1801-1900

FOURTH EDITION

Based on the original work of Chester L. Krause and Clifford Mishler

Colin R. Bruce II
Senior Editor

Thomas Michael
Market Analyst

George S. Cuhaj
Editor

Merna Dudley
Coordinating Editor

Randy Thern
Numismatic Cataloging Supervisor

Fred J. Borgmann
Technical Editor

Deborah McCue
Database Coordinator

Joel T. Edler
U.S. Market Analyst

Dennis Gill, Serge Huard, Paul Montz, Dana Roberts, Steven Tan
Special Contributors

UNCIRCULATED VALUATIONS

The uncirculated valuations represented in this edition are for typical quality specimens, for some of the more popularly collected series. Brilliant uncirculated (BU), or superior quality examples may easily command 10% to 50% premiums, or even greater where particularly popular or rare types or dates are concerned.

BULLION VALUE (BV) MARKET VALUATIONS

Valuations for all platinum, gold, pallidium or silver coins of the more common, basically bullion types, or those posessing only modest numismatic premiums are presented in this edition based on market values of $830 per ounce of platinum, $400 per ounce for gold, $210 per ounce for palladium and $6.25 per ounce for silver. Wherever the letters "BV"- Bullion Value - appear in a value column, that particular issue in the condition indicated generally trades at or near the bullion value of its precious metal content. Further information on using this catalog to evaluate platinum, gold, pallidium or silver coins amid fluctuating precious metal market conditions is presented in the introduction

Published by

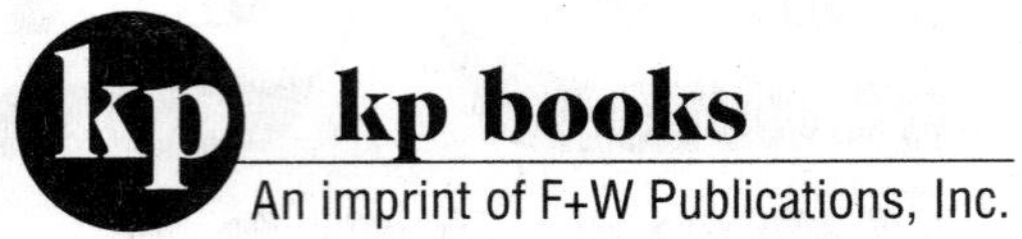

700 East State Street • Iola, WI 54990-0001
715-445-2214 • 888-457-2873

Our toll-free number to place an order or obtain a free catalog is (800) 258-0929.

Library of Congress Catalog Number: 2004093873

ISBN: 0-87349-798-8

Printed in the United States of America

TABLE OF CONTENTS

ADVERTISING INDEX

INTRODUCTION

Over 30 years have passed since the Standard Catalog of World Coins was nurtured to life in its first edition, compiled in 1971 and released to the collecting public in March 1972. Within its pages were listings organized in a logical format by denomination, date and mint of issue. Thus was our initial coverage presentation of the world's coinage from the mid-1800's through the 1960s. The collecting of world coins has never been the same since.

Prior to the release of that first Standard Catalog of World Coins, detailed world coin collecting information was available only to those who pursued their interests with the aid of specialized country catalogs, in whatever scope they existed. Generally speaking, they were available in English only for the most popular countries, with coverage restricted to the 19th and 20th centuries.

The Standard Catalog of World Coins changed all that. True to its stated objective of providing users a comprehensive one volume catalog, it literally replaces a shelf of often elusive specialized references, many of which were obscure, long out-of-print, non-English works. That original compilation listed the issues of all but a few countries in orderly, detailed arrangements. Several of those compilations were pioneering listings, just the first of a multitude to follow from edition to edition.

Research conducted by contributors and staff editors through the years gradually expanded the scope of the listings, embracing earlier eras and somewhat esoteric issues. Thus, the database from which annual editions of the Standard Catalog of World Coins have been drawn grew to include the first half of the 19th century, then the 18th and 17th centuries, successively, on a selective basis as useful and reliable listings could be generated.

Also folded into the listings were the more esoteric categories; patterns, piefort, trial strikes, medallic and pretender issues, related token issues, NCLTs, collector sets, and presentation sets - any "coins" an individual pursuing an interest in a given country might logically be expected to encounter -- which related to the circulation issue coinage of the respective countries. Early on, the resulting mass of the annual Standard Catalog of World Coins editions caused the volume to be reckoned as the "telephone book" or "bible" of the world coin field, be it the individual pursuit from the collector or dealer perspective.

The Standard Catalog quickly developed growing pains. As its distribution broadened, more suggestions and demands were visited upon the editors; the addressing of those needs and desires taxed the capability of the editors to incorporate the information in a manageable package. The editors welcomed and listened attentively to these appeals. There was no question, the additional information merited inclusion in the listings, and the annual edition progressively grew more voluminous and unwieldy.

Something had to give. As page counts continued to climb, effective with the 1984 edition, the editors began to systematically condense the listings, overlay large coin photos, and selectively eliminate esoteric categories. Effective with the 1988 edition, the scope of coverage was limited to issues of the 19th and 20th centuries.

KP Books has determined to best suit the needs of collectors and dealers alike, individual century volumes are the logical answer. The Standard Catalog of World Coins-19th Century, 4th edition is a result of that decision. This volume provides comprehensive, detailed coverage limited to the 19th century world coinage realm.

This newly revised 19th century edition is introduced shortly after the release of the 32nd edition Standard Catalog of World Coins-20th Century and the 18th and 17th Century Standard Catalogs. These new releases together represent years of research by our staff and many outside contributors to provide the most accurate and complete numismatic references in the world.

Welcome to the complete, one volume reference for 19th century world coins collecting information... "Basically, a compilation of the digested knowledge," as stated in the introduction to the first edition, "which students of the numismatic science have contributed to the coin collection hobby through the years," enhanced through the incorporation of original contributions that have substantially expanded the realm of awareness...a worthy successor to the ideals embodied in the publication of the first Standard Catalog of World Coins in 1972.

Clifford Mishler

ACKNOWLEDGMENTS

Many numismatists have contributed countless changes, which have been incorporated in this edition. While all cannot be acknowledged here, special appreciation is extended to the following individuals and organizations who have exhibited a special dedication – revising and verifying historical and technical data and coin listings, reviewing market valuations and loaning coins to photograph - for this edition.

Dr. Lawrence A. Adams
Stephen Album
Antonio Alessandrini
Don Bailey
Mitchell A. Battino
Allen G. Berman
Wolfgang Bertsch
Jack Beymer
Dr. Shailendra Bhandare
Joseph Boling
Larry Briggs
Klaus Bronny
Xavier Calicó
Ralph A. Cannito
Adolfo Cayón
Peter A. Chase
Liz Coggan
Scott E. Cordry
Freeman Craig
Jerry Crain
Lee Crane
Vincent Craven-Bartle
Jed Crump
A.J. Cunietti-Ferrando
Raymond Czahor
George D. Dean
Jean-Paul Divo
James R. Douglas
Sheridan Downey
Mike Dunigan
Graham P. Dyer
Wilhelm Eglseer
Esko Ekman
Jack Erb
George Falcke
John Ferm
George A. Fisher, Jr.
Thomas Fitzgerald
Luis Flores
Georg H. Förster
Donald T. Fox
Arthur Friedberg
Kent Froseth
Tom Galway
Vladimir Gamboa
Eng. Lajos Gergely
Dennis Gill
Lawrence S. Goldberg
Stan Goron
Brian Greer
Ron Guth
Marcel Häberling
Brian Hannon
Flemming Lyngbeck Hansen
Hans Herrli
Wade Hinderling
Serge Huard
Clyde Hubbard
Louis Hudson
Dr. Norman Jacobs
Ton Jacobs
Hector Carlos Janson
Lorenzo Jimenez
Robert Johnston
Francisco Jovel
Roberto Jovel
Robert W. Julian
Børge R. Juul
Alex Kaglyan
John Kallman
Craig Keplinger
Lawrence C. Korchnak
Peter Kraneveld
Prashant P. Kulkarni
Ronachai Krisadaolarn
Samson Kin Chiu Lai
Joseph Lang
Thomas Lautz
Nirat Lertchitvikul
Jan Lingen
Mike Locke
Jim Long
Rudi Lotter
Alan Luedeking
Ma Tak Wo
Enrico Manara
Harrington Manville
Jeff Means
Don Medcalf
Jurgen Mikeska
Harry Miller
Mario Gutierrez Minera
Juozas Minikevičius
Dr. William J.D. Mira
Dr. Richard Montrey
Paul Montz
Horst-Dieter Müller
Glenn Murray
Steve Musil
Hitoshi Nagai
Dr. Vladimir N. Nastich
Oen Nelson
N. Douglas Nicol
Jim O'Donnell
Leonard Novotny
David O'Harrow
Gus A. Pappas
Marc Pelletier
Juan Pena
Jens Pilegaard
Rick Ponterio
Kent Ponterio
Romain Probst
Kavan Ratnatunga
Jorge Emilio Restrepo
Dana Roberts
Joe Ross
John Sacher
Erwin Schäffer
Dr. Wolfgang Schuster
Daniel Frank Sedwick
Ladislav Sin
Richard Snow
Jørgen Sømod
William F. Spengler
Tom Steinmetz
Thomas Stohr
Richard Stuart
Vladimir Suchy
Alim A. Sumana
Steven Tan
Mark Teller
Anthony Tumonis
J. L. Van der Schueren
Robert van Bebber
Erik J. Van Loon
Helen Wallace
Justin C. Wang
Paul Welz
Stewart Westdal
J. Hugh Witherow

AUCTION HOUSES AND DISTRIBUTORS

David Akers Numismatics
Baldwin's Auctions Ltd.
Bonhams
Jean Elsen S.A.
Frankfurter Münzhandlung GmbH
Gorny & Mosch - Giessener Münzhandlung
Ronald J. Gillio Auctions
Heritage World Coin Auctions
Hess-Divo Ltd.
Gerhard Hirsch
Thomas Høiland Møntauktion
Fritz Rudolf Künker
Leu Numismatik AG
Münzhandlung Harald Möller GmbH
Noble Numismatics Pty. Ltd.
Ponterio & Associates
Laurens Schulman BV
Sotheby's
Spink America
Stack's – Coin Galleries
Superior Galleries
UBS, AG
World Wide Coins of California

SOCIETIES AND INSTITUTIONS

American Numismatic Association
American Numismatic Society
British Museum
Central American Numismatic Association
Chilean Numismatic Association
Numismatics International
Smithsonian Institution
Russian Numismatic Society

PUBLICATIONS

The Statesman's Yearbook – The Politics, Culture and Economies of the World, 2004. 140th Edition by Barry Turner, editor, Palgrave Macmillan Ltd., Houndsmills, Basingstoke, Hampshire, RG21 6XS, England. (Statistical and Historical Annual of the States of the World)

The World Factbook, 2003. by Central Intelligence Agency

SENDING SCANNED IMAGES BY EMAIL

Over the past 2 years or so, we have been receiving an ever-increasing flow of scanned images from sources worldwide. unfortunately, many of these scans could not be used due to the type of scan, or simple incompatability with our systems. We appreciate the effort it takes to produce these images and accuracy they add to the catalog listings.

Here are a few simple instructions to follow when producing scans for use in the standard catalog series. We encourage you to continue sending new images or upgrades to those currectly illustrated and please do not hesitate to ask questions about this process.

- Scan all images within a resolution range of 200 dpi to 300 dpi
- Size setting should be at 100%
- Scan in true 4-color
- Save images as 'jpeg' or 'tif' and name in such a way, which clearly identifies the country of origin of the item
- Email with a request to confirm receipt of the attachment
- Send images to **thernr@krause.com**

COUNTRY INDEX

HOW TO USE THIS CATALOG

This catalog series is designed to serve the needs of both the novice and advanced collectors. It provides a comprehensive guide to over 400 years of world coinage. It is generally arranged so that persons with no more than a basic knowledge of world history and a casual acquaintance with coin collecting can consult it with confidence and ease. The following explanations summarize the general practices used in preparing this catalog's listings. However, because of specialized requirements, which may vary by country and era, these must not be considered ironclad. Where these standards have been set aside, appropriate notations of the variations are incorporated in that particular listing.

ARRANGEMENT

Countries are arranged alphabetically. Political changes within a country are arranged chronologically. In countries where Rulers are the single most significant political entity a chronological arrangement by Ruler has been employed. Distinctive sub-geographic regions are listed alphabetically following the countries main listings. A few exceptions to these rules may exist. Refer to the Country Index.

Diverse coinage types relating to fabrication methods, revaluations, denomination systems, non-circulating categories and such have been identified, separated and arranged in logical fashion. Chronological arrangement is employed for most circulating coinage, i.e., Hammered coinage will normally precede Milled coinage, monetary reforms will flow in order of their institution. Non-circulating types such as Essais, Pieforts, Patterns, Trial Strikes, Mint and Proof sets will follow the main listings, as will Medallic coinage and Token coinage.

Within a coinage type coins will be listed by denomination, from smallest to largest. Numbered types within a denomination will be ordered by their first date of issue.

IDENTIFICATION

The most important step in the identification of a coin is the determination of the nation of origin. This is generally easily accomplished where English-speaking lands are concerned, however, use of the country index is sometimes required. The coins of Great Britain provide an interesting challenge. For hundreds of years the only indication of the country of origin was in the abbreviated Latin legends. In recent times there have been occasions when there has been no indication of origin. Only through the familiarity of the monarchical portraits, symbols and legends or indication of currency system are they identifiable.

The coins of many countries beyond the English-language realm, such as those of French, Italian or Spanish heritage, are also quite easy to identify through reference to their legends, which appear in the national languages based on Western alphabets. In many instances the name is spelled exactly the same in English as in the national language, such as France; while in other cases it varies only slightly, like Italia for Italy, Belgique or Belgie for Belgium, Brasil for Brazil and Danmark for Denmark.

This is not always the case, however, as in Norge for Norway, Espana for Spain, Sverige for Sweden and Helvetia for Switzerland. Some other examples include:

DEUTSCHES REICH - Germany 1873-1945

BUNDESREPUBLIC DEUTSCHLAND - Federal Republic of Germany.

DEUTSCHE DEMOKRATISCHE REPUBLIK - German Democratic Republic.

EMPIRE CHERIFIEN MAROC - Morocco.

ESTADOS UNIDOS MEXICANOS - United Mexican States (Mexico).

ETAT DU GRAND LIBAN - State of Great Lebanon (Lebanon).

Thus it can be seen there are instances in which a little schooling in the rudiments of foreign languages can be most helpful. In general, colonial possessions of countries using the Western alphabet are similarly identifiable as they often carry portraits of their current rulers, the familiar lettering, sometimes in combination with a companion designation in the local language.

Collectors have the greatest difficulty with coins that do not bear legends or dates in the Western systems. These include coins bearing Cyrillic lettering, attributable to Bulgaria, Russia, the Slavic states and Mongolia, the Greek script peculiar to Greece, Crete and the Ionian Islands; The Amharic characters of Ethiopia, or Hebrew in the case of Israel. Dragons and sunbursts along with the distinctive word characters attribute a coin to the Oriental countries of China, Japan, Korea, Tibet, Viet Nam and their component parts.

The most difficult coins to identify are those bearing only Persian or Arabic script and its derivatives, found on the issues of nations stretching in a wide swath across North Africa and East Asia, from Morocco to Indonesia, and the Indian subcontinent coinages which surely are more confusing in their vast array of Nagari, Sanskrit, Ahom, Assamese and other local dialects found on the local issues of the Indian Princely States. Although the task of identification on the more modern issues of these lands is often eased by the added presence of Western alphabet legends, a feature sometimes adopted as early as the late 19th Century, for the earlier pieces it is often necessary for the uninitiated to laboriously seek and find.

Except for the cruder issues, however, it will be found that certain characteristics and symbols featured in addition to the predominant legends are typical on coins from a given country or group of countries. The toughra monogram, for instance, occurs on some of the coins of Afghanistan, Egypt, the Sudan, Pakistan, Turkey and other areas of the late Ottoman Empire. A predominant design feature on the coins of Nepal is the trident; while neighboring Tibet features a lotus blossom or lion on many of their issues.

To assist in identification of the more difficult coins, we have assembled the Instant Identifier section presented on the following pages designed to provide a point of beginning for collectors by allowing them to compare unidentified coins with photographic details from typical issues.

We also suggest reference to the comprehensive Country Index.

DATING

Coin dating is the final basic attribution consideration. Here, the problem can be more difficult because the reading of a coin date is subject not only to the vagaries of numeric styling, but to calendar variations caused by the observance of various religious eras or regal periods from country to country, or even within a country. Here again with the exception of the sphere from North Africa through the Orient, it will be found that most countries rely on Western date numerals and Christian (AD) era reckoning, although in a few instances, coin dating has been tied to the year of a reign or government. The Vatican, for example dates its coinage according to the year of reign of the current pope, in addition to the Christian-era date.

Countries in the Arabic sphere generally date their coins to the Muslim era (AH), which commenced on July 16, 622 AD (Julian calendar), when the prophet Mohammed fled from Mecca to Medina. As their calendar is reckoned by the lunar year of 354 days, which is about three percent (precisely 2.98%) shorter than the Christian year, a formula is required to convert AH dating to its Western equivalent. To convert an AH date to the approximate AD date, subtract three percent of the AH date (round to the closest whole number) from the AH date and add 622. A chart converting all AH years from 1010 (July 2, 1601) to 1421 (May 25, 2028) is presented as the Heijra Chart elsewhere in this volume.

The Muslim calendar is not always based on the lunar year (AH), however, causing some confusion, particularly in Afghanistan and Iran, where a calendar based on the solar year (SH) was introduced around 1920. These dates can be converted to AD by simply adding 621. In 1976 the government of Iran implemented a new solar calendar based on the foundation of the Iranian monarchy in 559 BC. The first year observed on the new calendar was 2535 (MS), which commenced March 20, 1976. A reversion to the traditional SH dating standard occurred a few years later.

Several different eras of reckoning, including Christian and Muslim (AH), have been used to date coins of the Indian subcontinent. The two basic systems are the Vikrama Samvat (VS), which dates from Oct. 18, 58 BC, and the Saka era, the origin of which is reckoned from March 3, 78 AD. Dating according to both eras appears on various coins of the area.

Coins of Thailand (Siam) are found dated by three different eras. The most predominant is the Buddhist era (BE), which originated in 543 BC. Next is the Bangkok or Ratanakosindsok (RS) era, dating from 1781 AD; followed by the Chula- Sakarat (CS) era, dating from 638 AD. The latter era originated in Burma and is used on that country's coins.

Other calendars include that of the Ethiopian era (EE), which commenced seven years, eight months after AD dating; and that of the Jewish people, which commenced on Oct. 7, 3761 BC. Korea claims a legendary dating from 2333 BC, which is acknowledged in some of its coin dating. Some coin issues of the Indonesian area carry dates determined by the Javanese Aji Saka era (AS), a calendar of 354 days (100 Javanese years equal 97 Christian or Gregorian calendar years), which can be matched to AD dating by comparing it to AH dating.

The following table indicates the year dating for the various eras, which correspond to 2003 in Christian calendar reckoning, but it must be remembered that there are overlaps between the eras in some instances.

Christian era (AD)	2003
Muslim era (AH)	AH1424
Solar year (SH)	SH1381
Monarchic Solar era (MS)	MS2562
Vikrama Samvat (VS)	VS2060
Saka era (SE)	SE1925
Buddhist era (BE)	BE2546
Bangkok era (RS)	RS222
Chula-Sakarat era (CS)	CS1365
Ethiopian era (EE)	EE1997
Korean era	4336
Javanese Aji Saka era (AS)	AS1936
Fasli era (FE)	FE1413
Jewish era (JE)	JE5763

Coins of Asian origin - principally Japan, Korea, China, Turkestan and Tibet and some modern gold issues of Turkey - are generally dated to the year of the government, dynasty, reign or cyclic eras, with the dates indicated in Asian characters which usually read from right to left. In recent years, however, some dating has been according to the Christian calendar and in Western numerals. In Japan, Asian character dating was reversed to read from left to right in Showa year 23 (1948 AD).

More detailed guides to less prevalent coin dating systems, which are strictly local in nature, are presented with the appropriate listings.

Some coins carry dates according to both locally observed and Christian eras. This is particularly true in the Arabic world, where the Hejira date may be indicated in Arabic numerals and the Christian date in Western numerals, or both dates in either form.

The date actually carried on a given coin is generally cataloged here in the first column (Date). Dates listed alone in the date column which do not actually appear on a given coin, or dates which are known, but do not appear on the coin, are generally enclosed by parentheses with 'ND' at the left, for example ND(1926).

Timing differentials between some era of reckoning, particularly the 354-day Mohammedan and 365-day Christian years, cause situations whereby coins which carry dates for both eras exist bearing two year dates from one calendar combined with a single date from another.

Countermarked Coinage is presented with both 'Countermark Date' and 'Host Coin' date for each type. Actual date representation follows the rules outlined above.

NUMBERING SYSTEM

Some catalog numbers assigned in this volume are based on established references. This practice has been observed for two reasons: First, when world coins are listed chronologically they are basically self-cataloging; second, there was no need to confuse collectors with totally new numeric designations where appropriate systems already existed. As time progressed we found many of these established systems incomplete and inadequate and have now replaced many with new KM numbers. When numbers change appropriate cross-referencing has been provided.

Some of the coins listed in this catalog are identified or cross-referenced by numbers assigned by R.S. Yeoman (Y#), or slight adaptations thereof, in his Modern World Coins, and Current Coins of the World. For the pre-Yeoman dated issues, the numbers assigned by William D. Craig (C#) in his Coins of the World (1750- 1850 period), 3rd edition, have generally been applied.

In some countries, listings are cross-referenced to Robert Friedberg's (FR#) Gold Coins of the World or Coins of the British World. Major Fred Pridmore's (P#) studies of British colonial coinage are also referenced, as are W.H. Valentine's (V#) references on the Modern Copper Coins of the Muhammadan States. Coins issued under the Chinese sphere of influence are assigned numbers from E. Kann's (K#) Illustrated Catalog of Chinese Coins and T.K. Hsu's (Su) work of similar title. In most cases, these cross- reference numbers are presented in the descriptive text for each type.

DENOMINATIONS

The second basic consideration to be met in the attribution of a coin is the determination of denomination. Since denominations are usually expressed in numeric, rather than word form on a coin, this is usually quite easily accomplished on coins from nations, which use Western numerals, except in those instances where issues are devoid of any mention of face value, and denomination must be attributed by size, metallic composition or weight. Coins listed in this volume are generally illustrated in actual size. Where size is critical to proper attribution, the coin's millimeter size is indicated.

The sphere of countries stretching from North Africa through the Orient, on which numeric symbols generally unfamiliar to Westerners are employed, often provide the collector with a much greater challenge. This is particularly true on nearly all pre-20th Century issues. On some of the more modern issues and increasingly so as the years progress, Western-style numerals usually presented in combination with the local numeric system are becoming more commonplace on these coins.

Determination of a coin's currency system can also be valuable in attributing the issue to its country of origin.

The included table of Standard International Numeral Systems presents charts of the basic numeric designations found on coins of non- Western origin. Although denomination numerals are generally prominently displayed on coins, it must be remembered that these are general representations of characters, which individual coin engravers may have rendered in widely varying styles. Where numeric or script denominations designation forms peculiar to a given coin or country apply, such as the script used on some Persian (Iranian) issues. They are so indicated or illustrated in conjunction with the appropriate listings.

MINTAGES

Quantities minted of each date are indicated where that information is available, generally stated in millions, and usually rounded off to the nearest 10,000 pieces. On quantities of a few thousand or less, actual mintages are generally indicated. For combined mintage figures the abbreviation Inc. Above " means Included Above, while "Inc. Below" means Included Below. "Est." beside a mintage figure indicates the number given is an estimate or mintage limit.

MINT AND PRIVY MARKS

The presence of distinctive, but frequently inconspicuously placed, mintmarks indicates the mint of issue for many of the coins listed in this catalog. An appropriate designation in the date listings notes the presence, if any, of a mint mark on a particular coin type by incorporating the letter or letters of the mint mark adjoining the date, i.e., 1883CC or 1890H.

The presence of mint and/or mintmaster's privy marks on a coin in non-letter form is indicated by incorporating the mint letter in lower case within parentheses adjoining the date; i.e. 1827(a). The corresponding mark is illustrated or identified in the introduction of the country.

In countries such as France and Mexico, where many mints may be producing like coinage in the same denomination during the same time period, divisions by mint have been employed. In these cases the mint mark may appear next to the individual date listings and/or the mint name or mint mark may be listed in the Note field of the type description.

Where listings incorporate mintmaster initials, they are always presented in capital letters separated from the date by one character space; i.e., 1850 MF. The different mintmark and mintmaster letters found on the coins of any country, state or city of issue are always shown at the beginning of listings.

METALS

Each numbered type listing will contain a description of the coins metallic content. The traditional coinage metals and their symbolic chemical abbreviations sometimes used in this catalog are:

Platinum - (PT)	Copper - (Cu)
Gold - (Au)	Brass -
Silver - (Ag)	Copper-nickel- (CN)
Billion -	Lead - (Pb)
Nickel - (Ni)	Steel -
Zinc - (Zn)	Tin - (Sn)
Bronze - (Ae)	Aluminum - (Al)

During the 18th and 19th centuries, most of the world's coins were struck of copper or bronze, silver and gold. Commencing in the early years of the 20th century, however, numerous new coinage metals, primarily non-precious metal alloys, were introduced. Gold has not been widely used for circulation coinages since World War I, although silver remained a popular coinage metal in most parts of the world until after World War II. With the disappearance of silver for circulation coinage, numerous additional compositions were introduced to coinage applications.

OFF-METAL STRIKES

Off-metal strikes previously designated by "(OMS)" which also included the wide range of error coinage struck in other than their officially authorized compositions have been incorporated into Pattern listings along with special issues, which were struck for presentation or other reasons.

Collectors of Germanic coinage may be familiar with the term "Abschlag" which quickly identifies similar types of coinage.

PRECIOUS METAL WEIGHTS

Listings of weight, fineness and actual silver (ASW), gold (AGW), platinum or palladium (APW) content of most machine-struck silver, gold, platinum and palladium coins are provided in this edition. This information will be found incorporated in each separate type listing, along with other data related to the coin.

The ASW, AGW and APW figures were determined by multiplying the gross weight of a given coin by its known or tested fineness and converting the resulting gram or grain weight to troy ounces, rounded to the nearest ten-thousandth of an ounce. A silver coin with a 24.25-gram weight and .875 fineness for example, would have a fine weight of approximately 21.2188 grams, or a .6822 ASW, a factor that can be used to accurately determine the intrinsic value for multiple examples.

The ASW, AGW or APW figure can be multiplied by the spot price of each precious metal to determine the current intrinsic value of any coin accompanied by these designations.

Coin weights are indicated in grams (abbreviated "g") along with fineness where the information is of value in differentiating between types. These weights are based on 31.103 grams per troy (scientific) ounce, as opposed to the avoirdupois (commercial) standard of 28.35 grams. Actual coin weights are generally shown in hundredths or thousands of a gram; i.e., 2.9200 g., SILVER, 0.500 oz.

WEIGHTS AND FINENESSES

As the silver and gold bullion markets have advanced and declined sharply in recent years, the fineness and total precious metal content of coins has become especially significant where bullion coins - issues which trade on the basis of their intrinsic metallic content rather than numismatic value - are concerned. In many instances, such issues have become worth more in bullion form than their nominal collector values or denominations indicate.

Establishing the weight of a coin can also be valuable for determining its denomination. Actual weight is also necessary to ascertain the specific gravity of the coin's metallic content, an important factor in determining authenticity.

TROY WEIGHT STANDARDS

24 Grains = 1 Pennyweight
480 Grains = 1 Ounce
31.103 Grams = 1 Ounce

UNIFORM WEIGHTS

15.432 Grains = 1 Gram
0.0648 Gram = 1 Grain

AVOIRDUPOIS STANDARDS

27-11/32 Grains = 11 Dram
437-1/2 Grains = 1 Ounce
28.350 Grams = 1 Ounce

HOMELAND TYPES

Homeland types are coins which colonial powers used in a colony, but do not bear that location's name. In some cases they were legal tender in the homeland, in others not. They are listed under the homeland and cross-referenced at the colony listing.

COUNTERMARKS/COUNTERSTAMPS

There is some confusion among collectors over the terms "countermark" and "counterstamp" when applied to a coin bearing an additional mark or change of design and/or denomination.

To clarify, a countermark might be considered similar to the "hall mark" applied to a piece of silverware, by which a silversmith assured the quality of the piece. In the same way, a countermark assures the quality of the coin on which it is placed, as, for example, when the royal crown of England was countermarked (punched into) on segmented Spanish reales, allowing them to circulate in commerce in the British West Indies. An additional countermark indicating the new denomination may also be encountered on these coins.

Countermarks are generally applied singularly and in most cases indiscriminately on either side of the "host" coin.

Counterstamped coins are more extensively altered. The counterstamping is done with a set of dies, rather than a hand punch. The coin being counterstamped is placed between the new dies and struck as if it were a blank planchet as found with the Manila 8 reales issue of the Philippines.

PHOTOGRAPHS

To assist the reader in coin identification, every effort has been made to present actual size photographs of every coinage type listed. Obverse and reverse are illustrated, except when a change in design is restricted to one side, and the coin has a diameter of 39mm or larger, in which case only the side required for identification of the type is generally illustrated. All coins up to 60mm are illustrated actual size, to the nearest 1/2mm up to 25mm, and to the nearest 1mm thereafter. Coins larger than 60mm diameter are illustrated in reduced size, with the actual size noted in the descriptive text block. Where slight change in size is important to coin type identification, actual millimeter measurements are stated.

TRADE COINS

From approximately 1750-1940, a number of nations, particularly European colonial powers and commercial traders, minted trade coins to facilitate commerce with the local populace of Africa, the Arab countries, the Indian subcontinental, Southeast Asia and the Far East. Such coins generally circulated at a value based on the weight and fineness of their silver or gold content, rather than their stated denomination. Examples include the sovereigns of Great Britain and the gold ducat issues of Austria, Hungary and the Netherlands. Trade coinage will sometimes be found listed at the end of the domestic issues.

VALUATIONS

Values quoted in this catalog represent the current market and are compiled from recommendations provided and verified through various source documents and specialized consultants. It should be stressed, however, that this book is intended

COIN ALIGNMENT

MEDAL ALIGNMENT

COIN VS MEDAL ALIGNMENT

Some coins are struck with obverse and reverse aligned at a rotation of 180 degrees from each other. When a coin is held for vertical viewing with the obverse design aligned upright and the index finger and thumb at the top and bottom, upon rotation from left to right for viewing the reverse, the latter will be upside down. Such alignment is called "coin rotation." Other coins are struck with the obverse and reverse designs mated on an alignment of zero or 360 degrees. If such an example is held and rotated as described, the reverse will appear upright. This is the alignment, which is generally observed in the striking of medals, and for that reason coins produced in this manner are considered struck in "medal rotation". In some instances, often through error, certain coin issues have been struck to both alignment standards, creating interesting collectible varieties, which will be found noted in some listings. In addition, some countries are now producing coins with other designated overse to reverse alignments which are considered standard for this type.

to serve only as an aid for evaluating coins, actual market conditions are constantly changing and additional influences, such as particularly strong local demand for certain coin series, fluctuation of international exchange rates and worldwide collection patterns must also be considered. Publication of this catalog is not intended as a solicitation by the publisher, editors or contributors to buy or sell the coins listed at the prices indicated.

All valuations are stated in U.S. dollars, based on careful assessment of the varied international collector market. Valuations for coins priced below $100.00 are generally stated in full amounts - i.e. 37.50 or 95.00 - while valuations at or above that figure are rounded off in even dollars - i.e. $125.00 is expressed 125. A comma is added to indicate thousands of dollars in value.

It should be noted that when particularly select uncirculated or proof-like examples of uncirculated coins become available they can be expected to command proportionately high premiums. Such examples in reference to choice Germanic Thalers are referred to as "erst schlage" or first strikes.

TOKEN COINAGE

At times local economic conditions have forced regular coinage from circulation or found mints unable to cope with the demand for coinage, giving rise to privately issued token coinage substitutes. British tokens of the late 1700s and early 1880s, and the German and French and French Colonial emergency emissions of the World War I era are examples of such tokens being freely accepted in monetary transactions over wide areas. Tokens were likewise introduced to satisfy specific restricted needs, such as the leper colony issues of Brazil, Colombia and the Philippines.

This catalog includes introductory or detailed listings with "Tn" prefixes of many token coinage issues, particularly those which enjoyed wide circulation and where the series was limited in diversity. More complex series, and those more restricted in scope of circulation are generally not listed, although a representative sample may be illustrated and a specialty reference provided.

MEDALLIC ISSUES

Select medallic issues are segregated following the regular issue listings. Grouped there are coin- type issues, which can generally be identified as commemoratives produced to the country's established coinage standards but without the usual indicator of denomination. These pieces may or may not feature designs adapted from the country's regular issue or commemorative coinage, and may or may not have been issued in conjunction with related coinage issues. Additional medallic issues can be found listed in our Unusual World Coins catalog.

RESTRIKES, COUNTERFEITS

Deceptive restrike and counterfeit (both contemporary and modern) examples exist of some coin issues. Where possible, the existence of restrikes is noted. Warnings are also incorporated in instances where particularly deceptive counterfeits are known to exist. Collectors who are uncertain about the authenticity of a coin held in their collection, or being offered for sale, should take the precaution of having it authenticated by the American Numismatic Association Authentication Bureau, 818 N. Cascade, Colorado Springs, CO 80903. Their reasonably priced certification tests are widely accepted by collectors and dealers alike.

EDGE VARIETIES

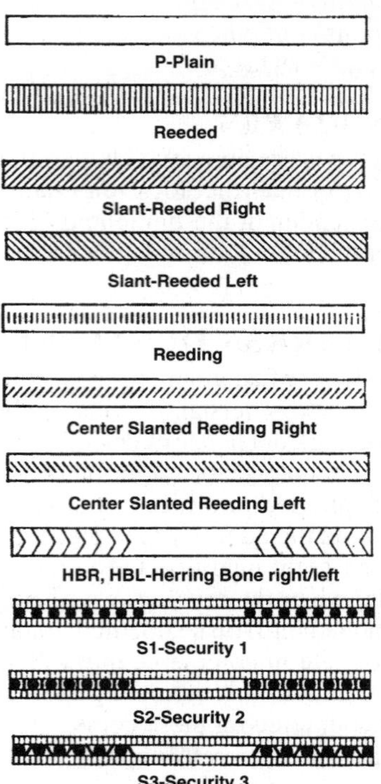

SETS

Listings in this catalog for specimen, proof and mint sets are for official, government-produced sets. In many instances privately packaged sets also exist.

Mint Sets/Fleur de Coin Sets: Specially prepared by worldwide mints to provide banks, collectors and government dignitaries with examples of current coinage. Usually subjected to rigorous inspection to insure that top quality specimens of selected business strikes are provided. One of the most popular mint set is that given out by the monarch of Great Britain each year on Maunday Thursday. This set contains four special coins in denominations of 1, 2, 3 and 4 pence, struck in silver and contained in a little pouch. They have been given away in a special ceremony for the poor for more than two centuries.

Specimen Sets: Forerunners of today's proof sets. In most cases the coins were specially struck, perhaps even double struck, to produce a very soft or matte finish on the effigies and fields, along with high, sharp, "wire" rims. The finish is rather dull to the naked eye.

The original purpose of these sets was to provide VIPs, monarchs and mintmasters around the world with samples of the highest quality workmanship of a particular mint. These were usually housed in elaborate velvet-lined leather and metal cases.

Proof Sets: This is undoubtedly among the most misused terms in the hobby, not only by collectors and dealers, but also by many of the world mints.

A true proof set must be at least double-struck on specially prepared polished planchets and struck using dies (often themselves polished) of the highest quality.

Listings for proof sets in this catalog are for officially issued proof sets so designated by the issuing authority, and may or may not possess what are considered modern proof quality standards.

It is necessary for collectors to acquire the knowledge to allow them to differentiate true proof sets from would-be proof sets and proof- like sets which may be encountered.

CONDITIONS/GRADING

Wherever possible, coin valuations are given in four or five grades of preservation. For modern commemoratives, which do not circulate, only uncirculated values are usually sufficient. Proof issues are indicated by the word "Proof" next to the date, with valuation proceeded by the word "value" following the mintage. For very recent circulating coins and coins of limited value, one, two or three grade values are presented.

There are almost no grading guides for world coins. What follows is an attempt to help bridge that gap until a detailed, illustrated guide becomes available.

In grading world coins, there are two elements to look for: 1) Overall wear, and 2) loss of design details, such as strands of hair, feathers on eagles, designs on coats of arms, etc.

The age, rarity or type of a coin should not be a consideration in grading.

Grade each coin by the weaker of the two sides. This method appears to give results most nearly consistent with conservative American Numismatic Association standards for U.S. coins. Split grades, i.e., F/VF for obverse and reverse, respectively, are normally no more than one grade apart. If the two sides are more than one grade apart, the series of coins probably wears differently on each side and should then be graded by the weaker side alone.

Grade by the amount of overall wear and loss of design detail evident on each side of the coin. On coins with a moderately small design element, which is prone to early wear, grade by that design alone. For example, the 5-ore (KM#554) of Sweden has a crown above the monogram on which the beads on the arches show wear most clearly. So, grade by the crown alone.

For Brilliant Uncirculated (BU) grades there will be no visible signs of wear or handling, even under a 30-power microscope. Full mint luster will be present. Ideally no bags marks will be evident.

For Uncirculated (Unc.) grades there will be no visible signs of wear or handling, even under a 30-power microscope. Bag marks may be present.

For Almost Uncirculated (AU), all detail will be visible. There will be wear only on the highest point of the coin. There will often be half or more of the original mint luster present.

On the Extremely Fine (XF or EF) coin, there will be about 95% of the original detail visible. Or, on a coin with a design with no inner detail to wear down, there will be a light wear over nearly all the coin. If a small design is used as the grading area, about 90% of the original detail will be visible. This latter rule stems from the logic that a smaller amount of detail needs to be present because a small area is being used to grade the whole coin.

The Very Fine (VF) coin will have about 75% of the original detail visible. Or, on a coin with no inner detail, there will be moderate wear over the entire coin. Corners of letters and numbers may be weak. A small grading area will have about 66% of the original detail.

For Fine (F), there will be about 50% of the original detail visible. Or, on a coin with no inner detail, there will be fairly heavy wear over all of the coin. Sides of letters will be weak. A typically uncleaned coin will often appear as dirty or dull. A small grading area will have just under 50% of the original detail.

On the Very Good (VG) coin, there will be about 25% of the original detail visible. There will be heavy wear on all of the coin.

The Good (G) coin's design will be clearly outlined but with substantial wear. Some of the larger detail may be visible. The rim may have a few weak spots of wear.

On the About Good (AG) coin, there will typically be only a silhouette of a large design. The rim will be worn down into the letters if any.

Strong or weak strikes, partially weak strikes, damage, corrosion, attractive or unattractive toning, dipping or cleaning should be described along with the above grades. These factors affect the quality of the coin just as do wear and loss of detail, but are easier to describe.

In the case of countermarked/counterstamped coins, the condition of the host coin will have a bearing on the end valuation. The important factor in determining the grade is the condition, clarity and completeness of the countermark itself. This is in reference to countermarks/counterstamps having raised design while being struck in a depression.

Incuse countermarks cannot be graded for wear. They are graded by the clarity and completeness including the condition of the host coin which will also have more bearing on the final grade/valuation determined.

STANDARD INTERNATIONAL GRADING TERMINOLOGY AND ABBREVIATIONS

	PROOF	UNCIRCULATED	EXTREMELY FINE	VERY FINE	FINE	VERY GOOD	GOOD	POOR
U.S. and ENGLISH SPEAKING LANDS	PRF	UNC	EF or XF	VF	F	VG	G	PR
BRAZIL	—	(1)FDC or FC	(3) S	(5) MBC	(7) BC	(8) BC/R	(9) R	UT GeG
DENMARK	M	0	01	1+	1	1÷	2	3
FINLAND	00	0	01	1+	1	1?	2	3
FRANCE	FB Flan Bruni	FDC Fleur de Coin	SUP Superbe	TTB Très très beau	TB Très beau	B Beau	TBC Très Bien Conservée	BC Bien Conservée
GERMANY	PP Polierte Platte	STG Stempelglanz	VZ Vorzüglich	SS Sehr schön	S Schön	S.G.E. Sehr gut erhalten	G.E. Gut erhalten	Gering erhalten
ITALY	FS Fondo Specchio	FDC Fior di Conio	SPL Splendido	BB Bellissimo	MB Molto Bello	B Bello	M	—
JAPAN	—	未使用	極美品	美品	並品	—	—	—
NETHERLANDS	— Proef	FDC Fleur de Coin	Pr. Prachtig	Z.f. Zeer fraai	Fr. Fraai	Z.g. Zeer goed	G	—
NORWAY	M	0	01	1+	1	1÷	2	3
PORTUGAL	—	Soberba	Bela	MBC	BC	MREG	REG	MC
SPAIN	Prueba	SC	EBC	MBC	BC+	BC	RC	MC
SWEDEN	Polerad	0	01	1+	1	1?	2	—

FOREIGN EXCHANGE TABLE

The latest foreign exchange fixed rates below apply to trade with banks in the country of origin. The left column shows the number of units per U.S. dollar at the official rate. The right column shows the number of units per dollar at the free market rate.

Country	Official #/$	Market #/$
Afghanistan (New Afghani)	43	–
Albania (Lek)	104	–
Algeria (Dinar)	72	–
Andorra uses Euro	.83	–
Angola (Readjust Kwanza)	85	–
Anguilla uses E.C.Dollar	2.67	–
Antigua uses E.C.Dollar	2.67	–
Argentina (Peso)	3	–
Armenia (Dram)	520	–
Aruba (Florin)	1.79	–
Australia (Dollar)	1.447	–
Austria (Euro)	.83	–
Azerbaijan (Manat)	4,910	–
Bahamas (Dollar)	1.00	–
Bahrain Is.(Dinar)	.377	–
Bangladesh (Taka)	60	–
Barbados (Dollar)	1.99	–
Belarus (Ruble)	2,165	–
Belgium (Euro)	.83	–
Belize (Dollar)	1.97	–
Benin uses CFA Franc West	545	–
Bermuda (Dollar)	1.00	–
Bhutan (Ngultrum)	47.6	–
Bolivia (Boliviano)	7.95	–
Bosnia-Herzegovina (Deutschmark)	1.59	–
Botswana (Pula)	4.8	–
British Virgin Islands uses U.S.Dollar	1.00	–
Brazil (Real)	2.93	–
Brunei (Dollar)	1.70	–
Bulgaria (Lev)	1.62	–
Burkina Faso uses CFA Fr.West	545	–
Burma (Kyat)	6.42	1,250
Burundi (Franc)	1,075	–
Cambodia (Riel)	3,850	–
Cameroon uses CFA Franc Central	545	–
Canada (Dollar)	1.302	–
Cape Verde (Escudo)	92	–
Cayman Is.(Dollar)	0.82	–
Central African Rep.	545	–
CFA Franc Central	545	–
CFA Franc West	545	–
CFP Franc	98.7	–
Chad uses CFA Franc Central	545	–
Chile (Peso)	620	–
China, P.R. (Renminbi Yuan)	8.278	–
Colombia (Peso)	2,550	–
Comoros (Franc)	400	–
Congo uses CFA Franc Central	545	–
Congo-Dem.Rep. (Congolese Franc)	545	–
Cook Islands (Dollar)	1.73	–
Costa Rica (Colon)	445	–
Croatia (Kuna)	6.1	–
Cuba (Peso)	1.00	27
Cyprus (Pound)	.48	–
Czech Republic (Koruna)	26.3	–
Denmark (Danish Krone)	6.17	–
Djibouti (Franc)	170	–
Dominica uses E.C.Dollar	2.67	–
Dominican Republic (Peso)	34.8	–
East Caribbean (Dollar)	2.67	–
Ecuador uses U.S. Dollar	1.00	–
Egypt (Pound)	6.19	–
El Salvador uses U.S. Dollar	1.00	–
Equatorial Guinea uses CFA Franc Central	545	–
Eritrea (Nafka)	9.6	–
Estonia (Kroon)	12.9	–
Ethiopia (Birr)	8.7	–
Euro	.83	–
Falkland Is. (Pound)	.563	–
Faroe Islands (Krona)	6.17	–
Fiji Islands (Dollar)	1.77	–
Finland (Euro)	.83	–
France (Euro)	.83	–
French Polynesia uses CFP Franc	98.7	–
Gabon (CFA Franc)	545	–
Gambia (Dalasi)	29.8	–
Georgia (Lari)	1.7	–
Germany (Euro)	.83	–
Ghana (Cedi)	9,000	–
Gibraltar (Pound)	.563	–
Greece (Euro)	.83	–
Greenland uses Danish Krone	6.17	–
Grenada uses E.C.Dollar	2.67	–
Guatemala (Quetzal)	7.9	–
Guernsey (Pound Sterling)	.563	–
Guinea Bissau (CFA Franc)	545	–
Guinea Conakry (Franc)	2,570	–
Guyana (Dollar)	180	–
Haiti (Gourde)	34.2	–
Honduras (Lempira)	18.4	–
Hong Kong (Dollar)	7.80	–
Hungary (Forint)	205	–
Iceland (Krona)	72.5	–
India (Rupee)	46.3	–
Indonesia (Rupiah)	9,275	–
Iran (Rial)	8,750	–
Iraq (Dinar)	1,450	1,935
Ireland (Euro)	.83	–
Isle of Man (Pound Sterling)	.563	–
Israel (New Sheqalim)	4.52	–
Italy (Euro)	.83	–
Ivory Coast uses CFA Franc West	545	–
Jamaica (Dollar)	61.3	–
Japan (Yen)	110	–
Jersey (Pound Sterling)	.563	–
Jordan (Dinar)	.71	–
Kazakhstan (Tenge)	135	–
Kenya (Shilling)	80.3	–
Kiribati uses Australian Dollar	1.447	–
Korea-PDR (Won)	2.2	500
Korea-Rep. (Won)	1,150	–
Kuwait (Dinar)	.295	–
Kyrgyzstan (Som)	42.8	–
Laos (Kip)	7,840	–
Latvia (Lat)	.54	–
Lebanon (Pound)	1,515	–
Lesotho (Maloti)	6.5	–
Liberia (Dollar) "JJ"	1.00	20.00
"Liberty"	–	40.00
Libya (Dinar)	1.21	–
Liechtenstein uses Swiss Franc	1.27	–
Lithuania (Litas)	2.86	–
Luxembourg (Euro)	.83	–
Macao (Pataca)	8.01	–
Macedonia (New Denar)	50	–
Madagascar (Franc)	10,275	–
Malawi (Kwacha)	110	–
Malaysia (Ringgit)	3.8	–
Maldives (Rufiya)	12.9	–
Mali uses CFA Franc West	545	–
Malta (Lira)	.35	–
Marshall Islands uses U.S.Dollar	1.00	–
Mauritania (Ouguiya)	270	–
Mauritius (Rupee)	28.5	–
Mexico (Peso)	11.51	–
Moldova (Leu)	12	–
Monaco uses Euro	.83	–
Mongolia (Tugrik)	1,200	–
Montenegro uses Euro	.83	–
Montserrat uses E.C.Dollar	2.67	–
Morocco (Dirham)	9.08	–
Mozambique (Metical)	21,900	–
Myanmar (Burma) (Kyat)	6.42	1,250
Namibia (Rand)	6.61	–
Nauru uses Australian Dollar	1.447	–
Nepal (Rupee)	72	–
Netherlands (Euro)	.83	–
Netherlands Antilles (Gulden)	1.78	–
New Caledonia uses CFP Franc	98.7	–
New Zealand (Dollar)	1.547	–
Nicaragua (Cordoba Oro)	15.9	–
Niger uses CFA Franc West	545	–
Nigeria (Naira)	130	–
Northern Ireland (Pound Sterling)	.563	–
Norway (Krone)	6.91	–
Oman (Rial)	.385	–
Pakistan (Rupee)	58.9	–
Palau uses U.S.Dollar	1.00	–
Panama (Balboa) uses U.S.Dollar	1.00	–
Papua New Guinea (Kina)	3.04	–
Paraguay (Guarani)	5,920	–
Peru (Nuevo Sol)	3.4	–
Philippines (Peso)	56.1	–
Poland (Zloty)	3.65	–
Portugal (Euro)	.83	–
Qatar (Riyal)	3.64	–
Romania (Leu)	33,925	–
Russia (New Ruble)	29.2	–
Rwanda (Franc)	565	–
St.Helena (Pound)	.563	–
St.Kitts uses E.C.Dollar	2.67	–
St.Lucia uses E.C.Dollar	2.67	–
St.Vincent uses E.C.Dollar	2.67	–
San Marino uses Euro	.83	–
Sao Tome e Principe (Dobra)	8,825	–
Saudi Arabia (Riyal)	3.75	–
Scotland (Pound Sterling)	.563	–
Senegal uses CFA Franc West	545	–
Serbia (Dinar)	61.4	–
Seychelles (Rupee)	5.18	6.40
Sierra Leone (Leone)	2,450	–
Singapore (Dollar)	1.70	–
Slovakia (Sk. Koruna)	33.3	–
Slovenia (Tolar)	200	–
Solomon Is.(Dollar)	7.49	–
Somalia (Shilling)	2,750	–
Somaliland (Somali Shilling)	1,800	4,000
South Africa (Rand)	6.61	–
Spain (Euro)	.83	–
Sri Lanka (Rupee)	103	–
Sudan (Dinar)	260	300
Surinam (Guilder)	2,515	–
Swaziland (Lilangeni)	6.50	–
Sweden (Krona)	7.56	–
Switzerland (Franc)	1.27	–
Syria (Pound)	51.7	–
Taiwan (NT Dollar)	33.9	–
Tajikistan (Somoni)	3.08	–
Tanzania (Shilling)	1,075	–
Thailand (Baht)	41.6	–
Togo uses CFAFranc West	545	–
Tonga (Paíanga)	2.0	–
Transdniestra (Ruble)	6.51	–
Trinidad & Tobago (Dollar)	6.23	–
Tunisia (Dinar)	1.27	–
Turkey (Lira)	1,520,000	–
Turkmenistan (Manat)	5,150	–
Turks &Caicos uses U.S.Dollar	1.00	–
Tuvalu uses Australian Dollar	1.447	–
Uganda (Shilling)	1,720	–
Ukraine (Hryvnia)	5.32	–
United Arab Emirates (Dirham)	3.673	–
United Kingdom (Pound Sterling)	.563	–
Uruguay (Peso Uruguayo)	28.4	–
Uzbekistan (Som)	1,030	–
Vanuatu (Vatu)	117	–
Vatican City uses Euro	.83	–
Venezuela (Bolivar)	1,920	–
Vietnam (Dong)	15,775	–
Western Samoa (Tala)	2.75	–
Yemen (Rial)	185	–
Zambia (Kwacha)	4,750	–
Zimbabwe (Dollar)	5,600	–

INSTANT IDENTIFIER

Aachen (German States)

Albania

Austria

Baden (German States)

Brandenburg Ansbach (German States)

Finland

Jever (German States)

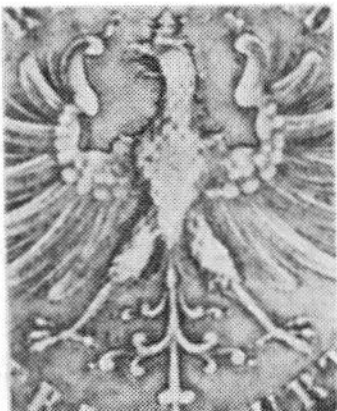
Frankfurt (German States)

Furstenberg (German States)

Geneva (Swiss Cantons)

German Empire

Montenegro (Yugoslavia)

Nürnberg (German States)

Milan (Italian States)

Prussia (German States)

Russia (Czarist) Russian Poland

Schwarzburg-Rudolstadt (German States)

Schwarzburg-Sondershausen (German States)

Serbia (Yugoslavia)

Teutonic Order (German States)

Genoa (Italian States)

Syrian Arab Republic

United Arab Republic (Egypt, Syria)

Arab Republic of Egypt Libya

Yemen Arab Republic

Bulgaria

Burma (Myanmar)

Ethiopia

Finland

Norway

Gorizia (Italian States)

Hannover (German States)

Hesse-Darmstadt (German States)

Hohenlohe-Neuenstein-Oehringen (German States)

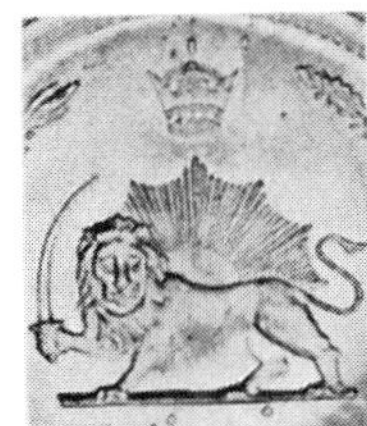
Iran (Persia)

Morocco

Siberia

Tibet (China)

Nepal

Morocco (AH1371-1951AD)

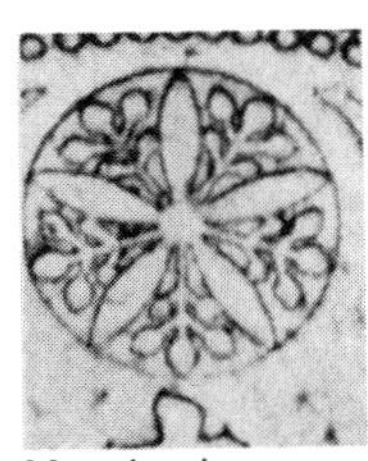
Manchoukuo (Puppet State-China)

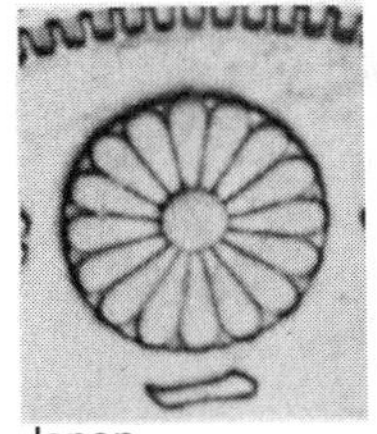
Japan

INSTANT IDENTIFIER

Hanau-Munzenberg (German States)

Nassau (German States)

Hesse-Cassel (German States)

Sri Lanka (Ceylon)

Tibet (China)

Utrecht (Netherlands)

Venice (Italian States)

Neuchatel (Swiss Cantons)

China (Empire-Provincial)

China (Empire-Provincial)

Japan

Japan

African States

Bretzenheim (German States)

Hall in Swabia (German States)

Greenland

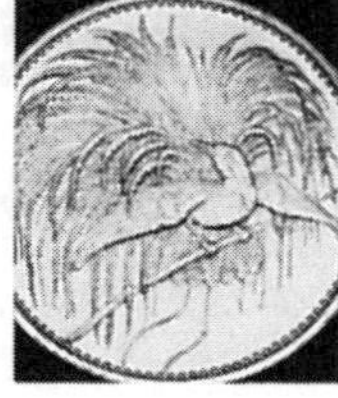
German New Guinea (Papua New Guinea)

Lithuania

Mongolia

Sudan

Algeria

Lowenstein-Wertheim (German States)

Maldive Islands

Afghanistan

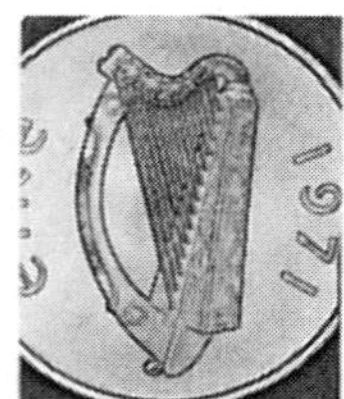
Ireland

Israel

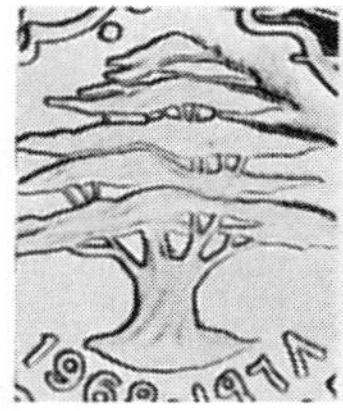
Lebanon

Papal States (Italian States)

Regensburg (German States)

Sweden

North Korea

CCCP-Russia

CCCP-Russia

Yugoslavia

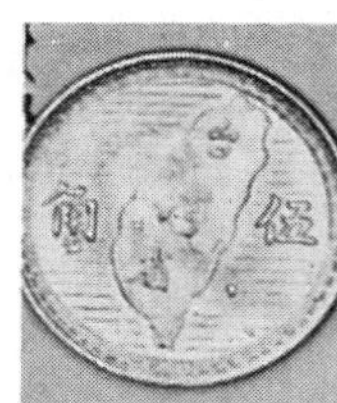
Taiwan (Rep. of China)

Mainz (German States)

Solms-Laubach (German States)

Ticino (Swiss Cantons)

Fugger (German States)

Naples & Sicily (Italian States)

Saxe-Saalfeld (German States)

Stolberg-Stolberg (German States)

INSTANT IDENTIFIER

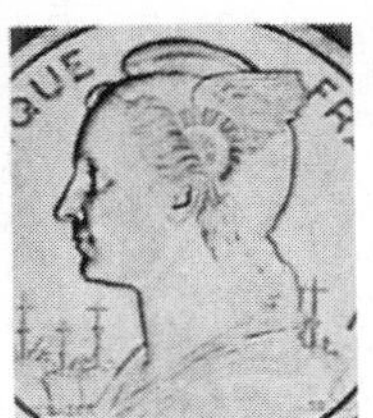
French Colonial

French Colonial

French Colonial

Bangladesh

Isle of Man
Sicily

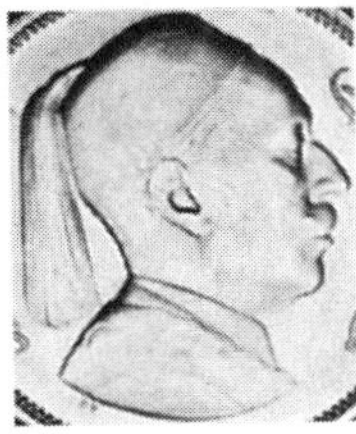
Libya

Anhalt-Bernburg
(German States)

Aargau
(Swiss Cantons)

Augsburg
(German States)

Basel
(Swiss Cantons)

Bavaria
(German States)

Brazil

Bremen
(German States)

Luzern
(Swiss Cantons)

Chur Pfalz
(German States)

Fulda
(German States)

Glarus
(Swiss Cantons)

Grand Duchy
of Warsaw
(Poland)

Graubunden
(Swiss Cantons)

Hamburg
(German States)

Lucca
(Italian States)

Hesse-Cassel
(German States)

Hesse-Homburg
(German States)

Hildesheim
(German States)

Hohenzollern-
Hechingen
(German States)

Hungary

Julich-Berg
(German States)

Gelderland
(Netherlands)

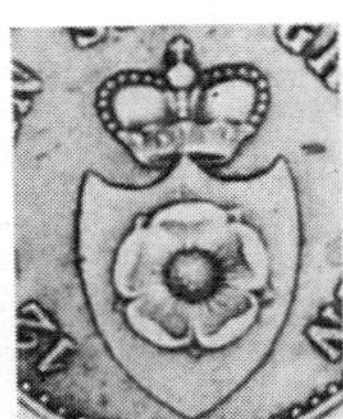
Lippe-Detmold
(German States)

Lübeck
(German States)

Mecklenburg-
Strelitz
(German States)

Oldenburg
(German States)

Passau
(German States)

Portugal

Vaud
(Swiss Cantons)

Anhalt
(Joint Coinage)
(German States)

Oldenburg
(German States)

Schwarzenberg
(German States)

Schaffhausen
(Swiss Cantons)

Paderborn
(German States)

Thurgau
(Swiss Cantons)

Westfrisia
(Netherlands)

INSTANT IDENTIFIER

Arenberg (German States)

Rhenish Confederation (German States)

Reuss-Greiz (German States)

Sardinia (Italian States)

Saxony (German States)

Schaumburg-Lippe (German States)

Schleswig-Holstein (German States)

St. Gall (Swiss Cantons)

Slovakia

Solothurn (Swiss Cantons)

Unterwalden (Nidwalden) (Swiss Cantons)

Württemberg (German States)

Würzburg (German States)

Zurich (Swiss Cantons)

Waldeck-Pyrmont (German States)

Iraq

Pakistan

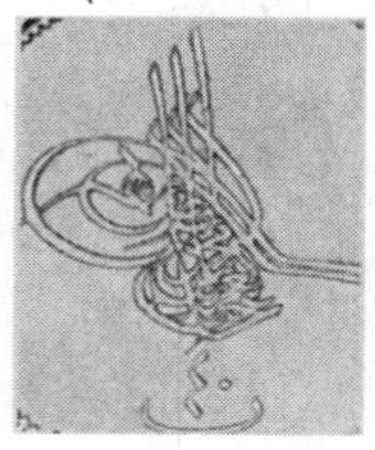
Turkey-Egypt Sudan, Algeria (Ottoman Empire)

Muscat & Oman, Oman

Saudi Arabia

Tunisia

Wismar (German States)

Order of Malta

Bamberg (German States)

Brunswick-Wolfenbüttel (German States)

Brunswick-Lüneburg (German States

Erfurt Mainz (German States)

Hannover (German States)

Eichstätt (German States)

Greece

Serbia

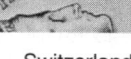

Switzerland

Albania

Thailand (Siam)

Israel

Japan (Dai Nippon)

South Korea

Sitten (Swiss Cantons)

Rostock (German States)

Saint Alban (German States)

English East India Co. (Sumatra)

China, Japan, Annam, Korea
(All Holed 'cash' coins look quite similar.)

Japan

Korea

STANDARD INTERNATIONAL NUMERAL SYSTEMS

PREPARED ESPECIALLY FOR THE STANDARD CATALOG OF WORLD COINS

WESTERN	0	½	1	2	3	4	5	6	7	8	9	10	50	100	500	1000
ROMAN			I	II	III	IV	V	VI	VII	VIII	IX	X	L	C	D	M
ARABIC-TURKISH	٠	١/٢	١	٢	٣	٤	٥	٦	٧	٨	٩	١٠	٥٠	١٠٠	٥٠٠	١٠٠٠
MALAY-PERSIAN	٠	١/٢	۱	۲	۳	۴	۵	٦ or ۶	۷	۸	۹	۱۰	۵۰	۱۰۰	۵۰۰	۱۰۰۰
EASTERN ARABIC	۰	۱/۲	۱	۲	۳	۴	۵	۶	۷	۸	۹	۱۰	۵۰	۱۰۰	۵۰۰	۱۰۰۰
HYERBAD ARABIC	٠	١/٢	١	٢	٣	۴	۵	۶	٧	٨	٩	١٠	۵٠	١٠٠	۵٠٠	١٠٠٠
INDIAN (Sanskrit)	०	१/२	१	२	३	४	५	६	७	८	९	१०	५०	१००	५००	१०००
ASSAMESE	০	১/২	১	২	৩	৪	৫	৬	৭	৮	৯	১০	৫০	১০০	৫০০	১০০০
BENGALI	০	১/২	১	২	৩	৪	৫	৬	৭	৮	৯	১০	৫০	১০০	৫০০	১০০০
GUJARATI	૦	૧/૨	૧	૨	૩	૪	૫	૬	૭	૮	૯	૧૦	૫૦	૧૦૦	૫૦૦	૧૦૦૦
KUTCH	०	१/२	१	२	३	४	५	६	७	८	९	१०	५०	१००	५००	१०००
DEVAVNAGRI	०	१/२	१	२	३	४	५	६ or ६	७	८	९ or ९	१०	५०	१००	५००	१०००
NEPALESE	०	१/२	१ or १	२	३	४	५ or ५	६	७	८ or ८	९ or ९	१०	५०	१००	५००	१०००
TIBETAN	༠	༡/༢	༡	༢	༣	༤	༥	༦	༧	༨	༩	༡༠	༥༠	༡༠༠	༥༠༠	༡༠༠༠
MONGOLIAN	᠐	᠑/᠒	᠑	᠒	᠓	᠔	᠕	᠖	᠗	᠘	᠙	᠑᠐	᠕᠐	᠑᠐᠐	᠕᠐᠐	᠑᠐᠐᠐
BURMESE	၀	၁/၂	၁	၂	၃	၄	၅	၆	၇	၈	၉	၁၀	၅၀	၁၀၀	၅၀၀	၁၀၀၀
THAI-LAO	๐	๑/๒	๑	๒	๓	๔	๕	๖	๗	๘	๙	๑๐	๕๐	๑๐๐	๕๐๐	๑๐๐๐
JAVANESE	꧐		꧑	꧒	꧓	꧔	꧕	꧖	꧗	꧘	꧙	꧑꧐	꧕꧐	꧑꧐꧐	꧕꧐꧐	꧑꧐꧐꧐
ORDINARY CHINESE JAPANESE-KOREAN	零	半	一	二	三	四	五	六	七	八	九	十	十五	百	百五	千
OFFICIAL CHINESE			壹	貳	叄	肆	伍	陸	柒	捌	玖	拾	拾伍	佰	佰伍	仟
COMMERCIAL CHINESE			〡	〢	〣	〤	〥	〦	〧	〨	〩	十	〥十	〡百	〥百	〡千
KOREAN		반	일	이	삼	사	오	육	칠	팔	구	십	오십	백	오백	천
GEORGIAN			ა	ბ	გ	დ	ე	ვ	ზ	ჱ	თ	ი	ნ	რ	ფ	ჩ
			11 ი	20 კ	30 ლ	40 მ	50 ნ	60 ჲ	70 ო	80 პ	90 ჟ	100 რ	200 ს 300 ტ	400 უ	600 ქ 700 ღ	800 ყ
ETHIOPIAN	◆		፩	፪	፫	፬	፭	፮	፯	፰	፱	፲	፶	፻	፭፻	፲፻
				20 ፳	30 ፴	40 ፵		60 ፷	70 ፸	80 ፹	90 ፺					
HEBREW			א	ב	ג	ד	ה	ו	ז	ח	ט	י	נ	ק	תק	
				20 כ	30 ל	40 מ		60 ס	70 ע	80 פ	90 צ		200 ר 300 ש	400 ת	600 תר 700 תש	800 תת
GREEK			Α	Β	Γ	Δ	Ε	ΣΤ	Ζ	Η	Θ	Ι	Ν	Ρ	Φ	Α
				20 Κ	30 Λ	40 Μ	60 Ξ	70 Ο	80 Π		200 Σ	300 Τ	400 Υ	600 Χ	700 Ψ	800 Ω

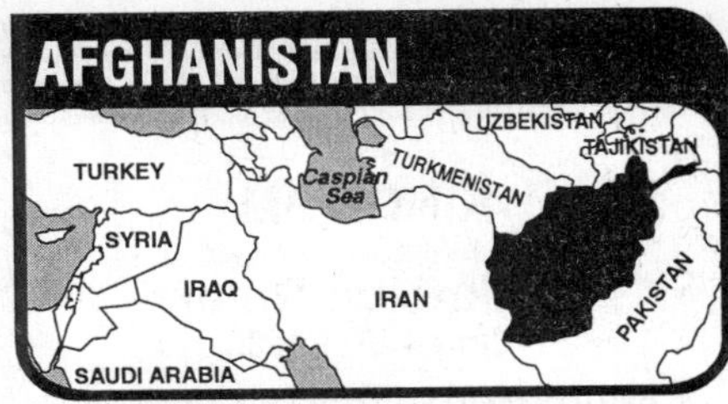

The Islamic State of Afghanistan, which occupies a mountainous region of Southwest Asia, has an area of 251,825 sq. mi. (652,090 sq. km.). Capital: Kabul. It is bordered by Iran, Pakistan, Turkmenistan, Uzbekistan, Tajikistan, and China's Sinkiang Province.

Because of its strategic position astride the ancient land route to India, Afghanistan (formerly known as Aryana and Khorasan) was invaded by Darius I, Alexander the Great, various Scythian tribes, the White Huns, the Arabs, the Turks, Genghis Khan, Tamerlane, the Mughals, the Persians, and in more recent times by Great Britain. It was a powerful empire under the Kushans, Hephthalites, Ghaznavids and Ghorids. The name Afghanistan, "Land of the Afghans," came into use in the eighteenth and nineteenth centuries to describe the realm of the Afghan kings. For a short period, this mountainous region was the easternmost frontier of the Iranian world, with strong cultural influences from the Turks and Mongols to the north and India to the south.

Previous to 1747, Afghan Kings ruled not only in Afghanistan, but also in India, of which Sher Shah Suri was one. Ahmad Shah Abdali, founder of the Durrani dynasty, established his rule at Qandahar in 1747. His clan was known as Saddozai. He conquered large territories in India and eastern Iran, which were lost by his grandson Shah Zaman. A new family, the Barakzai, drove the Durrani king out of Kabul, the capital, in 1819, but the Durranis were not eliminated completely until 1858. Further conflicts among the Barakzai prevented full unity until the reign of Abdur Rahman beginning in 1880.

Afghanistan's traditional coinage was much like that of its neighbors Iran and India. There were four major mints: Kabul, Qandahar, Balkh and Herat. The early Durranis also controlled mints in Iran and India. On gold and silver coins, the inscriptions in Persian (called *Dari* in Afghanistan) included the name of the mint city and, normally, of the ruler recognized there, but some issues are anonymous. The arrangement of the inscriptions, and frequently the name of the ruler, was different at each mint. Copper coins were controlled locally and usually did not name any ruler. For these reasons the coinage of each mint is treated separately. The relative values of gold, silver, and copper coins were not fixed but were determined in the marketplace.

In 1891 Abdur Rahman had a modern mint set up in Kabul using British minting machinery and the help of British advisors. The other mints were closed down, except for the issue of local coppers. The new system had 60 paisa equal one rupee; intermediate denominations also had special names. In 1901 the name Afghanistan appeared on coins for the first time. A decimal system, 100 puls to the afghani, was introduced in 1925. The gold amani, rated at 20 afghanis, was a bullion coin.

The national symbol on most coins of the kingdom is a stylized mosque, within which is seen the *mihrab*, a niche indicating the direction of Mecca, and the *minbar*, the pulpit, with a flight of steps leading up to it. Inscriptions in Pashtu were first used under the rebel Habibullah, but did not become standard until 1950.

Until 1919, coins were dated by the lunar Islamic Hejira calendar (AH), often with the king's regnal year as a second date.

RULERS

Names of rulers are shown in Perso-Arabic script in the style usually found on their coins; they are not always in a straight line.

DURRANI OR SADDOZAI DYNASTY

شاه زمان

Shah Zaman, AH1207-1216/1793-1801AD

شاه شجاع الملک

Shah Shuja al-Mulk, 1st reign, AH1216/1801AD (no coins)

محمود شاه

Mahmud Shah, 1st reign, AH1216-1218/1801-1803AD

قیصر شاه

Qaisar Shah, AH1218/1803AD

Shah Shuja al-Mulk, 2nd reign, AH1218-1224/1803-1808AD

Mahmud Shah, 2nd reign, AH1224-1233/1808-1817AD

ایوب شاه

Ayyub Shah, Puppet of Dost Muhammad, AH1233-1245/1817-1829AD

Sherdil Khan, AH1240-1242/1824-1826AD

Purdil Khan, AH1242-1245/1826-1829AD

سلطان محمد

Sultan Muhammad, at Peshawar AH1247-1250/1831-1834AD

کهندل خان

Kohandil Khan, 1st reign, at Qandahar AH1245-1254/1829-1838AD

Shah Shuja al-Mulk, as nominee of British East India Co., 3rd reign, AH1255-1258/1839-1842AD

فتح جنگ

Fath Jang AH1258/1842AD

شاپور شاه

Shahpur Shah AH1258/1842AD

Kohandil Khan, 2nd reign AH1259-1272/1843-1855AD

Rahamdil Khan, AH1272/1855AD

Succession at Kashmir, AH1221-1234

Qaisar Shah, AH1221-1223/1806-1808AD

شاه نورالدین

Ata Muhammad, called Shah Nur al-Din on coins, AH1223-1228/1808-1813AD

Azim Khan, coins in name of Mahmud Shah, AH1228-1234/1813-1818AD

Succession at Herat, AH1216-1298

Mahmud Shah, AH1216-1245/1801-1829AD

کامران شاه

Kamran Shah, AH1245-1258/1829-1842AD

یار محمد خان بارکزای

Yar Muhammad Khan Barakzai, AH1258-1267/1842-1851AD

محمد یوسف خان سادوزای

Muhammad Yusuf Khan Sadozai, AH1267-1272/1851-1856AD

Iranian Occupation of Herat (coins in name of Nasir al-Din Shah): AH1272-1280/1856-1863AD

Sher Ali, AH1280-1296/1863-1879AD

محمد یعقوب

Muhammad Yaqub AH1296-1298/1879-1881AD thereafter, as in the rest of Afghanistan

BARAKZAI DYNASTY

دوست محمد

Dost Muhammad, 1st reign, anonymous coinage, AH1239-1255/1824-1839AD

British Occupation, AH1255-1258/1839-1842AD

اکبر امیر

Dost Muhammad, at Qandahar, 2nd reign, "Akbar Amir" (Great King) in center of obv., AH1272-1280/1855-1863AD

شیر علی

Sher Ali, 1st reign, AH1280-1283/1863-1866AD

محمد افضل

Muhammad Afzal, AH1283-1284/1866-1867AD

محمد اعظم

Muhammad A'zam, AH1283-1285/1866-1868AD

Sher Ali, 2nd reign, AH1285-1296/1868-1879AD

Muhammad Yaqub, AH1296-1297/1879-1880AD

والی محمد

Wali Muhammad, at Kabul, AH1297/1880AD

والی شیر علی

Wali Sher Ali, at Qandahar, AH1297/1880AD

عبد الرحمن

Abdur Rahman, AH1297-1319/1880-1901AD

محمد اسحاق

Muhammad Ishaq, rebel in Balkh, AH1305-1306/1889AD

MINT NAMES

Coins were struck at numerous mints in Afghanistan and adjacent lands. These are listed below, together with their honorific titles, and shown in the style ordinarily found on the coins.

افغانستان

Afghanistan

احمد پور

Ahmadpur, see Bahawalpur

احمد شاهی

Ahmadshahi, see Qandahar

اشرف البلاد

'Ashraf al-Bilad', Most Noble of Cities

Ashraf-al-Bilad

Until AH1273, this mint was almost always given on the coins as *Ahmadshahi*, a name given it by Ahmad Shah in honor of himself in AH1171, often with the honorific *Ashraf al-Bilad* (meaning Most Noble of Cities'). On later issues, after AH1271, the traditional name *Qandahar* is generally used.

بد خشان

Badakhshan

بها ولپور

Bahawalpur

دار السرور

'Dar as-Surur', Abode of Happiness

بكهر

Bhakar

بلخ

Balkh,

ام البلاد

'Umm al-Bilad', Mother of Cities

Located in northern Afghanistan, Balkh bore the honorary epithet of *Umm al-Bilad*, 'Mother of Cities', because of its great age. It was taken by Ahmad Shah from the Amir of Bukhara in AH1180 (1765AD) and lost by Taimur Shah to the Uzbeks in AH1206 (1792AD).

ديره

Dera, Dera Ghazi Khan

The mint of Dera was located at Dera Ghazi Khan, taken by the Sikhs in AH1235 (1819AD), and now within Pakistan.

ديره جات

Derajat, Dera Isma'il Khan

The mint of Derajat was located at Dera Ismail Khan, which fell to the Sikhs in (AH1236) 1820-21AD. Issues in the name of Mahmud Shah dated AH1236 and later are actually Sikh issues. The Sikhs formally annexed Derajat in 1835AD (AH1281).

غزني

Ghazni

هرات

Herat

دارالنصرت

'Dar al-Nusrat', Seat of Victory

After AH1254, rupees ceased to be coined at Herat. Later emissions, beginning with anonymous issues of Yar Muhammad Khan, were 1/2 rupees. From AH1272-80 (1856-63AD), Herat was occupied by the Persians, who struck coins there in the name of Nasir al-Din Shah. The mint was closed in AH1308 (1891AD), except for a few later coins in copper.

دار السلطنة

'Dar as-Sultanat', Abode of the Sultanate

جلا ل ا باد

Jalalabad

كابل

Kabul,

دار الملك

'Dar al-Mulk', Abode of the King

'Dar as-Sultanat', see Herat

كشمير

Kashmir

خان اباد

Khanabad

لداخ

Ladakh, (Not usually clear on coins)

مشهد

Mashhad

Mashhad, entitled Muqaddas (holy), was the chief city of Iranian Khorasan. From AH1161/1748AD until AH1218/1803AD, it was the capital of the Afsharid principality, which remained under nominal Durrani suzerainty from AH1163/1750AD onwards. Coins were struck in the name of Durrani rulers in AH1163, 1168-1186, 1198-1218. Issues in the name of Iranian rulers will be listed in a future edition of this catalog under Iran.

ملتان

Multan,

دار الامان

'Dar al-Aman', Abode of Security

Multan was annexed by Ahmad Shah in AH1165/1752AD, and held under Afghan rule until lost to the Sikhs in AH1233/1818AD, except for an interval of Maratha control in AH1173/1759AD and Sikh control from AH1185-1194/1771-1780AD.

پشاور

Peshawar

Peshawar passed to Ahmad Shah after the death of Nadir Shah Afshar, who had seized it from the Mughals in AH1151/1738AD. It was lost to the Sikhs in AH1250/1834AD. Although the winter capital of the Durranis, it was never granted an honorific epithet.

قندهار

Qandahar, see Ahmadshahi

سرپل

Sar-i Pol

تاش قورغان

Tashqurghan

ANONYMOUS COPPER COINAGE

Afghan copper coins, prior to the beginning of machine-struck coinage in 1891, were not regulated by the central authorities. Mintmasters produced many types of hand-struck coinage including the use of old Afghan coins as blanks. Consequently, weights are quite random, and there are no denominations in the true sense of the term. All were known as falus or paisas, and lots of mixed sizes were accounted by weight. Every few years, sometimes every year, coppers were recalled and recoined, at a fee, often substantial, which was paid to the mintmaster and formed his salary. This accounts for the large number of overstruck pieces, which are generally less desirable than clear singly struck specimens.

Hundreds of varieties were issued at the principal mints of Kabul and Ahmadshahi/Qandahar, and the following listing is only a representation of what exists. It is arranged chronologically by mint, to the extent that coins bear dates. A more detailed, but still very fragmentary listing is given by W.H. Valentine, in Modern Copper Coins of the Muhammadan States. No attempt at a complete listing has ever been undertaken.

Prices are for well-struck specimens with clear design and date. Partial or overstruck coins are worth considerably less. Unrepresented types are worth about the same as listed pieces of the same mint.

IMPORTANT: Most types were used at one time or other at all mints. The type cannot therefore be used to determine the mint, which can ordinarily be ascertained only by reading the Persian inscription.

NOTE: Copper coins bearing the name of the issuing ruler are included under Named Hammered Coinage, below, by mint. For later anonymous issues, see the local coppers listed after the milled coinage.

NAMED HAMMERED COINAGE

Unlike the anonymous copper coinage, which was purely local, the silver and gold coins, as well as some of the early copper coins, bear the name or characteristic type of the ruler. Because the sequence of rulers often varied at different mint cities, each ruled by different princes, the coins are best organized according to mint. Each mint employed characteristic types and calligraphy, which continued from one ruler to the next. It is hoped that this system will facilitate identification of these coins.

The following listings include not only the mints situated in contiguous territories under Durrani and Barakzai rule for extended periods of time, but also mints in Kashmir or in other parts of India which the Afghans occupied for relatively brief intervals.

KINGDOM

Unknown Ruler
Circa 1801 - 1900

ANONYMOUS COPPER COINAGE

Mint: Kabul
KM# B79 FALUS
Copper, 20 mm. **Obv:** Arrowhead

Date	Mintage	Good	VG	F	VF	XF
AH1285	—	7.50	12.50	20.00	35.00	—

Mint: Ahmadshahi
KM# 11 FALUS
Copper **Obv:** Lion right

Date	Mintage	Good	VG	F	VF	XF
AH1227	—	8.00	15.00	25.00	40.00	—

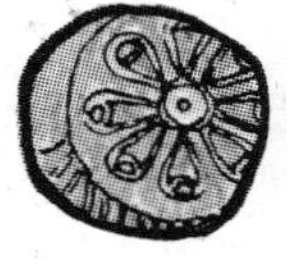

Mint: Ahmadshahi
KM# 14 FALUS
Copper **Obv:** 8-petalled flower

Date	Mintage	Good	VG	F	VF	XF
AH1240	—	8.00	15.00	25.00	40.00	—

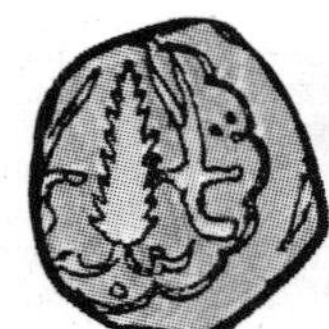

Mint: Ahmadshahi
KM# 15 FALUS
Copper **Obv:** Leaf between swords

Date	Mintage	Good	VG	F	VF	XF
AH1240	—	8.00	15.00	25.00	40.00	—

Mint: Ahmadshahi
KM# 16 FALUS
Copper **Obv:** Flower between swords

Date	Mintage	Good	VG	F	VF	XF
AH1241	—	8.00	15.00	25.00	40.00	—

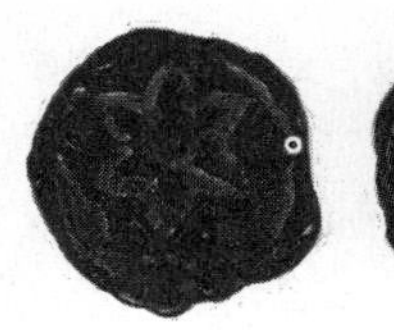

Mint: Ahmadshahi
KM# A20 FALUS
Copper **Obv:** Six-pointed star

Date	Mintage	Good	VG	F	VF	XF
AH(1)250	—	8.00	15.00	25.00	40.00	—

Mint: Ahmadshahi
KM# 20 FALUS
Copper **Obv:** Three swords

Date	Mintage	Good	VG	F	VF	XF
AH1249	—	9.00	17.00	27.00	45.00	—

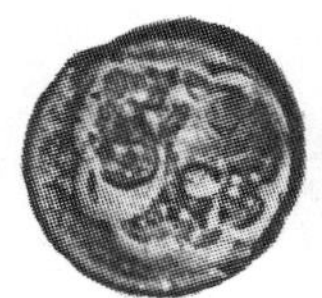

Mint: Ahmadshahi
KM# A21 FALUS
Copper **Obv. Legend:** "Falus" **Rev:** Mintname and date in toughra

Date	Mintage	Good	VG	F	VF	XF
AH1251	—	9.00	17.00	27.00	45.00	—

Mint: Ahmadshahi
KM# 21 FALUS
Copper **Obv:** Flower

Date	Mintage	Good	VG	F	VF	XF
AH1252	—	8.00	15.00	25.00	40.00	—

Mint: Ahmadshahi
KM# 22 FALUS
Copper **Obv:** Sunface

Date	Mintage	Good	VG	F	VF	XF
AH1253	—	8.00	15.00	25.00	40.00	—

Mint: Ahmadshahi
KM# 23 FALUS
Copper **Obv:** Crossed swords

Date	Mintage	Good	VG	F	VF	XF
ND	—	8.00	15.00	25.00	40.00	—
AH1253	—	8.00	15.00	25.00	40.00	—

Mint: Ahmadshahi
KM# 24 FALUS
Copper **Obv:** Leaf between two swords

Date	Mintage	Good	VG	F	VF	XF
AH1254	—	8.00	15.00	25.00	40.00	—

Mint: Ahmadshahi
KM# 25 FALUS
Copper **Obv:** Ornate borders

Date	Mintage	Good	VG	F	VF	XF
AH1255	—	8.00	15.00	25.00	45.00	—

Mint: Ahmadshahi
KM# 26 FALUS
Copper **Obv:** Two-bladed sword

Date	Mintage	Good	VG	F	VF	XF
AH1255	—	7.00	13.00	20.00	35.00	—

Mint: Ahmadshahi
KM# 27 FALUS
Copper **Obv:** Sword between two leaves

Date	Mintage	Good	VG	F	VF	XF
AH1256	—	7.00	13.00	20.00	35.00	—
AH1257	—	7.00	13.00	20.00	35.00	—

Mint: Ahmadshahi
KM# A28 FALUS
Copper **Obv:** Sword between two flowers

Date	Mintage	Good	VG	F	VF	XF
AH1262	—	9.00	15.00	25.00	45.00	—

Mint: Ahmadshahi
KM# 28 FALUS
Copper **Obv:** Bird

Date	Mintage	Good	VG	F	VF	XF
ND	—	7.00	13.00	20.00	35.00	—

Mint: Ahmadshahi
KM# 29 FALUS
Copper

Date	Mintage	Good	VG	F	VF	XF
AH1264	—	7.00	13.00	20.00	35.00	—

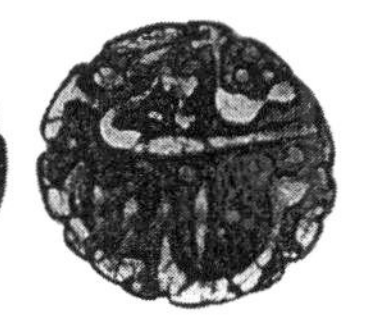

Mint: Ahmadshahi
KM# 29A FALUS
Copper **Obv:** Flower between two swords

Date	Mintage	Good	VG	F	VF	XF
AH1265	—	9.00	17.00	27.00	45.00	—

Mint: Badakhshan
KM# 30 FALUS
Copper **Rev. Legend:** "Badakhshan"

Date	Mintage	Good	VG	F	VF	XF
ND	—	10.00	20.00	32.00	50.00	—

Mint: Badakhshan
KM# 30A FALUS
Copper **Note:** Dated on both sides.

Date	Mintage	Good	VG	F	VF	XF
AH1302	—	8.00	15.00	25.00	45.00	—

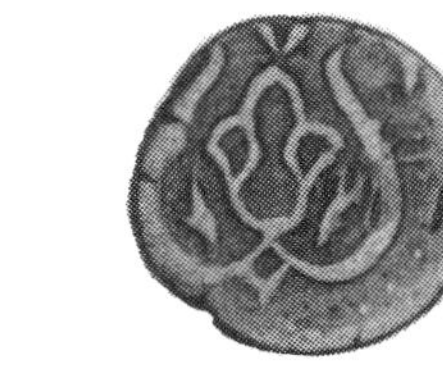

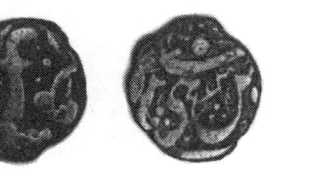

Mint: Balkh
KM# 31 FALUS
Copper **Obv:** Small flower within flower bulb

Date	Mintage	Good	VG	F	VF	XF
AH1221	—	9.00	17.00	27.00	45.00	—

Mint: Balkh
KM# 32 FALUS
Copper **Obv:** Flower between two swowrds

Date	Mintage	Good	VG	F	VF	XF
AH1228	—	6.00	12.00	20.00	35.00	—
AH1233	—	6.00	12.00	20.00	35.00	—
AH1234	—	6.00	12.00	20.00	35.00	—
AH1238	—	6.00	12.00	20.00	35.00	—

Mint: Balkh
KM# 35 FALUS
Copper **Obv:** Tiger right

Date	Mintage	Good	VG	F	VF	XF
AH1267	—	7.00	13.00	20.00	35.00	—

Mint: Balkh
KM# 36 FALUS
Copper **Obv:** Tiger right

Date	Mintage	Good	VG	F	VF	XF
AH1276	—	9.00	17.00	27.00	45.00	—

Mint: Balkh
KM# 37 FALUS
Copper **Obv:** Plant between two swords

Date	Mintage	Good	VG	F	VF	XF
AH1274	—	7.00	13.00	20.00	35.00	—
AH1275	—	7.00	13.00	20.00	35.00	—
AH1277	—	7.00	13.00	20.00	35.00	—
AH1278	—	7.00	13.00	20.00	35.00	—

Mint: Balkh
KM# 38.1 FALUS
Copper **Obv:** Small standing lion left **Rev:** Date

Date	Mintage	Good	VG	F	VF	XF
AH1295	—	7.00	13.00	20.00	35.00	—

Mint: Balkh
KM# 38.2 FALUS
Copper **Obv:** Mintname, small lion standing right **Note:** This type struck by machine over a number of years without change of date. Lion usually faces right, rarely left.

Date	Mintage	Good	VG	F	VF	XF
AH1295	—	4.00	8.00	12.00	16.00	—

Mint: Ghazni
KM# 39 FALUS
Copper

Date	Mintage	Good	VG	F	VF	XF
ND(ca 1860-80)	—	8.00	15.00	25.00	40.00	—

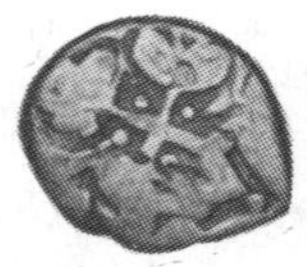

Mint: Ghazni
KM# 40 FALUS
Copper **Obv:** Floral design

Date	Mintage	Good	VG	F	VF	XF
ND	—	8.00	15.00	25.00	40.00	—

Mint: Herat
KM# 43 FALUS
Copper **Obv:** Leaf and two swords

Date	Mintage	Good	VG	F	VF	XF
AH1224	—	7.00	13.00	20.00	35.00	—
AH1226	—	7.00	13.00	20.00	35.00	—

Mint: Herat
KM# 44 FALUS
Copper **Obv:** Sunface

Date	Mintage	Good	VG	F	VF	XF
AH1227	—	7.00	13.00	20.00	35.00	—

Mint: Herat
KM# 45 FALUS
Copper **Obv:** Crab

Date	Mintage	Good	VG	F	VF	XF
AH(12)95	—	7.00	13.00	20.00	35.00	—

Mint: Herat
KM# 46 FALUS
Copper **Obv:** Floral scroll

Date	Mintage	Good	VG	F	VF	XF
AH1296	—	4.00	8.00	12.00	18.00	—

Mint: Herat
KM# 47 FALUS
Copper **Obv:** Fish ?

Date	Mintage	Good	VG	F	VF	XF
AH1297	—	4.00	8.00	12.00	18.00	—

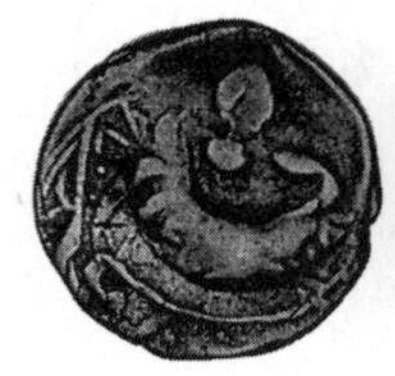

Mint: Herat
KM# 48 FALUS
Copper **Obv:** Crab **Rev:** Mintname and date

Date	Mintage	Good	VG	F	VF	XF
AH1297	—	4.00	8.00	12.00	18.00	—

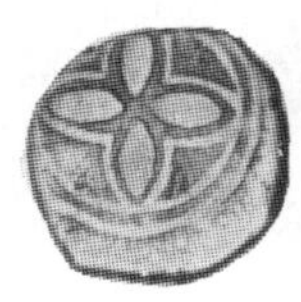

Mint: Herat
KM# 50 FALUS
Copper **Obv:** Four ovals in the shape of a cross within double circle

Date	Mintage	Good	VG	F	VF	XF
AH1304	—	5.00	9.00	15.00	25.00	—
AH1305	—	5.00	9.00	15.00	25.00	—

Mint: Jalalabad
KM# 52 FALUS
Copper **Obv:** Large flower

Date	Mintage	Good	VG	F	VF	XF
AHxxxx	—	15.00	30.00	50.00	75.00	—

Note: Crudely overstruck on earlier types

Mint: Kabul
KM# 53 FALUS
Copper **Obv:** Lily blossom

Date	Mintage	Good	VG	F	VF	XF
AH(1)222	—	8.00	15.00	25.00	40.00	—

Mint: Kabul
KM# A54 FALUS
Copper **Obv:** Leaf and two swords

Date	Mintage	Good	VG	F	VF	XF
AH1227	—	8.00	15.00	25.00	40.00	—

Mint: Kabul
KM# 54 FALUS
Copper **Obv:** Leaf and swords, "J" in center, large size

Date	Mintage	Good	VG	F	VF	XF
AH1229	—	8.00	15.00	25.00	40.00	—

Mint: Kabul
KM# 55.1 FALUS
Copper **Obv:** Flower

Date	Mintage	Good	VG	F	VF	XF
AH1232	—	8.00	15.00	25.00	40.00	—

Mint: Kabul
KM# 55.2 FALUS
Copper **Obv:** Two leaves between sword

Date	Mintage	Good	VG	F	VF	XF
AH1232	—	8.00	15.00	25.00	40.00	—

Mint: Kabul
KM# 55.3 FALUS
Copper **Obv:** Two ducks, necks intertwined within leaf **Rev. Legend:** "Falus..."

Date	Mintage	Good	VG	F	VF	XF
AH123x	—	10.00	20.00	35.00	50.00	—

Mint: Kabul
KM# 56 FALUS
Copper **Obv:** Crossed swords

Date	Mintage	Good	VG	F	VF	XF
AH1234	—	8.00	15.00	25.00	40.00	—

Mint: Kabul
KM# 57 FALUS
Copper **Obv:** Katar between two letter forms

Date	Mintage	Good	VG	F	VF	XF
AH1235	—	8.00	15.00	25.00	40.00	—

Mint: Kabul
KM# 58 FALUS
Copper **Obv:** Crossed swords

Date	Mintage	Good	VG	F	VF	XF
AH1236	—	8.00	15.00	25.00	40.00	—

Mint: Kabul
KM# 59 FALUS
Copper **Obv:** Star between two swords

Date	Mintage	Good	VG	F	VF	XF
AH1236	—	8.00	15.00	25.00	40.00	—
ND	—	8.00	15.00	25.00	40.00	—

Mint: Kabul
KM# 60 FALUS
Copper **Obv:** Flower between two leaves

Date	Mintage	Good	VG	F	VF	XF
AH1236	—	8.00	16.00	27.00	45.00	—

Mint: Kabul
KM# 62 FALUS
Copper **Obv:** Two ducks, necks intertwined

Date	Mintage	Good	VG	F	VF	XF
AH1238	—	9.00	17.00	30.00	50.00	—

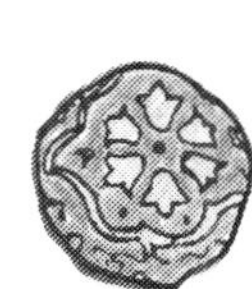

Mint: Kabul
KM# 66 FALUS
Copper **Obv:** Floral pattern

Date	Mintage	Good	VG	F	VF	XF
AH12xx	—	7.00	13.00	20.00	35.00	—
ND	—	7.00	13.00	20.00	35.00	—

Mint: Kabul
KM# 67 FALUS
Copper **Obv:** Flower between two swords

Date	Mintage	Good	VG	F	VF	XF
AH1249	—	9.00	17.00	27.00	45.00	—

Mint: Kabul
KM# 68 FALUS
Copper **Obv:** Sword and stars

Date	Mintage	Good	VG	F	VF	XF
AH1252	—	8.00	15.00	25.00	40.00	—
AH126x	—	8.00	15.00	25.00	40.00	—
ND	—	8.00	15.00	25.00	40.00	—

Mint: Kabul
KM# 69 FALUS
Copper **Obv:** Sword right

Date	Mintage	Good	VG	F	VF	XF
AH1258	—	8.00	15.00	25.00	40.00	—

Mint: Kabul
KM# 70 FALUS
Copper **Obv:** Sword and floral ornaments

Date	Mintage	Good	VG	F	VF	XF
AH1254	—	8.00	15.00	25.00	40.00	—
AH1258	—	8.00	15.00	25.00	40.00	—

Mint: Kabul
KM# 71 FALUS
Copper **Obv:** Flower

Date	Mintage	Good	VG	F	VF	XF
AH1254	—	8.00	15.00	25.00	40.00	—

Mint: Kabul
KM# 72 FALUS
Copper **Obv:** Flower and swords

Date	Mintage	Good	VG	F	VF	XF
AH1257	—	8.00	15.00	25.00	40.00	—
AH1258	—	8.00	15.00	25.00	40.00	—

Mint: Kabul
KM# 73 FALUS
Copper **Obv:** Sword

Date	Mintage	Good	VG	F	VF	XF
AH1254	—	8.00	15.00	25.00	40.00	—

Mint: Kabul
KM# 75 FALUS
Copper **Obv:** Flower and swords

Date	Mintage	Good	VG	F	VF	XF
AH1261	—	8.00	15.00	25.00	40.00	—
AH1265	—	8.00	15.00	25.00	40.00	—

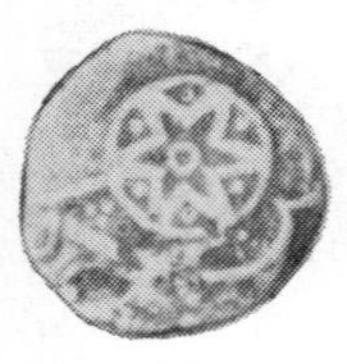

Mint: Kabul
KM# A76 FALUS
Copper **Obv:** Star within circle

Date	Mintage	Good	VG	F	VF	XF
AHxxxx	—	8.00	15.00	25.00	40.00	—

Mint: Kabul
KM# 76 FALUS
Copper **Obv:** Flower within chevron border

Date	Mintage	Good	VG	F	VF	XF
AH1261	—	9.00	17.00	27.00	45.00	—

Mint: Kabul
KM# A77 FALUS
Copper **Obv:** Flower within star

Date	Mintage	Good	VG	F	VF	XF
AH1262	—	9.00	17.00	27.00	45.00	—

Mint: Kabul
KM# 77 FALUS
Copper **Obv:** Floral spray

Date	Mintage	Good	VG	F	VF	XF
AH1267	—	9.00	17.00	27.00	45.00	—

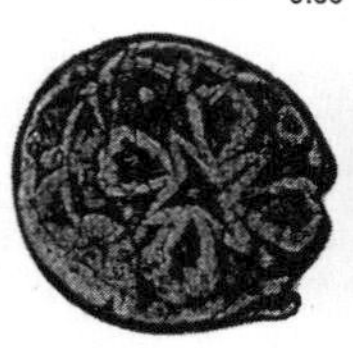

Mint: Kabul
KM# A78 FALUS
Copper **Obv:** Four-petalled flower

Date	Mintage	Good	VG	F	VF	XF
AH1268	—	9.00	17.00	27.00	45.00	—

Mint: Kabul
KM# B78 FALUS
Copper **Obv:** Three-petalled flower

Date	Mintage	Good	VG	F	VF	XF
AH1268	—	8.00	15.00	25.00	40.00	—

Mint: Kabul
KM# 78 FALUS
Copper **Obv:** Branch in cartouche

Date	Mintage	Good	VG	F	VF	XF
AH1271	—	9.00	17.00	27.00	45.00	—

Mint: Kabul
KM# A79 FALUS
Copper **Obv:** "Mihrabi" in square

Date	Mintage	Good	VG	F	VF	XF
AH1285	—	9.00	17.00	27.00	45.00	—

Mint: Kabul
KM# 79 FALUS
Copper **Obv:** Flower

Date	Mintage	Good	VG	F	VF	XF
ND	—	9.00	17.00	27.00	45.00	—

Mint: Khanabad
KM# 80 FALUS
Copper

Date	Mintage	Good	VG	F	VF	XF
AH1301	—	12.50	25.00	40.00	60.00	—
AH1302	—	12.50	25.00	40.00	60.00	—

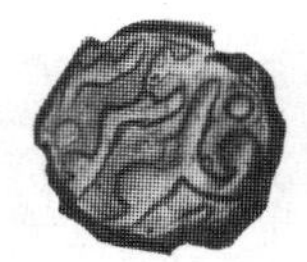

Mint: Khanabad
KM# 81 FALUS
Copper

Date	Mintage	Good	VG	F	VF	XF
AH(1)302	—	9.00	17.00	27.00	45.00	—

Mint: Khanabad
KM# 84A FALUS
Copper

Date	Mintage	Good	VG	F	VF	XF
ND	—	9.00	17.00	27.00	45.00	—

Mint: Peshawar
KM# 83 FALUS
Copper **Obv:** Four-petalled flower

Date	Mintage	Good	VG	F	VF	XF
AH1249	—	9.00	17.00	27.00	45.00	—

Mint: Peshawar
KM# 84 FALUS
Copper

Date	Mintage	Good	VG	F	VF	XF
ND	—	9.00	17.00	27.00	45.00	—

Mint: Qandahar
KM# A85 FALUS
Copper **Obv:** Flower between two swords

Date	Mintage	Good	VG	F	VF	XF
AH1202	—	12.50	25.00	40.00	60.00	—

Mint: Qandahar
KM# 85 FALUS
Copper **Obv:** Large date and legend

Date	Mintage	Good	VG	F	VF	XF
AH1228	—	7.00	13.00	20.00	35.00	—

Mint: Qandahar
KM# A87 FALUS
Copper **Obv:** Leaf between two swords **Rev:** Mint name and date

Date	Mintage	Good	VG	F	VF	XF
AH1230	—	7.00	13.00	20.00	35.00	—

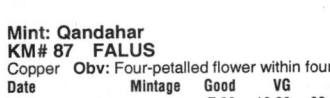

Mint: Qandahar
KM# 87 FALUS
Copper **Obv:** Four-petalled flower within four swords

Date	Mintage	Good	VG	F	VF	XF
ND	—	7.00	13.00	20.00	35.00	—

Mint: Qandahar
KM# 88 FALUS
Copper **Obv:** Three flowers on one stem **Rev:** Sword

Date	Mintage	Good	VG	F	VF	XF
ND	—	8.00	15.00	25.00	40.00	—

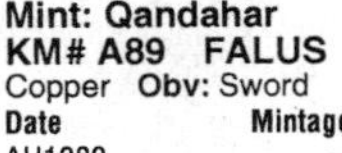

Mint: Qandahar
KM# A89 FALUS
Copper **Obv:** Sword

Date	Mintage	Good	VG	F	VF	XF
AH1282	—	8.00	15.00	25.00	40.00	—

Mint: Qandahar
KM# 90 FALUS
Copper **Obv:** Flower within wreath

Date	Mintage	Good	VG	F	VF	XF
AH1294	—	4.00	8.00	12.00	18.00	—

Mint: Qandahar
KM# 91 FALUS
Copper **Obv:** Hand of Ali?

Date	Mintage	Good	VG	F	VF	XF
AH1295	—	4.00	8.00	12.00	18.00	—

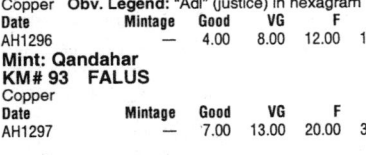

Mint: Qandahar
KM# 95 FALUS
Copper **Obv. Legend:** "Adl" (justice) in hexagram

Date	Mintage	Good	VG	F	VF	XF
AH1296	—	4.00	8.00	12.00	18.00	—

Mint: Qandahar
KM# 93 FALUS
Copper

Date	Mintage	Good	VG	F	VF	XF
AH1297	—	7.00	13.00	20.00	35.00	—

Mint: Qandahar
KM# 96 FALUS
Copper **Obv:** Peacock

Date	Mintage	Good	VG	F	VF	XF
AH1297	—	4.00	8.00	12.00	18.00	—

Mint: Qandahar
KM# 97 FALUS
Copper **Obv:** Flower

Date	Mintage	Good	VG	F	VF	XF
AH1300	—	8.00	15.00	25.00	40.00	—

Mint: Qandahar
KM# A101.1 FALUS
Copper **Note:** Crude large flan; issued during the British Occupation of Qandahar 1878-79.

Date	Mintage	Good	VG	F	VF	XF
AH1296	—	20.00	40.00	65.00	100	—

Mint: Qandahar
KM# A101.2 FALUS
Copper **Note:** Crude large flan; issued during the British Occupation of Qandahar 1878-79.

Date	Mintage	Good	VG	F	VF	XF
AH(1296)	—	21.50	42.50	70.00	110	—

Mint: Qandahar
KM# B101 FALUS
Copper **Obv:** Four leaves joined

Date	Mintage	Good	VG	F	VF	XF
AH1307	—	6.00	12.00	20.00	35.00	—

Mint: Qandahar
KM# D101 FALUS
Copper **Obv:** Crown

Date	Mintage	Good	VG	F	VF	XF
AH1308	—	18.00	35.00	60.00	90.00	—

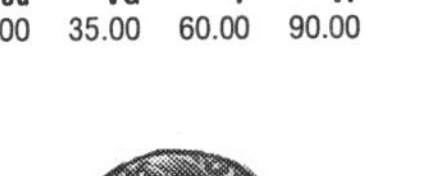

Mint: Qandahar
KM# 89 FALUS
Copper **Obv:** Flower with fancy border **Note:** Issued during the British Occupation of Qandahar 1878-79.

Date	Mintage	Good	VG	F	VF	XF
AH1289	—	11.00	22.00	35.00	55.00	—

Note: This type evidently served as the prototype for the British Occupation issue dated AH1296, KM#94

Mint: Qandahar
KM# 94 FALUS
Copper **Obv:** Crown **Note:** Issued during the British Occupation of Qandahar 1878-79.

Date	Mintage	Good	VG	F	VF	XF
AH1296	—	18.00	35.00	55.00	90.00	—

Mint: Qandahar
KM# C101 FALUS
Copper **Obv:** Five-pointed star **Note:** Several varieties exist.

Date	Mintage	Good	VG	F	VF	XF
AH1308	—	6.00	12.00	20.00	35.00	—

Mint: Qandahar
KM# 92 FALUS
Copper **Obv:** Leaf between two swords **Note:** Size varies 17-22 mm.

Date	Mintage	Good	VG	F	VF	XF
AH1295	—	4.00	8.00	12.00	18.00	—

Mint: Sar-i Pol
KM# 98 FALUS
Copper **Obv:** Lion

Date	Mintage	Good	VG	F	VF	XF
AH1297	—	12.50	25.00	40.00	60.00	—
ND	—	12.50	25.00	40.00	60.00	—

Mint: Tashqurghan
KM# 99 FALUS
Copper **Obv:** Stem and leaves

Date	Mintage	Good	VG	F	VF	XF
AH1300	—	11.00	22.00	35.00	55.00	—

Mint: Tashqurghan
KM# 100 FALUS
Copper **Obv:** Flower

Date	Mintage	Good	VG	F	VF	XF
AH1300	—	15.00	27.50	45.00	70.00	—

Taimur Shah
AH1186-1207 / 1772-1793AD - King
HAMMERED COINAGE

Mint: Herat
KM# 383.2 RUPEE
Silver **Rev:** Mint and epithet **Note:** Postumous issue struck by Mahmud Shah; weight varies: 11.20-11.60 grams.

Date	Mintage	Good	VG	F	VF	XF
AH1216	—	—	6.00	12.00	20.00	30.00
AH1221	—	—	6.00	12.00	20.00	30.00

Mint: Herat
KM# 384 RUPEE
Silver **Note:** Postumous issue struck by Mahmud Shah; weight varies: 11.20-11.60 grams.

Date	Mintage	Good	VG	F	VF	XF
AH1216	—	—	—	—	—	—

Shah Zaman
AH1207-1216 / 1793-1801AD
HAMMERED COINAGE

Mint: Bakhar
KM# 303 RUPEE
Silver **Note:** Weight varies: 11.40-11.60 grams.

Date	Mintage	Good	VG	F	VF	XF
AH1216	—	—	12.00	24.00	40.00	60.00

Mint: Derajat
KM# 358 RUPEE
Silver **Note:** Weight varies: 10.80-11.20 grams.

Date	Mintage	Good	VG	F	VF	XF
AH1215//8	—	—	12.50	30.00	40.00	50.00

Mint: Kabul Mint
KM# B444 RUPEE
Silver **Obv:** First couplet with new arrangement in inscription **Note:** Occasionally found on wide planchets. Weight varies 11.40-11.65 grams.

Date	Mintage	Good	VG	F	VF	XF
AH1215//7	—	2.50	6.00	12.00	20.00	30.00
AH1215//8	—	2.50	6.00	12.00	20.00	30.00
AH1216//8	—	2.50	6.00	12.00	20.00	30.00

Mint: Peshawar
KM# 713 RUPEE
Silver **Obv:** First couplet in circle, second in margin **Note:** Weight varies: 11.40-11.60 grams.

Date	Mintage	Good	VG	F	VF	XF
AH1215//9	—	3.50	9.00	18.00	30.00	45.00
AH1216//9	—	3.50	9.00	18.00	30.00	45.00

Mahmud Shah
AH1216-1218 / 1801-1803AD First reign
HAMMERED COINAGE

Mint: Kashmir
KM# 580 FRACTIONAL FALUS
Copper **Note:** Weight varies: 3.80-4.40 grams.

Date	Mintage	Good	VG	F	VF	XF
AH1217//2	—	8.00	12.00	18.00	30.00	—

Mint: Kashmir
KM# 583 FALUS
10.2000 g., Copper, 25.5 mm.

Date	Mintage	Good	VG	F	VF	XF
AH1216//1	—	9.00	14.00	20.00	35.00	—

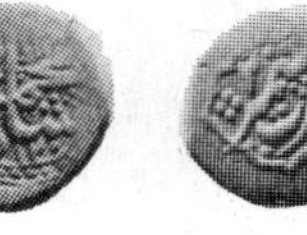

Mint: Kashmir
KM# 586 1/4 RUPEE
Silver **Note:** Weight varies: 2.50-2.60 grams.

Date	Mintage	Good	VG	F	VF	XF
AH1217//2	—	7.00	17.50	35.00	60.00	90.00

Mint: Ahmadpur
KM# 108 LIGHT RUPEE
Silver **Note:** Weight varies: 8.20-8.40 grams.

Date	Mintage	Good	VG	F	VF	XF
AH1217	—	6.00	15.00	30.00	50.00	75.00
AH121x	—	6.00	15.00	30.00	50.00	75.00

Note: Posthumous issue; Reverse only shown

Mint: Ahmadshahi
KM# 143 RUPEE
Silver **Note:** Weight varies: 11.40-11.60 grams.

Date	Mintage	Good	VG	F	VF	XF
AH1216	—	5.50	13.50	30.00	45.00	65.00
AH1217//2	—	5.50	13.50	27.00	45.00	65.00
AH1217//3	—	5.50	13.50	27.00	45.00	65.00
AH1218//3	—	5.50	13.50	27.00	45.00	65.00

Mint: Bahawalpur
KM# 243 RUPEE
Silver **Rev:** Mintname and "Julus" formula **Note:** Weight varies: 11.40-11.60 grams.

Date	Mintage	Good	VG	F	VF	XF
AH1217//1	—	5.50	13.50	27.00	45.00	65.00
AH1217//2	—	5.50	13.50	27.00	45.00	65.00
AH1218//2	—	5.50	13.50	27.00	45.00	65.00

Mint: Bahawalpur - Dar as-Surur
KM# 242 RUPEE
Silver **Rev:** Mintname and epithet **Note:** Weight varies: 11.40-11.60 grams.

Date	Mintage	Good	VG	F	VF	XF
AH1217	—	8.00	20.00	40.00	65.00	100

Mint: Bakhar
KM# 308 RUPEE

Silver **Note:** Weight varies: 11.40-11.60 grams. Broad flan, nazarana style.

Date	Mintage	Good	VG	F	VF	XF
ND(1801-03)	—	18.00	45.00	90.00	150	225

Mint: Dera - Dera Ghazi Khan
KM# 338 RUPEE
Silver **Note:** Weight varies: 11.40-11.60 grams.

Date	Mintage	Good	VG	F	VF	XF
AH1216//1	—	5.50	12.50	27.00	45.00	65.00
AH1217//2	—	5.50	12.50	27.00	45.00	65.00

Mint: Derajat
KM# 363 RUPEE
Silver **Note:** Weight varies: 11.00-11.20 grams.

Date	Mintage	Good	VG	F	VF	XF
AH1216//1	—	6.00	15.00	30.00	50.00	75.00
AH1217//2	—	6.00	15.00	30.00	50.00	75.00

Mint: Kabul
KM# 448 RUPEE
Silver **Note:** Weight varies: 11.40-11.60 grams.

Date	Mintage	Good	VG	F	VF	XF
AH1216//1	—	4.00	10.00	20.00	35.00	52.50
AH1217//1	—	4.00	10.00	20.00	35.00	52.50
AH1217//2	—	4.00	10.00	20.00	35.00	52.50
AH1218//2	—	4.00	10.00	20.00	35.00	52.50

Mint: Kashmir
KM# 588 RUPEE
Silver **Note:** Weight varies: 10.80-11.00 grams.

Date	Mintage	Good	VG	F	VF	XF
AH1216//1	—	4.50	10.00	15.00	25.00	37.50
AH1217//2	—	4.50	10.00	15.00	25.00	37.50
AH1218//3	—	4.50	10.00	15.00	25.00	37.50

Mint: Kashmir
KM# 589 RUPEE
Silver **Note:** Weight varies: 10.80-11.00 grams.

Date	Mintage	Good	VG	F	VF	XF
AH1218//3	—	4.50	10.00	18.00	30.00	45.00

Mint: Multan - Dar al-Aman
KM# 668 RUPEE
Silver **Note:** Weight varies: 11.50-11.60 grams.

Date	Mintage	Good	VG	F	VF	XF
AH1216//1	—	7.00	17.50	35.00	60.00	90.00
AH1218//1	—	7.00	17.50	35.00	60.00	90.00

Mint: Peshawar
KM# 718 RUPEE
Silver **Rev:** Mint name with "Julus" formula **Note:** Weight varies: 11.40-11.60 grams.

Date	Mintage	Good	VG	F	VF	XF
AH1216//1	—	2.50	6.00	12.00	20.00	30.00

Mint: Peshawar
KM# 719 RUPEE
Silver **Rev:** Mint name **Note:** Weight varies: 11.40-11.60 grams.

Date	Mintage	Good	VG	F	VF	XF
AH1217//2	—	2.50	6.00	12.00	20.00	30.00
AH1218//3	—	2.50	6.00	12.00	20.00	30.00

Mint: Bahawalpur
KM# 244 2 RUPEES
Silver **Note:** Weight varies: 23.00-23.20 grams.

Date	Mintage	Good	VG	F	VF	XF
AH1217//1	—	25.00	60.00	120	200	300

Note: Regnal year written as numeral, not "Ahad"

Mint: Ahmadshahi
KM# 144 ASHRAFI
3.5000 g., Gold, 25 mm.

Date	Mintage	Good	VG	F	VF	XF
AH1218//3 Rare	—	—	—	—	—	—

Mint: Ahmadshahi
KM# 145 MOHUR
10.9000 g., Gold

Date	Mintage	Good	VG	F	VF	XF
AH1218//2	—	—	150	250	400	600
AH1218//3	—	—	150	250	400	600

Mint: Bahawalpur
KM# 245 MOHUR
11.0000 g., Gold

Date	Mintage	Good	VG	F	VF	XF
AH1218//2	—	—	200	325	500	800

Mint: Kabul
KM# 450 MOHUR
Gold **Note:** Weight varies: 10.80-11.00 grams.

Date	Mintage	Good	VG	F	VF	XF
AH-//1	—	—	220	350	550	800
AH1218//3	—	—	220	350	550	800

Mint: Bahawalpur
KM# 246 2 MOHURS
Gold **Note:** Weight varies: 22.00-22.20 grams.

Date	Mintage	Good	VG	F	VF	XF
AH1217//1	—	—	700	1,150	1,750	2,500
AH1217//2	—	—	700	1,150	1,750	2,500
AH1218//2	—	—	700	1,150	1,750	2,500

Qaisar Shah
AH1218 / 1803AD

HAMMERED COINAGE

Mint: Ahmadshahi
KM# 148 RUPEE
Silver **Note:** Rebel issue; weight varies: 11.50-11.60 grams.

Date	Mintage	Good	VG	F	VF	XF
AH1218//1	—	8.50	21.50	42.50	70.00	110

Mint: Ahmadshahi
KM# 149 MOHUR
10.9000 g., Gold **Note:** Rebel issue.

Date	Mintage	Good	VG	F	VF	XF
AH1218	—	—	600	1,000	1,500	1,750

Shah Shuja al-Mulk
AH1218-1224 / 1803-1808AD Second reign

HAMMERED COINAGE

Mint: Balkh
KM# 274 FALUS
Copper

Date	Mintage	F	VF	XF	Unc
AH1218 Rare	—	—	—	—	—

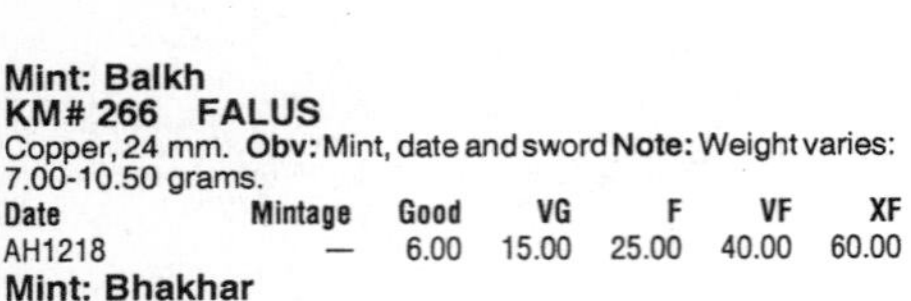

Mint: Balkh
KM# 266 FALUS
Copper, 24 mm. **Obv:** Mint, date and sword **Note:** Weight varies: 7.00-10.50 grams.

Date	Mintage	Good	VG	F	VF	XF
AH1218	—	6.00	15.00	25.00	40.00	60.00

Mint: Bhakhar
KM# 308a FALUS
Copper

Date	Mintage	Good	VG	F	VF	XF
AH1218	—	3.50	7.00	15.00	25.00	40.00
AH1222	—	3.50	7.00	15.00	25.00	40.00

Mint: Kashmir
KM# 594 FALUS
Copper **Rev:** Sword **Note:** Weight varies: 7.40-9.00 grams.

Date	Mintage	Good	VG	F	VF	XF
AH1218//1	—	8.00	12.00	20.00	35.00	—
AH-//2	—	8.00	12.00	20.00	35.00	—

Mint: Kashmir
KM# A595 FALUS
Copper **Rev:** Two swords **Note:** Weight varies: 7.40-9.00 grams.

Date	Mintage	Good	VG	F	VF	XF
AH1219	—	10.00	15.00	25.00	35.00	—

Mint: Kashmir
KM# 595 FALUS
Copper **Rev:** Crossed swords **Note:** Weight varies: 7.40-9.00 grams.

Date	Mintage	Good	VG	F	VF	XF
AH(12)19	—	8.00	12.00	20.00	35.00	—

Mint: Kashmir
KM# 596 FALUS
Copper **Note:** Weight varies: 7.40-9.00 grams.

Date	Mintage	Good	VG	F	VF	XF
AH1220//3	—	8.00	12.00	20.00	35.00	—

Mint: Kashmir
KM# 597 FALUS
Copper **Rev:** Sword **Note:** Weight varies: 7.40-9.00 grams.

Date	Mintage	Good	VG	F	VF	XF
AH1221//4	—	8.00	12.00	20.00	35.00	—

Mint: Peshawar
KM# 720 1/10 RUPEE
1.0000 g., Silver

Date	Mintage	Good	VG	F	VF	XF
AH1227//7 Rare	—	—	—	—	—	—

Mint: Ahmadshahi
KM# 151 1/4 RUPEE
Silver **Note:** Weight varies: 2.80-3.00 grams.

Date	Mintage	Good	VG	F	VF	XF
AH1218//2	—	7.00	17.50	35.00	60.00	90.00

Mint: Ahmadshahi
KM# 153 RUPEE
Silver **Note:** Weight varies: 11.40-11.60 grams. Varieties of the obverse exist.

Date	Mintage	Good	VG	F	VF	XF
AH1218//3	—	2.50	6.00	12.00	20.00	30.00
AH1219//1	—	2.50	6.00	12.00	20.00	30.00
AH1220//2	—	2.50	6.00	12.00	20.00	30.00
AH1221//3	—	2.50	6.00	12.00	20.00	30.00
AH1222	—	2.50	6.00	12.00	20.00	30.00
AH1223	—	2.50	6.00	12.00	20.00	30.00
AH1224	—	2.50	6.00	12.00	20.00	30.00

Mint: Bahawalpur
KM# 253 RUPEE
Silver **Note:** Weight varies: 11.20-11.60 grams.

Date	Mintage	Good	VG	F	VF	XF
AH1218//1	—	6.00	15.00	30.00	50.00	75.00
AH1218//2	—	6.00	15.00	30.00	50.00	75.00
AH1219//1	—	6.00	15.00	30.00	50.00	75.00
AH1220	—	6.00	15.00	30.00	50.00	75.00
AH1221	—	6.00	15.00	30.00	50.00	75.00
AH1212	—	6.50	16.50	35.00	55.00	82.50
Note: Error for 1221						
AH1222	—	6.00	15.00	30.00	50.00	75.00

Mint: Bakhar
KM# 309.1 RUPEE
Silver **Note:** Weight varies: 11.40-11.60 grams.

Date	Mintage	Good	VG	F	VF	XF
AH1218	—	5.00	12.50	25.00	40.00	52.50
AH1219	—	5.00	12.50	25.00	40.00	52.50
AH1220	—	5.00	12.50	25.00	40.00	52.50
AH1221//12	—	5.00	12.50	25.00	40.00	52.50
AH1222	—	5.00	12.50	25.00	40.00	52.50
AH1223	—	5.00	12.50	25.00	40.00	52.50
AH1224	—	5.00	12.50	25.00	40.00	52.50

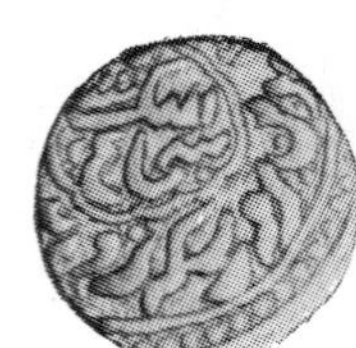 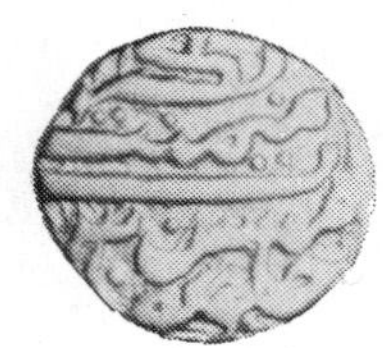

Mint: Bakhar
KM# 309.2 RUPEE
Silver **Obv:** King's name circle within couplet **Note:** Weight varies: 11.40-11.60 grams.

Date	Mintage	Good	VG	F	VF	XF
AH1223	—	18.00	45.00	90.00	150	225

Mint: Dera - Dera Ghazi Khan
KM# 343 RUPEE
Silver **Note:** Weight varies: 11.40-11.60 grams.

Date	Mintage	Good	VG	F	VF	XF
ND(1803-04)//1	—	5.00	13.50	27.50	45.00	67.50
ND(1807-08)//4	—	5.00	13.50	27.50	45.00	67.50
ND(1808-09)//5	—	5.00	13.50	27.50	45.00	67.50

Mint: Derajat
KM# 368 RUPEE
Silver, 20-21.5 mm. **Note:** Weight varies: 10.80-11.20 grams. Size varies.

Date	Mintage	Good	VG	F	VF	XF
AH1218//1	—	3.50	9.00	18.00	30.00	45.00
AH1218//2	—	3.50	9.00	18.00	30.00	45.00
AH1219//2	—	3.50	9.00	18.00	30.00	45.00
AH1220//2	—	3.50	9.00	18.00	30.00	45.00
AH1220//3	—	3.50	9.00	18.00	30.00	45.00
AH1221//3	—	3.50	9.00	18.00	30.00	45.00
AH1221//4	—	3.50	9.00	18.00	30.00	45.00
AH1221//5	—	3.50	9.00	18.00	30.00	45.00
AH122x//6	—	3.50	9.00	18.00	30.00	45.00
AH1223	—	3.50	9.00	18.00	30.00	45.00

Mint: Kabul
KM# 457 RUPEE
Silver **Note:** Weight varies: 11.50-11.60 grams.

Date	Mintage	Good	VG	F	VF	XF
AH1218//1	—	3.00	7.50	25.00	40.00	60.00
AH1219//2	—	3.00	7.50	25.00	40.00	60.00
AH1220	—	3.00	7.50	25.00	40.00	60.00
AH1222	—	3.00	7.50	25.00	40.00	60.00
AH1223	—	3.00	7.50	25.00	40.00	60.00

Mint: Kashmir
KM# 598 RUPEE
Silver **Note:** Weight varies: 10.80-11.20 grams.

Date	Mintage	Good	VG	F	VF	XF
AH1218//1	—	3.50	9.00	12.00	20.00	30.00
AH1219//2	—	3.50	9.00	12.00	20.00	30.00
AH1220//3	—	3.50	9.00	12.00	20.00	30.00
AH1221//4	—	3.50	9.00	12.00	20.00	30.00
AH1222//5	—	3.50	9.00	12.00	20.00	30.00
AH1223//6	—	4.00	10.00	15.00	25.00	40.00

Mint: Multan - Dar al-Aman
KM# 673 RUPEE
Silver, 20.5 mm. **Note:** Weight varies: 11.40-11.60 grams.

Date	Mintage	Good	VG	F	VF	XF
AH1218//1	—	7.00	17.50	35.00	60.00	90.00
AH1219	—	7.00	17.50	35.00	60.00	90.00

Mint: Peshawar
KM# 724 RUPEE
Silver **Note:** This coin may be distinguished from KM#722 and 723 by the octagon and calligraphy of the reverse and by the date. Weight varies: 11.40-11.60 grams.

Date	Mintage	Good	VG	F	VF	XF
AH1233//1	—	15.00	35.00	60.00	100	150
AH1234//1	—	15.00	35.00	60.00	100	150

Mint: Peshawar
KM# 722 RUPEE
Silver **Note:** Weight varies: 11.40-11.60 grams.

Date	Mintage	Good	VG	F	VF	XF
AH1218//1	—	3.50	8.50	12.00	20.00	30.00
AH1219//2	—	3.50	8.50	12.00	20.00	30.00
AH1220//3	—	3.50	8.50	12.00	20.00	30.00
AH1221//4	—	3.50	8.50	12.00	20.00	30.00
AH1222//5	—	3.50	8.50	12.00	20.00	30.00
AH1223//6	—	3.50	8.50	12.00	20.00	30.00
AH1224//7	—	3.50	8.50	12.00	20.00	30.00

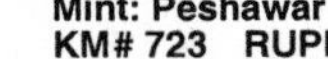

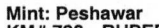

Mint: Peshawar
KM# 723 RUPEE
Silver **Note:** Weight varies: 11.40-11.60 grams.

Date	Mintage	Good	VG	F	VF	XF
AH1227//1	—	12.00	30.00	60.00	100	150

Mint: Bahawalpur
KM# 254 2 RUPEES
23.0000 g., Silver

Date	Mintage	Good	VG	F	VF	XF
AH1218//1	—	25.00	60.00	120	200	300
AH1219 Unique	—	—	—	—	—	—

Mint: Ahmadshahi
KM# 154 ASHRAFI
Gold **Note:** Weight varies: 3.00-3.50 grams.

Date	Mintage	Good	VG	F	VF	XF
AH1220//3 Rare	—	—	—	—	—	—
AH1222 Rare	—	—	—	—	—	—

Mint: Ahmadshahi
KM# 155 MOHUR
10.9000 g., Gold

Date	Mintage	Good	VG	F	VF	XF
AH-//2	—	—	250	400	600	850
AH1220//3	—	—	250	400	600	850
AH1222	—	—	250	400	600	850

Mint: Bahawalpur
KM# 255 MOHUR
Gold **Note:** Weight varies: 11.00-11.10 grams.

Date	Mintage	Good	VG	F	VF	XF
AH1218//1	—	65.00	165	325	550	850

Mint: Dera - Dera Ghazi Khan
KM# 345 MOHUR
Gold **Note:** Weight varies 10.9-11 grams.

Date	Mintage	Good	VG	F	VF	XF
AH1218//1 Rare	—	—	—	—	—	—

Mint: Herat - Dar as-Sultanat
KM# 399 MOHUR
10.9000 g., Gold

Date	Mintage	VG	F	VF	XF	Unc
AH1218	—	175	300	450	650	—

Mint: Kabul
KM# 459 MOHUR
10.9500 g., Gold

Date	Mintage	Good	VG	F	VF	XF
AH1222//4	—	65.00	200	325	550	850
AH1223	—	65.00	165	325	550	850

Mint: Kabul
KM# 487 MOHUR
Gold **Note:** Weight varies: 10.70-10.80 grams.

Date	Mintage	Good	VG	F	VF	XF
AH1255	—	55.00	135	275	450	775
AH1258	—	55.00	135	275	450	775

Mint: Multan - Dar al-Aman
KM# 675 MOHUR
Gold **Note:** Weight varies: 10.90-11.00 grams.

Date	Mintage	Good	VG	F	VF	XF
AH1218//1 Rare	—	—	—	—	—	—
AH1224//8 Rare	—	—	—	—	—	—

Mint: Qandahar
KM# 749 MOHUR
Gold **Note:** Weight varies: 10.80-10.90 grams.

Date	Mintage	Good	VG	F	VF	XF
AH1219 Rare	—	—	—	—	—	—

Mint: Bahawalpur
KM# 256 2 MOHURS
22.0000 g., Gold

Date	Mintage	Good	VG	F	VF	XF
AH1218//1	—	—	700	1,150	1,750	2,500

Qaisar Shah

AH1221-1223 / 1806-1808AD

HAMMERED COINAGE

Mint: Kabul
KM# 453 RUPEE
11.6500 g., Silver **Note:** Rebel issue.

Date	Mintage	Good	VG	F	VF	XF
AH1222//1	—	27.50	45.00	90.00	150	225

Mint: Kashmir
KM# 600 RUPEE
Silver **Note:** Rebel issue; weight varies: 11.00-11.20 grams.

Date	Mintage	VG	F	VF	XF	Unc
AH1222//1	—	17.50	35.00	60.00	90.00	—
AH1223//1	—	17.50	35.00	60.00	90.00	—
AH1223//2	—	17.50	35.00	60.00	90.00	—

Mint: Kabul
KM# 455 MOHUR
11.0000 g., Gold **Note:** Rebel issue.

Date	Mintage	Good	VG	F	VF	XF
AH1222 Rare	—	—	—	—	—	—

Ata Muhammad - Bamizai Khan
AH1223-1228 / 1808-1813AD
HAMMERED COINAGE

Mint: Kashmir
KM# 601 FALUS
7.5000 g., Copper, 16.5 mm.

Date	Mintage	Good	VG	F	VF	XF
AH1225//3	—	7.00	14.00	23.50	35.00	—
AH1228	—	7.00	14.00	23.50	35.00	—

Mint: Kashmir
KM# 603 RUPEE
Silver **Note:** Weight varies: 10.70-11.10 grams.

Date	Mintage	Good	VG	F	VF	XF
AH1223//1	—	—	10.00	15.00	20.00	30.00
AH1224//1	—	—	10.00	15.00	20.00	30.00
AH1224//2	—	—	10.00	15.00	20.00	30.00
AH1225//2	—	—	10.00	15.00	20.00	30.00
AH1225//3	—	—	10.00	15.00	20.00	30.00
AH1226//4	—	—	10.00	15.00	20.00	30.00
AH1227//4	—	—	10.00	15.00	20.00	30.00
AH1227//5	—	—	10.00	15.00	20.00	30.00
AH1228//5	—	—	10.00	15.00	20.00	30.00

Mint: Kashmir
KM# 604 HEAVY RUPEE
14.5000 g., Silver

Date	Mintage	Good	VG	F	VF	XF
AH1223//1	—	30.00	75.00	150	250	375
AH1225 Rare	—	—	—	—	—	—

Mint: Kashmir
KM# 607 2 MOHURS
Gold **Note:** Weight varies: 21.60-21.80 grams.

Date	Mintage	Good	VG	F	VF	XF
AH1225//2	—	—	—	—	5,000	6,500

Mint: Kashmir
KM# 608 2 MOHURS
Gold **Note:** Weight varies: 21.60-21.80 grams.

Date	Mintage	Good	VG	F	VF	XF
AH1225//3	—	—	2,000	3,250	5,000	6,500

Mahmud Shah
AH1224-1245 / 1808-1817AD Second reign
HAMMERED COINAGE

Mint: Kashmir
KM# 581 FRACTIONAL FALUS
Copper, 20 mm. **Obv:** King's name in toughra style **Note:** Weight varies: 7.20-7.80 grams.

Date	Mintage	Good	VG	F	VF	XF
AH-//1	—	8.00	12.00	18.00	30.00	—

Mint: Derajat
KM# 370 FALUS
Copper

Date	Mintage	Good	VG	F	VF	XF
AH124(9)	—	10.00	15.00	25.00	40.00	—

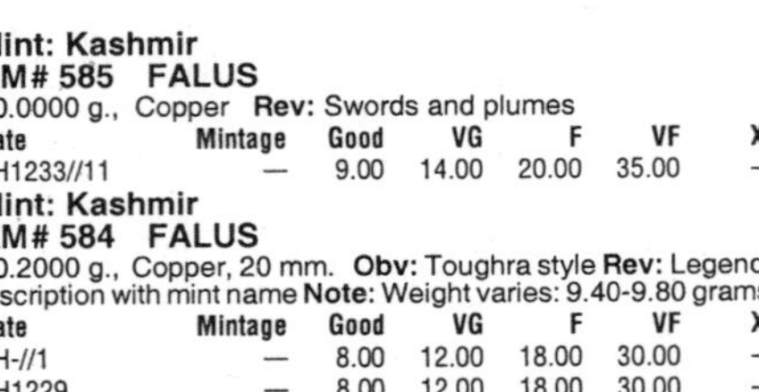

Mint: Kashmir
KM# 585 FALUS
10.0000 g., Copper **Rev:** Swords and plumes

Date	Mintage	Good	VG	F	VF	XF
AH1233//11	—	9.00	14.00	20.00	35.00	—

Mint: Kashmir
KM# 584 FALUS
10.2000 g., Copper, 20 mm. **Obv:** Toughra style **Rev:** Legend; inscription with mint name **Note:** Weight varies: 9.40-9.80 grams.

Date	Mintage	Good	VG	F	VF	XF
AH-//1	—	8.00	12.00	18.00	30.00	—
AH1229	—	8.00	12.00	18.00	30.00	—
AH1230//6	—	8.00	12.00	18.00	30.00	—

Mint: Multan - Dar al-Aman
KM# 677 FALUS
Copper **Note:** Issues dated after AH1233 are posthumous issues struck by the Sikhs. Weight varies: 11.60-12.80 grams.

Date	Mintage	Good	VG	F	VF	XF
AH1226//1	—	7.50	10.00	15.00	22.00	—
AH1227//1	—	7.50	10.00	15.00	22.00	—
AH1227//2	—	7.50	10.00	15.00	22.00	—
AH1228//3	—	7.50	10.00	15.00	22.00	—
AH1228//5	—	7.50	10.00	15.00	22.00	—
AH1229	—	7.50	10.00	15.00	22.00	—
AH1230//7	—	7.50	10.00	15.00	22.00	—
AH1231//7	—	7.50	10.00	15.00	22.00	—
AH1235	—	7.50	10.00	15.00	22.00	—
AH1253	—	7.50	10.00	15.00	22.00	—
AH1254	—	7.50	10.00	15.00	22.00	—
AH1257	—	7.50	10.00	15.00	22.00	—
AH1260	—	7.50	10.00	15.00	22.00	—
AH1263	—	7.50	10.00	15.00	22.00	—
AH1264	—	7.50	10.00	15.00	22.00	—
AH1267	—	7.50	10.00	15.00	22.00	—
AH1270	—	7.50	10.00	15.00	22.00	—

Mint: Peshawar
KM# 726 FALUS
11.4000 g., Copper

Date	Mintage	Good	VG	F	VF	XF
AH1232//8 Rare	—	—	—	—	—	—

Mint: Herat - Dar as-Sultanat
KM# 392 1/12 RUPEE
0.9000 g., Silver

Date	Mintage	Good	VG	F	VF	XF
AH1230	—	—	15.00	35.00	50.00	65.00

Mint: Herat - Dar as-Sultanat
KM# 393 1/6 RUPEE
1.8000 g., Silver

Date	Mintage	Good	VG	F	VF	XF
AH1225	—	6.00	15.00	30.00	50.00	75.00
AH1238	—	6.00	15.00	30.00	50.00	75.00

Mint: Herat - Dar as-Sultanat
KM# 395 1/4 RUPEE
2.8000 g., Silver, 11.5 mm.

Date	Mintage	Good	VG	F	VF	XF
AH1225	—	9.00	22.50	45.00	75.00	110
AH1242	—	9.00	22.50	45.00	75.00	110

Mint: Ahmadshahi
KM# 156 1/2 RUPEE
Silver **Note:** Weight varies: 5.40-5.80 grams.

Date	Mintage	Good	VG	F	VF	XF
AH1224	—	8.00	20.00	40.00	65.00	100

Mint: Herat - Dar as-Sultanat
KM# A396 1/2 RUPEE
Silver **Rev:** Mint name and date in small circle **Note:** Weight varies: 5.00-5.60 grams.

Date	Mintage	Good	VG	F	VF	XF
AH1230 Rare	—	—	—	—	—	—

Mint: Herat - Dar as-Sultanat
KM# 396 1/2 RUPEE
Silver **Note:** Weight varies: 5.00-5.60 grams.

Date	Mintage	Good	VG	F	VF	XF
AH1242	—	7.00	17.50	35.00	60.00	90.00
AH1243	—	7.00	17.50	35.00	60.00	90.00

Mint: Ahmadshahi
KM# A157 RUPEE
Silver **Obv:** KM#157 **Rev:** KM#153 **Note:** Mule; weight varies 11.40 - 11.60 grams.

Date	Mintage	Good	VG	F	VF	XF
AH1222	—	3.00	7.50	15.00	25.00	37.50

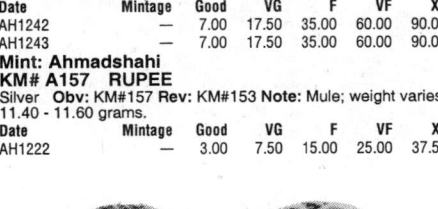

Mint: Ahmadshahi
KM# 158.1 RUPEE
Silver **Rev:** In toughra **Note:** Weight varies: 10.20-10.40 grams.

Date	Mintage	Good	VG	F	VF	XF
AH1229	—	2.00	5.00	10.00	16.00	25.00
AH1230	—	2.00	5.00	10.00	16.00	25.00
AH1231	—	2.00	5.00	10.00	16.00	25.00
AH1232	—	2.00	5.00	10.00	16.00	25.00

Mint: Ahmadshahi
KM# 158.2 RUPEE
Silver **Rev:** Legend in a circle **Note:** Weight varies: 10.20-10.40 grams.

Date	Mintage	Good	VG	F	VF	XF
AH1232	—	3.00	8.00	15.00	25.00	35.00
AH1233	—	3.00	8.00	15.00	25.00	35.00
AH1234	—	3.00	8.00	15.00	25.00	35.00

Mint: Ahmadshahi
KM# 157 RUPEE
Silver **Rev:** In cartouche or circle **Note:** Weight varies: 11.40-11.60 grams.

Date	Mintage	Good	VG	F	VF	XF
AH1223	—	2.50	6.00	12.00	20.00	30.00
AH1224	—	2.50	6.00	12.00	20.00	30.00

Date	Mintage	Good	VG	F	VF	XF
AH1225	—	2.50	6.00	12.00	20.00	30.00
AH1226	—	2.50	6.00	12.00	20.00	30.00
AH1227	—	2.50	6.00	12.00	20.00	30.00
AH1228	—	2.50	6.00	12.00	20.00	30.00
AH1229	—	2.50	6.00	12.00	20.00	30.00
AH1230	—	2.50	6.00	12.00	20.00	30.00
AH1232	—	2.50	6.00	12.00	20.00	30.00

Mint: Bahawalpur
KM# 263 RUPEE
Silver **Note:** Coins dated after AH1233 are struck in Mahmud's name by the virtually independent Nawabs of Bahawalpur. Weight varies: 11.00-11.20 grams. Size varies 21.5-26 mm.

Date	Mintage	Good	VG	F	VF	XF
AH1224//1	—	9.00	22.50	45.00	75.00	110
AH1239	—	5.00	12.50	25.00	40.00	60.00
AH1240	—	5.00	12.50	25.00	40.00	60.00
AH1241	—	5.00	12.50	25.00	40.00	60.00
AH1242	—	5.00	12.50	25.00	40.00	60.00
AH1244	—	5.00	12.50	25.00	40.00	60.00
AH1244//1245	—	5.00	12.50	25.00	40.00	60.00
AH1249	—	5.00	12.50	25.00	40.00	60.00
AH1249//1250	—	5.00	12.50	25.00	40.00	60.00
AH1250	—	5.00	12.50	25.00	40.00	60.00

Mint: Bhakhar
KM# 307 RUPEE
Silver **Note:** Weight varies: 11.40-11.60 grams.

Date	Mintage	Good	VG	F	VF	XF
AH1228	—	—	15.00	25.00	35.00	50.00
AH1229	—	—	15.00	25.00	35.00	50.00

Mint: Derajat
KM# 373 RUPEE
Silver **Note:** Coins after AH1235 (1819-20) were issued under Sikh protectorate. Weight varies: 10.60-11.20 grams.

Date	Mintage	Good	VG	F	VF	XF
AH1224//1	—	5.00	12.50	25.00	40.00	60.00
AH1226//3	—	5.00	12.50	25.00	40.00	60.00
AH1227//3	—	5.00	12.50	25.00	40.00	60.00
AH1228//4	—	5.00	12.50	25.00	40.00	60.00
AH1229	—	5.00	12.50	25.00	40.00	60.00
AH1230	—	5.00	12.50	25.00	40.00	60.00
AH1231//4	—	3.00	7.50	15.00	25.00	50.00
AH1232	—	3.00	7.50	15.00	25.00	50.00
AH1233	—	3.00	7.50	15.00	25.00	50.00
AH1234	—	3.00	7.50	15.00	25.00	50.00
AH1236	—	3.00	7.50	15.00	25.00	50.00
AH1237	—	3.00	7.50	15.00	25.00	50.00
AH1238//14	—	3.00	7.50	15.00	25.00	50.00
AH1239	—	3.00	7.50	15.00	25.00	50.00
AH1240	—	3.00	7.50	15.00	25.00	50.00
AH1241	—	3.00	7.50	15.00	25.00	50.00
AH1242	—	3.00	7.50	15.00	25.00	50.00
AH1243	—	3.00	7.50	15.00	25.00	50.00
AH1244	—	3.00	7.50	15.00	25.00	50.00
AH1245	—	3.00	7.50	15.00	25.00	50.00
AH1246	—	3.00	7.50	15.00	25.00	50.00
AH1247	—	3.00	7.50	15.00	25.00	50.00
AH1248	—	3.00	7.50	15.00	25.00	50.00
AH1249	—	3.00	7.50	15.00	25.00	50.00
AH1250	—	3.00	7.50	15.00	25.00	50.00
AH1251	—	3.00	7.50	15.00	25.00	50.00
AH1252	—	3.00	7.50	15.00	25.00	50.00

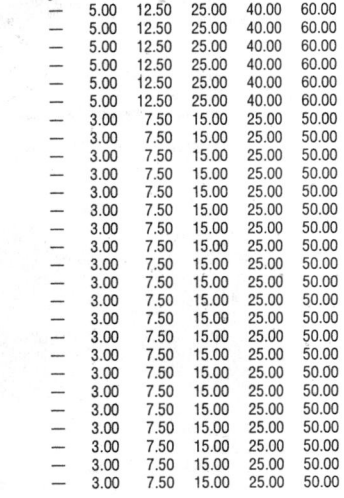

Mint: Herat - Dar as-Sultanat
KM# 398.1 RUPEE
Silver **Note:** Weight varies: 11.00-11.60 grams.

Date	Mintage	Good	VG	F	VF	XF
AH1216	—	2.50	6.00	12.00	20.00	30.00
AH1217	—	2.50	6.00	12.00	20.00	30.00
AH1218	—	2.50	6.00	12.00	20.00	30.00
AH1219	—	2.50	6.00	12.00	20.00	30.00

Mint: Herat - Dar as-Sultanat
KM# 398.2 RUPEE
Silver **Note:** Weight varies: 11.00-11.60 grams.

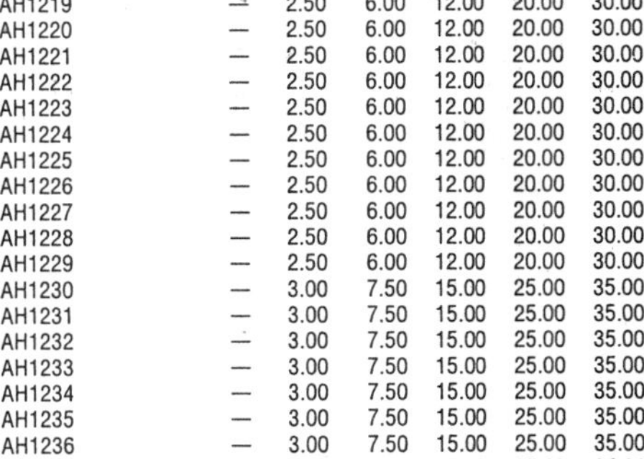

Date	Mintage	Good	VG	F	VF	XF
AH1219	—	2.50	6.00	12.00	20.00	30.00
AH1220	—	2.50	6.00	12.00	20.00	30.00
AH1221	—	2.50	6.00	12.00	20.00	30.00
AH1222	—	2.50	6.00	12.00	20.00	30.00
AH1223	—	2.50	6.00	12.00	20.00	30.00
AH1224	—	2.50	6.00	12.00	20.00	30.00
AH1225	—	2.50	6.00	12.00	20.00	30.00
AH1226	—	2.50	6.00	12.00	20.00	30.00
AH1227	—	2.50	6.00	12.00	20.00	30.00
AH1228	—	2.50	6.00	12.00	20.00	30.00
AH1229	—	2.50	6.00	12.00	20.00	30.00
AH1230	—	3.00	7.50	15.00	25.00	35.00
AH1231	—	3.00	7.50	15.00	25.00	35.00
AH1232	—	3.00	7.50	15.00	25.00	35.00
AH1233	—	3.00	7.50	15.00	25.00	35.00
AH1234	—	3.00	7.50	15.00	25.00	35.00
AH1235	—	3.00	7.50	15.00	25.00	35.00
AH1236	—	3.00	7.50	15.00	25.00	35.00
AH1237	—	3.00	7.50	15.00	25.00	35.00
AH1238	—	3.00	7.50	15.00	25.00	35.00
AH1240	—	3.00	7.50	15.00	25.00	35.00

Mint: Herat - Dar as-Sultanat
KM# 398.3 RUPEE
Silver **Note:** Weight varies: 11.00-11.60 grams.

Date	Mintage	Good	VG	F	VF	XF
AH1242	—	2.50	6.00	12.00	20.00	30.00
AH1243	—	2.50	6.00	12.00	20.00	30.00
AH1244	—	2.50	6.00	12.00	20.00	30.00
AH1254	—	2.50	6.00	12.00	20.00	30.00

Note: Error for 1245

Mint: Kabul
KM# 462.1 RUPEE
Silver **Note:** Small, thick flan. Weight varies: 10.75-11.60 grams.

Date	Mintage	Good	VG	F	VF	XF
AH1227/4	—	—	9.00	18.00	25.00	35.00

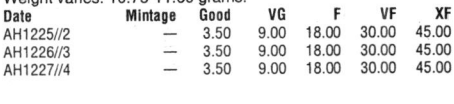

Mint: Kabul
KM# 461.1 RUPEE
Silver **Rev:** Mint name as on previous reign, KM#457 **Note:** Weight varies: 10.75-11.60 grams.

Date	Mintage	Good	VG	F	VF	XF
AH1225//2	—	3.50	9.00	18.00	30.00	45.00
AH1226//3	—	3.50	9.00	18.00	30.00	45.00
AH1227//4	—	3.50	9.00	18.00	30.00	45.00

Mint: Kabul
KM# 461.2 RUPEE
Silver **Note:** Weight varies: 10.75-11.60 grams.

Date	Mintage	Good	VG	F	VF	XF
AH122x//6	—	3.50	9.00	18.00	30.00	45.00

Mint: Kabul
KM# 462.2 RUPEE
Silver **Rev:** Mint name in small circle **Note:** Weight varies: 10.75-11.60 grams.

Date	Mintage	Good	VG	F	VF	XF
AH1228//5	—	3.00	7.50	15.00	25.00	35.00

Mint: Kabul
KM# 463 RUPEE
Silver **Rev:** Mint name in toughra form **Note:** Weight varies: 10.75-11.60 grams.

Date	Mintage	Good	VG	F	VF	XF
AH(122)6	—	3.50	9.00	18.00	30.00	45.00
AH1228	—	3.50	9.00	18.00	30.00	45.00
AH1230	—	3.50	9.00	18.00	30.00	45.00
AH1231//8	—	3.50	9.00	18.00	30.00	45.00
AH1232	—	3.50	9.00	18.00	30.00	45.00
AH1233//10	—	3.50	9.00	18.00	30.00	45.00

Mint: Kashmir
KM# 591 RUPEE
Silver **Note:** The sequence of regnal years at Kashmir is very confused. Weight varies: 10.80-11.00 grams.

Date	Mintage	Good	VG	F	VF	XF
AH1228//6	—	4.00	9.00	15.00	25.00	40.00
AH1229//6	—	4.00	9.00	15.00	25.00	40.00
AH1229//7	—	4.00	9.00	15.00	25.00	40.00
AH1230//7	—	4.00	9.00	15.00	25.00	40.00
AH1230//8	—	4.00	9.00	15.00	25.00	40.00
AH1230//10	—	4.00	9.00	15.00	25.00	40.00
AH1232//10	—	4.00	9.00	15.00	25.00	40.00
AH1233//10	—	5.00	12.00	18.00	30.00	45.00
AH1233//11	—	5.00	12.00	18.00	30.00	45.00

Mint: Peshawar
KM# A727 RUPEE
Silver **Rev:** Legend with beaded circle **Note:** Weight varies: 10.60-11.50 grams.

Date	Mintage	Good	VG	F	VF	XF
AH1224//1	—	6.50	16.50	32.50	50.00	80.00

Mint: Peshawar
KM# 727.1 RUPEE
Silver **Obv:** Linear legends **Rev:** Legend in octagon **Note:** Weight varies: 10.60-11.50 grams.

Date	Mintage	Good	VG	F	VF	XF
AH1225//1	—	2.50	7.50	11.00	18.00	27.00
AH1226//2	—	2.50	7.50	11.00	18.00	27.00
AH1227//2	—	2.50	7.50	11.00	18.00	27.00
AH(122)7//3	—	2.50	7.50	11.00	18.00	27.00

Mint: Peshawar
KM# 727.2 RUPEE
Silver **Note:** Weight varies: 10.60-11.50 grams.

Date	Mintage	Good	VG	F	VF	XF
AH1224//1	—	2.50	7.50	11.00	18.00	27.00
AH1227//3	—	2.50	7.50	11.00	18.00	27.00
AH1227//4	—	2.50	7.50	11.00	18.00	27.00
AH1228//4	—	2.50	7.50	11.00	18.00	27.00
AH1228//5	—	2.50	7.50	11.00	18.00	27.00
AH1229//5	—	2.50	7.50	11.00	18.00	27.00
AH1229//6	—	2.50	7.50	11.00	18.00	27.00
AH1230//6	—	2.50	7.50	11.00	18.00	27.00
AH1230//7	—	2.50	7.50	11.00	18.00	27.00
AH1231//7	—	2.50	7.50	11.00	18.00	27.00
AH1231//8	—	2.50	7.50	11.00	18.00	27.00

Mint: Peshawar
KM# 727.3 RUPEE
Silver **Rev:** Legend within square **Note:** Weight varies: 10.60-11.50 grams.

Date	Mintage	Good	VG	F	VF	XF
AH1227//7	—	4.00	10.00	20.00	35.00	50.00

Mint: Peshawar
KM# 728 RUPEE
Silver **Obv:** Circular legend around central cartouche **Note:** Weight varies: 10.60-11.50 grams.

Date	Mintage	Good	VG	F	VF	XF
AH1231//8	—	3.50	9.00	18.00	30.00	45.00
AH1232//8	—	3.50	9.00	18.00	30.00	45.00
AH1232//9	—	3.50	9.00	18.00	30.00	45.00
AH1233//6	—	5.00	9.00	20.00	35.00	50.00
Note: Error for regnal year 9						
AH1233//9	—	3.50	9.00	18.00	30.00	45.00
AH1233//10	—	3.50	9.00	18.00	30.00	45.00

Mint: Kabul
KM# 464 2 RUPEES
Silver **Note:** Weight varies: 23.00-23.20 grams.

Date	Mintage	Good	VG	F	VF	XF
AH1225//1	—	18.00	45.00	90.00	150	225

Mint: Ahmadshahi
KM# 159 ASHRAFI
2.4000 g., Gold, 28 mm.

Date	Mintage	Good	VG	F	VF	XF
AH1224 Rare	—	—	—	—	—	—
AH1226 Rare	—	—	—	—	—	—

Mint: Bahawalpur
KM# 265 MOHUR
11.0000 g., Gold, 21.5 mm.

Date	Mintage	Good	VG	F	VF	XF
AH1225//1 Rare	—	—	—	—	—	—

Mint: Kabul
KM# 465 MOHUR
Gold **Note:** Weight varies: 10.90-11.00 grams.

Date	Mintage	Good	VG	F	VF	XF
AH1224//2	—	—	250	425	650	1,000
AH122x//8	—	—	250	425	650	1,000

Muhammad A'zim
AH1228-1234 / 1813-1819AD
Governor for Ayub Shah

HAMMERED COINAGE

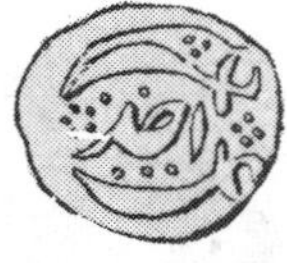

Mint: Kashmir
KM# 609 FALUS
7.5000 g., Copper

Date	Mintage	Good	VG	F	VF	XF
AH1228//1	—	10.00	15.00	25.00	40.00	—

Ayyub Shah
AH1233-1245 / 1817-1829

HAMMERED COINAGE

Mint: Ahmadshahi
KM# 165 FALUS
Bronze

Date	Mintage	Good	VG	F	VF	XF
AH1240	—	16.50	32.50	55.00	90.00	135
AH1241	—	16.50	32.50	55.00	90.00	135
AH1243	—	16.50	32.50	55.00	90.00	135

Mint: Kashmir
KM# 610 FALUS
Copper **Note:** Weight varies: 7.00-8.00 grams.

Date	Mintage	Good	VG	F	VF	XF
AH1233	—	10.00	15.00	25.00	40.00	—

Mint: Peshawar
KM# 730 FALUS
Copper **Note:** Weight varies: 10.40-12.20 grams.

Date	Mintage	Good	VG	F	VF	XF
AH1234//2	—	12.00	18.00	26.00	40.00	—
AH123x//3	—	12.00	18.00	26.00	40.00	—
AH1236//4	—	12.00	18.00	26.00	40.00	—
AH1237	—	10.00	15.00	25.00	35.00	—
AH1238//6	—	10.00	15.00	25.00	35.00	—
AH1239	—	10.00	15.00	25.00	35.00	—
AH1240	—	13.00	20.00	30.00	45.00	—

Mint: Ahmadshahi
KM# 166 1/2 RUPEE
Bronze **Note:** Date off flan.

Date	Mintage	Good	VG	F	VF	XF
ND(AH1240//1)	—	8.00	20.00	40.00	65.00	100

Mint: Ahmadshahi
KM# 162 RUPEE
Silver **Rev:** Mint in center circled by Kalimah

Date	Mintage	Good	VG	F	VF	XF
AH1234 Rare	—	—	—	—	—	—
AH1235 Rare	—	—	—	—	—	—

Mint: Ahmadshahi
KM# 168 RUPEE
Silver **Obv:** Kalimah **Rev:** Mint name **Note:** Minor variations exist on both sides.

Date	Mintage	Good	VG	F	VF	XF
AH1242	—	4.00	10.00	20.00	32.50	50.00
AH1243	—	4.00	10.00	20.00	32.50	50.00
AH1244	—	2.50	6.00	12.00	20.00	30.00
AH1245	—	2.00	4.50	9.00	15.00	25.00
AH1246	—	—	4.50	9.00	15.00	25.00
AH1247	—	2.00	4.50	9.00	15.00	25.00
AH1248	—	2.00	4.50	9.00	15.00	25.00
AH1249	—	2.00	4.00	8.00	13.00	23.00
AH1250	—	2.00	4.00	8.00	13.00	23.00
AH1251	—	2.00	4.00	8.00	13.00	23.00
AH1252	—	2.50	6.00	12.00	20.00	30.00
AH1253	—	2.50	6.00	12.00	20.00	30.00
AH1254	—	2.50	6.00	12.00	20.00	30.00

Mint: Ahmadshahi
KM# 164 RUPEE
Silver **Rev:** Kalima, date and mint **Note:** Weight varies: 11.20-11.60 grams.

Date	Mintage	Good	VG	F	VF	XF
AH1237	—	11.00	27.50	55.00	90.00	135
AH1239	—	11.00	27.50	55.00	90.00	135

Mint: Ahmadshahi
KM# 163 RUPEE
Silver **Note:** Weight varies: 11.20-11.60 grams. Reverses differ each year. Coins dated AH1239 are struck in debased silver.

Date	Mintage	Good	VG	F	VF	XF
AH1235	—	5.00	12.50	25.00	40.00	60.00
AH1236	—	5.00	12.50	25.00	40.00	60.00
AH1237	—	5.00	12.50	25.00	40.00	60.00
AH1239	—	5.00	12.50	25.00	40.00	60.00

Mint: Kabul
KM# 468 RUPEE
Silver **Note:** Various arrangements of obverse legend. Weight varies: 10.70-11.40 grams.

Date	Mintage	Good	VG	F	VF	XF
AH1234	—	5.00	12.50	25.00	40.00	60.00
AH1234//1	—	5.00	12.50	25.00	40.00	60.00
AH1235//2	—	5.00	12.50	25.00	40.00	60.00
AH1236//2	—	5.00	12.50	25.00	40.00	60.00
AH1236//2	—	5.00	12.50	25.00	40.00	60.00
AH1237//3	—	5.00	12.50	25.00	40.00	60.00
AH1237//2	—	5.00	12.50	25.00	40.00	60.00
AH1238//3	—	5.00	12.50	25.00	40.00	60.00
AH1239//4	—	5.00	12.50	25.00	40.00	60.00

Mint: Kabul
KM# 473 RUPEE
Silver **Obv:** Kalimah **Note:** Weight varies: 10.70-11.40 grams.

Date	Mintage	Good	VG	F	VF	XF
AH1239//4	—	6.00	15.00	30.00	50.00	75.00

Mint: Kashmir
KM# 614 RUPEE
Silver **Rev:** Mint, regnal year and "Julus" formula **Note:** Kashmir fell to the Sikhs in AH1234 (1819AD), ending the Durrani dominion in India. Weight varies: 11.00-11.20 grams.

Date	Mintage	Good	VG	F	VF	XF
AH1234//2	—	6.00	15.00	30.00	50.00	75.00

Mint: Kashmir
KM# 613 RUPEE
Silver **Rev:** Mint name and regnal year **Note:** Weight varies: 11.00-11.20 grams.

Date	Mintage	Good	VG	F	VF	XF
AH1233//1	—	6.00	15.00	30.00	50.00	75.00
AH1234//1	—	5.00	12.50	25.00	40.00	60.00

Mint: Peshawar
KM# 738 RUPEE
10.4000 g., Silver, 23 mm. **Note:** Dated on both sides.

Date	Mintage	Good	VG	F	VF	XF
AH1246	—	10.00	25.00	47.50	80.00	120
AH1247	—	10.00	25.00	47.50	80.00	120
AH1248	—	10.00	25.00	47.50	80.00	120
AH1249	—	10.00	25.00	47.50	80.00	120

Mint: Peshawar
KM# 732 RUPEE
Silver **Obv:** Ruler's name in fancy diamond **Note:** Weight varies: 10.40-10.60 grams.

Date	Mintage	Good	VG	F	VF	XF
AH1233//1	—	8.00	20.00	40.00	65.00	100

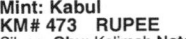

Mint: Peshawar
KM# 733 RUPEE
Silver **Obv:** Couplet in three lines **Note:** Weight varies: 10.40-10.60 grams.

Date	Mintage	Good	VG	F	VF	XF
AH1233//1	—	2.50	6.00	13.00	20.00	30.00
AH1233//2	—	2.50	6.00	13.00	20.00	30.00
AH1234/1	—	2.50	6.00	13.00	20.00	30.00

Date	Mintage	Good	VG	F	VF	XF
AH1234//2	—	2.50	6.00	13.00	20.00	30.00
AH(123)4//6	—	2.50	6.00	13.00	20.00	30.00
AH1235//2	—	2.50	6.00	13.00	20.00	30.00
AH1235//3	—	2.50	6.00	13.00	20.00	30.00
AH1236//3	—	2.50	6.00	13.00	20.00	30.00
AH1236//4	—	2.50	6.00	13.00	20.00	30.00
AH1237//4	—	2.50	6.00	13.00	20.00	30.00
AH1237//5	—	2.50	6.00	13.00	20.00	30.00
AH1238//5	—	2.50	6.00	13.00	20.00	30.00
AH1238//6	—	2.50	6.00	13.00	20.00	30.00
AH1239//6	—	2.50	6.00	13.00	20.00	30.00
AH1239//7	—	2.50	6.00	13.00	20.00	30.00
AH1240//6	—	2.50	6.00	13.00	20.00	30.00
AH1240//7	—	2.50	6.00	13.00	20.00	30.00
AH1240//8	—	2.50	6.00	13.00	20.00	30.00
AH1241//7	—	2.50	6.00	13.00	20.00	30.00
AH1242//9	—	2.50	6.00	13.00	20.00	30.00
AH1243//9	—	2.50	6.00	13.00	20.00	30.00
AH1243//10	—	2.50	6.00	13.00	20.00	30.00
AH1244//11	—	2.50	6.00	13.00	20.00	30.00
AH1245//11	—	2.50	6.00	8.50	14.00	20.00

Mint: Peshawar
KM# 734 RUPEE
Silver **Obv:** Name in foliated diamond **Note:** Weight varies: 10.40-10.60 grams.

Date	Mintage	Good	VG	F	VF	XF
AH124x//12	—	8.00	20.00	40.00	65.00	100

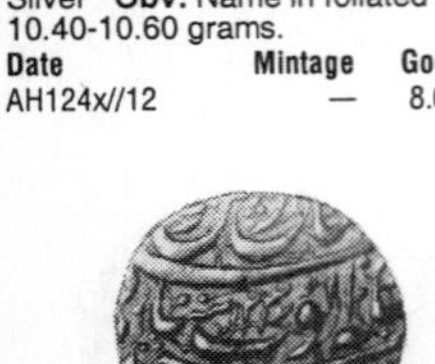

Mint: Kabul
KM# 469 MOHUR
10.7900 g., Gold

Date	Mintage	Good	VG	F	VF	XF
AH1237	—	—	—	—	1,600	2,000

Mint: Peshawar
KM# 735 MOHUR
Gold, 21.5 mm. **Note:** Weight varies: 10.50-10.60 grams.

Date	Mintage	Good	VG	F	VF	XF
AH-//6	—	—	400	650	1,000	1,750
AH-//7	—	—	400	650	1,000	1,750

Dost Muhammad

AH1240-1255 / 1824-1839AD

HAMMERED COINAGE

Mint: Kabul
KM# 475 RUPEE
Silver

Date	Mintage	Good	VG	F	VF	XF
AH1239	—	9.00	22.50	45.00	75.00	100

Kamran Shah

AH1245-1258 / 1829-1842AD

HAMMERED COINAGE

Mint: Ahmadshahi
KM# 18 FALUS
Copper **Obv:** Three flowers on one stem

Date	Mintage	Good	VG	F	VF	XF
AH1245	—	7.50	15.00	25.00	40.00	—

Mint: Herat - Dar as-Sultanat
KM# 400 1/6 RUPEE
1.8000 g., Silver

Date	Mintage	Good	VG	F	VF	XF
AH1257	—	12.00	30.00	60.00	100	150

Mint: Herat - Dar as-Sultanat
KM# 401 1/4 RUPEE
Silver **Note:** Weight varies: 2.60-2.80 grams.

Date	Mintage	Good	VG	F	VF	XF
AH1248	—	12.00	30.00	60.00	100	150

Mint: Herat - Dar as-Sultanat
KM# 402 1/2 RUPEE
Silver **Note:** Weight varies: 5.20-5.60 grams.

Date	Mintage	Good	VG	F	VF	XF
AH125x	—	6.00	15.00	30.00	50.00	75.00

Mint: Herat - Dar as-Sultanat
KM# 403 RUPEE
Silver **Note:** Weight varies: 10.20-11.00 grams.

Date	Mintage	Good	VG	F	VF	XF
AH1244	—	11.00	27.50	55.00	90.00	135
AH1245	—	11.00	27.50	55.00	90.00	135
AH1246	—	11.00	27.50	55.00	90.00	135
AH1248	—	11.00	27.50	55.00	90.00	135
AH1249	—	11.00	27.50	55.00	90.00	135
AH1251	—	11.00	27.50	55.00	90.00	135
AH1252	—	11.00	27.50	55.00	90.00	135
AH1254	—	11.00	27.50	55.00	90.00	135
AH1255	—	11.00	27.50	55.00	90.00	135

Sultan Muhammad

AH1247-1250 / 1831-1834AD at Peshawar

HAMMERED COINAGE

Mint: Peshawar
KM# 739 RUPEE
Silver **Note:** Peshawar fell to the Sikhs in AH1250/1834AD.

Date	Mintage	Good	VG	F	VF	XF
AH1247	—	5.00	12.50	25.00	40.00	60.00
AH1248	—	5.00	12.50	25.00	40.00	60.00
AH1249	—	5.00	12.50	25.00	40.00	60.00

Shah Shuja al-Mulk

AH1255-1258 / 1839-1842AD Third reign

HAMMERED COINAGE

Mint: Ahmadshahi
KM# 171 1/4 RUPEE
2.3000 g., Silver

Date	Mintage	Good	VG	F	VF	XF
AH1255	—	6.00	15.00	30.00	50.00	75.00

Mint: Ahmadshahi
KM# 172 1/2 RUPEE
Silver

Date	Mintage	Good	VG	F	VF	XF
AH1255	—	6.00	15.00	30.00	50.00	75.00

Mint: Ahmadshahi
KM# 173 RUPEE
Silver **Note:** Weight varies: 9.00-9.20 grams.

Date	Mintage	Good	VG	F	VF	XF
AH1255	—	3.00	7.50	15.00	25.00	35.00
AH1256	—	5.00	12.50	25.00	40.00	60.00
AH1257 Rare	—	—	—	—	—	—
AH1258	—	6.00	15.00	30.00	50.00	75.00

Mint: Bhakhar
KM# A310 RUPEE
Silver **Note:** Weight varies: 11.40-11.60 grams.

Date	Mintage	Good	VG	F	VF	XF
AH1234	—	—	—	—	—	—

Mint: Kabul
KM# 483 RUPEE
9.2000 g., Silver **Obv:** Long inscription

Date	Mintage	Good	VG	F	VF	XF
AH1255//1	—	3.00	7.50	15.00	25.00	37.50

Mint: Kabul
KM# 482 RUPEE
11.5000 g., Silver **Obv:** Short inscription, title "Sultan" **Note:** Broad flan.

Date	Mintage	Good	VG	F	VF	XF
AH1255 Rare	—	—	—	—	—	—
AH1256 Rare	—	—	—	—	—	—

Mint: Kabul
KM# 484.1 RUPEE
Silver **Obv:** Short inscription, title "Sultan" **Note:** Varieties exist, some on broad planchets. Weight varies: 9.20-9.50 grams.

Date	Mintage	Good	VG	F	VF	XF
AH1255	—	2.25	5.00	11.00	18.00	28.00
AH1256	—	2.25	5.00	11.00	18.00	28.00
AH1257	—	2.50	6.00	12.00	20.00	30.00
AH1258	—	2.50	6.00	12.00	20.00	30.00

Mint: Kabul
KM# 484.2 RUPEE
Silver **Obv:** "Dur-e-Duran" above "Sultan" **Note:** Weight varies: 9.20-9.50 grams.

Date	Mintage	Good	VG	F	VF	XF
AH1255	—	2.50	6.00	12.00	20.00	30.00

Mint: Kabul
KM# 485 RUPEE
Silver **Note:** Weight varies: 9.20-9.50 grams.

Date	Mintage	Good	VG	F	VF	XF
AH1257	—	4.50	11.50	22.50	36.00	55.00

Mint: Kabul
KM# 486 RUPEE
Silver **Note:** Weight varies: 9.20-9.50 grams.

Date	Mintage	Good	VG	F	VF	XF
AH1258	—	6.00	15.00	30.00	50.00	75.00

Kohandil Khan
AH1256-1271 / 1840-1855AD
HAMMERED COINAGE

Mint: Ahmadshahi
KM# 182.2 1/2 RUPEE
Silver **Obv:** Similar to 1 Rupee, KM#183 **Rev:** Similar to 1 Rupee, KM#183

Date	Mintage	Good	VG	F	VF	XF
AH1264	—	8.50	21.50	42.50	70.00	110
AH1265	—	8.50	21.50	42.50	70.00	110
AH1267	—	8.50	21.50	42.50	70.00	110
AH1269	—	6.00	15.00	30.00	50.00	75.00
AH1270	—	4.00	10.00	20.00	35.00	55.00

Mint: Ahmadshahi
KM# 182.1 1/2 RUPEE
Silver **Note:** Both sides have legends arranged differently in different years.

Date	Mintage	Good	VG	F	VF	XF
AH1260	—	2.00	4.00	8.50	14.00	20.00
AH1261	—	2.00	4.00	8.50	14.00	20.00
AH1262	—	2.00	4.00	8.50	14.00	20.00
AH1263	—	2.00	4.00	8.50	14.00	20.00
AH1264	—	2.00	4.00	8.50	14.00	20.00
AH1265	—	2.00	4.00	8.50	14.00	20.00
AH1267	—	2.50	6.00	12.00	20.00	30.00
AH1268	—	3.00	7.00	15.00	25.00	75.00
AH1269	—	3.00	7.00	15.00	25.00	75.00
AH1270	—	3.00	7.00	15.00	25.00	75.00
AH1271	—	3.00	7.00	15.00	25.00	75.00
AH1272	—	3.00	7.00	15.00	25.00	75.00

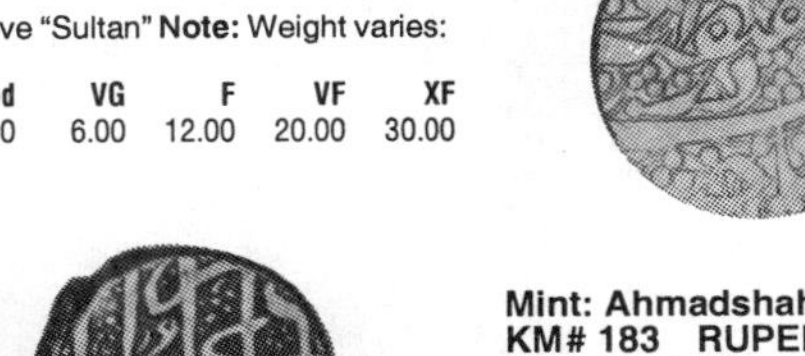

Mint: Ahmadshahi
KM# 183 RUPEE
Silver

Date	Mintage	Good	VG	F	VF	XF
AH1259	—	4.00	10.00	20.00	35.00	55.00

Dost Muhammad
AH1258-1280 / 1842-1863AD
ANONYMOUS COPPER COINAGE

Mint: Peshawar
KM# 84B FALUS
Copper, 24 mm. **Obv:** Flower

Date	Mintage	Good	VG	F	VF	XF
AH1265	—	5.00	12.50	25.00	40.00	—

HAMMERED COINAGE

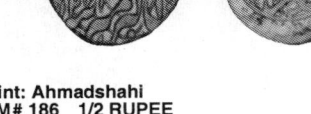

Mint: Ahmadshahi
KM# 186 1/2 RUPEE
Silver

Date	Mintage	Good	VG	F	VF	XF
AH1272	—	2.00	3.00	6.00	10.00	15.00
AH1273	—	2.00	3.00	6.00	10.00	15.00
AH1273//1272	—	2.00	3.00	6.00	10.00	15.00

Note: Dated on both sides.

Mint: Ahmadshahi
KM# 188 1/2 RUPEE
Silver **Note:** Dated on both sides.

Date	Mintage	Good	VG	F	VF	XF
AH1272//1272	—	4.00	10.00	20.00	35.00	55.00
AH1273//1273	—	4.00	10.00	20.00	35.00	55.00

Mint: Qandahar
KM# 187.1 1/2 RUPEE
Silver

Date	Mintage	Good	VG	F	VF	XF
AH1272//1272	—	2.00	3.00	6.00	10.00	15.00
AH1273//1273	—	2.00	3.00	6.00	10.00	15.00
AH1274//1274	—	2.00	3.00	6.00	10.00	15.00
AH1275//1275	—	2.00	3.00	6.00	10.00	15.00
AH1276//1276	—	2.00	3.75	7.50	12.00	18.00
AH1277//1277	—	2.00	3.75	7.50	12.00	18.00
AH1278//1278	—	2.00	3.75	7.50	12.00	18.00

Mint: Qandahar
KM# 187.2 1/2 RUPEE
Silver **Obv:** "Qandahar" above, "Duriba" below **Note:** Dated on both sides. Posthumous issue.

Date	Mintage	Good	VG	F	VF	XF
AH1281//1281	—	6.00	15.00	30.00	50.00	75.00

Mint: Kabul
KM# 476 RUPEE
Silver

Date	Mintage	Good	VG	F	VF	XF
AH1239//1	—	9.00	22.50	45.00	75.00	110

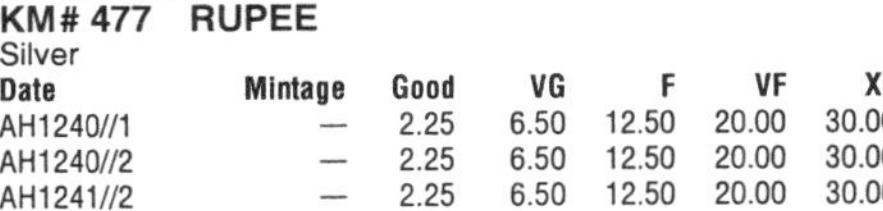

Mint: Kabul
KM# 477 RUPEE
Silver

Date	Mintage	Good	VG	F	VF	XF
AH1240//1	—	2.25	6.50	12.50	20.00	30.00
AH1240//2	—	2.25	6.50	12.50	20.00	30.00
AH1241//2	—	2.25	6.50	12.50	20.00	30.00

Mint: Kabul
KM# 478 RUPEE
Silver **Obv:** Cartouche in center

Date	Mintage	Good	VG	F	VF	XF
AH1241	—	2.00	4.50	9.00	15.00	22.50
AH1242	—	2.00	4.50	9.00	15.00	22.50
AH1243	—	2.00	4.50	9.00	15.00	22.50
AH1244	—	2.00	4.50	9.00	15.00	22.50

Mint: Kabul
KM# 479 RUPEE
Silver **Rev:** Mint name in ordinary form

Date	Mintage	Good	VG	F	VF	XF
AH1244	—	2.50	6.50	13.50	22.50	35.00
AH1245	—	2.50	6.50	13.50	22.50	35.00

Mint: Kabul
KM# 480.2 RUPEE
Silver

Date	Mintage	Good	VG	F	VF	XF
AH1247	—	2.00	4.00	8.00	13.00	20.00
AH1248	—	2.00	4.00	8.00	13.00	20.00

Mint: Kabul
KM# 481 RUPEE
Silver

Date	Mintage	Good	VG	F	VF	XF
AH1250	—	2.50	5.00	8.00	13.00	20.00
AH1251	—	2.50	5.00	8.00	13.00	20.00
AH1252	—	2.50	5.00	8.00	13.00	20.00
AH1253	—	2.50	5.00	8.00	13.00	20.00
AH1254	—	2.50	5.00	8.00	13.00	20.00
AH1255	—	2.50	5.00	8.00	13.00	20.00

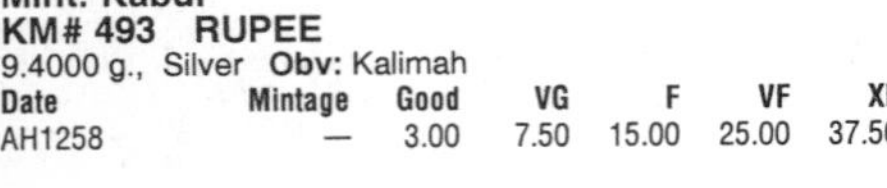

Mint: Kabul
KM# 493 RUPEE
9.4000 g., Silver **Obv:** Kalimah

Date	Mintage	Good	VG	F	VF	XF
AH1258	—	3.00	7.50	15.00	25.00	37.50

Mint: Kabul
KM# 496 RUPEE
9.4000 g., Silver **Obv:** Long couplet

Date	Mintage	Good	VG	F	VF	XF
AH1259	—	7.50	13.50	30.00	40.00	55.00

Mint: Kabul
KM# 497.2 RUPEE
Silver **Obv:** One leaf in field in 2-4 o'clock margin **Rev:** Two leaves facing each other at bottom

Date	Mintage	Good	VG	F	VF	XF
AH1271	—	2.00	4.00	7.50	12.00	18.00
AH1272	—	2.00	4.00	7.50	12.00	18.00
AH1273	—	2.00	4.00	7.50	12.00	18.00
AH1274	—	2.00	4.00	7.50	12.00	18.00
AH1277	—	2.00	4.00	7.50	12.00	18.00

Mint: Kabul
KM# 497.1 RUPEE
9.4000 g., Silver **Obv:** Couplet ending "Khaliq-i-Akbar" **Note:** Mulings exist with different dates on obverse and reverse.

Date	Mintage	Good	VG	F	VF	XF
AH1259	—	3.25	8.00	15.00	22.50	40.00
AH1262	—	3.00	7.00	12.00	15.00	25.00
AH1263	—	2.00	4.00	7.50	12.00	18.00
AH1264	—	2.00	4.00	7.50	12.00	18.00
AH1265	—	2.00	4.00	7.50	12.00	18.00
AH1266	—	2.00	4.00	7.50	12.00	18.00
Note: Five-pointed star on obverse						
AH1266	—	2.00	4.50	8.00	12.00	18.00
Note: Five-pointed star on both sides						
AH1267	—	2.00	4.00	7.50	12.00	18.00
AH1268	—	2.00	4.50	8.00	13.00	20.00
AH1269	—	2.00	4.00	7.50	12.00	18.00
AH1270	—	2.00	4.00	7.50	12.00	18.00
AH1271	—	2.00	4.00	7.50	12.00	18.00
AH1272	—	2.00	4.00	7.50	12.00	18.00
AH1273	—	2.00	4.00	7.50	12.00	18.00
AH1274	—	2.00	4.00	7.50	12.00	18.00
AH1275	—	2.00	4.00	7.50	12.00	18.00
AH1276	—	2.00	4.00	7.50	12.00	18.00
AH1277	—	2.00	4.00	7.50	12.00	18.00
AH1278	—	2.00	4.00	7.50	12.00	18.00
AH1279	—	2.00	4.00	7.50	12.00	18.00
AH1280	—	4.00	10.00	20.00	30.00	50.00

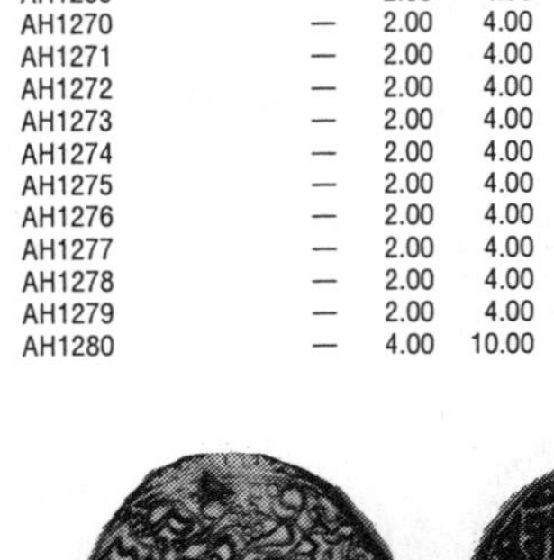

Mint: Kabul
KM# 480.1 RUPEE
Silver **Note:** Various arrangements of obverse couplet and various borders on reverse.

Date	Mintage	Good	VG	F	VF	XF
AH1245	—	2.00	3.50	7.00	13.00	20.00
AH1246	—	2.00	3.50	7.00	13.00	20.00
AH1247	—	2.00	3.50	7.00	13.00	20.00
AH1248	—	2.00	3.50	7.00	13.00	20.00
AH1249	—	2.00	3.50	7.00	13.00	20.00
AH1250	—	2.00	3.50	7.00	13.00	20.00

Mint: Kabul
KM# 499 TILLA
Gold

Date	Mintage	Good	VG	F	VF	XF
AH1269 Rare	—	—	—	—	—	—

Fath Jang
AH1285 / 1842AD
HAMMERED COINAGE

Mint: Ahmadshahi
KM# 178 RUPEE
Silver **Note:** Weight varies: 9.15-9.35 grams.

Date	Mintage	Good	VG	F	VF	XF
AH1258	—	10.00	25.00	50.00	80.00	120

Mint: Kabul
KM# 488.1 RUPEE
Silver **Obv:** Couplet, "Fath Jung" at top **Note:** Weight varies: 9.30-9.40 grams.

Date	Mintage	Good	VG	F	VF	XF
AH1258	—	7.00	18.00	35.00	60.00	90.00

Mint: Kabul
KM# 488.2 RUPEE
Silver **Obv:** Couplet, name "Fath Jung" in center **Note:** Weight varies: 9.30-9.40 grams.

Date	Mintage	Good	VG	F	VF	XF
AH1258	—	8.50	21.50	42.50	70.00	110

Mint: Kabul
KM# 488.3 RUPEE
Silver **Obv:** Name only with title "Dur-e-Duran" **Note:** Weight varies: 9.30-9.40 grams.

Date	Mintage	Good	VG	F	VF	XF
AH1258	—	7.00	18.00	35.00	60.00	90.00

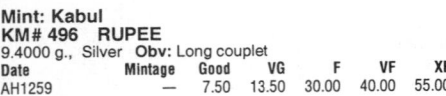

Mint: Kabul
KM# 488.4 RUPEE
Silver **Obv:** Name only with title "Padshah-i Ghazi" **Note:** Weight varies: 9.30-9.40 grams.

Date	Mintage	Good	VG	F	VF	XF
AH1258	—	7.00	18.00	35.00	60.00	90.00

Shahpur Shah
AH1258 / 1842AD
HAMMERED COINAGE

Mint: Kabul
KM# 489 RUPEE
9.4000 g., Silver

Date	Mintage	Good	VG	F	VF	XF
AH1258	—	13.00	32.50	65.00	100	150

Yar Muhammad Khan Sadozai
AH1258-1267 / 1842-1851AD
HAMMERED COINAGE

Mint: Herat - Dar as-Sultanat
KM# 404 1/6 RUPEE
Silver **Obv:** Kalima

Date	Mintage	Good	VG	F	VF	XF
AH1258	—	6.00	15.00	30.00	50.00	75.00
AH1259	—	6.00	15.00	30.00	50.00	75.00
AH1260	—	6.00	15.00	30.00	50.00	75.00

Mint: Herat - Dar as-Sultanat
KM# 405.1 1/2 RUPEE
Silver **Obv:** Kalima

Date	Mintage	Good	VG	F	VF	XF
AH1261	—	4.00	10.00	20.00	35.00	50.00
AH1262	—	4.00	10.00	20.00	35.00	50.00
AH1263	—	4.00	10.00	20.00	35.00	50.00
AH1264	—	5.00	12.50	25.00	40.00	60.00
AH1265	—	5.00	12.50	25.00	40.00	60.00
AH1266	—	5.00	12.50	25.00	40.00	60.00

Mint: Herat - Dar as-Sultanat
KM# 405.2 1/2 RUPEE
Silver **Rev:** Legend in circle

Date	Mintage	Good	VG	F	VF	XF
AH1269 (sic)	—	6.00	15.00	30.00	50.00	75.00

Mint: Herat - Dar as-Sultanat
KM# 405.3 1/2 RUPEE
Silver **Obv:** Kalimah in small double circle

Date	Mintage	Good	VG	F	VF	XF
AH1267	—	7.00	17.50	35.00	60.00	90.00

Muhammad Yusuf Khan Sadozai
AH1267-1272 / 1851-1856AD
HAMMERED COINAGE

Mint: Herat - Dar as-Sultanat
KM# A406 1/2 RUPEE
Silver **Obv:** Kalimah in circle

Date	Mintage	Good	VG	F	VF	XF
AH1269	—	10.00	25.00	50.00	80.00	120
AH1270	—	10.00	25.00	50.00	80.00	120

Mint: Herat - Dar as-Sultanat
KM# 406 1/2 RUPEE
Silver **Obv:** Kalimah **Rev:** Mint name in ornate circle

Date	Mintage	Good	VG	F	VF	XF
AH1271	—	10.00	25.00	50.00	80.00	120

Mint: Herat - Dar as-Sultanat
KM# 407 1/2 RUPEE
Silver **Obv:** Kalimah **Rev:** Mint name in square

Date	Mintage	Good	VG	F	VF	XF
AH1271	—	11.00	27.50	55.00	90.00	135

Mint: Herat - Dar as-Sultanat
KM# 408 1/2 RUPEE
Silver **Obv:** Kalimah

Date	Mintage	Good	VG	F	VF	XF
AH1272	—	11.00	27.50	55.00	90.00	135

Mint: Herat - Dar as-Sultanat
KM# 409 TILLA
Gold **Obv:** Kalimah

Date	Mintage	Good	VG	F	VF	XF
AH1272	—	—	—	300	450	650

Rahamdil Khan
AH1272-1273 / 1855-1856AD
HAMMERED COINAGE

Mint: Ahmadshahi
KM# 184 1/2 RUPEE
Silver

Date	Mintage	Good	VG	F	VF	XF
AH1271	—	6.00	15.00	30.00	50.00	75.00
AH1272	—	6.00	15.00	30.00	50.00	75.00

Sher Ali
AH1280-1283 / 1863-1866AD First reign
HAMMERED COINAGE

Mint: Qandahar
KM# 191 1/2 RUPEE
Silver **Obv:** Couplet **Rev:** Title of ruler and mint

Date	Mintage	Good	VG	F	VF	XF
AH1280	—	2.50	6.00	12.00	20.00	30.00
AH1281	—	3.50	9.00	18.00	30.00	45.00
AH1282	—	2.50	6.00	12.00	20.00	30.00
AH1283 Rare	—	—	—	—	—	—
AH1285	—	3.50	9.00	18.00	30.00	45.00

Mint: Qandahar
KM# 192 1/2 RUPEE
Silver **Obv:** Couplet **Rev:** Mint only **Note:** Arrangement of reverse legend varies.

Date	Mintage	Good	VG	F	VF	XF
AH1282	—	3.50	9.00	18.00	30.00	45.00
AH1283	—	3.50	9.00	18.00	30.00	45.00

Mint: Kabul
KM# 502 RUPEE
Silver **Obv:** New couplet, "Bi-Valayi Amir"

Date	Mintage	Good	VG	F	VF	XF
AH1280 Rare	—	—	—	—	—	—

Mint: Kabul
KM# 504 RUPEE
Silver

Date	Mintage	Good	VG	F	VF	XF
AH1282	—	5.00	12.50	20.00	35.00	55.00

Mint: Kabul
KM# 503 RUPEE
Silver **Obv:** Couplet starting "Za Aini Marhamat..." **Note:** Two obverse varieties exist.

Date	Mintage	Good	VG	F	VF	XF
AH1280	—	2.00	4.00	8.00	13.00	20.00
AH1281	—	2.00	4.00	8.00	13.00	20.00
AH1282	—	2.00	4.00	8.00	13.00	20.00

Mint: Qandahar
KM# 194 TILLA
Gold

Date	Mintage	Good	VG	F	VF	XF
AH1283	—	—	275	450	700	1,000
AH1284	—	—	275	450	700	1,000
AH1285	—	—	275	450	700	1,000

Mint: Kabul
KM# 524 TOMAN
3.4500 g., Gold

Date	Mintage	Good	VG	F	VF	XF
AH1294	—	—	225	400	600	850
AH1295	—	—	225	400	600	850
AH1296	—	—	225	400	600	850

Muhammad A'zam

AH1283-1285 / 1866-1868AD

HAMMERED COINAGE

Mint: Qandahar
KM# 201 1/2 RUPEE
Silver

Date	Mintage	Good	VG	F	VF	XF
AH1283	—	9.00	22.50	45.00	75.00	110
AH1284	—	9.00	22.50	45.00	75.00	110

Mint: Kabul
KM# 508.1 RUPEE
Silver **Obv:** "A'zam" above "Amir"

Date	Mintage	Good	VG	F	VF	XF
AH1284	—	2.50	6.00	12.00	20.00	30.00
AH1285	—	2.50	6.00	12.00	20.00	30.00

Mint: Kabul
KM# 508.2 RUPEE
Silver **Obv:** "A'zam" above "Muhammad"

Date	Mintage	Good	VG	F	VF	XF
AH1284	—	5.50	13.50	27.50	45.00	67.50

Mint: Kabul
KM# 509 RUPEE
Silver

Date	Mintage	Good	VG	F	VF	XF
AH1285	—	4.00	10.00	20.00	35.00	52.50

Muhammad Afzal

AH1283-1284 / 1866-1867AD

HAMMERED COINAGE

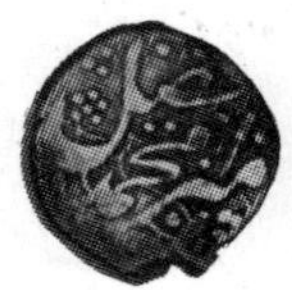

Mint: Ahmadshahi
KM# 196 1/2 RUPEE
Silver

Date	Mintage	Good	VG	F	VF	XF
AH1283	—	9.00	22.50	45.00	75.00	110

Mint: Qandahar
KM# 197 1/2 RUPEE
Silver **Obv:** KM#196 **Rev:** KM#201

Date	Mintage	Good	VG	F	VF	XF
AH1283	—	12.00	30.00	60.00	100	150
AH1284	—	12.00	30.00	60.00	100	150

Mint: Kabul
KM# 507 RUPEE
Silver **Note:** Two AH1283 varieties are known.

Date	Mintage	Good	VG	F	VF	XF
AH1283	—	3.50	9.00	18.00	30.00	45.00
AH1284	—	5.00	12.50	25.00	40.00	60.00

Sher Ali

AH1285-1296 / 1868-1879AD Second reign

HAMMERED COINAGE

Mint: Kabul
KM# 511 1/6 RUPEE
1.5000 g., Silver

Date	Mintage	Good	VG	F	VF	XF
AH1287	—	8.00	20.00	40.00	90.00	100

Mint: Herat - Dar as-Sultanat
KM# 410.1 1/2 RUPEE
Silver **Rev:** Legend in square

Date	Mintage	Good	VG	F	VF	XF
AH1280	—	4.00	10.00	20.00	35.00	55.00

Mint: Herat - Dar as-Sultanat
KM# 410.2 1/2 RUPEE
Silver **Rev:** Legend in "Mehrabi" square

Date	Mintage	Good	VG	F	VF	XF
AH1280	—	4.00	10.00	20.00	35.00	55.00

Mint: Herat - Dar as-Sultanat
KM# 411 1/2 RUPEE
Silver **Obv:** "Amir" at top **Rev:** Date

Date	Mintage	Good	VG	F	VF	XF
AH1280	—	4.00	10.00	20.00	35.00	55.00
AH1281	—	4.00	10.00	20.00	35.00	55.00

Mint: Herat - Dar as-Sultanat
KM# 414 1/2 RUPEE
Silver **Obv:** "Amir" at top, legend rearranged

Date	Mintage	Good	VG	F	VF	XF
AH1287	—	6.00	15.00	30.00	50.00	75.00
AH1288	—	5.00	12.50	25.00	40.00	60.00
AH1289	—	5.00	12.50	25.00	40.00	60.00
AH1290	—	5.00	12.50	25.00	40.00	60.00

Mint: Herat - Dar as-Sultanat
KM# 412 1/2 RUPEE

Silver **Obv:** "Amir" at bottom, date both sides **Note:** Mules exist bearing varieties combinations of these dates.

Date	Mintage	Good	VG	F	VF	XF
AH1281	—	3.50	9.00	18.00	30.00	45.00
AH1282	—	3.50	9.00	18.00	30.00	45.00
AH1283	—	3.50	9.00	18.00	30.00	45.00
AH1284	—	3.50	9.00	18.00	30.00	45.00
AH1287	—	3.50	9.00	18.00	30.00	45.00

Mint: Herat - Dar as-Sultanat
KM# 413 1/2 RUPEE
Silver **Obv:** Shorter inscription; (ruler's name only) **Note:** Several varieties exist. A tilla dated AH1284 of Sher Ali has been reported.

Date	Mintage	Good	VG	F	VF	XF
AH1292	—	3.50	9.00	18.00	30.00	45.00
AH1295	—	2.00	3.75	7.50	12.00	18.00

Mint: Kabul
KM# 513 1/2 RUPEE
Silver **Note:** Large, thin planchet, fine engraving.

Date	Mintage	Good	VG	F	VF	XF
AH1292	—	2.00	3.75	7.50	12.00	18.00

Mint: Kabul
KM# 514 1/2 RUPEE
Silver **Note:** Small, thick planchet, course engraving.

Date	Mintage	Good	VG	F	VF	XF
AH1295	—	2.00	3.00	6.00	10.00	15.00

Mint: Qandahar
KM# 205.3 1/2 RUPEE
Silver **Rev:** Legend within wreath

Date	Mintage	Good	VG	F	VF	XF
AH1285	—	5.00	12.50	25.00	40.00	60.00

Mint: Qandahar
KM# 206 1/2 RUPEE
Silver

Date	Mintage	Good	VG	F	VF	XF
AH1277	—	2.50	6.00	12.50	20.00	30.00
Note: Error for 1288						
AH1288	—	2.00	3.00	6.00	10.00	15.00
AH1289	—	2.50	6.00	12.50	20.00	30.00

Mint: Qandahar
KM# 207.1 1/2 RUPEE
Silver

Date	Mintage	Good	VG	F	VF	XF
AH1290	—	2.00	4.00	6.00	10.00	15.00
AH1291	—	2.00	4.00	6.00	10.00	15.00
AH1292	—	2.00	4.00	6.00	10.00	15.00
AH1293	—	2.00	4.00	6.00	10.00	15.00
Note: Varietiy of 1293 exists with double leaf at bottom of obverse						
AH1295	—	2.00	4.00	6.00	10.00	15.00

Mint: Qandahar
KM# 207.2 1/2 RUPEE
Silver **Obv:** Teardrop design

Date	Mintage	Good	VG	F	VF	XF
AH1294	—	2.00	4.00	6.00	10.00	15.00
AH1295	—	2.00	4.00	6.00	10.00	15.00

Mint: Qandahar
KM# 208 1/2 RUPEE
Silver

Date	Mintage	Good	VG	F	VF	XF
AH1295	—	3.00	7.50	15.00	25.00	37.50

Mint: Qandahar
KM# 205.2 1/2 RUPEE
Silver

Date	Mintage	Good	VG	F	VF	XF
AH1287	—	3.50	9.00	18.00	30.00	45.00

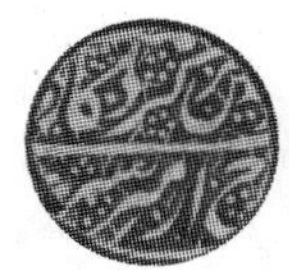

Mint: Qandahar
KM# 205.1 1/2 RUPEE
Silver **Note:** Resumption of type identical to KM#191 of first reign.

Date	Mintage	Good	VG	F	VF	XF
AH1284	—	2.50	6.00	12.00	20.00	30.00
AH1285	—	2.50	6.00	12.00	20.00	30.00

Mint: Kabul
KM# 516 RUPEE
Silver **Obv:** Couplet starting "Za Iltifat-i..."

Date	Mintage	Good	VG	F	VF	XF
AH1285	—	2.50	6.00	12.50	20.00	30.00

Mint: Kabul
KM# 517 RUPEE
Silver **Obv:** Three-stem toughra

Date	Mintage	Good	VG	F	VF	XF
AH1285	—	3.25	8.00	16.00	27.50	40.00
AH1286	—	2.00	5.00	8.00	13.00	20.00
AH1286//1287	—	2.00	5.00	10.00	16.50	25.00
AH1287	—	2.00	5.00	10.00	16.50	25.00

Mint: Kabul
KM# 518 RUPEE
Silver **Obv:** Five-stem toughra

Date	Mintage	Good	VG	F	VF	XF
AH1285	—	12.00	30.00	60.00	100	150
AH1286	—	11.00	27.50	55.00	90.00	135

Mint: Kabul
KM# 521 RUPEE
Silver **Note:** Course style.

Date	Mintage	Good	VG	F	VF	XF
AH1293	—	2.50	4.50	7.50	12.00	18.00
AH1294	—	2.50	4.50	7.50	12.00	18.00
AH1295	—	2.50	4.50	7.50	12.00	18.00

Mint: Kabul
KM# 520 RUPEE
Silver **Note:** Fine style.

Date	Mintage	Good	VG	F	VF	XF
AH1292	—	3.50	6.50	9.00	15.00	25.00
AH1293	—	3.50	6.50	9.00	15.00	25.00

Mint: Kabul
KM# 519 RUPEE
Silver **Note:** Other examples bearing different obverse and reverse dates exist.

Date	Mintage	Good	VG	F	VF	XF
AH1287	—	2.50	4.50	8.00	12.00	18.00
AH1288	—	2.00	3.50	6.50	10.00	15.00
AH1289	—	2.00	3.50	6.50	10.00	15.00
AH1290	—	2.00	3.50	6.50	10.00	15.00
AH1291	—	2.00	3.50	6.50	10.00	15.00
AH1292	—	2.00	3.50	6.50	10.00	15.00
AH1293	—	2.00	3.50	6.50	10.00	15.00
AH1294	—	2.00	3.50	6.50	10.00	15.00
AH1295	—	2.00	3.50	6.50	10.00	15.00
AH1295//1296	—	2.00	3.50	6.50	10.00	15.00
AH1296	—	2.50	5.00	10.00	16.00	24.00

Mint: Kabul
KM# 525 MOHUR
10.9000 g., Gold

Date	Mintage	Good	VG	F	VF	XF
AH1288	—	—	250	425	650	900

Muhammad Yaqub
AH1296-1298 / 1879-1880AD
HAMMERED COINAGE

Mint: Herat - Dar as-Sultanat
KM# 415 1/6 RUPEE
1.8000 g., Silver, 11 mm.

Date	Mintage	Good	VG	F	VF	XF
AH1297 Rare	—	—	—	—	—	—

Mint: Kabul
KM# 531 1/3 RUPEE
Silver

Date	Mintage	Good	VG	F	VF	XF
AH1296	—	9.00	22.50	45.00	75.00	110

Mint: Herat - Dar as-Sultanat
KM# 417 1/2 RUPEE
Silver

Date	Mintage	Good	VG	F	VF	XF
AH1296	—	2.00	3.00	6.00	10.00	15.00
AH1297	—	2.00	3.00	6.00	10.00	15.00
AH1298	—	2.00	3.00	6.00	10.00	15.00

Mint: Herat - Dar as-Sultanat
KM# 416 1/2 RUPEE
Silver **Obv:** Date below **Rev:** Date in "b" of Zarb

Date	Mintage	Good	VG	F	VF	XF
AH1298	—	—	—	—	—	—

Mint: Qandahar
KM# 212 1/2 RUPEE
Silver **Note:** Mules exist bearing both dates.

Date	Mintage	Good	VG	F	VF	XF
AH1296	—	3.00	7.50	15.00	25.00	37.50
AH1297	—	4.50	11.50	22.50	37.50	55.00

Mint: Kabul
KM# 533 RUPEE
Silver

Date	Mintage	Good	VG	F	VF	XF
AH1296	—	2.00	4.00	6.50	8.00	16.00

Wali Sher Ali
AH1297 / 1880AD
HAMMERED COINAGE

Mint: Qandahar
KM# 217 1/2 RUPEE
Silver

Date	Mintage	Good	VG	F	VF	XF
AH1297//1297	—	3.00	7.50	15.00	25.00	37.50

Mint: Qandahar
KM# 221 1/2 RUPEE
Silver **Obv. Legend:** "Al-Mulk Lillah"

Date	Mintage	Good	VG	F	VF	XF
AH1297//1297	—	3.50	9.00	18.00	30.00	45.00

Note: It is not known under whose authority this type was struck

Mint: Qandahar
KM# 218 RUPEE
Silver **Rev:** Date

Date	Mintage	Good	VG	F	VF	XF
AH1297	—	5.00	12.50	25.00	40.00	60.00

Mint: Qandahar
KM# 219 TILLA
Gold

Date	Mintage	Good	VG	F	VF	XF
AH1297	—	—	400	650	1,000	1,350

Abdur Rahman
AH1297-1319 / 1880-1901AD
HAMMERED COINAGE

Mint: Herat - Dar as-Sultanat
KM# 418 1/8 RUPEE
Silver, 13 mm.

Date	Mintage	Good	VG	F	VF	XF
AH1307 Rare	—	—	—	—	—	—

Mint: Kabul
KM# 541 1/3 RUPEE
Silver, 15 mm.

Date	Mintage	Good	VG	F	VF	XF
AH1297	—	11.00	27.50	55.00	90.00	135
AH1298	—	9.00	22.50	45.00	75.00	110

Mint: Ahmadshahi
KM# 222 1/2 RUPEE
Silver

Date	Mintage	Good	VG	F	VF	XF
AH1298	—	5.00	12.50	25.00	40.00	60.00

Mint: Herat - Dar as-Sultanat
KM# 419 1/2 RUPEE

Silver **Note:** Many coins of this type KM#419 are found with blundered dates. Such coins are worth the same as normal dates. Mulings of dates exist.

Date	Mintage	Good	VG	F	VF	XF
AH1297	—	1.25	3.00	6.00	10.00	15.00
AH1298	—	2.00	5.00	10.00	6.00	25.00
AH1299	—	2.50	6.00	12.00	20.00	30.00
AH1300	—	1.25	3.00	6.00	10.00	15.00
AH1301	—	1.25	3.00	6.00	10.00	15.00
AH1302	—	1.25	3.00	6.00	10.00	15.00
AH1303	—	1.00	2.00	5.00	8.00	12.00
AH1304	—	1.00	2.00	5.00	8.00	12.00
AH1305	—	1.00	2.00	5.00	8.00	12.00
AH1306	—	1.00	2.00	5.00	8.00	12.00
AH1307	—	1.00	2.00	5.00	8.00	12.00
AH1308	—	1.00	2.00	5.00	8.00	12.00

Mint: Qandahar
KM# 225 1/2 RUPEE
Silver

Date	Mintage	Good	VG	F	VF	XF
AH1298	—	6.00	15.00	30.00	50.00	75.00
AH1304	—	6.00	15.00	30.00	50.00	75.00

Mint: Ahmadshahi
KM# 223.1 RUPEE
Silver **Obv:** Two leaves, date **Rev:** Mint name **Note:** Struck at Ahmadshahi Mint.

Date	Mintage	Good	VG	F	VF	XF
AH1298	—	—	—	—	—	—

Mint: Kabul
KM# 543 RUPEE
Silver **Obv:** Rudimentary toughra

Date	Mintage	Good	VG	F	VF	XF
AH1297	—	7.00	17.50	35.00	60.00	90.00

Mint: Kabul
KM# A544 RUPEE
Silver **Obv:** Name of ruler in fancy border

Date	Mintage	Good	VG	F	VF	XF
AH1297	—	7.00	17.50	35.00	60.00	90.00

Mint: Kabul
KM# B544 RUPEE
Silver **Obv:** Ornate toughra

Date	Mintage	Good	VG	F	VF	XF
AH1298	—	11.00	27.50	55.00	90.00	135

Mint: Kabul
KM# C544 RUPEE
Silver **Obv:** Name of ruler within dotted circle

Date	Mintage	Good	VG	F	VF	XF
AH1297	—	11.00	27.50	55.00	90.00	135

Mint: Kabul
KM# D544 RUPEE
Silver **Obv:** Date above **Rev:** Date in "b" of "Zarb"

Date	Mintage	Good	VG	F	VF	XF
AH1297	—	12.00	30.00	60.00	100	150

Mint: Kabul
KM# 544.2 RUPEE
Silver **Obv:** Floral and legend varieties

Date	Mintage	Good	VG	F	VF	XF
AH1304	—	5.00	12.50	25.00	40.00	60.00

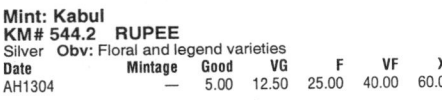

Mint: Kabul
KM# 544.1 RUPEE
Silver **Obv:** Name of ruler in plain border **Note:** Obverses are often muled with reverses bearing a different date. For machine-struck coins dated AH1303//1304 and 1304//1304, see KM#805.

Date	Mintage	Good	VG	F	VF	XF
AH1297	—	2.00	4.50	7.50	12.00	18.00

Note: The year AH1297 has been observed struck over an 1876 British India 1/4 rupee, probably a mint sport

Date	Mintage	Good	VG	F	VF	XF
AH1298	—	2.00	4.50	9.00	15.00	25.00
AH1299	—	3.50	9.00	18.00	30.00	45.00
AH1300	—	3.00	7.50	15.00	25.00	37.50
AH1301	—	2.00	4.50	7.50	12.00	18.00
AH1302	—	2.00	4.50	7.50	12.00	18.00
AH1303	—	2.00	4.50	7.50	12.00	18.00
AH1304	—	2.00	4.50	7.50	12.00	18.00
AH1305	—	2.00	4.50	7.50	12.00	18.00
AH1306	—	2.00	4.50	7.50	12.00	18.00
AH1307	—	2.00	4.50	7.50	12.00	18.00
AH1308	—	2.50	5.00	10.00	16.00	25.00

Mint: Qandahar
KM# 224 RUPEE
Silver

Date	Mintage	Good	VG	F	VF	XF
AH1299//3	—	3.50	9.00	18.00	30.00	45.00
AH1298	—	2.50	6.00	12.50	20.00	30.00
AH1300	—	3.50	9.00	18.00	30.00	45.00
AH1301	—	3.50	9.00	18.00	30.00	45.00
AH1302	—	3.50	9.00	18.00	30.00	45.00
AH1303	—	2.00	5.00	10.00	16.00	25.00
AH1304	—	2.00	3.75	7.50	12.00	18.00
AH1305	—	2.00	3.75	7.50	12.00	18.00
AH1306	—	2.00	3.75	7.50	12.00	18.00
AH1307	—	2.00	3.75	7.50	12.00	18.00
AH1308	—	2.00	3.75	7.50	12.00	18.00

Mint: Qandahar
KM# 223.2 RUPEE
Silver **Obv:** Two leaves, date **Rev:** Mint name, date **Note:** Variety with only one leaf on obverse exist.

Date	Mintage	Good	VG	F	VF	XF
AH1298	—	11.00	27.50	55.00	90.00	135
AH1299	—	11.00	27.50	55.00	90.00	135

Mint: Kabul
KM# 545 NAZARANA RUPEE
Silver

Date	Mintage	Good	VG	F	VF	XF
AH1303	—	9.00	22.50	45.00	75.00	110

Mint: Qandahar
KM# 226 TILLA
Gold

Date	Mintage	Good	VG	F	VF	XF
AH1298 Rare	—	—	—	—	—	—

MILLED COINAGE

10 Dinar = 1 Paisa; 5 Paise = 1 Shahi; 2 Shahi = 1 Sanar; 2 Sanar = 1 Abbasi; 1-1/2 Abbasi = 1 Qiran; 2 Qiran = 1 Kabuli Rupee; 1 Tilla = 10 Rupees

Mint: Kabul
KM# 800 PAISA
Bronze, 24 mm.

Date	Mintage	Good	VG	F	VF	XF
AH1309	—	18.00	45.00	100	200	400

Mint: Kabul
KM# 802 PAISA
Bronze or Brass, 21-21.5 mm. **Note:** Coins dated AH1313 and 1317 are known in two varieties. Three varieties are known for AH1314. Size varies.

Date	Mintage	Good	VG	F	VF	XF
AH1309	—	1.00	2.50	5.00	7.50	20.00
AH1312	—	0.75	2.00	4.00	6.50	15.00
AH1313	—	1.00	2.50	5.00	7.50	20.00
AH1314	—	0.75	2.00	4.00	6.50	15.00
AH1316	—	1.25	3.00	5.00	7.50	20.00
AH1317	—	1.50	4.00	6.00	10.00	30.00

Mint: Kabul
KM# 828 PAISA
Bronze or Brass **Obv:** KM#827 **Rev:** KM#802 **Note:** Mule.

Date	Mintage	Good	VG	F	VF	XF
AH1317	—	4.00	10.00	15.00	30.00	50.00

Mint: Kabul
KM# 801.1 PAISA
Bronze, 20 mm. **Note:** Smaller variety of KM#802.

Date	Mintage	Good	VG	F	VF	XF
AH1309	—	8.00	20.00	40.00	70.00	100

Mint: Kabul
KM# 801.2 PAISA
Bronze, 20.4 mm. **Note:** Thicker variety.

Date	Mintage	Good	VG	F	VF	XF
AH1309	—	10.00	25.00	50.00	100	150

Mint: Kabul
KM# 827 PAISA
Bronze or Brass **Note:** Two varieties are known.

Date	Mintage	Good	VG	F	VF	XF
AH1317	—	1.35	3.50	6.00	12.00	35.00

Mint: Kabul
KM# 803 SHAHI
Copper or Brass

Date	Mintage	Good	VG	F	VF	XF
AH1309	—	6.00	15.00	25.00	55.00	140

Mint: Kabul
KM# 809 100 DINARS
Copper

Date	Mintage	Good	VG	F	VF	XF
AH1311	—	100	250	400	600	800

Mint: Kabul
KM# 823 SANAR
1.5500 g., 0.5000 Silver .0249 oz. ASW **Obv:** Date in loop of toughra

Date	Mintage	Good	VG	F	VF	XF
AH1315	—	2.75	7.00	10.00	20.00	40.00
ND	—	3.50	8.50	13.00	25.00	45.00

Mint: Kabul
KM# 824 SANAR
1.5500 g., 0.5000 Silver .0249 oz. ASW **Rev:** Date below mosque

Date	Mintage	Good	VG	F	VF	XF
AH1315	—	3.50	9.00	14.00	25.00	45.00
ND	—	3.25	8.50	13.50	25.00	45.00

Mint: Kabul
KM# 810 ABBASI
3.1100 g., 0.5000 Silver .0499 oz. ASW **Obv:** Date above toughra

Date	Mintage	Good	VG	F	VF	XF
AH1313	—	1.35	3.00	5.00	8.00	14.00

Mint: Kabul
KM# 811 ABBASI
3.1100 g., 0.5000 Silver .0499 oz. ASW **Rev:** Date below mosque

Date	Mintage	Good	VG	F	VF	XF
AH1313	—	2.75	7.00	12.50	22.50	45.00

Mint: Kabul
KM# 816 ABBASI
3.1100 g., 0.5000 Silver .0499 oz. ASW **Rev:** New style mosque

Date	Mintage	Good	VG	F	VF	XF
AH1314	—	1.25	3.00	6.00	13.50	22.50

Mint: Kabul
KM# 804 1/2 RUPEE
4.6500 g., 0.5000 Silver .0747 oz. ASW **Rev:** Star above mosque

Date	Mintage	Good	VG	F	VF	XF
AH1308	—	2.00	5.00	7.50	10.00	20.00
AH1309	—	2.00	5.00	8.00	12.00	25.00
AH1310	—	2.00	5.00	8.00	12.00	25.00

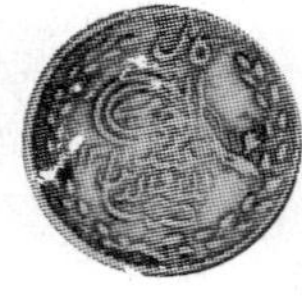

Mint: Kabul
KM# 825 1/2 RUPEE
4.6500 g., 0.5000 Silver .0747 oz. ASW **Rev:** Crossed swords and cannons below mosque

Date	Mintage	Good	VG	F	VF	XF
AH1316	—	1.75	4.50	8.50	15.00	30.00

Mint: Kabul
KM# 812 1/2 RUPEE
4.6500 g., 0.5000 Silver .0747 oz. ASW **Rev:** Star above mosque

Date	Mintage	Good	VG	F	VF	XF
AH1313	—	2.50	6.00	8.50	12.50	27.50

Mint: Kabul
KM# 817 1/2 RUPEE
4.6500 g., 0.5000 Silver .0747 oz. ASW **Rev:** "Yak Mesqhal" above mosque

Date	Mintage	Good	VG	F	VF	XF
AH1314	—	3.00	7.50	13.50	28.00	60.00

Note: The Half Rupee dated AH1314 bears the denomination of 1 Qiran

Mint: Birmingham
KM# 805 RUPEE
Silver **Note:** Similar to KM#544.1. These machine struck Rupees were produced by the Birmingham Mint as patterns.

Date	Mintage	Good	VG	F	VF	XF
AH1304/3	—	10.00	25.00	35.00	55.00	115
AH1304	—	10.00	25.00	35.00	55.00	115

Mint: Kabul
KM# 830 RUPEE
9.2000 g., 0.5000 Silver .0755 oz. ASW **Obv:** Date at right of toughra **Rev:** New style mosque

Date	Mintage	Good	VG	F	VF	XF
AH1318	—	2.00	5.00	8.00	12.50	25.00

Mint: Kabul
KM# 813 RUPEE
9.2000 g., 0.9000 Silver .2662 oz. ASW **Rev:** "Kabul" to right of mosque

Date	Mintage	Good	VG	F	VF	XF
AH1313	—	2.00	5.00	7.50	10.00	20.00

Mint: Kabul
KM# 814 RUPEE
9.2000 g., 0.9000 Silver .2662 oz. ASW **Rev:** "Kabul" above mosque

Date	Mintage	Good	VG	F	VF	XF
AH1312	—	4.00	10.00	20.00	50.00	75.00
AH1313	—	2.00	5.00	7.00	9.00	20.00

Mint: Kabul
KM# 818 RUPEE
9.2000 g., 0.9000 Silver .2662 oz. ASW **Rev:** "Du Mesqal" above mosque

Date	Mintage	Good	VG	F	VF	XF
AH1314	—	2.50	6.00	10.00	20.00	40.00

Mint: Kabul
KM# 819.1 RUPEE
9.2000 g., 0.5000 Silver .0755 oz. ASW **Obv:** "Kabul" above toughra, undivided dates

Date	Mintage	Good	VG	F	VF	XF
AH1314	—	1.50	4.00	10.00	17.50	35.00
AH1315	—	1.50	4.00	5.50	9.00	20.00

Mint: Kabul
KM# 819.2 RUPEE
9.2000 g., 0.5000 Silver .0755 oz. ASW **Obv:** Divided dates, last tow digits right of toughra

Date	Mintage	Good	VG	F	VF	XF
AH1315	—	8.00	20.00	50.00	100	150
AH1316	—	2.00	5.00	8.00	15.00	30.00

Mint: Kabul
KM# 819.4 RUPEE
9.2000 g., 0.5000 Silver .0755 oz. ASW **Obv:** Divided dates, "17" below toughra

Date	Mintage	Good	VG	F	VF	XF
AH1317	—	8.00	20.00	50.00	100	150

Mint: Kabul
KM# 819.3 RUPEE
9.2000 g., 0.5000 Silver .0755 oz. ASW **Obv:** Date at right of toughra

Date	Mintage	Good	VG	F	VF	XF
AH1317	—	6.00	15.00	40.00	60.00	110

Mint: Kabul
KM# 829 RUPEE
9.2000 g., 0.5000 Silver .0755 oz. ASW **Obv:** Three stars above toughra, date in toughra

Date	Mintage	Good	VG	F	VF	XF
AH1317	—	2.50	6.00	10.00	25.00	50.00

Mint: Kabul
KM# 806 RUPEE
9.2000 g., 0.9000 Silver .2662 oz. ASW **Obv:** Star above toughra **Rev:** Star above, "Kabul" below mosque **Note:** Two varieties each are known for dates AH1311-13.

Date	Mintage	Good	VG	F	VF	XF
AH1308	—	2.00	5.00	8.00	14.00	25.00
AH1309	—	1.50	4.00	6.00	10.00	20.00
AH1310	—	2.00	5.00	8.00	14.00	25.00
AH1311	—	1.50	4.00	6.00	10.00	20.00
AH1311/09	—	1.50	4.00	6.00	10.00	20.00
AH1312/1/9	—	1.50	4.00	7.00	14.00	25.00
AH1312/1	—	1.50	4.00	6.00	10.00	20.00
AH1312	—	1.50	4.00	6.00	10.00	20.00
AH1313	—	1.50	4.00	6.00	10.00	20.00
AH1391 Error	—	4.00	10.00	15.00	17.50	25.00

Mint: Kabul
KM# 820 5 RUPEES
46.0500 g., 0.9000 Silver 1.3325 oz. ASW

Date	Mintage	Good	VG	F	VF	XF
AH1314	—	8.00	20.00	30.00	60.00	115

Mint: Kabul
KM# 826 5 RUPEES
45.6000 g., 0.9000 Silver 1.3194 oz. ASW **Obv:** Similar to KM#820

Date	Mintage	Good	VG	F	VF	XF
AH1316	—	7.00	17.50	27.50	50.00	110

Mint: Without Mint Name
KM# 821 TILLA
4.6000 g., 0.9000 Gold .1331 oz. AGW **Rev:** Date below mosque

Date	Mintage	VG	F	VF	XF	Unc
AH1314	—	70.00	100	125	200	—
AH1316	—	80.00	115	140	225	—

Mint: Kabul
KM# 807 TILLA
4.6000 g., 0.9000 Gold .1331 oz. AGW, 22 mm. **Rev:** Legend above mosque **Rev. Legend:** "Allah Akbar"

Date	Mintage	Good	VG	F	VF	XF
AH1309	—	—	75.00	100	150	250

Mint: Kabul
KM# 815 TILLA
4.6000 g., 0.9000 Gold .1331 oz. AGW, 19 mm. **Rev:** Legend above **Rev. Legend:** "Allah Akbar"

Date	Mintage	Good	VG	F	VF	XF
AH1313	—	—	95.00	125	200	280

Mint: Kabul
KM# 822 TILLA
4.6000 g., 0.9000 Gold .1331 oz. AGW **Obv:** Date below toughra

Date	Mintage	Good	VG	F	VF	XF
AH1314	—	—	70.00	110	135	215
AH1316	—	—	70.00	110	135	215

Mint: Kabul
KM# 808 2 TILLAS
9.2000 g., 0.9000 Gold .2661 oz. AGW

Date	Mintage	Good	VG	F	VF	XF
AH1309	—	—	100	140	210	265

Wali Muhammad
AH1297 / 1880AD
HAMMERED COINAGE

Mint: Kabul
KM# 538 RUPEE
Silver

Date	Mintage	Good	VG	F	VF	XF
AH1297	—	3.25	8.00	16.00	27.50	40.00

Muhammad Ishaq
AH1305-1306 / 1889AD
HAMMERED COINAGE

Mint: Balkh
KM# 548 NAZARANA RUPEE

Silver **Obv:** Without "Alif" before "Ishaq" **Rev:** Mint name across center **Note:** Struck at Balkh, but inscribed "Kabul".

Date	Mintage	Good	VG	F	VF	XF
AH1305	—	12.00	30.00	60.00	100	150
AH1306	—	10.00	25.00	50.00	80.00	120

Mint: Kabul

KM# 549 NAZARANA RUPEE

Silver **Obv:** "Alif" before "Ishaq" **Rev:** Mint name at top, date at bottom **Note:** Mules of KM#548 obverse and KM#549 reverse exist.

Date	Mintage	Good	VG	F	VF	XF
AH1305	—	12.00	30.00	60.00	100	150
AH1306	—	12.00	30.00	60.00	100	150

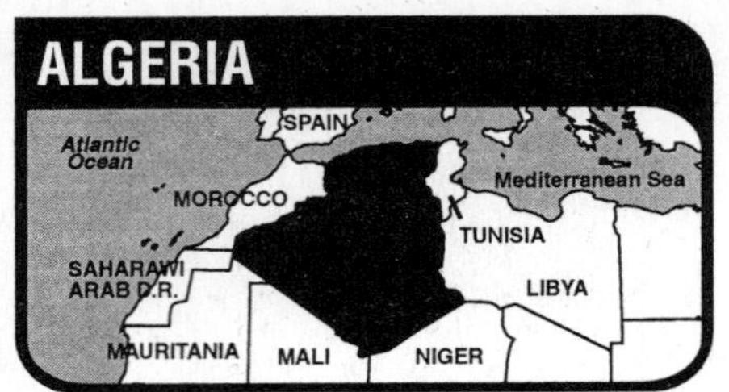

Algiers, the capital and chief seaport of Algeria, was the site of Phoenician and Roman settlements before the present Moslem city was founded about 950. Nominally part of the sultanate of Tilimsan, Algiers had a large measure of independence under the amirs of its own. In 1492 the Jews and Moors who had been expelled from Spain settled in Algiers and enjoyed an increasing influence until the imposition of Turkish control in 1518. For the following three centuries, Algiers was the headquarters of the notorious Barbary pirates as Turkish control became more and more nominal. The French took Algiers in 1830, and after a long and wearisome war completed the conquest of Algeria and annexed it to France, 1848.

RULERS

Ottoman, until 1830
Abd-el-Kader (rebel), AH1250-1264/1834-1847AD

ALGIERS

MINT NAMES

جزاير

Jaza'ir

al-Mascara

During revolt of Abd-el-Kader
AH1250-1264/1834-1847AD

مديه

Medea

AH1246/1830AD

قسنطينة

Qusantinah
Constantine

AH1245-1254/1830-1837AD

تاقدمت

Taqidemt

During revolt of Abd-el-Kader
AH1250-1264/1834-1847AD

NOTE: The dots above and below the letters are integral parts of the letters, but for stylistic reasons, are occasionally omitted.

MONETARY SYSTEM

(Until 1847)

14-1/2 Asper (Akche, Dirham Saghir)
= 1 Kharub
2 Kharuba = 1 Muzuna
24 Muzuna = 3 Batlaka (Pataka) = 1 Budju

NOTE: Coin denominations are not expressed on the coins, and are best determined by size and weight. The silver Budju weighed about 13.5 g until AH1236/1821AD, when it was reduced to about 10.0 g. The fractional pieces varied in proportion to the Budju. They had secondary names, which are given in the text. In 1829 three new silver coins were introduced and Budju became Tugrali-rial, Tugrali-batlaka = 1/3 Rial = 8 Muzuna and Tugrali-nessflik = 1/2 Batlaka = 4 Muzuna. The gold Sultani was officially valued at 108 Muzuna, but varied in accordance with the market price of gold expressed in silver. It weighed 3.20-3.40 g. The Zer-i Mahbub was valued at 80 Muzuna & weighed 2.38-3.10 g.

OTTOMAN

Selim III

AH1203-1222/1789-1807AD

HAMMERED COINAGE

KM# 52 FELS

1.7300 g., Copper **Obv:** Legend has Sultan Selim **Rev:** Mint name Jaza'ir within octagram

Date	Mintage	Good	VG	F	VF	XF
AH122x	—	45.00	90.00	150	—	—

Note: Some experts believe this strike to be a contemporary counterfeit of KM#47

KM# 40 1/8 BUDJU (3 Mazuna)

Silver **Note:** Weight varies: 1.65-1.70 grams.

Date	Mintage	VG	F	VF	XF	Unc
AH1216	—	20.00	40.00	60.00	100	—
AH1217	—	20.00	40.00	60.00	100	—
AH1218	—	20.00	40.00	60.00	100	—
AH1220	—	20.00	40.00	60.00	100	—

KM# 47 1/8 BUDJU (3 Mazuna)

Silver **Rev:** Mint name within octagram

Date	Mintage	VG	F	VF	XF	Unc
AH1221	—	40.00	60.00	125	175	225
AH1222	—	40.00	60.00	125	175	225

KM# 42 1/4 BUDJU

Silver **Note:** Weight varies: 2.90-3.40 grams. Size varies: 19-20 millimeters.

Date	Mintage	VG	F	VF	XF	Unc
AH1204	—	20.00	35.00	60.00	100	—
AH1205	—	20.00	35.00	60.00	100	—
AH1206	—	20.00	35.00	60.00	100	—
AH1207	—	20.00	35.00	60.00	100	—
AH1208	—	20.00	35.00	60.00	100	—
AH1209	—	20.00	35.00	60.00	100	—
AH1210	—	20.00	35.00	60.00	100	—
AH1211	—	20.00	35.00	60.00	100	—
AH1212	—	20.00	35.00	60.00	100	—
AH1213	—	20.00	35.00	60.00	100	—
AH1214	—	20.00	35.00	60.00	100	—
AH1215	—	20.00	35.00	60.00	100	—
AH1216	—	20.00	35.00	60.00	100	—
AH1217	—	20.00	35.00	60.00	100	—
AH1218	—	20.00	35.00	60.00	100	—
AH1219	—	20.00	35.00	60.00	100	—
AH1220	—	20.00	35.00	60.00	100	—

KM# 48 1/4 BUDJU

Silver **Rev:** Mint name within octagram **Note:** Weight varies: 2.90-3.40 grams. Size varies: 19-20 millimeters.

Date	Mintage	VG	F	VF	XF	Unc
AH1221	—	40.00	75.00	125	175	—
AH1222	—	40.00	75.00	125	175	—
AH1223	—	40.00	75.00	125	175	—

KM# 45 1/2 BUDJU

Silver **Note:** Weight varie:s 5.80-6.80 grams.

Date	Mintage	VG	F	VF	XF	Unc
AH1216	—	60.00	100	150	225	—
AH1217	—	60.00	100	150	225	—
AH1218	—	60.00	100	150	225	—
AH1219	—	60.00	100	150	225	—
AH1220	—	60.00	100	150	225	—

KM# 44 1/4 SULTANI

0.8500 g., Gold **Obv:** Legend has 2 lines **Rev:** Mint name above date. **Note:** Size varies: 15-16 millimeters.

Date	Mintage	VG	F	VF	XF	Unc
AH1217	—	65.00	100	200	250	—
AH1219	—	65.00	100	200	250	—
AH1222	—	65.00	100	200	250	—

KM# 49 1/4 SULTANI

0.8500 g., Gold **Rev:** Mint name within octagram

Date	Mintage	VG	F	VF	XF	Unc
AH1221	—	150	225	300	375	—
AH1222	—	150	225	300	375	—

KM# 46 1/2 SULTANI
Gold **Note:** Weight varies: 1.54-1.70 grams. SIze varies: 18-19 millimeters.

Date	Mintage	VG	F	VF	XF	Unc
AH1216	—	100	150	200	275	—
AH1217	—	100	150	200	275	—
AH1218	—	100	150	200	275	—
AH1219	—	100	150	200	275	—
AH1220	—	100	150	200	275	—

KM# 50 1/2 SULTANI
Gold **Rev:** Mint name within octagram

Date	Mintage	VG	F	VF	XF	Unc
AH1221	—	200	275	375	500	—
AH1222	—	200	275	375	500	—

KM# 41 SULTANI
Gold **Obv:** Star of Solomon **Note:** Weight varies: 3.25-3.40 grams. Size varies: 22-25 millimeters.

Date	Mintage	VG	F	VF	XF	Unc
AH1216	—	200	275	375	500	—
AH1217	—	200	275	375	500	—
AH1218	—	200	275	375	500	—
AH1219	—	200	275	375	500	—
AH1220	—	200	275	375	500	—
AH1221	—	200	275	375	500	—
AH1222	—	200	275	375	500	—

KM# 51 SULTANI
3.1000 g., Gold **Rev:** Mint name with octagram

Date	Mintage	VG	F	VF	XF	Unc
AH1221 Rare	—	—	—	—	—	—
AH1222 Rare	—	—	—	—	—	—

Mustafa IV
AH1222-1223/1807-1808AD

HAMMERED COINAGE

KM# 53 1/8 BUDJU (3 Mazuna)
1.4800 g., Silver **Note:** Mint name in octagram.

Date	Mintage	VG	F	VF	XF	Unc
AH1222	—	100	150	250	350	—
AH1223	—	100	150	250	350	—

KM# 54 1/4 BUDJU
Silver **Note:** Weight varies: 2.88-3.40 grams. Mint name in octagram.

Date	Mintage	VG	F	VF	XF	Unc
AH1222	—	100	150	250	350	—
AH1223	—	100	150	250	350	—

KM# 55 1/4 SULTANI
0.8000 g., Gold **Note:** Mint name in octagram.

Date	Mintage	VG	F	VF	XF	Unc
AH1222 Rare	—	—	—	—	—	—
AH1223 Rare	—	—	—	—	—	—

KM# 56 1/2 SULTANI
Gold **Note:** Weight varies: 1.60-1.73 grams. Mint name in octagram.

Date	Mintage	VG	F	VF	XF	Unc
AH1222 Rare	—	—	—	—	—	—
AH1223 Rare	—	—	—	—	—	—

KM# 57 SULTANI
Gold **Note:** Weight varies: 3.15-3.40 grams. Mint name in octagram.

Date	Mintage	VG	F	VF	XF	Unc
AH1222 Rare	—	—	—	—	—	—
AH1223 Rare	—	—	—	—	—	—

Mahmud II
AH1223-1252/1808-1839AD

HAMMERED COINAGE

KM# 70 2 ASPER
0.8000 g., Copper

Date	Mintage	VG	F	VF	XF	Unc
AH1237	—	15.00	25.00	36.50	70.00	—
AH1238	—	15.00	25.00	36.50	70.00	—
AH1240	—	15.00	25.00	36.50	70.00	—
AH1242	—	15.00	25.00	36.50	70.00	—
AH1243	—	15.00	25.00	36.50	70.00	—
AH1244	—	15.00	25.00	36.50	70.00	—

KM# 81 2 ASPER
0.8000 g., Copper **Note:** Varieties exist.

Date	Mintage	Good	VG	F	VF	XF
AH1247	—	40.00	60.00	90.00	135	—
AH1248	—	40.00	60.00	90.00	135	—
AH1250	—	40.00	60.00	90.00	135	—

KM# 71 5 ASPER
Copper **Note:** Weight varies: 1.80-2.20 grams. The 5 Aspers formerly listed as C#140 is probably an example of the 1/8 Budja, KM#74, of very base metal.

Date	Mintage	VG	F	VF	XF	Unc
AH1237	—	12.50	22.50	35.00	50.00	—
AH1238	—	12.50	22.50	35.00	50.00	—
AH1239	—	12.50	22.50	35.00	50.00	—
AH1240	—	15.00	25.00	40.00	60.00	—
AH1244	—	10.00	20.00	30.00	45.00	—

KM# 72 10 ASPER
Copper

Date	Mintage	Good	VG	F	VF	XF
AH1237 Rare	—	—	—	—	—	—

Note: Possibly a pattern issue

KM# 73 KHARUB
Billon **Note:** Weight varies: 0.70-0.80 grams.

Date	Mintage	VG	F	VF	XF	Unc
AH1237	—	10.00	15.00	30.00	75.00	—
AH1238	—	10.00	15.00	30.00	75.00	—
AH1240	—	10.00	15.00	30.00	75.00	—
AH1242	—	10.00	15.00	30.00	75.00	—

KM# 76 KHARUB
Billon **Note:** Weight varies: 0.70-0.90 grams.

Date	Mintage	VG	F	VF	XF	Unc
AH1245	—	50.00	100	175	275	—
AH1246	—	50.00	100	175	275	—
AH1247	—	50.00	100	175	275	—

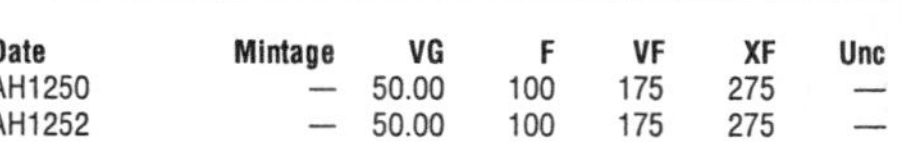

Date	Mintage	VG	F	VF	XF	Unc
AH1250	—	50.00	100	175	275	—
AH1252	—	50.00	100	175	275	—

KM# A61 1/8 BUDJU (Suman Budju)
1.6100 g., Silver **Note:** Mint name in octagram. Similar to 1/4 Budja, KM#54, but with Mahmud's name.

Date	Mintage	VG	F	VF	XF	Unc
AH1223	—	150	200	225	250	—
AH1224	—	150	200	225	250	—

KM# 61 1/8 BUDJU (Suman Budju)
Silver **Note:** Weight varies: 1.65-1.70 grams.

Date	Mintage	VG	F	VF	XF	Unc
AH1225	—	25.00	45.00	75.00	125	—
AH1226	—	25.00	45.00	75.00	125	—
AH1227	—	25.00	45.00	75.00	125	—
AH1228	—	25.00	45.00	75.00	125	—
AH1229	—	25.00	45.00	75.00	125	—
AH1230	—	25.00	45.00	75.00	125	—
AH1231	—	25.00	45.00	75.00	125	—
AH1232	—	25.00	45.00	75.00	125	—
AH1233	—	25.00	45.00	75.00	125	—
AH1234	—	25.00	45.00	75.00	125	—
AH1235	—	25.00	45.00	75.00	125	—

KM# 74 1/8 BUDJU (Suman Budju)
Silver **Note:** Reduced standard. Weight varies: 1.20-1.30 grams.

Date	Mintage	VG	F	VF	XF	Unc
AH1229	—	10.00	15.00	30.00	65.00	—
AH1237	—	10.00	15.00	30.00	65.00	—
AH1238	—	10.00	15.00	30.00	65.00	—
AH1239	—	10.00	15.00	30.00	65.00	—
AH1240	—	10.00	15.00	30.00	65.00	—
AH1242	—	10.00	15.00	30.00	65.00	—
AH1243	—	10.00	15.00	30.00	65.00	—
AH1244	—	10.00	15.00	30.00	65.00	—
AH1245	—	10.00	15.00	30.00	65.00	—

KM# 77 1/6 BUDJU (Tugrali-ness-flik)
1.5000 g., Silver

Date	Mintage	F	VF	XF	Unc
AH1245	—	35.00	70.00	120	200

KM# 82 1/6 BUDJU (Tugrali-ness-flik)
Silver or Billon **Note:** Weight varies: 1.40-1.50 grams. Size varies: 18-19 millimeters.

Date	Mintage	VG	F	VF	XF	Unc
AH1247	—	50.00	100	175	250	—
AH1248	—	50.00	100	175	250	—
AH1252	—	50.00	100	175	250	—

KM# 67 1/4 BUDJU (6 Mazuna)
2.4000 g., Silver

Date	Mintage	F	VF	XF	Unc
AH1229	—	15.00	30.00	55.00	90.00
AH1231	—	15.00	30.00	55.00	90.00
AH1234	—	15.00	30.00	55.00	90.00
AH1235	—	15.00	30.00	55.00	90.00
AH1236	—	15.00	30.00	55.00	90.00
AH1237	—	12.50	22.00	35.00	60.00
AH1238	—	12.50	22.00	35.00	60.00
AH1239	—	12.50	22.00	35.00	60.00

Date	Mintage	F	VF	XF	Unc
AH1240	—	12.50	22.00	35.00	60.00
AH1241	—	12.50	22.00	35.00	60.00
AH1242	—	12.50	22.00	35.00	60.00
AH1243	—	12.50	22.00	35.00	60.00
AH1244	—	12.50	22.00	35.00	60.00
AH1245	—	15.00	27.50	50.00	85.00
AH1246	—	20.00	35.00	60.00	100

KM# 80.1 1/4 BUDJU (6 Mazuna)

2.0300 g., Silver

Date	Mintage	VG	F	VF	XF	Unc
AH1246 Rare	—	—	—	—	—	—

KM# 80.2 1/4 BUDJU (6 Mazuna)

2.0000 g., Silver **Obv:** Ornament and Sultan's name around **Rev:** Similar to KM#67

Date	Mintage	VG	F	VF	XF	Unc
AH1246 Rare	—	—	—	—	—	—

KM# 59 1/3 BUDJU (Tugrali-batlaka)

Silver **Note:** Mint name is octagram type.

Date	Mintage	VG	F	VF	XF	Unc
AH1223	—	40.00	75.00	125	200	—
AH1224	—	75.00	90.00	125	200	—
AH1225	—	75.00	90.00	125	200	—
AH1226	—	35.00	60.00	100	150	—
AH1227	—	35.00	60.00	100	150	—
AH1228	—	35.00	60.00	100	150	—
AH1229	—	35.00	60.00	100	150	—

KM# 62 1/3 BUDJU (Tugrali-batlaka)

Silver **Note:** Mint name not in octagram.

Date	Mintage	VG	F	VF	XF	Unc
AH1226	—	35.00	60.00	100	150	—
AH1227	—	35.00	60.00	100	150	—
AH1228	—	35.00	60.00	100	150	—
AH1230	—	35.00	60.00	100	150	—
AH1231	—	35.00	60.00	100	150	—
AH1232	—	35.00	60.00	100	150	—
AH1233	—	35.00	60.00	100	150	—
AH1234	—	35.00	60.00	100	150	—
AH1235	—	75.00	90.00	125	200	—

KM# 78 1/3 BUDJU (Tugrali-batlaka)

3.1000 g., Silver **Note:** Toughra type. Varieties exist.

Date	Mintage	F	VF	XF	Unc
AH1245	—	45.00	75.00	135	245

KM# A68.1 1/2 BUDJU

5.3500 g., Silver **Note:** Toughra type.

Date	Mintage	VG	F	VF	XF	Unc
AH1223/13 Rare	—	—	—	—	—	—

KM# A68.2 1/2 BUDJU

4.8900 g., Silver

Date	Mintage	VG	F	VF	XF	Unc
AH1223/13 Rare	—	—	—	—	—	—

KM# B68 1/2 BUDJU

3.7700 g., Silver

Date	Mintage	VG	F	VF	XF	Unc
AH1246	—	—	—	—	—	—

KM# 68 BUDJU

Silver **Note:** Weight varies: 9.80-10.10 grams.

Date	Mintage	F	VF	XF	Unc
AH1236	—	20.00	45.00	100	175
AH1237	—	16.00	30.00	65.00	110
AH1238	—	16.00	30.00	65.00	110
AH1239	—	16.00	30.00	65.00	110
AH1240	—	16.00	30.00	65.00	110
AH1241	—	16.00	30.00	65.00	110
AH1242	—	20.00	30.00	65.00	110
AH1243	—	25.00	45.00	100	175
AH1244	—	40.00	45.00	100	175
AH1245	—	45.00	100	200	350

KM# 79 BUDJU (Tugrali-rial)

10.0200 g., Silver

Date	Mintage	VG	F	VF	XF	Unc
AH1245	—	70.00	175	350	750	—

KM# 83 BUDJU (Tugrali-rial)

Silver or Billon **Note:** Weight varies: 7.90-9.80 grams.

Date	Mintage	VG	F	VF	XF	Unc
AH1247	—	100	150	350	750	—
AH1248	—	100	150	350	750	—
AH1249	—	100	170	380	900	—
AH1250	—	100	170	380	900	—
AH1251	—	200	500	600	900	—
AH1253	—	100	150	350	750	—

KM# 75 2 BUDJU (Zudj Budju)

Silver **Note:** Weight varies: 19.50-20.00 grams. Varieties exist.

Date	Mintage	F	VF	XF	Unc
AH1236	—	50.00	80.00	120	220
AH1237	—	50.00	80.00	120	220
AH1238	—	50.00	80.00	120	220
AH1239	—	50.00	80.00	120	220

Date	Mintage	F	VF	XF	Unc
AH1240	—	60.00	90.00	130	230
AH1241	—	50.00	80.00	120	220
AH1242	—	50.00	80.00	120	220
AH1243	—	60.00	100	175	2,785
AH1244	—	95.00	170	275	375

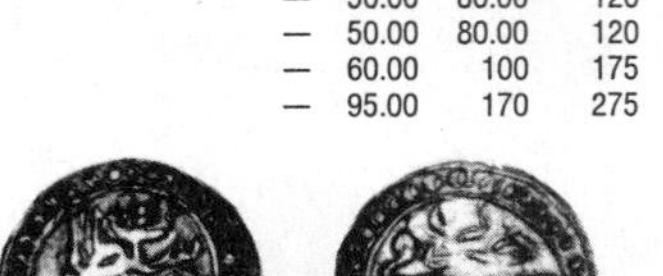

KM# 63 1/4 SULTANI

Gold **Obv. Legend:** Legend is Sultan Mahmud **Note:** Weight varies: 0.78-0.85 grams. Size varies: 14-15 millimeters.

Date	Mintage	VG	F	VF	XF	Unc
AH1224 Rare	—	—	—	—	—	—
AH1228 Rare	—	—	—	—	—	—
AH1231	—	85.00	125	175	250	—
AH1232	—	85.00	125	175	250	—
AH1234 Rare	—	—	—	—	—	—
AH1238	—	85.00	125	175	250	—
AH1240	—	85.00	125	175	250	—
AH1243	—	85.00	125	175	250	—

KM# 64 1/4 SULTANI

0.7050 g., Gold

Date	Mintage	VG	F	VF	XF	Unc
AH1246 Rare	—	—	—	—	2,500	—

KM# 65 1/2 SULTANI

Gold **Note:** Weight varies: 1.15-1.60 grams. Varieties exist.

Date	Mintage	VG	F	VF	XF	Unc
AH1230	—	100	140	200	275	—
AH1231	—	100	140	200	275	—
AH1232	—	100	140	200	275	—
AH1234	—	100	140	200	275	—
AH1236	—	100	140	200	275	—
AH1237	—	100	140	200	275	—
AH1238	—	100	140	200	275	—
AH1239	—	100	140	200	275	—
AH1240	—	100	140	200	275	—

KM# 60 SULTANI

3.2000 g., Gold **Rev:** Year in fourth line **Note:** Size varies: 22-24 millimeters.

Date	Mintage	VG	F	VF	XF	Unc
AH1223	—	250	350	450	575	—
AH1224	—	250	350	450	575	—
AH1225	—	250	350	450	575	—
AH1226	—	250	350	450	575	—
AH1228	—	250	350	450	575	—
AH1231	—	250	350	450	575	—
AH1232	—	250	350	450	575	—
AH1234	—	250	350	450	575	—

KM# 66 SULTANI

3.2000 g., Gold **Rev:** Year in third line

Date	Mintage	VG	F	VF	XF	Unc
AH1235	—	165	225	300	400	—
AH1236	—	165	225	300	400	—
AH1237	—	165	225	300	400	—
AH1238	—	165	225	300	400	—
AH1239	—	165	225	300	400	—
AH1240	—	165	225	300	400	—
AH1241	—	165	225	300	400	—
AH1243	—	165	225	300	400	—
AH3421 (Error)	—	165	225	300	400	—
AH1244	—	165	225	300	400	—
AH1245	—	275	400	550	750	—

KM# 69 SULTANI

2.3800 g., Gold **Obv:** Toughra **Rev:** 4-line legend with 20 above ibn

Date	Mintage	VG	F	VF	XF	Unc
AH1246	—	—	—	—	—	—

Note: The regnal year 20 is probably an error for 23

FRENCH COLONIAL

Abdel Kader
AH1250-1264/1834-1847AD

LOCAL COINAGE

KM# 85 5 ASPER/KHARUBA
Copper-Billon **Note:** Weight varies: 0.73-1.30 grams. Size varies: 12-18 millimeters.

Date	Mintage	VG	F	VF	XF	Unc
AH1250	—	25.00	40.00	60.00	120	—
AH1252	—	25.00	40.00	60.00	120	—
AH1253	—	25.00	40.00	60.00	120	—
AH1254 Arabic 4	—	22.50	35.00	45.00	90.00	—
AH1254 Persian 4	—	22.50	35.00	45.00	90.00	—
AH1255	—	22.50	35.00	45.00	90.00	—
AH1256	—	22.50	35.00	45.00	90.00	—
AH1257	—	25.00	40.00	60.00	120	—

KM# 87 KHARUBA
Billon

Date	Mintage	VG	F	VF	XF	Unc
AH1254	—	70.00	100	150	250	—

KM# 86 KHARUBA
Billon **Obv:** Different legend **Note:** Weight varies: 0.40-0.70 grams.

Date	Mintage	VG	F	VF	XF	Unc
AH1254	—	7.50	25.00	55.00	110	—
AH1255	—	20.00	40.00	60.00	110	—
AH1258	—	17.50	35.00	55.00	110	—

KM# 88 1/6 BUDJU (3 Mazuna-Nasfia)
1.0000 g., Billon

Date	Mintage	VG	F	VF	XF	Unc
AH1254	—	100	160	285	465	—
AH1255	—	—	—	—	—	—

KM# 90 1/2 BUDJU
2.8800 g., Silver **Obv. Inscription:** Nasr min/Allah wa fath/garib (Victory of God and Conquest is Near)

Date	Mintage	VG	F	VF	XF	Unc
AH1256 Rare	—	—	—	—	—	—

KM# 89 BUDJU
Silver **Obv:** Three lines **Rev:** Four lines **Note:** Denomination uncertain. Varieties exist.

Date	Mintage	VG	F	VF	XF	Unc
AH1256	—	150	300	600	900	—

Note: This coin has also been considered to be a 1/2 Budju, but its weight apparently indicates a reduced Budju in debased metal

PATTERNS

Including off metal strikes

KM#	Date	Mintage	Identification	Mkt Val
Pn1	AH1223	—	1/2 Budju.	—

KM#	Date	Mintage	Identification	Mkt Val
Pn2	AH1223	—	1/2 Sultani. White Metal.	175

KM#	Date	Mintage	Identification	Mkt Val
Pn3	AH1223	—	2 Sultani. White Metal. 16.7500 g. Similar to KM#616/617, Rumi Altin.	450

ANDAMAN ISLANDS

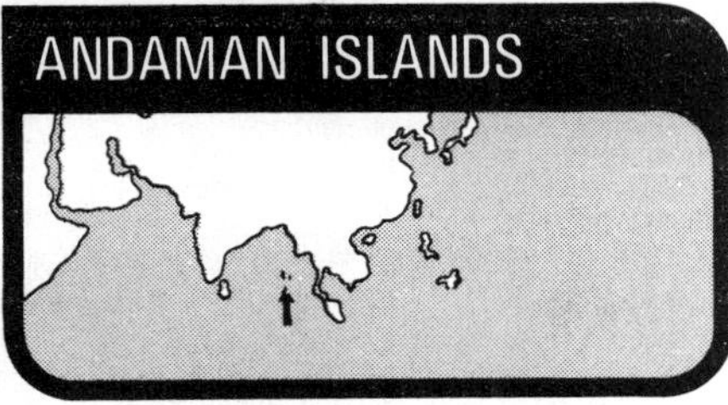

The Andaman Islands are the northern group of 204 volcanic and coral isles in the east part of the Bay of Bengal about 400 miles directly west of the coast of lower Burma. It has an area of 2,508 sq. mi.

In 1789 the first British settlement was established at Port Blair. It was relocated at Port Cornwallis on North Andaman in 1791 and abandoned in 1796. A penal colony on South Andaman was re-established at the place now known as Port Blair. In 1872 the islands were merged with the nearby Nicobar Islands to form a single administrative unit. No prisoners were sent here after 1921 and the penal colony was closed just after World War II.

RULERS
British, until 1947

PENAL COLONY

TOKEN COINAGE

KM# Tn1 RUPEE
Copper

Date	Mintage	VG	F	VF	XF	Unc
1861	Est. 20,000	1,000	1,500	2,250	3,750	—

KM# Tn1c RUPEE
Copper **Obv:** KM#Tn2 **Rev:** KM#Tn1 **Note:** Mule with center hole.

Date	Mintage	VG	F	VF	XF	Unc
1861	—	1,250	1,750	2,500	4,000	—

KM# Tn1b RUPEE
Copper **Obv:** KM#Tn2 **Rev:** KM#Tn1 **Note:** Mule without center hole.

Date	Mintage	VG	F	VF	XF	Unc
1861 Proof, rare	—	—	—	—	—	—

KM# Tn1a RUPEE
Copper **Note:** Without center hole.

Date	Mintage	VG	F	VF	XF	Unc
1861	—	—	—	—	—	4,000

KM# Tn2 RUPEE
Copper

Date	Mintage	VG	F	VF	XF	Unc
1866	Est. 21,000	1,500	2,000	2,750	4,500	—

Note: Recalled from circulation in 1870 with 17,788 pieces outstanding for both types

ANGOLA

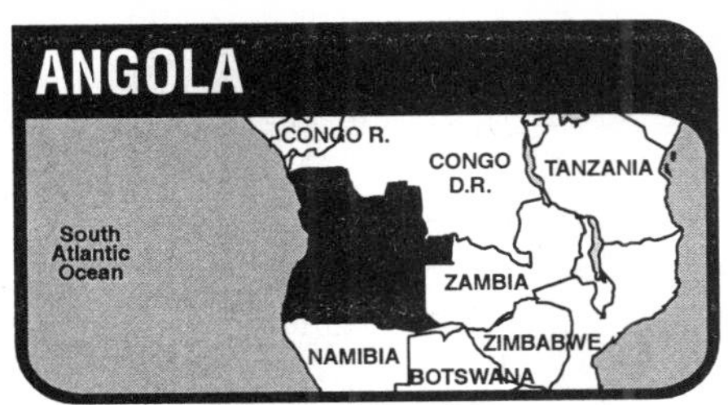

Angola, a country on the west coast of southern Africa bounded by Congo Democratic Republic, Zambia, and Namibia (Southwest Africa), has an area of 481,351 sq. mi. (1,246,700 sq. km.). Capital: Luanda. Most of the people are engaged in subsistence agriculture. However, important oil and mineral deposits make Angola potentially one of the richest countries in Africa. Iron and diamonds are exported.

The Portuguese navigator, Diogo Cao, discovered Angola in 1482 Angola. Portuguese settlers arrived in 1491, and established Angola as a major slaving center, which sent about 3 million slaves to the New World.

RULERS
Portuguese until 1975

MINT MARKS
KN - King's Norton

MONETARY SYSTEM
(Until 1860)
50 Reis = 1 Macuta

PORTUGUESE COLONY

COLONIAL COINAGE

KM# 44 1/4 MACUTA
Copper

Date	Mintage	VG	F	VF	XF	Unc
1814	—	10.00	25.00	45.00	85.00	120
1815	—	200	300	500	1,000	—

KM# 45 1/2 MACUTA
Copper

Date	Mintage	VG	F	VF	XF	Unc
1814	—	12.00	28.00	48.00	90.00	—
1815	18,000	200	350	600	900	—
1819 Rare	—	—	—	—	—	—

KM# 56 1/2 MACUTA
Copper

Date	Mintage	VG	F	VF	XF	Unc
1848	417,000	8.00	25.00	115	170	—

KM# 58 1/2 MACUTA
Copper **Obv. Legend:** PETRUS V D.G...

Date	Mintage	VG	F	VF	XF	Unc
1858	226,000	4.00	12.00	30.00	60.00	—
1860	398,000	4.00	14.00	35.00	65.00	—

KM# 46 MACUTA
Copper **Note:** Lightweight coins exist weighing 10.96 grams.

Date	Mintage	VG	F	VF	XF	Unc
1814	—	7.00	25.00	45.00	85.00	—
Note: Lightweight coins exist weighing 10.96 grams.						
1816	6,110	35.00	75.00	175	300	—
1819 Rare	—	—	—	—	—	—

KM# 59 MACUTA
Copper **Note:** Similar to 1/2 Macuta, KM#42.

Date	Mintage	VG	F	VF	XF	Unc
1860	194,000	7.00	15.00	30.00	65.00	135

KM# 47 2 MACUTAS
Copper **Note:** Similar to 1 Macuta, KM#40.

Date	Mintage	VG	F	VF	XF	Unc
1815	—	40.00	90.00	180	300	—
1816	3,175	60.00	120	220	400	—
1819 Rare	—	—	—	—	—	—

COUNTERMARKED COINAGE

1809

An order of April 18, 1809 provided for the use of an arms countermark to be applied to various circulating coinage. The mark doubled the host coin's face value.

KM# 38 5 REIS
Copper **Countermark:** Arms **Note:** Countermark on V Reis, KM#7.

CM Date	Host Date	Good	VG	F	VF	XF
ND(1809)	1752	25.00	50.00	160	250	—
ND(1809)	1753	6.00	12.00	28.00	55.00	—
ND(1809)	1757	10.00	22.00	45.00	85.00	—

KM# 39 5 REIS
Copper **Countermark:** Arms **Note:** Countermark on X Reis, KM#2.

CM Date	Host Date	Good	VG	F	VF	XF
ND(1809)	1694	12.00	25.00	60.00	150	—
ND(1809)	1696	10.00	20.00	50.00	120	—
ND(1809)	1697	7.00	15.00	45.00	90.00	—
ND(1809)	1699	7.00	15.00	55.00	100	—

KM# 40 5 REIS
Copper **Countermark:** Arms **Note:** Countermark on X Reis, KM#8.

CM Date	Host Date	Good	VG	F	VF	XF
ND(1809)	1752	25.00	50.00	125	375	—
ND(1809)	1753	6.00	12.00	28.00	55.00	—
ND(1809)	1757	6.00	12.00	28.00	55.00	—

KM# 41 5 REIS
Copper **Countermark:** Arms **Note:** Countermark on XX Reis, KM#1.

CM Date	Host Date	Good	VG	F	VF	XF
ND(1809)	1693	12.00	25.00	60.00	150	—
ND(1809)	1694	9.00	17.00	45.00	100	—
ND(1809)	1695	9.00	17.00	45.00	100	—
ND(1809)	1697	7.00	15.00	40.00	90.00	—
ND(1809)	1698	7.00	15.00	40.00	90.00	—
ND(1809)	1699	7.00	15.00	40.00	90.00	—

KM# 42 5 REIS
Copper **Countermark:** Arms **Note:** Countermark on XX Reis, KM#6.

CM Date	Host Date	Good	VG	F	VF	XF
ND(1809)	1752	15.00	30.00	100	250	—
ND(1809)	1753	5.00	10.00	50.00	125	—
ND(1809)	1757	4.00	8.00	40.00	100	

KM# 43 80 REIS
Copper **Countermark:** Arms **Note:** Countermark on XL Reis, KM#9.

CM Date	Host Date	Good	VG	F	VF	XF
ND(1809)	1753	9.00	17.00	35.00	70.00	—
ND(1809)	1757	9.00	17.00	35.00	70.00	—

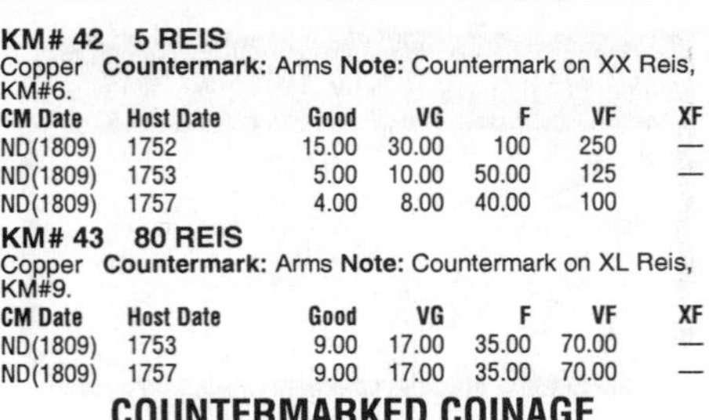

COUNTERMARKED COINAGE

1837

The Edict of March 21, 1837 initiated the use of crowned arms countermarks on various circulating coinage. The mark doubled the host coin's face value. A second edict was issued March 1, 1853 extending the use of these marks for the same purpose of doubling face value.

KM# 48 5 REIS (V)
Copper **Countermark:** Crowned arms **Note:** Countermark on 5 Reis, KM#19.

CM Date	Host Date	Good	VG	F	VF	XF
ND(1837)	1770	25.00	45.00	110	250	—
ND(1837)	1771	25.00	45.00	110	250	—

KM# 49.1 1/2 MACUTA
Copper **Countermark:** Crowned arms **Note:** Countermark on 1/4 Macuta, KM#10.

CM Date	Host Date	Good	VG	F	VF	XF
ND(1837)	1762	3.50	7.00	16.00	35.00	—
ND(1837)	1763	2.50	5.00	12.00	25.00	—
ND(1837)	1770	2.50	5.00	12.00	25.00	—
ND(1837)	1771	7.00	15.00	30.00	60.00	—

KM# 49.2 1/2 MACUTA
Copper **Countermark:** Crowned arms **Note:** Countermark on 1/4 Macuta, KM#27.

CM Date	Host Date	Good	VG	F	VF	XF
ND(1837)	1785	3.50	7.00	16.00	35.00	—

KM# 49.3 1/2 MACUTA
Copper **Countermark:** Crowned arms **Note:** Countermark on 1/4 Macuta, KM#29.

CM Date	Host Date	Good	VG	F	VF	XF
ND(1837)	1789	4.00	8.00	17.00	35.00	—

KM# 50.1 MACUTA
Copper **Countermark:** Crowned arms **Note:** Countermark on 1/2 Macuta, KM#11.

CM Date	Host Date	Good	VG	F	VF	XF
ND(1837)	1762	15.00	25.00	40.00	80.00	—
ND(1837)	1763	4.00	8.00	17.00	35.00	—
ND(1837)	1770	4.00	8.00	17.00	35.00	—

KM# 50.2 MACUTA
Copper **Countermark:** Crowned arms **Note:** Countermark on 1/2 Macuta, KM#28.

CM Date	Host Date	Good	VG	F	VF	XF
ND(1837)	1785	5.00	9.00	18.00	37.00	—
ND(1837)	1786	5.00	9.00	18.00	37.00	—

KM# 50.3 MACUTA
Copper **Countermark:** Crowned arms **Note:** Countermark on 1/2 Macuta, KM#30.

CM Date	Host Date	Good	VG	F	VF	XF
ND(1837)	1789	5.00	9.00	18.00	38.00	—

KM# 53 MACUTA
Copper **Countermark:** Crowned arms **Note:** Countermark on 1/2 Macuta, KM#39.

CM Date	Host Date	Good	VG	F	VF	XF
ND(1853)	1814	50.00	160	250	450	—

KM# 51.1 2 MACUTAS
Copper **Countermark:** Crowned arms **Note:** Countermark on 1 Macuta, KM#12.

CM Date	Host Date	Good	VG	F	VF	XF
ND(1837)	1762	40.00	135	225	425	—
ND(1837)	1763	6.00	12.00	22.00	45.00	—
ND(1837)	1770	5.00	10.00	20.00	40.00	—

KM# 51.2 2 MACUTAS
Copper **Countermark:** Crowned arms **Note:** Countermark on 1 Macuta, KM#20.

CM Date	Host Date	Good	VG	F	VF	XF
ND(1837)	1783	50.00	135	250	475	—
ND(1837)	1785	6.00	12.00	22.00	45.00	—
ND(1837)	1786	7.50	15.00	28.00	55.00	—

KM# 51.3 2 MACUTAS
Copper **Countermark:** Crowned arms **Note:** Countermark on 1 Macuta, KM#31.

CM Date	Host Date	Good	VG	F	VF	XF
ND(1837)	1789	6.00	12.00	22.00	45.00	—

KM# 54 2 MACUTAS
Copper **Countermark:** Crowned arms **Note:** Countermark on 1 Macuta, KM#40.

CM Date	Host Date	Good	VG	F	VF	XF
ND(1853)	1814	30.00	60.00	100	200	—
ND(1853)	1816	30.00	60.00	100	200	—

KM# 55 4 MACUTAS
Copper **Countermark:** Countermark on 2 Macutas, KM#41. **Note:** Countermark on 2 Macutas, KM#41.

CM Date	Host Date	Good	VG	F	VF	XF
ND(1853)	1815	40.00	80.00	150	300	—
ND(1853)	1816	40.00	80.00	150	300	—

PATTERNS

Including off metal strikes

KM#	Date	Mintage	Identification	Mkt Val
Pn1	1831	—	1/4 Macuta. Copper. 54 beads in circle.	—
Pn2	1831	—	1/4 Macuta. Copper. 64 beads in circle.	—
Pn3	1831	—	1/2 Macuta. Copper.	—
Pn4	1831	—	Macuta. Copper.	—
Pn5	1831	—	2 Macutas. Copper.	—

KM#	Date	Mintage	Identification	Mkt Val

KM#	Date	Mintage	Identification	Mkt Val
Pn6	1886	—	Bronze.	—

Antigua and Barbuda are located on the eastern edge of the Leeward Islands in the Caribbean Sea, have an area of 170 sq. mi. (440 sq. km.). Capital: St. John's. Prior to 1967, Antigua and its dependencies Barbuda and Redonda, comprised a presidency of the Leeward Islands.

Antigua was discovered by Columbus in 1493, settled by British colonists from St. Kitts in 1632, occupied by the French in 1666, and ceded to Britain in 1667.

Spanish silver coinage and French colonial "Black Dogs" were used throughout the islands' early history; however, late in the seventeeth century the introduction of British tin farthings was attempted with complete lack of success. In 1822, British colonial Anchor Money was introduced.

From 1825 to 1955, Antigua was on the sterling standard and used British coins.

RULERS
British

BRITISH ADMINISTRATION

STERLING POUND COINAGE

KM# Tn1 FARTHING
Copper **Issuer:** Hannay and Coltart, merchants **Note:** Although dated 1836, this was issued about 1850 in St. John. Five die varieties exist. Occasionally found countermarked with incuse 3 or 4.

Date	Mintage	F	VF	XF	Unc	BU
1836	—	22.50	45.00	90.00	185	—
1836 Proof	—	Value: 320				

Argentina was discovered in 1516 by the Spanish navigator Juan de Solis. A permanent Spanish colony was established at Buenos Aires in 1580, but the colony developed slowly. When Napoleon conquered Spain, the Argentines set up their own government on May 25, 1810. Independence was formally declared on July 9, 1816. A strong tendency toward local autonomy, fostered by difficult transportation, resulted in a federalized union with much authority left to the states or provinces, which resulted in the coinage of 1817-1867.

Internal conflict through the first half century of Argentine independence resulted in a provisional national coinage, chiefly of crown-sized silver. This was supplemented by provincial issues, mainly of minor denominations.

RULERS

Spanish until 1810

MINT MARKS

A = Korea
B = Great Britain
BA = Buenos Aires
CORDOBA, CORDOVA
C = France
PTS = Potosi monogram (Bolivia)
R, RA, RIOJA, RIOXA
SE = Santiago del Estero
T, TM = Tucuman
TIERRA DEL FUEGO

In the Colonial era, Potosi-struck coinage was used in Argentina (see Bolivia for these issues). During the War for Independence Potosi was held and used to strike coinage by both the Royalist and Independence forces. The mint was captured in 1813 by Independence forces who held it for eight months, using the facilities and some remaining workers to strike their new coinage until it was retaken in 1814 by Royalist forces. The Royalists set about recalling the Independence coinage and using the mint to strike coins of the old type with the King's portrait. Royalists abandoned the mint in April 1815 with the reappearance of Independence forces who again occupied and made use of the mint until it was retaken by the Spanish army in November 1815. The Royalists held the mint and used it to strike the King's coinage until 1824 when Independence was finally secured.

MONETARY SYSTEM

8 Reales = 8 Soles = 1/2 Escudo
16 Reales or Soles = 1 Escudo
10 Decimos = 1 Real
100 Centavos = 1 Peso
10 Pesos = 1 Argentino

PROVINCIAS DEL RIO DE LA PLATA

REAL COINAGE

KM# A1 1/4 REAL

Silver **Note:** 1/4 Real of Rondeau.

Date	Mintage	VG	F	VF	XF	Unc
ND(1815-16) 4-6pcs; Rare	—	—	—	—	—	—

KM# 1.1 1/2 REAL

1.6915 g., 0.8960 Silver .0487 oz. **Obv:** Flame tips end counter clockwise **Note:** Mint mark in monogram.

Date	Mintage	VG	F	VF	XF	Unc
1813PTS J	—	15.00	35.00	75.00	150	—

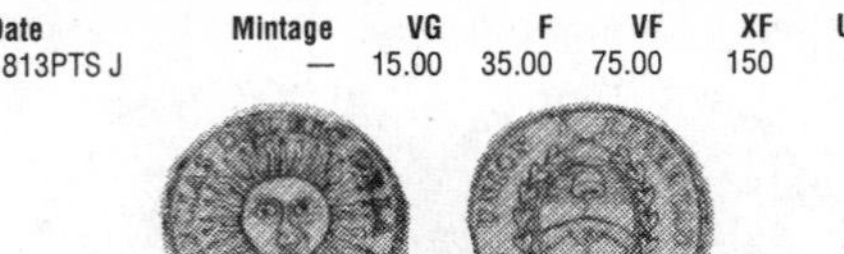

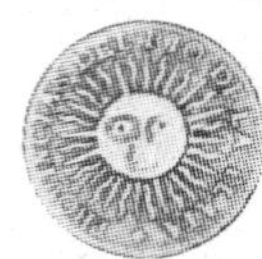

KM# 1.2 1/2 REAL

1.6915 g., 0.8960 Silver .0487 oz. **Obv:** Flame tips end clockwise **Note:** Mint mark in monogram.

Date	Mintage	VG	F	VF	XF	Unc
1815PTS F	—	13.00	30.00	70.00	150	—

KM# 10 1/2 SOL

1.6915 g., 0.8960 Silver .0487 oz. **Note:** Mint mark in monogram. Medal rotation.

Date	Mintage	VG	F	VF	XF	Unc
1815PTS FL	—	30.00	60.00	150	300	—

KM# 2 REAL

3.3830 g., 0.8960 Silver .0974 oz. **Note:** Mint mark in monogram. Medal rotation.

Date	Mintage	VG	F	VF	XF	Unc
1813PTS J	—	20.00	40.00	100	200	—
1815PTS F	—	25.00	50.00	110	225	—

KM# 17 REAL

3.3830 g., 0.8960 Silver .0974 oz. **Note:** Similar to 2 Soles, KM#18.

Date	Mintage	VG	F	VF	XF	Unc
1824RA DS	—	60.00	120	275	550	—
Note: Medal rotation						
1825RA CA Rare	—	—	—	—	—	—
Note: Almost all known specimens of the 1825 CA are false						

KM# 11 SOL

Silver **Note:** Similar to 1/2 Sol, KM#10; mint mark in monogram.

Date	Mintage	VG	F	VF	XF	Unc
1815PTS FL	—	40.00	70.00	175	475	—

KM# 3 2 REALES

6.7660 g., 0.8960 Silver .1949 oz. **Note:** Mint mark in monogram.

Date	Mintage	VG	F	VF	XF	Unc
1813PTS J	—	60.00	150	400	800	—
1815PTS F	—	60.00	150	400	800	—

KM# 12 2 SOLES

Silver **Note:** Similar to 2 Reales, KM#3; mint mark in monogram.

Date	Mintage	VG	F	VF	XF	Unc
1815PTS FL	—	60.00	120	275	750	—

KM# 18 2 SOLES

Silver

Date	Mintage	VG	F	VF	XF	Unc
1824RA DS	—	12.00	25.00	65.00	150	—
1825RA CA	—	25.00	55.00	125	350	—
1825RA CA DE B. AS.	—	15.00	30.00	70.00	200	—
1826/5RA P	—	16.00	35.00	80.00	250	—
1826RA	—	12.00	25.00	65.00	150	—
Note: "P" omitted from reverse legend						
1826RA P Medal alignment	—	14.00	25.00	65.00	150	—
1826RA P Coin alignment	—	20.00	40.00	90.00	265	—

KM# 4 4 REALES

13.5320 g., 0.8960 Silver .3898 oz. **Note:** Mint mark in monogram.

Date	Mintage	VG	F	VF	XF	Unc
1813PTS J	—	150	400	800	2,000	—
1815PTS F	—	200	450	900	2,200	—
Note: Size of sunface varies for 1815 dated coins						

KM# 13 4 SOLES

Silver **Note:** Mint mark in monogram.

Date	Mintage	VG	F	VF	XF	Unc
1815PTS FL	—	150	400	800	2,000	—

KM# 22 4 SOLES

Silver

Date	Mintage	VG	F	VF	XF	Unc
1828RA FL Coin alignment	—	30.00	75.00	150	350	—
1828RA P Coin alignment	—	30.00	75.00	150	350	—
1828RA P Medal alignment	—	35.00	85.00	175	425	—
1832RA P Coin alignment	—	30.00	75.00	150	350	—

KM# 5 8 REALES

27.0640 g., 0.8960 Silver .7795 oz. **Obv:** Flame tips end clockwise **Note:** Mint mark in monogram. Traces of earlier Spanish colonial edge designs are occasionally encountered and are considered rare.

Date	Mintage	VG	F	VF	XF	Unc
1813PTS J	—	65.00	150	300	750	1,500
1813PTS J Rare	—	—	—	—	—	—
Note: Error: PRORVINCIAS						

KM# 14 8 REALES
27.0640 g., 0.8960 Silver .7795 oz. **Obv:** Flame tips end counterclockwise **Note:** Mint mark in monogram.

Date	Mintage	VG	F	VF	XF	Unc
1815PTS F	—	60.00	150	300	750	1,500
1815PTS F	—	150	275	550	1,000	—

Note: Error: PROVICIAS

KM# 20 8 REALES
27.0640 g., 0.8960 Silver .7793 oz.

Date	Mintage	VG	F	VF	XF	Unc
1826RA P 7 laurel pairs	—	100	250	600	1,500	—
1826RA P 6 laurel pairs	—	150	300	700	1,650	—
1827RA P 7 laurel pairs	—	160	325	750	1,750	—
1827RA P 6 laurel pairs	—	100	250	650	1,550	—
1828RA P	—	35.00	80.00	175	350	700
1830RA P	—	125	275	675	1,600	—
1831/0RA P	—	100	250	600	1,500	—
1831RA P	—	90.00	225	450	1,350	—
1832RA P	—	35.00	85.00	200	400	850
1833RA P	—	35.00	85.00	200	375	800
1834RA P	—	35.00	85.00	200	375	800
1835RA P	—	35.00	85.00	200	375	800
1836RA P	—	35.00	80.00	175	350	700
1837RA P	—	35.00	80.00	175	350	700

KM# 15 8 SOLES
Silver **Note:** Mint mark in monogram.

Date	Mintage	VG	F	VF	XF	Unc
1815PTS FL	—	60.00	120	200	450	1,000
1815PTS FL S/R	—	75.00	150	300	750	1,500

KM# 6 ESCUDO
3.3750 g., 0.8750 Gold .0949 oz. **Note:** Mint mark in monogram.

Date	Mintage	VG	F	VF	XF	Unc
1813PTS Rare	—	—	—	—	—	—

KM# 7 2 ESCUDOS
6.7500 g., 0.8750 Gold .1899 oz. **Note:** Mint mark in monogram.

Date	Mintage	VG	F	VF	XF	Unc
1813PTS J Rare	—	—	—	—	—	—

KM# 19.1 2 ESCUDOS
6.7500 g., 0.8750 Gold .1899 oz.

Date	Mintage	VG	F	VF	XF	Unc
1824RA DS	—	185	325	550	1,000	—
1825RA CA DE B AS	—	185	325	550	1,000	—
1826RA P	—	185	285	475	900	—

KM# 19.2 2 ESCUDOS
6.7500 g., 0.8750 Gold .1899 oz. **Rev:** P omitted from legend **Note:** Struck in medal and coin alignment.

Date	Mintage	VG	F	VF	XF	Unc
1826RA	—	185	285	475	900	—

KM# 8 4 ESCUDOS
13.5000 g., 0.8750 Gold .3798 oz. **Note:** Mint mark in monogram.

Date	Mintage	VG	F	VF	XF	Unc
1813PTS J	—	—	—	—	—	—

Note: Reported, not confirmed

KM# 9 8 ESCUDOS
27.0000 g., 0.8750 Gold .7596 oz. **Note:** Mint mark in monogram.

Date	Mintage	VG	F	VF	XF	Unc
1813PTS J	—	5,000	7,000	10,000	20,000	—

Note: Superior Casterline sale 5-89 choice VF realized $11,000

KM# 21 8 ESCUDOS
27.0000 g., 0.8750 Gold .7596 oz.

Date	Mintage	VG	F	VF	XF	Unc
1826RA P	—	650	1,350	2,000	3,000	—
1826/6RA P	—	800	1,500	2,500	4,000	—
1828RA P	—	650	1,350	2,000	3,000	—
1829RA P Rare	—	—	—	—	—	—
1830RA P	—	1,650	3,500	5,500	8,000	—
1831/0RA	—	1,200	2,000	3,000	5,000	—
1831RA P	—	650	1,350	2,000	3,000	—
1832RA P	—	600	1,250	1,900	2,850	—
1833RA P	—	700	1,350	2,150	3,200	—
1834RA P	—	700	1,350	2,150	3,200	—
1835RA P	—	700	1,350	2,150	3,200	—

CONFEDERACION ARGENTINA

DECIMAL COINAGE

KM# 23 CENTAVO
5.0000 g., Copper, 21-22 mm. **Obv:** Sunface, date **Rev:** Denomination **Note:** Struck at Birmingham, England, most likely by Boulton & Watt.

Date	Mintage	VG	F	VF	XF	Unc
1854	—	2.50	5.00	17.50	40.00	—

KM# 24 2 CENTAVOS
10.0000 g., Copper, 29-30 mm. **Obv:** Sunface, date **Rev:** Denomination **Note:** Struck in medal and coin alignment.

Date	Mintage	VG	F	VF	XF	Unc
1854	—	3.00	7.50	22.00	50.00	—

KM# 25 4 CENTAVOS
20.0000 g., Copper, 35-36 mm. **Obv:** Sunface, date **Rev:** Denomination **Note:** Struck in medal and coin alignment.

Date	Mintage	VG	F	VF	XF	Unc
1854	—	7.00	15.00	37.50	85.00	—

REPUBLIC

DECIMAL COINAGE

KM# 32 CENTAVO

Bronze **Obv:** Arms **Rev:** Capped liberty head **Note:** Prev. KM#7.

Date	Mintage	F	VF	XF	Unc	BU
1882	108,000	6.50	13.50	25.00	50.00	—
1883	786,000	1.00	1.75	4.50	25.00	—
1884	4,604,000	1.00	1.75	4.00	20.00	—
1885	1,314,000	1.00	1.75	4.00	25.00	—
1886	444,000	1.00	1.75	4.50	28.00	—
1888	413,000	1.00	2.25	5.50	30.00	—
1889	568,000	1.00	2.25	5.50	30.00	—
1890	2,137,000	0.75	1.50	4.00	15.00	—
1891	605,000	1.00	1.75	4.50	25.00	—
1892	205,000	1.00	2.25	5.50	30.00	—
1893	754,000	1.00	1.75	4.50	25.00	—
1894	532,000	1.00	1.75	4.50	25.00	—
1895	423,000	1.00	2.25	5.50	25.00	—
1896	174,000	4.50	11.00	16.00	40.00	—

KM# 33 2 CENTAVOS

Bronze **Obv:** Arms **Rev:** Capped liberty head **Note:** Prev. KM#8.

Date	Mintage	F	VF	XF	Unc	BU
1882	88,000	7.00	15.00	30.00	70.00	—
1883	1,389,000	1.00	2.00	4.50	20.00	—
1884	5,667,000	0.75	1.75	3.00	15.00	—
1885	3,065,000	0.75	1.75	3.50	20.00	—
1887	363,000	4.50	11.50	18.00	45.00	—
1888	659,000	1.75	3.50	8.50	30.00	—
1889	2,391,000	0.75	1.75	3.50	15.00	—
1890	3,609,000	0.75	1.75	3.50	15.00	—
1891	8,050,000	0.50	1.75	3.00	15.00	—
1892	3,497,000	0.75	1.75	3.50	15.00	—
1893	5,473,000	0.75	1.75	3.50	15.00	—
1894	2,233,000	0.75	1.75	3.50	15.00	—
1895	593,000	1.25	3.50	15.00	40.00	—
1896	596,000	1.75	4.50	16.50	45.00	—

KM# 34 5 CENTAVOS

Copper-Nickel **Obv:** Capped liberty head **Rev:** Denomination **Note:** Prev. KM#9.

Date	Mintage	F	VF	XF	Unc	BU
1896	1,499,000	1.50	4.00	8.00	30.00	—
1897	3,981,000	0.50	1.00	4.00	22.00	—
1898	2,661,000	0.50	1.00	4.00	22.00	—
1899	2,835,000	0.25	0.50	3.00	18.00	—

KM# 26 10 CENTAVOS

2.5000 g., 0.9000 Silver .0723 oz. **Obv:** Arms **Rev:** Capped liberty head **Note:** Prev. KM#1.

Date	Mintage	F	VF	XF	Unc	BU
1881	1,020	75.00	150	225	375	—
1882	778,000	7.00	15.00	30.00	75.00	—
1883	2,786,000	5.00	10.00	20.00	50.00	—

KM# 35 10 CENTAVOS

Copper-Nickel **Obv:** Capped liberty head **Rev:** Denomination **Note:** Prev. KM#10.

Date	Mintage	F	VF	XF	Unc	BU
1896	1,877,000	2.00	7.50	20.00	45.00	—
1897	8,582,000	0.50	1.50	6.50	26.00	—
1898	8,534,000	0.50	1.50	6.50	26.00	—
1899	8,889,000	0.50	1.50	6.50	26.00	—

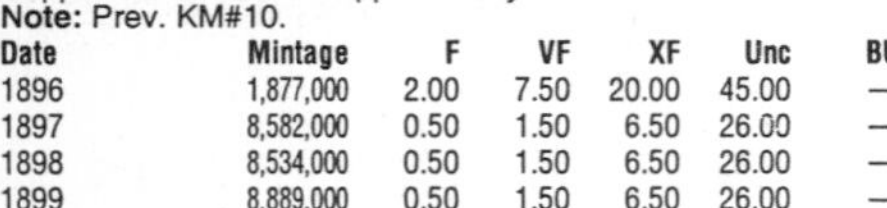

KM# 27 20 CENTAVOS

5.0000 g., 0.9000 Silver .1446 oz. **Obv:** Arms **Rev:** Capped liberty head **Note:** Prev. KM#2.

Date	Mintage	F	VF	XF	Unc	BU
1881	2,018	50.00	80.00	145	250	—
1882	762,000	8.00	15.00	35.00	80.00	—
1883/2	1,511,000	10.00	20.00	50.00	100	—
Note: Inverted 2						
1883	Inc. above	5.00	10.00	20.00	45.00	—

KM# 36 20 CENTAVOS

Copper-Nickel **Obv:** Capped liberty head **Rev:** Denomination **Note:** Prev. KM#11.

Date	Mintage	F	VF	XF	Unc	BU
1896	2,030,000	2.00	8.00	20.00	60.00	90.00
1897	5,263,000	1.50	6.00	12.00	50.00	—
1898	1,264,000	2.00	8.00	20.00	60.00	—
1899	840,000	20.00	55.00	100	200	—

KM# 28 50 CENTAVOS

12.5000 g., 0.9000 Silver .3617 oz. **Obv:** Arms **Rev:** Capped liberty head **Note:** Prev. KM#3.

Date	Mintage	F	VF	XF	Unc	BU
1881	1,020	125	225	375	650	—
1882	476,000	25.00	40.00	75.00	160	185
1883	2,273,000	10.00	20.00	40.00	85.00	—

KM# 29 PESO

25.0000 g., 0.9000 Silver .7234 oz. **Obv:** Arms **Rev:** Capped liberty head **Note:** Prev.KM#4.

Date	Mintage	F	VF	XF	Unc	BU
1881	62,000	100	150	250	500	—
1882	414,000	50.00	95.00	200	425	—
1883	98,000	100	150	225	450	—

KM# 30 1/2 ARGENTINO

4.0322 g., 0.9000 Gold .1167 oz. **Obv:** Arms **Rev:** Capped liberty head, right **Note:** Prev. KM#5.

Date	Mintage	F	VF	XF	Unc	BU
1881 Rare	9	—	—	—	—	—
1884	421	550	900	1,250	1,850	—

KM# 31 ARGENTINO

8.0645 g., 0.9000 Gold .2334 oz. **Obv:** Arms **Rev:** Capped liberty head, right **Note:** Prev. KM#6.

Date	Mintage	F	VF	XF	Unc	BU
1881	37,000	125	145	185	285	—
1882	252,000	100	120	145	220	—
1883	906,000	100	120	145	220	—
1884	448,000	100	120	145	220	—
1885	204,000	100	120	145	220	—
1886	398,000	100	120	145	220	—
1887	1,835,000	100	115	135	200	—
1888	1,663,000	100	115	135	200	—
1889	404,000	175	275	400	550	—
1896	197,000	100	120	145	220	—

ESSAIS

KM#	Date	Mintage	Identification	Mkt Val

E1	1878	—	Centavo. Copper.	125

E2	1878	—	2 Centavos. Copper.	150

E3	1879	—	20 Centavos Fuertes. Silver.	1,150
E3a	1879	—	20 Centavos Fuertes. Bronze.	950

E4	1879	—	40 Centavos Fuertes. Silver.	1,500
E4a	1879	—	40 Centavos Fuertes. Bronze.	1,100

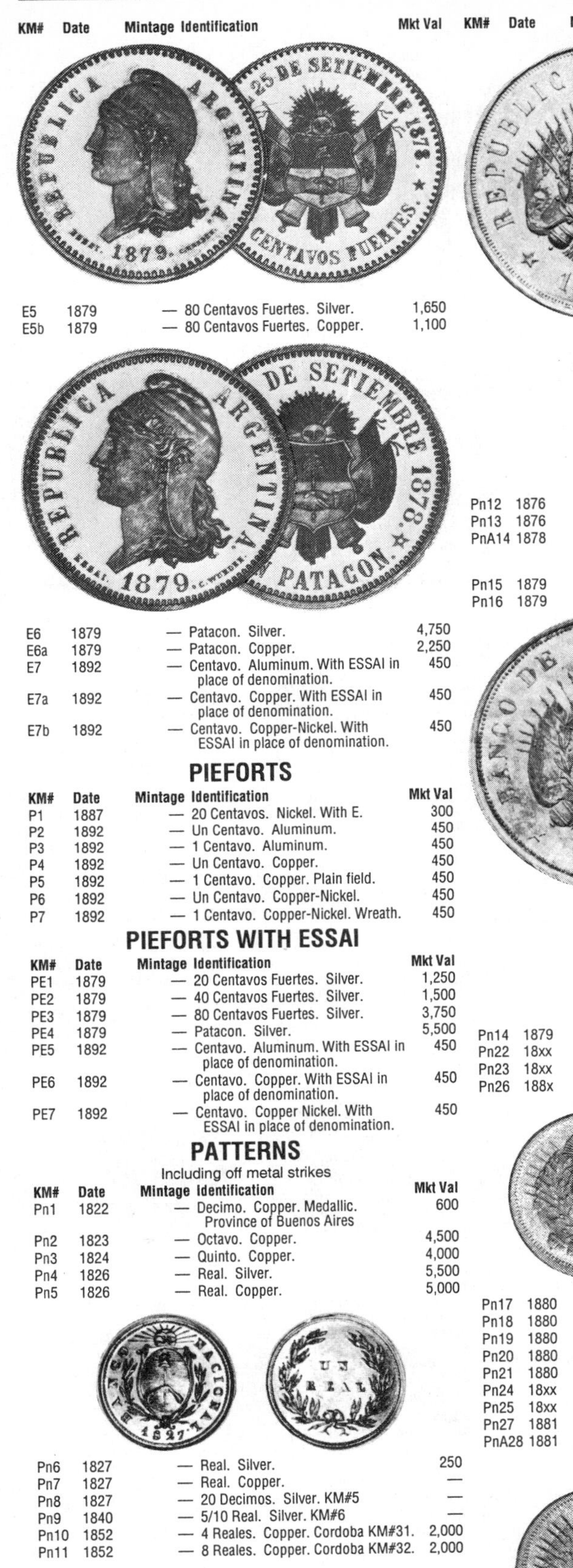

KM#	Date	Mintage	Identification	Mkt Val
E5	1879	—	80 Centavos Fuertes. Silver.	1,650
E5b	1879	—	80 Centavos Fuertes. Copper.	1,100
E6	1879	—	Patacon. Silver.	4,750
E6a	1879	—	Patacon. Copper.	2,250
E7	1892	—	Centavo. Aluminum. With ESSAI in place of denomination.	450
E7a	1892	—	Centavo. Copper. With ESSAI in place of denomination.	450
E7b	1892	—	Centavo. Copper-Nickel. With ESSAI in place of denomination.	450

PIEFORTS

KM#	Date	Mintage	Identification	Mkt Val
P1	1887	—	20 Centavos. Nickel. With E.	300
P2	1892	—	Un Centavo. Aluminum.	450
P3	1892	—	1 Centavo. Aluminum.	450
P4	1892	—	Un Centavo. Copper.	450
P5	1892	—	1 Centavo. Copper. Plain field.	450
P6	1892	—	Un Centavo. Copper-Nickel.	450
P7	1892	—	1 Centavo. Copper-Nickel. Wreath.	450

PIEFORTS WITH ESSAI

KM#	Date	Mintage	Identification	Mkt Val
PE1	1879	—	20 Centavos Fuertes. Silver.	1,250
PE2	1879	—	40 Centavos Fuertes. Silver.	1,500
PE3	1879	—	80 Centavos Fuertes. Silver.	3,750
PE4	1879	—	Patacon. Silver.	5,500
PE5	1892	—	Centavo. Aluminum. With ESSAI in place of denomination.	450
PE6	1892	—	Centavo. Copper. With ESSAI in place of denomination.	450
PE7	1892	—	Centavo. Copper Nickel. With ESSAI in place of denomination.	450

PATTERNS

Including off metal strikes

KM#	Date	Mintage	Identification	Mkt Val
Pn1	1822	—	Decimo. Copper. Medallic. Province of Buenos Aires	600
Pn2	1823	—	Octavo. Copper.	4,500
Pn3	1824	—	Quinto. Copper.	4,000
Pn4	1826	—	Real. Silver.	5,500
Pn5	1826	—	Real. Copper.	5,000

KM#	Date	Mintage	Identification	Mkt Val
Pn6	1827	—	Real. Silver.	250
Pn7	1827	—	Real. Copper.	—
Pn8	1827	—	20 Decimos. Silver. KM#5	—
Pn9	1840	—	5/10 Real. Silver. KM#6	—
Pn10	1852	—	4 Reales. Copper. Cordoba KM#31.	2,000
Pn11	1852	—	8 Reales. Copper. Cordoba KM#32.	2,000

KM#	Date	Mintage	Identification	Mkt Val
Pn12	1876	—	Peso. Silver.	3,500
Pn13	1876	—	Peso. Copper.	—
PnA14	1878	—	2 Centavos. Copper. 9.5000 g. 30 mm. Arms, date below. Bust left, legend around.	135
Pn15	1879	—	Peso. Copper.	—
Pn16	1879	—	Peso. Tin.	—

KM#	Date	Mintage	Identification	Mkt Val
Pn14	1879	—	Peso. Silver.	3,500
Pn22	18xx	—	Centavo. Copper.	500
Pn23	18xx	—	Centavo. Silver.	600
Pn26	188x	—	50 Centavos. Silver.	350

KM#	Date	Mintage	Identification	Mkt Val
Pn17	1880	—	Centavo. Copper. With E; KM#7.	120
Pn18	1880	—	2 Centavos. Copper. With E; KM#8.	130
Pn19	1880	—	50 Centavos. Silver. KM#3.	—
Pn20	1880	—	Peso. Silver. KM#4.	—
Pn21	1880	—	Peso. Silver. UN PESO PLATA.	—
Pn24	18xx	—	Centavo. Gold.	—
Pn25	18xx	—	20 Centavos. Silver.	—
Pn27	1881	9	Gold.	—
PnA28	1881	—	Argentino. Copper. 4.0000 g. Arms, date below. Bust right, legend around.	900

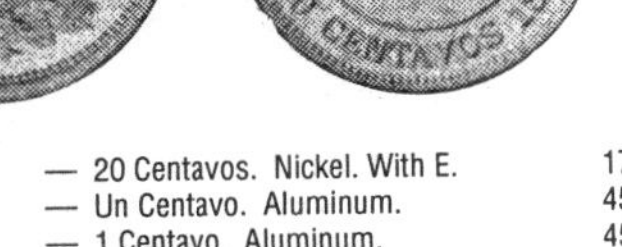

KM#	Date	Mintage	Identification	Mkt Val
Pn28	1887	—	20 Centavos. Nickel. With E.	175
Pn29	1892	—	Un Centavo. Aluminum.	450
Pn30	1892	—	1 Centavo. Aluminum.	450
Pn31	1892	—	Un Centavo. Copper.	450
Pn32	1892	—	1 Centavo. Copper.	450

KM#	Date	Mintage	Identification	Mkt Val
Pn33	1892	—	Un Centavo. Copper-Nickel.	450
Pn34	1892	—	1 Centavo. Copper-Nickel.	450

BUENOS AIRES

Buenos Aires, a city and province in eastern Argentina, was the first province to have coins made outside the country. Governor Martin Rodriguez initiated negotiations with Boulton & Watt (Soho Mint) in 1821. The Banco Nacional was dissolved in 1836 and the Casa de Moneda took its place.

NOTE: National Bank 5/10 reales are frequently struck over Soho decimos of 1822-1823. Pieces w/prominent showing of the under-type legend or divices can command a premium.

MONETARY SYSTEM
10 Decimos = 1 Real

PROVINCE

DECIMAL / REAL COINAGE

KM# 1 DECIMO
Copper, 23.5 mm. **Note:** Weight range 6.0-7.0g. Values given are for coin rotation examples, medal rotation pieces command a strong premium; officially retired in 1827 in favor of Banco Nacional issue KM#2-5.

Date	Mintage	VG	F	VF	XF	Unc
1822	—	2.00	5.00	16.50	40.00	100
1823	—	1.50	3.50	15.00	35.00	—

KM# 2 1/4 REAL
Copper, 20 mm. **Obv:** Fraction in shaded circle **Rev:** BUENOS AYRES 1827 within branches **Note:** Weight range 3.0-3.5g.

Date	Mintage	VG	F	VF	XF	Unc
1827	—	15.00	30.00	60.00	120	—

KM# 3 5/10 REAL
Copper, 22-28 mm. **Note:** Struck in medal and coin alignment. Weight range 4.5-8g.

Date	Mintage	VG	F	VF	XF	Unc
1827	—	2.00	4.00	10.00	25.00	75.00
1828	—	2.00	4.00	10.00	25.00	75.00
1830	—	3.00	5.00	12.50	30.00	—
1831/27	—	—	—	—	—	—
1831	—	2.00	4.00	10.00	25.00	75.00

KM# 6 5/10 REAL
2.5000 g., Copper, 22-23 mm.

Date	Mintage	VG	F	VF	XF	Unc
1840	—	5.00	12.00	25.00	55.00	—

KM# 4 10 DECIMOS
Copper, 28-32 mm. **Note:** Struck in medal and coin alignment. Weight range 12-15g

Date	Mintage	VG	F	VF	XF	Unc
1827	—	5.00	15.00	30.00	60.00	—
1828	—	15.00	30.00	60.00	120	—
1830	—	5.00	15.00	30.00	60.00	—

KM# 7 REAL
Copper, 26-27 mm. **Note:** Weight range 3-4g

Date	Mintage	VG	F	VF	XF	Unc
1840	—	2.00	8.00	20.00	50.00	175

KM# 10 REAL
Copper, 26-27 mm. **Note:** Weight range 4-5g. Examples known struck over cut down 2 reales 1853-1855 KM#9.

Date	Mintage	VG	F	VF	XF	Unc
1854	—	4.00	12.00	25.00	65.00	—

KM# 5 20 DECIMOS
Copper, 31-36 mm. **Note:** Struck in medal and coin alignment. Weight range 16-28g.

Date	Mintage	VG	F	VF	XF	Unc
1827	—	5.00	15.00	35.00	65.00	—
1830	—	4.00	10.00	30.00	60.00	—
1831	—	15.00	37.50	75.00	170	—

KM# 8 2 REALES
Copper, 31-32 mm. **Note:** Weight range 6-8g.

Date	Mintage	VG	F	VF	XF	Unc
1840	—	8.00	20.00	60.00	100	—
1844	—	8.00	20.00	60.00	100	—

KM# 9 2 REALES
Copper, 31-32 mm. **Note:** Weight range 6-8g.

Date	Mintage	VG	F	VF	XF	Unc
1853	—	3.00	10.00	20.00	65.00	—
1854	—	3.00	10.00	25.00	70.00	—
1855	—	3.00	10.00	20.00	65.00	—
1856	—	5.00	15.00	30.00	80.00	—

KM# 11 2 REALES
Copper, 31-32 mm. **Note:** Weight range 7-8g.

Date	Mintage	VG	F	VF	XF	Unc
1860	—	8.00	20.00	60.00	100	—
1861	—	9.00	22.00	65.00	110	—

CORDOBA

Cordoba, a city and province in central Argentina, was the most prolific of the provincial issuers. The provincial government contracted with concessionaires to make coins. The contractors for 1833 are not known, but all the private makers' coinage is relatively crude and replete with variations, die-sinking incongruities and minor errors. On many pieces it is almost impossible to find the same pairing of dies, i.e., 1/4 Reales, 1/2 Reales and 1 Reales of the 1839-41 type.

On February 2, 1844 a provincial mint was authorized by Governor Manuel Lopez. It operated from 1844 to 1852.

CONCESSIONAIRES

Letter	Date	Name
PP, PNP	1839-41	Pedro Nolasco Pizarro
JPP	1841-44	Jose Policarpo Patino

PROVINCE

REAL COINAGE

KM# 1.1 1/4 REAL
Silver **Obv:** Castle, date below **Rev:** Sun face

Date	Mintage	VG	F	VF	XF	Unc
1833	—	30.00	50.00	80.00	150	—
1838	—	25.00	40.00	65.00	125	—

KM# 1.2 1/4 REAL
Silver **Obv:** Wide castle, without date

Date	Mintage	VG	F	VF	XF	Unc
ND	—	2,250	3,750	—	—	—

KM# 2.1 1/4 REAL
Silver **Obv:** Castle flanked by prize cup

Date	Mintage	VG	F	VF	XF	Unc
1839	—	1,000	2,000	—	—	—
Note: Large eight, small sun face						
1839	—	1,500	3,000	—	—	—
Note: Small eight, large sun face						

KM# 2.2 1/4 REAL
Silver **Obv:** Castle flanked by P-P, date below **Note:** Many legend and die varieties exist.

Date	Mintage	VG	F	VF	XF	Unc
1839 PP	—	10.00	20.00	35.00	75.00	—
1840 PP	—	15.00	35.00	80.00	190	—
1841 PP	—	25.00	45.00	90.00	200	—

KM# 33.2 1/4 REAL
Silver **Rev:** Ten point sun

Date	Mintage	VG	F	VF	XF	Unc
ND	—	125	225	425	700	—

KM# 33.1 1/4 REAL
Silver **Obv:** Fraction **Rev:** Eight point sun

Date	Mintage	VG	F	VF	XF	Unc
ND	—	15.00	25.00	40.00	75.00	—

KM# 3 1/2 REAL
Silver **Obv:** Arms in wreath **Obv. Legend:** EN UNION Y LIBERTAD **Rev:** Sun face **Rev. Legend:** PROVINCIA DE CORDOVA

Date	Mintage	VG	F	VF	XF	Unc
1839 PNP	—	22.50	50.00	80.00	150	—
1839 PNP	—	25.00	55.00	90.00	175	—
Note: LIVERTAD						
1839 PNP	—	40.00	80.00	165	275	—
Note: CORDOBA on reverse						
1840 PNP	—	22.50	50.00	90.00	175	—
Note: LIVERTAD						
1840 PNP	—	60.00	120	200	—	—
Note: LIVEITAD						

KM# 4 1/2 REAL
Silver **Obv. Legend:** EN UNION Y LIBERTAD **Rev. Legend:** CONFEDERADA

Date	Mintage	VG	F	VF	XF	Unc
1839 PNP	—	40.00	85.00	175	300	—

KM# 5 1/2 REAL
Silver **Obv. Legend:** CONFEDERADA **Rev. Legend:** PROVINCIA DE CORDOVA

Date	Mintage	VG	F	VF	XF	Unc
1840 PNP	—	65.00	135	250	400	—

KM# 6 1/2 REAL
Silver **Obv:** Banner above castle, date below **Obv. Legend:** CORDOVA **Rev:** Sun face **Rev. Legend:** CONFEDERADA

Date	Mintage	VG	F	VF	XF	Unc
1840 PNP	—	60.00	120	200	—	—
Note: Crossed lances below castle						

KM# 16 1/2 REAL
Silver **Obv. Legend:** CONFEDERADA **Rev. Legend:** PROVINCIA DE CORDOVA

Date	Mintage	VG	F	VF	XF	Unc
1841 PNP	—	60.00	120	200	—	—
1841	—	60.00	120	200	—	—

KM# 15 1/2 REAL
Silver **Obv. Legend:** PROVINCIA DE CORDOVA **Rev. Legend:** PROVINCIA DE CORDOVA

Date	Mintage	VG	F	VF	XF	Unc
1841 PNP	—	65.00	135	250	400	—
1841	—	65.00	135	250	400	—

KM# 29 1/2 REAL
Silver **Obv:** Denomination **Rev:** Sun face **Note:** Many legend and die varieties exist.

Date	Mintage	VG	F	VF	XF	Unc
1850	—	12.00	25.00	50.00	90.00	—
1850	—	9.00	20.00	40.00	80.00	—
Note: Error: CONFEDRRADA						
1851	—	65.00	135	285	500	—
1853	—	7.00	15.00	35.00	80.00	—
1854	—	7.00	15.00	40.00	90.00	200

KM# 8 REAL
Silver **Obv. Legend:** PROVINCIA DE CORDOVA **Rev. Legend:** PROVINCIA DE CORDOVA

Date	Mintage	VG	F	VF	XF	Unc
1840 PNP	—	30.00	60.00	120	225	—
1841 PNP	—	30.00	60.00	120	225	—

KM# 9 REAL
Silver **Obv. Legend:** PROVINCIA DE CORDOVA **Rev. Legend:** EN UNION Y LIBERTAD

Date	Mintage	VG	F	VF	XF	Unc
1840 PNP	—	6.00	12.00	25.00	50.00	—
1841 PNP	—	6.00	12.00	25.00	50.00	—
1841 PNP CORDOBA	—	30.00	50.00	85.00	150	—

KM# 7 REAL
Silver **Obv:** Arms (shaded) in wreath, date below **Obv. Legend:** PROVINCIA DE CORDOVA **Rev:** Sun face **Rev. Legend:** CONFEDERADA **Note:** Many legend and die varieties exist.

Date	Mintage	VG	F	VF	XF	Unc
1840 PNP	—	5.00	10.00	20.00	45.00	—
1841/0 PNP	—	—	—	—	—	—
1841 PNP	—	5.00	10.00	20.00	45.00	—
1841 PNP	—	40.00	70.00	120	250	—
Note: CORDOBA						
1841 PNP	—	35.00	60.00	100	225	—
Note: CORDOBA and inverted 4						
1841 JPP	—	5.00	10.00	20.00	45.00	—
1842 JPP	—	5.00	10.00	20.00	45.00	—
Note: Also reported with PROVINCIA/VINCA						
1842 JPP	—	—	—	—	—	—
Note: PROVINCI						
1842 JPP	—	8.00	16.00	35.00	75.00	—
Note: PROVINCA						
1843 JPP	—	5.00	10.00	20.00	45.00	—
1843 JPP	—	6.50	12.50	25.00	55.00	—

Date	Mintage	VG	F	VF	XF	Unc
Note: Inverted 3						
3481 JPP	—	18.00	35.00	65.00	120	—
Note: Error for 1843						
1843 JPP	—	7.50	15.00	30.00	60.00	—
Note: PROVICIA						
1843 JPP	—	8.00	16.00	35.00	75.00	—
Note: CORDOV						
4481 JPP	—	30.00	60.00	100	200	—
Note: Error for 1844						

KM# 14 REAL

Silver **Obv:** Banner above castle **Obv. Legend:** PROVINCIA DE CORDOVA **Rev:** Sun face **Rev. Legend:** CONFEDERADA **Note:** Many legend and die varieties exist.

Date	Mintage	VG	F	VF	XF	Unc
1840 PNP	—	50.00	90.00	175	300	—
1841 PNP	—	8.00	18.00	35.00	75.00	—
1841 PNP	—	35.00	65.00	145	250	—
Note: CORDOBA						
1841 PNP	—	65.00	125	250	400	—
Note: CORDOBA, inverted 4						
1841 PNP	—	20.00	40.00	85.00	150	—
Note: CORDOV, inverted 4						
1841 PNP	—	7.00	15.00	30.00	60.00	—
Note: Inverted 4						
1841 PNP	—	10.00	20.00	40.00	85.00	—
Note: CORDOV						

KM# 10 REAL

Silver **Obv. Legend:** CONFEDERADA **Rev. Legend:** CONFEDERADA

Date	Mintage	VG	F	VF	XF	Unc
1840	—	30.00	65.00	130	250	—

KM# 11 REAL

Silver **Obv. Legend:** CONFEDERADA **Rev. Legend:** PROVINCIA DE CORDOVA

Date	Mintage	VG	F	VF	XF	Unc
1840 PNP	—	30.00	65.00	130	250	—

KM# 12 REAL

Silver **Obv. Legend:** EN UNION Y LIBERTAD **Rev. Legend:** PROVINCIA DE CORDOVA

Date	Mintage	VG	F	VF	XF	Unc
1840 PNP	—	35.00	75.00	150	275	—

KM# 13 REAL

Silver **Obv. Legend:** EN UNION Y LIBERTAD **Rev. Legend:** CONFEDERADA

Date	Mintage	VG	F	VF	XF	Unc
1840 PNP	—	50.00	100	200	350	—

KM# 17 REAL

Silver **Obv:** Arms without shading and 2 rosettes **Obv. Legend:** PROVINCIA DE CORDOVA **Rev:** Sun face **Rev. Legend:** CONFEDERADA

Date	Mintage	VG	F	VF	XF	Unc
1841 PNP	—	5.00	10.00	20.00	45.00	—
1843 JPP	—	5.00	10.00	20.00	45.00	—
1843 JPP	—	8.00	16.00	35.00	75.00	—
Note: PROVINCI						
1843 JPP	—	6.00	12.00	25.00	50.00	—
Note: CONFEDERDA						
1843 JPP	—	5.00	10.00	20.00	45.00	—
Note: CORDOV						

KM# 18 REAL

Silver **Obv. Legend:** PROVINCIA DE CORDOVA **Rev. Legend:** EN UNION Y LIBERTAD

Date	Mintage	VG	F	VF	XF	Unc
1841 PNP	—	35.00	65.00	145	250	—

KM# 19 REAL

Silver **Obv. Legend:** PROVINCIA DE CORDOVA **Rev. Legend:** PROVINCIA DE CORDOVA

Date	Mintage	VG	F	VF	XF	Unc
1841	—	40.00	80.00	160	285	—
Note: Rosette below castle						

KM# 21 REAL

Silver **Obv:** Arms without shading, date below **Obv. Legend:** PROVINCIA DE CORDOVA **Rev:** Sun face **Rev. Legend:** CONFEDERADA **Note:** Many legend and die varieties exist.

Date	Mintage	VG	F	VF	XF	Unc
1843 JPP	—	20.00	40.00	65.00	110	—
Note: CONFEDERDA						
1843 JPP	—	18.00	35.00	60.00	100	—
Note: CORDOV						
1843 JPP	—	30.00	60.00	100	200	—
Note: CORDOV and CONFEDERDA						
1843 JPP	—	20.00	40.00	70.00	120	—
Note: CORDOV and PROVINCI						
1843 JPP	—	18.00	35.00	60.00	100	—
Note: CORDO						
1843 JPP	—	18.00	35.00	60.00	100	—
Note: CORDO and CONFEDERDA						
1843 JPP	—	18.00	35.00	60.00	100	—
1844 JPP	—	35.00	75.00	150	275	—
1844 JPP	—	35.00	75.00	150	275	—
Note: CORDOV						

KM# 20 REAL

Silver **Rev. Legend:** LIBRE YNDEPENDIENTE

Date	Mintage	VG	F	VF	XF	Unc
1843 JPP	—	10.00	20.00	45.00	90.00	—

KM# 22 REAL

Silver **Obv. Legend:** PROVINCIA DE CORDOVA **Rev. Legend:** LIBRE YNDEPENDIENTE **Note:** Many legend and die varieties exist.

Date	Mintage	VG	F	VF	XF	Unc
1843 JPP	—	10.00	20.00	45.00	90.00	—

KM# 26.3 REAL

Silver **Rev:** Ten point sun

Date	Mintage	VG	F	VF	XF	Unc
1848 Medal rotation	—	35.00	70.00	150	250	—
1848 Coin rotation	—	7.50	15.00	30.00	60.00	—

KM# 26.1 REAL

Silver **Obv:** Denomination **Obv. Legend:** PROVINCIA DE CORDOBA **Rev:** Eight point sun face, date below **Rev. Legend:** CONFEDERADA

Date	Mintage	VG	F	VF	XF	Unc
1848	—	6.50	12.50	25.00	50.00	—

KM# 26.2 REAL

Silver **Rev:** Nine point sun

Date	Mintage	VG	F	VF	XF	Unc
1848	—	20.00	35.00	65.00	125	—

KM# 23 2 REALES

0.7500 Silver **Obv:** Castle among flags in sprays **Obv. Legend:** PROVINCIA DE CORDOBA **Rev:** Sun face in sprays, date below **Rev. Legend:** CONFEDERADA **Note:** Many legend and die varieties exist, including a rare 1844 CONFEDRADA with reverse medallic die alignment.

Date	Mintage	VG	F	VF	XF	Unc
1844	—	10.00	20.00	45.00	90.00	—
1844 CONFEDRADA	—	75.00	150	300	500	—
1845	—	10.00	20.00	40.00	80.00	—

KM# 25 2 REALES

0.7500 Silver **Note:** Many legend and die varieties exist.

Date	Mintage	VG	F	VF	XF	Unc
1846	—	10.00	20.00	45.00	90.00	—

KM# 27 2 REALES

0.7500 Silver **Rev:** Seven point sun

Date	Mintage	VG	F	VF	XF	Unc
1849	—	8.00	16.00	32.00	65.00	—
1850	—	10.00	20.00	45.00	90.00	—

KM# 28 2 REALES

0.7500 Silver **Rev:** Eight point sun **Note:** Many legend and die varieties exist.

Date	Mintage	VG	F	VF	XF	Unc
1848 Rare	—	—	—	—	—	—
1849	—	9.00	18.00	35.00	70.00	—

KM# 30 2 REALES

0.7500 Silver **Note:** Similar to 4 Reales, KM#31.

Date	Mintage	VG	F	VF	XF	Unc
1852	—	65.00	125	275	450	—
1854	—	60.00	100	225	400	—

KM# 24.1 4 REALES

0.7500 Silver **Note:** Reverse weight: 9 Ds; die varieties exist.

Date	Mintage	VG	F	VF	XF	Unc
1844	—	300	600	1,200	2,000	—

KM# 24.2 4 REALES

0.7500 Silver **Note:** Larger dies.

Date	Mintage	VG	F	VF	XF	Unc
1845	—	85.00	175	350	650	—
Note: Obverse with portcullis						
1845	—	22.50	40.00	75.00	150	—
Note: Obverse without portcullis						
1846	—	100	200	375	700	—
Note: Die of 1845						

KM# 24.3 4 REALES

0.7500 Silver

Date	Mintage	VG	F	VF	XF	Unc
1846	—	35.00	70.00	150	300	—
Note: Laureate edge						
1846	—	65.00	110	235	420	—
Note: Milled edge						
1847	—	20.00	35.00	65.00	125	—
1850	—	20.00	35.00	65.00	125	—
1851	—	20.00	30.00	55.00	100	—
Note: Small 5mm sunface, weight: 9 D						
1851	—	20.00	35.00	65.00	125	—
Note: Large 6.5mm sunface, weight: 9 D						

KM# A31 4 REALES

0.7500 Silver **Rev:** Flatter sunface with even length sunburst **Note:** This sunburst was struck utilizing dies from the La Rioja Mint; die and edge varieties exist.

Date	Mintage	VG	F	VF	XF	Unc
1852	—	30.00	60.00	120	275	500

KM# 31 4 REALES

0.7500 Silver **Note:** Struck from dies prepared in France.

Date	Mintage	VG	F	VF	XF	Unc
1852	—	50.00	100	200	350	—

KM# 32 8 REALES
0.7500 Silver **Obv:** High spear tips at left **Note:** Struck from dies prepared in France.

Date	Mintage	VG	F	VF	XF	Unc
1852	—	50.00	80.00	150	300	—

Note: 9 known varieties of obverses with differences in width of base, size of and distance between leaves and positions of flag poles in relation to letters in inscription. Spelling differences are known with CORDOBA the common one and Cordova the rare one

ENTRE RIOS

Entre Rios (Colonia San Jose) was a settlement of Swiss and Italian families in northeast Argentina on the Uruguayan border. General Urquiza (deposer of Rosas) was a political power in the province. As governor, during the war with Paraguay, he authorized an Italian, Pablo Cataldi, to make coins for the settlement during a coin shortage in 1867

PROVINCE

REAL COINAGE

KM# 1 1/2 REAL
Silver

Date	Mintage	VG	F	VF	XF	Unc
1867	—	60.00	90.00	150	275	—

LA RIOJA

La Rioja (Rioxa), a city and province in northwest Argentina, was the source of rich mineral wealth. In this province the city of Chilecito was significant as the spot where gold and silver mines within the Famatina Mountains had been worked since colonial times. After independence was gained from Spain, Governor Nicolas Davila authorized a mint at Chilecito, which was established in 1820. The first attempts at coinage came in 1821 and were nothing more than poor imitations of the Potosi 2 real cobs of Ferdinand VII, crude in all respects because the mint had no machinery with which to make proper dies, punches for collars. No examples of these types are distinguishable today as they are in essence identical to all other contemporary cob copies of the period. However, some experts believe that the presence of the letter A on provisional cobs of this type can be considered a mint mark or assayer initial tying the coins to the Chilecito mint.

The next coins to emerge from Chilecito were cob types dated 1821, 1822, and 1823, bearing the legend RIOXA. All of these cob coins circulated in the area until the middle of 1824 when they were officially recalled. These rare types were well received in their day as they were made of good silver. They can be distinguished today by their crude and uneven strike quality as opposed to the well made, attractive look of modern fakes.

In 1824 the mint at Chilecito was transferred to the capital of La Rioja where minting continued from 1824 to 1860. Chilecito's mines at Famatina Mountain continued to produce gold and silver for the new mint and Famatina is featured as a central design on many coins of the period.

NOTE: Virtually all of the early pieces are false. All pieces dated between 1820 and 1824 should only be bought with certification of two or more authorities.

PROVINCE

REAL COINAGE

KM# 3 1/2 REAL
Silver **Note:** Cob type with RIOXA.

Date	Mintage	Good	VG	F	VF	XF
1822 Rare	—	—	—	—	—	—

KM# 18 1/2 REAL
Silver **Obv:** Arms in branches **Rev:** Sun above mountain

Date	Mintage	Good	VG	F	VF	XF
1844 B	—	3.50	8.00	17.00	35.00	75.00

KM# 25 1/2 REAL
Silver **Rev. Legend:** CRED. PUB. DE LA RIOJA

Date	Mintage	Good	VG	F	VF	XF
1854 B	71,000	2.50	7.00	15.00	30.00	75.00
1860 B	—	4.00	9.00	20.00	40.00	—

KM# 22 1/2 REAL
Silver **Obv. Legend:** REPUB. ARGENT. CONFEDERADA **Rev. Legend:** PROV. DE LA RIOJA

Date	Mintage	Good	VG	F	VF	XF
1854 B	17,000	3.00	8.00	17.00	35.00	75.00

KM# 23 1/2 REAL
Silver **Rev. Legend:** CRED. PUB. DE LA RIOJA

Date	Mintage	Good	VG	F	VF	XF
1854 B	5,940	4.00	9.00	20.00	40.00	—

KM# 24 1/2 REAL
Silver **Obv. Legend:** CONFEDERACION ARGENTINA **Rev. Legend:** PROV. DE LA. RIOJA

Date	Mintage	Good	VG	F	VF	XF
1854 B	24,000	3.00	8.00	17.00	35.00	—

KM# 4 REAL
Silver **Note:** Struck at Chilecito; cob type with RIOXA; 1821 dated coins are counterfeit.

Date	Mintage	Good	VG	F	VF	XF
1822 Rare	—	—	—	—	—	—

KM# 5 REAL
Silver **Obv:** Sun above arms **Rev. Legend:** SVR AMERICA RIOXA **Note:** Struck at La Rioja.

Date	Mintage	Good	VG	F	VF	XF
ND(1823) Rare	—	—	—	—	—	—

KM# 6 REAL
Silver **Rev. Legend:** SUD AMERICA 1823 RIOXA **Note:** Struck at La Rioja.

Date	Mintage	Good	VG	F	VF	XF
1823 Rare	—	—	—	—	—	—

KM# 1 2 REALES
Silver **Obv:** Pillars, RIOXA, date **Rev:** Castles and lions **Note:** Cob type.

Date	Mintage	Good	VG	F	VF	XF
(1)821 Rare	—	—	—	—	—	—
(1)822 Rare	—	—	—	—	—	—
(1)823 Rare	—	—	—	—	—	—

KM# 12 2 REALES
Silver **Note:** General Rosas.

Date	Mintage	Good	VG	F	VF	XF
1842	—	25.00	40.00	65.00	135	—

KM# 16 2 REALES
Silver **Note:** Mountain and sun type; struck in coin and medal rotation.

Date	Mintage	Good	VG	F	VF	XF
1843 RB	—	30.00	60.00	125	225	—
1844 RB	—	40.00	75.00	165	285	—

KM# 15 2 REALES
Silver **Note:** Mountain type.

Date	Mintage	Good	VG	F	VF	XF
1843 RB	—	10.00	20.00	50.00	100	200

KM# 26 2 REALES
Silver

Date	Mintage	Good	VG	F	VF	XF
1859 B	—	25.00	60.00	125	250	600
1860 B	—	15.00	30.00	60.00	125	—

KM# 2.1 4 REALES
Silver **Obv:** Pillars, RIOXA, date. **Rev:** Castles and lions **Note:** Cob type.

Date	Mintage	Good	VG	F	VF	XF
(1)821	—	200	400	750	1,250	—
(1)822 Rare	—	—	—	—	—	—

KM# 2.2 4 REALES
Silver **Obv:** Without RIOXA

Date	Mintage	Good	VG	F	VF	XF
(1)823	—	200	400	750	1,250	—

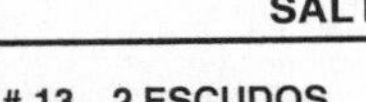

KM# 20 4 REALES
Silver

Date	Mintage	VG	F	VF	XF	Unc
1846 RV	—	15.00	25.00	45.00	85.00	—
1849 RV	—	—	—	—	—	—
1849 RB	—	15.00	35.00	65.00	100	—
1850 RB	—	20.00	50.00	100	200	—

KM# 21 4 REALES
Silver

Date	Mintage	VG	F	VF	XF	Unc
1852 B	—	60.00	90.00	200	400	—

KM# 8 8 REALES
Silver

Date	Mintage	VG	F	VF	XF	Unc
1838 R Coin rotation	—	45.00	85.00	175	350	—
1838 R Medal rotation	—	135	275	550	1,000	—
1839 R	—	50.00	90.00	185	375	—
1840 R	—	45.00	85.00	175	350	—

KM# 10 8 REALES
Silver **Obv. Legend:** REPUBLICA ARGENTINA

Date	Mintage	VG	F	VF	XF	Unc
1840 R	—	550	1,000	2,000	3,750	—

KM# 7 ESCUDO
3.3750 g., 0.8750 Gold .0949 oz. **Obv:** Sun above arms in branches **Rev:** Legend in wreath **Rev. Legend:** SUD AMERICA 1823 RIOXA

Date	Mintage	VG	F	VF	XF	Unc
1823 Rare	—	—	—	—	—	—

KM# 13 2 ESCUDOS
6.7500 g., 0.8750 Gold .1899 oz. **Note:** General Rosas.

Date	Mintage	VG	F	VF	XF	Unc
1842 R	—	250	450	800	1,500	—

KM# 17 2 ESCUDOS
6.7500 g., 0.8750 Gold .1899 oz.

Date	Mintage	VG	F	VF	XF	Unc
1843 RB	—	200	350	550	900	—

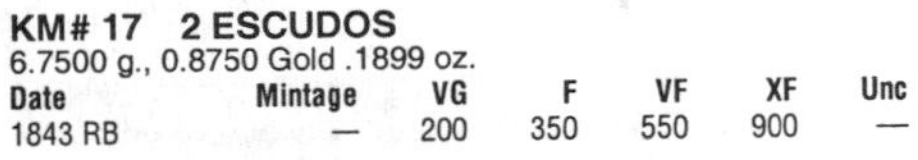

KM# A9 8 ESCUDOS
27.0000 g., 0.8750 Gold .7596 oz. **Note:** General Rosas.

Date	Mintage	VG	F	VF	XF	Unc
1836 R Rare	—	—	—	—	—	—

KM# 9 8 ESCUDOS
27.0000 g., 0.8750 Gold .7596 oz. **Note:** General Rosas.

Date	Mintage	VG	F	VF	XF	Unc
1838 R	—	650	1,150	2,000	3,750	—
1840 R	—	750	1,250	2,250	4,500	—

KM# 11 8 ESCUDOS
27.0000 g., 0.8750 Gold .7596 oz. **Obv. Legend:** REPUBLICA ARGENTINA

Date	Mintage	VG	F	VF	XF	Unc
1840 R	—	850	1,350	2,250	4,000	—

KM# 14 8 ESCUDOS
27.0000 g., 0.8750 Gold .7596 oz. **Note:** General Rosas.

Date	Mintage	VG	F	VF	XF	Unc
1842 R Rare	—	—	—	—	—	—

Note: Superior Heifetz sale 12-89 VF realized $18,700

KM# 19 8 ESCUDOS
27.0000 g., 0.8750 Gold .7596 oz.

Date	Mintage	VG	F	VF	XF	Unc
1845 B	—	1,200	1,800	2,700	5,000	—

MENDOZA

Mendoza, a province in western Argentina, was one of the first to make coins designed to resemble the Spanish Colonial cobs of Potosi. The mint was established in 1822, under Governor Pedro Molina. These local cobs were put in circulation in December 1823 and retired from circulation less than a year later.

In 1835 Molina again saw that coins were needed, and decided to award contracts for production rather than have the provincial mint make them. Abel Bucci and Manuel Espeys, who had the contract failed to supply any volume of coinage for circulation and were retired in 1836.

PROVINCE

REAL COINAGE

KM# 4 DECIMO
Copper **Obv:** MENDOZA, date and denomination within wreath **Rev:** Arms within branches

Date	Mintage	Good	VG	F	VF	XF
1823 Unique	—	—	—	—	—	—

KM# 5 1/8 REAL
Copper

Date	Mintage	Good	VG	F	VF	XF
1835 Rare	—	—	—	—	—	—

KM# 6 1/4 REAL
Silver **Obv:** Arms divide value **Rev:** Small animal

Date	Mintage	Good	VG	F	VF	XF
1836 Unique	—	—	—	—	—	—

SALTA

Salta, a province in northwest Argentina, was a frequent battleground during the War of Independence. Governor Martin Guemes fought the Spaniards without help from the patriotic forces in Buenos Aires. There was no money with which to pay the troops and what was circulating was counterfeit. Low morale and frequent desertions were one result. In desperation, Guemes decided to countermark the false coins with the word PATRIA and to guarantee them as genuine.

When this action became known to the patriot government in Buenos Aires, it was declared to be a violation of national laws and all the pieces were to be withdrawn.

Meanwhile, Guemes had gained valuable time, culminating with a victory at Castanares which finally rid the north of Spanish influence.

All genuine Salta countermarks are only found on counterfeit Potosi cobs.

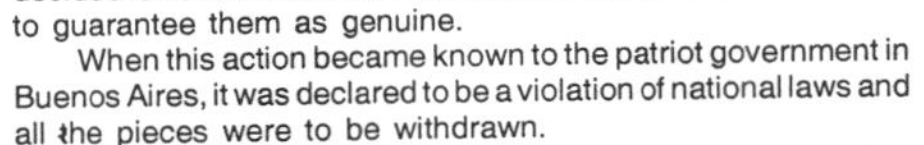

c/m: PATRIA monogram in wreath.

PROVINCE

COUNTERMARKED COINAGE

KM# 2 2 REALES
Silver **Countermark:** PATRIA monogram in wreath **Note:** Countermark on Potosi Mint cobs.

CM Date	Host Date	Good	VG	F	VF	XF
ND	ND	100	200	350	—	—

KM# 3 4 REALES
Silver **Countermark:** PATRIA monogram in wreath **Note:** Countermark on Potosi Mint cobs.

CM Date	Host Date	Good	VG	F	VF	XF
ND	ND Rare	—	—	—	—	—

SANTIAGO DEL ESTERO

Santiago del Estero is a province in north central Argentina. In 1823, during the governorship of Felipe Ibarra, coinage began in an effort to replace the fast-disappearing cob coins of the Potosi mint. The pieces were not well received and coining was soon halted. Another effort, in 1836, faired no better.

NOTE: Contemporary and more recent counterfeits are known of nearly all this province's coinage.

PROVINCE

REAL COINAGE

KM# 1 1/2 REAL
Base Silver **Obv:** SoEo in angles of crossed arrows, date below **Rev:** Sun in branches

Date	Mintage	Good	VG	F	VF	XF
(1)823 Unique	—	—	—	—	—	—

KM# 2 1/2 REAL
Base Silver **Obv:** S E in angles of crossed arrows, date below

Date	Mintage	Good	VG	F	VF	XF
(1)823	—	75.00	150	225	375	—

KM# 3 REAL
Base Silver **Obv:** SoEo in angles of crossed arrows, date below **Rev:** Cross

Date	Mintage	Good	VG	F	VF	XF
(1)823 Unique	—	—	—	—	—	—

KM# 4 REAL
Base Silver **Obv:** SoEo in angles of crossed arrows, date below **Rev:** Sun in branches

Date	Mintage	Good	VG	F	VF	XF
(1)823	—	250	400	700	1,200	—

KM# 5 REAL
Base Silver **Obv:** S E in angles of crossed arrows, date below **Rev:** Sun in branches

Date	Mintage	Good	VG	F	VF	XF
(1)823	—	50.00	100	150	275	—

KM# 6 REAL
Base Silver **Obv:** S E in angles of crossed arrows, date below **Rev:** Sun above Liberty cap in branches

Date	Mintage	Good	VG	F	VF	XF
(1)836	—	35.00	75.00	125	265	—

TIERRA DEL FUEGO

The largest island in the archipelago south of the tip of South America.The western part is under Chilean rule, the eastern part is under Argentine rule. Julius Popper was a Romanian born Jewish engineer/adventurer who was given permission to mine gold and strike coins on the Argentine side of the island. Popper's company was named Lavaderos de Oro del Sud (Gold Washers of the South) and his first mine was named El Paramo. In 1889 Popper hand-engraved dies and struck 2 varieties each of 1 Gramo and 5 Gramo tokens. The results of this effort were unsatisfactory, so Popper later used a government connection to have at least 10kg of gold tokens struck at Casa de Moneda (the Buenos Aires mint). The first 1 Gramo dies from this effort broke after only 6 tokens were struck. Another variety of 1 Gramo token of unknown origin is known in both bronze and gold and may be a pattern or contemporary counterfeit. Popper died in Buenos Aires in 1893 under mysterious circumstances while under house arrest for suspicion of murdering island natives.

NOTE: In 1995 Museo del Fin del Mundo in USHUAIA borrowed the surviving pair of Casa de Moneda 1 Gramo dies and struck 100 tokens with an outer ring marked USHUAIA. Additional tokens have been struck by oversize copy dies, also with an outer ring marked USHUAIA. Caution is advised, as these could be cut down and passed as genuine. Although rare and collectible, these restrike tokens are not priced in this catalog. Please refer to the fourth edition of *Unusual World Coins* by Colin R. Bruce II for detailed listings of these types.

TERRITORY

TOKEN COINAGE

KM# Tn1 GRAMO
Gold **Issuer:** Julius Popper **Obv:** POPPER 1 **Rev:** 1G **Note:** Struck from hand engraved dies.

Date	Mintage	F	VF	XF	Unc	BU
ND(1889) Rare	—	—	—	—	—	—

KM# Tn2 GRAMO
Gold **Issuer:** Julius Popper **Obv:** Legend and date flanked by stars **Rev:** Legend and mining tools **Note:** Struck from hand engraved dies.

Date	Mintage	F	VF	XF	Unc	BU
1889 Rare	—	—	—	—	—	—

KM# Tn3 GRAMO
Gold **Issuer:** Julius Popper **Obv:** Legend and date flanked by dots **Rev. Designer:** Legend and mining tools **Note:** Struck from hand engraved dies.

Date	Mintage	F	VF	XF	Unc	BU
.1889. Rare	—	—	—	—	—	—

KM# Tn4 GRAMO
Gold **Issuer:** Julius Popper, Buenos Aires issue **Obv:** Date and legend, similar to Tn5 **Rev:** Mining tools and legend, similar to Tn5 **Note:** First Buenos Aires die with small letters on obverse and reverse.

Date	Mintage	F	VF	XF	Unc	BU
1889 Unique	—	—	—	—	—	—

KM# Tn5 GRAMO
Gold **Issuer:** Julius Popper, Buenos Aires issue **Note:** Second Buenos Aires die with large letters on obverse and reverse.

Date	Mintage	F	VF	XF	Unc	BU
1889	—	—	—	650	1,000	—

KM# Tn6 5 GRAMOS
Gold **Issuer:** Julius Popper **Obv:** POPPER above date flanked by stars **Rev:** Denomination and legend **Note:** Struck from hand engraved dies with large letters on obverse and reverse.

Date	Mintage	F	VF	XF	Unc	BU
1889 Rare	—	—	—	—	—	—

KM# Tn7 5 GRAMOS
Gold **Issuer:** Julius Popper **Obv:** POPPER over crossed mining tools above date flanked by stars **Rev:** Denomination and legend **Note:** Struck from hand engraved dies with small letters on obverse and reverse.

Date	Mintage	F	VF	XF	Unc	BU
1889 Rare	—	—	—	—	—	—

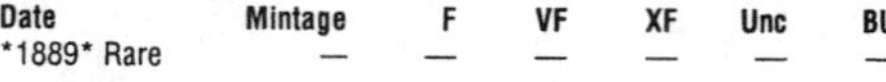

KM# Tn8 5 GRAMOS
Gold **Issuer:** Julius Popper, Buenos Aires issue

Date	Mintage	F	VF	XF	Unc	BU
1889	—	—	—	3,000	4,750	—

TUCUMAN

Tucuman is a province in northwestern Argentina. Due to the large quantity of false Potosi cobs circulating in the province, Governor Bernabe Araoz established a mint in 1823 to make cobs that would be distinctive to the area. Their circulation was brief due to the introduction of Confederation coins.

PROVINCE

COB COINAGE

KM# 1 2 REALES
Silver **Note:** Struck between 1820 and 1824. Similar in appearance to Potosi cob 2 Reales.

Date	Mintage	Good	VG	F	VF	XF
752TN	—	35.00	75.00	120	200	—

The Commonwealth of Australia, the smallest continent and largest island in the world, is located south of Indonesia between the Indian and Pacific oceans. It has an area of 2,967,893 sq. mi. (7,686,850 sq. km.). Capital: Canberra. Due to its early and sustained isolation, Australia is the habitat of such curious and unique fauna as the kangaroo, koala, platypus, wombat, echidna and frilled-necked lizard. The continent possesses extensive mineral deposits, the most important of which are iron ore, coal, gold, silver, nickel, uranium, lead and zinc. Livestock raising, mining and manufacturing are the principal industries. Chief exports are wool, meat, wheat, iron ore, coal and nonferrous metals.

The first caucasians to see Australia probably were Portuguese and Spanish navigators of the late 16th century. In 1770, Captain James Cook explored the east coast and annexed it for Great Britain. Following the loss of British North America, New South Wales was established as a penal colony by Capt. Arthur Phillip on January 26, 1788, a date now celebrated as Australia Day. Dates of creation of the six colonies that now comprise the states of the Australian Commonwealth are: New South Wales, 1823; Tasmania, 1825; Western Australia, 1838; South Australia, 1842; Victoria, 1851; Queensland, 1859. A constitution providing for federation of the colonies was approved by the British Parliament in 1900.

RULERS

British

MINT MARKS

M - Melbourne
P - Perth
S - Sydney
(sy) - Sydney

MONETARY SYSTEM

(Until 1966)

12 Pence = 1 Shilling
20 Shillings = 1 Pound

BRITISH COLONY

TRADE COINAGE

KM# 1 1/2 SOVEREIGN

3.9940 g., 0.9170 Gold .1177 oz. **Obv:** Fillet head

Date	Mintage	F	VF	XF	Unc	BU
1855(sy)	21,000	7,500	15,000	40,000	90,000	—
1856(sy)	478,000	400	1,350	3,750	10,000	—

KM# 3 1/2 SOVEREIGN

3.9940 g., 0.9170 Gold .1177 oz. **Obv:** Hair tied with banksia wreath

Date	Mintage	F	VF	XF	Unc	BU
1857(sy)	537,000	175	325	1,500	4,750	—
1857(sy) Proof	—	Value: 40,000				
1858(sy)	483,000	175	325	1,750	7,000	—
1858(sy) (Error)	—	—	—	—	—	—
1859(sy)	341,000	175	325	2,000	9,000	—
1860(sy)	156,000	350	1,500	5,000	14,250	—
1861(sy)	186,000	175	335	1,750	6,000	—
1862(sy)	210,000	165	335	2,000	7,000	—
1863(sy)	348,000	150	325	2,000	7,000	—
1864(sy)	141,000	175	600	2,200	9,200	—
1865(sy)	62,000	250	550	2,000	9,000	—
1866(sy)	154,000	200	550	2,000	9,000	—
1866(sy) Proof	—	Value: 30,000				

KM# 5 1/2 SOVEREIGN

3.9940 g., 0.9170 Gold .1177 oz. **Obv:** Young head, date below **Rev:** Mint mark below shield

Date	Mintage	F	VF	XF	Unc	BU
1871S	180,000	80.00	160	750	2,250	—
1871S Proof	—	Value: 13,500				
1872S	356,000	80.00	160	750	2,250	—
1873M	165,000	80.00	160	850	2,500	—
1875S	252,000	80.00	160	750	2,250	—
1877M	140,000	100	175	850	2,500	—
1879S	220,000	80.00	160	600	1,850	—
1880S	80,000	80.00	185	1,000	2,750	—
1880S Proof	—	Value: 12,000				
1881S	62,000	80.00	185	1,100	3,000	—
1881M	42,000	90.00	225	1,250	3,500	—
1881 Proof	—	Value: 12,000				
1882S	52,000	125	250	1,750	6,000	—
1882M	106,000	80.00	175	800	2,250	—
1883S	220,000	75.00	150	500	1,500	—
1883S Proof	—	Value: 12,000				
1884M	48,000	90.00	225	1,500	4,500	—
1884M Proof	—	Value: 12,000				
1885M	11,000	250	550	2,500	8,000	—
1886S	82,000	80.00	160	800	2,500	—
1886M	38,000	80.00	175	1,000	2,750	—
1886 Proof	—	Value: 12,000				
1887S	134,000	80.00	160	700	2,250	—
1887S Proof	—	Value: 12,000				
1887M	64,000	125	250	1,750	6,000	—

KM# 9 1/2 SOVEREIGN

3.9940 g., 0.9170 Gold .1177 oz. **Obv:** Jubilee head **Rev:** Date and mint mark below shield

Date	Mintage	F	VF	XF	Unc	BU
1887S	Inc. above	70.00	110	250	750	—
1887S Proof	—	Value: 10,000				
1887M	Inc. above	80.00	120	300	850	—
1887M Proof	—	Value: 10,000				
1888M Proof	—	Value: 11,500				
1889S	64,000	80.00	120	450	1,350	—
1889M Proof	—	Value: 11,500				
1890M Proof	—	Value: 11,500				
1891S With J.E.B.	154,000	90.00	150	650	2,000	—
1891S Without J.E.B.	Inc. above	80.00	120	450	1,350	—
1891M Proof	—	Value: 11,500				
1892S Proof	—	Value: 11,500				
1892M Proof	—	Value: 11,500				
1893S Proof	—	Value: 11,500				
1893M	110,000	70.00	110	400	1,250	—
1893M Proof	—	Value: 5,500				

KM# 12 1/2 SOVEREIGN

3.9940 g., 0.9170 Gold .1177 oz. **Obv:** Older veiled head of Queen Victoria left **Rev:** Mint mark above date

Date	Mintage	F	VF	XF	Unc	BU
1893S	250,000	65.00	90.00	250	1,250	—
1893S Proof	—	Value: 10,000				
1893M	—	1,000	—	—	—	—
1893M Proof	—	Value: 11,500				
1894M Proof	—	Value: 11,500				
1895M Proof	—	Value: 11,500				
1896M	218,000	70.00	120	300	1,500	—
1896M Proof	—	Value: 10,000				
1897S	230,000	65.00	90.00	250	1,350	—
1897M Proof	—	Value: 11,500				
1898M Proof	—	Value: 11,500				
1899M	90,000	70.00	120	400	1,500	—
1899M Proof	—	Value: 10,000				
1899P Proof	—	—	—	—	—	—
1900S	260,000	65.00	90.00	250	1,350	—
1900M	113,000	70.00	120	400	1,500	—
1900M Proof	—	Value: 10,000				
1900P	119,000	70.00	120	400	1,500	—
1901M Proof	—	Value: 11,500				
1901P Proof	—	Value: 20,000				

KM# 2 SOVEREIGN

7.9881 g., 0.9170 Gold .2354 oz. **Obv:** Filet head

Date	Mintage	F	VF	XF	Unc	BU
1855(sy)	502,000	1,000	3,000	7,500	25,000	—
1856(sy)	981,000	1,000	3,000	7,500	25,000	—

KM# 4 SOVEREIGN

7.9881 g., 0.9170 Gold .2354 oz. **Obv:** Hair tied with banksia wreath **Note:** 51,202,600 pieces reported in 1869 are dated 1868.

Date	Mintage	F	VF	XF	Unc	BU
1857(sy)	499,000	225	475	1,500	4,500	—
1857(sy) Plain or milled edge; Proof	—	Value: 60,000				
1858(sy)	1,101,000	265	600	1,750	7,000	—
1859(sy)	1,050,000	235	550	1,650	4,500	—
1860(sy)	1,573,000	325	750	2,250	7,500	—
1861(sy)	1,626,000	175	350	1,000	2,800	—
1862(sy)	2,477,000	225	475	1,650	4,500	—
1863(sy)	1,255,000	175	400	1,250	3,650	—
1864(sy)	2,698,000	125	250	650	2,250	—
1865(sy)	2,130,000	135	300	1,000	3,250	—
1866(sy)	2,911,000	125	250	550	1,750	—
1866(sy) Proof	—	Value: 55,000				
1867/6(sy)	Inc. above	—	—	—	—	—
1867(sy)	2,370,000	125	250	550	1,750	—
1868(sy)	3,522,000	125	250	550	1,750	—
1870(sy)	1,220,000	125	225	450	1,250	—
1870(sy) Proof	—	Value: 70,000				

KM# 6 SOVEREIGN

7.9881 g., 0.9170 Gold .2354 oz. **Obv:** Young head, date below **Rev:** Mint mark below shield **Note:** Mintage figures include St. George and shield types. No separate mintage figures are known. Mint mark placement varies.

Date	Mintage	F	VF	XF	Unc	BU
1871S Incuse ww	2,814,000	BV	100	200	650	—
1871S Raised ww	Inc. above	BV	100	200	650	—
1871S Proof	—	Value: 13,500				
1872S	1,815,000	BV	100	200	700	—
1872/1M	748,000	225	400	650	2,000	—
1872M	Inc. above	BV	100	200	625	—
1873S	1,478,000	BV	100	200	625	—
1874M	1,373,000	BV	100	200	700	—
1875S	2,122,000	BV	90.00	185	575	—
1875S Proof	—	Value: 13,000				
1877S	1,590,000	BV	90.00	185	575	—
1878S	1,259,000	BV	90.00	185	575	—
1879S	1,366,000	BV	90.00	185	575	—
1880S	1,459,000	BV	90.00	185	575	—
1880S Proof	—	Value: 13,000				
1880M	3,053,000	450	950	2,250	7,000	—
1880M Proof	—	Value: 12,500				
1881S	1,360,000	BV	90.00	170	425	—
1881M	2,324,000	BV	125	300	1,200	—
1882S	1,298,000	BV	90.00	170	425	—
1882M	2,466,000	BV	90.00	170	425	—
1883S	1,108,000	BV	90.00	170	425	—
1883S Proof	—	Value: 12,500				
1883M	2,049,999	125	300	875	2,250	—
1883M Proof	—	Value: 12,500				
1884S	1,595,000	BV	90.00	170	400	—
1884M	2,942,000	BV	90.00	170	400	—
1884M Proof	—	Value: 12,500				
1885S	1,486,000	BV	90.00	170	400	—
1885M	2,957,000	BV	90.00	170	400	—
1885M Proof	—	Value: 12,500				

Date	Mintage	F	VF	XF	Unc	BU
1886S	1,677,000	BV	90.00	170	425	—
1886S Proof	—	Value: 12,500				
1886M	2,902,000	1,400	2,800	5,750	9,000	—
1886M Proof	—	Value: 14,000				
1887S	1,000,000	BV	100	275	600	—
1887S Proof	—	Value: 12,500				
1887M	1,915,000	600	1,200	2,800	5,500	—
1887M Proof	—	Value: 12,500				

KM# 7 SOVEREIGN

7.9881 g., 0.9170 Gold .2354 oz. **Obv:** Young head, mint mark below **Rev:** St. George slaying dragon, date below **Note:** Mintage figures include St. George and shield types. No separate mintage figures are known.

Date	Mintage	F	VF	XF	Unc	BU
1871S	2,814,000	—	BV	350	1,000	—
1871S Proof	—	Value: 13,500				
1872S	1,815,000	—	BV	275	900	—
1872M	748,000	—	225	650	1,850	—
1873S	1,478,000	—	BV	250	850	—
1873M	752,000	—	BV	225	650	—
1873M Proof	—	Value: 12,000				
1874S	1,899,000	—	BV	225	750	—
1874M	1,373,000	—	BV	200	600	—
1874M Proof	—	Value: 12,000				
1875S	2,122,000	—	BV	175	600	—
1875M	1,888,000	—	BV	175	600	—
1875M Proof	—	Value: 12,000				
1876S	1,613,000	—	BV	125	475	—
1876M	2,124,000	—	BV	125	475	—
1877S Rare	2	—	—	—	—	—
1877M	1,487,000	—	BV	125	475	—
1878M	2,171,000	—	BV	125	450	—
1879S	1,366,000	—	BV	350	1,650	—
1879M	2,740,000	—	BV	125	425	—
1880S	1,459,000	—	BV	175	575	—
1880S Proof	—	Value: 12,000				
1880M	3,053,000	—	BV	125	400	—
1881S	1,360,000	—	BV	175	575	—
1881M	2,324,000	—	BV	125	450	—
1881M Proof	—	Value: 12,000				
1882S	1,298,000	—	BV	125	400	—
1882M	2,466,000	—	BV	125	450	—
1883S	1,108,000	—	BV	125	450	—
1883M	2,050,000	—	BV	125	450	—
1883M Proof	—	Value: 12,000				
1884S	1,595,000	—	BV	125	400	—
1884M	2,942,000	—	BV	125	400	—
1884M Proof	—	Value: 12,000				
1885S	1,486,000	—	BV	125	400	—
1885M	2,957,000	—	BV	125	400	—
1885M Proof	—	Value: 12,000				
1886S	1,677,000	—	BV	125	400	—
1886M	2,902,000	—	BV	125	400	—
1886M Proof	—	Value: 12,000				
1887S	1,000,000	—	BV	175	575	—
1887M	1,915,000	—	BV	175	575	—
1887M Proof	—	Value: 12,000				

KM# 10 SOVEREIGN

7.9881 g., 0.9170 Gold .2354 oz. **Obv:** Jubilee head **Rev:** Mint mark above date **Note:** Designers initials on reverse omitted on some pieces 1880S-1882S and 1881M-1882M. Mint mark placement varies.

Date	Mintage	F	VF	XF	Unc	BU
1887S	1,002,000	BV	185	400	950	—
1887S Proof	—	Value: 11,000				
1887M	940,000	—	BV	125	275	—
1887M Proof	—	Value: 10,000				
1888S	2,187,000	—	BV	100	200	—
1888M	2,830,000	—	BV	100	200	—
1888M Proof	—	Value: 10,000				
1889S	3,262,000	—	BV	100	200	—
1889M	2,732,000	—	BV	100	200	—
1889M Proof	—	Value: 10,000				
1890S	2,808,000	—	BV	100	200	—
1890M	2,473,000	—	BV	100	200	—
1890M Proof	—	Value: 10,000				
1891S	2,596,000	—	BV	100	200	—
1891M	2,749,000	—	BV	100	200	—
1892S	2,837,000	—	BV	100	200	—
1892M	3,488,000	—	BV	100	200	—
1893S	1,498,000	—	BV	100	200	—
1893S Proof	—	Value: 10,000				
1893M	1,649,000	—	BV	100	200	—
1893M Proof	—	Value: 10,000				

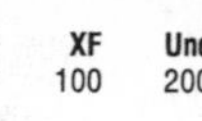
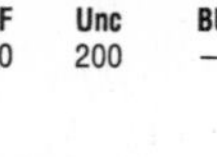
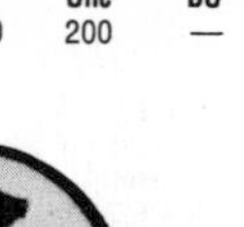
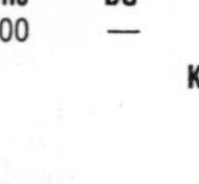

KM# 13 SOVEREIGN

7.9881 g., 0.9170 Gold .2354 oz. **Obv:** Older veiled head **Rev:** Similar to KM#12

Date	Mintage	F	VF	XF	Unc	BU
1893S	1,346,000	—	BV	85.00	175	—
1893S Proof	—	Value: 10,000				
1893M	1,914,000	—	BV	85.00	175	—
1893M Proof	—	Value: 10,000				
1894S	3,067,000	—	BV	85.00	155	—
1894S Proof	—	Value: 10,000				
1894M	4,166,000	—	BV	85.00	155	—
1894M Proof	—	Value: 10,000				
1895S	2,758,000	—	BV	85.00	165	—
1895M	4,165,000	—	BV	85.00	155	—
1895M Proof	—	Value: 10,000				
1896S	2,544,000	—	BV	85.00	165	—
1896M	4,456,000	—	BV	85.00	165	—
1896M Proof	—	Value: 10,000				
1897S	2,532,000	—	BV	85.00	180	—
1897M	5,130,000	—	BV	85.00	165	—
1897M Proof	—	Value: 10,000				
1898S	2,548,000	—	BV	85.00	180	—
1898M	5,509,000	—	BV	85.00	165	—
1898M Proof	—	Value: 10,000				
1899S	3,259,000	—	BV	85.00	130	—
1899M	5,579,000	—	BV	85.00	130	—
1899M Proof	—	Value: 10,000				
1899P	690,000	BV	135	350	750	—
1899P Proof	—	Value: 12,500				
1900S	3,586,000	—	BV	85.00	130	—
1900M	4,305,000	—	BV	85.00	130	—
1900M Proof	—	Value: 10,000				
1900P	1,886,000	—	BV	85.00	160	—

KM# 8 2 POUNDS

15.9761 g., 0.9170 Gold .4707 oz. **Subject:** 50th Anniversary of Reign

Date	Mintage	F	VF	XF	Unc	BU
1887S Proof	Est. 11	Value: 45,000				

Note: Spink Australia Sale #30 11-89 nearly FDC realized $16,940

KM# 11 5 POUNDS

39.9403 g., 0.9170 Gold 1.1771 oz. **Subject:** 50th Anniversary of Reign

Date	Mintage	F	VF	XF	Unc	BU
1887 Proof; Rare	Est. 3	—	—	—	—	—

Note: Spink AUstralia Sale #30 11-89 nearly FDC realized $62,370. David Akers Numismatics Pittman sale 8-99 Choice Proof realized $103,500

PATTERNS

Including off metal strikes

KM#	Date	Mintage	Identification	Mkt Val
Pn1	1853	—	1/2 Sovereign. Gold. T. 1.	60,000
Pn2	1853	—	Sovereign. Gold. T. 1.	75,000
Pn3	1855	—	1/2 Sovereign. Gold. Milled edge. T. 2.	49,500
Pn4	1855	—	Sovereign. Gold. Milled edge. T. 2.	55,000
Pn5	1856	—	1/2 Sovereign. Gold. Plain edge. T. 2.	25,000
Pn6	1856	—	Sovereign. Gold. Plain edge. T. 2.	55,000

PRIVATE TOKEN ISSUES

The first copper token of penny value was issued in Melbourne in 1849. With the increase in population following the discovery of gold in the early 1850s a large number of traders tokens were used in the colonies. Most of these were of copper and were valued as pennies or halfpennies. A few were of silver and valued at a higher rate. The greatest number appeared between 1857 and 1863. The total number exceeded 530 and they were issued by some 126 firms. About 1860 British bronze coins began to arrive in the colonies in quantity and with their use the tokens became unpopular. Victoria declared tokens illegal in 1863 and the other colonies took similar action in the following years, the last being West Australia in 1878. These are listed in The Coins and Tokens of British Oceania by Robert L. Clarke.

Other references are Dr. Andrews Australasian Coins and Tokens and Unofficial Coins of Colonial Australia and New Zealand by G. C. Heyde.

NOTE: An F designation indicates a fabrication. Most of these pieces show major die deterioration such as cracks and flaws, unlike restrikes which show only minor die deterioration from surface rust. Restrikes were made using original die combinations. Fabrications were made using die combinations that are not known on original pieces.

Lewis Abrahams
Hobart, Tasmania

KM# Tn6 1/2 PENNY
Copper, 27.5 mm. **Obv. Legend:** LEWIS ABRAHAMS... **Rev:** Legend above emu and kangaroo **Rev. Legend:** TASMANIA

Date	Mintage	VG	F	VF	XF	Unc
1855	—	20.00	40.00	75.00	140	245

KM# Tn7 PENNY
Copper, 34 mm. **Obv:** Similar to KM#Tn6 **Rev:** Similar to KM#Tn6

Date	Mintage	VG	F	VF	XF	Unc
1855	—	30.00	60.00	125	225	325

Adamson, Watts, McKechnie & Co.
Melbourne, Victoria

KM# Tn8.1 1/2 PENNY
Copper, 28 mm.

Date	Mintage	VG	F	VF	XF	Unc
1855	—	80.00	170	325	500	—

KM# Tn8.2 1/2 PENNY
Copper **Note:** Thick flan.

Date	Mintage	VG	F	VF	XF	Unc
1855 Restrike	—	—	—	—	600	—

John Allen
Kaima, New South Wales

KM# Tn9 PENNY
Copper, 34 mm.

Date	Mintage	Good	VG	F	VF	XF
1855 5 known	—	3,000	5,000	7,500	10,000	—

William Allen
Jamberoo, New South Wales

KM# Tn10 PENNY
Copper, 34 mm.

Date	Mintage	VG	F	VF	XF	Unc
1855 est. 25 known	—	750	2,000	3,500	5,000	—

John Andrew & Co.
Melbourne, Victoria

KM# TnA11 1/2 PENNY
Copper, 27.5 mm. **Obv:** Legend around crowned lion **Obv. Legend:** JOHN ANDREW & CO... **Rev:** Legend above seated justice **Rev. Legend:** MELBOURNE VICTORIA

Date	Mintage	VG	F	VF	XF	Unc
1860	—	50.00	100	180	375	600

KM# Tn11 PENNY
Copper, 34 mm. **Rev:** Seated figure

Date	Mintage	VG	F	VF	XF	Unc
1860	—	35.00	75.00	145	285	500

Jno Andrew & Co.
Melbourne, Victoria

KM# Tn12 1/2 PENNY
Copper, 27.5 mm. **Rev:** Seated figure

Date	Mintage	VG	F	VF	XF	Unc
1860	—	2,000	4,000	6,000	—	—

KM# Tn13 1/2 PENNY
Copper, 27.5 mm. **Rev:** Emu and kangaroo

Date	Mintage	VG	F	VF	XF	Unc
1862	—	35.00	75.00	145	285	500

KM# Tn14 PENNY
Copper, 34 mm. **Rev:** Seated figure

Date	Mintage	VG	F	VF	XF	Unc
1860	—	1,300	2,000	3,500	5,000	—

KM# Tn15 PENNY
Copper, 34 mm. **Rev:** Emu and kangaroo

Date	Mintage	VG	F	VF	XF	Unc
1862	—	35.00	75.00	145	285	500

Annand, Smith & Co.
Melbourne, Victoria

KM# Tn16.1 PENNY
Copper, 34 mm. **Rev:** Eleven leaves to branch, H&S on rock

Date	Mintage	VG	F	VF	XF	Unc
ND(1849)	45,000	50.00	100	180	325	600

KM# Tn16.2 PENNY
Copper, 34 mm. **Rev:** Fourteen leaves to branch, no H&S on rock

Date	Mintage	VG	F	VF	XF	Unc
ND(1849)	45,000	50.00	100	180	325	600

Barraclough
Richmond, Victoria

KM# Tn19.1 PENNY
Copper, 35 mm. **Rev:** Vertical leaf point between E and S in STOKES

Date	Mintage	VG	F	VF	XF	Unc
1862	—	50.00	170	325	500	—

KM# Tn19.2 PENNY
Copper, 35 mm. **Rev:** Vertical leaf point above last S in STOKES

Date	Mintage	VG	F	VF	XF	Unc
1862	—	150	300	600	1,000	—

William Bateman Junr. & Co.
Warnambool, Victoria

KM# Tn20 PENNY
Copper

Date	Mintage	VG	F	VF	XF	Unc
1855	—	50.00	100	180	325	600

Battle & Weight

Sydney, New South Wales

KM# Tn21 PENNY
Copper, 34 mm.

Date	Mintage	VG	F	VF	XF	Unc
ND	—	35.00	75.00	145	285	500

Bell & Gardner

Rockhampton, Queensland

KM# Tn22 PENNY
Copper, 34 mm.

Date	Mintage	VG	F	VF	XF	Unc
ND	—	750	1,500	2,000	3,000	—

I. Booth

Melbourne, Victoria

KM# Tn23 PENNY
Copper, 34 mm. **Obv. Legend:** I. BOOTH... **Rev:** Legend avove seated Britannia **Rev. Legend:** BRITANNIA

Date	Mintage	VG	F	VF	XF	Unc
ND	—	35.00	75.00	145	285	500

Joseph Brickhill

Campbelltown, Tasmania

KM# Tn24 PENNY
Copper, 34 mm. **Obv. Legend:** JOSEPH BRICKHILL... **Rev. Legend:** ONE PENNY TOKEN...

Date	Mintage	VG	F	VF	XF	Unc
1856	—	30.00	60.00	125	225	325

Brookes

Brisbane, Queensland

KM# Tn25.1 PENNY
Copper, 34 mm. **Obv:** Legend in fancy lettering **Obv. Legend:** IRONMONGERS BROOKES BRISBANE **Rev:** Legend in fancy lettering **Rev. Legend:** IRONMONGERS BROOKES BRISBANE

Date	Mintage	VG	F	VF	XF	Unc
ND	—	50.00	100	180	325	600

KM# Tn25.2 PENNY
Copper, 34 mm. **Obv:** Similar to KM#Tn25.1 but plain lettering **Rev:** Similar to KM#Tn25.1 but plain lettering **Note:** Two varieties exist.

Date	Mintage	VG	F	VF	XF	Unc
ND	—	50.00	100	180	325	600

W & B Brookes

Brisbane, Queensland

KM# Tn26 PENNY
Copper, 34 mm. **Obv. Legend:** W & B BROOKES... **Rev:** Legend above Australian arms **Rev. Legend:** QUEENSLAND

Date	Mintage	VG	F	VF	XF	Unc
1863	—	35.00	75.00	145	285	500

T. Butterworth & Co.

Castlemaine, Victoria

KM# Tn28 PENNY
Copper, 34 mm. **Obv. Legend:** T. BUTTERWORTH & CO... **Rev. Legend:** WHOLESALE & RETAIL... **Note:** Three varieties exist.

Date	Mintage	VG	F	VF	XF	Unc
ND	—	50.00	100	180	325	600

KM# Tn29 PENNY
Copper, 34 mm. **Obv. Legend:** T. BUTTERWORTH & CO... **Rev:** Seated justice

Date	Mintage	VG	F	VF	XF	Unc
1859	—	35.00	75.00	145	285	500

J. W. Buxton

Brisbane, Queensland

KM# Tn30 PENNY
Copper, 34 mm.

Date	Mintage	VG	F	VF	XF	Unc
ND	—	120	245	500	750	—

R. Calder

Castlemaine, Victoria

KM# Tn31 PENNY
Copper, 34 mm. **Rev:** M in MAKER in legend above T in EAST

Date	Mintage	VG	F	VF	XF	Unc
1862	—	120	245	500	750	—

KM# TnF31 PENNY
Copper, 34 mm. **Rev:** M in MAKER in legend above AS in EAST **Note:** Fabrication.

Date	Mintage	VG	F	VF	XF	Unc
ND As struck	—	—	—	—	450	—

James Campbell

Morpeth, New South Wales

KM# Tn32 1/2 PENNY
Copper, 27 mm. **Obv. Legend:** JAMES CAMPBELL... **Rev:** Legend above standing justice **Rev. Legend:** TASMANIA

Date	Mintage	VG	F	VF	XF	Unc
ND	—	35.00	75.00	145	285	500

KM# Tn33 PENNY
Copper, 34 mm. **Obv:** Similar to KM#Tn32 **Rev:** Similar to KM#Tn32 **Note:** Two varieties exist, but replicas in copper are 31mm.

Date	Mintage	VG	F	VF	XF	Unc
ND	—	35.00	75.00	145	285	500

KM# Tn34 THREEPENCE
Silver **Rev:** Denomination below rising sun **Note:** Estimated 12 examples known.

Date	Mintage	VG	F	VF	XF	Unc
ND	400	1,000	1,500	2,750	4,000	—

Collins & Co.
Bathurst, New South Wales

KM# Tn35 PENNY
Copper

Date	Mintage	VG	F	VF	XF	Unc
1864	—	120	245	500	750	—

W. C. Cook
Sandridge, Melbourne, Victoria

KM# Tn36 PENNY
Copper, 34 mm.

Date	Mintage	VG	F	VF	XF	Unc
1862	—	50.00	170	325	500	—

KM# Tn37 PENNY
Copper, 34 mm. **Obv. Legend:** SUGAR WORKS BY W. COOK... **Rev. Legend:** SUGAR WORKS BY W. COOK... **Note:** Legends counterstamped on Great Britain penny.

Date	Mintage	VG	F	VF	XF	Unc
ND	—	150	200	300	—	—

Thomas H. Cope
South Yarra, Victoria

KM# Tn38.1 PENNY
Copper, 34 mm. **Rev. Legend:** R in MAKER in legend above E in MELBOURNE

Date	Mintage	VG	F	VF	XF	Unc
1862	—	50.00	100	150	360	750

KM# Tn38.2 PENNY
Copper, 34 mm. **Rev:** R in MAKER in legend above L in MELBOURNE

Date	Mintage	VG	F	VF	XF	Unc
1862	—	50.00	100	150	360	750

Crocker & Hamilton
Adelaide, South Australia

KM# Tn39 1/2 PENNY
Copper, 28 mm.

Date	Mintage	VG	F	VF	XF	Unc
1857	—	35.00	75.00	145	285	500

KM# Tn40 PENNY
Copper, 34 mm. **Obv. Legend:** CROCKER & HAMILTON... **Rev. Legend:** DRAPERS...

Date	Mintage	VG	F	VF	XF	Unc
ND	—	50.00	100	180	325	600

Crombie, Clapperton & Findlay
Melbourne, Victoria

KM# Tn41 1/2 PENNY
Copper, 28 mm. **Obv. Legend:** CROMBIE, CLAPPERTON & FINDLAY... **Rev:** Legend above kangaroo **Rev. Legend:** MELBOURNE **Note:** Two varieties exist.

Date	Mintage	VG	F	VF	XF	Unc
ND	—	50.00	100	150	300	550

Crothers & Co.
Stawell, Victoria

KM# Tn42 1/2 PENNY
Copper, 24 mm. **Obv:** Similar to KM#Tn43 **Rev:** Similar to KM#Tn43

Date	Mintage	VG	F	VF	XF	Unc
ND	—	80.00	170	325	500	—

KM# Tn43 PENNY
Copper, 31 mm. **Note:** Two varieties exist.

Date	Mintage	VG	F	VF	XF	Unc
ND	—	80.00	170	325	500	—

Note: KM#Tn42 and Tn43 are known also in brass

Jas. Davey & Co.
Sale, Victoria

KM# Tn44 PENNY
Copper, 34 mm.

Date	Mintage	VG	F	VF	XF	Unc
1862	—	150	300	600	1,000	—

A. Davidson
Melbourne, Victoria

KM# Tn45.1 PENNY
Copper, 34 mm. **Rev:** Lower right leaf touches R in MAKER

Date	Mintage	VG	F	VF	XF	Unc
1862	—	80.00	170	325	500	—

KM# Tn45.2 PENNY
Copper, 34 mm. **Rev:** Lower right leaf doesn't touch R in MAKER

Date	Mintage	VG	F	VF	XF	Unc
1862	—	150	300	600	1,000	—

KM# TnF46 PENNY
Copper, 34 mm. **Obv:** Similar to KM#Tn45 **Rev:** VICTORIA 1862 above Australian arms

Date	Mintage	F	VF	XF	Unc	BU
1862 Fabrication; as struck	—	—	—	—	450	—

Alfred Davies
Fremantle, Western Australia

KM# Tn47 PENNY
Copper, 31 mm.

Date	Mintage	VG	F	VF	XF	Unc
1865	—	35.00	75.00	145	285	500

Davies, Alexander & Co.

Goulbourn, New South Wales

KM# Tn48 PENNY
Copper, 34 mm. **Obv:** Legend above Golden Fleece **Obv. Legend:** DAVIES, ALEXANDER & CO... **Rev:** Legend above arm **Rev. Legend:** AUSTRALIAN STORES... **Note:** Three varieties exist.

Date	Mintage	VG	F	VF	XF	Unc
ND	—	30.00	60.00	125	225	325

E. F. Dease

Launceston, Tasmania

KM# Tn50 1/2 PENNY
Copper, 28 mm. **Note:** Similar to 1 Penny, KM#Tn25.

Date	Mintage	VG	F	VF	XF	Unc
ND	—	50.00	100	180	325	600

KM# Tn51 1/2 PENNY
Copper, 28 mm. **Obv:** Tn#50 **Rev:** New Zealand H. J. Hall 1/2 Penny, KM#Tn25 **Note:** Mule. Specimen striking, made for collectors.

Date	Mintage	F	VF	XF	Unc	BU
ND	—	—	—	1,200	1,800	—

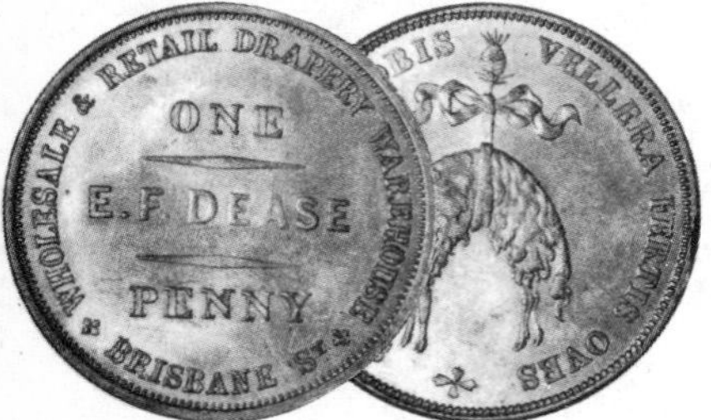

KM# Tn52.1 PENNY
Copper, 36 mm. **Rev:** Six spikes on pineapple

Date	Mintage	VG	F	VF	XF	Unc
ND	—	35.00	75.00	145	285	500

KM# Tn52.2 PENNY
Copper, 36 mm. **Rev:** Seven spikes on pineapple

Date	Mintage	VG	F	VF	XF	Unc
ND 2 known	—	—	1,500	2,000	3,000	—

Edwd. De Carle & Co.

Melbourne, Victoria

KM# Tn53 PENNY
Copper **Obv. Legend:** EDWD. DE'CARLE & CO... **Rev:** Legend above seated Justice **Rev. Legend:** TASMANIA

Date	Mintage	VG	F	VF	XF	Unc
1855	—	35.00	75.00	145	285	500

KM# Tn54 PENNY
Copper, 34 mm. **Obv. Legend:** E. DE CARLE & CO... **Rev:** Legend above seated Britannia **Rev. Legend:** BRITANNIA

Date	Mintage	VG	F	VF	XF	Unc
ND	—	35.00	75.00	145	285	500

KM# Tn55 PENNY
Copper, 34 mm. **Obv:** Lion **Rev:** Seated justice **Rev. Legend:** MELBOURNE VICTORIA

Date	Mintage	VG	F	VF	XF	Unc
1855	—	30.00	60.00	125	225	325

KM# Tn56 PENNY
Copper, 33 mm. **Obv:** Head of Lord Raglan left **Rev:** Similar to KM#Tn53 **Note:** Believed to be a pattern.

Date	Mintage	VG	F	VF	XF	Unc
1855 2 known	—	—	—	30,000	—	—

S. Deeble

Melbourne, Victoria

KM# Tn57.1 PENNY
Copper, 34 mm. **Rev:** M in MARKER above S in EAST

Date	Mintage	VG	F	VF	XF	Unc
1862	—	80.00	170	325	500	—

KM# Tn57.2 PENNY
Copper, 34 mm. **Rev:** M in MARKER above AS in EAST

Date	Mintage	VG	F	VF	XF	Unc
1862	—	80.00	170	325	500	750

KM# Tn58 PENNY
Copper, 34 mm. **Obv:** Similar to KM#Tn57 **Rev:** Legend above wheat sheaf **Rev. Legend:** ADVANCE AUSTRALIA

Date	Mintage	VG	F	VF	XF	Unc
1862	—	50.00	100	180	325	600

KM# Tn59 PENNY
Copper, 34 mm. **Obv:** Similar to KM#Tn57 **Rev:** Legend above EMU **Rev. Legend:** VICTORIA 1862

Date	Mintage	VG	F	VF	XF	Unc
1862	—	150	300	600	1,000	—

James Dixon

Wangaratta, Victoria

KM# TnF60 PENNY
Copper, 34 mm. **Obv:** Similar to KM#TnF61 **Rev:** M of MAKER above AS in EAST **Rev. Legend:** Large VICTORIA

Date	Mintage	VG	F	VF	XF	Unc
1862 Fabrication, as struck	—	—	—	—	2,000	—

KM# TnF61 PENNY
Copper, 34 mm. **Rev. Legend:** Small VICTORIA

Date	Mintage	VG	F	VF	XF	Unc
1862 Fabrication, as struck	—	—	—	—	1,500	—

KM# TnF62 PENNY
Copper, 34 mm. **Rev:** Legend below vine **Rev. Legend:** T. STOKES MAKER

Date	Mintage	VG	F	VF	XF	Unc
1862 Fabrication, as struck	—	—	—	—	1,500	—

KM# TnF63.1 PENNY
Copper, 34 mm. **Rev:** Stem of vine at right points down

Date	Mintage	VG	F	VF	XF	Unc
1862 Fabrication, as struck	—	—	—	—	1,500	—

KM# TnF63.2 PENNY
Copper, 34 mm. **Rev:** Stem of vine at right points up

Date	Mintage	VG	F	VF	XF	Unc
1862 Fabrication, as struck	—	—	—	—	1,500	—

KM# TnF64 PENNY
Copper, 34 mm. **Rev:** Legend above emu **Rev. Legend:** VICTORIA 1862

Date	Mintage	VG	F	VF	XF	Unc
1862 Fabrication, as struck	—	—	—	—	2,000	—

Evans & Foster

Wangaratta, Victoria

KM# Tn65 PENNY
Copper, 34 mm. **Rev:** Legend with dot, 13 long rays **Rev. Legend:** VICTORIA 1862

Date	Mintage	VG	F	VF	XF	Unc
1862	—	40.00	125	250	500	—

KM# TnF65 PENNY
Copper, 34 mm. **Rev:** Legend without dot, 15 long rays **Rev. Legend:** VICTORIA 1862

Date	Mintage	VG	F	VF	XF	Unc
1862 Fabrication, as struck	—	—	—	—	650	—

Fenwick Brothers
Melbourne, Victoria

KM# Tn66 PENNY
Brass, 34 mm. **Rev:** Head within circle

Date	Mintage	VG	F	VF	XF	Unc
ND	—	120	245	500	750	—

KM# Tn66a PENNY
Brass, 34 mm. **Rev:** Head within circle

Date	Mintage	VG	F	VF	XF	Unc
ND	—	120	245	500	750	—

KM# Tn67 PENNY
Bronze, 34 mm. **Rev:** Head not in circle

Date	Mintage	VG	F	VF	XF	Unc
ND	—	50.00	100	180	325	600

KM# Tn67a PENNY
Brass, 34 mm. **Rev:** Head not in circle

Date	Mintage	VG	F	VF	XF	Unc
ND	—	50.00	100	180	325	600

Fisher
South Yarra, Melbourne, Victoria

KM# Tn68 1/2 PENNY
Copper, 28 mm.

Date	Mintage	VG	F	VF	XF	Unc
1857	—	35.00	75.00	145	285	500

Flavelle Bros. & Co.
Sydney, New South Wales and Brisbane, Queensland

KM# Tn69.1 PENNY
Copper, 33 mm. **Rev:** Thick foilage behind kangaroo's tail

Date	Mintage	VG	F	VF	XF	Unc
ND	—	35.00	75.00	145	285	500

KM# Tn69.2 PENNY
Copper, 33 mm. **Rev:** Tall thin foilage behind kangaroo's tail **Note:** Specimen striking, made for collectors

Date	Mintage	F	VF	XF	Unc	BU
ND	—	—	—	750	1,000	—

KM# Tn70 PENNY
Copper, 33 mm. **Obv:** Legend below "ONE PENNY" **Obv. Legend:** OPTICIANS & JEWELERS **Rev:** Similar to KM#Tn69 **Note:** Varieties exist

Date	Mintage	VG	F	VF	XF	Unc
ND	—	35.00	75.00	145	285	500

J. G. Fleming
Hobart, Tasmania

KM# Tn71.1 PENNY
Copper, 31 mm. **Obv:** Scroll at right points to dot **Obv. Legend:** J. G. FLEMING... **Rev:** Top of leaf points to right of R of SUGAR **Rev. Legend:** SUGAR LOAF...

Date	Mintage	VG	F	VF	XF	Unc
1874	—	20.00	40.00	75.00	140	245

KM# Tn71.2 PENNY
Copper, 31 mm. **Obv:** Scroll at right points to R of DEALER **Rev:** Top of leaf points to R of SUGAR

Date	Mintage	VG	F	VF	XF	Unc
1874	—	50.00	100	180	325	600

I. Friedman
Hobart, Tasmania

KM# Tn72 1/2 PENNY
Copper, 27 mm. **Obv. Legend:** I. FRIEDMAN... **Rev:** Legend above seated Justice **Rev. Legend:** TASMANIA **Note:** Three varieties exist.

Date	Mintage	VG	F	VF	XF	Unc
1857	—	30.00	60.00	125	225	325

KM# Tn73 PENNY
Copper, 34 mm. **Note:** Similar to 1/2 Penny, KM#Tn72. Four varieties exist.

Date	Mintage	VG	F	VF	XF	Unc
1857	—	30.00	60.00	125	225	325

W. Froomes
Castlemaine, Victoria

KM# Tn74 PENNY
Copper, 34 mm.

Date	Mintage	VG	F	VF	XF	Unc
1862	—	50.00	100	180	325	600

Gipps Land Hardware Company
Port Albert & Sale, Victoria

KM# Tn75 PENNY
Copper, 34 mm. **Rev:** Arms

Date	Mintage	VG	F	VF	XF	Unc
1862	—	35.00	75.00	145	285	500

KM# TnF75 PENNY
Copper, 34 mm. **Obv:** "Gippsland" all one word

Date	Mintage	VG	F	VF	XF	Unc
1862 Fabrication, as struck	—	—	—	—	1,000	—

KM# Tn76 PENNY
Copper, 34 mm. **Rev:** Plough

Date	Mintage	VG	F	VF	XF	Unc
ND	—	50.00	100	180	325	600

R. Grieve
Eagle Hawk, Victoria

KM# Tn77 PENNY
Copper, 34 mm. **Rev:** M in MAKER above T of EAST in legend

Date	Mintage	VG	F	VF	XF	Unc
1862	—	50.00	100	180	325	600

KM# TnF77 PENNY
Copper, 34 mm. **Rev:** M in MAKER above AS of EAST in legend

Date	Mintage	VG	F	VF	XF	Unc
1862 Fabrication, as struck	—	—	—	—	300	—

J. R. Grundy
Ballarat, Victoria

KM# Tn78.1 PENNY
Copper, 34 mm. **Rev:** 7mm between I of INDUSTRIA and V of VICTORIA in legend

Date	Mintage	VG	F	VF	XF	Unc
1861	—	35.00	75.00	145	285	500

KM# Tn78.2 PENNY
Copper, 34 mm. **Rev:** 5.5mm between I of INDUSTRIA and V of VICTORIA in legend

Date	Mintage	VG	F	VF	XF	Unc
1861	—	50.00	100	180	325	600

KM# Tn79.1 PENNY
Copper, 34 mm. **Obv:** Top petal to R **Rev:** Raised rim

Date	Mintage	VG	F	VF	XF	Unc
1861	—	50.00	100	180	325	600

KM# Tn79.2 PENNY
Copper, 34 mm. **Obv:** Top petal to C **Rev:** Raised rim

Date	Mintage	VG	F	VF	XF	Unc
1861	—	80.00	170	325	500	—

Hanks and Compy.
Sydney, New South Wales

KM# Tn80 1/2 PENNY
Copper, 28 mm. **Obv. Legend:** AUSTRIALIAN TEA MART... **Rev:** Legend above Australian arms **Rev. Legend:** PEACE & PLENTY

Date	Mintage	VG	F	VF	XF	Unc
1857	—	35.00	75.00	145	285	500

KM# Tn81 PENNY
Copper, 34 mm. **Note:** Similar to 1/2 Penny, KM#Tn80.

Date	Mintage	VG	F	VF	XF	Unc
1857	—	30.00	60.00	125	225	325

Hanks and Lloyd
Sydney, New South Wales

KM# Tn82 1/2 PENNY
Copper, 28 mm. **Obv. Legend:** AUSTRIALIA TEA MART... **Rev. Legend:** TO COMMEMORATE...

Date	Mintage	VG	F	VF	XF	Unc
1855	—	30.00	60.00	125	225	325

KM# Tn83.1 1/2 PENNY
Copper, 28 mm. **Obv. Legend:** ...AND (5.5mm long), ".SYDNEY." **Rev:** Legend above Australian arms **Rev. Legend:** PEACE & PLENTY

Date	Mintage	VG	F	VF	XF	Unc
1857	—	50.00	100	180	325	600

KM# Tn83.2 1/2 PENNY
Copper, 28 mm. **Obv. Legend:** ...AND (7mm long), "SYDNEY"

Date	Mintage	VG	F	VF	XF	Unc
1857	—	35.00	75.00	145	285	500

KM# Tn84 PENNY
Copper, 34 mm. **Note:** Similar to 1/2 Penny, KM#Tn82.

Date	Mintage	VG	F	VF	XF	Unc
1855	—	30.00	60.00	125	225	325

KM# Tn85.1 PENNY
Copper, 34 mm. **Rev:** 1 millimeter between LL of LLOYD; SYDNEY 2.5 millimeters high **Note:** Similar to 1/2 Penny, KM#Tn83.

Date	Mintage	VG	F	VF	XF	Unc
1857	—	35.00	75.00	145	285	500

KM# Tn85.2 PENNY
Copper, 34 mm. **Rev:** .5 millimeters between LL of LLOYD; SYDNEY 3 millimeters high

Date	Mintage	VG	F	VF	XF	Unc
1857	—	35.00	75.00	145	285	500

KM# Tn85.3 PENNY
Copper, 34 mm. **Rev:** 1 millimeter between LL of LLOYD; SYDNEY 3 millimeters high

Date	Mintage	VG	F	VF	XF	Unc
1857	—	50.00	100	180	325	600

Harrold Brothers
Adelaide, South Australia

KM# Tn86 PENNY
Copper, 34 mm.

Date	Mintage	VG	F	VF	XF	Unc
1858	—	80.00	170	325	500	1,000

O. H. Hedberg
Hobart, Tasmania

KM# Tn87 1/2 PENNY
Copper, 28 mm. **Note:** Six varieties exist.

Date	Mintage	VG	F	VF	XF	Unc
ND	—	30.00	60.00	125	225	325

KM# Tn88 1/2 PENNY
Copper, 28 mm. **Obv:** Similar to obverse, KM#Tn87 **Rev:** Similar to obverse, KM#Tn87 **Note:** Mule. Specimen striking, made for collectors.

Date	Mintage	VG	F	VF	XF	Unc
ND	—	—	—	—	1,000	1,250

KM# Tn89 1/2 PENNY
Copper, 28 mm. **Obv:** KM#Tn87 **Rev:** New Zealand Lipman Levy 1/2 Penny, KM#Tn38 **Note:** Mule. Specimen striking, made for collectors.

Date	Mintage	F	VF	XF	Unc	BU
ND	—	—	—	750	1,000	—

KM# Tn90 1/2 PENNY
Copper, 28 mm. **Obv:** Similar to reverse 1/2 Penny, KM#Tn87 **Rev:** Golden fleece, E.F. Dease, KM#Tn50 **Note:** Specimen striking, made for collectors.

Date	Mintage	F	VF	XF	Unc	BU
ND	—	—	—	1,000	1,250	—

KM# Tn91 PENNY
Copper, 34 mm. **Rev:** One Penny **Note:** Four varieties exist.

Date	Mintage	VG	F	VF	XF	Unc
ND	—	30.00	60.00	125	225	325

KM# Tn93 PENNY
Copper, 34 mm. **Rev:** Seated Britannia, heavy rim **Note:** Specimen striking, made for collectors.

Date	Mintage	F	VF	XF	Unc	BU
ND	—	—	—	1,200	1,800	—

KM# Tn94 PENNY
Copper, 34 mm. **Rev:** Seated Britannia, date in exergue **Note:** Specimen striking, made for collectors.

Date	Mintage	F	VF	XF	Unc	BU
1860	—	—	—	600	1,000	—

KM# Tn96.1 PENNY
Copper, 34 mm. **Rev:** Britannia's staff points to I **Note:** Three varieties exist. Specimen striking, made for collectors.

Date	Mintage	F	VF	XF	Unc	BU
ND	—	—	—	750	1,200	—

KM# Tn96.2 PENNY
Copper, 34 mm. **Rev:** Britannia's staff points to right of I, waves across baseline **Note:** Specimen striking, made for collectors.

Date	Mintage	F	VF	XF	Unc	BU
ND	—	—	2,000	2,500	3,000	—

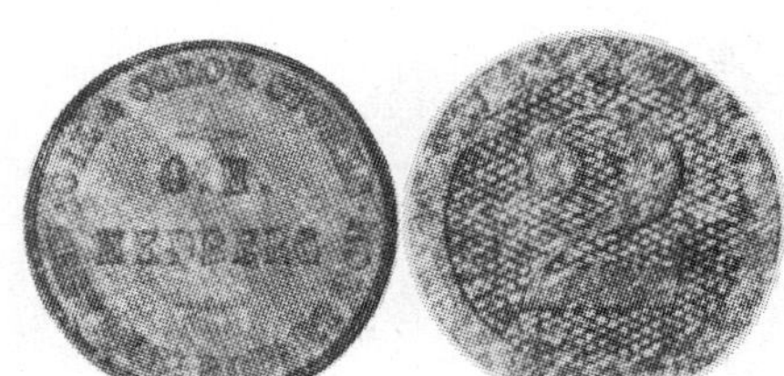

KM# Tn97 2 PENCE
White Metal, 34 mm. **Note:** Specimen striking, made for collectors.

Date	Mintage	F	VF	XF	Unc	BU
ND 2 known	—	—	—	5,000	—	—

KM# Tn98 4 PENCE
White Metal, 34 mm. **Obv:** Similar to Penny, KM#Tn93 **Rev:** FOUR PENCE on raised rim above large 4 in legend **Note:** Mule. Specimen striking, made for collectors.

Date	Mintage	F	VF	XF	Unc	BU
ND 2 known	—	—	—	5,000	—	—

John Henderson

Fremantle, Western Australia

KM# Tn99.1 PENNY
Copper, 34 mm. **Rev:** N of TOKEN on roof

Date	Mintage	VG	F	VF	XF	Unc
1874	—	50.00	100	180	325	600

KM# Tn99.2 PENNY
Copper, 34 mm. **Rev:** N of TOKEN above roof

Date	Mintage	VG	F	VF	XF	Unc
1874	—	50.00	100	180	325	600

KM# Tn100.1 PENNY
Copper, 31 mm. **Obv:** N of JOHN below kangaroo's ear

Date	Mintage	VG	F	VF	XF	Unc
ND	—	50.00	100	180	325	600

KM# Tn100.2 PENNY
Copper, 31 mm. **Obv:** N of JOHN ends on kangaroo's ear

Date	Mintage	VG	F	VF	XF	Unc
ND	—	35.00	75.00	145	285	500

KM# Tn100.3 PENNY
Copper, 31 mm. **Obv:** N of JOHN begins on kangaroo's ear

Date	Mintage	VG	F	VF	XF	Unc
ND	—	35.00	75.00	145	285	500

Note: KM#Tn99.1 through Tn100.3 are known also in brass

R. Henry

Hobart, Tasmania

KM# Tn101 PENNY
Copper, 33 mm. **Obv. Legend:** R. HENRY **Rev:** Legend above tools **Rev. Legend:** ONE PENNY TOKEN **Edge:** milled

Date	Mintage	VG	F	VF	XF	Unc
ND	—	50.00	100	180	325	600

Samuel Henry

Deloraine, Tasmania

KM# Tn102 PENNY
Copper, 34 mm.

Date	Mintage	VG	F	VF	XF	Unc
1857	—	50.00	100	180	325	600

Hide & De Carle

Melbourne, Victoria

KM# Tn103 1/2 PENNY
Copper, 28 mm. **Obv:** Legend above crowned lion in center **Obv. Legend:** HIDE & DE CARLE **Rev:** Legend above seated Justice **Rev. Legend:** MELBOURNE VICTORIA **Note:** Three varieties exist for 1857.

Date	Mintage	VG	F	VF	XF	Unc
1857	—	35.00	75.00	145	285	500
1858	—	50.00	100	180	325	600

KM# Tn104 PENNY
Copper, 34 mm. **Note:** Similar to 1/2 Penny, KM#Tn103.

Date	Mintage	VG	F	VF	XF	Unc
1857	—	30.00	60.00	125	225	325
Note: 5 varieties exist						
1858	—	30.00	60.00	125	225	325
Note: 7 varieties exist						

A. G. Hodgson

Melbourne, Victoria

KM# Tn107 1/2 PENNY
Copper, 28 mm.

Date	Mintage	VG	F	VF	XF	Unc
1860	—	35.00	75.00	145	285	500

KM# Tn108 1/2 PENNY
Copper, 28 mm. **Obv:** Legend above A. G. HODGSON, as Tn112 **Obv. Legend:** MELBOURNE **Rev:** Similar to 1/2 Penny, KM#Tn107 **Note:** Possible pattern.

Date	Mintage	VG	F	VF	XF	Unc
1860 3 known	—	—	1,500	2,000	3,000	—

KM# Tn109 1/2 PENNY
Copper, 28 mm. **Obv:** Similar to Penny, KM#Tn112 **Rev:** Similar to Penny, KM#Tn112

Date	Mintage	VG	F	VF	XF	Unc
1862	—	80.00	170	325	500	—

KM# Tn110 PENNY
Copper, 34 mm. **Obv. Legend:** Inner: LONSDALE STREET WEST

Date	Mintage	VG	F	VF	XF	Unc
1860	—	50.00	100	180	325	500

KM# Tn111 PENNY
Copper, 34 mm. **Obv. Legend:** Inner: LONSDALE STREET

Date	Mintage	VG	F	VF	XF	Unc
1860	—	150	300	600	1,000	—

KM# Tn112 PENNY
Copper, 34 mm.

Date	Mintage	VG	F	VF	XF	Unc
1862	—	80.00	170	325	500	—

KM# Tn113 PENNY
Copper **Obv:** Similar to KM#Tn112 **Rev:** Similar to KM#Tn111

Date	Mintage	VG	F	VF	XF	Unc
1860	—	—	—	1,800	2,750	—

Hodgson Bros.

Bendigo, Victoria

KM# Tn114.1 PENNY
Copper, 34 mm. **Obv:** 5mm gap at bottom in legend

Date	Mintage	VG	F	VF	XF	Unc
1862	—	150	300	600	1,000	—

KM# Tn114.2 PENNY
Copper, 34 mm. **Obv:** 9mm gap at bottom in legend

Date	Mintage	VG	F	VF	XF	Unc
1862	—	150	300	600	1,000	—

KM# TnF115.1 PENNY
Copper, 34 mm. **Obv:** Similar to KM#Tn114.1 **Rev:** VICTORIA 1862 above Australian arms

Date	Mintage	VG	F	VF	XF	Unc
1862 Fabrication, as struck	—	—	—	—	400	—

KM# TnF115.2 PENNY
Copper, 34 mm. **Obv:** Similar to KM#Tn114.2 **Rev:** Similar to KM#Tn115.1

Date	Mintage	VG	F	VF	XF	Unc
1862 Fabrication, as struck	—	—	—	—	400	—

Hogarth, Erichsen & Co.

Sydney, New South Wales

KM# Tn116.1 3 PENCE
Silver, 16 mm. **Obv:** Curved groundline above curved SYDNEY **Rev:** 3 (7mm high)

Date	Mintage	VG	F	VF	XF	Unc
1858	—	400	650	1,800	2,750	—

KM# Tn116.2 3 PENCE
Silver, 16 mm. **Obv:** Curved groundline above curved SYDNEY **Rev:** 3 (8mm high)

Date	Mintage	VG	F	VF	XF	Unc
1858	—	150	300	600	1,000	—

KM# Tn116.3 3 PENCE
Silver, 16 mm. **Obv:** Straight "low" groundline above curved SYDNEY

Date	Mintage	VG	F	VF	XF	Unc
1858	—	200	400	1,200	1,800	—

KM# Tn117.1 3 PENCE
Silver, 16 mm. **Obv:** Straight "high" groundline above curved SYDNEY **Rev:** 3 (7mm high)

Date	Mintage	VG	F	VF	XF	Unc
1858	—	200	400	1,200	1,800	—

KM# Tn117.2 3 PENCE
Silver, 16 mm. **Obv:** Straight "high" groundline above straight SYDNEY **Rev:** Emu at left, kangaroo at right

Date	Mintage	VG	F	VF	XF	Unc
1858	—	200	400	1,200	1,800	—

KM# Tn118 3 PENCE
Silver, 16 mm. **Obv:** Small 3 **Rev:** Kangaroos at left, emu at right

Date	Mintage	VG	F	VF	XF	Unc
1860	—	80.00	175	380	750	—

KM# Tn119 4 PENCE
Silver, 16 mm. **Obv:** Aborigine

Date	Mintage	VG	F	VF	XF	Unc
1860	—	5,000	7,500	12,500	18,000	—

J. Hosie

Melbourne, Victoria

KM# Tn121.1 PENNY
Copper, 34 mm. **Obv:** Without bars **Rev:** Emu, M of MAKER above AS of EAST

Date	Mintage	VG	F	VF	XF	Unc
1862	—	35.00	75.00	145	285	500

KM# Tn121.2 PENNY
Copper, 34 mm. **Obv:** With bars before 10 and after 12 **Rev:** Emu, M of MAKER above ST of EAST

Date	Mintage	VG	F	VF	XF	Unc
1862	—	50.00	100	180	325	600

KM# Tn122 PENNY
Copper, 34 mm. **Rev:** Vine branch

Date	Mintage	VG	F	VF	XF	Unc
1862	—	50.00	100	180	325	600

KM# Tn123.1 PENNY
Copper, 34 mm. **Obv:** Without bars before 10 and after 12 **Rev:** Legend above Australian arms, M of MAKER above ST of EAST, small letters **Rev. Legend:** VICTORIA 1862

Date	Mintage	VG	F	VF	XF	Unc
1862	—	80.00	170	325	500	—

KM# Tn123.2 PENNY
Copper, 34 mm. **Rev:** Australian arms, M of MAKER above S of EAST

Date	Mintage	VG	F	VF	XF	Unc
1862	—	50.00	100	180	325	600

KM# Tn123.3 PENNY
Copper, 34 mm. **Rev:** Australian arms, M of MAKER above S of EAST, large letters

Date	Mintage	VG	F	VF	XF	Unc
1862	—	80.00	170	325	500	750

John Howell

Adelaide, South Australia

KM# Tn128.1 PENNY
Copper, 34 mm. **Obv:** Legend with dash below T of ST **Obv. Legend:** RUNDLE ST

Date	Mintage	VG	F	VF	XF	Unc
ND	—	50.00	100	150	325	600

KM# Tn128.2 PENNY
Copper, 34 mm. **Obv:** Legend with dot below T of ST **Obv. Legend:** RUNDLE ST

Date	Mintage	VG	F	VF	XF	Unc
ND	—	35.00	75.00	145	285	325

KM# Tn129 PENNY
Copper, 34 mm. **Obv. Legend:** HINDLEY ST.

Date	Mintage	VG	F	VF	XF	Unc
ND	—	50.00	100	180	325	500

G. Hutton
Hobart, Tasmania

KM# Tn130 1/2 PENNY
Copper, 28 mm. **Note:** Similar to Penny, KM#Tn131.

Date	Mintage	VG	F	VF	XF	Unc
ND	—	30.00	60.00	125	225	325

KM# Tn131 PENNY
Copper, 34 mm.

Date	Mintage	VG	F	VF	XF	Unc
ND	—	35.00	75.00	145	285	500

Robert Hyde & Co.
Melbourne, Victoria

KM# Tn132 1/2 PENNY
Copper, 28 mm.

Date	Mintage	VG	F	VF	XF	Unc
1857	—	35.00	75.00	145	285	500
Note: 3 varieties exist for 1857						
1861	—	35.00	75.00	145	285	500
Note: 4 varieties exist for 1861						

KM# Tn133 PENNY
Copper, 34 mm.

Date	Mintage	VG	F	VF	XF	Unc
1857	—	30.00	60.00	125	225	325
1861	—	30.00	60.00	125	225	325
Note: 2 varieties exist for 1861						

Iredale & Co.
Sydney, New South Wales

KM# Tn134 PENNY
Copper, 34 mm. **Rev:** Seated figure **Rev. Legend:** BRITANNIA

Date	Mintage	VG	F	VF	XF	Unc
ND	—	125	245	500	750	1,200

KM# Tn135 PENNY
Copper, 34 mm. **Obv:** Similar to Penny, KM#Tn134 **Rev:** Legend above standing Justice **Rev. Legend:** AUSTRALIA **Note:** Six varieties exist.

Date	Mintage	VG	F	VF	XF	Unc
ND	—	20.00	40.00	75.00	140	245

W. W. Jamieson & Co.
Warnambool, Victoria

KM# Tn136 PENNY
Copper, 34 mm.

Date	Mintage	VG	F	VF	XF	Unc
1862	—	80.00	170	325	500	—

William Andrew Jarvey
Hobart, Tasmania

KM# Tn137.1 PENNY
Copper, 33 mm. **Rev:** Bar points to OK of TOKEN

Date	Mintage	VG	F	VF	XF	Unc
ND	—	80.00	170	325	500	—

KM# Tn137.2 PENNY
Copper, 33 mm. **Rev:** Bar points to T of TOKEN **Note:** Two varieties exist.

Date	Mintage	VG	F	VF	XF	Unc
ND	—	150	300	600	1,000	—

KM# Tn137.3 PENNY
Copper, 33 mm. **Rev:** Balls supported on bars

Date	Mintage	VG	F	VF	XF	Unc
ND	—	35.00	75.00	145	285	500

David Jones
Ballarat, Victoria

KM# Tn138 PENNY
Copper, 32 mm. **Note:** Replicas exist in copper and in silver piedforts. Authenticity can be verified by reverse roof supports and struts.

Date	Mintage	VG	F	VF	XF	Unc
1862	—	35.00	75.00	145	285	500

T. H. Jones & Co.
Ipswich, Queensland

KM# Tn139 PENNY
Copper, 34 mm. **Obv. Legend:** IRONMONGERS & GENERAL IMPORTERS... **Note:** Three varieties eixst.

Date	Mintage	VG	F	VF	XF	Unc
ND	—	35.00	75.00	145	285	500

R. Josephs
New Town, Tasmania

KM# Tn140 1/2 PENNY
Copper, 28 mm.

Date	Mintage	VG	F	VF	XF	Unc
1855	—	30.00	60.00	125	225	325

KM# Tn141 PENNY
Copper, 34 mm. **Note:** Similar to 1/2 Penny, KM#Tn140.

Date	Mintage	VG	F	VF	XF	Unc
1855	—	20.00	40.00	75.00	140	245

Larcombe & Compy.

Brisbane, Queensland

KM# Tn142 PENNY
Copper, 33 mm.

Date	Mintage	VG	F	VF	XF	Unc
ND	—	35.00	75.00	145	285	500

KM# Tn143 PENNY
Copper, 33 mm.

Date	Mintage	F	VF	XF	Unc	BU
ND	—	—	—	2,750	3,500	—

S. & S. Lazarus

Melbourne, Victoria

KM# Tn144.1 PENNY
Copper, 35 mm. **Obv:** E of WHOLESALE above I of RETAIL, S of QUEENS below 7 of 70

Date	Mintage	VG	F	VF	XF	Unc
ND	—	150	300	600	1,000	—

KM# Tn144.2 PENNY
Copper, 35 mm. **Obv:** E of WHOLESALE above L of RETAIL, S of QUEENS to right of 7 of 70

Date	Mintage	VG	F	VF	XF	Unc
ND	—	200	400	1,200	1,800	—

KM# Tn144.3 PENNY
Copper, 35 mm. **Obv:** E of WHOLESALE above I of RETAIL, S of QUEENS to below left of 7 of 70

Date	Mintage	VG	F	VF	XF	Unc
ND	—	200	400	1,200	1,800	—

J. D. Leeson

Sale, Victoria

KM# Tn145 PENNY
Copper, 34 mm.

Date	Mintage	VG	F	VF	XF	Unc
1862	—	120	245	500	750	—

J. M. Leigh

Sydney, New South Wales

KM# Tn146 PENNY
Copper, 33 mm. **Obv. Legend:** J. M. LEIGH... **Rev:** Legend above seated Britannia **Rev. Legend:** BRITANNIA

Date	Mintage	VG	F	VF	XF	Unc
ND	—	30.00	60.00	125	225	325

Levy Brothers

Melbourne, Victoria

KM# Tn147 PENNY
Copper, 34 mm.

Date	Mintage	VG	F	VF	XF	Unc
1855	—	120	245	500	750	—

H. Lipscombe

Hobart, Tasmania

KM# Tn148 PENNY
Copper, 33 mm. **Obv:** Legend around fruit **Obv. Legend:** H. LIPSCOMBE. MURRAY STREET... **Rev. Legend:** SHIPPING SUPPLIED... **Note:** Two varieties exist.

Date	Mintage	VG	F	VF	XF	Unc
ND	—	30.00	60.00	125	225	325

W. F. & D. L. Lloyd

Wollongong, New South Wales

KM# Tn149 1/2 PENNY
Copper, 28 mm.

Date	Mintage	Good	VG	F	VF	XF
1859	—	150	300	600	1,000	—

KM# Tn150 PENNY
Copper, 34 mm.

Date	Mintage	Good	VG	F	VF	XF
1859	—	80.00	170	325	500	—

Love & Roberts

Wagga Wagga, New South Wales

KM# Tn151.1 PENNY
Copper, 34 mm. **Obv:** V of LOVE at cetner of S of STOREKEEPERS **Rev:** Plough handles point to N of FARMING

Date	Mintage	VG	F	VF	XF	Unc
1865	—	120	245	500	750	—

KM# Tn151.2 PENNY
Copper, 34 mm. **Rev:** Plough handles point to NG of FARMING

Date	Mintage	VG	F	VF	XF	Unc
1865	—	80.00	170	325	500	—

KM# TnF151 PENNY
Copper, 34 mm. **Obv:** V of LOVE at center of S of STOREKEEPERS **Rev:** Plough handles point to N of FARMING, similar to Penny, KM#Tn151.1

Date	Mintage	VG	F	VF	XF	Unc
1865 Fabrication, as struck	—	—	—	—	450	—

KM# Tn151.3 PENNY
Copper, 34 mm. **Obv:** V of LOVE at top of S of STOREKEEPERS **Rev:** Plough handles point to NG of FARMING

Date	Mintage	VG	F	VF	XF	Unc
1865	—	150	300	600	1,000	—

J. MacGregor
Sydney, New South Wales

KM# Tn152 1/2 PENNY
Bronze, 25 mm. **Obv. Legend:** THE CITY TEA WAREHOUSE... **Rev:** Legend above Australian arms **Rev. Legend:** THE SULTAN'S STEAM COFFEE WORKS...

Date	Mintage	VG	F	VF	XF	Unc
ND	—	—	75.00	145	285	500

KM# Tn153 PENNY
Bronze, 31 mm. **Note:** Similar to 1/2 Penny, KM#Tn149.

Date	Mintage	VG	F	VF	XF	Unc
ND(1865)	—	—	60.00	125	225	325

Macintosh & Degraves
Hobart, Tasmania

KM# Tn154 SHILLING
Silver, 22 mm.

Date	Mintage	VG	F	VF	XF	Unc
1823	—	1,500	4,000	5,250	7,500	—

H. J. Marsh & Brother
Hobart, Tasmania

KM# Tn155 1/2 PENNY
Copper, 27 mm. **Obv. Legend:** H. J. MARSH & BROTHER ... **Rev:** Legend above sailing ship **Rev. Legend:** HALFPENNY TOKEN

Date	Mintage	VG	F	VF	XF	Unc
ND	—	35.00	75.00	145	285	500

KM# Tn156 PENNY
Copper, 34 mm. **Obv:** MURRY

Date	Mintage	VG	F	VF	XF	Unc
ND	—	35.00	75.00	145	285	500

KM# Tn157 PENNY
Copper, 33 mm. **Obv:** MURRAY **Rev:** Spade handle to left

Date	Mintage	VG	F	VF	XF	Unc
ND	—	35.00	75.00	145	285	500

KM# Tn158.1 PENNY
Copper, 33 mm. **Obv:** I of IRONMONGERS above bottom of J of H. J. **Rev:** Spade handle to right

Date	Mintage	VG	F	VF	XF	Unc
ND	—	120	245	500	750	—

KM# Tn158.2 PENNY
Copper, 33 mm. **Obv:** I of IRONMONGERS below bottom of J of H. J. **Rev:** Spade handle to right

Date	Mintage	VG	F	VF	XF	Unc
ND	—	35.00	75.00	145	285	500

John Martin
Adelaide, South Australia

KM# Tn159 PENNY
Copper, 34 mm.

Date	Mintage	VG	F	VF	XF	Unc
ND	—	50.00	100	180	325	600

Martin & Sach
Adelaide, South Australia

KM# Tn160 PENNY
Copper, 34 mm. **Obv. Legend:** MARTIN & SACH... **Rev:** Legend above standing Justice with scales in right hand **Rev. Legend:** AUSTRALIA **Note:** Three varieties exist.

Date	Mintage	VG	F	VF	XF	Unc
ND	—	80.00	170	325	500	—

Mason & Culley
Williamstown, Victoria

KM# Tn162 PENNY
Copper, 34 mm.

Date	Mintage	VG	F	VF	XF	Unc
ND	—	—	—	4,000	5,000	—

Note: Approximatley 12 known

R. Andrew Mather
Hobart, Tasmania

KM# Tn163 PENNY
Copper, 34 mm. **Note:** Three varieties exist.

Date	Mintage	VG	F	VF	XF	Unc
ND	—	20.00	40.00	75.00	140	245

J. McFarlane
Melbourne, Victoria

KM# Tn164 PENNY
Copper, 34 mm. **Obv. Legend:** CORNER OF ELIZABETH &... **Rev:** Legend above standing Peace, lion, and sheep **Rev. Legend:** PEACE AND PLENTY...

Date	Mintage	VG	F	VF	XF	Unc
ND	—	35.00	75.00	145	285	500

Merry & Bush
Brisbane, Queensland

KM# Tn165 PENNY
Copper, 34 mm.

Date	Mintage	VG	F	VF	XF	Unc
1863	—	50.00	100	180	325	600

T. F. Merry & Co.
Toowoomba, Queensland

KM# Tn166 1/2 PENNY
Copper, 28 mm. **Note:** Similar to 1 Penny, KM#Tn167.

Date	Mintage	VG	F	VF	XF	Unc
ND	—	80.00	170	325	500	—

KM# Tn167.1 PENNY
Copper, 34 mm. **Obv:** A of TOOWOOMBA slightly under S of MERCHANTS

Date	Mintage	VG	F	VF	XF	Unc
ND(1863)	—	35.00	75.00	140	280	500

KM# Tn167.2 PENNY
Copper, 34 mm. **Obv:** A of TOOWOOMBA beyond S of MERCHANTS

Date	Mintage	VG	F	VF	XF	Unc
ND	—	150	300	600	1,000	—

Metcalfe & Lloyd

Sydney, New South Wales

KM# Tn168 1/2 PENNY
Copper, 28 mm. **Obv. Legend:** SHIPPING AND FAMILY GROCERS... **Rev. Legend:** PURVEYORS OF THE...

Date	Mintage	VG	F	VF	XF	Unc
1863	—	50.00	100	180	325	600

KM# Tn169 PENNY
Copper, 34 mm. **Note:** Similar to 1/2 Penny, KM#Tn168.

Date	Mintage	VG	F	VF	XF	Unc
1863	—	30.00	60.00	125	225	325

Miller Brothers

Melbourne, Victoria

KM# Tn170.1 PENNY
Copper, 34 mm. **Rev:** R of MAKER touches leaf

Date	Mintage	VG	F	VF	XF	Unc
1862	—	50.00	100	180	325	600

KM# Tn170.2 PENNY
Copper, 34 mm. **Rev:** R of MAKER away from leaf

Date	Mintage	VG	F	VF	XF	Unc
1862	—	80.00	170	325	500	750

KM# Tn171 PENNY
Copper, 34 mm. **Obv:** Similar to Penny, KM#Tn170 **Rev:** Legend above Australian arms **Rev. Legend:** VICTORIA 1862

Date	Mintage	VG	F	VF	XF	Unc
1862	—	50.00	100	180	325	600

KM# Tn172 PENNY
Copper, 34 mm. **Obv:** Similar to Penny, KM#Tn170 **Rev:** Legend above Emu **Rev. Legend:** VICTORIA 1862

Date	Mintage	VG	F	VF	XF	Unc
1862	—	50.00	100	180	325	600

Miller & Dismorr

Melbourne, Victoria

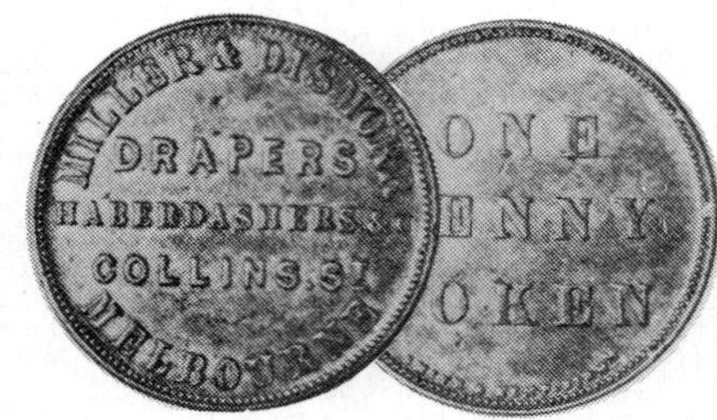

KM# Tn173 PENNY
Copper, 34 mm.

Date	Mintage	VG	F	VF	XF	Unc
ND	—	80.00	170	325	500	750

Joseph Moir

Hobart, Tasmania

KM# Tn174 PENNY
Copper, 34 mm.

Date	Mintage	VG	F	VF	XF	Unc
ND	—	35.00	75.00	145	285	500

William Morgan

Adelaide, South Australia

KM# Tn175 PENNY
Copper, 34 mm. **Note:** Two varieties exist.

Date	Mintage	VG	F	VF	XF	Unc
1858	—	50.00	100	180	325	600

Moubray, Lush & Co.

Melbourne, Victoria

KM# Tn176 PENNY
Copper, 34 mm.

Date	Mintage	VG	F	VF	XF	Unc
ND	—	80.00	170	325	500	750

D. T. Mulligan

Rockhampton, Queensland

KM# Tn177 1/2 PENNY
Copper, 28 mm. **Obv. Legend:** QUEENSLAND STORES... **Rev:** Legend above Australian arms **Rev. Legend:** QUEENSLAND **Note:** Two varieties exist.

Date	Mintage	VG	F	VF	XF	Unc
1863	—	35.00	75.00	145	285	500

KM# Tn178 PENNY
Copper, 34 mm. **Note:** Similar to 1/2 Penny, KM#Tn177.

Date	Mintage	VG	F	VF	XF	Unc
1863	—	35.00	75.00	145	285	500

Murray and Christie

Castlemaine, Victoria

KM# Tn179 PENNY
Copper, 34 mm. **Note:** Two varieties exist.

Date	Mintage	VG	F	VF	XF	Unc
ND	—	50.00	100	180	325	600

KM# Tn180 PENNY
Copper, 34 mm. **Obv:** As reverse of Tn179 **Rev:** Legend above Australian arms **Rev. Legend:** AUSTRALIA 1862 **Note:** Mule.

Date	Mintage	VG	F	VF	XF	Unc
1862	—	50.00	100	180	325	600

A. Nicholas

Hobart, Tasmania

KM# Tn183 PENNY
Copper, 33 mm. **Rev:** Arms of Liverpool, England

Date	Mintage	VG	F	VF	XF	Unc
ND	—	5,000	7,000	10,000	—	—

Alfred Nicholas

Hobart, Tasmania

KM# Tn181 1/2 PENNY
Copper, 33 mm. **Obv. Legend:** ALFRED NICHOLAS... **Rev:** Legend above seated Britannia **Rev. Legend:** BRITANNIA

Date	Mintage	VG	F	VF	XF	Unc
ND	—	50.00	100	180	350	600

KM# Tn182.1 PENNY
Copper, 33 mm. **Rev:** Center prong of trident slightly right of N of BRITANNIA

Date	Mintage	VG	F	VF	XF	Unc
ND	—	35.00	75.00	150	275	500

KM# Tn182.2 PENNY
Copper, 33 mm. **Rev:** Center prong of trident below N of BRITANNIA

Date	Mintage	VG	F	VF	XF	Unc
ND	—	35.00	75.00	150	275	500

George Nichols

Melbourne, Victoria

KM# Tn184.1 PENNY
Copper, 35 mm. **Obv. Legend:** BOOKSELLER AND STATIONER... **Rev:** Legend above Australian arms with ear of kangaroo below T of VICTORIA **Rev. Legend:** VICTORIA 1862

Date	Mintage	VG	F	VF	XF	Unc
1862	—	80.00	170	325	500	750

KM# Tn184.2 PENNY
Copper, 35 mm. **Rev:** Ear of kangaroo above T of VICTORIA

Date	Mintage	VG	F	VF	XF	Unc
1862	—	50.00	100	180	325	600

James Nokes

Melbourne, Victoria

KM# Tn185 1/2 PENNY
Copper, 28 mm. **Obv. Legend:** JAMES NOKES GROCER... **Rev. Legend:** IN COMMEMORATION OF...

Date	Mintage	VG	F	VF	XF	Unc
ND	—	30.00	60.00	125	225	325

KM# Tn186 1/2 PENNY
Copper, 28 mm. **Obv:** Similar to 1/2 Penny, KM#Tn185 **Rev:** Legend above seated figure **Rev. Legend:** AUSTRALIA

Date	Mintage	VG	F	VF	XF	Unc
ND	—	80.00	170	325	500	750

B. Palmer

Sydney, New South Wales

KM# Tn187 PENNY
Copper, 34 mm. **Obv. Legend:** WHOLESALE WINE &... **Rev:** Legend around dove **Rev. Legend:** LIVERPOOL ARMS

Date	Mintage	VG	F	VF	XF	Unc
ND	—	30.00	60.00	125	225	325

R. Parker

Geelong, Victoria

KM# Tn188 PENNY
Copper, 34 mm. **Note:** Seven varieties exist at 34mm, four varieties exist at 35mm.

Date	Mintage	VG	F	VF	XF	Unc
ND	—	30.00	60.00	125	225	350

Hugh Peck

Melbourne, Victoria

KM# Tn189 PENNY
Copper, 34 mm.

Date	Mintage	VG	F	VF	XF	Unc
ND	—	80.00	170	325	500	750

KM# Tn190 PENNY
Copper, 34 mm. **Obv:** Similar to 1 Penny, KM#Tn189 **Rev:** Legend above Australian arms **Rev. Legend:** VICTORIA 1862

Date	Mintage	VG	F	VF	XF	Unc
1862	—	50.00	100	175	350	600

Peek & Campbell Tea Stores

Sydney, New South Wales

KM# Tn191.1 1/2 PENNY
Copper, 29 mm. **Obv:** Left side of building with horizontal bricks raised and joints sunken

Date	Mintage	VG	F	VF	XF	Unc
1852	—	50.00	100	175	350	600

KM# Tn191.2 1/2 PENNY
Copper, 29 mm. **Obv:** Lower left side of building as KM#Tn191.1 except brick courses in perspective

Date	Mintage	VG	F	VF	XF	Unc
1852	—	100	175	350	550	750

KM# Tn191.3 1/2 PENNY
Copper, 29 mm. **Obv:** Smaller bricks and sunken joints raised

Date	Mintage	VG	F	VF	XF	Unc
1852	—	50.00	100	175	350	600

KM# Tn192.1 PENNY
Copper, 34 mm. **Obv:** S of ESTABLISHED above S of large SYDNEY

Date	Mintage	VG	F	VF	XF	Unc
1852	—	125	250	500	1,500	—
1853	—	50.00	100	200	625	—

KM# Tn192.2 PENNY
Copper, 34 mm. **Obv:** E of ESTABLISHED above S of small SYDNEY

Date	Mintage	VG	F	VF	XF	Unc
1852	—	3,500	5,000	6,500	—	—

KM# Tn193 PENNY
Copper, 34 mm. **Obv:** Similar to Penny, KM#Tn192 but lower legend in two lines **Rev:** Legend above seated Britannia **Rev. Legend:** BRITANNIA **Note:** Mule.

Date	Mintage	Good	VG	F	VF	XF
1852	—	1,500	3,000	4,500	7,500	12,500

KM# Tn194 PENNY
Copper, 34 mm. **Obv:** 1 Penny, KM#Tn192 **Rev:** Legend above Australian arms, as Tn250 **Rev. Legend:** ADVANCE AUSTRALIA

Date	Mintage	Good	VG	F	VF	XF
1854	—	500	750	2,500	—	—

John Pettigrew & Co.

Ipswich, Queensland

KM# Tn195 1/2 PENNY
Bronze, 26 mm.

Date	Mintage	VG	F	VF	XF	Unc
1865	—	80.00	175	325	500	—

KM# Tn196 PENNY
Bronze, 31 mm. **Note:** Similar to 1/2 Penney, KM#Tn195.

Date	Mintage	VG	F	VF	XF	Unc
1865	—	35.00	75.00	150	300	600

Geo. Petty

Melbourne, Victoria

KM# Tn197.1 PENNY
Copper, 35 mm. **Rev:** Bottom of V of VICTORIA above scale bar

Date	Mintage	VG	F	VF	XF	Unc
ND	—	35.00	75.00	150	300	500

KM# Tn197.2 PENNY
Copper, 35 mm. **Rev:** Bottom of V of VICTORIA below scale bar

Date	Mintage	VG	F	VF	XF	Unc
ND	—	80.00	175	350	550	750

KM# Tn198 PENNY
Copper, 35 mm. **Obv:** Similar to 1 Penny, KM#Tn197 **Rev:** Legend above seated Justice **Rev. Legend:** MELBOURNE VICTORIA **Note:** Specimen striking made for collectors.

Date	Mintage	F	VF	XF	Unc	BU
1860	—	—	—	2,000	2,500	—

KM# Tn199 PENNY
Copper, 35 mm. **Obv:** Similar to 1 Penny, KM#Tn197 **Rev:** Legend around Golden Fleece **Rev. Legend:** SIC VOS NON... **Note:** Specimen striking, made for collectors.

Date	Mintage	F	VF	XF	Unc	BU
ND	—	—	—	2,000	2,500	—

R. B. Ridler

Richmond, Victoria

KM# Tn200 PENNY
Copper, 34 mm. **Rev:** Emu, legend with dot after Victoria **Rev. Legend:** VICTORIA. 1862

Date	Mintage	VG	F	VF	XF	Unc
1862	—	80.00	170	325	500	750

KM# TnF200 PENNY
Copper, 34 mm. **Rev:** Legend without dot after Victoria **Rev. Legend:** VICTORIA 1862

Date	Mintage	VG	F	VF	XF	Unc
1862 Fabrication, as struck	—	—	—	—	400	—

KM# TnF201 PENNY
Copper, 34 mm. **Obv:** Similarto Penny, KM#Tn200 **Rev:** Legend around grape vine **Rev. Legend:** VICTORIA 1862

Date	Mintage	F	VF	XF	Unc	BU
1862 Fabrication, as struck	—	—	—	—	400	—

KM# Tn202 PENNY
Copper, 34 mm.

Date	Mintage	VG	F	VF	XF	Unc
1862	—	50.00	100	175	325	600

KM# TnF202 PENNY
Copper, 34 mm.

Date	Mintage	VG	F	VF	XF	Unc
1862 Fabrication, as struck	—	—	—	—	400	—

KM# Tn209 PENNY
Copper, 34 mm. **Rev:** Legend above wheat sheaf **Rev. Legend:** ADVANCE AUSTRALIA

Date	Mintage	VG	F	VF	XF	Unc
1862	—	200	400	1,200	1,800	—

Robison Bros. & Co.

Melbourne, Victoria

KM# Tn203 PENNY
Copper, 34 mm. **Obv. Legend:** VICTORIA COPPER WORKS... **Rev:** Similar to 1 Penny, KM#Tn200 **Note:** Four varieties exist.

Date	Mintage	VG	F	VF	XF	Unc
1862	—	35.00	75.00	150	300	500

KM# Tn204 PENNY
Copper, 34 mm. **Obv:** Similar to 1 Penny, KM#Tn203 **Rev:** Australian arms, similar to 1 Penny, KM#Tn202

Date	Mintage	VG	F	VF	XF	Unc
1862	—	50.00	100	180	325	600

KM# Tn205 PENNY
Copper, 34 mm. **Obv:** Similar to 1 Penny, KM#Tn203 **Rev:** Legend around grape vine **Rev. Legend:** VICTORIA 1862

Date	Mintage	VG	F	VF	XF	Unc
1862	—	80.00	175	350	500	750

G. & W. H. Rocke

Melbourne, Victoria

KM# Tn206 PENNY
Copper, 34 mm. **Obv:** Crowned lion in center of legend **Obv. Legend:** G. 7 W. H. Rocke **Rev:** Legend above seated Justice **Rev. Legend:** MELBOURNE VICTORIA **Note:** Four varieties exist.

Date	Mintage	VG	F	VF	XF	Unc
1859	—	35.00	75.00	150	285	350

G. Ryland

Castlemaine, Victoria

KM# Tn207 PENNY
Copper, 34 mm.

Date	Mintage	VG	F	VF	XF	Unc
1862	—	75.00	170	325	500	750

J. Sawyer

Brisbane, Queensland

KM# Tn208 PENNY
Copper, 35 mm.

Date	Mintage	VG	F	VF	XF	Unc
1864	—	30.00	60.00	125	225	325

Smith, Peate & Co.

Sydney, New South Wales

KM# Tn210 1/2 PENNY
Copper, 28 mm. **Obv. Legend:** SMITH, PEATE & CO. ... **Rev:** Legend above standing Justice **Rev. Legend:** ESTABLISHED **Note:** Seven varieties exist.

Date	Mintage	VG	F	VF	XF	Unc
1856	—	35.00	75.00	150	300	550

KM# Tn211 PENNY
Copper, 34 mm. **Note:** Similar to 1.2 Penny, KM#Tn210. Four varieties exist.

Date	Mintage	VG	F	VF	XF	Unc
1856	—	35.00	75.00	150	300	500

Southward & Sumpton

Ballarat, Victoria

KM# Tn212 PENNY
Copper, 34 mm.

Date	Mintage	VG	F	VF	XF	Unc
ND	—	50.00	100	175	350	600

Stead Brothers

Sandhurst, Victoria

KM# Tn213 PENNY

Copper, 34 mm.

Date	Mintage	VG	F	VF	XF	Unc
1862	—	75.00	175	350	500	750
1862 Restrike	—	—	—	—	150	—

KM# Tn214 PENNY

Copper, 34 mm.

Date	Mintage	VG	F	VF	XF	Unc
1862	—	200	400	1,000	1,800	—
1862 Restrike	—	—	—	—	150	—

Stewart & Hemmant

Brisbane & Rockhampton, Queensland

KM# Tn215 PENNY

Copper, 33 mm. **Obv. Legend:** STEWART & HEMMANT... **Rev:** Legend above emu **Rev. Legend:** CRITERION... **Note:** Two varieties exist.

Date	Mintage	VG	F	VF	XF	Unc
ND	—	35.00	75.00	150	300	500

KM# Tn216 PENNY

Copper, 30 mm. **Obv:** Legend around CRITERION **Obv. Legend:** STEWART & HEMMANT...

Date	Mintage	VG	F	VF	XF	Unc
ND	—	125	250	500	750	1,200

T. Stokes

Melbourne, Victoria

KM# Tn217 1/2 PENNY

Copper, 28 mm. **Obv. Legend:** T. STOKES DIE SINKERS... **Rev. Legend:** MILITARY ORNAMENTS & BUTTON...

Date	Mintage	VG	F	VF	XF	Unc
ND	—	125	250	500	750	—

KM# TnF219 PENNY

Copper, 34 mm. **Obv. Legend:** CHECK & TOKEN MAKER...

Date	Mintage	VG	F	VF	XF	Unc
1862 Fabrication, as struck	—	—	—	—	1,000	—

KM# Tn221.1 PENNY

Copper, 34 mm. **Obv. Legend:** THOMAS STOKES MAKER. **Rev:** Legend above Australian arms with rose leaf pointing left of S of STOKES **Rev. Legend:** VICTORIA. 1862

Date	Mintage	VG	F	VF	XF	Unc
1862	—	35.00	75.00	145	285	500

KM# Tn221.2 PENNY

Copper, 34 mm. **Rev:** Large letters, wtih tendrill pointing to E of MAKER

Date	Mintage	VG	F	VF	XF	Unc
1862	—	35.00	75.00	150	300	500

KM# Tn222 PENNY

Copper, 34 mm. **Obv:** Similar to 1 Penny, KM#Tn221 **Rev:** Legend above emu **Rev. Legend:** VICTORIA. 1862

Date	Mintage	VG	F	VF	XF	Unc
1862	—	80.00	175	325	500	750

KM# Tn223 PENNY

Copper, 34 mm. **Obv:** Similar to 1 Penny, KM#Tn221, but H of Thomas above C of Collins **Rev. Legend:** DIE SINKER SEAL ENGRAVER... **Note:** Considered a pattern.

Date	Mintage	VG	F	VF	XF	Unc
ND(1862) Four known	—	—	—	3,000	5,000	—

KM# Tn224 PENNY

Copper, 34 mm. **Obv. Legend:** LETTER CUTTER BUTTON CHECK & ... **Rev:** Legend above grape vine **Rev. Legend:** VICTORIA 1862

Date	Mintage	VG	F	VF	XF	Unc
1862	—	80.00	175	325	500	750

KM# Tn225.1 PENNY

Copper, 34 mm. **Obv:** Similar to 1 Penny, KM#Tn224 **Rev:** Legend above emu **Rev. Legend:** VICTORIA. 1862

Date	Mintage	VG	F	VF	XF	Unc
1862	—	120	245	500	750	—

KM# Tn225.2 PENNY

Copper, 34 mm. **Obv. Legend:** LETTER CUTTER - BUTTON CHECK

Date	Mintage	VG	F	VF	XF	Unc
1862	—	150	300	600	1,000	—

KM# Tn226 PENNY

Copper, 34 mm. **Obv. Legend:** LETTER CUTTER SEAL ENGRAVER ... **Rev:** Legend above grape vine **Rev. Legend:** VICTORIA 1862

Date	Mintage	VG	F	VF	XF	Unc
1862	—	35.00	75.00	150	300	500

KM# Tn227 PENNY

Copper, 34 mm. **Obv:** Similar to 1 Penny, KM#Tn226 **Rev:** Emu-A

Date	Mintage	VG	F	VF	XF	Unc
1862	—	50.00	100	175	325	600

KM# Tn228 PENNY

Copper, 34 mm. **Obv. Legend:** LETTER CUTTER. SEAL ENGRAVER. TOKEN MAKER. **Note:** Three varieties exist.

Date	Mintage	VG	F	VF	XF	Unc
1862	—	35.00	75.00	150	300	500

KM# TnF229 PENNY

Copper, 34 mm. **Obv. Legend:** ... ENGRAVER-TOKEN MAKER **Rev:** Legend above Australian arms **Rev. Legend:** VICTORIA 1862

Date	Mintage	VG	F	VF	XF	Unc
1862 Fabrication, as struck 150	—	—	—	—	1,000	—

KM# TnF230 PENNY

Copper, 34 mm. **Obv:** Outer legend compressed **Obv. Legend:** ... ENGRAVER-TOKEN MAKER **Rev:** Emu arms

Date	Mintage	VG	F	VF	XF	Unc
1862 Fabrication, as struck	—	—	—	—	1,000	—

KM# Tn231 PENNY

Copper, 34 mm. **Obv:** Similar to 1 Penny, KM#Tn229 **Rev:** Legend above grape vine, leaf does not touch R in MAKER **Rev. Legend:** VICTORIA 1862

Date	Mintage	VG	F	VF	XF	Unc
1862	—	35.00	75.00	150	300	500

KM# TnF232 PENNY

Copper, 34 mm. **Obv. Legend:** ... ENGRAVER - TOKEN MAKER **Rev:** Legend above Australian arms **Rev. Legend:** VICTORIA 1862

Date	Mintage	VG	F	VF	XF	Unc
1862 Fabrication, as struck	—	—	—	—	1,000	—

KM# Tn233 PENNY

Copper, 34 mm. **Obv. Legend:** MILITARY ORNAMENT BUTTON & ... **Note:** Two varieties exist.

Date	Mintage	VG	F	VF	XF	Unc
1862	—	50.00	100	175	325	600

KM# Tn234 PENNY
Copper, 34 mm. **Obv. Legend:** LETTERCUTTER • SEAL ENGRAVER • TOKEN MAKER

Date	Mintage	VG	F	VF	XF	Unc
1862	—	35.00	75.00	150	300	500

KM# Tn235 PENNY
Copper, 34 mm. **Obv. Legend:** T. STOKES, TOKEN MAKER

Date	Mintage	VG	F	VF	XF	Unc
1862	—	125	250	500	750	—

KM# Tn236.1 PENNY
Copper, 34 mm. **Note:** Mule. Arms, vine. Eight varieties exist.

Date	Mintage	VG	F	VF	XF	Unc
1862	—	30.00	60.00	125	225	325

KM# Tn236.2 PENNY
Copper, 34 mm. **Note:** Mule. Emu, vine. Three varieties exist.

Date	Mintage	VG	F	VF	XF	Unc
1862	—	35.00	75.00	150	300	500

KM# Tn237 PENNY
Copper, 34 mm. **Obv:** Legend above wheat sheaf **Obv. Legend:** ADVANCE AUSTRALIA **Rev:** Similar to 1 Penny reverse, KM#Tn236.1 **Note:** Mule. Six varieties exist.

Date	Mintage	VG	F	VF	XF	Unc
1862	—	35.00	75.00	150	300	500

Stokes & Martin

Melbourne, Victoria

KM# Tn238 PENNY
Copper, 31 mm.

Date	Mintage	VG	F	VF	XF	Unc
ND	—	80.00	175	325	500	750

Alfred Taylor

Adelaide, South Australia

KM# Tn239 PENNY
Copper, 34 mm.

Date	Mintage	VG	F	VF	XF	Unc
ND	—	50.00	100	175	325	600

J. Taylor

Ballarat, Victoria

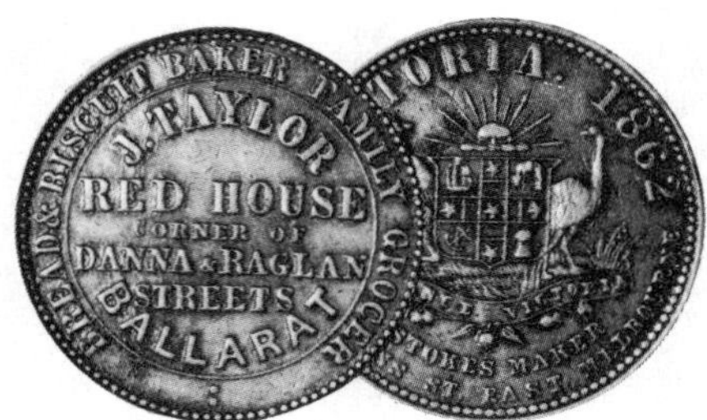

KM# Tn240 PENNY
Copper, 34 mm. **Rev:** Arms

Date	Mintage	VG	F	VF	XF	Unc
1862	—	80.00	175	325	500	750

KM# Tn241 PENNY
Copper, 34 mm. **Obv:** As KM#Tn240 **Rev:** Wheat sheaf

Date	Mintage	VG	F	VF	XF	Unc
1862	—	80.00	175	325	500	750

KM# Tn242 PENNY
Copper, 34 mm. **Obv:** Similar to 1 Penny, KM#Tn240 **Rev:** Legend above grape vines **Rev. Legend:** VICTORIA 1862

Date	Mintage	VG	F	VF	XF	Unc
1862	—	80.00	175	325	500	750

W. J. Taylor

Melbourne, Victoria

KM# Tn243 1/2 PENNY
Copper, 28 mm. **Obv:** Legend below kangaroo **Obv. Legend:** W. J. TAYLOR, MEDALLIST TO THE GREAT EXIBITION **Rev:** Kangaroo office **Note:** Restrikes known.

Date	Mintage	VG	F	VF	XF	Unc
1851	—	—	—	5,000	7,500	—

KM# Tn244 1/2 PENNY
Copper, 28 mm.

Date	Mintage	VG	F	VF	XF	Unc
1851	—	30.00	60.00	125	225	325

KM# Tn245 1/2 PENNY
Copper, 28 mm. **Rev:** Similar to Tn244 **Rev. Legend:** UNITED STATES **Note:** Specimen striking, made for collectors.

Date	Mintage	VG	F	VF	XF	Unc
1857	—	—	—	1,750	2,500	—

KM# Tn246 2 PENCE
Copper, 28 mm. **Note:** Specimen striking, made for collectors.

Date	Mintage	VG	F	VF	XF	Unc
1851	—	—	—	—	2,500	—

KM# Tn247 2 PENCE
Copper, 28 mm. **Obv:** Like KM#Tn243 **Rev:** Similar to KM#Tn246 but with large 2 in relief on plain field **Note:** Specimen striking, made for collectors.

Date	Mintage	VG	F	VF	XF	Unc
1851	—	—	—	—	2,500	—

T. W. Thomas & Co.

Melbourne, Victoria

KM# Tn248 1/2 PENNY
Copper **Obv. Legend:** T. W. THOMAS & CO. ... **Rev. Legend:** IN COMMERMORATION OF THE... **Note:** Three varieties known.

Date	Mintage	VG	F	VF	XF	Unc
1854	—	50.00	100	175	325	500

J. C. Thornthwaite

Sydney, New South Wales

KM# Tn249.1 1/2 PENNY
Copper, 28 mm. **Obv. Legend:** ...MEDALIST (sic)

Date	Mintage	Good	VG	F	VF	XF
1854	—	200	400	750	1,500	—

KM# Tn249.2 1/2 PENNY
Copper, 28 mm. **Obv. Legend:** ....MEDALLISIT (error)

Date	Mintage	Good	VG	F	VF	XF
1854	—	250	500	900	1,800	—

KM# TnP250 PENNY
Copper, 33 mm. **Note:** A pattern using 1/2 penny die on obverse and reverse of Penny, KM#250. Previously listed as 1/2 Penny KM#Tn249.3.

Date	Mintage	VG	F	VF	XF	Unc
1854 Unique	—	—	—	—	10,000	—

KM# Tn250 PENNY
Copper, 35 mm.

Date	Mintage	VG	F	VF	XF	Unc
1854	—	250	500	1,500	—	—

KM# Tn251 3 PENCE
Silver, 16 mm. **Rev:** Large sunburst above 3 **Note:** Two varieties exist.

Date	Mintage	VG	F	VF	XF	Unc
1854	—	1,000	1,500	2,000	3,500	—

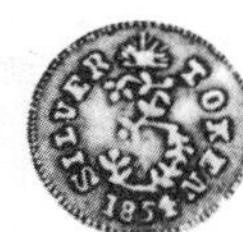

KM# Tn252 3 PENCE
Silver, 16 mm. **Obv:** Similar to 3 Pence, KM#Tn251 **Rev:** Small sunburst above floral 3

Date	Mintage	VG	F	VF	XF	Unc
1854	—	—	5,000	7,500	10,000	—

KM# Tn253 3 PENCE
Silver, 16 mm. **Obv:** Similar to 3 Pence, KM#Tn251 **Rev:** Without sun date or J.C.T. **Rev. Legend:** SILVER 3 TOKEN

Date	Mintage	VG	F	VF	XF	Unc
1854	—	1,000	2,000	4,000	—	—

Thrale & Cross

Melbourne, Victoria

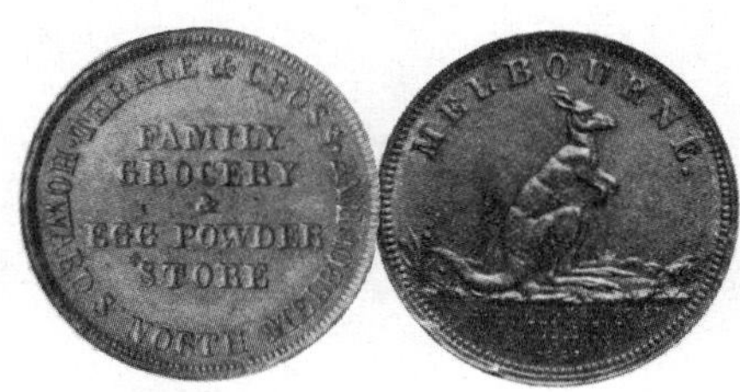

KM# Tn254 1/2 PENNY
Copper, 28 mm.

Date	Mintage	VG	F	VF	XF	Unc
1851	—	75.00	175	325	500	—

KM# Tn255 1/2 PENNY
Copper, 28 mm. **Obv:** Similar to 1/2 Penny, KM#Tn254 **Rev:** Legend above seated woman **Rev. Legend:** AUSTRALIA **Note:** Thick flan variety.

Date	Mintage	VG	F	VF	XF	Unc
ND	—	100	250	400	600	—

A. Toogood

Sydney, New South Wales

KM# Tn256 PENNY
Copper, 34 mm. **Obv. Legend:** A. TOOGOOD MERCHANT... **Rev:** Legend above seated Justice **Rev. Legend:** AUSTRALIA **Note:** Two varieties exist.

Date	Mintage	VG	F	VF	XF	Unc
1855	—	30.00	60.00	125	225	325

T. Warburton

Melbourne, Victoria

KM# Tn257 PENNY
Copper, 34 mm. **Obv. Legend:** IRON & ZINC SPOUTING... **Rev:** Legend above emu **Rev. Legend:** VICTORIA 1862 **Note:** Two varieties exist.

Date	Mintage	VG	F	VF	XF	Unc
1862	—	80.00	175	325	500	—

KM# Tn258 PENNY
Copper, 34 mm. **Obv:** Similar to 1 Penny, KM#Tn257 **Rev:** Legend above grape vine **Rev. Legend:** VICTORIA 1862 **Note:** Two varieties exist.

Date	Mintage	VG	F	VF	XF	Unc
1862	—	75.00	175	325	500	—

KM# Tn259 PENNY
Copper, 34 mm. **Obv:** Similar to 1 Penny, KM#Tn257 **Rev:** Legend above Australian arms **Rev. Legend:** VICTORIA 1862

Date	Mintage	VG	F	VF	XF	Unc
1862	—	35.00	75.00	150	285	500

KM# Tn260 PENNY
Copper, 34 mm. **Obv:** Similar to 1 Penny, KM#Tn257 **Rev:** Legend above wheat sheaf **Rev. Legend:** ADVANCE AUSTRALIA **Note:** Two varieties exist.

Date	Mintage	VG	F	VF	XF	Unc
1862	—	75.00	175	350	500	—

Warnock Bros.

Melbourne and Maldon, Victoria

KM# Tn261 1/2 PENNY
Copper, 28 mm. **Note:** Similar to 1 Penny, KM#Tn263.

Date	Mintage	VG	F	VF	XF	Unc
1861	—	50.00	100	180	325	500

KM# Tn262 PENNY
Copper, 34 mm. **Note:** Similar to 1 Penny, KM#Tn263.

Date	Mintage	VG	F	VF	XF	Unc
1861	—	35.00	75.00	145	285	450

KM# Tn263 PENNY
Bronze, 31 mm. **Note:** Two varieties exist.

Date	Mintage	VG	F	VF	XF	Unc
1863	—	35.00	75.00	145	285	450

R. S. Waterhouse

Hobart, Tasmania

KM# Tn264 1/2 PENNY
Copper, 26 mm. **Obv. Legend:** R. S. WATERHOUSE DRAPERY... **Rev:** Legend around baby ski jumper **Rev. Legend:** FOR READY MONEY... **Note:** Two varieties exist.

Date	Mintage	VG	F	VF	XF	Unc
ND	—	35.00	75.00	150	300	500

KM# Tn265 PENNY
Copper, 33 mm. **Note:** Similar to 1/2 Penny, KM#Tn264.

Date	Mintage	VG	F	VF	XF	Unc
ND	—	35.00	75.00	145	285	400

W. R. Watson & Co.

Ballarat, Victoria

KM# Tn266.1 PENNY
Copper, 34 mm. **Rev:** Vine leaf touches R of MAKER

Date	Mintage	VG	F	VF	XF	Unc
1862	—	50.00	100	180	325	500

KM# Tn266.2 PENNY
Copper, 34 mm. **Rev:** Vine leaf does not touch R of MAKER

Date	Mintage	VG	F	VF	XF	Unc
1862	—	150	300	600	1,000	—

W. Watson & Co.

Ballarat, Victoria

KM# TnF293 PENNY
Copper, 34 mm. **Rev:** Coat of arms

Date	Mintage	VG	F	VF	XF	Unc
1862 Fabrication, as struck	—	—	—	—	1,000	—

KM# TnF294 PENNY
Copper, 34 mm. **Rev:** Vine and branch

Date	Mintage	VG	F	VF	XF	Unc
1862 Fabrication, as struck	—	—	—	—	1,000	—

Weight & Johnson
Sydney, New South Wales

KM# Tn267 1/2 PENNY
Copper, 28 mm. **Obv. Legend:** LIVERPOOL & LONDON... **Rev:** Standing Justice **Note:** Four varieties exist.

Date	Mintage	VG	F	VF	XF	Unc
ND	—	35.00	75.00	150	300	500

KM# Tn268 PENNY
Copper, 34 mm.

Date	Mintage	VG	F	VF	XF	Unc
ND	—	50.00	100	175	325	500

Thomas White and Son
Westbury, Tasmania

KM# Tn269 1/2 PENNY
Copper, 28 mm. **Obv. Legend:** THOMAS WHITE AND SON... **Rev:** Legend above emu and kangaroo **Rev. Legend:** TASMANIA

Date	Mintage	VG	F	VF	XF	Unc
1855	—	75.00	175	325	500	750

KM# Tn270 PENNY
Copper, 34 mm.

Date	Mintage	VG	F	VF	XF	Unc
1855	—	35.00	75.00	145	285	450
1857	—	35.00	75.00	150	300	450

Note: Beware of modern replicas in bright copper of KM#Tn269 and Tn270 dated 1855; Key points - kangaroo's ears

Whitty & Brown
Sydney, New South Wales

KM# Tn271 PENNY
Copper, 33 mm. **Obv:** Bust **Rev:** Standing Justice **Note:** Varieties exist.

Date	Mintage	VG	F	VF	XF	Unc
ND	—	50.00	100	175	325	500

J. W. & G. Williams
Eaglehawk, Victoria

KM# Tn272 PENNY
Copper, 34 mm.

Date	Mintage	VG	F	VF	XF	Unc
ND	—	75.00	170	325	500	750

W. D. Wood
Hobart, Tasmania

KM# Tn273 1/2 PENNY
Copper, 28 mm.

Date	Mintage	VG	F	VF	XF	Unc
ND	—	30.00	60.00	125	225	350

KM# Tn274 PENNY
Copper, 34 mm.

Date	Mintage	VG	F	VF	XF	Unc
ND	—	35.00	75.00	150	300	500

KM# Tn275 PENNY
Copper, 34 mm. **Obv. Legend:** MONTPELIER RETREAT... **Rev:** Legend above building with date below **Rev. Legend:** HOBART TOWN

Date	Mintage	VG	F	VF	XF	Unc
1855	—	30.00	60.00	125	225	350

FOREIGN TOKEN ISSUES

Charles Harrold & Co., Late Joseph Lane & Son
Birmingham, England

The following tokens although struck abroad were circulated in Australia

KM# Tn290 1/2 PENNY
Copper, 29 mm.

Date	Mintage	VG	F	VF	XF	Unc
ND	—	—	—	—	6,000	—

Note: Noble Numismatics sale No. 75, 4-04, nearly XF realized approximately $6050.

Charles Harrold & Co.
Birmingham, England

KM# Tn291 1/2 PENNY
Copper, 29.5 mm. **Note:** Flan thickness: 3mm.

Date	Mintage	VG	F	VF	XF	Unc
ND	—	—	—	900	1,250	1,500

William Hodgins
Clochjordan, Ireland

KM# Tn276 PENNY
Copper

Date	Mintage	VG	F	VF	XF	Unc
1858	—	50.00	100	150	300	500

Professor Holloway
London, England

KM# Tn277.1 1/2 PENNY
Copper, 28 mm. **Obv:** J. Moore incuse on truncation of neck **Rev:** J.M. on base, border on dress

Date	Mintage	VG	F	VF	XF	Unc
1857	—	20.00	50.00	75.00	150	250
1858	—	20.00	50.00	75.00	150	250

KM# Tn277.2 1/2 PENNY
Copper, 28 mm. **Obv:** J. Moore in raised letters on trucation of neck **Rev:** Without J.M. on base **Note:** Specimen striking, made for collectors.

Date	Mintage	F	VF	XF	Unc	BU
1857	—	—	—	250	350	500

KM# Tn278.1 PENNY
Copper, 34 mm. **Obv:** J. Moore incuse on trucation of neck **Rev:**

J.M. on base, border of dress **Note:** Five varieties exist for 1857. Four varieties exist for 1858.

Date	Mintage	VG	F	VF	XF	Unc
1857	—	20.00	50.00	75.00	175	300
1858	—	20.00	50.00	75.00	175	300

KM# Tn278.2 PENNY
Copper, 34 mm. **Obv:** J. Moore in raised letters on truncation of neck **Rev:** Without J. M. on base **Note:** Specimen striking, made for collectors.

Date	Mintage	F	VF	XF	Unc	BU
1857	—	—	—	250	350	500

Joseph Lane & Son
Birmingham, England

KM# Tn279 1/2 PENNY
Copper, 29 mm. **Note:** Known in three thicknesses.

Date	Mintage	VG	F	VF	XF	Unc
ND	—	—	—	300	500	750

T. Pope & Co.
Birmingham, England

KM# Tn280 PENNY
Copper, 34 mm.

Date	Mintage	VG	F	VF	XF	Unc
ND	—	75.00	150	325	500	750

UNNAMED TOKEN ISSUES
Advance Australia

KM# Tn281 PENNY
Copper, 35 mm. **Issuer:** (J.C. Thornthwaite), Sydney **Obv:** Australian arms **Note:** A crudely struck pattern.

Date	Mintage	VG	F	VF	XF	Unc
1850 1 known	—	—	—	—	—	—

Note: In the Museum of Victoria collection

KM# Tn282.1 PENNY
Copper, 34 mm. **Issuer:** (W. J. Taylor) **Obv:** Large crosses below legend **Obv. Legend:** ADVANCE AUSTRALIA around ONE PENNY **Rev:** Emu and kangaroo with tall thin foliage behind tail

Date	Mintage	VG	F	VF	XF	Unc
ND	—	30.00	60.00	100	175	350

KM# Tn282.2 PENNY
Copper, 34 mm. **Issuer:** (W. J. Tayior) **Rev:** Thick foliage behind kangaroo's tail **Note:** Specimen stiking, made for collectors.

Date	Mintage	VG	F	VF	XF	Unc
ND	—	—	—	1,000	1,500	2,000

KM# Tn282.3 PENNY
Copper, 33 mm. **Issuer:** (Whitty & Brown), (Sydney) **Obv:** Small crosses below **Rev:** Kangaroo and emu one millimeter apart at exergue **Note:** Two varieties exist. All specimens crudely struck.

Date	Mintage	VG	F	VF	XF	Unc
ND	—	125	250	500	750	—

KM# Tn283 PENNY
Copper, 33 mm. **Issuer:** (Whitty & Brown), (Sydney) **Rev:** Drapery extends to right elbow and hangs below horizon **Note:** Varieties exist. All specimens crudely struck.

Date	Mintage	VG	F	VF	XF	Unc
ND	—	20.00	40.00	75.00	125	250

KM# Tn284 PENNY
Copper, 33 mm. **Issuer:** (Whitty & Brown), (Sydney) **Rev:** Drapery ends before right elbow and hangs above horizon **Note:** Varieties exist. All specimens crudely struck. Numerous degrees of die rotation.

Date	Mintage	VG	F	VF	XF	Unc
ND	—	35.00	75.00	150	300	500

Peace & Plenty
Melbourne, Victoria

KM# Tn285.1 PENNY
Copper, 34 mm. **Issuer:** (Heaton & Son) **Obv:** Without date **Rev:** Date and legend **Note:** Four varieties exist.

Date	Mintage	VG	F	VF	XF	Unc
1858	—	30.00	60.00	100	150	300

KM# Tn285.2 PENNY
Copper, 34 mm. **Issuer:** (Heaton & Son) **Obv:** Date **Rev:** Date without legend **Note:** Two varieties exist.

Date	Mintage	VG	F	VF	XF	Unc
1859	—	35.00	75.00	150	200	350

Peace and Plenty (Whitty & Brown)
Sydney, New South Wales

KM# Tn286.1 PENNY
Bronze, 34 mm. **Obv:** Ram, no projections from land base

Date	Mintage	VG	F	VF	XF	Unc
ND 1 known	—	—	—	750	—	—

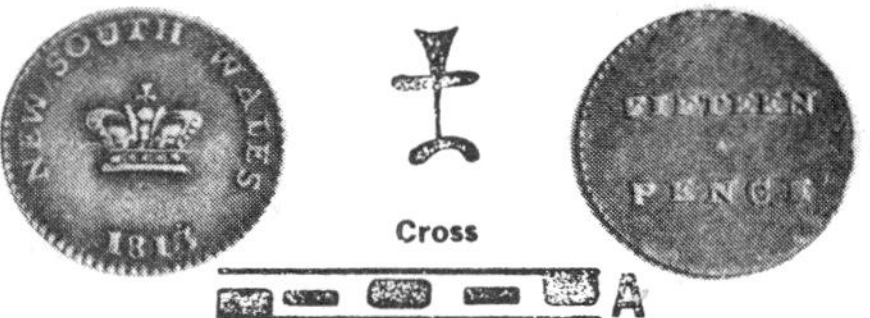

KM# Tn286.2 PENNY
Bronze, 34 mm. **Obv:** Ram, one diagonal projection from lower right of land base **Note:** All specimens crudely struck.

Date	Mintage	VG	F	VF	XF	Unc
ND	—	35.00	75.00	125	250	350

KM# Tn286.3 PENNY
Bronze, 34 mm. **Obv:** Ram, two diagonal projections from land base, one at center and one at right **Note:** All specimens crudely struck.

Date	Mintage	VG	F	VF	XF	Unc
ND	—	35.00	75.00	125	250	350

KM# Tn286.4 PENNY
Bronze, 34 mm. **Obv:** Ram, three or more diagonal projections from land base, one at center and one at right, etc. **Note:** All specimens crudely struck.

Date	Mintage	VG	F	VF	XF	Unc
ND	—	35.00	75.00	125	250	350

PROOF SETS

KM#	Date	Mintage	Identification	Issue Price	Mkt Val
PSA1	1887 (4)	2	KM#8-11 Rare	—	—

NEW SOUTH WALES
COLONY
CUT AND COUNTERMARKED COINAGE

Cross

A

KM# 1.1 15 PENCE (Dump)
0.9030 Silver **Rev. Inscription:** FIFTEEN/PENCE with 4.5 millimeters spacing **Note:** Mira type A/1.

CM Date	Host Date	Good	VG	F	VF	XF
1813	ND	2,000	3,250	5,750	9,000	—

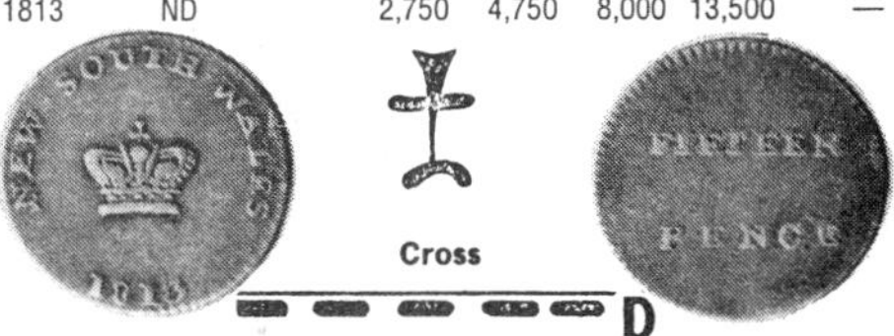

Cross

C

KM# 1.2 15 PENCE (Dump)
0.9030 Silver **Rev. Inscription:** FIFTEEN/PENCE with 4.0 millimeter spacing **Note:** Mira type C/4.

CM Date	Host Date	Good	VG	F	VF	XF
1813	ND	2,750	4,750	8,000	13,500	—

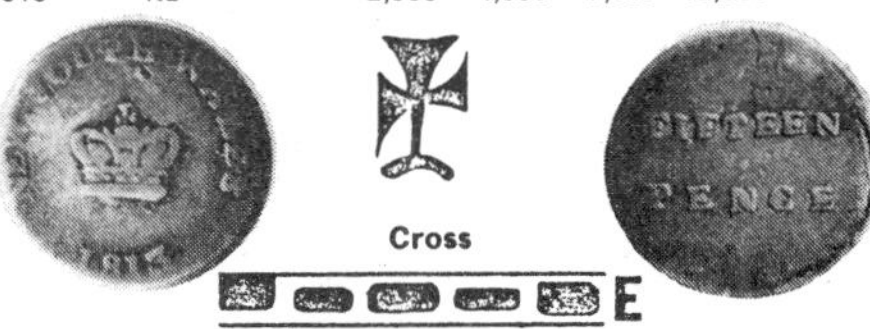

Cross

D

KM# 1.3 15 PENCE (Dump)
0.9030 Silver **Rev. Inscription:** FIFTEEN/PENCE with 5.0 millimeter spacing **Note:** Mira type D/2.

CM Date	Host Date	Good	VG	F	VF	XF
1813	ND	2,500	4,500	7,500	12,500	—

Cross

E

KM# 1.4 15 PENCE (Dump)
0.9030 Silver **Rev. Inscription:** FIFTEEN/PENCE with 3.5 millimeter spacing **Note:** Mira type E/3.

CM Date	Host Date	Good	VG	F	VF	XF
1813	ND	2,000	3,250	5,750	9,000	—

Note: Estimated original mintage; Reference: "A Classification of the New South Wales Dumps", 1977 by Dr. W. J. D. Mira.

KM# 2.1 5 SHILLING (Holey Dollar)
0.9030 Silver **Counterstamp:** NEW SOUTH WALES - 1813//FIVE SHILLINGS **Note:** Counterstamp on Bolivia, Potosi 8 Reales, KM#55.

CM Date	Host Date	Good	VG	F	VF	XF
1813	(1773-89) Rare	—	—	—	—	—

KM# 2.3 5 SHILLING (Holey Dollar)
0.9030 Silver **Counterstamp:** NEW SOUTH WALES - 1813//FIVE SHILLINGS **Note:** Counterstamp on holed Bolivia, Potosi 8 Reales, KM#73.

CM Date	Host Date	Good	VG	F	VF	XF
1813	(1791-1808) Rare	—	—	—	—	—

KM# 2.5 5 SHILLING (Holey Dollar)
0.9030 Silver **Counterstamp:** NEW SOUTH WALES - 1813//FIVE SHILLINGS **Note:** Counterstamp on holed Mexico City 8 Reales, KM#104.

CM Date	Host Date	Good	VG	F	VF	XF
1813	(1757) 1 known	—	—	—	—	—

Note: Spink Noble Numismatics sale 43, 11-93 nearly fine realized $16,080

KM# 2.6 5 SHILLING (Holey Dollar)
0.9030 Silver **Counterstamp:** NEW SOUTH WALES - 1813//FIVE SHILLINGS **Note:** Counterstamp on holed Mexico City 8 Reales, KM#106.

CM Date	Host Date	Good	VG	F	VF	XF
1813	(1772-89) Rare	—	—	—	—	—

KM# 2.7 5 SHILLING (Holey Dollar)
0.9030 Silver **Counterstamp:** NEW SOUTH WALES - 1813//FIVE SHILLINGS **Note:** Counterstamp on holed Mexico City 8 Reales, KM#107.

CM Date	Host Date	Good	VG	F	VF	XF
1813	(1789-90) Rare	—	—	—	—	—

KM# 2.9 5 SHILLING (Holey Dollar)
0.9030 Silver **Counterstamp:** NEW SOUTH WALES - 1813//FIVE SHILLINGS **Note:** Counterstamp on holed Mexico City 8 Reales, KM#109.

CM Date	Host Date	Good	VG	F	VF	XF
1813	(1791-1808) Rare	—	—	—	—	—

Note: Noble Numismatics sale No.75, 4-04, 1804 host nearly vf, counterstamp good vf realized approximately $87,250 and 1797 host, good fine/nearly fine realized approximately $41,000

KM# 2.10 5 SHILLING (Holey Dollar)
0.9030 Silver **Counterstamp:** NEW SOUTH WALES - 1813//FIVE SHILLINGS **Note:** Counterstamp on holed Mexico City 8 Reales, KM#110.

CM Date	Host Date	Good	VG	F	VF	XF
1813	(1809-10) Rare	—	—	—	—	—

KM# 2.11 5 SHILLING (Holey Dollar)
0.9030 Silver **Counterstamp:** NEW SOUTH WALES - 1813//FIVE SHILLINGS **Note:** Counterstamp on holed Peru, Lima 8 Reales, KM#78.

CM Date	Host Date	Good	VG	F	VF	XF
1813	(1772-89) Rare	—	—	—	—	—

KM# 2.13 5 SHILLING (Holey Dollar)
0.9030 Silver **Counterstamp:** NEW SOUTH WALES - 1813//FIVE SHILLINGS **Note:** Counterstamp on holed Peru, Lima 8 Reales, KM#97.

CM Date	Host Date	Good	VG	F	VF	XF
1813	(1791-1808) Rare	—	—	—	—	—

KM# 2.14 5 SHILLING (Holey Dollar)
0.9030 Silver **Counterstamp:** NEW SOUTH WALES - 1813//FIVE SHILLINGS **Note:** Counterstamp on holed Peru, Lima 8 Reales, KM#106.2.

CM Date	Host Date	Good	VG	F	VF	XF
ND	(1810) 2 known	—	—	—	—	—

KM# 2.15 5 SHILLING (Holey Dollar)
0.9030 Silver **Counterstamp:** NEW SOUTH WALES - 1813//FIVE SHILLINGS **Note:** Counterstamp on holed Spain, Madrid 8 Reales, C#71.1.

CM Date	Host Date	Good	VG	F	VF	XF
1813	(1788-1808) Rare	—	—	—	—	—

KM# 2.16 5 SHILLING (Holey Dollar)
0.9030 Silver **Counterstamp:** NEW SOUTH WALES - 1813//FIVE SHILLINGS **Note:** Counterstamp on holed Spain, Seville 8 Reales, C#71.2.

CM Date	Host Date	Good	VG	F	VF	XF
1813	(1788-1808) Rare	—	—	—	—	—

SOUTH AUSTRALIA

BRITISH COLONY

STANDARD COINAGE

KM# 1 ADELAIDE POUND
8.7500 g., 0.9170 Gold .2579 oz.

Date	Mintage	F	VF	XF	Unc	BU
1852 20-50 pieces	—	—	22,500	40,000	65,000	—

Note: Noble Numismatics sale No. 61 (Part A), 8-99, XF realized $37,500.

KM# 2 ADELAIDE POUND
8.7500 g., 0.9170 Gold .2579 oz. **Rev:** Dentilated inner circle

Date	Mintage	F	VF	XF	Unc	BU
1852	25,000	5,500	11,000	22,500	37,500	—

Note: David Akers Numismatics Pittman sale 8-99 AU realized $13,800. Noble Numismatic sale No. 75, 4-04, good vf with scratch realized approximately $18,700. Noble Numismatics sale No. 73, 7-03, good xf realized approximately $25,800 and nearly uncirculated realized approximately $36,500.

INGOTS

GOLD

The Gold Bullion Act of 1852 allowed for necessity ingots to be produced for banking purposes. Only eight Adeliade Assay office ingots are known, with only two remaining in private collections. Each of the known pieces displays unique weight and characteristics.

This example was sold through The David Akers Numismatics John Jay Pitman sale of 8-1999 realizing $149,500.

PATTERNS

Including off metal strikes

KM#	Date	Mintage	Identification	Mkt Val
Pn1	1852	7	5 Pounds. 0.9170 Gold. Restrike. The below restrike was produced at the Melbourne branch of the Royal Mint in 1921.	65,000
Pn1a	1852	2	5 Pounds. 0.9170 Silver. Restrike. Origin undocumented.	—

VICTORIA

TRIAL STRIKES

KM#	Date	Mintage	Identification	Mkt Val
TS1	1853	—	Ounce. Bronze. 6.4800 g. Milled edge.	—
TS2	1853	—	2 Ounces. Copper. 15.1800 g. Milled edge.	—
TS3	1853	—	2 Ounces. Lead. 20.2900 g.	—
TS4	1853	—	2 Ounces. Lead. 22.3200 g.	—

PRIVATE PATTERNS

Hodgkin, Taylor and Tyndall Series

Port Phillip, Kangaroo Office

These extremely rare gold patterns originated from a commercial venture set up by Messrs. Hodgkin, Taylor and Tyndall of England. Their idea was to buy up gold dust and use it to strike their own gold of 1/4, 1/2, 1 and 2 ounces which they proposed to pass on as bullion currency from their store in Melbourne. The dies were cut by W. J. Taylor and the machinery provided. This equipment arrived at Hobson's Bay on October 23, 1853, but before it could be removed and set up at the store, known as the Kangaroo Office, the availability of the British sovereign pre-empted the venture.

KM#	Date	Mintage	Identification	Mkt Val
Pn1	1853	—	1/4 Ounce. Gold. Uniface gilt copper electrotypes of both obverses and reverses of all denominations, with the exception of the 1/2 Ounce obverse, are known to exist for Pn1-Pn4e. Values range from $100 to $200. Bonded pairs have been noted.	—

Note: P.J. Downie Sale 5-87 AXF realized $23,100

KM#	Date	Mintage	Identification	Mkt Val
Pn1b	1853	—	1/4 Ounce. Copper. Milled edge.	—

KM#	Date	Mintage	Identification	Mkt Val
Pn2	1853	—	1/2 Ounce. Gold.	—

Note: Spink Australia Sale 10-77 XF realized $27,100

KM#	Date	Mintage	Identification	Mkt Val
Pn2b	1853	—	1/2 Ounce. Gilt. 6.3300 g. Restrike.	—
Pn2c	1853	—	1/2 Ounce. Copper. Milled edge.	1,500

KM#	Date	Mintage	Identification	Mkt Val
Pn3	1853	—	Ounce. Gold.	—
Pn3b	1853	—	Ounce. Gilt Lead. 24.0800 g.	—
Pn3c	1853	—	Ounce. Brass. Milled edge.	—
Pn3d	1853	—	Ounce. Copper. Milled edge.	—

KM#	Date	Mintage	Identification	Mkt Val
Pn4	1853	—	2 Ounces. Gold.	—
Pn4a	1853	—	2 Ounces. Gilt Copper.	—
Pn4b	1853	—	2 Ounces. Copper.	—
Pn4c	1853	—	2 Ounces. Pewter. Milled edge.	—
Pn4d	1854	—	2 Ounces. Copper. Milled edge.	—
Pn4e	1854	—	2 Ounces. Lead. Milled edge. Uniface gilt copper electrotypes of both obverses and reverses of all denominations, with the exception of the 1/2 Ounce obverse, are known to exist. Values range from $100 to $200. Bonded pairs have been noted.	—

KM#	Date	Mintage	Identification	Mkt Val
Pn5	ND(1855)	—	4 Pence. Copper.	—
Pn5a	ND(1855)	—	4 Pence. Gold. 41.0000 g. 35 mm.	—

Note: Noble Numismatics sale No. 73, 7-03, as struck realized approximately $35,600.

KM#	Date	Mintage	Identification	Mkt Val
Pn6	ND(1855)	—	6 Pence. Copper. Milled edge.	8,000
Pn6a	ND(1855)	—	6 Pence. Copper. Plain edge.	7,500
Pn6b	ND(1855)	—	6 Pence. Copper. Milled edge.	8,000
Pn6c	ND(1855)	—	6 Pence. Aluminum. Milled edge.	6,000
Pn6d	ND(1855)	—	6 Pence. Silver. Milled edge.	9,500
Pn6e	ND(1855)	—	6 Pence. Silver. Plain edge.	—
Pn6f	ND(1855)	—	6 Pence. Gold. Milled edge.	—
Pn6g	ND(1855)	—	6 Pence. Gold. Plain edge.	—

KM#	Date	Mintage	Identification	Mkt Val
Pn7	ND(1855)	—	Shilling. Copper. Milled edge.	7,500
Pn7a	ND(1855)	—	Shilling. Copper. Plain edge.	6,500
Pn7b	ND(1855)	—	Shilling. Silver Plated Tin. Milled edge. Tin, silver plated.	6,000
Pn7c	ND(1855)	—	Shilling. Aluminum. Milled edge.	6,000
Pn7d	ND(1855)	—	Shilling. Silver. Milled edge.	9,000
Pn7e	ND(1855)	—	Shilling. Silver. Plain edge.	7,750
Pn7f	ND(1855)	—	Shilling. Gold. Milled edge.	—
Pn7g	ND(1855)	—	Shilling. Gold. Plain edge.	—

KM#	Date	Mintage	Identification	Mkt Val
Pn8	ND(1860)	—	Shilling. Copper. Coronet bust. DEI GRATIA.	6,500
Pn8a	ND(1860)	—	Shilling. Copper. Coronet bust. DEI GRATIA. Plain edge.	6,000
Pn8b	ND(1860)	—	Shilling. Silver. Coronet bust. DEI GRATIA. Milled edge.	8,000
Pn8c	ND(1860)	—	Shilling. Silver. Coronet bust. DEI GRATIA. Plain edge.	6,500
Pn8d	ND(1860)	—	Shilling. Gold. Coronet bust. DEI GRATIA. Milled edge.	—
Pn8e	ND(1860)	—	Shilling. Gold. Coronet bust. DEI GRATIA. Plain edge.	—

KM#	Date	Mintage	Identification	Mkt Val
Pn9	ND(1860)	—	Shilling. Copper. Laureate bust. DEI GRATIA. Milled edge.	6,000
Pn9a	ND(1860)	—	Shilling. Copper. Laureate bust. DEI GRATIA. Plain edge.	6,000
Pn9b	ND(1860)	—	Shilling. Silver. Laureate bust. DEI GRATIA. Milled edge.	7,500
Pn9c	ND(1860)	—	Shilling. Silver. Laureate bust. DEI GRATIA. Plain edge.	6,000
Pn9d	ND(1860)	—	Shilling. Gold. Laureate bust. DEI GRATIA.	—

KM#	Date	Mintage	Identification	Mkt Val
Pn10	ND(1860)	—	Shilling. Silver. Coronet bust. REGINA. Plain edge.	7,500

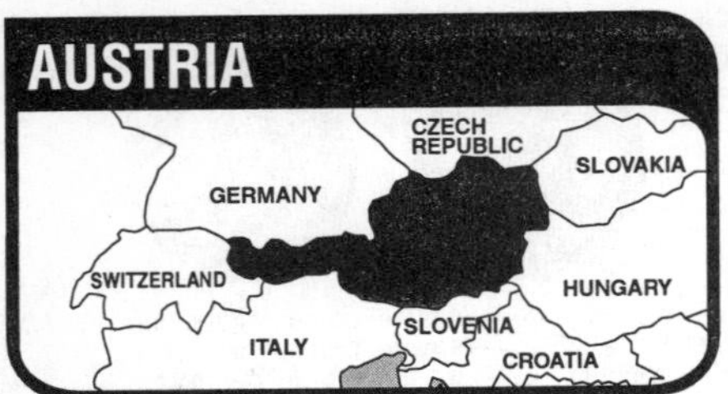

The Republic of Austria, a parliamentary democracy located in mountainous central Europe, has an area of 32,374 sq. mi. (83,850 sq. km.). Capital: Wien (Vienna). Austria is primarily an industrial country. Machinery, iron, steel, textiles, yarns and timber are exported.

The territories later to be known as Austria were overrun in pre-Roman times by various tribes, including the Celts. Upon the fall of the Roman Empire, the country became a margravate of Charlemagne's Empire. Premysl II of Otaker, King of Bohemia, gained possession in 1252, only to lose the territory to Rudolf of Habsburg in 1276. Thereafter, until World War I, the story of Austria was conducted by the ruling Habsburgs.

During the 17th century, Austrian coinage reflected the geopolitical strife of three wars. From 1618-1648, the Thirty Years' War between northern Protestants and southern Catholics produced low quality, "kipperwhipper" strikes of 12, 24, 30, 60, 75 and 150 Kreuzer. Later, during the Austrian-Turkish War, 1660-1664, coinages used to maintain soldier's salaries also reported the steady division of Hungarian territories. Finally, between 1683 and 1699, during the second Austrian-Turkish conflict, new issues of 3, 6 and 15 Kreuzers were struck, being necessary to help defray mounting expenses of the war effort.

During World War I, the Austro-Hungarian Empire was one of the Central Powers with Germany, Bulgaria and Turkey. At the end of the war, the Empire was dismembered and Austria established as an independent republic. In March, 1938, Austria was incorporated into Hitler's short-lived Greater German Reich. Allied forces of both East and West occupied Austria in April 1945, and subsequently divided it into 4 zones of military occupation. On May 15, 1955, the 4 powers formally recognized Austria as a sovereign independent democratic state.'

Francis I died on August 18, 1765. His wife Maria Theresa, decreed on July 21, 1766 that coins would be issued with the portrait of Francis and bearing the year of his death (1765). Also to be included were letters of the alphabet to indicate the actual year of issue: i.e. A-1766, G-1772, P-1780.

The posthumous coins were issued rather erratically as to denominations, years and mints. 5 denominations were made and 7 mints were used. Only the Ducat and 20 Kreuzer were made until 1780, the year in which Maria Theresa died. The other denominations were 3, 10 and 17 Kreuzer.

RULERS

Franz II (I), 1792-1835
(as Franz II, Holy Roman Emperor, 1792-1806)
(as Franz I, Austrian Emperor, 1806-1835)
Ferdinand I, 1835-1848
Franz Joseph I, 1848-1916

MINT MARKS

A, W, WI - Vienna (Wien)
(a) - Vienna (Wien)
AI,AL-IV,C-A,E,GA - Karlsburg (Alba Iulia, Transylvania)
B,K,KB - Kremnica (Kremnitz, Hungary)
BE,BE/V,BEZ,B.T. - Bistrice (Romania)
CB,CI,CI-BI(NI),CW,H,HS - Hermannstadt (Sibiu) (Transylvania)
CV (1693-94),FT,KV (1694-1700) - Klausenburg (Cluy, Transylvania)
D - Salzburg
D,G,GR - Graz (Styria)
F, HA - Hall
G,H,P-R - Gunzburg
GM - Mantua (Mantova)
(h) Shield - Vienna (Wien)
M - Milan (Milano, Lombardy)
MB 1693-1697, 1702 - Breh (Brzeg)
NB - Nagybanya (Baia Mare, Hungary)
O - Olmutz (Olomouc)
O - Oravicza (Oravita, Hungary)
S - Schmollnitz (Smolnik, Hungary)
V - Venice (Venice, Venetia)
(v) Eagle - Hall
W - Breslau (Wroclaw, Vratislav, Poland)

MINT IDENTIFICATION

To aid in determining an Austrian (Habsburg) coin's mint it is necessary to first check the coat of arms. In some cases the coat of arms will dominate the reverse. The Hungarian Madonna and child is a prime example. On more traditional Austrian design types the provincial coat of arms will be the only one on the imperial eagle's breast. When a more complicated coat of arms is used the provincial arms will usually be found in the center or at the top center usually overlapping neighboring arms.

Legend endings frequently reflect the various provincial coats of arms. Sometimes mint marks appear on coins such as the letter W for Breslau. Mintmaster's and mint officials' initials or symbols also appear and can be used to confirm the mint identity.

The following pages will present the mint name, illustrate or describe the provincial coats of arms, legend endings, mint marks, and mint officials' initials or symbols with which the mint identity can be determined.

KARLSBURG MINT

(in Transylvania)
For coat of arms and legend endings, see Hermannstadt.

MINT MARKS

E - 1797, 1819-1824, 1830-1833, 1857-1868

Nagybanya Mint

(Baia Mare)
(Hungary)

Hungarian coat of arms on imperial eagle's breast.

MINT MARKS

G – 1797, 1813-1814, 1819-1826

Salzburg Mint

Initials	Date	Name
M	1803-06	Franz Xavier Matzenkopf

MONETARY SYSTEM

Before 1857

8 Heller = 4 Pfennig = 1 Kreuzer

60 Kreuzer = 1 Florin (Gulden)

2 Florin = 1 Species or Convention Thaler

EMPIRE

UNIFORM COINAGE

KM# 2106 1/4 KREUZER

Copper

Date	Mintage	F	VF	XF	Unc
1812A	—	2.00	4.00	8.00	25.00
1812B	1,725,000	3.00	6.00	12.50	35.00
1812S	—	—	—	—	—

Note: Reported, not confirmed

KM# 2107 1/4 KREUZER

Copper **Note:** Struck until 1852 with 1816 date.

Date	Mintage	F	VF	XF	Unc
1816A	—	1.50	2.50	5.00	30.00
1816B	6,652,000	1.50	2.50	5.00	30.00
1816E Rare	—	—	—	—	—
1816G Rare	—	—	—	—	—
1816O	—	3.00	6.00	12.00	35.00
1816S	—	1.00	2.00	4.00	25.00

KM# 2180 1/4 KREUZER

Copper

Date	Mintage	F	VF	XF	Unc
1851A	—	0.50	1.00	2.00	7.50
1851B	9,637,000	1.00	3.50	6.00	10.00
1851G	—	30.00	90.00	180	300

KM# 2109 1/2 KREUZER

Copper

Date	F	VF	XF	Unc
1812A	2.00	6.00	12.00	40.00
1812B Rare	—	—	—	—
1812S	3.00	8.00	20.00	50.00

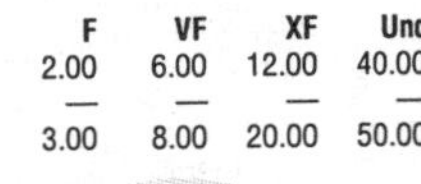

KM# 2110 1/2 KREUZER

Copper **Note:** Struck until 1852 with 1816 date.

Date	Mintage	F	VF	XF	Unc
1816A	—	1.00	2.00	4.00	25.00
1816B	6,652,000	1.50	5.00	10.00	40.00
1816E Rare	—	—	—	—	—
1816G Rare	—	—	—	—	—
1816O	—	3.00	10.00	30.00	60.00
1816S	—	2.00	6.00	12.50	40.00

KM# 2181 1/2 KREUZER

Copper

Date	Mintage	F	VF	XF	Unc
1851A	—	1.00	2.00	4.00	10.00
1851B	27,733,000	1.00	2.00	5.00	11.00
1851C	—	100	150	300	600
1851G	—	20.00	60.00	120	200

KM# 2182 5/10 KREUZER

1.6700 g., Copper **Obverse:** Small eagle

Date	Mintage	F	VF	XF	Unc
1858A	—	1.50	3.00	6.00	9.00
1858B	11,058,000	2.00	3.00	6.50	10.00
1858E	—	15.00	35.00	60.00	130
1858M	—	3.50	8.00	20.00	35.00
1858V	—	5.00	10.00	20.00	40.00
1859A	—	0.75	1.50	3.00	7.00
1859B	13,397,000	3.50	6.50	10.00	20.00
1859E	—	15.00	30.00	60.00	120
1859M	—	8.00	16.00	24.00	40.00
1859V	—	15.00	30.00	60.00	100
1860A	—	1.00	3.00	7.50	15.00
1860E	—	15.00	30.00	60.00	120
1860V	—	5.00	7.50	18.00	40.00
1861A	—	5.00	10.00	25.00	50.00
1861B	3,474,000	3.50	7.50	15.00	30.00
1863B	—	6.00	12.00	20.00	40.00
1864A	—	2.00	5.00	10.00	25.00
1864B	7,598,000	2.50	5.00	10.00	20.00
1864V	—	15.00	30.00	60.00	100
1865A	—	2.00	5.00	10.00	20.00
1865B	7,182,000	6.50	13.50	22.50	50.00
1866A	—	2.00	5.00	10.00	20.00

KM# 2183 5/10 KREUZER

1.6700 g., Copper

Date	Mintage	F	VF	XF	Unc
1877	—	5.00	15.00	20.00	40.00
1881	4,200,000	2.00	4.00	6.00	10.00
1885	2,000,000	0.75	1.50	3.00	7.00

KM# 2184 5/10 KREUZER
1.6000 g., Copper **Obverse:** Large eagle

Date	Mintage	F	VF	XF	Unc
1885	Inc. above	0.50	1.00	2.00	5.00
1891	2,000,000	3.00	6.00	12.50	15.00

KM# 2112 KREUZER
Copper

Date	Mintage	F	VF	XF	Unc
1812A	—	3.00	6.00	15.00	40.00
1812B	92,163,000	2.00	4.00	10.00	30.00
1812C	—	—	—	—	—
Note: Reported, not confirmed					
1812E	—	6.00	20.00	35.00	65.00
1812G	—	3.00	8.00	20.00	42.00
1812O	—	6.00	20.00	35.00	65.00
1812S	—	2.00	4.00	12.00	35.00

KM# 2113 KREUZER
Copper **Note:** Struck until 1852 with 1816 date.

Date	Mintage	F	VF	XF	Unc
1816A	—	1.00	2.00	4.00	25.00
1816B	54,516,000	1.00	2.00	5.00	25.00
1816E	—	7.50	15.00	35.00	110
1816G	—	2.00	6.00	12.00	32.00
1816O	—	2.00	6.00	12.00	35.00
1816S	—	2.00	6.00	12.00	35.00
1816S.	—	2.00	6.00	12.00	35.00

KM# 2185 KREUZER
Copper

Date	Mintage	F	VF	XF	Unc
1851A	—	0.50	0.75	1.50	5.00
1851B	106,458,000	1.00	1.50	3.00	6.00
1851C	—	40.00	60.00	120	250
1851E	—	8.00	15.00	30.00	80.00
1851G Small G	—	2.00	5.00	20.00	60.00
1851G Large G	—	2.00	5.00	20.00	60.00

KM# 2186 KREUZER
Copper **Obverse:** Small eagle

Date	Mintage	F	VF	XF	Unc
1858A	—	0.50	1.00	2.00	4.00
1858B	23,497,000	1.00	2.00	3.00	5.00
1858E	—	5.00	10.00	20.00	45.00
1858M	—	4.00	7.00	15.00	40.00
1858V	—	11.00	20.00	40.00	75.00
1859A	—	0.50	1.00	2.00	4.00
1859B	93,406,000	1.00	2.00	3.50	6.00
1859E	—	2.50	5.00	10.00	17.50
1859M	—	2.50	5.00	12.00	20.00
1859V	—	7.00	14.00	25.00	45.00
1860A	—	0.50	1.00	2.00	4.00
1860B	87,955,000	0.50	1.00	2.00	4.00
1860E	—	5.00	10.00	20.00	45.00
1860V	—	4.00	9.00	20.00	35.00
1861A	—	0.75	1.50	2.50	5.00
1861B	54,201,000	0.50	1.00	3.00	5.00
1861E	—	2.50	6.00	12.50	27.50
1862B	11,599,000	5.00	10.00	25.00	50.00
1862E	—	10.00	20.00	40.00	90.00
1863E	—	15.00	35.00	75.00	160
1873A	—	2.00	4.00	7.00	15.00
1878	—	0.50	1.00	2.00	4.00
1879	—	0.50	1.00	2.00	4.00
1881	37,900,000	0.25	0.50	1.50	3.00

KM# 2187 KREUZER
Copper **Obverse:** Large eagle

Date	Mintage	F	VF	XF	Unc
1885	29,000,000	0.25	0.50	1.25	3.00
1891	23,800,000	0.25	0.50	1.25	3.00

KM# 2188 2 KREUZER
Copper **Note:** Revolution 1848-1849

Date	Mintage	F	VF	XF	Unc
1848A	7,755,000	5.00	10.00	17.50	45.00

KM# 2189 2 KREUZER
Copper **Note:** 1851C is a pattern.

Date	Mintage	F	VF	XF	Unc
1851A	—	3.00	7.50	15.00	30.00
1851B	22,419,000	3.50	8.00	16.00	32.50
1851G Large G	—	8.00	15.00	30.00	85.00
1851G Small G	—	8.00	15.00	30.00	85.00

KM# 2114 3 KREUZER
0.3460 Silver **Obverse:** Bust of Franz II right **Reverse:** Crowned imperial eagle

Date	F	VF	XF	Unc
1801E	30.00	60.00	120	225
1810A	—	—	—	—
Note: Reported, not confirmed				

KM# 2115.3 3 KREUZER
8.7500 g., Copper **Obverse:** Bust of Franz II right **Obv. Legend:** REX. **Reverse:** Crowned imperial eagle **Note:** Varieties of tail feathers and heads exist.

Date	Mintage	F	VF	XF	Unc
1801E	—	15.00	30.00	75.00	150
1801F	2,762,000	10.00	15.00	35.00	100
1803F	—	20.00	40.00	60.00	140

KM# 2116 3 KREUZER
8.7500 g., Copper

Date	Mintage	F	VF	XF	Unc
1812A	—	10.00	20.00	30.00	125
1812B	13,594,000	2.00	4.00	8.00	25.00
1812B Error UH	—	8.00	17.50	25.00	75.00
1812E	—	5.00	10.00	20.00	60.00
1812G	—	4.00	10.00	20.00	60.00
1812O	—	4.00	10.00	20.00	60.00
1812S	—	3.00	6.00	12.00	35.00

KM# 2117 3 KREUZER
1.7000 g., 0.3440 Silver .0188 oz. ASW

Date	F	VF	XF	Unc
1814A Rare	—	—	—	—
1815A	7.50	15.00	30.00	60.00
1815B	10.00	20.00	40.00	90.00
1815V	7.50	15.00	30.00	60.00

KM# 2118 3 KREUZER
0.3460 Silver

Date	Mintage	F	VF	XF	Unc
1817A	—	50.00	80.00	150	300
1818B	538,000	12.00	25.00	40.00	90.00
1818V Rare	—	—	—	—	—
1819A	—	12.00	25.00	50.00	100
1820A	—	7.50	15.00	30.00	55.00
1820B	1,457,000	7.50	15.00	30.00	55.00
1820V Rare	—	—	—	—	—
1820G	—	—	—	—	—
1821A	—	7.50	15.00	30.00	60.00
1821B	4,894,000	7.50	15.00	30.00	60.00
1821E	—	25.00	50.00	75.00	200
1821G	—	25.00	50.00	75.00	175
1822A	79,000	12.00	25.00	50.00	100
1823A	35,000	25.00	45.00	75.00	150
1823B Rare	Inc. above	—	—	—	—
1824A Rare	37,000	—	—	—	—
1824G	Inc. above	25.00	50.00	75.00	175

KM# 2119 3 KREUZER
0.3460 Silver

Date	Mintage	F	VF	XF	Unc
1825A	51,000	25.00	50.00	75.00	175
1826A	—	8.00	15.00	30.00	50.00
1826B	375,000	8.00	15.00	30.00	60.00
1826E	—	25.00	40.00	75.00	175
1827A	118,000	40.00	80.00	150	250
1827B	—	45.00	75.00	150	250
1828A	—	8.00	15.00	30.00	50.00
1828B	965,000	8.00	15.00	30.00	60.00
1828E	—	35.00	60.00	120	200
1828G	—	40.00	70.00	140	225
1829A	—	8.00	15.00	30.00	50.00
1829B	133,000	22.50	40.00	75.00	160
1829E	—	17.50	30.00	60.00	140
1829G	—	40.00	70.00	140	225
1830A	—	8.00	15.00	30.00	55.00
1830B	76,000	40.00	80.00	150	250
1830E	—	40.00	70.00	140	225
1831A	—	—	—	—	—
Note: Reported, not confirmed					

KM# 2121 3 KREUZER
0.3460 Silver **Obverse:** Larger head

Date	F	VF	XF	Unc
1831A	30.00	50.00	80.00	175
Note: Reported, not confirmed				
1832A	5.00	10.00	20.00	50.00
1833A	5.00	10.00	20.00	50.00
1833C	8.00	15.00	30.00	60.00
1834A	20.00	40.00	70.00	130
1834C	30.00	50.00	80.00	175
1835A	8.00	15.00	30.00	60.00

KM# 2120 3 KREUZER
0.3460 Silver **Obverse:** Short braids **Note:** Struck in a collar.

Date	F	VF	XF	Unc
1831A Rare	—	—	—	—

KM# 2190 3 KREUZER
0.3460 Silver **Obverse:** Head of Ferdinand I right **Reverse:** Eagle, value on chest

Date	F	VF	XF	Unc
1835A	20.00	30.00	65.00	140
1835E	30.00	50.00	125	250
1836A	15.00	25.00	55.00	120
1836E	30.00	50.00	125	250

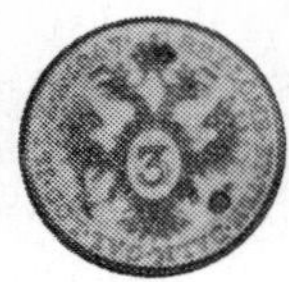

KM# 2191 3 KREUZER
0.3460 Silver

Date	Mintage	F	VF	XF	Unc
1837A	—	3.50	7.50	15.00	40.00
1837C	—	25.00	40.00	75.00	150
1837E	—	25.00	40.00	75.00	150
1838A	—	3.50	7.50	15.00	45.00
1838B	130,000	15.00	25.00	40.00	100
1838C	—	10.00	20.00	35.00	75.00
1838E	—	15.00	25.00	50.00	110
1839A	—	4.00	8.00	15.00	40.00
1839C	—	12.50	25.00	50.00	100
1839E	—	12.50	25.00	50.00	100
1840A	—	2.50	5.00	10.00	30.00
1840E	—	12.50	25.00	45.00	90.00
1841A	—	15.00	25.00	50.00	110
1841E	—	35.00	60.00	100	175
1842A	—	6.00	12.00	20.00	50.00
1842E	—	15.00	25.00	50.00	110
1843A	—	10.00	15.00	30.00	80.00
1843E	—	15.00	25.00	50.00	110
1844A	—	6.00	10.00	20.00	50.00
1844E	—	15.00	25.00	50.00	110
1845A	—	3.00	7.50	15.00	35.00
1845E	—	15.00	30.00	55.00	120
1846A	—	2.50	5.00	12.50	30.00
1846E	—	15.00	30.00	55.00	120
1847A	—	2.50	5.00	12.50	30.00
1847C	—	5.00	10.00	20.00	45.00
1847E	—	15.00	30.00	55.00	120
1848/5A	—	3.50	7.00	15.00	35.00
1848A	—	2.50	5.00	12.50	30.00
1848E	—	35.00	60.00	100	175

KM# 2192 3 KREUZER
0.3460 Silver **Note:** This issue was struck in Mantua by the Austrian garrison under General Josef Radetzky during the siege of March 18-22, 1848 by Italian rebels.

Date	F	VF	XF	Unc
1848GM	400	500	800	1,500
Note: Swan above mint mark				
1848GM	400	500	800	1,500
Note: Without swan above mint mark				

KM# 2193 3 KREUZER
Copper **Note:** Varieties of size of mint mark exist.

Date	Mintage	F	VF	XF	Unc
1851A	—	6.00	12.00	25.00	100
1851B	7,173,000	6.00	12.50	25.00	150
1851G	—	10.00	20.00	55.00	160

KM# 2194 4 KREUZER
Copper

Date	Mintage	F	VF	XF	Unc
1860A	—	2.00	6.00	12.00	40.00
1860B	—	2.00	6.00	12.00	35.00
1860E	—	10.00	25.00	60.00	160
1861A	—	2.00	6.00	12.00	35.00
1861B	18,470,000	2.00	6.00	12.00	35.00
1861E	—	7.00	20.00	50.00	140
1862B	383,000	3.00	9.00	16.00	40.00
1864B	6,666,000	2.00	6.00	12.00	35.00

KM# 2122 5 KREUZER
0.4380 Silver

Date	F	VF	XF	Unc
1815A	10.00	20.00	30.00	60.00

KM# 2123 5 KREUZER
0.4380 Silver

Date	Mintage	F	VF	XF	Unc
1817A	—	25.00	40.00	75.00	175
1818A	—	10.00	20.00	30.00	75.00
1818B	538,000	10.00	20.00	30.00	75.00
1819A Rare	—	—	—	—	—
1820A	—	10.00	20.00	30.00	75.00
1820B	1,457,000	10.00	20.00	30.00	75.00
1820G Rare	—	—	—	—	—
1820V	—	15.00	35.00	60.00	125
1821A	—	10.00	20.00	30.00	75.00
1821B	4,894,000	10.00	25.00	40.00	90.00
1821E	—	25.00	50.00	75.00	175
1821G	—	20.00	40.00	70.00	140
1822E Rare	5,791	—	—	—	—
1822G	—	30.00	50.00	75.00	125
1823A	—	30.00	50.00	75.00	125
1824A Rare	—	—	—	—	—
1824G	—	30.00	50.00	75.00	125

KM# 2124 5 KREUZER
0.4380 Silver **Obverse:** Bust with short hair, one ribbon on neck

Date	Mintage	F	VF	XF	Unc
1825A	15,000	75.00	100	200	400
1826A	53,000	60.00	90.00	175	350
1826E Rare	Inc. above	—	—	—	—
1827A Rare	18,000	—	—	—	—
1828A	44,000	60.00	90.00	175	350
1830A	—	60.00	90.00	175	350

KM# 2125 5 KREUZER
0.4380 Silver **Obverse:** Bust with short hair, both ribbons on neck

Date	F	VF	XF	Unc
1831A Rare	—	—	—	—

KM# 2126 5 KREUZER
0.4380 Silver **Obverse:** Larger head

Date	Mintage	F	VF	XF	Unc
1832A	—	20.00	35.00	60.00	125
1833A	29,000	20.00	40.00	70.00	150
1834A	31,000	20.00	35.00	60.00	125
1835A	—	15.00	25.00	50.00	100

KM# 2195 5 KREUZER
0.4380 Silver

Date	F	VF	XF	Unc
1835A	25.00	50.00	100	185
1836A	12.50	25.00	50.00	110

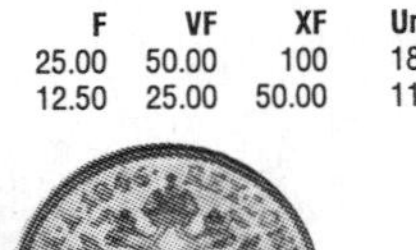

KM# 2196 5 KREUZER
0.4380 Silver

Date	Mintage	F	VF	XF	Unc
1837A	—	5.00	10.00	20.00	45.00
1838A	—	5.00	10.00	20.00	45.00
1838B	130,000	—	—	—	—
Note: Reported, not confirmed					
1839A	—	5.00	10.00	20.00	45.00
1839C	—	7.50	17.50	35.00	75.00
1840A	—	7.50	17.50	35.00	75.00
1840C	—	5.00	10.00	20.00	45.00
1842A	—	15.00	30.00	60.00	125

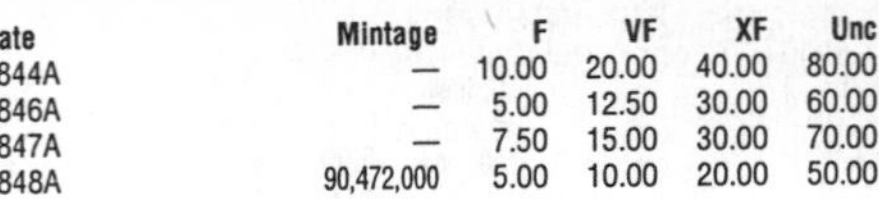

Date	Mintage	F	VF	XF	Unc
1844A	—	10.00	20.00	40.00	80.00
1846A	—	5.00	12.50	30.00	60.00
1847A	—	7.50	15.00	30.00	70.00
1848A	90,472,000	5.00	10.00	20.00	50.00

KM# 2197 5 KREUZER
1.3333 g., 0.3750 Silver .0161 oz. ASW

Date	Mintage	F	VF	XF	Unc
1858A	—	2.00	3.50	7.50	15.00
1858B	851	250	350	600	1,100
1858V	—	200	300	450	750
1859A	—	2.00	3.50	7.50	15.00
1859M	—	10.00	15.00	25.00	40.00
1859V	—	10.00	15.00	25.00	40.00
1860A	—	—	—	—	—
1860B	851	250	350	600	1,100
1860V	—	50.00	75.00	100	175
1863A	1,013,000	5.00	8.00	16.00	40.00
1864A	1,922,000	2.00	3.50	7.50	15.00

KM# 2198 5 KREUZER
1.3333 g., 0.3750 Silver .0161 oz. ASW **Obverse:** Head with heavier whiskers

Date	Mintage	F	VF	XF	Unc
1867A	69,000	125	150	350	750

KM# 2128 6 KREUZER
Copper **Obverse:** Bust of Franz II right

Date	F	VF	XF	Unc
1803F Rare	—	—	—	—

KM# 2199 6 KREUZER
2.2300 g., 0.4280 Silver .0306 oz. ASW **Note:** Revolution 1848-1849

Date	Mintage	F	VF	XF	Unc
1848A	90,400,000	3.00	5.00	10.00	20.00
1848B	—	25.00	40.00	75.00	140
1848C	—	5.00	10.00	20.00	50.00

KM# 2200 6 KREUZER
1.1900 g., 0.4380 Silver .0268 oz. ASW **Note:** The 1849 dated issues were struck from 1849-1852 and restruck again in 1859-1870.

Date	F	VF	XF	Unc
1849A	1.50	3.50	7.50	15.00
1849B	15.00	30.00	75.00	140
1849C	5.00	10.00	20.00	50.00

KM# 2129 7 KREUZER
4.6800 g., 0.2500 Silver .0376 oz. ASW **Note:** Overstruck on 1795 dated 12 Kreuzer pieces, KM#2137.

Date	Mintage	F	VF	XF	Unc
1802A	—	5.00	10.00	20.00	60.00
1802B	102,034,000	5.00	10.00	20.00	60.00
1802C	—	5.00	10.00	25.00	75.00
1802E	—	20.00	40.00	65.00	200
1802F	—	25.00	50.00	80.00	225
1802G	—	17.50	35.00	60.00	130

KM# 2131 10 KREUZER
0.5000 Silver **Obverse:** Crowned bust in wreath **Reverse:** Eagle **Rev. Legend:** ...D. LO. SAL. WIRC.

Date	F	VF	XF	Unc
1809A	40.00	75.00	160	275
1810A	35.00	70.00	140	225

KM# 2132 10 KREUZER
0.5000 Silver **Rev. Legend:** ...LO: WI: ET IN FR: D:

Date	Mintage	F	VF	XF	Unc
1814A Rare	—	—	—	—	—
1815A	—	15.00	30.00	60.00	120
1815B	1,800,000	15.00	30.00	60.00	120
1815C	—	20.00	40.00	75.00	160

KM# 2133 10 KREUZER
0.5000 Silver **Rev. Legend:** ...GAL. LOD. IL. REX. A. A.

Date	Mintage	F	VF	XF	Unc
1817A	—	45.00	80.00	150	275
1818A Rare	—	—	—	—	—
1818B Rare	—	—	—	—	—
1818G Rare	—	—	—	—	—
1818V	—	25.00	50.00	100	175
1819A	12,000	75.00	150	225	375
1820A Rare	—	—	—	—	—
1820B Rare	—	—	—	—	—
1820G Rare	—	—	—	—	—
1821B Rare	—	—	—	—	—
1821G	—	50.00	90.00	150	275
1821V Rare	—	—	—	—	—
1822G	—	75.00	150	225	375
1823A	—	30.00	50.00	80.00	175
1823G	—	30.00	60.00	120	225
1824A	—	30.00	60.00	100	200
1824G Rare	—	—	—	—	—

KM# 2134 10 KREUZER
0.5000 Silver **Obverse:** Older head of Franz II right, one ribbon on neck **Reverse:** Eagle, value below

Date	Mintage	F	VF	XF	Unc
1825A	—	40.00	80.00	160	265
1826A	—	35.00	70.00	140	225
1827A	—	35.00	70.00	140	225
1828A	—	35.00	70.00	140	200
1828E	—	45.00	90.00	175	300
1829A Rare	20,000	—	—	—	—
1829E	Inc. above	35.00	75.00	150	250
1830A	—	35.00	75.00	150	250
1830B	45,000	150	275	350	450
1830E	—	40.00	80.00	160	265

KM# 2135 10 KREUZER
0.5000 Silver **Obverse:** Both ribbons on neck

Date	F	VF	XF	Unc
1831A	—	—	—	—

Note: Reported, not confirmed

KM# 2136 10 KREUZER
0.5000 Silver **Obverse:** Larger head

Date	F	VF	XF	Unc
1832A	20.00	30.00	60.00	135
1833A	20.00	30.00	65.00	150
1834A	20.00	30.00	70.00	160
1835A	35.00	60.00	120	250

KM# 2201 10 KREUZER
0.5000 Silver **Obverse:** Head of Ferdinand I right **Reverse:** Eagle, value below

Date	F	VF	XF	Unc
1835A	20.00	35.00	70.00	175
1835E Rare	—	—	—	—
1836/5A	20.00	30.00	60.00	160
1836A	10.00	20.00	40.00	120
1836E Rare	—	—	—	—

KM# 2202 10 KREUZER
0.5000 Silver

Date	F	VF	XF	Unc
1837A	7.00	15.00	30.00	60.00
1837C	10.00	20.00	40.00	80.00
1837E	17.50	35.00	65.00	150
1838A	17.50	35.00	65.00	150
1838C	8.00	20.00	40.00	70.00
1839A	7.50	15.00	30.00	60.00
1839C	5.00	10.00	20.00	50.00
1839E	20.00	40.00	70.00	160
1840A	5.00	12.50	25.00	60.00
1840E	22.00	45.00	75.00	200
1841E	17.50	35.00	65.00	150
1842A	5.00	12.50	25.00	60.00
1842E	15.00	30.00	50.00	120
1843/2A	5.00	10.00	20.00	50.00
1843A	5.00	10.00	20.00	50.00
1843E	17.50	35.00	65.00	150
1844A	5.00	10.00	20.00	50.00
1844E	17.50	35.00	65.00	150
1845A	5.00	10.00	20.00	50.00
1845E	10.00	25.00	50.00	100
1846A	5.00	10.00	20.00	50.00
1846E	15.00	30.00	50.00	120
1847A	7.00	15.00	30.00	60.00
1847E	20.00	40.00	70.00	160
1848A	20.00	40.00	70.00	160
1848E	20.00	40.00	70.00	160

KM# 2203 10 KREUZER
2.1600 g., 0.9000 Silver .0625 oz. ASW

Date	Mintage	F	VF	XF	Unc
1852A	—	20.00	40.00	80.00	120
1853A	—	7.50	15.00	30.00	50.00
1853B	31,000	25.00	50.00	100	160
1854A	—	15.00	30.00	50.00	90.00
1855A	—	7.50	15.00	25.00	50.00

KM# 2204 10 KREUZER
2.0000 g., 0.5000 Silver .0322 oz. ASW

Date	Mintage	F	VF	XF	Unc
1858A	—	6.00	12.00	25.00	37.50
1858V	—	100	150	250	500
1859A	—	—	—	—	—
1859M	—	5.00	10.00	20.00	40.00
1859V	—	8.00	16.00	30.00	60.00
1860V	—	9.00	18.00	40.00	75.00
1861V	—	15.00	30.00	50.00	110
1862V	—	30.00	50.00	80.00	180
1863A	—	7.00	15.00	30.00	45.00
1864A	1,050,000	10.00	20.00	30.00	65.00
1864V	36,000	150	250	400	650
1865V	1,198,000	10.00	20.00	30.00	80.00

KM# 2205 10 KREUZER
2.0000 g., 0.5000 Silver .0322 oz. ASW **Obverse:** Head of Franz Joseph right with heavier whiskers

Date	Mintage	F	VF	XF	Unc
1867A	59,000	150	260	450	700

KM# 2206 10 KREUZER
1.6667 g., 0.4000 Silver .0214 oz. ASW

Date	Mintage	F	VF	XF	Unc
1868	12,000,000	0.75	1.00	3.00	8.00
1869	30,000,000	0.75	1.00	3.00	10.00
1870	35,000,000	0.75	1.00	2.50	8.00
1871	2,000,000	12.50	25.00	60.00	100
1872	70,000,000	0.25	0.50	1.00	6.00

KM# 2138 15 KREUZER
Copper

Date	Mintage	F	VF	XF	Unc
1807A	—	3.00	5.00	10.00	50.00
1807B	22,007,000	3.00	5.00	10.00	50.00
1087B	—	100	150	250	500

Date	Mintage	F	VF	XF	Unc
1807E	—	10.00	20.00	45.00	150
1807G	—	15.00	30.00	75.00	275
1807S	—	3.00	5.00	10.00	55.00

KM# 2139 20 KREUZER
6.6800 g., 0.5830 Silver .1252 oz. ASW

Date	Mintage	F	VF	XF	Unc
1802A	—	9.00	20.00	40.00	90.00
1802B	1,359,000	7.00	15.00	27.50	60.00
1802C	—	7.00	15.00	27.50	60.00
1802E	—	15.00	35.00	60.00	120
1802G	—	12.00	25.00	50.00	90.00
1802H	—	9.00	20.00	40.00	85.00
1803A	—	7.00	15.00	27.50	55.00
1803B	8,469,000	7.00	15.00	27.50	60.00
1803C	5,925,000	7.00	15.00	30.00	70.00
1803E	—	7.00	15.00	30.00	75.00
1803F	—	7.00	15.00	30.00	70.00
1803G	—	9.00	20.00	40.00	80.00
1803H	—	12.00	25.00	50.00	100
1804A	—	9.00	20.00	40.00	80.00
1804B	5,693,000	7.00	15.00	27.50	60.00
1804C	566,000	7.00	15.00	30.00	70.00
1804E	—	7.00	15.00	27.50	65.00
1804F	651,000	7.00	15.00	30.00	70.00
1804G	—	7.00	15.00	30.00	60.00

KM# 2140 20 KREUZER
6.6800 g., 0.5830 Silver .1252 oz. ASW **Rev. Legend:** ...D. LOTH. VEN. SAL.

Date	Mintage	F	VF	XF	Unc
1804A	—	25.00	45.00	80.00	175
1804F Rare	—	—	—	—	—
Note: Mintage included in KM#2139					
1804H Rare	—	—	—	—	—
1805A	—	6.00	12.00	25.00	60.00
1805B	8,402,000	5.00	10.00	20.00	60.00
1805C	1,993,000	7.00	15.00	30.00	80.00
1805E	—	7.00	15.00	25.00	60.00
1805G	—	10.00	20.00	40.00	90.00
1806A	—	5.00	10.00	20.00	55.00
1806B	19,090,000	5.00	10.00	20.00	60.00
1806C	2,977,000	6.00	12.00	25.00	60.00
1806D	—	10.00	20.00	40.00	85.00
1806E Rare	—	—	—	—	—
1806G	—	10.00	20.00	40.00	90.00

KM# 2141 20 KREUZER
6.6800 g., 0.5830 Silver .1252 oz. ASW **Rev. Legend:** ...D. LO. SAL. WIRC.

Date	Mintage	F	VF	XF	Unc
1806A	—	7.00	15.00	30.00	75.00
1806B	—	15.00	30.00	60.00	120
Note: Mintage included in.KM#2140					
1806C	—	25.00	55.00	100	175
1807A	—	7.00	15.00	30.00	75.00
1807B	6,723,000	12.00	25.00	45.00	95.00
1807C	2,421,000	12.00	25.00	45.00	95.00
1807D	—	12.00	25.00	45.00	100
1808A	—	5.00	10.00	20.00	50.00
1808B	3,235,000	7.00	15.00	30.00	75.00
1808C	1,188,000	5.00	10.00	20.00	55.00
1808D	—	10.00	20.00	40.00	80.00
1808E	—	7.00	15.00	35.00	80.00

Date	Mintage	F	VF	XF	Unc
1808G	—	7.00	15.00	30.00	70.00
1809A	—	5.00	10.00	20.00	55.00
1809B	7,239,000	7.00	15.00	27.50	65.00
1809C	2,381,000	7.00	15.00	27.50	60.00
1809D	—	12.00	25.00	50.00	100
1809E	—	7.00	15.00	35.00	80.00
1809G	—	5.00	10.00	20.00	50.00
1810A	—	5.00	10.00	20.00	50.00
1810C	714,000	—	—	—	—
1810E	—	50.00	100	150	200
1810G	—	12.00	25.00	50.00	100
1812C	92,000	—	—	—	—
1813C	55,000	—	—	—	—
1814C Rare	—	—	—	—	—

KM# 2142 20 KREUZER

6.6800 g., 0.5830 Silver .1252 oz. ASW **Rev. Legend:** ...LO WI: ET. IN FR D.

Date	Mintage	F	VF	XF	Unc
1811A	—	5.00	10.00	20.00	45.00
1811B	580,000	9.00	20.00	40.00	80.00
1811E	—	12.00	25.00	50.00	100
1812A	—	5.00	10.00	20.00	45.00
1812B	774,000	20.00	40.00	80.00	120
1812E	—	10.00	20.00	40.00	80.00
1812G	—	10.00	20.00	40.00	80.00
1813A	—	5.00	10.00	20.00	50.00
1813B	1,103,000	6.00	12.00	25.00	50.00
1813E	—	6.00	12.00	25.00	55.00
1813G	—	100	150	200	300
1814A	—	5.00	10.00	20.00	45.00
1814B	1,020,999	7.00	15.00	35.00	70.00
1814C	—	7.00	15.00	30.00	60.00
1814E	—	10.00	20.00	40.00	80.00
1814G	—	7.00	15.00	35.00	70.00
1815A	—	5.00	10.00	20.00	45.00
1815B	1,042,999	4.00	8.00	15.00	45.00
1815C	128,000	6.00	12.00	25.00	50.00
1815E	—	7.00	15.00	30.00	65.00
1815G	—	6.00	12.00	25.00	50.00
1815	—	15.00	30.00	60.00	120
1816B	5,773,000	10.00	20.00	40.00	80.00
1816C	785,000	—	—	—	—

Note: Reported, not confirmed

KM# 2143 20 KREUZER

6.6800 g., 0.5830 Silver .1252 oz. ASW **Rev. Legend:** ...GAL. LOD. IL. REX. A. A.

Date	Mintage	F	VF	XF	Unc
1817A	—	5.00	10.00	20.00	45.00
1818A	—	5.00	10.00	20.00	45.00
1818B	2,703,000	5.00	10.00	20.00	55.00
1818C	33,000	10.00	20.00	40.00	80.00
1818E	—	7.00	15.00	30.00	60.00
1818G	—	10.00	20.00	40.00	80.00
1818V	—	6.00	12.00	25.00	55.00
1818V FNANCISCUS (error)	—	60.00	100	150	375
1819A	—	5.00	10.00	20.00	45.00
1819C	81,000	25.00	45.00	75.00	140
1819E	—	8.00	15.00	30.00	60.00
1819M	—	7.00	15.00	25.00	50.00
1820A	—	5.00	10.00	20.00	45.00
1820B	1,118,000	12.00	25.00	50.00	100
1820C	28,000	10.00	20.00	40.00	80.00
1820E	—	7.00	15.00	30.00	65.00
1820G	—	25.00	45.00	75.00	140
1821A	—	6.00	12.00	25.00	55.00
1821B	1,075,000	10.00	20.00	40.00	80.00
1821C	116,000	20.00	40.00	70.00	130
1821E	—	7.00	15.00	30.00	70.00
1821G	—	25.00	45.00	75.00	140
1822A	—	6.00	12.00	25.00	55.00
1822B	269,000	10.00	20.00	40.00	80.00
1822C	165,000	20.00	40.00	70.00	130
1822E	—	7.00	15.00	30.00	75.00
1822G	—	12.00	25.00	45.00	85.00
1823A	—	5.00	10.00	20.00	45.00
1823B	324,000	25.00	45.00	75.00	140
1823C	96,000	30.00	50.00	90.00	150
1823E	—	6.00	12.00	25.00	55.00
1823G	—	12.00	25.00	50.00	100
1824A	—	5.00	10.00	20.00	45.00
1824B	14,000	40.00	60.00	90.00	175
1824E	—	6.00	12.00	25.00	60.00
1824G	—	6.00	12.00	25.00	55.00

KM# 2144 20 KREUZER

6.6800 g., 0.5830 Silver .1252 oz. ASW **Obverse:** Small bust with short hair

Date	Mintage	F	VF	XF	Unc
1825A	—	3.50	7.00	15.00	35.00
1825B	373,000	20.00	40.00	70.00	120
1825E	—	6.00	12.00	25.00	50.00
1826A	—	3.50	7.00	15.00	35.00
1826B	—	6.00	12.00	25.00	50.00
1826C	—	—	—	—	—
Note: Reported, not confirmed					
1826E	—	6.00	12.00	25.00	50.00
1826G Rare	—	—	—	—	—
1827A	—	3.50	7.00	15.00	35.00
1827B	1,053,000	7.00	15.00	30.00	60.00
1827C	924,000	5.00	10.00	20.00	40.00
1827E	—	6.00	12.00	25.00	50.00
1827G	—	7.00	15.00	30.00	60.00
1828A	—	3.50	7.00	15.00	35.00
1828B	2,402,000	6.00	12.00	25.00	50.00
1828E	—	6.00	12.00	25.00	50.00

KM# 2145 20 KREUZER

6.6800 g., 0.5830 Silver .1252 oz. ASW **Obverse:** Large bust with short hair

Date	Mintage	F	VF	XF	Unc
1829A	—	5.00	10.00	15.00	30.00
1829B	2,319,000	6.00	12.50	17.50	45.00
1829E	—	10.00	25.00	80.00	150
1830A	—	5.00	10.00	15.00	35.00
1830B Small	2,348,000	5.00	10.00	15.00	30.00
1830B Large	Inc. above	5.00	10.00	15.00	30.00
1830C	1,754,000	5.00	10.00	15.00	30.00
1830E	—	5.00	10.00	15.00	30.00

KM# 2146 20 KREUZER

6.6800 g., 0.5830 Silver .1252 oz. ASW **Obverse:** Ribbons on wreath forward across neck

Date	F	VF	XF	Unc
1831A	40.00	80.00	175	300

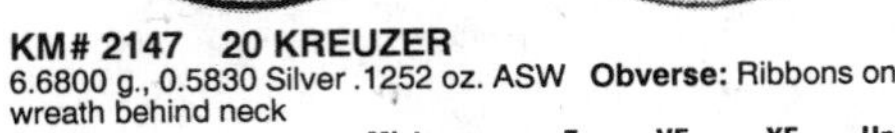

KM# 2147 20 KREUZER

6.6800 g., 0.5830 Silver .1252 oz. ASW **Obverse:** Ribbons on wreath behind neck

Date	Mintage	F	VF	XF	Unc
1831A	—	3.00	6.00	12.00	30.00
1831C	—	10.00	20.00	40.00	80.00
1831M	—	8.00	17.00	30.00	60.00
1831V	—	12.00	25.00	45.00	90.00
1832A	—	3.00	6.00	12.00	25.00
1832B	—	100	150	250	400
1832C	5,122,000	5.00	10.00	20.00	45.00
1832M	—	7.00	15.00	30.00	60.00
1833A	—	6.00	12.00	25.00	50.00
1833B	—	7.00	15.00	30.00	60.00
1833C	1,818,000	6.00	12.00	25.00	50.00
1833E	—	8.00	17.00	30.00	70.00
1834A	—	3.50	7.00	15.00	40.00
1834B	—	6.00	12.00	25.00	50.00
1834C	1,517,000	6.00	12.00	25.00	50.00
1834E	—	6.00	12.00	25.00	50.00
1835A	—	5.00	10.00	20.00	45.00
1835B	—	5.00	10.00	20.00	45.00
1835C	1,489,000	6.00	12.00	25.00	50.00
1835E	—	5.00	10.00	20.00	45.00

KM# 2207 20 KREUZER

6.6800 g., 0.5830 Silver .1252 oz. ASW

Date	Mintage	F	VF	XF	Unc
1835A	—	20.00	40.00	75.00	150
1835C	295,000	25.00	50.00	90.00	180
1835E	—	35.00	75.00	125	250
1836A	—	10.00	20.00	45.00	90.00
1836E	—	32.00	70.00	115	230

KM# 2208 20 KREUZER

6.6800 g., 0.5830 Silver .1252 oz. ASW

Date	Mintage	F	VF	XF	Unc
1837A	—	5.00	10.00	20.00	45.00
1837B	—	7.50	15.00	30.00	60.00
1837C	484,000	10.00	20.00	40.00	80.00
1837E	—	10.00	22.00	45.00	100
1837M	—	40.00	75.00	150	250
1838A	—	5.00	10.00	20.00	45.00
1838B	—	5.00	10.00	20.00	45.00
1838C	625,000	10.00	20.00	40.00	80.00
1838/7E	—	8.00	16.50	35.00	80.00
1838E	—	6.00	12.00	25.00	60.00
1838M	—	30.00	60.00	100	225
1839A	—	5.00	10.00	20.00	45.00
1839B	—	25.00	50.00	75.00	150
1839C	220,000	15.00	30.00	60.00	120
1839E	—	4.00	9.00	20.00	60.00
1840A	—	3.00	5.00	10.00	30.00
1840C	1,122,000	3.00	7.00	15.00	35.00
1840E	—	10.00	20.00	40.00	80.00
1840M	—	25.00	50.00	90.00	160
1841A	—	2.50	4.00	8.00	30.00
1841C	2,543,000	5.00	10.00	20.00	45.00
1841E	—	4.00	9.00	20.00	60.00
1842A	—	2.50	5.00	10.00	35.00
1842C	644,000	5.00	10.00	20.00	45.00
1842E	—	12.00	25.00	50.00	100
1842M	—	10.00	20.00	40.00	80.00
1843A	—	20.00	40.00	70.00	130
1843C	1,257,000	5.00	10.00	20.00	45.00
1843E	—	5.00	15.00	30.00	80.00
1843M	—	5.00	10.00	20.00	45.00
1844A	—	3.00	5.00	10.00	30.00
1844C	1,492,000	5.00	10.00	20.00	45.00
1844E	—	4.00	9.00	20.00	80.00
1844M	—	7.00	15.00	30.00	60.00
1845A	—	2.50	5.00	10.00	35.00
1845C	1,461,000	3.00	6.00	14.00	35.00
1845E	—	9.00	18.00	35.00	90.00
1845M	—	7.00	15.00	30.00	60.00
1846A	—	2.50	5.00	10.00	35.00
1846C	1,549,000	3.00	6.00	14.00	35.00
1846/5E	—	15.00	35.00	60.00	135
1846E	—	13.50	27.50	50.00	120
1846M	—	7.00	15.00	35.00	70.00
1847A	—	3.00	6.00	10.00	30.00
1847C	1,528,000	3.00	6.00	15.00	35.00
1847E	—	7.00	15.00	30.00	70.00
1847M	—	25.00	50.00	90.00	150
1848A	13,632,000	3.00	6.00	10.00	30.00
1848C	2,241,000	3.00	6.00	10.00	30.00
1848E	—	12.00	25.00	45.00	100

KM# 2209 20 KREUZER

6.6800 g., 0.5830 Silver .1252 oz. ASW **Note:** This issue was struck in Mantus by the Austrian garrison under General Josef Radetzky during the seige of March 18-22, 1848 by Italian rebels.

Date	Mintage	F	VF	XF	Unc
1848GM	7,799	200	350	450	900

KM# 2211 20 KREUZER

4.3200 g., 0.9000 Silver .1250 oz. ASW

Date	Mintage	F	VF	XF	Unc
1852A	—	4.00	8.00	18.00	30.00
1852B	4,926,000	5.00	8.00	15.00	32.00
1852C	1,687,000	50.00	100	150	325
1852E	—	75.00	150	275	650
1853A	—	4.00	8.00	18.00	35.00
1853C	1,590,000	5.50	11.00	22.00	45.00
1853E	—	12.50	25.00	50.00	90.00
1854A	—	4.00	8.00	18.00	30.00
1854B	2,287,000	5.00	8.00	18.00	40.00
1854C	2,098,000	6.50	13.00	25.00	50.00
1854E	—	10.00	20.00	40.00	75.00
1855A	—	4.00	8.00	18.00	35.00
1855B	2,198,000	5.00	8.00	15.00	30.00
1855C	1,904,000	10.00	20.00	30.00	47.50
1855E	—	10.00	20.00	35.00	65.00
1856A	—	20.00	35.00	50.00	100
1856B	3,654,000	5.00	8.00	15.00	30.00
1856C	48,000	35.00	75.00	115	225
1856E	—	10.00	20.00	37.50	65.00

KM# 2210 20 KREUZER

6.6800 g., 0.5830 Silver .1252 oz. ASW

Date	Mintage	F	VF	XF	Unc
1852A	—	40.00	65.00	120	200
1852C	114,000	60.00	100	200	400

KM# 2212 20 KREUZER

2.6667 g., 0.5000 Silver .0429 oz. ASW

Date	Mintage	F	VF	XF	Unc
1868	30,000,000	1.00	2.00	5.00	16.00
1869	30,000,000	1.00	2.00	4.00	14.00
1870	30,000,000	1.00	2.00	4.00	12.00
1872	576,000	15.00	30.00	55.00	125

KM# 2149 30 KREUZER

Copper **Note:** Struck until 1811.

Date	Mintage	F	VF	XF	Unc
1807A	—	4.00	8.00	16.00	45.00
1807B	15,787,000	5.00	10.00	25.00	70.00
1807B	—	40.00	70.00	120	250
Note: (Error) Inverted C in ERBLAENDISCH					
1807E	—	15.00	30.00	60.00	175
1807G	—	15.00	35.00	65.00	175
1807S	—	4.00	8.00	16.00	45.00

KM# 2213 1/4 FLORIN

5.3450 g., 0.5200 Silver .0893 oz. ASW

Date	Mintage	F	VF	XF	Unc
1857A	—	7.50	15.00	25.00	40.00
1857B	—	12.00	22.50	37.50	60.00
1857E	—	35.00	70.00	100	140
1857M	—	50.00	75.00	125	250
1857V	—	22.00	40.00	60.00	140
1858A	31,197,000	5.00	10.00	20.00	35.00
1858B	2,982,000	6.50	13.00	25.00	50.00
1858E	Inc. above	6.50	13.00	20.00	35.00
1858M	Inc. above	25.00	45.00	80.00	160
1858V	—	25.00	45.00	80.00	160
1859M	27,415,000	45.00	75.00	115	200

KM# 2214 1/4 FLORIN

5.3450 g., 0.5200 Silver .0893 oz. ASW

Date	Mintage	F	VF	XF	Unc
1859A	27,415,000	3.00	7.00	15.00	25.00
1859B	13,109,000	3.00	6.00	10.00	25.00
1859E	—	4.00	8.00	15.00	25.00
1859M	—	30.00	60.00	125	300
1859V	—	9.00	20.00	40.00	80.00
1860A	—	11.50	23.00	40.00	55.00
1860B	21,247,000	3.00	5.00	10.00	25.00
1860E	—	35.00	60.00	90.00	180
1860V	—	10.00	20.00	40.00	80.00
1861A	—	3.00	7.00	15.00	40.00
1861B	1,656,000	30.00	50.00	80.00	120
1861E	—	90.00	180	250	425
1861V	—	15.00	40.00	70.00	150
1862A	—	3.00	7.00	15.00	40.00
1862B	2,796,000	7.50	15.00	25.00	75.00
1862E	—	8.00	16.00	30.00	75.00
1862V	—	10.00	20.00	40.00	90.00
1863A	—	15.00	35.00	60.00	120
1863V	800,000	17.50	35.00	60.00	140
1864A	4,843,000	3.00	7.00	15.00	30.00
1864V	165,000	17.50	30.00	50.00	120
1865A	80,000	27.50	50.00	80.00	135

KM# 2215 1/4 FLORIN

5.3450 g., 0.5200 Silver .0893 oz. ASW **Obverse:** Head of Franz Joseph right with heavier whiskers **Reverse:** Eagle, value below

Date	F	VF	XF	Unc
1866A	150	250	400	850
1866V	120	225	450	950

KM# 2216 1/4 FLORIN

5.3450 g., 0.5200 Silver .0893 oz. ASW **Rev. Legend:** HUNGAR, BOHEM. GAL. - LOD. ILL...

Date	Mintage	F	VF	XF	Unc
1867A	—	100	200	550	800
1868A	—	65.00	110	200	315
1869A	—	55.00	90.00	150	250
1870A	7,956	130	350	750	1,000
1871A	—	125	325	600	850

KM# 2217 1/4 FLORIN

5.3450 g., 0.5200 Silver .0893 oz. ASW

Date	Mintage	F	VF	XF	Unc
1872	100,000	65.00	125	250	400
1873	50,000	50.00	100	200	325
1874	100,000	100	175	275	450
1875	20,000	125	300	500	800

KM# 2219 FLORIN

12.3400 g., 0.9000 Silver .3571 oz. ASW **Note:** Varieties exist.

Date	Mintage	F	VF	XF	Unc
1857A	—	20.00	35.00	70.00	150
1857B	—	100	210	350	600
1857E	—	100	225	375	675
1857V	—	135	240	400	775
1858A	—	7.50	15.00	22.50	35.00
1858B	1,920,000	9.00	18.00	27.50	45.00
1858E	—	15.00	25.00	40.00	75.00
1858M	—	20.00	45.00	90.00	200
1858V	—	14.00	30.00	60.00	120
1859A	—	5.00	7.00	14.00	30.00
1859B	7,537,000	6.00	11.00	25.00	40.00
1859E	—	10.00	20.00	35.00	60.00
1859M	—	12.00	18.00	45.00	125
1859V	—	12.50	25.00	45.00	90.00
1860A	—	3.00	5.00	10.00	25.00
1860B	1,883,000	12.50	25.00	40.00	70.00
1860E	—	10.00	20.00	35.00	50.00
1860V	—	17.50	30.00	60.00	120
1861A	—	3.00	5.00	10.00	25.00
1861B	815,000	75.00	150	300	500
1861E	—	15.00	30.00	60.00	120
1861V	—	20.00	35.00	75.00	150
1862A	—	6.00	10.00	15.00	27.50
1862B	314,000	11.00	25.00	50.00	90.00
1862E	—	60.00	150	225	450
1862V	—	25.00	60.00	95.00	190
1863A	—	7.00	12.00	17.50	35.00
1863B	287,000	17.50	35.00	60.00	100
1863E	—	17.50	32.50	65.00	95.00
1863V	—	17.50	37.50	65.00	130
1864A	—	15.00	30.00	50.00	120
1864B	340,000	40.00	75.00	140	350
1864E	150,000	40.00	100	175	275
1864V	130,000	55.00	110	200	400
1865A	—	15.00	30.00	50.00	120
1865B	291,000	20.00	35.00	65.00	110
1865E	—	15.00	32.50	70.00	100
1865V	31,000	120	240	400	675

KM# 2220 FLORIN

12.3400 g., 0.9000 Silver .3571 oz. ASW **Obverse:** Head of Franz Joseph right with heavier side whiskers **Reverse:** Eagle, value below

Date	Mintage	F	VF	XF	Unc
1866A	—	25.00	50.00	85.00	150
1866B	359,000	27.50	60.00	90.00	150
1866E	—	70.00	150	250	450
1866V	—	80.00	150	250	450

KM# 2221 FLORIN

12.3400 g., 0.9000 Silver .3571 oz. ASW **Rev. Legend:** HUNGAR, BOHEN. GAL. - LOD. ILL...

Date	Mintage	F	VF	XF	Unc
1867A	—	25.00	40.00	80.00	150
1867B	714,000	15.00	30.00	50.00	85.00
1867E	—	150	250	400	650
1868A	—	30.00	50.00	90.00	160
1869A	—	22.50	35.00	70.00	150
1870A	—	15.00	30.00	50.00	90.00
1871A	—	12.50	27.50	45.00	80.00
1872A	—	150	250	400	800

KM# 2222 FLORIN

12.3400 g., 0.9000 Silver .3571 oz. ASW

Date	Mintage	F	VF	XF	Unc
1872	4,725,000	12.50	25.00	40.00	100
1873	7,880,000	8.00	16.00	30.00	75.00
1874	2,479,000	22.50	40.00	70.00	100
1875/3	5,053,000	—	—	—	—
1875	Inc. above	6.00	10.00	15.00	30.00
1876	7,283,000	6.00	9.00	14.00	27.50
1877	13,963,000	5.00	8.00	13.00	25.00
1878	18,963,000	5.00	8.00	13.00	25.00
1878	—	—	—	—	—
Note: Plain edge					
1879	37,485,000	5.00	8.00	13.00	25.00
1880	6,505,000	7.50	12.00	20.00	35.00
1881	6,128,000	7.50	12.00	20.00	35.00
1882	5,476,000	9.00	15.00	25.00	45.00
1883	6,036,000	7.00	10.00	14.00	25.00
1884	4,303,000	7.00	10.00	14.00	25.00
1885	3,395,000	7.00	12.00	16.00	25.00
1886	6,710,000	6.00	10.00	14.00	25.00
1887	5,692,000	6.00	10.00	14.00	25.00
1888	6,572,000	6.00	10.00	14.00	25.00
1889	5,053,000	6.00	10.00	14.00	25.00
1890	4,164,000	6.00	10.00	14.00	25.00

Date	Mintage	F	VF	XF	Unc
1891	4,235,000	6.00	10.00	14.00	25.00
1892	2,504,000	10.00	15.00	25.00	50.00

KM# 2230 2 FLORIN
24.6900 g., 0.9000 Silver .7145 oz. ASW

Date	Mintage	F	VF	XF	Unc
1859A	—	75.00	125	175	275
1859B	511,000	40.00	70.00	120	200
1860A	—	550	950	1,500	2,250
1860V	—	175	350	700	1,100
1861A	—	—	—	—	—
1862A	15,000	100	180	300	450
1863A	24,000	50.00	90.00	150	250
1864A	31,000	50.00	90.00	150	250
1865A	72,000	50.00	90.00	150	250
1866A	—	—	—	—	—

Note: Reported, not confirmed

KM# 2231 2 FLORIN
24.6900 g., 0.9000 Silver .7145 oz. ASW **Obverse:** With heavier side whiskers

Date	Mintage	F	VF	XF	Unc
1866A	11,000	175	350	700	1,100

KM# 2232 2 FLORIN
24.6900 g., 0.9000 Silver .7145 oz. ASW **Rev. Legend:** HUNGAR. BOHEM. GAL. -LOD. ILL...

Date	Mintage	F	VF	XF	Unc
1867A	45,000	50.00	100	150	250
1868A	—	50.00	100	150	250
1869A	—	40.00	75.00	125	200
1870A	—	40.00	75.00	125	200
1871A	—	50.00	100	150	250
1872A	—	75.00	150	250	375

KM# 2233 2 FLORIN
24.6900 g., 0.9000 Silver .7145 oz. ASW

Date	Mintage	F	VF	XF	Unc
1872	45,000	35.00	70.00	125	225
1873	99,000	35.00	75.00	140	250
1874	79,000	25.00	50.00	85.00	175
1875	106,000	30.00	60.00	90.00	175
1876	92,000	35.00	65.00	100	190
1877	105,000	25.00	55.00	85.00	175
1878	147,000	30.00	60.00	85.00	175
1879	501,000	25.00	50.00	75.00	175
1880	83,000	30.00	60.00	85.00	150
1881	104,000	30.00	60.00	85.00	150
1882	121,000	25.00	50.00	75.00	140
1883	70,000	35.00	65.00	100	175
1884	87,000	25.00	50.00	75.00	150
1885	78,000	25.00	50.00	75.00	160
1886	93,000	25.00	50.00	75.00	160
1887	117,000	25.00	50.00	75.00	160
1888	73,000	25.00	50.00	75.00	160
1889	147,000	35.00	65.00	100	190
1890	104,000	35.00	65.00	100	175
1891	117,000	35.00	65.00	100	175
1892	32,000	30.00	60.00	80.00	160

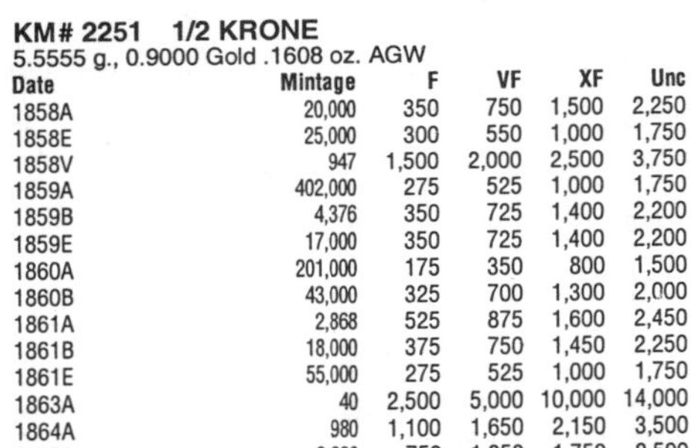

KM# 2251 1/2 KRONE
5.5555 g., 0.9000 Gold .1608 oz. AGW

Date	Mintage	F	VF	XF	Unc
1858A	20,000	350	750	1,500	2,250
1858E	25,000	300	550	1,000	1,750
1858V	947	1,500	2,000	2,500	3,750
1859A	402,000	275	525	1,000	1,750
1859B	4,376	350	725	1,400	2,200
1859E	17,000	350	725	1,400	2,200
1860A	201,000	175	350	800	1,500
1860B	43,000	325	700	1,300	2,000
1861A	2,868	525	875	1,600	2,450
1861B	18,000	375	750	1,450	2,250
1861E	55,000	275	525	1,000	1,750
1863A	40	2,500	5,000	10,000	14,000
1864A	980	1,100	1,650	2,150	3,500
1865A	2,690	750	1,250	1,750	2,500

KM# 2252 1/2 KRONE
5.5555 g., 0.9000 Gold .1608 oz. AGW **Obverse:** Large bust right

Date	Mintage	F	VF	XF	Unc
1866A	4,000	750	1,250	1,800	3,000

KM# 2253 KRONE
11.1111 g., 0.9000 Gold .3215 oz. AGW

Date	Mintage	F	VF	XF	Unc
1858A	47,000	500	1,000	1,500	2,750
1858E	31,000	350	600	1,000	1,850
1858V	600	1,150	1,850	2,750	4,500
1859A	10,000	450	800	1,500	2,750
1859M	3,974	750	1,500	3,000	5,000
1859V	1,885	1,000	2,000	4,000	6,000
1860A	557	1,250	2,500	3,250	5,500
1861A	2,010	650	1,100	1,850	2,850
1863A	1,000	750	1,350	2,150	3,500
1864A	1,530	650	1,150	1,950	3,000
1865A	2,800	650	1,150	1,950	3,000

KM# 2255 KRONE
11.1111 g., 0.9000 Gold .3215 oz. AGW **Obverse:** Large bust

Date	Mintage	F	VF	XF	Unc
1866A	3,000	1,150	1,850	2,750	4,500

KM# A2149 1/2 THALER
14.0300 g., 0.8330 Silver .3757 oz. ASW **Obv. Legend:** FRANCISCVS II. D. G. R. IMP...

Date	F	VF	XF	Unc
1801A	60.00	125	350	500
1802A	60.00	125	250	400
1803A	100	175	250	400
1804A	60.00	125	250	400

KM# 2150 1/2 THALER
14.0300 g., 0.8330 Silver .3757 oz. ASW **Obv. Legend:** FRANCISCVS II. D. G. ROM ET...

Date	F	VF	XF	Unc
1804A Rare	—	—	—	—
1805A	150	250	400	750
1805V	—	—	—	—
1806A	120	225	375	700

KM# 2151 1/2 THALER
14.0300 g., 0.8330 Silver .3757 oz. ASW **Obv. Legend:** FRANCISCVS I. D. G. AVSTRIAE... **Rev. Legend:** ...D. LO. SAL. WIRC.

Date	F	VF	XF	Unc
1807A Rare	—	—	—	—
1808A	125	200	400	675
1809A	125	200	400	675
1809C	150	225	450	750
1810A	150	225	450	750

KM# 2152 1/2 THALER
14.0300 g., 0.8330 Silver .3757 oz. ASW **Rev. Legend:** ... LO: WI: ET IN. FR: DVX

Date	Mintage	F	VF	XF	Unc
1811A	2,186	60.00	100	150	250
1812A	1,930	65.00	110	175	275
1813A	1,718	65.00	110	175	275
1814A	1,533	50.00	80.00	125	225
1815A	7,849	35.00	60.00	100	175
1815B	57,000	40.00	70.00	130	200

KM# 2153 1/2 THALER
14.0300 g., 0.8330 Silver .3757 oz. ASW **Rev. Legend:** ... GAL. LOD. IL. REX. A. A.

Date	Mintage	F	VF	XF	Unc
1817A	12,000	40.00	70.00	115	175
1818A	3,695	50.00	80.00	125	185
1818B	—	50.00	80.00	125	185
1818V	—	35.00	60.00	100	150
1819A	—	40.00	65.00	110	165
1819B Rare	15,000	—	—	—	—
1819C	—	45.00	75.00	125	185
1819E Rare	—	—	—	—	—
1819G	—	50.00	80.00	135	200
1820A	—	40.00	70.00	115	175
1820B Rare	23,000	—	—	—	—
1820C	—	40.00	70.00	115	175

Date	Mintage	F	VF	XF	Unc
1820E	—	50.00	80.00	125	185
1820G Rare	—	—	—	—	—
1821A	—	40.00	70.00	115	175
1821B	9,650	40.00	70.00	115	175
1821C	—	35.00	60.00	100	150
1821E	—	50.00	80.00	125	185
1821G	—	50.00	80.00	125	185
1821V Rare	—	—	—	—	—
1822A	—	35.00	60.00	100	150
1822B Rare	13,000	—	—	—	—
1822C	—	40.00	70.00	115	175
1822E	—	50.00	80.00	125	185
1822G	—	50.00	80.00	125	185
1823A	—	35.00	60.00	100	150
1823B	15,000	50.00	80.00	125	185
1823C	—	50.00	80.00	125	185
1823E	—	50.00	80.00	125	185
1823G	—	35.00	65.00	110	165
1824A	—	35.00	60.00	100	150
1824B	13,000	40.00	70.00	115	175
1824C	—	30.00	55.00	100	135
1824G	—	65.00	115	150	225

KM# 2154 1/2 THALER

14.0300 g., 0.8330 Silver .3757 oz. ASW **Obverse:** Bust with short hair

Date	Mintage	F	VF	XF	Unc
1825A	—	50.00	80.00	125	185
1825B	15,000	50.00	80.00	125	185
1825C	—	50.00	80.00	125	185
1826A	—	30.00	60.00	100	185
1826B	13,000	40.00	70.00	115	175
1826C	—	35.00	60.00	100	150
1826G	—	80.00	400	600	900
1827A	—	25.00	60.00	150	175
1827B Rare	5,230	—	—	—	—
1827C	—	60.00	400	600	900
1828A	—	30.00	60.00	100	175
1829A	—	30.00	60.00	100	175
1830A	—	25.00	60.00	100	175
1830E Rare	—	—	—	—	—

KM# 2155 1/2 THALER

14.0300 g., 0.8330 Silver .3757 oz. ASW **Obverse:** Ribbons on wreath forward across neck

Date	F	VF	XF	Unc
1831A	75.00	125	225	350

KM# 2156 1/2 THALER

14.0300 g., 0.8330 Silver .3757 oz. ASW

Date	F	VF	XF	Unc
1832A	40.00	75.00	125	200
1832A	—	—	—	—
Note: Plain edge				
1833A	40.00	75.00	125	200
1833A	—	—	—	—
Note: Plain edge				
1833E Rare	—	—	—	—
1834A	40.00	75.00	125	200
1835A	35.00	60.00	100	175

KM# 2224 1/2 THALER

14.0300 g., 0.8330 Silver .3757 oz. ASW **Obverse:** Head of Ferdinand right **Reverse:** Eagle

Date	F	VF	XF	Unc
1835A	125	225	450	1,100
1835C Rare	—	—	—	—
1836A	100	200	300	900
1836C	275	550	1,100	1,700

KM# 2225 1/2 THALER

14.0300 g., 0.8330 Silver .3757 oz. ASW

Date	Mintage	F	VF	XF	Unc
1837A	—	50.00	100	200	400
1838A	—	50.00	100	200	400
1839A	—	45.00	90.00	175	350
1840A	—	30.00	65.00	135	275
1841A	—	45.00	90.00	175	350
1842A	—	40.00	80.00	160	300
1843A	—	40.00	80.00	160	300
1844A	—	45.00	90.00	175	350
1845A	—	40.00	80.00	160	300
1846A	—	30.00	65.00	135	275
1847A	—	30.00	65.00	135	275
1848A	3,964	50.00	100	225	500

KM# 2227 1/2 THALER

14.0300 g., 0.8330 Silver .3757 oz. ASW **Obverse:** Young head of Franz Josef left **Note:** This issue was struck in Mantua by the Austrian garrison under General Josef Radetzky during the siege of March 18-22, 1848 by Italian rebels.

Date	F	VF	XF	Unc
1848A	700	1,450	2,000	3,250
1849A	700	1,450	2,000	3,250
1850A	850	1,750	2,250	3,750
1851A	650	1,250	1,800	3,000

KM# 2226 1/2 THALER

14.0300 g., 0.8330 Silver .3757 oz. ASW **Note:** This issue was struck in Mantua by the Austrian garrison under General Josef Radetzky during the siege of March 18-22, 1848 by Italian rebels.

Date	Mintage	F	VF	XF	Unc
1848GM	3,947	275	450	750	1,500

KM# 2228.1 1/2 THALER

12.9920 g., 0.9000 Silver **Obverse:** Young head of Franz Josef right **Edge Lettering:** VIRIBVS VNITIS

Date	F	VF	XF	Unc
1852A	125	250	400	800
1853A	200	375	500	1,000
1854A	200	375	500	1,000
1855A	150	325	450	950
1856A	150	325	425	900

KM# 2228.2 1/2 THALER

12.9920 g., 0.9000 Silver **Edge Lettering:** VIRIBUS-VIRIBUS

Date	F	VF	XF	Unc
1856A	150	275	450	750

KM# 2158 THALER

28.0600 g., 0.8330 Silver .7514 oz. ASW **Obv. Legend:** FRANCISCVS II. D. G. R. IMP. S.A... **Note:** Dav. #1178.

Date	F	VF	XF	Unc
1801A	85.00	175	325	650
1802A	110	225	450	850
1803A	125	250	475	950
1804A	75.00	150	275	550

KM# 2159 THALER

28.0600 g., 0.8330 Silver .7514 oz. ASW **Obv. Legend:** FRANCISCVS II D. G. ROM. ET...

Date	F	VF	XF	Unc
1804A	60.00	150	375	525
1805A	60.00	150	375	525
1806A	60.00	175	400	600

KM# 2160 THALER

28.0600 g., 0.8330 Silver .7514 oz. ASW **Obv. Legend:** FRANCISCVS I. D. G. AVSTRIAE... **Rev. Legend:** ...D. LO. SAL. WIRC.

Date	F	VF	XF	Unc
1806A Rare	—	—	—	—
1807A	40.00	80.00	160	325
1808A	40.00	80.00	160	325
1809A	40.00	80.00	160	325
1809B Restrike 1841	—	—	—	—
1809C	35.00	70.00	140	275
1810A	30.00	60.00	120	150

Note: 1810A exists as a klippe

KM# 2161 THALER
28.0600 g., 0.8330 Silver .7514 oz. ASW **Rev. Legend:** ...LO: WI: ET IN. FR: DVX.

Date	F	VF	XF	Unc
1811A	30.00	65.00	130	250
1811C	30.00	65.00	130	250
1812A	175	350	725	1,100
1812C	175	350	725	1,100
1813A	50.00	100	200	400
1813C	175	350	725	1,100
1813G	55.00	100	200	325
1814A	35.00	75.00	130	250
1814B Rare	—	—	—	—
1814C	40.00	80.00	160	325
1814G	55.00	100	200	325
1815A	35.00	75.00	130	250
1815B	50.00	110	225	325
1815C	35.00	75.00	150	250

KM# 2162 THALER
28.0600 g., 0.8330 Silver .7514 oz. ASW **Rev. Legend:** ...GAL. LOD. IL. RES. A. A.

Date	Mintage	F	VF	XF	Unc
1817A	—	25.00	50.00	100	250
1818A	—	25.00	50.00	100	250
1818B	—	30.00	55.00	110	200
1818V	—	35.00	70.00	150	275
1819A	—	35.00	70.00	135	300
1819B Rare	153,000	—	—	—	—
1819C	—	35.00	70.00	150	275
1819E	—	35.00	70.00	150	275
1819G	—	30.00	60.00	125	250
1819M	—	45.00	90.00	180	300
1820A	—	20.00	40.00	80.00	200
1820B Rare	250,000	—	—	—	—
1820C	—	30.00	55.00	100	200
1820E	—	50.00	100	200	325
1820G	—	65.00	130	250	375
1820M	—	30.00	60.00	125	250
1821A	—	25.00	50.00	100	250
1821B	150,000	20.00	40.00	85.00	150
1821C	—	20.00	40.00	85.00	150
1821E	—	27.50	55.00	125	225
1821G	—	25.00	50.00	100	200
1821M	—	50.00	100	200	300
1821V	—	45.00	80.00	175	275
1822A	—	20.00	40.00	80.00	200
1822B	215,000	25.00	50.00	100	200
1822C	—	25.00	50.00	100	200
1822E	—	30.00	60.00	125	250
1822G	—	25.00	50.00	100	200
1822M	—	50.00	100	200	400
1822V Rare	—	—	—	—	—
1823A	—	20.00	40.00	80.00	200
1823B	201,000	25.00	50.00	100	200
1823C	—	35.00	70.00	150	275
1823E	—	30.00	60.00	125	250
1823G	—	30.00	60.00	125	250
1824A	—	25.00	50.00	100	250
1824B	282,000	25.00	50.00	100	200
1824C	—	30.00	60.00	125	250
1824E	—	35.00	70.00	150	275
1824G	—	30.00	60.00	125	250

KM# 2163 THALER
28.0600 g., 0.8330 Silver .7514 oz. ASW **Obverse:** Bust with short hair

Date	Mintage	F	VF	XF	Unc
1824C 1	—	—	—	—	—
1824A	—	40.00	80.00	155	250
1825A	—	30.00	60.00	125	250
1825B 1	336,000	30.00	60.00	125	250
1825C 2	—	35.00	70.00	145	270
1825G 3	—	30.00	60.00	125	250
1826A	—	25.00	55.00	100	225
1826B 1	269,000	30.00	60.00	125	250
1826C 2	—	30.00	60.00	125	250
1826G 3	—	35.00	70.00	145	275
1827A	—	30.00	60.00	125	250
1827B 1	89,000	125	300	700	1,000
1827C 2	—	25.00	50.00	100	200
1828A	—	25.00	50.00	100	225
1829A 0	—	25.00	50.00	100	225
1830A	—	20.00	50.00	95.00	200
1830E 1	—	30.00	60.00	125	250

KM# 2164 THALER
28.0600 g., 0.8330 Silver .7514 oz. ASW **Obverse:** Ribbons on wreath forward across neck

Date	F	VF	XF	Unc
1831A	40.00	80.00	175	325

KM# 2165 THALER
28.0600 g., 0.8330 Silver .7514 oz. ASW **Obverse:** Ribbons on wreath hang behind neck

Date	F	VF	XF	Unc
1831A	400	800	1,200	1,800
1832A	40.00	80.00	175	325
1833A	50.00	100	200	350
1833A Error	100	200	325	525
Note: Edge: FUNDAMENIVM				
1833B	350	750	1,000	1,700
1833E	50.00	100	200	350
1834A	42.50	85.00	175	325
1835A	50.00	100	200	350

KM# 2238 THALER
28.0600 g., 0.8330 Silver .7514 oz. ASW **Obverse:** Head of Ferdinand I with oval loop in knot of wreath

Date	F	VF	XF	Unc
1835A	125	250	400	800
1835C Rare	—	—	—	—
1836A	100	175	275	550
1836C	250	400	800	1,500

KM# 2239 THALER
28.0600 g., 0.8330 Silver .7514 oz. ASW **Obverse:** Head of Ferdinand I with sharp-cornered loop in knot of wreath

Date	F	VF	XF	Unc
1835A	375	600	1,100	1,700

KM# 2240 THALER
28.0600 g., 0.8330 Silver .7514 oz. ASW

Date	Mintage	F	VF	XF	Unc
1837A	—	50.00	100	200	350
1837M	—	275	500	800	1,500
1838A	—	50.00	100	200	350
1838M	—	275	500	800	1,500
1839A	—	50.00	100	200	350
1840A	—	45.00	90.00	175	325
1841A	—	40.00	80.00	150	275
1842A	—	40.00	80.00	150	275
1843A	—	40.00	80.00	150	275
1844A	—	40.00	80.00	150	275
1845A	—	40.00	80.00	150	275
1846A	—	40.00	80.00	150	275
1847A	—	40.00	80.00	150	275
1848A	119,000	30.00	60.00	100	225

KM# 2241 THALER

28.0600 g., 0.8330 Silver .7514 oz. ASW **Obv. Legend:** FRANC. IOS. I. D. G. AVSTR. IMP. HVNG. BOH. REX. **Reverse:** Similar to KM#2240

Date	F	VF	XF	Unc
1848A	500	1,000	1,500	2,250
1849A	500	1,000	1,500	2,250
1850A	700	1,350	1,950	2,650
1851A	500	1,000	1,500	2,250

KM# 2242 THALER

28.0600 g., 0.8330 Silver .7514 oz. ASW **Obv. Legend:** ...AVSTRIAE. IMPERATOR. **Reverse:** Similar to KM#2240

Date	F	VF	XF	Unc
1852A	800	1,400	2,250	3,000

KM# 2243.1 THALER

25.9900 g., 0.9000 Silver .7520 oz. ASW **Edge Lettering:** VIRIBVS VNITIS

Date	F	VF	XF	Unc
1852A	60.00	120	225	350
1853A	50.00	100	200	300
1853B	160	275	450	700
1854A	50.00	100	200	375
1855A	50.00	100	200	350
1856A	50.00	100	200	350

KM# 2243.2 THALER

25.9900 g., 0.9000 Silver .7520 oz. ASW **Edge Lettering:** VIRIBUS-VIRIBUS

Date	F	VF	XF	Unc
1856A	—	—	—	—

KM# 2244 THALER

18.5186 g., 0.9000 Silver .5359 oz. ASW **Note:** Vereins Thaler. Varieties in asterisk size on edge exist on 1863 and 1864 dated coins.

Date	Mintage	F	VF	XF	Unc
1857A	9,154,000	15.00	30.00	60.00	100
1857A	—	—	—	—	—
Note: Restrike 1994-1996 Jablonec Mint					
1857B	—	50.00	100	200	425
1857E	—	40.00	80.00	165	325
1857V	—	100	225	550	900
1858A	Inc. above	15.00	30.00	60.00	100
1858B	—	20.00	40.00	80.00	150
1858E	—	50.00	100	200	425
1858M	—	37.50	75.00	150	300
1858V	—	37.50	100	200	350
1859A	4,949,000	20.00	40.00	70.00	125
1859B	—	20.00	40.00	80.00	150
1859E	—	40.00	80.00	160	350
1859M	—	37.50	75.00	150	300
1860A	1,620,000	20.00	40.00	70.00	150
1860V	43,000	37.50	100	200	350
1861A	3,140,000	20.00	40.00	70.00	150
1861B	—	20.00	40.00	75.00	150
1861E	—	20.00	40.00	75.00	150
1861V	—	25.00	100	200	350
1862A	998,000	25.00	50.00	90.00	175
1862B	—	25.00	50.00	85.00	175
1862V	—	25.00	100	200	350
1863A	2,209,000	20.00	40.00	70.00	125
1863B	—	25.00	50.00	85.00	175
1863E	—	25.00	50.00	90.00	175
1863V	—	25.00	100	200	350
1864A	2,636,000	17.50	35.00	65.00	110
1864B	—	27.50	55.00	100	200
1864E	556,000	17.50	35.00	65.00	125
1864V	107,000	62.50	125	250	450
1865A	2,085,000	17.50	35.00	65.00	110
1865B	—	20.00	40.00	75.00	125
1865E	—	17.50	35.00	60.00	100
1865V	—	75.00	150	275	525

KM# 2245 THALER

18.5186 g., 0.9000 Silver .5359 oz. ASW **Obverse:** Head with heavier whiskers

Date	Mintage	F	VF	XF	Unc
1866A	1,236,000	25.00	60.00	100	175
1866B	Inc. above	35.00	60.00	100	175
1866E	Inc. above	40.00	80.00	150	275
1867A	850,000	30.00	75.00	125	225
1867B	Inc. above	40.00	85.00	150	275
1867E	Inc. above	40.00	80.00	150	275
1868E	168,000	—	—	—	—
Note: Reported, not confirmed					

KM# 2246.2 2 THALER

37.0371 g., 0.9000 Silver 1.0718 oz. ASW **Obverse:** Wreath tips point between "AI" of "KAISER"

Date	F	VF	XF	Unc
1857A	500	1,200	2,000	2,750

KM# 2246.1 2 THALER

37.0371 g., 0.9000 Silver 1.0718 oz. ASW **Subject:** Opening of Viena-Trieste Railway **Obverse:** Wreath tips point between "KA" of "KAISER" **Note:** Varieties exist.

Date	Mintage	F	VF	XF	Unc
1857A	1,644	500	1,200	2,000	2,750

KM# 2249 2 THALER

37.0371 g., 0.9000 Silver 1.0718 oz. ASW

Date	Mintage	F	VF	XF	Unc
1865A	7,425	400	1,000	1,750	2,500

KM# 2250 2 THALER

37.0371 g., 0.9000 Silver 1.0718 oz. ASW

Date	Mintage	F	VF	XF	Unc
1866A	10,000	200	400	750	1,100
1867A	8,300	200	400	750	1,100

TRADE COINAGE

Uniform

KM# 1886 DUCAT

3.4909 g., 0.9860 Gold .1106 oz. AGW **Obverse:** Bust right **Obv. Legend:** FRANC. II. D. G. R... **Reverse:** Crowned imperial eagle **Note:** Prev. KM#2166.

Date	F	VF	XF	Unc
1801A	120	200	290	450
1802A	110	180	260	400
1802B	100	160	250	375
1802G	110	170	250	375
1803A	120	200	290	450
1804A	110	180	260	400
1804E	100	160	250	375

KM# 2167 DUCAT

3.4909 g., 0.9860 Gold .1106 oz. AGW **Obv. Legend:** FRANCISCVS II D. G. ROM... **Rev. Legend:** ...D. LOTH. VEN. SAL.

Date	F	VF	XF	Unc
1804A	325	650	1,000	1,750
1805A	325	650	1,000	1,750
1806A	300	600	900	1,600
1806B	325	650	1,000	1,750
1806C	750	1,500	2,250	3,000
1806D	325	650	1,000	1,750

KM# 2168 DUCAT

3.4909 g., 0.9860 Gold .1106 oz. AGW **Rev. Legend:** ... D. LO. SAL. WIRC.

Date	F	VF	XF	Unc
1806A	160	250	375	550
1806D	750	1,250	1,500	2,000
1807A	125	200	275	450
1807C	180	275	425	650
1808A	125	200	275	450
1808D Rare	—	—	—	—
1809A	125	200	275	450
1809B	160	250	375	575
1809D	500	700	950	1,200
1810A	125	200	275	450

KM# 2169 DUCAT

3.4909 g., 0.9860 Gold .1106 oz. AGW **Rev. Legend:** ...LO: I: ET IN. FR: DVX.

Date	F	VF	XF	Unc
1811A	80.00	120	200	300
1811B	80.00	120	200	300
1812A	80.00	120	200	300
1812B	80.00	120	200	300
1812G Rare	—	—	—	—
1813A	100	140	225	325
1813B	80.00	120	200	300
1813E	100	140	225	325
1813G Rare	—	—	—	—
1814A	80.00	120	200	300
1814B	100	140	225	325
1814E	100	140	225	325
1814G Rare	—	—	—	—
1815A	80.00	120	200	300
1815B	80.00	120	200	300
1815E	80.00	120	200	300
1815G	100	150	250	350

KM# 2170 DUCAT

3.4909 g., 0.9860 Gold .1106 oz. AGW **Rev. Legend:** ...GAL. LOD. IL. REX. A. A.

Date	F	VF	XF	Unc
1816A	80.00	120	200	300
1817A	80.00	120	200	300
1818A	80.00	120	200	300
1818B	80.00	120	200	300
1818E	80.00	120	200	300
1818G	100	140	225	325
1819A	80.00	120	200	300
1819B	100	140	225	325
1819E	80.00	120	200	300
1819G	100	140	225	325
1819V	350	525	700	1,050
1820A	80.00	120	200	300
1820B	80.00	120	200	300
1820E	80.00	120	200	300
1820G	80.00	120	200	300
1821A	80.00	120	200	300
1821B	80.00	120	200	300
1821E	80.00	120	200	300
1821G	80.00	120	200	300
1822A	80.00	120	200	300
1822B	80.00	120	200	300
1822E	80.00	120	200	300
1822G	80.00	120	200	300
1823A	80.00	120	200	300
1823B	80.00	120	200	300
1823E	80.00	120	200	300
1823G	80.00	120	200	300
1824A	80.00	120	200	300
1824B	80.00	120	200	300
1824E	80.00	120	200	300
1824G	100	140	225	325
1824V	350	525	700	1,050

KM# 2171 DUCAT

3.4909 g., 0.9860 Gold .1106 oz. AGW **Obverse:** Ribbons on wreath forward across neck

Date	F	VF	XF	Unc
1825A	80.00	120	200	300
1825B	100	130	225	325
1825E	110	160	250	375
1825G	—	—	—	—
1826A	80.00	120	200	300
1826B	110	160	250	375
1826E	90.00	130	200	300
1826G Rare	—	—	—	—
1827A	80.00	120	200	300
1827B	110	160	250	375
1827E	110	160	250	375
1828A	100	140	225	325
1828B	80.00	120	200	300
1828E	80.00	120	200	300
1829A	80.00	120	180	275
1829B	80.00	120	200	300
1829E	80.00	120	200	300
1830A	80.00	120	180	275
1830B	100	130	200	300
1830E	90.00	130	200	300
1831A	1,100	1,600	2,400	3,200

KM# 2172 DUCAT

3.4909 g., 0.9860 Gold .1106 oz. AGW **Obverse:** Ribbons on wreath behind neck

Date	F	VF	XF	Unc
1831A	110	160	250	375
1832A	100	120	200	300
1832B	100	120	200	300
1833A	100	120	200	300
1833B	100	120	200	300
1833E	110	160	250	375
1834A	100	120	200	300
1834B	100	120	200	300
1834E	110	160	250	375
1835A	100	120	200	300
1835B	100	120	200	300
1835E	110	160	250	375

KM# 2262 DUCAT

3.4909 g., 0.9860 Gold .1106 oz. AGW **Obverse:** ...AVSTRI. IMP.

Date	F	VF	XF	Unc
1837A	60.00	80.00	130	200
1837B	80.00	115	190	275
1837E	80.00	115	190	275
1838A	60.00	80.00	180	275
1838B	80.00	115	190	275
1838E	80.00	115	190	275
1839A	60.00	80.00	130	200
1839B	80.00	115	200	275
1839E	80.00	115	200	275
1840A	60.00	80.00	130	200
1840B	60.00	80.00	130	200
1840E	60.00	80.00	140	225
1840V	475	650	975	1,275
1841A	60.00	80.00	130	200
1841B	60.00	80.00	110	180
1841E	60.00	80.00	110	180
1841V	250	350	525	725
1842A	65.00	100	160	250
1842B	100	130	200	350
1842E	60.00	80.00	110	180
1842V	200	275	700	1,000
1843A	60.00	80.00	110	180
1843B	60.00	80.00	130	200
1843E	60.00	80.00	130	200
1843V	200	275	700	1,350
1844A	60.00	80.00	110	180
1844B	60.00	80.00	110	180
1844E	60.00	80.00	110	180
1844V	200	275	700	1,350
1845A	60.00	80.00	110	180
1845B	60.00	80.00	110	180
1845E	60.00	80.00	130	200
1845V	200	275	700	1,200
1846A	60.00	80.00	130	200
1846B	60.00	80.00	130	200
1846E	60.00	80.00	130	200
1846V	200	275	700	1,000
1847A	60.00	80.00	110	180
1847B	60.00	80.00	110	180
1847E	80.00	100	180	250
1847V	250	350	550	775
1848A	60.00	80.00	110	180
1848B	60.00	80.00	110	180
1848E	60.00	80.00	110	180
1848V	250	350	550	775

KM# 2268 DUCAT

3.4909 g., 0.9860 Gold .1106 oz. AGW **Subject:** 50th Jubilee **Reverse:** Second date below eagle

Date	Mintage	F	VF	XF	Unc
1848/1898A	27,000	150	250	350	500
1849/1898A	2,292	500	1,000	1,300	1,800
1850/1898A	2,292	500	1,000	1,300	1,800
1851/1898A	2,292	500	1,000	1,300	1,800

KM# 2263 DUCAT

3.4909 g., 0.9860 Gold .1106 oz. AGW

Date	Mintage	F	VF	XF	Unc
1852A	—	80.00	100	160	225
1853A	—	90.00	120	180	250
1853B	114,000	90.00	110	180	250
1853E	—	100	130	200	250
1854A	—	60.00	80.00	120	180
1854B	87,000	110	135	225	350
1854E	—	100	130	200	250
1854V	—	350	600	1,000	1,750
1855A	—	60.00	80.00	120	180
1855B	133,000	160	225	350	550
1855E	—	90.00	110	180	250
1855V	—	250	450	800	1,200
1856A	—	60.00	80.00	140	200
1856B	121,000	80.00	110	180	250
1856E	—	60.00	80.00	140	200
1856V	—	250	450	800	1,200
1857A	—	60.00	80.00	130	180
1857B	86,000	60.00	80.00	130	200
1857E	—	100	140	225	350
1857V	—	250	450	800	1,200
1858A	—	60.00	80.00	110	160
1858B	71,000	100	130	180	250
1858E	—	90.00	110	180	250
1858M	—	300	1,000	2,000	2,750
1858V	—	250	450	800	1,200
1859A	—	60.00	80.00	110	160
1859B	34,000	60.00	80.00	140	200
1859E	—	60.00	80.00	110	180
1859V	—	250	450	800	1,200

KM# 2264 DUCAT

3.4909 g., 0.9860 Gold .1106 oz. AGW

Date	Mintage	F	VF	XF	Unc
1860A	—	70.00	100	140	225
1860B	56,000	80.00	120	180	275
1860E	—	100	140	200	325
1860V	—	250	400	800	1,200
1861A	—	60.00	80.00	120	200
1861B	121,000	60.00	100	160	250
1861E	—	90.00	120	200	325
1861V	—	325	800	1,750	2,500
1862A	—	60.00	80.00	120	225
1862B	68,000	60.00	90.00	140	225
1862E	—	60.00	100	160	225
1862V	—	200	400	800	1,200
1863A	—	60.00	80.00	120	225
1863B	58,000	60.00	80.00	120	225
1863E	—	60.00	80.00	120	225
1863V	—	175	375	600	1,000
1864A	—	60.00	100	160	250
1864B	99,000	75.00	120	180	275
1864E	—	60.00	100	160	250
1864V	—	275	800	1,750	2,500
1865A	—	60.00	100	160	250
1865B	81,000	60.00	100	160	250
1865E	—	60.00	100	160	250
1865V	—	250	475	800	1,200

KM# 2265 DUCAT

3.4909 g., 0.9860 Gold .1106 oz. AGW **Obverse:** Head of Franz Joseph right with heavier side whiskers

Date	Mintage	F	VF	XF	Unc
1866A	—	75.00	115	200	350
1866B	76,000	75.00	140	225	400
1866E	—	75.00	115	200	350
1866V	—	275	575	1,100	1,700

KM# 2266 DUCAT

3.4909 g., 0.9860 Gold .1106 oz. AGW

Date	Mintage	F	VF	XF	Unc
1867A	—	60.00	90.00	130	180
1867B	112,000	60.00	100	140	200
1867E	—	70.00	110	160	225
1868A	—	60.00	90.00	130	180
1869A	—	60.00	90.00	130	180
1870A	—	60.00	90.00	130	180
1871A	—	60.00	90.00	130	180
1872A	—	60.00	90.00	130	180

KM# 2267 DUCAT

3.4909 g., 0.9860 Gold .1106 oz. AGW **Ruler:** Franz Joseph I **Note:** 996,721 pieces were struck from 1920-1936.

Date	Mintage	F	VF	XF	Unc
1872	460,000	60.00	100	125	175
1873	516,000	60.00	100	125	175
1874	353,000	60.00	100	125	175
1875	184,000	60.00	100	125	175
1876	680,000	60.00	80.00	125	150
1877	823,000	60.00	80.00	125	175
1878	281,000	60.00	80.00	125	175
1879	362,000	60.00	80.00	125	175
1880	341,000	60.00	100	150	225
1881	477,000	60.00	80.00	125	175
1882	390,000	60.00	100	125	175
1883	409,000	60.00	100	125	175
1884	238,000	60.00	80.00	125	175
1885	257,000	60.00	80.00	125	150
1886	291,000	60.00	80.00	125	150
1887	223,000	60.00	80.00	100	150
1888	309,000	60.00	80.00	100	150
1889	335,000	60.00	80.00	100	150
1890	374,000	60.00	80.00	100	150
1891	325,000	60.00	80.00	100	150

KM# 1888 2 DUCAT

7.0000 g., 0.9860 Gold .2219 oz. AGW **Obverse:** Head right **Reverse:** Crowned imperial eagle **Note:** Prev. KM#2173.

Date	F	VF	XF	Unc
1803A Rare	—	—	—	—

KM# 2179 2 DUCAT

7.0000 g., 0.9860 Gold .2219 oz. AGW **Note:** Similar to 1 Ducat KM#2167.

Date	F	VF	XF	Unc
1804A Rare	—	—	—	—

KM# 1887 4 DUCAT

14.0000 g., 0.9860 Gold .4438 oz. AGW **Obv. Legend:** FRANCISCVS II. D. G. R. IMP... **Rev. Legend:** ...LOTH. M. D. HET. **Note:** Prev. KM#2174.

Date	F	VF	XF	Unc
1801A	300	750	1,800	2,500
1802A	300	800	2,000	3,000
1803A	300	750	1,800	2,500
1804A	300	750	1,800	2,500

KM# 2175 4 DUCAT

14.0000 g., 0.9860 Gold .4438 oz. AGW **Obv. Legend:** FRANCISCVS II. D. G. ROM. ET... **Rev. Legend:** ...D. LOTH. VEN. SAL.

Date	F	VF	XF	Unc
1804A	400	1,250	2,000	2,750
1805A	400	1,250	1,750	2,000
1806A	350	900	1,500	2,000

KM# 2176 4 DUCAT

14.0000 g., 0.9860 Gold .4438 oz. AGW **Obv. Legend:** ...AVSTRIAE IMPERATOR. **Rev. Legend:** ...D. LO. SAL. WIRC.

Date	F	VF	XF	Unc
1807A	350	1,100	2,500	3,500
1808A	325	1,000	2,400	3,100
1809A	300	800	2,250	2,750
1810A	350	1,000	2,500	3,500

KM# 2177 4 DUCAT

14.0000 g., 0.9860 Gold .4438 oz. AGW **Rev. Legend:** ...LO: WI: ET IN. FR: DVX.

Date	F	VF	XF	Unc
1811A	300	750	1,600	2,200
1812A	350	800	1,800	2,500
1813A	300	750	1,600	2,200
1814A	350	800	1,800	2,500
1815A	300	750	1,600	2,200

KM# 2178 4 DUCAT

14.0000 g., 0.9860 Gold .4438 oz. AGW **Rev. Legend:** ...GAL. LOD. IL. REX. A. A.

Date	F	VF	XF	Unc
1816A	300	550	1,500	2,500
1817A	300	550	1,500	2,500
1818A	325	675	1,800	2,750

Date	F	VF	XF	Unc
1819A	300	550	1,500	2,500
1820A	300	550	1,500	2,500
1821A	300	550	1,500	2,500
1822A	300	550	1,500	2,500
1823A	300	550	1,500	2,500
1824A	300	550	1,500	2,500
1825A	250	500	1,200	2,000
1826A	300	550	1,500	2,500
1827A	300	550	1,500	2,500
1828A	250	500	1,275	2,000
1829A	250	500	1,275	2,000
1830A	250	500	1,275	2,000

KM# 2270 4 DUCAT
13.9636 g., 0.9860 Gold .4430 oz. AGW

Date	Mintage	F	VF	XF	Unc
1835A Rare	—	—	—	—	—
1837A	—	250	400	1,000	2,000
1838A	—	250	400	1,000	2,000
1839A	—	250	400	1,000	2,000
1840A	—	250	400	1,000	2,000
1841A	—	250	400	1,000	2,000
1842A	—	250	400	1,000	2,000
1843A	—	250	400	1,000	2,000
1844A	—	250	400	1,000	2,000
1845A	—	250	400	1,000	2,000
1846A	—	250	400	1,000	2,000
1847A	—	250	400	1,000	2,000
1848A	4,411	250	400	1,000	2,000
1848E	—	250	500	1,250	2,500

KM# 2271.1 4 DUCAT
13.9636 g., 0.9860 Gold .4430 oz. AGW

Date	Mintage	F	VF	XF	Unc
1852A	—	—	—	—	—
Note: No specimens known					
1853A	—	—	—	—	—
Note: No specimens known					
1854A	—	250	500	1,250	2,500
1855A	—	250	500	1,250	2,500
1856A	—	250	500	1,250	2,500
1857A	—	250	400	1,000	2,000
1858A	—	250	400	1,000	2,000
1859A	13,000	250	400	1,000	2,000

KM# 2271.2 4 DUCAT
13.9636 g., 0.9860 Gold .4430 oz. AGW **Obverse:** Laurel wreath without berries

Date	F	VF	XF	Unc
1854A	350	850	1,750	2,100
1855A Rare	—	—	—	—
1857V	800	1,600	3,000	4,000

KM# 2272 4 DUCAT
13.9636 g., 0.9860 Gold .4430 oz. AGW

Date	Mintage	F	VF	XF	Unc
1860A	6,303	250	600	1,500	2,750
1861A	7,664	250	600	1,500	2,750
1862A	8,944	250	500	1,250	2,250
1863A	22,000	250	400	1,000	2,000
1864A	45,000	250	400	1,000	2,000
1864V	4,463	600	1,250	2,500	3,500
1865A	13,000	250	400	1,000	2,000
1865V	10,000	600	1,250	2,500	3,500

KM# 2273 4 DUCAT
13.9636 g., 0.9860 Gold .4430 oz. AGW **Obverse:** Laureate bust with heavier side whiskers

Date	Mintage	F	VF	XF	Unc
1866A	8,463	350	750	1,750	2,750

KM# 2274 4 DUCAT
13.9636 g., 0.9860 Gold .4430 oz. AGW

Date	F	VF	XF	Unc
1867A	300	600	1,750	2,750
1868A	300	600	1,750	2,750
1869A	300	600	1,750	2,750
1870A	300	600	1,750	2,750
1871A	300	600	1,750	2,750
1872A	300	600	1,750	2,750

KM# 2276 4 DUCAT
13.9636 g., 0.9860 Gold .4430 oz. AGW **Ruler:** Franz Joseph I **Obverse:** Similar to 4 Ducat, KM#2272, but without mint

Date	F	VF	XF	Unc
1872	250	525	725	1,200
1873	225	400	600	1,000
1874	225	325	600	1,000
1875	225	325	600	1,000
1876	250	450	800	1,300
1877	250	450	800	1,300
1878	225	325	550	800
1879	225	325	550	800
1880	225	325	550	800
1881	225	325	550	800
1882	225	325	550	800
1883	225	325	550	800
1884	225	325	550	800
1885	225	325	550	800
1886	225	300	525	800
1887	225	300	525	800
1888	225	300	525	800
1889	225	300	525	800
1890	225	300	525	750
1891	225	300	525	750
1892	225	300	525	750
1893	225	275	550	800
1894	225	275	550	800
1895	225	275	550	800
1896	225	250	500	800
1897	225	275	550	800
1898	225	250	500	800
1899	225	250	500	600

KM# 2260 4 FLORIN 10 FRANCS
3.2258 g., 0.9000 Gold .0933 oz. AGW

Date	Mintage	F	VF	XF	Unc
1870	7,440	60.00	100	160	250
1871	6,665	60.00	100	160	250
1872	4,960	60.00	90.00	140	225
1877	3,004	80.00	160	250	350
1878	6,820	55.00	90.00	140	225
1881	8,370	55.00	90.00	140	200
1883	3,720	65.00	120	180	325
1884	7,518	55.00	90.00	115	200
1885	38,000	55.00	60.00	110	165
1888	4,145	55.00	100	140	250
1889	5,707	55.00	90.00	135	225
1890	2,947	65.00	120	180	300
1891	11,000	55.00	65.00	90.00	175
1892 Restrike	—	—	—	BV	55.00

KM# 2269 8 FLORINS - 20 FRANCS
6.4516 g., 0.9000 Gold .1867 oz. AGW **Obverse:** Joseph, value below

Date	Mintage	F	VF	XF	Unc
1870	25,000	BV	100	175	250
1871	34,000	BV	100	150	200
1872	5,185	400	1,000	1,750	2,250
1873	23,000	BV	100	175	250

Date	Mintage	F	VF	XF	Unc
1874	42,000	BV	100	150	200
1875	86,000	BV	100	150	200
1876	146,000	BV	100	150	200
1877	125,000	BV	100	150	200
1878	125,000	BV	100	150	200
1879	43,000	BV	100	175	250
1880	62,000	BV	100	150	200
1881	62,000	BV	100	150	200
1882	115,000	BV	100	150	200
1883	31,000	BV	100	150	200
1884	91,000	BV	100	150	200
1885	178,000	BV	100	150	200
1886	140,000	BV	100	150	200
1887	174,000	BV	100	150	200
1888	114,000	BV	100	150	200
1889	208,000	BV	100	150	175
1890	43,000	BV	100	150	200
1891	19,000	100	150	225	325
1892 Restrike	—	—	—	BV	110

TRADE COINAGE

Restrikes

KM# T1 THALER
28.0668 g., 0.8330 Silver .7517 oz. ASW

Date	F	VF	XF	Unc
1780 SF	—	—	—	7.00
Note: Restrike - 1853-present				
1780 SF	—	Value: 9.00		
Note: Proof; restrike				

REFORM COINAGE

100 Heller = 1 Corona

KM# 2800 HELLER
Bronze **Ruler:** Franz Joseph I

Date	Mintage	F	VF	XF	Unc
1892	—	35.00	75.00	150	350
1893	29,000,000	0.20	0.35	0.50	4.00
1894	30,100,000	0.20	0.35	0.50	4.00
1895	49,500,000	0.20	0.35	0.50	3.00
1896	15,600,000	0.35	1.50	3.00	8.00
1897	12,400,000	0.35	2.00	4.00	10.00
1898	6,780,000	5.00	10.00	20.00	35.00
1899	1,901,000	3.00	12.00	25.00	60.00
1900	26,981,000	0.20	0.50	1.50	4.00

KM# 2801 2 HELLER
Bronze **Ruler:** Franz Joseph I

Date	Mintage	F	VF	XF	Unc
1892	260,000	50.00	100	200	450
1893	41,507,000	0.20	0.50	1.75	5.00
1894	78,036,000	0.15	0.25	0.75	3.00
1895	25,610,000	0.20	0.50	2.25	6.25
1896	43,080,000	0.15	0.25	0.75	3.50
1897	98,000,000	0.15	0.25	0.75	3.00
1898	10,720,000	0.75	1.50	4.00	12.00
1899	42,734,000	0.15	0.25	1.00	4.00
1900	7,942,000	0.50	1.00	3.00	9.00

KM# 2802 10 HELLER
Nickel **Ruler:** Franz Joseph I

Date	Mintage	F	VF	XF	Unc
1892	—	125	250	450	1,150
1892 Proof	—	Value: 1,500			
1893	43,524,000	0.25	0.50	1.50	4.00
1894	45,558,000	0.25	0.50	1.25	4.00
1895	79,918,000	0.25	0.50	1.00	3.50

KM# 2803 20 HELLER
Nickel **Ruler:** Franz Joseph I

Date	Mintage	F	VF	XF	Unc
1892	1,500,000	7.50	15.00	35.00	75.00
1892 Proof	—	Value: 250			
1893	41,457,000	0.25	0.65	1.50	7.00
1894	50,116,000	0.25	0.65	1.50	7.00
1895	32,927,000	0.25	0.65	1.50	7.00

KM# 2804 CORONA
5.0000 g., 0.8350 Silver .1342 oz. ASW **Ruler:** Franz Joseph I
Obverse: Laureate bust

Date	Mintage	F	VF	XF	Unc
1892	235,000	80.00	160	275	700
1893	50,124,000	1.75	3.00	5.00	10.00
1894	28,003,000	1.75	3.00	5.00	12.00
1895	15,115,000	3.75	6.00	15.00	35.00
1896	3,068,000	7.50	15.00	25.00	55.00
1897	2,142,000	20.00	30.00	60.00	150
1898	5,855,000	2.50	5.00	8.00	25.00
1899	11,820,000	1.75	2.75	5.00	10.00
1900	3,745,000	2.50	5.00	8.00	14.00

KM# 2807 5 CORONA
24.0000 g., 0.9000 Silver .6945 oz. ASW **Ruler:** Franz Joseph I

Date	Mintage	F	VF	XF	Unc
1900	8,525,000	8.00	12.50	30.00	75.00

KM# 2805 10 CORONA
3.3875 g., 0.9000 Gold .0980 oz. AGW **Ruler:** Franz Joseph I
Obverse: Laureate head of Franz Joseph I right **Reverse:** Eagle with value and date below

Date	Mintage	F	VF	XF	Unc
1892	—	1,000	1,500	2,500	3,500
1893 Rare	—	—	—	—	—
1896	211,000	BV	50.00	60.00	85.00
1897	1,803,000	BV	50.00	60.00	85.00
1905	1,933,230	BV	50.00	60.00	85.00
1906	1,081,161	BV	50.00	60.00	85.00

KM# 2806 20 CORONA
6.7751 g., 0.9000 Gold .1960 oz. AGW **Ruler:** Franz Joseph I

Date	Mintage	F	VF	XF	Unc
1892	653,000	—	BV	125	150
1893	7,872,000	—	BV	90.00	110
1894	6,714,000	—	BV	90.00	110
1895	2,266,000	—	BV	90.00	110
1896	6,868,000	—	BV	90.00	110
1897	5,133,000	—	BV	90.00	110
1898	1,874,000	—	BV	90.00	110
1899	98,000	100	110	130	150
1900	27,000	200	400	600	800

PATTERNS

Including off metal strikes

KM#	Date	Mintage	Identification	Mkt Val
Pn37	1851	—	1/4 Kreuzer.KM#2180	—
Pn38	1851	—	2 Kreuzer. KM#2189	2,150
Pn39	1851	—	3 Kreuzer. KM#2193	2,750
Pn40	1851	—	1/4 Kreuzer. KM#2180	1,400
Pn41	1851	—	1/2 Kreuzer. KM#2181	2,250
Pn42	1851	—	2 Kreuzer. KM#2189	2,500
Pn43	1851	—	3 Kreuzer. KM#2193	2,150
Pn44	1852	—	20 Kreuzer. KM#2210	1,750
Pn45	1853	—	1/2 Thaler. KM#2228	5,500
Pn46	1854	—	Gulden. Aluminum. KM#2218	1,200
Pn47	1855	—	5 Gulden. Gold.	—
Pn48	1855	—	10 Gulden. Gold.	—
Pn49	1855	—	20 Gulden. Gold.	—
Pn50	1855	—	Ducat. Gold. KM#2263	—
Pn51	1857	—	1/4 Gulden. Aluminum.	—
Pn52	1858	—	3 Kreuzer.	—
Pn53	1858	—	3 Kreuzer. Lead.	—
Pn54	1858	—	3 Kreuzer. Lead.	—
Pn56	1858	—	2 Florin. KM#2230	—
Pn55	1858	—	10 Kreuzer.	950
Pn58	1859	—	Krone. Gold. KM#2253	32,000
Pn57	1859	—	5 Kreuzer. Aluminum. KM#2197	—
Pn59	1866	—	2 Florin. Copper. Without mint mark, KM#2230	700
Pn60	1867	—	10 Kreuzer. Without mint mark, KM#2205	1,600
Pn61	1868	—	10 Kreuzer. Copper. KM#2206	—
Pn62	1868	—	Thaler. Copper. KM#2246	—
Pn63	1870	—	20 Kreuzer. Copper. KM#2212	—
Pn64	1871	—	Florin. Aluminum. Without mint mark, KM#2221	750
Pn65	1875	—	Florin. Copper. KM#2223	160
Pn66	1887	—	2 Florin. Copper. KM#2237	2,200
Pn67	1887	—	2 Florin. Bronze. KM#2237	2,000

AUERSPERG

The Auersperg princes were princes of estates in Austrian Carniola, a former duchy with estates in Laibach and Silesia, a former province in southwestern Poland and Swabia, one of the stem-duchies of medieval Germany. They were elevated to princely rank in 1653, and the following year were made dukes of Muensterberg, which they ultimately sold to Prussia.

RULERS
Wilhelm, 1800-1822

MONETARY SYSTEM
120 Kreuzer = 1 Convention Thaler

PRINCIPALITY

STANDARD COINAGE

KM# 5 THALER
28.0600 g., 0.8330 Silver **Ruler:** Wilhelm **Note:** Convention Thaler.

Date	Mintage	VG	F	VF	XF	Unc
1805	—	80.00	175	275	500	—

GURK

A bishopric in the Austrian Alpine province of Carinthia. It was founded in 1071. In 1806 it was mediatized and assigned to Austria.

RULERS
Franz Xavier V, Count Salm-Reifferscheid, (later Prince), 1783-1822

BISHROPRIC

STANDARD COINAGE

KM# 1 20 KREUZER
6.6800 g., 0.5830 Silver, 28.3 mm. **Ruler:** Franz Xavier V Count Salm-Reifferscheid (later Prince)

Date	Mintage	VG	F	VF	XF	Unc
1806	—	37.50	75.00	90.00	125	—

KM# 2 THALER (Convention)
28.0600 g., 0.8330 Silver **Ruler:** Franz Xavier V Count Salm-Reifferscheid (later Prince)

Date	Mintage	VG	F	VF	XF	Unc
1801	—	100	200	325	500	—

TRADE COINAGE

KM# 3 DUCAT
3.5000 g., 0.9860 Gold .1109 oz. **Ruler:** Franz Xavier V Count Salm-Reifferscheid (later Prince) **Obv:** Bust of Franz Xavier right **Rev:** Crowned and mantled arms

Date	Mintage	VG	F	VF	XF	Unc
1806	—	350	750	1,450	2,650	—

OLMUTZ

In Moravia

Olmutz (Olomouc), a town in the eastern part of the Czech Republic which was, until 1640, the recognized capital of Moravia, obtained the right to mint coinage in 1144, but exercised it sparingly until the 17th century, when it became an archbishopric.

RULERS
Anton Theodor, Count von Colloredo, 1777-1811
Maria Thaddaus, Count von Trauttmansdorf, 1811-1819
Rudolph Johann, Archduke of Austria, 1819-1831

BISHOPRIC

STANDARD COINAGE

KM# 195 20 KREUZER
6.6800 g., 0.5830 Silver, 28.3 mm. **Ruler:** Rudolph Johann

Date	Mintage	VG	F	VF	XF	Unc
1820	—	20.00	35.00	60.00	100	—

KM# 196 1/2 CONVENTION THALER
14.0300 g., 0.8330 Silver **Ruler:** Rudolph Johann

Date	Mintage	VG	F	VF	XF	Unc
1820	—	50.00	90.00	150	220	—

KM# 197 THALER
28.0600 g., 0.8330 Silver **Ruler:** Rudolph Johann

Date	Mintage	VG	F	VF	XF	Unc
1820	—	100	200	400	700	—

TRADE COINAGE

KM# 198 DUCAT
3.5000 g., 0.9860 Gold .1109 oz. **Ruler:** Rudolph Johann

Date	Mintage	VG	F	VF	XF	Unc
1820	—	225	450	950	1,600	—

SALZBURG

A town on the Austro-Bavarian frontier which grew up around a monastery and bishopric that was founded circa 700. It was raised to the rank of archbishopric in 798. In 1803 Salzburg was secularized and given to an archduke of Austria. In 1803 it was annexed to Austria but years later passed to Bavaria, returning to Austria in 1813. It became a crown land in 1849, remaining so until becoming part of the Austrian Republic in 1918.

RULERS
Hieronymus, 1772-1803
Ferdinand, Elector, 1803-1805

ENGRAVERS INITIALS
FM, M - Franz Xavier Matzenkopf, Jr., 1755-1805

MONETARY SYSTEM
4 Pfenning = 1 Kreutzer
120 Kreutzer = 1 Convention Thaler

ARCHBISHOPRIC

STANDARD COINAGE

KM# 474 PFENNING
Copper **Ruler:** Hieronymus **Rev:** Crossed palm branches below date

Date	Mintage	VG	F	VF	XF	Unc
1801	—	3.00	5.00	9.00	18.00	—
1802	—	3.00	5.00	9.00	18.00	—

KM# 480 PFENNING
Copper **Ruler:** Hieronymus

Date	Mintage	VG	F	VF	XF	Unc
1802	—	5.00	7.00	10.00	20.00	—

KM# 488 PFENNING
Copper **Ruler:** Ferdinand Elector **Rev:** 1 PFENNING

Date	Mintage	VG	F	VF	XF	Unc
1804	—	5.00	7.00	12.00	30.00	—

KM# 489 PFENNING
Copper **Ruler:** Ferdinand Elector **Rev:** EIN PFENNING **Note:** Varieties exist.

Date	Mintage	VG	F	VF	XF	Unc
1804	—	1.50	3.00	7.00	22.00	—
1805	—	1.50	3.00	7.00	22.00	—

KM# 472 2 PFENNING
Copper **Ruler:** Hieronymus **Rev:** II Pfenning

Date	Mintage	VG	F	VF	XF	Unc
1801	—	3.00	6.00	12.00	25.00	—

KM# 481 2 PFENNING
Copper **Ruler:** Hieronymus **Rev:** 2 Pfenning

Date	Mintage	VG	F	VF	XF	Unc
1802	—	5.00	8.50	17.00	38.00	—

KM# 490 2 PFENNING
Copper **Ruler:** Ferdinand Elector **Rev:** II PFENNING

Date	Mintage	VG	F	VF	XF	Unc
1804	—	5.00	9.00	20.00	45.00	—

KM# 493 2 PFENNING
Copper **Ruler:** Ferdinand Elector **Rev:** ZWEI PFENNING

Date	Mintage	VG	F	VF	XF	Unc
1805	—	3.50	7.50	16.50	40.00	—
1806	—	3.50	7.50	16.50	40.00	—

KM# 470 KREUZER
Copper **Ruler:** Hieronymus

Date	Mintage	VG	F	VF	XF	Unc
1801	—	2.00	3.00	5.00	16.00	—
1802	—	2.00	3.00	5.00	16.00	—

KM# 482 KREUZER
Copper **Ruler:** Hieronymus

Date	Mintage	VG	F	VF	XF	Unc
1802	—	5.00	10.00	20.00	42.00	—

KM# 491 KREUZER
Copper **Ruler:** Ferdinand Elector

Date	Mintage	VG	F	VF	XF	Unc
1804	—	3.00	6.00	12.00	30.00	—
1805	—	1.50	4.00	10.00	25.00	—
1806	—	1.50	4.00	10.00	25.00	—

KM# 483 3 KREUZER
Copper **Ruler:** Ferdinand Elector

Date	Mintage	VG	F	VF	XF	Unc
1803	—	10.00	20.00	40.00	80.00	—
1804	—	10.00	20.00	40.00	80.00	—

KM# 494 3 KREUZER
Copper **Ruler:** Ferdinand Elector **Rev:** Date in lozenge **Note:** Varieties exist with and without mint mark.

Date	Mintage	VG	F	VF	XF	Unc
1805	—	10.00	20.00	40.00	85.00	—

KM# 477 5 KREUZER
Billon **Ruler:** Hieronymus

Date	Mintage	VG	F	VF	XF	Unc
1801	—	7.50	20.00	50.00	130	—
1802	—	7.50	20.00	50.00	130	—

KM# 484 6 KREUZER
Billon **Ruler:** Ferdinand Elector

Date	Mintage	VG	F	VF	XF	Unc
1803	—	10.00	30.00	65.00	140	—
1804	—	10.00	30.00	60.00	130	—
1805	—	10.00	25.00	50.00	115	—

KM# 495 6 KREUZER
Billon **Ruler:** Ferdinand Elector **Rev:** Date in lozenge

Date	Mintage	VG	F	VF	XF	Unc
1805	—	10.00	30.00	60.00	130	—
1806	—	10.00	30.00	60.00	130	—

KM# 464 10 KREUZER
3.8900 g., 0.5000 Silver .0625 oz. **Ruler:** Hieronymus

Date	Mintage	VG	F	VF	XF	Unc
1801 M	—	15.00	30.00	55.00	110	—
1802 M	—	15.00	30.00	55.00	110	—

KM# 460 20 KREUZER
6.6800 g., 0.5830 Silver .1252 oz. **Ruler:** Hieronymus **Note:** Varieties exist.

Date	Mintage	VG	F	VF	XF	Unc
1801 M	—	3.00	6.00	15.00	40.00	—
1802 M	—	3.00	6.00	15.00	40.00	—
1803 M	—	5.00	15.00	20.00	55.00	—

KM# 492 20 KREUZER
6.6800 g., 0.5830 Silver .1252 oz. **Ruler:** Ferdinand Elector

Date	Mintage	VG	F	VF	XF	Unc
1804 M	—	10.00	20.00	40.00	90.00	—

KM# 496 20 KREUZER
6.6800 g., 0.5830 Silver .1252 oz. **Ruler:** Ferdinand Elector

Date	Mintage	VG	F	VF	XF	Unc
1805 M	—	10.00	25.00	50.00	100	—
1806 M	—	10.00	25.00	50.00	100	—

KM# 461 1/2 THALER
14.0300 g., 0.8330 Silver .3757 oz. **Ruler:** Hieronymus

Date	Mintage	VG	F	VF	XF	Unc
1802 M	—	50.00	100	175	325	—

KM# 465 THALER
28.0600 g., 0.8330 Silver .7515 oz. **Ruler:** Hieronymus **Rev:** Crowned and mantled spade arms **Note:** Varieties exist. Dav.#1265.

Date	Mintage	F	VF	XF	Unc	BU
1801 M	—	65.00	110	150	325	—
1802 M	—	75.00	120	165	350	—
1803 M	—	100	150	250	550	—

KM# 485 THALER
28.0600 g., 0.8330 Silver .7515 oz. **Ruler:** Ferdinand Elector

Date	Mintage	F	VF	XF	Unc	BU
1803	—	100	175	400	750	—

KM# 497 THALER
28.0600 g., 0.8330 Silver .7515 oz. **Ruler:** Ferdinand Elector

Date	Mintage	F	VF	XF	Unc	BU
1805 M	—	150	250	450	850	—

KM# 499 THALER
28.0600 g., 0.8330 Silver .7515 oz. **Ruler:** Ferdinand Elector **Rev. Legend:** ... PAS ETBER S R IP ELECTOR

Date	Mintage	F	VF	XF	Unc	BU
1806 M	—	200	300	550	1,000	—

TRADE COINAGE

KM# 463 DUCAT
3.5000 g., 0.9860 Gold .1109 oz. **Ruler:** Hieronymus **Obv:** Bust right **Rev:** Crowned, mantled arms

Date	Mintage	VG	F	VF	XF	Unc
1801 M	—	75.00	125	250	450	—
1802 M	—	75.00	125	250	450	—

KM# 486 DUCAT
3.5000 g., 0.9860 Gold .1109 oz. **Ruler:** Hieronymus **Note:** Similar to KM#463. Varieties exist.

Date	Mintage	VG	F	VF	XF	Unc
1803 M	—	350	750	2,250	4,000	—

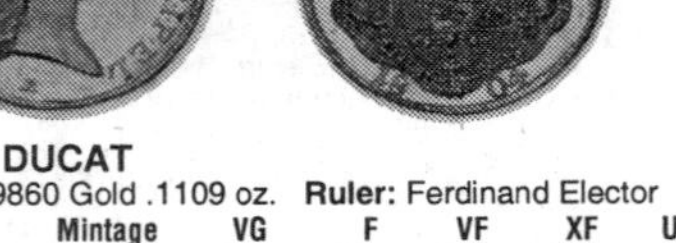

KM# 487 DUCAT
3.5000 g., 0.9860 Gold .1109 oz. **Ruler:** Ferdinand Elector

Date	Mintage	VG	F	VF	XF	Unc
1803 M	—	100	250	800	1,300	—
1804 M	—	125	275	850	1,400	—

KM# 498 DUCAT
3.5000 g., 0.9860 Gold .1109 oz. **Ruler:** Ferdinand Elector

Date	Mintage	VG	F	VF	XF	Unc
1805 M	—	100	250	750	1,250	—
1806 M	—	100	250	750	1,250	—

TYROL

Tirol

A princely county situated in Austria between Germany and Italy. In 1363 Margaret Maultasch, countess of Tyrol, handed over Tyrol to Rudolph, Duke of Austria. Except for a period of Bavarian occupation, 1805-14, Tyrol remained a Hapsburg possession until the breakup of the Austrian Empire at the end of World War I. The world's first dollar-size silver crown was struck at Hall, Tyrol, in 1486.

RULERS

Maximilian Joseph I, (Bavaria), 1805-1814
Andreas Hofer, Rebellion, 1809
Franz I, (Austria), 1814-1835
Ferdinand, (Austria), 1835-1848
Franz Joseph, (Austria), 1848-1916

MINT MARKS

F, FH, G, H, HA - Hall

MONETARY SYSTEM

120 Kreuzer = 1 Convention Thaler

COUNTY

INSURRECTION COINAGE

1809

KM# 148 KREUZER (Ein)
Copper **Issuer:** Andreas Hofer **Note:** Varieties exist.

Date	Mintage	VG	F	VF	XF	Unc
1809	—	10.00	15.00	35.00	85.00	—

KM# 149 20 KREUZER
Silver **Issuer:** Andreas Hofer **Note:** Three varieties exist.

Date	Mintage	VG	F	VF	XF	Unc
1809	—	15.00	25.00	50.00	100	—

AZERBAIJAN

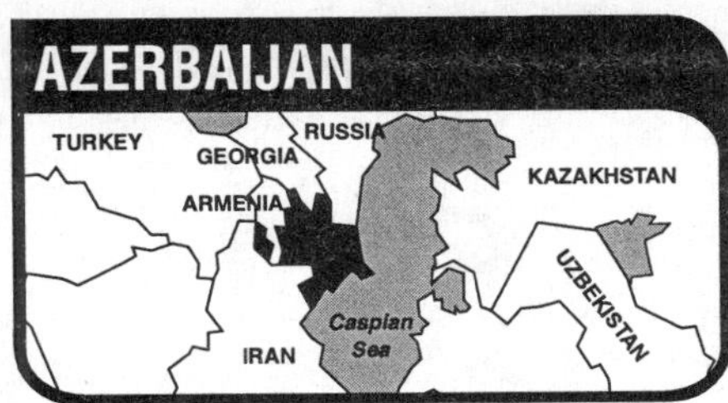

The Republic of Azerbaijan (formerly Azerbaijan S.S.R.) includes the Nakhichevan Autonomous Republic. Situated in the eastern area of Transcaucasia, it is bordered in the west by Armenia, in the north by Georgia and Dagestan, to the east by the Caspian Sea and to the south by Iran. It has an area of 33,430 sq. mi. (86,600 sq. km.). Capital: Baku. The area is rich in mineral deposits of aluminum, copper, iron, lead, salt and zinc, with oil as its leading industry. Agriculture and livestock follow in importance.

Ancient home of Scythian tribes and known under the Romans as Albania and to the Arabs as Arran, the country of Azerbaijan was formed at the time of its invasion by Seliuk Turks and grew into a prosperous state under Persian suzerainty. From the 16th century the country was a theatre of fighting and political rivalry between Turkey, Persia and later Russia. Baku was first annexed to Russia by Czar Peter I in 1723 and remained under Russian rule for 12 years. After the Russian retreat the whole of Azerbaijan north of the Aras River became a khanate under Persian control. Czar Alexander I, after an eight-year war with Persia, annexed it in 1813 to the Russian empire. Until the Russian Revolution of 1905, there was no political life in Azerbaijan.

MINT NAMES

Ganja (Genge) (Elisabethpol, Kirovabad)
Nakhjavan (Nackhchawan)
Shamakhi
Shirvan

DARBAND

Darband (Derbent) is the principal city in Daghistan, now the extreme southeastern portion of Russia. Generally connected to Iran from early Islamic time, it was conquered by the Russians in 1722 but restored to Iran in 1735 under Nadir Shah., After the death of Nadir in 1747, Darband became quasi-independent, adjoined with Qubba, and seems to have begun its local coinage around 1780. Darband was briefly seized by the Russians in 1796 and finally conquered on July 3, 1806 (16 Rabi' II 1221).

The coinage of Darband between 1780 and 1806 never mentions the local ruler, but bears the Arabic phrase, ya'alî.

MINT

Darband

CITY

ANONYMOUS HAMMERED COINAGE

KM# 1 ABBASI

2.3000 g., Silver **Obv:** Ya Sahib al-Zaman **Rev:** Mint, date and inscription **Rev. Inscription:** Ya' Aziz **Note:** Additional dates are said to exist in the Baku Museum.

Date	Mintage	Good	VG	F	VF	XF
ND	—	25.00	40.00	70.00	—	—
AH1219	—	40.00	70.00	125	—	—
AH1221	—	40.00	70.00	125	—	—

GANJA

Ganja has been an important city since pre-Islamic times, and became an Islamic mint about 705 AD. It was part of the Safavid Empire, though occasionally occupied by the Ottomans for short intervals. After the death of Nadir Shah in 1747, it gained independence under Shah Verdi Khan, and local coinage started about 1755. It remained independent until 1805, when acquired by Russia, though it was briefly under Georgian control 1780-1783 and partially under Iranian control between 1790 and 1802.

RULERS

(Part of Iran until AH1137/1724AD)

OTTOMAN

Ahmed III, AH1137-1143/1724-1730AD
Mahmud I, AH1143-1148/1730-1735AD
(Once again under Iran, AH1148-1168/1735-1755AD)

LOCAL RULERS

Shah Verdi Khan, AH1160-1174/1747-1760 AD (effectively independent from 1168/1755)
Muhammad Shah Khan, AH1174-1195/1760-1780AD
(Georgian occupation, AH1193-1198/1780-1783AD)
Hajji Beg, AH1198-1200/1783-1785AD
Ja'far al-Jawwad, ca. 1200-1220/1785-1805AD (partly under Iranian control 1204-1217, see types KM632, 738 and 724 under Iran).

MINT

Sanja

CITY

Muhammad Hasan Khan

AH1174-1195 / 1760-1780AD

HAMMERED COINAGE

KM# 100.8 KAZBEG

Copper **Note:** Unknown type; normal weight varies 7 - 9 grams.

Date	Mintage	Good	VG	F	VF	XF
AH1216	—	—	—	—	—	—

Note: Struck from before AH1181 until at least AH1216

ANONYMOUS HAMMERED COINAGE

Struck from before AH1181 until at least AH1216

KM# 35 1/2 ABBASI

1.5000 g., Silver **Note:** Issued in the name of Fath Ali Shah; rectangular flan.

Date	Mintage	Good	VG	F	VF	XF
AH1216 Rare	—	—	—	—	—	—

KM# 100.7 KAZBEG

Copper **Obv:** 2-blade sword **Rev:** Mint & date **Note:** Weight varies 7 - 9 grams.

Date	Mintage	Good	VG	F	VF	XF
AH1216 (1801)	—	—	12.50	20.00	30.00	—

KARABAGH

Karabagh, a former Khanate in Azerbaijan was under the control of the Ottomans until 996AD when Persia regained control. The principal mint was located in Panahabad, now the town of Shusha. The hereditary Jewanshir family then broke away from Persia in the second half of the 1700's and abandoned their principality to the Russians in 1822. For the remainder of the Czarist period it formed part of the Muslim governorship of Baker until 1868, when it was transfered to Elizabetpol.

It now forms part of The Nagorno-Karabakh-Oblast which was established as an autonomous region with Azerbaijan in 1923. They elected for independence in the C.I.S. in 1991.

RULERS

Ibrahim Khalil Khan, AH1177-1221/1763-1806AD
Mahdi Quli Khan Muzatfar, AH1221-1235/1806-1822AD

MINT NAME

بناه باد

Panahabad (Shusha)

MONETARY SYSTEM

Derived from the Safavid Persian System

1 Bisti = 20 Dinars
1 Abbasi = 200 Dinars

All coins are anonymous except KM#5, which is in the name of Fath'ali Shah of Iran.

The silver abbasi of Karabagh circulated widely in Iran, where it came to be known as a "Panabadi", a term later used for the half Kran in Iran.

KHANATE

Ibrahim Khalil Khan

AH1177-1221 / 1763-1806AD

HAMMERED COINAGE

KM# 5 ABBASI

4.4500 g., Silver **Obv:** Inscription, mintname and date **Obv. Inscription:** "Fath'ali Shah" **Rev:** Shiite formula

Date	Mintage	Good	VG	F	VF	XF
AH1216	—	45.00	60.00	85.00	125	—

KM# 4 ABBASI

Silver **Note:** Weight is about 4.5 grams.

Date	Mintage	Good	VG	F	VF	XF
AH1216	—	—	—	50.00	75.00	120

Note: These are generally found holed or looped

Mahdi Quli Khan Muzatfar

AH1221-1235 / 1806-1819AD

HAMMERED COINAGE

KM# 7 ABBASI

Silver **Obv:** Shiite formula **Rev:** Mint name, formula "ya allah". The date may appear on either side

Date	Mintage	Good	VG	F	VF	XF
AH1221	—	12.00	18.00	40.00	65.00	—
AH1222	—	27.50	35.00	47.50	65.00	—
AH1224	—	27.50	35.00	47.50	65.00	—
AH1226	—	30.00	40.00	55.00	75.00	—
AH1228	—	30.00	40.00	55.00	75.00	—
ND Date missing	—	10.00	15.00	20.00	27.50	—

KM# 6 ABBASI

Silver **Obv:** Crown above date **Rev:** Shiite formula, mint name

Date	Mintage	Good	VG	F	VF	XF
AH1222	—	40.00	55.00	75.00	110	—

KM# 8 ABBASI

Silver **Obv:** Unread couplet mentioning "sahib al-zaman" & date **Rev:** Mint and date with "ya allah" above **Note:** The below listings of types is incomplete. In addition, more dates of the listed type likely exist; AH1236 - 1238 dates were struck posthumously.

Date	Mintage	Good	VG	F	VF	XF
AH1236	—	30.00	40.00	55.00	75.00	—
AH1237	—	20.00	27.50	37.50	50.00	—
AH1238	—	20.00	27.50	37.50	50.00	—
ND Date missing	—	10.00	12.50	17.50	25.00	—

QUBBA

Qubba is now the upland city of Kuba in the north of Azerbaijan. It was part of Daghistan and frequently associated with Darband, from time to time partially or fully independent. The local ruler, Fath 'Ali Khan (1771-1203/1758-1788AD), acquired Darband, probably about 1775, but Darband regained its autonomy after his death. Coinage commenced in the late 1770's. Like Darband, Qubba was briefly seized by the Russians in 1796, and then formally acquired in July 1806. However, unlike Darband it was apparently permitted to continue its local coinage until AH1223/1808AD.

Coins of Qubba can readily be distinguished from that of Darband by the name of the mint and phrase "a 'aziz" instead of "ya 'alî".

MINT

Qubba

CITY

ANONYMOUS HAMMERED COINAGE

KM# 1 ABBASI

2.3000 g., Silver **Obv. Inscription:** "Ya sahib al-zaman" **Rev:** Mint, date and inscription **Rev. Inscription:** ya'ali **Note:** Other dates may exist for this type, but are yet unreported.

Date	Mintage	Good	VG	F	VF	XF
AH1221	—	40.00	70.00	125	—	—
AH1223	—	50.00	80.00	140	—	—
ND (date missing)	—	20.00	40.00	70.00	—	—

Note: The Baku Museum is said to contain examples dated AH1215-1222, as well as AH1223, which is illustrated in their catalog

SHEKI

Sheki, with its capital Nukha was a former khanate in Russian Caucasia, and in 1578 was part of Shirwan (under Ottoman rule). It was occupied in 1806 when the Russians invested Ja'far Quli Khan as governor and then annexed by Russia in 1819. Sheki is now part of Azerbaijan, which joined the Commonwealth of Independent States in December 1991.

RULERS

Muhammad Hasan, AH1198-1221/1783-1806AD
Ja'far Quli Khan, AH1221-1230/1806-1815AD
Ismail Khan, AH1230-1234/1815-1819AD
Annexed to Russia in 1819

MINT NAME

Nukha

MONETARY SYSTEM

200 Dinars = 1 Abbasi
20 Dinars = 1 Bisti

KHANATE

Muhammad Hasan Khan

AH1212-1217 / 1797-1802AD

HAMMERED COINAGE

KM# 3 ABBASI

2.2000 g., Silver **Obv:** The couplet of Karim Khan Zand **Rev:** Mint name and date

Date	Mintage	Good	VG	F	VF	XF
AH1216	—	20.00	30.00	50.00	80.00	—
AH1217	—	20.00	30.00	50.00	80.00	—

Mustafa Khan

AH1217-1221 / 1802-1806AD

HAMMERED COINAGE

KM# 6 ABBASI

2.3000 g., Silver **Obv. Inscription:** "Ya sahib al-zaman" **Rev:** Mint name and date

Date	Mintage	Good	VG	F	VF	XF
AH1220	—	25.00	35.00	55.00	90.00	—
AH1221	—	25.00	35.00	55.00	90.00	—

KM# 7 ABBASI

2.3000 g., Silver **Obv. Inscription:** "Ya sahib al-zaman" **Rev:** Mint name and date

Date	Mintage	Good	VG	F	VF	XF
AH1220 Rare	—	—	—	—	—	—

KM# 5 ABBASI

2.2000 g., Silver **Obv:** The couplet of Karim Khan Zand **Rev:** Mint name and date **Note:** Weight varies 2.10-2.30 grams.

Date	Mintage	Good	VG	F	VF	XF
AH1218	—	20.00	30.00	50.00	80.00	—
AH1219	—	20.00	30.00	50.00	80.00	—
AH1220	—	20.00	30.00	50.00	80.00	—

Ja'Far Quli Khan

AH1221-1230 / 1806-1815AD

HAMMERED COINAGE

KM# 10 BISTI

18.0000 g., Copper **Obv:** Crown above date with various symbols (star, rosette, sprig, etc.) below **Rev. Inscription:** "Zarb fulus nukhwi"

Date	Mintage	Good	VG	F	VF	XF
AH1221	—	40.00	60.00	90.00	175	—
AH1222	—	40.00	60.00	90.00	175	—
AH1223	—	40.00	60.00	90.00	175	—
AH1226	—	40.00	60.00	90.00	175	—
AH1228	—	40.00	60.00	90.00	175	—
AH1229	—	40.00	60.00	90.00	175	—

KM# 12 BISTI

Copper **Obv:** Large crown above date in cartouche **Rev. Inscription:** "Zarb fulus nukhwi" **Note:** Size varies 30-32 millimeters; weight is about 18 grams.

Date	Mintage	Good	VG	F	VF	XF
AH1228	—	35.00	50.00	90.00	165	—
AH1233	—	45.00	65.00	100	185	—

KM# 11 ABBASI

2.0500 g., Silver **Obv:** Crown above date **Rev:** Mint name

Date	Mintage	Good	VG	F	VF	XF
AH1222	—	25.00	35.00	55.00	90.00	—
AH1223	—	25.00	35.00	55.00	90.00	—
AH1225	—	25.00	35.00	55.00	90.00	—
AH1226	—	25.00	35.00	55.00	90.00	—
AH1227	—	25.00	35.00	55.00	90.00	—
AH1228	—	25.00	35.00	55.00	90.00	—
AH1229	—	25.00	35.00	55.00	90.00	—
AH1230	—	25.00	35.00	55.00	90.00	—
AH1231	—	25.00	35.00	55.00	90.00	—

Ismail Khan

AH1230-1234 / 1815-1819AD

HAMMERED COINAGE

KM# 16 ABBASI

2.0500 g., Silver **Obv:** Crown above date **Rev:** Mint name **Note:** Weight varies 2.10-2.30 grams.

Date	Mintage	Good	VG	F	VF	XF
AH1232	—	30.00	45.00	70.00	100	—
AH1233	—	30.00	45.00	70.00	100	—

PERSIAN OCCUPATION

AH1241-1242 / 1825-1826AD

HAMMERED COINAGE

KM# 20 BISTI

Copper **Obv:** Lion right **Rev:** Mint name and date **Note:** Weight is about 20 grams.

Date	Mintage	Good	VG	F	VF	XF
AH1242	—	100	130	175	250	—

KM# 24 ABBASI

1.8000 g., Silver **Obv. Inscription:** "Fath Ali Shah"

Date	Mintage	Good	VG	F	VF	XF
AH1241	—	—	—	50.00	75.00	100
AH1242	—	—	—	50.00	75.00	100

SHEMAKHI

Schemakhi, later the capital of Shirwan, is a former khanate located in Azerbaijan. It was taken by the Ottomans in 1578. Restored to Persian rule in 1607, it remained so throughout much of its later history until the Khan Mustafa submitted to the Russians in 1805 and later occupied by the Russians who annexed the khanate in 1813. After destruction in 1859 by earthquake, it came under the government of Baker. Presently it is part of Azerbaijan, C.I.S.

RULERS

Persian until annexed to Russia in 1813 by the Peace of Gulistan

MINT NAME

شماخه

Shamakha

شماخ

Shamakhi

MONETARY SYSTEM

20 Dinars = 1 Bisti
10 Bisti = 1 Abbasi

KHANATE

AH1177-1220

ANONYMOUS HAMMERED COINAGE

KM# 11 ABBASI

2.3000 g., Silver **Obv:** Persian text. **Obv. Inscription:** Ya Sâheb oz-Zamân. **Rev:** Persian text, mint name and date.

Date	Mintage	Good	VG	F	VF	XF
AH1216 (1801)	—	15.00	28.00	42.50	65.00	—
AH1217 (1802)	—	15.00	28.00	42.50	65.00	—
AH1218 (1803)	—	15.00	28.00	42.50	65.00	—
AH1219 (1804)	—	15.00	28.00	42.50	65.00	—
AH1220 (1805)	—	15.00	28.00	42.50	65.00	—
AH1221 (1806)	—	15.00	28.00	42.50	65.00	—
AH1222 (1807)	—	15.00	28.00	42.50	65.00	—
AH1223 (1808)	—	17.50	30.00	45.00	75.00	—
AH1226 (1811)	—	17.50	30.00	45.00	75.00	—
AH1227 (1812)	—	15.00	28.00	42.50	65.00	—
AH1228 (1812)	—	15.00	28.00	42.50	65.00	—
AH1229 (1813)	—	15.00	28.00	42.50	65.00	—
AH1230 (1814)	—	15.00	28.00	42.50	65.00	—
AH1231 (1815)	—	15.00	28.00	42.50	65.00	—
AH1232 (1816)	—	15.00	28.00	42.50	65.00	—
AH1233 (1817)	—	15.00	28.00	42.50	65.00	—
AH1234 (1818)	—	15.00	28.00	42.50	65.00	—
AH1235 (1819)	—	15.00	28.00	42.50	65.00	—
AH1236 (1820)	—	15.00	28.00	42.50	65.00	—

Mustafa Khan

AH1209-1235 / 1794-1820AD

ANONYMOUS HAMMERED COINAGE

KM# 15 KAZBEG

Copper **Obv:** Various designs **Rev:** Mint name and date

Date	Mintage	Good	VG	F	VF	XF
AH1218 Unknown design	—	—	—	—	—	—
AH1222 Lion and sun	—	—	17.50	27.50	45.00	—
ND Date off flan	—	—	10.00	17.50	30.00	—

HAMMERED COINAGE

KM# 20 ABBASI

Silver **Note:** Weight approximately 2.25 grams (3/6 mithqal), heavier weight of pre-AH1209 restored; similar to KM#5.

Date	Mintage	Good	VG	F	VF	XF
AH1216	—	—	18.50	25.00	35.00	55.00
AH1217	—	—	18.50	25.00	35.00	55.00
AH1218	—	—	18.50	25.00	35.00	55.00
AH1219	—	—	18.50	25.00	35.00	55.00
AH1220	—	—	18.50	25.00	35.00	55.00
AH1221	—	—	18.50	25.00	35.00	55.00
AH1222	—	—	18.50	25.00	35.00	55.00
AH1223	—	—	18.50	25.00	35.00	55.00
AH1224	—	—	18.50	25.00	35.00	55.00
AH1225	—	—	18.50	25.00	35.00	55.00
AH1227	—	—	18.50	25.00	35.00	55.00
AH1228	—	—	18.50	25.00	35.00	55.00
AH1230	—	—	22.50	30.00	45.00	65.00
AH1231	—	—	22.50	30.00	45.00	65.00
AH1232	—	—	22.50	30.00	45.00	65.00
AH1233	—	—	22.50	30.00	45.00	65.00
AH1234	—	—	22.50	30.00	45.00	65.00
AH1235	—	—	22.50	30.00	45.00	65.00

AZORES

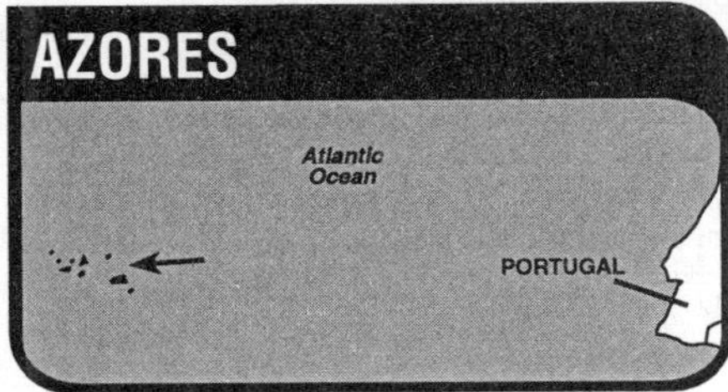

The Azores, an archipelago of nine islands of volcanic origin, are located in the Atlantic Ocean 740 miles (1,190 km.) west of Cape de Roca, Portugal. They are the westernmost region of Europe under the administration of Portugal and have an area of 902 sq. mi. (2,305 sq. km.). Principal city: Ponta Delgada. The natives are mainly of Portuguese descent and earn their livelihood by fishing, wine making, basket weaving and the growing of fruit, grains and sugar cane. Pineapples are the chief item of export. The climate is particularly temperate, making the islands a favorite winter resort.

The Azores were discovered about 1427 by the Portuguese navigator Diogo de Sevill. Portugal secured the islands in the 15th century and established the first settlement on Santa Maria about 1439. From 1580 to 1640 the Azores were subject to Spain.

The Azores' first provincial coinage was ordered by law of August 19, 1750. Copper coins were struck for circulation in both the Azores and Madeira Islands. Keeping the same technical specifications but with different designs. In 1795 a second provincial coinage was introduced but the weight was reduced by 50 percent.

Angra on Terceira Island became the capital of the captaincy-general of the Azores in 1766 and it was here in 1826 that the constitutionalists set up a pro-Pedro government in opposition to King Miguel in Lisbon. The whole Portuguese fleet attacked Terceira and was repelled at Praia, after which Azoreans, Brazilians and British mercenaries defeated Miguel in Portugal. Maria de Gloria, Pedro's daughter, was proclaimed queen of Portugal on Terceira in 1828.

RULERS

Portuguese

MONETARY SYSTEM

1000 Reis (Insulanos) = 1 Milreis

PORTUGUESE ADMINISTRATION

PROVINCIAL COINAGE

KM# 10 5 REIS
Copper **Subject:** Maria II

Date	Mintage	VG	F	VF	XF	Unc
1843	—	3.00	7.00	20.00	45.00	—

KM# 13 5 REIS
Copper **Subject:** Luiz I

Date	Mintage	F	VF	XF	Unc	BU
1865	90,000	8.00	20.00	45.00	110	—
1866	60,000	25.00	50.00	100	200	—
1880	40,000	3.00	6.00	18.00	35.00	—

KM# 11 10 REIS
Copper **Subject:** Maria II

Date	Mintage	VG	F	VF	XF	Unc
1843	—	4.00	9.00	30.00	120	—

KM# 14 10 REIS
Copper **Subject:** Luiz I

Date	Mintage	F	VF	XF	Unc	BU
1865	350,000	3.50	8.00	25.00	65.00	—
1866	175,000	75.00	150	350	600	—

KM# 12 20 REIS
Copper **Subject:** Maria II

Date	Mintage	VG	F	VF	XF	Unc
1843	—	3.00	7.00	22.00	65.00	—

KM# 15 20 REIS
Copper **Subject:** Luiz I **Note:** Varieties exist with points separating the reverse legend.

Date	Mintage	F	VF	XF	Unc	BU
1865	178,000	6.00	12.00	25.00	60.00	—
1866	150,000	7.00	15.00	30.00	70.00	—

COUNTERMARKED COINAGE

Decree of June 14, 1871

This first decree ordained that the circulating Brazilian Patacas of 2000 Reis, including the fractions of 1000, 500 and 200 Reis, which at the time locally had a value of 1200, 600, 300, and 120 Reis (Portuguese)respectively, were to be countermarked with a royal crown. These were eventually to be replaced or exchanged by current Portuguese coinage upon their entry into the public treasury. This countermark is also known on copper coins and on various silver coins of other nations that were circulating at the time. The following list is a basic guide with samples of known examples. Grades noted are for the basic coin as the countermark is normally found in better condition.

KM# 30 10 REIS
Copper **Countermark:** Crown **Note:** Countermark on Azores 5 Reis, KM#9.

CM Date	Host Date	Good	VG	F	VF	XF
ND(1871)	ND(1795-99)	10.00	18.00	35.00	65.00	—

KM# 18.1 20 REIS
Copper **Countermark:** Crown **Note:** Countermark on Azores, Terceira Island X Reis, KM#6.

CM Date	Host Date	Good	VG	F	VF	XF
ND(1871)	ND(1830)	10.00	20.00	40.00	85.00	—

KM# 18.2 20 REIS
Copper **Countermark:** Crown **Note:** Countermark on Portuguese X Reis, KM#481.

CM Date	Host Date	Good	VG	F	VF	XF
ND(1871)	ND(1852)	10.00	20.00	40.00	85.00	—

KM# 18.3 20 REIS
Copper **Countermark:** Crown **Note:** Countermark on St. Thomas 20 Reis, KM#D1.

CM Date	Host Date	Good	VG	F	VF	XF
ND(1871)	ND(1819)	10.00	20.00	40.00	85.00	—

KM# 22.1 40 REIS
Copper **Countermark:** Crown **Note:** Countermark on St. Thomas 40 Reis, KM#E1.

CM Date	Host Date	Good	VG	F	VF	XF
ND(1871)	ND(1819)	10.00	20.00	40.00	85.00	—
ND(1871)	ND(1825)	10.00	20.00	40.00	85.00	—

KM# 22.2 40 REIS
Copper **Countermark:** Crown **Note:** Countermark on Mozambique 40 Reis, KM#22.

CM Date	Host Date	Good	VG	F	VF	XF
ND(1871)	ND(1840)	10.00	20.00	40.00	85.00	—

KM# 19.3 120 REIS
Copper **Countermark:** Crown **Note:** Countermark on Angola Macuta, KM#12.

CM Date	Host Date	Good	VG	F	VF	XF
ND(1871)	ND(1762-70)	20.00	30.00	60.00	110	—

KM# 19.4 120 REIS
Copper **Countermark:** Crown **Note:** Countermark on Azores, Terceira Island 80 Reis, KM#4.2.

CM Date	Host Date	Good	VG	F	VF	XF
ND(1871)	ND(1829)	20.00	30.00	60.00	110	—

KM# 19.1 120 REIS
Silver **Countermark:** Crown **Note:** Countermark on Brazilian 200 Reis, KM#469.

CM Date	Host Date	Good	VG	F	VF	XF
ND	ND(1854-67)	10.00	20.00	30.00	50.00	—

KM# 19.2 120 REIS
Silver **Countermark:** Crown **Note:** Countermark on Brazilian 200 Reis, KM#471.

CM Date	Host Date	Good	VG	F	VF	XF
ND(1871)	ND(1867-69)	10.00	20.00	30.00	50.00	—

KM# 20.1 300 REIS
Silver **Countermark:** Crown **Note:** Countermark on Brazilian 500 Reis, KM#458.

CM Date	Host Date	Good	VG	F	VF	XF
ND(1871)	ND(1848-52)	12.50	25.00	40.00	60.00	—

KM# 20.2 300 REIS

Silver **Countermark:** Crown **Note:** Countermark on Brazilian 500 Reis, KM#464.

CM Date	Host Date	Good	VG	F	VF	XF
ND(1871)	ND(1853-67)	12.50	25.00	40.00	60.00	—

KM# 20.3 300 REIS

Silver **Countermark:** Crown **Note:** Countermark on Brazilian 500 Reis, KM#472.

CM Date	Host Date	Good	VG	F	VF	XF
ND(1871)	ND(1867-68)	12.50	25.00	40.00	60.00	—

KM# 28.1 600 REIS

Silver **Countermark:** Crown **Note:** Countermark on Brazilian 1000 Reis, KM#459.

CM Date	Host Date	Good	VG	F	VF	XF
ND(1871)	ND(1849-52)	15.00	27.50	45.00	65.00	—

KM# 28.2 600 REIS

Silver **Countermark:** Crown **Note:** Countermark on Brazilian 1000 Reis, KM#465.

CM Date	Host Date	Good	VG	F	VF	XF
ND(1871)	ND(1853-66)	15.00	27.50	45.00	65.00	—

KM# 28.3 600 REIS

Silver **Countermark:** Crown **Note:** Countermark on Brazilian 1000 Reis, KM#476.

CM Date	Host Date	Good	VG	F	VF	XF
ND(1871)	ND(1869)	17.50	30.00	50.00	75.00	—

KM# 28.4 600 REIS

Silver **Countermark:** Crown **Note:** Countermark on East India Co. Bengal Rupee, KM#108.

CM Date	Host Date	Good	VG	F	VF	XF
ND(1871)	ND(1819-32)	12.00	30.00	60.00	100	—

KM# 21.1 1200 REIS

Silver **Countermark:** Crown **Note:** Countermark on Austria-Burgau Thaler, KM#23.

CM Date	Host Date	Good	VG	F	VF	XF
ND(1871)	ND(1780*SF)	20.00	40.00	75.00	145	—

KM# 21.4 1200 REIS

Silver **Countermark:** Crown **Note:** Countermark on Brazilian 1200 Reis, KM#454.

CM Date	Host Date	Good	VG	F	VF	XF
ND(1871)	ND(1834)	100	165	275	450	—

KM# 21.2 1200 REIS

Silver **Countermark:** Crown **Note:** Countermark on Brazilian 2000 Reis, KM#462.

CM Date	Host Date	Good	VG	F	VF	XF
ND(1871)	ND(1851-52)	30.00	55.00	110	200	—

KM# 21.3 1200 REIS

Silver **Countermark:** Crown **Note:** Countermark on Brazilian 2000 Reis, KM#466.

CM Date	Host Date	Good	VG	F	VF	XF
ND(1871)	ND(1853-67)	30.00	55.00	110	200	—

COUNTERMARKED COINAGE

Decree of March 31, 1887

This second decree ordained that all foreign silver and copper coinage circulating in the Azores was to be countermarked with a crowned G.P. (Governo Portugues) within a circle. These also were eventually to be replaced or exchanged by current Portuguese coinage upon their entry into the public treasury. This countermark for general use is found on a profusion of Portuguese, Brazilian, and foreign issues. The largest crown or dollar size includes the Portuguese 1000 Reis, Brazilian 2000 Reis, obsolete 960 Reis, 1200 Reis, Austrian Thaler, English 5 Shilling or Crown, Spanish American 8 Reales and Spanish 2 Escudos for comparison to the United States dollar. This countermark has been heavily counterfeited and should be approached with caution. The following list is a basic guide with samples of known examples. Grades noted are for the basic coin and the countermark is normally found in better condition than the coin bearing it.

KM# 23 15 REIS

Copper **Countermark:** Crowned G.P. **Note:** Countermark on Portuguese India (Goa) 15 Reis, KM#263.

CM Date	Host Date	Good	VG	F	VF	XF
ND(1887)	ND(1834-53)	10.00	20.00	35.00	70.00	—

KM# A24 40 REIS

1.5000 g., Silver, 16.3 mm. **Counterstamp:** Crown over GP **Note:** Countermark on Portugese 40 reis KM-101

CM Date	Host Date	Good	VG	F	VF	XF
	ND (1887)	—	—	—	—	—

KM# 24.1 120 REIS

Silver **Countermark:** Crowned G.P. **Note:** Countermark on Spanish or Spanish Colonial Real.

CM Date	Host Date	Good	VG	F	VF	XF
ND(1887)	ND(1717-1821)	8.00	16.00	30.00	60.00	—

KM# 24.2 120 REIS

Silver **Countermark:** Crowned G.P. **Note:** Countermark on various Portuguese 80 Reis.

CM Date	Host Date	Good	VG	F	VF	XF
ND(1887)	ND(1689-1701)	15.00	25.00	40.00	80.00	—

KM# 25.1 300 REIS

Silver **Countermark:** Crowned G.P. **Note:** Countermark on Spanish or Spanish Colonial 2 Reales.

CM Date	Host Date	Good	VG	F	VF	XF
ND(1887)	ND(1717-1830)	12.00	22.00	37.50	75.00	—

KM# 25.2 300 REIS

Silver **Countermark:** Crowned G.P. **Note:** Countermark on various Portuguese 200 Reis.

CM Date	Host Date	Good	VG	F	VF	XF
ND(1887)	ND(1683-92)	20.00	30.00	50.00	90.00	—

KM# 26.1 600 REIS

Silver **Countermark:** Crowned G.P. **Note:** Countermark on Bolivia 4 Reales, KM#54.

CM Date	Host Date	Good	VG	F	VF	XF
ND(1887)	ND(1773-89)	30.00	50.00	85.00	145	—

KM# 26.2 600 REIS

Silver **Countermark:** Crowned G.P. **Note:** Countermark on Portuguese 400 Reis, KM#331.

CM Date	Host Date	Good	VG	F	VF	XF
ND(1887)	ND(1802-16)	25.00	45.00	75.00	125	—

KM# 26.3 600 REIS

Silver **Countermark:** Crowned G.P. **Note:** Countermark on Portuguese 400 Reis, KM#386.

CM Date	Host Date	Good	VG	F	VF	XF
ND(1887)	ND(1828-34)	35.00	60.00	110	165	—

KM# 29.1 1200 REIS

Silver **Countermark:** Crowned G.P. **Note:** Countermark on Brazilian (Minas Gerais) 960 Reis, KM#242.

CM Date	Host Date	Good	VG	F	VF	XF
ND(1887)	ND(1791-1808)	55.00	90.00	145	225	—

KM# 29.2 1200 REIS
Silver **Countermark:** Crowned G.P. **Note:** Countermark on Brazilian 960 Reis, KM#307.1.

CM Date	Host Date	Good	VG	F	VF	XF
ND(1887)	ND(1809-18)	—	40.00	60.00	115	175

KM# 29.3 1200 REIS
Silver **Countermark:** Crowned G.P. **Note:** Countermark on Peruvian 8 Reales, KM#142.3.

CM Date	Host Date	Good	VG	F	VF	XF
ND(1887)	ND(1828-40)	—	40.00	60.00	115	175

KM# 29.4 1200 REIS
Silver **Countermark:** Crowned G.P. **Note:** Countermark on Spanish 20 Reales, C#92.

CM Date	Host Date	Good	VG	F	VF	XF
ND(1887)	ND(1808-13)	65.00	100	185	325	—

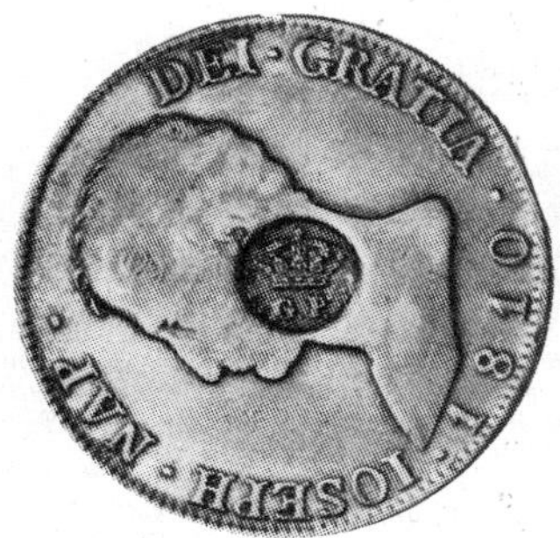

KM# 29.5 1200 REIS
Silver **Countermark:** Crowned G.P. **Note:** Countermark on Brazilian 960 Reis, KM#326.1.

CM Date	Host Date	Good	VG	F	VF	XF
ND(1887)	ND(1818-22)	—	40.00	60.00	115	175

PATTERNS

Including off metal strikes

KM#	Date	Mintage	Identification	Mkt Val
Pn3	1865	—	20 Reis. Copper.	—

KM#	Date	Mintage	Identification	Mkt Val
Pn4	ND	—	5 Reis. Copper. Similar to KM#16 but without obverse legend.	—

TRIAL STRIKES

KM#	Date	Mintage	Identification	Mkt Val
TS2	1843	—	10 Reis. Copper. Uniface.	500

TERCEIRA ISLAND

On the death of John VI in 1826 the constitutionalists on Terceira supported Pedro, the Brazilian emperor and oldest son of John VI, for the Portuguese throne in opposition to Miguel, Pedro's younger brother who was proclaimed king in 1828. After repelling the attack of the entire Portuguese fleet at Praia, the constitutionalists with their British mercenaries invaded Portugal and defeated Miguel in 1834. Maria da Gloria, daughter of Pedro, was then proclaimed Queen of Portugal.

TOKEN COINAGE

KM# Tn1 LXXX (80) REIS
Copper **Obv:** AZORES INDEPENDEN. ILHA TERCEIRA

Date	Mintage	G	VG	F	VF	XF
1826	4 known	750	1250	2000	3000	—

MARIA II IN EXILE

In 1828 Pedro declined the Portuguese throne in favor of his daughter, Maria da Gloria, who was therefore forced to live in exile 1828-1834 until Miguel was completely defeated.

STANDARD COINAGE

KM# 5 5 REIS
Copper

Date	Mintage	VG	F	VF	XF	Unc
1830	—	6.00	12.00	25.00	50.00	—

KM# 6 10 REIS
Copper

Date	Mintage	VG	F	VF	XF	Unc
1830	—	7.00	14.00	28.00	55.00	—

KM# 4.1 80 REIS
Bronze **Rev:** Large legend and large stars

Date	Mintage	VG	F	VF	XF	Unc
1829	—	40.00	75.00	100	200	—

KM# 4.2 80 REIS
Bronze **Rev:** Small legend and small stars

Date	Mintage	VG	F	VF	XF	Unc
1829	—	40.00	60.00	75.00	165	—

Note: Cast from gun or bell metal with varying degrees of planchet thickness and porosity

PATTERNS

Including off metal strikes

KM#	Date	Mintage	Identification	Mkt Val
Pn1	1829	—	40 Reis. Copper.	—
Pn2	1829	—	40 Reis. Lead.	—

KM#	Date	Mintage	Identification	Mkt Val
Pn3	1829	—	80 Reis. Bronze.	—

KM#	Date	Mintage	Identification	Mkt Val
Pn4	1829	—	80 Reis. Bronze.	—
Pn5	1829	—	600 Reis. Copper.	—

KM#	Date	Mintage	Identification	Mkt Val
Pn6	1829	—	800 Reis. Cast Silver.	—

KM#	Date	Mintage	Identification	Mkt Val

Pn7	1833	—	20 Reis. Copper.	—

Pn8	1833	—	50 Reis. Copper.	—

BAHAMAS

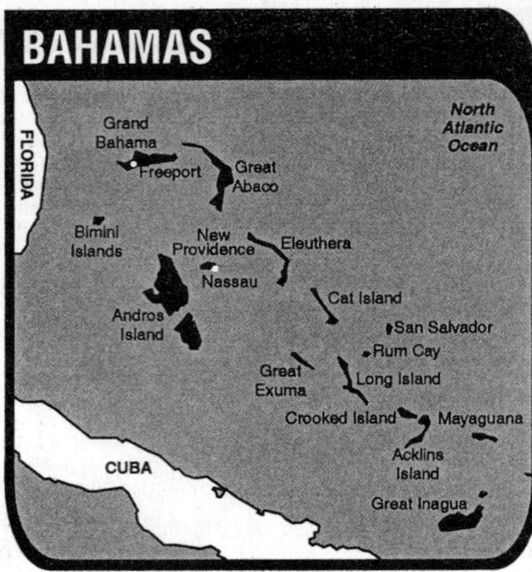

The Commonwealth of the Bahamas is an archipelago of about 3,000 islands, cays and rocks located in the Atlantic Ocean east of Florida and north of Cuba. The total land area of the 800 mile (1,287 km.) long chain of islands is 5,382 sq. mi. (13,935 sq. km.). Capital: Nassau. The Bahamas import most of their food and manufactured products and export cement, refined oil, pulpwood and lobsters. Tourism is the principal industry.

The Bahamas were discovered by Columbus October, 1492, upon his sighting of the island of San Salvador, but Spain made no attempt to settle them. British influence began in 1626 when Charles I granted them to the lord proprietors of Carolina, with settlements in 1629 at New Providence by colonists from the northern territory. Although the Bahamas were temporarily under Spanish control in 1641 and 1703, they continued under British proprietors until 1717, when, as the result of political and economic mismanagement, the civil and military governments were surrendered to the King and the islands designated a British Crown Colony. Full international agreement on British possession of the islands resulted from the Treaty of Versailles in 1783.

The coinage of Great Britain was legal tender in the Bahamas from 1825.

RULERS
British

MONETARY SYSTEM
12 Pence = 1 Shilling
20 Shillings = 1 Pound

BRITISH COLONY

REGULAR COINAGE

KM# 1 PENNY
Copper

Date	Mintage	F	VF	XF	Unc	BU
1806 Engrailed edge	120,000	35.00	65.00	160	275	—
1806 Engrailed edge; proof	—	Value: 300				
1806 Restrike; plain edge; proof	—	Value: 175				
1807 Engrailed edge; proof	—	Value: 3,000				

KM# 1a PENNY
Gilt

Date	Mintage	F	VF	XF	Unc	BU
1806 Engrailed edge; restrike	—	—	—	—	350	—

BELGIUM

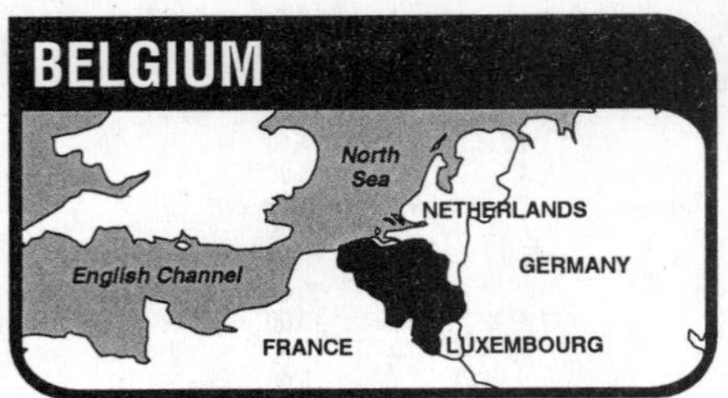

The Kingdom of Belgium, a constitutional monarchy in northwest Europe, has an area of 11,780 sq. mi. (30,519 sq. km.). Chiefly Dutch-speaking Flemish and French-speaking Walloons. Capital: Brussels. Agriculture, dairy farming, and the processing of raw materials for re-export are the principal industries. Beurs voor Diamant in Antwerp is the world's largest diamond trading center. Iron and steel, machinery motor vehicles, chemicals, textile yarns and fabrics comprise the principal exports.

The Celtic tribe called Belgae', from which Belgium derived its name, was described by Caesar as the most courageous of all the tribes of Gaul. The Belgae eventually capitulated to Rome and the area remained for centuries as a part of the Roman Empire known as Belgica.

The eastern part of today's Belgium lies in the Duchy of Lower Lorraine while much of the western parts eventually became the County of Flanders. After further divisions the area came under the control of the Duke of Burgundy from whence it passed under Hapsburg control. Charles and Ferdinand, sons of Philip and Johanna, began the separate Spanish and Austrian lines of the Hapsburg family. The Burgundian lands, along with the northern provinces that make up present day Netherlands, became the Spanish Netherlands. The northern provinces successfully rebelled and broke away from Hapsburg rule in the late 16th century and early 17th century. The southern provinces along with the Duchy of Luxembourg remained under the influence of Spain until the year 1700 when Charles II, last of the Spanish Hapsburg line, died without leaving an heir and the Spanish crown went to the Bourbon family of France. The Spanish Netherlands then reverted to the control of the Austrian line of Hapsburgs and became the Austrian Netherlands. The Austrian Netherlands along with the Bishopric of Liege fell to the French Republic in 1794.

At the Congress of Vienna in 1815 the area was reunited with the Netherlands, but in 1830 independence was gained and the constitutional monarchy of Belgium was established. A large part of the Duchy of Luxembourg was incorporated into Belgium and the first king was Leopold I of Saxe-Coburg-Gotha.

RULERS
Leopold I, 1831-1865
Leopold II, 1865-1909

MINT MARKS
Angel head - Brussels

MONETARY SYSTEM
100 Centimes = 1 Franc
1 Ecu - 1 Euro

LEGENDS

Belgian coins are usually inscribed either in Dutch, French or both. However some modern coins are being inscribed in Latin or German. The language used is best told by noting the spelling of the name of the country.

(Fr) French: BELGIQUE or BELGES
(Du) Dutch: BELGIE or BELGEN
(La) Latin: BELGICA
(Ge) German: BELGIEN

Many Belgian coins are collected by what is known as Position A and Position B edges. Some dates command a premium depending on the position which are as follows:

Position A: Coins with portrait side down having upright edge lettering.

Position B: Coins with portrait side up having upright edge lettering.

KINGDOM

DECIMAL COINAGE

KM# 1.1 CENTIME
Copper **Note:** Wide rims.

Date	Mintage	VG	F	VF	XF	Unc
1832	—	20.00	60.00	300	500	—
1833/2	5,007,000	2.50	12.00	75.00	140	200
1833	Inc. above	2.00	8.00	45.00	100	—
1835/2	4,367,000	2.50	10.00	75.00	150	200
1835	Inc. above	2.50	8.00	50.00	125	—

KM# 1.2 CENTIME

Copper **Note:** Narrow rims.

Date	Mintage	VG	F	VF	XF	Unc
1835/2	Inc. above	3.00	14.00	120	180	—
1835	Inc. above	1.25	4.00	25.00	65.00	—
1836/2	4,256,000	1.25	6.00	50.00	100	—
1836	Inc. above	1.25	5.00	35.00	80.00	120
1837	—	22.50	90.00	450	750	—
1838	—	22.50	90.00	450	750	—
1841	—	22.50	90.00	450	750	—
1844	1,822,000	2.75	10.00	80.00	160	250
1845	8,324,000	0.75	3.00	15.00	50.00	100
1846/1	8,241,000	1.50	5.00	30.00	75.00	—
1846	Inc. above	0.75	3.50	15.00	45.00	—
1847	5,138,000	0.75	5.00	30.00	85.00	150
1848/1	383,000	70.00	175	750	2,000	—
1848	Inc. above	70.00	175	750	2,000	—
1849	1,218,000	1.50	12.50	50.00	140	—
1850	2,309,000	1.50	8.00	40.00	90.00	135
1855	2,428,000	50.00	120	300	500	—
1856	Inc. above	0.75	7.50	40.00	90.00	150
1857	948,000	3.00	10.00	55.00	140	250
1858	916,000	3.00	10.00	55.00	140	225
1859	982,000	3.00	12.00	65.00	165	250
1860	1,581,000	1.00	3.00	20.00	50.00	80.00
1861	1,696,000	1.00	3.00	20.00	50.00	75.00
1862	11,907,000	0.50	1.50	10.00	30.00	50.00
1863	Inc. above	40.00	100	400	800	—

KM# 1.3 CENTIME

Copper **Rev:** Without dash below CENT.

Date	Mintage	VG	F	VF	XF	Unc
1857	Inc. above	6.00	15.00	70.00	140	—
1858	Inc. above	6.00	15.00	70.00	140	—
1859	Inc. above	4.00	10.00	50.00	125	150
1860	Inc. above	3.00	5.00	30.00	90.00	—

KM# 1.4 CENTIME

Copper **Rev:** Without stop in signature

Date	Mintage	VG	F	VF	XF	Unc
1862	Inc. above	2.00	2.00	10.00	30.00	—

Until 1838 these were often struck over Netherlands 1/2 Cent, KM# 51. If the date of the Netherlands coin is still visible, add up to 50 percent to the value, except for the dates 1837 and 1838 which are extremely rare.

KM# 33.1 CENTIME

Copper **Obv:** Legend in French **Obv. Legend:** DES BELGES

Date	Mintage	F	VF	XF	Unc	BU
1869	5,064,000	1.00	7.00	20.00	45.00	—
1870	3,930,000	1.00	7.00	20.00	45.00	—
1873	2,036,000	1.00	7.00	20.00	45.00	—
1874	3,907,000	1.00	7.00	20.00	45.00	—
1875	2,970,000	1.00	7.00	20.00	45.00	—
1876	2,966,000	1.00	7.00	20.00	45.00	—
1882	5,000,000	0.25	2.00	7.50	17.50	—
1883	—	60.00	125	450	1,000	—
1899	2,500,000	0.50	2.00	6.00	12.00	—

KM# 33.2 CENTIME

Copper **Note:** Thin flan.

Date	Mintage	F	VF	XF	Unc	BU
1882	Inc. above	0.50	1.50	6.00	15.00	—
1901	Inc. above	1.00	1.50	4.00	12.50	—
1902	Inc. above	1.00	1.50	6.00	15.00	—

KM# 34.1 CENTIME

Copper **Obv:** Legend in Dutch **Obv. Legend:** DER BELGEN

Date	Mintage	F	VF	XF	Unc	BU
1882	Inc. above	50.00	150	325	550	—
1887	5,000,000	0.50	2.50	6.00	15.00	—
1892	—	30.00	100	400	900	—
1894	5,000,000	0.50	2.50	6.00	15.00	—
1899	2,500,000	0.50	2.00	6.00	12.00	—

KM# 34.2 CENTIME

Copper **Note:** Thin flan.

Date	Mintage	F	VF	XF	Unc	BU
1887	Inc. above	3.00	4.50	12.00	35.00	—

KM# 4.3 2 CENTIMES

Copper **Note:** Medal alignment.

Date	Mintage	VG	F	VF	XF	Unc
1833	Inc. above	10.00	20.00	110	300	—
1834	Inc. above	20.00	30.00	170	400	—

KM# 4.1 2 CENTIMES

Copper **Note:** Wide rims.

Date	Mintage	VG	F	VF	XF	Unc
1833	16,748,000	2.50	5.00	40.00	90.00	150
1834	3,268,000	3.00	10.00	75.00	200	350
1835	26,774,000	2.50	8.00	50.00	150	285

KM# 4.2 2 CENTIMES

Copper **Note:** Narrow rims.

Date	Mintage	VG	F	VF	XF	Unc
1835/3	Inc. above	4.00	10.00	40.00	100	—
1835	Inc. above	0.75	2.00	10.00	25.00	—
.1835.	Inc. above	6.50	15.00	50.00	120	—
1836/3	27,539,000	5.00	3.00	15.00	45.00	—
1836	Inc. above	0.75	2.00	10.00	25.00	—
1837	—	30.00	65.00	400	600	—
18.8/7	—	70.00	100	500	900	—
1838	—	30.00	65.00	300	500	—
1841	2,226,000	1.50	6.00	35.00	85.00	200
1842	2,824,000	1.50	6.00	35.00	85.00	300
1844	1,802,000	1.00	8.00	45.00	150	400
1845 Large date	8,324,000	0.75	2.50	10.00	30.00	80.00
1845 Small date	Inc. above	0.75	2.50	10.00	30.00	80.00
1846	8,007,999	0.75	2.50	10.00	30.00	80.00
1847	3,432,000	1.00	3.50	15.00	40.00	100
1848	420,000	12.00	25.00	135	400	900
1849	3,690,000	1.00	3.50	15.00	40.00	150
1850	404,000	20.00	100	600	1,500	—
1851	2,407,000	1.00	4.00	25.00	75.00	150
1852 Large date	731,000	5.00	12.00	70.00	180	—
1852 Small date	Inc. above	5.00	12.00	70.00	180	—
1853	466,000	12.00	30.00	150	375	900
1855	172,000	20.00	40.00	250	700	1,500
1856 Large date	6,255,000	0.75	2.00	10.00	27.00	75.00
1856 Small date	Inc. above	0.75	2.00	10.00	27.00	75.00
1857	4,612,000	0.75	3.00	14.00	35.00	100
1857	Inc. above	5.00	10.00	40.00	100	—
1858/47	3,177,000	1.50	3.00	15.00	35.00	—
1858/57	Inc. above	1.50	8.00	25.00	65.00	—
1858	Inc. above	0.75	3.00	12.00	40.00	—
1859	4,074,000	0.75	3.00	12.00	40.00	75.00
1860 Large date	3,070,000	0.75	2.00	20.00	50.00	75.00
1860 Small date	Inc. above	0.75	2.00	20.00	50.00	75.00
1861	2,924,000	0.75	2.00	15.00	40.00	75.00
1862 Large date	6,586,000	0.50	2.50	17.50	45.00	75.00
1862 Small date	Inc. above	0.50	2.50	17.50	45.00	75.00
1863/2	18,621,000	0.75	2.50	9.00	25.00	50.00
1863	Inc. above	0.50	1.00	6.00	15.00	40.00
1864/1	16,840,000	1.00	2.00	12.50	35.00	70.00
1864	Inc. above	0.50	1.00	6.00	20.00	40.00
1865	2,447,000	0.50	2.00	8.00	25.00	50.00

KM# 4.4 2 CENTIMES

Copper **Rev:** Without stop in signature

Date	Mintage	VG	F	VF	XF	Unc
1844	Inc. above	1.00	8.00	45.00	150	—
1845	Inc. above	0.75	2.50	10.00	30.00	—
1851	Inc. above	0.75	4.00	25.00	75.00	—
1861	Inc. above	0.75	2.00	15.00	40.00	—

KM# 4.2a 2 CENTIMES

Bronze

Date	Mintage	VG	F	VF	XF	Unc
1845	Inc. above	30.00	40.00	200	400	—
1859	Inc. above	30.00	40.00	200	400	—

KM# 84 2 CENTIMES

Copper **Counterstamp:** Script LII **Note:** Counterstamp in monogram on Netherlands 1 Cent, KM#47.

Date	Mintage	VG	F	VF	XF	Unc
ND	—	120	450	900	1,400	—

KM# 35.1 2 CENTIMES

Copper **Obv:** Legend in French **Obv. Legend:** DES BELGES

Date	Mintage	F	VF	XF	Unc	BU
1869 Plain edge; restrike	—	—	—	—	—	—
1869	2,972,000	10.00	60.00	125	200	—
1870	5,654,000	0.25	1.00	7.00	12.00	—
1870/1	Inc. above	1.25	2.00	12.50	30.00	—
1871 Inc.1870	—	0.25	5.00	20.00	70.00	—
1873	7,491,000	0.25	1.00	5.00	12.00	—
1874 Small wide date	7,876,000	0.25	1.00	5.00	12.00	—
1874 Large narrow date	Inc. above	0.25	1.00	5.00	12.00	—
1875	7,932,000	0.25	1.00	5.00	12.00	—
1876	10,472,000	0.25	1.00	3.00	10.00	—

KM# 5.1 5 CENTIMES

Copper

Date	Mintage	VG	F	VF	XF	Unc
1811 Error	—	100	250	700	1,600	—
1833	4,437,000	2.50	5.00	27.50	85.00	175
1834	2,515,000	3.00	8.00	45.00	135	220
1835	—	60.00	200	700	1,800	3,000
1837	12,038,000	1.00	3.00	10.00	25.00	65.00
1838	Inc. above	60.00	125	300	1,200	—
1841 Narrow 1	2,509,000	2.00	4.00	25.00	75.00	165
1841 Wide 1	Inc. above	2.00	4.00	25.00	75.00	165
1842	5,536,000	1.00	3.00	15.00	40.00	120
1847	1,131,000	4.00	10.00	40.00	120	250
1848	1,845,000	2.50	7.00	35.00	100	150
1849 Large 9	1,447,000	2.50	8.00	40.00	115	175
1849 Small 9	Inc. above	2.50	8.00	40.00	115	175
1850	2,689,000	1.50	3.00	18.00	55.00	150
Note: 5 with ball top, round 0, with wide center						
1850	Inc. above	1.50	3.00	18.00	55.00	150
Note: 5 with less curved top, 0 tall with narrow center						
1851	2,381,000	1.50	3.00	18.00	55.00	100
1852	1,943,000	2.00	5.00	30.00	85.00	175
1853	705,000	10.00	15.00	90.00	250	400
1855 Large 5	265,000	25.00	50.00	275	700	1,500
1855 Small 5	Inc. above	25.00	50.00	275	700	1,500
1856	5,656,000	1.00	2.00	12.00	40.00	75.00
1857	2,299,000	1.50	4.00	25.00	75.00	140
1858	2,712,000	1.50	5.00	30.00	100	175
1858 Without cross on crown	Inc. above	5.00	8.00	45.00	120	200
1859	2,591,000	1.50	8.00	45.00	120	200
1859 Without cross on crown	Inc. above	—	14.00	75.00	225	300
1860	199,000	60.00	125	600	1,800	—
1861	Inc. above	70.00	200	700	2,000	—

KM# 5.1a 5 CENTIMES

Bronze

Date	Mintage	VG	F	VF	XF	Unc
1833	Inc. above	80.00	125	600	1,200	—
1834 Reported, not confirmed	—	—	—	—	—	—
1837 Reported, not confirmed	—	—	—	—	—	—
1848	Inc. above	35.00	75.00	250	800	—
1850	Inc. above	50.00	120	600	1,200	—
1858	Inc. above	45.00	100	325	900	—
1859	Inc. above	40.00	80.00	275	800	—

KM# 5.2 5 CENTIMES

Copper **Rev:** Without stop in signature

Date	Mintage	VG	F	VF	XF	Unc
1833	Inc. above	2.50	5.00	27.50	85.00	—
1834	Inc. above	3.00	8.00	45.00	135	—
1837	Inc. above	1.00	3.00	10.00	25.00	—
1841	Inc. above	2.00	4.00	25.00	75.00	—
1842	Inc. above	1.00	2.00	15.00	40.00	—
1847	Inc. above	5.00	10.00	40.00	120	—
1848	Inc. above	3.00	7.00	35.00	100	—
1849	Inc. above	3.00	8.00	40.00	115	—
1850	Inc. above	1.00	3.00	18.00	55.00	—
1851	Inc. above	1.00	3.00	18.00	55.00	—
1852	Inc. above	2.00	5.00	30.00	85.00	—

KM# 5.3 5 CENTIMES

Copper **Rev:** Large S in CENTS

Date	Mintage	VG	F	VF	XF	Unc
1858	Inc. above	2.00	3.00	20.00	65.00	—
1859	Inc. above	3.00	6.00	30.00	85.00	—

KM# 21 5 CENTIMES

Copper-Nickel **Note:** Varieties exist.

Date	Mintage	VG	F	VF	XF	Unc
1861	8,259,000	0.15	1.00	10.00	20.00	—
1862/1	14,149,000	0.25	2.00	15.00	35.00	—
1862	Inc. above	0.15	0.50	2.00	7.00	20.00
1863/2	16,055,000	0.25	3.00	18.00	40.00	—
1863	Inc. above	0.25	0.75	3.00	9.00	25.00
1864	2,513,000	4.00	10.00	60.00	120	175

KM# 40.1 5 CENTIMES

Copper-Nickel **Obv:** Legend in French **Obv. Legend:** DES BELGES

Date	Mintage	F	VF	XF	Unc	BU
1894	3,111,000	1.00	3.00	9.00	20.00	—
1895	3,693,000	1.00	3.00	9.00	20.00	—

Date	Mintage	F	VF	XF	Unc	BU
1898	1,004,000	6.00	20.00	50.00	100	—
1900/891	1,666,000	7.00	12.00	55.00	125	—
1900	Inc. above	5.00	20.00	45.00	85.00	—

KM# 41 5 CENTIMES

Copper-Nickel **Obv:** Legend in Dutch **Obv. Legend:** DER BELGEN

Date	Mintage	F	VF	XF	Unc	BU
1894	1,658,000	2.00	12.00	25.00	40.00	—
1895/4	—	2.00	5.00	15.00	25.00	—
1895	4,957,000	1.00	3.00	9.00	20.00	—
1898	985,000	8.00	25.00	60.00	120	—
1900	1,670,000	5.00	20.00	45.00	85.00	—

KM# 40.2 5 CENTIMES

Copper-Nickel **Obv:** Legend in Dutch **Obv. Legend:** DER BELGEN

Date	Mintage	F	VF	XF	Unc	BU
1895	—	—	—	—	—	—

Note: Less than 100 known

KM# 2.1 10 CENTIMES

Copper

Date	Mintage	VG	F	VF	XF	Unc
1832	993,000	9.00	25.00	130	325	450
1833	994,000	9.00	40.00	170	350	475
1835	—	125	250	1,200	2,500	—
1838	—	125	300	1,300	2,700	—
1841	—	125	250	1,200	2,500	—
1847/37	135,000	16.00	45.00	175	350	500
1847	Inc. above	30.00	80.00	200	550	—
1848/38	777,000	15.00	35.00	180	400	500
1848	Inc. above	25.00	75.00	150	400	500
1849/39	Inc. above	150	275	1,700	4,000	8,000
1849	Inc. above	125	200	1,400	3,500	7,000
1855	191,000	40.00	70.00	225	600	1,200
1856	Inc. above	200	300	1,500	3,000	6,500

KM# 2.2 10 CENTIMES

Copper **Note:** Medal alignment.

Date	Mintage	VG	F	VF	XF	Unc
1832	Inc. above	75.00	140	600	1,400	—

KM# 22 10 CENTIMES

Copper-Nickel

Date	Mintage	VG	F	VF	XF	Unc
1861	9,080,000	0.25	0.75	4.00	12.00	25.00
1862/61	15,129,000	1.00	4.00	20.00	40.00	—
1862	Inc. above	0.10	0.50	3.00	6.00	20.00
1862 Dot after PREMIER	Inc. above	1.00	3.00	20.00	50.00	—
1863	14,482,000	0.10	0.50	6.00	20.00	25.00
1864	3,202,000	2.50	3.00	18.00	35.00	100

KM# 42 10 CENTIMES

Copper-Nickel **Obv:** Legend in French **Obv. Legend:** DES BELGES

Date	Mintage	F	VF	XF	Unc	BU
1894	11,886,000	0.75	3.00	7.00	25.00	—
1895/4	736,000	30.00	50.00	125	175	—

Date	Mintage	F	VF	XF	Unc	BU
1895	Inc. above	15.00	50.00	125	175	—
1898	3,499,000	3.00	8.00	18.00	45.00	—

KM# 43 10 CENTIMES

Copper-Nickel **Obv:** Legend in Dutch **Obv. Legend:** DER BELGEN

Date	Mintage	F	VF	XF	Unc	BU
1894	9,209,000	0.75	3.00	7.00	25.00	—
1895/4	3,529,000	9.00	35.00	120	225	—
1895	Inc. above	1.00	8.00	18.00	35.00	—
1898	3,500,000	3.00	8.00	18.00	35.00	—

KM# 19 20 CENTIMES

1.0000 g., 0.9000 Silver .0289 oz.

Date	Mintage	VG	F	VF	XF	Unc
1852 With periods	301,000	8.00	20.00	85.00	125	200
1852 Without periods	Inc. above	10.00	25.00	90.00	135	215
1853 With periods	1,965,000	3.00	10.00	35.00	70.00	100
1853 Without periods	Inc. above	5.00	12.00	40.00	80.00	125
1858	865,000	30.00	75.00	250	500	1,000

KM# 20 20 CENTIMES

Copper-Nickel

Date	Mintage	VG	F	VF	XF	Unc
1860	1,804,000	7.00	15.00	65.00	200	300
1860 I.	Inc. above	90.00	50.00	350	600	1,000
1861	Inc. above	1.00	3.00	10.00	32.00	100

KM# 26 50 CENTIMES

2.5000 g., 0.8350 Silver .0671 oz. **Obv:** Legend in French **Obv. Legend:** DES BELGES

Date	Mintage	F	VF	XF	Unc	BU
1866	6,806,000	2.00	30.00	100	150	—
1867	1,014,000	3.00	75.00	275	400	—
1868	1,076,000	100	400	1,800	3,000	—
1881/61	200,000	15.00	200	850	1,200	—
1881/66	Inc. above	15.00	200	850	1,200	—
1881	Inc. above	15.00	225	900	1,300	—
1886/61	1,250,000	2.00	35.00	140	200	—
1886/66	Inc. above	2.00	25.00	100	150	—
1886	Inc. above	1.00	20.00	90.00	140	—
1898	499,000	1.00	25.00	95.00	145	—
1899	500,000	1.00	25.00	100	160	—

KM# 27 50 CENTIMES

2.5000 g., 0.8350 Silver .0671 oz. **Obv:** Legend in Dutch **Obv. Legend:** DER BELGEN

Date	Mintage	F	VF	XF	Unc	BU
1866 Restrike	—	—	—	—	—	—
1886	3,750,000	1.00	15.00	30.00	100	—
1898	501,000	2.00	20.00	95.00	145	—
1899	500,000	2.00	25.00	100	155	—

KM# 8 1/4 FRANC

1.2500 g., 0.9000 Silver .0362 oz. **Note:** Varieties exist with and without periods in signature.

Date	Mintage	VG	F	VF	XF	Unc
1834 Signature	762,000	15.00	30.00	120	220	350
1834 Without signature	Inc. above	20.00	50.00	220	325	—
1835 Signature	640,000	15.00	35.00	150	250	400
1835 Without signature	Inc. above	20.00	50.00	220	400	—
1841	8,000	175	300	1,200	2,000	3,000
1843	Inc. above	50.00	100	300	500	750
1844	966,000	8.00	20.00	120	200	300

KM# 14 1/4 FRANC

1.2500 g., 0.9000 Silver .0362 oz.

Date	Mintage	VG	F	VF	XF	Unc
1849	101,000	150	275	1,250	2,000	3,000
1850	Inc. above	85.00	175	850	1,800	2,800

KM# 6 1/2 FRANC

2.5000 g., 0.9000 Silver .0723 oz. **Note:** Varieties exist.

Date	Mintage	VG	F	VF	XF	Unc
1833	58,000	50.00	150	600	800	1,500
1834	1,578,000	15.00	30.00	150	300	600
1835	805,000	20.00	40.00	225	500	700
1838	550,000	25.00	50.00	275	550	750
1840	347,000	30.00	75.00	325	600	900
1841	Inc. above	125	250	1,200	2,000	3,750
1843	366,000	30.00	50.00	275	550	750
1844	1,584,000	15.00	30.00	150	300	600

KM# 15 1/2 FRANC

2.5000 g., 0.9000 Silver .0723 oz.

Date	Mintage	VG	F	VF	XF	Unc
1847 Restrike	—	—	—	—	—	—
1849	210,000	150	300	1,500	2,500	4,000
1850	Inc. above	125	400	1,200	2,200	4,000

KM# 7.1 FRANC

5.0000 g., 0.9000 Silver .1447 oz.

Date	Mintage	VG	F	VF	XF	Unc
1833	61,000	75.00	120	600	1,400	2,500
1834	482,000	20.00	40.00	200	400	700
1835	861,000	25.00	50.00	280	600	900
1838	525,000	35.00	75.00	340	700	1,000
1838 Large star	Inc. above	65.00	100	500	1,200	1,500
1840	261,000	40.00	90.00	350	800	1,000
1841	Inc. above	135	375	1,500	3,200	—
1843	2,196,000	65.00	225	900	1,800	—
1844	Inc. above	20.00	40.00	200	375	700

KM# 7.2 FRANC

5.0000 g., 0.9000 Silver .1447 oz. **Note:** Medal alignment.

Date	Mintage	VG	F	VF	XF	Unc
1833	Inc. above	100	300	1,000	2,000	—

KM# 16.1 FRANC
5.0000 g., 0.9000 Silver .1447 oz. **Note:** Edge varieties exist.

Date	Mintage	VG	F	VF	XF	Unc
1849	41,000	250	450	1,750	2,850	5,000
1850	162,000	125	300	1,100	2,100	4,000

KM# 16.2 FRANC
5.0000 g., 0.9000 Silver .1447 oz. **Obv:** Without period in signature

Date	Mintage	VG	F	VF	XF	Unc
1850	Inc. above	150	350	1,400	2,500	3,000

KM# 28.1 FRANC
5.0000 g., 0.8350 Silver .1342 oz. **Obv:** Legend in French **Obv. Legend:** DES BELGES

Date	Mintage	F	VF	XF	Unc	BU
1866	3,041,000	2.00	25.00	150	225	—
1867	6,652,000	1.50	20.00	120	170	—
1868	675,000	200	500	1,500	6,000	7,500
1869	1,394,000	3.00	45.00	300	400	—
1881/61	119,000	100	225	1,400	1,800	—
1881/67	Inc. above	25.00	500	1,400	1,700	—
1881	Inc. above	15.00	225	1,100	1,400	—
1886/66	1,250,000	2.50	25.00	120	175	—
1886	Inc. above	3.00	40.00	150	200	—
1886 Proof	—	Value: 450				

KM# 38 FRANC
5.0000 g., 0.8350 Silver .1342 oz. **Subject:** 50th Anniversary of Independence

Date	Mintage	F	VF	XF	Unc	BU
1880	545,000	4.00	35.00	100	140	—

KM# 28.2 FRANC
5.0000 g., 0.8350 Silver .1342 oz. **Obv:** Without period in signature

Date	Mintage	F	VF	XF	Unc	BU
1886	Inc. above	2.00	30.00	75.00	150	—

KM# 29.1 FRANC
5.0000 g., 0.8350 Silver .1342 oz. **Obv:** Legend in Dutch **Obv. Legend:** DER BELGEN

Date	Mintage	F	VF	XF	Unc	BU
1886	1,026,000	1.50	20.00	120	150	—
1887	2,724,000	1.00	20.00	120	150	—

KM# 29.2 FRANC
5.0000 g., 0.8350 Silver .1342 oz. **Obv:** Without period in signature

Date	Mintage	F	VF	XF	Unc	BU
1886	Inc. above	2.50	35.00	175	225	—
1887	Inc. above	1.00	20.00	100	150	—

KM# 9.1 2 FRANCS (2 Frank)
10.0000 g., 0.9000 Silver .2894 oz. **Note:** Edge inscription inclined to left.

Date	Mintage	VG	F	VF	XF	Unc
1834 Position A	276,000	100	175	1,000	2,000	—
1834 Postition A; Proof	—	Value: 3,500				
1834 Position B	Inc. above	100	180	1,000	2,000	—
1835 Position A	225,000	160	240	1,250	2,500	4,000
1835 Position B	Inc. above	160	240	1,250	2,500	4,000
1838 Position A	—	175	300	1,400	3,000	—
1838 Position B	—	175	300	1,400	3,000	—
1840 Position A	236,000	125	225	1,300	2,600	5,000
1840 Position B	Inc. above	125	225	1,250	2,500	5,000
1841 Position A	—	300	600	2,000	6,000	10,000
1843 Position A	735,000	100	175	1,000	2,200	—
1843 Position B	Inc. above	100	175	1,000	2,200	—
1844 Position A	483,000	125	225	1,200	2,600	—
1844 Position B	Inc. above	125	225	1,200	2,600	—

KM# 9.2 2 FRANCS (2 Frank)
10.0000 g., 0.9000 Silver .2894 oz. **Note:** Edge inscription inclined to right.

Date	Mintage	VG	F	VF	XF	Unc
1834 Position A	Inc. above	75.00	150	750	1,700	3,000
1834 Position B	Inc. above	75.00	150	750	1,700	3,000
1835 Position A	Inc. above	100	250	750	2,000	4,000
1835 Position B	Inc. above	100	250	900	2,100	—
1838 Position A	300,000	125	250	1,400	3,000	5,000
1838 Position B	Inc. above	125	250	1,400	3,000	5,000
1840 Position A	Inc. above	100	200	900	2,200	—
1840 Position B	Inc. above	100	200	900	2,200	—
1841 Position A	—	325	750	2,500	3,200	—
1843 Position A	Inc. above	100	150	800	1,600	2,500
1843 Position B	Inc. above	100	150	800	1,600	2,500
1844 Position A	Inc. above	100	200	1,000	2,200	—
1844 Position B	Inc. above	100	200	1,000	2,200	—

KM# 10 2 FRANCS (2 Frank)
10.0000 g., 0.9000 Silver .2894 oz. **Note:** This coin was not officially released into circulation.

Date	Mintage	VG	F	VF	XF	Unc
1848 Restrike	—	—	—	—	—	—
1849	—	400	900	3,500	5,000	8,000
1865	—	450	1,100	5,500	10,000	—

KM# 30.1 2 FRANCS (2 Frank)
10.0000 g., 0.8350 Silver .2685 oz. **Obv:** Legend in French **Obv. Legend:** DES BELGES **Note:** Edge varieties exist.

Date	Mintage	F	VF	XF	Unc	BU
1866	1,942,000	7.00	90.00	400	550	—
1867	3,789,000	5.00	80.00	325	425	—
1868	2,164,000	10.00	140	550	700	—

KM# 30.2 2 FRANCS (2 Frank)
10.0000 g., 0.8350 Silver .2685 oz. **Rev:** Without cross on crown

Date	Mintage	VG	F	VF	XF	Unc
1866	Inc. above	12.00	25.00	150	500	750
1867	Inc. above	6.00	20.00	125	450	600
1868	Inc. above	15.00	30.00	200	650	800

KM# 39 2 FRANCS (2 Frank)
10.0000 g., 0.8350 Silver .2685 oz. **Subject:** 50th Anniversary of Independence **Rev:** Legend in French **Rev. Legend:** DE BELGIQUE

Date	Mintage	F	VF	XF	Unc	BU
1880	118,000	15.00	75.00	200	500	—

KM# 31 2 FRANCS (2 Frank)
10.0000 g., 0.8350 Silver .2685 oz. **Obv:** Legned in Dutch **Obv. Legend:** DER BELGEN **Rev:** Cross on crown **Note:** Edge varieties exist.

Date	Mintage	F	VF	XF	Unc	BU
1887	150,000	35.00	300	1,300	2,200	—

KM# 11 2-1/2 FRANCS
12.5000 g., 0.9000 Silver .3617 oz. **Obv:** Legend in French **Obv. Legend:** ROI DES BELGES

Date	Mintage	VG	F	VF	XF	Unc
1848	559,000	35.00	100	300	600	900
1849	2,003,000	20.00	50.00	175	300	600

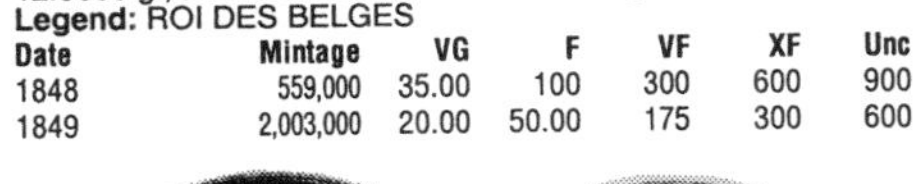

KM# 12 2-1/2 FRANCS
12.5000 g., 0.9000 Silver .3617 oz. **Note:** Larger head.

Date	Mintage	VG	F	VF	XF	Unc
1848	Inc. above	125	350	1,600	3,500	—
1849	Inc. above	30.00	80.00	300	700	1,000
1849 Proof	—	Value: 1,500				
1850	65,000	100	200	1,400	3,000	—
1865	—	350	800	3,000	8,000	—

Note: Coins dated 1865 were not released into circulation

KM# 3.1 5 FRANCS (5 Frank)
25.0000 g., 0.9000 Silver .7234 oz. **Note:** Incuse lettered edge.

Date	Mintage	VG	F	VF	XF	Unc
1832 Position A	37,000	50.00	125	800	1,800	4,000
1832 Position B	Inc. above	40.00	110	700	1,600	3,500
1833 Position A	1,126,000	16.00	30.00	100	550	750
1833 Position B	Inc. above	17.50	35.00	110	600	850
1834 Position A	350,000	30.00	75.00	550	1,300	3,500
1834 Position B	Inc. above	30.00	75.00	550	1,300	3,500
1835 Position A	370,000	45.00	90.00	600	1,400	4,000
1835 Position B	Inc. above	45.00	90.00	600	1,400	4,000
1838 Position A	5,203	200	400	3,000	6,500	9,000

Date	Mintage	VG	F	VF	XF	Unc
1838 Position B	Inc. above	200	400	3,000	6,500	9,000
1840	—	500	1,000	5,000	9,000	12,000
1841	—	500	1,000	5,000	9,000	12,000
1844 Position A	483,000	60.00	120	800	1,800	3,000
1844 Position B	Inc. above	60.00	120	800	1,800	3,000

KM# 3.2 5 FRANCS (5 Frank)
25.0000 g., 0.9000 Silver .7234 oz. **Note:** Raised lettered edge

Date	Mintage	VG	F	VF	XF	Unc
1847	700,000	20.00	40.00	150	400	1,200
1848	2,516,000	10.00	18.00	100	250	500
1849	3,014,000	9.00	12.00	80.00	200	400

KM# 17 5 FRANCS (5 Frank)
25.0000 g., 0.9000 Silver .7234 oz.

Date	Mintage	VG	F	VF	XF	Unc
1849	3,909,000	7.00	10.00	35.00	120	200
1850 Dot above date	5,265,000	10.00	15.00	40.00	125	300
1850 Without dot above date	Inc. above	7.00	10.00	35.00	100	200
1850 Proof	—	Value: 500				
1851/0	3,708,000	10.00	16.00	40.00	135	—
1851 Dot above date	Inc. above	10.00	17.50	50.00	150	—
1851	Inc. above	7.00	10.00	35.00	100	200
1852/1	4,605,000	15.00	25.00	75.00	200	—
1852	Inc. above	7.00	15.00	45.00	150	—
1853	2,427,000	12.00	20.00	50.00	200	400
1858	18,000	35.00	75.00	150	400	900
1865/15 Broken M in PREMIER	907,000	15.00	20.00	90.00	275	—
1865/55	Inc. above	8.00	25.00	90.00	275	—
1865/55 Dot after F	Inc. above	10.00	30.00	100	325	—
1865	Inc. above	10.00	15.00	50.00	150	300
1865 Dot after F on reverse	Inc. above	10.00	20.00	80.00	250	—

KM# 24 5 FRANCS (5 Frank)
25.0000 g., 0.9000 Silver .7234 oz. **Obv:** Smaller head, engraver's name near rim, below truncation

Date	Mintage	F	VF	XF	Unc	BU
1865 Inc. 1867	—	100	400	600	1,200	—
1866 Inc. 1867	—	150	500	800	1,600	—
1866 Inc. 1867; Dot after F on reverse	—	110	350	500	1,200	—
1867	3,693,000	7.50	25.00	70.00	110	—
1867 Dot after F on reverse	Inc. above	10.00	50.00	175	225	—
1868 Position A	6,751,000	7.00	10.00	35.00	75.00	—
1868 Position B	Inc. above	35.00	100	330	600	—
1869	12,658,000	6.50	8.00	30.00	65.00	—
1870	10,486,000	6.50	8.00	30.00	65.00	—
1871	4,783,000	6.50	8.00	35.00	70.00	—
1872	2,045,000	7.00	10.00	45.00	75.00	—
1873 Position A	22,341,000	6.50	8.00	25.00	60.00	—
1873 Position B	Inc. above	10.00	17.50	35.00	100	—
1874	2,400,000	6.50	8.00	40.00	100	—
1875	2,981,000	6.50	8.00	35.00	75.00	—
1876	2,160,000	7.00	9.00	40.00	100	—
1878 3 known	—	—	—	—	—	—

KM# 25 5 FRANCS (5 Frank)
25.0000 g., 0.9000 Silver .7234 oz. **Obv:** Larger head, engraver's name below truncation

Date	Mintage	F	VF	XF	Unc	BU
1865	Inc. above	450	1,800	3,500	5,000	—
1866	Inc. above	400	1,600	3,200	4,000	—
1867	Inc. above	275	1,400	2,500	3,000	—
1868	Inc. above	300	1,500	3,000	3,500	—

KM# 18 10 FRANCS (10 Frank)
3.1662 g., 0.9000 Gold .0916 oz. **Note:** 54,890 pieces dated 1849 and 1850 were withdrawn from circulation.

Date	Mintage	F	VF	XF	Unc	BU
1849	37,000	400	1,000	2,000	3,200	—
1850	63,000	500	1,200	2,000	3,000	—

KM# A33 10 FRANCS (10 Frank)
3.1662 g., 0.9000 Gold .0916 oz.

Date	Mintage	F	VF	XF	Unc	BU
1865 Restrike	—	—	—	—	—	—
1867	—	1,800	3,200	6,500	11,000	—

KM# A23.1 20 FRANCS (20 Frank)
6.4516 g., 0.9000 Gold .1867 oz. **Edge:** Lettered

Date	Mintage	F	VF	XF	Unc	BU
1834	—	950	4,800	8,000	13,000	—
1835	—	1,200	6,000	10,000	15,000	—
1838 1 known	—	—	—	—	—	—
1841	—	1,300	6,500	12,000	17,000	—

KM# A23.2 20 FRANCS (20 Frank)
6.4516 g., 0.9000 Gold .1867 oz. **Edge:** Milled

Date	Mintage	F	VF	XF	Unc	BU
1834 Restrike	—	—	—	—	—	—
1835 Restrike	—	—	—	—	—	—
1838 Restrike	—	—	—	—	—	—
1841 Restrike	—	—	—	—	—	—

KM# A23.3 20 FRANCS (20 Frank)
6.4516 g., 0.9000 Gold .1867 oz. **Edge:** Plain

Date	Mintage	F	VF	XF	Unc	BU
1834 Restrike	—	—	—	—	—	—
1835 Restrike	—	—	—	—	—	—
1838 Restrike	—	—	—	—	—	—
1841 Restrike	—	—	—	—	—	—

KM# 23 20 FRANCS (20 Frank)
6.4516 g., 0.9000 Gold .1867 oz. **Note:** Approximately 1/3 of the 1865 mintage was struck in 1866. Each variety of name below the bust exists both in positon A and position B, with values being the same.

Date	Mintage	F	VF	XF	Unc	BU
1865 L. WIENER	1,548,000	BV	70.00	95.00	150	300
1865 L WIENER	Inc. above	BV	70.00	95.00	150	250
1865 L WINNER Error	Inc. above	150	375	600	1,200	2,000

KM# 32 20 FRANCS (20 Frank)
6.4516 g., 0.9000 Gold .1867 oz. **Obv:** Heavy coarser beard

Date	Mintage	F	VF	XF	Unc	BU
1867	1,341,000	—	BV	70.00	85.00	100
1868	1,382,000	—	BV	70.00	85.00	100
1869 Position A	1,234,000	—	BV	70.00	95.00	125
1869 Position B	Inc. above	80.00	110	175	250	375
1870	3,191,000	BV	55.00	70.00	90.00	150

KM# 37 20 FRANCS (20 Frank)
6.4516 g., 0.9000 Gold .1867 oz. **Obv:** Finer beard

Date	Mintage	F	VF	XF	Unc	BU
1870 Position A	Inc. above	—	BV	70.00	90.00	—
1870 Position B	Inc. above	75.00	100	200	300	—
1871 Long beard	Inc. above	BV	80.00	115	150	—
1871	2,259,000	—	BV	70.00	90.00	—
1874	3,046,000	—	BV	70.00	90.00	—
1875	4,134,000	—	BV	70.00	90.00	—
1876 Position A	2,070,000	—	BV	70.00	90.00	—
1876 Position B	Inc. above	150	300	450	550	—
1877	5,906,000	—	BV	70.00	90.00	—
1878	2,505,000	—	BV	70.00	90.00	—
1882	522,000	—	BV	70.00	90.00	—

KM# 13.1 25 FRANCS
7.9155 g., 0.9000 Gold .2291 oz. **Note:** 16.5% of the total mintage of KM#13.1 and 13.2 was melted. Actual number melted per date is unavailable.

Date	Mintage	F	VF	XF	Unc	BU
1848	321,000	500	1,100	1,800	3,000	—
1849	150,000	900	2,000	4,000	6,000	—

KM# 13.2 25 FRANCS
7.9155 g., 0.9000 Gold .2291 oz. **Obv:** Larger head

Date	Mintage	F	VF	XF	Unc	BU
1850	74,000	700	1,800	3,000	4,500	—

KM# B23.1 40 FRANCS (40 Frank)
12.9032 g., 0.9000 Gold .3734 oz. **Edge:** Lettered

Date	Mintage	F	VF	XF	Unc	BU
1834	—	2,500	8,000	14,000	22,000	—
1835	—	2,500	8,000	14,000	22,000	—
1838	—	3,500	9,500	17,000	26,000	—
1841	—	2,500	9,000	15,000	23,000	—

KM# B23.2 40 FRANCS (40 Frank)
12.9032 g., 0.9000 Gold .3734 oz. **Note:** Medal alignment.

Date	Mintage	F	VF	XF	Unc	BU
1834	—	1,500	8,000	13,000	22,000	—

PATTERNS

Including off metal strikes

KM#	Date	Mintage	Identification	Mkt Val
Pn1	1832	—	Centime. Copper.	—
Pn3	1834	—	40 Francs. Bronze. KM#B23.1	300
Pn5	1835	—	5 Centimes. Copper.	—
Pn6	1835	—	10 Centimes. Copper.	—
Pn7	1835	—	20 Francs. Bronze. KM#A23.1	250
Pn10	1837	—	Centime. Copper.	—
Pn11	1837	—	2 Centimes. Copper.	—
Pn12	1838	—	Centime. Copper.	—
Pn13	1838	—	2 Centimes. Copper.	—
Pn14	1838	—	5 Centimes. Copper.	—
Pn15	1838	—	10 Centimes. Copper.	—
Pn16	1838	—	1/4 Franc. Silver.	—
Pn20	1840	—	5 Francs. Silver.	—
Pn21	1841	—	Centime. Copper.	—
Pn22	1841	—	10 Centimes. Copper.	—
Pn23	1841	—	1/4 Franc. Silver.	—
Pn24	1841	—	1/2 Franc. Silver.	—

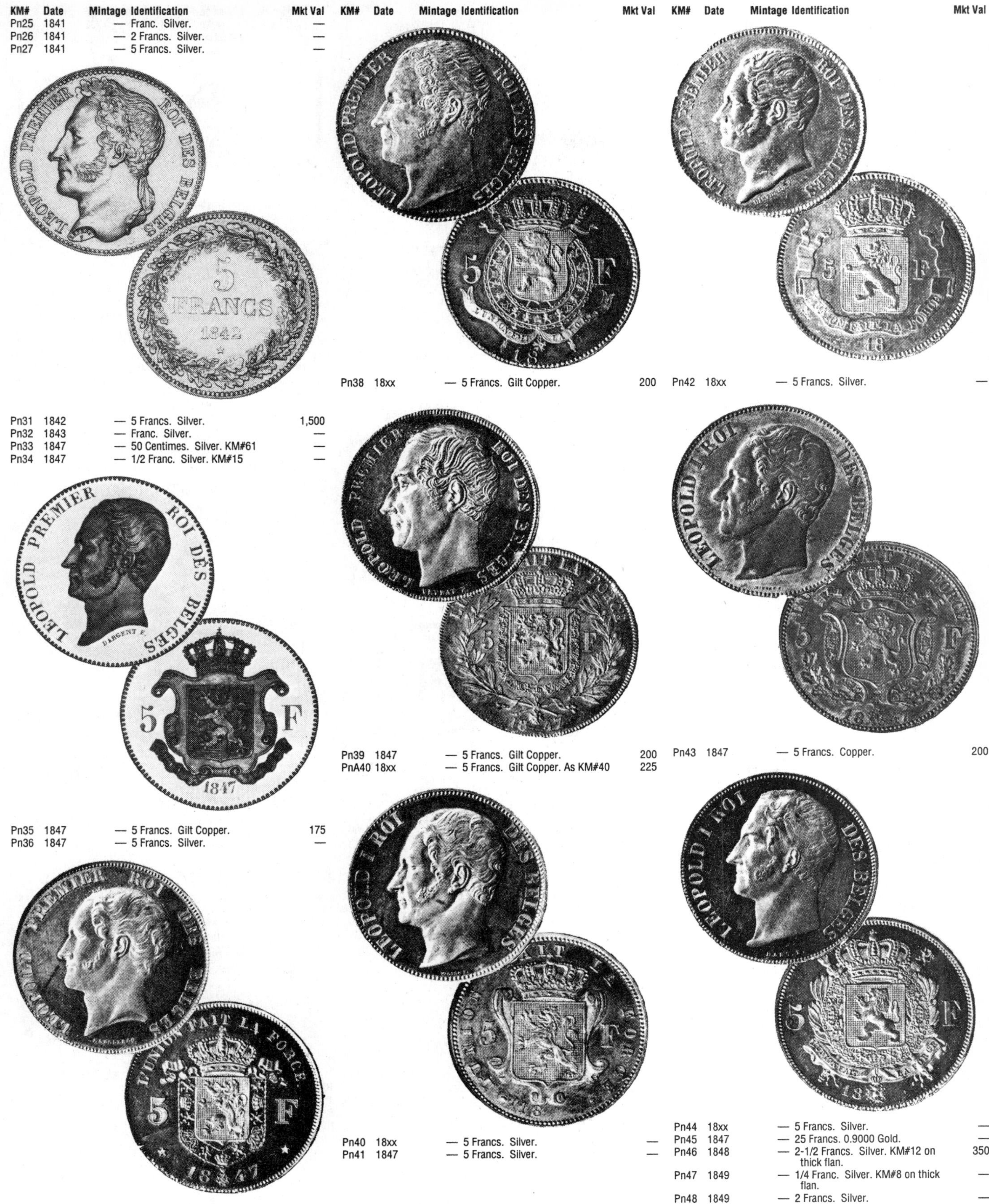

KM#	Date	Mintage	Identification	Mkt Val
Pn25	1841	—	Franc. Silver.	—
Pn26	1841	—	2 Francs. Silver.	—
Pn27	1841	—	5 Francs. Silver.	—
Pn31	1842	—	5 Francs. Silver.	1,500
Pn32	1843	—	Franc. Silver.	—
Pn33	1847	—	50 Centimes. Silver. KM#61	—
Pn34	1847	—	1/2 Franc. Silver. KM#15	—
Pn35	1847	—	5 Francs. Gilt Copper.	175
Pn36	1847	—	5 Francs. Silver.	—
Pn37	1847	—	5 Francs. Gilt Copper.	200
Pn38	18xx	—	5 Francs. Gilt Copper.	200
Pn39	1847	—	5 Francs. Gilt Copper.	200
PnA40	18xx	—	5 Francs. Gilt Copper. As KM#40	225
Pn40	18xx	—	5 Francs. Silver.	—
Pn41	1847	—	5 Francs. Silver.	—
Pn42	18xx	—	5 Francs. Silver.	—
Pn43	1847	—	5 Francs. Copper.	200
Pn44	18xx	—	5 Francs. Silver.	—
Pn45	1847	—	25 Francs. 0.9000 Gold.	—
Pn46	1848	—	2-1/2 Francs. Silver. KM#12 on thick flan.	350
Pn47	1849	—	1/4 Franc. Silver. KM#8 on thick flan.	—
Pn48	1849	—	2 Francs. Silver.	—

KM#	Date	Mintage	Identification	Mkt Val
Pn49	1854	—	100 Francs. Gold.	—
Pn50	1855	—	Centime. Copper.	—
Pn51	1858	—	20 Centimes. Silver.	—
Pn52	1859	—	2 Centimes. Aluminum.	—
Pn53	1859	—	10 Centimes. Nickel Clad Copper. ESSAI	100
Pn54	1859	—	1/2 Franc. Silver.	200
Pn55	1859	—	Franc. Silver.	200
Pn56	1860	—	20 Centimes. Brass Coated Nickel.	125
Pn57	1860	—	20 Centimes. Silver.	250
Pn58	1860	—	20 Centimes. Copper-Nickel.	175
Pn59	1860	—	20 Centimes. Copper-Iron Alloy. KM#20.	—
Pn60	1861	—	5 Centimes. Copper.	—
Pn61	1861	—	20 Centimes. Copper.	—
Pn62	1861	—	20 Centimes. Copper-Nickel. By Breamt.	—
Pn63	1861	—	20 Centimes. Copper-Nickel. By Weiner.	—
PnA64	1862	—	20 Francs. Gold. KM#23	20,000
PnB64	1864	—	20 Francs. Gold. KM#23	8,000
Pn64	1865	—	2 Francs. Silver.	—
Pn65	1865	—	5 Francs. Silver. Portrait Leopold II by Jouvenel. ESSAI/MONETAIRE.	—
Pn66	1865	—	5 Francs. Silver. KM#24	—
Pn67	1865	—	5 Francs. Silver. KM#25	—
Pn68	1866	—	50 Centimes. Silver. KM#27	—
Pn69	1866	—	5 Francs. Silver. KM#24	—
Pn70	1866	—	5 Francs. Silver. KM#25	—
Pn71	1866	—	20 Francs. Gold. KM#32	7,000
Pn72	1867	—	10 Francs. Gold.	3,000
Pn73	1869	—	Centime. Copper. Reeded edge. Thick flan, KM#33.1	—
Pn74	1870	—	Centime. Copper. Reeded edge. Thick flan, KM#33.1	—
Pn75	1870	—	10 Francs. Gold.	3,000
Pn76	1872	—	2 Centimes. Copper.	—
Pn77	1874	—	Centime. Nickel. Reeded edge. KM#33.1	—
Pn78	1882	—	Centime. Copper.	—
Pn79	1882	—	Centime. Copper. KM#34.1. KM#33.1.	300
Pn80	1887	—	Centime. Copper.	—
Pn81	1892	—	Centime. Copper.	—
Pn82	1892	—	5 Centimes. Copper-Nickel.	—
Pn83	1892	—	10 Centimes. Copper-Nickel. ESSAI	—
Pn84	1894	—	5 Centimes. Copper. KM#40	—
Pn85	1894	—	5 Centimes. Copper. KM#40. KM#41.	400
Pn86	1894	—	10 Centimes. Nickel.	—
Pn87	1895	—	5 Centimes. Copper. KM#40	—
Pn88	1896	—	5 Francs. Silver.	850
Pn89	1898	—	5 Centimes. Copper. KM#41	—
Pn90	19xx	—	Franc.	450
Pn91	1901	—	Centime. Copper. KM#33.3	—
Pn92	1901	—	5 Centimes. Pewter.	—

PIEFORTS

KM#	Date	Mintage	Identification	Mkt Val
P1	1849	—	10 Francs. KM#18.	—
P2	1859	—	20 Centimes. Silver. Piefort	—
P3	1859	—	20 Centimes. Silver. Double piefort	2,500
P4	1912	—	10 Francs. Gold. Plain edge.	1,900
P5	1912	—	10 Francs. Silver. Plain edge.	—

TRIAL STRIKES

KM#	Date	Mintage	Identification	Mkt Val
TS1	1860	—	20 Centimes. Bronze. Uniface.	—
TS2	ND(1866)	—	2 Francs. Copper. Uniface.	—
TS3	1872	—	2 Centimes. Pewter. Uniface.	—
TS4	1872	—	2 Centimes. Pewter. Uniface.	—

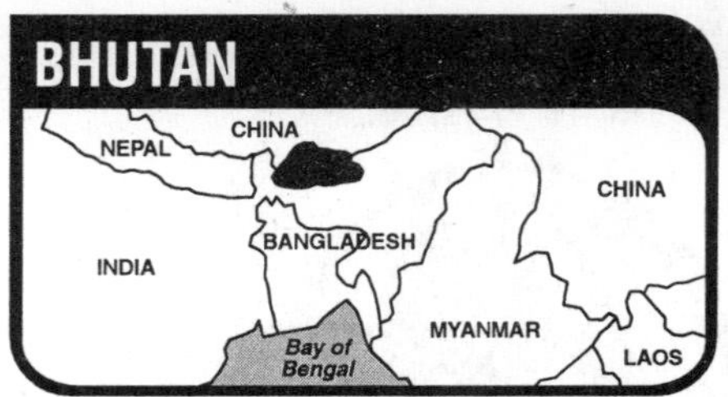

The Kingdom of Bhutan, a landlocked Himalayan country bordered by Tibet and India, has an area of 18,150 sq. mi. (47,000 sq. km.). Capital: Thimphu. Virtually the entire population is engaged in agricultural and pastoral activities. Rice, wheat, barley, and yak butter are produced in sufficient quantity to make the country self-sufficient in food. The economy of Bhutan is primitive and many transactions are conducted on a barter basis.

Bhutan's early history is obscure, but is thought to have resembled that of rural medieval Europe. The country was conquered by Tibet in the 9th century, and a dual temporal and spiritual rule developed which operated until the mid-19th century, when the southern part of the country was occupied by the British and annexed to British India. Bhutan was established as a hereditary monarchy in 1907, and in 1910 agreed to British control of its external affairs. In 1949, India and Bhutan concluded a treaty whereby India assumed Britain's role in subsidizing Bhutan and guiding its foreign affairs. In 1971 Bhutan became a full member of the United Nations.

KINGDOM

Under British Adminstration

HAMMERED COINAGE

Period I, 1790-1820AD

'Ma'

KM# 1 1/2 RUPEE (Deb)
Silver

Date	Mintage	Good	VG	F	VF	XF
ND(1790-1820)	—	6.00	9.00	15.00	25.00	—

'Sa'

KM# 2 1/2 RUPEE (Deb)
Silver

Date	Mintage	Good	VG	F	VF	XF
ND(1790-1820)	—	6.00	9.00	15.00	25.00	—

'Ma'

KM# A23 RUPEE
11.6000 g., Silver

Date	Mintage	Good	VG	F	VF	XF
ND	—	—	—	—	400	—

HAMMERED COINAGE

Period II, 1820-1835AD

'Sa'

KM# 3 1/2 RUPEE (Deb)
Silver, Lead Alloying

Date	Mintage	Good	VG	F	VF	XF
ND(1820-35)	—	3.50	4.50	7.00	10.00	—

KM# 4.1 1/2 RUPEE (Deb)
Silver, Copper Alloying

Date	Mintage	Good	VG	F	VF	XF
ND(1820-35)	—	3.50	4.50	7.00	10.00	—

KM# 4.2 1/2 RUPEE (Deb)
Silver, Copper Alloying **Obv:** Dot added

Date	Mintage	Good	VG	F	VF	XF
ND(1820-35)	—	3.50	4.50	7.00	10.00	—

KM# 4.3 1/2 RUPEE (Deb)
Silver, Copper Alloying **Obv:** Small "Sa" added

Date	Mintage	Good	VG	F	VF	XF
ND(1820-35)	—	3.50	4.50	7.00	10.00	—

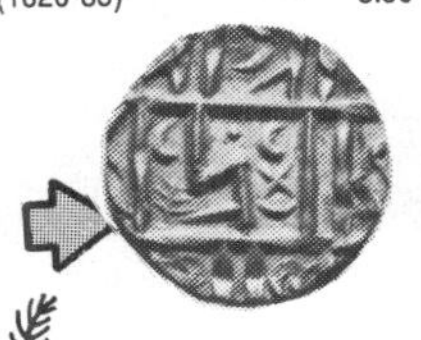

KM# 5 1/2 RUPEE (Deb)
Silver, Copper Alloying **Obv:** Leaf spray

Date	Mintage	Good	VG	F	VF	XF
ND(1820-35)	—	3.50	4.50	7.00	10.00	—

KM# 6 1/2 RUPEE (Deb)
Silver, Copper Alloying **Obv:** Swastika **Rev:** Center inscription retrograde

Date	Mintage	Good	VG	F	VF	XF
ND(1820-35)	—	3.50	5.00	8.50	12.50	—

KM# B23 RUPEE
9.8000 g., Silver **Note:** Similar to KM#4.

Date	Mintage	Good	VG	F	VF	XF
ND	—	—	—	—	350	—

HAMMERED COINAGE

Period III, 1835-1910AD

'Sa'

KM# A7 1/2 RUPEE (Deb)
Copper Or Brass **Obv:** Small "Sa" at upper right

Date	Mintage	Good	VG	F	VF	XF
ND(1835-1910)	—	1.00	2.25	4.50	7.50	—

'Sa'

KM# 7.1 1/2 RUPEE (Deb)
Copper Or Brass **Obv:** "Sa" at lower left

Date	Mintage	Good	VG	F	VF	XF
ND(1835-1910)	—	1.00	1.50	3.00	6.00	—

KM# 7.1a 1/2 RUPEE (Deb)
1.8500 g., Copper Or Brass **Obv. Inscription:** "Sa" at lower left **Note:** Small flan.

Date	Mintage	Good	VG	F	VF	XF
ND(1835-1910)	—	1.00	1.50	3.00	6.00	—

KM# 7.2 1/2 RUPEE (Deb)
Copper Or Brass **Obv:** Dots added

Date	Mintage	Good	VG	F	VF	XF
ND(1835-1910)	—	1.00	1.50	3.00	6.00	—

KM# 7.3 1/2 RUPEE (Deb)
Copper Or Brass **Obv:** "Sa" at upper right

Date	Mintage	Good	VG	F	VF	XF
ND(1835-1910)	—	1.00	1.50	3.00	6.00	—

KM# 7.4 1/2 RUPEE (Deb)
Copper Or Brass **Obv:** Large "Sa" below 5 pellets

Date	Mintage	Good	VG	F	VF	XF
ND(1835-1910)	—	1.00	1.50	3.00	6.00	—

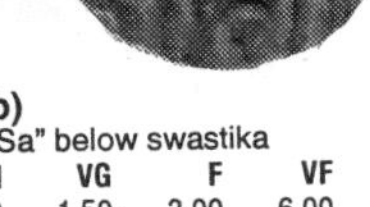

KM# 7.5 1/2 RUPEE (Deb)
Copper Or Brass **Obv:** Large "Sa" below swastika

Date	Mintage	Good	VG	F	VF	XF
ND(1835-1910)	—	1.00	1.50	3.00	6.00	—

KM# 7.6 1/2 RUPEE (Deb)
Copper Or Brass **Obv:** Branch

Date	Mintage	Good	VG	F	VF	XF
ND(1835-1910)	—	1.00	1.50	3.00	6.00	—

KM# A8.1 1/2 RUPEE (Deb)
Copper Or Brass **Obv. Inscription:** Retrograde **Rev. Inscription:** Retrograde

Date	Mintage	Good	VG	F	VF	XF
ND(1835-1910)	—	1.00	2.00	3.50	7.00	—

KM# A8.2 1/2 RUPEE (Deb)
Copper Or Brass **Rev:** Dots added

Date	Mintage	Good	VG	F	VF	XF
ND(1835-1910)	—	1.00	1.50	3.00	6.00	—

KM# A8.3 1/2 RUPEE (Deb)
Copper Or Brass **Rev:** Four pellets

Date	Mintage	Good	VG	F	VF	XF
ND(1835-1910)	—	1.00	1.50	3.00	6.00	—

KM# A8.4 1/2 RUPEE (Deb)
Copper Or Brass **Obv:** Two dots above crescent

Date	Mintage	Good	VG	F	VF	XF
ND(1835-1910)	—	1.00	1.50	3.00	6.00	—

KM# 8.1 1/2 RUPEE (Deb)
Copper Or Brass **Obv:** X above crescent

Date	Mintage	Good	VG	F	VF	XF
ND(1835-1910)	—	1.00	1.50	3.00	6.00	—

KM# 8.2 1/2 RUPEE (Deb)
Copper Or Brass **Obv:** One or two dots in center inscription

Date	Mintage	Good	VG	F	VF	XF
ND(1835-1910)	—	0.50	1.00	2.00	4.00	—

KM# 8.3 1/2 RUPEE (Deb)
Copper Or Brass **Obv:** Crescent above "+" at left

Date	Mintage	Good	VG	F	VF	XF
ND(1835-1910)	—	1.00	2.00	3.50	7.00	—

KM# 8.4 1/2 RUPEE (Deb)
Copper Or Brass **Obv:** "+" above crescent

Date	Mintage	Good	VG	F	VF	XF
ND(1835-1910)	—	1.00	2.00	3.50	7.00	—

KM# 8.6 1/2 RUPEE (Deb)
Copper Or Brass **Obv:** Low "x" at left

Date	Mintage	Good	VG	F	VF	XF
ND(1835-1910)	—	1.00	2.00	3.50	7.00	—

KM# 8.7 1/2 RUPEE (Deb)
Copper Or Brass **Obv:** Three pellets at left, low "x" at right

Date	Mintage	Good	VG	F	VF	XF
ND(1835-1910)	—	1.00	2.00	3.50	7.00	—

KM# 8.8 1/2 RUPEE (Deb)
Copper Or Brass **Obv:** "Hooks" added **Rev:** Four pellets

Date	Mintage	Good	VG	F	VF	XF
ND(1835-1910)	—	1.00	2.00	3.50	7.00	—

KM# 8.9 1/2 RUPEE (Deb)
Copper Or Brass **Obv:** Two rows of pellets, high "x" at right

Date	Mintage	Good	VG	F	VF	XF
ND(1835-1910)	—	1.00	2.00	3.50	7.00	—

KM# 9.1 1/2 RUPEE (Deb)
Copper Or Brass **Obv:** Swastika

Date	Mintage	Good	VG	F	VF	XF
ND(1835-1910)	—	2.00	3.00	5.00	9.00	—

KM# 9.2 1/2 RUPEE (Deb)
Copper Or Brass **Obv:** Swastika reversed

Date	Mintage	Good	VG	F	VF	XF
ND(1835-1910)	—	2.00	3.00	5.00	9.00	—

KM# 10 1/2 RUPEE (Deb)
Copper Or Brass **Obv:** "Wang"

Date	Mintage	Good	VG	F	VF	XF
ND(1835-1910)	—	3.00	5.00	8.00	12.00	—

KM# 11 1/2 RUPEE (Deb)
Copper Or Brass **Obv:** "Sa dar"

Date	Mintage	Good	VG	F	VF	XF
ND(1835-1910)	—	3.00	5.00	8.00	12.00	—

KM# 11a 1/2 RUPEE (Deb)
Copper Or Brass

Date	Mintage	Good	VG	F	VF	XF
ND(1835-1910)	—	3.00	5.00	8.00	12.00	—

KM# 11b 1/2 RUPEE (Deb)
Copper Or Brass

Date	Mintage	Good	VG	F	VF	XF
ND(1835-1910)	—	3.00	5.00	8.00	12.00	—

KM# 12 1/2 RUPEE (Deb)
Copper Or Brass **Obv:** Rosette **Rev:** Swastika

Date	Mintage	Good	VG	F	VF	XF
ND(1835-1910)	—	3.00	5.00	8.00	12.00	—

KM# 13 1/2 RUPEE (Deb)
Copper Or Brass **Obv:** Rosette **Rev:** Two fish

Date	Mintage	Good	VG	F	VF	XF
ND(1835-1910)	—	3.00	5.00	8.00	12.00	—

KM# 14 1/2 RUPEE (Deb)
Copper Or Brass **Rev:** Two fish **Note:** Varieties exist.

Date	Mintage	Good	VG	F	VF	XF
ND(1835-1910)	—	2.00	3.00	5.00	9.00	—

KM# 15 1/2 RUPEE (Deb)
Copper Or Brass **Obv:** Knot **Rev:** Conch shell

Date	Mintage	Good	VG	F	VF	XF
ND(1835-1910)	—	1.50	2.50	4.00	8.00	—

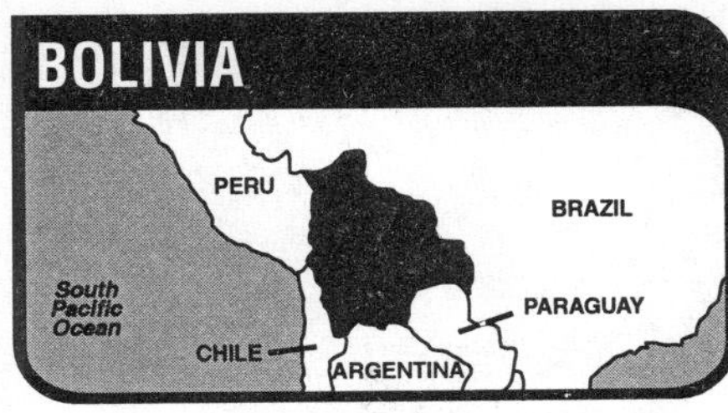

The Republic of Bolivia, a landlocked country in west central South America, has an area of 424,165 sq. mi. (1,098,580 sq. km).

Much of present day Bolivia was first dominated by the Tiahuanaco Culture ca.400 BC. It had in turn been incorporated into the Inca Empire by 1440AD prior to the arrival of the Spanish in 1535 who reduced the Indian population to virtual slavery. When Joseph Napoleon was placed upon the throne of occupied Spain in 1809, a fervor of revolutionary activity quickened throughout Alto Peru - culminating in the 1809 Proclamation of Liberty. Sixteen bloody years of struggle ensued before the republic, named for the famed liberator Simon Bolivar, was established on August 6, 1825. Since then Bolivia has survived more than 16 constitutions, 78 Presidents, 3 military juntas and over 160 revolutions.

The Imperial City of Potosi, founded by Villarroel in 1546, was established in the midst of what is estimated to have been the world's richest silver mines (having produced in excess of 2 billion dollars worth of silver).

The first mint, early in 1574, used equipment brought over from Lima. Before that it had been used at La Plata where the operation failed. The oldest type was a cob with the Hapsburg arms on the obverse and cross with quartered castles and lions on the reverse. To the heraldic right of the shield (at the left as one faces it) is a "p" and, under it, the assayer's initial, although in some early examples the "P" and assayer can appear to the right of the shield. While production at the "Casa de Moneda" was enormous, the quality of the coinage was at times so poor that some 50 were condemned to death by their superiors.

Therefore, by royal decree of February 17, 1651, the design was changed to the quartered castles and lions for the obverse and two crowned pillars of Hercules floating above the waves of the sea for the reverse. A new transitional series was introduced in 1651-1652 followed by a new standard design in 1652 and as the last cob type continued on for several years along with the milled pillars and bust pieces from 1767 through 1773. In the final years under Charles III the planchet is compact and dumpy, very irregular and of poor style, contrasting sharply with their counterpart denominations of the pillar and bust types.

Rarely, and at very high prices, we may be offered almost perfectly round cobs, with the dies well-centered, showing the legend and date completely. These have gained importance in the last decades and are known as "royal" or "presentation" pieces. Every year a few of these specimens were coined, using dies in excellent condition and a specially prepared round planchet, to prove the quality of the minting to the Viceroy or even to the King. Another very unusual and rare variety is specially struck specimens on heart-shaped flans. While many heart-shaped examples are encountered in today's market, a careful examination will reveal that most are underweight and were created after striking for jewelry and souvenir purposes. Most surviving specimens are holed, plugged or countermarked as found in Guatemala listings. The rest of the production was of primitive quality due to the shortage of equipment, skilled laborers and the volume to be struck.

Most pre-decimal coinage of independent Bolivia carries the assayers' initials on the reverse near the rim to the left of the date, in 4 to 5 o'clock position. The mint mark or name appears in the 7 to 8 o'clock area.

RULERS

Spanish until 1825

MINT MARKS

A - Paris
(a) - Paris, privy marks only
CHI - Valcambia
H - Heaton
KN - Kings' Norton
PTA monogram - La Plata (Sucre)
OR monogram – Oruro

ASSAYERS' INITIALS

Letter	Date	Name
F	1815	Francisco Jose de Matos
F	1830, 1848-67	Fortunato Equivar
FE	1867-90	Fortunato Equivar
J	1803-12, 1814-32	Juan Palomo y Sierra
J	1813	Jose Antonio de Sierra
J	1853-62	Joaquin Zemborain
L	1825-26	Leandro Osio
L	1825, 1830-43	Luis de Aquilar
M	1826-29, 1833-39	Digo Miguel Lopez
M	1848-55	Manuel Berrios
P	1776-1802	Pedro de Mazondo
P	1795-1824	Pedro Martin de Albizu
R	1839-47	Rafael Mariano Bustillo
R	1848	Manuel Telesforo Ramires

COLONIAL

MILLED COINAGE

KM# 82 1/4 REAL

0.8458 g., 0.8960 Silver .0244 oz. **Obv:** Castle **Rev:** Lion **Note:** There is a variety of 1802 with base of 2 not struck up and frequently miscataloged as 1809.

Date	Mintage	VG	F	VF	XF	Unc
1801PTS	17,000	35.00	90.00	175	350	—
1802PTS	165,000	10.00	25.00	50.00	100	—
1803PTS	29,000	13.50	35.00	75.00	150	—
1804PTS	5,724	50.00	135	245	475	—
1805PTS	11,000	50.00	135	245	475	—
1806PTS	30,000	12.50	30.00	60.00	120	—
1807PTS	10,000	25.00	60.00	120	250	—
1808PTS	8,161	12.50	30.00	50.00	100	200
1809PTS	—	100	250	400	800	—

KM# 69 1/2 REAL

1.6917 g., 0.8960 Silver .0487 oz. **Obv. Legend:** CAROLUS • IIII • DEI • GRATIA • **Note:** Mint mark in monogram.

Date	Mintage	VG	F	VF	XF	Unc
1801PTS PP	190,000	10.00	20.00	40.00	70.00	—
1802PTS PP	98,000	10.00	20.00	40.00	70.00	—
1803PTS PJ	66,000	10.00	20.00	40.00	70.00	—
1804PTS PJ	58,000	10.00	20.00	40.00	70.00	—
1805PTS PJ	84,000	10.00	20.00	40.00	70.00	—
1806PTS PJ	94,000	10.00	20.00	40.00	70.00	—
1807PTS PJ	114,000	10.00	20.00	35.00	60.00	300
1808/7PTS PJ	239,000	10.00	20.00	35.00	60.00	300
1808PTS PI Rare	—	—	—	—	—	—
Note: Assayer error with PI						
1808PTS PJ	Inc. above	10.00	20.00	35.00	60.00	300
1809PTS PJ	—	27.50	55.00	90.00	150	500

KM# 90 1/2 REAL

1.6917 g., 0.8960 Silver .0487 oz. **Ruler:** Ferdinand VII **Obv. Legend:** FERDIN • VII • DEI • GRATIA • **Note:** Mint mark in monogram.

Date	Mintage	VG	F	VF	XF	Unc
1814PTS PJ	—	27.50	55.00	90.00	150	—
1815PTS PJ	—	27.50	55.00	90.00	150	—
1816PTS PJ	74,000	15.00	30.00	50.00	100	—
1817PTS PJ	93,000	9.00	17.50	30.00	75.00	250
1818PTS PJ	106,000	9.00	17.50	30.00	75.00	250
1819PTS PJ	—	9.00	17.50	30.00	75.00	250
1820PTS PJ	—	9.00	17.50	30.00	75.00	250
1821PTS PJ	—	9.00	17.50	30.00	75.00	250
1822PTS PJ	—	9.00	17.50	30.00	75.00	250
1823PTS PJ	—	7.50	15.00	27.50	75.00	250
1823PTS JL	—	3.50	6.00	20.00	75.00	250
1824PTS PJ	—	9.00	17.50	30.00	75.00	250
1825PTS PJ Rare	—	—	—	—	—	—
1825PTS JL	—	9.00	17.50	30.00	75.00	250

KM# 70 REAL

3.3834 g., 0.8960 Silver .0975 oz. **Ruler:** Charles IIII **Obv:** Bust of Charles IIII **Note:** Mint mark in monogram.

Date	Mintage	VG	F	VF	XF	Unc
1801PTS PP	309,000	12.50	25.00	45.00	85.00	—
1802PTS PP	197,000	14.00	28.50	55.00	95.00	—
1803PTS PP	143,000	17.50	35.00	70.00	145	—
1803PTS PJ	Inc. above	12.50	25.00	45.00	85.00	—
1804PTS PJ	143,000	8.50	17.50	35.00	60.00	—
1805PTS PJ	72,000	12.50	25.00	45.00	90.00	—
1806PTS PJ	90,000	12.50	25.00	45.00	90.00	—
1807PTS PJ	107,000	12.50	25.00	45.00	80.00	300
1808/7PTS PJ	—	12.50	25.00	42.50	70.00	250
1808PTS PJ	238,000	12.50	25.00	40.00	65.00	250
1808/9PTS PJ	Inc. above	40.00	80.00	135	225	—
1809PTS PJ	—	32.50	65.00	110	185	—

KM# 87 REAL

3.3841 g., 0.8960 Silver .0975 oz. **Ruler:** Ferdinand VII **Obv:** Bust of Ferdinand VII **Obv. Legend:** FERDIN•VII• **Note:** Mint mark in monogram.

Date	Mintage	VG	F	VF	XF	Unc
1813PTS PJ	—	12.50	25.00	45.00	85.00	—
1816PTS PJ	38,000	8.00	16.50	30.00	55.00	—
1817PTS PJ	46,000	8.00	16.50	30.00	55.00	—
1818PTS PJ	56,000	8.00	16.50	30.00	55.00	—
1819/8PTS PJ	—	8.00	16.50	30.00	55.00	—
1819PTS PJ	—	8.00	16.50	30.00	55.00	—
1820PTS PJ	—	8.00	16.50	30.00	55.00	—
1821PTS PJ	—	8.00	16.50	30.00	55.00	—
1822/1PTS PJ	—	8.00	16.50	30.00	55.00	—
1822P PJ	—	8.00	16.50	30.00	55.00	—
1823PTS PJ	—	8.00	16.50	27.50	45.00	175
1824PTS PJ	—	8.00	16.50	30.00	55.00	—
1825/3PTS JL Rare	—	—	—	—	—	—
1825PTS JL	—	8.00	16.50	27.50	45.00	175

KM# 71 2 REALES

6.7668 g., 0.8960 Silver .1949 oz. **Ruler:** Charles IIII **Obv:** Bust of Charles IIII **Obv. Legend:** CAROLUS • IIII • DEI • GRATIA • **Rev:** Crowned arms between pillars **Rev. Legend:** HISPAN • ET IND • REX • **Note:** Mint mark in monogram.

Date	Mintage	VG	F	VF	XF	Unc
1801PTS PP	168,000	12.50	30.00	55.00	100	—
1802PTS PP	46,000	12.50	30.00	55.00	100	—
1803/2PTS PJ	48,000	16.50	42.50	70.00	125	—
1803PTS PJ	Inc. above	12.50	30.00	55.00	100	—
1804PTS PJ	52,000	12.50	30.00	55.00	100	—
1805/4PTS PJ	—	12.50	30.00	55.00	100	—
1805PTS PJ	43,000	12.50	30.00	55.00	100	—
1806PTS PJ	54,000	12.50	30.00	55.00	100	—
1807PTS PJ	98,000	12.50	30.00	55.00	100	—
1808PTS PJ	203,000	12.50	30.00	55.00	100	—

KM# 83 2 REALES

6.7668 g., 0.8960 Silver .1949 oz. **Ruler:** Ferdinand VII **Obv:** Bust of Ferdinand VII **Obv. Legend:** FERDIN • VII • DEI • GRATIA • **Rev:** Crowned arms between pillars **Rev. Legend:** HISPAN • ET IND • REX • **Note:** Mint mark in monogram.

Date	Mintage	VG	F	VF	XF	Unc
1808PTS PJ	Inc. above	17.50	45.00	80.00	150	—
1809PTS PJ	—	11.50	27.50	50.00	90.00	—
1813PTS PJ	—	11.50	27.50	50.00	90.00	—
1814PTS PJ	—	11.50	27.50	50.00	90.00	—
1816PTS PJ	48,000	12.50	30.00	55.00	100	—
1817PTS PJ	66,000	12.50	30.00	55.00	100	—
1818/7PTS PJ	—	18.50	42.50	75.00	135	—
1818PTS PJ	64,000	12.50	30.00	55.00	100	—
1819/8PTS PJ	—	11.50	27.50	50.00	90.00	—
1819PTS PJ	—	11.50	27.50	50.00	90.00	—
1820PTS PJ	—	12.50	30.00	55.00	100	—
1821PTS PJ	—	11.50	27.50	50.00	90.00	—
1822PTS PJ	—	11.50	27.50	50.00	90.00	—
1823PTS PJ	—	11.50	27.50	50.00	90.00	—
1824PTS PJ	—	11.50	27.50	50.00	90.00	—
1825PTS PJ	—	30.00	75.00	125	200	—
1825PTS J	—	65.00	15.00	275	400	—
1825PTS JL	—	22.50	55.00	95.00	185	—

KM# 72 4 REALES

13.5337 g., 0.8960 Silver .3899 oz. **Ruler:** Charles IIII **Obv:** Bust of Charles IIII **Obv. Legend:** CAROLUS • IIII • DEI • GRATIA • **Rev:** Crowned arms between pillars **Rev. Legend:** HISPAN • ET IND • REX • **Note:** Mint mark in monogram.

Date	Mintage	VG	F	VF	XF	Unc
1801PTS PP	90,000	30.00	60.00	175	350	—
1802PTS PP	53,000	30.00	60.00	175	350	—
1803PTS PJ	30,000	30.00	60.00	175	350	—
1804PTS PJ	53,000	30.00	60.00	175	350	800
1805PTS PJ	49,000	32.50	67.50	185	375	—
1806/5PTS PJ	59,000	32.50	67.50	185	375	—
1806PTS PJ	Inc. above	30.00	60.00	175	350	—
1807PTS PJ	101,000	30.00	60.00	175	350	—
1808PTS PJ	102,000	30.00	60.00	175	350	—
1808/9PTS PJ	Inc. above	30.00	60.00	175	350	—
1809PTS PJ	—	50.00	100	300	750	—

KM# 88 4 REALES

13.5337 g., 0.8960 Silver .3899 oz. **Ruler:** Ferdinand VII **Obv:** Bust of Ferdinand VII **Obv. Legend:** FERDIN • VII • DEI • GRATIA

• Rev: Crowned arms between pillars **Rev. Legend:** HISPAN • ET IND • REX • **Note:** Mint mark in monogram.

Date	Mintage	VG	F	VF	XF	Unc
1816PTS PJ	31,000	30.00	60.00	133	265	—
1817PTS PJ	33,000	30.00	60.00	133	265	—
1818PTS PJ	34,000	32.50	67.50	138	275	—
1819PTS PJ	—	32.50	67.50	138	275	—
1820PTS PJ	—	32.50	67.50	138	275	—
1821PTS PJ	—	37.50	75.00	150	300	—
1822PTS PJ	—	32.50	67.50	138	275	—
1823PTS PJ	—	30.00	60.00	133	265	—
1824PTS PJ	—	37.50	75.00	150	300	—
1825PTS PJ	—	250	425	600	850	—
1825PTS J	—	200	350	500	700	—
1825PTS JL	—	42.50	87.50	175	350	—

KM# 73 8 REALES

27.0674 g., 0.8960 Silver .7797 oz. **Ruler:** Charles III **Obv:** Bust of Charles IIII **Obv. Legend:** CAROLUS • IIII • DEI • GRATIA • **Rev:** Crowned arms between pillars **Rev. Legend:** HISPAN • ET IND • REX • **Note:** Mint mark in monogram. Prev. KM#73.1.

Date	Mintage	VG	F	VF	XF	Unc
1801PTS PP	3,965,000	32.50	55.00	95.00	175	—
1802PTS PP	2,083,000	32.50	55.00	95.00	175	—
1803PTS PJ	2,310,000	32.50	55.00	95.00	175	—
1804PTS PJ	3,074,000	32.50	55.00	95.00	175	—
1805/4PTS PJ	—	32.50	55.00	95.00	175	—
1805PTS PJ	3,199,000	32.50	55.00	95.00	175	—
1806/5PTS PJ	3,101,000	42.50	72.50	120	250	—
1806PTS PJ	Inc. above	32.50	55.00	100	200	—
1807PTS PJ	3,588,000	32.50	55.00	95.00	175	—
1808PTS PJ	3,299,000	32.50	55.00	100	200	—

KM# 84 8 REALES

27.0674 g., 0.8960 Silver .7797 oz. **Obv:** Bust of Ferdinand VII facing right **Obv. Legend:** FERDIN VII... **Rev:** Crowned arms between pillars **Note:** Mint mark in monogram.

Date	Mintage	VG	F	VF	XF	Unc
1808PTS PJ	Inc. above	42.50	75.00	125	245	—
1809PTS PJ	—	35.00	60.00	110	225	—
1813PTS PJ FERDIN IIV (error)	—	250	450	750	1,350	—
1813PTS PJ	—	27.50	45.00	75.00	150	—
1814/13PTS OH	—	22.00	45.00	95.00	200	—
1814PTS PJ	—	30.00	47.50	80.00	165	—
1815PTS PJ	—	30.00	47.50	80.00	165	—
1816PTS PJ	1,877,000	30.00	47.50	80.00	165	—
1817PTS PJ	1,906,000	30.00	47.50	80.00	165	—
1818PTS PJ	1,649,000	30.00	47.50	80.00	165	—
1819PTS PJ	—	30.00	47.50	80.00	165	—
1820PTS PJ	—	30.00	47.50	80.00	165	—
1821PTS PJ	—	30.00	47.50	80.00	165	—
1822PTS PJ	—	30.00	47.50	80.00	165	—
1823/2PTS PJ	—	90.00	150	250	450	—
1823PTS PJ	—	30.00	47.50	80.00	165	—
1823PTS JP	—	42.50	75.00	125	245	—
1824PTS PJ	—	47.50	80.00	135	275	—
1824PTS J	—	200	350	650	1,250	—
1825PTS J	—	125	250	500	1,000	—
1825PTS JL	—	20.00	35.00	60.00	150	300

Note: 1825 JL are also struck with coin rotation

Date	Mintage	VG	F	VF	XF	Unc
1825PTS JL Rare	—	—	—	—	—	—

Note: Without pomegranate or fleur-de-lis in arms

KM# 78 ESCUDO

3.3834 g., 0.8750 Gold .0952 oz. **Obv:** Bust of Charles IIII **Obv. Legend:** CAROL • IIII • D • G • HISP • ET IND • R • **Rev:** Similar to 2 Escudos, KM#79 **Note:** Mint mark in monogram.

Date	Mintage	VG	F	VF	XF	Unc
1801PTS PP	1,363	150	200	275	475	—
1802PTS PP	376	150	200	275	475	—
1803PTS PJ	410	150	200	275	600	—
1804PTS PJ	476	150	200	275	600	—
1805PTS PJ	613	150	200	275	600	—
1806PTS PJ	204	150	200	275	600	—
1807PTS PJ	1,123	150	200	275	600	—
1808PTS PJ	884	150	200	275	600	—

KM# 92 ESCUDO

3.3834 g., 0.8750 Gold .0952 oz. **Obv:** Bust of Ferdinand VII **Obv. Legend:** FERDIN • VII • D • G • HISP • ET IND • R • **Note:** Mint mark in monogram.

Date	Mintage	VG	F	VF	XF	Unc
1822PTS PJ	—	200	300	450	1,250	—
1823PTS PJ	—	250	400	650	1,500	—
1824PTS PJ	—	300	500	850	1,800	—

KM# 79 2 ESCUDOS

6.7668 g., 0.8750 Gold .1904 oz. **Obv:** Bust of Charles IIII **Obv. Legend:** CAROLUS • IIII • D • G • HISP • ET IND • R • **Note:** Mint mark in monogram.

Date	Mintage	VG	F	VF	XF	Unc
1801PTS PP	545	250	400	525	1,000	—
1802PTS PP	273	400	550	700	1,300	—
1803PTS PJ	273	400	550	700	1,300	—
1804PTS PJ	204	250	400	550	1,100	—
1805PTS PJ	306	325	475	700	1,300	—
1806PTS PJ	476	400	550	800	1,300	—
1807PTS PJ	748	250	350	525	850	—
1808PTS PJ	647	325	475	700	1,100	—

KM# 80 4 ESCUDOS

13.5337 g., 0.8750 Gold .3807 oz. **Obv:** Bust of Charles IIII **Obv. Legend:** CAROL • IIII • D • G • HISP • ET IND • R • **Note:** Mint mark in monogram.

Date	Mintage	VG	F	VF	XF	Unc
1801PTS PP	13,000	400	550	950	2,450	—
1802PTS PP	698	475	600	1,100	2,500	—
1803PTS PJ	408	800	1,100	1,600	3,550	—
1804PTS PJ	187	950	1,300	1,750	3,750	—
1805PTS PJ	255	500	700	1,100	2,500	—
1806PTS PJ	221	500	700	1,100	2,500	—
1807PTS PJ	527	475	600	950	2,450	—
1808PTS PJ	323	475	600	950	2,450	—

KM# 81 8 ESCUDOS

27.0674 g., 0.8750 Gold .7615 oz. **Obv:** Bust of Charles IIII **Obv. Legend:** CAROL • IIII • D • G • HISP • ET IND • R • **Note:** Mint mark in monogram.

Date	Mintage	VG	F	VF	XF	Unc
1801PTS PP	29,000	375	425	650	950	—
1802PTS PP	20,000	375	425	650	950	—
1803PTS PJ	17,000	375	425	650	950	—
1804PTS PJ	22,000	375	425	650	950	—
1805PTS PJ	49,000	375	425	650	950	—
1806PTS PJ	38,000	375	425	650	950	—
1807PTS PJ	39,000	375	425	650	950	—
1808PTS PJ	35,000	375	425	650	950	—

KM# 86 8 ESCUDOS

27.0674 g., 0.8750 Gold .7615 oz. **Obv:** Uniformed bust of Ferdinand VII **Obv. Legend:** FERDIN • VII • D • G • HISP • ET IND • R • **Note:** Mint mark in monogram.

Date	Mintage	VG	F	VF	XF	Unc
1809PTS PJ	—	—	—	—	—	—

KM# 91 8 ESCUDOS

27.0730 g., 0.8750 Gold .7616 oz. **Obv. Legend:** FERDIN. VII... **Rev:** Crowned arms in order chain **Note:** Mint mark in monogram. This type is most often encountered with a weak strike, fully struck coins with good bust detail command a strong premium.

Date	Mintage	VG	F	VF	XF	Unc
1822PTS PJ	—	375	450	850	1,450	—
1823PTS PJ	—	400	550	1,000	2,500	—
1824PTS PJ	—	400	500	900	2,000	—

REPUBLIC

MONETARY SYSTEM

8 Soles = 1 Peso

16 Soles = 1 Scudo

NOTE: The low quality of steel used for production of dies from the beginning of Republican coinage thru the late 1890s resulted in most series having multiple dies with differences in spacing, dots and even style of letters and numbers. Only major differences or errors will be listed.

SOL / SCUDO COINAGE

KM# 111 1/4 SOL

0.8500 g., 0.6670 Silver .0182 oz. **Obv:** Llama in plain field, POTOSI below **Edge:** Reeded **Note:** Three different die pairs known.

Date	Mintage	VG	F	VF	XF	Unc
1852	—	7.00	15.00	50.00	100	200

KM# 117 1/4 SOL

0.8500 g., 0.6670 Silver .0182 oz. **Obv:** Branches flank llama **Note:** The values listed are for holed coins, unholed specimens command a premium of 1-1/2 to 2 times these figures.

Date	Mintage	VG	F	VF	XF	Unc
1853	—	50.00	125	200	350	700

KM# 93.1 1/2 SOL

1.5000 g., 0.9030 Silver .0435 oz. **Rev:** 6-pointed stars in field **Rev. Legend:** ....CONSTITUCCI **Note:** Mint mark in monogram.

Date	Mintage	VG	F	VF	XF	Unc
1827PTS JM	—	8.00	20.00	45.00	90.00	200
1828/7PTS JM	—	9.00	20.00	45.00	90.00	200

KM# 93.2 1/2 SOL

1.5000 g., 0.9030 Silver .0435 oz. **Rev. Legend:** ... CONSTITUC **Note:** Mint mark in monogram.

Date	Mintage	VG	F	VF	XF	Unc
1827PTS JM	—	8.00	20.00	50.00	150	300
1828/7PTS JM	—	6.00	15.00	40.00	100	250
1828PTS JM	—	3.00	8.00	25.00	60.00	150
1829PTS JM	—	3.00	8.00	25.00	60.00	150

KM# 93.2a 1/2 SOL

1.5000 g., 0.6670 Silver .0322 oz. **Obv:** Six 6-pointed stars in arc above arms **Note:** Mint mark in monogram.

Date	Mintage	VG	F	VF	XF	Unc
1830PTS J Wide date, large star	—	2.50	7.00	15.00	50.00	—
1830PTS J Narrow date, small star	—	2.50	7.00	15.00	50.00	—
1830PTS J	—	4.00	9.00	30.00	75.00	—

Note: Error inverted N in CONSTITUC

Date	Mintage	VG	F	VF	XF	Unc
1830PTS JF	—	2.50	4.00	7.00	25.00	—
1830PTS JL	—	1.00	2.00	3.50	18.00	35.00
1830PTS JL Error CONSTITU(C/.)	—	2.50	5.00	9.00	35.00	—

KM# 93.3 1/2 SOL

1.5000 g., 0.6670 Silver .0322 oz. **Rev:** 5-pointed stars in field **Note:** Mint mark in monogram. Believed to have been struck after 1853.

Date	Mintage	VG	F	VF	XF	Unc
1830PTS JL	—	7.00	15.00	30.00	65.00	—

KM# 118.1 1/2 SOL

1.5000 g., 0.6670 Silver .0322 oz. **Obv:** Without value, nine 5-pointed stars in arc above arms **Rev:** BOLIVAR on truncation **Note:** Mint mark in monogram.

Date	Mintage	VG	F	VF	XF	Unc
1853PTS FP	—	4.00	10.00	20.00	50.00	150
1853PTS FP	—	—	—	—	—	—
Note: Inverted A for V in BOLIVIANA						
1854PTS MJ	—	4.00	10.00	20.00	50.00	150
1855PTS MJ	—	4.00	10.00	20.00	50.00	150
1856PTS FJ	—	4.00	10.00	20.00	50.00	150
1856PTS MJ	—	5.00	11.00	20.00	60.00	175

KM# 118.2 1/2 SOL

1.5000 g., 0.6670 Silver .0322 oz. **Obv:** Denomination added **Note:** Mint mark in monogram. Varieties exist with and without period after CONSTITUCION, and with variance in bust size.

Date	Mintage	VG	F	VF	XF	Unc
1856PTS FJ	—	3.00	7.00	18.00	40.00	125
1857/6PTS FJ	—	3.50	7.00	18.00	40.00	125
1857PTS FJ	—	3.00	7.00	18.00	40.00	125
1857PTS FJ	—	5.00	11.00	25.00	65.00	—
Note: Error, LIBRE POCA?R LA						
1858/7PTS FJ	—	3.00	8.00	20.00	50.00	135
1858PTS FJ	—	3.00	9.00	25.00	60.00	145
Note: No R in BOLIVAR under bust						

KM# 118.3 1/2 SOL

1.5000 g., 0.6670 Silver .0322 oz. **Rev:** BOLIVAR below truncation **Note:** Mint mark in monogram.

Date	Mintage	VG	F	VF	XF	Unc
1859PTS FJ	—	8.00	20.00	50.00	120	300
1859PTS FJ	—	15.00	35.00	70.00	150	350
Note: Error, BOLIVRA with inverted V for A						

KM# 127 1/2 SOL

1.5000 g., 0.6670 Silver .0322 oz. **Rev:** Crude "La Paz style" head **Note:** Usually found holed. The prices here are for unholed pieces.

Date	Mintage	VG	F	VF	XF	Unc
1855PAZ P	—	10.00	25.00	60.00	150	300
1856/5PAZ P	—	15.00	35.00	75.00	175	350
1856PAZ P	—	10.00	25.00	60.00	150	—

KM# A132 1/2 SOL

1.5000 g., 0.6670 Silver 0.0322 oz. **Obv:** KM#127 **Rev:** KM#132, crude so-called "ugly head"

Date	Mintage	VG	F	VF	XF	Unc
1855PAZ P Rare	—	—	—	—	—	—

KM# 132 1/2 SOL

1.5000 g., 0.6670 Silver .0322 oz. **Rev:** Crude so-called "ugly head"

Date	Mintage	VG	F	VF	XF	Unc
1858/7PAZ P	—	10.00	22.00	55.00	140	—
1858PAZ P	—	8.00	20.00	50.00	125	300
1859PAZ P Rare	2	—	—	—	—	—

KM# 133.1 1/2 SOL

1.3000 g., 0.6670 Silver .0279 oz. **Rev. Legend:** PESO 25 Gs **Note:** Mint mark in monogram.

Date	Mintage	VG	F	VF	XF	Unc
1859PTS FJ	—	15.00	40.00	100	250	—

KM# 133.2 1/2 SOL

1.3000 g., 0.9030 Silver .0377 oz. **Rev. Legend:** 25 G. **Note:** Mint mark in monogram.

Date	Mintage	VG	F	VF	XF	Unc
1859PTS FJ	—	8.00	18.00	45.00	100	—
1860PTS FJ	—	5.00	7.50	25.00	55.00	100
1861PTS FJ	—	5.00	7.50	30.00	60.00	150
1861PTS FJ	—	10.00	15.00	30.00	90.00	—
Note: With P/T for POTOSI monogram						
1862/1PTS FP	—	6.00	15.00	35.00	90.00	—
1862PTS FP	—	5.00	12.00	30.00	80.00	175
1863/2PTS FP	—	5.00	7.50	20.00	50.00	—
1863PTS FP	—	5.00	12.00	30.00	60.00	150
Note: Large stars, small head						
1863PTS FP	—	5.00	12.00	30.00	60.00	150
Note: Small stars, large head						

KM# 94 SOL

3.0000 g., 0.9030 Silver .0871 oz. **Obv:** Six 6-pointed stars in arc above arms **Rev:** BOLIVAR in truncation **Note:** Mint mark in monogram.

Date	Mintage	VG	F	VF	XF	Unc
1827PTS JM	—	10.00	25.00	100	500	1,000
1828PTS JM	—	10.00	25.00	100	500	—
1829PTS JM	—	8.00	20.00	75.00	200	800

KM# 94a SOL

3.0000 g., 0.6670 Silver .0643 oz. **Note:** Mint mark in monogram. The prices listed are for holed coins, unholed specimens command a substantial premium.

Date	Mintage	VG	F	VF	XF	Unc
1830PTS J	—	5.00	15.00	35.00	60.00	—
1830PTS JL	—	3.50	10.00	20.00	40.00	—

KM# 119.1 SOL

3.0000 g., 0.6670 Silver .0643 oz. **Obv:** Without value, nine 5-pointed stars in arc above arms **Rev:** BOLIVAR on truncation **Note:** Mint mark in monogram.

Date	Mintage	VG	F	VF	XF	Unc
1853PTS FP	—	7.50	15.00	40.00	100	300
1853PTS FP	—	6.00	12.50	30.00	70.00	—
Note: Error, BOLIVLANA						
1854PTS MJ	—	5.00	15.00	40.00	80.00	—

KM# 119.2 SOL

3.0000 g., 0.6670 Silver .0643 oz. **Obv:** Value added **Note:** Mint mark in monogram.

Date	Mintage	VG	F	VF	XF	Unc
1855PTS MJ	—	6.00	12.00	35.00	100	250
1856/5PTS (F/M) J	—	10.00	20.00	50.00	130	350
1856PTS FJ	—	6.00	12.00	35.00	100	250
1857/6PTS FJ	—	10.00	20.00	50.00	130	350
1857PTS FJ	—	6.00	12.00	35.00	100	300
1858/7PTS FJ	—	10.00	20.00	50.00	130	350
1858PTS FJ	—	6.00	12.00	35.00	100	250

KM# 120 SOL

3.0000 g., 0.6670 Silver .0643 oz. **Rev:** "Potosi style" laureate head **Note:** The prices listed are for holed coins, unholed specimens command a substantial premium.

Date	Mintage	VG	F	VF	XF	Unc
1855PAZ P	—	10.00	25.00	50.00	100	—
1855PAZ F	—	10.00	25.00	50.00	100	—

KM# 128 SOL

3.0000 g., 0.6670 Silver .0643 oz. **Rev:** Crude "La Paz style" head **Note:** The prices listed are for holed coins, unholed specimens command a substantial premium.

Date	Mintage	VG	F	VF	XF	Unc
1855PAZ F	—	30.00	75.00	100	150	—
1856PAZ P	—	20.00	35.00	65.00	100	—

KM# 131 SOL

3.0000 g., 0.6670 Silver .0643 oz. **Rev:** Crude, so-called "ugly head" **Note:** The prices listed are for holed coins, unholed specimens command a substantial premium.

Date	Mintage	VG	F	VF	XF	Unc
1857PAZ P	—	15.00	35.00	75.00	120	—
1858/7PAZ	—	20.00	40.00	75.00	150	—
1858PAZ P	—	15.00	30.00	70.00	120	—
1859/7PAZ P 5 known; Rare	—	—	—	—	—	—
1859PAZ P	—	15.00	30.00	70.00	120	—

KM# 134.1 SOL

2.5000 g., 0.6670 Silver .0536 oz. **Rev. Legend:** PESO 50 Gs **Note:** Mint mark in monogram.

Date	Mintage	VG	F	VF	XF	Unc
1859PTS FJ	—	12.00	25.00	55.00	100	—
1859PTS FJ	—	20.00	40.00	90.00	200	450
Note: Error R(E/R)P(U/B)BLICA, all A's are inverted V's						

KM# 119.3 SOL

3.0000 g., 0.6670 Silver .0643 oz. **Rev:** BOLIVAR below truncation **Note:** Mint mark in monogram.

Date	Mintage	VG	F	VF	XF	Unc
1859PTS FJ	—	15.00	30.00	60.00	120	300
1859PTS FJ	—	15.00	30.00	60.00	120	—
Note: Error, A's are inverted V's						

KM# 134.2 SOL

2.5000 g., 0.9030 Silver .0726 oz. **Rev. Legend:** 50 G or 50 Gs **Note:** Mint mark in monogram.

Date	Mintage	VG	F	VF	XF	Unc
1860PTS FJ Rare	—	—	—	—	—	—
Note: Denomination divided by a period						
1860PTS FJ	—	4.00	9.00	20.00	45.00	100
1860PTS (F/J) J	—	5.00	11.00	30.00	70.00	175
1861PTS FJ	—	4.00	9.00	20.00	45.00	100
1862/1PTS FP	—	9.00	20.00	50.00	100	250
1862PTS FJ	—	9.00	20.00	50.00	100	250
1862PTS FP	—	4.00	9.00	20.00	45.00	100
1863/2PTS FP	—	5.00	11.00	30.00	70.00	175
1863PTS FP	—	3.50	9.00	20.00	45.00	—
Note: Large stars, small head						
1863PTS FP	—	3.50	9.00	20.00	45.00	—
Note: Small stars, large head						

KM# 95 2 SOLES

6.2000 g., 0.9030 Silver .1799 oz. **Note:** Mint mark in monogram.

Date	Mintage	VG	F	VF	XF	Unc
1827PTS JM	—	15.00	40.00	100	250	1,000
1828/7PTS JM	—	35.00	50.00	120	300	—
1828PTS JM	—	10.00	25.00	50.00	125	—
1829PTS JM	—	15.00	40.00	100	250	—

KM# 95a 2 SOLES

6.2000 g., 0.6670 Silver .1324 oz. **Note:** Mint mark in monogram.

Date	Mintage	VG	F	VF	XF	Unc
1830/27PTS J	—	20.00	35.00	75.00	150	—
1830PTS J	—	10.00	25.00	40.00	80.00	—
1830PTS JF	—	10.00	25.00	45.00	90.00	—
1830/20PTS JL	—	20.00	35.00	55.00	110	—
1830PTS JL	—	5.00	10.00	25.00	60.00	150
1830PTS JL	—	17.00	30.00	50.00	100	—
Note: Error CONSTITU (C/I) ION						
1831PTS J Rare	—	—	—	—	—	—

KM# 121.1 2 SOLES

6.2000 g., 0.6670 Silver .1324 oz. **Obv:** Without value **Note:** Mint mark in monogram. Varieties with or without period after CONSTITUTION exist.

Date	Mintage	VG	F	VF	XF	Unc
1853PTS FP	—	20.00	45.00	90.00	125	300

KM# 122 2 SOLES

6.2000 g., 0.6670 Silver .1324 oz. **Rev:** Bare head

Date	Mintage	VG	F	VF	XF	Unc
1853PAZ J	—	1,500	2,000	3,500	5,000	—

Note: Five known, three are damaged

KM# 126 2 SOLES

6.2000 g., 0.6670 Silver .1324 oz. **Rev:** "Potosi style" laureate head

Date	Mintage	VG	F	VF	XF	Unc
1854PAZ F	—	100	175	300	500	1,000

KM# 121.2 2 SOLES

6.2000 g., 0.6670 Silver .1324 oz. **Obv:** Value added **Note:** Mint mark in monogram. Varieties with or without period after CONSTITUTION exist.

Date	Mintage	VG	F	VF	XF	Unc
1854PTS MJ	—	8.00	20.00	50.00	125	400
1855PTS MJ	—	8.00	20.00	50.00	125	300
1856/5PTS MJ	—	10.00	25.00	60.00	150	—
1856PTS MJ	—	10.00	25.00	60.00	150	—
1857PTS MJ	—	8.00	20.00	50.00	125	—
1857PTS FJ	—	8.00	20.00	50.00	125	—
1858/7PTS FJ Rare	—	—	—	—	—	—
1858PTS FJ	—	10.00	25.00	60.00	150	500

KM# 129 2 SOLES

6.2000 g., 0.6670 Silver .1324 oz. **Rev:** Crude "La Paz style" head

Date	Mintage	VG	F	VF	XF	Unc
1855PAZ F 4 known	—	300	650	1,500	2,000	—
1856PAZ P 10 known	—	175	400	800	1,200	—

KM# 121.3 2 SOLES

6.2000 g., 0.6670 Silver .1324 oz. **Rev:** BOLIVAR below truncation **Note:** Mint mark in monogram.

Date	Mintage	VG	F	VF	XF	Unc
1859/8/7PTS FJ	—	20.00	30.00	75.00	150	300
1859/7PTS FJ	—	20.00	30.00	75.00	150	300
1859PTS FJ	—	20.00	30.00	75.00	150	—

KM# 135.1 2 SOLES

6.2000 g., 0.6670 Silver .1324 oz. **Rev:** Crude "La Paz style" head **Rev. Legend:** PESO 100 Gs **Note:** Mint mark in monogram. Varieties with or without period after CONSTITUTION exist.

Date	Mintage	VG	F	VF	XF	Unc
1859/7PTS FJ	—	15.00	35.00	75.00	165	—
1859/8PTS FJ	—	20.00	40.00	90.00	200	—
1859PTS FJ	—	—	—	—	—	—

KM# 135.2 2 SOLES

4.5000 g., 0.9030 Silver .1306 oz. **Rev. Legend:** 100 Gs **Note:** Mint mark in monogram. Varieties with or without period after CONSTITUTION exist.

Date	Mintage	VG	F	VF	XF	Unc
1860PTS FJ	—	7.50	15.00	25.00	40.00	75.00
1860PTS FJ large Bolivar letters	—	15.00	35.00	60.00	90.00	—
1860PTS FJ	—	15.00	35.00	60.00	90.00	150
Note: Error, 60 over smaller 60, large 100						
1861PTS FJ	—	7.50	15.00	25.00	40.00	—
1862/1PTS JF large head, large 100	—	7.50	15.00	25.00	40.00	—
1862/1PTS FJ	—	6.00	10.00	17.00	35.00	—
1862PTS FJ	—	7.50	15.00	25.00	40.00	—
1862/1PTS FP	—	5.00	8.00	16.00	35.00	—
1862PTS FP	—	4.50	7.50	15.00	30.00	—
1863/2PTS FP	—	10.00	20.00	40.00	75.00	—
1863PTS FP	—	5.00	8.00	15.00	30.00	—
Note: Large stars, small head						
1863PTS FP	—	5.00	8.00	15.00	30.00	—
Note: Small stars, large head						

KM# 96 4 SOLES

13.5000 g., 0.9030 Silver .3918 oz. **Edge:** Reeded, incuse lettering **Edge Lettering:** AYACUCHO * SUCRE *1824* **Note:** Mint mark in monogram.

Date	Mintage	VG	F	VF	XF	Unc
1827PTS JM	—	20.00	60.00	150	300	—
1828/7PTS JM	—	22.00	65.00	160	325	—
1828PTS JM	—	20.00	60.00	150	250	—
1829PTS JM	—	20.00	60.00	150	250	—

KM# 96a.1 4 SOLES

13.5000 g., 0.6670 Silver .2895 oz. **Note:** Mint mark in monogram.

Date	Mintage	VG	F	VF	XF	Unc
1830PTS J	—	4.00	10.00	25.00	50.00	100
1830/20PTS JL	—	5.00	12.00	28.00	60.00	—
1830/27PTS JL	—	4.00	10.00	25.00	50.00	—
1830PTS JL	—	3.50	9.00	17.00	35.00	—

KM# 96a.2 4 SOLES

13.5000 g., 0.6670 Silver .2895 oz. **Obv:** Additional mint mark on lower part of island **Note:** Mint mark in monogram.

Date	Mintage	VG	F	VF	XF	Unc
1830PTS JL	—	5.00	12.00	28.00	60.00	—
1830/3PTS JL	—	7.00	20.00	50.00	120	—

KM# 96a.3 4 SOLES

13.5000 g., 0.6670 Silver .2895 oz. **Obv:** Additional mint mark on upper part of island **Note:** Mint mark in monogram.

Date	Mintage	VG	F	VF	XF	Unc
1830PTS JL	—	5.00	12.00	28.00	60.00	—

KM# A124 4 SOLES

12.5100 g., 0.7500 Silver 0.3017 oz. **Note:** Mint mark ORURO in monogram

Date	Mintage	VG	F	VF	XF	Unc
1849OR JM Unique	—	—	—	—	—	—

KM# 124.1 4 SOLES

13.5000 g., 0.6670 Silver .2895 oz.

Date	Mintage	VG	F	VF	XF	Unc
1853PAZ J	—	100	200	400	1,000	3,000

KM# 124.2 4 SOLES

13.4500 g., 0.6000 Silver .2595 oz. **Note:** Mint mark in monogram.

Date	Mintage	VG	F	VF	XF	Unc
1853PTA J Unique	—	—	—	—	—	—

KM# 125 4 SOLES

13.5000 g., 0.6670 Silver .2895 oz. **Rev:** "Potosi style" laureate head

Date	Mintage	VG	F	VF	XF	Unc
1853PAZ J	—	20.00	45.00	100	200	400
1854/3PAZ F	—	20.00	45.00	90.00	175	300
1854PAZ F	—	17.00	35.00	75.00	150	—
1855PAZ F	—	12.00	30.00	65.00	135	—

KM# 123.1 4 SOLES

13.5000 g., 0.6670 Silver .2895 oz. **Obv:** Without value **Note:** Mint mark in monogram. Varieties with or without period after CONSTITUTION exist.

Date	Mintage	VG	F	VF	XF	Unc
1853PTS FP	—	7.50	17.00	40.00	95.00	—

KM# 123.2 4 SOLES

13.5000 g., 0.6670 Silver .2895 oz. **Obv:** Value added **Note:** Mint mark in monogram. Varieties with or without period after CONSTITUTION exist.

Date	Mintage	VG	F	VF	XF	Unc
1853PTS MF	—	5.00	12.00	30.00	75.00	150
1854PTS MF	—	5.00	12.00	30.00	75.00	150
1854PTS MJ	—	5.00	12.00	30.00	75.00	150
1855PTS MJ	—	5.00	12.00	30.00	75.00	150
1855PTS MJ	—	100	250	500	700	—
Note: Error CONSTITUCIN, no dot after						
1855PTS FJ	—	10.00	25.00	45.00	90.00	—
1856PTS FJ	—	5.00	12.00	30.00	75.00	150
1856/5PTS MJ	—	5.00	12.00	30.00	75.00	—
1856PTS MJ	—	5.00	12.00	30.00	75.00	150
1857PTS FJ	—	5.00	12.00	30.00	75.00	150
1857PTS FJ	—	10.00	25.00	45.00	90.00	—
Note: Error V in BOLIVIANA inverted A						
1857/FPTS FJ	—	12.00	35.00	65.00	125	—
1857PTS FJ	—	125	250	400	750	—
Note: Error CONSTITUCIO						
1858PTS FJ	—	8.00	20.00	40.00	90.00	175

KM# 123.3 4 SOLES

13.5000 g., 0.6670 Silver .2895 oz. **Rev:** BOLIVAR below truncation **Note:** Mint mark in monogram. Varieties with or without period after CONSTITUTION exist.

Date	Mintage	VG	F	VF	XF	Unc
1859PTS FJ	—	15.00	35.00	75.00	165	—
1859PTS FJ	—	12.00	30.00	65.00	150	300

Note: Error, A in BOLIVAR inverted V

KM# 136 4 SOLES

13.5000 g., 0.6670 Silver .2895 oz.

Date	Mintage	VG	F	VF	XF	Unc
1859PAZ P	—	150	250	400	600	—

KM# 130 4 SOLES

13.5000 g., 0.6670 Silver .2895 oz. **Rev:** Crude "La Paz style" head

Date	Mintage	VG	F	VF	XF	Unc
1855PAZ F	—	12.50	30.00	45.00	90.00	—
Note: Varieties of bust, tree sizes, and dots (near, medium, far) from N exist						
1855PAZ F	—	30.00	60.00	90.00	160	—
Note: BOLIVIANA with IVI/VIA						
1(8/S)56PAZ P (A/P) Z	—	30.00	60.00	90.00	160	—
1856/5PAZ P/F	—	15.00	25.00	45.00	90.00	—
1856PAZ P	—	12.50	30.00	45.00	90.00	200
1857/6PAZ P	—	30.00	50.00	80.00	125	250
1857PAZ P	—	100	200	350	550	800
1858PAZ P	—	100	200	350	550	—

KM# 139 4 SOLES

13.5000 g., 0.9030 Silver .3918 oz. **Obv:** Without value **Note:** Mint mark in monogram. Weight indicated as 200 Gs.

Date	Mintage	VG	F	VF	XF	Unc
1860PTS FJ	—	150	250	400	600	900

KM# 97 8 SOLES

27.0000 g., 0.9030 Silver .7836 oz. **Edge:** Reeded **Edge Lettering:** AYACUCHO*SUCRE *1824* **Note:** Using the alpaca (llama-like animal) at the right as a guide, the overall size from bottom of legs to tip of ears is+/-8.3mm vs + /-7.2mm; Mint mark in monogram.

Date	Mintage	VG	F	VF	XF	Unc
1827PTS JM	—	15.00	25.00	45.00	75.00	—
1827PTS JM Large alpacas	—	20.00	35.00	60.00	100	—
1828PTS JM	—	15.00	25.00	45.00	75.00	—
1829PTS JM	—	15.00	25.00	45.00	75.00	—
1829PTS JM	—	30.00	50.00	225	350	—
Note: V in BOLIVIANA inverted A						
1830/20PTS JF	—	30.00	50.00	80.00	190	—
1830PTS JF	—	15.00	25.00	45.00	75.00	—
1830PTS JF/J	—	35.00	55.00	95.00	125	—
1830PTS J	—	25.00	35.00	55.00	100	—
1830PTS J	—	30.00	50.00	225	350	—
Note: V in BOLIVIANA inverted A						
1831PTS JF	—	20.00	35.00	60.00	125	—
1831PTS JL	—	15.00	25.00	45.00	75.00	—
1832PTS JL	—	15.00	25.00	45.00	75.00	—
1833PTS L	—	150	225	325	450	—
1833PTS LM	—	15.00	25.00	45.00	75.00	—
1834PTS LM	—	15.00	25.00	45.00	75.00	—
1835PTS LM	—	20.00	30.00	50.00	90.00	—
1836/5PTS LM	—	20.00	30.00	50.00	90.00	—
1836/6PTS LM	—	20.00	30.00	50.00	90.00	—
1836PTS LM	—	15.00	25.00	45.00	75.00	—
1837PTS LM	—	15.00	25.00	45.00	75.00	—
1838PTS LM	—	15.00	25.00	45.00	75.00	—
1839PTS LM	—	15.00	25.00	45.00	75.00	—
1839PTS LR	—	25.00	35.00	55.00	100	—
1840PTS LR 4 over inverted 4	—	30.00	50.00	90.00	220	—
1840PTS LR	—	15.00	25.00	45.00	75.00	—

KM# A103 8 SOLES

27.0000 g., 0.9030 Silver .7836 oz. **Obv:** Obverse of KM#97 **Rev:** KM#103 **Note:** Mule. Mint mark in monogram.

Date	Mintage	VG	F	VF	XF	Unc
1841PTS LR	—	—	—	—	—	—
1846PTS R	—	17.50	30.00	75.00	100	—
1847PTS R	—	17.50	30.00	75.00	100	—
1848PTS R	—	50.00	100	200	300	—
1848PTS M Rare	—	—	—	—	—	—
1848PTS M/R Rare	—	—	—	—	—	—

KM# 103 8 SOLES

27.0000 g., 0.9030 Silver .7836 oz. **Note:** Mint mark in monogram.

Date	Mintage	VG	F	VF	XF	Unc
1841PTS LR	—	15.00	25.00	45.00	75.00	—
1841PTS LR	—	150	250	350	600	—
Note: Error: CONSTITUCIN						
1842PTS LR	—	15.00	25.00	45.00	75.00	—
1843/2PTS LR	—	20.00	35.00	55.00	100	—
1843PTS LR	—	17.50	30.00	50.00	80.00	—
1844PTS R	—	17.50	30.00	50.00	80.00	—
1845PTS R	—	20.00	35.00	55.00	100	—
Note: LA/L in reverse legend						
1845PTS R	—	15.00	25.00	45.00	75.00	—
1846/5PTS R	—	25.00	45.00	75.00	155	—

KM# 109 8 SOLES

27.0000 g., 0.9030 Silver .7836 oz. **Obv:** Without value **Rev:** Bare head **Note:** Mint mark in monogram.

Date	Mintage	VG	F	VF	XF	Unc
1848PTS FM Large date	—	15.00	22.50	35.00	70.00	—
1848PTS FM Small date	—	15.00	22.50	35.00	70.00	—
1849PTS FM	—	15.00	22.50	35.00	70.00	—
1850PTS FM	—	10.00	20.00	32.50	65.00	—
1851/0PTS FM	—	20.00	30.00	50.00	100	—
1851PTS FM	—	17.50	25.00	45.00	80.00	—
1851PTS FR	—	75.00	125	175	300	—

KM# 112.1 8 SOLES

27.0000 g., 0.9030 Silver .7836 oz. **Rev:** Laureate head **Note:** Mint mark in monogram.

Date	Mintage	VG	F	VF	XF	Unc
1852PTS FM	—	25.00	35.00	50.00	100	—
1853PTS FP	—	40.00	80.00	125	200	—
1854PTS M	—	40.00	80.00	125	200	—
1856PTS FJ	—	25.00	45.00	85.00	140	—

KM# 112.2 8 SOLES

27.0000 g., 0.9030 Silver .7836 oz. **Obv:** Value added **Note:** Mint mark in monogram.

Date	Mintage	VG	F	VF	XF	Unc
1854PTS MJ Small S	—	17.50	27.50	50.00	90.00	—
1854PTS MJ Ball top 5	—	20.00	30.00	55.00	100	—
1855/4PTS MJ	—	17.50	25.00	50.00	90.00	—
1855PTS MJ	—	12.50	20.00	35.00	75.00	—

KM# 137 8 SOLES

27.0000 g., 0.9030 Silver .7836 oz. **Note:** Mint mark in monogram.

Date	Mintage	VG	F	VF	XF	Unc
1859PTS FJ	—	400	600	1,250	1,750	—

KM# 138.1 8 SOLES

20.0000 g., 0.9030 Silver .5807 oz. **Rev. Legend:** Po 400 Gs **Note:** Mint mark in monogram.

Date	Mintage	VG	F	VF	XF	Unc
1859PTS FJ	—	1,500	2,000	2,800	—	—

KM# 138.2 8 SOLES

20.0000 g., 0.9030 Silver .5807 oz. **Rev. Legend:** PESO/Po 400 Gs **Note:** Mint mark in monogram.

Date	Mintage	VG	F	VF	XF	Unc
1859PTS FJ	—	50.00	100	175	—	—

KM# 138.3 8 SOLES

20.0000 g., 0.9030 Silver .5807 oz. **Rev. Legend:** PESO 400 Gs **Note:** Mint mark in monogram.

Date	Mintage	VG	F	VF	XF	Unc
1859PTS FJ	—	25.00	50.00	100	150	—
1859PTS F.J.	—	25.00	50.00	100	150	—

KM# 138.6 8 SOLES
20.0000 g., 0.9030 Silver .5807 oz. **Rev. Legend:** 400 Gs **Note:** Mint mark in monogram.

Date	Mintage	VG	F	VF	XF	Unc
1859PTS FJ	—	75.00	125	200	350	—
1860PTS FJ	—	10.00	15.00	30.00	65.00	—
1861PTS FJ	—	10.00	15.00	30.00	65.00	—
1861PTS FJ	—	15.00	25.00	40.00	85.00	—
Note: Inverted A for V in Bolivar						
1862/1PTS FJ	—	10.00	15.00	30.00	65.00	—
1862PTS FJ	—	10.00	15.00	30.00	65.00	—
1862PTS FP	—	10.00	15.00	30.00	65.00	—
1863/2PTS FP	—	10.00	15.00	35.00	70.00	—
1863PTS FP	—	10.00	15.00	35.00	70.00	—
1863PTS FP	—	50.00	110	250	500	—
Note: Error REPUBLICA BOLIVANA						

KM# 138.4 8 SOLES
20.0000 g., 0.9030 Silver .5807 oz. **Rev. Legend:** 400 Gs **Note:** Mint mark in monogram.

Date	Mintage	VG	F	VF	XF	Unc
1859PTS FJ	—	150	250	500	900	—

KM# 138.5 8 SOLES
20.0000 g., 0.9030 Silver .5807 oz. **Obv:** Tree divides 10Ds-20Gs **Rev. Legend:** Po 400 Gs **Note:** Mint mark in monogram.

Date	Mintage	VG	F	VF	XF	Unc
1860PTS FJ	—	300	500	1,000	1,700	—

KM# 100 1/2 SCUDO
1.7000 g., 0.8750 Gold .0478 oz. **Note:** Mint mark in monogram.

Date	Mintage	VG	F	VF	XF	Unc
1834PTS LM Rare	—	—	—	—	—	—
1838PTS LM	—	80.00	140	210	400	—
1839PTS LM	—	80.00	130	200	375	—
1840PTS LR	—	80.00	140	210	400	—

KM# 104 1/2 SCUDO
1.7000 g., 0.8750 Gold .0478 oz. **Note:** Mint mark in monogram.

Date	Mintage	VG	F	VF	XF	Unc
1841PTS LR/PL	—	55.00	75.00	100	165	—
1841PTS LR	—	55.00	75.00	100	165	—

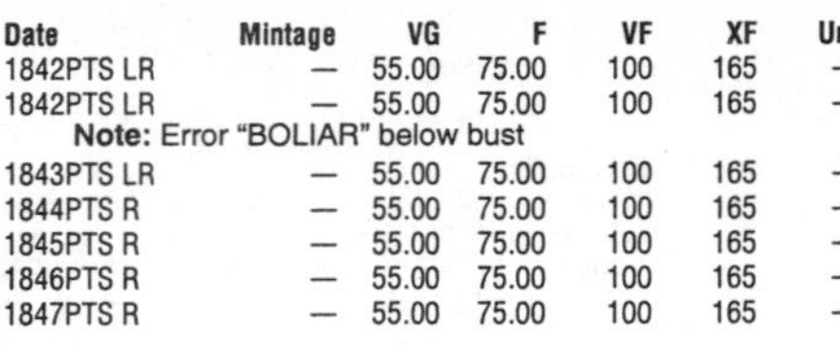

Date	Mintage	VG	F	VF	XF	Unc
1842PTS LR	—	55.00	75.00	100	165	—
1842PTS LR	—	55.00	75.00	100	165	—
Note: Error "BOLIAR" below bust						
1843PTS LR	—	55.00	75.00	100	165	—
1844PTS R	—	55.00	75.00	100	165	—
1845PTS R	—	55.00	75.00	100	165	—
1846PTS R	—	55.00	75.00	100	165	—
1847PTS R	—	55.00	75.00	100	165	—

KM# 113 1/2 SCUDO
1.7000 g., 0.8750 Gold .0478 oz. **Note:** Mint mark in monogram.

Date	Mintage	F	VF	XF	Unc	BU
1852/1PTS FP	—	85.00	150	200	400	—
1852PTS MJ	—	70.00	125	175	325	—
1852PTS FP	—	65.00	120	170	300	—
1853PTS FP	—	65.00	120	170	300	—
1854PTS FP	—	70.00	125	175	325	—
1855PTS MF/FJ	—	65.00	120	170	300	—
1855PTS FP	—	65.00	120	170	300	—
1855PTS M	—	65.00	120	170	300	—
1855PTS NJ	—	65.00	120	170	300	—
1855PTS FS	—	65.00	120	170	300	—
1856PTS FJ	—	65.00	120	170	300	—
1856PTS FS	—	65.00	120	170	300	—

KM# 140 1/2 SCUDO
1.2500 g., 0.9000 Gold .0361 oz.

Date	Mintage	F	VF	XF	Unc	BU
1868 FE	—	300	550	650	1,000	—

KM# 98 SCUDO
3.4000 g., 0.8750 Gold .0956 oz. **Note:** Mint mark in monogram.

Date	Mintage	VG	F	VF	XF	Unc
1831PTS JL	—	85.00	120	220	325	—
1832/1PTS JL	—	100	150	275	400	—
1832PTS JL	—	85.00	120	220	300	—
1833PTS JL	—	85.00	120	220	325	—
1833PTS LM	—	85.00	120	220	325	—
1834PTS JL	—	70.00	100	200	300	—
1834PTS LM	—	85.00	120	220	325	—
1835PTS LM	—	85.00	120	220	325	—
1836PTS LM	—	85.00	120	220	325	—
1837PTS LM	—	85.00	120	220	325	—
1838PTS LM	—	85.00	120	220	325	—
1839PTS LM	—	85.00	120	220	325	—
1840PTS LR	—	120	165	300	485	—

KM# 105 SCUDO
3.4000 g., 0.8750 Gold .0956 oz. **Note:** Mint mark in monogram.

Date	Mintage	VG	F	VF	XF	Unc
1841PTS LR	—	85.00	120	220	325	—
1842PTS LR	—	85.00	120	220	325	—
1846PTS R	—	85.00	120	220	325	—

KM# 114 SCUDO
3.4000 g., 0.8750 Gold .0956 oz. **Note:** Mint mark in monogram.

Date	Mintage	F	VF	XF	Unc	BU
1852PTS FP	—	80.00	120	200	350	—
1853PTS FP	—	80.00	120	200	350	—
1855PTS LM/J	—	80.00	120	200	350	—
1856PTS FJ	—	80.00	120	220	350	—

KM# 141 SCUDO
2.5000 g., 0.9000 Gold .0723 oz.

Date	Mintage	F	VF	XF	Unc	BU
1868 FE	—	200	300	450	800	—

KM# 101 2 SCUDOS
6.8000 g., 0.8750 Gold .1913 oz. **Note:** Mint mark in monogram.

Date	Mintage	VG	F	VF	XF	Unc
1834PTS LM	—	225	350	575	900	—
1835PTS LM	—	200	300	500	800	—

KM# 106 2 SCUDOS
6.8000 g., 0.8750 Gold .1913 oz. **Note:** Mint mark in monogram.

Date	Mintage	VG	F	VF	XF	Unc
1841PTS LR	—	400	550	850	1,500	—

KM# 102 4 SCUDOS
13.5000 g., 0.8750 Gold .3798 oz. **Note:** Mint mark in monogram.

Date	Mintage	VG	F	VF	XF	Unc
1834 LM Rare	—	—	—	—	—	—
1834PTS JL	—	650	1,000	1,750	3,500	—

KM# 107 4 SCUDOS
13.5000 g., 0.8750 Gold .3798 oz. **Note:** Mint mark in monogram.

Date	Mintage	VG	F	VF	XF	Unc
1841PTS LR	—	900	1,500	2,500	4,000	—

KM# 99 8 SCUDOS
27.0000 g., 0.8750 Gold .7596 oz. **Note:** Mint mark in monogram.

Date	Mintage	VG	F	VF	XF	Unc
1831PTS JL	—	550	675	950	1,650	—
1832PTS JL	—	550	675	950	1,650	—
1833PTS JL	—	550	675	950	1,650	—
1833PTS LM	—	550	675	950	1,650	—
1834PTS JL	—	550	675	950	1,650	—

Date	Mintage	VG	F	VF	XF	Unc
1834PTS JM	—	650	775	1,000	1,750	—
1834PTS LM	—	550	675	950	1,650	—
1835PTS JM	—	550	675	950	1,650	—
1835PTS LM	—	550	675	950	1,650	—
1836PTS LM	—	650	775	1,000	1,750	—
1837PTS LM	—	500	625	900	1,500	—
1838PTS LM	—	600	675	950	1,650	—
1839PTS LM	—	500	625	900	1,500	—
1840PTS LR	—	500	625	900	1,500	—

KM# 108.1 8 SCUDOS
27.0000 g., 0.8750 Gold .7596 oz. **Note:** Large bust, mint mark in monogram.

Date	Mintage	VG	F	VF	XF	Unc
1841PTS LR	—	600	700	950	1,650	—

KM# 108.2 8 SCUDOS
27.0000 g., 0.8750 Gold .7596 oz. **Note:** Mint mark in monogram.

Date	Mintage	VG	F	VF	XF	Unc
1841PTS LR	—	450	550	650	1,000	—
1842PTS LR	—	450	550	650	1,000	—
1843PTS LR	—	450	550	650	1,000	—
1844PTS LR	—	450	550	650	1,000	—
1844PTS R	—	625	750	1,000	1,750	—
1845PTS R	—	625	750	1,000	1,750	—
1846PTS R	—	625	750	1,000	1,750	—
1847PTS R	—	625	750	1,000	1,750	—

KM# 110 8 SCUDOS
27.0000 g., 0.8750 Gold .7596 oz. **Note:** Mint mark in monogram.

Date	Mintage	VG	F	VF	XF	Unc
1851PTS MF	—	900	1,500	2,750	4,500	—

KM# 115 8 SCUDOS
27.0000 g., 0.8750 Gold .7596 oz. **Note:** Mint mark in monogram.

Date	Mintage	F	VF	XF	Unc	BU
1852PTS FP	—	3,500	6,000	8,500	12,500	—

KM# 116 8 SCUDOS
27.0000 g., 0.8750 Gold .7596 oz. **Note:** Mint mark in monogram.

Date	Mintage	F	VF	XF	Unc	BU
1852PTS FP	—	450	650	1,000	1,850	—
1853/2PTS	—	450	650	1,000	1,850	—
1853PTS FP	—	450	650	1,000	1,850	—
1854PTS M	—	450	650	1,000	1,750	—
1854PTS MJ	—	450	650	1,000	1,750	—
1855PTS LM	—	450	650	1,000	1,750	—
1855PTS MJ	—	450	650	1,000	1,750	—
1856PTS FJ/MJ	—	450	650	1,000	1,750	—
1856PTS FJ	—	450	650	1,000	1,750	—
1857/6PTS FJ	—	450	650	1,000	1,750	—
1857PTS FJ	—	450	650	1,000	1,750	—

MELGAREJO COINAGE

KM# 144 1/4 MELGAREJO
5.0000 g., 0.6660 Silver .1071 oz.

Date	Mintage	VG	F	VF	XF	Unc
1865	—	8.00	15.00	25.00	90.00	—

KM# 145.1 1/2 MELGAREJO
10.0000 g., 0.6660 Silver .2141 oz. **Obv:** Long beards

Date	Mintage	VG	F	VF	XF	Unc
1865	—	10.00	20.00	30.00	80.00	200

KM# 145.2 1/2 MELGAREJO
10.0000 g., 0.6660 Silver .2141 oz. **Obv:** Short beards

Date	Mintage	VG	F	VF	XF	Unc
1865	—	10.00	20.00	30.00	80.00	200
1865 Error MELGREJO	—	20.00	40.00	70.00	135	—
1865 Error CATERIA	—	20.00	40.00	70.00	120	—
1868	—	275	400	—	—	—

KM# 146 MELGAREJO
20.0000 g., 0.6660 Silver .4282 oz.

Date	Mintage	VG	F	VF	XF	Unc
1865 FP	—	40.00	60.00	100	225	700

DECIMAL COINAGE

100 Centecimos = 1 Boliviano

KM# 147 CENTECIMO
Copper **Edge:** Reeded

Date	Mintage	VG	F	VF	XF	Unc
1864	10,000	100	200	300	500	800

KM# 148 2 CENTECIMOS
Copper **Edge:** Reeded

Date	Mintage	VG	F	VF	XF	Unc
1864	150,000	75.00	150	300	600	—

KM# 149 1/20 BOLIVIANO
1.2500 g., 0.9000 Silver .0361 oz. **Obv:** Legend around oval shield above 9 stars **Obv. Legend:** REPUBLICA BOLIVIANA **Rev:** Legend around wreath, with dots below S's **Rev. Legend:** LA UNION ES LA FUERZA **Rev. Inscription:** 1/20/BOLIVIANO/25GS/9. DSFINO. **Edge:** Reeded **Note:** Mint mark in monogram.

Date	Mintage	F	VF	XF	Unc	BU
1864PTS FP	—	10.00	30.00	50.00	150	300
1864PTS FP	—	50.00	75.00	100	200	—
Note: Error, 1st N in UNION inverted						
1865/4PTS FP	—	25.00	50.00	35.00	175	350
1865PTS FP	—	15.00	25.00	30.00	150	—

KM# 150 1/10 BOLIVIANO
2.5000 g., 0.9000 Silver .0723 oz. **Obv:** Legend around oval shield above 9 stars **Obv. Legend:** REPUBLICA BOLIVIANA **Rev:** With dots below S's. **Rev. Legend:** LA UNION ES LA FUERZA **Rev. Inscription:** 1/10/BOLIVIANO/50. GS/9. FS FINO. **Note:** Mint mark in monogram.

Date	Mintage	F	VF	XF	Unc	BU
1864PTS FP	—	5.00	10.00	50.00	150	—
1865/4PTS FP	—	15.00	25.00	100	200	—
1865PTS FP	—	5.00	10.00	50.00	150	—
1867PTS FP	—	22.50	45.00	75.00	125	—

KM# 151.1 1/5 BOLIVIANO
5.0000 g., 0.9000 Silver .1446 oz. **Obv:** Widely spaced stars **Note:** Mint mark in monogram.

Date	Mintage	VG	F	VF	XF	Unc
1864PTS FP	—	5.00	12.00	30.00	75.00	300
1864PTS FP	—	7.00	15.00	35.00	85.00	—
Note: Error 9. (D/I)s FINO						

KM# 151.2 1/5 BOLIVIANO

5.0000 g., 0.9000 Silver .1446 oz. **Obv:** Smaller, closely spaced stars **Note:** Mint mark in monogram.

Date	Mintage	VG	F	VF	XF	Unc
1864PTS FP	—	5.00	12.00	30.00	75.00	—
1865PTS FP	—	4.00	10.00	25.00	50.00	—
1866/5PTS FP	—	10.00	25.00	50.00	100	—
1866PTS FP	—	4.00	10.00	25.00	50.00	—

KM# 152.1 BOLIVIANO

25.0000 g., 0.9000 Silver .7234 oz. **Obv:** 9 stars **Rev:** I/BOLIVIANO/500 Gs/ 9 Ds FINO inside wide wreath **Rev. Legend:** BOLIVIA LIBRE E INDEPENDIENTE 1825 **Edge:** Raised **Note:** Some dates medal rotation strikes; Mint mark in monogram.

Date	Mintage	VG	F	VF	XF	Unc
1864PTS FP	—	25.00	50.00	90.00	185	—
Note: Error inverted P						
1864PTS FP	—	350	600	975	1,500	—
Note: Error BOLIVIAN(A/O)						
1864PTS FP	—	18.00	30.00	55.00	125	—
Note: P/inverted P						
1864PTS FP	—	12.00	17.00	30.00	65.00	—
1865/1PTS FP	—	15.00	25.00	55.00	100	—
Note: Error 9. (D/reversed D)						
1865/4PTS FP	—	15.00	25.00	55.00	100	—
1865PTS FP	—	10.00	15.00	30.00	60.00	—
1866/5PTS FP	—	12.00	15.00	30.00	60.00	—
1866PTS FP (F/p)P	—	18.00	30.00	55.00	125	—
1866PTS FP	—	10.00	15.00	30.00	60.00	—
1866PTS PF Inverted FP	—	150	250	450	800	—
1867/6PTS FP	—	13.00	22.00	40.00	80.00	—
1867PTS FP	—	13.00	20.00	35.00	75.00	—
1868PTS FP Rare	—	—	—	—	—	—

KM# 152.2 BOLIVIANO

25.0000 g., 0.9000 Silver .7234 oz., 35 mm. **Obv:** 11 stars **Note:** Reduced size. Some dates medal rotation strikes; Mint mark in monogram.

Date	Mintage	VG	F	VF	XF	Unc
1867/6PTS FP	—	11.50	17.50	25.00	55.00	—
1867/6PTS FE/P	—	10.00	15.00	22.00	50.00	—
1867PTS FE/P	—	11.50	17.50	25.00	55.00	—
1867PTS FE	—	300	500	850	1,300	—
Note: Error REPUBLICA BOLIVIANO						
1867PTS FE	—	9.00	14.00	20.00	45.00	—
1867PTS FP	—	10.00	16.00	30.00	65.00	—
1868/7PTS FE	720,000	11.50	18.00	30.00	65.00	—
1868PTS FE	Inc. above	9.00	14.00	20.00	45.00	—
1868PTS FP	—	9.00	14.00	20.00	45.00	—
1869PTS FE	260,000	10.00	16.00	30.00	65.00	—
1869/8PTS FE	—	12.50	20.00	35.00	75.00	—
1869PTS FP	—	12.50	20.00	35.00	70.00	—

KM# 142 ONZA

32.4000 g., 0.9000 Gold .9375 oz. **Note:** Mint mark in monogram.

Date	Mintage	F	VF	XF	Unc	BU
1868PTS FE Rare	—	—	—	—	—	—
Note: Stack's Hammel sale 9-82 AU realized $13,000., Pacific Coast Auction Galleries, Long Beach sale 6-86 AU realized $15,500., Superior Parker/Casterline sale 12-89 AU realized $15,400						
1868PTS FP Rare	—	—	—	—	—	—

REFORM COINAGE

1870 - 1951

KM# 162 CENTAVO

Copper

Date	Mintage	VG	F	VF	XF	Unc
1878	—	100	250	350	650	—

KM# 163 CENTAVO

Copper **Obv:** Value below condor **Rev:** "LA UNION ES LA FUERZA" in wreath, date below

Date	Mintage	VG	F	VF	XF	Unc
1878	—	125	250	350	650	—

KM# 167 CENTAVO

Copper **Rev:** Cornucopia and fasces flank date

Date	Mintage	F	VF	XF	Unc	BU
1883/73A	500,000	5.00	12.00	30.00	60.00	—
1883A	Inc. above	3.50	10.00	25.00	50.00	75.00

KM# 164.1 2 CENTAVOS

Copper **Rev:** 2 CENTAVOS

Date	Mintage	VG	F	VF	XF	Unc
1878	—	50.00	100	200	350	700

KM# 164.2 2 CENTAVOS

Copper **Rev:** 2 Cents

Date	Mintage	VG	F	VF	XF	Unc
1878 Unique	1	—	—	—	—	—

KM# 165 2 CENTAVOS

Copper **Rev:** Value 2 Cents beneath condor

Date	Mintage	VG	F	VF	XF	Unc
1878	—	200	400	750	1,100	—

KM# 168 2 CENTAVOS

Copper **Rev:** Cornucopia and fasces flank date

Date	Mintage	VG	F	VF	XF	Unc
1883A	250,000	3.50	7.50	15.00	50.00	85.00

KM# 156.1 5 CENTAVOS

1.2500 g., 0.9000 Silver .0361 oz. **Obv:** Legend around rectangular shield with 11 stars beneath **Obv. Legend:** REPUBLICA DE BOLIVIA **Rev:** With dots below S's **Rev. Legend:** LA UNION HACE LA FUERZA **Rev. Inscription:** CINCO CS/1G. Y 5CS/9 DS FINO.

Date	Mintage	VG	F	VF	XF	Unc
1871/0 ER Rare	—	—	—	—	—	—
1871 ER	—	30.00	50.00	100	150	350
1871 ER	—	20.00	35.00	70.00	120	—
Note: Without dots in inscription						
1871 FP Rare	6	—	—	—	—	—

KM# 156.2 5 CENTAVOS

1.1500 g., 0.9000 Silver .0333 oz. **Rev. Inscription:** CINCO/CENT. /9 D. FINO.

Date	Mintage	VG	F	VF	XF	Unc
1871 ER	—	5.00	10.00	30.00	60.00	150
1872 ER Rare	2	—	—	—	—	—
1872/1 FE	—	10.00	20.00	40.00	80.00	—
1872 FE Rare	3	—	—	—	—	—

KM# 156.3 5 CENTAVOS

1.1500 g., 0.9000 Silver .0333 oz. **Obv:** 9 stars at bottom

Date	Mintage	VG	F	VF	XF	Unc
1872 FE	—	4.00	9.00	20.00	50.00	75.00

KM# 157.1 5 CENTAVOS

1.1500 g., 0.9000 Silver .0333 oz. **Obv:** Legend around oval shield above 9 stars **Obv. Legend:** REPUBLICA BOLIVIANA **Rev. Legend:** LA UNION ES LA FUERZA

Date	Mintage	VG	F	VF	XF	Unc
1872 FE CR	—	2.00	3.50	9.00	20.00	50.00
1872 FE MR	—	4.00	10.00	20.00	40.00	100
1873 FE	—	1.50	2.50	5.00	12.00	25.00
1874 FE	—	2.00	4.00	9.00	20.00	30.00
1875 FE	—	1.50	2.50	5.00	12.00	25.00
1875 FE	—	3.00	6.00	12.00	25.00	50.00
Note: Without dot after CENT						
1875 FE	—	4.00	7.00	15.00	35.00	—
Note: Error RE(P/E)(U/P)LICA						
1876 FE	—	4.00	7.00	15.00	30.00	—
Note: Without periods						
1876 FE With periods	—	4.00	7.00	15.00	30.00	50.00
1876 FE	—	3.00	6.00	12.00	25.00	—
Note: Error F(U/E)ERZA with periods						
1877 FE	—	2.00	3.00	7.00	15.00	25.00
1878 FE	—	2.50	3.50	7.00	15.00	25.00
1878 FE	—	2.50	3.50	9.00	18.00	40.00
Note: V in BOLIVIANA inverted A						
1879 FE	—	3.50	5.00	12.00	20.00	—
1879 FE	—	5.00	10.00	17.50	40.00	65.00
Note: V in BOLIVIANA inverted A						
1880 FE	—	3.00	6.00	12.00	25.00	—
1881 FE	—	2.00	3.50	7.00	15.00	25.00
1882/1 FE	—	4.00	9.00	17.00	40.00	—
1882 FE	—	3.75	7.00	15.00	30.00	—
1883 FE	—	4.00	9.00	17.00	40.00	—
Note: Error RE (F/P) UBLICA						
1883 FE	—	3.00	5.00	10.00	20.00	35.00
1884 FE	—	4.00	6.00	10.00	20.00	40.00
1884/3 FE	—	4.50	8.50	16.00	35.00	60.00

KM# 169.1 5 CENTAVOS

Copper-Nickel **Rev:** Cornucopia and fasces flank star **Note:** KM#169.1 was withdrawn from circulation due to confusion with contemporary silver 10 centavos. Eventually most of these Paris Mint pieces were officially hole punched and released back into circulation as KM#169.2.

Date	Mintage	F	VF	XF	Unc	BU
1883A	2,200,000	12.00	25.00	50.00	110	150
1883A Proof	—	—	—	—	—	—

KM# 169.2 5 CENTAVOS

Copper-Nickel **Note:** Hole punched.

Date	Mintage	F	VF	XF	Unc	BU
1883A	Inc. above	3.00	8.00	18.00	40.00	60.00

KM# 157.2 5 CENTAVOS

1.1500 g., 0.9000 Silver .0333 oz. **Rev:** Bar between CENT and 9 D, FINO **Note:** Mint mark in monogram.

Date	Mintage	VG	F	VF	XF	Unc
1884PTS FE Proof, Rare	—	—	—	—	—	—
1885PTS FE	—	3.00	5.00	9.00	18.00	30.00
1886/5PTS FE	—	3.00	5.00	9.00	18.00	—
1886PTS FE	—	2.75	4.00	6.00	15.00	25.00
1887PTS FE	—	2.75	4.00	6.00	15.00	25.00
1888PTS FE Large date	—	4.00	9.00	15.00	40.00	60.00
1888PTS FE Small date	—	4.00	9.00	15.00	40.00	60.00
1889/8PTS FE	—	7.50	15.00	20.00	30.00	50.00
1889PTS FE	—	5.00	8.00	11.50	20.00	40.00
1890PTS CB	—	2.00	5.00	7.50	15.00	25.00
1891/0PTS CB	—	10.00	20.00	30.00	50.00	—
1891PTS CB	—	3.00	6.50	10.00	18.00	30.00
1893/83PTS CB	—	2.50	4.00	9.00	18.00	30.00
1893PTS CB	70,000	2.00	4.00	9.00	20.00	35.00
1895PTS ES/CB	—	10.00	20.00	30.00	50.00	—
1895PTS ES	20,000	5.00	15.00	20.00	40.00	50.00
1899PTS MM	—	2.50	5.00	8.00	16.00	25.00
1900PTS MM	50,000	2.00	4.00	6.00	12.00	20.00

KM# 171 5 CENTAVOS

Copper-Nickel **Note:** Medal rotation strike.

Date	Mintage	F	VF	XF	Unc	BU
1892H	2,000,000	3.00	6.00	18.00	35.00	75.00
1892H Proof	—	Value: 300				

KM# 173.1 5 CENTAVOS

Copper-Nickel **Note:** Coins dated 1893, 1918 and 1919 medal rotation were struck at the Heaton Mint.

Date	Mintage	F	VF	XF	Unc	BU
1893	2,500,000	5.00	10.00	20.00	45.00	60.00
1893 Proof	—	Value: 350				
1899	2,000,000	2.00	7.00	15.00	35.00	50.00

KM# 173.2 5 CENTAVOS

Copper-Nickel **Rev:** Cornucopia and fasces flank date

Date	Mintage	F	VF	XF	Unc	BU
1895	2,000,000	5.00	10.00	20.00	45.00	—

KM# 173.3 5 CENTAVOS

Copper-Nickel **Rev:** Cornucopia and torch flank date

Date	Mintage	F	VF	XF	Unc	BU
1897(a)	1,500,000	2.00	8.00	20.00	25.00	40.00

KM# 153.1 10 CENTAVOS

2.5000 g., 0.9000 Silver .0723 oz. **Obv:** Legend around rectangular shield above 11 stars **Obv. Legend:** REPUBLICA DE BOLIVIA **Rev:** Inscription with dots below S's in DS **Rev. Legend:** LA UNION HACE LA FUERZA **Rev. Inscription:** DIEZ CTS/2 GMS Y 5 Ds/9 Ds FINO.

Date	Mintage	VG	F	VF	XF	Unc
1870 ER	—	2.00	6.00	12.00	30.00	80.00
1870 ER	—	4.00	10.00	25.00	50.00	—
Note: Error LA VION HACE						
1871 ER	—	2.00	6.00	12.00	30.00	—
1871 ER	—	2.50	9.00	20.00	40.00	—
Note: A in REPUBLICA inverted V and BOLI(V/L)IA						
1871 FP	—	4.00	10.00	25.00	50.00	—
1871 FP	—	3.00	11.00	22.00	45.00	—
Note: A in REPUBLICA inverted V and BOLI(V/L)IA						

KM# 153.2 10 CENTAVOS

2.3000 g., 0.9000 Silver .0666 oz. **Rev:** Inscription with dot below S **Rev. Inscription:** DIEZ/CENT./9 Ds FINO.

Date	Mintage	VG	F	VF	XF	Unc
1871 ER	—	2.00	6.00	12.00	30.00	80.00

KM# 153.3 10 CENTAVOS

2.3000 g., 0.9000 Silver .0666 oz. **Obv:** 9 stars at bottom

Date	Mintage	VG	F	VF	XF	Unc
1871 ER	—	2.00	4.00	10.00	25.00	—
1872 FE	—	2.00	4.00	10.00	25.00	50.00
1872 FE	—	2.00	6.00	12.00	30.00	—
Note: Error V in BOLIVIA inverted A						

KM# 158.1 10 CENTAVOS

2.3000 g., 0.9000 Silver .0666 oz. **Obv:** Legend around larger oval shield above 9 stars **Obv. Legend:** REPUBLICA BOLIVIA **Rev:** Legend around wreath, inscription **Rev. Legend:** LA UNION ES LA FUERZA **Rev. Inscription:** DIEZ/CENTs/9 Ds. FINO

Date	Mintage	VG	F	VF	XF	Unc
1872 FE	—	2.00	4.00	10.00	25.00	50.00
1873 FE	—	2.00	4.00	10.00	25.00	50.00
1874 FE	—	2.50	5.00	10.00	30.00	60.00
1875 FE	—	3.00	6.00	12.00	35.00	—

KM# 158.2 10 CENTAVOS

2.3000 g., 0.9000 Silver .0666 oz. **Rev. Inscription:** DIEZ/CENTs/9D. FINO

Date	Mintage	VG	F	VF	XF	Unc
1875 FE	—	1.25	2.00	7.00	15.00	30.00
1875 FE	—	5.00	10.00	20.00	40.00	—
Note: Error LA UNIO ES						
1876 FE	—	1.25	2.00	7.00	15.00	30.00
1877 FE	—	1.25	2.00	7.00	15.00	30.00
1878 FE	—	2.00	5.00	12.00	25.00	50.00
1879 FE	—	1.25	2.00	7.00	15.00	30.00
1880 FE	—	1.25	3.00	9.00	18.00	35.00
1881 FE	—	1.25	2.00	7.00	15.00	30.00
1882 FE	—	1.50	2.50	7.00	15.00	30.00
1883/2 FE	—	2.00	3.50	10.00	20.00	—
1883 FE	—	2.00	4.00	10.00	20.00	40.00
Note: Error (F/E) E						
1883 FE	—	1.50	2.50	5.00	10.00	—

KM# 170.1 10 CENTAVOS

Copper-Nickel **Rev:** Cornucopia and fasces flank star **Note:** KM#170.1 was withdrawn from circulation due to confusion with contemporary silver 20 Centavos. Eventually most of these Paris Mint pieces were officially hole punched and released back into circulation as KM#170.2.

Date	Mintage	F	VF	XF	Unc	BU
1883A Proof, Rare	—	—	—	—	—	—
1883A	800,000	18.00	35.00	75.00	150	—
1884A Prooflike, 2 known	—	—	—	—	2,550	—

KM# 170.2 10 CENTAVOS

Copper Nickel

Date	Mintage	F	VF	XF	Unc	BU
1883A	Inc. above	4.00	10.00	25.00	75.00	—

KM# 158.3 10 CENTAVOS

2.3000 g., 0.9000 Silver .0666 oz. **Obv:** Smaller oval shield **Rev:** Reduced size lettering, bar between CENTS and 9D **Note:** Mint mark in monogram.

Date	Mintage	VG	F	VF	XF	Unc
1884PTS FE Proof; Rare	—	—	—	—	—	—
1884PTS FE	—	—	—	—	—	—
1885PTS FE	—	1.50	2.50	7.00	15.00	30.00
1886PTS FE	—	1.25	2.00	7.00	15.00	30.00
1887PTS FE	—	5.00	10.00	20.00	35.00	60.00
1888PTS FE	—	5.00	12.00	25.00	45.00	70.00
1889PTS FE	—	2.50	7.00	15.00	30.00	55.00
1890PTS FE	—	2.50	7.00	15.00	30.00	55.00
1890PTS CB	—	7.50	20.00	35.00	70.00	100
Note: 1 over horizontal bar						
1890PTS CB	—	2.50	7.00	15.00	30.00	55.00
1891PTS CB	—	1.50	3.00	9.00	18.00	35.00
1893PTS CB	50,000	1.50	3.00	9.00	18.00	35.00
1895PTS ES	20,000	4.00	10.00	20.00	35.00	60.00
1899PTS MM	—	1.50	10.00	20.00	35.00	60.00
1900PTS MM	30,000	2.00	4.00	10.00	25.00	50.00

KM# 158.4 10 CENTAVOS

2.3000 g., 0.9000 Silver .0666 oz. **Obv:** Larger oval shield similar to KM#158.1 & KM#158.2 **Rev. Legend:** DIEZ/CENT. /9D. FINO

Date	Mintage	VG	F	VF	XF	Unc
1884/3 FE	—	10.00	30.00	70.00	150	—
Note: Error, A in REPUBLICA inverted V						

KM# 172 10 CENTAVOS

Copper Nickel **Note:** Medal rotation strike.

Date	Mintage	F	VF	XF	Unc	BU
1892H	1,000,000	9.00	20.00	50.00	150	—
1892H Proof	—	Value: 450				

KM# 174.1 10 CENTAVOS

Copper-Nickel **Rev:** Without privy marks **Note:** Coins dated 1893, 1918 and 1919 medal rotation were struck at the Heaton Mint.

Date	Mintage	F	VF	XF	Unc	BU
1893	1,250,000	6.00	12.00	25.00	70.00	—
1893 Proof	—	Value: 450				
1899	3,000,000	3.00	9.00	20.00	45.00	—

KM# 174.2 10 CENTAVOS

Copper Nickel **Rev:** Cornucopia and fasces flank date

Date	Mintage	F	VF	XF	Unc	BU
1895	1,000,000	7.00	15.00	30.00	60.00	—

KM# 174.3 10 CENTAVOS
Copper-Nickel **Rev:** Cornucopia and torch flank date

Date	Mintage	F	VF	XF	Unc	BU
1897	2,250,000	3.00	8.00	20.00	45.00	60.00

KM# 154.1 20 CENTAVOS
5.0000 g., 0.9000 Silver .1446 oz. **Obv:** 11 stars at bottom **Rev:** Weight **Rev. Legend:** LA UNION HACE LA FUERZA

Date	Mintage	VG	F	VF	XF	Unc
1870 ER	—	25.00	35.00	75.00	150	—
1871 ER	—	20.00	30.00	50.00	80.00	—
1871 ER	—	30.00	50.00	90.00	175	—
Note: Error: LA (UN/LA)ION						
1871 FP Rare, 2 known	—	—	—	—	—	—

KM# 154.2 20 CENTAVOS
4.6000 g., 0.9000 Silver .1331 oz. **Obv:** 11 stars **Rev:** Without weight

Date	Mintage	VG	F	VF	XF	Unc
1871 ER	—	15.00	40.00	100	175	—
1871 ER	—	25.00	50.00	120	250	—
Note: Reverse rotated at 90 degrees						

KM# 154.3 20 CENTAVOS
4.6000 g., 0.9000 Silver .1331 oz. **Obv:** 9 stars at bottom

Date	Mintage	VG	F	VF	XF	Unc
1871 ER	—	8.00	15.00	30.00	55.00	100
1872 ER	—	10.00	20.00	40.00	65.00	—
1872FE MR	—	10.00	20.00	45.00	75.00	115
1872 FE	—	2.50	7.00	18.00	45.00	75.00

KM# 159.1 20 CENTAVOS
4.6000 g., 0.9000 Silver .1331 oz. **Rev. Legend:** LA UNION ES LA FUERZA **Note:** Mint mark in monogram.

Date	Mintage	VG	F	VF	XF	Unc
1872PTS FE	—	30.00	60.00	100	200	—
1873PTS FE	—	1.50	3.00	8.00	20.00	50.00
1874PTS FE	—	4.00	7.00	18.00	45.00	70.00
1875PTS FE	—	2.25	3.00	7.00	18.00	45.00
1876PTS FE Large date	—	2.25	3.00	8.00	20.00	50.00
1876PTS FE Small date	—	2.25	3.00	8.00	20.00	50.00
1876PTS FE	—	6.50	9.00	15.00	35.00	—
Note: Error UNI(O/N)N						
1877PTS FE	—	2.25	3.00	7.00	18.00	45.00
1878PTS FE	—	2.25	3.00	7.00	18.00	45.00
1878PTS FE	—	7.50	10.00	22.00	55.00	—
Note: Error BOLI(V/inverted V)IANA						
1879/8PTS FE	—	3.00	6.00	12.00	25.00	—
1879PTS FE	—	2.25	3.00	7.00	18.00	45.00
1880PTS FE	—	6.00	12.00	25.00	50.00	—
Note: Error REPUB(L/B)ICA						
1880PTS FE	—	2.25	3.00	7.00	18.00	—
1881PTS FE	—	2.25	3.00	7.00	18.00	45.00
1882PTS FE	—	2.25	3.00	7.00	18.00	45.00
1883PTS FE	—	2.25	3.00	7.00	18.00	45.00
1883PTS EF 3 to 5 known	—	50.00	90.00	145	—	—
1884/3PTS FE	—	4.00	6.00	12.50	25.00	—
1884PTS FE	—	2.25	3.00	7.00	18.00	—
1884PTS FE	—	7.00	15.00	30.00	60.00	—

Date	Mintage	VG	F	VF	XF	Unc
Note: Error VE(I/N)NTE						
1885PTS FE	—	2.00	3.00	7.00	18.00	45.00

KM# 166 20 CENTAVOS
4.6000 g., 0.9000 Silver .1331 oz. **Rev:** Daza

Date	Mintage	VG	F	VF	XF	Unc
1879	—	12.50	27.50	35.00	60.00	—
1879	—	15.00	30.00	50.00	80.00	—
Note: Error A's in DAZA inverted V's						

KM# 159.2 20 CENTAVOS
4.6000 g., 0.9000 Silver .1331 oz. **Note:** Reduced size dates and lettering, bar below CENTS. The small bar usually found below "S" in "9DS" is missing in the 1886-1888 and 1902 dates, Mint mark in monogram.

Date	Mintage	VG	F	VF	XF	Unc
1884PTS FE Proof, Rare	—	—	—	—	—	—
1885PTS FE	—	2.25	3.00	7.00	18.00	45.00
1886PTS FE	—	2.25	3.00	8.00	20.00	50.00
1887PTS FE	—	2.25	3.00	7.00	18.00	45.00
1888PTS FE	—	2.25	3.00	7.00	18.00	45.00
1889PTS FE	—	2.25	3.00	8.00	20.00	55.00
1889/8PTS FE	—	2.50	4.00	8.00	20.00	55.00
1890PTS FE	—	2.25	3.00	7.00	18.00	75.00
1890/80PTS CB	—	2.50	4.00	8.00	20.00	55.00
1890PTS CB	—	2.25	3.00	7.00	18.00	45.00
1891PTS CB	—	2.25	3.50	8.00	20.00	50.00
1891PTS CB Error C B/E	—	3.00	5.00	8.00	16.00	—
1892/82PTS CB	—	2.25	3.50	6.00	9.00	—
1892PTS CB	—	2.25	3.50	8.00	20.00	50.00
1893PTS CB	500,000	2.25	3.00	7.00	18.00	45.00
1894PTS ES	490,000	2.25	4.50	12.00	30.00	75.00
1894PTS ES Error E S/B	—	3.00	5.00	14.00	35.00	—
1895PTS ES	—	2.25	3.50	8.00	20.00	50.00
1896PTS ES	100,000	2.25	3.00	7.00	18.00	45.00
1896PTS CB	Inc. above	6.50	10.00	25.00	60.00	—
1897PTS CB	170,000	2.25	3.00	7.00	18.00	45.00
1898PTS CB	—	10.00	20.00	35.00	80.00	—
1899PTS CB Rare	—	—	—	—	—	—
1899PTS MM	—	2.25	3.50	8.00	20.00	50.00
1900PTS MM	170,000	2.25	3.50	8.00	20.00	50.00

KM# 161.1 50 CENTAVOS (1/2 Boliviano)
12.5000 g., 0.9000 Silver .3617 oz. **Rev. Legend:** 12 GS. 500 MS. 9 DS. FINO **Note:** Mint mark in monogram.

Date	Mintage	VG	F	VF	XF	Unc
1873PTS	—	7.50	18.00	45.00	100	350

KM# 161.2 50 CENTAVOS (1/2 Boliviano)
12.5000 g., 0.9000 Silver .3617 oz. **Rev. Legend:** 12 GMS 500 MMS **Note:** Mint mark in monogram.

Date	Mintage	VG	F	VF	XF	Unc
1873PTS FE	—	20.00	40.00	85.00	200	400

KM# 161.3 50 CENTAVOS (1/2 Boliviano)
12.5000 g., 0.9000 Silver .3617 oz. **Rev:** Without 50 Cents and weight **Note:** Mint mark in monogram.

Date	Mintage	VG	F	VF	XF	Unc
1879/7PTS FE	—	50.00	100	200	450	—
1879PTS FE	—	50.00	100	165	500	—
1882PTS FE	—	50.00	100	165	475	—

KM# 161.4 50 CENTAVOS (1/2 Boliviano)
11.5000 g., 0.9000 Silver .3328 oz. **Rev:** Reduced size lettering with weight **Note:** Mint mark in monogram.

Date	Mintage	VG	F	VF	XF	Unc
1884PTS FE Proof, Rare	—	—	—	—	—	—
1887PTS FE Rare	—	—	—	—	—	—
1889PTS MM Rare	—	—	—	—	—	—
1891PTS CB	—	125	250	500	1,000	—

KM# 161.5 50 CENTAVOS (1/2 Boliviano)
11.5000 g., 0.9000 Silver .3328 oz. **Rev:** Reduced size lettering without weight **Note:** Mint mark in monogram.

Date	Mintage	VG	F	VF	XF	Unc
1891PTS CB	—	BV	4.00	9.00	20.00	50.00
1892PTS CB	—	BV	4.00	9.00	20.00	50.00
1893PTS CB	3,150,000	BV	4.00	9.00	20.00	50.00
1894/1PTS CB	2,470,000	BV	6.00	12.00	35.00	—
1894PTS CB	Inc. above	BV	4.00	9.00	20.00	50.00
1894/84PTS ES	—	BV	7.00	15.00	45.00	—
1894PTS ES	Inc. above	BV	5.00	10.00	25.00	60.00
1895/85PTS ES	—	BV	7.00	15.00	45.00	—
1895PTS ES	3,390,000	BV	4.00	9.00	20.00	50.00
1896PTS ES	2,980,000	BV	4.00	9.00	20.00	50.00
1897PTS CB	2,300,000	BV	4.00	9.00	20.00	50.00
1897PTS ES	—	BV	5.00	10.00	25.00	60.00
1898/7PTS CB	—	BV	5.00	10.00	25.00	—
1898PTS CB	—	BV	4.00	9.00	20.00	50.00
1899PTS CB	—	BV	4.00	9.00	20.00	50.00
1899/69PTS MM	—	BV	5.00	10.00	25.00	60.00
Note: First 9 over inverted 9						
1899PTS MM	—	BV	4.00	9.00	20.00	50.00
1900PTS MM	3,820,000	BV	5.00	10.00	25.00	50.00

KM# 175.1 50 CENTAVOS (1/2 Boliviano)
11.5000 g., 0.9000 Silver .3328 oz. **Note:** Mint mark in monogram.

Date	Mintage	VG	F	VF	XF	Unc
1900PTS MM	Inc. above	BV	4.00	10.00	20.00	50.00

KM# 175.2 50 CENTAVOS (1/2 Boliviano)
11.5000 g., 0.9000 Silver .3328 oz.

Date	Mintage	VG	F	VF	XF	Unc
1900So	900,000	BV	8.00	15.00	35.00	90.00

KM# 155.1 BOLIVIANO
25.0000 g., 0.9000 Silver .7234 oz. **Obv:** Legend around rectangular shield, 11 stars below **Obv. Legend:** REPUBLICA DE BOLIVIA **Rev:** Wide wreath, inscription **Rev. Legend:** LA UNION HACE LA FUERZA **Rev. Inscription:** UN/BOLIVIANO/ 25G 9D FINO

Date	Mintage	VG	F	VF	XF	Unc
1870 ER	—	40.00	60.00	120	180	—

KM# 155.3 BOLIVIANO
25.0000 g., 0.9000 Silver .7234 oz. **Rev:** Line and dot under MS and S, normal wreath **Note:** Mint mark in monogram.

Date	Mintage	VG	F	VF	XF	Unc
1870PTS ER	—	10.00	17.00	25.00	50.00	—
1870PTS ER Proof	—	Value: 1,000				
1871/0PTS ER	—	15.00	25.00	35.00	65.00	—
1871PTS ER	—	13.00	20.00	30.00	60.00	—
1871PTS FP	—	13.00	20.00	30.00	60.00	—

KM# 155.4 BOLIVIANO
25.0000 g., 0.9000 Silver .7234 oz. **Obv:** 9 stars at bottom **Note:** Mint mark in monogram.

Date	Mintage	VG	F	VF	XF	Unc
1870PTS ER	—	15.00	25.00	35.00	65.00	—
1871PTS ER	—	12.50	17.50	25.00	55.00	—
1871PTS FP	—	12.50	17.50	25.00	55.00	—
1871PTS EF	—	12.50	17.50	25.00	55.00	—
1872PTS FE	—	20.00	30.00	40.00	70.00	—
1872PTS FE	—	20.00	40.00	60.00	100	—

Note: Error REPUB(L/B)ICA

KM# 155.2 BOLIVIANO
25.0000 g., 0.9000 Silver .7234 oz. **Rev:** Dot under MS **Rev. Legend:** UN/BOLIVIANO/25Gms 9Ds FINO **Note:** Wide wreaths have four leaves at top while normal size wreaths have two leaves at top. Mint mark in monogram.

Date	Mintage	VG	F	VF	XF	Unc
1870PTS ER	—	10.00	12.50	20.00	30.00	—

KM# 160.1 BOLIVIANO
25.0000 g., 0.9000 Silver .7234 oz. **Obv:** Legend around oval wreath, 9 stars below **Obv. Legend:** REPUBLICA BOLIVIANA **Rev. Legend:** LA UNION ES LA FUERZA **Note:** Mint mark in monogram.

Date	Mintage	VG	F	VF	XF	Unc
1872PTS FE	—	10.00	15.00	25.00	40.00	—
1872PTS FE	—	50.00	80.00	160	250	—
Note: Error ES (L/E)A FUERZA						
1873PTS FE	—	15.00	20.00	35.00	50.00	—
1874PTS FE	—	15.00	20.00	35.00	50.00	—
1875PTS FE	—	15.00	20.00	35.00	50.00	—
1877/5PTS FE	—	100	175	250	500	—
1877PTS FE	—	45.00	65.00	120	200	—

KM# 160.2 BOLIVIANO
25.0000 g., 0.9000 Silver .7234 oz. **Rev:** With line under s's **Rev. Legend:** 25 Gs 9Ds FINO

Date	Mintage	VG	F	VF	XF	Unc
1879 F.E.	—	60.00	120	225	375	—

KM# 160.3 BOLIVIANO
25.0000 g., 0.9000 Silver .7234 oz. **Rev:** Horizontal bar between value and weight **Rev. Legend:** 25 GMS **Note:** Mint mark in monogram.

Date	Mintage	VG	F	VF	XF	Unc
1884PTS FE Proof, Rare	—	—	—	—	—	—
1887PTS FE Rare	—	—	—	—	—	—
1893PTS CB	—	—	1,000	1,500	2,500	—

ESSAIS

Standard metals unless otherwise noted

KM#	Date	Mintage	Identification	Mkt Val
E1	1883A	—	Centavo. Bronze. KM167.	150

KM#	Date	Mintage	Identification	Mkt Val
E2	1883 EG	—	Centavo. Bronze. KM167.	200
E3	1883A	—	2 Centavos. Bronze. KM168.	120
E4	1883 EG	—	2 Centavos. Bronze. KM168.	150
E5	1883A	—	5 Centavos. Copper Nickel. KM169.	200

KM#	Date	Mintage	Identification	Mkt Val
E6	1883 EG	—	5 Centavos. Copper-Nickel. KM169.	250
E7	1883A	—	10 Centavos. Copper-Nickel. KM170.	200

KM#	Date	Mintage	Identification	Mkt Val
E8	1883 EG	—	10 Centavos. Copper-Nickel. KM170.	250

PATTERNS

Including off metal strikes

KM#	Date	Mintage	Identification	Mkt Val
Pn1	1827 JM	—	4 Soles. Silver. Struck at Potosi. Bare head right.	6,000
Pn2	1852 FM	—	2 Soles. Silver. Struck at Potosi. KM#121.1.	—
Pn3	1852 FM	—	4 Soles. Silver. Struck at Potosi. With hole. KM#123.1.	—

KM#	Date	Mintage	Identification	Mkt Val
Pn4	1854 MJ	—	1/2 Sol. Brass. 16.77 mm. Struck at Potosi. KM#118.1.	—
Pn5	1865	—	1/4 Melgarejo. Copper. Struck at Potosi. KM#144.	30.00
Pn6	1865	—	1/2 Melgarejo. Copper. Struck at Potosi. KM#145.	71.50
Pn7	1865 FP	—	Onza. Gold. Struck at Potosi.	25,000

KM#	Date	Mintage	Identification	Mkt Val
Pn8	1868 CT	—	Boliviano. Silver. Reeded edge. Struck at Potosi.	3,000
Pn9	1868 CT	—	Boliviano. Silver. Plain edge. Struck at Potosi.	2,500
Pn10	1868 CT	—	Boliviano. Copper. Reeded edge. Struck at Potosi. Without E.	700
Pn11	1868 CT	—	Boliviano. Gold. Reeded edge. Struck at Potosi.	20,900
Pn12	1868 FE	—	1/2 Scudo. Silver. Struck at Potosi. KM#140.	450

KM#	Date	Mintage	Identification	Mkt Val
Pn13	1868 FE	—	Onza. Silver. Struck at Potosi.	2,150

KM#	Date	Mintage	Identification	Mkt Val
Pn14	1868 CT	—	5 Centavos. Silver. Struck at La Paz.	—

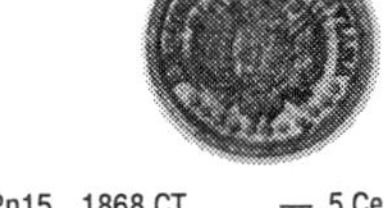

KM#	Date	Mintage	Identification	Mkt Val
Pn15	1868 CT	—	5 Centavos. Silver. Reeded edge. Struck at La Paz.	500
Pn16	1868 CT	—	5 Centavos. Gold. Struck at La Paz.	—

KM#	Date	Mintage	Identification	Mkt Val
Pn17	1868 CT	—	10 Centavos. Silver. Reeded edge. Struck at La Paz.	500
Pn18	1868 CT	—	10 Centavos. Gold. Struck at La Paz.	—

KM#	Date	Mintage	Identification	Mkt Val
Pn19	1868 CT	—	20 Centavos. Copper. Plain edge. Struck at La Paz.	400
Pn20	1868 CT	—	20 Centavos. Silver. Reeded edge. Struck at La Paz.	550
Pn21	1868 CT	—	20 Centavos. Silver. Plain edge. Struck at La Paz.	400
Pn22	1868 CT	—	20 Centavos. Gold. Struck at La Paz.	—
Pn23	1868 CT	—	Boliviano. Copper. Plain edge. Struck at La Paz. Without E.	500
Pn24	1868 CT	—	Boliviano. Copper. Reeded edge. Struck at La Paz.	500

Note: Many varieties exist with a mixture of the following: CT, E, UN, 1; reeded edge and plain edge. At least 11 different varieties are known.

KM#	Date	Mintage	Identification	Mkt Val
Pn25	1868 CT	—	Boliviano. Silver. Reeded edge. Struck at La Paz. With E.	—
Pn26	1868 CT	—	Boliviano. Silver. Reeded edge. Struck at La Paz. Without E.	2,100
Pn27	1868	—	Un Bolivano, w/E Copper, plain edge	—
Pn28	1868	—	Boliviano. Copper. Plain edge. Struck at La Paz. Without E.	500
Pn29	868	—	Boliviano. Silver. Reeded edge. Struck at La Paz. Without E.	3,000
Pn30	1868	—	Boliviano. Copper. Plain edge. Struck at La Paz.	500
Pn31	1868 CT	—	Boliviano. Copper. Plain edge. Struck at La Paz.	500
Pn32	1868 CT	—	Boliviano. Copper. Reeded edge. Struck at La Paz.	500
Pn33	1868 CT	—	Boliviano. Copper. Reeded edge. Struck at La Paz. With E.	500
Pn34	1868 CT	—	Boliviano. Copper. Plain edge. Struck at La Paz. With E.	500
Pn35	1868 CT	—	Boliviano. Silver. Plain edge. Struck at La Paz. Without E	1,750
Pn36	1868	—	Boliviano. Silver. Reeded edge. Struck at La Paz. Without E.	1,600
Pn37	1868	—	Boliviano. Silver. Reeded edge. Struck at La Paz. With E.	2,500
Pn38	1870 ER	—	Boliviano. Copper. Struck at La Paz. Ex Farouk.	1,100
Pn39	1872 FE	—	5 Cents. Silver. Struck at La Paz. Proof Medal turn.	800
PnA40	1884	—	Boliviano. Copper. Plain edge. Struck at La Paz. With E. Prev. KM#Pn27.	500
Pn40	1884 F.E.	—	5 Centavos. Silver. Struck at La Paz.	500
Pn41	1884 F.E.	—	10 Centavos. Silver. Struck at La Paz. Medal alignment.	800
Pn42	1884 F.E.	—	10 Centavos. Silver. Struck at La Paz.	850
Pn43	1884 F.E.	—	20 Centavos. Silver. Struck at La Paz.	1,250
Pn44	1884 F.E.	—	50 Centavos. Silver. Smaller size than on the normal KM-161.4. Struck at La Paz.	2,000
Pn45	1884 F.E.	—	Boliviano. Silver. Including the date is smaller than on the normal issue KM-160.3. Struck at La Paz.	3,500
Pn46	1887 F.E.	—	Escudo. Silver. Struck at La Paz.	1,500
Pn47	1887 F.E.	—	Escudo. Gold. Struck at La Paz.	2,500
Pn48	1887 F.E.	—	1/2 Bolivar. Gold. Struck at La Paz.	—
Pn49	1887 F.E.	—	Bolivar. Gold. Struck at La Paz.	—
Pn50	1897 C.B.	—	20 Centavos. Brass. Struck at La Paz. KM#159.2.	—
Pn51	1900	—	20 Centavos. Silver. Struck at La Paz.	1,000
Pn52	1900 MM	—	20 Centavos. Brass. Struck at La Paz.	100
Pn53	1900 So	—	50 Centavos. 0.9000 Gold. Struck at La Paz. KM#175.2	7,000
PnA54	1900	1	50 Centavos. Silver. without So mintmark	—

PIEFORTS

KM#	Date	Mintage	Identification	Issue Price	Mkt Val
P1	1855 MJ	—	Escudo. Silver.	—	275
P2	1856 FJ	—	Escudo. Silver.	—	285
P3	1865 FP	—	1/10 Boliviano. Silver.	—	400
PA3	1865/4 FP	—	1/20 Boliviano. Silver. Medal alignment.	—	1,500
PB3	1865/4 FP	—	1/10 Boliviano. Silver. Reeded edge. Medal alignment.	—	2,000
PC3	1865/4 FP	—	1/10 Boliviano. Silver. Plain edge. Medal alignment.	—	2,500
PE3	1865/4 FP	—	1/5 Boliviano. Silver. Plain edge. Medal alignment.	—	2,500
P4	1868 CT	—	10 Centavos. Silver. Proof.	—	500
P5	1868 CT	—	20 Centavos. Silver.	—	400
P6	1868 CT	—	Boliviano. Silver. Same as Pn8. Proof.	—	4,000
P7	1868 FE	—	Escudo. Silver.	—	275
P8	1868 FE	—	1/2 Escudo. Silver.	—	275

The Federative Republic of Brazil, which comprises half the continent of South America and is the only Latin American country deriving its culture and language from Portugal, has an area of 3,286,488 sq. mi. (8,511,965 sq. km.). Capital: Brasilia.

Brazil was discovered and claimed for Portugal by Admiral Pedro Alvares Cabral in 1500. Portugal established a settlement in 1532 and proclaimed the area a royal colony in 1549. During the Napoleonic Wars, Dom Joao VI established the seat of Portuguese government in Rio de Janeiro. When he returned to Portugal, his son Dom Pedro I declared Brazil's independence on Sept. 7, 1822, and became emperor of Brazil. The Empire of Brazil was maintained until 1889 when the federal republic was established. The Federative Republic was established in 1946 by terms of a constitution drawn up by a constituent assembly. Following a coup in 1964 the armed forces retained overall control under a dictatorship until civilian government was restored on March 15, 1985. The current constitution was adopted in 1988.

RULERS

Portuguese

Maria I Widow, 1786-1816
Joao, Prince Regent, 1799-1818
Joao VI, 1818-1822

Brazilean

Pedro I, 1822-1831
Pedro II, 1831-1889

MINT MARKS

(a) - Paris, privy marks only
B - Bahia
C - Cuiaba (Mato Grosso) 1823-1833
G - Goias 1823-1833
M - Minas Gerais 1823-1828
P - Pernambuco
R - Rio de Janeiro
SP - Sao Paulo 1825-1832
W/o mint mark - Lisbon 1715-1805

MONETARY SYSTEM

(Until 1833)

120 Reis = 1 Real
6400 Reis 1 Peca (Dobra = Johannes (Joe) = 4 Escudos

(1833-1942)

1000 Reis = 1 Milreis

NOTE: KM#307.1-307.3, 313 and 326.1-326.2 are usually found struck over Spanish Colonial 8 Reales. Specimens of Spanish types with original elements visible command the following approximate premiums: 30% for mint mark, 40% for mint mark and assayer initial and 55% for mint mark, assayer initial and date. Specimens of Spanish Colonial types with original elements visible command the following approximate premiums: 10% for mint mark, 20% for mint mark and assayer initial and 35% for mint mark, assayer initial and date. In addition KM#326.1 and 326.2 are sometimes found struck over early South American Republic Peso and 8 Reales types. Specimens of Republic issues with original elements visible command the following approximate premiums: 25% for mint mark, 50% for mint mark and assayer initial and 100% for mint mark, assayer initial and date.

PORTUGUESE COLONY

MILLED COINAGE

KM# 232.1 10 REIS
Copper **Obv. Legend:** JOANNES. D. G. P. E. BRASILIAE.. **Note:** Struck at Lisbon Mint but without mint mark.

Date	Mintage	VG	F	VF	XF	Unc
1802	612,000	10.00	15.00	30.00	50.00	—
1803	1,167,000	3.00	7.00	15.00	25.00	—
1805	1,248,000	3.00	7.00	15.00	25.00	—

KM# 232.3 10 REIS
Copper

Date	Mintage	VG	F	VF	XF	Unc
1805R	400,000	10.00	15.00	30.00	50.00	—
1806R	1,136,000	3.00	8.00	12.00	20.00	—
1812R	—	—	—	—	—	—
1814R	66,000	15.00	30.00	75.00	150	—
1815R	302,000	10.00	15.00	30.00	50.00	—

KM# 232.2 10 REIS
Copper

Date	Mintage	VG	F	VF	XF	Unc
1815B	—	3.00	7.50	15.00	30.00	—
1816B	413,000	6.50	12.50	20.00	45.00	—
1818B	—	6.50	12.50	20.00	30.00	—

KM# 314.1 10 REIS
Copper **Obv. Legend:** JOANNES VI. D. G. PORT..

Date	Mintage	VG	F	VF	XF	Unc
1818R Cross on crown	496,000	4.00	9.00	17.50	35.00	—
1819R Star and cross on crown	1,440,000	3.00	6.00	12.50	22.00	—
1820R Star and cross on crown	1,646,000	3.00	6.00	12.50	22.00	—
1821/0R Star and cross on crown	—	3.50	7.00	15.00	30.00	—
1821R Star and cross on crown	2,003,000	3.00	6.00	12.50	22.00	—
1822R Cross and crown	1,839,000	3.00	6.00	12.50	22.00	—

KM# 314.2 10 REIS
Copper **Note:** Mint mark: B

Date	Mintage	VG	F	VF	XF	Unc
1821B	—	2.50	5.00	10.00	20.00	—
1822B	—	2.50	5.00	10.00	20.00	—
1822/29B	—	10.00	20.00	40.00	90.00	—
1823B	—	2.50	5.00	10.00	18.00	—

KM# 233.1 20 REIS
Copper **Obv. Legend:** JOANNES D. G. PORT. ET. BRAS. P. REGENS.. **Rev:** Globe **Note:** Struck at Lisbon without mint mark.

Date	Mintage	VG	F	VF	XF	Unc
1802	788,000	5.00	10.00	15.00	25.00	—
1803	1,920,000	2.50	5.00	10.00	20.00	—

KM# 233.2 20 REIS
Copper

Date	Mintage	VG	F	VF	XF	Unc
1812B	—	3.00	6.00	15.00	30.00	—
1813B	160,000	10.00	15.00	20.00	50.00	—
1815B Cross on crown	448,000	7.50	12.50	17.50	35.00	—
1816B	700,000	5.00	10.00	15.00	25.00	—

KM# 233.3 20 REIS
Copper

Date	Mintage	VG	F	VF	XF	Unc
1812R	12,000	10.00	20.00	35.00	75.00	—
1813R	717,000	5.00	10.00	15.00	25.00	—
1813/14R	—	10.00	20.00	35.00	75.00	—
1814R	1,164,000	3.00	6.00	12.50	20.00	—
1815R Star on crown	302,000	7.50	14.00	25.00	35.00	—
1817R	116,000	7.50	14.00	25.00	45.00	—
1818R	60,000	8.00	15.00	30.00	60.00	—

KM# 309 20 REIS
Copper **Obv. Legend:** JOANNES D. G. PORT. BRAS. ET ALG

Date	Mintage	VG	F	VF	XF	Unc
1816R	206,000	5.00	70.00	20.00	45.00	—

KM# 316.1 20 REIS
Copper **Obv. Legend:** JOANNES. VI. D. G. PORT...

Date	Mintage	VG	F	VF	XF	Unc
1818R Star on crown	174,000	5.00	10.00	20.00	45.00	—
1819R Star and cross on crown	1,440,000	3.00	6.00	12.50	25.00	—
1820R Star and cross on crown	4,872,000	2.50	5.00	10.00	20.00	—
1821R Star on crown	10,828,000	—	500	10.00	20.00	—
1821R Cross on crown	—	3.00	6.00	10.00	25.00	—
1822R Star and cross on crown	7,046,000	2.50	5.00	9.00	17.50	—

KM# 315 20 REIS
Copper **Obv:** Crowned value **Obv. Legend:** JOANNES D. G. P. E.. **Rev:** Globe **Rev. Legend:** PECUNIA. TOTUM. CIRCUMIT.. **Note:** Minted for Goias and Mato Grosso.

Date	Mintage	VG	F	VF	XF	Unc
1818	—	8.00	16.00	35.00	70.00	—

KM# 316.2 20 REIS
Copper

Date	Mintage	VG	F	VF	XF	Unc
1820B	—	2.50	5.00	10.00	20.00	—
1821B Cross on crown	—	2.50	5.00	10.00	20.00	—

KM# 317.2 37-1/2 REIS
Copper

Date	Mintage	VG	F	VF	XF	Unc
1818R Rare	—	—	—	—	—	—

KM# 317.1 37-1/2 REIS
Copper **Obv. Legend:** JOANNES. VI. D. G. PORT. BRAS.. **Rev. Legend:** PECUNIA. TOTUM. CIRCUMIT.. **Note:** Minted for Minas Gerais.

Date	Mintage	VG	F	VF	XF	Unc
1818M	200,000	20.00	35.00	75.00	125	—
1819M	—	20.00	35.00	75.00	125	—
1821M	—	20.00	35.00	75.00	125	—

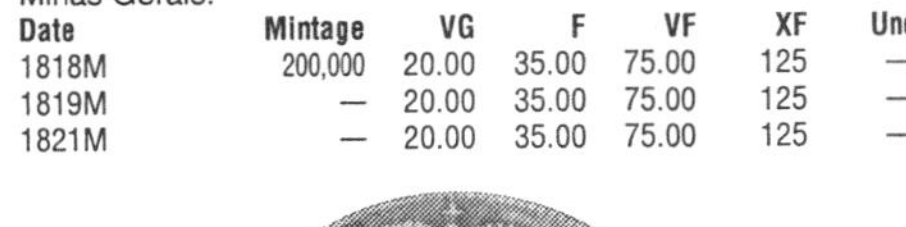

KM# 234.1 40 REIS
Copper **Obv. Legend:** JOANNES D. G. P. ET. BRASILAE... **Rev:** Similar to 10 Reis, KM#232.1 **Note:** Struck at Lisbon without mint mark; crown varieties exist for both dates.

Date	Mintage	VG	F	VF	XF	Unc
1802	584,000	5.00	10.00	20.00	50.00	—
1803	1,143,000	2.50	6.50	12.50	30.00	—

KM# 234.2 40 REIS
Copper

Date	Mintage	VG	F	VF	XF	Unc
1809B	—	7.50	15.00	25.00	50.00	—
1810B	—	7.50	15.00	25.00	50.00	—
1811B	—	3.00	7.50	15.00	35.00	—
1812B Ball on crown	—	3.00	7.50	15.00	30.00	—
1814B	132,000	5.00	10.00	20.00	45.00	—
1816B Cross on crown	286,000	5.00	10.00	20.00	45.00	—

KM# 234.3 40 REIS
Copper

Date	Mintage	VG	F	VF	XF	Unc
1812R	252,000	5.00	10.00	17.50	35.00	—
1813R	307,000	5.00	10.00	17.50	35.00	—
1815R	131,000	5.00	10.00	17.50	35.00	—
1816R	453,000	3.50	7.50	12.50	30.00	—
1817R	379,000	6.00	15.00	25.00	50.00	—

KM# 311 40 REIS
Copper **Obv. Legend:** JOANNES. D. G. PORT. BRAS. ET. ALG..

Date	Mintage	VG	F	VF	XF	Unc
1816R	—	5.00	10.00	20.00	45.00	—

KM# 319.1 40 REIS
Copper

Date	Mintage	VG	F	VF	XF	Unc
1818R Star on crown	687,000	3.50	7.50	20.00	35.00	—
1819R	2,500,000	5.00	10.00	22.00	45.00	—
1820R Star on crown	2,018,000	2.50	6.50	15.00	25.00	—
1821R Cross on crown	5,307,000	2.50	6.50	15.00	25.00	—
1822R	4,583,000	2.50	6.50	15.00	25.00	—

KM# 318 40 REIS
Copper **Obv. Legend:** JOANNES. D. G. P. E **Rev. Legend:** PECUNIA. TOTUM. CIRCUMIT.. **Note:** Minted for Goias and Mato Grosso.

Date	Mintage	VG	F	VF	XF	Unc
1818	—	15.00	40.00	100	150	—

KM# 319.2 40 REIS
Copper

Date	Mintage	VG	F	VF	XF	Unc
1820B	—	3.50	8.50	22.00	35.00	—
1821B	—	3.50	8.50	22.00	35.00	—
1822B	—	3.50	8.50	22.00	35.00	—
1823B	—	3.50	8.50	25.00	50.00	—

KM# 340 40 REIS
Copper **Obv. Legend:** JOANNES. VI. D. G. PORT. BRAS **Note:** Minted for Goias and Mato Grosso.

Date	Mintage	VG	F	VF	XF	Unc
1820	—	45.00	90.00	175	275	—
1821	—	45.00	90.00	175	275	—
1822	—	45.00	90.00	175	275	—
1822	—	5.00	35.00	100	150	—

KM# 320 75 REIS
Copper **Obv. Legend:** JOANNES. VI. D. G. PORT. BRAS.. **Rev:** Arms on globe **Rev. Legend:** PECUNIA. TOTUM. CIRCUMIT.. **Note:** Minted for Minas Gerais.

Date	Mintage	VG	F	VF	XF	Unc
1818M	269,000	15.00	30.00	75.00	110	—
1819M	—	15.00	30.00	80.00	120	—
1821M	—	15.00	30.00	75.00	110	—

KM# 305 80 REIS
2.2400 g., 0.9170 Silver .0660 oz. **Obv. Legend:** JOANNES. D. G. PORT. P. REGENS..

Date	Mintage	VG	F	VF	XF	Unc
1810R Rare	—	—	—	—	—	—
1814R	—	30.00	70.00	150	300	—
1816R	—	25.00	50.00	120	200	—

KM# 308 80 REIS
Copper **Note:** Similar to 10 Reis, KM#232.2.

Date	Mintage	VG	F	VF	XF	Unc
1811	13,000	25.00	60.00	125	300	—
1812	13,000	20.00	50.00	100	250	—

KM# 321.2 80 REIS
Copper

Date	Mintage	VG	F	VF	XF	Unc
1818R	—	6.00	17.50	35.00	60.00	—

KM# 322.1 80 REIS
2.2400 g., 0.9170 Silver .0660 oz. **Obv:** Crowned 80 within wreath **Obv. Legend:** JOANNES. VI. D. G. PORT. BRAS..

Date	Mintage	VG	F	VF	XF	Unc
1818R	—	30.00	60.00	125	250	—

KM# 321.1 80 REIS
Copper **Obv:** Crowned value **Obv. Legend:** JOANNES D. G. PORT.. **Rev:** Globe **Rev. Legend:** PECUNIA. TOTUM. CIRCUMIT.. **Note:** Minted for Goias and Mato Grosso.

Date	Mintage	VG	F	VF	XF	Unc
1818B	—	8.00	20.00	50.00	85.00	—

KM# 341 80 REIS
Copper **Obv:** Crowned value **Obv. Legend:** JOANNES. VI. D. G. PORT.. **Rev:** Arms on globe **Note:** Minted for Goias and Mato Grosso.

Date	Mintage	VG	F	VF	XF	Unc
1820R	—	10.00	20.00	40.00	95.00	—

KM# 342.1 80 REIS
Copper

Date	Mintage	VG	F	VF	XF	Unc
1820B	—	7.50	15.00	25.00	45.00	—
1821B	—	7.50	15.00	25.00	45.00	—
1822/1B	—	10.00	20.00	40.00	95.00	—
1822B	—	7.50	15.00	30.00	60.00	—
1823/1B	—	10.00	20.00	40.00	95.00	—
1823B	—	7.50	15.00	30.00	60.00	—

KM# 342.2 80 REIS
Copper

Date	Mintage	VG	F	VF	XF	Unc
1821R	210,000	7.50	15.00	25.00	45.00	—
1822R	617,000	6.00	12.00	20.00	40.00	—

KM# 322.2 80 REIS
2.2400 g., 0.9170 Silver .0660 oz.

Date	Mintage	VG	F	VF	XF	Unc
1821B	125,000	25.00	45.00	100	200	—

KM# 306.1 160 REIS
4.4800 g., 0.9170 Silver .1320 oz. **Obv:** Crowned value **Obv. Legend:** JOANNES. D. G. PORT. P. REGENS.. **Rev:** Globe

Date	Mintage	VG	F	VF	XF	Unc
1810R	—	17.50	35.00	80.00	160	—
1813R	—	6.00	10.00	25.00	50.00	—
1813R/B	—	8.50	17.50	30.00	50.00	—
1815R	—	12.50	25.00	35.00	60.00	—

KM# 306.3 160 REIS
4.4800 g., 0.9170 Silver .1320 oz. **Note:** Medal strike.

Date	Mintage	VG	F	VF	XF	Unc
1810R	—	17.00	40.00	80.00	180	—
1813R	—	17.00	40.00	80.00	180	—

KM# 306.2 160 REIS
4.4800 g., 0.9170 Silver .1320 oz.

Date	Mintage	VG	F	VF	XF	Unc
1811B Rare	—	—	—	—	—	—
1812B	—	150	350	700	1,500	—

KM# 323.1 160 REIS
4.4509 g., 0.9170 Silver .1312 oz. **Obv. Legend:** JOANNES. VI. D. G. PORT. BRAS..

Date	Mintage	VG	F	VF	XF	Unc
1818R R/F	—	12.50	27.50	45.00	90.00	—
1818R	—	10.00	25.00	40.00	80.00	—
1820R Rare	—	—	—	—	—	—

KM# 323.2 160 REIS
4.4509 g., 0.9170 Silver .1312 oz.

Date	Mintage	VG	F	VF	XF	Unc
1821B	5,639	40.00	80.00	120	150	—

KM# 221.3 320 REIS
8.9018 g., 0.9170 Silver .2623 oz. **Obv. Legend:** MARIA. I. D. G. PORT. REGINA.. **Note:** Similar to KM#255.1 but obverse legend: MARIA. I. D. G...

Date	Mintage	VG	F	VF	XF	Unc
1800R	—	11.00	20.00	27.50	40.00	—
1802R	—	11.00	20.00	27.50	45.00	—

KM# 255.1 320 REIS
8.9600 g., 0.9170 Silver .2641 oz. **Obv. Legend:** JOANNES. D. G. PORT. P. REGENS..

Date	Mintage	VG	F	VF	XF	Unc
1809R	—	11.50	22.50	30.00	45.00	—
1812R	—	9.00	18.00	28.00	40.00	—
1813R	—	9.00	18.00	28.00	40.00	—
1817R	—	15.00	30.00	50.00	75.00	—

KM# 255.2 320 REIS
8.9600 g., 0.9170 Silver .2641 oz.

Date	Mintage	VG	F	VF	XF	Unc
1810B	—	17.50	40.00	90.00	160	—
1816B	—	65.00	110	200	350	—

KM# 255.3 320 REIS
8.9600 g., 0.9170 Silver .2641 oz.

Date	Mintage	VG	F	VF	XF	Unc
1812M	—	60.00	130	220	460	—
1814M	—	75.00	200	350	750	—
1816M	—	75.00	200	350	750	—

KM# 255.4 320 REIS
8.9600 g., 0.9170 Silver .2641 oz. **Note:** Medal strike.

Date	Mintage	VG	F	VF	XF	Unc
1813R	—	30.00	50.00	100	250	—

KM# 324.2 320 REIS
8.9600 g., 0.9170 Silver .2641 oz.

Date	Mintage	VG	F	VF	XF	Unc
1818R	—	11.00	20.00	50.00	100	—
1819R	—	17.50	35.00	60.00	125	—
1820R Star on crown	—	12.00	18.00	35.00	70.00	—

KM# 324.1 320 REIS
8.9600 g., 0.9170 Silver .2641 oz. **Obv:** JOANNES. VI. D. G. PORT. BRAS..

Date	Mintage	VG	F	VF	XF	Unc
1818M	—	1,500	2,800	5,000	8,000	—

KM# 324.3 320 REIS
8.9600 g., 0.9170 Silver .2641 oz.

Date	Mintage	VG	F	VF	XF	Unc
1821B	—	18.50	37.50	55.00	125	—

KM# 231.2 640 REIS
17.7600 g., 0.9170 Silver .5233 oz. **Rev. Legend:** SUBQ..

Date	Mintage	VG	F	VF	XF	Unc
1801B	—	18.50	25.00	40.00	75.00	—
1802B	—	18.50	25.00	40.00	75.00	—
1803B	—	18.50	25.00	40.00	75.00	—
1804B	—	18.50	25.00	40.00	75.00	—
1805B	—	35.00	75.00	150	275	—

KM# 222.2 640 REIS
17.7600 g., 0.9170 Silver .5233 oz. **Obv:** High crown **Obv. Legend:** MARIA.I.D.G.PORT.REGINA... **Note:** Similar to KM#231 but obverse legend differs.

Date	Mintage	VG	F	VF	XF	Unc
1802R	56,126,000	15.00	20.00	40.00	85.00	—

KM# 237 640 REIS
17.9200 g., 0.9170 Silver .5280 oz. **Obv. Legend:** JOANNES. D. G. PORT. P. REGENS..

Date	Mintage	VG	F	VF	XF	Unc
1806B	—	30.00	75.00	150	350	—
1807B	—	30.00	75.00	150	350	—
1808/7B	—	20.00	35.00	60.00	75.00	—
1808B	—	16.50	25.00	35.00	70.00	—

KM# 256.1 640 REIS
17.9200 g., 0.9170 Silver .5280 oz.

Date	Mintage	VG	F	VF	XF	Unc
1809B	—	16.50	25.00	35.00	70.00	—
1810B	—	17.50	27.50	40.00	80.00	—
1816B Rare	—	—	—	—	—	—

KM# 256.2 640 REIS
17.9200 g., 0.9170 Silver .5280 oz.

Date	Mintage	VG	F	VF	XF	Unc
1809R	—	18.50	35.00	45.00	75.00	—
1811R	—	18.50	35.00	45.00	75.00	—
1812R	—	25.00	80.00	175	350	—
1813R	—	50.00	125	250	450	—
1814R	—	55.00	150	300	650	—
1815R	—	55.00	150	300	650	—
1816R	—	55.00	150	300	650	—

KM# 256.3 640 REIS
17.9200 g., 0.9170 Silver .5280 oz.

Date	Mintage	VG	F	VF	XF	Unc
1810M Rare	—	—	—	—	—	—
1811M	—	50.00	120	250	500	—
1812M	—	70.00	150	275	600	—
1813M	—	70.00	150	300	700	—
1816M	—	70.00	175	400	1,000	—

KM# 325.1 640 REIS
19.3200 g., 0.9170 Silver .5693 oz. **Obv. Legend:** JOANNES. VI

Date	Mintage	VG	F	VF	XF	Unc
1818M	—	350	1,250	3,750	6,000	—

KM# 325.2 640 REIS
19.3200 g., 0.9170 Silver .5693 oz.

Date	Mintage	VG	F	VF	XF	Unc
1818R	—	17.50	45.00	90.00	180	—
1819R	—	25.00	50.00	100	200	—
1820R	—	16.50	25.00	45.00	65.00	—
1821R	—	16.50	25.00	45.00	65.00	—
1822R	—	25.00	75.00	250	400	—

KM# 325.3 640 REIS
19.3200 g., 0.9170 Silver .5693 oz.

Date	Mintage	VG	F	VF	XF	Unc
1821B	—	40.00	75.00	140	350	—

KM# 307.1 960 REIS
26.8900 g., 0.8960 Silver .7746 oz.

Date	Mintage	VG	F	VF	XF	Unc
1810B	—	17.50	27.50	40.00	60.00	—
1810B Small crown; Rare	—	—	—	—	—	—
1810B P. REGENES...	—	50.00	80.00	180	350	—
1811B	—	25.00	40.00	60.00	100	—
1812B	—	17.50	27.50	40.00	65.00	—
1813B	—	17.50	27.50	40.00	65.00	—
1813B P. REGENES...	—	50.00	80.00	150	300	—
1814B	—	17.50	27.50	40.00	65.00	—
1815B	—	17.50	27.50	40.00	65.00	—
1816B	—	17.50	27.50	40.00	65.00	—
1817B	—	17.50	27.50	40.00	65.00	—

KM# 307.2 960 REIS
26.8900 g., 0.8960 Silver .7746 oz.

Date	Mintage	VG	F	VF	XF	Unc
1810M Rare	—	—	—	—	—	—
1816M Rare	—	—	—	—	—	—

KM# 307.3 960 REIS
26.8900 g., 0.8960 Silver .7746 oz.

Date	Mintage	VG	F	VF	XF	Unc
1810R	—	17.50	27.50	40.00	65.00	—
1811R	—	17.50	27.50	40.00	65.00	—
1812R	—	17.50	27.50	40.00	65.00	—
1812/1R	—	—	—	—	120	—
1813/2R	—	20.00	30.00	50.00	85.00	—
1813R	—	17.50	27.50	40.00	65.00	—
1814R	—	17.50	27.50	40.00	65.00	—
1815R	—	17.50	27.50	40.00	65.00	—
1815R ...STAB. NATA.; Rare	—	—	—	—	—	—
1816R	—	17.50	27.50	40.00	65.00	—
1817R	—	17.50	27.50	40.00	65.00	—
1818R Star on crown	—	17.50	27.50	40.00	65.00	—

KM# 313 960 REIS
27.0700 g., 0.9030 Silver .7859 oz. **Obv:** Legend ends: ... BRAS. ET. ALG. P. REGENS

Date	Mintage	VG	F	VF	XF	Unc
1816R	—	30.00	70.00	150	250	—

KM# 326.1 960 REIS
27.0700 g., 0.9030 Silver .7859 oz.

Date	Mintage	VG	F	VF	XF	Unc
1818R	—	17.50	27.50	40.00	65.00	—
1819R	—	17.50	27.50	40.00	65.00	—
1820R	—	17.50	27.50	40.00	65.00	—
1820R Small castle within zero of denomination	—	750	1,350	1,850	—	—
1821R	—	17.50	27.50	40.00	65.00	—
1822R	—	25.00	45.00	85.00	140	—

KM# 326.2 960 REIS
27.0700 g., 0.9030 Silver .7859 oz.

Date	Mintage	VG	F	VF	XF	Unc
1819B Rare	—	—	—	—	—	—
1920B Rare	—	—	—	—	—	—
1820B	—	17.50	25.00	35.00	60.00	—
1820B BARS. ET...	—	25.00	40.00	60.00	100	—
1821B	—	17.50	25.00	35.00	60.00	—
1821/0B	—	20.00	30.00	40.00	70.00	—
1821B	—	20.00	35.00	45.00	75.00	—
1822B	—	400	1,000	2,500	4,000	—

KM# 225.2 4000 REIS
8.0683 g., 0.9170 Gold .2378 oz. **Obv. Legend:** MARIA I. D. G.. **Note:** Struck at Bahia without mint mark.

Date	Mintage	F	VF	XF	Unc	BU
1801	3,705	150	260	400	600	—
1802	7,738	150	260	400	600	—
1803	7,807	150	260	400	600	—
1804/2	Inc. above	150	260	400	600	—
1805/2	Inc. below	150	260	400	600	—

KM# 235.1 4000 REIS
8.0683 g., 0.9170 Gold .2378 oz. **Obv:** Large crown **Obv. Legend:** JOANNES. D. G.. **Rev:** Dots on either side of date **Note:** Struck at Bahia without mint mark.

Date	Mintage	F	VF	XF	Unc	BU
1805	10,000	125	225	375	500	—
1806	12,000	125	225	375	500	—
1807	7,725	125	225	375	500	—
1808	37,000	125	225	375	500	—
1809/8	19,000	125	225	375	500	—
1809	Inc. above	125	225	375	500	—
1810	18,000	125	225	375	500	—
1811	19,000	125	225	375	500	—
1811 Flowers at date	Inc. above	125	225	375	500	—
1813	11,000	125	225	375	500	—
1814	9,494	125	225	375	500	—
1815	—	125	225	375	500	—
1816	7,522	125	225	375	500	—

KM# 235.2 4000 REIS
8.0683 g., 0.9170 Gold .2378 oz. **Obv:** Small crown **Rev:** Flower on either side of date **Note:** Struck at Rio de Janiero without mint mark.

Date	Mintage	F	VF	XF	Unc	BU
1808	128,000	125	225	375	500	—
1809/8	94,000	125	225	375	500	—
1809	Inc. above	125	225	375	500	—
1810/09	66,000	125	225	400	500	—
1810	Inc. above	125	225	400	500	—
1811/10	87,000	125	225	400	500	—
1811	Inc. above	125	225	400	500	—
1812	124,000	125	225	400	500	—
181.2	Inc. above	125	275	400	500	—
1812 Error: PROT	Inc. above	150	275	500	700	—
1813/2	148,000	125	225	400	500	—
1813	Inc. above	125	225	400	500	—
1814/3	102,000	125	225	400	500	—
1814	Inc. above	125	225	400	500	—
1815	83,000	125	225	400	500	—
1816	91,000	125	225	400	500	—
1817	71,000	125	225	400	500	—

KM# 235.3 4000 REIS
8.0683 g., 0.9170 Gold .2378 oz. **Obv. Legend:** PORT. ET. BRAS (error) **Note:** Struck at Rio de Janiero without mint mark.

Date	Mintage	F	VF	XF	Unc	BU
1812	Inc. above	150	275	450	600	—

KM# 312 4000 REIS
8.0683 g., 0.9170 Gold .2378 oz. **Obv. Legend:** PORT. BRAS. ET. ALG **Rev. Legend:** PRINCEPS. REGENS.. **Note:** Struck at Rio de Janiero without mint mark.

Date	Mintage	F	VF	XF	Unc	BU
1816	Inc. above	200	650	1,200	2,000	—

KM# 327.1 4000 REIS
8.0683 g., 0.9170 Gold .2378 oz. **Obv:** 6-petal flower on either side of date **Note:** Struck at Rio de Janiero without mint mark.

Date	Mintage	F	VF	XF	Unc	BU
1818	64,000	140	300	500	700	—
1819	49,000	200	400	500	700	—
1820	87,000	140	300	500	700	—
1821/0	35,000	140	300	500	700	—
1821	Inc. above	140	300	500	700	—
1822/0	54,000	150	320	510	710	—
1822/1	Inc. above	150	320	510	710	—
1822	Inc. above	150	320	510	710	—

KM# 327.2 4000 REIS
8.0683 g., 0.9170 Gold .2378 oz. **Obv:** 4-petal flower on either side of date **Note:** Struck at Rio de Janiero without mint mark.

Date	Mintage	F	VF	XF	Unc	BU
1819	Inc. above	150	300	500	700	—

KM# 327.3 4000 REIS
8.0683 g., 0.9170 Gold .2378 oz. **Obv:** Date between crosses **Note:** Struck at Bahia without mint mark.

Date	Mintage	F	VF	XF	Unc	BU
1819	1,864	600	1,200	2,000	2,500	—
1820	4,374	850	1,500	2,500	3,000	—

KM# 226.1 6400 REIS
14.3436 g., 0.9170 Gold .4229 oz. **Obv:** Bust right with bejeweled headdress **Rev:** Crowned arms

Date	Mintage	F	VF	XF	Unc	BU
1801R	185,000	250	325	450	650	—
1802R	168,000	250	325	450	650	—
1803R	176,000	250	325	450	650	—
1804R	128,000	250	325	450	650	—
1805R	109,000	250	325	450	650	—

KM# 226.2 6400 REIS
14.3436 g., 0.9170 Gold .4229 oz.

Date	Mintage	F	VF	XF	Unc	BU
1801B	12,000	260	375	550	700	—
1802B	3,324	260	375	550	700	—
1803B	3,743	260	375	550	700	—
1804B	3,539	260	375	550	700	—

KM# 236.1 6400 REIS
14.3436 g., 0.9170 Gold .4229 oz. **Obv. Legend:** JOANNES. D. G. PORT. ET. ALG. P. REGENS

Date	Mintage	F	VF	XF	Unc	BU
1805R	Inc. above	260	350	500	800	—
1806R	96,000	260	350	500	800	—
1807R	59,000	260	350	500	800	—
1808/7R	133,000	260	350	500	800	—
1808R	Inc. above	280	350	500	800	—
1809/8R	188,000	280	350	500	800	—
1809R	Inc. above	300	350	500	800	—
1810/09R	159,000	300	350	500	800	—
1810R	Inc. above	300	400	600	1,000	—
1811/10R	82,000	350	400	600	1,000	—
1811R	Inc. above	350	400	600	1,000	—
1812R	64,000	350	450	600	1,000	—
1813R	53,000	350	450	600	1,000	—
1814/3R	42,000	360	475	750	1,000	—
1814R	Inc. above	360	475	750	1,200	—
1815R	40,000	400	450	750	1,200	—
1816R	39,000	420	500	1,000	2,800	—
1817R	32,000	450	500	1,000	3,500	—

KM# 236.2 6400 REIS
14.3436 g., 0.9170 Gold .4229 oz. **Obv. Legend:** PORT. BRAS. ET. ALG. P. REG

Date	Mintage	F	VF	XF	Unc	BU
1816R	Inc. above	2,800	3,500	4,500	6,000	—

KM# 328 6400 REIS
14.3436 g., 0.9170 Gold .4229 oz. **Obv. Legend:** JOANNES. VI. D. G. PORT. BRAS. ET. ALG. REX

Date	Mintage	F	VF	XF	Unc	BU
1818R	14,000	1,000	2,000	2,500	3,000	—
1819R	9,227	2,000	3,000	4,000	4,500	—
1820R	3,286	2,700	4,000	5,000	5,500	—
1821R Unique	2,122	—	—	—	—	—
1822R Rare	599	—	—	—	—	—

COUNTERMARKED COINAGE

Shield Countermark

Authorized on April 18, 1809.

The purpose of the shield countermark was to double the value of the earlier Colonial copper coinage and raise the value of the earlier silver coinage. Other Portuguese and Portuguese Colonial coins are known with this countermark. There are basically 8 types of shields that vary in size from 7mm x 7mm to 11mm x 11mm

75 = 80 Reis 300 = 320 Reis
150 = 160 Reis 600 = 640 Reis

KM# 260 10 REIS
Copper **Countermark:** Shield **Note:** Countermark on 5 Reis, KM#142.5.

CM Date	Host Date	Good	VG	F	VF	XF
ND(1809)	1749	2.50	6.00	12.50	25.00	—

KM# 261 10 REIS
Copper **Countermark:** Shield **Note:** Countermark on 5 Reis, KM#173.1.

CM Date	Host Date	Good	VG	F	VF	XF
ND(1809)	1752	10.00	25.00	70.00	140	—
ND(1809)	1753	3.00	7.00	15.00	30.00	—
ND(1809)	1768	2.50	6.50	7.50	25.00	—
ND(1809)	1773	2.50	6.50	7.50	25.00	—
ND(1809)	1774	2.50	6.50	7.50	25.00	—

KM# 262 10 REIS
Copper **Countermark:** Shield **Note:** Countermark on 5 Reis, KM#188.

CM Date	Host Date	Good	VG	F	VF	XF
ND(1809)	1762B	2.50	5.00	10.00	20.00	—
ND(1809)	1763B	2.50	5.00	10.00	20.00	—
ND(1809)	1764B	2.50	5.00	10.00	20.00	—
ND(1809)	1766B	2.50	5.00	10.00	20.00	—
ND(1809)	1767B	2.50	5.00	10.00	20.00	—
ND(1809)	1768B	2.50	5.00	10.00	20.00	—
ND(1809)	1769B	2.50	5.00	10.00	20.00	—

KM# 263 10 REIS
Copper **Countermark:** Shield **Note:** Countermark on 5 Reis, KM#200.

CM Date	Host Date	Good	VG	F	VF	XF
ND(1809)	1778	2.50	5.00	10.00	20.00	—
ND(1809)	1781	2.50	5.00	10.00	20.00	—
ND(1809)	1782	2.50	5.00	10.00	20.00	—
ND(1809)	1784	2.50	5.00	10.00	20.00	—
ND(1809)	1785	2.50	5.00	10.00	20.00	—

KM# 264.2 10 REIS
Copper **Countermark:** Shield **Note:** Countermark on 5 Reis, with high full arch, KM#214.2

CM Date	Host Date	Good	VG	F	VF	XF
ND(1809)	1786	2.50	5.00	12.50	25.00	—
ND(1809)	1787	2.50	5.00	12.50	25.00	—
ND(1809)	1790	2.50	5.00	12.50	25.00	—
ND(1809)	1791	2.50	5.00	12.50	25.00	—

KM# 264.1 10 REIS
Copper **Countermark:** Shield **Note:** Countermark on 5 Reis, with low flat arch crown, KM#214.1

CM Date	Host Date	Good	VG	F	VF	XF
ND(1809)	1786	2.50	5.00	12.50	25.00	—
ND(1809)	1787	2.50	5.00	12.50	25.00	—
ND(1809)	1790	2.50	5.00	12.50	25.00	—
ND(1809)	1791	2.50	5.00	12.50	25.00	—
ND(1809)	1797	7.50	15.00	25.00	45.00	—

KM# 266 20 REIS
Copper **Countermark:** Shield **Note:** Countermark on 10 Reis, KM#107.

CM Date	Host Date	Good	VG	F	VF	XF
ND(1809)	ND	30.00	45.00	85.00	160	—

KM# 267 20 REIS
Copper **Countermark:** Shield **Note:** Countermark on 10 Reis, KM#108.

CM Date	Host Date	Good	VG	F	VF	XF
ND(1809)	1715	2.50	5.00	12.50	25.00	—
ND(1809)	1718	2.50	5.00	12.50	25.00	—
ND(1809)	1719	2.50	5.00	12.50	25.00	—
ND(1809)	1720	2.50	5.00	12.50	25.00	—

KM# 268.1 20 REIS
Copper **Countermark:** Shield **Note:** Countermark on 10 Reis, KM#142.1.

CM Date	Host Date	Good	VG	F	VF	XF
ND(1809)	1729B	2.50	5.00	7.50	15.00	—
ND(1809)	1730B	2.50	5.00	7.50	15.00	—
ND(1809)	1731B	2.50	5.00	7.50	15.00	—

KM# 268.2 20 REIS
Copper **Countermark:** Shield **Note:** Countermark on 10 Reis, KM#142.2.

CM Date	Host Date	Good	VG	F	VF	XF
ND(1809)	1729	2.50	5.00	10.00	20.00	—
ND(1809)	1730	2.50	5.00	10.00	20.00	—
ND(1809)	1731	2.50	5.00	10.00	20.00	—
ND(1809)	1732	2.50	5.00	10.00	20.00	—
ND(1809)	1747	10.00	17.50	25.00	45.00	—
ND(1809)	1748	20.00	50.00	80.00	150	—

KM# 268.3 20 REIS
Copper **Countermark:** Shield **Note:** Countermark on 10 Reis, KM#142.3.

CM Date	Host Date	Good	VG	F	VF	XF
ND(1809)	1735	2.50	5.00	10.00	20.00	—
ND(1809)	1736	2.50	5.00	10.00	20.00	—
ND(1809)	1746	2.50	5.00	10.00	20.00	—

KM# 268.4 20 REIS
Copper **Countermark:** Shield **Note:** Countermark on 10 Reis, KM#142.4.

CM Date	Host Date	Good	VG	F	VF	XF
ND(1809)	1746	2.50	5.00	10.00	20.00	—

KM# 268.5 20 REIS
Copper **Countermark:** Shield **Note:** Countermark on 10 Reis, KM#142.5.

CM Date	Host Date	Good	VG	F	VF	XF
ND(1809)	1749	2.50	5.00	10.00	20.00	—

KM# 269 20 REIS
Copper **Countermark:** Shield **Note:** Countermark on 10 Reis, KM#165.1.

CM Date	Host Date	Good	VG	F	VF	XF
ND(1809)	1751	20.00	40.00	85.00	150	—

KM# 270 20 REIS
Copper **Countermark:** Shield **Note:** Countermark on 10 Reis, KM#174.1.

CM Date	Host Date	Good	VG	F	VF	XF
ND(1809)	1752	4.00	10.00	20.00	35.00	—
ND(1809)	1753	2.50	5.00	9.00	18.00	—
ND(1809)	1773	3.00	10.00	20.00	35.00	—
ND(1809)	1774	2.50	5.00	9.00	18.00	—
ND(1809)	1775	2.50	5.00	9.00	18.00	—
ND(1809)	1776	2.50	5.00	9.00	18.00	—

KM# 271 20 REIS
Copper **Countermark:** Shield **Note:** Countermark on 10 Reis, KM#174.2.

CM Date	Host Date	Good	VG	F	VF	XF
ND(1809)	1762B	2.50	5.00	10.00	20.00	—

KM# 272 20 REIS
Copper **Countermark:** Shield **Note:** Countermark on 10 Reis, KM#201.

CM Date	Host Date	Good	VG	F	VF	XF
ND(1809)	1778	2.50	5.00	7.50	14.50	—
ND(1809)	1781	2.50	5.00	7.50	14.50	—
ND(1809)	1782	2.50	5.00	7.50	14.50	—
ND(1809)	1784	2.50	5.00	7.50	14.50	—
ND(1809)	1785	2.50	5.00	7.50	14.50	—

KM# 265 20 REIS
Copper **Countermark:** Shield **Note:** Countermark on 10 Reis, KM#71.

CM Date	Host Date	Good	VG	F	VF	XF
ND(1809)	1694P	10.00	30.00	55.00	90.00	—
ND(1809)	1696P	10.00	17.50	30.00	55.00	—
ND(1809)	1697P	7.50	15.00	25.00	50.00	—
ND(1809)	1699P	7.50	15.00	25.00	50.00	—

KM# 273.2 20 REIS
Copper **Countermark:** Shield **Note:** Countermark on 10 Reis, with high full arch crown, KM#215.2.

CM Date	Host Date	Good	VG	F	VF	XF
ND(1809)	1786	2.50	5.00	10.00	20.00	—
ND(1809)	1787	2.50	5.00	10.00	20.00	—
ND(1809)	1790	2.50	5.00	10.00	20.00	—

KM# 274 20 REIS
Copper **Countermark:** Shield **Note:** Countermark on 10 Reis, with high full arch crown, KM#288.

CM Date	Host Date	Good	VG	F	VF	XF
ND(1809)	1799	5.00	10.00	20.00	50.00	—

KM# 273.1 20 REIS
Copper **Countermark:** Shield **Note:** Countermark on 10 Reis, with low flat arch crown, KM#215.1.

CM Date	Host Date	Good	VG	F	VF	XF
ND(1809)	1786	2.50	5.00	10.00	20.00	—
ND(1809)	1787	2.50	5.00	10.00	20.00	—
ND(1809)	1790	2.50	5.00	10.00	20.00	—
ND(1809)	1796	2.50	5.00	10.00	20.00	—

KM# 276 40 REIS
Copper **Countermark:** Shield **Note:** Countermark on 20 Reis, KM#109.

CM Date	Host Date	Good	VG	F	VF	XF
ND(1809)	1715	5.00	7.50	10.00	20.00	—
ND(1809)	1718	5.00	7.50	10.00	20.00	—
ND(1809)	1719	5.00	7.50	10.00	20.00	—
ND(1809)	1729	5.00	7.50	10.00	20.00	—

KM# 277 40 REIS
Copper **Countermark:** Shield **Note:** Countermark on 20 Reis, KM#110.

CM Date	Host Date	Good	VG	F	VF	XF
ND(1809)	1722	5.00	7.50	10.00	20.00	—

KM# 278.1 40 REIS
Copper **Countermark:** Shield **Note:** Countermark on 20 Reis, KM#143.1.

CM Date	Host Date	Good	VG	F	VF	XF
ND(1809)	1729B	2.50	5.00	10.00	20.00	—
ND(1809)	1730B	2.50	5.00	10.00	20.00	—
ND(1809)	1731B	2.50	5.00	10.00	20.00	—
ND(1809)	1748B	17.00	35.00	85.00	150	—

KM# 278.2 40 REIS
Copper **Countermark:** Shield **Note:** Countermark on 20 Reis, KM#143.2.

CM Date	Host Date	Good	VG	F	VF	XF
ND(1809)	1729B	2.50	5.00	10.00	22.50	—
ND(1809)	1730B	2.50	5.00	10.00	22.50	—
ND(1809)	1731B	2.50	5.00	10.00	22.50	—

KM# 278.3 40 REIS
Copper **Countermark:** Shield **Note:** Countermark on 20 Reis, KM#143.3.

CM Date	Host Date	Good	VG	F	VF	XF
ND(1809)	1735	2.50	5.00	7.50	15.00	—
ND(1809)	1736	2.50	5.00	7.50	15.00	—

KM# 278.4 40 REIS
Copper **Countermark:** Shield **Note:** Countermark on 20 Reis, KM#143.4.

CM Date	Host Date	Good	VG	F	VF	XF
ND(1809)	1735	2.50	4.50	7.50	15.00	—
ND(1809)	1736	2.50	4.50	7.50	15.00	—
ND(1809)	1746	2.50	4.50	7.50	15.00	—

KM# 278.5 40 REIS
Copper **Countermark:** Shield **Note:** Countermark on 20 Reis, KM#143.5.

CM Date	Host Date	Good	VG	F	VF	XF
ND(1809)	1749	2.50	5.00	10.00	22.50	—

KM# 279 40 REIS
Copper **Countermark:** Shield **Note:** Countermark on 20 Reis, KM#166.1

CM Date	Host Date	Good	VG	F	VF	XF
ND(1809)	1751	10.00	25.00	55.00	90.00	—
ND(1809)	1752	5.00	7.50	15.00	25.00	—

KM# 280.1 40 REIS
Copper **Countermark:** 11mm shield **Note:** Countermark on 20 Reis, KM#175.1.

CM Date	Host Date	Good	VG	F	VF	XF
ND(1809)	1752	2.50	5.00	10.00	20.00	—
ND(1809)	1753	2.50	5.00	10.00	20.00	—
ND(1809)	1773	2.50	5.00	10.00	20.00	—
ND(1809)	1774	2.50	5.00	10.00	20.00	—
ND(1809)	1775	2.50	5.00	10.00	20.00	—
ND(1809)	1776	2.50	5.00	10.00	20.00	—

KM# 280.2 40 REIS
Copper **Countermark:** 8mm shield **Note:** Countermark on 20 Reis, KM#175.1.

CM Date	Host Date	Good	VG	F	VF	XF
ND(1809)	1776	10.00	15.00	25.00	45.00	—

KM# 281 40 REIS
Copper **Countermark:** Shield **Note:** Countermark on 20 Reis, KM#175.2.

CM Date	Host Date	Good	VG	F	VF	XF
ND(1809)	1761B	5.00	7.50	12.50	25.00	—

KM# 282 40 REIS
Copper **Countermark:** Shield **Note:** Countermark on 20 Reis, KM#202.

CM Date	Host Date	Good	VG	F	VF	XF
ND(1809)	1778	2.50	5.00	8.50	16.50	—
ND(1809)	1781	2.50	5.00	8.50	16.50	—
ND(1809)	1782	2.50	5.00	8.50	16.50	—
ND(1809)	1784	2.50	5.00	8.50	16.50	—

KM# 284 40 REIS
Copper **Countermark:** Shield **Note:** Countermark on 20 Reis, KM#229.

CM Date	Host Date	Good	VG	F	VF	XF
ND(1809)	1799	5.00	10.00	20.00	40.00	—

KM# 285 40 REIS
Copper **Countermark:** Shield **Note:** Countermark on 20 Reis, KM#233.1.

CM Date	Host Date	Good	VG	F	VF	XF
ND(1809)	1802	2.50	5.00	10.00	20.00	—
ND(1809)	1803	2.50	5.00	10.00	20.00	—

KM# 275 40 REIS
Copper **Countermark:** Shield **Note:** Countermark on 20 Reis, KM#70.

CM Date	Host Date	Good	VG	F	VF	XF
ND(1809)	1693P	20.00	35.00	75.00	125	—
ND(1809)	1694P	10.00	20.00	40.00	75.00	—
ND(1809)	1695P	10.00	15.00	30.00	60.00	—
ND(1809)	1697P	7.50	12.50	25.00	45.00	—
ND(1809)	1698P	7.50	12.50	25.00	45.00	—
ND(1809)	1699P	7.50	12.50	25.00	45.00	—

KM# 283.2 40 REIS
Copper **Countermark:** Shield **Note:** Countermark on 20 Reis, with high full arch crown, KM#216.2.

CM Date	Host Date	Good	VG	F	VF	XF
ND(1809)	1786	2.50	5.00	8.00	15.00	—
ND(1809)	1787	2.50	5.00	8.00	15.00	—
ND(1809)	1790	2.50	5.00	8.00	15.00	—
ND(1809)	1799	2.50	5.00	8.00	15.00	—

KM# 283.1 40 REIS
Copper **Countermark:** Shield **Note:** Countermark on 20 Reis, with low flat arch crown, KM#216.1.

CM Date	Host Date	Good	VG	F	VF	XF
ND(1809)	1786	2.50	5.00	9.00	18.00	—
ND(1809)	1787	2.50	5.00	9.00	18.00	—
ND(1809)	1790	2.50	5.00	9.00	18.00	—
ND(1809)	1796	2.50	5.00	9.00	18.00	—
ND(1809)	1799	2.50	5.00	9.00	18.00	—

KM# 290.2 80 REIS

Copper **Countermark:** 11mm shield **Note:** Countermark on 40 Reis with high full arch crown, KM#217.2.

CM Date	Host Date	Good	VG	F	VF	XF
ND(1809)	1786	4.00	7.00	10.00	20.00	—
ND(1809)	1787	4.00	7.00	10.00	20.00	—
ND(1809)	1790	4.00	7.00	10.00	20.00	—
ND(1809)	1791	4.00	7.00	10.00	20.00	—

KM# 290.4 80 REIS

Copper **Countermark:** 8mm shield **Note:** Countermark on 40 Reis with high full arch crown, KM#217.2.

CM Date	Host Date	Good	VG	F	VF	XF
ND(1809)	1787	10.00	15.00	25.00	50.00	—

KM# 290.1 80 REIS

Copper **Countermark:** 11mm shield **Note:** Countermark on 40 Reis with low flat arch crown, KM#217.1.

CM Date	Host Date	Good	VG	F	VF	XF
ND(1809)	1786	4.00	7.00	10.00	20.00	—
ND(1809)	1790	4.00	7.00	10.00	25.00	—
ND(1809)	1791	10.00	15.00	25.00	35.00	—
ND(1809)	1796	4.00	7.00	10.00	20.00	—

KM# 290.3 80 REIS

Copper **Countermark:** 8mm shield **Note:** Countermark on 40 Reis with low flat arch crown, KM#217.1.

CM Date	Host Date	Good	VG	F	VF	XF
ND(1809)	1796	10.00	15.00	25.00	45.00	—

KM# 286 80 REIS

Copper **Countermark:** Shield **Note:** Countermark on 40 Reis, KM#111.

CM Date	Host Date	Good	VG	F	VF	XF
ND(1809)	1722	5.00	7.50	15.00	25.00	—

KM# 287 80 REIS

Copper **Countermark:** Shield **Note:** Countermark on 40 Reis, KM#184.1.

CM Date	Host Date	Good	VG	F	VF	XF
ND(1809)	1753	2.50	5.00	8.50	16.50	—
ND(1809)	1760	2.50	5.00	8.50	16.50	—
ND(1809)	1774	2.50	5.00	8.50	16.50	—

KM# 288 80 REIS

Copper **Countermark:** Shield **Note:** Countermark on 40 Reis, KM#189.

CM Date	Host Date	Good	VG	F	VF	XF
ND(1809)	1762B	2.50	5.00	8.50	16.50	—

KM# 289 80 REIS

Copper **Countermark:** Shield **Note:** Countermark on 40 Reis, KM#203.

CM Date	Host Date	Good	VG	F	VF	XF
ND(1809)	1778	2.50	5.00	8.50	16.50	—
ND(1809)	1781	2.50	5.00	8.50	16.50	—
ND(1809)	1784	2.50	5.00	8.50	16.50	—

KM# 291 80 REIS

Copper **Countermark:** Shield **Note:** Countermark on 40 Reis, KM#230.

CM Date	Host Date	Good	VG	F	VF	XF
ND(1809)	1799	10.00	17.50	35.00	75.00	—

KM# 292 80 REIS

Copper **Countermark:** Shield **Note:** Countermark on 40 Reis, KM#234.1.

CM Date	Host Date	Good	VG	F	VF	XF
ND(1809)	1802	5.00	7.50	10.00	20.00	—
ND(1809)	1803	5.00	7.50	10.00	20.00	—

KM# 293 80 REIS

2.2600 g., 0.9170 Silver .0666 oz. **Countermark:** Shield **Note:** Countermark on 75 Reis, KM#176.1.

CM Date	Host Date	Good	VG	F	VF	XF
ND(1809)	1752B	50.00	150	650	1,000	—
ND(1809)	1753B	7.00	30.00	125	200	—
ND(1809)	1754B	7.00	30.00	125	200	—

KM# 294 80 REIS

2.2600 g., 0.9170 Silver .0666 oz. **Countermark:** Shield **Note:** Countermark on 75 Reis, KM#176.2.

CM Date	Host Date	Good	VG	F	VF	XF
ND(1809)	1754R	20.00	45.00	75.00	200	—
ND(1809)	1755R	20.00	45.00	75.00	200	—
ND(1809)	1760R	27.00	60.00	150	400	—

KM# 301 80 REIS

Copper **Countermark:** Shield **Note:** Countermark on Angola XL Reis, KM#9.

CM Date	Host Date	Good	VG	F	VF	XF
ND(1809)	1757	25.00	40.00	60.00	90.00	—

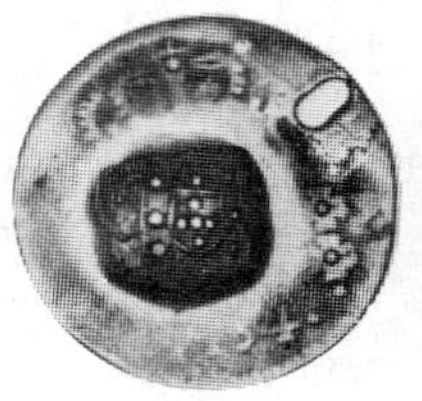

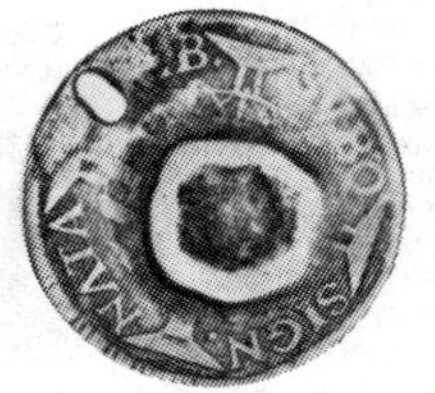

KM# 295 160 REIS

4.5200 g., 0.9170 Silver .1332 oz. **Countermark:** Shield **Note:** Countermark on 150 Reis, KM#177.

CM Date	Host Date	Good	VG	F	VF	XF
ND(1809)	1752B	9.00	60.00	250	1,200	—
ND(1809)	1753B	9.00	45.00	75.00	200	—
ND(1809)	1754B	9.00	45.00	75.00	200	—
ND(1809)	1756B	70.00	150	400	1,500	—
ND(1809)	1768B Rare	—	—	—	—	—

KM# 296 160 REIS

4.5200 g., 0.9170 Silver .1332 oz. **Countermark:** Shield **Note:** Countermark on 150 Reis, KM#185.

CM Date	Host Date	Good	VG	F	VF	XF
ND(1809)	1754R	9.00	30.00	70.00	125	—
ND(1809)	1754 R ATAN NGIS	10.00	40.00	80.00	130	—
ND(1809)	1755R	9.00	18.00	40.00	80.00	—
ND(1809)	1758R	9.00	18.00	40.00	80.00	—
ND(1809)	1760R	40.00	85.00	150	300	—
ND(1809)	1771R	30.00	75.00	100	200	—

KM# 297 320 REIS

9.0500 g., 0.9170 Silver .2668 oz. **Countermark:** Shield **Note:** Countermark on 300 Reis, KM#178.

CM Date	Host Date	Good	VG	F	VF	XF
ND(1809)	1752B	25.00	45.00	85.00	160	—
ND(1809)	1753B	19.00	35.00	65.00	120	—
ND(1809)	1754B	19.00	35.00	65.00	120	—
ND(1809)	1756B	25.00	45.00	85.00	200	—
ND(1809)	1757B	25.00	50.00	90.00	240	—
ND(1809)	1768B Rare	—	—	—	—	—

KM# 298 320 REIS

9.0500 g., 0.9170 Silver .2668 oz. **Countermark:** Shield **Note:** Countermark on 300 Reis, KM#186.

CM Date	Host Date	Good	VG	F	VF	XF
ND(1809)	1754R	12.50	30.00	45.00	85.00	—
ND(1809)	1755R	12.50	30.00	45.00	85.00	—
ND(1809)	1756R	12.50	30.00	45.00	85.00	—
ND(1809)	1757R	12.50	30.00	45.00	85.00	—
ND(1809)	1758R	12.50	30.00	45.00	85.00	—
ND(1809)	1764R	12.50	30.00	45.00	85.00	—
ND(1809)	1771R	15.00	35.00	50.00	90.00	—

KM# 299 640 REIS

18.1100 g., 0.9170 Silver .5339 oz. **Countermark:** Shield **Note:** Countermark on 600 Reis, KM#179.

CM Date	Host Date	Good	VG	F	VF	XF
ND(1809)	1752B	100	350	500	800	—
ND(1809)	1754B	30.00	60.00	105	350	—
ND(1809)	1756B	30.00	60.00	105	300	—
ND(1809)	1757B	35.00	65.00	110	200	—
ND(1809)	1758B	30.00	60.00	100	150	—
ND(1809)	1760B	50.00	200	350	680	—
ND(1809)	1768B Rare	—	—	—	—	—

KM# 300 640 REIS

18.1100 g., 0.9170 Silver .5339 oz. **Countermark:** Shield **Note:** Countermark on 600 Reis, KM#187.

CM Date	Host Date	Good	VG	F	VF	XF
ND(1809)	1754R	25.00	45.00	90.00	140	—
ND(1809)	1755R	30.00	50.00	100	150	—
ND(1809)	1756R	30.00	50.00	100	150	—
ND(1809)	1758R	30.00	50.00	100	150	—
ND(1809)	1760R	80.00	150	250	550	—
ND(1809)	1764R	25.00	30.00	50.00	75.00	—
ND(1809)	1765R	65.00	95.00	140	320	—
ND(1809)	1770R	40.00	60.00	120	220	—
ND(1809)	1771R	30.00	50.00	100	200	—
ND(1809)	1774R	30.00	50.00	100	200	—

EMPIRE

COPPER COINAGE

Regional Standard

The imperial copper coins of Brazil (1823-1833) were struck to several different standards simultaneously, each intended for a different part of the empire. The following table shows the standards used at each mint:

Weights of Imperial Brazilian copper coins in oitavos:

MINT MARK DENOMINATION (Reis)

	MARK	10	20	40	80	37½	75
Rio De Janeiro	R	1	2	4	8	—	—
Bahia	B	1	2	4	8	—	—
Goias	G	—	1	2	4	—	4
Cuiaba	C	—	1	2	4	—	—
Minas Gerais	M	—	—	—	—	2	—
Sao Paulo	SP	—	—	—	5⅓	—	—

NOTE: 1 Oitavo = 3.586 g; 8 Oitavos = 1 Onza (28.68 g); thus 5-1/3 Oitavos plus 1 Escropalo is precisely 2/3 Onza (ounce).

Lightweight Coins: Many coppers are found as much as 15 percent or more below the official weights, and even heavy specimens are occasionally observed. Most of the above coins were counterfeited, as their face value exceeded the cost of the metal and minting. Though usually crude and carelessly engraved, some counterfeits are of decent workmanship, and entirely undistinguishable from government issues. Brazilian collectors generally accept these contemporary counterfeits as collectable, due to their historical value. Before Pedro I began his regular coinage, colonial coppers were revalued with a special countermark, probably in 1822.

KM# 371.1 10 REIS

Copper

Date	Mintage	Good	VG	F	VF	XF
1824R	235,000	3.00	7.50	15.00	25.00	—

KM# 371.2 10 REIS

Copper

Date	Mintage	Good	VG	F	VF	XF
1827B	104,000	5.00	10.00	17.50	30.00	—
1828B	728,000	2.50	5.00	12.50	20.00	—

KM# 360.1 20 REIS
7.1700 g., Copper **Ruler:** Pedro I

Date	Mintage	Good	VG	F	VF	XF
1822R Counterfeit	—	—	—	—	—	—
1823R Cross on crown	1,700,000	2.00	3.00	7.00	15.00	—
1824R	4,956,000	2.00	3.00	7.00	15.00	—
1824R BRSA	Inc. above	7.00	10.00	20.00	60.00	—
1825R	9,054,000	2.00	3.00	7.00	15.00	—
1826R	4,419,000	2.00	3.00	7.00	15.00	—
1827R	4,648,000	2.00	3.00	7.00	15.00	—
1828R	4,474,000	2.00	3.00	7.00	15.00	—
1829R	6,806,000	2.00	3.00	7.00	15.00	—
1830R	—	2.00	3.00	7.00	15.00	—
1831R Counterfeit	—	—	—	—	—	—

KM# 360.2 20 REIS
Copper **Ruler:** Pedro I

Date	Mintage	VG	F	VF	XF	Unc
1825B	582,000	3.00	5.00	10.00	20.00	—
1827B	44,000	5.00	7.50	15.00	35.00	—
1828B	585,000	3.00	5.00	10.00	20.00	—
1830B	316,000	3.00	5.00	10.00	20.00	—

KM# 375.1 20 REIS
3.5900 g., Copper

Date	Mintage	Good	VG	F	VF	XF
1825C	—	15.00	30.00	80.00	150	—

KM# 375.2 20 REIS
3.5900 g., Copper **Ruler:** Pedro I

Date	Mintage	Good	VG	F	VF	XF
1829G Counterfeit	—	—	—	—	—	—

KM# 380 20 REIS
7.1700 g., Copper **Ruler:** Pedro II

Date	Mintage	Good	VG	F	VF	XF
1832R	14,000	35.00	75.00	150	250	—

KM# 362 37-1/2 REIS
7.1700 g., Copper **Ruler:** Pedro I

Date	Mintage	Good	VG	F	VF	XF
1823M	—	15.00	30.00	55.00	100	—
1824M	—	10.00	22.00	45.00	90.00	—
1825M	—	10.00	22.00	45.00	90.00	—
1826M	—	10.00	22.00	45.00	90.00	—
1827M	—	10.00	22.00	45.00	90.00	—
1828M	—	10.00	22.00	45.00	90.00	—

KM# 363.1 40 REIS
14.3400 g., Copper **Ruler:** Pedro I

Date	Mintage	Good	VG	F	VF	XF
1823R	920,000	—	5.00	7.50	15.00	25.00
1824R	9,170,000	—	2.50	5.00	7.50	20.00
1825R	6,774,000	—	2.50	5.00	7.50	20.00
1826R Cross on crown	10,507,000	—	2.50	5.00	7.50	20.00
1826R	Inc. above	—	15.00	30.00	50.00	90.00
1827R	17,892,000	—	2.50	5.00	10.00	20.00
1828R	15,570,000	—	2.50	5.00	10.00	20.00
1829R	8,924,000	—	2.50	5.00	10.00	20.00
1830R	—	—	2.50	5.00	10.00	20.00
1831/0R	—	—	5.00	7.50	15.00	35.00
1831R	—	—	2.50	5.00	10.00	20.00

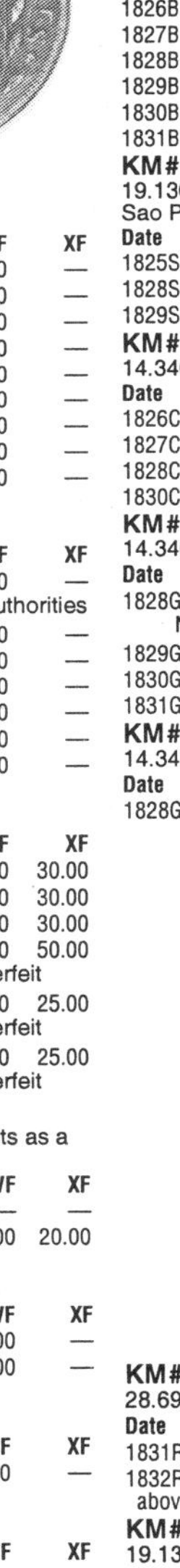

KM# 364.1 40 REIS
7.1700 g., Copper **Ruler:** Pedro I

Date	Mintage	Good	VG	F	VF	XF
1823C	—	7.50	15.00	20.00	35.00	—
1824C	—	5.00	9.00	15.00	30.00	—
1825C	—	5.00	9.00	15.00	30.00	—
1826C	—	5.00	9.00	15.00	30.00	—
1827C	—	5.00	9.00	15.00	30.00	—
1828C	—	5.00	9.00	15.00	30.00	—
1829C	—	5.00	9.00	15.00	30.00	—
1830C	—	5.00	9.00	15.00	30.00	—
1831C	—	7.50	15.00	20.00	35.00	—

KM# 364.2 40 REIS
7.1700 g., Copper **Ruler:** Pedro I

Date	Mintage	Good	VG	F	VF	XF
1823G	—	7.50	12.50	25.00	50.00	—

Note: 1823C is considered a counterfeit by many authorities

Date	Mintage	Good	VG	F	VF	XF
1825G	—	5.00	7.50	15.00	30.00	—
1826G	—	7.50	12.50	25.00	50.00	—
1827G	—	5.00	7.50	15.00	30.00	—
1828G	—	5.00	7.50	15.00	30.00	—
1829G	—	5.00	7.50	15.00	30.00	—
1830G	—	5.00	7.50	15.00	30.00	—

KM# 363.2 40 REIS
14.3400 g., Copper **Ruler:** Pedro I

Date	Mintage	Good	VG	F	VF	XF
1824B	230,000	—	5.00	7.50	15.00	30.00
1825B	Inc. above	—	5.00	7.50	15.00	30.00
1827B	161,000	—	5.00	7.50	15.00	30.00
1828B	51,000	—	7.50	12.50	20.00	50.00

Note: Most known examples of 1828R are counterfeit

Date	Mintage	Good	VG	F	VF	XF
1829B	2,052,000	—	2.50	5.00	10.00	25.00

Note: Most known examples of 1829R are counterfeit

Date	Mintage	Good	VG	F	VF	XF
1830B	1,032,000	—	2.50	5.00	10.00	25.00

Note: Most known examples of 1830R are counterfeit

KM# 378 40 REIS
14.3400 g., Copper **Ruler:** Pedro II **Note:** 1833R exists as a pattern.

Date	Mintage	Good	VG	F	VF	XF
1831R Counterfeit	—	—	—	—	—	—
1832R	816,000	—	2.50	5.00	10.00	20.00

KM# 381.1 40 REIS
7.1700 g., Copper **Ruler:** Pedro II

Date	Mintage	Good	VG	F	VF	XF
1832G Petrus II	—	5.00	10.00	25.00	50.00	—
1832G Petrus 2.0	—	7.50	15.00	35.00	75.00	—

KM# 381.2 40 REIS
7.1700 g., Copper **Ruler:** Pedro II

Date	Mintage	Good	VG	F	VF	XF
1833C	—	5.00	10.00	20.00	45.00	—

KM# 365 75 REIS
14.3400 g., Copper **Ruler:** Pedro I

Date	Mintage	Good	VG	F	VF	XF
1823G	—	25.00	50.00	100	200	—

KM# 366.1 80 REIS
28.6900 g., Copper **Ruler:** Pedro I

Date	Mintage	Good	VG	F	VF	XF
1823R	100,000	—	10.00	15.00	25.00	50.00
1824R	825,000	—	7.50	10.00	15.00	30.00
1825R	1,026,999	—	7.50	10.00	15.00	30.00
1826R	10,507,000	—	2.50	5.00	10.00	25.00
1827R	17,892,000	—	2.50	5.00	10.00	25.00
1828R	26,524,000	—	2.50	5.00	10.00	25.00
1829R	20,180,000	—	2.50	5.00	10.00	25.00
1830R	—	—	2.50	5.00	10.00	25.00
1831R	—	—	2.50	5.00	10.00	25.00

KM# 366.2 80 REIS
28.6900 g., Copper **Ruler:** Pedro I **Note:** Coins with P mint mark are all counterfeit. Counterfeits of the 1831 B are common.

Date	Mintage	Good	VG	F	VF	XF
1824B	879,000	—	5.00	8.00	15.00	30.00
1825B	Inc. above	—	5.00	8.00	15.00	30.00
1826B	695,000	—	5.00	8.00	15.00	30.00
1827B	352,000	—	5.00	10.00	17.50	40.00
1828B	2,539,000	—	3.50	7.00	15.00	30.00
1829B	3,993,000	—	3.50	7.00	15.00	30.00
1830B	359,000	—	5.00	8.50	16.50	35.00
1831B	—	—	10.00	20.00	60.00	120

KM# 376 80 REIS
19.1300 g., Copper **Ruler:** Pedro I **Note:** Many varieties of the Sao Paulo coins exist.

Date	Mintage	Good	VG	F	VF	XF
1825SP	—	10.00	17.50	35.00	75.00	—
1828SP	—	5.00	8.50	16.50	35.00	—
1829SP	—	7.50	12.50	20.00	45.00	—

KM# 377.1 80 REIS
14.3400 g., Copper **Ruler:** Pedro I

Date	Mintage	Good	VG	F	VF	XF
1826C	—	5.00	7.50	15.00	35.00	—
1827C	—	15.00	25.00	40.00	90.00	—
1828C	—	7.50	10.00	20.00	45.00	—
1830C	—	10.00	30.00	60.00	100	—

KM# 377.2 80 REIS
14.3400 g., Copper **Ruler:** Pedro I

Date	Mintage	Good	VG	F	VF	XF
1828G	—	7.50	12.50	17.50	40.00	—

Note: Coins dated 1826G are believed to be counterfeit

Date	Mintage	Good	VG	F	VF	XF
1829G	—	7.50	12.50	17.50	40.00	—
1830G	—	7.50	12.50	17.50	40.00	—
1831G	—	10.00	15.00	25.00	65.00	—

KM# 377.3 80 REIS
14.3400 g., Copper **Ruler:** Pedro I **Rev:** Arms without stars

Date	Mintage	Good	VG	F	VF	XF
1828G	—	30.00	50.00	70.00	100	—

KM# 379 80 REIS
28.6900 g., Copper **Ruler:** Pedro II **Rev:** Similar to KM#366.1

Date	Mintage	Good	VG	F	VF	XF
1831R	—	—	5.00	7.50	15.00	35.00
1832R Cross above crown	6,119,000	—	2.50	5.00	12.50	25.00

KM# 382 80 REIS
19.1300 g., Copper **Ruler:** Pedro II

Date	Mintage	Good	VG	F	VF	XF
1832SP	—	30.00	70.00	120	200	—

Note: The 1832SP is considered a counterfeit by many authorities

KM# 383 80 REIS
14.3400 g., Copper **Ruler:** Pedro II

Date	Mintage	Good	VG	F	VF	XF
1832G	—	5.00	7.50	15.00	30.00	—
1833G	—	5.00	7.50	15.00	30.00	—
1833G	—	50.00	90.00	150	225	—

SILVER COINAGE

National Standard

KM# 372 80 REIS
2.2400 g., 0.9170 Silver .0660 oz. **Obv:** Around value in floral circle **Obv. Legend:** PETRUS I D.G.. **Rev:** Crowned arms in branches

Date	Mintage	F	VF	XF	Unc	BU
1824R	—	200	450	1,100	2,000	—
1826R	—	200	450	1,200	2,250	—

KM# 388 80 REIS
2.2400 g., 0.9170 Silver .0660 oz. **Rev. Legend:** PETRUS II D.G..

Date	Mintage	F	VF	XF	Unc	BU
1833R	418	180	300	750	1,500	—

KM# 373 160 REIS
4.4800 g., 0.9170 Silver .1320 oz. **Obv. Legend:** PETRUS I D.G..

Date	Mintage	F	VF	XF	Unc	BU
1824R	—	200	400	850	2,000	—
1826R	—	200	400	850	2,000	—

KM# 389 160 REIS
4.4800 g., 0.9170 Silver .1320 oz. **Obv. Legend:** PETRUS II D.G..

Date	Mintage	F	VF	XF	Unc	BU
1833R	492	300	600	1,350	2,500	—

KM# 374 320 REIS
8.9600 g., 0.9170 Silver .2640 oz. **Obv. Legend:** PETRUS I D.G..

Date	Mintage	F	VF	XF	Unc	BU
1824R Rare	642	—	—	—	—	—
1825R Cross above crown	18,000	20.00	40.00	90.00	175	—
1826R	—	800	1,450	2,250	—	—
1827R Unique	—	—	—	—	—	—
1830R Rare	4,190	—	—	—	—	—

KM# 390 320 REIS
8.9600 g., 0.9170 Silver .2640 oz. **Obv. Legend:** PETRUS II D.G..

Date	Mintage	F	VF	XF	Unc	BU
1833R Rare	22	—	—	—	—	—

KM# 367 640 REIS
17.9200 g., 0.9170 Silver .5280 oz. **Obv. Legend:** PETRUS I D.G..

Date	Mintage	F	VF	XF	Unc	BU
1823R Counterfeit	—	—	—	—	—	—
1824/3R	80,000	10.00	25.00	50.00	85.00	—
1824R	Inc. above	10.00	25.00	50.00	85.00	—
1825R	353,000	10.00	25.00	50.00	85.00	—
1826R	9,472	500	1,000	2,550	3,850	—
1827R	Inc. above	600	1,250	2,800	4,000	—

KM# 384 640 REIS
17.9200 g., 0.9170 Silver .5280 oz. **Obv. Legend:** PETRUS II D.G..

Date	Mintage	F	VF	XF	Unc	BU
1832R Rare	118	—	—	—	—	—
1833R Rare	5	—	—	—	—	—

KM# 368.1 960 REIS
26.8900 g., 0.8960 Silver .7746 oz. **Note:** KM#368 is occasionally found struck over Spanish Colonial 8 Reales. Specimens having the original elements visible command a premium. Discernable mint mark, assayer initial and date all factor into premium values. See note for Colonial 960 Reis, KM#326.2 for additional information.

Date	Mintage	F	VF	XF	Unc	BU
1823R SIGNO above crown	395,000	12.50	25.00	45.00	85.00	—
1823R IGNO above crown	Inc. above	150	350	650	1,000	—
1824R	600,000	12.50	25.00	45.00	85.00	—
1825R Small 960	600,000	12.50	25.00	50.00	90.00	—
1825R Large 960	Inc. above	50.00	160	400	600	—
1826R Cross above crown	500,000	12.50	25.00	50.00	90.00	—
1827R	18,000	1,450	2,750	4,500	—	—
1828R Counterfeit	—	—	—	—	—	—

KM# 368.2 960 REIS
26.8900 g., 0.8960 Silver .7746 oz. **Note:** KM#368 is occasionally found struck over Spanish Colonial 8 Reales. Specimens having the original elements visible command a premium. Discernable mint mark, assayer initial and date all factor into premium values. See note for Colonial 960 Reis, KM#326.2 for additional information.

Date	Mintage	F	VF	XF	Unc	BU
1824B	—	40.00	80.00	140	200	—
1825B	—	40.00	80.00	140	200	—
1826B	—	200	450	1,000	1,750	—

KM# 385 960 REIS
26.8900 g., 0.8960 Silver .7746 oz.

Date	Mintage	F	VF	XF	Unc	BU
1832R	3,039	450	850	1,750	3,000	—
1833R	Inc. above	850	1,750	3,500	6,000	—
1834R	154	2,000	4,500	8,500	14,500	—

GOLD COINAGE

National Standard

KM# 369.1 4000 REIS
8.2000 g., 0.9170 Gold .2417 oz.

Date	Mintage	F	VF	XF	Unc	BU
1823R	21,000	250	450	650	1,200	—
1824R	38,000	250	450	650	1,200	—
1825R	20,000	250	450	650	1,400	—
1826R	9,142	350	650	1,450	2,000	—
1827/6R	7,771	3,000	6,000	12,000	—	—
1827R	Inc. above	3,000	6,000	12,000	—	—

KM# 369.2 4000 REIS
8.2000 g., 0.9170 Gold .2417 oz.

Date	Mintage	F	VF	XF	Unc	BU
1825B	—	1,200	2,500	6,000	12,500	—
1826B	—	1,500	3,000	7,000	15,000	—
1828B	—	3,000	5,000	—	—	—

KM# 386.1 4000 REIS
8.2000 g., 0.9170 Gold .2417 oz.

Date	Mintage	F	VF	XF	Unc	BU
1832B Rare	64	—	—	—	—	—
Note: Spink America Norweb sale 3-97 Unc realized $14,300						
1833/2R	257	4,500	7,500	12,500	—	—

KM# 386.2 4000 REIS
8.2000 g., 0.9170 Gold .2417 oz. **Obv:** AZEVEDO below bust

Date	Mintage	F	VF	XF	Unc	BU
1832 Rare, 5 known	—	—	—	—	—	—

KM# 361 6400 REIS
14.3400 g., 0.9170 Gold .4228 oz. **Subject:** Pedro I Coronation

Date	Mintage	F	VF	XF	Unc	BU
1822 Rare	64	—	—	—	—	—

Note: Spink London sale No. 52, 6-86 near XF realized $87,000. Spink America Norweb sale 3-97 choice VF realized $82,500

KM# 370.1 6400 REIS
14.3400 g., 0.9170 Gold .4228 oz.

Date	Mintage	F	VF	XF	Unc	BU
1823R	931	1,200	4,500	6,000	9,000	—
1824R	235	2,000	5,000	8,000	12,500	—
1825R	776	1,500	4,500	6,500	11,500	—
1827R	637	1,500	4,500	6,500	11,500	—
1828R	650	1,500	4,500	6,500	11,500	—
1830R Unique	—	—	—	—	—	—

KM# 370.2 6400 REIS
14.3400 g., 0.9170 Gold .4228 oz.

Date	Mintage	F	VF	XF	Unc	BU
1825B	—	3,000	5,500	9,000	13,500	—
1826B	—	3,000	5,500	9,000	13,500	—
1828B	423	3,000	5,500	9,000	13,500	—

KM# 387.1 6400 REIS
14.3400 g., 0.9170 Gold .4228 oz.

Date	Mintage	F	VF	XF	Unc	BU
1832R	30,000	450	850	1,650	2,500	—
1833R	11,000	450	850	1,650	2,500	—

KM# 387.2 6400 REIS
14.3400 g., 0.9170 Gold .4228 oz. **Obv:** AZEVEDO below bust

Date	Mintage	F	VF	XF	Unc	BU
1832R	4,101	500	1,500	3,000	4,500	—

COUNTERMARKED COINAGE

Imperial Countermarks

These countermarks consist of a crowned 20, 40, or 80 within a wreath in a circle and opposite a shield in a circle is used.

KM# 355 20 REIS
Copper **Countermark:** Crowned 20 in sprays **Note:** Countermark on various Colonial 10 Reis.

CM Date	Host Date	Good	VG	F	VF	XF
ND(1822)	ND	900	1,500	2,500	3,750	—

Note: Many authorities consider all known examples of KM#355 to be counterfeit

KM# 358 40 REIS
Copper **Countermark:** Crowned 40 **Note:** Countermark on various 10 Reis.

CM Date	Host Date	Good	VG	F	VF	XF
ND(1822)	ND	750	1,250	2,000	3,500	—

KM# 356 40 REIS
Copper **Countermark:** Crowned 40 in sprays **Note:** Countermark on various Colonial 20 Reis.

CM Date	Host Date	Good	VG	F	VF	XF
ND(1822)	ND	700	1,150	1,850	2,750	—

Note: Three of eight known dies are believed counterfeit

KM# 359 80 REIS
Copper **Countermark:** Crowned 80 **Note:** Countermark on 75 Reis.

CM Date	Host Date	Good	VG	F	VF	XF
ND(1822)	ND Rare	—	—	—	—	—

KM# 354 80 REIS
Copper **Countermark:** 80 **Note:** Countermark on Colonial 20 Reis.

CM Date	Host Date	Good	VG	F	VF	XF
ND(1822)	ND	1,250	2,250	3,500	5,500	—

KM# 357 80 REIS
Copper **Countermark:** Crowned 80 in sprays **Note:** Countermark on various Colonial 40 Reis.

CM Date	Host Date	Good	VG	F	VF	XF
ND(1822)	ND	1,500	2,500	4,200	6,500	—

Note: One of 11 known dies is believed counterfeit

COUNTERMARKED COINAGE

National - 1835

In order to prevent chaotic conditions resulting from local and private countermarking, the government passed Law #54 of 6 October 1835 ordering all coppers countermarked according to the following standards:

2 Oitavos = 7.18 g = 10 Reis
4 Oitavos = 14.34 g = 20 Reis
8 Oitavos = 28.69 g = 40 Reis

The countermarks consist of neat numerals within a circle, having a plain or shaded field. These countermarks were applied to various Brazilian coinage from 1799-1833. In addition, wrong countermarks are occasionally found, as well as various Portuguese, Angolan, San Tome, Mozambiquean, and pre-1799 Brazilian coins.

KM# 418 10 REIS
Copper **Countermark:** 10 **Note:** Countermark on XX (20) Reis, KM#309.

CM Date	Host Date	Good	VG	F	VF	XF
ND(1835)	1817	3.50	7.00	14.00	28.00	—
ND(1835)	1816	3.50	7.00	14.00	28.00	—
ND(1835)	1818	5.00	10.00	18.00	35.00	—

KM# 417.3 10 REIS
Copper **Countermark:** 10 **Note:** Countermark on XX (20) Reis, KM#233.1.

CM Date	Host Date	Good	VG	F	VF	XF
ND(1835)	1812R	3.50	7.00	14.00	28.00	—
ND(1835)	1813R	3.50	7.00	14.00	28.00	—
ND(1835)	1814R	3.50	7.00	14.00	28.00	—
ND(1835)	1815R	3.50	7.00	14.00	28.00	—

KM# 417.1 10 REIS
Copper **Countermark:** 10 **Note:** Countermark on XX (20) Reis, KM#233.1.

CM Date	Host Date	Good	VG	F	VF	XF
ND(1835)	1802	2.75	5.50	12.00	20.00	—
ND(1835)	1803	2.75	5.50	12.00	20.00	—
ND(1835)	1805	2.75	5.50	12.00	20.00	—

KM# 417.2 10 REIS
Copper **Countermark:** 10 **Note:** Countermark on XX (20) Reis, KM#233.1.

CM Date	Host Date	Good	VG	F	VF	XF
ND(1835)	1812B	3.50	6.50	12.50	20.00	—
ND(1835)	1813B	2.75	5.50	8.00	18.00	—

CM Date	Host Date	Good	VG	F	VF	XF
ND(1835)	1815B	2.75	5.50	8.00	18.00	—
ND(1835)	1816B	2.75	5.50	8.00	18.00	—

KM# 427.2 10 REIS
Copper **Countermark:** 10 **Note:** Countermark on 40 Reis of Pedro I, KM#364.2.

CM Date	Host Date	Good	VG	F	VF	XF
ND(1835)	1823G	5.00	7.50	15.00	30.00	—
ND(1835)	1825G	5.00	7.50	15.00	30.00	—
ND(1835)	1826G	5.00	7.50	15.00	30.00	—
ND(1835)	1827G	2.50	5.00	12.50	20.00	—
ND(1835)	1828G	2.50	5.00	12.50	20.00	—
ND(1835)	1829G	2.50	5.00	12.50	20.00	—
ND(1835)	1830G	2.50	5.00	12.50	20.00	—

KM# 428.1 10 REIS
Copper **Countermark:** 10 **Note:** Countermark on 40 Reis of Pedro II, KM#81.1.

CM Date	Host Date	Good	VG	F	VF	XF
ND(1835)	1832 PETRUS II	3.00	7.50	12.50	20.00	—
ND(1835)	1832 Petrus 2.0	3.00	7.50	12.50	20.00	—

KM# 429 10 REIS
Copper **Countermark:** 10 **Note:** Countermark on Mozambique 40 Reis, KM#19.

CM Date	Host Date	Good	VG	F	VF	XF
ND(1835)	1819C	5.00	10.00	15.00	30.00	—
ND(1835)	1820C	5.00	10.00	15.00	30.00	—
ND(1835)	1821C	5.00	10.00	15.00	30.00	—
ND(1835)	1822C	5.00	10.00	17.50	45.00	—
ND(1835)	1825C	5.00	10.00	17.50	45.00	—

KM# 419 10 REIS
Copper **Countermark:** 10 **Note:** Countermark on XL (40) Reis, KM#318.

CM Date	Host Date	Good	VG	F	VF	XF
ND(1835)	1818	15.00	20.00	30.00	45.00	—

KM# 428.2 10 REIS
Copper **Countermark:** 10

CM Date	Host Date	Good	VG	F	VF	XF
ND(1835)	1833C	5.00	7.50	15.00	35.00	—

KM# 423.2 10 REIS
Copper **Countermark:** 10 **Note:** Countermark on 20 Reis of Pedro I, KM#360.2.

CM Date	Host Date	Good	VG	F	VF	XF
ND(1835)	1825B	3.00	5.00	9.00	17.50	—
ND(1835)	1827B	3.00	5.00	9.00	17.50	—
ND(1835)	1828B	3.00	5.00	9.00	17.50	—
ND(1835)	1830B	3.00	5.00	9.00	17.50	—

KM# 424.2 10 REIS
Copper **Countermark:** 10 **Note:** Countermark on 20 Reis of Pedro I, KM#375.1.

CM Date	Host Date	Good	VG	F	VF	XF
ND(1835)	1827G	20.00	32.50	50.00	100	—

KM# 424.1 10 REIS
Copper **Countermark:** 10 **Note:** Countermark on 20 Reis of Pedro I, KM#375.1. The below two pieces were not supposed to have been countermarked, as they only weigh one oitavo-3.59 grams.

CM Date	Host Date	Good	VG	F	VF	XF
ND(1835)	1825C	50.00	100	150	240	—

KM# 425 10 REIS
Copper **Countermark:** 10 **Note:** Countermark on 20 Reis of Pedro II, KM#380.

CM Date	Host Date	Good	VG	F	VF	XF
ND(1835)	1832R	30.00	70.00	120	200	—

KM# 423.1 10 REIS
Copper **Countermark:** 10 **Note:** Countermark on 20 Reis, Pedro I, KM#360.1.

CM Date	Host Date	Good	VG	F	VF	XF
ND(1835)	1823R	2.50	4.50	7.50	15.00	—
ND(1835)	1824R	2.50	4.50	7.50	15.00	—
ND(1835)	1825R	2.50	4.50	7.50	15.00	—
ND(1835)	1826R	2.50	4.50	7.50	15.00	—
ND(1835)	1827R	2.50	4.50	7.50	15.00	—
ND(1835)	1828R	2.50	4.50	7.50	15.00	—
ND(1835)	1829R	2.50	4.50	7.50	15.00	—
ND(1835)	1830R	2.50	4.50	7.50	15.00	—

KM# 426 10 REIS
Copper **Countermark:** 10 **Note:** Countermark on 37-1/2 Reis of Pedro I.

CM Date	Host Date	Good	VG	F	VF	XF
ND(1835)	1823M	10.00	22.00	45.00	85.00	—
ND(1835)	1824M	10.00	22.00	45.00	85.00	—
ND(1835)	1825M	10.00	22.00	45.00	85.00	—
ND(1835)	1826M	10.00	22.00	45.00	85.00	—
ND(1835)	1827M	10.00	22.00	45.00	85.00	—

KM# 427.1 10 REIS

Copper **Countermark:** 10 **Note:** Countermark on 40 Reis of Pedro I, KM#364.1.

CM Date	Host Date	Good	VG	F	VF	XF
ND(1835)	1824C	2.50	5.00	7.50	15.00	—
ND(1835)	1825C	2.50	5.00	7.50	15.00	—
ND(1835)	1826C	2.50	5.00	7.50	15.00	—
ND(1835)	1827C	2.50	5.00	7.50	15.00	—
ND(1835)	1828C	2.50	5.00	7.50	15.00	—
ND(1835)	1829C	2.50	5.00	7.50	15.00	—
ND(1835)	1830C	2.50	5.00	7.50	15.00	—
ND(1835)	1831C	2.50	5.00	7.50	15.00	—
ND(1835)	1832C	4.50	7.50	12.50	20.00	—

KM# 420.1 10 REIS

Copper **Countermark:** 10 **Note:** Countermark on XX (20) Reis, KM#316.1.

CM Date	Host Date	Good	VG	F	VF	XF
ND(1835)	1818	2.75	5.50	8.00	18.00	—
ND(1835)	1819	2.75	5.50	8.00	18.00	—
ND(1835)	1820	2.75	5.50	8.00	18.00	—
ND(1835)	1821	2.75	5.50	8.00	18.00	—
ND(1835)	1822	2.75	5.50	8.00	18.00	—

KM# 420.2 10 REIS

Copper **Countermark:** 10 **Note:** Countermark on XX (20) Reis, KM#316.1.

CM Date	Host Date	Good	VG	F	VF	XF
ND(1835)	1820B	3.50	6.50	12.50	20.00	—
ND(1835)	1821B	3.50	6.50	12.50	20.00	—

KM# 421.2 10 REIS

Copper **Countermark:** 10 **Note:** Countermark on XX (20) Reis, KM#316.1.

CM Date	Host Date	Good	VG	F	VF	XF
ND(1835)	1818	12.50	30.00	50.00	110	—

KM# 422 10 REIS

Copper **Countermark:** 10 **Note:** Without mint mark. Countermark on XL (40) Reis, KM#340.

CM Date	Host Date	Good	VG	F	VF	XF
ND(1835)	1820	25.00	75.00	100	150	—

KM# 416 10 REIS

Copper **Countermark:** 10 **Note:** Without mint mark. Countermark on XX (20) Reis, KM#229.

CM Date	Host Date	Good	VG	F	VF	XF
ND(1835)	1799	6.00	10.00	20.00	40.00	—

KM# 431.2 20 REIS

Copper **Countermark:** 20

CM Date	Host Date	Good	VG	F	VF	XF
ND(1835)	1809B	3.00	6.00	12.00	25.00	—
ND(1835)	1810B	3.00	6.00	12.00	25.00	—
ND(1835)	1811B	2.50	4.50	9.00	18.00	—
ND(1835)	1812B	2.50	3.50	6.00	12.00	—
ND(1835)	1814B	2.50	3.50	6.00	12.00	—
ND(1835)	1816B	2.50	3.50	6.00	12.00	—

KM# 436.1 20 REIS

Copper **Countermark:** 20 **Note:** Countermark on 40 Reis of Pedro I, KM#363.1.

CM Date	Host Date	Good	VG	F	VF	XF
ND(1835)	1823R	2.50	5.00	7.50	15.00	—
ND(1835)	1824R	2.50	5.00	7.50	15.00	—
ND(1835)	1825R	2.50	5.00	7.50	15.00	—
ND(1835)	1826R	2.50	5.00	7.50	15.00	—
ND(1835)	1827R	2.50	5.00	7.50	15.00	—
ND(1835)	1828R	2.50	5.00	7.50	15.00	—
ND(1835)	1829R	2.50	5.00	7.50	15.00	—
ND(1835)	1830R	2.50	5.00	7.50	15.00	—
ND(1835)	1831R	2.50	5.00	7.50	15.00	—

KM# 436.2 20 REIS

Copper **Countermark:** 20 **Note:** Countermark on 40 Reis of Pedro I, KM#363.1.

CM Date	Host Date	Good	VG	F	VF	XF
ND(1835)	1824B	2.50	5.00	8.00	16.00	—
ND(1835)	1825B	2.50	5.00	8.00	16.00	—
ND(1835)	1827B	2.50	5.00	8.00	16.00	—
ND(1835)	1828B	2.50	5.00	8.00	16.00	—
ND(1835)	1829B	2.50	5.00	8.00	16.00	—
ND(1835)	1830B	2.50	5.00	8.00	16.00	—

KM# 437 20 REIS

Copper **Countermark:** 20 **Note:** Countermark on 40 Reis of Pedro II, KM#378.

CM Date	Host Date	Good	VG	F	VF	XF
ND(1835)	1831R	2.50	5.00	7.50	15.00	—
ND(1835)	1832R	2.50	5.00	7.50	15.00	—

KM# 438 20 REIS

Copper **Countermark:** 20 **Note:** Countermark on 75 Reis of Pedro I, KM#365.

CM Date	Host Date	Good	VG	F	VF	XF
ND(1835)	1823G	10.00	25.00	40.00	75.00	—

KM# 434 20 REIS

Copper **Countermark:** 20 **Note:** Countermark on 75 Reis, KM#320.

CM Date	Host Date	Good	VG	F	VF	XF
ND(1835)	1818M	7.50	15.00	30.00	65.00	—
ND(1835)	1819M	7.50	15.00	30.00	65.00	—
ND(1835)	1819M Medal strike	7.50	15.00	30.00	60.00	—
ND(1835)	1821M	7.50	15.00	30.00	60.00	—

KM# 439.1 20 REIS

Copper **Countermark:** 20 **Note:** Countermark on 80 Reis of Pedro I, KM#377.1.

CM Date	Host Date	Good	VG	F	VF	XF
ND(1835)	1826C	5.00	7.50	10.00	15.00	—
ND(1835)	1827C	7.50	10.00	15.00	35.00	—
ND(1835)	1828C	5.00	7.50	10.00	17.50	—
ND(1835)	1830C	5.00	7.50	10.00	17.50	—

KM# 439.2 20 REIS

Copper **Countermark:** 20 **Note:** Countermark on 80 Reis of Pedro I, KM#377.1.

CM Date	Host Date	Good	VG	F	VF	XF
ND(1835)	1826G	3.50	5.00	7.50	20.00	—
ND(1835)	1828G	3.50	5.00	7.50	15.00	—
ND(1835)	1829G	3.50	5.00	7.50	15.00	—
ND(1835)	1830G	3.50	5.00	7.50	15.00	—
ND(1835)	1831G	7.50	12.50	20.00	50.00	—

KM# 440 20 REIS

Copper **Countermark:** 20 **Note:** Countermark on 80 Reis of Pedro II, KM#383.

CM Date	Host Date	Good	VG	F	VF	XF
ND(1835)	1832G	3.50	5.00	7.50	15.00	—
ND(1835)	1833G	3.50	5.00	7.50	15.00	—
ND(1835)	1833G Petrus I	10.00	25.00	50.00	100	—

KM# 441 20 REIS

Countermark: 20 **Note:** Countermark on Mozambique 80 Reis, KM#20.

CM Date	Host Date	Good	VG	F	VF	XF
ND(1835)	1819G	7.50	15.00	25.00	50.00	—
ND(1835)	1820G	7.50	15.00	25.00	50.00	—

KM# 431.1 20 REIS

Copper **Countermark:** 20 **Note:** Countermark on XL (40) Reis, KM#234.1.

CM Date	Host Date	Good	VG	F	VF	XF
ND(1835)	1802	2.50	3.50	6.00	12.00	—
ND(1835)	1803	2.50	3.50	6.00	12.00	—

KM# 431.3 20 REIS

Copper **Countermark:** 20 **Note:** Countermark on XL (40) Reis, KM#234.1.

CM Date	Host Date	Good	VG	F	VF	XF
ND(1835)	1812R	2.50	5.50	12.00	25.00	—
ND(1835)	1813R	2.50	5.50	12.00	25.00	—
ND(1835)	1815R	2.50	5.50	12.00	25.00	—

KM# 432 20 REIS

Copper **Countermark:** 20 **Note:** Countermark on XL (40) Reis, KM#311.

CM Date	Host Date	Good	VG	F	VF	XF
ND(1835)	1816R	2.50	5.50	12.00	25.00	—
ND(1835)	1817R	2.50	5.50	12.00	25.00	—

KM# 433.1 20 REIS

Copper **Countermark:** 20 **Note:** Countermark on XL (40) Reis, KM#319.1.

CM Date	Host Date	Good	VG	F	VF	XF
ND(1835)	1818R	2.50	4.50	9.00	18.00	—
ND(1835)	1819R	2.50	4.50	9.00	18.00	—
ND(1835)	1820R	2.50	4.50	9.00	18.00	—
ND(1835)	1821R	2.50	4.50	9.00	18.00	—
ND(1835)	1822R	2.50	4.50	9.00	18.00	—

KM# 433.2 20 REIS

Copper **Countermark:** 20 **Note:** Countermark on XL (40) Reis, KM#319.1.

CM Date	Host Date	Good	VG	F	VF	XF
ND(1835)	1820B	3.00	6.00	12.00	25.00	—
ND(1835)	1821B	3.00	6.00	12.00	25.00	—
ND(1835)	1822B	3.00	6.00	12.00	25.00	—
ND(1835)	1823B	5.00	8.00	15.00	30.00	—

KM# 435 20 REIS

Copper **Countermark:** 20 **Note:** Without mint mark. countermark on LXXX (80) Reis, KM#341.

CM Date	Host Date	Good	VG	F	VF	XF
ND(1835)	1820	7.50	15.00	25.00	50.00	—

KM# 430 20 REIS

Copper **Countermark:** 20 **Note:** Without mint mark. Countermark on XL (40) Reis, KM#230.

CM Date	Host Date	Good	VG	F	VF	XF
ND(1835)	1799	5.00	8.00	14.00	25.00	—

KM# 444.1 40 REIS

Copper **Countermark:** 40 **Note:** Countermark on 80 Reis of Pedro I, KM#366.1.

CM Date	Host Date	Good	VG	F	VF	XF
ND(1835)	1823R	5.00	7.50	10.00	20.00	—
ND(1835)	1824R	2.50	5.00	7.50	12.50	—
ND(1835)	1825R	2.50	5.00	7.50	12.50	—
ND(1835)	1826R	2.50	5.00	7.50	12.50	—
ND(1835)	1827R	2.50	5.00	7.50	12.50	—
ND(1835)	1828R	2.50	5.00	7.50	12.50	—
ND(1835)	1829R	2.50	5.00	7.50	12.50	—
ND(1835)	1830R	2.50	5.00	7.50	12.50	—
ND(1835)	1831R	2.50	5.00	7.50	12.50	—

KM# 444.2 40 REIS

Copper **Countermark:** 40 **Note:** Countermark on 80 Reis of Pedro I, KM#366.1.

CM Date	Host Date	Good	VG	F	VF	XF
ND(1835)	1824B	2.50	5.00	7.50	12.50	—
ND(1835)	1825B	2.50	5.00	7.50	12.50	—
ND(1835)	1826B	2.50	5.00	7.50	12.50	—
ND(1835)	1827B	2.50	5.00	7.50	12.50	—
ND(1835)	1828B	2.50	5.00	7.50	12.50	—
ND(1835)	1829B	2.50	5.00	7.50	12.50	—
ND(1835)	1830B	2.50	5.00	7.50	12.50	—
ND(1835)	1831B	3.50	7.50	12.50	25.00	—

KM# 445 40 REIS

Copper **Countermark:** 40 **Note:** Countermark on 80 Reis of Pedro I, KM#376.

CM Date	Host Date	Good	VG	F	VF	XF
ND(1835)	1825SP	7.50	12.50	17.50	35.00	—
ND(1835)	1828SP	7.50	12.50	17.50	35.00	—
ND(1835)	1829SP	7.50	12.50	17.50	35.00	—

KM# 446 40 REIS

Copper **Countermark:** 40 **Note:** Countermark on 80 Reis of Pedro II, KM#379.

CM Date	Host Date	Good	VG	F	VF	XF
ND(1835)	1831R	7.50	12.50	20.00	30.00	—
ND(1835)	1832R	5.00	7.50	10.00	20.00	—

KM# 447 40 REIS

Copper **Countermark:** 40 **Note:** Countermark on 80 Reis of Pedro II, KM#382.

CM Date	Host Date	Good	VG	F	VF	XF
ND(1835)	1832SP	40.00	75.00	125	180	—

KM# 442 40 REIS

Copper **Countermark:** 40 **Note:** Countermark on LXXX (80) Reis, KM#308.

CM Date	Host Date	Good	VG	F	VF	XF
ND(1835)	1811R	4.50	9.00	15.00	30.00	—
ND(1835)	1812R	4.50	9.00	15.00	30.00	—

KM# 443.1 40 REIS

Copper **Countermark:** 40 **Note:** Countermark on LXXX (80) Reis, KM#342.1.

CM Date	Host Date	Good	VG	F	VF	XF
ND(1835)	1820B	2.50	5.00	10.00	20.00	—
ND(1835)	1821B	2.50	5.00	10.00	20.00	—
ND(1835)	1822B	2.50	5.00	10.00	20.00	—
ND(1835)	1823B	2.50	5.00	10.00	20.00	—

KM# 443.2 40 REIS

Copper **Countermark:** 40 **Note:** Countermark on LXXX (80) Reis, KM#342.1.

CM Date	Host Date	Good	VG	F	VF	XF
ND(1835)	CD1821R	2.50	5.50	11.50	25.00	—
ND(1835)	1822R	2.50	5.50	11.50	25.00	—

KM# 421.1 160 REIS

Copper **Countermark:** 10 **Note:** Countermark on XX (20) Reis, KM#316.1.

CM Date	Host Date	Good	VG	F	VF	XF
ND(1835)	1818M	3.00	9.00	16.00	25.00	—
ND(1835)	1819M	3.00	9.00	16.00	25.00	—
ND(1835)	1821M	3.00	9.00	16.00	25.00	—
ND(1835)	1819M Medal strike	3.50	12.00	20.00	28.00	—
ND(1835)	1821M Medal strike	3.00	9.00	16.00	25.00	—

REFORM COINAGE

1834-1889

KM# 473 10 REIS

Bronze **Obv:** CL below bust

Date	Mintage	F	VF	XF	Unc	BU
1868	89,604,000	0.50	2.00	4.00	7.00	—
1869	Inc. above	0.50	2.00	4.00	7.00	—
1870	—	0.50	2.00	6.00	18.00	—

KM# 474 20 REIS

Bronze **Obv:** CL below bust **Note:** Varieties exist on 1869 dated coins.

Date	Mintage	F	VF	XF	Unc	BU
1868	90,360,000	1.50	2.25	4.00	7.00	—
1869	Inc. above	1.50	2.25	4.00	7.00	—
1870	—	1.75	3.50	7.50	20.00	—

KM# 479 40 REIS

Bronze **Obv:** ESRC below bust

Date	Mintage	F	VF	XF	Unc	BU
1873	3,750,000	1.00	2.50	15.00	65.00	—
1874	890,000	1.00	2.50	15.00	65.00	—
1875	1,208,000	1.00	2.50	15.00	65.00	—
1876	549,000	1.00	4.00	25.00	125	—
1877	465,000	1.00	3.00	15.00	70.00	—
1878	1,223,000	1.00	2.50	15.00	70.00	—
1879	2,771,000	1.00	2.50	15.00	70.00	—
1880	1,569,000	1.00	2.50	15.00	70.00	—

KM# 482 50 REIS

Copper-Nickel

Date	Mintage	F	VF	XF	Unc	BU
1886	590,000	1.00	2.00	7.00	17.50	—
1887	Inc. above	1.00	2.50	7.00	20.00	—
1888	153,000	1.00	2.50	7.00	35.00	—

KM# 452 100 REIS

2.2400 g., 0.9170 Silver .0660 oz. **Obv:** Value in floral circle **Rev:** Crowned arms in branches

Date	Mintage	F	VF	XF	Unc	BU
1834	7,709	20.00	45.00	85.00	150	—
1835	Inc. above	20.00	45.00	85.00	150	—
1836	5,592	400	700	1,200	2,750	—
1837	9,562	20.00	45.00	85.00	150	—
1840	910	100	175	275	600	—
1844 Rare	—	—	—	—	—	—
1846	4,699	20.00	45.00	85.00	140	—
1847/4	682	100	180	250	450	—
1848	486	300	500	800	1,750	—

KM# 477 100 REIS

Copper-Nickel

Date	Mintage	F	VF	XF	Unc	BU
1871	4,000,000	0.50	1.25	3.00	50.00	—
1872	100	600	900	1,800	3,000	—
1874	—	0.75	2.50	20.00	80.00	—
1875	—	5.00	30.00	150	600	—
1876/4	—	3.50	25.00	145	600	—
1876	—	2.50	20.00	135	600	—
1877	—	0.75	2.50	20.00	80.00	—
1878	—	1.00	3.00	30.00	200	—
1879	—	1.00	2.50	20.00	80.00	—
1880	—	1.50	5.00	100	500	—
1881	—	0.75	2.50	15.00	70.00	—
1882	—	0.75	2.50	15.00	70.00	—
1883	2,700	0.75	2.50	15.00	70.00	—
1884	—	0.75	2.50	15.00	70.00	—
1885	—	0.75	2.50	15.00	70.00	—

KM# 483 100 REIS

Copper-Nickel

Date	Mintage	F	VF	XF	Unc	BU
1886	877,000	0.75	2.00	10.00	70.00	—
1887	—	0.75	2.00	10.00	70.00	—
1888	1,696,000	0.75	2.00	10.00	70.00	—
1889	862,000	0.75	2.00	10.00	70.00	—

KM# 455 200 REIS

4.4800 g., 0.9170 Silver .1320 oz.

Date	Mintage	F	VF	XF	Unc	BU
1835	4,894	20.00	50.00	100	300	—
1837	5,007	20.00	50.00	100	300	—
1840	624	125	300	500	800	—
1844	893	100	200	300	500	—
1846	406	150	300	450	500	—
1847	2,936	25.00	60.00	125	300	—
1848/7	501	250	450	850	1,200	—
1848	Inc. above	250	450	850	1,200	—

KM# 469 200 REIS

2.5500 g., 0.9170 Silver .0752 oz.

Date	Mintage	F	VF	XF	Unc	BU
1854	37,000	6.00	10.00	30.00	100	—
1855 Spikes on crown	—	3.00	6.00	10.00	25.00	—
1855 Beads on crown	228,000	3.00	6.00	10.00	25.00	—
1856/5 Spikes on crown	—	3.00	6.00	10.00	25.00	—
1856/5 Beads on crown	103,000	3.00	6.00	10.00	25.00	—
1856 Spikes on crown	—	3.00	6.00	10.00	25.00	—
1856 Beads on crown	Inc. above	3.00	6.00	10.00	25.00	—
1857	128,000	3.00	6.00	10.00	25.00	—
1858	245,000	3.00	6.00	10.00	25.00	—
1859	152,000	3.00	6.00	10.00	25.00	—
1860	28,000	3.00	6.00	10.00	25.00	—
1861	—	4.00	10.00	30.00	100	—
1862	—	3.00	6.00	10.00	25.00	—
1863	—	3.00	5.00	10.00	25.00	—
1864	—	3.00	6.00	10.00	25.00	—
1865/4	—	—	—	—	—	—
1865	—	3.00	6.00	10.00	25.00	—
1866	—	3.00	6.00	10.00	25.00	—
1867	—	3.00	6.00	10.00	25.00	—

KM# 471 200 REIS

2.5000 g., 0.8350 Silver .0671 oz. **Obv:** Globe and cross flank date **Rev:** Caduceus and scales flank denomination

Date	Mintage	F	VF	XF	Unc	BU
1867	—	2.50	5.00	10.00	25.00	—
1868	—	2.50	5.00	10.00	25.00	—
1869	—	5.00	12.50	25.00	50.00	—

KM# 478 200 REIS

Copper-Nickel

Date	Mintage	F	VF	XF	Unc	BU
1871	3,650,000	0.50	1.50	12.00	60.00	—
1874	—	1.00	2.50	15.00	90.00	—
1875	—	3.00	12.00	60.00	250	—
1876	—	1.00	2.50	15.00	90.00	—
1877	—	1.00	2.50	15.00	90.00	—
1878	—	1.00	3.50	20.00	100	—
1880	—	1.00	3.50	18.00	90.00	—
1882	—	1.00	3.50	18.00	90.00	—
1884	—	1.00	1.50	18.00	90.00	—

KM# 484 200 REIS

Copper-Nickel

Date	Mintage	F	VF	XF	Unc	BU
1886	177,000	4.50	25.00	100	300	—
1887	—	1.00	2.50	15.00	70.00	—
1888	967,000	1.00	2.50	15.00	70.00	—
1889	511,000	1.50	3.00	16.00	75.00	—

KM# 453 400 REIS

8.9600 g., 0.9170 Silver .2640 oz. **Obv:** Value in floral circle **Rev:** Crowned arms in branches

Date	Mintage	F	VF	XF	Unc	BU
1834	6,197	50.00	100	175	325	—
1835	Inc. above	50.00	100	175	325	—
1837	7,837	50.00	100	175	325	—
1840	—	100	300	700	1,200	—
1841	—	200	600	1,000	1,800	—
1843	161	400	850	1,600	2,500	—
1844	649	100	300	600	1,100	—
1845	179	250	650	1,200	2,250	—
1847/0	878	100	275	500	1,000	—
1847	Inc. above	100	275	500	1,000	—
1848	510	200	600	1,000	1,800	—

KM# 458 500 REIS
6.3750 g., 0.9170 Silver .1880 oz.

Date	Mintage	F	VF	XF	Unc	BU
1848 Rare	—	—	—	—	—	—
1849	26,000	25.00	50.00	80.00	200	—
1850	67,000	7.50	10.00	18.00	50.00	—
1851	95,000	7.50	10.00	18.00	50.00	—
1852	167,000	7.50	10.00	18.00	50.00	—

KM# 464 500 REIS
6.3750 g., 0.9170 Silver .1880 oz.

Date	Mintage	F	VF	XF	Unc	BU
1853	241,000	5.00	8.50	12.00	35.00	—
1854	317,000	5.00	8.50	12.00	35.00	—
1855	212,000	5.00	8.50	12.00	35.00	—
1856/5	—	5.00	9.00	15.00	40.00	—
1856	223,000	5.00	8.50	12.00	35.00	—
1857	265,000	5.00	7.50	10.00	35.00	—
1858	791,000	5.00	7.50	10.00	35.00	—
1859	152,000	5.00	7.50	10.00	35.00	—
1860/50	Est. 108,000	5.00	9.00	18.00	50.00	—

Note: The 1860 mintage figure includes only first six month's production

Date	Mintage	F	VF	XF	Unc	BU
1860	Inc. above	5.00	7.50	10.00	35.00	—

Note: The 1860 mintage figure includes only first six month's production

Date	Mintage	F	VF	XF	Unc	BU
1861	—	5.00	7.50	10.00	35.00	—
1862	—	5.00	7.50	10.00	35.00	—
1863	—	5.00	7.50	10.00	35.00	—
1864	—	5.00	7.50	10.00	35.00	—
1865	—	5.00	7.50	10.00	35.00	—
1866	—	5.00	7.50	10.00	35.00	—
1867	—	5.00	7.50	10.00	35.00	—

KM# 472 500 REIS
6.2500 g., 0.8350 Silver .1678 oz. **Obv:** CL below truncation, globe and cross flank date **Rev:** Caduceus and scales flank denomination

Date	Mintage	F	VF	XF	Unc	BU
1867	—	5.00	7.50	10.00	35.00	—
1868	—	5.00	7.50	10.00	35.00	—

KM# 480 500 REIS
6.3750 g., 0.9170 Silver .1879 oz. **Obv:** Without CL **Rev. Legend:** DECRETO DE 1870

Date	Mintage	F	VF	XF	Unc	BU
1876	76,000	4.50	10.00	20.00	50.00	—
1886	5,283	50.00	100	150	350	—
1887	768	180	250	400	600	—
1888	333,000	4.50	7.00	10.00	35.00	—
1889	278,000	4.50	7.00	10.00	35.00	—

KM# 456 800 REIS
17.9300 g., 0.9170 Silver .5283 oz.

Date	Mintage	F	VF	XF	Unc	BU
1835	1,698	300	600	1,000	2,350	—
1838	497	500	900	1,200	2,500	—
1840	145	600	1,000	2,000	4,000	—
1843	127	2,500	4,500	7,000	10,000	—
1844	628	500	850	1,150	2,400	—
1846	672	500	850	1,150	2,400	—

KM# 459 1000 REIS
12.7500 g., 0.9170 Silver .3757 oz.

Date	Mintage	F	VF	XF	Unc	BU
1849	965	200	400	600	1,800	—
1850	169,000	6.00	8.00	20.00	60.00	—
1851	99,000	6.00	8.00	20.00	65.00	—
1852	196,000	6.00	8.00	20.00	60.00	—

KM# 465 1000 REIS
12.7500 g., 0.9170 Silver .3757 oz.

Date	Mintage	F	VF	XF	Unc	BU
1853	266,000	6.00	8.00	20.00	40.00	—
1854	228,000	6.00	8.00	20.00	40.00	—
1855	312,000	6.00	8.00	20.00	40.00	—
1856	426,000	6.00	8.00	20.00	40.00	—
1857	512,000	6.00	8.00	20.00	40.00	—
1858	430,000	6.00	8.00	20.00	40.00	—
1859	996,000	6.00	8.00	20.00	40.00	—
1860/50	387,000	8.00	12.00	30.00	60.00	—
1860	Inc. above	6.00	8.00	20.00	40.00	—
1861	—	6.00	8.00	20.00	40.00	—
1862	—	6.00	8.00	20.00	40.00	—
1863	—	6.00	8.00	20.00	40.00	—
1864	—	6.00	8.00	20.00	40.00	—
1865	—	6.00	8.00	20.00	40.00	—
1866	—	6.00	8.00	20.00	40.00	—

KM# 476 1000 REIS
12.5000 g., 0.9000 Silver .3617 oz. **Obv:** LUSTER F below truncation, globe and cross flank date **Rev:** Caduceus and scales flank denomination

Date	Mintage	F	VF	XF	Unc	BU
1869	—	15.00	25.00	50.00	85.00	—

KM# 481 1000 REIS
12.7500 g., 0.9170 Silver .3759 oz. **Obv:** Without LUSTER F **Rev. Legend:** DECRETO DE 1870

Date	Mintage	F	VF	XF	Unc	BU
1876	194,000	7.50	12.50	20.00	60.00	—
1877	12,000	15.00	20.00	35.00	100	—
1878	47,000	12.50	17.50	30.00	90.00	—
1879	35,000	12.50	17.50	30.00	85.00	—
1880	20,000	12.50	17.50	30.00	90.00	—
1881	20,000	20.00	40.00	75.00	140	—
1882	18,000	25.00	45.00	85.00	175	—
1883	31,000	12.50	17.50	30.00	80.00	—
1884	22,000	20.00	35.00	65.00	150	—
1885	11,000	30.00	40.00	75.00	175	—
1886	48,000	8.50	17.50	35.00	100	—
1887	9,875	35.00	60.00	85.00	175	—
1888	100,000	7.50	12.50	20.00	65.00	—
1889	89,000	50.00	70.00	100	200	—

KM# 454 1200 REIS
26.8900 g., 0.9170 Silver .7924 oz. **Note:** 1841 and 1842 dates of this type are counterfeit.

Date	Mintage	F	VF	XF	Unc	BU
1834	891	75.00	200	350	600	—
1835	10,000	75.00	175	325	600	—
1837	6,304	75.00	175	325	600	—
1839	186	2,000	3,500	6,000	9,000	—
1840/37	633	200	400	650	1,500	—
1840	Inc. above	200	350	550	850	—
1843	1,803	100	250	500	1,150	—
1845	292	350	650	1,000	2,000	—
1846	1,898	200	450	800	1,800	—
1847	10,000	75.00	175	350	750	—

KM# 462 2000 REIS
25.5000 g., 0.9170 Silver .7514 oz.

Date	Mintage	F	VF	XF	Unc	BU
1851	256,000	10.00	15.00	30.00	100	—
1852	277,000	10.00	15.00	30.00	100	—

KM# 466 2000 REIS
25.5000 g., 0.9170 Silver .7514 oz.

Date	Mintage	F	VF	XF	Unc	BU
1853	145,000	10.00	20.00	35.00	80.00	—
1854	86,000	20.00	30.00	60.00	125	—
1855	300,000	10.00	20.00	35.00	100	—
1856	229,000	10.00	20.00	35.00	80.00	—
1857	105,000	20.00	30.00	50.00	80.00	—
1858	22,000	35.00	65.00	100	200	—
1859	41,000	200	400	650	1,150	—
1863	—	10.00	20.00	35.00	80.00	—
1864	—	35.00	65.00	100	300	—
1865	—	20.00	30.00	50.00	80.00	—
1866	—	200	400	650	1,150	—
1867	—	200	400	650	1,150	—

KM# 475 2000 REIS
25.0000 g., 0.9000 Silver .7234 oz. **Obv:** LUSTER F below truncation, globe and cross flank date **Rev:** Caduceus and scales flank denomination

Date	Mintage	F	VF	XF	Unc	BU
1868	—	20.00	30.00	80.00	200	—
1869	—	15.00	20.00	50.00	150	—

KM# 475a 2000 REIS
25.5000 g., 0.9170 Silver .7515 oz.

Date	Mintage	F	VF	XF	Unc	BU
1875	—	15.00	25.00	50.00	150	—
1876	—	75.00	125	250	500	—

KM# 485 2000 REIS
25.5000 g., 0.9170 Silver .7515 oz. **Obv:** Without LUSTER F **Rev. Legend:** DECRETO DE 1870

Date	Mintage	F	VF	XF	Unc	BU
1886	1,190	200	300	500	1,150	—
1887	43,000	15.00	30.00	65.00	125	—
1888	906,000	9.00	15.00	30.00	60.00	—
1889	—	9.00	15.00	30.00	60.00	—

KM# 470 5000 REIS
4.4824 g., 0.9170 Gold .1321 oz.

Date	Mintage	F	VF	XF	Unc	BU
1854	21,000	75.00	100	125	200	—
1855	47,000	90.00	120	150	250	—
1856	27,000	75.00	100	125	200	—
1857	4,631	800	1,200	2,000	2,500	—
1858	1,146	2,000	4,000	7,000	12,000	—
1859	493	3,000	5,000	8,000	—	—

KM# 451 10000 REIS
14.3400 g., 0.9170 Gold .4228 oz.

Date	Mintage	F	VF	XF	Unc	BU
1833	7,304	200	500	700	1,000	—
1834	5,617	200	500	700	1,000	—
1835	13,000	200	500	700	1,000	—
1836	11,000	300	550	750	1,150	—
1838	482	650	1,250	2,500	4,000	—
1839	567	650	1,250	2,500	4,000	—
1840	4,462	200	700	1,450	2,200	—

KM# 457 10000 REIS
14.3400 g., 0.9170 Gold .4228 oz. **Obv:** Military bust

Date	Mintage	F	VF	XF	Unc	BU
1841	3,454	700	1,500	3,500	7,000	—
1842	1,146	700	1,500	3,500	7,000	—
1843	544	2,000	3,500	6,500	10,000	—
1844	1,989	700	1,500	3,500	7,000	—
1845	3,834	700	1,500	3,500	7,000	—
1847	26,000	450	900	2,000	4,000	—
1848	4,567	500	1,000	2,500	5,000	—

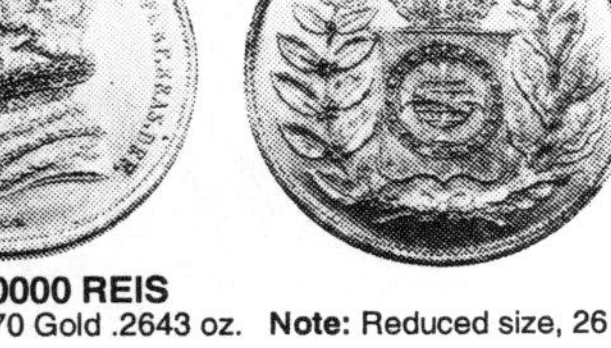

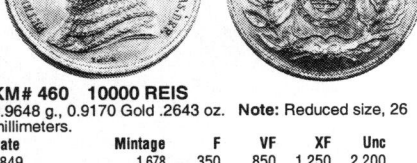

KM# 460 10000 REIS
8.9648 g., 0.9170 Gold .2643 oz. **Note:** Reduced size, 26 millimeters.

Date	Mintage	F	VF	XF	Unc	BU
1849	1,678	350	850	1,250	2,200	—
1850	7,359	150	250	350	500	—
1851	11,000	150	250	350	500	—

KM# 467 10000 REIS
8.9648 g., 0.9170 Gold .2643 oz.

Date	Mintage	F	VF	XF	Unc	BU
1853	40,000	—	140	180	300	—
1854	163,000	—	140	180	300	—
1855	41,000	—	140	180	300	—
1856	208,000	—	140	180	300	—
1857	98,000	—	140	180	300	—
1858	55,000	—	140	180	300	—
1859	16,000	400	1,000	2,000	3,000	—
1861	—	—	140	180	300	—
1863	—	400	1,000	2,000	3,000	—
1865	—	—	140	180	300	—
1866	—	—	140	180	300	—
1867	—	—	140	180	300	—
1871	—	—	160	300	400	—
1872	—	—	160	300	400	—
1873	—	—	160	300	400	—
1874	—	—	160	300	400	—
1875	—	—	160	300	400	—
1876	20,000	—	160	300	400	—
1877	3,441	—	200	320	420	—
1878	10,000	—	150	320	420	—
1879	6,431	—	150	320	420	—
1880	9,806	—	200	350	500	—
1882	4,671	—	220	350	500	—
1883	10,000	—	240	350	500	—
1884	11,000	—	240	350	500	—
1885	7,955	100	300	400	600	—
1886	3,782	—	300	400	600	—
1887	1,180	150	450	700	1,200	—
1888	5,359	—	350	500	800	—
1889	—	100	400	600	900	—

KM# 461 20000 REIS
17.9296 g., 0.9170 Gold .5286 oz.

Date	Mintage	F	VF	XF	Unc	BU
1849	6,464	275	500	700	900	—
1850	42,000	240	300	450	650	—
1851	303,000	240	300	450	650	—

KM# 463 20000 REIS
17.9296 g., 0.9170 Gold .5286 oz.

Date	Mintage	F	VF	XF	Unc	BU
1851	Inc. above	230	270	350	600	—
1852	186,000	230	270	350	600	—

KM# 468 20000 REIS
17.9296 g., 0.9170 Gold .5286 oz. **Obv:** Larger bust

Date	Mintage	F	VF	XF	Unc	BU
1853	246,000	—	260	300	550	—
1854	26,000	—	320	450	650	—
1855	48,000	—	260	300	550	—
1856	262,000	—	260	300	550	—
1857/6	315,000	—	260	300	550	—
1857	Inc. above	—	260	300	550	—
1858	32,000	—	260	300	550	—
1859	47,000	—	260	300	550	—
1860	—	—	275	400	750	—
1861	—	—	275	400	750	—
1862 Rare	—	—	—	—	—	—
Note: Spink America Norweb sale 3-97 VF realized $11,000						
1863	—	425	500	700	1,000	—
1864	—	300	500	700	1,000	—
1865	—	—	275	400	700	—
1867	—	—	275	400	700	—
1889	—	—	275	400	700	—

REPUBLIC

DECIMAL COINAGE

1889-1942

KM# 490 20 REIS
Bronze

Date	Mintage	F	VF	XF	Unc	BU
1889	630,000	1.00	4.50	9.50	20.00	—
1893	250,000	1.00	4.50	9.50	20.00	—
1894	Inc. above	1.00	4.50	9.50	25.00	—
1895	2,118,000	1.00	2.00	4.50	9.00	—
1896	490,000	4.50	18.00	38.00	95.00	—
1897	273,000	1.00	4.50	9.50	20.00	—
1898	300,000	2.75	7.50	17.50	38.00	—
1899	1,065,000	2.75	7.50	17.50	38.00	—
1900	1,718,000	1.00	4.50	9.50	20.00	—

KM# 491 40 REIS
Bronze **Rev:** FC above star

Date	Mintage	F	VF	XF	Unc	BU
1889	1,781,000	0.50	1.00	2.00	15.00	—
1893	1,085,000	1.50	3.00	5.00	22.50	—
1894	770,000	1.50	3.00	5.00	22.50	—
1895	Inc. above	2.00	3.50	6.00	25.00	—
1896	191,000	10.00	40.00	80.00	300	—
1897	1,236,000	0.75	2.00	3.50	17.50	—
1898	300,000	10.00	20.00	40.00	85.00	—
1900	2,115,000	0.75	2.50	4.50	20.00	—

KM# 492 100 REIS
Copper-Nickel

Date	Mintage	F	VF	XF	Unc	BU
1889	7,686,000	0.75	2.50	8.00	28.00	—
1893	3,589,000	1.00	2.50	8.00	28.00	—
1894	1,881,000	1.00	2.50	8.00	28.00	—
1895	2,308,000	1.00	2.50	8.00	28.00	—
1896	3,390,000	1.00	2.50	8.00	28.00	—
1897	2,875,000	3.00	6.00	11.50	38.00	—
1898	3,685,000	3.00	6.00	11.50	38.00	—
1899	2,990,000	3.00	6.00	11.50	38.00	—
1900	539,000	15.00	40.00	200	—	—

KM# 493 200 REIS
Copper-Nickel

Date	Mintage	F	VF	XF	Unc	BU
1889	4,829,000	1.50	3.00	10.00	62.50	—
1893	2,586,000	2.00	4.50	12.50	62.50	—
1894	1,562,000	2.00	4.50	12.50	62.50	—
1895	1,633,000	2.00	4.50	12.50	72.50	—
1896	2,850,000	2.50	5.00	15.00	72.50	—
1897	2,405,000	2.50	5.50	16.50	72.50	—
1898	3,925,000	2.50	5.00	15.00	72.50	—
1899	2,724,000	3.00	6.00	18.50	72.50	—
1900	330,000	15.00	50.00	220	—	—

KM# 499 400 REIS
5.1000 g., 0.9170 Silver .1503 oz. **Subject:** 400th Anniversary of Discovery **Edge:** Reeded

Date	Mintage	F	VF	XF	Unc	BU
1900	55,000	10.00	25.00	40.00	80.00	—

KM# 494 500 REIS
6.3750 g., 0.9170 Silver .1879 oz. **Obv:** FC below bust **Edge:** Reeded

Date	Mintage	F	VF	XF	Unc	BU
1889	4,541,000	3.50	12.00	23.50	42.50	—

KM# 495 1000 REIS
12.7500 g., 0.9170 Silver .3758 oz.

Date	Mintage	F	VF	XF	Unc	BU
1889	296,000	12.00	20.00	40.00	80.00	—

KM# 500 1000 REIS
12.7500 g., 0.9170 Silver .3758 oz. **Subject:** 400th Anniversary of Discovery

Date	Mintage	F	VF	XF	Unc	BU
1900	33,000	40.00	65.00	80.00	120	—

KM# 498 2000 REIS
25.5000 g., 0.9170 Silver .7515 oz.

Date	Mintage	F	VF	XF	Unc	BU
1891	40,000	500	1,200	2,500	4,000	—
1896	10,000	500	1,200	2,500	4,000	—
1897	160,000	200	500	800	2,000	—

KM# 501 2000 REIS
25.5000 g., 0.9170 Silver .7515 oz. **Subject:** 400th Anniversary of Discovery **Obv:** Ship

Date	Mintage	F	VF	XF	Unc	BU
1900	20,000	60.00	100	200	300	—

KM# 502.1 4000 REIS
51.0000 g., 0.9170 Silver 1.5030 oz. **Subject:** 400th Anniversary of Discovery **Rev:** Pedro Alvares Cabbai and stars with 16 rays

Date	Mintage	F	VF	XF	Unc	BU
1900	6,850	125	300	500	700	—

KM# 502.2 4000 REIS
51.0000 g., 0.9170 Silver 1.5030 oz. **Rev:** Pedro Alvares Cabbai and stars with 20 rays

Date	Mintage	F	VF	XF	Unc	BU
1900	Inc. above	125	300	500	700	—

KM# 496 10000 REIS
8.9645 g., 0.9170 Gold .2643 oz.

Date	Mintage	F	VF	XF	Unc	BU
1889	7,302	150	250	600	1,000	—
1892 Rare	2,289	—	—	—	—	—
1893	—	150	250	600	1,000	—
1895	306	150	250	700	1,150	—
1896 Rare	383	—	—	—	—	—
1897	421	150	250	650	1,100	—
1898	216	250	500	1,500	2,000	—
1899	238	150	250	700	1,150	—

KM# 497 20000 REIS
17.9290 g., 0.9170 Gold .5286 oz.

Date	Mintage	F	VF	XF	Unc	BU
1889	91,000	BV	300	550	1,100	—
1892 Rare	7,738	—	—	—	—	—
1893	4,303	BV	300	550	1,100	—
1894	4,267	BV	300	550	1,100	—
1895	4,811	BV	300	550	1,100	—
1896	7,043	BV	300	550	1,100	—
1897	11,000	BV	300	550	1,100	—
1898	14,000	BV	300	550	1,100	—
1899	9,558	BV	300	550	1,100	—
1900	7,551	BV	300	550	1,100	—

PATTERNS

Including off metal strikes

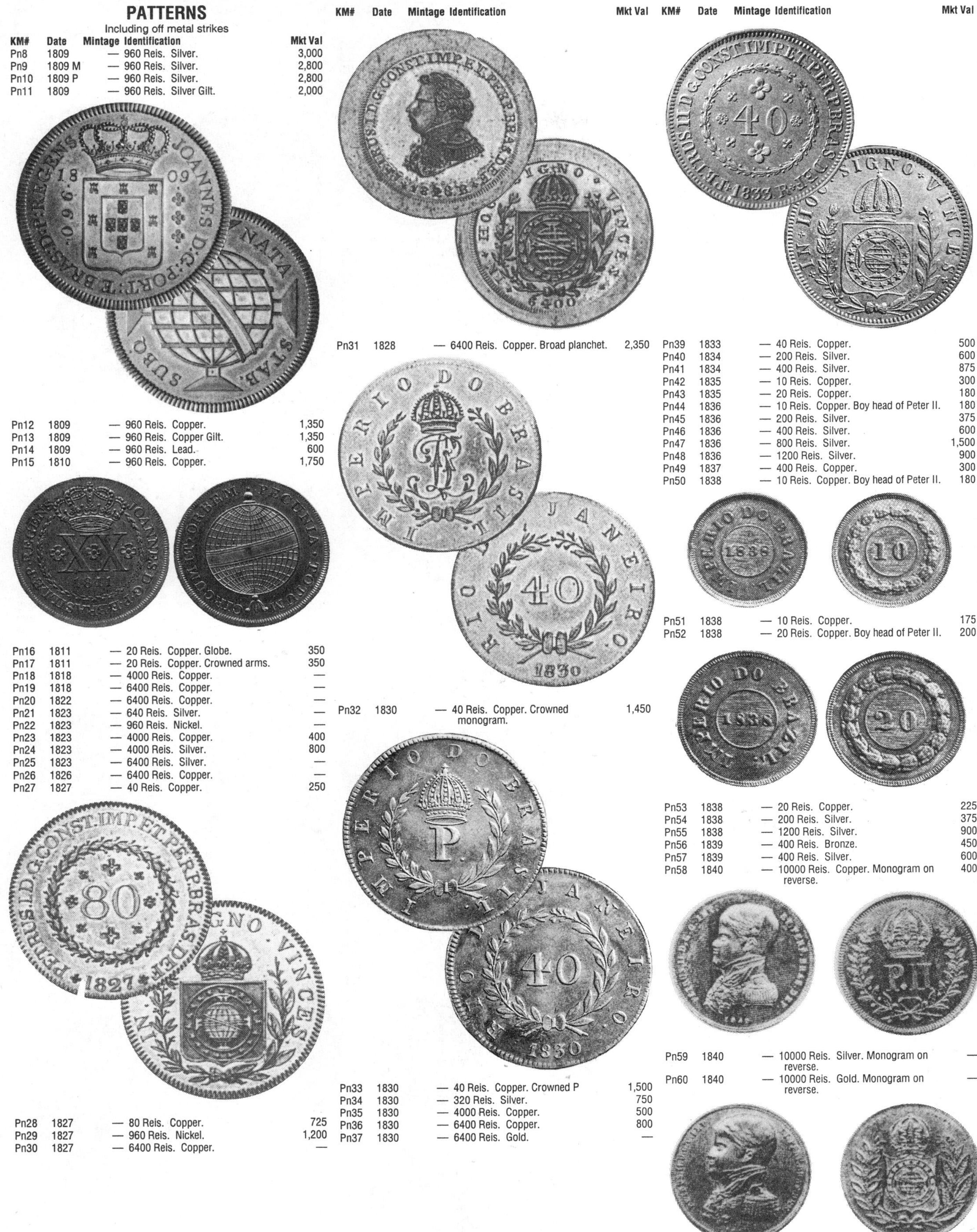

KM#	Date	Mintage	Identification	Mkt Val
Pn8	1809	—	960 Reis. Silver.	3,000
Pn9	1809 M	—	960 Reis. Silver.	2,800
Pn10	1809 P	—	960 Reis. Silver.	2,800
Pn11	1809	—	960 Reis. Silver Gilt.	2,000
Pn12	1809	—	960 Reis. Copper.	1,350
Pn13	1809	—	960 Reis. Copper Gilt.	1,350
Pn14	1809	—	960 Reis. Lead.	600
Pn15	1810	—	960 Reis. Copper.	1,750
Pn16	1811	—	20 Reis. Copper. Globe.	350
Pn17	1811	—	20 Reis. Copper. Crowned arms.	350
Pn18	1818	—	4000 Reis. Copper.	—
Pn19	1818	—	6400 Reis. Copper.	—
Pn20	1822	—	6400 Reis. Copper.	—
Pn21	1823	—	640 Reis. Silver.	—
Pn22	1823	—	960 Reis. Nickel.	—
Pn23	1823	—	4000 Reis. Copper.	400
Pn24	1823	—	4000 Reis. Silver.	800
Pn25	1823	—	6400 Reis. Silver.	—
Pn26	1826	—	6400 Reis. Copper.	—
Pn27	1827	—	40 Reis. Copper.	250
Pn28	1827	—	80 Reis. Copper.	725
Pn29	1827	—	960 Reis. Nickel.	1,200
Pn30	1827	—	6400 Reis. Copper.	—

KM#	Date	Mintage	Identification	Mkt Val
Pn31	1828	—	6400 Reis. Copper. Broad planchet.	2,350
Pn32	1830	—	40 Reis. Copper. Crowned monogram.	1,450
Pn33	1830	—	40 Reis. Copper. Crowned P	1,500
Pn34	1830	—	320 Reis. Silver.	750
Pn35	1830	—	4000 Reis. Copper.	500
Pn36	1830	—	6400 Reis. Copper.	800
Pn37	1830	—	6400 Reis. Gold.	—

KM#	Date	Mintage	Identification	Mkt Val
Pn39	1833	—	40 Reis. Copper.	500
Pn40	1834	—	200 Reis. Silver.	600
Pn41	1834	—	400 Reis. Silver.	875
Pn42	1835	—	10 Reis. Copper.	300
Pn43	1835	—	20 Reis. Copper.	180
Pn44	1836	—	10 Reis. Copper. Boy head of Peter II.	180
Pn45	1836	—	200 Reis. Silver.	375
Pn46	1836	—	400 Reis. Silver.	600
Pn47	1836	—	800 Reis. Silver.	1,500
Pn48	1836	—	1200 Reis. Silver.	900
Pn49	1837	—	400 Reis. Copper.	300
Pn50	1838	—	10 Reis. Copper. Boy head of Peter II.	180
Pn51	1838	—	10 Reis. Copper.	175
Pn52	1838	—	20 Reis. Copper. Boy head of Peter II.	200
Pn53	1838	—	20 Reis. Copper.	225
Pn54	1838	—	200 Reis. Silver.	375
Pn55	1838	—	1200 Reis. Silver.	900
Pn56	1839	—	400 Reis. Bronze.	450
Pn57	1839	—	400 Reis. Silver.	600
Pn58	1840	—	10000 Reis. Copper. Monogram on reverse.	400
Pn59	1840	—	10000 Reis. Silver. Monogram on reverse.	—
Pn60	1840	—	10000 Reis. Gold. Monogram on reverse.	—
Pn61	1840	—	10000 Reis. Copper. Arms.	175
Pn62	1840	—	10000 Reis. Silver. Arms.	—

KM#	Date	Mintage	Identification	Mkt Val
Pn63	1840	—	10000 Reis. Gold. Arms.	—
Pn64	1841	—	100 Reis. Silver.	900
Pn65	1841	—	200 Reis. Silver.	600
Pn66	1841	—	800 Reis. Silver.	1,500
Pn67	1841	—	1200 Reis. Silver.	900
Pn68	1842	—	10 Reis. Copper.	250
Pn69	1842	—	20 Reis. Copper.	200
Pn70	1842	—	1200 Reis. Silver.	900
Pn71	1844	—	1200 Reis. Silver.	900
Pn72	1845	—	800 Reis. Silver.	1,500
Pn73	1847	—	800 Reis. Silver.	1,500
Pn74	1848	—	10 Reis. Bronze.	250
Pn75	1848	—	200 Reis. Copper.	600
Pn76	1848	—	200 Reis. Copper.	600
Pn77	1848	—	800 Reis. Silver.	1,500
Pn78	1848	—	1200 Reis. Silver.	900
Pn79	1849	—	100 Reis. Silver.	750
Pn80	1849	—	200 Reis. Silver.	600
Pn81	1849	—	400 Reis. Silver.	900
Pn82	1849	—	1200 Reis. Silver.	900
Pn83	1849	—	2000 Reis. Silver.	1,250
Pn84	1850	—	2000 Reis. Silver.	1,250
Pn85	1855	—	1000 Reis. Silver.	350
Pn86	1855	—	20000 Reis. Gold.	2,500
Pn87	1859	—	2000 Reis. Silver.	500
Pn88	1860	—	20 Reis. Copper.	165
Pn89	1860	—	1000 Reis. Copper.	125
Pn90	1861	—	20 Reis. Copper.	150
Pn91	1861	—	200 Reis. Nickel-Silver.	100
Pn92	1862	—	20 Reis. Copper.	100
Pn93	1862	—	40 Reis. Copper.	100
Pn94	1862	—	40 Reis. Nickel.	100
Pn95	1862	—	1000 Reis. Nickel.	125
Pn96	1862	—	2000 Reis. Copper. 2$000.	600
Pn97	1862	—	2000 Reis. Copper. 2,000.	600
Pn98	1862	—	2000 Reis. Silver. 2$000.	1,500
Pn99	1862	—	2000 Reis. Silver. 2000.	1,500
Pn100	1863	—	10 Reis. Copper.	150
Pn101	1863	—	10 Reis. Copper. Without legend.	150
Pn102	1863	—	10 Reis. Silver. With raised border.	165

KM#	Date	Mintage	Identification	Mkt Val
Pn103	1863	—	10 Reis. Silver. Without raised border.	165
Pn104	1863	—	10 Reis. Palladium.	550
Pn105	1863	—	20 Reis. Copper. Small planchet.	165
Pn106	1863	—	20 Reis. Copper. Large planchet.	165
Pn107	1863	—	20 Reis. Nickel.	165
Pn108	1863	—	40 Reis. Copper. Small date.	165
Pn109	1863	—	40 Reis. Copper Gilt. Large date.	165
Pn110	1863	—	40 Reis. Nickel.	140
Pn111	1863	—	2000 Reis. Copper. 2$000.	1,000
Pn112	1863	—	2000 Reis. Copper. 2000.	1,000
Pn113	1863	—	2000 Reis. Silver. 2$000.	2,550
Pn114	1863	—	2000 Reis. Silver. 2000.	2,550
Pn115	1864	—	10 Reis. Copper.	80.00
Pn116	1864	—	10 Reis. Silver.	80.00
Pn117	1864	—	10 Reis. Bronze.	80.00
Pn118	1864	—	20 Reis. Bronze.	175
Pn119	1864	—	20 Reis. Silver.	200
Pn120	1865	—	10 Reis. Silver.	125
Pn121	1865	—	40 Reis. Copper.	125
Pn122	1865	—	40 Reis. Nickel.	125
Pn123	1865	—	40 Reis. Silver.	150
Pn124	1865	—	100 Reis. Copper.	200
Pn125	1865	—	100 Reis. Nickel.	225
PnA126	1865	—	100 Reis. Silvered Copper.	125

KM#	Date	Mintage	Identification	Mkt Val
Pn126	1865	—	100 Reis. Silver.	100
Pn127	1865	—	1000 Reis. Silver.	300
Pn128	1866	—	10 Reis. Copper.	200
Pn129	1866	—	40 Reis. Copper.	275
Pn130	1867	—	500 Reis. Silver.	400
Pn131	1867	—	1000 Reis. Silver.	400
Pn132	1867	—	20000 Reis. Wood.	400
Pn133	1869	—	10 Reis. Nickel.	125
Pn134	1869	—	10 Reis. Nickel Gilt.	150
Pn135	1869	—	20 Reis. Nickel.	150
Pn136	1869	—	20 Reis. Nickel Gilt.	150
Pn137	1869	—	1000 Reis. Copper.	250
Pn138	1870	—	200 Reis. Silver.	375
Pn139	1870	—	500 Reis. Silver.	600
Pn140	1870	—	1000 Reis. Silver.	600
Pn141	1870	—	2000 Reis. Wood.	600
Pn142	1870	—	2000 Reis. Silver.	800
Pn143	1871	—	50 Reis. Copper-Nickel.	3,500
Pn144	1871	—	100 Reis. Copper.	280
Pn145	1871	—	100 Reis. Bronze.	150
Pn146	1871	—	100 Reis. Nickel.	280
Pn147	1871	—	200 Reis. Copper.	200
Pn148	1872	—	10 Reis. Copper.	500
Pn149	1872	—	100 Reis. Bronze.	200
Pn150	1875	—	2000 Reis. Silver.	1,200
Pn151	1876	—	100 Reis. Wood.	325
Pn152	1876	—	500 Reis. Wood.	350
PnA153	1876	—	2000 Reis. Wood.	375
Pn153	1881	—	100 Reis. Zinc.	180
Pn154	1884	—	20 Reis. Silver.	300
Pn155	1884	—	10000 Reis. Wood.	375
Pn156	1885	—	1000 Reis. Wood.	375
Pn157	1886	—	50 Reis. Wood.	300

KM#	Date	Mintage	Identification	Mkt Val
Pn158	1886	—	100 Reis. Wood.	300
Pn159	1886	—	100 Reis. Zinc.	250
Pn160	1886	—	200 Reis. Wood.	200
Pn161	1886	—	500 Reis. Wood.	450
Pn162	1886	—	1000 Reis. Wood.	600
Pn163	1886	—	2000 Reis. Wood.	600
Pn164	1887	—	500 Reis. Wood.	800
Pn165	1887	—	1000 Reis. Wood.	500
Pn166	1887	—	2000 Reis. Wood.	500
Pn167	1888	—	100 Reis. Copper.	280
Pn168	1888	—	100 Reis. Nickel.	280
Pn169	1888	—	200 Reis. Copper-Nickel.	280
Pn170	1888	—	5000 Reis. Silver. Small planchet.	200
Pn171	1889	—	40 Reis. Copper. Value in center.	350
Pn172	1889	—	40 Reis. Copper. Value at bottom.	225
Pn173	1889	—	200 Reis. Nickel.	225
Pn174	1891	—	2000 Reis. Copper.	4,500
Pn175	1893	—	40 Reis. Nickel.	250
Pn176	1893	—	40 Reis. Silver.	350
Pn177	1899	—	200 Reis. Nickel.	400
Pn178	1899	—	400 Reis. Nickel.	400

TRIAL STRIKES

KM#	Date	Mintage	Identification	Mkt Val
TS3	1831	—	6400 Reis. Copper. Uniface.	—

MATO GROSSO

A large state in the center of Brazil. One of the issuers of the counterstamps of the 1808 law. The name of the province appears below the arms on the obverse.

STATE

COUNTERSTAMPED COINAGE

A large state in the center of Brazil. One of the issuers of the counterstamps of the 1808 law. The name of the province appears below the arms on the obverse.

Type A

Authorized November 4, 1818

Counterstamps: The obverse is a crowned shield above MATO GROSSO.

The reverse counterstamp is a banded globe.

NOTE: The c/s having the crown made up of close large pearls is considered a counterfeit.

KM# 330 960 REIS

Silver **Counterstamp:** Type A **Note:** Counterstamp on Argentina 8 Reales, KM#5.

CS Date	Host Date	Good	VG	F	VF	XF
ND(1818)	1813-1815	—	3,000	5,000	7,500	—

KM# 331.1 960 REIS

Silver **Counterstamp:** Type A **Note:** Counterstamp on Bolivia 8 Reales, KM#73.

CS Date	Host Date	Good	VG	F	VF	XF
ND(1818)	1791-1808	—	2,000	4,000	7,000	—

KM# 331.2 960 REIS

Silver **Counterstamp:** Type A **Note:** Counterstamp on Bolivia 8 Reales, KM#84.

CS Date	Host Date	Good	VG	F	VF	XF
ND(1818)	1808-18	—	2,000	4,000	—	—

CUIABA

Cuiaba is the present capital of the Mato Grosso state. In 1820, this city name appeared as "CUYABA" or "C" on a counterstamp appearing on Spanish-American 8 Reales coins. This is the rarest Brazilian counterstamp.

CITY

COUNTERSTAMPED COINAGE

Type B

Authorized 1820

Obv. c/s: Crowned shield above CUYABA.

Rev. c/s: Banded globe.

Type C

Authorized in January, 1821

Obv. c/s: Crowned 960/C (C. or .C. or C) within branches.

Rev. c/s: shield on globe.

KM# 345 960 REIS
Silver **Counterstamp:** Type B **Note:** Counterstamp on Spanish Colonial 8 Reales.

CS Date	Host Date	Good	VG	F	VF	XF
ND(1820)	1808	—	3,200	5,500	7,500	—

KM# 351.1 960 REIS
Silver **Counterstamp:** Type C **Note:** Counterstamp on Argentina 8 Reales, KM#5.

CS Date	Host Date	Good	VG	F	VF	XF
ND(1821)	1813	—	550	950	1,650	2,700

KM# 351.2 960 REIS
Silver **Counterstamp:** Type C **Note:** Counterstamp on Argentina 8 Reales, KM#14.

CS Date	Host Date	Good	VG	F	VF	XF
ND(1821)	1815	—	550	950	1,650	2,700

KM# 350 960 REIS
Silver **Counterstamp:** Type C **Note:** Counterstamp on Bolivia 8 Reales, KM#73.

CS Date	Host Date	Good	VG	F	VF	XF
ND(1821)	1791-1808	—	450	850	1,500	2,500

KM# 352 960 REIS
Silver **Counterstamp:** Type C **Note:** Counterstamp on Bolivia 8 Reales, KM#84.

CS Date	Host Date	Good	VG	F	VF	XF
ND(1821)	1808-1818	—	300	550	800	1,600

KM# A353 960 REIS
Silver **Counterstamp:** Type C **Note:** Counterstamp on Chile 8 Reales, KM#80.

CS Date	Host Date	Good	VG	F	VF	XF
ND(1821)	1812-1817	—	450	850	1,500	2,500

KM# 353 960 REIS
Silver **Counterstamp:** Type C **Note:** Counterstamp on Peru 8 Reales, KM#97.

CS Date	Host Date	Good	VG	F	VF	XF
ND(1821)	1791-1808	—	550	950	1,650	2,700

MINAS GERAIS

Minas Gerais is a state in eastern Brazil. In September of 1808 an edict was issued for the authorization of various counterstamps to be used on the many circulating Spanish 8 Reales in the country. The Minas Gerais counterstamp was issued both with and w/o the M on the reverse. The silver value was 750 to 800 Reis per coin but they were stamped and passed at 960 Reis giving the government a nice profit.

STATE

COUNTERSTAMPED COINAGE

Sept. 1, 1808 until 1810

Obv. c/s: Crowned shield in branches /960.

Rev. c/s: Banded globe with cross.

KM# 240 960 REIS
Silver **Counterstamp:** Obverse: Crowned shield in branches/960; Reverse: Banded globe with cross **Note:** Counterstamp on Bolivia 8 Reales, KM#55.

CS Date	Host Date	Good	VG	F	VF	XF
ND(1808)	1773-1789	—	—	550	1,000	1,500

KM# 241 960 REIS
Silver **Counterstamp:** Obverse: Crowned shield in branches/960; Reverse: Banded globe with cross **Note:** Counterstamp on Bolivia 8 Reales, KM#64.

CS Date	Host Date	Good	VG	F	VF	XF
ND(1808)	1789-1791	—	—	450	650	1,200

KM# 242 960 REIS
Silver **Counterstamp:** Obverse: Crowned shield in branches/960; Reverse: Banded globe with cross **Note:** Counterstamp on Bolivia 8 Reales, KM#73.

CS Date	Host Date	Good	VG	F	VF	XF
ND(1808)	1791-1808	—	—	80.00	170	300

KM# 243 960 REIS
Silver **Counterstamp:** Obverse: Crowned shield in branches/960; Reverse: Banded globe with cross **Note:** Counterstamp on Chile 8 Reales, KM#51.

CS Date	Host Date	Good	VG	F	VF	XF
ND(1808)	1791-1808	—	—	350	550	800

KM# 244 960 REIS
Silver **Counterstamp:** Obverse: Crowned shield in branches/960; Reverse: Banded globe with cross **Note:** Counterstamp on Guatemala 8 Reales.

CS Date	Host Date	Good	VG	F	VF	XF
ND(1808)	ND Rare	—	—	—	—	—

KM# 245 960 REIS
Silver **Counterstamp:** Obverse: Crowned shield in branches/960; Reverse: Banded globe with cross **Note:** Counterstamp on Mexico City 8 Reales, KM#105.

CS Date	Host Date	Good	VG	F	VF	XF
ND(1808)	1760-1772 Rare	—	—	—	—	—

KM# 246 960 REIS
Silver **Counterstamp:** Obverse: Crowned shield in branches/960; Reverse: Banded globe with cross **Note:** Counterstamp on Mexico City 8 Reales, KM#106.

CS Date	Host Date	Good	VG	F	VF	XF
ND(1808)	1772-1789	—	—	650	1,000	1,500

KM# 247 960 REIS
Silver **Counterstamp:** Obverse: Crowned shield in branches/960; Reverse: Banded globe with cross **Note:** Counterstamp on Mexico City 8 Reales, KM#107.

CS Date	Host Date	Good	VG	F	VF	XF
ND(1808)	1789-1790	—	—	400	600	1,100

KM# A248 960 REIS
Silver **Counterstamp:** Obverse: Crowned shield in branches/960; Reverse: Banded globe with cross **Note:** Counterstamp on Mexico City 8 Reales, KM#108.

CS Date	Host Date	Good	VG	F	VF	XF
ND(1808)	1790	—	—	1,500	2,000	—

KM# 248 960 REIS
Silver **Counterstamp:** Obverse: Crowned shield in branches/960; Reverse: Banded globe with cross **Note:** Counterstamp on Mexico City 8 Reales, KM#109.

CS Date	Host Date	Good	VG	F	VF	XF
ND(1808)	1791-1808	—	—	400	600	1,150

KM# 249 960 REIS
Silver **Counterstamp:** Obverse: Crowned shield in branches/960; Reverse: Banded globe with cross **Note:** Counterstamp on Peru 8 Reales, KM#78.

CS Date	Host Date	Good	VG	F	VF	XF
ND(1808)	1772-1789	—	—	450	650	1,200

KM# 250 960 REIS
Silver **Counterstamp:** Obverse: Crowned shield in branches/960; Reverse: Banded globe with cross **Note:** Counterstamp on Peru 8 Reales, KM#87.

CS Date	Host Date	Good	VG	F	VF	XF
ND(1808)	1789-1791	—	—	100	200	350

KM# 251 960 REIS
Silver **Counterstamp:** Obverse: Crowned shield in branches/960; Reverse: Banded globe with cross **Note:** Counterstamp on Peru 8 Reales, KM#97.

CS Date	Host Date	Good	VG	F	VF	XF
ND(1808)	1791-1808	—	—	80.00	170	300

KM# 252 960 REIS
Silver **Counterstamp:** Obverse: Crowned shield in branches/960; Reverse: Banded globe with cross **Note:** Counterstamp on Spanish 8 Reales.

CS Date	Host Date	Good	VG	F	VF	XF
ND(1808)	ND Rare	—	—	—	—	—

CEARA

Ceara is a state in northeastern Brazil. Due to coin shortages a law was passed October 3, 1833 that copper coins would be countermarked and pass for 1/2 of their face value. In November of 1834 legislation was passed to stop the star countermarks.

STATE

COUNTERMARKED COINAGE

(1833-34)

Coins of 10, 20, 40, and 80 Reis were countermarked CEARA in a 5-pointed star to indicate a 50 percent reduction in value (to 5, 10, 20, and 40 Reis). NOTE: Values given are for most common host coins.

KM# 395 5 REIS
Copper **Countermark:** Star **Note:** Countermark on 10 Reis.

CM Date	Host Date	Good	VG	F	VF	XF
ND(1833-34)	ND Rare	—	—	—	—	—

KM# 396 10 REIS
Copper **Countermark:** Star **Note:** Countermark on various 20 Reis.

CM Date	Host Date	Good	VG	F	VF	XF
ND(1833-34)	ND	10.00	15.00	22.00	35.00	—

KM# 397 20 REIS
Copper **Countermark:** Star **Note:** Countermark on various 40 Reis.

CM Date	Host Date	Good	VG	F	VF	XF
ND(1833-34)	ND	12.00	18.00	25.00	40.00	—

KM# 398 40 REIS
Copper **Countermark:** Star **Note:** Countermark on various 80 Reis.

CM Date	Host Date	Good	VG	F	VF	XF
ND(1833-34)	ND	15.00	20.00	30.00	50.00	—

Note: A few silver coins bearing this countermark are considered trial pieces and are rare. Many imitations of this countermark exist on various silver coins and are listed in Unusual World Coins

MARANHAO

Maranhao is a state in northeastern Brazil. Coin shortages caused 2 issues of countermarked coins. The first was to make the coins pass for 1/4 their face value. These had M and the new value in Roman numerals.Trial impressions of unadopted designs using M and the new value in Arabic numerals are also known. The second issue was to make the coins pass for 1/2 the face value. These were countermarked with an M. These too were soon recalled.

NOTE: Values given are for most common host coins. Host coins with National countermarks are known for this series and command a 50% premium.

Second Series Countermarks:

Second series countermarks are found struck over coins which already have the first series countermark. They are worth about 50 percent more than ordinary second series coins.

STATE

COUNTERMARKED COINAGE

KM# 401 5 REIS
Copper **Series:** First (1834) **Countermark:** M/V **Obv:** M and denomination in Roman numerals within a rectangle **Note:** Countermark on various 20 Reis.

CM Date	Host Date	Good	VG	F	VF	XF
ND(1834)	ND	12.00	18.00	30.00	50.00	—

KM# 402 10 REIS
Copper **Series:** First (1834) **Countermark:** M/X **Obv:** M and denomination in Roman numerals within a rectangle **Note:** Countermark on various 40 Reis.

CM Date	Host Date	Good	VG	F	VF	XF
ND(1834)	ND	10.00	15.00	25.00	40.00	—

KM# 404 10 REIS
Copper **Series:** Second (1835) **Countermark:** M **Rev:** Large M on coin **Note:** Countermark on various 20 Reis.

CM Date	Host Date	Good	VG	F	VF	XF
ND(1835)	ND	7.50	12.50	25.00	40.00	—

KM# 403 20 REIS
Copper **Series:** First (1834) **Countermark:** M/XX **Obv:** M and denomination in Roman numerals within a rectangle **Note:** Countermark on various 80 Reis.

CM Date	Host Date	Good	VG	F	VF	XF
ND(1834)	ND	10.00	15.00	28.00	55.00	—

KM# 405 20 REIS
Copper **Series:** Second (1835) **Countermark:** M **Rev:** Large M on coin **Note:** Countermark on various 40 Reis.

CM Date	Host Date	Good	VG	F	VF	XF
ND(1835)	ND	7.50	12.50	25.00	40.00	—

KM# 406 40 REIS
Copper **Series:** Second (1835) **Countermark:** M **Rev:** Large M on coin **Note:** Countermark on various 80 Reis.

CM Date	Host Date	Good	VG	F	VF	XF
ND(1835)	ND	20.00	40.00	80.00	120	—

PARA

Para is a state in northern Brazil. Two series of countermarks were issued from this state. On January 14, 1835 Governor Malcher authorized a law for the countermarking of the recently withdrawn Mato Grosso coppers to 1/4 of their previous value. On March 6, 1835 Governor Vinagre authorized the countermarking of coppers at 1/2 their face value. Although heavily counterfeited because of their crudeness these coins stayed in circulation until 1868 and even later.

STATE

COUNTERMARKED COINAGE

Crude Arabic 10, 20, or 40 countermarked on obverse of coins weighing 2, 4, and 8 Oitavos, respectively. The numerals are quite crude and styles vary and are easily distinguished from the general countermarks. Examples of the Para marks are:

10 20 40

NOTE: Values given are for most common host coins. Host coins with National countermarks are known for this series and command a 50 percent premium.

KM# 407 10 REIS
Copper **Countermark:** 10 **Note:** Countermark on various Colonial XX (20) Reis.

CM Date	Host Date	Good	VG	F	VF	XF
ND(1835)	ND	5.00	7.50	10.00	20.00	—

KM# 408 10 REIS
Copper **Countermark:** 10 **Note:** Countermark on Imperial 20 Reis, R or B mints.

CM Date	Host Date	Good	VG	F	VF	XF
ND(1835)	ND	5.00	7.50	10.00	20.00	—

KM# 409 10 REIS
Copper **Countermark:** 10 **Note:** Countermark on Imperial 40 Reis, C or G mints, KM#364.1 and KM#364.2.

CM Date	Host Date	Good	VG	F	VF	XF
ND(1835)	ND	7.50	10.00	15.00	35.00	—

KM# 410 20 REIS
Copper **Countermark:** 20 **Note:** Countermark on Colonial XL (40) Reis.

CM Date	Host Date	Good	VG	F	VF	XF
ND(1835)	ND	5.00	7.50	12.50	30.00	—

KM# 411 20 REIS

Copper **Countermark:** 20 **Note:** Countermark on Imperial 40 Reis, R or B mints.

CM Date	Host Date	Good	VG	F	VF	XF
ND(1835)	ND	5.00	7.50	12.50	30.00	—

KM# 412 20 REIS

Copper **Countermark:** 20 **Note:** Countermark on Imperial 80 Reis, C or G mints, KM#377.1 and KM#377.2.

CM Date	Host Date	Good	VG	F	VF	XF
ND(1835)	ND	7.50	12.50	20.00	40.00	—

KM# 413 40 REIS

Copper **Countermark:** 40 **Note:** Countermark on Colonial LXXX (80) Reis.

CM Date	Host Date	Good	VG	F	VF	XF
ND(1835)	ND	12.00	20.00	30.00	45.00	—

KM# 414 40 REIS

Copper **Countermark:** 40 **Note:** Countermark on Imperial 80 Reis, R or B mints.

CM Date	Host Date	Good	VG	F	VF	XF
ND(1835)	ND	10.00	15.00	25.00	40.00	—

REPUBLIC OF PIRATINI

As a result of a revolt in 1835 in the southern Brazilian state of Rio Grande do Sol the "Republic of Piratini" was briefly established and all coins then circulating in the province were countermarked with the arms of the new republic. This series is probably the most counterfeited of all of the elaborate countermarks.

REPUBLIC

COUNTERMARKED COINAGE

1835-1845

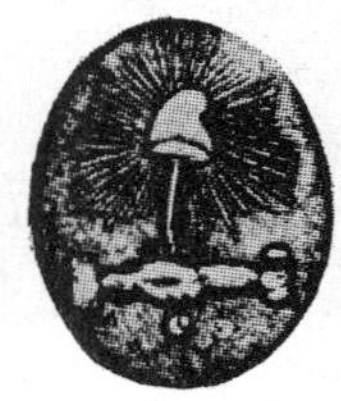

Two hands grasping a sword with Liberty cap on point within oval. Similar countermarks with either the date 1835 or PIRATINI at the bottom or date divided are considered to be fantasies.

KM# A415 20 REIS

Copper **Note:** Countermark on various 20 Reis.

CM Date	Host Date	Good	VG	F	VF	XF
ND(1835)	ND	—	50.00	100	175	250

KM# B415 40 REIS

Copper **Note:** Countermark on various 40 Reis.

CM Date	Host Date	Good	VG	F	VF	XF
ND(1835)	ND	—	50.00	100	175	250

KM# C415 80 REIS

Copper **Note:** Countermark on various 80 Reis.

CM Date	Host Date	Good	VG	F	VF	XF
ND(1835)	ND	—	50.00	100	185	265

KM# E415 320 REIS

Silver **Note:** Countermark on 320 Reis, KM#374.

CM Date	Host Date	Good	VG	F	VF	XF
ND(1835)	1825R	—	450	750	1,250	2,000

KM# F415 640 REIS

Silver **Note:** Countermark on 640 Reis, KM#367.

CM Date	Host Date	Good	VG	F	VF	XF
ND(1835)	1825R Rare	—	—	—	—	—

KM# G415 960 REIS

Silver **Note:** Countermark on Columbia-Cundinamarca 8 Reales, KM#6.

CM Date	Host Date	Good	VG	F	VF	XF
ND(1835)	1821 Rare	—	—	—	—	—

KM# H415 960 REIS

Silver **Note:** Countermark on Spain 8 Reales, C#93.

CM Date	Host Date	Good	VG	F	VF	XF
ND(1835)	1809 IG Rare	—	—	—	—	—

KM# I415 960 REIS

Silver **Note:** Countermark on Brazil 960 Reis, KM#368.1.

CM Date	Host Date	Good	VG	F	VF	XF
ND(1835)	1826R Rare	—	—	—	—	—

GOLD BARS

Extensive gold mining in various outlaying districts of Brazil eventually led to the use of gold dust as a virtually legal tender commodity in the early 18th century. The assay and production of individual gold bars was instituted to extend a greater control over the gold trade. Governmental control increased to the point of establishing specific foundries where miners were forced to bring their gold for processing. These foundries would assay the gold of miners, retaining the required "Royal fifth" or 20% in value for taxes, and returning the remainder to the miner in gold bar form. The miner also received a certificate attesting to personal ownership, and indicating that the "Royal fifth" taxes had been collected.

Cuiaba

Actual size 89x18mm.

Counterstamp: CUYABA below crown in branches.
Known dates: 1821, 1822

Goias

Illustration reduced. Actual size: 112 x 18mm.

Countermark: GOIAS in an incuse rectangle.
Known dates: 1790, 1801, 1813, 1814, 1817, 1819, 1820, 1821, 1822, 1823.

Mato Grosso

Illustration reduced. Actual size: 83x17mm.

Counterstamp: MATO GROSSO above crown in branches.
Known dates: 1784, 1800, 1811, 1812, 1813, 1815, 1816, 1817, 1818, 1819, 1820.

Rio Das Mortes

Illustration reduced. Actual size: 64x16mm.

Counterstamp: RIO DAS M. below crowned arms in branches.

Known dates: 1796, 1800, 1804, 1817, 1818.

Sabara

Illustration reduced. Actual size:
Top – 78x20mm, Bottom – 66x13mm.

Counterstamp: SABARA or V.DO SABARA below or V.DO-SAB above crowned arms.

Known dates: 1778, 1792, 1794, 1796, 1801, 1804, 1805, 1806, 1807, 1808, 1809, 1810, 1811, 1812, 1813, 1814, 1815, 1816, 1817, 1818, 1819, 1828, 1832, 1833.

NOTE: UBS Auction 48, 1-00, 1815 Sabara, XF realized $34,430.

Serro Frio

Both illustrations reduced. Actual size:
Top – 80x17mm, Bottom – 55x12mm.

Counterstamp S.-F. above or SERRO FRIO below

Crowned arms and AAB monogram in beaded circle.

Known dates: 1809, 1810, 1811, 1812, 1813, 1814, 1816, 1818, 1820, 1829, 1830, 1831, 1832.

Vila Rica

Illustration reduced. Actual size: 107 x 17mm

Counterstamp: Crowned arms or crowned arms with V.-R. above. Countermark: Script VCR monogram.

Known dates: 1786, 1796, 1799, 1802, 1804, 1807, 1808, 1809, 1810, 1811, 1812, 1813, 1814, 1815, 1816, 1817, 1818, 1828.

NOTE: UBS Auction 48, 1-00, 1807 Vila Rica, XF realized $38,825; 1811 Vila Rica, XF realized $41,750.

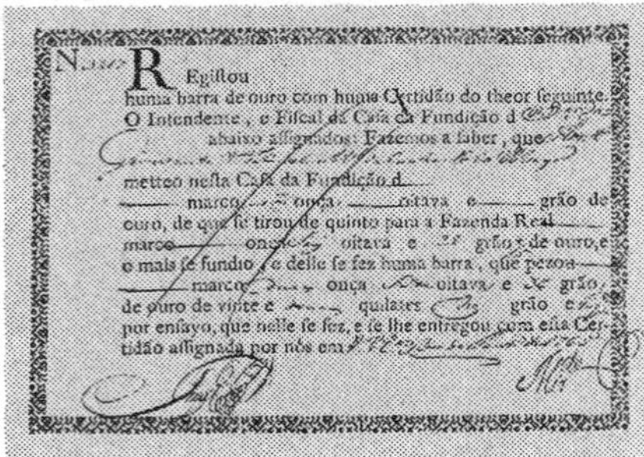

N.
Registou
huma barra de ouro com huma Certidão do theor seguinte.
O Intendente, e Fiscal da Casa da Fundição d
abaixo assignados: Fazemos a saber, que
metteo nesta Casa da Fundição d
marco onça oitava e grão de
ouro, de que se tirou de quinto para a Fazenda Real
marco onça oitava e grão de ouro, e
e mais se fundio, e delle se fez huma barra, que pesou
marco onça oitava e grão
de ouro de vinte e quilates grão e
por ensayo, que nelle se fez, e se lhe entregou com esta Certidão assignada por nós em

A receipt for a gold bar.

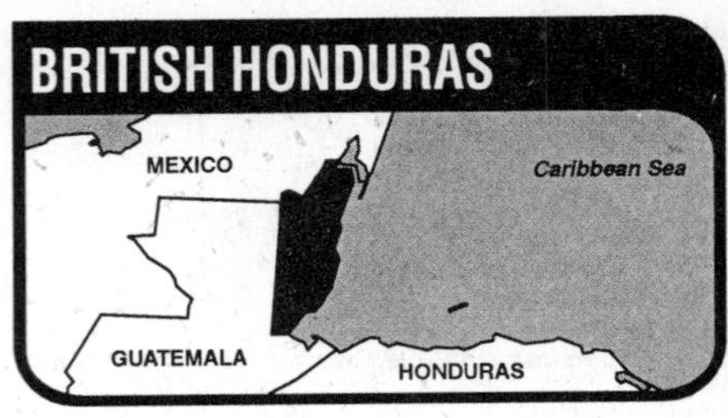

British Honduras is situated in Central America south of Mexico and east and north of Guatemala, with an area of 8,867 sq. mi. (22,960 sq. km.). Capital: Belmopan.

The area, site of the ancient Mayan civilization, was sighted by Columbus in 1502, and settled by shipwrecked English seamen in 1638. British buccaneers settled the former capital of Belize in the 17th century. Britain claimed administrative right over the area after the emancipation of Central America from Spain. In 1825, Imperial coins were introduced into the colony and were rated against the Spanish dollar and Honduran currency. It was declared a colony subordinate to Jamaica in 1862 and was established as the separate Crown Colony of British Honduras in 1884. In May, 1885 an order in Council authorized coins for the colony, with the first shipment arriving in July. While the Guatemalan peso was originally the standard of value, in 1894 the colony changed to the gold standard, based on the U.S. gold dollar.

RULERS
British, until 1981

MINT MARKS
H - Birmingham Mint
No mm - Royal Mint

MONETARY SYSTEM

Circa 1765-1855
6 Shillings 8 Pence (Jamaican) = 8 Reales
1855-1864
1 Dollar = 8 Rials = 4 Shillings (Sterling)
Commencing 1864
100 Cents = 1 Dollar

BRITISH COLONY

DECIMAL COINAGE

KM# 6 CENT

Bronze

Date	Mintage	F	VF	XF	Unc	BU
1885	72,000	4.50	10.00	25.00	75.00	—
1885 Proof	—	Value: 250				
1888	100,000	3.50	8.50	25.00	85.00	—
1888 Proof	—	Value: 275				
1889	50,000	6.00	15.00	40.00	90.00	—
1889 Proof	—	Value: 275				
1894	50,000	8.00	20.00	50.00	275	—
1894 Proof	Est. 25	Value: 300				

KM# 7 5 CENTS

1.1620 g., 0.9250 Silver .0346 oz.

Date	Mintage	F	VF	XF	Unc	BU
1894	128,000	5.00	15.00	30.00	75.00	—
1894 Proof	Est. 25	Value: 350				

KM# 8 10 CENTS

2.3240 g., 0.9250 Silver .0691 oz.

Date	Mintage	F	VF	XF	Unc	BU
1894	126,000	6.00	20.00	60.00	150	—
1894 Proof	Est. 25	Value: 450				

KM# 9 25 CENTS
5.8100 g., 0.9250 Silver .1728 oz.

Date	Mintage	F	VF	XF	Unc	BU
1894	48,000	10.00	20.00	65.00	285	—
1894 Proof	Est. 25	Value: 650				
1895	47,000	15.00	25.00	75.00	300	—
1897	40,000	15.00	25.00	85.00	375	—

KM# 10 50 CENTS
11.6200 g., 0.9250 Silver .3456 oz.

Date	Mintage	F	VF	XF	Unc	BU
1894	38,000	15.00	35.00	100	375	—
1894 Proof	Est. 25	Value: 1,500				
1895	36,000	15.00	40.00	120	400	—
1897	20,000	16.00	45.00	165	550	—

TOKEN COINAGE

KM# Tn1 1/4 RIAL
Brass **Issuer:** John Jex **Obv:** Indian head

Date	Mintage	F	VF	XF	Unc	BU
1871	—	175	300	500	—	—

KM# Tn2 1-1/2 PENCE
Copper **Issuer:** Henry Gansz

Date	Mintage	F	VF	XF	Unc	BU
1885	—	—	—	600	900	—

COUNTERMARKED COINAGE

It is generally believed that the crowned "GR" monogram was placed on certain coins to make them acceptable as trade items with local indigenous peoples. This mark did not affect their currency status, although in light of the Revolutionary War of 1810-20 it may have been an attempt to localize and keep coins in the colony at a time when the supply of Spanish coins dwindled.

KM# 1.1 6 SHILLING 1 PENNY
0.9160 Silver **Countermark:** Crowned script GR in rectangular indent **Note:** Countermark on Mexico City 8 Reales, KM#109.

CM Date	Host Date	Good	VG	F	VF	XF
ND(1810-18)	ND(1791-1808)	85.00	175	275	450	—

KM# 1.2 6 SHILLING 1 PENNY
0.9160 Silver **Countermark:** Crowned script GR in rectangular indent **Note:** Countermark on Mexico City 8 Reales, KM#110

CM Date	Host Date	Good	VG	F	VF	XF
ND(1810-18)	ND(1808-11)	85.00	175	275	450	—

KM# 2 6 SHILLING 1 PENNY
0.9160 Silver **Countermark:** Crowned script GR in oval indent **Note:** Countermark on Mexico City 8 Reales, KM#111.

CM Date	Host Date	Good	VG	F	VF	XF
ND(1810-18)	ND(1811-18)	70.00	140	200	350	—

KM# 3 6 SHILLING 1 PENNY
0.9160 Silver **Countermark:** Crowned script GR in oval indent **Note:** Countermark on France 5 Francs, C#138.

CM Date	Host Date	Good	VG	F	VF	XF
ND(1810-18)	ND	100	200	300	500	—

KM# 4 6 SHILLING 1 PENNY
0.9160 Silver **Countermark:** Incuse crowned script GR **Note:** Countermark on Mexico City 8 Reales, KM#111.

CM Date	Host Date	Good	VG	F	VF	XF
ND(1810-18)	ND(1811-18)	75.00	150	250	400	—

Note: KM#4 is considered a local issue. The countermark crowned GR in octagonal indent is considered a modern fabrication. Refer to Unusual World Coins, third edition, Krause Publications

KM# 5 6 SHILLING 1 PENNY
0.9160 Silver **Countermark:** Crowned script GR in rectangular indent **Note:** Countermark on Peru (Lima) 8 Reales, KM#97.

CM Date	Host Date	Good	VG	F	VF	XF
ND(1810-18)	ND(1791-1808)	80.00	165	250	400	—

PROOF SETS

KM#	Date	Mintage	Identification	Issue Price	Mkt Val
PS1	1894 (5)	25	KM#6-10	—	3,000

BRITISH NORTH BORNEO

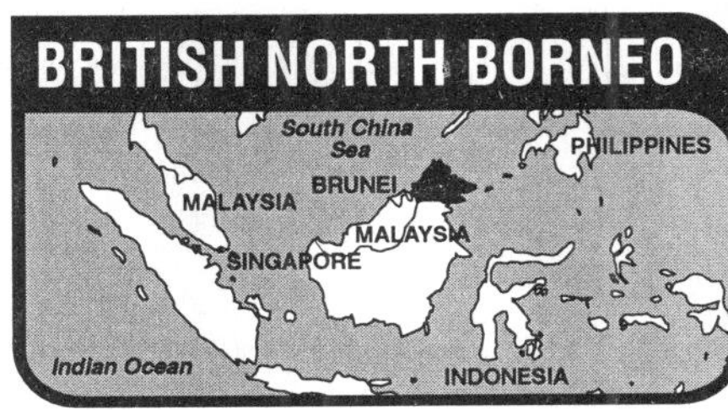

British North Borneo (now known as *Sabah*), a former British protectorate and crown colony, occupies the northern tip of the island of Borneo. The island of Labuan, which lies 6 miles off the northwest coast of the island of Borneo, was attached to Singapore settlement in 1907. It became an independent settlement of the Straits Colony in 1912 and was incorporated with British North Borneo in 1946. In 1963 it became part of Malaysia.

RULERS
British

MINT MARKS
H - Heaton, Birmingham

MONETARY SYSTEM
100 Cents = 1 Straits Dollar

BRITISH PROTECTORATE

STANDARD COINAGE

KM# 1 1/2 CENT
Bronze

Date	Mintage	F	VF	XF	Unc	BU
1885H	1,000,000	8.00	22.50	60.00	150	—
1885H Proof	—	Value: 320				
1886H	1,000,000	8.00	22.50	60.00	150	—
1886H Proof	—	Value: 320				
1887H	500,000	8.00	18.00	55.00	120	—
1891H	2,000,000	6.00	16.00	45.00	120	—
1891H Proof	—	Value: 320				
1907H Proof	—	Value: 350				

KM# 2 CENT
Bronze

Date	Mintage	F	VF	XF	Unc	BU
1882H	2,000,000	4.00	10.00	25.00	110	—
1882H Proof	—	Value: 230				
1884H	2,000,000	4.00	10.00	25.00	110	—
1884H Proof	—	Value: 230				
1885H	1,000,000	8.00	12.00	32.00	115	—
1886H	5,000,000	5.00	9.00	30.00	100	—
1886H Proof	—	Value: 230				
1887H	6,000,000	5.00	9.00	30.00	100	—
1887H Proof	—	Value: 230				
1888H	6,000,000	5.00	9.00	30.00	100	—
1888H Proof	—	Value: 230				
1889H	9,000,000	4.00	8.00	26.00	100	—
1890H	8,003,000	4.00	8.00	26.00	100	—
1890H Proof	—	Value: 220				
1891H	3,000,000	4.00	8.00	26.00	100	—
1891H Proof	—	Value: 220				
1894H	1,000,000	25.00	60.00	110	200	—
1896H	1,000,000	25.00	60.00	110	200	—

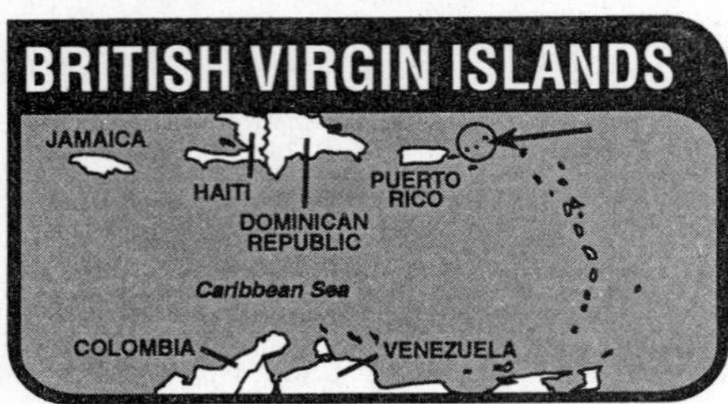

The Colony of the Virgin Islands, a British colony situated in the Caribbean Sea northeast of Puerto Rico and west of the Leeward Islands, has an area of 59 sq. mi. (155 sq. km.) and a population of 13,000. Capital: Road Town. The principal islands of the 36-island group are Tortola, Virgin Gorda, Anegada, and Jost Van Dyke. The chief industries are fishing and stock raising. Fish, livestock and bananas are exported.

The Virgin Islands were discovered by Columbus in 1493, and named by him, Las Virgienes, in honor of St. Ursula and her companions. The British Virgin Islands were formerly part of the administration of the Leeward Islands but received a separate administration as a Crown Colony in 1950. A new constitution promulgated in 1967 provided for a ministerial form of government headed by the Governor.

The Government of the British Virgin Islands issued the first official coinage in its history on June 30, 1973, in honor of 300 years of constitutional government in the islands. U.S. coins and currency continue to be the primary medium of exchange, though the coinage of the British Virgin Islands is legal tender.

TORTOLA

Tortola, which has an area of about 24 sq. mi. (62 sq. km.), is the largest of 36 islands which comprise the British Virgin Islands. It was settled by the Dutch in 1648 and was occupied by the British in 1666. They have held it ever since.

MONETARY SYSTEM
8 Shillings, 3 Pence = 11 Bits = 8 Reales

LEEWARD ISLANDS ADMINISTRATION

COUNTERMARKED COINAGE

Type I: TORTOLA in odd shaped rectangle.

Market valuations listed for TORTOLA c/m issues are just for the TORTOLA c/m and do not take into consideration any other c/m that may be encountered on the same piece.

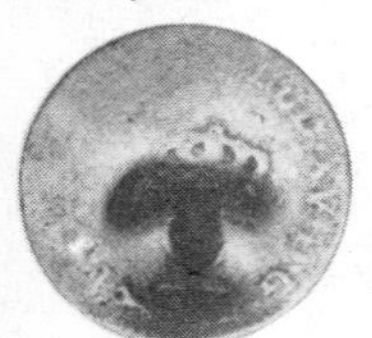

KM# 3 1-1/2 PENCE (Black Dog)
Billon **Countermark:** Incuse T **Note:** Countermark on French and French Guiana, Colony of Cayenne 2 Sous.

CM Date	Host Date	Good	VG	F	VF	XF
ND(1801)	ND	22.50	40.00	75.00	135	—

KM# 4 9 PENCE (Bit)
Silver **Countermark:** Type I **Note:** Countermark on 1/2 cut of Spanish or Spanish Colonial 2 Reales.

CM Date	Host Date	Good	VG	F	VF	XF
ND(1801)	ND	45.00	95.00	185	275	—

KM# 5 SHILLING
Silver **Countermark:** Type I **Note:** Countermark on 1/8 cut of Spanish or Spanish Colonial 8 Reales.

CM Date	Host Date	Good	VG	F	VF	XF
ND(1801)	ND	80.00	135	225	300	—

KM# 6 2 SHILLING
Silver **Countermark:** Type I **Note:** Countermark on 1/4 cut of Spanish or Spanish Colonial 8 Reales.

CM Date	Host Date	Good	VG	F	VF	XF
ND(1801)	ND	75.00	150	275	400	—

KM# 7 4 SHILLING 1-1/2 PENCE
Silver **Countermark:** Type I **Note:** Countermark on 1/2 cut of Spanish or Spanish Colonial 8 Reales.

CM Date	Host Date	Good	VG	F	VF	XF
ND(1801)	ND	100	200	375	750	—

COUNTERMARKED COINAGE

Type II: TORTOLA in rectangle.

KM# 8 SHILLING
Silver **Countermark:** Type II **Note:** Type II: TORTOLA in rectangle. Countermark on 1/8 cut of Spanish or Spanish Colonial 8 Reales.

CM Date	Host Date	Good	VG	F	VF	XF
ND(1801-05)	ND	100	200	320	475	—

KM# 9 2 SHILLING
Silver **Countermark:** Type II **Note:** Countermark on 1/4 cut of Spanish or Spanish Colonial 8 Reales.

CM Date	Host Date	Good	VG	F	VF	XF
ND(1801-05)	ND	40.00	80.00	150	285	—

KM# 10 4 SHILLING 1-1/2 PENCE
Silver **Countermark:** Type II **Note:** Countermark 1/2 cut of Spanish or Spanish Colonial 8 Reales.

CM Date	Host Date	Good	VG	F	VF	XF
ND(1801-05)	ND	50.00	100	200	375	—

PRIVATE COUNTERMARKED COINAGE

KM# 11 1-1/2 PENCE (Black Dog)
Billon **Countermark:** Small 3 millimeter incuse H **Note:** Countermark in square indent on French and French Guiana, Colony of Cayenne 2 Sous.

Date	Mintage	Good	VG	F	VF	XF
ND	—	—	12.50	25.00	40.00	80.00

KM# 12 1-1/2 PENCE (Black Dog)
Billon **Countermark:** Large 5 millimeter incuse H **Note:** Countermark in square indent on French and French Guiana, Colony of Cayenne 2 Sous.

Date	Mintage	Good	VG	F	VF	XF
ND	—	12.00	22.50	37.50	75.00	—

COUNTERMARKED COINAGE

Type III: TIRTILA

KM# 13 9 PENCE (Bit)
Silver **Countermark:** Type III **Note:** Countermark on 1/2 cut of Spanish or Spanish Colonial 2 Reales.

CM Date	Host Date	Good	VG	F	VF	XF
ND(1805-24)	ND	125	185	280	450	—

KM# 15 SHILLING
Silver **Countermark:** Type III **Note:** Countermark on 1/8 cut of Spanish or Spanish Colonial 8 Reales.

CM Date	Host Date	Good	VG	F	VF	XF
ND(1805-24)	ND	125	185	280	450	—

KM# 17 2 SHILLING
Silver **Countermark:** Type III **Note:** Countermark on 1/4 cut of Spanish or Spanish Colonial 8 Reales.

CM Date	Host Date	Good	VG	F	VF	XF
ND(1805-24)	ND	85.00	120	200	300	—

KM# 19 4 SHILLING 1-1/2 PENCE
Silver **Countermark:** Type III **Note:** Countermark on 1/2 cut of Spanish or Spanish Colonial 8 Reales.

CM Date	Host Date	Good	VG	F	VF	XF
ND(1805-24)	ND	125	175	275	450	—

COUNTERMARKED COINAGE

Type IV: TIRTILA w/inverted V for A.

Market valuations listed for TIRTOLA c/m issues are just for the TIRTOLA c/m and do not take into consideration any other c/m that may be encountered on the same piece. Multiple c/m issues tend to have a higher market value.

KM# 14 9 PENCE (Bit)
Silver **Countermark:** Type IV **Note:** Countermark on 1/2 cut of Spanish or Spanish Colonial 2 Reales.

CM Date	Host Date	Good	VG	F	VF	XF
ND(1805-24)	ND	150	225	350	575	—

KM# 16 SHILLING
Silver **Countermark:** Type IV **Note:** Countermark on 1/8 cut of Spanish or Spanish Colonial 8 Reales.

CM Date	Host Date	Good	VG	F	VF	XF
ND(1805-24)	ND	125	185	280	450	—

KM# 18 2 SHILLING
Silver **Countermark:** Type IV **Note:** Countermark on 1/4 cut of Spanish or Spanish Colonial 8 Reales.

CM Date	Host Date	Good	VG	F	VF	XF
ND(1805-24)	ND	85.00	120	200	300	—

KM# 20 4 SHILLING 1-1/2 PENCE
Silver **Countermark:** Type IV **Note:** Countermark on 1/2 cut of Spanish or Spanish Colonial 8 Reales.

CM Date	Host Date	Good	VG	F	VF	XF
ND(1805-24)	ND	125	175	275	450	—

BRITISH WEST INDIES

The 'Anchor Coins' catalogued under this heading do not bear a particular place identification. They were issued for use in various British colonies in both the New World and the Orient. Coins of this type dated 1820 are traditionally assigned to Mauritius and other holdings in the Indian Ocean. Those of 1822 were initially struck for Mauritius but after the introduction of sterling as the denomination of public accounts in Mauritius, they found their widest circulation in Canada and colonies in the Caribbean Sea. In Jamaica they were limited to military transactions only. In the Leeward Islands they were used on all the islands except the Virgin Islands, Windward Islands, Barbados, Tobago and Trinidad.

RULERS
British

BRITISH COLONY

ANCHOR COINAGE

KM# 1 1/16 DOLLAR
0.8920 Silver

Date	Mintage	F	VF	XF	Unc	BU
1820	162,000	12.50	30.00	60.00	165	—
1820 Proof	—	Value: 350				
1820/1	142,000	15.00	35.00	65.00	185	—
1822	Inc. above	7.50	15.00	30.00	125	—
1822 Proof	—	Value: 350				

KM# 2 1/8 DOLLAR
0.8920 Silver

Date	Mintage	F	VF	XF	Unc	BU
1820	120,000	15.00	35.00	75.00	225	—
1820 Proof	—	Value: 375				
1822/0	142,000	12.50	30.00	60.00	200	—
1822/1	Inc. above	10.00	20.00	45.00	175	—
1822	Inc. above	7.50	18.00	40.00	165	—
1822 Proof	—	Value: 375				

KM# 3 1/4 DOLLAR
0.8920 Silver

Date	Mintage	F	VF	XF	Unc	BU
1820	100,000	30.00	50.00	100	275	—
1820 Proof	—	Value: 450				
1822/1	71,000	10.00	20.00	45.00	225	—
1822	Inc. above	7.50	18.00	40.00	200	—
1822 Proof	—	Value: 450				

KM# 4 1/2 DOLLAR
0.8920 Silver

Date	Mintage	F	VF	XF	Unc	BU
1821 Proof, Unique	—	—	—	—	—	—
1822/1	89,000	120	250	550	800	—
1822	Inc. above	85.00	175	300	600	—
1822	—	Value: 800				

PATTERNS

Including off metal strikes

KM#	Date	Mintage	Identification	Mkt Val
Pn1	1820	—	1/16 Dollar. Silver. As KM1 but George III in legend, 17-19mm.	—
Pn2	1820	—	1/8 Dollar. Silver. As KM2 but George III in legend, 21-22mm.	—
Pn3	1820	—	1/4 Dollar. Silver. As KM3 but George III in legend, 27-28mm.	—

KM#	Date	Mintage	Identification	Mkt Val
Pn4	1823	—	1/100 Dollar. Copper.	2,250

KM#	Date	Mintage	Identification	Mkt Val
Pn5	1823	—	1/50 Dollar. Copper.	2,750

BRUNEI

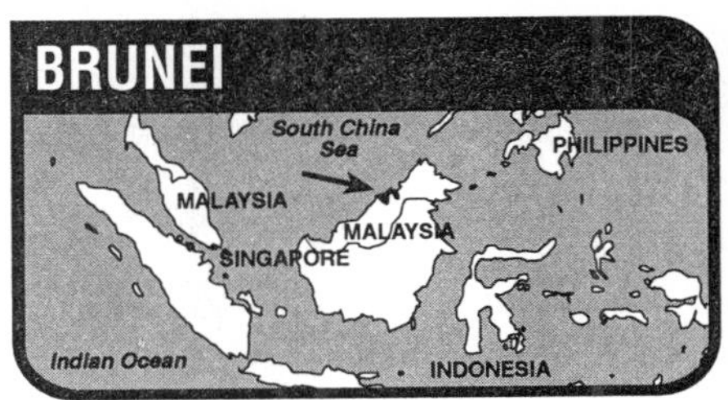

Negara Brunei Darussalam (State of Brunei), an independent sultanate on the northwest coast of the island of Borneo, has an area of 2,226 sq. mi. (5,765 sq. km.) and a population of *326,000. Capital: Bandar Seri Begawan. Crude oil and rubber are exported.

Magellan was the first European to visit Brunei in 1521. It was a powerful state, ruling over northern Borneo and adjacent islands from the 16th to the 19th century. Brunei became a British protectorate in 1888 and a British dependency in 1905. The Constitution of 1959 restored control over internal affairs to the sultan, while delegating responsibility for defense and foreign affairs to Britain. On January 1, 1984 it became independent.

TITLES

Negri Brunei

RULERS
Sultan Muhammad Tajuddin, 1795-1804
Sultan Muhammad Jamalul Alam I, 1804
Sultan Muhammad Tajuddin, 1804-1807
Sultan Muhammad Kanzul Alam, 1807-1826
Sultan Muhammad Alam, 1826-1828
Sultan Omar Ali Saifuddin II, 1828-1852
Sultan Abdul Mumin, 1852-1885
Sultan Hashim Jalal, 1885-1906

MONETARY SYSTEM
100 Cents = 1 Straits Dollar
100 Sen = 1 Dollar

SULTANATE

STANDARD COINAGE

KM# 1 1/2 PITIS
Tin, 24 mm.

Date	Mintage	Good	VG	F	VF	XF
AH1285	—	25.00	40.00	65.00	100	—

KM# 2.1 PITIS
Tin **Obv:** Flag at top to right

Date	Mintage	Good	VG	F	VF	XF
AH1285	—	20.00	30.00	50.00	95.00	—

KM# 2.2 PITIS
Tin **Obv:** Flag at top to left

Date	Mintage	Good	VG	F	VF	XF
AH1285	—	20.00	30.00	50.00	95.00	—

KM# 3 CENT
Copper

Date	Mintage	F	VF	XF	Unc	BU
AH1304	1,000,000	12.50	25.00	65.00	135	—
AH1304 Proof	—	Value: 470				

BULGARIA

The Republic of Bulgaria, formerly the Peoples Republic of Bulgaria, a Balkan country on the Black Sea in southeastern Europe, has an area of 42,855 sq. mi. (110,910 sq. km.). Capital: Sofia. Agriculture remains a key component of the economy but industrialization, particularly heavy industry, has been emphasized since the late 1940s.

The area now occupied by Bulgaria was conquered by the Bulgars, an Asiatic tribe, in the 7th century. Bulgarian kingdoms continued to exist on the Bulgarian peninsula until it came under Turkish rule in 1395. In 1878, after nearly 500 years of Turkish rule, Bulgaria was made a principality under Turkish suzerainty. Union seven years later with Eastern Rumelia created a Balkan state with borders approximating those of present-day Bulgaria. A Bulgarian kingdom, fully independent of Turkey, was proclaimed Sept. 22, 1908.

RULERS
Alexander I, as Prince, 1879-1886
Ferdinand I, as Prince, 1887-1908

MINT MARKS
KB - Kormoczbanya

MONETARY SYSTEM
100 Stotinki = 1 Lev

TURKISH PRINCIPALITY

STANDARD COINAGE

KM# 1 2 STOTINKI
Bronze **Ruler:** Alexander I as Prince **Rev:** HEATON below wreath

Date	Mintage	F	VF	XF	Unc	BU
1881	4,996,345	3.00	6.00	14.00	36.00	—
1881 Proof	—	Value: 95.00				

KM# 8 2-1/2 STOTINKI
Copper-Nickel **Ruler:** Ferdinand I as Prince

Date	Mintage	F	VF	XF	Unc	BU
1888	11,646,666	2.00	6.00	15.00	36.00	—
1888 Proof	—	Value: 85.00				

KM# 2 5 STOTINKI
Bronze **Ruler:** Alexander I as Prince **Rev:** HEATON below ribbon bow

Date	Mintage	F	VF	XF	Unc	BU
1881	10,000,000	2.00	5.00	14.00	40.00	—
1881 Proof	—	Value: 120				

KM# 9 5 STOTINKI
Copper-Nickel **Ruler:** Ferdinand I as Prince

Date	Mintage	F	VF	XF	Unc	BU
1888	14,000,000	1.00	3.00	12.00	26.00	—
1888 Proof	—	Value: 70.00				

KM# 3 10 STOTINKI
Bronze **Ruler:** Alexander I as Prince **Rev:** HEATON below ribbon bow

Date	Mintage	F	VF	XF	Unc	BU
1881	15,000,000	1.50	3.50	8.00	35.00	—
1881 Proof	—	Value: 80.00				

KM# 10 10 STOTINKI
Copper-Nickel **Ruler:** Ferdinand I as Prince

Date	Mintage	F	VF	XF	Unc	BU
1888	10,000,000	1.00	2.50	9.00	24.00	—

KM# 11 20 STOTINKI
Copper-Nickel **Ruler:** Ferdinand I as Prince

Date	Mintage	F	VF	XF	Unc	BU
1888	5,000,000	2.00	6.00	14.00	32.00	—
1888 Proof	—	Value: 80.00				

KM# 6 50 STOTINKI
2.5000 g., 0.8350 Silver .0671 oz. **Ruler:** Alexander I as Prince

Date	Mintage	F	VF	XF	Unc	BU
1883	3,000,000	1.50	2.50	7.00	22.00	—

KM# 12 50 STOTINKI
2.5000 g., 0.8350 Silver .0671 oz. **Ruler:** Ferdinand I as Prince

Date	Mintage	F	VF	XF	Unc	BU
1891KB	2,000,000	1.50	2.50	8.00	25.00	—

KM# 4 LEV
5.0000 g., 0.8350 Silver .1342 oz. **Ruler:** Alexander I as Prince

Date	Mintage	F	VF	XF	Unc	BU
1882	4,500,015	2.00	5.00	12.00	30.00	—

KM# 13 LEV
5.0000 g., 0.8350 Silver .1342 oz. **Ruler:** Ferdinand I as Prince

Date	Mintage	F	VF	XF	Unc	BU
1891KB	4,000,000	2.00	6.00	15.00	35.00	—

KM# 16 LEV
5.0000 g., 0.8350 Silver .1342 oz. **Ruler:** Ferdinand I as Prince

Date	Mintage	F	VF	XF	Unc	BU
1894KB	1,000,013	2.50	7.00	19.00	42.00	—

KM# 5 2 LEVA
10.0000 g., 0.8350 Silver .2685 oz. **Ruler:** Alexander I as Prince

Date	Mintage	F	VF	XF	Unc	BU
1882	2,000,000	3.00	7.50	20.00	52.00	—

KM# 14 2 LEVA
10.0000 g., 0.8350 Silver .2685 oz. **Ruler:** Ferdinand I

Date	Mintage	F	VF	XF	Unc	BU
1891KB	1,500,000	3.00	7.50	22.00	55.00	—

KM# 17 2 LEVA
10.0000 g., 0.8350 Silver .2685 oz. **Ruler:** Ferdinand I as Prince

Date	Mintage	F	VF	XF	Unc	BU
1894	1,000,000	3.50	9.00	22.00	60.00	—
1894 Proof	—	Value: 320				

KM# 7 5 LEVA
25.0000 g., 0.9000 Silver .7234 oz. **Ruler:** Alexander I as Prince

Date	Mintage	F	VF	XF	Unc	BU
1884	512,473	10.00	20.00	65.00	300	—
1885	1,426,000	8.00	14.00	55.00	275	—

KM# 15 5 LEVA
25.0000 g., 0.9000 Silver .7234 oz. **Ruler:** Ferdinand I as Prince

Date	Mintage	F	VF	XF	Unc	BU
1892KB	1,001,375	8.00	12.50	40.00	260	—
1892KB Proof	—	Value: 1,750				

KM# 18 5 LEVA
25.0000 g., 0.9000 Silver .7234 oz. **Ruler:** Ferdinand I as Prince
Obv: Legend rearranged

Date	Mintage	F	VF	XF	Unc	BU
1894KB	1,800,000	6.00	12.00	30.00	225	—
1894KB Proof	—	Value: 1,750				

KM# 19 10 LEVA
3.2258 g., 0.9000 Gold .0933 oz. **Ruler:** Ferdinand I as Prince

Date	Mintage	F	VF	XF	Unc	BU
1894KB	75,000	50.00	100	150	320	—
1894KB Proof	—	Value: 2,000				

KM# 20 20 LEVA
6.4516 g., 0.9000 Gold .1867 oz. **Ruler:** Ferdinand I as Prince

Date	Mintage	F	VF	XF	Unc	BU
1894KB	100,000	80.00	130	180	450	—
1894KB Proof	—	Value: 4,500				

KM# 21 100 LEVA
32.2580 g., 0.9000 Gold .9334 oz. **Ruler:** Ferdinand I as Prince

Date	Mintage	F	VF	XF	Unc	BU
1894KB	2,500	450	650	1,250	2,750	—

TURKISH SUZERAINTY

ESSAIS

KM#	Date	Mintage	Identification	Mkt Val
E1	1880 O.M.	8	10 Santim. Copper.	220
E2	1880	1	10 Santim. Silver.	—
E3	1887 A.B.	8	10 Santim. Copper.	250
E4	1887 A.D.	8	10 Stotinki. Copper.	—
E5	1894	—	Lev. Tin. Plain edge. KM#16.	—
E6	1894	2	2 Leva. Tin. Plain edge. KM#17.	—
E7	1894	1	5 Leva. Tin. Plain edge. KM#18.	—
E8	1894	1	20 Leva. Tin. Plain edge. KM#20.	—

PIEFORTS

KM#	Date	Mintage	Identification	Mkt Val
P1	1888	—	5 Stotinki. Nickel Alloy.	—
P2	1888	—	10 Stotinki. Nickel Alloy.	—

PATTERNS

Including off metal strikes

KM#	Date	Mintage	Identification	Mkt Val
Pn1	1887 A.B.	8	10 Santim. Copper.	—
Pn2	1887 A.D.	—	10 Stotinki. Copper.	—
PnA3	1888	—	10 Stotinki. Nickel Alloy. Plain edge. Thick planchet.	—
Pn3	1889	—	10 Stotinki. Copper. Broad flan.	—

BURMA (Myanmar)

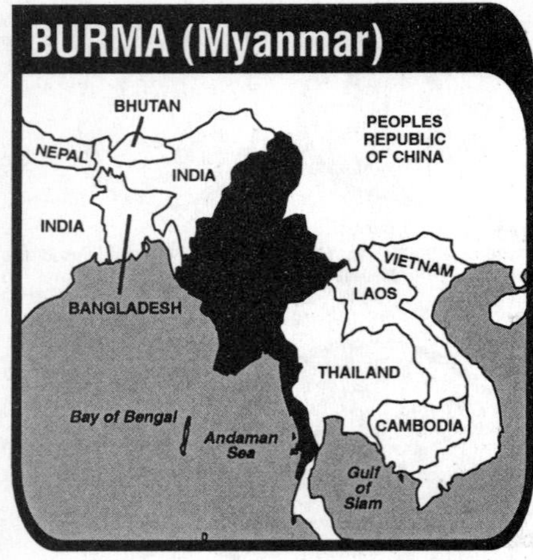

Burma, a country of Southeast Asia fronting on the Bay of Bengal and the Andaman Sea, had an area of 261,218 sq. mi. (678,500 sq. km.).

The first European to reach Burma, in about 1435, was Nicolo Di Conti, a Venetian merchant. During the beginning of the reign of Bodawpaya (1781-1819AD) the kingdom comprised most of the same area as it does today including Arakan which was taken over in 1784-85. The British East India Company, while unsuccessful in its 1612 effort to establish posts along the Bay of Bengal, was enabled by the Anglo-Burmese Wars of 1824-86 to expand to the whole of Burma and to secure its annexation to British India.

The coins issued by kings Mindon and Thibaw between 1852 and 1885 circulated in Upper Burma. Indian coins were current in Lower Burma, which was annexed in 1852. Burmese coins are frequently known by the equivalent Indian denominations, although their values are inscribed in Burmese units. Upper Burma was annexed in 1885 and the Burmese coinage remained in circulation until 1889, when Indian coins became current throughout Burma. Coins were again issued in the old Burmese denominations after independence in 1948, but these were replaced by decimal issues in 1952. The Chula-Sakarat (CS) dating is sometimes referred to as BE-Burmese Era and began in 638AD.

RULERS

Bodawpaya, CS1143-1181/1782-1819AD
Bagyidaw, CS1181-1198/1819-1837AD
Tharawaddy, CS1198-1207/1837-46AD
Pagan, CS1207-1214/1846-53AD
Mindon, CS1214-1240/1853-78AD
Thibaw, CS1240-1248/1880-85AD
British, 1886-1948

MONETARY SYSTEM

(Until 1952)

4 Pyas = 1 Pe
2 Pe = 1 Mu
2 Mu = 1 Mat
5 Mat = 1 Kyat

NOTE: Originally 10 light Mu = 1 Kyat, eventually 8 heavy Mu = 1 Kyat.

Indian Equivalents

1 Silver Kyat = 1 Rupee = 16 Annas
1 Gold Kyat = 1 Mohur = 16 Rupees

STANDARD COINAGE

KM# 22.1 1/8 PYA
Lead

Date	Mintage	Good	VG	F	VF	XF
BE1230 (1868) Rare	—	—	—	—	—	—

KM# 22.2 1/8 PYA
Lead **Obv:** Legend closer together

Date	Mintage	Good	VG	F	VF	XF
BE1231 (1869)	—	30.00	50.00	75.00	125	—

KM# 23 1/4 PYA
Lead, 21-22 mm. **Obv:** Hare crouching left **Rev:** Legend in wreath

Date	Mintage	Good	VG	F	VF	XF
CS1231 (1869)	—	25.00	40.00	60.00	100	—

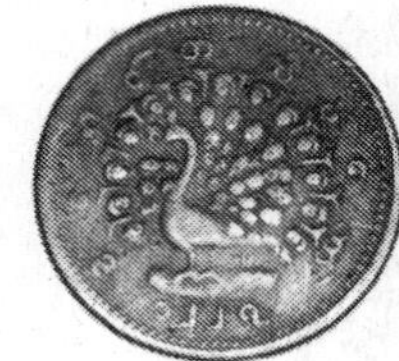

KM# 17 1/4 PE (Pice)
Copper

Date	Mintage	Good	VG	F	VF	XF
CS1227 (1865)	—	2.50	4.50	7.50	15.00	—

KM# 18 1/4 PE (Pice)
Copper **Rev:** Without stars above and below legend

Date	Mintage	Good	VG	F	VF	XF
CS1227 (1865)	—	2.50	4.50	8.50	17.50	—

KM# 18a 1/4 PE (Pice)
Iron

Date	Mintage	Good	VG	F	VF	XF
CS1227 (1865)	—	22.50	35.00	55.00	85.00	—

KM# 25.1 1/4 PE (Pice)
Copper **Rev:** Flower petals at the top of wreath upright

Date	Mintage	Good	VG	F	VF	XF
CS1240 (1878)	—	2.50	4.50	12.00	28.00	—

KM# 25.2 1/4 PE (Pice)
Copper **Rev:** Flower petals at the top of wreath diagonal

Date	Mintage	Good	VG	F	VF	XF
CS1240 (1878)	—	2.50	4.50	12.00	28.00	—

KM# 25a 1/4 PE (Pice)
Brass

Date	Mintage	Good	VG	F	VF	XF
CS1240 (1878)	—	7.50	12.50	22.50	38.00	—

KM# 25b 1/4 PE (Pice)
Tin

Date	Mintage	Good	VG	F	VF	XF
CS1240 (1878)	—	—	—	—	—	—

KM# 24 2 PYAS
10.9400 g., Copper

Date	Mintage	Good	VG	F	VF	XF
CS1231 (1869)	—	17.50	30.00	55.00	90.00	—

KM# 6.1 PE
0.7300 g., 0.9170 Silver .0215 oz.

Date	Mintage	F	VF	XF	Unc	BU
CS1214 (1852)	—	12.50	27.50	60.00	125	—

KM# 6.2 PE
0.7300 g., 0.9170 Silver .0215 oz. **Note:** Accent mark omitted from value.

Date	Mintage	F	VF	XF	Unc	BU
CS1214 (1852)	—	12.50	27.50	60.00	125	—

KM# 6.3 PE
0.7300 g., 0.9170 Silver .0215 oz. **Note:** Figure J omtted from date.

Date	Mintage	F	VF	XF	Unc	BU
CS1214 (1852)	—	12.50	27.50	60.00	125	—

KM# 6.4 PE
0.7300 g., 0.9170 Silver .0215 oz. **Note:** 2 dots omitted from value.

Date	Mintage	F	VF	XF	Unc	BU
CS1214 (1852)	—	12.50	27.50	60.00	125	—

KM# 6.5 PE
0.7300 g., 0.9170 Silver .0215 oz. **Note:** Accent marks and 2 dots omitted.

Date	Mintage	F	VF	XF	Unc	BU
CS1214 (1852)	—	12.50	27.50	60.00	125	—

KM# 13 PE
0.9000 Gold **Obv:** Facing peacock **Rev:** Value in sprays

Date	Mintage	Good	VG	F	VF	XF
CS1214 (1852)	—	35.00	60.00	90.00	150	—

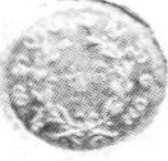

KM# 19 PE
0.6700 g., Gold

Date	Mintage	Good	VG	F	VF	XF
CS1228 (1866)	—	35.00	60.00	100	185	—

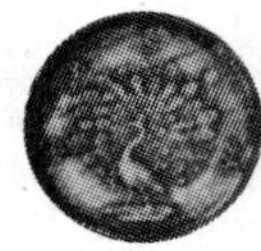

KM# 7.1 MU
1.4580 g., 0.9170 Silver .0430 oz.

Date	Mintage	F	VF	XF	Unc	BU
CS1214 (1852)	—	5.00	10.00	20.00	100	—

KM# 7.2 MU
1.4580 g., 0.9170 Silver .0430 oz. **Rev:** Dot above top left character in denomination

Date	Mintage	F	VF	XF	Unc	BU
CS1214 (1852)	—	Value: 450				

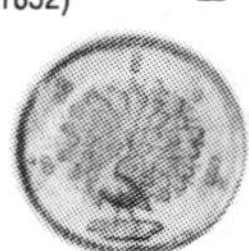
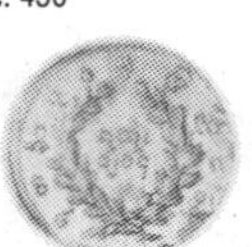

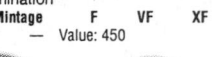

KM# 14 MU
0.9000 Gold **Obv:** Facing peacock **Rev:** Value in wreath

Date	Mintage	Good	VG	F	VF	XF
CS1214 (1852)	—	60.00	100	150	250	—

KM# A20 MU
1.2600 g., Gold **Obv:** Chinz standing left **Rev:** Value in sprays

Date	Mintage	VG	F	VF	XF	Unc
CS1228 (1866)	—	1,000	1,500	2,000	—	—

KM# 8.1 MAT
2.9160 g., 0.9170 Silver .0860 oz.

Date	Mintage	F	VF	XF	Unc	BU
CS1214 (1852)	—	7.50	12.50	50.00	125	—
CS1214 (1852)	—	—	—	—	—	—

KM# 8.2 MAT
2.9160 g., 0.9170 Silver .0860 oz. **Note:** Tail omitted from last digit of date.

Date	Mintage	F	VF	XF	Unc	BU
CS1214 (1852)	—	7.50	12.50	50.00	125	—

KM# 15 KYAT (Rupee)
16.4500 g., Silver **Obv:** Shwepyizoe bird **Rev:** Legend above date

Date	Mintage	Good	VG	F	VF	XF
BE2396 (0)	—	—	—	—	—	—

KM# 10 KYAT (Rupee)
11.6638 g., 0.9170 Silver .3436 oz.

Date	Mintage	F	VF	XF	Unc	BU
CS1214 (1852)	—	10.00	20.00	60.00	225	—
CS1214 (1852)	—	—	—	—	—	—

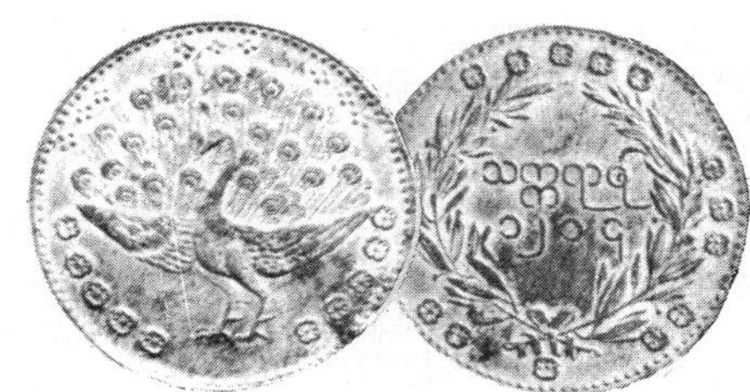

KM# 11 KYAT (Rupee)
16.2300 g., Silver **Obv:** Peacock with spread tail, flanked by two groups of 5 rosettes

Date	Mintage	Good	VG	F	VF	XF
CS1214 (1852)	—	150	350	500	850	—

KM# 12 KYAT (Rupee)
16.2300 g., Silver **Obv:** Peacock in full display with circular feather ends

Date	Mintage	Good	VG	F	VF	XF
CS1214 (1852)	—	250	500	1,000	1,500	—

KM# 16 KYAT (Rupee)
15.7500 g., Silver **Obv:** Peacock with folded tail flanked by floral garlands

Date	Mintage	Good	VG	F	VF	XF
CS1222 (1860)	—	—	—	—	—	—

KM# 20 2 MU 1 PE
2.7500 g., Gold **Obv:** Chinze

Date	Mintage	VG	F	VF	XF	Unc
CS1228 (1866)	—	125	175	275	475	—

KM# 26 5 MU (1/2 Mohur)
5.8500 g., Gold **Obv:** Chinze

Date	Mintage	VG	F	VF	XF	Unc
CS1240 (1878)	—	—	—	—	—	—

KM# 9 5 MU (1/2 Rupee)
5.8319 g., 0.9170 Silver .1718 oz.

Date	Mintage	F	VF	XF	Unc	BU
CS1214 (1852)	—	12.50	22.50	70.00	175	—
CS1214 (1852)	—	—	—	—	—	—

KM# 21 KYAT (Mohur)
11.9400 g., Gold **Obv:** Chinze

Date	Mintage	VG	F	VF	XF	Unc
CS1228 (1866)	—	—	—	—	—	—

PATTERNS

Including off metal strikes

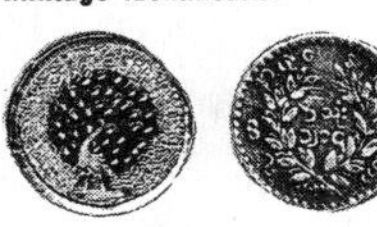

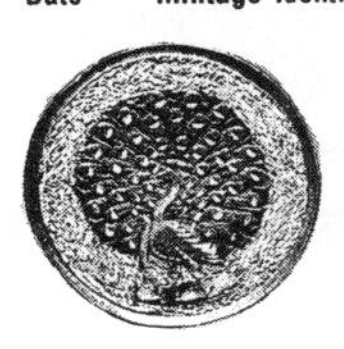

KM#	Date	Mintage	Identification	Mkt Val
Pn1	CS1214	—	Pe. Silver. Stippled field.	550
Pn2	CS1214	—	Mu. Silver. Stippled field.	450
Pn3	CS1214	—	Mat. Silver. Stippled field.	500
Pn4	CS1214	—	5 Mu. Silver. Stippled field.	700
Pn5	CS1214	—	5 Mu. Copper. KM9.	—
Pn6	CS1214	—	Kyat. Silver. Stippled field.	800
Pn7	CS1214	—	Kyat. Gold. KM#10. Restrike.	—
Pn8	CS1214	3	Kyat. Silver.	1250
Pn9	CS1214	—	Kyat. Copper.	900

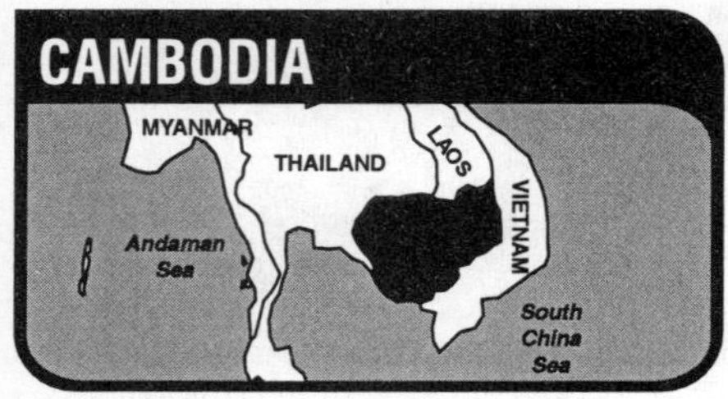

The State of Cambodia, formerly Democratic Kampuchea and the Khmer Republic, a land of paddy fields and forest-clad hills located on the Indo-Chinese peninsula, fronting on the Gulf of Thailand, has an area of 70,238 sq. mi. (181,040 sq. km.). Capital: Phnom Penh. Agriculture is the basis of the economy, with rice the chief crop.

The region was the nucleus of the Khmer Empire which flourished from the 5th to the 12th century and attained an excellence in art and architecture still evident in the magnificent ruins at Angkor. The Khmer empire once ruled over much of Southeast Asia, but began to decline in the 13th century as the Thai and Vietnamese invaded the region and attached its territories. At the request of the Cambodian king, a French protectorate attached to Cochin-China was established over the country in 1863, saving it from dissolution, and in 1885, Cambodia was included in the French Union of Indo-China.

RULERS

Kings of Cambodia

Norodom I, 1835-1904

MONETARY SYSTEM

(Until 1860)

2 Att = 1 Pe (Pey)
4 Pe = 1 Fuang (Fuong)
8 Fuang = 1 Tical
4 Salong = 1 Tical

(Commencing 1860)

100 Centimes = 1 Franc

FRENCH PROTECTORATE

TOKEN COINAGE

KM# Tn5 CENTIME

Brass **Issuer:** Pnom-Pehn Merchants **Note:** Round, center hole.

Date	Mintage	F	VF	XF	Unc	BU
ND	—	45.00	85.00	175	—	—

KM# Tn6 CENTIME

Brass **Issuer:** Pnom-Pehn Merchants **Note:** Without center hole.

Date	Mintage	F	VF	XF	Unc	BU
ND	—	50.00	95.00	200	—	—

KM# Tn7 CENTIME

Brass **Issuer:** Pnom-Pehn Merchants **Note:** Square center hole.

Date	Mintage	F	VF	XF	Unc	BU
ND	—	60.00	100	175	285	—

KINGDOM

TICAL COINAGE

KM# 1 ATT

Copper **Note:** Varieties exist. Weight varies: 1.40-2.50 grams. Uniface. Similar to 1 Pe, KM#2.

Date	Mintage	VG	F	VF	XF	Unc
CS1208 (1847)	—	4.00	6.50	12.00	25.00	—

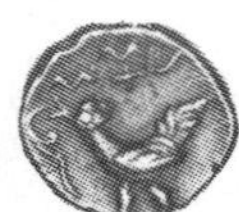

KM# 2 PE

Copper **Note:** Weight varies: 4.00-4.60 grams. Uniface. Hamza bird left.

Date	Mintage	VG	F	VF	XF	Unc
CS1208 (1847)	—	9.00	15.00	27.50	55.00	—

Note: With or without silver wash

KM# 3.1 PE

Copper-Billon **Note:** Weight varies: 0.20-0.90 grams. Uniface. Size varies: 8-9 millimeters. Counter-clockwise coiled lotus seed.

Date	Mintage	VG	F	VF	XF	Unc
ND	—	6.00	8.50	12.50	27.50	—

KM# 3.2 PE

Copper-Billon **Note:** Weight varies: 0.20-0.90 grams. Uniface. Size varies: 8-9 millimeters. Clockwise-coiled lotus seed. Varieties exist in tail design.

Date	Mintage	VG	F	VF	XF	Unc
ND (1847)	—	—	—	—	—	—

KM# 4 PE

Copper-Billon **Note:** Varieties exist. Size varies: 10-11 millimeters. Uniface. Cocoa bean.

Date	Mintage	VG	F	VF	XF	Unc
ND (1847)	—	6.00	9.00	15.00	30.00	—

KM# 5 PE

Copper-Billon **Note:** Size varies: 6-7 millimeters. Uniface. Crab, similar to 2 PE, KM#19.

Date	Mintage	VG	F	VF	XF	Unc
ND (1847)	—	9.00	15.00	27.50	50.00	—

KM# 7 2 PE (1/2 Fuang)

Copper-Billon **Note:** Weight varies: 1.00-2.00 grams. Uniface. Size varies: 13-15 millimeters. Rooster left.

Date	Mintage	VG	F	VF	XF	Unc
ND (1847)	—	3.00	4.50	8.00	20.00	—

KM# 9 2 PE (1/2 Fuang)

Copper-Billon **Note:** Peacock right, uniface.

Date	Mintage	VG	F	VF	XF	Unc
ND (1847)	—	5.00	8.00	15.00	35.00	—

KM# 11 2 PE (1/2 Fuang)

Copper-Billon **Note:** "Chi" (=luck) above Hamza bird, uniface.

Date	Mintage	VG	F	VF	XF	Unc
ND (1847)	—	3.00	6.00	10.00	15.00	—

Note: Some copper specimens show light silver wash; Varieties in style of tail feathers, dots and dashes

KM# 13 2 PE (1/2 Fuang)

Copper-Billon **Note:** Cobra

Date	Mintage	VG	F	VF	XF	Unc
ND (1847)	—	4.00	7.00	12.00	22.50	—

KM# 14 2 PE (1/2 Fuang)

Copper-Billon **Note:** Lotus, uniface.

Date	Mintage	VG	F	VF	XF	Unc
ND (1847)	—	4.00	7.00	—	22.50	12.00

KM# 15 2 PE (1/2 Fuang)

Copper-Billon **Note:** Goat left, uniface.

Date	Mintage	VG	F	VF	XF	Unc
ND (1847)	—	5.50	8.00	12.50	27.50	—

KM# 17 2 PE (1/2 Fuang)

Copper-Billon **Note:** Horse right, uniface.

Date	Mintage	VG	F	VF	XF	Unc
ND (1847)	—	5.50	8.00	12.50	27.50	—

KM# 19 2 PE (1/2 Fuang)

Copper-Billon **Note:** Crab, uniface.

Date	Mintage	VG	F	VF	XF	Unc
ND (1847)	—	10.00	15.00	27.50	55.00	—

KM# 21 2 PE (1/2 Fuang)

Copper-Billon **Note:** Weight varies: 1.00-2.00 grams. Uniface. Size varies: 13-15 millimeters. Hyppogriff right.

Date	Mintage	VG	F	VF	XF	Unc
ND (1847)	—	10.00	15.00	27.50	55.00	—

KM# 23 2 PE (1/2 Fuang)

Copper-Billon **Note:** Weight varies: 1.00-2.00 grams. Uniface. Size varies: 13-15 millimeters. Elephant right.

Date	Mintage	VG	F	VF	XF	Unc
ND (1847)	—	10.00	15.00	27.50	55.00	—

KM# 25 2 PE (1/2 Fuang)

Copper-Billon **Rev. Legend:** Cambodian script **Note:** Weight varies: 1.00-2.00 grams. Uniface. Size varies: 13-15 millimeters. Garuda bird facing left.

Date	Mintage	VG	F	VF	XF	Unc
ND (1847)	—	5.00	8.00	15.00	35.00	—

Note: KM#3's through 25 were hand struck between 1650 and 1850.

KM# 28 2 PE (1/2 Fuang)

1.8500 g., Silver **Note:** Uniface. Similar to KM#25, but without snake in hand.

Date	Mintage	VG	F	VF	XF	Unc
ND (1847)	—	—	—	—	300	—

KM# 26 2 PE (1/2 Fuang)

Copper-Billon **Obv:** Garuda bird facing left without border **Note:** Weight varies: 1.00-2.00 grams. Uniface. Size varies: 13-15 millimeters.

Date	Mintage	VG	F	VF	XF	Unc
ND (1880)	—	3.00	6.00	10.00	15.00	—

Note: Varieties exist in style of denticles

KM# 30 2 PE (1/2 Fuang)

Brass Or Copper **Obv:** Garuda bird facing left but without border around bird **Rev:** 3-line legend

Date	Mintage	VG	F	VF	XF	Unc
ND (1880)	—	50.00	100	125	175	—

KM# 30a 2 PE (1/2 Fuang)

1.4600 g., Billon

Date	Mintage	VG	F	VF	XF	Unc
ND (1880)	—	—	50.00	70.00	90.00	—

Note: The precise status is undetermined. It is probably a token issue

KM# 27 FUANG

Silver Or Billon **Obv:** Circle at left **Note:** Weight varies: 2.70-5.60 grams (heavy issue). Uniface. Large flan. Size varies: 18-22 millimeters. Hand struck.

Date	Mintage	VG	F	VF	XF	Unc
ND (1847)	—	50.00	100	180	250	—

KM# 29 FUANG

Silver Or Billon **Obv:** Hippogriff walking to right **Note:** Similar to 2 Pe, KM#21.

Date	Mintage	VG	F	VF	XF	Unc
ND (1847)	—	50.00	100	180	250	—

Note: KM#'s 1 through 29 are believed to have been struck at Battambang except KM#25 which is thought to have been made at Siam Reap

KM# 32.1 1/8 TICAL (1 Fuang)
Copper-Billon **Obv:** Hamza bird **Note:** Weight varies: 1.50-1.80 grams (light issue). Small flan. Size varies: 11-15 millimeters. Uniface.

Date	Mintage	VG	F	VF	XF	Unc
ND (1847)	—	4.50	7.00	12.50	27.50	—

KM# 32.2 1/8 TICAL (1 Fuang)
Copper-Billon **Obv:** Hamza bird without small circle at left **Note:** Light issue, weight varies: 1.50-1.80 grams. Small flan. Size varies: 11-15 millimeters. Uniface.

Date	Mintage	VG	F	VF	XF	Unc
ND (1847)	—	4.00	7.00	12.50	27.50	—

Note: Many varieties exist, copper strikes with silver wash known

KM# 33 1/8 TICAL (1 Fuang)
Silver **Note:** Modern counterfeits exist in copper, silver, and gold.

Date	Mintage	F	VF	XF	Unc	BU
ND (1847)	—	125	225	350	—	—

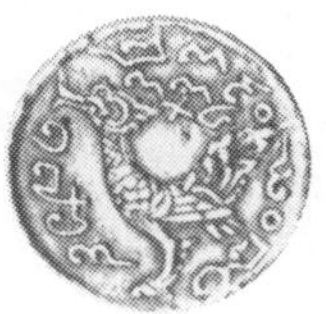

KM# 34 1/4 TICAL (1 Salong)
3.2000 g., Silver

Date	Mintage	F	VF	XF	Unc	BU
CS1208 (1847)	—	350	550	800	—	—

KM# 35 1/4 TICAL (1 Salong)
3.6000 g., Silver

Date	Mintage	F	VF	XF	Unc	BU
CS1208 (1847)	—	250	400	550	—	—

KM# 39 1/4 TICAL (1 Salong)
3.6000 g., Silver

Date	Mintage	F	VF	XF	Unc	BU
CS1209 (1848)	—	—	—	—	—	—

KM# 36 TICAL
15.2580 g., Silver **Note:** Thick flan.

Date	Mintage	F	VF	XF	Unc	BU
CS1208 (1847)	—	100	200	500	—	—

KM# 37 TICAL
14.2090 g., Silver **Note:** Thin flan.

Date	Mintage	F	VF	XF	Unc	BU
CS1208 (1847)	—	75.00	150	350	—	—

Note: Various local merchant countermarks in Chinese or other scripts are known to exist for KM#36-37

KM# 38 TICAL
60.5000 g., Silver

Date	Mintage	F	VF	XF	Unc	BU
CS1209 (1848) Rare	—	—	—	—	—	—

FRANC COINAGE

KM# 42.1 CENTIME
Bronze

Date	Mintage	F	VF	XF	Unc	BU
1860	11,467,000	5.00	12.00	35.00	75.00	—
1860 Proof	—	Value: 100				

KM# 42.2 CENTIME
Bronze

Date	Mintage	F	VF	XF	Unc	BU
1860 Restrike	—	—	10.00	30.00	65.00	—

KM# 43.1 CENTIME
Bronze

Date	Mintage	F	VF	XF	Unc	BU
1860 Proof	—	Value: 185				
1860	10,267,000	6.00	15.00	45.00	95.00	—

KM# 43.2 CENTIME
Bronze

Date	Mintage	F	VF	XF	Unc	BU
1860 Restrike	—	—	12.00	35.00	75.00	—

KM# 43.3 CENTIME
Bronze

Date	Mintage	F	VF	XF	Unc	BU
1860	—	15.00	40.00	75.00	150	—

KM# 44.1 25 CENTIMES
1.2500 g., 0.9000 Silver .0361 oz.

Date	Mintage	F	VF	XF	Unc	BU
1860	—	10.00	30.00	100	250	—
1860 Proof	—	Value: 500				

KM# 44.2 25 CENTIMES
1.2500 g., 0.9000 Silver .0361 oz. **Note:** Reduced weight.

Date	Mintage	F	VF	XF	Unc	BU
1860 Restrike	—	—	15.00	30.00	75.00	—

KM# 45.1 50 CENTIMES
2.5000 g., 0.9000 Silver .0723 oz.

Date	Mintage	F	VF	XF	Unc	BU
1860	—	20.00	60.00	125	300	—

KM# 45.2 50 CENTIMES
1.7000 g., 0.9000 Silver .0723 oz. **Note:** Reduced weight.

Date	Mintage	F	VF	XF	Unc	BU
1860 Restrike	—	—	20.00	40.00	100	—

KM# 46.1 FRANC
5.0000 g., 0.9000 Silver .1446 oz.

Date	Mintage	F	VF	XF	Unc	BU
1860	—	25.00	70.00	175	400	—
1860 Proof	—	Value: 700				

KM# 46.2 FRANC
3.5000 g., 0.9000 Silver .1446 oz. **Note:** Reduced weight.

Date	Mintage	F	VF	XF	Unc	BU
1860 Restrike	—	—	35.00	60.00	125	—

KM# 47.1 FRANC
10.0000 g., 0.9000 Silver .2893 oz.

Date	Mintage	F	VF	XF	Unc	BU
1860	—	45.00	125	250	500	—
1860 Proof	—	Value: 850				

KM# 47.2 FRANC
8.0000 g., 0.9000 Silver .2893 oz. **Note:** Reduced weight.

Date	Mintage	F	VF	XF	Unc	BU
1860	—	—	45.00	75.00	225	—

KM# 48.1 4 FRANCS
20.0000 g., 0.9000 Silver .5786 oz.

Date	Mintage	F	VF	XF	Unc	BU
1860	—	85.00	225	375	700	—
1860 Proof	—	Value: 1,650				

KM# 48.2 4 FRANCS
15.6000 g., 0.9000 Silver .5786 oz. **Note:** Reduced weight.

Date	Mintage	F	VF	XF	Unc	BU
1860	—	—	60.00	120	350	—

KM# 49 PIASTRE
27.0000 g., 0.9000 Silver .7812 oz.

Date	Mintage	F	VF	XF	Unc	BU
1860	—	325	650	1,400	2,750	—
1860 Proof	—	Value: 3,250				

TOKEN COINAGE

KM# Tn1 10 CENTIMES
Brass, 26 mm. **Issuer:** Panom Penh Royal Palace **Obv. Legend:** SOMDACH PREA NÒRÔDOM...

Date	Mintage	F	VF	XF	Unc	BU
ND(1875-1904)	—	—	125	145	175	—

KM# Tn2 15 CENTIMES
Brass, 26 mm. **Issuer:** Panom Penh Royal Palace **Obv. Legend:** SOMDACH PREA NÒRÔDOM...

Date	Mintage	F	VF	XF	Unc	BU
ND(1875-1904)	—	—	175	200	225	—

KM# Tn3 20 CENTIMES
Brass, 26 mm. **Issuer:** Panom Penh Royal Palace **Obv. Legend:** SOMDACH PREA NÒRÔDOM...

Date	Mintage	F	VF	XF	Unc	BU
ND(1875-1904)	—	—	175	200	225	—

KM# Tn4 25 CENTIMES
Brass, 26 mm. **Issuer:** Panom Penh Royal Palace **Obv. Legend:** SOMDACH PREA NÒRÔDOM...

Date	Mintage	F	VF	XF	Unc	BU
ND(1875-1904)	—	—	200	225	250	—

ESSAIS

KM#	Date	Mintage	Identification	Issue Price	Mkt Val
E1	1860	—	5 Centimes. Large bust, E left of truncation.	—	125
E2	1860	—	5 Centimes. Small bust, ESSAI below truncation.	—	150
E2a	1860	—	10 Centimes. Silver.	—	250
EA3	1860	—	10 Centimes. Silver. Large bust, E left of truncation.	—	125
E3	1860	—	25 Centimes.	—	200
E4	1860	—	50 Centimes.	—	250
E5	1860	—	Franc.	—	350
E6	1860	—	2 Francs.	—	450
E7	1860	—	4 Francs. With E.	—	1,000
E8	1860	—	Piastre.	—	5,000

PATTERNS

Including off metal strikes

KM#	Date	Mintage	Identification	Mkt Val
Pn1	CS1208	—	3 Tical. White Metal.	5,000
Pn2	CS1208	—	3 Tical. White Metal.	5,000
PnA3	ND	—	2 Pe. Gold. 2.9800 g. KM#26.	1,200
Pn3	1860	—	5 Centimes. Gold. KM#42.	—
Pn4	1860	—	10 Centimes. Gold. Plain edge.	—
Pn5	1860	—	10 Centimes. Gold. KM#43.	3,000
Pn7	1860	—	50 Centimes. Gold. KM#45.	1,000
Pn8	1860	—	Franc. Gold. KM46.	1,250
Pn9	1860	—	2 Francs. Gold. KM47.	2,250
Pn10	1860	—	4 Francs. Gold. KM48.	4,000
Pn11	1860	—	Piastre. Gold. KM49.	—
Pn12	1860	—	Piastre. Silver. KM49.	1,000
Pn13	1860	—	Piastre. Copper. Reeded edge. KM49.	650
Pn14	1860	—	Piastre. Copper. Plain edge. KM49.	650

PIEFORTS

Double thickness

Standard metals unless otherwise noted

KM#	Date	Mintage	Identification	Issue Price	Mkt Val
P1	1860	110	5 Centimes.	—	300
P2	1860	110	10 Centimes.	—	400
P3	1860	—	20 Centimes.	—	500
P4	1860	—	50 Centimes.	—	600
P5	1860	—	Franc.	—	700
P6	1860	—	2 Francs.	—	800
P7	1860	—			1,500
P8	1860	—	Piastre.	—	6,000

CANADA

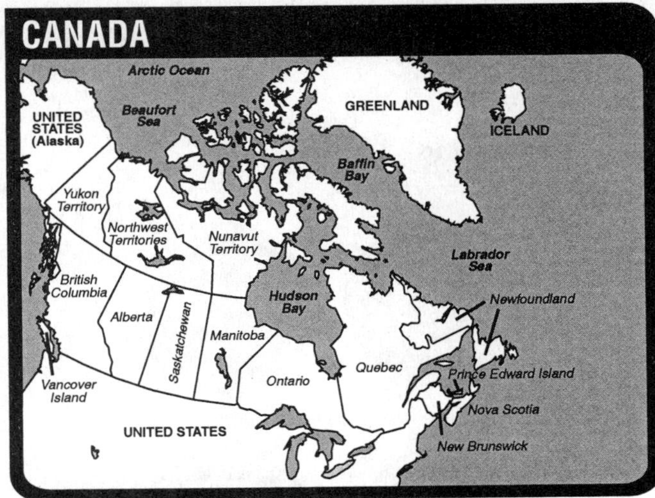

Canada is located to the north of the United States, and spans the full breadth of the northern portion of North America from Atlantic to Pacific oceans, except for the State of Alaska. It has a total area of 3,850,000 sq. mi. (9,971,550 sq. km.) and a population of 30.29 million. Capital: Ottawa.

Jacques Cartier, a French explorer, took possession of Canada for France in 1534, and for more than a century the history of Canada was that of a French colony. Samuel de Champlain helped to establish the first permanent colony in North America, in 1604 at Port Royal, Acadia – now Annapolis Royal, Nova Scotia. Four years later he founded the settlement in Quebec.

The British settled along the coast to the south while the French, motivated by a grand design, pushed into the interior. France's plan for a great American empire was to occupy the Mississippi heartland of the country, and from there to press in upon the narrow strip of English coastal settlements from the west. Inevitably, armed conflict erupted between the French and the British; consequently, Britain acquired Hudson Bay, Newfoundland and Nova Scotia from the French in 1713. British control of the rest of New France was secured in 1763, largely because of James Wolfe's great victory over Montcalm near Quebec in 1759.

During the American Revolution, Canada became a refuge for great numbers of American Royalists, most of whom settled in Ontario, thereby creating an English majority west of the Ottawa River. The ethnic imbalance contravened the effectiveness of the prevailing French type of government, and in 1791 the Constitutional act was passed by the British parliament, dividing Canada at the Ottawa River into two parts, each with its own government: Upper Canada, chiefly English and consisting of the southern section of what is now Ontario; and Lower Canada, chiefly French and consisting principally of the southern section of Quebec. Subsequent revolt by dissidents in both sections caused the British government to pass the Union Act, July 23, 1840, which united Lower and Upper Canada (as Canada East and Canada West) to form the Province of Canada, with one council and one assembly in which the two sections had equal numbers.

The union of the two provinces did not encourage political stability; the equal strength of the French and British made the task of government all but impossible. A further change was made with the passage of the British North American Act, which took effect on July 1, 1867, and established Canada as the first federal union in the British Empire. Four provinces entered the union at first: Upper Canada as Ontario, Lower Canada as Quebec, Nova Scotia and New Brunswick. The Hudson Bay Company's territories were acquired in 1869 out of which were formed the provinces of Manitoba, Saskatchewan and Alberta. British Columbia joined in 1871 and Prince Edward Island in 1873. Canada took over the Arctic Archipelago in 1895. In 1949 Newfoundland came into the confederation.

In the early years, Canada's coins were struck in England at the Royal Mint in London or at the Heaton Mint in Birmingham. Issues struck at the Royal Mint do not bear a mint mark, but those produced by Heaton carry an "H". All Canadian coins have been struck since January 2, 1908, at the Royal Canadian Mints at Ottawa and recently at Winnipeg except for some 1968 pure nickel dimes struck at the U.S. Mint in Philadelphia, and do not bear mint marks. Ottawa's mint mark (C) does not appear on some 20th Century Newfoundland issues, however, as it does on English type sovereigns struck there from 1908 through 1918.

Canada is a member of the Commonwealth of Nations. Elizabeth II is Head of State as Queen of Canada.

RULERS:
British 1763-

MONETARY SYSTEM
1 Dollar = 100 Cents

CONFEDERATION

CIRCULATION COINAGE

KM# 1 CENT Weight: 3.2400 g. **Composition:** Bronze

Date	Mintage	VG-8	F-12	VF-20	XF-40	MS-60	MS-63	Proof
1858	421,000	50.00	60.00	80.00	120	300	1,250	—
1859/8 Wide 9	Inc. above	25.00	35.00	60.00	90.00	250	1,350	—
1859 Narrow 9	9,579,000	2.25	3.00	5.00	7.00	35.00	175	—
1859 Double punched narrow 9 type I	Inc. above	175	250	350	540	1,150	3,000	—
1859 Double punched narrow 9 type II	Inc. above	35.00	70.00	95.00	150	325	1,600	—

KM# 7 CENT Weight: 3.2400 g. **Composition:** Bronze

Date	Mintage	VG-8	F-12	VF-20	XF-40	MS-60	MS-63	Proof
1876H	4,000,000	2.00	2.75	4.00	7.50	45.00	190	—
1881H	2,000,000	3.00	4.00	9.00	14.00	60.00	250	—
1882H	4,000,000	2.00	2.75	4.00	7.50	32.00	170	—
1884	2,500,000	2.25	3.00	5.00	8.50	60.00	225	—
1886	1,500,000	3.75	5.00	10.00	20.00	90.00	350	—
1887	1,500,000	2.75	4.00	6.00	11.00	55.00	215	—
1888	4,000,000	2.00	3.00	5.00	7.50	35.00	160	—
1890H	1,000,000	5.00	8.00	13.00	25.00	100	400	—
1891 Large date	1,452,000	5.50	9.00	13.50	30.00	125	420	—
1891 S.D.L.L.	Inc. above	50.00	75.00	110	160	620	2,150	—
1891 S.D.S.L.	Inc. above	35.00	50.00	65.00	95.00	225	650	—
1892	1,200,000	4.00	7.00	10.00	13.50	55.00	220	—
1893	2,000,000	2.50	3.00	5.00	7.50	35.00	125	—
1894	1,000,000	8.00	12.00	17.00	30.00	90.00	265	—
1895	1,200,000	4.00	7.00	10.00	16.00	55.00	225	—
1896	2,000,000	2.00	2.75	5.00	7.50	40.00	150	—
1897	1,500,000	2.50	4.00	5.00	9.00	45.00	165	—
1898H	1,000,000	5.00	7.00	12.00	18.00	75.00	250	—
1899	2,400,000	2.25	3.00	4.00	7.00	35.00	100	—
1900	1,000,000	5.00	9.00	15.00	22.00	85.00	400	—
1900H	2,600,000	2.00	2.50	4.00	5.50	30.00	75.00	—
1901	4,100,000	2.25	3.00	4.50	5.50	30.00	80.00	—

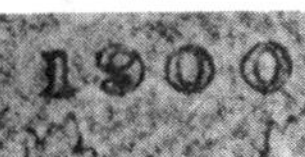

KM# 2 5 CENTS Weight: 1.1620 g. **Composition:** 0.9250 Silver 0.0346 oz. ASW

Date	Mintage	VG-8	F-12	VF-20	XF-40	MS-60	MS-63	Proof
1858 Small date	1,500,000	12.00	20.00	35.00	55.00	250	525	—
1858 Large date over small date	Inc. above	125	200	325	550	1,350	3,000	—
1870 Flat rim	2,800,000	13.50	22.50	40.00	60.00	250	650	—
1870 Wire rim	Inc. above	10.00	20.00	35.00	55.00	225	525	—
1871	1,400,000	13.50	22.50	40.00	70.00	275	600	—
1872H	2,000,000	9.00	16.00	35.00	55.00	250	750	—
1874H Plain 4	800,000	15.00	35.00	75.00	120	400	950	—
1874H Crosslet 4	Inc. above	14.00	30.00	60.00	120	450	1,100	—
1875H Large date	1,000,000	170	275	425	875	2,750	7,000	—
1875H Small date	Inc. above	90.00	175	285	500	1,750	4,550	—
1880H	3,000,000	5.00	8.00	18.00	40.00	250	600	—
1881H	1,500,000	6.00	10.00	20.00	45.00	265	650	—
1882H	1,000,000	8.00	15.00	25.00	55.00	275	700	—
1883H	600,000	15.00	30.00	70.00	150	750	2,000	—
1884	200,000	85.00	165	275	650	2,850	7,250	—
1885 Small 5	1,000,000	10.00	20.00	40.00	90.00	500	1,800	—
1885 Large 5	Inc. above	11.50	22.50	45.00	100	550	2,000	—
1885 Large 5 over small 5	Inc. above	50.00	100	175	450	2,850	2,750	—
1886 Small 6	1,700,000	7.00	15.00	25.00	50.00	300	900	—
1886 Large 6	Inc. above	9.00	16.00	28.00	60.00	350	1,000	—
1887	500,000	16.00	30.00	55.00	120	400	825	—
1888	1,000,000	5.00	9.00	18.00	35.00	165	425	—
1889	1,200,000	20.00	35.00	75.00	125	475	1,200	—
1890H	1,000,000	6.00	12.00	22.00	50.00	200	450	—
1891	1,800,000	5.00	8.00	15.00	30.00	150	385	—
1892	860,000	6.00	10.00	20.00	50.00	250	675	—
1893	1,700,000	4.00	7.00	14.00	30.00	175	400	—
1894	500,000	12.00	25.00	50.00	100	300	1,100	—
1896	1,500,000	5.00	7.00	14.00	35.00	175	375	—
1897	1,319,283	4.50	6.50	13.50	30.00	150	325	—
1898	580,717	10.00	20.00	35.00	70.00	250	750	—
1899	3,000,000	4.50	6.50	12.00	25.00	115	300	—
1900 Oval 0's	1,800,000	4.50	6.50	12.00	25.00	115	325	—
1900 Round 0's	Inc. above	15.00	35.00	50.00	110	300	800	—
1901	2,000,000	4.50	6.50	12.00	30.00	125	345	—

KM# 3 10 CENTS Weight: 2.3240 g. **Composition:** 0.9250 Silver 0.0691 oz. ASW
Obverse: Victoria bust left

Date	Mintage	VG-8	F-12	VF-20	XF-40	MS-60	MS-63	Proof
1858/5		475	775	1,250	1,850	4,550	—	—
1858	1,250,000	20.00	35.00	65.00	100	325	850	—
1870 Narrow 0	1,600,000	18.00	30.00	75.00	125	375	900	—
1870 Wide 0	Inc. above	25.00	50.00	100	200	500	1,150	—
1871	800,000	22.00	40.00	90.00	175	500	1,800	—
1871H	1,870,000	22.00	40.00	95.00	200	550	1,250	—
1872H	1,000,000	90.00	150	300	550	1,750	3,350	—
1874H	600,000	12.00	22.00	45.00	100	350	900	—

Date	Mintage	VG-8	F-12	VF-20	XF-40	MS-60	MS-63	Proof
1875H	1,000,000	200	375	650	1,350	4,500	9,500	—
1880H	1,500,000	12.00	22.00	45.00	85.00	300	800	—
1881H	950,000	17.50	30.00	60.00	110	375	1,000	—
1882H	1,000,000	17.50	30.00	60.00	110	385	1,100	—
1883H	300,000	45.00	85.00	185	325	900	2,000	—
1884	150,000	165	345	635	1,400	5,150	12,000	—
1885	400,000	40.00	75.00	185	425	1,700	4,500	—
1886 Small 6	800,000	20.00	40.00	85.00	185	800	2,250	—
1886 Large 6	Inc. above	30.00	50.00	100	215	925	2,150	—
1887	350,000	45.00	85.00	175	375	1,150	3,000	—
1888	500,000	10.00	22.00	45.00	85.00	300	800	—
1889	600,000	450	900	1,550	3,200	10,000	18,500	—
1890H	450,000	20.00	35.00	80.00	175	425	950	—
1891 21 leaves	800,000	20.00	35.00	85.00	175	450	1,150	—
1891 22 leaves	Inc. above	20.00	35.00	85.00	175	435	1,000	—
1892/1	520,000	120	220	425	675	2,350	3,250	—
1892	Inc. above	20.00	35.00	75.00	145	425	950	—
1893 Flat-top 3	500,000	30.00	55.00	110	200	675	1,750	—
1893 Round-top 3	Inc. above	500	975	1,800	3,200	8,000	17,500	—
1894	500,000	25.00	45.00	85.00	150	400	1,150	—
1896	650,000	12.00	22.00	40.00	75.00	275	650	—
1898	720,000	12.00	24.00	45.00	80.00	300	700	—
1899 Small 9's	1,200,000	8.50	16.00	35.00	75.00	210	575	—
1899 Large 9's	Inc. above	16.00	28.00	60.00	120	400	1,100	—
1900	1,100,000	8.50	16.00	35.00	70.00	200	550	—
1901	1,200,000	8.50	16.00	35.00	70.00	200	550	—

KM# 4 20 CENTS **Weight:** 4.6480 g. **Composition:** 0.9250 Silver 0.1382 oz. ASW

Date	Mintage	VG-8	F-12	VF-20	XF-40	MS-60	MS-63	Proof
1858	750,000	45.00	60.00	90.00	170	725	1,950	—

KM# 5 25 CENTS **Weight:** 5.8100 g. **Composition:** 0.9250 Silver 0.1728 oz. ASW

Date	Mintage	VG-8	F-12	VF-20	XF-40	MS-60	MS-63	Proof
1870	900,000	14.00	30.00	75.00	150	550	1,500	—
1871	400,000	22.00	40.00	90.00	225	800	2,100	—
1871H	748,000	25.00	45.00	115	250	700	1,650	—
1872H	2,240,000	10.00	20.00	40.00	90.00	425	1,250	—
1874H	1,600,000	10.00	20.00	40.00	90.00	375	1,100	—
1875H	1,000,000	275	550	1,350	2,750	10,000	17,500	—
1880H Narrow 0	400,000	40.00	85.00	220	400	1,150	2,750	—
1880H Wide 0	Inc. above	60.00	185	350	800	2,350	4,750	—
1880H Wide/narrow 0	Inc. above	100	225	400	950	2,800	—	—
1881H	820,000	20.00	45.00	90.00	250	1,000	2,300	—
1882H	600,000	20.00	45.00	110	265	1,000	2,150	—
1883H	960,000	16.00	32.00	70.00	150	500	1,250	—
1885	192,000	100	200	450	950	3,500	7,500	—
1886/3	540,000	35.00	80.00	150	375	1,500	3,200	—
1886	Inc. above	20.00	40.00	110	285	1,100	2,800	—
1887	100,000	85.00	225	450	1,000	4,250	8,000	—
1888	400,000	20.00	40.00	80.00	185	650	1,550	—
1889	66,324	100	250	500	1,000	3,500	8,500	—
1890H	200,000	25.00	50.00	125	275	950	2,250	—
1891	120,000	65.00	125	320	625	1,600	2,500	—
1892	510,000	15.00	25.00	65.00	175	675	1,600	—
1893	100,000	90.00	185	375	700	1,750	3,000	—
1894	220,000	20.00	40.00	90.00	250	700	1,600	—
1899	415,580	8.00	20.00	55.00	150	600	1,350	—
1900	1,320,000	7.00	16.00	40.00	95.00	425	975	—
1901	640,000	7.00	16.00	45.00	140	450	975	—

KM# 6 50 CENTS **Weight:** 11.6200 g. **Composition:** 0.9250 Silver .3456 oz. ASW

Date	Mintage	VG-8	F-12	VF-20	XF-40	MS-60	MS-63	Proof
1870	450,000	500	850	1,700	3,400	15,500	38,500	—
1870 LCW	Inc. above	45.00	75.00	165	375	3,500	10,000	—
1871	200,000	50.00	120	250	500	4,200	11,500	—
1871H	45,000	90.00	175	375	850	6,700	14,000	—
1872H	80,000	45.00	75.00	175	400	3,800	10,250	—
1872H Inverted A for V in Victoria	Inc. above	150	400	900	2,200	7,750	13,500	—
1881H	150,000	45.00	85.00	200	450	4,250	10,500	—
1888	60,000	175	300	600	1,100	5,600	13,500	—
1890H	20,000	650	1,250	2,000	4,000	12,250	22,500	—
1892	151,000	50.00	95.00	320	500	6,000	11,500	—
1894	29,036	250	450	950	2,100	9,000	17,500	—
1898	100,000	50.00	120	250	450	4,750	11,500	—
1899	50,000	100	200	450	1,100	9,000	17,500	—
1900	118,000	45.00	75.00	165	375	4,000	10,500	—
1901	80,000	48.00	80.00	175	400	4,200	10,500	—

PATTERNS

Including off metal strikes

KM	Date	Mintage	Identification	Mkt Val
Pn1	1858	—	Cent. Bronze. Uniface, wide date.	—
Pn2	1858	—	Cent. Bronze. Uniface, close date.	—
Pn3	1858	—	Cent. Bronze.	—
Pn4	1858	—	20 Cents. Silver. Plain edge.	15,000
Pn5	1859	—	Cent. Bronze. Mule with Great Britain 1/2 penny reverse.	—
PnA6	1859	—	Cent. Copper-Nickel. Mule with Great Britain 1/2 penny reverse.	—
Pn7	1871	—	20 Cents. Silver. Plain edge.	—
Pn8	1871	—	20 Cents. Silver. Reeded edge. Without H.	—
Pn9	1875	—	5 Cents. Without H.	—
Pn10	1876	—	Cent. Bronze. Without H.	—
Pn11	1876	—	Cent. Copper-Nickel.	12,500
Pn12	1876	—	Cent. Bronze. Head of '58.	—
Pn13	1876	—	10 Cents. Bronze. Engraved B. Reeded edge. Unique.	—

TRIAL STRIKES

KM	Date	Mintage	Identification	Mkt Val
TS1	1858	—	Cent. Copper-Nickel. Double thickness.	—
TS2	1858	—	Cent. Copper-Nickel. 2 known.	—

SPECIMEN SETS (SS)

KM	Date	Mintage	Identification	Issue Price	Mkt Val
SS1	1858	I.A.	KM1-4, Reeded edge	—	9,000
SS2	1858	I.A.	KM1-4, Plain edge	—	6,000
SS3	1858	I.A.	KM1-4; Double Set	—	15,000
SS4	1858	I.A.	KM1 (overdate), 2-4; Double Set	—	15,000
SS5	1870	100	KM2, 3, 5, 6 (reeded edges)	—	28,500
SS6	1870	I.A.	KM2, 3, 5, 6; Double Set (plain edges)	—	55,000
SS7	1872	I.A.	KM2, 3, 5, 6	—	12,500
SS8	1875	I.A.	KM2 (Large date), 3, 5	—	65,000
SS9	1880	I.A.	KM2, 3, 5 (Narrow 0)	—	35,000
SS10	1881	I.A.	KM7, 2, 3, 5, 6	—	26,500
SS11	1892	I.A.	KM3, 5	—	10,000

BRITISH COLUMBIA

PATTERNS

KM	Date	Mintage	Identification	Mkt Val
Pn1	1862	—	10 Dollars. Silver. 5-10 pieces.	32,500

Note: Bowers and Merena Norweb Sale 11-96, Specimen 58 realized $18,700; David Akers Pittman Sale 8-99, Choice AU realized $32,200

KM	Date	Mintage	Identification	Mkt Val
Pn2	1862	—	10 Dollars. Gold.	—
Pn3	1862	—	20 Dollars. Silver. 5-10 pieces.	38,500

Note: Bowers and Merena Norweb Sale 11-96, Specimen 61 realized $25,300

KM	Date	Mintage	Identification	Mkt Val
Pn4	1862	—	20 Dollars. Gold. 5 pieces.	—

Note: Bowers and Merena Norweb Sale 11-96, Specimen 61 realized $143,000; David Akers Pittman sale 8-99, AU realized $149,500

LOWER CANADA

BRITISH ADMINISTRATION

TOKEN COINAGE

Bouquet Sous

KM# Tn1 SOU Composition: Copper **Obv. Legend:** TRADE & AGRICULTURE LOWER CANADA **Rev. Legend:** BANK TOKEN MONTREAL

Date	Mintage	VG	F	VF	XF	Unc
ND	—	2.50	6.00	12.50	—	150

KM# Tn2 SOU Composition: Copper **Obv. Legend:** TRADE & AGRICULTURE LOWER CANADA **Rev. Legend:** BANK OF MONTREAL TOKEN

Date	Mintage	VG	F	VF	XF	Unc
ND	—	3.00	6.50	12.50	—	225

KM# Tn3 SOU Composition: Copper **Obv. Legend:** Star - AGRICULTURE & COMMERCE - star **Reverse:** Leaves surround denomination **Rev. Legend:** Star - BANQUE DU PEUPLE - Liberty cap

Date	Mintage	VG	F	VF	XF	Unc
ND	—	5.00	15.00	30.00	—	185

KM# Tn4 SOU Composition: Copper **Obv. Legend:** AGRICULTURE & COMMERCE **Reverse:** Without star and liberty cap **Rev. Legend:** BANQUE DU PEUPLE

Date	Mintage	VG	F	VF	XF	Unc
ND	—	2.00	3.50	9.00	—	125

KM# Tn4a SOU Composition: Brass **Obv. Legend:** AGRICULTURE & COMMERCE **Reverse:** Without star and liberty cap **Rev. Legend:** BANQUE DU PEUPLE

Date	Mintage	VG	F	VF	XF	Unc
ND	—	2.50	4.00	10.00	—	130

KM# Tn5 SOU Composition: Copper **Obv. Legend:** Star - AGRICULTURE & COMMERCE - star **Reverse:** Wreath surrounds denomination **Rev. Legend:** TOKEN/MONTREAL
Note: Many varieties of Tn#5 exist. All are inscribed TOKEN-MONTREAL and were privately struck during the period 1837-38.

Date	Mintage	VG	F	VF	XF	Unc
ND	—	2.50	4.00	10.00	—	175

TOKEN COINAGE

Quebec

The Bouquet Sous of 1835-37 were followed by the Quebec Habitant tokens of 1837, the Bank of Montreal tokens of 1842-45, and the Quebec Bank tokens of 1852.

The Habitant tokens were so named because they show on obverse a Canadian habitant in traditional winter garb. For years the habitant was popularly identified with the rebel and politician Louis Joseph Papineau and the tokens known as 'Papineaus', but there is no valid reason for the association. The Habitants were struck by Boulton & Watt in denominations of penny and halfpenny.

After Upper and Lower Canada were united as the Province of Canada, the Bank of Montreal was granted the right to coin copper and ordered the 'Side View' tokens bearing a side view of the bank in 1837-38 which were rejected, being returned to the Mint of Cotterill, Hill & Co. of Walsall, England. It later issued in 1842-45, a series of tokens bearing a front view of the bank, and commonly known as the 'Front View' tokens. The tokens were struck by Boulton & Watt in denominations of penny and halfpenny.

In 1852 the Quebec Bank was granted the authority to coin copper because of a severe shortage of copper coin in the province, and issued an exceptionally attractive Colonial issue with the habitant obverse and reverse depicting the arms of the city of Quebec. They were struck by Ralph Heaton & Sons in denominations of penny and halfpenny.

KM# Tn6 SOU (1/2 PENNY) **Composition:** Copper **Obv. Legend:** PROVINCE DU BAS CANADA **Reverse:** CITY BANK on ribbon

Date	Mintage	VG	F	VF	XF	Unc
1837	240,000	2.00	4.00	9.00	—	150
1837 Proof	—	Value: 500				

KM# Tn7 SOU (1/2 PENNY) **Composition:** Copper **Reverse:** QUEBEC BANK on ribbon

Date	Mintage	VG	F	VF	XF	Unc
1837	240,000	2.00	4.00	9.00	—	150
1837 Proof	—	Value: 1,100				

KM# Tn8 SOU (1/2 PENNY) **Composition:** Copper **Reverse:** BANQUE DU PEUPLE on ribbon

Date	Mintage	VG	F	VF	XF	Unc
1837	240,000	3.50	7.00	15.00	—	175
1837 Proof	—	Value: 1,100				

KM# Tn9 SOU (1/2 PENNY) **Composition:** Copper **Reverse:** BANK OF MONTREAL on ribbon

Date	Mintage	VG	F	VF	XF	Unc
1837	480,000	3.50	6.50	12.50	—	165
1837 Proof	—	Value: 450				

M# Tn10 2 SOUS (PENNY) **Composition:** Copper **Obverse:** Standing figure **Obv. Legend:** PROVINCE DU BAS CANADA **Reverse:** CITY BANK on ribbon

Date	Mintage	VG	F	VF	XF	Unc
1837	120,000	3.50	7.00	15.00	—	200

KM# Tn11 2 SOUS (PENNY) **Composition:** Copper **Obverse:** Standing figure **Obv. Legend:** PROVINCE DU BAS CANADA. **Reverse:** QUEBEC BANK on ribbon

Date	Mintage	VG	F	VF	XF	Unc
1837	120,000	3.00	6.00	13.50	—	185

KM# Tn12 2 SOUS (PENNY) **Composition:** Copper **Obverse:** Standing figure **Obv. Legend:** PROVINCE DU BAS CANADA. **Reverse:** BANQUE DU PEUPLE on ribbon

Date	Mintage	VG	F	VF	XF	Unc
1837	120,000	7.00	15.00	35.00	—	250

KM# Tn13 2 SOUS (PENNY) **Composition:** Copper **Obverse:** Standing figure **Obv. Legend:** PROVINCE DU BAS CANADA. **Reverse:** BANK OF MONTREAL on ribbon

Date	Mintage	VG	F	VF	XF	Unc
1837	240,000	5.00	10.00	22.50	—	225

KM# Tn14 2 SOUS (PENNY) **Composition:** Copper **Obverse:** Front view of bank **Obv. Legend:** PROVINCE OF CANADA-BANK OF MONTREAL. **Reverse:** CITY BANK on ribbon

Date	Mintage	VG	F	VF	XF	Unc
1837	—	100	150	185	—	475
1837 Proof	—	Value: 700				

KM# Tn15 SOU (1/2 PENNY) **Composition:** Copper **Obverse:** Side view of bank, leg: BANK OF MONTREAL **Reverse:** BANK OF MONTREAL on ribbon **Note:** These issues were never officially released to circulation. Most of the mintage was returned to the mint for melting.

Date	Mintage	VG	F	VF	XF	Unc
1838	240,000,000	200	400	800	—	1,850
1839	240,000,000	200	400	750	—	1,750

KKM# Tn17 2 SOUS (PENNY) **Composition:** Copper **Obverse:** Side view of bank **Obv. Legend:** BANK OF MONTREAL **Reverse:** BANQUE DU PEUPLE on ribbon **Note:** Never officially released to circulation.

Date	Mintage	VG	F	VF	XF	Unc
1839 Rare	—	—	—	—	—	—

KM# Tn18 SOU (1/2 PENNY) **Composition:** Copper **Obverse:** Front view of Bank **Obv. Legend:** PROVINCE OF CANADA-BANK OF MONTREAL **Note:** NOTE: 3 varieties of trees exist for 1842 and 1844 tokens.

Date	Mintage	VG	F	VF	XF	Unc
1842	480,000	5.00	9.00	15.00	—	150
1844	1,440,000	2.50	4.50	7.50	—	175
1844 Proof	—	Value: 700				
1845 Rare, 2 known	—	—	—	—	—	—

KM# Tn19 2 SOUS (PENNY) **Composition:** Copper **Obverse:** Front view of bank **Obv. Legend:** PROVINCE OF CANADA-BANK OF MONTREAL **Reverse:** BANK OF MONTREAL on ribbon

Date	Mintage	VG	F	VF	XF	Unc
1842	240,000	4.00	8.00	17.50	—	200

KM# Tn20 SOU (1/2 PENNY) **Composition:** Copper **Obverse:** Standing figure **Obv. Legend:** PROVINCE DU CANADA. **Reverse:** Seated figure **Rev. Legend:** QUEBEC BANK TOKEN.

Date	Mintage	VG	F	VF	XF	Unc
1852	—	2.50	5.00	10.00	—	175

KM# Tn20a SOU (1/2 PENNY) **Composition:** Bronze **Obverse:** Standing figure **Obv. Legend:** PROVINCE DU CANADA. **Reverse:** Seated figure **Rev. Legend:** QUEBEC BANK TOKEN.

Date	Mintage	VG	F	VF	XF	Unc
1852 Proof, Rare	—	—	—	—	—	—

KM# Tn21 2 SOUS (PENNY) **Composition:** Copper **Obverse:** Standing figure **Obv. Legend:** PROVINCE DU CANADA. **Reverse:** Seated figure **Rev. Legend:** QUEBEC BANK TOKEN. **Note:** Similar to Sou Km#Tn20.

Date	Mintage	VG	F	VF	XF	Unc
1852	—	5.00	10.00	20.00	—	225

KM# Tn21a 2 SOUS (PENNY) **Composition:** Bronze **Obverse:** Standing figure **Obv. Legend:** PROVINCE DU CANADA. **Reverse:** Seated figure **Rev. Legend:** QUEBEC BANK TOKEN. **Note:** Similar to Sou Km#Tn20.

Date	Mintage	VG	F	VF	XF	Unc
1852 Proof, Rare	—	—	—	—	—	—

UPPER CANADA

In 1849, rioting mobs, angered by the passage of the French Rebellion Losses bill, burned the Parliament Buildings at Montreal. The capital was then transferred to Toronto and the Bank of Upper Canada was granted the right to coin copper. Penny and halfpenny tokens struck by Ralph Heaton and Sons were issued during the period of 1850-57. Because of their design, these attractive tokens are frequently called the St. George' tokens. The initials RK & CO on obverse are those of Rowe, Kentish & Co., London, the agents through whom the token orders were placed for Ralph Heaton, Birmingham Mint.

BRITISH ADMINISTRATION

TOKEN COINAGE

KM# Tn1 1/2 PENNY Composition: Copper **Obverse:** Laureate bust of George III left **Obv. Legend:** PROVINCE OF UPPER CANADA **Reverse:** Britannia seated with shield

Date	Mintage	VG	F	VF	XF	Unc
1832	—	10.00	20.00	40.00	—	375

KM# Tn2 1/2 PENNY Composition: Copper **Obverse:** St. George on horseback slaying a dragon **Obv. Legend:** BANK OF UPPER CANADA **Reverse:** Bank arms

Date	Mintage	VG	F	VF	XF	Unc
1850	1,500,000	2.50	4.00	6.50	—	135
1850 Proof	—	Value: 500				
1852	1,500,000	2.50	4.00	6.50	—	120
1854	1,500,000	2.50	4.00	6.50	—	120
1854 crosslet 4	Inc. above	8.00	16.00	30.00	—	225
1857	3,000,000	2.50	4.00	6.50	—	120

KM# Tn2a 1/2 PENNY Composition: Bronze **Obverse:** St. George on horseback slaying a dragon **Obv. Legend:** BANK OF UPPER CANADA **Reverse:** Bank arms

Date	Mintage	VG	F	VF	XF	Unc
1857 Proof	—	Value: 450				

KM# Tn3 PENNY Composition: Copper **Obverse:** St. George on horseback slaying a dragon **Obv. Legend:** BANK OF UPPER CANADA **Reverse:** Bank arms **Note:** 4 varieties exist in "2" of 1852

Date	Mintage	VG	F	VF	XF	Unc
1850	750,000	3.00	6.00	10.00	—	150
1850 dot between cornucopias	Inc. above	5.00	10.00	20.00	—	225
1852	750,000,000	2.00	4.00	8.00	—	145
1852 Proof	—	Value: 500				
1854	750,000	2.00	3.50	7.00	—	140
1854 crosslet 4	Inc. above	6.00	12.00	22.00	—	225
1857	1,500,000	2.00	3.50	7.00	—	140

KM# Tn3a PENNY Composition: Bronze **Issuer:** Bank of Upper Canada **Obverse:** St. George on horseback slaying a dragon **Reverse:** Bank arms

Date	Mintage	VG	F	VF	XF	Unc
1854	1,854	—	—	—	—	—
1857	—	—	—	—	—	—

NEW BRUNSWICK

New Brunswick is a Canadian province, one of the Maritime Provinces. Bordered on the north by Quebec, on the east by the Gulf of St. Lawrence and Northumberland Strait and on the south by Bay of Fundy, and on the west by Maine. Evidence of early habitation throughout the region. Micmac, Malecite and Passamaquoddy tribes were there at the time of European colonization. The westrn boundary settled by treaty with U.S. in 1842; joined Nova Scotia, Quebec, and Ontario to form Dominion of Canada in 1867.

COLONIAL

STERLING COINAGE

KM# 1 HALFPENNY TOKEN Composition: Copper

Date	Mintage	VG-8	F-12	VF-20	XF-40	MS-60	MS-63	Proof
1843	480,000	3.00	6.00	11.50	30.00	110	265	—
1843 Proof	—	—	—	—	—	—	—	750

KM# 3 HALFPENNY TOKEN Composition: Copper

Date	Mintage	VG-8	F-12	VF-20	XF-40	MS-60	MS-63	Proof
1854	864,000	3.00	6.00	11.50	30.00	100	265	—

KM# 3a HALFPENNY TOKEN Composition: Bronze

Date	Mintage	VG-8	F-12	VF-20	XF-40	MS-60	MS-63	Proof
1854 Proof	—	—	—	—	—	—	—	400

KM# 2 1 PENNY TOKEN Composition: Copper

Date	Mintage	VG-8	F-12	VF-20	XF-40	MS-60	MS-63	Proof
1843	480,000	3.75	7.50	15.00	37.50	165	325	—
1843 Proof	—	—	—	—	—	—	—	800

KM# 4 1 PENNY TOKEN Composition: Copper

Date	Mintage	VG-8	F-12	VF-20	XF-40	MS-60	MS-63	Proof
1854	432,000	3.75	7.50	15.00	40.00	175	350	—

DECIMAL COINAGE

KM# 5 HALF CENT Composition: Bronze

Date	Mintage	VG-8	F-12	VF-20	XF-40	MS-60	MS-63	Proof
1861	222,800	60.00	90.00	150	200	375	800	—
1861 Proof	—	—	—	—	—	—	—	2,200

KM# 6 CENT Composition: Bronze

Date	Mintage	VG-8	F-12	VF-20	XF-40	MS-60	MS-63	Proof
1861	1,000,000	2.25	4.00	8.00	13.00	100	250	—
1861 Proof	—	—	—	—	—	—	—	450
1864 short 6	1,000,000	2.25	4.00	8.00	13.00	110	245	—
1864 long 6	Inc. above	2.25	4.00	8.00	13.00	110	245	—

KM# 7 5 CENTS Weight: 1.1620 g. **Composition:** 0.9250 Silver .0346 oz. ASW

Date	Mintage	VG-8	F-12	VF-20	XF-40	MS-60	MS-63	Proof
1862	100,000	35.00	65.00	150	300	1,500	3,200	—
1862 Proof	—	—	—	—	—	—	—	3,500
1864 small 6	100,000	35.00	65.00	150	300	1,500	3,200	—

KM# 8 10 CENTS Weight: 2.3240 g. Composition: 0.9250 Silver .0691 oz. ASW

Date	Mintage	VG-8	F-12	VF-20	XF-40	MS-60	MS-63	Proof
1862	150,000	35.00	65.00	150	300	975	2,450	—
1862 recut 2	Inc. above	42.50	85.00	250	500	2,000	3,250	—
1862 Proof	—	—	—	—	—	—	—	2,850
1864	100,000	35.00	65.00	150	300	1,500	2,750	—

KM# 9 20 CENTS Weight: 4.6480 g. Composition: 0.9250 Silver .1382 oz. ASW

Date	Mintage	VG-8	F-12	VF-20	XF-40	MS-60	MS-63	Proof
1862	150,000	14.00	30.00	60.00	200	1,000	2,350	—
1862 Proof	—	—	—	—	—	—	—	2,850
1864	150,000	14.00	30.00	60.00	200	1,000	2,500	—

PATTERNS

KM	Date	Mintage	Identification	Mkt Val
Pn1	1861	—	Cent. Bronze.	4,000
PnA2	1862	—	10 Cents. Silver. Plain edge.	3,500

KM	Date	Mintage	Identification	Mkt Val
Pn2	1862	—	10 Cents. Silver. Reeded edge.	—
Pn3	1862	—	20 Cents. Silver. G. W. Wyon on obverse.	—
Pn4	1870	—	5 Cents. Silver.	10,000
Pn5	1870	—	10 Cents. Silver. Reeded edge.	—
PnA6	1870	—	10 Cents. Silver. Plain edge.	—

Note: Bowers and Merena Norweb Sale 11-96, Specimen 63 realized $17,600

KM	Date	Mintage	Identification	Mkt Val
Pn6	1871	—	10 Cents. Silver. Reeded edge.	—
Pn7	1871	—	20 Cents. Silver. Plain edge.	—
Pn8	1871	—	20 Cents. Silver. Milled edge.	—
Pn9	1875	—	5 Cents. Silver.	9,000
Pn10	1875	—	5 Cents. Silver.	—

TRIAL STRIKES

KM	Date	Mintage	Identification	Mkt Val
TS1	1862	—	Cent. Bronze.	—

NEWFOUNDLAND

Island which along with Labrador became a province of Canada. Prehistoric inhabitants left evidence of an early presence on the island. Norsemen briefly settled on the island but officially discovered in 1497 by Italian explorer John Cabot. English settlements were sporadic and disputed by France. The English settled along the east coast and the French along the west coast of the island. With the treaty of Utrecht in 1713, it officially became English, but the fishing rights went to France. Controversies continued through the 19th century. Boundaries were set in 1927, colonial government reestablished 1934, became a province of Canada 1949.

BRITISH COLONY

CIRCULATION COINAGE

KM# 1 CENT (Large) Composition: Bronze

Date	Mintage	VG-8	F-12	VF-20	XF-40	MS-60	MS-63	Proof
1865	240,000	2.25	3.50	6.00	20.00	120	550	—
1872H	200,000	2.50	4.00	7.00	15.00	60.00	160	—
1872H Proof	—	—	—	—	—	—	—	800
1873	200,025	2.50	4.50	13.00	40.00	300	1,100	—
1873 Proof	—	—	—	—	—	—	—	3,000
1876H	200,000	2.50	7.00	15.00	40.00	300	1,100	—
1876H Proof, reported not confirmed	—	—	—	—	—	—	—	—
1880 round O, even date	400,000	2.00	3.00	6.00	20.00	90.00	300	—
1880 round O, low O	Inc. above	2.25	8.00	20.00	50.00	400	1,300	—
1880 oval 0	Inc. above	125	200	300	450	1,100	1,600	—
1880 oval 0 Proof	—	—	—	—	—	—	—	2,500
1885	40,000	20.00	50.00	75.00	125	500	1,250	—
1885 Proof	—	—	—	—	—	—	—	2,500
1888	50,000	30.00	50.00	80.00	175	700	1,970	—
1890	200,000	2.25	6.00	15.00	45.00	300	1,100	—
1894	200,000	2.25	5.00	10.00	25.00	140	700	—
1894 Proof	—	—	—	—	—	—	—	1,500
1896	200,000	2.25	3.50	7.00	18.00	120	350	—
1896 Proof	—	—	—	—	—	—	—	1,500

KM# 2 5 CENTS Weight: 1.1782 g. Composition: 0.9250 Silver .0350 oz. ASW

Date	Mintage	VG-8	F-12	VF-20	XF-40	MS-60	MS-63	Proof
1865	80,000	25.00	50.00	100	200	775	1,500	—
1865 Proof	—	—	—	—	—	—	—	4,000
1870	40,000	45.00	85.00	150	300	1,100	2,000	—
1870 Proof	—	—	—	—	—	—	—	4,000
1872H	40,000	22.00	45.00	85.00	175	600	1,400	—
1873	44,260	60.00	100	250	700	1,750	2,850	—
1873H	Inc. above	650	1,000	1,875	3,300	8,200	12,500	—
1873 Proof	—	—	—	—	—	—	—	10,000
1876H	20,000	65.00	100	175	325	1,100	2,750	—
1880	40,000	30.00	65.00	100	200	1,000	1,850	—
1880 Proof	—	—	—	—	—	—	—	5,000
1881	40,000	30.00	65.00	100	300	1,200	2,200	—
1881 Proof	—	—	—	—	—	—	—	5,000
1882H	60,000	15.00	27.00	50.00	125	800	1,500	—
1882H Proof	—	—	—	—	—	—	—	2,000
1885	16,000	110	175	275	600	2,000	4,500	—
1885 Proof	—	—	—	—	—	—	—	7,500
1888	40,000	35.00	70.00	125	350	1,800	2,450	—
1888 Proof	—	—	—	—	—	—	—	7,500
1890	160,000	6.00	12.00	30.00	85.00	800	1,500	—
1890 Proof	—	—	—	—	—	—	—	5,000
1894	160,000	6.50	12.50	30.00	75.00	800	1,500	—
1894 Proof	—	—	—	—	—	—	—	5,000
1896	400,000	4.00	8.00	20.00	45.00	700	1,350	—
1896 Proof	—	—	—	—	—	—	—	5,000

KM# 3 10 CENTS Weight: 2.3564 g. Composition: 0.9250 Silver .0701 oz. ASW

Date	Mintage	VG-8	F-12	VF-20	XF-40	MS-60	MS-63	Proof
1865	80,000	15.00	30.00	75.00	180	1,100	2,250	—
1865 plain edge, Proof	—	—	—	—	—	—	—	5,500
1870	30,000	120	190	335	725	2,350	5,000	—
1870 Proof	—	—	—	—	—	—	—	10,000
1872H	40,000	13.50	20.00	50.00	135	800	1,700	—
1873 flat 3	23,614	30.00	60.00	150	345	1,675	2,900	—
1873 round 3	Inc. above	30.00	60.00	150	345	1,675	2,900	—
1873 Proof	—	—	—	—	—	—	—	12,000
1876H	10,000	30.00	60.00	125	300	1,400	2,500	—
1880/70	10,000	30.00	60.00	125	350	1,800	2,950	—
1880 Proof	—	—	—	—	—	—	—	7,500
1882H	20,000	25.00	50.00	125	450	2,185	3,410	—
1882H Proof	—	—	—	—	—	—	—	3,000
1885	8,000	60.00	110	200	475	2,100	4,250	—
1885 Proof	—	—	—	—	—	—	—	8,000
1888	30,000	30.00	65.00	175	700	2,185	2,500	—
1888 Proof	—	—	—	—	—	—	—	8,000
1890	100,000	5.50	11.50	35.00	100	1,100	1,550	—
1890 Proof	—	—	—	—	—	—	—	5,000
1894	100,000	5.50	11.50	25.00	85.00	700	1,550	—
1894 Proof	—	—	—	—	—	—	—	5,000
1896	230,000	5.00	10.00	25.00	85.00	600	1,500	—
1896 Proof	—	—	—	—	—	—	—	5,000

KM# 4 20 CENTS Weight: 4.7127 g. Composition: 0.9250 Silver .1401 oz. ASW

Date	Mintage	VG-8	F-12	VF-20	XF-40	MS-60	MS-63	Proof
1865	100,000	11.00	20.00	60.00	150	950	2,000	—
1865 plain edge, Proof	—	—	—	—	—	—	—	6,500
1865 reeded edge, Proof	—	—	—	—	—	—	—	10,000
1870	50,000	12.00	30.00	100	250	1,250	2,500	—
1870 plain edge, Proof	—	—	—	—	—	—	—	6,500
1870 reeded edge, Proof	—	—	—	—	—	—	—	6,500
1872H	90,000	7.00	14.00	40.00	140	750	1,800	—
1873	45,797	18.00	40.00	125	300	1,500	3,000	—
1873 Proof	—	—	—	—	—	—	—	12,000
1876H	50,000	15.00	30.00	80.00	200	1,350	2,700	—
1880/70	30,000	15.00	35.00	100	250	1,350	3,000	—
1880 Proof	—	—	—	—	—	—	—	8,000
1881	60,000	12.00	25.00	80.00	200	1,200	1,900	—
1881 Proof	—	—	—	—	—	—	—	8,000
1882H	100,000	5.00	12.00	35.00	140	1,000	1,900	—

Date	Mintage	VG-8	F-12	VF-20	XF-40	MS-60	MS-63	Proof
1882H Proof	—	—	—	—	—	—	—	3,500
1885	40,000	12.00	25.00	75.00	200	1,300	2,600	—
1885 Proof	—	—	—	—	—	—	—	10,000
1888	75,000	6.00	15.00	45.00	150	900	2,200	—
1888 Proof	—	—	—	—	—	—	—	10,000
1890	100,000	6.00	15.00	45.00	150	625	1,600	—
1890 Proof	—	—	—	—	—	—	—	6,500
1894	100,000	6.00	15.00	30.00	100	650	1,700	—
1894 Proof	—	—	—	—	—	—	—	6,500
1896 large 96	Inc. above	7.00	15.00	50.00	200	725	1,900	—
1896 small 96	125,000	5.00	10.00	30.00	100	700	1,800	—
1896 large 96, Proof	—	—	—	—	—	—	—	6,500
1899 hook 99	125,000	15.00	30.00	75.00	200	1,000	2,200	—
1899 large 99	Inc. above	5.00	8.00	30.00	125	700	1,900	—
1900	125,000	5.00	7.00	25.00	80.00	700	1,900	—
1900 Proof	—	—	—	—	—	—	—	6,500

KM# 6 50 CENTS **Weight:** 11.7818 g. **Composition:** 0.9250 Silver .3504 oz. ASW

Date	Mintage	VG-8	F-12	VF-20	XF-40	MS-60	MS-63	Proof
1870	50,000	12.00	30.00	100	600	1,400	3,600	—
1870 plain edge, Proof	—	—	—	—	—	—	—	25,000
1870 reeded edge, Proof	—	—	—	—	—	—	—	25,000
1872H	48,000	10.00	20.00	50.00	225	1,250	3,600	—
1873	37,675	40.00	70.00	175	600	4,350	6,000	—
1873 Proof	—	—	—	—	—	—	—	40,000
1874	80,000	25.00	40.00	125	500	2,500	5,000	—
1874 Proof	—	—	—	—	—	—	—	40,000
1876H	28,000	30.00	40.00	125	400	2,250	5,250	—
1880	24,000	25.00	40.00	150	450	2,500	5,250	—
1880 Proof	—	—	—	—	—	—	—	40,000
1881	50,000	20.00	35.00	135	400	2,250	5,250	—
1881 Proof	—	—	—	—	—	—	—	40,000
1882H	100,000	12.00	17.00	55.00	200	1,600	3,600	—
1882H Proof	—	—	—	—	—	—	—	8,000
1885	40,000	20.00	35.00	125	400	2,250	5,500	—
1885 Proof	—	—	—	—	—	—	—	40,000
1888	20,000	35.00	75.00	200	900	2,500	5,500	—
1888 Proof	—	—	—	—	—	—	—	40,000
1894	40,000	7.00	17.00	75.00	30.00	2,000	3,800	—
1896	60,000	7.00	15.00	65.00	225	1,400	3,600	—
1896 Proof	—	—	—	—	—	—	—	25,000
1898	76,607	7.00	12.00	60.00	200	1,700	3,600	—
1899 wide 9's	150,000	7.00	12.00	60.00	200	1,500	3,600	—
1899 narrow 9's	Inc. above	7.00	12.00	45.00	125	1,500	3,600	—
1900	150,000	7.00	12.00	45.00	175	1,500	3,600	—

KM# 5 2 DOLLARS **Weight:** 3.3284 g. **Composition:** 0.9170 Gold .0981 oz. AGW

Date	Mintage	F-12	VF-20	XF-40	AU-50	MS-60	MS-63
1865	10,000	125	150	210	350	1,050	4,950
1865 plain edge, Specimen-63, $15,000.	Est. 10	—	—	—	—	—	—
1870	10,000	125	150	225	350	1,050	5,850
1870 reeded edge, Specimen-63 $20,000.	Est. 5	—	—	—	—	—	—
1872	6,050	150	275	300	590	2,100	8,650
1872 Specimen-63 $12,500.	Est. 10	—	—	—	—	—	—
1880	2,500	775	950	1,150	2,300	4,650	14,250
1880/70	—	—	—	—	—	—	—

Note: Specimen. Bowers and Merena Norweb sale 11-96, specimen 64 realized $70,400.

Date	Mintage	F-12	VF-20	XF-40	AU-50	MS-60	MS-63
1881 Specimen; Rare	—	—	—	—	—	—	—
1881	10,000	110	145	180	300	1,100	4,750
1882H	25,000	105	140	175	200	375	1,300
1882H Specimen $4,250.	—	—	—	—	—	—	—
1885	10,000	110	145	180	300	475	1,900
1885 Specimen	—	—	—	—	—	—	—

Note: Bowers and Merena Norweb sale 11-96, specimen 66 realized $44,000

Date	Mintage	F-12	VF-20	XF-40	AU-50	MS-60	MS-63
1888	25,000	105	140	175	200	365	1,550
1888 Specimen; Rare	—	—	—	—	—	—	—

PATTERNS

KM	Date	Mintage	Identification	Mkt Val
Pn1	1864	—	Cent. Bronze.	—
Pn2	1864	—	Cent. Bronze. VICTORIA QUEEN.	—
Pn3	1864	—	5 Cents. Bronze.	—
Pn4	1864	—	10 Cents. Bronze.	—
Pn5	1864	—	20 Cents. Bronze.	4,000
Pn6	1864	—	2 Dollars. Bronze.	13,500
Pn7	1865	—	Cent. Bronze.	3,000
Pn8	1865	—	5 Cents. Silver.	—
Pn9	1865	—	5 Cents. Silver.	6,500
Pn10	1865	—	10 Cents. Silver.	—
Pn11	1865	—	10 Cents. Silver.	11,500
Pn12	1865	—	20 Cents. Silver.	—
PnA13	1865	—	20 Cents. Bronze. 1 Known.	—
Pn13	1865	—	20 Cents. Silver.	—
Pn14	1865	—	2 Dollars. Gold.	—

KM	Date	Mintage	Identification	Mkt Val

KM	Date	Mintage	Identification	Mkt Val
Pn15	1865	—	2 Dollars. Gold.	—

Note: Bowers and Merena Norweb Sale 11-96, Specimen 63 realized $39,600

KM	Date	Mintage	Identification	Mkt Val
Pn16	1870	—	50 Cents. Bronze.	—

TRIAL STRIKES

KM	Date	Mintage	Identification	Mkt Val
TS1	1864	—	Cent. Bronze.	—
TS2	1882	—	50 Cents. Silver. Without H.	—

MAGDALEN ISLAND

A group of 13 islands in the Gulf of St. Lawrence north of Prince Edward Island and west of Newfoundland. The island was awarded to Sir Isaac Coffin after the American Revolution. In an effort to exercise his authority on his property Coffin had 1 penny tokens made at Birmingham, England in 1815. The British government felt this was overstepping his authority and revoked his grant of the island. Today it is a part of the province of Quebec.

PRIVATE ESTATE

Under Administration of Quebec - Lower Canada.

TOKEN COINAGE

KM# Tn1 PENNY Composition: Copper **Issuer:** Sir Isaac Coffin **Obverse:** Seal on ice **Reverse:** Butchered seal carcass **Size:** 33.5 mm.

Date	Mintage	VG	FINE	VF	XF	AU	UNC
1815	—	60.00	125	275	650	—	1,850

NOVA SCOTIA

Province of Canada, one of the Maritime Provinces. Peninsula province about 375 mi. (605 km.) long by 50 to 100 mi. (80-160 km.) wide and joined to continent by isthmus of Chignecto. Coast may have been reached by Norsemen in 11th century, inhabited by Micmacs prior to European settlement. Another territory contested by the French and English for hundreds of years. Entered Confederation in 1867.

PROVINCE

STERLING COINAGE

KM# 1a HALFPENNY TOKEN Composition: Copper

Date	Mintage	VG-8	F-12	VF-20	XF-40	MS-60	MS-63	Proof
1382 1382 (error)	—	500	700	1,650	—	—	—	—
1832/1382	—	6.00	15.00	50.00	100	—	—	—
1832 (imitation)	—	3.00	6.00	18.00	40.00	50.00	100	—

KM# 1 HALFPENNY TOKEN Composition: Copper

Date	Mintage	VG-8	F-12	VF-20	XF-40	MS-60	MS-63	Proof
1823	400,000	3.00	5.00	8.00	20.00	75.00	150	—
1823 without hyphen	Inc. above	5.00	10.00	20.00	35.00	170	350	—
1824	118,636	3.00	5.00	12.50	25.00	150	225	—

Date	Mintage	VG-8	F-12	VF-20	XF-40	MS-60	MS-63	Proof
1832	800,000	3.00	5.00	7.50	15.00	60.00	150	—

KM# 3 HALFPENNY TOKEN Composition: Copper

Date	Mintage	VG-8	F-12	VF-20	XF-40	MS-60	MS-63	Proof
1840 small 0	300,000	3.50	5.00	10.00	22.00	115	165	—
1840 medium 0	Inc. above	2.50	4.00	7.50	15.00	95.00	125	—
1840 large 0	Inc. above	4.00	6.00	12.50	27.50	125	185	—
1843	300,000	3.00	5.00	12.00	25.00	85.00	160	—

KM# 5 HALFPENNY TOKEN Composition: Copper

Date	Mintage	VG-8	F-12	VF-20	XF-40	MS-60	MS-63	Proof
1856 without LCW	720,000	2.00	4.00	7.50	15.00	70.00	175	—
1856 without LCW, Proof	—	—	—	—	—	—	—	600
1856 without LCW, inverted A for V in PROVINCE, Proof	—	—	—	—	—	—	—	600

KM# 5a HALFPENNY TOKEN Composition: Bronze

Date	Mintage	VG-8	F-12	VF-20	XF-40	MS-60	MS-63	Proof
1856 with LCW, Proof	—	—	—	—	—	—	—	600

KM# 2 1 PENNY TOKEN Composition: Copper

Date	Mintage	VG-8	F-12	VF-20	XF-40	MS-60	MS-63	Proof
1824	217,776	3.00	6.00	10.00	25.00	100	250	—
1832	200,000	3.00	6.00	10.00	22.50	80.00	230	—

KM# 2a 1 PENNY TOKEN Composition: Copper

Date	Mintage	VG-8	F-12	VF-20	XF-40	MS-60	MS-63	Proof
1832 (imitation)	—	3.75	7.50	22.50	42.50	—	—	—

KM# 4 1 PENNY TOKEN Composition: Copper **Size:** 32 mm.

Date	Mintage	VG-8	F-12	VF-20	XF-40	MS-60	MS-63	Proof
1840	150,000	2.50	5.00	7.50	20.00	100	175	—
1843/0	150,000	12.00	20.00	40.00	80.00	150	—	—
1843	Inc. above	3.00	6.00	10.00	22.50	110	200	—

KM# 6 1 PENNY TOKEN Composition: Copper

Date	Mintage	VG-8	F-12	VF-20	XF-40	MS-60	MS-63	Proof
1856 without LCW	360,000	2.50	5.00	8.50	19.00	110	135	—
1856 with LCW	Inc. above	2.50	5.00	7.00	15.00	85.00	115	—

KM# 6a 1 PENNY TOKEN Composition: Bronze

Date	Mintage	VG-8	F-12	VF-20	XF-40	MS-60	MS-63	Proof
1856 Proof	—	—	—	—	—	—	—	400

DECIMAL COINAGE

KM# 7 HALF CENT Composition: Bronze

Date	Mintage	VG-8	F-12	VF-20	XF-40	MS-60	MS-63	Proof
1861	400,000	3.00	5.00	8.00	12.00	60.00	165	—
1864	400,000	3.00	5.00	8.00	12.00	55.00	165	—
1864 Proof	—	—	—	—	—	—	—	300

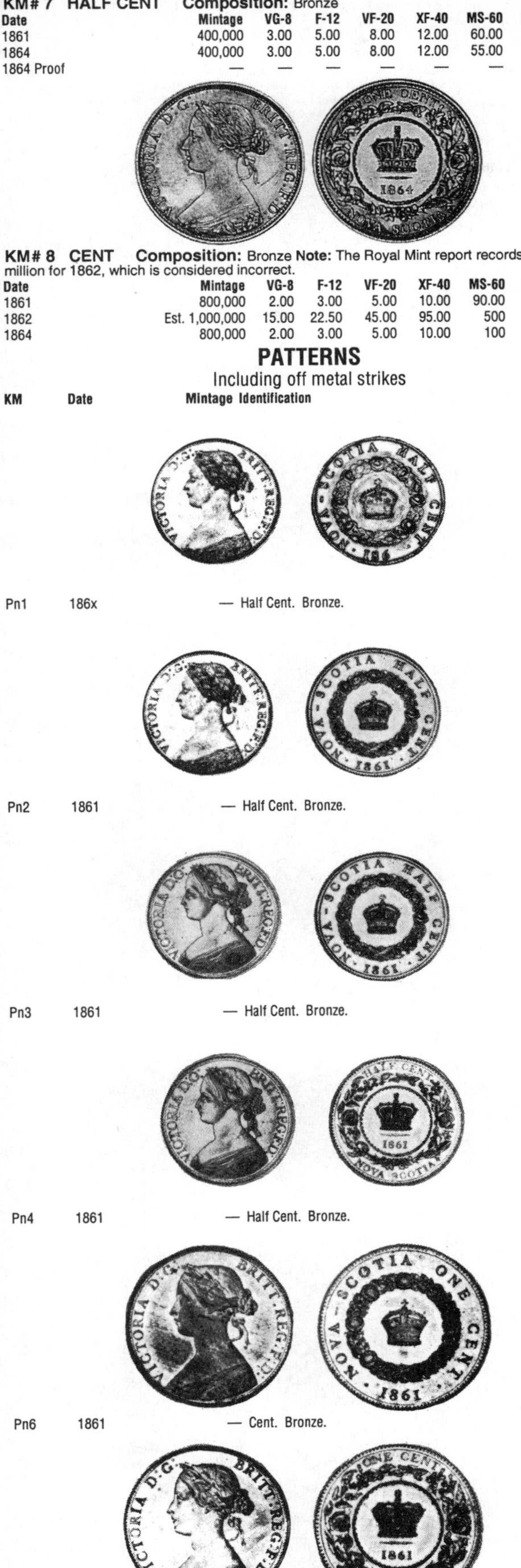

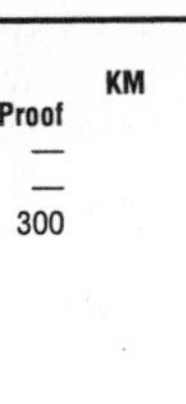

KM# 8 CENT Composition: Bronze **Note:** The Royal Mint report records mintage of 1 million for 1862, which is considered incorrect.

Date	Mintage	VG-8	F-12	VF-20	XF-40	MS-60	MS-63	Proof
1861	800,000	2.00	3.00	5.00	10.00	90.00	215	—
1862	Est. 1,000,000	15.00	22.50	45.00	95.00	500	1,300	—
1864	800,000	2.00	3.00	5.00	10.00	100	225	—

PATTERNS

Including off metal strikes

KM	Date	Mintage Identification	Mkt Val
Pn1	186x	— Half Cent. Bronze.	4,000
Pn2	1861	— Half Cent. Bronze.	4,000
Pn3	1861	— Half Cent. Bronze.	4,000
Pn4	1861	— Half Cent. Bronze.	3,000
Pn6	1861	— Cent. Bronze.	5,500
Pn7	1861	— Cent. Bronze.	5,500

KM	Date	Mintage Identification	Mkt Val
Pn8	1861	— Cent. Bronze.	5,000

KM	Date	Mintage Identification	Mkt Val
Pn9	1861	— Cent. Bronze.	5,250
Pn10	186x	— Cent. Bronze.	5,500

PRINCE EDWARD ISLAND

Island province of Canada in the Gulf of St. Lawrence, 2184 sq. mi. (5657 sq. km.). It is separated from New Brunswick and Nova Scotia by Northumberland Strait. Settled by Scottish immigrants at beginning of 19th century, entered Confederation 1873. It was named after Edward, duke of Kent in 1799.

PROVINCE

DECIMAL COINAGE

KM# 4 CENT Composition: Bronze

Date	Mintage	VG-8	F-12	VF-20	XF-40	MS-60	MS-63	Proof
1871	2,000,000	1.75	2.50	4.50	10.50	75.00	185	—
1871 Proof	—	—	—	—	—	—	—	2,000

CUT & COUNTERMARKED COINAGE

ca. 1813

KM# 1 SHILLING Composition: Silver **Countermark:** Sunburst **Note:** Countermark on center plug of Spanish or Spanish Colonial 8 Reales.

Date	Mintage	VG-8	F-12	VF-20	XF-40	MS-60	MS-63	Proof
ND	1,000	2,000	3,000	5,000	—	—	—	—

KM# 3 5 SHILLING Composition: Silver **Countermark:** Sunburst **Note:** Countermark on holed Lima 8 Reales, C#96.

Date	Mintage	VG-8	F-12	VF-20	XF-40	MS-60	MS-63	Proof
ND	1,000	1,000	1,750	3,000	—	—	—	—

KM# 2 5 SHILLING Composition: Silver **Countermark:** Sunburst **Note:** Countermark on holed Mexico City 8 Reales, KM#109.

Date	Mintage	VG-8	F-12	VF-20	XF-40	MS-60	MS-63	Proof
1791-1808	—	800	1,350	2,250	—	—	—	—

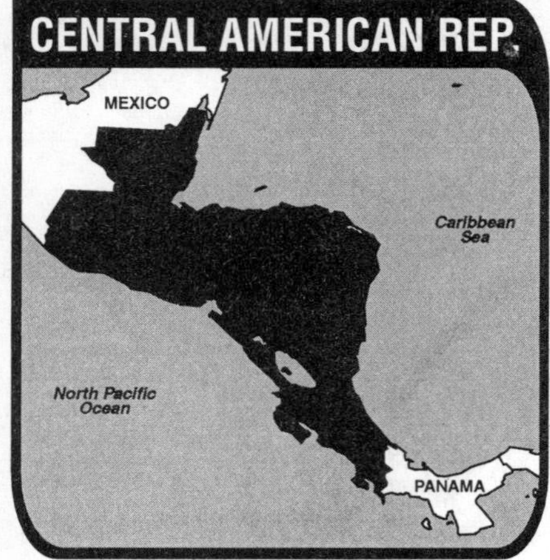

The Central American Republic (Provincias Unidas del Centro de America, Republic of the United States of Central America, Central American Confederation) was an 1823-39 confederation of the former provinces of the Captaincy General of Guatemala - Guatemala, Honduras, El Salvador, Nicaragua and Costa Rica - formed from the southernmost provinces of the short-lived Mexican empire of Augustin de Iturbide. The confederation, which included all Central America between Mexico and Panama, had a population of fewer than 1.5 million.

On Sept. 15, 1821, the leaders of the Captaincy General that governed the five provinces of Central America for Spain, declared Central America independent. The following year, Iturbide crowned himself Augustin I of Mexico and invited the Central Americans to join his empire. Guatemala, Honduras, Nicaragua and Costa Rica did so. El Salvador, which desired to become a part of the United States, refused and was invaded and conquered for Mexico by Vicente Filisola, the military governor Iturbide had sent to Guatemala. But almost before El Salvador had been forced into the Mexican empire, Iturbide was ousted. Filisola then reconvened the National Constituent Assembly that had been established by the Central American declaration of independence of 1821. On July 1, 1823, the Assembly issued a second declaration of independence, from Mexico as well as Spain, and established the Central American Republic.

Historically the confederation, which lasted 15 years, was an anomaly for a government: It had neither permanent capital, army nor treasury and was all but powerless to raise funds. Its written constitution, was as unsatisfactory as the first constitution of the United States, the Articles of Confederation.

Divided by geography as well as religious and class animosity the citizens of the Republic had no sense of nationhood. By 1827 the entire Republic was embroiled in civil war. By 1839 every state but El Salvador had seceded from the union; interestingly, Costa Rica, Guatemala and Honduras continued to strike coins in the confederation style - until 1850, 1851 and 1861, respectively. Costa Rica then countermarked many coins of this series for continued circulation within its boundaries.

MINT MARKS

CR - San Jose, Costa Rica
G, NG - Guatemala
T - Tegucigalpa, Honduras

MONETARY SYSTEM

16 Reales = 1 Escudo

REPUBLIC

STANDARD COINAGE

KM# 1 1/4 REAL
0.8500 g., 0.9030 Silver .0246 oz.

Date	Mintage	F	VF	XF	Unc	BU
1824G	—	10.00	20.00	40.00	90.00	—
1826G	—	6.00	12.50	25.00	60.00	—
1828G Rare	—	—	—	—	—	—
1831G	—	6.00	12.50	30.00	65.00	—
1833G Rare	—	—	—	—	—	—
1837G	—	5.00	12.50	28.00	42.50	—
1838G Rare	—	—	—	—	—	—
1840/30G	—	4.50	12.50	27.50	37.50	—
1841G Rare	—	—	—	—	—	—
1842/29G	—	3.50	9.00	18.50	40.00	—
1842/37G	—	3.50	9.00	17.50	35.00	—
1843G	—	4.00	12.00	20.00	45.00	—
1844G	—	3.50	9.00	17.50	35.00	—
1845G	—	70.00	125	250	—	—
1846G	—	7.00	15.00	27.50	50.00	—

Note: 1846 date exists with both coin and medal alignment

Date	Mintage	F	VF	XF	Unc	BU
1847G Rare	—	—	—	—	—	—
1848G Rare	—	—	—	—	—	—
1850G	—	15.00	35.00	60.00	120	—
1851G Rare	—	—	—	—	—	—

KM# 23 1/4 REAL
0.8500 g., 0.9030 Silver .0246 oz.

Date	Mintage	F	VF	XF	Unc	BU
1845CR	—	75.00	155	235	500	—

Note: Caution, counterfeits are known

KM# 2 1/2 REAL
1.6900 g., 0.9030 Silver .0490 oz.

Date	Mintage	F	VF	XF	Unc	BU
1824NG M	—	13.50	28.00	65.00	180	—

KM# 18 1/2 REAL
1.6900 g., 0.9030 Silver .0490 oz. **Note:** Similar to KM#2.

Date	Mintage	VG	F	VF	XF	Unc
1830T F Rare, 3-4 known	—	—	—	—	—	—

KM# 20 1/2 REAL
1.6900 g., 0.9030 Silver .0490 oz.

Date	Mintage	VG	F	VF	XF	Unc
1831CR E	—	6.00	16.50	35.00	60.00	—
1831CR F	—	4.50	12.50	25.00	42.50	—
1843CR M	—	3.00	7.50	20.00	45.00	—
1845CR B	—	15.00	35.00	75.00	150	—

KM# 20a 1/2 REAL
1.6900 g., 0.7500 Silver .0407 oz.

Date	Mintage	VG	F	VF	XF	Unc
1846CR JB Cresca	—	6.00	15.00	30.00	65.00	—
1846CR JB Crezca	—	20.00	45.00	85.00	180	—
1847CR JB Cresca	—	20.00	45.00	80.00	170	—
1847CR JB Crezca	—	5.00	12.50	27.50	55.00	—
1848CR JB	—	3.00	8.50	22.50	47.50	—
1849CR JB	—	15.00	35.00	75.00	150	—

KM# 3 REAL
3.3800 g., 0.9030 Silver .0981 oz.

Date	Mintage	F	VF	XF	Unc	BU
1824NG M	—	15.00	33.50	60.00	165	250
1828NG M	—	60.00	130	235	—	—

KM# 19.1 REAL
3.3800 g., 0.9030 Silver .0981 oz. **Obv. Legend:** REP. DEL CENT. DE AMER. **Rev. Legend:** LIB. CRESC. FEC.

Date	Mintage	F	VF	XF	Unc	BU
1824T NR Rare, 3-5 known	—	—	—	—	—	—

KM# 19.2 REAL
3.3800 g., 0.9030 Silver .0981 oz. **Obv. Legend:** REPUBLIC DEL CENTRO DE AMER. **Rev. Legend:** LIBRE CRESCA FECUNDO

Date	Mintage	F	VF	XF	Unc	BU
1825T M Unique	—	—	—	—	—	—
1830T F	—	10.00	25.00	55.00	300	—

Note: Planchets can vary widely in diameter and levelness or flatness, resulting in considerable differences between struck coins

KM# 21 REAL
3.3800 g., 0.9030 Silver .0981 oz. **Obv. Legend:** REPUBLIC DEL CENTRO DE AMER. **Rev. Legend:** LIBRE CRESCA FECUNDO

Date	Mintage	VG	F	VF	XF	Unc
1831CR E	—	15.50	28.50	67.50	150	—
1831CR F	—	13.00	25.00	55.00	115	—

KM# 21a REAL
3.3800 g., 0.7500 Silver .0815 oz.

Date	Mintage	VG	F	VF	XF	Unc
1848CR JB	—	27.50	60.00	125	220	—
1849CR JB	—	12.50	28.50	50.00	115	—

KM# 9.3 2 REALES
6.7700 g., 0.9030 Silver .1965 oz. **Obv. Legend:** REPUBLICA DEL CENTRO DE AMER. **Rev. Legend:** LIBRE CRESCA FECUNDO.

Date	Mintage	VG	F	VF	XF	Unc
1831T F	—	5.00	9.00	22.50	40.00	85.00
1832T F	—	15.00	30.00	50.00	135	—

KM# 9.1 2 REALES
6.7700 g., 0.9030 Silver .1965 oz. **Obv. Legend:** REPUBLICA DE CENTRO AMERIC. **Rev. Legend:** LIBRE CRESCA FECUNDO.

Date	Mintage	VG	F	VF	XF	Unc
1825T M Rare	—	—	—	—	—	—

KM# 9.2 2 REALES
6.7700 g., 0.9030 Silver .1965 oz. **Obv. Legend:** REPUBLICA DEL CENTRO AMER. **Rev. Legend:** LIBRE CRESCA FECUND.

Date	Mintage	VG	F	VF	XF	Unc
1825T M Rare	—	—	—	—	—	—

KM# 10 2 REALES
6.7700 g., 0.9030 Silver .1965 oz. **Obv. Legend:** REP. D. CENT. D. AMER. **Rev. Legend:** LIB. CRESC. FEC.

Date	Mintage	Good	VG	F	VF	XF
1825T JD Rare	—	—	—	—	—	—
1825T NR	—	60.00	110	250	400	—

KM# 24 2 REALES
6.5000 g., 0.7500 Silver .1567 oz.

Date	Mintage	VG	F	VF	XF	Unc
1849CR JB	4-6	250	475	950	1,600	—

KM# 4 8 REALES
27.0700 g., 0.9030 Silver .7859 oz.

Date	Mintage	F	VF	XF	Unc	BU
1824NG M	—	25.00	50.00	125	750	—
1825NG M	—	25.00	50.00	125	750	—
1826/5NG M	—	30.00	60.00	150	750	—
1826NG M CRES/CCA	—	275	475	800	1,250	—
1826NG M	—	25.00	50.00	125	750	—
1827NG M	—	25.00	60.00	150	750	—
1828NG M	—	25.00	70.00	175	750	—
1829NG M	—	25.00	50.00	125	750	—
1830NG M	—	250	500	900	—	—
Note: Reverse of 1830						
1830NG M	—	300	600	1,000	—	—
Note: Reverse of 1831, two crossed marks below 8						
1831NG M	—	400	750	1,200	—	—
1834NG M	—	120	200	350	800	—
1835NG M coin	—	25.00	50.00	125	750	—
1835NG M medal	—	25.00	50.00	125	750	—
1836NG M	—	25.00	50.00	125	750	—
1836NG BA	—	25.00	60.00	150	750	—
1837NG BA	—	25.00	50.00	125	750	—
1839/7NG MA/BA	—	60.00	100	250	750	—
1840/37NG MA/BA	—	25.00	65.00	150	750	—
1840/39NG MA	—	25.00	50.00	125	750	—
1840NG MA	—	25.00	50.00	125	750	—
1841/37NG MA/BA	—	125	250	500	900	—
1841NG MA	—	100	200	400	850	—
1842/37NG MA/BA	—	25.00	60.00	150	750	—
1842/0NG MA	—	25.00	60.00	150	750	—
1842NG MA	—	25.00	50.00	125	750	—
1846NG MA	—	75.00	150	400	950	—
1846/2NG AE/MA	—	40.00	75.00	200	750	—
Note: With CREZCA over CRESCA						
1846NG A	—	25.00	65.00	150	750	—
1847NG A	—	40.00	75.00	200	750	—

KM# 22 8 REALES
27.0700 g., 0.9030 Silver .7859 oz.

Date	Mintage	F	VF	XF	Unc	BU
1831CR E	—	2,000	4,000	7,500	15,000	—
1831CR F	—	400	1,000	2,500	—	—

KM# 5 1/2 ESCUDO
1.6875 g., 0.8750 Gold .0474 oz.

Date	Mintage	VG	F	VF	XF	Unc
1824NG M	—	35.00	55.00	100	200	—
1825/4NG M	—	40.00	60.00	115	180	—
1825NG M	—	30.00	45.00	85.00	150	—
1826NG M	—	40.00	60.00	115	180	—
1843NG M	—	70.00	120	225	325	—

KM# 11 1/2 ESCUDO
1.6875 g., 0.8750 Gold .0474 oz. **Note:** Provisional issue.

Date	Mintage	VG	F	VF	XF	Unc
1825CR MU Rare	—	—	—	—	—	—

KM# 13.1 1/2 ESCUDO
1.6875 g., 0.8750 Gold .0474 oz.

Date	Mintage	VG	F	VF	XF	Unc
1828CR F	4,435	75.00	125	200	350	—
1843CR M	593	90.00	180	360	600	—
1846CR JB	13,000	30.00	50.00	80.00	140	—
1847CR JB	23,000	30.00	50.00	80.00	140	—
1848CR JB	14,000	30.00	50.00	80.00	140	—
1849CR JB	Inc. above	90.00	180	350	550	—

KM# 13.2 1/2 ESCUDO
1.6875 g., 0.8750 Gold .0474 oz. **Note:** Inverted "C" in mint mark.

Date	Mintage	VG	F	VF	XF	Unc
1847CR JB	Inc. above	30.00	50.00	80.00	140	—
1848CR JB	Inc. above	30.00	50.00	80.00	140	—

KM# 6 ESCUDO
3.3750 g., 0.8750 Gold .0949 oz.

Date	Mintage	VG	F	VF	XF	Unc
1824NG M	—	100	300	750	1,200	—
1825NG M	—	70.00	175	350	800	—

KM# 14 ESCUDO
3.3750 g., 0.8750 Gold .0949 oz.

Date	Mintage	VG	F	VF	XF	Unc
1828CR F Rare	—	—	—	—	—	—
1833CR E	10,000	40.00	100	150	250	—
1844CR M	6,353	40.00	100	150	260	—
1845CR JB	8,672	40.00	150	250	375	—
1846CR JB	2,722	40.00	100	175	275	—
1847CR JB	3,510	40.00	100	175	275	—
1848CR JB	10,000	40.00	80.00	150	225	—
1849CR JB	13,000	40.00	90.00	150	225	—

KM# 12 2 ESCUDOS
6.7500 g., 0.8750 Gold .1899 oz.

Date	Mintage	VG	F	VF	XF	Unc
1825NG M	—	90.00	180	320	500	—
1826NG M	—	90.00	180	320	500	—
1827NG M	—	90.00	180	320	500	—
1828NG M	—	90.00	180	320	500	—
1830NG M	—	90.00	250	400	600	—
1834NG M	—	90.00	375	750	1,000	—
1835NG M	—	90.00	190	320	500	—
1836NG M	—	100	200	400	550	—
1837NG BA	—	100	200	425	800	—
1840NG MA Rare	—	—	—	—	—	—
1842NG MA	—	100	200	400	775	—
1844NG B	—	100	200	425	800	—
1846NG A	—	100	200	400	600	—
1847NG A	—	100	200	400	650	—

KM# 15 2 ESCUDOS
6.7500 g., 0.8750 Gold .1899 oz.

Date	Mintage	VG	F	VF	XF	Unc
1828CR F	2,750	90.00	190	350	700	—
1835CR F	5,452	80.00	170	275	550	—
1843CR M	4,482	90.00	190	350	700	—
1850CR JB	7,432	BV	125	200	400	—

KM# 7 4 ESCUDOS
13.5000 g., 0.8750 Gold .3798 oz.

Date	Mintage	VG	F	VF	XF	Unc
1824NG M	—	700	1,450	2,500	4,500	—
1825NG M	—	950	1,700	2,800	4,800	—

KM# 16 4 ESCUDOS
13.5000 g., 0.8750 Gold .3798 oz.

Date	Mintage	VG	F	VF	XF	Unc
1828CR F	3,048	400	600	1,150	2,750	—
1835CR F	697	275	500	1,000	2,500	—
1837CR E	11,000	275	525	1,100	2,750	—
1837CR F Rare	Inc. above	—	—	—	—	—
1849CR JB	441	1,200	2,000	3,750	6,000	—

KM# 8 8 ESCUDOS
27.0000 g., 0.8750 Gold .7596 oz.

Date	Mintage	VG	F	VF	XF	Unc
1824NG M	—	1,000	2,000	4,000	7,500	—
Note: Stack's Hammel sale 9-82 Unc 1824 M realized $27,000						
1825NG M	—	1,500	3,500	7,000	12,000	—

KM# 17 8 ESCUDOS
27.0000 g., 0.8750 Gold .7596 oz.

Date	Mintage	VG	F	VF	XF	Unc
1828CR F	5,302	500	1,000	2,000	3,200	—
Note: Stack's Hammel sale 9-82 AU 1828 F realized $9,500						
1833CR F	4,459	500	1,000	2,000	3,200	—
1837CR E	2,028	950	1,550	3,250	5,500	—
1837CR F	Inc. above	1,200	2,100	4,000	6,500	—

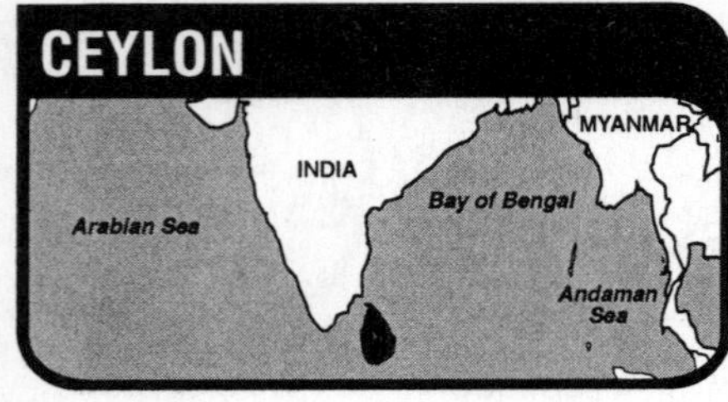

The earliest known inhabitants of Ceylon, the Veddahs, were subjugated by the Sinhalese from northern India in the 6th century B.C. Sinhalese rule was maintained until 1408, after which the island was controlled by China for 30 years. The Portuguese came to Ceylon in 1505 and maintained control of the coastal area for 150 years. The Dutch supplanted them in 1658, which were in turn supplanted by the British who seized the Dutch colonies in 1796, and made them a Crown Colony in 1802. In 1815, the British conquered the independent Kingdom of Kandy in the central part of the island. Constitutional changes in 1931 and 1946 granted the Ceylonese a measure of autonomy and a parliamentary form of government. Britain granted Ceylon independence as a self-governing state within the British Commonwealth on Feb. 4, 1948. On May 22, 1972, the Ceylonese adopted a new Constitution, which declared Ceylon to be the Republic of Sri Lanka –'Resplendent Island'

RULERS
British, 1796-1948

MINT MARKS
H – Heaton, Birmingham
B – Bombay

MONETARY SYSTEM
4 Pies = 1 Stiver
4 Stivers = 1 Fanam
12 Fanams = 1 Rixdollar = 1 Rupee = 1-1/2 Shillings
2 Rupees = 3 Shillings

HOMELAND COINAGE
4 Farthings = 1 Penny

1/4 FARTHING

Copper and Bronze

NOTE: From 1839 through 1868 homeland type 1/4 Farthings were issued by Great Britain for circulation in Ceylon. These are listed under Great Britain.

1/2 FARTHING

Copper and Bronze

NOTE: From 1828 through 1868 homeland type 1/2 Farthings were issued by Great Britain for circulation in Ceylon. These are listed under Great Britain.

1-1/2 PENCE

SILVER

NOTE: From 1834 through 1870 homeland type 1-1/2 Pence were issued by Great Britain for circulation in Ceylon and Jamaica. These are listed under Great Britain.

BRITISH COLONIAL

HAMMERED COINAGE

KM# 72 1/4 PICE (1/256 Rixdaler)
Copper **Obv:** C. G., date **Rev:** Value

Date	Mintage	Good	VG	F	VF	XF
1813 Rare	—	—	—	—	—	—

KM# 63 1/48 RIXDOLLAR
Copper **Rev:** Elephant faces left

Date	Mintage	Good	VG	F	VF	XF
1801	—	5.00	10.00	17.50	35.00	—
1802	—	5.00	10.00	17.50	35.00	—
1803	—	5.00	10.00	17.50	35.00	—
1811	—	6.50	12.00	22.50	45.00	—
1812	—	6.50	12.00	20.00	40.00	—
1813	—	8.50	15.00	22.50	45.00	—
1814	—	8.50	15.00	22.50	45.00	—
1815	—	8.50	15.00	22.50	45.00	—
1816	—	75.00	125	185	275	—

KM# 66 1/48 RIXDOLLAR
Copper **Obv:** Two parallel lines under "48"

Date	Mintage	Good	VG	F	VF	XF
1802	—	65.00	175	325	450	—

KM# 69 1/48 RIXDOLLAR
Copper **Rev:** Elephant faces right

Date	Mintage	Good	VG	F	VF	XF
1803 Unique	—	—	—	—	—	—

KM# 64 1/24 RIXDOLLAR
Copper

Date	Mintage	Good	VG	F	VF	XF
1801	—	10.00	22.50	35.00	60.00	—
1802	—	7.00	18.50	40.00	65.00	—
1803	—	6.00	17.50	30.00	55.00	—
1805	—	10.00	18.50	45.00	70.00	—
1811	—	7.00	16.50	30.00	55.00	—
1812	—	7.00	18.50	30.00	55.00	—
1813	—	7.00	18.50	35.00	60.00	—
1814	—	12.50	23.50	45.00	70.00	—
1815	—	12.50	22.50	45.00	70.00	—
1816	—	25.00	60.00	100	185	—

KM# 67 1/24 RIXDOLLAR
Copper **Obv:** Two parallel lines under "24"

Date	Mintage	Good	VG	F	VF	XF
1802	—	65.00	175	325	450	—

KM# 70 1/24 RIXDOLLAR
Copper **Rev:** Elephant faces right

Date	Mintage	Good	VG	F	VF	XF
1803	—	60.00	140	225	350	—
1805	—	60.00	140	225	350	—

KM# 65 1/12 RIXDOLLAR
Copper **Rev:** Elephant faces left

Date	Mintage	Good	VG	F	VF	XF
1801	—	10.00	25.00	35.00	65.00	—
1802	—	8.00	16.50	25.00	45.00	—
1803	—	8.00	16.50	25.00	45.00	—
1804	—	12.50	25.00	35.00	65.00	—
1805	—	12.50	25.00	35.00	65.00	—
1811	—	12.50	25.00	35.00	65.00	—
1812	—	9.00	22.50	35.00	60.00	—
1813	—	9.00	30.00	45.00	70.00	—
1814	—	9.00	27.50	45.00	70.00	—
1815	—	9.00	22.50	35.00	65.00	—

KM# 68 1/12 RIXDOLLAR
Copper **Obv:** Two parallel lines under "12"

Date	Mintage	Good	VG	F	VF	XF
1802 Rare	—	—	—	—	—	—

KM# 71 1/12 RIXDOLLAR
Copper **Rev:** Elephant faces right

Date	Mintage	Good	VG	F	VF	XF
1803	—	100	200	375	550	—

KM# 76 24 STIVERS
0.8920 Silver

Date	Mintage	VG	F	VF	XF	Unc
1803	—	17.50	35.00	70.00	135	—
1804	—	20.00	40.00	80.00	145	—
1805	—	35.00	70.00	120	190	—
1808	—	25.00	60.00	110	175	—
1809	—	35.00	70.00	115	185	—

KM# 77 48 STIVERS
0.8920 Silver

Date	Mintage	VG	F	VF	XF	Unc
1803	—	30.00	60.00	125	175	—
1804	—	30.00	60.00	125	175	—
1805	—	30.00	60.00	125	175	—
1808	—	30.00	60.00	125	175	—
1809	—	25.00	50.00	100	150	—

KM# 78 48 STIVERS
0.8920 Silver **Rev:** Elephant faces right

Date	Mintage	VG	F	VF	XF	Unc
1803	—	85.00	185	300	500	—

KM# 79 96 STIVERS
0.8330 Silver

Date	Mintage	VG	F	VF	XF	Unc
1808	—	45.00	90.00	150	225	—
1809	—	50.00	100	185	275	—

KM# 83 FANAM TOKEN
0.5800 g., 0.8330 Silver **Obv:** Circular legends, FANAM **Rev:** TOKEN

Date	Mintage	VG	F	VF	XF	Unc
ND(1814-15)	2,095,000	4.00	8.00	15.00	30.00	—

Note: There are two known varieties: with or without dot in center of reverse circle

MILLED COINAGE

KM# 80 1/2 STIVER
Copper

Date	Mintage	F	VF	XF	Unc	BU
1815	2,400,000	5.00	15.00	35.00	175	—
1815 Proof	—	Value: 350				

KM# 81 STIVER
Copper

Date	Mintage	F	VF	XF	Unc	BU
1815	2,800,000	5.00	15.00	35.00	175	—
1815 Proof	—	Value: 400				

KM# 82.1 2 STIVERS
Copper **Obv:** Without rose below bust

Date	Mintage	F	VF	XF	Unc	BU
1815	1,920,000	6.00	18.00	60.00	250	—
1815 Proof	—	Value: 550				

KM# 82.2 2 STIVERS
Copper **Obv:** Rose below bust

Date	Mintage	F	VF	XF	Unc	BU
1815 Proof	—	Value: 950				

KM# 73 1/192 RIXDOLLAR
Copper

Date	Mintage	F	VF	XF	Unc	BU
1802	3,600,000	2.50	7.50	20.00	70.00	—
1802 Proof	—	Value: 120				
1802 Gilt Proof	—	—	—	—	100	—
1804 Proof	—	Value: 200				
1804 Gilt Proof	—	—	—	—	200	—

KM# 73a 1/192 RIXDOLLAR
Gilt Silver **Obv:** Denomination and legend **Rev:** Elephant and date

Date	Mintage	F	VF	XF	Unc	BU
1802 Proof	—	—	—	—	—	—

KM# 74 1/96 RIXDOLLAR
Copper

Date	Mintage	F	VF	XF	Unc	BU
1802	1,800,000	4.00	8.00	22.50	85.00	—
1802 Proof	—	Value: 150				
1802 Gilt Proof	—	—	—	—	125	—

KM# 74a 1/96 RIXDOLLAR
Gilt Silver **Obv:** Denomination and legend **Rev:** Elephant and date

Date	Mintage	F	VF	XF	Unc	BU
1802 Proof	—	—	—	—	—	—

KM# 75 1/48 RIXDOLLAR
Copper

Date	Mintage	F	VF	XF	Unc	BU
1802	2,700,000	5.00	10.00	25.00	90.00	—
1802 Proof	—	Value: 175				
1802 Gilt Proof	—	—	—	—	150	—
1804 Proof	—	Value: 250				
1804 Gilt Proof	—	—	—	—	250	—

KM# 75a 1/48 RIXDOLLAR
Gilt Silver **Obv:** Denomination and legend **Rev:** Elephant and date

Date	Mintage	F	VF	XF	Unc	BU
1802 Proof	—	—	—	—	—	—

KM# 84 RIXDOLLAR
0.8920 Silver

Date	Mintage	F	VF	XF	Unc	BU
1821	400,000	12.00	28.00	80.00	225	—
1821 Proof	—	Value: 275				

COUNTERMARKED COINAGE

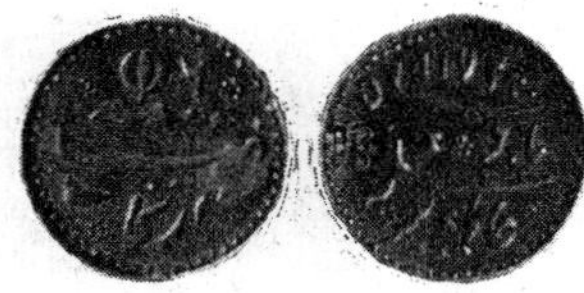

KM# 85 1/3 RIXDOLLAR
Silver **Countermark:** Crown **Note:** Countermark on Madras Arcot 1/4 Rupee, KM#413.

CM Date	Host Date	Good	VG	F	VF	XF
ND	AH1172//6	—	22.50	50.00	90.00	160

KM# 86 1-1/3 RIXDOLLAR (16 Fanams)
Silver **Countermark:** Crown **Note:** Countermark on Madras Arcot Rupee, KM#415.

CM Date	Host Date	Good	VG	F	VF	XF
ND	AH1172//6	—	80.00	160	250	375

DECIMAL COINAGE

100 Cents = 1 Rupee

KM# 90 1/4 CENT
Copper

Date	Mintage	F	VF	XF	Unc	BU
1870	200,000	1.50	3.00	5.00	12.00	—
1870 Proof	—	Value: 100				
1890	200,000	1.50	3.00	5.00	12.00	—
1890 Proof	—	Value: 100				
1891 Proof	—	Value: 150				
1892 Proof	—	Value: 150				
1898	160,000	2.50	5.00	8.00	16.00	—
1898 Proof	—	Value: 100				

KM# 90a 1/4 CENT
Silver

Date	Mintage	F	VF	XF	Unc	BU
1870 Proof	—	Value: 250				
1891 Proof	—	Value: 250				
1892 Proof	—	Value: 250				
1898 Proof	—	Value: 250				

KM# 90b 1/4 CENT
Gold

Date	Mintage	F	VF	XF	Unc	BU
1870 Proof	—	Value: 1,250				
1891 Proof	—	Value: 1,250				

KM# 91 1/2 CENT
Copper

Date	Mintage	F	VF	XF	Unc	BU
1870	3,040,000	1.00	1.50	3.00	8.00	—
1870 Proof	—	Value: 120				
1890	400,000	1.50	3.50	8.00	16.00	—
1890 Proof	—	Value: 125				
1891	1,000,000	1.25	2.75	4.00	12.00	—
1891 Proof	—	Value: 125				
1892 Proof	—	Value: 225				
1895	4,040,000	1.00	1.75	3.00	8.00	—
1895 Proof	—	Value: 120				
1898	4,000,000	1.25	2.50	4.00	10.00	—
1898 Proof	—	Value: 120				

KM# 91a 1/2 CENT
Silver

Date	Mintage	F	VF	XF	Unc	BU
1870 Proof	—	Value: 300				
1891 Proof	—	Value: 300				
1892 Proof	—	Value: 300				
1895 Proof	—	Value: 300				
1898 Proof	—	Value: 300				

KM# 91b 1/2 CENT
Gold

Date	Mintage	F	VF	XF	Unc	BU
1870 Proof	—	Value: 1,250				
1891 Proof	—	Value: 1,250				
1895 Proof	—	Value: 1,250				

KM# 92 CENT
Copper

Date	Mintage	F	VF	XF	Unc	BU
1870	7,055,000	1.50	3.00	6.00	15.00	—
1870 Proof	—	Value: 125				
1890	4,940,000	1.50	3.00	5.00	12.00	—
1890 Proof	—	Value: 125				
1891	1,328,000	2.00	4.00	8.00	20.00	—
1891 Proof	—	Value: 125				
1892	5,000,000	1.50	3.00	6.00	15.00	—
1892 Proof	—	Value: 125				
1900	1,000,000	2.50	5.00	10.00	22.00	—
1900 Proof	—	Value: 175				

KM# 92a CENT
Silver

Date	Mintage	F	VF	XF	Unc	BU
1870 Proof	—	Value: 425				
1890 Proof	—	Value: 425				
1891 Proof	—	Value: 425				
1892 Proof	—	Value: 425				

KM# 92b CENT
Gold

Date	Mintage	F	VF	XF	Unc	BU
1870 Proof	—	Value: 1,350				
1891 Proof	—	Value: 1,350				

KM# 93 5 CENTS
Copper

Date	Mintage	F	VF	XF	Unc	BU
1870	7,009,000	5.00	10.00	30.00	80.00	—
1870 Proof	—	Value: 175				
1890	1,001,000	7.50	20.00	50.00	110	—
1890 Proof	—	Value: 200				
1891 Proof	—	Value: 350				
1892	1,000,000	7.50	20.00	50.00	110	—
1892 Proof	—	Value: 200				

KM# 93b 5 CENTS
Gold

Date	Mintage	F	VF	XF	Unc	BU
1870 Proof	—	Value: 1,500				
1891 Proof	—	Value: 1,500				

KM# 93a 5 CENTS
Silver

Date	Mintage	F	VF	XF	Unc	BU
1891 Proof	—	Value: 500				
1892 Proof	—	Value: 500				

KM# 94 10 CENTS
1.1664 g., 0.8000 Silver .0300 oz.

Date	Mintage	F	VF	XF	Unc	BU
1892	2,500,000	1.50	3.50	7.00	15.00	—
1892 Proof	—	Value: 150				
1893	2,500,000	1.50	3.50	7.00	15.00	—
1893 Proof	—	Value: 150				
1894	3,000,000	1.50	3.50	7.00	15.00	—
1894 Proof	—	Value: 150				
1897	1,500,000	1.50	3.50	9.00	20.00	—
1899	1,000,000	1.75	4.00	10.00	25.00	—
1900	1,000,000	1.75	4.00	10.00	25.00	—

KM# 95 25 CENTS
2.9160 g., 0.8000 Silver .0750 oz.

Date	Mintage	F	VF	XF	Unc	BU
1892	500,000	5.00	10.00	22.00	50.00	—
1892 Proof	—	Value: 150				
1893	1,500,000	3.00	7.00	15.00	35.00	—
1893 Proof	—	Value: 150				
1895	1,200,000	3.00	7.00	15.00	35.00	—
1899	600,000	5.00	10.00	22.00	50.00	—
1900	400,000	6.00	12.00	25.00	60.00	—

KM# 96 50 CENTS
5.8319 g., 0.8000 Silver .1500 oz.

Date	Mintage	F	VF	XF	Unc	BU
1892	250,000	10.00	20.00	40.00	80.00	—
1892 Proof	—	Value: 200				
1893	750,000	6.00	12.00	27.50	45.00	—
1893 Proof	—	Value: 175				
1895	450,000	5.00	8.00	30.00	60.00	—
1899	100,000	12.50	30.00	50.00	100	—
1900	200,000	5.00	10.00	30.00	70.00	—

PATTERNS

Including off metal strikes

KM#	Date	Mintage	Identification	Mkt Val
Pn3	1812	—	Rixdollar. Silver.	5,000

KM#	Date	Mintage	Identification	Mkt Val
Pn4	1812	—	2 Rixdollars. Silver.	10,000

KM#	Date	Mintage	Identification	Mkt Val
Pn5	1815	—	Fanam. Bronze. Struck over Dutch Doit.	1,250
Pn6	1815	—	Fanam. Lead.	1,550

KM#	Date	Mintage	Identification	Mkt Val
Pn7	1815	—	Rixdollar. Silver.	2,250

CHILE

The Republic of Chile, a ribbon-like country on the Pacific coast of southern South America, has an area of 292,135 sq. mi. (756,950 sq. km.). Capital: Santiago. Historically, the economic base of Chile has been the rich mineral deposits of its northern provinces. Copper has accounted for more than 75 percent of Chile's export earnings in recent years. Other important mineral exports are iron ore, iodine and nitrate of soda. Fresh fruits and vegetables, as well as wine are increasingly significant in inter-hemispheric trade.

Diego de Almargo was the first Spaniard to attempt to wrest Chile from the Incas and Araucanian tribes in 1536. He failed, and was followed by Pedro de Valdivia, a favorite of Pizarro, who founded Santiago in 1541. When the Napoleonic Wars involved Spain, leaving the constituent parts of the Spanish Empire to their own devices, Chilean patriots formed a national government and proclaimed the country's independence, Sept. 18, 1810. Independence however, was not secured until Feb. 12, 1818, after a bitter struggle led by Bernardo O'Higgins and San Martin. Despite a long steady history of monetary devaluation, reflected in declining weight and fineness in its currency, Chile developed a strong democracy. This was displaced when rampant inflation characterized chaotic and subsequently repressive governments in the mid to late 20th century.

RULERS
Spanish until 1818

MINT MARKS
So - Santiago

MINT MASTERS' INITIALS

AJ	1800-01	Agustin de Infante y Prado and Jose Maria de Bobadilla
D	1773-99	Domingo Eizaguirre
F	1803-17	Francisco Rodriguez Brochero
FJ, JF	1803-17	Francisco Rodriguez Brochero and Jose Maria de Bobadilla
J	1800-17	Jose Maria de Bobadilla

MONETARY SYSTEM
16 Reales = 1 Escudo

COLONIAL

MILLED COINAGE

KM# 63 1/4 REAL
0.8458 g., 0.8960 Silver .0244 oz., 12 mm. **Obv:** Lion **Rev:** Castle between denomination at right and mint mark at left, date below **Note:** Struck at Santiago Mint, mint mark So.

Date	Mintage	VG	F	VF	XF	Unc
1801So	57,000	10.00	25.00	60.00	100	—
1802So	56,000	10.00	25.00	60.00	100	—
1803/1So	—	12.00	30.00	70.00	120	—
1803So	54,000	10.00	25.00	60.00	100	—
1804So	56,000	10.00	25.00	60.00	100	—
1805So	56,000	10.00	25.00	60.00	100	—
1806/5So	54,000	10.00	25.00	60.00	100	—
1806So	Inc. above	10.00	25.00	60.00	100	—
1807So	57,000	10.00	25.00	60.00	100	—
1808/6So	—	12.00	30.00	70.00	120	—
1808So	57,000	10.00	25.00	60.00	100	—

KM# 73 1/4 REAL
0.8458 g., 0.8960 Silver .0244 oz., 12 mm. **Obv:** Lion **Rev:** Castle between denomination at right and mint mark at left **Note:** Struck at Santiago Mint, mint mark So. Varieties with and without dots flanking the date.

Date	Mintage	VG	F	VF	XF	Unc
1810	54,000	10.00	25.00	60.00	100	—
1811	54,000	10.00	25.00	60.00	100	—
1812	71,000	10.00	25.00	60.00	100	—
1813	63,000	10.00	25.00	60.00	100	—
1814	67,000	10.00	25.00	60.00	100	—

Date	Mintage	VG	F	VF	XF	Unc
1815	54,000	10.00	25.00	60.00	100	—
1816/5	82,000	10.00	25.00	60.00	100	—
1816	Inc. above	10.00	25.00	60.00	100	—
1817	—	10.00	20.00	50.00	90.00	—
Note: 1817 and 1818 dated coins struck under the Republic						
1818/6	403,000	10.00	25.00	65.00	110	—
1818	Inc. above	10.00	25.00	65.00	110	—
Note: Specially minted for the patriots after the defeat of Spain						

KM# 57 1/2 REAL

1.6917 g., 0.8960 Silver .0487 oz., 17 mm. **Obv:** Bust of Charles IV **Obv. Legend:** CAROLUS IIII **Rev:** Similar to KM#64 **Note:** Struck at Santiago Mint, mint mark So.

Date	Mintage	VG	F	VF	XF	Unc
1801 AJ	59,000	8.00	20.00	45.00	100	—
1801 AI Broken J	Inc. above	8.00	20.00	45.00	100	—
1802 JJ	78,000	8.00	20.00	45.00	100	—
1803 FJ	36,000	15.00	30.00	70.00	140	—
1804/3 FJ	58,000	9.00	22.00	65.00	125	—
1804 FJ	Inc. above	8.00	20.00	60.00	100	—
1805 FJ	28,000	10.00	25.00	75.00	150	—
1806/5 FJ	—	8.00	22.00	65.00	125	—
1806 FJ	59,000	8.00	20.00	45.00	100	—
1807 FJ	40,000	8.00	20.00	45.00	100	—
1808/7 FJ	58,000	8.00	22.00	65.00	125	—
1808 FJ	Inc. above	8.00	20.00	45.00	100	—

KM# 64 1/2 REAL

1.6917 g., 0.8960 Silver .0487 oz., 16.5 mm. **Obv:** Bust of Charles IV **Obv. Legend:** FERDIN VII **Note:** Struck at Santiago Mint, mint mark So.

Date	Mintage	VG	F	VF	XF	Unc
1808 FJ	Inc. above	8.00	20.00	45.00	100	—
1809/8 FJ	51,000	8.00	30.00	60.00	125	—
1809/8/7 FJ	Inc. above	10.00	35.00	70.00	125	—
1809 FJ	Inc. above	8.00	20.00	45.00	100	—
1810 FJ	50,000	8.00	20.00	45.00	100	—
1811 FJ	18,000	8.00	20.00	45.00	100	—
1812 FJ	125,000	8.00	20.00	45.00	100	—
1813 FJ	218,000	8.00	20.00	45.00	100	—
1814 FJ	77,000	8.00	20.00	45.00	100	—
1815 FJ	99,000	8.00	20.00	45.00	100	—
1816/5 FJ	—	8.00	30.00	60.00	120	—
1816 FJ	119,000	8.00	20.00	45.00	100	—
1817 FJ	—	8.00	30.00	60.00	100	—
1817 FD	—	20.00	40.00	80.00	190	—
1817 FI	—	—	—	—	—	—

KM# 58 REAL

3.3834 g., 0.8960 Silver .0975 oz., 21 mm. **Obv:** Bust of Charles IV **Obv. Legend:** CAROLUS IIII... **Rev:** Similar to KM#65 **Note:** Struck at Santiago Mint, mint mark So.

Date	Mintage	VG	F	VF	XF	Unc
1801 AJ/DA	—	—	—	—	—	—
1801 AJ	53,000	8.00	30.00	60.00	100	—
1801 AI Broken J	Inc. above	8.00	30.00	60.00	100	—
1802 JJ	81,000	8.00	28.00	55.00	90.00	—
1803 FJ	18,000	45.00	85.00	165	—	—
1804/1 FJ	—	—	—	—	—	—
1804/2 FJ	—	—	—	—	—	—
1804 FJ	35,000	8.00	28.00	55.00	90.00	—
1804 FJ/JJ	Inc. above	10.00	35.00	75.00	125	—
1805 FJ	19,000	9.00	32.00	65.00	110	—
1806/5 FJ	—	—	—	—	—	—
1806 FJ	38,000	10.00	35.00	75.00	125	—
1807/1796 FJ/DA	—	—	—	—	—	—
1807/6 FJ	23,000	10.00	35.00	75.00	125	—
1807 FJ	Inc. above	9.00	32.00	70.00	120	—
1808/7 FJ	34,000	9.00	32.00	70.00	120	—
1808 FJ	Inc. above	9.00	32.00	65.00	110	—

KM# 65 REAL

3.3841 g., 0.8960 Silver .0975 oz., 21 mm. **Obv:** Bust of Charles IV **Obv. Legend:** FERDIN. VII... **Note:** Struck at Santiago Mint, mint mark So.

Date	Mintage	VG	F	VF	XF	Unc
1808/7 FJ	—	20.00	40.00	75.00	150	—
1808 FJ	Inc. above	20.00	40.00	75.00	150	—
1809/1798 FJ	—	—	—	—	—	—
1809/08 FJ Ferdin VII/Carolus IIII; Rare	—	—	—	—	—	—
1809/8 FJ	29,000	8.00	30.00	60.00	100	—
1809 FJ	Inc. above	8.00	30.00	60.00	100	—
1810 FJ	79,000	8.00	30.00	60.00	100	—
1811 FJ	20,000	9.00	32.00	65.00	110	—
1812/1 FJ	43,000	10.00	35.00	75.00	125	—
1812 FJ	Inc. above	8.00	30.00	60.00	100	—

Date	Mintage	VG	F	VF	XF	Unc
1813/2 FJ	—	8.00	30.00	60.00	150	—
1813 FJ	213,000	8.00	30.00	60.00	100	—
1814 FJ	54,000	8.00	30.00	60.00	100	—
1815/4 FJ	—	8.00	30.00	60.00	100	—
1815 FJ	41,000	8.00	30.00	60.00	100	—
1816/5 FJ	—	8.00	30.00	60.00	100	—
1816 FJ	123,000	8.00	30.00	60.00	100	—
1817 FJ	—	8.00	30.00	60.00	100	—

KM# 59 2 REALES

6.7668 g., 0.8960 Silver .1949 oz., 28.5 mm. **Obv:** Bust of Charles IV **Obv. Legend:** CAROLUS IIII **Note:** Struck at Santiago Mint, mint mark So.

Date	Mintage	VG	F	VF	XF	Unc
1801 AJ	39,000	12.00	40.00	80.00	160	—
1802 JJ/AJ	—	15.00	45.00	90.00	175	—
1802 JJ	28,000	12.00	40.00	80.00	160	—
1803 FJ	25,000	12.00	40.00	80.00	160	—
1803 FJ/JJ	Inc. above	15.00	45.00	90.00	175	—
1804 FJ	28,000	12.00	40.00	80.00	160	—
1804 FJ Inverted mm	Inc. above	15.00	45.00	90.00	175	—
1805 FJ	24,000	12.00	40.00	80.00	160	—
1806/5 FJ	66,000	15.00	45.00	90.00	175	—
1806 FJ Inverted mm	Inc. above	15.00	45.00	90.00	175	—
1806 FJ	Inc. above	12.00	40.00	80.00	160	—
1807 FJ	42,000	12.00	40.00	80.00	160	—
1808 FJ	54,000	12.00	40.00	80.00	160	—

KM# 66 2 REALES

6.7668 g., 0.8960 Silver .1949 oz., 27.5 mm. **Obv:** Bust of Charles IV **Obv. Legend:** FERDIN. VII **Note:** Struck at Santiago Mint, mint mark So.

Date	Mintage	VG	F	VF	XF	Unc
1808 FJ	Inc. below	—	—	—	—	—
1809 FJ	41,000	12.00	40.00	80.00	160	—

KM# 74 2 REALES

6.7668 g., 0.8960 Silver .1949 oz., 27.5 mm. **Obv:** Imaginary laureate military bust **Obv. Legend:** FERDIN. VII... **Note:** Struck at Santiago Mint, mint mark So. Struck for exclusive use in Chile.

Date	Mintage	VG	F	VF	XF	Unc
1810 FJ	45,000	30.00	75.00	175	350	—
1810 FJ Inverted A for V in VII	Inc. above	35.00	85.00	—	—	—
1811 FJ	27,000	30.00	80.00	185	365	—

KM# 79 2 REALES

6.7668 g., 0.8960 Silver .1949 oz., 27.5 mm. **Obv:** Bust of Ferdinand **Obv. Legend:** FERDIN. VII... **Note:** Struck at Santiago Mint, mint mark So.

Date	Mintage	VG	F	VF	XF	Unc
1812 FJ	69,000	10.00	35.00	65.00	125	—
1813 FJ	136,000	10.00	35.00	65.00	125	—

Date	Mintage	VG	F	VF	XF	Unc
1813 FJ Inverted mm	Inc. above	10.00	35.00	65.00	125	—
1814 FJ	4,000	80.00	150	250	—	—
1815 FJ	24,000	12.00	40.00	75.00	150	—
1816 FJ	67,000	10.00	35.00	65.00	125	—
1817/16 FH	—	15.00	45.00	85.00	175	—
1817 FH	—	10.00	35.00	65.00	125	—

KM# 60 4 REALES

13.5337 g., 0.8960 Silver .3899 oz., 35 mm. **Obv:** Bust of Charles IV **Obv. Legend:** CAROLUS IIII... **Note:** Struck at Santiago Mint, mint mark So.

Date	Mintage	VG	F	VF	XF	Unc
1801 AJ	2,000	90.00	150	220	450	—
1802 JJ	18,000	65.00	115	175	375	—
1803 FJ	9,000	65.00	115	175	375	—
1804/3 FJ	6,000	65.00	115	175	375	—
1804 FJ	Inc. above	60.00	100	150	300	—
Note: Two varieties nown with flat forehead/flat nose in one line or with round nose						
1805 FJ	9,000	65.00	115	175	375	—
1806 FJ	20,000	60.00	100	150	300	—
1807 FJ	48,000	60.00	100	150	300	—
1808/7 FJ	25,000	60.00	100	150	300	—
1808 FJ	Inc. above	60.00	100	150	325	—

KM# 67 4 REALES

13.5337 g., 0.8960 Silver .3899 oz., 34 mm. **Obv:** Bust of Charles IV **Obv. Legend:** FERDIN. VII... **Note:** Struck at Santiago Mint, mint mark So.

Date	Mintage	VG	F	VF	XF	Unc
1808/7 FJ Inverted J	Inc. above	60.00	100	150	300	—
1808 FJ	Inc. above	60.00	100	150	300	—
1808 FJ Inverted J	Inc. above	60.00	100	150	300	—
1809 FJ	15,000	75.00	125	200	450	—
1810 FJ	10,000	60.00	100	150	325	—
1811 FJ	6,000	60.00	100	150	325	—
1811 FJ Inverted J	Inc. above	60.00	100	150	325	—
1812 FJ	27,000	60.00	100	150	300	—
1813 FJ	34,000	60.00	100	150	300	—
1813 FJ Inverted J	Inc. above	60.00	100	150	300	—
1815 FJ	10,000	85.00	135	220	500	—

KM# 51 8 REALES

27.0674 g., 0.8960 Silver .7797 oz., 40 mm. **Obv:** Bust of Charles IIII **Obv. Legend:** CAROLUS IIII **Note:** Struck at Santiago Mint, mint mark So.

Date	Mintage	VG	F	VF	XF	Unc
1801 AJ	185,000	125	175	275	550	—
1802/1 JJ/AJ	—	150	200	325	650	—
1802 JJ	160,000	125	175	275	550	—
1803/2 FJ/JJ	111,000	150	200	325	650	—

Date	Mintage	VG	F	VF	XF	Unc
1803 FJ	Inc. above	150	200	325	650	—
1804/3/2 FJ	—	350	450	550	750	—
1804/3 FJ	129,000	350	450	550	800	—
1804 FJ	Inc. above	150	200	300	600	—
1805 FJ	159,000	150	200	300	600	—
1806/5 FJ	155,000	150	200	325	650	—
1806 FJ	Inc. above	150	200	325	650	—
1807 FJ	94,000	150	200	325	650	—
1808 FJ	134,000	250	350	450	750	—

KM# 68 8 REALES
27.0674 g., 0.8960 Silver .7797 oz., 40.5 mm. **Obv:** Imaginary military bust **Obv. Legend:** FERDIN. VII **Note:** Struck at Santiago Mint for exclusive use in Chile, mint mark So.

Date	Mintage	VG	F	VF	XF	Unc
1808 FJ	Inc. below	—	2,000	3,500	6,000	—
1809 FJ	123,000	200	400	650	1,250	—

KM# 75 8 REALES
27.0674 g., 0.8960 Silver .7797 oz., 40.5 mm. **Obv:** Imaginary laureate military bust **Obv. Legend:** FERDIN. VII **Note:** Struck at Santiago Mint for exclusive use in Chile, mint mark So.

Date	Mintage	VG	F	VF	XF	Unc
1810 FJ	126,000	150	300	600	1,000	—
1811	97,000	150	300	600	1,000	—

KM# 80 8 REALES
27.0674 g., 0.8960 Silver .7797 oz. **Obv:** Bust of Ferdinand **Obv. Legend:** FERDIN. VII **Note:** Struck at Santiago Mint, mint mark So.

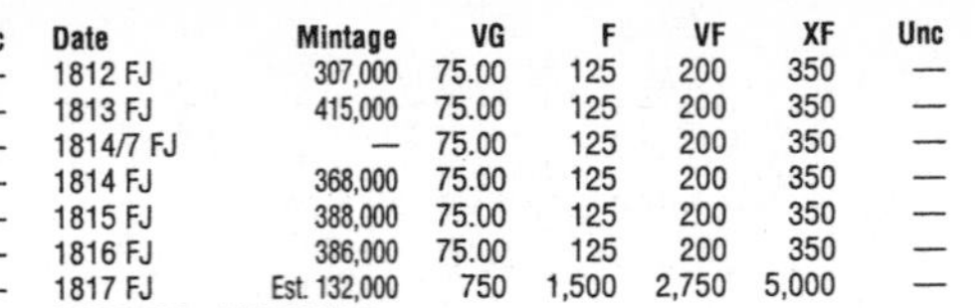

Date	Mintage	VG	F	VF	XF	Unc
1812 FJ	307,000	75.00	125	200	350	—
1813 FJ	415,000	75.00	125	200	350	—
1814/7 FJ	—	75.00	125	200	350	—
1814 FJ	368,000	75.00	125	200	350	—
1815 FJ	388,000	75.00	125	200	350	—
1816 FJ	386,000	75.00	125	200	350	—
1817 FJ	Est. 132,000	750	1,500	2,750	5,000	—

KM# 61 ESCUDO
3.3834 g., 0.8750 Gold .0952 oz., 19 mm. **Obv:** Bust of Charles IV **Obv. Legend:** CAROL IIII... **Rev:** Arms in order chain **Note:** Struck at Santiago Mint, mint mark So.

Date	Mintage	VG	F	VF	XF	Unc
1801 AJ	1,088	125	200	450	950	—
1802 JJ	748	160	250	425	900	—
1803 FJ/JJ	1,156	250	450	850	1,500	—
1803 FJ	Inc. above	140	185	300	600	—
1804 FJ	1,428	140	185	300	600	—
1805 FJ/JJ	816	200	350	700	1,250	—
1805 FJ	Inc. above	140	185	300	600	—
1806 FJ	544	150	200	375	775	—
1807 FJ	544	150	200	375	775	—
1808 FJ	2,448	140	185	300	600	—

KM# 69 ESCUDO
3.3841 g., 0.9040 Gold 0.0984 oz. **Obv:** Imaginary military bust **Obv. Legend:** FERDIN. VII... **Rev:** Arms

Date	Mintage	VG	F	VF	XF	Unc
1808 Rare	3,986	—	—	—	—	—
1809 Rare	5,026	—	—	—	—	—

KM# 76 ESCUDO
3.3841 g., 0.8750 Gold .0952 oz., 19 mm. **Obv:** Bust of Charles IV **Obv. Legend:** FERDIN. VII. D. G.... **Rev:** Arms in order chain **Note:** Struck at Santiago Mint, mint mark So. An additional 17,860 pieces were struck between 1818-1823; the actual date on the coin is unknown.

Date	Mintage	VG	F	VF	XF	Unc
1808 FJ	3,986,000	185	275	500	1,000	—
1809 FJ	5,026,000	150	200	325	750	—
1810 FJ	816	150	200	350	775	—
1811 FJ	680	150	200	350	775	—
1812/1 FJ	952	150	225	375	825	—
1812 FJ	Inc. above	150	200	325	750	—
1813 FJ	4,556	125	175	300	700	—
1814 FJ	1,152	150	200	350	775	—
1815 FJ	816	150	200	350	775	—
1816 FJ	408	200	350	700	1,250	—
1817 FJ	22,000	125	175	300	700	—
1817 JF MM to right	Inc. above	450	750	1,150	1,750	—

KM# 53 2 ESCUDOS
6.7668 g., 0.8750 Gold .1904 oz., 23 mm. **Obv:** Bust of Charles III **Obv. Legend:** CAROL. IIII... **Rev:** Arms **Note:** Struck at Santiago Mint, mint mark So.

Date	Mintage	VG	F	VF	XF	Unc
1801 AJ	680	350	550	775	1,350	—
1802 JJ	374	325	500	700	1,250	—
1803 FJ	578	350	550	775	1,350	—
1804 FJ	544	325	500	700	1,250	—
1805 FJ	646	325	500	700	1,250	—
1806 FJ	306	350	550	850	1,600	—
1807 FJ	340	350	550	850	1,600	—
1808/7 FJ	1,020	300	450	600	1,000	—
1808 FJ	Inc. above	175	250	350	750	—

KM# 70 2 ESCUDOS
6.7668 g., 0.8750 Gold .1904 oz., 23 mm. **Obv:** Bust of Charles III **Obv. Legend:** FERDIN. VII... **Rev:** Arms in order chain **Note:** Struck at Santiago Mint, mint mark So.

Date	Mintage	VG	F	VF	XF	Unc
1810 FJ	Inc. above	325	500	700	1,250	—
1811 FJ	Inc. above	500	900	1,200	2,000	—

KM# 81 2 ESCUDOS
6.7668 g., 0.8750 Gold .1904 oz., 22.5 mm. **Obv:** Bust of Charles IV **Obv. Legend:** FERDIN. VII... **Rev:** Arms in order chain **Note:** Struck at Santiago Mint, mint mark So. An additional 19,876 pieces were struck between 1818-1823; the actual dates of these coins are unknown.

Date	Mintage	VG	F	VF	XF	Unc
1813 FJ	Inc. below	600	1,000	1,300	2,250	—
1814 FJ	682	325	500	700	1,250	—
1815 FJ	408	325	500	700	1,250	—
1816 FJ	608	400	750	1,100	1,750	—
1817 FJ	168	300	450	600	1,000	—

KM# 62 4 ESCUDOS
13.5337 g., 0.8750 Gold .3807 oz., 30.5 mm. **Obv:** Bust of Charles IV **Obv. Legend:** CAROL. IIII... **Rev:** Arms in order chain **Note:** Struck at Santiago Mint, mint mark So.

Date	Mintage	VG	F	VF	XF	Unc
1801 AJ	340	500	750	1,100	1,750	—
1802 JJ	374	500	750	1,100	1,750	—
1803 FJ	476	500	750	1,100	1,750	—
1804 FJ	255	700	1,150	1,500	2,750	—
1805 FJ	323	500	750	1,100	1,750	—
1806 FJ	204	500	750	1,100	1,750	—
1807 FJ	187	800	1,250	1,600	3,000	—
1808/7 FJ	1,207	550	800	1,150	2,000	—
1808 FJ	Inc. above	500	750	1,100	1,750	—

KM# 77 4 ESCUDOS
13.5337 g., 0.8750 Gold .3807 oz., 30.5 mm. **Obv:** Bust of Charles IV **Obv. Legend:** FERDIN VII... **Rev:** Arms in order chain **Note:** Struck at Santiago Mint, mint mark So. An additional 6,560 pieces were struck between 1818-1823; the actual date on the coin is unknown.

Date	Mintage	VG	F	VF	XF	Unc
1810 FJ	272	425	700	1,250	2,000	—
1811 FJ	170	475	750	1,300	2,100	—
1812 FJ	254	375	650	1,150	1,900	—
1813 FJ	1,462	375	650	1,150	1,900	—
1816 FJ	100	650	1,000	1,500	2,500	—
1817 FJ	68	425	700	1,250	2,000	—

KM# 54 8 ESCUDOS
27.0674 g., 0.8750 Gold .7615 oz., 37.5 mm. **Obv:** Bust of Charles III **Obv. Legend:** CAROL. IIII... **Rev:** Arms in order chain **Rev. Legend:** IN UTROQ FELIX AUSPICE DEO **Note:** Struck at Santiago Mint, mint mark So.

Date	Mintage	VG	F	VF	XF	Unc
1800 AJ	Inc. above	375	550	700	1,000	—
1801 AJ	46,000	375	525	650	900	—
1802 JJ	49,000	375	525	650	900	—
1803/2 FJ/JJ	44,000	375	600	750	1,100	—
1803 FJ	Inc. above	375	525	650	900	—
1804 FJ	40,000	375	525	650	900	—
1805 FJ	44,000	375	525	650	900	—
1806/5 FJ	40,000	375	525	650	900	—

Date	Mintage	VG	F	VF	XF	Unc
1806 FJ	Inc. above	375	525	650	900	—
1806 JF	Inc. above	600	1,000	1,500	2,500	—
1807 FJ	39,000	375	550	650	900	—
1807 JF	Inc. above	375	550	650	900	—
1808 FJ	39,000	375	550	650	900	—

KM# 72 8 ESCUDOS
27.0674 g., 0.8750 Gold .7615 oz., 38 mm. **Obv:** Imaginary military bust of Ferdinand VII **Obv. Legend:** FERDIN. VII... **Rev:** Arms in order chain **Note:** Struck at Santiago Mint for exclusive use in Chile, mint mark So.

Date	Mintage	VG	F	VF	XF	Unc
1808 FJ	Inc. below	700	1,200	1,500	2,750	—
1809 FJ	41,000	400	650	950	1,600	—
1810 FJ	55,000	400	650	950	1,600	—
1810 FJ Inverted mint mark	Inc. above	500	850	1,200	2,000	—
1811 FJ	44,000	400	650	950	1,600	—

KM# 78 8 ESCUDOS
27.0730 g., 0.8750 Gold .7616 oz., 38 mm. **Obv:** Bust of Charles IV **Obv. Legend:** FERDIN VII... **Rev:** Arms in order chain **Note:** Struck at Santiago Mint for exclusive use in Chile, mint mark So.

Date	Mintage	VG	F	VF	XF	Unc
1811 FJ	—	1,500	3,000	4,500	7,500	—
1812 FJ	48,000	375	525	650	900	—
1813/2 FT	37,000	375	525	650	900	—
1813 FJ	Inc. above	375	525	650	900	—
1814 FJ	29,000	375	525	650	900	—
1815 FN	39,000	375	525	650	900	—
1816 FJ	30,000	375	525	650	900	—
1817/6 FJ	11,000	375	525	650	900	—
1817/8 FJ	Inc. above	400	550	700	1,000	—
1817 FJ	Inc. above	375	525	650	900	—

REPUBLIC

PESO COINAGE

Coinage according to decree of June 9, 1817 and February 6, 1824, based on the standards of the Spanish system

KM# 82.1 PESO
0.9020 Silver 27 oz., 39.5 mm. **Obv:** Volcano **Rev:** Y above pillar

Date	Mintage	VG	F	VF	XF	Unc
1817	—	125	210	650	1,500	—

KM# 82.2 PESO
0.9020 Silver 27 oz., 39.5 mm. **Obv:** Volcano **Rev:** Y to left of pillar

Date	Mintage	VG	F	VF	XF	Unc
1817 FJ	—	40.00	85.00	150	300	—
1817 FD	—	55.00	120	275	500	—
1818/7 FD	371,000	65.00	135	300	550	—
1818 FD	Inc. above	65.00	135	300	550	—
1819/8 FD	236,000	65.00	135	300	550	—
1819 FD	Inc. above	60.00	125	275	500	—
1820 FD	116,000	45.00	95.00	200	350	—
1821 FD	126,000	100	200	450	750	—
1822 FI	148,000	40.00	85.00	175	350	—
1823 FI	45,000	60.00	125	250	475	—
1824 I	11,000	200	350	800	1,400	—
1825 I	3,400	150	300	750	1,350	—
1826 I Rare	6,111	—	—	—	—	—
1830 I	6,868	200	400	950	1,700	—
1831 I	51,000	65.00	135	275	500	—
1832 I	40,000	55.00	110	250	475	—
1833 I	88,000	40.00	85.00	175	350	—
1834 I	43,000	80.00	180	375	650	—
1834 IJ	Inc. above	120	250	500	900	—

KM# 88 PESO
0.9020 Silver **Obv:** Volcano **Rev:** Similar to KM#82.2

Date	Mintage	VG	F	VF	XF	Unc
1828 TH Rare	—	—	—	—	—	—

Note: Akers Pittman sale 8-99, XF-AU realized $23,000

COUNTERMARKED COINAGE

1833 — Chiloe

KM# A106 REAL
Silver **Countermark:** Mountains/CHIL **Note:** Countermark on Argentina 1 Real, KM#2.

CM Date	Host Date	Good	VG	F	VF	XF
ND(1833)	1815	—	1,250	—	—	—

Note: Sold Bank Leu #51, Bostonian Collection 10-90

KM# B106 2 REALES
Silver **Countermark:** Mountains/CHIL **Note:** Countermark on Argentina 2 Reales, KM#3.

CM Date	Host Date	Good	VG	F	VF	XF
ND(1833)	1813 Rare	—	—	—	—	—

KM# 106.1 8 REALES
Silver **Countermark:** Mountains/CHIL **Note:** Countermark on Argentina 8 Reales, KM#5.

CM Date	Host Date	Good	VG	F	VF	XF
ND(1833)	1813 Rare	—	—	—	—	—

KM# 106.2 8 REALES
Silver **Countermark:** Mountains/CHIL **Note:** Countermark on Argentina 8 Reales, KM#14.

CM Date	Host Date	Good	VG	F	VF	XF
ND(1833)	1815 Rare	—	—	—	—	—

KM# 106.3 8 REALES
Silver **Countermark:** Mountains/CHIL **Note:** Countermark on Argentina 8 Soles, KM#15.

CM Date	Host Date	Good	VG	F	VF	XF
ND(1833)	1815 Rare	—	—	—	—	—

COUNTERMARKED COINAGE

1833 — Concepcion

KM# 107.1 8 REALES
Silver **Countermark:** Mountains/CON **Note:** Countermark on Argentina 8 Reales, KM#5.

CM Date	Host Date	Good	VG	F	VF	XF
ND(1833)	1813 Rare	—	—	—	—	—

KM# 107.2 8 REALES
Silver **Countermark:** Mountains/CON **Note:** Countermark on Argentina 8 Reales, KM#14.

CM Date	Host Date	Good	VG	F	VF	XF
ND(1833)	1815 Rare	—	—	—	—	—

COUNTERMARKED COINAGE

1833 — Santiago

KM# A108 2 REALES
Silver **Countermark:** Mountains/SAN **Note:** Countermark on Argentina 2 Reales, KM#3.

CM Date	Host Date	Good	VG	F	VF	XF
ND(1833)	1813 Rare	—	—	—	—	—

KM# B108 4 REALES
Silver **Countermark:** Mountains/SAN **Note:** Countermark on Argentina 4 Reales, KM#4.

CM Date	Host Date	Good	VG	F	VF	XF
ND(1833)	1815	—	—	—	—	9,500

Note: Offered by D.A. Perry in WOrld Coin News 9-97

KM# 108.1 8 REALES
Silver **Countermark:** Countermark on Argentina 8 Reales, KM#5 **Note:** Countermark on Argentina 8 Reales, KM#5.

CM Date	Host Date	Good	VG	F	VF	XF
ND(1833)	1813	—	—	—	—	—

KM# 108.2 8 REALES
Silver **Countermark:** Mountains/SAN **Note:** Countermark no Argentina 8 Reales, KM#14.

CM Date	Host Date	Good	VG	F	VF	XF
ND(1833)	1815	—	—	—	—	—

COUNTERMARKED COINAGE

1833 — Serena

KM# 113 4 REALES
Silver **Countermark:** Mountains/SER **Note:** Countermark on Argentina 4 Soles, KM#13.

CM Date	Host Date	Good	VG	F	VF	XF
ND(1833)	1815	—	3,500	—	—	—

Note: Sold Bank Leu #51, Bostonian Cllection 10-90

KM# 109.1 8 REALES
Silver **Countermark:** Mountains/SER **Note:** Countermark on Argentina 8 Reales, KM#5.

CM Date	Host Date	Good	VG	F	VF	XF
ND(1833)	1813	175	300	475	750	—

Note: Known examples are likely counterfeits

KM# 109.2 8 REALES
Silver **Countermark:** Mountains/SER **Note:** Countermark on Argentina 8 Reales, KM#15.

CM Date	Host Date	Good	VG	F	VF	XF
ND(1833)	1815	175	300	475	750	—

Note: Known examples are likely counterfeits

KM# A109 8 ESCUDOS
Gold **Countermark:** Mountains/SER **Note:** Countermark on Argentina 8 Escudos, KM#9.

CM Date	Host Date	Good	VG	F	VF	XF
ND(1833)	1813 Rare	—	—	—	—	—

COUNTERMARKED COINAGE

1833 — Valdivia

KM# 110 4 REALES
Silver **Countermark:** Mountains/VALD **Note:** Countermark on Argentina 4 Reales, KM#4. Known examples are likely counterfeits.

CM Date	Host Date	Good	VG	F	VF	XF
ND(1833)	1813	225	400	700	1,200	—
ND(1833)	1815	225	400	700	1,200	—

KM# 111.1 8 REALES
Silver **Countermark:** Mountains/VALD **Note:** Countermark on Argentina 8 Reales, KM#5.

CM Date	Host Date	Good	VG	F	VF	XF
ND(1833)	1813	225	400	700	1,200	—

Note: Known examples are likely counterfeits

KM# 111.2 8 REALES
Silver **Countermark:** Mountains/VALD **Note:** Countermark on Argentina 8 Reales, KM#14.

CM Date	Host Date	Good	VG	F	VF	XF
ND(1833)	1815	225	400	700	1,200	—

Note: Known examples are likely counterfeits

COUNTERMARKED COINAGE

1833 — Valparaiso

KM# A112 4 SOLES
Silver **Countermark:** Mountains/VALP **Note:** Countermark on Argentina 4 Soles, KM#13.

CM Date	Host Date	Good	VG	F	VF	XF
ND(1833)	1815 Rare	—	—	—	—	—

KM# 112.1 8 REALES
Silver **Countermark:** Mountains/VALP **Note:** Countermark on Argentina 8 Reales, KM#5.

CM Date	Host Date	Good	VG	F	VF	XF
ND(1833)	1813	225	400	700	1,200	—

Note: Known examples are likely counterfeits

KM# 112.2 8 REALES
Silver **Countermark:** Mountains/VALP **Note:** Countermark on Argentina 8 Reales, KM#14.

CM Date	Host Date	Good	VG	F	VF	XF
ND(1833)	1815	225	400	700	1,200	—

Note: Known examples are likely counterfeits

REAL/ESCUDO COINAGE

KM# 89 1/4 REAL
0.9000 g., 0.9010 Silver, 11 mm. **Note:** Struck at Santiago Mint, mint mark So. Approved by the Congress on April 21, 1831, legalized June 24, 1831.

Date	Mintage	VG	F	VF	XF	Unc
1832/1	54,000	13.50	27.50	55.00	100	—
1832	Inc. above	13.50	27.50	55.00	100	—
1833	82,000	13.50	27.50	55.00	100	—
1834	134,000	100	200	300	500	—

KM# 90 1/2 REAL
1.7000 g., 0.9020 Silver, 17.5 mm. **Note:** Intended issue published June 9, 1817. Legalized February 6, 1824.

Date	Mintage	VG	F	VF	XF	Unc
1833 I	14,000	13:50	22.50	40.00	80.00	—
1834/3 I	22,000	15.00	27.50	45.00	85.00	—
Note: 1834 dated coins are medal rotation strikes						
1834 I	Inc. above	13.50	22.50	40.00	80.00	—
Note: 1834 dated coins are medal rotation strikes						

KM# 98.1 1/2 REAL
1.6000 g., 0.9020 Silver, 17 mm. **Rev. Legend:** POR LA RAZ. Y LA FUER

Date	Mintage	VG	F	VF	XF	Unc
1838 IJ	15,000	20.00	38.50	75.00	115	—
1840 IJ	14,000	18.50	35.00	57.50	100	—

KM# 98.3 1/2 REAL
1.6000 g., 0.9020 Silver, 17 mm. **Rev. Legend:** POR LA RAZON Y LA FUERZA

Date	Mintage	VG	F	VF	XF	Unc
1841 IJ	16,000	18.50	37.50	75.00	125	—
1842 IJ	27,000	15.00	33.50	65.00	110	—

KM# 98.2 1/2 REAL
1.6000 g., 0.9020 Silver, 15.5 mm. **Note:** Struck by law of August 18, 1843, decree of December 5, 1843.

Date	Mintage	VG	F	VF	XF	Unc
1844 IJ RAZON V (Y) LA	—	3.50	7.00	16.50	28.00	—
1845 IJ	—	3.50	8.00	18.50	32.50	—
1846/5 IJ	—	6.00	13.00	25.00	45.00	—
1846 IJ	—	3.50	8.00	18.50	32.50	—
1847 IJ	—	3.50	8.00	18.50	32.50	—
1848 JM	—	65.00	145	200	—	—
1849 ML	—	4.00	9.00	20.00	35.00	—
1851 LA	—	6.00	13.00	22.50	45.00	—

KM# 91 REAL
3.5000 g., 0.9020 Silver .1015 oz., 20-21 mm. **Note:** Intended issue published June 9, 1817. Legalized February 6, 1824.

Date	Mintage	VG	F	VF	XF	Unc
1834 IJ	16,000	17.50	35.00	67.50	175	—

KM# 94.1 REAL
3.3500 g., 0.9020 Silver .0972 oz., 21.5 mm. **Obv:** Large plumes, large shield, pointed sprays **Note:** Law 1117 of October 24, 1834 authorized coinage for dates 1836, 1838, 1840 and 1842 only.

Date	Mintage	VG	F	VF	XF	Unc
1838 IJ	12,000	15.00	28.50	60.00	185	—
1840 IJ	6,800	17.50	32.50	70.00	160	—

KM# 94.3 REAL
3.3500 g., 0.9020 Silver .0972 oz., 21.5 mm. **Obv:** Small shield, blunt sprays with berries **Note:** Law 1117 of October 24, 1834 authorized coinage for dates 1836, 1838, 1840 and 1842 only.

Date	Mintage	VG	F	VF	XF	Unc
1841 IJ	7,928	20.00	42.50	75.00	165	—

KM# 94.4 REAL
3.3500 g., 0.9020 Silver .0972 oz., 21.5 mm. **Obv:** Small shield, blunt sprays without berries **Edge:** Reeded **Note:** Law 1117 of October 24, 1834 authorized coinage for dates 1836, 1838, 1840 and 1842 only.

Date	Mintage	VG	F	VF	XF	Unc
1842 IJ	4,768	25.00	50.00	80.00	175	—

KM# 94.2 REAL
3.0000 g., 0.9020 Silver .0870 oz., 19 mm. **Note:** Two different dies exist for all dates.

Date	Mintage	VG	F	VF	XF	Unc
1843 IJ	—	3.50	8.00	16.00	30.00	—
1844 IJ	—	3.50	8.00	16.00	30.00	—
1845 IJ	—	3.50	8.00	16.00	30.00	—
1846 IJ	—	3.50	8.00	16.00	30.00	—
1847 IJ	—	17.50	35.00	60.00	100	—
1848/7/6 JM	—	8.00	16.50	30.00	52.50	—
1848 JM	—	4.50	9.00	16.50	35.00	—
1848/7 JM	—	4.00	8.00	16.50	32.50	—
1849 ML	—	11.00	22.50	45.00	70.00	—
1850/9 LA/ML	—	6.50	13.50	25.50	62.50	—
1850 LA	—	4.00	8.00	16.00	30.00	—

KM# 92 2 REALES
6.5500 g., 0.9020 Silver .1900 oz., 28 mm. **Note:** Intended issue published June 9, 1817. Legalized February 6, 1824.

Date	Mintage	VG	F	VF	XF	Unc
1834 IJ	3,740	25.00	47.50	100	185	—

KM# 100.1 2 REALES
5.7000 g., 0.9020 Silver .1653 oz., 24.5 mm.

Date	Mintage	VG	F	VF	XF	Unc
1843 IJ	—	8.50	16.50	35.00	75.00	—

KM# 100.2 2 REALES
5.7000 g., 0.9020 Silver .1653 oz. **Note:** Size varies 23-23.5 millimeters.

Date	Mintage	VG	F	VF	XF	Unc
1843 IJ	—	6.50	13.00	25.00	52.50	—
1844 IJ	—	3.00	5.50	12.00	23.50	—
1845/3 IJ	—	13.50	27.50	40.00	—	—
1845/4 IJ	—	13.50	27.50	40.00	—	—
1845 IJ	—	3.00	6.50	12.00	27.50	—
1846/5 IJ	—	12.00	27.50	38.50	—	—
1846/6 IJ	—	12.00	27.50	38.50	—	—
1846 IJ	—	3.00	6.00	12.00	22.50	—
1847 IJ	—	3.00	6.00	12.00	22.50	—
1848/7 JM	—	3.50	6.50	11.50	22.50	—
1848 JM	—	3.00	6.50	11.50	22.50	—
1849 ML	—	6.00	12.00	18.50	35.00	—
1850/49 LA/ML	—	8.00	13.50	20.00	37.50	—
1850 LA	—	9.00	16.50	30.00	55.00	—
1850 LA/ML	—	8.00	12.50	18.50	32.50	—
1851 LA	—	10.00	20.00	35.00	50.00	—
1851 LA (Error) GHILE	—	10.00	20.00	35.00	50.00	—
1852 LA	—	10.00	22.50	37.50	55.00	—

KM# 96.1 8 REALES
26.7000 g., 0.9020 Silver .7743 oz., 39 mm.

Date	Mintage	VG	F	VF	XF	Unc
1837 IJ Rare	5,404	—	—	—	—	—
1839 IJ	205,000	45.00	75.00	125	375	—
1840 IJ	4,556	850	1,250	1,650	2,850	—

KM# 96.2 8 REALES
26.6000 g., 0.9020 Silver .7714 oz., 38.5 mm. **Rev:** Similar to KM#96.1 but with larger leg **Note:** Reduced size.

Date	Mintage	VG	F	VF	XF	Unc
1848 JM	—	40.00	75.00	125	350	—
1849 ML	—	50.00	90.00	150	400	—

KM# 85 ESCUDO
3.3000 g., 0.8750 Gold .0928 oz., 19 mm. **Obv:** Sun above mountains in wreath **Rev:** Crossed flags behind pillar in wreath, date below

Date	Mintage	VG	F	VF	XF	Unc
1824 I	3,400	95.00	135	175	350	—
1825 I	2,920	95.00	135	175	350	—
1826 I	4,280	95.00	135	175	350	—
1827 I	408	150	240	300	500	—
1828 I	4,488	95.00	135	175	350	—
1830 I	3,328	95.00	135	175	350	—
1832 I	2,338	95.00	135	175	350	—
1833/0 I	2,620	130	200	250	450	—
1833 I	Inc. above	115	180	225	400	—
1834 I	10,614	115	180	225	400	—

KM# 99 ESCUDO
3.3000 g., 0.8750 Gold .0928 oz., 18.5 mm. **Obv:** Plumed and supported arms, date below **Rev:** Hand on book below sun rays **Note:** Issued by law 1117 of October 24, 1834.

Date	Mintage	VG	F	VF	XF	Unc
1838 IJ	6,122	125	185	225	400	—

KM# 101.1 ESCUDO
3.3000 g., 0.8750 Gold .0928 oz., 18.5 mm. **Rev:** Liberty standing, column at left, fasces and cornucopia at right **Note:** Decree of January 17, 1839 authorized the change of coin type.

Date	Mintage	VG	F	VF	XF	Unc
1839 IJ	4,946	100	135	175	325	—
1840 IJ	4,312	100	135	175	325	—
1841 IJ	3,992	100	135	175	325	—
1842 IJ	5,076	100	135	175	325	—
1843 IJ	4,632	100	135	175	325	—
1844 IJ	—	100	135	175	325	—
1845 IJ	—	100	135	175	325	—

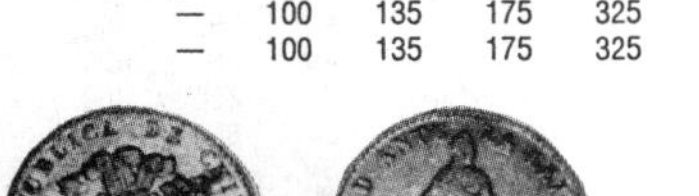

KM# 101.2 ESCUDO
3.3000 g., 0.8750 Gold .0928 oz., 18.5 mm. **Rev:** Liberty standing scene rendered on smaller scale

Date	Mintage	VG	F	VF	XF	Unc
1846 IJ	—	150	200	350	550	—
1847 IJ	—	125	175	225	400	—
1848 JM	—	100	135	185	350	—
1849 ML	—	100	135	185	350	—
1850 LA	—	100	135	185	350	—
1851 LA	—	125	175	225	400	—

KM# 86 2 ESCUDOS
6.7000 g., 0.8750 Gold .1885 oz., 22 mm. **Rev:** Crossed flags behind pillar

Date	Mintage	VG	F	VF	XF	Unc
1824 I	1,700	150	200	350	500	—
1825 I	1,460	150	200	350	500	—
1826 I	1,936	150	200	350	500	—
1827 I	204	200	300	400	650	—
1832 I	493	200	300	400	650	—
1833 I	224	150	200	350	550	—
1834 IJ	4,648	120	175	225	450	—

KM# 97 2 ESCUDOS
6.7000 g., 0.8750 Gold .1885 oz., 22.5 mm. **Rev:** Hand on book, sun rays above **Note:** Authorized by law 1117 October 24, 1834.

Date	Mintage	VG	F	VF	XF	Unc
1837 IJ	331	200	250	400	650	—
1838 IJ	3,449	120	175	225	450	—

KM# 102.1 2 ESCUDOS
6.7000 g., 0.8750 Gold .1885 oz., 23 mm. **Rev:** Liberty standing, column at left, fasces and cornucopia at right

Date	Mintage	VG	F	VF	XF	Unc
1839 IJ	3,064	150	200	350	500	—
1840 IJ	2,396	150	200	350	500	—
1841 IJ	2,552	135	185	325	500	—
1842 IJ	2,986	135	185	325	500	—
1843 IJ	2,464	135	185	325	500	—
1844 IJ	—	135	185	325	500	—
1845 IJ	—	135	185	325	500	—

KM# 102.2 2 ESCUDOS
6.7000 g., 0.8750 Gold .1885 oz., 22.5 mm. **Rev:** Liberty standing scene rendered on smaller scale

Date	Mintage	VG	F	VF	XF	Unc
1846 IJ	—	135	185	325	500	—
1847 IJ	—	135	185	325	500	—
1848 JM	—	135	185	325	500	—
1849 ML	—	135	185	325	500	—
1850 LA	—	135	185	325	500	—
1851 LA	—	135	185	325	500	—

KM# 87 4 ESCUDOS
13.5000 g., 0.8750 Gold .3798 oz., 30 mm. **Rev:** Crossed flags behind pillar

Date	Mintage	VG	F	VF	XF	Unc
1824 FD	1,530	325	450	700	1,350	—
1825 I	986	350	550	900	1,600	—
1826 I	1,326	325	450	700	1,350	—
1833 I	321	375	600	950	1,750	—
1834 IJ	2,564	325	450	700	1,350	—

KM# 95 4 ESCUDOS
13.5000 g., 0.8750 Gold .3798 oz., 29 mm. **Rev:** Hand on book, sun rays above

Date	Mintage	VG	F	VF	XF	Unc
1836 IJ	1,389	275	400	600	1,000	—
1837 IJ	321	375	600	950	1,750	—

KM# 103 4 ESCUDOS
13.5000 g., 0.8750 Gold .3798 oz., 29 mm. **Rev:** Liberty standing, column at left, fasces and cornucopia at right

Date	Mintage	VG	F	VF	XF	Unc
1839 IJ	—	1,500	2,500	3,500	—	—
1840 IJ Rare	108	—	—	—	—	—
1841 IJ Rare	100	—	—	—	—	—

KM# 84 8 ESCUDOS
27.0000 g., 0.8750 Gold .7596 oz., 37 mm. **Rev:** Crossed flags behind pillar **Note:** Published June 9, 1817, legalized February 6, 1824.

Date	Mintage	VG	F	VF	XF	Unc
1818 FD Constit	29,000	BV	350	400	850	—
1818 FD Constitu	Inc. above	BV	375	500	950	—
1819 FD	37,000	BV	350	400	850	—
1820 FD	35,000	BV	350	400	850	—
1821 FD	16,000	BV	350	400	850	—
1822 FI	31,000	BV	350	400	850	—
1823 FI	19,000	BV	350	400	850	—
1824 I	10,000	BV	350	400	850	—
1825 I	8,483	BV	350	400	800	—
1826 I	7,607	BV	350	400	800	—
1827 I	2,176	BV	350	400	800	—

Date	Mintage	VG	F	VF	XF	Unc
1828/7 I	4,250	400	700	1,200	2,500	—
1828 I	Inc. above	BV	350	400	850	—
1829 I	—	BV	350	400	800	—
1830 I	3,068	BV	350	400	800	—
1831 I	1,745	BV	375	500	900	—
1832/1 I	11,000	BV	350	400	800	—
1832 I	Inc. above	BV	350	400	800	—
1833/2 I	25,000	BV	500	800	1,400	—
1833 I	Inc. above	BV	350	400	800	—
1834 IJ	31,000	BV	350	400	750	—

KM# 93 8 ESCUDOS
27.0000 g., 0.8750 Gold .7596 oz., 37.5 mm. **Rev:** Hand on book, sun rays above **Note:** Issued by law 1117 of October 24, 1834. KM#93 has been rarely encountered struck over KM#84.

Date	Mintage	VG	F	VF	XF	Unc
1835 IJ	28,000	BV	350	450	900	—
1836 IJ	27,000	BV	350	450	900	—
1837 IJ	17,000	BV	350	450	900	—
1838 IJ	33,000	BV	350	450	900	—

KM# 104.1 8 ESCUDOS
27.0000 g., 0.8750 Gold .7596 oz., 36 mm. **Rev:** Liberty standing, column at left, fasces and cornucopia at right **Edge:** Reeded

Date	Mintage	VG	F	VF	XF	Unc
1839 IJ	27,000	BV	350	400	700	—
1840 IJ	25,000	BV	350	400	700	—
1841 IJ	25,000	BV	350	400	700	—
1842 IJ	27,000	BV	350	400	700	—
1843/2 IJ	27,000	BV	400	500	800	—
1843 IJ	Inc. above	BV	350	400	700	—

KM# 104.2 8 ESCUDOS
27.0000 g., 0.8750 Gold .7596 oz., 35.5 mm. **Rev:** Liberty standing, column at left, fasces and cornucopia at right **Edge:** Lettered **Note:** Edge lettering includes month of issue.

Date	Mintage	VG	F	VF	XF	Unc
1843 IJ	—	BV	400	550	850	—
1844 IJ	—	BV	400	550	850	—
1845 IJ	—	BV	400	550	850	—

KM# 105 8 ESCUDOS
27.0000 g., 0.8750 Gold .7596 oz., 35.5 mm. **Rev:** Liberty standing scene rendered on smaller scale **Note:** Edge lettering includes month of issue.

Date	Mintage	VG	F	VF	XF	Unc
1846 IJ	—	BV	350	400	700	—
1847 IJ	—	BV	350	400	700	—
1848/7 JM	—	BV	350	400	700	—
1848 JM	—	BV	350	400	700	—
1849 ML	—	BV	350	400	700	—
1850 LA	—	BV	350	400	700	—
1851 LA	—	BV	350	400	700	—

DECIMAL COINAGE

KM# 114 1/2 CENTAVO
8.9000 g., Copper, 22 mm. **Obv:** 5 pointed flat star **Rev:** Laurel wreaths surround MEDIO CENTAVO **Edge:** Plain **Note:** Thick planchet. Coin alignment. Varieties exist. Struck in England, Chilean law of October 24, 1834.

Date	Mintage	VG	F	VF	XF	Unc
1835	2,000,000	1.00	2.00	3.50	20.00	—
1835 Proof	Inc. above	Value: 235				

KM# 114.2 1/2 CENTAVO
8.6000 g., Copper, 22 mm. **Obv:** 5 pointed star **Edge:** Plain **Note:** Thin planchet. Medal alignment. Struck in England, Chilean law of October 24, 1834.

Date	Mintage	VG	F	VF	XF	Unc
1835	Inc. above	2.00	4.00	8.00	27.50	—
1835 Proof	Inc. above	Value: 250				
1835 Proof, thin planchet	Inc. above	—	—	—	—	—

KM# 117.1 1/2 CENTAVO
5.0000 g., Copper, 22 mm. **Obv:** 5-pointed flat star, small stars flank high date **Obv. Legend:** REPUBLICA DE CHILE **Rev:** Laurel wreaths surround MEDIO CENTAVO **Rev. Legend:** ECONOMIA ES RIQUEZA between dots **Note:** All 1851 and 1853 issues in copper were minted in England and the United States. Struck by law of January 9, 1851.

Date	Mintage	VG	F	VF	XF	Unc
1851	1,620,000	2.00	4.00	6.00	25.00	—

KM# 117.2 1/2 CENTAVO
Copper **Obv:** 5-pointed flat star, large stars flank low date **Obv. Legend:** REPUBLICA DE CHILE **Rev:** Laurel wreaths surround MEDIO CENTAVO **Rev. Legend:** ECONOMIA ES RIQUEZA between dots **Note:** All 1851 and 1853 issues in copper were minted in England and the United States. Struck by law of January 9, 1851.

Date	Mintage	VG	F	VF	XF	Unc
1851	Inc. above	2.00	4.00	6.00	25.00	—

KM# 117.3 1/2 CENTAVO
Copper **Obv:** 5-pointed flat star, small stars flank high date **Obv. Legend:** REPUBLICA DE CHILE **Rev:** Laurel wreaths surround MEDIO CENTAVO **Rev. Legend:** ECONOMIA ES RIQUEZA between stars **Note:** All 1851 and 1853 issues in copper were minted in England and the United States. Struck by law of January 9, 1851.

Date	Mintage	VG	F	VF	XF	Unc
1851	Inc. above	2.00	4.00	6.00	25.00	—

KM# 117.4 1/2 CENTAVO
Copper **Obv:** 5-pointed flat star, small stars flank high and off-centered date **Obv. Legend:** REPUBLICA DE CHILE **Rev:** Laurel wreaths surround MEDIO CENTAVO **Rev. Legend:** ECONOMIA ES RIQUEZA between stars **Note:** All 1851 and 1853 issues in copper were minted in England and the United States. Struck by law of January 9, 1851.

Date	Mintage	VG	F	VF	XF	Unc
1851	Inc. above	20.00	4.00	6.00	25.00	—

KM# 117.5 1/2 CENTAVO
Copper **Obv:** 5-pointed flat star, doubled stars flank high date **Obv. Legend:** REPUBLICA DE CHILE **Rev:** Laurel wreaths surround MEDIO CENTAVO between stars **Note:** All 1851 and 1853 issues in copper were minted in England and the United States. Struck by law of January 9, 1851.

Date	Mintage	VG	F	VF	XF	Unc
1851	Inc. above	2.00	4.00	6.00	25.00	—

KM# 118 1/2 CENTAVO
Copper **Obv:** Raised star, dots flank date **Rev:** Diamond below crossed wreath stems **Note:** All 1851 and 1853 issues in copper were minted in England and the United States. Struck by law of January 9, 1851.

Date	Mintage	VG	F	VF	XF	Unc
1851	2,200,000	1.00	2.00	4.00	20.00	—

KM# 126 1/2 CENTAVO
Copper **Obv:** Raised star, dots flank date **Rev:** Refined wreath **Note:** All 1851 and 1853 issues in copper were minted in England and the United States. Struck by law of January 9, 1851.

Date	Mintage	VG	F	VF	XF	Unc
1853	2,667,000	1.00	2.00	4.00	20.00	—
1853 Proof	—	—	—	—	—	—

KM# 148 1/2 CENTAVO
5.0000 g., Copper-Nickel, 21 mm. **Note:** Issued under law of October 25, 1879, struck at Santiago Mint.

Date	Mintage	VG	F	VF	XF	Unc
1871	133,000	2.00	4.50	9.00	17.50	—
1872/1	506,000	2.00	4.50	9.00	17.50	—
1872	Inc. above	3.50	6.00	12.00	22.50	—
1873/1	—	2.00	4.50	9.00	17.50	—
1873	1,265,000	2.00	4.50	9.00	17.50	—

KM# 148a 1/2 CENTAVO
3.0000 g., Copper, 19 mm. **Note:** Struck at Santiago Mint.

Date	Mintage	VG	F	VF	XF	Unc
1883/73	714,000	1.50	3.00	5.00	12.00	—
1883	Inc. above	1.00	2.00	3.50	10.00	—
1884/3	—	1.50	3.00	6.00	15.00	—
1884	104,000	1.50	3.00	6.00	15.00	—
1885	132,000	1.00	2.00	3.50	10.00	—
1886/76	—	1.25	2.50	5.00	12.00	—
1886	469,000	1.00	2.00	3.50	10.00	—
1888/78	294,000	1.25	2.50	5.00	12.00	—
1888	Inc. above	1.50	3.00	6.00	15.00	—
1890/70	70,000	2.00	4.00	7.00	16.00	—
1890	Inc. above	3.25	6.00	10.00	22.50	—
1890/73	Inc. above	2.50	5.00	8.50	18.00	—
1893/88	71,000	2.50	5.00	8.50	18.00	—
1893	Inc. above	2.00	4.00	6.00	14.50	—
1894	251,000	1.00	2.00	3.50	10.00	—

KM# 115 CENTAVO
17.9000 g., Copper, 30 mm. **Note:** Thick flan, weight varies 17.80-18.01 grams. Coin alignment. Struck in England, Chilean law of October 24, 1834.

Date	Mintage	VG	F	VF	XF	Unc
1835	2,000,000	2.00	4.00	8.00	22.50	—
1835 Proof	—	Value: 185				

KM# 116 CENTAVO
Copper **Note:** Thin flan, weight varies 13.35-13.40 grams. Medal alignment.

Date	Mintage	VG	F	VF	XF	Unc
1835 Proof; Rare	—	—	—	—	—	—

KM# 120 CENTAVO
Copper **Obv:** Raised star, dots flank date **Rev:** Diamond below wreath

Date	Mintage	VG	F	VF	XF	Unc
1851	3,300,000	3.00	8.00	17.50	45.00	—

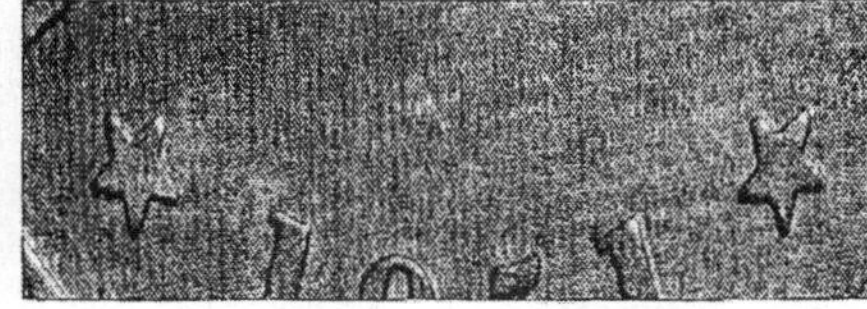

No "H" mm in left star on obverse.

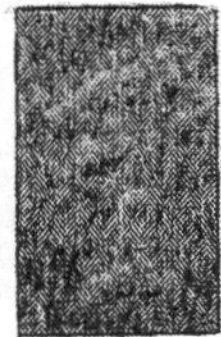

Pointed-top 1 in date on obverse.

KM# 119.1 CENTAVO

Copper

Date	Mintage	VG	F	VF	XF	Unc
1851	2,430,000	25.00	50.00	90.00	—	—

Note: The above attributes of variety 119.1 are only found on coins minted in Santiago

An "H" mm in the left star on obverse.

Flat-top 1 in date on obverse.

Double loop in the knot on reverse.

KM# 119.2 CENTAVO

Copper

Date	Mintage	VG	F	VF	XF	Unc
1851	Inc. above	2.50	5.00	12.50	30.00	—

Note: This type of Q is the most common on all 1851 pieces with flat 5-pointed star. The double loop on this variety belongs to the coins minted abroad. (England)

KM# 119.3 CENTAVO

Copper **Obv:** No mint mark on left star, 5-pointed star, flat-top 1 in date **Rev:** 2 laurel wreaths with double loop in knot surround UN CENTAVO, short leg below Q in RIQUEZA in legend

Date	Mintage	VG	F	VF	XF	Unc
1851	Inc. above	2.50	5.00	12.50	30.00	—

Note: Minted in USA

KM# 119.4 CENTAVO

Copper **Obv:** No mint mark on left star, 5-pointed flat star, flat-top 1 in date **Rev:** 2 laurel wreaths with double loop in knot surround UN CENTAVO,leg traversing the Q in RIQUEZA in legend

Date	Mintage	VG	F	VF	XF	Unc
1851	Inc. above	5.00	10.00	25.00	60.00	—

Note: Minted in USA. Pieces having this type of the letter Q are extremely scarce

KM# 127 CENTAVO

Copper **Rev:** Different sprays **Note:** The 1853 coins were struck with coin and medal rotation.

Date	Mintage	VG	F	VF	XF	Unc
1853	2,667,000	2.00	5.00	15.00	35.00	—
1853 Proof	—	Value: 150				

KM# 146 CENTAVO

Copper Nickel

Date	Mintage	VG	F	VF	XF	Unc
1870/60	—	—	—	—	—	—
1871	1,687,000	1.50	3.00	5.50	12.00	—
1872/1	690,000	2.50	4.50	7.50	20.00	—
1872	Inc. above	2.00	4.00	6.00	17.50	—
1873/1	779,000	10.00	20.00	35.00	50.00	—
1873/2	Inc. above	2.00	4.00	6.00	17.50	—
1873	Inc. above	10.00	20.00	35.00	50.00	—
1874/1	263,000	3.50	6.00	10.00	25.00	—
1874/3	Inc. above	3.50	6.00	10.00	25.00	—
1874	Inc. above	3.00	5.00	7.50	19.00	—
1875/1	113,000	3.50	6.50	8.50	22.00	—
1875	Inc. above	3.00	5.00	8.00	20.00	—
1876	22,000	12.00	20.00	35.00	60.00	—
1877	16,000	15.00	30.00	50.00	75.00	—

KM# 146a CENTAVO

Copper **Note:** Varieties exist.

Date	Mintage	VG	F	VF	XF	Unc
1878/1	—	2.25	3.50	7.00	15.00	—
1878	177,000	2.00	4.00	7.00	25.00	—
1879	793,000	1.50	3.00	5.50	15.00	—
1880/70	478,000	1.50	3.00	5.50	15.00	—
1880/79	Inc. above	2.00	4.00	6.00	20.00	—
1880	Inc. above	2.00	4.00	6.00	20.00	—
1881	318,000	1.75	3.25	6.00	16.00	—
1882	492,000	1.50	3.00	5.50	15.00	—
1883	274,000	2.00	4.00	6.00	20.00	—
1884/3	171,000	2.25	4.50	7.50	25.00	—
1884	Inc. above	2.00	4.00	6.00	20.00	—
1885	205,000	1.50	3.00	5.50	15.00	—
1886	510,000	1.50	3.00	5.50	15.00	—
1887/4	231,000	1.75	3.50	7.00	18.00	—
1887/1	Inc. above	1.75	3.50	7.00	18.00	—
1887	Inc. above	1.50	3.00	5.50	15.00	—
1888	141,000	2.00	4.00	6.00	20.00	—
1890	47,000	4.25	8.50	15.00	28.00	—
1891/0	99,000	4.25	8.50	15.00	30.00	—
1891	Inc. above	2.50	5.00	10.00	25.00	—
1891/81	Inc. above	15.00	30.00	50.00	80.00	—
1891/88	Inc. above	15.00	30.00	50.00	80.00	—
1893	115,000	1.50	3.00	5.50	15.00	—
1894/3	244,000	1.75	3.50	7.00	18.00	—
1894	Inc. above	1.00	2.00	4.00	8.00	—
1895	449,000	1.00	2.00	3.50	7.00	—
1895 1 over inverted 1	Inc. above	4.50	9.00	16.00	30.00	—
1896/5	139,000	1.75	3.50	7.00	18.00	—
1896	Inc. above	1.25	2.50	4.00	8.00	—
1898/1	1,605,000	1.00	2.00	3.50	7.00	—
1898/81	Inc. above	1.00	2.00	3.50	7.00	—
1898/888	Inc. above	1.00	2.00	3.50	7.00	—
1898	Inc. above	0.50	1.00	2.00	5.00	—

KM# 147 2 CENTAVOS

7.0000 g., Copper-Nickel, 25 mm. **Note:** Authorized by law of October 25, 1870.

Date	Mintage	F	VF	XF	Unc	BU
1870/60	—	5.00	9.00	18.00	35.00	—
1871	639,000	3.50	7.50	15.00	30.00	—
1872/1	207,000	12.00	20.00	30.00	60.00	—
1872	Inc. above	3.50	7.50	15.00	30.00	—
1873/2	461,000	7.50	15.00	30.00	—	—
1873	Inc. above	3.50	7.50	15.00	30.00	—
1874	263,000	5.00	9.00	18.00	35.00	—
1875	294,000	5.00	9.00	18.00	35.00	—
1876/5	108,000	20.00	30.00	60.00	—	—
1876	Inc. above	12.00	20.00	30.00	60.00	—
1877	21,000	15.00	35.00	50.00	120	—

KM# 147a 2 CENTAVOS

Copper **Note:** Authorized by law of October 25, 1870.

Date	Mintage	F	VF	XF	Unc	BU
1878/6	112,000	10.00	20.00	35.00	65.00	—
1878	Inc. above	5.00	9.00	15.00	45.00	—
1879	479,000	2.50	6.00	10.00	30.00	—
1880/70	—	3.00	7.00	12.00	35.00	—
1880	278,000	2.50	6.00	10.00	30.00	—
1881	172,000	3.00	7.00	12.00	35.00	—
1882	361,000	2.50	6.00	10.00	30.00	—
1883/73	405,000	3.00	7.00	12.00	35.00	—
1883/2	Inc. above	2.50	6.00	10.00	30.00	—
1883	Inc. above	2.00	5.00	8.00	25.00	—
1884	182,000	2.50	6.00	10.00	30.00	—
1885	146,000	2.50	6.00	10.00	30.00	—
1886	494,000	2.00	5.00	8.00	25.00	—
1887	106,000	2.50	6.00	10.00	30.00	—
1888	186,000	3.00	7.00	12.00	35.00	—
1890	155,000	5.00	9.00	15.00	45.00	—
1891/8 Rare	89,000	—	—	—	—	—
1891	Inc. above	8.00	20.00	30.00	60.00	—
1893/1	141,000	2.50	6.00	10.00	30.00	—
1893	Inc. above	2.50	6.00	10.00	30.00	—
1894	190,000	3.00	7.00	12.00	35.00	—

KM# 150 2-1/2 CENTAVOS (Dos I Medio)

8.0000 g., Copper, 27 mm. **Note:** Issued under law of August 10, 1886.

Date	Mintage	F	VF	XF	Unc	BU
1886	381,000	2.50	6.00	18.00	45.00	—
1887/6	500,000	5.00	10.00	25.00	65.00	—
1887	Inc. above	2.75	7.00	18.00	45.00	—
1895/85	366,000	5.00	10.00	25.00	65.00	—
1895	Inc. above	2.50	6.00	18.00	45.00	—
1896/86	172,000	2.75	7.00	18.00	50.00	—
1896	Inc. above	3.00	8.00	20.00	50.00	—
1898/86	21,770,000	3.00	8.00	20.00	50.00	—
1898/85	Inc. above	3.00	8.00	20.00	50.00	—
1898/88	Inc. above	2.50	6.00	18.00	45.00	—
1898/5	Inc. above	3.00	8.00	20.00	50.00	—
1898/87	Inc. above	3.00	8.00	20.00	50.00	—
1898	Inc. above	3.00	8.00	20.00	50.00	—

KM# 121 1/2 DECIMO

1.2500 g., 0.9000 Silver .0361 oz. **Rev:** Condor with spread wings **Edge:** Reeded **Note:** Struck under law of January 9, 1851 and decree of March 19, 1851.

Date	Mintage	VG	F	VF	XF	Unc
1851	233,000	200	300	400	600	—
1853	Inc. above	3.00	5.00	9.00	20.00	—
1854	122,000	20.00	35.00	55.00	80.00	—
1855/3	1,257,000	3.50	6.00	12.00	25.00	—
1855/4	Inc. above	3.00	5.00	9.00	20.00	—
1855	Inc. above	—	—	—	—	—
1856/5	767,000	3.50	6.00	12.00	25.00	—
1856	Inc. above	4.00	7.00	15.00	30.00	—
1857	1,655,000	3.00	5.00	9.00	20.00	—
1858	318,000	3.50	6.00	12.00	25.00	—

Date	Mintage	VG	F	VF	XF	Unc
1859/8	41,000	3.00	5.00	10.00	22.00	—
1859	Inc. above	20.00	35.00	55.00	90.00	—

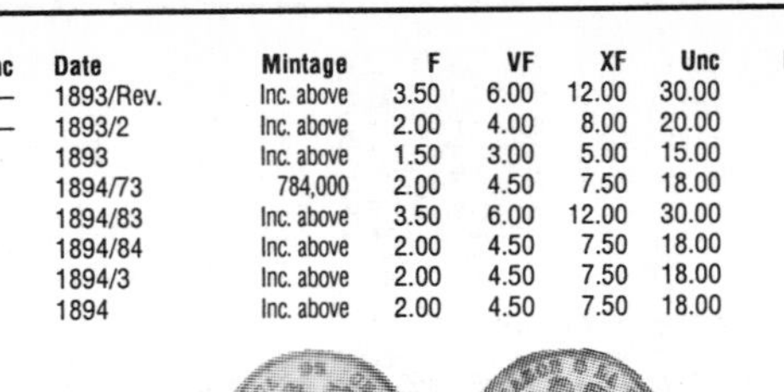

KM# 121a 1/2 DECIMO
1.1500 g., 0.9000 Silver .0332 oz. **Note:** Struck under law of July 28, 1860 and decree of August 20, 1860.

Date	Mintage	VG	F	VF	XF	Unc
1860/59	372,000	10.00	20.00	27.50	55.00	—
1860	Inc. above	7.00	15.00	22.00	50.00	—
1861	338,000	5.00	10.00	18.00	45.00	—
1862 Rare	4,400	—	—	—	—	—

KM# 137.1 1/2 DECIMO
1.1500 g., 0.9000 Silver .0332 oz. **Rev:** Condor with infolded wings **Note:** Issued by decree of August 5, 1864.

Date	Mintage	VG	F	VF	XF	Unc
1865	40,000	17.50	30.00	45.00	90.00	—
1866	82,000	10.00	20.00	32.50	50.00	—

KM# 137.2 1/2 DECIMO
1.2500 g., 0.8350 Silver .0336 oz., 15 mm. **Note:** Struck by law of Ocyober 21, 1865.

Date	Mintage	VG	F	VF	XF	Unc
1867	28,000	4.00	8.00	20.00	35.00	—
1868	181,000	2.00	4.00	6.00	12.50	—
1868 Proof	—	Value: 200				
1869	293,000	1.50	3.00	4.75	9.50	—
1870/69	540,000	1.25	2.50	4.00	8.00	—
1870	Inc. above	1.25	2.00	3.25	6.50	—
1871/0	171,000	1.50	3.00	5.00	10.00	—
1871	Inc. above	3.00	5.00	7.50	15.00	—
1872	286,000	2.00	4.00	7.00	12.50	—
1873/2	170,000	3.00	5.00	7.50	15.00	—
1873/9	Inc. above	5.00	10.00	30.00	50.00	—
1873	Inc. above	5.00	10.00	30.00	50.00	—
1874/3	588,000	3.00	7.00	15.00	20.00	—
1874	Inc. above	2.00	4.00	7.00	12.50	—
1875/2	97,000	3.00	7.00	12.00	20.00	—
1875/3	Inc. above	3.00	7.00	12.00	20.00	—
1875/4	Inc. above	3.00	7.00	12.00	20.00	—
1875	Inc. above	5.00	8.00	12.50	25.00	—
1876	82,000	3.00	7.00	12.00	16.00	—
1877	327,000	2.00	6.00	9.00	14.00	—
1878	306,000	2.00	6.50	10.00	15.00	—
1880	194,000	3.00	7.00	12.00	16.00	—
1881	264,000	3.00	7.00	12.00	16.00	—

KM# 137.3 1/2 DECIMO
1.2500 g., 0.5000 Silver .0200 oz. **Obv. Legend:** 0.5 added **Note:** Varieties exist.

Date	Mintage	F	VF	XF	Unc	BU
1879	916,000	2.00	3.00	6.00	20.00	—
1880	1,205,000	1.50	3.00	5.00	15.00	—
1881	1,687,000	1.50	3.00	5.00	15.00	—
1882	235,000	2.50	5.00	8.00	20.00	—
1883/2	117,000	3.00	6.00	12.00	25.00	—
1883	Inc. above	3.75	7.50	12.50	25.00	—
1884	664,000	2.50	3.50	6.50	20.00	—
1885/2	489,000	2.00	3.00	5.50	18.00	—
1885/3	Inc. above	3.00	6.00	12.00	25.00	—
1885/4/3	Inc. above	2.00	3.00	5.50	18.00	—
1885/4	Inc. above	2.50	5.00	8.00	20.00	—
1885	Inc. above	2.50	3.50	6.50	20.00	—
1887	3,081,000	1.50	3.00	5.00	15.00	—
1888/7	2,448,000	2.50	3.50	6.50	20.00	—
1888	Inc. above	1.50	3.00	5.00	15.00	—
1892/72	1,684,000	5.00	10.00	30.00	60.00	—
1892/82	Inc. above	3.50	6.50	12.50	35.00	—
1892/82/72	Inc. above	2.50	3.50	8.00	20.00	—
1892/88/72	Inc. above	2.50	3.50	8.00	20.00	—
1892	Inc. above	3.50	6.50	12.50	35.00	—
1893/73	850,000	3.50	6.00	12.00	30.00	—
1893/78	Inc. above	3.50	6.00	12.00	30.00	—
1893/8/7	Inc. above	3.50	6.00	12.00	30.00	—
1893/83	Inc. above	3.50	6.00	12.00	30.00	—
1893/Rev.	Inc. above	3.50	6.00	12.00	30.00	—
1893/2	Inc. above	2.00	4.00	8.00	20.00	—
1893	Inc. above	1.50	3.00	5.00	15.00	—
1894/73	784,000	2.00	4.50	7.50	18.00	—
1894/83	Inc. above	3.50	6.00	12.00	30.00	—
1894/84	Inc. above	2.00	4.50	7.50	18.00	—
1894/3	Inc. above	2.00	4.50	7.50	18.00	—
1894	Inc. above	2.00	4.50	7.50	18.00	—

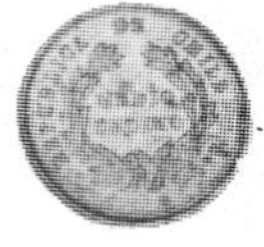 

KM# 149 1/2 DECIMO
1.2500 g., 0.5000 Silver .0200 oz. **Obv:** KM#137.2 **Rev:** KM#137.3 **Note:** Mule

Date	Mintage	F	VF	XF	Unc	BU
1884	—	—	—	20.00	50.00	—

KM# 155.1 5 CENTAVOS
1.0000 g., 0.8350 Silver .0268 oz., 14.5 mm. **Obv:** O.ROTY on stone below condor **Rev:** Hammer and sickle **Note:** Struck by law No. 277 of February 11, 1895, called the "Metal Conversion Law".

Date	Mintage	F	VF	XF	Unc	BU
1896 Large 6	888,000	3.00	6.00	10.00	20.00	—
1896 Small 6	Inc. above	3.00	6.00	10.00	20.00	—
1899 2nd 9/inverted 6	Inc. above	—	—	—	—	—

KM# 155.2 5 CENTAVOS
1.0000 g., 0.5000 Silver .0160 oz., 14 mm. **Obv:** 0.5 below condor **Note:** Varieties exist with 0.5, 0.5., 0/5.5., 0,5 or 05. below condor.

Date	Mintage	F	VF	XF	Unc	BU
1899	1,794,000	2.00	3.00	5.00	15.00	—
1901/896	Inc. above	3.00	6.00	15.00	30.00	—
1904/891/9	—	3.50	7.50	15.00	35.00	—

KM# 124 DECIMO
2.5000 g., 0.9000 Silver .0723 oz., 18 mm. **Rev:** Condor with spread wings **Note:** Struck by law of January 9, 1851 and decree of March 19, 1851.

Date	Mintage	VG	F	VF	XF	Unc
1851	—	—	—	—	—	—
Note: Reported, not confirmed						
1852	211,000	—	2.50	5.00	15.00	50.00
1853	Inc. above	—	2.50	5.00	15.00	50.00
1855	585,000	—	2.50	5.00	15.00	50.00
1856/5	580,000	—	2.50	5.00	12.00	35.00
1856	Inc. above	—	2.50	5.00	15.00	50.00
1857	1,481,000	—	2.50	5.00	12.00	35.00
1858	540,000	—	2.50	5.00	15.00	50.00
1859	20,000	—	40.00	65.00	100	—
1860/59	—	—	5.00	10.00	30.00	60.00

KM# 124a DECIMO
2.3000 g., 0.9000 Silver .0665 oz., 18 mm. **Rev:** Condor with spread wings **Note:** Struck by law of July 28, 1860 and decree of August 20, 1860.

Date	Mintage	VG	F	VF	XF	Unc
1860/50	382,000	6.00	12.50	22.00	55.00	—
1860	Inc. above	2.50	6.00	12.50	30.00	—
1861	236,000	2.50	6.00	12.50	30.00	—
1862	95,000	3.00	7.00	15.00	40.00	—

KM# 136.1 DECIMO
2.3000 g., 0.9000 Silver .0665 oz., 18 mm. **Rev:** Condor with open wings **Note:** Issued by decree of August 5, 1864.

Date	Mintage	VG	F	VF	XF	Unc
1864 Thick flan	96,000	5.50	10.00	22.00	40.00	—
1864 Thin flan	Inc. above	—	—	—	—	—
1865/4	222,000	6.00	9.00	15.00	30.00	—
1865 Inverted 5	Inc. above	6.00	9.00	15.00	30.00	—
1865	Inc. above	6.00	9.00	15.00	30.00	—
1866/5	—	6.00	10.00	22.00	40.00	—
1866	96,000	5.50	10.00	22.00	40.00	—

KM# 136.2 DECIMO
2.5000 g., 0.8350 Silver .0671 oz., 18 mm.

Date	Mintage	VG	F	VF	XF	Unc
1867	20,000	7.00	12.00	20.00	40.00	—
1868	207,000	2.00	3.00	5.00	10.00	—
1868 Proof	—	Value: 300				
1869/8	245,000	—	—	—	—	—
1869	Inc. above	2.00	3.00	5.00	10.00	—
1870/60	192,000	3.00	4.00	7.00	15.00	—
1870/69	Inc. above	3.00	4.00	7.00	15.00	—
1870	Inc. above	2.50	3.50	6.00	12.00	—
1871	91,000	2.50	3.50	6.00	12.00	—
1872/1	288,000	—	—	—	—	—
1872	Inc. above	2.00	3.00	5.00	10.00	—
1873/2	305,000	—	—	—	—	—
1873/8	Inc. above	—	—	—	—	—
1873/9	Inc. above	—	—	—	—	—
1873	Inc. above	2.00	3.00	5.00	10.00	—
1874/64	271,000	—	—	—	—	—
1874	Inc. above	2.00	3.00	5.00	10.00	—
1875/4	50,000	3.00	5.00	9.00	16.50	—
1875	Inc. above	5.00	10.00	20.00	40.00	—
1876	100,000	2.25	3.25	5.50	11.00	—
1877/6	96,000	3.00	5.00	9.00	16.50	—
1877	Inc. above	2.25	3.25	5.50	11.00	—
1878	512,000	2.00	3.00	5.00	10.00	—
1880/70	243,000	—	—	—	—	—
1880/79	Inc. above	—	—	—	—	—
1880	Inc. above	2.00	3.00	5.00	10.00	—

KM# 136.3 DECIMO
2.5000 g., 0.5000 Silver .0401 oz., 18 mm. **Obv. Legend:** 0.5 added **Note:** Issued under change of alloy law of June 14, 1879.

Date	Mintage	F	VF	XF	Unc	BU
1879/8	1,268,000	1.25	2.25	3.50	8.00	—
1879	Inc. above	1.00	2.00	3.00	7.50	—
1880/70	705,000	1.50	3.00	5.00	10.00	—
1880	Inc. above	1.00	2.00	5.00	10.00	—
1881	2,186,000	1.00	2.00	5.00	10.00	—
1882/1	233,000	2.00	5.00	10.00	15.00	—
1882/2	Inc. above	2.00	5.00	10.00	15.00	—
1882	Inc. above	1.00	2.00	5.00	10.00	—
1883/2	178,000	2.00	5.00	10.00	15.00	—
1883	Inc. above	1.00	2.00	5.00	10.00	—
1884/2	319,000	5.00	10.00	17.00	25.00	—
1884	Inc. above	1.00	2.00	5.00	10.00	—
1885/4	—	6.00	12.00	18.00	25.00	—
1885	116,000	6.00	12.00	18.00	25.00	—
1887/6	1,514,000	1.25	2.25	3.50	8.00	—
1887 R/B in Republica	Inc. above	1.25	2.25	3.50	8.00	—
Note: 1 in 10 pieces dated 1887 has R/B in REPUBLICA						
1887	Inc. above	1.00	2.00	3.00	7.50	—
1891 Rare	—	—	—	—	—	—
1892/82/1	—	1.00	2.00	5.00	10.00	—
1892/82	994,000	1.00	2.00	3.00	7.50	—
1892/0	Inc. above	1.00	2.00	5.00	10.00	—
1892	Inc. above	3.00	6.00	12.00	20.00	—
1893/83	516,000	3.50	5.50	10.00	18.00	—
1893/inverted	Inc. above	1.00	2.00	3.00	7.50	—
1893	Inc. above	1.25	2.25	3.50	8.00	—
1894/84	826,000	1.00	2.00	3.00	7.50	—
1894/3	Inc. above	1.25	2.25	3.50	8.00	—
1894/3 E/R in REPUBLICA	Inc. above	1.00	2.00	3.50	7.50	—
1894	Inc. above	1.00	2.00	3.00	7.50	—

KM# 136.3a DECIMO
2.0000 g., 0.5000 Silver .0321 oz.

Date	Mintage	F	VF	XF	Unc	BU
1891/81	264,000	35.00	80.00	160	300	—
1891	Inc. above	35.00	80.00	160	300	—

KM# 156.1 10 CENTAVOS
2.0000 g., 0.8350 Silver .0536 oz., 17 mm. **Obv:** O. ROTY on

stone below condor **Rev:** Hammer and sickle **Note:** Issued under law No. 277 of February 11, 1895.

Date	Mintage	F	VF	XF	Unc	BU
1896	2,561,000	2.00	3.50	7.00	16.50	—

KM# 156.2 10 CENTAVOS

2.0000 g., 0.5000 Silver .0321 oz., 17 mm. **Obv:** 0.5 below condor **Note:** Obverse varieties exist with 0.5, 0,5, 0.5. or 0.5/9 below condor. Struck by law of January 19, 1899.

Date	Mintage	F	VF	XF	Unc	BU
1899	2,013,000	2.00	3.50	7.00	16.50	—
1900/896	104,000	20.00	35.00	50.00	85.00	—

KM# 125 20 CENTAVOS

5.0000 g., 0.9000 Silver .1446 oz., 23 mm. **Rev:** Condor with spread wings **Edge:** Reeded **Note:** Issued by law of January 9, 1851 and decree of March 19, 1851.

Date	Mintage	VG	F	VF	XF	Unc
1852	77,000	10.00	15.00	20.00	40.00	—
1853	906,000	5.00	6.50	11.00	22.50	—
1854	417,000	5.00	6.50	11.00	22.50	—
1854 Inverted 1	Inc. above	5.00	6.50	11.00	22.50	—
1855/4	Inc. above	6.00	8.00	12.50	25.00	—
1855	325,000	5.00	6.50	12.00	25.00	—
1856/5	396,000	6.00	8.00	12.50	25.00	—
1856	Inc. above	5.00	6.50	11.00	22.50	—
1857	748,000	5.00	6.50	11.00	22.50	—
1858/7	532,000	6.00	8.00	12.50	25.00	—
1858	Inc. above	7.50	10.00	15.00	28.00	—
1859/8	120,000	15.00	25.00	50.00	80.00	—
1859	Inc. above	50.00	75.00	—	—	—

KM# 125a 20 CENTAVOS

4.6000 g., 0.9000 Silver .1331 oz., 23 mm. **Note:** Issue authorized by law of July 28, 1860 and decree of August 20, 1860.

Date	Mintage	VG	F	VF	XF	Unc
1860/50	388,000	—	—	—	—	—
1860/59	Inc. above	3.00	6.00	10.00	20.00	—
1860	Inc. above	3.00	6.00	10.00	20.00	—
1861/51	1,471,000	5.00	7.00	10.00	22.50	—
1861/58	Inc. above	5.00	7.00	10.00	25.00	—
1861/91	Inc. above	5.00	7.00	10.00	25.00	—
1861	Inc. above	5.00	7.00	10.00	22.50	—
1862/52	324,000	5.00	7.00	10.00	22.50	—
1862	Inc. above	5.00	7.00	10.00	25.00	—

KM# 135 20 CENTAVOS

4.6000 g., 0.9000 Silver .1331 oz., 23 mm.

Date	Mintage	VG	F	VF	XF	Unc
1863/55	160,000	—	—	—	—	—
1863	Inc. above	5.00	7.50	11.50	22.50	—
1864	226,000	4.50	6.00	10.00	17.00	—
1865/4	1,505,000	2.00	3.00	5.00	9.00	—
1865	Inc. above	2.00	3.00	5.00	9.00	—
1866/4	4,298,000	2.00	3.00	5.00	9.00	—
1866	Inc. above	2.00	3.00	5.00	9.00	—
1867	—	10.00	15.00	25.00	42.00	—

KM# 138.1 20 CENTAVOS

5.0000 g., 0.8350 Silver .1343 oz., 23 mm. **Obv:** Smaller sprays **Note:** Varieties exist.

Date	Mintage	VG	F	VF	XF	Unc
1867	286,000	4.50	6.00	8.00	14.00	—
1868	197,000	2.00	3.50	5.00	8.00	—
1869/8	163,000	3.00	5.00	7.00	12.00	—
1869	Inc. above	2.00	3.50	5.00	8.00	—
1870/60	992,000	3.00	5.00	7.00	10.00	—
1870	Inc. above	2.00	3.50	5.00	8.00	—
1871/0	1,144,000	—	—	—	—	—
1871	Inc. above	2.00	3.50	5.00	8.00	—
1872/0	1,979,000	—	—	—	—	—
1872	Inc. above	2.00	3.50	5.00	8.00	—
1873/2 O over horizontal) in OLA	—	2.00	3.50	5.00	8.00	—
1873	Inc. above	—	—	—	—	—
1874 Wide date	1,256,000	2.00	3.50	5.00	8.00	—
1874 Narrow date	Inc. above	2.00	3.50	5.00	8.00	—
1875	120,000	5.00	7.50	15.00	28.00	—
1876 Large stars	749,000	2.75	4.50	6.00	9.00	—
1876 Small stars	Inc. above	2.75	4.50	6.00	9.00	—
1877	549,000	2.75	4.50	6.00	9.00	—
1878/7	2,639,000	2.75	4.50	6.00	9.00	—
1878	Inc. above	2.75	4.50	6.00	9.00	—
1879	9,645	60.00	100	175	250	—

KM# 138.2 20 CENTAVOS

5.0000 g., 0.5000 Silver .0803 oz., 23 mm. **Obv. Legend:** 0.5 added, without dash below S in CENTS in legend **Note:** Law of June 14, 1879 authorized change of silver alloy from 0.9 to 0.5 silver.

Date	Mintage	VG	F	VF	XF	Unc
1879/0	5,073,000	2.75	4.50	7.00	12.00	—
1879	Inc. above	2.50	4.00	6.00	10.00	—
1880/70	6,846,000	2.75	4.50	7.00	12.00	—
1880/79	Inc. above	2.75	4.50	7.00	12.00	—
1880	Inc. above	2.50	4.00	6.00	10.00	—
1881	6,408,000	2.50	4.00	6.00	10.00	—
1882	—	2.50	4.00	6.00	10.00	—
1893/2	1,397,000	2.75	4.50	7.00	12.00	—
1893	Inc. above	2.50	4.00	6.00	10.00	—

KM# 138.2a 20 CENTAVOS

4.0000 g., 0.5000 Silver .0643 oz., 23 mm. **Obv:** Dash below S in CENTS in legend

Date	Mintage	VG	F	VF	XF	Unc
1890	—	—	—	—	—	—
1891/81	2,953,000	—	—	—	—	—
1891	Inc. above	3.00	6.00	15.00	25.00	—

KM# 138.4 20 CENTAVOS

5.0000 g., 0.5000 Silver .0803 oz., 23 mm. **Obv:** Dash below S in CENTS **Obv. Legend:** 0.5

Date	Mintage	VG	F	VF	XF	Unc
1891	—	3.00	5.00	9.00	16.00	—
1892/82 0.5/0.2	3,719,000	2.75	4.50	7.00	12.50	—
1892	Inc. above	2.50	4.00	6.00	11.50	—
1893	Inc. above	2.50	4.00	6.00	11.50	—

KM# 138.3 20 CENTAVOS

4.6000 g., 0.2000 Silver .0296 oz. **Obv. Legend:** 0.2 added **Note:** Varieties exist for 1891/81 with 0.2 and 0.2/5.

Date	Mintage	VG	F	VF	XF	Unc
1891/81	787,000	10.00	15.00	20.00	50.00	—
1891	Inc. above	10.00	15.00	20.00	50.00	—

KM# 151.1 20 CENTAVOS

4.0000 g., 0.8350 Silver .1073 oz., 21.5 mm. **Obv:** O. ROTY below condor **Rev:** Hammer and sickle

Date	Mintage	VG	F	VF	XF	Unc
1895	146,000	12.50	20.00	30.00	70.00	—

KM# 151.2 20 CENTAVOS

4.0000 g., 0.5000 Silver .0643 oz., 21.5 mm. **Obv:** 0.5 below condor **Note:** Obverse varieties with 0.5 or 0.5. exist. Issued by law of January 19, 1899.

Date	Mintage	F	VF	XF	Unc	BU
1899/69	4,343,000	4.00	9.00	18.00	30.00	—
1899/7	Inc. above	—	—	—	—	—
1899/8	Inc. above	—	—	—	—	—
1899	Inc. above	1.00	2.00	3.00	7.50	—
1899/ Sideways 9	Inc. above	—	—	—	—	—
1900/899	334,000	75.00	100	—	—	—
1900/895	Inc. above	30.00	40.00	80.00	150	—
1906/806	—	2.50	6.00	12.00	25.00	—
1907/807	—	2.00	5.00	10.00	20.00	—

KM# 128 50 CENTAVOS

12.5000 g., 0.9000 Silver .3617 oz., 30 mm. **Edge:** Reeded **Note:** Struck under law of January 9, 1851 and decree of March 19, 1851.

Date	Mintage	VG	F	VF	XF	Unc
1853	769,000	7.50	10.00	22.00	80.00	—
1854	551,000	7.50	10.00	22.00	80.00	—
1855	1,354,000	7.50	10.00	20.00	75.00	—
1856/5	606,000	7.50	10.00	22.00	80.00	—
1856	Inc. above	12.00	20.00	40.00	110	—
1856 1/inverted 1	Inc. above	12.00	20.00	35.00	100	—
1858	245,000	14.00	22.00	45.00	120	—
1859	489,000	10.00	15.00	30.00	90.00	—
1860/59 Rare	20,000	—	—	—	—	—
1860	Inc. above	250	350	450	600	—
1862/52	123,000	25.00	40.00	75.00	185	—
1862	Inc. above	20.00	30.00	60.00	160	—

KM# 134 50 CENTAVOS

12.5000 g., 0.9000 Silver .3617 oz., 30 mm. **Obv:** Large sprays **Rev:** Eagle with shield **Note:** Issued by decree of November 25, 1862.

Date	Mintage	VG	F	VF	XF	Unc
1862	Inc. above	22.00	30.00	45.00	90.00	—
1863/2	80,000	13.00	22.00	32.00	55.00	—
1863	Inc. above	12.00	20.00	30.00	50.00	—
1864/3	68,000	12.00	20.00	30.00	50.00	—
1864	Inc. above	12.00	20.00	30.00	50.00	—
1865/4	287,000	6.50	11.00	18.00	30.00	—
1865	Inc. above	7.00	12.00	20.00	32.50	—
1866/5	200,000	6.50	11.00	18.00	30.00	—
1866/55	Inc. above	6.50	11.00	18.00	30.00	—
1866	Inc. above	9.00	13.00	22.00	35.00	—
1867/6	47,000	35.00	60.00	90.00	150	—
1867	Inc. above	35.00	60.00	90.00	150	—

KM# 139 50 CENTAVOS

12.5000 g., 0.9000 Silver .3617 oz., 30 mm. **Obv:** Smaller sprays

Date	Mintage	VG	F	VF	XF	Unc
1867	Inc. above	15.00	22.00	30.00	55.00	—
1867 Proof	—	Value: 600				
1868	147,000	7.00	9.00	11.00	22.00	—
1870/60	271,000	5.50	7.00	9.00	18.00	—
1870/68	Inc. above	10.00	15.00	22.00	45.00	—
1870/68/7	Inc. above	10.00	15.00	22.00	45.00	—
1870	Inc. above	10.00	15.00	22.00	45.00	—
1872/0	104,000	7.00	9.00	11.00	22.00	—
1872	Inc. above	7.00	9.00	11.00	22.00	—

KM# 129 PESO
25.0000 g., 0.9000 Silver .7234 oz., 37 mm. **Rev:** Condor with shield at right **Edge:** Reeded **Note:** Struck under law of January 9, 1851 and decree of March 19, 1851.

Date	Mintage	VG	F	VF	XF	Unc
1853	394,000	15.00	30.00	70.00	200	—
1854	567,000	15.00	30.00	70.00	200	—
1855	683,000	15.00	30.00	70.00	200	—
1856/5	406,000	25.00	40.00	85.00	275	—
1858	51,000	25.00	45.00	100	300	—
1859/8	330,000	15.00	30.00	70.00	200	—
1859	Inc. above	18.50	35.00	75.00	220	—
1862	103,000	50.00	100	250	450	—

KM# 133 PESO
1.5235 g., 0.9000 Gold .0441 oz., 14 mm. **Note:** Crude style. Struck under law of July 28, 1860 and decree of August 20, 1860.

Date	Mintage	F	VF	XF	Unc	BU
1860	156,000	30.00	45.00	75.00	120	—
1861	176,000	30.00	45.00	75.00	120	—
1862	11,000	40.00	60.00	80.00	130	—
1863	55,000	30.00	45.00	75.00	120	—
1864	29,000	40.00	60.00	80.00	130	—

KM# 140 PESO
1.5235 g., 0.9000 Gold .0441 oz., 14 mm. **Note:** Fine style. Struck under law of July 28, 1860 and decree of August 20, 1860.

Date	Mintage	F	VF	XF	Unc	BU
1867	949	75.00	100	250	425	—
1873	16,000	40.00	60.00	80.00	130	—

KM# 141 PESO
25.0000 g., 0.9000 Silver .7234 oz., 37 mm. **Obv:** Value: 1 Peso **Rev:** Eagle with shield at left **Note:** Struck by decree of November 25, 1862.

Date	Mintage	F	VF	XF	Unc	BU
1867	Inc. below	600	1,500	2,500	6,000	—

Note: Mintage is included in KM#142.1, 1867.

KM# 142.1 PESO
25.0000 g., 0.9000 Silver .7234 oz., 37 mm. **Obv:** Value: UN PESO **Note:** Struck by law of October 21, 1865.

Date	Mintage	F	VF	XF	Unc	BU
1867	220,000	20.00	40.00	60.00	400	800
1868	1,037,000	8.00	12.00	30.00	150	200
1868 Proof	—	Value: 800				
1869	467,000	10.00	15.00	30.00	150	200
1870/60	566,000	10.00	15.00	30.00	150	200
1870/69	Inc. above	10.00	15.00	30.00	150	200
1870	Inc. above	10.00	15.00	30.00	75.00	95.00
1871	795,000	25.00	45.00	60.00	200	250
1872/0	Inc. above	10.00	17.50	30.00	75.00	95.00
1872	Inc. above	10.00	17.50	30.00	75.00	95.00
1873/2	323,000	20.00	35.00	65.00	100	150
1873	Inc. above	8.00	12.00	20.00	60.00	80.00
1874	1,204,000	8.00	12.00	20.00	60.00	80.00
1875/0	2,128,000	8.00	12.00	20.00	60.00	80.00
1875/4	Inc. above	8.00	12.00	20.00	60.00	80.00
1875	Inc. above	8.00	12.00	20.00	60.00	80.00
1875 NM	Inc. above	10.00	20.00	35.00	90.00	120
1876 NM	Inc. above	10.00	20.00	35.00	90.00	120
1876	1,508,000	8.00	12.00	20.00	60.00	80.00
1877/66	1,930,000	8.00	12.00	20.00	60.00	80.00
1877/67	Inc. above	8.00	12.00	20.00	60.00	80.00
1877/6	Inc. above	8.00	12.00	20.00	60.00	80.00
1877/7	Inc. above	8.00	12.00	20.00	60.00	80.00
1877	Inc. above	8.00	12.00	20.00	60.00	80.00
1877 M	Inc. above	10.00	20.00	35.00	90.00	120
1878	950,000	8.00	12.00	20.00	60.00	80.00
1879/69	780,000	10.00	15.00	25.00	70.00	90.00
1879/8	Inc. above	8.00	12.00	20.00	60.00	80.00
1879	Inc. above	8.00	12.00	20.00	60.00	80.00
1880/70/60	693,000	10.00	15.00	25.00	70.00	90.00
1880	Inc. above	8.00	12.00	20.00	60.00	80.00
1881	1,420,000	8.00	12.00	20.00	60.00	80.00
1882/1	1,648,000	10.00	15.00	25.00	75.00	95.00
1882	Inc. above	10.00	15.00	25.00	75.00	95.00
1883/2	1,397,000	—	—	—	—	—
1883/8	Inc. above	—	—	—	—	—
1883 Round-top 3	Inc. above	8.00	12.00	20.00	60.00	80.00
1884	1,812,000	8.00	12.00	20.00	60.00	80.00
1885/3	528,000	12.50	20.00	40.00	115	165
1885/4	Inc. above	12.50	20.00	40.00	115	165
1885	Inc. above	10.00	158	30.00	95.00	125
1886/5	966,000	10.00	15.00	25.00	70.00	90.00
1886	Inc. above	10.00	15.00	25.00	70.00	90.00
1887	23,000	350	750	1,100	1,500	1,800
1889	241,000	20.00	35.00	55.00	160	200
1890/80	109,000	25.00	45.00	65.00	190	245
1890/89	Inc. above	20.00	35.00	55.00	160	200
1890	Inc. above	25.00	45.00	65.00	190	245
1891/0	109,000	50.00	100	200	650	1,000
1891	Inc. above	50.00	100	200	650	1,000

KM# 152.1 PESO
20.0000 g., 0.8350 Silver .5369 oz., 35 mm. **Note:** Issued under law No. 277 of February 11, 1895.

Date	Mintage	F	VF	XF	Unc	BU
1895/4	6,086,000	15.00	25.00	40.00	70.00	—
1895	Inc. above	8.00	12.50	18.50	42.50	—
1896	1,556,000	10.00	15.00	28.00	55.00	—
1897	37,000	25.00	40.00	55.00	90.00	—

KM# 142.2 PESO
25.0000 g., 0.9000 Silver .7234 oz. **Rev:** Flat top 3 **Note:** Medal alignment.

Date	Mintage	F	VF	XF	Unc	BU
1883(1925)	712,000	—	150	350	1,400	2,000

KM# 142.3 PESO
25.0000 g., 0.9000 Silver .7234 oz. **Rev:** Flat top 3 **Note:** Coin alignment. Minted in 1925-6 and most coins were melted down in 1927.

Date	Mintage	F	VF	XF	Unc	BU
1883(1926)	149,000	—	150	300	465	550

KM# 132 2 PESOS
3.0506 g., 0.9000 Gold .0882 oz., 17 mm. **Note:** Fine style, bold letters. Struck by law of January 9, 1851.

Date	Mintage	F	VF	XF	Unc	BU
1856	—	120	250	350	—	—
1857	207,000	BV	50.00	90.00	175	—
1858/7	56,000	BV	65.00	100	150	—
1858	Inc. above	BV	50.00	80.00	165	—
1859	97,000	BV	50.00	80.00	165	—
1860	78,000	BV	50.00	80.00	165	—
1862	10,000	BV	50.00	90.00	175	—
1865	—	BV	250	350	—	—

KM# 143 2 PESOS
3.0506 g., 0.9000 Gold .0882 oz. **Note:** Modified arms. Fine letters.

Date	Mintage	F	VF	XF	Unc	BU
1867	841	175	350	600	950	—
1873	54,000	BV	50.00	75.00	145	—
1874	61,000	BV	50.00	75.00	145	—
1875	37,000	45.00	60.00	85.00	170	—

KM# 122 5 PESOS
7.6265 g., 0.9000 Gold .2207 oz., 22.5 mm. **Note:** Crude style, bold letters. Struck by law of January 9, 1851.

Date	Mintage	F	VF	XF	Unc	BU
1851	3,735	BV	135	160	275	—
1852	20,000	BV	125	150	250	—
1853	5,987	BV	135	160	275	—

KM# 130 5 PESOS
7.6265 g., 0.9000 Gold .2207 oz. **Note:** Fine style, fine letters. Struck by law of January 9, 1851.

Date	Mintage	F	VF	XF	Unc	BU
1854 Rare	953	—	—	—	—	—
1855	7,609	BV	135	160	265	—
1856/5	4,753	125	225	300	450	—
1856	Inc. above	BV	135	160	275	—
1857/6	25,000	BV	150	200	320	—
1857	Inc. above	BV	125	150	235	—
1858	11,000	BV	125	150	235	—
1859/8	66,000	BV	125	150	235	—
1859	Inc. above	BV	125	150	235	—
1862	6,738	BV	135	160	265	—
1865	5,110	BV	135	160	265	—
1866/5	6,249	BV	135	160	265	—
1866	Inc. above	BV	150	200	320	—
1867	10,000	BV	125	150	235	—

KM# 144 5 PESOS
7.6265 g., 0.9000 Gold .2207 oz. **Note:** Modified arms. Struck by law of January 9, 1851.

Date	Mintage	F	VF	XF	Unc	BU
1867 Rare	Inc. above	—	—	—	—	—
1868	4,065	BV	135	160	265	—
1869	5,913	BV	135	160	265	—
1870	13,000	BV	125	150	235	—
1872	23,000	BV	125	150	235	—
1873	50,000	BV	125	150	225	—

KM# 153 5 PESOS
2.9955 g., 0.9170 Gold .0883 oz., 16.5 mm. **Note:** Issued under law 277 of June 22, 1891.

Date	Mintage	F	VF	XF	Unc	BU
1895	3,002,000	BV	50.00	60.00	90.00	—
1896	24,000	BV	85.00	175	275	—

KM# 159 5 PESOS

2.9955 g., 0.9170 Gold .0883 oz., 16.5 mm.

Date	Mintage	F	VF	XF	Unc	BU
1897 Rare	—	—	—	—	—	—
1898	426,000	BV	50.00	65.00	100	—

KM# 123 10 PESOS

15.2530 g., 0.9000 Gold .4414 oz. **Note:** Crude style. Issued under law of February 9, 1851.

Date	Mintage	F	VF	XF	Unc	BU
1851	50,000	BV	225	265	365	—
1852	135,000	BV	225	265	365	—
1853	206,000	BV	225	250	300	—

KM# 131 10 PESOS

15.2530 g., 0.9000 Gold .4414 oz. **Note:** Fine style. Issued under law of February 9, 1851.

Date	Mintage	F	VF	XF	Unc	BU
1854	195,000	BV	225	265	365	—
1855	61,000	BV	225	265	365	—
1856	66,000	BV	225	265	365	—
1857	20,000	BV	225	265	365	—
1858/7	52,000	BV	225	265	365	—
1858	Inc. above	BV	225	265	365	—
1859	281,000	BV	225	265	365	—
1860	31,000	BV	225	265	365	—
1861	15,000	BV	225	265	365	—
1862	21,000	BV	225	265	365	—
1863/2	25,000	BV	225	265	365	—
1863	Inc. above	BV	225	265	365	—
1864	26,000	BV	225	265	365	—
1865	45,000	BV	225	265	365	—
1866	66,000	BV	225	265	365	—
1867/6	121,000	BV	225	265	365	—
1867	Inc. above	BV	225	265	365	—

KM# 145 10 PESOS

15.2530 g., 0.9000 Gold .4414 oz. **Obv:** Modified arms **Note:** Issued under law of February 9, 1851.

Date	Mintage	F	VF	XF	Unc	BU
1867	Inc. above	BV	225	265	365	—
1868	54,000	BV	225	265	365	—
1869	36,000	BV	225	265	365	—
1870	76,000	BV	225	265	365	—
1871	41,000	BV	225	265	365	—
1872	235,000	BV	225	265	365	—
1873	112,000	BV	225	265	365	—
1874	1,277	BV	235	285	400	—
1876	2,106	BV	235	285	400	—
1877	8,208	BV	235	285	385	—
1877 Proof	—	Value: 2,500				
1878	7,983	BV	235	285	385	—
1879	9,805	BV	235	285	385	—
1880	11,000	BV	225	265	365	—
1881	13,000	BV	225	265	365	—
1882	14,000	BV	225	265	365	—
1883	8,381	BV	235	285	385	—
1884	9,888	BV	235	285	385	—
1885	7,758	BV	235	285	385	—
1886	3,721	BV	235	285	385	—
1887	5,236	BV	235	285	385	—
1888	4,217	BV	235	285	385	—
1889	4,650	BV	235	285	385	—
1890	2,344	BV	235	285	400	—
1892	1,192	BV	235	285	400	—

KM# 154 10 PESOS

5.9910 g., 0.9170 Gold .1766 oz.

Date	Mintage	F	VF	XF	Unc	BU
1895	808,000	—	BV	100	165	—

KM# 157 10 PESOS

5.9910 g., 0.9170 Gold .1766 oz.

Date	Mintage	F	VF	XF	Unc	BU
1896	1,163,000	—	BV	90.00	125	—
1898	276,000	—	BV	100	145	—

KM# 158 20 PESOS

11.9821 g., 0.9170 Gold .3532 oz., 27 mm.

Date	Mintage	F	VF	XF	Unc	BU
1896	149,000	—	BV	165	250	—

PATTERNS

Including off metal strikes

KM#	Date	Mintage	Identification	Mkt Val
Pn1	1819	—	Peso. Silver.	9,000
PnA2	ND	—	8 Escudos. Copper. Similar to KM#84.	175
Pn2	1828	—	1/2 Real. Silver. Coquimbo mint.	—
Pn3	ND(1835)	—	8 Escudos. Copper.	175
PnA3	ND	—	8 Reales. Copper.	550
PnA4	ND(1835)	—	8 Escudos. Brass.	250
Pn4	1836 I.J.	—	8 Escudos. Copper.	165
Pn5	1836 I.J.	—	8 Escudos. Copper Gilt.	275
PnA6	1836 I.J.	—	8 Escudos. Silver Plated Copper.	220
Pn6	1836 I.J.	—	8 Escudos. Silver.	450
Pn7	ND(1842) R.N.	—	8 Escudos. Copper.	—

KM#	Date	Mintage	Identification	Mkt Val
Pn15	1868	—	Peso. Copper. KM#141.	1,750
Pn16	1868	—	Peso. Copper. KM#140.	200
Pn17	1868	—	Peso. Gold-Plated Copper. KM#140.	250
PnA18	1868	—	Peso. Copper. KM#142.	1,150
Pn18	1868	—	2 Pesos. Copper. KM#143.	235
Pn19	1868	—	2 Pesos. Gold-Plated Copper. KM#143.	350
Pn20	1868	—	5 Pesos. Copper. KM#144.	375
Pn21	1868	—	5 Pesos. Gold-Plated Copper. KM#145.	400
Pn22	1868	—	10 Pesos. Copper. KM#145.	450
Pn23	1868	—	10 Pesos. Gold-Plated Copper. KM#145.	475

KM#	Date	Mintage	Identification	Mkt Val
Pn8	ND	—	8 Escudos. Copper.	—
PnA8	ND	—	Real. Silver. Without legend or date	500
PnA9	1851	—	1/2 Decimo. Silver. Similar to Pn9, Essai.	375

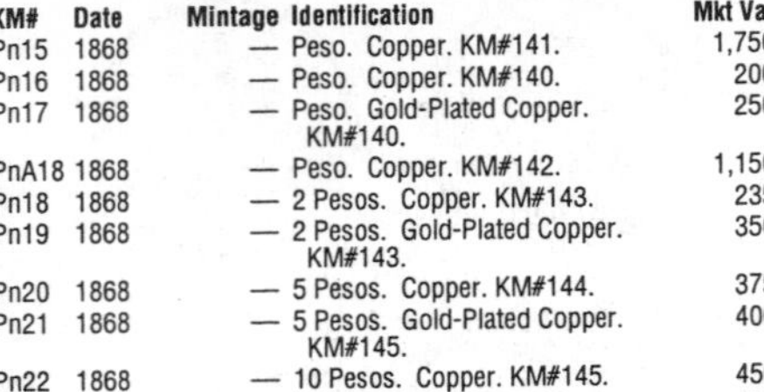

KM#	Date	Mintage	Identification	Mkt Val
Pn9	1851	—	Peso. Copper. Bust. Legend. Plain edge. Essai.	500

KM#	Date	Mintage	Identification	Mkt Val
PnA10	1851	—	Peso. Lead. Wreath. Head of Ceres. Essai.	400
Pn10	1851	—	5 Pesos. Copper. Bust. Legend.	400
PnA11	1866	—	Peso. Silver. KM#141.	—
Pn11	1867	—	20 Centavos. Copper. KM#138.	600
PnA12	1867	—	20 Centavos. Silver. Plain edge.	700
Pn12	1867	—	50 Centavos. Copper. KM#139.	800

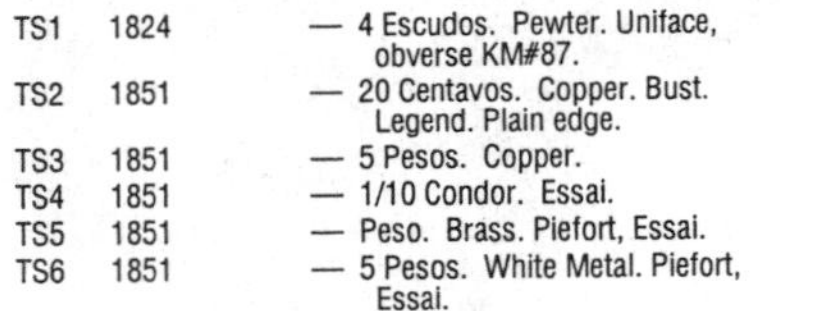

KM#	Date	Mintage	Identification	Mkt Val
PnA13	1867	—	Peso. Bronze.	650
PnB13	1867	—	Peso. Silver.	750
Pn13	1868	—	1/2 Decimo. Copper. KM#137.2.	320
Pn14	1868	—	Decimo. Copper. KM#136.2.	400

KM#	Date	Mintage	Identification	Mkt Val
PnA24	1878//1876	—	10 Pesos. Copper. Arms. Liberty.	—
Pn24	1894	—	Peso. Silver. Essai, KM#152.1.	1,500
Pn25	1895	—	5 Pesos. Copper.	—

PIEFORTS

KM#	Date	Mintage	Identification	Mkt Val
P1	1835	—	1/2 Centavo. Copper. KM#114.	150
P2	1851	—	Centavo. Copper.	300
P3	1867	—	Peso. Bronze.	800

TRIAL STRIKES

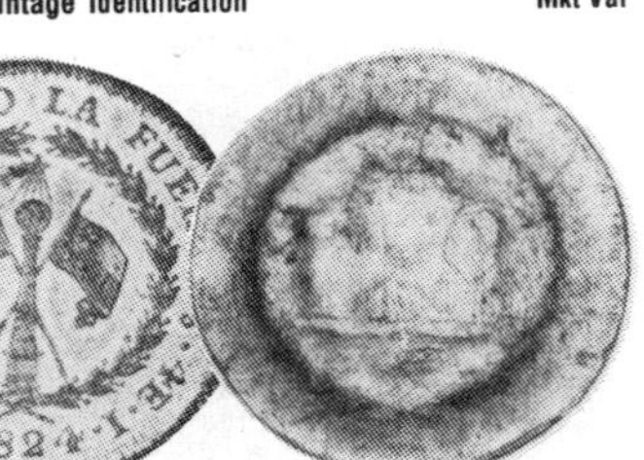

KM#	Date	Mintage	Identification	Mkt Val
TS1	1824	—	4 Escudos. Pewter. Uniface, obverse KM#87.	275
TS2	1851	—	20 Centavos. Copper. Bust. Legend. Plain edge.	175
TS3	1851	—	5 Pesos. Copper.	—
TS4	1851	—	1/10 Condor. Essai.	150
TS5	1851	—	Peso. Brass. Piefort, Essai.	150
TS6	1851	—	5 Pesos. White Metal. Piefort, Essai.	100

CHILOE

Chiloe is an island off the southwest coast of Chile. The island was the last outpost of the Spanish in their effort to deny Chilean independence. Antonio Quintanilla had coins cast to show that the empire of Ferdinand VII of Spain still exerted some authority in the New World.

COLONIAL

COUNTERMARKED COINAGE

Royalist Issues of Antonio Quintanilla

KM# 1 8 REALES

Cast Silver **Countermark:** Chi-loe **Note:** Countermark on sand cast copy of Peru-Lima 8 Reales.

CM Date	Host Date	Good	VG	F	VF	XF
ND	1818	900	1,500	2,500	4,500	—

Note: The authenticity of these pieces has been questioned by leading authorities

KM# 2 8 REALES

23.5000 g., Cast Silver, 38 mm. **Countermark:** Chi-loe **Obv:** Bust of Ferdinand VII flanked by Chi-Loe **Note:** Countermark on sand cast copy of Bolivia-Potosi 8 reales.

CM Date	Host Date	Good	VG	F	VF	XF
ND	1822	900	1,500	2,500	4,500	—
ND	1825	900	1,500	2,500	4,500	—

VALDIVIA

Emergency coinage issued by Don Antonio Adriazola by order of the Governor during a shortage of coin with which to pay the local garrison.

REPUBLIC

PROVISIONAL COINAGE

KM# 1 REAL

Billon **Obv:** Value / V A / date **Rev:** Stars around column

Date	Mintage	VG	F	VF	XF	Unc
1822	—	200	400	750	1,300	—

KM# 2 2 REALES

Billon **Obv:** Value /V A / date **Rev:** Stars around column

Date	Mintage	VG	F	VF	XF	Unc
1822	—	200	400	750	1,250	—

KM# 3 8 REALES

Billon **Obv:** Value / V A / date **Rev:** Stars around column

Date	Mintage	VG	F	VF	XF	Unc
1822	—	500	750	1,250	3,500	—

COUNTERMARKED COINAGE

KM# 4 REAL
Billon **Countermark:** APDLVA **Note:** Countermark in monogram on KM#1.

CM Date	Host Date	Good	VG	F	VF	XF
ND	1822	—	200	400	750	1,300

KM# 5 2 REALES
Billon **Countermark:** APDLVA **Note:** Countermark in monogram on KM#2.

CM Date	Host Date	Good	VG	F	VF	XF
ND	1822	—	200	400	750	1,250

KM# 6 8 REALES
Billon **Countermark:** APDLVA **Note:** Countermark in monogram on KM#3.

CM Date	Host Date	Good	VG	F	VF	XF
ND	1822	—	500	750	1,250	3,500

COPIAPO

REVOLUTION OF 1859

REVOLUTIONARY COINAGE

Issued by Don Pedro Leon Gallo

KM# 1.1 50 CENTAVOS
10.2000 g., Silver, 29 mm. **Obv:** Uniface, with star and denomination **Note:** Star in relief, small shield pointing down.

Date	Mintage	VG	F	VF	XF	Unc
ND(1859)	—	—	60.00	80.00	120	—

KM# 1.2 50 CENTAVOS
Silver **Obv:** Uniface, with star in relief, wide body shield pointing down

Date	Mintage	VG	F	VF	XF	Unc
ND(1859)	—	—	50.00	75.00	90.00	—

KM# 1.3 50 CENTAVOS
Silver **Obv:** Uniface, with star flat, small shield pointing down

Date	Mintage	VG	F	VF	XF	Unc
ND(1859)	—	—	50.00	75.00	90.00	—

KM# 1.4 50 CENTAVOS
Silver **Obv:** Uniface, with star flat, wide shield pointing down

Date	Mintage	VG	F	VF	XF	Unc
ND(1859)	—	—	50.00	75.00	90.00	—

KM# 2.1 PESO
22.3000 g., Silver, 37 mm. **Note:** Uniface.

Date	Mintage	VG	F	VF	XF	Unc
ND(1859)	—	—	50.00	65.00	95.00	—

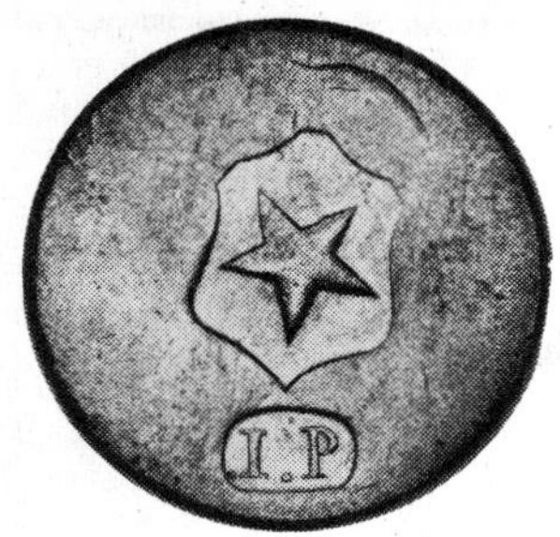

KM# 2.2 PESO
Silver **Note:** Inverted shield.

Date	Mintage	VG	F	VF	XF	Unc
ND(1859)	—	—	50.00	65.00	95.00	—

KM# 2.3 PESO
Silver **Note:** Similar to 50 Centavos, KM#1. Other varieties exist.

Date	Mintage	VG	F	VF	XF	Unc
ND(1859)	—	—	50.00	65.00	95.00	—

Note: Denomination appears as either 1.P or I.P

BLOCKADE OF PUERTO DE CALDERA

SIEGE COINAGE

Issued during the War of 1865 with Spain

KM# 3 50 CENTAVOS
11.0000 g., 0.9700 Silver, 27 mm. **Obv:** Legend around shield, denomination flanking **Obv. Legend:** COPIAPO-CHILE **Rev:** Date

Date	Mintage	VG	F	VF	XF	Unc
1865 7 known	—	—	—	350	500	—

Note: All known 50 Centavos are restrikes made from original dies circa 1909 by Medina

KM# 4 PESO
22.0000 g., 0.9700 Silver, 35 mm.

Date	Mintage	VG	F	VF	XF	Unc
1865 Restrike	—	—	40.00	60.00	75.00	—

SAN BERNARDO DE MAYPO

REPUBLIC

TOKEN COINAGE

KM# 1 1/4 REAL
Copper **Obv:** Mountains, with volcano in center, in circle **Rev:** Trout swimming right **Note:** Counterfeits have been reported.

Date	Mintage	VG	F	VF	XF	Unc
1821	—	135	280	450	750	—

Note: Struck to pay canal workers

TARAPACA

Tarapaca is the northernmost province of Chile. It was annexed to Chile from Peru in 1885 after a war between those two countries, in which Chile was the victor. In that same year the Liberal Party came to power in Chile, instituting reforms. In response to these reforms the Conservative Party rebelled and formed a provisional government, and within a few years defeated the Liberals.

REPUBLIC

REVOLUTIONARY COINAGE

Struck at Iquique by the revolutionary Junta.

KM# 1 PESO
25.0000 g., 0.6200 Silver .4983 oz. **Rev. Legend:** 25 GRs/620 FINO **Note:** Struck at Iquique by the revolutionary Junta.

Date	Mintage	F	VF	XF	Unc	BU
1891	—	250	500	1,000	1,850	—

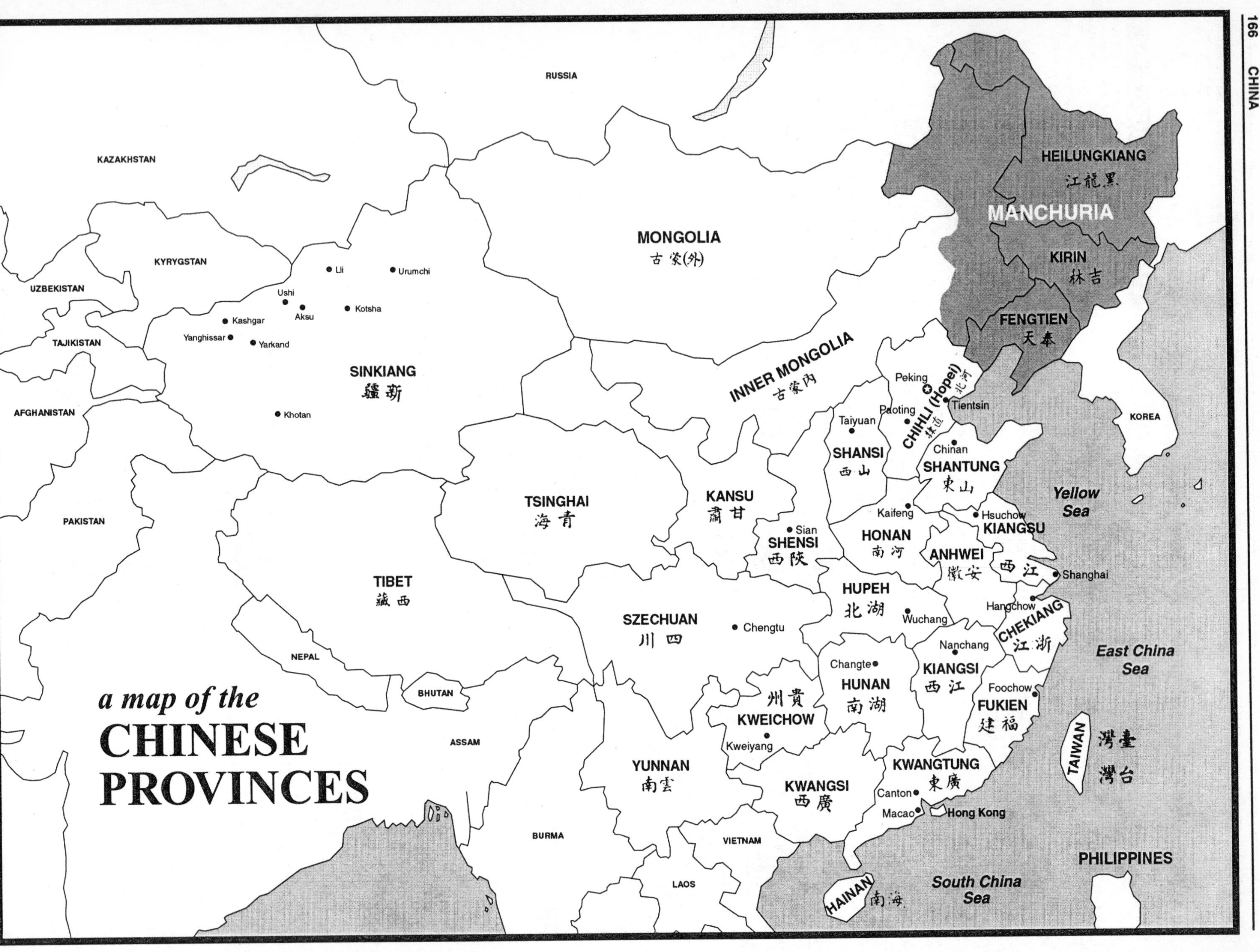
a map of the
CHINESE
PROVINCES
RUSSIA
KAZAKHSTAN
KYRYGSTAN
UZBEKISTAN
TAJIKISTAN
AFGHANISTAN
PAKISTAN
MONGOLIA
SINKIANG
Lli
Urumchi
Ushi
Aksu
Kotsha
Kashgar
Yanghissar
Yarkand
Khotan
INNER MONGOLIA
MANCHURIA
HEILUNGKIANG
KIRIN
FENGTIEN
KOREA
Peking
Tientsin
Paoting
CHIHLI (Hopei)
Taiyuan
SHANSI
Chinan
SHANTUNG
Yellow Sea
TSINGHAI
KANSU
Kaifeng
Hsuchow
KIANGSU
Sian
SHENSI
HONAN
ANHWEI
Shanghai
TIBET
HUPEH
Wuchang
Hangchow
CHEKIANG
SZECHUAN
Chengtu
NEPAL
BHUTAN
Nanchang
East China Sea
Changte
HUNAN
KIANGSI
Foochow
FUKIEN
KWEICHOW
Kweiyang
TAIWAN
ASSAM
YUNNAN
KWANGSI
KWANGTUNG
Canton
Macao
Hong Kong
BURMA
VIETNAM
PHILIPPINES
LAOS
HAINAN
South China Sea

Before 1912, China was ruled by an imperial government. The republican administration which replaced it was itself supplanted on the Chinese mainland by a communist government in 1949, but it has remained in control of Taiwan and other offshore islands in the China Sea with a land area of approximately 14,000 square miles and a population of more than 14 million. The People's Republic of China administers some 3.7 million square miles and an estimated 1.19 billion people. This communist government, officially established on October 1, 1949, was admitted to the United Nations, replacing its nationalist predecessor, the Republic of China, in 1971.

Cast coins in base metals were used in China many centuries before the Christian era, but locally struck coinages of the western type in gold, silver, copper and other metals did not appear until 1888. In spite of the relatively short time that modern coins have been in use, the number of varieties is exceptionally large.

Both Nationalist and Communist China, as well as the pre-revolutionary Imperial government and numerous provincial or other agencies, including some foreign-administered agencies and governments, have issued coins in China. Most of these have been in dollar (yüan) or dollar-fraction denominations, based on the internationally used dollar system, but coins in tael denominations were issued in the 1920's and earlier. The striking of coins nearly ceased in the late 1930's through the 1940's due to the war effort and a period of uncontrollable inflation while vast amounts of paper currency were issued by the Nationalist, Communist and Japanese occupation institutions.

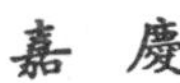

Chia-ch'ing (Jen-tsung)
1796-1820

Type A

嘉慶通寶

Chia-ch'ing T'ung-pao

Chia-ch'ing - Born November 13, 1760 in Peking. He was proclaimed emperor and assumed the reign title in 1796. The White Lotus Rebellion, 1796-1804, broke out in central and western China. Capable generals were appointed to quell the rebellion, but it took the depleted Ch'ing armies five years to put it down. Chia-ch'ing made efforts to restore the finances of the imperial treasury but corruption may have increased as a result of the practice of selling high office as a means of collecting more revenue.
Chia-ch'ing died on September 2, 1820, as one of the most unpopular emperors of the Ch'ing dynasty.

Tao-kuang (Hsüan-tsung)
1821-1851

Type A

道光通寶

Tao-kuang T'ung-pao

Tao-kuang - The sixth emperor of the Ch'ing dynasty, born September 16, 1782, in Peking, ascended the throne in 1820. He tried to restore the nation's finances by personal austerity. In 1838 the Emperor's attempts to stop the opium trade carried out by Western merchants resulted in the first Opium War between Britain and China, 1839-42.

Tao-kuang died February 25, 1850 just as the Taiping Rebellion (1850-64) was beginning to sweep South China.

Hsien-fêng (Wen-tsung)
1851-1861

Type A

道光通寶

Hsien-feng T'ung-pao

Type B-1

咸豐重寶

Hsien-fêng Chung-pao

Type B-2
Left character *Pao* in another style, called Chen Pao.

咸豐重寶

Hsien-fêng Chung-pao

Type C

咸豐元寶

Hsien-fêng Yüan-pao

Hsien-fêng - The 7th emperor in the Ch'ing dynasty was born in 1831, the 4th son of Tao-kuang. He took Yehonala as his concubine and she later became the Empress Dowager Tz'u-hsi. Her son T'ung-chih was Hsien-fêng's successor. The T'ai-p'ing Rebellion (1850-1864) occurred during his reign. The Treaty of Tientsin, a result of war with England, in 1858 opened 11 ports to western trade. He fled to Jehol in 1860.

祺祥

Ch'i-hsiang (Mu-tsung), 1st reign
1861

Type A-1

祺祥通寶

Ch'i-hsiang T'ung-pao

Type B-1

祺祥重寶

Ch'i-hsiang Chung-pao, 1st reign

同治

T'ung-chih, (Mu-tsung), 2nd reign
1862-1875

Type A-2

同治通寶

T'ung-chih T'ung-pao

Type B-2

同治重寶

T'ung-chih Chung-pao

T'ung-chih - Born on April 27, 1856, T'ung-chih ascended the throne at the age of six with the reign-title Ch'i-hsiang and very few coins were struck with this title. He ruled under the regency of a triumvirate headed by his mother, the Empress Dowager Tz'u-hsi (1835-1908), in whose reign the Taiping rebels were suppressed and the government began attempts to understand and deal with the West. He assumed personal control of the government in 1873 when he was 17. T'ung-chih was a weak ruler whose affairs were constantly scrutinized by the Empress Dowager. He died January 12, 1875, in Peking.

光緒

Kuang-hsü (Te-tsung)
1875-1908

Type A

光緒通寶

Kuang-hsü T'ung-pao

Type B

光緒重寶

Kuang-hsü Chung-pao

Kuang-hsü - When the previous emperor died, his mother, the Empress Dowager Tz'u-hsi, chose her four-year-old nephew, born August 14, 1871, as emperor. She adopted the boy so that she could act as regent and on February 25, 1875, the young prince ascended the throne, taking the reign title of Kuang-hsü. In 1898 he tried to assert himself and collected a group of progressive officials around him. He issued a series of edicts for revamping of the military, abolition of civil service examinations, improvement of agriculture and restructuring of administrative procedures. During Kuang-hsü's reign (1875-1908) the Empress Dowager totally dominated the government. She confined the emperor to his palace and spread rumors that he was deathly ill. Foreign powers let it be known they would not take kindly to the Emperor's death. This saved his life but thereafter he had no power over the government. On November 15, 1908, Tz'u-hsi died under highly suspicious circumstances and the usually healthy emperor was announced as having died the previous day.

PROVINCIAL MINT NAMES

(and other source indicators)

Provincial names throughout the catalog are based on the Wade-Giles transliteration of the Chinese word. Current spellings, known as the "Pinyin" form, are widely adopted by the printed media. Example: Sinkiang = Xinjiang.

The column at left illustrates the full name as used on most provincial coinage while the column at right illustrates the abbreviated name that appears in the center of the obverse of the Tai-Ch'ing-Ti-Kuo copper coinage.

Full Name Right to Left reading	Single Character (1)
徽安 ANHWEI	皖 Huan

Also An-hwi, Anhui, now Anhui

江浙 CHEKIANG	浙 Che

Also Cheh-kiang, now Zhejiang

隸直 CHIHLI	直 Chih

Also Hopei (after 1928) now Hebei

清大
CH'ING DYNASTY

Tai Ch'ing, also Tsing Dynasty now Qing Dynasty

江清 CHING-KIANG	淮 Huai

Also Tsing-kiang now Qingjiang

天奉 FENGTIEN	奉 Feng

Also Fung-tien, Fun-tien Shengching, Manchurian Provinces, now Liaoning

建福 FUKIEN	閩 Min

Also Foo-kien, F.K., now Fujian

江龍黑 HEILUNGKIANG	黑 Hei

Also Hei Lung Kiang, now Heilongjiang

南河 HONAN	豫 Yu

Also Ho-nan, now Henan

北河 HOPEH	冀 Chi

Also Chihli, Hopei, now Hebei

南湖 HUNAN	湘 Hsiang

Also Hu-nan

北湖 HUPEH	 O

Also Hupei, Hu-peh, now Hubei

部戶 HU PU (Board of Revenue)	 Hu

Also Hu Poo, Hoo Poo

肅甘 KANSU	甘 Kan

Now Gansu

南江 KIANGNAN	 Ning

Also Kiang Nan, now Jiangnan

西江 KIANGSI	 Kan	or	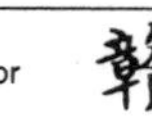

Also Kiang-si, Kiang-see, now Jiangxi

蘇江 KIANGSU	 Su

Also Kiang-soo, now Jiangsu

林吉 KIRIN	 Chi

Also Chi-lin, now Jilin

西廣 KWANGSI, KWANGSEA	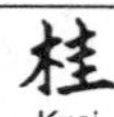 Kuei

Also Kwang-si, now Guangxi

東廣 KWANGTUNG	 Yüeh

Also Kwang-tung, now Guangdong

州貴 KWEICHOW	 Ch'ien

Also Kweichou, now Guizhou

洋北
PEIYANG MINT (Tientsin)

Also Pei Yang

西山 SHANSI	山 Shan

Now Shanxi (Chin)

西陝 SHENSI	陝 Shan

Also Shen-si, now Shaanxi

東山 SHANTUNG	東

Also Shang-tung, Shan-tung, now Shandong (Lu)

SIKANG

疆新 SINKIANG (Chinese Turkestan)	新 Hsin

Also Sin-kiang, Hsin-kiang Sungarei, now Xinjiang

川四 SZECHUAN	川 Ch'uan	蜀

Also Szechwan Szechuen, now Sichuan (Shu)

灣臺 TAIWAN	臺 T'ai

Also Tai-wan, now Taiwan

灣台 TAIWAN	台 T'ai

(Alternate)

南雲 YÜNNAN	雲 Yün	滇 (Alternate) (Tien)

Also Yün-nan, now Yunnan

TUNG SAN SHENG

Manchuria

滇川
YUNNAN-SZECHUAN

ADDITIONAL CHARACTERS

The additional characters illustrated and defined below are found on the reverse of cast bronze cash coins, usually above the square center hole. In the period covered by this catalog the following mints produced cash coins with these additional marks: Board of Revenue and Board of Works in Peking, Kweichow, Aksu and Ili in Sinkiang, Shantung, Szechuan, and all three mints listed in Yünnan.

CHARACTERS

一	I, YI	十	Shih I	心	Hsin
二	Erh	合	Ho	宇	Yu
三	San	工	Kung	宙	Chou
四	Szu	主	Chu	來	Lai
五	Wu	川	Ch'uan	往	Wang
六	Liu	之	Chih	晋	Chin
七	Ch'i	正	Cheng	村	Ts'un

八	Pa	又	Yu	日	Jih
九	Chiu	山	Shan	列	Lieh
十	Shih	大	Ta	仁	Jen
中	Chung	丰	Feng	上	Shang
順	Shun	云	Yun	手	Shou
天	T'ien	利	Li	穴	Kung
分	Fen				

MINT MARK IDENTIFIER

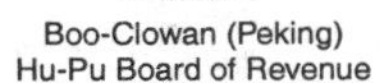

Boo-Clowan (Peking)
Hu-Pu Board of Revenue

Boo-Yuwan (Peking)
Kung-Pu Board of Public Works

Boo-hu
Hu Mint
ANHWEI

Boo-Je
Chê Mint
Hangchow
CHEKIANG

Boo-Jiyen
Chih Mint
Paoting
CHIHLI

Boo-GI
Chi Mint
Chichou
CHIHLI

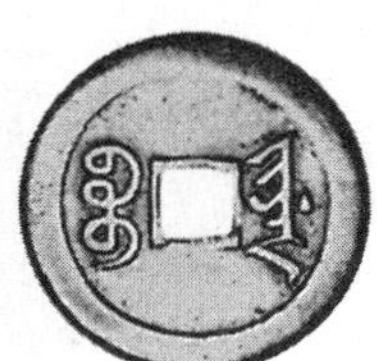

Boo-Jiyen
Ching Mint
Tientsin
CHIHLI

Boo-De
Ch'eng-te (Chengde) Mint
Jehol
CHIHLI
(Through Hsien-Feng era)

Boo-Fung
Fung Mint
FENGTIEN

Boo-Fu
Fu Mint
Fuchou
FUKIEN

Boo-Ho
Ho Mint
K'aifeng
HONAN

Boo-Nan
Nan Mint
Ch'ang-sha
HUNAN

Boo-De
Teh Mint
Chengte
CHIHLI

Boo-U
Wu Mint
Wuch'ang
HUPEH

Boo-Gung
Kung Mint
Kungchang
KANSU

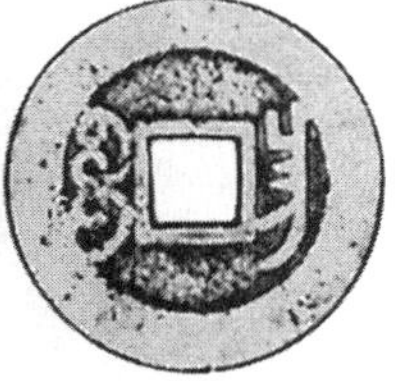

Boo-ch'ang
Ch'ang Mint
Nanchang
KIANGSI

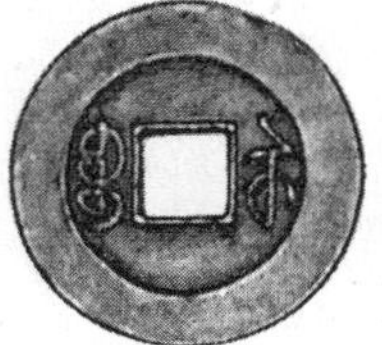

Boo-Su
Su Mint
Soohow
KIANGSU

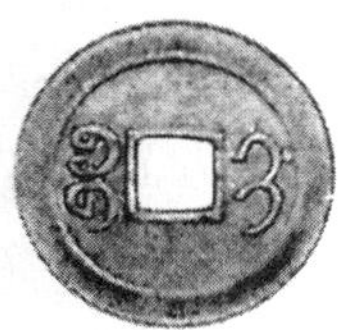

Boo-Gi
Chi Mint

KIRIN

Boo-Gui
Kue Mint
Kuelin
KWANGSI

Boo-Guwang
Kuang Mint
Canton
KWANGTUNG

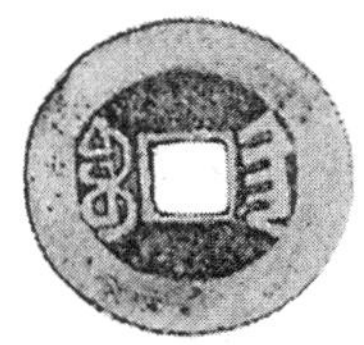

Boo-Giyan
Kwei Mint
Kweiyang
KWEICHOW

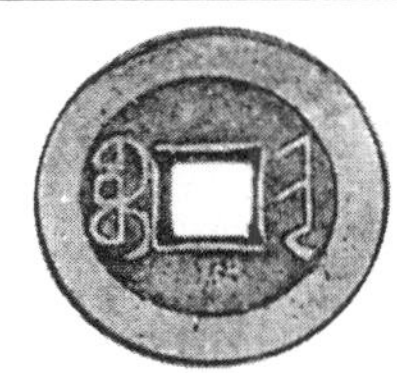

Boo-Jin
Chin Mint
Taiyuan
SHANSI

Boo-Ji
Chi Mint
Chinan
SHANTUNG

Boo-Cuwan
Chuan Mint
Chengtu
SZECHUAN

Boo-San
Shan Mint
Sian
SHENSI

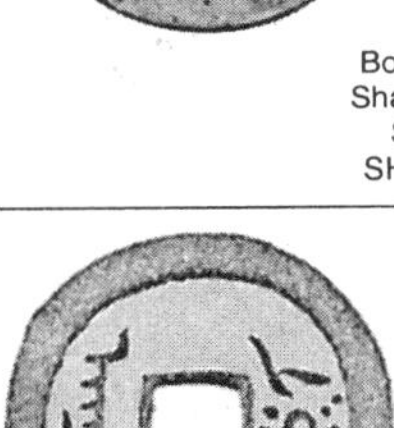

Aksu (Hocheng)
SINKIANG

Boo-Yi
Ili (Hweiyuan)
SINKIANG

Kotsha (Kuche)
SINKIANG

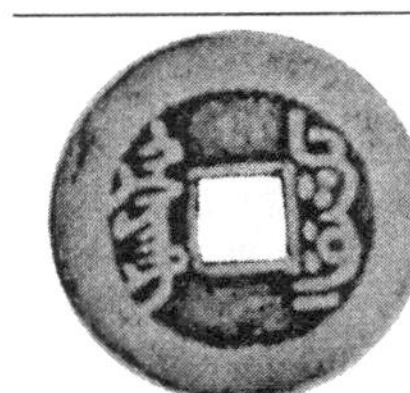

Kashgar (Shufu)
SINKIANG

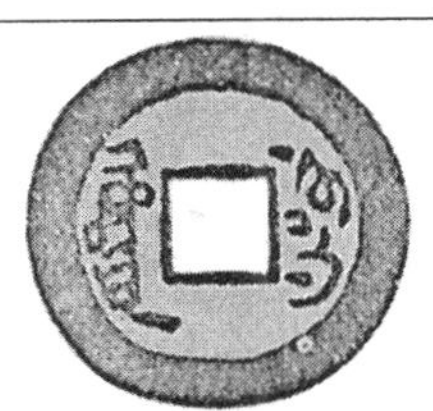

Khotan (Hotien)
SINKIANG

Boo-Di
Di Mint
Urumchi (Tihwa)
SINKIANG

Ushi (Wushih)
SINKIANG

Yarkand (Soche)
SINKIANG

Boo-Tai
Tai Mint
TAIWAN

Boo-Yôn
Yûn Mint
Yûnnan Fu
YUNNAN

Boo-Dong
Tung Mint
Tungch'uan
YUNNAN

Boo-Gu
Ku Mint
Taku Naval Arsenal
TIENTSIN, CHIHLI

Boo-Fu
Fu Mint
Fuchow
YUNNAN

Boo-Jing
Ching Mint
Chingchow Fu
HUPEH

ENGRAVED MASTER COINS

Not to be confused with actual patterns. Illustrated is a One Cash engraved master for the Kung-pu Board of Public Works Mint.

After a new coin design is drawn up, a master coin is engraved from quality copper and presented to the emperor for inspection and approval. The aperture is left unfinished, with only a small hole bored through the center, called 'Golden mouth'. Upon approval, the aperture is processed into the commonly seen square hole with rims around it; the golden mouth is now 'opened' and the finished master coin is ready to imprint molds for casting mother coins. The engraved masters are also called 'Grandparents' coins. (Courtesy of David Jen, author of *Chinese Cash*, ©2000 Krause Publications.)

NON-CIRCULATING ISSUES

Along with regular circulation coinage produced by the various mints certain cash types were cast in various sizes with the emperor's reign title on the obverse but with various characters and/or symbols not found in our mint identifiers. This listing is not complete but it will benefit the collector as an aid to proper identification.

PALACE ISSUES

(Palace Cash)

Usually 1-6 mace in weight, made of 60" copper and 40" zinc. Made for distribution in the palace during new year. Usually given to eunuchs and guards. Recipients hung them under lamps - "lamp 'hanging' money."

Tao-kuang, 1821-1851

"Unify the whole country"
Obv. inscription: Hsien-fêng T'ung-pao
Rev. inscription: I-t'ung T'ien-hsia

Hsien-fêng, 1851-1861

"Unify the whole country"
Obv. inscription: Hsien-fêng T'ung-pao
Rev. inscription: I-t'ung T'ien-hsia

T'ung-chih, 1862-1875

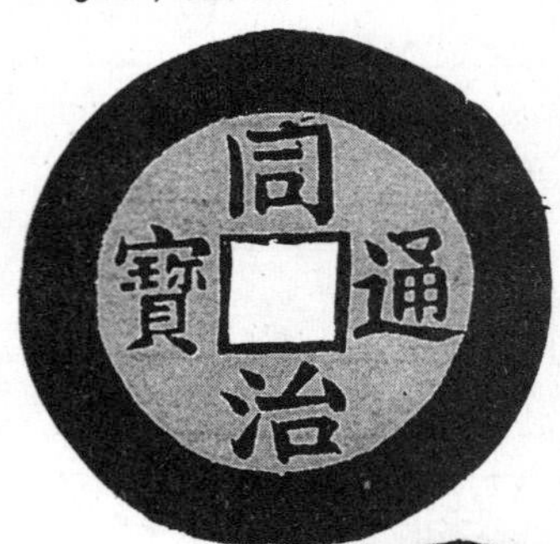

"Peace under heaven"
Obv. inscription: T'ung-chih T'ung-pao
Rev. inscription: T'ien-hsia T'ai-ping

Kuang-hsü, 1875-1908

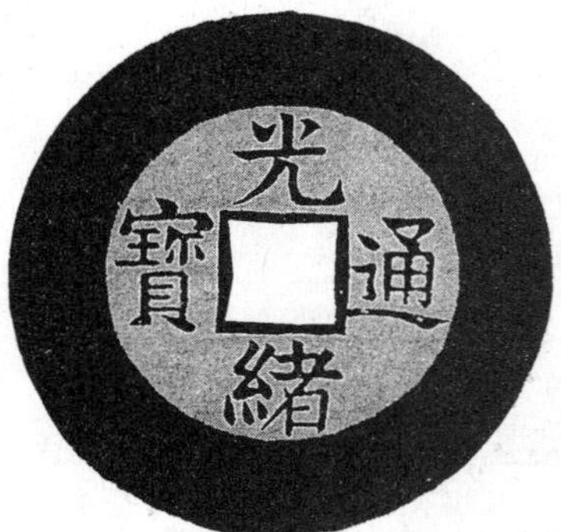

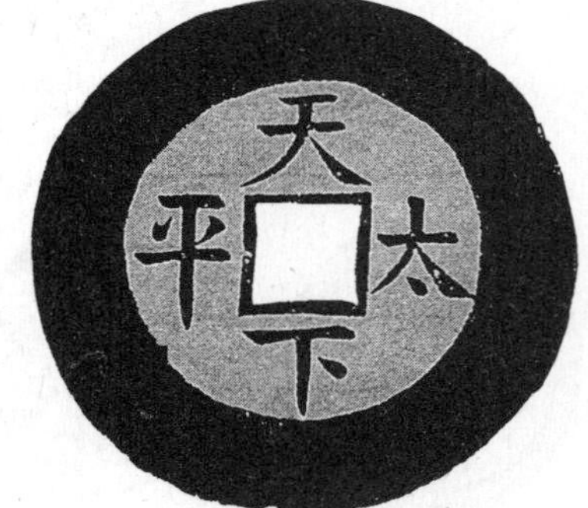

"Peace under heaven"
Obv. inscription: Kuang-hsü T'ung-pao
Rev. inscription: T'ien-hsia T'ai-ping

BIRTHDAY CASH

壽福

These issues have the normal reign title on the obverse but the reverse has two Chinese characters *Fu* in normal or seal script (happiness), at right and *Shou* (birthday) at left. The market value is about $60.00-100.00 in F/VF condition. Some are palaceissues, but most are made by private sources as good luck amulets

Hsien-fêng

T'ung-chih

Kuang-hsü

AMULETS

Eight Trigrams

The eight trigrams (Pa Kua) of the Book of Changes (I Ching). This book, one of the Five Classics, consists of a set of sixty-four figures known as "trigrams". The trigram is composed of combinations of pairs of eight trigrams each of which represents some power in nature, either active or passive, such as fire, water, thunder, earth, etc. These trigrams are said to have been invented 2000 years and more B.C. by the legendary monarch Fu Hsi, who copied them from the back of a tortoise. Attached to each hexagram are explanatory notes and expository comments. The notes are said to have been written by the Chou King Wen Wang and the comments by Confucius. The notes are made in symbolic language which only mystics could understand, but the comments are written in plain language. These comments have lifted the Book of Changes from a primitive book of divination and oracles to an ethical and philosophical importance. The market value is about $30.00-40.00 in VF condition. Many cash coins have been privately decorated with engraved designs on the rims, in the fields, or both, to convert them to amulets.

NUMERALS

NUMBER	CONVENTIONAL	FORMAL	COMMERCIAL
1	一 元	壹 弌	〡
2	二	弍 貳	〢
3	三	叁 弎	〣
4	四	肆	〤
5	五	伍	〥
6	六	陸	〦
7	七	柒	〧
8	八	捌	〨
9	九	玖	〩
10	十	拾 什	十
20	十 二 or 廿	拾貳	〢十
25	五 十 二 or 五廿	伍拾貳	〢十〥
30	十 三 or 卅	拾叁	〣十
100	百 一	佰壹	〡百
1,000	千 一	仟壹	〡千
10,000	萬 一	萬壹	〡万
100,000	萬十 億 一	萬拾 億壹	十万
1,000,000	萬百一	萬佰壹	〡百万

NOTE: This table has been adapted from *Chinese Bank Notes* by Ward Smith and Brian Matravers.

MONETARY UNITS

Dollar Amounts		
DOLLAR *(Yuan)*	元 or 員	圓 or 圜
HALF DOLLAR *(Pan Yuan)*	圓 半	元中
50¢ *(Chiao/Hao)*	角伍	毫伍
10¢ *(Chiao/Hao)*	角壹	毫壹
1¢ *(Fen/Hsien)*	分壹	仙壹

Copper and Cash Coin Amounts			
COPPER *(Mei)*	枚	CASH *(Wen)*	文

Tael Amounts	
1 TAEL *(Liang)*	兩
HALF TAEL *(Pan Liang)*	兩半
5 MACE *(Wu Ch'ien)*	錢伍
1 MACE *(I Ch'ien)*	錢壹
1 CANDEREEN *(I Fen)*	分壹

Common Prefixes			
COPPER *(T'ung)*	銅	GOLD *(Chin)*	金
SILVER *(Yin)*	銀	Ku Ping *(Tael)**	平庫

NOTE: This table has been adapted from Chinese Bank Notes by Ward Smith and Brian Matravers.

MONETARY SYSTEM

Cash Coin System

800-1600 Cash = 1 Tael
400 Sinkiang 'red' cash = 1 Tael

In theory, 1000 cash were equal to a tael of silver, but in actuality the rate varied from time to time and place to place.

Dollar System

10 Cash (Wen, Ch'ien) = 1 Cent (Fen, Hsien)
10 Cents = 1 Chiao (Hao)
100 Cents = 1 Dollar (Yuan)
1 Dollar = 0.72 Tael

Imperial silver coins normally bore no denomination, but were inscribed with their weights as follows:

1 Dollar = 7 Mace and 2 Candareens
50 Cents = 3 Mace and 6 Candareens
20 Cents = 1 Mace and 4.4 Candareens
10 Cents = 7.2 Candareens
5 Cents = 3.6 Candareens

NOTE: *Candareen* is spelled *Candarin* and misspelled as *Caindarin* on Kirin Province Imperial coinage.

Tael System

10 Li = 1 Fen (Candareen)
10 Fen (Candareen) = 1 Ch'ien (Mace)
10 Ch'ien (Mace) = 1 Liang (Tael)

CYCLICAL DATES

	庚	辛	壬	癸	甲	乙	丙	丁	戊	己
戌	1850 1910		1862 1922		1874 1934		1886 1946		1838 1898	
亥		1851 1911		1863 1923		1875 1935		1887 1947		1839 1899
子	1840 1900		1852 1912		1864 1924		1876 1936		1888 1948	
丑		1841 1901		1853 1913		1865 1925		1877 1937		1889 1949
寅	1830 1890		1842 1902		1854 1914		1866 1926		1878 1938	
卯		1831 1891		1843 1903		1855 1915		1867 1927		1879 1939
辰	1880 1940		1832 1892		1844 1904		1856 1916		1868 1928	
巳		1881 1941		1833 1893		1845 1905		1857 1917		1869 1929
午	1870 1930		1882 1942		1834 1894		1846 1906		1858 1918	
未		1871 1931		1883 1943		1835 1895		1847 1907		1859 1919
申	1860 1920		1872 1932		1884 1944		1836 1896		1848 1908	
酉		1861 1921		1873 1933		1885 1945		1837 1897		1849 1909

NOTE: This table has been adapted from *Chinese Bank Notes* by Ward Smith and Brian Matravers.

GRADING

Chinese coins should not be graded entirely by western standards. In addition to Fine, Very Fine, Extremely Fine (XF), and Uncirculated, the type of strike should be considered weak, medium or sharp strike. China had no rigid minting rules as we know them. For instance, Kirin (Jilin) and Sinkiang (Xinjiang) Provinces used some dies made of iron - hence, they wore out rapidly. Some communist army issues were apparently struck by crude hand methods on soft dies (it is hard to find two coins of the same die!). In general, especially for some minor coins, dies were used until they were worn well beyond western standards. Subsequently, one could have an uncirculated coin struck from worn dies with little of the design or letters still visible, but still uncirculated! All prices quoted are for well-struck (sharp struck), well-centered specimens. Most silver coins can be found from very fine to uncirculated. Some copper coins are difficult to find except in poorer grades.

REFERENCES

The following references have been used for this section:

K - Edward Kann - Illustrated Catalog of Chinese Coins.

Hsu - T.K. Hsu - Illustrated Catalog of Chinese Coins, 1981 edition.

W - A.M. Tracey Woodward - "The Minted Ten-Cash Coins of China".

RACKATEER COINAGE

NOTE: The die struck 10 and 20 Cash coins are often found silver plated. This was not done at the mint. They were apparently plated to be passed to the unwary as silver coins.

IDENTIFICATION

(1900)
Made in Kiangnan Province

Candareens/2/Mace/7/Treasury Scales

Central leg: Kuang Hsü Yuan Pao
Coin of Kuang Hsü

DRAGON TYPES

(Chinese Imperial Coins)

Side View Dragon-left (Silver Coins)

First used by the Kwangtung Mint in 1889. This was the standard (though not the only) dragon used on silver coins. Normally there is no circle around the dragon. Note the fireball beneath the dragon's chin. Normally there are seven flames on the fireball.

Side View Dragon-left (Copper Coins)

First used on copper coins in 1901 or 1902. The dragon may be circled or uncircled. Many varieties exist, with three to seven flames on the fireball.

Side View Dragon-right (Silver Coins)

First appears on the second series of Fukien. The dragon is redesigned with the dragon's body reversed.

Flying Dragon

Introduced in 1901. Copied from the dragon on Japanese coins. China used this dragon only on copper coins (with one rare exception). Note that the clouds around the dragon's body are curly and snake-like instead of puffy like those around the side-view dragon. The fireball now appears as a pearl which the dragon is about to grasp, and normally has no flames. This dragon is normally circled.

Front View Dragon

Introduced about 1904, this type of dragon was not used by many mints. The dragon is usually uncircled and has few clouds around its body. Note the tiny mountain under the cloud beneath the fireball.

Tai Ch'ing Ti Kuo Dragon

In 1905 China carried out a coinage reform which standardized the designs of copper coins. All mints were ordered to use the same obverse and reverse designs, but to place a mint mark in the center of the obverse.

Sycee (Ingots)

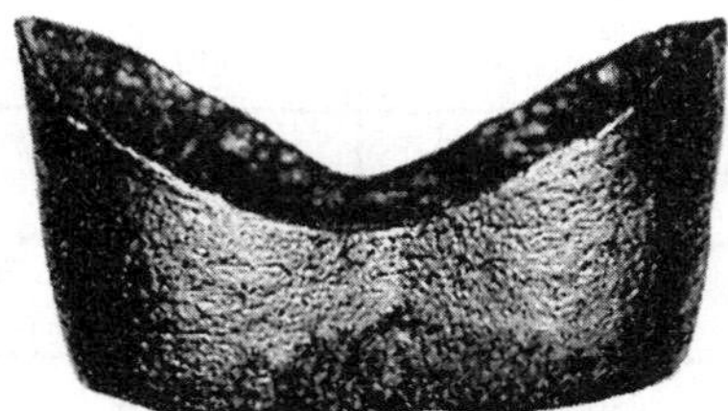

Prior to 1889 the general coinage issued by the Chinese government was the copper-alloy cash coin. Despite occasional shortlived experiments with silver and gold coinage, and disregarding paper money which tended to be unreliable, the government expected the people to get by solely with cash coins. This system worked well for individuals making purchases for themselves, but was unsatisfactory for trade and large business transactions, since a dollar's worth of cash coins weighed about four pounds. As a result, a private currency consisting of silver ingots, usually stamped by the firm which made them, came into use. These were the sycee ingots.

It is not known when these ingots first came into use. Some sources date them to the Yuan (Mongol) dynasty but they are certainly much older. Examples are known from as far back as the Han dynasty (206 BC - 220 AD) but prior to the Sung era (960 - 1280AD) they were used mainly for hoarding wealth. The development of commerce by the Sung dynasty, however, required the use of silver or gold to pay for large purchases. By the Mongol period (1280-1368) silver ingots and paper money had become the dominant currencies, especially for trade. The western explorers who traveled to China during this period (such as Marco Polo) mention both paper money and sycee but not a single one refers to cash coins.

During the Ming dynasty (1368-1644) trade fell off and the use of silver decreased. But toward the end of that dynasty, Dutch and British ships began a new China trade and sycee once again became common. During the 19th and early 20th centuries, the trade in sycee became enormous. Most of the sycee around today are from this period. In 1935 the Chinese government and in 1939 Sinkiang banned the use of sycee and it soon disappeared.

The word sycee (pronounced "sigh - see") is a western corruption of the Chinese word hsi-szu ("fine silk") or hsi yin ("fine silver") and is first known to have appeared in the English language in the late 1600's. By the early 1700's the word appeared regularly in the records of the British East India Company. Westerners also called these ingots "boat money" or "shoe money" owing to the fact that the most common type of ingot resembles a Chinese shoe. The Chinese, however, called the ingots by a variety of names, the most common of which were yuan pao, wen -yin (fine silver) and yin-ting (silver ingot).

The ingots were cast in molds (giving them their characteristic shapes) and while the metal was still semi-liquid, the inscription was impressed. It was due to this procedure that the sides of some sycee are higher than the center. The manufacturers were usually silver firms, often referred to as lu fang's, and after the sycee was finished it was occasionally tested and marked by the kung ku (public assayer).

Sycee were not circulated as we understand it. One didn't usually carry a sycee to market and spend it. Usually the ingots were used as a means of carrying a large amount of money on trips (as we would carry $100 bills instead of $5 bills) or for storing wealth. Large transactions between merchants or banks were paid by means of crates of sycee - each containing 60 fifty tael ingots.

Sycee are known in a variety of shapes the most common of which are the shoe or boat shaped, drum shaped, and loaf shaped (rectangular or hourglass-shaped, with a generally flat surface). Other shapes include one that resembles a double headed axe (this is the oldest type known), one that is square and flat, and others that are "fancy" (in the form of fish, butterflies, leaves, etc.).

Sycee have no denominations as they were simply ingots that passed by weight. Most are in more or less standard weights, however, the most common being 1, 5, 10 and 50 taels. Other weights known include 1/10, 1/5, 1/4, 1/3, 1/2, 2/3, 72/100 (this is the weight of a dollar), 3/4, 2, 3, 4, 6, 7, 8 and 25 taels. Most of the pieces weighing less than 5 taels were used as gifts or souvenirs.

The actual weight of any given value of sycee varied considerably due to the fact that the tael was not a single weight but a general term for a wide range of local weight standards. The weight of the tael varied depending upon location and type of tael in question. For example in one town, the weight of a tael of rice, of silver and of stones may each be different. In addition, the fineness of silver also varied depending upon location and type of tael in question. It was not true, as westerners often wrote, that sycee were made of pure silver. For most purposes, a weight of 37 grams may be used for the tael.

Weights and Current Market Value of Sycee

(Weights are approximate)

1/2 Tael	17-19 grams	26.00
72/100 Tael	25-27 grams	36.00
1 Tael	35-38 grams	46.00
2 Taels	70-75 grams	70.00
3 Taels	100-140 grams	85.00
5 Taels	175-190 grams	110.00
7 Taels	240-260 grams	125.00
10 Taels	350-380 grams	250.00
25 Taels	895-925 grams	3500.00
50 Taels	1790-1850 grams	2000.00
50 Taels, square	1790-1850 grams	1600.00

REFERENCE

Catalog reference Schjöth #: "Chinese Currency" by Fredrik Schjöth c.1965 by Virgil Hancock, published by Krause Publications, Iola, Wisconsin, U.S.A.

EMPIRE

CH'ING DYNASTY

Manchu, 1644 - 1911

Chia-ch'ing

CAST COINAGE

KM# 440.1 CASH

Cast Brass **Obv. Inscription:** Chia-ch'ing T'ung-pao. **Reverse:** Manchu "Boo-ciowan" **Mint:** Hu-pu Board of Revenue

Date	Mintage	Good	VG	F	VF	XF
ND(1796-1820)	—	0.20	0.35	0.50	0.75	—

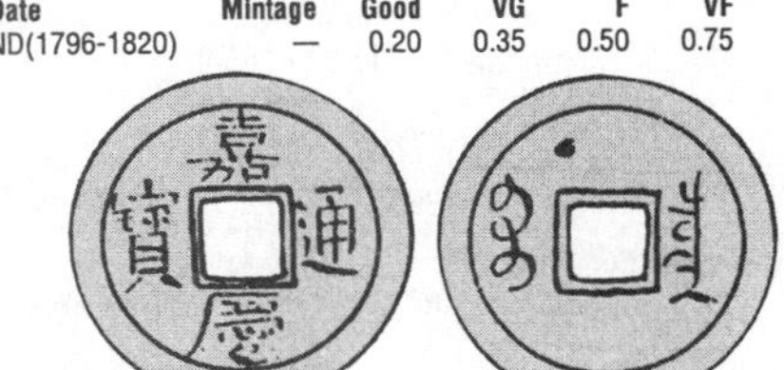

KM# 440.2 CASH
Cast Brass **Obv. Inscription:** Chia-ch'ing T'ung-pao. **Reverse:** Manchu Boo-ciowan" with dot at upper left. **Mint:** Hupu **Note:** Schjöth #1489.

Date	Mintage	Good	VG	F	VF	XF
ND(1796-1820)	—	2.00	3.50	5.00	7.00	—

KM# 440.3 CASH
Cast Brass **Obv. Inscription:** Chia-ch'ing T'ung-pao. **Reverse:** Manchu "Boo-ciowan" with dot below. **Mint:** Hu-pu Board of Revenue

Date	Mintage	Good	VG	F	VF	XF
ND(1796-1820)	—	2.00	3.50	5.00	7.00	—

KM# 441 CASH
Cast Brass **Obv. Inscription:** Chia-ch'ing T'ung-pao. **Reverse:** Manchu "Boo-ciowan". **Mint:** Hu-pu Board of Revenue **Note:** Size varies 28-30mm.

Date	Mintage	Good	VG	F	VF	XF
ND(1796-1820)	—	10.00	17.50	25.00	35.00	—

KM# 442.1 CASH
Cast Brass **Obv. Inscription:** Chia-ch'ing T'ung-pao. **Reverse:** Manchu "Boo-yuwan". **Mint:** Kungpu **Note:** Schjöth #1490.

Date	Mintage	Good	VG	F	VF	XF
ND(1796-1820)	—	0.20	0.30	0.50	0.75	—

KM# 442.2 CASH
Cast Brass, 24 mm. **Obv. Inscription:** Chia-ch'ing T'ung-pao. **Reverse:** Manchu "Boo-yuwan" with dot above. **Mint:** Kungpu **Note:** Schjöth #1489.

Date	Mintage	Good	VG	F	VF	XF
ND(1796-1820)	—	2.00	3.00	5.00	7.50	—

KM# 442.3 CASH
Cast Brass **Obv. Inscription:** Chia-ch'ing T'ung-pao. **Reverse:** Manchu "Boo-yuwan" with dot below. **Mint:** Kungpu **Note:** Schjöth #1491.

Date	Mintage	Good	VG	F	VF	XF
ND(1796-1820)	—	2.00	3.00	5.00	7.50	—

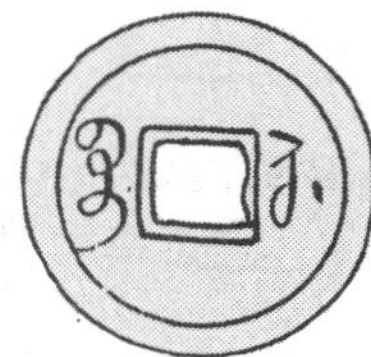

KM# 446 CASH
Cast Brass **Obv. Inscription:** Chia-ch'ing T'ung-pao. **Reverse:** Manchu "Boo-su". **Mint:** Soochow **Note:** Schjöth #1492.

Date	Mintage	Good	VG	F	VF	XF
ND(1796-1820)	—	0.85	1.35	2.00	3.00	—

KM# 447a CASH
Cast Brass **Obv. Inscription:** Chia-ch'ing T'ung-pao **Note:** Wide rims.

Date	Mintage	Good	VG	F	VF	XF
ND(1796-1820)	—	35.00	60.00	85.00	120	—

KM# 449 CASH
Cast Brass **Obv. Inscription:** Chia-ch'ing T'ung-pao. **Reverse:** Manchu "Boo-guwang". **Mint:** Kuangtung **Note:** Schjöth #1493.

Date	Mintage	Good	VG	F	VF	XF
ND(1796-1820)	—	0.85	1.35	2.00	3.00	—

KM# 449a CASH
Cast Iron **Obv. Inscription:** Chia-ch'ing T'ung-pao. **Reverse:** Manchu "Boo-guwang". **Mint:** Kuang

Date	Mintage	Good	VG	F	VF	XF
ND(1796-1820) Rare	—	—	—	—	—	—

KM# 451 CASH
Cast Brass **Obv. Inscription:** Chia-ch'ing T'ung-pao. **Reverse:** Manchu "Boo-nan". **Mint:** Ch'angsha **Note:** Schjöth #1494.

Date	Mintage	Good	VG	F	VF	XF
ND(1796-1820)	—	1.50	2.50	3.50	5.00	—

KM# 453.1 CASH
Cast Brass **Obverse:** Type A **Obv. Inscription:** Chia-ch'ing T'ung-pao. **Reverse:** Manchu "Boo-yôn". **Mint:** Yünnan-fu **Note:** Schjöth #1495.

Date	Mintage	Good	VG	F	VF	XF
ND(1796-1820)	—	0.40	0.70	1.00	1.50	—

KM# 453.2 CASH
Cast Brass **Obv. Inscription:** Chia-ch'ing T'ung-pao. **Reverse:** Manchu "Boo-yôn" with dot at upper right. **Mint:** Yünnan-fu **Note:** Schjöth #1496.

Date	Mintage	Good	VG	F	VF	XF
ND(1796-1820)	—	1.25	2.00	2.75	4.00	—

KM# 453.3 CASH
Cast Brass **Obv. Inscription:** Chia-ch'ing T'ung-pao. **Reverse:** Manchu "Boo-yôn" with crescent above. **Mint:** Yünnan-fu **Note:** Schjöth #1497.

Date	Mintage	Good	VG	F	VF	XF
ND(1796-1820)	—	1.75	3.00	4.25	6.00	—

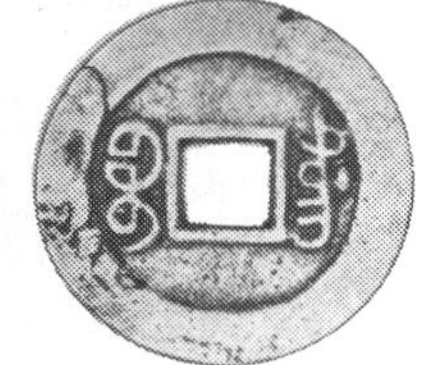

KM# 455 CASH
Cast Brass **Obverse:** Type A-1 **Obv. Inscription:** Chia-ch'ing T'ung-pao. **Reverse:** Type 1 mint mark, Manchu "Boo-dung". **Mint:** Tungch'uan **Note:** Schjöth #1498.

Date	Mintage	Good	VG	F	VF	XF
ND(1796-1820)	—	1.75	3.00	4.25	6.00	—

KM# 456 CASH
Cast Brass **Obv. Inscription:** Chia-ch'ing T'ung-pao. **Reverse:** Type 2 mint mark, Manchu "Boo-dung". **Mint:** Tungch'uan

Date	Mintage	Good	VG	F	VF	XF
ND(1796-1820)	—	10.00	17.50	25.00	35.00	—

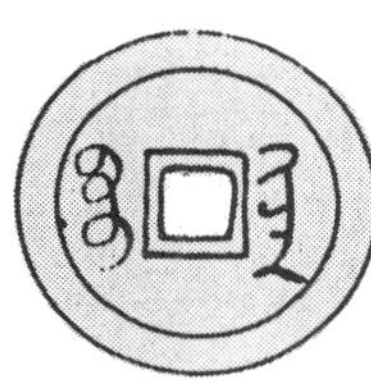

KM# 458.1 CASH
Cast Brass **Obv. Inscription:** Chia-ch'ing T'ung-pao. **Reverse:** Manchu "Boo-kiyan" **Mint:** Kweiyang **Note:** Schjöth #1499.

Date	Mintage	Good	VG	F	VF	XF
ND(1796-1820)	—	1.25	2.00	2.75	4.00	—

KM# 458.2 CASH
Cast Brass **Obv. Inscription:** Chia-ch'ing T'ung-pao. **Reverse:** Manchu "Boo-kiyan" with dot above. **Mint:** Kweiyang

Date	Mintage	Good	VG	F	VF	XF
ND(1796-1820)	—	1.50	2.50	3.50	5.00	—

KM# 460 CASH
Cast Brass **Obv. Inscription:** Chia-ch'ing T'ung-pao. **Reverse:** Manchu "Boo-kiyan" with Chinese "Êrh". **Mint:** Kweiyang

Date	Mintage	Good	VG	F	VF	XF
ND(1796-1820)	—	7.50	12.50	17.50	25.00	—

KM# 462 CASH
Cast Brass **Obv. Inscription:** Chia-ch'ing T'ung-pao. **Reverse:** Wide Manchu "Boo-fu". **Mint:** Foochou **Note:** Schjöth #1500.

Date	Mintage	Good	VG	F	VF	XF
ND(1796-1820)	—	0.85	1.35	2.00	3.00	—

KM# 463 CASH
Cast Brass **Obv. Inscription:** Chia-ch'ing T'ung-pao. **Reverse:** Thin Manchu "Boo-fu" at right. **Mint:** Fuchou

Date	Mintage	Good	VG	F	VF	XF
ND(1796-1820)	—	1.75	3.00	4.25	6.00	—

KM# 464 CASH
Cast Brass **Obv. Inscription:** Chia-ch'ing T'ung-pao. **Reverse:** Different Manchu "Boo-fu" at right. **Mint:** Fuchou

Date	Mintage	Good	VG	F	VF	XF
ND(1796-1820)	—	1.50	2.50	3.50	5.00	—

KM# 465 CASH
Cast Brass **Obverse:** Type A **Obv. Inscription:** Chia-ch'ing T'ung-pao. **Reverse:** Manchu Boo-jiyen **Mint:** Chih **Note:** Size varies 25-26mm. Schjöth #1501.

Date	Mintage	Good	VG	F	VF	XF
ND(1796-1820)	—	0.85	1.35	2.00	3.00	—

KM# 466 CASH
Cast Brass, 31 mm. **Obv. Inscription:** Chia-ch'ing T'ung-pao. **Reverse:** Manchu "Boo-j'i". **Mint:** Chihli

Date	Mintage	Good	VG	F	VF	XF
ND(1796-182)	—	60.00	100	140	200	—

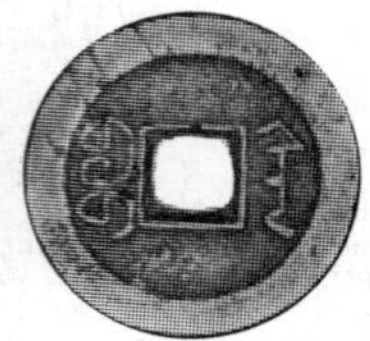

KM# 468 CASH
Cast Brass **Obverse:** Type A **Obv. Inscription:** Chia-ch'ing T'ung-pao. **Reverse:** Manchu "Boo-san". **Mint:** Sian **Note:** Schjöth #1502.

Date	Mintage	Good	VG	F	VF	XF
ND(1796-1820)	—	2.25	3.75	5.50	8.00	—

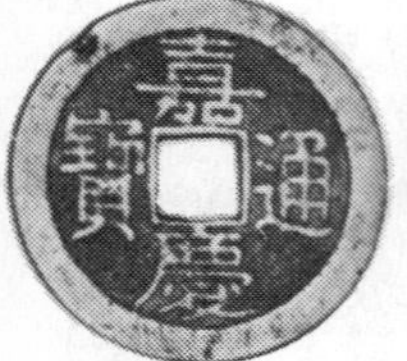

KM# 470.1 CASH
Cast Brass **Obv. Inscription:** Chia-ch'ing T'ung-pao. **Reverse:** Large mint mark and normal rims, Manchu "Boo-je". **Mint:** Hangchow **Note:** Schjöth #1503.

Date	Mintage	Good	VG	F	VF	XF
ND(1796-1820)	—	0.50	0.90	1.35	2.00	—

KM# 470.2 CASH
Cast Brass **Obv. Inscription:** Chia-ch'ing T'ung-pao. **Reverse:** Manchu "Boo-je" with dot at bottom. **Mint:** Hangchow

Date	Mintage	Good	VG	F	VF	XF
ND(1796-1820)	—	3.50	6.00	8.50	12.00	—

KM# 470a CASH
Cast Iron **Obv. Inscription:** Chia-ch'ing T'ung-pao. **Reverse:** Manchu "Boo-je". **Mint:** Hangchow

Date	Mintage	Good	VG	F	VF	XF
ND(1796-1820) Rare	—	—	—	—	—	—

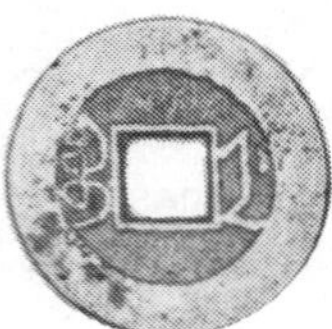

KM# 471 CASH
Cast Brass **Obv. Inscription:** Chia-ch'ing T'ung-pao. **Reverse:** Manchu "Boo-je" with small mint mark and wide rims. **Mint:** Hangchow

Date	Mintage	Good	VG	F	VF	XF
ND(1796-1820)	—	0.50	0.90	1.35	2.00	—

KM# 474.1 CASH
Cast Brass **Obv. Inscription:** Chia-ch'ing T'ung-pao. **Reverse:** Manchu "Boo-u". **Mint:** Wuch'ang **Note:** Schjöth #1504.

Date	Mintage	Good	VG	F	VF	XF
ND(1796-1820)	—	1.75	3.00	4.25	6.00	—

KM# 474.2 CASH
Cast Brass **Obv. Inscription:** Chia-ch'ing T'ung-pao. **Reverse:** Manchu "Wu" with circle above. **Mint:** Wuch'ang **Note:** Schjöth #1505.

Date	Mintage	Good	VG	F	VF	XF
ND(1796-1820)	—	4.00	6.50	9.00	12.00	—

KM# 474.3 CASH
Cast Brass **Obv. Inscription:** Chia-ch'ing T'ung-pao. **Reverse:** Manchu "Boo-u" with crescent above, dot below. **Mint:** Wuch'ang **Note:** Schjöth #1506.

Date	Mintage	Good	VG	F	VF	XF
ND(1796-1820)	—	4.00	7.00	10.00	15.00	—

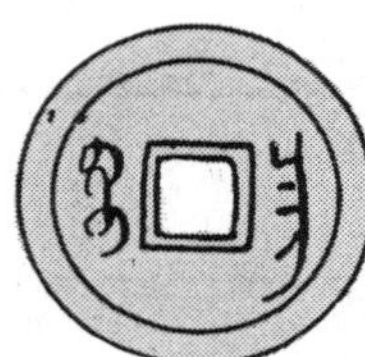

KM# 476.1 CASH
Cast Brass **Obv. Inscription:** Chia-ch'ing T'ung-pao. **Reverse:** Manchu "Boo-cang". **Mint:** Nanch'ang **Note:** Schjöth #1507.

Date	Mintage	Good	VG	F	VF	XF
ND(1796-1820)	—	0.50	0.90	1.35	2.00	—

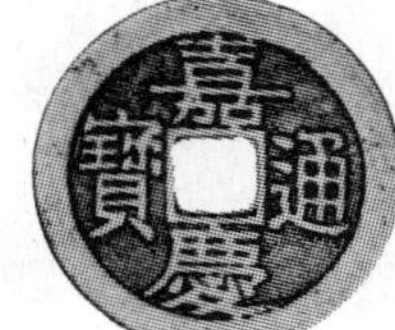

KM# 476.2 CASH
Cast Brass **Obv. Inscription:** Chia-ch'ing T'ung-pao. **Reverse:** Manchu "Boo-cang" with dot in upper left corner. **Mint:** Nanch'ang **Note:** Schjöth #1508 variation.

Date	Mintage	Good	VG	F	VF	XF
ND(1796-1820)	—	3.00	5.00	7.00	10.00	—

KM# 478 CASH
Cast Brass **Obv. Inscription:** Chia-ch'ing T'ung-pao. **Reverse:** Manchu "Boo-qui". **Mint:** Kuelin **Note:** Schjöth #1509.

Date	Mintage	Good	VG	F	VF	XF
ND(1796-1820)	—	0.75	1.00	1.75	3.00	—

KM# 480 CASH
Cast Brass **Obv. Inscription:** Chia-ch'ing T'ung-pao. **Reverse:** Manchu "Boo-cuwan". **Mint:** Chengtu **Note:** Schjöth #1510.

Date	Mintage	Good	VG	F	VF	XF
ND(1796-1820)	—	1.00	1.75	3.00	4.00	—

KM# 482 CASH
Cast Brass **Obv. Inscription:** Chia-ch'ing T'ung-pao. **Reverse:** Manchu "Boo-jin". **Mint:** T'aiyüan **Note:** Schjöth #1511.

Date	Mintage	Good	VG	F	VF	XF
ND(1796-1820)	—	1.25	2.00	2.75	4.00	—

Tao-kuang

Daoguang, 1821-1850

GENERAL CAST COINAGE

C# 2-3 CASH
Cast Brass **Obv. Inscription:** Tao-kuang T'ung-pao **Mint:** Kung-pu Board of Public Works

Date	Mintage	Good	VG	F	VF	XF
ND(1821-51)	—	0.30	0.40	0.60	1.00	—

C# 2-3.1 CASH
Cast Brass **Obv. Inscription:** Tao-kuang T'ung-pao **Reverse:** Dot above **Mint:** Kung-pu Board of Public Works

Date	Mintage	Good	VG	F	VF	XF
ND(1821-51)	—	2.50	4.00	6.00	7.50	—

C# 2-3.2 CASH
Cast Brass **Obv. Inscription:** Tao-kuang T'ung-pao **Reverse:** Dot below **Mint:** Kung-pu Board of Public Works

Date	Mintage	Good	VG	F	VF	XF
ND(1821-51)	—	2.50	4.00	6.00	7.50	—

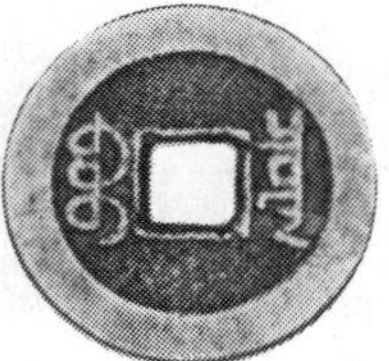

C# 1-3 CASH
Cast Brass **Obv. Inscription:** Tao-kuang T'ung-pao **Mint:** Hu-pu Board of Revenue **Note:** Schjöth #1512. Size varies: 20-26mm.

Date	Mintage	Good	VG	F	VF	XF
ND(1821-51)	—	0.20	0.30	0.40	0.75	—

C# 1-3.1 CASH
Cast Brass **Obv. Inscription:** Tao-kuang T'ung-pao **Mint:** Hu-pu Board of Revenue **Note:** Size varies: 28-30mm.

Date	Mintage	Good	VG	F	VF	XF
ND(1821-51)	—	10.00	14.00	18.00	24.00	—

C# 1-3.2 CASH
Cast Brass **Obv. Inscription:** Tao-kuang T'ung-pao **Reverse:** Dot above **Mint:** Hu-pu Board of Revenue **Note:** Schöth #1513.

Date	Mintage	Good	VG	F	VF	XF
ND(1821-51)	—	1.75	3.00	4.50	8.00	—

C# 1-3.3 CASH
Cast Brass **Obv. Inscription:** Tao-kuang T'ung-pao **Reverse:** Dot below **Mint:** Hu-pu Board of Revenue

Date	Mintage	Good	VG	F	VF	XF
ND(1821-51)	—	1.75	3.00	4.50	8.00	—

Hsien-fêng

GENERAL CAST COINAGE

C# 1-4b CASH
Cast Zinc **Obv. Inscription:** Hsien-fêng T'ung-pao **Mint:** Hu-pu Board of Revenue

Date	Mintage	Good	VG	F	VF	XF
ND1851-61) Rare	—	—	—	—	—	—

C# 2-4a CASH
Cast Iron **Obv. Inscription:** Hsien-fêng T'ung-pao **Mint:** Kung-pu Board of Public Works

Date	Mintage	Good	VG	F	VF	XF
ND(1851-61)	—	30.00	50.00	65.00	80.00	—

C# 2-4b CASH
Cast Zinc **Obv. Inscription:** Hsien-fêng T'ung-pao **Mint:** Kung-pu Board of Public Works

Date	Mintage	Good	VG	F	VF	XF
ND(1851-61) Rare	—	—	—	—	—	—

C# 1-4 CASH
Cast Brass **Obv. Inscription:** Hsien-fêng T'ung-pao **Mint:** Hu-pu Board of Revenue **Note:** Schjöth #1534.

Date	Mintage	Good	VG	F	VF	XF
ND(1851-61)	—	0.60	1.00	2.50	4.00	—

C# 2-4.1 CASH
Cast Brass **Obv. Inscription:** Hsien-fêng T'ung-pao **Mint:** Kung-pu Board of Public Works **Note:** Size varies: 20-24mm.

Date	Mintage	Good	VG	F	VF	XF
ND(1851-61)	—	1.00	1.50	3.00	4.00	—

C# 2-4 CASH
Cast Brass **Obv. Inscription:** Hsien-fêng T'ung-pao **Mint:** Kung-pu Board of Public Works **Note:** Wide rims.

Date	Mintage	Good	VG	F	VF	XF
ND(1851-61)	—	3.00	5.00	9.00	14.00	—

C# 1-4a CASH
Cast Iron **Obv. Inscription:** Hsien-fêng T'ung-pao **Mint:** Hu-pu Board of Revenue **Note:** Struck at Board of Revenue (Peking).

Date	Mintage	Good	VG	F	VF	XF
ND(1851-61)	—	7.50	10.00	15.00	30.00	—

C# 1-4.2a CASH
Cast Iron **Obv. Legend:** "Hsien-fêng T'ung-pao" **Note:** Struck at Board of Revenue (Peking).

Date	Mintage	Good	VG	F	VF	XF
ND(1851-61)	—	—	—	—	—	—

C# 1-5 5 CASH
Cast Brass **Obv. Inscription:** Hsien-feng Chung-pao **Mint:** Hu-pu Board of Revenue

Date	Mintage	Good	VG	F	VF	XF
ND(1851-61) Rare	—	—	—	—	—	—

C# 2-5a 5 CASH
Cast Brass **Obv. Inscription:** Hsien-fêng Chung-pao **Mint:** Kung-pu Board of Public Works **Note:**

Date	Mintage	Good	VG	F	VF	XF
ND(1851-61)	—	—	—	—	—	—

C# 2-5.1 5 CASH
Cast Brass **Obv. Inscription:** Hsien-fêng Chung-pao **Mint:** Kung-pu Board of Public Works **Note:** Size varies: 23-26mm.

Date	Mintage	Good	VG	F	VF	XF
ND(1851-61)	—	10.00	20.00	30.00	50.00	—

C# 2-5 5 CASH
Cast Brass **Obv. Inscription:** Hsien-fêng Chung-pao **Mint:** Kung-pu Board of Public Works **Note:** Size varies: 28-32mm.

Date	Mintage	Good	VG	F	VF	XF
ND(1851-61)	—	10.00	12.50	17.50	35.00	—

C# 2-6a 10 CASH
Cast Iron **Obverse:** Type B-2 **Obv. Inscription:** Hsien-fêng Chung-pao **Mint:** Kung-pu Board of Public Works

Date	Mintage	Good	VG	F	VF	XF
ND(1851-61) Rare	—	—	—	—	—	—

C# 1-6.1 10 CASH
Cast Brass **Obv. Inscription:** Hsien-fêng Chung-pao **Mint:** Hu-pu Board of Revenue **Note:** Size varies: 27-35mm.

Date	Mintage	Good	VG	F	VF	XF
ND(1851-61)	—	3.00	5.00	6.00	8.00	—

C# 2-6.1 10 CASH
Cast Brass **Obv. Inscription:** Hsien-fêng Chung-pao **Mint:** Kung-pu Board of Public Works **Note:** Size varies: 29-31mm.

Date	Mintage	Good	VG	F	VF	XF
ND(1851-61)	—	2.50	5.00	8.00	18.00	—

C# 2-6 10 CASH
Cast Brass **Obverse:** Type B-1 **Obv. Inscription:** Hsien-fêng Chung-pao **Mint:** Kung-pu Board of Public Works **Note:** Size varies: 33-38mm.

Date	Mintage	Good	VG	F	VF	XF
ND(1851-61)	—	2.50	5.00	8.00	18.00	—

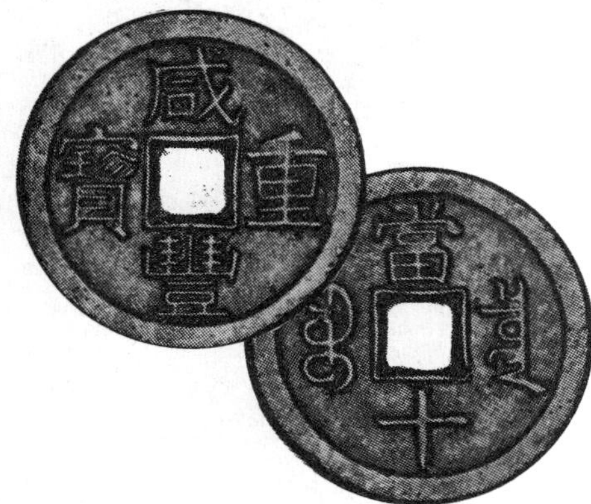

C# 1-6.2a 10 CASH
Cast Iron **Obverse:** Type B-2 **Obv. Inscription:** Hsien-fêng Chung-pao **Mint:** Hu-pu Board of Revenue **Note:** Size varies: 35-36mm. Varieties exist.

Date	Mintage	Good	VG	F	VF	XF
ND(1851-61)	—	30.00	45.00	75.00	225	—

C# 1-6 10 CASH
Cast Brass **Obverse:** Type B-1 **Obv. Inscription:** Hsien-fêng Chung-pao **Mint:** Hu-pu Board of Revenue **Note:** Size varies: 36-39mm.

Date	Mintage	Good	VG	F	VF	XF
ND(1851-61)	—	4.00	5.00	7.00	9.00	—

C# 1-6a 10 CASH
Cast Iron **Obv. Inscription:** Hsien-fêng Chung-pao **Mint:** Hu-pu Board of Revenue **Note:** Size varies: 37-39mm.

Date	Mintage	Good	VG	F	VF	XF
ND(1851-61)	—	10.00	15.00	25.00	40.00	—

C# 1-7.2 50 CASH
Cast Brass **Obv. Inscription:** Hsien-fêng Chung-pao **Reverse:** Dot upper right, crescent upper left **Mint:** Hu-pu Board of Revenue

Date	Mintage	Good	VG	F	VF	XF
ND(1851-61)	—	15.00	30.00	60.00	100	—

Note: Marked with a dot and crescent to indicate that they were issued by Ch'ing-hui, the Hereditary Prince of K'o-ch'in

C# 1-7a 50 CASH
Cast Iron **Obv. Inscription:** Hsien-fêng Chung-pao **Mint:** Hu-pu Board of Revenue

Date	Mintage	Good	VG	F	VF	XF
ND(1851-61) Rare	—	—	—	—	—	—

C# 1-7.1 50 CASH
Cast Brass **Obv. Inscription:** Hsien-fêng Chung-pao **Mint:** Hu-pu Board of Revenue **Note:** Size varies: 40-48mm.

Date	Mintage	Good	VG	F	VF	XF
ND(1851-61)	—	10.00	15.00	25.00	40.00	—

C# 2-7.1 50 CASH
Cast Brass **Obv. Inscription:** Hsien-fêng Chung-pao **Mint:** Kung-pu Board of Public Works **Note:** Size varies: 42-45mm.

Date	Mintage	Good	VG	F	VF	XF
ND(1851-61)	—	10.00	15.00	25.00	50.00	—

C# 2-7 50 CASH
Cast Brass **Obv. Inscription:** Hsien-fêng Chung-pao **Mint:** Kung-pu Board of Public Works **Note:** Size varies: 51-57mm.

Date	Mintage	Good	VG	F	VF	XF
ND(1851-61)	—	15.00	20.00	30.00	65.00	—

C# 1-7 50 CASH
Cast Brass **Obv. Inscription:** Hsien-fêng Chung-pao **Mint:** Hu-pu Board of Revenue **Note:** Size varies: 54-58mm.

Date	Mintage	Good	VG	F	VF	XF
ND(1851-61)	—	12.50	20.00	30.00	45.00	—

C# 1-8a 100 CASH
Cast Iron **Obv. Inscription:** Hsien-fêng Yüan-pao **Mint:** Hu-pu Board of Revenue

Date	Mintage	Good	VG	F	VF	XF
ND(1851-61) Rare	—	—	—	—	—	—

C# 1-8 100 CASH
Cast Brass **Obv. Inscription:** Hsien-fêng Yüan-pao **Mint:** Hu-pu Board of Revenue

Date	Mintage	Good	VG	F	VF	XF
ND(1851-61)	—	7.50	12.00	17.50	35.00	—

C# 1-8.1 100 CASH
Cast Brass **Obv. Inscription:** Hsien-fêng Yüan-pao **Mint:** Hu-pu Board of Revenue

Date	Mintage	Good	VG	F	VF	XF
ND(1851-61)	—	60.00	100	125	200	—

Note: Marked with a dot and crescent to indicate that they were issued by Ch'ing-hui, the hereditary Prince of K'o-ch'in

C# 2-8 100 CASH
50.4000 g., Cast Brass **Obv. Inscription:** Hsien-fêng Yüan-pao **Mint:** Kung-pu Board of Public Works **Note:** Size varies: 49-50mm.

Date	Mintage	Good	VG	F	VF	XF
ND(1851-61)	—	13.50	18.00	22.50	50.00	—

C# A1-10 300 CASH
Cast Brass **Mint:** Board of Revenue

Date	Mintage	Good	VG	F	VF	XF
ND(1851-61)	—	—	—	—	—	—

C# 1-10 500 CASH
Cast Copper, 55 mm. **Obv. Inscription:** Hsien-fêng Yüan-pac **Mint:** Hu-pu Board of Revenue

Date	Mintage	Good	VG	F	VF	X
ND(1851-61)	—	35.00	70.00	90.00	120	-

C# 1-10.2 500 CASH
Cast Brass **Obv. Inscription:** Hsien-fêng Yüan-pao **Reverse:** Dot at upper right and crescent at upper left **Mint:** Hu-pu Board of Revenue

Date	Mintage	Good	VG	F	VF	XF
ND(1851-61)	—	25.00	50.00	70.00	120	—

Note: Additional dot and crescent in reverse field to indicate they were issued by Ch'ing-hui, the hereditary Prince of K'o-ch'in

C# 2-9 500 CASH
Cast Brass **Obv. Inscription:** Hsien-fêng Yüan-pao **Mint:** Kung-pu Board of Public Works

Date	Mintage	Good	VG	F	VF	XF
ND(1851-61)	—	30.00	50.00	75.00	130	—

C# 2-9.1 500 CASH
Cast Copper **Obv. Inscription:** Hsien-fêng Yüan-pao **Mint:** Kung-pu Board of Public Works

Date	Mintage	Good	VG	F	VF	XF
ND(1851-61)	—	60.00	100	175	250	—

C# 1-10a 500 CASH
Cast Brass **Obv. Inscription:** Hsien-fêng Yüan-pao **Mint:** Hu-pu Board of Revenue **Note:** Size varies: 45-46mm.

Date	Mintage	Good	VG	F	VF	XF
ND(1851-61)	—	40.00	80.00	110	150	—

C# 1-10.1 500 CASH
Cast Brass **Obv. Inscription:** Hsien-fêng Yüan-pao **Mint:** Hu-pu Board of Revenue **Note:** Size varies: 56-58mm.

Date	Mintage	Good	VG	F	VF	XF
ND(1851-61)	—	25.00	35.00	55.00	85.00	—

C# 1-11.1 1000 CASH
Cast Brass **Obv. Inscription:** Hsien-fêng Yüan-pao **Reverse:** Dot at upper right and crescent at upper left **Mint:** Hu-pu Board of Revenue

Date	Mintage	Good	VG	F	VF	XF
ND(1851-61)	—	100	150	200	300	—

Note: Additional dot and crescent in reverse field to indicate they were issued by Ch'ing-hui, the hereditary Prince of K'o-ch'in.

C# 2-10 1000 CASH
Cast Brass **Obv. Inscription:** Hsien-fêng Yüan-pao **Mint:** Kung-pu Board of Public Works

Date	Mintage	Good	VG	F	VF	XF
ND(1851-61)	—	100	150	200	280	—

C# 1-11 1000 CASH
Cast Brass **Obv. Inscription:** Hsien-fêng Yüan-pao **Mint:** Hu-pu Board of Revenue **Note:** Size varies: 63-64mm.

Date	Mintage	Good	VG	F	VF	XF
ND(1851-61)	—	50.00	100	140	200	—

Ch'i-hsiang
1861
GENERAL CAST COINAGE

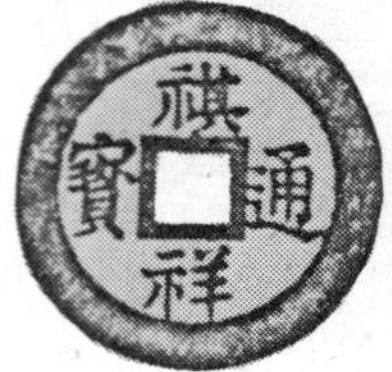

C# 1-12 CASH
Cast Brass **Obv. Inscription:** Ch'i-hsiang T'ung-pao **Mint:** Hu-pu Board of Revenue

Date	Mintage	Good	VG	F	VF	XF
ND(1861)	—	600	1,000	1,400	2,000	—

C# 2-11 CASH
Cast Brass **Obv. Inscription:** Ch'i-hsiang T'ung-pao **Mint:** Kung-pu Board of Public Works

Date	Mintage	Good	VG	F	VF	XF
ND(1861)	—	600	1,000	1,400	2,000	—

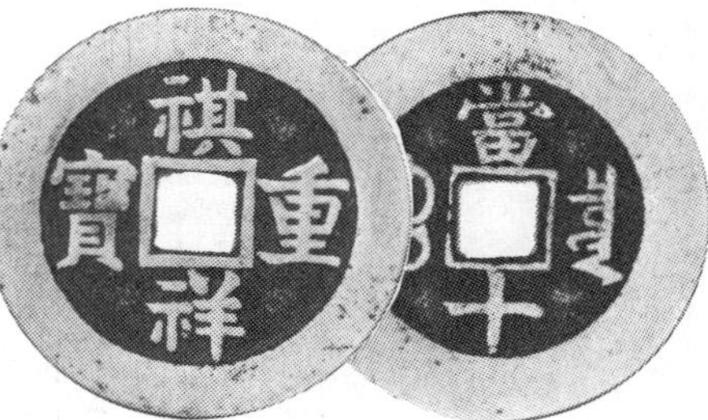

C# 1-13 10 CASH
Cast Brass **Obverse:** Type B-1 **Obv. Inscription:** Ch'i-hsiang T'ung-pao **Mint:** Hu-pu Board of Revenue

Date	Mintage	Good	VG	F	VF	XF
ND(1861)	—	700	1,250	1,800	2,500	—

C# 2-12 10 CASH
Cast Brass **Obv. Inscription:** Ch'i-hsiang Chung-pao **Mint:** Kung-pu Board of Public Works **Note:** Size varies: 34-35mm.

Date	Mintage	Good	VG	F	VF	XF
ND(1861)	—	300	500	700	1,000	—

T'ung-chih
GENERAL CAST COINAGE

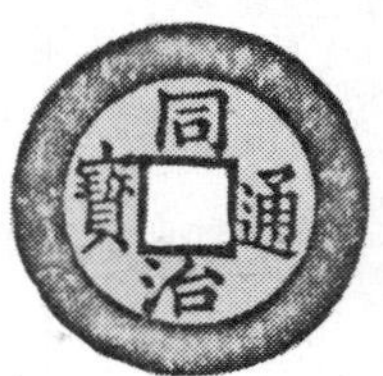

C# 1-14 CASH
Cast Brass **Obv. Inscription:** T'ung-chih T'ung-pao **Mint:** Hu-pu Board of Revenue

Date	Mintage	Good	VG	F	VF	XF
ND(1862-74)	—	3.50	5.50	8.50	15.00	—

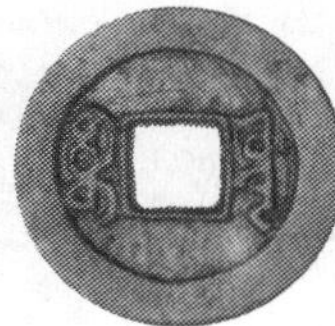

C# 2-13 CASH
Cast Brass **Obv. Inscription:** T'ung-chih T'ung-pao **Mint:** Kung-pu Board of Public Works

Date	Mintage	Good	VG	F	VF	XF
ND(1862-74)	—	0.60	1.00	1.40	2.00	—

C# 1-15.1 10 CASH
Cast Brass **Obv. Inscription:** T'ung-chih Chung-pao **Mint:** Hu-pu Board of Revenue **Note:** Size varies: 23-27mm.

Date	Mintage	Good	VG	F	VF	XF
ND(1862-74)	—	1.50	3.00	5.50	8.00	—

C# 1-15 10 CASH
Cast Brass **Obv. Inscription:** T'ung-chih Chung-pao **Mint:** Hu-pu Board of Revenue **Note:** Size varies: 28-33mm.

Date	Mintage	Good	VG	F	VF	XF
ND(1862-74)	—	1.50	3.00	5.50	10.00	—

C# 2-14 10 CASH
Cast Brass **Obv. Inscription:** T'ung-chih Chung-pao **Mint:** Kung-pu Board of Public Works **Note:** Size varies: 32-33mm.

Date	Mintage	Good	VG	F	VF	XF
ND(1862-74)	—	4.50	7.50	12.00	25.00	—

Kuang-hsü

GENERAL CAST COINAGE

C# 1-16 CASH
Cast Brass **Obv. Inscription:** Kuang-hsü T'ung-pao **Mint:** Hu-pu Board of Revenue

Date	Mintage	Good	VG	F	VF	XF
ND(1875-1908)	—	1.50	2.00	2.75	4.00	—

Note: For crude cast, red copper issues, see Sinkiang General coinage

C# 1-16.2 CASH
Cast Brass **Series:** Thousand Character Classic **Obv. Inscription:** Kuang-hsü T'ung-pao **Reverse:** "Chou" above **Mint:** Hu-pu Board of Revenue

Date	Mintage	Good	VG	F	VF	XF
ND(1875-1908)	—	6.00	9.00	13.50	20.00	—

C# 1-16.3 CASH
Cast Brass **Series:** Thousand Character Classic **Obv. Inscription:** Kuang-hsü T'ung-pao **Reverse:** "Jih" above **Mint:** Hu-pu Board of Revenue

Date	Mintage	Good	VG	F	VF	XF
ND(1875-1908)	—	6.00	9.00	13.50	20.00	—

C# 1-16.4 CASH
Cast Brass **Series:** Thousand Character Classic **Obv. Inscription:** Kuang-hsü T'ung-pao **Reverse:** "Lai" above **Mint:** Hu-pu Board of Revenue

Date	Mintage	Good	VG	F	VF	XF
ND(1875-1908)	—	6.00	9.00	13.50	20.00	—

C# 1-16.5 CASH
Cast Brass **Series:** Thousand Character Classic **Obv. Inscription:** Kuang-hsü T'ung-pao **Reverse:** "Lieh" above **Mint:** Hu-pu Board of Revenue

Date	Mintage	Good	VG	F	VF	XF
ND(1875-1908)	—	6.00	9.00	13.50	20.00	—

C# 1-16.6 CASH
Cast Brass **Series:** Thousand Character Classic **Obv. Inscription:** Kuang-hsü T'ung-pao **Reverse:** "Wang" above **Mint:** Hu-pu Board of Revenue

Date	Mintage	Good	VG	F	VF	XF
ND(1875-1908)	—	6.00	9.00	13.50	20.00	—

C# 1-16.7 CASH
Cast Brass **Series:** Thousand Character Classic **Obv. Inscription:** Kuang-hsü T'ung-pao **Reverse:** "Yu" above **Mint:** Hu-pu Board of Revenue

Date	Mintage	Good	VG	F	VF	XF
ND(1875-1908)	—	6.00	9.00	13.50	20.00	—

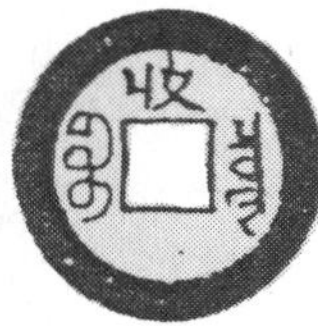

C# 1-16.10 CASH
Cast Brass **Series:** Thousand Character Classic **Obv. Inscription:** Kuang-hsü T'ung-pao **Reverse:** "Shou" above **Mint:** Hu-pu Board of Revenue

Date	Mintage	Good	VG	F	VF	XF
ND(1875-1908)	—	6.00	9.00	13.50	20.00	—

C# 1-16.1 CASH
Cast Brass **Series:** Thousand Character Classic **Obv. Inscription:** Kuang-hsü T'ung-pao **Reverse:** "Chin" above **Mint:** Hu-pu Board of Revenue

Date	Mintage	Good	VG	F	VF	XF
ND(1875-1908)	—	6.00	9.00	13.50	20.00	—

C# 2-15 CASH
Cast Brass **Obv. Inscription:** Kuang-hsü T'ung-pao **Mint:** Kung-pu Board of Public Works **Note:** Size varies: 25-26mm.

Date	Mintage	Good	VG	F	VF	XF
ND(1875-1908)	—	1.50	3.00	6.00	7.00	—

Note: For crude cast copper strikes, see Sinkiang General Coinage

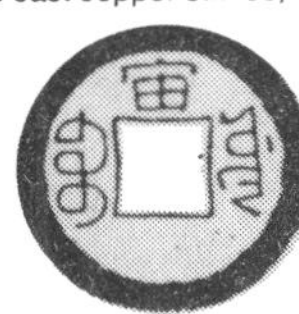

C# 2-15.1 CASH
Cast Brass **Series:** Thousand Character Classic **Obv. Inscription:** Kuang-hsü T'ung-pao **Reverse:** "Chou" above **Mint:** Kung-pu Board of Public Works **Note:** Size varies: 19-20mm.

Date	Mintage	Good	VG	F	VF	XF
ND(1899-1901)	—	6.00	10.00	15.00	20.00	—

C# 2-15.2 CASH
Cast Brass **Series:** Thousand Character Classic **Obv. Inscription:** Kuang-hsü T'ung-pao **Reverse:** "Lai" above **Mint:** Kung-pu Board of Public Works

Date	Mintage	Good	VG	F	VF	XF
ND(1899-1901)	—	6.00	10.00	15.00	20.00	—

C# 2-15.3 CASH
Cast Brass **Series:** Thousand Character Classic **Obv. Inscription:** Kuang-hsü T'ung-pao **Reverse:** "Lieh" above **Mint:** Kung-pu Board of Public Works

Date	Mintage	Good	VG	F	VF	XF
ND(1899-1901	—	6.00	10.00	15.00	20.00	—

C# 2-15.4 CASH
Cast Brass **Series:** Thousand Character Classic **Obv. Inscription:** Kuang-hsü T'ung-pao **Reverse:** "Yu" above **Mint:** Kung-pu Board of Public Works

Date	Mintage	Good	VG	F	VF	XF
ND(1899-1901)	—	6.00	10.00	15.00	20.00	—

C# 2-15.5 CASH
Cast Brass, 20 mm. **Series:** Thousand Character Classic **Obv. Inscription:** Kuang-hsü T'ung-pao **Reverse:** "Jih" above **Mint:** Kung-pu Board of Public Works

Date	Mintage	Good	VG	F	VF	XF
ND(1899-1901)	—	6.00	10.00	15.00	20.00	—

C# 2-15.6 CASH
Cast Brass **Series:** Thousand Character Classic **Obv. Inscription:** Kuang-hsü T'ung-pao **Reverse:** "Wang" above **Mint:** Kung-pu Board of Public Works

Date	Mintage	Good	VG	F	VF	XF
ND(1899-1901)	—	6.00	10.00	15.00	20.00	—

C# 2-15.7 CASH
Cast Brass **Series:** Thousand Character Classic **Obv. Inscription:** Kuang-hsü T'ung-pao **Reverse:** "Jih" above, dot below **Mint:** Kung-pu Board of Public Works

Date	Mintage	Good	VG	F	VF	XF
ND(1899-1901)	—	6.00	10.00	15.00	20.00	—

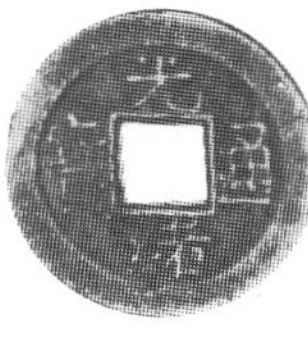
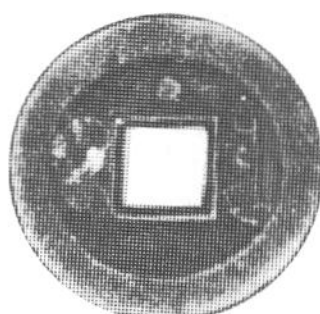

C# 1-16.9 CASH
Cast Brass **Obv. Inscription:** Kuang-hsü T'ung-pao **Reverse:** Dot above **Mint:** Hu-pu Board of Revenue

Date	Mintage	Good	VG	F	VF	XF
ND(1899-1901)	—	1.75	3.00	4.00	6.00	—

C# 1-16.8 CASH

Cast Brass **Obv. Inscription:** Kuang-hsü T'ung-pao **Reverse:** Dot below **Mint:** Hu-pu Board of Revenue

Date	Mintage	Good	VG	F	VF	XF
ND(1899-1901)	—	1.75	3.00	4.00	6.00	—

C# 2-16 5 CASH

Cast Brass **Obv. Inscription:** Kuang-hsü T'ung-pao **Mint:** Kung-pu Board of Public Works

Date	Mintage	Good	VG	F	VF	XF
ND(1875-1908)	—	200	350	500	700	—

C# 1-17 10 CASH

Cast Brass, 30 mm. **Obv. Inscription:** Kuang-hsü Chung-pao **Reverse:** Normal "Shih" for 10 below **Mint:** Hu-pu Board of Revenue

Date	Mintage	Good	VG	F	VF	XF
ND(1875-1908)	—	3.00	5.00	8.00	10.00	—

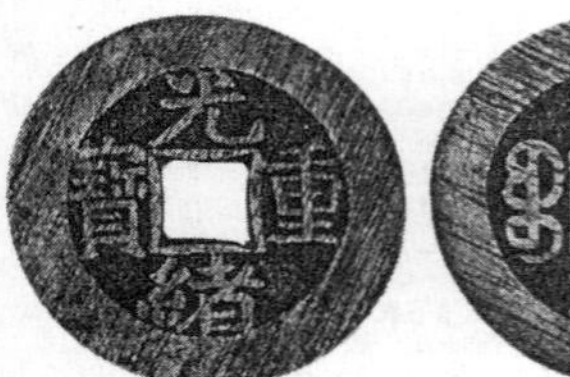

C# 1-18 10 CASH

Cast Brass, 28 mm. **Obv. Inscription:** Kuang-hsü Chung-pao **Reverse:** Official "Shih" for 10 below **Mint:** Hu-pu Board of Revenue

Date	Mintage	Good	VG	F	VF	XF
ND(1875-1908)	—	4.50	7.50	10.00	15.00	—

C# 1-18.1 10 CASH

Cast Brass, 22 mm. **Obv. Inscription:** Kuang-hsü Chung-pao **Reverse:** Official "Shih" for 10 below **Mint:** Hu-pu Board of Revenue

Date	Mintage	Good	VG	F	VF	XF
ND(1875-1908)	—	6.00	9.00	15.00	20.00	—

C# 2-17 10 CASH

Cast Brass **Obv. Inscription:** Kuang-hsü T'ung-pao **Reverse:** Normal Shih (10) below **Mint:** Kung-pu Board of Public Works **Note:** Size varies: 31-32mm.

Date	Mintage	Good	VG	F	VF	XF
ND(1875-1908)	—	4.50	7.50	10.00	25.00	—

C# 2-18 10 CASH

Cast Brass **Obv. Inscription:** Kuang-hsü T'ung-pao **Reverse:** Official Shih (10) below **Mint:** Kung-pu Board of Public Works

Date	Mintage	Good	VG	F	VF	XF
ND(1880-1908)	—	6.00	10.00	15.00	35.00	—

PATTERNS

Peking Dollar Series

There are two theories concerning the origin of the Peking coins. One asserts that a few sets of all five denominations were minted during 1900 at the mint erected in Peking the previous year, with equipment partly from the Hangchow Chekiang Mint, and partly from Germany. The second theory alleges that some 10- and 20-cent pieces may have been minted in 1900, but that the rest of the set was restruck sometime later by private parties using original dies looted from the mint during the Boxer uprising. The 10 Cash pieces struck in copper and brass are considered fantasies.

KM#	Date	Mintage	Identification	Mkt Val

KM#	Date	Mintage	Identification	Mkt Val
Pn285	ND(1900)	—	5 Cents. Silver. K237.	1,500
Pn286	ND(1900)	—	10 Cents. Silver. K236.	1,500

KM#	Date	Mintage	Identification	Mkt Val
Pn287	ND(1900)	—	20 Cents. Silver. K235.	1,500

KM#	Date	Mintage	Identification	Mkt Val
Pn288	ND(1900)	—	50 Cents. Silver. K234.	2,500

KM#	Date	Mintage	Identification	Mkt Val
Pn289	ND(1900)	—	Dollar. Silver. K233.	4,000

PATTERNS

Including off metal strikes

KM#	Date	Mintage	Identification	Mkt Val
Pn31	ND(1821)	—	Cash. Cast Brass. "Boo-ili"	500
Pn32	ND(1821)	—	Cash. Cast Brass. Manchu and Turki "Aksu"	300
Pn35	ND(1851)	—	Cash. Cast Brass. "Boo-Ciowan"	300
Pn36	ND(1851)	—	Cash. Cast Brass. "Boo-Ciowan"	200
Pn37	ND(1851)	—	Cash. Cast Brass. "Boo-Ciowan"	300
Pn38	ND(1851)	—	10 Cash. Cast Brass. "Boo-Ciowan"	150
Pn39	ND(1851)	—	10 Cash. Cast Brass. "Boo-Ciowan"	120

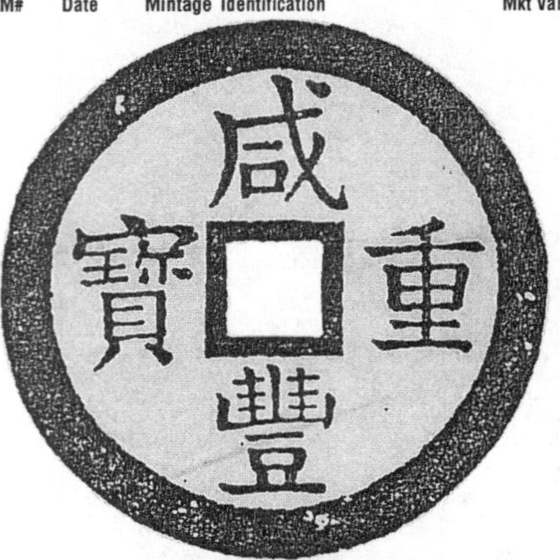

KM#	Date	Mintage	Identification	Mkt Val
Pn40	ND(1851)	—	50 Cash. Cast Brass. "Boo-Ciowan"	200

KM#	Date	Mintage	Identification	Mkt Val
Pn41	ND(1851)	—	100 Cash. Cast Brass. "Boo-Ciowan"	250

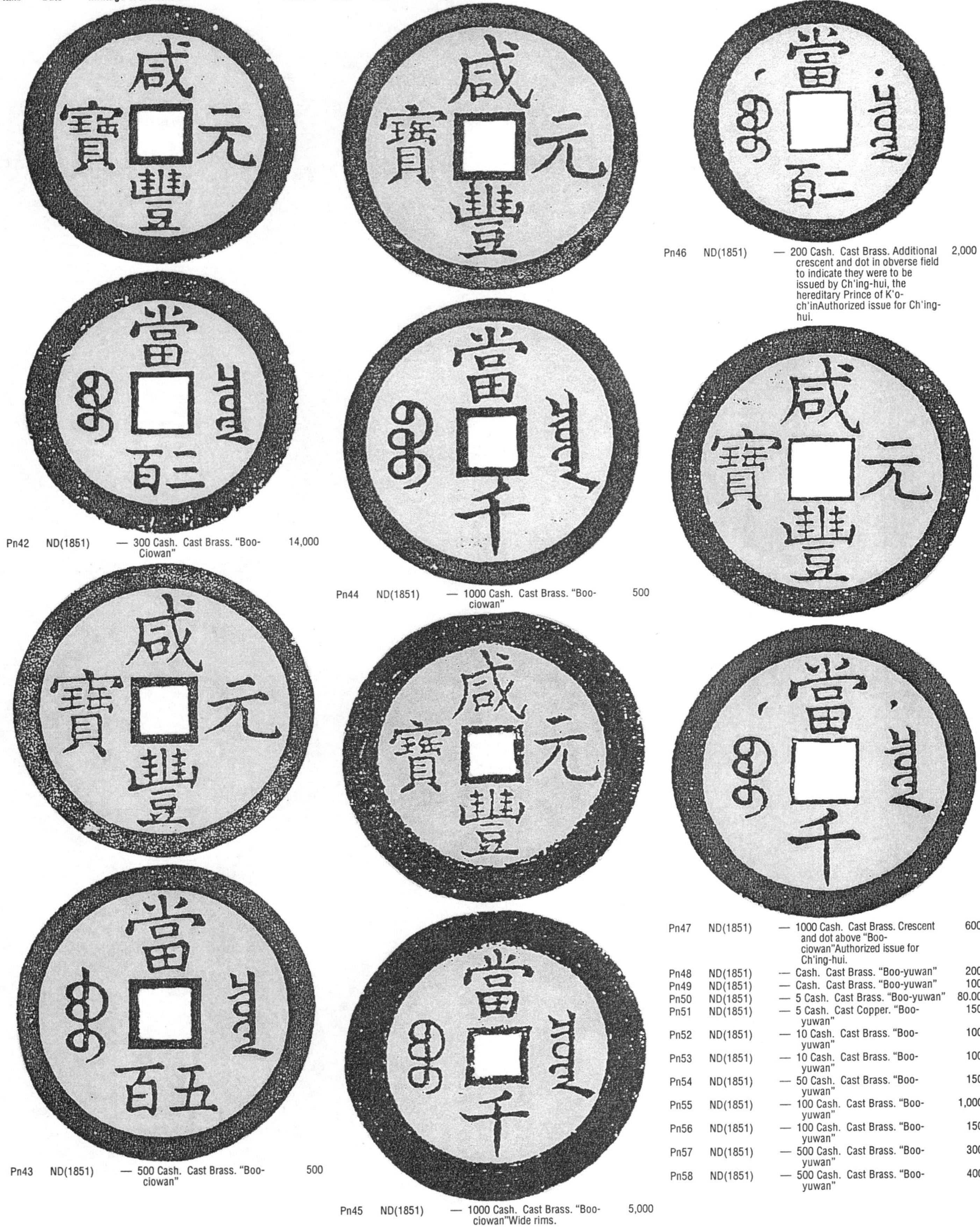

KM#	Date	Mintage	Identification	Mkt Val
Pn42	ND(1851)	—	300 Cash. Cast Brass. "Boo-Ciowan"	14,000
Pn43	ND(1851)	—	500 Cash. Cast Brass. "Boo-ciowan"	500
Pn44	ND(1851)	—	1000 Cash. Cast Brass. "Boo-ciowan"	500
Pn45	ND(1851)	—	1000 Cash. Cast Brass. "Boo-ciowan"Wide rims.	5,000
Pn46	ND(1851)	—	200 Cash. Cast Brass. Additional crescent and dot in obverse field to indicate they were to be issued by Ch'ing-hui, the hereditary Prince of K'o-ch'inAuthorized issue for Ch'ing-hui.	2,000
Pn47	ND(1851)	—	1000 Cash. Cast Brass. Crescent and dot above "Boo-ciowan"Authorized issue for Ch'ing-hui.	600
Pn48	ND(1851)	—	Cash. Cast Brass. "Boo-yuwan"	200
Pn49	ND(1851)	—	Cash. Cast Brass. "Boo-yuwan"	100
Pn50	ND(1851)	—	5 Cash. Cast Brass. "Boo-yuwan"	80.00
Pn51	ND(1851)	—	5 Cash. Cast Copper. "Boo-yuwan"	150
Pn52	ND(1851)	—	10 Cash. Cast Brass. "Boo-yuwan"	100
Pn53	ND(1851)	—	10 Cash. Cast Brass. "Boo-yuwan"	100
Pn54	ND(1851)	—	50 Cash. Cast Brass. "Boo-yuwan"	150
Pn55	ND(1851)	—	100 Cash. Cast Brass. "Boo-yuwan"	1,000
Pn56	ND(1851)	—	100 Cash. Cast Brass. "Boo-yuwan"	150
Pn57	ND(1851)	—	500 Cash. Cast Brass. "Boo-yuwan"	300
Pn58	ND(1851)	—	500 Cash. Cast Brass. "Boo-yuwan"	400

KM#	Date	Mintage	Identification	Mkt Val
Pn59	ND(1851)	—	1000 Cash. Cast Brass. "Boo-yuwan"	500
Pn60	ND(1851)	—	1000 Cash. Cast Brass. "Boo-yuwan"	400
Pn61	ND(1851)	—	Cash. Cast Brass. "Boo-ji"	300
Pn62	ND(1851)	—	5 Cash. Cast Brass. "Boo-ji"	1,000
Pn63	ND(1851)	—	10 Cash. Cast Brass. "Boo-ji"	150
Pn64	ND(1851)	—	50 Cash. Cast Brass. "Boo-ji"	300
Pn65	ND(1851)	—	100 Cash. Cast Brass. "Boo-ji"	200

KM#	Date	Mintage	Identification	Mkt Val
Pn66	ND(1851)	—	10 Cash. Cast Brass. "Boo-gi"	500
Pn67	ND(1851)	—	100 Cash. Cast Brass. "Boo-gi"	1,500
Pn69	ND(1851)	—	50 Cash. Cast Brass. "Boo-de"	300
Pn71	ND(1851)	—	10 Cash. Cast Brass. "Boo-ho"	300
Pn72	ND(1851)	—	50 Cash. Cast Brass. "Boo-ho"	400
Pn73	ND(1851)	—	100 Cash. Cast Brass. "Boo-ho"	400
Pn74	ND(1851)	—	500 Cash. Cast Brass. "Boo-ho"	1,600

KM#	Date	Mintage	Identification	Mkt Val
Pn75	ND(1851)	—	1000 Cash. Cast Brass. "Boo-ho"	2,000

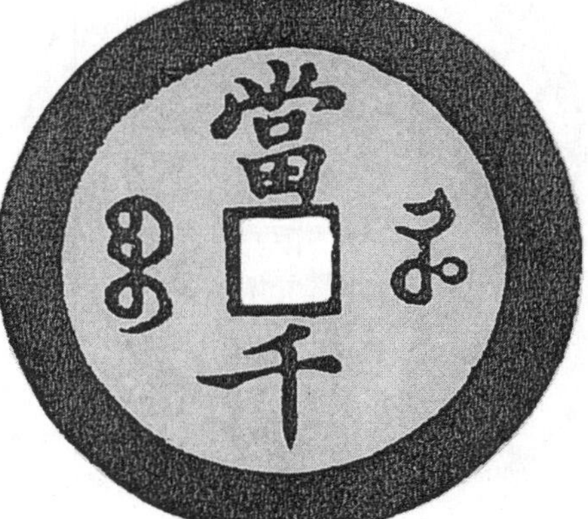

KM#	Date	Mintage	Identification	Mkt Val
Pn76	ND(1851)	—	1000 Cash. Cast Brass. "Boo-ho"	2,500
Pn78	ND(1851)	—	Cash. Cast Brass. "Boo-gin" (by Hu-pu)	200
Pn80	ND(1851)	—	Cash. Cast Brass. "Boo-san"	200
Pn81	ND(1851)	—	Cash. Cast Brass. "Boo-san" (by Hu-pu)	250
Pn82	ND(1851)	—	10 Cash. Cast Brass. "Boo-san"	400

KM#	Date	Mintage	Identification	Mkt Val
Pn83	ND(1851)	—	50 Cash. Cast Brass. "Boo-san"	200

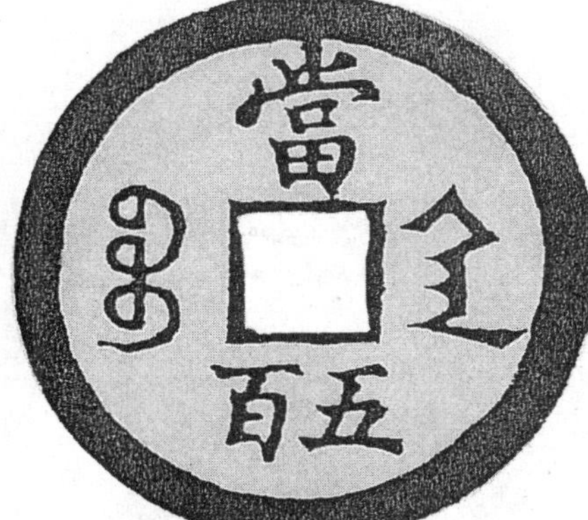

KM#	Date	Mintage	Identification	Mkt Val
Pn84	ND(1851)	—	500 Cash. Cast Brass. "Boo-san"	1,000
Pn86	ND(1851)	—	Cash. Cast Brass. "Boo-gung"	100
Pn87	ND(1851)	—	Cash. Cast Copper. "Boo-gung"	100

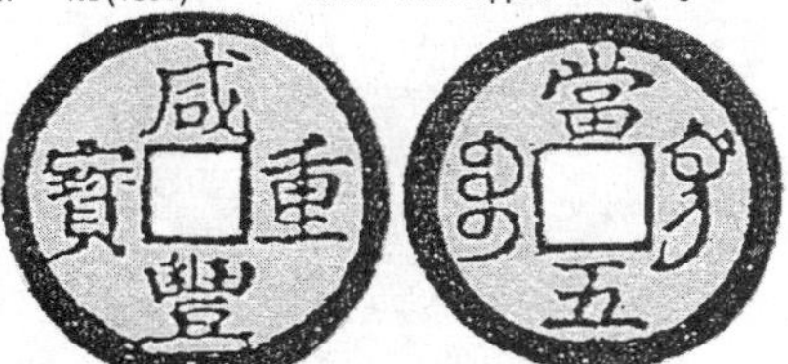

KM#	Date	Mintage	Identification	Mkt Val
Pn88	ND(1851)	—	5 Cash. Cast Brass. "Boo-gung"	150
Pn89	ND(1851)	—	10 Cash. Cast Brass. "Boo-gung"	150

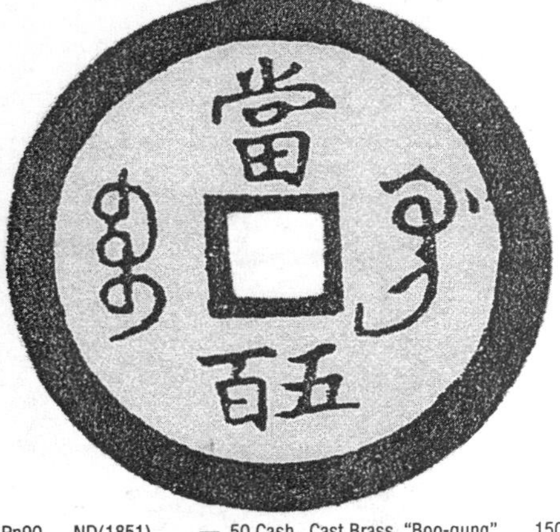

KM#	Date	Mintage	Identification	Mkt Val
Pn90	ND(1851)	—	50 Cash. Cast Brass. "Boo-gung"	150
Pn91	ND(1851)	—	500 Cash. Cast Brass. "Boo-gung"	1,600

KM#	Date	Mintage	Identification	Mkt Val
Pn92	ND(1851)	—	1000 Cash. Cast Brass. "Boo-gung"	2,000
Pn94	ND(1851)	—	Cash. Cast Brass. "Boo-su" (by Hu-pu)	200

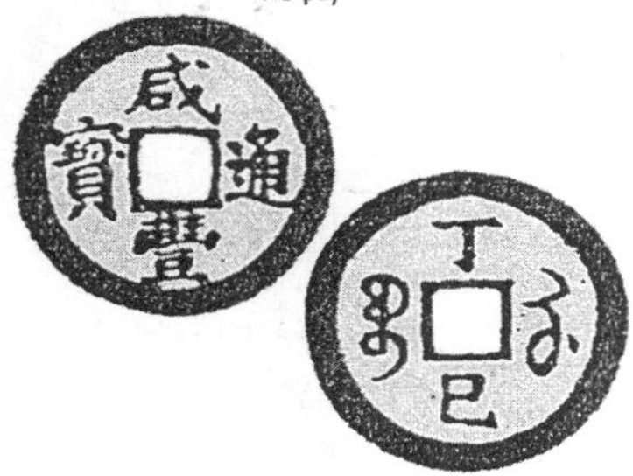

KM#	Date	Mintage	Identification	Mkt Val
Pn95	ND(1851)	—	Cash. Cast Copper. "Ting-szu Boo-su"	1,000
Pn96	ND(1851)	—	10 Cash. Cast Brass. "Boo-su"	200
Pn97	ND(1851)	—	10 Cash. Cast Brass. "Boo-su"	200

KM#	Date	Mintage	Identification	Mkt Val
Pn98	ND(1851)	—	10 Cash. Cast Brass. "Boo-su"	250

KM#	Date	Mintage	Identification	Mkt Val
Pn99	ND(1851)	—	50 Cash. Cast Brass. "Boo-su"	400
Pn100	ND(1851)	—	50 Cash. Cast Brass. "Boo-su"	400
Pn101	ND(1851)	—	50 Cash. Cast Brass. "Boo-su"	600

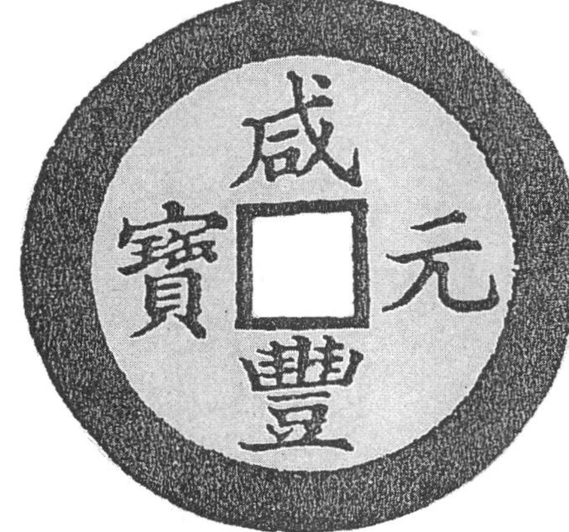

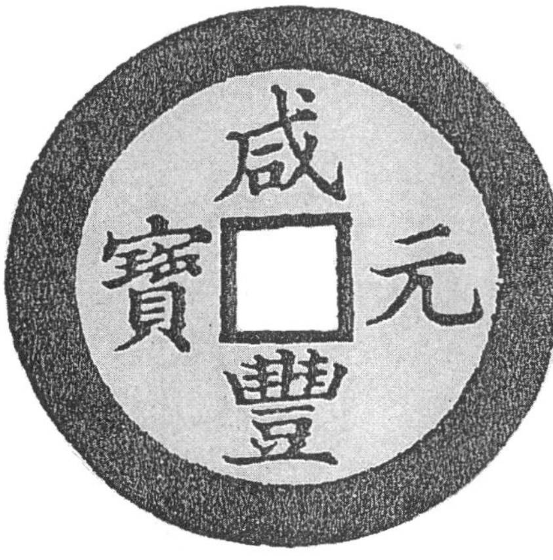

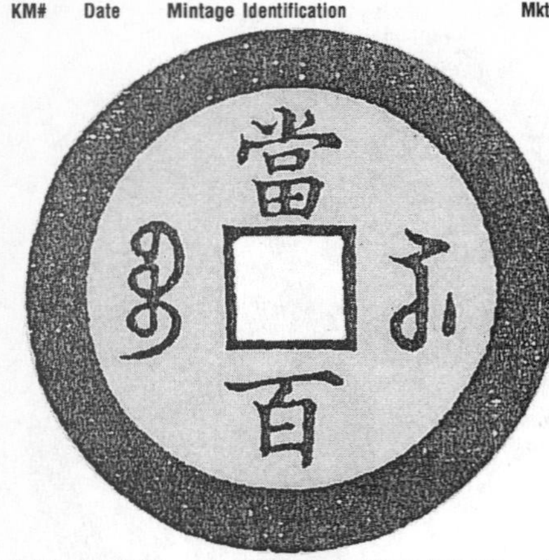

KM#	Date	Mintage	Identification	Mkt Val
Pn102	ND(1851)	—	100 Cash. Cast Brass. "Boo-su"	250

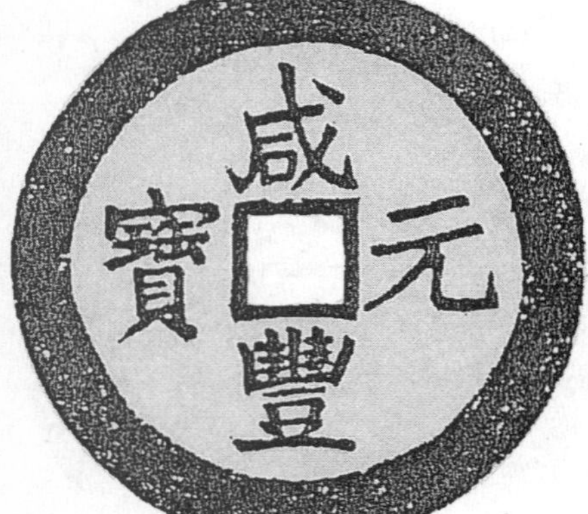

KM#	Date	Mintage	Identification	Mkt Val
Pn103	ND(1851)	—	100 Cash. Cast Brass. "Boo-su"	250
Pn105	ND(1851)	—	Cash. Cast Brass. "Boo-je"	200
Pn106	ND(1851)	—	5 Cash. Cast Brass. "Boo-je"	8,000
Pn107	ND(1851)	—	10 Cash. Cast Brass. "Boo-je"	200
Pn108	ND(1851)	—	10 Cash. Cast Brass. "Je-chê"	1,400
Pn109	ND(1851)	—	20 Cash. Cast Brass. "Je-chê"	1,400

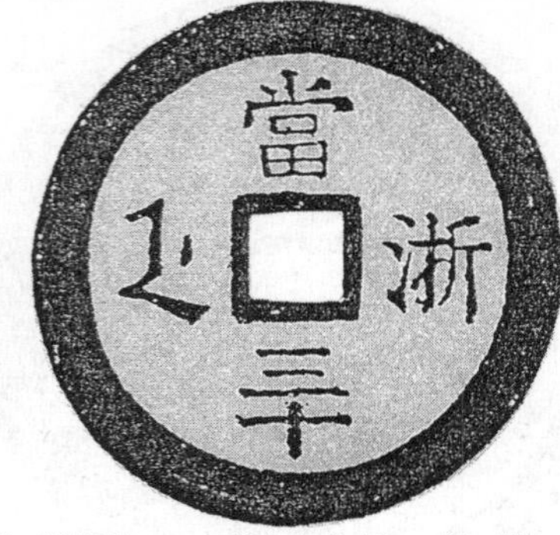

KM#	Date	Mintage	Identification	Mkt Val
Pn110	ND(1851)	—	30 Cash. Cast Brass. "Je-chê"	1,600

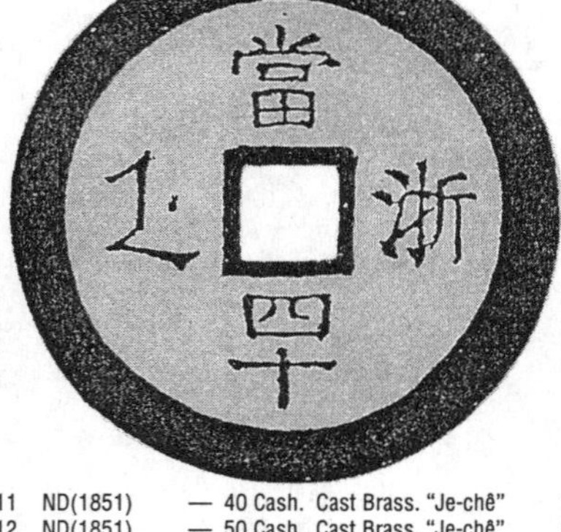

KM#	Date	Mintage	Identification	Mkt Val
Pn111	ND(1851)	—	40 Cash. Cast Brass. "Je-chê"	1,600
Pn112	ND(1851)	—	50 Cash. Cast Brass. "Je-chê"	1,600

KM#	Date	Mintage	Identification	Mkt Val
Pn113	ND(1851)	—	100 Cash. Cast Brass. "Je-chê"	2,000

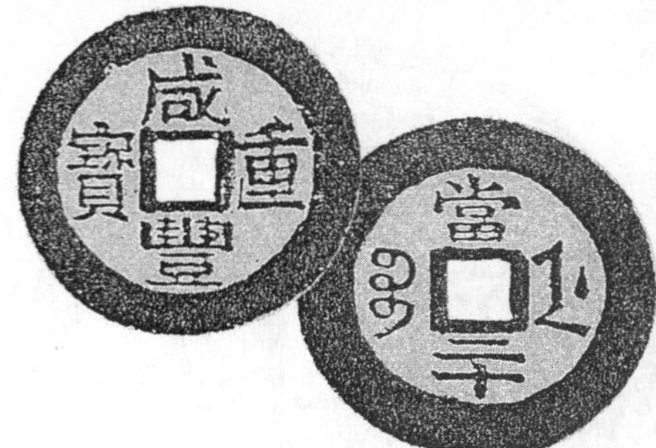

KM#	Date	Mintage	Identification	Mkt Val
Pn114	ND(1851)	—	20 Cash. Cast Brass. "Boo-je"	1,200
Pn115	ND(1851)	—	30 Cash. Cast Brass. "Boo-je"	1,400

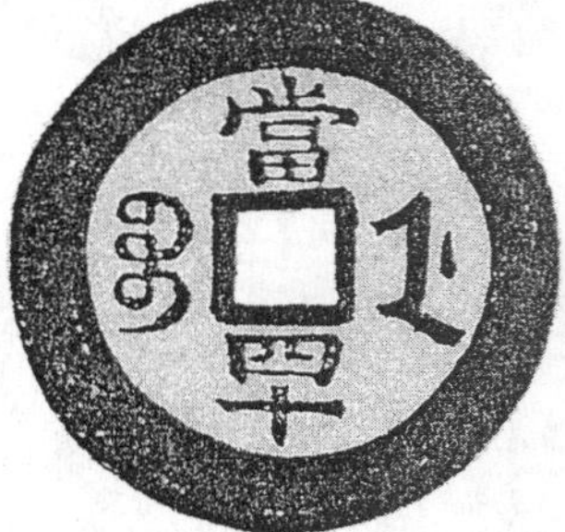

KM#	Date	Mintage	Identification	Mkt Val
Pn116	ND(1851)	—	40 Cash. Cast Brass. "Boo-je"	1,500
Pn117	ND(1851)	—	50 Cash. Cast Brass. "Boo-je"	1,400
Pn118	ND(1851)	—	50 Cash. Cast Brass. "Boo-je"	1,600
Pn119	ND(1851)	—	10 Cash. Cast Brass. "Boo-je"	8,000

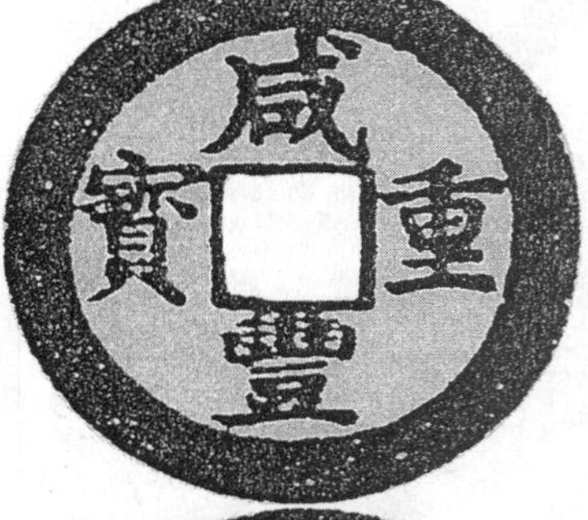

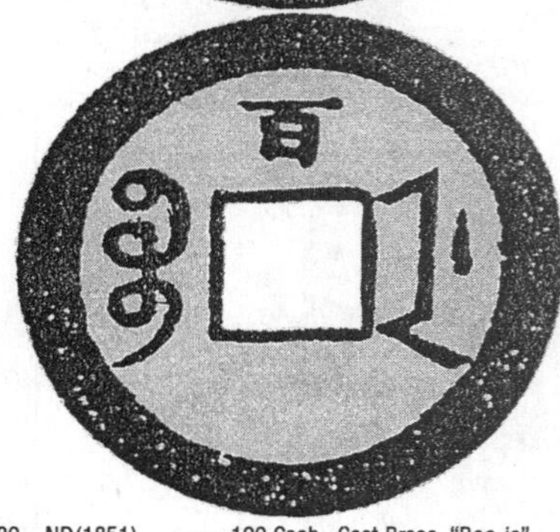

KM#	Date	Mintage	Identification	Mkt Val
Pn120	ND(1851)	—	100 Cash. Cast Brass. "Boo-je"	3,000
Pn121	ND(1851)	—	50 Cash. Cast Brass. "Boo-je"	2,000
Pn123	ND(1851)	—	Cash. Cast Brass. "Boo-ch'ang"	250
Pn124	ND(1851)	—	50 Cash. Cast Brass. "Boo-ch'ang"	250
Pn126	ND(1851)	—	Cash. Cast Brass. "Boo-fu"	250
Pn127	ND(1851)	—	10 Cash. Cast Brass. "Boo-fu"	200
Pn128	ND(1851)	—	20 Cash. Cast Brass. "Boo-fu"	300
Pn130	ND(1851)	—	Cash. Cast Brass. "Boo-u"	300
Pn132	ND(1851)	—	Cash. Cast Brass. "Boo-nan"	500
Pn133	ND(1851)	—	10 Cash. Cast Brass. "Boo-nan"	2,000

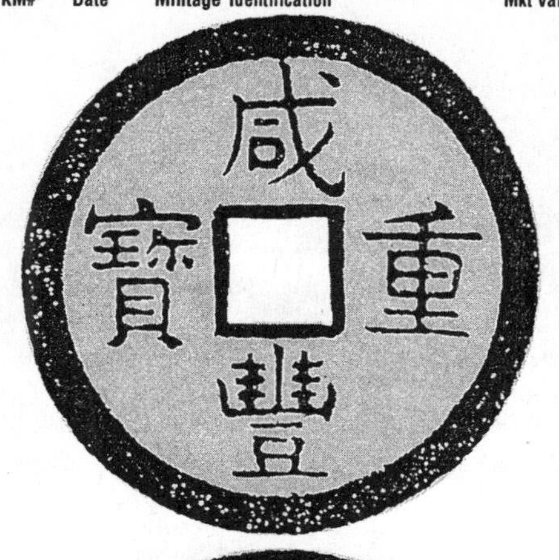

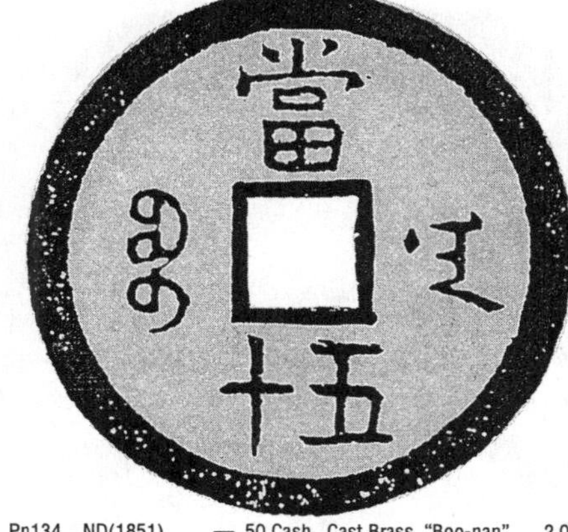

KM#	Date	Mintage	Identification	Mkt Val
Pn134	ND(1851)	—	50 Cash. Cast Brass. "Boo-nan" (by Hu-pu)	2,000
Pn136	ND(1851)	—	Cash. Cast Brass. "Boo-guwang" (by Hu-pu)	300
Pn137	ND(1851)	—	10 Cash. Cast Brass. "Boo-guwang" (by Hu-pu)	2,000
Pn139	ND(1851)	—	Cash. Cast Brass. "Boo-gui" (by Hu-pu)	200
Pn141	ND(1851)	—	Cash. Cast Brass. "Boo-cuwan" (by Hu-pu)	200
Pn142	ND(1851)	—	10 Cash. Cast Brass. "Boo-cuwan"	150
Pn143	ND(1851)	—	10 Cash. Cast Brass. "Boo-cuwan"	1,500
Pn144	ND(1851)	—	50 Cash. Cast Brass. "Boo-cuwan"	250
Pn145	ND(1851)	—	50 Cash. Cast Brass. "Boo-cuwan"	1,200

KM#	Date	Mintage	Identification	Mkt Val
Pn146	ND(1851)	—	100 Cash. Cast Brass. "Boo-cuwan"	1,000
Pn148	ND(1851)	—	Cash. Cast Brass. "Boo-yôn" (by Hu-pu)	300
Pn149	ND(1851)	—	10 Cash. Cast Brass. "Boo-yôn"	300
Pn150	ND(1851)	—	50 Cash. Cast Brass. "Boo-yôn" (by Hu-pu)"	2,000
Pn152	ND(1851)	—	Cash. Cast Brass. "Boo-giyan" (by Hu-pu)"	300
Pn154	ND(1851)	—	8 Cash. Cast Brass. "Boo-di"	300
Pn156	ND(1851)	—	Cash. Cast Brass. "Boo-yi" (by Hu-pu)Prev. KM#Pn1.	500

KM#	Date	Mintage	Identification	Mkt Val
Pn157	ND(1851)	—	100 Cash. Cast Brass. . "Boo-yi"	500
Pn158	ND(1851)	—	500 Cash. Cast Brass. . "Boo-yi"	10,000
Pn169	ND(1851)	—	10 Cash. Cast Brass. . "Boo-on"	2,000
Pn170	ND(1851)	—	50 Cash. Cast Brass. . "Boo-on"	2,000
Pn175	ND(1861)	—	Cash. Cast Brass. . "Boo-yôn"	500
Pn176	ND(1861)	—	Cash. Cast Brass. . "Boo-gung"	10,000
Pn177	ND(1861)	—	Cash. Cast Brass. . "Boo-su"	6,000
Pn179	ND(1862)	—	Cash. Cast Brass. . "Boo-yuwan"	200
Pn181	ND(1862)	—	Cash. Cast Brass. . "Boo-c'y"	60.00

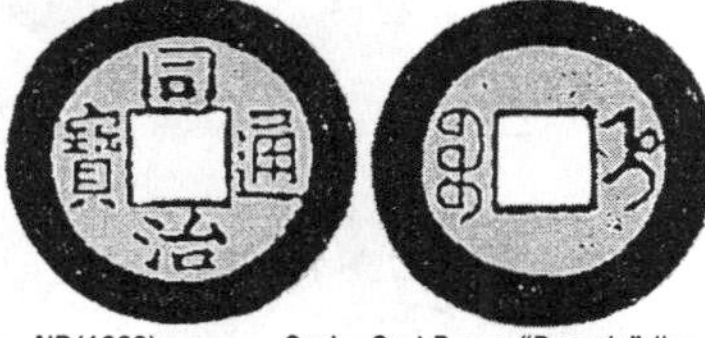

KM#	Date	Mintage	Identification	Mkt Val
Pn180	ND(1862)	—	Cash. Cast Brass. "Boo-c'y" (by Hu-pu)	300
PnA182	ND(1862)	—	Cash. Cast Brass. "Boo-je"	200
Pn182	ND(1862)	—	Cash. Cast Brass. "Boo-nan" (by Hu-pu)	300
Pn183	ND(1862)	—	Cash. Cast Brass. "Boo-u" (by Hu-pu)	300
Pn184	ND(1862)	—	Cash. Cast Brass. "Boo-fu" (by Hu-pu)	300
Pn185	ND(1862)	—	Cash. Cast Brass. "Boo-giyan" (by Hu-pu)	300
Pn186	ND(1862)	—	Cash. Cast Brass. "Boo-jin" (by Hu-pu)	300
Pn187	ND(1862)	—	Cash. Cast Brass. "Boo-san" (by Hu-pu)C23-11.	300
Pn188	ND(1862)	—	Cash. Cast Brass. "Boo-guwang" (by Hu-pu)	300
Pn189	ND(1862)	—	Cash. Cast Brass. "Boo-ji"	200

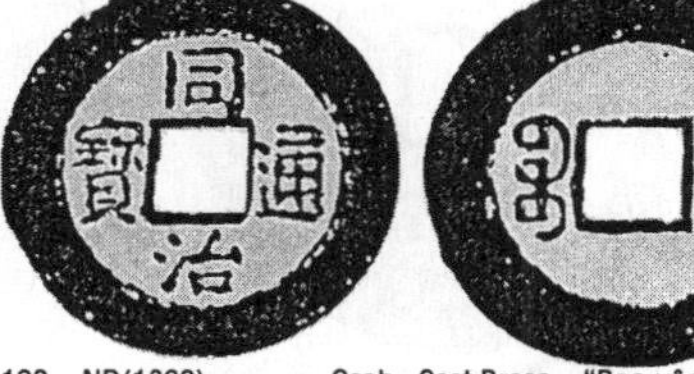

KM#	Date	Mintage	Identification	Mkt Val
Pn190	ND(1862)	—	Cash. Cast Brass. . "Boo-yôn"	150

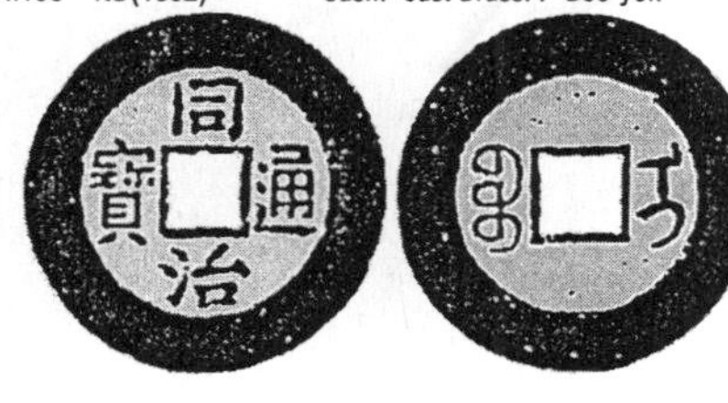

KM#	Date	Mintage	Identification	Mkt Val
Pn191	ND(1862)	—	Cash. Cast Brass. "Boo-yi" (by Hu-pu)	500
Pn194	ND(1862)	—	10 Cash. Cast Brass. "Boo-yi" (by Hu-pu), C28-9	700
Pn195	ND(1862)	—	5 Cash. Cast Brass. "Boo-gung"	800
Pn197	ND(1862)	—	10 Cash. Cast Brass. "Boo-yuwan", C2-14	300

KM#	Date	Mintage	Identification	Mkt Val
Pn198	ND(1862)	—	10 Cash. Cast Brass. "Boo-yôn", C2-14	500

KM#	Date	Mintage	Identification	Mkt Val
Pn199	ND(1862)	—	10 Cash. Cast Brass."Boo-ji", C5-9	500

KM#	Date	Mintage	Identification	Mkt Val
Pn200	ND(1862)	—	10 Cash. Cast Brass. "Boo-cang", C15-8	500

KM#	Date	Mintage	Identification	Mkt Val
Pn201	ND(1862)	—	10 Cash. Cast Brass. "Boo-je", C4-18	500

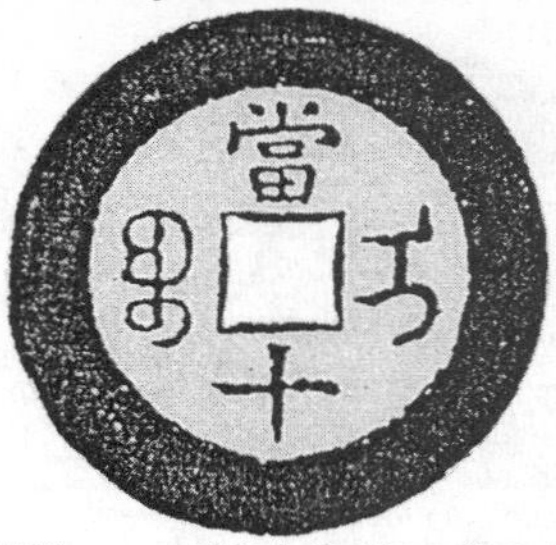

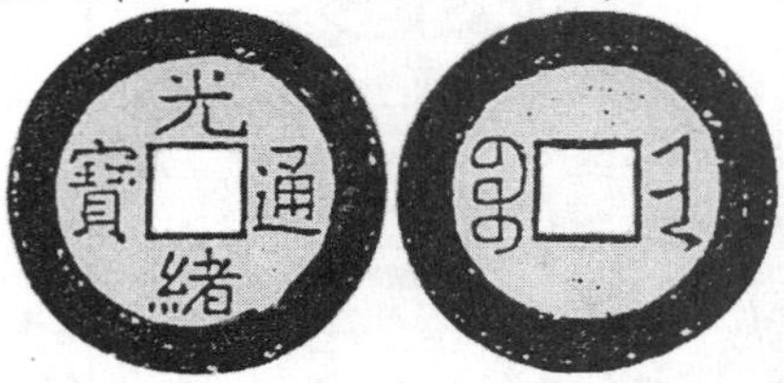

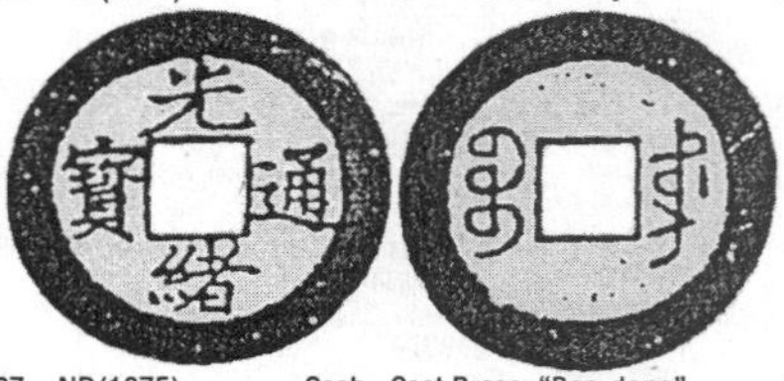

KM#	Date	Mintage	Identification	Mkt Val
Pn202	ND(1862)	—	10 Cash. Cast Brass. "Boo-su" (by Hu-pu)	500
Pn203	ND	—	10 Cash. Cast Brass. "Boo-fu" (by Hu-pu), C10-23	500
Pn204	ND	—	10 Cash. Cast Brass. "Boo-an" (by Hu-pu), C4-18	500
Pn205	ND(1862)	—	10 Cash. Cast Brass. "Boo-yuwan" C2-14	500
Pn206	ND(1862)	—	10 Cash. Cast Brass. "Boo-u" (by Hu-pu), C13-10	500
Pn207	ND(1862)	—	10 Cash. Cast Brass. "Boo-guwang" (by Hu-pu), C19-6	500
Pn208	ND(1862)	—	10 Cash. Cast Brass. "Boo-nan" (by Hu-pu), C12-6	500
Pn209	ND(1862)	—	10 Cash. Cast Brass. "Boo-san" (by Hu-pu)	500
Pn210	ND(1862)	—	10 Cash. Cast Brass. "Boo-giyan" (by Hu-pu), C20-8	500
Pn211	ND(1862)	—	10 Cash. Cast Brass. "Boo-jin" (by Hu-pu), C21-7	500
Pn212	ND(1862)	—	10 Cash. Cast Brass. "Boo-gui" (by Hu-pu), C18-8	500
Pn213	ND(1862)	—	10 Cash. Cast Brass. "Boo-yi" (by Hu-pu)	500
Pn217	ND(1875)	—	Cash. Cast Brass. "Boo-su"	150
Pn218	ND(1875)	—	Cash. Cast Brass. "Boo-fu", dot above	60.00
Pn219	ND(1875)	—	Cash. Cast Brass. "Boo-fu" (by Hupu)	250
Pn220	ND(1875)	—	Cash. Cast Brass. "Boo-guwang"	120
Pn221	ND(1875)	—	Cash. Brass. "Boo-guwang"	300
Pn222	ND(1875)	—	Cash. Cast Brass. "Boo-jin"	100
Pn223	ND(1875)	—	Cash. Cast Brass. "Boo-jin" (by Hupu)	240
Pn224	ND(1875)	—	Cash. Cast Brass. "Boo-san" (by Hupu)	240
Pn225	ND(1875)	—	Cash. Cast Brass. "Boo-cuwan" (by Hupu)	240
Pn226	ND(1875)	—	Cash. Cast Brass. "Boo-yôn"	60.00
Pn227	ND(1875)	—	Cash. Cast Brass. "Boo-dong"	160
Pn228	ND(1875)	—	Cash. Cast Brass. "Boo-dong"	240
Pn229	ND(1875)	—	Cash. Cast Brass. "Boo-yi" (by Hupu)	400
Pn231	ND(1875)	—	Cash. Cast Brass. "Boo-ku"	160
Pn232	ND(1875)	—	10 Cash. Cast Brass. "Boo-yuwan", C2-17	200
Pn233	ND(1875)	—	10 Cash. Cast Brass. "Boo-ji" (by Hupu), C5-11	400

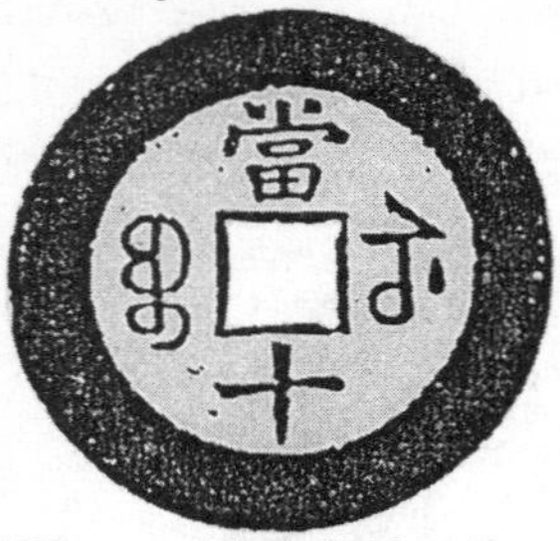

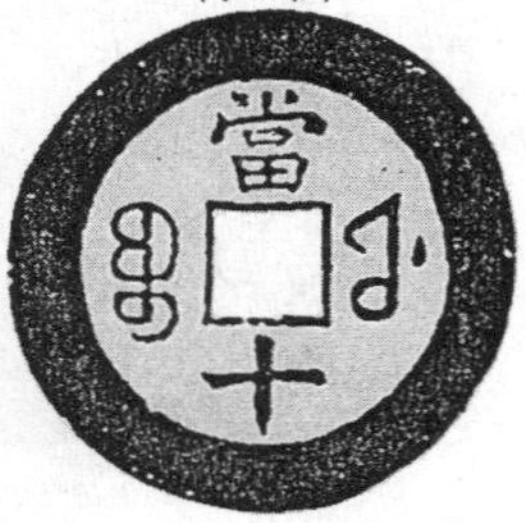

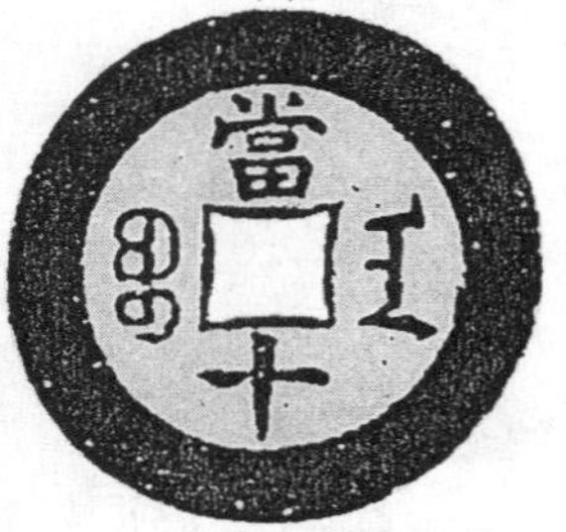

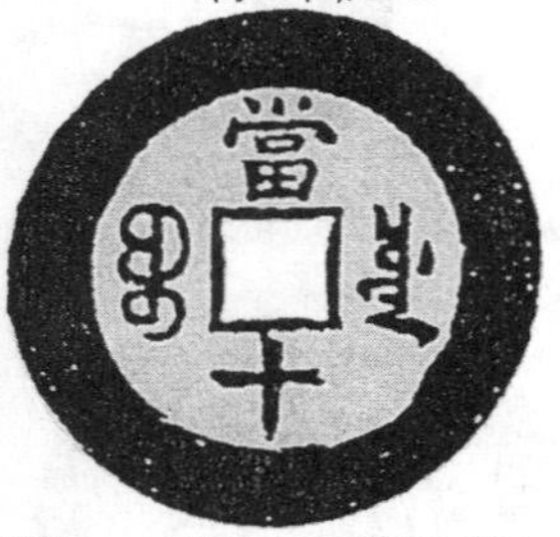

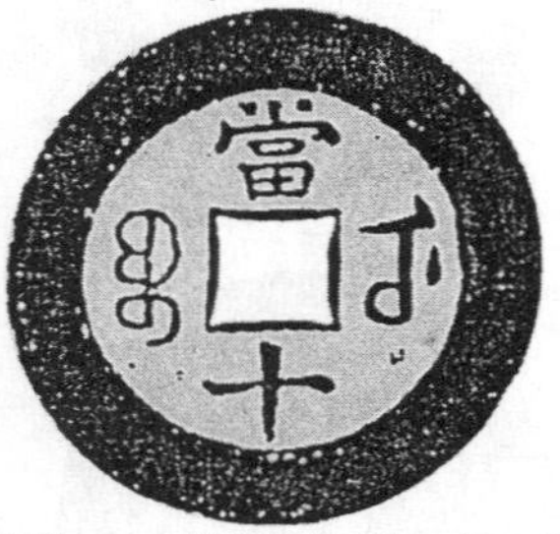

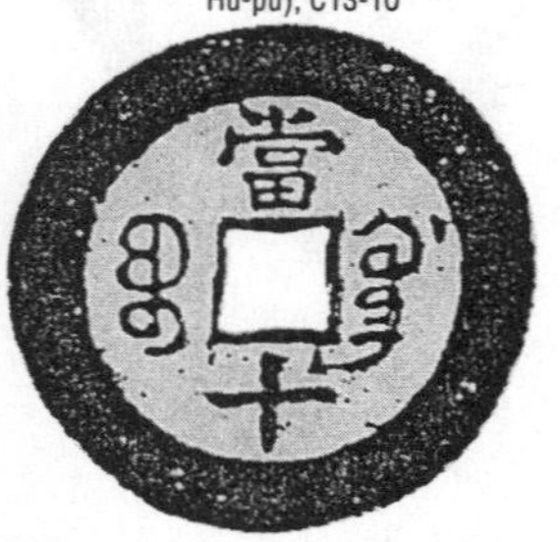

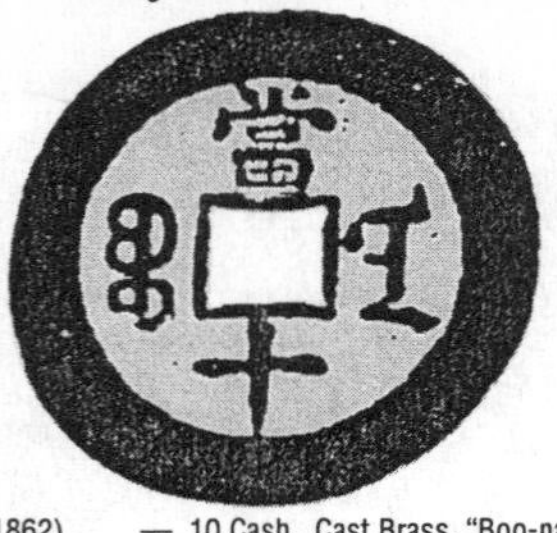

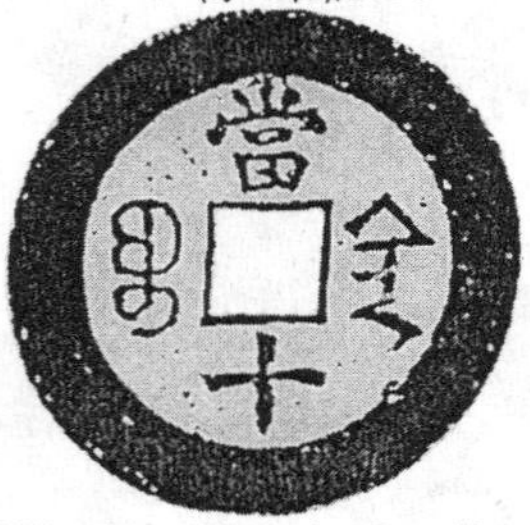

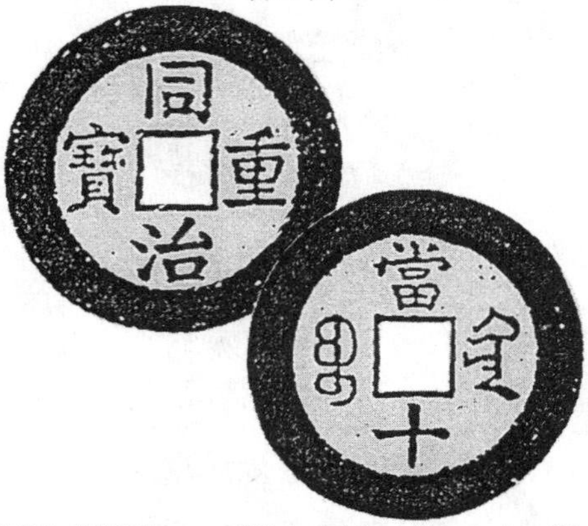

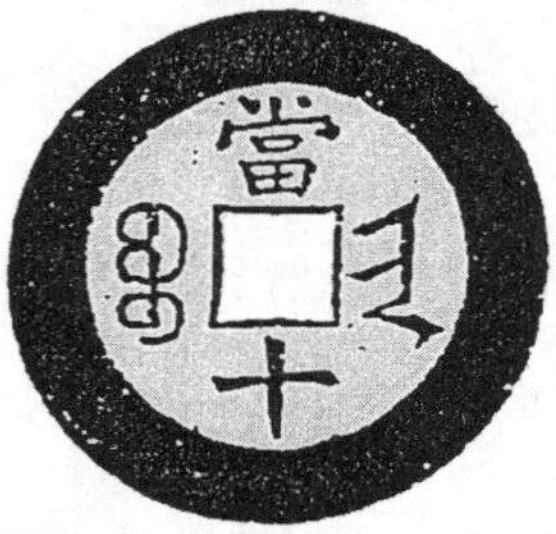

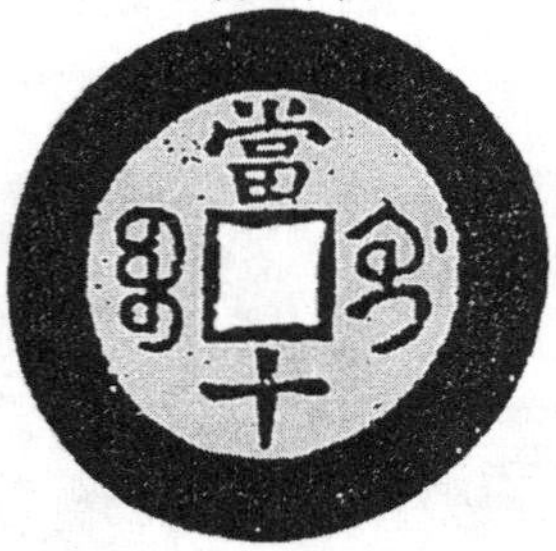

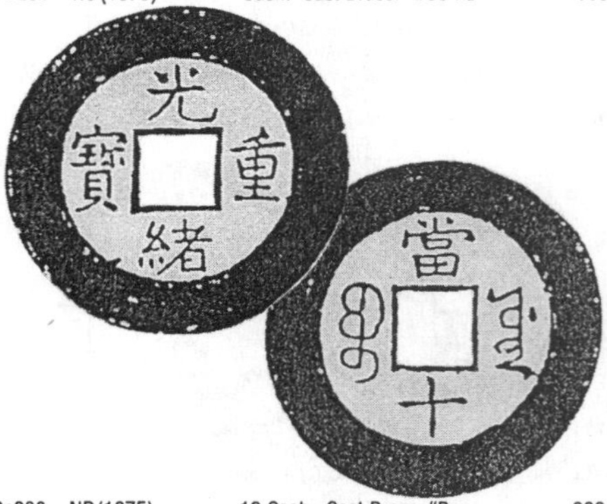

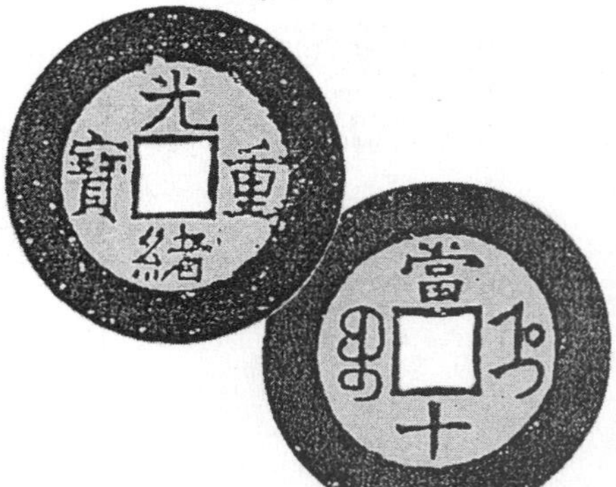

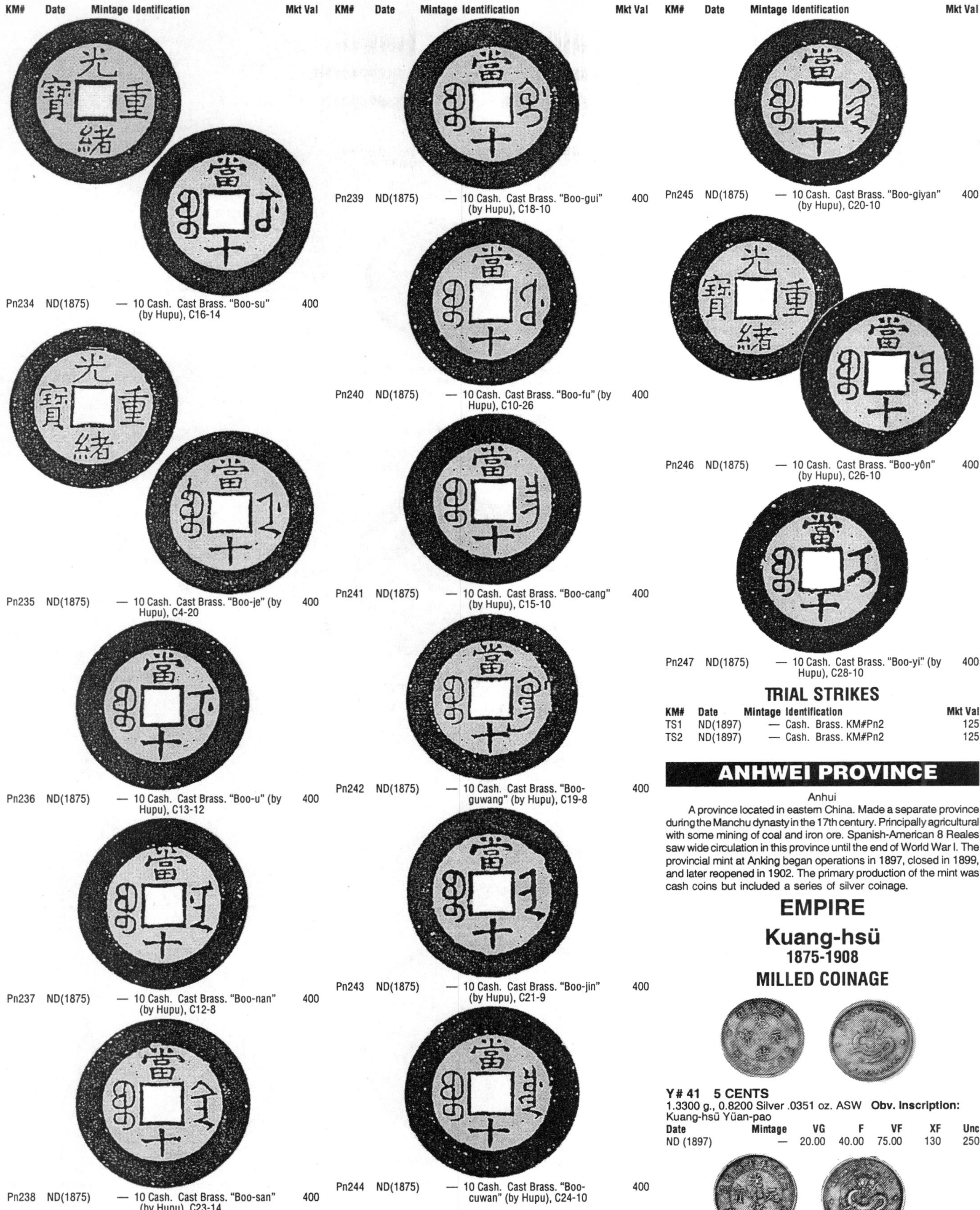

KM#	Date	Mintage	Identification	Mkt Val
Pn234	ND(1875)	—	10 Cash. Cast Brass. "Boo-su" (by Hupu), C16-14	400
Pn235	ND(1875)	—	10 Cash. Cast Brass. "Boo-je" (by Hupu), C4-20	400
Pn236	ND(1875)	—	10 Cash. Cast Brass. "Boo-u" (by Hupu), C13-12	400
Pn237	ND(1875)	—	10 Cash. Cast Brass. "Boo-nan" (by Hupu), C12-8	400
Pn238	ND(1875)	—	10 Cash. Cast Brass. "Boo-san" (by Hupu), C23-14	400
Pn239	ND(1875)	—	10 Cash. Cast Brass. "Boo-gui" (by Hupu), C18-10	400
Pn240	ND(1875)	—	10 Cash. Cast Brass. "Boo-fu" (by Hupu), C10-26	400
Pn241	ND(1875)	—	10 Cash. Cast Brass. "Boo-cang" (by Hupu), C15-10	400
Pn242	ND(1875)	—	10 Cash. Cast Brass. "Boo-guwang" (by Hupu), C19-8	400
Pn243	ND(1875)	—	10 Cash. Cast Brass. "Boo-jin" (by Hupu), C21-9	400
Pn244	ND(1875)	—	10 Cash. Cast Brass. "Boo-cuwan" (by Hupu), C24-10	400
Pn245	ND(1875)	—	10 Cash. Cast Brass. "Boo-giyan" (by Hupu), C20-10	400
Pn246	ND(1875)	—	10 Cash. Cast Brass. "Boo-yôn" (by Hupu), C26-10	400
Pn247	ND(1875)	—	10 Cash. Cast Brass. "Boo-yi" (by Hupu), C28-10	400

TRIAL STRIKES

KM#	Date	Mintage	Identification	Mkt Val
TS1	ND(1897)	—	Cash. Brass. KM#Pn2	125
TS2	ND(1897)	—	Cash. Brass. KM#Pn2	125

ANHWEI PROVINCE

Anhui

A province located in eastern China. Made a separate province during the Manchu dynasty in the 17th century. Principally agricultural with some mining of coal and iron ore. Spanish-American 8 Reales saw wide circulation in this province until the end of World War I. The provincial mint at Anking began operations in 1897, closed in 1899, and later reopened in 1902. The primary production of the mint was cash coins but included a series of silver coinage.

EMPIRE

Kuang-hsü

1875-1908

MILLED COINAGE

Y# 41 5 CENTS

1.3300 g., 0.8200 Silver .0351 oz. ASW **Obv. Inscription:** Kuang-hsü Yüan-pao

Date	Mintage	VG	F	VF	XF	Unc
ND (1897)	—	20.00	40.00	75.00	130	250

Y# 41.1 5 CENTS

1.3300 g., 0.8200 Silver .0351 oz. ASW **Obv. Inscription:** Kuang-hsü Yüan-pao

Date	Mintage	VG	F	VF	XF	Unc
25 (1899)	—	17.50	35.00	60.00	100	200

Y# 42 10 CENTS
2.6500 g., 0.8200 Silver .0699 oz. ASW **Obverse:** Rosettes divide legend **Obv. Inscription:** Kuang-hsü Yüan-pao

Date	Mintage	VG	F	VF	XF	Unc
ND (1897)	—	5.00	12.50	30.00	65.00	135

Y# 42.1 10 CENTS
2.6500 g., 0.8200 Silver .0699 oz. ASW **Obverse:** Without rosettes dividing legend **Obv. Inscription:** Kuang-hsü Yüan-pao

Date	Mintage	VG	F	VF	XF	Unc
24 (1898)	—	4.00	10.00	25.00	50.00	120

Y# 42.2 10 CENTS
2.6500 g., 0.8200 Silver .0699 oz. ASW **Obverse:** Rosettes divide legend **Obv. Inscription:** Kuang-hsü Yüan-pao

Date	Mintage	VG	F	VF	XF	Unc
24 (1898)	—	4.00	10.00	25.00	50.00	120

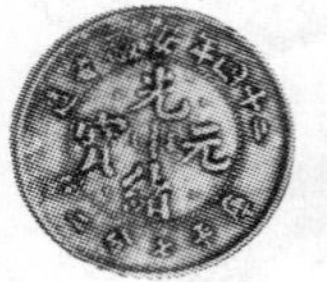

Y# 42.3 10 CENTS
2.6500 g., 0.8200 Silver .0699 oz. ASW **Obverse:** A S T C in field Obv. Designer: Kuang-hsü Yüan-pao

Date	Mintage	VG	F	VF	XF	Unc
24 (1898)	—	4.00	10.00	25.00	50.00	135

Y# 42.4 10 CENTS
2.6500 g., 0.8200 Silver .0699 oz. ASW **Obv. Legend:** Six characters at top **Obv. Inscription:** Kuang-hsü Yüan-pao

Date	Mintage	VG	F	VF	XF	Unc
CD (1898)	—	6.00	15.00	30.00	70.00	150

Y# 43 20 CENTS
5.3000 g., 0.8200 Silver .1397 oz. ASW **Obv. Inscription:** Kuang-hsü Yüan-pao **Reverse:** Large dragon and small English legend

Date	Mintage	VG	F	VF	XF	Unc
ND (1897)	—	10.00	20.00	40.00	80.00	185

Y# 43.1 20 CENTS
5.3000 g., 0.8200 Silver .1397 oz. ASW **Obv. Inscription:** Kuang-hsü Yüan-pao **Reverse:** Smaller dragon and larger English legend

Date	Mintage	VG	F	VF	XF	Unc
ND (1897)	—	10.00	20.00	40.00	80.00	185

Y# 43.2 20 CENTS
5.3000 g., 0.8200 Silver .1397 oz. ASW **Obv. Inscription:** Kuang-hsü Yüan-pao

Date	Mintage	VG	F	VF	XF	Unc
23 (1897)	2	—	—	—	—	—

Note: D.K.E. Ching Sale 6-91 AU realized $2,200

Y# 43.3 20 CENTS
5.3000 g., 0.8200 Silver .1397 oz. ASW **Obv. Inscription:** Kuang-hsü Yüan-pao

Date	Mintage	VG	F	VF	XF	Unc
24 (1898)	—	10.00	20.00	40.00	80.00	200

Y# 43.4 20 CENTS
5.3000 g., 0.8200 Silver .1397 oz. ASW **Obverse:** A S T C in field **Obv. Inscription:** Kuang-hsü Yüan-pao

Date	Mintage	VG	F	VF	XF	Unc
24 (1898)	—	10.00	20.00	40.00	80.00	200

Y# 44.1 50 CENTS
13.5000 g., 0.8600 Silver .3733 oz. ASW **Obverse:** A S T C in field **Obv. Inscription:** Kuang-hsü Yüan-pao

Date	Mintage	VG	F	VF	XF	Unc
24 (1898)	—	50.00	100	185	300	850

Y# 44.2 50 CENTS
13.5000 g., 0.8600 Silver .3733 oz. ASW **Obv. Inscription:** Kuang-hsü Yüan-pao

Date	Mintage	VG	F	VF	XF	Unc
24 (1898)	—	50.00	100	185	275	650

Note: Struck from reworked dies; Usually ASTC is faintly discernable

Y# 45 DOLLAR
27.1000 g., 0.9000 Silver .7842 oz. ASW **Obv. Inscription:** Kuang-hsü Yüan-pao

Date	Mintage	VG	F	VF	XF	Unc
ND (1897)	—	—	200	300	500	1,500

Y# 45.1 DOLLAR
27.1000 g., 0.9000 Silver .7842 oz. ASW **Obv. Inscription:** Kuang-hsü Yüan-pao

Date	Mintage	VG	F	VF	XF	Unc
23 (1897)	—	—	—	—	17,500	25,000

Y# 45.2 DOLLAR
27.1000 g., 0.9000 Silver .7842 oz. ASW **Obverse:** Tall Chinese character "4" in date **Obv. Inscription:** Kuang-hsü Yüan-pao **Reverse:** Similar to Y#45

Date	Mintage	VG	F	VF	XF	Unc
24 (1898)	—	—	125	200	500	1,400

Y# 45.3 DOLLAR
27.1000 g., 0.9000 Silver .7842 oz. ASW **Obverse:** Tall Chinese character "4" in date, A S T C in field **Obv. Inscription:** Kuang-hsü Yüan-pao **Reverse:** Similar to Y#45

Date	Mintage	F	VF	XF	Unc
24 (1898)	—	100	200	400	1,200

Y# 45.5 DOLLAR
27.1000 g., 0.9000 Silver .7842 oz. ASW **Obverse:** Short Chinese character "4" in date **Obv. Inscription:** Kuang-hsü Yüan-pao **Reverse:** Similar to Y#45

Date	Mintage	VG	F	VF	XF	Unc
24 (1898)	—	—	125	200	500	1,400

Y# 45.4 DOLLAR
26.9000 g., 0.9000 Silver .7842 oz. ASW **Obv. Legend:** Six characters at top **Obv. Inscription:** Kuang-hsü Yüan-pao **Reverse:** Similar to Y#45.1

Date	Mintage	VG	F	VF	XF	Unc
CD (1898)	—	—	200	300	500	1,600

PATTERNS

Including off metal strikes

KM#	Date	Mintage	Identification	Mkt Val
Pn1	CD23	—	Dollar. Silver Plated Bronze. Y#45.1.	18,500
Pn2	CD24	—	50 Cents. Brass. Y#44.	1,000

CHEKIANG PROVINCE

Zhejiang

A province located along the east coast of China. Although the smallest of the Chinese mainland provinces, it is one of the most densely populated. Economic interests are mostly agricultural with iron and coal mining and some fishing. A small mint opened in 1897. This was replaced by a larger mint which operated briefly 1898-99. Other mints opened in 1903 and 1905. These were merged with the Fukien Mint in 1906-07.

EMPIRE

Tao-kuang
1821-1851

PROVINCIAL CAST COINAGE

C# 4-3 CASH
Obverse: Type A **Reverse:** Large mint mark **Mint:** Chê **Note:** Size varies: 23-25mm.

Date	Mintage	Good	VG	F	VF	XF
ND(1820-51)	—	0.35	0.60	0.75	1.50	—

C# 4-3.1 CASH
Reverse: Small mint mark **Mint:** Chê **Note:** Size varies: 21-23mm.

Date	Mintage	Good	VG	F	VF	XF
ND(1820-51)	—	0.35	0.75	1.00	2.00	—

Hsien-fêng
1851-1861

PROVINCIAL CAST COINAGE

C# 4-3.5 CASH
Obverse: Type A **Note:** Size varies: 21-25mm.

Date	Mintage	Good	VG	F	VF	XF
ND(1851-61)	—	1.00	2.00	3.00	6.00	—

C# 4-3.6 CASH
Mint: Chê **Note:** Size varies: 16-20mm.

Date	Mintage	Good	VG	F	VF	XF
ND(1851-61)	—	1.00	2.00	3.00	6.00	—

C# 4-3.6a CASH
Cast Iron **Mint:** Chê

Date	Mintage	Good	VG	F	VF	XF
ND(1851-61)	—	5.00	10.00	20.00	40.00	—

C# 4-4 10 CASH
Cast Brass **Obverse:** Type B-1 **Reverse:** Manchu mint mark at right, value "Shih" (10) below **Mint:** Chê

Date	Mintage	Good	VG	F	VF	XF
ND(1851-61)	—	3.00	4.50	6.00	10.00	—

C# 4-4a 10 CASH
Cast Iron, 36 mm. **Mint:** Chê

Date	Mintage	Good	VG	F	VF	XF
ND(1851-61)	—	—	—	—	—	—

C# 4-9 10 CASH
Cast Brass **Reverse:** "Shih" (10) above **Mint:** Chê

Date	Mintage	Good	VG	F	VF	XF
ND(1851-61) Rare	—	—	—	—	—	—

C# 4-11 10 CASH
Cast Brass **Reverse:** Manchu mint mark left and Chinese mint mark right, "Shih" (10) at bottom **Mint:** Chê

Date	Mintage	Good	VG	F	VF	XF
ND(1851-61)	—	425	600	800	1,250	—

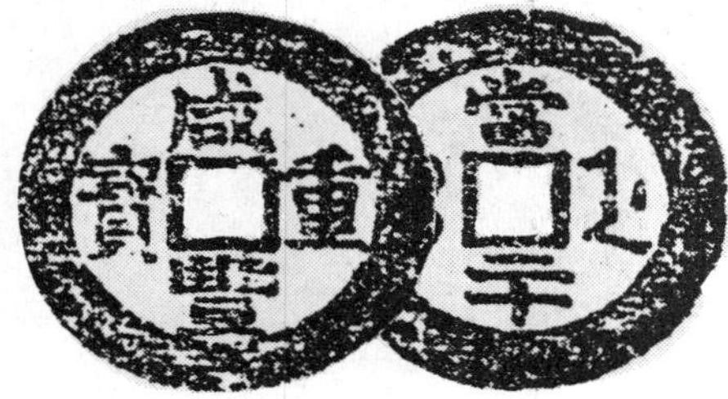

C# 4-5 20 CASH
Cast Brass **Obverse:** Type B-1 **Mint:** Chê

Date	Mintage	Good	VG	F	VF	XF
ND(1851-61)	—	425	600	850	1,250	—

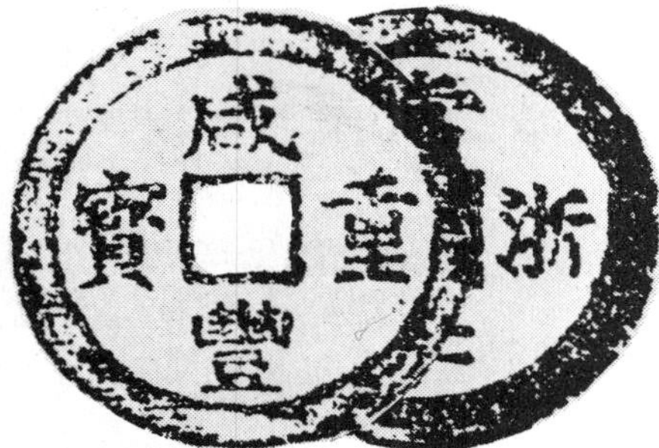

C# 4-12 20 CASH
Cast Brass **Reverse:** Manchu mint mark at left, Chinese at right **Mint:** Chê

Date	Mintage	Good	VG	F	VF	XF
ND(1851-61)	—	450	700	1,000	1,400	—

C# 4-6 30 CASH
Cast Brass **Obverse:** Type B-1 **Reverse:** Similar to 10 Cash, C#4-4 **Mint:** Chê

Date	Mintage	Good	VG	F	VF	XF
ND(1851-61)	—	525	750	1,100	1,600	—

C# 4-13 30 CASH
Cast Brass **Reverse:** Manchu mint mark at left, Chinese at right **Mint:** Chê

Date	Mintage	Good	VG	F	VF	XF
ND(1851-61)	—	450	700	1,000	1,400	—

C# 4-7 40 CASH
Cast Brass **Obverse:** Type B-1 **Mint:** Chê

Date	Mintage	Good	VG	F	VF	XF
ND(1851-61)	—	450	700	1,000	1,500	—

C# 4-14 40 CASH
Cast Brass **Reverse:** Manchu mint mark at left, Chinese at right **Mint:** Chê

Date	Mintage	Good	VG	F	VF	XF
ND(1851-61)	—	500	750	1,100	1,600	—

C# 4-8 50 CASH
Cast Brass **Obverse:** Type B-1 **Reverse:** Manchu mint mark at left, Chinese at right **Mint:** Chê

Date	Mintage	Good	VG	F	VF	XF
ND(1851-61)	—	100	200	350	500	—

C# 4-15 50 CASH
Cast Brass **Reverse:** Manchu mint mark at left, Chinese at right **Mint:** Chê

Date	Mintage	Good	VG	F	VF	XF
ND(1851-61)	—	80.00	150	250	350	—

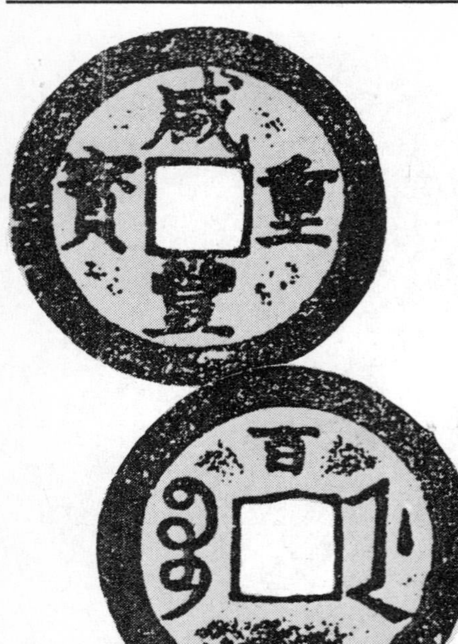

C# 4-10 100 CASH
Cast Brass **Obverse:** Type B-1 **Mint:** Chê

Date	Mintage	Good	VG	F	VF	XF
ND(1851-61)	—	1,000	1,500	2,100	3,000	—

C# 4-16 100 CASH
Cast Brass **Reverse:** Manchu mint mark at left, Chinese at right **Mint:** Chê

Date	Mintage	Good	VG	F	VF	XF
ND(1851-61)	—	100	165	275	400	—

T'ung-chih
1862-1875

PROVINCIAL CAST COINAGE

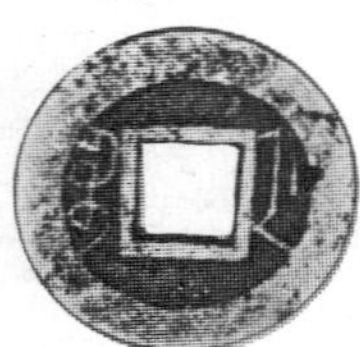

C# 4-17 CASH
Cast Brass **Obverse:** Type A-2 **Mint:** Chê

Date	Mintage	Good	VG	F	VF	XF
ND(1862-74)	—	1.25	2.50	4.00	8.00	—

Kuang-hsü
1875-1908

PROVINCIAL CAST COINAGE

C# 4-19 CASH
Cast Brass **Obverse:** Type A **Mint:** Chê **Note:** Size varies: 21-22mm.

Date	Mintage	Good	VG	F	VF	XF
ND(1875-1908)	—	3.00	4.50	6.50	12.00	—

C# 4-19.1 CASH
Cast Brass **Reverse:** More angular mint mark

Date	Mintage	Good	VG	F	VF	XF
ND(1875-1908)	—	2.00	3.00	4.00	6.00	—

MILLED COINAGE

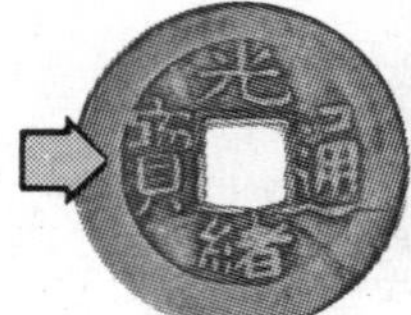

HSU# 151 CASH
Brass **Obverse:** Type A, large "Pao" at left **Obv. Inscription:** Kuang-hsü Yüan-pao **Mint:** Chê

Date	Mintage	VG	F	VF	XF	Unc
ND(1887)	—	35.00	50.00	65.00	80.00	—

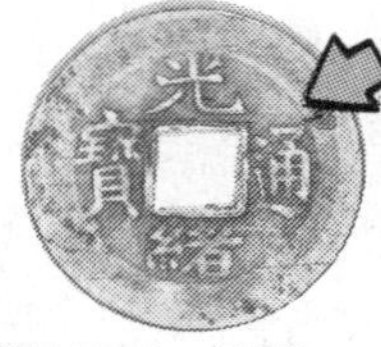
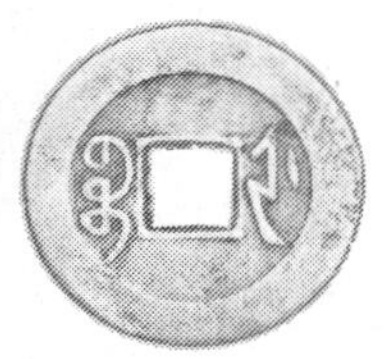

HSU# 151.1 CASH
Brass **Obverse:** Top part of "T'ung" shaped like a triangle **Mint:** Chê

Date	Mintage	VG	F	VF	XF	Unc
ND(1897-98)	—	35.00	50.00	60.00	80.00	—

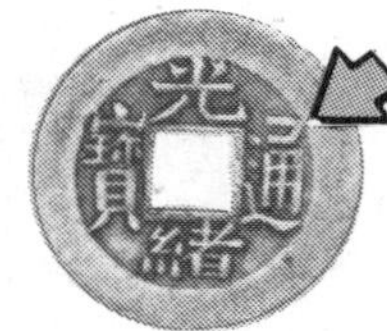
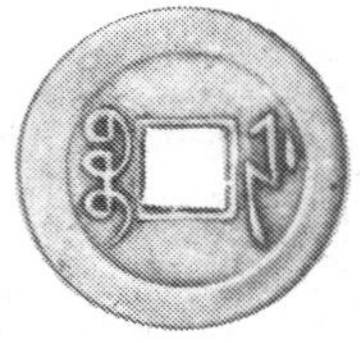

HSU# 151.2 CASH
Brass **Obverse:** Top part of "T'ung" shaped like a box **Mint:** Chê

Date	Mintage	VG	F	VF	XF	Unc
ND(1897-98)	—	35.00	50.00	60.00	80.00	—

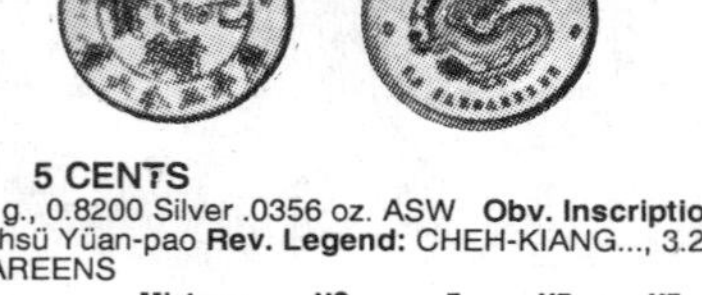

Y# 51 5 CENTS
1.3500 g., 0.8200 Silver .0356 oz. ASW **Obv. Inscription:** Kuang-hsü Yüan-pao **Rev. Legend:** CHEH-KIANG..., 3.2 CANDAREENS

Date	Mintage	VG	F	VF	XF	Unc
ND (1898)	—	6.00	15.00	25.00	40.00	100

Y# 52.2 10 CENTS
2.7000 g., 0.8200 Silver .0712 oz. ASW **Obv. Inscription:** Kuang-hsü Yüan-pao **Reverse:** Denomination reads 2.7 instead of 7.2

Date	Mintage	F	VF	XF	Unc
22(1896)	—	75.00	200	350	500

Y# 52 10 CENTS
2.7000 g., 0.8200 Silver .0712 oz. ASW **Obv. Inscription:** Kuang-hsü Yüan-pao **Rev. Legend:** CHEH-KIANG...

Date	Mintage	F	VF	XF	Unc
22 (1896)	—	100	250	400	600

Y# 52.1 10 CENTS
2.7000 g., 0.8200 Silver .0712 oz. ASW **Obv. Inscription:** Kuang-hsü Yüan-pao **Reverse:** Retrograde "N's" in legend

Date	Mintage	F	VF	XF	Unc
22 (1896)	—	100	250	400	600

Y# 52.3 10 CENTS
2.7000 g., 0.8200 Silver .0712 oz. ASW **Obv. Inscription:** Kuang-hsü Yüan-pao

Date	Mintage	F	VF	XF	Unc
23(1897)	—	100	250	450	600

Y# 52.4 10 CENTS
2.7000 g., 0.8200 Silver .0712 oz. ASW **Obv. Inscription:** Kuang-hsü Yüan-pao

Date	Mintage	F	VF	XF	Unc
ND(1898-99)	—	15.00	25.00	35.00	75.00

Y# 53 20 CENTS
5.4000 g., 0.8200 Silver .1424 oz. ASW **Obv. Inscription:** Kuang-hsü Yüan-pao **Reverse:** Six rows of scales on dragon

Date	Mintage	F	VF	XF	Unc
22(1896)	—	100	300	450	650

Y# 53.1 20 CENTS
5.4000 g., 0.8200 Silver .1424 oz. ASW **Obv. Inscription:** Kuang-hsü Yüan-pao **Reverse:** Letter "E" retrograde in legend **Rev. Legend:** CHEH-KIANG

Date	Mintage	F	VF	XF	Unc
22(1896)	—	100	300	450	650

Y# 53.2 20 CENTS
5.4000 g., 0.8200 Silver .1424 oz. ASW **Obv. Inscription:** Kuang-hsü Yüan-pao **Reverse:** Additional cross-strokes in letter "H" in legend, eight rows of scales on dragon **Rev. Legend:** CHEH-KIANG

Date	Mintage	F	VF	XF	Unc
22(1896)	—	100	300	450	650

Y# 53.3 20 CENTS
5.4000 g., 0.8200 Silver .1424 oz. ASW **Obv. Inscription:** Kuang-hsü Yüan-pao **Reverse:** Legend without hyphen **Rev. Legend:** CHEH KIANG

Date	Mintage	F	VF	XF	Unc
22(1896)	—	100	300	450	650

Y# 53.4 20 CENTS
5.4000 g., 0.8200 Silver .1424 oz. ASW **Obv. Inscription:** Kuang-hsü Yüan-pao **Reverse:** Dot in legend **Rev. Legend:** CHEH.KIANG

Date	Mintage	F	VF	XF	Unc
22(1896)	—	100	300	450	650

Y# 53.5 20 CENTS
5.4000 g., 0.8200 Silver .1424 oz. ASW **Obv. Inscription:** Kuang-hsü Yüan-pao **Reverse:** Rosettes made of seven dots dividing legend

Date	Mintage	F	VF	XF	Unc
23(1897)	—	125	300	450	700

Y# 53.6 20 CENTS
5.4000 g., 0.8200 Silver .1424 oz. ASW **Obv. Inscription:** Kuang-hsü Yüan-pao **Reverse:** Rosettes replaced by a cross **Rev. Legend:** MACE misspelled NACE

Date	Mintage	F	VF	XF	Unc
23(1897)	—	125	300	450	700

Y# 53.7 20 CENTS
5.4000 g., 0.8200 Silver .1424 oz. ASW **Obv. Inscription:** Kuang-hsü Yüan-pao **Rev. Legend:** CHEH-KIANG...

Date	Mintage	F	VF	XF	Unc
ND(1898-99)	—	15.00	30.00	50.00	150

Y# 54 50 CENTS
13.5000 g., 0.8600 Silver .3733 oz. ASW **Obv. Inscription:** Kuang-hsü Yüan-pao **Rev. Legend:** CHEH-KIANG...

Date	Mintage	F	VF	XF	Unc
ND(1898-99)	—	175	350	650	1,200

Y# 56 DOLLAR
27.5000 g., 0.9000 Silver .7958 oz. ASW **Obv. Inscription:** Kuang-hsü Yüan-pao **Rev. Legend:** CHEH-KIANG...

Date	Mintage	F	VF	XF	Unc
23(1897) Rare	—	—	—	—	—

Note: Superior Goodman Sale 6-91 AU realized $46,200

Y# 55 DOLLAR
27.5000 g., 0.9000 Silver .7958 oz. ASW **Obv. Inscription:** Kuang-hsü Yüan-pao

Date	Mintage	F	VF	XF	Unc
ND(1898-99)	—	—	—	9,900	13,500

PATTERNS

Including off metal strikes

KM#	Date	Mintage	Identification	Mkt Val
Pn2	ND23(1897)	—	5 Cents. Silver.	1,200
Pn3	ND23(1897)	—	5 Cents. Brass.	500

CHIHLI PROVINCE

Hebei, Hopei

A province located in northeastern China which contains the eastern end of the Great Wall. An important producer of coal and some iron ore. In 1928 the provincial name was changed from Chihli to Hopei. The Paoting mint was established in 1745 and only produced cast cash coins.

A mint for struck cash was established in 1888 and the mint for the Peiyang silver coinage was added in 1896. This was destroyed during the Boxer Rebellion. A replacement mint was built in 1902 for the provincial coinage and merged with the Tientsin (Tianjin) Central mint in 1910.

EMPIRE

Tao-Kuang
1821-1851

PROVINCIAL CAST COINAGE

C# 5-3 CASH
Cast Brass **Obverse:** Type A **Obv. Inscription:** Tao-kuang T'ung-pao **Mint:** Paoting

Date	Mintage	Good	VG	F	VF	XF
ND(1820-51)	—	0.60	0.90	1.50	2.50	—

C# 5-3.1 CASH
Cast Brass **Obv. Inscription:** Tao-kuang T'ung-pao **Reverse:** Dot below **Mint:** Paoting

Date	Mintage	Good	VG	F	VF	XF
ND(1820-51)	—	2.50	3.50	6.00	10.00	—

Hsien-fêng
1851-1861

PROVINCIAL CAST COINAGE

C# 5-4 CASH
Cast Brass **Obverse:** Type A **Obv. Inscription:** Hsien-fêng T'ung-pao **Mint:** Paoting

Date	Mintage	Good	VG	F	VF	XF
ND(1851-61)	—	2.00	3.50	6.00	10.00	—

C# 5-4a CASH
Cast Iron **Obv. Inscription:** Hsien-fêng T'ung-pao **Mint:** Paoting

Date	Mintage	Good	VG	F	VF	XF
ND(1851-61)	—	11.50	18.50	30.00	55.00	—

C# 6-1 CASH
Cast Brass **Obverse:** Type A **Obv. Inscription:** Hsien-fêng T'ung-pao **Mint:** Ch'eng-te

Date	Mintage	Good	VG	F	VF	XF
ND(1851-61)	—	45.00	65.00	75.00	110	—

C# 6-1a CASH
Cast Iron **Obv. Inscription:** Hsien-fêng T'ung-pao **Mint:** Ch'eng-te

Date	Mintage	Good	VG	F	VF	XF
ND(1851-61)	—	20.00	30.00	50.00	80.00	—

C# 6-2 5 CASH
Cast Brass **Obv. Inscription:** Hsien-fêng Chung-pao **Mint:** Ch'eng-te

Date	Mintage	Good	VG	F	VF	XF
ND(1851-61)	—	450	800	1,150	1,600	—

C# 6-2a 5 CASH
Cast Iron **Obv. Inscription:** Hsien-fêng Chung-pao **Mint:** Ch'eng-te

Date	Mintage	Good	VG	F	VF	XF
ND(1851-61)	—	20.00	30.00	50.00	90.00	—

C# 7-1 5 CASH
Cast Brass **Obverse:** Type B-1 **Obv. Inscription:** Hsien-fêng Chung-pao **Mint:** Chi

Date	Mintage	Good	VG	F	VF	XF
ND(1851-61)	—	27.50	45.00	75.00	125	—

C# 7-1a 5 CASH
Cast Iron **Obv. Inscription:** Hsien-fêng Chung-pao **Mint:** Chi

Date	Mintage	Good	VG	F	VF	XF
ND(1851-61)	—	11.50	18.50	30.00	50.00	—

C# 5-5 10 CASH
Cast Brass **Obverse:** Type B-1 **Obv. Inscription:** Hsien-fêng Chung-pao **Mint:** Paoting

Date	Mintage	Good	VG	F	VF	XF
ND(1851-61)	—	10.00	17.50	30.00	50.00	—

C# 5-5.1 10 CASH
Cast Brass **Obv. Inscription:** Hsien-fêng Chung-pao **Reverse:** Dot above **Mint:** Paoting

Date	Mintage	Good	VG	F	VF	XF
ND(1851-61)	—	13.50	21.50	37.50	60.00	—

C# 5-5a 10 CASH
Cast Iron **Obv. Inscription:** Hsien-fêng Chung-pao **Mint:** Paoting

Date	Mintage	Good	VG	F	VF	XF
ND(1851-61)	—	30.00	45.00	75.00	125	—

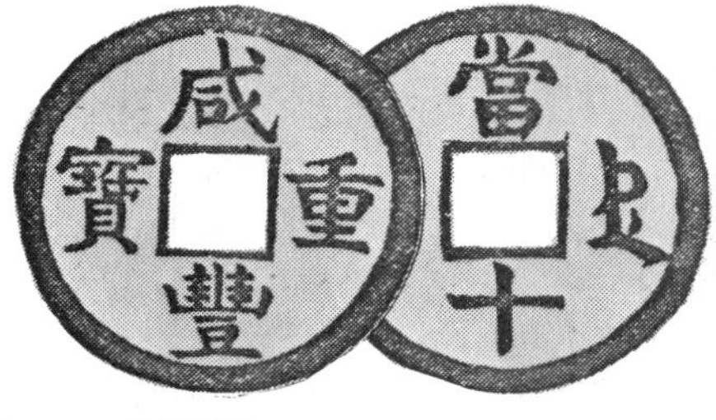

C# 6-3 10 CASH
Cast Brass **Obverse:** Type B-1 **Obv. Inscription:** Hsien-fêng Chung-pao **Mint:** Chengde

Date	Mintage	Good	VG	F	VF	XF
ND(1851-61)	—	15.00	20.00	32.50	50.00	—

C# 6-3a 10 CASH
Cast Iron **Obv. Inscription:** Hsien-fêng Chung-pao **Mint:** Ch'eng-te

Date	Mintage	Good	VG	F	VF	XF
ND(1851-61)	—	30.00	40.00	90.00	150	—

C# 7-2 10 CASH
Cast Brass, 36 mm. **Obv. Inscription:** Hsien-fêng Chung-pao **Mint:** Chi **Note:** Large size.

Date	Mintage	Good	VG	F	VF	XF
ND(1851-61)	—	90.00	150	185	250	—

C# 7-2.1 10 CASH
Cast Brass, 27 mm. **Obv. Inscription:** Hsien-fêng Chung-pao **Mint:** Chi **Note:** Small size.

Date	Mintage	Good	VG	F	VF	XF
ND(1851-61)	—	8.00	18.00	25.00	35.00	—

C# 7-2a 10 CASH
Cast Iron **Obv. Inscription:** Hsien-fêng Chung-pao **Mint:** Chi

Date	Mintage	Good	VG	F	VF	XF
ND(1851-61)	—	27.50	45.00	75.00	125	—

C# 5-6 50 CASH
Cast Brass **Obverse:** Type B-1 **Obv. Inscription:** Hsien-fêng Chung-pao **Mint:** Paoting

Date	Mintage	Good	VG	F	VF	XF
ND(1851-61)	—	25.00	40.00	65.00	130	—

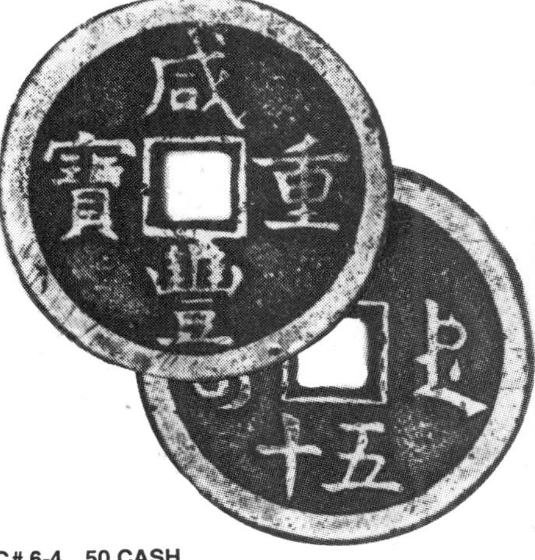

C# 6-4 50 CASH
Cast Brass **Obverse:** Type B-1 **Obv. Inscription:** Hsien-fêng Chung-pao **Mint:** Ch'eng-te

Date	Mintage	Good	VG	F	VF	XF
ND(1851-61)	—	13.50	30.00	42.50	60.00	—

C# 7-3 50 CASH
Cast Brass **Obv. Inscription:** Hsien-fêng Chung-pao **Mint:** Chi

Date	Mintage	Good	VG	F	VF	XF
ND(1851-61)	—	20.00	32.50	55.00	100	—

C# 5-7 100 CASH
Cast Brass **Obverse:** Type C **Obv. Inscription:** Hsien-fêng Yüan-pao **Mint:** Paoting

Date	Mintage	Good	VG	F	VF	XF
ND(1851-61)	—	22.50	35.00	50.00	70.00	—

C# 6-5 100 CASH
Cast Brass **Obv. Inscription:** Hsien-fêng Yüan-pao **Mint:** Ch'eng-te

Date	Mintage	Good	VG	F	VF	XF
ND(1851-61)	—	27.50	50.00	62.50	80.00	—

C# 7-4 100 CASH
Cast Brass **Obv. Inscription:** Hsien-fêng Yüan-pao **Mint:** Chi

Date	Mintage	Good	VG	F	VF	XF
ND(1851-61)	—	175	300	425	600	—

Note: This mint mark was later transferred to the Kirin Mint; the Chichow Mint operated through the reign of Hsien-fêng

T'ung-chih
1862-1875

PROVINCIAL CAST COINAGE

C# 5-8 CASH
Cast Brass **Obverse:** Type A-2 **Obv. Inscription:** T'ung-chih T'ung-pao **Mint:** Paoting

Date	Mintage	Good	VG	F	VF	XF
ND(1862-74)	—	3.50	6.00	10.00	16.50	—

Kuang-hsü
1875-1908

PROVINCIAL CAST COINAGE

C# 3-1.1 CASH
Cast Brass, 23 mm. **Obv. Inscription:** Kuang-hsü T'ung-pao **Reverse:** Type 1 mint mark, Manchu inscription **Rev. Inscription:** Boo-gu **Mint:** Taku

Date	Mintage	Good	VG	F	VF	XF
ND(1875-1908)	—	90.00	125	200	300	—

C# 3-1.2 CASH
Cast Brass, 22 mm. **Obv. Inscription:** Kuang-hsü T'ung-pao **Reverse:** Type 2 mint mark, Manchu inscription **Rev. Inscription:** Boo-gu **Mint:** Taku

Date	Mintage	Good	VG	F	VF	XF
ND(1875-1908)	—	20.00	30.00	50.00	75.00	—

C# 5-10 CASH
Cast Brass **Obverse:** Type A **Obv. Inscription:** Kuang-hsü T'ung-pao **Mint:** Paoting **Note:** Schjöth #1572.

Date	Mintage	Good	VG	F	VF	XF
ND(1875-86)	—	3.50	6.00	10.00	16.50	—

C# 5-10.1 CASH
Cast Brass **Obv. Inscription:** Kuang-hsü T'ung-pao **Reverse:** Dot above **Mint:** Paoting **Note:** Schjöth #1568.

Date	Mintage	Good	VG	F	VF	XF
ND(1875-86)	—	4.50	7.50	12.50	25.00	—

C# 5-10.2 CASH
Cast Brass **Obv. Inscription:** Kuang-hsü T'ung-pao **Reverse:** Crescent above **Mint:** Paoting

Date	Mintage	Good	VG	F	VF	XF
ND(1875-86)	—	4.50	7.50	12.00	20.00	—

Note: The crescent is known in various positions above the center hole

C# 5-10.3 CASH
Cast Brass **Obv. Inscription:** Kuang-hsü T'ung-pao **Reverse:** Circle above **Mint:** Paoting

Date	Mintage	Good	VG	F	VF	XF
ND(1875-86)	—	4.50	7.50	12.50	25.00	—

C# 5-10.4 CASH
Cast Brass **Obv. Inscription:** Kuang-hsü T'ung-pao **Reverse:** Dot below **Mint:** Paoting

Date	Mintage	Good	VG	F	VF	XF
ND(1875-86)	—	3.50	6.00	10.00	16.00	—

C# 5-10.5 CASH
Cast Brass **Obv. Inscription:** Kuang-hsü T'ung-pao **Reverse:** Circle below **Mint:** Paoting

Date	Mintage	Good	VG	F	VF	XF
ND(1875-86)	—	4.50	7.50	12.00	20.00	—

C# 5-10.6 CASH
Cast Brass **Obv. Inscription:** Kuang-hsü T'ung-pao **Reverse:** Dash above **Mint:** Paoting

Date	Mintage	Good	VG	F	VF	XF
ND(1875-86)	—	4.50	7.50	12.00	20.00	—

C# 5-10.7 CASH
Cast Brass **Obv. Inscription:** Kuang-hsü T'ung-pao **Reverse:** Dash below **Mint:** Paoting

Date	Mintage	Good	VG	F	VF	XF
ND(1875-86)	—	4.50	7.50	12.00	20.00	—

C# 5-10.8 CASH
Cast Brass **Obv. Inscription:** Kuang-hsü T'ung-pao **Reverse:** Dot upper left **Mint:** Paoting

Date	Mintage	Good	VG	F	VF	XF
ND(1875-86)	—	4.50	7.50	12.50	25.00	—

C# 5-10.9 CASH
Cast Brass **Obv. Inscription:** Kuang-hsü T'ung-pao **Reverse:** Dot upper right **Mint:** Paoting

Date	Mintage	Good	VG	F	VF	XF
ND(1875-86)	—	4.50	7.50	12.50	25.00	—

C# 8-1 CASH
Cast Brass, 23 mm. **Obv. Inscription:** Kuang-hsü T'ung-pao **Reverse:** Manchu inscription **Mint:** Chih

Date	Mintage	Good	VG	F	VF	XF
ND(1875-1908)	—	2.50	4.50	7.50	12.00	—

C# 8-1.1 CASH
Cast Brass **Obv. Inscription:** Kuang-hsü T'ung-pao **Reverse:** Dot above, Manchu inscription **Rev. Inscription:** Boo-jiyen **Mint:** Chih

Date	Mintage	Good	VG	F	VF	XF
ND(1875-1908)	—	2.75	4.50	7.50	15.00	—

C# 8-1.2 CASH
Cast Brass **Obv. Inscription:** Kuang-hsü T'ung-pao **Reverse:** Dot below, Manchu inscription **Rev. Inscription:** Boo-jiyen **Mint:** Chih

Date	Mintage	Good	VG	F	VF	XF
ND(1875-1908)	—	2.00	3.50	6.00	10.00	—

C# 8-1.3 CASH
Cast Brass **Obv. Inscription:** Kuang-hsü T'ung-pao **Reverse:** 2 dots below, Manchu inscription **Rev. Inscription:** Boo-jiyen **Mint:** Chih

Date	Mintage	Good	VG	F	VF	XF
ND(1875-1908)	—	3.50	5.50	9.00	15.00	—

C# 8-1.4 CASH
Cast Brass **Obv. Inscription:** Kuang-hsü T'ung-pao **Reverse:** Circle above Manchu inscription **Rev. Inscription:** Boo-jiyen **Mint:** Chih

Date	Mintage	Good	VG	F	VF	XF
ND(1875-1908)	—	3.50	5.50	9.00	18.00	—

C# 8-1.5 CASH
Cast Brass **Obv. Inscription:** Kuang-hsü T'ung-pao **Reverse:** Circle below Manchu inscription **Rev. Inscription:** Boo-jiyen **Mint:** Chih

Date	Mintage	Good	VG	F	VF	XF
ND(1875-1908)	—	3.50	5.50	9.00	18.00	—

C# 8-1.6 CASH
Cast Brass **Obv. Inscription:** Kuang-hsü T'ung-pao **Reverse:** Crescent above Manchu inscription **Rev. Inscription:** Boo-jiyen **Mint:** Chih

Date	Mintage	Good	VG	F	VF	XF
ND(1875-1908)	—	3.50	5.50	9.00	18.00	—

C# 8-1.7 CASH
Cast Brass **Obv. Inscription:** Kuang-hsü T'ung-pao **Reverse:** Crescent below Manchu inscription **Rev. Inscription:** Boo-jiyen **Mint:** Chih

Date	Mintage	Good	VG	F	VF	XF
ND(1875-1908)	—	2.00	3.75	7.50	17.00	—

C# 8-1.8 CASH
Cast Brass **Obv. Inscription:** Kuang-hsü T'ung-pao **Reverse:** Dash below Manchu inscription **Rev. Inscription:** Boo-jiyen **Mint:** Chih

Date	Mintage	Good	VG	F	VF	XF
ND(1875-1908)	—	2.00	3.75	7.50	15.00	—

Note: Varieties exist with dots and crescents in different corners on reverse and also with incuse dots.

MILLED COINAGE

HSU# 410 CASH
Brass **Obverse:** Small characters **Obv. Inscription:** Kuang-hsü T'ung-pao **Reverse:** Large characters

Date	Mintage	VG	F	VF	XF	Unc
ND(1888-89)	—	40.00	50.00	75.00	120	—

HSU# 410.1 CASH
Brass **Obverse:** Large characters **Obv. Inscription:** Kuang-hsü T'ung-pao **Reverse:** Small characters

Date	Mintage	VG	F	VF	XF	Unc
ND(1888-89)	—	40.00	50.00	75.00	120	—

HSU# 410.2 CASH
Brass **Obverse:** Small characters **Obv. Inscription:** Kuang-hsü T'ung-pao **Reverse:** Small characters

Date	Mintage	VG	F	VF	XF	Unc
ND(1888-89)	—	40.00	50.00	75.00	120	—

HSU# 410.3 CASH
Brass **Obverse:** Large characters **Obv. Inscription:** Kuang-hsü T'ung-pao **Reverse:** Large characters

Date	Mintage	VG	F	VF	XF	Unc
ND(1888-89)	—	40.00	50.00	75.00	120	—

Y# 61 5 CENTS
1.3200 g., 0.8200 Silver .0348 oz. ASW **Obv. Inscription:** Kuang-hsü Yüan-pao

Date	Mintage	VG	F	VF	XF	Unc
22(1896)	7,000	100	200	250	300	650

Y# 61.1 5 CENTS
1.3200 g., 0.8200 Silver .0348 oz. ASW **Obv. Legend:** "TAI TSING..." **Obv. Inscription:** Kuang-hsü Yüan-pao

Date	Mintage	VG	F	VF	XF	Unc
23(1897)	Inc. above	12.50	25.00	50.00	85.00	225

Y# 61.2 5 CENTS
1.3200 g., 0.8200 Silver .0348 oz. ASW **Obv. Inscription:** Kuang-hsü Yüan-pao **Reverse:** Redesigned dragon

Date	Mintage	VG	F	VF	XF	Unc
23(1897)	39,000	10.00	20.00	35.00	55.00	120
24(1898)	231,000	7.50	18.00	30.00	40.00	100

Y# 69 5 CENTS
1.3200 g., 0.8200 Silver .0348 oz. ASW **Obv. Inscription:** Kuang-hsü Yüan-pao

Date	Mintage	VG	F	VF	XF	Unc
25(1899)	97,000	10.00	20.00	50.00	75.00	125
26(1900)	—	62.50	125	250	500	1,000

Y# 62 10 CENTS
2.6500 g., 0.8200 Silver .0699 oz. ASW **Obv. Inscription:** Kuang-hsü Yüan-pao

Date	Mintage	VG	F	VF	XF	Unc
22(1896)	5,000	50.00	100	150	250	600

Y# 62.1 10 CENTS
2.6500 g., 0.8200 Silver .0699 oz. ASW **Obv. Legend:** "TAI TSING..." **Obv. Inscription:** Kuang-hsü Yüan-pao

Date	Mintage	Good	VG	F	VF	XF
23(1897)	148,000	—	7.50	15.00	30.00	50.00
24(1898)	614,000	—	6.50	12.00	25.00	40.00

Y# 70 10 CENTS
2.6500 g., 0.8200 Silver .0699 oz. ASW **Obv. Inscription:** Kuang-hsü Yüan-pao

Date	Mintage	Good	VG	F	VF	XF
25(1899)	153,000	—	10.00	20.00	50.00	75.00

Y# 63.1 20 CENTS
5.3000 g., 0.8200 Silver .1397 oz. ASW **Obv. Inscription:** Kuang-hsü Yüan-pao

Date	Mintage	VG	F	VF	XF	Unc
22(1896)	12,000	50.00	100	225	400	750

Y# 63.2 20 CENTS
5.3000 g., 0.8200 Silver .1397 oz. ASW **Obv. Legend:** "TAI TSING..." **Obv. Inscription:** Kuang-hsü Yüan-pao

Date	Mintage	Good	VG	F	VF	XF
23(1897)	147,000	6.50	16.50	30.00	45.00	120
24(1898)	350,000	—	6.00	15.00	25.00	40.00

Y# 71 20 CENTS
5.3000 g., 0.8200 Silver .1397 oz. ASW **Obv. Inscription:** Kuang-hsü Yüan-pao **Reverse:** Side view dragon, legend at bottom **Rev. Legend:** PEI YANG

Date	Mintage	VG	F	VF	XF	Unc
25(1899)	152,000	12.50	25.00	50.00	100	300
26(1900)	—	250	500	650	900	1,500

Y# 64 50 CENTS
13.3000 g., 0.8600 Silver .3678 oz. ASW **Obv. Inscription:** Kuang-hsü Yüan-pao

Date	Mintage	VG	F	VF	XF	Unc
22(1896)	2,500	200	400	800	1,500	3,000

Y# 64.1 50 CENTS
13.3000 g., 0.8600 Silver .3678 oz. ASW **Obv. Legend:** "TAI TSING..." **Obv. Inscription:** Kuang-hsü Yüan-pao **Reverse:** Dragon with beady eyes

Date	Mintage	VG	F	VF	XF	Unc
23(1897)	21,000	15.00	30.00	65.00	150	300
24(1898)	Inc. above	15.00	30.00	65.00	150	300

Y# 64.2 50 CENTS
13.3000 g., 0.8600 Silver .3678 oz. ASW **Obv. Inscription:** Kuang-hsü Yüan-pao **Reverse:** Dragon with eyelids

Date	Mintage	VG	F	VF	XF	Unc
24(1898)	176,000	10.00	20.00	50.00	90.00	240

Y# 72 50 CENTS
13.3000 g., 0.8600 Silver .3678 oz. ASW **Obv. Inscription:** Kuang-hsü Yüan-pao

Date	Mintage	VG	F	VF	XF	Unc
25(1899)	56,000	37.50	75.00	140	225	400

Y# 65 DOLLAR
26.7000 g., 0.9000 Silver .7727 oz. ASW **Obv. Inscription:** Kuang-hsü Yüan-pao

Date	Mintage	VG	F	VF	XF	Unc
22(1896)	3,000	500	1,000	2,000	4,000	8,000

Y# 65.1 DOLLAR
26.7000 g., 0.9000 Silver .7727 oz. ASW **Obv. Inscription:** Kuang-hsü Yüan-pao **Reverse:** Dragon with beady eyes

Date	Mintage	VG	F	VF	XF	Unc
23(1897)	1,120,000	30.00	60.00	150	400	1,000

Y# 65.2 DOLLAR
26.7000 g., 0.9000 Silver .7727 oz. ASW **Obv. Inscription:** Kuang-hsü Yüan-pao **Reverse:** Dragon with eyelids

Date	Mintage	VG	F	VF	XF	Unc
24(1898)	2,806,000	30.00	60.00	150	400	1,000

Y# 73 DOLLAR
26.7000 g., 0.9000 Silver .7727 oz. ASW **Obv. Inscription:** Kuang-hsü Yüan-pao **Reverse:** Side view dragon, legend at bottom **Rev. Legend:** PEI YANG **Mint:** Chih

Date	Mintage	VG	F	VF	XF	Unc
25(1899)	1,566,000	12.50	25.00	40.00	75.00	450
26(1900)	—	20.00	40.00	75.00	125	750
29(1903)	22,018,000	5.00	12.50	17.00	42.50	200

PATTERNS

Including off metal strikes

KM#	Date	Mintage	Identification	Mkt Val
Pn5	25(1899)	—	5 Cents. Copper. Y#69.	—

KM#	Date	Mintage	Identification	Mkt Val
Pn1	(c.1900)	—	Cash. Brass.	—

Note: Mint mark "Boo-ting" produced at the Birmingham Mint, England

KM#	Date	Mintage	Identification	Mkt Val
Pn2	(c.1900)	—	Cash. Copper.	650

Note: Mint mark "Boo-gu" for Taku Mint produced at the Imperial Naval Ship Yard

KM#	Date	Mintage	Identification	Mkt Val
Pn3	(c.1900)	—	Tael. Copper.	300
Pn4	(c.1900)	—	10 Taels. Brass.	400

FENGTIEN PROVINCE

(Fungtien)
Liaoning

The southernmost province of the Three Eastern Provinces was known by a variety of names including Fengtien, Shengching, and Liaoning. The modern Mukden (Fengtien Province) Mint operated from 1897 to 1931.

EMPIRE

Kuang-hsü
1875-1908

PROVINCIAL CAST COINAGE

C# 9-1 CASH
Cast Brass **Obverse:** Type A **Obv. Inscription:** Kuang-hsü T'ung-pao **Reverse:** Manchu inscription **Rev. Inscription:** Boo-fung **Mint:** Fung

Date	Mintage	Good	VG	F	VF	XF
ND(1875-1908)	—	20.00	30.00	50.00	80.00	—

MILLED COINAGE

Y# 81 10 CASH
Copper **Obv. Inscription:** Kuang-hsü T'ung-pao

Date	Mintage	VG	F	VF	XF	Unc
ND(c.1899)	—	40.00	60.00	90.00	200	—

Note: 7 varieties exist

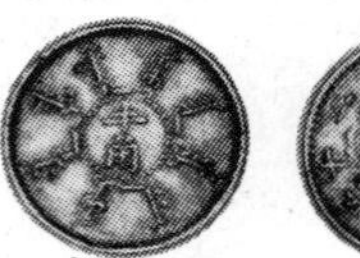

Y# 83 5 CENTS
1.2000 g., Silver **Obv. Inscription:** Tai-ch'ing T'ung-pi

Date	Mintage	VG	F	VF	XF	Unc
25(1899)	—	—	20.00	50.00	80.00	200

Y# 84 10 CENTS
Silver **Obv. Inscription:** Tai-ch'ing T'ung-pi

Date	Mintage	VG	F	VF	XF	Unc
24(1898)	—	—	20.00	50.00	80.00	200

Y# 85 20 CENTS
5.2000 g., Silver **Obv. Inscription:** Tai-ch'ing T'ung-pi **Reverse:** Four rows of scales on dragon, clockwise spiral on pearl

Date	Mintage	VG	F	VF	XF	Unc
24(1898)	—	—	15.00	30.00	55.00	160

Y# 85.1 20 CENTS
5.2000 g., Silver **Obv. Inscription:** Tai-ch'ing T'ung-pi **Reverse:** Five rows of scales on dragon, counter-clockwise spiral on pearl

Date	Mintage	VG	F	VF	XF	Unc
24(1898)	—	—	15.00	30.00	55.00	160

Y# 86 50 CENTS
13.1000 g., Silver **Obv. Inscription:** Kuang-hsü Yüan-pao

Date	Mintage	VG	F	VF	XF	Unc
32(1897) Rare	—	—	—	—	—	—

Note: Error - Year 32 should read year 23 (1897); Workmanship on this coin is inferior to that of the succeeding years

Date	Mintage	VG	F	VF	XF	Unc
24(1898)	—	—	100	150	250	500
25(1899)	—	—	200	350	500	800

Y# 87 DOLLAR
26.4000 g., 0.8500 Silver .7215 oz. ASW **Obv. Inscription:** Kuang-hsü Yüan-pao

Date	Mintage	VG	F	VF	XF	Unc
24(1898)	—	—	125	250	400	750
25(1899)	—	—	300	450	650	1,000

Y# 87.1 DOLLAR
26.4000 g., 0.8500 Silver .7215 oz. ASW **Obverse:** "Yi Yan" within double circle, one of dots around one solid **Obv. Inscription:** Kuang-hsü Yüan-pao

Date	Mintage	VG	F	VF	XF	Unc
25(1899)	—	—	250	400	600	900

PATTERNS

Including off metal strikes

KM#	Date	Mintage	Identification	Mkt Val
Pn1	(c.1899)	—	Cash. Copper. "Szu (4) Fen" below hole. HSU#456.1.	200
Pn2	(c.1899)	—	Cash. Copper. Without characters below hole.	—

FUKIEN PROVINCE

Fujian

A province located on the southeastern coast of China, including the island of Taiwan until it became its own separate province in 1885. Although known mainly as an agricultural area, forestry and some mining, particularly iron ore and coal, are also important to the economy. The Foochow Mint operated throughout the Manchu dynasty. The Viceroy's or City mint was opened in 1896 for struck coinage. Two other mints were established in 1905, the Mamoi Arsenal Mint which struck the Custom-House issues until it closed in 1906, and the West Mint which later became the main Fukien (Fujian) Mint. It closed between 1914 and 1920. Various subsidiary mints were in operation from 1924 to 1925.

EMPIRE

MILLED COINAGE

K# 5 DOLLAR
27.2000 g., Silver **Obverse:** Lower character written in different style

Date	Mintage	Good	VG	F	VF	XF
ND(1844)	—	1,500	3,000	4,000	5,000	7,500

K# 6 DOLLAR
25.7000 g., Silver **Obverse:** Four characters at top **Obv. Inscription:** Changchow Soldier's Pay

Date	Mintage	Good	VG	F	VF	XF
ND(c.1844)	—	900	1,800	2,500	3,000	4,500

K# 7 DOLLAR
26.2000 g., Silver **Obverse:** Two rosettes, 2 characters at top **Obv. Inscription:** Soldier's Pay **Reverse:** Two rosettes

Date	Mintage	Good	VG	F	VF	XF
ND(1844)	—	175	350	700	1,200	2,500

K# 7c DOLLAR
26.2000 g., Silver **Obverse:** Two rosettes and two five-petalled flowers

Date	Mintage	VG	F	VF	XF	Unc
ND(1844)	—	850	1,250	1,500	3,000	—

Tao-kuang
1821-1851

PROVINCIAL CAST COINAGE

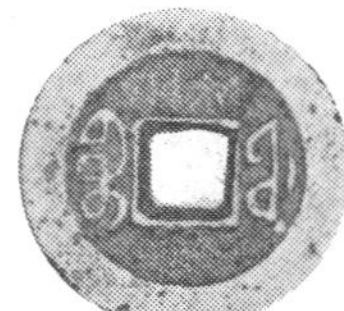

C# 10-3 CASH
Cast Copper Or Brass **Obv. Inscription:** Tao-kuang T'ung-pao **Mint:** Fu

Date	Mintage	Good	VG	F	VF	XF
ND(1821-51)	—	1.00	2.50	3.00	4.50	—

C# 10-4 CASH
Cast Copper Or Brass, 26 mm. **Obv. Inscription:** Tao-kuang T'ung-pao **Reverse:** Line right of mint mark **Mint:** Fu

Date	Mintage	Good	VG	F	VF	XF
ND(1851-61)	—	2.00	3.00	4.00	10.00	—

C# 10-4.1 CASH
Cast Copper Or Brass **Obv. Inscription:** Tao-kuang T'ung-pao **Reverse:** Dot right of mint mark **Mint:** Fu **Note:** Size varies: 22-24mm.

Date	Mintage	Good	VG	F	VF	XF
ND(1851-61)	—	2.50	3.50	5.50	12.50	—

Hsien-fêng
1851-1861

PROVINCIAL CAST COINAGE

C# 10-4a.1 CASH
Cast Iron **Obv. Inscription:** Hsien-fêng T'ung-pao **Mint:** Fu

Date	Mintage	Good	VG	F	VF	XF
ND(1851-61)	—	15.00	27.00	37.50	60.00	—

C# 10-4a.2 CASH
Cast Iron **Obv. Inscription:** Hsien-fêng T'ung-pao **Mint:** Fu **Note:** Larger size. Wide rims.

Date	Mintage	Good	VG	F	VF	XF
ND(1851-61)	—	20.00	35.00	50.00	75.00	—

C# 10-5 5 CASH
Cast Brass, 31 mm. **Obv. Inscription:** Hsien-fêng Chung-pao **Reverse:** Weight on the rim similar to 20 Cash, C#10-12 **Mint:** Fu

Date	Mintage	Good	VG	F	VF	XF
ND(1851-61)	—	50.00	100	150	200	—

C# 10-5.1 5 CASH
Cast Brass **Obv. Inscription:** Hsien-fêng Chung-pao **Reverse:** "Wen" at top **Mint:** Fu

Date	Mintage	Good	VG	F	VF	XF
ND(1854) Rare	—	—	—	—	—	—

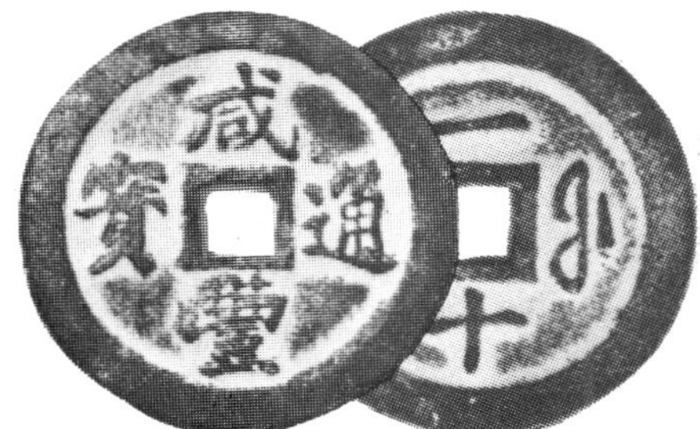

C# 10-6 10 CASH
Cast Brass **Obverse:** Type A **Obv. Inscription:** Hsien-fêng Chung-pao **Mint:** Fu **Note:** Size varies: 35-40mm.

Date	Mintage	Good	VG	F	VF	XF
ND(1851-61)	—	4.00	8.00	17.00	30.00	—

C# 10-6.1 10 CASH

Cast Brass, 35-40 mm. **Obv. Inscription:** Hsien-fêng Chung-pao **Reverse:** Characters "Ta Ch'ing" appear at upper right and left **Mint:** Fu **Note:** Size varies: 35-40mm.

Date	Mintage	Good	VG	F	VF	XF
ND(1851-61)	—	2,000	3,000	4,250	—	—

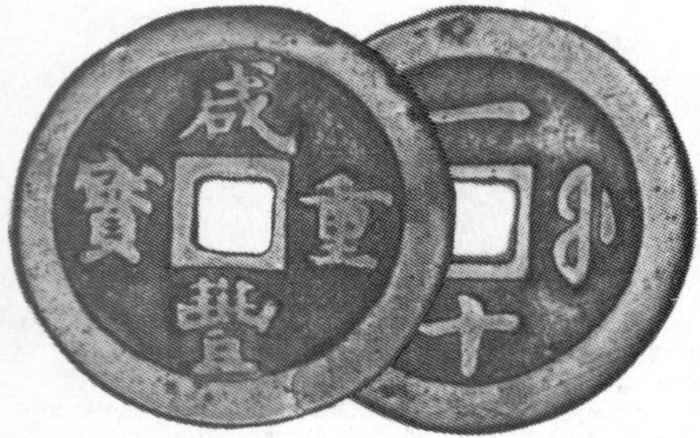

C# 10-7 10 CASH

Cast Brass **Obverse:** Type B-1 **Obv. Inscription:** Hsien-fêng Chung-pao **Mint:** Fu **Note:** Size varies: 35-40mm.

Date	Mintage	Good	VG	F	VF	XF
ND(1851-61)	—	8.50	15.00	18.50	35.00	—

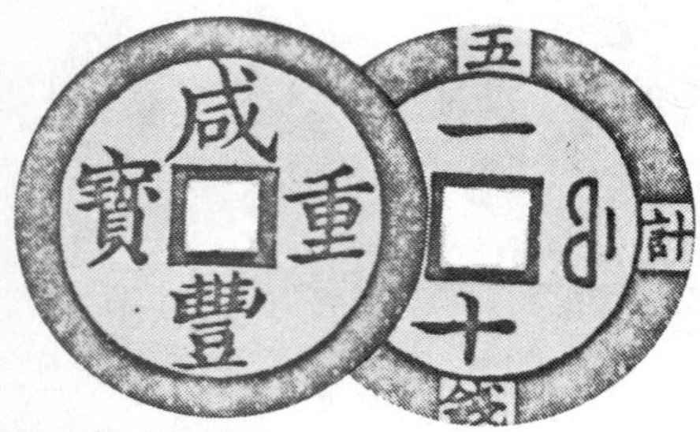

C# 10-8 10 CASH

Cast Brass **Obv. Inscription:** Hsien-fêng Chung-pao **Reverse:** Four characters weight of Wu (5) Mace on rim **Mint:** Fu **Note:** Size varies: 35-40mm.

Date	Mintage	Good	VG	F	VF	XF
ND(1851-61)	—	13.50	20.00	30.00	42.50	—

C# 10-8a 10 CASH

Cast Iron **Obv. Inscription:** Hsien-fêng Chung-pao **Mint:** Fu **Note:** Size varies: 35-40mm.

Date	Mintage	Good	VG	F	VF	XF
ND(1851-61)	—	20.00	50.00	70.00	100	—

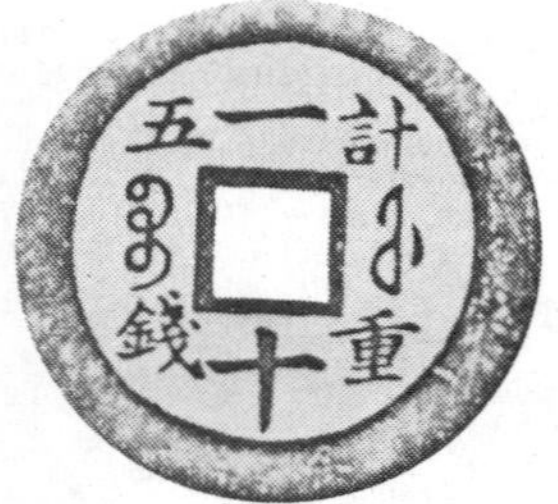

C# 10-9 10 CASH

Cast Brass **Obv. Inscription:** Hsien-fêng Chung-pao **Reverse:** Four characters weight of Wu (5) Mace in field **Mint:** Fu **Note:** Size varies: 35-40mm.

Date	Mintage	Good	VG	F	VF	XF
ND(1851-61)	—	350	500	700	1,000	—

C# 10-9.1 10 CASH

Cast Brass, 42 mm. **Obv. Inscription:** Hsien-fêng Chung-pao **Reverse:** Four characters at top, four different characters at bottom; mint mark (at right) has a crescent at right instead of a dot **Mint:** Fu

Date	Mintage	Good	VG	F	VF	XF
ND(1851-61)	—	600	850	1,250	1,850	—

C# 10-9.2 10 CASH

Cast Brass, 35 mm. **Obv. Inscription:** Hsien-fêng Chung-pao **Reverse:** Chinese mint mark at right, Manchu mint mark at left **Mint:** Fu **Note:** Not an official issue.

Date	Mintage	Good	VG	F	VF	XF
ND(1851-61)	—	450	700	1,000	1,500	—

C# 10-10 20 CASH

Cast Brass **Obverse:** Type A **Obv. Inscription:** Hsien-fêng Chung-pao **Mint:** Fu **Note:** Size varies: 45-46mm.

Date	Mintage	Good	VG	F	VF	XF
ND(1851-61)	—	7.00	10.00	15.00	22.50	—

C# 10-10a 20 CASH

Cast Iron **Obv. Inscription:** Hsien-fêng Chung-pao **Mint:** Fu

Date	Mintage	Good	VG	F	VF	XF
ND(1851-61)	—	13.50	20.00	30.00	42.50	—

C# 10-11 20 CASH

Cast Brass **Obverse:** Type B-1 **Obv. Inscription:** Hsien-fêng Chung-pao **Reverse:** Large characters **Mint:** Fu

Date	Mintage	Good	VG	F	VF	XF
ND(1851-61)	—	100	140	200	300	—

C# 10-13 20 CASH

Cast Copper, 46 mm. **Obv. Inscription:** Hsien-fêng Chung-pao **Reverse:** Eight characters in the field **Mint:** Fu

Date	Mintage	Good	VG	F	VF	XF
ND(1851-61)	—	100	175	250	350	—

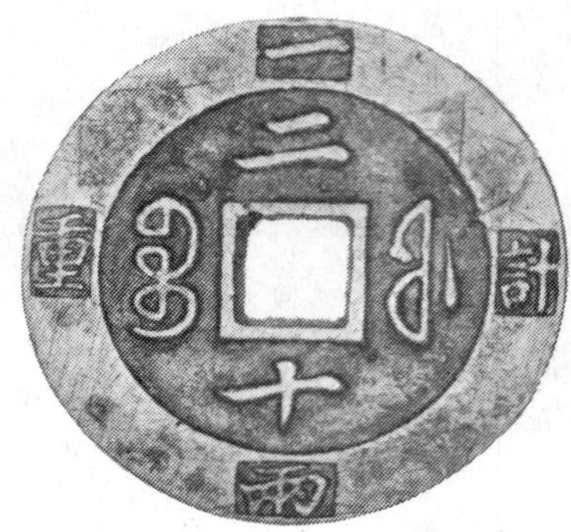

C# 10-12 20 CASH

Cast Brass **Obv. Inscription:** Hsien-fêng Chung-pao **Reverse:** Four characters Yi (1) Tael appearing on rim **Mint:** Fu **Note:** Schjöth #1591.

Date	Mintage	Good	VG	F	VF	XF
ND(1851-61)	—	13.50	20.00	35.00	50.00	—

C# 10-14 50 CASH

Cast Copper **Obverse:** Type A **Obv. Inscription:** Hsien-fêng Chung-pao **Reverse:** Four characters **Mint:** Fu **Note:** Size varies: 55-57mm.

Date	Mintage	Good	VG	F	VF	XF
ND(1851-61)	—	15.00	25.00	30.00	60.00	—

C# 10-14.1 50 CASH

Cast Copper, 68 mm. **Obv. Inscription:** Hsien-fêng Chung-pao **Reverse:** Mint mark with long vertical stroke at right instead of dot **Mint:** Fu

Date	Mintage	Good	VG	F	VF	XF
ND(1851-61)	—	300	500	725	1,000	—

C# 10-15 50 CASH

Cast Copper, 55 mm. **Obverse:** Type B-1 **Obv. Inscription:** Hsien-fêng Chung-pao **Reverse:** Four characters **Mint:** Fu

Date	Mintage	Good	VG	F	VF	XF
ND(1851-61)	—	25.00	40.00	55.00	100	—

C# 10-16 50 CASH

Cast Copper **Obv. Inscription:** Hsien-fêng Chung-pao **Reverse:** Weight in four characters Erh (2) Tael Wu (5) Mace appearing on rim **Mint:** Fu

Date	Mintage	Good	VG	F	VF	XF
ND(1851-61)	—	50.00	85.00	150	250	—

C# 10-17 50 CASH

Cast Copper **Obv. Inscription:** Hsien-fêng Chung-pao **Reverse:** Weight in additional four characters in field Erh (2) Tael Wu (5) Mace **Mint:** Fu

Date	Mintage	Good	VG	F	VF	XF
ND(1851-61)	—	550	850	1,250	1,800	—

C# 10-18 100 CASH

Cast Copper, 70 mm. **Obverse:** Type A **Obv. Inscription:** Hsien-fêng Yüan-pao **Reverse:** Four characters **Mint:** Fu

Date	Mintage	Good	VG	F	VF	XF
ND(1851-61)	—	100	150	210	300	—

C# 10-18.1 100 CASH
Cast Copper, 74 mm. **Obv. Inscription:** Hsien-fêng Yüan-pao **Reverse:** Mint mark with long vertical stroke at right instead of dot **Mint:** Fu

Date	Mintage	Good	VG	F	VF	XF
ND(1851-61)	—	350	700	1,000	1,400	—

C# 10-18a 100 CASH
Cast Iron **Obv. Inscription:** Hsien-fêng Yüan-pao **Mint:** Fu

Date	Mintage	Good	VG	F	VF	XF
ND(1851-61) Rare	—	—	—	—	—	—

C# 10-18b 100 CASH
Cast Iron **Obv. Inscription:** Hsien-fêng Yüan-pao **Mint:** Fu **Note:** Prev. C#10-18a.

Date	Mintage	Good	VG	F	VF	XF
ND(1851-61) Rare	—	—	—	—	—	—

Note: Composition of this coin is reportedly a mixture of zinc, lead, and tin; The coin is blue-gray in color and has a large mint mark, written differently from any of the above

C# 10-19 100 CASH
Cast Copper **Obverse:** Type B-1 **Obv. Inscription:** Hsien-fêng Yüan-pao **Reverse:** Four characters **Mint:** Fu

Date	Mintage	Good	VG	F	VF	XF
ND(1851-61)	—	25.00	40.00	55.00	90.00	—

C# 10-19a 100 CASH
Cast Iron **Obv. Inscription:** Hsien-fêng Yüan-pao **Mint:** Fu

Date	Mintage	Good	VG	F	VF	XF
ND(1851-61) Rare	—	—	—	—	—	—

C# 10-20 100 CASH
Cast Copper **Obv. Inscription:** Hsien-fêng Yüan-pao **Reverse:** Four characters appearing on rim and small characters in field **Mint:** Fu

Date	Mintage	Good	VG	F	VF	XF
ND(1851-61)	—	75.00	125	175	250	—

C# 10-20.1 100 CASH
Cast Copper, 78 mm. **Obv. Inscription:** Hsien-fêng Yüan-pao **Reverse:** Larger characters in field **Mint:** Fu

Date	Mintage	Good	VG	F	VF	XF
ND(1851-61)	—	35.00	50.00	75.00	125	—

C# 10-21 100 CASH
Cast Copper, 68 mm. **Obv. Inscription:** Hsien-fêng Yüan-pao **Reverse:** Weight in additional 4 characters in field **Mint:** Fu

Date	Mintage	Good	VG	F	VF	XF
ND(1851-61)	—	350	700	1,000	1,400	—

T'ung-chih
1862-1875

PROVINCIAL CAST COINAGE

C# 10-22 CASH
Cast Brass **Obverse:** Type A-2 **Obv. Inscription:** T'ung-chih T'ung-pao **Mint:** Fu **Note:** Schjöth #1557.

Date	Mintage	Good	VG	F	VF	XF
ND(1862-74)	—	1.25	2.50	4.00	6.00	—

Kuang - hsü
1875-1908

PROVINCIAL CAST COINAGE

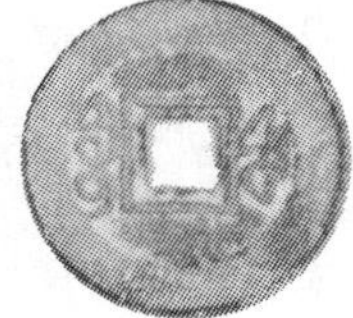

C# 10-25 CASH
Cast Brass **Obv. Inscription:** Kuang hsü T'ung-pao **Reverse:** Manchu inscription **Rev. Inscription:** Boo-fu **Mint:** Fu **Note:** Schjöth #1581.

Date	Mintage	Good	VG	F	VF	XF
ND(1875-1908)	—	0.85	1.50	2.50	3.50	—

C# 10-25.1 CASH
Cast Brass **Obv. Inscription:** Kuang hsü T'ung-pao **Reverse:** Dot at top of hole, Manchu inscription **Rev. Inscription:** Boo-fu **Mint:** Fu

Date	Mintage	Good	VG	F	VF	XF
ND(1875-1908)	—	2.50	4.00	6.50	10.00	—

C# 10-25.2 CASH
Cast Brass **Obv. Inscription:** Kuang-hsü T'ung-pao **Reverse:** Inverted Manchu inscription **Rev. Inscription:** Boo-fu **Mint:** Fu

Date	Mintage	Good	VG	F	VF	XF
ND(1875-1908)	—	—	—	—	—	—

MILLED COINAGE

Y# 102 5 CENTS
1.3500 g., 0.8200 Silver .0356 oz. ASW **Obverse:** Legend with 5 characters at top, inscription **Obv. Inscription:** Kuang-hsü Yüan-pao **Reverse:** Side view dragon left **Mint:** Fu

Date	Mintage	VG	F	VF	XF	Unc
ND(1896-1903)	—	2.25	7.00	13.00	22.50	60.00

Y# 103 10 CENTS
2.7000 g., 0.8200 Silver .0712 oz. ASW **Obverse:** Legend with 5 characters at top, inscription **Obv. Inscription:** Kuang-hsü Yüan-pao **Reverse:** Rosette at either side of side view dragon left **Mint:** Fu

Date	Mintage	VG	F	VF	XF	Unc
ND(1896-1903)	13,425,000	1.75	5.00	9.00	17.50	35.00

Y# 103.1 10 CENTS
2.7000 g., 0.8200 Silver .0712 oz. ASW **Obv. Inscription:** Kuang-hsü Yüan-pao **Reverse:** Dot at either side of side view dragon left **Mint:** Fu

Date	Mintage	VG	F	VF	XF	Unc
ND(1896-1903)	Inc. above	3.25	8.00	15.00	30.00	60.00

Y# 104 20 CENTS
5.4000 g., 0.8200 Silver .1424 oz. ASW **Obverse:** Legend has 5 characters at top, inscription **Obv. Inscription:** Kuang-hsü Yüan-pao **Reverse:** Dot at either side of side view dragon left **Mint:** Fu

Date	Mintage	VG	F	VF	XF	Unc
ND(1896-1903)	31,772,000	1.00	3.00	6.00	12.50	30.00

Y# 104.1 20 CENTS
5.4000 g., 0.8200 Silver .1424 oz. ASW **Obv. Inscription:** Kuang-hsü Yüan-pao **Reverse:** Rosette at either side of side view dragon left **Mint:** Fu

Date	Mintage	VG	F	VF	XF	Unc
ND(1898-1903)	Inc. above	1.00	3.00	6.00	12.50	30.00

Y# 105 DOLLAR
27.0000 g., Silver **Obv. Inscription:** Kuang-hsü Yüan-pao **Reverse:** Dragon

Date	Mintage	F	VF	XF	Unc
ND(c.1899) Rare	—	—	—	—	—

HONAN PROVINCE

Henan

A province in east-central China. As well as being one of the most densely populated provinces it is also one of the most important agriculturally. It is the area of earliest settlement in China and has housed the capital during various dynasties. The Kaifeng Mint issued coins from its opening in 1647 through most of the rulers of the Manchu dynasty. In 1905 a modern mint opened at Kaifeng but closed in 1914. A mint in Loyang opened in 1924.

EMPIRE

Hsien-fêng
1851-1861

PROVINCIAL CAST COINAGE

C# 11-1 CASH
Cast Brass **Obverse:** Type A **Obv. Inscription:** Hsien-fêng T'ung-pao **Reverse:** Type 1 **Mint:** Ho

Date	Mintage	Good	VG	F	VF	XF
ND(1851-61)	—	20.00	30.00	40.00	60.00	—

C# 11-1.1 CASH
Cast Brass **Obv. Inscription:** Hsien-fêng T'ung-pao **Reverse:** Crescent above **Mint:** Ho

Date	Mintage	Good	VG	F	VF	XF
ND(1851-61)	—	20.00	30.00	40.00	60.00	—

C# 11-1.2 CASH
Cast Brass **Obv. Inscription:** Hsien-fêng T'ung-pao **Reverse:** Circle above **Mint:** Ho

Date	Mintage	Good	VG	F	VF	XF
ND(1851-61)	—	20.00	30.00	40.00	60.00	—

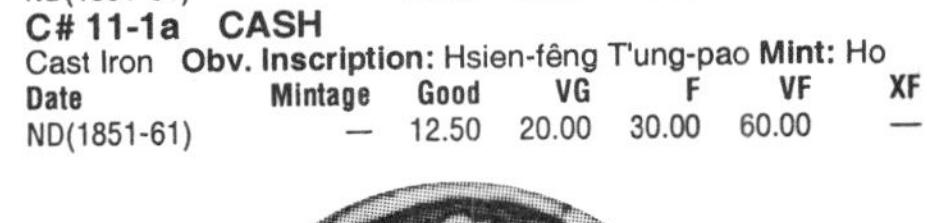

C# 11-1a CASH
Cast Iron **Obv. Inscription:** Hsien-fêng T'ung-pao **Mint:** Ho

Date	Mintage	Good	VG	F	VF	XF
ND(1851-61)	—	12.50	20.00	30.00	60.00	—

C# 11-2 10 CASH
Cast Brass **Obverse:** Type B-1 **Obv. Inscription:** Hsien-fêng Chung-pao **Mint:** Ho **Note:** Size varies: 35-38mm.

Date	Mintage	Good	VG	F	VF	XF
ND(1851-61)	—	6.00	10.00	15.00	20.00	—

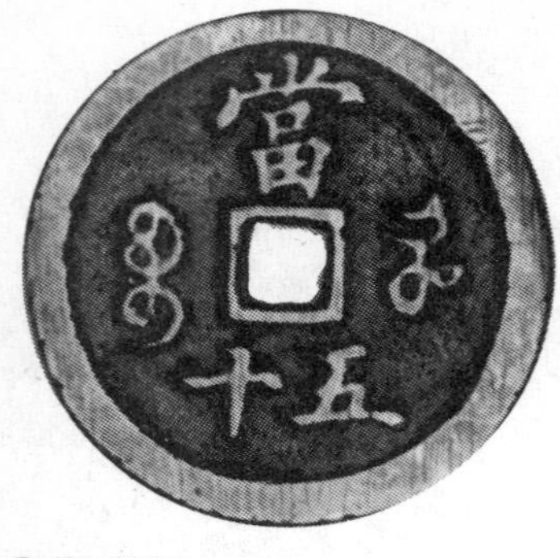

C# 11-5 50 CASH
Cast Brass **Obverse:** Type B-1 **Obv. Inscription:** Hsien-fêng Chung-pao **Mint:** Ho

Date	Mintage	Good	VG	F	VF	XF
ND(1851-61)	—	8.00	15.00	25.00	50.00	—

C# 11-6 100 CASH
Cast Brass **Obverse:** Type C **Obv. Inscription:** Hsien-fêng Yüan-pao **Mint:** Ho **Note:** Size varies: 48-50mm.

Date	Mintage	Good	VG	F	VF	XF
ND(1851-61)	—	7.00	15.00	20.00	30.00	—

C# 11-7 500 CASH
Cast Brass, 55 mm. **Obverse:** Type C **Obv. Inscription:** Hsien-fêng Yüan-pao **Mint:** Ho

Date	Mintage	Good	VG	F	VF	XF
ND(1851-61)	—	75.00	150	220	300	—

C# 11-8 1000 CASH
Cast Brass, 60 mm. **Obverse:** Type C **Obv. Inscription:** Hsien-fêng Yüan-pao **Mint:** Ho

Date	Mintage	Good	VG	F	VF	XF
ND(1851-61)	—	200	300	400	500	—

Kuang-hsü
1875-1908

PROVINCIAL CAST COINAGE

C# 3-1.1a CASH
Cast Zinc **Obv. Inscription:** Kuang-hsü T'ung-pao **Reverse:** Dot at upper left, Manchu inscription **Rev. Inscription:** Boo-ho **Mint:** Ho

Date	Mintage	Good	VG	F	VF	XF
ND(1875-1908) Rare	—	—	—	—	—	—

C# 11-9 CASH
Cast Brass **Obv. Inscription:** Kuang-hsü T'ung-pao **Reverse:** Manchu inscription **Rev. Inscription:** Boo-ho **Mint:** Ho

Date	Mintage	Good	VG	F	VF	XF
ND(1875-1908)	—	4.00	8.00	10.00	12.00	—

C# 11-9.1 CASH
Cast Brass **Obv. Inscription:** Kuang-hsü T'ung-pao **Reverse:** Circle above, Manchu inscription **Rev. Inscription:** Boo-ho **Mint:** Ho

Date	Mintage	Good	VG	F	VF	XF
ND(1875-1908)	—	5.00	9.00	13.50	35.00	—

C# 11-9.2 CASH
Cast Brass **Obv. Inscription:** Kuang-hsü T'ung-pao **Reverse:** Circle below, Manchu inscription **Rev. Inscription:** Boo-ho **Mint:** Ho

Date	Mintage	Good	VG	F	VF	XF
ND(1875-1908)	—	5.00	9.00	13.50	25.00	—

C# 11-9.3 CASH
Cast Brass **Obv. Inscription:** Kuang-hsü T'ung-pao **Reverse:** Crescent above, Manchu inscription **Rev. Inscription:** Boo-ho **Mint:** Ho

Date	Mintage	Good	VG	F	VF	XF
ND(1875-1908)	—	5.00	9.00	13.50	25.00	—

C# 11-9.4 CASH
Cast Brass **Obv. Inscription:** Kuang-hsü T'ung-pao **Reverse:** Crescent below, Manchu inscription **Rev. Inscription:** Boo-ho **Mint:** Ho

Date	Mintage	Good	VG	F	VF	XF
ND(1875-1908)	—	5.00	9.00	13.50	25.00	—

C# 11-9.5 CASH
Cast Brass **Obv. Inscription:** Kuang-hsü T'ung-pao **Reverse:** Crescent above, dot below, Manchu inscription **Rev. Inscription:** Boo-ho **Mint:** Ho **Note:** Schjöth #1571.

Date	Mintage	Good	VG	F	VF	XF
ND(1875-1908)	—	5.00	9.00	13.50	25.00	—

C# 11-9.6 CASH
Cast Brass **Obv. Inscription:** Kuang-hsü T'ung-pao **Reverse:** Dot above, Manchu inscription **Rev. Inscription:** Boo-ho **Mint:** Ho

Date	Mintage	Good	VG	F	VF	XF
ND(1875-1908)	—	5.00	9.00	13.50	20.00	—

C# 11-9.7 CASH
Cast Brass **Obv. Inscription:** Kuang-hsü T'ung-pao **Reverse:** Dot below, Manchu inscription **Rev. Inscription:** Boo-ho **Mint:** Ho

Date	Mintage	Good	VG	F	VF	XF
ND(1875-1908)	—	5.00	9.00	13.50	20.00	—

C# 11-9.8 CASH
Cast Brass **Obv. Inscription:** Kuang-hsü T'ung-pao **Reverse:** Dot at upper left, Manchu inscription **Rev. Inscription:** Boo-ho **Mint:** Ho **Note:** Crescent and dot varieties exist.

Date	Mintage	Good	VG	F	VF	XF
ND(1875-1908)	—	5.00	9.00	13.50	20.00	—

C# 11-9.9 CASH
Cast Brass **Obv. Inscription:** Kuang-hsü T'ung-pao **Reverse:** Crescent above, circle below **Mint:** Ho

Date	Mintage	Good	VG	F	VF	XF
ND(1875-1908)	—	10.00	17.50	25.00	35.00	—

C# 11-9.10 CASH
Cast Brass **Obv. Inscription:** Kuang-hsü T'ung-pao **Reverse:** Dot in circle below **Mint:** Ho

Date	Mintage	Good	VG	F	VF	XF
ND(1875-1908)	—	15.00	25.00	35.00	50.00	—

HUNAN PROVINCE

A province in south-central China. Mining of coal, antimony, tungsten and tin is important as well as raising varied agricultural products. The Changsha Mint produced Cash coins from early in the Manchu dynasty. Its facility for struck coinage opened in 1897, and two further copper mints were added in 1905. All three mints were closed down in 1907, but one mint was reopened at a later date and produced vast quantities of republican copper coinage until 1926.

EMPIRE

Tao-Kuang
1821-1851

PROVINCIAL CAST COINAGE

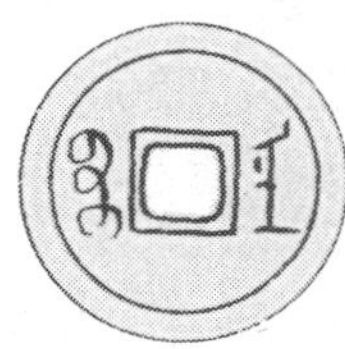

C# 12-3 CASH
Cast Brass **Obverse:** Type A **Obv. Inscription:** Tao-kuang T'ung-pao **Mint:** Nan **Note:** Schjöth #1532.

Date	Mintage	Good	VG	F	VF	XF
ND(1821-50)	—	2.00	4.00	6.50	10.00	—

Hsien-fêng
1851-1861

PROVINCIAL CAST COINAGE

C# 12-4 CASH
Cast Brass **Obverse:** Type A **Obv. Inscription:** Hsien-fêng T'ung-pao **Mint:** Nan **Note:** Schjöth #1543.

Date	Mintage	Good	VG	F	VF	XF
ND(1851-61)	—	2.00	4.00	6.50	10.00	—

T'ung-chih
1862-1875

PROVINCIAL CAST COINAGE

C# 12-5 CASH
Cast Brass **Obverse:** Type A-2 **Obv. Inscription:** T'ung-chih T'ung-pao **Mint:** Nan

Date	Mintage	Good	VG	F	VF	XF
ND(1862-74)	—	6.00	12.50	18.50	25.00	—

Kuang-hsü
1875-1908

PROVINCIAL CAST COINAGE

C# 12-7 CASH
Cast Brass **Obv. Inscription:** Kuang-hsü T'ung-pao **Reverse:** Manchu inscription **Rev. Inscription:** Boo-nan **Mint:** Nan

Date	Mintage	Good	VG	F	VF	XF
ND(1875-1908)	—	7.50	15.00	21.50	30.00	—

MILLED COINAGE

Y# 114 5 CENTS
1.3000 g., 0.8200 Silver .0343 oz. ASW **Obv. Inscription:** Kuang-hsü Yüan-pao **Mint:** Nan **Note:** Kann #164.

Date	Mintage	F	VF	XF	Unc
ND(c.1902) Rare	—	—	—	—	—

Y# 115.1 10 CENTS
2.5000 g., 0.8200 Silver .0659 oz. ASW **Obverse:** One rosette at both sides **Obv. Inscription:** Kuang-hsü Yüan-pao **Mint:** Nan

Date	Mintage	F	VF	XF	Unc
ND(1897)	—	14.00	25.00	45.00	120
CD(1898)	—	17.50	35.00	60.00	150
CD(1899)	—	22.50	45.00	75.00	175

Y# 115 10 CENTS
2.5000 g., 0.8200 Silver .0659 oz. ASW **Obverse:** Two rosettes at both sides **Obv. Inscription:** Kuang-hsü Yüan-pao **Mint:** Nan

Date	Mintage	F	VF	XF	Unc
ND(c.1902)	—	7.00	15.00	25.00	100

Y# 116 20 CENTS
5.3000 g., 0.8200 Silver .1397 oz. ASW **Obv. Inscription:** Kuang-hsü Yüan-pao **Mint:** Nan

Date	Mintage	F	VF	XF	Unc
ND(c.1902)	—	35.00	75.00	125	250

PATTERNS

Including off metal strikes

KM#	Date	Mintage	Identification	Mkt Val
Pn1	ND(1897)	—	10 Cents. Antimony. Y#115.	—

KM#	Date	Mintage	Identification	Mkt Val
Pn2	ND(1897)	—	50 Cents. Silver.	7,500

KM#	Date	Mintage	Identification	Mkt Val
Pn3	ND(1897)	—	Dollar. Silver.	25,000

Note: The dollar and half dollar above were produced at the Heaton Mint, Birmingham, England as trials before sending the dies and machinery to China; about 6 pieces of each denomination exist

HUPEH PROVINCE

Hubei

A province located in east-central China. Hilly, with some lakes and swamps, it has rich coal and iron deposits plus a varied agricultural program. The Wuchang Mint had been active from early in the Manchu dynasty and its modern equipment began operations in 1895. It probably closed in 1929.

EMPIRE

Tao-kuang
1821-1851

PROVINCIAL CAST COINAGE

C# 13-3 CASH
Cast Brass **Obverse:** Type A **Obv. Inscription:** Tao-kuang T'ung-pao **Mint:** Wu

Date	Mintage	Good	VG	F	VF	XF
ND(1821-50)	—	1.00	2.00	3.00	5.00	—

Hsien-fêng
1851-1861

PROVINCIAL CAST COINAGE

C# 13-4 CASH
Cast Brass **Obverse:** Type A **Obv. Inscription:** Hsien-fêng T'ung-pao **Mint:** Wu

Date	Mintage	Good	VG	F	VF	XF
ND(1851-61)	—	3.00	6.00	7.50	10.00	—

C# 13-5 5 CASH
Cast Brass **Obverse:** Type B-1 **Obv. Inscription:** Hsien-fêng Chung-pao **Mint:** Wu

Date	Mintage	Good	VG	F	VF	XF
ND(1851-61)	—	40.00	70.00	100	130	—

C# 13-6 10 CASH
Cast Brass **Obverse:** Type B-1 **Obv. Inscription:** Hsien-fêng Chung-pao **Mint:** Wu

Date	Mintage	Good	VG	F	VF	XF
ND(1851-61)	—	6.00	12.50	25.00	60.00	—

C# 13-6.1 10 CASH
Cast Brass **Obv. Inscription:** Hsien-fêng Chung-pao **Reverse:** Crescent in upper right corner **Mint:** Wu

Date	Mintage	Good	VG	F	VF	XF
ND(1851-61)	—	10.00	20.00	30.00	60.00	—

C# 13-7 50 CASH
Cast Brass, 48 mm. **Obverse:** Type B-1; large characters **Obv. Inscription:** Hsien-fêng Chung-pao **Reverse:** Large characters **Mint:** Wu

Date	Mintage	Good	VG	F	VF	XF
ND(1851-61)	—	10.00	20.00	35.00	60.00	—

C# 13-7.1 50 CASH
Cast Brass **Obv. Inscription:** Hsien-fêng Chung-pao **Reverse:** Crescent in upper right corner **Mint:** Wu

Date	Mintage	Good	VG	F	VF	XF
ND(1851-61)	—	52.50	85.00	110	175	—

C# 13-8 100 CASH
Cast Brass **Obverse:** Type C **Obv. Inscription:** Hsien-fêng Yüan-pao **Mint:** Wu

Date	Mintage	Good	VG	F	VF	XF
ND(1851-61)	—	10.00	20.00	30.00	70.00	—

C# 13-8.1 100 CASH
Cast Brass **Obv. Inscription:** Hsien-fêng Yüan-pao **Reverse:** Crescent in upper right corner **Mint:** Wu

Date	Mintage	Good	VG	F	VF	XF
ND(1851-61)	—	35.00	55.00	75.00	110	—

T'ung-chih
1862-1875

PROVINCIAL CAST COINAGE

C# 13-9 CASH
Cast Brass **Obverse:** Type A-2 **Obv. Inscription:** T'ung-chih T'ung-pao **Mint:** Wu

Date	Mintage	Good	VG	F	VF	XF
ND(1862-74)	—	3.50	7.50	11.50	16.50	—

Kuang-hsü
1875-1908

PROVINCIAL CAST COINAGE

C# 13-11 CASH
Cast Brass **Obv. Inscription:** Kuang-hsü T'ung-pao **Rev. Inscription:** Manchu Boo-ching **Mint:** Ching

Date	Mintage	Good	VG	F	VF	XF
ND(1875-1908)	—	12.50	20.00	30.00	45.00	—

C# 13-11.1 CASH
Cast Brass **Obv. Inscription:** Kuang-hsü T'ung-pao **Rev. Inscription:** Manchu Boo-ching **Mint:** Ching **Note:** Attribution of this mint mark to Chingchow is uncertain. Some authorities claim the Taku (Dagu) Mint in Tientsin struck this coin.

Date	Mintage	Good	VG	F	VF	XF
ND(1875-1908)	—	12.00	15.00	22.50	30.00	—

MILLED COINAGE

HSU# 181 CASH
Brass, 22.5 mm. **Obverse:** Small characters

Date	Mintage	VG	F	VF	XF	Unc
ND(1898)	—	22.50	40.00	50.00	85.00	—

HSU# 182 CASH
Brass, 20.5 mm. **Obverse:** Larger characters

Date	Mintage	VG	F	VF	XF	Unc
ND(1898)	—	—	—	—	—	—

HSU# A182 CASH
Brass **Obverse:** Small characters **Reverse:** Larger characters **Note:** Mule.

Date	Mintage	VG	F	VF	XF	Unc
ND(1898)	—	—	—	—	—	—

Y# 123 5 CENTS
1.3500 g., 0.8200 Silver .0356 oz. ASW **Obv. Inscription:** Kuang-hsü Yüan-pao **Reverse:** Dragon **Rev. Legend:** Kuang-hsü Nien-tsao, TAI-CHING-TI-KUO ... **Mint:** Ching

Date	Mintage	VG	F	VF	XF	Unc
ND(1895-1905)	4,278,000	17.50	50.00	100	150	250

Y# 124 10 CENTS
2.7000 g., 0.8200 Silver .0712 oz. ASW **Obv. Inscription:** Kuang-hsü Yüan-pao **Reverse:** Character at either side of dragon "Pen Sheng" indicating coin was for provincial use **Rev. Legend:** Kuang-hsü Nien-tsao, TAI-CHING-TI-KUO ... **Mint:** Ching

Date	Mintage	F	VF	XF	Unc
ND(1894)	—	300	700	1,300	2,000

Y# 124.1 10 CENTS
2.7000 g., 0.8200 Silver .0712 oz. ASW **Obv. Inscription:** Kuang-hsü Yüan-pao **Reverse:** Without characters beside dragon **Rev. Legend:** Kuang-hsü Nien-tsao, TAI-CHING-TI-KUO ... **Mint:** Ching

Date	Mintage	VG	F	VF	XF	Unc
ND(1895-1907)	—	0.65	2.00	4.00	7.50	20.00

Note: 2 varieties of edge milling exist

Y# 125 20 CENTS
5.3000 g., 0.8200 Silver .1397 oz. ASW **Obv. Inscription:** Kuang-hsü Yüan-pao **Reverse:** Character at either side of dragon "Pen Sheng" indicating coin was for provincial use **Mint:** Ching

Date	Mintage	F	VF	XF	Unc
ND(1894)	—	1,500	3,500	4,000	5,000

Y# 125.1 20 CENTS
5.3000 g., 0.8200 Silver .1397 oz. ASW **Obv. Inscription:** Kuang-hsü Yüan-pao **Reverse:** Without characters beside dragon **Mint:** Ching

Date	Mintage	VG	F	VF	XF	Unc
ND(1895-1907)	—	1.75	5.00	10.00	15.00	30.00

Y# 127 DOLLAR
26.7000 g., 0.9000 Silver .7727 oz. ASW **Obv. Inscription:** "Kuang-hsü Yüan-pao" **Reverse:** Characters "Pen Sheng" at either side of dragon indicating coin was for provincial use

Date	Mintage	F	VF	XF	Unc
ND(1894)	—	7,500	10,000	15,000	25,000

Y# 127.1 DOLLAR
26.7000 g., 0.9000 Silver .7727 oz. ASW **Obv. Inscription:** Kuang-hsü Yüan-pao **Reverse:** Without "Pen Sheng" at either side of dragon **Mint:** Ching

Date	Mintage	VG	F	VF	XF	Unc
ND(1895-1907)	19,935,000	6.50	20.00	30.00	50.00	250

Hsüan-t'ung
1908-1911
MILLED COINAGE

Y# 126 50 CENTS
13.5000 g., 0.8600 Silver .3733 oz. ASW **Obv. Inscription:** Kuang-hsü Yüan-pao **Reverse:** Dragon **Mint:** Ching

Date	Mintage	VG	F	VF	XF	Unc
ND(1895-1905)	—	15.00	40.00	80.00	120	250

PATTERNS
Including off metal strikes

KM#	Date	Mintage	Identification	Mkt Val
Pn1	ND(1895)	—	5 Cents. Copper. Y#123.	—
Pn2	ND(1895)	—	10 Cents. Copper. Y#124.1.	—
Pn3	ND(1895)	—	20 Cents. Copper. Y#125.1.	—
Pn4	ND(1895)	—	20 Cents. Copper. Y#126.	—
Pn5	ND(1895)	—	Dollar. Copper. Y#127.1.	350

KANSU PROVINCE
Gansu

A province located in north-central China with a contrast of mountains and sandy plains. The west end of the Great Wall with its branches lies in Kansu (Gansu). Kansu (Gansu) was the eastern end of the "Silk Road" that led to central and western Asia. Two mints issued Cash coins. It has been reported, but not confirmed, that the Lanchow Mint operated as late as 1949.

EMPIRE
Hsien-fêng
1851-1861
PROVINCIAL CAST COINAGE

C# 14-1 CASH
Cast Brass **Obv. Inscription:** Hsien-fêng T'ung-pao **Mint:** Kung

Date	Mintage	Good	VG	F	VF	XF
ND(1851-61)	—	15.00	30.00	45.00	67.50	—

C# 14-2 5 CASH
Cast Brass **Obverse:** Type B-1 **Obv. Inscription:** Hsien-fêng Chung-pao **Mint:** Kung

Date	Mintage	Good	VG	F	VF	XF
ND(1851-61)	—	20.00	30.00	50.00	75.00	—

C# 14-2.1 5 CASH
Cast Brass **Obv. Inscription:** Hsien-fêng Chung-pao **Reverse:** Large Manchu **Mint:** Kung

Date	Mintage	Good	VG	F	VF	XF
ND(1851-61)	—	30.00	50.00	75.00	95.00	—

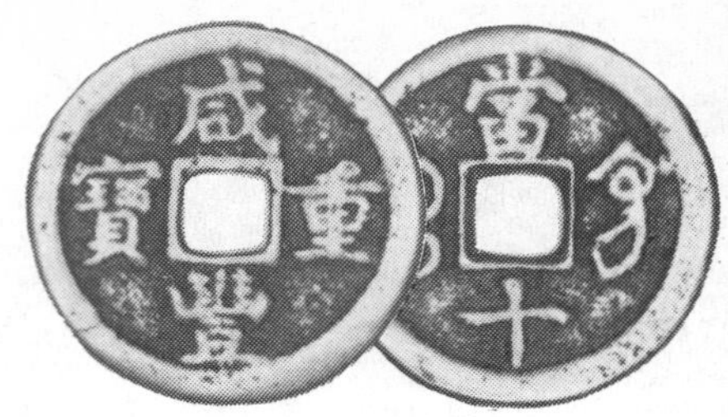

C# 14-3 10 CASH
Cast Brass **Obverse:** Type B **Obv. Inscription:** Hsien-fêng Chung-pao **Mint:** Kung

Date	Mintage	Good	VG	F	VF	XF
ND(1851-61)	—	7.00	10.00	20.00	35.00	—

C# 14-4 50 CASH
Cast Brass, 48 mm. **Obverse:** Type B-1 **Obv. Inscription:** Hsien-fêng Chung-pao **Mint:** Kung

Date	Mintage	Good	VG	F	VF	XF
ND(1851-61)	—	10.00	14.00	20.00	30.00	—

C# 14-4.1 50 CASH
Cast Brass, 42 mm. **Obv. Inscription:** Hsien-fêng Chung-pao **Mint:** Kung

Date	Mintage	Good	VG	F	VF	XF
ND(1851-61)	—	10.00	14.00	20.00	30.00	—

C# 14-4.2 50 CASH
Cast Brass, 48 mm. **Obverse:** Type B-1 with wide rims **Obv. Inscription:** Hsien-fêng Chung-pao **Reverse:** Wide rims **Mint:** Kung

Date	Mintage	Good	VG	F	VF	XF
ND(1851-61)	—	13.50	20.00	35.00	50.00	—

C# 14-5 100 CASH
Cast Brass **Obverse:** Type C **Obv. Inscription:** Hsien-fêng Yüan-pao **Mint:** Kung

Date	Mintage	Good	VG	F	VF	XF
ND(1851-61)	—	20.00	25.00	35.00	50.00	—

C# 14-6 500 CASH
Cast Brass **Obverse:** Type C **Obv. Inscription:** Hsien-fêng Yüan-pao **Mint:** Kung

Date	Mintage	Good	VG	F	VF	XF
ND(1851-61)	—	110	225	350	500	—

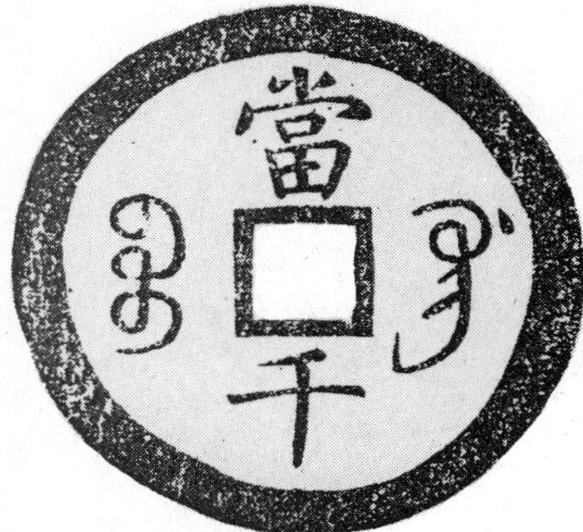

C# 14-7 1000 CASH
Cast Copper, 66 mm. **Obverse:** Type C **Obv. Inscription:** Hsien-fêng Yüan-pao **Mint:** Kung **Note:** Illustration reduced.

Date	Mintage	Good	VG	F	VF	XF
ND(1851-61)	—	400	600	850	1,250	—

T'ung-chih
1862-1875
PROVINCIAL CAST COINAGE

C# 14-8 CASH
Cast Brass **Obv. Inscription:** T'ung-chih T'ung-pao **Mint:** Kung

Date	Mintage	Good	VG	F	VF	XF
ND(1862-74)	—	8.00	16.00	25.00	35.00	—

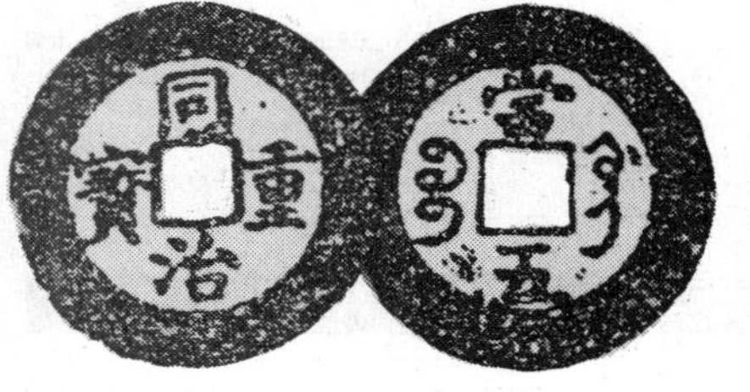

C# 14-9 5 CASH
Cast Brass **Obverse:** Type B **Obv. Inscription:** T'ung-chih T'ung-pao **Mint:** Kung

Date	Mintage	Good	VG	F	VF	XF
ND(1862-74)	—	80.00	130	200	300	—

C# 14-10 10 CASH
Cast Brass, 25 mm. **Obverse:** Type B **Obv. Inscription:** T'ung-chih T'ung-pao **Mint:** Kung

Date	Mintage	Good	VG	F	VF	XF
ND(1862-74)	—	1.40	2.00	3.25	5.00	—

KIANGNAN

A district in eastern China made up of Anhwei (Anhui) and Kiangsu (Jiangsu) provinces. In 1667 the province of Kiangnan was divided into the present provinces of Anhwei (Anhui) and Kiangsu (Jiangsu). In 1723 Nanking, formerly the capital of Kiangnan, was made the capital of Liang-Chiang Chiang (an administrative area consisting of Anhwei (Anhui), Kiangsu (Jiangsu), and Kiangsi (Jiangxi) provinces).

Always highly regarded because of location, agriculture and manufacturing, Kiangnan has frequently been sought after by contending forces.

The Nanking Mint had been active during imperial times. Modern minting facilities began operations in 1897. A second mint was planned for the Kiangnan Arsenal in Shanghai in 1905. Mints for copper coins also operated in Chingkiang (Qingjiang) in central Kiangsu and at Soochow which is further south. A silver mint was planned for Shanghai in 1921. The Nanking Mint, the most important of the group, burned down in 1929. The Nationalist Government Central Mint was completed in Shanghai in 1930 and opened in 1933.

EMPIRE
Kuang-hsü
1875-1908
MILLED COINAGE

The initials HAH, SY, CH and TH are those of mint officials and were placed on the coins as a guarantee of the coin's fineness. The 5-, 10-, and 20-cent coins are often found without a decimal point between the numbers on the reverse. The 1904 dated dollar was restruck during Republican times.

Y# 133 CASH
Brass **Obverse:** Large inscription **Obv. Inscription:** "Kuang-hsü T'ung-pao" **Mint:** Nanking **Note:** HSU #261.

Date	Mintage	Good	VG	F	VF	XF
ND(1898)	—	6.00	15.00	25.00	35.00	75.00

Note: This coin has been erroneously attributed to Ningpo in Chekiang (Zhejang) and to Changchow in Fukien (Fujian); The coin was minted at Nanking from dies produced by the Heaton Mint

Y# 134 CASH
Brass **Obverse:** Small inscription **Obv. Inscription:** Kuang-hsü T'ung-pao **Reverse:** Mint mark written differently **Mint:** Nanking

Date	Mintage	Good	VG	F	VF	XF
ND(1898)	—	45.00	90.00	135	200	325

Y# 141a 5 CENTS
13.0000 g., 0.8200 Silver .0343 oz. ASW **Obv. Inscription:** Kuang-hsü Yüan-pao **Reverse:** Without circle around dragon

Date	Mintage	VG	F	VF	XF	Unc
ND(1898)	Inc. above	2.50	10.00	15.00	30.00	50.00
CD(1899)	3,812	17.50	50.00	100	150	300
CD(1900)	618,000	3.00	10.00	15.00	30.00	50.00
CD(1901)	—	17.50	50.00	75.00	150	275

Y# 141 5 CENTS
1.3000 g., 0.8200 Silver .0343 oz. ASW **Obv. Inscription:** Kuang-hsü Yüan-pao **Reverse:** Circled dragon

Date	Mintage	VG	F	VF	XF	Unc
ND(1898)	100,000	10.00	20.00	30.00	80.00	180
ND(1898) Proof	—	Value: 700				

Y# 142 10 CENTS
2.6000 g., 0.8200 Silver .0686 oz. ASW **Obv. Inscription:** Kuang-hsü Yüan-pao **Reverse:** Circled dragon

Date	Mintage	F	VF	XF	Unc
ND(1898)	8,000,000	12.00	25.00	50.00	150
ND(1898) Proof	—	Value: 700			

Y# 142.1 10 CENTS
2.6000 g., 0.8200 Silver .0686 oz. ASW **Obv. Inscription:** Kuang-hsü Yüan-pao

Date	Mintage	F	VF	XF	Unc
CD(1898)	Inc. above	7.00	15.00	25.00	45.00

Y# 142a 10 CENTS
2.6000 g., 0.8200 Silver .0686 oz. ASW **Obv. Inscription:** Kuang-hsü Yüan-pao **Reverse:** Without circle around dragon with small rosettes at sides

Date	Mintage	F	VF	XF	Unc
CD(1898)	Inc. above	3.50	7.00	15.00	30.00

Y# 142a.1 10 CENTS
2.6000 g., 0.8200 Silver .0686 oz. ASW **Obv. Inscription:** Kuang-hsü Yüan-pao **Reverse:** Large rosettes at sides of dragon

Date	Mintage	F	VF	XF	Unc
CD(1898)	Inc. above	3.50	7.00	15.00	30.00

Y# 142a.2 10 CENTS
2.6000 g., 0.8200 Silver .0686 oz. ASW **Obverse:** Large characters in center, small characters in outer ring **Obv. Inscription:** Kuang-hsü Yüan-pao

Date	Mintage	F	VF	XF	Unc
CD(1899)	10,784,000	2.25	4.50	9.00	30.00

Y# 142a.3 10 CENTS
2.6000 g., 0.8200 Silver .0686 oz. ASW **Obverse:** Small characters in center, large characters in outer ring **Obv. Inscription:** Kuang-hsü Yüan-pao

Date	Mintage	F	VF	XF	Unc
CD(1899)	Inc. above	2.25	4.50	9.00	30.00

Y# 142a.4 10 CENTS
2.6000 g., 0.8200 Silver .0686 oz. ASW **Obv. Inscription:** Kuang-hsü Yüan-pao

Date	Mintage	F	VF	XF	Unc
CD(1900)	5,460,000	2.50	5.00	10.00	35.00

Y# 143 20 CENTS
5.3000 g., 0.8200 Silver .1397 oz. ASW **Obverse:** Rosettes at 2 and 10 o'clock **Obv. Inscription:** Kuang-hsü Yüan-pao **Reverse:** Circle around dragon

Date	Mintage	VG	F	VF	XF	Unc
CD(1898)	7,000,000	7.01	17.50	40.00	70.00	180

Y# 143.1 20 CENTS
5.3000 g., 0.8200 Silver .1397 oz. ASW **Obv. Inscription:** Kuang-hsü Yüan-pao

Date	Mintage	F	VF	XF	Unc
CD(1898)	Inc. above	15.00	35.00	65.00	100

Y# 143a 20 CENTS
5.3000 g., 0.8200 Silver .1397 oz. ASW **Obverse:** Large characters in outer ring **Obv. Inscription:** Kuang-hsü Yüan-pao **Reverse:** Large English letters, without circle around dragon

Date	Mintage	F	VF	XF	Unc
CD(1898)	Inc. above	3.75	7.50	15.00	35.00

Y# 143a.1 20 CENTS
5.3000 g., 0.8200 Silver .1397 oz. ASW **Obverse:** Small characters in outer ring **Obv. Inscription:** Kuang-hsü Yüan-pao **Reverse:** Small English letters

Date	Mintage	F	VF	XF	Unc
CD(1898)	Inc. above	3.75	7.50	15.00	35.00

Y# 143a.2 20 CENTS
5.3000 g., 0.8200 Silver .1397 oz. ASW **Obv. Inscription:** Kuang-hsü Yüan-pao **Reverse:** Old type dragon with long face, flanked by short rosettes

Date	Mintage	F	VF	XF	Unc
CD(1899)	11,096,000	3.50	7.50	15.00	35.00

Y# 143a.3 20 CENTS
5.3000 g., 0.8200 Silver .1397 oz. ASW **Obv. Inscription:** Kuang-hsü Yüan-pao **Reverse:** New type dragon with shorter face and larger forehead, flanked by long rosettes

Date	Mintage	F	VF	XF	Unc
CD(1899)	Inc. above	5.00	10.00	25.00	60.00

Y# 143a.4 20 CENTS
5.3000 g., 0.8200 Silver .1397 oz. ASW **Obv. Inscription:** Kuang-hsü Yüan-pao **Reverse:** Old type dragon with long face, flanked by long rosettes

Date	Mintage	F	VF	XF	Unc
CD(1900)	5,796,000	5.00	10.00	25.00	60.00

Y# 143a.5 20 CENTS
5.3000 g., 0.8200 Silver .1397 oz. ASW **Obv. Inscription:** Kuang-hsü Yüan-pao **Reverse:** New type dragon with shorter face and larger forehead

Date	Mintage	F	VF	XF	Unc
CD(1900)	Inc. above	10.00	25.00	50.00	100

Y# 144 50 CENTS
13.2000 g., 0.8600 Silver .3650 oz. ASW **Obv. Inscription:** Kuang-hsü Yüan-pao **Reverse:** Circled dragon

Date	Mintage	VG	F	VF	XF	Unc
ND(1898)	100,000	87.50	175	325	500	1,200
ND(1898) Proof	—	Value: 2,500				

Y# 144a 50 CENTS
13.2000 g., 0.8600 Silver .3650 oz. ASW **Obv. Inscription:** Kuang-hsü Yüan-pao **Reverse:** Without circle around dragon

Date	Mintage	F	VF	XF	Unc
CD(1899)	155	500	1,000	2,000	3,500
CD(1900)	—	500	1,000	1,750	3,000

Y# 145a.2 DOLLAR
27.0000 g., 0.9000 Silver .7814 oz. ASW **Obv. Inscription:** Kuang-hsü Yüan-pao **Note:** Similar to Y#145a.1 but with smaller letters.

Date	Mintage	VG	F	VF	XF	Unc
CD(1898)	Inc. above	50.00	100	175	300	800
CD(1899)	2,039,000	15.00	30.00	75.00	150	600

Y# 145 DOLLAR
27.0000 g., 0.9000 Silver .7814 oz. ASW **Obv. Inscription:** Kuang-hsü Yüan-pao **Reverse:** Circled dragon **Edge:** Normal reeding

Date	Mintage	VG	F	VF	XF	Unc
ND(1898)	1,603,000	100	200	400	800	1,500

Y# 145.1 DOLLAR
27.0000 g., 0.9000 Silver .7814 oz. ASW **Obv. Inscription:** Kuang-hsü Yüan-pao **Edge:** Ornamented

Date	Mintage	VG	F	VF	XF	Unc
ND(1898)	Inc. above	62.50	125	175	300	800

Y# 145a.1 DOLLAR
27.0000 g., 0.9000 Silver .7814 oz. ASW **Obv. Inscription:** Kuang-hsü Yüan-pao **Reverse:** Without circle around old style dragon

Date	Mintage	VG	F	VF	XF	Unc
CD(1898)	Inc. above	12.50	25.00	75.00	150	600

Y# 145a.18 DOLLAR
27.0000 g., 0.9000 Silver .7814 oz. ASW **Obverse:** Chinese date characters "Wu Shu" reversed **Obv. Inscription:** Kuang-hsü Yüan-pao

Date	Mintage	VG	F	VF	XF	Unc
CD(1898)	Inc. above	750	1,500	2,750	—	—

Y# 145a.3 DOLLAR
27.0000 g., 0.9000 Silver .7814 oz. ASW **Obv. Inscription:** Kuang-hsü Yüan-pao **Reverse:** Redesigned dragon with shorter face and larger forehead, similar to 1900

Date	Mintage	VG	F	VF	XF	Unc
CD(1899)	Inc. above	50.00	100	150	250	750

Y# 145a.4 DOLLAR
26.7000 g., 0.9000 Silver .7814 oz. ASW **Obv. Inscription:** Kuang-hsü Yüan-pao **Reverse:** Large scales on dragon

Date	Mintage	VG	F	VF	XF	Unc
CD(1900)	2,531,000	15.00	30.00	75.00	150	600

Y# 145a.20 DOLLAR
26.7000 g., 0.9000 Silver .7814 oz. ASW **Obv. Inscription:** Kuang-hsü Yüan-pao **Reverse:** Small scales on dragon

Date	Mintage	VG	F	VF	XF	Unc
CD(1900)	Inc. above	11.50	22.50	50.00	125	600

PATTERNS

Including off metal strikes

KM#	Date	Mintage	Identification	Mkt Val
Pn1	CD(1898)	—	Dollar. Silver. Plain edgeY#145	5,500
Pn2	CD(1898)	—	Dollar. Copper. Y#145.	1,200

KIANGSI PROVINCE

Jiangxi, Kiangsee

A province located in southeastern China. Mostly hilly with some mountains on the borders that produce coal and tungsten. Some of China's finest porcelain comes from this province. Kiangsi was visited by Marco Polo. A mint was opened in Nanchang in 1729, closed in 1733, reopened in 1736 and operated with reasonable continuity from that time. Modern machinery was introduced in 1901 although it only produced copper coins. The mint closed amidst internal problems in the 1920's.

EMPIRE

Tao-kuang
1821-1851

PROVINCIAL CAST COINAGE

C# 15-3 CASH
Cast Brass **Obv. Inscription:** Tao-kuang T'ung-pao **Mint:** Ch'ang

Date	Mintage	Good	VG	F	VF	XF
ND(1821-51)	—	0.50	0.85	1.50	2.00	—

C# 15-3a CASH
Cast Zinc **Obv. Inscription:** Tao-kuang T'ung-pao **Mint:** Ch'ang

Date	Mintage	Good	VG	F	VF	XF
ND(1821-51) Rare	—	—	—	—	—	—

Hsien-fêng
1851-1861

PROVINCIAL CAST COINAGE

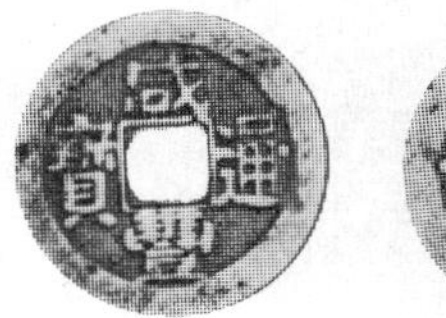

C# 15-4 CASH
Cast Brass **Obverse:** Type A **Obv. Inscription:** Hsien-fêng T'ung-pao **Mint:** Ch'ang

Date	Mintage	Good	VG	F	VF	XF
ND(1821-61)	—	1.00	2.00	3.00	4.00	—

C# 15-5 10 CASH
Cast Brass **Obverse:** Type B-1 **Obv. Inscription:** Hsien-fêng Chung-pao **Mint:** Ch'ang

Date	Mintage	Good	VG	F	VF	XF
ND(1851-61)	—	3.00	6.00	10.00	30.00	—

C# 15-6 50 CASH
Cast Copper **Obverse:** Type B-1 **Obv. Inscription:** Hsien-fêng Chung-pao **Mint:** Ch'ang

Date	Mintage	Good	VG	F	VF	XF
ND(1851-61)	—	8.00	16.00	30.00	60.00	—

C# 15-6.1 50 CASH
Cast Brass, 52 mm. **Obv. Inscription:** Hsien-fêng Chung-pao **Mint:** Ch'ang

Date	Mintage	Good	VG	F	VF	XF
ND(1851-61)	—	6.00	12.00	18.00	35.00	—

T'ung-chih
1862-1875

PROVINCIAL CAST COINAGE

C# 15-7 CASH
Cast Brass **Obverse:** Type A **Obv. Inscription:** T'ung-chih T'ung-pao **Mint:** Ch'ang

Date	Mintage	Good	VG	F	VF	XF
ND(1862-74)	—	1.20	3.00	4.00	5.00	—

Kuang-hsü
1875-1908

PROVINCIAL CAST COINAGE

C# 15-9 CASH
Cast Brass **Obv. Inscription:** Kuang-hsü T'ung-pao **Reverse:** Manchu Boo-ch'ang type 1 mint mark **Mint:** Ch'ang

Date	Mintage	Good	VG	F	VF	XF
ND(1875-86)	—	4.50	6.50	12.00	15.00	—

KIANGSU-KIANGSOO PROVINCE

Jiangsu

A province located on the east coast of China. One of the smallest and most densely populated of all Chinese provinces. A mint opened in Soochow in 1667, but closed shortly after in 1670. A new mint opened in 1734 for producing cast coins and had continuous operation until about 1870. Modern equipment was introduced in 1898 and a second mint was opened in 1904. Both mints closed down production in 1906. Taels were produced in Shanghai by local silversmiths as early as 1856. These saw limited circulation in the immediate area.

EMPIRE

SHANGHAI COINAGE

An important port city in Kiangsu (Jiangsu) province. Although there was no mint in Shanghai prior to the 1930's, a number of coins were minted for Shanghai by silversmiths.

Kann ##900-903 are known as 'Silversmith' Taels because each bears the name of a silver smelting firm in Shanghai. The engravers' names are all given names; their surnames are unknown. The coins were authorized by the Taotai (a government official) of Shanghai to facilitate foreign trade and to replace the vanishing Mexican 8 Reales which had become very scarce due to hoarding.

K# 907 5 CH'IEN
18.4000 g., Silver **Issuer:** Yu Sheng-Sheng **Note:** Engraved by Wang Shou.

Date	Mintage	Good	VG	F	VF	XF
6(1856)	—	—	—	—	500	800

K# 908 5 CH'IEN
18.4000 g., Silver **Issuer:** Wang Yung-sheng **Note:** Engraved by Wan Ch'uan. Similar to Kann#902.

Date	Mintage	Good	VG	F	VF	XF
6(1856)	—	—	—	—	600	900

K# 910 5 CH'IEN
18.4000 g., Silver **Issuer:** Ching Cheng-chi **Note:** Engraved by Wan Ch'uan.

Date	Mintage	Good	VG	F	VF	XF
6(1856)	—	—	—	—	500	800

K# 900 LIANG (Tael)
36.7000 g., Silver **Issuer:** Wang Yung-sheng **Note:** Engraved by Wan Ch'uan.

Date	Mintage	Good	VG	F	VF	XF
6(1856)	—	—	—	—	800	1,300

K# 901 LIANG (Tael)
36.7000 g., Silver **Issuer:** Yu Sen-sheng **Note:** Engraved by Feng-nien.

Date	Mintage	Good	VG	F	VF	XF
6(1856)	—	—	—	—	700	1,000

K# 902 LIANG (Tael)
36.7000 g., Silver **Issuer:** Yu Sen-sheng **Note:** Engraved by P'ing Cheng.

Date	Mintage	Good	VG	F	VF	XF
6(1856)	—	—	—	—	700	1,000

K# 903 LIANG (Tael)
36.7000 g., Silver **Issuer:** Ching Cheng-chi **Note:** Engraved by Feng-nien.

Date	Mintage	Good	VG	F	VF	XF
6(1856)	—	—	—	—	700	1,000

Tao-kuang
1821-1851

PROVINCIAL CAST COINAGE

C# 16-3 CASH
Cast Brass **Obv. Inscription:** Tao-kuang T'ung-pao **Mint:** Su **Note:** Narrow rims. Schjöth #1515.

Date	Mintage	Good	VG	F	VF	XF
ND(1821-51)	—	0.50	1.00	2.00	4.00	—

C# 16-3.1 CASH
Cast Brass **Obv. Inscription:** Tao-kuang T'ung-pao **Mint:** Su **Note:** Medium rims.

Date	Mintage	Good	VG	F	VF	XF
ND(1821-51)	—	0.50	1.00	2.00	4.00	—

C# 16-3.2 CASH
Cast Brass **Obv. Inscription:** Tao-kuang T'ung-pao **Mint:** Su **Note:** Wide rims.

Date	Mintage	Good	VG	F	VF	XF
ND(1821-51)	—	30.00	50.00	70.00	110	—

Hsien-fêng
1851-1861

PROVINCIAL CAST COINAGE

C# 16-4 CASH
Cast Brass **Obv. Inscription:** Hsien-fêng T'ung-pao **Mint:** Su **Note:** Narrow rims. Schjöth #1536.

Date	Mintage	Good	VG	F	VF	XF
ND(1851-61)	—	1.00	2.00	3.00	4.50	—

C# 16-4.1 CASH
Cast Brass **Obv. Inscription:** Hsien-fêng T'ung-pao **Mint:** Su **Note:** Medium rims.

Date	Mintage	Good	VG	F	VF	XF
ND(1851-61)	—	1.00	2.00	3.00	4.50	—

C# 16-4.2 CASH
Cast Brass **Obv. Inscription:** Hsien-fêng T'ung-pao **Mint:** Su **Note:** Wide rims.

Date	Mintage	Good	VG	F	VF	XF
ND(1851-61)	—	18.50	37.50	75.00	150	—

C# 16-4.3 CASH
Cast Brass **Obv. Inscription:** Hsien-fêng T'ung-pao **Reverse:** Crescent above **Mint:** Su

Date	Mintage	Good	VG	F	VF	XF
ND(1851-61)	—	4.25	8.50	17.50	35.00	—

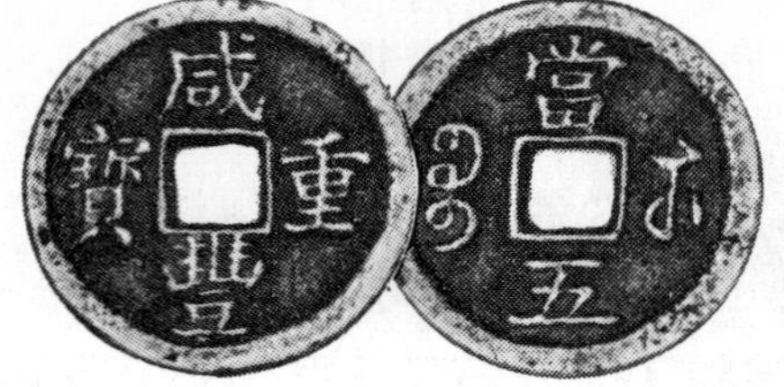

C# 16-5 5 CASH
Cast Brass **Obverse:** Type B-1 **Obv. Inscription:** Hsien-fêng Chung-pao **Mint:** Su

Date	Mintage	Good	VG	F	VF	XF
ND(1851-61)	—	30.00	45.00	65.00	100	—

C# 16-5a 5 CASH
Cast Iron **Obv. Inscription:** Hsien-fêng Chung-pao **Mint:** Su

Date	Mintage	Good	VG	F	VF	XF
ND(1851-61)	—	40.00	55.00	80.00	120	—

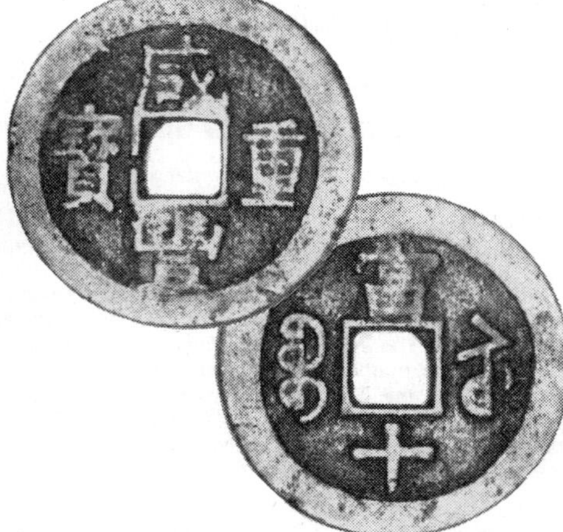

C# 16-6 10 CASH
Cast Brass **Obverse:** Type B-1 **Obv. Inscription:** Hsien-fêng Chung-pao **Mint:** Su **Note:** Size varies: 36-40mm.

Date	Mintage	Good	VG	F	VF	XF
ND(1851-61)	—	5.00	7.50	15.00	25.00	—

C# 16-6.1 10 CASH
Cast Brass **Obv. Inscription:** Hsien-fêng Chung-pao **Mint:** Su **Note:** Schjöth #1594. Size varies: 30-34mm.

Date	Mintage	Good	VG	F	VF	XF
ND(1851-61)	—	5.00	7.50	10.00	20.00	—

C# 16-6a 10 CASH
Cast Iron **Obv. Inscription:** Hsien-fêng Chung-pao **Mint:** Su

Date	Mintage	Good	VG	F	VF	XF
ND(1851-61)	—	27.50	50.00	75.00	100	—

C# 16-7 20 CASH
Cast Brass, 39 mm. **Obverse:** Type B-1 **Obv. Inscription:** Hsien-fêng Chung-pao **Mint:** Su

Date	Mintage	Good	VG	F	VF	XF
ND(1851-61)	—	35.00	55.00	75.00	100	—

C# 16-8 30 CASH
Cast Brass, 46 mm. **Obverse:** Type B-1 **Obv. Inscription:** Hsien-fêng Chung-pao **Mint:** Su

Date	Mintage	Good	VG	F	VF	XF
ND(1851-61)	—	85.00	120	150	200	—

C# 16-9.1 50 CASH
Cast Copper, 55 mm. **Obverse:** Type B-1 **Obv. Inscription:** Hsien-fêng Chung-pao **Reverse:** Small characters **Mint:** Su

Date	Mintage	Good	VG	F	VF	XF
ND(1851-61)	—	8.00	22.00	35.00	60.00	—

C# 16-9.2 50 CASH
Cast Copper **Obv. Inscription:** Hsien-fêng Chung-pao **Reverse:** Large characters **Mint:** Su

Date	Mintage	Good	VG	F	VF	XF
ND(1851-61)	—	8.00	22.00	35.00	60.00	—

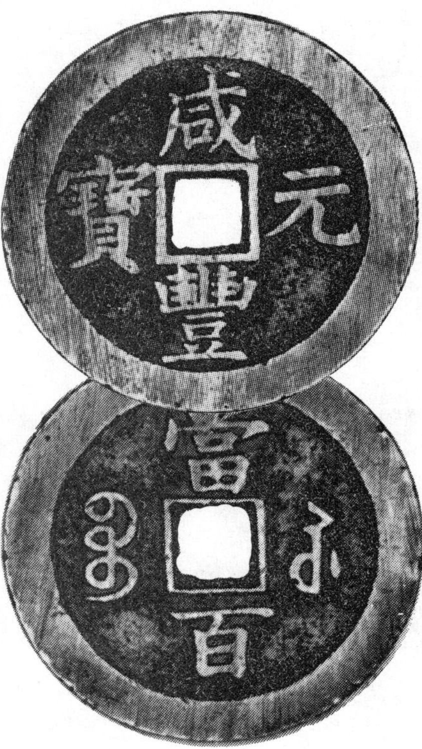

C# 16-10 100 CASH
Cast Brass **Obverse:** Type C; small characters **Obv. Inscription:** Hsien-fêng Yüan-pao **Reverse:** Small characters **Mint:** Su

Date	Mintage	Good	VG	F	VF	XF
ND(1851-61)	—	10.00	25.00	35.00	85.00	—

C# 16-10.1 100 CASH
Cast Brass **Obverse:** Large characters **Obv. Inscription:** Hsien-fêng Yüan-pao **Reverse:** Large characters **Mint:** Su **Note:** Schjöth #1589.

Date	Mintage	Good	VG	F	VF	XF
ND(1851-61)	—	10.00	25.00	35.00	85.00	—

T'ung-chih
1862-1875

PROVINCIAL CAST COINAGE

C# 16-11 CASH
Cast Brass **Obv. Inscription:** T'ung-chih T'ung-pao **Mint:** Su **Note:** Schjöth #1556.

Date	Mintage	Good	VG	F	VF	XF
ND(1862-74)	—	2.75	5.50	9.00	15.00	—

Kuang-hsü
1875-1908

PROVINCIAL CAST COINAGE

C# 16-12 CASH
Cast Brass **Obv. Inscription:** Kuang-hsü T'ung-pao **Reverse:** Manchu inscription **Rev. Inscription:** Boo-su **Mint:** Su

Date	Mintage	Good	VG	F	VF	XF
ND(1875-1908)	—	2.25	4.50	8.00	13.00	—

C# 16-12.1 CASH
Cast Brass **Obv. Inscription:** Kuang-hsü T'ung-pao **Reverse:** Manchu inscription **Rev. Inscription:** Boo-su **Mint:** Su

Date	Mintage	Good	VG	F	VF	XF
ND(1875-1908)	—	3.00	6.00	10.00	16.00	—

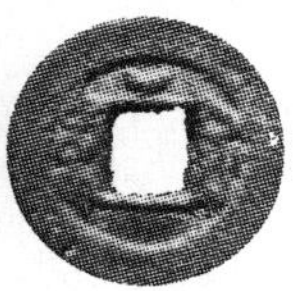

C# 16-12.2 CASH
Cast Brass **Obv. Inscription:** Kuang-hsü T'ung-pao **Reverse:** Manchu inscription **Rev. Inscription:** Boo-su **Mint:** Su

Date	Mintage	Good	VG	F	VF	XF
ND(1875-1908)	—	3.00	6.00	10.00	16.00	—

C# 16-13 5 CASH
Cast Brass **Obv. Inscription:** Kuang-hsü Chung-pao **Reverse:** Manchu inscription **Rev. Inscription:** Boo-su **Mint:** Su

Date	Mintage	Good	VG	F	VF	XF
ND(1875-86)	—	25.00	40.00	55.00	75.00	—

MILLED COINAGE

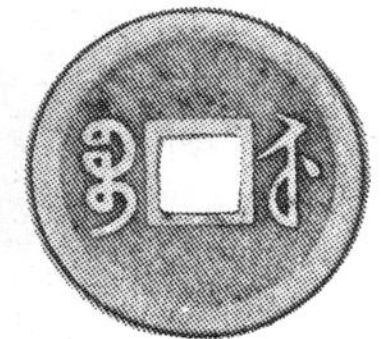

HSU# 85 CASH
Brass **Obv. Inscription:** Kuang-hsü T'ung-pao

Date	Mintage	VG	F	VF	XF	Unc
ND(c.1890)	—	17.50	35.00	55.00	90.00	120

Y# A158 10 CASH
Brass **Note:** Prev. Y#148.

Date	Mintage	VG	F	VF	XF	Unc
ND(1898) Rare	—	—	—	—	—	—

PATTERNS
Including off metal strikes

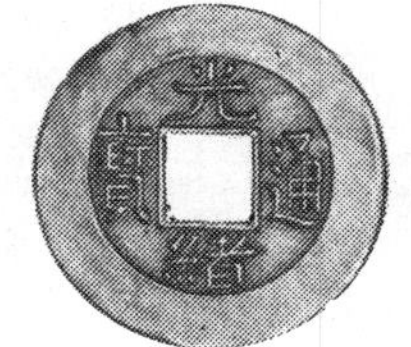
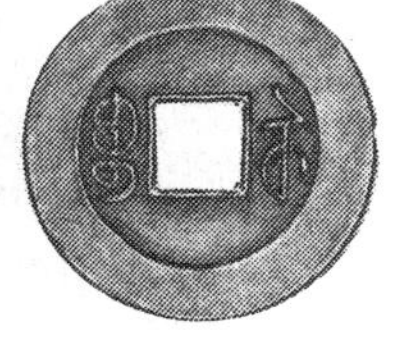

KM#	Date	Mintage	Identification	Mkt Val
Pn1	ND(c.1890)	—	Cash. Brass. Hsu#85.1.	—

KIRIN PROVINCE

Jilin

A province of northeast China that was formed in 1945. Before that it was one of the three original provinces of Manchuria. Besides growing corn, wheat and tobacco, there is also coal mining. An arsenal in Kirin (Jilin) opened in 1881 and was chosen as a source for coinage attempts. In 1884 Tael trials were struck and regular coinage began in 1895. Modern equipment was installed in a new mint in Kirin (Jilin) in 1901. The issues of this mint were very prolific and many varieties exist due to the use of hand cut dies for the earlier issues. The mint burned down in 1911.

EMPIRE

Kuang-hsü
1875-1908

PROVINCIAL CAST COINAGE

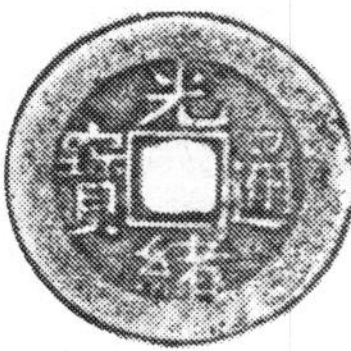
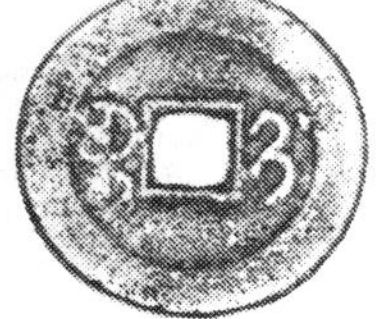

C# 17-1 CASH
Cast Brass **Obv. Inscription:** Kuang-hsü T'ung-pao **Mint:** Chi

Date	Mintage	Good	VG	F	VF	XF
ND(1875-80)	—	15.00	25.00	35.00	50.00	—

Note: This coin is sometimes erroneously attributed to Chi-chou (Chichow) in Chihli (Hebei) province, which used this mint mark in the Hsien-fêng and earlier reigns

MILLED COINAGE

Errors in the English legends are very common in the Kirin coinage. It has been estimated there are over 2500 die varieties of Kirin (Jilin) silver coins and more than 1000 varieties of copper 10 Cash. Listed here are basic types and major varieties only.

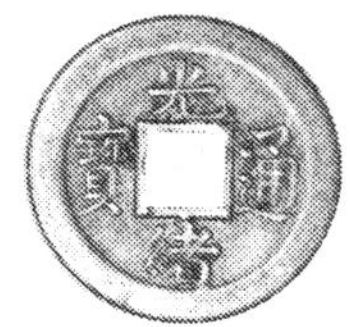
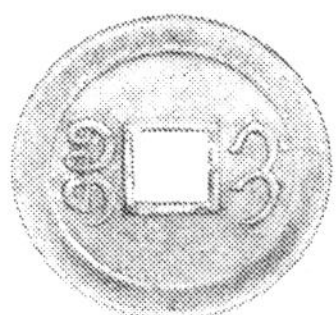

HSU# 481 CASH
Brass **Obv. Inscription:** Kuang-hsü T'ung-pao

Date	Mintage	VG	F	VF	XF	Unc
ND(ca.1900)	—	10.00	30.00	50.00	75.00	100

Note: This coin is sometimes erroneously attributed to Chi-chou (Chichow) in Chihli (Hebei) province, which used this mint mark in the Hsien-fêng and earlier reigns. Four minor varieties exist.

Y# 179.1 5 CENTS
1.2700 g., Silver **Obv. Inscription:** Kuang-hsü Yüan-pao **Reverse:** Side view dragon; without crosses flanking weight **Note:** Kann #394, 416, 549

Date	Mintage	VG	F	VF	XF	Unc
ND(ca.1898)	—	1.75	5.00	10.00	20.00	50.00
CD(1899)	—	2.25	6.50	12.50	25.00	60.00
CD(1900)	—	3.50	10.00	20.00	30.00	75.00
CD(1906)	—	2.25	6.50	12.50	25.00	60.00
CD(1907)	—	2.75	8.00	15.00	25.00	60.00
CD(1908) Rare	—	—	—	—	—	—

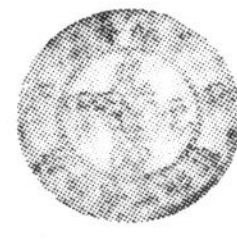
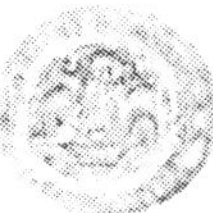

Y# 179 5 CENTS
1.2700 g., Silver **Obverse:** Flower vase center **Obv. Inscription:** Kuang-hsü Yüan-pao **Reverse:** Side view dragon; cross before and after weight: "CANDARINS .36"

Date	Mintage	F	VF	XF	Unc
ND(ca.1898)	—	10.00	25.00	45.00	85.00

Y# 179a 5 CENTS
1.2700 g., Silver **Obverse:** Yin-yang in center **Obv. Inscription:** Kuang-hsü Yüan-pao **Reverse:** Side view dragon **Note:** Kann #444,465, 481, 510, 533.

Date	Mintage	VG	F	VF	XF	Unc
CD(1900)	—	2.50	7.50	15.00	30.00	60.00
CD(1901)	—	1.85	5.50	11.50	25.00	50.00
CD(1902)	—	2.25	6.50	12.50	25.00	60.00
CD(1903)	—	4.50	12.50	25.00	50.00	100
CD(1904)	—	3.50	10.00	15.00	30.00	70.00
CD(1905)	—	2.50	7.50	15.00	30.00	65.00

Y# 180.1 10 CENTS
2.5500 g., Silver **Obverse:** Large flower vase center **Obv. Inscription:** Kuang-hsü Yüan-pao **Reverse:** Side view dragon; without crosses flanking weight **Note:** Kann #393, 416, 546.

Date	Mintage	VG	F	VF	XF	Unc
ND(ca.1898)	—	1.85	5.50	11.50	22.50	50.00
CD(1899)	—	2.25	6.50	12.50	25.00	60.00
CD(1900)	—	2.25	6.50	12.50	25.00	60.00

Y# 180 10 CENTS
2.5500 g., Silver **Obverse:** Small flower vase center **Obv. Inscription:** Kuang-hsü Yüan-pao **Reverse:** Side view dragon; cross before and after weight: "CANDARINS .76"

Date	Mintage	F	VF	XF	Unc
ND(ca.1898)	—	5.50	11.50	22.50	65.00

Y# 180a 10 CENTS
2.5500 g., Silver **Obverse:** Yin-yang in center **Obv. Inscription:** Kuang-hsü Yüan-pao **Reverse:** Side view dragon

Date	Mintage	VG	F	VF	XF	Unc
CD(1900)	—	2.50	7.50	15.00	30.00	75.00

Y# 181 20 CENTS
5.1000 g., Silver **Obverse:** Flower vase center **Obv. Inscription:** Kuang-hsü Yüan-pao **Reverse:** Side view dragon

Date	Mintage	VG	F	VF	XF	Unc
ND(ca.1898)	—	2.50	7.50	15.00	30.00	60.00
CD(1899)	—	2.25	6.50	12.50	25.00	50.00
CD(1900)	—	2.50	7.50	15.00	30.00	60.00

Y# 181a 20 CENTS
5.1000 g., Silver **Obverse:** Yin-yang in center **Obv. Inscription:** Kuang-hsü Yüan-pao **Reverse:** Side view dragon

Date	Mintage	VG	F	VF	XF	Unc
CD(1900)	—	2.50	7.50	15.00	30.00	60.00

Y# 182 50 CENTS
13.1000 g., Silver **Obverse:** Flower vase center with rosette at either side **Obv. Inscription:** Kuang-hsü Yüan-pao **Reverse:** Side view dragon; without crosses flanking weight

Date	Mintage	F	VF	XF	Unc
ND(ca.1898)	—	15.00	25.00	50.00	150

Y# 182.1 50 CENTS
13.1000 g., Silver **Obverse:** Rosette at either side **Obv. Inscription:** Kuang-hsü Yüan-pao **Reverse:** Side view dragon; crosses before and after weight: "CANDARENS 6"

Date	Mintage	F	VF	XF	Unc
ND(ca.1898)	—	15.00	25.00	50.00	150

Y# 182.2 50 CENTS
13.1000 g., Silver **Obverse:** Without rosettes **Obv. Inscription:** Kuang-hsü Yüan-pao **Reverse:** Side view dragon; without crosses flanking weight

Date	Mintage	F	VF	XF	Unc
ND(ca.1898)	—	—	—	—	—

Y# 182.3 50 CENTS
13.1000 g., Silver **Obv. Inscription:** Kuang-hsü Yüan-pao **Reverse:** Side view dragon

Date	Mintage	VG	F	VF	XF	Unc
CD(1899)	—	8.50	25.00	45.00	80.00	200
CD(1900)	—	6.50	20.00	35.00	60.00	150

Y# 182a 50 CENTS
13.1000 g., Silver **Obverse:** Figure-8 yin-yang in center **Obv. Inscription:** Kuang-hsü Yüan-pao **Reverse:** Side view dragon

Date	Mintage	F	VF	XF	Unc
CD(1900)	—	20.00	35.00	60.00	150

Y# 183 DOLLAR
26.1000 g., Silver **Obverse:** Flower vase center **Obv. Inscription:** Kuang-hsü Yüan-pao **Reverse:** Side view dragon; small rosettes before and after weight: 7 CANDARINS 2 or 7 CAINDARINS 2

Date	Mintage	VG	F	VF	XF	Unc
ND(ca.1898)	—	20.00	60.00	100	250	500
CD(1899)	—	20.00	60.00	100	250	500
CD(1900)	—	20.00	60.00	100	300	600

Y# 183a DOLLAR
26.1000 g., Silver **Obverse:** Figure "8" Yin-yang in center **Obv. Inscription:** Kuang-hsü Yüan-pao **Reverse:** Side view dragon

Date	Mintage	F	VF	XF	Unc
CD(1900)	—	100	200	350	850

BULLION TAEL COINAGE

Y# 169 CH'IEN (Mace)
3.6000 g., Silver **Obverse:** Facing stylized dragons **Reverse:** Numeral 1 in simple Chinese **Note:** Kann #919.

Date	Mintage	VG	F	VF	XF	Unc
10(1885)	—	—	—	—	500	750

Y# 169.1 CH'IEN (Mace)
3.6000 g., Silver **Obverse:** Facing stylized dragons **Reverse:** Different, more complicated character for 1 **Note:** Kann #920.

Date	Mintage	VG	F	VF	XF	Unc
10(1885)	—	—	—	—	400	650

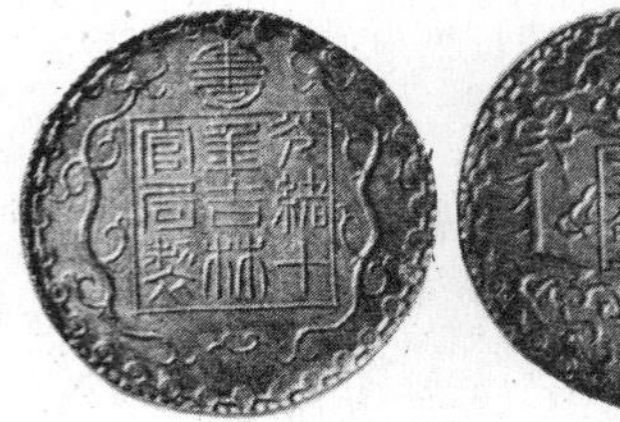

Y# 170 3 CH'IEN
10.8000 g., Silver **Obverse:** Facing stylized dragons **Edge:** Vertical reeding **Note:** Kann #918.

Date	Mintage	VG	F	VF	XF	Unc
10(1884)	—	—	—	—	500	750

Y# 170.1 3 CH'IEN
10.8000 g., Silver **Obverse:** Facing stylized dragons **Edge:** Diagonal reeding **Note:** Kann #918b.

Date	Mintage	VG	F	VF	XF	Unc
10(1885)	—	—	—	—	500	750

Y# 171 5 CH'IEN (1/2 Tael)
17.8000 g., Silver **Obverse:** Facing stylized dragons **Note:** Kann #917.

Date	Mintage	VG	F	VF	XF	Unc
10(1885)	—	—	—	—	850	1,500

Y# 172 7 CH'IEN
25.4000 g., Silver **Obverse:** Facing stylized dragons **Note:** Kann #916.

Date	Mintage	VG	F	VF	XF	Unc
10(1885)	—	—	—	—	3,500	5,000

Y# 173 TAEL
35.5000 g., Silver **Obverse:** Facing stylized dragons **Note:** Kann #915.

Date	Mintage	VG	F	VF	XF	Unc
10(1885) Rare	—	—	—	—	—	—

Note: Superior Goodman sale 6-91 AU realized $35,200

PATTERNS

Including off metal strikes

KM#	Date	Mintage	Identification	Mkt Val
Pn1	8(1882)	—	Tael. Silver. K#914.	—
Pn2	8(1882)	—	Tael. Copper. K#914x.	—
Pn3	10(1884)	—	Ch'len. White Metal. K#920.	—
Pn4	10(1884)	—	3 Ch'len. White Metal. K#918.	—
Pn5	10(1884)	—	3 Ch'len. Brass. K#918.	1,500
Pn6	10(1884)	—	5 Ch'len. White Metal. K#917.	—
Pn7	10(1884)	—	7 Ch'len. White Metal. K#916.	—
Pn8	10(1884)	—	Tael. White Metal. K#915.	—

KWANGSI-KWANGSEA

Guangxi

A hilly region in southeast China with many forests. Large amounts of rice are grown adjacent to the many rivers. A mint opened in Kweilin in 1667, closed in 1670, reopened in 1679, closed again in 1681. It reopened in the mid-1700's and was a rather prolific issuer of Cash coins. In 1905 the government allowed modern mints to be established in Kwangsi (Guangxi) at Nanning (1905) and Kweilin (1905). The Nanning Mint began operation in 1919 and closed in 1923. In 1920 a new mint was opened at Wuchow and operated sporadically until 1929. In 1938 part of the Shanghai Central Mint was moved to Kweilin where it operated until at least 1945 and perhaps as late as 1949.

EMPIRE

Tao-kuang
1821-1851

PROVINCIAL CAST COINAGE

C# 18-3 CASH

Cast Brass **Obverse:** Type A **Obv. Inscription:** Tao-kuang T'ung-pao **Mint:** Kue

Date	Mintage	Good	VG	F	VF	XF
ND(1821-51)	—	0.50	1.00	1.75	3.00	—

C# 18-3.1 CASH

Cast Brass **Obv. Inscription:** Tao-kuang T'ung-pao **Reverse:** Dot below left **Mint:** Kue

Date	Mintage	Good	VG	F	VF	XF
ND(1821-51)	—	0.60	1.00	2.00	3.00	—

Hsien-fêng
1851-1861

PROVINCIAL CAST COINAGE

C# 18-4 CASH

Cast Brass **Obverse:** Type A **Obv. Inscription:** Hsien-fêng T'ung-pao **Mint:** Kue

Date	Mintage	Good	VG	F	VF	XF
ND(1851-61)	—	1.00	2.00	3.00	5.00	—

C# 18-5 10 CASH

Cast Brass **Obverse:** Type B-1 **Obv. Inscription:** Hsien-fêng Chung-pao **Mint:** Kue

Date	Mintage	Good	VG	F	VF	XF
ND(1851-61)	—	3.00	7.00	9.00	15.00	—

C# 18-6 50 CASH

Cast Brass **Obverse:** Type B-1 **Obv. Inscription:** Hsien-fêng Chung-pao **Mint:** Kue

Date	Mintage	Good	VG	F	VF	XF
ND(1851-61)	—	40.00	60.00	80.00	165	—

T'ung-chih
1862-1875

PROVINCIAL CAST COINAGE

C# 18-7 CASH

Cast Brass **Obverse:** Type A-2 **Obv. Inscription:** T'ung-chih T'ung-pao **Reverse:** Large Manchu script **Mint:** Kue

Date	Mintage	Good	VG	F	VF	XF
ND(1862-74)	—	2.50	3.50	6.50	9.00	—

C# 18-7.1 CASH

Cast Brass **Obv. Inscription:** T'ung-chih T'ung-pao **Reverse:** Small Manchu script **Mint:** Kue

Date	Mintage	Good	VG	F	VF	XF
ND(1862-74)	—	2.50	3.50	6.50	9.00	—

C# 18-7.2 CASH

Cast Brass **Obv. Inscription:** T'ung-chih T'ung-pao **Reverse:** Circle above **Mint:** Kue **Note:** Schjöth #1566.

Date	Mintage	Good	VG	F	VF	XF
ND(1862-74)	—	5.50	8.50	13.50	25.00	—

Kuang-hsü
1875-1908

PROVINCIAL CAST COINAGE

C# 18-9 CASH

Cast Brass **Obv. Inscription:** Kuang-hsü T'ung-pao **Reverse:** Manchu inscription **Rev. Inscription:** Boo-gui **Mint:** Kue

Date	Mintage	Good	VG	F	VF	XF
ND(1875-1908)	—	5.50	8.50	13.50	25.00	—

KWANGTUNG PROVINCE

Guangdong

A province located on the southeast coast of China. Kwangtung (Guangdong) lies mostly in the tropics and has both mountains and plains. Its coastline is nearly 800 miles long and provides many good harbors. Because of the location of Guangzhou (Canton) in the province, Kwangtung (Guangdong) was the first to be visited by seaborne foreign traders. Hong Kong was ceded to Great Britain after the First Opium War in 1841. Kowloon was later ceded to Britain in 1860 and the New Territories (100 year lease) in 1898 and Macao to Portugal in 1887, Kwangchowwan was leased to France in 1898 (a property was restored in 1946). A modern mint opened in Guangzhou (Canton) in 1889 with Edward Wyon as superintendent. The mint was a large issuer of coins until it closed in 1931. The Nationalists reopened the mint briefly in 1949, striking a few silver dollars, before abandoning the mainland for their retreat to Taiwan.

The large island of Hainan was split off from Kwangtung (Guangdong) Province in 1988 and established as a separate province.

Hong Kong was returned to China by Britain on July 1, 1997 and established as a special administrative region, retaining its own coinage.

EMPIRE

Tao-kuang
1821-1851

PROVINCIAL CAST COINAGE

C# 19-3 CASH

Cast Brass **Obverse:** Type A **Obv. Inscription:** Tao-kuang T'ung-pao **Mint:** Kuang **Note:** Schjöth #1522.

Date	Mintage	Good	VG	F	VF	XF
ND(1821-51)	—	0.25	0.50	1.00	2.00	—

Hsien-fêng
1851-1861

PROVINCIAL CAST COINAGE

C# 19-4 CASH

Cast Brass **Obverse:** Type A **Obv. Inscription:** Hsien-fêng T'ung-pao **Mint:** Kuang **Note:** Schjöth #1542.

Date	Mintage	Good	VG	F	VF	XF
ND(1851-61)	—	7.50	12.50	20.00	30.00	—

T'ung-chih
1862-1875

PROVINCIAL CAST COINAGE

C# 19-5 CASH

Cast Brass **Obverse:** Type A-2 **Obv. Inscription:** T'ung-chih T'ung-pao **Mint:** Kuang

Date	Mintage	Good	VG	F	VF	XF
ND(1862-74)	—	200	350	500	800	—

Kuang-hsü
1875-1908

PROVINCIAL CAST COINAGE

C# 19-7 CASH

Cast Brass **Obv. Inscription:** Kuang-hsü T'ung-pao **Reverse:** Manchu inscription **Rev. Inscription:** Boo-guwang **Mint:** Kuang

Date	Mintage	Good	VG	F	VF	XF
ND(1875-1908)	—	12.00	22.00	32.00	45.00	—

MILLED COINAGE

Y# 189 CASH
Brass **Obverse:** Type B **Obv. Inscription:** Kuang-hsü T'ung-pao **Mint:** Kuang

Date	Mintage	VF	XF	Unc
ND(1889) Proof	—	Value: 275		
ND(1889)	— 0.25	0.45	0.85	3.00

Y# 189.1 CASH
Brass **Obverse:** "Kuang" in a different style **Obv. Inscription:** Kuang-hsü T'ung-pao **Mint:** Kuang

Date	Mintage	VG	F	VF	XF	Unc
ND(1889)	—	10.00	20.00	25.00	40.00	75.00

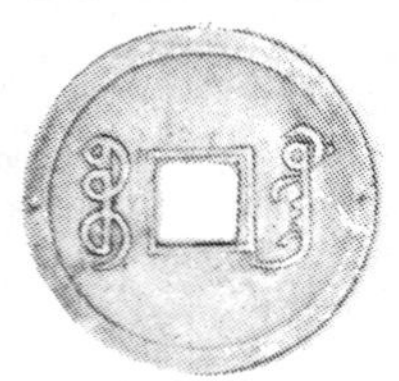

Y# 190 CASH
Brass **Obverse:** "Kuang" in a different style **Obv. Inscription:** Kuang-hsü T'ung-pao **Reverse:** Manchu inscription **Rev. Inscription:** Boo-guwang **Mint:** Kuang

Date	Mintage	VG	F	VF	XF	Unc
ND(1890-1908)	1,059,253,000	—	0.10	0.25	1.00	2.00

Y# A192 CENT (10 Cash)
Copper **Obverse:** Y#192 **Obv. Inscription:** Kuang-hsü Yüan-pao **Reverse:** Chihli 10 Cash, Y#67, dragon **Note:** Mule.

Date	Mintage	VG	F	VF	XF	Unc
ND	—	8.50	25.00	35.00	50.00	125

Y# 192 CENT (10 Cash)
Copper **Obv. Legend:** Six characters at bottom **Obv. Inscription:** Kuang-hsü Yüan-pao **Reverse:** Dragon, ONE CENT

Date	Mintage	VG	F	VF	XF	Unc
ND(1900-06)	—	0.25	0.75	1.50	3.00	20.00

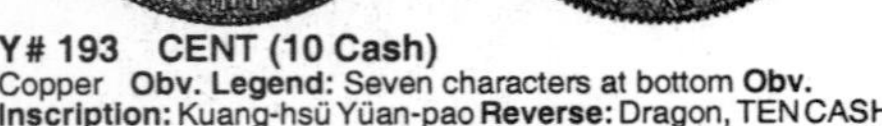

Y# 193 CENT (10 Cash)
Copper **Obv. Legend:** Seven characters at bottom **Obv. Inscription:** Kuang-hsü Yüan-pao **Reverse:** Dragon, TEN CASH

Date	Mintage	VG	F	VF	XF	Unc
ND(1900-06)	—	0.35	1.00	2.00	4.00	20.00

Note: Varieties in lettering exist, including spacing of characters.

Y# 194 5 CENTS
1.3000 g., 0.8200 Silver .0343 oz. ASW **Obverse:** 3.65 CANDAREENS **Obv. Inscription:** Kuang-hsü Yüan-pao **Reverse:** Chinese characters around dragon

Date	Mintage	F	VF	XF	Unc
ND(1889)	—	150	400	600	1,000

Y# 194.1 5 CENTS
1.3000 g., 0.8200 Silver .0343 oz. ASW **Obverse:** 3.6 CANDAREENS **Obv. Inscription:** Kuang-hsü Yüan-pao

Date	Mintage	F	VF	XF	Unc
ND(1899)	—	275	700	1,000	1,500

Y# 199 5 CENTS
1.3000 g., 0.8200 Silver .0343 oz. ASW **Obv. Inscription:** Kuang-hsü Yüan-pao **Reverse:** English legend around dragon

Date	Mintage	VG	F	VF	XF	Unc
ND(1890-1905)	—	1.00	3.50	6.00	10.00	30.00

Y# 195 10 CENTS
2.7000 g., 0.8200 Silver .0712 oz. ASW **Obverse:** 7 3/10 CANDAREENS **Obv. Inscription:** Kuang-hsü Yüan-pao

Date	Mintage	F	VF	XF	Unc
ND(1889)	—	100	175	275	500
ND(1889) Proof	—	—	—	—	—

Y# 195.1 10 CENTS
2.7000 g., 0.8200 Silver .0712 oz. ASW **Obverse:** 7.2 CANDAREENS **Obv. Inscription:** Kuang-hsü Yüan-pao

Date	Mintage	F	VF	XF	Unc
ND(1889)	—	2,000	3,000	4,500	—

Y# 200 10 CENTS
2.7000 g., 0.8200 Silver .0712 oz. ASW **Obv. Inscription:** Kuang-hsü Yüan-pao **Reverse:** English legends around dragon **Mint:** Kuang

Date	Mintage	VG	F	VF	XF	Unc
ND(1890-1908)	—	0.65	2.00	4.00	6.00	15.00

Y# 196 20 CENTS
5.3000 g., 0.8200 Silver .1397 oz. ASW **Obverse:** 1 MACE AND 4 3/5 CANDAREENS **Obv. Inscription:** Kuang-hsü Yüan-pao

Date	Mintage	F	VF	XF	Unc
ND(1889)	—	125	225	375	600
ND(1889) Proof	—	—	—	—	—

Y# 196.1 20 CENTS
5.3000 g., 0.8200 Silver .1397 oz. ASW **Obverse:** 1 MACE AND 4.4 CANDAREENS **Obv. Inscription:** Kuang-hsü Yüan-pao

Date	Mintage	F	VF	XF	Unc
ND(1889)	—	2,500	3,500	5,000	—

Y# 201 20 CENTS
5.5000 g., 0.8000 Silver .1415 oz. ASW **Obv. Inscription:** Kuang-hsü Yüan-pao **Reverse:** Dragon

Date	Mintage	VG	F	VF	XF	Unc
ND(1890-1908)	—	0.50	1.50	2.50	3.50	10.00
ND(1890-1908) Proof, 10 known	—	Value: 400				

Y# 197 50 CENTS
13.8000 g., 0.8600 Silver .3816 oz. ASW **Obverse:** 3 MACE AND 6-1/2 CANDAREENS **Obv. Inscription:** Kuang-hsü Yüan-pao

Date	Mintage	F	VF	XF	Unc
ND(1889)	—	325	625	900	1,600

Y# 197.1 50 CENTS
13.8000 g., 0.8600 Silver .3816 oz. ASW **Obverse:** 3 MACE AND 6 CANDAREENS **Obv. Inscription:** Kuang-hsü Yüan-pao

Date	Mintage	F	VF	XF	Unc
ND(1889)	—	—	6,500	10,000	15,000

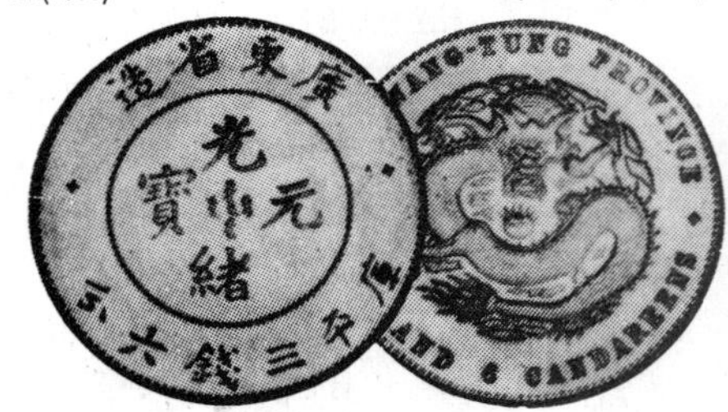

Y# 202 50 CENTS
13.5000 g., 0.8600 Silver .3733 oz. ASW **Obv. Inscription:** Kuang-hsü Yüan-pao **Reverse:** English legends around dragon

Date	Mintage	VG	F	VF	XF	Unc
ND(1890-1905)	—	6.50	20.00	40.00	75.00	250
ND(1890-1905) Proof	—	Value: 650				

Y# 198 DOLLAR

27.4000 g., 0.9000 Silver .7929 oz. ASW **Obverse:** 7 MACE AND 3 CANDAREENS **Obv. Inscription:** Kuang-hsü Yüan-pao **Reverse:** Dragon

Date	Mintage	F	VF	XF	Unc
ND(1889)	—	1,250	1,750	2,500	4,800
ND(1889) Proof	—	Value: 10,000			

Y# 198.1 DOLLAR

27.4000 g., 0.9000 Silver .7929 oz. ASW **Obverse:** 7 MACE AND 2 CANDAREENS **Obv. Inscription:** Kuang-hsü Yüan-pao **Reverse:** Dragon **Note:** Considered a pattern.

Date	Mintage	F	VF	XF	Unc
ND(1889)	—	—	—	—	35,000

Y# 203 DOLLAR

27.0000 g., 0.9000 Silver .7814 oz. ASW **Obv. Inscription:** Kuang-hsü Yüan-pao **Reverse:** English legends around dragon

Date	Mintage	VG	F	VF	XF	Unc
ND(1890-1908)	—	5.00	15.00	25.00	50.00	350
ND(1890-1908) Proof	—	Value: 1,000				

PATTERNS

Including off metal strikes

KM#	Date	Mintage	Identification	Mkt Val
Pn1	ND(c.1888)	—	5 Cash. Brass.	—

KM#	Date	Mintage	Identification	Mkt Val
Pn3	ND(c.1888)	—	10 Cash. Brass.	1,200
Pn4	ND(1889)	—	10 Cents. Copper. Y#195.	3,500

KM#	Date	Mintage	Identification	Mkt Val
Pn5	ND(1889)	—	20 Cents. Copper. Y#196.	5,500
Pn6	ND(1889)	—	50 Cents. Copper. Y#197.	7,500
Pn7	ND(1889)	—	50 Cents. Copper. Y#197.1.	7,500
Pn8	ND(1889)	—	Dollar. Copper. Y#198.1.	12,500
Pn9	ND(1890)	—	5 Cents. Copper. Y#199.	—
Pn10	ND(1890)	—	10 Cents. Copper. Y#200.	—
Pn11	ND(1890)	—	10 Cents. Brass. Y#200.	—
Pn12	ND(1890)	—	20 Cents. Copper. Y#201.	—
Pn13	ND(1890)	—	20 Cents. Brass. Y#201.	—
Pn14	ND(1890)	—	50 Cents. Copper. Y#202.	—
Pn15	ND(1890)	—	Dollar. Copper. Y#203.	—

SPECIMEN SETS (SS)

KM#	Date	Mintage	Identification	Issue Price	Mkt Val
SS1	1889 (10)	—	Y#189, Y#195-198 (2 each)	—	—
SS2	1890 (7)	—	Y#189-190, 199-203	—	2,000

KWEICHOW PROVINCE

Guizhou

A province located in southern China. It is basically a plateau region that is somewhat remote from the general traffic of China. The Kweichow Mint opened in 1730 and produced Cash coins until the end of the reign of Kuang Hsu. The Republic issues for this province are enigmatic as to their origin, as a mint supposedly did not exist in Kweichow (Guizhou) at this time.

The Kweichow (Guizhou) coins, (Kann #9, 10, 11, 12, 13), obviously copied from contemporary Japanese coins, are still a mystery. Even as late as the 1920's, Kweichow (Guizhou) was a very primitive area. It is highly unlikely that the coins were made there in the 1880's and 1890's. It is possible that they were minted elsewhere, possibly in one of the central coastal provinces.

EMPIRE

Tao-kuang

1821-1850

PROVINCIAL CAST COINAGE

C# 20-3 CASH

Cast Brass **Obverse:** Type A **Obv. Inscription:** Tao-kuang T'ung-pao **Mint:** Kuei **Note:** Schjöth #1527.

Date	Mintage	Good	VG	F	VF	XF
ND(1821-50)	—	2.00	3.00	4.00	6.00	—

C# 20-3.1 CASH

Cast Brass **Reverse:** Crescent above **Mint:** Kuei **Note:** Schjöth #1529.

Date	Mintage	Good	VG	F	VF	XF
ND(1821-50)	—	3.50	6.00	9.00	13.50	—

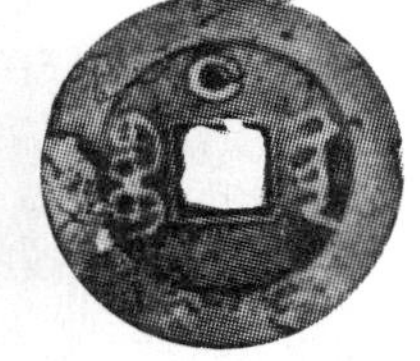

C# 20-3.2 CASH

Cast Brass **Obv. Inscription:** Tao-kuang T'ung-pao **Reverse:** Circle above **Mint:** Kuei **Note:** Schjöth #1528.

Date	Mintage	Good	VG	F	VF	XF
ND(1821-50)	—	3.50	6.00	9.00	18.00	—

C# 20-3.3 CASH

Cast Brass **Obv. Inscription:** Tao-kuang T'ung-pao **Reverse:** Dot inside circle above **Mint:** Kuei

Date	Mintage	Good	VG	F	VF	XF
ND(1821-50)	—	2.50	5.00	6.50	9.00	—

C# 20-3.4 CASH

Cast Brass **Obv. Inscription:** Tao-kuang T'ung-pao **Reverse:** Dot above **Mint:** Kuei

Date	Mintage	Good	VG	F	VF	XF
ND(1821-50)	—	2.50	5.00	6.50	9.00	—

C# 20-3.5 CASH

Cast Brass **Obv. Inscription:** Tao-kuang T'ung-pao **Reverse:** "X" above **Mint:** Kuei **Note:** Schjöth #1530.

Date	Mintage	Good	VG	F	VF	XF
ND(1821-50)	—	5.50	8.50	13.50	20.00	—

C# 20-3.6 CASH

Cast Brass **Obv. Inscription:** Tao-kuang T'ung-pao **Reverse:** A triangle above **Mint:** Kuei

Date	Mintage	Good	VG	F	VF	XF
ND(1821-50)	—	5.50	8.50	13.50	20.00	—

C# 20-3.7 CASH

Cast Brass **Obv. Inscription:** Tao-kuang T'ung-pao **Reverse:** Character "Yi" (one) above **Mint:** Kuei **Note:** Schjöth #1531.

Date	Mintage	Good	VG	F	VF	XF
ND(1821-50)	—	5.50	8.50	13.50	20.00	—

C# 20-3.8 CASH

Cast Brass **Obv. Inscription:** Tao-kuang T'ung-pao **Reverse:** Character "Ta" (large) above **Mint:** Kuei

Date	Mintage	Good	VG	F	VF	XF
ND(1821-50)	—	5.50	8.50	13.50	20.00	—

Note: This coin and C#20-3.14 are difficult to distinguish

C# 20-3.9 CASH

Cast Brass **Obv. Inscription:** Tao-kuang T'ung-pao **Reverse:** Crescent below **Mint:** Kuei

Date	Mintage	Good	VG	F	VF	XF
ND(1821-50)	—	3.50	6.00	9.00	13.50	—

C# 20-3.10 CASH

Cast Brass **Obv. Inscription:** Tao-kuang T'ung-pao **Reverse:** "X" below **Mint:** Kuei

Date	Mintage	Good	VG	F	VF	XF
ND(1821-50)	—	5.50	50.00	13.50	25.00	—

C# 20-3.11 CASH

Cast Brass **Obv. Inscription:** Tao-kuang T'ung-pao **Reverse:** Dot below **Mint:** Kuei

Date	Mintage	Good	VG	F	VF	XF
ND(1821-50)	—	3.00	5.50	8.00	11.50	—

C# 20-3.12 CASH

Cast Brass **Obv. Inscription:** Tao-kuang T'ung-pao **Reverse:** Inverted triangle below **Mint:** Kuei

Date	Mintage	Good	VG	F	VF	XF
ND(1821-50)	—	5.50	8.50	13.50	20.00	—

C# 20-3.13 CASH

Cast Brass **Obv. Inscription:** Tao-kuang T'ung-pao **Reverse:** "Yi" (one) below **Mint:** Kuei

Date	Mintage	Good	VG	F	VF	XF
ND(1821-50)	—	5.50	8.50	13.50	20.00	—

C# 20-3.14 CASH

Cast Brass **Obv. Inscription:** Tao-kuang T'ung-pao **Reverse:** "Liu" (six) above **Mint:** Kuei

Date	Mintage	Good	VG	F	VF	XF
ND(1821-50)	—	5.50	8.50	13.50	20.00	—

Note: This coin and C#20-3.8 are difficult to distinguish

C# 20-3.15 CASH
Cast Brass **Obv. Inscription:** Tao-kuang T'ung-pao **Reverse:** "Ch'i" (seven) below **Mint:** Kuei

Date	Mintage	Good	VG	F	VF	XF
ND(1821-50)	—	5.50	8.50	13.50	20.00	—

Hsien-fêng
1851-1861
PROVINCIAL CAST COINAGE

C# 20-4 CASH
Cast Brass **Obverse:** Type A **Obv. Inscription:** Hsien-fêng T'ung-pao **Mint:** Kuei

Date	Mintage	Good	VG	F	VF	XF
ND(1851-61)	—	1.50	2.50	4.00	6.00	—

C# 20-4.1 CASH
Cast Brass **Obv. Inscription:** Hsien-fêng T'ung-pao **Reverse:** Dot above **Mint:** Kuei

Date	Mintage	Good	VG	F	VF	XF
ND(1851-61)	—	2.50	4.00	5.00	7.00	—

C# 20-4.2 CASH
Cast Brass **Obv. Inscription:** Hsien-fêng T'ung-pao **Reverse:** Two vertical lines above **Mint:** Kuei

Date	Mintage	Good	VG	F	VF	XF
ND(1851-61)	—	5.50	8.50	13.50	25.00	—

C# 20-4.3 CASH
Cast Brass **Obv. Inscription:** Hsien-fêng T'ung-pao **Reverse:** Three vertical lines above **Mint:** Kuei

Date	Mintage	Good	VG	F	VF	XF
ND(1851-61)	—	5.50	8.50	13.50	25.00	—

C# 20-4.4 CASH
Cast Brass **Obv. Inscription:** Hsien-fêng T'ung-pao **Reverse:** "X" above **Mint:** Kuei

Date	Mintage	Good	VG	F	VF	XF
ND(1851-61)	—	5.50	8.50	13.50	25.00	—

C# 20-4.5 CASH
Cast Brass **Obv. Inscription:** Hsien-fêng T'ung-pao **Reverse:** Character "Ch'i" (seven) above **Mint:** Kuei

Date	Mintage	Good	VG	F	VF	XF
ND(1851-61)	—	5.50	8.50	13.50	25.00	—

C# 20-4.6 CASH
Cast Brass **Obv. Inscription:** Hsien-fêng T'ung-pao **Reverse:** Character "Shih" (ten) above **Mint:** Kuei

Date	Mintage	Good	VG	F	VF	XF
ND(1851-61)	—	5.50	8.50	13.50	25.00	—

C# 20-4.7 CASH
Cast Brass **Obv. Inscription:** Hsien-fêng T'ung-pao **Reverse:** Character "Wen" (unit) lying on its side **Mint:** Kuei

Date	Mintage	Good	VG	F	VF	XF
ND(1851-61)	—	5.50	8.50	13.50	25.00	—

C# 20-4.8 CASH
Cast Brass **Obv. Inscription:** Hsien-fêng T'ung-pao **Reverse:** Character "Shih" above and crescent below **Mint:** Kuei

Date	Mintage	Good	VG	F	VF	XF
ND(1851-61)	—	5.50	8.50	13.50	25.00	—

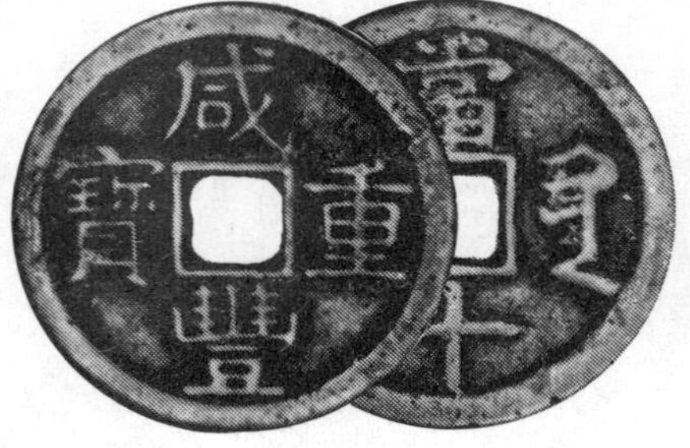

C# 20-5 10 CASH
Cast Brass, 38 mm. **Obverse:** Type B-1 **Obv. Inscription:** Hsien-fêng Chung-pao **Mint:** Kuei

Date	Mintage	Good	VG	F	VF	XF
ND(1851-61)	—	18.00	25.00	35.00	60.00	—

C# 20-5.1 10 CASH
Cast Brass, 25 mm. **Obv. Inscription:** Hsien-fêng Chung-pao **Mint:** Kuei

Date	Mintage	Good	VG	F	VF	XF
ND(1851-61)	—	35.00	55.00	75.00	100	—

C# 20-6 50 CASH
Cast Brass **Obverse:** Type B-1 **Obv. Inscription:** Hsien-fêng Chung-pao **Mint:** Kuei

Date	Mintage	Good	VG	F	VF	XF
ND(1851-61)	—	60.00	85.00	110	165	—

T'ung-chih
1862-1874
PROVINCIAL CAST COINAGE

C# 20-7 CASH
Cast Brass **Obverse:** Type A-2 **Obv. Inscription:** T'ung-chih T'ung-pao **Mint:** Kuei

Date	Mintage	Good	VG	F	VF	XF
ND(1862-74)	—	90.00	140	200	300	—

Kuang-hsü
1875-1908
PROVINCIAL CAST COINAGE

C# 20-9 CASH
Cast Brass **Obv. Inscription:** Kuang-hsü T'ung-pao **Reverse:** Manchu inscription **Rev. Inscription:** Boo-jiyan **Mint:** Kuei

Date	Mintage	Good	VG	F	VF	XF
ND(1875-1908)	—	4.00	7.50	10.00	15.00	—

C# 20-9.1 CASH
Cast Brass **Obv. Inscription:** Kuang-hsü T'ung-pao **Reverse:** Manchu inscription **Rev. Inscription:** Boo-jiyan **Mint:** Kuei

Date	Mintage	Good	VG	F	VF	XF
ND(1875-1908)	—	5.00	9.00	12.50	18.50	—

C# 20-9.2 CASH
Cast Brass **Obv. Inscription:** Kuang-hsü T'ung-pao **Reverse:** Manchu inscription **Rev. Inscription:** Boo-jiyan **Mint:** Kuei

Date	Mintage	Good	VG	F	VF	XF
ND(1875-1905)	—	8.50	11.50	16.50	25.00	—

MILLED COINAGE

K# 10 50 CENTS
Silver

Date	Mintage	VG	F	VF	XF	Unc
14(1888) Rare	—	—	—	—	—	—

K# 9 DOLLAR
24.8000 g., Silver

Date	Mintage	VG	F	VF	XF	Unc
14(1888) Rare	—	—	—	—	—	—

Note: Superior Goodman Sale 6-91 Choice XF realized $46,200

K# 11 DOLLAR
24.8000 g., Silver

Date	Mintage	VG	F	VF	XF	Unc
14(1888) Rare	—	—	—	—	—	—

K# 12 DOLLAR
22.6000 g., Silver

Date	Mintage	VG	F	VF	XF	Unc
16(1890) Rare	—	—	—	—	—	—

K# 13 DOLLAR
22.6000 g., Silver

Date	Mintage	VG	F	VF	XF	Unc
16(1890) Rare	—	—	—	—	—	—

SHANSI PROVINCE

Shanxi

A province located in northeastern China that has some of the richest coal deposits in the world. Parts of the Great Wall cross the province. Extensive agriculture of early China started here. Cited as a "model province" in the new Chinese Republic. Intermittently active mints from 1645. The modern mint was established in 1919. It operated until the mid-1920's and closed because of the public's resistance against the coins that were being produced.

EMPIRE

Tao-Kuang
1821-1851

PROVINCIAL CAST COINAGE

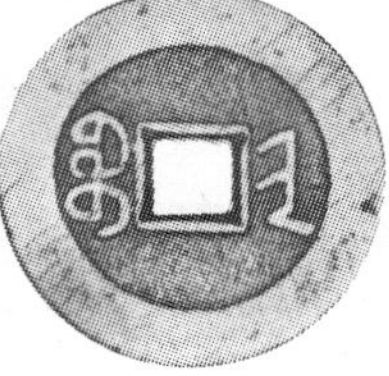

C# 21-3 CASH
Cast Brass **Obverse:** Type A **Obv. Inscription:** Tao-kuang T'ung-pao **Mint:** Chin

Date	Mintage	Good	VG	F	VF	XF
ND(1821-50)	—	1.25	2.50	3.00	6.00	—

Hsien-fêng
1851-1861

PROVINCIAL CAST COINAGE

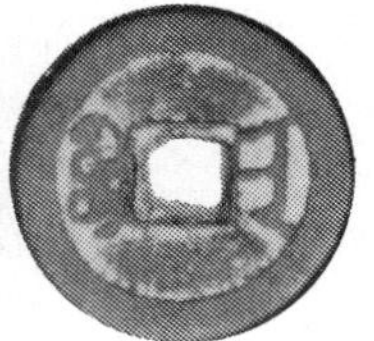

C# 21-4 CASH
Cast Brass **Obverse:** Type A **Obv. Inscription:** Hsien-fêng T'ung-pao **Mint:** Chin

Date	Mintage	Good	VG	F	VF	XF
ND(1851-61)	—	18.50	27.50	37.50	45.00	—

C# 21-5 10 CASH
Cast Brass **Obverse:** Type B-1 **Obv. Inscription:** Hsien-fêng Chung-pao **Mint:** Chin

Date	Mintage	Good	VG	F	VF	XF
ND(1851-61)	—	12.00	20.00	27.50	50.00	—

T'ung-chih
1862-1875

PROVINCIAL CAST COINAGE

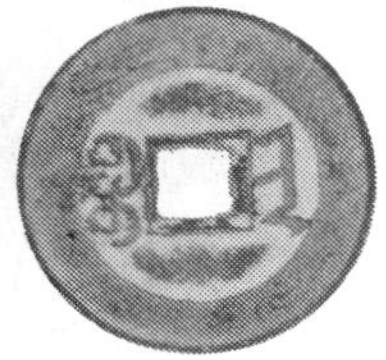

C# 21-6 CASH
Cast Brass **Obverse:** Type A-2 **Obv. Inscription:** T'ung-chih T'ung-pao **Mint:** Chin

Date	Mintage	Good	VG	F	VF	XF
ND(1862-74)	—	8.50	17.50	25.00	40.00	—

Kuang-hsü
1875-1908

PROVINCIAL CAST COINAGE

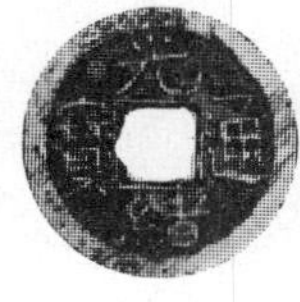
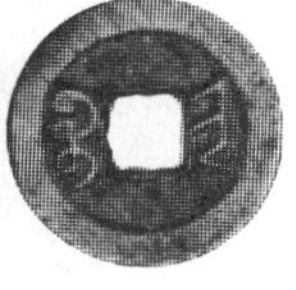

C# 21-8 CASH
Cast Brass **Obverse:** Manchu inscription **Obv. Inscription:** Kuang-hsü T'ung-pao **Rev. Inscription:** Boo-Jin **Mint:** Chin

Date	Mintage	Good	VG	F	VF	XF
ND(1875-1908)	—	6.50	11.50	17.50	35.00	—

PATTERNS

Including off metal strikes

KM#	Date	Mintage	Identification	Mkt Val
Pn1	16(1890)	—	Tael. Silver. K#922.	—

Note: The authenticity of K922 was questioned by Kann and other authorities, however, two specimens were sold in the Superior Goodman sale 6-91; an AU plain edge realized $19,25, and an XF milled edge realized $11,000

SHANTUNG PROVINCE

Shandong

A province located on the northeastern coast of China. Confucius was born in this province. Parts of the province were leased to Great Britain and to Germany. Farming, fishing and mining are the chief occupations. A mint was opened at Tsinan in 1647 and was an intermittent producer for the empire. A modern mint was opened at Tsinan in 1905, but closed in 1906. Patterns were prepared between 1926-1933 in anticipation of a new coinage, but none were struck for circulation.

EMPIRE

Hsien-fêng
1851-1861

PROVINCIAL CAST COINAGE

C# 22-2 CASH
Cast Brass **Obverse:** Type A **Obv. Inscription:** Hsien-fêng T'ung-pao **Reverse:** Manchu inscription **Rev. Inscription:** Boo-ji **Mint:** Chi

Date	Mintage	Good	VG	F	VF	XF
ND(1851-61)	—	16.50	30.00	45.00	60.00	—

T'ung-chih
1862-1875

PROVINCIAL CAST COINAGE

C# 22-5 CASH
Cast Brass **Obverse:** Type A-2 **Obv. Inscription:** T'ung-chih T'ung-pao **Mint:** Chi

Date	Mintage	Good	VG	F	VF	XF
ND(1862-74)	—	30.00	50.00	85.00	125	—

Kuang-hsü
1875-1908

PROVINCIAL CAST COINAGE

C# 22-6 CASH
Cast Brass **Obv. Inscription:** Kuang-hsü T'ung-pao **Reverse:** Type 1 mint mark **Rev. Inscription:** Boo-ji **Mint:** Chi

Date	Mintage	Good	VG	F	VF	XF
ND(1875-1908)	—	10.00	18.50	27.50	40.00	—

Note: Refer to Tungch'uan, Yünnan Province, for one-cash C#27 series coins previously listed here.

PATTERNS

Including off metal strikes

KM#	Date	Mintage	Identification	Mkt Val
Pn1	ND(1851)	—	10 Cash. Cast Brass. C22-7.	—
Pn2	ND(1851)	—	50 Cash. Cast Brass. C22-3.	—
Pn3	ND(1851)	—	100 Cash. Cast Brass. C22-4.	—

KM#	Date	Mintage	Identification	Mkt Val

KM#	Date	Mintage	Identification	Mkt Val
Pn4	ND16(1890)	—	5 Mace. Silver. K924	—
Pn5	ND16(1890)	—	5 Mace. Copper. K924x.	—

KM#	Date	Mintage	Identification	Mkt Val
Pn6	ND16(1890)	—	Tael. Silver. K923.	—

Note: Superior Goodman sale 6-91 VF realized $45,100

SHENSI PROVINCE

Shaanxi

A province located in central China that is a rich agricultural area. A very important province in the early development of China. An active imperial mint was located at Sian (Xi'an).

EMPIRE

Tao-kuang
1821-1851

PROVINCIAL CAST COINAGE

C# 23-3 CASH
Cast Brass Or Copper **Obverse:** Type A **Obv. Inscription:** Tao-kuang T'ung-pao **Mint:** Shan **Note:** Schjöth #1520.

Date	Mintage	Good	VG	F	VF	XF
ND(1821-50)	—	2.50	5.00	7.50	12.50	—

Hsien-fêng
1851-1861

PROVINCIAL CAST COINAGE

C# 23-4 CASH
Cast Brass Or Copper **Obverse:** Type A **Obv. Inscription:** Hsien-fêng T'ung-pao **Mint:** Shan **Note:** Schjöth #1550.

Date	Mintage	Good	VG	F	VF	XF
ND(1851-61)	—	4.00	7.00	12.00	20.00	—

C# 23-4a CASH
Cast Iron **Obv. Inscription:** Hsien-fêng T'ung-pao **Mint:** Shan

Date	Mintage	Good	VG	F	VF	XF
ND(1851-61)	—	10.00	20.00	40.00	—	—

C# 23-5 10 CASH
Cast Brass, 43 mm. **Obverse:** Type B-1 **Obv. Inscription:** Hsien-fêng Chung-pao **Mint:** Shan

Date	Mintage	Good	VG	F	VF	XF
ND(1851-61)	—	10.00	15.00	25.00	45.00	—

C# 23-5.1 10 CASH
Cast Brass, 36 mm. **Obv. Inscription:** Hsien-fêng Chung-pao **Mint:** Shan

Date	Mintage	Good	VG	F	VF	XF
ND(1851-61)	—	6.00	10.00	15.00	28.00	—

C# 23-6 10 CASH
Cast Brass **Obv. Inscription:** Hsien-fêng Chung-pao **Reverse:** Character "Shan" (for Shensi) above hole **Mint:** Shan

Date	Mintage	Good	VG	F	VF	XF
ND(1851-61)	—	150	225	350	500	—

C# 23-7 50 CASH
Cast Brass **Obverse:** Type B-1 **Obv. Inscription:** Hsien-fêng Chung-pao **Mint:** Shan

Date	Mintage	Good	VG	F	VF	XF
ND(1851-61)	—	14.00	20.00	35.00	50.00	—

C# 23-8.1 100 CASH
Cast Brass **Obverse:** Type C **Obv. Inscription:** Hsien-fêng Yüan-pao **Mint:** Shan **Note:** Size varies: 57-58mm.

Date	Mintage	Good	VG	F	VF	XF
ND(1851-61)	—	35.00	55.00	75.00	125	—

C# 23-8.2 100 CASH
Cast Brass **Obv. Inscription:** Hsien-fêng Yüan-pao **Mint:** Shan **Note:** Size varies: 48-49mm.

Date	Mintage	Good	VG	F	VF	XF
ND(1851-61)	—	10.00	17.50	25.00	45.00	—

C# 23-9 500 CASH
Cast Copper **Obverse:** Type C **Obv. Inscription:** Hsien-fêng Yüan-pao **Mint:** Shan

Date	Mintage	Good	VG	F	VF	XF
ND(1851-61)	—	75.00	110	150	200	—

C# 23-9.1 500 CASH
Cast Copper, 65 mm. **Obv. Inscription:** Hsien-fêng Yüan-pao **Reverse:** Character "Kuan" (official) cast on rim at top **Mint:** Shan

Date	Mintage	Good	VG	F	VF	XF
ND(1851-61)	—	300	600	850	1,200	—

C# 23-10 1000 CASH
Cast Bronze **Obverse:** Type C **Obv. Inscription:** Hsien-fêng Yüan-pao **Mint:** Shan

Date	Mintage	Good	VG	F	VF	XF
ND(1851-61)	—	90.00	135	175	250	—

C# 23-10.1 1000 CASH
Cast Copper, 74 mm. **Obv. Inscription:** Hsien-fêng Yüan-pao **Reverse:** Character "Kuan" cast on rim at bottom **Mint:** Shan **Note:** Illustration reduced.

Date	Mintage	Good	VG	F	VF	XF
ND(1851-61)	—	400	700	1,000	1,500	—

C# 23-10a 1000 CASH
Cast Copper **Obv. Inscription:** Hsien-fêng Yüan-pao **Mint:** Shan

Date	Mintage	Good	VG	F	VF	XF
ND(1851-61)	—	75.00	110	150	200	—

Kuang-hsü
1875-1908

PROVINCIAL CAST COINAGE

C# 23-13 CASH
Cast Brass **Obverse:** Type A

Date	Mintage	Good	VG	F	VF	XF
ND(1875-1908)	—	20.00	35.00	50.00	75.00	—

PATTERNS

Including off metal strikes

KM#	Date	Mintage	Identification	Mkt Val
Pn1	ND(1898)	—	5 Cents. Silver. K#159.	2,600
Pn2	ND(1898)	—	10 Cents. Silver. K#158.	—

KM#	Date	Mintage	Identification	Mkt Val
Pn3	ND(1898)	—	20 Cents. Silver. K#157.	3,000

KM#	Date	Mintage	Identification	Mkt Val
Pn4	ND(1898)	—	50 Cents. Silver. K#156.	6,000

KM#	Date	Mintage	Identification	Mkt Val
Pn5	ND(1898)	—	Dollar. Silver. K#155.	35,000

Note: The Shensi (Shaanxi) patterns above were made at the Heaton Mint, Birmingham, England as samples to be sent, along with the dies and machinery, to Shensi (Shaanxi). The machinery never reached the province, having been diverted instead to the Hupeh Mint. Beware of forgeries.

SINKIANG PROVINCE

Hsinkiang, Xinjiang
"New Dominion"

An autonomous region in western China, often referred to as Chinese Turkestan. High mountains surround 2000 ft. tableland on three sides with a large desert in center of this province. Many salt lakes, mining and some farming and oil. Inhabited by early man and was referred to as the "Silk Route" to the West. Sinkiang (Xinjiang) has been historically under the control of many factions, including Genghis Khan. It became a province in 1884. China has made claim to Sinkiang (Xinjiang) for many, many years. This rule has been more nominal than actual. Sinkiang (Xinjiang) had eight imperial mints, only three of which were in operation toward the end of the reign of Kuang Hsu. Only two mints operated during the early years of the republic. In 1949, due to a drastic coin shortage and lack of confidence in the inflated paper money, it was planned to mint some dollars in Sinkiang (Xinjiang). These did not see much circulation, however, due to the defeat of the nationalists, though they have recently appeared in considerable numbers in today's market.

PATTERNS

NOTE: A number of previously listed cast coins of Sinkiang Province are now known to be patterns - "mother" cash or "seed" cash for which no circulating issues are known. The following coins are, therefore, no longer listed. Most were probably manufactured in Beijing. They are generally made of brass rather than the purer copper usual to Sinkiang. The following coins are, therefore, no longer listed here: Craig #30-9, 30-11a, 30-12a, 30-14, 30-15a, 30-16, 30-17, 28-4.1, 28-8a, 28-9a, 28-9c, 28-10, 31-1a, 31-1v, 31-2, 32-4, 32-5, 33-12, 33-21, 34-2, 34-3, 35-5a and 35-6.

MONETARY SYSTEM

2 Pul = 1 Cash
2 Cash = 5 Li
4 Cash = 10 Li = 1 Fen
25 Cash = 10 Fen = 1 Miscal = 1 Ch'ien, Mace, Tanga
10 Miscals (Mace) = 1 Liang (Tael or Sar)
20 Miscals (Tangas) = 1 Tilla

MINT NAMES

LOCAL MINT NAMES AND MARKS

MINT	CHINESE	TURKI	MANCHU
Aksu	城阿	اقصو	
Ili, now Yining	犂伊	الي	
Kashgar, now Kashi	什喀	كشقر	
Khotan, now Hotan	闐和	خوتن	
Kotsha (Kuche)		كوتشر	
Kuche, now Kuqa	車庫	كوچا	
Ti-hua, now Dihua, refer to Urumchi	化廸		
Urumchi, now Urumqi	化廸	ارومجي	
Ushi, now Wushi (Uqturpan)	什烏	اوش	
Yangihissar, now Yengisar	沙吉英		
Yarkand, now Shache (Yarkant)	羌爾葉	يارقند	

EMPIRE

Ghazi Rashid

AH1279-84/1862-67AD

REBEL COINAGE

In 1864 the Xinjiang peasants revolted, overthrew the local Ch'ing authorities and set up their own government. Ghazi Rashid, a member of the upper clergy, seized control, proclaimed himself khagan. He was slain by the invading Yakub Beg in 1867.

C# 36-1 CASH

Cast Copper, 25 mm. **Obverse:** Turki legend **Obv. Legend:** SEYYID GHAZI RASHID KHAN **Reverse:** Turki legend **Rev. Legend:** MINTED AT THE CAPITAL, KUCHE **Mint:** Yarkand **Note:** Small legends.

Date	Mintage	Good	VG	F	VF	XF
AH128(0)	—	8.50	15.00	25.00	40.00	—

Note: Exists with coin or medal rotation

C# 36-2 CASH

Cast Copper, 25 mm. **Obverse:** Turki legend **Obv. Legend:** SEYYID GHAZI RASHID KHAN **Reverse:** Turki legend **Rev. Legend:** MINTED AT THE CAPITAL, KUCHE **Mint:** Yarkand **Note:** Large legends.

Date	Mintage	Good	VG	F	VF	XF
AH128(0)	—	8.50	15.00	25.00	40.00	—

Note: The date of C#36-1 and 36-2 is found at the top of the reverse. These coins are usually undated or with the date illegible. Even in clearly dated specimens, which are worth a substantial premium, the "0" never seems to be detectable.

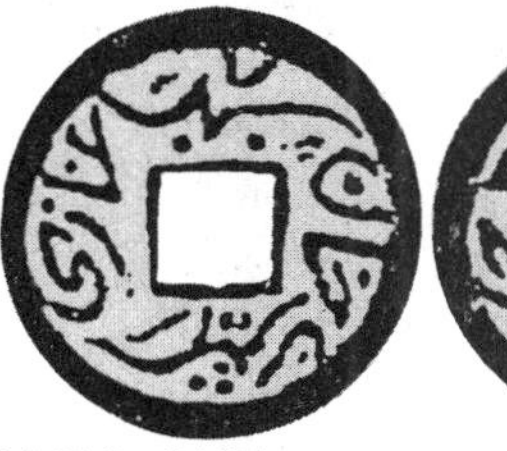

C# 36-3 CASH

Cast Copper, 29 mm. **Obverse:** Turki legend **Obv. Legend:** SEYYID GHAZI RASHID KHAN **Reverse:** Turki legend **Rev. Legend:** MINTED AT THE CAPITAL, KUCHE **Mint:** Kuche

Date	Mintage	Good	VG	F	VF	XF
AH128(0)	—	65.00	125	185	250	—

C# 36-4 10 CASH

Cast Copper, 25 mm. **Obverse:** Barbaric inscription **Reverse:** Chinese inscription (10) at bottom, Turki inscription at right **Rev. Inscription:** SHIH (10), AKSU **Mint:** Aksu **Note:** Prev. C#36-3.

Date	Mintage	G	VG	F	VF	XF
ND(1864-67)	—	75.00	150	225	300	—

C# 36-5 TENGA

Silver **Mint:** Khotan

Date	Mintage	VG	F	VF	XF	Unc
AH1283	—	100	165	250	350	—

Yakub Beg

AH1281-1294/1864-1877AD

REBEL COINAGE

Most of these coins were struck at Kashgar (Kashi) in the name of the Ottoman Sultan Abdul Aziz by the rebel Yakub Beg, who controlled much of Sinkiang (X

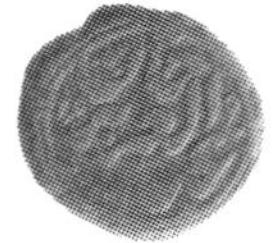 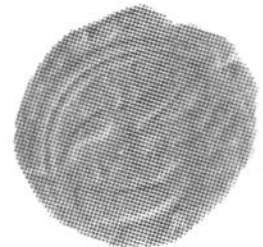

C# 37-4 FALUS

Copper **Obverse:** Date **Obv. Inscription:** Abdul Aziz **Reverse:** Date **Mint:** Kashgar

Date	Mintage	Good	VG	F	VF	XF
AH1290	—	20.00	32.50	40.00	50.00	—
AH1292	—	20.00	32.50	40.00	50.00	—

C# 37-5 FALUS

Copper **Obverse:** Date **Obv. Inscription:** Abdul Aziz **Mint:** Kashgar

Date	Mintage	Good	VG	F	VF	XF
AH1291	—	20.00	32.50	40.00	50.00	—
AH1293	—	20.00	32.50	40.00	50.00	—
AH1294	—	20.00	32.50	40.00	50.00	—

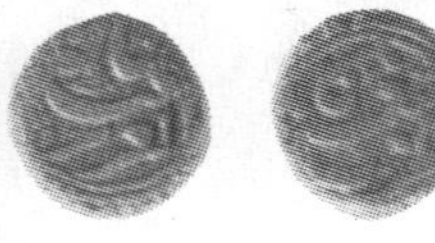

C# 37-6 FALUS
Copper **Obv. Inscription:** Abdul Aziz **Reverse:** Date **Mint:** Kashgar

Date	Mintage	Good	VG	F	VF	XF
AH1292	—	20.00	32.50	40.00	50.00	—

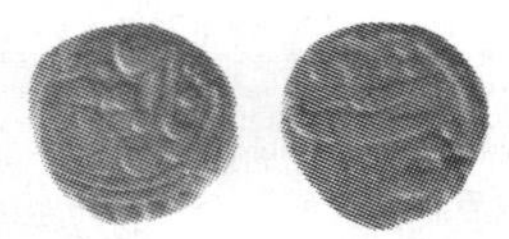

C# 37-7 FALUS
Copper **Obv. Inscription:** Abdul Aziz **Mint:** Kashgar

Date	Mintage	Good	VG	F	VF	XF
ND(1878)	—	15.00	21.50	30.00	40.00	—

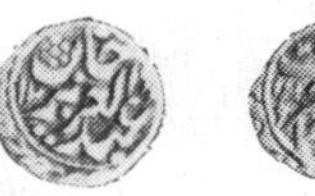

C# 37-1.1 1/2 MISCAL (Mace)
Silver **Obverse:** Aziz above Abd **Obv. Inscription:** Abdul Aziz **Reverse:** "K" (of Kashpar) left to Zarb **Mint:** Kashgar

Date	Mintage	Good	VG	F	VF	XF
ND(c.1874)	—	3.50	9.00	15.00	25.00	40.00
AH1290//1291	—	3.50	9.00	15.00	25.00	40.00
AH1291	—	3.50	9.00	15.00	25.00	40.00
AH1291/1292	—	3.50	9.00	15.00	25.00	40.00
AH1292	—	3.50	9.00	15.00	25.00	40.00
AH1293	—	3.00	9.00	15.00	25.00	40.00
AH1294	—	5.00	9.00	15.00	25.00	40.00

C# 37-1.2 1/2 MISCAL (Mace)
Silver **Obverse:** Aziz on bottom below Abd **Obv. Inscription:** Abdul Aziz **Mint:** Kashgar

Date	Mintage	Good	VG	F	VF	XF
ND(c.1874)	—	3.50	9.00	15.00	25.00	40.00
AH1291	—	3.50	9.00	15.00	25.00	40.00
AH1292	—	3.50	9.00	15.00	25.00	40.00
AH1292//1293	—	3.50	9.00	15.00	25.00	40.00
AH1293	—	3.50	9.00	15.00	25.00	40.00
AH1293//1294	—	3.50	9.00	15.00	25.00	40.00
AH1294	—	3.50	9.00	15.00	25.00	40.00

C# 37-2.1 TILLA
4.5000 g., Gold **Rev. Inscription:** Zarb Mahrusa Kashgar **Mint:** Kashgar

Date	Mintage	VG	F	VF	XF	Unc
AH1290	—	120	225	400	650	—

C# 37-2.2 TILLA
4.5000 g., Gold **Obv. Inscription:** Abdul Aziz **Rev. Inscription:** Zarb Dar us-Sultanat Kashgar **Mint:** Kashgar

Date	Mintage	VG	F	VF	XF	Unc
AH1291//1290	—	135	245	450	750	—
AH1291	—	100	210	350	550	—

C# 37-2.3 TILLA
4.5000 g., Gold **Obverse:** Inscription within dotted border within circles **Obv. Inscription:** Abdul Aziz **Reverse:** Inscription within circle **Mint:** Kashgar

Date	Mintage	VG	F	VF	XF	Unc
AH1291	—	100	210	350	550	—

C# 37-2.4 TILLA
4.5000 g., Gold **Reverse:** Inscription within segmented circles **Mint:** Kashgar

Date	Mintage	VG	F	VF	XF	Unc
AH1291	—	100	210	350	550	—

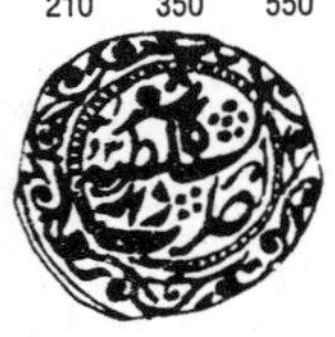

C# 37-2.6 TILLA
4.5000 g., Gold **Obverse:** Inscription within segmented circles with loop **Obv. Inscription:** Abdul Aziz **Reverse:** Inscription within segmented circles

Date	Mintage	VG	F	VF	XF	Unc
AH1292	—	90.00	180	300	500	—
AH1293	—	120	225	400	650	—
AH1294	—	120	225	400	650	—
AH1295	—	120	225	400	650	—

C# 37-2.5 TILLA
4.5000 g., Gold **Obverse:** Inscription within dotted border within circles with loop **Obv. Inscription:** Abdul Aziz **Reverse:** Inscription within dotted border within circles **Mint:** Kashgar

Date	Mintage	VG	F	VF	XF	Unc
AH1292	—	120	225	400	650	—

C# 37-3 TILLA
4.5000 g., Gold **Obv. Inscription:** Abdulhamid II **Mint:** Kashgar

Date	Mintage	VG	F	VF	XF	Unc
AH12xx	—	—	—	—	—	—

MILLED COINAGE

Y# A7.14 1/2 MISCAL
1.4500 g., Silver **Mint:** Yangihissar

Date	Mintage	VG	F	VF	XF	Unc
ND(c.1878)	—	55.00	90.00	150	250	—

K# 1000 MISCAL (Mace)
Silver **Obv. Legend:** "Tsu Yin I Ch'ien" (Pure silver 1 Mace)

Date	Mintage	VG	F	VF	XF	Unc
ND(1876)	—	150	250	425	800	—

Note: Kann #1000 was minted at the Arsenal of Lanchowfu in Kansu (Gansu) by order of General Tso Tsung-tang when he was campaigning against Yakub Beg's Sinkiang (Xinjiang) armies. It was struck circa 1876.

Y# A13 MISCAL (Mace)
3.5000 g., Silver **Mint:** Aksu **Note:** Similar to 3 Miscals, Y#14.

Date	Mintage	VG	F	VF	XF	Unc
AH1310	—	275	450	750	1,250	—

Y# 13 2 MISCALS (2 Mace)
7.2000 g., Silver **Mint:** Aksu **Note:** Similar to 3 Miscals, Y#14.

Date	Mintage	VG	F	VF	XF	Unc
AH1310	—	40.00	80.00	150	225	—
AH1311	—	30.00	60.00	100	165	—

Y# 14 3 MISCALS (3 Mace)
10.5000 g., Silver **Mint:** Aksu

Date	Mintage	VG	F	VF	XF	Unc
AH1310	—	40.00	80.00	140	225	—
AH1311	—	32.50	65.00	110	200	—
AH1312	—	32.50	65.00	110	200	—

HAMMERED COINAGE

Y# A7.3 1/2 MISCAL (5 Fen)
1.4500 g., Silver **Obverse:** Turki inscription **Obv. Inscription:** Gumush **Reverse:** Turki inscription without mint name **Rev. Inscription:** Besh Fung (5 Fen)

Date	Mintage	VG	F	VF	XF	Unc
AH1294	—	7.50	12.50	18.50	30.00	—
ND	—	7.50	12.50	18.50	30.00	—
AH1295	—	7.50	12.50	18.50	30.00	—

Y# A7.1 1/2 MISCAL (5 Fen)
Silver **Obverse:** Turki inscription in square **Obv. Inscription:** Obdan Gumush, 1294 **Reverse:** Turki inscription **Rev. Inscription:** Besh Fung (5 Fen), 1294 **Note:** Weight varies: 1.50-1.65 grams.

Date	Mintage	VG	F	VF	XF	Unc
AH1294 Rare	—	—	—	—	—	—

Y# A7.2 1/2 MISCAL (5 Fen)
1.6500 g., Silver **Obverse:** Turki inscription **Obv. Inscription:** Obdan **Reverse:** Turki inscription **Rev. Inscription:** Gumush 1294

Date	Mintage	VG	F	VF	XF	Unc
AH1294 Rare	—	—	—	—	—	—

Y# A7.25 1/2 MISCAL (5 Fen)
1.4500 g., Silver **Obverse:** Turki inscription **Reverse:** Turki inscription **Mint:** Aksu **Note:** Prev. Y#A7.4.

Date	Mintage	VG	F	VF	XF	Unc
AH1296	—	27.50	45.00	75.00	125	—
ND(c.1878)	—	27.50	45.00	75.00	125	—

Y# A7.4 1/2 MISCAL (5 Fen)
1.4500 g., Silver **Obv. Inscription:** Chu **Reverse:** Turki inscription **Rev. Inscription:** Besh Fung **Mint:** Aksu

Date	Mintage	VG	F	VF	XF	Unc
AH1295	—	32.50	55.00	90.00	150	—

Y# A7.6 1/2 MISCAL (5 Fen)
1.4500 g., Silver **Obverse:** Legend with Manchu, Chinese and Manchu with outer border of S's at rim without square in center **Reverse:** Turki legend **Mint:** Kashgar

Date	Mintage	VG	F	VF	XF	Unc
AH(12)95	—	15.00	25.00	40.00	65.00	—

Y# A7.27 1/2 MISCAL (5 Fen)
1.4500 g., Silver **Obverse:** Turki inscription **Reverse:** Manchu inscription **Mint:** Aksu **Note:** Prev. Y#A7.5.

Date	Mintage	VG	F	VF	XF	Unc
ND(c.1879) Rare	—	—	—	—	—	—

Ch'ien-lung

LOCAL CAST COINAGE

C# 30-4 CASH
Cast Copper **Obverse:** Type A-1 **Obv. Inscription:** Ch'ien-lung T'ung-pao **Reverse:** Character "Chiu" (nine) above **Mint:** Aksu

Date	Mintage	Good	VG	F	VF	XF
ND(1883)	—	13.50	18.50	25.00	35.00	—

Note: Cast as a commemorative of the establishment of Sinkiang (Xinjiang) Province (1884)

Chia-ch'ing

1796-1820

LOCAL CAST COINAGE

C# 28-2 CASH
Cast Copper **Obv. Inscription:** Chia-ch'ing T'ung-pao. **Reverse:** Manchu inscription **Mint:** Ili

Date	Mintage	Good	VG	F	VF	XF
ND(1796-1820)	—	15.00	30.00	55.00	100	—

C# 28-2.1 CASH
Cast Copper **Obv. Inscription:** Chia-ch'ing T'ung-pao. **Reverse:** Vertical line above and below. **Mint:** Ili

Date	Mintage	Good	VG	F	VF	XF
ND(1796-1820)	—	30.00	50.00	85.00	125	—

C# 28-2.2 CASH
Cast Copper **Obv. Inscription:** Chia-ch'ing T'ung-pao. **Reverse:** Vertical line above. **Mint:** Ili

Date	Mintage	Good	VG	F	VF	XF
ND(1796-1820)	—	7.50	15.00	30.00	60.00	—

Tao-kuang

1821-1851

LOCAL CAST COINAGE

C# 28-3 CASH
Cast Copper **Obverse:** Type A **Mint:** Ili

Date	Mintage	Good	VG	F	VF	XF
ND(1821-50)	—	25.00	35.00	50.00	85.00	—

C# 28-3.1 CASH
Cast Copper **Obv. Inscription:** Tao-kuang T'ung-pao **Reverse:** Dot above **Mint:** Ili

Date	Mintage	Good	VG	F	VF	XF
ND(1821-50)	—	30.00	50.00	85.00	125	—

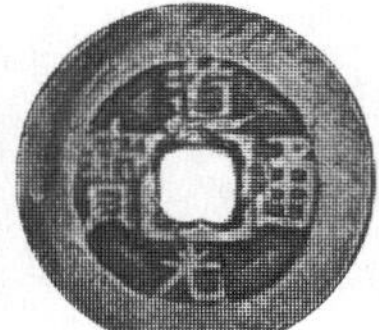

C# 28-3.2 CASH
Cast Copper **Obv. Inscription:** Tao-kuang T'ung-pao **Reverse:** Vertical line above **Mint:** Ili

Date	Mintage	Good	VG	F	VF	XF
ND(1821-50)	—	30.00	50.00	85.00	125	—

C# 28-3.3 CASH
Cast Copper **Obv. Inscription:** Tao-kuang T'ung-pao **Reverse:** Character "Shih" (10) above **Mint:** Ili

Date	Mintage	Good	VG	F	VF	XF
ND(1821-50)	—	60.00	75.00	110	150	—

C# 28-3.4 CASH
Cast Copper **Obv. Inscription:** Tao-kuang T'ung-pao **Reverse:** Short vertical lines above and below **Mint:** Ili

Date	Mintage	Good	VG	F	VF	XF
ND(1821-50)	—	35.00	55.00	95.00	140	—

C# 30-6 CASH
Cast Copper **Obverse:** Type A **Obv. Inscription:** Tao-kuang T'ung-pao **Mint:** Aksu

Date	Mintage	Good	VG	F	VF	XF
ND(1821-50)	—	1.00	2.00	3.50	6.00	—

C# 30-7 5 CASH
Cast Copper **Obverse:** Type A **Obv. Inscription:** Tao-kuang T'ung-pao **Reverse:** Characters "Pa Nien" (= year = 1828) above **Mint:** Aksu

Date	Mintage	Good	VG	F	VF	XF
8(1828)	—	1.50	3.00	6.00	10.00	—

Note: C#30-7 and 30-8 are commemoratives marking the supression of a revolt in Sinkiang in 1828. Numerous counterfeits, presumably contemporary, have recently come on the market. Many of these modern counterfeits have coin alignment. Refer to page 28 of Ch'en Hung-hsi's 1987 "Hsinchiang Hung Ch'ien Chiako Mulu" for illustrations.

C# 30-8 10 CASH
Cast Copper **Obverse:** Type A **Obv. Inscription:** T'ung-chih T'ung-pao **Reverse:** Characters "Pa Nien" (= year 8 = 1828) above **Mint:** Aksu

Date	Mintage	Good	VG	F	VF	XF
8(1828)	—	1.00	1.75	2.75	5.50	—

Note: C#30-7 and 30-8 are commemoratives marking the supression of a revolt in Sinkiang in 1828. Numerous counterfeits, presumably contemporary, have recently come on the market. Many of these modern counterfeits have coin alignment. Refer to page 28 of Ch'en Hung-hsi's 1987 "Hsinchiang Hung Ch'ien Chiako Mulu" for illustrations.

PROVINCIAL CAST COINAGE

C# 33-6 10 CASH
Cast Copper **Obv. Inscription:** Tao-kuang T'ung-pao **Reverse:** Character "K'u" (Kuche) above **Mint:** Kuche

Date	Mintage	Good	VG	F	VF	XF
ND(1821-50)	—	2.50	4.00	10.00	18.00	—

Note: This coin was struck during a later reign beginning in 1875

KM# 3 10 CASH
Cast Copper **Obv. Inscription:** Tao-kuang T'ung-pao **Reverse:** "Pao Ku" with "Hsin" (new) above **Mint:** Kuche

Date	Mintage	Good	VG	F	VF	XF
ND(1886-)	—	5.50	9.00	15.00	25.00	—

Note: Cast by the Kuche Mint for the Tihwa (Ürümqi) or Bao Xin (Hsin), Mint

Hsien-fêng

1851-1861

LOCAL CAST COINAGE

C# 28-4 CASH
Cast Brass **Obverse:** Type A **Obv. Inscription:** Hsien-fêng T'ung-pao **Mint:** Ili **Note:** Narrow rims.

Date	Mintage	Good	VG	F	VF	XF
ND(1851-61)	—	40.00	80.00	125	250	—

C# 28-5 4 CASH
Cast Copper, 33 mm. **Obverse:** Type B-2 **Obv. Inscription:** Hsien-fêng Chung-pao **Mint:** Ili

Date	Mintage	Good	VG	F	VF	XF
ND(1851-61)	—	22.50	30.00	42.50	90.00	—

C# 30-10 5 CASH
Cast Copper **Obv. Inscription:** Hsien-fêng T'ung-pao **Mint:** Aksu

Date	Mintage	Good	VG	F	VF	XF
ND(1851-61)	—	0.65	1.25	2.50	3.50	—

C# 28-6 10 CASH
Cast Copper, 35 mm. **Obverse:** Type B-2 **Obv. Inscription:** Hsien-fêng Chung-pao **Mint:** Ili

Date	Mintage	Good	VG	F	VF	XF
ND(1851-61)	—	25.00	37.50	55.00	80.00	—

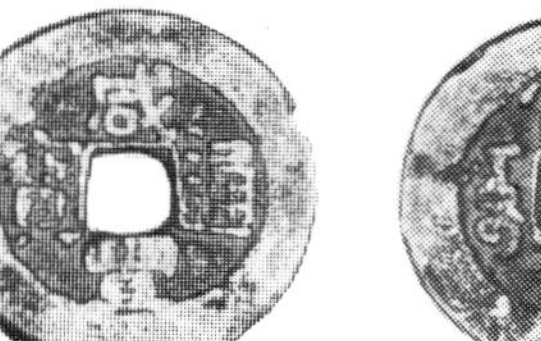

C# 30-11 10 CASH
Cast Copper, 25 mm. **Obverse:** Type A **Obv. Inscription:** Hsien-fêng T'ung-pao **Mint:** Aksu

Date	Mintage	Good	VG	F	VF	XF
ND(1851-61)	—	3.00	5.00	8.00	15.00	—

C# 28-7 50 CASH
Cast Copper **Obv. Inscription:** Hsien-fêng Chung-pao **Mint:** Ili

Date	Mintage	Good	VG	F	VF	XF
ND(1851-61)	—	100	150	220	300	—

C# 30-12 50 CASH
Cast Copper, 36-37 mm. **Obverse:** Type B-1 **Obv. Inscription:** Hsien-fêng Chung-pao **Mint:** Aksu

Date	Mintage	Good	VG	F	VF	XF
ND(1851-61)	—	100	150	200	300	—

C# 28-8 100 CASH
Cast Copper **Obverse:** Type C **Obv. Inscription:** Hsien-fêng Yüan-pao **Mint:** Ili

Date	Mintage	Good	VG	F	VF	XF
ND(1851-61)	—	20.00	30.00	45.00	70.00	—

Note: Numerous counterfeits of C28-8, presumably contemporary, have recently come on the market. Refer to page 39 of Ch'en Hung-hsi's 1987 Hsinchiang Hung "Ch'ien Chiako Mulu" for illustrations. The characters for "Feng" and "Pao" on the obverse are greatly abbreviated, and the bottom horizontal line of the box at the bottom of "Tang" at the top on the reverse is merged with the upper hole frame line.

C# 28-8a 100 CASH
Cast Brass **Obv. Inscription:** Hsien-fêng Yüan-pao **Mint:** Ili

Date	Mintage	Good	VG	F	VF	XF
ND(1851-61)	—	35.00	55.00	75.00	100	—

C# 30-13 100 CASH
Cast Copper **Obverse:** Type C **Obv. Inscription:** Hsien-fêng Yüan-pao **Mint:** Aksu **Note:** Size varies: 44-45mm.

Date	Mintage	Good	VG	F	VF	XF
ND(1851-61)	—	35.00	50.00	70.00	100	—

C# 30-13.1 100 CASH
Cast Copper **Obv. Inscription:** Hsien-fêng Yüan-pao **Mint:** Aksu **Note:** Size varies: 40-41mm.

Date	Mintage	Good	VG	F	VF	XF
ND(1851-61)	—	14.00	20.00	28.50	40.00	—

PROVINCIAL CAST COINAGE

C# 33-8 5 CASH
Cast Copper **Obverse:** Type A **Obv. Inscription:** Hsien-fêng T'ung-pao **Mint:** Kuche

Date	Mintage	Good	VG	F	VF	XF
ND(1851-61)	—	50.00	75.00	100	175	—

C# 29-1 8 CASH
Cast Copper **Obverse:** Type B-1 **Obv. Inscription:** Hsien-fêng Chung-pao **Mint:** Urumqi

Date	Mintage	Good	VG	F	VF	XF
ND(1851-61)	—	100	150	225	300	—

C# 29-2 10 CASH
Cast Copper, 33 mm. **Obverse:** Type B-1 **Obv. Inscription:** Hsien-fêng Chung-pao **Mint:** Ti-hua

Date	Mintage	Good	VG	F	VF	XF
ND(1851-61)	—	35.00	50.00	70.00	100	—

C# 29-2.1 10 CASH
Cast Copper, 27 mm. **Obverse:** Type B-1 **Obv. Inscription:** Hsien-fêng Chung-pao **Mint:** Urumqi

Date	Mintage	Good	VG	F	VF	XF
ND(1851-61)	—	6.50	10.00	15.00	22.50	—

C# 32-2 10 CASH
Cast Copper **Obverse:** Type A **Mint:** Kashgar

Date	Mintage	Good	VG	F	VF	XF
ND(1851-61)	—	12.00	17.50	35.00	55.00	—

C# 33-9 10 CASH
Cast Copper **Obverse:** Type A **Obv. Inscription:** Hsien-fêng T'ung-pao **Mint:** Kuche

Date	Mintage	Good	VG	F	VF	XF
ND(1851-61)	—	2.00	3.00	9.00	16.00	—

C# 35-3 10 CASH
Cast Copper, 25 mm. **Obv. Inscription:** Hsien-fêng T'ung-pao **Mint:** Yarkand

Date	Mintage	Good	VG	F	VF	XF
ND(1851-61)	—	4.00	7.00	10.00	16.00	—

C# 32-3.1 50 CASH
Cast Copper, 32 mm. **Obverse:** Type B-2 **Obv. Inscription:** Hsien-fêng Chung-pao **Reverse:** Stylized Turki mint name legend **Mint:** Kashgar

Date	Mintage	Good	VG	F	VF	XF
ND(1851-61)	—	90.00	150	250	350	—

C# 33-10 50 CASH
Cast Copper **Obv. Inscription:** Hsien-fêng Chung-pao **Mint:** Kuche

Date	Mintage	Good	VG	F	VF	XF
ND(1851-61)	—	100	150	250	400	—

C# 35-4 50 CASH
Cast Copper, 37 mm. **Obverse:** Type B-1 **Obv. Inscription:** Hsien-fêng Chung-pao **Mint:** Yarkand

Date	Mintage	Good	VG	F	VF	XF
ND(1851-61)	—	80.00	135	175	250	—

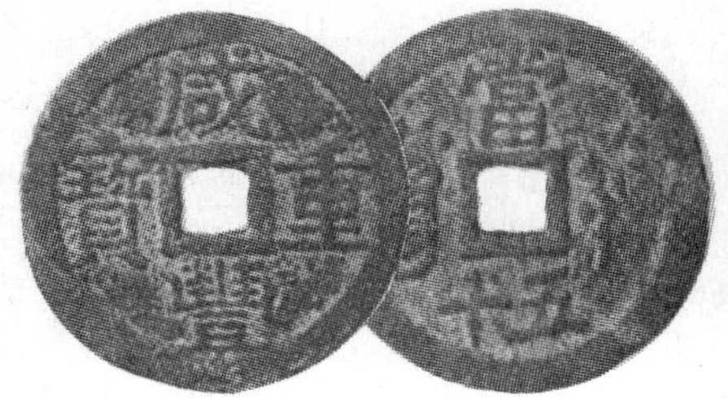

C# 35-4.1 50 CASH
Cast Copper, 32 mm. **Obv. Inscription:** Hsien-fêng Chung-pao **Mint:** Yarkand

Date	Mintage	Good	VG	F	VF	XF
ND(1851-61)	—	65.00	115	140	200	—

C# 29-5 80 CASH
Cast Brass, 50 mm. **Obverse:** Type C **Obv. Inscription:** Hsien-fêng Yüan-pao **Mint:** Ti-hua

Date	Mintage	Good	VG	F	VF	XF
ND(1851-61)	—	275	500	850	1,350	—

Note: Smaller 40mm examples, sometimes described as local issues, are considered counterfeits

C# 32-4 100 CASH
Cast Copper **Obverse:** Type B-2 **Obv. Inscription:** Hsien-fêng Yüan-pao **Reverse:** Stylized Turki mint name **Mint:** Kashgar

Date	Mintage	Good	VG	F	VF	XF
ND(1851-61)	—	100	160	265	375	—

C# 33-11 100 CASH
Cast Copper, 34 mm. **Obv. Inscription:** Hsien-fêng Yüan-pao **Mint:** Kuche

Date	Mintage	Good	VG	F	VF	XF
ND(1851-61)	—	60.00	75.00	90.00	125	—

C# 35-5.1 100 CASH
Cast Copper **Obverse:** Type C **Obv. Inscription:** Hsien-fêng Yüan-pao **Mint:** Yarkand **Note:** Size varies: 50-56mm.

Date	Mintage	Good	VG	F	VF	XF
ND(1851-61)	—	85.00	100	140	200	—

C# 35-5.2 100 CASH
Cast Copper, 45 mm. **Obv. Inscription:** Hsien-fêng Yüan-pao **Mint:** Yarkand

Date	Mintage	Good	VG	F	VF	XF
ND(1851-61)	—	85.00	125	200	400	—

T'ung-chih
1862-1875

LOCAL CAST COINAGE

C# 28-9 4 CASH
Cast Copper **Obv. Inscription:** T'ung-chih Chung-pao **Mint:** Ili

Date	Mintage	Good	VG	F	VF	XF
ND(1862-74)	—	70.00	100	150	225	—

C# 30-A15 5 CASH
Cast Copper **Obv. Inscription:** T'ung-chih T'ung-pao **Mint:** Aksu

Date	Mintage	Good	VG	F	VF	XF
ND(1862-74)	—	7.00	10.00	15.00	77.50	—

C# 30-15 10 CASH
Cast Copper, 25 mm. **Obverse:** Type A **Obv. Inscription:** T'ung-chih T'ung-pao **Mint:** Aksu

Date	Mintage	Good	VG	F	VF	XF
ND(1862-74)	—	3.00	5.00	8.00	15.00	—

PROVINCIAL CAST COINAGE

C# 33-22 5 CASH
Cast Copper **Obverse:** Type A-2 **Obv. Inscription:** T'ung-chih T'ung-pao **Mint:** Kuche

Date	Mintage	Good	VG	F	VF	XF
ND(1862-74)	—	135	225	350	500	—

C# 33-13 10 CASH
Cast Copper **Obverse:** Type A-2 **Obv. Inscription:** T'ung-chih T'ung-pao **Mint:** Kuche

Date	Mintage	Good	VG	F	VF	XF
ND(1862-74)	—	1.50	3.00	9.00	16.00	—

C# 33-14 10 CASH
Cast Copper **Obv. Inscription:** T'ung-chih T'ung-pao **Reverse:** Character "K'u" (Kuche) above **Mint:** Kuche

Date	Mintage	Good	VG	F	VF	XF
ND(1862-74)	—	4.00	6.00	12.00	20.00	—

C# 33-20 10 CASH
Cast Copper **Obv. Inscription:** T'ung-chih T'ung-pao **Reverse:** Manchu inscription at left and right, "K'u" above **Rev. Inscription:** Boo Yuan **Mint:** Kuche

Date	Mintage	Good	VG	F	VF	XF
ND(1862-74)	—	7.50	14.00	22.00	32.50	—

C# 35-7 10 CASH
Cast Copper **Obverse:** Type A-2 **Obv. Inscription:** T'ung-chih T'ung-pao **Mint:** Yarkand

Date	Mintage	Good	VG	F	VF	XF
ND(1862-74)	—	4.00	7.00	10.00	16.00	—

KM# 5 10 CASH
Cast Copper **Obv. Inscription:** T'ung-chih T'ung-pao **Reverse:** Inscription with "Hsin" (new) above **Rev. Inscription:** Boo-kuce **Mint:** Kuche

Date	Mintage	Good	VG	F	VF	XF
ND(1886-)	—	5.50	9.00	15.00	25.00	—

Note: Cast by the Kuche Mint for the Tihwa (Ürümqi) or Bao Xin, Mint

Kuang-hsü
1875-1908
LOCAL CAST COINAGE

C# 30-18 10 CASH
Cast Copper **Obv. Inscription:** Kuang-hsü Chung-pao **Reverse:** Character "A" (for Aksu) above center hole, "Aksu" in Turki at right, in Manchu at left **Mint:** Aksu

Date	Mintage	Good	VG	F	VF	XF
ND(1875-1908)	—	1.50	2.50	4.00	8.00	—

C# 30-18.1 10 CASH
Cast Copper **Reverse:** "Asku" in Manchu at right, in Turki at left **Mint:** Aksu

Date	Mintage	Good	VG	F	VF	XF
ND(1875-1908)	—	7.50	12.50	19.00	35.00	—

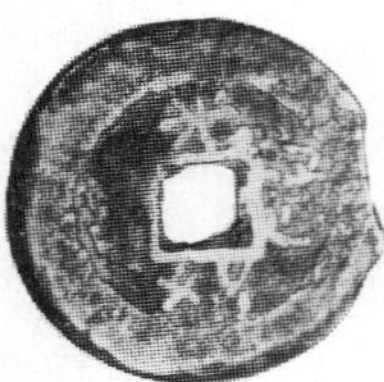

C# 30-19 10 CASH
Cast Copper **Obv. Inscription:** Kuang-hsü T'ung-pao **Reverse:** Character "K'a" (for Kashgar) above **Mint:** Aksu

Date	Mintage	Good	VG	F	VF	XF
ND(1886-1908)	—	2.00	4.50	6.50	13.50	—

Note: Cast in the Aksu Mint for the Kashgar Mint, beginning in 1886 during the reign of Kuang-Hsü

PROVINCIAL CAST COINAGE

KM# 10 CASH
Cast Copper **Obv. Inscription:** Kuang-hsü T'ung-pao **Reverse:** Manchu inscription for Hu-pu Board of Revenue **Rev. Inscription:** Boo Ciowan **Mint:** Kuche

Date	Mintage	Good	VG	F	VF	XF
ND(1875-1908)	—	1.50	3.50	6.00	9.50	—

KM# 11 CASH
Cast Copper **Reverse:** Similar to KM#10 but entire reverse is in inverted mirror image **Mint:** Kuche

Date	Mintage	Good	VG	F	VF	XF
ND(1875-1908)	—	3.50	6.00	9.00	13.50	—

KM# 12 CASH
Cast Copper **Obv. Inscription:** Kuang-hsü T'ung-pao **Reverse:** Similar to KM#11 **Mint:** Kuche

Date	Mintage	Good	VG	F	VF	XF
ND(1875-1908)	—	1.50	3.50	6.00	9.50	—

KM# 13 CASH
Cast Copper **Obv. Inscription:** Kuang-hsü T'ung-pao **Reverse:** Illiterate Manchu inscription **Rev. Inscription:** Boo Chuan or Yuan **Mint:** Kuche

Date	Mintage	Good	VG	F	VF	XF
ND(1875-1908)	—	1.50	3.50	6.00	9.50	—

KM# 14 CASH
Cast Copper **Obv. Inscription:** Kuang-hsü T'ung-pao **Reverse:** Illiterate Manchu inscription **Rev. Inscription:** Boo-Chuan **Mint:** Kuche

Date	Mintage	Good	VG	F	VF	XF
ND(1875-1908)	—	1.50	3.00	5.00	8.50	—

Note: The five one-cash varieties listed above could be confused with Beijing issues C1-16 or C2-15, but they are much more crudely cast, and are made of red copper rather than brass; see Landon Ross, 1986, Numismatics International Bulletin 20(3) for a more detailed review

C# 33-23 CASH
Cast Copper **Obv. Inscription:** Kuang-hsü T'ung-pao **Mint:** Kuche

Date	Mintage	Good	VG	F	VF	XF
ND(1875-1908)	—	6.00	8.00	12.00	20.00	—

KM# 7.1 10 CASH
Cast Copper **Obv. Inscription:** Kuang-hsü T'ung-pao **Reverse:** "Pao Ku" with "K'u" (for Kuche) above **Mint:** Kuche

Date	Mintage	Good	VG	F	VF	XF
ND(1875-1908)	—	1.50	3.00	5.00	10.00	—

KM# 7.2 10 CASH
Cast Copper **Obv. Inscription:** Kuang-hsü T'ung-pao **Reverse:** "Pao" (for Kuche) at left reversed **Mint:** Kuche

Date	Mintage	Good	VG	F	VF	XF
ND(1875-1908)	—	7.50	13.50	22.50	35.00	—

KM# 8 10 CASH
Cast Copper **Obv. Inscription:** Kuang-hsü T'ung-pao **Reverse:** "Manchu Boo Hsin" with "Hsin" (new, but here standing for the Tihwa (now Urumqi) Mint) above **Mint:** Urumqi

Date	Mintage	Good	VG	F	VF	XF
ND(1875-1908)	—	3.50	5.00	7.50	15.00	—

KM# 9 10 CASH
Cast Copper **Obv. Inscription:** Kuang-hsü T'ung-pao **Reverse:** "Manchu Boo Hsin" (for Tihwa Mint) with "Hsin" (new) above **Mint:** Urumqi

Date	Mintage	Good	VG	F	VF	XF
ND(1875-1908)	—	3.00	4.50	7.00	15.00	—

C# 32-6 10 CASH
Cast Copper **Obv. Inscription:** Kuang-hsü T'ung-pao **Reverse:** "Kashgar" in Turki at left, in Manchu at right, "K'a" (Kashgar) above **Mint:** Kashgar

Date	Mintage	Good	VG	F	VF	XF
ND(1875-1908)	—	5.00	9.50	15.00	25.00	—

C# 32-6.1 10 CASH
Cast Copper **Obv. Inscription:** Kuang-hsü T'ung-pao **Reverse:** Manchu inscription (right-left) **Rev. Inscription:** Boo-Kashgar **Mint:** Kashgar

Date	Mintage	Good	VG	F	VF	XF
ND(1875-1908)	—	5.00	9.50	15.00	25.00	—

C# 33-16 10 CASH
Cast Copper **Obv. Inscription:** Kuang-hsü T'ung-pao **Mint:** Kuche

Date	Mintage	Good	VG	F	VF	XF
ND(1875-1908)	—	10.00	20.00	30.00	50.00	—

C# 33-18 10 CASH
Cast Copper **Obv. Inscription:** Kuang-hsü T'ung-pao **Reverse:** Character "K'u" above **Mint:** Kuche

Date	Mintage	Good	VG	F	VF	XF
ND1875-1908)	—	7.50	12.00	17.50	35.00	—

C# 33-19 10 CASH
Cast Copper **Obv. Inscription:** Kuang-hsü T'ung-pao **Reverse:** Manchu inscription, "kuce" in simple style **Rev. Inscription:** Boo-kuce **Mint:** Kuche

Date	Mintage	Good	VG	F	VF	XF
ND(1875-1908)	—	2.00	3.00	10.00	18.00	—

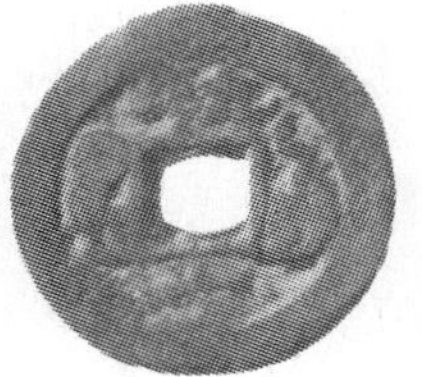

C# 33-17 10 CASH
Cast Copper **Obv. Inscription:** Kuang-hsü T'ung-pao **Reverse:** Character "Chiu Nien" (year 9 = 1883) above **Mint:** Kuche

Date	Mintage	Good	VG	F	VF	XF
9(1883)	—	10.00	17.50	25.50	45.00	—

Note: Cast as a commemorative of the 1884 establishment of Hsinchiang (Xinjiang) as a province

KM# 6 10 CASH
Cast Copper **Obverse:** Type A **Obv. Inscription:** Kuang-hsü T'ung-pao **Reverse:** "Pao Ku" with "K'u" (for Kuche) above **Mint:** Kuche

Date	Mintage	Good	VG	F	VF	XF
ND(1886-)	—	5.50	8.00	14.00	22.50	—

Note: Cast by the Kucha Mint for the Kashgar Mint. KM#3, 5, and 6 were cast in the reign of Kuang Hsü (1875-1908), beginning in 1886

MILLED COINAGE

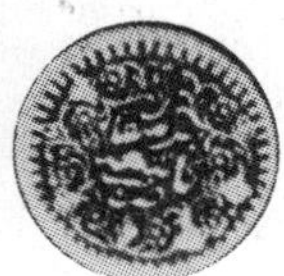

Y# 16 MISCAL (Mace)
Silver **Obverse:** Inscription between value **Obv. Inscription:** Kuang-hsü Yin-yüan **Reverse:** Wreath around Turki legend **Mint:** Kashgar

Date	Mintage	VG	F	VF	XF	Unc
ND(c.1891)	—	50.00	75.00	150	250	—
AH1309	—	50.00	75.00	150	250	—
AH1310	—	50.00	75.00	150	250	—
AH1311	—	50.00	75.00	150	250	—

Y# D16 MISCAL (Mace)
Silver **Obv. Inscription:** Kuang-hsü Yin-yüan **Reverse:** Wreath around Turki legend **Mint:** Kashgar

Date	Mintage	VG	F	VF	XF	Unc
AH1310	—	150	250	400	650	—

Y# A16 MISCAL (Mace)
Silver **Obv. Inscription:** Kuang-hsü Yin-yüan **Reverse:** Without wreath **Mint:** Kashgar

Date	Mintage	VG	F	VF	XF	Unc
ND(c.1892)	—	90.00	150	250	400	—
AH1310	—	90.00	150	250	400	—

Y# 17 2 MISCALS (2 Mace)
7.2000 g., Silver **Obverse:** Inscription between value **Obv. Inscription:** Kuang-hsü Yin-yüan **Reverse:** Turki in flowering wreath **Mint:** Kashgar

Date	Mintage	VG	F	VF	XF	Unc
ND(c.1892)	—	60.00	100	175	300	—
AH1310	—	16.50	27.50	45.00	75.00	—
AH1311	—	12.00	20.00	30.00	50.00	—
AH1312	—	10.00	14.00	30.00	65.00	—
AH1313	—	17.50	30.00	45.00	75.00	—

Y# 17a 2 MISCALS (2 Mace)
7.2000 g., Silver **Obverse:** Inscription between Kashgar and value **Obv. Inscription:** Kuang-hsü Yin-yüan **Mint:** Kashgar

Date	Mintage	VG	F	VF	XF	Unc
AH1311	—	—	—	—	—	—
Note: Error						
AH1312	—	12.50	22.50	32.50	50.00	—
AH1313	—	12.50	22.50	32.50	50.00	—
AH1314	—	12.50	22.50	32.50	50.00	—
AH1315	—	12.50	22.50	32.50	50.00	—
AH1317	—	12.50	22.50	32.50	50.00	—
AH1319	—	12.50	22.50	32.50	50.00	—
AH1320	—	17.50	30.00	45.00	75.00	—

Y# A18 3 MISCALS
10.5000 g., Silver **Obverse:** Inscription between Turki and Manchu **Obv. Inscription:** Kuang-hsü Yin-yüan **Reverse:** Dragon

Date	Mintage	Good	VG	F	VF	XF
AH1307	—	750	1,250	2,250	3,750	5,500

Y# 18 3 MISCALS
10.5000 g., Silver **Obverse:** Inscription between value **Obv. Inscription:** Kuang-hsü Yin-yüan **Reverse:** Turki in sprays, flower above **Mint:** Kashgar

Date	Mintage	Good	VG	F	VF	XF
ND(c.1892) Rare	—	—	—	—	—	—
AH1310	—	6.00	15.00	25.00	40.00	65.00
AH1311	—	7.00	17.50	30.00	45.00	75.00
AH1312	—	10.00	20.00	35.00	55.00	100

Y# 18a 3 MISCALS
10.5000 g., Silver **Obverse:** Inscription between Kashgar and value **Obv. Inscription:** Kuang-hsü Yin-yüan **Reverse:** Turki in floral wreath **Mint:** Kashgar

Date	Mintage	VG	F	VF	XF	Unc
AH1311 Error	—	—	—	—	—	—
AH1313	—	10.00	20.00	32.50	65.00	—
AH1314	—	10.00	20.00	32.50	65.00	—
AH1315	—	10.00	20.00	32.50	65.00	—
AH1316	—	10.00	20.00	32.50	65.00	—
AH1317	—	10.00	20.00	32.50	65.00	—
AH1319	—	10.00	20.00	32.50	65.00	—
AH1320	—	10.00	20.00	32.50	65.00	—

K# 1040 5 MISCALS
10.5000 g., Silver **Obverse:** Inscription above value between Turki and Manchu **Obv. Inscription:** Kuang-hsü Yin-yüan **Reverse:** Dragon

Date	Mintage	VG	F	VF	XF	Unc
AH1307	—	1,250	2,000	3,500	5,000	—

Y# 19 5 MISCALS
10.5000 g., Silver **Obverse:** Inscription between value **Obv. Inscription:** Kuang-hsü Yin-yüan **Rev. Inscription:** Turki within sprays **Mint:** Kashgar

Date	Mintage	VG	F	VF	XF	Unc
AH1310	—	17.50	30.00	55.00	100	—
AH1311	—	10.00	20.00	35.00	70.00	—
AH1312	—	15.00	27.50	45.00	90.00	—
AH1313	—	15.00	27.50	45.00	90.00	—
AH1315	—	15.00	27.50	45.00	90.00	—

Y# 19a 5 MISCALS
17.2000 g., Silver **Obverse:** Inscription between "Kashgar" and value; Chinese characters "K'a Shih" at right **Obv. Inscription:** Kuang-hsü Yin-yüan **Rev. Inscription:** Turki within sprays **Mint:** Kashgar

Date	Mintage	VG	F	VF	XF	Unc
AH1311 Error	—	—	—	—	—	—
AH1313	—	17.50	25.00	40.00	70.00	—
AH1314	—	17.50	25.00	40.00	70.00	—
AH1315	—	17.50	25.00	40.00	70.00	—
AH1316	—	17.50	25.00	40.00	70.00	—
AH1317	—	17.50	25.00	40.00	70.00	—
AH1319	—	17.50	25.00	40.00	70.00	—
AH1320	—	17.50	25.00	40.00	70.00	—

Y# 15 5 MISCALS (5 Mace)
17.5000 g., Silver **Mint:** Aksu

Date	Mintage	VG	F	VF	XF	Unc
AH1310	—	55.00	110	190	325	—
AH1311	—	40.00	100	165	275	—
AH1312	—	40.00	80.00	150	250	—

HAMMERED COINAGE

Y# A7.12 1/2 MISCAL
1.4500 g., Silver **Reverse:** "Zarb Khotan" in Arabic **Mint:** Khotan

Date	Mintage	VG	F	VF	XF	Unc
ND(c.1878)	—	27.50	45.00	72.50	120	—

Y# A7.11 1/2 MISCAL (5 Fen)
1.4500 g., Silver **Reverse:** "Kho-tan" in Arabic; retrograde and inverted Chinese "5" **Mint:** Khotan

Date	Mintage	VG	F	VF	XF	Unc
ND(c.1878)	—	27.50	45.00	72.50	120	—

Y# A7.7 1/2 MISCAL (5 Fen)
1.4500 g., Silver **Obverse:** Square in center **Reverse:** Square in center **Rev. Legend:** Manchu, Chinese official "5" above Turki **Mint:** Kashgar

Date	Mintage	VG	F	VF	XF	Unc
ND(1877-78)	—	15.00	25.00	40.00	65.00	—
AH1295	—	15.00	25.00	40.00	65.00	—

Y# A7.26 1/2 MISCAL (5 Fen)
1.4500 g., Silver **Mint:** Kuche **Note:** Prev. #YA7.2.

Date	Mintage	VG	F	VF	XF	Unc
ND(1877-78)	—	5.50	9.00	15.00	25.00	—
4(1878)	—	16.50	27.50	45.00	75.00	—
AH1295	—	5.50	9.00	15.00	25.00	—

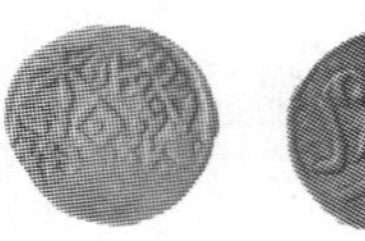

Y# A7.13 1/2 MISCAL (5 Fen)
1.4500 g., Silver **Mint:** Kuche

Date	Mintage	VG	F	VF	XF	Unc
ND(1877) Rare	—	—	—	—	—	—

Y# A7.5 1/2 MISCAL (5 Fen)
1.4500 g., Silver **Obverse:** Large Chinese "Kuang" above square with Turki legend below **Reverse:** Turki legend

Date	Mintage	VG	F	VF	XF	Unc
AH1296	—	55.00	90.00	150	250	—
AH1297	—	11.50	18.50	30.00	50.00	—
AH1298//1297	—	11.50	18.50	30.00	50.00	—
AH1298	—	11.50	18.50	30.00	50.00	—

Y# A7.15 1/2 MISCAL (5 Fen)
1.4500 g., Silver **Reverse:** Turki mintname and Chinese value **Mint:** Yarkand

Date	Mintage	VG	F	VF	XF	Unc
ND(c.1878)	—	20.00	35.00	60.00	100	—

Y# A7.16 1/2 MISCAL (5 Fen)
1.4500 g., Silver **Reverse:** Date at left **Mint:** Yarkand

Date	Mintage	VG	F	VF	XF	Unc
AH1295	—	45.00	75.00	120	200	—

Y# A7.17 1/2 MISCAL (5 Fen)
1.4500 g., Silver **Reverse:** Date at right **Mint:** Yarkand

Date	Mintage	VG	F	VF	XF	Unc
AH1295	—	55.00	90.00	150	250	—

Y# A7.19 1/2 MISCAL (5 Fen)
1.4500 g., Silver **Mint:** Kashgar

Date	Mintage	VG	F	VF	XF	Unc
ND(1878) Rare	—	—	—	—	—	—

Note: Believed to be degenerate copy of Y#A7.7 by certain authority

Y# A7.23 1/2 MISCAL (5 Fen)
1.4500 g., Silver **Mint:** Kashgar **Note:** Similar to Y#A7.7 but with normal "5" above.

Date	Mintage	VG	F	VF	XF	Unc
ND(1878)	—	15.00	25.00	40.00	65.00	—

Y# A7.24 1/2 MISCAL (5 Fen)
1.4500 g., Silver **Obverse:** "Kuang" in unusual script, dot in central square **Mint:** Kashgar

Date	Mintage	VG	F	VF	XF	Unc
ND(1878)	—	15.00	25.00	40.00	65.00	—

Y# A7.18 1/2 MISCAL (5 Fen)
1.4500 g., Silver **Reverse:** Turki, Chinese, and Manchu legend **Mint:** Yarkand

Date	Mintage	VG	F	VF	XF	Unc
ND(c.1879)	—	15.00	25.00	40.00	65.00	—

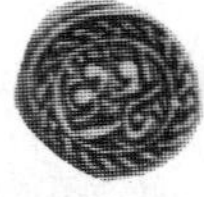 

Y# A7.8 1/2 MISCAL (5 Fen)
1.4500 g., Silver **Obverse:** Without square in center, Turki inscription **Reverse:** Without square in center, Chinese inscription for 5 Fen **Mint:** Kashgar

Date	Mintage	VG	F	VF	XF	Unc
AH1313	—	100	175	300	500	—

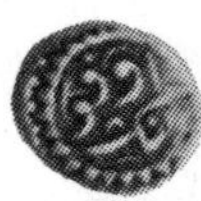 

Y# A7.9 1/2 MISCAL (5 Fen)
1.4500 g., Silver **Mint:** Kashgar

Date	Mintage	VG	F	VF	XF	Unc
ND(c.1896)	—	100	175	300	500	—

Y# A7.10 1/2 MISCAL (5 Fen)
1.4500 g., Silver **Obverse:** Arabesque, wreath and flower replaces Turki inscription **Reverse:** Chinese inscription for 5 Fen **Mint:** Kashgar

Date	Mintage	VG	F	VF	XF	Unc
ND(c.1896)	—	100	175	300	500	—

Y# A7.20 1/2 MISCAL (5 Fen)
1.4500 g., Silver **Obverse:** Turki inscription **Obv. Inscription:** Besh Fen **Reverse:** Turki inscription **Rev. Inscription:** Darb Kashgar **Mint:** Kashgar

Date	Mintage	VG	F	VF	XF	Unc
ND(c.1896)	—	9.00	15.00	25.00	40.00	—

Y# B7 MISCAL (Mace)
2.9000 g., Silver **Reverse:** Inscription in Chinese, Turki and Manchu **Mint:** Kashgar

Date	Mintage	VG	F	VF	XF	Unc
AH1292	—	250	400	700	1,200	—
AH1295	—	250	400	700	1,200	—

PATTERNS

Including off metal strikes

KM#	Date	Mintage	Identification	Mkt Val
Pn1	AH(1851)	—	Cash. Cast Brass. C#30-9.	350

KM#	Date	Mintage	Identification	Mkt Val
Pn2	AH(1851)	—	Cash. Cast Brass. Wide rims. C#28-4.1.	600
Pn3	AH(1851)	—	Cash. Cast Brass.	350
Pn4	AH(1851)	—	Cash. Cast Brass.	350
Pn5	AH(1851)	—	Cash. Cast Brass.	350
Pn6	AH(1851)	—	Cash. Cast Brass.	350
Pn7	AH(1851)	—	Cash. Cast Brass.	400
Pn8	AH(1851)	—	10 Cash. Cast Brass. C#30-11a.	350
Pn9	AH(1851)	—	10 Cash. Cast Brass.	200

KM#	Date	Mintage	Identification	Mkt Val
Pn10	AH(1851)	—	50 Cash. Cast Brass. 54 mm. C#30-12a.	350
Pn11	AH(1851)	—	100 Cash. Cast Brass.	400

KM#	Date	Mintage	Identification	Mkt Val
Pn12	AH(1851)	—	100 Cash. Cast Copper. C#31-1v.	750

KM#	Date	Mintage	Identification	Mkt Val

KM#	Date	Mintage	Identification	Mkt Val
Pn13	AH(1851)	—	100 Cash. Cast Brass. C#34-2.	350
Pn14	AH(1851)	—	100 Cash. Cast Brass.	500
Pn15	AH(1851)	—	100 Cash. Cast Brass.	600
Pn16	AH(1851)	—	500 Cash. Cast Brass.	500
Pn17	AH(1851)	—	500 Cash. Cast Copper. C#31-1a.	900
Pn18	AH(1851)	—	500 Cash. Cast Copper. C#33-21	500
Pn19	AH(1851)	—	500 Cash. Cast Brass. C#34-3.	500
Pn21	AH(1851)	—	500 Cash. Cast Copper. C#35-5a.	500
Pn22	AH(1851)	—	1000 Cash. Cast Copper. C#31-2.	900
Pn23	AH(1851)	—	1000 Cash. Cast Copper. C#33-12	500
Pn24	AH(1851)	—	1000 Cash. Cast Brass.	600
Pn25	AH(1851)	—	1000 Cash. Cast Copper. C#35-6.	500
Pn20	AH(1851)	—	500 Cash. Cast Brass.	600
Pn26	AH(1861)	—	Cash. Cast Brass.	500
Pn27	AH(1861)	—	Cash. Cast Brass.	500

KM#	Date	Mintage	Identification	Mkt Val
Pn28	AH(1862)	—	Cash. Cast Brass. C#30-14.	350

KM#	Date	Mintage	Identification	Mkt Val
Pn29	AH(1862)	—	Cash. Cast Brass. C#28-8a.	500

KM#	Date	Mintage	Identification	Mkt Val
Pn30	AH(1862)	—	10 Cash. Cast Brass. C#30-15a.	—

KM#	Date	Mintage	Identification	Mkt Val
Pn31	AH(1862)	—	10 Cash. Cast Brass. C#28-9a.	600

KM#	Date	Mintage	Identification	Mkt Val
Pn32	AH(1875)	—	Cash. Cast Brass. C#30-16.	350

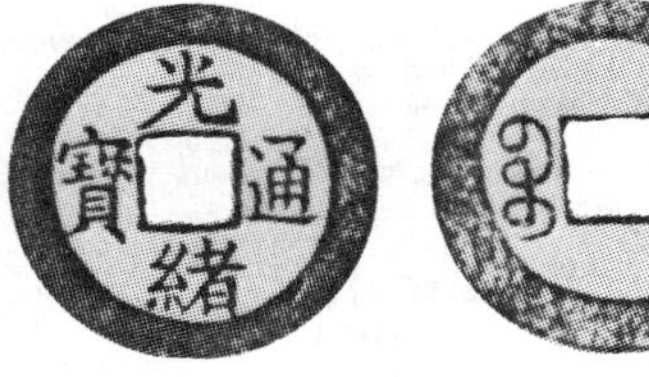

KM#	Date	Mintage	Identification	Mkt Val
Pn33	AH(1875)	—	Cash. Cast Brass. C#28-9c.	500

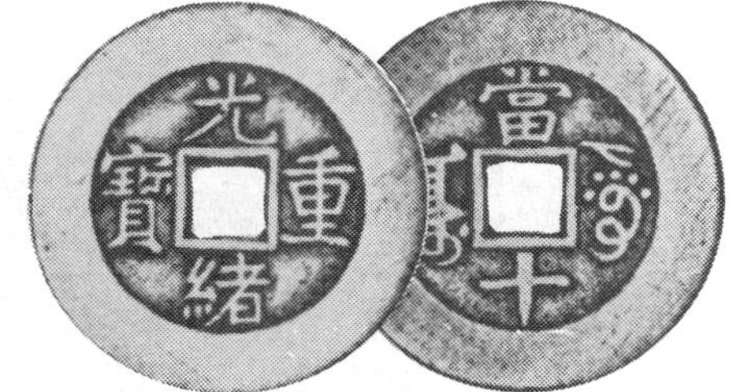

KM#	Date	Mintage	Identification	Mkt Val
Pn34	AH(1875)	—	10 Cash. Cast Brass. C#30-17.	350
Pn35	AH(1875)	—	10 Cash. Cast Brass. C#28-10.	600

SZECHUAN PROVINCE

Sichuan

A province located in south-central China. The largest of the traditional Chinese provinces, Szechuan (Sichuan) is a plateau region watered by many rivers. These rivers carry much trading traffic. Agriculture or mining are the occupational choices of most of the populace. In World War II the national capital was moved to Chungking in Szechuan (Sichuan). Chengtu was an active imperial mint that opened in 1732 and was in practically continuous operation until the advent of modern equipment. Modern minting was introduced in the province when Chengtu began milled coinage in 1898. A mint was authorized for Chungking in 1905 but it did not begin operations until 1913. The Chengtu Mint was looted by soldiers in 1925. The last republic issues from Szechuan (Sichuan) were dated 1932.

The machinery for the first Szechuan (Sichuan) Mint was produced in New Jersey and the dies were engraved in Philadelphia. The mint was opened in 1898, but closed within a few months and did not reopen until 1901. There is no doubt now that Y#234-238 (K#145-149) were the first issues of this mint, contrary to the Kann listings.

EMPIRE

Tao-kuang
1821-1851

PROVINCIAL CAST COINAGE

C# 24-3 CASH

Cast Copper **Obv. Inscription:** Tao-kuang T'ung-pao **Mint:** Chuan

Date	Mintage	Good	VG	F	VF	XF
ND(1821-50)	—	1.00	1.75	2.50	4.00	—

Hsien-fêng
1851-1861

PROVINCIAL CAST COINAGE

C# 24-4 CASH

Cast Copper **Obv. Inscription:** Hsien-fêng T'ung-pao **Mint:** Chuan

Date	Mintage	Good	VG	F	VF	XF
ND(1851-61)	—	4.50	7.50	11.50	18.00	—

C# 24-4.1 CASH

Cast Copper **Obv. Inscription:** Hsien-fêng T'ung-pao **Reverse:** Character "Shih" above **Mint:** Chuan

Date	Mintage	Good	VG	F	VF	XF
ND(1851-61)	—	5.00	8.00	12.50	20.00	—

C# 24-4.2 CASH

Cast Copper **Obv. Inscription:** Hsien-fêng T'ung-pao **Reverse:** Character "Wen" above **Mint:** Chuan

Date	Mintage	Good	VG	F	VF	XF
ND(1851-61)	—	5.00	8.00	12.50	20.00	—

C# 24-4.3 CASH

Cast Copper **Obv. Inscription:** Hsien-fêng T'ung-pao **Reverse:** Character "Kung" (work) above **Mint:** Chuan

Date	Mintage	Good	VG	F	VF	XF
ND(1851-61)	—	5.00	8.00	12.50	20.00	—

C# 24-4.4 CASH

Cast Copper **Obv. Inscription:** Hsien-fêng T'ung-pao **Reverse:** Character "Erh" (two) above **Mint:** Chuan

Date	Mintage	Good	VG	F	VF	XF
ND(1851-61)	—	5.00	8.00	12.50	20.00	—

C# 24-4.5 CASH

Cast Copper **Obv. Inscription:** Hsien-fêng T'ung-pao **Reverse:** Circle above **Mint:** Chuan

Date	Mintage	Good	VG	F	VF	XF
ND(1851-61)	—	5.00	8.00	12.50	20.00	—

C# 24-4.6 CASH

Cast Copper **Obv. Inscription:** Hsien-fêng T'ung-pao **Reverse:** Crescent standing on end above **Mint:** Chuan

Date	Mintage	Good	VG	F	VF	XF
ND(1851-61)	—	5.00	8.00	12.50	20.00	—

C# 24-4.7 CASH

Cast Copper **Obv. Inscription:** Hsien-fêng T'ung-pao **Reverse:** Two horizontal and one vertical line above **Mint:** Chuan

Date	Mintage	Good	VG	F	VF	XF
ND(1851-61)	—	5.00	8.00	12.50	20.00	—

C# 24-4.8 CASH

Cast Copper **Obv. Inscription:** Hsien-fêng T'ung-pao **Reverse:** Two figures above, possibly 15 **Mint:** Chuan

Date	Mintage	Good	VG	F	VF	XF
ND(1851-61)	—	5.00	8.00	12.50	20.00	—

C# 24-4.9 CASH

Cast Copper **Obv. Inscription:** Hsien-fêng T'ung-pao **Reverse:** Crescent below **Mint:** Chuan

Date	Mintage	Good	VG	F	VF	XF
ND(1851-61)	—	5.00	8.00	12.50	20.00	—

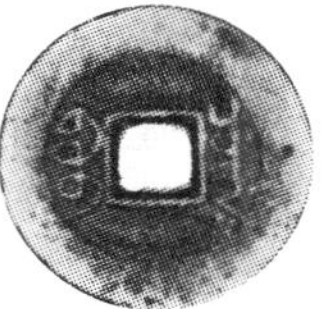

C# 24-4a CASH

Cast Copper **Obv. Inscription:** Hsien-fêng T'ung-pao **Mint:** Chuan **Note:** Reduced size.

Date	Mintage	Good	VG	F	VF	XF
ND(1851-61)	—	1.50	3.00	4.00	5.00	—

C# 24-5 10 CASH
Cast Brass **Obverse:** Type B-1 **Obv. Inscription:** Hsien-fêng Chung-pao **Reverse:** Type 1 mint mark **Mint:** Chuan

Date	Mintage	Good	VG	F	VF	XF
ND(1851-61)	—	15.00	25.00	35.00	60.00	—

C# 24-5.1 10 CASH
Cast Brass **Obv. Inscription:** Hsien-fêng Chung-pao **Reverse:** Type II mint mark **Mint:** Chuan

Date	Mintage	Good	VG	F	VF	XF
ND(1851-61)	—	35.00	45.00	60.00	85.00	—

C# 24-6 50 CASH
Cast Brass **Obverse:** Type B-1 **Obv. Inscription:** Hsien-fêng Chung-pao **Reverse:** Type II mint mark **Mint:** Chuan

Date	Mintage	Good	VG	F	VF	XF
ND(1851-61)	—	55.00	75.00	100	135	—

C# 24-7 100 CASH
Cast Brass **Obverse:** Type C **Obv. Inscription:** Hsien-fêng Yüan-pao **Reverse:** Type II mint mark **Mint:** Chuan

Date	Mintage	Good	VG	F	VF	XF
ND(1851-61)	—	22.50	35.00	50.00	72.50	—

T'ung-chih
1862-1875

PROVINCIAL CAST COINAGE

C# 24-8 CASH
Cast Copper **Obverse:** Type A-2 **Obv. Inscription:** T'ung-chih T'ung-pao **Mint:** Chuan

Date	Mintage	Good	VG	F	VF	XF
ND(1862-74)	—	5.00	8.00	12.50	20.00	—

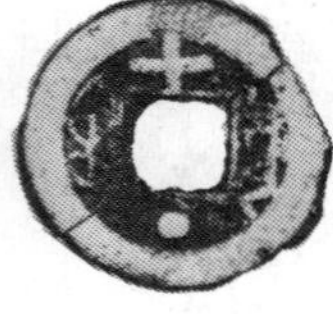

C# 24-8.1 CASH
Cast Copper **Obv. Inscription:** T'ung-chih T'ung-pao **Reverse:** Character "Shih" (ten) above and dot below **Mint:** Chuan

Date	Mintage	Good	VG	F	VF	XF
ND(1862-74)	—	5.00	8.00	12.50	20.00	—

C# 24-8.2 CASH
Cast Copper **Obv. Inscription:** T'ung-chih T'ung-pao **Reverse:** Character "Shih" (ten) above and crescent on end below **Mint:** Chuan

Date	Mintage	Good	VG	F	VF	XF
ND(1862-74)	—	5.00	8.00	12.50	20.00	—

C# 24-8.3 CASH
Cast Copper **Obv. Inscription:** T'ung-chih T'ung-pao **Reverse:** Character "Shih" above and "San" below **Mint:** Chuan

Date	Mintage	Good	VG	F	VF	XF
ND(1862-74)	—	5.00	8.00	12.50	20.00	—

C# 24-8.4 CASH
Cast Copper **Obv. Inscription:** T'ung-chih T'ung-pao **Reverse:** Character "Shih" above and "Lin" below **Mint:** Chuan

Date	Mintage	Good	VG	F	VF	XF
ND(1862-74)	—	5.00	8.00	12.50	20.00	—

C# 24-8.5 CASH
Cast Copper **Obv. Inscription:** T'ung-chih T'ung-pao **Reverse:** Character "Wen" above and "Yi" below **Mint:** Chuan

Date	Mintage	Good	VG	F	VF	XF
ND(1862-74)	—	5.00	8.00	12.50	20.00	—

C# 24-8.6 CASH
Cast Copper **Obv. Inscription:** T'ung-chih T'ung-pao **Reverse:** Character "Wen" above and "Ch'i" below **Mint:** Chuan

Date	Mintage	Good	VG	F	VF	XF
ND(1862-74)	—	5.00	8.00	12.50	20.00	—

C# 24-8.7 CASH
Cast Copper **Obv. Inscription:** T'ung-chih T'ung-pao **Reverse:** Character "Wen" above and "Ch'uan" below **Mint:** Chuan

Date	Mintage	Good	VG	F	VF	XF
ND(1862-74)	—	5.00	8.00	12.50	20.00	—

Note: Refer to "Additional Characters" chart in the introduction to China

Kuang-hsü
1875-1908

PROVINCIAL CAST COINAGE

C# 24-9 CASH
Cast Brass **Obv. Inscription:** Kuang-hsü T'ung-pao **Reverse:** Manchu inscription **Rev. Inscription:** Boo-Cuwan **Mint:** Chuan
Note: Struck at Chuan (Cheng tu)

Date	Mintage	Good	VG	F	VF	XF
ND(1875-1908)	—	4.50	7.50	11.50	22.50	—

C# 24-10 10 CASH
Cast Brass **Obv. Inscription:** Kuang-hsü Chung-pao **Reverse:** Type I mint mark **Mint:** Chuan

Date	Mintage	Good	VG	F	VF	XF
ND(1875-80) Rare	—	—	—	—	—	—

MILLED COINAGE

Y# 234 5 CENTS
1.3000 g., 0.8200 Silver .0343 oz. ASW **Obv. Inscription:** Kuang-hsü Yüan-pao

Date	Mintage	VG	F	VF	XF	Unc
ND(1898; 1901-08)	671,000	4.50	12.50	17.50	30.00	80.00

Y# 235 10 CENTS
2.6000 g., 0.8200 Silver .0686 oz. ASW **Obv. Inscription:** Kuang-hsü Yüan-pao

Date	Mintage	VG	F	VF	XF	Unc
ND(1898; 1901-08)	1,274,000	3.50	10.00	20.00	30.00	90.00

Y# 236 20 CENTS
5.3000 g., 0.8200 Silver .1397 oz. ASW **Obv. Inscription:** Kuang-hsü Yüan-pao **Reverse:** Five flames on pearl

Date	Mintage	VG	F	VF	XF	Unc
ND(1898; 1901-08)	897,000	3.50	10.00	20.00	40.00	100

Y# 236.1 20 CENTS
5.3000 g., 0.8200 Silver .1397 oz. ASW **Obv. Inscription:** Kuang-hsü Yüan-pao **Reverse:** Six flames on pearl

Date	Mintage	VG	F	VF	XF	Unc
ND(1898; 1901-08)	Inc. above	3.50	10.00	20.00	40.00	100

Y# 236.2 20 CENTS
5.3000 g., 0.8200 Silver .1397 oz. ASW **Obv. Inscription:** Kuang-hsü Yüan-pao **Reverse:** Seven flames on pearl

Date	Mintage	VG	F	VF	XF	Unc
ND(1898; 1901-08)	Inc. above	3.50	10.00	20.00	40.00	100

Y# 237 50 CENTS
13.2000 g., 0.8600 Silver .3650 oz. ASW **Obv. Inscription:** Kuang-hsü Yüan-pao **Reverse:** Dragon with narrow face, small cross at either side, large fireball

Date	Mintage	VG	F	VF	XF	Unc
ND(1898; 1901-08)	474,000	7.50	22.50	40.00	100	300

PATTERNS

Including off metal strikes

KM#	Date	Mintage	Identification	Mkt Val
Pn4	ND(1896)	—	30 Cash. Copper. Front view dragon. Y#233.	—
Pn5	ND(1896)	—	30 Cash. Brass. Y#233.	—
Pn6	ND(1896)	—	30 Cash. Copper. Flying dragon.	—
Pn7	ND(1896)	—	30 Cash. Brass.	—
Pn8	ND(1898)	—	5 Cents. Brass. Y#234.	350
Pn9	ND(1898)	—	10 Cents. Brass. Y#235.	350
Pn10	ND(1898)	—	20 Cents. Silver. K#142.	1,500
Pn11	ND(1898)	—	20 Cents. Brass. Y#236.	—
Pn12	ND(1898)	—	50 Cents. Silver. K#141.	3,500
Pn13	ND(1898)	—	50 Cents. Brass. Y#237.	550

KM#	Date	Mintage	Identification	Mkt Val
Pn14	ND(1898)	—	Dollar. Silver. K#140.	10,000
Pn15	ND(1898)	—	Dollar. Brass. Y#238.	850

PIEFORTS

KM#	Date	Mintage	Identification	Mkt Val
P1	ND(1898)	—	5 Cents. White Metal. Y#234.	350

TAIWAN

Chinese migration to Taiwan began as early as the sixth century. The Dutch established a base on the island in 1624 and held it until 1661, when they were driven out by supporters of the Ming dynasty who used it as a base for their unsuccessful attempt to displace the ruling Manchu dynasty of mainland China. After being occupied by Manchu forces in 1683, Taiwan remained under the suzerainty of China until its cession to Japan in 1895. The island was part of the province of Fukien (Fujian) until established as a separate province in the period 1885-1895. (It took 10 years to complete the conversion to a full-fledged province.)

EMPIRE

Tao-kuang
1821-1851

REBEL COINAGE
1837-1845

Issued by Chang Wen in the town of Chiayi, Taiwan (Formosa)

C# 25-3 DOLLAR
26.8000 g., Silver **Obverse:** "Old Man", God of Longevity **Reverse:** Sacrificial vase **Note:** Kann #1.

Date	Mintage	VG	F	VF	XF	Unc
ND(1837-45)	—	350	600	1,200	2,500	—

Hsien-fêng
1851-1861

PROVINCIAL CAST COINAGE

C# 25-6 CASH
Cast Brass **Obverse:** Type A **Obv. Inscription:** Hsien-fêng T'ung-pao **Mint:** Tai

Date	Mintage	Good	VG	F	VF	XF
ND(1851-61)	—	4.00	10.00	16.00	25.00	—

REBEL COINAGE
1853

Issued by Lin Kung in Fung-shan District, Taiwan (Formosa) as military pay.

C# 25-4 DOLLAR
26.8000 g., Silver **Obverse:** Floral vase **Reverse:** Crossed lotus flowers **Note:** Kann #2.

Date	Mintage	VG	F	VF	XF	Unc
ND(1853)	—	300	600	1,200	3,500	—

Note: This coin usually comes with two maker's chops (one being a Chinese numeral "six") on the reverse

Tung-chih
1862-1875

PROVINCIAL CAST COINAGE

 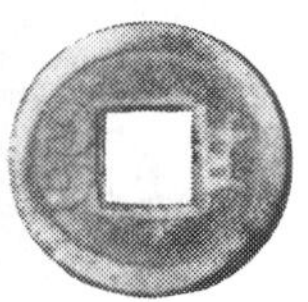

C# 25-9 CASH
Cast Brass **Obv. Inscription:** T'ung-chih T'ung-pao **Mint:** Tai

Date	Mintage	Good	VG	F	VF	XF
ND(1862-74)	—	8.00	20.00	32.50	50.00	—

REBEL COINAGE
1862

Issued by General Tai Chou-chung in Taiwan (Formosa)

K# 3 DOLLAR
25.0000 g., Silver **Obverse:** God of Longevity, Chinese inscription **Obv. Inscription:** Chia Yi Hsien Tsao

Date	Mintage	VG	F	VF	XF	Unc
1(1862)	—	1,800	3,000	4,500	6,500	—

Note: Market valuations for the dollar coins above are for specimens with a few light chops, for unchopped specimens add 10 percent, and for heavily chopped specimens deduct 20 percent

C# 25-5 DOLLAR
25.3000 g., Silver **Obverse:** Floral vase **Reverse:** Crossed brushes **Note:** Kann #4.

Date	Mintage	VG	F	VF	XF	Unc
ND(1862)	—	300	700	1,500	3,700	—

Note: The market values shown for C#25-3/25-5 are for coins which have been lightly chopmarked; Attribution of C#25-4 and C#25-5 to Taiwan is not fully accepted; Other sources attribute these coins to Chihli (Hebei) Province

Kuang-hsü
1875-1908

MILLED COINAGE

Y# 246 5 CENTS
1.3000 g., 0.8200 Silver .0343 oz. ASW **Mint:** Taiwan **Note:** Similar to 10 Cents, Y#247.

Date	Mintage	F	VF	XF	Unc
ND(1893-94)	—	200	350	500	1,000

Y# 247 10 CENTS
2.7000 g., 0.8200 Silver .0712 oz. ASW **Obverse:** Four Chinese characters above meaning: "Made in Taiwan"; large characters in outside circle; small characters inside **Mint:** Taiwan

Date	Mintage	F	VF	XF	Unc
ND(1893-94)	—	80.00	175	400	600

Y# 247.1 10 CENTS
2.7000 g., 0.8200 Silver .0712 oz. ASW **Obverse:** Smaller characters in outside circle, larger characters inside circle **Mint:** Taiwan

DateT	Mintage	F	VF	XF	Unc
ND(1893-94)	—	80.00	175	400	600

Y# 247.2 10 CENTS
2.7000 g., 0.8200 Silver .0712 oz. ASW **Obverse:** Four Chinese characters above meaning: "Made in Tai Province" **Mint:** Taiwan

Date	Mintage	F	VF	XF	Unc
ND(1893-94)	—	150	250	500	750

Y# 248 20 CENTS
5.4000 g., 0.8200 Silver .1424 oz. ASW **Obverse:** Four Chinese characters above meaning "Made in Taiwan" **Mint:** Taiwan

Date	Mintage	F	VF	XF	Unc
ND(1894) Rare	—	—	—	—	—

Y# 248.1 20 CENTS
5.4000 g., 0.8200 Silver .1424 oz. ASW **Obverse:** Four Chinese characters above meaning "Made in Tai Province" **Mint:** Taiwan

Date	Mintage	F	VF	XF	Unc
ND(1894) Rare	—	—	—	—	—

YUNNAN PROVINCE

A province located in south China bordering Burma, Laos and Vietnam. It is very mountainous with many lakes. Yunnan was the home of various active imperial mints. A modern mint was established at Kunming in 1905 and the first struck copper coins were issued in 1906 and the first struck silver coins in 1908. General Tang Chi-yao issued coins in gold, silver and copper with his portrait in 1919. The last Republican coins were struck here in 1949.

EMPIRE

Tao-kuang
1821-1851

PROVINCIAL CAST COINAGE

C# 27-2 CASH
Cast Brass **Obv. Inscription:** Tao-kuang T'ung-pao **Reverse:** Type 1 mint mark **Mint:** Tung

Date	Mintage	Good	VG	F	VF	XF
ND(1821-50)	—	0.50	1.00	1.50	2.50	—

C# 27-2.1 CASH
Cast Brass **Obv. Inscription:** Tao-kuang T'ung-pao **Reverse:** Type 3 mint mark **Mint:** Tung

Date	Mintage	Good	VG	F	VF	XF
ND(1821-51)	—	0.50	1.00	1.50	2.50	—

C# 26-3 CASH
Cast Brass **Obv. Inscription:** Tao-kuang T'ung-pao **Mint:** Yün

Date	Mintage	Good	VG	F	VF	XF
ND(1821-51)	—	0.25	0.50	0.75	1.25	—

C# 26-3.1 CASH
Cast Brass **Obv. Inscription:** Tao-kuang T'ung-pao **Reverse:** Crescent above **Mint:** Yün

Date	Mintage	Good	VG	F	VF	XF
ND(1821-51)	—	2.50	3.50	5.00	7.50	—

C# 26-3.2 CASH
Cast Brass **Obv. Inscription:** Tao-kuang T'ung-pao **Reverse:** Horizontal line above **Mint:** Yün

Date	Mintage	Good	VG	F	VF	XF
ND(1821-51)	—	1.50	2.00	4.00	6.00	—

Hsien-fêng
1851-1861

PROVINCIAL CAST COINAGE

KM# 1 CASH
Cast Brass **Obverse:** Type A-2 **Obv. Inscription:** Hsien-fêng T'ung-pao **Reverse:** Crescent above **Mint:** Chou

Date	Mintage	Good	VG	F	VF	XF
ND(1851-61)	—	10.00	15.00	20.00	25.00	—

KM# 2 CASH
Cast Brass **Obv. Inscription:** Hsien-fêng T'ung-pao **Reverse:** Circle above **Mint:** Chou

Date	Mintage	Good	VG	F	VF	XF
ND(1851-61)	—	10.00	15.00	20.00	25.00	—

C# 26-4 CASH
Cast Brass, 24 mm. **Obverse:** Type A **Obv. Inscription:** Hsien-fêng T'ung-pao **Mint:** Yün

Date	Mintage	Good	VG	F	VF	XF
ND(1851-61)	—	0.50	1.00	1.50	2.50	—

C# 26-4.1 CASH
Cast Brass **Obv. Inscription:** Hsien-fêng T'ung-pao **Reverse:** Crescent above **Mint:** Yün **Note:** Size varies: 20-22mm.

Date	Mintage	Good	VG	F	VF	XF
ND(1851-61)	—	5.00	7.50	10.00	15.00	—

C# 26-4.2 CASH
Cast Brass **Obv. Inscription:** Hsien-fêng T'ung-pao **Reverse:** Crescent below **Mint:** Yün **Note:** Size varies: 20-22mm.

Date	Mintage	Good	VG	F	VF	XF
ND(1851-61)	—	5.00	7.50	10.00	15.00	—

C# 26-4.3 CASH
Cast Brass **Obv. Inscription:** Hsien-fêng T'ung-pao **Reverse:** Crescent standing on end above **Mint:** Yün **Note:** Size varies: 20-22mm.

Date	Mintage	Good	VG	F	VF	XF
ND(1851-61)	—	5.00	7.50	10.00	15.00	—

C# 26-4.4 CASH
Cast Brass **Obv. Inscription:** Hsien-fêng T'ung-pao **Reverse:** Dot within crescent above (Pregnant Moon) **Mint:** Yün **Note:** Size varies: 20-22mm.

Date	Mintage	Good	VG	F	VF	XF
ND(1851-61)	—	5.00	7.50	10.00	15.00	—

C# 26-4.5 CASH
Cast Brass **Obv. Inscription:** Hsien-fêng T'ung-pao **Reverse:** Circle above **Mint:** Yün **Note:** Size varies: 20-22mm.

Date	Mintage	Good	VG	F	VF	XF
ND(1851-61)	—	5.00	7.50	10.00	15.00	—

C# 26-4.6 CASH
Cast Brass **Obv. Inscription:** Hsien-fêng T'ung-pao **Reverse:** Circle below **Mint:** Yün **Note:** Size varies: 20-22mm.

Date	Mintage	Good	VG	F	VF	XF
ND(1851-61)	—	5.00	7.50	10.00	15.00	—

C# 26-4.7 CASH
Cast Brass Obv. Designer: Hsien-fêng T'ung-pao **Reverse:** Dot within circle above **Mint:** Yün **Note:** Size varies: 20-22mm.

Date	Mintage	Good	VG	F	VF	XF
ND(1851-61)	—	5.00	7.50	10.00	15.00	—

C# 26-4.8 CASH
Cast Brass **Obv. Inscription:** Hsien-fêng T'ung-pao **Reverse:** Dot within circle below **Mint:** Yün **Note:** Size varies: 20-22mm.

Date	Mintage	Good	VG	F	VF	XF
ND(1851-61)	—	5.00	7.50	10.00	15.00	—

C# 26-4.9 CASH
Cast Brass **Obv. Inscription:** Hsien-fêng T'ung-pao **Reverse:** An X above the center **Mint:** Yün **Note:** Size varies: 20-22mm.

Date	Mintage	Good	VG	F	VF	XF
ND(1851-61)	—	5.00	7.50	10.00	15.00	—

C# 26-4.10 CASH
Cast Brass **Obv. Inscription:** Hsien-fêng T'ung-pao **Reverse:** Character "Ho" above and circle below **Mint:** Yün **Note:** Size varies: 20-22mm.

Date	Mintage	Good	VG	F	VF	XF
ND(1851-61)	—	5.00	7.50	10.00	15.00	—

C# 26-4.11 CASH
Cast Brass **Obv. Inscription:** Hsien-fêng T'ung-pao **Reverse:** Character "Ho" above and dot within circle below **Mint:** Yün **Note:** Size varies: 20-22mm.

Date	Mintage	Good	VG	F	VF	XF
ND(1851-61)	—	5.00	7.50	10.00	15.00	—

C# 26-4.12 CASH
Cast Brass **Obv. Inscription:** Hsien-fêng T'ung-pao **Reverse:** Character "Kung" above **Mint:** Yün **Note:** Size varies: 20-22mm.

Date	Mintage	Good	VG	F	VF	XF
ND(1851-61)	—	5.00	7.50	10.00	15.00	—

C# 26-4.13 CASH
Cast Brass **Obv. Inscription:** Hsien-fêng T'ung-pao **Reverse:** Character "Yi" (one) above **Mint:** Yün **Note:** Size varies: 20-22mm.

Date	Mintage	Good	VG	F	VF	XF
ND(1851-61)	—	5.00	7.50	10.00	15.00	—

C# 26-4.14 CASH
Cast Brass **Obv. Inscription:** Hsien-fêng T'ung-pao **Reverse:** Character "Erh" above **Mint:** Yün **Note:** Size varies: 20-22mm.

Date	Mintage	Good	VG	F	VF	XF
ND(1851-61)	—	—	—	—	—	—

Note: Reported, not confirmed

C# 26-4.15 CASH
Cast Brass **Obv. Inscription:** Hsien-fêng T'ung-pao **Reverse:** Character "San" (three) above **Mint:** Yün **Note:** Size varies: 20-22mm.

Date	Mintage	Good	VG	F	VF	XF
ND(1851-61)	—	5.00	7.50	10.00	15.00	—

C# 26-4.16 CASH
Cast Brass **Obv. Inscription:** Hsien-fêng T'ung-pao **Reverse:** Character "Szu" (four) above **Mint:** Yün **Note:** Size varies: 20-22mm.

Date	Mintage	Good	VG	F	VF	XF
ND(1851-61)	—	5.00	7.50	10.00	15.00	—

C# 26-4.17 CASH
Cast Brass **Obv. Inscription:** Hsien-fêng T'ung-pao **Reverse:** Character above probably meaning "five" **Mint:** Yün **Note:** Size varies: 20-22mm.

Date	Mintage	Good	VG	F	VF	XF
ND(1851-61)	—	5.00	7.50	10.00	15.00	—

C# 26-4.18 CASH
Cast Brass **Obv. Inscription:** Hsien-fêng T'ung-pao **Reverse:** Character "Shih" (ten) above and a crescent below **Mint:** Yün **Note:** Size varies: 20-22mm.

Date	Mintage	Good	VG	F	VF	XF
ND(1851-61)	—	5.00	7.50	10.00	15.00	—

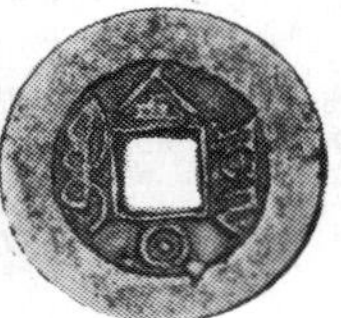

C# 26-4.19 CASH
Cast Brass **Obv. Inscription:** Hsien-fêng T'ung-pao **Reverse:** Character "Chin" above and dot in circle below **Mint:** Yün **Note:** Size varies: 20-22mm.

Date	Mintage	Good	VG	F	VF	XF
ND(1851-61)	—	5.00	7.50	10.00	15.00	—

C# 26-4.20 CASH
Cast Brass **Obv. Inscription:** Hsien-fêng T'ung-pao **Reverse:** Manchu words above **Mint:** Yün **Note:** Size varies: 20-22mm.

Date	Mintage	Good	VG	F	VF	XF
ND(1851-61)	—	5.00	7.50	10.00	15.00	—

C# 26-4.22 CASH
Cast Brass **Obv. Inscription:** Hsien-fêng T'ung-pao **Reverse:** "Yuan" above and inverted crescent below hole **Mint:** Yün **Note:** Size varies: 20-22mm.

Date	Mintage	Good	VG	F	VF	XF
ND(1851-61)	—	5.00	7.50	10.00	15.00	—

C# 27-3 CASH
Cast Brass **Obverse:** Type A **Obv. Inscription:** Hsien-fêng T'ung-pao **Mint:** Tung

Date	Mintage	Good	VG	F	VF	XF
ND(1851-61)	—	2.00	4.00	5.00	7.00	—

C# 27-3.1 CASH
Cast Brass **Obv. Inscription:** Hsien-fêng T'ung-pao **Reverse:** Character "Cheng" above **Mint:** Tung

C# 26-5 10 CASH
Cast Brass **Obverse:** Type B-1 **Obv. Inscription:** Hsien-fêng Chung-pao **Mint:** Yün **Note:** Size varies: 37-39mm.

Date	Mintage	Good	VG	F	VF	XF
ND(1851-61)	—	2.00	5.00	7.00	15.00	—

C# 26-5.1 10 CASH
Cast Brass **Obv. Inscription:** Hsien-fêng Chung-pao **Reverse:** Dot at upper left **Mint:** Yün **Note:** Size varies: 37-39mm.

Date	Mintage	Good	VG	F	VF	XF
ND(1851-61)	—	20.00	40.00	70.00	90.00	—

C# 27-4 10 CASH
Cast Brass **Obverse:** Type B-1 **Obv. Inscription:** Hsien-fêng Chung-pao **Mint:** Tung

Date	Mintage	Good	VG	F	VF	XF
ND(1851-61)	—	5.00	9.00	16.00	30.00	—

C# 26-6 50 CASH
Cast Brass **Obv. Inscription:** Hsien-fêng Chung-pao **Mint:** Yün

Date	Mintage	Good	VG	F	VF	XF
ND(1851-61)	—	50.00	60.00	70.00	90.00	—

T'ung-chih
1862-1875

PROVINCIAL CAST COINAGE

KM# 46 CASH
Cast Brass **Obv. Inscription:** T'ung-chih T'ung-pao **Reverse:** Character "Ts'ai" above **Mint:** Chou

Date	Mintage	Good	VG	F	VF	XF
ND(1862-74)	—	12.00	20.00	35.00	50.00	—

KM# 22 CASH
Cast Brass **Obv. Inscription:** T'ung-chih T'ung-pao **Reverse:** Character "Cheng" above and circle below **Mint:** Chou

Date	Mintage	Good	VG	F	VF	XF
ND(1862-74)	—	12.00	20.00	35.00	50.00	—

KM# 23 CASH
Cast Brass **Obv. Inscription:** T'ung-chih T'ung-pao **Reverse:** Character "Chih" above **Mint:** Chou

Date	Mintage	Good	VG	F	VF	XF
ND(1862-74)	—	12.00	20.00	35.00	50.00	—

KM# 10 CASH
Cast Brass **Obverse:** Type A-2 **Obv. Inscription:** T'ung-chih T'ung-pao **Reverse:** Without characters above or below center hole **Mint:** Chou

Date	Mintage	Good	VG	F	VF	XF
ND(1862-74)	—	5.00	12.00	20.00	25.00	—

C# 26-7.9 CASH
Cast Brass **Obv. Inscription:** T'ung-chih T'ung-pao **Reverse:** Character "Ta" above **Mint:** Yün

Date	Mintage	Good	VG	F	VF	XF
ND(1862-74)	—	5.00	7.50	10.00	15.00	—

C# 26-7 CASH
Cast Brass **Obverse:** Type A-2 **Obv. Inscription:** T'ung-chih T'ung-pao **Mint:** Yün **Note:** Varieties with wide and narrow rims exist.

Date	Mintage	Good	VG	F	VF	XF
ND(1862-74)	—	1.50	3.00	4.00	6.00	—

KM# 11 CASH
Cast Brass **Obv. Inscription:** T'ung-chih T'ung-pao **Reverse:** Crescent above **Mint:** Chou

Date	Mintage	Good	VG	F	VF	XF
ND(1862-74)	—	5.00	12.00	20.00	25.00	—

C# 26-7.1 CASH
Cast Brass **Obv. Inscription:** T'ung-chih T'ung-pao **Reverse:** Circle above **Mint:** Yün

Date	Mintage	Good	VG	F	VF	XF
ND(1862-74)	—	5.00	7.50	10.00	15.00	—

C# 26-7.2 CASH
Cast Brass **Obv. Inscription:** T'ung-chih T'ung-pao **Reverse:** Dot within circle above **Mint:** Yün

Date	Mintage	Good	VG	F	VF	XF
ND(1862-74)	—	5.00	7.50	10.00	15.00	—

 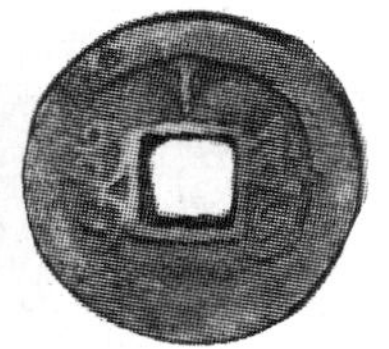

KM# 12 CASH
Cast Brass **Obv. Inscription:** T'ung-chih T'ung-pao **Reverse:** Vertical line above **Mint:** Chou

Date	Mintage	Good	VG	F	VF	XF
ND(1862-74)	—	12.00	20.00	35.00	50.00	—

KM# 13 CASH
Cast Brass **Obv. Inscription:** T'ung-chih T'ung-pao **Reverse:** Vertical line below **Mint:** Chou

Date	Mintage	Good	VG	F	VF	XF
ND(1862-74)	—	12.00	20.00	35.00	50.00	—

C# 26-7.3 CASH
Cast Brass **Obv. Inscription:** T'ung-chih T'ung-pao **Reverse:** Dot within crescent above **Mint:** Yün

Date	Mintage	Good	VG	F	VF	XF
ND(1862-74)	—	5.00	7.50	10.00	15.00	—

KM# 14 CASH
Cast Brass **Obv. Inscription:** T'ung-chih T'ung-pao **Reverse:** Dot above **Mint:** Chou

Date	Mintage	Good	VG	F	VF	XF
ND(1862-74)	—	12.00	20.00	35.00	50.00	—

C# 26-7.4 CASH
Cast Brass **Obv. Inscription:** T'ung-chih T'ung-pao **Reverse:** Crescent below **Mint:** Yün

Date	Mintage	Good	VG	F	VF	XF
ND(1862-74)	—	5.00	7.50	10.00	15.00	—

C# 26-7.5 CASH
Cast Brass **Obv. Inscription:** T'ung-chih T'ung-pao **Reverse:** Vertical line above **Mint:** Yün

Date	Mintage	Good	VG	F	VF	XF
ND(1862-74)	—	5.00	7.50	10.00	15.00	—

KM# 15 CASH
Cast Brass **Obv. Inscription:** T'ung-chih T'ung-pao **Reverse:** Dot below **Mint:** Chou

Date	Mintage	Good	VG	F	VF	XF
ND(1862-74)	—	12.00	20.00	35.00	50.00	—

KM# 16 CASH
Cast Brass **Obv. Inscription:** T'ung-chih T'ung-pao **Reverse:** With "X" above **Mint:** Chou

Date	Mintage	Good	VG	F	VF	XF
ND(1862-74)	—	12.00	20.00	35.00	50.00	—

C# 26-7.6 CASH
Cast Brass **Obv. Inscription:** T'ung-chih T'ung-pao **Reverse:** Vertical line below **Mint:** Yün

Date	Mintage	Good	VG	F	VF	XF
ND(1862-74)	—	5.00	7.50	10.00	15.00	—

C# 26-7.7 CASH
Cast Brass **Obv. Inscription:** T'ung-chih T'ung-pao **Reverse:** Character "Kung" above center **Mint:** Yün

Date	Mintage	Good	VG	F	VF	XF
ND(1862-74)	—	5.00	7.50	10.00	15.00	—

 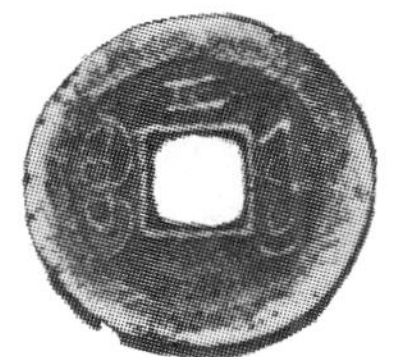

KM# 21 CASH
Cast Brass **Obv. Inscription:** T'ung-chih T'ung-pao **Reverse:** Character "Cheng" above **Mint:** Chou

Date	Mintage	Good	VG	F	VF	XF
ND(1862-74)	—	12.00	20.00	35.00	50.00	—

KM# 25 CASH
Cast Brass **Obv. Inscription:** T'ung-chih T'ung-pao **Reverse:** Character "Chu" above **Mint:** Chou

Date	Mintage	Good	VG	F	VF	XF
ND(1862-74)	—	12.00	20.00	35.00	50.00	—

C# 26-7.8 CASH
Cast Brass **Obv. Inscription:** T'ung-chih T'ung-pao **Reverse:** Character "Ho" above **Mint:** Yün

Date	Mintage	Good	VG	F	VF	XF
ND(1862-74)	—	5.00	7.50	10.00	15.00	—

KM# 27 CASH
Cast Brass **Obv. Inscription:** T'ung-chih T'ung-pao **Reverse:** Character "Ch'uan" above **Mint:** Chou

Date	Mintage	Good	VG	F	VF	XF
ND(1862-74)	—	12.00	20.00	35.00	50.00	—

Cast Brass **Obv. Inscription:** T'ung-chih T'ung-pao **Reverse:** Character "Ch'uan" above **Mint:** Chou

Date	Mintage	Good	VG	F	VF	XF
ND(1862-74)	—	12.00	20.00	35.00	50.00	—

KM# 29 CASH

Cast Brass **Obv. Inscription:** T'ung-chih T'ung-pao **Reverse:** Character "Chung" above **Mint:** Chou

Date	Mintage	Good	VG	F	VF	XF
ND(1862-74)	—	12.00	20.00	35.00	50.00	—

C# 26-7.10 CASH

Cast Brass **Obv. Inscription:** T'ung-chih T'ung-pao **Reverse:** Character "Shan" above **Mint:** Yün

Date	Mintage	Good	VG	F	VF	XF
ND(1862-74)	—	5.00	7.50	10.00	15.00	—

C# 26-7.11 CASH

Cast Brass **Obv. Inscription:** T'ung-chih T'ung-pao **Reverse:** Character "Ch'uan" below **Mint:** Yün

Date	Mintage	Good	VG	F	VF	XF
ND(1862-74)	—	5.00	7.50	10.00	15.00	—

KM# 31 CASH

Cast Brass **Obv. Inscription:** T'ung-chih T'ung-pao **Reverse:** Character "Feng" above **Mint:** Chou

Date	Mintage	Good	VG	F	VF	XF
ND(1862-74)	—	12.00	20.00	35.00	50.00	—

KM# 33 CASH

Cast Brass **Obv. Inscription:** T'ung-chih T'ung-pao **Reverse:** Character "Ho" above **Mint:** Chou

Date	Mintage	Good	VG	F	VF	XF
ND(1862-74)	—	12.00	20.00	35.00	50.00	—

C# 26-7.12 CASH

Cast Brass **Obv. Inscription:** T'ung-chih T'ung-pao **Reverse:** Character "Yi" (one) below **Mint:** Yün

Date	Mintage	Good	VG	F	VF	XF
ND(1862-74)	—	5.00	7.50	10.00	15.00	—

C# 26-7.13 CASH

Cast Brass **Obv. Inscription:** T'ung-chih T'ung-pao **Reverse:** Character "Wu" (five) inverted below **Mint:** Tung

Date	Mintage	Good	VG	F	VF	XF
ND(1862-74)	—	5.00	7.50	10.00	15.00	—

KM# 35 CASH

Cast Brass **Obv. Inscription:** T'ung-chih T'ung-pao **Reverse:** Character "Jen" above **Mint:** Chou

Date	Mintage	Good	VG	F	VF	XF
ND(1862-74)	—	12.00	20.00	35.00	50.00	—

KM# 37 CASH

Cast Brass **Obv. Inscription:** T'ung-chih T'ung-pao **Reverse:** Character "Kung" above **Mint:** Chou

Date	Mintage	Good	VG	F	VF	XF
ND(1862-74)	—	12.00	20.00	35.00	50.00	—

C# 26-7.14 CASH

Cast Brass **Obv. Inscription:** T'ung-chih T'ung-pao **Reverse:** Character "Liu" (six) above **Mint:** Yün

Date	Mintage	Good	VG	F	VF	XF
ND(1862-74)	—	5.00	7.50	10.00	15.00	—

C# 26-7.15 CASH

Cast Brass **Obv. Inscription:** T'ung-chih T'ung-pao **Reverse:** Character "Liu" (six) above, but sideways **Mint:** Yün

Date	Mintage	Good	VG	F	VF	XF
ND(1862-74)	—	5.00	7.50	10.00	15.00	—

KM# 39 CASH

Cast Brass **Obv. Inscription:** T'ung-chih T'ung-pao **Reverse:** Character "Shang" above **Mint:** Chou

Date	Mintage	Good	VG	F	VF	XF
ND(1862-74)	—	12.00	20.00	35.00	50.00	—

KM# 41 CASH

Cast Brass **Obv. Inscription:** T'ung-chih T'ung-pao **Reverse:** Character "Shun" above **Mint:** Chou

Date	Mintage	Good	VG	F	VF	XF
ND(1862-74)	—	12.00	20.00	35.00	50.00	—

C# 26-7.16 CASH

Cast Brass **Obv. Inscription:** T'ung-chih T'ung-pao **Reverse:** Character "Pa" (eight) above **Mint:** Yün

Date	Mintage	Good	VG	F	VF	XF
ND(1862-74)	—	5.00	7.50	10.00	15.00	—

C# 26-7.17 CASH

Cast Brass **Obv. Inscription:** T'ung-chih T'ung-pao **Reverse:** Character "Shih" (ten) above **Mint:** Yün

Date	Mintage	Good	VG	F	VF	XF
ND(1862-74)	—	5.00	7.50	10.00	15.00	—

KM# 43 CASH

Cast Brass **Obv. Inscription:** T'ung-chih T'ung-pao **Reverse:** Character "Hsin" above **Mint:** Chou

Date	Mintage	Good	VG	F	VF	XF
ND(1862-74)	—	12.00	20.00	35.00	50.00	—

KM# 45 CASH

Cast Brass **Obv. Inscription:** T'ung-chih T'ung-pao **Reverse:** Character "Ta" above **Mint:** Chou

Date	Mintage	Good	VG	F	VF	XF
ND(1862-74)	—	12.00	20.00	35.00	50.00	—

C# 26-7.18 CASH

Cast Brass **Obv. Inscription:** T'ung-chih T'ung-pao **Reverse:** Character "Shih" (ten) above, crescent below **Mint:** Yün

Date	Mintage	Good	VG	F	VF	XF
ND(1862-74)	—	5.00	7.50	10.00	15.00	—

C# 26-7.19 CASH

Cast Brass **Obv. Inscription:** T'ung-chih T'ung-pao **Reverse:** Character "Shih Yi" (eleven) above **Mint:** Yün

Date	Mintage	Good	VG	F	VF	XF
ND(1862-74)	—	5.00	7.50	10.00	15.00	—

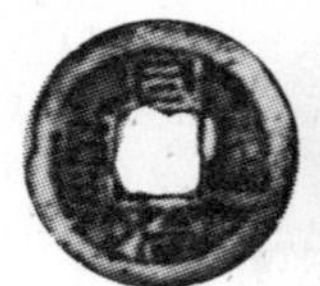

C# 26-7.20 CASH

Cast Brass **Obv. Inscription:** T'ung-chih T'ung-pao **Reverse:** Character "Shih" (ten) above and "Yi" (one) below **Mint:** Yün

Date	Mintage	Good	VG	F	VF	XF
ND(1862-74)	—	5.00	7.50	10.00	15.00	—

KM# 47 CASH

Cast Brass **Obv. Inscription:** T'ung-chih T'ung-pao **Reverse:** Character "Yu" above **Mint:** Chou

Date	Mintage	Good	VG	F	VF	XF
ND(1862-74)	—	12.00	20.00	35.00	50.00	—

KM# 49 CASH

Cast Brass **Obv. Inscription:** T'ung-chih T'ung-pao **Reverse:** Character "Yun" above **Mint:** Chou

Date	Mintage	Good	VG	F	VF	XF
ND(1862-74)	—	12.00	20.00	35.00	50.00	—

C# 26-7.21 CASH

Cast Brass **Obv. Inscription:** T'ung-chih T'ung-pao **Reverse:** Character "Shih" (ten) above and "San" (three) below **Mint:** Yün

Date	Mintage	Good	VG	F	VF	XF
ND(1862-74)	—	5.00	7.50	10.00	15.00	—

C# 26-7.22 CASH

Cast Brass **Obv. Inscription:** T'ung-chih T'ung-pao **Reverse:** Character "Jen" above **Mint:** Yün

Date	Mintage	Good	VG	F	VF	XF
ND(1862-74)	—	5.00	7.50	10.00	15.00	—

KM# 61 CASH

Cast Brass **Obv. Inscription:** T'ung-chih T'ung-pao **Reverse:** Character "Yi" (one) above **Mint:** Chou

Date	Mintage	Good	VG	F	VF	XF
ND(1862-74)	—	12.00	20.00	35.00	50.00	—

KM# 62 CASH

Cast Brass **Obv. Inscription:** T'ung-chih T'ung-pao **Reverse:** Character "Erh" (two) above **Mint:** Chou

Date	Mintage	Good	VG	F	VF	XF
ND(1862-74)	—	12.00	20.00	35.00	50.00	—

C# 26-7.23 CASH

Cast Brass **Obv. Inscription:** T'ung-chih T'ung-pao **Reverse:** Inverted crescent above **Mint:** Yün

Date	Mintage	Good	VG	F	VF	XF
ND(1862-74)	—	5.00	7.50	10.00	15.00	—

C# 27-5 CASH

Cast Brass **Obverse:** Type A-2 **Obv. Inscription:** T'ung-chih T'ung-pao **Mint:** Tung

Date	Mintage	Good	VG	F	VF	XF
ND(1862-74)	—	5.00	9.00	12.00	18.00	—

KM# 63 CASH

Cast Brass **Obv. Inscription:** T'ung-chih T'ung-pao **Reverse:** Character "San" (three) above **Mint:** Chou

Date	Mintage	Good	VG	F	VF	XF
ND(1862-74)	—	12.00	20.00	35.00	50.00	—

KM# 65 CASH

Cast Brass **Obv. Inscription:** T'ung-chih T'ung-pao **Reverse:** Character "Wu" (five) above **Mint:** Chou

Date	Mintage	Good	VG	F	VF	XF
ND(1862-74)	—	12.00	20.00	35.00	50.00	—

C# 27-5.1 CASH

Cast Brass **Obv. Inscription:** T'ung-chih T'ung-pao **Reverse:** Character "Cheng" above and crescent below **Mint:** Tung

Date	Mintage	Good	VG	F	VF	XF
ND(1862-74)	—	5.00	7.50	10.00	15.00	—

C# 27-5.2 CASH

Cast Brass **Obv. Inscription:** T'ung-chih T'ung-pao **Reverse:** Character "Cheng" above, dot below **Mint:** Tung

Date	Mintage	Good	VG	F	VF	XF
ND(1862-74)	—	5.00	7.50	10.00	15.00	—

KM# 70 CASH

Cast Brass **Obv. Inscription:** T'ung-chih T'ung-pao **Reverse:** Character "Shih" (ten) above **Mint:** Chou

Date	Mintage	Good	VG	F	VF	XF
ND(1862-74)	—	12.00	20.00	35.00	50.00	—

Note: Other varieties probably exist. Refer to "Additional Characters" chart in the introduction

C# 26-8 10 CASH

Cast Brass, 37 mm. **Obv. Inscription:** T'ung-chih Chung-pao **Mint:** Yün

Date	Mintage	Good	VG	F	VF	XF
ND(1862-74)	—	30.00	40.00	45.00	60.00	—

C# 26-8.1 10 CASH

Cast Brass, 35 mm. **Obv. Inscription:** T'ung-chih Chung-pao **Mint:** Yün

Date	Mintage	Good	VG	F	VF	XF
ND(1862-74)	—	30.00	40.00	45.00	60.00	—

Kuang-hsü
1875-1908

PROVINCIAL CAST COINAGE

C# 27-6 CASH

Cast Brass **Obv. Inscription:** Kuang-hsü T'ung-pao **Reverse:** Manchu inscription **Rev. Inscription:** Boo-dong **Mint:** Tung

Date	Mintage	Good	VG	F	VF	XF
ND(1875-1908)	—	4.00	6.50	9.00	15.00	—

C# 26-9 CASH

Cast Brass **Obv. Inscription:** Kuang-hsü T'ung-pao **Reverse:** Manchu inscription **Rev. Inscription:** Boo-yôn **Mint:** Yün

Date	Mintage	Good	VG	F	VF	XF
ND(1875-1908)	—	2.00	4.00	6.50	9.00	—

C# 26-9.1 CASH

Cast Brass **Obv. Inscription:** Kuang-hsü T'ung-pao **Reverse:** Manchu inscription, "Kung" above **Rev. Inscription:** Boo-yôn **Mint:** Yün

Date	Mintage	Good	VG	F	VF	XF
ND(1875-1908)	—	2.00	5.00	7.50	10.00	—

C# 26-9.2 CASH

Cast Brass **Obv. Inscription:** Kuang-hsü T'ung-pao **Reverse:** Manchu inscription, "Szu" (four) above **Rev. Inscription:** Boo-yôn **Mint:** Yün

Date	Mintage	Good	VG	F	VF	XF
ND(1875-1908)	—	2.50	5.00	7.50	10.00	—

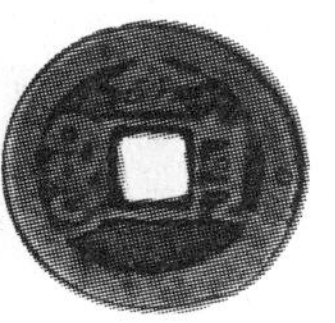

C# 26-9.3 CASH

Cast Brass **Obv. Inscription:** Kuang-hsü T'ung-pao **Reverse:** Manchu inscription, "Chin" above **Rev. Inscription:** Boo-yôn **Mint:** Yün

Date	Mintage	Good	VG	F	VF	XF
ND(1875-1908)	—	2.50	5.00	7.50	10.00	—

C# 26-9.4 CASH

Cast Brass **Obv. Inscription:** Kuang-hsü T'ung-pao **Reverse:** Manchu inscription, crescent above, dot below **Rev. Inscription:** Boo-yôn **Mint:** Yün

Date	Mintage	Good	VG	F	VF	XF
ND(1875-1908)	—	2.50	5.00	7.50	12.00	—

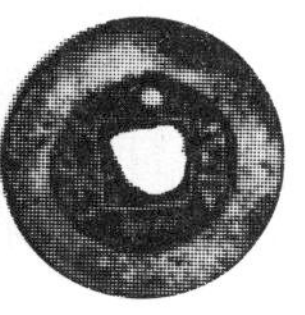

C# 26-9.5 CASH

Cast Brass **Obv. Inscription:** Kuang-hsü T'ung-pao **Reverse:** Manchu inscription, dot above hole **Rev. Inscription:** Boo-yôn **Mint:** Yün

Date	Mintage	Good	VG	F	VF	XF
ND(1875-1908)	—	2.50	5.00	7.50	12.00	—

C# 27-6.1 CASH

Cast Brass **Obv. Inscription:** Kuang-hsü T'ung-pao **Reverse:** Manchu inscription, "Chin" above **Rev. Inscription:** Boo-dong **Mint:** Tung

Date	Mintage	Good	VG	F	VF	XF
ND(1875-1908)	—	5.00	7.50	10.00	15.00	—

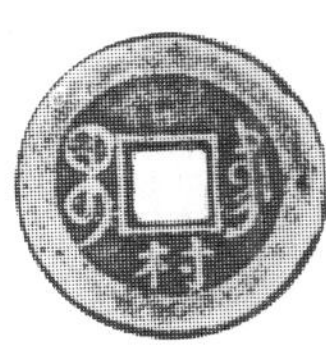

C# 27-6.2 CASH

Cast Brass **Obv. Inscription:** Kuang-hsü T'ung-pao **Reverse:** Manchu inscription, "Ts'un" below **Rev. Inscription:** Boo-dong **Mint:** Tung

Date	Mintage	Good	VG	F	VF	XF
ND(1875-1908)	—	5.00	7.50	10.00	15.00	—

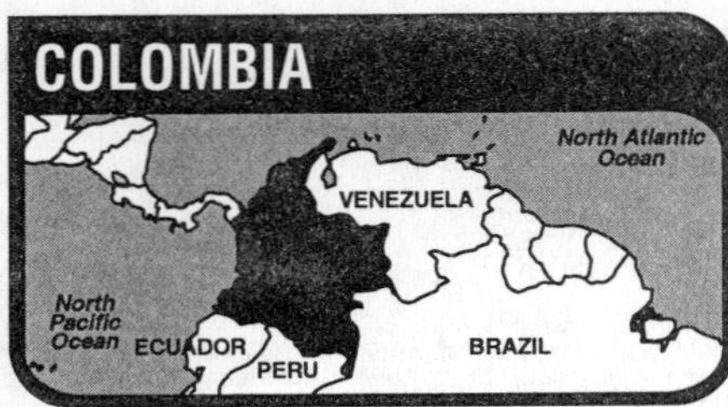

The Republic of Colombia, in the northwestern corner of South America, has an area of 440,831 sq. mi. (1,138,910 sq. km.). Capital: Bogota. The economy is primarily agricultural with a mild, rich coffee being the chief crop. Colombia has the world's largest platinum deposits and important reserves of coal, iron ore, petroleum and limestone; other precious metals and emeralds are also mined. Coffee, crude oil, bananas, sugar and emeralds are exported.

The northern coast of present Colombia was one of the first parts of the American continent to be visited by Spanish navigators. At Darien in Panama is the site of the first permanent European settlement on the American mainland in 1510. New Granada, as Colombia was known until 1861, stemmed from the settlement of Santa Marta in 1525. New Granada was established as a Spanish colony in 1549. Independence was declared in 1810, and secured in 1819 when Simon Bolivar united Colombia, Venezuela, Panama and Ecuador as the Republic of Gran Colombia. Venezuela withdrew from the Republic in 1829; Ecuador in 1830; and Panama in 1903.

RULERS

Spanish, until 1819

MINT MARKS

C, NER, NR, NRE, R, RN, S - Cartagena
B, F, FS, N, NR, S, SF - Nuevo Reino (Bogota)
A, M - Medellin (capital), Antioquia (state)
H – Heaton (Birm. England)
M, (m) - Medellin, w/o mint mark
(Mo) - Mexico City
P, PN, Pn POPAYAN - Popayan
caduceus - Bogota
floral spray - Popayan

COLONIAL

MILLED COINAGE

KM# 63 1/4 REAL

0.8458 g., 0.8960 Silver .0244 oz. **Obv:** Castle **Rev:** Lion

Date	Mintage	VG	F	VF	XF	Unc
1801/0NR	—	12.00	25.00	50.00	90.00	—
1801NR	—	10.00	20.00	40.00	100	—
1802/1NR	—	12.00	25.00	50.00	90.00	—
1802NR	—	20.00	40.00	70.00	150	—
1803/2NR	—	12.00	25.00	45.00	90.00	—
1803NR	—	15.00	30.00	50.00	90.00	—
1804NR	—	10.00	20.00	35.00	80.00	—
1805NR	—	12.00	25.00	45.00	90.00	—
1806NR	—	15.00	30.00	50.00	90.00	—
1808/6NR	—	20.00	40.00	65.00	110	—
1808NR	—	10.00	20.00	35.00	80.00	—

KM# 67.1 1/4 REAL

0.8458 g., 0.8960 Silver .0244 oz. **Obv:** Castle **Rev:** Lion

Date	Mintage	VG	F	VF	XF	Unc
1809/8NR	—	60.00	120	200	400	—
1809NR	—	30.00	60.00	100	185	—
1810/09NR	—	20.00	35.00	60.00	100	—
1810NR	—	10.00	20.00	40.00	75.00	—
1812NR	—	15.00	30.00	50.00	100	—
1816NR	—	25.00	45.00	90.00	165	—
1817NR	—	15.00	30.00	50.00	100	—
1818/7NR	—	35.00	65.00	125	185	—
1819NR	—	20.00	40.00	60.00	100	—

KM# 67.2 1/4 REAL

0.8458 g., 0.8960 Silver .0244 oz. **Note:** Similar to KM# 63.

Date	Mintage	VG	F	VF	XF	Unc
1816/26PN	—	200	400	700	1,000	—
1816PN	—	15.00	30.00	50.00	90.00	—
1816NR	—	15.00	30.00	50.00	90.00	—

KM# 57 1/2 REAL

1.6917 g., 0.8960 Silver .0487 oz. **Obv:** Bust of Charles IV

Date	Mintage	VG	F	VF	XF	Unc
1801NR JJ	—	75.00	125	200	300	—

KM# 69.1 1/2 REAL

1.6917 g., 0.8960 Silver .0487 oz. **Obv:** Bust of Charles IV **Obv. Legend:** FERND. VII..

Date	Mintage	VG	F	VF	XF	Unc
1810NR JJ	—	65.00	120	170	285	—
1812 JF Denomination, MR	—	100	200	300	500	—
1816NR FJ	—	32.50	55.00	90.00	175	—
1818NR FJ	—	32.50	55.00	90.00	175	—

KM# 69.2 1/2 REAL

1.6917 g., 0.8960 Silver .0487 oz. **Obv:** Bust of Charles IV **Obv. Legend:** FERND. VII..

Date	Mintage	VG	F	VF	XF	Unc
1810P JF	—	18.00	35.00	90.00	185	—

KM# 58 REAL

3.3834 g., 0.8960 Silver .0975 oz. **Obv:** Bust of Charles IV

Date	Mintage	VG	F	VF	XF	Unc
1801/797NR JJ	—	20.00	50.00	150	300	—
1801/9NR	—	20.00	50.00	150	300	—
1801NR JJ	—	12.00	25.00	120	250	—
1802NR JJ	—	12.00	25.00	120	250	—
1804NR JJ	—	35.00	70.00	165	250	—

KM# 68.1 REAL

3.3834 g., 0.8960 Silver .0975 oz. **Obv:** Bust of Charles IV **Obv. Legend:** FERDND VII..

Date	Mintage	VG	F	VF	XF	Unc
1810/9NR FJ	—	50.00	100	200	300	—
1810NR JF	—	10.00	25.00	70.00	150	—
1810NR JJ	—	60.00	120	250	500	—
1812NR JF	—	15.00	40.00	80.00	165	—
1816NR FJ	—	10.00	25.00	70.00	150	—
1817NR FJ	—	12.00	30.00	75.00	150	—
1818NR FJ	—	15.00	30.00	60.00	120	—
1819NR FJ	—	10.00	20.00	45.00	100	—
1819NR FJ Inverted J	—	10.00	20.00	45.00	100	—
1819NR J	—	10.00	20.00	45.00	100	—

KM# 68.2 REAL

3.3834 g., 0.8960 Silver .0975 oz. **Obv:** Bust of Charles IV **Obv. Legend:** FERDND VII..

Date	Mintage	VG	F	VF	XF	Unc
1810P JF	—	18.00	35.00	90.00	170	—
Note: 1810 commonly found on especially broad planchets						
1813/0P JF	—	150	275	650	1,200	—

KM# 70.2 2 REALES

6.7668 g., 0.8960 Silver .1949 oz. **Obv:** Bust of Charles IV **Obv. Legend:** FERDND VII..

Date	Mintage	VG	F	VF	XF	Unc
1810P JF	—	25.00	40.00	80.00	250	—
1811/0P JF	—	60.00	90.00	150	350	—
1811P JF	—	45.00	75.00	110	300	—
1813P JF	—	45.00	75.00	110	300	—
1814/3P JF	—	150	300	500	1,000	—
1814P JF	—	100	200	400	800	—
1818P MF	—	40.00	70.00	100	250	—
1819P MF	—	25.00	40.00	80.00	200	—
1820/10P MF	—	70.00	150	300	600	—
1820P MF	—	35.00	60.00	90.00	225	—
1820P FM	—	35.00	65.00	90.00	225	—

KM# 70.1 2 REALES

6.7668 g., 0.8960 Silver .1949 oz. **Obv:** Bust of Charles IV **Obv. Legend:** FERDND VII..

Date	Mintage	VG	F	VF	XF	Unc
1816NR FJ	—	30.00	75.00	150	250	—
1816NR FJ/JJ	—	35.00	90.00	175	300	—
1817NR FJ	—	35.00	75.00	150	250	—
1818NR FJ	—	30.00	60.00	135	220	—
1819NR FJ	—	27.50	60.00	135	220	—

KM# 74 2 REALES

6.7668 g., 0.8960 Silver .1949 oz. **Obv:** Bust of Charles IV **Obv. Legend:** FERDND.7.D.G.ET.CONST

Date	Mintage	VG	F	VF	XF	Unc
1822P O	—	40.00	67.50	120	200	—

Note: The P mint mark on this coin has been traditionally attributed to Popayan, but recently recognized information supports the belief this P may stand for Pasto, making this the first coin of Ecuador. In 1820, Pasto was simply a city in the newly-organized Gran Colombia or United Provinces of Nueva Granada. It was not until 1830 that Ecuador withdrew from Bolivar's visionary unified government for all of northern-most South America. This is the only regular issue coin of Spain's New World Empire to

KM# 71 8 REALES

27.0674 g., 0.9170 Silver .7797 oz. **Obv:** Bust of Charles IV **Obv. Legend:** FERDND VII..

Date	Mintage	VG	F	VF	XF	Unc
1810P JF Rare	—	—	—	—	—	—
1811P JF	—	1,000	2,000	4,250	7,500	—
1812P JF	—	1,800	2,500	3,500	6,000	—
1813/2P JF	—	2,000	3,000	5,000	9,000	—
1813P JF	—	2,000	3,000	5,000	9,000	—
1814/3P JF	—	450	800	1,600	3,000	—
1814P JF	—	500	900	1,800	3,500	—
1816P F	—	1,200	2,200	3,500	5,000	—
1820P MF Rare	—	—	—	—	—	—

KM# 56.2 ESCUDO
3.3834 g., 0.8750 Gold .0952 oz. **Obv:** Bust of Charles IV

Date	Mintage	VG	F	VF	XF	Unc
1801P JF	—	65.00	100	135	200	—
1802P JF	—	65.00	100	135	200	—
1803P JF	—	65.00	100	135	200	—
1804P JF	—	65.00	100	135	200	—
1804P JT	—	100	150	225	350	—
1805P JT	—	65.00	100	135	200	—
1805P JF	—	100	150	225	350	—
1806P JT	—	65.00	100	135	200	—
1806P JF	—	65.00	100	135	200	—
1807P JF	—	65.00	100	135	200	—
1808/7P JF	—	65.00	100	135	200	—

KM# 56.1 ESCUDO
3.3834 g., 0.8750 Gold .0952 oz. **Obv:** Bust of Charles IV

Date	Mintage	VG	F	VF	XF	Unc
1802/1NR JJ	—	75.00	125	185	275	—
1802NR JJ	—	50.00	100	150	220	—
1803NR JJ	—	50.00	100	150	220	—
1804/3NR JJ	—	80.00	125	200	275	—
1804NR JJ	—	50.00	100	150	220	—
1805NR JJ	—	50.00	100	150	220	—
1806NR JJ	—	75.00	125	185	275	—
1807NR JJ	—	100	150	225	325	—

KM# 64.1 ESCUDO
3.3834 g., 0.8750 Gold .0952 oz. **Obv:** Bust of Charles IV **Obv. Legend:** FERDND VII.. **Rev:** Arms, Order chain

Date	Mintage	VG	F	VF	XF	Unc
1808NR JF	—	55.00	90.00	135	220	—
1809NR JF	—	55.00	90.00	135	220	—
1810NR JF	—	50.00	85.00	125	220	—
1811NR JJ	—	55.00	90.00	135	220	—
1811NR JF	—	55.00	90.00	135	220	—
1812/1NR JJ	—	55.00	90.00	135	220	—
1812NR JF	—	50.00	85.00	135	200	—
1813NR JF	—	50.00	85.00	125	200	—
1814NR JF	—	50.00	85.00	125	200	—
1815NR JF	—	50.00	85.00	125	200	—
1816NR JF	—	50.00	85.00	125	200	—
1817NR JF	—	50.00	85.00	125	200	—
1818NR JF	—	50.00	85.00	125	200	—
1819NR JF	—	50.00	85.00	125	200	—
1820NR JF	—	55.00	90.00	135	220	—

KM# 64.2 ESCUDO
3.3834 g., 0.8750 Gold .0952 oz. **Obv:** Bust of Charles IV **Obv. Legend:** FERDND VII.. **Rev:** Arms, Order chain

Date	Mintage	VG	F	VF	XF	Unc
1808P JF	—	50.00	85.00	125	200	—
1809P JF	—	50.00	85.00	125	200	—
1810P JF	—	50.00	85.00	125	200	—
1812P JF	—	50.00	85.00	125	200	—
1813/2P JF	—	50.00	85.00	125	200	—
1813P JF	—	50.00	85.00	125	200	—
1814/3P JF	—	50.00	85.00	125	200	—
1814P JF	—	50.00	85.00	125	200	—
1816P JF	—	55.00	90.00	135	220	—
1816P FM	—	50.00	85.00	125	200	—
1816P F	—	50.00	85.00	125	200	—
1817P FM	—	50.00	85.00	125	200	—
1818P FM	—	50.00	85.00	125	200	—
1819P FM	—	50.00	85.00	125	200	—

KM# 64.3 ESCUDO
3.3834 g., 0.8750 Gold .0952 oz. **Obv:** Bust of Charles IV **Obv. Legend:** FERDND VII.. **Rev:** Arms, Order chain

Date	Mintage	VG	F	VF	XF	Unc
1815PN FR	—	80.00	150	250	300	—
1816PN FR	—	55.00	90.00	140	225	—

KM# 60.1 2 ESCUDOS
6.7668 g., 0.8750 Gold .1904 oz. **Obv:** Bust right **Rev:** Crowned arms, Order chain

Date	Mintage	VG	F	VF	XF	Unc
1801NR JJ	—	125	200	275	350	—
1803NR JJ	—	175	225	300	375	—
1804NR JJ	—	200	275	325	450	—
1805NR JJ	—	100	150	225	300	—
1806/5NR JJ	—	325	400	500	750	—
1806/5NR JJ	—	275	350	450	700	—
1806NR JJ	—	100	150	225	300	—

KM# 60.2 2 ESCUDOS
6.7668 g., 0.8750 Gold .1904 oz. **Obv:** Bust right **Rev:** Crowned arms, Order chain

Date	Mintage	VG	F	VF	XF	Unc
1802P JF	—	90.00	175	225	350	—
1804P JF	—	100	185	200	375	—

KM# 65.1 2 ESCUDOS
6.7668 g., 0.8750 Gold .1904 oz. **Obv:** Bust of Charles IV **Obv. Legend:** FERDND VII.. **Rev:** Arms, Order chain

Date	Mintage	VG	F	VF	XF	Unc
1808NR JF	—	200	275	350	525	—
1809NR JJ	—	125	200	275	450	—
1811NR JF	—	200	275	350	550	—
1811NR JF/J	—	200	275	350	550	—

KM# 65.2 2 ESCUDOS
6.7668 g., 0.8750 Gold .1904 oz. **Obv:** Bust of Charles IV **Obv. Legend:** FERDND VII.. **Rev:** Arms, Order chain

Date	Mintage	VG	F	VF	XF	Unc
1817P FM	—	225	300	500	650	—
1818P FM	—	225	300	500	850	—
1819P FM	—	225	300	500	850	—

KM# 61.1 4 ESCUDOS
13.5337 g., 0.8750 Gold .3807 oz. **Obv:** Bust of Charles IV **Obv. Legend:** CAROL IIII..

Date	Mintage	VG	F	VF	XF	Unc
1801NR JJ	—	225	450	550	1,100	—
1803NR JJ	—	225	450	550	1,100	—
1804/3NR JJ	—	225	450	650	1,300	—
1805NR JJ	—	225	450	600	1,250	—
1806NR JJ	—	225	450	600	1,250	—
1807NR JJ	—	350	650	1,000	1,650	—

KM# 61.2 4 ESCUDOS
13.5337 g., 0.8750 Gold .3807 oz. **Obv:** Bust of Charles IV **Obv. Legend:** CAROL IIII.. **Rev:** Crowned arms in Order chain

Date	Mintage	VG	F	VF	XF	Unc
1801P JF	—	300	550	750	1,400	—

KM# 72 4 ESCUDOS
13.5337 g., 0.8750 Gold .3807 oz. **Obv:** Bust of Charles IV **Obv. Legend:** FERDND VII.. **Rev:** Arms, Order chain

Date	Mintage	VG	F	VF	XF	Unc
1818NR JF	—	400	800	1,500	2,750	—
1819NR JF	—	400	800	1,500	2,750	—

KM# 62.1 8 ESCUDOS
27.0674 g., 0.8750 Gold .7615 oz. **Obv:** Bust of Charles IV **Obv. Legend:** CAROL IIII.. **Rev:** Crowned arms, Order chain

Date	Mintage	VG	F	VF	XF	Unc
1801/0NR JJ	—	350	525	675	850	—
1801NR JJ	—	350	525	675	850	—
1802/1NR JJ	—	350	525	675	850	—
1802NR JJ	—	350	525	675	850	—
1803/2NR JJ	—	350	525	675	850	—
1803NR JJ	—	350	525	675	850	—
1804/3NR JJ	—	350	525	675	850	—
1804NR JJ	—	350	525	675	850	—
1805/4NR JJ	—	350	525	675	850	—
1805NR JJ	—	350	525	675	850	—
1806NR JJ	—	350	525	675	850	—
1807NR JJ	—	350	525	675	850	—
1808NR JJ	—	350	525	675	850	—
1808NR JJ D:G	—	350	525	675	850	—

KM# 62.2 8 ESCUDOS
27.0674 g., 0.8750 Gold .7615 oz. **Obv:** Bust of Charles IV **Obv. Legend:** CAROL IIII.. **Rev:** Crowned arms, Order chain

Date	Mintage	VG	F	VF	XF	Unc
1801P JF	—	350	525	675	850	—
1802P JF	—	350	525	675	850	—
1803P JF	—	350	525	675	850	—
1804P JT	—	1,500	2,500	3,500	4,500	—
1804P JF	—	350	525	675	850	—
1805P JF	—	750	1,500	2,000	3,000	—
1805/4P JT	—	350	525	675	850	—
1805P JT	—	350	525	675	850	—
1806/5P JF	—	350	525	675	850	—
1806P JF	—	350	525	675	850	—
1807/6P JF	—	350	525	675	850	—
1807P JF	—	350	525	675	850	—
1808P JF	—	350	525	675	850	—

KM# 66.1 8 ESCUDOS
27.0674 g., 0.8750 Gold .7615 oz. **Obv:** Bust of Charles IV **Obv. Legend:** FERDND. VII..

Date	Mintage	VG	F	VF	XF	Unc
1808NR JJ	—	450	700	1,200	1,800	—
1808NR JF/JJ	—	400	600	800	1,000	—
1809/8NR JF/JJ	—	450	650	900	1,200	—
1809NR JF/JJ	—	350	500	700	850	—
1809NR JF	—	350	500	650	775	—
1810/9NR JF	—	350	500	700	850	—
1810NR JF	—	350	500	700	850	—
1811/0NR JF	—	350	500	700	850	—
1811NR JF	—	350	500	700	850	—
1812/1/0NR JF	—	350	500	700	850	—
1812/1NR JF	—	350	500	700	850	—
1812NR JF	—	350	500	700	850	—
1813/2NR JF	—	350	500	700	850	—
1813NR JF	—	350	500	700	850	—
1814/3NR JF	—	350	500	700	850	—

Date	Mintage	VG	F	VF	XF	Unc
1814NR J	—	350	500	700	850	—
1815/4NR JF	—	350	500	700	850	—
1815NR JF	—	350	500	700	850	—
1816/4NR JF	—	350	500	700	850	—
1816/5NR JF	—	350	500	700	850	—
1816NR JF	—	350	500	700	850	—
1817/6NR	—	350	500	700	850	—
1817NR JF	—	350	500	700	850	—
1818NR JF	—	350	500	700	850	—
1819NR JF	—	350	500	700	850	—
1819/29NR JF	—	350	500	700	850	—
1820NR JF	—	350	500	700	850	—

KM# 66.2 8 ESCUDOS
27.0674 g., 0.8750 Gold .7615 oz. **Obv:** Bust of Charles IV **Obv. Legend:** FERDND. VII..

Date	Mintage	VG	F	VF	XF	Unc
1808P JF	—	350	500	700	850	—
1809/8P JF	—	350	500	700	850	—
1809P JF	—	350	500	700	850	—
1810/09P JF	—	350	500	700	850	—
1810P JF	—	350	500	700	850	—
1811/0P JF	—	350	500	700	850	—
1811P JF	—	350	500	700	850	—
1812/11P JF	—	350	500	700	850	—
1812P JF	—	350	500	700	850	—
1813P JF	—	350	500	700	850	—
1814P JF	—	350	500	700	850	—
1815P JF	—	350	500	700	850	—
1816P JF	—	900	1,500	2,000	3,000	—
1816P F	—	600	1,000	1,300	1,800	—
1816P FM	—	450	700	1,000	1,500	—
1817P FM	—	350	500	650	775	—
1818P FM	—	350	500	650	775	—
1819P FM	—	350	500	650	775	—
1820P FM	—	350	500	650	750	—

KM# 66.3 8 ESCUDOS
27.0674 g., 0.8750 Gold .7615 oz. **Obv:** Bust of Charles IV **Obv. Legend:** FERDND. VII..

Date	Mintage	VG	F	VF	XF	Unc
1814 Pn FR	—	550	900	1,500	2,500	—
1815 Pn FR	—	1,500	2,500	4,000	6,000	—
1816 Pn FR	—	450	700	1,000	1,500	—
1820 Pn FM	—	450	700	1,000	1,500	—

POPAYAN

A city located in Southwest Colombia south of Cali at the foot of Mt. Purace. Founded in 1537. During the colonial era it was a center of a mining region and an important residential, administrative and religious center.

ROYALIST PROVISIONAL COINAGE

1813

KM# B1 1/2 REAL
Copper **Obv:** P/ANO/1813 **Rev:** Value **Note:** Previous Popayan KM#1.

Date	Mintage	VG	F	VF	XF	Unc
1813 5 known	—	300	500	800	1,800	—

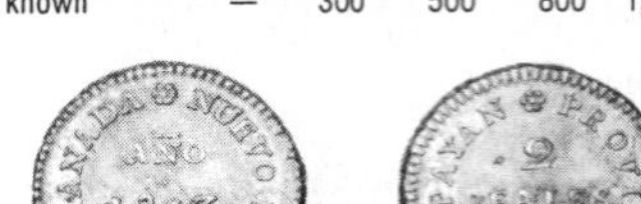

KM# B2 2 REALES
Copper **Obv. Legend:** ANO/1813 NUEVO REYNO DE GRANADA **Rev:** Value **Rev. Legend:** PROVINCIA DE POPAYAN **Note:** Previous Popayan KM#2.

Date	Mintage	VG	F	VF	XF	Unc
1813	—	30.00	65.00	115	170	—

KM# B3 8 REALES
Copper **Obv:** ANO/1813 **Obv. Legend:** NUEVO REYNO DE GRANADA **Rev:** Value **Rev. Legend:** PROVINCIA DE POPAYAN **Note:** Previous Popayan KM#3.

Date	Mintage	VG	F	VF	XF	Unc
1813	—	45.00	100	175	285	—

SANTA MARTA

A city on the shore of the Caribbean Sea, founded in 1525, it is the oldest in Colombia. Santa Marta was one of several areas in Colombia that remained under Spanish rule longer. Besieged by Republican forces, Royalists made a necessity coinage that reflects certain design elements of Spanish Imperial issues.

ROYALIST SIEGE COINAGE

KM# C1 1/4 REAL
Copper **Obv:** NR, star, denomination **Rev:** Lion **Note:** Previous Santa Marta KM#1.

Date	Mintage	Good	VG	F	VF	XF
ND(1812-13)	—	120	300	500	—	—

KM# C2 1/4 REAL
Copper **Obv:** F.VII, date below **Rev:** SM. **Note:** Previous Santa Marta KM#2.

Date	Mintage	Good	VG	F	VF	XF
1813	—	32.50	55.00	75.00	110	—
ND(1813)	—	20.00	45.00	67.50	80.00	—

KM# B4 1/4 REAL
Copper **Obv:** Crown above; castle, denomination, sword, pyramid of cannon balls; date below **Rev:** Cross with S, M, castle, sword and cannon balls in quarters **Note:** Medal alignment. Previous Santa Marta KM#4.

Date	Mintage	VG	F	VF	XF	Unc
1820	—	12.50	22.50	42.50	85.00	—

KM# C3 1/2 REAL
Copper **Obv:** Crude bust of Ferdinand VII **Rev:** Date above denomination **Note:** Previous Santa Marta KM#3.

Date	Mintage	Good	VG	F	VF	XF
1813	—	1,650	2,250	—	—	—

KM# B5 2 REALES
Silver **Obv:** Crowned pillars and worlds, denomination flanking, date below **Rev:** Cross with S, M, castle, sword and cannon balls in quarters **Note:** Previous Santa Marta KM#5.

Date	Mintage	Good	VG	F	VF	XF
1820	—	550	1,000	2,000	3,000	—

ROYALIST COUNTERMARKED COINAGE

KM# B6 8 REALES
27.0700 g., 0.9030 Silver .7859 oz. **Countermark:** S. M. and VPB **Note:** Previous Santa Marta KM#6.

CM Date	Host Date	Good	VG	F	VF	XF
ND	1809 TH	350	500	750	1,100	—

PRE-REPUBLICAN - CARTAGENA

This port city on Colombia's northern coast was very important for the Spanish colonies and was heavily fortified to ward off British and French privateers. Cartagena was the first major city in Colombia to declare independence from Spain – November 11, 1811. In 1815, after a four month siege, it fell to the Royalists. In the interim the besieged Republicans struck coins for local use. All these coins are crude in die-work, planchets and striking.

SIEGE COINAGE

KM# D2 1/2 REAL
Copper **Note:** Previous Cartagena KM#2.
NOTE: Most examples of KM#D1 and KM#D2 are poorly struck. Fully struck-up pieces are worth about 20%-25% more, while pieces with non-struck areas are generally worth a percent less equivalent to the area of poor striking

Date	Mintage	Good	VG	F	VF	XF
ND(1811)	—	5.00	9.00	15.00	30.00	—
1811 Rare	—	—	—	—	—	—
1812	—	7.50	13.50	25.00	45.00	—
Note: Medal alignment						
1813	—	8.00	16.50	30.00	50.00	—
1814 Rare	—	—	—	—	—	—

KM# D1 2 REALES
Copper **Note:** Previous Cartagena KM#1.

Date	Mintage	Good	VG	F	VF	XF
ND(1811)	—	5.00	10.00	20.00	40.00	—
1811	—	15.00	32.50	55.00	100	—

Date	Mintage	Good	VG	F	VF	XF
1812	—	10.00	22.50	45.00	80.00	—
1813	—	10.00	22.50	45.00	80.00	—
Note: Coin alignment						
1814	—	15.00	32.50	55.00	100	—

PRE-REPUBLICAN - CUNDINAMARCA

This province in central Colombia, with Bogota as its capital, was the first to declare independence – July 16, 1813. Spain regained control in 1816 and held on until 1819. After the battle of Boyaca, the province was again free. Coins made before and after the Spanish re-occupation, 1814-16 and 1819-23, when the Gran Colombia plan was put into effect , bear the provincial designation. Imperial Spanish types were struck during the Spanish re-occupation.

PROVINCIAL COINAGE

KM# F2 1/4 REAL
0.7000 g., 0.5830 Silver .0131 oz. **Note:** Previous Cundinamarca KM#2.

Date	Mintage	Good	VG	F	VF	XF
1814	—	40.00	75.00	180	385	—
1815	—	55.00	125	270	450	—

KM# D3 1/2 REAL
Silver **Obv:** Indian head **Rev:** Pomegranate **Note:** Previous Cundinamarca KM#3.

Date	Mintage	Good	VG	F	VF	XF
1814 JF	—	120	250	375	500	—

KM# F1 REAL
2.5000 g., 0.5830 Silver .0468 oz. **Note:** Previous Cundinamarca KM#1.

Date	Mintage	Good	VG	F	VF	XF
1813 JF	—	25.00	55.00	130	250	—
1814 JF	—	37.50	85.00	175	325	—
1815 JF	—	37.50	85.00	170	320	—
1816 JF	—	25.00	55.00	125	235	—

KM# C4 2 REALES
4.9000 g., 0.5830 Silver .0918 oz. **Note:** Previous Cundinamarca KM#4.

Date	Mintage	Good	VG	F	VF	XF
1815 JF	—	18.50	37.50	85.00	180	—
1816/5 JF	—	35.00	72.50	150	275	—
1816/6 JF Over horizontal 6	—	80.00	150	275	500	—
1816 JF	—	37.50	80.00	150	280	—

PRE-REPUBLICAN - REPUBLIC OF COLOMBIA

PROVINCIAL COINAGE

KM# F8 1/2 REAL
1.3000 g., 0.6660 Silver .0278 oz. **Issuer:** Cundinamarca **Note:** Previous Republic of Colombia KM#8.

Date	Mintage	Good	VG	F	VF	XF
1821 Ba JF	—	25.00	55.00	115	175	—

KM# B9 REAL
2.7800 g., 0.6660 Silver .0595 oz. **Issuer:** Cundinamarca **Note:** Previous Republic of Colombia KM#9.

Date	Mintage	Good	VG	F	VF	XF
1821 Ba JF	—	6.00	16.50	35.00	65.00	—

KM# C5 2 REALES
4.9800 g., 0.6660 Silver .1066 oz. **Issuer:** Cundinamarca **Note:** Previous Republic of Colombia KM#5.

Date	Mintage	Good	VG	F	VF	XF
1820 JF	—	37.50	80.00	170	280	—
1820 Ba JF Rare	—	—	—	—	—	—
1821 Ba JF	—	4.00	6.50	20.00	47.50	—
Note: Numerous punctuation variations are known						
1821 JF	—	25.00	65.00	165	275	—
1823 JF	—	200	455	950	1,500	—

KM# D7 8 REALES
23.0000 g., 0.6660 Silver .4924 oz. **Issuer:** Cundinamarca **Obv:** Like KM#C6 **Note:** Mule. Previous Republic of Colombia KM#7.

Date	Mintage	Good	VG	F	VF	XF
1820 JF	—	1,000	1,500	2,000	2,500	—

KM# C6 8 REALES
23.0000 g., 0.6660 Silver .4924 oz. **Issuer:** Cundinamarca **Note:** Previous Republic of Colombia KM#6.

Date	Mintage	Good	VG	F	VF	XF
1820 JF	—	10.00	30.00	50.00	110	—
1820 Ba JF	—	50.00	75.00	125	250	—
1821 JF	—	10.00	25.00	45.00	100	—
1821 Ba JF	—	10.00	30.00	50.00	110	—

UNITED PROVINCES OF NUEVA GRANADA

COUNTERMARKED COINAGE

KM# 73 8 REALES
Silver **Counterstamp:** Pomegranate **Note:** Countermark on 8 Reales, KM#C6. Modern counterfeit countermarks of this type are known, caution is advised.

CM Date	Host Date	Good	VG	F	VF	XF
ND	1820 JF	50.00	85.00	150	250	—
ND	1821 JF	50.00	85.00	150	250	—
ND	1821 Ba JF	50.00	85.00	150	250	—

PROVISIONAL COINAGE

KM# 79.1 1/4 REAL
0.7000 g., 0.6660 Silver .0149 oz. **Obv:** Liberty cap **Rev:** Pomegranate

Date	Mintage	Good	VG	F	VF	XF
1820	—	15.00	25.00	45.00	100	—
1821	—	22.50	38.50	70.00	125	—

KM# 79.2 1/4 REAL
0.7000 g., 0.6660 Silver .0149 oz. **Obv:** Liberty cap **Rev:** Pomegranate

Date	Mintage	Good	VG	F	VF	XF
1821BA	—	12.50	22.50	37.50	60.00	—

KM# 79.3 1/4 REAL
0.7000 g., 0.6660 Silver .0149 oz. **Obv:** Liberty cap **Rev:** Pomegranate

Date	Mintage	Good	VG	F	VF	XF
1822 Pn Rare	—	—	—	—	—	—

KM# 75 REAL
3.1500 g., 0.6660 Silver .0674 oz. **Obv:** Legend around indian head **Obv. Legend:** LIBERTAD AMERICANA **Rev:** Legend around pomegranate **Rev. Legend:** NUEVA GRANADA

Date	Mintage	Good	VG	F	VF	XF
1819 JF	—	22.50	45.00	90.00	185	—

KM# 76 2 REALES
5.9000 g., 0.6660 Silver .1263 oz.

Date	Mintage	Good	VG	F	VF	XF
1819 JF	—	13.50	30.00	55.00	120	—

KM# 77 2 REALES
5.9000 g., 0.6660 Silver .1263 oz. **Rev:** Pomegranate divides value

Date	Mintage	Good	VG	F	VF	XF
1819 JF	—	50.00	115	250	500	—
1820 JF	—	45.00	80.00	175	375	—

KM# 78 8 REALES
23.0000 g., 0.6660 Silver .4924 oz.

Date	Mintage	Good	VG	F	VF	XF
1819 JF	—	25.00	45.00	90.00	175	—
1820/19 JF	—	30.00	50.00	100	200	—
1820 JF	—	25.00	45.00	90.00	175	—

REPUBLIC OF COLOMBIA

MILLED COINAGE

KM# 85.1 1/4 REAL

0.7000 g., 0.6660 Silver .0149 oz. **Rev:** Mint mark and initials below 1/4

Date	Mintage	Good	VG	F	VF	XF
1826B TR	—	60.00	135	300	650	—

Note: Contemporary counterfeits of the above type with initials RS are reported for 1825-27

KM# 85.2 1/4 REAL

0.7000 g., 0.6660 Silver .0149 oz. **Rev:** Mint mark above 1/4, initials

Date	Mintage	Good	VG	F	VF	XF
1826B RS	—	15.00	30.00	55.00	90.00	—
1827B RS	—	8.50	16.50	30.00	50.00	—
1828B RS	—	10.00	20.00	35.00	60.00	—
1829B RS	—	7.00	15.00	27.50	45.00	—
1833B RS	—	50.00	95.00	180	300	—
1834B RS	—	7.00	15.00	27.50	45.00	—
1835B RS	—	50.00	100	200	325	—
1836B RS	—	8.50	16.50	30.00	50.00	—

KM# 85.3 1/4 REAL

0.7000 g., 0.6660 Silver .0149 oz. **Rev:** Mint mark above 1/4, initials

Date	Mintage	Good	VG	F	VF	XF
1826P RU	—	8.00	17.50	35.00	60.00	—
1832P RU Rare	—	—	—	—	—	—
1833P RU	—	12.00	25.00	45.00	80.00	—
1834P RU	—	8.50	16.50	30.00	50.00	—
1836P RU	—	10.00	20.00	42.00	75.00	—

KM# 88.1 1/2 REAL

1.5500 g., 0.6660 Silver .0331 oz. **Obv:** Faces between crossed cornucopias **Rev:** Value in wreath

Date	Mintage	Good	VG	F	VF	XF
1833B RS	—	15.00	27.50	50.00	90.00	—
1834B RS	—	10.00	18.50	35.00	60.00	—
1835B RS	—	12.50	25.00	47.50	80.00	—

KM# 88.2 1/2 REAL

1.5500 g., 0.6660 Silver .0331 oz. **Obv:** Faces between crossed cornucopias **Rev:** Value in wreath

Date	Mintage	Good	VG	F	VF	XF
1834P RU	—	9.00	16.50	28.50	55.00	—
1835P RU	—	12.50	25.00	45.00	75.00	—
1836P RU	—	7.00	12.00	25.00	45.00	—

KM# 87.2 REAL

3.1000 g., 0.6660 Silver .0663 oz.

Date	Mintage	Good	VG	F	VF	XF
1827PN RU	—	18.00	35.00	75.00	165	—
1828/7PN RU	—	7.00	13.50	27.50	65.00	—
1828PN MF	—	9.00	18.50	37.50	75.00	—
1828PN RU	—	5.00	10.00	20.00	40.00	—
1828PN RU/MF	—	20.00	40.00	90.00	200	—
1829PN MF	—	7.00	15.00	32.50	65.00	—
1829PN RU	—	4.00	7.00	18.00	37.50	—
1830PN RU	—	3.50	7.00	18.00	37.50	—
1831PN RU	—	3.00	7.00	18.00	37.50	—
1832PN RU	—	3.50	7.00	18.00	37.50	—
1833PN RU	—	4.00	9.00	18.50	40.00	—
1834PN RU	—	20.00	42.50	85.00	180	—

KM# 87.1 REAL

3.1000 g., 0.6660 Silver .0663 oz. **Note:** Mint mark B or BA

Date	Mintage	Good	VG	F	VF	XF
1827B RR	—	2.75	7.00	16.00	35.00	—
1828 RR	—	3.00	7.50	20.00	45.00	—
1828 RS	—	12.50	27.50	60.00	135	—
1829 RS	—	25.00	45.00	85.00	175	—
1833/29 RS	—	5.00	12.00	25.00	45.00	—
1833 RS	—	2.50	7.50	15.00	32.50	—
1834 RS	—	15.00	30.00	67.50	145	—
1835/4 RS	—	6.00	15.00	35.00	67.50	—
1835 RS	—	3.00	7.00	16.50	35.00	—
1836/5 RS	—	3.50	7.00	15.00	32.50	—
1836 RS	—	2.50	5.25	9.00	15.00	—

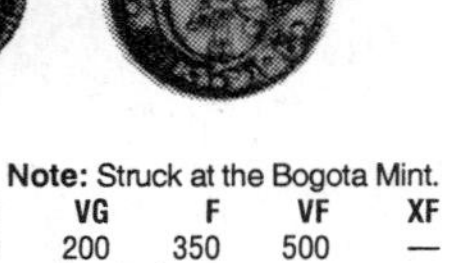

KM# 89 8 REALES

27.0200 g., 0.8350 Silver .7253 oz.

Date	Mintage	Good	VG	F	VF	XF
1834 RS	—	25.00	55.00	150	300	—
1835/4 RS	—	18.50	40.00	80.00	175	—
1835 RS	—	22.50	50.00	135	275	—
1836 RS	—	18.50	40.00	80.00	175	—

KM# 80 PESO

1.6875 g., 0.8750 Gold .0474 oz. **Note:** Struck at the Bogota Mint.

Date	Mintage	Good	VG	F	VF	XF
1821 JF	—	100	200	350	500	—

Note: Authenticity currently under study

KM# 84 PESO

1.6875 g., 0.8750 Gold .0474 oz.

Date	Mintage	VG	F	VF	XF	Unc
1825 JF	—	55.00	60.00	80.00	125	—
1826 JF	—	55.00	60.00	80.00	125	—
1826/5 JF	—	55.00	60.00	80.00	125	—
1826 JR	—	55.00	60.00	80.00	125	—
1826 PJ	—	55.00	60.00	80.00	125	—
1827 JF	—	55.00	60.00	80.00	125	—
1827 RR	—	55.00	60.00	80.00	125	—
1829/7 PJ	—	55.00	60.00	80.00	125	—
1829 JF	—	55.00	60.00	80.00	125	—
1829 RS	—	55.00	60.00	80.00	125	—
1830 RS	—	55.00	60.00	80.00	125	—
1834 RS	—	55.00	60.00	80.00	125	—
1835 RS	—	55.00	60.00	80.00	125	—
1836 RS	—	55.00	60.00	80.00	125	—

KM# 81.2 ESCUDO

3.3841 g., 0.8750 Gold .0952 oz.

Date	Mintage	VG	F	VF	XF	Unc
1823 FM	—	55.00	65.00	115	175	—
1824 FM	—	55.00	65.00	100	150	—
1825 FM	—	55.00	65.00	100	150	—
1826 FM	—	55.00	65.00	100	150	—
1827 FM	—	55.00	65.00	100	150	—
1827 RU	—	55.00	65.00	115	175	—
1828 RU	—	55.00	65.00	115	175	—
1829 RU	—	55.00	65.00	100	150	—
1830 RU	—	55.00	65.00	100	150	—
1831/21 RM	—	65.00	75.00	125	200	—
1831 RU	—	65.00	75.00	125	200	—
1832 RU	—	55.00	65.00	100	150	—
1833/2 RU	—	55.00	65.00	115	175	—
1834 RU	—	55.00	65.00	115	175	—
1836/4 RU	—	55.00	65.00	115	175	—
1836 RU	—	55.00	65.00	115	175	—

KM# 81.1 ESCUDO

3.3841 g., 0.8750 Gold .0952 oz. **Note:** An 1821 dated piece is known and considered to be a contemporary counterfeit. Struck at the Bogota Mint.

Date	Mintage	VG	F	VF	XF	Unc
1823 JF	—	100	125	225	350	—
1825 JF	—	—	—	—	—	—

KM# 83 2 ESCUDOS

6.7682 g., 0.8750 Gold .1904 oz. **Note:** Struck at the Bogota Mint.

Date	Mintage	VG	F	VF	XF	Unc
1823 JF	—	150	250	400	600	—
1824 JF	—	135	235	375	550	—
1825 JF	—	135	235	375	550	—
1826 JF	—	135	235	375	550	—
1829 JF	—	150	250	400	600	—
1829 PJ	—	150	250	400	600	—
1829 RS	—	125	225	350	500	—
1836 RS	—	125	225	350	500	—

KM# 86 4 ESCUDOS

13.5365 g., 0.8750 Gold .3808 oz. **Note:** Struck at the Bogota Mint.

Date	Mintage	VG	F	VF	XF	Unc
1826 JF	—	1,550	2,150	3,650	—	—

KM# 82.1 8 ESCUDOS

27.0730 g., 0.8750 Gold .7616 oz. **Note:** Struck at the Bogota Mint.

Date	Mintage	VG	F	VF	XF	Unc
1822 JF	—	400	600	850	1,350	—
1823 JF	—	375	425	625	850	—
1824/3 JF	—	375	425	625	850	—
1824 JF	—	375	425	625	850	—
1825 JF	—	375	425	625	850	—
1826 JF	—	375	425	625	850	—
1827 JF	—	375	450	675	950	—
1827 RR	—	400	550	800	1,250	—
1828 RR	—	400	550	800	1,250	—
1828 RS	—	375	425	625	850	—
1829 RS	—	375	425	625	850	—

Date	Mintage	VG	F	VF	XF	Unc
1830 RS	—	375	425	625	850	—
1831 RS	—	375	425	625	850	—
1832 RS	—	375	425	625	850	—
1833 RS	—	375	425	625	850	—
1834 RS	—	375	425	625	850	—
1835 RS	—	375	425	625	850	—
1836 RS	—	375	425	625	850	—

KM# 82.2 8 ESCUDOS
27.0730 g., 0.8750 Gold .7616 oz. **Note:** Struck at the Popayan Mint.

Date	Mintage	VG	F	VF	XF	Unc
1822 FM	—	400	600	850	1,350	—
1823 FM	—	375	425	625	900	—
1824 FM	—	375	425	625	850	—
1825 FM	—	375	425	625	850	—
1826 FM	—	375	425	625	850	—
1827 FM	—	375	425	625	900	—
1827 UR	—	400	500	750	1,150	—
1828 FM	—	375	425	625	900	—
1829 FM	—	400	550	750	1,150	—
1829 UR	—	375	425	625	850	—
1830 FW M inverted	—	400	600	1,000	1,500	—
1830 FM	—	400	600	1,000	1,500	—
1830 UR	—	375	425	625	850	—
1831 UR	—	400	600	1,000	1,500	—
1832/1 UR	—	375	425	625	850	—
1832 UR	—	375	425	625	850	—
1833/22 UR	—	425	650	1,250	2,000	—
1833 UR	—	375	425	625	850	—
1834/3 UR	—	500	850	1,650	2,500	—
1834 UR	—	425	650	1,250	2,000	—
1835 UR	—	375	425	625	850	—
1836 UR	—	375	425	625	850	—
1838 UR Rare	—	—	—	—	—	—

REPUBLIC OF NUEVA GRANADA

MILLED COINAGE

KM# 90.1 1/4 REAL
0.6800 g., 0.6660 Silver .0145 oz. **Note:** Struck at the Bogota Mint.

Date	Mintage	Good	VG	F	VF	XF
1837	—	20.00	42.50	100	180	—
1838	—	7.00	15.00	32.50	65.00	—
1839	—	4.00	9.00	20.00	42.50	—
1840	—	4.00	9.00	20.00	45.00	—
1841	—	5.00	13.50	30.00	85.00	—
1842	—	6.00	15.00	35.00	100	—
1843	—	4.00	10.00	22.00	45.00	—
1844	—	3.75	10.00	18.50	40.00	—
1845	—	20.00	45.00	100	180	—
1846	—	4.00	10.00	20.00	45.00	—
1847	—	3.50	9.00	20.00	42.50	—
1848	—	27.50	55.00	125	200	—

KM# 90.2 1/4 REAL
0.6800 g., 0.6660 Silver .0145 oz. **Note:** Struck at the Popayan Mint.

Date	Mintage	Good	VG	F	VF	XF
1838	—	150	325	—	—	—
1841	—	—	—	—	—	—
Note: At present only one known						
1842	—	—	—	—	—	—
Note: Reported, not confirmed						
1843	—	150	325	—	—	—
1844	—	40.00	85.00	200	375	—
1845	—	125	300	—	—	—
1846	—	37.50	75.00	175	335	—

KM# 96.1 1/2 REAL
1.2600 g., 0.6660 Silver 0.269 oz. **Note:** Struck at the Bogota Mint.

Date	Mintage	Good	VG	F	VF	XF
1838 RS Rare	—	—	—	—	—	—
Note: 2-4 pieces known						
1839 RS	—	4.50	12.50	20.00	37.50	—
1840/39 RS	—	4.50	12.50	20.00	37.50	—
1840 RS	—	4.50	12.50	20.00	37.50	—
1842 RS	—	4.50	12.50	20.00	37.50	—
1843 RS	—	4.50	12.50	20.00	37.50	—
1844/3 RS	—	4.00	11.00	18.50	35.00	—
1844 RS	—	4.00	11.00	18.50	35.00	—
1845 RS	—	4.50	13.00	22.00	40.00	—
1846 RS	—	4.00	11.00	18.50	35.00	—
1847/6 RS	—	4.50	12.50	20.00	37.50	—
1847 RS	—	2.50	6.25	12.50	22.50	—

KM# 96.2 1/2 REAL
1.2600 g., 0.6660 Silver 0.269 oz. **Note:** Struck at the Popayan Mint.

Date	Mintage	Good	VG	F	VF	XF
1838 RU	—	2.50	6.25	12.50	22.50	—
1839 RU	—	2.50	6.25	12.50	22.50	—
1840 RU	—	5.50	12.00	17.50	32.50	—
1841 RU	—	5.50	12.00	17.50	32.50	—
1841 VU	—	12.50	17.50	40.00	80.00	—
1842 UM	—	5.50	12.00	17.50	35.00	—
1843 UM	—	7.50	13.00	22.00	45.00	—
1844 UE	—	3.00	7.50	13.50	25.00	—
1844 UM Rare	—	—	—	—	—	—
1845 UE	—	4.50	11.00	17.50	35.00	—
1846/5 UE	—	4.50	10.00	15.00	30.00	—
1846 UE	—	1.75	4.00	9.00	17.50	—
1846 UM	—	2.50	5.00	11.00	20.00	—
1848 UE	—	18.00	32.50	47.50	85.00	—
1848 UE	—	—	—	—	—	—
Note: Star over last 8 in date; Rare, with only one currently known						

KM# 91.1 REAL
2.7000 g., 0.6660 Silver .0578 oz. **Note:** Struck at the Bogota Mint.

Date	Mintage	Good	VG	F	VF	XF
1837 RS	—	2.50	5.00	10.00	17.50	—
1838 RS	—	2.50	5.00	10.00	17.50	—
1839 RS	—	2.50	5.00	10.00	17.50	—
184/30 RS	—	4.50	10.00	18.00	30.00	—
1840/39 RS	—	5.00	11.00	17.50	35.00	—
1841 RS	—	150	270	380	575	—
1843 RS	—	2.50	5.00	10.00	17.50	—
1844 RS	—	2.50	5.00	10.00	17.50	—
1845 RS	—	4.50	12.00	22.50	45.00	—
1846 RS	—	5.00	12.50	27.50	60.00	—

KM# 91.2 REAL
2.7000 g., 0.6660 Silver .0578 oz. **Note:** Struck at the Popayan Mint.

Date	Mintage	Good	VG	F	VF	XF
1839 RU	—	—	—	—	—	—
Note: Reported, not confirmed						
1840 RU	—	5.50	13.50	25.00	45.00	—
1841 VU/RU	—	15.00	35.00	65.00	125	—
1844 UM	—	7.50	20.00	35.00	70.00	—
1845 UM	—	4.00	7.50	20.00	35.00	70.00
1846/4 UM	—	7.50	20.00	35.00	70.00	—
1846 UM	—	7.50	20.00	37.50	75.00	—

KM# 97.1 2 REALES
5.5000 g., 0.6660 Silver .1177 oz. **Note:** Struck at the Bogota Mint.

Date	Mintage	Good	VG	F	VF	XF
1839 RS	—	45.00	85.00	175	360	—
1840 RS	—	2.00	4.50	9.00	18.50	—
1841/0 RS	—	15.00	45.00	100	175	—
1841 RS	—	15.00	45.00	100	175	—
1843 RS	—	2.00	4.00	7.50	15.00	—
1844/3 RS	—	10.00	25.00	45.00	80.00	—
1844 RS	—	2.00	4.00	9.00	22.00	—
1845 RS	—	16.50	45.00	100	175	—
1846/5 RS	—	30.00	65.00	130	225	—

KM# 97.2 2 REALES
5.5000 g., 0.6660 Silver .1177 oz. **Note:** Struck at the Popayan Mint.

Date	Mintage	Good	VG	F	VF	XF
1840 RU	—	7.00	18.50	38.00	85.00	—
1841 VU	—	30.00	62.50	135	200	—
1842/0/1 UM	—	30.00	62.50	135	200	—
1842 VU	—	2.75	6.00	11.00	22.50	—
1842 UM	—	30.00	62.50	135	200	—
1843/2 UM	—	6.00	15.00	37.50	75.00	—
1843 UM	—	8.50	20.00	40.00	80.00	—
1844/3 UM	—	20.00	42.50	85.00	155	—
1844 UM	—	2.75	6.00	11.00	22.50	—
1846 UM Rare	—	—	—	—	—	—
1849 UM	—	100	175	250	—	—

KM# 92 8 REALES
Silver

Date	Mintage	VG	F	VF	XF	Unc
1837 RS	—	75.00	200	425	850	—
1838 RS Rare; 1 known	—	—	—	—	—	—

KM# 98 8 REALES
Silver

Date	Mintage	VG	F	VF	XF	Unc
1839 RS	—	13.50	30.00	60.00	—	—
1840 RS	—	15.00	35.00	70.00	—	—
1841 RS	—	17.50	40.00	80.00	—	—
1842 RS	—	17.50	40.00	80.00	—	—
1843 RS	—	15.00	35.00	70.00	—	—
1844 RS	—	17.50	40.00	80.00	—	—
1845 RS	—	17.50	40.00	80.00	—	—
1846/4 RS	—	20.00	45.00	90.00	—	—
1846/5 RS	—	20.00	45.00	90.00	—	—
1846 RS	—	17.50	40.00	80.00	—	—

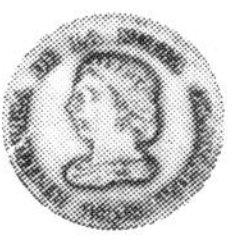

KM# 93 PESO
1.6875 g., 0.8750 Gold .0474 oz. **Note:** Struck at the Bogota Mint.

Date	Mintage	VG	F	VF	XF	Unc
1837 RS	—	40.00	60.00	90.00	150	—
1838 RS	—	60.00	90.00	135	225	—
1839 RS	—	60.00	90.00	135	225	—
1840/39 RS	—	50.00	80.00	120	200	—
1840 RS	—	45.00	70.00	100	175	—
1842 RS	—	40.00	60.00	90.00	150	—
1844 RS	—	45.00	70.00	100	175	—
1846 RS	—	40.00	60.00	90.00	150	—

KM# 95 2 PESOS
3.3750 g., 0.9000 Gold .0976 oz. **Note:** Struck at the Popayan Mint.

Date	Mintage	VG	F	VF	XF	Unc
1838 RU	—	55.00	80.00	120	200	—
1842 VU	—	55.00	80.00	160	275	—
1843 UM	—	55.00	80.00	120	200	—
1843 VU	—	55.00	80.00	160	275	—
1844 UM	—	55.00	80.00	130	225	—
1845 UM	—	55.00	80.00	120	200	—
1845 UE	—	55.00	80.00	160	275	—
1846 UE	—	55.00	80.00	120	200	—
1846 UM	—	55.00	80.00	120	200	—

KM# 99 2 PESOS
3.2258 g., 0.9000 Gold .0933 oz. **Note:** Struck at the Bogota Mint.

Date	Mintage	VG	F	VF	XF	Unc
1849	—	400	650	950	1,550	—
1851	—	600	1,200	1,800	2,700	—

KM# 94.1 16 PESOS (Diez I Seis)
27.0000 g., 0.8750 Gold .7596 oz. **Note:** Struck at the Bogota Mint.

Date	Mintage	VG	F	VF	XF	Unc
1837 RS	—	300	350	400	625	—
1838/7 RS	—	325	375	450	700	—
1838 RS	—	300	350	400	625	—
1839/8 RS	—	325	375	450	700	—
1839 RS	—	300	350	400	625	—
1840 RS	—	300	350	400	625	—
1841 RS	—	300	350	400	625	—
1842 RS	—	300	350	400	625	—
1843 RS	—	300	350	400	625	—
1844 RS	—	300	350	400	625	—
1845 RS	—	300	350	400	625	—
1846 RS	—	300	350	400	625	—
1847 RS	—	300	350	400	625	—
1848 RS	—	400	500	650	900	—
1849 RS	—	425	600	950	1,350	—

KM# 94.2 16 PESOS (Diez I Seis)
27.0000 g., 0.8750 Gold .7596 oz. **Note:** Struck at the Popayan Mint.

Date	Mintage	VG	F	VF	XF	Unc
1837 RU	—	300	350	400	625	—
1838 RU	—	300	350	400	625	—
1839 RU	—	300	350	400	625	—
1840 RU	—	300	350	425	650	—
1841/0 RU	—	450	—	—	—	—
1841 RU	—	425	650	—	—	—
1841 VU	—	300	350	400	625	—
1842 VU	—	300	350	400	625	—
1842 UM	—	300	350	400	625	—
1843 UM	—	300	350	400	625	—
1844 UM	—	300	350	400	625	—
1845 UM	—	300	350	400	625	—
1846 UM	—	300	350	425	650	—
1846 UE	—	425	650	950	—	—
1846 UR	—	300	350	400	625	—

KM# 100 16 PESOS (Diez I Seis)
25.8064 g., 0.9000 Gold .7468 oz. **Note:** Struck at the Bogota Mint.

Date	Mintage	VG	F	VF	XF	Unc
1848	—	400	800	1,500	3,000	—
1849	—	400	800	1,500	3,000	—
1850	—	400	800	1,500	3,000	—
1851	—	600	1,200	2,000	4,000	—
1852	—	400	800	1,500	3,000	—
1853	—	400	800	1,500	3,000	—

DECIMAL COINAGE

10 Decimos de Real = 1 Real (1847-53)

KM# 101 1/2 DECIMO DE REAL (1/20 Real)
Copper

Date	Mintage	F	VF	XF	Unc	BU
1847	—	3.00	7.00	22.50	60.00	—
1847 Proof	—	Value: 100				
1848	—	7.50	18.50	50.00	90.00	—

KM# 102 DECIMO DE REAL (1/10 Real)
Copper

Date	Mintage	F	VF	XF	Unc	BU
1847	—	3.00	7.50	22.50	60.00	—
1847 Proof	—	Value: 135				
1848	—	12.00	25.00	65.00	100	—

KM# 114 1/2 DECIMO
1.5000 g., 0.9000 Silver .0434 oz. **Note:** Struck at the Bogota Mint.

Date	Mintage	VG	F	VF	XF	Unc
1853	—	5.00	10.00	20.00	32.50	—
1854	—	9.00	18.50	30.00	55.00	—
1855	—	8.00	16.00	27.50	47.50	—
1856	—	7.00	14.00	25.00	42.50	—
1857	—	7.00	14.00	25.00	42.50	—
1858/4	—	8.00	16.50	24.00	40.00	—
1858	—	6.50	12.50	22.00	35.00	—

KM# 115 DECIMO
2.5000 g., 0.9000 Silver .0723 oz. **Note:** Struck at the Bogota Mint.

Date	Mintage	VG	F	VF	XF	Unc
1853	—	4.00	7.50	12.50	30.00	—
1854	—	2.75	4.50	9.00	22.00	—
1855/3	—	10.00	16.50	30.00	—	—
1855/4/3	—	10.00	20.00	35.00	—	—
1855/4	—	5.00	9.50	15.00	32.50	—
1855	—	2.75	4.50	8.00	22.00	—
1856	—	2.25	4.00	7.50	20.00	—
1857	—	6.50	10.00	16.50	35.00	—
1858/6	—	7.50	13.00	25.00	50.00	—
1858/7	—	4.00	7.50	12.50	30.00	—
1858	—	8.50	20.00	37.50	85.00	—

KM# 117 2 DECIMOS
5.0000 g., 0.9000 Silver .1447 oz. **Note:** Struck at the Bogota Mint.

Date	Mintage	VG	F	VF	XF	Unc
1854/3	—	7.50	18.50	42.50	85.00	—
1854	—	6.00	12.00	27.50	65.00	—
1855/3	—	4.50	9.00	35.00	75.00	—
1855	—	3.50	7.50	16.50	30.00	—
1856/5	—	5.50	12.00	38.00	75.00	—
1857	—	4.00	9.00	22.00	47.50	—
1858/7	—	12.50	27.50	60.00	125	—

KM# 108.1 1/4 REAL
0.9000 g., 0.9000 Silver .0260 oz. **Note:** Struck at the Bogota Mint.

Date	Mintage	VG	F	VF	XF	Unc
1850	—	6.50	15.00	27.50	55.00	—
1851	—	7.50	18.50	32.50	70.00	—
1852 Rare	—	—	—	—	—	—

KM# 108.2 1/4 REAL
0.9000 g., 0.9000 Silver .0260 oz. **Edge:** Plain **Note:** Struck at the Popayan Mint.

Date	Mintage	VG	F	VF	XF	Unc
1849	—	3.00	7.00	15.00	35.00	—
1850	—	2.50	6.50	15.00	35.00	—
1851	—	3.50	8.00	17.50	50.00	—
1852	—	4.50	10.00	22.50	55.00	—
1853	—	3.00	7.00	15.00	35.00	—
1855	—	6.50	12.00	25.00	57.50	—
1856	—	8.00	15.00	28.50	60.00	—
1858	—	17.50	32.50	47.50	100	—

KM# 113 1/4 REAL
0.9000 g., 0.9000 Silver .0260 oz. **Obv:** Similar to KM#108.1 **Rev:** Caduceus at each side of "1/4" instead of 3 stars below **Note:** Struck at the Bogota Mint.

Date	Mintage	VG	F	VF	XF	Unc
1852	—	13.50	35.00	75.00	165	—
1858 Rare	—	—	—	—	—	—

KM# 110 1/2 REAL
1.4000 g., 0.9000 Silver .0405 oz. **Note:** Struck at the Bogota Mint.

Date	Mintage	VG	F	VF	XF	Unc
1850	—	7.50	16.00	25.00	60.00	—
1851	—	3.75	10.00	17.50	40.00	—
1852/1	—	4.00	10.00	18.50	50.00	—
1852	—	4.00	9.00	16.00	37.50	—
1853	—	4.00	8.50	15.00	35.00	—

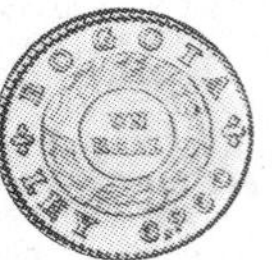

KM# 103 REAL
2.7000 g., 0.9000 Silver .0781 oz. **Edge:** Reeded **Note:** Struck at the Bogota Mint.

Date	Mintage	VG	F	VF	XF	Unc
1847	—	5.00	10.00	18.50	37.50	—

KM# 112 REAL
2.5000 g., 0.9000 Silver .0723 oz.

Date	Mintage	VG	F	VF	XF	Unc
1851	—	4.00	8.50	18.50	40.00	—
1852	—	2.50	5.50	10.00	17.50	—
1853	—	2.75	6.00	15.50	38.00	—

KM# 105 2 REALES
5.0000 g., 0.9000 Silver .1447 oz. **Obv:** Date below shield

Date	Mintage	VG	F	VF	XF	Unc
1847	—	4.00	8.00	17.50	35.00	—
1848	—	2.25	4.00	8.00	17.50	—
1849	—	2.25	4.00	8.00	16.50	—

KM# 104 2 REALES
5.0000 g., 0.9000 Silver .1447 oz. **Obv:** Date above shield **Note:** Struck at the Bogota Mint.

Date	Mintage	VG	F	VF	XF	Unc
1847 Rare	—	—	—	—	—	—

Note: Probably a pattern

KM# 109 2 REALES
5.0000 g., 0.9000 Silver .1447 oz. **Obv:** Date below shield

Date	Mintage	VG	F	VF	XF	Unc
1849 Rare	—	—	—	—	—	—
1850	—	3.50	7.00	15.00	37.50	—
1851	—	3.50	7.00	15.00	37.50	—
1852	—	5.00	9.00	20.00	42.50	—
1853	—	6.00	9.00	20.00	42.50	—

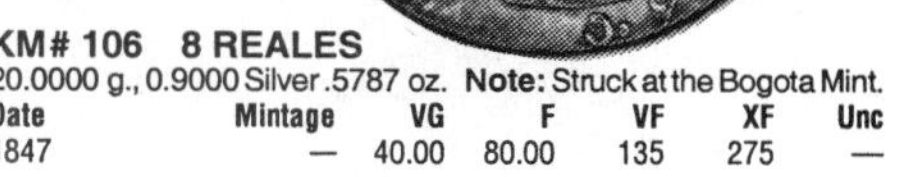

KM# 106 8 REALES
20.0000 g., 0.9000 Silver .5787 oz. **Note:** Struck at the Bogota Mint.

Date	Mintage	VG	F	VF	XF	Unc
1847	—	40.00	80.00	135	275	—

KM# 107 10 REALES
25.0000 g., 0.9000 Silver .7234 oz. **Note:** Struck at Bogota and Popayan without mint marks.

Date	Mintage	VG	F	VF	XF	Unc
1847	—	25.00	50.00	90.00	225	—
1848	—	20.00	35.00	65.00	185	—
1849/8	—	30.00	60.00	120	270	—
1849	—	25.00	55.00	100	240	—

KM# 111 10 REALES
25.0000 g., 0.9000 Silver .7234 oz. **Note:** Struck at the Bogota Mint.

Date	Mintage	VG	F	VF	XF	Unc
1850	—	25.00	50.00	100	225	—
1851	—	25.00	50.00	100	225	—

KM# 118 PESO
25.0000 g., 0.9000 Silver .7234 oz.

Date	Mintage	VG	F	VF	XF	Unc
1855/1	—	18.00	37.50	75.00	125	—
1855	—	15.00	30.00	45.00	65.00	—
1856/5	—	17.50	32.50	50.00	70.00	—
1856	—	12.50	25.00	40.00	60.00	—
1857/6	—	15.00	30.00	45.00	65.00	—
1857	—	12.50	25.00	40.00	60.00	—
1858/7	—	15.00	30.00	45.00	65.00	—
1858	—	12.50	25.00	40.00	60.00	—
1859/6	—	18.00	35.00	65.00	115	—

KM# 119 PESO
1.6875 g., 0.8750 Gold .0474 oz. **Note:** Similar to 2 Pesos, KM#121.

Date	Mintage	VG	F	VF	XF	Unc
1856	—	65.00	150	300	500	—
1858	—	65.00	150	300	500	—

KM# 121 2 PESOS
3.2258 g., 0.9000 Gold .0933 oz. **Rev:** Value in wreath

Date	Mintage	VG	F	VF	XF	Unc
1857P	—	60.00	100	175	300	—
1858/48P	—	70.00	120	200	350	—
1858P	—	60.00	100	175	300	—

KM# 120.1 5 PESOS
8.0648 g., 0.9000 Gold .2333 oz.

Date	Mintage	VG	F	VF	XF	Unc
1849B Unique	—	—	—	—	—	—
1857B	—	175	400	850	1,350	—

KM# 120.2 5 PESOS
8.0648 g., 0.9000 Gold .2333 oz. **Rev:** PESOS in small letters

Date	Mintage	VG	F	VF	XF	Unc
1858	—	200	500	1,000	1,750	—

KM# 116.1 10 PESOS
16.4000 g., 0.9000 Gold .4745 oz. **Note:** Struck at the Bogota Mint.

Date	Mintage	VG	F	VF	XF	Unc
1853	—	450	800	1,450	1,850	—
1854	—	350	650	1,250	1,500	—
1855	—	350	650	1,250	1,500	—
1856	—	350	650	1,250	1,500	—
1857	—	350	650	1,250	1,500	—

KM# 116.2 10 PESOS
16.4000 g., 0.9000 Gold .4745 oz. **Note:** Struck at the Popayan Mint.

Date	Mintage	VG	F	VF	XF	Unc
1853	—	250	400	600	1,000	—
1856	—	450	800	1,450	1,850	—
1857	—	—	—	800	1,250	—

KM# 122.2 10 PESOS
16.1290 g., 0.9000 Gold .4667 oz. **Rev. Legend:** DIEZ PESOS **Note:** Struck at the Popayan Mint.

Date	Mintage	VG	F	VF	XF	Unc
1857	—	225	325	500	900	—
1858	—	225	325	500	900	—

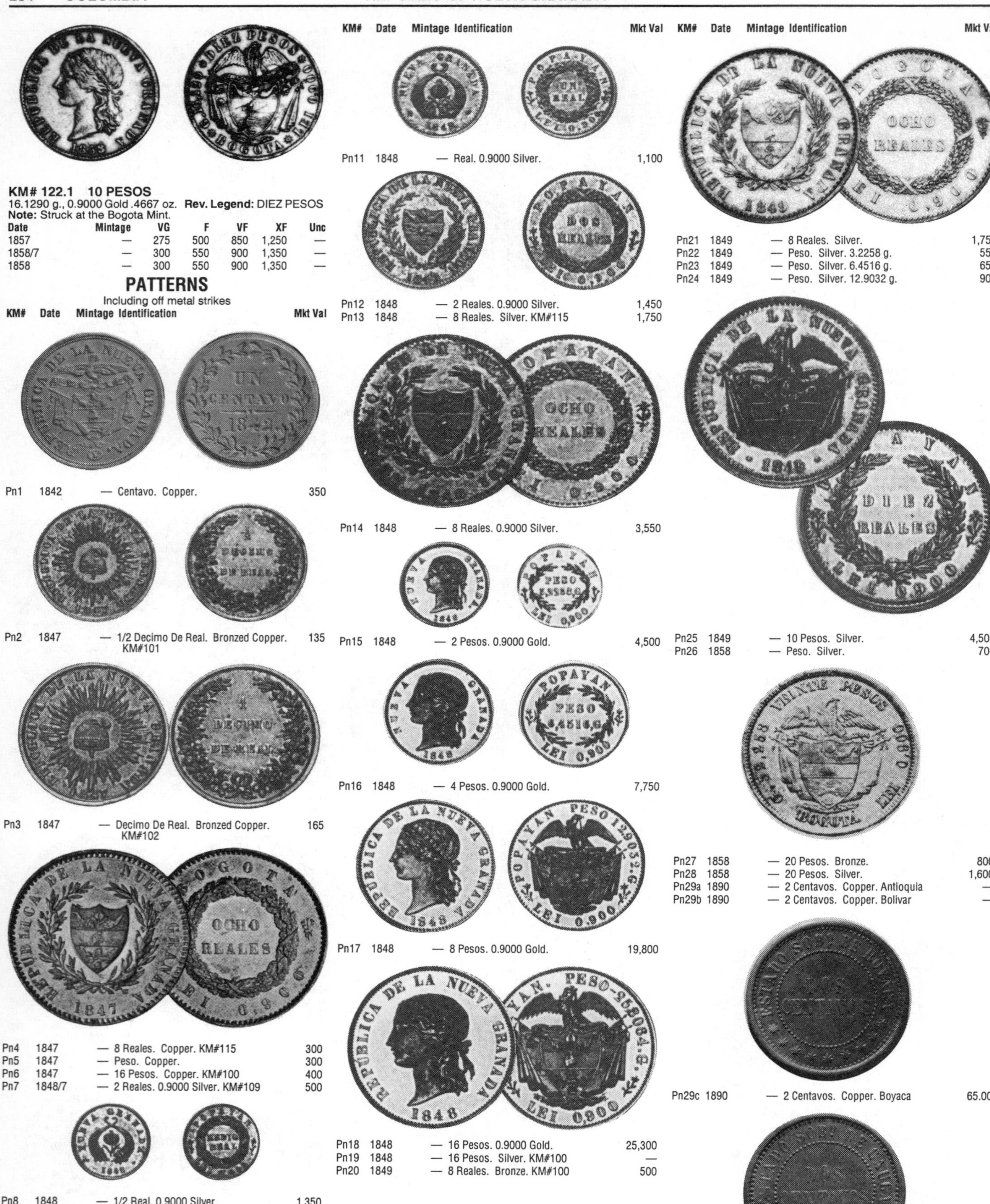

KM# 122.1 10 PESOS

16.1290 g., 0.9000 Gold .4667 oz. **Rev. Legend:** DIEZ PESOS
Note: Struck at the Bogota Mint.

Date	Mintage	VG	F	VF	XF	Unc
1857	—	275	500	850	1,250	—
1858/7	—	300	550	900	1,350	—
1858	—	300	550	900	1,350	—

PATTERNS

Including off metal strikes

KM#	Date	Mintage	Identification	Mkt Val
Pn1	1842	—	Centavo. Copper.	350
Pn2	1847	—	1/2 Decimo De Real. Bronzed Copper. KM#101	135
Pn3	1847	—	Decimo De Real. Bronzed Copper. KM#102	165
Pn4	1847	—	8 Reales. Copper. KM#115	300
Pn5	1847	—	Peso. Copper.	300
Pn6	1847	—	16 Pesos. Copper. KM#100	400
Pn7	1848/7	—	2 Reales. 0.9000 Silver. KM#109	500
Pn8	1848	—	1/2 Real. 0.9000 Silver.	1,350
Pn9	1848	—	1/2 Real. 0.9000 Silver. Piefort, KM#109.	350
Pn10	1848	—	Real. Silver. KM#112	450
Pn11	1848	—	Real. 0.9000 Silver.	1,100
Pn12	1848	—	2 Reales. 0.9000 Silver.	1,450
Pn13	1848	—	8 Reales. Silver. KM#115	1,750
Pn14	1848	—	8 Reales. 0.9000 Silver.	3,550
Pn15	1848	—	2 Pesos. 0.9000 Gold.	4,500
Pn16	1848	—	4 Pesos. 0.9000 Gold.	7,750
Pn17	1848	—	8 Pesos. 0.9000 Gold.	19,800
Pn18	1848	—	16 Pesos. 0.9000 Gold.	25,300
Pn19	1848	—	16 Pesos. Silver. KM#100	—
Pn20	1849	—	8 Reales. Bronze. KM#100	500
Pn21	1849	—	8 Reales. Silver.	1,750
Pn22	1849	—	Peso. Silver. 3.2258 g.	550
Pn23	1849	—	Peso. Silver. 6.4516 g.	650
Pn24	1849	—	Peso. Silver. 12.9032 g.	900
Pn25	1849	—	10 Pesos. Silver.	4,500
Pn26	1858	—	Peso. Silver.	700
Pn27	1858	—	20 Pesos. Bronze.	800
Pn28	1858	—	20 Pesos. Silver.	1,600
Pn29a	1890	—	2 Centavos. Copper. Antioquia	—
Pn29b	1890	—	2 Centavos. Copper. Bolivar	—
Pn29c	1890	—	2 Centavos. Copper. Boyaca	65.00
Pn29d	1890	—	2 Centavos. Copper. Cauca	65.00

KM#	Date	Mintage	Identification	Mkt Val
Pn29e	1890	—	2 Centavos. Copper. Cundinamarca	70.00
Pn29f	1890	—	2 Centavos. Copper. Magdalena	250
Pn29g	1890	—	2 Centavos. Copper. Santander	70.00
Pn29h	1890	—	2 Centavos. Copper. Tolima	65.00
Pn30	1871	—	5 Decimos. 0.8350 Silver. Small Liberty head.	—
Pn31	1871	—	5 Decimos. Copper. LEI .835	—
Pn32	1871	—	2 Pesos. Copper.	—
Pn33	1872	—	2 Pesos. Copper.	—
Pn34	1872	—	20 Pesos. Gold. ESSAI. ESSAI.	12,500
Pn35	1873	—	1/2 Decimo. Silver.	—
Pn36	1873	—	Decimo. Silver. ESSAI.	—
Pn37	1873	—	Decimo. Silver. ESSAI.	—
Pn38	1873	—	2 Decimos. Silver. ESSAI.	350
Pn39	1873	—	50 Centavos. 0.8350 Silver. Small Liberty head, ESSAI, A.B.	—
Pn40	1873	—	50 Centavos. Copper. LEI .835.	—
Pn41	1873	—	5 Decimos. Silver.	3,000
Pn42	1873	—	Peso. Silver. Bust by Barre without legend or date.	—
Pn43	1873	—	Peso. Silver. Bust by Wyon. Plain edge.	—
Pn44	1873	—	2 Decimos. ESSAI.	—
Pn45	1873	—	2 Decimos. ESSAI.	—
Pn46	1873	—	10 Pesos. Copper. Medellin.	400
Pn47	1873	—	10 Pesos. Gold.	—
Pn48	1873	—	10 Pesos. Gold. ESSAI on both sides.	10,000
Pn49	1873	—	20 Pesos. Gold. ESSAI on both sides.	12,500
Pn50	1873	—	20 Pesos. Copper.	800
Pn51	1873	—	20 Pesos. Silver.	1,400
Pn52	1874	—	1-1/4 Centavos. Copper.	—
Pn53	1874	—	50 Centavos. Silver Plated Copper. Small Liberty head.	—
Pn54	1874	—	50 Centavos. 0.8350 Silver. Small Liberty head.	2,750
Pn55	1875	—	50 Centavos. 0.8350 Silver. Small Liberty head.	—
Pn56	1881	—	2-1/2 Centavos. Aluminum. KM#179; 14-14.5mm.	200
Pn57	1881	—	2-1/2 Centavos. Copper. KM#179; 14-14.5mm.	200
Pn58	1881	—	2-1/2 Centavos. Copper-Nickel. KM#179; 14-14.5mm.	200
Pn59	1881	—	2-1/2 Centavos. Silver. KM#179; 14-14.5mm.	1,000
Pn60	1881	—	2-1/2 Centavos. Copper. Flat base on cap.	250
Pn61	1881	—	2-1/2 Centavos. Copper-Nickel. Flat base on cap.	250
Pn62	1881	—	2-1/2 Centavos. Silver. Flat base on cap.	1,250
Pn63	1881	—	2-1/2 Centavos. Copper. Slanted base on cap.	300
Pn64	1881	—	2-1/2 Centavos. Copper-Nickel. Slanted base on cap.	300
Pn65	1881	—	2-1/2 Centavos. Silver. Slanted base on cap.	1,500
Pn66	1881	—	5 Centavos. Copper.	250
Pn67	1881	—	5 Centavos. Copper-Nickel.	300
Pn68	1881	—	5 Centavos. Copper-Nickel. Without stars.	—
Pn69	1881	—	5 Centavos. Copper-Nickel. Wide bust, tall 5.	—
Pn70	1886	—	Centavo. Copper.	—
Pn71	1886	—	2-1/2 Centavos. Copper-Nickel.	—
Pn72	1886	—	5 Centavos. Copper-Nickel.	—
Pn73	1891	—	50 Centavos. Copper.	—
Pn74	1891	—	50 Centavos. 0.8350 Silver. Small bust and condor.	—
Pn75	1891	—	50 Centavos. 0.8350 Silver.	—
Pn76	1900	—	5 Centavos. Copper-Nickel.	275
Pn77	1900	—	10 Centavos. Copper-Nickel. Straight or curved neckline	300
Pn78	1900	—	10 Centavos. Copper-Nickel. ESSAI MONETAIRE.	400
Pn79	1900	—	10 Centavos. Copper-Nickel. Quartefoil.	100
Pn80	1900	—	10 Centavos. Silver. Reeded edge.	—
Pn81	1900	—	20 Centavos. Silver. Reeded edge.	—
Pn82	1900	—	50 Centavos. 0.8350 Silver. Plain edge.	—
Pn83	1900	—	50 Centavos. 0.8350 Silver. Reeded edge.	—

GRANADINE CONFEDERATION

DECIMAL COINAGE

10 Decimos = 1 Peso (1859-62)

KM# 131 1/4 DECIMO

0.9000 g., 0.6660 Silver .0192 oz. **Rev:** Caducei flanking fraction **Note:** Struck at the Bogota mint.

Date	Mintage	Good	VG	F	VF	XF
1860	—	6.50	15.00	32.50	55.00	—

KM# 132.2 1/4 DECIMO

0.9000 g., 0.6660 Silver .0192 oz. **Rev:** 9 stars below fraction **Note:** Struck at the Popayan mint.

Date	Mintage	Good	VG	F	VF	XF
1860	—	9.00	22.50	40.00	90.00	—

KM# 132.1 1/4 DECIMO

0.9000 g., 0.6660 Silver .0192 oz. **Rev:** 9 stars below fraction **Note:** Struck at the Bogota mint.

Date	Mintage	Good	VG	F	VF	XF
1861	—	6.50	13.50	27.50	50.00	—
1862	—	10.00	22.50	40.00	85.00	—

KM# 124 1/2 DECIMO

1.2500 g., 0.9000 Silver .0362 oz. **Note:** Struck at the Bogota mint.

Date	Mintage	VG	F	VF	XF	Unc
1859	—	7.50	18.50	32.50	80.00	—
1860/59	—	8.00	20.00	35.00	85.00	—
1860	—	6.00	14.00	25.00	55.00	—
1861	—	7.50	18.50	32.50	80.00	—

KM# 125 DECIMO

2.5000 g., 0.9000 Silver .0723 oz. **Note:** Struck at the Bogota mint.

Date	Mintage	VG	F	VF	XF	Unc
1859	—	4.00	9.00	22.50	50.00	—
1860	—	7.50	18.50	37.50	85.00	—

KM# 123 1/4 REAL
0.9000 g., 0.6660 Silver .0192 oz. **Rev:** 3 stars **Note:** Struck at the Popayan mint.

Date	Mintage	Good	VG	F	VF	XF
1859	—	8.00	30.00	65.00	160	—
1860	—	3.50	7.50	15.00	35.00	—
1861	—	3.50	7.50	15.00	35.00	—
1862/1	—	—	—	—	—	—
1862	—	10.00	35.00	75.00	175	—

KM# 133 1/2 REAL
1.2500 g., 0.9000 Silver .0362 oz. **Note:** Struck at the Popayan mint.

Date	Mintage	Good	VG	F	VF	XF
1862	—	7.00	13.50	30.00	57.50	—
1862/48	—	7.00	12.50	27.50	55.00	—

KM# 134 2 REALES
5.0000 g., 0.9000 Silver .1447 oz. **Note:** These are struck from reworked dies of KM#109. Struck at the Popayan mint.

Date	Mintage	VG	F	VF	XF	Unc
1862/48/47	—	6.00	15.00	27.50	62.50	—
1862/48	—	5.50	13.50	25.00	60.00	—
1862/49	—	4.50	10.00	22.50	55.00	—
1862/52	—	25.00	45.00	85.00	130	—
1862	—	7.00	15.00	27.50	60.00	—

KM# 126 PESO
25.0000 g., 0.9000 Silver .7234 oz. **Note:** Struck at the Bogota mint.

Date	Mintage	VG	F	VF	XF	Unc
1859	—	15.00	25.00	50.00	100	—
1860	—	15.00	25.00	50.00	100	—
1861	—	25.00	50.00	100	200	—

KM# 135 PESO
1.6129 g., 0.9000 Gold .0466 oz.

Date	Mintage	VG	F	VF	XF	Unc
1862M Rare; 2 known	—	—	—	—	—	—

KM# 127 2 PESOS
3.2258 g., 0.9000 Gold .0933 oz.

Date	Mintage	VG	F	VF	XF	Unc
1859P	—	75.00	150	300	550	—
1860P	—	125	250	550	1,000	—

KM# 128 5 PESOS
8.0645 g., 0.9000 Gold .2333 oz.

Date	Mintage	VG	F	VF	XF	Unc
1859P	—	—	—	—	5,000	—

KM# 136 5 PESOS
8.0645 g., 0.9000 Gold .2333 oz.

Date	Mintage	VG	F	VF	XF	Unc
1862M	—	—	—	—	6,000	—

KM# 129.1 10 PESOS
16.1290 g., 0.9000 Gold .4667 oz. **Note:** Struck at the Bogota mint.

Date	Mintage	VG	F	VF	XF	Unc
1859	3,481	250	350	600	1,000	—
1860	9,687	225	300	500	900	—
1861	834	275	450	750	1,200	—

KM# 129.2 10 PESOS
16.1290 g., 0.9000 Gold .4667 oz. **Note:** Struck at the Popayan mint.

Date	Mintage	VG	F	VF	XF	Unc
1858	—	225	300	500	900	—
1859/58	—	250	350	600	1,000	—
1859	—	225	300	500	900	—
1860	—	250	350	600	1,000	—
1861	—	275	400	700	1,100	—
1862	—	250	350	600	1,000	—

KM# 130 20 PESOS
32.2580 g., 0.9000 Gold .9335 oz. **Note:** Struck at the Bogota mint.

Date	Mintage	VG	F	VF	XF	Unc
1859	2,002	900	1,750	3,000	5,000	—

ESTADOS UNIDOS DE NUEVA GRANADA

DECIMAL COINAGE

10 Decimos = 1 Peso (1861-62)

KM# 137 DECIMO
2.5000 g., 0.9000 Silver .0723 oz. **Note:** Struck at the Bogota mint.

Date	Mintage	VG	F	VF	XF	Unc
1861	—	22.50	60.00	125	250	—

KM# 138 PESO
25.0000 g., 0.9000 Silver .7234 oz. **Note:** Struck at the Bogota mint.

Date	Mintage	VG	F	VF	XF	Unc
1861	—	125	250	400	700	—

ESTADOS UNIDOS DE COLOMBIAE

DECIMAL COINAGE

10 Decimos = 1 Peso (1862-86)

KM# 143.1 1/4 DECIMO
0.8500 g., 0.9000 Silver .0245 oz. **Note:** Struck at the Bogota mint.

Date	Mintage	VG	F	VF	XF	Unc
1863	48,000	3.00	6.00	11.00	25.00	—
1864	435,000	2.00	5.00	9.50	20.00	—
1865	206,000	2.00	5.00	10.00	22.00	—
1866	267,000	2.00	5.00	10.00	22.00	—
1867	208,000	2.00	5.00	10.00	22.00	—

KM# 143.2 1/4 DECIMO
0.8500 g., 0.9000 Silver .0245 oz. **Note:** Struck at the Popayan mint.

Date	Mintage	VG	F	VF	XF	Unc
1863	—	4.50	8.00	13.50	30.00	—
1864	504,000	4.00	7.50	12.50	28.00	—
1865/3	—	6.00	13.50	22.50	42.50	—
1865	291,000	4.50	10.00	18.50	35.00	—
1866	157,000	7.50	16.50	35.00	55.00	—
1867	55,000	7.50	16.50	35.00	55.00	—

KM# 143.2a 1/4 DECIMO
0.8500 g., 0.6660 Silver .0182 oz. **Note:** Date varieties exist for 1880 and 1881. Struck at the Popayan mint.

Date	Mintage	VG	F	VF	XF	Unc
1868	—	8.50	20.00	42.50	67.50	—
1869	—	4.00	7.50	15.00	37.50	—
1870	—	4.00	7.50	15.00	37.50	—
1871	155,000	6.00	14.00	20.00	45.00	—
1872/1	41,000	9.00	18.00	32.50	55.00	—
1872	Inc. above	4.00	7.50	15.00	35.00	—
1873/2	—	9.00	18.00	30.00	55.00	—
1873	—	4.00	7.50	15.00	35.00	—
1874	—	6.50	16.50	27.50	55.00	—
1875	—	4.50	9.00	22.50	37.50	—
1876	—	7.00	16.00	27.50	50.00	—
1877	25,000	4.50	9.00	25.00	40.00	—
1878	25,000	8.50	20.00	42.50	65.00	—
1879	—	12.50	27.50	60.00	135	—
1880 Narrow date	—	4.50	9.00	25.00	40.00	—
1880 Wide date	—	4.50	9.00	25.00	40.00	—
1881 Narrow date	—	4.50	9.00	25.00	40.00	—
1888 Rare	—	—	—	—	—	—

KM# 143.1a 1/4 DECIMO
0.8500 g., 0.6660 Silver .0182 oz. **Note:** Struck at the Bogota mint.

Date	Mintage	VG	F	VF	XF	Unc
1868	23,000	40.00	75.00	135	200	—
1869	183,000	5.00	10.00	16.50	32.50	—
1870	92,000	6.00	12.00	18.00	35.00	—
1871	413,000	4.50	10.00	16.50	32.50	—
1873 Rare; including KM#169	—	—	—	—	—	—
1881 Including KM#169	—	7.50	16.50	25.00	45.00	—

KM# 143.3 1/4 DECIMO
0.8500 g., 0.6660 Silver .0182 oz. **Note:** Struck at the Medellin mint.

Date	Mintage	VG	F	VF	XF	Unc
1874	—	8.00	18.00	30.00	60.00	—

KM# 144 1/2 DECIMO
1.2500 g., 0.9000 Silver .0362 oz. **Note:** Struck at the Bogota mint.

Date	Mintage	VG	F	VF	XF	Unc
1863	28,000	10.00	20.00	40.00	85.00	—
1864	Inc. above	10.00	22.50	55.00	100	—
1865	29,000	15.00	30.00	65.00	150	—

KM# 144a 1/2 DECIMO
1.2500 g., 0.6660 Silver .0268 oz. **Note:** Struck at the Bogota mint.

Date	Mintage	VG	F	VF	XF	Unc
1867 Reverse .666/.900	363,000	10.00	18.50	37.50	72.50	—

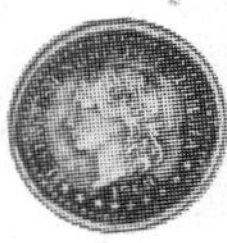

KM# 150.1 1/2 DECIMO
1.2500 g., 0.6660 Silver .0268 oz. **Note:** Struck at the Bogota mint.

Date	Mintage	VG	F	VF	XF	Unc
1868 Including KM#144a	—	4.50	12.50	22.50	37.50	—
1869 Rare	173,000	—	—	—	—	—
1870	140,000	6.00	13.50	26.50	47.50	—
1871	100,000	8.50	17.50	32.50	52.50	—

KM# 150.2 1/2 DECIMO

1.2500 g., 0.6660 Silver .0268 oz. **Note:** Struck at the Medellin mint.

Date	Mintage	VG	F	VF	XF	Unc
1868	62,000	8.00	18.50	37.50	57.50	—
1869	26,000	10.00	22.50	40.00	75.00	—

KM# 150.3 1/2 DECIMO

1.2500 g., 0.6660 Silver .0268 oz. **Note:** Struck at the Popayan mint.

Date	Mintage	VG	F	VF	XF	Unc
1868	—	20.00	45.00	100	185	—
1869	—	6.50	15.00	30.00	50.00	—
1870	382,000	6.50	15.00	30.00	50.00	—
1873 Rare	—	—	—	—	—	—
1874	—	7.50	16.50	36.50	70.00	—
1875	573,000	6.50	15.00	30.00	50.00	—
1876	—	8.00	20.00	40.00	80.00	—
1878	—	20.00	38.50	80.00	150	—

KM# 150.2a 1/2 DECIMO

1.2500 g., 0.8350 Silver .0336 oz. **Obv:** Small bust **Note:** Struck at the Medellin mint.

Date	Mintage	VG	F	VF	XF	Unc
1870	Inc. above	12.50	25.00	37.50	50.00	—
1871	61,000	4.50	10.00	22.50	37.50	—
1872/1	Inc. above	4.00	9.00	20.00	35.00	—
1872 .835/.666	—	4.00	9.00	20.00	35.00	—

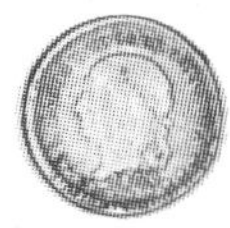
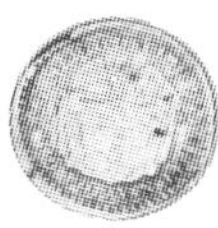

KM# 150.3a 1/2 DECIMO

1.2500 g., 0.8350 Silver .0336 oz. **Obv:** AB below Barre bust **Note:** Struck at the Popayan mint.

Date	Mintage	VG	F	VF	XF	Unc
1872 Reverse with 0.835/0.666	Inc. above	5.00	12.00	25.00	50.00	—
1875/65	—	10.00	25.00	40.00	85.00	—
1875	Inc. above	25.00	40.00	70.00	135	—

KM# 150.4 1/2 DECIMO

1.2500 g., 0.8350 Silver .0336 oz. **Obv:** AB below Barre bust **Note:** Struck at the Medellin mint.

Date	Mintage	VG	F	VF	XF	Unc
1873 Rare	—	—	—	—	—	—
1874/3	—	18.00	35.00	75.00	150	—

KM# 145.1 DECIMO

2.5000 g., 0.9000 Silver .0723 oz. **Note:** Struck at the Bogota mint.

Date	Mintage	VG	F	VF	XF	Unc
1863	96,000	5.00	11.00	22.00	45.00	—
1864	39,000	6.00	12.50	25.00	55.00	—
1866	112,000	5.00	11.00	18.00	40.00	—

KM# 145.2 DECIMO

2.5000 g., 0.9000 Silver .0723 oz. **Note:** The overdates appear to have been struck from recut dies of 1 Real, 1848 Popayan, Pn7 with stars over 1848 on obverse and 1863 or 1864 on reverse. Struck at the Popayan mint.

Date	Mintage	VG	F	VF	XF	Unc
1863//1848	—	7.00	15.00	30.00	60.00	—
1864//1848	28,000	10.00	18.50	36.50	67.50	—
1864	—	10.00	22.50	42.50	90.00	—

KM# 145.2a DECIMO

2.5000 g., 0.8350 Silver .0671 oz. **Note:** Some, or all, appear to have been struck from recut dies of 1 Real, 1848 Popayan, Pn7 with stars over 1848 on obverse and 1866 on reverse. Struck at the Popayan mint.

Date	Mintage	VG	F	VF	XF	Unc
1866	34,000	12.50	27.50	52.50	115	—

KM# 145.1a DECIMO

2.5000 g., 0.8350 Silver .0671 oz. **Note:** Struck at the Bogota mint.

Date	Mintage	VG	F	VF	XF	Unc
1866	606,000	5.00	12.00	22.50	40.00	—

KM# 151.1 DECIMO

2.5000 g., 0.8350 Silver .0671 oz. **Note:** Struck at the Bogota mint.

Date	Mintage	VG	F	VF	XF	Unc
1868	146,000	4.00	10.00	25.00	55.00	—
1869	82,000	4.00	10.00	25.00	55.00	—
1870 Rare	—	—	—	—	—	—
1871	144,000	2.50	6.50	17.50	37.50	—
1872	133,000	2.50	6.50	17.50	37.50	—

KM# 151.2 DECIMO

2.5000 g., 0.8350 Silver .0671 oz. **Obv:** AB below Barre bust **Note:** Struck at the Medellin mint.

Date	Mintage	VG	F	VF	XF	Unc
1874/3	—	35.00	75.00	145	300	—

KM# 149 2 DECIMOS

5.0000 g., 0.9000 Silver .1447 oz. **Note:** Struck at the Bogota mint.

Date	Mintage	VG	F	VF	XF	Unc
1865	—	35.00	75.00	135	225	—

KM# 149a.1 2 DECIMOS

5.0000 g., 0.8350 Silver .1342 oz. **Note:** Struck at the Bogota mint.

Date	Mintage	VG	F	VF	XF	Unc
1866	—	4.00	10.00	18.50	38.50	—
1867	—	4.00	10.00	18.50	38.50	—

KM# 149b 2 DECIMOS

5.0000 g., 0.8350 Silver .1342 oz.

Date	Mintage	VG	F	VF	XF	Unc
1867 Error: reverse 0.666	—	10.00	22.50	35.00	60.00	—
1867 Reverse: 0.835/0.666	—	12.50	27.50	55.00	85.00	—

KM# 149a.2 2 DECIMOS

5.0000 g., 0.8350 Silver .1342 oz. **Note:** Large and small star varieties. Struck at the Popayan mint.

Date	Mintage	VG	F	VF	XF	Unc
1867 Reverse 0.835/0.900	—	6.00	13.50	27.50	62.50	—

KM# 155.2 2 DECIMOS

5.0000 g., 0.8350 Silver .1342 oz. **Note:** Each date of KM#155.2 has slightly different head, with 2 varieties for 1872. Legend spacings also vary. Struck at the Medellin mint.

Date	Mintage	VG	F	VF	XF	Unc
1870	15,000	8.00	18.50	32.50	55.00	—
1871	36,000	15.00	35.00	65.00	150	—
1872	45,000	6.00	12.50	27.50	40.00	—

KM# 155.1 2 DECIMOS

5.0000 g., 0.8350 Silver .1342 oz. **Note:** Struck at the Bogota mint.

Date	Mintage	VG	F	VF	XF	Unc
1872	24,000	22.50	37.50	65.00	120	—

KM# 159 2 DECIMOS

5.0000 g., 0.8350 Silver .1342 oz.

Date	Mintage	VG	F	VF	XF	Unc
1873 Rare	800	—	—	—	—	—

KM# 160 2 DECIMOS

5.0000 g., 0.8350 Silver .1342 oz. **Obv:** Large head **Rev:** Arms **Note:** Struck at the Medellin mint.

Date	Mintage	VG	F	VF	XF	Unc
1874	—	1.25	3.25	9.50	27.50	—

KM# 153.1 5 DECIMOS

12.5000 g., 0.8350 Silver .3356 oz. **Edge Lettering:** DIOS LEI LIBERTAD **Note:** Struck at the Bogota mint.

Date	Mintage	VG	F	VF	XF	Unc
1868	9,161	35.00	60.00	130	225	—
1869	187,000	8.00	18.00	45.00	100	—
1870	206,000	8.00	18.00	45.00	90.00	—
1871	273,000	10.00	20.00	60.00	120	—

KM# 153.2 5 DECIMOS

12.5000 g., 0.8350 Silver .3356 oz. **Edge Lettering:** DIOS LEI LIBERTAD **Note:** Struck at the Medellin mint.

Date	Mintage	VG	F	VF	XF	Unc
1868 Rare; 5 known	—	—	—	—	—	—
1869	1,054	275	500	750	1,000	—

KM# 153.6 5 DECIMOS

12.5000 g., 0.8350 Silver .3356 oz. **Obv:** Small round head **Rev:** Fineness faces out **Edge Lettering:** DIOS LEI LIBERTAD **Note:** Struck at the Popayan mint.

Date	Mintage	Good	VG	F	VF	XF
1869 Rare; 1 known	—	—	—	—	—	—
1870	Inc. above	55.00	115	185	300	—
1871	—	57.50	125	220	400	—
1873	Inc. above	45.00	100	175	275	—
1873/69 Rare	7,743	—	—	—	—	—
1874	11,000	125	275	450	750	—
Note: 1874 dated coins with 0,835/0,900 overprint are known						
1878	3,158	85.00	175	300	500	—
1880 Rare; 2 known	—	—	—	—	—	—

KM# 153.3 5 DECIMOS

12.5000 g., 0.8350 Silver .3356 oz. **Edge Lettering:** DIOS LEI LIBERTAD **Note:** Struck at the Medellin mint.

Date	Mintage	VG	F	VF	XF	Unc
1872	30,000	20.00	45.00	85.00	150	—
1873	90,000	9.00	22.50	45.00	90.00	—

KM# 153.4 5 DECIMOS

12.5000 g., 0.8350 Silver .3356 oz. **Obv:** Small round head **Rev:** Small arms, fineness faces in **Edge Lettering:** DIOS LEI LIBERTAD **Note:** Struck at the Medellin mint.

Date	Mintage	VG	F	VF	XF	Unc
1873	Inc. above	35.00	75.00	150	250	—
1874	185,000	8.00	16.00	40.00	85.00	—
1875/4	197,000	8.00	16.00	40.00	85.00	—

KM# 153.5 5 DECIMOS

12.5000 g., 0.8350 Silver .3356 oz. **Obv:** Small round head **Rev:** Fineness faces out **Edge:** Lettered **Note:** Varieties exist. Struck at the Medellin mint.

Date	Mintage	VG	F	VF	XF	Unc
1875	Inc. above	7.00	15.00	35.00	75.00	—
1876/5	—	12.50	25.00	50.00	100	—
1876	—	7.00	15.00	40.00	85.00	—
1877 Rare; 2 known	—	—	—	—	—	—

KM# 161.1 5 DECIMOS

12.5000 g., 0.8350 Silver .3356 oz. **Obv:** Large head **Rev:** Large arms **Edge Lettering:** DIOS LEI LIBERTAD **Note:** Date varieties exist. Struck at the Medellin mint.

Date	Mintage	VG	F	VF	XF	Unc
1877/4	168,000	9.00	18.00	45.00	110	—
1878/4	318,000	7.00	17.50	35.00	75.00	—
1878/4 Large 8; rare	Inc. above	—	—	—	—	—
1879/4 Pointed-tail 9	379,000	6.00	15.00	28.00	60.00	—
1879/4 Ball-tailed 9	Inc. above	8.00	22.00	45.00	90.00	—
1880/74	411,000	22.50	55.00	115	245	—
1880	Inc. above	4.00	8.00	16.00	40.00	—
1881	379,000	5.00	10.00	20.00	45.00	—
1882	—	3.00	7.00	14.00	35.00	—
1883	1,096,000	3.00	7.00	14.00	35.00	—
1884/3	1,429,000	40.00	80.00	135	225	—
1884	Inc. above	3.00	7.00	14.00	35.00	—
Note: Narrow and wide date varieties exist						
1885	—	4.00	8.00	16.00	40.00	—

KM# 161.2 5 DECIMOS

12.5000 g., 0.8350 Silver .3356 oz. **Obv:** 8-pointed stars, different head **Rev:** Large arms **Edge Lettering:** DIOS LEI LIBERTAD **Note:** Struck at the Medellin mint.

Date	Mintage	VG	F	VF	XF	Unc
1880 Rare; 2 known	—	—	—	—	—	—
1882 Rare	—	—	—	—	—	—
1883 Rare	—	—	—	—	—	—

KM# 161.3 5 DECIMOS

12.2000 g., Silver **Obv:** Square Liberty head **Edge Lettering:** DIOS LEI LIBERTAD

Date	Mintage	VG	F	VF	XF	Unc
1881 Including KM#161.1	—	50.00	85.00	140	245	—

KM# 161.2a 5 DECIMOS

12.2000 g., Silver **Obv:** 8-pointed stars, different head **Rev:** Large arms **Edge Lettering:** DIOS LEI LIBERTAD **Note:** 0.500/0.835. Struck at the Medellin mint.

Date	Mintage	VG	F	VF	XF	Unc
1886/4	—	65.00	140	250	425	—
1886/6 Rare	—	—	—	—	—	—

KM# 161.2b 5 DECIMOS

12.2000 g., Silver **Obv:** 8-pointed stars, different head **Rev:** Large arms **Edge Lettering:** DIOS PATRIA LIBERTAD **Note:** 0.500/0.835. Struck at the Medellin mint.

Date	Mintage	VG	F	VF	XF	Unc
1886	—	45.00	125	225	340	—
Note: First A in PATRIA is inverted V						

KM# 161.2c 5 DECIMOS

12.2000 g., Silver **Obv:** 8-pointed stars, different head **Rev:** 4 stars **Edge Lettering:** DIOS PATRIA LIBERTAD **Note:** 0.500/0.835. Struck at the Medellin mint.

Date	Mintage	VG	F	VF	XF	Unc
1886	—	100	200	350	550	—

KM# 161.1a 5 DECIMOS

12.5000 g., 0.8350 Silver .3356 oz. **Obv:** Large head **Rev:** Large arms **Edge Lettering:** DIOS PATRIA LIBERTAD **Note:** Struck at the Medellin mint.

Date	Mintage	VG	F	VF	XF	Unc
1886	—	25.00	60.00	120	250	—
1886 Round-top 3 in fineness; rare	—	—	—	—	—	—

KM# 164.3 5 DECIMOS

12.5000 g., Silver **Obv:** Modified head with curl on top, 5-pointed stars **Rev:** Without stars or dots **Rev. Legend:** LEI **Edge Lettering:** DIOS LEI LIBERTAD **Note:** Struck at the Medellin mint.

Date	Mintage	VG	F	VF	XF	Unc
1886 Rare; 1 known	—	—	—	—	—	—

KM# 164.1 5 DECIMOS

12.5000 g., 0.5000 Silver .2009 oz. **Obv:** Modified head with curl on top, 5-pointed stars **Rev:** 2 stars and 2 dots **Rev. Legend:** LEV **Edge Lettering:** DIOS LEI LIBERTAD **Note:** Struck at the Medellin mint.

Date	Mintage	VG	F	VF	XF	Unc
1886 Rare	—	—	—	—	—	—

KM# 164.2 5 DECIMOS

12.5000 g., 0.5000 Silver .2009 oz. **Obv:** Modified head with curl on top, 5-pointed stars **Rev:** Without stars or dots **Rev. Legend:** LEI **Edge Lettering:** DIOS LEI LIBERTAD **Note:** Struck at the Medellin mint.

Date	Mintage	VG	F	VF	XF	Unc
1886 Rare	—	—	—	—	—	—

KM# 152 1/2 PESO

12.5000 g., Silver .3356 oz. **Edge Lettering:** DIOS LEI LIBERTAD **Note:** 0.835/0.900. Struck at the Medellin mint.

Date	Mintage	VG	F	VF	XF	Unc
1868 Rare	—	—	—	—	—	—

KM# 162 2 REALES

5.0000 g., 0.8350 Silver .1342 oz. **Note:** Struck at the Popayan mint.

Date	Mintage	VG	F	VF	XF	Unc
1880	3,000	55.00	100	185	300	—
Note: Apparently struck from heavily recut dies of 2 Decimos, 1854-1858						

KM# 139.1 PESO

25.0000 g., 0.9000 Silver .7234 oz. **Note:** Struck at the Bogota mint.

Date	Mintage	VG	F	VF	XF	Unc
1862	55,000	12.50	35.00	60.00	115	—
1863	18,000	10.00	30.00	55.00	100	—
1864	104,000	9.00	25.00	50.00	90.00	—
1865	122,000	9.00	25.00	50.00	90.00	—
1866	91,000	9.00	25.00	50.00	90.00	—
1867	44,000	12.50	35.00	60.00	115	—
1868	17,000	12.50	35.00	60.00	115	—

KM# 139.2 PESO

25.0000 g., 0.9000 Silver .7234 oz. **Note:** Struck at the Popayan mint.

Date	Mintage	VG	F	VF	XF	Unc
1863	—	200	500	700	1,000	—

KM# 146.1 PESO

1.6129 g., 0.9000 Gold .0466 oz. **Obv. Legend:** ESTADOS UNIDOS DE COLOMBIA **Note:** Struck at the Medellin mint.

Date	Mintage	VG	F	VF	XF	Unc
1863	11,000	90.00	175	275	500	—

KM# 146.2 PESO
1.6129 g., 0.9000 Gold .0466 oz. **Obv. Legend:** COLOMBIA **Note:** Struck at the Medellin mint.

Date	Mintage	VG	F	VF	XF	Unc
1864	1,072	500	850	1,250	1,650	—

KM# 154.1 PESO
25.0000 g., 0.9000 Silver .7234 oz. **Note:** Struck at the Bogota mint.

Date	Mintage	VG	F	VF	XF	Unc
1868	—	300	500	800	1,350	—
1869 Rare	—	—	—	—	—	—
1870	46,000	55.00	100	165	350	—
1871	40,000	42.50	85.00	150	325	—

KM# 154.2 PESO
25.0000 g., 0.9000 Silver .7234 oz. **Note:** Struck at the Medellin mint.

Date	Mintage	VG	F	VF	XF	Unc
1869	3,598	65.00	135	200	450	—
1870/69	48,000	75.00	150	225	500	—
1870	Inc. above	50.00	100	165	350	—
1871	55,000	40.00	75.00	135	325	—

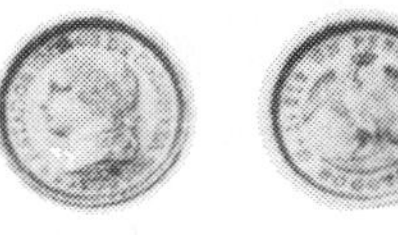

KM# 157.2 PESO
1.6129 g., 0.9000 Gold .0466 oz. **Rev:** Condor **Note:** Struck at the Bogota mint.

Date	Mintage	VG	F	VF	XF	Unc
1871	—	60.00	120	200	400	—

Note: The 1871 date is more commonly encountered as a counterfeit than an authentic striking

Date	Mintage	VG	F	VF	XF	Unc
1872	—	30.00	50.00	75.00	115	—
1873	3,374	30.00	50.00	75.00	115	—
1874	14,000	30.00	50.00	80.00	125	—
1875	7,002	30.00	50.00	80.00	125	—
1878	—	75.00	150	250	350	—

KM# 156 PESO
1.6129 g., 0.9000 Gold .0466 oz. **Rev:** Arms **Note:** Struck at the Medellin mint.

Date	Mintage	VG	F	VF	XF	Unc
1872/1	62,000	45.00	75.00	115	175	—
1872	Inc. above	30.00	60.00	90.00	125	—
1873	18,000	45.00	75.00	115	175	—

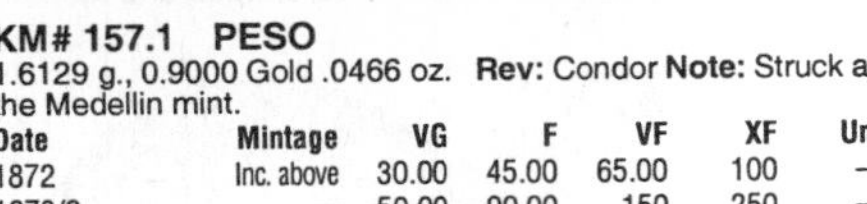

KM# 157.1 PESO
1.6129 g., 0.9000 Gold .0466 oz. **Rev:** Condor **Note:** Struck at the Medellin mint.

Date	Mintage	VG	F	VF	XF	Unc
1872	Inc. above	30.00	45.00	65.00	100	—
1873/2	—	50.00	90.00	150	250	—
1873	—	50.00	90.00	150	250	—

KM# 147 2 PESOS
3.2258 g., 0.9000 Gold .0933 oz. **Note:** Struck at the Medellin mint.

Date	Mintage	VG	F	VF	XF	Unc
1863	2,996	150	280	450	700	—

KM# A154 2 PESOS
3.2258 g., 0.9000 Gold .0933 oz. **Note:** Struck at the Medellin mint.

Date	Mintage	VG	F	VF	XF	Unc
1871	66,000	55.00	65.00	80.00	125	—
1872	30,000	65.00	80.00	120	175	—
1876	—	80.00	100	140	200	—

KM# A154a 2 PESOS
3.2258 g., 0.6660 Gold .0690 oz. **Note:** Struck at the Medellin mint.

Date	Mintage	VG	F	VF	XF	Unc
1885/74 Rare	—	—	—	—	—	—

KM# 140 5 PESOS
8.0645 g., 0.9000 Gold .2333 oz. **Obv. Legend:** ESTADOS UNIDOS DE COLOMBIA **Note:** Struck at the Medellin mint.

Date	Mintage	VG	F	VF	XF	Unc
1863	29,000	1,500	2,500	4,000	5,750	—

KM# A148 5 PESOS
8.0645 g., 0.9000 Gold .2333 oz. **Obv:** KM#140 **Rev:** KM#48 **Note:** Mule. Struck at the Medellin mint.

Date	Mintage	VG	F	VF	XF	Unc
1864 Unique	—	—	—	—	—	—

KM# 148 5 PESOS
8.0645 g., 0.9000 Gold .2333 oz. **Obv. Legend:** COLOMBIA above **Note:** Struck at the Medellin mint.

Date	Mintage	VG	F	VF	XF	Unc
1864	8,035	2,000	3,000	4,750	6,500	—

KM# 163 5 PESOS
8.0645 g., 0.6660 Gold .1728 oz. **Note:** Struck at the Medellin mint.

Date	Mintage	VG	F	VF	XF	Unc
1885 Inverted 5	—	800	1,350	1,750	2,850	—
1885/74	—	800	1,350	1,750	2,850	—

KM# 141.1 10 PESOS
16.1290 g., 0.9000 Gold .4667 oz. **Note:** Struck at the Bogota mint.

Date	Mintage	VG	F	VF	XF	Unc
1862	11,000	250	450	750	1,200	—
1863	17,000	250	450	750	1,150	—
1864	—	600	1,000	2,000	3,000	—
1866	—	1,000	2,000	3,500	5,000	—

KM# 141.3 10 PESOS
16.1290 g., 0.9000 Gold .4667 oz. **Obv:** Small date, inverted LEI 0.900 **Rev:** Small Phrygian cap **Note:** Struck at the Popayan mint.

Date	Mintage	VG	F	VF	XF	Unc
1863	—	250	375	650	900	—
1864	10,000	225	325	450	750	—
1865	8,727	250	375	650	900	—
1866	13,000	225	325	450	750	—
1867	—	300	400	700	1,000	—
1869	—	300	400	700	1,000	—
1870	—	600	1,000	2,000	3,000	—

KM# 141.2 10 PESOS
16.1290 g., 0.9000 Gold .4667 oz. **Note:** Varieties exist. Struck at the Medellin mint.

Date	Mintage	VG	F	VF	XF	Unc
1864	—	300	475	775	1,250	—
1867	14,000	250	350	600	900	—
1868	18,000	225	325	500	800	—
1869	18,000	225	325	500	800	—
1870	7,786	250	350	600	900	—
1871	6,018	250	350	600	900	—

KM# 141.4 10 PESOS
16.1290 g., 0.9000 Gold .4667 oz. **Obv:** Small date, inverted LEI 0.900 **Rev:** Small Phrygian cap **Note:** Varieties exist.

Date	Mintage	VG	F	VF	XF	Unc
1873	8,623	250	375	650	1,000	—
1874	—	250	350	625	950	—
1875	—	225	325	550	850	—
1876/5	—	225	325	550	850	—
1876	—	225	325	550	850	—

KM# 141.2a 10 PESOS
16.1290 g., 0.6660 Gold .3453 oz. **Obv:** Small date, inverted LEI 0.900 **Rev:** Small Phrygian cap

Date	Mintage	VG	F	VF	XF	Unc
1886/74 Rare	—	—	—	—	—	—

KM# 142.1 20 PESOS
32.2580 g., 0.9000 Gold .9335 oz. **Note:** Struck at the Bogota mint.

Date	Mintage	VG	F	VF	XF	Unc
1862	—	450	575	1,000	1,850	—
1863	—	450	575	1,000	1,850	—
1867	—	700	1,200	2,000	3,250	—
1868	—	500	650	1,250	2,150	—
1869	—	500	650	1,250	2,150	—

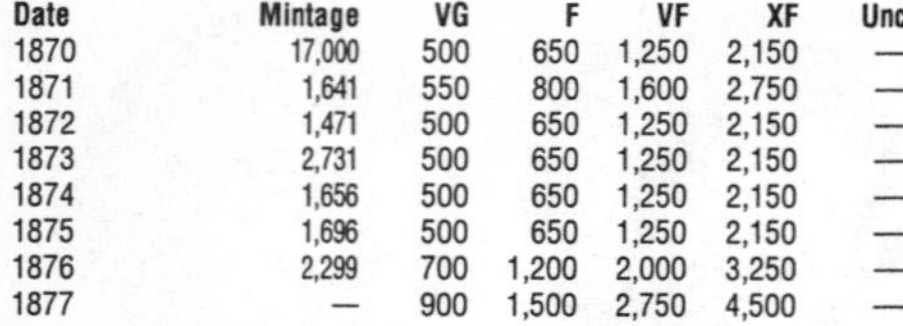

Date	Mintage	VG	F	VF	XF	Unc
1870	17,000	500	650	1,250	2,150	—
1871	1,641	550	800	1,600	2,750	—
1872	1,471	500	650	1,250	2,150	—
1873	2,731	500	650	1,250	2,150	—
1874	1,656	500	650	1,250	2,150	—
1875	1,696	500	650	1,250	2,150	—
1876	2,299	700	1,200	2,000	3,250	—
1877	—	900	1,500	2,750	4,500	—

KM# 142.3 20 PESOS

32.2580 g., 0.9000 Gold .9335 oz. **Note:** Struck at the Popayan mint.

Date	Mintage	VG	F	VF	XF	Unc
1863	—	475	600	1,100	1,700	—
1868	—	475	600	1,100	1,700	—
1869	—	475	600	1,100	1,700	—
1870	8,247	475	550	1,000	1,600	—
1871	5,885	475	600	1,100	1,700	—
1872	—	475	600	1,100	1,700	—
1873	—	475	600	1,100	1,700	—
1874/3	5,352	475	600	1,100	1,700	—
1874	Inc. above	475	600	1,100	1,700	—
1875	5,240	475	600	1,100	1,700	—
1877	1,219	900	1,500	2,750	5,000	—
1878	2,873	500	650	1,400	2,250	—

1868

1869

KM# 142.2 20 PESOS

32.2580 g., 0.9000 Gold .9335 oz. **Note:** On 1868, arrows in shield on reverse point between zeros in 0.900. On 1869, arrows point at zeros in 0.900. Struck at the Medellin mint.

Date	Mintage	VG	F	VF	XF	Unc
1867	—	2,000	3,500	6,000	9,500	—
1868	7,984	450	550	1,000	1,500	—
1869/8	7,313	450	550	1,000	1,500	—
1869	Inc. above	450	550	1,000	1,500	—
1871	5,996	650	1,100	2,250	3,800	—
1872	17,000	450	550	1,000	1,600	—

KM# 158 20 PESOS

32.2580 g., 0.9000 Gold .9335 oz. **Note:** Modified design. Struck at the Medellin mint.

Date	Mintage	VG	F	VF	XF	Unc
1873	—	1,000	2,000	4,000	6,500	—

DECIMAL COINAGE

100 Centavos = 1 Peso

KM# 173 1-1/4 CENTAVOS

Copper-Nickel **Edge:** Plain **Note:** Struck at the Bogota mint.

Date	Mintage	F	VF	XF	Unc	BU
1874 Proof, rare	—	—	—	—	—	—
Note: Proof-like or specimen strikes are sometimes mistaken for Proofs						
1874	2,400,000	1.00	2.00	4.50	—	—

KM# 169 2-1/2 CENTAVOS

0.9000 g., 0.6660 Silver .0192 oz. **Note:** Date varieties exist. Struck at the Bogota mint.

Date	Mintage	VG	F	VF	XF	Unc
1872	328,000	3.00	6.00	10.00	16.50	—
1873	302,000	2.00	4.00	7.50	20.00	—
1874	75,000	2.50	5.00	8.50	20.00	—
1875	56,000	2.50	5.00	10.00	25.00	—
1876	71,000	2.50	5.00	9.00	22.50	—
1877	78,000	2.50	5.00	8.50	20.00	—
1878	347,000	2.00	3.25	7.50	18.00	—
1879	402,000	2.00	3.25	7.50	18.00	—
1880	123,000	2.00	3.25	7.50	18.00	—
1881	123,000	3.50	8.00	15.50	30.00	—

KM# 180 2-1/2 CENTAVOS

Copper-Nickel

Date	Mintage	F	VF	XF	Unc	BU
1881H	4,000,000	0.65	1.75	3.00	20.00	—

KM# 179 2-1/2 CENTAVOS

Copper-Nickel **Note:** 14-14.5 milimeters.

Date	Mintage	F	VF	XF	Unc	BU
1881(W)	24,000,000	0.10	0.25	0.75	4.50	—

KM# 181 2-1/2 CENTAVOS

Copper **Edge:** Reeded **Note:** Many die varieties exist, including 1 or I in 1/2 of denomination.

Date	Mintage	F	VF	XF	Unc	BU
1885(B)	—	1.50	3.50	7.50	32.00	—

KM# 182 2-1/2 CENTAVOS

Copper **Edge:** Plain

Date	Mintage	F	VF	XF	Unc	BU
1886H	12,000,000	0.35	0.85	2.00	6.50	—

KM# 170 5 CENTAVOS

1.2500 g., 0.6660 Silver .0268 oz. **Note:** Struck at the Bogota mint.

Date	Mintage	VG	F	VF	XF	Unc
1872	—	3.00	7.00	12.50	27.50	—
1873	89,000	3.00	7.00	12.50	27.50	—
1874	276,000	2.00	5.00	9.00	20.00	—

KM# 174 5 CENTAVOS

1.2300 g., 0.8350 Silver .0330 oz. **Note:** Struck at the Medellin mint.

Date	Mintage	VG	F	VF	XF	Unc
1874	—	18.50	37.50	65.00	100	—

KM# 174a.2 5 CENTAVOS

1.2500 g., 0.6660 Silver .0268 oz. **Note:** Struck at the Medelllin mint.

Date	Mintage	VG	F	VF	XF	Unc
1875	—	25.00	55.00	100	225	—

KM# 174a.1 5 CENTAVOS

1.2500 g., 0.6660 Silver .0268 oz. **Note:** Struck at the Bogota mint.

Date	Mintage	VG	F	VF	XF	Unc
1875	77,000	1.50	3.00	5.00	15.00	—
1876	19,000	3.50	9.00	16.00	27.50	—
1877	94,000	2.00	5.00	8.50	18.00	—
1878	190,000	1.00	2.75	5.00	15.00	—
1879/8	177,000	1.00	2.75	5.00	15.00	—
1879	Inc. above	1.00	2.75	5.00	15.00	—
1880	44,000	1.75	3.75	7.00	16.50	—
1881	219,000	2.50	7.50	15.00	28.00	—
1882/1	—	2.50	7.50	15.00	28.00	—
1882	—	1.25	3.00	5.00	15.00	—
1883	412,000	1.25	3.00	5.00	15.00	—
1884	220,000	1.25	3.00	5.00	15.00	—
1885	—	1.50	3.50	6.50	15.00	—

KM# 171 10 CENTAVOS

2.5000 g., 0.8350 Silver .0671 oz. **Note:** Struck at the Bogota mint.

Date	Mintage	VG	F	VF	XF	Unc
1872	Inc. above	4.00	9.00	22.50	47.50	—
1873	43,000	2.75	6.00	12.50	23.50	—
1874	Inc. below	2.00	4.50	10.00	18.50	—

KM# 175.1 10 CENTAVOS

2.5000 g., 0.8350 Silver .0671 oz. **Note:** Struck at the Bogota mint.

Date	Mintage	VG	F	VF	XF	Unc
1874	179,000	1.75	4.00	8.50	16.50	—
1875	265,000	1.50	3.00	6.00	13.50	—
1878	419	1.50	3.00	6.00	15.00	—
1879	Inc. above	0.75	2.00	4.25	10.00	—
1880/79	134,000	5.00	12.00	17.50	30.00	—
1880	Inc. above	4.00	10.00	17.50	30.00	—
1881	20,000	1.25	2.75	4.00	8.75	—
1882	—	2.50	4.00	6.00	15.00	—
1882 (0.835/0.500)	—	3.50	7.50	17.50	27.50	—
1883	202,000	2.00	3.25	4.50	10.00	—
1884/3	—	2.25	5.00	11.00	22.50	—
1884	—	1.25	3.00	4.00	10.00	—

KM# 175.2 10 CENTAVOS

2.5000 g., 0.8350 Silver .0671 oz. **Note:** Struck at the Medellin mint.

Date	Mintage	VG	F	VF	XF	Unc
1885 (0.835)	—	8.00	17.50	32.50	65.00	—
1885 (0.835/0.500)	—	10.00	20.00	35.00	70.00	—

KM# 175.2a 10 CENTAVOS

2.5000 g., 0.5000 Silver .0402 oz. **Note:** Struck at the Medellin mint.

Date	Mintage	VG	F	VF	XF	Unc
1885 (0.500)	—	12.00	20.00	36.50	75.00	—
1885 (0.500/0.835)	—	13.50	22.50	37.50	85.00	—
1886	—	15.00	32.50	50.00	100	—

KM# 176.1 20 CENTAVOS

5.0000 g., 0.8350 Silver .1342 oz. **Obv:** Large head **Rev. Legend:** GRAM 5 **Note:** Struck at the Medellin mint.

Date	Mintage	VG	F	VF	XF	Unc
1874	—	10.00	25.00	55.00	115	—

KM# 176.2 20 CENTAVOS

5.0000 g., 0.8350 Silver .1342 oz. **Obv:** Large head **Rev. Legend:** GRAMOS 5 **Note:** Struck at the Medellin mint.

Date	Mintage	VG	F	VF	XF	Unc
1874	—	30.00	55.00	85.00	150	—
1882/74	—	16.50	30.00	45.00	90.00	—

KM# 178.1 20 CENTAVOS

5.0000 g., 0.8350 Silver .1342 oz. **Obv:** Small head **Rev. Legend:** GRAM 5 **Note:** Size of stars varies. Struck at the Medellin mint.

Date	Mintage	VG	F	VF	XF	Unc
1875	—	10.00	18.50	37.50	85.00	—
1876	—	2.00	3.75	8.00	20.00	—
1877	—	4.50	10.00	17.50	32.50	—
1882	—	2.00	3.75	8.00	20.00	—

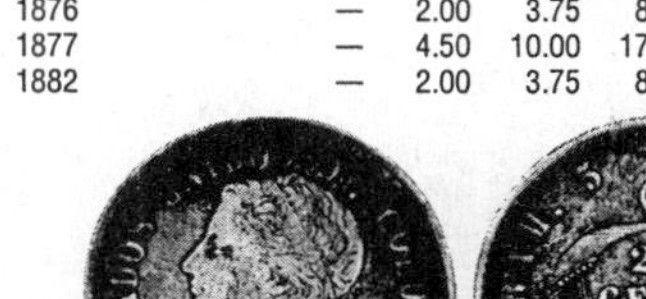 

KM# 178.2 20 CENTAVOS

5.0000 g., 0.8350 Silver .1342 oz. **Obv:** Small head, tiny B in O of ESTADOS **Note:** Struck at the Medellin mint.

Date	Mintage	VG	F	VF	XF	Unc
1875	—	12.50	22.50	35.00	75.00	—
1876/5	—	10.00	18.50	27.50	50.00	—
1876	—	10.00	18.50	27.50	50.00	—

KM# 178.3 20 CENTAVOS

5.0000 g., 0.8350 Silver .1342 oz. **Obv:** Small head **Rev. Legend:** GRAMOS 5 **Note:** Struck at the Medellin mint.

Date	Mintage	VG	F	VF	XF	Unc
1882/1	—	2.50	5.50	10.00	15.00	—
1882	—	2.00	3.50	7.50	13.50	—
1884	—	2.50	5.00	10.00	15.00	—
1885/4	—	13.50	30.00	52.50	95.00	—
1885	—	18.50	42.50	70.00	115	—
1885/4 (0.835/0.500)	—	17.50	35.00	65.00	110	—
1885 (0.835/0.500)	—	20.00	42.50	85.00	140	—

KM# 176.3 20 CENTAVOS

5.0000 g., 0.8350 Silver .1342 oz. **Obv:** Small head **Rev. Legend:** GRAMOS 5 **Note:** Struck at the Bogota mint.

Date	Mintage	VG	F	VF	XF	Unc
1884/3	—	10.00	17.50	36.50	85.00	—
1884	—	9.00	16.50	35.00	80.00	—

KM# 178.3a 20 CENTAVOS

5.0000 g., 0.5000 Silver .0804 oz. **Obv:** Small head **Rev. Legend:** GRAMOS 5 **Note:** Struck at the Medellin mint.

Date	Mintage	VG	F	VF	XF	Unc
1886 (0.500)	—	35.00	75.00	135	220	—
1886 (0.500/0.835)	—	35.00	75.00	135	220	—

KM# 172.1 50 CENTAVOS

12.5000 g., 0.8350 Silver .3356 oz. **Obv:** Small letters **Rev:** Small letters, "50" in numerals **Edge Lettering:** DIOS LEI LIBERTAD **Note:** Struck at the Bogota mint.

Date	Mintage	VG	F	VF	XF	Unc
1872	27,000	12.50	35.00	65.00	125	—
1873	101,000	7.00	17.50	35.00	75.00	—

KM# 177.1 50 CENTAVOS

12.5000 g., 0.8350 Silver .3356 oz. **Rev:** CINCUENTA for denomination **Note:** Struck at the Bogota mint.

Date	Mintage	VG	F	VF	XF	Unc
1874	Inc. above	3.00	7.50	15.00	28.00	—
1875	621,000	2.50	7.00	13.00	25.00	—
1876	259,000	3.75	10.00	20.00	50.00	—
1877/6 Rare	133,000	—	—	—	—	—
1877	Inc. above	3.75	9.50	20.00	45.00	—
1878	264,000	3.75	9.50	20.00	45.00	—
1879	307,000	3.00	8.00	14.00	28.00	—
1880	1,249,000	2.50	6.00	12.00	24.00	—
1881	1,086,000	2.50	6.00	12.00	24.00	—
1882/1 Rare	—	—	—	—	—	—
1882	—	2.50	7.00	13.00	25.00	—
1883	221,000	2.50	7.50	14.00	28.00	—
1884	993,000	2.50	6.00	12.00	24.00	—
1885	—	8.50	20.00	40.00	85.00	—

KM# 172.2 50 CENTAVOS

12.5000 g., 0.8350 Silver .3356 oz. **Obv:** Large letters **Rev:** Large letters, "50" in numerals **Edge Lettering:** DIOS LEI LIBERTAD **Note:** Varieties exist. Struck at the Bogota mint.

Date	Mintage	VG	F	VF	XF	Unc
1874	280,000	5.00	12.00	22.00	55.00	—
1875 Rare	—	—	—	—	—	—

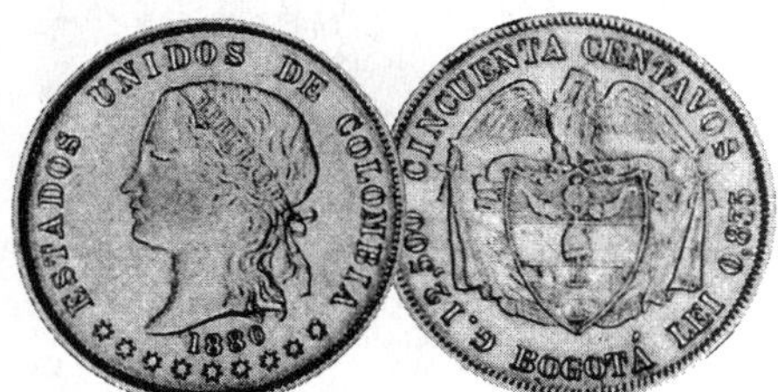

KM# 177.2 50 CENTAVOS

12.5000 g., 0.8350 Silver .3356 oz. **Rev:** CINCUENTA for denomination **Note:** Struck at the Popayan mint.

Date	Mintage	VG	F	VF	XF	Unc
1880	—	150	265	450	800	—

KM# 177a.1 50 CENTAVOS

12.5000 g., 0.5000 Silver .2009 oz. **Rev:** CINCUENTA for denomination **Note:** Struck at the Bogota mint.

DateE	Mintage	VG	F	VF	XF	Unc
1885	—	3.00	7.50	15.00	32.00	—
1886/76 Rare	—	—	—	—	—	—
1886/5 Rare	—	—	—	—	—	—
1886	—	5.00	15.00	25.00	50.00	—

KM# 177a.2 50 CENTAVOS

12.5000 g., 0.5000 Silver .2009 oz. **Rev:** CINCUENTA for denomination **Edge Lettering:** DIOS LEI LIBERTAD **Note:** Struck at the Medellin mint.

Date	Mintage	VG	F	VF	XF	Unc
1886	—	125	25.00	500	700	—

KM# 177a.3 50 CENTAVOS

12.5000 g., 0.5000 Silver .2009 oz. **Rev:** CINCUENTA for denomination **Edge Lettering:** DIOS PATRIA LIBERTAD

Date	Mintage	VG	F	VF	XF	Unc
1886	—	65.00	135	275	600	—

KM# A183 50 CENTAVOS

12.5000 g., 0.5000 Silver .2009 oz. **Obv:** KM#161.1a **Rev:** KM#177a.2

Date	Mintage	VG	F	VF	XF	Unc
1886 Rare	—	—	—	—	—	—

REPUBLIC

DECIMAL COINAGE

100 Centavos = 1 Peso

KM# 190 2-1/2 CENTAVOS

Copper-Nickel

Date	Mintage	F	VF	XF	Unc	BU
1900(W) Rare	—	—	—	—	—	—

KM# 183.1 5 CENTAVOS

Copper-Nickel **Rev:** Large top 5 **Edge:** Plain

Date	Mintage	F	VF	XF	Unc	BU
1886(W)	1,000,000	0.25	0.75	2.00	10.00	—

KM# 183.2 5 CENTAVOS

Copper-Nickel **Rev:** Small top 5 **Edge:** Plain

Date	Mintage	F	VF	XF	Unc	BU
1886(W)	—	0.25	0.75	2.00	10.00	—
1886(W) Rare	—	Value: 165				
1888(W)	—	0.25	0.75	2.00	10.00	—

KM# 184 5 CENTAVOS
Copper-Nickel

Date	Mintage	F	VF	XF	Unc	BU
1886/5(W)	Inc. above	3.00	7.50	15.00	25.00	—
1886(W)	Inc. above	0.30	0.85	2.75	11.50	—

KM# 188 10 CENTAVOS
2.5000 g., 0.6660 Silver .0536 oz.

Date	Mintage	F	VF	XF	Unc	BU
1897 (Brussels)	2,642,000	0.75	1.50	3.00	8.50	—

KM# 189 20 CENTAVOS
5.0000 g., 0.6660 Silver .1072 oz.

Date	Mintage	F	VF	XF	Unc	BU
1897 (Brussels)	1,441,000	1.25	2.50	5.50	11.00	—

KM# 185 50 CENTAVOS
12.5000 g., 0.5000 Silver .2009 oz. **Edge Lettering:** DIOS LEI LIBERTAD **Note:** Struck at the Bogota Mint.

Date	Mintage	VG	F	VF	XF	Unc
1887	1,764,000	6.00	13.50	32.50	100	—
1888 Rare	—	—	—	—	—	—

KM# 186.1 50 CENTAVOS
12.5000 g., 0.5000 Silver .2009 oz. **Note:** Similar to KM#186.1a.

Date	Mintage	VG	F	VF	XF	Unc
1888	—	70.00	120	220	400	—

KM# 186.1a 50 CENTAVOS
12.5000 g., 0.8350 Silver .3356 oz. **Edge Lettering:** DIOS LEI LIBERTAD

Date	Mintage	VG	F	VF	XF	Unc
1889	130,000	13.50	30.00	60.00	140	—
1898	—	12.00	25.00	47.50	120	—
1899	—	55.00	125	250	525	—

KM# 187.1 50 CENTAVOS
12.5000 g., 0.8350 Silver .3356 oz. **Subject:** 400th Anniversary of Columbus' Discovery of America **Obv:** Tip of cap points to left side of A in REPUBLICA **Note:** 30.4mm.

Date	Mintage	F	VF	XF	Unc	BU
1892	4,826,000	7.50	15.00	35.00	175	—

KM# 187.2 50 CENTAVOS
12.5000 g., 0.8350 Silver .3356 oz. **Subject:** 400th Anniversary of Columbus' Discovery of America **Obv:** Tip of cap points to right side of A in REPUBLICA **Note:** 29.6mm.

Date	Mintage	F	VF	XF	Unc	BU
1892	Inc. above	5.00	10.00	23.50	80.00	—
1892 Proof; 3 known	—	Value: 1,750				

KM# 165 5 DECIMOS
12.5000 g., 0.5000 Silver .2009 oz. **Obv:** So-called Greek profile **Edge Lettering:** DIOS PATRIA LIBERTAD

Date	Mintage	VG	F	VF	XF	Unc
1887	84,000	35.00	70.00	150	300	—
1888	—	50.00	100	250	500	—

KM# 166 5 DECIMOS
12.5000 g., 0.5000 Silver .2009 oz. **Obv:** Large head **Edge Lettering:** DIOS LEI LIBERTAD

Date	Mintage	VG	F	VF	XF	Unc
1888	—	30.00	60.00	125	250	—
1889 Rare	—	—	—	—	—	—

KM# 167 5 DECIMOS
12.5000 g., 0.5000 Silver .2009 oz. **Obv:** Long-necked Liberty head **Edge Lettering:** DIOS LEI LIBERTAD

Date	Mintage	VG	F	VF	XF	Unc
1888 Rare	—	—	—	—	—	—

KM# 168 5 DECIMOS
12.5000 g., 0.8350 Silver .3356 oz. **Obv:** Large head **Rev:** 2 stars and 2 dots **Edge Lettering:** DIOS PATRIA LIBERTAD

Date	Mintage	VG	F	VF	XF	Unc
1889 Rare	—	—	—	—	—	—

PIEFORTS

KM#	Date	Mintage	Identification	Mkt Val
P1	1848	—	1/2 Real. 0.9000 Silver. KM#110; Bogota.	—
P2	1848	—	Real. 0.9000 Silver. KM#112.	—

TRIAL STRIKES

KM#	Date	Mintage	Identification	Mkt Val
TS1	1873	—	1/2 Decimo. Silver.	350
TS2	1873	—	1/2 Decimo. Silver.	350
TS3	1873	—	Decimo. Silver Plated Bronze.	175
TS4	ND	—	Decimo. Silver Plated Bronze.	175
TS5	1873	—	2 Decimos. Silver Plated Bronze.	175
TS6	ND	—	2 Decimos. Silver Plated Bronze.	175

KM#	Date	Mintage	Identification	Mkt Val
TS7	1873	—	Peso. Silver.	600

KM#	Date	Mintage	Identification	Mkt Val
TS8	ND	—	Peso. Silver.	600

KM#	Date	Mintage	Identification	Mkt Val
TS9	1873	—	10 Pesos. Gold Plated Bronze.	400
TS10	ND	—	10 Pesos. Gold Plated Bronze.	400

KM#	Date	Mintage	Identification	Mkt Val
TS11	1873	—	20 Pesos. Gold Plated Bronze.	450

KM#	Date	Mintage	Identification	Mkt Val

KM#	Date	Mintage	Identification	Mkt Val
TS12	ND	—	20 Pesos. Gold Plated Bronze.	450
TS13	ND	—	50 Centavos. Lead.	—

COMOROS

The Federal Islamic Republic of the Comoros, a volcanic archipelago located in the Mozambique Channel of the Indian Ocean 300 miles (483 km.) northwest of Madagascar, has an area of 719 sq. mi. (2,171 sq. km.). Capital: Moroni. The economy of the islands is based on agriculture. There are practically no mineral resources. Vanilla, essence for perfumes, copra, and sisal are exported.

Ancient Phoenician traders were probably the first visitors to the Comoro Islands, but the first detailed knowledge of the area was gathered by Arab sailors. Arab dominion and culture were firmly established when the Portuguese, Dutch, and French arrived in the 16th century. In 1843 a Malagasy ruler ceded the island of Mayotte to France; the other three principal islands of the archipelago-Anjouan, Moheli, and Grand Comore came under French protection in 1886. The islands were joined administratively with Madagascar in 1912. The Comoros became partially autonomous, with the status of a French overseas territory, in 1946, and achieved complete internal autonomy in 1961. On Dec. 31, 1975, after 133 years of French association, the Comoro Islands became the independent Republic of the Comoros.

Mayotte retained the option of determining its future ties and in 1976 voted to remain French. Its present status is that of a French Territorial Collectivity. French currency now circulates there.

TITLES

دولة انجزنجية

Daulat Anjazanchiyah

RULERS

Said Ali ibn Said Amr, regnant, 1890
French, 1886-1975

MINT MARKS

(a) - Paris, privy marks only
A - Paris

MONETARY SYSTEM

100 Centimes = 1 Franc

GRANDE COMORE SULTANATE
(Njazidja)

STANDARD COINAGE

KM# 1.1 5 CENTIMES
Bronze **Rev:** Privy mark: Fasces

Date	Mintage	F	VF	XF	Unc	BU
AH1308A	100,000	6.50	12.50	30.00	110	—

KM# 1.2 5 CENTIMES
Bronze **Rev:** Privy mark: Torch

Date	Mintage	F	VF	XF	Unc	BU
AH1308A	200,000	6.50	12.50	32.00	125	—

KM# 2.1 10 CENTIMES
Bronze **Rev:** Privy mark: Fasces

Date	Mintage	F	VF	XF	Unc	BU
AH1308A	50,000	9.00	18.00	70.00	200	—

KM# 2.2 10 CENTIMES
Bronze **Rev:** Privy mark: Torch

Date	Mintage	F	VF	XF	Unc	BU
AH1308A	100,000	9.00	18.00	75.00	210	—

KM# 3 5 FRANCS
0.9000 Silver **Rev:** Privy mark: Torch

Date	Mintage	F	VF	XF	Unc	BU
AH1308A	2,050	300	600	1,250	2,000	—

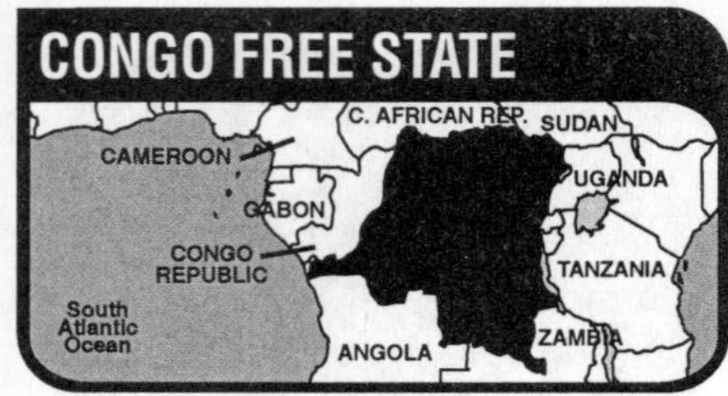

In ancient times the territory comprising former Zaire was occupied by Negrito peoples (Pygmies) pushed into the mountains by Bantu and Nilotic invaders. The interior was first explored by the American correspondent Henry Stanley, who was subsequently commissioned by King Leopold II of Belgium to conclude development treaties with the local chiefs. The Berlin conference of 1885 awarded the area to Leopold, who administered and exploited it as his private property until it was annexed to Belgium in 1908.

RULER
Leopold II

ROYAL DOMAIN
1865-1909
STANDARD COINAGE

KM# 1 CENTIME
Copper **Ruler:** Leopold II

Date	Mintage	F	VF	XF	Unc	BU
1887	180,000	1.50	3.00	10.00	22.00	—
1888	Inc. above	1.00	2.00	4.00	10.00	—

KM# 2 2 CENTIMES
Copper **Ruler:** Leopold II

Date	Mintage	F	VF	XF	Unc	BU
1887	130,000	1.50	3.00	10.00	20.00	—
1888	Inc. above	1.00	2.00	4.00	10.00	—

KM# 3 5 CENTIMES
Copper

Date	Mintage	F	VF	XF	Unc	BU
1887	180,000	2.00	4.00	15.00	25.00	—
1888/7	Inc. above	1.50	3.00	8.00	15.00	—
1888	Inc. above	1.50	3.00	10.00	20.00	—
1894	150,000	2.00	4.00	15.00	30.00	—

KM# 4 10 CENTIMES
Copper

Date	Mintage	F	VF	XF	Unc	BU
1887	40,000	6.00	12.00	35.00	75.00	—
1888	Inc. above	2.00	3.50	15.00	30.00	—
1889	100,000	3.00	7.00	25.00	45.00	—
1894	150,000	2.50	5.00	22.00	38.00	—

KM# 5 50 CENTIMES
2.5000 g., 0.8350 Silver .0671 oz.

Date	Mintage	F	VF	XF	Unc	BU
1887	20,000	10.00	20.00	45.00	95.00	—
1887 Proof	—	Value: 250				
1891	60,000	12.00	22.00	50.00	110	—
1894	40,000	12.00	25.00	60.00	125	—
1896	200,000	12.00	20.00	45.00	95.00	—

KM# 6 FRANC
5.0000 g., 0.8350 Silver .1342 oz.

Date	Mintage	F	VF	XF	Unc	BU
1887	20,000	12.00	25.00	55.00	135	—
1891	70,000	15.00	30.00	70.00	150	—
1894	70,000	15.00	30.00	75.00	175	—
1896	160,000	12.00	25.00	50.00	135	—

KM# 7 2 FRANCS
10.0000 g., 0.8350 Silver .2685 oz.

Date	Mintage	F	VF	XF	Unc	BU
1887	20,000	25.00	45.00	125	250	—
1891	30,000	30.00	60.00	165	325	—
1894	80,000	30.00	50.00	150	300	—
1896	100,000	30.00	50.00	125	250	—

KM# 8.1 5 FRANCS
25.0000 g., 0.9000 Silver .7234 oz. **Obv. Legend:** LEOPOLD II R. D. BELGES...

Date	Mintage	F	VF	XF	Unc	BU
1887	8,000	95.00	160	300	650	—
1891	30,000	100	175	345	750	—
1894	50,000	100	175	345	750	—
1896	110,000	90.00	150	275	625	—

KM# 8.2 5 FRANCS
25.0000 g., 0.9000 Silver .7234 oz. **Obv. Legend:** LEOPOLD II ROI DES BELGES...

Date	Mintage	F	VF	XF	Unc	BU
1887	100	1,000	2,500	4,250	6,500	—

PATTERNS
Including off metal strikes

KM#	Date	Mintage	Identification	Mkt Val
Pn1	1887	—	10 Centimes. Without dots or rays.	450
Pn2	1887	—	50 Centimes. Brass.	125
Pn3	1887	—	Franc. Brass.	175
Pn4	1887	—	2 Francs. Brass.	250

KM#	Date	Mintage	Identification	Mkt Val
Pn5	1896	—	5 Francs. Lead And Tin Alloy.	—
Pn6	1896	—	5 Francs. 0.9000 Lead And Tin Alloy. Milled edge.	1,100
Pn7	1896	—	5 Francs. 0.9000 Lead And Tin Alloy. Plain edge.	1,100
Pn8	1896	—	5 Francs. 0.9000 Lead And Tin Alloy. Lettered edge.	1,250

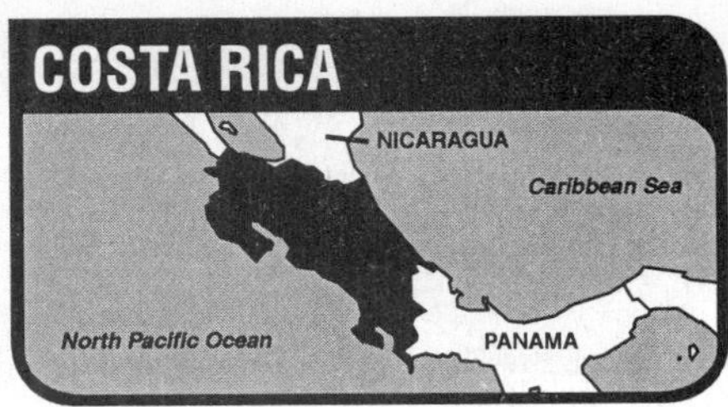

The Republic of Costa Rica, located in southern Central America between Nicaragua and Panama, has an area of 19,730 sq. mi. (51,100 sq. km.) and a population of 3.4 million. Capital: San Jose. Agriculture predominates; tourism and coffee, bananas, beef and sugar contribute heavily to the country's export earnings.

Costa Rica was discovered by Christopher Columbus in 1502, during his last voyage to the New World, and was a colony of Spain from 1522 until independence in 1821. Columbus named the territory Nueva Cartago; the name Costa Rica wasn't generally applied until 1540. Bartholomew Columbus attempted the first settlement but was driven off by Indian attacks and the country wasn't subdued until 1530. After centuries, as part of the Spanish Captaincy-General of Guatemala, Costa Rica was absorbed into the Mexican Empire of Augustin de Iturbide from 1821-1823. From 1823 to 1848, it was a constituent state of the Central American Republic (q.v.). Established as a republic in 1848, Costa Rica adopted democratic reforms in the 1870's and 80's. Today, Costa Rica remains a model of orderly democracy in Latin America, although, like most of the hemisphere - its economy is in stress.

MINT MARKS

CR - San Jose 1825-1947
HEATON - Heaton, Birmingham, England, 1889-93
BIRMm - Heaton, Birmingham, England, 1889-93

ASSAYERS INITIALS

MM – Miguel Mora, 1842
JB – Juan Barth, 1847-1864
GW - Guillermo Witting, 1854-1890

MONETARY SYSTEM

8 Reales = 1 Peso
16 Pesos = 8 Escudos = 1 Onza

REPUBLIC

REAL/ESCUDO COINAGE

KM# 32 1/2 REAL
1.5000 g., 0.9030 Silver .0435 oz. **Obv:** Radiant 6-pointed star in circle above branches **Rev:** Tobacco plant and value in circle, date below **Note:** Struck at San Jose.

Date	Mintage	VG	F	VF	XF	Unc
1842 MM	—	25.00	50.00	100	185	—

Note: Holed examples are valued at about 40% of the above figures

KM# 65 REAL
2.9000 g., 0.9030 Silver .0842 oz. **Obv:** Coffee tree **Rev:** Female bust **Note:** Struck at San Jose.

Date	Mintage	VG	F	VF	XF	Unc
1847 JB	—	5.75	10.00	18.50	37.50	—
1847 JB	—	6.50	12.50	20.00	40.00	—

Note: Error backwards B

KM# 66 REAL
2.9000 g., 0.7500 Silver .0699 oz. **Obv:** Coffee tree **Rev:** Female bust **Note:** Struck at San Jose.

Date	Mintage	VG	F	VF	XF	Unc
1849 JB	—	2.50	6.50	10.00	27.50	—
1850 JB	—	3.75	8.00	15.00	35.00	—

KM# 97 1/2 ESCUDO
1.6000 g., 0.8750 Gold .0450 oz. **Obv:** Ornate arms **Rev:** Indian woman leaning against column **Note:** Struck at San Jose.

Date	Mintage	VG	F	VF	XF	Unc
1850 JB	3,388	38.50	65.00	100	150	—
1851 JB	6,565	38.50	65.00	100	150	—
1853 JB	8,491	38.50	65.00	100	150	—
1854 JB	4,663	38.50	65.00	100	150	—
1855 JB	8,822	38.50	65.00	100	150	—
1855 GW	Inc. above	38.50	65.00	100	150	—
1864 JB	9,018	38.50	65.00	100	150	—

KM# 33.1 ESCUDO
3.0000 g., 0.8750 Gold .0844 oz. **Obv:** Radiant star **Rev:** Tree **Note:** Struck at San Jose.

Date	Mintage	VG	F	VF	XF	Unc
1842 MM	10,000	300	600	1,200	2,000	—

KM# 33.2 ESCUDO
3.1000 g., 0.8750 Gold .872 oz. **Obv:** Radiant star **Rev:** Tree **Note:** Struck at San Jose.

Date	Mintage	VG	F	VF	XF	Unc
1842 MM	Inc. above	350	800	1,500	2,250	—

KM# 98 ESCUDO
3.1000 g., 0.8750 Gold .872 oz. **Obv:** Ornate arms in sprays **Rev:** Indian woman leaning against column **Note:** Struck at San Jose.

Date	Mintage	VG	F	VF	XF	Unc
1850 JB	6,167	55.00	100	150	265	—
1851 JB	4,388	55.00	100	150	265	—
1853 JB	2,979	65.00	150	250	500	—
1855 JB	4,095	60.00	125	200	350	—

KM# 99 2 ESCUDOS
6.3000 g., 0.8750 Gold .1772 oz. **Obv:** Ornate arms in sprays **Rev:** Indian woman leaning against column **Note:** Struck at San Jose.

Date	Mintage	VG	F	VF	XF	Unc
1850 JB	3,641	100	150	200	400	—
1854 JB	Inc. above	100	150	200	400	—
1854 GW	Inc. above	100	150	200	400	—
1855 JB	60,000	100	125	175	400	—
1855 GW	Inc. above	100	150	200	400	—
1858 GW	17,000	100	125	175	400	—
1862 GW	5,896	110	200	325	550	—
1863 GW	5,632	110	200	325	550	—

KM# 100 1/2 ONZA (4 Escudos)
12.6000 g., 0.8750 Gold .3545 oz. **Obv:** Ornate arms in sprays **Rev:** Indian woman leaning against column **Note:** Struck at San Jose.

Date	Mintage	VG	F	VF	XF	Unc
1850 JB	18,000	200	300	400	800	—
1850 JB Proof	—	Value: 4,200				

COUNTERMARKED COINAGE

Type I • 1841-1842

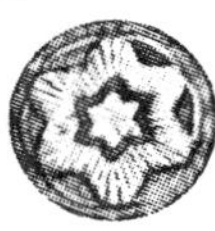

Countermark: Radiant 6-pointed star in 7mm circle.

NOTE: An additional plug was cut from each coin to pay for the work. Market valuations are for holed coins.

KM# 1 1/2 REAL
Silver **Countermark:** Type I **Note:** Countermark on Mexico 1/2 Real, KM#72.

CM Date	Host Date	Good	VG	F	VF	XF
ND(1841-42)	1792-1808	150	200	350	—	—

KM# 4 REAL
Silver **Countermark:** Type I **Note:** Countermark on Mexico 1 Real, KM#77.

CM Date	Host Date	Good	VG	F	VF	XF
ND(1841-42)	1760-71	150	200	350	—	—

KM# 7 2 REALES
Silver **Countermark:** Type I **Note:** Countermark on Bolivia (Potosi) 2 Reales, KM#53.

CM Date	Host Date	Good	VG	F	VF	XF
ND(1841-42)	1773-89	15.00	30.00	60.00	90.00	—

KM# 8 2 REALES
Silver **Countermark:** Type I **Note:** Countermark on Guatemala 2 Reales, KM#34.1.

CM Date	Host Date	Good	VG	F	VF	XF
ND(1841-42)	1772-76	15.00	30.00	60.00	90.00	—

KM# 12 2 REALES
Silver **Countermark:** Type I **Note:** Countermark on Mexico 2 Reales, KM#91.

CM Date	Host Date	Good	VG	F	VF	XF
ND(1841-42)	1800	15.00	30.00	60.00	90.00	—

KM# 9 2 REALES
Silver **Countermark:** Type I **Note:** Countermark on Mexico 2 Reales, KM#92.

CM Date	Host Date	Good	VG	F	VF	XF
ND(1841-42)	1809-12	15.00	30.00	60.00	90.00	—

KM# 10 2 REALES
Silver **Countermark:** Type I **Note:** Countermark on Mexico 2 Reales, KM#372.8.

CM Date	Host Date	Good	VG	F	VF	XF
ND(1841-42)	1825-41	15.00	30.00	60.00	90.00	—

KM# 11 2 REALES
Silver **Countermark:** Type I **Note:** Countermark on Peru 2 Reales, KM#141.1.

CM Date	Host Date	Good	VG	F	VF	XF
ND(1841-42)	1825-40	15.00	30.00	60.00	90.00	—

KM# 13 2 REALES
Silver **Countermark:** Type I **Note:** Countermark on Peru 2 Reales, KM#95.

CM Date	Host Date	Good	VG	F	VF	XF
ND(1841-42)	1791-1808	15.00	30.00	60.00	90.00	—

KM# 14 4 REALES
Silver **Countermark:** Type I **Note:** Countermark on Bolivia (Potosi) 4 Reales, KM#54.

CM Date	Host Date	Good	VG	F	VF	XF
ND(1841-42)	1773-89	150	275	425	1,000	—

KM# 15 4 REALES
Silver **Countermark:** Type I **Note:** Countermark on Bolivia (Potosi) 4 Reales, KM#72.

CM Date	Host Date	Good	VG	F	VF	XF
ND(1841-42)	1791-1808	150	275	425	1,000	—

KM# 16 4 REALES
Silver **Countermark:** Type I **Note:** Countermark on Guatemala, 4 Reales, KM#35.1.

CM Date	Host Date	Good	VG	F	VF	XF
ND(1841-42)	1772-76	750	1,250	2,500	—	—

KM# 19 8 REALES
Silver **Countermark:** Type I **Note:** Countermark on Mexico 8 Reales, KM#106.

CM Date	Host Date	Good	VG	F	VF	XF
ND(1841-42)	1772-89	150	275	425	950	—

KM# 20 8 REALES
Silver **Countermark:** Type I **Note:** Countermark on Mexico 8 Reales, KM#376.

CM Date	Host Date	Good	VG	F	VF	XF
ND(1841-42)	1823-25	200	300	450	1,000	—

KM# 21 8 REALES
Silver **Countermark:** Type I **Note:** Countermark on Mexico 8 Reales, KM#377.

CM Date	Host Date	Good	VG	F	VF	XF
ND(1841-42)	1824-41	150	250	400	900	—

KM# 22 8 REALES
Silver **Countermark:** Type I **Note:** Countermark on Peru 8 Reales, KM#78.

CM Date	Host Date	Good	VG	F	VF	XF
ND(1841-42)	1772-89	150	275	425	950	—

KM# 23 8 REALES
Silver **Countermark:** Type I **Note:** Countermark on Peru 8 Reales, KM#142.1.

CM Date	Host Date	Good	VG	F	VF	XF
ND(1841-42)	1825-28	150	250	400	900	—

KM# 24 8 REALES
Silver **Countermark:** Type I **Note:** Countermark on Peru 8 Reales, KM#142.3.

CM Date	Host Date	Good	VG	F	VF	XF
ND(1841-42)	1828-40	150	250	400	900	—

KM# 25 8 REALES
Silver **Countermark:** Type I **Note:** Countermark on North Peru 8 Reales, KM#155.

CM Date	Host Date	Good	VG	F	VF	XF
ND(1841-42)	1836-39	150	275	425	950	—

KM# 26 8 REALES
Silver **Countermark:** Type I **Note:** Countermark on Spanish 8 Reales, C#136.

CM Date	Host Date	Good	VG	F	VF	XF
ND(1841-42)	1809-30	150	275	425	950	—

KM# 27 8 REALES
Silver **Countermark:** Type I **Note:** Countermark on Mexico 8 Reales, KM#111.

CM Date	Host Date	Good	VG	F	VF	XF
ND(1841-42)	1812-22	—	—	—	2,500	—

COUNTERMARKED COINAGE

Type II • 1841-1842

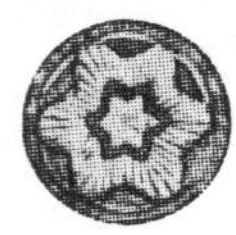

Countermark: Radiant 6-pointed star in 4mm circle

KM# 28 2 ESCUDOS
Gold **Countermark:** Type II **Note:** Countermark on Central American Republic 2 Escudos, KM#15.

CM Date	Host Date	Good	VG	F	VF	XF
ND(1841-42)	1825-37 Rare	—	—	—	—	—

KM# 29 4 ESCUDOS
Gold **Countermark:** Type II **Note:** Countermark on Central American Republic 4 Escudos, KM#16.

CM Date	Host Date	Good	VG	F	VF	XF
ND(1841-42)	1828-37 Rare	—	—	—	—	—

COUNTERSTAMPED COINAGE

Type III • 1845

Obverse counterstamp: COSTA RICA and 2 R. around female head.

Reverse counterstamp: HABILITADA POR EL GOB. around tree

KM# 35 2 REALES
Silver **Countermark:** Type III **Note:** Counterstamped on Spanish (Seville) 2 Reales.

CS Date	Host Date	Good	VG	F	VF	XF
ND(1845)	1732	20.00	35.00	60.00	100	—

KM# 36 2 REALES
Silver **Countermark:** Type III **Note:** Counterstamped on Cuba 2 Reales, KM#1.

CS Date	Host Date	Good	VG	F	VF	XF
ND(1845)	1772-88	8.50	16.00	30.00	60.00	—

Note: The coin illustrated above also has the (1841) lattice countermark of Cuba and thus would command a premium

KM# 37 2 REALES
Silver **Countermark:** Type III **Note:** Counterstamped on Spanish (Madrid) 2 Reales, C#69.

CS Date	Host Date	Good	VG	F	VF	XF
ND(1845)	1788-1808	8.50	16.00	30.00	60.00	—

KM# 38 2 REALES
Silver **Countermark:** Type III **Note:** Counterstamped on Spanish (Seville) 2 Reales, C#69.

CS Date	Host Date	Good	VG	F	VF	XF
ND(1845)	1793-1808	8.50	16.00	30.00	60.00	—

KM# 39 2 REALES

Silver **Countermark:** Type III **Note:** Counterstamped on Spanish 2 Reales, C#89.

CS Date	Host Date	Good	VG	F	VF	XF
ND(1845)	1811-13	15.00	25.00	45.00	75.00	—

KM# 40 2 REALES

Silver **Countermark:** Type III **Note:** Counterstamped on Spanish 4 Reales, C#90.

CS Date	Host Date	Good	VG	F	VF	XF
ND(1845)	1808-13	10.00	18.50	35.00	70.00	—

KM# 41 2 REALES

Silver **Countermark:** Type III **Note:** Counterstamped on Spanish (Madrid) 2 Reales, C#134.

CS Date	Host Date	Good	VG	F	VF	XF
ND(1845)	1814-33	10.00	18.50	32.50	65.00	—

KM# 42 2 REALES

Silver **Countermark:** Type III **Note:** Counterstamped on Spanish (Seville) 2 Reales, C#134.

CS Date	Host Date	Good	VG	F	VF	XF
ND(1845)	1815-33	10.00	18.50	32.50	65.00	—

KM# 43 2 REALES

Silver **Countermark:** Type III **Note:** Counterstamped on Spanish 4 Reales, C#135.

CS Date	Host Date	Good	VG	F	VF	XF
ND(1845)	1811-33	25.00	50.00	95.00	160	—

KM# 44 2 REALES

Silver **Countermark:** Type III **Note:** Counterstamped on Trinidad, Cuba counterstamped on Spanish (Seville) 2 Reales, KM#12.

CS Date	Host Date	Good	VG	F	VF	XF
ND(1845)	1793-1808	14.00	22.00	42.00	70.00	—

Note: The coin illustrated above also has the (1841) lattice countermark of Cuba and thus would command a premium

COUNTERSTAMPED COINAGE

Type IV • 1846

Obverse counterstamp: REPUB. DE CENT. DE AMER. 1846 around sun above mountains in a 14mm circle.

Reverse counterstamp: HABILITADA EN COSTA RICA J.B... around tree, 1-R

KM# 47 REAL

Silver **Countermark:** Type IV **Note:** Counterstamped on Spanish American "cob" 1 Real.

CS Date	Host Date	Good	VG	F	VF	XF
1846	1607-1753	12.50	25.00	40.00	75.00	—

KM# 50 4 REALES

Silver **Countermark:** Type IV **Note:** Counterstamped with additional countermark 4 in square on Guatemala "cob" 4 Reales, KM#5.

CS Date	Host Date	Good	VG	F	VF	XF
1846	1733-46G J	250	400	600	800	—

KM# 51.1 4 REALES

Silver **Countermark:** Type IV **Note:** Counterstamped with additional countermark 4 in square on United States Capped Bust 50 Cents.

CS Date	Host Date	Good	VG	F	VF	XF
1846	1809	1,250	2,750	5,000	8,000	—

KM# 51.2 4 REALES

Silver **Countermark:** Type IV **Note:** Counterstamped with additional countermark in square on United States Capped Bust 50 Cents.

CS Date	Host Date	Good	VG	F	VF	XF
1846	1837	850	1,750	3,250	5,000	—

KM# 52 4 REALES

Silver **Countermark:** Type IV **Note:** Counterstamped with additional countermark 4 in square on United States Seated Liberty 50 cents.

CS Date	Host Date	Good	VG	F	VF	XF
1846	1843	850	1,750	3,250	5,000	—

COUNTERSTAMPED COINAGE

Type V • 1846

Obverse counterstamp: REPUB. DE CENT. DE AMER. 1846 around sun above mountains in a 14mm circle.

Reverse counterstamp: HABILITADA EN COSTA RICA J-B around tree, 2-R

KM# 54 2 REALES

Silver **Countermark:** Type V **Note:** Counterstamped on Bolivia (Potosi) "cob" 2 Reales, KM#29.

CS Date	Host Date	Good	VG	F	VF	XF
1846	1700-46	20.00	35.00	65.00	100	—

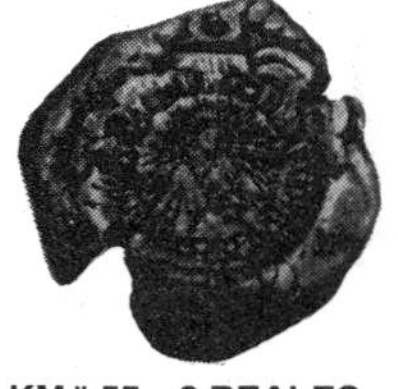

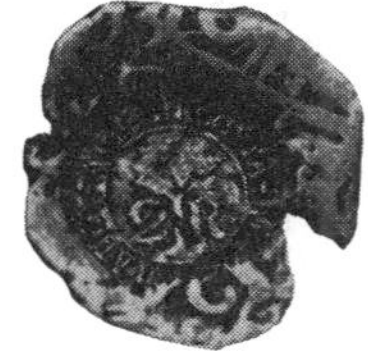

KM# 55 2 REALES

Silver **Countermark:** Type V **Note:** Counterstamped on Peru (Lima) "cob" 2 Reales, KM#30.

CS Date	Host Date	Good	VG	F	VF	XF
1846	1700-46	20.00	35.00	65.00	100	—

KM# 56 2 REALES

Silver **Countermark:** Type V **Note:** Counterstamped on Guatemula 2 Reales proclamation medal.

CS Date	Host Date	Good	VG	F	VF	XF
1846	1808	150	350	550	900	—

KM# 58 8 REALES

Silver **Countermark:** Type V **Note:** Counterstamped with additional countermark 8 in circle on Bolivia (Potosi) "cob" 8 Reales, KM#31.

CS Date	Host Date	Good	VG	F	VF	XF
1846	1700-46	400	700	1,250	2,000	—

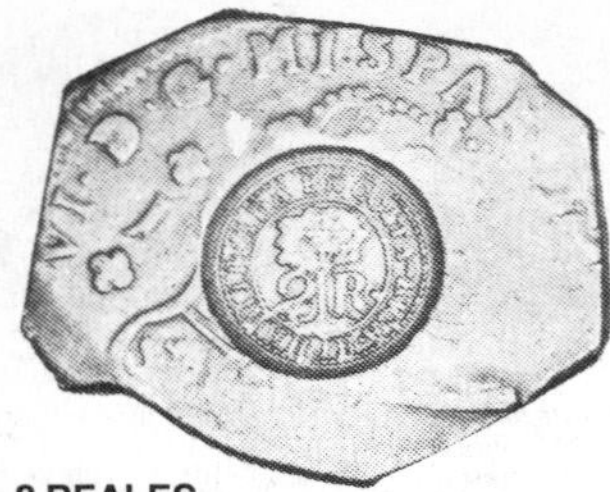

KM# 59 8 REALES

Silver **Countermark:** Type V **Note:** Counterstamped on Guatemala "cob" 8 Reales, KM#12.

CS Date	Host Date	Good	VG	F	VF	XF
1846	1747-53	400	700	1,250	2,000	—

KM# 60 8 REALES

Silver **Countermark:** Type V **Note:** Counterstamped on Peru (Lima) "cob" 8 Reales of Charles II.

CS Date	Host Date	Good	VG	F	VF	XF
1846	1665-1700	400	700	1,250	2,000	—

KM# 61 8 REALES

Silver **Countermark:** Type V **Note:** Counterstamped on Peru (Lima) "cob" 8 Reales, KM#34.

CS Date	Host Date	Good	VG	F	VF	XF
1846	1700-46	400	700	1,250	2,000	—

KM# 62 8 REALES

Silver **Countermark:** Type V **Note:** Counterstamped on Mexico City "klippe" 8 Reales, KM#48.

CS Date	Host Date	Good	VG	F	VF	XF
1846	1733-34	400	700	1,250	2,000	—

COUNTERMARKED COINAGE

Type VI • 1849-1857

Countermark: HABILITADA PO EL GOBIERNO around lion in 5mm circle

KM# 67 1/2 REAL

Silver **Countermark:** Type VI **Note:** Countermarked on Central American Republic 1/2 Real, KM#20. Values listed for KM#67-69 are for unholed pieces, holed examples are worth substantially less.

CM Date	Host Date	Good	VG	F	VF	XF
ND(1849-57)	1831 E	5.00	9.00	15.00	22.00	—
ND(1849-57)	1831 F	5.00	9.00	15.00	22.00	—
ND(1849-57)	1843 M	4.00	6.00	11.00	20.00	—
ND(1849-57)	1845 B	4.00	6.00	11.00	20.00	—

KM# 68 1/2 REAL

Silver **Countermark:** Type VI **Note:** Countermarked on Central American Republic 1/2 Real, KM#20a.

CM Date	Host Date	Good	VG	F	VF	XF
ND(1849-57)	1846 JB "CRESCA"	3.50	5.00	10.00	17.50	—
ND(1849-57)	1846 JB "CRESCA"	3.50	5.00	10.00	17.50	—
ND(1849-57)	1847 JB "CRESCA"	3.50	5.00	10.00	17.50	—
ND(1849-57)	1847 JB "CRESCA"	3.50	5.00	10.00	17.50	—
ND(1849-57)	1848 JB	3.50	5.00	10.00	17.50	—
ND(1849-57)	1849 JB	3.50	7.00	12.00	22.00	—

KM# 69 1/2 REAL

Silver **Countermark:** Type VI **Note:** Countermarked on Costa Rica 1/2 Real, KM#32.

CM Date	Host Date	Good	VG	F	VF	XF
ND(1849-57)	1842	12.00	17.50	32.50	55.00	—

KM# 72 REAL

Silver **Countermark:** Type VI **Note:** Countermarked on Central American Republic 1 Real, KM#21. Values listed for KM#72-74 are for unholed pieces, holed examples are worth substantially less.

CM Date	Host Date	Good	VG	F	VF	XF
ND(1849-57)	1831	7.50	12.50	27.50	47.50	—
ND(1849-57)	1831 F	6.00	9.50	25.00	42.50	—
ND(1849-57)	1848 JB	9.00	18.00	32.50	50.00	—

KM# 72a REAL

Silver **Countermark:** Type VI **Note:** Countermarked on Central American Republic 1 Real, KM#21a.

CM Date	Host Date	Good	VG	F	VF	XF
ND(1849-57)	1848 JB	9.00	18.00	30.00	50.00	—
ND(1849-57)	1849 JB	5.50	10.00	25.00	42.50	—

KM# 74 REAL

Silver **Countermark:** Type VI **Note:** Countermarked on Costa Rica 1 Real, KM#66.

CM Date	Host Date	Good	VG	F	VF	XF
ND(1849-57)	1849 JB	13.50	25.00	42.50	70.00	—
ND(1849-57)	1850 JB	14.00	30.00	47.50	72.50	—

KM# 73 REAL

Silver **Countermark:** Type VI **Note:** Countermarked on Costa Rica 1 Real, KM#65.

CM Date	Host Date	Good	VG	F	VF	XF
ND(1849-57)	1847 JB	13.50	25.00	42.50	65.00	—
ND(1849-57)	1847 JB	15.00	30.00	55.00	75.00	—

Note: Error, backwards B

KM# 87 REAL

Silver **Countermark:** Type VI **Note:** Countermark on Great Britain 6 Pence, KM#665.

CM Date	Host Date	Good	VG	F	VF	XF
ND(1849-57)	1816-20	7.50	11.00	17.50	30.00	—

KM# 88 REAL

Silver **Countermark:** Type VI **Note:** Countermark on Great Britain 6 Pence, KM#698.

CM Date	Host Date	Good	VG	F	VF	XF
ND(1849-57)	1826-29	8.50	17.50	32.50	55.00	—

KM# 89 REAL

Silver **Countermark:** Type VI **Note:** Countermark on Great Britain 6 Pence, KM#712.

CM Date	Host Date	Good	VG	F	VF	XF
ND(1849-57)	1831, 1834-37	7.50	13.50	27.50	45.00	—

KM# 90 REAL

Silver **Countermark:** Type VI **Note:** Countermark on Great Britain 6 Pence, KM#733.

CM Date	Host Date	Good	VG	F	VF	XF
ND(1849-57)	1838-46, 1848-49	6.00	10.00	17.50	30.00	—

KM# 77 2 REALES

Silver **Countermark:** Type VI **Note:** Countermarked on Central American Republic 2 Reales, KM#24. Values listed for KM#77 are for unholed pieces, holed examples are worth substantially less.

CM Date	Host Date	Good	VG	F	VF	XF
ND(1849-57)	1849 JB	4.75	10.00	18.50	32.50	—

KM# 93 2 REALES

Silver **Countermark:** Type VI **Note:** Countermark on Great Britain Shilling, KM#666.

CM Date	Host Date	Good	VG	F	VF	XF
ND(1849-57)	1816-20	7.50	12.50	22.50	37.50	—

KM# 94 2 REALES

Silver **Countermark:** Type VI **Note:** Countermark on Great Britain Shilling, KM#734.

CM Date	Host Date	Good	VG	F	VF	XF
ND(1849-57)	1838-46, 1849	6.50	12.00	20.00	35.00	—

KM# 80 1/2 ESCUDO

Gold **Countermark:** Type VI **Note:** Countermark on Central American Republic 1/2 Escudo, KM#13.

CM Date	Host Date	Good	VG	F	VF	XF
ND(1849-57)	1828CR F	—	50.00	100	150	225
ND(1849-57)	1843CR M	—	50.00	100	150	225
ND(1849-57)	1846CR JB	—	40.00	80.00	125	200
ND(1849-57)	1847CR JB	—	40.00	80.00	125	200
ND(1849-57)	1848CR JB	—	40.00	80.00	125	200
ND(1849-57)	1849CR JB	—	50.00	100	150	225

KM# 81 1/2 ESCUDO

Gold **Countermark:** Type VI **Note:** Countermark on Central American Republic 1/2 Escudo, KM#5.

CM Date	Host Date	Good	VG	F	VF	XF
ND(1849-57)	1825NG M	—	—	—	—	—

KM# 84 ESCUDO

Gold **Countermark:** Type VI **Note:** Countermark on Central American Republic 1 Escudo, KM#14.

CM Date	Host Date	Good	VG	F	VF	XF
ND(1849-57)	1833CR E	—	90.00	175	275	375
ND(1849-57)	1833CR F	—	90.00	175	275	375
ND(1849-57)	1844CR M	—	55.00	125	225	325
ND(1849-57)	1845CR JB	—	90.00	175	275	375
ND(1849-57)	1846CR JB	—	65.00	125	225	325
ND(1849-57)	1847CR JB	—	65.00	125	225	325
ND(1849-57)	1848CR JB	—	65.00	125	225	325
ND(1849-57)	1849CR JB	—	65.00	125	225	325

PESO COINAGE

KM# 101 1/16 PESO

1.4600 g., 0.9030 Silver .0423 oz. **Obv:** Arms in sprays **Rev:** Tree **Edge:** Reeded

Date	Mintage	VG	F	VF	XF	Unc
1850 JB	—	8.50	20.00	37.50	77.50	—
1855/0 JB	—	11.00	22.50	45.00	90.00	—
1855 JB	—	6.50	17.50	32.50	75.00	—
1862 JB Rare	—	—	—	—	—	—
1862 GW	—	30.00	50.00	87.50	185	—

KM# 102 1/8 PESO

2.9500 g., 0.9030 Silver .0856 oz. **Obv:** Arms in sprays **Rev:** Tree

Date	Mintage	VG	F	VF	XF	Unc
1850 JB	—	6.50	15.00	27.50	57.50	—
1853 JB	—	8.00	18.50	40.00	85.00	—
1855 JB	—	5.50	13.50	25.00	52.50	—

KM# 103 1/4 PESO

6.4000 g., 0.9030 Silver .1858 oz. **Obv:** Arms in sprays **Rev:** Tree

Date	Mintage	VG	F	VF	XF	Unc
1850 JB	—	5.00	11.00	22.50	52.50	—
1853 JB	—	9.00	20.00	42.50	88.00	—
1855 JB	—	13.50	30.00	55.00	100	—

DECIMAL COINAGE

100 Centavos = 1 Peso

KM# 108 1/4 CENTAVO

0.8000 g., Copper-Nickel **Edge:** Plain

Date	Mintage	VG	F	VF	XF	Unc
ND(1865)	20,000	35.00	62.50	100	200	—

Note: Deceptive counterfeits reported

KM# 109 CENTAVO

3.8000 g., Copper-Nickel **Obv:** Arms

Date	Mintage	VG	F	VF	XF	Unc
1865	33,000	4.00	11.50	25.00	42.50	—
1866	39,000	6.50	13.50	27.50	55.00	—
1867	44,000	8.00	20.00	35.00	70.00	—
1868	20,000	3.75	8.50	15.00	32.50	—

KM# 120 CENTAVO

3.8000 g., Copper-Nickel

Date	Mintage	F	VF	XF	Unc	BU
1874	32,000	2.25	4.00	8.00	15.00	—

KM# 110 5 CENTAVOS

1.2680 g., 0.7500 Silver .0305 oz. **Obv:** Arms in sprays **Rev:** Tree **Edge:** Reeded

Date	Mintage	VG	F	VF	XF	Unc
1865 GW	233,000	2.50	6.00	15.00	32.50	—
1869 GW	—	3.50	10.00	25.00	60.00	—
1870 GW	27,000	12.50	27.50	60.00	125	—
1871 GW	328,000	7.50	20.00	45.00	87.50	—
1872 GW	Inc. above	9.00	22.00	47.50	110	—
1875/1 GW	Inc. above	2.00	6.00	14.50	35.00	—
1875 GW	Inc. above	1.75	5.00	12.00	28.00	—

KM# 125 5 CENTAVOS

1.2680 g., 0.7500 Silver .0305 oz. **Obv:** Arms in sprays **Rev:** Denomination in wreath

Date	Mintage	F	VF	XF	Unc	BU
1885 GW	180,000	1.50	3.50	8.00	22.00	—
1886/5 GW	251,000	2.50	6.00	13.50	35.00	—
1887 GW	491,000	1.25	3.00	7.00	20.00	—

KM# 128 5 CENTAVOS

1.2000 g., 0.7500 Silver .0289 oz. **Obv:** Arms in sprays

Date	Mintage	F	VF	XF	Unc	BU
1889HEATON	520,000	0.65	1.75	4.00	15.00	—
1889HEATON Proof	—	Value: 150				
1890HEATON	431,000	0.65	1.75	4.00	15.00	—
1892HEATON	280,000	0.75	2.00	4.50	18.00	—

KM# 111 10 CENTAVOS

2.5360 g., 0.7500 Silver .0611 oz. **Obv:** Arms in sprays **Rev:** Tree

Date	Mintage	VG	F	VF	XF	Unc
1865 GW	185,000	4.00	10.00	20.00	50.00	—
1868 GW	10,000	60.00	150	285	—	—
1870 GW	48,000	20.00	40.00	80.00	150	—
1872 GW	18,000	50.00	115	235	—	—

KM# 121 10 CENTAVOS

2.5360 g., 0.7500 Silver .0611 oz. **Obv:** Arms in sprays **Rev:** Tree

Date	Mintage	VG	F	VF	XF	Unc
1875 GW	286,000	2.25	5.50	13.50	35.00	—

KM# 126 10 CENTAVOS

2.5000 g., 0.7500 Silver .0602 oz. **Obv:** "CB" below arms in sprays **Rev:** Value in wreath

Date	Mintage	F	VF	XF	Unc	BU
1886 GW	120,000	3.00	7.00	16.50	40.00	—
1887 GW	245,000	2.25	5.00	12.50	32.50	—

KM# 129 10 CENTAVOS

2.5000 g., 0.7500 Silver .0602 oz. **Obv:** Arms in sprays **Rev:** Value in wreath

Date	Mintage	F	VF	XF	Unc	BU
1889HEATON	260,000	1.00	2.50	4.50	15.00	—
1889HEATON Proof	—	Value: 200				
1890HEATON	215,000	1.00	2.75	5.00	18.00	—
1892HEATON	140,000	1.25	3.00	6.50	20.00	—

KM# 105 25 CENTAVOS

6.2500 g., 0.7500 Silver .1507 oz. **Obv:** Arms in sprays **Rev:** Tree divides small "25 Cs"

Date	Mintage	VG	F	VF	XF	Unc
1864 GW	223,000	6.00	22.50	57.50	140	—

KM# 106 25 CENTAVOS

6.2500 g., 0.7500 Silver .1507 oz. **Obv:** Arms in sprays **Rev:** Tree divides large "25 Cs"

Date	Mintage	VG	F	VF	XF	Unc
1864 GW	Inc. above	13.50	35.00	90.00	200	—
1865 GW	42,000	6.00	13.50	35.00	87.50	—
1875 GW	121,000	3.00	10.00	22.50	65.00	—

KM# 127.1 25 CENTAVOS

6.2500 g., 0.7500 Silver .1507 oz. **Obv:** Arms in sprays **Rev:** GW 9Ds below wreath enclosing denomination

Date	Mintage	F	VF	XF	Unc	BU
1886 GW	100,000	5.00	9.00	16.50	45.00	—
1887 GW	200,000	5.75	13.50	22.50	50.00	—

Note: CB below arms in sprays

KM# 127.2 25 CENTAVOS

6.2500 g., 0.7500 Silver .1507 oz. **Obv:** Arms in sprays **Rev:** 9Ds GW below wreath enclosing denomination

Date	Mintage	F	VF	XF	Unc	BU
1886 GW	Inc. above	7.50	15.00	22.50	60.00	—

Note: C below arms in sprays

Date	Mintage	F	VF	XF	Unc	BU
1887 GW	Inc. above	3.50	8.75	20.00	47.50	—

Note: CB below arms in sprays

KM# 130 25 CENTAVOS

6.3000 g., 0.7500 Silver .1519 oz. **Obv:** Arms in sprays

Date	Mintage	F	VF	XF	Unc	BU
1889/8HEATON	410,000	1.25	2.75	5.75	16.50	—
1889/93HEATON	Inc. above	1.25	3.00	6.00	17.50	—
1889/99HEATON	Inc. above	1.25	3.75	7.50	20.00	—
1889HEATON	Inc. above	1.25	2.75	5.75	16.50	—
1889HEATON Proof	—	Value: 250				
1890/80HEATON	395,000	1.25	3.50	7.50	20.00	—
1890HEATON	Inc. above	1.25	2.75	5.75	16.50	—
1892HEATON	440,000	1.25	2.75	5.75	16.50	—
1893HEATON	670,000	1.25	2.25	4.00	13.50	—

KM# 112 50 CENTAVOS

12.5000 g., 0.7500 Silver .3014 oz. **Obv:** Arms in sprays **Rev:** Tree divides "50-Cs"

Date	Mintage	Good	VG	F	VF	XF
1865 GW	29,000	7.00	17.50	45.00	115	—
1866/5 GW	117,000	8.00	20.00	50.00	125	—
1866 GW	Inc. above	7.50	18.50	55.00	135	—
1867 GW	5,168	60.00	90.00	250	400	—
1870 GW	6,267	100	155	350	—	—
1872 GW	Inc. above	120	255	—	—	—
1875 GW	69,000	4.50	12.50	35.00	90.00	—

KM# 124 50 CENTAVOS
12.5000 g., 0.7500 Silver .3014 oz. **Obv:** Arms in sprays **Rev:** Denomination within wreath

Date	Mintage	F	VF	XF	Unc	BU
1880 GW	389,000	6.00	13.00	27.50	70.00	—
1885 GW	152,000	7.00	15.00	25.00	65.00	—
Note: With and without CB below ribbon						
1886 GW	97,000	7.00	15.00	32.50	80.00	—
1887 GW	208,000	6.50	13.50	25.00	67.50	—
1890/80 GW	58,000	6.00	12.00	25.00	70.00	—
Note: Inverted N in CENTAVOS						
1890 GW	Inc. above	6.50	12.50	25.00	70.00	—

KM# 131 50 CENTAVOS
12.5000 g., 0.7500 Silver .3014 oz. **Obv:** Arms in sprays

Date	Mintage	F	VF	XF	Unc	BU
1889 GW Rare	205,000	—	—	—	—	—

Note: Not released for circulation. Eventually used as bullion to strike the 1890 dated KM#124 50 Centavos at San Jose. Only a few examples of the 1889 are known

KM# 107.1 PESO
1.5253 g., 0.8750 Gold .0429 oz. **Obv:** Arms in sprays

Date	Mintage	VG	F	VF	XF	Unc
1864 GW	6,383	35.00	70.00	100	135	—
1866 GW	35,000	27.50	55.00	85.00	115	—
1868 GW	—	45.00	85.00	120	160	—

KM# 107.2 PESO
1.5253 g., 0.8750 Gold .0429 oz. **Obv:** Arms in sprays **Rev:** Large UN in center of wreath

Date	Mintage	VG	F	VF	XF	Unc
1866 GW	Inc. above	27.50	55.00	85.00	115	—

KM# 107.3 PESO
1.5253 g., 0.8750 Gold .0429 oz. **Obv:** Arms in sprays **Rev:** Small UN, fineness omitted

Date	Mintage	VG	F	VF	XF	Unc
1866 GW	Inc. above	27.50	55.00	85.00	115	—

KM# 116 PESO
1.5253 g., 0.8750 Gold .0429 oz. **Obv:** Arms in sprays **Note:** Design modified.

Date	Mintage	VG	F	VF	XF	Unc
1871 GW	11,000	28.50	52.50	80.00	115	—
1872 GW	37,000	28.50	52.50	80.00	115	—

KM# 113 2 PESOS (Dos)
2.9355 g., 0.8750 Gold .0825 oz. **Obv:** Arms in sprays

Date	Mintage	VG	F	VF	XF	Unc
1866 GW	13,000	45.00	70.00	115	150	—
1867 GW	—	60.00	100	155	200	—
1868 GW	—	45.00	70.00	115	150	—

KM# 122 2 PESOS (Dos)
2.9355 g., 0.8750 Gold .0825 oz. **Obv:** Arms in sprays **Note:** Design modified (19 millimeters).

Date	Mintage	VG	F	VF	XF	Unc
1876 GW Rare	2,161	—	—	—	—	—

KM# 114 5 PESOS (Cinco)
7.3387 g., 0.8750 Gold .2064 oz. **Obv:** Arms in sprays

Date	Mintage	VG	F	VF	XF	Unc
1867 GW	39,000	100	125	165	250	—
1868 GW	6,752	100	125	165	250	—
1869 GW	11,000	100	125	165	250	—
1870 GW	15,000	100	125	165	250	—

KM# 117 5 PESOS (Cinco)
7.3387 g., 0.8750 Gold .2064 oz. **Obv:** Arms in sprays

Date	Mintage	VG	F	VF	XF	Unc
1873 GW	5,167	165	300	650	1,000	—
1875 GW	Inc. above	165	300	650	1,000	—

KM# 118 5 PESOS (Cinco)
8.0645 g., 0.9000 Gold .2333 oz. **Obv:** Arms in sprays

Date	Mintage	VG	F	VF	XF	Unc
1873 GW	Inc. above	1,500	2,000	2,500	3,000	—

KM# 115 10 PESOS
14.6774 g., 0.8750 Gold .4129 oz. **Obv:** Arms in sprays

Date	Mintage	VG	F	VF	XF	Unc
1870 GW	20,000	225	300	400	600	—
1871 GW	30,000	250	325	425	650	—
1872 GW	4,555	300	400	550	800	—

KM# 123 10 PESOS
14.6774 g., 0.8750 Gold .4129 oz. **Obv:** Arms in sprays **Note:** Design modified.

Date	Mintage	VG	F	VF	XF	Unc
1876 GW	3,389	500	1,000	1,600	2,250	—

KM# 119 20 PESOS
32.2580 g., 0.9000 Gold .9334 oz. **Obv:** Arms in sprays

Date	Mintage	F	VF	XF	Unc	BU
1873 Rare	—	—	—	—	—	—

Note: Stack's Hammel sale 9-82 AU realized $16,000., Pacific Coast Auction Galleries, Long Beach sale 6-86 AU realized $17,000, Superior Galleries Casterline sale 5-89 XF realized $16,500

COUNTERSTAMPED COINAGE

Type VII • 1889

Necessity issue undertaken in 1889 (and 1890) consequent to supply, by Heaton Mint of underweight 50 Centavo coinage of the general type of the Heaton-made 5, 10, and 25 Centavos of 1889-93. The host coins were particularly available, due to the adoption by Colombia of a .500 fine debasement of its silver coinage under President Nunez in 1886. This led to runaway inflation, rampant printing press money and hoarding of good (.835-.902 fine) silver. The Colombian Peso declined in value to about 1 Centavo of the old silver and gold currency.

Obverse counterstamp: COSTA RICA above national arms. Reverse counterstamp: HABILITADA POR EL GOBIERNO around lion/CR in 7mm circle

KM# 133.1 50 CENTAVOS
12.5000 g., 0.8350 Silver .3356 oz. **Countermark:** Type VII **Note:** Counterstamped on Colombia (Bogota) 50 Centavos.

CS Date	Host Date	Good	VG	F	VF	XF
ND(1889)	1872	25.00	50.00	100	225	—
ND(1889)	1873	20.00	40.00	85.00	200	—

KM# 136 50 CENTAVOS
12.5000 g., 0.8350 Silver .3356 oz. **Countermark:** Type VII **Note:** Counterstamped on Colombia (Bogota) Cinco Decimos, KM#153.1

CS Date	Host Date	Good	VG	F	VF	XF
ND(1889)	1868	40.00	80.00	160	320	—
ND(1889)	1870	30.00	60.00	120	250	—

KM# 134 50 CENTAVOS
12.5000 g., 0.8350 Silver .3356 oz. **Countermark:** Type VII **Note:** Counterstamped on Colombia (Bogota) Cincuenta Centavos, KM#1771.

CS Date	Host Date	Good	VG	F	VF	XF
ND(1889)	1874	20.00	40.00	85.00	70.00	—
ND(1889)	1875	20.00	40.00	85.00	70.00	—
ND(1889)	1876	20.00	40.00	85.00	70.00	—
ND(1889)	1877	20.00	40.00	85.00	70.00	—
ND(1889)	1878	20.00	40.00	85.00	200	—
ND(1889)	1879	18.00	35.00	75.00	200	—
ND(1889)	1880	18.00	35.00	75.00	200	—
ND(1889)	1881	18.00	35.00	75.00	200	—
ND(1889)	1882	18.00	35.00	75.00	200	—
ND(1889)	1883	18.00	35.00	75.00	185	—
ND(1889)	1884	18.00	35.00	75.00	185	—
ND(1889)	1885	30.00	60.00	120	250	—

KM# 135.5 50 CENTAVOS
12.5000 g., 0.8350 Silver .3356 oz. **Countermark:** Type VII **Note:** Counterstamped on Colombia (Medellin) Cinco Decimos, KM#153.3.

CS Date	Host Date	Good	VG	F	VF	XF
ND(1889)	1872	25.00	50.00	100	225	—

KM# 135.1 50 CENTAVOS
12.5000 g., 0.8350 Silver .3356 oz. **Countermark:** Type VII **Note:** Counterstamped on Colombia (Medellin) Cinco Decimos, KM#153.6.

CS Date	Host Date	Good	VG	F	VF	XF
ND(1889)	1874 C.B.	20.00	40.00	85.00	200	—
ND(1889)	1875 C.B.	20.00	40.00	85.00	200	—
ND(1889)	1876 C.B.	20.00	40.00	85.00	200	—

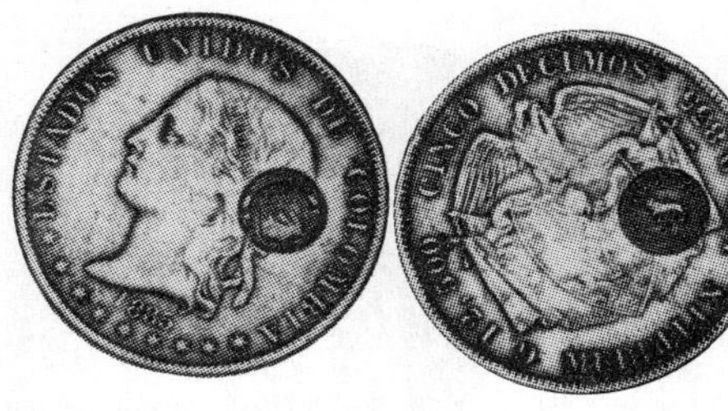

KM# 135.2 50 CENTAVOS

12.5000 g., 0.8350 Silver .3356 oz. **Countermark:** Type VII **Note:** Counterstamped on Colombia (Medellin) Cinco Decimos, KM#161.1.

CS Date	Host Date	Good	VG	F	VF	XF
ND(1889)	1877/4 C.B.	20.00	40.00	85.00	200	—
ND(1889)	1878/4 C.B.	20.00	40.00	85.00	200	—
ND(1889)	1879/4 C.B.	20.00	40.00	85.00	200	—
ND(1889)	1880 C.B.	20.00	40.00	85.00	200	—
ND(1889)	1881 C.B.	18.00	35.00	75.00	185	—
ND(1889)	1882 C.B.	18.00	35.00	75.00	185	—
ND(1889)	1883 C.B.	18.00	35.00	75.00	185	—
ND(1889)	1884 C.B.	16.00	30.00	65.00	175	—
ND(1889)	1885 C.B.	16.00	30.00	65.00	175	—
ND(1889)	1886 C.B.	45.00	75.00	150	300	—

KM# 133.2 50 CENTAVOS

12.5000 g., 0.8350 Silver .3356 oz. **Countermark:** Type VII **Note:** Counterstamped on Colombia (Bogota) 50 Centavos, KM#172.2.

CS Date	Host Date	Good	VG	F	VF	XF
ND(1889)	1874	18.00	35.00	75.00	185	—

KM# 135.3 50 CENTAVOS

12.5000 g., 0.8350 Silver .3356 oz. **Countermark:** Type VII **Note:** Counterstamped on Colombia (Medellin) Cinco Decimos, KM#153.4

CS Date	Host Date	Good	VG	F	VF	XF
ND(1889)	1874	25.00	50.00	100	225	—

KM# 135.4 50 CENTAVOS

12.5000 g., 0.8350 Silver .3356 oz. **Countermark:** Type VII **Note:** Counterstamped on Colombia (Medellin) Cinco Decimos, KM#153.5

CS Date	Host Date	Good	VG	F	VF	XF
ND1889	1875	25.00	50.00	100	225	—

Note: Counterstamps appear on coins dated 1875.

REFORM COINAGE

1897, 100 Centimos = 1 Colon

KM# 139 2 COLONES

1.5560 g., 0.9000 Gold .0456 oz. **Obv:** Ornate arms **Rev:** Bust of Christopher Colombus

Date	Mintage	F	VF	XF	Unc	BU
1897 Proof	500	Value: 1,500				
1900	45,000	25.00	35.00	45.00	70.00	—

KM# 142 5 COLONES

3.8900 g., 0.9000 Gold .1125 oz. **Obv:** Ornate arms **Rev:** Bust of Christopher Colombus

Date	Mintage	F	VF	XF	Unc	BU
1899	100,000	BV	60.00	75.00	125	—
1900	100,000	BV	60.00	75.00	125	—

KM# 140 10 COLONES

7.7800 g., 0.9000 Gold .2251 oz. **Obv:** Ornate arms **Rev:** Bust of Christopher Colombus

Date	Mintage	F	VF	XF	Unc	BU
1897	60,000	BV	115	125	185	—
1899	50,000	BV	115	125	185	—
1900	140,000	BV	115	125	185	—

KM# 141 20 COLONES

15.5600 g., 0.9000 Gold .4502 oz. **Obv:** Ornate arms **Rev:** Bust of Christopher Colombus

Date	Mintage	F	VF	XF	Unc	BU
1897	20,000	BV	225	275	450	—
1899	25,000	BV	225	275	450	—
1900	5,000	BV	250	375	700	—

ESSAIS

KM#	Date	Mintage	Identification	Mkt Val
E1	1872	—	5 Centavos. Nickel.	375
E2	1872	—	10 Centavos. Nickel.	400

PATTERNS

KM#	Date	Mintage	Identification	Mkt Val
Pn1	1850	—	1/2 Peso. White Metal. Similar to 1/4 Peso KM#103.	—

KM#	Date	Mintage	Identification	Mkt Val
PnA2	1850	—	White Metal.	—
Pn2	1850	—	White Metal.	—
Pn3	1850	—	Onza. Tin. Prev.# KMPnB2.	150

KM#	Date	Mintage	Identification	Mkt Val
Pn4	1850	—	Onza. Gold. Prev.# KMPn2.	—
Pn5	1888HEATON	—	50 Centavos. White Metal. Similar to 25 Centavos KM#130.	—
Pn6	1892	—	Centavo. Copper-Nickel. Prev.# KMPn4.	300
Pn7	1892	—	Centavo. Copper. Prev.# KMPn5.	—
Pn8	1892	—	Centavo. Copper. Arms. Value and wreath. Prev.# KMPn6.	—
Pn9	1897	—	10 Colones. Copper. KM#140.	—
Pn10	1897	—	10 Colones. Yellow Silver.	—

PIEFORTS

KM#	Date	Mintage	Identification	Mkt Val
P1	1892	—	Centavo. Copper. Type of Pn7.	—
P3	1892	—	Centavo. Bronze.	—
P4	1892	—	Centavo. Nickel.	—
P5	1892	—	Centavo. Aluminum. Type of Pn6	—
P2	1892	—	Centavo. Nickel. Type of Pn6.	750

PROOF SETS

KM#	Date	Mintage	Identification	Issue Price	Mkt Val
PS1	1889 (4)	—	KM#128-131	—	—

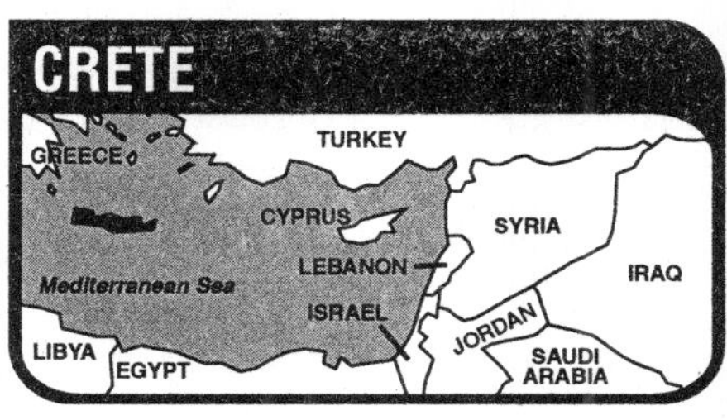

The island of Crete (Kriti), located 60 miles southeast of the Peloponnesus, was the center of a brilliant civilization that flourished before the advent of Greek culture. After being conquered by the Romans, Byzantines, Moslems and Venetians, Crete became part of the Turkish Empire in 1669. As a consequence of the Greek Revolution of the 1820s, it was ceded to Egypt. Egypt returned the island to the Turks in 1840, and they ceded it to Greece in 1913, after the Second Balkan War.

RULERS

Prince Geqrge, 1898-1906

MINT MARKS

A - Paris

(a) - Paris (privy marks only)

TURKISH EMPIRE

STANDARD COINAGE

KM# 1.1 LEPTON

Bronze, 15 mm. **Note:** Diameter 15mm

Date	Mintage	F	VF	XF	Unc	BU
1900A	289,283	7.00	15.00	50.00	350	—

KM# 2 2 LEPTA

Bronze

Date	Mintage	F	VF	XF	Unc	BU
1900A	793,079	6.00	12.50	40.00	150	—

KM# 3 5 LEPTA

Copper-Nickel

Date	Mintage	F	VF	XF	Unc	BU
1900A	4,000,000	5.00	10.00	50.00	300	—

KM# 4.1 10 LEPTA

Copper-Nickel

Date	Mintage	F	VF	XF	Unc	BU
1900A	2,000,000	5.00	10.00	50.00	350	—

KM# 4.2 10 LEPTA

Copper-Nickel **Note:** Medal strike.

Date	Mintage	F	VF	XF	Unc	BU
1900A	—	25.00	50.00	300	1,000	—

KM# 5 20 LEPTA

Copper-Nickel

Date	Mintage	F	VF	XF	Unc	BU
1900A	1,250,000	5.00	10.00	75.00	350	—

Note: For coins similar to the five listings above, but dated 1893-95, see Greece

CROATIA

The Republic of Croatia, (Hrvatska) bordered on the west by the Adriatic Sea and the northeast by Hungary, has an area of 21,829 sq. mi. (56,538 sq. km.) and a population of 4.7 million. Capital: Zagreb.

The country was attached to the Kingdom of Hungary until Dec. 1, 1918, when it joined with the Serbs and Slovenes to form the Kingdom of the Serbs, Croats and Slovenes, which changed its name to the Kingdom of Yugoslavia on Oct. 3, 1929. On April 6, 1941, Hitler, angered by the coup d'etat that overthrew the pro-Nazi regime of regent Prince Paul, sent the Nazi armies crashing across the Yugoslav borders from Germany, Hungary, Romania and Bulgaria. Within a week the army of the Balkan Kingdom was prostrate and broken. Yugoslavia was dismembered to reward Hitler's Balkan allies. Croatia, reconstituted as a nominal kingdom, was given to the administration of an Italian princeling, who wisely decided to remain in Italy. By 1947 it was again totally part of the 6 Yugoslav Socialist Republics.

Croatia proclaimed their independence from Yugoslavia on Oct. 8, 1991.

Local Serbian forces, supported by the Yugoslav Federal Army, had developed a military stronghold and proclaimed an independent "SRPSKEKRAJINA" State in the area around Knin, located in southern Croatia having an estimated population of 350,000 Croat Serbs. In September 1995, Croat forces overwhelmed Croat Serb forces ending the short life of their proclaimed Serbian Republic.

NOTE: Coin dates starting with 1994 are followed with a period. Example: 1994.

MONETARY SYSTEM

100 Banica = 1 Kuna

The word kunas', related to the Russian Kunitsa, which means marten, reflects the use of furs for money in medieval Eastern Europe.

PATTERNS

Including off metal strikes

KM#	Date	Mintage	Identification	Mkt Val
Pn1	1848	—	Forint. Silver. 9.5000 g. Portrait right. Star and crescent.	—
Pn2	1848	—	2 Forint.	—
Note: Reported, not confirmed				
Pn3	1849	46	Kreuzer. Copper. Crowned triune arms. Star, legend, date. JEDEN/KRIZAR.	—
Pn4	1849	—	20 Kreuzer. Silver. Issued in Zagreb by Governor Jelacic in 1849. Destroyed by decree of Franz Joseph.	—

ZARA

(Zadar)

Zara, a port and fortress in Dalmatia, Croatia, was occupied by the French during the period of 1807-13. While the Fren ch defenders of the city were under siege in 1813, they issued a silver emergency coinage.

FRENCH OCCUPATION

FRENCH SIEGE COINAGE

KM# 1 4 FRANCS (60 Centimes)

30.5900 g., Silver

Date	Mintage	VG	F	VF	XF	Unc
1813	—	750	900	1,200	1,800	—

KM# 2 9 FRANCS (20 Centimes)

61.1200 g., Silver

Date	Mintage	VG	F	VF	XF	Unc
1813	—	850	1,300	1,800	2,500	—

KM# 3 18 FRANCS (40 Centimes)

122.3800 g., Silver **Obv:** Large stamp

Date	Mintage	VG	F	VF	XF	Unc
1813	—	1,600	2,100	3,800	5,500	—

KM# 4 18 FRANCS (40 Centimes)

122.3800 g., Silver **Obv:** Small stamp

Date	Mintage	VG	F	VF	XF	Unc
1813	—	1,600	2,100	3,800	5,600	—

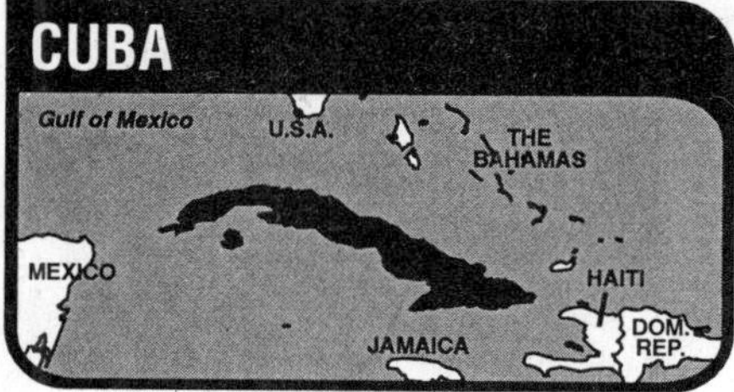

The Republic of Cuba, situated at the northern edge of the Caribbean Sea about 90 miles (145 km.) south of Florida, has an area of 42,804 sq. mi. (110,860 sq. km.). Capital: Havana. The Cuban economy is based on the cultivation and refining of sugar, which provides 80 percent of export earnings.

Discovered by Columbus in 1492 and settled by Diego Velasquez in the early 1500s, Cuba remained a Spanish possession until 1898, except for a brief British occupancy of Havana in 1762-63. Cuban attempts to gain freedom were crushed, even while Spain was granting independence to its other American possessions. Ten years of warfare, 1868-78, between Spanish troops and Cuban rebels exacted guarantees of rights which were never implemented. The final revolt, begun in 1895, evoked American sympathy, and with the aid of U.S. troops independence was proclaimed on May 20, 1902. Fulgencio Batista seized the government in 1952 and established a dictatorship. Opposition to Batista, led by Fidel Castro, drove him into exile on Jan. 1, 1959. A communist-type, 25-member collective leadership headed by Castro was inaugurated in March, 1962.

RULERS

Spanish, until 1898

COLONIAL

COUNTERMARKED COINAGE

1841

The loss of the Spanish Colonial mints in the new world caused a severe shortage of coinage in Cuba. Clandestine traders introduced the silver inflationary "reales de vellom" of Spain. The ratio was 2-1/2 New Reales to 1 Old Colonial Real. They were accepted easily by the Cuban public, ignorant of the devaluation in Spain where the silver "Peso" was now divided into 20 Reales.

In 1827 the Spanish governor of Cuba banned their importation. Various exchange rates were used until March 22, 1841 when a Royal Order decreed all will be recalled, counted and recorded with receipts issued and devalued with a countermark in the provinces Trinidad, Santiago de Cuba and Puerto Principe. Fifty punches were prepared.

KM# 1.1 2 REALES
0.9030 Silver **Countermark:** Lattice **Note:** Countermark on Spanish (Madrid) 2 Reales, KM#412.1.

CM Date	Host Date	Good	VG	F	VF	XF
ND(1841)	1772-88	12.50	22.50	35.00	55.00	—

KM# 1.2 2 REALES
0.9030 Silver **Countermark:** Lattice **Note:** Countermark on Spanish (Seville) 2 Reales, KM#412.2.

CM Date	Host Date	Good	VG	F	VF	XF
ND(1841)	1773-88	12.50	22.50	35.00	60.00	—

KM# 2 2 REALES
0.9030 Silver **Countermark:** Lattice **Note:** Countermark on Spanish (Madrid) 2 Reales, KM#430.1.

CM Date	Host Date	Good	VG	F	VF	XF
ND(1841)	1788-1808	10.00	20.00	30.00	60.00	—

KM# 3 2 REALES
0.9030 Silver **Countermark:** Lattice **Note:** Countermark on Spanish (Seville) 2 Reales, KM#430.2.

CM Date	Host Date	Good	VG	F	VF	XF
ND(1841)	1788-1808	10.00	20.00	30.00	50.00	—

KM# 4.1 2 REALES
0.9030 Silver **Countermark:** Lattice **Note:** Countermark on Spanish (Catalonia) 2 Reales, KM#464.

CM Date	Host Date	Good	VG	F	VF	XF
ND(1841)	1811-14	13.50	27.00	40.00	75.00	—

KM# 4.2 2 REALES
0.9030 Silver **Countermark:** Lattice **Note:** Countermark on Spanish (Cadiz) 2 Reales, KM#460.1.

CM Date	Host Date	Good	VG	F	VF	XF
ND(1841)	1810-12	13.50	27.00	40.00	75.00	—

KM# 5 2 REALES
0.9030 Silver **Countermark:** Lattice **Note:** Countermark on Spanish (Madrid) 2 Reales, KM#460.2.

CM Date	Host Date	Good	VG	F	VF	XF
ND(1841)	1814-33	10.00	20.00	30.00	50.00	—

KM# 6 2 REALES
0.9030 Silver **Countermark:** Lattice **Note:** Countermark on Spanish (Seville) 2 Reales, KM#460.3.

CM Date	Host Date	Good	VG	F	VF	XF
ND(1841)	1815-33	10.00	20.00	30.00	50.00	—

KM# 9 2 REALES
0.9030 Silver **Countermark:** Lattice **Note:** Countermark on Spanish (Madrid) 2 Reales, KM#474.3.

CM Date	Host Date	Good	VG	F	VF	XF
ND(1841)	1812-14	10.00	20.00	30.00	75.00	—

KM# 7 4 REALES
0.9030 Silver **Countermark:** Lattice **Note:** Countermark on Spanish (Madrid) 4 Reales, KM#540.1.

CM Date	Host Date	Good	VG	F	VF	XF
ND(1841)	1808-13	10.00	20.00	30.00	50.00	—

KM# 10 4 REALES
0.9030 Silver **Countermark:** Lattice **Note:** Countermark on Spanish (Madrid) 4 Reales, KM#562.2.

CM Date	Host Date	Good	VG	F	VF	XF
ND(1841)	1822	10.00	20.00	30.00	65.00	—
ND(1841)	1823	10.00	20.00	30.00	75.00	—

KM# 8 4 REALES
0.9030 g., Silver **Countermark:** Lattice **Note:** Countermark on Spanish (Seville) 4 Reales, KM#540.2.

CM Date	Host Date	Good	VG	F	VF	XF
ND(1841)	1810	10.00	20.00	30.00	50.00	—
ND(1841)	1811	10.00	20.00	30.00	50.00	—
ND(1841)	1812	10.00	20.00	30.00	50.00	—

KM# 11 4 REALES
0.9030 Silver **Countermark:** Lattice **Note:** Countermark on Spanish (Valencia) 4 Reales, KM#567.

CM Date	Host Date	Good	VG	F	VF	XF
ND(1841)	1823	13.50	27.00	40.00	65.00	—

KM# 12 4 REALES
0.9030 Silver **Countermark:** Lattice **Note:** Countermark on Spanish (Madrid) Proclamation medal of Charles IV.

CM Date	Host Date	Good	VG	F	VF	XF
ND(1841)	1789	—	—	—	—	—

COUNTERMARKED COINAGE

Real Series - 1872-77 Revolutionary Fund

It is thought that these countermarks were most likely used 1872-1877 by the Cuban revolutionary troops as a fund raising device. Commonly encountered on Mexican coins.

Key Countermark Varieties:

A-Short and thick

B-Long and thin

Values for these pieces vary according to the rarity of the date and type of coin on which the countermark is found. Prices listed here are for the most common host coins.

KM# R1 2 REALES
0.9030 Silver **Countermark:** Key **Note:** Countermark on Mexican 2 Reales, KM#374.

CM Date	Host Date	Good	VG	F	VF	XF
ND(1872-77)	1825-70	15.00	25.00	40.00	60.00	—

KM# R2 4 REALES
0.9030 Silver **Countermark:** Key **Note:** Countermark on Mexican 4 Reales, KM#375.

CM Date	Host Date	Good	VG	F	VF	XF
ND(1872-77)	1827-70	20.00	30.00	45.00	70.00	—

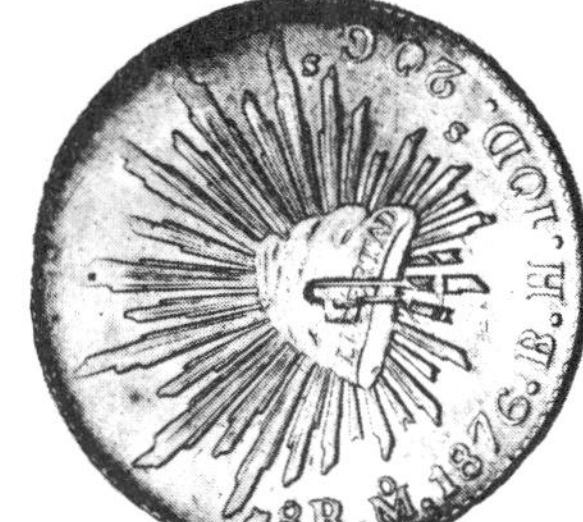

KM# R3 8 REALES
0.9030 Silver **Countermark:** Key **Note:** Countermark on Mexican 8 Reales, KM#377.

CM Date	Host Date	Good	VG	F	VF	XF
ND(1872-77)	1824-77	30.00	45.00	65.00	100	—

COUNTERMARKED COINAGE

Decimal Series

KM# R4.1 25 CENTAVOS
0.9030 Silver **Countermark:** Key **Note:** Countermark on Mexican 25 Centavos, KM#406.

CM Date	Host Date	Good	VG	F	VF	XF
ND(1872-77)	1869-77	15.00	20.00	30.00	55.00	—

KM# R4.2 25 CENTAVOS
0.9030 Silver **Countermark:** Key **Note:** Countermark on United States Liberty Seated Quarter.

CM Date	Host Date	Good	VG	F	VF	XF
ND(1872-77)	1853	65.00	125	185	285	—

KM# R4.3 25 CENTAVOS

0.9030 Silver **Countermark:** Key **Note:** Countermark on United States Liberty Seated Quarter.

CM Date	Host Date	Good	VG	F	VF	XF
ND(1872-77)	1858	65.00	125	185	285	—

Note: Countermarks appear on coins ranging in date from 1840-66.

KM# R4.4 25 CENTAVOS

0.9030 Silver **Countermark:** Key **Note:** Countermark on United States Capped Bust quarter.

CM Date	Host Date	Good	VG	F	VF	XF
ND(1872-77)	1835	65.00	125	185	285	—

KM# R5.1 50 CENTAVOS

0.9030 Silver **Countermark:** Key **Note:** Countermark on Mexican 50 Centavos, KM#407.

CM Date	Host Date	Good	VG	F	VF	XF
ND(1872-77)	1869-77	20.00	30.00	40.00	60.00	—

KM# R5.2 50 CENTAVOS

0.9030 Silver **Countermark:** Key **Note:** Countermark on United States Bust Half Dollar, KM#32.

CM Date	Host Date	Good	VG	F	VF	XF
ND(1872-77)	1833	550	—	—	—	—

KM# R6 PESO

0.9030 Silver **Countermark:** Key **Note:** Countermark on Mexican Peso, KM#388.

CM Date	Host Date	Good	VG	F	VF	XF
ND(1872-77)	1866-67	40.00	75.00	125	225	—

KM# R7 PESO

0.9030 Silver **Countermark:** Key **Note:** Countermark on Mexican Peso, KM#408.

CM Date	Host Date	Good	VG	F	VF	XF
ND(1872-77)	1869-77	30.00	55.00	80.00	125	—

PRE-REPUBLIC

DECIMAL COINAGE

KM# A8 PESO

22.5500 g., 0.9000 Silver .6526 oz. **Obv:** Arms **Rev:** Bust

Date	Mintage	F	VF	XF	Unc	BU
1898	1,000	300	750	1,650	3,200	4,000
1898 Proof	—	Value: 5,000				

PIEFORTS

KM#	Date	Mintage	Identification	Mkt Val
P1	1870 PCT	—	Peso. Silver.	7,500
P2	1870 PCT	—	Peso. Copper.	5,000

PATTERNS

Including off metal strikes

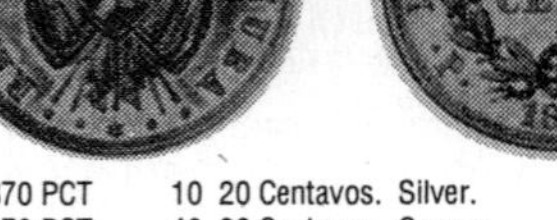

KM#	Date	Mintage	Identification	Mkt Val
Pn1	1870 PCT	10	5 Centavos. Silver.	2,500
Pn1a	1870 PCT	40	5 Centavos. Copper.	500
Pn2	1870 PCT	10	10 Centavos. Silver.	4,000
Pn2a	1870 PCT	40	10 Centavos. Copper.	600
Pn3	1870 PCT	10	20 Centavos. Silver.	4,500
Pn3a	1870 PCT	40	20 Centavos. Copper.	750
Pn4	1870 PCT	10	1/2 Peso. Silver.	4,200
Pn4a	1870 PCT	40	1/2 Peso. Copper.	2,550
Pn5	1870 PCT	10	Peso. Silver.	6,500
Pn5a	1870 PCT	40	Peso. Copper.	4,500
Pn9	1898	—	20 Centavos. Silver.	900
PnB10	1898	—	Peso. Copper.	5,000

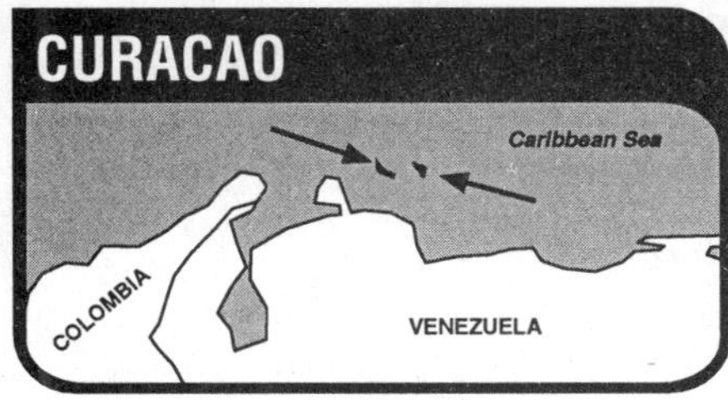

The island of Curacao, the largest of the Netherlands Antilles, which is an autonomous part of the Kingdom of the Netherlands located in the Caribbean Sea 40 miles off the coast of Venezuela, has an area of 173 sq. mi. (472 sq. km.).

Curacao was discovered by Spanish navigator Alonsode Ojeda in 1499 and was settled by Spain in 1527. The Dutch West India Company took the island from Spain in 1634 and administered it until 1787, when it was surrendered to the United Netherlands. The Dutch held it thereafter except for two periods during the Napoleonic Wars, 1800-1803 and 1807-16, when it was occupied by the British. During the second occupation of the Napoleonic period, the British created an emergency coinage for Curacao by cutting the Spanish dollar into 5 equal segments and countermarking each piece with a rosette indent.

MINT MARKS

D - Denver
P - Philadelphia
(u) - Utrecht

BATAVIAN REPUBLIC

MONETARY SYSTEM

1 Cent (U.S.) = 2-1/2 Stuivers
6 Stuivers = 1 Reaal
8 Realen = 1 Peso, 1793-1801
12 Realen = 1 Peso, 1801-18
7-1/2 Pesos = 1 Johannes (unmarked), 1793-99
6 Pesos = 1 Johannes (unmarked), 1799-1815
8 Pesos = 1 Johannes (c/m), 1799-1815
7-1/2 Pesos = 1 Johannes (c/m), 1815-27

COUNTERMARKED COINAGE

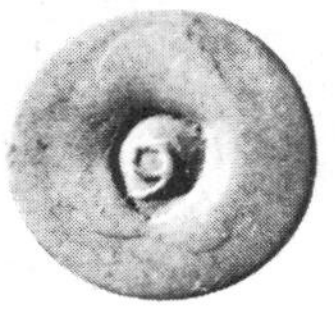

KM# 4 9 STUIVERS
Silver **Countermark:** 9 **Note:** Countermark in oval indent on Spanish Colonial 1 Real.

CM Date	Host Date	Good	VG	F	VF	XF
ND	ND	150	200	265	345	—

Note: The above coins along with similar coins bearing the numbers 3, 5, 14-18 are of questionable origin. Thus, they are not listed in Craig. Pridmore states these as unattributable

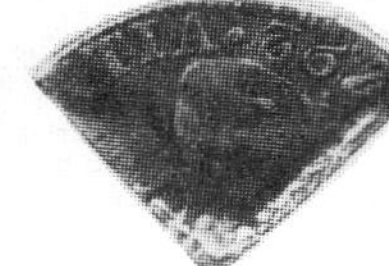

KM# 7 3 REAAL
Silver **Note:** Countermark 5-petalled rosace in circle on 1/4 cut of Spanish or Spanish Colonial 8 Reales.

CM Date	Host Date	Good	VG	F	VF	XF
	ND(c.1810)	—	600	1,200	1,850	2,250

BRITISH OCCUPATION

COUNTERMARKED COINAGE

KM# 13 3 REAAL
Silver **Note:** Partial reconstruction, 4 out of 5 segments; countermark 5-petalled rosace in circle on 1/5 cut of Spanish or Spanish Colonial 8 Reales.

CM Date	Host Date	Good	VG	F	VF	XF
ND	ND(1815)	—	35.00	50.00	85.00	145

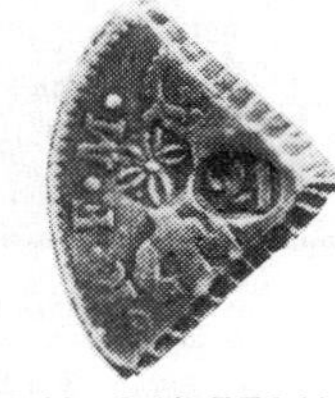

KM# 16 3-1/2 REAAL
Silver **Note:** Countermark: additional 21 in oval indent on KM#13.

CM Date	Host Date	Good	VG	F	VF	XF
ND	ND(1814)	—	700	1,200	1,600	3,500

KM# 19 6 PESOS
Gold **Countermark:** W **Obv:** Countermark: GI, L, MH and B at edges, GH in center on false Brazil 6400 Reis type of KM#172.2. **Rev:** Countermark

CM Date	Host Date	Good	VG	F	VF	XF
ND	ND(1815) Unique	—	—	—	—	—

KM# 20 6 PESOS
Gold **Countermark:** W **Obv:** Countermark: GI, L, MH and B at edges, GH in center on false Brazil 6400 Reis type of KM#199.1 **Rev:** Countermark

CM Date	Host Date	Good	VG	F	VF	XF
ND	ND(1815) Unique	—	—	—	—	—

NETHERLANDS RESTORED

1816

MONETARY REFORM

15 Realen = 1 Peso, 1818-22
7 Stuivers = 1 Reaal, 1822-27
10 Stuivers = 1 Franc, 1822-27
5 Francs = 1 Dollar
20 Stuivers = 1 Gulden, 1827-99
2/5 Peso = 1 Gulden, 1827-96
5/7 Peso = 1 Gulden, 1896-97
1 Peso = 1 Gulden, 1897-99

REFORM COINAGE

KM# 24 STUIVER
0.3000 Silver

Date	Mintage	F	VF	XF	Unc	BU
1822	529,000	30.00	50.00	90.00	170	—

Note: Struck also in 1840-41, circulating at that time as a 2 Cent piece

KM# 25 1/4 REAAL
Silver

Date	Mintage	F	VF	XF	Unc	BU
1821 Unique?	—	—	—	—	—	—

KM# 26.1 REAAL
Silver **Rev:** 4 acorns

Date	Mintage	F	VF	XF	Unc	BU
1821	121,000	50.00	75.00	135	225	—

KM# 26.2 REAAL
Silver **Rev:** 7 acorns

Date	Mintage	F	VF	XF	Unc	BU
1821	Inc. above	50.00	75.00	135	225	—

KM# 26.3 REAAL
Silver **Rev:** 8 acorns

Date	Mintage	F	VF	XF	Unc	BU
1821	Inc. above	50.00	75.00	135	225	—

KM# 26.4 REAAL
Silver **Rev:** 9 acorns

Date	Mintage	F	VF	XF	Unc	BU
1821	Inc. above	50.00	75.00	135	225	—

KM# 26.5 REAAL
Silver **Rev:** 12 acorns

Date	Mintage	F	VF	XF	Unc	BU
1821	Inc. above	50.00	75.00	135	225	—

KM# 28 3 REAAL
Silver **Countermark:** 3 **Note:** Reconstructed 5 segment, countermark in circle on 1/5 cut of Spanish or Spanish Colonial 8 Reales.

Date	Mintage	VG	F	VF	XF	Unc
ND(1818)	78,000	40.00	70.00	120	200	—

KM# 29 3 REAAL
Silver **Countermark:** 3 **Note:** Countermark in dentilated circle on 1/5 cut of Spanish or Spanish Colonial 8 Reales.

Date	Mintage	VG	F	VF	XF	Unc
ND(1819-25)	—	35.00	60.00	110	185	—

KM# 30 5 REAAL
Silver **Countermark:** 5 **Note:** Countermark in circle on 1/3 cut of Spanish or Spanish Colonial 8 Reales.

Date	Mintage	VG	F	VF	XF	Unc
ND(1818)	3,000	3,500	6,000	9,000	14,500	—

KM# 27 1/4 GUILDER
Silver **Countermark:** C **Note:** Reconstructed 4 segment, countermark in oval indent on 1/4 cut of Netherlands 1 Guilden.

Date	Mintage	VG	F	VF	XF	Unc
ND(1838)	24,000	60.00	100	185	300	—

TOKEN COINAGE

All of these tokens are known with the counterstamp of a letter C and were used by the S.E.L. Maduro Co. as coal loading tokens.

KM# Tn1 STUIVER
Copper-Nickel-Zinc **Issuer:** Jesurun and Co. **Obv:** 1 STUIVER in 2 lines **Rev:** J x Co.

Date	Mintage	F	VF	XF	Unc	BU
ND(c. 1880)	—	10.00	20.00	35.00	60.00	—

KM# Tn2 STUIVER
Copper-Nickel-Zinc **Issuer:** J. J. Naar **Obv:** 1 STUIVER in 2 lines **Rev:** J.J.N

Date	Mintage	F	VF	XF	Unc	BU
ND(c. 1880)	—	10.00	20.00	35.00	60.00	—

KM# Tn3 STUIVER
Copper-Nickel-Zinc **Issuer:** Leyba and Co. **Obv:** 1 STUIVER in 2 lines **Rev:** L x C

Date	Mintage	F	VF	XF	Unc	BU
ND(c. 1880)	—	15.00	25.00	45.00	75.00	—

MODERN COINAGE

100 Cents = 1 Gulden

KM# 35 1/4 GULDEN
3.5800 g., 0.6400 Silver .0736 oz.

Date	Mintage	F	VF	XF	Unc	BU
1900 (u)	480,000	12.00	20.00	35.00	65.00	—
1900 (u) Proof	40	Value: 200				

PROOF SETS

KM#	Date	Mintage	Identification	Issue Price	Mkt Val
PS1	1901 (2)	40	KM36(1901), KM35(1900)	—	400

CYPRUS

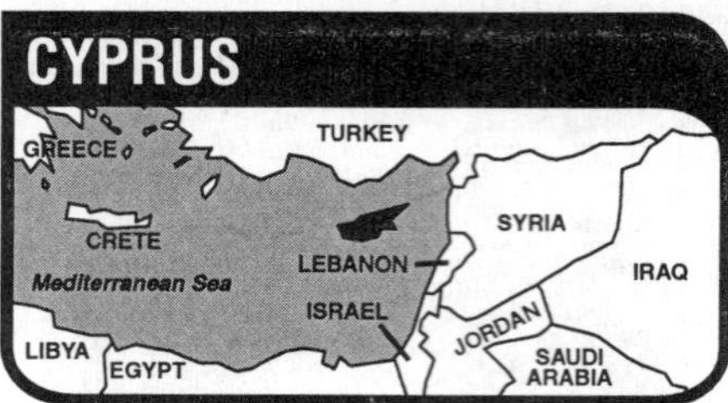

The island of Cyprus lies in the eastern Mediterranean Sea 44 miles (71 km.) south of Turkey and 60 miles (97 km.) off the Syrian coast. It is the third largest island in the Mediterranean Sea, having an area of 3,572 sq. mi. (9,251 sq. km.). Capital: Nicosia.

The importance of Cyprus dates from the Bronze Age when it was desired as a principal source of copper (from which the island derived its name) and as a strategic trading center. It was during this period that large numbers of Greeks settled on the island and gave it the predominantly Greek character. Its role as an international marketplace made it a prime disseminator of the then prevalent cultures, a role that still influences the civilization of Western man. Because of its fortuitous position and influential role, Cyprus was conquered by a succession of empires: the Assyrian, Egyptian, Persian, Macedonian, Ptolemaic, Roman and Byzantine. It was taken from Isaac Comnenus by Richard the Lion-Heart in 1191, sold to the Templar Knights and for the following 7 centuries was ruled by the Franks, the Venetians and the Ottomans. During the Ottoman period Cyprus acquired its Turkish community (18 percent of its population). In 1878 the island fell to the British.

RULERS
British, until 1960

MINT MARKS
no mint mark - Royal Mint, London, England
H - Birmingham, England

MONETARY SYSTEM
9 Piastres = 1 Shilling
20 Shillings = 1 Pound

BRITISH COLONY

PIASTRE COINAGE

KM# 1.1 1/4 PIASTRE
Bronze

Date	Mintage	F	VF	XF	Unc	BU
1879	150,000	5.00	15.00	30.00	100	—
1879 Proof	—	Value: 850				
1880	72,000	10.00	25.00	50.00	120	—
1880 Proof	—	Value: 375				
1881	72,000	10.00	25.00	50.00	120	—
1881 Proof	—	Value: 350				
1881H	108,000	5.50	16.00	40.00	110	—
1881H Proof	—	Value: 300				
1882H	36,000	15.00	30.00	90.00	165	—
1884	72,000	10.00	25.00	65.00	160	—
1885	36,000	20.00	50.00	125	200	—
1887	60,000	12.50	32.50	80.00	150	—
1887 Proof	—	Value: 360				
1895	72,000	12.00	30.00	80.00	150	—
1898	72,000	12.00	30.00	80.00	150	—

KM# 1.2 1/4 PIASTRE
Bronze, 21 mm. **Obv:** Bust of King Edward VII **Rev:** Denomination

Date	Mintage	F	VF	XF	Unc	BU
1900	36,000	25.00	55.00	120	240	—
1900 Proof	—	Value: 600				

KM# 2 1/2 PIASTRE
Bronze

Date	Mintage	F	VF	XF	Unc	BU
1879	250,000	7.50	15.00	45.00	165	—
1879 Proof	—	Value: 850				
1881	54,000	15.00	25.00	80.00	250	—
1881 Proof	—	Value: 500				
1881H	72,000	10.00	20.00	55.00	140	—
1881H Proof	—	Value: 325				
1882H	54,000	10.00	20.00	60.00	180	—
1882H Proof	—	Value: 325				
1884	36,000	20.00	50.00	120	275	—
1884 Proof	—	Value: 325				
1885	54,000	15.00	30.00	90.00	260	—
1886	122,000	7.50	15.00	45.00	165	—
1887	60,000	10.00	20.00	70.00	200	—
1887 Proof	—	Value: 325				
1889	54,000	15.00	35.00	125	380	—
1890	180,000	20.00	50.00	100	300	—
1890 Proof	—	Value: 400				
1891	108,000	27.50	75.00	150	300	—
1896	36,000	35.00	110	200	450	—
1900	36,000	35.00	110	200	450	—
1900	—	Value: 700				

KM# 3.1 PIASTRE
Bronze **Rev:** Thin "1"

Date	Mintage	F	VF	XF	Unc	BU
1879	250,000	8.00	25.00	50.00	150	—
1879 Proof	—	Value: 950				
1881	36,000	15.00	35.00	150	325	—
1881 Proof	—	Value: 600				
1881H	36,000	15.00	35.00	150	500	—
1881H	—	Value: 650				

KM# 3.2 PIASTRE
Bronze **Obv:** Bust of Queen Victoria left **Rev:** Thick "1" in denomination

Date	Mintage	F	VF	XF	Unc	BU
1881 Proof	Inc. above	Value: 1,000				
1881H	Inc. above	10.00	35.00	120	500	—
1881H Proof	—	Value: 900				
1882H	18,000	135	225	450	1,250	—
1882H Proof	—	Value: 2,000				
1884	18,000	135	225	450	1,250	—
1884 Proof	—	Value: 1,800				
1885	54,000	25.00	70.00	115	275	—
1885 Proof	—	Value: 1,220				
1886	227,000	10.00	30.00	85.00	175	—
1887	45,000	10.00	32.50	100	200	—
1889	27,000	30.00	90.00	250	500	—
1890	90,000	20.00	70.00	150	350	—
1891	54,000	25.00	80.00	200	400	—
1891 Proof	—	Value: 780				
1895	54,000	25.00	80.00	200	400	—
1896	54,000	25.00	80.00	200	400	—
1900	27,000	35.00	100	250	500	—
1900 Proof	—	Value: 1,900				

TRIAL STRIKES

KM#	Date	Mintage	Identification	Mkt Val
TS1	1879	—	Piastre. 0.9170 Gold. 40.0000 g. Uniface.	2,500

PROOF SETS

KM#	Date	Mintage	Identification	Issue Price	Mkt Val
PS1	1879 (3)	—	KM1.1, 2, 3.1	—	3,000
PS2	1881 (3)	—	KM1.1, 2, 3.1	—	1,800
PS3	1900 (3)	—	KM1.1, 2, 3.2	—	3,500

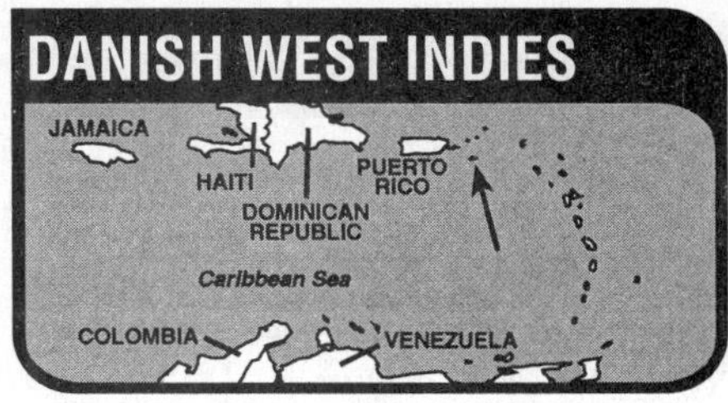

The Danish West Indies (now the U.S. organized unincorporated territory of the Virgin Islands of the United States) consisted of the islands of St. Thomas, St. John, St. Croix, and 62 islets in the Caribbean Sea roughly 40 miles (64 km.) east of Puerto Rico. The islands have a combined area of 133 sq. mi. (352 sq. km.) and a population of *106,000. Capital: Charlotte Amalie. Tourism is the principal industry. Watch movements, costume jewelry, pharmaceuticals, and rum are exported.

The Virgin Islands were discovered by Columbus in 1493, during his second voyage to America. During the 17th century, individual islands, actually the peaks of a submerged mountain range, were held by Spain, Holland, England, France and Denmark. These islands were also the favorite resorts of the buccaneers operating in the Caribbean and the coastal waters of eastern North America. Control of most of the 100-island group finally passed to Denmark, with England securing the easterly remainder. The Danish islands had their own coinage from the early 18th century, based on but unequal to, Denmark's homeland system. In the late 18th and early 19th centuries, Danish minor copper and silver coinage augmented the islands currency. The Danish islands were purchased by the United States in 1917 for $25 million, mainly to forestall their acquisition by Germany and because they command the Anegada Passage into the Caribbean Sea, a strategic point on the defense perimeter of the Panama Canal.

RULERS

Danish, until 1917

MINT MARKS

(a) - Altona - tall, widely spaced crown
(c) - Copenhagen - symetrical crown
(h) - Copenhagen - heart
(o) - Altona – orb

MINTMASTERS' INITIALS

See Denmark

MONETARY SYSTEM

(Until 1849)

96 Skilling = 1 Daler

NOTE: The 2 Skillings, Danish coins exported to the Danish West Indies, were minted from old dies in 1805.

DANISH COLONY

COLONIAL COINAGE

KM# 13 2 SKILLING
1.2180 g., 0.2500 Silver .0098 oz. **Ruler:** Frederik VI **Obv:** Crowned arms **Rev:** Value and date **Edge:** Reeded

Date	Mintage	VG	F	VF	XF	Unc
1816	96,000	7.50	15.00	27.50	85.00	—
1837 Flat top 3	493,000	6.50	12.00	25.00	57.50	—
1837 Round top 3	Inc. above	11.00	18.50	35.00	67.50	—

KM# 18 2 SKILLING
1.2180 g., 0.2500 Silver .0098 oz. **Ruler:** Christian VIII **Edge:** Plain

Date	Mintage	VG	F	VF	XF	Unc
1847	244,000	6.50	12.00	25.00	60.00	—

KM# 19 2 SKILLING
1.2180 g., 0.2500 Silver .0098 oz. **Ruler:** Frederik VII **Edge:** Plain

Date	Mintage	VG	F	VF	XF	Unc
1848	958,000	5.50	9.50	17.50	42.50	—

KM# 14 10 SKILLING
2.4360 g., 0.6250 Silver .0489 oz. **Ruler:** Frederik VI **Edge:** Engrailed

Date	Mintage	VG	F	VF	XF	Unc
1816	Est. 80,000	8.50	20.00	45.00	90.00	—

KM# 16 10 SKILLING
2.4360 g., 0.6250 Silver .0489 oz. **Ruler:** Christian VIII **Edge:** Engrailed

Date	Mintage	VG	F	VF	XF	Unc
1840	103,000	6.75	14.00	27.50	57.50	—
1845	97,000	6.50	13.50	25.00	55.00	—
1845 Proof	—	—	—	—	—	—
1847	109,000	9.00	20.00	38.50	85.00	—

KM# 20.1 10 SKILLING
2.4360 g., 0.6250 Silver .0489 oz. **Ruler:** Frederik VII **Edge:** Engrailed

Date	Mintage	VG	F	VF	XF	Unc
1848	389,000	7.50	17.50	32.50	75.00	—
1848 Proof	—	—	—	—	—	—

KM# 20.2 10 SKILLING
2.4360 g., 0.6250 Silver .0489 oz. **Ruler:** Frederik VII **Edge:** Plain

Date	Mintage	VG	F	VF	XF	Unc
1848	85,000	7.00	15.00	32.50	75.00	—

Note: Struck in 1856; fixed date of 1848

KM# 15 20 SKILLING
4.8720 g., 0.6250 Silver .0979 oz. **Ruler:** Frederik VI **Obv:** Crowned arms **Rev:** Value and date **Edge:** Engrailed

Date	Mintage	VG	F	VF	XF	Unc
1816	Est. 20,000	15.00	35.00	100	200	—

KM# 17 20 SKILLING
4.8720 g., 0.6250 Silver .0979 oz. **Ruler:** Christian VIII **Obv:** Crowned arms **Rev:** Value and date **Edge:** Engrailed

Date	Mintage	VG	F	VF	XF	Unc
1840	Est. 50,000	13.50	27.50	70.00	150	—
1845	Est. 55,000	13.50	27.50	70.00	150	—
1847	Est. 50,000	13.50	27.50	70.00	150	—

KM# 21.1 20 SKILLING
4.8720 g., 0.6250 Silver .0979 oz. **Ruler:** Frederik VII **Edge:** Engrailed

Date	Mintage	VG	F	VF	XF	Unc
1848	71,000	12.00	22.50	70.00	155	—
1848 Proof	—	Value: 385				

KM# 21.2 20 SKILLING
4.8720 g., 0.6250 Silver .0979 oz. **Ruler:** Frederik VII **Edge:** Plain

Date	Mintage	VG	F	VF	XF	Unc
1848	40,000	18.50	37.50	115	220	—

Note: Struck in 1856; fixed date 1848

COUNTERMARKED COINAGE

U.S. Series - 1850

KM# 26 25 CENTS
0.9000 Silver **Countermark:** Crowned FRVII **Note:** Countermark on U.S.A. Liberty Seated 25 Cent.

CM Date	Host Date	Good	VG	F	VF	XF
ND(1850)	1849 10 Known	—	—	—	4,000	—

KM# 27 50 CENTS
0.9000 Silver **Countermark:** Crowned FRVII **Note:** Countermark on U.S.A. Liberty Seated 50 Cent.

CM Date	Host Date	Good	VG	F	VF	XF
ND(1850)	1848 4-5 known	—	—	—	6,000	—
ND(1850)	1849 4-5 known	—	—	—	6,000	—
ND(1850)	1850 6 known	—	—	—	5,000	—

DECIMAL COINAGE

20 Cents = 1 Franc

KM# 63 CENT
Bronze

Date	Mintage	VG	F	VF	XF	Unc
1859(o)	216,000	1.50	3.50	8.00	17.50	—
1859(o) Prooflike	10	—	—	—	—	265
1860(o)	250,000	2.00	4.00	9.00	30.00	—

KM# 68 CENT
Bronze

Date	Mintage	VG	F	VF	XF	Unc
1868(c)	240,000	1.50	3.50	8.00	17.50	—
1868(c) Prooflike	—	—	—	—	—	265
1878(h)	20,000	3.00	7.50	15.00	35.00	—
1879(h)	40,000	125	220	315	550	—
1883(h)	210,000	1.75	5.00	12.00	25.00	—

KM# 64 3 CENTS
1.0440 g., 0.6250 Silver .0210 oz.

Date	Mintage	VG	F	VF	XF	Unc
1859(o)	291,000	2.50	6.00	14.00	35.00	—
1859(o) Prooflike	10	—	—	—	—	325

KM# 65 5 CENTS
1.7400 g., 0.6250 Silver .0349 oz.

Date	Mintage	VG	F	VF	XF	Unc
1859(c)	150,000	2.25	4.50	12.50	30.00	—
1859(c) Prooflike	10	—	—	—	—	325

KM# 69 5 CENTS
1.7400 g., 0.6250 Silver .0349 oz.

Date	Mintage	VG	F	VF	XF	Unc
1878(h)	500,000	5.00	15.00	25.00	60.00	—
1878(h) Prooflike	—	—	—	—	—	425
1879(h)	Inc. above	5.00	15.00	30.00	80.00	—
1879(h) Prooflike	—	—	—	—	—	350

KM# 66 10 CENTS
3.4850 g., 0.6250 Silver .0699 oz.

Date	Mintage	VG	F	VF	XF	Unc
1859(c)	250,000	3.00	5.75	13.50	32.50	—
1859(c) Prooflike	10	—	—	—	—	325
1862(c)	140,000	5.00	10.00	17.50	40.00	—
1862(c) Prooflike	—	—	—	—	—	350

KM# 70 10 CENTS
3.4850 g., 0.6250 Silver .0699 oz.

Date	Mintage	VG	F	VF	XF	Unc
1878(h)	80,000	6.50	14.50	30.00	60.00	—
1878(h) Prooflike	—	—	—	—	—	325
1879(h)	120,000	12.50	27.50	60.00	100	—
1879(h) Prooflike	—	—	—	—	—	425

KM# 67 20 CENTS
6.9610 g., 0.6250 Silver .1399 oz.

Date	Mintage	VG	F	VF	XF	Unc
1859(c)	430,000	7.50	16.50	25.00	60.00	—
1859(c) Prooflike	10	—	—	—	—	450
1862(c)	560,000	8.00	17.50	28.50	62.50	—
1862(c) Prooflike	—	—	—	—	—	425

KM# 71 20 CENTS
6.9610 g., 0.6250 Silver .1399 oz.

Date	Mintage	VG	F	VF	XF	Unc
1878(h)	200,000	13.50	22.50	42.50	100	—
1878(h) Prooflike	—	—	—	—	—	500
1879(h)	300,000	40.00	100	200	325	—

PROOF-LIKE SETS (PL)

KM#	Date	Mintage	Identification	Issue Price	Mkt Val
PL1	1859 (5)	10	KM#63-67	—	—
PL2	1862 (2)	—	KM#66-67	—	—
PL3	1878 (3)	—	KM#69-71	—	—

DANZIG

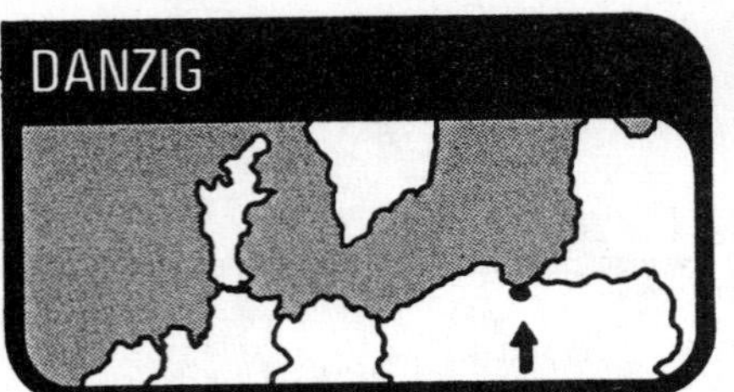

Danzig is an important seaport on the northern coast of Poland with access to the Baltic Sea. It has at different times belonged to the Teutonic Knights, Pomerania, Russia, and Prussia. It was part of the Polish Kingdom from 1587-1772.

RULERS
Friedrich Wilhelm III (of Prussia), 1797-1840
Marshal Lefebvre (as Duke), 1807-1814

MINT MARKS
A - Berlin

MINT OFFICIALS' INITIALS

Initial	Date	Name
M	1808-12	Johann Ludwig Meyer

MONETARY SYSTEM
3 Schilling (Szelag) = 1 Groschen (Grosz)

KINGDOM

STANDARD COINAGE

KM# 135 SZELAG (12 Danarii)
Copper

Date	Mintage	VG	F	VF	XF	Unc
1801A	—	6.00	12.00	28.00	65.00	—

KM# 136 SZELAG (12 Danarii)
Copper

Date	Mintage	VG	F	VF	XF	Unc
1808 M	—	7.50	15.00	35.00	85.00	—
1812 M	—	7.50	15.00	35.00	85.00	—

KM# 137 GROSZ
Copper

Date	Mintage	VG	F	VF	XF	Unc
1809 M	—	7.50	15.00	32.00	75.00	—
1812 M	—	7.50	15.00	32.00	75.00	—

PATTERNS

Including off metal strikes

KM#	Date	Mintage	Identification	Mkt Val
Pn34	1808	—	1 Schilling, Copper, KM136	—
Pn35	1808	—	1 Schilling, silver, KM136	225.00
Pn36	1808	—	1 Schilling, Gold, KM136	3500.
Pn37	1808	—	1/5 Gulden, Silver	700.00
Pn38	1809M	—	1 Groschen, Silver, KM137	275.00
Pn39	1809M	—	1/5 Gulden, Silver	500.00
Pn40	1812M	—	1 Schilling, Silver, KM136	200.00
Pn41	1812M	—	1 Groschen, Silver, KM137	275.00
Pn42	1812M	—	1 Groschen, Gold, KM137	4500.

DENMARK

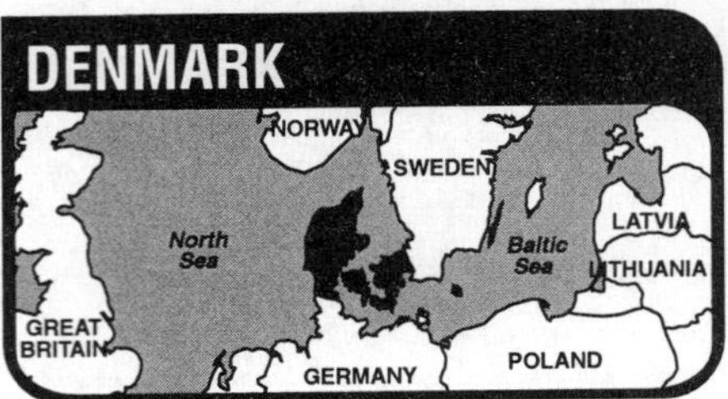

The Kingdom of Denmark (Danmark), a constitutional monarchy located at the mouth of the Baltic Sea, has an area of 16,639 sq. mi. (43,070 sq. km.) and a population of 5.2 million. Capital: Copenhagen. Most of the country is arable. Agriculture, is conducted by large farms served by cooperatives. The largest industries are food processing, iron and metal, and fishing. Machinery, meats (chiefly bacon), dairy products and chemicals are exported.

Denmark, a great power during the Viking period of the 9th-11th centuries, conducted raids on western Europe and England, and in the 11th century united England, Denmark and Norway under the rule of King Canute. Despite a struggle between the crown and the nobility (13th-14th centuries) which forced the King to grant a written constitution, Queen Margaret (Margrethe) (1387-1412) succeeded in uniting Denmark, Norway, Sweden, Finland and Greenland under the Danish crown, placing all of Scandinavia under the rule of Denmark. An unwise alliance with Napoleon contributed to the dismembering of the empire and fostered a liberal movement which succeeded in making Denmark a constitutional monarchy in 1849.

In 1864, Denmark lost Schleswig and Holstein to Prussia. In 1920, Denmark regained North-Schleswig by plebiscite.

The present decimal system of coinage was introduced in 1874.

RULERS
Christian VII, 1766-1808
Frederik VI, 1808-1839
Christian VIII, 1839-1848
Frederik VII, 1848-1863
Christian IX, 1863-1906

MINT MARKS
(a) - Altona (1842 issues), apple
(c) - Copenhagen (Kobenhavn), crown
(h) - Copenhagen, heart
(o) - Altona, orb
KM - Copenhagen
Gluckstadt
S – Rendsborg

NOTE: (ch) - crossed hammers - Kongsberg.

MINT OFFICIALS' INITIALS

Altona

This mint closed in 1863.

Initial	Date	Name
MJ	1786-1816	Michael Flor
CB	1817-19	Cajus Branth
FF, IFF	1819-56	Johan Friedrich Freund
TA	1848-51	Theodor Andersen
FA	1856-63	Hans Frederik Alsing

Copenhagen

NOTE: The letter P was only used on Danish West Indies coins.

Initial	Date	Name
HIAB	1797-1810	Hans Jacob Arnold Branth
None	1810-21	Ole Varberg
CFG	1821-31	Conrad Frederik Gerlach
VS, WS	1835-61	Georg Wilhelm Svendsen
RH	1861-69	Rasmus Hinnerup
CS	1869-93	Diderik Christian Andreas Svendsen
*P, VBP	1893-1918	Vilhelm Burchard Poulsen

MONEYERS' INITIALS

Altona

Initial	Date	Name
FA	1825-55	Hans Frederik Alsing
FK	1841-63	Frederik Christopher Krohn
HL	1848-51	Carl Heinrich Lorenz
PP	1852-63	Peter Petersen

Copenhagen

Initial	Date	Name
D I ADLER FE	1808	Daniel Jensen Adzer
PG	1798-1807	Peter Leonard Gianelli
IC, ICF	1810-13, 1823-41	Johannes Conradsen
M	1813	Christian Andreas Muller
CC	1836	Christen Christensen
FK	1841-73	Frederik Christopher Krohn
HC	1873-1901	Harald Conradsen

MONETARY SYSTEM

(Until 1813)

4 Penning = 1 Huid = 1/4 Skilling
6 Penning = 1 Sosling = 1/2 Skilling
16 Skillings = 1 Mark
64 Skilling Danske = 4 Mark = 1 Krone
96 Skilling Danske = 6 Mark = 1 Daler Specie
12 Mark = 1 Ducat
10 Ducat = 1 Portugaloser

KINGDOM

STANDARD COINAGE

Thru 1813

KM# 662 SKILLING
0.9230 g., 0.1380 Silver .0041 oz. **Ruler:** Frederik VI **Obv:** Crowned FR VI monogram **Rev:** Value, DANSK, date **Note:** Struck at Altona.

Date	Mintage	VG	F	VF	XF	Unc
1808 MF	—	2.25	7.50	15.00	27.50	65.00
1809 MF	—	1.75	3.50	9.00	17.50	45.00
1810 MF Unique	—	—	—	—	—	—
1819 MF Error; unique	—	—	—	—	—	—

KM# 671 SKILLING
0.7800 g., Copper, 15 mm. **Ruler:** Frederik VI **Obv:** Crowned FR VI monogram **Rev:** Value, DANSK, date

Date	Mintage	VG	F	VF	XF	Unc
1812 MF	—	1.25	2.50	6.00	9.00	15.00

KM# 660.1 2 SKILLING
1.5000 g., 0.2500 Silver .0121 oz. **Obv:** Crowned CVIIR monogram **Rev:** Value, date **Note:** Struck at Copenhagen.

Date	Mintage	VG	F	VF	XF	Unc
1801 HIAB	—	2.50	5.00	12.00	30.00	—

KM# 660.2 2 SKILLING
1.5000 g., 0.2500 Silver .0121 oz. **Ruler:** C hristian VII **Obv:** Crowned CVIIIR monogram **Rev:** Value, date **Note:** Struck at Altona.

Date	Mintage	VG	F	VF	XF	Unc
1801 MF	—	6.00	10.00	15.00	30.00	—
1805 MF	—	5.00	7.50	12.50	30.00	—

KM# 663 2 SKILLING
Copper **Ruler:** Frederik VI **Obv:** Head right, truncation in a curved line **Rev:** Crowned arms, date below

Date	Mintage	VG	F	VF	XF	Unc
1809 IC	—	1.75	4.50	12.50	25.00	50.00
1810	—	1.75	4.50	12.50	25.00	50.00

KM# 670 2 SKILLING
Copper **Ruler:** Frederik VI **Obv:** Head right, truncation in a broken curved line **Rev:** Crowned arms, date below

Date	Mintage	VG	F	VF	XF	Unc
1810 IC	—	2.25	4.50	9.50	22.50	50.00
1811 IC	—	2.75	5.00	13.00	24.00	50.00

KM# 672 3 SKILLING
2.4400 g., Copper **Ruler:** Frederik VI **Obv:** Head right **Rev. Designer:** Crowned arms, date below

Date	Mintage	VG	F	VF	XF	Unc
1812	—	1.25	3.00	6.00	17.50	35.00

KM# 661 4 SKILLING
2.5980 g., 0.2500 Silver .0209 oz. **Ruler:** Christian VII **Obv:** Crowned C&R monogram **Rev:** Value, date **Note:** Struck at Altona.

Date	Mintage	VG	F	VF	XF	Unc
1807 MF	—	2.25	7.50	15.00	27.50	—

KM# 673.1 12 SKILLING
Copper **Ruler:** Frederik VI **Obv:** Head right **Rev:** Crowned arms **Note:** Struck over 1 Skilling, KM#616. Add a premium if the undertype is clearly visible.

Date	Mintage	VG	F	VF	XF	Unc
1812 IC	—	7.50	17.50	40.00	70.00	140

KM# 673.2 12 SKILLING
Copper **Ruler:** Frederik VI **Obv:** Head right **Rev:** Crowned arms **Note:** Struck over Schleswig-Holstein 1 Sechsling, 1787, C#2. Add a premium if the undertype is clearly visible.

Date	Mintage	VG	F	VF	XF	Unc
1812 3 Known	—	—	—	—	1,350	—

KM# 664 1/6 RIGSDALER
5.0490 g., 0.4060 Silver .0659 oz. **Ruler:** Frederik VI **Subject:** Offering for Fatherland **Obv:** Crowned FVI monogram **Obv. Legend:** GANGBAR 1/6 RIGSDALER SANSK COURANT **Rev:** Legend within oak wreath **Rev. Legend:** FRIVILLIGT OFFER TIL FÆDRENE LANDET **Note:** 1/6 Rigsdaler Courant. Struck at Altona. Varieties exist.

Date	Mintage	VG	F	VF	XF	Unc
1808 MF	—	6.00	15.00	30.00	55.00	125

KM# 651.1 SPECIEDALER
28.8930 g., 0.8750 Silver .8128 oz. **Obv:** Head of Christian VII right **Rev:** Crowned oval arms **Note:** Dav. #1313.

Date	Mintage	VG	F	VF	XF	Unc
1801 MF; B	—	250	450	750	1,000	—

KM# 650 DUCAT SPECIE
3.4900 g., 0.9790 Gold .1098 oz. **Rev:** Five-line legend in square tablet

Date	Mintage	F	VF	XF	Unc	BU
1802	—	400	850	1,600	1,900	—

REFORM COINAGE

1813-1854

Monetary System:

96 Rigsbankskilling = 1 Rigsbankdaler

30 Schilling Courant = 1 Rigsbankdaler

2 Rigsbankdaler = 1 Speciedaler

5 Speciedaler = 1 D'Or

KM# 723 1/5 RIGSBANKSKILLING
1.4620 g., Copper **Ruler:** Christian VIII **Obv:** Head right **Rev:** Crown above crossed sword and sceptre **Note:** Struck at Altona. Value spelled out in full.

Date	Mintage	VG	F	VF	XF	Unc
1842 (o)FF	—	5.50	11.00	22.50	60.00	100

KM# 724 1/5 RIGSBANKSKILLING
1.4620 g., Copper **Ruler:** Christian VIII **Obv:** Head right **Rev:** Crown above crossed sword and sceptre **Note:** Struck at Altona. Value as 1/8 R.B.S.

Date	Mintage	VG	F	VF	XF	Unc
1842(o) FF	—	1.75	4.50	10.00	20.00	40.00

KM# 715 1/2 RIGSBANKSKILLING
3.6540 g., Copper **Ruler:** Frederik VI **Obv:** Crowned FVIR monogram **Rev:** Large value

Date	Mintage	VG	F	VF	XF	Unc
1838	—	1.75	3.00	10.00	30.00	60.00

KM# 725 1/2 RIGSBANKSKILLING
3.6540 g., Copper **Ruler:** Christian VIII **Obv:** Head right **Obv. Legend:** CHRISTIANVS VIII D G DANIÆ V G REX **Rev:** Crown above crossed sword and sceptre **Note:** Struck at Copenhagen.

Date	Mintage	VG	F	VF	XF	Unc
1842(c) FK//VS	—	3.00	6.00	14.00	50.00	120

KM# 753 1/2 RIGSBANKSKILLING
3.6540 g., Copper **Ruler:** Frederik VII **Obv:** Crowned CVII within oak branches **Rev:** Large value

Date	Mintage	VG	F	VF	XF	Unc
1852(c) FK//VS	—	2.25	5.00	10.00	27.50	75.00

KM# 680 RIGSBANKSKILLING
4.8720 g., Copper **Ruler:** Frederik VI **Obv:** Head right **Obv. Legend:** FRIDERICUS VI DEI GRATIA REX **Rev:** Value and date

Date	Mintage	VG	F	VF	XF	Unc
1813	—	1.75	3.25	5.00	12.50	30.00

KM# 688 RIGSBANKSKILLING
7.3080 g., Copper **Ruler:** Frederik VI **Obv:** Crowned oval arms **Rev:** Value and date

Date	Mintage	VG	F	VF	XF	Unc
1818	—	1.75	3.75	15.00	32.50	60.00

KM# 726.1 RIGSBANKSKILLING
7.3080 g., Copper **Ruler:** Christian VIII **Obv:** Crowned oval arms **Rev:** Value and date **Note:** Struck at Altona.

Date	Mintage	VG	F	VF	XF	Unc
1842(o) FK//FF	—	3.25	7.00	15.00	40.00	75.00

KM# 726.2 RIGSBANKSKILLING
7.3080 g., Copper **Ruler:** Christian VIII **Obv:** Crowned oval arms **Rev:** Value and date

Date	Mintage	VG	F	VF	XF	Unc
1842(c) FK//VS	—	3.25	7.00	15.00	40.00	75.00

KM# 754 RIGSBANKSKILLING
7.3080 g., Copper **Ruler:** Frederik VII **Obv:** Large bust right **Note:** Struck at Copenhagen.

Date	Mintage	VG	F	VF	XF	Unc
1852 FK//VS	—	3.00	9.00	30.00	85.00	175

KM# 756 RIGSBANKSKILLING
Copper **Ruler:** Frederik VII **Obv:** Medium bust right

Date	Mintage	VG	F	VF	XF	Unc
1853(c) FK//VS	—	2.75	6.50	12.50	27.50	55.00

KM# 689 2 RIGSBANKSKILLING
14.6160 g., Copper **Obv:** Crowned oval arms **Rev:** Value and date

Date	Mintage	VG	F	VF	XF	Unc
1818	—	3.50	10.00	45.00	90.00	225

KM# 710 2 RIGSBANKSKILLING
1.1120 g., 0.2080 Silver .0074 oz. **Ruler:** Frederik VI **Obv:** Crowned FVIR monogram **Rev:** Value and date **Note:** Struck at Altona.

Date	Mintage	VG	F	VF	XF	Unc
1836 IFF	152,000	1.75	9.00	17.50	13.50	40.00

KM# 728 2 RIGSBANKSKILLING
14.6160 g., Copper **Ruler:** Christian VIII **Obv:** Head right **Obv. Legend:** CHRISTIANVS VIII D G DANIÆ V G REX **Rev:** Large crown above crossed sword and sceptre **Note:** Struck at Copenhagen.

Date	Mintage	VG	F	VF	XF	Unc
1842(c) FK//VS	—	16.00	45.00	125	225	500

KM# 711 3 RIGSBANKSKILLING
1.5190 g., 0.2290 Silver .0112 oz. **Ruler:** Frederik VI **Obv:** Crowned FVIIR monogram **Rev:** Value and date **Note:** Struck at Altona.

Date	Mintage	VG	F	VF	XF	Unc
1836 IFF	130,000	7.25	15.00	50.00	100	200

KM# 729 3 RIGSBANKSKILLING
1.5190 g., 0.2290 Silver .0112 oz. **Ruler:** Christian VIII

Date	Mintage	VG	F	VF	XF	Unc
1842(o) K//FF	—	3.50	7.00	17.50	45.00	75.00

KM# A730 3 RIGSBANKSKILLING
1.5190 g., 0.2290 Silver .0112 oz. **Ruler:** Christian VIII **Obv:** Head right **Obv. Legend:** CHRISTIANVS VIII D G DANIÆ V G REX **Rev:** Large crown above crossed sword and sceptre **Note:** Prev. KM#730.

Date	Mintage	VG	F	VF	XF	Unc
1842(o) K//FF	—	3.50	7.00	20.00	50.00	100

KM# 712 4 RIGSBANKSKILLING
1.8560 g., 0.2500 Silver .0149 oz. **Ruler:** Frederik VI **Obv:** Crowned FVIR monogram **Rev:** Value and date **Note:** Struck at Altona.

Date	Mintage	VG	F	VF	XF	Unc
1836 IFF	73,000	10.00	22.50	55.00	150	225

KM# 721.1 4 RIGSBANKSKILLING
1.8560 g., 0.2500 Silver .0149 oz. **Obv:** Head right **Obv. Legend:** CHRISTIANVS VIII D G DANIÆ V G REX **Rev:** Large crown with crossed sword and sceptre **Note:** Struck at Copenhagen. Dual denominated in consideration of Schleswig-Holstein.

Date	Mintage	VG	F	VF	XF	Unc
1841(h) FK	—	2.25	5.50	12.50	32.50	85.00

KM# 721.2 4 RIGSBANKSKILLING
1.8560 g., 0.2500 Silver .0149 oz. **Ruler:** Christian VIII **Obv:** Head right **Rev:** Large crown with crossed sword and sceptre **Note:** Struck at Copenhagen. Dual denominated in consideration of Schleswig-Holstein.

Date	Mintage	VG	F	VF	XF	Unc
1842(c) FK//VS	—	2.25	5.50	11.00	30.00	85.00

KM# 721.3 4 RIGSBANKSKILLING
1.8560 g., 0.2500 Silver .0149 oz. **Obv:** Head right **Rev:** Large crown with crossed sword and sceptre **Note:** Struck at Altona. Dual denominated in consideration for Schleswig-Holstein.

Date	Mintage	VG	F	VF	XF	Unc
1842(o) FK//FF Rare	—	—	—	—	—	—

KM# 737 8 RIGSBANKSKILLING
2.8090 g., 0.3750 Silver .0339 oz. **Ruler:** Christian VIII **Obv:** Head right **Rev:** Crowned and draped arms **Note:** Struck at Altona. Dual denominated in consideration of use in Schleswig-Holstein.

Date	Mintage	VG	F	VF	XF	Unc
1843(o) FK//FF	—	12.50	30.00	80.00	165	275

KM# 733 16 RIGSBANKSKILLING
4.2140 g., 0.5000 Silver .0677 oz. **Ruler:** Christian VIII **Obv:** Head right **Rev:** Crowned draped arms **Note:** Struck at Copenhagen. Dual denominated in consideration of Schleswig-Holstein.

Date	Mintage	VG	F	VF	XF	Unc
1842(c) FK//VS	—	22.50	45.00	85.00	165	—
1844(c) FK//VS	—	450	600	—	—	—

KM# 690.1 32 RIGSBANKSKILLING
6.1290 g., 0.6870 Silver .1354 oz. **Ruler:** Frederik VI **Obv:** Crowned FVIR monogram **Rev:** Value and date **Note:** Struck at Altona.

Date	Mintage	VG	F	VF	XF	Unc
1818 CB Rare	—	—	—	—	—	—

KM# 690.2 32 RIGSBANKSKILLING
6.1290 g., 0.6870 Silver .1354 oz. **Ruler:** Frederik VI **Obv:** Crowned FVIR monogram **Rev:** Value and date

Date	Mintage	VG	F	VF	XF	Unc
1820 IFF	—	25.00	85.00	160	275	550

KM# 734 32 RIGSBANKSKILLING
6.1290 g., 0.6870 Silver .1354 oz. **Ruler:** Christian VIII **Obv:** Head right **Rev:** Crowned draped arms **Note:** Struck at Altona. Dual denominated in consideration of Schleswig-Holstein.

Date	Mintage	VG	F	VF	XF	Unc
1842 FF//FK	—	22.50	45.00	90.00	200	375
1843 FF//FK	—	22.50	45.00	90.00	200	360
1843 FF//FF (error)	—	100	200	300	—	—

KM# 683.2 RIGSBANKDALER
14.4470 g., 0.8750 Silver .4064 oz. **Ruler:** Frederik VI **Obv:** Head right **Obv. Legend:** FREDERICUS VI DEI GRATIA REX **Rev:** Value above crowned arms

Date	Mintage	VG	F	VF	XF	Unc
1813 IC	—	25.00	50.00	110	250	400

KM# 683.3 RIGSBANKDALER
14.4470 g., 0.8750 Silver .4064 oz. **Ruler:** Frederik VI **Obv:** Head right **Rev:** Value above crowned arms

Date	Mintage	VG	F	VF	XF	Unc
1813 IC//MF	—	45.00	75.00	180	360	600

KM# 683.1 RIGSBANKDALER

14.4470 g., 0.8750 Silver .4064 oz. **Ruler:** Frederik VI **Obv:** Head right **Rev:** Value above crowned arms **Note:** Struck at Copenhagen.

Date	Mintage	VG	F	VF	XF	Unc
1813 M	—	70.00	175	350	625	1,000

KM# 683.4 RIGSBANKDALER

14.4470 g., 0.8750 Silver .4064 oz. **Ruler:** Frederik VI **Obv:** Head right **Rev:** Value above crowned arms

Date	Mintage	VG	F	VF	XF	Unc
1818 IC; CB	—	47.50	60.00	175	265	425

KM# 683.5 RIGSBANKDALER

14.4470 g., 0.8750 Silver .4064 oz. **Ruler:** Frederik VI **Obv:** Head right **Rev:** Value above crowned arms

Date	Mintage	VG	F	VF	XF	Unc
1819 IC; FF	—	45.00	75.00	175	300	600

KM# 696.1 RIGSBANKDALER

14.4470 g., 0.8750 Silver .4064 oz. **Ruler:** Frederik VI **Obv:** Head right **Obv. Legend:** FREDERICUS VI D G DAN V G REX **Rev:** Crowned arms **Note:** Struck at Altona.

Date	Mintage	VG	F	VF	XF	Unc
1826 FA//FF	—	45.00	100	250	400	625
1827 FA//FF	—	55.00	115	275	450	650
1828 FA//FF	—	55.00	115	275	450	650
1833 FA//FF	—	45.00	100	250	400	625
1834 FA//FF	—	130	265	450	625	—

KM# 706.1 RIGSBANKDALER

14.4470 g., 0.8750 Silver .4064 oz. **Ruler:** Frederik VI **Obv:** Large head with a curved, broken neckline **Rev:** Crowned arms **Note:** Struck at Altona.

Date	Mintage	VG	F	VF	XF	Unc
1833 FA//FF	—	50.00	120	275	450	650
1834 FA//FF	—	150	265	450	625	—
1835 FA//FF	—	150	265	450	625	—
1836 FA//FF	—	60.00	135	300	475	700
1839 FA//FF	—	55.00	125	275	450	650

KM# 696.2 RIGSBANKDALER

14.4470 g., 0.8750 Silver .4064 oz. **Ruler:** Frederik VI **Rev:** Crowned arms **Note:** Struck at Copenhagen.

Date	Mintage	VG	F	VF	XF	Unc
1833 FA//KM	—	85.00	175	300	500	700
1834 FA//KM	—	85.00	175	300	500	700

KM# 706.2 RIGSBANKDALER

14.4470 g., 0.8750 Silver .4064 oz. **Ruler:** Frederik VI **Rev:** Crowned arms **Note:** Struck at Copenhagen.

Date	Mintage	VG	F	VF	XF	Unc
1834 FA//KM	—	85.00	175	300	500	750

KM# 706.3 RIGSBANKDALER

14.4470 g., 0.8750 Silver .4064 oz. **Ruler:** Frederik VI **Rev:** Crowned arms

Date	Mintage	VG	F	VF	XF	Unc
1835 FA//WS	—	175	325	525	700	—
1838 FA//WS	—	30.00	75.00	175	425	650

KM# 735.1 RIGSBANKDALER

14.4470 g., 0.8750 Silver .4064 oz. **Ruler:** Christian VIII **Obv:** Head right **Obv. Legend:** CHRISTIANVS VIII D G DANIÆ V G REX **Rev:** Large crown above crossed sword and sceptre **Note:** Struck at Copenhagen. Dual denominated in consideration of Schleswig-Holstein.

Date	Mintage	VG	F	VF	XF	Unc
1842 FK//VS	—	25.00	60.00	85.00	175	400
1843 FK//VS	—	25.00	60.00	95.00	200	360
1843 FK//VS Proof; Rare	—	—	—	—	—	—
1846 FK//VS	—	30.00	65.00	95.00	200	360
1847 FK//VS	—	25.00	60.00	85.00	175	300
1847 FK//VS Proof; Rare	—	—	—	—	—	—
1848 FK//VS	—	25.00	60.00	85.00	175	300

KM# 735.2 RIGSBANKDALER

14.4470 g., 0.8750 Silver .4064 oz. **Ruler:** Christian VIII **Obv:** Head right **Obv. Legend:** CHRISTIANVS VIII D G DANIÆ V G REX **Rev:** Large crown above crossed sword and sceptre **Note:** Struck at Altona. Dual denominated in consideration of Schleswig-Holstein.

Date	Mintage	VG	F	VF	XF	Unc
1844(o) FK//FF	—	35.00	70.00	125	225	400
1845(o) FK//FF	—	25.00	60.00	100	200	350
1847(o) FK//FF	—	25.00	60.00	100	200	350

KM# 743 RIGSBANKDALER

14.4470 g., 0.8750 Silver .4064 oz. **Ruler:** Frederik VII **Obv:** Head right **Obv. Legend:** FREDERICUS VII D G DANIÆ V G REX **Rev:** Crowned draped arms **Note:** Struck at Copenhagen. Dual denominated in consideration of Schleswig-Holstein.

Date	Mintage	VG	F	VF	XF	Unc
1849 FK//VS	—	50.00	125	225	500	1,000
1851 FK//VS	—	40.00	100	200	425	850

KM# 693 SPECIEDALER

28.8930 g., 0.8750 Silver .8128 oz. **Ruler:** Frederik VI **Obv:** Head right **Rev:** Crowned arms **Note:** Struck at Altona. Last coin with the Norwegian lion in the arms.

Date	Mintage	VG	F	VF	XF	Unc
1819 ICF//IFF	—	275	775	1,900	3,000	4,400

KM# 695.1 SPECIEDALER

28.8930 g., 0.8750 Silver .8128 oz. **Ruler:** Frederik VI **Obv:** Head right **Rev:** National Arms **Note:** Struck at Altona.

Date	Mintage	VG	F	VF	XF	Unc
1820 IC//FF	—	42.50	80.00	185	300	—
1822 IC//FF	—	42.50	80.00	185	300	—
1824 IC//FF	—	42.50	80.00	185	300	—
1825 IC//FF	—	35.00	70.00	160	270	—
1826 IC//FF	—	42.50	80.00	185	300	—
1827 IC//FF	—	42.50	80.00	185	300	—
1828 IC//FF	—	35.00	70.00	175	270	—
1829 IC//FF	—	42.50	80.00	185	300	—
1833 IC//FF	—	42.50	80.00	185	300	—
1834 IC//FF	—	35.00	70.00	175	270	—
1835 IC//FF	—	42.50	80.00	185	300	—
1838 IC//FF	—	35.00	70.00	160	270	—
1839 IC//FF	—	35.00	70.00	160	270	—

KM# 695.2 SPECIEDALER

28.8930 g., 0.8750 Silver .8128 oz. **Ruler:** Frederik VI **Obv:** Head right **Rev:** National Arms **Note:** Struck at Copenhagen.

Date	Mintage	VG	F	VF	XF	Unc
1820 IC//CFG	—	55.00	115	265	370	—
1822 IC//CFG	—	55.00	115	265	370	—
1824 IC//CFG	—	37.50	80.00	200	300	—
1825 IC//CFG	—	75.00	140	275	450	—

KM# 695.3 SPECIEDALER

28.8930 g., 0.8750 Silver .8128 oz. **Obv:** Head right **Rev:** National arms **Note:** Struck at Copenhagen.

Date	Mintage	VG	F	VF	XF	Unc
1833 IC//KM	—	35.00	70.00	155	200	—
1834 IC//KM	—	35.00	70.00	155	200	—

KM# 695.4 SPECIEDALER

28.8930 g., 0.8750 Silver .8128 oz. **Ruler:** Frederik VI **Obv:** Head right **Rev:** National arms **Note:** Struck at Copenhagen

Date	Mintage	VG	F	VF	XF	Unc
1835 IC//WS	—	37.50	80.00	185	300	—
1837 IC//WS	—	37.50	80.00	185	300	—
1838 IC//SW (error)	—	—	—	—	—	—
1838 IC//WS	—	35.00	70.00	160	250	—
1839 IC//WS	—	35.00	70.00	160	250	—

KM# 720.1 SPECIEDALER

28.8930 g., 0.8750 Silver .8128 oz. **Ruler:** Christian VIII **Obv:** Head right **Rev:** Crowned supported and draped arms **Note:** Struck at Altona.

Date	Mintage	VG	F	VF	XF	Unc
1840 FF	—	42.50	95.00	180	300	500
1844 (o)FF	—	50.00	100	200	300	525
1845 (o)FF	—	40.00	80.00	165	300	475
1847 (o)FF	—	42.50	85.00	165	300	475

KM# 720.2 SPECIEDALER

28.8930 g., 0.8750 Silver .8128 oz. **Ruler:** Christian VIII **Obv:** Head right **Rev:** Crowned supported and draped arms **Note:** Struck at Copenhagen.

Date	Mintage	VG	F	VF	XF	Unc
1840(h)	—	42.50	95.00	180	300	525
1841(h)	—	250	350	550	—	—

KM# 720.3 SPECIEDALER

28.8930 g., 0.8750 Silver .8128 oz. **Ruler:** Christian VIII **Obv:** Head right **Rev:** Crowned supported and draped arms **Note:** Struck at Copenhagen.

Date	Mintage	VG	F	VF	XF	Unc
1840(c) Unique	—	—	—	—	—	—
1843(h) VS	—	500	700	900	1,400	2,500
1843(c) VS	—	50.00	100	185	325	525
1845(h) VS	—	500	700	900	1,400	2,500
1845(c) VS	—	40.00	80.00	140	300	450
1846(c) VS	—	40.00	80.00	140	300	450

KM# 741 SPECIEDALER

28.8930 g., 0.8750 Silver .8128 oz. **Ruler:** Christian VIII **Obv:** Head right **Rev:** Crowned supported and draped arms **Note:** Struck at Copenhagen.

Date	Mintage	VG	F	VF	XF	Unc
1846(c) VS	—	42.50	95.00	180	325	525
1847(c) VS	—	42.50	95.00	180	325	525
1848(c) VS	—	47.50	110	200	325	525

KM# 742 SPECIEDALER
28.8930 g., 0.8750 Silver .8128 oz. **Ruler:** Frederik VII **Subject:** Christian VIII Death and Accession of Frederik VII **Note:** Struck at Copenhagen

Date	Mintage	VG	F	VF	XF	Unc
1848(c) FK//VS	47,000	42.50	90.00	180	325	700

KM# 744.1 SPECIEDALER
28.8930 g., 0.8750 Silver .8128 oz. **Ruler:** Frederik VII **Obv:** Head right **Rev:** Crowned arms within oak wreath **Note:** Struck at Copenhagen.

Date	Mintage	VG	F	VF	XF	Unc
1849(c) FK//VS	—	50.00	100	225	450	700
1853(c) FK//VS	—	62.50	110	250	450	700
1854(c) FK//VS	—	300	500	850	1,200	—

KM# 744.2 SPECIEDALER
28.8930 g., 0.8750 Silver .8128 oz. **Ruler:** Frederik VII **Obv:** Head right **Rev:** Crowned arms within oak wreath **Note:** Struck at Altona.

Date	Mintage	VG	F	VF	XF	Unc
1851(o) FK//FF	—	350	550	—	—	—
1853(o) FK//FF	—	75.00	125	325	575	875

REFORM COINAGE

1854-1874

Monetary System

96 Skilling Rigsmont = 1 Rigsdaler Rigsmont

1 (old) Speciedaler = 2 Rigsdaler Rigsmont

10 Rigsdaler Rigsmont = 1 D'Or

KM# 767 1/2 SKILLING RIGSMONT
Bronze **Ruler:** Frederik VII **Obv:** Crowned FVII monogram above oak branches **Rev:** Value

Date	Mintage	VG	F	VF	XF	Unc
1857(o)	—	1.25	2.25	4.50	11.00	20.00
1857(c)	—	—	—	—	200	300

KM# 776 1/2 SKILLING RIGSMONT
Bronze **Ruler:** Christian IX **Obv:** Crowned CIX monogram above oak branches **Rev:** Value

Date	Mintage	VG	F	VF	XF	Unc
1868(c)	—	1.25	3.50	7.00	11.50	24.00

KM# 763 SKILLING RIGSMONT
Bronze **Ruler:** Frederik VII **Obv:** Crowned FVII monogram above oak branches **Rev:** Value

Date	Mintage	VG	F	VF	XF	Unc
1856(o)	—	0.75	1.50	5.50	11.00	24.00
1856(c)	—	—	—	—	275	350
1860(o)	—	1.00	2.00	6.50	12.00	20.00
1863(c)	—	1.00	3.00	8.00	15.00	27.50

KM# 774 SKILLING RIGSMONT
Bronze **Ruler:** Christian IX **Obv:** Crowned CIX monogram above oak branches **Rev:** Value

Date	Mintage	VG	F	VF	XF	Unc
1867(c)	—	0.75	1.75	6.00	11.00	24.00
1869(c)	—	1.25	3.25	8.00	15.00	30.00
1870(c)	—	1.75	5.00	11.00	22.50	40.00
1871(c)	—	3.00	7.00	17.50	30.00	60.00
1872(c)	—	1.25	3.00	6.00	12.00	30.00

KM# 758.1 4 SKILLING RIGSMONT
1.8560 g., 0.2500 Silver .0149 oz. **Ruler:** Frederik VII **Obv:** Head right **Rev:** Value within oak wreath **Note:** Struck at Altona.

Date	Mintage	VG	F	VF	XF	Unc
1854(o) FF	—	1.25	6.00	17.50	50.00	100
1854(o) FF Proof; Rare	—	—	—	—	—	—

KM# 758.2 4 SKILLING RIGSMONT
1.8560 g., 0.2500 Silver .0149 oz. **Ruler:** Frederik VII **Obv:** Head right **Rev:** Value within oak wreath **Note:** Struck at Copenhagen.

Date	Mintage	VG	F	VF	XF	Unc
1856(c) VS	—	1.25	4.50	10.00	27.50	65.00
1856(c) VS Proof	—	—	—	—	—	—

KM# 775.1 4 SKILLING RIGSMONT
1.8560 g., 0.2500 Silver .0149 oz. **Ruler:** Christian IX **Obv:** Head right **Rev:** Value within oak wreath **Note:** Struck at Copenhagen.

Date	Mintage	VG	F	VF	XF	Unc
1867(c) RH	—	1.25	6.50	12.50	30.00	65.00
1867(c) RH Proof; Rare	—	—	—	—	—	—

KM# 775.2 4 SKILLING RIGSMONT
1.8560 g., 0.2500 Silver .0149 oz. **Ruler:** Christian IX **Obv:** Head right **Rev:** Value within oak wreath

Date	Mintage	VG	F	VF	XF	Unc
1869(c) CS	—	2.75	8.00	17.50	45.00	75.00
1870(c) CS	—	2.75	8.00	17.00	35.00	65.00
1871(c) CS	—	2.25	6.50	12.00	27.50	62.50
1872(c) CS	—	2.25	7.00	16.00	35.00	65.00
1873(c) CS	—	5.00	10.00	23.00	45.00	75.00
1874(c) CS	—	15.00	27.50	50.00	125	200

KM# 765 16 SKILLING RIGSMONT
3.8980 g., 0.5000 Silver .0626 oz. **Ruler:** Frederik VII **Note:** Struck at Copenhagen.

Date	Mintage	VG	F	VF	XF	Unc
1856(c) VS reeded edge	—	1.75	5.00	12.00	32.50	62.50
1856(c) VS plain edge	—	—	—	—	800	—
1857(c) VS	—	1.75	6.00	13.50	32.50	57.50
1858(c) VS	—	3.75	10.00	25.00	50.00	80.00

KM# 759 1/2 RIGSDALER
7.2240 g., 0.8750 Silver .2032 oz. **Ruler:** Frederik VII **Obv:** Head right **Obv. Legend:** FREDERICUS VII D G DANIÆ V G REX **Rev:** Value within oak wreath

Date	Mintage	VG	F	VF	XF	Unc
1854(c) FK//VS	—	8.00	22.00	50.00	75.00	150
1855(c) FK//VS	—	8.00	22.00	50.00	75.00	150

KM# 760.1 RIGSDALER
14.4470 g., 0.8750 Silver .4064 oz. **Ruler:** Frederik VII **Obv:** Head right **Rev:** Value within oak wreath **Note:** Struck at Copenhagen.

Date	Mintage	VG	F	VF	XF	Unc
1854(c) FK/VS	—	17.50	37.50	70.00	125	300
1855(c) FK/VS	—	17.50	40.00	90.00	165	375

KM# 760.2 RIGSDALER
14.4470 g., 0.8750 Silver .4064 oz. **Ruler:** Frederik VII **Obv:** Head right **Rev:** Value within oak wreath **Note:** Struck at Altona.

Date	Mintage	VG	F	VF	XF	Unc
1855(o) FK/FF	—	17.50	37.50	70.00	125	300

KM# 761.1 2 RIGSDALER
28.8930 g., 0.8750 Silver .8128 oz. **Ruler:** Frederik VII **Obv:** Head right **Rev:** Value within oak wreath **Note:** Struck at Altona.

Date	Mintage	VG	F	VF	XF	Unc
1854(o) FK//FF	—	42.50	80.00	175	285	525
1855(o) FK//FF	—	47.50	90.00	200	300	550
1856(o) FK//FF	—	450	600	750	1,000	—

KM# 761.2 2 RIGSDALER
28.8930 g., 0.8750 Silver .8128 oz. **Ruler:** Frederik VII **Note:** Struck at Copenhagen.

Date	Mintage	VG	F	VF	XF	Unc
1854(c) FK//VS	—	47.50	95.00	190	300	550
1855(c) FK//VS	—	47.50	95.00	190	300	550

KM# 770 2 RIGSDALER
28.8930 g., 0.8750 Silver .8128 oz. **Ruler:** Christian IX **Subject:** Frederik VII Death and Accession of Christian IX

Date	Mintage	VG	F	VF	XF	Unc
1863 HC//FK//RH	101,000	42.50	95.00	200	360	525

KM# 761.3 2 RIGSDALER
28.8930 g., 0.8750 Silver .8128 oz. **Ruler:** Frederik VII **Obv:** Head right **Rev:** Value within oak wreath

Date	Mintage	VG	F	VF	XF	Unc
1863(c) FK//RH	360,000	57.50	125	300	525	850

KM# 772.1 2 RIGSDALER

28.8930 g., 0.8750 Silver .8128 oz. **Ruler:** Christian IX **Obv:** Head right **Obv. Legend:** CHRISTIANVS IX D G DANIÆ V G REX **Rev:** Value within oak wreath

Date	Mintage	VG	F	VF	XF	Unc
1864 HC//RH	237,000	100	200	340	625	975
1868 HC//RH	261,000	110	220	360	675	975

KM# 772.2 2 RIGSDALER

28.8930 g., 0.8750 Silver .8128 oz. **Ruler:** Christian IX **Obv:** Head right **Rev:** Value within oak wreath

Date	Mintage	VG	F	VF	XF	Unc
1871 HC//CS	586,000	125	225	400	700	975
1872 HC//CS	149,000	125	225	400	700	975

GOLD COINAGE

1840-1874

KM# 698 FR(EDERIKS) D'OR

6.6420 g., 0.8960 Gold .1913 oz. **Ruler:** Frederik VI **Obv:** Head right **Obv. Legend:** FREDERICUS VI REX DANIÆ **Rev:** Value and date **Note:** Struck at Altona.

Date	Mintage	VG	F	VF	XF	Unc
1827 IC//IFF	—	600	1,200	2,500	3,900	—

KM# 699 FR(EDERIKS) D'OR

6.6420 g., 0.8960 Gold .1913 oz. **Ruler:** Frederik VI **Obv:** Head right **Obv. Legend:** FREDERICUS VI REX DANIÆ **Rev:** Crowned arms

Date	Mintage	VG	F	VF	XF	Unc
1828 IC//FF	21,000	450	900	180	3,200	—

KM# 701 FR(EDERIKS) D'OR

6.6420 g., 0.8960 Gold .1913 oz. **Ruler:** Frederik VI **Obv:** Modified head right

Date	Mintage	VG	F	VF	XF	Unc
1829 FA//FF	7,625	300	550	1,300	2,450	—
1830 FA//FF Rare	12,000	—	800	—	—	—
1831 FA//FF	—	300	550	1,300	2,200	—
1833 FA//FF	—	300	575	1,500	2,200	—
1834 FA//FF	—	400	900	2,500	2,000	—
1835 FA//FF	—	300	500	1,200	2,000	4,100

Date	Mintage	VG	F	VF	XF	Unc
1837 FA//FF	—	300	500	1,200	2,000	—
1838 FA//FF	—	300	550	1,400	2,200	—

KM# 757 FR(EDERIKS) D'OR

6.6420 g., 0.8960 Gold .1913 oz. **Ruler:** Frederik VII **Obv:** Head right **Obv. Legend:** FREDERICUS VII D G DANIÆ V G REX **Rev:** Crowned supported draped arms

Date	Mintage	VG	F	VF	XF	Unc
1853 FK//FF	678	400	775	2,450	3,800	—

KM# 730 CHR(ISTIANS) D'OR

6.6420 g., 0.8960 Gold .1913 oz. **Ruler:** Christian VIII **Obv:** Head right **Obv. Legend:** CHRISTIANVS VIII D G DANIÆ V G REX **Rev:** Crowned supported and draped arms **Note:** Struck at Altona.

Date	Mintage	VG	F	VF	XF	Unc
1843(o) FK//FF	38,000	235	475	1,200	2,250	—
1844(o) FK//FF	Inc. above	300	750	1,500	2,500	—
1845(o) FK//FF	Inc. above	250	550	1,200	2,500	—
1847(o) FK//FF	Inc. above	350	875	1,700	3,250	—

KM# 778 CHR(ISTIANS) D'OR

6.6420 g., 0.8960 Gold .1913 oz. **Ruler:** Christian IX **Obv:** Head right **Obv. Legend:** CHRISTIANVS IX D G DANIÆ V G REX **Rev:** Crowned supported and draped arms **Note:** Struck at Copenhagen.

Date	Mintage	VG	F	VF	XF	Unc
1869 HC//CS	539	800	1,500	3,250	6,000	—

KM# 697 2 FR(EDERIKS) D'OR

13.2840 g., 0.8960 Gold .3827 oz. **Ruler:** Frederik VI **Obv:** Head left **Obv. Legend:** FREDERICUS IV REX DANIÆ **Rev:** Value and date **Note:** Struck at Altona.

Date	Mintage	VG	F	VF	XF	Unc
1826 IC//IFF Unique	—	—	—	—	—	—
1827 IC//IFF	—	750	1,550	3,600	5,000	6,500

KM# 700 2 FR(EDERIKS) D'OR

13.2840 g., 0.8960 Gold .3827 oz. **Ruler:** Frederik VI **Obv:** Head left **Obv. Legend:** FREDERICUS VI REX DANIÆ **Rev:** Crowned arms **Note:** Struck at Altona.

Date	Mintage	VG	F	VF	XF	Unc
1828 IC//FF	168,000	375	550	1,500	2,600	—
1829 IC//FF	96,000	400	600	1,750	3,000	—
1830 IC//FF	105,000	300	475	1,150	2,100	—
1833 IC//FF	—	375	550	1,500	2,800	—
1834 IC//FF	—	375	550	1,500	2,750	—
1835 IC//FF	—	350	525	1,400	2,500	—
1836 IC//FF Rare	—	—	—	—	—	—

KM# 713.1 2 FR(EDERIKS) D'OR

13.2840 g., 0.8960 Gold .3827 oz. **Ruler:** Frederik VI **Obv:** Head right **Obv. Legend:** FREDERICUS VI REX DANIÆ **Rev:** Crowned supported and draped arms **Note:** Struck at Altona.

Date	Mintage	VG	F	VF	XF	Unc
1836 CC//FF	—	350	700	1,500	2,700	—
1837 CC//FF	—	300	625	1,400	2,500	—
1838 CC//FF	—	300	625	1,400	2,500	—
1839 CC//FF	—	325	650	1,500	3,000	—

KM# 713.2 2 FR(EDERIKS) D'OR

13.2840 g., 0.8960 Gold .3827 oz. **Ruler:** Frederik VI **Obv:** Head right **Obv. Inscription:** FREDERUCUS VI REX DANIÆ **Rev:** Crowned supported and draped arms **Note:** Struck at Copenhagen.

Date	Mintage	VG	F	VF	XF	Unc
1838 CC//WS	—	400	800	1,950	3,000	—

KM# 750.1 2 FR(EDERIKS) D'OR

13.2840 g., 0.8960 Gold .3827 oz. **Ruler:** Frederik VII **Obv:** Head right **Obv. Legend:** FREDERICUS VII D G DANIÆ V G REX **Rev:** Crowned supported and draped arms **Note:** Struck at Copenhagen. Total mintage 1850VS and 1863RH 31,000.

Date	Mintage	VG	F	VF	XF	Unc
1850 FK//VS	—	250	600	2,000	3,000	—

KM# 750.2 2 FR(EDERIKS) D'OR

13.2840 g., 0.8960 Gold .3827 oz. **Ruler:** Frederik VII **Obv:** Head right **Obv. Legend:** FREDERICUS VII D G DANIÆ V G REX **Rev:** Crowned supported and draped arms **Note:** Struck at Altona.

Date	Mintage	VG	F	VF	XF	Unc
1851 FK//FF	1,205,000	325	700	2,000	3,100	—
1852 FK//FF	Inc. above	325	700	2,000	3,100	—
1853 FK//FF	Inc. above	300	600	1,650	2,700	—
1854 FK//FF	Inc. above	325	650	1,800	3,000	—
1855 FK//FF	Inc. above	325	650	1,800	3,000	—

KM# 750.3 2 FR(EDERIKS) D'OR

13.2840 g., 0.8960 Gold .3827 oz. **Ruler:** Frederik VII **Obv:** Head right **Obv. Legend:** FREDERICUS VII D G DANIÆ V G REX **Rev:** Crowned supported and draped arms **Note:** Struck at Altona.

Date	Mintage	VG	F	VF	XF	Unc
1856 FK//FA	Inc. above	325	650	1,800	3,000	—
1857 FK//FA	Inc. above	300	600	1,650	2,700	—
1859 FK//FA	Inc. above	300	650	1,800	3,000	—

KM# 750.4 2 FR(EDERIKS) D'OR

13.2840 g., 0.8960 Gold .3827 oz. **Ruler:** Frederik VII **Obv:** Head right **Rev:** Crowned supported and draped arms **Note:** Struck at Copenhagen. Total mintage 1850VS and 1863RH 31,000.

Date	Mintage	VG	F	VF	XF	Unc
1863(c) FK//RH	—	350	700	2,000	3,000	—

KM# 722.1 2 CHR(ISTIANS) D'OR

13.2840 g., 0.8960 Gold .3827 oz. **Ruler:** Christian VIII **Obv:** Head right **Obv. Legend:** CHRISTIANVS VIII D G DANIÆ V G REX **Rev:** Crowned supported and draped arms **Note:** Struck at Copenhagen.

Date	Mintage	VG	F	VF	XF	Unc
1841 CC	—	350	700	1,200	2,500	—

Note: Total mintage 1841(h) and 1844(c) 9,222.

KM# 722.2 2 CHR(ISTIANS) D'OR

13.2840 g., 0.8960 Gold .3827 oz. **Ruler:** Christian VIII **Note:** Struck at Altona.

Date	Mintage	VG	F	VF	XF	Unc
1842(o) CC//FF	551,000	350	750	1,500	2,500	—
1844(o) CC//FF	Inc. above	300	525	1,400	2,350	—
1845(o) CC//FF	Inc. above	300	750	1,500	2,750	—
1847(o) CC//FF	Inc. above	300	550	1,350	2,350	—

KM# 722.3 2 CHR(ISTIANS) D'OR

13.2840 g., 0.8960 Gold .3827 oz. **Ruler:** Christian VIII **Obv:** Head right **Note:** Struck at Copenhagen.

Date	Mintage	VG	F	VF	XF	Unc
1844(c) CC//VS	—	300	600	1,400	2,400	3,600

Note: Total mintage 1841(h) and 1844(c) 9,222.

KM# 773.1 2 CHR(ISTIANS) D'OR

13.2840 g., 0.8960 Gold .3827 oz. **Ruler:** Christian IX **Obv:** Head right **Obv. Legend:** CHRISTIANVS IX D G DANIÆ V G REX **Rev:** Crowned supported and draped arms **Note:** Struck at Copenhagen.

Date	Mintage	VG	F	VF	XF	Unc
1866(c) HC//RH	42,000	400	800	2,400	4,500	—
1867(c) HC//RH Rare	Inc. above	—	—	—	—	—

KM# 773.2 2 CHR(ISTIANS) D'OR

13.2840 g., 0.8960 Gold .3827 oz. **Ruler:** Christian IX **Obv:** Head right **Obv. Legend:** CHRISTIANVS IX D G DANIÆ V G REX **Rev:** Crowned supported and draped arms

Date	Mintage	VG	F	VF	XF	Unc
1869(c) HC//CS	Inc. above	400	800	2,250	4,400	—
1870(c) HC//CS Rare	Inc. above	—	—	—	—	—

DECIMAL COINAGE

100 Øre = 1 Krone; 1874-present

KM# 792.1 ORE

2.0000 g., Bronze **Ruler:** Christian IX **Obv:** Crowned CIX monogram **Rev:** Value above porpoise and barley ear

Date	Mintage	F	VF	XF	Unc	BU
1874(h) CS	5,540,000	9.50	24.00	47.50	90.00	—
1875(h) CS	2,361,000	9.00	24.00	55.00	120	—
1876(h) CS	1,483,000	400	750	975	1,500	—
1878(h) CS	1,016,000	70.00	115	250	600	—
1879(h) CS	1,491,000	37.50	75.00	185	550	—
1880(h) CS	1,989,000	12.50	30.00	65.00	140	—
1881(h) CS	260,000	750	1,500	2,000	3,000	—
1882(h) CS	1,782,000	10.00	23.00	50.00	125	—
1883(h) CS	2,989,000	6.00	16.00	37.50	90.00	—
1886(h) CS	997,000	20.00	75.00	160	300	—
1887(h) CS	3,007,000	10.00	26.50	45.00	100	—
1888(h) CS	1,505,000	22.50	37.50	60.00	130	—
1889(h) CS	2,999,000	4.50	850	24.00	55.00	—
1891(h) CS	4,488,000	2.75	5.00	8.00	37.50	—
1892(h) CS	492,000	85.00	200	375	575	—

KM# 792.2 ORE

2.0000 g., Bronze **Ruler:** Christian IX **Obv:** Crowned CIX monogram, date at lower left, initials at lower right **Rev:** Value above porpoise and barley ear

Date	Mintage	F	VF	XF	Unc	BU
1894(h) VBP	4,982,000	2.25	4.75	7.50	25.00	—
1897/4(h) VBP	2,988,000	4.75	10.00	20.00	47.50	—
1897(h) VBP	Inc. above	4.25	8.50	18.00	42.50	—
1899/7(h) VBP	5,012,000	2.00	4.00	8.00	24.00	—
1899(h) VBP	Inc. above	1.75	3.50	7.25	20.00	—

KM# 793.1 2 ORE

4.0000 g., Bronze **Ruler:** Christian IX **Obv:** Crowned CIX monogram **Rev:** Value above porpoise and barley ear

Date	Mintage	F	VF	XF	Unc	BU
1874(h) CS	8,828,000	4.25	9.50	15.00	47.50	—
1875(h) CS	2,817,000	7.25	24.00	65.00	150	—
1876(h) CS	231,000	100	265	475	1,100	—
1880(h) CS	1,012,000	20.00	47.50	110	275	—
1881(h) CS	1,484,000	16.00	30.00	65.00	150	—
1883(h) CS	1,990,000	7.50	16.00	35.00	125	—
1886(h) CS	1,493,000	13.50	27.50	75.00	250	—
1887(h) CS	Inc. above	60.00	130	275	600	—
1889/7(h) CS	1,993,000	7.00	9.75	25.00	95.00	—
1889(h) CS	Inc. above	7.00	9.75	25.00	95.00	—
1891(h) CS	1,903,000	4.00	7.25	16.00	80.00	—
1892(h) CS	573,000	35.00	80.00	150	525	—

KM# 793.2 2 ORE

4.0000 g., Bronze **Ruler:** Christian IX **Obv:** Crowned CIX monogram, date at lower left, initials at lower right **Rev:** Value above porpoise and barley ear

Date	Mintage	F	VF	XF	Unc	BU
1894(h) VBP	2,486,000	3.50	6.00	12.50	60.00	—
1897/4(h) VBP	2,479,000	4.25	6.50	14.00	70.00	—
1897(h) VBP	Inc. above	3.50	5.75	10.00	45.00	—
1899/7(h) VBP	2,504,000	2.50	5.25	10.00	37.50	—
1899(h) VBP	Inc. above	2.50	5.25	10.00	37.50	—

KM# 794.1 5 ORE

8.0000 g., Bronze **Ruler:** Christian IX **Obv:** Crowned CIX monogram **Rev:** Value above porpoise and barley ear

Date	Mintage	F	VF	XF	Unc	BU
1874(h) CS	2,762,000	7.50	15.00	70.00	220	—
1875(h) CS	207,000	55.00	90.00	185	475	—
1882(h) CS	76,000	37.50	75.00	135	465	—
1884(h) CS	321,000	18.50	37.50	125	465	—
1890(h) CS	598,000	140	225	425	1,100	—
1891(h) CS	787,000	12.50	27.50	95.00	250	—

KM# 794.2 5 ORE

8.0000 g., Bronze **Ruler:** Christian IX **Obv:** Crowned CIX monogram, date at lower left, initials at lower right **Rev:** Value above porpoise and barley ear

Date	Mintage	F	VF	XF	Unc	BU
1894(h) VBP	595,000	16.00	35.00	95.00	250	—
1898(h) VBP	397,000	25.00	50.00	100	300	—
1899(h) VBP	601,000	16.00	35.00	90.00	250	—

KM# 795.1 10 ORE

1.4500 g., Bronze **Ruler:** Christian IX **Obv:** Head right **Rev:** Value above porpoise and barley ear, star at top

Date	Mintage	F	VF	XF	Unc	BU
1874(h) CS	8,975,000	9.00	35.00	70.00	250	—
1875(h) CS	1,387,000	16.00	35.00	75.00	240	—
1882(h) CS	1,057,000	67.50	100	165	250	—
1884(h) CS	1,019,000	70.00	110	170	285	—
1886(h) CS	508,000	105	170	250	375	—
1888(h) CS	306,000	135	225	300	475	—
1889(h) CS	1,030,000	17.50	32.50	55.00	100	—
1891(h) CS	1,507,000	9.50	20.00	37.50	75.00	—

KM# 795.2 10 ORE

1.4500 g., 0.4000 Silver .0186 oz. **Ruler:** Christian IX **Obv:** Head of Christian IX, date, mint mark and initials **Rev:** Value above porpoise and barley ear, star at top

Date	Mintage	F	VF	XF	Unc	BU
1894(h) VBP	1,521,000	11.00	22.50	35.00	70.00	—
1897(h) VBP	2,044,000	6.00	12.50	22.50	50.00	—
1899(h) VBP	2,049,999	6.50	12.50	20.00	47.50	—

KM# 796.1 25 ORE

2.4200 g., 0.6000 Silver .0467 oz. **Ruler:** Christian IX **Obv:** Head right **Rev:** Value above porpoise and barley ear, star at top

Date	Mintage	F	VF	XF	Unc	BU
1874(h) CS	8,139,000	14.00	45.00	100	250	—
1874(h) CS Proof	—	Value: 300				
1891(h) CS	1,214,000	20.00	45.00	75.00	150	—

KM# 796.2 25 ORE

2.4200 g., 0.6000 Silver .0467 oz. **Ruler:** Christian IX **Obv:** Head of Christian IX, date, mint mark and initials **Rev:** Value above porpoise and barley ear, star at top

Date	Mintage	F	VF	XF	Unc	BU
1894(h) VBP	1,206,000	20.00	42.50	70.00	140	—
1900/800(h) VBP	1,206,000	22.50	42.50	67.50	140	—
1900(h) VBP	Inc. above	21.00	40.00	65.00	135	—

KM# 797.1 KRONE

7.5000 g., 0.8000 Silver .1929 oz. **Ruler:** Christian IX **Obv:** Head right **Rev:** Crowned arms, porpoise and barley ear flanking

Date	Mintage	F	VF	XF	Unc	BU
1875(h) HC//CS	4,040,000	7.50	62.50	165	450	—
1875(h) HC//CS Proof	—	Value: 550				
1876(h) HC//CS	1,284,000	25.00	125	340	650	—
1892(h) HC//CS	701,000	20.00	42.50	65.00	140	—

KM# 797.2 KRONE

7.5000 g., 0.8000 Silver .1929 oz. **Ruler:** Christian IX **Obv:** Head right **Rev:** Crowned arms, porpoise and barley ear flanking

Date	Mintage	F	VF	XF	Unc	BU
1898(h) HC//VBP	201,000	60.00	100	150	235	—

KM# 798.1 2 KRONER

15.0000 g., 0.8000 Silver .3858 oz. **Ruler:** Christian IX **Obv:** Head right **Rev:** Crowned arms, porpoise and barley ear flanking

Date	Mintage	F	VF	XF	Unc	BU
1875(h) HC//CS	3,396,000	8.00	62.50	115	340	—
1876(h) HC//CS	1,381,000	9.75	62.50	125	280	—
1876(h) HC//CS Proof	—	Value: 500				

KM# 799 2 KRONER

15.0000 g., 0.8000 Silver .3858 oz. **Ruler:** Christian IX **Subject:** 25th Anniversary of Reign **Obv:** Head right **Rev:** King's motto in center

Date	Mintage	F	VF	XF	Unc	BU
1888(h) HC/CS	101,000	8.00	24.00	42.50	70.00	135

KM# 800 2 KRONER

15.0000 g., 0.8000 Silver .3858 oz. **Ruler:** Christian IX **Subject:**

Golden Wedding Anniversary **Obv:** Heads of Christian IX and Queen Louise **Rev:** Wedding date with myrtle wreath

Date	Mintage	F	VF	XF	Unc	BU
1892(h) CONRADSEN/CS	101,000	8.00	24.00	42.50	75.00	135

KM# 798.2 2 KRONER
15.0000 g., 0.8000 Silver .3858 oz.

Date	Mintage	F	VF	XF	Unc	BU
1897(h) HC/VBP	151,000	100	150	225	350	—
1899(h) HC/VBP	152,000	70.00	130	175	250	—

KM# 790.1 10 KRONER
4.4803 g., 0.9000 Gold .1296 oz.

Date	Mintage	F	VF	XF	Unc	BU
1873(h) HC/CS	369,000	BV	70.00	155	275	—
1874(h) HC/CS	Inc. above	BV	85.00	165	300	—
1877(h) HC/CS	98,000	BV	125	180	375	—
1890(h) HC/CS	151,000	BV	80.00	155	250	—

KM# 790.2 10 KRONER
4.4803 g., 0.9000 Gold .1296 oz. **Ruler:** Christian IX

Date	Mintage	F	VF	XF	Unc	BU
1898(h) HC/VBP	100,000	BV	95.00	165	270	—
1900(h) HC/VBP	204,000	BV	70.00	110	200	—

KM# 791.1 20 KRONER
8.9606 g., 0.9000 Gold .2592 oz.

Date	Mintage	F	VF	XF	Unc	BU
1873(h) HC/CS	1,153,000	BV	110	165	230	—
1874(h) HC/CS	Inc. above	800	1,500	2,250	3,500	—
1876(h) HC/CS	351,000	BV	115	170	280	—
1877(h) HC/CS	Inc. above	BV	150	285	380	—
1890(h) HC/CS	102,000	BV	150	285	380	—

KM# 791.2 20 KRONER
8.9606 g., 0.9000 Gold .2592 oz. **Ruler:** Christian IX

Date	Mintage	F	VF	XF	Unc	BU
1900(h) CS/VBP	100,000	BV	130	230	340	—

TOKEN COINAGE

National Bank Tokens (Rigsbank Tegn) were issued after the reorganization of Denmarks Monetary System

KM# Tn4 2 SKILLING
1.5000 g., 0.2500 Silver .0121 oz. **Obv:** Crowned arms of Denmark, Norway and Holstein **Rev:** Value and date

Date	Mintage	VG	F	VF	XF	Unc
1815	—	1.00	2.75	9.00	27.50	60.00

KM# Tn5 3 SKILLING
3.7500 g., Copper **Obv:** Crowned arms of Denmark, Norway and Holstein **Rev:** Value and date

Date	Mintage	VG	F	VF	XF	Unc
1815	—	1.50	3.75	24.00	50.00	95.00

KM# Tn6 4 SKILLING
9.7500 g., Copper **Obv:** Crowned arms of Denmark, Norway and Holstein **Rev:** Value and date

Date	Mintage	VG	F	VF	XF	Unc
1815	—	3.50	7.00	27.50	45.00	120

KM# Tn1 6 SKILLING
7.0000 g., Copper **Obv:** Crowned arms of Denmark, Norway and Holstein **Rev:** Value and date **Note:** Similar type with very monor differences also struck at Kongsberg Mint and listed under Norway as KM#282.

Date	Mintage	VG	F	VF	XF	Unc
1813	—	3.50	9.50	30.00	70.00	140

KM# Tn2 12 SKILLING
10.0000 g., Copper **Obv:** Crowned arms of Denmark, Norway and Holstein **Rev:** Value and date **Note:** Similar type with very monor differences also struck at Kongsberg Mint and listed under Norway as KM#283.

Date	Mintage	VG	F	VF	XF	Unc
1813	—	3.50	9.50	30.00	70.00	140

KM# Tn3 16 SKILLING
15.0000 g., Copper **Obv:** Crowned national arms **Rev:** Value and date

Date	Mintage	VG	F	VF	XF	Unc
1814	—	3.50	9.50	35.00	100	250

PATTERNS

Including off metal strikes

KM#	Date	Mintage	Identification	Mkt Val
PnC52	1813	—	Rigsbankskilling. Silver. KM#680	—
Pn48	1809	—	Skilling. Copper.	500
PnA49	1810	—	2 Skilling. Silver. KM#670	—
PnB49	1811	—	2 Skilling. Silver. KM#670	—
PnB50	1811	—	3 Skilling. Silver.	—

KM#	Date	Mintage	Identification	Mkt Val
Pn49	1811	—	3 Skilling. Copper.	450
PnA50	1811	—	3 Skilling. Pewter.	400

KM#	Date	Mintage	Identification	Mkt Val
Pn51	1812	—	6 Skilling. Copper.	500
PnB51	1812/1813	—	3 Skilling. Silver. Mule of PnA51 reverse/KM680 reverse	800
PnC50	1812	—	Skilling. Silver. KM#671	—
PnD50	1812	—	3 Skilling. Silver. KM#672	—
Pn50	1812	—	4 Skilling. Copper.	—
PnA51	1812	—	6 Skilling. Copper. Uniface, reverse KM#Pn51	—
PnA52	1812	—	6 Skilling. Silver.	—
PnB52	1812	—	12 Skilling. Pewter. KM#673	—

KM#	Date	Mintage	Identification	Mkt Val
Pn52	1818	—	2 Rigsbankskilling. Copper.	500
PnA53	1822	—	Rigsdaler Species. Copper center. Pewter ring. Bimetallic. Struck at Altona.	—
PnB53	1822	—	Rigsdaler Species. Pewter. Struck at Altona.	—
PnC53	1824	—	Rigsdaler Species. Copper. Struck at Copenhagen.	—
PnD53	1825	—	2 Fr(Ederiks) D'Or. Pewter. Struck at Altona.	—
PnE53	1826	—	Rigsdaler Species. Pewter. Struck at Copenhagen.	—
PnF53	1826	—	Rigsdaler Species. Copper. Struck at Copenhagen.	—
PnFA53	1826	—	Rigsdaler Species. Copper. Struck at Altoona.	2,500
PnG53	1827	—	Fr(Ederiks) D'Or. Silver.	—

KM#	Date	Mintage	Identification	Mkt Val
Pn53	1833	—	1/4 Rigsbankdaler. Silver.	1,000
PnA54	1835	—	Fr(Ederiks) D'Or. Silver. Struck at Altona.	—
PnB54	1835	—	2 Fr(Ederiks) D'Or. Pewter. Struck at Altona.	—
PnC54	1836	—	2 Fr(Ederiks) D'Or. Pewter. Struck at Altona.	—
PnH53	ND	—	2 Fr(Ederiks) D'Or. Pewter. Uniface obverse.	—
PnCB54	ND	—	2 Fr(Ederiks) D'Or. Lead. Uniface reverse.	—
PnDB54	1840	—	Uniface reverse. Pewter.	
PnD54	1840	—	Rigsdaler Species. Pewter. Struck at Copenhagen.	—
PnDA54	1840	—	Rigsdaler Species. Pewter. Uniface obverse.	500
PnBA55	1841	—	2 Chr(Istians) D'Or. Pewter. KM#722.1	—
PnE54	1842	—	1/5 Rigsbankskilling. Gold Plated Silver.	—
PnA55	1842	—	32 Rigsbankskilling. Copper. Struck at Altona.	—
PnB55	1842	—	2 Chr(Istians) D'Or. Silver.	—
Pn54	1842	—	Rigsbankskilling. Copper.	1,000
PnAA55	1842	—	32 Rigsbankskilling. Pewter. Uniface obverse.	100
PnAB55	1842	—	32 Rigsbankskilling. Pewter. Uniface reverse.	100
PnC55	1843	—	Chr(Istians) D'Or. Copper. Reverse only. Struck at Copenhagen.	—
PnD55	1852	—	Rigsbankskilling. Copper. KM#755	3,000
PnDA55	1853	—	Rigsbankskilling. Copper. 1.5mm thick planchet (thin)	—
Pn55	1854	—	1/2 Rigsmontskilling. Copper.	1,200

KM#	Date	Mintage	Identification	Mkt Val
Pn56	1854	—	Rigsmontskilling. Copper.	1,000
Pn57	1854	—	16 Rigsmontskilling. Silver.	600
PnF55	1854	—	1/2 Rigsbankskilling. Copper. Uniface, thick planchet, 5.66 grams, 20mm.	750
Pn58	1856	—	Skilling.	—
Pn59	1857	—	1/2 Skilling. Silver.	—
Pn61	1857	—	2 Rigsdaler. Copper. Straight foot on 2.	—
PnA61	1857	—	2 Rigsdaler. Copper. Curved foot on 2.	2,500
PnA60	1857	—	2 Rigsdaler. Silver.	2,500
Pn60	1857	—	2 Rigsdaler. Silver. Straight foot on 2.	800
PnA63	1875	—	Krone. Silver. No HC on neck.	—

TRIAL STRIKES

KM#	Date	Mintage	Identification	Mkt Val
TS1	ND(1839)	—	Daler Specie. Fredericus VI. Uniface.	—

KM#	Date	Mintage	Identification	Mkt Val
TS2	ND(1839)	—	Daler Specie. Crowned arms, wildmen at sides. Uniface.	—

DOMINICA

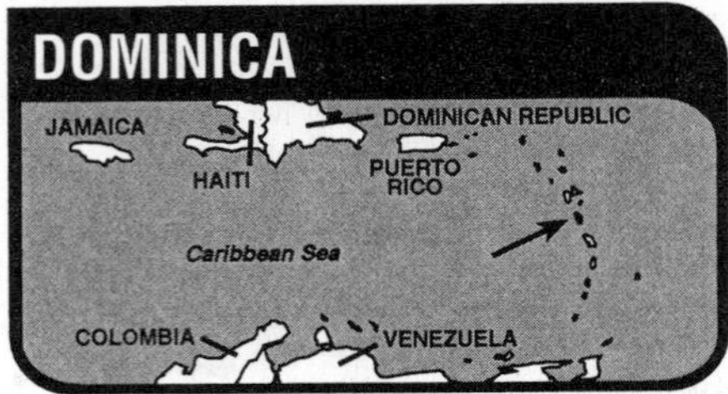

The island of Dominica, situated in the Lesser Antilles midway between Guadeloupe to the north and Martinique to the south, has an area of 290 sq. mi. (750 sq. km.) and a population of 82,608. Capital: Roseau. Agriculture is the chief economic activity of the mountainous island. Bananas are the chief export.

Columbus discovered and named the island on Nov. 3, 1493. Spain neglected it and it was finally colonized by the French in 1632. The British drove the French from the island in 1756. Thereafter it changed hands between the French and British a dozen or more times before becoming permanently British in 1805. Around 1761, pierced or mutilated silver from Martinique was used on the island. A council in 1798 acknowledged and established value for these mutilated coins and ordered other cut and countermarked to be made in Dominica. These remained in use until 1862, when they were demonetized and sterling became the standard. Throughout the greater part of its British history, Dominica was a presidency of the Leeward Islands. In 1940 its administration was transferred to the Windward Islands and it was established as a separate colony with considerable local autonomy. From 1955, Dominica was a member of the currency board of the British Caribbean Territories (Eastern Group), which issued its own coins until 1965. Dominica became a West Indies associated state with a built in option for independence in 1967. Full independence was attained on Nov. 3, 1978. Dominica, which has a republican form of government, is a member of the Commonwealth of Nations.

RULERS
British, until 1978

COLONY

COUNTERMARKED COINAGE

1813

KM# 4 3 BITS
Silver **Countermark:** Crowned 3 on 1/2 of 23-millimeter center plug cut from Spanish or Spanish Colonial 8 Reales

CM Date	Host Date	Good	VG	F	VF	XF
ND(1813)	ND	100	200	320	525	—

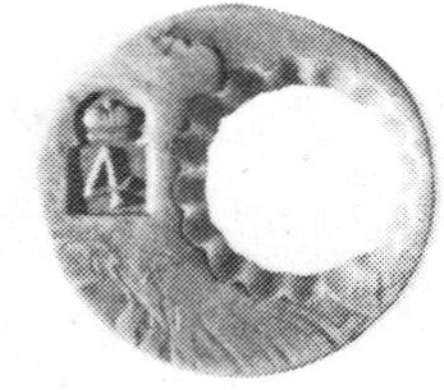

KM# 5 4 BITS
Silver **Countermark:** Crowned "4" on center-ring segment of Spanish or Spanish Colonial 8 Reales

CM Date	Host Date	Good	VG	F	VF	XF
ND(1813)	ND	200	400	850	1,500	—

KM# 6 6 BITS
Silver **Countermark:** Crowned "6" on obverse or reverse of center plug cut from Spanish or Spanish Colonial 8 Reales

CM Date	Host Date	Good	VG	F	VF	XF
ND(1813)	ND	35.00	60.00	125	275	—

KM# 7 12 BITS
Silver **Countermark:** Crowned 12 on holed Peru-Lima 8 Reales, KM#97 **Note:** Modern copies are common.

CM Date	Host Date	Good	VG	F	VF	XF
ND(1813)	1791-1808 Rare	—	—	—	—	—

KM# 8.1 16 BITS
Silver **Countermark:** Crowned "16" on obverse of holed Mexico City 8 Reales, KM#107

CM Date	Host Date	Good	VG	F	VF	XF
ND(1813)	1789-90	600	1,250	4,000	7,500	—

KM# 8.2 16 BITS
Silver **Countermark:** Crowned "16" on obverse and reverse of Mexico City 8 Reales, KM#108

CM Date	Host Date	Good	VG	F	VF	XF
ND(1813)	1790	600	1,250	4,000	7,000	—

KM# 8.3 16 BITS
Silver **Countermark:** Crowned "16" on obverse and reverse of holed Mexico City 8 Reales, KM#109

CM Date	Host Date	Good	VG	F	VF	XF
ND(1813)	1791-1808	500	1,150	3,500	7,000	—

COUNTERMARKED COINAGE

1816

KM# 9 2 BITS
Silver **Note:** Holed Spanish or Spanish Colonial 2 Reales.

CM Date	Host Date	Good	VG	F	VF	XF
ND(1816)	ND	100	180	225	350	—

KM# 10 2 SHILLING (6 Pence)
Silver **Countermark:** "2.6" on 1/4 segment of Spanish or Spanish Colonial 8 Reales

CM Date	Host Date	Good	VG	F	VF	XF
ND(1816-18)	ND	150	275	400	700	—

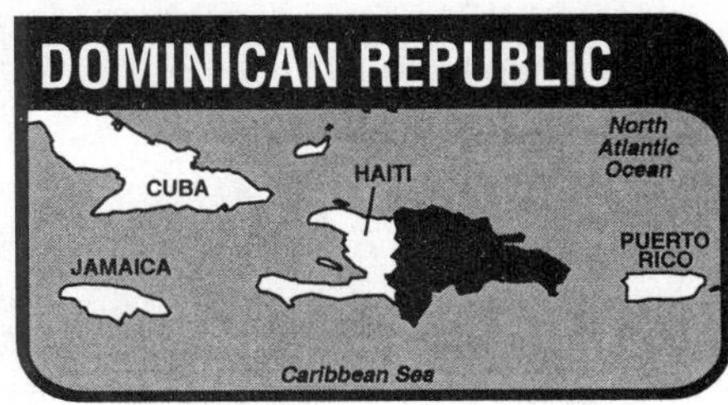

The Dominican Republic occupies the eastern two-thirds of the island of Hispaniola.

Columbus discovered Hispaniola in 1492, and named it La Isla Espanola - 'the Spanish Island'. Santo Domingo, the oldest white settlement in the Western Hemisphere, was the base from which Spain conducted its exploration of the New World. Later, French buccaneers settled the western third of Hispaniola, naming the colony St. Dominique, which in 1697, was ceded to France by Spain. In 1804, following a bloody revolt by former slaves, the French colony became the Republic of Haiti - mountainous country'. The Spanish called their part of Hispaniola Santo Domingo. In 1822, the Haitians conquered the entire island and held it until 1844, when Juan Pablo Duarte, the national hero of the Dominican Republic, drove them out of Santo Domingo and established an independent Dominican Republic. The republic returned voluntarily to Spanish dominion from 1861 to 1865, after being rejected by France, Britain and the United States. Independence was reclaimed in 1866.

MINT MARKS

A - Paris
(a) - Berlin
(c) - Stylized maple leaf, Royal Canadian Mint
H - Heaton, Birmingham, England
Mo - Mexico
(o) - CHI in oval - Valcambi, Chiasso, Italy
(t) - Tower, Tower Mint, London

RULERS

Spanish, until 1822, 1861-1865
Haiti, 1822-1844

MONETARY SYSTEM

8 Reales = 1 Peso
16 Reales = 1 Escudo

REPUBLIC

REAL COINAGE

8 Reales = 1 Peso

KM# 1 1/4 REAL
Bronze

Date	Mintage	F	VF	XF	Unc	BU
1844	1,600,000	6.00	13.50	37.50	—	—

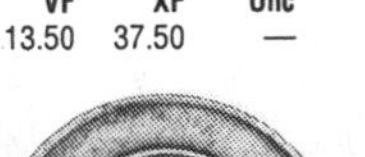

KM# 2 1/4 REAL
Brass **Note:** Many varieties exist.

Date	Mintage	F	VF	XF	Unc	BU
1844	—	3.75	8.50	22.50	75.00	—
1848 plain 4	—	3.75	8.50	22.50	75.00	—
1848 crosslet 4	—	3.75	8.50	22.50	75.00	—

DECIMAL COINAGE

100 Centavos = 1 Peso

KM# 3 CENTAVO
Brass

Date	Mintage	F	VF	XF	Unc	BU
1877	1,000,000	0.50	1.50	2.75	6.00	8.50

KM# 6 1-1/4 CENTAVOS
Copper-Nickel

Date	Mintage	F	VF	XF	Unc	BU
1882	400,000	7.00	13.50	32.50	80.00	—
1888A	500,000	2.50	5.00	12.50	40.00	—
1888A Proof	—	Value: 300				

KM# 4 2-1/2 CENTAVOS
Copper-Nickel

Date	Mintage	F	VF	XF	Unc	BU
1877	21,000	17.50	25.00	47.50	90.00	125
1877 Proof	—	—	—	—	—	—

KM# 7.1 2-1/2 CENTAVOS
Copper-Nickel **Obv:** Small book on shield

Date	Mintage	F	VF	XF	Unc	BU
1882	—	4.50	9.00	22.50	70.00	—

KM# 7.2 2-1/2 CENTAVOS
Copper-Nickel **Obv:** Large book with thin cross on shield, small date

Date	Mintage	F	VF	XF	Unc	BU
1888A	950,000	1.25	3.00	8.00	45.00	—
1888A Proof	—	Value: 275				

KM# 7.3 2-1/2 CENTAVOS
Copper-Nickel **Obv:** Large book with thick cross on shield, large date **Rev:** On the "1888HH", the star is flanked by H's

Date	Mintage	F	VF	XF	Unc	BU
1888A	8,000,000	0.75	2.00	6.00	40.00	—
1888A Proof	—	Value: 275				
1888H H	4,000,000	0.75	2.00	6.00	40.00	—
1888H H Proof	—	Value: 325				

KM# 5 5 CENTAVOS
Copper-Nickel

Date	Mintage	F	VF	XF	Unc	BU
1877	130,000	10.00	20.00	32.50	80.00	—

REFORM DECIMAL COINAGE

1891

KM# 8 5 CENTESIMOS
Bronze

Date	Mintage	F	VF	XF	Unc	BU
1891A	400,000	1.75	5.00	16.50	42.50	55.00
1891A Proof	—	—	—	—	—	—

KM# 9 10 CENTESIMOS
Bronze

Date	Mintage	F	VF	XF	Unc	BU
1891A	300,000	2.00	6.00	22.00	45.00	70.00
1891A Proof	—	—	—	—	—	—

KM# 10 50 CENTESIMOS
2.5000 g., 0.8350 Silver .0671 oz.

Date	Mintage	F	VF	XF	Unc	BU
1891A	150,000	5.00	13.50	32.50	100	—
1891A Proof	—	—	—	—	—	—

KM# 11 FRANCO
5.0000 g., 0.8350 Silver .1342 oz.

Date	Mintage	F	VF	XF	Unc	BU
1891A	125,000	11.50	18.50	40.00	150	—
1891A Proof	—	—	—	—	—	—

KM# 12 5 FRANCOS
25.0000 g., 0.9000 Silver .7234 oz.

Date	Mintage	F	VF	XF	Unc	BU
1891A	150,000	45.00	90.00	175	675	—
1891A Proof	—	—	—	—	—	—

REFORM DECIMAL COINAGE

1897

KM# 13 10 CENTAVOS
2.5000 g., 0.3500 Silver .0281 oz.

Date	Mintage	F	VF	XF	Unc	BU
1897A	764,000	2.50	9.50	22.50	135	—

KM# 14 20 CENTAVOS
5.0000 g., 0.3500 Silver .0563 oz.

Date	Mintage	F	VF	XF	Unc	BU
1897A	1,395,000	1.75	7.50	22.50	125	—

KM# 15 1/2 PESO
12.5000 g., 0.3500 Silver .1407 oz.

Date	Mintage	F	VF	XF	Unc	BU
1897A	917,000	4.50	16.50	45.00	385	—

KM# 16 PESO

25.0000 g., 0.3500 Silver .2813 oz.

Date	Mintage	F	VF	XF	Unc	BU
1897A	1,455,000	25.00	75.00	185	775	—

PATTERNS

Including off metal strikes

KM#	Date	Mintage	Identification	Mkt Val
Pn1	1855	—	10 Reales. 0.8350 Silver.	15,000
Pn2	1855	—	10 Reales. Copper.	10,000
Pn3	1877	—	Centavo. Brass. Small date.	—
Pn4	1877	—	Centavo. Nickel. Normal date.	—
Pn6	1937	—	50 Centavos. Silver. Obverse only.	—

ESSAIS

KM#	Date	Mintage	Identification	Mkt Val
E1	1874	—	2 Centavos. Bronze.	100
E2.1	1877	—	Centavo. Bronze. E below spray, Unc.. ... LIBERTAT.	70.00
E2.2	1877	—	Centavo. Bronze. E below spray, Proof. ... LIBERTAT.	175
E3	1877	—	Centavo. Gilt Bronze.	—
E4	1877	—	Centavo. Nickel.	—

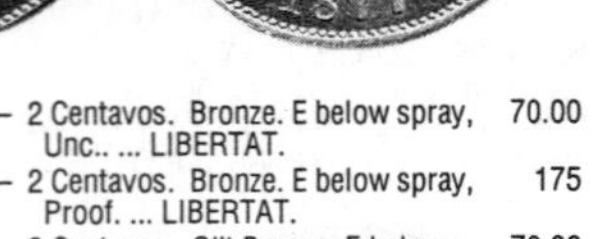

KM#	Date	Mintage	Identification	Mkt Val
E5.1	1877	—	2 Centavos. Bronze. E below spray, Unc.. ... LIBERTAT.	70.00
E5.2	1877	—	2 Centavos. Bronze. E below spray, Proof. ... LIBERTAT.	175
E6	1877	—	2 Centavos. Gilt Bronze. E below spray. ... LIBERTAT.	70.00
E7	1877	—	2 Centavos. Nickel.	—

KM#	Date	Mintage	Identification	Mkt Val
E8.1	1878	—	Centavo. Bronze. E below spray, Unc.. ... LIBERTAD.	60.00
E8.2	1878	—	Centavo. Bronze. E below spray, Proof. ... LIBERTAD.	150
E9	1878	—	Centavo. Nickel.	—

KM#	Date	Mintage	Identification	Mkt Val
E10.1	1878	—	Centavo. Bronze. E below spray. Wreath. ... LIBERTAD. Unc.	60.00
E10.2	1878	—	Centavo. Bronze. E below spray. Wreath. ... LIBERTAD. Proof.	175
E11	1878	—	Centavo. Nickel.	—

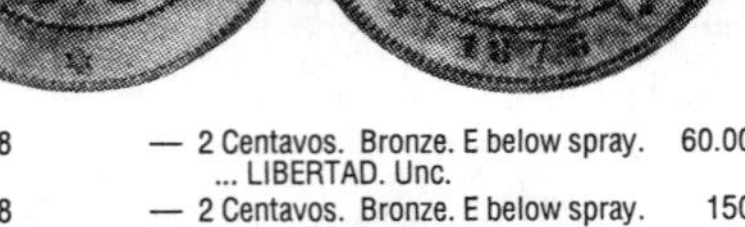

KM#	Date	Mintage	Identification	Mkt Val
E12.1	1878	—	2 Centavos. Bronze. E below spray. ... LIBERTAD. Unc.	60.00
E12.2	1878	—	2 Centavos. Bronze. E below spray. ... LIBERTAD. Proof.	150

KM#	Date	Mintage	Identification	Mkt Val
E13	1878	—	2 Centavos. Nickel.	—
E14.1	1878	—	2 Centavos. Bronze. E below spray, Unc.. Wreath. ... LIBERTAD.	60.00
E14.2	1878	—	2 Centavos. Bronze. E below spray, Proof. Wreath. ... LIBERTAD.	150
E15	1878	—	2 Centavos. Nickel.	—
E16	1887	—	1-1/4 Centavos. Copper-Nickel. KM#6.	300
E17	1887	—	2-1/2 Centavos. Copper-Nickel. KM#7.	300
E18	1892	—	Centavo. Copper-Nickel.	500
E19	1892	—	Centavo. Copper-Nickel.	500
E20	1892	—	Centavo. Copper. Essai de Monnaie	500
E21	1892	—	Centavo. Copper. Piefort, Essai de Monnaie	500
E22	1892	—	Centavo. Aluminum. Essai de Monnaie	500
E23	1892	—	Centavo. Aluminum. Piefort, Essais de Monnaie	500

SANTO DOMINGO

(Hispaniola – Española)

The first coinage for circulation in Santo Domingo and other possessions in the New World was ordered by Fernando the Catholic on April 15, 1505 to be acquired from the Seville Mint. A second issue was acquired from the Burgos Mint.

Rulers

Ferdinand II & Elizabeth, 1479-1504
Charles & Johanna, 1516-1556
Philip II, 1556-1598

Mint Marks

B – Burgos
B-B – Burgos
S-S – Seville
SDo monogram – Santo Domingo

Assayers

F, oF – Francisco Rodriguez 1542-1578
X – Cristobal Medina 1578

SPANISH COLONIAL

Loyalist - ca.1810 - 1822

COLONIAL COINAGE

KM# 2 1/4 REAL

Copper **Note:** Several varieties exist of fraction and letter arrangement on reverse and crowned F.7 on obverse. Planchet sizes and weights vary, but values given are for well struck specimens which carry the full design.

Date	Mintage	Good	VG	F	VF	XF
ND(ca.1810-20)	—	12.50	22.50	37.50	55.00	—

KM# 4.1 REAL

Silver **Obv:** Large rude bust between F and 7 **Rev:** Crowned arms

Date	Mintage	Good	VG	F	VF	XF
ND(ca.1810-20)	—	200	300	450	700	—

KM# 4.2 REAL

Silver **Obv:** Small rude bust between F and 7 **Rev:** Crowned arms

Date	Mintage	Good	VG	F	VF	XF
ND(ca.1810-20)	—	200	300	450	700	—

KM# 5 2 REALES

Silver **Obv:** Rude bust between F and 7 **Rev:** Crowned arms

Date	Mintage	Good	VG	F	VF	XF
ND(ca.1810-20)	—	400	600	900	1,350	—

COUNTERMARKED COINAGE

ca. 1820

KM# 8 REAL

0.9030 Copper **Countermark:** Crowned F.7o **Note:** Countermark on Mexico City 1 Real, KM#75.

CM Date	Host Date	Good	VG	F	VF	XF
ND(1820)	ND(1732-47)	45.00	75.00	125	200	—

KM# 11 8 REALES

0.9030 Silver **Countermark:** Crowned F.7o **Note:** Countermark on Mexico City 8 Reales, KM#109

CM Date	Host Date	Good	VG	F	VF	XF
ND(1820)	ND(1796)	250	400	650	900	—
ND(1820)	ND(1807)	350	500	750	1,100	—

EAST AFRICA

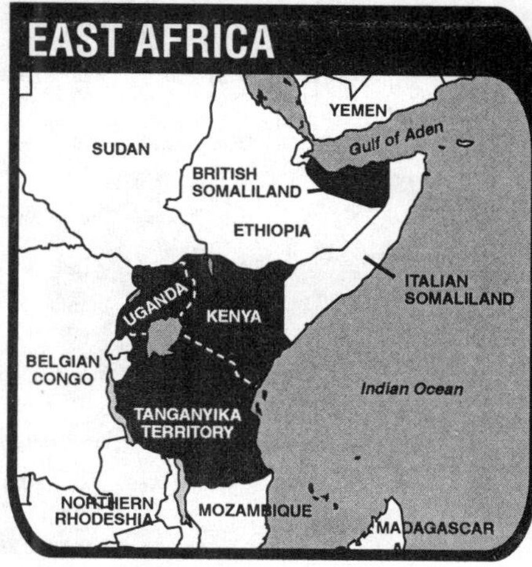

East Africa was an administrative grouping of five separate British territories: Kenya, Uganda, the Sultanate of Zanzibar and British Somaliland.

The common interest of Kenya, Tanganyika and Uganda invited cooperation in economic matters and consideration of political union. The territorial governors, organized as the East Africa High Commission, met periodically to administer such common activities as taxation, industrial development and education. The authority of the Commission did not infringe upon the constitution and internal autonomy of the individual colonies. A common coinage and banknotes, which were also legal tender in Aden, were provided for use of the member colonies by the East Africa Currency Board. The coinage through 1919 had the legend "East Africa and Uganda Protectorate".

NOTE: For later coinage see Kenya, Tanzania and Uganda.

RULERS

British

MINT MARKS

A - Ackroyd & Best, Morley
I - Bombay Mint
H - Heaton Mint, Birmingham, England
K, KN - King's Norton Mint, Birmingham, England
SA - Pretoria Mint, South Africa
no mint mark – British Royal Mint, London

EAST AFRICA PROTECTORATE

DECIMAL COINAGE

50 Cents = 1 Shilling; 100 Cents = 1 Florin

KM# 1 PICE

Bronze **Ruler:** Victoria

Date	Mintage	F	VF	XF	Unc	BU
1897	640,000	6.00	12.50	55.00	90.00	—
1897 Proof	—	Value: 200				
1898	6,400,000	4.00	10.00	45.00	80.00	—
1898 Proof	—	Value: 200				
1899	3,200,000	4.00	10.00	45.00	80.00	—
1899 Proof	—	Value: 200				

PATTERNS

Including off metal strikes

KM#	Date	Mintage	Identification	Mkt Val
Pn1	1897	—	Pice. Silver. KM#1.	750
Pn2	1897	—	Pice. Gold. KM#1.	2,500
Pn3	1898	—	Pice. Silver. KM#1.	650
Pn4	1899	—	Pice. Silver. KM#1.	650
Pn5	1899	—	Pice. Gold. KM#1.	2,500

ECUADOR

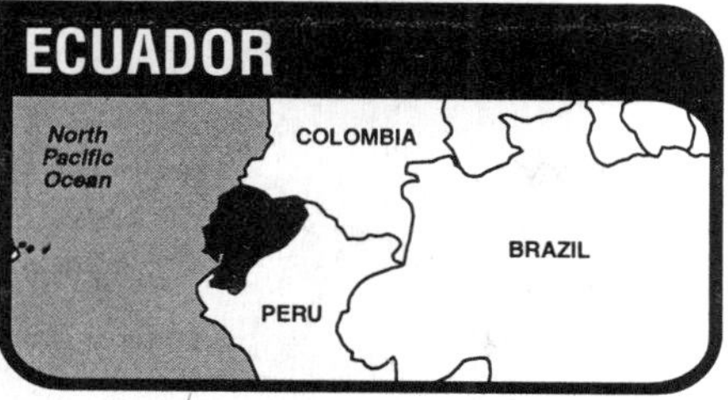

The Republic of Ecuador, located astride the equator on the Pacific Coast of South America, has an area of 105,037 sq. mi. (283,560 sq. km.). Capital: Quito. Agriculture is the mainstay of the economy but there are appreciable deposits of minerals and petroleum. It is one of the world's largest exporters of bananas and balsa wood. Coffee, cacao, sugar and petroleum are also valuable exports.

Ecuador was first sighted in 1526 by Francisco Pizarro. Conquest was undertaken by Sebastian de Benalcazar, who founded Quito in 1534. Ecuador was part of the Viceroyalty of New Granada through the 16th and 17th centuries. After previous attempts to attain independence were crushed, Antonio Sucre, the able lieutenant of Bolivar, secured Ecuador's freedom in the Battle of Pinchincha, May 24, 1822. It then joined Venezuela and Colombia in a confederation known as Gran Colombia, and became an independent republic when it left the confederacy in 1830.

MINT MARKS

BIRMm - Birmingham, Heaton
Birmingham - Birmingham
D - Denver
H - Heaton, Birmingham
HEATON - Heaton, Birmingham
HEATON BIRMINGHAM
HF - LeLocle (Swiss)
LIMA - Lima
Mo - Mexico
PHILA.U.S.A. - Philadelphia
PHILADELPHIA - Philadelphia
PHILA - Philadelphia
QUITO - Quito
SANTIAGO – Chile

ASSAYER'S INITIALS

FP - Feliciano Paredes
GJ - Guillermo Jameson
MV - Miguel Vergara
ST - Santiago Taylor

MONETARY SYSTEM

16 Reales = 1 Escudo

REPUBLIC

COUNTERMARKED COINAGE

M.D.Q. - Moneda de Quito - 1831

KM# 1 1/4 REAL

Silver **Countermark:** MDQ monogram **Note:** Countermark on Colombia (Nueva Granada) 1/4 Real, KM#79.1.

CM Date	Host Date	Good	VG	F	VF	XF
ND(1831)	1820 Rare	—	—	—	—	—
ND(1831)	1821 Rare	—	—	—	—	—

KM# 2 1/4 REAL

Silver **Countermark:** MDQ monogram **Note:** Countermark on Colombia (Nueva Granada)1/4 Real, KM#79.2.

CM Date	Host Date	Good	VG	F	VF	XF
ND(1831)	1821Ba Rare	—	—	—	—	—

KM# 3 1/2 REAL

Silver **Countermark:** MDQ monogram **Note:** Countermark on Colombia (Cundinamarca) 1/2 Real, KM#8.

CM Date	Host Date	Good	VG	F	VF	XF
ND(1831)	1821Ba JF Rare	—	—	—	—	—

KM# 5 REAL

Silver **Countermark:** MDQ monogram **Note:** Countermark on Colombia (Cundinamarca) Real, KM#9.

CM Date	Host Date	Good	VG	F	VF	XF
ND(1831)	1821Ba JF Rare	—	—	—	—	—

KM# 4 REAL

Silver **Countermark:** MDQ monogram **Note:** Countermark on Colombia (Nueva Granada) Real, KM#75.

CM Date	Host Date	Good	VG	F	VF	XF
ND(1831)	1819 JF Rare	—	—	—	—	—

KM# 6 2 REALES

Silver **Countermark:** MDQ monogram **Note:** Countermark on Colombia (Nueva Granada) 2 Reales, KM#76.

CM Date	Host Date	Good	VG	F	VF	XF
ND(1831)	1819 JF Rare	—	—	—	—	—

KM# A6 2 REALES

Silver **Countermark:** MDQ monogram **Note:** Countermark on Colombia 2 Reales, KM#4.

CM Date	Host Date	Good	VG	F	VF	XF
ND(1831)	1815 JF Rare	—	—	—	—	—

KM# 7 2 REALES

Silver **Countermark:** MDQ monogram **Note:** Countermark on Colombia (Nueva Granada) 2 Reales, KM#77.

CM Date	Host Date	Good	VG	F	VF	XF
ND(1831)	1819 JF Rare	—	—	—	—	—
ND(1831)	1820 JF Rare	—	—	—	—	—

KM# 8 2 REALES

Silver **Countermark:** MDQ monogram **Note:** Countermark on Colombia 2 Reales, KM#5.

CM Date	Host Date	Good	VG	F	VF	XF
ND(1831)	1820 JF Rare	—	—	—	—	—
ND(1831)	1821Ba JF	200	425	850	—	—
ND(1831)	1823 JF Rare	—	—	—	—	—
ND(1831)	1820Ba JF Rare	—	—	—	—	—
ND(1831)	1821 JF	100	150	—	—	—

KM# 9 8 REALES

Silver **Countermark:** MDQ monogram **Note:** Countermark on Colombia (Nueva Granada) 8 Reales, KM#78.

CM Date	Host Date	Good	VG	F	VF	XF
ND(1831)	1819 JF Rare	—	—	—	—	—
ND(1831)	1820/19 JF Rare	—	—	—	—	—
ND(1831)	1820 JF Rare	—	—	—	—	—

KM# 10 8 REALES

Silver **Countermark:** MDQ monogram **Note:** Countermark on Colombia (Cundinamarca) 8 Reales, KM#6.

CM Date	Host Date	Good	VG	F	VF	XF
ND(1831)	1820Ba JF Rare	—	—	—	—	—
ND(1831)	1820 JF Rare	—	—	—	—	—
ND(1831)	1821Ba JF	200	350	600	1,250	—
ND(1831)	1821 JF	150	200	325	800	—

KM# 11 8 REALES

Silver **Countermark:** MDQ monogram **Note:** Countermark on Colombia (Cundinamarca) 8 Reales, KM#7.

CM Date	Host Date	Good	VG	F	VF	XF
ND(1831)	1820 JF Rare	—	—	—	—	—

GENERAL COINAGE

KM# 25 1/4 REAL

0.3330 Silver **Rev:** Fortress and 2 eliptical lines **Note:** Weight varies 0.72-0.83 grams.

Date	Mintage	VG	F	VF	XF	Unc
1842 MV	—	350	600	900	1,750	—

KM# 26 1/4 REAL

0.3330 Silver **Rev:** Fortress on hill with bird above **Note:** Weight varies 0.72-0.83 grams. The "A" and "S" are found on the hill below the fortress.

Date	Mintage	VG	F	VF	XF	Unc
1842 MV-S	—	125	275	450	700	—
1843 MV	—	85.00	175	275	400	—
1843 MV-A	—	50.00	120	225	350	—

KM# 36 1/4 REAL
0.6670 Silver

Date	Mintage	VG	F	VF	XF	Unc
1849 GJ	—	10.00	20.00	45.00	75.00	—
1850 GJ	—	40.00	80.00	150	250	—
1851 GJ	—	10.00	20.00	45.00	75.00	—
1852 GJ	—	10.00	20.00	45.00	75.00	—
1855 GJ	—	12.00	25.00	50.00	85.00	—
1856 GJ	—	12.00	25.00	50.00	85.00	—
1862 GJ	—	425	750	1,150	2,200	—

KM# 12.1 1/2 REAL
1.3000 g., 0.6670 Silver **Obv. Legend:** EL ECUADOR EN COLOMBIA **Rev:** Denomination MoR (Medio Real)

Date	Mintage	VG	F	VF	XF	Unc
1833 GJ	—	100	175	300	600	—

KM# 12.2 1/2 REAL
1.3000 g., 0.6670 Silver **Rev:** Denomination 1/2 R

Date	Mintage	VG	F	VF	XF	Unc
1833 GJ	—	175	300	650	—	—
1835 GJ Rare	—	—	—	—	—	—

KM# 22 1/2 REAL
1.3000 g., 0.6670 Silver **Obv. Legend:** REPUBLICA DEL ECUADOR

Date	Mintage	VG	F	VF	XF	Unc
1838 ST	—	30.00	60.00	120	250	—
1840 MV	—	35.00	65.00	135	285	—
1840 WV (W is inverted M)	—	40.00	90.00	150	300	—

KM# 35 1/2 REAL
0.6670 Silver **Obv:** Flag draped arms **Rev:** Bust of Liberty **Note:** Weight varies 1.55-1.85 g., size varies 15-17 mm.

Date	Mintage	VG	F	VF	XF	Unc
1848 GJ	—	7.50	15.00	30.00	60.00	—
1849 GJ	—	10.00	20.00	40.00	80.00	—

KM# 13 REAL
0.6670 Silver **Obv. Legend:** EL ECUADOR EN COLOMBIA **Note:** Weight varies 3.00-3.40 g.

Date	Mintage	VG	F	VF	XF	Unc
1833 GJ	—	15.00	35.00	75.00	200	—
1834 GJ	—	15.00	30.00	70.00	175	—
1835 GJ	—	17.50	45.00	90.00	225	—

KM# 17 REAL
0.6670 Silver **Obv. Legend:** REPUBLICA DEL ECUADOR **Note:** Weight varies 3.40-3.92 g.

Date	Mintage	VG	F	VF	XF	Unc
1836 GJ	—	35.00	75.00	150	250	—
1836 FP	—	37.50	80.00	165	275	—
1837 FP	—	300	500	850	—	—
1838 ST	—	15.00	40.00	85.00	175	—

Date	Mintage	VG	F	VF	XF	Unc
1838 MV	—	45.00	120	225	400	—
1839 MV	—	13.50	32.50	75.00	165	—
1840 MV	—	13.50	32.50	75.00	165	—
1841 MV	—	500	800	1,600	—	—

KM# 20 REAL
0.6670 Silver **Note:** Weight varies 3.40-3.92 g.; obverse and reverse legends transposed.

Date	Mintage	VG	F	VF	XF	Unc
1837 FP	—	200	350	550	800	—
1838 ST	—	120	250	400	650	—

KM# 14 2 REALES
0.6670 Silver **Obv. Legend:** EL ECUADOR EN COLOMBIA **Note:** Weight varies 5.17-5.60 g., size varies 25-27 mm.

Date	Mintage	VG	F	VF	XF	Unc
1833 GJ	—	250	450	700	1,200	—
1834 GJ	—	17.50	35.00	75.00	235	—
1835 GJ	—	16.50	30.00	70.00	225	—
1836 GJ	—	100	200	350	650	—

KM# 18 2 REALES
0.6670 Silver **Obv. Legend:** REPUBLICA DEL ECUADOR **Note:** Weight varies 5.80-6.10 g.

Date	Mintage	VG	F	VF	XF	Unc
1836 GJ	—	13.50	25.00	45.00	120	—
1836 FP	—	15.00	32.50	55.00	140	—
1837 FP	—	400	650	—	—	—
1838 ST	—	20.00	40.00	80.00	200	—
1838 MV	—	13.50	25.00	45.00	120	—
1839/8 MV	—	30.00	50.00	—	—	—
1839 MV	—	17.50	35.00	60.00	150	—
1839 MV (A is inverted V in LA)	—	30.00	55.00	95.00	225	—
1840 MV	—	17.50	35.00	60.00	150	—
1840 MV (V is inverted A)	—	30.00	55.00	100	250	—
1841 MV	—	30.00	55.00	95.00	225	—

KM# 21 2 REALES
0.6670 Silver **Note:** Weight varies 5.80-6.10 g.; obverse and reverse legends transposed.

Date	Mintage	VG	F	VF	XF	Unc
1837 FP	—	30.00	60.00	120	270	—
1838 ST	—	200	300	450	650	—

KM# 33 2 REALES
0.6670 Silver **Obv:** Flag draped arms **Rev:** Bust of Liberty **Note:** Weight varies 5.50-6.05 g.

Date	Mintage	VG	F	VF	XF	Unc
1847 GJ	—	12.50	25.00	50.00	150	—
1848/7 GJ	—	12.50	25.00	65.00	200	—
1849 GJ	—	15.00	27.50	65.00	185	—
1850 GJ	—	12.50	25.00	50.00	150	—
1851 GJ	—	12.50	25.00	50.00	150	—
1852 GJ	—	12.50	25.00	50.00	150	—

KM# 38 2 REALES
0.6670 Silver **Obv:** Flag draped arms **Rev:** Bust of Liberty **Note:** Weight varies 5.50-6.05 g.

Date	Mintage	VG	F	VF	XF	Unc
1857 GJ Unique	—	—	—	—	—	—
1862 GJ Rare	—	—	—	—	—	—

Note: Ponterio C.I.C.F. sale #86 4-97 AU-58 realized $24,000

KM# 40 2 REALES
6.7600 g., 0.6660 Silver .1447 oz. **Obv:** Liberty head with short hair **Rev:** Flag draped arms

Date	Mintage	VG	F	VF	XF	Unc
1862 GJ Rare	—	—	—	—	—	—

Note: Ponterio C.I.C.F. sale #86 4-97 MS-62 realized $8,000

KM# 24 4 REALES
0.6670 Silver **Note:** 12.30-12.75 g.

Date	Mintage	VG	F	VF	XF	Unc
1841 MV	—	15.00	35.00	85.00	370	—
1841 MV (V is inverted A)	—	25.00	50.00	100	400	—
1842 MV	—	15.00	32.50	75.00	350	—
1843 MV	—	15.00	32.50	75.00	350	—

KM# 24a 4 REALES
15.3400 g., 0.8924 Silver 0.4192 oz., 31.8 mm. **Edge:** Lettered "YNDUSTRIA ----- MORAL"

Date	Mintage	F	VF	XF	Unc	BU
1841MVQUITO	—	—	—	—	7,500	—

KM# 27 4 REALES
12.3000 g., 0.6670 Silver **Obv:** Arms in sprays **Rev:** Bust of Bolivar **Note:** The A is found on the condor's breast.

Date	Mintage	VG	F	VF	XF	Unc
1844 MV-A	—	225	425	750	1,800	—

KM# 29 4 REALES
11.7000 g., 0.6670 Silver **Obv:** Arms in sprays **Rev:** Bust of Bolivar **Note:** The A is found on the condor's breast.

Date	Mintage	VG	F	VF	XF	Unc
1845 MV-A	—	225	425	800	1,850	—

KM# 37 4 REALES
13.3500 g., 0.6670 Silver **Obv:** Flag draped arms **Rev:** Bust of Liberty

Date	Mintage	VG	F	VF	XF	Unc
1855 GJ	—	22.50	57.50	185	375	—
1857 GJ	—	17.50	42.50	90.00	220	—

KM# 37a 4 REALES
13.4300 g., 0.6660 Silver .2876 oz. **Obv:** Flag draped arms **Rev:** Bust of Liberty

Date	Mintage	VG	F	VF	XF	Unc
1862 GJ	—	2,000	4,000	7,000	11,500	—

KM# 41 4 REALES
13.4300 g., 0.6660 Silver .2876 oz. **Obv:** Flag draped arms **Rev:** Large head of Liberty.

Date	Mintage	VG	F	VF	XF	Unc
1862	—	67.50	150	350	750	—

KM# 32 8 REALES
25.0000 g., 0.9000 Silver .7234 oz. **Obv:** Flag draped arms **Rev:** Bust of Liberty

Date	Mintage	VG	F	VF	XF	Unc
1846 GJ	—	750	1,250	2,250	4,750	—
1846 GJ Proof, Rare	—	—	—	—	—	—

KM# 39 5 FRANCOS
25.0000 g., 0.9000 Silver .7234 oz. **Obv:** Flag draped arms **Rev:** Bust of Liberty

Date	Mintage	VG	F	VF	XF	Unc
1858 GJ	—	125	250	350	750	—

KM# 15 ESCUDO
3.3000 g., 0.8750 Gold .0928 oz. **Obv:** Bust of Liberty **Rev:** Sun face over two volcanoes

Date	Mintage	VG	F	VF	XF	Unc
1828	—	—	—	—	—	—
Note: 1828-dated coins are considered contemporary counterfeits						
1833 GJ	—	175	425	850	1,500	—
1834 GJ	—	100	275	400	600	—
1835 GJ	—	200	450	900	1,600	—
1845 GJ	—	—	—	—	—	—
Note: 1845-dated coins are suspicious						

KM# 16 2 ESCUDOS (Double)
6.7666 g., 0.8750 Gold .1903 oz. **Obv:** Bust of Liberty **Rev:** Sun face over two volcanoes

Date	Mintage	VG	F	VF	XF	Unc
1833 GJ Rare	—	—	—	—	—	—
1834 GJ	—	550	900	1,500	—	—
1835 GJ	—	250	425	650	1,550	—
1835 FP 3 known	—	—	—	—	—	—

KM# 19 4 ESCUDOS
13.5000 g., 0.8750 Gold .3798 oz. **Obv:** Sun face on banner over three volcanoes **Rev:** Bust of Liberty **Note:** Engraver's initial A in front drape of bust.

Date	Mintage	VG	F	VF	XF	Unc
1836 FP-A	—	250	375	600	1,000	—
1837 FP-A	—	250	375	650	1,150	—
1838 FP-A	—	700	1,350	2,200	3,650	—
1838 ST-A 3-4 known	—	—	2,500	4,000	—	—
1838 MV-A	—	425	900	1,450	2,500	—
1839 MV-A	—	350	650	1,000	1,400	—
1841 MV-A 2 known	—	—	—	6,000	—	—

KM# 23.1 8 ESCUDOS
27.0640 g., 0.8750 Gold .7614 oz. **Obv:** Sun face on banner over three volcanoes **Rev:** Bust of Liberty **Note:** Engraver's initial A in front drape of bust.

Date	Mintage	VG	F	VF	XF	Unc
1838 ST-A	—	650	1,250	1,850	3,250	—
1838 MV-A	—	850	2,200	3,500	5,000	—
1839 MV-A	—	550	1,000	1,750	3,000	—
1840 MV-A	—	450	750	1,600	2,500	—
1841 MV-A	—	400	700	1,500	2,250	—

KM# 23.2 8 ESCUDOS
0.8750 Gold **Obv:** Sun face on banner over three volcanoes **Rev:** Bust of Liberty **Note:** Reduced size. Engraver's initial S sideways in back drape of bust.

Date	Mintage	VG	F	VF	XF	Unc
1841 MV-S	—	750	2,000	3,000	4,000	—
1842 MV-S	—	450	750	1,550	2,500	—
1843 MV-S	—	450	750	1,600	2,600	—

KM# 28 8 ESCUDOS
0.8750 Gold **Obv:** Flag draped arms with cannons **Rev:** Bust of Bolivar

Date	Mintage	VG	F	VF	XF	Unc
1844 MV Rare	—	—	—	—	—	—
Note: Stack's Hammel sale 9-82 VF/G 1844 MV realized $32,000						
1845 MV Rare	—	—	—	—	—	—

KM# 30 8 ESCUDOS
0.8750 Gold **Obv:** Flag draped arms with cannons **Rev:** Bust of Bolivar

Date	Mintage	VG	F	VF	XF	Unc
1845 MV	—	3,000	4,500	5,750	8,500	—

KM# 31 8 ESCUDOS
0.8750 Gold **Obv:** Flag draped arms with cannons **Rev:** Bust of Bolivar

Date	Mintage	VG	F	VF	XF	Unc
1845 MV	—	2,500	4,000	5,500	8,500	—

KM# 34.1 8 ESCUDOS
0.8750 Gold **Obv:** Flag draped arms **Rev:** Larger bust of Bolivar

Date	Mintage	VG	F	VF	XF	Unc
1847 GJ	—	—	2,250	3,250	5,000	—
1848 GJ	—	—	2,500	3,500	5,500	—
1849/7 GJ Rare	—	—	—	—	—	—
Note: Smith & Daughter sale No. 2 9-96 choice AU 1849/7 GJ realized $23,000						
1850 GJ	—	—	1,800	3,000	5,000	—
1852/0 GJ	—	—	1,150	1,650	2,250	—
1854 GJ	—	—	1,250	1,750	2,500	—
1855/2 GJ	—	—	1,000	1,500	2,000	—
1855 GJ	—	—	1,250	1,750	2,500	—

KM# 34.2 8 ESCUDOS
0.8750 Gold **Obv:** Flag draped arms **Rev:** Larger bust of Bolivar

Date	Mintage	VG	F	VF	XF	Unc
1856 GJ	—	—	1,250	1,750	2,500	—

DECIMAL COINAGE

10 Centavos = 1 Decimo; 10 Decimos = 1 Sucre;
25 Sucres = 1 Condor

KM# 47 1/2 CENTAVO (Medio)
Copper-Nickel **Obv:** Flag draped arms **Rev:** Denomination in laurels

Date	Mintage	F	VF	XF	Unc	BU
1884H	600,000	10.00	15.00	32.00	75.00	—
1884H Proof	—	Value: 200				

KM# 54 1/2 CENTAVO (Medio)
Copper **Obv:** Flag draped arms **Rev:** Denomination in laurels

Date	Mintage	F	VF	XF	Unc	BU
1890H	2,000,000	8.00	15.00	30.00	60.00	—
1890H Proof	—	Value: 210				

KM# 45 CENTAVO (Un)
Copper **Obv:** Flag draped arms **Rev:** Denomination in laurels

Date	Mintage	F	VF	XF	Unc	BU
1872HEATON	—	12.50	20.00	50.00	100	135
1872HEATON Proof	—	Value: 225				
1890H	2,000,000	6.00	12.00	25.00	75.00	—
1890H Proof	—	Value: 210				

KM# 48 CENTAVO (Un)
Copper-Nickel **Obv:** Flag draped arms **Rev:** Denomination in laurels

Date	Mintage	F	VF	XF	Unc	BU
1884HEATON BIRMINGHAM	500,000	7.50	20.00	45.00	100	—
1884HEATON BIRMINGHAM Proof	—	Value: 210				
1886HEATON BIRMINGHAM	1,000,000	5.00	12.50	25.00	55.00	—
1886HEATON BIRMINGHAM Proof	—	—	—	—	—	—

KM# 46 2 CENTAVOS (Dos)
Copper **Obv:** Flag draped arms **Rev:** Denomination in laurels

Date	Mintage	F	VF	XF	Unc	BU
1872HEATON	—	18.00	35.00	70.00	150	200
1872HEATON Proof	—	Value: 250				

KM# 49 1/2 DECIMO (Medio)
Copper-Nickel **Obv:** Flag draped arms **Rev:** Denomination in laurels

Date	Mintage	F	VF	XF	Unc	BU
1884HEATON BIRMINGHAM	600,000	8.50	17.50	35.00	75.00	—
1884HEATON BIRMINGHAM Proof	—	Value: 200				
1886HEATON BIRMINGHAM	600,000	8.50	17.50	35.00	75.00	—
1886HEATON BIRMINGHAM Proof	—	Value: 250				

KM# 55.1 1/2 DECIMO (Medio)
1.2500 g., 0.9000 Silver .0361 oz. **Obv:** Denomination in laurels **Rev:** Flag draped arm

Date	Mintage	F	VF	XF	Unc	BU
1893LIMA TF rev: "G. 1.250"	1,718,000	1.00	2.00	7.00	16.50	—
1893LIMA TF rev: "G. 1:250"	Inc. above	1.00	2.00	7.00	16.50	—
1894/3LIMA TF	243,000	3.00	5.00	12.00	30.00	—
1897LIMA JF	800,000	2.00	4.00	10.00	25.00	—
1899/87LIMA JF	560,000	3.00	5.00	15.00	45.00	—
1899/7LIMA	—	3.00	5.00	12.00	35.00	—
1899LIMA JF	Inc. above	—	3.00	8.50	17.50	—
1899LIMA JF	Inc. above	3.00	5.00	12.00	35.00	—
Note: ECUADO. R (obverse error)						

KM# 50.1 DECIMO (Un)
2.5000 g., 0.9000 Silver .0723 oz. **Obv:** Head of Sucre **Rev:** Flag draped arms with LEI in legend

Date	Mintage	VG	F	VF	XF	Unc
1884HEATON BIRMINGHAM	50,000	4.00	9.00	25.00	80.00	—
1884HEATON BIRMINGHAM Proof	—	Value: 350				
1889HEATON BIRMINGHAM	100,000	2.00	5.00	18.00	40.00	—
1890HEATON BIRMINGHAM	150,000	2.00	5.00	18.00	40.00	—
1890HEATON BIRMINGHAM Proof	—	Value: 150				

KM# 50.2 DECIMO (Un)
2.5000 g., 0.9000 Silver .0723 oz. **Obv:** Head of Sucre **Rev:** Flag draped arms

Date	Mintage	VG	F	VF	XF	Unc
1889/789SANTIAGO DT	1,000,000	6.00	10.00	25.00	65.00	—
1889SANTIAGO DT	Inc. above	3.00	5.00	10.00	25.00	—

KM# 50.3 DECIMO (Un)
2.5000 g., 0.9000 Silver .0723 oz. **Obv:** Head of Sucre left, legend without LEY **Rev. Legend:** Flag draped arms

Date	Mintage	VG	F	VF	XF	Unc
1892/89LIMA TF	—	—	—	—	—	—
1892LIMA TF	350,000	—	3.00	7.00	15.00	30.00
1893LIMA TF	848,000	—	1.50	3.00	8.00	20.00
1894/3LIMA JF/TF	206,000	—	3.00	7.00	15.00	30.00
1894LIMA TF	Inc. above	—	1.50	3.00	8.00	22.00
1899/4LIMA JF/TF	220,000	—	2.50	6.00	14.00	30.00
1899LIMA JF/TF	Inc. above	—	2.50	6.00	14.00	30.00
1899LIMA JF	Inc. above	—	4.00	7.50	16.50	45.00
1900LIMA F	—	—	—	—	—	—
1900LIMA JF/TF	480,000	—	2.00	5.50	11.50	27.50
Note: JR below fasces on reverse						
1900LIMA JF	Inc. above	—	1.50	4.50	10.00	22.00
1900LIMA JF	Inc. above	—	2.00	5.00	10.00	25.00
Note: Without JR below fasces on reverse						

KM# 51.1 2 DECIMOS (Dos)
5.0000 g., 0.9000 Silver .1446 oz. **Obv:** Head of Sucre **Rev:** Flag draped arms with LEI in legend

Date	Mintage	F	VF	XF	Unc	BU
1884HEATON BIRMINGHAM	25,000	6.00	12.00	25.00	45.00	—
1884HEATON BIRMINGHAM Proof	—	Value: 550				
1889HEATON BIRMINGHAM	50,000	6.00	12.00	27.50	50.00	—
1890HEATON BIRMINGHAM	75,000	4.00	7.50	12.50	37.50	—
1890HEATON BIRMINGHAM Proof	—	Value: 200				

KM# 51.2 2 DECIMOS (Dos)
5.0000 g., 0.9000 Silver .1446 oz. **Obv:** Head of Sucre **Rev:** Flag draped arms with LEI in legend

Date	Mintage	F	VF	XF	Unc	BU
1889SANTIAGO DT	1,000,000	3.00	5.00	10.00	28.00	—
1891SANTIAGO DT	230,000	4.00	10.00	15.00	35.00	—

KM# 51.3 2 DECIMOS (Dos)
5.0000 g., 0.9000 Silver .1446 oz. **Obv:** Head of Sucre left **Rev:** Flag draped arms; legend without LEY

Date	Mintage	F	VF	XF	Unc	BU
1889 TF	75,000	4.00	10.00	20.00	50.00	—
1891/81 TF	25,000	3.00	7.00	15.00	30.00	—
1891/89 TF	Inc. above	7.00	15.00	35.00	65.00	—
1892/89 TF	1,138,000	2.00	6.00	12.00	25.00	—
1892 TF	Inc. above	6.00	15.00	30.00	65.00	—
1893/89 TF	390,000	2.50	6.50	13.50	37.50	—
1893 TF	—	—	—	—	—	—
1894/89 TF	409,000	2.00	6.00	12.50	40.00	—
1895/89 TF	160,000	3.00	7.00	15.00	42.50	—
1895 TF Proof, rare	—	—	—	—	—	—
1896/89 TF	109,000	3.50	8.00	16.00	45.00	—

KM# 51.4 2 DECIMOS (Dos)
5.0000 g., 0.9000 Silver .1446 oz. **Obv:** Head of Sucre **Rev:** Flag draped arms

Date	Mintage	F	VF	XF	Unc	BU
1895PHILADELPHIA TF	5,000,000	1.50	3.00	7.00	15.00	—
1895PHILADELPHIA TF Proof	—	Value: 500				

KM# 52 1/2 SUCRE (Medio)

12.5000 g., 0.9000 Silver .3617 oz. **Obv:** Head of Sucre **Rev:** Flag draped arms

Date	Mintage	VG	F	VF	XF	Unc
1884HEATON BIRMINGHAM	20,000	25.00	40.00	75.00	250	—
1884HEATON BIRMINGHAM Proof	—	Value: 2,500				

KM# 53.1 SUCRE (Un)

25.0000 g., 0.9000 Silver .7234 oz. **Obv:** Head of Sucre **Rev:** Flag draped arms

Date	Mintage	F	VF	XF	Unc	BU
1884HEATON BIRMINGHAM	250,000	6.50	12.50	22.00	45.00	—
1884HEATON BIRMINGHAM Proof	—	Value: 3,000				
1888HEATON BIRMINGHAM	100,000	10.00	20.00	35.00	85.00	—
1889HEATON BIRMINGHAM	150,000	6.50	12.50	22.00	45.00	—
1890HEATON BIRMINGHAM	12,000	30.00	55.00	125	300	—
1892HEATON BIRMINGHAM	60,000	20.00	35.00	65.00	150	—
1895HEATON BIRMINGHAM	102,000	10.00	20.00	32.00	65.00	—

KM# 53.2 SUCRE (Un)

25.0000 g., 0.9000 Silver .7234 oz. **Obv:** Head of Sucre **Rev:** Flag draped arms

Date	Mintage	F	VF	XF	Unc	BU
1888SANTIAGO DT	373,000	6.50	12.50	25.00	55.00	—
1889SANTIAGO DT	327,000	6.50	12.50	25.00	55.00	—

KM# 53.3 SUCRE (Un)

25.0000 g., 0.9000 Silver .7234 oz. **Obv:** Head of Sucre **Rev:** Flag draped arms

Date	Mintage	F	VF	XF	Unc	BU
1890LIMA TF	287,000	6.50	12.50	18.50	38.00	—
1891LIMA TF	143,000	6.50	12.50	18.50	38.00	—
1892LIMA TF	58,000	15.00	30.00	55.00	120	—
1895LIMA TF	174,000	6.50	12.50	18.50	38.00	—
1896LIMA TF	148,000	12.00	25.00	45.00	100	—
1896LIMA F	Inc. above	10.00	20.00	40.00	90.00	—
1897LIMA JF	462,000	6.50	12.50	18.50	38.00	—

KM# 56 10 SUCRES (Diez)

8.1360 g., 0.9000 Gold .2354 oz. **Obv:** Head of Sucre **Rev:** Flag draped arms **Note:** Most KM#56 mintages are held in reserve in the Banco Central del Ecuador vaults.

Date	Mintage	F	VF	XF	Unc	BU
1899Birmingham JM	50,000	85.00	115	145	285	—
1900Birmingham JM	50,000	85.00	115	145	285	—

PATTERNS

Including off metal strikes

KM#	Date	Mintage	Identification	Mkt Val
Pn1	1832	—	2 Reales. Copper. KM#14	—
Pn2	ND(1833) (GJ)	—	1/2 Real. Silver. Similar to KM#12.	—
Pn3	1833 GJ	—	Escudo. Silver. Reeded edge. KM#15. Thick planchet.	—
Pn4	1835 GJ	—	Escudo. Silver. 1.9200 g. Plain edge. KM#15.	1,450

KM#	Date	Mintage	Identification	Mkt Val
Pn5	1836 GJ	—	2 Reales. Lead. KM#18.	300

KM#	Date	Mintage	Identification	Mkt Val
Pn6	1862 GJ	—	2 Reales. Silver.	12,000
Pn7	1862	—	4 Reales.	—

KM#	Date	Mintage	Identification	Mkt Val
Pn8	1862	—	8 Reales. Silver. Plain edge.	—
Pn9	1862	—	8 Reales. Silver. Reeded edge.	—

KM#	Date	Mintage	Identification	Mkt Val
Pn10	1862 GJ	—	50 Francos. 0.9000 Gold.	—

PROOF SETS

KM#	Date	Mintage	Identification	Issue Price	Mkt Val
PS1	1884 (8)	—	Unique. KM#50.1, 51.1, 52, 53.1 (2 of each)	—	—

GALAPAGOS ISLANDS

The Galapagos Islands, a territory of Ecuador situated in the Pacific Ocean 650 miles west of Ecuador, have an area of 3,028 sq. mi. (7,842 sq. km.) and a population of 3,100. Capital: San Cristobal, on the island of that name. The archipelago of more than 60 islands scattered over 23,000 sq. mi. of the Pacific was discovered by the Spaniards early in the 16th century, and became part of Ecuador in 1832. The islands are notable for their unique plant and animal life, including 15 species of giant tortoise which are the longest-lived animals on earth, with life spans of more than 200 years.

Countermarked Coinage

Countermark: Script RA on 1/2 Decimo, KM#55.
Countermark: Script RA on 1 Decimo, KM#50.
Countermark: Script RA on 2 Decimos, KM#51.
Countermark: Script RA on 1/2 Sucre, KM#52.
Countermark: Script RA on Un Sucre, KM#53.

Until recently the script RA countermarks, believed to be initials of a well-known merchant, Rogelio Alvarado, of Guayaquil, were attributed to the Galapagos Islands. It has been reported that these countermarks were applied in the 1920's to 1930's. The coins were said to have been used to pay prisoners in a penal colony. Without formal documentation however, these pieces cannot be positively attributed.

The Arab Republic of Egypt, located on the northeastern corner of Africa, has an area of 385,229 sq. mi. (1,1001,450 sq. km.). Capital: Cairo. Although Egypt is an almost rainless expanse of desert, its economy is predominantly agricultural. Cotton, rice and petroleum are exported. Other main sources of income are revenues from the Suez Canal, remittances of Egyptian workers abroad and tourism.

Egyptian history dates back to about 3000 B.C. when the empire was established by uniting the upper and lower kingdoms. Following its 'Golden Age' (16th to 13th centuries B.C.), Egypt was conquered by Persia (525 B.C.) and Alexander the Great (332 B.C.). The Ptolemies, descended from one of Alexander's generals, ruled until the suicide of Cleopatra (30 B.C.) when Egypt became the private domain of the Roman emperor, and subsequently part of the Byzantine world. Various Muslim dynasties ruled Egypt from 641 on, including Ayyubid Sultans to 1250 and Mamluks to 1517, when it was conquered by the Ottoman Turks, interrupted by the occupation of Napoleon (1798-1801). A semi-independent dynasty was founded by Muhammad Ali in 1805 which lasted until 1952. Turkish rule became increasingly casual, permitting Great Britain to inject its influence by purchasing shares in the Suez Canal. British troops occupied Egypt in 1882, becoming the de facto rulers. On Dec. 14, 1914, Egypt was made a protectorate of Britain. British occupation ended on Feb. 28, 1922, when Egypt became a sovereign, independent kingdom. The monarchy was abolished and a republic proclaimed on June 18, 1953.

RULERS

Ottoman, until 1882
Local Viceroys
- Muhammad Ali, 1805-1848
- Ibrahim Pasha, 1848
- Abbas I Pasha, 1848-1854
- Sa'id Pasha, 1854-1863

Local Khedives
- Isma'il Pasha, 1863-1879
- Mohammed Tewfik Pasha, 1879--

French, 1798-1801
British, 1882-1922
Local Khedives
- Mohammed Tewfik Pasha, 1882-
- Abbas II Hilmi, 1892-1914

MONETARY SYSTEM

40 Paras = 1 Qirsh (Piastre)
(1885-1916)
10 Ushr-al-Qirsh = 1 Piastre

MINT MARKS

Egyptian coins issued prior to the advent of the British Protectorate series of Sultan Hussein Kamil introduced in 1916 were very similar to Turkish coins of the same period. They can best be distinguished by the presence of the Arabic word *Misr* Egypt) on the reverse, which generally appears immediately above the Muslim accession date of the ruler, which is presented in Arabic numerals. Each coin is individually dated according to the regnal years.

BP - Budapest, Hungary
H - Birmingham, England
KN - King's Norton, England

ENGRAVER

W - Emil Weigand, Berlin

INITIAL LETTERS

Letters, symbols and numerals were placed on coins during the reigns of Mustafa II (1695) until Selim III (1789). They have been observed in various positions but the most common position being over *bin* in the third row of the obverse. In Egypt these letters and others used on the Paras (Medins) above the word *duribe* on the reverse during this period.

INITIAL LETTERS, NUMERALS

Alif ا i	ba ب ii	ha ح iii	ha حـ iv	dal د v
ra ر vi	sin س vii	sad ص viii	(?) sm صم ix	ta ط x
tha ظ xi	'ain ع xii	(hamza) ء xiii	kaf ق xiv	mim م xv
noon ن xvi	noon w/o dot ں xvii	ha هو xviii	(?) ra ر xix	ah اح xx
es اس xxi	ba با xxii	bkr بكر xxiii	ha حا xxiv	raa را xxv
ragib راغب xxvi	sma سا xxvii	msi صبي xxviii	'aa عا xxvix	gha غا xxx
'ab عب xxxi	'abd عبد xxxii	'ad عد xxxiii	'an عن xxxiv	md مد xxxv
mr مر xxxvi	mk مط xxxvii	mdm مصر xxxviii	mha حلا xxxix	ha ده xl
ya يا xli	42a ١٣٤ xlii	md6 مد٦ xliii	6md ٦مد xliv	6mdm ٦مصر xlv

REGNAL YEAR IDENTIFICATION

4
Duriba fi

Misr — Accession Date

DENOMINATIONS

Para

Qirsh

NOTE: The unit of value on coins of this period is generally presented on the obverse immediately below the toughra, as shown in the illustrations above.

TITLES

المملكة — al-Mamlaka

المصرية — al-Misriya

OTTOMAN EMPIRE

Selim III

First Reign AH1203-1212/1789-1798AD, Regnal Years 1-12; Second Reign AH1216-1222/1801-1807AD, Regnal Years 15-21

FIRST TOUGHRA SERIES

Heavy coinage based on a Piastre weighing approximately 19.20 g with first Toughra.

The first Toughra inscribed: *Han Selim bin-Mustafa al-Muzaffer Dai'ma.*

SECOND TOUGHRA SERIES

Light coinage based on a Piastre weighing approximately 12.80 g with second Toughra.

The second Toughra inscribed: *Selim Han bin-Mustafa al-Muzaffer Dai'ma.*

HAMMERED COINAGE

KM# 134 PARA

0.3500 g., Billon **Note:** For similar coins with regnal year 13 refer to French Occupation.

Date	Mintage	Good	VG	F	VF	XF
AH1203//15	—	3.00	4.50	6.50	10.00	—
AH1203//16	—	3.00	4.50	6.50	10.00	—
AH1203//17	—	3.00	6.00	10.00	20.00	—
AH1203//18	—	3.00	6.00	10.00	20.00	—
AH1203//19	—	3.00	6.00	10.00	25.00	—

KM# 135 5 PARA

1.6000 g., Billon

Date	Mintage	Good	VG	F	VF	XF
AH1203//16	—	50.00	100	150	250	—

Note: For regnal yr. 13, see French Occupation.

KM# 136 10 PARA
2.4500 g., Billon

Date	Mintage	Good	VG	F	VF	XF
AH1203//16	—	300	600	1,000	1,400	—

KM# 137 20 PARA
6.9000 g., Billon **Note:** Weight varies 27.5-29 millimeters. Similar to 5 Para, KM#135. For similar coins with regnal year 13 refer to French Occupation.

Date	Mintage	Good	VG	F	VF	XF
AH1203//15	—	150	200	300	500	—
AH1203//16	—	120	180	250	400	—

KM# 138 QIRSH (40 Para)
12.8000 g., Billon

Date	Mintage	Good	VG	F	VF	XF
AH1203//16	—	30.00	50.00	90.00	180	—

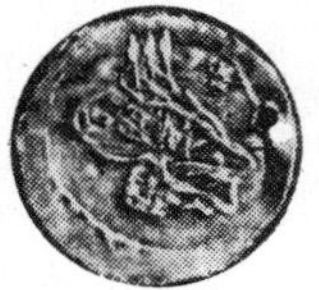

KM# 139 1/4 ZERI MAHBUB (Rubiya)
Gold, 16 mm. **Note:** Weight varies .50-0.90 grams.

Date	Mintage	Good	VG	F	VF	XF
ND	—	60.00	100	180	250	—

KM# 140 1/2 ZERI MAHBUB
Gold **Note:** Weight varies .95-1.30 grams.

Date	Mintage	VG	F	VF	XF	Unc
AH1203//20	—	50.00	100	200	400	—
AH1203//21	—	50.00	100	200	400	—

KM# 141 ZERI MAHBUB
Gold **Note:** Weight varies 2.50-2.60 grams.

Date	Mintage	VG	F	VF	XF	Unc
AH1203 I and VII	—	70.00	120	200	275	—
AH1203 VIII	—	70.00	120	200	275	—
AH1203//15	—	70.00	120	200	275	—
AH1203//16	—	70.00	120	200	275	—

KM# 142 2 ZERI MAHBUB
Gold **Note:** Weight varies 3.76-5.00 grams.

Date	Mintage	VG	F	VF	XF	Unc
AH1203 I and VII	—	200	300	500	900	—

FRENCH OCCUPATION
AH1212-16/1798-1801AD
OCCUPATION COINAGE

KM# 145 PARA
0.2247 g., Billon, 16 mm.

Date	Mintage	VG	F	VF	XF	Unc
AH1203//13	160,830,000	12.50	30.00	45.00	65.00	—
AH1203//14	—	12.50	30.00	45.00	65.00	—
AH1204//15	—	12.50	30.00	45.00	65.00	—

KM# 146 5 PARA
Billon

Date	Mintage	VG	F	VF	XF	Unc
AH1203//13	—	275	375	500	600	—

KM# 147 10 PARA
3.5000 g., Billon, 20 mm.

Date	Mintage	VG	F	VF	XF	Unc
AH1203//13	—	300	600	1,000	1,400	—

KM# 148 20 PARA
6.1580 g., Billon, 28 mm.

Date	Mintage	VG	F	VF	XF	Unc
AH1203//13	90,000	325	450	600	750	—
AH1203//14	—	325	450	600	750	—

KM# 149 PIASTRE
12.3160 g., Billon **Note:** Varieties exist with ornaments.

Date	Mintage	VG	F	VF	XF	Unc
AH1203//13	31,000	400	800	1,200	1,600	—

KM# 150 1/4 ZERI MAHBUB
0.6480 g., 0.6850 Gold .0143 oz. AGW, 17 mm. **Note:** Initial letter was for Bonaparte

Date	Mintage	VG	F	VF	XF	Unc
AH1203//13	—	100	150	200	250	—
AH1203 II	—	150	250	325	400	—
AH1203//14	—	—	—	—	—	—

KM# 151 1/2 ZERI MAHBUB
1.2960 g., 0.6850 Gold .0285 oz. AGW, 19 mm. **Note:** Initial letter was for Bonaparte.

Date	Mintage	VG	F	VF	XF	Unc
AH1203//13	—	275	350	425	500	—
AH1203 II	—	350	425	500	575	—
AH1203//14	—	800	1,000	1,200	1,500	—

KM# 152 ZERI MAHBUB
2.5920 g., 0.6850 Gold .0570 oz. AGW **Note:** Initial letter was for Bonaparte.

Date	Mintage	VG	F	VF	XF	Unc
AH1203 II	—	175	250	325	400	—
AH1203//13	—	100	150	200	250	—
AH1203//14	—	200	300	450	600	—
AH1203//15	—	200	300	450	600	—

KM# 153 2 ZERI MAHBUB
Gold, 35 mm. **Note:** Weight varies 4.76-5.00 grams.

Date	Mintage	VG	F	VF	XF	Unc
AH1203//14	—	200	300	500	900	—

KM# 154 3 ZERI MAHBUB
7.7000 g., Gold, 35 mm.

Date	Mintage	VG	F	VF	XF	Unc
AH1203//14	—	350	500	1,000	1,500	—

OTTOMAN EMPIRE
Resumed
Mustafa IV
AH1222-1223/1807-1808AD
HAMMERED COINAGE

KM# 155 PARA
Billon **Obv:** Toughra **Rev:** Mint name above date **Note:** Weight varies: 0.20-0.40 grams. Size varies: 13-14 millimeters.

Date	Mintage	Good	VG	F	VF	XF
AH1222//1 (1807)	—	10.00	20.00	35.00	60.00	—

KM# 156 20 PARA
Billon

Date	Mintage	VG	F	VF	XF	Unc
AH1222//1 (1807)	—	500	800	1,300	2,150	—

KM# 157 QIRSH (40 Para)

10.6500 g., Billon

Date	Mintage	VG	F	VF	XF	Unc
AH1222//1 (1807)	—	550	1,000	1,800	3,200	—

KM# 158 1/2 ZERI MAHBUB

1.6500 g., Gold, 20 mm.

Date	Mintage	VG	F	VF	XF	Unc
AH1222//1 (1807)	—	350	500	800	1,350	—

KM# 159 ZERI MAHBUB

2.3000 g., Gold

Date	Mintage	VG	F	VF	XF	Unc
AH1222//1 (1807)	—	275	400	700	1,100	—

KM# 160 2 ZERI MAHBUB

4.7000 g., Gold, 32 mm.

Date	Mintage	VG	F	VF	XF	Unc
AH1222//1 (1807)	—	400	600	900	1,550	—

Mahmud II

AH1223-1255/1808-1839AD

HAMMERED COINAGE

KM# AA161 ASPER

Brass **Note:** Uniface.

Date	Mintage	Good	VG	F	VF	XF
AH1223//28	—	50.00	80.00	110	150	—

Note: The precise status of this piece is undetermined

KM# A161 AKCHEH

Billon **Note:** Weight varies: 0.10-0.13 grams. Size varies: 11-12 millimeters.

Date	Mintage	Good	VG	F	VF	XF
AH1223//15 (1821)	—	1.00	2.00	3.00	10.00	—
AH1223//16 (1822)	—	1.00	2.00	3.00	10.00	—
AH1223//17 (1823)	—	1.00	2.00	3.00	10.00	—
AH1223//18 (1824)	—	1.00	2.00	3.00	10.00	—
AH1223//19 (1825)	—	1.00	2.00	3.00	10.00	—
AH1223//20 (1826)	—	1.00	2.00	3.00	10.00	—
AH1223//21 (1827)	—	1.00	2.00	3.00	10.00	—

KM# 161 PARA

Billon **Note:** Weight varies: 0.15-0.28 grams. Size varies: 12-15 millimeters.

Date	Mintage	Good	VG	F	VF	XF
AH1223//1 (1808)	—	0.75	1.50	4.00	8.50	—
AH1223//2 (1809)	—	0.75	1.50	4.00	8.50	—
AH1223//3 (1810)	—	0.75	1.50	4.00	8.50	—
AH1223//4 (1811)	—	0.75	1.50	4.00	—	—
AH1223//5 (1812)	—	0.75	1.50	4.00	8.50	—
AH1223//6 (1813)	—	0.75	1.50	4.00	8.50	—
AH1223//7 (1813)	—	0.75	1.50	4.00	8.50	—
AH1223//8 (1814)	—	0.75	1.50	4.00	8.50	—
AH1223//9 (1815)	—	0.75	1.50	4.00	8.50	—
AH1223//10 (1816)	—	0.75	1.50	4.00	8.50	—
AH1223//11 (1817)	—	0.75	1.50	4.00	8.50	—
AH1223//12 (1818)	—	0.75	1.50	4.00	8.50	—
AH1223//13 (1819)	—	0.75	1.50	4.00	8.50	—
AH1223//14 (1820)	—	0.75	1.50	4.00	8.50	—
AH1223//15 (1821)	—	0.75	1.50	4.00	8.50	—
AH1223//16 (1822)	—	0.75	1.50	4.00	8.50	—
AH1223//17 (1823)	—	1.00	3.00	10.00	15.00	—
AH1223//18 (1824)	—	1.00	3.00	10.00	15.00	—
AH1223//19 (1825)	—	2.00	4.00	15.00	20.00	—
AH1223//20 (1826)	—	—	—	—	—	—
AH1223//25 (1831)	—	—	—	—	—	—

KM# 165 5 PARA

Billon **Note:** Weight varies: 0.50-0.70 grams. Size varies: 15-16 millimeters.

Date	Mintage	Good	VG	F	VF	XF
AH1223//5 (1812)	—	15.00	20.00	40.00	90.00	—
AH1223//6 (1813)	—	15.00	20.00	40.00	90.00	—
AH1223//7 (1813)	—	15.00	20.00	40.00	90.00	—
AH1223//8 (1814)	—	15.00	20.00	40.00	90.00	—
AH1223//9 (1815)	—	10.00	15.00	35.00	70.00	—
AH1223//10 (1816)	—	10.00	15.00	35.00	70.00	—
AH1223//11 (1817)	—	10.00	15.00	35.00	70.00	—
AH1223//12 (1818)	—	10.00	15.00	35.00	70.00	—
AH1223//13 (1819)	—	10.00	15.00	35.00	70.00	—
AH1223//14 (1820)	—	10.00	15.00	35.00	70.00	—
AH1223//15 (1821)	—	10.00	15.00	35.00	70.00	—
AH1223//16 (1822)	—	10.00	15.00	35.00	70.00	—
AH1223//17 (1823)	—	10.00	15.00	35.00	70.00	—
AH1223//18 (1824)	—	10.00	15.00	35.00	70.00	—
AH1223//19 (1825)	—	10.00	15.00	35.00	70.00	—
AH1223//20 (1826)	—	10.00	15.00	35.00	70.00	—
AH1223//21 (1827)	—	10.00	15.00	35.00	70.00	—

KM# A166 5 PARA

Billon **Obv:** Beaded circle around toughra and legend **Rev:** Beaded circle around toughra and legend

Date	Mintage	Good	VG	F	VF	XF
AH1223//18 (1824)	—	35.00	60.00	120	200	—

KM# 166 5 PARA

0.4000 g., Billon **Obv:** Rose added to right of toughra

Date	Mintage	Good	VG	F	VF	XF
AH1223//21 (1827)	—	7.00	20.00	40.00	85.00	—
AH1223//22 (1828)	—	5.00	15.00	30.00	65.00	—
AH1223//23 (1829)	—	5.00	15.00	30.00	65.00	—
AH1223//24 (1830)	—	5.00	15.00	30.00	65.00	—
AH1223//25 (1831)	—	5.00	15.00	30.00	65.00	—
AH1223//26 (1832)	—	7.00	20.00	40.00	85.00	—
AH1223//27 (1833)	—	45.00	70.00	120	185	—
AH1223//28 (1834)	—	45.00	70.00	120	185	—

KM# 175 20 PARA

Billon **Obv:** Mint name and date below toughra

Date	Mintage	Good	VG	F	VF	XF
AH1223//5 (1812)	—	50.00	100	200	400	—

KM# 179.1 QIRSH

9.2000 g., Billon **Note:** Size varies: 29-31 millimeters.

Date	Mintage	Good	VG	F	VF	XF
AH1223//1 (1808)	—	25.00	50.00	100	165	—

KM# 179.2 QIRSH

7.0000 g., Billon **Note:** Varieties exist.

Date	Mintage	Good	VG	F	VF	XF
AH1223//3 (1810)	—	15.00	40.00	50.00	100	—
AH1223//5 (1812)	—	15.00	40.00	50.00	100	—
AH1223//6 (1813)	—	12.50	30.00	45.00	85.00	—
AH1223//7 (1813)	—	12.50	30.00	45.00	85.00	—
AH1223//8 (1814)	—	15.00	35.00	50.00	95.00	—

KM# 179.3 QIRSH

Billon **Obv:** Flower right of toughra

Date	Mintage	Good	VG	F	VF	XF
AH1223//7 (1813) Rare	—	—	—	—	—	—

MILLED COINAGE

KM# 162 PARA

Copper

Date	Mintage	Good	VG	F	VF	XF
AH1223//28 (1834)	—	8.00	20.00	45.00	100	—
AH1223//29 (1835)	—	8.00	20.00	45.00	100	—

KM# 164 PARA

Copper **Note:** Size varies: 15-17 millimeters. With denomination.

Date	Mintage	Good	VG	F	VF	XF
AH1223//29 (1835)	—	8.00	20.00	45.00	100	—
AH1223//30 (1836)	—	8.00	20.00	45.00	100	—
AH1223//31 (1837)	—	8.00	20.00	45.00	100	—
AH1223//32 (1838)	—	8.00	20.00	45.00	100	—

KM# 163 PARA

Copper, 15 mm. **Note:** Without denomination.

Date	Mintage	Good	VG	F	VF	XF
AH1223//29 (1835)	—	8.00	20.00	45.00	100	—

KM# 167 5 PARA

Copper **Note:** Floral designs in wreath. Weight varies: 6.14-7.41 grams. Size varies: 22-24 millimeters.

Date	Mintage	Good	VG	F	VF	XF
AH1223//28 (1834)	—	5.00	10.00	20.00	40.00	—
AH1223//29 (1835)	—	5.00	10.00	20.00	40.00	—

KM# 168.1 5 PARA

Copper **Note:** Without wreath and denomination.

Date	Mintage	Good	VG	F	VF	XF
AH1223//29 (1835)	—	15.00	25.00	40.00	75.00	—

KM# 168.2 5 PARA

Copper **Rev:** Larger legend

Date	Mintage	Good	VG	F	VF	XF
AH1223//29 (1835)	—	15.00	25.00	40.00	75.00	—

KM# 169 5 PARA

Copper **Obv:** Denomination added below toughra

Date	Mintage	Good	VG	F	VF	XF
AH1223//29 (1835)	—	2.00	5.00	10.00	20.00	—
AH1223//30 (1836)	—	2.00	5.00	10.00	20.00	—
AH1223//31 (1837)	—	2.00	5.00	10.00	20.00	—
AH1223//32 (1838)	—	3.00	7.00	15.00	25.00	—

KM# 170.1 10 PARA

Billon **Note:** Plain dotted borders. Border varieties exist. Weight varies: 0.90-1.40 grams. Size varies: 17-18 millimeters.

Date	Mintage	Good	VG	F	VF	XF
AH1223 (1808) Rare	—	—	—	—	—	—
AH1223//8 (1814)	—	20.00	40.00	80.00	160	—
AH1223//9 (1815)	—	10.00	20.00	50.00	100	—
AH1223//10 (1816)	—	10.00	20.00	50.00	100	—
AH1223//11 (1817)	—	10.00	20.00	50.00	100	—
AH1223//12 (1818)	—	10.00	20.00	50.00	100	—
AH1223//15 (1821)	—	10.00	20.00	50.00	100	—

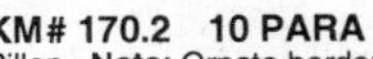

KM# 170.2 10 PARA

Billon **Note:** Ornate borders.

Date	Mintage	Good	VG	F	VF	XF
AH1223//18 (1824)	—	5.00	15.00	35.00	70.00	—
AH1223//19 (1825)	—	5.00	15.00	35.00	70.00	—
AH1223//20 (1826)	—	5.00	15.00	35.00	70.00	—
AH1223//21 (1827)	—	5.00	15.00	35.00	70.00	—

KM# 171 10 PARA

Billon **Note:** Wavy borders. Weight varies: 0.75-0.78 grams.

Date	Mintage	Good	VG	F	VF	XF
AH1223//21 (1827)	—	6.00	15.00	25.00	50.00	—
AH1223//22 (1828)	—	5.00	12.50	20.00	40.00	—
AH1223//23 (1829)	—	5.00	12.50	20.00	40.00	—
AH1223//24 (1830)	—	5.00	12.50	20.00	40.00	—
AH1223//25 (1831)	—	5.00	12.50	20.00	40.00	—
AH1223//26 (1832)	—	13.50	30.00	75.00	150	—
AH1223//27 (1833)	—	25.00	55.00	120	200	—

 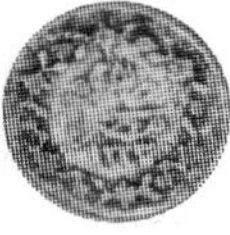

KM# 172 10 PARA

0.3000 g., Billon, 12 mm. **Obv:** "Adli" right of toughra, wreath borders **Note:** Varieties exist.

Date	Mintage	Good	VG	F	VF	XF
AH1223//28 (1834)	—	30.00	60.00	135	280	—
AH1223//29 (1835)	—	25.00	45.00	95.00	200	—

KM# 173 10 PARA

0.3500 g., Silver, 14 mm. **Obv:** Denomination below toughra

Date	Mintage	VG	F	VF	XF	Unc
AH1223//29 (1835)	—	50.00	100	180	300	—
AH1223//30 (1836)	—	50.00	100	180	300	—
AH1223//31 (1837)	—	50.00	100	180	300	—
AH1223//32 (1838)	—	50.00	100	180	300	—

KM# 174 20 PARA

Billon **Rev:** Date **Note:** Weight varies: 2.40-3.80 grams. Size varies: 22-24 millimeters.

Date	Mintage	Good	VG	F	VF	XF
AH1223//1 (1808)	—	65.00	115	200	320	—
AH1223//5 (1812)	—	45.00	65.00	100	170	—
AH1223//6 (1813)	—	45.00	65.00	100	170	—
AH1223//7 (1813)	—	45.00	65.00	100	170	—
AH1223//8 (1814)	—	45.00	65.00	100	170	—
AH1223//9 (1815)	—	45.00	65.00	100	170	—
AH1223//10 (1816)	—	45.00	65.00	100	170	—
AH1223//11 (1817)	—	45.00	65.00	100	170	—

KM# 176 20 PARA

Billon, 21 mm. **Note:** Weight varies: 1.38-1.62 grams.

Date	Mintage	Good	VG	F	VF	XF
AH1223//21 (1827)	—	20.00	35.00	60.00	100	—
AH1223//22 (1828)	—	20.00	35.00	60.00	100	—
AH1223//23 (1829)	—	20.00	35.00	60.00	100	—
AH1223//24 (1830)	—	20.00	35.00	60.00	100	—
AH1223//25 (1830)	—	20.00	35.00	60.00	100	—
AH1223//26 (1832)	—	40.00	80.00	150	275	—
AH1223//27 (1833)	—	40.00	65.00	100	170	—

KM# 177 20 PARA

Billon, 15 mm. **Obv:** "Adli" right of toughra **Note:** Weight varies: 0.58-0.62 grams. Varieties exist.

Date	Mintage	Good	VG	F	VF	XF
AH1223//28 (1834)	—	12.00	25.00	70.00	120	—
AH1223//29 (1835)	—	12.00	25.00	70.00	120	—

KM# 178 20 PARA

0.8330 Silver **Obv:** Denomination below toughra **Note:** Weight varies: 0.68-0.70 grams. Size varies: 15-16 millimeters.

Date	Mintage	VG	F	VF	XF	Unc
AH1223//29 (1835)	—	20.00	40.00	80.00	160	—
AH1223//30 (1836)	—	20.00	40.00	80.00	160	—
AH1223//31 (1837)	—	20.00	40.00	80.00	160	—
AH1223//32 (1838)	—	20.00	40.00	80.00	160	—

KM# 180 QIRSH

Billon **Obv:** Mint name and date below toughra

Date	Mintage	Good	VG	F	VF	XF
AH1223//5 (1812)	—	40.00	70.00	140	260	—

KM# 181 QIRSH

Billon **Obv:** Mint name and date below toughra **Note:** Wavy borders. Weight varies: 2.67-3.15 grams. Size varies: 26-27 millimeters. Coins with accession date 1213H, 1223H, and regnal year 13, are jewelry imitations.

Date	Mintage	Good	VG	F	VF	XF
AH1223//21 (1827)	—	10.00	20.00	45.00	80.00	—
AH1223//22 (1828)	—	10.00	20.00	45.00	80.00	—
AH1223//23 (1829)	—	10.00	20.00	45.00	80.00	—
AH1223//24 (1830)	—	10.00	20.00	45.00	80.00	—
AH1223//25 (1831)	—	10.00	20.00	45.00	80.00	—
AH1223//26 (1832)	—	10.00	20.00	45.00	80.00	—
AH1223//27 (1833)	—	15.00	25.00	50.00	100	—

KM# 182 QIRSH

Billon, 19 mm. **Obv:** "Adli" right of toughra **Note:** Wreath borders. Weight varies: 1.00-1.31 grams. Varieties exist.

Date	Mintage	Good	VG	F	VF	XF
AH1223//28 (1834)	—	15.00	20.00	45.00	70.00	—
AH1223//29 (1835)	—	15.00	20.00	45.00	70.00	—

KM# 183 QIRSH
1.4000 g., 0.8330 Silver **Obv:** Denomination below toughra **Note:** Size varies: 19-20 millimeters.

Date	Mintage	VG	F	VF	XF	Unc
AH1223//29 (1835)	—	15.00	45.00	75.00	135	—
AH1223//30 (1836)	—	15.00	45.00	75.00	135	—
AH1223//31 (1837)	—	15.00	45.00	75.00	135	—
AH1223//32 (1838)	—	15.00	45.00	75.00	135	—

KM# 184 5 QIRSH
7.0000 g., 0.8330 Silver **Note:** Size varies: 24-26 millimeters.

Date	Mintage	VG	F	VF	XF	Unc
AH1223//29 (1835)	—	100	200	600	900	—
AH1223//30 (1836)	—	200	300	600	900	—
AH1223//31 (1837)	—	200	300	600	900	—

KM# 185 10 QIRSH
0.8330 Silver, 30 mm. **Note:** Weight varies: 13.75-14.00 grams.

Date	Mintage	VG	F	VF	XF	Unc
AH1223//29 (1835)	—	—	—	6,500	7,500	—

KM# 186 20 QIRSH
0.8330 Silver, 37 mm. **Note:** Weight varies: 27.15-28.06 grams.

Date	Mintage	VG	F	VF	XF	Unc
AH1223//29 (1835)	—	400	700	1,000	1,500	—
AH1223//30 (1836)	—	425	750	1,250	1,750	—
AH1223//31 (1837)	—	350	650	900	1,400	—
AH1223//32 (1838)	—	550	900	1,400	1,950	—

PRE-REFORM COINAGE

Prior to AH1251 (1834AD)

The basic unit was the 'Mahbub' or 'Zer Mahbub' (Zer = Gold), which weighed approximately 2.35 g from AH1223 until 1247 (Yr. 15), when it was reduced to about 1.6 g. Fractional denominations were Halves (Nisfiya) and Quarters (Rubiya). The value of the Mahbub in terms of silver Piastres fluctuated according to the relative value of gold and silver, and the price of debased Egyptian silver coin.

KM# 194 1/2 ZERI MAHBUB (Nisfiya)
0.8750 Gold **Note:** Weight varies: 1.15-1.20 grams. Size varies: 19-20 millimeters.

Date	Mintage	VG	F	VF	XF	Unc
AH1223//1 (1808)	—	75.00	135	350	650	—
AH1223//5 (1812)	—	75.00	135	350	650	—
AH1223//8 (1814)	—	75.00	135	350	650	—

KM# 195 1/2 ZERI MAHBUB (Khayriya)
0.8750 Gold, 16 mm. **Note:** Weight varies: 0.70-0.80 grams.

Date	Mintage	VG	F	VF	XF	Unc
AH1223//21 (1827)	—	20.00	30.00	75.00	150	—
AH1223//22 (1828)	—	20.00	30.00	60.00	125	—
AH1223//23 (1829)	—	20.00	30.00	60.00	125	—
AH1223//24 (1830)	—	20.00	30.00	60.00	125	—
AH1223//25 (1831)	—	20.00	30.00	60.00	125	—
AH1223//26 (1832)	—	20.00	30.00	75.00	150	—
AH1223//27 (1833)	—	30.00	40.00	100	200	—
AH1223//28 (1834)	—	40.00	50.00	125	250	—

KM# 197 ZERI MAHBUB (Altin)
0.8750 Gold **Note:** Crude flan. Weight varies: 2.19-2.38 grams. Size varies: 23-26 millimeters.

Date	Mintage	VG	F	VF	XF	Unc
AH1223//1 (1808)	—	90.00	175	350	600	—
AH1223//1 (1808)	—	—	—	—	—	—
Note: Dot right of toughra						
AH1223//2 (1809)	—	100	200	400	750	—
AH1223//3 (1810)	—	90.00	175	350	600	—
AH1223//5 (1812)	—	90.00	175	350	600	—
AH1223//7 (1813)	—	150	250	425	800	—
AH1223//8 (1814)	—	150	250	425	800	—
AH1223//10 (1816)	—	150	250	425	800	—
Note: Dot next to toughra						
AH1223//10 (1816)	—	180	300	425	800	—
Note: Rose branch next to toughra						
AH1223//11 (1817)	—	90.00	175	350	600	—
AH1223//12 (1818)	—	—	—	—	—	—
Note: Rose branch right of toughra						
AH1223//13 (1819)	—	150	250	350	600	—
AH1223//14 (1820)	—	90.00	175	350	600	—

KM# 199 ZERI MAHBUB (Altin)
0.8750 Gold **Note:** Without "Azza Nashruhu".

Date	Mintage	VG	F	VF	XF	Unc
AH1223//5 (1812)	—	100	200	375	700	—

KM# 198 ZERI MAHBUB (Altin)
2.3500 g., 0.8750 Gold, 23 mm. **Note:** Thicker and well-shaped flan.

Date	Mintage	VG	F	VF	XF	Unc
AH1223//15 (1821)	—	120	220	425	1,000	—

KM# 189 1/4 MAHBUB (Rubiya)
0.8750 Gold **Rev. Legend:** "Azze Nashruhu Duribe Fi..." **Note:** Plain borders of dots. Weight varies: 0.35-0.60 grams. Size varies: 13-14 millimeters.

Date	Mintage	VG	F	VF	XF	Unc
AH1223 (1808)	—	150	225	300	450	—

KM# 190 1/4 MAHBUB (Rubiya)
0.8750 Gold

Date	Mintage	VG	F	VF	XF	Unc
AH1223//7 (1813)	—	35.00	55.00	85.00	110	—
AH1223//8 (1814)	—	35.00	55.00	85.00	110	—
AH1223//9 (1815)	—	35.00	55.00	85.00	110	—
AH1223//10 (1816)	—	35.00	55.00	85.00	110	—
AH1223//11 (1817)	—	35.00	55.00	85.00	110	—
AH1223//12 (1818)	—	35.00	55.00	85.00	110	—
AH1223//13 (1819)	—	35.00	55.00	85.00	110	—
AH1223//14 (1820)	—	35.00	55.00	85.00	110	—

KM# 191 1/4 MAHBUB (Rubiya)
0.8750 Gold **Note:** Plain border of dots. Weight varies: 0.35-0.40 grams. Size varies: 12-13 millimeters.

Date	Mintage	VG	F	VF	XF	Unc
AH1223//15 (1821)	—	25.00	40.00	60.00	85.00	—
AH1223//16 (1822)	—	17.50	27.50	45.00	65.00	—
AH1223//17 (1823)	—	25.00	40.00	60.00	85.00	—
AH1223//18 (1824)	—	17.50	27.50	45.00	65.00	—
AH1223//19 (1825)	—	20.00	35.00	55.00	80.00	—
AH1223//20 (1826)	—	20.00	35.00	55.00	80.00	—
AH1223//21 (1827)	—	20.00	35.00	55.00	80.00	—

KM# 192 1/4 MAHBUB (Saadiya)
0.8750 Gold **Note:** Ornamental borders.

Date	Mintage	VG	F	VF	XF	Unc
AH1223//19 (1825)	—	30.00	50.00	65.00	75.00	—
AH1223//20 (1826)	—	40.00	65.00	90.00	115	—
AH1223//21 (1827)	—	60.00	90.00	115	140	—

KM# 201 1/4 MAHBUB (Coyrek Rumi)
0.8750 Gold **Note:** Different design and without year.

Date	Mintage	VG	F	VF	XF	Unc
AH1223 (1808)	—	—	—	—	—	—

KM# 193 1/4 MAHBUB (Coyrek Rumi)
0.8750 Gold **Note:** Vine-like borders.

Date	Mintage	VG	F	VF	XF	Unc
AH1223//21 (1827)	—	25.00	35.00	50.00	100	—
AH1223//22 (1828)	—	25.00	35.00	50.00	100	—
AH1223//23 (1829)	—	25.00	35.00	50.00	100	—
AH1223//24 (1830)	—	25.00	35.00	50.00	100	—
AH1223//25 (1831)	—	25.00	35.00	50.00	100	—
AH1223//26 (1832)	—	20.00	30.00	40.00	90.00	—
AH1223//27 (1833)	—	30.00	40.00	70.00	150	—
AH1223//28 (1834)	—	100	175	275	375	—

KM# 200 2 ZERI MAHBUB
0.8750 Gold, 28 mm. **Note:** Weight varies: 3.25-3.60 grams.

Date	Mintage	VG	F	VF	XF	Unc
AH1223//5 (1812)	—	300	500	850	1,750	—

Note: The above piece may be a medal, token or jewelry piece

KM# 202 TEK RUMI
2.3500 g., 0.8750 Gold, 23 mm. **Note:** Similar to 1/4 Mahbub, KM#193.

Date	Mintage	VG	F	VF	XF	Unc
AH1223//11 (1817) Rare	—	—	—	—	—	—

KM# 203 CHIFTE RUMI
3.6000 g., 0.8750 Gold, 28 mm. **Note:** Similar to 1/4 Mahbub, KM#193.

Date	Mintage	VG	F	VF	XF	Unc
AH1223//5 (1812) Rare	—	—	—	—	—	—

REFORM COINAGE

KM# 210 5 QIRSH
0.8750 Gold **Note:** Weight varies: 0.30-0.35 grams.

Date	Mintage	VG	F	VF	XF	Unc
AH1223//28 (1834)	—	80.00	135	210	320	—
AH1223//29 (1835)	—	60.00	90.00	135	225	—

KM# 211 5 QIRSH
0.4200 g., 0.8750 Gold **Obv:** Without value below toughra

Date	Mintage	VG	F	VF	XF	Unc
AH1223//29 (1835)	—	50.00	90.00	135	225	—

KM# 212 5 QIRSH
0.4200 g., 0.8750 Gold **Obv:** Denomination added below toughra

Date	Mintage	VG	F	VF	XF	Unc
AH1223//29 (1835)	—	50.00	90.00	135	185	—
AH1223//30 (1836)	—	50.00	90.00	135	185	—
AH1223//31 (1837)	—	50.00	90.00	135	185	—
AH1223//32 (1838)	—	50.00	90.00	135	185	—

KM# 213 10 QIRSH
0.8750 Gold **Note:** Weight varies: 0.70-0.75 grams.

Date	Mintage	VG	F	VF	XF	Unc
AH1223//28 (1834)	—	30.00	50.00	125	200	—
AH1223//29 (1835)	—	30.00	50.00	125	200	—

KM# 214 10 QIRSH
0.8500 g., 0.8750 Gold, 15 mm. **Obv:** Denomination beneath toughra

Date	Mintage	VG	F	VF	XF	Unc
AH1223//29 (1835)	—	50.00	90.00	180	325	—
AH1223//30 (1836)	—	50.00	90.00	180	325	—
AH1223//32 (1838)	—	50.00	90.00	180	325	—

KM# 215 20 QIRSH
1.7000 g., 0.8750 Gold, 18 mm.

Date	Mintage	VG	F	VF	XF	Unc
AH1223//29 (1835)	—	50.00	90.00	135	285	—
AH1223//30 (1836)	—	50.00	90.00	135	285	—
AH1223//31 (1837)	—	50.00	90.00	135	285	—
AH1223//32 (1838)	—	50.00	90.00	135	285	—

KM# 216 20 QIRSH
1.7000 g., 0.8750 Gold **Obv:** Four roses around edge **Rev:** Four roses around edge

Date	Mintage	VG	F	VF	XF	Unc
AH1223//32 (1838)	—	70.00	120	185	375	—

KM# 217 100 QIRSH (Pound)
8.4000 g., 0.8750 Gold, 22 mm.

Date	Mintage	VG	F	VF	XF	Unc
AH1223//30 (1836)	—	750	1,000	2,000	3,000	—
AH1223//31 (1837)	—	750	1,000	2,000	3,000	—

Abdul Mejid
AH1255-1277/1839-1861AD

REFORM COINAGE

KM# 220 PARA
1.2000 g., Copper, 16 mm.

Date	Mintage	Good	VG	F	VF	XF
AH1255//1 (1839)	—	12.00	30.00	75.00	150	—
AH1255//2 (1840)	—	9.00	18.00	45.00	100	175
AH1255//4 (1842)	—	9.00	18.00	45.00	100	175
AH1255//5 (1843)	—	9.00	18.00	45.00	100	175
AH1255//6 (1844)	—	9.00	18.00	45.00	100	175
(1839-45) (1845) Proof; Common date	—	—	—	—	—	—
AH1255//7 (1845) Unique	—	—	—	—	—	—

KM# 221 PARA
Copper, 15 mm.

Date	Mintage	Good	VG	F	VF	XF
AH1255//8 (1845) Rare	—	—	—	—	—	—

KM# 222 5 PARA
6.4000 g., Copper, 21 mm. **Note:** Varieties of size of toughra exist.

Date	Mintage	Good	VG	F	VF	XF
AH1255//1 (1839)	—	1.00	2.00	5.00	12.50	—
AH1255//2 (1840)	—	1.00	2.00	5.00	12.50	—
AH1255//3 (1841)	—	1.00	2.00	5.00	12.50	—
AH1255//4 (1842)	—	1.00	2.00	5.00	12.50	—
AH1255//5 (1843)	—	1.00	2.00	5.00	12.50	—
AH1255//6 (1844)	—	1.00	2.00	5.00	12.50	—

KM# 224.1 5 PARA
6.4000 g., Copper **Note:** Similar to KM#224.2.

Date	Mintage	Good	VG	F	VF	XF
AH1255//8 (1845)	—	4.00	10.00	20.00	35.00	—

KM# 223 5 PARA
6.4000 g., Copper

Date	Mintage	Good	VG	F	VF	XF
AH1255//7 (1845)	—	1.00	2.00	5.00	16.00	—
AH1255//8 (1845)	—	4.50	8.50	15.00	27.50	—

KM# 224.2 5 PARA
6.4000 g., Copper

Date	Mintage	Good	VG	F	VF	XF
AH1255//13 (1850)	—	2.00	5.00	12.50	25.00	—
AH1255//14 (1851)	—	1.00	2.50	10.00	20.00	—
AH1255//15 (1852)	—	1.00	2.00	7.50	15.00	25.00
AH1255//16 (1853)	—	1.00	2.00	7.50	15.00	25.00
(1847-54) (1854) Proof; Common date	—	—	—	—	—	—

KM# 225 10 PARA
0.3700 g., 0.8330 Silver, 15 mm.

Date	Mintage	VG	F	VF	XF	Unc
AH1255//1 (1839)	—	14.00	28.00	60.00	90.00	—
AH1255//2 (1840)	—	14.00	28.00	60.00	75.00	—
AH1255//3 (1841)	—	11.50	23.50	50.00	75.00	—
AH1255//4 (1842)	—	11.50	23.50	50.00	75.00	—
AH1255//5 (1843)	—	11.50	23.50	50.00	75.00	—
AH1255//6 (1844)	—	11.50	23.50	50.00	75.00	—
AH1255//7 (1845)	—	11.50	23.50	50.00	75.00	—
AH1255//8 (1845)	—	11.50	23.50	50.00	75.00	—
AH1255//9 (1846)	—	11.50	23.50	50.00	75.00	—
AH1255//10 (1847)	—	14.00	28.00	60.00	90.00	—
AH1255//11 (1848)	—	14.00	28.00	60.00	90.00	—
AH1255//12 (1849)	—	14.00	28.00	60.00	90.00	—
AH1255//13 (1850)	—	30.00	60.00	120	180	—
AH1255//14 (1851)	—	14.00	28.00	60.00	90.00	—
AH1255//15 (1852)	—	14.00	28.00	60.00	90.00	—
AH1255//18 (1855)	—	16.50	32.50	65.00	100	—
AH1255//19 (1856)	—	16.50	32.50	65.00	100	—
AH1255//20 (1857)	—	16.50	32.50	65.00	100	—
AH1255//23 (1860)	—	14.00	28.00	60.00	90.00	—

KM# 226 10 PARA
12.9000 g., Copper, 29 mm. **Note:** Varieties of size of toughra exist.

Date	Mintage	VG	F	VF	XF	Unc
AH1255//15 (1852)	—	4.50	8.00	15.00	45.00	—
AH1255//16 (1853)	—	6.00	15.00	22.00	60.00	—

KM# 227 20 PARA
0.6800 g., 0.8330 Silver, 16 mm.

Date	Mintage	VG	F	VF	XF	Unc
AH1255//1 (1839)	—	13.50	27.50	50.00	75.00	150
AH1255//2 (1840)	—	13.50	27.50	50.00	75.00	150
AH1255//3 (1841)	—	13.50	27.50	50.00	75.00	150
AH1255//4/3 (1842)	—	16.50	32.50	60.00	90.00	—
AH1255//4 (1842)	—	13.50	27.50	50.00	75.00	150
AH1255//5 (1843)	—	13.50	27.50	50.00	75.00	150
AH1255//6 (1844)	—	13.50	27.50	50.00	75.00	150
AH1255//7 (1845)	—	13.50	27.50	50.00	75.00	150
AH1255//8 (1845)	—	13.50	27.50	50.00	75.00	150
AH1255//9 (1846)	—	13.50	27.50	50.00	75.00	150
AH1255//10 (1847)	—	13.50	27.50	50.00	75.00	150
AH1255//11 (1848)	—	16.50	32.50	60.00	90.00	—
AH1255//12 (1849)	—	16.50	35.00	60.00	90.00	—
AH1255//13 (1850)	—	16.50	32.50	60.00	90.00	—
AH1255//14 (1851)	—	16.50	32.50	60.00	90.00	—
AH1255//15 (1852)	—	16.50	32.50	60.00	90.00	—
AH1255//18/6 (1855)	—	20.00	40.00	70.00	110	—
AH1255//18 (1855)	—	20.00	40.00	70.00	110	—
AH1255//19 (1856)	—	30.00	60.00	90.00	150	—
AH1255//20 (1857)	—	20.00	40.00	70.00	110	—
AH1255//21 (1858)	—	20.00	40.00	70.00	110	—
AH1255//22 (1859)	—	20.00	40.00	70.00	110	—
AH1255//23 (1860)	—	16.50	32.50	60.00	90.00	—
(1839-61) (1861) Proof; Common date	—	—	—	—	—	150

KM# 228 QIRSH
1.4200 g., 0.8330 Silver

Date	Mintage	VG	F	VF	XF	Unc
AH1255//1 (1839)	—	13.50	27.50	50.00	85.00	150
AH1255//2 (1840)	—	13.50	27.50	50.00	85.00	150
AH1255//3 (1841)	—	13.50	27.50	50.00	85.00	150
AH1255//4 (1842)	—	16.50	32.50	60.00	100	—
AH1255//5 (1843)	—	13.50	27.50	50.00	85.00	150
AH1255//6 (1844)	—	13.50	27.50	50.00	85.00	150
AH1255//8 (1845)	—	16.50	32.50	60.00	100	—
AH1255//7 (1845)	—	16.50	32.50	60.00	100	—
AH1255//8/7 (1845)	—	16.50	32.50	60.00	100	—
AH1255//9 (1846)	—	16.50	32.50	60.00	100	—
AH1255//10 (1847)	—	16.50	32.50	60.00	100	—
AH1255//11 (1848)	—	16.50	32.50	60.00	100	—
AH1255//12 (1849)	—	16.50	32.50	60.00	100	—
AH1255//13 (1850)	—	16.50	32.50	60.00	100	—
AH1255//14 (1851)	—	16.50	32.50	60.00	100	—
AH1255//15 (1852)	—	16.50	32.50	60.00	100	—
AH1255//16 (1853)	—	16.50	32.50	60.00	100	—

Date	Mintage	VG	F	VF	XF	Unc
AH1255//17 (1854)	—	22.50	45.00	75.00	125	—
AH1255//18 (1855)	—	22.50	45.00	75.00	125	—
AH1255//19 (1856)	—	22.50	45.00	75.00	125	—
AH1255//20 (1857)	—	22.50	45.00	75.00	125	—
AH1255//22 (1859)	—	22.50	45.00	75.00	125	—
AH1255//23 (1860)	—	16.50	32.50	65.00	110	—
(1839-61) (1861) Proof; Common date	—	—	—	—	—	150

KM# 230 5 QIRSH
0.4270 g., 0.8750 Gold

Date	Mintage	VG	F	VF	XF	Unc
AH1255//1 (1839)	—	16.50	28.00	40.00	75.00	—
AH1255//2 (1840)	—	16.50	28.00	40.00	75.00	—
AH1255//3 (1841)	—	16.50	28.00	40.00	75.00	—
AH1255//4 (1842)	—	16.50	28.00	40.00	75.00	—
AH1255//5 (1843)	—	16.50	28.00	40.00	75.00	—
AH1255//6 (1844)	—	16.50	28.00	40.00	75.00	—
AH1255//7 (1845)	—	16.50	28.00	40.00	75.00	—
AH1255//8 (1845)	—	16.50	28.00	40.00	75.00	—
AH1255//9 (1846)	—	16.50	28.00	40.00	75.00	—
AH1255//10 (1847)	—	16.50	28.00	40.00	75.00	—
AH1255//11 (1848)	—	16.50	28.00	40.00	75.00	—
AH1255//12 (1849)	—	16.50	28.00	40.00	75.00	—
AH1255//13 (1850)	—	20.00	35.00	55.00	120	—
AH1255//14 (1851)	—	16.50	28.00	40.00	75.00	—
AH1255//15 (1852)	—	16.50	28.00	40.00	75.00	—
AH1255//16 (1853)	—	16.50	28.00	40.00	75.00	—
AH1255//18 (1855)	—	16.50	28.00	40.00	75.00	—
AH1255//19 (1856)	—	16.50	28.00	40.00	75.00	—
AH1255//20 (1857)	—	16.50	28.00	40.00	75.00	—
AH1255//22 (1859)	—	16.50	28.00	40.00	75.00	—
AH1255//23 (1860)	—	16.50	28.00	40.00	75.00	—

KM# 229 5 QIRSH
0.8330 Silver **Note:** Weight varies: 6.80-7.00 grams. Size varies: 25-26 millimeters.

Date	Mintage	VG	F	VF	XF	Unc
AH1255//1 (1839)	—	150	250	500	800	—
AH1255//2 (1840)	—	150	250	500	800	—
AH1255//3 (1841)	—	150	250	500	800	—
AH1255//4 (1842)	—	150	250	500	800	—
AH1255//5 (1843)	—	150	250	500	800	—
AH1255//6 (1844)	—	150	250	500	800	—
AH1255//16 (1853)	—	200	300	750	1,250	—
(1839-61) (1861)	—	—	—	—	—	—

KM# 231a 10 QIRSH
0.8400 g., 0.8750 Gold .0236 oz. AGW, 15 mm.

Date	Mintage	VG	F	VF	XF	Unc
AH1255//1 (1839)	—	—	—	—	—	—

KM# 231 10 QIRSH
0.8330 Silver .3749 oz. ASW **Note:** Oblique or vertical milled edges. Weight varies: 13.60-14.00 grams. Size varies: 29-30 millimeters.

Date	Mintage	VG	F	VF	XF	Unc
AH1255//1 (1839)	—	200	350	800	1,500	—
AH1255//2 (1840)	—	175	350	800	1,500	—
AH1255//3 (1841)	—	175	350	800	1,500	—
AH1255//4 (1842)	—	175	350	800	1,500	—
AH1255//5 (1843)	—	200	350	800	1,500	—
AH1255//6 (1844)	—	240	400	900	1,800	—
(1839-54) (1854)	—	—	—	—	—	—

KM# 233 20 QIRSH
1.7100 g., 0.8750 Gold .0481 oz. AGW

Date	Mintage	VG	F	VF	XF	Unc
AH1255//1 (1839)	—	400	650	1,250	1,800	—

KM# 232 20 QIRSH
0.8330 Silver .7498 oz. ASW **Note:** Weight varies: 27.70-28.00 grams. Size varies: 36-38 millimeters.

Date	Mintage	VG	F	VF	XF	Unc
AH1255//1 (1839)	—	350	650	1,150	1,600	—
AH1255//2 (1840)	—	325	600	1,100	1,550	—
AH1255//3 (1841)	—	375	700	1,350	1,850	—
AH1255//4 (1842)	—	325	600	1,100	1,550	—
(1839-43) (1843) Proof; Common date	—	—	—	—	—	3,500

KM# 234.1 50 QIRSH (1/2 Pound)
4.2720 g., 0.8750 Gold .1202 oz. AGW **Note:** Beaded border.

Date	Mintage	VG	F	VF	XF	Unc
AH1255//1 (1839)	550	185	285	550	750	—
AH1255//2 (1840)	—	90.00	135	275	450	—
AH1255//3 (1841)	—	90.00	115	225	375	—
AH1255//4 (1842)	—	70.00	90.00	180	285	—
AH1255//5 (1843)	—	70.00	90.00	180	285	—

KM# 234.2 50 QIRSH (1/2 Pound)
4.2720 g., 0.8750 Gold .1202 oz. AGW **Note:** Toothed border.

Date	Mintage	VG	F	VF	XF	Unc
AH1255//6 (1844)	—	70.00	115	225	375	—
AH1255//7 (1845)	—	70.00	135	275	450	—
AH1255//8 (1845)	—	70.00	135	275	450	—
AH1255//9 (1846)	—	70.00	135	275	450	—
AH1255//11 (1848)	—	70.00	135	275	450	—
AH1255//15 (1852)	—	40.00	70.00	140	235	—
AH1255//16 (1853)	—	70.00	90.00	180	325	—

KM# 235.1 100 QIRSH (Pound)
8.5440 g., 0.8750 Gold .2404 oz. AGW **Note:** Beaded border.

Date	Mintage	VG	F	VF	XF	Unc
AH1255//1 (1839)	—	BV	180	265	450	—
AH1255//2 (1840)	—	BV	135	225	425	—
Note: For crude copy of regnal year 2 see Sudan KM#3						
AH1255//3 (1841)	—	BV	110	200	400	—
AH1255//4 (1842)	—	BV	100	180	375	—
AH1255//5 (1843)	—	BV	100	180	375	—

KM# 235.2 100 QIRSH (Pound)
8.5440 g., 0.8750 Gold .2404 oz. AGW **Note:** Toothed border.

Date	Mintage	VG	F	VF	XF	Unc
AH1255//6 (1844)	—	BV	100	110	250	—
AH1255//7 (1845)	—	BV	110	135	320	—
AH1255//8 (1845)	—	BV	110	135	320	—
AH1255//9 (1846)	—	120	180	265	450	—
AH1255//10 (1847)	—	120	180	265	450	—
AH1255//11 (1848)	—	BV	110	135	320	—
AH1255//12 (1849)	—	BV	110	135	320	—
AH1255//13 (1850)	—	BV	110	135	320	—
AH1255//14 (1851)	—	BV	110	135	320	—
AH1255//15 (1852)	—	BV	100	110	225	—
AH1255//16 (1853)	—	BV	100	120	250	—
AH1255//17 (1854)	—	BV	110	135	320	—

Abdul Aziz
AH1277-1293/1861-1876AD
REFORM COINAGE

KM# 240 4 PARA
2.2600 g., Bronze, 22 mm.

Date	Mintage	F	VF	XF	Unc
AH1277//4 (1863)	—	2.50	5.00	10.00	25.00

KM# 243 10 PARA
0.8330 Silver, 16 mm. **Note:** Weight varies: 0.29-0.33 grams.

Date	Mintage	F	VF	XF	Unc
AH1277//2 (1861)	—	15.00	30.00	70.00	160
AH1277//3 (1862)	—	10.00	20.00	50.00	125
AH1277//4 (1863)	—	10.00	20.00	50.00	125
AH1277//5 (1864)	—	12.00	25.00	60.00	150
AH1277//6 (1865)	—	8.00	16.00	35.00	75.00
AH1277//7 (1866)	—	6.00	12.00	30.00	60.00
AH1277//8 (1867)	—	5.00	10.00	22.00	45.00
AH1277//9 (1868)	—	5.00	10.00	25.00	50.00

KM# 243a 10 PARA
0.9000 Silver **Note:** Weight varies: 0.30-0.33 grams.

Date	Mintage	F	VF	XF	Unc
AH1277/10 (1869)	—	4.00	8.00	22.00	45.00
AH1277//11 (1870)	—	4.00	8.00	22.00	45.00
AH1277//12 (1871)	—	7.00	15.00	32.00	65.00
AH1277//13 (1872)	—	7.00	15.00	32.00	65.00
AH1277//14 (1873)	—	10.00	20.00	45.00	100
AH1277//15 (1874)	—	15.00	30.00	65.00	140
AH1277//16 (1875)	—	17.00	25.00	60.00	120

KM# 241 10 PARA
Bronze, 30 mm. **Obv:** Without flower at right of toughra **Note:** Weight varies: 6.10-6.60 grams.

Date	Mintage	F	VF	XF	Unc
AH1277//4 (1863)	—	1.00	2.50	10.00	25.00
AH1277//5 (1864)	—	1.00	2.50	10.00	25.00

Date	Mintage	F	VF	XF	Unc
AH1277//6 (1865)	—	2.00	3.50	12.00	35.00
AH1277//7 (1866)	—	2.00	3.50	12.00	40.00
AH1277//9 (1868)	—	1.00	2.50	10.00	25.00
AH1277//10 (1869)	—	2.00	3.50	12.00	35.00

KM# 242 10 PARA

5.8000 g., Copper **Obv:** Flower added at right of toughra

Date	Mintage	F	VF	XF	Unc
AH1277//8 (1867)	204,000	400	700	1,550	—
AH1277//9 (1868)	—	300	600	1,400	—
AH1277//11 (1870)	200	—	—	—	5,000

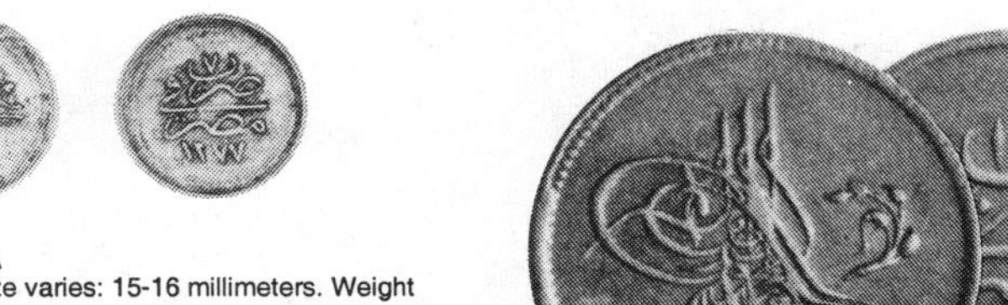

KM# 247 20 PARA

0.8330 Silver **Note:** Size varies: 15-16 millimeters. Weight varies: 0.65-0.70 grams.

Date	Mintage	F	VF	XF	Unc
AH1277//1 (1861)	—	40.00	90.00	175	350
AH1277//2 (1861)	—	20.00	45.00	100	175
AH1277//3 (1862)	—	10.00	20.00	50.00	125
AH1277//4 (1863)	—	8.00	16.00	45.00	100
AH1277//5 (1864)	—	10.00	25.00	60.00	135
AH1277//6 (1865)	—	8.00	16.00	45.00	100
AH1277//7 (1866)	—	6.00	12.00	35.00	85.00
AH1277//8 (1867)	—	5.00	10.00	20.00	50.00
AH1277//9 (1868)	—	5.00	10.00	20.00	50.00

KM# 247a 20 PARA

0.9000 Silver **Note:** Weight varies: 0.65-0.70 grams.

Date	Mintage	F	VF	XF	Unc
AH1277//10 (1869)	—	5.00	10.00	22.00	50.00
AH1277//11 (1870)	—	5.00	10.00	22.00	50.00
AH1277//12 (1871)	—	5.00	10.00	22.00	50.00
AH1277//13 (1872)	—	7.00	15.00	40.00	80.00
AH1277//14 (1873)	—	7.00	15.00	40.00	80.00
AH1277//15 (1874)	—	18.00	35.00	75.00	150

KM# 244 20 PARA

Bronze **Obv:** Without flower at right of toughra **Note:** Weight varies: 12.10-12.70 grams. Size varies: 29.5-32 millimeters.

Date	Mintage	F	VF	XF	Unc
AH1277//3 (1862)	—	2.50	6.00	20.00	50.00
AH1277//4 (1863)	—	2.50	6.00	20.00	50.00
AH1277//5 (1864)	—	1.50	4.00	15.00	35.00
AH1277//6 (1865)	—	1.50	4.00	15.00	35.00
AH1277//7 (1866) Rare	—	—	—	—	—
AH1277//8 (1867)	—	2.00	5.00	17.50	45.00
AH1277//9 (1868)	—	1.00	3.00	12.00	35.00
AH1277//10 (1869)	—	2.00	5.00	17.50	45.00

KM# 246 20 PARA

12.5000 g., Copper **Obv:** Flower at right of toughra

Date	Mintage	F	VF	XF	Unc
AH1277//7 (1866) Rare	—	—	—	—	—
AH1277//8 (1867)	2,395,000	13.50	28.00	65.00	180
AH1277//9 (1868)	3,089,000	8.50	20.00	55.00	140
AH1277//10 (1869)	966,000	13.50	30.00	80.00	180
AH1277//11 (1870) Rare	200	—	—	—	2,500

KM# 245 20 PARA

12.5000 g., Bronze, 29 mm. **Note:** Similar, but crude and thick. Struck at Cairo.

Date	Mintage	F	VF	XF	Unc
AH1277//7 (1866)	1,190,000	200	300	600	1,250

KM# 249 40 PARA (Qirsh)

24.0000 g., Copper, 36 mm. **Obv:** Flower added at right of toughra

Date	Mintage	F	VF	XF	Unc
AH1277//9 (1868)	125	—	—	—	5,000
AH1277//10 (1869)	150,000	600	900	1,700	3,000

Note: An example of year 10 struck in gold is reported, not confirmed

Date	Mintage	F	VF	XF	Unc
AH1277//11 (1870)	200	—	—	—	5,000

KM# 248 40 PARA (Qirsh)

25.6300 g., Bronze, 37 mm. **Note:** Exists with large or small toughra, wide and narrow rim.

Date	Mintage	F	VF	XF	Unc
AH1277//10 (1869)	—	3.00	10.00	30.00	100

KM# 250 QIRSH

0.8330 Silver, 18 mm. **Note:** Weight varies: 1.18-1.25 grams.

Date	Mintage	F	VF	XF	Unc
AH1277//1 (1861)	—	25.00	45.00	100	250
AH1277//2 (1861)	—	15.00	30.00	75.00	150
AH1277//3 (1862)	—	12.00	22.00	50.00	100
AH1277//4 (1863)	—	12.00	22.00	50.00	100
AH1277//5 (1864)	—	15.00	30.00	75.00	150
AH1277//6 (1865)	—	10.00	20.00	45.00	90.00
AH1277//7 (1866)	—	7.00	15.00	40.00	80.00
AH1277//8 (1867)	—	4.00	8.00	20.00	50.00
AH1277//9 (1868)	—	4.00	8.00	20.00	50.00

KM# 250a QIRSH

0.9000 Silver **Note:** Weight varies: 1.18-1.23 grams.

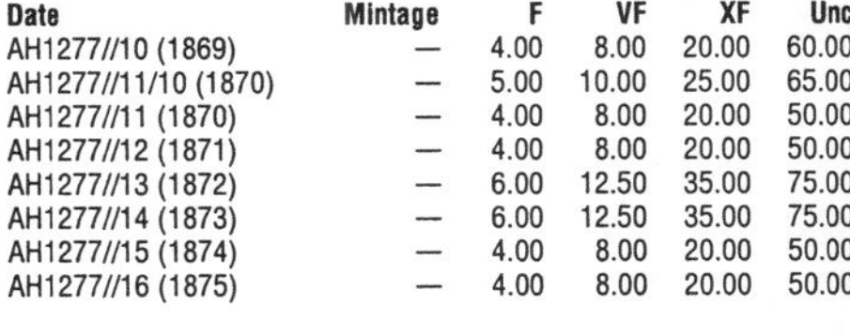

Date	Mintage	F	VF	XF	Unc
AH1277//10 (1869)	—	4.00	8.00	20.00	60.00
AH1277//11/10 (1870)	—	5.00	10.00	25.00	65.00
AH1277//11 (1870)	—	4.00	8.00	20.00	50.00
AH1277//12 (1871)	—	4.00	8.00	20.00	50.00
AH1277//13 (1872)	—	6.00	12.50	35.00	75.00
AH1277//14 (1873)	—	6.00	12.50	35.00	75.00
AH1277//15 (1874)	—	4.00	8.00	20.00	50.00
AH1277//16 (1875)	—	4.00	8.00	20.00	50.00

KM# 251 2-1/2 QIRSH

3.1500 g., 0.8330 Silver .0844 oz. ASW, 20 mm. **Obv:** Without flower at right of toughra

Date	Mintage	F	VF	XF	Unc
AH1277//4 (1863)	3,803,000	40.00	80.00	175	350

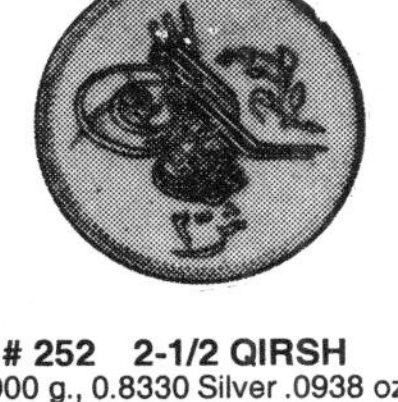

KM# 252 2-1/2 QIRSH

3.5000 g., 0.8330 Silver .0938 oz. ASW **Obv:** Flower at right of toughra

Date	Mintage	F	VF	XF	Unc
AH1277//8 (1867)	—	185	325	650	1,000
AH1277//9 (1868)	—	185	325	650	1,000

KM# 252a 2-1/2 QIRSH

3.6000 g., 0.9000 Silver .1013 oz. ASW

Date	Mintage	F	VF	XF	Unc
AH1277//10 (1869)	—	225	450	750	1,100
AH1277//11 (1870)	—	275	550	1,000	1,800
AH1277//12 (1871)	—	400	750	1,500	2,750
AH1277//13 (1872)	—	400	750	1,500	2,750
AH1277//15 (1874)	—	600	1,000	1,800	3,000

KM# 254 5 QIRSH

6.2000 g., 0.8330 Silver .1661 oz. ASW **Obv:** Flower at right of toughra **Note:** Weight varies: 6.60-7.00 grams.

Date	Mintage	F	VF	XF	Unc
AH1277//1 (1861)	—	250	550	900	1,400
AH1277//2 (1861)	—	200	450	850	1,200
AH1277//3 (1862)	—	200	450	850	1,200
AH1277//4 (1863)	—	200	450	850	1,400
AH1277//5 (1864)	—	250	600	950	2,000
AH1277//6 (1865)	—	250	600	950	2,000
AH1277//7 (1866)	—	250	600	950	2,000
AH1277//8 (1867)	—	200	450	875	1,250
AH1277//9 (1868)	—	200	450	875	1,250
AH1277//10 (1869)	—	250	600	950	2,000

KM# 255 5 QIRSH

0.4272 g., 0.8750 Gold .0120 oz. AGW

Date	Mintage	VG	F	VF	XF	Unc
AH1277//3 (1862)	—	18.00	28.00	35.00	60.00	—
AH1277//4 (1863)	—	18.00	28.00	35.00	60.00	—
AH1277//5 (1864)	—	18.00	28.00	35.00	60.00	—
AH1277//6 (1865)	—	18.00	28.00	35.00	60.00	—
AH1277//7 (1866)	—	18.00	28.00	35.00	60.00	—
AH1277//8 (1867)	—	18.00	28.00	35.00	60.00	—
AH1277//9 (1868)	—	18.00	28.00	35.00	60.00	—
AH1277//10 (1869)	—	18.00	28.00	35.00	60.00	—
AH1277//11 (1870)	—	18.00	28.00	35.00	60.00	—
AH1277//12 (1871)	—	18.00	28.00	35.00	60.00	—
AH1277//13 (1872)	—	18.00	28.00	35.00	60.00	—
AH1277//14 (1873)	—	18.00	28.00	35.00	60.00	—
AH1277//15 (1874)	—	18.00	28.00	35.00	60.00	—

KM# 253.1 5 QIRSH
6.2000 g., 0.8330 Silver .1661 oz. ASW **Obv:** Without flower at right of toughra

Date	Mintage	F	VF	XF	Unc
AH1277//4 (1863)	4,108,000	40.00	100	185	375

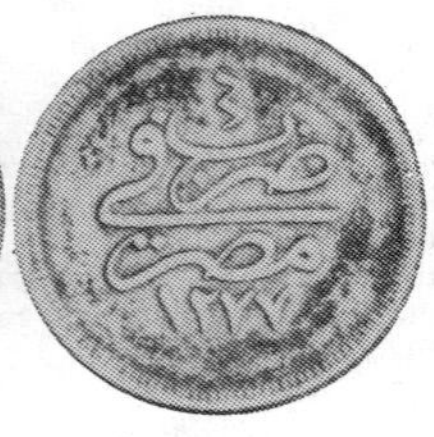

KM# 253.2 5 QIRSH
6.2000 g., 0.8330 Silver .1661 oz. ASW **Rev:** Regnal year retrograde

Date	Mintage	F	VF	XF	Unc
AH1277//4 (1863)	Inc. above	60.00	150	285	550

KM# 254a 5 QIRSH
6.2000 g., 0.8330 Silver .1661 oz. ASW **Note:** Weight varies: 6.60-7.00 grams.

Date	Mintage	F	VF	XF	Unc
AH1277//10 (1869)	—	200	450	850	1,250
AH1277//11 (1870)	—	300	600	950	1,800
AH1277//12 (1871)	—	400	700	1,350	3,000
AH1277//13 (1872)	—	400	700	1,350	3,000
AH1277//15 (1874)	—	400	700	1,350	3,000

KM# 256 10 QIRSH
14.0000 g., 0.9000 Silver .4051 oz. ASW **Obv:** Flower at right of toughra

Date	Mintage	VG	F	VF	XF	Unc
AH1277//2 (1861)	—	250	400	650	1,400	—
AH1277//3 (1862)	—	250	400	650	1,400	—
AH1277//4 (1863)	—	250	400	650	1,400	—

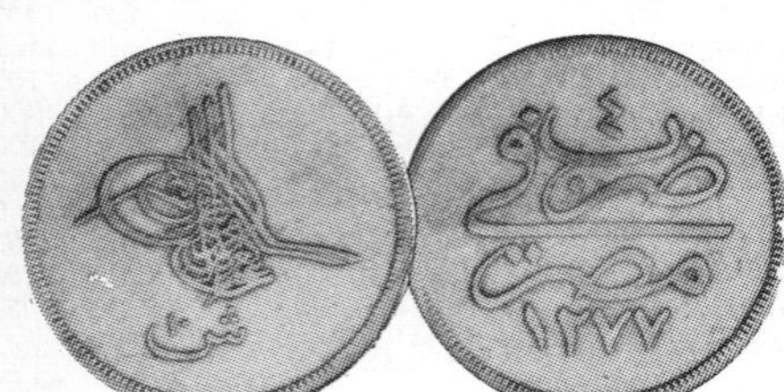

KM# 257 10 QIRSH
12.5000 g., 0.8330 Silver .3617 oz. ASW **Obv:** Without flower at right of toughra

Date	Mintage	F	VF	XF	Unc
AH1277//4 (1863)	3,803,000	60.00	120	220	500

KM# 258 10 QIRSH
14.0000 g., 0.9000 Silver .4051 oz. ASW **Note:** Similar to KM#256.

Date	Mintage	VG	F	VF	XF	Unc
AH1277//10 (1869)	—	400	800	1,400	3,000	—
AH1277//11 (1870)	—	—	—	—	—	7,500

KM# 259 10 QIRSH
0.8554 g., 0.8750 Gold .0240 oz. AGW

Date	Mintage	VG	F	VF	XF	Unc
AH1277//10 (1869)	—	45.00	65.00	80.00	110	—
AH1277//11 (1870)	—	45.00	65.00	80.00	110	—
AH1277//12 (1871)	—	45.00	65.00	80.00	110	—
AH1277//14 (1873)	—	45.00	65.00	80.00	110	—

KM# 260 20 QIRSH
28.0000 g., 0.8330 Silver .7500 oz. ASW **Obv:** Flower at right of toughra

Date	Mintage	VG	F	VF	XF	Unc
AH1277//1 (1861)	—	325	525	1,150	1,650	—
AH1277//2 (1861)	—	350	575	1,400	1,900	—

KM# 260a 20 QIRSH
28.0000 g., 0.9000 Silver .8103 oz. ASW

Date	Mintage	VG	F	VF	XF	Unc
AH1277//11 (1870)	—	—	—	—	—	12,500

KM# 261 25 QIRSH
2.1360 g., 0.8750 Gold .0601 oz. AGW

Date	Mintage	VG	F	VF	XF	Unc
AH1277//8 (1867)	—	30.00	45.00	70.00	140	—
AH1277//9 (1868)	—	30.00	45.00	70.00	140	—
AH1277//10 (1869)	—	30.00	45.00	70.00	140	—
AH1277//11 (1870)	—	30.00	45.00	70.00	140	—
AH1277//12 (1871)	—	30.00	45.00	70.00	140	—
AH1277//13 (1872)	—	45.00	70.00	115	185	—
AH1277//14 (1873)	—	45.00	70.00	115	185	—
AH1277//15 (1874)	—	45.00	70.00	115	185	—

KM# 262 50 QIRSH (1/2 Pound)
4.2740 g., 0.8750 Gold .1202 oz. AGW

Date	Mintage	VG	F	VF	XF	Unc
AH1277//11 (1870)	—	90.00	135	315	450	—
AH1277//12 (1871)	—	70.00	100	200	300	—
AH1277//13 (1872)	—	90.00	120	275	400	—
AH1277//14 (1873)	—	70.00	100	200	300	—
AH1277//15 (1874)	—	70.00	100	200	300	—
AH1277//16 (1875)	—	70.00	100	200	300	—

KM# 263 100 QIRSH (Pound)
8.5440 g., 0.8750 Gold .2404 oz. AGW **Obv:** Flower at right of toughra

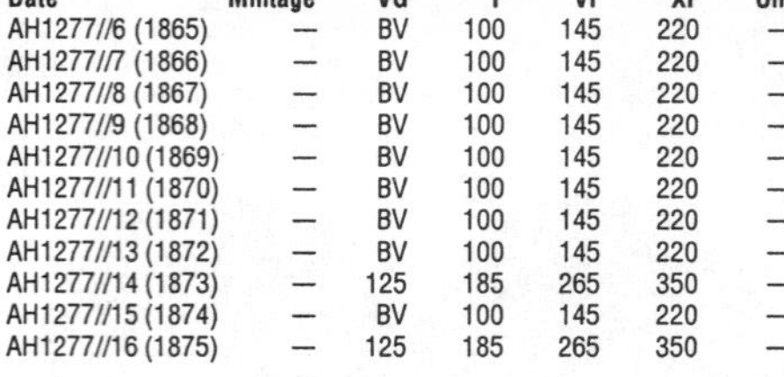

Date	Mintage	VG	F	VF	XF	Unc
AH1277//2 (1861)	—	125	165	225	300	—
AH1277//4 (1863)	—	BV	100	145	220	—
AH1277//5 (1864)	—	BV	100	145	220	—
AH1277//6 (1865)	—	BV	100	145	220	—
AH1277//7 (1866)	—	BV	100	145	220	—
AH1277//8 (1867)	—	BV	100	145	220	—
AH1277//9 (1868)	—	BV	100	145	220	—
AH1277//10 (1869)	—	BV	100	145	220	—
AH1277//11 (1870)	—	BV	100	145	220	—
AH1277//12 (1871)	—	BV	100	145	220	—
AH1277//13 (1872)	—	BV	100	145	220	—
AH1277//14 (1873)	—	125	185	265	350	—
AH1277//15 (1874)	—	BV	100	145	220	—
AH1277//16 (1875)	—	125	185	265	350	—

KM# 264 100 QIRSH (Pound)
8.5440 g., 0.8750 Gold .2404 oz. AGW **Obv:** Without flower at right of toughra

Date	Mintage	VG	F	VF	XF	Unc
AH1277//4 (1863)	20,000	150	300	600	1,000	—

KM# 265 500 QIRSH (5 Pounds)
42.7200 g., 0.8750 Gold 1.2018 oz. AGW

Date	Mintage	F	VF	XF	Unc
AH1277//[illegible] (18[illegible])	118	3,500	7,500	12,500	17,500
AH1277//9 (1868)	Inc. above	3,000	6,000	10,000	15,000
AH1277//11 (1870)	200	3,000	6,000	10,000	15,000
Note: Spink Zurich Auction 31 6-89 AU realized $13,400					
AH1277//15 (1874)	56	3,000	6,000	10,000	15,000

TOKEN COINAGE

The following token issues were struck for firms participating in the construction of the Suez Canal, and were used as currency by the company employees. All are multi-sided and appear round if the edge is not examined.

KM# Tn1 20 CENTIMES
Copper, 15 mm. **Issuer:** Ch. & A. Bazin **Note:** 16-sided.

Date	Mintage	VG	F	VF	XF	Unc
1865	—	50.00	75.00	135	220	—

KM# Tn5 20 CENTIMES
Brass **Issuer:** Borel Lavalley et Cie **Note:** 20-sided.

Date	Mintage	VG	F	VF	XF	Unc
1865	—	40.00	65.00	95.00	185	—

KM# Tn2 50 CENTIMES
Copper **Issuer:** Ch. & A. Bazin **Note:** 18-sided.

Date	Mintage	VG	F	VF	XF	Unc
1865	—	125	150	200	320	—

KM# Tn6 50 CENTIMES
Brass **Issuer:** Borel Lavalley et Cie **Note:** 24-sided.

Date	Mintage	VG	F	VF	XF	Unc
1865	—	35.00	60.00	90.00	175	—

KM# Tn3 FRANC
Copper, 5 mm. **Issuer:** Ch. & A. Bazin **Note:** 24-sided.

Date	Mintage	VG	F	VF	XF	Unc
1865	—	125	150	200	320	—

KM# Tn7 FRANC
Brass **Issuer:** Borel Lavalley et Cie **Note:** 24-sided.

Date	Mintage	VG	F	VF	XF	Unc
1865	—	65.00	100	150	265	—

KM# Tn8 5 FRANCS
Brass **Issuer:** Borel Lavalley et Cie

Date	Mintage	VG	F	VF	XF	Unc
1865 Rare	—	—	—	—	—	—

Note: The only known example of KM#Tn8 was illustrated in Wayte Raymond's "Coins of the World" nineteenth century issues and is not to be confused with the modern fantasies encountered in today's market

KM# Tn4 5 FRANCS
Copper **Issuer:** Ch. & A. Bazin **Note:** 29-sided.

Date	Mintage	VG	F	VF	XF	Unc
1865	—	250	350	550	900	—

Murad V
AH1293/1876AD

REFORM COINAGE

KM# 270 QIRSH
0.900 Silver 1.2000 oz. AGW **Obv:** Toughra of Murad V

Date	Mintage	F	VF	XF	Unc
AH1293//1 (1876)	—	100	150	300	500

KM# 271 50 QIRSH (1/2 Pound)
4.2740 g., 0.8750 Gold .1202 oz. AGW **Obv:** Toughra of Murad V

Date	Mintage	VG	F	VF	XF	Unc
AH1293//1 (1876)	—	375	650	1,000	1,500	—

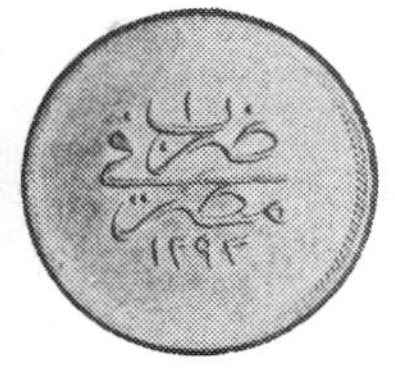

KM# 272 100 QIRSH (Pound)
8.5440 g., 0.8750 Gold .2402 oz. AGW **Obv:** Toughra of Murad V

Date	Mintage	VG	F	VF	XF	Unc
AH1293//1 (1876)	—	400	750	1,250	1,750	—

Abdul Hamid II
AH1293-1327/1876-1909AD

REFORM COINAGE

KM# 275 10 PARA
0.8330 Silver **Note:** Mintname, Misr.

Date	Mintage	F	VF	XF	Unc
AH1293/1 (1876)	—	60.00	100	140	320
AH1293/2 (1877)	—	70.00	110	175	425
AH1293/3 (1878)	—	60.00	100	140	320

KM# 287 1/40 QIRSH
Bronze **Note:** Mintname Misr.

Date	Mintage	F	VF	XF	Unc
AH1293/10 (1884)	1,669,000	1.00	2.50	5.00	15.00
AH1293/12 (1886)	2,476,000	1.00	2.50	4.00	15.00
AH1293/18 (1892)	—	40.00	60.00	100	160
AH1293/19 (1893)	—	1.00	2.50	5.00	15.00
AH1293/20 (1894)	—	5.00	10.00	20.00	40.00
AH1293/24 (1898)	1,601,000	1.00	2.50	5.00	15.00
AH1293/26 (1900)	1,999,000	1.00	2.00	4.00	15.00

KM# 288 1/20 QIRSH
Bronze **Note:** Mintname Misr.

Date	Mintage	F	VF	XF	Unc
AH1293/10 (1884)	4,105,000	1.00	2.00	4.00	12.00
AH1293/12 (1886)	4,457,000	1.00	2.00	4.00	12.00
AH1293/18 (1892)	—	10.00	20.00	30.00	75.00
AH1293/19 (1893)	—	2.50	5.00	10.00	20.00
AH1293/20 (1894)	—	8.00	15.00	30.00	75.00
AH1293/21 (1895)	—	2.00	3.50	10.00	20.00
AH1293/24 (1898)	801,000	1.00	3.00	5.00	15.00
AH1293/26 (1900)	1,405,000	1.00	2.00	3.00	12.00

KM# 289 1/10 QIRSH
Copper-Nickel **Note:** Mintname Misr.

Date	Mintage	F	VF	XF	Unc
AH1293/10 (1884)	2,307,000	1.00	1.50	4.00	12.50
AH1293/12 (1886)	3,435,000	1.00	1.50	4.00	12.50
AH1293/18 (1892)	—	6.00	12.00	30.00	75.00
AH1293/19 (1893)	—	1.00	1.50	5.00	15.00
AH1293/20 (1894)	—	1.00	1.50	5.00	15.00
AH1293/21 (1895)	—	1.00	1.50	5.00	15.00
AH1293/22 (1896)	—	4.00	10.00	20.00	60.00
AH1293/23 (1897)	—	1.00	1.50	6.00	17.50
AH1293/24 (1898)	1,004,999	1.00	1.50	4.00	12.50
AH1293/25 (1899)	2,000,000	1.00	1.50	5.00	15.00
AH1293/27-35 (1901) Proof	—	Value: 100			

Note: Above value for common date proof

KM# 290 2/10 QIRSH
Copper-Nickel **Note:** Mintname Misr.

Date	Mintage	F	VF	XF	Unc
AH1293/10 (1884)	3,201,000	1.00	3.00	6.00	20.00
AH1293/12 (1886)	2,009,000	1.00	3.00	6.00	20.00
AH1293/20 (1894)	—	8.00	15.00	30.00	75.00
AH1293/21 (1895)	500,000	2.00	6.00	12.00	40.00
AH1293/24 (1898)	500,000	1.00	3.00	6.00	20.00
AH1293/25 (1899)	250,000	3.00	5.00	10.00	35.00

KM# 276 20 PARA
0.5500 g., 0.8330 Silver 0.147 oz. ASW **Note:** Mintname, Misr.

Date	Mintage	F	VF	XF	Unc
AH1293/1 (1876)	—	65.00	110	150	400
AH1293/2 (1877)	—	60.00	100	125	375
AH1293/3 (1878)	—	65.00	110	150	400
AH1293/5 (1879)	—	—	—	750	1,000

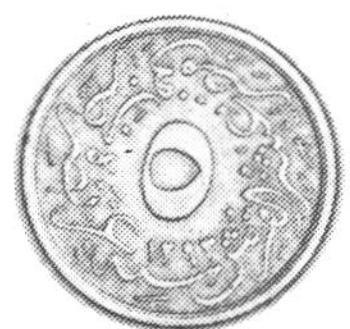

KM# 291 5/10 QIRSH
Copper-Nickel **Note:** Mintname Misr.

Date	Mintage	F	VF	XF	Unc
AH1293/10 (1884)	7,003,000	2.00	4.00	12.50	40.00
AH1293/11 (1885)	10,005,000	0.50	2.00	6.00	20.00
AH1293/13 (1887)	5,003,000	0.50	2.00	6.00	20.00
AH1293/20 (1894)	1,002,000	3.00	10.00	20.00	60.00
AH1293/21 (1895)	3,404,000	0.65	2.50	7.50	25.00
AH1293/23 (1897)	1,000,000	2.50	5.00	12.50	40.00
AH1293/24 (1898)	3,605,000	0.45	2.00	6.00	20.00
AH1293/25 (1899)	1,998,000	0.45	2.00	6.00	20.00
AH1293/27-33 (1901) Proof	—	Value: 145			

Note: Above value for common date proof

KM# 277 QIRSH
0.8330 Silver

Date	Mintage	F	VF	XF	Unc
AH1293//1 (1876)	—	3.00	10.00	20.00	65.00
AH1293//2 (1877)	—	3.00	10.00	18.00	55.00
AH1293//3 (1878)	—	2.50	8.00	15.00	45.00
AH1293//4 (1878)	—	3.00	10.00	18.00	55.00
AH1293//5 (1879)	—	4.00	12.00	20.00	65.00

KM# A278 QIRSH
0.9000 Silver **Obv:** KM#250a **Rev:** KM#270 **Note:** Mule. Weight varies: 1.18-1.23 grams.

Date	Mintage	F	VF	XF	Unc
AH1293//1 (1876) Rare	—	—	—	—	—

KM# 292 QIRSH
1.4000 g., 0.8330 Silver .0375 oz. ASW **Note:** Mintname Misr.

Date	Mintage	F	VF	XF	Unc
AH1293/10 (1884) W	8,192,000	1.00	3.00	7.50	20.00
AH1293/17 (1891) W	546,000	1.00	4.00	10.00	30.00

KM# 299 QIRSH
Copper-Nickel **Note:** Mintname Misr.

Date	Mintage	F	VF	XF	Unc
AH1293/22 (1896)	200,000	10.00	25.00	45.00	100
AH1293/23 (1897)	1,500,000	2.00	6.00	20.00	50.00
AH1293/25 (1899)	751,000	3.00	8.00	30.00	60.00

KM# 293 2 QIRSH

2.8000 g., 0.8330 Silver **Obv:** Flower to right of toughra **Note:** Mintname Misr.

Date	Mintage	F	VF	XF	Unc
AH1293/10 (1884) W	4,011,000	1.00	3.00	7.50	30.00
AH1293/11 (1885) W	989,000	2.00	5.00	12.50	35.00
AH1293/17 (1891) W	540,000	2.00	5.00	12.50	35.00
AH1293/20 (1894) W	1,113,000	2.00	5.00	12.50	40.00
AH1293/24 (1898) W	500,000	2.00	5.00	12.50	50.00
AH1293/17-33 (1901) Proof	—	Value: 145			

Note: Above value for common date of proof

KM# 278 2-1/2 QIRSH

3.4600 g., 0.8330 Silver .0927 oz. ASW **Note:** Mintname, Misr

Date	Mintage	F	VF	XF	Unc
AH1293/6 (1880)	2	—	—	—	4,500

KM# 280 5 QIRSH

0.4200 g., 0.8750 Gold .0118 oz. AGW **Obv:** Flower at right of toughra

Date	Mintage	VG	F	VF	XF	Unc
AH1293//2 (1877)	—	90.00	180	375	750	—
AH1293//3 (1878)	—	35.00	60.00	75.00	100	—
AH1293//5 (1879)	—	90.00	135	185	250	—
AH1293//6 (1880)	—	135	225	350	650	—
AH1293//7 (1881)	—	35.00	60.00	75.00	100	—
AH1293//22 (1896)	—	90.00	135	185	285	—

KM# 279 5 QIRSH

6.9200 g., 0.8330 Silver .1854 oz. ASW **Obv:** Flower at right of toughra **Note:** Mintname, Misr

Date	Mintage	F	VF	XF	Unc
AH1293/2 (1877)	—	700	1,200	1,800	—
AH1293/6 (1880)	2	—	—	—	4,000

KM# A299 5 QIRSH

0.4200 g., 0.8750 Gold .0118 oz. AGW **Rev:** Legend in wreath

Date	Mintage	VG	F	VF	XF	Unc
AH1293//15 (1889)	—	100	200	350	600	—

KM# 298 5 QIRSH

0.4200 g., 0.8750 Gold .0118 oz. AGW **Obv:** "Al-Ghazi" at right of toughra

Date	Mintage	VG	F	VF	XF	Unc
AH1293//15 (1889)	—	—	—	—	—	—
AH1293//16 (1890)	—	—	—	—	—	—
AH1293//18 (1892)	—	—	—	—	—	—
AH1293//24 (1898)	—	—	—	—	—	—
AH1293//26 (1900)	—	—	—	—	—	—
AH1293//34 (1908)	8,000	—	—	—	—	—

KM# A282 10 QIRSH

0.8544 g., 0.8750 Gold .0240 oz. AGW **Obv:** Flower at right of toughra

Date	Mintage	VG	F	VF	XF	Unc
AH1293//4 (1878)	—	300	500	900	1,500	—

KM# 281 10 QIRSH

14.0000 g., 0.8330 Silver .3749 oz. ASW **Obv:** Flower at right of toughra

Date	Mintage	F	VF	XF	Unc
AH1293//6 (1880)	2	—	—	—	6,000

KM# 295 10 QIRSH

14.0000 g., 0.8330 Silver .3749 oz. ASW **Obv:** Flower at right of toughra **Note:** Mintname Misr.

Date	Mintage	F	VF	XF	Unc
AH1293/10 (1884) W	4,030,000	5.00	10.00	35.00	100
AH1293/11 (1885) W	Inc. above	8.00	15.00	40.00	100
AH1293/15 (1889) W	300,000	15.00	30.00	65.00	150
AH1293/15 (1889) W Proof	—	Value: 450			
AH1293/16 (1890) W	602,000	8.00	15.00	45.00	125
AH1293/17 (1891) W	380,000	10.00	20.00	55.00	150
AH1293/20 (1894) W	340,000	15.00	30.00	55.00	150
AH1293/21 (1895) W	420,000	10.00	20.00	45.00	125
AH1293/22 (1896) W	600,000	10.00	20.00	45.00	125
AH1293/24 (1898) W	500,000	10.00	20.00	45.00	125

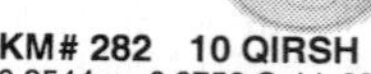

KM# 282 10 QIRSH

0.8544 g., 0.8750 Gold .0240 oz. AGW **Obv:** Al-Ghazi at right of toughra **Note:** Mintname: Misr.

Date	Mintage	VG	F	VF	XF	Unc
AH1293/17 (1891)	—	20.00	40.00	65.00	110	—
AH1293/18 (1892)	—	25.00	50.00	75.00	115	—
AH1293/23 (1897)	—	35.00	55.00	85.00	130	—

KM# 283 20 QIRSH

27.5700 g., 0.8330 Silver .7385 oz. ASW

Date	Mintage	VG	F	VF	XF	Unc
AH1293//1 (1876)	—	550	900	1,500	2,000	—
AH1293//5 (1879)	—	650	1,750	2,500	3,500	—
AH1293//6 (1880)	2	—	—	—	12,500	—

KM# 296 20 QIRSH

28.0000 g., 0.8330 Silver .7499 oz. ASW **Note:** Mintname Misr.

Date	Mintage	VG	F	VF	XF	Unc
AH1293/10 W	874,000	—	12.00	25.00	70.00	375
AH1293/11 W	126,000	—	15.00	40.00	100	425
AH1293/15 W	29,000	—	17.50	50.00	150	500
AH1293/16 W	55,000	—	15.00	40.00	100	425
AH1293/17 W	54,000	—	17.50	50.00	150	500
AH1293/17 W Proof	—	Value: 800				
AH1293/20 W	172,000	—	12.00	40.00	100	425
AH1293/21 W	158,000	—	12.00	30.00	85.00	400
AH1293/22 W	287,000	—	12.00	30.00	85.00	400
AH1293/24 W	500,000	—	12.00	30.00	85.00	400

KM# A284 25 QIRSH

2.1360 g., 0.8750 Gold .0601 oz. AGW **Obv:** Flower at right of toughra

Date	Mintage	F	VF	XF	Unc
AH1293//2 (1877)	—	—	—	—	—
Note: Reported, not confirmed					
AH1293//6 (1880)	2	—	—	—	8,500

KM# 284 50 QIRSH (1/2 Pound)

4.2720 g., 0.8750 Gold .1202 oz. AGW

Date	Mintage	VG	F	VF	XF	Unc
AH1293//6 (1880)	2	—	—	—	9,000	—

KM# 285 100 QIRSH (Pound)

8.5440 g., 0.8750 Gold .2404 oz. AGW **Obv:** Toughra of Abdul Hamid II

Date	Mintage	F	VF	XF	Unc
AH1293//1 (1876)	—	400	800	1,350	2,250
AH1293//4 (1878)	—	400	800	1,350	2,250
AH1293//6 (1880)	4	—	—	—	9,500
AH1293//8 (1882) Rare	—	—	—	—	—

KM# 297 100 QIRSH (Pound)

8.5000 g., 0.8750 Gold .2391 oz. AGW **Note:** Floral border.

Date	Mintage	F	VF	XF	Unc
AH1293//12 (1886)	52,000	120	150	185	280

KM# 286 500 QIRSH (5 Pounds)

42.7400 g., 0.8750 Gold 1.2024 oz. AGW

Date	Mintage	F	VF	XF	Unc
AH1293//1 (1876)	—	1,450	3,250	5,000	8,000
AH1293//6 (1880)	5	3,000	6,000	10,000	15,000

Note: Spinks & Son Zurich Auction 18 2-86 super Unc. realized $14,520; Although the mint report documents only five pieces, perhaps ten pieces are thought to exist

TOKEN COINAGE

The following token issues were struck for firms participating in the construction of the Suez Canal, and were used as currency by the company employees. All are multi-sided and appear round if the edge is not examined.

KM# Tn13 5 CENTIMES

Aluminum, 17.5 mm. **Issuer:** Societe Cooperative du Canal de Suez **Note:** Similar to 1 Franc Tn11, but octagonal.

Date	Mintage	F	VF	XF	Unc
1892	—	—	—	—	—

KM# Tn9 10 CENTIMES

Aluminum, 20.5 mm. **Issuer:** Societe Cooperative du Canal de Suez **Note:** Similar to 1 Franc Tn11, but octagonal.

Date	Mintage	F	VF	XF	Unc
1892	—	100	200	300	500

KM# Tn10 50 CENTIMES

Aluminum, 24.5 mm. **Issuer:** Societe Cooperative du Canal de Suez **Note:** Similar to 1 Franc Tn11, but octagonal.

Date	Mintage	F	VF	XF	Unc
1892	—	125	225	350	550

KM# Tn11 FRANC

Aluminum **Issuer:** Societe Cooperative du Canal de Suez

Date	Mintage	F	VF	XF	Unc
1892	—	—	—	1,200	—

Note: 1 known.

KM# Tn12 2 FRANCS

Aluminum, 26 mm. **Issuer:** Societe Cooperative du Canal de Suez **Note:** Similar to 1 Franc Tn11.

Date	Mintage	F	VF	XF	Unc
1892	—	150	250	375	600

KM# Tn14 5 FRANCS

Aluminum, 32 mm. **Issuer:** Societe Cooperative du Canal de Suez **Note:** Similar to 1 Franc Tn11.

Date	Mintage	F	VF	XF	Unc
1892	—	—	—	—	—

PATTERNS

Including off metal strikes

KM#	Date	Mintage	Identification	Mkt Val
Pn2	1277//4	—	4 Para. Bronze. ESSAI.	350
Pn4	1277//4	—	25 Qirsh. 0.8750 Gold. Plain edge. Without flower.	—
Pn5	1277//4	—	50 Qirsh. 0.8750 Gold. Plain edge. Without flower.	—

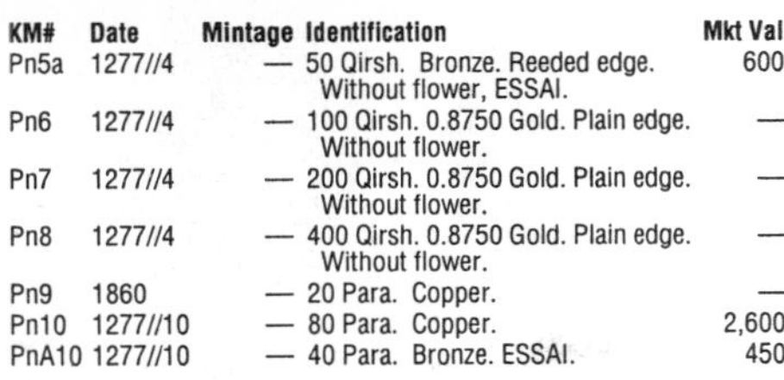

KM#	Date	Mintage	Identification	Mkt Val
Pn5a	1277//4	—	50 Qirsh. Bronze. Reeded edge. Without flower, ESSAI.	600
Pn6	1277//4	—	100 Qirsh. 0.8750 Gold. Plain edge. Without flower.	—
Pn7	1277//4	—	200 Qirsh. 0.8750 Gold. Plain edge. Without flower.	—
Pn8	1277//4	—	400 Qirsh. 0.8750 Gold. Plain edge. Without flower.	—
Pn9	1860	—	20 Para. Copper.	—
Pn10	1277//10	—	80 Para. Copper.	2,600
PnA10	1277//10	—	40 Para. Bronze. ESSAI.	450

KM#	Date	Mintage	Identification	Mkt Val
Pn11	1277//10	—	80 Para. Bronze. Struck on France, 10 Centimes, Y#21.3.	—

KM#	Date	Mintage	Identification	Mkt Val
Pn12	1279	—	20 Para. Said Pasha.	450
Pn13	1293//9	—	1/40 Qirsh. Bronze.	—
Pn14	1293//9	—	1/20 Qirsh. Bronze.	1,100
Pn15	1293//9	—	1/10 Qirsh. Nickel.	1,600
Pn16	1293//9	—	2/10 Qirsh. Nickel.	1,600
Pn17	1293//9	—	5/10 Qirsh. Nickel.	1,600
Pn18	1293//9	—	Qirsh. Nickel.	1,600
Pn19	1293//9	—	2 Qirsh. Silver.	1,600
Pn20	1293//9	—	5 Qirsh. Silver.	1,600
Pn21	1293//9	—	10 Qirsh. Silver.	2,600

KM#	Date	Mintage	Identification	Mkt Val
Pn22	1293//9	—	20 Qirsh. Silver.	2,600
Pn23	1293//11	—	100 Qirsh. Copper.	500
Pn24	1293//15	—	5 Qirsh. Gold.	750
Pn25	1293//19	—	1/40 Qirsh. Silver. KM#287.	550

PIEFORTS

KM#	Date	Mintage	Identification	Mkt Val
PA1	1277//10	—	80 Para. Nickel. 16.8000 g.Three millimeters thick.	450

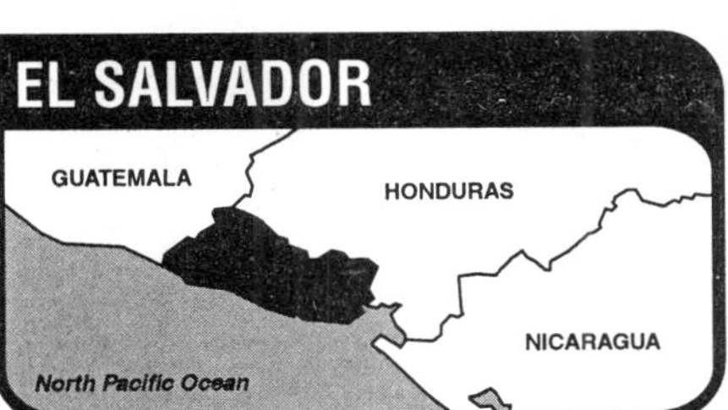

The Republic of El Salvador, a Central American country bordered by Guatemala, Honduras and the Pacific Ocean, has an area of 8,124 sq. mi. (21,040 sq. km.) and a population of 6.0 million. Capital: San Salvador. This most intensely cultivated of Latin America countries produces coffee (the major crop), sugar and balsam for export. Gold, silver and other metals are largely unexploited.

The first Spanish attempt to subjugate the area was undertaken in 1523 by Pedro de Alvarado, Cortes' lieutenant. He was forced to retreat by Indian forces, but returned in 1525 and succeeded in bringing the region under control of the Captaincy General of Guatemala. In 1821, El Salvador and the other Central American provinces jointly declared independence from Spain. In 1823, the Republic of Central America was formed by the five Central American states; this federation dissolved in 1839. El Salvador then became an independent republic in 1841.

MINT MARKS

C.A.M. - Central American Mint, San Salvador
H - Heaton Mint, Birmingham
S - San Francisco
Mo - Mexico

STATE OF EL SALVADOR

Under the Central American Federation 1828-1840

PROVISIONAL COINAGE

16 Reales = 1 Escudo

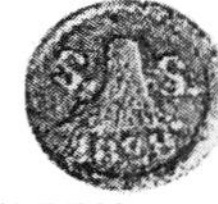

KM# 1 1/4 REAL

0.9030 Silver .0305 oz. **Obv:** Volcano between S.-S., date below **Rev:** Column with liberty cap on top between 1/4-1/4 **Note:** Issued during the siege of San Salvador, from March to October 1828.

Date	Mintage	Good	VG	F	VF	XF
1828 3 known; Rare	—	—	—	—	—	—

KM# 14 1/2 REAL

1.5000 g., 0.6330 Silver .0305 oz. **Obv:** Star above volcano within branches **Obv. Legend:** POR LA LIVERTAD DEL SAL **Rev:** Halo above column within branches **Rev. Legend:** MONEDA PROVISIONAL

Date	Mintage	Good	VG	F	VF	XF
1833	—	250	450	800	1,350	—

KM# 21.1 1/2 REAL

1.2000 g., 0.7000 Silver .0270 oz. **Obv:** S - volcano - S above water within circle **Obv. Legend:** POR LA LIBERTAD DEL SAL **Rev:** Liberty cap over 1. - column - 1/2 over water

Date	Mintage	Good	VG	F	VF	XF
1835	—	185	375	700	1,150	—

KM# 21.2 1/2 REAL

1.2000 g., 0.7000 Silver .0270 oz. **Obv:** S - volcano - S above water within circle **Obv. Legend:** POR LA LIBERTAD DEL SAL

Date	Mintage	Good	VG	F	VF	XF
1835	—	200	400	725	1,200	—
1835 retrograde 2 in 1/2	—	220	425	750	1,250	—

KM# 21.3 1/2 REAL

1.2000 g., 0.7000 Silver .0270 oz. **Obv:** Star above S - volcano - S above water **Obv. Legend:** POR LA LIBERTAD DEL SALVA **Rev:** Liberty cap over column: 1 - column - M **Rev. Legend:** MONEDA PROVISIONAL

Date	Mintage	Good	VG	F	VF	XF
1835	—	185	375	700	1,150	—

KM# 17 REAL
2.7000 g., 0.6330 Silver .0550 oz. **Obv:** Star above volcano within branches **Obv. Legend:** ESTADO DEL SALVADOR **Rev:** Star in branches above 1. - column - R. within branches **Rev. Legend:** MONEDA PROVISIONAL IND*

Date	Mintage	Good	VG	F	VF	XF
1833	—	75.00	150	250	375	—

KM# 18.1 REAL
3.4000 g., 0.6330 Silver .0692 oz. **Obv. Legend:** POR LA LIVERTAD DEL SALVADOR **Rev:** 1. - (thin) column - R. within branches

Date	Mintage	Good	VG	F	VF	XF
1833	—	50.00	100	175	300	—

KM# 18.2 REAL
3.4000 g., 0.6330 Silver .0692 oz. **Obv:** Similar to KM#18.1 **Rev:** 1. - (thick) column - R. within branches

Date	Mintage	Good	VG	F	VF	XF
1833	—	50.00	100	175	300	—

KM# 18.3 REAL
3.4000 g., 0.6330 Silver .0692 oz. **Obv. Legend:** POR LA LIVERTAD DEL SALVADOR* **Rev:** Similar to KM#18.2

Date	Mintage	Good	VG	F	VF	XF
1833	—	50.00	100	175	300	—

KM# 18.4 REAL
3.4000 g., 0.6330 Silver .0692 oz. **Obv:** Star above volcano above water in 1/2 circle of stars

Date	Mintage	Good	VG	F	VF	XF
1833	—	75.00	150	250	375	—

KM# 18.5 REAL
2.7000 g., 0.6330 Silver .0550 oz. **Obv:** Volcano within branches **Obv. Legend:** POR LA LIVERTAD DE SAL **Rev:** Column within branches **Rev. Legend:** MONEDA PROVISIONAL IND

Date	Mintage	Good	VG	F	VF	XF
1834	—	75.00	150	250	375	—

KM# 18.6 REAL
2.4000 g., 0.7000 Silver .0540 oz. **Obv:** Star above S. - volcano - S. within circle **Obv. Legend:** POR LA LIVERTAD DEL SAL **Rev:** Liberty cap above I. - column - R., water below thin circle **Rev. Legend:** MONEDA PROVISIONAL

Date	Mintage	Good	VG	F	VF	XF
1835	—	50.00	115	175	300	—

KM# 18.7 REAL
2.4000 g., 0.7000 Silver .0540 oz. **Obv. Legend:** POR LA LIVERTAD DEL SAL

Date	Mintage	Good	VG	F	VF	XF
1835 NA	—	75.00	150	250	375	—
ND	—	—	—	—	—	—

KM# 18.8 REAL
2.4000 g., 0.7000 Silver .0540 oz. **Obv:** Star above S - volcano - S above water within circle **Obv. Legend:** POR LIBERTAD DEL SAL **Note:** Varieties also exist with 2 or 3 dots after SAL.

Date	Mintage	Good	VG	F	VF	XF
1835	—	50.00	115	175	300	—

KM# 18.9 REAL
2.4000 g., 0.7000 Silver .0540 oz. **Obv. Legend:** POR LA LIBERTAD DEL SAL

Date	Mintage	Good	VG	F	VF	XF
1835	—	50.00	115	175	300	—

KM# 18.10 REAL
2.4000 g., 0.7000 Silver .0540 oz. **Obv:** Star above S - volcano - S above water within circle **Obv. Legend:** POR LA LIBERTAD DEL SA:

Date	Mintage	Good	VG	F	VF	XF
1835	—	50.00	115	200	325	—

KM# 18.11 REAL
2.4000 g., 0.7000 Silver .0540 oz. **Obv:** Star above S - volcano - S above water within circle **Obv. Legend:** POR LA LIBERTAD DE SALV

Date	Mintage	Good	VG	F	VF	XF
1835	—	50.00	115	175	300	—

KM# 4 2 REALES
4.7000 g., 0.9030 Silver .1365 oz. **Obv:** Liberty cap above 2. column - R. above water **Obv. Legend:** POR LA LIVERTAD. SALV **Rev:** Volcano **Rev. Legend:** MONEDA PROVISIONAL **Note:** Issued during siege of San Salvador by Federation and Guatemalan armies, from March to October 1828.

Date	Mintage	Good	VG	F	VF	XF
1828 FP	—	30.00	55.00	100	185	—

KM# 5.1 2 REALES
4.7000 g., 0.9030 Silver .1365 oz. **Obv:** Inner circle added **Note:** Issued during siege of San Salvador, from March to October 1828.

Date	Mintage	Good	VG	F	VF	XF
1828 FP	—	30.00	55.00	100	185	—
1828 F	—	35.00	65.00	125	225	—

KM# 5.2 2 REALES
4.7000 g., 0.9030 Silver .1365 oz. **Obv. Legend:** POR LA LIBERTAD. SALB. **Note:** Issued during siege of San Salvador, from March to October 1828.

Date	Mintage	Good	VG	F	VF	XF
1828 FP	—	30.00	55.00	100	185	—

KM# 6.1 2 REALES
4.7000 g., 0.9030 Silver .1365 oz. **Obv. Legend:** POR LA LIBERTAD SALVAD **Rev. Legend:** MONEDA PROBISIONAL

Date	Mintage	Good	VG	F	VF	XF
1829 RL	—	35.00	75.00	150	250	—

KM# 6.2 2 REALES
4.7000 g., 0.9030 Silver .1365 oz. **Obv. Legend:** POR LA LIBERTAD SALVAD **Note:** Previous KM#5.4.

Date	Mintage	Good	VG	F	VF	XF
1829 RL	—	35.00	65.00	125	280	—

KM# 6.3 2 REALES
4.7000 g., 0.9030 Silver .1365 oz. **Obv. Legend:** POR LA LIBERTAD SALVADOR **Note:** Previous KM#5.5.

Date	Mintage	Good	VG	F	VF	XF
1829	—	35.00	65.00	125	200	—

KM# 6.4 2 REALES
4.7000 g., 0.9030 Silver .1365 oz. **Obv:** Without waves beneath volcano **Obv. Legend:** POR LA LIBERTAD SALVADOR **Note:** Previous KM#5.5.

Date	Mintage	Good	VG	F	VF	XF
1829 RL	—	40.00	80.00	150	250	—

KM# 11.1 2 REALES
0.7500 Silver **Obv:** Star above S - volcano - S. above water **Obv. Legend:** POR LA LIBERTAD DEL SALVADR **Rev:** Liberty cap above 2 - column - R **Note:** Weight varies 5.6-6.3 g.

Date	Mintage	Good	VG	F	VF	XF
1832	—	35.00	65.00	125	200	—

KM# 11.2 2 REALES
0.7500 Silver **Obv. Legend:** POR LA LIBERTAD DEL SALVADOR **Rev:** Liberty cap above 2 - column - R between sprays within dotted circle

Date	Mintage	Good	VG	F	VF	XF
1832 RL	—	35.00	65.00	125	200	—

KM# 11.3 2 REALES
0.7500 Silver **Rev:** 2 - column - R within solid circle

Date	Mintage	Good	VG	F	VF	XF
1832 RL	—	35.00	65.00	125	200	—

KM# 11.4 2 REALES
0.7500 Silver **Obv. Legend:** POR LA LIBERTAD SALVADORE

Date	Mintage	Good	VG	F	VF	XF
1832	—	35.00	65.00	125	200	—

KM# 11.5 2 REALES
0.7500 Silver **Obv. Legend:** POR LA LIBERTAD DEL SALVADO

Date	Mintage	Good	VG	F	VF	XF
1832 RL	—	35.00	65.00	125	200	—

KM# 11.6 2 REALES
5.4000 g., 0.6330 Silver .1099 oz. **Obv:** Star above retrograde S - volcano - S above water **Obv. Legend:** POR LA LIVERTAD DEL SALV **Rev:** Liberty cap above 2. - column - R within branches

Date	Mintage	Good	VG	F	VF	XF
1833	—	35.00	65.00	125	200	—
1834/3T	—	40.00	80.00	150	250	—

KM# 11.7 2 REALES
5.4000 g., 0.6330 Silver .1099 oz. **Obv:** Regular S' recut above retrograde S'

Date	Mintage	Good	VG	F	VF	XF
1834/3	—	40.00	80.00	150	250	—

KM# 11.8 2 REALES
5.4000 g., 0.6330 Silver .1099 oz. **Obv:** Star above S - volcano - S above water **Obv. Legend:** POR LA LIBERTAD DEL SALVA **Note:** Varieties exist with 2 or 3 dots after SALVA.

Date	Mintage	Good	VG	F	VF	XF
1833 RL	—	35.00	65.00	125	200	—

KM# 11.9 2 REALES
5.4000 g., 0.6330 Silver .1099 oz. **Obv. Legend:** POR LA LIBERTAD DEL SALVAD

Date	Mintage	Good	VG	F	VF	XF
1833/2 RL	—	40.00	80.00	150	250	—
1833 RL	—	35.00	65.00	125	200	—

KM# 11.10 2 REALES
5.4000 g., 0.6330 Silver .1099 oz. **Obv. Legend:** POR LA LIBERTAD DEL SALV

Date	Mintage	Good	VG	F	VF	XF
1833 L	—	35.00	65.00	125	200	—

KM# 11.11 2 REALES
5.4000 g., 0.6330 Silver **Obv. Legend:** LIBERTAD SALVO DORENO

Date	Mintage	Good	VG	F	VF	XF
1833	—	35.00	65.00	125	200	—

KM# 11.12 2 REALES
5.4000 g., 0.6330 Silver .1099 oz. **Obv. Legend:** POR LA LIBERTAD DEL SALVADOR

Date	Mintage	Good	VG	F	VF	XF
1833 RL	—	35.00	65.00	125	200	—

KM# 11.13 2 REALES
5.4000 g., 0.6330 Silver .1099 oz. **Obv. Legend:** POR LA LIBERTAD DEL SALV **Rev. Legend:** MONEDA PROVISIONAL with retrograde "S"

Date	Mintage	Good	VG	F	VF	XF
1834	—	40.00	75.00	135	240	—

KM# 11.14 2 REALES
5.4000 g., 0.6330 Silver .1099 oz. **Obv. Legend:** POR LA LIBERTAD DEL SALV **Rev. Legend:** MONEDA PROVISIONAL with retrograde "N" **Note:** The one known example of this variety grades G/VG.

Date	Mintage	Good	VG	F	VF	XF
1834 1 known	—	300	485	—	—	—

KM# 11.16 2 REALES
0.7500 Silver **Obv:** Without waves beneath volcano, denomination flanks volcano, within dotted circle **Obv. Legend:** POR LA LIBERTAD SALVADOR

Date	Mintage	Good	VG	F	VF	XF
1832	—	40.00	80.00	150	250	—

KM# 8.1 4 REALES
9.4000 g., 0.9030 Silver .2729 oz. **Obv:** Liberty cap above column between retrograde R. - 4 **Obv. Legend:** POR LA LIBERTAD SALV **Note:** Issued during the siege of San Salvador, from March to October 1828.

Date	Mintage	Good	VG	F	VF	XF
1828	—	1,000	2,000	3,250	5,750	—

KM# 8.2 4 REALES
9.4000 g., 0.9030 Silver .2729 oz. **Obv:** Corrected 4. - R **Obv. Legend:** POR LA LIBERTAD DEL SALV **Rev. Legend:** MONEDA PROVISIONAL **Note:** Issued during the siege of San Salvador, from March to October 1828.

Date	Mintage	Good	VG	F	VF	XF
1828 F	—	1,250	2,250	3,500	6,000	—

COUNTERMARKED COINAGE

SAP Monogram

No documentary evidence has been found linking the SAP monogram to El Salvador as yet. While this monogram has previously been attributed to El Salvador and to some Caribbean Islands as well, its inclusion here is for reference purposes only.

KM# 24.1 2 REALES
Silver **Countermark:** SAP monogram **Note:** Countermark on El Salvador 2 Reales, KM#5.

CM Date	Host Date	Good	VG	F	VF	XF
ND(ca.1836)	ND1828 FP	—	—	—	—	—
ND(ca.1836)	ND1829 RL	—	—	—	—	—

KM# 25 2 REALES
Silver **Countermark:** SAP monogram **Note:** Countermark on Central American Republic 2 Reales, KM#9.

CM Date	Host Date	Good	VG	F	VF	XF
ND(ca.1836)	ND1831 F	100	200	400	600	—

KM# 26 2 REALES
Silver **Countermark:** SAP monogram **Note:** Countermark on 2 Reales, KM#11.6.

CM Date	Host Date	Good	VG	F	VF	XF
ND(ca.1836)	ND1833	50.00	100	200	300	—
ND(ca.1836)	ND1834	50.00	100	200	300	—

COUNTERMARKED COINAGE

Type I — 1830 Volcano

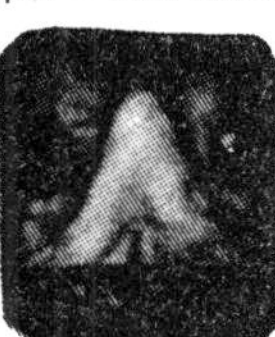

Countermark: Volcano, S on either side, 1830 below in rectangle.

A decree dated October 27, 1830 authorized countermarking 4 Real and 1 Peso coins of legal Silver weight and fineness.

KM# 27 4 REALES
13.5400 g., 0.9030 Silver .3931 oz. **Countermark:** Type I **Note:** Countermark on Mexico 4 Reales, KM#97.

CM Date	Host Date	Good	VG	F	VF	XF
1830	1772-89 Rare	—	—	—	—	—

COUNTERMARKED COINAGE

Type II — 1834 Zig-Zag Test Mark

Through a decree dated December 18, 1834, Salvadorian Provisional coins were to be tested to ascertain their legitamacy. The zig-zag test mark was used for this purpose in late 1834 to mid-1835.

KM# 101.1 2 REALES
Silver **Countermark:** Type II **Note:** Countermark on El Salvador 2 Reales, KM#11.7.

CM Date	Host Date	Good	VG	F	VF	XF
ND(1834-35)	1834/3	60.00	85.00	125	185	—

KM# 101.2 2 REALES
Silver **Countermark:** Type II **Note:** Countermark on El Salvador 2 Reales, KM#11.10.

CM Date	Host Date	Good	VG	F	VF	XF
ND(1834-35)	1833 L	60.00	85.00	125	175	—

KM# 101.3 2 REALES
Silver **Countermark:** Type II **Note:** Countermark on El Salvador 2 Reales, KM#11.13.

CM Date	Host Date	Good	VG	F	VF	XF
ND(1834-35)	1834	60.00	85.00	125	175	—

KM# 102 2 REALES
Silver **Countermark:** Type II **Note:** Countermark on Guatemala 2 Reales, KM#82 (Peru 2 Reales).

CM Date	Host Date	Good	VG	F	VF	XF
ND(1834-35)	1825-35	60.00	85.00	125	185	—

KM# 103 2 REALES
Silver **Countermark:** Type II **Note:** Countermark on Peru 2 Reales, KM#141.1.

CM Date	Host Date	Good	VG	F	VF	XF
ND(1834-35)	1825-35	60.00	85.00	125	185	—

KM# 104 4 REALES
Silver **Countermark:** Type II **Note:** Countermark on Guatemala 4 Reales, KM#92 (Bolivia 4 Soles).

CM Date	Host Date	Good	VG	F	VF	XF
ND(1834-35)	1827-30	60.00	85.00	125	185	—

COUNTERMARKED COINAGE

Type III — 1839 Volcano

Countermark: Volcano, 1839 below, in rectangle. Exists with normal 3 and retrograde 3 in date.

Debased fractional coins of the Peru-Bolivian Confederation (1835-1839) were rejected. A decree of January 13, 1840 ordered all Peruvian and Bolivian coins of legal Silver weight and fineness issued before 1835 to be countermarked to indicate their legitmacy. This countermarking was done in 1840, using a counterpunch bearing a 1839 date.

KM# 30 1/2 REAL
Silver **Countermark:** Type III **Note:** Countermark on Chile 1/2 Real, KM#90.

CM Date	Host Date	Good	VG	F	VF	XF
1839 (1840)	1833-4 Rare	—	—	—	—	—

KM# 33 REAL
Silver **Countermark:** Type III **Note:** Countermark on Peru Real, KM#145.1.

CM Date	Host Date	Good	VG	F	VF	XF
1839 (1840)	1826-36 Rare	—	—	—	—	—

KM# 36 2 REALES
Silver **Countermark:** Type III **Note:** Countermark on Peru (Lima) 2 Reales, KM#141.1.

CM Date	Host Date	Good	VG	F	VF	XF
1839 (1840)	1825-36	100	200	300	—	—

KM# 37 2 REALES
Silver **Countermark:** Type III **Note:** Countermark on South Peru 2 Reales, KM#169.1

CM Date	Host Date	Good	VG	F	VF	XF
1839 (1840)	1837 Rare	—	—	—	—	—

KM# 40 8 REALES
Silver **Countermark:** Type III **Note:** Countermark on South Peru 8 Reales, KM#170.2.

CM Date	Host Date	Good	VG	F	VF	XF
1839 (1840)	1837-39 Rare	—	—	—	—	—

REPUBLIC OF EL SALVADOR

COUNTERMARKED COINAGE

Type IV — R in beaded 5mm circle

In late 1862 and early 1863 Guatemalan coins were countermarked with a R (for revalidated) to certify their legitamacy for circulation in El Salvador.

Copper coins of Brazil have also been reported with the Type IV countermark. An 1827 20 Reis and an 1820 80 Reis countermarked 40. These copper pieces are not genuine.

KM# 83 1/2 REAL
1.5500 g., 0.9030 Silver .0449 oz. **Countermark:** Type IV **Note:** Countermark on Guatemala 1/2 Real, KM#131.

CM Date	Host Date	Good	VG	F	VF	XF
ND(1862-63)	1859	100	150	200	300	—
ND(1862-63)	1860	100	150	200	300	—
ND(1862-63)	1861	100	150	200	300	—

KM# 84 1/2 REAL
1.5500 g., 0.9030 Silver .0449 oz. **Countermark:** Type IV **Note:** Countermark on Guatemala 1/2 Real, KM#138.

CM Date	Host Date	Good	VG	F	VF	XF
ND(1862-63)	1862	60.00	100	150	275	—
ND(1862-63)	1863	60.00	100	150	275	—

KM# 87 REAL
Silver **Countermark:** R in rectangular indent **Note:** Countermark on Colombia Real, KM#87. This is a different style R countermark on a non-Guatemala host coin, making initial attribution to this section doubtful.

CM Date	Host Date	Good	VG	F	VF	XF
ND(1862-63)	1827-36	—	—	—	—	—

KM# 88 REAL
3.0000 g., 0.9030 Silver .0870 oz. **Countermark:** Type IV **Note:** Countermark on Guatemala Real, KM#132.

CM Date	Host Date	Good	VG	F	VF	XF
ND(1862-63)	1859	15.00	22.00	30.00	50.00	—
ND(1862-63)	1860	15.00	22.00	30.00	50.00	—

KM# 89 REAL
3.0000 g., 0.9030 Silver .0870 oz. **Countermark:** Type IV **Note:** Countermark on Guatemala Real, KM#137.

CM Date	Host Date	Good	VG	F	VF	XF
ND(1862-63)	1862	15.00	22.00	30.00	50.00	—
ND(1862-63)	1863	15.00	22.00	30.00	50.00	—

KM# 91 2 REALES
6.3000 g., 0.9030 Silver .1829 oz. **Countermark:** Type IV **Note:** Countermark on Guatemala 2 Reales, KM#133.

CM Date	Host Date	Good	VG	F	VF	XF
ND(1862-63)	1859	200	300	450	—	—

KM# 92 2 REALES
6.2000 g., 0.9030 Silver .18 oz. **Countermark:** Type IV **Note:** Countermark on Guatemala 2 Reales, KM#134.

CM Date	Host Date	Good	VG	F	VF	XF
ND(1862-63)	1860	17.50	25.00	32.50	55.00	—
ND(1862-63)	1861	17.50	25.00	32.50	55.00	—

KM# 93 2 REALES
Silver **Countermark:** Type IV **Note:** Countermark on Guatemala 2 Reales, KM#139.

CM Date	Host Date	Good	VG	F	VF	XF
ND(1862-63)	1861	17.50	25.00	32.50	55.00	—

CM Date	Host Date	Good	VG	F	VF	XF
ND(1862-63)	1862	17.50	25.00	32.50	55.00	—
ND(1862-63)	1863	17.50	25.00	32.50	55.00	—

KM# 96 4 REALES
12.5000 g., 0.9030 Silver .3629 oz. **Countermark:** Type IV **Note:** Countermark on Guatemala 4 Reales, KM#136.

CM Date	Host Date	Good	VG	F	VF	XF
ND(1862-63)	1860	75.00	150	225	350	—
ND(1862-63)	1861	75.00	150	225	350	—

KM# 99 8 REALES
25.0000 g., 0.9030 Silver .7258 oz. **Countermark:** Type IV **Note:** Countermark on Guatemala Peso, KM#178.

CM Date	Host Date	Good	VG	F	VF	XF
ND(1862-63)	1859	2,000	2,500	3,500	4,500	—

COUNTERMARKED COINAGE

Type V — 1868 - Arms on Milled Spanish-American Coins

Plain Liberty cap above shield on draped flags within 10mm circle.

Radiant Liberty cap above shield on draped flags within 12mm circle.

Liberty cap above shield within branches in 12mm circle.

A decree on September 28, 1868 ordered all worn, Spanish-American, 1 and 2 Real milled coins counterstamped with this mark, to distinguish them from debased Spanish Provincial coins.

KM# 47 REAL
Silver **Countermark:** Type V **Note:** Countermark on Bolivia (Potosi) Real, KM#52.

CM Date	Host Date	Good	VG	F	VF	XF
ND(1868)	1773-89	15.00	20.00	30.00	50.00	—

KM# 48 REAL
Silver **Countermark:** Type V **Note:** Countermark on (Santiago) Chile Real, KM#65.

CM Date	Host Date	Good	VG	F	VF	XF
ND(1868)	1808-17	17.50	25.00	40.00	60.00	—

KM# 49 REAL
Silver **Countermark:** Type V **Note:** Countermark on Colombia Real, KM#91.1.

CM Date	Host Date	Good	VG	F	VF	XF
ND(1868)	1837-46	17.50	25.00	40.00	60.00	—

KM# 50 REAL
Silver **Countermark:** Type V **Note:** Countermark on Mexico Charles and Johanna Real, KM#0009.

CM Date	Host Date	Good	VG	F	VF	XF
ND(1868)	1536-72	20.00	30.00	45.00	75.00	—

KM# 51 REAL
Silver **Countermark:** Type V **Note:** Countermark on Mexico City Philip II Real, KM#27.

CM Date	Host Date	Good	VG	F	VF	XF
ND(1868)	1556-98	20.00	30.00	45.00	75.00	—

KM# 52 REAL
Silver **Countermark:** Type V **Note:** Countermark on Spain Real, KM#412.

CM Date	Host Date	Good	VG	F	VF	XF
ND(1868)	1772-88	15.00	22.50	35.00	55.00	—

KM# A53 REAL
Silver **Countermark:** Type V **Note:** Countermark on Mexico Real, KM#81.

CM Date	Host Date	Good	VG	F	VF	XF
ND(1868)	1801-08	15.00	22.50	35.00	55.00	—

KM# B53 REAL
Silver **Countermark:** Type V **Note:** Countermark on Mexico Real, KM#82.

CM Date	Host Date	Good	VG	F	VF	XF
ND(1868)	1809-14	15.00	22.50	35.00	55.00	—

KM# 53 REAL
Silver **Countermark:** Type V **Note:** Countermark on Peru Real, KM#114.

CM Date	Host Date	Good	VG	F	VF	XF
ND(1868)	1839	15.00	22.50	35.00	55.00	—

KM# 54 2 REALES
Silver **Countermark:** Type V **Note:** Countermark on Guatemala 2 Reales, KM#34.2.

CM Date	Host Date	Good	VG	F	VF	XF
ND(1868)	1787 M	35.00	60.00	85.00	150	—

KM# 55 2 REALES
Silver **Countermark:** Type V **Note:** Countermark on Bolivia (Potosi) 2 Reales, KM#53.

CM Date	Host Date	Good	VG	F	VF	XF
ND(1868)	1773-89	20.00	30.00	45.00	75.00	—

KM# 56 2 REALES
Silver **Countermark:** Type V **Note:** Countermark on Colombia 2 Reales, KM#97.

CM Date	Host Date	Good	VG	F	VF	XF
ND(1868)	1837-46	22.50	35.00	50.00	85.00	—

KM# 57 2 REALES
Silver **Countermark:** Type V **Note:** Countermark on Mexico 2 Reales, KM#86.

CM Date	Host Date	Good	VG	F	VF	XF
ND(1868)	1747-60	22.50	35.00	50.00	85.00	—

KM# 58 2 REALES
Silver **Countermark:** Type V **Note:** Countermark on Mexico 2 Reales, KM#89.

CM Date	Host Date	Good	VG	F	VF	XF
ND(1868)	1789-90	20.00	30.00	45.00	75.00	—

KM# 59 2 REALES
Silver **Countermark:** Type V **Note:** Countermark on Mexico 2 Reales, KM#90.

CM Date	Host Date	Good	VG	F	VF	XF
ND(1868)	1790	25.00	37.50	55.00	90.00	—

KM# 60 2 REALES
Silver **Countermark:** Type V **Note:** Countermark on Mexico 2 Reales, KM#91.

CM Date	Host Date	Good	VG	F	VF	XF
ND(1868)	1792-1808	20.00	30.00	45.00	75.00	—

KM# 61 2 REALES
Silver **Countermark:** Type V **Note:** Countermark on Mexico 2 Reales, KM#93.

CM Date	Host Date	Good	VG	F	VF	XF
ND(1868)	1812-21	20.00	30.00	45.00	75.00	—

KM# 62 2 REALES
Silver **Countermark:** Type V **Note:** Countermark on (Lima) Peru 2 Reales, KM#53.

CM Date	Host Date	Good	VG	F	VF	XF
ND(1868)	1752-59	20.00	30.00	45.00	75.00	—

KM# 63 2 REALES
Silver **Countermark:** Type V **Note:** Countermark on Peru (Lima) 2 Reales, KM#95.

CM Date	Host Date	Good	VG	F	VF	XF
ND(1868)	1791-1808	15.00	22.50	35.00	55.00	—

KM# 64 2 REALES
Silver **Countermark:** Type V **Note:** Countermark on Spanish 2 Reales, C#134.

CM Date	Host Date	Good	VG	F	VF	XF
ND(1868)	1810-33	17.50	25.00	40.00	60.00	—

KM# 65 2 REALES
Silver **Countermark:** Type V **Note:** Countermark on Mexico Iturbide 2 Reales, KM#303.

CM Date	Host Date	Good	VG	F	VF	XF
ND(1868)	1823 JM	50.00	100	175	300	—

KM# 68 4 REALES
Silver **Countermark:** Type V **Note:** Countermark on Mexico Sombrerte 4 Reales, KM#175.

CM Date	Host Date	Good	VG	F	VF	XF
ND(1868)	1812 Rare	—	—	—	—	—

KM# 71 8 REALES
Silver **Countermark:** Type V **Note:** Countermark on (Santiago) Chile 8 Reales, KM#31.

CM Date	Host Date	Good	VG	F	VF	XF
ND(1868)	1773-89 Rare	—	—	—	—	—

KM# 72 8 REALES
Silver **Countermark:** Type V **Note:** Countermark on (Lima) Peru 8 Reales, KM#A64.2.

CM Date	Host Date	Good	VG	F	VF	XF
ND(1868)	1765 Rare	—	—	—	—	—

COUNTERMARKED COINAGE

Type V — 1869 - Arms on Spanish-American Cobs

A decree of April 7, 1869 ordered all legitimate cob coins to be countermarked with the coat of arms counterpunch.

KM# 43 1/2 REAL
Silver **Countermark:** Type V **Note:** Countermark on Guatemala 1/2 Real Cob, KM#2.

CM Date	Host Date	Good	VG	F	VF	XF
ND(1869)	ND	35.00	50.00	75.00	125	—

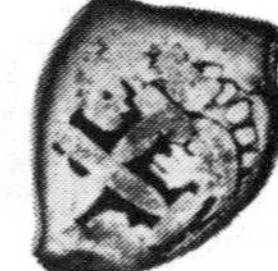

KM# 46 REAL
Silver **Countermark:** Type V **Note:** Countermark on Bolivia (Potosi) Cob Real, KM#42 or Mecixo Cob Real, KM#29 or KM#30.

CM Date	Host Date	Good	VG	F	VF	XF
ND(1869)		17.50	25.00	45.00	75.00	—

KM# 67 4 REALES
Silver **Countermark:** Type V **Note:** Countermark on Guatemala 4 Reales Cob, KM#76.1.

CM Date	Host Date	Good	VG	F	VF	XF
ND(1869)	1747-53 Rare	—	—	—	—	—

COUNTERMARKED COINAGE

Type V — 1873 - Arms on English Sterling Coins

English coins were ordered countermarked with the same coat of arms counterpunch to certify their legitimacy, following the September 28, 1868 decree.

KM# 74 6 PENCE
0.9250 Silver **Countermark:** Type V **Note:** Countermark on Great Britain 6 Pence, KM#394.

CM Date	Host Date	Good	VG	F	VF	XF
ND(1873)	1816-20	22.00	30.00	45.00	60.00	—

KM# 75 6 PENCE
0.9250 Silver **Countermark:** Type V **Note:** Countermark on Great Britain 6 Pence, KM#425.

CM Date	Host Date	Good	VG	F	VF	XF
ND(1873)	1831-37	22.00	30.00	45.00	60.00	—

KM# 78 SHILLING
0.9250 Silver **Countermark:** Type V **Note:** Countermark on Great Britain Shilling, KM#395.

CM Date	Host Date	Good	VG	F	VF	XF
ND(1873)	1816-20	25.00	32.50	47.50	65.00	—

KM# 79 SHILLING
0.9250 Silver **Countermark:** Type V **Note:** Countermark on Great Britain Shilling, KM#409 or KM#666.

CM Date	Host Date	Good	VG	F	VF	XF
ND(1873)	1823-25	25.00	32.50	47.50	65.00	—

KM# 80 SHILLING
0.9250 Silver **Countermark:** Type V **Note:** Countermark on Great Britain Shilling, KM#414.

CM Date	Host Date	Good	VG	F	VF	XF
ND(1873)	1825-29	25.00	32.50	47.50	65.00	—

DECIMAL COINAGE

100 Centavos = 1 Peso

KM# 106 CENTAVO
2.5000 g., Copper-Nickel **Obv:** Francisco Morazan **Rev:** Denomination **Note:** Medal rotation.

Date	Mintage	F	VF	XF	Unc	BU
1889H	1,500,000	1.00	2.50	5.00	20.00	—
1889H Proof	—	Value: 150				
1913H	2,500,000	1.50	3.50	6.00	35.00	—

KM# 108 CENTAVO
Copper

Date	Mintage	F	VF	XF	Unc	BU
1892/1	182,000	45.00	80.00	120	225	—
Note: Only 14,000 were put into circulation, the rest were melted.						
1892	Inc. above	25.00	45.00	65.00	100	—
1892 Proof	10	Value: 750				
1893	446,000	250	400	650	1,250	—
Note: Never placed in circulation.						

KM# 107 3 CENTAVOS
3.3000 g., Copper-Nickel **Obv:** Francisco Morazan **Rev:** Denomination **Note:** Medal rotation.

Date	Mintage	F	VF	XF	Unc	BU
1889H	333,000	1.50	6.00	15.00	30.00	—
1889H Proof	—	Value: 200				
1913H	1,000,000	2.00	8.00	20.00	60.00	—

KM# 109 5 CENTAVOS
1.2500 g., 0.8350 Silver .0336 oz. **Obv:** Arms **Rev:** Denomination

Date	Mintage	F	VF	XF	Unc	BU
1892C.A.M.	80,000	6.00	12.50	25.00	50.00	—
1892C.A.M. Proof	—	Value: 500				
1893C.A.M.	Inc. above	6.00	12.50	25.00	50.00	—

KM# 110 10 CENTAVOS
2.5000 g., 0.8350 Silver .0671 oz. **Obv:** Arms **Rev:** Denomination

Date	Mintage	F	VF	XF	Unc	BU
1892C.A.M.	12,020	25.00	50.00	80.00	200	—
1892C.A.M. Proof	—	Value: 500				

KM# 111 20 CENTAVOS
5.0000 g., 0.8350 Silver .1342 oz. **Obv:** Arms **Rev:** Denomination

Date	Mintage	F	VF	XF	Unc	BU
1892C.A.M.	146,000	10.00	25.00	50.00	125	—
1892C.A.M. Proof	—	Value: 350				

KM# 112 50 CENTAVOS
12.5000 g., 0.9000 Silver .3617 oz. **Obv:** Arms **Rev:** Flag

Date	Mintage	F	VF	XF	Unc	BU
1892C.A.M.	43,000	25.00	60.00	200	450	—
Note: Recalled from circulation and melted.						
1892C.A.M. Proof	—	Value: 750				

KM# 113 50 CENTAVOS
12.5000 g., 0.9000 Silver .3617 oz. **Obv:** Arms **Rev:** Columbus

Date	Mintage	F	VF	XF	Unc	BU
1892C.A.M.	55,000	10.00	20.00	50.00	200	—
1893C.A.M.	285,000	10.00	20.00	50.00	175	—
1894C.A.M.	163,000	14.00	27.50	75.00	300	—

KM# 114 PESO (Colon)

25.0000 g., 0.9000 Silver .7234 oz. **Obv:** Arms **Rev:** Flag

Date	Mintage	F	VF	XF	Unc	BU
1892C.A.M.	41,000	40.00	85.00	150	700	—

Note: Recalled from circulation and melted.

Date	Mintage	
1892C.A.M. Proof	—	Value: 2,000

KM# 115.1 PESO (Colon)

25.0000 g., 0.9000 Silver .7234 oz. **Obv:** Arms **Rev:** Columbus

Date	Mintage	F	VF	XF	Unc	BU
1892C.A.M.	250,500	20.00	40.00	80.00	250	—
1893/2C.A.M.	Inc. below	12.50	30.00	50.00	150	—
1893C.A.M.	354,500	7.50	15.00	30.00	120	—
1894C.A.M.	2,249,800	7.50	15.00	30.00	150	—
1895C.A.M.	2,161,700	7.50	15.00	30.00	175	—
1896C.A.M.	—	75.00	150	400	—	—

Note: Just a few hundred minted before closing the C.A.M.

KM# 116 2-1/2 PESOS

4.0323 g., 0.9000 Gold .1167 oz.

Date	Mintage	F	VF	XF	Unc	BU
1892C.A.M.	597	225	450	650	1,400	—
1892C.A.M. Proof	—	Value: 1,750				

KM# 117 5 PESOS

8.0645 g., 0.9000 Gold .2334 oz.

Date	Mintage	F	VF	XF	Unc	BU
1892C.A.M.	558	300	600	900	1,850	—
1892C.A.M. Proof	—	Value: 3,000				

KM# 118 10 PESOS

16.1290 g., 0.9000 Gold .4667 oz.

Date	Mintage	F	VF	XF	Unc	BU
1892C.A.M.	321	500	800	1,400	3,500	—
1892C.A.M. Proof	—	Value: 3,750				

KM# 119 20 PESOS

32.2580 g., 0.9000 Gold .9334 oz.

Date	Mintage	F	VF	XF	Unc	BU
1892C.A.M.	300	1,000	1,500	2,500	6,500	—
1892C.A.M. Proof	—	Value: 8,000				

ESSAIS

KM#	Date	Mintage	Identification	Mkt Val
E1	1892	—	Centavo. Copper. Arms. Value in wreath. ESSAI/DE/MONNAIE.	—

PATTERNS

Including off metal strikes

KM#	Date	Mintage	Identification	Mkt Val
Pn1	1861	—	25 Centavos. Brass. Well-worn examples of Pn1 exist and are valued accordingly. A VG piece sold in 1997 for $130.	600
Pn2	1861	—	Peso. Bronze.	—
Pn3	1861	—	Peso. Silver.	2,500
Pn7	1892	—	5 Centavos. Copper.	—
Pn13	1892	—	20 Centavos. Copper Silvered.	—
Pn26	1892	—	5 Pesos. Bronze Gilt. Reeded edge.	—
Pn14	1892	—	50 Centavos. Copper.	—
Pn15	1892	—	50 Centavos. White Metal.	—
Pn22	1892	—	2-1/2 Pesos. Bronze Gilt. Reeded edge.	—
Pn24	1892	—	2-1/2 Pesos. Copper Gilt.	—
Pn32	1892	—	20 Pesos. Bronze Gilt. Reeded edge.	—
Pn33	1892	—	20 Pesos. Copper Gilt.	—
Pn19	1892	—	Peso. Copper Silvered.	—
Pn27	1892	—	5 Pesos. Copper Gilt.	—
Pn10	1892	—	10 Centavos. Copper Silvered.	—
Pn12	1892	—	20 Centavos. Copper.	—
Pn16	1892	—	50 Centavos. Copper Silvered.	—
Pn20	1892	—	Peso. Copper.	—
Pn30	1892	—	10 Pesos. Copper Gilt.	—
Pn31	1892	—	20 Pesos. Copper.	—
Pn4	1892	—	Centavo. White Metal. KM#108.	650
Pn28	1892C.A.M.	—	10 Pesos. Copper. KM#118. Prev. KM#Pn9.	1,100
Pn29	1892C.A.M.	—	20 Pesos. Gilt Bronze. KM#119. Prev. KM#Pn10.	1,200
Pn5	1892	—	Centavo. Copper. Date within wreath.	—
Pn6	1892C.A.M.	—	5 Centavos. White Metal. Prev. KM#A6.	300
Pn9	1892C.A.M.	—	10 Centavos. White Metal. Prev. KM#B6.	400
Pn11	1892C.A.M.	—	20 Centavos. White Metal. Prev. KM#PnC6.	600
Pn17	1892	—	Peso. Silver Plated Copper. KM#114. Prev. KM#6.	—
Pn18	1892C.A.M.	—	Peso. Copper. KM#115.1. Prev. KM#A7.	—
Pn21	1892C.A.M.	—	2-1/2 Pesos. 0.9000 Gold. KM#116. Prev. KM#Pn7.	—
Pn23	1892C.A.M.	—	2-1/2 Pesos. Copper. KM#116. Prev. KM#PnA8.	900
Pn25	1892C.A.M.	—	5 Pesos. Copper. KM#117. Prev. KM#Pn8.	1,000

KM#	Date	Mintage	Identification	Mkt Val
Pn8	1893	—	5 Centavos. Copper Silvered.	—
Pn35	1893	—	5 Centavos. Silver.	—
Pn39	1893	—	Peso. Copper Silvered.	—
Pn34	1893	—	Centavo.	—
Pn36	1893	—	20 Centavos. Silver.	—
Pn40	1893	—	Peso. Bronze.	—
Pn38	1893	—	Peso. Copper. Reeded edge.	—

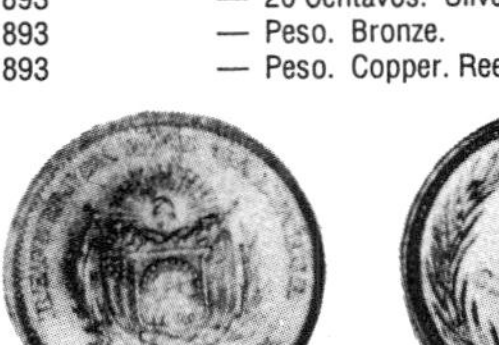

KM#	Date	Mintage	Identification	Mkt Val
Pn37	1893	—	25 Centavos. Silver. Prev. KM#Pn11.	1,250
Pn42	1894	—	50 Centavos. Copper. KM#113. Prev. KM#Pn12.	1,350
Pn45	1894	—	Peso. Copper Silvered. Reeded edge.	—
Pn41	1894	—	50 Centavos. Lead.	—
Pn43	1894	—	Peso. White Metal.	—
Pn44	1894	—	Peso. Bronze.	—
Pn46	1894	—	Peso. Copper. KM#115.1; Prev. KM#Pn13.	1,250
Pn48	1895	—	Peso. Bronze.	—
Pn47	1895	—	Peso. Copper. KM#115.1; Prev. KM#Pn14.	1,250
Pn50	1896	—	Peso. Silver. Reeded edge.	—
Pn49	1896	—	Peso. Copper.	—

PIEFORTS

KM#	Date	Mintage	Identification	Mkt Val
P1	1861	—	25 Centavos. Brass.	—
P2	1862	—	25 Centavos. Brass.	—

PROOF SETS

KM#	Date	Mintage	Identification	Issue Price	Mkt Val
PS1	1889H (2)	—	KM#106-107	—	350
PS2	1892 (10)	—	KM#108-112, 114, 116-119	—	16,000

ERITREA

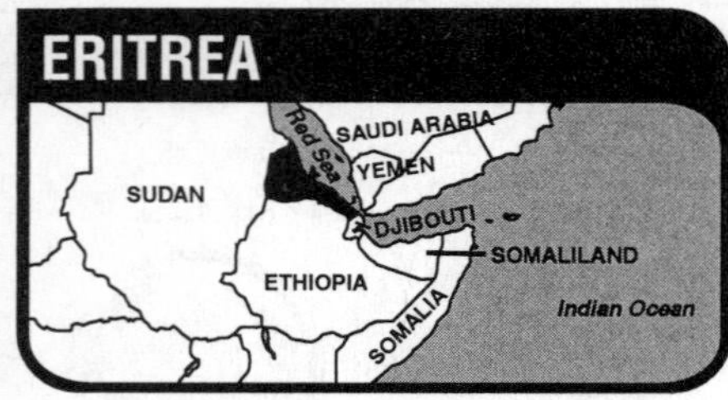

The State of Eritrea, a former Ethiopian province fronting on the Red Sea, has an area of 45,300 sq. mi. (117,600 sq. km.). It was an Italian colony from 1889 until its incorporation into Italian East Africa in 1936. It was under the British Military Administration from 1941 to Sept. 15, 1952, when the United Nations designated it an autonomous unit within the federation of Ethiopia and Eritrea. On Nov. 14, 1962, it was annexed with Ethiopia. In 1991 the Eritrean Peoples Liberation Front extended its control over the entire territory of Eritrea. Following 2 years of provisional government, Eritrea held a referendum on independence in May 1993. Overwhelming popular approval led to the proclamation of an independent Republic of Eritrea on May 24.

RULERS
Umberto I, 1889-1900
Vittorio Emanuele III, 1900-1945

MINT MARKS
M - Milan
R – Rome

MONETARY SYSTEM
100 Centesimi = 1 Lira
5 Lire = 1 Tallero

ITALIAN COLONY

COLONIAL COINAGE

KM# 1 50 CENTESIMI
2.5000 g., 0.8350 Silver .0671 oz.

Date	Mintage	F	VF	XF	Unc	BU
1890M	1,800,000	25.00	55.00	125	250	—

KM# 2 LIRA
5.0000 g., 0.8350 Silver .1342 oz.

Date	Mintage	F	VF	XF	Unc	BU
1890R	598,000	20.00	40.00	100	275	—
1891R	2,401,000	20.00	40.00	80.00	225	—
1896R	1,500,000	40.00	75.00	150	550	—

KM# 3 2 LIRE
10.0000 g., 0.8350 Silver .2685 oz.

Date	Mintage	F	VF	XF	Unc	BU
1890R	1,000,000	35.00	75.00	150	400	—
1896R	750,000	40.00	85.00	175	500	—

KM# 4 5 LIRE/TALLERO
28.1250 g., 0.8000 Silver .7235 oz.

Date	Mintage	F	VF	XF	Unc	BU
1891	196,000	100	250	550	1,400	—
1896	200,000	125	275	575	1,600	—

ESSEQUIBO & DEMERARY

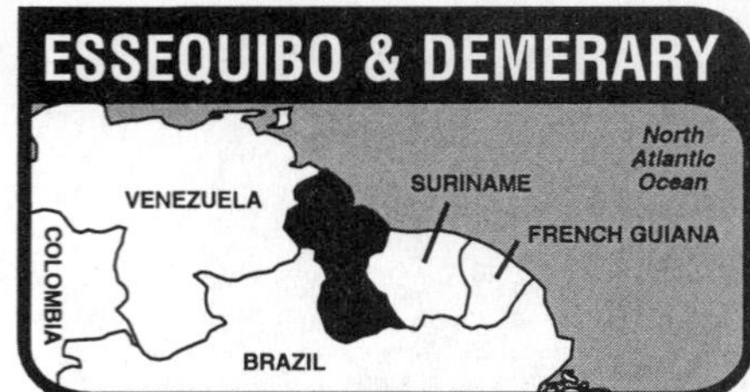

The original area of Essequibo and Demerary, which included present-day Suriname, French Guiana, and parts of Brazil and Venezuela was sighted by Columbus in 1498.The first European settlement was made late in the 16th century by the Dutch, however, the region was claimed for the British by Sir Walter Raleigh during the reign of Elizabeth I. For the next 150 years, possession alternated between the Dutch and the British, with a short interval of French control. The British exercised de facto control after 1796, although the area, which included the Dutch colonies of Essequibo, Demerary and Berbice, was not ceded to them by the Dutch until 1814. From 1803 to 1831, Essequibo and Demerary were administered separately from Berbice. The three colonies were united in the British Crown Colony of British Guiana in 1831. British Guiana won internal self-government in 1952 and full independence, under the traditional name of Guyana, on May 26,1966. Guyana became a republic on Feb. 23, 1970. It is a member of the Commonwealth of Nations. The president is the Chief of State. The prime minister is the Head of Government.

MONETARY SYSTEM

(Until 1839)
20 Stiver = 1 Guilder (Gulden)
3 Guilders = 12 Bits = 5 Shillings = 1 Dollar
(Commencing 1839)
3-1/8 Guilders = 50 Pence

NECESSITY COINAGE

1808 Emergency Issues

During the time of the countermarked coins of the Bank of England for George III, Spanish or Spanish Colonial 8 Reales were punched to form two new denominations. The plug or center was countermarked 3 Bits while the holed 8 Reales was countermarked 3 Guilders.

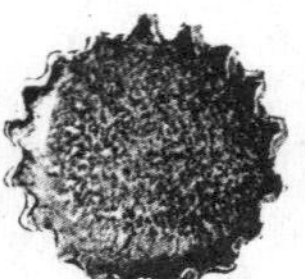

KM# 1 3 BITS
0.9030 Silver **Countermark:** E & D 3 Bit **Note:** Countermark on serrated cetner plug from 8 Reales.

Date	Mintage	VG	F	VF	XF	Unc
ND	—	950	1600	2650	3350	—

KM# 2 3 GUILDER
0.9030 Silver **Countermark:** E & D 3 G D **Note:** Countermark in dotted oval on Mexico City 8 Reales, KM#109.

Date	Mintage	VG	F	VF	XF	Unc
1791	—	2,000	3,250	5,500	7,000	—
1796	—	2,000	3,250	5,500	7,000	—
1803	—	2,000	3,250	5,500	7,000	—

COLONIAL COINAGE

KM# 9 1/2 STIVER
Copper

Date	Mintage	F	VF	XF	Unc	BU
1813	215,000	5.00	12.50	45.00	125	—
1813 Proof	—	Value: 350				

KM# 9a 1/2 STIVER
Copper-Gilt

Date	Mintage	F	VF	XF	Unc	BU
1813 Proof	—	Value: 650				

KM# 10 STIVER
Copper

Date	Mintage	F	VF	XF	Unc	BU
1813	215,000	6.50	15.00	50.00	175	—
1813 Proof	—	Value: 400				

KM# 10a STIVER
Copper-Gilt

Date	Mintage	F	VF	XF	Unc	BU
1813 Proof	—	Value: 600				

KM# 16 1/8 GUILDER
0.9700 g., 0.8160 Silver .0255 oz.

Date	Mintage	F	VF	XF	Unc	BU
1832	98,000	6.00	12.00	35.00	75.00	—
1832 Proof	—	Value: 250				
1835/1	71,000	10.00	19.00	37.50	95.00	—
1835/3/2	Inc. above	15.00	30.00	45.00	100	—
1835/3	Inc. above	10.00	19.00	37.50	95.00	—
1835	Inc. above	7.50	17.00	30.00	70.00	—
1835 Proof	—	Value: 300				
Note: Plain edge						
1835 Proof	—	Value: 400				
Note: Reeded edge						

KM# 4 1/4 GUILDER
1.9400 g., 0.8160 Silver .0510 oz. **Obv:** Similar to 2 Guilders, KM#7 **Rev:** Crown over denomination **Note:** Flan size varies.

Date	Mintage	F	VF	XF	Unc	BU
1809	124,000	12.50	25.00	65.00	175	—

KM# 11 1/4 GUILDER
1.9400 g., 0.8160 Silver .0510 oz.

Date	Mintage	F	VF	XF	Unc	BU
1816	43,000	12.50	25.00	70.00	185	—
1816 Proof	—	Value: 350				

KM# 17 1/4 GUILDER
1.9400 g., 0.8160 Silver .0510 oz.

Date	Mintage	F	VF	XF	Unc	BU
1832	39,000	12.50	22.50	50.00	165	—
1833	97,000	9.00	17.50	40.00	135	—
1833 Proof	—	Value: 575				
1835/3	73,000	9.00	17.50	40.00	135	—
1835	Inc. Above	7.00	12.00	27.50	110	—
1835 Proof	—	Value: 450				
Note: Plain edge						
1835 Proof	—	Value: 500				
Note: Reeded edge						

KM# 5 1/2 GUILDER
3.8800 g., 0.8160 Silver .1020 oz.

Date	Mintage	F	VF	XF	Unc	BU
1809	64,000	15.00	37.50	110	250	—

KM# 12 1/2 GUILDER
3.8800 g., 0.8160 Silver .1020 oz.

Date	Mintage	F	VF	XF	Unc	BU
1816	34,000	13.50	27.50	100	225	—
1816 Proof	—	Value: 350				

KM# 18 1/2 GUILDER
3.8800 g., 0.8160 Silver .1020 oz.

Date	Mintage	F	VF	XF	Unc	BU
1832	87,000	12.50	25.00	95.00	200	—
1832 Proof	—	Value: 350				
1835/5	36,000	13.50	27.50	100	210	—
1835	Inc. above	19.00	27.50	70.00	145	—
1835 Proof	—	Value: 400				
Note: Plain edge						
1835 Proof	—	Value: 500				
Note: Reeded edge						

KM# 6 GUILDER
7.7700 g., 0.8160 Silver .2040 oz.

Date	Mintage	F	VF	XF	Unc	BU
1809	32,000	18.00	35.00	120	375	—

KM# 13 GUILDER
7.7700 g., 0.8160 Silver .2040 oz.

Date	Mintage	F	VF	XF	Unc	BU
1816	34,000	15.00	30.00	110	325	—
1816 Proof	—	Value: 600				

KM# 19 GUILDER
7.7700 g., 0.8160 Silver .2040 oz. **Note:** 1932 dated coins exist with flat and round top 3.

Date	Mintage	F	VF	XF	Unc	BU
1832	47,000	20.00	45.00	90.00	300	—
1832 Proof	—	Value: 550				
1835	22,000	20.00	45.00	90.00	325	—
1835 Proof	—	Value: 550				
Note: Plain edge						
1835 Proof	—	Value: 600				
Note: Reeded edge						

KM# 7 2 GUILDER
15.5000 g., 0.8160 Silver .4079 oz.

Date	Mintage	F	VF	XF	Unc	BU
1809	16,000	100	200	500	1,800	—

KM# 14 2 GUILDER
15.5000 g., 0.8160 Silver .4079 oz.

Date	Mintage	F	VF	XF	Unc	BU
1816	15,000	60.00	135	300	900	—
1816 Proof, rare	—	—	—	—	—	—

KM# 20 2 GUILDER
15.5000 g., 0.8160 Silver .4079 oz.

Date	Mintage	F	VF	XF	Unc	BU
1832	14,000	75.00	165	425	1,550	—
1832 Proof, rare	—	—	—	—	—	—

KM# 8 3 GUILDER
23.3200 g., 0.8160 Silver .6118 oz.

Date	Mintage	F	VF	XF	Unc	BU
1809	21,000	200	400	850	2,500	—

KM# 15 3 GUILDER
23.3200 g., 0.8160 Silver .6118 oz.

Date	Mintage	F	VF	XF	Unc	BU
1816	10,000	175	325	550	1,600	—
1816 Proof, rare	—	—	—	—	—	—

KM# 21 3 GUILDER
23.3200 g., 0.8160 Silver .6118 oz.

Date	Mintage	F	VF	XF	Unc	BU
1832	7,156	250	600	1,500	4,000	—
1832 Proof, rare	—	—	—	—	—	—

ETHIOPIA

Legend claims that Menelik I, the son born to Solomon, King of Israel, by the Queen of Sheba, settled in Axum in North Ethiopia to establish the dynasty, which reigned with only brief interruptions until 1974. Modern Ethiopian history began with the reign of Emperor Menelik II (1889-1913) under whose guidance the country emerged from medieval isolation. Progress continued throughout the reigns of Menelik's daughter, Empress Zauditu, and her successor Emperor Haile Selassie I who was coronated in 1930.

No coins, patterns or presentation pieces are known bearing Emperor Lij Yasu's likeness or titles. Coins of Menelik II were struck during this period with dates frozen.

RULERS

Menelik II, 1889-1913

MINT MARKS

A – Paris
(a) – Paris, privy marks only

Coinage of Menelik II, 1889-1913

NOTE: The first national issue coinage, dated 1887 and 1888 E.E., carried a cornucopia, A, and fasces on the reverse. Subsequent dates have a torch substituted for the fasces, the A being dropped. All issues bearing these marks were struck at the Paris Mint. Coins without mint marks were struck in Addis Ababa.

MONETARY SYSTEM

(Until about 1903)
40 Besa = 20 Gersh = 1 Birr

DATING

Ethiopian coinage is dated by the Ethiopian Era calendar (E.E.), which commenced 7 years and 8 months after the advent of A.D. dating.

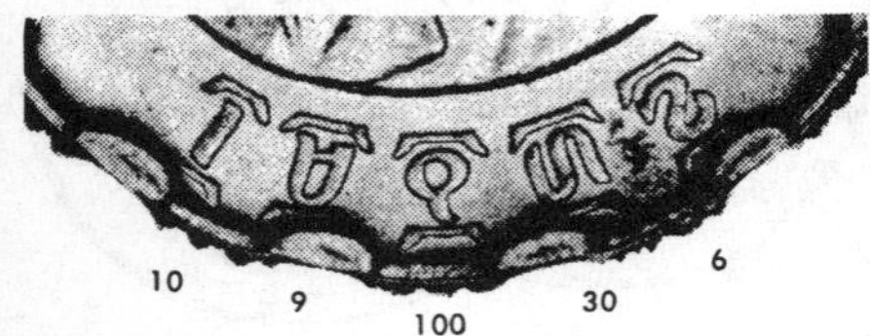

EXAMPLE

1900 (10 and 9 = 19 x 100)
36 (Add 30 and 6)
1936 E.E.
8 (Add)
1943/4 AD

EMPIRE OF ETHIOPIA

STANDARD COINAGE

KM# 1 MAHALEKI
1.4000 g., Silver **Obv:** Crown **Rev:** Date, denomination and Ethiopian script

Date	Mintage	F	VF	XF	Unc	BU
EE1885	—	85.00	145	250	350	—

Note: The above issue has been reported to be the last issue of the Harrar Mint following the capture of that city in 1887 by Menelik's forces

REFORM COINAGE

KM# 9 1/100 BIRR (Matonya)
Copper

Date	Mintage	F	VF	XF	Unc	BU
EE1889	500,000	5.00	10.00	25.00	50.00	—

KM# 6 1/4 GERSH
Copper, 26 mm.

Date	Mintage	F	VF	XF	Unc	BU
EE1888A	200	350	700	1,150	2,000	—

KM# 7 1/2 GERSH
Copper, 32 mm.

Date	Mintage	F	VF	XF	Unc	BU
EE1888A	200	225	375	650	1,250	—

First Issue

Enlargement (below lion)

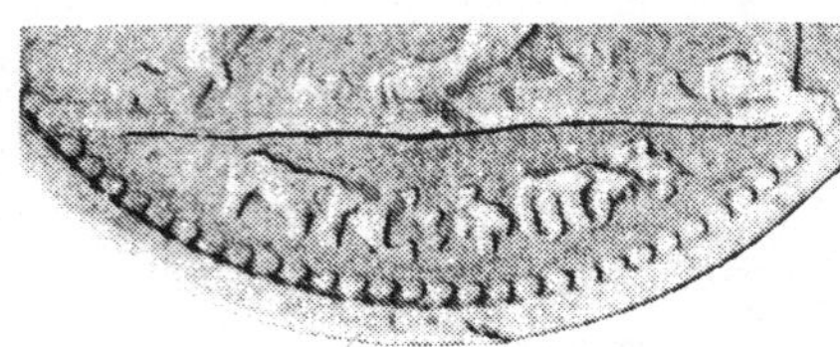

Defaced, with plain and rough edge.

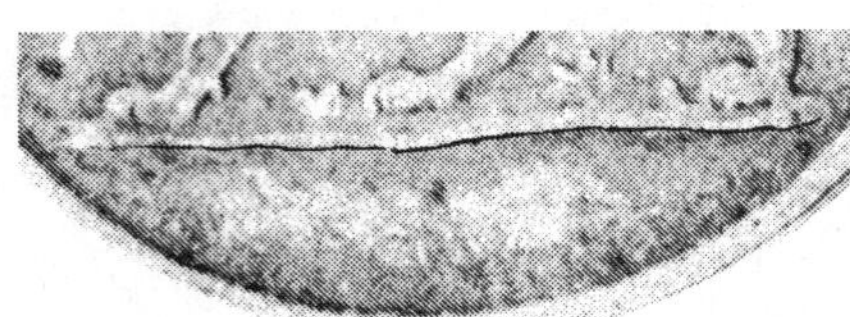

Obliterated, plain and reeded edge.

KM# 10 1/32 BIRR
Copper Or Brass

Date	Mintage	F	VF	XF	Unc	BU
EE1889	—	3.50	7.50	15.00	50.00	—

Note: This issue was struck from dies intended for a silver 1/8 Birr of the die series that included KM#13, 14 and 15. These are found with the denomination partially to almost totally effaced from beneath the lion

Second Issue

Enlargement (below lion)

KM# 11 1/32 BIRR
Copper Or Brass

Date	Mintage	F	VF	XF	Unc	BU
EE1889	3,353,000	4.00	10.00	20.00	60.00	—

Note: Struck at the Addis Ababa Mint in 1922, 1931 and 1933 from newly prepared dies having corrected denominations

KM# 8 GERSH
Copper, 38 mm.

Date	Mintage	F	VF	XF	Unc	BU
EE1888A	200	275	450	700	1,400	—

KM# 12 GERSH
1.4038 g., 0.8350 Silver .0377 oz. **Rev:** Lion's left foreleg raised

Date	Mintage	F	VF	XF	Unc	BU
EE1889A	1,000,000	6.00	12.00	20.00	40.00	—
EE1891A	4,000,000	4.00	6.50	12.00	22.00	—

KM# 13 GERSH
1.4038 g., 0.8350 Silver .0377 oz. **Rev:** Lion's right foreleg raised

Date	Mintage	F	VF	XF	Unc	BU
EE1889	—	60.00	100	165	375	—

KM# 2 1/8 BIRR
3.5094 g., 0.8350 Silver .0942 oz. **Rev:** Lion's left foreleg raised

Date	Mintage	F	VF	XF	Unc	BU
EE1887A	25,000	15.00	30.00	65.00	225	—
EE1887A Proof	—	Value: 650				
EE1888A	200	200	300	500	850	—

KM# 3 1/4 BIRR
7.1088 g., 0.8350 Silver .1884 oz. **Rev:** Lion's left foreleg raised

Date	Mintage	F	VF	XF	Unc	BU
EE1887A	15,000	10.00	20.00	40.00	135	—
EE1887A Proof	—	Value: 650				
EE1888A	200	150	250	400	750	—
EE1889A	400,000	7.00	15.00	30.00	100	—

KM# 14 1/4 BIRR
7.1088 g., 0.8350 Silver .1884 oz. **Rev:** Lion's right foreleg raised

Date	Mintage	F	VF	XF	Unc	BU
EE1889	—	25.00	45.00	75.00	250	—

KM# 4 1/2 BIRR

14.0375 g., 0.8350 Silver .3768 oz. **Rev:** Lion's left foreleg raised

Date	Mintage	F	VF	XF	Unc	BU
EE1887A	10,000	12.00	25.00	60.00	175	—
EE1887A Proof	—	Value: 650				
EE1888A	200	150	250	400	750	—
EE1889A	420,000	10.00	25.00	50.00	150	—

Note: Struck between 1897 and 1925

KM# 15 1/2 BIRR

14.0375 g., 0.8350 Silver .3768 oz. **Rev:** Lion's right foreleg raised

Date	Mintage	F	VF	XF	Unc	BU
EE1889	—	85.00	150	300	600	—

KM# 5 BIRR

28.0750 g., 0.8350 Silver .7537 oz. **Rev:** Lion's left foreleg raised

Date	Mintage	F	VF	XF	Unc	BU
EE1887A	20,000	20.00	40.00	100	325	—
EE1887A Proof	—	Value: 650				
EE1888A	200	—	—	—	—	—
EE1889A	418,000	15.00	30.00	85.00	275	—

KM# 19 BIRR

28.0750 g., 0.8350 Silver .7537 oz. **Rev:** Lion's right foreleg raised

Date	Mintage	F	VF	XF	Unc	BU
EE1892	401,000	15.00	30.00	90.00	325	—
EE1892 Proof	—	Value: 550				
EE1892 Matte Proof	—	Value: 450				

KM# 16 1/4 WERK

1.7500 g., 0.9000 Gold .0506 oz.

Date	Mintage	F	VF	XF	Unc	BU
EE1889	—	60.00	135	210	350	—

KM# 17 1/2 WERK

3.5000 g., 0.9000 Gold .1012 oz.

Date	Mintage	F	VF	XF	Unc	BU
EE1889	—	100	165	245	385	—

KM# 18 WERK

7.0000 g., 0.9000 Gold .2025 oz.

Date	Mintage	F	VF	XF	Unc	BU
EE1889	—	120	185	265	525	—

Note: KM#16-18 vary considerably in weight due to disparities in planchet thicknesses

PATTERNS

Including off metal strikes

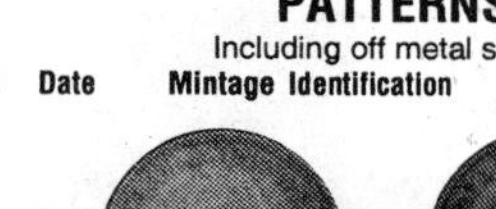

KM#	Date	Mintage	Identification	Mkt Val
Pn1	EE1889	—	Gersh. Gold. KM13.	2,400
Pn2	EE1889	—	1/4 Birr. Gold. 6.7500 g. Reeded edge. KM14.	2,500
Pn3	EE1889	—	1/4 Birr. Gold. 14.5000 g. Plain edge. KM14.	3,500
Pn4	EE1889	—	1/2 Birr. Gold. KM15.	2,200
Pn5	EE1889	—	Birr. Gold.	6,000

TRIAL STRIKES

KM#	Date	Mintage	Identification	Mkt Val
TS1	EE1887	—	Birr. Copper. KM5.	90.00
TS2	ND	—	Birr. Copper. KM5.	—
TS3	EE1889	—	1/4 Werk. Gold. KM16. Plain edge.	—
TS4	ND	—	1/4 Werk. Gold. KM16. Plain edge.	—
TS5	EE1889	—	1/2 Werk. Gold. KM17. Reeded edge.	—
TS6	ND	—	1/2 Werk. Gold. KM17. Reeded edge.	—
TS7	EE1889	—	Werk. Gold. KM18. Reeded edge.	—
TS8	ND	—	Werk. Gold. KM18. Plain edge.	—

PROOF SETS

KM#	Date	Mintage	Identification	Issue Price	Mkt Val
PS1	1894 (4)	—	KM2-5	—	2,600

HARAR

Harar, a province and city located in eastern Ethiopia, was founded by Arab immigrants from Yemen in the 7th century. The sultanate conquered Ethiopia in the mid-16th century, and was in turn conquered by Egypt in 1875 and by Ethiopia in 1887.

TITLES

al-Harar

RULERS

Ahmad II, AH1209-1236/AD1794-1821
Abd al-Rahman, AH1236-1240/AD1821-1825
Abd al-Karim, AH1240-1250/AD1825-1834
Abu Baker II, AH1250-1268/AD1834-1852
Muhammad II, AH1272-1292/AD1856-1875
Abdallah, AH1303-1304/AD1885-1887

MONETARY SYSTEM

Not known; 22 Mahallak were said to be equal to one Ashrafi. In the late 18th and the 19th century the Ashrafi in Harar was a fictitious medium used in accounts, which varied in value against the Maria Theresa Dollar. In the 1st half of the 19th century, 3 Ashrafi were thought to be one Maria Theresa Dollar.

The brass coins are of various sizes, but were probably all called Mahallak'. The denominations of the billon and silver are unknown.

SULTANATE

BRASS COINAGE

KM# 4 MAHALLAK
Copper-Brass **Ruler:** Ahmad II AD1794-1821 **Note:** 7-10mm, 0.13-0.26g. Anonymous strike, without name of ruler.

Date	Mintage	Good	VG	F	VF	XF
AH1222	—	10.00	15.00	25.00	40.00	—
AH1226	—	10.00	15.00	25.00	40.00	—
AH1227	—	10.00	15.00	25.00	40.00	—

Note: Other dates reported to exist

KM# 5 MAHALLAK
Brass **Ruler:** Abd al-Karim AD1825-34 **Note:** 5-7mm, 0.10-0.20g.

Date	Mintage	Good	VG	F	VF	XF
ND	—	4.00	7.50	12.50	22.00	—

Note: Believed to be an issue of 'Abd al-Karim

KM# 6 MAHALLAK
Brass **Ruler:** Abu Baker II AD1834-52 **Note:** Anonymous. About 10-11mm, 0.40-0.65g.

Date	Mintage	Good	VG	F	VF	XF
AH1257	—	8.00	15.00	25.00	40.00	—
AH1258	—	8.00	15.00	25.00	40.00	—

KM# 7 MAHALLAK
Copper-Brass **Ruler:** Muhammad II AD1856-75 **Obv:** *Sultan Muhammad bin Ali* **Rev:** *Al-Sultan abd-al Shakur and date* **Note:** In the name of Muhammad II. 9-11mm, 0.19-0.25g.

Date	Mintage	Good	VG	F	VF	XF
AH1274	—	6.00	12.00	20.00	30.00	—

KM# 8 MAHALLAK
Copper-Brass **Ruler:** Muhammad II AD1856-75 **Obv:** *Sultan Muhammad bin Ali and date* **Rev:** *City of al Harar* **Note:** 10-12mm, 0.35-0.48 g.

Date	Mintage	Good	VG	F	VF	XF
AH1279	—	7.00	14.00	22.00	35.00	—

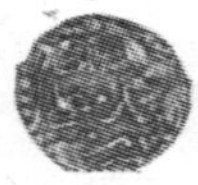

KM# 9 MAHALLAK
Copper-Brass **Ruler:** Muhammad II AD1856-75 **Obv:** *Sultan Muhammad bin Ali* **Rev:** *Struck at Harar and date* **Note:** 10-14mm, 0.35-0.70 g.

Date	Mintage	Good	VG	F	VF	XF
AH1284	—	3.00	6.00	12.00	20.00	—

KM# 11 MAHALLAK
Copper-Brass **Ruler:** Abdallah AD1885-87 **Note:** Anonymous, in name of "THE WEAK SLAVE'. 15-19mm, 0.85-1.55 g.

Date	Mintage	Good	VG	F	VF	XF
AH1303	—	3.00	6.00	9.00	15.00	—
AH1305	—	5.00	10.00	17.50	25.00	—

Note: Varieties exist

SILVER COINAGE

KM# 10 MAHALLAK
Silver **Obv. Inscription:** "Muhammad II" **Note:** Size varies: 9.5-10 mm; Weight varies: .05 - .12 grams.

Date	Mintage	Good	VG	F	VF	XF
AH1288	—	35.00	65.00	110	185	—

KM# 12 MAHALLAK
Silver **Note:** Weight varies: 3.25 - 3.67 grams.

Date	Mintage	Good	VG	F	VF	XF
AH1303	—	—	—	—	175	—
AH1305	—	—	—	—	175	—

FINLAND

The Republic of Finland, the third most northerly state of the European continent, has an area of 130,559 sq. mi. (338,127 sq. km.). Capital: Helsinki. Lumbering, shipbuilding, metal and woodworking are the leading industries. Paper, timber, wood pulp, plywood and metal products are exported.

The Finns, who probably originated in the Volga region of Russia, took Finland from the Lapps late in the 7th century. They were conquered in the 12th century by Eric IX of Sweden, and brought into contact with Western Christendom. In 1809, Sweden was conquered by Alexander I of Russia, and the peace terms gave Finland to Russia which became a grand duchy within the Russian Empire

RULERS
Alexander II, 1855-1881
Alexander III, 1881-1894
Nicholas II, 1894-1917

MONETARY SYSTEM
100 Pennia = 1 Markka

MINT MARKS
No mm – Helsinki

MINT OFFICIALS' INITIALS

Letter	Date	Name
L	1885-1912	Johan Conrad Lihr
S	1864-85	Aug. F. Soldan

GRAND DUCHY

DECIMAL COINAGE

KM# 1.1 PENNI
Copper **Note:** Dotted border; varieties exist.

Date	Mintage	F	VF	XF	Unc	BU
1864	30,000	1,500	2,000	3,000	4,500	—
1865	515,000	25.00	40.00	100	200	—
1866/5	3,673,000	35.00	70.00	120	250	—
1866	Inc. above	10.00	15.00	35.00	75.00	—
1867	3,843,000	10.00	15.00	35.00	75.00	—
1869/6	1,575,000	50.00	75.00	120	250	—
1869	Inc. above	20.00	30.00	60.00	100	—
1870	500,000	50.00	75.00	150	200	—
1871	1,500,000	10.00	15.00	35.00	75.00	—

KM# 1.2 PENNI
Copper **Note:** Dentilated border.

Date	Mintage	F	VF	XF	Unc	BU
1872	1,000,000	20.00	35.00	70.00	100	—
1873	2,000,000	7.00	10.00	30.00	60.00	—
1874	1,450,000	7.00	10.00	30.00	60.00	—
1875	1,550,000	7.00	10.00	30.00	60.00	—
1876	2,005,000	7.00	10.00	30.00	60.00	—

KM# 10 PENNI
Copper

Date	Mintage	F	VF	XF	Unc	BU
1881	600,000	10.00	15.00	30.00	75.00	—
1882	100,000	45.00	75.00	150	200	—
1883	3,900,000	1.00	3.00	6.00	20.00	—
1884	404,000	50.00	75.00	150	200	—
1888	2,290,000	1.00	3.00	5.00	15.00	—
1891	1,008,000	2.00	5.00	15.00	30.00	—
1892	1,510,000	1.00	3.00	10.00	20.00	—
1893	2,290,000	0.75	1.50	4.00	10.00	—
1893 Dot after date	Inc. above	0.75	1.50	4.00	10.00	—
1894	1,810,000	0.75	1.50	4.00	10.00	—

KM# 13 PENNI
1.2800 g., Copper, 15 mm. **Obv:** Monogram of Nicholas II **Rev:** Value, date

Date	Mintage	F	VF	XF	Unc	BU
1895	880,000	3.00	5.00	10.00	25.00	—
1898	1,430,000	0.75	1.25	3.00	10.00	—
1899	1,540,000	0.75	1.25	3.00	10.00	—
1900	3,550,000	0.50	1.00	2.00	7.00	—

KM# 4.1 5 PENNIA
Copper **Note:** Dotted border; varieties exist.

Date	Mintage	F	VF	XF	Unc	BU
1865	480,000	6.00	30.00	75.00	200	—
1866	2,490,000	1.00	7.00	45.00	100	—
1867	1,660,000	2.00	10.00	50.00	120	—
1870	300,000	7.00	25.00	100	250	—

KM# 4.2 5 PENNIA
Copper **Note:** Dentilated border.

Date	Mintage	F	VF	XF	Unc	BU
1872	500,000	5.00	25.00	75.00	200	—
1873	1,000,000	1.00	10.00	50.00	150	—
1875	1,000,000	1.00	10.00	50.00	150	—

KM# 11 5 PENNIA
Copper

Date	Mintage	F	VF	XF	Unc	BU
1888	600,000	2.00	10.00	50.00	120	—
1889	1,070,000	1.00	7.00	25.00	100	—
1892	330,000	3.00	10.00	50.00	150	—

KM# 15 5 PENNIA
6.4000 g., Copper, 25 mm. **Obv:** Monogram of Nicholas II **Rev:** Value, date

Date	Mintage	F	VF	XF	Unc	BU
1896	410,000	2.00	10.00	50.00	120	—
1897	590,000	1.00	7.00	35.00	100	—
1898	1,150,000	1.00	5.00	30.00	75.00	—
1899	860,000	1.00	5.00	30.00	75.00	—

KM# 5.1 10 PENNIA
Copper **Note:** Dotted border.

Date	Mintage	F	VF	XF	Unc	BU
1865	250,000	5.00	30.00	100	250	—
1866/5	850,000	10.00	35.00	75.00	220	—
1866	Inc. above	3.00	20.00	65.00	200	—
1867	1,440,000	3.00	25.00	75.00	200	—

KM# 5.2 10 PENNIA
Copper **Note:** Dentilated border; varieties exist.

Date	Mintage	F	VF	XF	Unc	BU
1875	100,000	60.00	200	500	—	—
1876	300,000	5.00	35.00	250	500	—

KM# 12 10 PENNIA
Copper

Date	Mintage	F	VF	XF	Unc	BU
1889	100,000	10.00	40.00	120	600	—
1890	106,000	8.00	40.00	120	600	—
1891	295,000	5.00	15.00	75.00	250	—

KM# 14 10 PENNIA
12.8000 g., Copper, 30 mm. **Obv:** Monogram of Nicholas II **Rev:** Value and date in wreath

Date	Mintage	F	VF	XF	Unc	BU
1895	210,000	3.00	15.00	100	300	—
1896	294,000	3.00	15.00	75.00	250	—
1897	502,000	1.50	10.00	50.00	125	—
1898	40,000	30.00	100	250	600	—
1899	440,000	1.50	10.00	50.00	150	—
1900	524,000	2.00	10.00	50.00	150	—

KM# 6.1 25 PENNIA
1.2747 g., 0.7500 Silver .0307 oz. **Note:** Dotted border; varieties exist.

Date	Mintage	F	VF	XF	Unc	BU
1865 S	705,000	15.00	50.00	100	200	—
1866 S	810,000	10.00	30.00	75.00	150	—
1867 S	400,000	350	700	1,200	2,500	—
1868 S	136,000	175	400	1,000	1,500	—
1869 S	264,000	35.00	100	175	350	—
1871 S	150,000	70.00	150	250	600	—

KM# 6.2 25 PENNIA
1.2747 g., 0.7500 Silver .0307 oz., 16 mm. **Obv:** Coat of arms **Rev:** Value and date in wreath **Note:** Dentilated border.

Date	Mintage	F	VF	XF	Unc	BU
1872 S	400,000	10.00	30.00	100	200	—
1873 S	800,000	5.00	20.00	50.00	100	—
1875 S	810,000	5.00	20.00	50.00	100	—
1876 S	1,200	1,250	2,500	4,000	7,000	—
1889 L	404,000	3.00	10.00	30.00	100	—
1890 L	800,000	2.00	7.00	20.00	70.00	—
1891 L	280,000	5.00	15.00	50.00	125	—
1894 L	820,000	2.00	7.00	20.00	70.00	—
1897 L	450,000	2.00	7.00	20.00	70.00	—
1898 L	444,000	1.50	5.00	20.00	60.00	—
1898 L Inverted L	Inc. above	15.00	40.00	100	250	—
1899 L	312,000	2.00	10.00	50.00	125	—

KM# 2.1 50 PENNIA
2.5495 g., 0.7500 Silver .0615 oz. **Note:** Dotted border.

Date	Mintage	F	VF	XF	Unc	BU
1864 S	104,000	7.00	30.00	150	500	—
1865 S	1,184,000	5.00	15.00	100	200	—
1866 S	363,000	20.00	75.00	250	500	—
1868 S	140,000	100	250	500	2,000	—
1869 S	144,000	20.00	75.00	200	500	—
1869 S Slanted 9	Inc. above	20.00	75.00	250	600	—
1871 S	320,000	3.00	15.00	50.00	200	—

KM# 2.2 50 PENNIA
2.5494 g., 0.7500 Silver .0615 oz., 18.6 mm. **Obv:** Coat of arms **Rev:** Value and date in wreath **Note:** Dentilated border.

Date	Mintage	F	VF	XF	Unc	BU
1872 S	Est. 200,000	5.00	20.00	70.00	350	—

Note: Some specimens may appear prooflike; Proofs were never made officially by the mint

Date	Mintage	F	VF	XF	Unc	BU
1874 S	402,000	2.50	15.00	50.00	150	—
1876 S	600	4,000	7,000	10,000	15,000	—
1889 L	312,000	2.50	10.00	50.00	120	—
1890 L	693,000	1.00	5.00	20.00	50.00	—
1891 L	282,000	1.00	5.00	20.00	75.00	—
1892 L	344,000	1.00	5.00	20.00	70.00	—
1893 L	400,000	1.00	5.00	20.00	70.00	—

KM# 3.1 MARKKA
5.1828 g., 0.8680 Silver .1446 oz. **Note:** Dotted border; varieties exist.

Date	Mintage	F	VF	XF	Unc	BU
1864 S	75,000	25.00	50.00	170	600	—
1865 S	1,673,000	2.50	10.00	40.00	100	—
1866 S	1,990,000	2.50	10.00	35.00	100	—
1867 S	852,000	15.00	30.00	100	500	—
1870 S 5 known	—	—	—	—	—	—

KM# 3.2 MARKKA
5.1828 g., 0.8680 Silver .1446 oz., 24 mm. **Obv:** Coat of arms, fineness around (text in Finnish) **Note:** Obverse text translates to: "94.48 pieces from one pound of fine silver." Dentilated border.

Date	Mintage	F	VF	XF	Unc	BU
1872 S	538,000	5.00	20.00	100	300	—
1874 S	1,002,000	2.50	10.00	25.00	80.00	—
1890 L	841,000	2.50	6.00	20.00	70.00	—
1892 L	484,000	2.50	6.00	20.00	80.00	—
1893 L	254,000	3.00	7.50	20.00	80.00	—

KM# 7.1 2 MARKKAA
10.3657 g., 0.8680 Silver .2893 oz. **Note:** Dotted border.

Date	Mintage	F	VF	XF	Unc	BU
1865 S	203,000	7.00	15.00	50.00	200	—
1866/5 S	820,000	12.00	30.00	100	350	—
1866 S	Inc. above	12.00	35.00	120	370	—
1867 S 8 known	—	—	—	—	—	—

Note: Helsingin Numismaattinen Yhdistys Auction 3-1990 VF-EF realized $45,000

Date	Mintage	F	VF	XF	Unc	BU
1870 S	500,000	7.00	15.00	50.00	200	—

KM# 7.2 2 MARKKAA
10.3657 g., 0.8680 Silver .2893 oz., 27.5 mm. **Obv:** Coat of arms, fineness around (Finnish text) **Note:** Obverse text translates to: "47.24 pieces from one pound of fine silver." Dentilated border.

Date	Mintage	F	VF	XF	Unc	BU
1872 S	250,000	7.00	15.00	50.00	200	—
1874 S	502,000	7.00	15.00	50.00	200	—

KM# 8.1 10 MARKKAA
3.2258 g., 0.9000 Gold .0933 oz. **Obv:** Narrow eagle **Note:** Regal issues; similar to 20 Markkaa, KM#9.2.

Date	Mintage	F	VF	XF	Unc	BU
1878 S	254,000	60.00	80.00	100	125	—

KM# 8.2 10 MARKKAA
3.2258 g., 0.9000 Gold .0933 oz., 18.9 mm. **Obv:** Wide eagle coat of arms **Rev:** Value and date, fineness around **Note:** Regal issues; similar to 20 Markkaa, KM#9.2.

Date	Mintage	F	VF	XF	Unc	BU
1879/0 S	—	1,500	3,000	5,000	—	—

Note: Only a few pieces known

Date	Mintage	F	VF	XF	Unc	BU
1879 S	200,000	60.00	80.00	100	125	—
1881 S	100,000	80.00	100	115	150	—
1882 S	386,000	60.00	80.00	100	115	—

KM# 9.1 20 MARKKAA
6.4516 g., 0.9000 Gold .1867 oz. **Obv:** Narrow eagle **Note:** Regal issues; similar to 10 Markkaa, KM#8.1.

Date	Mintage	F	VF	XF	Unc	BU
1878 S	Est. 235,000	130	160	200	250	—

Note: Some specimens may appear as proof-like. Proofs were never made officially by the mint

KM# 9.2 20 MARKKAA
6.4516 g., 0.9000 Gold .1867 oz., 21.3 mm. **Obv:** Wide eagle coat of arms **Rev:** Value and date, fineness around **Note:** Regal issues.

Date	Mintage	F	VF	XF	Unc	BU
1879 S	300,000	100	110	120	150	—
1880 S	90,000	250	350	500	650	—
1891 L	91,000	110	125	150	175	—

PATTERNS

Including off metal strikes

KM#	Date	Mintage	Identification	Mkt Val
Pn1	1863	—	Penni. Copper.	—
Pn2	1863	—	5 Pennia. Copper.	—
Pn3	1863	—	10 Pennia. Copper.	—
Pn4	1863	—	20 Pennia. Copper.	—
Pn5	1863	—	Tin.	—
PnA6	1863	—	2 Markkaa. Tin.	—

Note: Suomen Numismaattinen Yhdistys Auction 11-99 Unc realized $15,800

KM#	Date	Mintage	Identification	Mkt Val
Pn6	1866	—	20 Pennia. Silver.	—
Pn7	1867	—	10 Pennia. Gold.	—
Pn8	1867	8	2 Markkaa. Silver. KM7.1.	—
Pn9	1870	5	Silver. KM3.1.	—
Pn10	1890	—	10 Pennia. Copper-Nickel.	—

TRIAL STRIKES

KM#	Date	Mintage	Identification	Mkt Val
TS1	1866	—	2 Pennia. Copper.	3,000
TS2	1866	—	2 Pennia. Copper.	—
TS3	1866	—	20 Pennia. Silver.	—
TS4	1867	—	2 Markkaa. Tin.	—
TSA4	1867	—	10 Pennia. Gold.	—
TS5	1870	—	Markka. Tin.	—

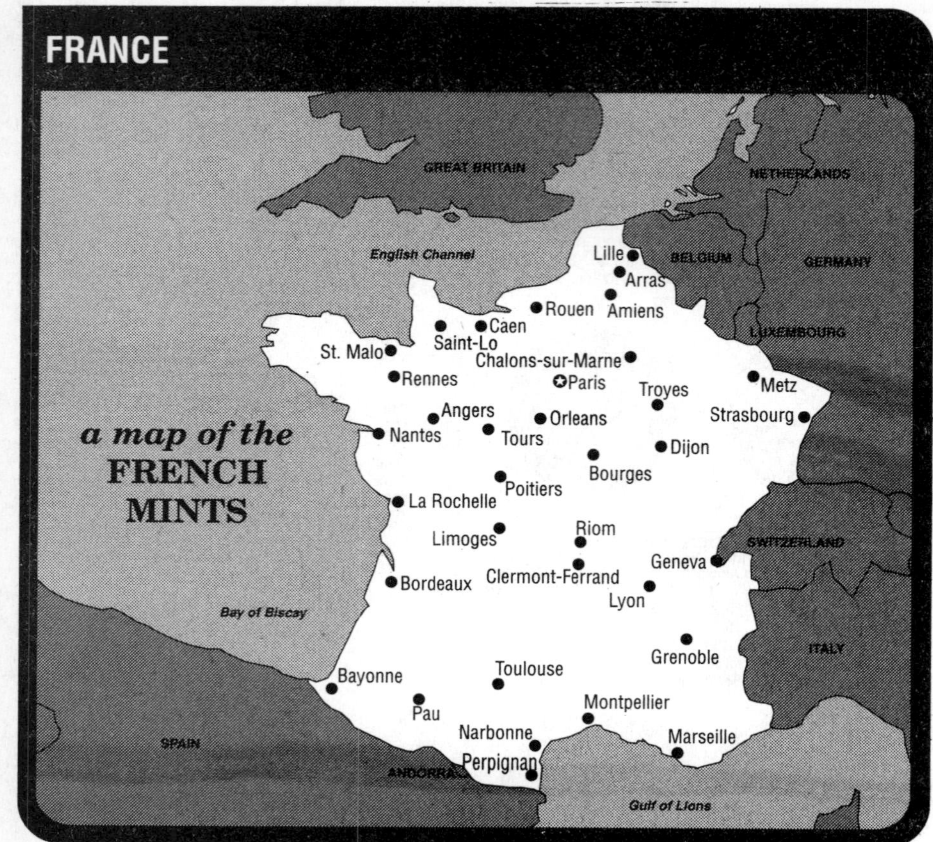

The French Republic, largest of the West European nations, has an area of 210,026 sq. mi. (547,030 sq. km.). Capital: Paris.

France, the Gaul of ancient times, emerged from the Renaissance as a modern centralized national state which reached its zenith during the reign of Louis XIV (1643-1715) when it became an absolute monarchy and the foremost power in Europe. Although his reign marks the golden age of French culture, the domestic abuses and extravagance of Louis XIV plunged France into a series of costly wars. This, along with a system of special privileges granted the nobility and other favored groups, weakened the monarchy and brought France to bankruptcy. This laid the way for the French Revolution of 1789-99 that shook Europe and affected the whole world.

The monarchy was abolished and the First Republic formed in 1793. The new government fell in 1799 to a coup led by Napoleon Bonaparte who, after declaring himself First Consul for life, in 1804 had himself proclaimed Emperor of France and King of Italy.

Napoleon's military victories made him master of much of Europe, but his disastrous Russian campaign of 1812 initiated a series of defeats that led to his abdication in 1814 and exile to the island of Elba. The monarchy was briefly restored under Louis XVIII. Napoleon returned to France in March 1815, but his efforts to uphold his power were totally crushed at the battle of Waterloo. He was exiled to the island of St. Helena where he died in 1821.

The monarchy under Louis XVIII was again restored in 1815, but the ultra reactionary regime of Charles X (1824-30) was overthrown by a liberal revolution and Louis Philippe of Orleans replaced him as monarch. The monarchy was ousted by the Revolution of 1848 and the Second Republic proclaimed. Louis Napoleon Bonaparte (nephew of Napoleon I) was elected president of the Second Republic. He was proclaimed emperor in 1852. As Napoleon III, he gave France two decades of prosperity under a stable, autocratic regime, but led it to defeat in the Franco-Prussian War of 1870, after which the Third Republic was established.

RULERS

Consulate, 1799-1803, L'an 8-11
Napoleon as First Consul, 1799-1804
Napoleon I as Emperor, L'AN 12 1804-1814 (first restoration)
Louis XVIII, 1814-1815
Napoleon I, March-June 1815 (second restoration)
Louis XVIII, 1815-1824
Charles X, 1824-1830
Louis Philippe, 1830-1848
Second Republic, 1848-1852
Napoleon III, 1852-1870
Government of National Defense, 1870-1871
Third Republic, 1871-1940

MINT MARKS AND PRIVY MARKS

In addition to the date and mint mark which are customary on western civilization coinage, most coins manufactured by the French Mints contain two or three small 'Marks or Differents' as the French call them. These privy marks represent the men responsible for the dies which struck the coins. One privy mark is sometimes for the Engraver General (since 1880 the title is Chief Engraver). The other privy mark is the signature of the Mint Director of each mint; another one is the different' of the local engraver. Three other marks appeared at the end of Louis XIV's reign: one for the Director General of Mints, one for the General Engineer of Mechanical edge-marking, one identifying over struck coins in 1690-1705 and in 1715-1723. Equally amazing and unique is that sometimes the local assayer's or Judge-custody's 'different' or 'secret pellet' appears. Since 1880 this privy mark has represented the office rather than the personage of both the Administration of Coins & Medals and the Mint Director, and a standard privy mark has been used (cornucopia).

For most dates these privy marks are important though minor features for advanced collectors or local researchers. During some issue dates, however, the marks changed. To be even more accurate sometimes the marks changed when the date didn't, even though it should have. These coins can be attributed to the proper mintage report only by considering the privy marks. Previous references (before G. Sobin and F. Droulers) have by and large ignored these privy marks. It is entirely possible that unattributed varieties may exist for any privy mark transition. All transition years which may have two or three varieties or combinations of privy marks have the known attribution indicated after the date (if it has been confirmed).

ENGRAVER GENERAL'S PRIVY MARKS

Mark	Desc.	Date	Name
	Bow shooting Artemise	1795-1803	Augustus Dupre
	Cursive initial	1803-75	Pierre-Joseph Tiolier
	Horse's head	1815-16	Pierre-Joseph Tiolier
	Horse's head	1816-17	Nicolaus-Pierre Tiolier
	Cursive initial (pointed)	1818-29	Nicolaus-Pierre Tiolier
	Cursive initial (simple)	1825-30	Nicolaus-Pierre Tiolier
	Star	1830-42	Nicolaus-Pierre Tiolier
	Dog's head (d)	1843-55	Jean-Jacques Barre
	Anchor (a)	1855-79	Albert-Désiré Barre
	Anchor w/bar	1878-79	Auguste Barre
	Fasces	1880-96	
	Torch	1896-1926	Henri Patey

MINT DIRECTORS' PRIVY MARKS

Some modern coins struck from dies produced at the Paris Mint have the 'A' mint mark. In the absence of a mint mark, the cornucopia privy mark serves to attribute a coin to Paris design.

A – Paris, Central Mint

Mark	Desc.	Date
	Cock	L'AN 6-1821
	Anchor	1822-42
	Prow of ship (p)	1843-45
	Hand (ha)	1845-60
	Bee (b)	1860-79
	(Commune), Trident (tr)	1871
	Cornucopia	1880

B - Rouen

Mark	Desc.	Date
	Vase	L'AN 5-7
	Sheep	L'AN 12 – 1844
	Hand	1845-46
	Pick & Shovel	1853-57

BB - Strasbourg

Mark	Desc.	Date
	Sheaf	L'AN 5 – 1825
	Beaver (ba)	1826-34
	Bee (be)	1834-60
	Cross (c)	1860-70

Legend ending BD, see PAU

CL - Genoa

Mark	Desc.	Date	Name
	Prow w/banner	1813-14	Podesta
	Prow of ship	1805, 1813-14	

D - Lyon

Mark	Desc.	Date
	Monogram	L'AN 8 – XI

Mark	Desc.	Date
	Bee (b)	L'AN XI – 1823
	Ark (a)	1823-39
	Tower (to)	1839-42
	Lion	1848-57

G - Geneve

Mark	Desc.	Date
	Lion	L'AN 8-12
	Fish left	L'AN 12

H – La Rochelle

Mark	Desc.	Date	Name
	Monogram T.G.F.S.	L'AN 12-1817	Jean-Gualbert-Francois Seguy
	Lyre	1817-25	Denis Bernard
	Trident	1825-35	Eugene Morel

I - Limoges

Mark	Desc.	Date	Name
	Horizontal clasped hands	L'AN 12 – 1822	Martial Parent
	Vertical clasped hands	1823-35	Jean Perant

K - Bordeaux

Mark	Desc.	Date	Name
	Antique oil lamp	L'AN 5-12	Laurent Bruno Lhoste, (AN 5-AN12; Guillaume Duthol, (AN 12 – AN13)
	Fish	L'AN 13 – 1809	Etienne Froidevaux
	Vine Leaf	1809-57	Hubert Vignes (1809-26); Alexander Vignes (1827-57)
	Pick & Hammer	1861-67	Ernest Dumas
	Slanted M in star	1870-71	Joseph Marchant Dupleny
	Trefoiled cross	1870-78	Henri Delbeque

L - Bayonne

Mark	Desc.	Date	Name
	Lion's head	L'AN 6-AN XI	Antoine Laa
	Tulip	L'AN XI – 1829	Pierre-Romain d'Arripe (AN XI – 1810); Pierre-Boniface d'Arripe (1810-29)

M - Toulouse

Mark	Desc.	Date	Name
	Hammer	L'AN 14 – 1812	Daumy
	Cursive monogram CT	1812-36	Carayon – Talpayrac, Sr. (1812-18); Carayon – Talpayrac, Jr. (1823-26)

Q - Perpignan

Mark	Desc.	Date	Name
	Grapes	L'AN 5 – 1837	Joseph Dastros
		AN 5 – 1829	Jean-Marie de Sainte-Croix
		(1829-35)	Abel de Lorme

R - London

Mark	Desc.	Date	Name
	Fleur-de-lis	1815	Wellesley

T - Nantes

Mark	Desc.	Date	Name
	Anchor	L'AN 5 – 1818	Pierre Athenas
	Key	1818-20	Alexandre Lepot
	Olive branch	1826-35	G. Laurent Olivier d'Assenoy

U - Turin

Mark	Desc.	Date	Name
	Heart	L'AN 12 – 1813	Vittorio Modesto Paroletti

W – Lille (See also "L")

Mark	Desc.	Date	Name
	Caduceus	L'AN 5 – 1840 (L'AN 6 – 1817)	Louis-Theophile – Francois Lepage; Alexandre Beausier (1817-40)
	Retort	1840-46	Charles-Louis Dierickx
	Ancient lamp	1853-57	Charles-Frideric Kuhlmann

M (MA) Monogram - Marseille

Mark	Desc.	Date	Name
	Star	L'AN 9 – 1809	Cyprian Gaillard
	Monogram VR	1809-23	Victor Regis
	Lean palm tree	1824-30	Joseph-Augusta Ricard
	Large palm tree	1830-39	Jacques-Henri Ricard
	Scallop	1853-57	Alexandre-Joseph Beaussier

Flag on mast w/banner - Utrecht

Mark	Desc.	Date	Name
	Fish	1812-13	Gideon Jan Langerak, Dumarchic Servaas

Crowned R – (R) Rome

Mark	Desc.	Date
	She-wolf suckling rombus	1812-13

CONSULSHIP

Napoleon as First Consul

DECIMAL COINAGE

KM# 653.1 1/4 FRANC

1.2500 g., 0.9000 Silver .0362 oz. ASW **Mint:** Paris **Obv. Legend:** BONAPARTE PR. CONSUL.

Date	Mintage	VG	F	VF	XF	Unc
AN12A	171,000	15.00	27.50	65.00	110	—

KM# 653.2 1/4 FRANC

1.2500 g., 0.9000 Silver .0362 oz. ASW **Mint:** Strasbourg

Date	Mintage	VG	F	VF	XF	Unc
AN12BB	1,565	60.00	120	300	550	—

KM# 653.3 1/4 FRANC

1.2500 g., 0.9000 Silver .0362 oz. ASW **Mint:** Lyon

Date	Mintage	VG	F	VF	XF	Unc
AN12D		60.00	120	300	550	—

KM# 653.4 1/4 FRANC

1.2500 g., 0.9000 Silver .0362 oz. ASW **Mint:** Limoges

Date	Mintage	VG	F	VF	XF	Unc
AN12I	41,000	22.50	45.00	110	225	—

KM# 653.5 1/4 FRANC

1.2500 g., 0.9000 Silver .0362 oz. ASW **Mint:** Bayonne

Date	Mintage	VG	F	VF	XF	Unc
AN12L	19,000	30.00	60.00	150	275	—

KM# 653.6 1/4 FRANC

1.2500 g., 0.9000 Silver .0362 oz. ASW **Mint:** Toulouse

Date	Mintage	VG	F	VF	XF	Unc
AN12M	39,000	17.50	32.50	80.00	200	—

KM# 653.7 1/4 FRANC

1.2500 g., 0.9000 Silver .0362 oz. ASW **Mint:** Marseille

Date	Mintage	VG	F	VF	XF	Unc
AN12MA	9,080	30.00	60.00	150	300	—

KM# 653.8 1/4 FRANC

1.2500 g., 0.9000 Silver .0362 oz. ASW **Mint:** Perpignan

Date	Mintage	VG	F	VF	XF	Unc
AN12Q	28,000	25.00	50.00	90.00	250	—

KM# 653.9 1/4 FRANC

1.2500 g., 0.9000 Silver .0362 oz. ASW **Mint:** Nantes

Date	Mintage	VG	F	VF	XF	Unc
AN12T	10,000	30.00	60.00	150	300	—

KM# 648.1 1/2 FRANC

2.2500 g., 0.9000 Silver .0723 oz. ASW **Mint:** Paris **Obv. Legend:** BONAPARTE PREMIER CONSUL

Date	Mintage	VG	F	VF	XF	Unc
ANXIA	31,000	20.00	50.00	150	275	—
AN12A	280,000	10.00	20.00	50.00	200	—

KM# 648.2 1/2 FRANC

2.2500 g., 0.9000 Silver .0723 oz. ASW **Mint:** Strasbourg **Obv. Legend:** BONAPARTE PREMIER CONSUL

Date	Mintage	VG	F	VF	XF	Unc
AN12BB	2,125	75.00	150	325	650	—

KM# 648.3 1/2 FRANC

2.2500 g., 0.9000 Silver .0723 oz. ASW **Mint:** Lyon **Obv. Legend:** BONAPARTE PREMIER CONSUL

Date	Mintage	VG	F	VF	XF	Unc
AN12D	15,000	25.00	60.00	175	300	—

KM# 648.4 1/2 FRANC

2.2500 g., 0.9000 Silver .0723 oz. ASW **Mint:** Geneve **Obv. Legend:** BONAPARTE PREMIER CONSUL

Date	Mintage	VG	F	VF	XF	Unc
AN12G	7,407	75.00	175	350	750	—

KM# 648.5 1/2 FRANC

2.2500 g., 0.9000 Silver .0723 oz. ASW **Mint:** La Rochelle **Obv. Legend:** BONAPARTE PREMIER CONSUL

Date	Mintage	VG	F	VF	XF	Unc
AN12H	1,988	100	175	350	800	—

KM# 648.6 1/2 FRANC

2.2500 g., 0.9000 Silver .0723 oz. ASW **Mint:** Limoges **Obv. Legend:** BONAPARTE PREMIER CONSUL

Date	Mintage	VG	F	VF	XF	Unc
AN12I	416,000	9.00	18.00	40.00	175	—

KM# 648.7 1/2 FRANC

2.2500 g., 0.9000 Silver .0723 oz. ASW **Mint:** Bordeaux **Obv. Legend:** BONAPARTE PREMIER CONSUL

Date	Mintage	VG	F	VF	XF	Unc
AN12K	12,000	30.00	70.00	200	375	—

KM# 648.8 1/2 FRANC

2.2500 g., 0.9000 Silver .0723 oz. ASW **Mint:** Bayonne **Obv. Legend:** BONAPARTE PREMIER CONSUL

Date	Mintage	VG	F	VF	XF	Unc
AN12L	67,000	10.00	25.00	65.00	200	—

KM# 648.9 1/2 FRANC

2.2500 g., 0.9000 Silver .0723 oz. ASW **Mint:** Toulouse **Obv. Legend:** BONAPARTE PREMIER CONSUL

Date	Mintage	VG	F	VF	XF	Unc
AN12M	136,000	10.00	20.00	50.00	200	—

KM# 648.10 1/2 FRANC

2.2500 g., 0.9000 Silver .0723 oz. ASW **Mint:** Marseille **Obv. Legend:** BONAPARTE PREMIER CONSUL

Date	Mintage	VG	F	VF	XF	Unc
AN12MA	26,000	20.00	50.00	125	250	—

KM# 648.11 1/2 FRANC

2.2500 g., 0.9000 Silver .0723 oz. ASW **Mint:** Perpignan **Obv. Legend:** BONAPARTE PREMIER CONSUL

Date	Mintage	VG	F	VF	XF	Unc
AN12Q	54,000	15.00	40.00	100	225	—

KM# 648.12 1/2 FRANC

2.5000 g., 0.9000 Silver .0723 oz. ASW **Mint:** Nantes **Obv. Legend:** BONAPARTE PREMIER CONSUL

Date	Mintage	VG	F	VF	XF	Unc
AN12T	17,000	25.00	50.00	175	300	—

KM# 648.13 1/2 FRANC

2.5000 g., 0.9000 Silver .0723 oz. ASW **Mint:** Turin **Obv. Legend:** BONAPARTE PREMIER CONSUL

Date	Mintage	VG	F	VF	XF	Unc
AN12U	3,150	80.00	200	400	850	—
1804U	—	Value: 1,804				

Note: Above value for common date uncirculated

KM# 649.1 FRANC
5.0000 g., 0.9000 Silver .1446 oz. ASW **Mint:** Paris **Obv. Legend:** BONAPARTE PREMIER CONSUL

Date	Mintage	VG	F	VF	XF	Unc
ANXIA	232,000	20.00	50.00	125	275	450
AN12A	1,311,000	15.00	30.00	90.00	250	425

KM# 649.2 FRANC
5.0000 g., 0.9000 Silver .1446 oz. ASW **Mint:** Strasbourg **Obv. Legend:** BONAPARTE PREMIER CONSUL

Date	Mintage	VG	F	VF	XF	Unc
AN12BB	5,737	100	200	400	800	—

KM# 649.3 FRANC
5.0000 g., 0.9000 Silver .1446 oz. ASW **Mint:** Lyon **Obv. Legend:** BONAPARTE PREMIER CONSUL

Date	Mintage	VG	F	VF	XF	Unc
ANXID	12,000	75.00	150	350	650	—
AN12D	53,000	35.00	60.00	150	350	—

KM# 649.4 FRANC
5.0000 g., 0.9000 Silver .1446 oz. ASW **Mint:** Poitiers **Obv. Legend:** BONAPARTE PREMIER CONSUL

Date	Mintage	VG	F	VF	XF	Unc
ANXIG	13,000	100	200	400	900	—
AN12G	7,397	125	280	500	1,000	—

KM# 649.5 FRANC
5.0000 g., 0.9000 Silver .1446 oz. ASW **Mint:** La Rochelle **Obv. Legend:** BONAPARTE PREMIER CONSUL

Date	Mintage	VG	F	VF	XF	Unc
AN12H	57,000	35.00	60.00	150	350	—

KM# 649.6 FRANC
5.0000 g., 0.9000 Silver .1446 oz. ASW **Mint:** Limoges **Obv. Legend:** BONAPARTE PREMIER CONSUL

Date	Mintage	VG	F	VF	XF	Unc
AN12I	279,000	20.00	45.00	100	250	—

KM# 649.7 FRANC
5.0000 g., 0.9000 Silver .1446 oz. ASW **Mint:** Bordeaux **Obv. Legend:** BONAPARTE PREMIER CONSUL

Date	Mintage	VG	F	VF	XF	Unc
AN12K	102,000	30.00	55.00	125	300	—

KM# 649.8 FRANC
5.0000 g., 0.9000 Silver .1446 oz. ASW **Mint:** Bayonne **Obv. Legend:** BONAPARTE PREMIER CONSUL

Date	Mintage	VG	F	VF	XF	Unc
ANXIL	22,000	40.00	75.00	200	500	—
AN12L	125,000	25.00	50.00	115	275	—

KM# 649.9 FRANC
5.0000 g., 0.9000 Silver .1446 oz. ASW **Mint:** Toulouse **Obv. Legend:** BONAPARTE PREMIER CONSUL

Date	Mintage	VG	F	VF	XF	Unc
AN12M	285,000	20.00	45.00	100	250	400

KM# 649.10 FRANC
5.0000 g., 0.9000 Silver .1446 oz. ASW **Mint:** Marseille **Obv. Legend:** BONAPARTE PREMIER CONSUL

Date	Mintage	VG	F	VF	XF	Unc
ANXIMA	12,000	45.00	90.00	250	600	—
AN12MA	141,000	25.00	50.00	115	275	—

KM# 649.11 FRANC
5.0000 g., 0.9000 Silver .1446 oz. ASW **Mint:** Perpignan **Obv. Legend:** BONAPARTE PREMIER CONSUL

Date	Mintage	VG	F	VF	XF	Unc
ANXIQ	34,000	40.00	75.00	200	500	—
AN12Q	140,000	25.00	50.00	115	275	—

KM# 649.12 FRANC
5.0000 g., 0.9000 Silver .1446 oz. ASW **Mint:** Nantes **Obv. Legend:** BONAPARTE PREMIER CONSUL

Date	Mintage	VG	F	VF	XF	Unc
AN12T	46,000	35.00	60.00	150	350	—

KM# 649.13 FRANC
5.0000 g., 0.9000 Silver .1446 oz. ASW **Mint:** Turin **Obv. Legend:** BONAPARTE PREMIER CONSUL

Date	Mintage	VG	F	VF	XF	Unc
AN12U	5,580	75.00	150	350	650	—

KM# 649.14 FRANC
5.0000 g., 0.9000 Silver .1446 oz. ASW **Mint:** Lille **Obv. Legend:** BONAPARTE PREMIER CONSUL

Date	Mintage	VG	F	VF	XF	Unc
ANXIW	5,756	75.00	150	350	650	—
AN12W	28,000	40.00	75.00	200	500	—
ANXI-12W	—	—	—	—	—	725

Note: Above value for common date uncirculated

KM# 657.1 2 FRANCS
10.0000 g., 0.9000 Silver .2893 oz. ASW **Mint:** Paris **Obv. Legend:** BONAPARTE PREMIER CONSUL

Date	Mintage	VG	F	VF	XF	Unc
AN12A	187,000	40.00	90.00	250	575	—
AN12A Proof	—	Value: 2,500				

KM# 657.2 2 FRANCS
10.0000 g., 0.9000 Silver .2893 oz. ASW **Mint:** Strasbourg **Obv. Legend:** BONAPARTE PREMIER CONSUL

Date	Mintage	VG	F	VF	XF	Unc
AN12BB	1,965	—	—	—	—	—

Note: One example known

KM# 657.3 2 FRANCS
10.0000 g., 0.9000 Silver .2893 oz. ASW **Mint:** Lyon **Obv. Legend:** BONAPARTE PREMIER CONSUL

Date	Mintage	VG	F	VF	XF	Unc
AN12D	2,672	—	—	—	—	—

Note: Reported, not confirmed

KM# 657.4 2 FRANCS
10.0000 g., 0.9000 Silver .2893 oz. ASW **Mint:** Poitiers **Obv. Legend:** BONAPARTE PREMIER CONSUL

Date	Mintage	VG	F	VF	XF	Unc
AN12G	2,859	100	250	400	900	—

KM# 657.5 2 FRANCS
10.0000 g., 0.9000 Silver .2893 oz. ASW **Mint:** La Rochelle **Obv. Legend:** BONAPARTE PREMIER CONSUL

Date	Mintage	VG	F	VF	XF	Unc
AN12H	12,000	50.00	115	250	650	—

KM# 657.6 2 FRANCS
10.0000 g., 0.9000 Silver .2893 oz. ASW **Mint:** Limoges **Obv. Legend:** BONAPARTE PREMIER CONSUL

Date	Mintage	VG	F	VF	XF	Unc
AN12I	102,000	40.00	90.00	200	500	—

KM# 657.7 2 FRANCS
10.0000 g., 0.9000 Silver .2893 oz. ASW **Mint:** Bordeaux **Obv. Legend:** BONAPARTE PREMIER CONSUL

Date	Mintage	VG	F	VF	XF	Unc
AN12K	26,000	45.00	100	225	450	—

KM# 657.8 2 FRANCS
10.0000 g., 0.9000 Silver .2893 oz. ASW **Mint:** Bayonne **Obv. Legend:** BONAPARTE PREMIER CONSUL

Date	Mintage	VG	F	VF	XF	Unc
AN12L	15,000	50.00	115	250	650	—

KM# 657.9 2 FRANCS
10.0000 g., 0.9000 Silver .2893 oz. ASW **Mint:** Toulouse **Obv. Legend:** BONAPARTE PREMIER CONSUL

Date	Mintage	VG	F	VF	XF	Unc
AN12M	66,000	40.00	90.00	200	500	—

KM# 657.10 2 FRANCS
10.0000 g., 0.9000 Silver .2893 oz. ASW **Mint:** Marseille **Obv. Legend:** BONAPARTE PREMIER CONSUL

Date	Mintage	VG	F	VF	XF	Unc
AN12MA	6,804	60.00	125	275	700	—

KM# 657.11 2 FRANCS
10.0000 g., 0.9000 Silver .2893 oz. ASW **Mint:** Perpignan **Obv. Legend:** BONAPARTE PREMIER CONSUL

Date	Mintage	VG	F	VF	XF	Unc
AN12Q	21,000	45.00	100	225	500	—

KM# 657.12 2 FRANCS
10.0000 g., 0.9000 Silver .2893 oz. ASW **Mint:** Nantes **Obv. Legend:** BONAPARTE PREMIER CONSUL

Date	Mintage	VG	F	VF	XF	Unc
AN12T	4,484	—	—	—	—	—

Note: One example known

KM# 657.13 2 FRANCS
10.0000 g., 0.9000 Silver .2893 oz. ASW **Mint:** Turin

Date	VG	F	VF	XF	Unc
AN12U Unique	—	—	—	—	—

KM# 657.14 2 FRANCS
10.0000 g., 0.9000 Silver .2893 oz. ASW **Mint:** Lille

Date	Mintage	VG	F	VF	XF	Unc
AN12W	5,850	65.00	135	300	775	—

KM# 639.1 5 FRANCS
25.0000 g., 0.9000 Silver .7234 oz. ASW **Mint:** Paris **Obverse:** Hercules with two maidens **Obv. Legend:** UNION ET FORCE.* **Rev. Legend:** REPUBLIQUE FRANCAISE **Edge Lettering:** GARANTIE NATIONALE **Note:** Dav. #1337.

Date	Mintage	VG	F	VF	XF	Unc
LAN 10 (1801-02)A	561,000	35.00	75.00	175	550	—
LAN 11 (1802-03)A	1,558,000	25.00	60.00	150	450	—

KM# 639.4 5 FRANCS
25.0000 g., 0.9000 Silver .7234 oz. ASW **Mint:** Poitiers

Date	Mintage	VG	F	VF	XF	Unc
LAN 10 (1801-02)G	4,447	125	300	600	22.00	—

KM# 639.5 5 FRANCS
25.0000 g., 0.9000 Silver .7234 oz. ASW **Mint:** Bordeaux

Date	Mintage	VG	F	VF	XF	Unc
LAN 10 (1801-02)K	60,000	40.00	100	250	600	900
LAN 11 (1802-03)K	29,000	60.00	100	250	600	900

KM# 639.6 5 FRANCS
25.0000 g., 0.9000 Silver .7234 oz. ASW **Mint:** Bayonne

Date	Mintage	VG	F	VF	XF	Unc
LAN 10 (1801-02)L	165,000	35.00	90.00	225	550	—
LAN 11 (1802-03)L	170,000	35.00	90.00	225	550	—

KM# 639.7 5 FRANCS
25.0000 g., 0.9000 Silver .7234 oz. ASW **Mint:** Marseille

Date	Mintage	VG	F	VF	XF	Unc
LAN 10 (1801-02)MA	39,000	50.00	125	300	1,150	—
LAN 11 (1802-03)MA	160,000	35.00	90.00	225	550	—

KM# 639.8 5 FRANCS
25.0000 g., 0.9000 Silver .7234 oz. ASW **Mint:** Perpignan

Date	Mintage	VG	F	VF	XF	Unc
LAN 10 (1801-02)Q	134,000	35.00	90.00	225	550	—
LAN 11 (1802-03)Q	360,000	30.00	80.00	200	500	—

KM# 639.9 5 FRANCS
25.0000 g., 0.9000 Silver .7234 oz. ASW **Mint:** Nantes

Date	Mintage	VG	F	VF	XF	Unc
LAN 10 (1801-02)T Reported, not confirmed	5,232	—	—	—	—	—
LAN 11 (1802-03)T	9,950	70.00	165	400	1,350	—

KM# 650.1 5 FRANCS
25.0000 g., 0.9000 Silver .7234 oz. ASW **Mint:** Paris **Obv. Legend:** BONAPARTE PREMIER CONSUL

Date	Mintage	VG	F	VF	XF	Unc
ANXIA	3,878,000	20.00	50.00	150	300	—
ANXIA	Inc. above	150	300	700	—	—

Note: Without dotts flanking privy mark

KM# 650.2 5 FRANCS
25.0000 g., 0.9000 Silver .7234 oz. ASW **Mint:** Lyon **Obv. Legend:** BONAPARTE PREMIER CONSUL

Date	Mintage	VG	F	VF	XF	Unc
ANXID	5,547	100	200	500	900	—

KM# 650.3 5 FRANCS
25.0000 g., 0.9000 Silver .7234 oz. ASW **Mint:** Bordeaux **Obv. Legend:** BONAPARTE PREMIER CONSUL

Date	Mintage	VG	F	VF	XF	Unc
ANXIK	31,000	50.00	125	300	800	—

KM# 650.4 5 FRANCS
25.0000 g., 0.9000 Silver .7234 oz. ASW **Mint:** Bayonne **Obv. Legend:** BONAPARTE PREMIER CONSUL

Date	Mintage	VG	F	VF	XF	Unc
ANXIL	119,000	35.00	90.00	225	550	—

KM# 650.5 5 FRANCS
25.0000 g., 0.9000 Silver .7234 oz. ASW **Mint:** Marseille **Obv. Legend:** BONAPARTE PREMIER CONSUL

Date	Mintage	VG	F	VF	XF	Unc
ANXIMA	206,000	30.00	80.00	200	500	—

KM# 650.6 5 FRANCS
25.0000 g., 0.9000 Silver .7234 oz. ASW **Mint:** Perpignan **Obv. Legend:** BONAPARTE PREMIER CONSUL

Date	Mintage	VG	F	VF	XF	Unc
ANXIQ	309,000	30.00	80.00	200	450	—

KM# 650.7 5 FRANCS
25.0000 g., 0.9000 Silver .7234 oz. ASW **Mint:** Nantes **Obv. Legend:** BONAPARTE PREMIER CONSUL

Date	Mintage	VG	F	VF	XF	Unc
ANXIT	18,000	75.00	200	400	650	—

KM# 659.1 5 FRANCS
25.0000 g., 0.9000 Silver .7234 oz. ASW **Mint:** Paris

Date	Mintage	VG	F	VF	XF	Unc
AN12A	3,454,000	20.00	40.00	125	300	—

KM# 659.2 5 FRANCS
25.0000 g., 0.9000 Silver .7234 oz. ASW **Mint:** Rouen

Date	Mintage	VG	F	VF	XF	Unc
AN12B	35,000	50.00	125	300	800	—

KM# 659.3 5 FRANCS
25.0000 g., 0.9000 Silver .7234 oz. ASW **Mint:** Strasbourg

Date	Mintage	VG	F	VF	XF	Unc
AN12BB	18,000	75.00	200	400	650	—

KM# 659.4 5 FRANCS
25.0000 g., 0.9000 Silver .7234 oz. ASW **Mint:** Lyon

Date	Mintage	VG	F	VF	XF	Unc
AN12D	116,000	35.00	90.00	225	550	—

KM# 659.5 5 FRANCS
25.0000 g., 0.9000 Silver .7234 oz. ASW **Mint:** Poitiers

Date	Mintage	VG	F	VF	XF	Unc
AN12G	14,000	200	500	1,000	3,000	—

KM# 659.6 5 FRANCS
25.0000 g., 0.9000 Silver .7234 oz. ASW **Mint:** La Rochelle

Date	Mintage	VG	F	VF	XF	Unc
AN12H	70,000	50.00	125	300	800	—

KM# 659.7 5 FRANCS
25.0000 g., 0.9000 Silver .7234 oz. ASW **Mint:** Limoges

Date	Mintage	VG	F	VF	XF	Unc
AN12I	422,000	30.00	80.00	200	350	—

KM# 659.8 5 FRANCS
25.0000 g., 0.9000 Silver .7234 oz. ASW **Mint:** Bordeaux

Date	Mintage	VG	F	VF	XF	Unc
AN12K	462,000	40.00	80.00	200	350	—

KM# 659.9 5 FRANCS
25.0000 g., 0.9000 Silver .7234 oz. ASW **Mint:** Bayonne

Date	Mintage	VG	F	VF	XF	Unc
AN12L	311,000	40.00	80.00	200	350	—

KM# 659.10 5 FRANCS
25.0000 g., 0.9000 Silver .7234 oz. ASW **Mint:** Toulouse

Date	Mintage	VG	F	VF	XF	Unc
AN12M	1,199,000	30.00	70.00	175	300	—

KM# 659.11 5 FRANCS
25.0000 g., 0.9000 Silver .7234 oz. ASW **Mint:** Marseille

Date	Mintage	VG	F	VF	XF	Unc
AN12MA	148,000	35.00	90.00	225	550	—

KM# 659.12 5 FRANCS
25.0000 g., 0.9000 Silver .7234 oz. ASW **Mint:** Perpignan

Date	Mintage	VG	F	VF	XF	Unc
AN12Q	578,000	40.00	80.00	200	350	—

KM# 659.13 5 FRANCS
25.0000 g., 0.9000 Silver .7234 oz. ASW **Mint:** Nantes

Date	Mintage	VG	F	VF	XF	Unc
AN12T	113,000	35.00	90.00	225	550	—

KM# 659.14 5 FRANCS
25.0000 g., 0.9000 Silver .7234 oz. ASW **Mint:** Turin

Date	Mintage	VG	F	VF	XF	Unc
AN12U	9,953	150	350	1,000	2,200	—

KM# 659.15 5 FRANCS
25.0000 g., 0.9000 Silver .7234 oz. ASW **Mint:** Lille

Date	Mintage	VG	F	VF	XF	Unc
AN12W	28,000	50.00	125	300	700	—

KM# 652 40 FRANCS
12.9039 g., 0.9000 Gold .3734 oz. AGW **Mint:** Paris

Date	Mintage	F	VF	XF	Unc
ANXIA	226,000	200	225	325	2,250
AN12A	253,000	200	225	325	1,850

FIRST EMPIRE
Napoleon as Emperor
DECIMAL COINAGE

KM# 689 5 CENTIMES
Copper **Mint:** Strasbourg

Date	Good	VG	F	VF	XF
1808BB	20.00	40.00	125	250	—

KM# 676.1 10 CENTIMES
Billon **Mint:** Paris

Date	Mintage	F	VF	XF	Unc
1807A	—	150	250	500	—
1808A	6,269,000	2.00	10.00	50.00	125
1809A	7,529,000	2.00	10.00	50.00	125
1810A Unique	—	—	—	—	—

KM# 676.2 10 CENTIMES
Billon **Mint:** Rouen

Date	Mintage	F	VF	XF	Unc
1808B	163,000	25.00	60.00	125	300
1809B	831,000	6.00	20.00	60.00	150
1810B	1,231,000	5.00	18.00	55.00	135

KM# 676.3 10 CENTIMES
Billon **Mint:** Strasbourg

Date	Mintage	F	VF	XF	Unc
1808BB	1,425,000	3.00	15.00	40.00	100
1809BB	695,000	6.00	20.00	60.00	150
1810BB Unique	—	—	—	—	—

KM# 676.4 10 CENTIMES
Billon **Mint:** La Rochelle

Date	Mintage	F	VF	XF	Unc
1808H	129,000	20.00	40.00	150	360
1809H	631,000	7.00	15.00	40.00	125
1810H	673,000	7.00	15.00	40.00	125

KM# 676.5 10 CENTIMES
Billon **Mint:** Limoges

Date	Mintage	F	VF	XF	Unc
1808I	1,062,000	4.00	10.00	25.00	95.00
1809I	3,473,000	3.00	7.00	20.00	75.00
1810I	3,066,000	3.00	7.00	20.00	75.00

KM# 676.6 10 CENTIMES
Billon **Mint:** Toulouse

Date	Mintage	F	VF	XF	Unc
1808M	860,000	7.00	15.00	40.00	125
1809M	1,070,000	4.00	10.00	25.00	90.00

KM# 676.7 10 CENTIMES
Billon **Mint:** Perpignan

Date	Mintage	F	VF	XF	Unc
1808Q Rare	—	—	—	—	—
1809Q	555,000	8.00	25.00	55.00	150
1810Q	130,000	25.00	60.00	125	250

KM# 676.8 10 CENTIMES
Billon **Mint:** Nantes

Date	Mintage	F	VF	XF	Unc
1808T	54,000	40.00	100	200	500
1809T	134,000	25.00	50.00	100	200
1810T	103,000	35.00	75.00	150	360

KM# 676.9 10 CENTIMES
Billon **Mint:** Lille

Date	Mintage	F	VF	XF	Unc
1808W	1,576,000	4.00	10.00	25.00	90.00
1809W	1,160,000	4.00	10.00	25.00	90.00

KM# 654.1 1/4 FRANC
1.2500 g., 0.9000 Silver .0362 oz. ASW **Mint:** Paris **Obv. Legend:** NAPOLEON EMPEREUR

Date	Mintage	VG	F	VF	XF	Unc
AN12A	19,000	25.00	45.00	85.00	225	—
AN13A	128,000	12.50	25.00	45.00	115	—
AN14A	—	—	—	—	—	—

Note: Reported, not confirmed

KM# 654.2 1/4 FRANC
1.2500 g., 0.9000 Silver .0362 oz. ASW **Mint:** Strasbourg

Date	Mintage	VG	F	VF	XF	Unc
AN13BB	2,194	60.00	115	235	480	—

KM# 654.3 1/4 FRANC
1.2500 g., 0.9000 Silver .0362 oz. ASW **Mint:** Lyon

Date	Mintage	VG	F	VF	XF	Unc
AN12D	5,156	45.00	100	175	400	—

KM# 654.4 1/4 FRANC
1.2500 g., 0.9000 Silver .0362 oz. ASW **Mint:** La Rochelle

Date	Mintage	VG	F	VF	XF	Unc
AN12H	12,000	30.00	60.00	145	350	—
AN13/12H	—	45.00	90.00	225	460	—
AN13H	2,744	45.00	90.00	225	460	—

KM# 654.5 1/4 FRANC
1.2500 g., 0.9000 Silver .0362 oz. ASW **Mint:** Limoges

Date	Mintage	VG	F	VF	XF	Unc
AN12I	32,000	20.00	40.00	85.00	225	—
AN13I	118,000	15.00	30.00	75.00	175	—

KM# 654.6 1/4 FRANC
1.2500 g., 0.9000 Silver .0362 oz. ASW **Mint:** Bordeaux

Date	Mintage	VG	F	VF	XF	Unc
AN12K	8,122	30.00	60.00	145	350	—
AN13K	18,000	25.00	45.00	100	225	—
AN14K	1,757	70.00	140	290	650	—

KM# 654.7 1/4 FRANC
1.2500 g., 0.9000 Silver .0362 oz. ASW **Mint:** Bayonne

Date	Mintage	VG	F	VF	XF	Unc
AN13L	25,000	25.00	45.00	85.00	280	—
AN14L	—	70.00	135	280	575	—

KM# 654.8 1/4 FRANC
1.2500 g., 0.9000 Silver .0362 oz. ASW **Mint:** Toulouse

Date	Mintage	VG	F	VF	XF	Unc
AN12M	16,000	25.00	45.00	115	280	—
AN13M	39,000	20.00	40.00	80.00	225	—

KM# 654.9 1/4 FRANC
1.2500 g., 0.9000 Silver .0362 oz. ASW **Mint:** Marseille

Date	Mintage	VG	F	VF	XF	Unc
AN13MA	8,114	30.00	60.00	145	350	—

KM# 654.10 1/4 FRANC
1.2500 g., 0.9000 Silver .0362 oz. ASW **Mint:** Nantes

Date	Mintage	VG	F	VF	XF	Unc
AN12T	3,606	60.00	115	200	425	—
AN13T	6,801	35.00	70.00	140	280	—

KM# 654.11 1/4 FRANC
1.2500 g., 0.9000 Silver .0362 oz. ASW **Mint:** Turin

Date	Mintage	VG	F	VF	XF	Unc
AN13U	14,000	60.00	115	280	575	—
AN14U	100	400	600	1,000	2,000	—
AN13-14U	100	—	—	—	—	325

Note: Above value for common date uncirculated

KM# 670.1 1/4 FRANC
1.2500 g., 0.9000 Silver .0362 oz. ASW **Mint:** Paris

Date	Mintage	VG	F	VF	XF	Unc
1806A	31,000	25.00	50.00	90.00	200	—
1807A	—	—	—	—	—	—

KM# 670.2 1/4 FRANC
1.2500 g., 0.9000 Silver .0362 oz. ASW **Mint:** Limoges

Date	Mintage	VG	F	VF	XF	Unc
1806I	4,583	35.00	70.00	140	280	—
1807I	8,356	30.00	60.00	115	225	—

KM# 670.3 1/4 FRANC
1.2500 g., 0.9000 Silver .0362 oz. ASW **Mint:** Bordeaux

Date	Mintage	VG	F	VF	XF	Unc
1806K	4,359	35.00	70.00	140	280	—
1807K	5,538	35.00	70.00	140	280	—

KM# 670.4 1/4 FRANC
1.2500 g., 0.9000 Silver .0362 oz. ASW **Mint:** Bayonne

Date	Mintage	VG	F	VF	XF	Unc
1806L	18,000	25.00	50.00	90.00	225	—
1807L	7,618	30.00	75.00	115	250	—

KM# 670.5 1/4 FRANC
1.2500 g., 0.9000 Silver .0362 oz. ASW **Mint:** Toulouse

Date	Mintage	VG	F	VF	XF	Unc
1807M	1,626	85.00	1,750	300	700	—

KM# 670.6 1/4 FRANC
1.2500 g., 0.9000 Silver .0362 oz. ASW **Mint:** Perpignan

Date	Mintage	VG	F	VF	XF	Unc
1806Q	8,948	30.00	60.00	115	225	—
1807Q	9,713	30.00	60.00	115	225	—

KM# 670.7 1/4 FRANC
1.2500 g., 0.9000 Silver .0362 oz. ASW **Mint:** Turin

Date	Mintage	VG	F	VF	XF	Unc
1806U	1,361	85.00	175	300	700	—
1807U	13,000	30.00	50.00	90.00	225	—

KM# 677 1/4 FRANC
1.2500 g., 0.9000 Silver .0362 oz. ASW **Mint:** Paris **Obverse:** Negro head

Date	Mintage	VG	F	VF	XF	Unc
1807A	41,000	45.00	100	250	425	—

KM# 678.1 1/4 FRANC
1.2500 g., 0.9000 Silver .0362 oz. ASW **Mint:** Paris **Obverse:** Laureate head

Date	Mintage	VG	F	VF	XF	Unc
1807A	17,000	45.00	100	225	400	—
1808A	—	50.00	125	250	650	—

KM# 678.2 1/4 FRANC
1.2500 g., 0.9000 Silver .0362 oz. ASW **Mint:** Limoges

Date	Mintage	VG	F	VF	XF	Unc
1808I	1,466	60.00	150	300	750	—

KM# 678.3 1/4 FRANC
1.2500 g., 0.9000 Silver .0362 oz. ASW **Mint:** Bayonne

Date	Mintage	VG	F	VF	XF	Unc
1808L	4,393	50.00	100	225	400	—

KM# 690 1/4 FRANC
1.2500 g., 0.9000 Silver .0362 oz. ASW **Mint:** Paris

Date	Mintage	VG	F	VF	XF	Unc
1809A	34,000	30.00	75.00	125	250	—

KM# 655.1 1/2 FRANC
2.5000 g., 0.9000 Silver .0723 oz. ASW **Mint:** Paris **Obv. Legend:** NAPOLEON EMPEREUR

Date	Mintage	VG	F	VF	XF	Unc
AN12A	39,000	12.00	25.00	60.00	250	—
AN13A	427,000	9.00	18.00	40.00	200	—
AN14A	20,000	25.00	50.00	125	350	—

KM# 655.2 1/2 FRANC
2.5000 g., 0.9000 Silver .0723 oz. ASW **Mint:** Strasbourg **Obv. Legend:** NAPOLEON EMPEREUR

Date	Mintage	VG	F	VF	XF	Unc
AN12BB	1,825	50.00	125	275	500	—
AN13BB	895	100	200	400	900	—

KM# 655.3 1/2 FRANC
2.5000 g., 0.9000 Silver .0723 oz. ASW **Mint:** Lyon **Obv. Legend:** NAPOLEON EMPEREUR

Date	Mintage	VG	F	VF	XF	Unc
AN13D	2,402	35.00	70.00	150	350	—

KM# 655.4 1/2 FRANC
2.5000 g., 0.9000 Silver .0723 oz. ASW **Mint:** Poitiers **Obv. Legend:** NAPOLEON EMPEREUR

Date	Mintage	VG	F	VF	XF	Unc
AN13G Rare	1,181	—	—	—	—	—

KM# 655.5 1/2 FRANC
2.5000 g., 0.9000 Silver .0723 oz. ASW **Mint:** La Rochelle **Obv. Legend:** NAPOLEON EMPEREUR

Date	Mintage	VG	F	VF	XF	Unc
AN12H	7,286	25.00	60.00	125	300	—
AN13H	5,036	30.00	75.00	150	350	—

KM# 655.6 1/2 FRANC
2.5000 g., 0.9000 Silver .0723 oz. ASW **Mint:** Limoges **Obv. Legend:** NAPOLEON EMPEREUR

Date	Mintage	VG	F	VF	XF	Unc
AN12I	22,000	20.00	50.00	100	225	—
AN13I	206,000	12.00	22.00	50.00	200	—

KM# 655.7 1/2 FRANC
2.5000 g., 0.9000 Silver .0723 oz. ASW **Mint:** Bordeaux **Obv. Legend:** NAPOLEON EMPEREUR

Date	Mintage	VG	F	VF	XF	Unc
AN12K	19,000	20.00	50.00	100	250	—
AN13K	37,000	18.00	40.00	80.00	200	—
AN14K Rare	1,757	—	—	—	—	—

KM# 655.8 1/2 FRANC
2.5000 g., 0.9000 Silver .0723 oz. ASW **Mint:** Bayonne **Obv. Legend:** NAPOLEON EMPEREUR

Date	Mintage	VG	F	VF	XF	Unc
AN13L	46,000	15.00	30.00	65.00	180	—
AN14L	3,889	50.00	100	225	500	—

KM# 655.9 1/2 FRANC
2.5000 g., 0.9000 Silver .0723 oz. ASW **Mint:** Toulouse **Obv. Legend:** NAPOLEON EMPEREUR

Date	Mintage	VG	F	VF	XF	Unc
AN12M	99,000	12.00	25.00	60.00	175	—
AN13M	212,000	10.00	20.00	50.00	150	—

KM# 655.10 1/2 FRANC
2.5000 g., 0.9000 Silver .0723 oz. ASW **Mint:** Marseille **Obv. Legend:** NAPOLEON EMPEREUR

Date	Mintage	VG	F	VF	XF	Unc
AN13MA	6,103	30.00	75.00	150	350	—

KM# 655.11 1/2 FRANC
2.5000 g., 0.9000 Silver .0723 oz. ASW **Mint:** Perpignan **Obv. Legend:** NAPOLEON EMPEREUR

Date	Mintage	VG	F	VF	XF	Unc
AN13Q	34,000	18.00	40.00	80.00	200	—

KM# 655.12 1/2 FRANC
2.5000 g., 0.9000 Silver .0723 oz. ASW **Mint:** Nantes **Obv. Legend:** NAPOLEON EMPEREUR

Date	Mintage	VG	F	VF	XF	Unc
AN12T	3,735	35.00	70.00	150	350	—
AN13T	6,140	30.00	70.00	140	300	—

KM# 655.13 1/2 FRANC
2.5000 g., 0.9000 Silver .0723 oz. ASW **Mint:** Turin **Obv. Legend:** NAPOLEON EMPEREUR

Date	Mintage	VG	F	VF	XF	Unc
AN13U	1,662	50.00	90.00	200	400	—
AN14U	—	100	200	400	800	—
AN13-14U	—	—	—	—	—	550

KM# 671.1 1/2 FRANC
2.5000 g., 0.9000 Silver .0723 oz. ASW **Mint:** Paris

Date	Mintage	VG	F	VF	XF	Unc
1806A	156,000	12.00	25.00	60.00	200	—

KM# 671.2 1/2 FRANC
2.5000 g., 0.9000 Silver .0723 oz. ASW **Mint:** Limoges

Date	Mintage	VG	F	VF	XF	Unc
1806I	7,027	30.00	75.00	150	350	—
1807I	3,848	40.00	90.00	175	400	—

KM# 671.3 1/2 FRANC
2.5000 g., 0.9000 Silver .0723 oz. ASW **Mint:** Bordeaux

Date	Mintage	VG	F	VF	XF	Unc
1806K	1,673	50.00	100	200	450	—
1807K	2,983	40.00	90.00	175	400	—

KM# 671.4 1/2 FRANC
2.5000 g., 0.9000 Silver .0723 oz. ASW **Mint:** Bayonne

Date	Mintage	VG	F	VF	XF	Unc
1806L	42,000	15.00	30.00	75.00	200	—
1807/6L	17,000	20.00	40.00	100	225	—
1807L	Inc. above	20.00	40.00	100	250	—

KM# 671.5 1/2 FRANC
2.5000 g., 0.9000 Silver .0723 oz. ASW **Mint:** Toulouse

Date	Mintage	VG	F	VF	XF	Unc
1807M	1,791	—	—	—	—	—

Note: Reported, not confirmed

KM# 671.6 1/2 FRANC
2.5000 g., 0.9000 Silver .0723 oz. ASW **Mint:** Perpignan

Date	Mintage	VG	F	VF	XF	Unc
1806Q	15,000	20.00	50.00	110	275	—
1807Q	14,000	20.00	50.00	110	275	—

KM# 671.7 1/2 FRANC
2.5000 g., 0.9000 Silver .0723 oz. ASW **Mint:** Turin

Date	Mintage	VG	F	VF	XF	Unc
1806U	9,592	30.00	75.00	150	350	—
1807U	4,448	40.00	90.00	175	400	—
1807U	—	—	—	—	—	500

KM# 679 1/2 FRANC
2.5000 g., 0.9000 Silver .0723 oz. ASW **Mint:** Paris **Note:** Negro head.

Date	Mintage	VG	F	VF	XF	Unc
1807A	58,000	75.00	175	450	950	—

KM# 680.1 1/2 FRANC
2.5000 g., 0.9000 Silver .0723 oz. ASW **Note:** Laureate head.

Date	Mintage	VG	F	VF	XF	Unc
1807	46,000	60.00	125	250	500	—
1808	6,606,000	5.00	10.00	20.00	75.00	—

KM# 680.2 1/2 FRANC
2.5000 g., 0.9000 Silver .0723 oz. ASW **Mint:** Rouen

Date	Mintage	VG	F	VF	XF	Unc
1808B	559,000	8.00	15.00	30.00	100	—

KM# 680.3 1/2 FRANC
2.5000 g., 0.9000 Silver .0723 oz. ASW **Mint:** Strasbourg

Date	Mintage	VG	F	VF	XF	Unc
1808BB	1,596,000	5.00	10.00	25.00	75.00	—

KM# 680.4 1/2 FRANC
2.5000 g., 0.9000 Silver .0723 oz. ASW **Mint:** Lyon

Date	Mintage	VG	F	VF	XF	Unc
1808D	871,000	6.00	12.00	30.00	90.00	—

KM# 680.5 1/2 FRANC
2.5000 g., 0.9000 Silver .0723 oz. ASW **Mint:** La Rochelle

Date	Mintage	VG	F	VF	XF	Unc
1808H	336,000	8.00	18.00	45.00	100	—

KM# 680.6 1/2 FRANC
2.5000 g., 0.9000 Silver .0723 oz. ASW **Mint:** Limoges

Date	Mintage	VG	F	VF	XF	Unc
1808I	298,000	10.00	20.00	40.00	100	—

KM# 680.7 1/2 FRANC
2.5000 g., 0.9000 Silver .0723 oz. ASW **Mint:** Bordeaux

Date	Mintage	VG	F	VF	XF	Unc
1808K	363,000	8.00	18.00	45.00	100	—

KM# 680.8 1/2 FRANC
2.5000 g., 0.9000 Silver .0723 oz. ASW **Mint:** Bayonne

Date	Mintage	VG	F	VF	XF	Unc
1808L	3,394	50.00	100	200	375	—

KM# 680.9 1/2 FRANC
2.5000 g., 0.9000 Silver .0723 oz. ASW **Mint:** Toulouse

Date	Mintage	VG	F	VF	XF	Unc
1808M	54,000	20.00	50.00	100	200	—

KM# 680.10 1/2 FRANC
2.5000 g., 0.9000 Silver .0723 oz. ASW **Mint:** Marseille

Date	Mintage	VG	F	VF	XF	Unc
1808MA	28,000	30.00	60.00	125	250	—

KM# 680.11 1/2 FRANC
2.5000 g., 0.9000 Silver .0723 oz. ASW **Mint:** Perpignan

Date	Mintage	VG	F	VF	XF	Unc
1808Q	289,000	10.00	20.00	40.00	100	—

KM# 680.12 1/2 FRANC
2.5000 g., 0.9000 Silver .0723 oz. ASW **Mint:** Nantes

Date	Mintage	VG	F	VF	XF	Unc
1808T	128,000	12.00	25.00	50.00	125	—

KM# 680.13 1/2 FRANC
2.5000 g., 0.9000 Silver .0723 oz. ASW **Mint:** Turin

Date	Mintage	VG	F	VF	XF	Unc
1808U	3,339	50.00	100	200	375	—

KM# 680.14 1/2 FRANC
2.5000 g., 0.9000 Silver .0723 oz. ASW **Mint:** Lille

Date	Mintage	VG	F	VF	XF	Unc
1808W	1,069,000	5.00	10.00	25.00	75.00	—
1808W	—	—	—	—	—	275

Note: Above value for common date proof

KM# 691.1 1/2 FRANC
2.5000 g., 0.9000 Silver .0723 oz. ASW **Mint:** Paris

Date	Mintage	VG	F	VF	XF	Unc
1809A	1,680,000	5.00	10.00	20.00	75.00	—
1810A	1,362,000	5.00	10.00	20.00	75.00	—
1811A	1,860,000	5.00	10.00	20.00	75.00	—
1812A	1,720,000	5.00	10.00	20.00	75.00	—
1813A	627,000	8.00	15.00	30.00	85.00	—
1814A	107,000	10.00	20.00	50.00	100	—

KM# 691.2 1/2 FRANC
2.5000 g., 0.9000 Silver .0723 oz. ASW **Mint:** Rouen

Date	Mintage	VG	F	VF	XF	Unc
1809B	14,000	15.00	30.00	90.00	225	—
1810B	285,000	8.00	15.00	35.00	100	—
1811B	252,000	8.00	15.00	35.00	100	—
1812B	192,000	9.00	18.00	40.00	115	—

KM# 691.3 1/2 FRANC
2.5000 g., 0.9000 Silver .0723 oz. ASW **Mint:** Strasbourg

Date	Mintage	VG	F	VF	XF	Unc
1810BB	11,000	20.00	40.00	100	250	—
1811BB	37,000	10.00	22.00	55.00	140	—

KM# 691.4 1/2 FRANC
2.5000 g., 0.9000 Silver .0723 oz. ASW **Mint:** Genoa

Date	Mintage	VG	F	VF	XF	Unc
1813CL	8,385	50.00	100	225	550	—

KM# 691.5 1/2 FRANC
2.5000 g., 0.9000 Silver .0723 oz. ASW **Mint:** Lyon

Date	Mintage	VG	F	VF	XF	Unc
1809D	43,000	10.00	20.00	45.00	125	—
1810D	71,000	9.00	18.00	40.00	115	—
1811D	221,000	8.00	15.00	35.00	100	—
1812D	155,000	8.00	15.00	35.00	100	—
1813D	110,000	8.00	18.00	45.00	125	—

KM# 691.6 1/2 FRANC
2.5000 g., 0.9000 Silver .0723 oz. ASW **Mint:** La Rochelle

Date	Mintage	VG	F	VF	XF	Unc
1810H	3,563	40.00	80.00	175	350	—
1811H	120,000	8.00	15.00	35.00	100	—
1812H	270,000	6.00	12.00	30.00	90.00	—
1813H	138,000	8.00	15.00	35.00	100	—

KM# 691.7 1/2 FRANC
2.5000 g., 0.9000 Silver .0723 oz. ASW **Mint:** Limoges

Date	Mintage	VG	F	VF	XF	Unc
1811I	134,000	8.00	15.00	35.00	100	—
1812I	137,000	8.00	15.00	35.00	100	—
1813I	97,000	9.00	18.00	40.00	115	—

KM# 691.8 1/2 FRANC
2.5000 g., 0.9000 Silver .0723 oz. ASW **Mint:** Bordeaux

Date	Mintage	VG	F	VF	XF	Unc
1809K	43,000	10.00	20.00	45.00	125	—
1810K	41,000	10.00	20.00	45.00	125	—
1811K	16,000	15.00	30.00	75.00	175	—
1812K	34,000	12.00	25.00	60.00	150	—
1813K	58,000	10.00	20.00	50.00	125	—

KM# 691.9 1/2 FRANC
2.5000 g., 0.9000 Silver .0723 oz. ASW **Mint:** Bayonne

Date	Mintage	VG	F	VF	XF	Unc
1810L	55,000	10.00	22.00	50.00	125	—
1810L (Tr)	Inc. above	—	—	—	—	—
Note: Reported, not confirmed						
1811L	95,000	8.00	17.50	40.00	100	—
1812L	52,000	10.00	20.00	50.00	125	—
1813L	44,000	10.00	22.00	55.00	140	—

KM# 691.10 1/2 FRANC
2.5000 g., 0.9000 Silver .0723 oz. ASW **Mint:** Toulouse

Date	Mintage	VG	F	VF	XF	Unc
1809M	21,000	12.00	25.00	65.00	160	—
1810M	33,000	12.00	25.00	60.00	150	—
1811M	49,000	10.00	22.00	55.00	140	—
1812M	105,000	8.00	17.50	40.00	110	—
1813M	159,000	7.00	15.00	35.00	100	—
1814M	36,000	40.00	75.00	150	350	—

KM# 691.11 1/2 FRANC
2.5000 g., 0.9000 Silver .0723 oz. ASW **Mint:** Marseille

Date	Mintage	VG	F	VF	XF	Unc
1809MA	3,176	40.00	75.00	150	400	—
1810MA	11,000	20.00	40.00	100	300	—
1811MA	69,000	10.00	20.00	50.00	125	—
1812MA	52,000	10.00	20.00	50.00	125	—
1813MA	70,000	8.00	17.50	45.00	120	—

KM# 691.12 1/2 FRANC
2.5000 g., 0.9000 Silver .0723 oz. ASW **Mint:** Perpignan

Date	Mintage	VG	F	VF	XF	Unc
1809	70,000	10.00	22.00	50.00	125	—
1811	126,000	7.50	15.00	35.00	100	—
1812	106,000	8.00	17.50	40.00	110	—
1813	44,000	10.00	22.00	50.00	140	—

KM# 691.13 1/2 FRANC
2.5000 g., 0.9000 Silver .0723 oz. ASW **Mint:** Nantes

Date	Mintage	VG	F	VF	XF	Unc
1811T	114,000	8.00	17.50	40.00	100	—
1812T	81,000	7.00	15.00	45.00	120	—
1813T	53,000	10.00	20.00	50.00	125	—

KM# 691.14 1/2 FRANC

2.5000 g., 0.9000 Silver .0723 oz. ASW **Mint:** Turin

Date	Mintage	VG	F	VF	XF	Unc
1809U	5,853	30.00	65.00	125	300	—
1811U	39,000	12.00	25.00	60.00	150	—

KM# 691.15 1/2 FRANC

2.5000 g., 0.9000 Silver .0723 oz. ASW **Mint:** Lille

Date	Mintage	VG	F	VF	XF	Unc
1809W	314,000	6.00	12.00	30.00	100	—
1810W	240,000	7.00	14.00	32.00	110	—
1811W	246,000	7.00	14.00	32.00	110	—
1812W	337,000	6.00	12.00	30.00	100	—
1813W	58,000	10.00	20.00	50.00	125	—

KM# 691.16 1/2 FRANC

2.5000 g., 0.9000 Silver .0723 oz. ASW **Mint:** Utrecht **Note:** Mint mark: Flag.

Date	Mintage	VG	F	VF	XF	Unc
1812	5,084	50.00	100	225	500	—
1813	6,894	50.00	100	225	500	—
1812-13	—	—	—	—	—	200

Note: Above price for common date uncirculated

KM# 656.1 FRANC

5.0000 g., 0.9000 Silver .1446 oz. ASW **Mint:** Paris **Obv. Legend:** NAPOLEON EMPEREUR

Date	Mintage	VG	F	VF	XF	Unc
AN12A	326,000	20.00	40.00	100	225	—
AN13A	2,454,000	15.00	30.00	85.00	200	—
AN14A	298,000	25.00	50.00	110	275	—

KM# 656.2 FRANC

5.0000 g., 0.9000 Silver .1446 oz. ASW **Mint:** Rouen **Obv. Legend:** NAPOLEON EMPEREUR

Date	Mintage	VG	F	VF	XF	Unc
AN12B	30,000	30.00	60.00	135	300	—
AN13B	2,906	65.00	125	275	600	—

KM# 656.3 FRANC

5.0000 g., 0.9000 Silver .1446 oz. ASW **Mint:** Strasbourg **Obv. Legend:** NAPOLEON EMPEREUR

Date	Mintage	VG	F	VF	XF	Unc
AN13BB	3,410	65.00	125	275	600	—
AN14BB	491	325	750	1,300	2,100	—

KM# 656.4 FRANC

5.0000 g., 0.9000 Silver .1446 oz. ASW **Mint:** Lyon **Obv. Legend:** NAPOLEON EMPEREUR

Date	Mintage	VG	F	VF	XF	Unc
AN12D	3,968	65.00	125	275	600	—
AN13D	10,000	40.00	75.00	175	350	—
AN14D	2,450	65.00	125	275	650	—

KM# 656.5 FRANC

5.0000 g., 0.9000 Silver .1446 oz. ASW **Mint:** Poitiers **Obv. Legend:** NAPOLEON EMPEREUR

Date	Mintage	VG	F	VF	XF	Unc
AN13G	11,000	125	250	550	1,250	—

KM# 656.6 FRANC

5.0000 g., 0.9000 Silver .1446 oz. ASW **Mint:** La Rochelle **Obv. Legend:** NAPOLEON EMPEREUR

Date	Mintage	VG	F	VF	XF	Unc
AN12H	4,398	65.00	125	275	500	800
AN13H	43,000	30.00	60.00	135	250	400
AN14H	7,164	65.00	125	275	500	800

KM# 656.7 FRANC

5.0000 g., 0.9000 Silver .1446 oz. ASW **Mint:** Limoges **Obv. Legend:** NAPOLEON EMPEREUR

Date	Mintage	VG	F	VF	XF	Unc
AN12I	43,000	30.00	60.00	135	300	—
AN13I	390,000	20.00	40.00	100	225	—
AN14I	2,847	100	200	400	800	—

KM# 656.8 FRANC

5.0000 g., 0.9000 Silver .1446 oz. ASW **Mint:** Bordeaux **Obv. Legend:** NAPOLEON EMPEREUR

Date	Mintage	VG	F	VF	XF	Unc
AN12K	24,000	35.00	65.00	150	350	—
AN13K	61,000	30.00	60.00	135	300	—
AN14K	1,526	100	200	400	900	—

KM# 656.9 FRANC

5.0000 g., 0.9000 Silver .1446 oz. ASW **Mint:** Bayonne **Obv. Legend:** NAPOLEON EMPEREUR

Date	Mintage	VG	F	VF	XF	Unc
AN12L	4,253	65.00	125	275	600	—
AN13L	73,000	30.00	60.00	135	300	—
AN14L	4,107	65.00	125	275	600	—

KM# 656.10 FRANC

5.0000 g., 0.9000 Silver .1446 oz. ASW **Mint:** Toulouse **Obv. Legend:** NAPOLEON EMPEREUR

Date	Mintage	VG	F	VF	XF	Unc
AN12M	300,000	20.00	40.00	100	225	—
AN13M	651,000	15.00	30.00	70.00	200	—
AN14M	1,096	100	200	400	900	—

KM# 656.11 FRANC

5.0000 g., 0.9000 Silver .1446 oz. ASW **Mint:** Marseille **Obv. Legend:** NAPOLEON EMPEREUR

Date	Mintage	VG	F	VF	XF	Unc
AN12MA	5,582	65.00	125	275	600	—
AN13MA	28,000	35.00	65.00	150	350	—
AN14MA	6,910	65.00	125	275	600	—

KM# 656.12 FRANC

5.0000 g., 0.9000 Silver .1446 oz. ASW **Mint:** Perpignan **Obv. Legend:** NAPOLEON EMPEREUR

Date	Mintage	VG	F	VF	XF	Unc
AN12Q	25,000	35.00	65.00	150	350	—
AN13Q	117,000	25.00	50.00	125	275	—

KM# 656.13 FRANC

5.0000 g., 0.9000 Silver .1446 oz. ASW **Mint:** Nantes **Obv. Legend:** NAPOLEON EMPEREUR

Date	Mintage	VG	F	VF	XF	Unc
AN12T	3,462	65.00	125	275	700	—
AN13T	13,000	40.00	75.00	175	350	—

KM# 656.14 FRANC

5.0000 g., 0.9000 Silver .1446 oz. ASW **Mint:** Turin **Obv. Legend:** NAPOLEON EMPEREUR

Date	Mintage	VG	F	VF	XF	Unc
AN12U	1,166	100	200	400	800	1,200
AN13U	15,000	60.00	120	250	650	950
AN14U	4,667	—	—	1,000	—	—

Note: 3 known

KM# 656.15 FRANC

5.0000 g., 0.9000 Silver .1446 oz. ASW **Mint:** Lille **Obv. Legend:** NAPOLEON EMPEREUR

Date	Mintage	VG	F	VF	XF	Unc
AN13W	17,000	40.00	75.00	175	350	—
AN14W	4,667	75.00	150	300	700	—
AN13-14W	—	—	—	—	—	1,000

Note: Above value for common date uncirculated

KM# 672.1 FRANC

5.0000 g., 0.9000 Silver .1446 oz. ASW **Mint:** Paris **Obv. Legend:** NAPOLEON EMPEREUR

Date	Mintage	VG	F	VF	XF	Unc
1806A	828,000	20.00	40.00	100	225	—

KM# 672.2 FRANC

5.0000 g., 0.9000 Silver .1446 oz. ASW **Mint:** Rouen

Date	Mintage	VG	F	VF	XF	Unc
1807B	3,465	65.00	125	275	600	—

KM# 672.3 FRANC

5.0000 g., 0.9000 Silver .1446 oz. ASW **Mint:** La Rochelle

Date	Mintage	VG	F	VF	XF	Unc
1806H	8,472	55.00	100	225	500	—
1807H	4,728	60.00	110	240	525	—

KM# 672.4 FRANC

5.0000 g., 0.9000 Silver .1446 oz. ASW **Mint:** Limoges

Date	Mintage	VG	F	VF	XF	Unc
1806I	34,000	35.00	65.00	150	350	—
1807I	11,000	50.00	100	200	450	—

KM# 672.5 FRANC

5.0000 g., 0.9000 Silver .1446 oz. ASW **Mint:** Bordeaux

Date	Mintage	VG	F	VF	XF	Unc
1806K	3,173	75.00	150	400	800	—
1807K	2,362	75.00	150	400	800	—

KM# 672.6 FRANC

5.0000 g., 0.9000 Silver .1446 oz. ASW **Mint:** Bayonne

Date	Mintage	VG	F	VF	XF	Unc
1806L	253,000	25.00	50.00	125	275	—
1807L	177,000	25.00	50.00	125	275	—

KM# 672.7 FRANC

5.0000 g., 0.9000 Silver .1446 oz. ASW **Mint:** Toulouse

Date	Mintage	VG	F	VF	XF	Unc
1806M	1,066	100	200	400	900	—
1807M	23,000	35.00	65.00	150	350	—

KM# 672.8 FRANC

5.0000 g., 0.9000 Silver .1446 oz. ASW **Mint:** Marseille

Date	Mintage	VG	F	VF	XF	Unc
1806MA	1,010	100	200	400	900	—
1807MA	1,493	100	200	400	900	—

KM# 672.9 FRANC

5.0000 g., 0.9000 Silver .1446 oz. ASW **Mint:** Perpignan

Date	Mintage	VG	F	VF	XF	Unc
1806Q	16,000	40.00	75.00	175	350	—
1807Q	9,659	50.00	100	225	450	—

KM# 672.10 FRANC

5.0000 g., 0.9000 Silver .1446 oz. ASW **Mint:** Turin

Date	Mintage	VG	F	VF	XF	Unc
1806U	15,000	40.00	75.00	175	350	—
1807U	11,000	50.00	100	225	450	—

KM# 672.11 FRANC

5.0000 g., 0.9000 Silver .1446 oz. ASW **Mint:** Lille

Date	Mintage	VG	F	VF	XF	Unc
1806W	28,000	35.00	65.00	150	350	—
1807W	15,000	40.00	75.00	175	350	—
1806-07W	—	—	—	—	—	800

Note: Above value for common date uncirculated

KM# 681 FRANC

5.0000 g., 0.9000 Silver .1446 oz. ASW **Mint:** Paris **Note:** Negro head.

Date	Mintage	VG	F	VF	XF	Unc
1807A	100,000	150	350	750	1,800	—

KM# 682.1 FRANC

5.0000 g., 0.9000 Silver .1446 oz. ASW **Mint:** Paris **Note:** Laureate head.

Date	Mintage	VG	F	VF	XF	Unc
1807A	50,000	100	200	350	900	—
1808A	4,599,000	6.00	12.00	55.00	175	—

KM# 682.2 FRANC

5.0000 g., 0.9000 Silver .1446 oz. ASW **Mint:** Rouen

Date	Mintage	VG	F	VF	XF	Unc
1808B	765,000	10.00	20.00	65.00	175	—

KM# 682.3 FRANC

5.0000 g., 0.9000 Silver .1446 oz. ASW **Mint:** Strasbourg

Date	Mintage	VG	F	VF	XF	Unc
1808BB	2,126,000	8.00	16.00	55.00	150	—

KM# 682.4 FRANC

5.0000 g., 0.9000 Silver .1446 oz. ASW **Mint:** Lyon

Date	Mintage	VG	F	VF	XF	Unc
1808D	752,000	10.00	20.00	65.00	175	—

KM# 682.5 FRANC

5.0000 g., 0.9000 Silver .1446 oz. ASW **Mint:** La Rochelle

Date	Mintage	VG	F	VF	XF	Unc
1808H	316,000	12.00	25.00	75.00	200	—

KM# 682.6 FRANC

5.0000 g., 0.9000 Silver .1446 oz. ASW **Mint:** Limoges

Date	Mintage	VG	F	VF	XF	Unc
1808I	256,000	12.00	25.00	75.00	200	—

KM# 682.7 FRANC

5.0000 g., 0.9000 Silver .1446 oz. ASW **Mint:** Bordeaux

Date	Mintage	VG	F	VF	XF	Unc
1808K	228,000	12.00	25.00	75.00	200	—

KM# 682.8 FRANC

5.0000 g., 0.9000 Silver .1446 oz. ASW **Mint:** Bayonne

Date	Mintage	VG	F	VF	XF	Unc
1808L	16,000	40.00	80.00	150	325	—

KM# 682.9 FRANC

5.0000 g., 0.9000 Silver .1446 oz. ASW **Mint:** Toulouse

Date	Mintage	VG	F	VF	XF	Unc
1808M	130,000	20.00	40.00	80.00	200	—

KM# 682.10 FRANC

5.0000 g., 0.9000 Silver .1446 oz. ASW **Mint:** Marseille

Date	Mintage	VG	F	VF	XF	Unc
1808MA	29,000	35.00	75.00	135	300	—

KM# 682.11 FRANC

5.0000 g., 0.9000 Silver .1446 oz. ASW **Mint:** Perpignan

Date	Mintage	VG	F	VF	XF	Unc
1808Q	64,000	30.00	65.00	125	275	—

KM# 682.12 FRANC

5.0000 g., 0.9000 Silver .1446 oz. ASW **Mint:** Nantes

Date	Mintage	VG	F	VF	XF	Unc
1808T	106,000	20.00	40.00	80.00	200	—

KM# 682.13 FRANC

5.0000 g., 0.9000 Silver .1446 oz. ASW **Mint:** Turin

Date	Mintage	VG	F	VF	XF	Unc
1808U	13,000	50.00	125	300	550	—

KM# 682.14 FRANC

5.0000 g., 0.9000 Silver .1446 oz. ASW **Mint:** Lille

Date	Mintage	VG	F	VF	XF	Unc
1808W	2,422,000	8.00	16.00	55.00	150	—
1808W	—	—	—	—	—	450

Note: Above value for common date uncirculated

KM# 692.1 FRANC

5.0000 g., 0.9000 Silver .1446 oz. ASW **Mint:** Paris

Date	Mintage	VG	F	VF	XF	Unc
1809A	980,000	8.00	16.00	55.00	150	—
1810A	1,676,000	8.00	16.00	55.00	150	—
1811A	1,347,000	8.00	16.00	55.00	150	—
1812A	563,000	10.00	20.00	45.00	140	—
1813A	446,000	10.00	20.00	45.00	140	—
1814A	42,000	35.00	75.00	135	300	—

KM# 692.2 FRANC

5.0000 g., 0.9000 Silver .1446 oz. ASW **Mint:** Rouen

Date	Mintage	VG	F	VF	XF	Unc
1809B	202,000	10.00	20.00	50.00	150	—
1810B	167,000	12.00	22.50	60.00	160	—
1811B	253,000	10.00	20.00	50.00	150	—
1812B	118,000	12.00	25.00	65.00	175	—
1813B	61,000	15.00	30.00	75.00	200	—

KM# 692.3 FRANC

5.0000 g., 0.9000 Silver .1446 oz. ASW **Mint:** Strasbourg

Date	Mintage	VG	F	VF	XF	Unc
1810BB	4,336	50.00	100	175	375	—
1811BB	12,000	40.00	80.00	150	325	—
1812BB	5,571	50.00	100	175	375	—

KM# 692.4 FRANC
5.0000 g., 0.9000 Silver .1446 oz. ASW **Mint:** Genoa

Date	Mintage	VG	F	VF	XF	Unc
1813CL	7,229	115	250	425	850	—

KM# 692.5 FRANC
5.0000 g., 0.9000 Silver .1446 oz. ASW **Mint:** Lyon

Date	Mintage	VG	F	VF	XF	Unc
1809D	47,000	30.00	65.00	125	275	—
1810D	39,000	30.00	65.00	125	275	—
1811D	242,000	10.00	20.00	50.00	150	—
1812D	147,000	12.00	22.50	65.00	170	—
1813D	78,000	15.00	30.00	75.00	200	—

KM# 692.6 FRANC
5.0000 g., 0.9000 Silver .1446 oz. ASW **Mint:** La Rochelle

Date	Mintage	VG	F	VF	XF	Unc
1809H	34,000	30.00	65.00	125	275	—
1810H	16,000	35.00	75.00	150	325	—
1811H	105,000	12.00	25.00	65.00	175	—
1812H	165,000	10.00	22.00	60.00	160	—
1813H	96,000	15.00	30.00	75.00	200	—

KM# 692.7 FRANC
5.0000 g., 0.9000 Silver .1446 oz. ASW **Mint:** Limoges

Date	Mintage	VG	F	VF	XF	Unc
1810I	18,000	40.00	80.00	150	325	—
1811I	85,000	15.00	30.00	75.00	200	—
1812I	91,000	15.00	30.00	75.00	200	—
1813I	76,000	15.00	30.00	75.00	200	—

KM# 692.8 FRANC
5.0000 g., 0.9000 Silver .1446 oz. ASW **Mint:** Bordeaux

Date	Mintage	VG	F	VF	XF	Unc
1809K	74,000	15.00	30.00	75.00	200	—
1810K	93,000	15.00	30.00	75.00	200	—
1811K	48,000	20.00	40.00	85.00	225	—
1812K	41,000	20.00	40.00	85.00	225	—
1813K	68,000	15.00	30.00	75.00	200	—

KM# 692.9 FRANC
5.0000 g., 0.9000 Silver .1446 oz. ASW **Mint:** Bayonne

Date	Mintage	VG	F	VF	XF	Unc
1809L	28,000	30.00	65.00	125	275	—
1810L (Tr)	47,000	30.00	65.00	125	275	—
1810L Unique	Inc. above	—	—	—	—	—
1811L	188,000	10.00	22.00	60.00	160	—
1812L	47,000	20.00	40.00	85.00	225	—
1813L	33,000	20.00	40.00	85.00	225	—

KM# 692.10 FRANC
5.0000 g., 0.9000 Silver .1446 oz. ASW **Mint:** Toulouse

Date	Mintage	VG	F	VF	XF	Unc
1809M	8,855	50.00	100	175	375	—
1810M	35,000	30.00	65.00	125	275	—
1811M	81,000	15.00	30.00	75.00	200	—
1812M	125,000	12.00	25.00	65.00	175	—
1813M	181,000	12.00	25.00	65.00	175	—
1814M	29,000	40.00	80.00	150	325	—

KM# 692.11 FRANC
5.0000 g., 0.9000 Silver .1446 oz. ASW **Mint:** Marseille

Date	Mintage	VG	F	VF	XF	Unc
1809MA	20,000	40.00	80.00	150	325	—
1810MA	28,000	30.00	65.00	125	275	—
1811MA	44,000	25.00	60.00	110	250	—
1812MA	36,000	25.00	60.00	110	250	—
1813MA	44,000	25.00	60.00	110	250	—

KM# 692.12 FRANC
5.0000 g., 0.9000 Silver .1446 oz. ASW **Mint:** Perpignan

Date	Mintage	VG	F	VF	XF	Unc
1809Q	163,000	12.00	25.00	65.00	175	—
1810Q	73,000	15.00	30.00	75.00	200	—
1811Q	161,000	12.00	25.00	65.00	175	—
1812Q	34,000	30.00	65.00	125	275	—
1813Q	75,000	15.00	30.00	75.00	200	—

KM# 692.13 FRANC
5.0000 g., 0.9000 Silver .1446 oz. ASW **Mint:** London

Date	Mintage	VG	F	VF	XF	Unc
1812R	12,000	75.00	150	350	700	—
1813R	779	325	550	925	1,450	—

KM# 692.14 FRANC
5.0000 g., 0.9000 Silver .1446 oz. ASW **Mint:** Nantes

Date	Mintage	VG	F	VF	XF	Unc
1811T	42,000	25.00	60.00	110	250	—
1812T	41,000	25.00	60.00	110	250	—
1813T	20,000	40.00	80.00	150	325	—

KM# 692.15 FRANC
5.0000 g., 0.9000 Silver .1446 oz. ASW **Mint:** Turin

Date	Mintage	VG	F	VF	XF	Unc
1809U	5,549	60.00	125	250	500	—
1810U	10,200	50.00	100	225	400	—
1812U	21,000	45.00	90.00	200	350	—
1813U	6,065	100	200	350	700	1,100

KM# 692.16 FRANC
5.0000 g., 0.9000 Silver .1446 oz. ASW **Mint:** Lille

Date	Mintage	VG	F	VF	XF	Unc
1809W	196,000	12.00	25.00	65.00	175	—
1810W	187,000	12.00	25.00	65.00	175	—
1811W	265,000	12.00	25.00	65.00	175	—
1812W	143,000	12.00	25.00	65.00	175	—
1813W	93,000	15.00	30.00	75.00	200	—

KM# 692.17 FRANC
5.0000 g., 0.9000 Silver .1446 oz. ASW **Mint:** Utrecht **Note:** Mint mark: Flag.

Date	Mintage	VG	F	VF	XF	Unc
1812	12,000	100	200	400	800	—
1813	69,000	75.00	150	300	650	—
1812-13	—	—	—	—	—	400

Note: Above value for common date uncirculated

KM# 658.1 2 FRANCS
10.0000 g., 0.9000 Silver .2893 oz. ASW **Mint:** Paris **Obv. Legend:** NAPOLEON EMPEREUR

Date	Mintage	VG	F	VF	XF	Unc
AN12A	60,000	60.00	125	225	525	—
AN13/2A	742,000	30.00	65.00	150	475	—
AN13A	Inc. above	30.00	60.00	125	450	—
AN14A	232,000	35.00	70.00	150	475	—
1806A	169,000	35.00	70.00	150	475	—

KM# 658.2 2 FRANCS
10.0000 g., 0.9000 Silver .2893 oz. ASW **Mint:** Rouen **Obv. Legend:** NAPOLEON EMPEREUR

Date	Mintage	VG	F	VF	XF	Unc
AN12B	14,000	45.00	115	225	500	—

KM# 658.3 2 FRANCS
10.0000 g., 0.9000 Silver .2893 oz. ASW **Mint:** Strasbourg **Obv. Legend:** NAPOLEON EMPEREUR

Date	Mintage	VG	F	VF	XF	Unc
AN12BB	1,798	—	—	—	—	—
AN13BB	4,341	150	—	—	—	—

KM# 658.4 2 FRANCS
10.0000 g., 0.9000 Silver .2893 oz. ASW **Mint:** Lyon **Obv. Legend:** NAPOLEON EMPEREUR

Date	Mintage	VG	F	VF	XF	Unc
AN13D	2,560	—	—	—	—	—
Note: Reported, not confirmed						
AN14D	204	—	—	—	—	—
Note: Reported, not confirmed						
1806D	530	—	—	—	—	—
Note: Reported, not confirmed						

KM# 658.5 2 FRANCS
10.0000 g., 0.9000 Silver .2893 oz. ASW **Mint:** Poitiers **Obv. Legend:** NAPOLEON EMPEREUR

Date	Mintage	VG	F	VF	XF	Unc
AN13G	13,000	200	350	600	1,200	—

KM# 658.6 2 FRANCS
10.0000 g., 0.9000 Silver .2893 oz. ASW **Mint:** La Rochelle **Obv. Legend:** NAPOLEON EMPEREUR

Date	Mintage	VG	F	VF	XF	Unc
AN13H	3,727	65.00	150	300	775	—
AN14H	1,063	200	350	600	1,200	—

KM# 658.7 2 FRANCS
10.0000 g., 0.9000 Silver .2893 oz. ASW **Mint:** Limoges **Obv. Legend:** NAPOLEON EMPEREUR

Date	Mintage	VG	F	VF	XF	Unc
AN13/2I	124,000	20.00	40.00	150	450	—
AN13I	Inc. above	35.00	70.00	175	500	—
AN14I	6,299	150	350	750	—	—
1806I	21,000	45.00	115	225	450	—
1807I	82,000	35.00	70.00	150	450	—

KM# 658.8 2 FRANCS
10.0000 g., 0.9000 Silver .2893 oz. ASW **Mint:** Bordeaux **Obv. Legend:** NAPOLEON EMPEREUR

Date	Mintage	VG	F	VF	XF	Unc
AN12K	10,000	45.00	115	225	450	—
AN13K	36,000	100	250	400	900	—
AN14K Rare	1,210	—	—	—	—	—
1807K	3,665	200	460	750	1,300	—

KM# 658.9 2 FRANCS
10.0000 g., 0.9000 Silver .2893 oz. ASW **Mint:** Bayonne **Obv. Legend:** NAPOLEON EMPEREUR

Date	Mintage	VG	F	VF	XF	Unc
AN12L	1,247	200	350	600	1,200	—
AN13L	22,000	100	250	400	950	—
AN14L	5,183	75.00	200	500	—	—
1806L	72,000	35.00	70.00	150	450	—
1807L	54,000	30.00	65.00	160	400	—

KM# 658.10 2 FRANCS
10.0000 g., 0.9000 Silver .2893 oz. ASW **Mint:** Toulouse **Obv. Legend:** NAPOLEON EMPEREUR

Date	Mintage	VG	F	VF	XF	Unc
AN12M	16,000	40.00	100	200	500	—
AN13M	334,000	35.00	70.00	150	450	—
1807M	8,878	65.00	150	300	775	—

KM# 658.11 2 FRANCS
10.0000 g., 0.9000 Silver .2893 oz. ASW **Mint:** Marseille **Obv. Legend:** NAPOLEON EMPEREUR

Date	Mintage	VG	F	VF	XF	Unc
AN13MA	11,000	45.00	115	225	450	—
AN14MA	—	200	400	800	—	—

KM# 658.12 2 FRANCS
10.0000 g., 0.9000 Silver .2893 oz. ASW **Mint:** Perpignan **Obv. Legend:** NAPOLEON EMPEREUR

Date	Mintage	VG	F	VF	XF	Unc
AN13Q	52,000	35.00	70.00	150	450	—
1806Q	42,000	45.00	115	225	450	—
1807Q	33,000	45.00	115	225	450	—

KM# 658.13 2 FRANCS
10.0000 g., 0.9000 Silver .2893 oz. ASW **Mint:** Nantes **Obv. Legend:** NAPOLEON EMPEREUR

Date	Mintage	VG	F	VF	XF	Unc
AN12T	1,444	200	350	600	1,200	2,500
AN13T	4,600	65.00	150	300	775	—

KM# 658.14 2 FRANCS
10.0000 g., 0.9000 Silver .2893 oz. ASW **Mint:** Turin **Obv. Legend:** NAPOLEON EMPEREUR

Date	Mintage	VG	F	VF	XF	Unc
AN13U	7,221	200	400	750	1,300	—
AN14U	—	200	400	800	—	—
1806U	10,000	125	300	600	1,200	—
1807U	10,000	125	300	600	1,200	—

KM# 658.15 2 FRANCS
10.0000 g., 0.9000 Silver .2893 oz. ASW **Mint:** Lille **Obv. Legend:** NAPOLEON EMPEREUR

Date	Mintage	VG	F	VF	XF	Unc
AN13W	11,000	45.00	115	225	450	—
AN14W	—	200	400	750	1,300	—
1806W	10,000	65.00	150	300	775	—
1807W	4,114	200	400	750	1,300	—

KM# 683 2 FRANCS
10.0000 g., 0.9000 Silver .2893 oz. ASW **Mint:** Paris **Obverse:** Negro head

Date	VG	F	VF	XF	Unc
1807A	300	650	1,200	2,750	—

KM# 684.1 2 FRANCS
10.0000 g., 0.9000 Silver .2893 oz. ASW **Obverse:** Laureate head

Date	Mintage	VG	F	VF	XF	Unc
1807	19,000	175	325	750	1,500	—
1808	1,100,000	30.00	60.00	150	400	—

KM# 684.2 2 FRANCS
10.0000 g., 0.9000 Silver .2893 oz. ASW **Mint:** Rouen

Date	Mintage	VG	F	VF	XF	Unc
1808B	161,000	40.00	80.00	175	450	—

KM# 684.3 2 FRANCS
10.0000 g., 0.9000 Silver .2893 oz. ASW **Mint:** Limoges

Date	Mintage	VG	F	VF	XF	Unc
1808I	106,000	45.00	90.00	175	400	—

KM# 684.4 2 FRANCS
10.0000 g., 0.9000 Silver .2893 oz. ASW **Mint:** Bordeaux

Date	Mintage	VG	F	VF	XF	Unc
1808K	38,000	55.00	90.00	200	450	—

KM# 684.5 2 FRANCS
10.0000 g., 0.9000 Silver .2893 oz. ASW **Mint:** Bayonne

Date	Mintage	VG	F	VF	XF	Unc
1808L	19,000	65.00	110	235	500	—

KM# 684.6 2 FRANCS
10.0000 g., 0.9000 Silver .2893 oz. ASW **Mint:** Toulouse

Date	Mintage	VG	F	VF	XF	Unc
1808M	28,000	55.00	90.00	200	450	—

KM# 684.7 2 FRANCS
10.0000 g., 0.9000 Silver .2893 oz. ASW **Mint:** Marseille

Date	Mintage	VG	F	VF	XF	Unc
1808MA	7,676	70.00	125	250	550	—

KM# 684.8 2 FRANCS
10.0000 g., 0.9000 Silver .2893 oz. ASW **Mint:** Perpignan

Date	Mintage	VG	F	VF	XF	Unc
1808Q	4,965	75.00	140	300	600	—

KM# 684.9 2 FRANCS
10.0000 g., 0.9000 Silver .2893 oz. ASW **Mint:** Turin

Date	Mintage	VG	F	VF	XF	Unc
1808U	2,297	150	300	550	1,200	—

KM# 684.10 2 FRANCS
10.0000 g., 0.9000 Silver .2893 oz. ASW **Mint:** Lille

Date	Mintage	VG	F	VF	XF	Unc
1808W	40,000	55.00	90.00	200	450	—
1808W	—	—	—	—	—	875

Note: Above value for common date uncirculated

KM# 693.1 2 FRANCS
10.0000 g., 0.9000 Silver .2893 oz. ASW **Mint:** Paris

Date	Mintage	VG	F	VF	XF	Unc
1809A	469,000	18.00	35.00	100	300	—
1810A	771,000	16.00	32.00	90.00	275	—
1811A	2,509,000	14.00	32.00	75.00	250	—
1812A	308,000	18.00	35.00	100	300	—
1813A	442,000	18.00	35.00	100	300	—
1814A	95,000	32.00	70.00	150	350	—

KM# 693.2 2 FRANCS
10.0000 g., 0.9000 Silver .2893 oz. ASW **Mint:** Rouen

Date	Mintage	VG	F	VF	XF	Unc
1809B	136,000	27.50	55.00	125	300	—
1810B	72,000	32.50	70.00	150	350	—
1811B	290,000	18.00	35.00	100	300	—
1812B	57,000	32.50	70.00	150	350	—
1813B	31,000	32.50	75.00	175	450	—

M# 693.3 2 FRANCS
10.0000 g., 0.9000 Silver .2893 oz. ASW **Mint:** Strasbourg

Date	Mintage	VG	F	VF	XF	Unc
1811BB	12,000	35.00	90.00	200	500	—

KM# 693.4 2 FRANCS
10.0000 g., 0.9000 Silver .2893 oz. ASW **Mint:** Genoa

Date	Mintage	VG	F	VF	XF	Unc
1813CL	906	400	800	1,500	3,250	—

KM# 693.5 2 FRANCS
10.0000 g., 0.9000 Silver .2893 oz. ASW **Mint:** Lyon

Date	Mintage	VG	F	VF	XF	Unc
1810D	18,000	35.00	90.00	200	450	—
1811D	37,000	32.50	75.00	175	425	—
1812D	61,000	32.50	70.00	150	350	—
1813D	33,000	32.50	75.00	175	425	—

KM# 693.6 2 FRANCS
10.0000 g., 0.9000 Silver .2893 oz. ASW **Mint:** La Rochelle

Date	Mintage	VG	F	VF	XF	Unc
1809H	4,534	75.00	150	250	600	—
1810H	5,710	75.00	150	250	575	—
1811H	44,000	32.00	70.00	150	350	—
1812H	81,000	32.00	70.00	150	350	—
1813H	80,000	32.00	70.00	150	350	—

KM# 693.7 2 FRANCS
10.0000 g., 0.9000 Silver .2893 oz. ASW **Mint:** Limoges

Date	Mintage	VG	F	VF	XF	Unc
1810I	29,000	32.00	75.00	175	425	—
1811I	137,000	27.50	55.00	125	300	—
1812I	209,000	18.00	35.00	100	300	—
1813I	98,000	32.00	70.00	150	335	—

KM# 693.8 2 FRANCS
10.0000 g., 0.9000 Silver .2893 oz. ASW **Mint:** Bordeaux

Date	Mintage	VG	F	VF	XF	Unc
1809K	3,451	100	225	350	725	—
1810K	3,518	100	225	350	725	—
1811K	28,000	32.00	75.00	175	425	—
1812K	21,000	32.00	75.00	175	425	—
1813K	27,000	32.00	75.00	175	425	—

KM# 693.9 2 FRANCS
10.0000 g., 0.9000 Silver .2893 oz. ASW **Mint:** Bayonne

Date	Mintage	VG	F	VF	XF	Unc
1809L	27,000	32.00	75.00	175	425	—
1810L	32,000	32.00	75.00	175	425	—
1811L	99,000	32.00	70.00	150	350	—
1812L	42,000	32.00	70.00	150	350	—
1813L	33,000	32.00	75.00	175	425	—

KM# 693.10 2 FRANCS
10.0000 g., 0.9000 Silver .2893 oz. ASW **Mint:** Toulouse

Date	Mintage	VG	F	VF	XF	Unc
1810M	11,000	50.00	100	225	425	—
1811M	124,000	20.00	40.00	100	300	—
1812M	145,000	20.00	40.00	100	300	—
1813M	221,000	30.00	60.00	125	300	—
1814M	46,000	35.00	75.00	150	350	—

KM# 693.11 2 FRANCS
10.0000 g., 0.9000 Silver .2893 oz. ASW **Mint:** Marseille

Date	Mintage	VG	F	VF	XF	Unc
1809MA	27,000	32.00	75.00	175	425	—
1810MA	8,843	45.00	90.00	225	500	—
1811MA	39,000	32.00	70.00	150	350	—
1812MA	16,000	35.00	90.00	200	450	—
1813MA	18,000	35.00	90.00	200	450	—

KM# 693.12 2 FRANCS
10.0000 g., 0.9000 Silver .2893 oz. ASW **Mint:** Perpignan

Date	Mintage	VG	F	VF	XF	Unc
1809Q	20,000	45.00	75.00	175	425	—
1810Q	4,857	75.00	150	250	600	—
1811Q	75,000	32.00	70.00	150	350	—
1812Q	86,000	32.00	70.00	150	350	—
1813Q	253,000	18.00	35.00	100	300	—
1814Q	16,000	45.00	90.00	225	525	—

KKM# 693.13 2 FRANCS
10.0000 g., 0.9000 Silver .2893 oz. ASW **Mint:** Nantes

Date	Mintage	VG	F	VF	XF	Unc
1811T	35,000	32.00	75.00	175	425	—
1812T	19,000	35.00	90.00	200	500	—
1813T	11,000	18.00	35.00	100	300	—

KM# 693.14 2 FRANCS
10.0000 g., 0.9000 Silver .2893 oz. ASW **Mint:** Turin

Date	Mintage	VG	F	VF	XF	Unc
1809U	3,149	100	200	400	850	—
1810U	3,077	100	200	400	850	—
1811U	3,893	100	200	400	850	—

KM# 693.15 2 FRANCS
10.0000 g., 0.9000 Silver .2893 oz. ASW **Mint:** Lille

Date	Mintage	VG	F	VF	XF	Unc
1809W	62,000	32.00	70.00	150	350	—
1810W	48,000	32.00	70.00	150	350	—
1811W	118,000	27.00	60.00	125	300	—
1812W	108,000	27.00	60.00	125	300	—
1813W	88,000	32.00	70.00	150	350	—

KM# 693.16 2 FRANCS
10.0000 g., 0.9000 Silver .2893 oz. ASW **Mint:** Utrecht **Note:** Mint mark: Flag.

Date	Mintage	VG	F	VF	XF	Unc
1812	9,493	150	300	600	1,350	—
1813/2	41,000	—	—	—	—	—
1813	Inc. above	100	200	400	900	—
1813	—	—	—	—	—	675

Note: Above value for common date uncirculated

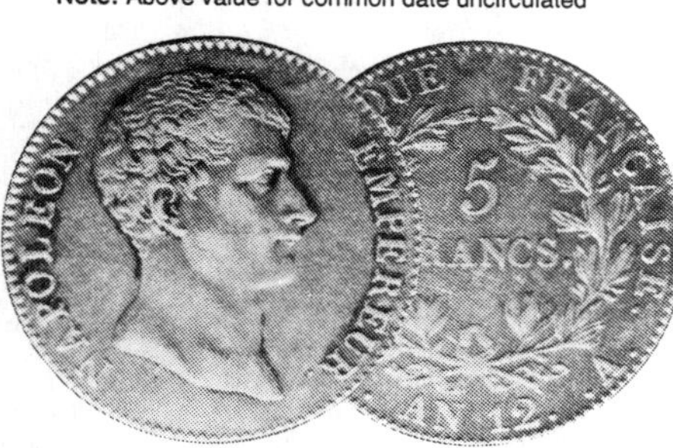

KM# 660.1 5 FRANCS
25.0000 g., 0.9000 Silver .7234 oz. ASW **Mint:** Paris **Obv. Legend:** NAPOLEON EMPEREUR

Date	Mintage	VG	F	VF	XF	Unc
AN12A	767,000	40.00	125	300	600	1,200

KM# 660.2 5 FRANCS
25.0000 g., 0.9000 Silver .7234 oz. ASW **Mint:** Rouen **Obv. Legend:** NAPOLEON EMPEREUR

Date	Mintage	VG	F	VF	XF	Unc
AN12B	10,000	60.00	150	400	800	1,500

KM# 660.3 5 FRANCS
25.0000 g., 0.9000 Silver .7234 oz. ASW **Mint:** Lyon **Obv. Legend:** NAPOLEON EMPEREUR

Date	Mintage	VG	F	VF	XF	Unc
AN12D	14,000	50.00	125	300	650	1,100

KM# 660.4 5 FRANCS
25.0000 g., 0.9000 Silver .7234 oz. ASW **Mint:** La Rochelle **Obv. Legend:** NAPOLEON EMPEREUR

Date	Mintage	VG	F	VF	XF	Unc
AN12H	15,000	50.00	125	300	800	—

KM# 660.5 5 FRANCS
25.0000 g., 0.9000 Silver .7234 oz. ASW **Mint:** Limoges **Obv. Legend:** NAPOLEON EMPEREUR

Date	Mintage	VG	F	VF	XF	Unc
AN12I	90,000	40.00	100	200	750	—

KM# 660.6 5 FRANCS
25.0000 g., 0.9000 Silver .7234 oz. ASW **Mint:** Bordeaux **Obv. Legend:** NAPOLEON EMPEREUR

Date	Mintage	VG	F	VF	XF	Unc
AN12K	71,000	40.00	100	200	750	—

KM# 660.7 5 FRANCS
25.0000 g., 0.9000 Silver .7234 oz. ASW **Mint:** Bayonne **Obv. Legend:** NAPOLEON EMPEREUR

Date	Mintage	VG	F	VF	XF	Unc
AN12L	16,000	50.00	125	300	800	—

KM# 660.8 5 FRANCS
25.0000 g., 0.9000 Silver .7234 oz. ASW **Mint:** Toulouse **Obv. Legend:** NAPOLEON EMPEREUR

Date	Mintage	VG	F	VF	XF	Unc
AN12M	427,000	40.00	100	200	725	—

KM# 660.9 5 FRANCS
25.0000 g., 0.9000 Silver .7234 oz. ASW **Mint:** Marseille **Obv. Legend:** NAPOLEON EMPEREUR

Date	Mintage	VG	F	VF	XF	Unc
AN12MA	2,030	—	—	—	—	—

Note: Reported, not confirmed

KM# 660.10 5 FRANCS
25.0000 g., 0.9000 Silver .7234 oz. ASW **Mint:** Perpignan **Obv. Legend:** NAPOLEON EMPEREUR

Date	Mintage	VG	F	VF	XF	Unc
AN12Q	55,000	40.00	100	200	750	—

KM# 660.11 5 FRANCS
25.0000 g., 0.9000 Silver .7234 oz. ASW **Mint:** Nantes **Obv. Legend:** NAPOLEON EMPEREUR

Date	Mintage	VG	F	VF	XF	Unc
AN12T	11,000	100	200	400	800	—

KM# 660.12 5 FRANCS
25.0000 g., 0.9000 Silver .7234 oz. ASW **Mint:** Lille **Obv. Legend:** NAPOLEON EMPEREUR

Date	Mintage	VG	F	VF	XF	Unc
AN12W	4,366	120	250	500	1,800	—

KM# 662.1 5 FRANCS
25.0000 g., 0.9000 Silver .7234 oz. ASW **Mint:** Paris **Obverse:** Monogram below bust

Date	Mintage	VG	F	VF	XF	Unc
AN13A	5,121,000	20.00	40.00	100	295	—
AN14A	1,855,000	25.00	50.00	135	365	—

KM# 662.2 5 FRANCS
25.0000 g., 0.9000 Silver .7234 oz. ASW **Mint:** Rouen **Obverse:** Monogram below bust

Date	Mintage	VG	F	VF	XF	Unc
AN13B	4,901	60.00	150	400	800	—

KM# 662.3 5 FRANCS
25.0000 g., 0.9000 Silver .7234 oz. ASW **Mint:** Strasbourg **Obverse:** Monogram below bust

Date	Mintage	VG	F	VF	XF	Unc
AN13BB	7,510	—	—	—	—	—
AN14BB	831,000	—	—	—	—	—

KM# 662.4 5 FRANCS
25.0000 g., 0.9000 Silver .7234 oz. ASW **Mint:** Lyon **Obverse:** Monogram below bust

Date	Mintage	VG	F	VF	XF	Unc
AN13D	24,000	40.00	100	200	500	—
AN14D	3,890	100	250	500	1,500	—

KM# 662.5 5 FRANCS
25.0000 g., 0.9000 Silver .7234 oz. ASW **Mint:** Geneve **Obverse:** Monogram below bust

Date	Mintage	VG	F	VF	XF	Unc
AN13G	6,487	200	400	1,000	2,500	—

KM# 662.6 5 FRANCS
25.0000 g., 0.9000 Silver .7234 oz. ASW **Mint:** La Rochelle **Obverse:** Monogram below bust

Date	Mintage	VG	F	VF	XF	Unc
AN13H	35,000	40.00	100	200	500	—
AN14H	3,780	100	250	500	1,150	—

KM# 662.7 5 FRANCS
25.0000 g., 0.9000 Silver .7234 oz. ASW **Mint:** Limoges **Obverse:** Monogram below bust

Date	Mintage	VG	F	VF	XF	Unc
AN13I	333,000	40.00	100	200	500	—
AN14I	12,000	—	—	—	—	—

KM# 662.8 5 FRANCS
25.0000 g., 0.9000 Silver .7234 oz. ASW **Mint:** Bordeaux **Obverse:** Monogram below bust

Date	Mintage	VG	F	VF	XF	Unc
AN13K	161,000	50.00	125	300	600	—
AN14K	2,113	200	400	700	2,000	—

KM# 662.9 5 FRANCS
25.0000 g., 0.9000 Silver .7234 oz. ASW **Mint:** Bayonne **Obverse:** Monogram below bust

Date	Mintage	VG	F	VF	XF	Unc
AN13L	207,000	40.00	110	275	475	—
AN14L	15,000	50.00	125	300	600	—

KM# 662.10 5 FRANCS
25.0000 g., 0.9000 Silver .7234 oz. ASW **Mint:** Toulouse **Obverse:** Monogram below bust

Date	Mintage	VG	F	VF	XF	Unc
AN13M	1,547,000	30.00	60.00	125	300	—
AN14M	40,000	40.00	100	200	500	—

KM# 662.11 5 FRANCS
25.0000 g., 0.9000 Silver .7234 oz. ASW **Mint:** Marseille **Obverse:** Monogram below bust

Date	Mintage	VG	F	VF	XF	Unc
AN13MA	64,000	40.00	100	200	450	—

KM# 662.12 5 FRANCS
25.0000 g., 0.9000 Silver .7234 oz. ASW **Mint:** Perpignan **Obverse:** Monogram below bust

Date	Mintage	VG	F	VF	XF	Unc
AN13Q	245,000	35.00	75.00	175	375	—

KM# 662.13 5 FRANCS
25.0000 g., 0.9000 Silver .7234 oz. ASW **Mint:** Nantes **Obverse:** Monogram below bust

Date	Mintage	VG	F	VF	XF	Unc
AN13T	25,000	40.00	100	200	500	—

KM# 662.14 5 FRANCS
25.0000 g., 0.9000 Silver .7234 oz. ASW **Mint:** Turin **Obverse:** Monogram below bust

Date	Mintage	VG	F	VF	XF	Unc
AN13U	21,000	100	200	400	800	—
AN14U	14,000	125	250	550	1,150	—

KM# 662.15 5 FRANCS
25.0000 g., 0.9000 Silver .7234 oz. ASW **Mint:** Lille **Obverse:** Monogram below bust

Date	Mintage	VG	F	VF	XF	Unc
AN13W	34,000	40.00	100	200	500	—
AN14W	14,000	50.00	125	300	600	—

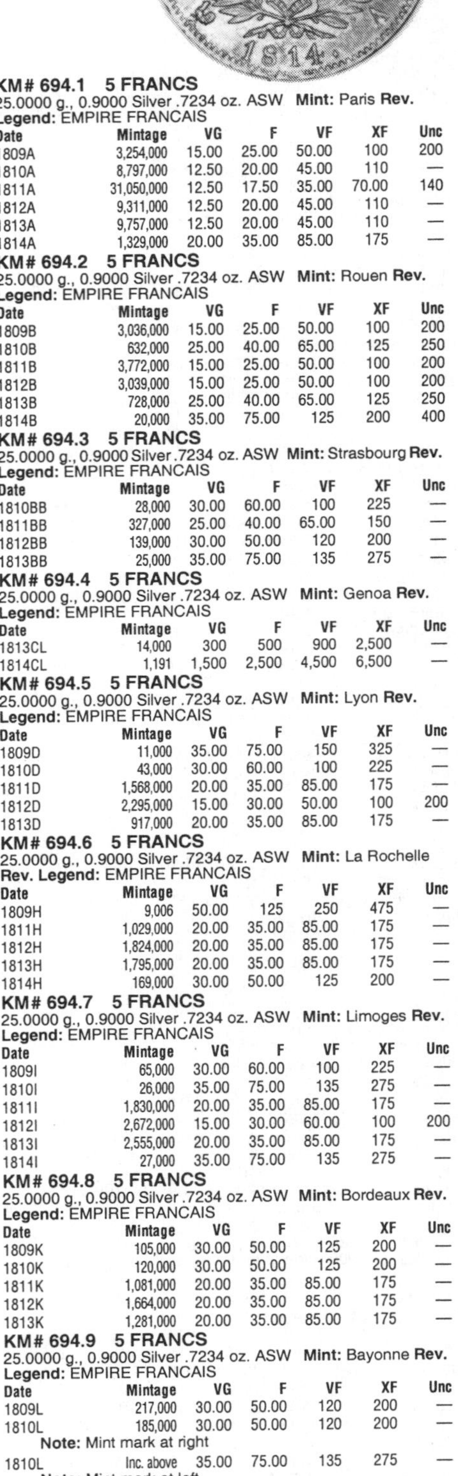

KM# 673.1 5 FRANCS

25.0000 g., 0.9000 Silver .7234 oz. ASW **Mint:** Paris **Obverse:** Bare head

Date	Mintage	VG	F	VF	XF	Unc
1806A	826,000	35.00	75.00	150	350	—

KM# 673.2 5 FRANCS

25.0000 g., 0.9000 Silver .7234 oz. ASW **Mint:** Rouen

Date	Mintage	VG	F	VF	XF	Unc
1806B	25,000	40.00	100	200	500	—
1807B	44,000	40.00	100	200	500	—

KM# 673.3 5 FRANCS

25.0000 g., 0.9000 Silver .7234 oz. ASW **Mint:** Strasbourg

Date	Mintage	VG	F	VF	XF	Unc
1806BB	660,000	35.00	75.00	150	350	—
1807BB	1,296	—	—	—	—	—

KM# 673.4 5 FRANCS

25.0000 g., 0.9000 Silver .7234 oz. ASW **Mint:** Lyon

Date	Mintage	VG	F	VF	XF	Unc
1806D	2,771	—	—	—	—	—
1807D	2,423	—	—	—	—	—

KM# 673.5 5 FRANCS

25.0000 g., 0.9000 Silver .7234 oz. ASW **Mint:** La Rochelle

Date	Mintage	VG	F	VF	XF	Unc
1806H	28,000	—	—	—	—	—
Note: Reported, not confirmed						
1807H	4,847	100	250	500	1,300	—

KM# 673.6 5 FRANCS

25.0000 g., 0.9000 Silver .7234 oz. ASW **Mint:** Limoges

Date	Mintage	VG	F	VF	XF	Unc
1806I	239,000	35.00	70.00	150	325	—
1807I	91,000	35.00	80.00	175	400	—

KM# 673.7 5 FRANCS

25.0000 g., 0.9000 Silver .7234 oz. ASW **Mint:** Bordeaux

Date	Mintage	VG	F	VF	XF	Unc
1806K	29,000	40.00	100	200	500	—
1807K	10,000	60.00	175	350	800	—

KM# 673.8 5 FRANCS

25.0000 g., 0.9000 Silver .7234 oz. ASW **Mint:** Bayonne

Date	Mintage	VG	F	VF	XF	Unc
1806L	551,000	35.00	75.00	150	350	—
1807L	375,000	35.00	70.00	150	325	—

KM# 673.9 5 FRANCS

25.0000 g., 0.9000 Silver .7234 oz. ASW **Mint:** Toulouse

Date	Mintage	VG	F	VF	XF	Unc
1806M	22,000	40.00	100	200	500	—
1807M	101,000	35.00	80.00	175	400	—

KM# 673.10 5 FRANCS

25.0000 g., 0.9000 Silver .7234 oz. ASW **Mint:** Perpignan

Date	Mintage	VG	F	VF	XF	Unc
1806Q	78,000	35.00	70.00	150	350	—
1807Q	25,000	40.00	100	200	500	—

KM# 673.11 5 FRANCS

25.0000 g., 0.9000 Silver .7234 oz. ASW **Mint:** Nantes

Date	Mintage	VG	F	VF	XF	Unc
1807T Rare	449	—	—	—	—	—

KM# 673.12 5 FRANCS

25.0000 g., 0.9000 Silver .7234 oz. ASW **Mint:** Turin

Date	Mintage	VG	F	VF	XF	Unc
1806U	31,000	100	200	400	800	—
1807U	30,000	125	250	500	1,400	—

KM# 673.13 5 FRANCS

25.0000 g., 0.9000 Silver .7234 oz. ASW **Mint:** Lille

Date	Mintage	VG	F	VF	XF	Unc
1806W	32,000	40.00	100	200	500	—
1807W	29,000	40.00	100	200	500	—

KM# 685 5 FRANCS

25.0000 g., 0.9000 Silver .7234 oz. ASW **Mint:** Paris **Obverse:** Similar to KM#662.1 **Reverse:** Similar to KM#686.1

Date	Mintage	VG	F	VF	XF	Unc
1807A	49,000	450	850	1,500	3,000	—

KM# 686.1 5 FRANCS

25.0000 g., 0.9000 Silver .7234 oz. ASW **Obverse:** Laureate head **Rev. Legend:** REPUBLIQUE FRANCAISE

Date	Mintage	VG	F	VF	XF	Unc
1807	41,000	350	700	1,300	2,000	—
1808	6,462,000	20.00	35.00	55.00	120	—
1808 Proof	—	Value: 5,000				

KM# 686.2 5 FRANCS

25.0000 g., 0.9000 Silver .7234 oz. ASW **Mint:** Rouen **Rev. Legend:** REPUBLIQUE FRANCAISE

Date	Mintage	VG	F	VF	XF	Unc
1808B	1,542,000	22.00	40.00	65.00	135	—

KM# 686.3 5 FRANCS

25.0000 g., 0.9000 Silver .7234 oz. ASW **Mint:** Strasbourg **Rev. Legend:** REPUBLIQUE FRANCAISE

Date	Mintage	VG	F	VF	XF	Unc
1808BB	68,000	35.00	70.00	150	325	—

KM# 686.4 5 FRANCS

25.0000 g., 0.9000 Silver .7234 oz. ASW **Mint:** Lyon **Rev. Legend:** REPUBLIQUE FRANCAISE

Date	Mintage	VG	F	VF	XF	Unc
1808D	65,000	35.00	70.00	150	325	—

KM# 686.5 5 FRANCS

25.0000 g., 0.9000 Silver .7234 oz. ASW **Mint:** La Rochelle **Rev. Legend:** REPUBLIQUE FRANCAISE

Date	Mintage	VG	F	VF	XF	Unc
1808H	7,204	—	—	—	—	—
Note: Reported, not confirmed						

KM# 686.6 5 FRANCS

25.0000 g., 0.9000 Silver .7234 oz. ASW **Mint:** Limoges **Rev. Legend:** REPUBLIQUE FRANCAISE

Date	Mintage	VG	F	VF	XF	Unc
1808I	107,000	35.00	70.00	150	300	—

KM# 686.7 5 FRANCS

25.0000 g., 0.9000 Silver .7234 oz. ASW **Mint:** Bordeaux **Rev. Legend:** REPUBLIQUE FRANCAISE

Date	Mintage	VG	F	VF	XF	Unc
1808K	54,000	35.00	70.00	150	325	—

KM# 686.8 5 FRANCS

25.0000 g., 0.9000 Silver .7234 oz. ASW **Mint:** Bayonne **Rev. Legend:** REPUBLIQUE FRANCAISE

Date	Mintage	VG	F	VF	XF	Unc
1808L	144,000	35.00	70.00	125	275	—

KM# 686.9 5 FRANCS

25.0000 g., 0.9000 Silver .7234 oz. ASW **Mint:** Toulouse **Rev. Legend:** REPUBLIQUE FRANCAISE

Date	Mintage	VG	F	VF	XF	Unc
1808M	351,000	25.00	40.00	65.00	150	—

KM# 686.10 5 FRANCS

25.0000 g., 0.9000 Silver .7234 oz. ASW **Mint:** Marseille **Rev. Legend:** REPUBLIQUE FRANCAISE

Date	Mintage	VG	F	VF	XF	Unc
1808MA	2,681	100	225	450	900	—

KM# 686.11 5 FRANCS

25.0000 g., 0.9000 Silver .7234 oz. ASW **Mint:** Perpignan **Rev. Legend:** REPUBLIQUE FRANCAISE

Date	Mintage	VG	F	VF	XF	Unc
1808Q	12,000	55.00	95.00	200	500	—

KM# 686.12 5 FRANCS

25.0000 g., 0.9000 Silver .7234 oz. ASW **Mint:** Nantes **Rev. Legend:** REPUBLIQUE FRANCAISE

Date	Mintage	VG	F	VF	XF	Unc
1808T	2,682	—	—	—	—	—
Note: Reported, not confirmed						

KM# 686.13 5 FRANCS

25.0000 g., 0.9000 Silver .7234 oz. ASW **Mint:** Turin **Rev. Legend:** REPUBLIQUE FRANCAISE

Date	Mintage	VG	F	VF	XF	Unc
1808U	14,000	75.00	200	400	750	—

KM# 686.14 5 FRANCS

25.0000 g., 0.9000 Silver .7234 oz. ASW **Mint:** Lille **Rev. Legend:** REPUBLIQUE FRANCAISE

Date	Mintage	VG	F	VF	XF	Unc
1808	550,000	25.00	40.00	65.00	150	—
1808	—	—	—	—	—	600
Note: Above value for common date uncirculated						

KM# 694.1 5 FRANCS

25.0000 g., 0.9000 Silver .7234 oz. ASW **Mint:** Paris **Rev. Legend:** EMPIRE FRANCAIS

Date	Mintage	VG	F	VF	XF	Unc
1809A	3,254,000	15.00	25.00	50.00	100	200
1810A	8,797,000	12.50	20.00	45.00	110	—
1811A	31,050,000	12.50	17.50	35.00	70.00	140
1812A	9,311,000	12.50	20.00	45.00	110	—
1813A	9,757,000	12.50	20.00	45.00	110	—
1814A	1,329,000	20.00	35.00	85.00	175	—

KM# 694.2 5 FRANCS

25.0000 g., 0.9000 Silver .7234 oz. ASW **Mint:** Rouen **Rev. Legend:** EMPIRE FRANCAIS

Date	Mintage	VG	F	VF	XF	Unc
1809B	3,036,000	15.00	25.00	50.00	100	200
1810B	632,000	25.00	40.00	65.00	125	250
1811B	3,772,000	15.00	25.00	50.00	100	200
1812B	3,039,000	15.00	25.00	50.00	100	200
1813B	728,000	25.00	40.00	65.00	125	250
1814B	20,000	35.00	75.00	125	200	400

KM# 694.3 5 FRANCS

25.0000 g., 0.9000 Silver .7234 oz. ASW **Mint:** Strasbourg **Rev. Legend:** EMPIRE FRANCAIS

Date	Mintage	VG	F	VF	XF	Unc
1810BB	28,000	30.00	60.00	100	225	—
1811BB	327,000	25.00	40.00	65.00	150	—
1812BB	139,000	30.00	50.00	120	200	—
1813BB	25,000	35.00	75.00	135	275	—

KM# 694.4 5 FRANCS

25.0000 g., 0.9000 Silver .7234 oz. ASW **Mint:** Genoa **Rev. Legend:** EMPIRE FRANCAIS

Date	Mintage	VG	F	VF	XF	Unc
1813CL	14,000	300	500	900	2,500	—
1814CL	1,191	1,500	2,500	4,500	6,500	—

KM# 694.5 5 FRANCS

25.0000 g., 0.9000 Silver .7234 oz. ASW **Mint:** Lyon **Rev. Legend:** EMPIRE FRANCAIS

Date	Mintage	VG	F	VF	XF	Unc
1809D	11,000	35.00	75.00	150	325	—
1810D	43,000	30.00	60.00	100	225	—
1811D	1,568,000	20.00	35.00	85.00	175	—
1812D	2,295,000	15.00	30.00	50.00	100	200
1813D	917,000	20.00	35.00	85.00	175	—

KM# 694.6 5 FRANCS

25.0000 g., 0.9000 Silver .7234 oz. ASW **Mint:** La Rochelle **Rev. Legend:** EMPIRE FRANCAIS

Date	Mintage	VG	F	VF	XF	Unc
1809H	9,006	50.00	125	250	475	—
1811H	1,029,000	20.00	35.00	85.00	175	—
1812H	1,824,000	20.00	35.00	85.00	175	—
1813H	1,795,000	20.00	35.00	85.00	175	—
1814H	169,000	30.00	50.00	125	200	—

KM# 694.7 5 FRANCS

25.0000 g., 0.9000 Silver .7234 oz. ASW **Mint:** Limoges **Rev. Legend:** EMPIRE FRANCAIS

Date	Mintage	VG	F	VF	XF	Unc
1809I	65,000	30.00	60.00	100	225	—
1810I	26,000	35.00	75.00	135	275	—
1811I	1,830,000	20.00	35.00	85.00	175	—
1812I	2,672,000	15.00	30.00	60.00	100	200
1813I	2,555,000	20.00	35.00	85.00	175	—
1814I	27,000	35.00	75.00	135	275	—

KM# 694.8 5 FRANCS

25.0000 g., 0.9000 Silver .7234 oz. ASW **Mint:** Bordeaux **Rev. Legend:** EMPIRE FRANCAIS

Date	Mintage	VG	F	VF	XF	Unc
1809K	105,000	30.00	50.00	125	200	—
1810K	120,000	30.00	50.00	125	200	—
1811K	1,081,000	20.00	35.00	85.00	175	—
1812K	1,664,000	20.00	35.00	85.00	175	—
1813K	1,281,000	20.00	35.00	85.00	175	—

KM# 694.9 5 FRANCS

25.0000 g., 0.9000 Silver .7234 oz. ASW **Mint:** Bayonne **Rev. Legend:** EMPIRE FRANCAIS

Date	Mintage	VG	F	VF	XF	Unc
1809L	217,000	30.00	50.00	120	200	—
1810L	185,000	30.00	50.00	120	200	—
Note: Mint mark at right						
1810L	Inc. above	35.00	75.00	135	275	—
Note: Mint mark at left						
1811L	1,123,000	20.00	35.00	85.00	175	—

Date	Mintage	VG	F	VF	XF	Unc
1812L	936,000	20.00	35.00	85.00	175	—
1813L	1,161,000	20.00	35.00	85.00	175	—

KM# 694.10 5 FRANCS
25.0000 g., 0.9000 Silver .7234 oz. ASW **Mint:** Toulouse **Rev. Legend:** EMPIRE FRANCAIS

Date	Mintage	VG	F	VF	XF	Unc
1809	34,000	30.00	60.00	100	225	—
1809M	12,000	30.00	60.00	100	225	—
1810M	12,000	30.00	60.00	100	225	—
1810	72,000	30.00	60.00	100	225	—
1811	1,101,000	20.00	35.00	85.00	175	—
1811M	671,000	20.00	35.00	85.00	175	—
1812M	612,000	20.00	35.00	85.00	175	—
1812	1,617,000	20.00	35.00	85.00	175	—
1813M	834,000	20.00	35.00	85.00	175	—
1814M	16,000	25.00	45.00	90.00	200	—

KM# 694.11 5 FRANCS
25.0000 g., 0.9000 Silver .7234 oz. ASW **Mint:** Marseille **Rev. Legend:** EMPIRE FRANCAIS

Date	Mintage	VG	F	VF	XF	Unc
1809MA	12,000	35.00	75.00	150	325	—
1810MA	12,000	35.00	75.00	150	325	—
1811MA	671,000	25.00	40.00	90.00	200	—
1812MA	612,000	25.00	40.00	90.00	200	—
1813MA	834,000	25.00	40.00	90.00	200	—
1814MA	16,000	40.00	85.00	120	300	—

KM# 694.12 5 FRANCS
25.0000 g., 0.9000 Silver .7234 oz. ASW **Mint:** Perpignan **Rev. Legend:** EMPIRE FRANCAIS

Date	Mintage	VG	F	VF	XF	Unc
1810Q	118,000	30.00	50.00	125	200	—
1811Q	1,213,000	20.00	35.00	85.00	175	—
1812Q	1,460,000	20.00	35.00	85.00	175	—
1813Q	1,826,000	20.00	35.00	85.00	175	—
1814Q	367,000	25.00	45.00	100	190	—

KM# 694.13 5 FRANCS
25.0000 g., 0.9000 Silver .7234 oz. ASW **Mint:** London **Rev. Legend:** EMPIRE FRANCAIS

Date	Mintage	VG	F	VF	XF	Unc
1812R /cr	49,000	100	250	550	1,100	—
1813R /cr	17,000	175	400	850	2,000	—

KM# 694.14 5 FRANCS
25.0000 g., 0.9000 Silver .7234 oz. ASW **Mint:** Nantes **Rev. Legend:** EMPIRE FRANCAIS

Date	Mintage	VG	F	VF	XF	Unc
1811T	724,000	20.00	35.00	85.00	175	—
1812T	926,000	20.00	35.00	85.00	175	—
1813T	564,000	20.00	35.00	85.00	175	—
1814T	8,745	55.00	125	275	500	—

KM# 694.15 5 FRANCS
25.0000 g., 0.9000 Silver .7234 oz. ASW **Mint:** Turin **Rev. Legend:** EMPIRE FRANCAIS

Date	Mintage	VG	F	VF	XF	Unc
1809U	16,000	100	200	450	900	—
1810U	14,000	100	250	500	950	1,450
1811U	169,000	30.00	60.00	100	225	—
1812/1U	—	75.00	150	250	500	—
1812U	105,000	30.00	60.00	100	225	—
1813U	60,000	35.00	75.00	150	325	—

KM# 694.16 5 FRANCS
25.0000 g., 0.9000 Silver .7234 oz. ASW **Mint:** Lille **Rev. Legend:** EMPIRE FRANCAIS

Date	Mintage	VG	F	VF	XF	Unc
1809W	1,221,000	20.00	35.00	85.00	175	—
1810W	297,000	30.00	50.00	120	200	—
1811W	3,290,000	15.00	30.00	60.00	125	—
1812W	4,342,000	15.00	30.00	60.00	125	—
1813W	1,824,000	20.00	35.00	85.00	175	—
1814W	33,000	35.00	75.00	150	325	—

KM# 694.17 5 FRANCS
25.0000 g., 0.9000 Silver .7234 oz. ASW **Mint:** Utrecht **Rev. Legend:** EMPIRE FRANCAIS **Note:** Mint mark: Flag.

Date	Mintage	VG	F	VF	XF	Unc
1812	55,000	150	300	650	1,300	—
1813	362,000	125	250	500	1,000	—
1813	—	—	—	—	—	450

Note: Above value for common date uncirculated

KM# 651 20 FRANCS
6.4516 g., 0.9000 Gold .1867 oz. AGW **Mint:** Paris **Obverse:** Bare head

Date	Mintage	F	VF	XF	Unc
ANXIA	58,000	150	225	450	1,400
AN12A	988,000	125	150	300	900
AN12A Proof	—	Value: 5,500			

KM# 661 20 FRANCS
6.4516 g., 0.9000 Gold .1867 oz. AGW **Mint:** Paris **Obv. Legend:** NAPOLEON EMPEREUR

Date	Mintage	F	VF	XF	Unc
AN12A	428,000	125	150	350	1,500

KM# 663.1 20 FRANCS
6.4516 g., 0.9000 Gold .1867 oz. AGW **Mint:** Paris **Obverse:** Redesigned head

Date	Mintage	F	VF	XF	Unc
AN13A	519,000	100	125	275	850
AN14A	148,000	125	150	350	900

KM# 663.2 20 FRANCS
6.4516 g., 0.9000 Gold .1867 oz. AGW **Mint:** Limoges **Obverse:** Redesigned head

Date	Mintage	F	VF	XF	Unc
AN13I	—	—	—	—	—
AN14I	1,646	750	1,250	2,500	—

KM# 663.3 20 FRANCS
6.4516 g., 0.9000 Gold .1867 oz. AGW **Mint:** Perpignan **Obverse:** Redesigned head

Date	Mintage	F	VF	XF	Unc
AN13Q	522	1,000	1,500	3,000	—
AN14Q	2,710	375	625	1,250	2,250

KM# 663.4 20 FRANCS
6.4516 g., 0.9000 Gold .1867 oz. AGW **Mint:** Nantes **Obverse:** Redesigned head

Date	Mintage	F	VF	XF	Unc
AN13T	918	875	1,400	2,750	—

KM# 663.5 20 FRANCS
6.4516 g., 0.9000 Gold .1867 oz. AGW **Mint:** Turin **Obverse:** Redesigned head

Date	Mintage	F	VF	XF	Unc
AN14U	1,755	500	800	1,500	—

KM# 663.6 20 FRANCS
6.4516 g., 0.9000 Gold .1867 oz. AGW **Mint:** Lille **Obverse:** Redesigned head

Date	F	VF	XF	Unc
AN14W	—	—	—	—

KM# 674.1 20 FRANCS
6.4516 g., 0.9000 Gold .1867 oz. AGW **Mint:** Paris

Date	Mintage	F	VF	XF	Unc
1806A	964,000	100	125	225	850

KM# 674.2 20 FRANCS
6.4516 g., 0.9000 Gold .1867 oz. AGW **Mint:** Limoges

Date	Mintage	F	VF	XF	Unc
1806I	8,143	200	400	800	1,500

KM# 674.4 20 FRANCS
6.4516 g., 0.9000 Gold .1867 oz. AGW **Mint:** Perpignan

Date	Mintage	F	VF	XF	Unc
1806Q	3,973	300	600	1,000	—

KM# 674.5 20 FRANCS
6.4516 g., 0.9000 Gold .1867 oz. AGW **Mint:** Turin

Date	Mintage	F	VF	XF	Unc
1806U	17,000	150	300	600	1,250

KM# 674.6 20 FRANCS
6.4516 g., 0.9000 Gold .1867 oz. AGW **Mint:** Lille

Date	Mintage	F	VF	XF	Unc
1806W	4,242	200	400	800	1,500

KM# A687.1 20 FRANCS
6.4516 g., 0.9000 Gold .1867 oz. AGW **Mint:** Paris

Date	Mintage	F	VF	XF	Unc
1807A	826,000	100	150	275	1,250

KM# A687.2 20 FRANCS
6.4516 g., 0.9000 Gold .1867 oz. AGW **Mint:** Toulouse

Date	Mintage	F	VF	XF	Unc
1807M	5,296	225	450	850	1,500

KM# A687.3 20 FRANCS
6.4516 g., 0.9000 Gold .1867 oz. AGW **Mint:** Turin

Date	Mintage	F	VF	XF	Unc
1807U	2,557	400	800	1,250	2,000

KM# A687.4 20 FRANCS
6.4516 g., 0.9000 Gold .1867 oz. AGW **Mint:** Lille

Date	Mintage	F	VF	XF	Unc
1807W	5,181	200	400	850	1,500

KM# 687.1 20 FRANCS
6.4516 g., 0.9000 Gold .1867 oz. AGW **Mint:** Paris **Obverse:** Laureate head

Date	Mintage	F	VF	XF	Unc
1807A	Inc. above	100	150	225	800
1808A	1,450,000	100	150	225	800

KM# 687.2 20 FRANCS
6.4516 g., 0.9000 Gold .1867 oz. AGW **Mint:** Bordeaux **Obverse:** Laureate head

Date	Mintage	F	VF	XF	Unc
1808K Rare	281	—	—	—	—

KM# 687.3 20 FRANCS
6.4516 g., 0.9000 Gold .1867 oz. AGW **Mint:** Toulouse **Obverse:** Laureate head

Date	Mintage	F	VF	XF	Unc
1808M	22,000	150	250	500	1,000

KM# 687.4 20 FRANCS
6.4516 g., 0.9000 Gold .1867 oz. AGW **Mint:** Perpignan **Obverse:** Laureate head

Date	Mintage	F	VF	XF	Unc
1808Q Rare	646	—	—	—	—

KM# 687.5 20 FRANCS
6.4516 g., 0.9000 Gold .1867 oz. AGW **Mint:** Turin **Obverse:** Laureate head

Date	Mintage	F	VF	XF	Unc
1808U	1,505	375	625	1,250	1,750

KM# 687.6 20 FRANCS
6.4516 g., 0.9000 Gold .1867 oz. AGW **Mint:** Lille **Obverse:** Laureate head

Date	Mintage	F	VF	XF	Unc
1808W	8,489	200	350	750	1,250

KM# 695.1 20 FRANCS
6.4516 g., 0.9000 Gold .1867 oz. AGW **Mint:** Paris

Date	Mintage	F	VF	XF	Unc
1809A	688,000	100	125	200	700
1810A	1,936,000	100	125	150	600
1811A	3,705,000	100	125	150	600
1812A	3,072,000	100	125	150	600
1813A	2,798,000	100	125	150	600
1814A	328,000	100	150	225	750

KM# 695.2 20 FRANCS
6.4516 g., 0.9000 Gold .1867 oz. AGW **Mint:** Genoa

Date	Mintage	F	VF	XF	Unc
1813CL	4,380	500	1,000	2,000	—
1814CL	887	750	1,500	3,000	—

KM# 695.3 20 FRANCS
6.4516 g., 0.9000 Gold .1867 oz. AGW **Mint:** La Rochelle

Date	Mintage	F	VF	XF	Unc
1809H	501	750	1,500	3,000	—
1810H	2,454	500	1,000	2,000	—
1811H	1,278	625	1,250	2,500	—

KM# 695.4 20 FRANCS
6.4516 g., 0.9000 Gold .1867 oz. AGW **Mint:** Bordeaux

Date	Mintage	F	VF	XF	Unc
1809K	3,614	250	500	1,000	1,500
1810K	15,000	225	450	900	1,750
1811K	11,000	225	450	900	1,750
1812K	2,650	375	750	1,500	—
1813K	869	600	1,200	2,250	—

KM# 695.5 20 FRANCS
6.4516 g., 0.9000 Gold .1867 oz. AGW **Mint:** Bayonne

Date	Mintage	F	VF	XF	Unc
1809L	2,383	325	650	1,250	—
1812L	18,000	125	175	300	800
1813L	19,000	125	175	300	800

KM# 695.6 20 FRANCS
6.4516 g., 0.9000 Gold .1867 oz. AGW **Mint:** Toulouse

Date	Mintage	F	VF	XF	Unc
1809M	5,007	225	450	900	1,750
1810M	1,983	300	600	1,200	2,400
1811M	4,971	250	400	850	1,750
1812M	6,498	175	300	650	1,400

KM# 695.7 20 FRANCS
6.4516 g., 0.9000 Gold .1867 oz. AGW **Mint:** Perpignan

Date	Mintage	F	VF	XF	Unc
1810Q	2,343	450	875	1,750	—
1812Q	5,470	250	500	1,000	2,000
1813Q	13,000	175	350	700	1,400
1814Q	3,289	300	600	1,200	—

KM# 695.8 20 FRANCS
6.4516 g., 0.9000 Gold .1867 oz. AGW **Mint:** London

Date	Mintage	F	VF	XF	Unc
1812R (c)	14,000	250	500	750	2,000
1813R	5,532	300	600	1,000	—

KM# 695.9 20 FRANCS
6.4516 g., 0.9000 Gold .1867 oz. AGW **Mint:** Turin

Date	Mintage	F	VF	XF	Unc
1809U	3,400	375	750	1,500	—
1810U	5,891	225	450	900	2,000
1811U	20,000	150	250	450	1,100
1812U	7,339	175	300	550	1,500
1813U	925	750	1,500	3,000	—

KM# 695.10 20 FRANCS
6.4516 g., 0.9000 Gold .1867 oz. AGW **Mint:** Lille

Date	Mintage	F	VF	XF	Unc
1809W	17,000	125	200	400	1,000
1810W	223,000	100	125	175	625
1811W	328,000	100	125	175	625
1812W	346,000	100	125	175	625
1813W	104,000	100	125	175	625
1814W	16,000	125	200	350	900

KM# 695.11 20 FRANCS
6.4516 g., 0.9000 Gold .1867 oz. AGW **Mint:** Utrecht **Note:** Mint mark: Flag.

Date	Mintage	F	VF	XF	Unc
1813	90,000	150	250	350	1,100

KM# 664.1 40 FRANCS
12.9039 g., 0.9000 Gold .3734 oz. AGW **Mint:** Paris

Date	Mintage	F	VF	XF	Unc
AN13A	252,000	200	225	400	1,750
AN13A Proof	—	Value: 10,000			
AN14A	121,000	200	225	350	1,600

KM# 664.2 40 FRANCS
12.9039 g., 0.9000 Gold .3734 oz. AGW **Mint:** Turin

Date	F	VF	XF	Unc
AN14U Rare	—	—	—	—

KM# 664.3 40 FRANCS
12.9039 g., 0.9000 Gold .3734 oz. AGW **Mint:** Lille

Date	F	VF	XF	Unc
AN14W Rare	—	—	—	—

KM# 675.1 40 FRANCS
12.9039 g., 0.9000 Gold .3734 oz. AGW **Mint:** Paris

Date	Mintage	F	VF	XF	Unc
1806A	196,000	200	225	400	1,500

KM# 675.2 40 FRANCS
12.9039 g., 0.9000 Gold .3734 oz. AGW **Mint:** Genoa

Date	F	VF	XF	Unc
1806CL Rare	—	—	—	—

KM# 675.3 40 FRANCS
12.9039 g., 0.9000 Gold .3734 oz. AGW **Mint:** Limoges

Date	Mintage	F	VF	XF	Unc
1806I	7,103	250	500	1,250	2,500

KM# 675.4 40 FRANCS
12.9039 g., 0.9000 Gold .3734 oz. AGW **Mint:** Toulouse

Date	F	VF	XF	Unc
1806M	—	—	—	—

KM# 675.5 40 FRANCS
12.9039 g., 0.9000 Gold .3734 oz. AGW **Mint:** Turin

Date	Mintage	F	VF	XF	Unc
1806U	59,000	200	275	500	2,000

KM# 675.6 40 FRANCS
12.9039 g., 0.9000 Gold .3734 oz. AGW **Mint:** Lille

Date	Mintage	F	VF	XF	Unc
1806W	4,336	300	650	1,450	—

KM# A688.1 40 FRANCS
12.9039 g., 0.9000 Gold .3734 oz. AGW **Mint:** Paris **Obverse:** Large plain bust

Date	Mintage	F	VF	XF	Unc
1807A	12,000	200	450	900	2,000

KM# A688.2 40 FRANCS
12.9039 g., 0.9000 Gold .3734 oz. AGW **Mint:** Limoges **Obverse:** Large plain bust

Date	Mintage	F	VF	XF	Unc
1807I	1,859	350	750	2,000	—

KM# A688.3 40 FRANCS
12.9039 g., 0.9000 Gold .3734 oz. AGW **Mint:** Toulouse **Obverse:** Large plain bust

Date	Mintage	F	VF	XF	Unc
1807M	4,994	300	650	1,450	2,600

KM# A688.4 40 FRANCS
12.9039 g., 0.9000 Gold .3734 oz. AGW **Mint:** Turin **Obverse:** Large plain bust

Date	Mintage	F	VF	XF	Unc
1807U	619	1,000	2,000	3,750	—

KM# A688.5 40 FRANCS
12.9039 g., 0.9000 Gold .3734 oz. AGW **Mint:** Lille **Obverse:** Large plain bust

Date	Mintage	F	VF	XF	Unc
1807W	6,043	300	650	1,450	—

KM# 688.1 40 FRANCS
12.9039 g., 0.9000 Gold .3734 oz. AGW **Mint:** Paris **Obverse:** Large laureate head left

Date	F	VF	XF	Unc
1807A	200	450	750	2,000
1808A	200	225	350	1,350

KM# 688.2 40 FRANCS
12.9039 g., 0.9000 Gold .3734 oz. AGW **Mint:** La Rochelle **Obverse:** Large laureate head left

Date	Mintage	F	VF	XF	Unc
1808H	12,000	225	450	900	2,250

KM# 688.3 40 FRANCS
12.9039 g., 0.9000 Gold .3734 oz. AGW **Mint:** Toulouse **Obverse:** Large laureate head left

Date	Mintage	F	VF	XF	Unc
1808M	4,226	300	500	1,000	—

KM# 688.4 40 FRANCS
12.9039 g., 0.9000 Gold .3734 oz. AGW **Mint:** Turin **Obverse:** Large laureate head left

Date	Mintage	F	VF	XF	Unc
1808U Rare	346	—	—	—	—

KM# 688.5 40 FRANCS
12.9039 g., 0.9000 Gold .3734 oz. AGW **Mint:** Lille **Obverse:** Large laureate head left

Date	Mintage	F	VF	XF	Unc
1808W	6,356	225	450	950	2,400

KM# 696.1 40 FRANCS
12.9039 g., 0.9000 Gold .3734 oz. AGW **Mint:** Paris

Date	Mintage	F	VF	XF	Unc
1809A	13,000	225	375	700	1,800
1809A Proof	—	Value: 10,000			
1811A	1,262,000	200	225	250	850
1812A	693,000	200	225	325	1,100
1813A	45,000	200	300	600	1,500

KM# 696.2 40 FRANCS
12.9039 g., 0.9000 Gold .3734 oz. AGW **Mint:** Genoa

Date	Mintage	F	VF	XF	Unc
1813CL	3,070	500	1,000	2,000	—

KM# 696.3 40 FRANCS
12.9039 g., 0.9000 Gold .3734 oz. AGW **Mint:** Bordeaux

Date	Mintage	F	VF	XF	Unc
1810K	886	650	1,250	2,500	—
1811K	6,333	300	625	1,250	2,500

KM# 696.4 40 FRANCS
12.9039 g., 0.9000 Gold .3734 oz. AGW **Mint:** Toulouse

Date	Mintage	F	VF	XF	Unc
1809M	1,402	500	1,000	1,750	—

KM# 696.5 40 FRANCS
12.9039 g., 0.9000 Gold .3734 oz. AGW **Mint:** Turin

Date	F	VF	XF	Unc
1809U Rare	—	—	—	—

KM# 696.6 40 FRANCS
12.9039 g., 0.9000 Gold .3734 oz. AGW **Mint:** Lille

Date	Mintage	F	VF	XF	Unc
1809W	5,925	300	600	1,200	—
1810W	57,000	200	250	450	1,500
1812W	14,000	200	275	550	1,700

STRASBOURG PROVISIONAL COINAGE

KM# 700 DECIME
Bronze **Mint:** Strasbourg

Date	Mintage	VG	F	VF	XF	Unc
1814	544,000	7.50	15.00	45.00	125	—
1814 DECIME.	Inc. above	15.00	35.00	90.00	225	400
1814.	Inc. above	10.00	20.00	50.00	145	—
1814. DECIME.	Inc. above	10.00	20.00	40.00	140	—
1815	Inc. above	12.50	25.00	55.00	150	—
1815. DECIME.	Inc. above	15.00	30.00	65.00	175	—

KM# 701 DECIME
Bronze **Mint:** Strasbourg

Date	Mintage	VG	F	VF	XF	Unc
1814	1,208,000	15.00	30.00	60.00	150	—
1814. DECIME.	Inc. above	15.00	30.00	60.00	150	—
1815	Inc. above	7.50	15.00	30.00	125	—
1815. DECIME.	Inc. above	10.00	20.00	40.00	140	—

SECOND KINGDOM

DECIMAL COINAGE

KM# 714.1 1/4 FRANC
1.2500 g., 0.9000 Silver .0362 oz. ASW **Mint:** Paris

Date	Mintage	F	VF	XF	Unc
1817A	100,000	10.00	25.00	75.00	150
1818A	28,000	20.00	50.00	100	275
1819A	11,000	25.00	60.00	150	325
1820A	12,000	25.00	60.00	150	325
1821A	22,000	20.00	50.00	100	275
1822A	36,000	20.00	50.00	100	200
1823A	44,000	20.00	50.00	100	200
1824A	83,000	15.00	30.00	75.00	150

KM# 714.2 1/4 FRANC
1.2500 g., 0.9000 Silver .0362 oz. ASW **Mint:** Rouen

Date	Mintage	F	VF	XF	Unc
1817B	21,000	22.50	50.00	100	250
1818B	16,000	25.00	60.00	110	300
1819B	15,000	25.00	60.00	110	300
1822B	30,000	22.50	50.00	100	275
1823B	13,000	25.00	60.00	150	350
1824B	18,000	22.50	55.00	110	300

KM# 714.3 1/4 FRANC
1.2500 g., 0.9000 Silver .0362 oz. ASW **Mint:** Strasbourg

Date	Mintage	F	VF	XF	Unc
1817BB	3,772	35.00	90.00	250	400

KM# 714.4 1/4 FRANC
1.2500 g., 0.9000 Silver .0362 oz. ASW **Mint:** Lyon

Date	Mintage	F	VF	XF	Unc
1817D	12,000	25.00	50.00	100	250

KM# 714.5 1/4 FRANC
1.2500 g., 0.9000 Silver .0362 oz. ASW **Mint:** Limoges

Date	Mintage	F	VF	XF	Unc
1817I	16,000	30.00	60.00	90.00	225
1823I	1,870	75.00	150	250	500

KM# 714.6 1/4 FRANC
1.2500 g., 0.9000 Silver .0362 oz. ASW **Mint:** Bayonne

Date	Mintage	F	VF	XF	Unc
1817L	14,000	25.00	50.00	100	250
1823L	12,000	25.00	50.00	100	250
1824L	31,000	20.00	40.00	100	250

KM# 714.7 1/4 FRANC
1.2500 g., 0.9000 Silver .0362 oz. ASW **Mint:** Toulouse

Date	Mintage	F	VF	XF	Unc
1817M	4,314	35.00	90.00	250	400
1823M	3,994	40.00	100	260	425
1824M	7,774	35.00	75.00	175	375

KM# 714.8 1/4 FRANC
1.2500 g., 0.9000 Silver .0362 oz. ASW **Mint:** Marseille

Date	Mintage	F	VF	XF	Unc
1817MA	2,132	60.00	125	225	400

KM# 714.9 1/4 FRANC
1.2500 g., 0.9000 Silver .0362 oz. ASW **Mint:** Perpignan

Date	Mintage	F	VF	XF	Unc
1817Q	13,000	25.00	60.00	150	325
1823Q	11,000	25.00	60.00	150	325

KM# 714.10 1/4 FRANC
1.2500 g., 0.9000 Silver .0362 oz. ASW **Mint:** Nantes

Date	Mintage	F	VF	XF	Unc
1817T	7,606	35.00	75.00	175	400

KM# 714.11 1/4 FRANC
1.2500 g., 0.9000 Silver .0362 oz. ASW **Mint:** Lille

Date	Mintage	F	VF	XF	Unc
1817W	14,000	25.00	60.00	150	325
1818W	3,294	40.00	100	260	475
1819W	3,170	40.00	100	260	475
1820W	5,894	35.00	75.00	145	400
1822W	4,486	40.00	100	175	450
1823W	16,000	25.00	50.00	120	275
1824W	11,000	25.00	60.00	150	325

KM# 722.1 1/4 FRANC
1.2500 g., 0.9000 Silver .0362 oz. ASW **Mint:** Paris

Date	Mintage	F	VF	XF	Unc
1825A	9,448	35.00	75.00	150	350
1826A	83,000	15.00	30.00	75.00	175
1827A	322,000	6.00	15.00	60.00	100
1828A	446,000	6.00	15.00	60.00	100
1829A	154,000	7.00	17.50	65.00	150
1830A	659,000	6.00	15.00	40.00	100
1830A	Inc. above	60.00	125	225	425

Note: Reeded edge

KM# 722.2 1/4 FRANC
1.2500 g., 0.9000 Silver .0362 oz. ASW **Mint:** Rouen

Date	Mintage	F	VF	XF	Unc
1826B	23,000	20.00	35.00	75.00	200
1827B	17,000	20.00	35.00	75.00	200

Date	Mintage	F	VF	XF	Unc
1828B	23,000	20.00	35.00	75.00	200
1829B	32,000	15.00	25.00	50.00	175

KM# 722.3 1/4 FRANC
1.2500 g., 0.9000 Silver .0362 oz. ASW **Mint:** Strasbourg

Date	Mintage	F	VF	XF	Unc
1827BB	1,567	60.00	175	300	550
1827BB	1,567	60.00	175	300	550
1829BB	14,000	25.00	60.00	150	300

KM# 722.4 1/4 FRANC
1.2500 g., 0.9000 Silver .0362 oz. ASW **Mint:** Lyon

Date	Mintage	F	VF	XF	Unc
1826D	13,000	25.00	60.00	150	300
1827D	7,820	35.00	75.00	175	350
1828D	13,000	25.00	60.00	150	300
1829D	52,000	15.00	25.00	50.00	175

KM# 722.5 1/4 FRANC
1.2500 g., 0.9000 Silver .0362 oz. ASW **Mint:** La Rochelle

Date	Mintage	F	VF	XF	Unc
1828H	16,000	20.00	35.00	75.00	225

KM# 722.6 1/4 FRANC
1.2500 g., 0.9000 Silver .0362 oz. ASW **Mint:** Limoges

Date	Mintage	F	VF	XF	Unc
1827I	828	—	—	—	—
1828I	2,226	45.00	125	250	385
1829I	10,000	20.00	50.00	100	275

KM# 722.7 1/4 FRANC
1.2500 g., 0.9000 Silver .0362 oz. ASW **Mint:** Bordeaux

Date	Mintage	F	VF	XF	Unc
1829K	27,000	20.00	35.00	75.00	200
1830K	21,000	20.00	35.00	75.00	200

KM# 722.8 1/4 FRANC
1.2500 g., 0.9000 Silver .0362 oz. ASW **Mint:** Bayonne

Date	Mintage	F	VF	XF	Unc
1826L	11,000	20.00	50.00	100	275
1827L	7,582	35.00	85.00	175	300
1828L	15,000	20.00	35.00	75.00	225
1829L	6,486	35.00	85.00	175	300
1830L	15,000	20.00	35.00	75.00	225

KM# 722.9 1/4 FRANC
1.2500 g., 0.9000 Silver .0362 oz. ASW **Mint:** Toulouse

Date	Mintage	F	VF	XF	Unc
1826M	4,861	40.00	100	175	350
1827M	4,292	40.00	100	175	350
1828M	48,000	15.00	30.00	65.00	200
1829M	14,000	20.00	35.00	75.00	225

KM# 722.10 1/4 FRANC
1.2500 g., 0.9000 Silver .0362 oz. ASW **Mint:** Perpignan

Date	Mintage	F	VF	XF	Unc
1826Q	7,534	35.00	85.00	175	320
1828Q	13,000	20.00	35.00	75.00	225

KM# 722.11 1/4 FRANC
1.2500 g., 0.9000 Silver .0362 oz. ASW **Mint:** Nantes

Date	Mintage	F	VF	XF	Unc
1826T	1,753	—	—	—	—
1828T	6,316	25.00	75.00	175	320
1829T	6,481	25.00	75.00	175	320

KM# 722.12 1/4 FRANC
1.2500 g., 0.9000 Silver .0362 oz. ASW **Mint:** Lille

Date	Mintage	F	VF	XF	Unc
1826W	15,000	20.00	35.00	75.00	225
1827W	22,000	20.00	35.00	75.00	200
1828W	47,000	15.00	30.00	65.00	200
1829W	108,000	10.00	20.00	50.00	125
1830W	74,000	15.00	25.00	60.00	150

KM# 740.1 1/4 FRANC
1.2500 g., 0.9000 Silver .0362 oz. ASW **Mint:** Paris

Date	Mintage	F	VF	XF	Unc
1831A	75,000	15.00	25.00	60.00	175
1832A	286,000	7.00	15.00	30.00	80.00
1833A	155,000	8.00	18.00	35.00	90.00
1834A	770,000	4.00	10.00	20.00	65.00
1835A	801,000	4.00	10.00	20.00	65.00
1836A	898,000	4.00	7.00	17.50	55.00
1837A	830,000	4.00	7.00	17.50	55.00
1838A	922,000	4.00	7.00	17.50	55.00
1839A	1,180,000	4.00	7.00	17.50	55.00
1840A	1,246,000	4.00	7.00	17.50	55.00
1841A	1,303,000	4.00	7.00	17.50	55.00
1842A	647,000	4.00	7.00	17.50	55.00
1843A	478,000	4.00	7.00	17.50	55.00
1844A	816,000	4.00	7.00	17.50	55.00
1845A	396,000	4.00	7.00	17.50	55.00

KM# 740.2 1/4 FRANC
1.2500 g., 0.9000 Silver .0362 oz. ASW **Mint:** Rouen

Date	Mintage	F	VF	XF	Unc
1831	52,000	6.00	12.00	32.50	80.00
1832	135,000	5.00	10.00	20.00	55.00
1833	80,000	5.00	10.00	20.00	65.00
1834	70,000	5.00	10.00	20.00	65.00
1835	—	—	500	—	—
Note: 3 known					
1835	Inc. above	—	—	400	—
Note: Error: PRANCAIS					
1836	8,413	20.00	40.00	100	200
1837	94,000	5.00	10.00	20.00	55.00
1838	49,000	10.00	20.00	40.00	90.00
1839	53,000	10.00	20.00	40.00	90.00
1840/30	—	—	750	—	—
Note: 1 known					
1840	53,000	10.00	20.00	40.00	90.00
1841	289,000	4.00	8.00	20.00	65.00
1842	642,000	4.00	8.00	17.50	55.00
1843	762,000	4.00	8.00	17.50	55.00
1844	18,000	10.00	20.00	40.00	90.00
1845	4,603,000	3.00	6.00	17.50	55.00

KM# 740.3 1/4 FRANC
1.2500 g., 0.9000 Silver .0362 oz. ASW **Mint:** Strasbourg

Date	Mintage	F	VF	XF	Unc
1831BB	3,629	30.00	65.00	125	250
1832BB	11,000	15.00	30.00	60.00	150
1833BB	7,890	20.00	40.00	100	200
1834BB	6,063	20.00	40.00	100	200
1835BB	10,000	10.00	20.00	40.00	100
1836BB	11,000	10.00	20.00	40.00	100
1837BB	9,762	20.00	40.00	100	200
1838BB	6,561	20.00	40.00	100	225
1839BB	13,000	10.00	20.00	45.00	110
1844BB	36,000	10.00	20.00	40.00	90.00
1845BB	51,000	10.00	20.00	40.00	90.00

KM# 740.4 1/4 FRANC
1.2500 g., 0.9000 Silver .0362 oz. ASW **Mint:** Lyon

Date	Mintage	F	VF	XF	Unc
1831D	34,000	10.00	20.00	40.00	90.00
1832D	141,000	6.00	12.00	28.00	75.00
1833D	16,000	15.00	30.00	60.00	150
1834D	30,000	6.00	12.00	27.50	75.00
1835D	28,000	6.00	12.00	27.50	75.00
1837D	8,352	20.00	40.00	100	225
1838D	6,199	20.00	40.00	100	225
1839D	5,163	25.00	50.00	125	250
1840D	15,000	15.00	30.00	60.00	150

KM# 740.5 1/4 FRANC
1.2500 g., 0.9000 Silver .0362 oz. ASW **Mint:** La Rochelle

Date	Mintage	F	VF	XF	Unc
1831H	26,000	10.00	20.00	50.00	115
1832H	40,000	10.00	20.00	40.00	90.00
1833H	14,000	15.00	30.00	60.00	150
1834H	46,000	10.00	20.00	40.00	90.00
1835H	9,989	20.00	40.00	100	225

KM# 740.6 1/4 FRANC
1.2500 g., 0.9000 Silver .0362 oz. ASW **Mint:** Limoges

Date	Mintage	F	VF	XF	Unc
1831I	967	—	—	—	—
1832I	34,000	10.00	20.00	50.00	115
1833I	24,000	10.00	20.00	50.00	115
1834I	40,000	6.00	12.00	27.50	75.00
1835I	44,000	6.00	12.00	27.50	75.00

KM# 740.7 1/4 FRANC
1.2500 g., 0.9000 Silver .0362 oz. ASW **Mint:** Bordeaux

Date	Mintage	F	VF	XF	Unc
1831K	36,000	6.00	12.00	27.50	75.00
1832K	20,000	6.00	12.00	27.50	75.00
1833K	22,000	6.00	12.00	27.50	75.00
1834K	36,000	6.00	12.00	27.50	75.00
1835K	41,000	6.00	12.00	27.50	75.00
1836K	9,500	25.00	50.00	110	250
1837K	11,000	15.00	30.00	60.00	150
1838K	16,000	15.00	30.00	60.00	150
1839K	16,000	15.00	30.00	60.00	150
1840K	30,000	10.00	20.00	40.00	90.00
1841K	92,000	8.00	15.00	35.00	80.00
1842K	23,000	10.00	20.00	50.00	115
1843K	27,000	10.00	20.00	50.00	115
1844K	23,000	10.00	20.00	50.00	115
1845K	16,000	12.00	25.00	60.00	125

KM# 740.8 1/4 FRANC
1.2500 g., 0.9000 Silver .0362 oz. ASW **Mint:** Bayonne

Date	Mintage	F	VF	XF	Unc
1831L	6,182	20.00	40.00	100	225
1832L	22,000	10.00	20.00	50.00	115
1833L	8,927	20.00	40.00	100	225
1834L	8,789	20.00	40.00	100	225

KM# 740.9 1/4 FRANC
1.2500 g., 0.9000 Silver .0362 oz. ASW **Mint:** Toulouse

Date	Mintage	F	VF	XF	Unc
1831M	6,831	20.00	40.00	100	225
1832M	35,000	6.00	12.00	27.50	75.00
1833M	17,000	15.00	30.00	60.00	150
1834M	8,218	20.00	40.00	100	225
1835M	11,000	15.00	30.00	60.00	150

KM# 740.10 1/4 FRANC
1.2500 g., 0.9000 Silver .0362 oz. ASW **Mint:** Marseille

Date	Mintage	F	VF	XF	Unc
1832MA Rare	—	—	—	—	—
1833MA	3,452	—	—	—	—

KM# 740.11 1/4 FRANC
1.2500 g., 0.9000 Silver .0362 oz. ASW **Mint:** Perpignan

Date	Mintage	F	VF	XF	Unc
1831Q	11,000	15.00	30.00	60.00	150
1832Q	18,000	12.00	25.00	50.00	125
1834Q	14,000	15.00	30.00	60.00	150

KM# 740.12 1/4 FRANC
1.2500 g., 0.9000 Silver .0362 oz. ASW **Mint:** Nantes

Date	Mintage	F	VF	XF	Unc
1832T	8,486	20.00	40.00	100	225
1833T	18,000	12.00	25.00	50.00	125
1834T	34,000	7.00	15.00	30.00	80.00

KM# 740.13 1/4 FRANC
1.2500 g., 0.9000 Silver .0362 oz. ASW **Mint:** Lille

Date	Mintage	F	VF	XF	Unc
1831W	160,000	5.00	10.00	20.00	50.00
1832W	218,000	5.00	10.00	20.00	60.00
1833W	141,000	5.00	10.00	20.00	60.00
1834W	404,000	4.00	8.00	18.00	45.00
1835W	133,000	5.00	10.00	20.00	55.00
1836W	89,000	6.00	12.00	30.00	70.00
1837W	168,000	5.00	10.00	20.00	55.00
1838/3W	100,000	—	—	—	—
1838W	Inc. above	5.00	10.00	20.00	55.00
1839W	114,000	5.00	10.00	20.00	55.00
1840W	42,000	10.00	20.00	40.00	90.00
1841W	168,000	5.00	10.00	20.00	55.00
1842W	91,000	5.00	10.00	20.00	55.00
1843W	73,000	5.00	10.00	20.00	55.00
1844W	367,000	4.00	8.00	17.50	50.00
1845W	330,000	4.00	8.00	17.50	50.00

KM# 708.1 1/2 FRANC
2.5000 g., 0.9000 Silver .0723 oz. ASW **Mint:** Paris

Date	Mintage	VG	F	VF	XF	Unc
1816A	261,000	8.00	16.00	40.00	125	—
1817A	236,000	8.00	16.00	40.00	125	—
1818A	50,000	10.00	20.00	50.00	135	300
1819A	47,000	10.00	20.00	50.00	135	300
1820A	43,000	10.00	22.00	55.00	140	320
1821A	82,000	8.00	17.50	45.00	125	—
1822A	584,000	6.00	12.00	35.00	90.00	—
1823A	500,000	6.00	12.00	35.00	90.00	—
1824A	613,000	6.00	12.00	35.00	90.00	—

KM# 708.2 1/2 FRANC
2.5000 g., 0.9000 Silver .0723 oz. ASW **Mint:** Rouen

Date	Mintage	VG	F	VF	XF	Unc
1816B	19,000	15.00	30.00	60.00	150	—
1817B	8,759	20.00	40.00	80.00	200	—
1818B	7,803	20.00	40.00	80.00	200	—
1822B	34,000	12.00	25.00	55.00	140	—
1823B	18,000	15.00	30.00	60.00	150	—
1824B	42,000	10.00	22.00	55.00	140	—

KM# 708.3 1/2 FRANC
2.5000 g., 0.9000 Silver .0723 oz. ASW **Mint:** Lyon

Date	Mintage	VG	F	VF	XF	Unc
1824D	18,000	15.00	30.00	60.00	150	—

KM# 708.4 1/2 FRANC
2.5000 g., 0.9000 Silver .0723 oz. ASW **Mint:** La Rochelle

Date	Mintage	VG	F	VF	XF	Unc
1817H	86,000	8.00	17.50	40.00	110	—
1818H	14,000	16.00	35.00	70.00	175	—
1819H	2,463	30.00	60.00	125	250	—
1822H	1,332	35.00	75.00	125	300	—
1823H	3,558	25.00	50.00	110	250	—
1824H	20,000	15.00	30.00	60.00	150	—

KM# 708.5 1/2 FRANC
2.5000 g., 0.9000 Silver .0723 oz. ASW **Mint:** Limoges

Date	Mintage	VG	F	VF	XF	Unc
1816I	2,692	30.00	60.00	125	250	—
1823I	3,113	25.00	50.00	110	250	—
1824I	11,000	16.00	35.00	70.00	165	—

KM# 708.6 1/2 FRANC
2.5000 g., 0.9000 Silver .0723 oz. ASW **Mint:** Bordeaux

Date	Mintage	VG	F	VF	XF	Unc
1817K	213,000	8.00	16.00	40.00	125	—
1820K	7,794	20.00	40.00	80.00	200	—
1823K	8,136	20.00	40.00	80.00	200	—
1824K	53,000	10.00	20.00	55.00	140	—

KM# 708.7 1/2 FRANC
2.5000 g., 0.9000 Silver .0723 oz. ASW **Mint:** Bayonne

Date	Mintage	VG	F	VF	XF	Unc
1816L	3,273	25.00	50.00	110	250	—
1817L	8,767	20.00	40.00	80.00	200	—
1818L	2,816	30.00	60.00	125	250	—
1823L	36,000	12.00	25.00	55.00	140	—
1824L	56,000	12.00	25.00	60.00	150	—

KM# 708.8 1/2 FRANC
2.5000 g., 0.9000 Silver .0723 oz. ASW **Mint:** Toulouse

Date	Mintage	VG	F	VF	XF	Unc
1816M	4,682	20.00	40.00	90.00	225	450
1823M	8,632	20.00	40.00	80.00	200	400
1824M	11,000	16.00	35.00	70.00	165	375

KM# 708.9 1/2 FRANC
2.5000 g., 0.9000 Silver .0723 oz. ASW **Mint:** Perpignan

Date	Mintage	VG	F	VF	XF	Unc
1816Q	12,000	16.00	35.00	70.00	165	—
1819Q	4,488	20.00	40.00	90.00	250	—
1820Q	17,000	15.00	30.00	60.00	150	—
1823Q	101,000	9.00	18.00	45.00	135	—
1824Q	170,000	8.00	16.00	40.00	125	—

KM# 708.10 1/2 FRANC
2.5000 g., 0.9000 Silver .0723 oz. ASW **Mint:** Nantes

Date	Mintage	VG	F	VF	XF	Unc
1816T	5,964	20.00	40.00	90.00	225	—
1819T	1,741	40.00	70.00	160	325	—

KM# 708.11 1/2 FRANC
2.5000 g., 0.9000 Silver .0723 oz. ASW **Mint:** Lille

Date	Mintage	VG	F	VF	XF	Unc
1816W	8,728	20.00	40.00	80.00	200	—
1817W	25,000	12.00	25.00	60.00	150	—
1818W	7,811	15.00	30.00	70.00	175	—
1819W	5,166	20.00	40.00	90.00	250	—
1821W	37,000	12.00	25.00	55.00	140	—
1822W	15,000	12.00	25.00	60.00	150	—
1823W	70,000	8.00	17.50	45.00	125	—
1824W	102,000	9.00	18.00	45.00	135	—
1824W	—	—	—	—	—	225

Note: Above value for common date uncirculated

KM# 723.1 1/2 FRANC
2.5000 g., 0.9000 Silver .0723 oz. ASW **Mint:** Paris

Date	Mintage	VG	F	VF	XF	Unc
1825A	11,000	30.00	60.00	125	250	—
1826A	361,000	6.00	12.00	35.00	90.00	—
1827A	786,000	4.00	10.00	25.00	75.00	—
1828A	508,000	6.00	12.00	27.00	80.00	—
1829A	538,000	4.00	10.00	25.00	75.00	—
1830A	377,000	5.00	12.00	30.00	80.00	—

KM# 723.2 1/2 FRANC
2.5000 g., 0.9000 Silver .0723 oz. ASW **Mint:** Rouen

Date	Mintage	VG	F	VF	XF	Unc
1826B	6,019	20.00	45.00	90.00	225	—
1827B	19,000	12.00	25.00	55.00	140	—
1828B	56,000	10.00	20.00	40.00	115	—
1829B	116,000	6.00	12.00	35.00	100	—

KM# 723.3 1/2 FRANC
2.5000 g., 0.9000 Silver .0723 oz. ASW **Mint:** Strasbourg

Date	Mintage	VG	F	VF	XF	Unc
1826BB	11,000	15.00	30.00	60.00	150	—
1827BB	2,476	30.00	60.00	120	250	—
1828BB	23,000	10.00	20.00	45.00	125	—
1829BB	22,000	10.00	20.00	45.00	125	—

KM# 723.4 1/2 FRANC
2.5000 g., 0.9000 Silver .0723 oz. ASW **Mint:** Lyon

Date	Mintage	VG	F	VF	XF	Unc
1826D	20,000	12.00	25.00	50.00	125	—
1827D	5,629	25.00	50.00	100	200	—
1828D	83,000	7.50	15.00	35.00	100	—
1829D	28,000	10.00	20.00	45.00	120	—

KM# 723.5 1/2 FRANC
2.5000 g., 0.9000 Silver .0723 oz. ASW **Mint:** La Rochelle

Date	Mintage	VG	F	VF	XF	Unc
1826H	23,000	10.00	20.00	45.00	120	—
1827H	14,000	15.00	30.00	60.00	150	—
1828H	26,000	10.00	20.00	45.00	120	—
1829H	58,000	7.50	15.00	35.00	100	—

KM# 723.6 1/2 FRANC
2.5000 g., 0.9000 Silver .0723 oz. ASW **Mint:** Limoges

Date	Mintage	VG	F	VF	XF	Unc
1826I	1,435	25.00	60.00	140	280	—
1827I	1,520	25.00	60.00	140	280	—
1828I	2,526	25.00	60.00	140	280	—
1829I	15,000	12.00	25.00	50.00	125	—

KM# 723.7 1/2 FRANC
2.5000 g., 0.9000 Silver .0723 oz. ASW **Mint:** Bordeaux

Date	Mintage	VG	F	VF	XF	Unc
1826K	17,000	12.00	25.00	50.00	125	—
1827K	9,597	22.00	45.00	80.00	200	—
1828K	27,000	10.00	20.00	45.00	125	—
1829K	37,000	8.00	17.50	40.00	110	—
1830K	22,000	10.00	20.00	45.00	125	—

KM# 723.8 1/2 FRANC
2.5000 g., 0.9000 Silver .0723 oz. ASW **Mint:** Bayonne

Date	Mintage	VG	F	VF	XF	Unc
1826L	36,000	8.00	17.50	40.00	100	—
1827L	31,000	8.00	17.50	40.00	110	—
1828L	27,000	10.00	20.00	45.00	120	—
1829L	16,000	14.00	30.00	55.00	130	—
1830L	18,000	12.00	25.00	50.00	125	—

KM# 723.9 1/2 FRANC
2.5000 g., 0.9000 Silver .0723 oz. ASW **Mint:** Toulouse

Date	Mintage	VG	F	VF	XF	Unc
1826M	9,192	20.00	40.00	75.00	200	—
1827M	7,288	22.00	45.00	85.00	225	—
1828M	72,000	7.50	15.00	35.00	100	—
1829M	16,000	12.00	25.00	50.00	125	—
1830M	7,826	22.00	45.00	85.00	225	—

KM# 723.10 1/2 FRANC
2.5000 g., 0.9000 Silver .0723 oz. ASW **Mint:** Marseille

Date	Mintage	VG	F	VF	XF	Unc
1829MA	32,000	10.00	22.00	50.00	125	—

KM# 723.11 1/2 FRANC
2.5000 g., 0.9000 Silver .0723 oz. ASW **Mint:** Perpignan

Date	Mintage	VG	F	VF	XF	Unc
1826Q	63,000	7.50	15.00	35.00	100	—
1827Q	11,000	15.00	30.00	60.00	150	—
1828Q	30,000	8.00	17.50	40.00	110	—
1829Q	19,000	10.00	20.00	50.00	125	—

KM# 723.12 1/2 FRANC
2.5000 g., 0.9000 Silver .0723 oz. ASW **Mint:** Nantes

Date	Mintage	VG	F	VF	XF	Unc
1827T	8,815	20.00	40.00	75.00	200	—
1828T	18,000	12.00	25.00	50.00	125	—
1829T	3,609	25.00	50.00	100	250	—

KM# 723.13 1/2 FRANC
2.5000 g., 0.9000 Silver .0723 oz. ASW **Mint:** Lille

Date	Mintage	VG	F	VF	XF	Unc
1826W	38,000	8.00	17.50	40.00	100	—
1827W	30,000	8.00	17.50	40.00	100	—
1828W	170,000	6.00	12.00	30.00	90.00	—
1829W	126,000	6.00	12.00	30.00	90.00	—
1830W	131,000	6.00	12.00	30.00	90.00	—
1830W	—	—	—	—	—	250

Note: Above value for common date uncirculated

KM# 741.1 1/2 FRANC
2.5000 g., 0.9000 Silver .0723 oz. ASW **Mint:** Paris

Date	Mintage	F	VF	XF	Unc
1831A	110,000	7.50	15.00	35.00	125
1832A	345,000	6.00	12.00	30.00	110
1833A	272,000	6.00	12.00	30.00	110
1834A	419,000	6.00	12.00	30.00	110
1835A	831,000	6.00	12.00	30.00	90.00
1836A	432,000	6.00	12.00	30.00	110
1837A	137,000	7.50	15.00	35.00	125
1838A	385,000	6.00	12.00	30.00	110
1839A	636,000	6.00	12.00	30.00	110
1840A	1,107,000	5.00	10.00	25.00	110
1841A	1,119,000	5.00	10.00	25.00	110
1842A	338,000	7.50	15.00	35.00	125
1843A	152,000	7.50	15.00	35.00	125
1844A	196,000	7.50	15.00	35.00	125
1845A	494,000	7.50	15.00	35.00	110

KM# 741.2 1/2 FRANC
2.5000 g., 0.9000 Silver .0723 oz. ASW **Mint:** Rouen

Date	Mintage	F	VF	XF	Unc
1831B	136,000	7.50	15.00	35.00	125
1832B	256,000	6.00	12.00	30.00	125
1833B	93,000	7.50	15.00	35.00	130
1834B	86,000	9.00	17.50	35.00	130
1835B	54,000	10.00	20.00	45.00	150
1836B	43,000	10.00	20.00	45.00	150
1837B	158,000	7.50	15.00	35.00	130
1838B	84,000	9.00	17.50	35.00	130
1839B	116,000	9.00	17.50	35.00	130
1840B	117,000	9.00	17.50	35.00	130
1841B	831,000	6.00	12.00	30.00	110
1842B	250,000	7.50	15.00	35.00	115
1843B	213,000	7.50	15.00	35.00	115
1844B	46,000	10.00	20.00	45.00	150
1845B	2,501,000	5.00	10.00	25.00	90.00

KM# 741.3 1/2 FRANC
2.5000 g., 0.9000 Silver .0723 oz. ASW **Mint:** Strasbourg

Date	Mintage	F	VF	XF	Unc
1831BB	2,767	30.00	60.00	120	250
1832BB	10,000	15.00	30.00	60.00	150
1833BB	29,000	10.00	20.00	45.00	125
1834BB	20,000	10.00	20.00	45.00	125
1835BB	5,346	22.00	45.00	85.00	225
1836BB	22,000	10.00	20.00	45.00	125
1837BB	5,952	22.00	45.00	85.00	225
1838BB	5,820	22.00	45.00	85.00	225
1839BB	6,896	20.00	40.00	75.00	200
1840BB	770	—	—	—	—
1841BB	10,000	15.00	30.00	60.00	150
1842BB	308,000	7.50	15.00	30.00	90.00
1844BB	25,000	10.00	20.00	45.00	150
1845BB	44,000	10.00	20.00	45.00	150

KM# 741.4 1/2 FRANC
2.5000 g., 0.9000 Silver .0723 oz. ASW **Mint:** Lyon

Date	Mintage	F	VF	XF	Unc
1831D	16,000	10.00	20.00	45.00	150
1832D	206,000	7.50	15.00	30.00	110
1833D	32,000	10.00	20.00	45.00	150
1834D	64,000	9.00	18.00	35.00	130
1835D	15,000	15.00	30.00	60.00	180
1836D	8,706	20.00	40.00	75.00	250
1837D	7,556	20.00	40.00	75.00	250
1838D	2,432	25.00	50.00	100	300
1840D	19,000	10.00	20.00	45.00	150

KM# 741.5 1/2 FRANC
2.5000 g., 0.9000 Silver .0723 oz. ASW **Mint:** La Rochelle

Date	Mintage	F	VF	XF	Unc
1831H	18,000	10.00	20.00	45.00	150
1832H	77,000	9.00	18.00	35.00	130
1833H	43,000	10.00	20.00	45.00	150
1834H	86,000	9.00	18.00	35.00	130

KM# 741.6 1/2 FRANC
2.5000 g., 0.9000 Silver .0723 oz. ASW **Mint:** Limoges

Date	Mintage	F	VF	XF	Unc
1831I	13,000	15.00	30.00	60.00	180
1832I	26,000	10.00	20.00	45.00	150
1833I	49,000	8.00	18.00	35.00	125
1834I	25,000	10.00	20.00	45.00	150
1835I	45,000	8.00	18.00	35.00	125

KM# 741.7 1/2 FRANC
2.5000 g., 0.9000 Silver .0723 oz. ASW **Mint:** Bordeaux

Date	Mintage	F	VF	XF	Unc
1831K	35,000	10.00	20.00	45.00	150
1832K	40,000	8.00	18.00	35.00	125
1833K	29,000	10.00	20.00	45.00	150
1834K	69,000	8.00	18.00	35.00	125
1835K	50,000	8.00	18.00	35.00	125
1836K	15,000	15.00	30.00	60.00	180
1837K	26,000	10.00	20.00	45.00	150
1838K	17,000	12.00	25.00	50.00	165
1839K	18,000	12.00	25.00	50.00	165
1840K	43,000	8.00	18.00	35.00	125
1841K	26,000	10.00	20.00	45.00	150
1842K	35,000	8.00	18.00	35.00	125
1843K	34,000	8.00	18.00	35.00	125
1844K	23,000	10.00	20.00	45.00	150
1845K	22,000	10.00	20.00	45.00	150

KM# 741.8 1/2 FRANC
2.5000 g., 0.9000 Silver .0723 oz. ASW **Mint:** Bayonne

Date	Mintage	F	VF	XF	Unc
1831L	4,723	22.00	45.00	85.00	275
1832L	34,000	8.00	18.00	35.00	125
1833L	16,000	12.00	25.00	50.00	160
1834L	10,000	15.00	30.00	60.00	180

KM# 741.9 1/2 FRANC
2.5000 g., 0.9000 Silver .0723 oz. ASW **Mint:** Toulouse

Date	Mintage	F	VF	XF	Unc
1831M	8,289	20.00	40.00	75.00	250
1832M	92,000	9.00	18.00	35.00	230
1833M	26,000	10.00	20.00	45.00	150
1834M	19,000	10.00	20.00	45.00	150
1835M	23,000	10.00	20.00	45.00	150
1836M	6,173	22.00	45.00	85.00	275

KM# 741.10 1/2 FRANC
2.5000 g., 0.9000 Silver .0723 oz. ASW **Mint:** Marseille

Date	Mintage	F	VF	XF	Unc
1831MA	—	400	—	—	—
1832MA	52,000	8.00	18.00	35.00	125
1834MA	—	—	—	—	—
1835MA	29,000	10.00	20.00	45.00	150

KM# 741.11 1/2 FRANC
2.5000 g., 0.9000 Silver .0723 oz. ASW **Mint:** Perpignan

Date	Mintage	F	VF	XF	Unc
1831Q	12,000	15.00	30.00	60.00	180
1832Q	21,000	10.00	20.00	45.00	150
1833Q	55,000	8.00	18.00	35.00	125
1834Q	1,824	200	400	—	—

KM# 741.12 1/2 FRANC
2.5000 g., 0.9000 Silver .0723 oz. ASW **Mint:** Nantes

Date	Mintage	F	VF	XF	Unc
1831T	5,573	22.00	45.00	85.00	275
1832T	33,000	8.00	18.00	35.00	125
1833T	14,000	15.00	30.00	60.00	180
1834T	55,000	8.00	18.00	35.00	125

KM# 741.13 1/2 FRANC
2.5000 g., 0.9000 Silver .0723 oz. ASW **Mint:** Lille

Date	Mintage	F	VF	XF	Unc
1831W	125,000	8.00	15.00	35.00	125
1832W	427,000	6.00	12.00	25.00	110
1833W	151,000	8.00	15.00	35.00	125
1834W	683,000	6.00	12.00	25.00	110
1835W	183,000	8.00	15.00	35.00	125
1836W	87,000	8.00	15.00	35.00	125
1837W	267,000	7.00	14.00	30.00	115
1838W	132,000	8.00	15.00	35.00	125
1839W	119,000	8.00	15.00	35.00	125
1840W	79,000	9.00	18.00	40.00	130
1841W	234,000	7.00	14.00	30.00	115
1842W	215,000	7.00	14.00	30.00	115
1843W	233,000	7.00	14.00	30.00	115
1844W	408,000	6.00	12.00	25.00	110
1845W	525,000	6.00	12.00	25.00	90.00

KM# 709.1 FRANC
5.0000 g., 0.9000 Silver .1446 oz. ASW **Mint:** Paris

Date	Mintage	VG	F	VF	XF	Unc
1816A	253,000	10.00	20.00	65.00	135	—
1817A	178,000	12.00	25.00	75.00	160	—
1818A	60,000	15.00	30.00	85.00	180	—
1819A	27,000	18.00	35.00	90.00	200	—
1820A	28,000	18.00	35.00	90.00	200	—
1821A	100,000	12.00	25.00	75.00	160	—
1822A	635,000	6.00	12.00	45.00	115	—
1823A	360,000	7.50	15.00	50.00	115	—
1824A	417,000	6.00	12.00	45.00	115	—

KM# 709.2 FRANC
5.0000 g., 0.9000 Silver .1446 oz. ASW **Mint:** Rouen

Date	Mintage	VG	F	VF	XF	Unc
1816B	16,000	20.00	40.00	100	225	—
1817B	31,000	18.00	35.00	90.00	200	—
1818B	3,866	25.00	60.00	150	350	750
1819B	10,000	20.00	40.00	100	225	—
1820B	16,000	20.00	40.00	100	225	—
1822B	31,000	18.00	35.00	90.00	190	—
1823B	7,577	20.00	50.00	125	275	—
1824B	66,000	12.00	25.00	75.00	160	—

KM# 709.3 FRANC
5.0000 g., 0.9000 Silver .1446 oz. ASW **Mint:** Lyon

Date	Mintage	VG	F	VF	XF	Unc
1817D	5,362	22.00	45.00	125	250	—
1823D	3,485	25.00	60.00	150	340	—
1824D	30,000	18.00	35.00	90.00	190	—

KM# 709.4 FRANC
5.0000 g., 0.9000 Silver .1446 oz. ASW **Mint:** La Rochelle

Date	Mintage	VG	F	VF	XF	Unc
1817H	48,000	12.00	25.00	75.00	160	—
1818H	8,477	20.00	50.00	115	250	—
1819H	8,141	20.00	50.00	115	250	—
1820H	6,709	22.00	50.00	115	250	—
1821H	5,083	22.00	50.00	115	250	—
1822H	16,000	20.00	40.00	100	225	—
1823H	14,000	20.00	40.00	100	225	—
1824H	33,000	18.00	35.00	90.00	190	—

KM# 709.5 FRANC
5.0000 g., 0.9000 Silver .1446 oz. ASW **Mint:** Limoges

Date	Mintage	VG	F	VF	XF	Unc
1816I	5,041	22.00	50.00	125	270	—
1823I	5,273	22.00	50.00	125	270	—
1824I	33,000	18.00	35.00	90.00	190	—

KM# 709.6 FRANC
5.0000 g., 0.9000 Silver .1446 oz. ASW **Mint:** Bordeaux

Date	Mintage	VG	F	VF	XF	Unc
1817K	307,000	10.00	20.00	65.00	135	—
1820K	20,000	20.00	40.00	100	225	—
1823K	5,173	22.00	50.00	125	275	—
1824K	123,000	10.00	20.00	65.00	135	—

KM# 709.7 FRANC
5.0000 g., 0.9000 Silver .1446 oz. ASW **Mint:** Bayonne

Date	Mintage	VG	F	VF	XF	Unc
1816L	5,770	22.00	50.00	125	275	—
1817L	5,059	22.00	50.00	125	275	—
1818L	1,450	40.00	85.00	200	360	—
1823L	36,000	18.00	35.00	90.00	190	—
1824L	54,000	12.00	25.00	75.00	160	—

KM# 709.8 FRANC
5.0000 g., 0.9000 Silver .1446 oz. ASW **Mint:** Toulouse

Date	Mintage	VG	F	VF	XF	Unc
1816M	70,000	12.00	25.00	75.00	160	—
1817M	21,000	20.00	40.00	100	225	—
1823M	36,000	18.00	35.00	90.00	190	—
1824M	59,000	12.00	25.00	75.00	160	—

KM# 709.9 FRANC
5.0000 g., 0.9000 Silver .1446 oz. ASW **Mint:** Marseille

Date	Mintage	VG	F	VF	XF	Unc
1824MA	7,209	20.00	50.00	125	255	—

KM# 709.10 FRANC
5.0000 g., 0.9000 Silver .1446 oz. ASW **Mint:** Perpignan

Date	Mintage	VG	F	VF	XF	Unc
1816Q	25,000	20.00	40.00	100	225	—
1817Q	5,045	22.00	50.00	125	275	—
1819Q	13,000	20.00	40.00	100	225	—
1820Q	22,000	18.00	35.00	90.00	190	—
1821Q	4,942	25.00	60.00	150	340	—
1822Q	3,838	25.00	60.00	150	340	—
1823Q	33,000	18.00	35.00	90.00	190	—
1824Q	52,000	12.00	25.00	75.00	160	—

KM# 709.11 FRANC
5.0000 g., 0.9000 Silver .1446 oz. ASW **Mint:** Nantes

Date	Mintage	VG	F	VF	XF	Unc
1816T	2,240	35.00	75.00	175	360	—
1818T	1,728	45.00	100	275	450	—
1819T	4,094	25.00	60.00	150	340	—

KM# 709.12 FRANC
5.0000 g., 0.9000 Silver .1446 oz. ASW **Mint:** Lille

Date	Mintage	VG	F	VF	XF	Unc
1816W	15,000	20.00	40.00	100	225	—
1817W	19,000	20.00	40.00	100	225	—
1818W	16,000	20.00	40.00	100	225	—
1819W	24,000	20.00	40.00	100	225	—
1820W	13,000	25.00	50.00	125	250	—
1821W	200,000	10.00	20.00	65.00	135	—
1822W	61,000	12.00	25.00	75.00	160	—
1823W	277,000	10.00	20.00	65.00	135	—
1824W	388,000	10.00	20.00	65.00	135	—
1816-24W	—	—	—	—	—	400

Note: Above value for common date uncirculated

KM# 724.1 FRANC
5.0000 g., 0.9000 Silver .1446 oz. ASW **Mint:** Paris

Date	Mintage	VG	F	VF	XF	Unc
1825A	335,000	10.00	20.00	55.00	135	—
1826A	326,000	10.00	20.00	55.00	135	—
1827A	431,000	10.00	20.00	55.00	135	—
1828A	517,000	10.00	20.00	55.00	135	—
1829A	290,000	10.00	20.00	55.00	135	—
1830A	234,000	10.00	20.00	55.00	135	—
1830A	—	100	200	450	1,000	—

Note: Reeded edge

KM# 724.2 FRANC
5.0000 g., 0.9000 Silver .1446 oz. ASW **Mint:** Rouen

Date	Mintage	VG	F	VF	XF	Unc
1825B	17,000	20.00	40.00	80.00	160	—
1826B	20,000	20.00	40.00	80.00	160	—
1827B	96,000	15.00	30.00	70.00	160	—
1828B	70,000	15.00	30.00	70.00	140	—
1829B	124,000	10.00	20.00	45.00	125	—
1830B	75,000	12.00	25.00	70.00	145	—

KM# 724.3 FRANC
5.0000 g., 0.9000 Silver .1446 oz. ASW **Mint:** Strasbourg

Date	Mintage	VG	F	VF	XF	Unc
1825BB	9,256	30.00	60.00	125	275	—
1826BB	12,000	25.00	50.00	100	225	—
1827BB	13,000	25.00	50.00	100	225	—
1828BB	24,000	20.00	40.00	80.00	175	—
1829BB	21,000	20.00	40.00	80.00	175	—

KM# 724.4 FRANC
5.0000 g., 0.9000 Silver .1446 oz. ASW **Mint:** Lyon

Date	Mintage	VG	F	VF	XF	Unc
1825D	40,000	15.00	30.00	70.00	155	—
1826D	28,000	20.00	40.00	80.00	180	—
1827D	36,000	15.00	30.00	70.00	155	—
1828D	76,000	12.00	25.00	65.00	135	—
1829D	31,000	20.00	40.00	80.00	180	—

KM# 724.5 FRANC
5.0000 g., 0.9000 Silver .1446 oz. ASW **Mint:** La Rochelle

Date	Mintage	VG	F	VF	XF	Unc
1825H	23,000	20.00	40.00	80.00	180	—
1826H	28,000	20.00	40.00	80.00	180	—
1827H	5,444	35.00	70.00	150	320	—
1828H	27,000	20.00	40.00	80.00	180	—
1829H	51,000	12.00	25.00	65.00	135	—

KM# 724.6 FRANC
5.0000 g., 0.9000 Silver .1446 oz. ASW **Mint:** Limoges

Date	Mintage	VG	F	VF	XF	Unc
1825I	6,663	35.00	70.00	150	320	—
1826I	4,206	35.00	70.00	150	320	—
1827I	6,850	35.00	70.00	150	320	—
1828I	5,236	35.00	70.00	150	320	—
1829I	20,000	20.00	40.00	80.00	180	—
1830I	1,025	60.00	125	250	450	—

KM# 724.7 FRANC
5.0000 g., 0.9000 Silver .1446 oz. ASW **Mint:** Bordeaux

Date	Mintage	VG	F	VF	XF	Unc
1825K	24,000	20.00	40.00	80.00	180	—
1826K	38,000	20.00	40.00	80.00	180	—
1827K	44,000	18.00	35.00	75.00	160	—
1828K	132,000	8.00	17.50	55.00	125	—
1829K	50,000	15.00	30.00	70.00	155	—
1830K	21,000	20.00	40.00	80.00	180	—

KM# 724.8 FRANC
5.0000 g., 0.9000 Silver .1446 oz. ASW **Mint:** Bayonne

Date	Mintage	VG	F	VF	XF	Unc
1825L	3,830	35.00	70.00	150	325	—
1826L	28,000	20.00	40.00	80.00	180	—
1827L	47,000	18.00	35.00	75.00	165	—
1828L	44,000	18.00	35.00	75.00	165	—
1829L	33,000	20.00	40.00	80.00	180	—
1830L	13,000	22.00	38.00	75.00	165	—

KM# 724.9 FRANC
5.0000 g., 0.9000 Silver .1446 oz. ASW **Mint:** Toulouse

Date	Mintage	VG	F	VF	XF	Unc
1825	6,069	35.00	70.00	150	325	—
1826	31,000	20.00	40.00	80.00	180	—
1827	24,000	20.00	40.00	80.00	180	—
1828	72,000	12.00	25.00	65.00	135	—
1829	46,000	18.00	35.00	75.00	165	—
1830	21,000	20.00	40.00	80.00	180	—

KM# 724.10 FRANC
5.0000 g., 0.9000 Silver .1446 oz. ASW **Mint:** Marseille

Date	Mintage	VG	F	VF	XF	Unc
1829MA	66,000	12.00	25.00	65.00	140	—

KM# 724.11 FRANC
5.0000 g., 0.9000 Silver .1446 oz. ASW **Mint:** Perpignan

Date	Mintage	VG	F	VF	XF	Unc
1825Q	5,653	35.00	70.00	150	325	—
1826Q	25,000	20.00	40.00	80.00	180	—
1827Q	20,000	20.00	40.00	80.00	180	—
1828Q	18,000	20.00	40.00	80.00	180	—
1829Q	13,000	22.00	45.00	90.00	200	—

KM# 724.12 FRANC
5.0000 g., 0.9000 Silver .1446 oz. ASW **Mint:** Nantes

Date	Mintage	VG	F	VF	XF	Unc
1826T	5,930	35.00	70.00	150	325	—
1827T	14,000	22.00	45.00	90.00	200	—
1828T	36,000	20.00	40.00	80.00	180	—
1829T	14,000	22.00	45.00	90.00	200	—
1830T	8,871	30.00	60.00	135	275	—

KM# 724.13 FRANC
5.0000 g., 0.9000 Silver .1446 oz. ASW **Mint:** Lille

Date	Mintage	VG	F	VF	XF	Unc
1825W	78,000	12.00	25.00	65.00	135	—
1826W	130,000	8.00	17.50	55.00	125	—
1827W	519,000	6.00	12.00	40.00	110	—
1828W	418,000	6.00	12.00	45.00	110	—
1829W	149,000	8.00	17.50	55.00	125	—
1830W	78,000	12.00	25.00	65.00	125	—
1825-30W	—	—	—	—	—	375

Note: Above value for common date uncirculated

KM# 742.1 FRANC
5.0000 g., 0.9000 Silver .1446 oz. ASW **Mint:** Paris

Date	Mintage	VG	F	VF	XF	Unc
1831A	202,000	30.00	85.00	200	375	—

KM# 742.2 FRANC
5.0000 g., 0.9000 Silver .1446 oz. ASW **Mint:** Rouen

Date	Mintage	VG	F	VF	XF	Unc
1831B	400,000	25.00	65.00	175	325	—

KM# 742.3 FRANC
5.0000 g., 0.9000 Silver .1446 oz. ASW **Mint:** Strasbourg

Date	Mintage	VG	F	VF	XF	Unc
1831BB	18,000	60.00	150	300	575	—

KM# 742.4 FRANC
5.0000 g., 0.9000 Silver .1446 oz. ASW **Mint:** Lyon

Date	Mintage	VG	F	VF	XF	Unc
1831D	127,000	40.00	110	225	375	—

KM# 742.5 FRANC
5.0000 g., 0.9000 Silver .1446 oz. ASW **Mint:** La Rochelle

Date	Mintage	VG	F	VF	XF	Unc
1831H	27,000	50.00	125	275	400	—

KM# 742.6 FRANC
5.0000 g., 0.9000 Silver .1446 oz. ASW **Mint:** Limoges

Date	Mintage	VG	F	VF	XF	Unc
1831I	21,000	50.00	125	275	400	—

KM# 742.7 FRANC
5.0000 g., 0.9000 Silver .1446 oz. ASW **Mint:** Bordeaux

Date	Mintage	VG	F	VF	XF	Unc
1831K	53,000	40.00	115	250	500	—

KM# 742.8 FRANC
5.0000 g., 0.9000 Silver .1446 oz. ASW **Mint:** Bayonne

Date	Mintage	VG	F	VF	XF	Unc
1831L	2,406	100	250	425	700	—

KM# 742.9 FRANC
5.0000 g., 0.9000 Silver .1446 oz. ASW **Mint:** Toulouse

Date	VG	F	VF	XF	Unc
1831M	45.00	125	250	500	—

KM# 742.10 FRANC
5.0000 g., 0.9000 Silver .1446 oz. ASW **Mint:** Perpignan

Date	Mintage	VG	F	VF	XF	Unc
1831Q	18,000	60.00	150	300	575	—

KM# 742.11 FRANC
5.0000 g., 0.9000 Silver .1446 oz. ASW **Mint:** Nantes

Date	Mintage	VG	F	VF	XF	Unc
1831T	43,000	40.00	115	250	500	—

KM# 742.12 FRANC
5.0000 g., 0.9000 Silver .1446 oz. ASW **Mint:** Lille

Date	Mintage	VG	F	VF	XF	Unc
1831W	453,000	30.00	75.00	175	325	—
1831W	—	—	—	—	—	600

Note: Above value for common date uncirculated

KM# 748.1 FRANC
5.0000 g., 0.9000 Silver .1446 oz. ASW **Mint:** Paris **Obverse:** Laureate head

Date	Mintage	F	VF	XF	Unc
1832A	379,000	10.00	35.00	75.00	250
1833A	114,000	12.00	40.00	90.00	300
1834A	330,000	10.00	35.00	75.00	225
1835A	483,000	10.00	35.00	75.00	225
1836A	138,000	15.00	40.00	85.00	175
1837A	241,000	12.00	35.00	75.00	225
1838A	183,000	15.00	40.00	85.00	175
1839A	243,000	12.00	35.00	75.00	250
1840A	481,000	10.00	35.00	75.00	225
1841A	623,000	10.00	35.00	75.00	250
1842A	130,000	15.00	40.00	85.00	175
1843A	74,000	18.00	40.00	80.00	225
1844A	72,000	18.00	40.00	80.00	225
1845A	215,000	15.00	40.00	85.00	175
1846A	1,225,000	8.00	18.00	40.00	175
1847A	2,401,000	8.00	18.00	40.00	175
1848A	228,000	15.00	40.00	85.00	175

KM# 748.2 FRANC
5.0000 g., 0.9000 Silver .1446 oz. ASW **Mint:** Rouen **Obverse:** Laureate head

Date	Mintage	F	VF	XF	Unc
1832B	197,000	15.00	45.00	90.00	200
1833B	98,000	12.00	35.00	70.00	200
1834B	146,000	10.00	25.00	50.00	200
1835B	103,000	12.00	30.00	60.00	200
1836B	93,000	12.00	35.00	70.00	200
1837B	212,000	12.00	30.00	60.00	200
1838B	145,000	12.00	30.00	60.00	200
1839B	184,000	12.00	30.00	60.00	200
1840B	148,000	10.00	25.00	50.00	200
1841B	663,000	8.00	18.00	40.00	175
1842B	158,000	12.00	30.00	60.00	200
1843B	130,000	12.00	30.00	60.00	200
1844B	45,000	15.00	45.00	90.00	200
1845B	882,000	8.00	18.00	40.00	175
1846B	818,000	8.00	18.00	40.00	175

KM# 748.3 FRANC

5.0000 g., 0.9000 Silver .1446 oz. ASW **Mint:** Strasbourg
Obverse: Laureate head

Date	Mintage	F	VF	XF	Unc
1832BB	42,000	15.00	45.00	90.00	200
1833BB	79,000	15.00	45.00	90.00	200
1834BB	68,000	15.00	45.00	90.00	200
1835BB	46,000	15.00	45.00	90.00	200
1836BB	50,000	15.00	45.00	90.00	220
1837BB	13,000	20.00	50.00	100	225
1838BB	24,000	15.00	40.00	80.00	175
1839BB	43,000	15.00	45.00	90.00	200
1840BB	17,000	20.00	50.00	100	225
1841BB	53,000	15.00	45.00	90.00	200
1842BB	244,000	12.00	30.00	60.00	175
1843BB	72,000	15.00	45.00	90.00	200
1844BB	76,000	15.00	45.00	90.00	200
1845BB	83,000	15.00	45.00	90.00	200
1846BB	24,000	15.00	40.00	80.00	175
1847BB	68,000	15.00	45.00	90.00	200
1848BB	21,000	25.00	60.00	125	275

KM# 748.4 FRANC

5.0000 g., 0.9000 Silver .1446 oz. ASW **Mint:** Lyon **Obverse:** Laureate head

Date	Mintage	F	VF	XF	Unc
1832D	127,000	10.00	25.00	50.00	175
1833D	24,000	15.00	40.00	80.00	175
1834D	59,000	15.00	45.00	95.00	235
1835D	52,000	15.00	45.00	95.00	235
1836D	19,000	25.00	60.00	125	275
1837D	2,531	40.00	100	200	550
1838D	12,000	20.00	50.00	95.00	235
1839D	11,000	20.00	50.00	95.00	235
1840D	7,130	40.00	80.00	175	375

KM# 748.5 FRANC

5.0000 g., 0.9000 Silver .1446 oz. ASW **Mint:** La Rochelle
Obverse: Laureate head

Date	Mintage	F	VF	XF	Unc
1832H	80,000	15.00	45.00	95.00	235
1833H	26,000	15.00	45.00	95.00	235
1834H	79,000	15.00	45.00	95.00	235
1835H	17,000	20.00	50.00	110	250

KM# 748.6 FRANC

5.0000 g., 0.9000 Silver .1446 oz. ASW **Mint:** Limoges
Obverse: Laureate head

Date	Mintage	F	VF	XF	Unc
1832I	37,000	15.00	45.00	95.00	235
1833I	34,000	15.00	45.00	95.00	235
1834I	45,000	15.00	45.00	95.00	235
1835I	48,000	15.00	45.00	95.00	235

KM# 748.7 FRANC

5.0000 g., 0.9000 Silver .1446 oz. ASW **Mint:** Bordeaux
Obverse: Laureate head

Date	Mintage	F	VF	XF	Unc
1832K	35,000	15.00	45.00	90.00	215
1833K	30,000	15.00	45.00	90.00	215
1834K	70,000	15.00	45.00	90.00	215
1835K	58,000	15.00	45.00	90.00	215
1836K	40,000	15.00	40.00	80.00	200
1837K	34,000	20.00	50.00	100	250
1838K	17,000	20.00	50.00	100	250
1839K	48,000	15.00	45.00	90.00	210
1840K	48,000	15.00	45.00	90.00	210
1841K	42,000	15.00	45.00	90.00	210
1842K	32,000	15.00	45.00	90.00	210
1843K	39,000	15.00	45.00	90.00	210
1844K	23,000	15.00	45.00	90.00	210
1845K	23,000	15.00	45.00	90.00	210
1846K	23,000	15.00	45.00	90.00	210
1847K	6,787	—	500	—	—

Note: One piece known

KM# 748.8 FRANC

5.0000 g., 0.9000 Silver .1446 oz. ASW **Mint:** Bayonne
Obverse: Laureate head

Date	Mintage	F	VF	XF	Unc
1832L	31,000	15.00	45.00	90.00	225
1833L	18,000	20.00	50.00	100	250
1834L	12,000	20.00	50.00	100	250
1835L	3,647	80.00	180	350	—

KM# 748.9 FRANC

5.0000 g., 0.9000 Silver .1446 oz. ASW **Mint:** Toulouse
Obverse: Laureate head

Date	Mintage	F	VF	XF	Unc
1832M	51,000	15.00	45.00	90.00	200
1833M	49,000	15.00	45.00	90.00	200
1834M	37,000	15.00	45.00	90.00	200
1835M	25,000	18.00	45.00	90.00	200

KM# 748.10 FRANC

5.0000 g., 0.9000 Silver .1446 oz. ASW **Mint:** Marseille
Obverse: Laureate head

Date	Mintage	F	VF	XF	Unc
1832MA	78,000	15.00	45.00	90.00	225
1833MA	57,000	15.00	45.00	90.00	225
1834MA	18,000	20.00	50.00	100	250
1835MA	12,000	20.00	50.00	100	250
1837MA Rare	—	—	—	—	—
1838MA	20,000	20.00	50.00	100	250

KM# 748.11 FRANC

5.0000 g., 0.9000 Silver .1446 oz. ASW **Mint:** Perpignan
Obverse: Laureate head

Date	Mintage	F	VF	XF	Unc
1832Q Rare	—	—	—	—	—
1833Q	19,000	25.00	65.00	125	275
1834Q	57,000	15.00	45.00	90.00	225

KM# 748.12 FRANC

5.0000 g., 0.9000 Silver .1446 oz. ASW **Mint:** Nantes **Obverse:** Laureate head

Date	Mintage	F	VF	XF	Unc
1832T	34,000	20.00	50.00	100	250
1833T	31,000	15.00	50.00	100	250
1834T	102,000	12.00	30.00	60.00	200
1835T	51,000	15.00	45.00	90.00	225

KM# 748.13 FRANC

5.0000 g., 0.9000 Silver .1446 oz. ASW **Mint:** Lille **Obverse:** Laureate head

Date	Mintage	F	VF	XF	Unc
1832W	155,000	12.00	30.00	60.00	200
1833W	213,000	12.00	30.00	60.00	200
1834W	608,000	8.00	18.00	40.00	175
1835W	206,000	12.00	30.00	60.00	200
1836W	49,000	15.00	45.00	90.00	225
1837W	266,000	12.00	30.00	60.00	200
1838W	162,000	12.00	30.00	60.00	200
1839W	120,000	12.00	30.00	60.00	200
1840W	79,000	15.00	45.00	85.00	215
1841W	321,000	12.00	30.00	55.00	175
1842W	195,000	12.00	30.00	55.00	175
1843W	271,000	12.00	30.00	55.00	175
1844W	381,000	10.00	25.00	50.00	175
1845W	478,000	10.00	25.00	50.00	175
1846W	74,000	15.00	45.00	90.00	225

KM# 703 2 FRANCS

10.0000 g., 0.9000 Silver .2893 oz. ASW **Mint:** Paris

Date	Mintage	VG	F	VF	XF	Unc
1815A	6,783	175	350	700	1,500	—
1815A Proof	—	Value: 3,500				

KM# 710.1 2 FRANCS

10.0000 g., 0.9000 Silver .2893 oz. ASW **Mint:** Paris

Date	Mintage	VG	F	VF	XF	Unc
1816A	61,000	25.00	55.00	150	375	—
1817A	214,000	20.00	40.00	100	350	—
1818A	13,000	35.00	75.00	185	475	—
1819A	2,334	50.00	100	225	525	—
1820A	53,000	25.00	55.00	150	375	—
1821A	139,000	22.00	45.00	125	350	—
1822A	421,000	20.00	40.00	100	300	—
1823A	268,000	20.00	40.00	100	250	—
1824A	284,000	20.00	40.00	100	250	—

KM# 710.2 2 FRANCS

10.0000 g., 0.9000 Silver .2893 oz. ASW **Mint:** Rouen

Date	Mintage	VG	F	VF	XF	Unc
1816B	4,398	40.00	85.00	250	500	—
1817B	15,000	35.00	75.00	175	450	—
1818B	3,039	45.00	90.00	225	500	—
1819B	12,000	35.00	75.00	175	450	—
1822B	30,000	30.00	65.00	150	400	—
1824B	71,000	25.00	50.00	145	375	—

KM# 710.3 2 FRANCS

10.0000 g., 0.9000 Silver .2893 oz. ASW **Mint:** Lyon

Date	Mintage	VG	F	VF	XF	Unc
1820D	2,282	—	—	—	—	—
1822D	2,181	50.00	100	250	500	—
1823D	7,251	40.00	85.00	250	500	—
1824D	108,000	22.00	45.00	120	350	—

KM# 710.4 2 FRANCS

10.0000 g., 0.9000 Silver .2893 oz. ASW **Mint:** La Rochelle

Date	Mintage	VG	F	VF	XF	Unc
1816H	7,037	40.00	85.00	250	500	—
1817H	37,000	30.00	65.00	150	400	—
1818H	8,530	40.00	85.00	250	500	—
1819H	5,309	40.00	85.00	250	500	—
1820H	2,801	—	—	—	—	—
1821H	2,897	45.00	90.00	225	500	—
1822H	9,806	40.00	85.00	250	500	—
1823H	20,000	30.00	65.00	150	400	—
1824H	27,000	30.00	65.00	150	400	—

KM# 710.5 2 FRANCS

10.0000 g., 0.9000 Silver .2893 oz. ASW **Mint:** Limoges

Date	Mintage	VG	F	VF	XF	Unc
1816I	3,956	45.00	90.00	225	500	—
1823I	10,000	40.00	85.00	250	500	—
1824I	53,000	25.00	55.00	150	375	—

KM# 710.6 2 FRANCS

10.0000 g., 0.9000 Silver .2893 oz. ASW **Mint:** Bordeaux

Date	Mintage	VG	F	VF	XF	Unc
1817K	213,000	20.00	40.00	100	250	—
1820K	11,000	40.00	85.00	250	500	—
1823K	2,545	—	—	—	—	—
1824K	38,000	30.00	65.00	150	400	—

KM# 710.7 2 FRANCS

10.0000 g., 0.9000 Silver .2893 oz. ASW **Mint:** Bayonne

Date	Mintage	VG	F	VF	XF	Unc
1816L	1,068	—	—	—	—	—
1817L	3,026	—	—	—	—	—
1818L	444	—	—	—	—	—
1823L	27,000	30.00	65.00	150	400	—
1824L	48,000	25.00	55.00	150	375	—

KM# 710.8 2 FRANCS

10.0000 g., 0.9000 Silver .2893 oz. ASW **Mint:** Toulouse

Date	Mintage	VG	F	VF	XF	Unc
1816M	1,699	—	—	—	—	—
1817M	30,000	30.00	65.00	150	400	—
1822M	1,496	—	—	—	—	—
1823M	94,000	25.00	55.00	150	375	—
1824M	132,000	22.00	45.00	125	350	—

KM# 710.9 2 FRANCS

10.0000 g., 0.9000 Silver .2893 oz. ASW **Mint:** Marseille

Date	Mintage	VG	F	VF	XF	Unc
1824MA	7,455	40.00	85.00	250	500	—

KM# 710.10 2 FRANCS

10.0000 g., 0.9000 Silver .2893 oz. ASW **Mint:** Perpignan

Date	Mintage	VG	F	VF	XF	Unc
1816Q	13,000	35.00	75.00	175	450	—
1817Q	47,000	25.00	55.00	150	400	—
1818Q	52,000	25.00	55.00	150	400	—
1819Q	64,000	25.00	55.00	150	400	—
1820Q	47,000	25.00	55.00	150	400	—
1821Q	28,000	30.00	65.00	150	400	—
1822Q	11,000	40.00	85.00	250	500	—
1823Q	3,399	50.00	100	250	500	—
1824Q	53,000	25.00	55.00	150	375	—

KM# 710.11 2 FRANCS

10.0000 g., 0.9000 Silver .2893 oz. ASW **Mint:** Nantes

Date	Mintage	VG	F	VF	XF	Unc
1817T	1,456	—	—	—	—	—

KM# 710.12 2 FRANCS

10.0000 g., 0.9000 Silver .2893 oz. ASW **Mint:** Lille

Date	Mintage	VG	F	VF	XF	Unc
1824W	—	—	—	200	500	1,000

Note: Above value for common date uncirculated

Date	Mintage	VG	F	VF	XF	Unc
1817W	8,504	40.00	85.00	250	500	—
1818W	3,208	—	—	—	—	—
1821W	22,000	30.00	65.00	150	400	—
1822W	102,000	22.00	45.00	125	350	—
1823W	265,000	20.00	30.00	75.00	225	—
1824W	460,000	20.00	30.00	75.00	225	—

KM# 725.1 2 FRANCS

10.0000 g., 0.9000 Silver .2893 oz. ASW **Mint:** Paris

Date	Mintage	VG	F	VF	XF	Unc
1825A	34,000	30.00	60.00	150	400	—
1826A	122,000	25.00	50.00	125	350	—
1827A	268,000	20.00	45.00	100	325	—
1828A	235,000	20.00	45.00	100	325	—
1829A	145,000	25.00	50.00	150	400	—
1830A	44,000	30.00	60.00	150	400	—
1830A	Inc. above	150	300	600	1,150	2,200

Note: Reeded edge

KM# 725.2 2 FRANCS
10.0000 g., 0.9000 Silver .2893 oz. ASW **Mint:** Rouen

Date	Mintage	VG	F	VF	XF	Unc
1825B	17,000	35.00	70.00	175	400	—
1826B	24,000	35.00	70.00	175	400	—
1827B	138,000	25.00	50.00	125	350	—
1828B	59,000	30.00	60.00	150	400	—
1829B	102,000	25.00	50.00	125	250	—
1830B	64,000	30.00	60.00	150	400	—

KM# 725.3 2 FRANCS
10.0000 g., 0.9000 Silver .2893 oz. ASW **Mint:** Strasbourg

Date	Mintage	VG	F	VF	XF	Unc
1825BB	5,856	40.00	80.00	200	500	—
1826BB	19,000	35.00	70.00	175	400	—
1827BB	19,000	35.00	70.00	175	400	—
1828BB	25,000	35.00	70.00	175	400	—
1829BB	18,000	35.00	70.00	175	400	—

KM# 725.4 2 FRANCS
10.0000 g., 0.9000 Silver .2893 oz. ASW **Mint:** Lyon

Date	Mintage	VG	F	VF	XF	Unc
1825D	27,000	35.00	70.00	175	400	—
1826D	72,000	30.00	60.00	150	400	—
1827D	116,000	25.00	50.00	125	250	—
1828D	108,000	25.00	50.00	125	250	—
1829D	96,000	30.00	60.00	150	400	—

KM# 725.5 2 FRANCS
10.0000 g., 0.9000 Silver .2893 oz. ASW **Mint:** La Rochelle

Date	Mintage	VG	F	VF	XF	Unc
1825H	3,215	—	—	—	—	—
1826H	19,000	35.00	70.00	175	400	—
1827H	19,000	35.00	70.00	175	400	—
1828H	16,000	35.00	70.00	175	400	—
1829H	49,000	30.00	60.00	150	400	—

KM# 725.6 2 FRANCS
10.0000 g., 0.9000 Silver .2893 oz. ASW **Mint:** Limoges

Date	Mintage	VG	F	VF	XF	Unc
1825I	6,239	40.00	80.00	200	500	—
1826I	32,000	30.00	60.00	150	400	—
1827I	22,000	35.00	70.00	175	400	—
1828I	4,863	45.00	100	200	500	—
1829I	16,000	35.00	70.00	175	400	—
1830I	5,635	45.00	100	200	500	—

KM# 725.7 2 FRANCS
10.0000 g., 0.9000 Silver .2893 oz. ASW **Mint:** Bordeaux

Date	Mintage	VG	F	VF	XF	Unc
1825K	11,000	35.00	70.00	175	400	—
1826K	11,000	35.00	70.00	175	400	—
1827K	33,000	30.00	60.00	150	400	—
1828K	81,000	30.00	60.00	150	400	—
1829K	33,000	30.00	60.00	150	400	—
1830K	14,000	35.00	70.00	175	400	—

KM# 725.8 2 FRANCS
10.0000 g., 0.9000 Silver .2893 oz. ASW **Mint:** Bayonne

Date	Mintage	VG	F	VF	XF	Unc
1825L	4,397	45.00	100	200	500	—
1826L	25,000	30.00	60.00	150	400	—
1827L	52,000	30.00	60.00	150	400	—
1828L	46,000	30.00	60.00	150	400	—
1829L	21,000	35.00	70.00	175	400	—
1830L	13,000	35.00	60.00	150	400	—

KM# 725.9 2 FRANCS
10.0000 g., 0.9000 Silver .2893 oz. ASW **Mint:** Toulouse

Date	Mintage	VG	F	VF	XF	Unc
1825M	6,770	40.00	80.00	200	500	—
1826M	40,000	30.00	60.00	150	400	—
1827M	31,000	30.00	60.00	150	400	—
1828M	120,000	25.00	50.00	125	250	—
1829M	49,000	30.00	60.00	150	400	—
1830M	16,000	35.00	70.00	175	400	—

KM# 725.10 2 FRANCS
10.0000 g., 0.9000 Silver .2893 oz. ASW **Mint:** Marseille

Date	Mintage	VG	F	VF	XF	Unc
1829MA	41,000	30.00	60.00	150	350	700

KM# 725.11 2 FRANCS
10.0000 g., 0.9000 Silver .2893 oz. ASW **Mint:** Perpignan

Date	Mintage	VG	F	VF	XF	Unc
1825Q	4,956	50.00	100	200	500	—
1826Q	21,000	40.00	60.00	150	400	—
1827Q	14,000	50.00	70.00	175	400	—
1828Q	24,000	50.00	70.00	175	400	—
1829Q	11,000	50.00	70.00	175	400	—
1830Q	6,688	60.00	125	200	500	—

KM# 725.12 2 FRANCS
10.0000 g., 0.9000 Silver .2893 oz. ASW **Mint:** Nantes

Date	Mintage	VG	F	VF	XF	Unc
1826T	9,189	45.00	100	200	500	—
1827T	43,000	30.00	60.00	150	400	—
1828T	31,000	30.00	60.00	150	400	—
1829T	50,000	30.00	60.00	150	400	—
1830T	12,000	35.00	70.00	175	400	—

KM# 725.13 2 FRANCS
10.0000 g., 0.9000 Silver .2893 oz. ASW **Mint:** Lille

Date	Mintage	VG	F	VF	XF	Unc
1825W	15,000	35.00	70.00	175	400	—
1826W	155,000	25.00	50.00	125	250	—
1827W	481,000	15.00	35.00	90.00	275	—
1828W	358,000	15.00	35.00	90.00	275	—
1829W	105,000	25.00	50.00	125	400	—
1830W	109,000	25.00	50.00	125	400	—
1825-30W	—	—	—	—	—	750

Note: Above value for common date uncirculated

KM# 743.1 2 FRANCS
10.0000 g., 0.9000 Silver .2893 oz. ASW **Mint:** Paris

Date	Mintage	F	VF	XF	Unc
1831A	10,000	45.00	100	275	600
1832A	688,000	18.00	45.00	125	400
1833A	194,000	22.00	60.00	135	450
1834A	493,000	18.00	45.00	100	375
1835A	452,000	18.00	45.00	125	400
1836A	112,000	22.00	60.00	135	450
1837A	104,000	22.00	60.00	135	450
1838A	93,000	22.00	60.00	135	450
1839A	36,000	40.00	85.00	200	500
1840A	42,000	40.00	85.00	200	500
1841A	68,000	40.00	85.00	200	500
1842A	17,000	45.00	100	275	600
1843A	68,000	40.00	85.00	200	500
1844A	30,000	40.00	85.00	200	500
1845A (p)	19,000	20.00	50.00	125	400
1845A (ha)	Inc. above	20.00	50.00	125	400
1846A	305,000	18.00	45.00	100	375
1847A	784,000	18.00	45.00	125	400
1848A	98,000	22.00	55.00	135	450

KM# 743.2 2 FRANCS
10.0000 g., 0.9000 Silver .2893 oz. ASW **Mint:** Rouen

Date	Mintage	F	VF	XF	Unc
1831B	49,000	40.00	85.00	200	500
1832B	384,000	18.00	45.00	90.00	375
1833B	105,000	25.00	50.00	125	400
1834B	296,000	18.00	45.00	90.00	375
1835B	66,000	40.00	85.00	200	500
1836B	113,000	25.00	50.00	125	400
1837B	256,000	18.00	45.00	90.00	375
1838B	156,000	20.00	50.00	100	375
1839B	102,000	25.00	50.00	125	400
1840B	121,000	25.00	50.00	125	400
1841B	22,000	20.00	50.00	125	400
1842B	147,000	20.00	50.00	100	375
1843B	67,000	40.00	85.00	200	500
1844B	13,000	45.00	120	300	650
1845B	155,000	20.00	50.00	100	375
1846B	46,000	40.00	85.00	200	500

KM# 743.3 2 FRANCS
10.0000 g., 0.9000 Silver .2893 oz. ASW **Mint:** Strasbourg

Date	Mintage	F	VF	XF	Unc
1832BB	55,000	40.00	85.00	200	500
1833BB	74,000	40.00	85.00	200	500
1834BB (ba)	77,000	40.00	85.00	200	500
1834BB (be)	Inc. above	40.00	85.00	200	500
1835BB	38,000	40.00	85.00	200	500
1836BB	73,000	40.00	85.00	200	500
1837BB	22,000	20.00	50.00	125	400
1838BB	82,000	40.00	85.00	200	500
1839BB	47,000	40.00	85.00	200	500
1840BB	64,000	40.00	85.00	200	500
1841BB	61,000	40.00	85.00	200	500
1842BB	26,000	20.00	50.00	125	400
1843BB	59,000	40.00	85.00	200	500
1844BB	86,000	40.00	85.00	200	500
1845BB	76,000	40.00	85.00	200	500
1846BB	44,000	40.00	85.00	200	500
1847BB	60,000	40.00	85.00	200	500
1848BB	27,000	20.00	50.00	125	400

KM# 743.4 2 FRANCS
10.0000 g., 0.9000 Silver .2893 oz. ASW **Mint:** Lyon

Date	Mintage	F	VF	XF	Unc
1832D	239,000	20.00	50.00	100	375
1833D	98,000	40.00	85.00	200	500
1834D	98,000	40.00	85.00	200	500
1835D	40,000	40.00	85.00	200	500
1836D	5,519	55.00	125	300	800
1837D	6,306	55.00	125	300	800
1838D	3,478	—	—	—	—
1839D (a)	7,299	50.00	110	300	750
1839D (t)	Inc. above	50.00	110	300	750
1840D	10,000	45.00	100	275	600
1848D	12,000	45.00	100	275	600

KM# 743.5 2 FRANCS
10.0000 g., 0.9000 Silver .2893 oz. ASW **Mint:** La Rochelle

Date	Mintage	F	VF	XF	Unc
1832H	186,000	25.00	50.00	125	400
1833H	22,000	20.00	50.00	125	400
1834H	72,000	40.00	85.00	200	500
1835H	23,000	20.00	50.00	125	400

KM# 743.6 2 FRANCS
10.0000 g., 0.9000 Silver .2893 oz. ASW **Mint:** Limoges

Date	Mintage	F	VF	XF	Unc
1831I	38,000	40.00	85.00	200	500
1832I	34,000	40.00	85.00	200	500
1833I	34,000	40.00	85.00	200	500
1834I	48,000	40.00	85.00	200	500
1835I	48,000	40.00	85.00	200	500

KM# 743.7 2 FRANCS
10.0000 g., 0.9000 Silver .2893 oz. ASW **Mint:** Bordeaux

Date	Mintage	F	VF	XF	Unc
1832K	76,000	40.00	85.00	200	500
1833K	23,000	20.00	50.00	125	400
1834K	57,000	40.00	85.00	200	500
1835K	42,000	40.00	85.00	200	500
1836K	20,000	40.00	100	350	700
1837K	36,000	40.00	85.00	200	500
1838K	19,000	40.00	100	350	700
1839K	31,000	40.00	85.00	200	500
1840K	39,000	40.00	85.00	200	500
1841K	29,000	40.00	85.00	200	500
1842K	33,000	40.00	85.00	200	500
1843K	37,000	40.00	85.00	200	500
1844K	31,000	40.00	85.00	200	500
1845K	18,000	40.00	100	350	700
1846K	18,000	40.00	100	350	700
1847K	6,504	55.00	125	300	800

KM# 743.8 2 FRANCS
10.0000 g., 0.9000 Silver .2893 oz. ASW **Mint:** Bayonne

Date	Mintage	F	VF	XF	Unc
1832L	24,000	20.00	50.00	125	400
1833L	14,000	45.00	100	275	600
1834L	15,000	45.00	100	275	600
1835L	2,669	—	—	—	—

KM# 743.9 2 FRANCS
10.0000 g., 0.9000 Silver .2893 oz. ASW **Mint:** Toulouse

Date	Mintage	F	VF	XF	Unc
1832M	69,000	40.00	85.00	200	500
1833M	50,000	40.00	85.00	200	500
1834M	78,000	40.00	85.00	200	500
1835M	41,000	40.00	85.00	200	500
1836M	6,733	55.00	125	300	800

KM# 743.10 2 FRANCS
10.0000 g., 0.9000 Silver .2893 oz. ASW **Mint:** Marseille

Date	Mintage	F	VF	XF	Unc
1832MA	64,000	45.00	85.00	200	500
1833MA	21,000	45.00	100	275	600
1834MA	19,000	45.00	100	275	600
1835MA	15,000	45.00	100	275	600
1837MA	—	250	550	1,000	1,900
1838MA	25,000	20.00	50.00	125	400

KM# 743.11 2 FRANCS
10.0000 g., 0.9000 Silver .2893 oz. ASW **Mint:** Perpignan

Date	Mintage	F	VF	XF	Unc
1832Q	22,000	45.00	100	275	600
1833Q	37,000	40.00	85.00	200	500
1834Q	69,000	40.00	85.00	200	500

KM# 743.12 2 FRANCS
10.0000 g., 0.9000 Silver .2893 oz. ASW **Mint:** Nantes

Date	Mintage	F	VF	XF	Unc
1832T	104,000	25.00	50.00	125	400
1833T	28,000	40.00	85.00	200	500
1834T	104,000	25.00	50.00	125	400
1835T	17,000	45.00	100	275	600

KM# 743.13 2 FRANCS
10.0000 g., 0.9000 Silver .2893 oz. ASW **Mint:** Lille

Date	Mintage	F	VF	XF	Unc
1831W	33,000	40.00	85.00	200	500
1832W	427,000	18.00	45.00	100	375
1833W	168,000	25.00	50.00	125	400
1834W	583,000	18.00	45.00	100	375
1835W	147,000	25.00	50.00	125	400
1836W	60,000	40.00	85.00	200	500
1837W	230,000	25.00	50.00	125	400
1838W	170,000	25.00	50.00	125	400
1839W	105,000	25.00	50.00	125	400
1840W	63,000	40.00	85.00	200	500
1840W	Inc. above	40.00	85.00	200	500
1841W	290,000	25.00	50.00	125	400
1842W	190,000	25.00	50.00	125	400
1843W	296,000	22.00	45.00	120	400
1844W	290,000	22.00	45.00	120	400
1845W	353,000	22.00	45.00	120	400
1846W	49,000	40.00	85.00	200	500

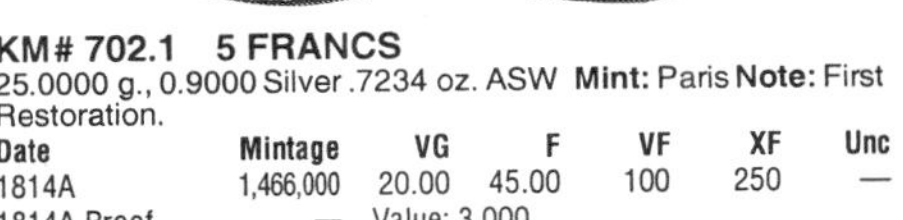

KM# 702.1 5 FRANCS
25.0000 g., 0.9000 Silver .7234 oz. ASW **Mint:** Paris **Note:** First Restoration.

Date	Mintage	VG	F	VF	XF	Unc
1814A	1,466,000	20.00	45.00	100	250	—
1814A Proof	—	Value: 3,000				

Date	Mintage	VG	F	VF	XF	Unc
Note: 4 known						
1815A	413,000	25.00	50.00	125	275	—

KM# 702.2 5 FRANCS
25.0000 g., 0.9000 Silver .7234 oz. ASW **Mint:** Rouen

Date	Mintage	VG	F	VF	XF	Unc
1814B	634,000	25.00	50.00	125	250	475
1815B	254,000	30.00	65.00	150	325	625

KM# 702.3 5 FRANCS
25.0000 g., 0.9000 Silver .7234 oz. ASW **Mint:** Strasbourg

Date	Mintage	VG	F	VF	XF	Unc
1814BB	4,913	75.00	175	400	900	—
1815BB	1,551	100	225	500	1,200	—

KM# 702.4 5 FRANCS
25.0000 g., 0.9000 Silver .7234 oz. ASW **Mint:** Lyon

Date	Mintage	VG	F	VF	XF	Unc
1814D	82,000	35.00	75.00	175	400	—
1815D	7,482	65.00	150	325	700	—

KM# 702.5 5 FRANCS
25.0000 g., 0.9000 Silver .7234 oz. ASW **Mint:** La Rochelle

Date	Mintage	VG	F	VF	XF	Unc
1814H	46,000	40.00	85.00	200	500	—
1815H	34,000	40.00	85.00	200	500	—

KM# 702.6 5 FRANCS
25.0000 g., 0.9000 Silver .7234 oz. ASW **Mint:** Limoges

Date	Mintage	VG	F	VF	XF	Unc
1814I	1,554,000	20.00	45.00	100	250	—
1815I	1,739,000	20.00	45.00	100	250	—

KM# 702.7 5 FRANCS
25.0000 g., 0.9000 Silver .7234 oz. ASW **Mint:** Bordeaux

Date	Mintage	VG	F	VF	XF	Unc
1814K	355,000	30.00	60.00	120	350	—
1815K	108,000	30.00	60.00	120	350	—

KM# 702.8 5 FRANCS
25.0000 g., 0.9000 Silver .7234 oz. ASW **Mint:** Bayonne

Date	Mintage	VG	F	VF	XF	Unc
1814L	1,902,000	20.00	45.00	100	250	—
1815L	1,130,000	20.00	45.00	100	250	—

KM# 702.9 5 FRANCS
25.0000 g., 0.9000 Silver .7234 oz. ASW **Mint:** Toulouse

Date	Mintage	VG	F	VF	XF	Unc
1814M	2,377,000	20.00	45.00	100	250	—
1815M	1,406,000	20.00	45.00	100	250	—

KM# 702.10 5 FRANCS
25.0000 g., 0.9000 Silver .7234 oz. ASW **Mint:** Marseille

Date	Mintage	VG	F	VF	XF	Unc
1814MA	99,000	35.00	75.00	135	300	—
1815MA	7,461	75.00	175	400	850	—

KM# 702.11 5 FRANCS
25.0000 g., 0.9000 Silver .7234 oz. ASW **Mint:** Perpignan

Date	Mintage	VG	F	VF	XF	Unc
1814	1,182,000	20.00	45.00	100	250	—
1815/4	925,000	30.00	50.00	75.00	200	—
1815	Inc. above	20.00	45.00	100	250	—

KM# 702.12 5 FRANCS
25.0000 g., 0.9000 Silver .7234 oz. ASW **Mint:** Nantes

Date	Mintage	VG	F	VF	XF	Unc
1814T	5,235	75.00	175	400	850	—

KM# 702.13 5 FRANCS
25.0000 g., 0.9000 Silver .7234 oz. ASW **Mint:** Lille

Date	Mintage	VG	F	VF	XF	Unc
1814	104,000	35.00	75.00	135	300	450
1815	114,000	35.00	75.00	135	300	450
1814-15	—	—	—	—	—	600

Note: Above value for common date uncirculated

KM# 704.1 5 FRANCS
25.0000 g., 0.9000 Silver .7234 oz. ASW **Mint:** Paris **Note:** The Hundred Days.

Date	Mintage	VG	F	VF	XF	Unc
1815A	473,000	80.00	165	300	700	—

KM# 704.2 5 FRANCS
25.0000 g., 0.9000 Silver .7234 oz. ASW **Mint:** Rouen

Date	Mintage	VG	F	VF	XF	Unc
1815B	93,000	100	200	350	1,000	—

KM# 704.3 5 FRANCS
25.0000 g., 0.9000 Silver .7234 oz. ASW **Mint:** Strasbourg

Date	Mintage	VG	F	VF	XF	Unc
1815BB	3,723	250	600	1,200	2,200	—

KM# 704.4 5 FRANCS
25.0000 g., 0.9000 Silver .7234 oz. ASW **Mint:** Limoges

Date	Mintage	VG	F	VF	XF	Unc
1815I	596,000	65.00	125	250	550	—

KM# 704.5 5 FRANCS
25.0000 g., 0.9000 Silver .7234 oz. ASW **Mint:** Bayonne

Date	Mintage	VG	F	VF	XF	Unc
1815L	97,000	90.00	200	350	1,000	—

KM# 704.6 5 FRANCS
25.0000 g., 0.9000 Silver .7234 oz. ASW **Mint:** Toulouse

Date	Mintage	VG	F	VF	XF	Unc
1815M	80,000	100	225	375	1,250	—

KM# 704.7 5 FRANCS
25.0000 g., 0.9000 Silver .7234 oz. ASW **Mint:** Perpignan

Date	Mintage	VG	F	VF	XF	Unc
1815Q	21,000	120	280	550	1,500	—

KM# 704.8 5 FRANCS
25.0000 g., 0.9000 Silver .7234 oz. ASW **Mint:** Lille

Date	Mintage	VG	F	VF	XF	Unc
1815W	21,000	120	280	550	1,500	—

KM# 711.1 5 FRANCS
25.0000 g., 0.9000 Silver .7234 oz. ASW **Mint:** Paris **Note:** Second Restoration.

Date	Mintage	VG	F	VF	XF	Unc
1816A	3,210,000	12.00	20.00	45.00	150	—
1817A	3,778,000	12.00	20.00	45.00	150	—
1818A	86,000	20.00	40.00	75.00	225	—
1819A	658,000	17.50	30.00	65.00	175	—
1820A	3,226,000	12.00	20.00	45.00	150	—
1821A	9,526,000	12.00	20.00	40.00	135	—
1822A	13,453,000	12.00	20.00	40.00	125	—
1823A	6,536,000	12.00	20.00	40.00	125	—
1824A	9,066,000	12.00	20.00	40.00	125	—

KM# 711.2 5 FRANCS
25.0000 g., 0.9000 Silver .7234 oz. ASW **Mint:** Rouen

Date	Mintage	VG	F	VF	XF	Unc
1816B	922,000	18.00	30.00	65.00	175	—
1817B	1,580,000	15.00	25.00	55.00	150	—
1818B	2,190,000	12.00	20.00	45.00	150	—
1819B	3,437,000	12.00	20.00	45.00	150	—
1820B	210,000	20.00	45.00	100	225	—
1821B	123,000	30.00	55.00	125	250	—
1822B	897,000	12.00	20.00	45.00	150	—
1823B	393,000	20.00	45.00	100	225	—
1824B	1,246,000	15.00	25.00	55.00	150	—

KM# 711.3 5 FRANCS
25.0000 g., 0.9000 Silver .7234 oz. ASW **Mint:** Strasbourg

Date	Mintage	VG	F	VF	XF	Unc
1816BB	8,115	40.00	75.00	150	475	—
1817BB	3,510	55.00	110	200	550	—
1818BB	1,119	55.00	110	200	550	—
1819BB	2,469	55.00	110	200	550	—
1820BB	1,976	55.00	110	200	550	—
1821BB	1,527	60.00	120	240	700	—
1823BB	3,712	55.00	110	200	550	—

KM# 711.4 5 FRANCS
25.0000 g., 0.9000 Silver .7234 oz. ASW **Mint:** Lyon

Date	Mintage	VG	F	VF	XF	Unc
1816D	6,446	35.00	65.00	125	400	—
1817D	3,605	35.00	65.00	125	450	—
1820D	17,000	—	45.00	75.00	300	—
1823D	994,000	12.00	20.00	45.00	150	—
1824D	2,448,000	12.00	20.00	45.00	150	—
1824D Rare	Inc. above	—	—	—	—	—
Note: Inverted D						

KM# 711.5 5 FRANCS
25.0000 g., 0.9000 Silver .7234 oz. ASW **Mint:** La Rochelle

Date	Mintage	VG	F	VF	XF	Unc
1816H	6,575	35.00	80.00	165	550	—
1817H	110,000	22.00	45.00	85.00	250	—
1818H	12,000	55.00	110	220	500	—
1819H	33,000	35.00	65.00	120	325	—
1820H	18,000	40.00	85.00	165	375	—
1821H	18,000	55.00	110	220	450	—
1822H	77,000	27.50	60.00	100	275	—
1823H	329,000	20.00	40.00	75.00	200	—
1824H	771,000	12.00	20.00	45.00	150	—

KM# 711.6 5 FRANCS
25.0000 g., 0.9000 Silver .7234 oz. ASW **Mint:** Limoges

Date	Mintage	VG	F	VF	XF	Unc
1816I	306,000	20.00	40.00	75.00	200	—
1817I	4,204	45.00	65.00	115	400	—
1818I	1,568	55.00	110	285	575	—
1819I	1,104	55.00	110	285	575	—
1820I	639	140	250	400	800	—
1821I	6,320	50.00	85.00	145	440	—
1822I	8,712	45.00	70.00	145	440	—
1823I	269,000	20.00	40.00	75.00	200	—
1824I	1,039,000	12.00	20.00	45.00	150	—

KM# 711.7 5 FRANCS
25.0000 g., 0.9000 Silver .7234 oz. ASW **Mint:** Bordeaux

Date	Mintage	VG	F	VF	XF	Unc
1816K	34,000	25.00	55.00	90.00	250	—
1817K	386,000	20.00	40.00	75.00	200	—
1818K	17,000	—	65.00	135	300	—
1820K	18,000	25.00	65.00	135	300	—
1822K	393,000	20.00	40.00	75.00	200	—
1823K	800,000	12.00	20.00	45.00	150	—
1824K	1,010,000	12.00	20.00	45.00	150	—

KM# 711.8 5 FRANCS
25.0000 g., 0.9000 Silver .7234 oz. ASW **Mint:** Bayonne

Date	Mintage	VG	F	VF	XF	Unc
1816L	1,001,000	12.00	20.00	45.00	150	—
1817L	377,000	20.00	40.00	75.00	200	—
1818L	10,000	35.00	75.00	150	250	—
1823L	898,000	12.00	20.00	45.00	150	—
1824L	1,068,000	12.00	20.00	45.00	150	—

KM# 711.9 5 FRANCS
25.0000 g., 0.9000 Silver .7234 oz. ASW **Mint:** Toulouse

Date	Mintage	VG	F	VF	XF	Unc
1816M	651,000	12.00	20.00	45.00	150	—
1817M	188,000	20.00	40.00	75.00	225	—
1818M	2,920	40.00	80.00	175	350	—
1823M	958,000	12.00	20.00	45.00	150	—
1824M	1,589,000	12.00	20.00	40.00	125	—

KM# 711.10 5 FRANCS
25.0000 g., 0.9000 Silver .7234 oz. ASW **Mint:** Marseille

Date	Mintage	VG	F	VF	XF	Unc
1816MA	18,000	35.00	75.00	150	350	—
1817MA	10,000	40.00	80.00	165	375	—
1818MA	7,805	50.00	100	200	500	—
1819MA	1,186	60.00	120	250	600	—
1820MA	440	100	200	350	750	—
1821MA	198	150	250	500	900	—
1823MA	3,847	55.00	110	225	550	—
1824MA	1,422,000	12.00	20.00	45.00	150	—

KM# 711.11 5 FRANCS
25.0000 g., 0.9000 Silver .7234 oz. ASW **Mint:** Perpignan

Date	Mintage	VG	F	VF	XF	Unc
1816Q	591,000	18.00	30.00	65.00	175	—
1817Q	105,000	20.00	40.00	75.00	225	—
1819Q	1,618	60.00	120	250	600	—
1820Q	2,770	55.00	110	225	550	—
1821Q	5,626	50.00	100	200	500	—
1822Q	20,000	35.00	75.00	150	350	—
1823Q	715,000	12.00	20.00	45.00	150	—
1824Q	1,006,000	12.00	20.00	45.00	150	—

KM# 711.12 5 FRANCS
25.0000 g., 0.9000 Silver .7234 oz. ASW **Mint:** Nantes

Date	Mintage	VG	F	VF	XF	Unc
1816T	11,000	40.00	80.00	165	325	—
1817T	25,000	35.00	70.00	135	300	—
1818T	24,000	35.00	70.00	135	300	—
1819T	20,000	35.00	70.00	135	300	—
1820T	11,000	40.00	80.00	165	325	—

KM# 711.13 5 FRANCS
25.0000 g., 0.9000 Silver .7234 oz. ASW **Mint:** Lille

Date	Mintage	VG	F	VF	XF	Unc
1816W	72,000	25.00	55.00	90.00	250	—
1817W	438,000	18.00	30.00	65.00	175	—
1818W	66,000	25.00	55.00	90.00	250	—
1819W	34,000	30.00	65.00	125	275	—
1820W	106,000	20.00	40.00	75.00	225	—
1821W	3,674,000	12.00	20.00	45.00	150	—
1822W	4,839,000	12.00	20.00	45.00	150	—
1823W	4,168,000	12.00	20.00	45.00	150	—
1824W	9,807,000	10.00	15.00	35.00	100	—
1816-24W	—	—	—	—	—	400

Note: Above value for common date uncirculated

KM# 720.1 5 FRANCS
25.0000 g., 0.9000 Silver .7234 oz. ASW **Mint:** Paris **Obverse:** Type I **Reverse:** Similar to KM#711

Date	Mintage	VG	F	VF	XF	Unc
1824A	408,000	60.00	125	275	800	—
1825A	2,492,000	10.00	15.00	35.00	90.00	—
1826A	7,171,000	10.00	15.00	35.00	90.00	—

KM# 720.2 5 FRANCS
25.0000 g., 0.9000 Silver .7234 oz. ASW **Mint:** Rouen **Obverse:** Type I **Reverse:** Similar to KM#711

Date	Mintage	VG	F	VF	XF	Unc
1825B	113,000	20.00	50.00	75.00	150	—
1826B	595,000	15.00	35.00	60.00	125	—

KM# 720.3 5 FRANCS
25.0000 g., 0.9000 Silver .7234 oz. ASW **Mint:** Strasbourg **Obverse:** Type I **Reverse:** Similar to KM#711

Date	Mintage	VG	F	VF	XF	Unc
1825BB	157,000	20.00	50.00	75.00	150	—
1826BB	411,000	15.00	35.00	60.00	125	—

KM# 720.4 5 FRANCS

25.0000 g., 0.9000 Silver .7234 oz. ASW **Mint:** Lyon **Obverse:** Type I **Reverse:** Similar to KM#711

Date	Mintage	VG	F	VF	XF	Unc
1825D	185,000	20.00	50.00	75.00	150	—
1826D	1,437,000	10.00	15.00	35.00	90.00	—

KM# 720.5 5 FRANCS

25.0000 g., 0.9000 Silver .7234 oz. ASW **Mint:** La Rochelle **Obverse:** Type I **Reverse:** Similar to KM#711

Date	Mintage	VG	F	VF	XF	Unc
1825H	157,000	20.00	50.00	75.00	150	—
1826H	573,000	15.00	35.00	60.00	125	—

KM# 720.6 5 FRANCS

25.0000 g., 0.9000 Silver .7234 oz. ASW **Mint:** Limoges **Obverse:** Type I **Reverse:** Similar to KM#711

Date	Mintage	VG	F	VF	XF	Unc
1825I	155,000	20.00	50.00	75.00	150	—
1826I	536,000	15.00	35.00	60.00	125	—

KM# 720.7 5 FRANCS

25.0000 g., 0.9000 Silver .7234 oz. ASW **Mint:** Bordeaux **Obverse:** Type I **Reverse:** Similar to KM#711

Date	Mintage	VG	F	VF	XF	Unc
1825K	326,000	15.00	35.00	60.00	115	—
1826K	429,000	15.00	35.00	60.00	115	—

KM# 720.8 5 FRANCS

25.0000 g., 0.9000 Silver .7234 oz. ASW **Mint:** Bayonne **Obverse:** Type I **Reverse:** Similar to KM#711

Date	Mintage	VG	F	VF	XF	Unc
1825L	227,000	15.00	35.00	60.00	125	—
1826L	720,000	10.00	15.00	35.00	90.00	—

KM# 720.9 5 FRANCS

25.0000 g., 0.9000 Silver .7234 oz. ASW **Mint:** Toulouse **Obverse:** Type I **Reverse:** Similar to KM#711

Date	Mintage	VG	F	VF	XF	Unc
1825M	154,000	20.00	50.00	75.00	150	—
1826M	670,000	10.00	15.00	35.00	90.00	—

KM# 720.10 5 FRANCS

25.0000 g., 0.9000 Silver .7234 oz. ASW **Mint:** Marseille **Obverse:** Type I **Reverse:** Similar to KM#711

Date	Mintage	VG	F	VF	XF	Unc
1825MA	176,000	20.00	50.00	75.00	150	—
1826MA	1,072,000	10.00	15.00	35.00	90.00	—

KM# 720.11 5 FRANCS

25.0000 g., 0.9000 Silver .7234 oz. ASW **Mint:** Perpignan **Obverse:** Type I **Reverse:** Similar to KM#711

Date	Mintage	VG	F	VF	XF	Unc
1825Q	163,000	20.00	50.00	75.00	150	—
1826Q	346,000	15.00	35.00	60.00	125	—

KM# 720.12 5 FRANCS

25.0000 g., 0.9000 Silver .7234 oz. ASW **Mint:** Nantes **Obverse:** Type I **Reverse:** Similar to KM#711

Date	Mintage	VG	F	VF	XF	Unc
1826T	203,000	15.00	35.00	60.00	125	—

KM# 720.13 5 FRANCS

25.0000 g., 0.9000 Silver .7234 oz. ASW **Mint:** Lille **Obverse:** Type I **Reverse:** Similar to KM#711

Date	Mintage	VG	F	VF	XF	Unc
1825W	1,104,000	10.00	15.00	35.00	90.00	—
1826W	3,583,000	10.00	15.00	35.00	90.00	—
1825-26W	—	—	—	—	—	450

Note: Above value for common date uncirculated

KM# 727 5 FRANCS

25.0000 g., 0.9000 Silver .7234 oz. ASW **Mint:** Paris

Date	VG	F	VF	XF	Unc
1830A	75.00	125	250	500	—

Note: Mintage included with KM720.1

KM# 728.1 5 FRANCS

25.0000 g., 0.9000 Silver .7234 oz. ASW **Mint:** Paris **Obverse:** Type II

Date	Mintage	VG	F	VF	XF	Unc
1827A	6,822,000	10.00	25.00	50.00	100	—
1828A	8,803,000	10.00	25.00	50.00	100	—
1829A	4,827,000	10.00	25.00	50.00	100	—
1830A	6,333,000	10.00	25.00	50.00	100	—

KM# 728.2 5 FRANCS

25.0000 g., 0.9000 Silver .7234 oz. ASW **Mint:** Rouen **Obverse:** Type II

Date	Mintage	VG	F	VF	XF	Unc
1827B	2,792,000	10.00	25.00	50.00	100	—
1828B	1,898,000	10.00	25.00	50.00	100	—
1829B	2,834,000	10.00	25.00	50.00	100	—
1830B	2,910,000	10.00	25.00	50.00	100	—

KM# 728.3 5 FRANCS

25.0000 g., 0.9000 Silver .7234 oz. ASW **Mint:** Strasbourg **Obverse:** Type II

Date	Mintage	VG	F	VF	XF	Unc
1827BB	393,000	20.00	45.00	75.00	125	—
1828BB	699,000	20.00	45.00	75.00	125	—
1829BB	548,000	20.00	45.00	75.00	125	—
1830BB	112,000	20.00	45.00	90.00	150	—

KM# 728.4 5 FRANCS

25.0000 g., 0.9000 Silver .7234 oz. ASW **Mint:** Lyon **Obverse:** Type II

Date	Mintage	VG	F	VF	XF	Unc
1827D	1,651,000	10.00	25.00	50.00	100	—
1828D	2,743,000	10.00	25.00	50.00	100	—
1829D	1,608,000	10.00	25.00	50.00	100	—
1830D	631,000	15.00	35.00	65.00	125	—

KM# 728.5 5 FRANCS

25.0000 g., 0.9000 Silver .7234 oz. ASW **Mint:** La Rochelle **Obverse:** Type II

Date	Mintage	VG	F	VF	XF	Unc
1827H	419,000	20.00	45.00	75.00	125	—
1828H	490,000	20.00	45.00	75.00	125	—
1829H	1,155,000	10.00	25.00	50.00	100	—
1830H	574,000	20.00	45.00	75.00	125	—

KM# 728.6 5 FRANCS

25.0000 g., 0.9000 Silver .7234 oz. ASW **Mint:** Limoges **Obverse:** Type II

Date	Mintage	VG	F	VF	XF	Unc
1827I	335,000	20.00	45.00	75.00	125	—
1828I	124,000	20.00	45.00	90.00	150	—
1829I	475,000	20.00	45.00	75.00	125	—
1830I	67,000	35.00	80.00	150	300	—

KM# 728.7 5 FRANCS

25.0000 g., 0.9000 Silver .7234 oz. ASW **Mint:** Bordeaux **Obverse:** Type II

Date	Mintage	VG	F	VF	XF	Unc
1827K	1,147,000	10.00	25.00	50.00	100	—
1828K	1,632,000	10.00	25.00	50.00	100	—
1829K	1,011,000	10.00	25.00	50.00	100	—
1830K	713,000	15.00	25.00	45.00	125	—

KM# 728.8 5 FRANCS

25.0000 g., 0.9000 Silver .7234 oz. ASW **Mint:** Bayonne **Obverse:** Type II

Date	Mintage	VG	F	VF	XF	Unc
1827L	1,144,000	10.00	25.00	50.00	100	—
1828L	1,083,000	10.00	25.00	50.00	100	—
1829L	857,000	10.00	25.00	50.00	100	—
1830L	399,000	20.00	45.00	75.00	125	—

KM# 728.9 5 FRANCS

25.0000 g., 0.9000 Silver .7234 oz. ASW **Mint:** Toulouse **Obverse:** Type II

Date	Mintage	VG	F	VF	XF	Unc
1827M	806,000	10.00	25.00	50.00	100	—
1828M	1,818,000	10.00	25.00	50.00	100	—
1829M	873,000	10.00	25.00	50.00	100	—
1830M	496,000	20.00	45.00	75.00	125	—

KM# 728.10 5 FRANCS

25.0000 g., 0.9000 Silver .7234 oz. ASW **Mint:** Marseille **Obverse:** Type II

Date	Mintage	VG	F	VF	XF	Unc
1827MA	1,531,000	10.00	25.00	50.00	100	—
1828MA	1,201,000	10.00	25.00	50.00	100	—
1829MA	1,258,000	10.00	25.00	50.00	100	—
1830MA	1,803,000	10.00	25.00	50.00	100	—

KM# 728.11 5 FRANCS

25.0000 g., 0.9000 Silver .7234 oz. ASW **Mint:** Perpignan **Obverse:** Type II

Date	Mintage	VG	F	VF	XF	Unc
1827Q	484,000	20.00	45.00	75.00	125	—
1828Q	394,000	20.00	45.00	75.00	125	—
1829Q	360,000	20.00	45.00	75.00	125	—
1830Q	151,000	20.00	45.00	90.00	150	—

KM# 728.12 5 FRANCS

25.0000 g., 0.9000 Silver .7234 oz. ASW **Mint:** Nantes **Obverse:** Type II

Date	Mintage	VG	F	VF	XF	Unc
1827T	865,000	10.00	25.00	50.00	100	—
1828T	933,000	10.00	25.00	50.00	100	—
1829T	888,000	10.00	25.00	50.00	100	—
1830T	137,000	20.00	35.00	55.00	125	—

KM# 728.13 5 FRANCS

25.0000 g., 0.9000 Silver .7234 oz. ASW **Mint:** Lille **Obverse:** Type II

Date	Mintage	VG	F	VF	XF	Unc
1827W	11,525,000	15.00	25.00	45.00	125	—
1828W	9,610,000	15.00	25.00	45.00	125	—
1829W	3,235,000	15.00	25.00	45.00	125	—
1830W	4,134,000	15.00	25.00	45.00	125	—
1827-30W	—	—	—	—	—	400

Note: Above value for common date uncirculated

KM# 735.1 5 FRANCS

25.0000 g., 0.9000 Silver .7234 oz. ASW **Mint:** Paris **Obv. Legend:** LOUIS PHILIPPE I ROI... **Edge:** Incused lettering

Date	Mintage	VG	F	VF	XF	Unc
1830A	2,421,000	12.00	25.00	50.00	175	—
1831A	11,785,000	10.00	20.00	35.00	90.00	—

KM# 735.2 5 FRANCS

25.0000 g., 0.9000 Silver .7234 oz. ASW **Mint:** Rouen **Obv. Legend:** LOUIS PHILIPPE I ROI... **Edge:** Incused lettering

Date	Mintage	VG	F	VF	XF	Unc
1830B	1,025,000	15.00	35.00	75.00	150	—
1831B	7,889,000	10.00	20.00	35.00	90.00	—

KM# 735.3 5 FRANCS

25.0000 g., 0.9000 Silver .7234 oz. ASW **Mint:** Strasbourg **Obv. Legend:** LOUIS PHILIPPE I ROI... **Edge:** Incused lettering

Date	Mintage	VG	F	VF	XF	Unc
1830BB	5,125	75.00	175	300	600	—
1831BB	983,000	15.00	35.00	75.00	150	—

KM# 735.4 5 FRANCS

25.0000 g., 0.9000 Silver .7234 oz. ASW **Mint:** Lyon **Obv. Legend:** LOUIS PHILIPPE I ROI... **Edge:** Incused lettering

Date	Mintage	VG	F	VF	XF	Unc
1830D	368,000	20.00	40.00	80.00	175	—
1831D	3,460,000	12.00	25.00	50.00	175	—

KM# 735.5 5 FRANCS

25.0000 g., 0.9000 Silver .7234 oz. ASW **Mint:** La Rochelle **Obv. Legend:** LOUIS PHILIPPE I ROI... **Edge:** Incused lettering

Date	Mintage	VG	F	VF	XF	Unc
1830H	30,000	35.00	75.00	175	375	—
1831H	843,000	15.00	35.00	75.00	150	—

KM# 735.6 5 FRANCS

25.0000 g., 0.9000 Silver .7234 oz. ASW **Mint:** Limoges **Obv. Legend:** LOUIS PHILIPPE I ROI... **Edge:** Incused lettering

Date	Mintage	VG	F	VF	XF	Unc
1830I	28,000	35.00	75.00	175	375	—
1831I	502,000	20.00	40.00	80.00	175	—

KM# 735.7 5 FRANCS

25.0000 g., 0.9000 Silver .7234 oz. ASW **Mint:** Bordeaux **Obv. Legend:** LOUIS PHILIPPE I ROI... **Edge:** Incused lettering

Date	Mintage	VG	F	VF	XF	Unc
1830K	123,000	25.00	50.00	100	200	—
1831K	1,523,000	15.00	35.00	75.00	175	—

KM# 735.8 5 FRANCS

25.0000 g., 0.9000 Silver .7234 oz. ASW **Mint:** Bayonne **Obv. Legend:** LOUIS PHILIPPE I ROI... **Edge:** Incused lettering

Date	Mintage	VG	F	VF	XF	Unc
1830L	8,931	40.00	100	200	400	—
1831L	430,000	20.00	40.00	80.00	175	—

KM# 735.9 5 FRANCS

25.0000 g., 0.9000 Silver .7234 oz. ASW **Mint:** Toulouse **Obv. Legend:** LOUIS PHILIPPE I ROI... **Edge:** Incused lettering

Date	Mintage	VG	F	VF	XF	Unc
1830M	50,000	35.00	75.00	125	275	—
1831M	1,337,000	15.00	35.00	75.00	175	—

KM# 735.10 5 FRANCS

25.0000 g., 0.9000 Silver .7234 oz. ASW **Mint:** Marseille **Obv. Legend:** LOUIS PHILIPPE I ROI... **Edge:** Incused lettering

Date	Mintage	VG	F	VF	XF	Unc
1830MA	65,000	35.00	75.00	125	275	—
1831MA	2,062,000	12.00	25.00	50.00	175	—

KM# 735.11 5 FRANCS

25.0000 g., 0.9000 Silver .7234 oz. ASW **Mint:** Perpignan **Obv. Legend:** LOUIS PHILIPPE I ROI... **Edge:** Incused lettering

Date	Mintage	VG	F	VF	XF	Unc
1830Q	12,000	40.00	80.00	175	375	—
1831Q	357,000	20.00	40.00	80.00	175	—

KM# 735.12 5 FRANCS

25.0000 g., 0.9000 Silver .7234 oz. ASW **Mint:** Nantes **Obv. Legend:** LOUIS PHILIPPE I ROI... **Edge:** Incused lettering

Date	Mintage	VG	F	VF	XF	Unc
1830T	125,000	25.00	50.00	100	200	—
1831T	1,261,000	15.00	35.00	75.00	175	—

KM# 735.13 5 FRANCS

25.0000 g., 0.9000 Silver .7234 oz. ASW **Mint:** Lille **Obv. Legend:** LOUIS PHILIPPE I ROI... **Edge:** Incused lettering

Date	Mintage	VG	F	VF	XF	Unc
1830	1,020,000	15.00	35.00	75.00	175	—
1831	8,226,000	12.00	20.00	35.00	85.00	—
1830-31	—	—	—	—	—	650

Note: Above value for common date circulated

KM# 736.1 5 FRANCS

25.0000 g., 0.9000 Silver .7234 oz. ASW **Mint:** Paris **Edge:** Raised lettering

Date	VG	F	VF	XF	Unc
1830A	15.00	45.00	90.00	275	—
1831A	15.00	45.00	90.00	275	—

KM# 736.2 5 FRANCS

25.0000 g., 0.9000 Silver .7234 oz. ASW **Mint:** Rouen **Edge:** Raised lettering

Date	VG	F	VF	XF	Unc
1831B	75.00	125	250	—	—

KM# 736.3 5 FRANCS

25.0000 g., 0.9000 Silver .7234 oz. ASW **Mint:** Lille **Edge:** Raised lettering

Date	VG	F	VF	XF	Unc
1830W	—	—	—	—	—
1831W	15.00	45.00	75.00	275	400

Note: 1 known (1830W)

KM# 737.1 5 FRANCS
25.0000 g., 0.9000 Silver .7234 oz. ASW **Mint:** Paris **Obv. Legend:** LOUIS PHILIPPE ROI... **Edge:** Incuse lettering

Date	VG	F	VF	XF	Unc
1830A	40.00	90.00	250	600	1,100

KM# 737.2 5 FRANCS
25.0000 g., 0.9000 Silver .7234 oz. ASW **Mint:** Rouen **Obv. Legend:** LOUIS PHILIPPE ROI... **Edge:** Incuse lettering

Date	VG	F	VF	XF	Unc
1830B	50.00	125	300	700	1,400

KM# 737.3 5 FRANCS
25.0000 g., 0.9000 Silver .7234 oz. ASW **Mint:** Lyon **Obv. Legend:** LOUIS PHILIPPE ROI... **Edge:** Incuse lettering

Date	VG	F	VF	XF	Unc
1830D	75.00	175	450	900	1,800

KM# 737.4 5 FRANCS
25.0000 g., 0.9000 Silver .7234 oz. ASW **Mint:** Lille **Obv. Legend:** LOUIS PHILIPPE ROI... **Edge:** Incuse lettering

Date	VG	F	VF	XF	Unc
1830W	50.00	125	300	700	1,400

KM# 738 5 FRANCS
25.0000 g., 0.9000 Silver .7234 oz. ASW **Mint:** Paris **Edge:** Raised lettering

Date	VG	F	VF	XF	Unc
1830A	100	225	450	900	—

KM# 744.1 5 FRANCS
25.0000 g., 0.9000 Silver .7234 oz. ASW **Mint:** Strasbourg **Edge:** Incuse lettering

Date	VG	F	VF	XF	Unc
1831BB	20.00	40.00	80.00	175	—

KM# 744.2 5 FRANCS
25.0000 g., 0.9000 Silver .7234 oz. ASW **Mint:** Lyon **Edge:** Incuse lettering

Date	VG	F	VF	XF	Unc
1831D	25.00	50.00	100	200	—

KM# 744.3 5 FRANCS
25.0000 g., 0.9000 Silver .7234 oz. ASW **Mint:** Limoges **Edge:** Incuse lettering

Date	VG	F	VF	XF	Unc
1831I	25.00	50.00	100	200	—

KM# 744.4 5 FRANCS
25.0000 g., 0.9000 Silver .7234 oz. ASW **Mint:** Bordeaux **Edge:** Incuse lettering

Date	VG	F	VF	XF	Unc
1831K	25.00	50.00	80.00	200	—

KM# 744.5 5 FRANCS
25.0000 g., 0.9000 Silver .7234 oz. ASW **Mint:** Toulouse **Edge:** Incuse lettering

Date	VG	F	VF	XF	Unc
1831M	20.00	40.00	100	175	—

KM# 744.6 5 FRANCS
25.0000 g., 0.9000 Silver .7234 oz. ASW **Mint:** Marseille **Edge:** Incuse lettering

Date	VG	F	VF	XF	Unc
1831MA	25.00	50.00	100	200	—

KM# 744.7 5 FRANCS
25.0000 g., 0.9000 Silver .7234 oz. ASW **Mint:** Perpignan **Edge:** Incuse lettering

Date	VG	F	VF	XF	Unc
1831Q	25.00	50.00	125	185	400

KM# 745.1 5 FRANCS
25.0000 g., 0.9000 Silver .7234 oz. ASW **Mint:** Paris **Edge:** Raised lettering

Date	VG	F	VF	XF	Unc
1831A	12.00	20.00	50.00	90.00	200

KM# 745.2 5 FRANCS
25.0000 g., 0.9000 Silver .7234 oz. ASW **Mint:** Rouen **Edge:** Raised lettering

Date	VG	F	VF	XF	Unc
1831B	12.00	20.00	50.00	90.00	200

KM# 745.3 5 FRANCS
25.0000 g., 0.9000 Silver .7234 oz. ASW **Mint:** Strasbourg **Edge:** Raised lettering

Date	VG	F	VF	XF	Unc
1831BB	20.00	45.00	75.00	125	—

KM# 745.4 5 FRANCS
25.0000 g., 0.9000 Silver .7234 oz. ASW **Mint:** Lyon **Edge:** Raised lettering

Date	VG	F	VF	XF	Unc
1831D	12.00	20.00	50.00	90.00	200

KM# 745.5 5 FRANCS
25.0000 g., 0.9000 Silver .7234 oz. ASW **Mint:** La Rochelle **Edge:** Raised lettering

Date	VG	F	VF	XF	Unc
1831H	20.00	45.00	75.00	125	—

KM# 745.6 5 FRANCS
25.0000 g., 0.9000 Silver .7234 oz. ASW **Mint:** Limoges **Edge:** Raised lettering

Date	VG	F	VF	XF	Unc
1831I	20.00	45.00	75.00	125	—

KM# 745.7 5 FRANCS
25.0000 g., 0.9000 Silver .7234 oz. ASW **Mint:** Bordeaux **Edge:** Raised lettering

Date	VG	F	VF	XF	Unc
1831K	20.00	45.00	75.00	125	—

KM# 745.8 5 FRANCS
25.0000 g., 0.9000 Silver .7234 oz. ASW **Mint:** Bayonne **Edge:** Raised lettering

Date	VG	F	VF	XF	Unc
1831L	25.00	50.00	125	225	—

KM# 745.9 5 FRANCS
25.0000 g., 0.9000 Silver .7234 oz. ASW **Mint:** Toulouse **Edge:** Raised lettering

Date	VG	F	VF	XF	Unc
1831M	20.00	45.00	75.00	125	—

KM# 745.10 5 FRANCS
25.0000 g., 0.9000 Silver .7234 oz. ASW **Mint:** Marseille **Edge:** Raised lettering

Date	VG	F	VF	XF	Unc
1831MA	20.00	45.00	75.00	125	—

KM# 745.11 5 FRANCS
25.0000 g., 0.9000 Silver .7234 oz. ASW **Mint:** Perpignan **Edge:** Raised lettering

Date	VG	F	VF	XF	Unc
1831Q	20.00	45.00	75.00	125	—

KM# 745.12 5 FRANCS
25.0000 g., 0.9000 Silver .7234 oz. ASW **Mint:** Nantes **Edge:** Raised lettering

Date	VG	F	VF	XF	Unc
1831T	20.00	45.00	75.00	125	—

KM# 745.13 5 FRANCS
25.0000 g., 0.9000 Silver .7234 oz. ASW **Mint:** Lille **Edge:** Raised lettering

Date	VG	F	VF	XF	Unc
1831W	12.00	20.00	50.00	90.00	200

KM# 749.1 5 FRANCS
25.0000 g., 0.9000 Silver .7234 oz. ASW **Mint:** Paris **Reverse:** Mint marks at edge outside wreath

Date	Mintage	F	VF	XF	Unc
1832A	7,800,000	9.00	25.00	50.00	210
1833A	8,211,000	9.00	25.00	50.00	210
1834A	11,307,000	9.00	25.00	50.00	210
1835A	5,807,000	9.00	25.00	50.00	210
1836A	1,940,000	9.00	25.00	50.00	210
1837A	6,884,000	9.00	25.00	50.00	210
1838A	4,805,000	9.00	25.00	50.00	210
1839A	5,071,000	9.00	25.00	50.00	210
1840A	4,769,000	9.00	25.00	50.00	210
1841A	1,005,000	9.00	25.00	50.00	165
1842A	755,000	15.00	50.00	85.00	300
1843A	1,838,000	9.00	25.00	50.00	210
1844A	1,971,000	9.00	25.00	50.00	210
1845A (p)	3,096,000	9.00	25.00	50.00	210
1845A (ha)	Inc. above	9.00	25.00	50.00	210
1846A	5,434,000	9.00	25.00	50.00	210
1847A	12,578,000	9.00	25.00	50.00	210
1848A	3,196,000	9.00	25.00	50.00	210
1848A Proof	—	Value: 1,700			

KM# 749.2 5 FRANCS
25.0000 g., 0.9000 Silver .7234 oz. ASW **Mint:** Rouen **Reverse:** Mint marks at edge outside wreath

Date	Mintage	F	VF	XF	Unc
1832B	2,852,000	9.00	25.00	50.00	210
1833B	3,791,000	9.00	25.00	50.00	210
1834B	4,453,000	9.00	25.00	50.00	210
1835B	2,793,000	9.00	25.00	50.00	210
1836B	2,631,000	9.00	25.00	50.00	210
1837B	6,075,000	9.00	25.00	50.00	210
1838B	4,002,000	9.00	25.00	50.00	210
1839B	3,467,000	9.00	25.00	50.00	210
1840B	3,337,000	9.00	25.00	50.00	210
1841B	1,652,000	9.00	25.00	50.00	210
1842B	3,489,000	9.00	25.00	50.00	210
1843B	2,472,000	9.00	25.00	50.00	210
1844B	361,000	15.00	50.00	85.00	275

KM# 749.3 5 FRANCS
25.0000 g., 0.9000 Silver .7234 oz. ASW **Mint:** Strasbourg **Reverse:** Mint marks at edge outside wreath

Date	Mintage	F	VF	XF	Unc
1832BB	1,725,000	9.00	25.00	50.00	210
1833BB	1,799,000	9.00	25.00	50.00	210
1834BB (b)	1,621,000	9.00	25.00	50.00	210
1834BB bee	Inc. above	15.00	25.00	50.00	210
1835BB	1,286,000	9.00	25.00	50.00	210
1836BB	1,188,000	9.00	25.00	50.00	210
1837BB	600,000	15.00	50.00	85.00	275
1838BB	1,535,000	9.00	25.00	50.00	210
1839BB	1,064,000	9.00	25.00	50.00	210
1840BB	1,186,000	9.00	25.00	50.00	210
1841BB	2,082,000	9.00	25.00	50.00	210
1842BB	2,471,000	9.00	25.00	50.00	210
1843BB	1,422,000	9.00	25.00	50.00	210
1844BB	1,890,000	9.00	25.00	50.00	210
1845BB	2,041,000	9.00	25.00	50.00	210
1846BB	840,000	12.00	30.00	65.00	225
1847BB	1,577,000	9.00	25.00	50.00	210
1848BB	935,000	12.00	30.00	65.00	225

KM# 749.4 5 FRANCS
25.0000 g., 0.9000 Silver .7234 oz. ASW **Mint:** Lyon **Reverse:** Mint marks at edge outside wreath

Date	Mintage	F	VF	XF	Unc
1832D	3,007,000	9.00	25.00	50.00	210
1833D	1,487,000	9.00	25.00	50.00	210
1834D	2,119,000	9.00	25.00	50.00	210
1835D	1,084,000	9.00	25.00	50.00	210
1836D	200,000	20.00	50.00	125	325
1837D	93,000	40.00	125	250	550
1838D	149,000	20.00	50.00	125	325
1839D (a)	519,000	15.00	30.00	60.00	275
1839D (t)	Inc. above	15.00	30.00	60.00	275
1840D	70,000	60.00	150	275	650

KM# 749.5 5 FRANCS
25.0000 g., 0.9000 Silver .7234 oz. ASW **Mint:** La Rochelle **Reverse:** Mint marks at edge outside wreath

Date	Mintage	F	VF	XF	Unc
1832H	900,000	9.00	25.00	50.00	210
1833/2H	844,000	15.00	30.00	60.00	275
1833H	Inc. above	9.00	25.00	50.00	210
1834H	2,184,000	9.00	25.00	50.00	210
1835H	467,000	15.00	30.00	60.00	275

KM# 749.6 5 FRANCS
25.0000 g., 0.9000 Silver .7234 oz. ASW **Mint:** Limoges **Reverse:** Mint marks at edge outside wreath

Date	Mintage	F	VF	XF	Unc
1832I	703,000	9.00	25.00	50.00	210
1833I	1,014,000	9.00	25.00	50.00	210
1834I	1,933,000	9.00	25.00	50.00	210
1835I	598,000	15.00	30.00	60.00	275

KM# 749.7 5 FRANCS
25.0000 g., 0.9000 Silver .7234 oz. ASW **Mint:** Bordeaux **Reverse:** Mint marks at edge outside wreath

Date	Mintage	F	VF	XF	Unc
1832K	602,000	15.00	30.00	60.00	275
1833K	749,000	9.00	25.00	50.00	210
1834K	2,157,000	9.00	25.00	50.00	211
1835K	928,000	9.00	25.00	50.00	210
1836K	296,000	20.00	50.00	125	325
1837K	813,000	9.00	25.00	50.00	210
1838K	450,000	15.00	30.00	60.00	275
1839K	897,000	9.00	25.00	50.00	210
1840K	1,186,000	9.00	25.00	50.00	210
1841K	995,000	9.00	25.00	50.00	210
1842K	1,026,000	9.00	25.00	50.00	210
1843K	794,000	9.00	25.00	50.00	210
1844K	398,000	15.00	30.00	60.00	275
1845K	537,000	15.00	30.00	60.00	275
1846K	511,000	15.00	30.00	60.00	275
1847K	167,000	20.00	50.00	125	325
1848K	166,000	20.00	50.00	125	325

KM# 749.8 5 FRANCS
25.0000 g., 0.9000 Silver .7234 oz. ASW **Mint:** Bayonne **Reverse:** Mint marks at edge outside wreath

Date	Mintage	F	VF	XF	Unc
1832L	567,000	20.00	50.00	125	325
1833L	378,000	20.00	50.00	125	325
1834L	359,000	20.00	50.00	125	325
1835L	64,000	50.00	125	250	650

KM# 749.9 5 FRANCS
25.0000 g., 0.9000 Silver .7234 oz. ASW **Mint:** Toulouse **Reverse:** Mint marks at edge outside wreath

Date	Mintage	F	VF	XF	Unc
1832M	729,000	20.00	50.00	125	325
1833M	669,000	20.00	50.00	125	325
1834M	889,000	20.00	50.00	125	325
1835M	412,000	20.00	50.00	125	325
1836M	72,000	50.00	125	250	650

KM# 749.10 5 FRANCS
25.0000 g., 0.9000 Silver .7234 oz. ASW **Mint:** Marseille **Reverse:** Mint marks at edge outside wreath

Date	Mintage	F	VF	XF	Unc
1832MA	1,184,000	9.00	50.00	125	325
1833MA	872,000	15.00	50.00	125	325
1834MA	489,000	15.00	30.00	60.00	275
1835MA	373,000	15.00	30.00	60.00	275
1836MA	362,000	15.00	30.00	60.00	275
1837MA	724,000	9.00	25.00	50.00	200
1838MA	2,116,000	9.00	25.00	50.00	200
1839MA	20,000	100	175	375	900

KM# 749.11 5 FRANCS

25.0000 g., 0.9000 Silver .7234 oz. ASW **Mint:** Perpignan **Reverse:** Mint marks at edge outside wreath

Date	Mintage	F	VF	XF	Unc
1832Q	716,000	9.00	25.00	50.00	200
1833Q	663,000	9.00	25.00	50.00	200
1834Q	982,000	9.00	25.00	50.00	200

KM# 749.12 5 FRANCS

25.0000 g., 0.9000 Silver .7234 oz. ASW **Mint:** Nantes **Reverse:** Mint marks at edge outside wreath

Date	Mintage	F	VF	XF	Unc
1832T	1,592,000	9.00	25.00	50.00	200
1833T	1,437,000	9.00	25.00	50.00	200
1834T	2,119,000	9.00	25.00	50.00	200
1835T	294,000	20.00	35.00	60.00	275

KM# 749.13 5 FRANCS

25.0000 g., 0.9000 Silver .7234 oz. ASW **Mint:** Lille **Reverse:** Mint marks at edge outside wreath

Date	Mintage	F	VF	XF	Unc
1832W	4,483,000	9.00	25.00	50.00	190
1833W	9,270,000	9.00	25.00	50.00	190
1834W	11,733,000	9.00	25.00	50.00	190
1835W	5,016,000	9.00	25.00	50.00	190
1836W	1,614,000	9.00	25.00	50.00	190
1837W	6,652,000	9.00	25.00	50.00	190
1838W	4,190,000	9.00	25.00	50.00	190
1839W	3,269,000	9.00	25.00	50.00	190
1840W (c)	1,714,000	9.00	25.00	50.00	190
1840W (r)	Inc. above	15.00	30.00	60.00	275
1841W	8,926,000	9.00	25.00	50.00	190
1842W	5,436,000	9.00	25.00	50.00	190
1843W	7,846,000	9.00	25.00	50.00	190
1844W	8,775,000	9.00	25.00	50.00	190
1845W	11,107,000	9.00	25.00	50.00	190
1846W	1,658,000	9.00	25.00	50.00	190

KM# 705.1 20 FRANCS

6.4516 g., 0.9000 Gold .1867 oz. AGW **Mint:** Paris **Note:** The Hundred Days.

Date	Mintage	F	VF	XF	Unc
1815A	436,000	120	200	300	900

KM# 705.2 20 FRANCS

6.4516 g., 0.9000 Gold .1867 oz. AGW **Mint:** Bayonne

Date	Mintage	F	VF	XF	Unc
1815L	18,000	150	200	400	1,100

KM# 705.3 20 FRANCS

6.4516 g., 0.9000 Gold .1867 oz. AGW **Mint:** Lille

Date	Mintage	F	VF	XF	Unc
1815W	9,369	200	350	700	1,500

KM# 706.1 20 FRANCS

6.4516 g., 0.9000 Gold .1867 oz. AGW **Mint:** Paris **Note:** Engraver: Tiolier.

Date	Mintage	F	VF	XF	Unc
1814A	2,684,000	100	125	150	425
1815A	2,113,000	100	125	150	425

KM# 706.2 20 FRANCS

6.4516 g., 0.9000 Gold .1867 oz. AGW **Mint:** Rouen

Date	Mintage	F	VF	XF	Unc
1815B	1,539	300	600	1,200	1,500

KM# 706.3 20 FRANCS

6.4516 g., 0.9000 Gold .1867 oz. AGW **Mint:** Bordeaux

Date	Mintage	F	VF	XF	Unc
1814K	63,000	100	150	200	600
1815K	30,000	100	150	200	600

KM# 706.4 20 FRANCS

6.4516 g., 0.9000 Gold .1867 oz. AGW **Mint:** Bayonne

Date	Mintage	F	VF	XF	Unc
1814L	45,000	100	150	200	600
1815L	34,000	100	150	200	600

KM# 706.5 20 FRANCS

6.4516 g., 0.9000 Gold .1867 oz. AGW **Mint:** Perpignan

Date	Mintage	F	VF	XF	Unc
1814Q	29,000	125	175	250	650
1815Q	39,000	100	150	200	600

KM# 706.6 20 FRANCS

6.4516 g., 0.9000 Gold .1867 oz. AGW **Mint:** Lille

Date	Mintage	F	VF	XF	Unc
1814W	60,000	100	150	200	600
1815W	88,000	100	150	200	600

KM# 707 20 FRANCS

6.4516 g., 0.9000 Gold .1867 oz. AGW **Mint:** London **Note:** Engraver: T. Wyon, Jr.

Date	Mintage	F	VF	XF	Unc
1815R	872,000	100	125	175	450

KM# 712.1 20 FRANCS

6.4516 g., 0.9000 Gold .1867 oz. AGW **Mint:** Paris

Date	Mintage	F	VF	XF	Unc
1816A	522,000	100	125	150	375
1817A	2,135,000	100	125	150	375
1818A	2,681,000	100	125	150	375
1819A	2,350,000	100	125	150	375
1820A	1,317,000	100	125	150	375
1821A	12,000	125	200	300	650
1822A	213,000	100	125	150	375
1823A	12,000	125	200	300	600
1824A	1,510,000	100	125	150	375

KM# 712.2 20 FRANCS

6.4516 g., 0.9000 Gold .1867 oz. AGW **Mint:** Rouen

Date	Mintage	F	VF	XF	Unc
1816B	22,000	—	—	—	—

KM# 712.3 20 FRANCS

6.4516 g., 0.9000 Gold .1867 oz. AGW **Mint:** La Rochelle

Date	Mintage	F	VF	XF	Unc
1822H	1,253	500	850	1,100	2,400

KM# 712.4 20 FRANCS

6.4516 g., 0.9000 Gold .1867 oz. AGW **Mint:** Bordeaux

Date	Mintage	F	VF	XF	Unc
1816K	4,947	—	—	—	—
1817K	4,803	175	275	475	900

KM# 712.5 20 FRANCS

6.4516 g., 0.9000 Gold .1867 oz. AGW **Mint:** Bayonne

Date	Mintage	F	VF	XF	Unc
1816L	22,000	—	—	—	—
1817L	36,000	125	200	300	650
1818L	5,394	150	225	350	850

KM# 712.6 20 FRANCS

6.4516 g., 0.9000 Gold .1867 oz. AGW **Mint:** Marseille

Date	Mintage	F	VF	XF	Unc
1824MA	2,001	625	1,250	1,500	3,000

KM# 712.7 20 FRANCS

6.4516 g., 0.9000 Gold .1867 oz. AGW **Mint:** Perpignan

Date	Mintage	F	VF	XF	Unc
1816Q	16,000	100	150	225	550
1817Q	97,000	100	125	200	500
1818Q	25,000	100	150	200	500
1819Q	34,000	100	125	225	550
1820Q	60,000	100	125	225	550
1824Q	12,000	100	150	275	650

KM# 712.8 20 FRANCS

6.4516 g., 0.9000 Gold .1867 oz. AGW **Mint:** Nantes

Date	Mintage	F	VF	XF	Unc
1818T	16,000	100	125	200	550
1819T	8,734	100	150	250	600
1820T	5,749	100	150	250	600

KM# 712.9 20 FRANCS

6.4516 g., 0.9000 Gold .1867 oz. AGW **Mint:** Lille

Date	Mintage	F	VF	XF	Unc
1816W	54,000	100	125	200	600
1817W	156,000	100	125	150	500
1818W	1,315,000	100	125	150	400
1819W	219,000	100	125	150	450
1820W	44,000	100	125	200	600
1821W	8,446	100	150	250	650
1822W	20,000	100	125	200	600
1823W	7,655	100	150	250	650
1824W	253,000	100	125	150	425

KM# 726.1 20 FRANCS

6.4516 g., 0.9000 Gold .1867 oz. AGW **Mint:** Paris

Date	Mintage	F	VF	XF	Unc
1825A	664,000	100	125	200	900
1826A	35,000	150	225	375	1,100
1827A	154,000	100	150	250	950
1828A	279,000	100	150	250	900
1829A	7,783	150	250	425	1,500
1830A	431,000	100	150	250	950

KM# 726.2 20 FRANCS

6.4516 g., 0.9000 Gold .1867 oz. AGW **Mint:** Perpignan

Date	Mintage	F	VF	XF	Unc
1826Q	4,574	500	1,000	1,250	2,400

KM# 726.3 20 FRANCS

6.4516 g., 0.9000 Gold .1867 oz. AGW **Mint:** Nantes

Date	Mintage	F	VF	XF	Unc
1828T	3,175	500	1,000	1,250	2,400

KM# 726.4 20 FRANCS

6.4516 g., 0.9000 Gold .1867 oz. AGW **Mint:** Lille

Date	Mintage	F	VF	XF	Unc
1825W	62,000	125	200	300	950
1826W	6,436	200	275	450	1,400
1827W	3,431	225	350	550	1,600
1828W	15,000	150	250	350	1,200
1829W	5,946	200	275	450	1,400
1830W	15,000	150	250	350	1,200

KM# A726 20 FRANCS

6.4516 g., 0.9000 Gold .1867 oz. AGW **Mint:** Paris **Edge:** Reeded

Date	Mintage	F	VF	XF	Unc
1830A	1,797	500	1,000	1,500	2,500

KM# 739.1 20 FRANCS

6.4516 g., 0.9000 Gold .1867 oz. AGW **Mint:** Paris **Edge:** Incuse lettering

Date	Mintage	F	VF	XF	Unc
1830A	18,000	125	200	300	1,000
1831A	2,162,000	100	125	150	900

KM# 739.2 20 FRANCS

6.4516 g., 0.9000 Gold .1867 oz. AGW **Mint:** Rouen

Date	Mintage	F	VF	XF	Unc
1831B	88,000	150	300	550	1,500

KM# 739.3 20 FRANCS

6.4516 g., 0.9000 Gold .1867 oz. AGW **Mint:** Lille

Date	Mintage	F	VF	XF	Unc
1831W	107,000	110	150	200	1,200

KM# 746.1 20 FRANCS

6.4516 g., 0.9000 Gold .1867 oz. AGW **Mint:** Paris **Edge:** Raised lettering

Date	F	VF	XF	Unc
1830A	175	240	450	800
1831A	110	150	200	800

KM# 746.2 20 FRANCS

6.4516 g., 0.9000 Gold .1867 oz. AGW **Mint:** Rouen

Date	F	VF	XF	Unc
1831B	125	175	250	950

KM# 746.3 20 FRANCS

6.4516 g., 0.9000 Gold .1867 oz. AGW **Mint:** Nantes

Date	F	VF	XF	Unc
1831T	500	800	1,250	—

KM# 746.4 20 FRANCS

6.4516 g., 0.9000 Gold .1867 oz. AGW **Mint:** Lille

Date	F	VF	XF	Unc
1831W	110	150	250	1,000

KM# 750.1 20 FRANCS

6.4516 g., 0.9000 Gold .1867 oz. AGW **Mint:** Paris

Date	Mintage	F	VF	XF	Unc
1832A	6,360	175	325	550	1,275
1832A Proof	—	Value: 4,500			
1833A	207,000	100	120	150	775
1834A	744,000	100	120	150	500
1835A	97,000	100	120	150	725
1836A	139,000	100	120	150	725
1837A	34,000	100	125	175	775
1838A	173,000	100	120	150	725
1839A	1,012,000	90.00	110	130	500
1840A	2,045,000	90.00	110	130	500
1841A	610,000	100	120	150	500
1842A	71,000	100	125	175	775
1843A	106,000	100	120	150	775
1844A	103,000	100	120	150	775
1845A	939	625	1,250	1,800	2,200
1846A	103,000	100	120	150	775
1847A	385,000	100	120	150	500
1848A	442,000	90.00	110	130	500

KM# 750.2 20 FRANCS

6.4516 g., 0.9000 Gold .1867 oz. AGW **Mint:** Rouen

Date	Mintage	F	VF	XF	Unc
1832B	15,000	100	125	175	775
1833B	155,000	100	120	150	775
1834B	77,000	100	120	150	775
1835B	26,000	100	125	185	775

KM# 750.3 20 FRANCS

6.4516 g., 0.9000 Gold .1867 oz. AGW **Mint:** Bayonne

Date	Mintage	F	VF	XF	Unc
1834L	21,000	100	125	175	775
1835L	856	625	1,250	2,000	—

KM# 750.4 20 FRANCS

6.4516 g., 0.9000 Gold .1867 oz. AGW **Mint:** Nantes

Date	Mintage	F	VF	XF	Unc
1832T	868	750	1,500	2,250	—

KM# 750.5 20 FRANCS

6.4516 g., 0.9000 Gold .1867 oz. AGW **Mint:** Lille

Date	Mintage	F	VF	XF	Unc
1832W	27,000	100	125	175	725
1833W	32,000	100	125	175	725
1834W	41,000	100	125	175	725
1835W	30,000	100	125	175	725
1836W	10,000	100	125	185	725
1837W	11,000	100	125	185	725
1838W	12,000	100	125	185	725
1839W	22,000	100	125	175	850
1840W	4,550	150	250	350	1,150
1841W	8,524	125	225	325	1,000
1842W	22,000	100	125	175	725
1843W	35,000	100	125	175	725
1844W	34,000	100	125	175	725
1845W	5,018	125	225	325	1,000
1846W	1,408	375	750	1,250	—

KM# 713.1 40 FRANCS

12.9039 g., 0.9000 Gold .3734 oz. AGW **Mint:** Paris

Date	Mintage	F	VF	XF	Unc
1816A	41,000	200	300	600	1,000
1817A	90,000	200	300	500	950
1818A	11,000	200	350	750	1,250
1820A	5,480	250	500	1,000	2,250
1822A Rare	373	—	—	—	—
1823A Rare	161	—	—	—	—
1824A	15,000	200	275	450	1,000

KM# 713.2 40 FRANCS

12.9039 g., 0.9000 Gold .3734 oz. AGW **Mint:** Rouen

Date	Mintage	F	VF	XF	Unc
1816B	767	1,000	2,000	3,500	—

KM# 713.3 40 FRANCS

12.9039 g., 0.9000 Gold .3734 oz. AGW **Mint:** La Rochelle

Date	Mintage	F	VF	XF	Unc
1822H	611	1,000	2,000	3,500	—

KM# 713.4 40 FRANCS

12.9039 g., 0.9000 Gold .3734 oz. AGW **Mint:** Bayonne

Date	Mintage	F	VF	XF	Unc
1816L	2,923	375	675	1,200	3,000
1817L Rare	377	—	—	—	—

KM# 713.5 40 FRANCS

12.9039 g., 0.9000 Gold .3734 oz. AGW **Mint:** Perpignan

Date	Mintage	F	VF	XF	Unc
1816Q	11,000	200	300	500	1,400

KM# 713.6 40 FRANCS

12.9039 g., 0.9000 Gold .3734 oz. AGW **Mint:** Lille

Date	Mintage	F	VF	XF	Unc
1816W	3,210	200	300	600	1,500
1818W	353,000	200	225	300	900
1819W	4,610	200	300	600	1,500

KM# 721.1 40 FRANCS

12.9039 g., 0.9000 Gold .3734 oz. AGW **Mint:** Paris

Date	Mintage	F	VF	XF	Unc
1824A	50,000	225	275	450	1,400
1826A Rare	62	—	—	—	—
1827A Rare	106	—	—	—	—
1828A	52,000	225	275	450	1,350
1829A	21,000	225	300	500	1,500
1830A	354,000	200	250	300	1,250
1830A	1,324	750	1,250	2,000	3,500

Note: Raised edge letters

KM# 721.2 40 FRANCS

12.9039 g., 0.9000 Gold .3734 oz. AGW **Mint:** Marseille

Date	Mintage	F	VF	XF	Unc
1830MA	1,026	750	1,500	2,500	—

KM# 747.1 40 FRANCS

12.9039 g., 0.9000 Gold .3734 oz. AGW **Mint:** Paris

Date	Mintage	F	VF	XF	Unc
1831A	63,000	200	250	500	1,200
1832A	22,000	200	275	500	1,200
1832A Proof	—	Value: 9,000			
1833A	221,000	200	250	450	1,200
1834A	303,000	200	225	400	1,200
1835A	36,000	200	275	500	1,200
1836A	53,000	200	275	500	1,200
1837A	28,000	200	275	500	1,200
1838A	31,000	200	275	500	1,250
1839A Rare	23	—	—	—	—

KM# 747.2 40 FRANCS

12.9039 g., 0.9000 Gold .3734 oz. AGW **Mint:** Rouen

Date	Mintage	F	VF	XF	Unc
1832B	3,947	300	450	900	2,200
1833B	1,392	450	900	1,750	—

KM# 747.3 40 FRANCS

12.9039 g., 0.9000 Gold .3734 oz. AGW **Mint:** Bayonne

Date	Mintage	F	VF	XF	Unc
1834L	12,000	225	325	600	1,800
1835L	856	600	1,200	2,000	—

SECOND REPUBLIC

DECIMAL COINAGE

KM# 754 CENTIME

Bronze **Mint:** Paris

Date	Mintage	F	VF	XF	Unc
1848A	8,615,000	2.00	5.00	10.00	22.00
1849A	8,664,000	2.00	5.00	10.00	22.00
1850A	2,721,000	6.00	12.00	30.00	60.00
1851A	2,712,000	4.00	8.00	25.00	45.00

KM# 758.1 20 CENTIMES

1.0000 g., 0.9000 Silver .0289 oz. ASW **Mint:** Paris

Date	Mintage	F	VF	XF	Unc
1849A	4,877	125	225	400	700
1850A	6,157,000	3.00	10.00	18.00	45.00
1851A	3,309,000	5.00	15.00	25.00	55.00

KM# 758.2 20 CENTIMES

1.0000 g., 0.9000 Silver .0289 oz. ASW **Mint:** Strasbourg

Date	Mintage	F	VF	XF	Unc
1850BB	48,000	40.00	75.00	200	450

KM# 758.3 20 CENTIMES

1.0000 g., 0.9000 Silver .0289 oz. ASW **Mint:** Bordeaux

Date	Mintage	F	VF	XF	Unc
1850K	344,000	20.00	35.00	85.00	210

KM# 755.1 25 CENTIMES

1.2500 g., 0.9000 Silver .0362 oz. ASW **Mint:** Paris

Date	Mintage	F	VF	XF	Unc
1845A	Inc. above	5.00	10.00	25.00	85.00
1846A	1,748,000	4.00	8.00	18.00	60.00
1847A	3,000,000	3.00	6.00	15.00	55.00
1848A	142,000	5.00	10.00	25.00	85.00

KM# 755.2 25 CENTIMES

1.2500 g., 0.9000 Silver .0362 oz. ASW **Mint:** Rouen

Date	F	VF	XF	Unc
1845B	3.00	6.00	12.50	55.00

KM# 755.3 25 CENTIMES

1.2500 g., 0.9000 Silver .0362 oz. ASW **Mint:** Strasbourg

Date	Mintage	F	VF	XF	Unc
1845BB	Inc. above	5.00	10.00	35.00	125
1846BB	7,922	20.00	40.00	100	250
1847BB	9,939	20.00	40.00	100	250
1848BB	5,886	25.00	75.00	150	300

KM# 755.4 25 CENTIMES

1.2500 g., 0.9000 Silver .0362 oz. ASW **Mint:** Bordeaux

Date	Mintage	F	VF	XF	Unc
1845K	Inc. above	15.00	30.00	70.00	200
1846K	12,000	20.00	40.00	100	275
1847K	3,905	30.00	75.00	200	350

KM# 755.5 25 CENTIMES

1.2500 g., 0.9000 Silver .0362 oz. ASW **Mint:** Lille

Date	Mintage	F	VF	XF	Unc
1845W	Inc. above	5.00	10.00	25.00	85.00
1846W	39,000	5.00	10.00	35.00	125

KM# 768.1 50 CENTIMES

2.5000 g., 0.9000 Silver .0723 oz. ASW **Mint:** Paris

Date	Mintage	F	VF	XF	Unc
1845A	494,000	10.00	20.00	40.00	90.00
1846A	3,165,000	7.50	15.00	30.00	80.00
1847A	3,437,000	7.50	15.00	30.00	80.00
1848A	218,000	10.00	20.00	40.00	90.00

KM# 768.2 50 CENTIMES

2.5000 g., 0.9000 Silver .0723 oz. ASW **Mint:** Rouen

Date	Mintage	F	VF	XF	Unc
1845B	—	7.50	15.00	30.00	75.00
Note: Mintage included in KM#741.2					
1846B	1,000,000	7.50	15.00	30.00	75.00

KM# 768.3 50 CENTIMES

2.5000 g., 0.9000 Silver .0723 oz. ASW **Mint:** Strasbourg

Date	Mintage	F	VF	XF	Unc
1845BB	—	12.00	25.00	50.00	135
Note: Mintage included in KM#741.3					
1846BB	17,000	12.00	25.00	50.00	135
1847BB	44,000	10.00	20.00	40.00	100
1848BB	18,000	12.00	25.00	50.00	135

KM# 768.4 50 CENTIMES

2.5000 g., 0.9000 Silver .0723 oz. ASW **Mint:** Bordeaux

Date	Mintage	F	VF	XF	Unc
1845K	—	35.00	70.00	150	300
Note: Mintage included KM#741.7					
1846K	22,000	10.00	20.00	45.00	125
1847K	8,915	25.00	50.00	110	250

KM# 768.5 50 CENTIMES

2.5000 g., 0.9000 Silver .0723 oz. ASW **Mint:** Lille

Date	Mintage	F	VF	XF	Unc
1845W	—	7.00	15.00	30.00	90.00
Note: Mintage included in KM#741.13					
1846W	70,000	10.00	25.00	40.00	100

KM# 769.1 50 CENTIMES

2.5000 g., 0.9000 Silver .0723 oz. ASW **Mint:** Paris

Date	Mintage	F	VF	XF	Unc
1849A	2,655	150	300	600	1,100
1850A	2,165,000	8.00	18.00	40.00	150
1851A	850,000	15.00	35.00	100	175
1851A Proof	—	Value: 800			

KM# 769.2 50 CENTIMES

2.5000 g., 0.9000 Silver .0723 oz. ASW **Mint:** Strasbourg

Date	Mintage	F	VF	XF	Unc
1850BB	40,000	40.00	110	250	450

KM# 769.3 50 CENTIMES

2.5000 g., 0.9000 Silver .0723 oz. ASW **Mint:** Bordeaux

Date	Mintage	F	VF	XF	Unc
1850K	31,000	60.00	125	275	600

KM# 793 50 CENTIMES

2.5000 g., 0.9000 Silver .0723 oz. ASW **Mint:** Paris **Note:** President Louis-Napoleon.

Date	Mintage	F	VF	XF	Unc
1852A	1,010,000	25.00	60.00	150	375

KM# 759.1 FRANC
5.0000 g., 0.9000 Silver .1446 oz. ASW **Mint:** Paris

Date	Mintage	F	VF	XF	Unc
1849A	1,289,000	20.00	45.00	90.00	200
1850A	1,041,000	25.00	60.00	115	225
1851A	638,000	40.00	100	175	300

KM# 759.2 FRANC
5.0000 g., 0.9000 Silver .1446 oz. ASW **Mint:** Strasbourg

Date	Mintage	F	VF	XF	Unc
1849BB	15,000	100	250	600	1,000
1850BB	213,000	60.00	150	300	600

KM# 759.3 FRANC
5.0000 g., 0.9000 Silver .1446 oz. ASW **Mint:** Bordeaux

Date	Mintage	F	VF	XF	Unc
1849K	19,000	100	250	600	1,000
1850K	35,000	75.00	200	375	700

KM# 760.1 2 FRANCS
10.0000 g., 0.9000 Silver .2893 oz. ASW **Mint:** Paris

Date	Mintage	F	VF	XF	Unc
1849A	665,000	100	275	650	1,100
1850A	857,000	85.00	250	600	1,000
1851A	351,000	110	300	700	1,250

KM# 760.2 2 FRANCS
10.0000 g., 0.9000 Silver .2893 oz. ASW **Mint:** Strasbourg

Date	Mintage	F	VF	XF	Unc
1849BB	14,000	250	500	1,000	2,000
1850BB	202,000	160	350	850	1,600

KM# 760.3 2 FRANCS
10.0000 g., 0.9000 Silver .2893 oz. ASW **Mint:** Bordeaux

Date	Mintage	F	VF	XF	Unc
1849K	17,000	250	500	1,000	2,000
1850K	9,914	275	650	1,500	—

KM# 756.1 5 FRANCS
25.0000 g., 0.9000 Silver .7234 oz. ASW **Mint:** Paris

Date	Mintage	F	VF	XF	Unc
1848A	16,648,000	10.00	20.00	75.00	200
1848A Proof	—	Value: 3,500			
Note: Plain edge					
1849A	29,338,000	8.00	15.00	65.00	150

KM# 756.2 5 FRANCS
25.0000 g., 0.9000 Silver .7234 oz. ASW **Mint:** Strasbourg

Date	Mintage	F	VF	XF	Unc
1848BB	2,300,000	15.00	40.00	125	275
1849BB	2,594,000	15.00	40.00	125	275

KM# 756.3 5 FRANCS
25.0000 g., 0.9000 Silver .7234 oz. ASW **Mint:** Lyon

Date	Mintage	F	VF	XF	Unc
1848D	136,000	100	200	400	900
1849D	9,711	300	650	1,500	3,500

KM# 756.4 5 FRANCS
25.0000 g., 0.9000 Silver .7234 oz. ASW **Mint:** Bordeaux

Date	Mintage	F	VF	XF	Unc
1848K	428,000	45.00	125	275	550
1849K	471,000	45.00	125	275	550

KM# 761.1 5 FRANCS
25.0000 g., 0.9000 Silver .7234 oz. ASW **Mint:** Paris

Date	Mintage	F	VF	XF	Unc
1849A	7,437,000	20.00	40.00	125	450
1850A	14,619,000	15.00	35.00	100	375
1851A	13,223,000	15.00	35.00	100	375

KM# 761.2 5 FRANCS
25.0000 g., 0.9000 Silver .7234 oz. ASW **Mint:** Strasbourg

Date	Mintage	F	VF	XF	Unc
1849BB	916,000	35.00	80.00	200	500
1850BB	1,169,000	30.00	70.00	175	450

KM# 761.3 5 FRANCS
25.0000 g., 0.9000 Silver .7234 oz. ASW **Mint:** Bordeaux

Date	Mintage	F	VF	XF	Unc
1850K	332,000	100	200	400	750

KM# 773.1 5 FRANCS
25.0000 g., 0.9000 Silver .7234 oz. ASW **Mint:** Paris

Date	Mintage	F	VF	XF	Unc
1852A	16,117,000	12.50	35.00	100	375
1852A	3,769	350	600	1,000	1,750
Note: Signature: J.J. Barre					
1852A Proof	—	Value: 3,000			

kM# 773.2 5 FRANCS
25.0000 g., 0.9000 Silver .7234 oz. ASW **Mint:** Strasbourg

Date	Mintage	F	VF	XF	Unc
1852BB	41,000	350	650	1,250	3,500

KM# 770 10 FRANCS
3.2258 g., 0.9000 Gold .0933 oz. AGW **Mint:** Paris

Date	Mintage	F	VF	XF	Unc
1850A	592,000	55.00	100	200	675
1850A Proof	—	Value: 4,000			
1851A	3,115,000	BV	65.00	150	575
1851A Proof	—	Value: 4,000			

KM# 757 20 FRANCS
6.4516 g., 0.9000 Gold .1867 oz. AGW **Mint:** Paris

Date	Mintage	F	VF	XF	Unc
1848A	1,543,000	100	125	175	500
1848A Proof	—	Value: 4,000			
1849A	1,303,000	100	125	175	500

KM# 762 20 FRANCS
6.4516 g., 0.9000 Gold .1867 oz. AGW **Mint:** Paris

Date	Mintage	F	VF	XF	Unc
1849A	53,000	100	125	200	750
1850A	3,964,000	BV	80.00	100	400
1850A Proof	—	Value: 3,750			
1851A	12,704,000	BV	75.00	90.00	350

SECOND EMPIRE

Napoleon III as Emperor

DECIMAL COINAGE

KM# 775.1 CENTIME
Bronze **Mint:** Paris

Date	Mintage	F	VF	XF	Unc
1853A	4,076,000	2.00	5.00	9.00	15.00
1854A	2,750,000	4.00	7.00	15.00	28.00
1855A (d)	6,034,000	3.00	5.00	12.00	25.00
1855A (a)	Inc. above	6.00	15.00	35.00	60.00
1855A (a) Proof	—	Value: 400			
1856A	2,878,000	4.00	10.00	23.00	40.00
1857A	2,000,000	5.00	12.00	27.00	50.00

KM# 775.2 CENTIME
Bronze **Mint:** Rouen

Date	Mintage	F	VF	XF	Unc
1853B	824,000	5.00	12.00	22.00	35.00
1854B	1,709,000	10.00	20.00	40.00	75.00
1855B (d)	1,971,000	10.00	20.00	40.00	75.00
1855B (a)	Inc. above	12.00	25.00	50.00	90.00
1856B	4,373,000	2.00	5.00	9.00	15.00
1857B	3,000,000	3.00	7.00	20.00	40.00

KM# 775.3 CENTIME
Bronze **Mint:** Strasbourg

Date	Mintage	F	VF	XF	Unc
1853BB	2,558,000	3.00	5.00	12.00	25.00
1854BB	1,447,000	4.00	7.00	15.00	28.00
1855BB (d)	248,000	15.00	30.00	75.00	150
1855BB (a)	Inc. above	15.00	30.00	75.00	150
1856BB	1,874,000	10.00	15.00	30.00	55.00
1857BB Rare	—	—	—	—	—

KM# 775.4 CENTIME
Bronze **Mint:** Lyon

Date	Mintage	F	VF	XF	Unc
1853D	964,000	3.00	6.00	18.00	30.00
Note: The 1853 dated coins exist with large and small D mint mark					
1854D	1,546,000	8.00	16.00	35.00	60.00
1855D (d)	2,466,000	6.00	15.00	30.00	50.00
1855D (a)	Inc. above	10.00	25.00	50.00	100
1856D	880,000	15.00	40.00	80.00	175
1857D	1,000,000	12.00	28.00	55.00	90.00

KM# 775.5 CENTIME
Bronze **Mint:** Bordeaux

Date	Mintage	F	VF	XF	Unc
1853K	405,000	8.00	18.00	45.00	75.00
1854K	1,150,000	6.00	14.00	35.00	65.00
1855K (d)	Inc. above	7.00	15.00	45.00	75.00
1855K (a)	1,455,000	10.00	20.00	50.00	95.00
1856K	2,062,000	4.00	8.00	20.00	45.00
1857K	1,000,000	8.00	18.00	40.00	65.00

KM# 775.6 CENTIME
Bronze **Mint:** Marseille **Note:** Mint mark: MA monogram.

Date	Mintage	F	VF	XF	Unc
1853	225,000	20.00	35.00	60.00	125
1854	1,976,000	3.00	6.00	15.00	35.00
1855 (d)	2,839,000	15.00	25.00	65.00	150
1855 (a)	Inc. above	3.00	7.00	15.00	35.00
1856	305,000	12.00	30.00	65.00	150
1857	1,500,000	3.00	10.00	20.00	45.00

KM# 775.7 CENTIME
Bronze **Mint:** Lille

Date	Mintage	F	VF	XF	Unc
1853W	1,634,000	2.00	5.00	12.00	25.00
1855W (d)	3,102,000	2.00	5.00	12.00	20.00
1855W (a)	Inc. above	5.00	15.00	30.00	55.00
1856W	2,707,000	3.00	8.00	20.00	35.00
1857W	2,500,000	3.00	10.00	22.00	40.00

KM# 795.1 CENTIME
Bronze **Mint:** Paris

Date	Mintage	F	VF	XF	Unc
1861A	7,398,000	0.50	2.00	5.00	10.00
1862A	15,561,000	0.50	1.00	3.00	7.00
1870A	1,000,000	5.00	18.00	30.00	60.00

KM# 795.2 CENTIME
Bronze **Mint:** Strasbourg

Date	Mintage	F	VF	XF	Unc
1861BB	3,012,000	1.00	3.00	9.00	15.00
1862BB	4,493,000	1.00	3.00	9.00	15.00

KM# 795.3 CENTIME

Bronze **Mint:** Bordeaux

Date	Mintage	F	VF	XF	Unc
1861K	1,999,000	2.00	5.00	10.00	20.00
1862K	7,431,000	0.50	1.00	3.00	7.50

KM# 776.1 2 CENTIMES

Bronze **Mint:** Paris

Date	Mintage	F	VF	XF	Unc
1853	610,000	4.00	10.00	18.00	30.00
1854	3,118,000	0.75	2.00	6.00	18.00
1855	5,417,000	0.25	2.00	6.00	12.00
1855A	Inc. above	0.25	2.00	6.00	12.00
1856	1,738,000	1.00	3.00	7.00	15.00
1857	1,250,000	1.50	5.00	10.00	20.00

KM# 776.2 2 CENTIMES

Bronze **Mint:** Rouen

Date	Mintage	F	VF	XF	Unc
1853B	539,000	5.00	12.00	20.00	35.00
1854B	1,995,000	1.00	3.00	7.00	15.00
1855B (d)	1,754,000	1.50	4.00	8.00	15.00
1855B (a)	Inc. above	1.50	4.00	8.00	15.00
1856B	4,324,000	0.25	2.00	6.00	12.00
1857B	2,000,000	1.50	5.00	15.00	25.00

KM# 776.3 2 CENTIMES

Bronze **Mint:** Strasbourg

Date	Mintage	F	VF	XF	Unc
1853BB	168,000	6.00	15.00	35.00	100
1854BB	2,003,000	1.00	3.00	7.00	15.00
1855BB (d)	2,135,000	1.00	3.00	7.00	15.00
1855BB (a)	Inc. above	2.00	5.00	9.00	18.00
1856BB	1,282,000	1.00	3.00	6.00	12.00

Small D

Large D

KM# 776.4 2 CENTIMES

Bronze **Mint:** Lyon

Date	Mintage	F	VF	XF	Unc
1853D Small D	—	10.00	25.00	40.00	90.00
1853D Large D	—	13.00	35.00	55.00	110
1854D Small D	2,524,000	7.00	12.00	25.00	50.00
1854D Large D	Inc. above	10.00	15.00	30.00	60.00
1855D (d) Small D	2,554,000	4.00	10.00	18.00	30.00
1855D (d) Large D	Inc. above	10.00	20.00	35.00	100
1855D (a) Small D	Inc. above	6.00	12.00	25.00	60.00
1855D (a) Large D	Inc. above	1.00	3.00	8.00	15.00
1856D	774,000	—	—	—	—
1857D Small D	1,000,000	10.00	20.00	50.00	125
1857D Large D	Inc. above	6.00	10.00	25.00	50.00

KM# 776.5 2 CENTIMES

Bronze **Mint:** Bordeaux

Date	Mintage	F	VF	XF	Unc
1853K	117,000	10.00	25.00	45.00	100
1854K	1,545,000	1.50	4.00	8.00	20.00
1855K (d)	1,068,000	2.50	6.00	15.00	30.00
1855K (a)	Inc. above	2.00	5.00	12.00	25.00
1856K	2,281,000	1.00	3.00	7.00	15.00
1857K	750,000	6.00	12.00	25.00	60.00

KM# 776.6 2 CENTIMES

Bronze **Mint:** Marseille

Date	Mintage	F	VF	XF	Unc
1853MA	163,000	6.00	16.00	35.00	100
1854MA	1,312,000	3.00	8.00	16.00	25.00
1855MA (d)	2,438,000	2.00	6.00	16.00	25.00
1855MA (a)	Inc. above	4.00	10.00	20.00	35.00
1856MA	2,781,000	1.00	3.00	7.00	15.00
1857MA	1,250,000	7.00	14.00	28.00	65.00

KM# 776.7 2 CENTIMES

Bronze **Mint:** Lille

Date	Mintage	F	VF	XF	Unc
1853W	70,000	20.00	40.00	100	135
1854W	3,402,000	1.00	3.00	7.00	15.00
1855W (d)	—	3.00	7.00	14.00	25.00
1855W(a)	939,340	3.00	7.00	14.00	25.00
1856W	2,581,000	1.00	3.00	7.00	15.00
1857W	2,250,000	1.00	3.00	7.00	15.00

KM# 796.1 2 CENTIMES

Bronze **Mint:** Paris **Obverse:** Bust points to 1 in date

Date	Mintage	F	VF	XF	Unc
1861A	4,054,000	0.50	1.50	3.00	7.00

KM# 796.2 2 CENTIMES

Bronze **Mint:** Strasbourg

Date	Mintage	F	VF	XF	Unc
1861BB	2,440,000	0.75	3.00	6.00	14.00

KM# 796.3 2 CENTIMES

Bronze **Mint:** Bordeaux

Date	Mintage	F	VF	XF	Unc
1861K	3,291,000	0.75	2.50	5.00	8.00

KM# 796.4 2 CENTIMES

Bronze **Mint:** Paris **Obverse:** Recut die (r), bust points to 8 in date

Date	Mintage	F	VF	XF	Unc
1861A (r)	Inc. above	1.00	3.00	5.00	10.00
1862A	7,515,000	0.50	1.50	3.00	5.00

KM# 796.5 2 CENTIMES

Bronze **Mint:** Strasbourg

Date	Mintage	F	VF	XF	Unc
1861BB (r)	Inc. above	1.00	3.00	5.00	10.00
1862BB	2,807,000	1.50	3.50	6.00	12.00

KM# 796.6 2 CENTIMES

Bronze **Mint:** Bordeaux

Date	Mintage	F	VF	XF	Unc
1861K (r)	Inc. above	0.25	2.00	4.00	10.00
1862K	13,692,000	0.10	1.50	3.00	5.00

KM# 777.1 5 CENTIMES

Bronze **Mint:** Paris

Date	Mintage	F	VF	XF	Unc
1853A	13,928,000	2.00	5.00	16.00	30.00
1854A	28,767,000	2.00	5.00	14.00	28.00
1855A (d)	26,932,000	1.00	4.00	12.00	25.00
1855A (a)	Inc. above	3.00	6.00	15.00	35.00
1856A	25,799,000	1.00	4.00	12.00	25.00
1857A	5,729,000	8.00	18.00	35.00	50.00

KM# 777.2 5 CENTIMES

Bronze **Mint:** Rouen

Date	Mintage	F	VF	XF	Unc
1853B	4,424,000	4.00	10.00	25.00	45.00
1854B	16,354,000	2.00	5.00	16.00	30.00
1855B (d)	18,290,000	2.00	5.00	16.00	30.00
1855B (a)	Inc. above	3.00	6.00	18.00	35.00
1856B	14,813,000	2.00	5.00	16.00	30.00
1857B	1,843,000	20.00	35.00	100	175

KM# 777.3 5 CENTIMES

Bronze **Mint:** Strasbourg

Date	Mintage	F	VF	XF	Unc
1853BB	4,148,000	4.00	10.00	25.00	45.00
1854BB	20,380,000	2.00	5.00	16.00	30.00
1855BB (d)	17,108,000	2.00	5.00	16.00	30.00
1855BB (a)	Inc. above	2.00	5.00	16.00	30.00
1856BB	10,372,000	2.00	5.00	14.00	28.00
1857BB	1,662,000	25.00	40.00	125	200

KM# 777.4 5 CENTIMES

Bronze **Mint:** Lyon

Date	Mintage	F	VF	XF	Unc
1853	5,013,000	3.00	6.00	18.00	35.00
1854	18,597,000	2.00	5.00	16.00	30.00
1855 (d) Small D	14,250,000	10.00	20.00	45.00	90.00
1855 (d) Large D	Inc. above	10.00	20.00	45.00	90.00
1855 (a) Small D	Inc. above	3.00	6.00	18.00	35.00
1855 (a) Large D	Inc. above	3.00	6.00	18.00	35.00
1856 Small D	7,669,000	2.00	6.00	15.00	30.00
1856 Large D	Inc. above	2.00	6.00	15.00	30.00
1857 Small D	1,531,000	25.00	40.00	125	200
1857 Large D	Inc. above	25.00	40.00	125	200

KM# 777.5 5 CENTIMES

Bronze **Mint:** Bordeaux

Date	Mintage	F	VF	XF	Unc
1853K	1,652,000	8.00	18.00	35.00	50.00
1854K	13,608,000	2.00	5.00	16.00	30.00
1855K (d)	15,761,000	10.00	20.00	40.00	75.00
1855K (a)	Inc. above	3.00	6.00	18.00	35.00
1856K	14,775,000	2.00	5.00	16.00	30.00
1857K	2,417,000	12.00	25.00	50.00	90.00

KM# 777.6 5 CENTIMES

Bronze **Mint:** Marseille

Date	Mintage	F	VF	XF	Unc
1853MA	1,654,000	8.00	18.00	35.00	50.00
1854MA	14,835,000	2.00	5.00	16.00	30.00
1855MA (d)	15,417,000	10.00	20.00	50.00	100
1855MA (a)	Inc. above	2.00	5.00	14.00	28.00
1856MA	16,997,000	2.00	5.00	16.00	30.00
1857MA	4,188,000	10.00	20.00	45.00	90.00

KM# 777.7 5 CENTIMES

Bronze **Mint:** Lille

Date	Mintage	F	VF	XF	Unc
1853W	5,398,000	4.00	10.00	25.00	50.00
1854W	14,957,000	2.00	5.00	15.00	30.00
1855W (d)	17,473,000	2.00	5.00	15.00	30.00
1855W (a)	Inc. above	2.00	5.00	15.00	30.00
1856W	15,472,000	2.00	5.00	15.00	30.00
1857W	1,842,000	25.00	40.00	125	200

KM# 797.1 5 CENTIMES

Bronze **Mint:** Paris

Date	Mintage	F	VF	XF	Unc
1861A	6,857,000	5.00	12.00	25.00	60.00
1862A	5,300,000	5.00	12.00	25.00	60.00
1863A	12,128,000	3.00	6.00	20.00	45.00
1864A	3,053,000	7.00	20.00	40.00	75.00
1865A	2,619,000	10.00	25.00	50.00	90.00

KM# 797.2 5 CENTIMES

Bronze **Mint:** Strasbourg

Date	Mintage	F	VF	XF	Unc
1861BB	7,124,000	4.00	10.00	20.00	50.00
1862BB	8,584,000	4.00	10.00	20.00	50.00
1863BB	2,323,000	20.00	40.00	75.00	125
1864BB	6,110,000	5.00	12.00	25.00	60.00
1865BB	7,226,000	4.00	10.00	20.00	50.00

KM# 797.3 5 CENTIMES

Bronze **Mint:** Bordeaux

Date	Mintage	F	VF	XF	Unc
1861K	6,582,000	5.00	12.00	25.00	60.00
1862K	7,065,000	4.00	10.00	20.00	50.00
1863K	9,437,000	3.00	8.00	18.00	40.00
1864K	5,831,000	5.00	12.00	25.00	60.00

KM# 771.1 10 CENTIMES

Bronze **Mint:** Paris

Date	Mintage	F	VF	XF	Unc
1852A	577,000	18.00	30.00	90.00	200
1853A	12,256,000	2.00	5.00	18.00	50.00
1854A	13,327,000	2.00	5.00	18.00	50.00
1855A (d)	14,816,000	2.00	5.00	18.00	45.00
1855A (a)	Inc. above	3.00	6.00	20.00	60.00
1856A	19,149,000	1.50	4.00	15.00	30.00
1857A	3,096,000	5.00	10.00	25.00	80.00

KM# 771.2 10 CENTIMES

Bronze **Mint:** Rouen

Date	Mintage	F	VF	XF	Unc
1853B	3,546,000	3.00	7.00	20.00	50.00
1854B	8,065,000	3.00	9.00	25.00	50.00
1855B (d)	9,960,000	3.00	10.00	30.00	75.00
1855B (a)	Inc. above	2.00	6.00	18.00	45.00
1856B	11,637,000	2.00	6.00	18.00	45.00
1857B	1,620,000	15.00	30.00	85.00	200

KM# 771.3 10 CENTIMES

Bronze **Mint:** Strasbourg

Date	Mintage	F	VF	XF	Unc
1853BB	4,582,000	3.00	7.00	20.00	50.00
1854BB	8,433,000	2.00	6.00	18.00	45.00
1855BB (d)	11,953,000	2.00	6.00	18.00	45.00
1855BB (a)	Inc. above	1.50	5.00	15.00	40.00
1856BB	7,781,000	2.00	6.00	18.00	45.00
1857BB	1,685,000	15.00	30.00	85.00	200

KM# 771.4 10 CENTIMES
Bronze **Mint:** Lyon

Date	Mintage	F	VF	XF	Unc
1853D	3,709,000	3.00	7.00	20.00	50.00
1854D	8,487,000	2.00	6.00	18.00	45.00
1855D (d)	12,099,000	5.00	10.00	30.00	100
1855D (a)	Inc. above	3.00	8.00	25.00	75.00
1856D	5,118,000	3.00	8.00	25.00	75.00

KM# 771.5 10 CENTIMES
Bronze **Mint:** Bordeaux

Date	Mintage	F	VF	XF	Unc
1853K	1,203,000	5.00	18.00	50.00	135
1854K	7,083,000	10.00	20.00	40.00	90.00
1855K (d)	11,797,000	5.00	10.00	30.00	100
1855K (a)	Inc. above	2.00	7.00	20.00	60.00
1856K	8,871,000	2.00	7.00	18.00	50.00
1857K	1,179,000	20.00	40.00	100	225

KM# 771.6 10 CENTIMES
Bronze **Mint:** Marseille

Date	Mintage	F	VF	XF	Unc
1853MA	889,000	15.00	30.00	60.00	135
1854MA	7,995,000	3.00	7.00	20.00	50.00
1855MA (d)	11,309,000	5.00	10.00	30.00	100
1855MA (a)	Inc. above	2.00	7.00	18.00	50.00
1856MA	10,937,000	1.50	5.00	15.00	40.00
1857MA	2,052,000	20.00	45.00	90.00	200

KM# 771.7 10 CENTIMES
Bronze **Mint:** Lille

Date	Mintage	F	VF	XF	Unc
1853W	3,107,000	2.00	8.00	20.00	60.00
1854W	8,242,000	2.00	7.00	18.00	50.00
1855W (d)	9,837,000	4.00	10.00	25.00	65.00
1855W (a)	Inc. above	2.00	7.00	18.00	50.00
1856W	11,402,000	1.50	5.00	15.00	40.00
1857W	1,858,000	10.00	20.00	60.00	125

KM# 798.1 10 CENTIMES
Bronze **Mint:** Paris

Date	Mintage	F	VF	XF	Unc
1861A	3,638,000	4.00	12.00	30.00	75.00
1862A	4,736,000	3.00	10.00	28.00	65.00
1863A	4,873,000	3.00	10.00	28.00	65.00
1864A	1,556,000	20.00	50.00	160	300
1865A	1,608,000	8.00	20.00	40.00	90.00

KM# 798.2 10 CENTIMES
Bronze **Mint:** Strasbourg

Date	Mintage	F	VF	XF	Unc
1861BB	4,625,000	3.00	10.00	28.00	65.00
1862BB	4,702,000	3.00	10.00	28.00	65.00
1863BB	1,340,000	6.00	15.00	35.00	80.00
1864BB	3,053,000	5.00	12.00	30.00	70.00
1865BB	4,797,000	3.00	10.00	28.00	65.00

KM# 798.3 10 CENTIMES
Bronze **Mint:** Bordeaux

Date	Mintage	F	VF	XF	Unc
1861K	4,363,000	3.00	10.00	28.00	65.00
1862K	5,244,000	2.00	10.00	25.00	60.00
1863K	4,521,000	3.00	10.00	28.00	65.00
1864K	3,075,000	4.00	12.00	30.00	75.00

KM# 778.1 20 CENTIMES
1.0000 g., 0.9000 Silver .0289 oz. ASW **Mint:** Paris

Date	Mintage	F	VF	XF	Unc
1853A Small head	680,000	10.00	20.00	50.00	100
1853A Large head	Inc. above	100	200	400	700
1854A	1,683,000	5.00	12.00	25.00	60.00
1855A (d)	362,000	10.00	25.00	45.00	100
1856A	603,000	8.00	17.50	40.00	80.00
1857A	840,000	6.00	15.00	35.00	70.00
1858A	704,000	10.00	20.00	40.00	80.00
1859A	3,620,000	3.00	10.00	20.00	45.00
1860/50A	6,536,000	6.00	15.00	40.00	85.00
1860A (h)	Inc. above	3.00	6.00	15.00	35.00
1862A	54,000	75.00	175	300	600

KM# 778.2 20 CENTIMES
1.0000 g., 0.9000 Silver .0289 oz. ASW **Mint:** Strasbourg

Date	Mintage	F	VF	XF	Unc
1856BB	13,000	125	275	450	800
1860BB (b)	2,986,000	5.00	12.00	25.00	80.00
1863BB	398,000	20.00	45.00	90.00	200

KM# 778.3 20 CENTIMES
1.0000 g., 0.9000 Silver .0289 oz. ASW **Mint:** Lyon

Date	Mintage	F	VF	XF	Unc
1856D	396,000	12.50	25.00	50.00	125

KM# 805.1 20 CENTIMES
1.0000 g., 0.8350 Silver .0268 oz. ASW **Mint:** Paris

Date	Mintage	F	VF	XF	Unc
1864A	268,000	10.00	25.00	75.00	175
1866A	1,460,000	5.00	10.00	30.00	65.00

KM# 805.2 20 CENTIMES
1.0000 g., 0.8350 Silver .0268 oz. ASW **Mint:** Strasbourg

Date	Mintage	F	VF	XF	Unc
1864BB	112,000	15.00	30.00	75.00	175
1866BB	843,000	7.00	15.00	35.00	75.00

KM# 805.3 20 CENTIMES
1.0000 g., 0.8350 Silver .0268 oz. ASW **Mint:** Bordeaux

Date	Mintage	F	VF	XF	Unc
1864K	58,000	30.00	60.00	150	260
1866K	413,000	10.00	25.00	55.00	150

KM# 808.1 20 CENTIMES
1.0000 g., 0.8350 Silver .0268 oz. ASW **Mint:** Paris

Date	Mintage	F	VF	XF	Unc
1867A	5,611,000	2.00	4.00	10.00	30.00
1868A	353,000	7.00	15.00	35.00	90.00

KM# 808.2 20 CENTIMES
1.0000 g., 0.8350 Silver .0268 oz. ASW **Mint:** Strasbourg

Date	Mintage	F	VF	XF	Unc
1867BB	3,114,000	2.50	5.00	12.00	30.00
1868BB	200,000	15.00	30.00	65.00	115
1869BB	Inc. above	—	—	—	—

KM# 808.3 20 CENTIMES
1.0000 g., 0.8350 Silver .0268 oz. ASW **Mint:** Bordeaux

Date	Mintage	F	VF	XF	Unc
1867K	91,000	20.00	50.00	125	250

KM# 794.1 50 CENTIMES
2.5000 g., 0.9000 Silver .0723 oz. ASW

Date	Mintage	F	VF	XF	Unc
1853	154,000	35.00	90.00	200	450
1854	1,080,000	15.00	30.00	75.00	175
1855	400,000	25.00	60.00	125	250
1856	1,436,000	15.00	30.00	75.00	175
1857	1,632,000	15.00	30.00	75.00	175
1858	5,559,000	8.00	18.00	40.00	150
1859	3,880,000	9.00	20.00	45.00	150
1860 (h)	2,657,000	10.00	22.00	50.00	150
1862	1,549,000	15.00	30.00	75.00	175

KM# 794.2 50 CENTIMES
2.5000 g., 0.9000 Silver .0723 oz. ASW **Mint:** Strasbourg

Date	Mintage	F	VF	XF	Unc
1856BB	1,196,000	15.00	30.00	75.00	175
1859BB	1,112,000	15.00	30.00	75.00	175
1860BB (be)	1,555,000	175	300	—	—
1860BB (c)	Inc. above	15.00	30.00	75.00	175
1861BB	355,000	30.00	80.00	175	400
1862BB	1,007,000	20.00	50.00	125	250
1863BB	137,000	45.00	120	250	500

KM# 794.3 50 CENTIMES
2.5000 g., 0.9000 Silver .0723 oz. ASW **Mint:** Lyon

Date	Mintage	F	VF	XF	Unc
1856D	1,246,000	15.00	30.00	75.00	175

KM# 814.1 50 CENTIMES
2.5000 g., 0.8350 Silver .0671 oz. ASW **Mint:** Paris

Date	Mintage	F	VF	XF	Unc
1864A	7,598,000	5.00	10.00	20.00	60.00
1865A	7,398,000	5.00	10.00	20.00	60.00
1866A	5,921,000	6.00	12.00	25.00	75.00
1867A	14,528,000	3.00	6.00	15.00	60.00
1868A	2,789,000	8.00	18.00	40.00	100

KM# 814.2 50 CENTIMES
2.5000 g., 0.8350 Silver .0671 oz. ASW **Mint:** Strasbourg

Date	Mintage	F	VF	XF	Unc
1864BB	4,626,000	6.00	12.00	25.00	75.00
1865BB	5,175,000	6.00	12.00	25.00	75.00
1866BB	5,256,000	6.00	12.00	25.00	75.00
1867BB	9,992,000	5.00	10.00	20.00	60.00
1868BB	Inc. below	45.00	110	225	500
1869BB	1,800,000	30.00	75.00	150	250

KM# 814.3 50 CENTIMES
2.5000 g., 0.8350 Silver .0671 oz. ASW **Mint:** Bordeaux

Date	Mintage	F	VF	XF	Unc
1864K	1,828,000	15.00	35.00	75.00	150
1865K	4,901,000	6.00	12.00	25.00	75.00
1866K	3,500,000	8.00	16.00	35.00	100
1867K	4,692,000	6.00	12.00	25.00	75.00

KM# 772 FRANC
5.0000 g., 0.9000 Silver .1446 oz. ASW **Mint:** Paris **Subject:** President Louis-Napoleon

Date	Mintage	F	VF	XF	Unc
1852A	1,015,000	45.00	80.00	185	475
1852A Proof	—	Value: 1,400			

KM# 779.1 FRANC
5.0000 g., 0.9000 Silver .1446 oz. ASW **Ruler:** Napoleon III

Date	Mintage	F	VF	XF	Unc
1853	183,000	150	400	750	1,400
Note: Large head					
1853 Proof	—	Value: 625			
Note: Large head					
1853	Inc. above	60.00	125	300	600
Note: Small head					
1854	764,000	25.00	50.00	150	350
1855 (d)	757,000	35.00	90.00	175	300
1855 (a)	Inc. above	75.00	150	225	500
1856	1,196,000	20.00	50.00	125	250
1857	1,681,000	20.00	40.00	100	250
1858	5,607,000	10.00	25.00	75.00	200
1859	3,830,000	15.00	35.00	90.00	225
1860 (h)	2,740,000	15.00	35.00	90.00	225
1860 (b)	Inc. above	15.00	35.00	90.00	225
1861	2,012,000	100	200	450	700
1863	19,000	325	600	900	1,300

KM# 779.2 FRANC
5.0000 g., 0.9000 Silver .1446 oz. ASW **Ruler:** Napoleon III **Mint:** Strasbourg

Date	Mintage	F	VF	XF	Unc
1856BB	1,635,000	20.00	50.00	125	250
1859BB	1,333,000	20.00	50.00	125	250
1860BB	Inc. above	20.00	50.00	125	250
1861BB	218,000	100	250	500	850
1862BB	1,124,000	80.00	200	400	800
1863BB	54,000	125	300	650	900

KM# 779.3 FRANC
5.0000 g., 0.9000 Silver .1446 oz. ASW **Ruler:** Napoleon III **Mint:** Lyon

Date	Mintage	F	VF	XF	Unc
1856D	1,227,000	20.00	50.00	725	250

KM# 806.1 FRANC
5.0000 g., 0.8350 Silver .1342 oz. ASW **Ruler:** Napoleon III **Mint:** Paris **Obverse:** Laureate head

Date	Mintage	F	VF	XF	Unc
1866A	14,638,000	5.00	12.00	25.00	75.00
1867A	12,131,000	5.00	12.00	25.00	75.00
1868A	14,942,000	5.00	12.00	25.00	75.00

Date	Mintage	F	VF	XF	Unc
1869A	2,935,000	10.00	25.00	75.00	150
1870A	788,000	—	—	—	—

KM# 806.2 FRANC
5.0000 g., 0.8350 Silver .1342 oz. ASW **Ruler:** Napoleon III **Mint:** Strasbourg **Obverse:** Laureate head

Date	Mintage	F	VF	XF	Unc
1866BB	7,204,000	6.00	15.00	30.00	90.00
1867BB	7,295,000	6.00	15.00	30.00	90.00
1868BB	10,230,000	5.00	12.00	25.00	75.00
1869BB	3,094,000	10.00	25.00	75.00	150
1870BB	1,992,000	15.00	40.00	90.00	200

KM# 806.3 FRANC
5.0000 g., 0.8350 Silver .1342 oz. ASW **Ruler:** Napoleon III **Mint:** Bordeaux **Obverse:** Laureate head

Date	Mintage	F	VF	XF	Unc
1866K	1,402,000	15.00	40.00	90.00	200
1867K	6,092,000	5.00	15.00	35.00	110
1868K	22,000	150	300	425	1,000

KM# 780.1 2 FRANCS
10.0000 g., 0.9000 Silver .2893 oz. ASW **Mint:** Paris

Date	Mintage	F	VF	XF	Unc
1853A	49,000	260	425	725	2,000
1854A Proof	—	—	—	—	—
1854A	215,000	190	350	600	1,600
1855A (d)	82,000	225	385	700	2,000
1856A	241,000	150	350	600	1,600
1857A	389,000	150	320	500	1,450
1858A	1,288	450	700	1,100	3,750
1858A Proof	Inc. above	Value: 4,000			
1859A	894	600	950	1,350	5,000

KM# 780.2 2 FRANCS
10.0000 g., 0.9000 Silver .2893 oz. ASW **Mint:** Strasbourg **Note:** Date varieties exist.

Date	Mintage	F	VF	XF	Unc
1856BB	693,000	150	275	900	1,500
Note: Large mint mark					
1856BB	Inc. above	150	275	900	1,500
Note: Small mint mark					

KM# 780.3 2 FRANCS
10.0000 g., 0.9000 Silver .2893 oz. ASW **Mint:** Lyon

Date	Mintage	F	VF	XF	Unc
1856D	289,000	150	275	600	1,600

KM# 807.1 2 FRANCS
10.0000 g., 0.9000 Silver .2893 oz. ASW **Mint:** Paris

Date	Mintage	F	VF	XF	Unc
1866A	3,226,000	10.00	25.00	75.00	225
1867A	3,695,000	10.00	25.00	75.00	225
1868A	3,762,000	10.00	25.00	75.00	225
1869A	1,104,000	20.00	40.00	90.00	275
1870A	3,187,000	10.00	25.00	75.00	225

KM# 807.2 2 FRANCS
10.0000 g., 0.9000 Silver .2893 oz. ASW **Mint:** Strasbourg

Date	Mintage	F	VF	XF	Unc
1866BB	3,090,000	10.00	25.00	75.00	225
1867BB	3,471,000	10.00	25.00	75.00	225
1868BB	733,000	30.00	75.00	175	400
1869BB	367,000	35.00	90.00	200	500
1870BB	1,001,000	—	—	—	—

KM# 807.3 2 FRANCS
10.0000 g., 0.9000 Silver .2893 oz. ASW **Mint:** Bordeaux

Date	Mintage	F	VF	XF	Unc
1866K	437,000	50.00	125	250	600
1867K	1,744,000	15.00	40.00	100	275
1868K	87,000	—	—	—	—

KM# 782.1 5 FRANCS
25.0000 g., 0.9000 Silver .7234 oz. ASW **Mint:** Paris

Date	Mintage	F	VF	XF	Unc
1854A	11,000	250	500	700	1,500
1855A	4,075,000	35.00	85.00	175	800
1856A	4,683,000	35.00	85.00	175	800
1856A Proof	—	Value: 2,000			
1857A	93,000	250	500	800	2,500
1858A	27,000	275	550	900	3,000
1859A	3,365	400	1,200	2,000	3,500

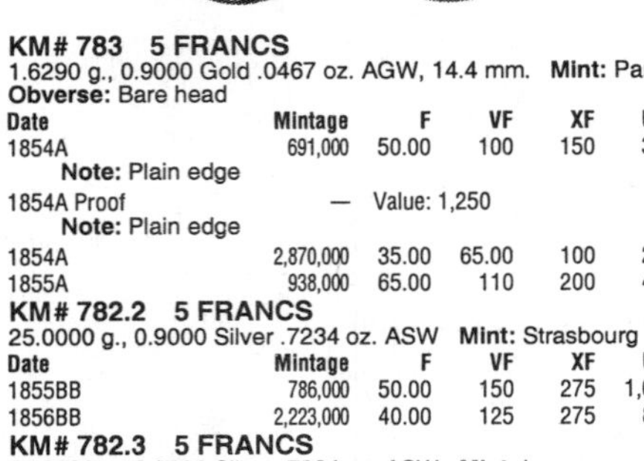

KM# 783 5 FRANCS
1.6290 g., 0.9000 Gold .0467 oz. AGW, 14.4 mm. **Mint:** Paris **Obverse:** Bare head

Date	Mintage	F	VF	XF	Unc
1854A	691,000	50.00	100	150	300
Note: Plain edge					
1854A Proof	—	Value: 1,250			
Note: Plain edge					
1854A	2,870,000	35.00	65.00	100	275
1855A	938,000	65.00	110	200	400

KM# 782.2 5 FRANCS
25.0000 g., 0.9000 Silver .7234 oz. ASW **Mint:** Strasbourg

Date	Mintage	F	VF	XF	Unc
1855BB	786,000	50.00	150	275	1,000
1856BB	2,223,000	40.00	125	275	800

KM# 782.3 5 FRANCS
25.0000 g., 0.9000 Silver .7234 oz. ASW **Mint:** Lyon

Date	Mintage	F	VF	XF	Unc
1855D	—	60.00	150	300	1,000
1856D	2,249,000	40.00	110	200	800

KM# 787.1 5 FRANCS
1.6290 g., 0.9000 Gold .0467 oz. AGW, 16.7 mm.

Date	Mintage	F	VF	XF	Unc
1856	2,960,000	30.00	40.00	65.00	225
1857	3,479,000	30.00	40.00	65.00	225
1858	2,983,000	30.00	40.00	65.00	225
1859	5,660,000	30.00	40.00	65.00	225
1860	4,798,000	30.00	40.00	65.00	225

KM# 787.2 5 FRANCS
1.6290 g., 0.9000 Gold .0467 oz. AGW **Mint:** Strasbourg

Date	Mintage	F	VF	XF	Unc
1858BB	—	65.00	125	200	450
1859BB	2,279,000	30.00	40.00	65.00	225
1860BB	2,022,000	30.00	40.00	65.00	225

KM# 799.1 5 FRANCS
25.0000 g., 0.9000 Silver .7234 oz. ASW **Mint:** Paris

Date	Mintage	F	VF	XF	Unc
1861A	22,000	225	450	850	1,900
1861A Proof	—	Value: 3,500			
1862A	21,000	225	450	850	2,000
1863A	22,000	225	450	850	2,000
1864A	32,000	225	450	850	2,000
1865A	25,000	225	450	850	2,000
1866A	38,000	225	450	850	2,000
1867A	6,586,000	10.00	20.00	90.00	275
1868A	6,634,000	10.00	20.00	90.00	275
1869A	2,056,000	15.00	30.00	125	325
1870A	6,620,000	10.00	20.00	90.00	275

KM# 799.2 5 FRANCS
25.0000 g., 0.9000 Silver .7234 oz. ASW **Mint:** Strasbourg

Date	Mintage	F	VF	XF	Unc
1865BB	73,000	225	450	900	2,000
1867BB	4,224,000	10.00	20.00	65.00	200
1868BB	12,090,000	8.00	15.00	50.00	175
1869BB	9,597,000	8.00	15.00	50.00	175
1870BB	2,055,000	12.00	30.00	90.00	275

KM# 803.1 5 FRANCS
1.6129 g., 0.9000 Gold .0467 oz. AGW **Mint:** Paris **Obverse:** Laureate head right

Date	Mintage	F	VF	XF	Unc
1862A	1,101,000	30.00	35.00	65.00	200
1863A	1,591,000	30.00	35.00	65.00	200
1864A	2,240,000	30.00	35.00	65.00	200
1865A	824,000	30.00	35.00	65.00	200
1866A	1,949,000	30.00	35.00	65.00	200
1867A	1,006,000	30.00	35.00	65.00	200
1868A	1,864,000	30.00	35.00	65.00	200

KM# 803.2 5 FRANCS
1.6129 g., 0.9000 Gold .0467 oz. AGW **Mint:** Strasbourg **Obverse:** Laureate head right

Date	Mintage	F	VF	XF	Unc
1862BB	882,000	30.00	35.00	65.00	200
1863BB	1,104,000	30.00	35.00	65.00	200
1864BB	1,000,000	30.00	35.00	65.00	200
1865BB	828,000	30.00	35.00	65.00	200
1866BB	1,388,000	30.00	35.00	65.00	200
1867BB	1,504,000	30.00	35.00	65.00	200
1868BB	439,000	30.00	35.00	70.00	225
1869BB	288,000	30.00	35.00	75.00	250

KM# 784.1 10 FRANCS
3.2258 g., 0.9000 Gold .0933 oz. AGW, 17.2 mm. **Mint:** Paris **Obverse:** Bare head

Date	Mintage	F	VF	XF	Unc
1854A	3,900,000	BV	75.00	200	800
1855A	6,117,000	BV	65.00	150	750

KM# 784.2 10 FRANCS
3.2258 g., 0.9000 Gold .0933 oz. AGW **Mint:** Paris **Obverse:** Bare head **Edge:** Plain

Date	Mintage	F	VF	XF	Unc
1854A		60.00	125	300	900
1854A Proof	—	Value: 1,750			

KM# 784.3 10 FRANCS
3.2258 g., 0.9000 Gold .0933 oz. AGW **Mint:** Paris **Obverse:** Bare head

Date	Mintage	F	VF	XF	Unc
1855A	6,117,000	BV	45.00	70.00	275
1856A	10,778,000	BV	45.00	70.00	275
1857A	14,498,000	BV	45.00	70.00	275
1858A	7,534,000	BV	45.00	70.00	275
1859A	10,111,000	BV	45.00	70.00	275
1860A	6,000,000	BV	45.00	70.00	275

KM# 784.4 10 FRANCS
3.2258 g., 0.9000 Gold .0933 oz. AGW **Mint:** Strasbourg **Obverse:** Bare head

Date	Mintage	F	VF	XF	Unc
1855BB	32,188	BV	100	150	500
1858BB	677,000	BV	45.00	80.00	275
1859BB	2,279	BV	45.00	80.00	275
1860BB	3,104,000	BV	45.00	80.00	275

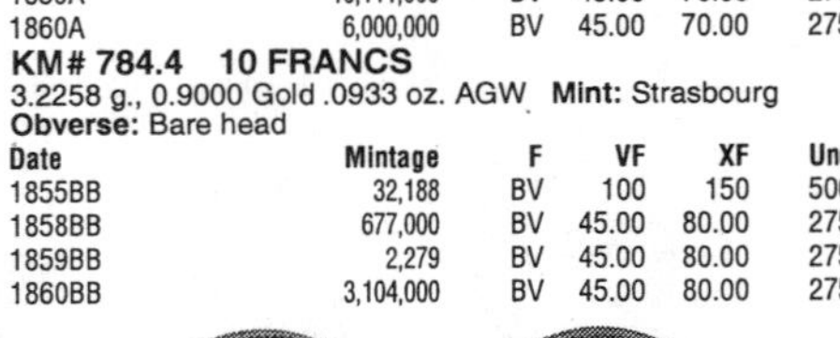

KM# 800.1 10 FRANCS
3.2258 g., 0.9000 Gold .0933 oz. AGW **Mint:** Paris **Obverse:** Laureate head

Date	Mintage	F	VF	XF	Unc
1861A	363,000	BV	75.00	125	300
1862A	2,844,000	BV	45.00	70.00	250
1863A	2,346,000	BV	45.00	70.00	250
1864A	3,339,000	BV	45.00	70.00	250
1865A	1,673,000	BV	45.00	70.00	250
1866A	3,720,000	BV	45.00	70.00	250

Date	Mintage	F	VF	XF	Unc
1867A	1,205,000	BV	45.00	70.00	250
aA	3,416,000	BV	45.00	70.00	250

KM# 800.2 10 FRANCS
3.2258 g., 0.9000 Gold .0933 oz. AGW **Mint:** Strasbourg
Obverse: Laureate head

Date	Mintage	F	VF	XF	Unc
1861BB	44,000	75.00	100	150	300
1862BB	1,462,000	BV	45.00	70.00	250
1863BB	1,905,000	BV	45.00	70.00	250
1864BB	1,449,000	BV	45.00	70.00	250
1865BB	1,576,000	BV	45.00	70.00	250
1866BB	2,776,000	BV	45.00	70.00	250
1867BB	2,346,000	BV	45.00	70.00	250
1868BB	1,117,000	BV	45.00	70.00	250
1869BB	109,000	50.00	75.00	125	250

KM# 774 20 FRANCS
6.4516 g., 0.9000 Gold .1867 oz. AGW **Mint:** Paris

Date	Mintage	F	VF	XF	Unc
1852A	10,494,000	BV	75.00	90.00	475
1852A Proof	—	Value: 3,250			

KM# 781.1 20 FRANCS
6.4516 g., 0.9000 Gold .1867 oz. AGW **Mint:** Paris

Date	Mintage	F	VF	XF	Unc
1853A	5,729,000	BV	70.00	80.00	170
1853A Proof	—	Value: 2,850			
1854A	23,486,000	BV	70.00	80.00	125
1854A Proof	—	Value: 2,600			
1855A (d)	16,595,000	BV	70.00	80.00	170
1855A (a)	Inc. above	BV	70.00	80.00	170
1856A	17,303,000	BV	70.00	80.00	170
1857A	19,193,000	BV	70.00	80.00	170
1858A	16,861,000	BV	70.00	80.00	170
1859A	20,295,000	BV	70.00	80.00	170
1860A	10,220,000	BV	70.00	80.00	170

KM# 781.2 20 FRANCS
6.4516 g., 0.9000 Gold .1867 oz. AGW **Mint:** Strasbourg

Date	Mintage	F	VF	XF	Unc
1855BB	1,760,000	BV	75.00	90.00	175
1856BB	1,125,000	BV	75.00	90.00	175
1858BB	2,017,000	BV	75.00	90.00	175
1859BB	5,871,000	BV	70.00	80.00	140
1860BB	5,727,000	BV	70.00	80.00	140

KM# 781.3 20 FRANCS
6.4516 g., 0.9000 Gold .1867 oz. AGW **Mint:** Lyon

Date	Mintage	F	VF	XF	Unc
1855D	45,000	100	100	150	400

KM# 801.1 20 FRANCS
6.4516 g., 0.9000 Gold .1867 oz. AGW **Mint:** Paris

Date	Mintage	F	VF	XF	Unc
1861A	2,607,000	BV	70.00	80.00	140
1861A Proof	—	Value: 3,000			
1862A	4,826,000	BV	70.00	80.00	140
1863A	3,920,000	BV	70.00	80.00	140
1864A	7,059,000	BV	70.00	80.00	140
1865A	2,951,000	BV	70.00	80.00	140
1866A	6,992,000	BV	70.00	80.00	140
1867A	2,923,000	BV	70.00	80.00	140
1868A	9,281,000	BV	70.00	80.00	140
1869A	4,046,000	BV	70.00	80.00	140
1870A	865,000	BV	70.00	80.00	150

KM# 801.2 20 FRANCS
6.4516 g., 0.9000 Gold .1867 oz. AGW **Mint:** Strasbourg

Date	Mintage	F	VF	XF	Unc
1861BB	1,423,000	BV	70.00	80.00	140
1862BB	2,907,000	BV	70.00	80.00	140
1863BB	4,753,000	BV	70.00	80.00	140
1864BB	3,323,000	BV	70.00	80.00	140
1865BB	3,088,000	BV	70.00	80.00	140
1866BB	6,979,000	BV	70.00	80.00	140
1867BB	4,516,000	BV	70.00	80.00	140
1868BB	4,829,000	BV	70.00	80.00	140

Date	Mintage	F	VF	XF	Unc
1869BB	7,317,000	BV	70.00	80.00	140
1870BB	1,853,000	BV	70.00	80.00	150

KM# 785.1 50 FRANCS
16.1290 g., 0.9000 Gold .4667 oz. AGW **Mint:** Paris **Obverse:** Bare head right

Date	Mintage	F	VF	XF	Unc
1855A	152,000	250	275	300	500
1856A	97,000	250	275	350	550
1857A	320,000	250	275	300	500
1858A	85,000	250	275	350	550
1859A	34,000	250	275	350	500

KM# 785.2 50 FRANCS
16.1290 g., 0.9000 Gold .4667 oz. AGW **Mint:** Strasbourg
Obverse: Bare head right

Date	Mintage	F	VF	XF	Unc
1855BB	3,051	250	350	600	1,000
1856BB	3,803	250	375	600	1,000
1858BB	9,135	250	350	550	1,000
1859BB	32,000	250	275	400	600
1860BB	29,000	—	—	—	—

KM# 804.1 50 FRANCS
16.1290 g., 0.9000 Gold .4667 oz. AGW **Mint:** Paris **Obverse:** Laureate head right

Date	Mintage	F	VF	XF	Unc
1862A	24,000	225	250	350	700
1862A Proof	—	Value: 7,500			
1864A	29,000	225	250	350	700
1865A	3,740	225	365	550	950
1866A	39,000	225	250	350	700
1867A	2,000	225	365	550	950
1868A	16,000	225	250	350	750

KM# 804.2 50 FRANCS
16.1290 g., 0.9000 Gold .4667 oz. AGW **Mint:** Strasbourg
Obverse: Laureate head right

Date	Mintage	F	VF	XF	Unc
1862BB	7,310	225	275	375	850
1863BB	8,251	225	275	375	850
1866BB	17,000	225	250	350	700
1867BB	20,000	225	250	350	700
1868BB	1,795	325	400	600	1,250

KM# 786.1 100 FRANCS
32.2581 g., 0.9000 Gold .9335 oz. AGW **Mint:** Paris

Date	Mintage	F	VF	XF	Unc
1855A	51,000	450	500	550	900
1856A	57,000	450	500	550	900
1857A	103,000	450	500	550	900
1858A	92,000	450	500	550	900
1859A	22,000	450	500	550	900

KM# 786.2 100 FRANCS
32.2581 g., 0.9000 Gold .9335 oz. AGW **Mint:** Strasbourg

Date	Mintage	F	VF	XF	Unc
1855BB	4,173	450	500	600	1,150
1856BB	876	600	1,000	1,500	3,000
1858BB	1,928	475	525	625	1,300
1859BB	9,305	450	500	550	1,100
1860BB	5,405	450	500	600	1,150

KM# 802.1 100 FRANCS
32.2581 g., 0.9000 Gold .9335 oz. AGW **Mint:** Paris

Date	Mintage	F	VF	XF	Unc
1861A Proof	—	Value: 10,000			
1862A	6,650	450	550	750	1,200
1864A	5,536	450	550	750	1,200
1865A	1,517	475	600	1,000	1,800
1866A	9,041	450	550	700	1,100
1867A	4,309	450	550	750	1,200
1868A	2,315	450	550	1,000	1,800
1869A	29,000	450	500	700	1,100
1870A	10,000	3,000	6,000	12,000	20,000

KM# 802.2 100 FRANCS
32.2581 g., 0.9000 Gold .9335 oz. AGW **Mint:** Strasbourg

Date	Mintage	F	VF	XF	Unc
1862BB	3,078	450	600	800	1,400
1863BB	3,745	450	600	800	1,400
1864BB	1,333	475	600	850	1,800
1866BB	3,075	450	600	850	1,600
1867BB	2,807	450	600	850	1,600
1868BB	789	525	800	1,200	2,000
1869BB	14,000	450	550	750	1,100

MODERN REPUBLICS

1870-

DECIMAL COINAGE

KM# 826.1 CENTIME
Bronze **Mint:** Paris **Note:** Third Republic, 1870-1940.

Date	Mintage	F	VF	XF	Unc
1872A	1,250,000	2.00	5.00	9.00	15.00
1874A	1,000,000	2.00	5.00	9.00	15.00
1875A	1,000,000	2.00	5.00	9.00	15.00
1877A	1,000,000	2.00	5.00	9.00	15.00
1878A	1,500,000	1.50	3.00	7.00	12.00
1879A (ab)	800,000	2.00	6.00	11.00	16.00
1882A	419,000	3.00	9.00	16.00	30.00
1884A	400,000	4.00	10.00	18.00	35.00
1885A	400,000	3.00	9.00	16.00	30.00
1886A	400,000	3.00	9.00	16.00	30.00
1887A	400,000	3.00	9.00	16.00	30.00
1888A	400,000	3.00	9.00	16.00	30.00
1889A	400,000	3.00	9.00	16.00	30.00
1890A	400,000	3.00	9.00	16.00	30.00
1891A	1,400,000	0.75	4.00	8.00	12.00
1892A	800,000	1.00	5.00	10.00	18.00
1893A	300,000	3.00	9.00	16.00	30.00
1894A	500,000	2.00	7.00	14.00	22.00
1895A	3,000,000	1.50	2.50	5.00	10.00
1896A (f)	3,000,000	1.50	2.50	5.00	10.00
1897A	2,000,000	2.00	3.00	6.00	12.00

KM# 826.2 CENTIME
Bronze **Mint:** Bordeaux **Note:** Third Republic, 1870-1940.

Date	Mintage	F	VF	XF	Unc
1872K	750,000	3.00	9.00	16.00	30.00
1875K	2,000,000	2.00	5.00	9.00	15.00
1878K	289,000	10.00	20.00	45.00	80.00

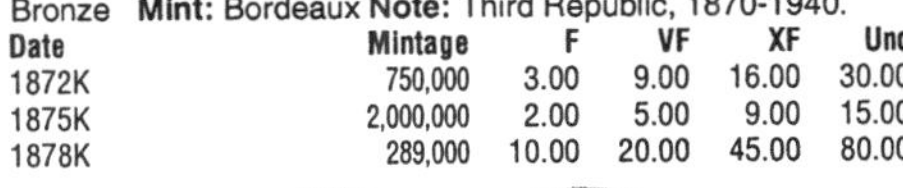

KM# 840 CENTIME
Bronze **Mint:** Paris **Note:** Without mint mark or privy mark. Struck at Paris Mint.

Date	Mintage	F	VF	XF	Unc
1898	250,000	3.00	8.00	15.00	25.00
1898 Proof	—	Value: 300			
1899	1,500,000	1.00	2.00	4.00	12.00
1900	221,000	15.00	30.00	55.00	100
1900 Proof	—	Value: 335			

KM# 827.1 2 CENTIMES

Bronze **Mint:** Paris **Note:** Third Republic.

Date	Mintage	F	VF	XF	Unc
1877A	500,000	3.00	6.00	10.00	18.00
1878A	750,000	2.00	4.00	8.00	15.00
1879A (ab)	600,000	2.00	4.00	8.00	15.00
1882A	290,000	4.00	8.00	18.00	35.00
1883A	500,000	3.00	6.00	10.00	18.00
1884A	300,000	4.00	8.00	15.00	25.00
1885A	300,000	4.00	8.00	15.00	25.00
1886A	300,000	4.00	8.00	15.00	25.00
1887A	300,000	4.00	8.00	15.00	25.00
1888A	400,000	3.00	6.00	12.00	18.00
1889A	600,000	2.00	4.00	8.00	15.00
1890A	300,000	4.00	8.00	15.00	25.00
1891A	300,000	4.00	8.00	15.00	25.00
1892A	500,000	3.00	6.00	10.00	18.00
1893A	250,000	8.00	15.00	35.00	50.00
1894A	150,000	10.00	20.00	40.00	70.00
1895A	1,000,000	1.00	3.00	5.00	10.00
1896A (f)	1,000,000	1.00	3.00	5.00	10.00
1897A	1,250,000	0.75	2.00	4.00	8.00

KM# 827.2 2 CENTIMES

Bronze **Mint:** Bordeaux

Date	Mintage	F	VF	XF	Unc
1878K	363,000	3.00	8.00	16.00	25.00

KM# 841 2 CENTIMES

Bronze **Mint:** Paris **Note:** Without mark mark or privy mark. Struck at Paris Mint.

Date	Mintage	F	VF	XF	Unc
1898	125,000	4.00	10.00	15.00	25.00
1898 Proof	—	Value: 300			
1899	750,000	2.00	5.00	10.00	20.00
1900	101,000	40.00	75.00	150	200
1900 Proof	—	Value: 325			

KM# 821.1 5 CENTIMES

Bronze **Mint:** Paris **Note:** Third Republic, 1870-1940.

Date	Mintage	F	VF	XF	Unc
1871A	2,238,000	3.00	8.00	18.00	40.00
1872A	4,263,000	2.00	5.00	10.00	20.00
1873A	1,492,000	4.00	10.00	20.00	50.00
1874A	1,730,000	4.00	10.00	20.00	50.00
1875A	1,193,000	4.00	10.00	20.00	50.00
1876A	2,481,000	2.00	5.00	12.00	25.00
1877A	766,000	10.00	25.00	40.00	100
1878A	300,000	25.00	50.00	100	175
1879A (a)	1,955,000	2.00	5.00	10.00	20.00
1879A Anchor with bar	Inc. above	30.00	50.00	125	200
1880A	1,172,000	4.00	10.00	20.00	50.00
1881A	2,502,000	2.00	5.00	10.00	20.00
1882A	1,600,000	3.00	8.00	18.00	40.00
1883A	2,400,000	2.00	5.00	10.00	20.00
1884A	1,680,000	3.00	8.00	18.00	40.00
1885A	2,000,000	2.00	5.00	10.00	20.00
1886A	1,680,000	3.00	8.00	18.00	40.00
1887A	1,008,000	4.00	10.00	20.00	50.00
1888A	1,660,000	2.00	5.00	12.00	25.00
1889A	1,660,000	2.00	5.00	12.00	25.00
1890A	1,680,000	2.00	5.00	12.00	25.00
1891A	1,600,000	2.00	5.00	12.00	25.00
1892A	1,600,000	2.00	5.00	12.00	25.00
1893A	1,600,000	2.00	5.00	12.00	25.00
1894A	2,240,000	1.50	4.00	8.00	18.00
1896A	6,695,000	1.00	2.00	5.00	12.00
1896A	Inc. above	40.00	85.00	200	400
1897A	12,600,000	1.00	2.00	5.00	12.00
1898A	1,200,000	4.00	10.00	20.00	50.00

KM# 821.2 5 CENTIMES

Bronze **Mint:** Bordeaux

Date	Mintage	F	VF	XF	Unc
1871K	16,000	100	200	300	500
1872K	4,064,000	2.00	5.00	10.00	20.00
1873K	1,997,000	4.00	10.00	20.00	50.00
1874K	1,326,000	5.00	12.00	22.00	55.00
1875K	760,000	10.00	25.00	40.00	100
1876K	1,597,000	5.00	12.00	22.00	55.00
1877K	1,193,000	6.00	15.00	25.00	65.00
1878K	166,000	40.00	85.00	175	325

KM# 842 5 CENTIMES

Bronze **Mint:** Paris **Note:** Without mint mark. Struck at Paris Mint.

Date	Mintage	F	VF	XF	Unc
1898	7,900,000	1.00	3.00	8.00	18.00
1898 Proof	—	Value: 350			
1899	7,400,000	1.00	3.00	8.00	18.00
1900	7,400,000	1.00	3.00	8.00	18.00
1900 Proof	—	Value: 350			

KM# 815.1 10 CENTIMES

Bronze **Mint:** Paris **Note:** Third Republic, 1870-1940.

Date	Mintage	F	VF	XF	Unc
1870A	889,000	3.00	10.00	28.00	65.00
1871A	1,840,000	2.00	8.00	20.00	45.00
1872A	4,399,000	1.00	4.00	8.00	25.00
1873A	2,096,000	1.50	5.00	10.00	30.00
1874A	1,194,000	2.50	7.00	20.00	45.00
1875A	1,434,000	30.00	65.00	175	300
1876A	458,000	8.00	25.00	50.00	90.00
1877A	392,000	12.00	35.00	65.00	135
1878A	150,000	15.00	40.00	75.00	160
1879A	823,000	4.00	12.00	28.00	55.00
1880A	1,414,000	2.00	6.00	18.00	40.00
1881A	749,000	4.00	12.00	28.00	55.00
1882A	1,100,000	2.00	8.00	20.00	45.00
1883A	700,000	6.00	20.00	40.00	80.00
1884A	1,060,000	2.00	8.00	20.00	45.00
1885A	900,000	2.50	7.00	20.00	45.00
1886A	1,060,000	2.00	8.00	20.00	45.00
1887A	874,000	2.50	7.00	20.00	45.00
1888A	1,050,000	2.00	8.00	20.00	45.00
1889A	1,010,000	2.00	8.00	20.00	45.00
1890A	1,060,000	2.00	8.00	20.00	45.00
1891A	1,000,000	2.00	8.00	20.00	45.00
1892A	1,020,000	2.00	8.00	20.00	45.00
1893A	1,120,000	2.00	8.00	20.00	45.00
1894A	800,000	2.50	10.00	25.00	50.00
1895A	600,000	3.00	8.00	28.00	55.00
1896A (f)	Inc. above	1.00	3.00	8.00	30.00
1896A (t)	Inc. above	30.00	75.00	250	450
1897A	7,250,000	0.50	3.00	6.00	15.00
1898A	1,400,000	2.00	6.00	18.00	40.00

KM# 815.2 10 CENTIMES

Bronze **Mint:** Bordeaux **Note:** Third Republic, 1870-1940.

Date	Mintage	F	VF	XF	Unc
1871K	27,000	75.00	175	300	650
1872K	4,359,000	1.00	4.00	8.00	25.00
1873K	2,001,000	2.00	6.00	18.00	40.00
1874K	1,337,000	6.00	20.00	40.00	80.00
1875K	430,000	6.00	20.00	40.00	80.00
1876K	601,000	5.00	18.00	35.00	75.00
1877K	403,000	6.00	20.00	40.00	80.00
1878K	100,000	40.00	100	175	300

KM# 843 10 CENTIMES

Bronze **Mint:** Paris **Note:** Without mint mark. Struck at Paris Mint.

Date	Mintage	F	VF	XF	Unc
1898	4,000,000	1.00	3.00	8.00	20.00
1898 Matte Proof	—	Value: 450			
1899	4,000,000	1.00	3.00	8.00	20.00
1900 (n)	5,000,000	1.00	3.00	8.00	20.00
1900 (n) Proof	—	Value: 425			

KM# 828.1 20 CENTIMES

1.0000 g., 0.9000 Silver .0289 oz. ASW, 15 mm. **Mint:** Paris

Date	Mintage	F	VF	XF	Unc
1878A	30	—	—	1,700	2,300

KM# 828.2 20 CENTIMES

1.0000 g., 0.9000 Silver .0289 oz. ASW, 16 mm. **Mint:** Paris **Note:** Considered an Essai.

Date	Mintage	F	VF	XF	Unc
1889	100	—	—	950	1,500

KM# 834.1 50 CENTIMES

2.5000 g., 0.8350 Silver .0671 oz. ASW **Mint:** Paris **Note:** Third Republic.

Date	Mintage	F	VF	XF	Unc
1871A	236,000	15.00	40.00	100	225
1872A	4,243,000	4.00	10.00	25.00	60.00
1873A	926,000	10.00	25.00	60.00	125
1874A	1,228,000	8.00	15.00	35.00	80.00
1878A Proof	30	Value: 2,400			
1881A	5,391,000	2.00	4.00	15.00	60.00
1882A	2,320,000	3.00	6.00	20.00	60.00
1886A	309,000	15.00	40.00	100	225
1887A	1,866,000	6.00	12.00	25.00	65.00
1888A	4,517,000	1.50	3.00	15.00	60.00
1889A Proof	100	Value: 2,000			
1894A	3,600,000	1.50	3.00	15.00	60.00
1895A	7,200,000	1.50	3.00	10.00	55.00

KM# 834.2 50 CENTIMES

2.5000 g., 0.8350 Silver .0671 oz. ASW **Mint:** Bordeaux **Note:** Third Republic.

Date	Mintage	F	VF	XF	Unc
1871K	723,000	8.00	15.00	40.00	85.00
1872K	1,643,000	7.00	14.00	30.00	70.00
1873K	166,000	100	250	450	800

KM# 854 50 CENTIMES

2.5000 g., 0.8350 Silver .0671 oz. ASW **Mint:** Paris **Note:** Without mint mark. Struck at Paris Mint.

Date	Mintage	F	VF	XF	Unc
1897	88,000	30.00	75.00	125	200
1897 Proof	—	Value: 300			
1898	30,000,000	1.00	2.00	10.00	20.00
1898 Proof	—	Value: 300			
1899	18,000,000	1.50	3.00	8.00	35.00
1900	9,195,000	3.00	6.00	15.00	45.00
1900 Proof	—	Value: 300			

KM# 822.1 FRANC

5.0000 g., 0.8350 Silver .1342 oz. ASW **Mint:** Paris **Note:** Third Republic.

Date	Mintage	F	VF	XF	Unc
1871A Small A	2,980,000	4.00	8.00	25.00	75.00
1871A Large A	Inc. above	3.00	6.00	20.00	70.00
1872A Small A	10,129,000	2.00	4.00	15.00	65.00
1872A Large A	Inc. above	10.00	25.00	50.00	100
1878A Proof	30	Value: 2,800			
1881A	2,010,000	4.00	8.00	25.00	75.00
1887A	3,292,000	4.00	8.00	25.00	75.00
1888A	3,244,000	4.00	8.00	25.00	75.00
1889A Proof	100	Value: 2,300			
1894A	1,600,000	4.00	8.00	25.00	75.00
1895A	3,200,000	4.00	8.00	25.00	75.00

KM# 822.2 FRANC

5.0000 g., 0.8350 Silver .1342 oz. ASW **Mint:** Bordeaux **Note:** Third Republic.

Date	Mintage	F	VF	XF	Unc
1871K Small K	1,252,000	4.00	8.00	25.00	75.00
1871K Large K	Inc. above	3.00	6.00	20.00	70.00
1872K Large K	5,779,000	15.00	35.00	65.00	150
1872K Small K	Inc. above	4.00	8.00	25.00	75.00
1873K	19,000	150	350	700	1,200

KM# 844.1 FRANC
5.0000 g., 0.8350 Silver .1342 oz. ASW **Mint:** Paris **Note:** Without mint mark. Struck at Paris Mint.

Date	Mintage	F	VF	XF	Unc
1898	15,000,000	1.50	2.50	5.00	30.00
1898 Proof	—	Value: 400			
1899	11,000,000	1.50	3.00	7.00	35.00
1900	99,000	125	225	450	850
1900 Proof	—	Value: 425			

KM# 816.1 2 FRANCS
10.0000 g., 0.9000 Silver .2893 oz. ASW **Mint:** Paris **Note:** Third Republic.

Date	Mintage	F	VF	XF	Unc
1870A	239,000	50.00	125	350	750

KM# 816.2 2 FRANCS
10.0000 g., 0.9000 Silver .2893 oz. ASW **Mint:** Bordeaux **Note:** Third Republic.

Date	Mintage	F	VF	XF	Unc
1870K (a)	560,000	50.00	100	275	600
1870K (s)	Inc. above	50.00	100	275	645
1871K	1,256,000	40.00	125	300	750

KM# 817.1 2 FRANCS
10.0000 g., 0.8350 Silver .2684 oz. ASW **Mint:** Paris **Note:** Third Republic.

Date	Mintage	F	VF	XF	Unc
1870A	1,324,000	8.00	18.00	50.00	175
Note: Large A					
1870A	Inc. above	10.00	20.00	60.00	200
Note: Small A					
1871A	4,757,000	7.00	15.00	40.00	175
Note: Large A					
1871A	Inc. above	7.00	15.00	40.00	175
Note: Small A					
1872A	2,306,000	7.00	15.00	40.00	175
1873A	528,000	30.00	75.00	175	400
1878A Proof	30	Value: 4,500			
1881A	1,014,000	10.00	30.00	75.00	200
1887A	2,343,000	7.00	15.00	40.00	150
1888A	131,000	65.00	150	300	650
1889A Proof	100	Value: 4,000			
1894A	300,000	15.00	40.00	100	200
1895A	600,000	12.00	30.00	75.00	175

KM# 817.2 2 FRANCS
10.0000 g., 0.8350 Silver .2684 oz. ASW **Mint:** Bordeaux **Note:** Third Republic.

Date	Mintage	F	VF	XF	Unc
1871K	1,215,000	15.00	40.00	100	250
Note: Large K					
1871K	Inc. above	12.00	30.00	75.00	200
Note: Small K					
1872K	1,467,000	12.00	30.00	75.00	200

KM# 845.1 2 FRANCS
10.0000 g., 0.8350 Silver .2684 oz. ASW **Mint:** Paris **Note:** Without mint mark.

Date	Mintage	F	VF	XF	Unc
1898	5,000,000	3.00	5.00	20.00	45.00
1898 Proof	—	Value: 425			
1899	3,500,000	4.00	7.00	25.00	50.00
1900	500,000	30.00	80.00	200	450
1900 Proof	—	Value: 400			

KM# 818.1 5 FRANCS
25.0000 g., 0.9000 Silver .7234 oz. ASW **Mint:** Paris **Obverse:** E. A. OUDINE F. below truncation

Date	Mintage	F	VF	XF	Unc
1870A (a)	64,000	50.00	125	450	850

KM# 818.2 5 FRANCS
25.0000 g., 0.9000 Silver .7234 oz. ASW **Mint:** Bordeaux **Obverse:** E. A. OUDINE F. below truncation

Date	Mintage	F	VF	XF	Unc
1870K (a)	544,000	60.00	150	550	1,000
1870K M/star	Inc. above	50.00	125	450	800
1871K M/star	630,000	45.00	110	400	700

KM# 818.3 5 FRANCS
25.0000 g., 0.9000 Silver .7234 oz. ASW **Mint:** Bordeaux **Obverse:** A. E. OUDINE F. (error) below truncation

Date	F	VF	XF	Unc
1870K M/star	300	650	1,200	1,800

KM# 818.4 5 FRANCS
25.0000 g., 0.9000 Silver .7234 oz. ASW **Mint:** Bordeaux **Obverse:** E. A. OUDI"J"E F. (error) below truncation

Date	F	VF	XF	Unc
1870K M/star	—	—	—	—

Note: Reported, not confirmed

KM# 819 5 FRANCS
25.0000 g., 0.9000 Silver .7234 oz. ASW **Mint:** Paris **Note:** Third Republic.

Date	Mintage	F	VF	XF	Unc
1870A	1,185,000	30.00	125	250	600

KM# 820.1 5 FRANCS
25.0000 g., 0.9000 Silver .7234 oz. ASW **Mint:** Paris **Obverse:** Similar to KM#823

Date	Mintage	F	VF	XF	Unc
1870A	261,000	45.00	125	275	500
1871A	238,000	50.00	150	300	600
1872A	57,000	45.00	125	275	500
1873A	27,077,000	7.00	9.00	12.00	25.00
1874A	7,999,000	8.00	10.00	25.00	60.00
1875A	13,339,000	8.00	10.00	18.00	50.00
Note: Varieties of mint mark size exist for 1875 dated coins					
1876A	8,800,000	8.00	10.00	25.00	60.00
1877A	2,632,000	12.00	20.00	40.00	90.00
1878A	1,154	600	1,200	2,000	4,000
1878A Proof	30	Value: 4,500			
1889A C Proof	20	Value: 8,000			

KM# 820.2 5 FRANCS
25.0000 g., 0.9000 Silver .7234 oz. ASW **Mint:** Bordeaux **Obverse:** Similar to KM#823

Date	Mintage	F	VF	XF	Unc
1871K	75,000	100	250	500	900
1872K	21,000	300	500	850	2,000
1873K	3,853,000	8.00	11.00	25.00	60.00
1874K	4,000,000	8.00	11.00	25.00	60.00
1875K	1,661,000	15.00	30.00	50.00	150
1876K	1,732,000	15.00	30.00	50.00	150

Date	Mintage	F	VF	XF	Unc
1877K	661,000	20.00	35.00	75.00	250
1878K	263,000	40.00	100	200	450

Trident

KM# 823 5 FRANCS
25.0000 g., 0.9000 Silver .7234 oz. ASW **Mint:** Paris **Edge Lettering:** DIEU PROTEGE LA FRANCE **Note:** Trident symbol - issued by commune.

Date	Mintage	F	VF	XF	Unc
1871A	75,000	200	350	675	1,500

KM# 829 5 FRANCS
1.6929 g., 0.9000 Gold .0467 oz. AGW **Mint:** Paris **Edge Lettering:** DIEU PROTEGE LA FRANCE

Date	Mintage	F	VF	XF	Unc
1878A Proof	30	Value: 6,500			
1889A Proof	40	Value: 5,250			

KM# 830 10 FRANCS
3.2258 g., 0.9000 Gold .0933 oz. AGW **Mint:** Paris

Date	Mintage	F	VF	XF	Unc
1878A Proof	30	Value: 5,250			
1889A Proof	100	Value: 4,750			
1895A	214,000	BV	45.00	60.00	200
1896A	585,000	BV	45.00	60.00	125
1899A	1,600,000	BV	45.00	60.00	125

KM# 846 10 FRANCS
3.2258 g., 0.9000 Gold .0933 oz. AGW **Mint:** Paris **Note:** Without mint mark. Struck at Paris Mint.

Date	Mintage	F	VF	XF	Unc
1899	699,000	BV	45.00	60.00	120
1899 Matte Proof	—	Value: 900			
1900	1,570,000	BV	42.00	52.00	80.00
1900 Proof	—	Value: 800			

KM# 825 20 FRANCS
6.4516 g., 0.9000 Gold .1867 oz. AGW **Mint:** Paris

Date	Mintage	F	VF	XF	Unc
1871A	2,508,000	BV	70.00	80.00	125
1874A	1,216,000	BV	70.00	80.00	135
1875A	11,746,000	BV	70.00	80.00	135
1876A	8,825,000	BV	70.00	80.00	135
1877A	12,759,000	BV	70.00	80.00	135
1878A	9,189,000	BV	70.00	80.00	135
1878A Proof	30	Value: 5,000			
1879A	1,038,000	BV	70.00	80.00	135
1886A	985,000	BV	70.00	80.00	135
1887A	1,231,000	BV	70.00	80.00	135
1887A Proof	—	Value: 5,250			

Date	Mintage	F	VF	XF	Unc
1888A	28,000	BV	100	150	275
1889A	873,000	BV	70.00	80.00	135
1889A Proof	100	Value: 4,250			
1890A	1,030,000	BV	70.00	80.00	135
1891A	871,000	BV	70.00	80.00	135
1892A	226,000	BV	70.00	80.00	135
1893A	2,517,000	BV	70.00	80.00	135
1894A	491,000	BV	70.00	80.00	135
1895A	5,293,000	BV	70.00	80.00	135
1896A	5,330,000	BV	70.00	80.00	135
1897A	11,069,000	BV	70.00	80.00	135
1898A	8,866,000	BV	70.00	80.00	120

KM# 847 20 FRANCS
6.4516 g., 0.9000 Gold .1867 oz. AGW **Edge Lettering:** DIEU PROTEGE LA FRANCE

Date	Mintage	F	VF	XF	Unc
1899	1,500,000	—	BV	80.00	135
1899 Proof	—	Value: 1,250			
1900	615,000	—	BV	80.00	125
1900 Proof	Inc. above	Value: 1,000			

KM# 831 50 FRANCS
16.1290 g., 0.9000 Gold .4467 oz. AGW **Mint:** Paris

Date	Mintage	F	VF	XF	Unc
1878A	5,294	350	700	1,350	2,000
1887A	301	550	1,250	2,250	3,700
1889A Proof	100	Value: 7,000			
1896A	800	450	900	1,800	2,800
1900A	200	650	1,500	2,500	4,500
1900A Proof	—	Value: 8,000			

KM# 832 100 FRANCS
32.2581 g., 0.9000 Gold .9335 oz. AGW **Mint:** Paris **Edge Lettering:** DIEU PROTEGE LA FRANCE

Date	Mintage	F	VF	XF	Unc
1878A	13,000	450	475	525	650
1878A Proof	30	Value: 14,000			
1879A	39,000	450	475	525	650
1881A	22,000	450	475	525	650
1882A	37,000	450	475	525	650
1885A	2,894	450	650	850	1,150
1886A	39,000	450	475	525	675
1887A	234	750	1,750	3,500	6,500
1889A Proof	100	Value: 12,000			
1894A	143	1,250	2,750	5,500	10,000
1896A	400	500	1,000	2,500	5,000
1899A	10,000	450	475	525	675

ESSAIS

Standard metals unless otherwise noted

KM#	Date	Mintage	Identification	Mkt Val
E5	(1815-24)	—	Non-Denominated. Bust of Louis XVIII left. Crowned arms in crossed branches above ESSAI	—
E6	(1815-24)	—	Non-Denominated. Uniformed bust of Louis XVIII left	—
E7	1816	—	1/4 Franc. Napoleon II left. Denomination within wreath, date below	—
E-A8	1816	—	5 Centimes. Napoleon II left. Denomination within wreath, date below	—
E8	1821A	—	10 Centimes. Bust of Louis XVIII left. Denomination above date	165
E9	1824A	—	20 Francs. Bust of Louis XVIII right. Crowned arms in branches above date, KM#726.1	150
E10	(ca.1840)	—	Decime. Laureate bust of Louis Philippe left. Denomination in wreath, ESSAI below	150
E11	1847	—	2 Centimes. Laureate bust of Louis Philippe left. Crown above branches, denomination and date below	120
E12	1848	—	5 Centimes. Liberty standing with shield and Liberty cap on pole. Denomination and ESSAI within wreath	135
E13	1848	—	20 Francs. Gold.	—
E14	1848A	—	20 Francs. Gold.	4,000
E15	1851	—	5 Centimes. Bronze. Crowned tablet divides CINQ-CENT. ESSAI/DE BRONZE/1851	—
E16	1851	—	10 Centimes. Bronze.	—
E17	1851	—	Decime. Bronze. Crowned tablet divides UN-DE	—
E18	1852	—	10 Centimes. KM#771.	200
E19	1854	—	100 Francs. Napoleon III, ESSAI and date below. Eagle on crowned and mantled shield	—
E20	(1855)	—	10 Centimes. Nickel. 10 CENTS in inner circle. ESSAI/DE/MONNAIES/EN/NICKEL	—
E-A21	1855	—	10 Francs. Gold. Bare head, date below. Denomination in wreath	1,250

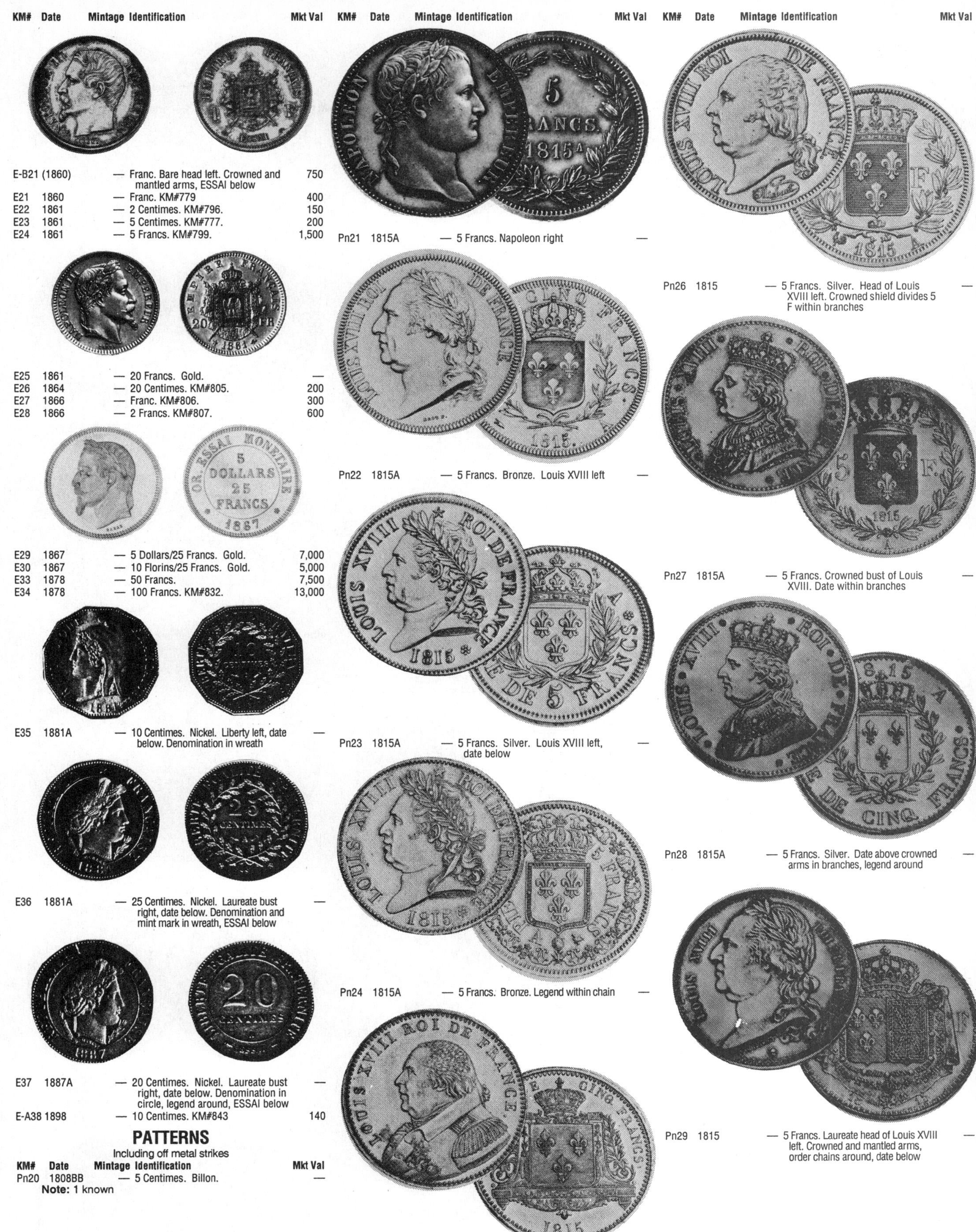

KM#	Date	Mintage	Identification	Mkt Val
E-B21	(1860)	—	Franc. Bare head left. Crowned and mantled arms, ESSAI below	750
E21	1860	—	Franc. KM#779	400
E22	1861	—	2 Centimes. KM#796.	150
E23	1861	—	5 Centimes. KM#777.	200
E24	1861	—	5 Francs. KM#799.	1,500
E25	1861	—	20 Francs. Gold.	—
E26	1864	—	20 Centimes. KM#805.	200
E27	1866	—	Franc. KM#806.	300
E28	1866	—	2 Francs. KM#807.	600
E29	1867	—	5 Dollars/25 Francs. Gold.	7,000
E30	1867	—	10 Florins/25 Francs. Gold.	5,000
E33	1878	—	50 Francs.	7,500
E34	1878	—	100 Francs. KM#832.	13,000
E35	1881A	—	10 Centimes. Nickel. Liberty left, date below. Denomination in wreath	—
E36	1881A	—	25 Centimes. Nickel. Laureate bust right, date below. Denomination and mint mark in wreath, ESSAI below	—
E37	1887A	—	20 Centimes. Nickel. Laureate bust right, date below. Denomination in circle, legend around, ESSAI below	—
E-A38	1898	—	10 Centimes. KM#843	140

PATTERNS

Including off metal strikes

KM#	Date	Mintage	Identification	Mkt Val
Pn20	1808BB	—	5 Centimes. Billon.	—
Pn21	1815A	—	5 Francs. Napoleon right	—
Pn22	1815A	—	5 Francs. Bronze. Louis XVIII left	—
Pn23	1815A	—	5 Francs. Silver. Louis XVIII left, date below	—
Pn24	1815A	—	5 Francs. Bronze. Legend within chain	—
Pn25	1815	—	5 Francs. Bronze. Uniformed bust of Louis XVIII. Ornately draped arms, date below	—
Pn26	1815	—	5 Francs. Silver. Head of Louis XVIII left. Crowned shield divides 5 F within branches	—
Pn27	1815A	—	5 Francs. Crowned bust of Louis XVIII. Date within branches	—
Pn28	1815A	—	5 Francs. Silver. Date above crowned arms in branches, legend around	—
Pn29	1815	—	5 Francs. Laureate head of Louis XVIII left. Crowned and mantled arms, order chains around, date below	—

Note: 1 known (Pn20)

KM#	Date	Mintage	Identification	Mkt Val
Pn30	1815	—	5 Francs. Tin. Plain head of Louis XVIII left, date below. Crowned round arms above denomination	—
Pn31	1815A	—	5 Francs. Bronze. Uniformed bust of Louis XVIII left. Crowned arms above crossed branches, date	—
Pn32	1824A	—	5 Francs. Bust of Charles X left. Crowned arms divide 5 F above branches, date below	—
Pn33	1830A	—	5 Francs. Gold. Galle	5,000
PnA34	1831A	—	5 Francs. Pewter.	175
PnB34	1831A	—	100 Francs. Pewter.	150
Pn34	1838	—	10 Centimes. LP monogram. Denomination above date in branches	135
Pn35	1840	—	Franc. Bust of Louis Philippe right. Denomination and date in wreath	—
Pn36	1847	—	5 Centimes. Louis Philippe left in inner circle. Crowned tablet divides 5-C, crossed swords behind	85.00
Pn37	1847	—	5 Centimes. Silver. Crowned tablet divides CINQ CENT	70.00
Pn38	1847	—	Decime. Silver. Louis Philippe left in inner circle, date below. Crowned tablet divides UNO-Dms, crossed swords behind	120
Pn39	1847	—	10 Centimes. Silver. Louis Philippe left in circle. Crowned tablet divides 10-Cmes	100
Pn40	1848	—	10 Centimes. Crowned laureate Liberty bust left, heart necklace. 10 CENTIMES and date within wreath, legend around at top	100
Pn41	1848	—	10 Centimes. Liberty left wearing crown of cherubs. 10 C and date within small circle, legend around, wreath	—
Pn42	1848	—	10 Centimes. Laureate bust of Liberty left with hair in back. 10 ENTIMES and date within wreath, legend at top	85.00

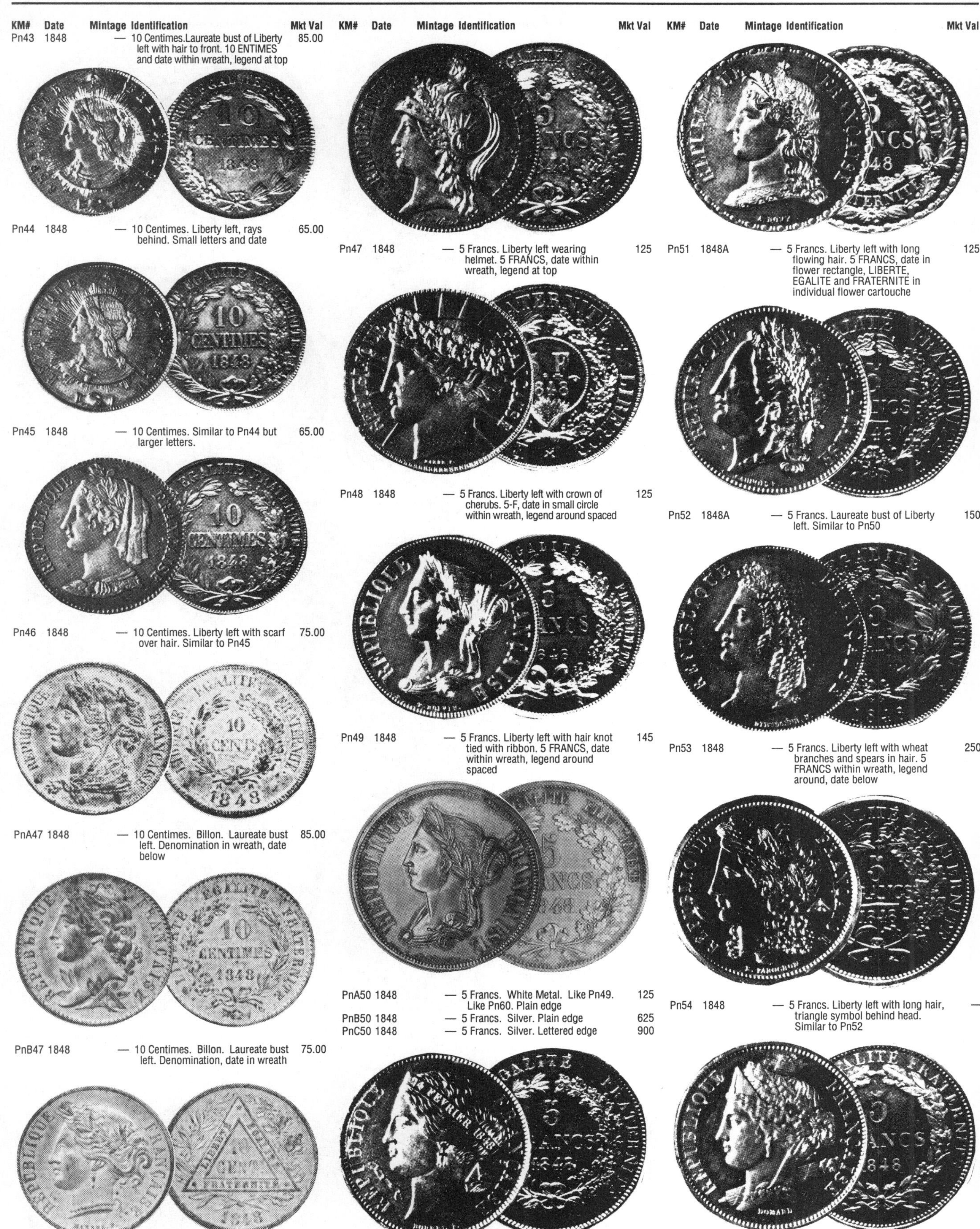

KM#	Date	Mintage	Identification	Mkt Val
Pn43	1848	—	10 Centimes.Laureate bust of Liberty left with hair to front. 10 ENTIMES and date within wreath, legend at top	85.00
Pn44	1848	—	10 Centimes. Liberty left, rays behind. Small letters and date	65.00
Pn45	1848	—	10 Centimes. Similar to Pn44 but larger letters.	65.00
Pn46	1848	—	10 Centimes. Liberty left with scarf over hair. Similar to Pn45	75.00
PnA47	1848	—	10 Centimes. Billon. Laureate bust left. Denomination in wreath, date below	85.00
PnB47	1848	—	10 Centimes. Billon. Laureate bust left. Denomination, date in wreath	75.00
PnC47	1848	—	10 Centimes. Billon. Laureate bust left. Denomination in triangle	65.00
Pn47	1848	—	5 Francs. Liberty left wearing helmet. 5 FRANCS, date within wreath, legend at top	125
Pn48	1848	—	5 Francs. Liberty left with crown of cherubs. 5-F, date in small circle within wreath, legend around spaced	125
Pn49	1848	—	5 Francs. Liberty left with hair knot tied with ribbon. 5 FRANCS, date within wreath, legend around spaced	145
PnA50	1848	—	5 Francs. White Metal. Like Pn49. Like Pn60. Plain edge	125
PnB50	1848	—	5 Francs. Silver. Plain edge	625
PnC50	1848	—	5 Francs. Silver. Lettered edge	900
Pn50	1848	—	5 Francs. Liberty left wearing band with 24 FEVRIER 1848. Similar to Pn30	145
Pn51	1848A	—	5 Francs. Liberty left with long flowing hair. 5 FRANCS, date in flower rectangle, LIBERTE, EGALITE and FRATERNITE in individual flower cartouche	125
Pn52	1848A	—	5 Francs. Laureate bust of Liberty left. Similar to Pn50	150
Pn53	1848	—	5 Francs. Liberty left with wheat branches and spears in hair. 5 FRANCS within wreath, legend around, date below	250
Pn54	1848	—	5 Francs. Liberty left with long hair, triangle symbol behind head. Similar to Pn52	—
Pn55	1848	—	5 Francs. Crowned laureate bust of Liberty left, hearts around neck. Similar to Pn47	120

KM#	Date	Mintage	Identification	Mkt Val
Pn56	1848	—	5 Francs. White Metal. Facing Liberty. Similar to Pn54	—
Pn57	1848	—	5 Francs. Liberty left with hair to front. Similar to Pn53	—
Pn58	1848	—	5 Francs.Laureate Liberty bust left with short hair. Similar to Pn57	145
Pn59	1848	—	5 Francs. Facing Liberty, band in hair, hair flowing over shoulders to front. Similar to Pn55 but without legend	—
Pn60	1848	—	5 Francs. Similar to Pn58. Similar to Pn59	165
Pn61	1848	—	5 Francs. Laureate bust with short hair left, beads around neck. Branches in field around 5 FRANCS and date	—
Pn62	1848	—	5 Francs. Laureate bust with flowing hair. Similar to Pn60	—
Pn63	1848	—	5 Francs. Similar to Pn62 but one symbol added below bust.	—
Pn64	1848	—	5 Francs.Similar to Pn62 but three symbols added below bust.	—
Pn65	1848	—	5 Francs. Laureate bust left with hair tied with bow, symbol above. Similar to Pn64 but wreath closer to bottom	—
Pn66	1848	—	5 Francs. Similar to Pn65 but larger wreath, date below.	—
Pn67	1848	—	5 Francs. Crowned laureate bust left with long hair. Similar to Pn65	125
Pn68	1848	—	5 Francs. White Metal. Laureate bust left, hair falling over shoulder. 5 FRANCS, date in branches, legend around spaced	—

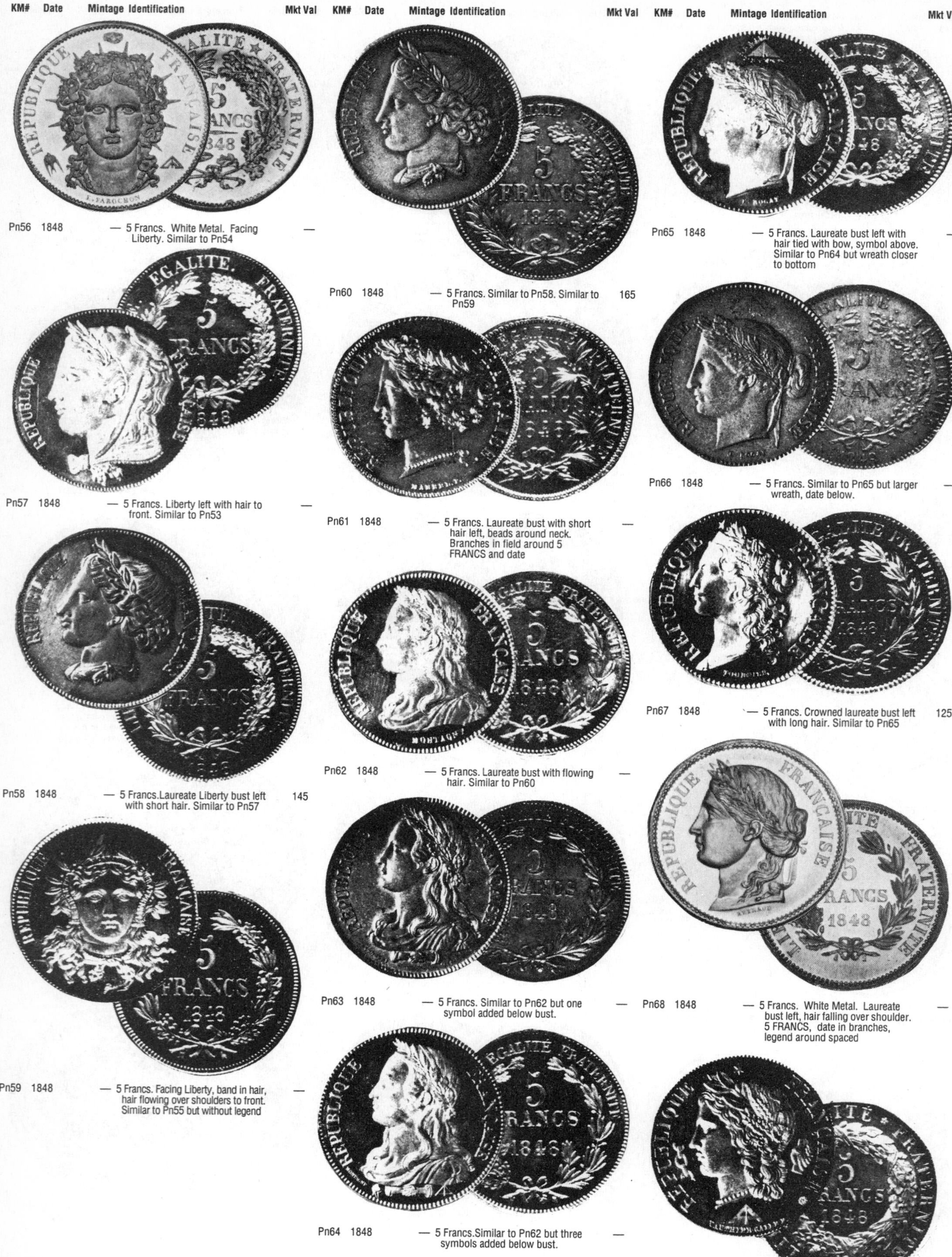

KM#	Date	Mintage	Identification	Mkt Val
Pn69	1848	—	5 Francs. Laureate bust with long hair left, three symbols around. 5 FRANCS, date in wreath	—
Pn70	1848	—	5 Francs. White Metal. Laureate bust with long hair showing at both sides, two symbols at front and back. Similar to Pn56	—
Pn71	1848A	—	5 Francs. White Metal. Laureate bust with hair hanging on shoulder. Outer legend spaced	—
Pn72	1848	—	5 Francs. Bust left with wide band in hair. Similar to Pn68 but symbol below crossed branches	200
Pn73	1848	—	5 Francs. White Metal. VG3063	300

KM#	Date	Mintage	Identification	Mkt Val
Pn74	1848	—	5 Francs. White Metal. VG3064	300
Pn75	1848	—	5 Francs. White Metal. VG3095	350
Pn76	1848	—	5 Francs. Gold. Reeded edge. KM#756.1.	6,000
Pn77	1848	—	5 Francs. Bronze. KM#756.1.	500
Pn78	1848	—	5 Francs. Laureate bust left. 5-F divided by fasces, date below	—
Pn79	(1848)	—	20 Francs. Bronze Gilt. Facing laureate bust. Legend in four lines in oak and laurel wreath	135
Pn80	1848	—	20 Francs. Bust wearing helmet left. 20 FRANCS, date in wreath	—
Pn81	1848	—	20 Francs. Laureate bust right	—

KM#	Date	Mintage	Identification	Mkt Val
Pn82	1848	—	20 Francs.	2,750
Pn83	1849	—	20 Centimes. Laureate bust left	—
Pn84	1849	—	5 Francs. Laureate bust left	—
Pn85	1849	—	5 Francs. Bronze. KM#756.1.	500
Pn86	1852	—	5 Francs. Louis Napoleon Bonaparte.	—
Pn87	1853	—	Centime. Eagle	—
Pn88	1853A	—	20 Centimes. Silver. Large head. KM#778.1.	375
Pn89	1853	—	20 Centimes. Silver. Large head. Plain edge. KM#778.1.	325
Pn90	1853	—	5 Francs. Napoleon III. Eagle on crowned and mantled shield	140

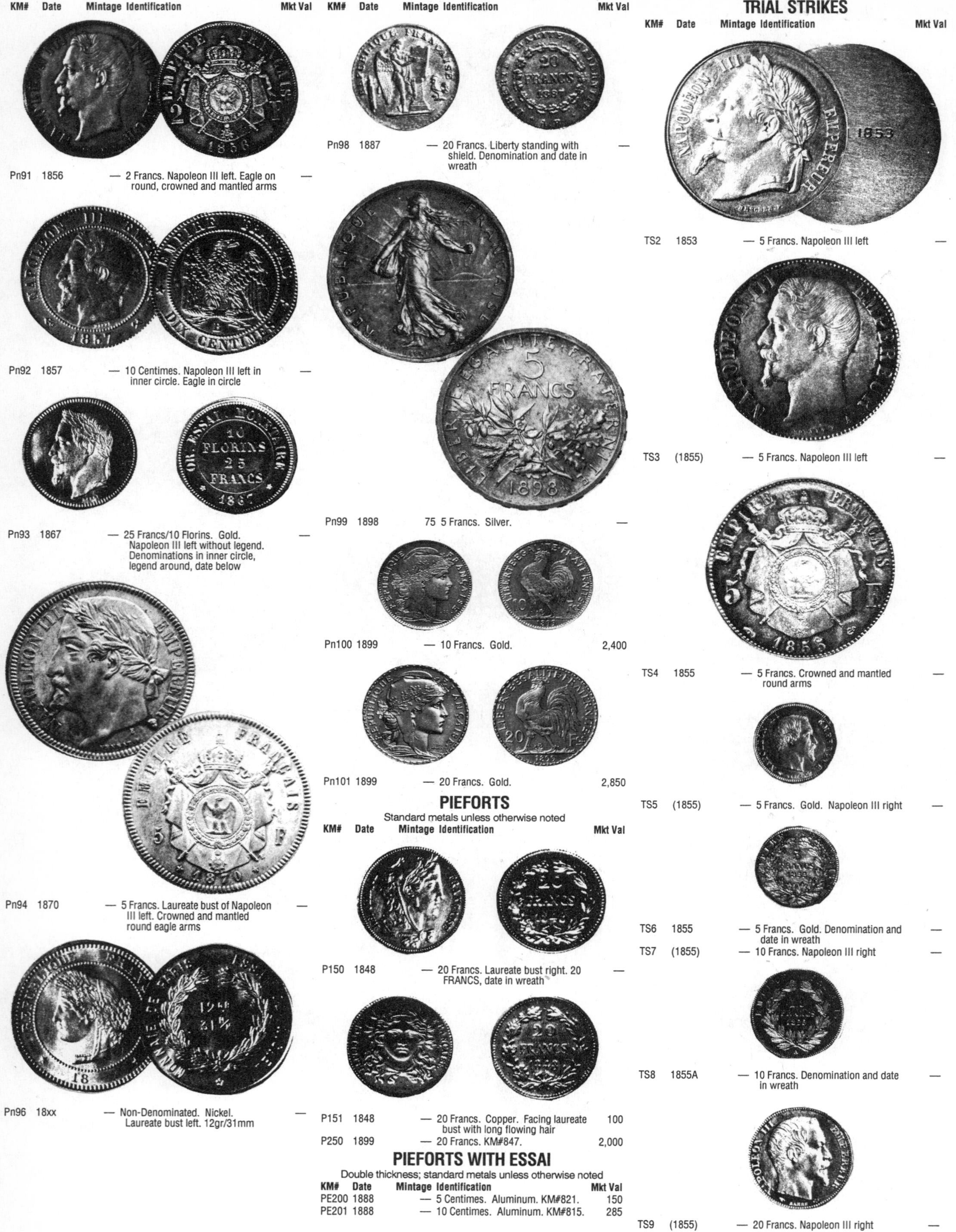

KM#	Date	Mintage	Identification	Mkt Val
Pn91	1856	—	2 Francs. Napoleon III left. Eagle on round, crowned and mantled arms	—
Pn92	1857	—	10 Centimes. Napoleon III left in inner circle. Eagle in circle	—
Pn93	1867	—	25 Francs/10 Florins. Gold. Napoleon III left without legend. Denominations in inner circle, legend around, date below	—
Pn94	1870	—	5 Francs. Laureate bust of Napoleon III left. Crowned and mantled round eagle arms	—
Pn96	18xx	—	Non-Denominated. Nickel. Laureate bust left. 12gr/31mm	—
Pn98	1887	—	20 Francs. Liberty standing with shield. Denomination and date in wreath	—
Pn99	1898	75	5 Francs. Silver.	—
Pn100	1899	—	10 Francs. Gold.	2,400
Pn101	1899	—	20 Francs. Gold.	2,850

PIEFORTS

Standard metals unless otherwise noted

KM#	Date	Mintage	Identification	Mkt Val
P150	1848	—	20 Francs. Laureate bust right. 20 FRANCS, date in wreath	—
P151	1848	—	20 Francs. Copper. Facing laureate bust with long flowing hair	100
P250	1899	—	20 Francs. KM#847.	2,000

PIEFORTS WITH ESSAI

Double thickness; standard metals unless otherwise noted

KM#	Date	Mintage	Identification	Mkt Val
PE200	1888	—	5 Centimes. Aluminum. KM#821.	150
PE201	1888	—	10 Centimes. Aluminum. KM#815.	285

TRIAL STRIKES

KM#	Date	Mintage	Identification	Mkt Val
TS2	1853	—	5 Francs. Napoleon III left	—
TS3	(1855)	—	5 Francs. Napoleon III left	—
TS4	1855	—	5 Francs. Crowned and mantled round arms	—
TS5	(1855)	—	5 Francs. Gold. Napoleon III right	—
TS6	1855	—	5 Francs. Gold. Denomination and date in wreath	—
TS7	(1855)	—	10 Francs. Napoleon III right	—
TS8	1855A	—	10 Francs. Denomination and date in wreath	—
TS9	(1855)	—	20 Francs. Napoleon III right	—

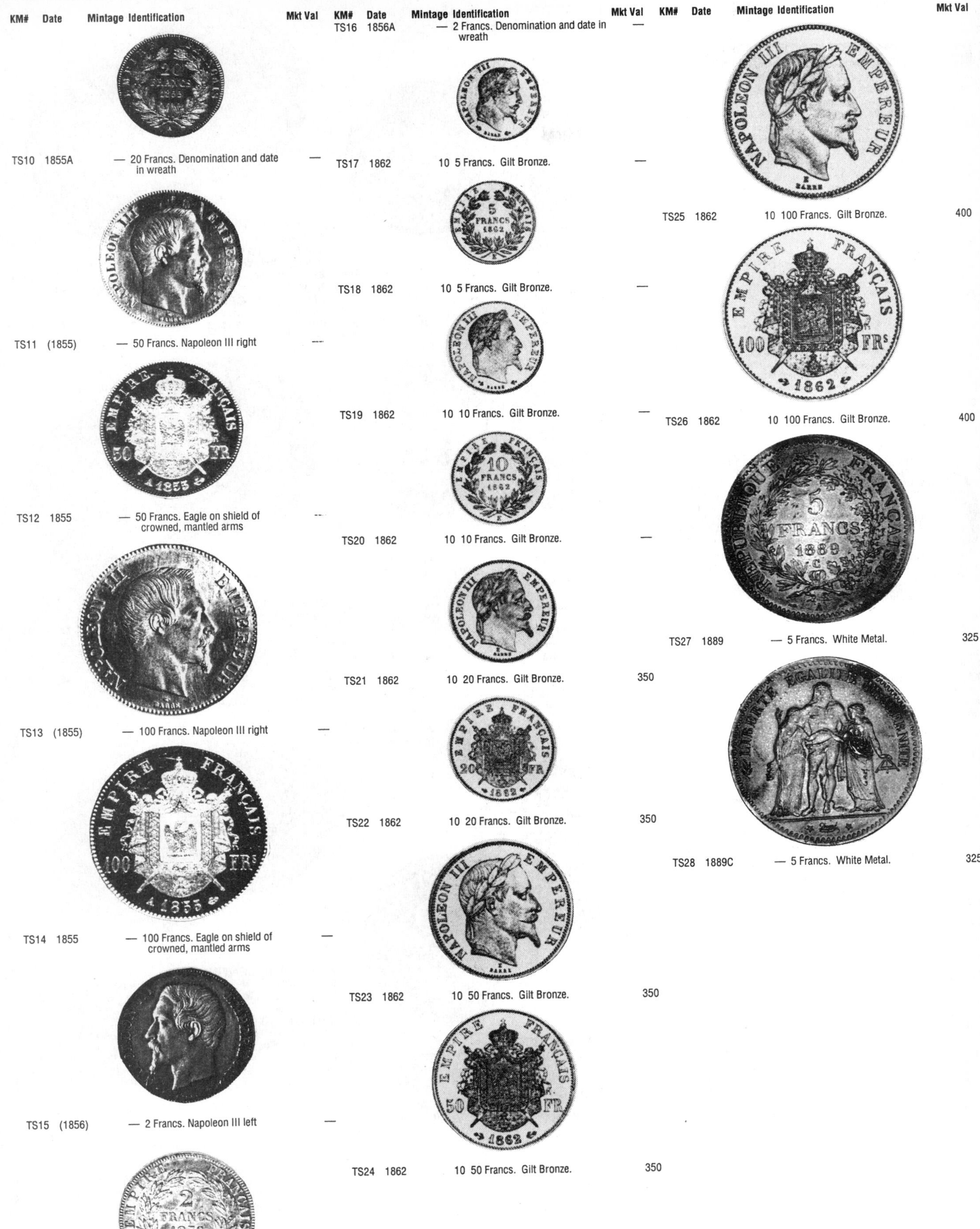

KM#	Date	Mintage	Identification	Mkt Val
TS10	1855A	—	20 Francs. Denomination and date in wreath	—
TS11	(1855)	—	50 Francs. Napoleon III right	—
TS12	1855	—	50 Francs. Eagle on shield of crowned, mantled arms	—
TS13	(1855)	—	100 Francs. Napoleon III right	—
TS14	1855	—	100 Francs. Eagle on shield of crowned, mantled arms	—
TS15	(1856)	—	2 Francs. Napoleon III left	—
TS16	1856A	—	2 Francs. Denomination and date in wreath	—
TS17	1862	10	5 Francs. Gilt Bronze.	—
TS18	1862	10	5 Francs. Gilt Bronze.	—
TS19	1862	10	10 Francs. Gilt Bronze.	—
TS20	1862	10	10 Francs. Gilt Bronze.	—
TS21	1862	10	20 Francs. Gilt Bronze.	350
TS22	1862	10	20 Francs. Gilt Bronze.	350
TS23	1862	10	50 Francs. Gilt Bronze.	350
TS24	1862	10	50 Francs. Gilt Bronze.	350
TS25	1862	10	100 Francs. Gilt Bronze.	400
TS26	1862	10	100 Francs. Gilt Bronze.	400
TS27	1889	—	5 Francs. White Metal.	325
TS28	1889C	—	5 Francs. White Metal.	325

FRENCH STATES

ANTWERP

ANVERS Antwerp, a town in Belgium, grew from a tiny walled marquisate under Godfrey of Bouillon, one of the leaders of the First Crusade in the 11th century, to the chief port and commercial center of 15th-century western Europe. Not only was it an acknowledged leader in trade and commerce, but also in the arts. The following centuries carried as much tragedy as triumph. Antwerp was plundered by Spain and its Protestant citizens murdered during the religious troubles of the 16th century. It served as the chief military harbor of Napoleon during the fall of the First Empire. It was the scene of the most famous siege of World War I, and was repeatedly battered by V-bombs during World War II. The French-auspice Antwerp coins of 1814-15 were a necessity money issued while Antwerp, under General Carnot, was besieged by the Allies.

ENGRAVERS INITIALS

JLGN - Jean-Louis Gagnepain
R - Ransonnet
V - Van Goor
W - Wolschot Foundry

CITY

SIEGE COINAGE

The following coins were minted from captured cannons by the French while besieged in Antwerp, Belgium. Some have an "N"; for Napoleon while others have a double "L" monogram for King Louis XVIII of France.

KM# 1 5 CENTIMES
18.0000 g., Bronze **Obv:** N in wreath **Note:** Size varies: 29-32 millimeters.

Date	Mintage	VG	F	VF	XF	Unc
1814	180	100	200	400	800	—

KM# 1a 5 CENTIMES
18.0000 g., Silver

Date	Mintage	VG	F	VF	XF	Unc
1814 Rare	—	—	—	—	—	—

KM# 2.2 5 CENTIMES
Bronze **Obv:** V above ribbon

Date	Mintage	VG	F	VF	XF	Unc
1814	11,000	20.00	45.00	90.00	200	350

KM# 2.2a 5 CENTIMES
Silver

Date	Mintage	VG	F	VF	XF	Unc
1814	—	—	—	350	600	1,200

KM# 2.3 5 CENTIMES
Bronze **Obv:** V below ribbon bow

Date	Mintage	VG	F	VF	XF	Unc
1814	2,800	50.00	120	270	600	—

KM# 2.4 5 CENTIMES
Bronze **Obv:** JLGN on ribbon

Date	Mintage	VG	F	VF	XF	Unc
1814	17,000	35.00	80.00	190	450	—

KM# 3.1 5 CENTIMES
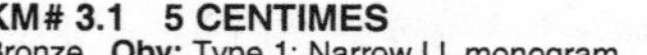
Bronze **Obv:** Type 1: Narrow LL monogram

Date	Mintage	VG	F	VF	XF	Unc
1814	10,000	—	—	—	—	—

Note: Reported, not confirmed

KM# 3.2 5 CENTIMES
Bronze **Obv:** V below ribbon bow

Date	Mintage	VG	F	VF	XF	Unc
1814	—	25.00	50.00	125	300	450

KM# 3.3 5 CENTIMES
Bronze **Obv:** JLGN on ribbon

Date	Mintage	VG	F	VF	XF	Unc
1814	31,000	—	—	—	—	—

Note: Reported, not confirmed

KM# 4.1 5 CENTIMES
Bronze **Obv:** Type II: Wide LL monogram, JLGN on ribbon

Date	Mintage	VG	F	VF	XF	Unc
1814	—	30.00	70.00	160	400	—

KM# 4.1a 5 CENTIMES
Silver

Date	Mintage	VG	F	VF	XF	Unc
1814	—	—	—	600	1,000	—

KM# 4.2 5 CENTIMES
Bronze **Obv:** V below ribbon

Date	Mintage	VG	F	VF	XF	Unc
1814	—	—	—	—	—	—

Note: Reported, not confirmed

KM# 2.1 5 CENTIMES
Bronze **Note:** Size varies: 29-30 millimeters. Weight varies: 12-15 grams.

Date	Mintage	VG	F	VF	XF	Unc
1814	—	25.00	50.00	110	250	—

KM# 5.1 10 CENTIMES
Bronze **Obv:** JEAN LOUIS//GAGNEPAIN on ribbon

Date	Mintage	VG	F	VF	XF	Unc
1814	18,000	60.00	120	275	600	—

KM# 5.1a 10 CENTIMES
Silver

Date	Mintage	VG	F	VF	XF	Unc
1814 Rare	—	—	—	—	—	—

KM# 5.2 10 CENTIMES
Bronze **Obv:** Without initials or name on ribbon

Date	Mintage	VG	F	VF	XF	Unc
1814	7,500	30.00	65.00	140	300	—

KM# 5.3 10 CENTIMES
Bronze **Obv:** R below ribbon bow

Date	Mintage	VG	F	VF	XF	Unc
1814	66,000	35.00	80.00	160	350	—

KM# 5.4 10 CENTIMES
Bronze **Obv:** W above ribbon bow

Date	Mintage	VG	F	VF	XF	Unc
1814	29,000	35.00	70.00	140	300	—

KM# 6.1 10 CENTIMES
Bronze **Obv:** Type I: Narrow LL monogram

Date	Mintage	VG	F	VF	XF	Unc
1814	—	—	—	—	—	—

Note: Reported, not confirmed

KM# 6.2 10 CENTIMES
Bronze **Obv:** JEAN LOUIS//GAGNEPAIN on ribbon

Date	Mintage	VG	F	VF	XF	Unc
1814	25,000	35.00	80.00	175	420	—

KM# 7.1 10 CENTIMES
Bronze **Obv:** Type II: Wide LL monogram, JEAN LOUIS GAGNEPAIN on ribbon

Date	Mintage	VG	F	VF	XF	Unc
1814	20,000	45.00	100	215	475	—

KM# 7.2 10 CENTIMES
Bronze **Obv:** R below ribbon bow

Date	Mintage	VG	F	VF	XF	Unc
1814	53,000	30.00	60.00	120	275	—

KM# 7.2a 10 CENTIMES
Silver

Date	Mintage	VG	F	VF	XF	Unc
1814	—	—	—	550	900	—

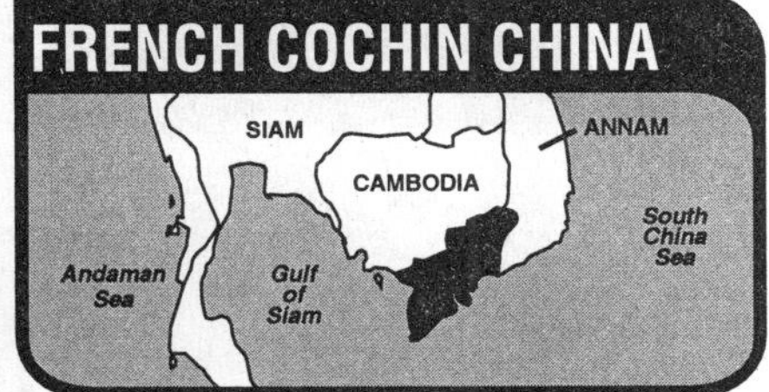

Cochin-China, a colony of France in Indo-China, now part of Viet Nam, occupied an alluvial plain of the Mekong Delta along the South China Sea. In its colonial period, Cochin-China had an area of 24,981 sq. mi. (63,701 sq. km.) and a population of about 5 million. Capital: Saigon. The region was (and is) one of Asia's chief rice-growing areas. Fishing is also an important economic activity. French Cochin-China exported rice, fish and timber.

The region, inhabited mainly by Vietnamese, was formerly part of the ancient Khmer empire and later of the Empire of Dai Viet. It was brought under French control in 1862-67 and made a colony. The Japanese occupied the area before World War II to use as a base for the invasion of Malaya. When France regained power of the area following World War II, Cochin-China was included in the Federation of Indo-China as an autonomous republic. It was attached to Viet Nam in 1949.

MINT MARKS
A - Paris
K – Bordeaux

MONETARY SYSTEM
5 Sapeques = 1 Cent
100 Cents = 1 Piastre

COLONY

MILLED COINAGE

KM# 1 SAPEQUE
Bronze **Note:** Center hole punched in France 1 Centime, Y#41.

Date	Mintage	F	VF	XF	Unc	BU
1875K	1,000,000	6.00	12.00	25.00	65.00	—

KM# 2 2 SAPEQUE
Bronze, 20 mm. **Obv. Legend:** COCHINCHINE FRANCAISE
Rev. Legend: Annam of Great France **Rev. Inscription:** "Equals 2"

Date	Mintage	F	VF	XF	Unc	BU
1879A	20,000,000	3.00	6.00	12.50	35.00	—
1879A Proof	—	Value: 200				
1885A Proof	100	Value: 450				

KM# 3 CENT
Bronze

Date	Mintage	F	VF	XF	Unc	BU
1879A	500,000	5.00	15.00	50.00	200	—
1879A Proof	—	—	—	—	—	—
Note: Reported, not confirmed						
1884A	444,000	6.00	25.00	65.00	300	—
1885A	255,000	7.00	30.00	100	475	—
1885A Proof	100	Value: 650				

KM# 4 10 CENTS
2.7216 g., 0.9000 Silver .0787 oz.

Date	Mintage	F	VF	XF	Unc	BU
1879A	400,000	20.00	35.00	90.00	325	—
1879A Proof	—	Value: 575				
1884A	510,000	25.00	60.00	125	375	—
1885A Proof	100	Value: 800				

KM# 5 20 CENTS
5.4431 g., 0.9000 Silver .1575 oz.

Date	Mintage	F	VF	XF	Unc	BU
1879A	350,000	30.00	60.00	150	425	—
1879A Proof	—	Value: 725				
1884A	320,000	40.00	70.00	185	475	—
1885A Proof	100	Value: 900				

KM# 6 50 CENTS
13.6078 g., 0.9000 Silver .3937 oz.

Date	Mintage	F	VF	XF	Unc	BU
1879A	180,000	90.00	150	300	1,250	—
1879A Proof	—	Value: 2,750				
1884A	10,000	500	750	1,000	3,000	—
1885A Proof	100	Value: 1,500				

KM# 7 PIASTRE
27.2156 g., 0.9000 Silver .7875 oz.

Date	Mintage	F	VF	XF	Unc	BU
1885A Proof, rare	100	—	—	—	—	—

Note: Superior Goodman sale 5-95 proof with tiny edge nick realized, $10,925

ESSAIS

Standard metals unless otherwise noted

KM#	Date	Mintage	Identification	Mkt Val
E1	1878	—	Sapeque.	250
E2	ND	—	Sapeque. As above, without date.	250
E3	1879	—	Sapeque. ESSAI. Without mint mark, filled square hole.	200

KM#	Date	Mintage	Identification	Mkt Val
E4	1879	—	Sapeque. ESSAI. Without mint mark, open square hole.	200
E5	1879	—	Sapeque. Without ESSAI. With mint mark, filled square hole.	200

KM#	Date	Mintage	Identification	Mkt Val
E11	1879	—	50 Cents. ESSAI below CENT. Mint mark between anchors.	2,450

KM#	Date	Mintage	Identification	Mkt Val
E12	1879A	—	Piastre. KM#7.	11,500
E13	1879	—	Piastre. (E) KM#7.	10,000
E14	1884A	—	Piastre. KM#7.	12,500
E15	1885A	—	Sapeque. Without ESSAI. With mint mark, open square hole.	—

PATTERNS

Including off metal strikes

KM#	Date	Mintage	Identification	Mkt Val
Pn1	1879A	—	Sapeque. Nickel-Silver.	300

PIEFORTS WITH ESSAI

Standard metals unless otherwise noted

KM#	Date	Mintage	Identification	Mkt Val
PE1	1879A	—	Cent. Bronze-Aluminum. KM#3.	1,400
PE2	1879A	—	Cent. Brass. KM#3.	600

TRIAL STRIKES

KM#	Date	Mintage	Identification	Mkt Val
TS1	1879	—	Sapeque. KM#2 over France 2 Centimes, Y#20.	250
TS2	1879	—	10 Cents. Aluminum. KM#4 obverse on 33.5 millimeter aluminum planchet.	450
TS3	1879	—	50 Cents. White Metal. KM#6 obverse.	375

PROOF SETS

KM#	Date	Mintage	Identification	Issue Price	Mkt Val
PS1	1879A (5)	—	KM#2-6; Reported, not confirmed	—	—
PS2	1885A (5)	—	KM#3-7	—	15,000

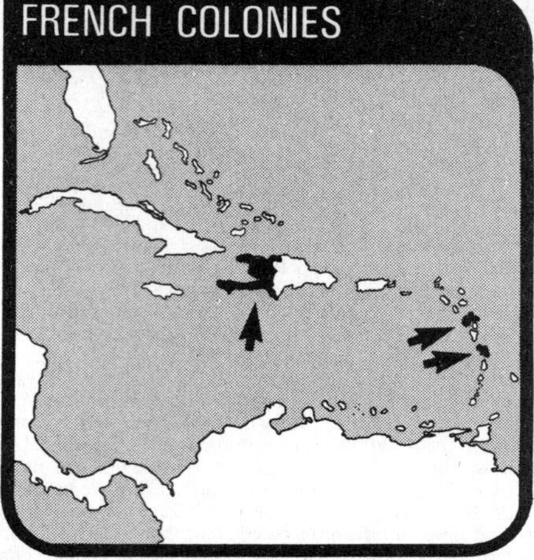

The coins catalogued under this heading were not issued for use in any particular colony but were intended for general use in the West Indies, particularly Martinique, Guadeloupe, and Saint-Dominique (western Hispaniola) until it attained independence as Haiti in 1804.

RULERS
French

MINT MARKS
A - Paris
H – LaRochelle

MONETARY SYSTEM
100 Centimes = 1 Franc

COLONIAL

MILLED COINAGE

KM# 10.1 5 CENTIMES

Bronze **Mint:** Paris

Date	Mintage	VG	F	VF	XF	Unc
1825A	607,000	2.50	6.00	20.00	55.00	—
1828A	501,000	3.00	7.50	25.00	68.00	—
1829A	299,000	5.00	15.00	45.00	95.00	—
1830A	402,000	4.50	9.00	35.00	80.00	—

KM# 10.2 5 CENTIMES

Bronze **Mint:** La Rochelle

Date	Mintage	VG	F	VF	XF	Unc
1827H	600,000	2.50	6.00	20.00	55.00	—

KM# 12 5 CENTIMES

Bronze **Mint:** Paris

Date	Mintage	VG	F	VF	XF	Unc
1839A	600,000	2.50	6.00	20.00	50.00	—
1839A Proof	—	Value: 300				
1841A	602,000	2.50	6.00	20.00	50.00	—
1843A	202,000	7.50	15.00	30.00	65.00	—
1844A	201,000	7.50	15.00	30.00	65.00	—

KM# 11.1 10 CENTIMES

Bronze **Mint:** Paris

Date	Mintage	VG	F	VF	XF	Unc
1825A	301,000	5.00	15.00	45.00	110	—
1828A	253,000	7.50	20.00	50.00	115	—
1829A	152,000	9.00	25.00	60.00	145	—

KM# 11.2 10 CENTIMES

Bronze **Mint:** La Rochelle

Date	Mintage	VG	F	VF	XF	Unc
1827H	300,000	5.00	15.00	35.00	90.00	—

KM# 13 10 CENTIMES

Bronze **Mint:** Paris

Date	Mintage	VG	F	VF	XF	Unc
1839A	300,000	5.00	10.00	25.00	60.00	—
1841A	301,000	5.00	10.00	25.00	60.00	—
1843A	101,000	9.00	17.50	50.00	125	325
1843A Proof	—	Value: 450				
1844A	100,000	9.00	17.50	50.00	125	325

ESSAIS

Standard metals unless otherwise noted

KM#	Date	Mintage	Identification	Mkt Val
E3	1817	—	Demi Sou. Bronze. 23 mm. Bust right. Denomination and date	350
E4	(1817)	—	Demi Sou. Bronze. 23 mm. Bust right. PIECE D'ESSAI	350

KM#	Date	Mintage	Identification	Mkt Val
E5	1817	—	Un Sou. Bronze. 25 mm. Bust right. Denomination and date	385
E6	1817	—	Un Sou. Bronze. 25 mm. PIECE D'ESSAI. Denomination and date	385

KM#	Date	Mintage	Identification	Mkt Val
E7	1817	—	2 Sous. Bronze. 31 mm. Bust left. Denomination and date	450
E8	1824A	—	5 Centimes. Bronze. 6.5000 g.	125

KM#	Date	Mintage	Identification	Mkt Val
E9	1824A	—	5 Centimes. Silver.	450
E10	1824A	—	10 Centimes. Bronze. 12.3000 g.	150
E11	1824A	—	10 Centimes. Silver.	500
E12	1839A	—	5 Centimes. Bronze.	325
E13	1839A	—	10 Centimes. Bronze.	500
E14	ND	—	Decime.	200

PIEFORTS WITH ESSAI

Standard metals unless otherwise noted

KM#	Date	Mintage	Identification	Mkt Val
PE1	1824A	—	5 Centimes. Silver.	850
PE2	1824A	—	5 Centimes. Bronze.	250
PE3	1824A	—	10 Centimes. Silver.	1,150
PE4	1824A	—	10 Centimes. Bronze.	700
PE5	1839A	—	10 Centimes. Bronze.	325

FRENCH GUIANA

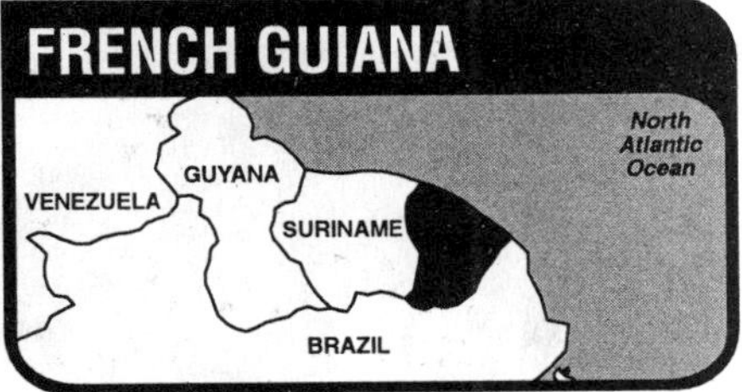

The French Overseas Department of Guiana, located on the northeast coast of South America, bordered by Surinam and Brazil, has an area of 33,399 sq. mi. (91,000 sq. km.). Capital: Cayenne. Placer gold mining and shrimp processing are the chief industries. Shrimp, lumber, gold, cocoa, and bananas are exported.

The coast of Guiana was sighted by Columbus in 1498 and explored by Amerigo Vespucci in 1499. The French established the first successful trading stations and settlements, and placed the area under direct control of the French Crown in 1674. Portuguese and British forces occupied French Guiana for five years during the Napoleonic Wars. Devil's Island, the notorious penal colony in French Guiana where Capt. Alfred Dreyfus was imprisoned, was established in 1852 and finally closed in 1947. When France adopted a new constitution in 1946, French Guiana voted to remain within the French Union as an Overseas Department. It now hosts some of the French and Common Market space and satellite stations.

In the late 18th century, a series of 2 sous coins was struck for the colony. It is probable that contemporary imitations of these issues, many emanating from Birmingham, England, outnumber the originals. These, both genuine and bogus, host coins for many West Indies counterstamps. As an Overseas Department, Guiana now uses the coins of metropolitan France, however, the franc used in the former colony was always distinct in value from that of the homeland as well as that used in the islands of the French West Indies.

RULERS
French

MINT MARKS
A – Paris

MONETARY SYSTEM
(Commencing 1794)
100 Centimes = 10 Decimes = 1 Franc

COLONY OF CAYENNE

COLONIAL COINAGE

KM# 3 2 SOUS
Billon

Date	Mintage	VG	F	VF	XF	Unc
1816A	—	40.00	80.00	175	360	—

KM# 2 3 SOUS
Billon

Date	Mintage	VG	F	VF	XF	Unc
1846A	—	100	175	400	850	—

DECIMAL COINAGE

KM# A1 10 CENTIMES
2.5000 g., Billon

Date	Mintage	VG	F	VF	XF	Unc
1818A	2,000,000	9.00	18.00	40.00	90.00	—

KM# A2 10 CENTIMES
2.5000 g., Billon

Date	Mintage	VG	F	VF	XF	Unc
1846	1,400,000	8.00	15.00	35.00	75.00	—

ESSAIS

KM#	Date	Mintage	Identification	Mkt Val
E1	1887	—	10 Centimes. Bronze. 10.0500 g. 30 mm. E below value.	275

KM#	Date	Mintage	Identification	Mkt Val
E2	1887	—	20 Centimes. Copper-Nickel-Zinc. 4.9200 g. 23 mm.	275

KM#	Date	Mintage	Identification	Mkt Val
E3	1887	—	5 Francs. 0.9000 Silver. 25.0000 g. 38 mm.	4,000
E4	1887	—	5 Francs. White Metal.	850

KM#	Date	Mintage	Identification	Mkt Val
E5	1889	—	10 Centimes. Bronze. 9.0800 g. 30 mm. E below bust.	725

PIEFORTS

KM#	Date	Mintage	Identification	Mkt Val
P2	1816A	—	2 Sous. Tin. 5.4000 g.	

KM#	Date	Mintage	Identification	Mkt Val
P3	ND(1817-18)A	—	10 Centimes. Tin. 4.9500 g. 22 mm.	400
P4	ND(1824-30)	—	10 Centimes. Tin. 6.4000 g. 22 mm.	—

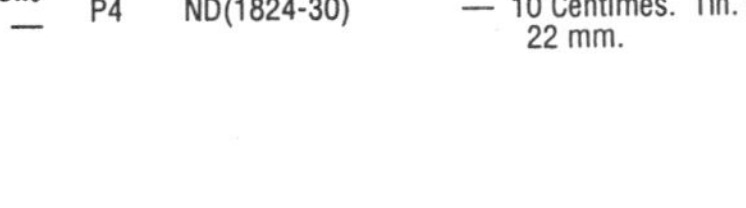

FRENCH INDO-CHINA

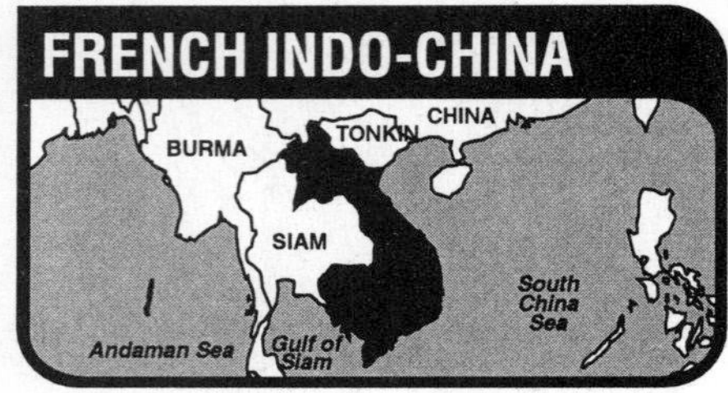

French Indo-China, made up of the protectorates of Annam, Tonkin, Cambodia and Laos and the colony of Cochin-China was located on the Indo-Chinese peninsula of Southeast Asia. The colony had an area of 286,194 sq. mi. (741,242 sq. km.). and a population of 30 million. Principal cities: Saigon, Haiphong, Vientiane, Pnom-Penh and Hanoi.

The forebears of the modern Indo-Chinese people originated in the Yellow River Valley of Northern China. From there, they were driven into the Indo-Chinese peninsula by the Han Chinese. The Chinese followed southward in the second century B.C., conquering the peninsula and ruling it until 938, leaving a lingering heritage of Chinese learning and culture. Indo-Chinese independence was basically maintained until the arrival of the French in the mid-19th century who established control over all of Vietnam, Laos and Cambodia. Activities directed toward obtaining self-determination accelerated during the Japanese occupation of World War II. The dependencies were changed from colonies to territories within the French Union in 1946, and all the inhabitants were made French citizens.

In Aug. of 1945, an uprising erupted involving the French and Vietnamese Nationalists, culminated in the French military disaster at Dien Bien Phu (May, 1954) and the subsequent Geneva Conference that brought an end to French colonial rule in Indo-China.

For later coinage see Kampuchea, Laos and Vietnam.

RULERS

French, until 1954

MINT MARKS

A - Paris
(a) - Paris, privy marks only
B - Beaumont-le-Roger
C - Castlesarrasin
H - Heaton, Birmingham
(p) - Thunderbolt - Poissy
S - San Francisco, U.S.A.
None - Osaka, Japan
None - Hanoi, Tonkin

MONETARY SYSTEM

5 Sapeques = 1 Cent
100 Cents = 1 Piastre

FRENCH COLONY

STANDARD COINAGE

KM# 6 SAPEQUE
Bronze **Mint:** Paris

Date	Mintage	F	VF	XF	Unc
1887A	5,000,000	1.50	3.00	12.00	38.00
1888A	5,000,000	3.00	6.00	16.00	45.00
1889A Proof	100	Value: 900			
1892A	1,636,000	60.00	160	375	550
1893A	864,000	50.00	140	340	500
1894A	2,500,000	6.00	15.00	40.00	85.00
1897A	2,829,000	6.00	15.00	40.00	85.00
1898A	2,171,000	50.00	125	270	400
1899A	5,000,000	2.50	7.50	15.00	35.00
1900A	2,657,000	10.00	30.00	75.00	135
1900A Proof	100	Value: 500			

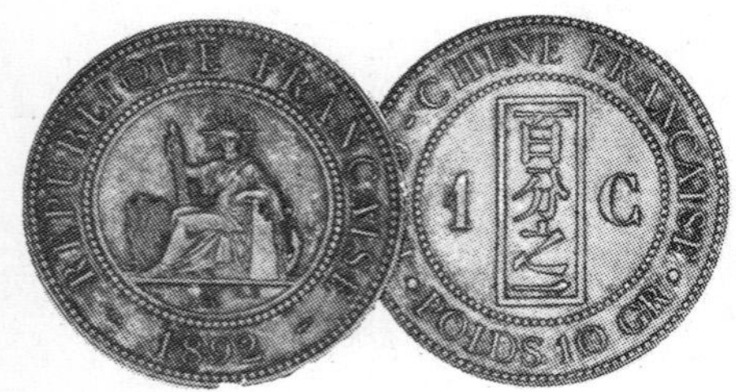

KM# 1 CENT
Bronze **Mint:** Paris

Date	Mintage	F	VF	XF	Unc
1885A	3,673,000	1.25	4.00	10.00	30.00
1885A Proof	—	Value: 600			
1886A	1,883,000	2.00	6.00	20.00	55.00
1887A	2,362,000	1.50	5.00	15.00	45.00
1888A	2,564,000	1.50	5.00	15.00	40.00
1889A	1,573,000	2.00	6.00	20.00	55.00
1889A Proof	100	Value: 550			
1892A	2,648,000	1.50	4.00	15.00	40.00
1893A	1,852,000	8.00	20.00	50.00	125
1894A	465,000	15.00	40.00	75.00	150

KM# 7 CENT
Bronze **Rev. Legend:** UN CENTIEME DE PIASTRE

Date	Mintage	F	VF	XF	Unc
1895	290,000	65.00	140	290	450

KM# 8 CENT
Bronze

Date	Mintage	F	VF	XF	Unc
1896	5,690,000	3.00	7.00	15.00	35.00
1897	11,055,000	2.00	5.00	10.00	25.00
1898	5,000,000	7.00	15.00	35.00	60.00
1899	8,000,000	2.00	4.00	10.00	30.00
1900	3,000,000	4.00	8.00	20.00	50.00
1900 Proof	100	Value: 750			

KM# 2 10 CENTS
2.7210 g., 0.9000 Silver .0787 oz. ASW **Mint:** Paris **Rev. Legend:** TITRE 0.900. POIDS 2.721

Date	Mintage	F	VF	XF	Unc
1885A	2,040,000	10.00	25.00	65.00	140
1885A Proof	—	Value: 850			
1888A	1,000,000	12.00	30.00	75.00	160
1889A Proof	100	Value: 1,250			
1892A	200,000	70.00	140	280	450
1893A	600,000	25.00	55.00	130	225
1894A	500,000	25.00	55.00	130	225
1895A	600,000	25.00	55.00	130	225

KM# 2a 10 CENTS
2.7000 g., 0.9000 Silver .0781 oz. ASW **Mint:** Paris **Rev. Legend:** TITRE 0.900. POIDS 2 GR. 7

Date	Mintage	F	VF	XF	Unc
1895A	300,000	150	300	500	1,000
1896A Fasces	650,000	40.00	80.00	175	270
1896A Torch	Inc. above	60.00	120	220	425
1897A	900,000	20.00	55.00	120	220

KM# 9 10 CENTS
2.7000 g., 0.8350 Silver .0725 oz. ASW **Rev. Legend:** TITRE 0.835. POIDS 2 GR. 7

Date	Mintage	F	VF	XF	Unc
1898	500,000	60.00	120	250	500
1899	4,100,000	4.00	10.00	30.00	75.00
1900	3,600,000	4.00	10.00	30.00	75.00
1900 Proof	100	Value: 1,350			

KM# 3 20 CENTS
5.4430 g., 0.9000 Silver .1575 oz. ASW **Mint:** Paris **Rev. Legend:** TITRE 0.900. POIDS 5.443 **Edge:** Plain

Date	Mintage	F	VF	XF	Unc
1885	1,280,000	18.00	45.00	130	250
1885 Proof	—	Value: 950			
1887	250,000	40.00	100	250	450
1887 Proof	—	Value: 700			
1889 Proof	100	Value: 2,000			
1892	200,000	60.00	125	300	525
1893	200,000	50.00	115	275	450
1894	250,000	50.00	115	275	450
1895	300,000	35.00	75.00	200	325

KM# 3a 20 CENTS
5.4000 g., 0.9000 Silver .1562 oz. ASW **Mint:** Paris **Rev. Legend:** TITRE 0.900. POIDS 5 GR. 4

Date	Mintage	F	VF	XF	Unc
1895A	250,000	125	275	525	875
1896A Fasces	300,000	100	225	480	775
1896A Torch	Inc. above	125	250	525	850
1897A	300,000	70.00	140	350	700

KM# 10 20 CENTS
5.4000 g., 0.8350 Silver .1450 oz. ASW

Date	Mintage	F	VF	XF	Unc
1898	250,000	50.00	120	250	475
1899	2,050,000	15.00	30.00	75.00	200
1900	1,750,000	30.00	70.00	180	325
1900 Proof	100	Value: 1,750			

KM# 4 50 CENTS
13.6070 g., 0.9000 Silver .3937 oz. ASW **Mint:** Paris **Rev. Legend:** TITRE 0.900. POIDS 13.607 GR.

Date	Mintage	F	VF	XF	Unc
1885A	40,000	100	225	450	900
1885A Proof	—	Value: 2,750			
1889A Proof	100	Value: 3,000			
1894A	100,000	60.00	140	300	650
1895A	100,000	60.00	140	320	675

KM# 4a.1 50 CENTS
13.5000 g., 0.9000 Silver .3906 oz. ASW **Mint:** Paris **Rev. Legend:** TITRE 0.900. POIDS 13 GR. 5

Date	Mintage	F	VF	XF	Unc
1896A	110,000	50.00	100	225	500
1900A	—	—	—	—	—
1900A Proof	100	Value: 4,750			

KM# 5 PIASTRE
27.2150 g., 0.9000 Silver .7875 oz. ASW **Mint:** Paris **Rev. Legend:** TITRE 0.900 POIDS 27.215 GR.

Date	Mintage	F	VF	XF	Unc
1885A	800,000	45.00	100	325	650
1885A Proof	—	Value: 6,000			
1886A	3,216,000	25.00	60.00	190	375
1886A Proof	—	Value: 4,000			
1887A	3,076,000	25.00	60.00	190	375
1888A	948,000	45.00	100	290	600
1889A	1,240,000	30.00	75.00	230	275
1889A Proof	100	Value: 4,500			
1890A	6,108	1,250	2,250	4,750	—
1893A	795,000	50.00	110	300	650
1894A	1,308,000	25.00	45.00	220	400
1895A	1,782,000	25.00	45.00	200	375

KM# 5a.1 PIASTRE
27.0000 g., 0.9000 Silver .7812 oz. ASW **Mint:** Paris **Rev. Legend:** TITRE 0.900 POIDS 27 GR.

Date	Mintage	F	VF	XF	Unc
1895A	3,798,000	15.00	45.00	125	260
1896A	11,858,000	12.00	30.00	100	175
1897A	2,511,000	20.00	50.00	150	320
1898A	4,304,000	15.00	45.00	125	275
1899A	4,681,000	15.00	45.00	125	275
1900A	13,319,000	12.00	30.00	100	225
1900A	100	Value: 6,500			

ESSAIS

Standard metals unless otherwise noted

KM#	Date	Mintage	Identification	Mkt Val
E1	1887(a)	—	Sapeque. Copper-Nickel. Without milimeter, 16-sided, KM#6.	300
E2	1895	—	Cent. Copper-Nickel. KM#7	450
E3	1896	—	Cent. Bronze. With ESSAI	550
E4	1896A	—	Cent. Silver.	1,000
E5	1896	—	Cent. Zinc. . ESSAIWithout mint mark, KM#4.	—
E6	1897A	—	Cent. Copper-Nickel. Without Essai; Y#3.	500

PIEFORTS

KM#	Date	Mintage	Identification	Mkt Val
P-A1	1876A	—	Sapeque. Bronze. 4.0000 g. 20 mm.	450
P1	1896A	—	Cent. Bronze. KM#8	350

FRENCH SOMALILAND

French Somaliland is located in northeast Africa at the Bab el Mandeb Strait connecting the Suez Canal and the Red Sea with the Gulf of Aden and the Indian Ocean. French interest in French Somaliland began in 1839 with concessions obtained by a French naval lieutenant from the provincial sultans. French Somaliland was made a protectorate in 1884 and its boundaries were delimited by the Franco-British and Ethiopian accords of 1887 and 1897. It became a colony in 1896 and a territory within the French Union in 1946. NOTE: For later coinage see French Afars & Issas.

MINT MARKS
(a) - Paris (privy marks only)

MONETARY SYSTEM
100 Centimes = 1 Franc

FRENCH COLONY

COUNTERMARKED COINAGE

Rupee-Taler (Riyal) Series

'Abd (al) Latif/
Bayya' al-Fudda/
bi Jibuti
(Abd al Latif, silver merchant in Djibouti)

Coins privately countermarked (c/m) around 1900 with 12 scalloped square with Arabic inscription. Sometimes coins have additional c/m's on the coin showing silver fineness .830.

KM# A1 1/4 RUPEE SIZE
0.9170 Silver **Note:** c/m on India 1/4 Rupee, KM#490.

CM Date	Host Date	Good	VG	F	VF	XF
ND(1900)	ND(1877-1900)	—	125	250	425	600

KM# 1 1/2 RUPEE SIZE
0.9170 Silver **Note:** c/m on India 1/2 Rupee, KM#491.

CM Date	Host Date	Good	VG	F	VF	XF
ND(1900)	ND(1877-1900)	—	75.00	150	275	500

KM# 2.1 RUPEE SIZE
0.9170 Silver **Note:** c/m on India Rupee, KM#450.

CM Date	Host Date	Good	VG	F	VF	XF
ND(1900)	ND(1835, 40)	—	150	260	400	680

KM# 2.2 RUPEE SIZE
0.9170 Silver **Note:** c/m on India Rupee, KM#457.

CM Date	Host Date	Good	VG	F	VF	XF
ND(1900)	ND(1840)	—	115	225	340	575

KM# 2.3 RUPEE SIZE
0.9170 Silver **Note:** c/m on India Rupee, KM#458.

CM Date	Host Date	Good	VG	F	VF	XF
(1900)	ND(1840)	—	115	225	340	575

KM# 2.4 RUPEE SIZE
0.9170 Silver **Note:** c/m on India Rupee, KM#473.

CM Date	Host Date	Good	VG	F	VF	XF
ND(1900)	ND(1862-1901)	—	150	260	425	680

KM# 2.6 RUPEE SIZE
Silver **Note:** c/m on Murshidabad Rupee, KM#99.

CM Date	Host Date	Good	VG	F	VF	XF
ND(1900)	ND(1793-1818)	—	120	200	350	600

KM# 3.1 RIYAL SIZE
0.8330 Silver **Note:** c/m on Austria M.T. Thaler, KM#T1.

CM Date	Host Date	Good	VG	F	VF	XF
ND(1900)	ND(1780)	—	145	275	550	900

KM# 3.2 RIYAL SIZE
0.8330 Silver **Note:** c/m with additional Arabic "830".

CM Date	Host Date	Good	VG	F	VF	XF
ND(1900)	ND(1780)	—	200	375	700	1,350

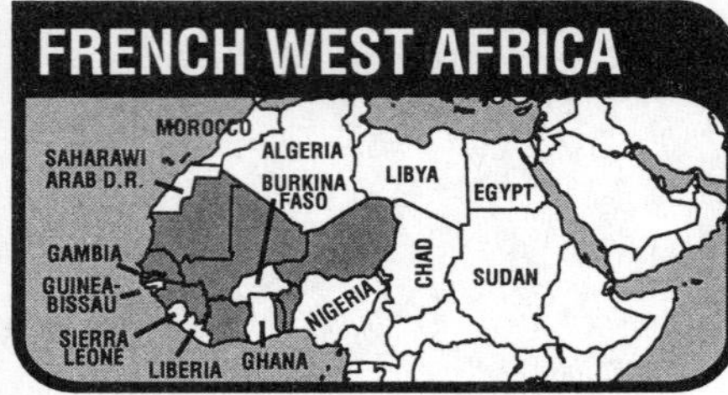

French West Africa (Afrique Occidentale Francaise), a former federation of French colonial territories on the northwest coast of Africa, had an area of 1,831,079 sq. mi. (4,742,495 sq. km.) and a population of about 17.4 million. Capital: Dakar. The constituent territories were Mauritania, Senegal, Dahomey, French Sudan, Ivory Coast, Upper Volta, Niger, French Guinea, and later on the mandated area of Togo. Peanuts, palm kernels, cacao, coffee and bananas were exported.

Prior to the mid-19th century, France, as the other European states, maintained establishments on the west coast of Africa for the purpose of trading in slaves and gum, but made no serious attempt at colonization. From 1854 onward, the coastal settlements were gradually extended into the interior until, by the opening of the 20th century, acquisition ended and organization and development began. French West Africa was formed in 1895 by grouping the several colonies under one administration (at Dakar) while retaining a large measure of autonomy to each of the constituent territories. The inhabitants of French West Africa were made French citizens in 1946. With the exception of French Guinea, all of the colonies voted in 1958 to become autonomous members of the new French Community. French Guinea voted to become the fully independent Republic of Guinea. The present-day independent states are members of the "Union Monetaire Ouest-Africaine". For later coinage see West African States.

RULERS

French

MONETARY SYSTEM

100 Centimes = 1 Franc
5 Francs = 1 Unit

FRENCH COLONY

TOKEN COINAGE

KM# Tn6 UNIT (5 Francs)

Brass **Note:** Similar to Tn7.

Date	Mintage	F	VF	XF	Unc	BU
1883	—	75.00	150	300	500	—

KM# Tn7 5 UNITS (25 Francs)

Brass

Date	Mintage	F	VF	XF	Unc	BU
1883	—	75.00	150	300	500	—

KM# Tn8 10 UNITS (50 Francs)

Brass **Note:** Similar to Tn7.

Date	Mintage	F	VF	XF	Unc	BU
1883	—	120	190	375	575	1,000

Georgia (formerly the Georgian Social Democratic Republic under the U.S.S.R.), is bounded by the Black Sea to the west and by Turkey, Armenia and Azerbaijan. It occupies the western part of Transcaucasia covering an area of 26,900 sq. mi. (69,700 sq. km.). Capitol: Tbilisi. Hydro-electricity, minerals, forestry and agriculture are the chief industries.

The Georgian dynasty first emerged after the Macedonian victory over the Achaemenid Persian Empire in the 4th century B.C. Roman "friendship" was imposed in 65 B.C. after Pompey's victory over Mithradates. The Georgians embraced Christianity in the 4th century A.D. During the next three centuries Georgia was involved in the ongoing conflicts between the Byzantine and Persian empires. The latter developed control until Georgia regained its independence in 450-503 A.D. but then it reverted to a Persian province in 533 A.D., then restored as a kingdom by the Byzantines in 562 A.D. It was established as an Arab emirate in the 8th century. The Seljuk Turks invaded but the crusades thwarted their interests. Over the following centuries, Turkish and Persian rivalries along with civil strife divided the area under the two influences.

Through significant contributions of Georgian kings (King David the Builder 1089-1124 and King Tamara 1136-1224), Georgia reached its peak of political, economic, and military development from the 11th to the 12th century. During these centuries the significant architectural and literary masterpieces that had won international recognition were created. Georgia had also regained territories that had been invaded by Islamic countries.

Czarist Russian interests increased and a treaty of alliance was signed on July 24, 1773 whereby Russia guaranteed Georgian independence and it acknowledged Russian suzerainty. Persia invaded again in 1795 leaving Tiflis in ruins. Russia slowly took over annexing piece-by-piece and soon developed total domination. After the Russian Revolution the Georgians, Armenians, and Azerbaijanis formed the short-lived Transcaucasian Federal Republic on Sept. 20, 1917, which broke up into three independent republics on May 26, 1918. A Germano-- Georgian treaty was signed on May 28, 1918, followed by a Turko-Georgian peace treaty on June 4. The end of WW I and the collapse of the central powers allowed free elections.

On May 20, 1920, Soviet Russia concluded a peace treaty, recognizing its independence, but later invaded on Feb. 11, 1921 and a soviet republic was proclaimed. On March 12, 1922 Stalin included Georgia in a newly formed Transcaucasian Soviet Federated Socialist Republic. On Dec. 5, 1936 the T.S.F.S.R. was dissolved and Georgia became a direct member of the U.S.S.R. The collapse of the U.S.S.R. allowed full transition to independence and on April 9, 1991 a unanimous vote declared the republic an independent state based on its original treaty of independence of May 1918.

RULERS

David, Regent
AH1215-1216/1801AD

Russian Issues

Struck under the authority of Alexander I (1801-25) and Nicholas I (1825-55) of Russia at the Tiflis (Tbilisi) mint.

Mint

Tiflis

MINT OFFICIALS' INITIALS

Initial	Date	Name
TT3	1804-06	Peter Zaitsev
AK	1806-24	Alexei Karpinski
AT	1810-31	Alexander Trifonov
BK	1831-33	Vasili Kleimenov

MONETARY SYSTEM

1 Puli = 5 Dinars = 1/2 Kopek
2 Puli = 1 Kopek
4 Puli = 1 Bisti = 2 Kopeks
20 Puli = 1/2 Abazi = 10 Kopeks
40 Puli = 1 Abazi = 20 Kopeks
80 Puli = 2 Abazi = 40 Kopeks

DATING

The dates are shown in a quantitive manner ex. 1000 plus 800 plus 10 plus 9 = 1819.

NOTE: The fine style 1 and 2 Abaze coins of 1828 are patterns struck at St. Petersburg.

RUSSIAN AUTHORITY

RUSSIAN COINAGE

Struck under the authority of Alexander I (1801-25) and Nicholas I (1825-55) of Russia at the Tiflis (Tbilisi) Mint.

KM# 70 PULI (1/2 Kopek)

Copper **Ruler:** David, as Regent

Date	Mintage	VG	F	VF	XF	Unc
1804 Rare	4,000	—	—	—	—	—
1805	Inc. above	75.00	150	185	275	—
1806	15,000	75.00	150	185	275	—

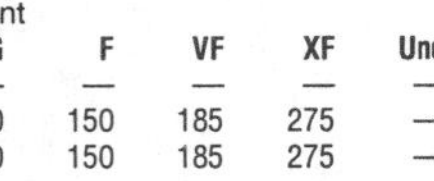

KM# 71 2 PULI (Kopek)

Copper **Ruler:** David, as Regent

Date	Mintage	VG	F	VF	XF	Unc
1804 Rare	3,000	—	—	—	—	—
1805	Inc. above	90.00	150	220	325	—
1806	34,000	50.00	80.00	100	150	—
1808	12,000	50.00	80.00	100	150	—
1810	50,000	50.00	70.00	100	150	—

KM# 72 BISTI (2 Kopeks)

Copper **Ruler:** David, as Regent

Date	Mintage	VG	F	VF	XF	Unc
1804 Rare	1,000	—	—	—	—	—
1805	Inc. above	90.00	150	185	275	—
1806	25,000	40.00	60.00	100	150	—
1808	20,000	40.00	60.00	100	150	—
1810	315,000	40.00	60.00	100	150	—

KM# 73 1/2 ABAZI (10 Kopeks)

1.5800 g., 0.9170 Silver **Ruler:** David, as Regent

Date	Mintage	VG	F	VF	XF	Unc
1804 "SI"	5,000	50.00	100	150	300	—
1805 "SI"	Inc. above	40.00	80.00	100	200	—
1806 AK Rare	1,070	—	—	—	—	—
1807 AK Rare	80	—	—	—	—	—
1810 AT Rare	398	—	—	—	—	—
1813 AT Rare	2,000	—	—	—	—	—
1820 AT	4,000	50.00	80.00	110	225	—
1821 AT	Inc. above	40.00	70.00	100	200	—
1822 AK	1,000	40.00	70.00	100	200	—
1823 AK	4,000	40.00	70.00	100	200	—
1824 AK	4,000	40.00	70.00	100	200	—
1826 AT	5,000	30.00	60.00	100	200	—
1827 AT	7,000	30.00	60.00	100	200	—
1828 AT	16,000	25.00	40.00	60.00	100	—
1831 AT	—	35.00	60.00	100	225	—
1832 BK	—	35.00	60.00	100	200	—
1833 BK	—	25.00	50.00	95.00	200	—

KM# 74 ABAZI (20 Kopeks)

3.1500 g., 0.9170 Silver, 19 mm. **Ruler:** David, as Regent

Date	Mintage	VG	F	VF	XF	Unc
1804 "SI"	—	40.00	100	175	325	—
1805 "SI"	19,000	30.00	50.00	65.00	95.00	—
1806 "SI"	23,000	30.00	50.00	65.00	95.00	—
1806 AK	Inc. above	30.00	50.00	65.00	95.00	—
1807 AK	9,000	30.00	50.00	65.00	95.00	—
1808 AK	14,000	30.00	50.00	65.00	95.00	—
1809 AK	17,000	30.00	50.00	65.00	95.00	—
1810 AT	4,000	35.00	65.00	95.00	140	—
1811 AT Rare	1,000	—	—	—	—	—
1812 AT	9,000	30.00	50.00	70.00	110	—
1813 AT	7,000	30.00	50.00	70.00	110	—
1814 AT	3,000	30.00	50.00	65.00	95.00	—
1815 AT	3,000	35.00	60.00	80.00	120	—
1816 AT	12,000	30.00	50.00	65.00	95.00	—
1817 AT Rare	—	—	—	—	—	—
1818 AT	8,000	30.00	50.00	65.00	95.00	—
1819 AT	10,000	30.00	50.00	65.00	95.00	—
1820 AT	12,000	30.00	50.00	65.00	95.00	—
1821 AT	14,000	30.00	50.00	65.00	95.00	—
1822 AT	5,000	35.00	60.00	80.00	120	—
1822 AK	Inc. above	30.00	50.00	65.00	95.00	—
1823 AK	5,000	30.00	50.00	65.00	95.00	—
1824 AK	5,000	30.00	50.00	65.00	95.00	—
1826 AT	5,000	30.00	50.00	65.00	95.00	—
1828 AT Rare	—	—	—	—	—	—
1830 AT	—	30.00	50.00	65.00	95.00	—
1831 AT	—	30.00	50.00	65.00	95.00	—

KM# 75 2 ABAZI (40 Kopeks)

6.3100 g., 0.9170 Silver, 23 mm. **Ruler:** David, as Regent

Date	Mintage	VG	F	VF	XF	Unc
1804 "SI"	33,000	45.00	85.00	175	325	—
1805 "SI"	Inc. above	30.00	40.00	70.00	95.00	—
1806 AK	42,000	30.00	40.00	70.00	95.00	—
1807 AK	71,000	30.00	40.00	70.00	95.00	—
1807 AT	Inc. above	40.00	70.00	110	200	—
1808 AK	65,000	30.00	40.00	70.00	95.00	—
1809 AK	86,000	30.00	40.00	70.00	95.00	—
1810 AK	20,000	35.00	45.00	75.00	100	—
1811 AT	5,000	35.00	50.00	80.00	110	—
1812 AT	59,000	30.00	40.00	70.00	95.00	—
1813 AT	48,000	30.00	40.00	70.00	95.00	—
1814 AT	20,000	30.00	40.00	70.00	95.00	—
1815 AT	21,000	30.00	40.00	70.00	95.00	—
1816 AT	79,000	30.00	40.00	70.00	95.00	—
1817 AT Rare	—	—	—	—	—	—
1818 AT	85,000	30.00	40.00	70.00	95.00	—
1819 AT	105,000	30.00	40.00	70.00	95.00	—
1820 AT	112,000	30.00	40.00	70.00	95.00	—
1821 AT	75,000	30.00	40.00	70.00	95.00	—
1822 AT	24,000	35.00	55.00	85.00	120	—
1822 AK	Inc. above	30.00	40.00	70.00	95.00	—
1823 AK	39,000	30.00	40.00	70.00	95.00	—
1824 AK	32,000	30.00	40.00	70.00	95.00	—
1826 AT	75,000	30.00	40.00	70.00	95.00	—
1827 AT	172,000	30.00	40.00	70.00	95.00	—
1828 AT	126,000	30.00	40.00	70.00	95.00	—
1829 AT	213,000	25.00	35.00	45.00	70.00	—
1830 AT	273,000	25.00	35.00	50.00	75.00	—
1831 AT	338,000	30.00	35.00	50.00	75.00	—
1831 BK	Inc. above	25.00	35.00	50.00	75.00	—
1832 BK	210,000	30.00	35.00	50.00	75.00	—
1833 BK	114,000	30.00	40.00	70.00	95.00	—

ESSAIS

Standard metals unless otherwise noted

KM#	Date	Mintage	Identification	Mkt Val
E1	1828	—	Abazi. Silver. No mintmaster initials. KM#74.	—
E2	1828	—	2 Abazi. Silver. No mintmaster initials. KM#75.	—

PATTERNS

Including off metal strikes

KM#	Date	Mintage	Identification	Mkt Val
Pn1	1804	—	Abazi. Silver. No mintmaster initials. 20 (Kopeks), KM#74.	—

GERMAN EAST AFRICA

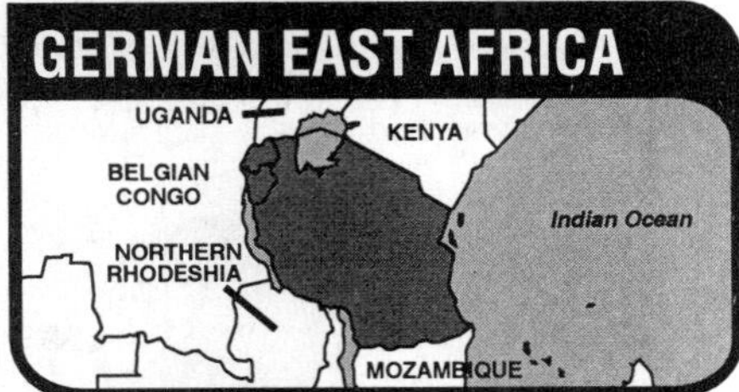

German East Africa (Tanganyika), located on the coast of east-central Africa between British East Africa (now Kenya) and Portuguese East Africa (now Mozambique), had an area of 362,284 sq. mi. (938,216 sq. km.). Chief products prior to German control were ivory and slaves; after German control, sisal, coffee, and rubber. Germany acquired control of the area by treaties with coastal chiefs in 1884, established it as a protectorate in 1891, and proclaimed it the Colony of German East Africa in 1897.
NOTE: For later coinage see East Africa.

TITLES

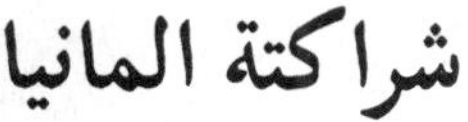

Sharaka(t) Almania

RULERS
Wilhelm II, 1888-1918

MINT MARKS
A - Berlin
J - Hamburg
T - Tabora

MONETARY SYSTEM
Until 1904
64 Pesa = 1 Rupie
Commencing 1904
100 Heller = 1 Rupie

COLONIAL

STANDARD COINAGE

64 Pesa = 1 Rupee until 1904; 100 Heller = 1 Rupie commencing 1904

KM# 1 PESA

Copper **Ruler:** Wihelm II

Date	Mintage	F	VF	XF	Unc	BU
1890	1,000,000	1.00	3.50	8.00	25.00	—
1890 Proof	—	Value: 210				
1891	12,551,000	1.50	4.00	12.00	30.00	—
1892	27,541,000	1.50	5.00	15.00	75.00	—

KM# 3 1/4 RUPIE

2.9160 g., 0.9170 Silver .0859 oz. **Ruler:** Wihelm II

Date	Mintage	F	VF	XF	Unc	BU
1891	77,000	7.00	20.00	50.00	135	—
1891 Proof	—	Value: 250				
1898	100,000	10.00	30.00	65.00	225	—

KM# 4 1/2 RUPIE

5.8319 g., 0.9170 Silver .1719 oz. **Ruler:** Wihelm II

Date	Mintage	F	VF	XF	Unc	BU
1891	68,000	15.00	42.50	110	250	—
1891 Proof	—	Value: 350				
1897	75,000	17.50	50.00	135	350	—

KM# 2 RUPIE

11.6638 g., 0.9170 Silver .3437 oz. **Ruler:** Wihelm II

Date	Mintage	F	VF	XF	Unc	BU
1890	154,000	10.00	20.00	45.00	125	—
1890 Proof	—	Value: 300				
1891	126,000	10.00	22.00	50.00	175	—
1891 Proof	—	Value: 300				
1892	360,000	10.00	25.00	50.00	200	—
1892 Proof	—	Value: 500				
1893	142,000	25.00	50.00	175	550	—
1894	48,000	100	250	450	950	—
1897	244,000	15.00	35.00	85.00	300	—
1898	357,000	15.00	35.00	85.00	300	—
1899	227,000	20.00	40.00	100	350	—
1900	209,000	20.00	45.00	125	400	—

KM# 5 2 RUPIEN

23.3200 g., 0.9170 Silver .6872 oz. **Ruler:** Wihelm II

Date	Mintage	F	VF	XF	Unc	BU
1893	33,000	150	285	650	2,000	—
1893 Proof	—	Value: 3,500				
1894	18,000	200	350	750	2,500	—

GERMAN NEW GUINEA

German New Guinea, now called Papua New Guinea occupies the eastern half of the island of New Guinea. It lies north of Australia near the equator and borders on West Irian. The country, which includes nearby Bismark archipelago, Buka and Bougainville, has an area of 178,260 sq. mi. (461,690 sq. km.) and a population that is divided into more than 1,000 separate tribes speaking more than 700 mutually unintelligible languages. Capital: Port Moresby. The economy is agricultural, and exports copra, rubber, cocoa, coffee, tea, gold and copper.

In 1884 Germany annexed the area known as German New Guinea (also Neu Guinea or Kaiser Wilhelmsland) comprising the northern section of eastern New Guinea, and granted its administration and development to the Neu-Guinea Compagnie. Administration reverted to Germany in 1899 following the failure of the company to exercise adequate administration. While a German protectorate, German New Guinea had an area of 92,159 sq. mi. (238,692 sq. km.) and a population of about 250,000. Capital: Herbertshohe, 1 of 4 capitals of German New Guinea. The seat of government was transferred to Rabaul in 1910. Copra was the chief crop.

Australian troops occupied German New Guinea in Aug. 1914, shortly after Great Britain declared war on Germany. It was mandated to Australia by the League of Nations in 1920, known as the Territory of New Guinea. The territory was invaded and most of it was occupied by Japan in 1942. Following the Japanese surrender, it came under U.N. trusteeship, Dec. 13, 1946, with Australia as the administering power.

RULERS

German, 1884-1914

MINT MARKS

A – Berlin

MONETARY SYSTEM

100 Pfennig = 1 Mark

GERMAN PROTECTORATE

STANDARD COINAGE

KM# 1 PFENNIG

Copper **Obv:** NEU-GUINEA COMPAGNIE above crossed palm branches **Rev:** denomination, with date in legend **Rev. Legend:** EIN NEU-GUINEA PFENNIG

Date	Mintage	F	VF	XF	Unc	BU
1894A	33,000	20.00	40.00	90.00	150	—
1894A Proof	—	Value: 400				

KM# 2 2 PFENNIG

Copper **Obv:** NEU-GUINEA COMPAGNIE above crossed palm branches **Rev:** denomination, with date in legend **Rev. Legend:** ZWEI NEU-GUINEA PFENNIG

Date	Mintage	F	VF	XF	Unc	BU
1894A	17,000	35.00	65.00	120	200	—
1894A Proof	—	Value: 550				

KM# 3 10 PFENNIG

Copper **Obv:** Denomination and date in palm wreath **Rev:** Bird of Paradise

Date	Mintage	F	VF	XF	Unc	BU
1894A	24,000	30.00	60.00	140	300	—
1894A Proof	—	Value: 1,250				

KM# 4 1/2 MARK

2.7780 g., 0.9000 Silver .0804 oz. **Obv:** Denomination and date in palm wreath **Rev:** Bird of Paradise

Date	Mintage	F	VF	XF	Unc	BU
1894A	16,000	50.00	100	200	350	—
1894A Proof	—	Value: 600				

KM# 5 MARK

5.5560 g., 0.9000 Silver 0.1608 oz. **Obv:** Denomination and date in palm wreath **Rev:** Bird of Paradise

Date	Mintage	F	VF	XF	Unc	BU
1894A	33,000	50.00	100	200	400	—
1894A Proof	—	Value: 700				

KM# 6 2 MARK

11.1110 g., 0.9000 Silver 0.3215 oz. **Obv:** Denomination and date in palm wreath **Rev:** Bird of Paradise

Date	Mintage	F	VF	XF	Unc	BU
1894A	13,000	125	250	465	950	—
1894A Proof	—	Value: 1,250				

KM# 7 5 MARK

27.7780 g., 0.9000 Silver 0.8038 oz. **Obv:** Denomination and date in palm wreath **Rev:** Bird of Paradise

Date	Mintage	F	VF	XF	Unc	BU
1894A	19,000	450	850	1,250	2,500	—
1894A Proof	—	Value: 3,750				

KM# 8 10 MARK

3.9820 g., 0.9000 Gold 0.1152 oz. **Obv:** Denomination and date in palm wreath **Rev:** Bird of Paradise

Date	Mintage	F	VF	XF	Unc	BU
1895A	2,000	—	4,000	8,250	12,000	—
1895A Proof	—	Value: 15,500				

KM# 9 20 MARK

7.9650 g., 0.9000 Gold 0.2305 oz. **Obv:** Denomination and date in palm wreath **Rev:** Bird of Paradise

Date	Mintage	F	VF	XF	Unc	BU
1895A	1,500	—	4,250	8,750	12,500	—
1895A Proof	—	Value: 16,500				

PROOF SETS

KM#	Date	Mintage	Identification	Issue Price	Mkt Val
PS1	1894 (7)	—	KM1-7	—	8,500

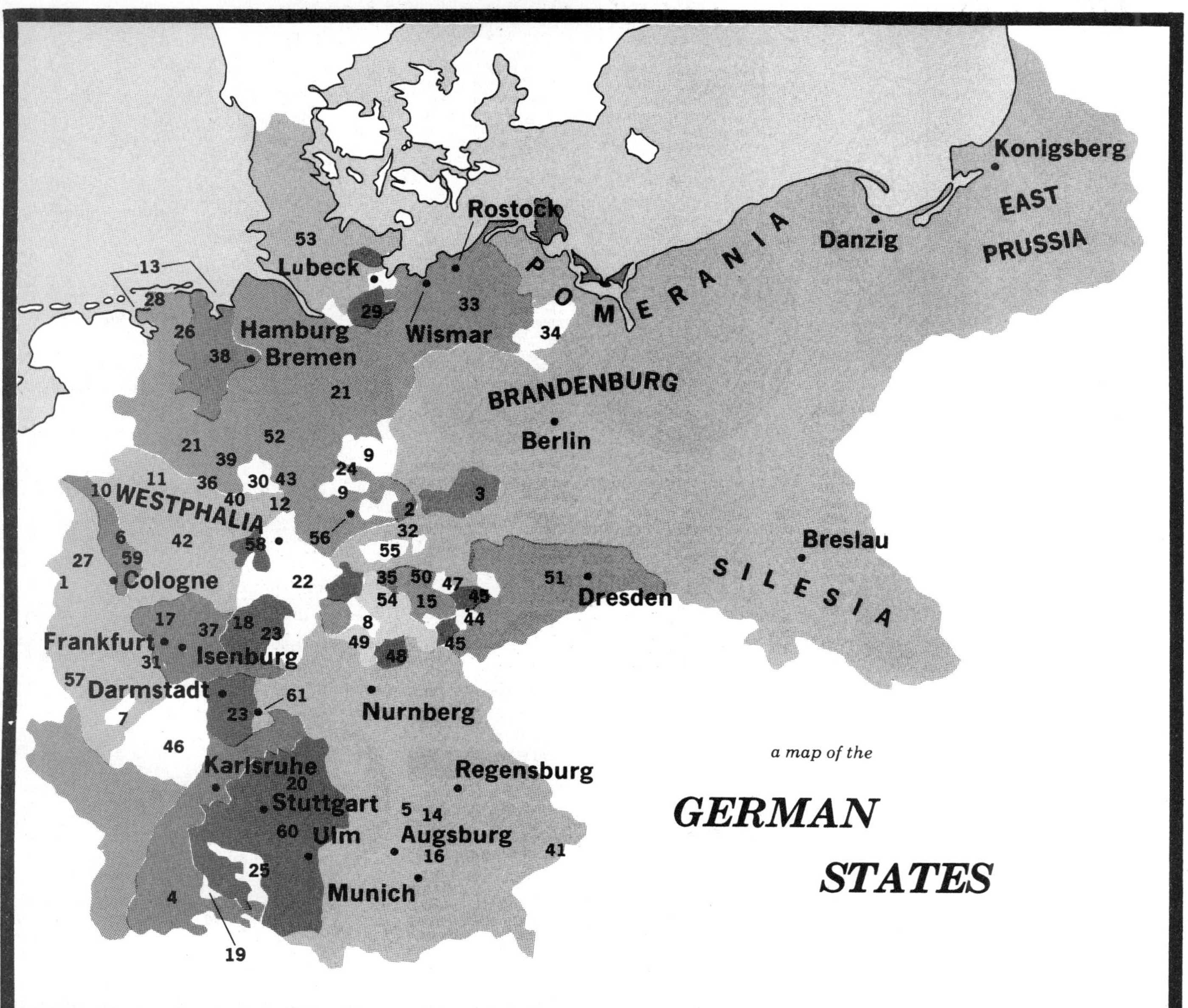

1 Aachen
2 Anhalt-Bernburg
3 Anhalt-Dessau
4 Baden
5 Bavaria
6 Berg
7 Birkenfeld
8 Brandenburg-Ansbach Bayreuth
9 Brunswick-Luneburg & Wolfenbuttel
10 Cleve
11 Coesfeld
12 Corvey
13 East Friesland
14 Eichstadt
15 Erfurt
16 Freising
17 Friedberg
18 Fulda
19 Furstenberg
20 Halle
21 Hannover
22 Hesse-Cassel
23 Hesse-Darmstadt
24 Hildesheim
25 Hohenzollern
26 Jever
27 Julich
28 Knyphausen
29 Lauenburg
30 Lippe-Detmold
31 Mainz
32 Mansfeld
33 Mecklenburg-Schwerin
34 Mecklenburg-Strelitz
35 Muhlhausen
36 Munster
37 Nassau
38 Oldenburg
39 Osnabruck
40 Paderborn
41 Passau
42 Prussia
43 Pyrmont
44 Reuss-Greiz
45 Reuss-Schleiz
46 Rhein-Pfalz
47 Saxe-Altenburg
48 Saxe-Coburg-Gotha
49 Saxe-Meiningen
50 Saxe-Weimar-Eisenach
51 Saxony
52 Schaumberg-Hessen & Lippe
53 Schleswig-Holstein
54 Schwarzburg-Rudolstadt
55 Schwarzburg Sonderhausen
56 Stolberg-Wernigerode
57 Trier
58 Wallmoden-Pyrmont
59 Wallmoden-Gimborn
60 Wurttemberg
61 Wurzburg

GERMAN STATES

Although the origin of the German Empire can be traced to the Treaty of Verdun that ceded Charlemagne's lands east of the Rhine to German Prince Louis, it was for centuries little more than a geographic expression, con- sisting of hundreds of effectively autonomous big and little states. Nominally the states owed their allegiance to the Holy Roman Emperor, who was also a German king, but as the Emperors exhibited less and less concern for Germany the actual power devolved on the lords of the individual states. The fragmentation of the empire climaxed with the tragic denouement of the Thirty Years War, 1618-48, which devastated much of Germany, destroyed its agriculture and medieval commercial eminence and ended the attempt of the Hapsburgs to unify Germany. Deprived of administrative capacity by a lack of resources, the imperial authority became utterly powerless. At this time Germany contained an estimated 1,800 individual states, some with a population of as little as 300. The German Empire of recent history (the creation of Bis- marck) was formed on April 14, 1871, when the king of Prussia became German Emperor William I. The new empire comprised 4 kingdoms, 6 grand duchies, 12 duchies and principalities, 3 free cities and the nonautonomous province of Alsace-Lorraine. The states had the right to issue gold and silver coins of higher value than 1 Mark; coins of 1 Mark and under were general issues of the empire.

MINT MARKS
A - Berlin, 1750-date
A - Clausthal (Hannover), 1833-1849
B - Bayreuth, Franconia (Prussia), 1796-1804
B - Breslau (Prussia, Silesia), 1750-1826
B - Brunswick (Brunswick), 1850-1860
B - Brunswick (Westphalia), 1809-1813
B - Dresden (Saxony), 1861-1872
B - Hannover (Brunswick), 1860-1871
B - Hannover (East Friesland), 1823-1825
B - Hannover (Germany) 1872-1878
B - Hannover (Hannover) 1821-1866
B - Hannover (Prussia) 1866-1873
B - Regensburg (Regensburg) 1809
B.H. Frankfurt (Free City of Frankfurt), 1808
B (rosette) H - Regensburg (Rhenish Confederation) 1802-1812
C - Cassel (Westphalia), 1810-1813
C - Clausthal (Brunswick)
C - Clausthal (Hannover), 1813-1834
C - Clausthal (Westphalia), 1810-1811
C - Dresden (Saxony), 1779-1804
C - Frankfurt (Germany), 1866-1879
D - Aurich (East Friesland under Prussia), 1750-1806
D - Dusseldorf, Rhineland (Prussia), 1816-1848
D - Munich (Germany), 1872-date
E - Dresden (Germany), 1872-1887
E - Muldenhutten (Germany), 1887-1953
F - Dresden (Saxony), 1845-1858
F - Magdeburg (Prussia), 1750-1806
F - Cassel (Hesse-Cassel), 1803-1807
F - Stuttgart (Germany) 1872-date
G - Dresden (Saxony), 1833-1844, 1850-1854
G - Glatz (Prussian Silesia) 1807-1809
G - Karlsruhe (Germany) 1872-date
G - Stettin In Pomerania (Prussia), 1750-1806
GN-BW - Bamberg (Bamberg)
H - Darmstadt (Germany) 1872-1882
H - Dresden (Saxony) 1804-1812
H.K. - Rostock (Rostock) 1862-1864
I - Hamburg (Germany)
J - Hamburg (Germany) 1873-date
J - Paris (Westphalia) 1808-1809
M.C. - Brunswick (Brunswick), 1813-14, 1820
P.R. - Dusseldorf (Julich-Berg), 1783-1804
S - Dresden (Saxony) 1813-1832
S - Hannover (Hannover) 1839-1844

MONETARY SYSTEM

Until 1871 the Mark (Marck) was a measure of weight.

North German States until 1837
2 Heller = 1 Pfennig
8 Pfennige = 1 Mariengroschen
12 Pfennige = 1 Groschen
24 Groschen = 1 Thaler
2 Gulden = 1-1/3 Reichsthaler
1 Speciesthaler (before 1753)
1 Convention Thaler (after 1753)

North German States after 1837
12 Pfennige = 1 Groschen
30 Groschen = 1 Thaler
1 Vereinsthaler (after 1857)

South German States until 1837
8 Heller = 4 Pfennige = 1 Kreuzer
24 Kreuzer Landmunze = 20 Kreuzer Convention Munze
120 Convention Kreuzer = 2 Convention Gulden = 1 Convention Thaler

South German States after 1837
8 Heller = 4 Pfennige = 1 Kreuzer

German States 1857-1871

As a result of the Monetary Convention of 1857, all the German States adopted a Vereinsthaler of uniform weight being 1/30 fine pound silver. They did continue to use their regional minor coin units to divide the Vereinsthaler for small change purposes.

After the German unification in 1871 when the old Thaler system was abandoned in favor of the Mark system (100 Pfennig = 1 Mark) the Vereinsthaler continued to circulate as a legal tender 3 Mark coin, and the double Thaler as a 6 Mark coin until 1908. In 1908 the Vereinsthalers were officially demonetized and the Thaler coinage was replaced by the new 3 Mark coin which had the same specifications as the old Vereinsthaler. The double Thaler coinage was not replaced as there was no great demand for a 6 Mark coin. Until the 1930's the German public continued to refer to the 3 Mark piece as a "Thaler".

Commencing 1871
100 Pfennig = 1 Mark

VERRECHNUNGS & GUTSCHRIFTS TOKENS

These were metallic indebtedness receipts used for commercial and banking purposes due to the lack of available subsidiary coinage. These tokens could be redeemed in sufficient quantities.

ANHALT-BERNBURG

Located in north-central Germany. Appeared as part of the patrimony of Albrecht the Bear of Brandenburg in 1170. Bracteates were first made in the 12th century. It was originally in the inheritance of Heinrich the Fat in 1252 and became extinct in 1468. The division of 1603, among the sons of Joachim Ernst, revitalized Anhalt-Bernburg. Bernburg passed to Dessau after the death of Alexander Carl in 1863.

RULERS
Alexius Friedrich Christian, 1796-1834
Alexander Carl, 1834-1863

MINT OFFICIALS' INITIALS

Initial	Date	Name
HS	1795-1821	Hans Schluter
Z	1821-48	Johann Carl Ludwig Zincken

DUCHY

REGULAR COINAGE

KM# 74 PFENNIG

Copper **Ruler:** Alexius Friedrich Christian **Obv:** Crowned AFC monogram **Rev:** I/PFENNIG

Date	Mintage	F	VF	XF	Unc	BU
1807	—	10.00	30.00	70.00	95.00	130

KM# 76 PFENNIG

Copper **Ruler:** Alexius Friedrich Christian **Rev. Inscription:** SCHEIDE/MUNTZ

Date	Mintage	F	VF	XF	Unc	BU
1808	—	5.00	15.00	65.00	100	135

KM# 77.1 PFENNIG

Copper **Ruler:** Alexius Friedrich Christian **Rev. Legend:** H ANH BERNE:SCHEIDEMUNZE **Rev. Inscription:** I/PFENNIG

Date	Mintage	F	VF	XF	Unc	BU
1822	—	10.00	15.00	45.00	115	140
1823	—	10.00	20.00	50.00	120	150
1827	—	10.00	20.00	50.00	120	150

KM# 77.2 PFENNIG

Copper **Ruler:** Alexius Friedrich Christian **Rev. Legend:** SCHEIDEMUNZE HZL ANHALT **Rev. Inscription:** I/PFENNIG

Date	Mintage	F	VF	XF	Unc	BU
1831 Z	—	10.00	15.00	45.00	65.00	80.00

KM# 78.1 4 PFENNIG

Copper **Ruler:** Alexius Friedrich Christian **Obv:** Crowned AFC monogram **Rev. Legend:** H ANH BERNB:SCHEIDE MUNZE **Rev. Inscription:** 4/PFENNIGE

Date	Mintage	F	VF	XF	Unc	BU
1822	—	15.00	30.00	75.00	120	150
1823	—	10.00	25.00	70.00	115	140

KM# 78.2 4 PFENNIG

Copper **Ruler:** Alexius Friedrich Christian **Rev. Inscription:** 4/PFENNIGE

Date	Mintage	F	VF	XF	Unc	BU
1831 Z	—	15.00	30.00	100	150	220

KM# 75 1/48 THALER

0.9700 g., 0.2500 Silver .0077 oz. **Ruler:** Alexius Friedrich Christian **Obv:** Crowned arms in branches **Rev:** Value

Date	Mintage	F	VF	XF	Unc	BU
1807	—	20.00	40.00	75.00	120	165

KM# 79 1/24 THALER

1.9800 g., 0.3500 Silver .0234 oz. **Ruler:** Alexius Friedrich Christian **Obv:** Crowned bear walking left on wall **Rev. Legend:** H ANH BERNB...

Date	Mintage	F	VF	XF	Unc	BU
1822	—	5.00	10.00	40.00	70.00	90.00
1823	—	10.00	20.00	60.00	90.00	120
1827	—	8.00	15.00	50.00	80.00	100

KM# 81 1/24 THALER

1.9800 g., 0.3500 Silver .0234 oz. **Ruler:** Alexius Friedrich Christian **Rev. Legend:** HZL. ANHALT...

Date	Mintage	F	VF	XF	Unc	BU
1831 Z	—	15.00	25.00	75.00	120	190

KM# 85 1/6 THALER

5.3400 g., 0.5200 Silver .0892 oz. **Ruler:** Alexander Carl **Obv:** Crowned bear walking right on wall **Obv. Legend:** HERZOGTHUM ANHALT-BERNBERG **Rev. Inscription:** 6/EINEN/THALER in sprays

Date	Mintage	F	VF	XF	Unc	BU
1856A	60,000	10.00	15.00	30.00	50.00	75.00

KM# 87 1/6 THALER

5.3400 g., 0.5200 Silver .0892 oz. **Ruler:** Alexander Carl **Obv:** Crowned bear walking right on wall **Obv. Legend:** HERZOFTHUM ANHALT • BERNBERG

Date	Mintage	F	VF	XF	Unc	BU
1861A	62,000	5.00	12.00	30.00	45.00	60.00
1862A	60,000	5.00	10.00	25.00	40.00	55.00

KM# 72 2/3 THALER
14.0300 g., 0.8330 Silver .3757 oz. **Ruler:** Alexius Friedrich Christian **Obv. Inscription:** XX/EINE FEINE/MARK in wreath **Rev:** Crowned bear walking left on wall **Rev. Legend:** ALEXIUS FRIEDRICH CHRISTIAN HERZOG ZU ANHALT..

Date	Mintage	F	VF	XF	Unc	BU
1806 HS	—	30.00	50.00	90.00	120	150
1808 HS	—	40.00	60.00	100	150	180
1809 HS	—	45.00	70.00	140	175	250

KM# 73 THALER
28.0600 g., 0.8330 Silver .7515 oz. **Ruler:** Alexius Friedrich Christian **Obv. Legend:** ALEXIUS FRIEDRICH CHRISTIAN... **Rev:** Crowned and mantled arms **Note:** Convention Thaler. Dav. #501.

Date	Mintage	F	VF	XF	Unc	BU
1806 HS	—	350	500	1,000	3,500	—
1809 HS	—	400	800	3,000	7,000	—

KM# 82 THALER
22.2700 g., 0.7500 Silver .5370 oz. **Ruler:** Alexius Friedrich Christian **Obv:** Crowned and mantled arms **Obv. Legend:** ALEXANDER CARL HERZOG ZU ANHALT **Note:** Mining Thaler. Dav. #502.

Date	Mintage	F	VF	XF	Unc	BU
1834	15,000	35.00	60.00	150	275	400

KM# 84 THALER
22.2700 g., 0.7500 Silver .5370 oz. **Ruler:** Alexander Carl **Obv. Legend:** ALEXANDER CARL HERZOG ZU ANHALT **Rev:** Crowned bear walking right on wall **Note:** Dav. #504.

Date	Mintage	F	VF	XF	Unc	BU
1846A	10,000	25.00	40.00	70.00	130	165
1852A	10,000	30.00	50.00	80.00	145	200
1855A	20,000	20.00	40.00	70.00	130	165

KM# 86 THALER
18.5200 g., 0.9000 Silver .5358 oz. **Ruler:** Alexander Carl **Obv:** Head of Alexander Carl left **Obv. Legend:** ALEXANDER CARL... **Rev:** Crowned arms with bear supporters **Note:** Vereins Thaler. Dav. #505.

Date	Mintage	F	VF	XF	Unc	BU
1859A	24,000	35.00	60.00	140	350	600

KM# 88 THALER
18.5200 g., 0.9000 Silver .5358 oz. **Ruler:** Alexander Carl **Obv. Legend:** ALEXANDER CARL... **Rev:** Crowned bear walking right on wall **Note:** Mining Thaler. Dav. #506.

Date	Mintage	F	VF	XF	Unc	BU
1861A	10,000	30.00	50.00	75.00	140	190
1862A	20,000	25.00	40.00	70.00	130	180

KM# 83 2 THALER (3-1/2 Gulden)
37.1200 g., 0.9000 Silver 1.0741 oz. **Ruler:** Alexander Carl **Obv:** Bust of Alexander Carl right **Obv. Legend:** ALEX.CARL HERZOG ZU ANHALT **Rev:** Crowned and mantled arms **Note:** Dav. #503.

Date	Mintage	F	VF	XF	Unc	BU
1840A	3,600	400	700	950	1,250	1,700
1845A	7,200	350	650	950	1,250	1,700
1855A	5,000	350	600	800	1,200	1,600

JOINT COINAGE

Under Alexander Carl for Anhalt-Cothen and Anhalt-Dessau

KM# 91 PFENNIG
Copper **Ruler:** Alexander Carl **Obv:** Crowned arms **Obv. Legend:** HRZGTH ANHALT **Rev. Legend:** 288 EINEN THALER

Date	Mintage	F	VF	XF	Unc	BU
1839	589,000	5.00	10.00	30.00	50.00	80.00
1840	654,000	5.00	15.00	35.00	55.00	100

KM# 96 PFENNIG
Copper **Ruler:** Alexander Carl **Obv:** Crowned arms **Obv. Legend:** HERZOGTHUM ANHALT

Date	Mintage	F	VF	XF	Unc	BU
1856A	360,000	5.00	8.00	12.00	30.00	55.00
1862A	360,000	5.00	8.00	15.00	35.00	65.00
1864A	300,000	5.00	8.00	13.00	35.00	50.00
1867B -	180,000	5.00	8.00	17.00	40.00	60.00

KM# 92 3 PFENNIGE
Copper **Ruler:** Alexander Carl **Obv:** Crowned arms **Obv. Inscription:** HRZGTH ANHALT

Date	Mintage	F	VF	XF	Unc	BU
1839	386,000	7.00	15.00	35.00	55.00	85.00
1840	292,000	7.00	10.00	35.00	55.00	85.00

KM# 98 3 PFENNIGE
Copper **Ruler:** Alexander Carl **Obv:** Crowned arms **Obv. Legend:** HERZOGTHUM ANHALT

Date	Mintage	F	VF	XF	Unc	BU
1861A	240,000	4.00	6.00	15.00	30.00	45.00
1864A	200,000	4.00	6.00	15.00	27.00	40.00
1867B	240,000	4.00	8.00	18.00	35.00	55.00

KM# 94 6 PFENNIGE
0.8100 g., 0.3750 Silver .0097 oz. **Ruler:** Alexander Carl **Obv:** Crowned arms **Obv. Legend:** HRZGTH ANHALT

Date	Mintage	F	VF	XF	Unc	BU
1840	322,000	8.00	15.00	30.00	55.00	95.00

KM# 93 GROSCHEN
1.6200 g., 0.3750 Silver .0195 oz. **Ruler:** Alexander Carl **Obv:** Crowned arms **Obv. Legend:** HRZGTH ANHALT **Rev. Legend:** 24 EINEN THALER

Date	Mintage	F	VF	XF	Unc	BU
1839	319,000	5.00	10.00	35.00	55.00	90.00
1840	Inc. above	5.00	10.00	35.00	55.00	90.00

KM# 95 SILBERGROSCHEN
2.1900 g., 0.2220 Silver .0156 oz. **Ruler:** Alexander Carl **Obv:** Crowned arms **Obv. Legend:** HERZOGTHUM ANHALT

Date	Mintage	F	VF	XF	Unc	BU
1851A	176,000	4.00	8.00	18.00	35.00	60.00
1852A	197,000	4.00	8.00	18.00	35.00	60.00
1855A	303,000	3.00	7.00	14.00	30.00	50.00
1859A	150,000	4.00	8.00	18.00	35.00	60.00
1862A	300,000	3.00	6.00	14.00	25.00	45.00

KM# 97 2-1/2 SILBERGROSCHEN
3.2400 g., 0.3750 Silver .0390 oz. **Ruler:** Alexander Carl **Obv:** Crowned arms **Obv. Legend:** HERZOGTHUM ANHALT

Date	Mintage	F	VF	XF	Unc	BU
1856A	120,000	5.00	10.00	25.00	50.00	80.00
1859A	60,000	7.00	15.00	30.00	60.00	110
1861A	120,000	5.00	10.00	25.00	50.00	80.00
1862A	240,000	5.00	8.00	20.00	45.00	75.00
1864A	120,000	5.00	10.00	25.00	50.00	80.00

TRADE COINAGE

KM# 80 DUCAT
3.5000 g., 0.9860 Gold .1109 oz. **Ruler:** Alexius Friedrich Christian **Obv. Legend:** ALEXIUS FRIED CHRIST... **Rev:** Crowned bear walking left on wall **Rev. Legend:** EX AURO ANHALTINO

Date	Mintage	F	VF	XF	Unc	BU
1825 Z	116	850	1,400	2,400	3,750	—

PATTERNS

Including off metal strikes

KM#	Date	Mintage	Identification	Mkt Val
Pn5	1825 Z	—	Ducat. Copper. KM#80.	450
Pn6	1862A	—	1/6 Thaler. Brass. KM#87.	225

ANHALT-COTHEN

Cothen has a checkered history after the patrimony of Heinrich the Fat in 1252. It was often ruled with other segments of the House of Anhalt. Founded as a separate line in 1603, became extinct in 1665 and passed to Plotzkau which changed the name to Cothen. It passed to Dessau after the death of Heinrich in 1847.

RULERS
Heinrich, 1830-1847

DUCHY

REGULAR COINAGE

KM# 39 2 THALER (3-1/2 Gulden)
37.1200 g., 0.9000 Silver 1.0743 oz. **Obv:** Head of Heinrich left **Obv. Legend:** HEINRICH HERZOG ZU ANHALT **Rev:** Crowned and mantled arms **Edge Lettering:** GOTT SEGNE ANHALT **Note:** Dav. #507.

Date	Mintage	F	VF	XF	Unc	BU
1840A	3,100	400	750	1,650	2,500	3,300

ANHALT-DESSAU

Dessau was part of the 1252 division that included Zerbst and Cothen. In 1396 Zerbst divided into Zerbst and Dessau. In 1508 Zerbst was absorbed into Dessau. Dessau was given to the eldest son of Joachim Ernst in the division of 1603. As other lines became extinct, they fell to Dessau, which united all branches in 1863.

RULERS
Leopold Friedrich Franz, 1751-1817
Leopold Friedrich, 1817-1871
Friedrich I, 1871-1904

DUCHY

REGULAR COINAGE

KM# 19 1/6 THALER
5.3400 g., 0.5200 Silver .0892 oz. **Obv:** Head of Leopold Friedrich left **Rev:** Crowned arms

Date	Mintage	F	VF	XF	Unc	BU
1865A	120,000	10.00	20.00	35.00	65.00	90.00

KM# 14 THALER (Vereins)
18.5200 g., 0.9000 Silver .5359 oz. **Ruler:** Leopold Friedrich **Obv:** Bust of Leopold Friedrich left **Obv. Legend:** LEOPOLD FRIEDRICH HERZOG ZU ANHALT **Rev:** Crowned arms supported by bears **Edge Lettering:** GOTT SEGNE ANHALT **Note:** Dav. #509.

Date	Mintage	F	VF	XF	Unc	BU
1858A	27,000	25.00	50.00	110	200	265

KM# 15 THALER (Vereins)
18.5200 g., 0.9000 Silver .5359 oz. **Subject:** Separation of Anhalt Duchies - 1603, Reunion of Anhalt Duchies - 1863 **Obv:** Bust of Leopold Friedrich left **Rev:** Crowned arms in sprays **Edge Lettering:** GOTT SEGNE ANHALT

Date	Mintage	F	VF	XF	Unc	BU
1863A	50,000	25.00	45.00	75.00	125	175

KM# 20 THALER (Vereins)
18.5200 g., 0.9000 Silver .5359 oz. **Obv:** Bust of Leopold Friedrich left **Obv. Legend:** LEOPOLD FRIEDRICH HERZOG VON ANHALT **Rev:** Crowned arms supported by bears

Date	Mintage	F	VF	XF	Unc	BU
1866A	30,880	40.00	60.00	120	200	265
1869A	31,527	30.00	50.00	100	180	230

KM# 13 2 THALER (3-1/2 Gulden)
37.1200 g., 0.9000 Silver 1.0741 oz. **Ruler:** Leopold Friedrich **Obv:** Bust of Leopold Friedrich right **Rev:** Crowned and mantled arms supported by bears **Edge Lettering:** GOTT SEGNE ANHALT **Note:** Dav. #508.

Date	Mintage	F	VF	XF	Unc	BU
1839A	4,700	300	450	750	1,350	1,850
1843A	4,700	400	500	850	1,600	2,500
1846A	4,700	350	450	800	1,350	1,900

REFORM COINAGE

KM# 22 2 MARK
11.1110 g., 0.9000 Silver .3215 oz. **Ruler:** Friedrich I **Obv:** Large head of Friedrich I right **Obv. Legend:** FRIEDRICH HERZOG V.ANHOLT **Rev:** Crowned German eagle

Date	Mintage	F	VF	XF	Unc	BU
1876A	200,000	125	225	700	1,400	1,750

KM# 23 2 MARK
11.1110 g., 0.9000 Silver .3215 oz. **Ruler:** Friedrich I **Subject:** 25th Year of Reign of Friedrich I **Obv:** Small head of Friedrich I right **Rev:** Crowned imperial German eagle

Date	Mintage	F	VF	XF	Unc	BU
1896A	50,000	200	350	500	800	900
1896A Proof	—	Value: 1,000				

KM# 24 5 MARK
27.7770 g., 0.9000 Silver .8038 oz. **Ruler:** Friedrich I **Subject:**

25th Year of Reign of Friedrich I **Obv:** Head of Friedrich I right **Rev:** Crowned imperial German eagle

Date	Mintage	F	VF	XF	Unc	BU
1896A	10,000	600	900	1,500	2,000	2,500
1896A Proof	—	Value: 2,600				

KM# 25 10 MARK
3.9820 g., 0.9000 Gold .1152 oz. **Ruler:** Friedrich I **Obv:** Head of Friedrich I right **Rev:** Crowned imperial German eagle

Date	Mintage	F	VF	XF	Unc	BU
1896A	20,000	600	1,000	1,600	2,250	2,600
1896A Proof	200	Value: 2,700				

KM# 21 20 MARK
7.9650 g., 0.9000 Gold .2304 oz. **Ruler:** Friedrich I **Obv:** Large head of Friedrich I right **Rev:** Crowned imperial German eagle

Date	Mintage	F	VF	XF	Unc	BU
1875A	25,000	500	900	1,350	2,000	2,500
1875A Proof	—	Value: 3,500				

KM# 26 20 MARK
7.9650 g., 0.9000 Gold .2304 oz. **Ruler:** Friedrich I **Obv:** Small head of Friedrich I right **Rev:** Crowned imperial German eagle

Date	Mintage	F	VF	XF	Unc	BU
1896A	15,000	600	900	1,600	2,000	2,500
1896A Proof	200	Value: 2,750				

AUGSBURG

FREE CITY

Founded as a Roman colony in the reign of Augustus, it was declared a Free City in 1276. The mint rights were granted in 1521 but the first coins are dated somewhat earlier. Augsburg was given to Bavaria in 1806.

REGULAR COINAGE

KM# 188 HELLER
Copper **Obv:** Crowned arms **Rev:** Value, date

Date	Mintage	VG	F	VF	XF	Unc
1801	—	2.00	5.00	10.00	28.00	—

KM# 190 HELLER
Copper **Ruler:** Clemens Wenzel Prince of Poland and Saxony **Obv:** State arms in oval shield **Rev:** Value and date

Date	Mintage	F	VF	XF	Unc	BU
1801	—	3.00	6.00	18.00	55.00	—
1803	—	3.00	6.00	18.00	55.00	—
1804	—	3.00	6.00	18.00	55.00	—
1805	—	3.00	6.00	18.00	55.00	—

KM# 189 PFENNING
Copper **Obv:** Arms in shield **Rev:** Inscription: STADTMYNZ

Date	Mintage	VG	F	VF	XF	Unc
1801	—	3.00	6.00	12.00	32.00	—
1802	—	3.00	6.00	12.00	32.00	—
1803	—	3.00	6.00	12.00	32.00	—

KM# 192 PFENNING
Copper **Obv:** Different arms

Date	Mintage	F	VF	XF	Unc	BU
1801	—	3.50	7.00	20.00	55.00	—
1803	—	3.00	6.00	16.00	55.00	—
1804	—	3.00	6.00	16.00	55.00	—
1805	—	3.00	6.00	16.00	55.00	—

KM# 191 PFENNING
Copper **Rev. Inscription:** STADT MUNZ

Date	Mintage	F	VF	XF	Unc	BU
1803	—	3.50	7.00	20.00	55.00	—
1804	—	3.50	7.00	20.00	55.00	—
1805	—	3.50	7.00	20.00	55.00	—

BADEN

The earliest rulers of Baden, in the southwestern part of Germany along the Rhine, descended from the dukes of Zähringen in the late 11th century. The first division of the territory occurred in 1190, when separate lines of margraves were established in Baden and in Hachberg. Immediately prior to its extinction in 1418, Hachberg was sold back to Baden, which underwent several minor divisions itself during the next century. Baden acquired most of the Countship of Sponheim from Electoral Pfalz near the end of the 15th century. In 1515, the most significant division of the patrimony took place, in which the Baden-Baden and Baden-(Pforzheim) Durlach lines were established.

UNITED BADEN LINE

REGULAR COINAGE

KM# 132 1/4 KREUZER
Copper

Date	Mintage	F	VF	XF	Unc	BU
1802	24,734	75.00	140	220	350	600

KM# 153 1/4 KREUZER
Copper **Obv:** Crowned shield **Rev:** Value, date within wreath

Date	Mintage	F	VF	XF	Unc	BU
1810 Rare	—	—	—	—	—	—

KM# 181 1/4 KREUZER
Copper

Date	Mintage	F	VF	XF	Unc	BU
1821	—	—	—	—	—	—
1824	128,000	10.00	60.00	100	175	290

KM# 133 1/2 KREUZER
Copper

Date	Mintage	F	VF	XF	Unc	BU
1803	27,000	30.00	70.00	125	500	850
1804	104,000	25.00	45.00	160	400	650
1805	157,000	20.00	40.00	125	350	575

KM# 139 1/2 KREUZER
Copper

Date	Mintage	F	VF	XF	Unc	BU
1809	877,000	10.00	25.00	90.00	150	300
1810	129,000	15.00	35.00	110	200	350
1812	105,000	20.00	40.00	135	225	325

KM# 164 1/2 KREUZER
Copper **Obv:** Crowned draped arms **Rev:** Similar to KM#165

Date	Mintage	F	VF	XF	Unc	BU
1814	78,000	20.00	50.00	100	175	275
1815	62,000	20.00	50.00	90.00	150	240
1816	39,000	20.00	50.00	100	175	275
1817	102,000	20.00	45.00	100	175	275

KM# 165 1/2 KREUZER
Copper **Obv:** Smaller crowned draped arms

Date	Mintage	F	VF	XF	Unc	BU
1814	Inc. above	20.00	50.00	90.00	150	240

KM# 171 1/2 KREUZER
Copper **Rev:** Value: 1/2 KREU/ZER

Date	Mintage	F	VF	XF	Unc	BU
1817	—	75.00	175	250	500	900

KM# 182 1/2 KREUZER
Copper

Date	Mintage	F	VF	XF	Unc	BU
1821	127,000	75.00	175	240	450	800

KM# 186 1/2 KREUZER
Copper

Date	Mintage	F	VF	XF	Unc	BU
1821	—	8.00	16.00	125	250	400
1822	109,000	8.00	16.00	125	225	325
1823	35,000	6.00	12.00	60.00	150	200
1824	66,000	6.00	12.00	60.00	175	225
1825	53,000	6.00	12.00	100	225	300
1826	191,000	6.00	8.00	50.00	100	165

KM# 188 1/2 KREUZER
Copper **Note:** Ludwig I

Date	Mintage	F	VF	XF	Unc	BU
1828	137,000	7.00	20.00	50.00	120	150
1829	204,000	4.00	14.00	30.00	60.00	90.00
1830	Inc. above	6.00	17.00	35.00	65.00	95.00

KM# 194 1/2 KREUZER
Copper **Obv:** D on truncation **Note:** Leopold I

Date	Mintage	F	VF	XF	Unc	BU
1830	24,000	7.00	15.00	50.00	80.00	120
1834	76,000	8.00	25.00	65.00	95.00	150
1835	28,000	8.00	25.00	65.00	95.00	150

KM# 213 1/2 KREUZER
Copper

Date	Mintage	F	VF	XF	Unc	BU
1842	101,000	4.00	8.00	30.00	50.00	75.00
1844	52,000	4.00	12.00	40.00	60.00	90.00
1845	74,000	4.00	8.00	25.00	40.00	60.00
1846	90,000	4.00	8.00	25.00	40.00	60.00
1847	256,000	4.00	8.00	25.00	40.00	60.00
1848	89,000	4.00	8.00	30.00	50.00	75.00
1849	102,000	4.00	8.00	25.00	40.00	60.00
1850	74,000	4.00	8.00	25.00	40.00	60.00
1851/0	87,000	4.00	8.00	25.00	40.00	60.00
1851	Inc. above	4.00	8.00	25.00	40.00	60.00
1852	227,000	4.00	8.00	20.00	35.00	50.00

KM# 230 1/2 KREUZER
Copper **Ruler:** Friedrich I as Grand Duke **Obv:** Bust right

Date	Mintage	F	VF	XF	Unc	BU
1856	195,000	4.00	8.00	20.00	40.00	60.00

KM# 241 1/2 KREUZER
Copper

Date	Mintage	F	VF	XF	Unc	BU
1859	219,000	3.00	6.00	15.00	22.00	30.00
1860	120,000	3.00	6.00	15.00	22.00	30.00
1861	109,000	3.00	6.00	15.00	22.00	30.00
1862	117,000	3.00	6.00	20.00	30.00	47.00
1863	298,000	3.00	6.00	15.00	22.00	30.00
1864	94,000	3.00	6.00	15.00	22.00	30.00
1865	349,000	3.00	6.00	15.00	22.00	30.00
1866	239,000	3.00	6.00	15.00	25.00	36.00
1867	—	5.00	10.00	50.00	—	—
1868	—	5.00	10.00	25.00	45.00	65.00
1870	38,000	3.00	6.00	15.00	25.00	35.00
1871	—	3.00	6.00	15.00	22.00	30.00

KM# 134 KREUZER
Copper

Date	Mintage	F	VF	XF	Unc	BU
1803	146,312	30.00	75.00	200	400	750
1805	95,564	50.00	90.00	250	600	950
1806 Rare	—	—	—	—	—	—

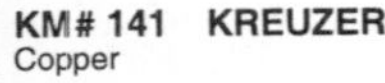

KM# 141 KREUZER
Copper

Date	Mintage	F	VF	XF	Unc	BU
1807	96,000	10.00	25.00	65.00	80.00	120
1808	1,704,000	8.00	20.00	50.00	70.00	110

KM# 147 KREUZER
Copper

Date	Mintage	F	VF	XF	Unc	BU
1809	1,263,000	10.00	50.00	80.00	125	175
1810	639,000	15.00	60.00	125	150	230
1811	125,000	7.00	40.00	65.00	100	125
1812	285,000	7.00	40.00	70.00	135	165

KM# 157 KREUZER
Copper **Obv:** Legend; crowned arms **Rev:** Value: 1 KREUZ/ER, date

Date	Mintage	F	VF	XF	Unc	BU
1813	—	30.00	75.00	150	300	600

KM# 158 KREUZER
Copper **Rev:** Value: 1 KREUZER/1813 within circle of dots

Date	Mintage	F	VF	XF	Unc	BU
1813	320,000	15.00	50.00	70.00	150	240

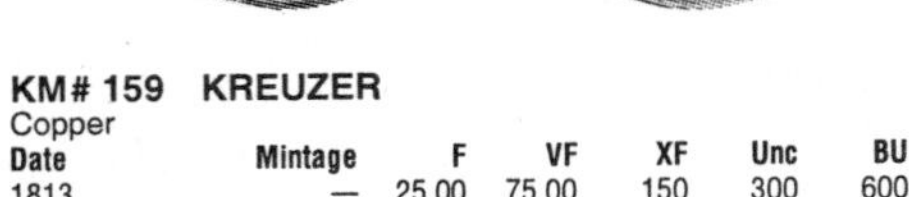

KM# 159 KREUZER
Copper

Date	Mintage	F	VF	XF	Unc	BU
1813	—	25.00	75.00	150	300	600

KM# 160 KREUZER
Copper

Date	Mintage	F	VF	XF	Unc	BU
1813	—	20.00	60.00	110	200	350

KM# 166.1 KREUZER
Copper **Obv:** Date between dots

Date	Mintage	F	VF	XF	Unc	BU
1814	489,000	20.00	70.00	120	200	375

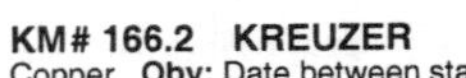

KM# 166.2 KREUZER
Copper **Obv:** Date between stars

Date	Mintage	F	VF	XF	Unc	BU
1814	Inc. above	10.00	35.00	70.00	110	170
1815	490,000	5.00	25.00	55.00	75.00	115
1816	464,000	10.00	30.00	60.00	110	140
1817	327,000	10.00	40.00	80.00	110	170

KM# 166.3 KREUZER
Copper **Obv:** Date between crosses

Date	Mintage	F	VF	XF	Unc	BU
1815	—	7.00	25.00	75.00	110	175

KM# 167 KREUZER
Copper **Rev:** Value: 1 KREU=/ZER

Date	Mintage	F	VF	XF	Unc	BU
1814	—	15.00	35.00	55.00	100	215
1815	490,000	10.00	25.00	45.00	100	140
1816	464,000	10.00	25.00	55.00	215	—
1817	Inc. above	5.00	15.00	35.00	100	120
1820	—	10.00	25.00	45.00	100	140

KM# 183 KREUZER
Copper

Date	Mintage	F	VF	XF	Unc	BU
1821	55,000	20.00	30.00	60.00	100	150
1822	197,000	15.00	25.00	60.00	100	150
1823	205,000	10.00	20.00	55.00	85.00	125
1824	253,000	8.00	15.00	55.00	85.00	125
1825	335,000	5.00	8.00	45.00	75.00	120
1826	—	15.00	25.00	60.00	100	150

KM# 189 KREUZER
Copper **Ruler:** Ludwig I **Obv:** Bust right

Date	Mintage	F	VF	XF	Unc	BU
1827	515,000	4.00	7.50	35.00	75.00	120
1827 D	Inc. above	2.50	7.50	16.00	75.00	—
1828	1,206,000	4.00	7.50	25.00	50.00	75.00
1828 D	Inc. above	2.50	7.50	16.00	75.00	—
1829	603,000	4.00	7.50	30.00	60.00	85.00
1829 D	Inc. above	2.50	7.50	16.00	75.00	—
1830	149,000	4.00	7.50	40.00	85.00	130
1830 D	Inc. above	2.50	7.50	16.00	75.00	—

KM# 197.1 KREUZER
Copper **Ruler:** Leopold I **Obv:** Period after BADEN in legend

Date	Mintage	F	VF	XF	Unc	BU
1831	227,000	4.00	8.00	15.00	30.00	45.00

KM# 197.2 KREUZER
Copper **Obv:** Without period after BADEN in legend

Date	Mintage	F	VF	XF	Unc	BU
1831	Inc. above	4.00	8.00	15.00	30.00	45.00
1832	172,000	4.00	8.00	15.00	30.00	45.00
1833	181,000	4.00	8.00	15.00	30.00	45.00
1834	250,000	4.00	8.00	15.00	30.00	45.00
1835	294,000	4.00	8.00	15.00	30.00	45.00
1836	163,000	4.00	8.00	15.00	30.00	45.00
1837	—	4.00	8.00	15.00	30.00	45.00

KM# 203 KREUZER
Copper **Obv:** Without D on truncation

Date	Mintage	F	VF	XF	Unc	BU
1836	321,000	3.00	6.00	15.00	35.00	50.00
1837	Inc. above	4.00	8.00	20.00	50.00	65.00
1838	642,000	3.00	6.00	15.00	35.00	50.00
1839	254,000	3.00	6.00	15.00	35.00	50.00
1840	573,000	3.00	6.00	15.00	35.00	50.00
1841	423,000	3.00	6.00	15.00	35.00	50.00
1842	865,000	3.00	6.00	15.00	35.00	50.00
1843	527,000	3.00	6.00	15.00	35.00	50.00
1844	663,000	3.00	6.00	15.00	35.00	50.00
1845	1,442,000	3.00	6.00	15.00	35.00	50.00

KM# 216 KREUZER
Copper **Subject:** Erection of Karl Friedrich's statue

Date	Mintage	F	VF	XF	Unc	BU
1844	54,000	3.00	5.00	15.00	35.00	55.00

KM# 218.1 KREUZER
Copper **Obv:** Without period after Baden

Date	Mintage	F	VF	XF	Unc	BU
1845	Inc. above	3.00	6.00	10.00	22.00	35.00
1846	452,000	3.00	6.00	10.00	22.00	35.00

KM# 218.2 KREUZER
Copper **Obv:** Period after Baden

Date	Mintage	F	VF	XF	Unc	BU
1847	639,000	3.00	6.00	10.00	22.00	35.00
1848	232,000	3.00	6.00	10.00	22.00	35.00
1849	872,000	3.00	6.00	10.00	22.00	35.00
1850	238,000	4.00	8.00	22.00	50.00	75.00
1851	1,208,000	3.00	6.00	10.00	22.00	35.00
1852	821,000	2.00	4.00	7.00	15.00	25.00

KM# 231 KREUZER
Copper **Ruler:** Friedrich I as Prince Regent **Obv:** Bust right

Date	Mintage	F	VF	XF	Unc	BU
1856	707,000	10.00	20.00	40.00	55.00	75.00

KM# 232 KREUZER
Copper **Ruler:** Friedrich I as Grand Duke

Date	Mintage	F	VF	XF	Unc	BU
1856	660,000	5.00	10.00	25.00	45.00	70.00

KM# 238 KREUZER
Copper **Subject:** Birth of Heir

Date	Mintage	F	VF	XF	Unc	BU
1857	12,000	5.00	15.00	25.00	40.00	65.00

KM# 242 KREUZER
Copper

Date	Mintage	F	VF	XF	Unc	BU
1859	898,000	3.00	5.00	8.00	15.00	24.00
1860	655,000	3.00	5.00	8.00	15.00	24.00
1861	726,000	3.00	5.00	8.00	15.00	24.00
1862	623,000	4.00	7.00	12.00	20.00	30.00
1863	765,000	3.00	5.00	8.00	15.00	24.00
1864	724,000	3.00	5.00	8.00	15.00	24.00
1865	778,000	3.00	5.00	8.00	15.00	24.00
1866	732,000	3.00	5.00	8.00	15.00	24.00
1867	698,000	3.00	5.00	8.00	15.00	24.00
1868	885,000	3.00	5.00	8.00	15.00	24.00
1869	858,000	3.00	5.00	8.00	15.00	24.00
1870	918,000	3.00	5.00	8.00	15.00	24.00
1871	—	3.00	5.00	8.00	15.00	24.00

KM# 244 KREUZER
Copper **Subject:** Leopold Memorial

Date	Mintage	F	VF	XF	Unc	BU
1861	—	5.00	20.00	40.00	55.00	75.00

KM# 250 KREUZER
Copper **Subject:** 50th Anniversary of Baden's Constitution

Date	Mintage	F	VF	XF	Unc	BU
1868	25,000	5.00	10.00	25.00	35.00	55.00

KM# 251 KREUZER
Copper **Subject:** Church at Seckenheim

Date	Mintage	F	VF	XF	Unc	BU
1869	1,000	30.00	50.00	100	160	240

KM# 252 KREUZER
Copper **Subject:** Victory in War with France

Date	Mintage	F	VF	XF	Unc	BU
1871	—	3.00	5.00	10.00	18.00	—

KM# 253 KREUZER
Copper **Obv:** SCHEIDE MUNZE below shield

Date	Mintage	F	VF	XF	Unc	BU
1871	—	5.00	10.00	20.00	30.00	45.00

KM# 254 KREUZER
Copper **Subject:** Buehl Commemorating Victory Over France

Date	Mintage	F	VF	XF	Unc	BU
1871	—	45.00	75.00	125	160	220

KM# 255 KREUZER
Copper **Subject:** Karlsruhe Commemorating Victory Over France
Obv: Arms **Rev:** Legend

Date	Mintage	F	VF	XF	Unc	BU
1871	76,000	7.00	15.00	20.00	50.00	75.00

KM# 256 KREUZER
Copper **Subject:** Offenburg Commemorating Victory Over France

Date	Mintage	F	VF	XF	Unc	BU
1871	2,100	20.00	45.00	90.00	145	210

KM# 135 3 KREUZER
1.4230 g., 0.3130 Silver .0143 oz.

Date	Mintage	F	VF	XF	Unc	BU
1803	189,000	50.00	90.00	175	475	900
1805	445,000	50.00	90.00	220	575	950
1806	126,000	30.00	75.00	150	375	725

KM# 144 3 KREUZER
1.4230 g., 0.3130 Silver .0143 oz. **Obv:** Lion in shield faces left

Date	Mintage	F	VF	XF	Unc	BU
1808	410,000	30.00	75.00	160	300	650

KM# 148.1 3 KREUZER
1.4230 g., 0.3130 Silver .0143 oz. **Obv:** Lion in shield faces right

Date	Mintage	F	VF	XF	Unc	BU
1809	208,000	20.00	50.00	140	300	700
1810	262,000	25.00	60.00	150	300	750
1811	316,000	10.00	30.00	100	300	600
1812	734,000	10.00	30.00	100	300	600
1813	273,000	20.00	50.00	140	300	700

KM# 148.2 3 KREUZER
1.4230 g., 0.3130 Silver .0143 oz. **Rev:** Z backwards in KREUZER

Date	Mintage	F	VF	XF	Unc	BU
1812	Inc. above	20.00	50.00	140	300	700

KM# 161 3 KREUZER
1.2470 g., 0.3130 Silver .0125 oz. **Rev:** Value: 3 KREUZER within branches

Date	Mintage	F	VF	XF	Unc	BU
1813	—	25.00	50.00	75.00	145	275
1814	280,000	20.00	40.00	70.00	140	215
1815	214,000	15.00	30.00	55.00	95.00	165
1816	243,000	20.00	40.00	70.00	140	215
1817	—	25.00	50.00	75.00	145	275

KM# 172 3 KREUZER
1.2470 g., 0.3130 Silver .0125 oz. **Rev:** Value: 3 KREU=/ZER

Date	Mintage	F	VF	XF	Unc	BU
1817	371,000	10.00	25.00	75.00	140	240
1818	593,000	10.00	25.00	90.00	175	275
1819	815,000	15.00	35.00	125	200	325
1820	Inc. above	15.00	35.00	110	190	300

KM# 178 3 KREUZER
1.2470 g., 0.3130 Silver .0125 oz. **Obv:** Larger shield, without drape

Date	Mintage	F	VF	XF	Unc	BU
1820	Inc. above	50.00	100	250	400	650
1821	65,000	50.00	100	250	350	600
1824	96,000	50.00	100	200	300	535
1825	73,000	50.00	100	225	350	600

KM# 191 3 KREUZER
1.1400 g., 0.3750 Silver .0134 oz. **Rev:** Value: DREI KREUZER

Date	Mintage	F	VF	XF	Unc	BU
1829	1,277,000	6.00	11.00	20.00	40.00	75.00
1830	1,009,000	4.00	8.00	15.00	40.00	60.00

KM# 199 3 KREUZER
1.1400 g., 0.3750 Silver .0134 oz. **Rev:** Value: 3 KREUZER

Date	Mintage	F	VF	XF	Unc	BU
1832	729,000	4.00	8.00	15.00	35.00	60.00
1833	846,000	4.00	8.00	15.00	35.00	60.00
1834	549,000	4.00	8.00	15.00	35.00	60.00
1835	476,000	4.00	8.00	15.00	35.00	60.00
1836	723,000	4.00	8.00	15.00	35.00	60.00
1837	—	7.00	12.00	40.00	75.00	110

KM# 211 3 KREUZER
1.2990 g., 0.3330 Silver .0139 oz.

Date	Mintage	F	VF	XF	Unc	BU
1841	328,000	3.00	6.00	15.00	40.00	65.00
1842	420,000	4.00	8.00	20.00	45.00	70.00
1843	168,000	5.00	10.00	25.00	50.00	80.00
1844	361,000	4.00	8.00	20.00	45.00	70.00
1845	385,000	4.00	8.00	20.00	45.00	70.00
1846	219,000	5.00	10.00	25.00	50.00	80.00
1847	392,000	4.00	8.00	20.00	45.00	70.00
1848	195,000	3.00	6.00	15.00	40.00	65.00
1849	397,000	4.00	8.00	20.00	45.00	70.00
1850	212,000	4.00	8.00	20.00	45.00	70.00
1851	196,000	4.00	8.00	20.00	45.00	70.00
1852	192,000	4.00	8.00	20.00	45.00	70.00
1853	—	3.00	6.00	15.00	40.00	70.00
1854	—	4.00	8.00	20.00	45.00	70.00
1855	—	3.00	6.00	15.00	40.00	65.00
1856	—	3.00	6.00	15.00	40.00	65.00

KM# 246 3 KREUZER
1.2320 g., 0.3500 Silver .0138 oz. **Obv:** SCHEIDE/MUNZE below arms

Date	Mintage	F	VF	XF	Unc	BU
1866	240,000	3.00	7.00	12.00	20.00	30.00
1867	389,000	3.00	7.00	12.00	20.00	30.00
1868	315,000	3.00	7.00	12.00	20.00	30.00
1869	285,000	3.00	7.00	12.00	20.00	30.00
1870	259,000	3.00	7.00	12.00	20.00	30.00
1871	—	5.00	9.00	15.00	25.00	36.00

KM# 137 6 KREUZER
2.3530 g., 0.3750 Silver .0283 oz.

Date	Mintage	F	VF	XF	Unc	BU
1804	55,000	100	150	1,000	1,750	2,500

KM# 138 6 KREUZER
2.3530 g., 0.3750 Silver .0283 oz.

Date	Mintage	F	VF	XF	Unc	BU
1804	Inc. above	30.00	100	300	600	900
1805	461,000	50.00	125	350	800	1,200

KM# 140 6 KREUZER
2.3530 g., 0.3750 Silver .0283 oz. **Obv:** Lion in arms facing left

Date	Mintage	F	VF	XF	Unc	BU
1806	131,000	25.00	45.00	140	250	475
1807	371,000	25.00	45.00	140	250	475
1808	1,118,000	15.00	30.00	120	200	475

KM# 149 6 KREUZER
2.3530 g., 0.3750 Silver .0283 oz. **Obv:** Lion in arms facing right **Obv. Legend:** G. H. BADEN...

Date	Mintage	F	VF	XF	Unc	BU
1809	539,000	350	750	975	1,700	3,000
1812	339,000	25.00	50.00	100	300	700
1813	559,000	25.00	50.00	100	300	700

KM# 162 6 KREUZER
2.3530 g., 0.3750 Silver .0283 oz. **Obv. Legend:** G. B. BADEN...

Date	Mintage	F	VF	XF	Unc	BU
1813	Inc. above	25.00	50.00	100	300	700

KM# 168 6 KREUZER
2.2270 g., 0.3750 Silver .0268 oz. **Rev:** Value: 6 KREUT=/ZER within olive branches

Date	Mintage	F	VF	XF	Unc	BU
1814	115,000	15.00	45.00	100	175	275
1815	244,000	10.00	40.00	80.00	125	225
1816	1,603,000	8.00	25.00	40.00	90.00	175
1817	563,000	10.00	40.00	90.00	160	250

KM# 170 6 KREUZER
2.2270 g., 0.3750 Silver .0268 oz. **Rev:** Value: 6 KREU=/ZER within olive branches

Date	Mintage	F	VF	XF	Unc	BU
1816	Inc. above	10.00	40.00	75.00	145	225
1817	Inc. above	8.00	30.00	65.00	130	200
1818	112,000	10.00	40.00	65.00	140	210

KM# 173 6 KREUZER
2.2270 g., 0.3750 Silver .0268 oz. **Ruler:** Ludwig I **Obv:** Bust right

Date	Mintage	F	VF	XF	Unc	BU
1819	390,000	60.00	95.00	300	900	1,600
1822	—	700	1,400	—	—	—

KM# 179 6 KREUZER
2.2270 g., 0.3750 Silver .0268 oz. **Obv:** Larger head right, hair combed forward **Rev:** Crowned shield

Date	Mintage	F	VF	XF	Unc	BU
1820	95,000	60.00	150	300	500	750

KM# 180 6 KREUZER
2.2270 g., 0.3750 Silver .0268 oz. **Rev:** Crowned shield within branches

Date	Mintage	F	VF	XF	Unc	BU
1820	Inc. above	60.00	160	350	700	1,000
1821	186,000	45.00	120	300	600	900

KM# 198.1 6 KREUZER
2.2270 g., 0.3750 Silver .0268 oz. **Ruler:** Leopold I **Obv:** D on truncation, head right

Date	Mintage	F	VF	XF	Unc	BU
1831	862,000	3.00	7.00	18.00	50.00	70.00
1832	929,000	3.00	7.00	18.00	40.00	60.00
1833	1,003,000	3.00	7.00	20.00	50.00	70.00
1834	898,000	3.00	7.00	17.00	50.00	70.00
1835	1,025,000	3.00	7.00	20.00	50.00	70.00
1836	917,000	3.00	7.00	20.00	50.00	70.00

KM# 198.2 6 KREUZER

2.2270 g., 0.3750 Silver .0268 oz. **Obv:** Without D on truncation

Date	Mintage	F	VF	XF	Unc	BU
1835	Inc. above	12.00	40.00	90.00	140	240
1836	Inc. above	12.00	50.00	140	170	300
1837	415,000	8.00	18.00	30.00	90.00	150

KM# 210 6 KREUZER

2.5980 g., 0.3330 Silver .0278 oz.

Date	Mintage	F	VF	XF	Unc	BU
1839	—	10.00	20.00	50.00	100	150
1840	1,317,000	4.00	8.00	25.00	40.00	65.00
1841	168,000	5.00	10.00	30.00	45.00	75.00
1842	612,000	5.00	10.00	30.00	45.00	75.00
1843	615,000	5.00	10.00	35.00	50.00	85.00
1844	757,000	5.00	10.00	30.00	45.00	75.00
1845	262,000	7.00	15.00	35.00	50.00	85.00
1846	368,000	5.00	10.00	30.00	45.00	75.00
1847	857,000	4.00	8.00	25.00	40.00	65.00
1848	377,000	4.00	8.00	25.00	40.00	65.00
1849	371,000	4.00	8.00	25.00	40.00	65.00
1850	200,000	10.00	20.00	55.00	75.00	120
1855	—	4.00	8.00	25.00	40.00	65.00
1856	—	4.00	8.00	25.00	40.00	65.00

KM# 145 10 KREUZER

3.8980 g., 0.5000 Silver .0626 oz. **Ruler:** Karl Friedrich as Grand Duke

Date	Mintage	F	VF	XF	Unc	BU
1808	68,000	75.00	175	700	1,400	2,200

KM# 150 10 KREUZER

3.8980 g., 0.5000 Silver .0626 oz.

Date	Mintage	F	VF	XF	Unc	BU
1809	Inc. above	250	750	1,100	1,600	2,500

KM# 192 10 KREUZER

2.7840 g., 0.5000 Silver .0447 oz. **Ruler:** Ludwig I

Date	Mintage	F	VF	XF	Unc	BU
1829	527,000	7.00	12.00	40.00	70.00	90.00
1830	510,000	4.00	8.00	30.00	55.00	75.00

KM# 142 20 KREUZER

6.6820 g., 0.5830 Silver .1252 oz. **Obv:** Karl Friedrich with long hair **Rev:** Lion in shield facing left

Date	Mintage	F	VF	XF	Unc	BU
1807 B	15,000	100	250	700	1,200	1,750

KM# 146 20 KREUZER

6.6820 g., 0.5830 Silver .1252 oz. **Rev:** Lion in shield facing right

Date	Mintage	F	VF	XF	Unc	BU
1808	—	75.00	150	250	450	900
1808 B	—	75.00	150	275	500	1,000

KM# 151 20 KREUZER

6.6820 g., 0.5830 Silver .1252 oz. **Obv:** Bust with short hair

Date	Mintage	F	VF	XF	Unc	BU
1809	—	300	800	1,250	1,700	2,800
1810	170,000	150	650	850	1,300	1,800

KM# 209 1/2 GULDEN

5.3030 g., 0.9000 Silver .1534 oz. **Ruler:** Leopold I **Obv:** Head right

Date	Mintage	F	VF	XF	Unc	BU
1838	1,044,000	10.00	25.00	50.00	90.00	130
1839	500,000	10.00	30.00	60.00	100	150
1840	511,000	10.00	25.00	55.00	95.00	135
1841	417,000	10.00	25.00	60.00	100	150
1842	362,000	10.00	25.00	60.00	100	150
1843	469,000	10.00	25.00	60.00	100	150
1844	274,000	10.00	25.00	60.00	100	150
1845	322,000	10.00	25.00	60.00	100	150
1846	118,000	15.00	30.00	85.00	225	360

KM# 221 1/2 GULDEN

5.3030 g., 0.9000 Silver .1534 oz. **Obv:** Without D on truncation, larger head`

Date	Mintage	F	VF	XF	Unc	BU
1845	—	10.00	45.00	80.00	140	185
1846	Inc. above	10.00	45.00	80.00	140	185
1847	537,000	8.00	35.00	65.00	90.00	150
1848	332,000	10.00	35.00	65.00	90.00	150
1849	69,000	10.00	35.00	65.00	90.00	150
1850	—	10.00	35.00	75.00	110	160
1851	122,000	10.00	45.00	90.00	150	210
1852	26,000	10.00	45.00	90.00	150	210

KM# 233 1/2 GULDEN

5.3030 g., 0.9000 Silver .1534 oz. **Obv:** Head of Friedrich I right

Date	Mintage	F	VF	XF	Unc	BU
1856	—	35.00	65.00	125	250	420

KM# 234 1/2 GULDEN

5.3030 g., 0.9000 Silver .1534 oz. **Obv:** VOIGHT below head

Date	Mintage	F	VF	XF	Unc	BU
1856	150,000	25.00	50.00	150	250	325
1860	342,000	20.00	45.00	100	160	210

KM# 243 1/2 GULDEN

5.2910 g., 0.9000 Silver .0850 oz.

Date	Mintage	F	VF	XF	Unc	BU
1860	Inc. above	25.00	50.00	85.00	145	190
1861	264,000	20.00	45.00	80.00	140	180
1862	233,000	20.00	45.00	80.00	140	180
1863	227,000	20.00	45.00	80.00	140	180
1864	117,000	20.00	45.00	80.00	140	180
1865	184,000	20.00	45.00	80.00	140	180

KM# 248 1/2 GULDEN

5.2910 g., 0.9000 Silver .0850 oz.

Date	Mintage	F	VF	XF	Unc	BU
1867	155,000	15.00	30.00	75.00	150	210
1868	70,000	15.00	35.00	100	200	275
1869	73,000	15.00	30.00	75.00	150	210

KM# 184 GULDEN

12.7270 g., 0.7500 Silver .3069 oz. **Obv:** Ludwig I with short hair

Date	Mintage	F	VF	XF	Unc	BU
1821	90,000	125	400	600	1,000	1,900
1822	45,000	200	450	700	1,200	2,100
1823	39,000	175	425	700	1,200	2,100
1824	50,000	210	475	700	1,200	2,100
1825	22,000	125	400	600	1,000	1,900

KM# 187 GULDEN

12.7270 g., 0.7500 Silver .3069 oz. **Obv:** Ludwig I with curly hair

Date	Mintage	F	VF	XF	Unc	BU
1826	94,000	400	700	1,600	2,500	3,500

KM# 207 GULDEN
12.7270 g., 0.7500 Silver .3069 oz. **Obv:** Ludwig I without period after BADEN

Date	Mintage	F	VF	XF	Unc	BU
1837	629,000	15.00	35.00	100	250	360
1838	210,000	10.00	30.00	60.00	100	180
1839	485,000	10.00	30.00	60.00	100	180
1840	468,000	10.00	30.00	60.00	100	180
1841	387,000	10.00	30.00	60.00	100	180

KM# 214 GULDEN
12.7270 g., 0.7500 Silver .3069 oz. **Obv:** Period after BADEN

Date	Mintage	F	VF	XF	Unc	BU
1842	390,000	10.00	30.00	70.00	110	190
1843	444,000	10.00	30.00	60.00	100	180
1844	585,000	10.00	30.00	70.00	110	190
1845	439,000	10.00	30.00	70.00	110	190

KM# 219 GULDEN
10.6060 g., 0.9000 Silver .3069 oz.

Date	Mintage	F	VF	XF	Unc	BU
1845	Inc. above	30.00	50.00	90.00	125	175
1846	—	40.00	75.00	150	250	425
1847	397,000	25.00	35.00	75.00	100	150
1848	116,000	30.00	50.00	90.00	125	175
1849	21,000	40.00	75.00	150	250	425
1850	8,652	30.00	50.00	90.00	125	185
1851	89,000	30.00	50.00	90.00	135	195
1852	33,000	30.00	50.00	110	150	210

KM# 224 GULDEN
10.6060 g., 0.9000 Silver .3069 oz. **Subject:** Blessing on the Baden Mines

Date	Mintage	F	VF	XF	Unc	BU
1852	Inc. above	35.00	55.00	100	150	220

KM# 235 GULDEN
10.5820 g., 0.9000 Silver .3062 oz. **Obv. Legend:** FRIEDRICH PRINZ...

Date	Mintage	F	VF	XF	Unc	BU
1856	149,000	60.00	110	250	450	600

KM# 236 GULDEN
10.5820 g., 0.9000 Silver .3062 oz. **Obv. Legend:** FRIEDRICH GROSHERZOG... **Rev:** Similar to KM#235

Date	Mintage	F	VF	XF	Unc	BU
1856	342,000	25.00	45.00	70.00	170	240
1859	195,000	30.00	55.00	100	240	350
1860	44,000	25.00	45.00	80.00	175	270

KM# 239 GULDEN
10.5820 g., 0.9000 Silver .3062 oz. **Subject:** Mint Visit

Date	Mintage	F	VF	XF	Unc	BU
1857	776	75.00	175	250	325	425

KM# 247 GULDEN
10.5820 g., 0.9000 Silver .3062 oz. **Subject:** First Shooting Festival at Mannheim

Date	Mintage	F	VF	XF	Unc	BU
1863	12,000	20.00	35.00	70.00	110	150

KM# 249 GULDEN
10.5820 g., 0.9000 Silver .3062 oz. **Subject:** Second Shooting Festival at Karlsruhe

Date	Mintage	F	VF	XF	Unc	BU
1867	14,000	45.00	90.00	175	250	—

KM# 185 2 GULDEN
25.4540 g., 0.7500 Silver .6138 oz. **Ruler:** Ludwig I

Date	Mintage	F	VF	XF	Unc	BU
1821	30,000	125	225	450	1,300	1,900
1822	20,000	75.00	150	375	850	1,500
1823	7,040	125	225	500	1,350	2,100
1824	17,000	100	175	400	900	1,550
1825	6,642	90.00	160	375	800	1,500

KM# 222 2 GULDEN
21.2100 g., 0.9000 Silver .6138 oz. **Ruler:** Leopold I

Date	Mintage	F	VF	XF	Unc	BU
1846	592,000	35.00	60.00	100	200	300
1847	232,000	40.00	70.00	125	190	325
1848	273,000	40.00	70.00	125	190	325
1849	41,000	50.00	100	200	400	600
1850	140,000	40.00	70.00	125	190	325
1851	124,000	40.00	70.00	125	190	325
1852	142,000	35.00	60.00	100	200	300

KM# 237 2 GULDEN
21.2100 g., 0.9000 Silver .6138 oz. **Rev:** Similar to KM#222
Note: Friedrich I

Date	Mintage	F	VF	XF	Unc	BU
1856	84,000	125	250	400	750	1,050

KM# 176.1 5 GULDEN
3.4390 g., 0.9030 Gold .0998 oz. **Ruler:** Ludwig I **Obv:** Head right

Date	Mintage	F	VF	XF	Unc	BU
1819 PH	3,000	500	1,000	1,500	2,200	—

KM# 176.2 5 GULDEN
3.4390 g., 0.9030 Gold .0998 oz. **Obv:** Without engraver's initials below head

Date	Mintage	F	VF	XF	Unc	BU
1819	695	650	1,000	1,500	2,200	—
1821	465	675	1,125	1,750	2,500	—
1822	1,718	525	875	1,500	2,200	—
1823	1,854	525	875	1,500	2,200	—
1824	2,763	450	750	1,350	1,850	—
1825	1,508	525	875	1,500	2,200	—
1826	887	600	1,000	1,650	2,450	—

KM# 190 5 GULDEN
3.4390 g., 0.9030 Gold .0998 oz. **Obv:** Curly hair

Date	Mintage	F	VF	XF	Unc	BU
1827	2,877	450	850	2,250	3,250	—
1828	2,317	450	850	2,250	3,250	—

KM# 177.1 10 GULDEN
6.8780 g., 0.9030 Gold .1997 oz. **Ruler:** Ludwig I **Obv:** Head right

Date	Mintage	F	VF	XF	Unc	BU
1819 PH	4,332	950	1,500	2,350	3,500	—

KM# 177.2 10 GULDEN
6.8780 g., 0.9030 Gold .1997 oz. **Obv:** Withhout engraver's initials below head

Date	Mintage	F	VF	XF	Unc	BU
1821	812	1,150	1,800	2,500	4,000	—
1823	373	1,250	2,000	2,750	4,250	—
1824	328	1,400	2,200	3,000	4,500	—
1825	Inc. above	1,400	2,200	3,000	4,500	—

KM# 136 THALER
28.0600 g., 0.8330 Silver .7515 oz. **Ruler:** Karl Friedrich as Elector **Obv:** Head right

Date	Mintage	F	VF	XF	Unc	BU
1803 FE HB	675	1,000	2,500	4,500	8,000	12,000

KM# 152 THALER
28.0600 g., 0.8330 Silver .7515 oz.

Date	Mintage	F	VF	XF	Unc	BU
1809 B E	6,219	350	750	1,700	3,200	6,000
1810 B	2,815	400	950	2,200	4,000	7,000
1811 B E	3,885	300	600	1,700	3,200	6,000

KM# 163 THALER (Krone)
59.5160 g., 0.8710 Silver .8266 oz.

Date	Mintage	F	VF	XF	Unc	BU
1813 D	—	125	250	600	1,200	1,700
1814 D	36,000	100	200	500	1,000	1,500

KM# 169 THALER (Krone)
59.5160 g., 0.8710 Silver .8266 oz. **Rev:** Without mintmaster's initial

Date	Mintage	F	VF	XF	Unc	BU
1814	Inc. above	125	200	475	850	1,200
1815	38,000	100	185	275	650	850
1816	36,000	90.00	165	250	600	750
1817	52,000	90.00	165	225	650	775
1818	39,000	100	175	275	700	850
1819	—	125	210	600	1,300	1,750

KM# 175.1 THALER (Krone)
59.5160 g., 0.8710 Silver .8266 oz. **Ruler:** Ludwig I **Obv:** WD monogram below bust

Date	Mintage	F	VF	XF	Unc	BU
1819	—	500	1,100	2,000	3,000	5,000

KM# 175.2 THALER (Krone)
59.5160 g., 0.8710 Silver .8266 oz. **Ruler:** Ludwig I **Obv:** DOELL on truncation

Date	Mintage	F	VF	XF	Unc	BU
1819	—	150	325	700	2,500	4,000
1820	38,000	225	500	800	3,500	5,000
1821	19,000	225	500	875	3,600	5,200

KM# 193 THALER (Krone)
18.1480 g., 0.8750 Silver .5105 oz. **Ruler:** Ludwig I

Date	Mintage	F	VF	XF	Unc	BU
1829	168,000	70.00	125	200	300	525
1830	101,000	50.00	100	150	270	475

KM# 195.1 THALER (Krone)
18.1480 g., 0.8750 Silver .5105 oz. **Ruler:** Leopold I **Rev:** Without dot after BADEN in legend

Date	Mintage	F	VF	XF	Unc	BU
1830	238,000	55.00	95.00	250	650	—
1831	168,000	25.00	75.00	180	450	—
1832	176,000	25.00	75.00	180	450	—
1832 Star	Inc. above	30.00	85.00	190	475	—

KM# 195.2 THALER (Krone)
18.1480 g., 0.8750 Silver .5105 oz. **Rev:** Dot after BADEN in legend

Date	Mintage	F	VF	XF	Unc	BU
1832 Star	Inc. above	30.00	85.00	190	475	—
1833 Star	115,000	30.00	85.00	190	325	410
1833	Inc. above	25.00	75.00	150	300	410
1834	36,000	30.00	85.00	150	310	425
1835	75,000	30.00	85.00	160	310	425
1836 Large 6	85,000	30.00	85.00	160	310	425
1837	—	50.00	95.00	235	375	500

KM# 195.3 THALER (Krone)
18.1480 g., 0.8750 Silver .5105 oz. **Rev:** Hyphen between KRONEN-THALER in legend

Date	Mintage	F	VF	XF	Unc	BU
1834	Inc. above	30.00	80.00	150	300	430
1836	Inc. above	30.00	80.00	150	300	430

KM# 200 THALER (Krone)
18.1480 g., 0.8750 Silver .5105 oz. **Subject:** Mint Visit

Date	Mintage	F	VF	XF	Unc	BU
1832	—	400	700	1,000	1,500	2,000

KM# 202 THALER (Krone)
18.1480 g., 0.8750 Silver .5105 oz. **Subject:** Blessings on the Baden Mines

Date	Mintage	F	VF	XF	Unc	BU
1834	6,517	200	300	500	900	1,500

KM# 204 THALER (Krone)
18.1480 g., 0.8750 Silver .5105 oz.

Date	Mintage	F	VF	XF	Unc	BU
1836	8,250	100	200	400	900	1,300

KM# 205 THALER (Krone)
18.1480 g., 0.8750 Silver .5105 oz. **Obv:** KM#195.2 **Rev:** KM#204 **Note:** Mule

Date	Mintage	F	VF	XF	Unc	BU
1836 Rare	—	—	—	—	—	—

KM# 206 THALER (Krone)
18.1480 g., 0.8750 Silver .5105 oz. **Rev:** Arms of Ten Customs Union States between 10 caduceus

Date	Mintage	F	VF	XF	Unc	BU
1836	18,000	65.00	90.00	135	175	270

KM# 240 THALER (Vereins)
18.1590 g., 0.9000 Silver .5359 oz. **Ruler:** Friedrich I as Grand Duke **Obv:** Head right

Date	Mintage	F	VF	XF	Unc	BU
1857	19,000	100	175	275	475	720
1858	232,000	35.00	60.00	95.00	150	270
1859	289,000	35.00	65.00	110	165	310
1860	174,000	40.00	75.00	125	225	350
1861	358,000	35.00	60.00	95.00	150	270
1862	400,000	35.00	60.00	90.00	175	270
1863	326,000	35.00	60.00	90.00	175	270
1864	322,000	35.00	60.00	90.00	175	270
1865	265,000	35.00	60.00	90.00	175	270

KM# 245 THALER (Vereins)
18.1590 g., 0.9000 Silver .5359 oz.

Date	Mintage	F	VF	XF	Unc	BU
1865	Inc. above	95.00	175	250	500	900
1866	149,000	45.00	65.00	90.00	190	300
1867	96,000	45.00	65.00	90.00	190	300
1868	102,000	45.00	65.00	90.00	190	300
1869	62,000	50.00	75.00	100	200	325
1870	22,000	65.00	85.00	135	275	475
1871	—	65.00	85.00	135	275	475

KM# 212 2 THALER (3-1/2 Gulden)
37.1200 g., 0.9000 Silver 1.0743 oz. **Ruler:** Leopold I **Obv:** Head right

Date	Mintage	F	VF	XF	Unc	BU
1841	231,000	125	175	300	550	845
1842	33,000	150	200	400	900	1,500
1843	35,000	150	250	500	1,250	1,650

KM# 217.1 2 THALER (3-1/2 Gulden)
37.1200 g., 0.9000 Silver 1.0743 oz. **Rev:** Monument of Karl Friedrich

Date	Mintage	F	VF	XF	Unc	BU
1844	4,323	75.00	125	200	350	480

KM# 217.2 2 THALER (3-1/2 Gulden)
37.1200 g., 0.9000 Silver 1.0743 oz. **Edge:** Plain

Date	Mintage	F	VF	XF	Unc	BU
1844 Rare	—	—	—	—	—	—

KM# 220 2 THALER (3-1/2 Gulden)
37.1200 g., 0.9000 Silver 1.0743 oz.

Date	Mintage	F	VF	XF	Unc	BU
1845	57,000	85.00	110	275	400	650
1846	1,130	100	250	600	1,200	1,800
1847	31,000	100	250	550	1,100	1,675
1852	60,000	75.00	100	200	375	550

KM# 225 2 THALER (3-1/2 Gulden)
37.1200 g., 0.9000 Silver 1.0743 oz. **Ruler:** Friedrich I as Prince Regent **Obv:** BALBACH below truncation

Date	Mintage	F	VF	XF	Unc	BU
1852 Rare	9	—	—	—	—	—
1854	85,000	450	750	1,500	3,000	4,200

KM# 229 2 THALER (3-1/2 Gulden)
37.1200 g., 0.9000 Silver 1.0743 oz. **Obv:** Modified head, without engraver's name below truncation

Date	Mintage	F	VF	XF	Unc	BU
1855 Rare	2	—	—	—	—	—

KM# 196 5 THALER (500 Kreuzer)
5.7320 g., 0.9030 Gold .1664 oz. **Ruler:** Ludwig I

Date	Mintage	F	VF	XF	Unc	BU
1830	1,788	800	1,250	2,000	3,000	—

REFORM COINAGE

KM# 265 2 MARK
11.1110 g., 0.9000 Silver .3215 oz. **Ruler:** Friedrich I as Grand Duke **Obv:** Head left

Date	Mintage	F	VF	XF	Unc	BU
1876G	1,739,000	35.00	100	800	1,600	2,000
1877G	764,000	35.00	100	700	1,600	2,100
1880G	74,000	70.00	175	1,000	2,500	3,500
1883G	45,000	75.00	175	850	2,500	3,000
1888G	75,000	60.00	140	1,000	2,000	2,500

KM# 269 2 MARK
11.1110 g., 0.9000 Silver .3215 oz. **Ruler:** Friedrich I as Grand Duke **Obv:** Head left

Date	Mintage	F	VF	XF	Unc	BU
1892G	107,000	35.00	95.00	350	1,000	1,200
1894G	107,000	35.00	95.00	350	1,000	1,200
1896G	214,000	35.00	95.00	350	1,000	1,200
1898G	87,000	35.00	95.00	350	1,000	1,300
1899G	327,000	35.00	95.00	350	1,000	1,200
1900G	222,000	35.00	95.00	350	1,000	1,200

KM# 263.1 5 MARK
27.7770 g., 0.9000 Silver .8038 oz. **Ruler:** Friedrich I as Grand Duke **Obv:** Head left

Date	Mintage	F	VF	XF	Unc	BU
1875G	314,000	35.00	75.00	900	4,000	6,500
1876G	473,000	35.00	75.00	1,000	4,000	6,500
1888G	30,000	300	750	2,000	5,000	9,500

KM# 263.2 5 MARK
27.7770 g., 0.9000 Silver .8038 oz. **Obv:** Inverted V for "A" of BADEN in legend

Date	Mintage	F	VF	XF	Unc	BU
1875G	Inc. above	35.00	75.00	800	3,000	5,000
1876G	Inc. above	35.00	75.00	1,100	3,000	5,000
1888G	Inc. above	50.00	110	800	3,000	5,000
(1875-88) Proof; common date	—	Value: 4,500				

KM# 266 5 MARK
1.9910 g., 0.9000 Gold .0576 oz.

Date	Mintage	F	VF	XF	Unc	BU
1877G	345,000	200	300	450	600	900
1877G Proof	—	Value: 1,500				

KM# 268 5 MARK
27.7770 g., 0.9000 Silver .8038 oz. **Ruler:** Friedrich I as Grand Duke

Date	Mintage	F	VF	XF	Unc	BU
1891G	43,000	250	500	2,000	6,000	9,000
Note: Inverted "V" for "A" in BADEN.						
1891G	Inc. above	30.00	90.00	425	2,250	3,000
Note: Normal "A" in BADEN						
1893G	43,000	30.00	75.00	400	2,000	3,000
1894G	61,000	30.00	70.00	300	2,000	2,800
1895G	73,000	30.00	70.00	300	2,000	3,000
1898G	131,000	30.00	70.00	300	2,000	2,800
1899G	61,000	30.00	75.00	425	2,000	3,000
1900G	128,000	30.00	75.00	425	2,000	2,800
(1891-1902)G Proof; common date	—	Value: 2,500				

KM# 260 10 MARK
3.9820 g., 0.9000 Gold .1152 oz. **Ruler:** Friedrich I as Grand Duke **Obv:** Head left **Rev:** Type I

Date	Mintage	F	VF	XF	Unc	BU
1872G	273,000	75.00	135	225	450	600
1873G	466,000	75.00	135	250	450	600
1873G Proof	—	Value: 1,750				

KM# 264 10 MARK
3.9820 g., 0.9000 Gold .1152 oz. **Rev:** Type II

Date	Mintage	F	VF	XF	Unc	BU
1875	339,000	75.00	160	225	400	600
1876G	1,396,000	75.00	125	225	425	625
1877G	159,000	75.00	160	275	400	600
1878G	236,000	75.00	160	225	400	600
1879G	98,000	100	200	350	475	675
1880G	1,169	7,500	15,000	20,000	30,000	50,000
1881G	196,000	75.00	175	300	450	650
1888G	122,000	75.00	160	300	400	600
(1876-88)G Proof; common date	—	Value: 1,300				

KM# 267 10 MARK
3.9820 g., 0.9000 Gold .1152 oz. **Ruler:** Friedrich I as Grand Duke **Obv:** Head left

Date	Mintage	F	VF	XF	Unc	BU
1890G	73,000	125	225	325	550	650
1891G	110,000	125	200	275	400	600
1893G	183,000	125	175	250	400	575
1896G	52,000	125	225	325	500	600
1897G	70,000	125	250	300	450	600
1898G	256,000	115	180	250	400	500
1900G	31,000	150	350	500	800	900
1900G Proof	—	Value: 5,000				

KM# 261 20 MARK
7.9650 g., 0.9000 Gold .2304 oz. **Ruler:** Friedrich I as Grand Duke **Obv:** Head left **Rev:** Type I

Date	Mintage	F	VF	XF	Unc	BU
1872G	398,000	125	150	250	450	650
1873G	517,000	125	160	250	400	600
(1872-73) Proof; common date	—	Value: 2,250				

KM# 262 20 MARK
7.9650 g., 0.9000 Gold .2304 oz. **Ruler:** Friedrich I as Grand Duke **Rev:** Type II

Date	Mintage	F	VF	XF	Unc	BU
1874G	155,000	225	375	600	1,000	1,300
1874G Proof	—	Value: 3,000				

KM# 270 20 MARK
7.9650 g., 0.9000 Gold .2304 oz. **Ruler:** Friedrich I as Grand Duke **Rev:** Type III

Date	Mintage	F	VF	XF	Unc	BU
1894G Small 4	400,000	135	160	250	400	500
1894G Large 4	400,000	135	160	250	400	500
1895G	100,000	135	225	325	450	550
(1894-95) Proof; common date	—	Value: 1,300				

TRADE COINAGE

KM# 143 DUCAT
3.6600 g., 0.9380 Gold .1103 oz. **Ruler:** Karl Friedrich as Grand Duke **Obv:** Head right

Date	Mintage	F	VF	XF	Unc	BU
1807	1,022	—	1,500	2,500	4,500	—

KM# 201 DUCAT
3.6600 g., 0.9380 Gold .1103 oz. **Ruler:** Leopold I **Obv:** Head right

Date	Mintage	F	VF	XF	Unc	BU
1832	6,631	—	1,000	1,500	2,250	—
1833	2,496	—	1,100	1,600	2,350	—
1834	1,992	—	1,150	1,650	2,450	—
1835	2,470	—	1,100	1,600	2,350	—
1836	1,777	—	1,150	1,650	2,450	—

KM# 208 DUCAT
3.6600 g., 0.9380 Gold .1103 oz. **Obv:** Without designer's initial or star below head

Date	Mintage	F	VF	XF	Unc	BU
1837	1,467	—	1,125	1,650	2,450	—
1838	2,095	—	1,125	1,650	2,450	—
1839	2,448	—	1,100	1,600	2,350	—
1840	2,044	—	1,125	1,650	2,450	—
1841	2,145	—	1,125	1,650	2,450	—
1842	2,130	—	1,125	1,650	2,450	—

KM# 215 DUCAT
3.6600 g., 0.9380 Gold .1103 oz.

Date	Mintage	F	VF	XF	Unc	BU
1843	1,350	—	1,300	1,700	2,500	—
1844	850	—	1,500	2,000	2,750	—
1845	2,097	—	1,200	1,600	2,350	—
1846	1,950	—	1,200	1,600	2,350	—

KM# 223.1 DUCAT
3.6600 g., 0.9380 Gold .1103 oz. **Obv:** Larger head

Date	Mintage	F	VF	XF	Unc	BU
1847	1,870	—	1,200	1,600	2,350	—
1848	1,590	—	1,200	1,600	2,350	—
1849	1,420	—	1,200	1,600	2,350	—
1850	1,390	—	1,200	1,600	2,350	—
1851	1,280	—	1,200	1,600	2,350	—
1852	1,450	—	1,350	1,750	2,550	—

KM# 223.2 DUCAT
3.6600 g., 0.9380 Gold .1103 oz. **Obv:** Star below head **Note:** Posthumous issue.

Date	Mintage	F	VF	XF	Unc	BU
1852	Inc. above	—	1,350	1,750	2,550	—

KM# 227 DUCAT
3.6600 g., 0.9380 Gold .1103 oz. **Ruler:** Friedrich I as Prince Regent **Obv:** Head right

Date	Mintage	F	VF	XF	Unc	BU
1854	1,820	—	1,500	3,000	4,750	—

PATTERNS

Including off metal strikes

KM#	Date	Mintage	Identification	Mkt Val
Pn21	ND(1805)	—	Ducat. Silver. KM#143.	—
Pn22	ND(1805)	—	Ducat. Copper. KM#143.	—

KM#	Date	Mintage	Identification	Mkt Val
Pn23	1808 A	—	5 Frank. Silver.	—
Pn24	1839	—	6 Kreuzer. 0.3330 Billon. KM#210.	—
Pn25	1842	—	Kreuzer. Gold. KM#203.	—
Pn26	1842	—	Kreuzer. Silver. KM#203.	—
Pn27	1844	—	Kreuzer. Gold. KM#203.	—
Pn28	1844	—	Kreuzer. Silver. KM#203.	—
Pn29	1844	—	Kreuzer. Nickel. KM#203.	—
Pn30	1874G	—	5 Mark. Silver. KM#263.1.	—

KM#	Date	Mintage	Identification	Mkt Val
Pn31	1875G	—	10 Mark. Copper. KM#264.	—

TRIAL STRIKES

KM#	Date	Mintage	Identification	Mkt Val
TSA1	ND(1860)	—	1/4 Gulden. Pewter. Previous KM#TS1.	—

KM#	Date	Mintage	Identification	Mkt Val
TSA2	1860	—	1/4 Gulden. Pewter. Previous KM#TS2.	—

BAMBERG

Bishopric in northern Bavaria. The See was founded in 1007 and the first coinage appeared soon after. The bishops were made princes of the empire in the mid-1200s. It was annexed to Bavaria in 1802.

RULERS
Christoph Franz, Freiherr von Buseck, Bishop, 1795-1802
Georg Karl, von Fechenbach, 1802-1803

BISHOPRIC

TRADE COINAGE

KM# 154 DUCAT
3.5000 g., 0.9860 Gold .1109 oz. **Subject:** Union of Bamberg with Bavaria

Date	Mintage	F	VF	XF	Unc	BU
1802	—	350	750	1,350	2,000	—

PATTERNS

Including off metal strikes

KM#	Date	Mintage	Identification	Mkt Val
Pn11	1802	—	Ducat. Silver. KM#154	—

BAVARIA

(Bayern)

Located in south Germany. In 1180 the Duchy of Bavaria was given to the Count of Wittelsbach by the emperor. He is the ancestor of all who ruled in Bavaria until 1918. Primogeniture was proclaimed in 1506 and in 1623 the dukes of Bavaria were given the electoral right. Bavaria, which had been divided for the various heirs, was reunited in 1799. The title of king was granted to Bavaria in 1805.

RULERS
Maximilian IV, Josef as Elector, 1799-1805
Maximilian IV, As King Maximilian I, Josef, 1806-1825
Ludwig I, 1825-1848
Maximilian II, 1848-1864
Ludwig II, 1864-1886
Otto, 1886-1913,
Prince Regent Luitpold, 1886-1912

MINT MARKS
M-Munich

DUCHY

REGULAR COINAGE

KM# 305 HELLER
Copper **Obv:** Shield and date in diamond **Rev:** Value: 1/HEL/LER in diamond

Date	Mintage	F	VF	XF	Unc	BU
1801	—	15.00	35.00	100	175	285
1802	—	10.00	30.00	80.00	150	260
1803	—	10.00	30.00	70.00	135	240
1804	—	10.00	30.00	60.00	125	215
1805	—	10.00	30.00	70.00	135	240

KM# 306 PFENNIG
Copper **Obv:** Bavarian shield in ornamental cartouche **Rev:** Value above date

Date	Mintage	F	VF	XF	Unc	BU
1801	—	15.00	30.00	75.00	150	300
1802	—	10.00	20.00	75.00	150	300
1803	—	10.00	20.00	75.00	150	300
1804	—	15.00	30.00	75.00	150	300
1805	—	15.00	30.00	75.00	150	300

KM# 307 2 PFENNIG
Copper

Date	Mintage	F	VF	XF	Unc	BU
1801	—	35.00	75.00	150	250	425
1802	—	35.00	75.00	150	250	—
1803	—	35.00	75.00	150	250	—
1804	—	20.00	50.00	100	225	360
1805	—	30.00	60.00	125	250	—

KM# 317 KREUZER
0.7700 g., 0.1870 Silver .0046 oz.

Date	Mintage	F	VF	XF	Unc	BU
1801	—	25.00	75.00	150	300	475
1802	—	25.00	75.00	150	300	475
1803	—	25.00	80.00	160	300	475

KM# 315 KREUZER
0.7700 g., 0.1870 Silver .0046 oz. **Obv. Legend:** MAX. IOS. H. I. B. C. **Rev:** Without numeric value

Date	Mintage	F	VF	XF	Unc	BU
1801	—	25.00	100	150	300	475
1802	—	25.00	100	150	300	475
1803	—	25.00	100	150	300	475
1806/0	—	25.00	110	160	325	500

KM# 308 KREUZER
0.7700 g., 0.1870 Silver .0046 oz. **Obv:** Head right, MAX. IOS. **Rev:** Crowned shield within palm branches

Date	Mintage	F	VF	XF	Unc	BU
1802	—	25.00	100	150	300	475
1803	—	25.00	100	150	300	475

KM# 329 KREUZER
0.7700 g., 0.1870 Silver .0046 oz. **Rev:** Numeral value separating date

Date	Mintage	F	VF	XF	Unc	BU
1804	—	25.00	100	150	300	475

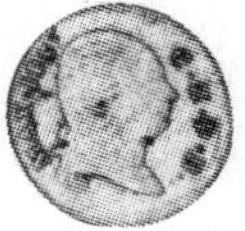

KM# 330 KREUZER
0.7700 g., 0.1870 Silver .0046 oz. **Obv. Legend:** MAX. IOS. C. Z. P. B. **Rev:** LAND MUNZ, oval arms separating value

Date	Mintage	F	VF	XF	Unc	BU
1804	—	25.00	80.00	190	375	540
1805	—	20.00	65.00	150	300	475

KM# 309 3 KREUZER (1 Groschen)
1.3500 g., 0.3330 Silver .0144 oz. **Obv:** Head right, legend **Obv. Legend:** MAX. IOS. P. B. **Rev:** Crowned oval arms separating value

Date	Mintage	F	VF	XF	Unc	BU
1801	—	40.00	60.00	175	375	540
1802	—	40.00	60.00	175	375	540

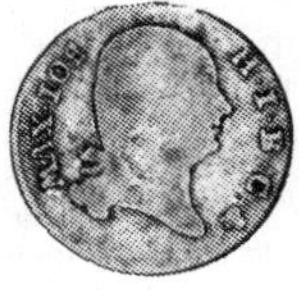

KM# 322 3 KREUZER (1 Groschen)
1.3500 g., 0.3330 Silver .0144 oz. **Obv. Legend:** MAX. IOS. H. I. B. C. &

Date	Mintage	F	VF	XF	Unc	BU
1803	—	75.00	150	300	400	660
1804	—	90.00	175	320	450	720

KM# 331 3 KREUZER (1 Groschen)
1.3500 g., 0.3330 Silver .0144 oz. **Obv. Legend:** MAX. IOS. C. Z. P. B.

Date	Mintage	F	VF	XF	Unc	BU
1804	—	75.00	150	250	400	650
1805	—	35.00	60.00	100	200	300

KM# 318 6 KREUZER
2.7000 g., 0.3330 Silver .0289 oz. **Obv. Legend:** MAX. IOS. H. I. B. C. &

Date	Mintage	F	VF	XF	Unc	BU
1801	—	100	200	400	600	900
1803	—	25.00	120	225	400	660
1804	—	25.00	120	225	400	660

KM# 310 6 KREUZER
2.7000 g., 0.3330 Silver .0289 oz. **Obv:** Head right **Obv. Legend:** MAX. IOS. P. B. **Rev:** Crowned arms, date below

Date	Mintage	F	VF	XF	Unc	BU
1802	—	25.00	120	250	400	660
1803	—	25.00	120	250	400	660

KM# 332 6 KREUZER
2.7000 g., 0.3330 Silver .0289 oz. **Obv. Legend:** MAX. IOS. C. Z. P. B.

Date	Mintage	F	VF	XF	Unc	BU
1804	—	25.00	120	225	425	660
1805	—	25.00	100	200	400	600

KM# 316 10 KREUZER (Convention)
3.9000 g., 0.5000 Silver .0626 oz. **Obv:** Maximilian IV Josef right in wreath **Rev:** Cfowned three-fold oval arms

Date	Mintage	F	VF	XF	Unc	BU
1801 Rare	—	—	—	—	—	—

KM# 319 10 KREUZER (Convention)
3.9000 g., 0.5000 Silver .0626 oz. **Rev. Legend:** POPOLO

Date	Mintage	F	VF	XF	Unc	BU
1801 Rare	—	—	—	—	—	—

KM# 311 20 KREUZER
6.6800 g., 0.5830 Silver .1252 oz. **Obv:** Maximilian IV Josef right within wreath **Rev:** Crowned arms within crossed branches, date and value below

Date	Mintage	F	VF	XF	Unc	BU
1801	—	65.00	120	275	500	725
1802	—	75.00	165	350	650	960
1803	—	75.00	150	300	600	900

KM# 333 20 KREUZER
6.6800 g., 0.5830 Silver .1252 oz.

Date	Mintage	F	VF	XF	Unc	BU
1804	—	65.00	120	250	550	725
1805	—	65.00	120	250	550	725

KM# 312 1/2 THALER
14.0300 g., 0.8330 Silver .3757 oz. **Note:** Similar to 1 Thaler, KM#313.

Date	Mintage	F	VF	XF	Unc	BU
1801	—	500	1,000	2,000	3,500	6,000
1802	—	500	1,000	2,000	3,500	6,000
1803	—	500	1,000	2,000	3,500	6,000

KM# 323 1/2 THALER
14.0300 g., 0.8330 Silver .3757 oz.

Date	Mintage	F	VF	XF	Unc	BU
1803	—	450	900	1,250	1,700	2,400
1804	—	450	900	1,250	1,700	2,400
1805	—	150	350	525	700	900

KM# 324 1/2 THALER (School prize without denomination)
14.0300 g., 0.8330 Silver .3757 oz.

Date	Mintage	F	VF	XF	Unc	BU
ND(1799-1805)	—	150	250	400	750	1,100

KM# 313 THALER
28.0000 g., 0.8330 Silver .7500 oz. **Obv:** Head of Maximilian IV Josef right **Note:** Cross-reference number Dav. #1975.

Date	Mintage	F	VF	XF	Unc	BU
1801	—	80.00	130	275	500	725
1802	—	95.00	140	300	700	960

KM# 320.1 THALER
28.0000 g., 0.8330 Silver .7500 oz. **Obv. Legend:** D. G. MAXIM. IOSEPH

Date	Mintage	F	VF	XF	Unc	BU
1802	—	1,000	2,000	4,500	7,000	9,600

KM# 320.2 THALER
28.0000 g., 0.8330 Silver .7500 oz. **Obv. Legend:** D. G. MAX. IOSEPH

Date	Mintage	F	VF	XF	Unc	BU
1802	—	5,000	7,000	9,000	11,500	14,400
1803	—	5,500	7,500	10,000	12,500	15,600

KM# 321 THALER
28.0000 g., 0.8330 Silver .7500 oz. **Obv:** Uniformed bust right **Obv. Legend:** MAXIMILIAN...

Date	Mintage	F	VF	XF	Unc	BU
1802	—	3,500	7,000	10,000	—	—

KM# 325 THALER
28.0000 g., 0.8330 Silver .7500 oz.

Date	Mintage	F	VF	XF	Unc	BU
1803	—	90.00	175	300	600	860

KM# 326 THALER
28.0000 g., 0.8330 Silver .7500 oz. **Rev. Legend:** GOTT UND DAS - VATERLAND

Date	Mintage	F	VF	XF	Unc	BU
1803	—	150	300	600	1,500	3,000
1804	—	120	250	500	1,200	2,400
1805	—	200	350	700	2,700	4,200

KM# 334 THALER
28.0000 g., 0.8330 Silver .7500 oz. **Rev. Legend:** FUR GOTT UND - VATERLAND

Date	Mintage	F	VF	XF	Unc	BU
1804	—	1,000	2,000	4,000	9,000	12,000
1805	—	100	175	300	600	900

TRADE COINAGE

KM# 314.1 DUCAT
3.4900 g., 0.9370 Gold .1051 oz. **Obv. Legend:** D. G. MAX. IOS... **Note:** Fr. #262.

Date	Mintage	F	VF	XF	Unc	BU
1801	—	750	1,250	2,250	2,850	—
1802	—	1,000	1,500	2,500	3,200	—

KM# 314.2 DUCAT
3.4900 g., 0.9370 Gold .1051 oz. **Obv. Legend:** D. G. MAXIM. IOSEPH

Date	Mintage	F	VF	XF	Unc	BU
1801	—	1,000	1,500	2,500	3,000	—
1802	—	1,000	1,500	2,500	3,000	—
1803	—	1,100	1,600	2,650	3,500	—

KM# 335 DUCAT
3.4900 g., 0.9370 Gold .1051 oz. **Obv. Legend:** MAXIMILIAN IOSEPH... **Note:** Fr. #263.

Date	Mintage	F	VF	XF	Unc	BU
1804	—	1,500	2,000	3,000	4,000	—
1805	—	1,250	1,500	2,500	3,250	—

KINGDOM

REGULAR COINAGE

KM# 340 HELLER
Copper **Edge:** Plain

Date	Mintage	F	VF	XF	Unc	BU
1806	—	5.00	15.00	30.00	50.00	90.00
1807	—	4.00	10.00	25.00	45.00	75.00
1808	—	5.00	15.00	30.00	50.00	90.00
1809	—	4.00	10.00	25.00	45.00	75.00
1810	—	5.00	15.00	30.00	50.00	90.00
1811	—	5.00	15.00	30.00	50.00	90.00
1812	—	5.00	15.00	30.00	50.00	90.00
1813	—	4.00	10.00	25.00	45.00	75.00
1814	—	4.00	10.00	25.00	45.00	75.00
1815	—	5.00	15.00	30.00	50.00	90.00
1816	—	4.00	10.00	25.00	45.00	75.00
1817	—	4.00	10.00	25.00	45.00	75.00
1818	—	5.00	15.00	30.00	50.00	90.00
1819	—	4.00	10.00	25.00	45.00	75.00
1820	—	4.00	10.00	25.00	45.00	75.00
1821	—	5.00	15.00	30.00	50.00	90.00
1822	—	4.00	10.00	25.00	45.00	75.00
1823	—	4.00	10.00	25.00	45.00	75.00
1824	—	4.00	10.00	25.00	45.00	75.00
1825	—	4.00	10.00	12.00	45.00	75.00
1828	—	4.00	10.00	12.00	45.00	75.00
1829	—	4.00	8.00	20.00	30.00	60.00

KM# 383 HELLER
Copper **Edge:** Reeded

Date	Mintage	F	VF	XF	Unc	BU
1829	—	7.00	15.00	40.00	150	—
1830	—	3.00	8.00	20.00	45.00	60.00
1831	—	3.00	8.00	20.00	45.00	60.00
1832	—	3.00	8.00	20.00	45.00	60.00
1833	—	3.00	8.00	20.00	45.00	60.00
1834	—	3.00	8.00	20.00	45.00	60.00
1835	—	3.00	8.00	20.00	45.00	60.00

KM# 419 HELLER
Copper

Date	Mintage	F	VF	XF	Unc	BU
1839	256,000	4.00	8.00	10.00	20.00	30.00
1840	169,000	4.00	8.00	10.00	20.00	30.00
1841	—	5.00	10.00	17.00	25.00	40.00
1842	—	5.00	10.00	17.00	25.00	40.00
1843	—	5.00	10.00	17.00	25.00	40.00
1844	190,000	5.00	10.00	17.00	25.00	40.00
1845	434,000	5.00	8.00	10.00	20.00	30.00
1846	—	4.00	8.00	10.00	20.00	30.00

Date	Mintage	F	VF	XF	Unc	BU
1847	74,000	5.00	10.00	17.00	20.00	30.00
1848	514,000	5.00	10.00	17.00	25.00	40.00
1849	346,000	4.00	8.00	12.00	20.00	30.00
1850	306,000	4.00	8.00	12.00	20.00	30.00
1851	437,000	5.00	10.00	17.00	25.00	30.00
1852	206,000	4.00	8.00	12.00	20.00	30.00
1853	279,000	5.00	10.00	17.00	25.00	30.00
1854	193,000	5.00	10.00	17.00	25.00	30.00
1855	132,000	5.00	10.00	17.00	25.00	40.00
1856	34,000	5.00	10.00	17.00	25.00	40.00

KM# 341 PFENNIG

Copper **Edge:** Plain

Date	Mintage	F	VF	XF	Unc	BU
1806	—	9.00	20.00	50.00	125	240
1807	—	5.00	10.00	20.00	40.00	75.00
1808	—	6.00	15.00	25.00	50.00	90.00
1809	—	5.00	10.00	20.00	40.00	75.00
1810	—	5.00	10.00	20.00	40.00	75.00
1811	—	9.00	20.00	45.00	100	175
1812	—	9.00	20.00	45.00	100	175
1813	—	5.00	10.00	20.00	40.00	75.00
1814	—	6.00	15.00	25.00	50.00	90.00
1815	—	5.00	10.00	20.00	40.00	75.00
1816	—	5.00	10.00	20.00	40.00	75.00
1817	—	6.00	15.00	25.00	50.00	90.00
1818	—	6.00	15.00	25.00	50.00	90.00
1819	—	6.00	15.00	25.00	50.00	90.00
1820	—	5.00	10.00	20.00	40.00	75.00
1821	—	6.00	15.00	25.00	50.00	90.00
1822	—	5.00	10.00	20.00	40.00	75.00
1823	—	5.00	10.00	20.00	40.00	75.00
1824	—	5.00	10.00	20.00	40.00	75.00
1825	—	5.00	10.00	20.00	40.00	75.00
1828	—	5.00	10.00	20.00	40.00	75.00
1829	—	5.00	10.00	20.00	40.00	75.00

KM# 384 PFENNIG

Copper **Edge:** Reeded

Date	Mintage	F	VF	XF	Unc	BU
1830	—	5.00	10.00	20.00	40.00	70.00
1831	—	3.00	8.00	15.00	35.00	60.00
1832	—	5.00	10.00	20.00	40.00	70.00
1833	—	3.00	8.00	15.00	35.00	65.00
1834	—	3.00	8.00	15.00	35.00	60.00
1835	—	3.00	8.00	15.00	35.00	60.00

KM# 420 PFENNIG

Copper

Date	Mintage	F	VF	XF	Unc	BU
1839	801,000	4.00	8.00	20.00	40.00	60.00
1840	732,000	4.00	8.00	15.00	30.00	45.00
1841	970,000	5.00	9.00	20.00	40.00	60.00
1842	817,000	4.00	8.00	20.00	40.00	60.00
1843	892,000	4.00	8.00	15.00	30.00	45.00
1844	645,000	5.00	9.00	20.00	40.00	60.00
1845	1,037,000	4.00	8.00	15.00	30.00	45.00
1846	1,487,000	5.00	9.00	20.00	40.00	60.00
1847	1,808,000	4.00	8.00	15.00	30.00	45.00
1848	1,815,000	5.00	10.00	22.00	35.00	65.00
1849	2,120,000	4.00	8.00	15.00	30.00	45.00
1850	2,494,000	4.00	8.00	15.00	30.00	45.00
1851	2,162,000	4.00	8.00	15.00	30.00	45.00
1852	2,634,000	4.00	8.00	15.00	30.00	45.00
1853	1,950,000	5.00	9.00	20.00	40.00	60.00
1854	1,842,000	4.00	8.00	15.00	30.00	45.00
1855	1,576,000	4.00	8.00	15.00	30.00	45.00
1856	1,530,000	4.00	8.00	15.00	30.00	45.00

KM# 471 PFENNIG

Copper

Date	Mintage	F	VF	XF	Unc	BU
1858	—	3.00	5.00	9.00	20.00	30.00
1859	—	3.00	5.00	9.00	20.00	30.00
1860	—	3.00	5.00	9.00	20.00	35.00
1861	—	3.00	5.00	9.00	20.00	30.00
1862	—	3.00	5.00	9.00	20.00	35.00
1863	2,284,000	3.00	5.00	9.00	20.00	30.00
1864	2,304,000	3.00	5.00	9.00	20.00	30.00
1865	1,401,000	3.00	5.00	9.00	20.00	35.00
1866	1,485,000	3.00	5.00	9.00	20.00	30.00
1867	1,633,000	3.00	5.00	9.00	20.00	30.00
1868	1,394,000	3.00	5.00	9.00	20.00	30.00
1869	1,474,000	3.00	5.00	9.00	20.00	30.00
1870	1,608,000	3.00	5.00	9.00	20.00	30.00
1871	1,534,000	3.00	5.00	9.00	20.00	30.00

KM# 342 2 PFENNIG

Copper **Edge:** Plain

Date	Mintage	F	VF	XF	Unc	BU
1806	—	10.00	25.00	50.00	90.00	175
1807	—	6.00	20.00	40.00	70.00	130
1808	—	9.00	25.00	50.00	80.00	140
1809	—	6.00	20.00	40.00	70.00	130
1810	—	9.00	25.00	40.00	70.00	130
1811	—	9.00	25.00	40.00	70.00	130
1812	—	10.00	25.00	50.00	90.00	175
1813	—	6.00	20.00	40.00	70.00	130
1814	—	6.00	20.00	40.00	70.00	130
1815	—	10.00	25.00	50.00	90.00	175
1816	—	6.00	20.00	40.00	70.00	130
1817	—	6.00	20.00	40.00	70.00	130
1818	—	10.00	25.00	50.00	90.00	175
1819	—	10.00	25.00	50.00	90.00	175
1820	—	10.00	25.00	50.00	90.00	175
1821	—	6.00	25.00	50.00	90.00	175
1822	—	6.00	20.00	40.00	70.00	130
1823	—	6.00	20.00	40.00	70.00	130
1824	—	6.00	20.00	40.00	70.00	130
1825	—	6.00	20.00	40.00	70.00	130
1828	—	9.00	25.00	40.00	70.00	130
1829	—	6.00	20.00	40.00	70.00	130

KM# 385 2 PFENNIG

Copper **Edge:** Reeded

Date	Mintage	F	VF	XF	Unc	BU
1830	—	15.00	35.00	45.00	55.00	75.00
1831	—	15.00	35.00	45.00	55.00	75.00
1832	—	15.00	35.00	45.00	55.00	75.00
1833	—	15.00	35.00	45.00	55.00	75.00
1834	—	15.00	35.00	40.00	50.00	70.00
1835	—	10.00	25.00	30.00	45.00	65.00

KM# 421 2 PFENNIG

Copper

Date	Mintage	F	VF	XF	Unc	BU
1839	320,000	4.00	8.00	25.00	50.00	75.00
1840	320,000	4.00	8.00	25.00	50.00	75.00
1841	442,000	4.00	8.00	25.00	50.00	75.00
1842	353,000	4.00	8.00	25.00	50.00	75.00
1843	203,000	5.00	10.00	30.00	60.00	90.00
1844	226,000	4.00	8.00	25.00	50.00	75.00
1845	242,000	4.00	8.00	25.00	50.00	75.00
1846	232,000	4.00	8.00	25.00	50.00	75.00
1847	663,000	4.00	8.00	25.00	50.00	75.00
1848	776,000	4.00	8.00	25.00	50.00	75.00
1849	454,000	4.00	8.00	25.00	50.00	75.00
1850	1,477,000	4.00	8.00	25.00	50.00	75.00

KM# 472 2 PFENNIG

Copper

Date	Mintage	F	VF	XF	Unc	BU
1858	—	4.00	8.00	14.00	20.00	30.00
1859	—	4.00	8.00	14.00	20.00	30.00
1860	—	4.00	8.00	14.00	20.00	30.00
1861	—	4.00	8.00	14.00	20.00	30.00
1862	—	4.00	8.00	14.00	20.00	30.00
1863	228,000	4.00	8.00	14.00	20.00	30.00
1864	589,000	4.00	8.00	14.00	20.00	30.00
1865	358,000	4.00	8.00	14.00	20.00	30.00
1866	234,000	4.00	8.00	14.00	20.00	30.00
1867	481,000	5.00	10.00	17.00	26.00	35.00
1868	208,000	4.00	8.00	14.00	20.00	30.00
1869	466,000	4.00	8.00	14.00	20.00	30.00
1870	476,000	5.00	10.00	17.00	26.00	35.00
1871	466,000	4.00	8.00	14.00	20.00	30.00

KM# 463 1/2 KREUZER

Copper

Date	Mintage	F	VF	XF	Unc	BU
1851	796,000	4.00	8.00	15.00	28.00	50.00
1852	981,000	4.00	8.00	20.00	28.00	65.00
1853	797,000	4.00	8.00	15.00	28.00	50.00
1854	528,000	4.00	8.00	15.00	28.00	50.00
1855	641,000	4.00	8.00	20.00	28.00	60.00
1856	462,000	4.00	8.00	12.00	28.00	45.00

KM# 343 KREUZER

Copper **Note:** Minted for use in Tyrol, then occupied by Bavaria.

Date	Mintage	F	VF	XF	Unc	BU
1806	145,000	20.00	50.00	100	300	—

KM# 344 KREUZER

0.7700 g., 0.1870 Silver .0046 oz.

Date	Mintage	F	VF	XF	Unc	BU
1806	—	8.00	15.00	25.00	45.00	75.00
1807	—	5.00	10.00	20.00	40.00	65.00
1808	—	5.00	10.00	20.00	40.00	65.00
1809	—	5.00	10.00	20.00	40.00	65.00
1810	—	5.00	10.00	20.00	40.00	65.00
1811	—	5.00	10.00	20.00	40.00	65.00
1812	—	5.00	10.00	20.00	40.00	65.00
1813	—	8.00	15.00	25.00	45.00	75.00
1814	—	5.00	10.00	20.00	40.00	65.00
1815	—	5.00	10.00	20.00	40.00	65.00
1816	—	5.00	10.00	20.00	40.00	65.00
1817	—	5.00	10.00	20.00	40.00	65.00
1818	—	8.00	15.00	25.00	45.00	75.00
1819	—	5.00	10.00	20.00	40.00	65.00
1820	—	5.00	10.00	20.00	40.00	65.00
1821	—	5.00	10.00	20.00	40.00	65.00
1822	—	5.00	10.00	20.00	40.00	65.00
1823	—	5.00	10.00	20.00	40.00	65.00
1824	—	5.00	10.00	20.00	40.00	65.00
1825	—	5.00	10.00	20.00	40.00	65.00

KM# 376 KREUZER
0.7700 g., 0.1870 Silver .0046 oz. **Obv. Legend:** LUDWIG KOENIG...

Date	Mintage	F	VF	XF	Unc	BU
1827	—	8.00	20.00	35.00	75.00	105
1828	—	5.00	10.00	20.00	35.00	50.00
1829	—	8.00	15.00	30.00	40.00	60.00
1830	—	15.00	35.00	60.00	85.00	130

KM# 390 KREUZER
0.7700 g., 0.1870 Silver .0046 oz. **Obv. Legend:** LUDWIG I KOENIG...

Date	Mintage	F	VF	XF	Unc	BU
1830	—	3.00	8.00	25.00	55.00	90.00
1831	—	3.00	8.00	20.00	40.00	65.00
1832	—	3.00	8.00	20.00	40.00	65.00
1833	—	3.00	8.00	20.00	40.00	65.00
1834	—	3.00	8.00	20.00	40.00	65.00
1835	—	3.00	8.00	16.00	30.00	45.00
1836	—	30.00	75.00	—	—	—
1852 Rare	—	—	—	—	—	—

KM# 422 KREUZER
0.8400 g., 0.1660 Silver .0044 oz.

Date	Mintage	F	VF	XF	Unc	BU
1839	1,474,000	2.00	5.00	10.00	15.00	24.00
1840	1,769,000	2.00	5.00	10.00	15.00	24.00
1841	1,591,000	2.00	5.00	10.00	15.00	24.00
1842	1,855,000	2.00	5.00	10.00	15.00	24.00
1843	1,373,000	2.00	5.00	10.00	15.00	24.00
1844	1,324,000	2.00	5.00	12.00	20.00	30.00
1845	1,660,000	2.00	5.00	12.00	20.00	35.00
1846	1,849,000	2.00	5.00	10.00	15.00	24.00
1847	1,519,000	2.00	5.00	10.00	15.00	24.00
1848	1,746,000	2.00	5.00	12.00	20.00	30.00
1849	1,971,000	2.00	5.00	10.00	15.00	24.00
1850	3,135,000	2.00	5.00	10.00	15.00	24.00
1851	2,084,000	2.00	5.00	10.00	15.00	24.00
1852	1,915,000	2.00	5.00	10.00	15.00	24.00
1853	1,528,000	2.00	5.00	12.00	20.00	30.00
1854	1,650,000	2.00	5.00	12.00	20.00	35.00
1855	1,510,000	2.00	5.00	10.00	15.00	24.00
1856	1,335,000	2.00	5.00	10.00	15.00	24.00

KM# 473 KREUZER
0.8400 g., 0.1660 Silver .0044 oz.

Date	Mintage	F	VF	XF	Unc	BU
1858	2,400,000	3.00	6.00	10.00	15.00	24.00
1859	—	3.00	6.00	10.00	15.00	24.00
1860	231,000	3.00	6.00	10.00	15.00	24.00
1861	3,276,000	3.00	6.00	10.00	15.00	24.00
1862	3,358,000	3.00	6.00	10.00	15.00	24.00
1863	3,356,000	3.00	5.00	8.00	12.00	18.00
1864	3,293,000	3.00	6.00	10.00	15.00	24.00

KM# 487 KREUZER
0.8400 g., 0.1660 Silver .0044 oz.

Date	Mintage	F	VF	XF	Unc	BU
1865	1,837,000	3.00	6.00	10.00	15.00	24.00
1866	2,542,000	3.00	6.00	10.00	15.00	24.00
1867	2,305,000	3.00	6.00	10.00	15.00	24.00
1868	2,526,000	3.00	6.00	10.00	15.00	24.00
1869	2,774,000	3.00	6.00	10.00	15.00	24.00
1870	2,199,000	3.00	6.00	10.00	15.00	24.00
1871	2,634,000	3.00	5.00	8.00	10.00	18.00

KM# 352 3 KREUZER
1.3500 g., 0.3330 Silver .0144 oz. **Obv:** Head right **Rev:** Shield with crown above crossed scepter and sword

Date	Mintage	F	VF	XF	Unc	BU
1807	—	8.00	15.00	30.00	75.00	150
1808	—	10.00	20.00	60.00	120	200
1809	—	8.00	15.00	30.00	85.00	175
1810	—	10.00	20.00	60.00	120	200
1811	—	8.00	15.00	30.00	85.00	175
1812	—	10.00	20.00	60.00	140	230
1813	—	8.00	15.00	30.00	85.00	175
1814	—	8.00	15.00	30.00	85.00	175
1815	—	10.00	20.00	60.00	120	200
1816	—	8.00	15.00	30.00	85.00	175
1817	—	8.00	15.00	30.00	75.00	150
1818	—	10.00	20.00	60.00	135	200
1819	—	8.00	15.00	30.00	75.00	150
1820	—	8.00	15.00	30.00	75.00	150
1821	—	8.00	15.00	30.00	75.00	150
1822	—	8.00	15.00	30.00	75.00	150
1823	—	8.00	15.00	30.00	75.00	150
1824	—	8.00	15.00	30.00	75.00	150
1825	—	8.00	15.00	30.00	55.00	120

KM# 377 3 KREUZER
1.3000 g., 0.3330 Silver .0139 oz. **Obv. Legend:** LUDWIG KOENIG...

Date	Mintage	F	VF	XF	Unc	BU
1827	—	5.00	15.00	60.00	125	210
1828	—	5.00	15.00	60.00	125	210
1829	—	5.00	15.00	60.00	125	210
1830	—	10.00	20.00	125	350	700

KM# 391 3 KREUZER
1.3000 g., 0.3330 Silver .0139 oz. **Obv. Legend:** LUDWIG I KOENIG...

Date	Mintage	F	VF	XF	Unc	BU
1830	—	8.00	20.00	40.00	60.00	90.00
1831	—	5.00	15.00	30.00	50.00	75.00
1832	—	5.00	15.00	30.00	50.00	75.00
1833	—	5.00	15.00	30.00	50.00	75.00
1834	—	5.00	15.00	30.00	50.00	75.00
1835	—	5.00	15.00	27.50	40.00	65.00
1836 Rare	—	—	—	—	—	—

KM# 423 3 KREUZER
1.3000 g., 0.3330 Silver .0139 oz.

Date	Mintage	F	VF	XF	Unc	BU
1839	456,000	5.00	10.00	15.00	20.00	35.00
1840	235,000	5.00	10.00	15.00	20.00	35.00
1841	337,000	5.00	10.00	17.00	25.00	40.00
1842	370,000	5.00	10.00	17.00	25.00	40.00
1843	337,000	5.00	10.00	15.00	20.00	35.00
1844	269,000	5.00	10.00	1,515	20.00	35.00
1845	361,000	5.00	10.00	17.00	20.00	35.00
1846	463,000	5.00	10.00	15.00	25.00	40.00
1847	563,000	5.00	10.00	15.00	20.00	35.00
1848	447,000	5.00	10.00	15.00	20.00	35.00
1849	373,000	5.00	10.00	15.00	20.00	35.00
1850	615,000	5.00	10.00	15.00	20.00	35.00
1851	582,000	5.00	10.00	15.00	20.00	35.00
1852	282,000	5.00	10.00	15.00	20.00	35.00
1853	280,000	5.00	10.00	15.00	20.00	35.00
1854	388,000	5.00	10.00	15.00	20.00	35.00
1855	285,000	5.00	10.00	15.00	20.00	35.00
1856	91,000	5.00	10.00	15.00	20.00	35.00

KM# 488 3 KREUZER
1.2300 g., 0.3500 Silver .0138 oz.

Date	Mintage	F	VF	XF	Unc	BU
1865	832,000	4.00	8.00	15.00	40.00	60.00
1866	566,000	5.00	10.00	20.00	50.00	75.00
1867	99,000	5.00	10.00	20.00	65.00	90.00
1868	65,000	5.00	10.00	20.00	50.00	75.00

KM# 345 6 KREUZER
2.7000 g., 0.3330 Silver .0289 oz. **Obv:** Head right **Rev:** Crowned arms with shield divided

Date	Mintage	F	VF	XF	Unc	BU
1806	—	15.00	45.00	200	400	700

KM# 346 6 KREUZER
2.7000 g., 0.3330 Silver .0289 oz.

Date	Mintage	F	VF	XF	Unc	BU
1806	—	10.00	25.00	45.00	75.00	130
1807	—	8.00	15.00	30.00	60.00	110
1808	—	8.00	15.00	30.00	60.00	110
1809	—	8.00	15.00	30.00	60.00	110
1810	—	8.00	15.00	30.00	60.00	110
1811	—	8.00	15.00	30.00	60.00	110
1812	—	8.00	15.00	30.00	60.00	110
1813	—	8.00	15.00	30.00	60.00	110
1814	—	8.00	15.00	30.00	60.00	110
1815	—	8.00	15.00	30.00	60.00	110
1816	—	8.00	15.00	30.00	60.00	110
1817	—	10.00	15.00	45.00	80.00	130
1818	—	10.00	25.00	55.00	100	175
1819	—	8.00	15.00	30.00	60.00	110
1820	—	8.00	15.00	40.00	60.00	110
1821/0	—	10.00	20.00	30.00	70.00	120
1821	—	8.00	15.00	30.00	60.00	110
1822	—	8.00	15.00	30.00	60.00	110
1823	—	8.00	15.00	30.00	60.00	110
1824	—	8.00	15.00	30.00	60.00	110
1825	—	8.00	15.00	25.00	50.00	90.00

KM# 378 6 KREUZER
2.6000 g., 0.3330 Silver .0278 oz. **Obv. Legend:** LUDWIG KOENIG...

Date	Mintage	F	VF	XF	Unc	BU
1827	—	10.00	35.00	75.00	150	240
1828	—	8.00	20.00	50.00	125	175
1829	—	10.00	35.00	75.00	150	240

KM# 392 6 KREUZER
2.6000 g., 0.3330 Silver .0278 oz. **Obv. Legend:** LUDWIG I KOENIG...

Date	Mintage	F	VF	XF	Unc	BU
1830	—	10.00	25.00	40.00	65.00	90.00
1831	—	10.00	25.00	40.00	65.00	90.00
1832	—	15.00	30.00	45.00	85.00	120
1833	—	10.00	25.00	35.00	65.00	90.00
1834	—	10.00	25.00	40.00	70.00	100
1835	—	5.00	15.00	25.00	40.00	65.00

KM# 424 6 KREUZER
2.6000 g., 0.3330 Silver .0278 oz.

Date	Mintage	F	VF	XF	Unc	BU
1839	800,000	10.00	20.00	50.00	125	175
1840	—	5.00	10.00	25.00	40.00	60.00
1841	—	8.00	15.00	30.00	55.00	90.00
1842	—	5.00	10.00	25.00	40.00	70.00
1843	—	8.00	15.00	35.00	60.00	100
1844	—	5.00	10.00	25.00	40.00	70.00
1845	—	5.00	10.00	25.00	40.00	70.00
1846	—	5.00	10.00	25.00	40.00	70.00
1847	—	5.00	10.00	20.00	35.00	55.00
1848	—	5.00	8.00	25.00	40.00	70.00
1849	—	5.00	10.00	25.00	40.00	70.00
1850	—	5.00	10.00	25.00	40.00	70.00
1851	—	5.00	10.00	25.00	40.00	70.00

Date	Mintage	F	VF	XF	Unc	BU
1852	—	5.00	10.00	25.00	40.00	70.00
1853	—	5.00	8.00	20.00	35.00	55.00
1854	—	5.00	10.00	25.00	40.00	70.00
1855	—	5.00	10.00	25.00	40.00	70.00
1856	—	5.00	10.00	25.00	40.00	70.00

KM# 491 6 KREUZER
2.4600 g., 0.3500 Silver .0276 oz. **Obv. Legend:** SCHEIDE MUNZE added

Date	Mintage	F	VF	XF	Unc	BU
1866	87,000	7.50	40.00	80.00	175	240
1867	24,000	10.00	100	200	275	360

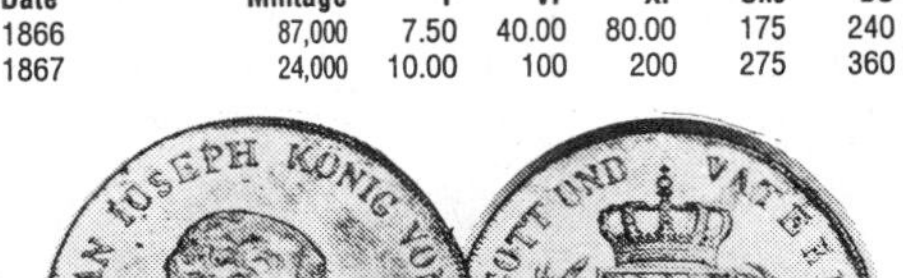

KM# 347 20 KREUZER
6.6800 g., 0.5830 Silver .1252 oz.

Date	Mintage	F	VF	XF	Unc	BU
1806	—	35.00	60.00	125	350	525
1807	—	35.00	60.00	125	350	525
1808	—	35.00	60.00	125	350	525
1809	—	25.00	50.00	90.00	125	175
1810	—	25.00	50.00	90.00	125	175
1811	—	20.00	40.00	80.00	120	165
1812	—	25.00	50.00	90.00	125	175
1813	—	25.00	50.00	90.00	125	175
1814	—	30.00	55.00	100	140	210
1815	—	25.00	50.00	90.00	125	175
1816	—	30.00	55.00	100	140	210
1817	—	25.00	50.00	90.00	125	175
1818	—	35.00	60.00	125	150	300
1819	—	30.00	55.00	100	125	210
1820	—	35.00	60.00	125	150	300
1821	—	30.00	55.00	100	125	210
1822	—	30.00	55.00	100	125	210
1823	—	30.00	55.00	100	125	210
1824	—	30.00	55.00	100	125	210
1825	—	30.00	55.00	100	125	210

KM# 417 1/2 GULDEN
5.3000 g., 0.9000 Silver .1533 oz. **Obv:** Head of Ludwig I right

Date	Mintage	F	VF	XF	Unc	BU
1838	1,750,000	10.00	20.00	35.00	60.00	90.00
1839	474,000	15.00	25.00	40.00	70.00	110
1840	233,000	15.00	30.00	60.00	100	150
1841	243,000	15.00	30.00	60.00	100	150
1842	508,000	15.00	25.00	40.00	70.00	110
1843	337,000	15.00	25.00	50.00	80.00	120
1844	1,452,000	10.00	20.00	40.00	70.00	100
1845	1,869,000	10.00	20.00	40.00	70.00	100
1846	1,181,000	10.00	20.00	40.00	70.00	100
1847	241,000	10.00	20.00	40.00	70.00	100
1848	407,000	10.00	20.00	40.00	70.00	100

KM# 444 1/2 GULDEN
5.3000 g., 0.9000 Silver .1533 oz. **Obv:** Head of Maximilian II right

Date	Mintage	F	VF	XF	Unc	BU
1848	Inc. above	15.00	25.00	45.00	90.00	115
1849	218,000	10.00	20.00	40.00	75.00	100

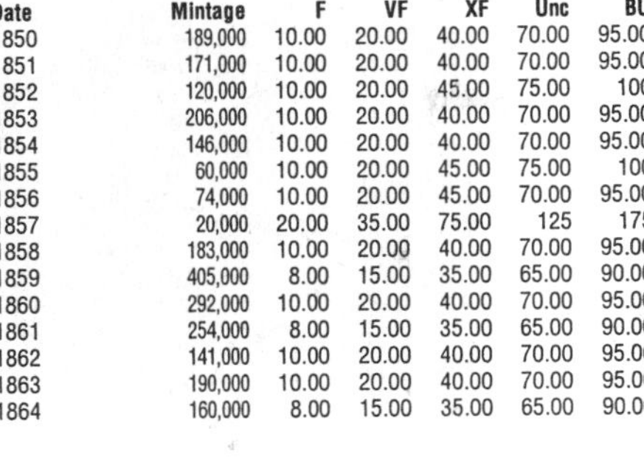

Date	Mintage	F	VF	XF	Unc	BU
1850	189,000	10.00	20.00	40.00	70.00	95.00
1851	171,000	10.00	20.00	40.00	70.00	95.00
1852	120,000	10.00	20.00	45.00	75.00	100
1853	206,000	10.00	20.00	40.00	70.00	95.00
1854	146,000	10.00	20.00	40.00	70.00	95.00
1855	60,000	10.00	20.00	45.00	75.00	100
1856	74,000	10.00	20.00	45.00	70.00	95.00
1857	20,000	20.00	35.00	75.00	125	175
1858	183,000	10.00	20.00	40.00	70.00	95.00
1859	405,000	8.00	15.00	35.00	65.00	90.00
1860	292,000	10.00	20.00	40.00	70.00	95.00
1861	254,000	8.00	15.00	35.00	65.00	90.00
1862	141,000	10.00	20.00	40.00	70.00	95.00
1863	190,000	10.00	20.00	40.00	70.00	95.00
1864	160,000	8.00	15.00	35.00	65.00	90.00

KM# 479 1/2 GULDEN
5.3000 g., 0.9000 Silver .1533 oz. **Obv:** Ludwig II with part in hair

Date	Mintage	F	VF	XF	Unc	BU
1864	Inc. above	45.00	75.00	250	600	725
1865	227,000	25.00	50.00	150	200	275
1866	101,000	35.00	65.00	20.00	300	475

KM# 492 1/2 GULDEN
5.3000 g., 0.9000 Silver .1533 oz. **Obv:** Without part in hair

Date	Mintage	F	VF	XF	Unc	BU
1866	Inc. above	25.00	45.00	150	210	270
1867	100,000	25.00	45.00	150	210	270
1868	121,000	20.00	40.00	130	175	240
1869	133,000	17.00	35.00	85.00	150	210
1870	111,000	25.00	45.00	140	175	240
1871	51,000	20.00	40.00	130	175	240

KM# 414 GULDEN
10.6000 g., 0.9000 Silver .3067 oz. **Obv:** Head of Ludwig I right

Date	Mintage	F	VF	XF	Unc	BU
1837	2,057,000	20.00	35.00	55.00	85.00	120
1838	2,045,000	15.00	30.00	45.00	75.00	105
1839	2,320,000	15.00	30.00	45.00	75.00	105
1840	3,591,000	15.00	30.00	40.00	60.00	90.00
1841	4,362,000	15.00	30.00	45.00	75.00	105
1842	1,449,000	15.00	30.00	40.00	65.00	90.00
1843	4,832,000	15.00	35.00	55.00	85.00	120
1844	3,491,000	15.00	30.00	40.00	65.00	90.00
1845	1,115,000	20.00	35.00	60.00	100	150
1846	686,000	20.00	35.00	50.00	80.00	115
1847	387,000	20.00	35.00	60.00	95.00	135
1848	437,000	20.00	35.00	60.00	95.00	135

KM# 445 GULDEN
10.6000 g., 0.9000 Silver .3067 oz. **Obv:** Head of Maximilian I right

Date	Mintage	F	VF	XF	Unc	BU
1848	Inc. above	15.00	25.00	75.00	160	210
1849	366,000	10.00	20.00	60.00	125	160
1850	343,000	10.00	20.00	60.00	125	160
1851	224,000	10.00	20.00	60.00	125	160
1852	453,000	10.00	20.00	60.00	125	160
1853	257,000	10.00	25.00	55.00	125	150
1854	513,000	150	35.00	75.00	160	210
1855	1,076,000	10.00	20.00	55.00	125	150
1856	455,000	8.00	15.00	50.00	110	135
1857	32,000	15.00	30.00	75.00	140	175
1858	144,000	10.00	20.00	60.00	125	160
1859	529,000	10.00	20.00	55.00	125	150
1860	452,000	10.00	20.00	55.00	125	150
1861	358,000	10.00	20.00	55.00	125	150
1862	266,000	10.00	20.00	55.00	125	150
1863	234,000	10.00	20.00	55.00	125	150
1864	414,000	10.00	20.00	55.00	125	150

KM# 480 GULDEN
10.6000 g., 0.9000 Silver .3067 oz. **Obv:** Ludwig II with part in hair

Date	Mintage	F	VF	XF	Unc	BU
1864	Inc. above	35.00	60.00	150	250	350
1865	167,000	40.00	75.00	170	300	400
1866	122,000	50.00	100	225	350	475

KM# 493 GULDEN
10.6000 g., 0.9000 Silver .3067 oz. **Obv:** Without part in hair

Date	Mintage	F	VF	XF	Unc	BU
1866	Inc. above	35.00	55.00	125	175	210
1867	86,000	40.00	60.00	150	275	360
1868	122,000	30.00	50.00	115	160	195
1869	122,000	30.00	50.00	115	160	195
1870	72,000	35.00	55.00	125	175	210
1871	35,000	40.00	60.00	150	250	335

KM# 438 2 GULDEN
21.2100 g., 0.9000 Silver .6138 oz. **Obv. Legend:** LUDWIG I KOENIG V. BAYERN.

Date	Mintage	F	VF	XF	Unc	BU
1845	883,000	30.00	50.00	65.00	100	145
1846	1,523,000	30.00	60.00	85.00	125	180
1847	1,491,000	30.00	50.00	75.00	100	155
1848	950,000	30.00	50.00	70.00	95.00	150

KM# 446 2 GULDEN
21.2100 g., 0.9000 Silver .6138 oz. **Obv. Legend:** MAXIMILIAN II KOENIG V. BAYERN. **Rev:** Similar to KM#438.

Date	Mintage	F	VF	XF	Unc	BU
1848	Inc. above	25.00	50.00	75.00	100	135
1849	741,000	20.00	40.00	65.00	85.00	125
1850	915,000	20.00	40.00	65.00	85.00	125
1851	1,157,000	20.00	40.00	65.00	85.00	125
1852	1,356,000	20.00	40.00	55.00	75.00	115
1853	634,000	20.00	40.00	65.00	85.00	125
1854	430,000	25.00	50.00	75.00	100	135
1855	585,000	20.00	40.00	65.00	85.00	125
1856	510,000	20.00	40.00	65.00	85.00	125

KM# 465 2 GULDEN
21.2100 g., 0.9000 Silver .6138 oz. **Subject:** Restoration of Madonna Column in Munich

Date	Mintage	F	VF	XF	Unc	BU
1855	1,000,000	15.00	25.00	45.00	70.00	90.00

KM# 348 1/2 THALER (School prize without denomination)
14.0300 g., 0.8330 Silver .3757 oz.

Date	Mintage	F	VF	XF	Unc	BU
ND(1806-08)	1,500	100	250	350	650	950

KM# 353 1/2 THALER (School prize without denomination)
14.0300 g., 0.8330 Silver .3757 oz. **Obv:** Script letters

Date	Mintage	F	VF	XF	Unc	BU
ND(1807-08)	—	125	350	550	950	1,400

KM# 357 1/2 THALER (School prize without denomination)
14.0300 g., 0.8330 Silver .3757 oz. **Obv:** Block or normal letters

Date	Mintage	F	VF	XF	Unc	BU
ND(1808-37)	25,000	75.00	150	275	350	500

KM# 349 THALER
28.0000 g., 0.8330 Silver .7500 oz.

Date	Mintage	F	VF	XF	Unc	BU
1806	—	150	250	450	750	1,000

KM# 350 THALER
28.0000 g., 0.8330 Silver .7500 oz. **Rev:** Crowned lions facing outward

Date	Mintage	F	VF	XF	Unc	BU
1806	—	1,000	1,600	3,000	5,000	9,000

KM# 354 THALER
28.0000 g., 0.8330 Silver .7500 oz. **Obv:** Bust with pigtail

Date	Mintage	F	VF	XF	Unc	BU
1807 Rare	100,000	—	—	—	—	—

KM# 355 THALER
28.0000 g., 0.8330 Silver .7500 oz.

Date	Mintage	F	VF	XF	Unc	BU
1807	Inc. above	50.00	110	210	450	650
1808	55,000	45.00	100	200	400	600
1809	8,932	55.00	125	275	600	900
1810	6,721	55.00	125	300	650	925
1811	11,000	55.00	125	275	600	850
1812	8,432	55.00	125	250	550	850
1813	5,888	55.00	125	250	550	900
1814	4,579	55.00	125	275	600	850
1815	6,913	55.00	125	250	550	850
1816	11,000	55.00	125	250	550	850
1817	4,638	55.00	125	250	550	900
1818	—	55.00	125	275	600	900
1819	—	55.00	125	275	600	900
1820	3,974	55.00	125	275	600	950
1821	3,826	60.00	135	300	650	950
1822	—	55.00	125	275	650	925

KM# 367 THALER
28.0600 g., 0.8680 Silver .7515 oz. **Rev:** Similar to KM#355

Date	Mintage	F	VF	XF	Unc	BU
1822	51,000	100	200	450	1,000	—
1823	47,000	150	350	750	1,800	—
1824	3,907	100	225	500	1,200	—
1825	1,932	100	200	450	1,000	—

KM# 370 THALER
28.0600 g., 0.8680 Silver .7515 oz. **Subject:** Coronation of Ludwig I

Date	Mintage	F	VF	XF	Unc	BU
1825	—	75.00	150	250	400	540

KM# 371 THALER
28.0600 g., 0.8680 Silver .7515 oz. **Subject:** Death of Reichenbach and Fraunhofer **Obv:** Similar to KM#370.

Date	Mintage	F	VF	XF	Unc	BU
1826	—	60.00	125	250	400	540

KM# 372 THALER

28.0600 g., 0.8680 Silver .7515 oz. **Subject:** Removal of Universtiy from Landshut to Munich **Obv:** Similar to KM#370.

Date	Mintage	F	VF	XF	Unc	BU
1826	—	75.00	150	250	400	540

KM# 380 THALER

28.0600 g., 0.8330 Silver .7515 oz. **Subject:** Founding of Order of Ludwig **Obv:** Similar to KM#370.

Date	Mintage	F	VF	XF	Unc	BU
1827	—	150	125	250	375	475

KM# 381 THALER

28.0600 g., 0.8330 Silver .7515 oz. **Subject:** Founding of Theresien Order **Obv:** Similar to KM#370.

Date	Mintage	F	VF	XF	Unc	BU
1827	—	150	125	250	375	475

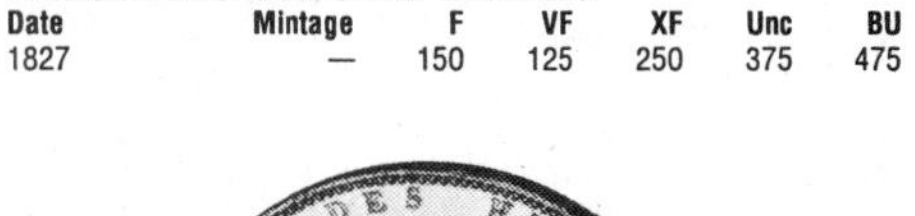

KM# 386 THALER

28.0600 g., 0.8330 Silver .7515 oz. **Subject:** Blessings of Heaven on Royal Family **Obv:** Similar to KM#370.

Date	Mintage	F	VF	XF	Unc	BU
1828	—	40.00	65.00	100	150	210

KM# 387 THALER

28.0600 g., 0.8330 Silver .7515 oz. **Subject:** Constitution Monument Dedication **Obv:** Similar to KM#370.

Date	Mintage	F	VF	XF	Unc	BU
1828	—	75.00	150	275	425	540

KM# 389 THALER

28.0600 g., 0.8330 Silver .7515 oz. **Subject:** Commercial Treaty Between Bavaria, Prussia, Hesse, and Wurttemberg **Obv:** Similar to KM#370.

Date	Mintage	F	VF	XF	Unc	BU
1829	—	75.00	125	250	375	500

KM# 393 THALER

28.0600 g., 0.8330 Silver .7515 oz. **Subject:** Loyalty of Bavarians to Royal Family **Obv:** Similar to KM#370.

Date	Mintage	F	VF	XF	Unc	BU
1830	—	75.00	125	250	350	475

KM# 402 THALER

28.0600 g., 0.8330 Silver .7515 oz. **Subject:** Prince Otto of Bavaria First King of Greece **Obv:** Similar to KM#370.

Date	Mintage	F	VF	XF	Unc	BU
1832	—	75.00	125	225	375	510

KM# 403 THALER

28.0600 g., 0.8330 Silver .7515 oz. **Subject:** Formation of Customs Union wtih Prussis, Saxony, Hesse, and Thuringia. **Obv:** Similar to KM#370.

Date	Mintage	F	VF	XF	Unc	BU
1833	—	75.00	150	225	375	510

KM# 404 THALER

28.0600 g., 0.8330 Silver .7515 oz. **Subject:** Monument for Bavarians Who Fell in Russia **Obv:** Similar to KM#370.

Date	Mintage	F	VF	XF	Unc	BU
1833	—	75.00	150	300	450	650

KM# 405 THALER

28.0600 g., 0.8330 Silver .7515 oz. **Subject:** Provincial Legislature **Obv:** Similar to KM#370.

Date	Mintage	F	VF	XF	Unc	BU
1834	—	75.00	145	225	375	510

KM# 406 THALER

28.0600 g., 0.8330 Silver .7515 oz. **Subject:** Erection of Monument at Oberwittelsbach **Obv:** Similar to KM#370.

Date	Mintage	F	VF	XF	Unc	BU
1834	—	75.00	125	250	400	540

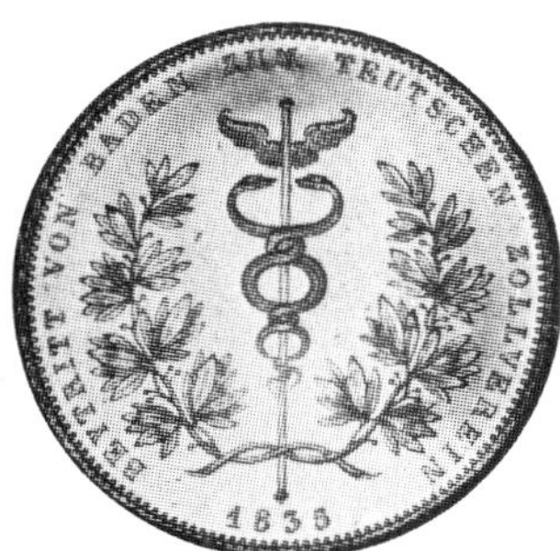

KM# 407 THALER

28.0600 g., 0.8330 Silver .7515 oz. **Subject:** Entry of Baden to German Customs Union **Obv:** Similar to KM#370.

Date	Mintage	F	VF	XF	Unc	BU
1835	—	75.00	150	260	410	540

KM# 408 THALER
28.0600 g., 0.8330 Silver .7515 oz. **Subject:** Established of Bavarian Mortgage Bank **Obv:** Similar to KM#370.

Date	Mintage	F	VF	XF	Unc	BU
1835	—	65.00	125	250	400	540

KM# 409 THALER
28.0600 g., 0.8330 Silver .7515 oz. **Subject:** Monument for King Otto Leaving his Mother **Obv:** Similar to KM#370.

Date	Mintage	F	VF	XF	Unc	BU
1835	—	65.00	125	275	425	650

KM# 410 THALER
28.0600 g., 0.8330 Silver .7515 oz. **Subject:** Construction of First Steam Railway **Obv:** Similar to KM#370.

Date	Mintage	F	VF	XF	Unc	BU
1835	—	65.00	125	250	350	475

KM# 411.1 THALER
28.0600 g., 0.8330 Silver .7515 oz. **Subject:** Monument in Munich to King Maximilian Josef

Date	Mintage	F	VF	XF	Unc	BU
1835	—	60.00	170	225	375	450

KM# 411.2 THALER
28.0600 g., 0.8330 Silver .7515 oz. **Rev:** Sceptre not beyond shoulder

Date	Mintage	F	VF	XF	Unc	BU
1835	—	75.00	150	225	375	510

KM# 412 THALER
28.0600 g., 0.8330 Silver .7515 oz. **Subject:** School Given to Benedictine Order

Date	Mintage	F	VF	XF	Unc	BU
1835	—	65.00	125	225	375	475

KM# 413 THALER
28.0600 g., 0.8330 Silver .7515 oz. **Subject:** Erection of Otto Chapel at Kiefersfelden **Obv:** Similar to KM#370.

Date	Mintage	F	VF	XF	Unc	BU
1836	—	60.00	115	225	375	475

KM# 415 THALER
28.0600 g., 0.8330 Silver .7515 oz. **Subject:** Order of St. Michael as Order of Merit **Obv:** Similar to KM#370

Date	Mintage	F	VF	XF	Unc	BU
1837	—	75.00	150	225	375	510

KM# 481 THALER
18.5200 g., 0.9000 Silver .5360 oz. **Obv:** Ludwig II with part in hair

Date	Mintage	F	VF	XF	Unc	BU
1864	Inc. above	45.00	65.00	250	450	600
1865	1,144,000	30.00	50.00	150	250	310
1866	1,075,000	35.00	55.00	160	275	360

KM# 489 THALER
18.5200 g., 0.9000 Silver .5360 oz. **Obv:** No part in hair **Rev:** Madonna with child, J. Reis below truncation

Date	Mintage	F	VF	XF	Unc	BU
ND(1865)	110,000	17.00	25.00	45.00	65.00	80.00
1866	Inc. above	17.00	25.00	45.00	65.00	80.00
1867	—	20.00	30.00	50.00	70.00	85.00
1868	—	17.00	25.00	45.00	65.00	80.00
1869	—	25.00	40.00	60.00	90.00	120
1870	263,500	12.00	25.00	45.00	65.00	80.00
1871	718,000	17.00	25.00	45.00	65.00	80.00

KM# 494.1 THALER
18.5200 g., 0.9000 Silver .5360 oz. **Rev:** Arms

Date	Mintage	F	VF	XF	Unc	BU
1866	Inc. above	35.00	55.00	100	140	195
1867	595,000	40.00	60.00	120	150	210
1868	312,000	45.00	65.00	130	160	220
1869	277,000	45.00	65.00	130	170	240
1870	264,000	45.00	65.00	130	160	220
1871	718,000	40.00	60.00	120	150	210

KM# 494.2 THALER
18.5200 g., 0.9000 Silver .5360 oz. **Rev:** New arabesques below arms

Date	Mintage	F	VF	XF	Unc	BU
1871	—	150	300	475	900	1,200

KM# 495 THALER
18.5200 g., 0.9000 Silver .5360 oz. **Obv:** J. REIS below truncation

Date	Mintage	F	VF	XF	Unc	BU
1871	Inc. above	85.00	160	300	750	1,000

KM# 496 THALER
18.5200 g., 0.9000 Silver .5360 oz. **Subject:** German Victory in Franco-Prussian War

Date	Mintage	F	VF	XF	Unc	BU
1871	150,000	18.00	25.00	60.00	90.00	120
1871 Proof	—	Value: 350				

KM# 361 THALER (Convention)
28.0600 g., 0.8680 Silver .7515 oz. **Subject:** Granting of Bavarian Constitution

Date	Mintage	F	VF	XF	Unc	BU
1818	40,000	30.00	75.00	100	150	210

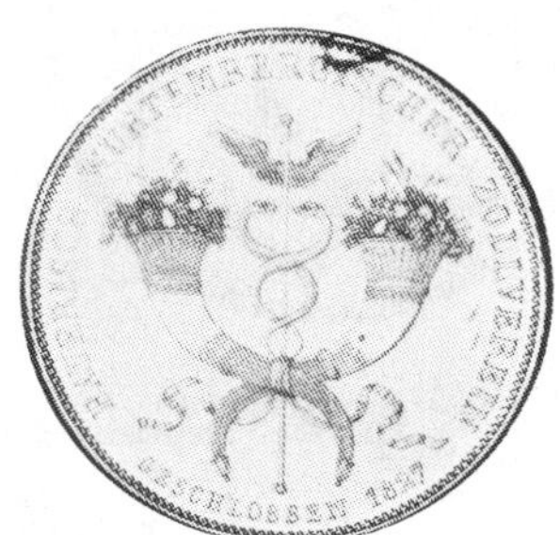

KM# 379 THALER (Convention)
28.0600 g., 0.8330 Silver .7515 oz. **Subject:** Bavaria-Wurttemberg Customs Treaty Signing **Obv:** Similar to KM#370.

Date	Mintage	F	VF	XF	Unc	BU
1827	—	100	135	250	375	500

KM# 401 THALER (Convention)
28.0600 g., 0.8330 Silver .7515 oz. **Subject:** Opening of Legislature **Obv:** Similar to KM#370.

Date	Mintage	F	VF	XF	Unc	BU
1831	—	90.00	175	300	500	650

KM# 358.1 THALER (Krone)
29.3400 g., 0.8680 Silver .8188 oz.

Date	Mintage	F	VF	XF	Unc	BU
1809	929,921	35.00	55.00	175	375	540
1810	648,777	40.00	60.00	175	400	600
1811	114,018	50.00	75.00	200	450	700
1812	1,160,605	35.00	55.00	125	375	540
1813	835,524	35.00	55.00	125	325	475
1814	1,015,406	35.00	55.00	125	300	450
1815	681,444	35.00	55.00	125	325	475
1816	2,261,286	30.00	50.00	125	275	410
1817	334,619	40.00	60.00	125	400	600
1818	163,619	40.00	60.00	200	400	600
1819	286,575	40.00	60.00	200	400	600
1820	115,937	45.00	65.00	200	425	625
1821	216,167	40.00	60.00	185	400	600
1822	29,475	45.00	65.00	200	425	650
1823	27,245	45.00	65.00	200	425	650
1824	41,593	45.00	65.00	200	425	650
1825	75,693	45.00	65.00	185	400	600

KM# 358.2 THALER (Krone)
29.3400 g., 0.8680 Silver .8188 oz. **Obv. Legend:** JOEPHUS (error)

Date	Mintage	F	VF	XF	Unc	BU
1813	Inc. above	250	300	550	1,100	1,500

KM# 373 THALER (Krone)
29.5400 g., 0.8710 Silver .8272 oz.

Date	Mintage	F	VF	XF	Unc	BU
1825 Rare	—	—	—	—	—	—
1826	51,000	75.00	110	175	375	650
1827	66,000	85.00	125	225	425	725
1828	79,000	55.00	100	150	300	500
1829	94,000	95.00	125	250	450	775

KM# 394 THALER (Krone)
29.5400 g., 0.8710 Silver .8272 oz.

Date	Mintage	F	VF	XF	Unc	BU
1830	78,386	90.00	140	200	375	500
1831	47,316	100	150	170	375	500
1832	54,697	90.00	140	200	360	475
1833	42,352	110	160	250	400	625
1834	14,649	100	150	210	376	500
1835	8,813	110	160	300	500	750
1836	49,604	90.00	140	200	325	475
1837	163,730	50.00	110	175	250	390

KM# 468 THALER (Vereins)
18.5200 g., 0.9000 Silver .5360 oz. **Obv:** Head of Maximilian II right

Date	Mintage	F	VF	XF	Unc	BU
1857	1,560,000	12.00	20.00	50.00	90.00	120
1858	2,283,000	12.00	20.00	50.00	90.00	120
1859	2,661,000	12.00	20.00	50.00	90.00	120
1860	2,471,000	12.00	20.00	50.00	90.00	120
1861	2,682,000	12.00	20.00	50.00	90.00	120
1862	2,587,000	12.00	20.00	50.00	90.00	120
1863	2,587,000	12.00	20.00	50.00	90.00	120
1864	1,458,000	15.00	25.00	60.00	90.00	130

KM# 416 2 THALER (3-1/2 Gulden)
37.1200 g., 0.9000 Silver 1.0743 oz. **Subject:** Monetary Union of Six South German States **Obv:** Head of Ludwig I right

Date	Mintage	F	VF	XF	Unc	BU
1837	—	85.00	115	250	375	450

KM# 418 2 THALER (3-1/2 Gulden)
37.1200 g., 0.9000 Silver 1.0743 oz. **Subject:** Reapportionment of Bavaria

Date	Mintage	F	VF	XF	Unc	BU
1838	—	90.00	125	375	650	725

KM# 425 2 THALER (3-1/2 Gulden)
37.1200 g., 0.9000 Silver 1.0743 oz. **Subject:** Maximilian I, Elector of Bavaira

Date	Mintage	F	VF	XF	Unc	BU
1839	—	125	175	300	400	510

KM# 426 2 THALER (3-1/2 Gulden)
37.1200 g., 0.9000 Silver 1.0743 oz. **Obv:** Similar to KM#416

Date	Mintage	F	VF	XF	Unc	BU
1839	113,000	60.00	125	325	100	1,500
1840	193,000	50.00	100	250	900	1,375
1841	450,000	70.00	175	450	1,200	1,800

KM# 427 2 THALER (3-1/2 Gulden)
37.1200 g., 0.9000 Silver 1.0743 oz. **Subject:** Albrecht Durer

Date	Mintage	F	VF	XF	Unc	BU
1840	—	100	165	300	450	540

KM# 429 2 THALER (3-1/2 Gulden)
37.1200 g., 0.9000 Silver 1.0743 oz. **Subject:** Jean Paul Friedrich Richter

Date	Mintage	F	VF	XF	Unc	BU
1841	—	125	200	325	550	625

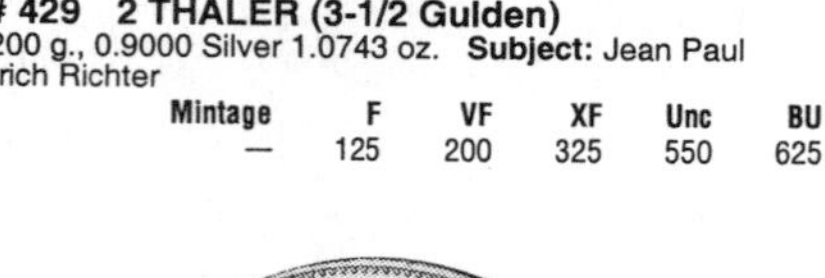

KM# 430 2 THALER (3-1/2 Gulden)
37.1200 g., 0.9000 Silver 1.0743 oz. **Subject:** Walhalla Commemorative

Date	Mintage	F	VF	XF	Unc	BU
1842	—	125	150	325	375	450

KM# 431.1 2 THALER (3-1/2 Gulden)
37.1200 g., 0.9000 Silver 1.0743 oz. **Subject:** Marriage of Crown Prince of Bavaria and Marie, Royal Princess of Prussia

Date	Mintage	F	VF	XF	Unc	BU
1842	—	90.00	125	250	400	450

KM# 431.2 2 THALER (3-1/2 Gulden)
37.1200 g., 0.9000 Silver 1.0743 oz. **Obv:** 1 OCTB. 1842 (error date)

Date	Mintage	F	VF	XF	Unc	BU
1842	—	100	125	250	400	450

KM# 432 2 THALER (3-1/2 Gulden)
37.1200 g., 0.9000 Silver 1.0743 oz.

Date	Mintage	F	VF	XF	Unc	BU
1842	85,000	75.00	175	450	750	900
1843	277,000	50.00	125	250	500	650
1844	122,000	60.00	145	300	600	720
1845	167,000	55.00	135	300	600	720
1846	132,000	65.00	150	425	700	840
1847	12,000	95.00	325	700	900	1,025
1848	192,000	60.00	145	300	600	720

KM# 434 2 THALER (3-1/2 Gulden)
37.1200 g., 0.9000 Silver 1.0743 oz. **Subject:** 100th Anniversary Academy of Erlangen

Date	Mintage	F	VF	XF	Unc	BU
1843	—	90.00	150	250	450	510

KM# 437 2 THALER (3-1/2 Gulden)
37.1200 g., 0.9000 Silver 1.0743 oz. **Subject:** Completion of the General's Hall in Munich

Date	Mintage	F	VF	XF	Unc	BU
1844	—	90.00	175	350	475	575

KM# 439 2 THALER (3-1/2 Gulden)
37.1200 g., 0.9000 Silver 1.0743 oz. **Subject:** Chancellor Baron von Kreittmayr

Date	Mintage	F	VF	XF	Unc	BU
1845	—	200	325	500	700	900

KM# 440 2 THALER (3-1/2 Gulden)
37.1200 g., 0.9000 Silver 1.0743 oz. **Subject:** Birth of Two Grandsons

Date	Mintage	F	VF	XF	Unc	BU
1845	—	90.00	160	300	600	775

KM# 441 2 THALER (3-1/2 Gulden)
37.1200 g., 0.9000 Silver 1.0743 oz. **Subject:** Completion of Canal Between Danube and Main Rivers

Date	Mintage	F	VF	XF	Unc	BU
1846	—	170	250	450	725	900

KM# 442 2 THALER (3-1/2 Gulden)
37.1200 g., 0.9000 Silver 1.0743 oz. **Subject:** Bishop Julius Echter von Mespelbrunn

Date	Mintage	F	VF	XF	Unc	BU
1847	—	145	255	475	700	900

KM# 443 2 THALER (3-1/2 Gulden)
37.1200 g., 0.9000 Silver 1.0743 oz. **Subject:** Abdication of Ludwig I for Maximilian

Date	Mintage	F	VF	XF	Unc	BU
1848	—	400	100	1,600	2,800	3,600

KM# 447.1 2 THALER (3-1/2 Gulden)
37.1200 g., 0.9000 Silver 1.0743 oz. **Subject:** New Constitution **Obv:** Maximilian II head right **Edge Lettering:** VEREINSMUNZE

Date	Mintage	F	VF	XF	Unc	BU
1848	—	175	245	400	850	1,200

KM# 447.2 2 THALER (3-1/2 Gulden)
37.1200 g., 0.9000 Silver 1.0743 oz. **Edge Lettering:** CONVENTION-VOM

Date	Mintage	F	VF	XF	Unc	BU
1848	—	175	275	400	775	1,025

KM# 448.1 2 THALER (3-1/2 Gulden)
37.1200 g., 0.9000 Silver 1.0743 oz. **Subject:** Johann Christoph von Gluck **Edge Lettering:** VEREINSMUNZE

Date	Mintage	F	VF	XF	Unc	BU
1848	—	500	1,150	1,750	2,500	3,350

KM# 447.3 2 THALER (3-1/2 Gulden)
37.1200 g., 0.9000 Silver 1.0743 oz. **Edge Lettering:** DREY EIN HALB GULDEN **Note:** Restrike post 1857.

Date	Mintage	F	VF	XF	Unc	BU
1848	—	150	245	500	700	1,025

KM# 448.2 2 THALER (3-1/2 Gulden)
37.1200 g., 0.9000 Silver 1.0743 oz. **Edge Lettering:** DREY EIN HALB GULDEN **Note:** Restrike post 1857.

Date	Mintage	F	VF	XF	Unc	BU
1848	—	500	1,250	1,700	3,000	3,600

KM# 455.1 2 THALER (3-1/2 Gulden)
37.1200 g., 0.9000 Silver 1.0743 oz. **Subject:** Orlando Di Lasso **Edge Lettering:** VEREINSMUNZE

Date	Mintage	F	VF	XF	Unc	BU
1849	—	700	1,250	1,750	3,000	3,700

KM# 455.2 2 THALER (3-1/2 Gulden)
37.1200 g., 0.9000 Silver 1.0743 oz. **Edge Lettering:** DREY EIN HALB GULDEN **Note:** Restrike post 1857.

Date	Mintage	F	VF	XF	Unc	BU
1849	—	700	1,250	2,100	3,200	4,200

KM# 456 2 THALER (3-1/2 Gulden)
37.1200 g., 0.9000 Silver 1.0743 oz.

Date	Mintage	F	VF	XF	Unc	BU
1849	—	150	250	500	800	900
1850	—	125	225	375	700	850
1851	—	100	200	300	500	600
1852	—	110	200	300	500	600
1853	—	110	210	330	600	775
1854	—	75.00	140	220	450	550
1855	417,000	75.00	140	220	450	550
1856	142,000	85.00	150	245	475	575

KM# 464.1 2 THALER (3-1/2 Gulden)
37.1200 g., 0.9000 Silver 1.0743 oz. **Subject:** Exibition of German Products in Crystal Palace **Edge Lettering:** VEREINS MUNZE

Date	Mintage	F	VF	XF	Unc	BU
1854	—	90.00	125	250	350	420

KM# 464.2 2 THALER (3-1/2 Gulden)
37.1200 g., 0.9000 Silver 1.0743 oz. **Edge Lettering:** CONVENTION-BOM

Date	Mintage	F	VF	XF	Unc	BU
1854	—	100	150	275	450	625

KM# 467 2 THALER (3-1/2 Gulden)
37.1200 g., 0.9000 Silver 1.0743 oz. **Subject:** Erection of Monument to King Maximilian II

Date	Mintage	F	VF	XF	Unc	BU
1856	1,152	300	350	600	900	1,200

KM# 474 2 THALER (Vereins)
37.0400 g., 0.9000 Silver 1.0717 oz.

Date	Mintage	F	VF	XF	Unc	BU
1859	28,000	350	1,750	2,500	4,000	5,400
1860	69,000	200	300	600	1,250	1,800

KM# 475 2 THALER (Vereins)
37.0400 g., 0.9000 Silver 1.0717 oz. **Obv:** Different hair style

Date	Mintage	F	VF	XF	Unc	BU
1861	29,000	175	300	700	1,100	1,450
1862	8,727	250	400	1,000	1,300	1,900
1863	11,000	200	350	800	1,150	1,550
1864	8,201	250	400	1,000	1,300	1,900

KM# 490 2 THALER (Vereins)
37.0400 g., 0.9000 Silver 1.0717 oz. **Obv:** Ludwig II head right

Date	Mintage	F	VF	XF	Unc	BU
1865	2,490	2,000	3,500	5,000	7,000	9,000
1867	1,760	2,500	4,000	5,500	8,000	11,000
1869	—	2,500	4,000	5,500	8,000	11,000

TRADE COINAGE

KM# 351 DUCAT
3.4900 g., 0.9370 Gold .1051 oz. **Note:** Fr. #264.

Date	Mintage	F	VF	XF	Unc	BU
1806	3,937	1,750	2,250	3,250	4,250	—

KM# 356 DUCAT
3.4900 g., 0.9370 Gold .1051 oz. **Note:** Fr. #265.

Date	Mintage	F	VF	XF	Unc	BU
1807	2,260	650	1,125	1,750	2,500	—
1808	1,465	500	1,050	1,600	2,250	—
1809	3,263	750	1,250	2,000	2,750	—
1810	3,124	850	1,350	2,250	3,000	—
1811	—	600	1,100	1,750	2,500	—
1812	—	850	1,350	2,250	3,000	—
1813	—	600	1,100	1,750	2,500	—
1814	—	600	1,100	1,750	2,500	—
1815	—	750	1,250	2,000	2,750	—
1816	—	600	1,000	1,600	2,250	—
1817	—	600	1,100	1,750	2,500	—
1818	—	600	1,100	1,750	2,500	—
1819	—	750	1,250	2,000	2,750	—
1820	—	600	1,100	1,750	2,500	—
1821	—	500	1,050	1,600	2,250	—
1822	—	600	1,100	1,750	2,500	—

KM# 362 DUCAT
3.4900 g., 0.9370 Gold .1051 oz. **Obv. Legend:** BAEIRN... **Note:** Fr. #265.

Date	Mintage	F	VF	XF	Unc	BU
1821	—	1,250	1,950	3,000	4,200	—
1822	—	750	1,250	1,850	2,650	—

KM# 363 DUCAT
3.4900 g., 0.9370 Gold .1051 oz. **Rev:** Legend above river god **Rev. Legend:** EX AURO DANUBIT **Note:** Fr. #266.

Date	Mintage	F	VF	XF	Unc	BU
1821	—	2,000	3,000	4,250	7,500	—

KM# 364 DUCAT
3.4900 g., 0.9370 Gold .1051 oz. **Rev:** Legend above river god **Rev. Legend:** EX AURO DENI **Note:** Fr. #267.

Date	Mintage	F	VF	XF	Unc	BU
1821	—	2,200	3,200	5,500	8,500	—

KM# 365 DUCAT
3.4900 g., 0.9370 Gold .1051 oz. **Subject:** Isar **Note:** Fr. #268.

Date	Mintage	F	VF	XF	Unc	BU
1821	—	1,500	2,850	5,000	7,750	—

KM# 366 DUCAT
3.4900 g., 0.9370 Gold .1051 oz. **Subject:** Rhine **Note:** Fr. #269.

Date	Mintage	F	VF	XF	Unc	BU
1821	—	1,000	1,750	3,250	4,750	—

KM# 368 DUCAT
3.4900 g., 0.9370 Gold .1051 oz. **Obv:** Older head

Date	Mintage	F	VF	XF	Unc	BU
1823	4,400	600	1,000	1,600	2,250	—
1824	19,000	750	1,250	2,000	2,750	—
1825	3,000	600	1,100	1,650	2,300	—

KM# 375 DUCAT
3.4900 g., 0.9370 Gold .1051 oz. **Obv:** Ludwig I head right **Note:** Fr. #270.

Date	Mintage	F	VF	XF	Unc	BU
1826	696	1,250	1,850	2,375	2,850	—
1827	4,200	1,750	2,500	3,250	3,850	—
1828	3,090	1,750	2,000	2,500	3,000	—

KM# 388.1 DUCAT
3.4900 g., 0.9370 Gold .1051 oz. **Obv. Legend:** LUDWIG I **Note:** Fr. #270a.

Date	Mintage	F	VF	XF	Unc	BU
1828	1,351	800	1,300	1,800	2,350	—
1829	1,143	600	1,000	1,500	2,150	—
1830	1,731	600	1,000	1,500	2,150	—
1831	3,907	1,000	1,500	2,100	2,600	—
1832	1,884	600	1,000	1,500	2,150	—
1833	1,230	1,000	1,500	2,100	2,600	—
1834	1,711	1,200	1,800	2,600	3,250	—

KM# 388.2 DUCAT
3.4900 g., 0.9370 Gold .1051 oz. **Note:** Struck in collared dies. Fr. #270b.

Date	Mintage	F	VF	XF	Unc	BU
1835	2,048	600	1,000	1,500	2,150	—

KM# 395.1 DUCAT
3.4900 g., 0.9370 Gold .1051 oz. **Rev:** Legend above river god **Rev. Legend:** EX AURO DANUBII **Note:** Fr. #272.

Date	Mintage	F	VF	XF	Unc	BU
1830	—	1,200	2,500	4,250	7,500	—

KM# 395.2 DUCAT
3.4900 g., 0.9370 Gold .1051 oz. **Rev:** Inverted "C" in date

Date	Mintage	F	VF	XF	Unc	BU
1830	—	1,200	2,550	4,350	8,000	—

KM# 396 DUCAT
3.4900 g., 0.9370 Gold .1051 oz. **Obv. Legend:** LUDWIG I...

Date	Mintage	F	VF	XF	Unc	BU
1830	—	1,200	2,500	4,250	7,500	—

KM# 397 DUCAT

3.4900 g., 0.9370 Gold .1051 oz. **Subject:** Inn **Note:** Fr. #273.

Date	Mintage	F	VF	XF	Unc	BU
1830	—	1,200	2,750	4,500	8,500	—

KM# 398 DUCAT

3.4900 g., 0.9370 Gold .1051 oz. **Subject:** Isar **Note:** Fr. #274.

Date	Mintage	F	VF	XF	Unc	BU
1830	—	1,200	2,500	4,250	7,500	—

KM# 399 DUCAT

3.4900 g., 0.9370 Gold .1051 oz. **Subject:** Rhine **Note:** Fr. #275.

Date	Mintage	F	VF	XF	Unc	BU
1830	—	1,000	2,250	4,000	7,000	—

KM# 400 DUCAT

3.4900 g., 0.9370 Gold .1051 oz. **Obv. Legend:** LUDWIG I...

Date	Mintage	F	VF	XF	Unc	BU
1830	—	1,000	2,250	4,000	7,000	—

KM# 428 DUCAT

3.4900 g., 0.9370 Gold .1051 oz. **Note:** Fr. #271.

Date	Mintage	F	VF	XF	Unc	BU
1840	5,000	600	1,000	1,500	2,150	—
1841	2,309	650	1,150	1,800	2,350	—
1842	810	650	1,150	1,800	2,350	—
1843	2,358	650	1,150	1,800	2,350	—
1844	4,259	850	1,500	2,350	3,150	—
1845	2,470	600	1,000	1,500	2,150	—
1846	3,642	650	1,150	1,800	2,350	—
1847	5,122	600	1,000	1,500	2,150	—
1848	1,470	600	1,000	1,500	2,150	—

KM# 433 DUCAT

3.4900 g., 0.9370 Gold .1051 oz. **Subject:** Rhine **Note:** Fr. #276.

Date	Mintage	F	VF	XF	Unc	BU
1842	—	500	1,250	2,250	3,500	—
1846	—	400	1,000	2,000	3,250	—

KM# 457 DUCAT

3.4900 g., 0.9370 Gold .1051 oz. **Obv:** Maximilian II head right **Obv. Legend:** ...KOENIG V BAYERN **Note:** Fr. #277.

Date	Mintage	F	VF	XF	Unc	BU
1849	1,470	750	1,250	1,750	2,250	—
1850	1,519	500	1,000	1,250	1,750	—
1851	3,815	400	600	900	1,200	—
1852	4,396	400	600	900	1,200	—
1853	5,603	400	600	900	1,200	—
1854	5,707	400	600	900	1,200	—
1855	1,540	500	1,000	1,250	1,750	—
1856	3,782	400	600	900	1,200	—

KM# 461 DUCAT

3.4900 g., 0.9370 Gold .1051 oz. **Obv. Legend:** ...BAVARIAE REX

Date	Mintage	F	VF	XF	Unc	BU
1850	100	1,750	2,250	3,500	5,250	—

KM# 462 DUCAT

3.4900 g., 0.9370 Gold .1051 oz. **Subject:** Rhine **Note:** Fr. #278.

Date	Mintage	F	VF	XF	Unc	BU
1850	—	500	1,000	1,700	2,000	—
1851	—	550	1,200	2,000	2,250	—
1852	—	500	1,000	1,700	2,000	—
1853	—	500	1,000	1,700	2,000	—
1854	—	425	900	1,500	1,800	—
1855	—	600	1,400	2,500	3,000	—
1856	—	425	900	1,500	1,800	—

KM# 466 DUCAT

3.4900 g., 0.9370 Gold .1051 oz. **Rev. Legend:** ...BERGBAU BEI GOLDKRONACH **Note:** Fr. #279.

Date	Mintage	F	VF	XF	Unc	BU
1855	—	12,500	17,500	25,000	35,000	—

KM# 477 DUCAT

3.4900 g., 0.9370 Gold .1051 oz. **Note:** Reduced size. Fr. #278.

Date	Mintage	F	VF	XF	Unc	BU
1863	—	1,500	2,500	4,000	5,000	—

REFORM COINAGE

KM# 505 2 MARK

11.1110 g., 0.9000 Silver .3215 oz. **Obv:** Ludwig II head right

Date	Mintage	F	VF	XF	Unc	BU
1876D	5,370,000	35.00	70.00	225	550	—
1877D	1,512,000	35.00	70.00	250	700	—
1880D	169,000	75.00	150	600	1,200	—
1883D	104,000	60.00	150	325	800	—

KM# 507 2 MARK

11.1110 g., 0.9000 Silver .3215 oz. **Obv:** Otto head left

Date	Mintage	F	VF	XF	Unc	BU
1888	172,000	150	300	700	1,200	—

KM# 511 2 MARK

11.1110 g., 0.9000 Silver .3215 oz. **Ruler:** Otto Prince Regent Luitpold **Note:** Open and closed curl varieties exist.

Date	Mintage	F	VF	XF	Unc	BU
1891D	246,000	15.00	35.00	100	240	300
1893D	246,000	20.00	40.00	100	250	350
1896D	492,000	15.00	30.00	90.00	175	275
1898D	201,000	50.00	110	250	600	1,000
1899D	753,000	12.00	28.00	50.00	140	200
1900D	722,000	12.00	30.00	50.00	130	190

KM# 502 5 MARK

27.7770 g., 0.9000 Silver .8038 oz. **Obv:** Ludwig II head right

Date	Mintage	F	VF	XF	Unc	BU
1874D	85,000	40.00	70.00	325	800	1,000
1875D	657,000	40.00	65.00	275	700	900
1876D	1,130,000	35.00	65.00	225	600	800

KM# 506 5 MARK

1.9910 g., 0.9000 Gold .0576 oz.

Date	Mintage	F	VF	XF	Unc	BU
1877	635,000	150	225	350	500	750
1877 Proof	—	Value: 1,500				
1878	128,000	400	700	1,000	1,300	1,600

KM# 508 5 MARK

27.7770 g., 0.9000 Silver .8038 oz. **Obv:** Otto

Date	Mintage	F	VF	XF	Unc	BU
1888D	69,000	200	300	800	1,000	1,250
1888D Proof	—	Value: 3,750				

KM# 512 5 MARK
27.7770 g., 0.9000 Silver .8038 oz. **Ruler:** Otto **Note:** Varieties in the hair locks and curls exist.

Date	Mintage	F	VF	XF	Unc	BU
1891D	98,000	17.50	40.00	110	400	600
1893D	98,000	25.00	50.00	120	400	600
1894D	141,000	17.50	40.00	120	400	600
1895D	141,000	22.50	45.00	120	400	600
1896D	28,000	55.00	135	600	1,250	1,750
1898D	303,000	15.00	30.00	75.00	300	500
1899D	141,000	25.00	40.00	100	325	525
1900D	295,000	15.00	30.00	95.00	300	500
(1891-1900)D Proof	—	Value: 1,000				

KM# 500 10 MARK
3.9820 g., 0.9000 Gold .1152 oz. **Obv:** Ludwig II head right; J. REIS below truncation **Rev:** Type I

Date	Mintage	F	VF	XF	Unc	BU
1872D	626,000	100	200	300	500	750
1872D Proof	—	Value: 1,600				
1873D	1,198,000	75.00	150	250	400	600
1873D Proof	—	Value: 1,600				

KM# 503 10 MARK
3.9820 g., 0.9000 Gold .1152 oz. **Rev:** Type II

Date	Mintage	F	VF	XF	Unc	BU
1874D	407,000	75.00	130	170	300	400
1874D Proof	—	Value: 1,350				
1875D	816,000	75.00	130	170	300	400
1876D	684,000	75.00	130	170	300	400
1877D	283,000	75.00	130	170	300	400
1878D	638,000	75.00	130	170	300	400
1879D	224,000	75.00	130	170	300	400
1880D	299,000	75.00	130	170	300	400
1881D	157,000	75.00	130	170	300	425
1881D Proof	—	Value: 1,350				

KM# 509 10 MARK
3.9820 g., 0.9000 Gold .1152 oz. **Obv:** Otto head left **Obv. Legend:** ...VON BAYERN **Rev:** Type II

Date	Mintage	F	VF	XF	Unc	BU
1888D	281,000	150	250	325	500	700
1888D Proof	—	Value: 1,350				

KM# 510 10 MARK
3.9820 g., 0.9000 Gold .1152 oz. **Rev:** Type III

Date	Mintage	F	VF	XF	Unc	BU
1890D	420,000	75.00	130	175	225	300
1893D	422,000	75.00	130	175	225	300
1896D	281,000	75.00	130	190	250	350
1898D	589,000	75.00	130	175	225	300
1900D	141,000	100	150	225	300	450
1900D Proof	—	Value: 700				

KM# 514 10 MARK
3.9820 g., 0.9000 Gold .1152 oz. **Ruler:** Otto **Obv. Legend:** ... V. BAYERN

Date	Mintage	F	VF	XF	Unc	BU
1900D	Inc. above	85.00	150	225	300	350
1900D Proof	—	Value: 900				

KM# 501 20 MARK
7.9650 g., 0.9000 Gold .2304 oz. **Obv:** Ludwig II head right **Rev:** Type I

Date	Mintage	F	VF	XF	Unc	BU
1872D	1,556,000	125	160	250	500	—
1872D Proof	—	Value: 1,600				
1873D	2,770,000	125	150	250	400	—
1873D Proof	—	Value: 1,700				

KM# 504 20 MARK
7.9650 g., 0.9000 Gold .2304 oz. **Rev:** Type II

Date	Mintage	F	VF	XF	Unc	BU
1874D	615,000	125	160	225	300	400
1875D	—	725	1,200	1,800	2,250	2,750
1875D Proof	—	Value: 1,500				
1876D	454,000	125	160	225	350	450
1878D	50,000	300	600	850	1,200	1,400
1878D Proof	—	Value: 1,600				

KM# 513 20 MARK
7.9650 g., 0.9000 Gold .2304 oz. **Ruler:** Otto **Obv:** Head left **Rev:** Type III

Date	Mintage	F	VF	XF	Unc	BU
1895D	501,000	100	140	185	265	—
1895D Proof	—	Value: 800				
1900D	501,000	100	150	185	265	—

KM# 469 1/2 KRONE
5.5550 g., 0.9000 Gold .1607 oz. **Obv:** Maximilian II head right

Date	Mintage	F	VF	XF	Unc	BU
1857	1,749	—	2,500	4,000	7,000	—
1858	1,020	—	3,000	4,500	7,500	—
1859	1,200	—	3,000	4,500	7,500	—
1860	—	—	—	8,000	12,000	—
1861	32	—	—	8,000	12,000	—
1863	—	—	—	8,000	12,000	—
1863 Proof	—	—	—	—	—	—
Note: Stack's Hammel sale 9/82 Proof realized $13,000						
1864	—	—	—	8,000	12,000	—

KM# 482 1/2 KRONE
5.0000 g., 0.9000 Gold .1446 oz. **Obv:** Ludwig II head right

Date	Mintage	F	VF	XF	Unc	BU
1864 Rare	—	—	—	—	—	—
1865 Rare	—	—	—	—	—	—
1866 Rare	—	—	—	—	—	—
1867 Rare	12	—	—	—	—	—
1868 Rare	—	—	—	—	—	—
1869 Rare	—	—	—	—	—	—
1869 Proof	—	—	—	—	—	—
Note: Stack's Hammel sale 9/82 Proof realized $17,000						

KM# 470 KRONE
11.1110 g., 0.9000 Gold .3215 oz. **Obv:** Maximilian II head right

Date	Mintage	F	VF	XF	Unc	BU
1857	771	—	5,000	8,000	12,000	—
1858	753	—	5,000	8,000	12,000	—
1859	200	—	6,000	10,000	15,000	—
1860	45	—	—	12,000	18,000	—
1861	65	—	—	12,000	18,000	—
1863	—	—	—	12,000	18,000	—
1864	—	—	—	12,000	18,000	—

KM# 483 KRONE
10.0000 g., 0.9000 Gold .2892 oz. **Obv:** Ludwig II head right

Date	Mintage	F	VF	XF	Unc	BU
1864	—	—	—	—	—	—
1865	—	—	—	—	—	—
1865 Proof	12	—	—	—	—	—
Note: Stack's Hammel sale 9/82 Proof realized $29,000						
1866	—	—	—	—	—	—
1867	12	—	—	—	—	—
1868	—	—	—	—	—	—
1869	—	—	—	—	—	—

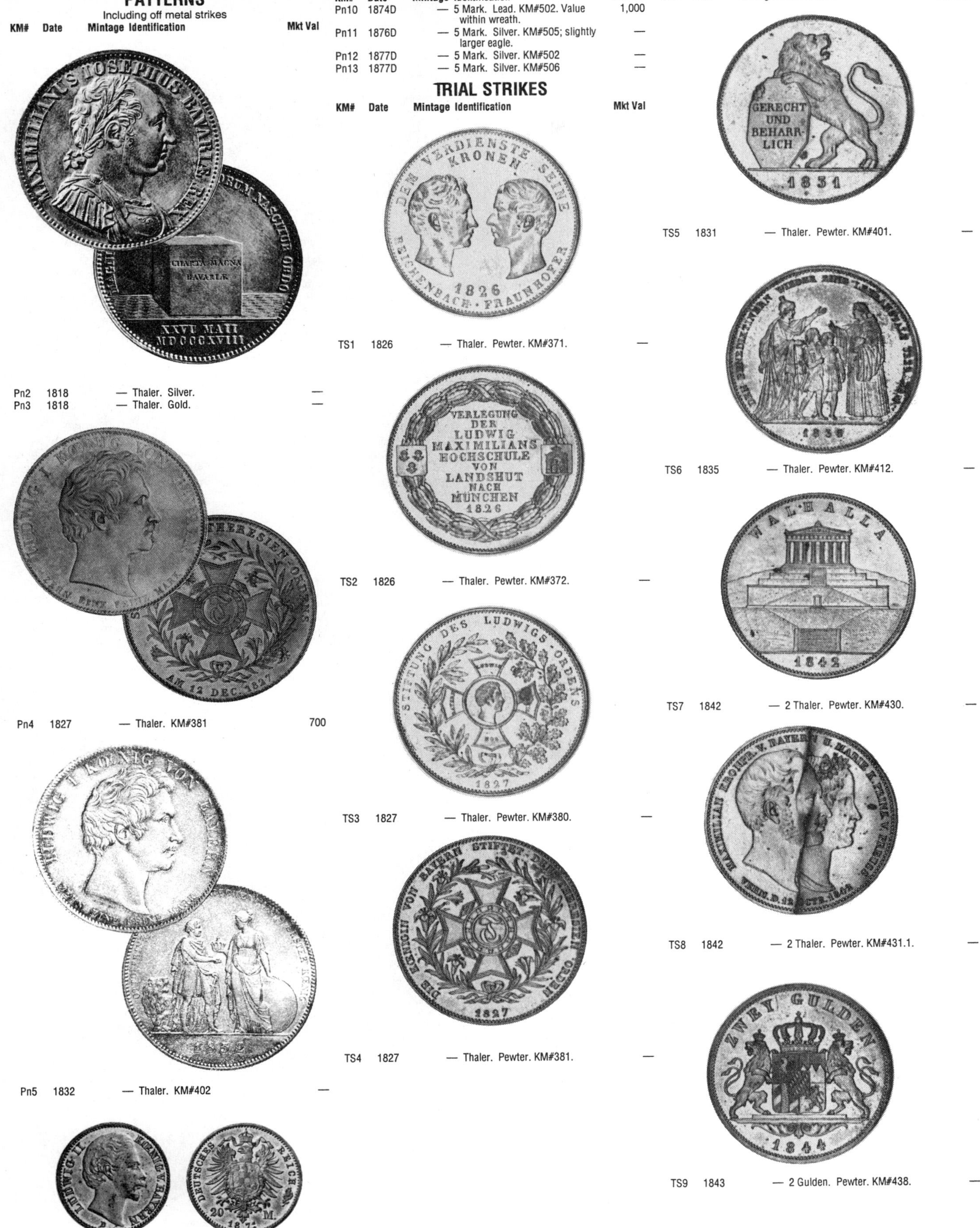

PATTERNS

Including off metal strikes

KM#	Date	Mintage	Identification	Mkt Val
Pn2	1818	—	Thaler. Silver.	—
Pn3	1818	—	Thaler. Gold.	—
Pn4	1827	—	Thaler. KM#381	700
Pn5	1832	—	Thaler. KM#402	—
Pn9	1871D	—	20 Mark. Tin. Like KM#501	—
Pn10	1874D	—	5 Mark. Lead. KM#502. Value within wreath.	1,000
Pn11	1876D	—	5 Mark. Silver. KM#505; slightly larger eagle.	—
Pn12	1877D	—	5 Mark. Silver. KM#502	—
Pn13	1877D	—	5 Mark. Silver. KM#506	—

TRIAL STRIKES

KM#	Date	Mintage	Identification	Mkt Val
TS1	1826	—	Thaler. Pewter. KM#371.	—
TS2	1826	—	Thaler. Pewter. KM#372.	—
TS3	1827	—	Thaler. Pewter. KM#380.	—
TS4	1827	—	Thaler. Pewter. KM#381.	—
TS5	1831	—	Thaler. Pewter. KM#401.	—
TS6	1835	—	Thaler. Pewter. KM#412.	—
TS7	1842	—	2 Thaler. Pewter. KM#430.	—
TS8	1842	—	2 Thaler. Pewter. KM#431.1.	—
TS9	1843	—	2 Gulden. Pewter. KM#438.	—

KM#	Date	Mintage	Identification	Mkt Val
TS10	ND	—	Thaler. Silver.	315

KM#	Date	Mintage	Identification	Mkt Val
TS11	1855	—	Ducat. Gold.	—

KM#	Date	Mintage	Identification	Mkt Val
TS12	ND	—	Ducat. Copper.	—

KM#	Date	Mintage	Identification	Mkt Val
TS13	1863	—	6 Kreuzer. Copper.	200
TS14	ND(1865)	—	Thaler. Gold.	—

BERG

The history of Berg from 1423 until the early 19th century follows that of the united Jülich-Cleves-Berg. France occupied these territories in 1801 and by the order of Napoleon, transformed into the Grand Duchy of Berg for Joachim Murat in 1806. Two years later, Murat was made the King of Naples and Berg became part of the Kingdom of Westphalia. At the conclusion of the Napoleonic Wars, Berg and the other territories were joined to Prussia as its western province.

RULERS

Maximilian IV, Joseph (of Bavaria), 1799-1806
Joachim Murat, 1806-1808

MINT OFFICIALS' INITIALS

Initial	Date	Name
PR, R.,.R.	1783-1804	Peter Rudesheim
TS, S, S., T:s, Sr.	1805-1818	Theodor Stockmar

DUCHY

REGULAR COINAGE

KM# 2 1/2 STUBER
Copper **Ruler:** Joseph Maximilian IV

Date	Mintage	F	VF	XF	Unc	BU
1802.R.	—	5.00	10.00	45.00	90.00	180
1803.R.	—	5.00	10.00	45.00	90.00	180
1804.R.	—	5.00	10.00	45.00	90.00	180
1805.R.	—	5.00	15.00	55.00	125	240

KM# 5 1/2 STUBER
Copper **Ruler:** Joseph Maximilian IV

Date	Mintage	F	VF	XF	Unc	BU
1805 S	—	5.00	35.00	60.00	125	225

KM# 6 1/2 STUBER
Copper **Ruler:** Joseph Maximilian IV **Obv:** Monogram without rosettes

Date	Mintage	F	VF	XF	Unc	BU
1805 s	—	25.00	50.00	100	175	300

KM# 1 3 STUBER
1.8500 g., 0.2200 Silver .0130 oz. **Ruler:** Joseph Maximilian IV

Date	Mintage	F	VF	XF	Unc	BU
1801.R.	—	15.00	20.00	50.00	90.00	110
1802.R.	—	10.00	15.00	40.00	75.00	90.00
1803.R.	—	10.00	15.00	40.00	75.00	90.00
1804.R.	—	15.00	20.00	50.00	85.00	105
1805.R.	—	15.00	20.00	55.00	95.00	120
1806.R.	—	10.00	15.00	40.00	75.00	90.00

KM# 7 3 STUBER
1.8500 g., 0.2200 Silver .0130 oz. **Ruler:** Joseph Maximilian IV

Date	Mintage	F	VF	XF	Unc	BU
1805 S	—	5.00	20.00	60.00	100	180
1806 S	—	5.00	20.00	50.00	90.00	150

KM# 9 3 STUBER
1.8500 g., 0.2200 Silver .0130 oz. **Ruler:** Joseph Maximilian IV
Obv: Royal crown

Date	Mintage	F	VF	XF	Unc	BU
1806	—	5.00	25.00	50.00	80.00	115

KM# 10 3 STUBER
1.8500 g., 0.2200 Silver .0130 oz. **Ruler:** Joseph Maximilian IV

Date	Mintage	F	VF	XF	Unc	BU
1806 S	—	10.00	25.00	45.00	140	240
1806 Sr	—	5.00	15.00	32.00	140	240
1807 S	—	10.00	45.00	70.00	240	260
1807 Sr	—	5.00	25.00	80.00	200	300

Note: KM#1, 9, and 10 were restruck officially in 1808-09 for circulation and were equal to 10 Centimes

KM# 4 1/2 THALER (Reichs)
9.7440 g., 0.7500 Silver .2349 oz. **Ruler:** Joseph Maximilian IV
Subject: Maximillian IV Joseph

Date	Mintage	F	VF	XF	Unc	BU
1803 R	—	125	400	800	1,200	1,500
1804 R	—	100	350	700	1,000	1,375

KM# 3 THALER (Reichs)
19.4880 g., 0.7500 Silver .4690 oz. **Ruler:** Joseph Maximilian IV
Subject: Maximillian IV Joseph

Date	Mintage	F	VF	XF	Unc	BU
1802 PR	—	150	350	700	1,500	2,400
1803 PR	—	150	350	700	1,500	2,400
1804 PR	—	150	350	700	1,500	2,400
1805 PR	—	250	450	800	2,100	3,000

KM# 8 THALER (Reichs)
19.4880 g., 0.7500 Silver .4690 oz. **Ruler:** Joseph Maximilian IV
Obv: T.S. below larger head

Date	Mintage	F	VF	XF	Unc	BU
1805 TS	9,396	200	325	1,000	1,800	2,650
1806 TS	7,044	225	400	1,200	2,000	3,000

KM# 11 THALER (Reichs)
19.4880 g., 0.7500 Silver .4690 oz. **Ruler:** Joseph Maximilian IV

Date	Mintage	F	VF	XF	Unc	BU
1806 TS	8,356	400	700	1,100	2,000	2,650

KM# 12 THALER (Cassa)
17.3230 g., 0.7510 Silver .4177 oz. **Ruler:** Joseph Maximilian IV

Date	Mintage	F	VF	XF	Unc	BU
1807 TS	784	500	900	2,500	3,500	4,500

KM# 13 THALER (Cassa)
17.3230 g., 0.7510 Silver .4177 oz. **Ruler:** Joseph Maximilian IV **Obv:** Similar to KM#12

Date	Mintage	F	VF	XF	Unc	BU
1807 TS	Inc. above	1,250	2,200	5,500	8,500	12,000

BIBERACH

Located in Württemberg 22 miles to the southwest of Ulm, Biberach became a free imperial city in 1312. The city came under the control of Baden in 1803 and then of Württemberg in 1806.

FREE CITY

TRADE COINAGE

KM# 20 DUCAT
3.5000 g., 0.9860 Gold .1109 oz. **Subject:** Peace of Luneville **Obv:** City god kneeling at altar, eye of God with rays above **Rev:** Nine-line inscription with Roman numeral date

Date	Mintage	VG	F	VF	XF	Unc
1801 Rare	—	—	—	—	—	—

PATTERNS

Including off metal strikes

KM#	Date	Mintage	Identification	Mkt Val
Pn3	1801	—	Ducat. Copper. KM#20	120
Pn4	1801	—	Ducat. Silver. KM#20	150

BIRKENFELD

Located in southwest Germany. For most of the time prior to 1801, Birkenfeld was in the possession of the Counts Palatine. It was a part of France from 1801-1814, Prussia from 1814-1817 and was made a principality in 1817 and given to the Duke of Oldenburg.

RULERS
Paul Friedrich August (of Oldenburg), 1829-1853
Nikolaus Friedrich Peter (of Oldenburg), 1853-1900

MINT MARKS
B - Hannover

COUNTSHIP

REGULAR COINAGE

KM# 1 PFENNIG
Silver **Ruler:** Paul Friedrich August of Oldenburg **Note:** Uniface. Schussel-type: Small arms of Pfalz-Veldenz (rampant lion left) on larger arms of Sponheim (checkerboard), SP above.

Date	Mintage	VG	F	VF	XF	Unc
ND	—	30.00	60.00	95.00	165	—

KM# 6 PFENNIG
Copper **Ruler:** Paul Friedrich August of Oldenburg

Date	Mintage	F	VF	XF	Unc	BU
1848	158,000	45.00	80.00	125	185	—

KM# 20 PFENNIG
Copper **Ruler:** Paul Friedrich August of Oldenburg

Date	Mintage	F	VF	XF	Unc	BU
1859B	72,000	25.00	60.00	90.00	160	—

KM# 7 2 PFENNIGE
Copper **Ruler:** Paul Friedrich August of Oldenburg

Date	Mintage	F	VF	XF	Unc	BU
1848	117,000	15.00	35.00	65.00	150	—

KM# 15 2 PFENNIGE
Copper **Ruler:** Paul Friedrich August of Oldenburg

Date	Mintage	F	VF	XF	Unc	BU
1858B	72,000	15.00	35.00	60.00	130	—

KM# 8 3 PFENNIGE
Copper **Ruler:** Paul Friedrich August of Oldenburg

Date	Mintage	F	VF	XF	Unc	BU
1848	121,000	17.00	37.50	75.00	155	—

KM# 16 3 PFENNIGE
Copper **Ruler:** Paul Friedrich August of Oldenburg **Obv:** Crowned NFP monogram

Date	Mintage	F	VF	XF	Unc	BU
1858B	72,000	17.00	37.50	75.00	160	—

KM# 2 ALBUS
Silver **Ruler:** Paul Friedrich August of Oldenburg **Obv:** Small shield of three-fold arms on larger shield of Sponheim arms **Rev:** I/ALB in center **Rev. Legend:** MONETA. NOVA. ARGENT BIRK

Date	Mintage	VG	F	VF	XF	Unc
ND	—	45.00	75.00	110	180	—

KM# 17 1/2 SILBER GROSCHEN
1.0900 g., 0.2200 Silver .0077 oz. **Ruler:** Paul Friedrich August of Oldenburg

Date	Mintage	F	VF	XF	Unc	BU
1858B	60,000	40.00	80.00	120	275	—

KM# 9 SILBER GROSCHEN
2.1900 g., 0.2200 Silver .0154 oz. **Ruler:** Paul Friedrich August of Oldenburg **Obv:** Crowned arms **Rev:** Value

Date	Mintage	F	VF	XF	Unc	BU
1848	63,000	35.00	70.00	110	225	—

KM# 18 SILBER GROSCHEN
2.1900 g., 0.2200 Silver .0154 oz. **Ruler:** Paul Friedrich August of Oldenburg **Obv:** Different arms

Date	Mintage	F	VF	XF	Unc	BU
1858	60,000	35.00	70.00	110	225	—

KM# 10 2-1/2 SILBER GROSCHEN (1/12 Thaler)
3.2200 g., 0.3750 Silver .0388 oz. **Ruler:** Paul Friedrich August of Oldenburg **Obv:** Crowned arms **Rev:** Value

Date	Mintage	F	VF	XF	Unc	BU
1848	23,000	35.00	70.00	110	225	—

KM# 19 2-1/2 SILBER GROSCHEN (1/12 Thaler)
3.2200 g., 0.3750 Silver .0388 oz. **Ruler:** Paul Friedrich August of Oldenburg **Obv:** Different arms

Date	Mintage	F	VF	XF	Unc	BU
1858	36,000	35.00	70.00	110	225	—

BRANDENBURG-ANSBACH-BAYREUTH

Held by Prussia from 1791 to 1805 and then given to Bavaria.

RULERS
Friedrich Wilhelm III of Prussia, 1797-1805

MARGRAVIATE

REGULAR COINAGE

KM# 17 PFENNIG
0.2600 g., 0.1110 Silver .0009 oz. **Obv:** Crowned FWR monogram **Rev:** Value

Date	Mintage	F	VF	XF	Unc	BU
1801B	616,000	4.00	8.00	17.50	50.00	—
1803B	984,000	4.00	8.00	17.50	50.00	—

KM# 18 KREUZER
0.7200 g., 0.1630 Silver .0037 oz.

Date	Mintage	F	VF	XF	Unc	BU
1802B	324,000	4.00	8.00	22.00	60.00	—
1803B	533,000	4.00	8.00	22.00	60.00	—
1804B	1,243,000	4.00	8.00	22.00	60.00	—

KM# 15 3 KREUZER
1.0500 g., 0.3360 Silver .0113 oz.

Date	Mintage	F	VF	XF	Unc	BU
1801B	1,335,000	8.00	16.00	35.00	110	—
1802B	1,330,000	8.00	16.00	35.00	110	—

KM# 16 6 KREUZER
2.4400 g., 0.3750 Silver .0294 oz.

Date	Mintage	F	VF	XF	Unc	BU
1801B	340,000	10.00	20.00	60.00	135	—
1802B	249,000	10.00	20.00	60.00	135	—

TRADE COINAGE

KM# 19 DUCAT
3.5000 g., 0.9860 Gold .1109 oz.

Date	Mintage	F	VF	XF	Unc	BU
1803B Rare	—	—	—	—	—	—

BREMEN

Established at about the same time as the bishopric in 787, Bremen was under the control of the bishops and archbishops until joining the Hanseatic League in 1276. Archbishop Albrecht II granted the mint right to the city in 1369, but this was not formalized by imperial decree until 1541. In 1646, Bremen was raised to free imperial status and continued to strike its own coins into the early 20th century. The city lost its free imperial status in 1803 and was controlled by France from 1806 until 1813. Regaining it independence in 1815, Bremen joined the North German Confederation in 1867 and the German Empire in 1871.

MINT OFFICIALS' INITIALS

Initials	Date	Name
B	1844-68	Th. W. Bruel in Hannover
OHK	1761-1805	Otto Heinrich Knorre
	1780-1811	Eberhard Christian Poppe, warden

ARMS: Key, often in shield

FREE CITY

REGULAR COINAGE

KM# 241 SCHWAREN
Copper

Date	Mintage	F	VF	XF	Unc	BU
1859	69,000	4.00	8.00	12.00	40.00	60.00

KM# 220 2-1/2 SCHWAREN
Copper **Rev:** D. B. in exergue

Date	Mintage	F	VF	XF	Unc	BU
1802	196,000	5.00	12.00	25.00	50.00	60.00

KM# 225 2-1/2 SCHWAREN
Copper

Date	Mintage	F	VF	XF	Unc	BU
1820	183,000	5.00	12.00	30.00	50.00	72.00

KM# 234 2-1/2 SCHWAREN
Copper

Date	Mintage	F	VF	XF	Unc	BU
1841	105,000	4.00	8.00	25.00	45.00	65.00
1853	142,000	4.00	8.00	25.00	45.00	65.00
1861	101,000	4.00	8.00	25.00	50.00	72.00
1866	72,000	4.00	8.00	25.00	50.00	72.00

KM# 236 1/2 GROTE
Copper **Note:** Mintage included in KM#234.

Date	Mintage	F	VF	XF	Unc	BU
1841	Inc. above	25.00	55.00	90.00	150	240

KM# 230 GROTEN
0.7700 g., 0.2810 Silver .0069 oz.

Date	Mintage	F	VF	XF	Unc	BU
1840	262,000	4.00	8.00	15.00	35.00	55.00

KM# 231 6 GROTE / 1/12 THALER
1.9440 g., 0.7400 Silver .0462 oz.

Date	Mintage	F	VF	XF	Unc	BU
1840	79,000	5.00	15.00	50.00	100	135

KM# 240 6 GROTE / 1/12 THALER
2.9200 g., 0.4940 Silver .0463 oz.

Date	Mintage	F	VF	XF	Unc	BU
1857	311,000	5.00	15.00	40.00	65.00	90.00

KM# 245 6 GROTE / 1/12 THALER
2.9200 g., 0.4940 Silver .0463 oz.

Date	Mintage	F	VF	XF	Unc	BU
1861	127,000	5.00	15.00	50.00	60.00	85.00

KM# 232 12 GROTE (1/6 Thaler)
3.8890 g., 0.7400 Silver .0925 oz.

Date	Mintage	F	VF	XF	Unc	BU
1840	193,000	7.00	20.00	45.00	75.00	110
1841	112,000	7.00	20.00	45.00	85.00	120
1845	63,000	7.00	20.00	55.00	95.00	125
1846	56,000	7.00	25.00	60.00	100	130

KM# 242 12 GROTE (1/6 Thaler)
3.8890 g., 0.7400 Silver .0925 oz. **Obv:** Crowned cornered arms

Date	Mintage	F	VF	XF	Unc	BU
1859	450,000	5.00	15.00	30.00	60.00	80.00
1860	150,000	5.00	15.00	40.00	70.00	90.00

KM# 233 36 GROTE (1/2 Thaler)
8.7700 g., 0.9860 Silver .2780 oz.

Date	Mintage	F	VF	XF	Unc	BU
1840	170,000	10.00	35.00	60.00	120	150
1841	44,000	10.00	45.00	85.00	145	190
1845	84,000	15.00	45.00	85.00	145	190
1846	85,000	15.00	45.00	85.00	145	190
1859	121,000	15.00	45.00	85.00	145	190

KM# 243 36 GROTE (1/2 Thaler)
8.7700 g., 0.9860 Silver .2780 oz.

Date	Mintage	F	VF	XF	Unc	BU
1859	50,000	10.00	35.00	75.00	110	150
1864	100,000	8.00	20.00	65.00	95.00	125

KM# 246 THALER (Vereins)
17.5390 g., 0.9860 Silver .5560 oz. **Subject:** 50th Anniversary - Liberation of Germany

Date	Mintage	F	VF	XF	Unc	BU
1863	20,000	20.00	35.00	60.00	125	150

KM# 248 THALER (Vereins)
17.5390 g., 0.9860 Silver .5560 oz. **Subject:** 2nd German Shooting Festival

Date	Mintage	F	VF	XF	Unc	BU
1865 B	50,000	20.00	35.00	55.00	75.00	90.00

KM# 249 THALER (Vereins)
17.5390 g., 0.9860 Silver .5560 oz. **Subject:** Victory Over France

Date	Mintage	F	VF	XF	Unc	BU
1871 B	61,000	20.00	35.00	60.00	90.00	120

PATTERNS

Including off metal strikes

KM#	Date	Mintage	Identification	Mkt Val
Pn38	1802	—	2-1/2 Schwaren. Silver. KM#220	170
Pn39	1840	—	Groten. Gold. KM#230	800

BRUNSWICK-LUNEBURG-CALENBERG-HANNOVER

Located in north-central Germany. The first duke began his rule in 1235. The first coinage appeared c. 1175. There was considerable shuffling of territory until 1692 when Ernst August became the elector of Hannover. George Ludwig became George I of England in 1714. There was separate coinage for Luneburg until during the reign of George III. The name was changed to Hannover in 1814.

RULERS

George III, (King of Great Britain), 1760-1814
After 1814 see Kingdom of Hannover

BRUNSWICK MINTS AND MINTMASTERS

Clausthal Mint

Initial	Date	Name
A	1833-49	Vacant Mintmastership
C	1751-53, 1790-92, 1800-02	Commission
GM, GFM	1802-07	Georg Friedrich Michaelis
IWL	1807-19	Johann Wilhelm Lunde
WAJA	1821-38	Wilhelm August Julius Albert

Hannover Mint

C	1800-06	Commission

NOTE: From 1715 on, the titles are changed on the coinage to reflect the ruler's elevation to "King of Great Britain, France and Ireland" as well as elector and duke of Brunswick and Luneburg.

DUCHY

REGULAR COINAGE

KM# 330.4 PFENNING
Copper **Ruler:** George III **Obv:** Wildman with tree in right hand, staff in left **Rev:** Value and date

Date	Mintage	F	VF	XF	Unc	BU
1804 GFM	—	10.00	20.00	40.00	80.00	—

KM# 360 PFENNING
Copper **Ruler:** George III

Date	Mintage	F	VF	XF	Unc	BU
1801 .C.	—	4.00	7.00	10.00	40.00	—
1802 .C.	—	4.00	7.00	10.00	40.00	—
1802 GFM	—	4.00	7.00	10.00	40.00	—
1803 GFM	—	4.00	7.00	10.00	40.00	—
1804 GFM	—	4.00	7.00	10.00	40.00	—
1806 GFM	—	4.00	7.00	10.00	40.00	—

KM# 360.1 PFENNING
Copper **Ruler:** George III **Obv:** Crowned GR monogram **Rev:** Denomination, PFENN

Date	Mintage	F	VF	XF	Unc	BU
1801 .C.	—	4.00	7.00	12.00	40.00	—

KM# 360.2 PFENNING
Copper **Obv:** Mint mark under monogram

Date	Mintage	F	VF	XF	Unc	BU
1814 H	—	4.00	7.00	10.00	40.00	—
1814 C	—	4.00	7.00	10.00	40.00	—

KM# 360.3 PFENNING
Copper **Rev:** Mint mark

Date	Mintage	F	VF	XF	Unc	BU
1814 C	—	4.00	7.00	10.00	40.00	—
1817 C	—	4.00	7.00	10.00	40.00	—
1818 C	—	4.00	7.00	10.00	40.00	—
1819 C	—	4.00	7.00	10.00	40.00	—
1820 C	—	4.00	7.00	10.00	40.00	—

KM# 380 PFENNING
Copper **Ruler:** George III

Date	Mintage	F	VF	XF	Unc	BU
1801 C	—	4.00	7.00	14.00	45.00	—
1802 C	—	4.00	7.00	14.00	45.00	—

KM# 402 2 PFENNING
Copper **Ruler:** George III

Date	Mintage	F	VF	XF	Unc	BU
1801 .C.	—	5.00	9.00	22.00	70.00	—
1802 GFM	—	5.00	9.00	22.00	70.00	—
1803 GFM	—	5.00	9.00	22.00	70.00	—
1804 GFM	—	5.00	9.00	22.00	70.00	—
1807 GFM	—	5.00	9.00	22.00	70.00	—

KM# 344 4 PFENNING
Billon **Ruler:** George III **Obv:** Crowned GR monogram **Rev:** Value, date

Date	Mintage	F	VF	XF	Unc	BU
1802 .C.	—	10.00	20.00	40.00	75.00	—
1804 GFM	—	10.00	20.00	40.00	75.00	—

KM# 345 MARIENGROSCHEN
Billon **Ruler:** George III **Obv:** Crowned GR monogram **Rev:** Value, date

Date	Mintage	F	VF	XF	Unc	BU
1802 .C.	—	5.00	12.00	25.00	50.00	—
1802 .C.	—	5.00	12.00	25.00	50.00	—
1803 GFM	—	5.00	12.00	25.00	50.00	—
1804 GFM	—	5.00	12.00	25.00	50.00	—

KM# 341 24 MARIENGROSCHEN
Silver **Ruler:** George III **Obv:** Crowned arms above 2/3 in oval **Rev:** Value above date

Date	Mintage	F	VF	XF	Unc	BU
1801 PLM	—	30.00	50.00	85.00	185	—

KM# 336 1/12 THALER (2 Groschen)
Silver **Ruler:** George III

Date	Mintage	F	VF	XF	Unc	BU
1801 PLM	—	4.00	10.00	20.00	65.00	—
1801 PLM	—	4.00	10.00	20.00	65.00	—
1801 EC	—	4.00	10.00	20.00	65.00	—
1801 .C.	8,780	4.00	10.00	20.00	65.00	—
1801 GFM	—	4.00	10.00	20.00	65.00	—
1802 .C.	—	4.00	10.00	20.00	65.00	—
1802 GFM	—	4.00	10.00	20.00	65.00	—
1803 GFM	—	4.00	10.00	20.00	65.00	—
1804 GFM	—	4.00	10.00	20.00	65.00	—
1805 GFM	—	4.00	10.00	20.00	65.00	—
1806 GFM	—	4.00	10.00	20.00	65.00	—
1807 GFM	—	4.00	10.00	20.00	65.00	—

KM# 415 1/6 THALER
Silver **Subject:** George III **Note:** Without French arms or titles.

Date	Mintage	F	VF	XF	Unc	BU
1802 C.	—	20.00	30.00	60.00	175	—
1802 GFM	—	20.00	30.00	60.00	175	—
1803 GFM	—	20.00	30.00	60.00	175	—
1804/3 GFM	—	37.50	65.00	120	250	—
1804 GFM	—	—	—	—	—	—

KM# 419 1/6 THALER
Silver

Date	Mintage	F	VF	XF	Unc	BU
1804 GFM	—	15.00	25.00	75.00	200	—

KM# 420 1/6 THALER
Silver

Date	Mintage	F	VF	XF	Unc	BU
1804 GFM	—	15.00	25.00	75.00	200	—

KM# 423 1/6 THALER
Silver

Date	Mintage	F	VF	XF	Unc	BU
1807 GM	—	15.00	20.00	40.00	125	—

KM# 417 1/3 THALER
Silver **Subject:** George III

Date	Mintage	F	VF	XF	Unc	BU
1803 GFM	—	30.00	50.00	115	260	—
1804 GFM	—	30.00	50.00	115	260	—

KM# 421 1/3 THALER
Silver

Date	Mintage	F	VF	XF	Unc	BU
1804 GFM	—	40.00	65.00	135	285	—

KM# 410 1/2 THALER (Cassen)
Silver **Subject:** George III **Rev:** Value: CASSEN GELD

Date	Mintage	F	VF	XF	Unc	BU
1801 C Rare	372	—	—	—	—	—

KM# 411 1/2 THALER (Cassen)
Silver **Rev:** Value: CASSEN=GELD

Date	Mintage	F	VF	XF	Unc	BU
1801 C	—	80.00	160	275	450	—

KM# 412 2/3 THALER
Silver **Subject:** George III

Date	Mintage	F	VF	XF	Unc	BU
1801 . C.	—	30.00	55.00	125	265	—
1802 . C.	—	30.00	55.00	125	265	—

KM# 413 2/3 THALER
Silver

Date	Mintage	F	VF	XF	Unc	BU
1801 . C.	—	30.00	50.00	110	245	—
1802	—	30.00	50.00	110	245	—
1802 . C.	—	30.00	50.00	110	245	—
1802 GFM	—	30.00	50.00	110	245	—
1803 GFM	—	30.00	50.00	110	245	—
1804 GFM	—	30.00	50.00	110	245	—
1805 GFM	—	30.00	50.00	110	245	—

KM# 422 2/3 THALER
Silver

Date	Mintage	F	VF	XF	Unc	BU
1805 GFM	—	30.00	50.00	110	245	—
1806 GFM	—	30.00	50.00	110	245	—
1807 GFM	—	30.00	50.00	110	245	—

KM# 414 THALER (Cassengeld)
Silver **Subject:** George III

Date	Mintage	F	VF	XF	Unc	BU
1801 C	126	400	750	1,250	2,000	—

TRADE COINAGE

KM# 416 DUCAT
3.5000 g., 0.9860 Gold .1109 oz. **Obv:** Large modified arms
Rev: Legend above horse **Rev. Legend:** EX AURO...

Date	Mintage	F	VF	XF	Unc	BU
1802 .C.	—	350	525	900	1,500	—
1802 GFM	—	400	600	1,000	1,650	—
1804 GFM	—	300	525	800	1,450	—

KM# 418 PISTOLE
6.6500 g., 0.9000 Gold .1924 oz.

Date	Mintage	F	VF	XF	Unc	BU
1803 C	—	350	650	1,100	2,000	—

BRUNSWICK-WOLFENBUTTEL

(Braunschweig-Wolfenbüttel)

Located in north-central Germany. Wolfenbüttel was annexed to Brunswick in 1257. One of the five surviving sons of Albrecht II founded the first line in Wolfenbüttel in 1318. A further division in Wolfenbüttel and Lüneburg was undertaken in 1373. Another division occurred in 1495, but the Wolfenbüttel duchy survived in the younger line. Heinrich IX was forced out of his territory during the religious wars of the mid-sixteenth century by Duke Johann Friedrich I of Saxony and Landgrave Philipp of Hessen in 1542, but was restored to his possessions in 1547. Duke Friedrich Ulrich was forced to cede the Grubenhagen lands, which had been acquired by Wolfenbüttel in 1596, to Lüneburg in 1617. When the succession died out in 1634, the lands and titles fell to the cadet line in Dannenberg. The line became extinct once again and passed to Brunswick-Bevern in 1735 from which a new succession of Wolfenbüttel dukes descended. The ducal family was beset by continual personal and political tragedy during the nineteenth century. Two of the dukes were killed in battles with Napoleon, the territories were occupied by the French and became part of the Kingdom of Westphalia, another duke was forced out by a revolt in 1823. From 1884 until 1913, Brunswick-Wolfenbüttel was governed by Prussia and then turned over to a younger prince of Brunswick who married a daughter of Kaiser Wilhelm II. His reign was short, however, as he was forced to abdicate at the end of World War I.

RULERS

Karl Wilhelm Ferdinand, 1780-1806
Friedrich Wilhelm, 1806-1815
Karl II (under regency of George III of Great Britain), 1815-1820
Karl II (under regency of George IV of Great Britain), 1820-1823
Karl II, 1823-1830
Wilhelm, 1831-1884
Prussian rule, 1884-1913

MINT OFFICIALS' INITIALS

Initial	Date	Name
B, LB	1844-66	Theodor Wilhelm Bruel in Hannover
B	1850-59	Johann W. Chr. Brumleu in Brunswick
CvC	1820-50	Cramer von Clausbruch in Brunswick
FR	1814-20	Friedrich Ritter in Brunswick
K	1776-1802	Christian Friedrich Krull, die-cutter in Brunswick
MC	1779-1806, 1820	Munz – Commission at Brunswick

DUCHY

REGULAR COINAGE

KM# 995 PFENNIG
Copper **Ruler:** Karl Wilhelm Ferdinand **Obv:** Horse left

Date	Mintage	F	VF	XF	Unc	BU
1801 MC	—	4.00	8.00	18.00	40.00	60.00
1802 MC	—	4.00	8.00	20.00	45.00	65.00
1803 MC	—	4.00	8.00	18.00	40.00	60.00
1804 MC	—	4.00	8.00	18.00	40.00	60.00
1805 MC	—	4.00	8.00	18.00	40.00	60.00
1806 MC	—	5.00	10.00	18.00	40.00	60.00

KM# 1050.1 PFENNIG
Copper **Ruler:** Fredrich Wilhelm **Obv:** M. C. below horse

Date	Mintage	F	VF	XF	Unc	BU
1813 MC	—	5.00	25.00	45.00	85.00	150
1814 MC	—	5.00	25.00	40.00	80.00	135

KM# 1050.2 PFENNIG
Copper **Ruler:** Fredrich Wilhelm **Obv:** F.R. below horse

Date	Mintage	F	VF	XF	Unc	BU
1814 FR	—	4.00	8.00	25.00	40.00	60.00
1815 FR	—	4.00	8.00	20.00	35.00	54.00

KM# 1068 PFENNIG
Copper **Ruler:** Karl II under regency of George III of Great Britain
Obv: F.R. below horse **Obv. Legend:** GEORG P.R.T.N.

Date	Mintage	F	VF	XF	Unc	BU
1816 FR	—	8.00	20.00	60.00	110	175
1818 FR	—	8.00	20.00	60.00	110	175

KM# 1069 PFENNIG
Copper **Ruler:** Karl II under regency of George III of Great Britain

Date	Mintage	F	VF	XF	Unc	BU
1816 FR	—	4.00	8.00	30.00	65.00	90.00
1817 FR	—	4.00	8.00	25.00	55.00	75.00
1818 FR	—	5.00	10.00	35.00	70.00	100
1819 FR	—	4.00	8.00	25.00	55.00	75.00
1820 FR	—	5.00	10.00	35.00	70.00	100

KM# 1075 PFENNIG
Copper **Ruler:** Karl II under regency of George III of Great Britain
Obv. Legend: FRIEDRICH WILHELM

Date	Mintage	F	VF	XF	Unc	BU
1818	—	15.00	30.00	60.00	140	—

KM# 1076 PFENNIG
Copper **Ruler:** Karl II under regency of George III of Great Britain
Obv. Legend: GEORG D.G.

Date	Mintage	F	VF	XF	Unc	BU
1818 FR	—	5.00	10.00	30.00	55.00	90.00

KM# 1077 PFENNIG
Copper **Ruler:** Karl II under regency of George III of Great Britain
Obv. Legend: GEORG T.N. . . begins at upper left

Date	Mintage	F	VF	XF	Unc	BU
1818 FR	—	5.00	10.00	40.00	65.00	110
1819 FR	—	5.00	10.00	30.00	55.00	90.00

KM# 1078 PFENNIG
Copper **Ruler:** Karl II under regency of George III of Great Britain
Obv. Legend: GEORG T.N. . . begins at lower left

Date	Mintage	F	VF	XF	Unc	BU
1819 FR	—	5.00	10.00	30.00	55.00	90.00

KM# 1079.1 PFENNIG
Copper **Ruler:** Karl II under regency of George III of Great Britain **Obv:** Without F. R. **Obv. Legend:** GEORG IV. R. TVT. . . **Rev:** MC below date

Date	Mintage	F	VF	XF	Unc	BU
1819 MC	—	5.00	10.00	40.00	65.00	110
1820 MC	—	5.00	10.00	35.00	55.00	90.00

KM# 1079.2 PFENNIG
Copper **Ruler:** Karl II under regency of George III of Great Britain **Obv. Legend:** GEORG IV D.G.R.T.N. CAROLI. . . **Rev:** MC below date

Date	Mintage	F	VF	XF	Unc	BU
1820 MC	—	5.00	10.00	40.00	65.00	110

KM# 1085 PFENNIG
Copper **Ruler:** Karl II under regency of George IV of Great Britain **Obv. Legend:** GEORG IV D.G.R. TVT. . .

Date	Mintage	F	VF	XF	Unc	BU
1820 MC	—	5.00	10.00	40.00	65.00	110
1822 MC	—	5.00	10.00	40.00	65.00	110
1823 MC	—	5.00	10.00	40.00	65.00	110

KM# 1094 PFENNIG
Copper **Ruler:** Karl II under regency of George IV of Great Britain **Obv. Legend:** GEORG IV D.G.R.T.N. . . ET. L.

Date	Mintage	F	VF	XF	Unc	BU
1822 CvC	—	5.00	10.00	30.00	55.00	90.00
1823 CvC	—	5.00	15.00	55.00	85.00	130

KM# 1098 PFENNIG
Copper **Ruler:** Karl II **Obv. Legend:** . . . BR. U. LUEN.

Date	Mintage	F	VF	XF	Unc	BU
1823 CvC	—	4.00	8.00	20.00	40.00	65.00
1824 CvC	—	4.00	8.00	30.00	50.00	90.00
1825 CvC	—	4.00	8.00	30.00	50.00	90.00
1826 CvC	—	4.00	8.00	30.00	45.00	80.00
1828 CvC	—	4.00	8.00	30.00	55.00	100
1829/8 CvC	—	4.00	8.00	40.00	65.00	110
1829 CvC	—	4.00	8.00	25.00	45.00	80.00
1830 CvC	—	4.00	8.00	30.00	50.00	90.00

KM# 1107 PFENNIG
Copper **Ruler:** Karl II **Obv. Legend:** . . . BR.U.L.

Date	Mintage	F	VF	XF	Unc	BU
1824 CvC	—	65.00	100	175	250	325

KM# 1120 PFENNIG
Copper **Ruler:** Wilhelm **Obv. Legend:** . . . BR. U. LUEN **Rev. Legend:** PFENNIG

Date	Mintage	F	VF	XF	Unc	BU
1831 CvC	—	4.00	8.00	25.00	40.00	60.00
1832 CvC	—	4.00	8.00	35.00	45.00	65.00
1833 CvC	—	4.00	8.00	30.00	45.00	65.00
1834 CvC	—	4.00	8.00	25.00	40.00	60.00

KM# 1127 PFENNIG
Copper **Ruler:** Wilhelm **Rev:** Value: PFENNIG

Date	Mintage	F	VF	XF	Unc	BU
1834 CvC	—	10.00	30.00	60.00	100	175

KM# 1142 PFENNIG
Copper **Ruler:** Wilhelm

Date	Mintage	F	VF	XF	Unc	BU
1851 B	—	5.00	10.00	18.00	45.00	65.00
1852 B	270,000	5.00	10.00	18.00	45.00	65.00
1853 B	139,000	5.00	10.00	18.00	40.00	60.00
1855 B	79,000	5.00	10.00	18.00	40.00	60.00
1856 B	514,000	5.00	10.00	18.00	40.00	60.00

KM# 1148 PFENNIG
Copper **Ruler:** Wilhelm **Rev:** Without B below date

Date	Mintage	F	VF	XF	Unc	BU
1854	126,000	4.00	8.00	20.00	40.00	55.00
1856	Inc. above	4.00	8.00	20.00	40.00	55.00

KM# 1154 PFENNIG
Copper **Ruler:** Wilhelm **Obv. Legend:** HERZOGTH. BRAUNSCHWEIG

Date	Mintage	F	VF	XF	Unc	BU
1859	103,000	4.00	8.00	20.00	35.00	60.00
1860	307,000	4.00	8.00	20.00	30.00	54.00

KM# 1056 2 PFENNIGE
Copper **Ruler:** Fredrich Wilhelm

Date	Mintage	F	VF	XF	Unc	BU
1814 FR	—	4.00	8.00	45.00	80.00	115
1815 FR	—	4.00	8.00	50.00	95.00	130

KM# 1064 2 PFENNIGE
Copper **Ruler:** Fredrich Wilhelm **Obv:** Without F.R. below monogram

Date	Mintage	F	VF	XF	Unc	BU
1815	—	5.00	10.00	60.00	140	210

KM# 1086 2 PFENNIGE
Copper **Ruler:** Karl II under regency of George IV of Great Britain **Rev:** M.C. below date

Date	Mintage	F	VF	XF	Unc	BU
1820 MC	—	5.00	10.00	30.00	60.00	90.00
1820 MC MVNZE	—	5.00	15.00	35.00	75.00	105

KM# 1099 2 PFENNIGE
Copper **Ruler:** Karl II under regency of George IV of Great Britain **Rev:** C. v. C. below date

Date	Mintage	F	VF	XF	Unc	BU
1823 CvC	—	5.00	15.00	50.00	100	150

KM# 1108 2 PFENNIGE
Copper **Ruler:** Karl II

Date	Mintage	F	VF	XF	Unc	BU
1824 CvC	—	4.00	8.00	30.00	55.00	75.00
1826 CvC	—	4.00	8.00	30.00	55.00	75.00

Date	Mintage	F	VF	XF	Unc	BU
1827 CvC	—	4.00	10.00	40.00	70.00	100
1828 CvC	—	4.00	8.00	30.00	55.00	75.00
1829 CvC	—	4.00	10.00	40.00	70.00	100
1830 CvC	—	4.00	8.00	35.00	65.00	100

KM# 1123 2 PFENNIGE
Copper **Ruler:** Wilhelm **Obv. Legend:** WILHELM. . .

Date	Mintage	F	VF	XF	Unc	BU
1832 CvC	—	4.00	8.00	40.00	75.00	90.00
1833 CvC	—	4.00	8.00	40.00	75.00	90.00
1834 CvC	—	4.00	8.00	40.00	75.00	95.00

KM# 1128 2 PFENNIGE
Copper **Ruler:** Wilhelm **Rev:** Value: PFENNIG

Date	Mintage	F	VF	XF	Unc	BU
1834 CvC	—	10.00	45.00	85.00	200	325

KM# 1143 2 PFENNIGE
Copper **Ruler:** Wilhelm

Date	Mintage	F	VF	XF	Unc	BU
1851 B	—	4.00	8.00	20.00	35.00	60.00
1852 B	135,000	4.00	8.00	20.00	45.00	70.00
1853 B	124,000	4.00	8.00	20.00	30.00	55.00
1854 B	63,000	4.00	8.00	25.00	45.00	70.00
1855 B	189,000	4.00	8.00	15.00	30.00	55.00
1855	—	—	—	—	—	—
1856 B	253,000	4.00	8.00	15.00	30.00	55.00

KM# 1155 2 PFENNIGE
Copper **Ruler:** Wilhelm

Date	Mintage	F	VF	XF	Unc	BU
1859	62,000	5.00	10.00	15.00	35.00	60.00
1860	147,000	5.00	10.00	13.00	32.00	55.00

KM# 997 4 PFENNIGE
Billon **Obv:** Horse **Rev:** Value

Date	Mintage	F	VF	XF	Unc	BU
1801 MC	—	10.00	20.00	30.00	50.00	80.00
1802 MC	—	8.00	15.00	30.00	50.00	80.00
1803 MC	—	10.00	20.00	35.00	55.00	85.00
1804 MC	—	8.00	15.00	25.00	45.00	70.00

KM# 1087 4 PFENNIGE
1.2300 g., 0.1870 Silver .0073 oz. **Obv:** Prancing horse left, 'F.R.' below **Obv. Legend:** Ends: BRIETL **Rev:** Value

Date	Mintage	F	VF	XF	Unc	BU
1820 FR	35,000	15.00	40.00	75.00	150	240

KM# 1100 4 PFENNIGE
1.2300 g., 0.1870 Silver .0073 oz. **Obv:** Without F.R. **Rev:** C.V.C. below date

Date	Mintage	F	VF	XF	Unc	BU
1823 CvC	63,000	5.00	15.00	60.00	110	225

KM# 1019 6 PFENNIGE
Billon **Obv:** Horse **Rev:** Value

Date	Mintage	F	VF	XF	Unc	BU
1802 MC	—	15.00	35.00	75.00	125	160
1804 MC	—	15.00	35.00	75.00	125	160

KM# 1057 6 PFENNIGE
1.3900 g., 0.2500 Silver .0111 oz. **Obv:** M. C. below horse

Date	Mintage	F	VF	XF	Unc	BU
1814 MC	—	5.00	10.00	75.00	165	240

KM# 1058 6 PFENNIGE
1.3900 g., 0.2500 Silver .0111 oz. **Obv:** B. instead of BR in legend

Date	Mintage	F	VF	XF	Unc	BU
1814 MC	—	25.00	75.00	120	190	270

KM# 1059 6 PFENNIGE
1.3900 g., 0.2500 Silver .0111 oz. **Obv:** F. R. below mound

Date	Mintage	F	VF	XF	Unc	BU
1814 FR	—	30.00	65.00	130	200	300
1815 FR	133,000	25.00	50.00	90.00	160	320

KM# 1070 6 PFENNIGE
Billon **Obv. Legend:** GEORG T. N. CAROLI D. BR.

Date	Mintage	F	VF	XF	Unc	BU
1816 FR	36,000	10.00	45.00	80.00	150	240
1819 FR	30,000	10.00	45.00	90.00	165	260

KM# 1101 6 PFENNIGE
Billon **Obv. Legend:** GEORG IV. . . **Rev:** C. V. C. below date

Date	Mintage	F	VF	XF	Unc	BU
1823 CvC	60,000	20.00	40.00	75.00	175	260

KM# 1116 6 PFENNIGE
Billon **Obv. Legend:** Ends: . . . BR U L.

Date	Mintage	F	VF	XF	Unc	BU
1828 CvC	—	5.00	10.00	55.00	125	175

KM# 1151 1/2 GROSCHEN (1/60 Thaler; Vereins)
1.0900 g., 0.2200 Silver .0077 oz.

Date	Mintage	F	VF	XF	Unc	BU
1858	576,000	4.00	8.00	20.00	55.00	—
1859	131,000	5.00	10.00	25.00	65.00	—
1860	313,000	4.00	8.00	20.00	55.00	—

KM# 1031 MARIENGROSCHEN
Billon **Obv:** Horse left **Rev:** Value date

Date	Mintage	F	VF	XF	Unc	BU
1802 MC	—	10.00	20.00	45.00	60.00	90.00
1803 MC	—	10.00	20.00	45.00	60.00	90.00
1804 MC	—	10.00	20.00	55.00	75.00	115
1805 MC	—	8.00	15.00	25.00	40.00	60.00
1806 MC	—	10.00	20.00	40.00	50.00	80.00

KM# 1080 MARIENGROSCHEN
1.9400 g., 0.3750 Silver .0233 oz. **Obv. Legend:** GEORG T. N. CAROLI D. BR:. **Rev:** Value

Date	Mintage	F	VF	XF	Unc	BU
1819 fr	58,000	10.00	35.00	65.00	125	195

KM# 1137 GROSCHEN (1/24 Thaler; Gutergroschen)
Silver

Date	Mintage	VG	F	VF	XF	Unc
1847 CVC	—	400	750	1,250	2,000	—

KM# 1150 GROSCHEN (1/30 Thaler; Vereins)
2.1900 g., 0.2200 Silver .0154 oz.

Date	Mintage	F	VF	XF	Unc	BU
1857	39,000	4.00	8.00	15.00	30.00	45.00
1858	713,000	4.00	8.00	15.00	30.00	45.00
1859	594,000	4.00	8.00	15.00	30.00	45.00
1860	95,000	5.00	10.00	20.00	35.00	55.00

KM# 1045 2 MARIENGROSCHEN
Billon

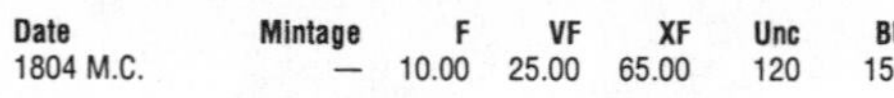

Date	Mintage	F	VF	XF	Unc	BU
1804 M.C.	—	10.00	25.00	65.00	120	150

KM# 1135 4 GUTE GROSCHEN
5.3500 g., 0.5210 Silver .0896 oz.

Date	Mintage	F	VF	XF	Unc	BU
1840 CvC	60,000	10.00	20.00	75.00	110	175

KM# 1026 8 GUTE GROSCHEN
Silver

Date	Mintage	F	VF	XF	Unc	BU
1801 MC	—	15.00	35.00	80.00	140	175
1803 MC	—	15.00	35.00	75.00	130	160
1804 MC	—	15.00	35.00	80.00	140	175
1805 MC	—	15.00	35.00	90.00	150	195

KM# 1020 16 GUTE GROSCHEN
Silver **Obv:** Arms **Rev:** Value

Date	Mintage	F	VF	XF	Unc	BU
1801 MC	—	35.00	85.00	150	220	300
1803 MC	—	60.00	160	300	425	575
1804 MC	—	55.00	150	275	400	540
1805 MC	—	35.00	100	150	250	360

KM# 1034 24 MARIENGROSCHEN (2/3 Thaler)
Silver

Date	Mintage	F	VF	XF	Unc	BU
1801 MC	—	25.00	65.00	100	240	330
1802 MC	—	30.00	75.00	155	270	360
1803 MC	—	25.00	65.00	110	200	270
1804 MC	—	30.00	75.00	155	270	360
1805 MC	—	25.00	60.00	125	225	300
1806 MC	—	25.00	70.00	150	250	345

KM# 1060 24 MARIENGROSCHEN (2/3 Thaler)
13.0800 g., 0.9930 Silver .4176 oz. **Obv. Legend:** FRIDERICVS. . .

Date	Mintage	F	VF	XF	Unc	BU
1814 FR	—	45.00	125	225	500	625
1815 FR	36,000	45.00	125	225	475	600

KM# 1065 24 MARIENGROSCHEN (2/3 Thaler)
13.0800 g., 0.9930 Silver .4176 oz.

Date	Mintage	F	VF	XF	Unc	BU
1815 FR	—	100	200	500	1,000	1,500
1816 FR	27,000	50.00	75.00	165	250	325
1817 FR	19,000	50.00	75.00	175	260	330
1818 FR	17,000	50.00	75.00	150	225	300

KM# 1088 24 MARIENGROSCHEN (2/3 Thaler)
13.0800 g., 0.9930 Silver .4176 oz. **Obv. Legend:** REX BRITANNIAR

Date	Mintage	F	VF	XF	Unc	BU
1820 MC	24,000	45.00	75.00	165	275	400

KM# 1091 24 MARIENGROSCHEN (2/3 Thaler)
13.0800 g., 0.9930 Silver .4176 oz. **Rev:** CvC below date

Date	Mintage	F	VF	XF	Unc	BU
1821 CvC	29,000	20.00	55.00	100	200	300
1823 CvC	30,000	25.00	75.00	175	350	425

KM# 1102 24 MARIENGROSCHEN (2/3 Thaler)
13.0800 g., 0.9930 Silver .4176 oz. **Obv. Legend:** ZU BRAUNS

Date	Mintage	F	VF	XF	Unc	BU
1823 CvC	—	55.00	100	350	550	775
1824 CvC	—	45.00	80.00	275	500	650
1825 CvC	—	55.00	100	275	500	650
1826 CvC	40,000	55.00	100	275	475	600
1828 CvC	34,000	55.00	100	350	550	780
1829 CvC	34,000	50.00	90.00	200	400	540

KM# 1109 24 MARIENGROSCHEN (2/3 Thaler)
13.0800 g., 0.9930 Silver .4176 oz. **Obv. Legend:** ZU BRAUNSCHW

Date	Mintage	F	VF	XF	Unc	BU
1824 CvC	32,000	30.00	65.00	115	175	270
1825 CvC	32,000	30.00	50.00	100	150	240
1826 CvC	—	25.00	45.00	85.00	140	195
1828 CvC	—	30.00	50.00	100	150	210
1829 CvC	—	25.00	45.00	85.00	140	195

KM# 1124 24 MARIENGROSCHEN (2/3 Thaler)
13.0800 g., 0.9930 Silver .4176 oz.

Date	Mintage	F	VF	XF	Unc	BU
1832 CvC	32,000	35.00	55.00	125	225	270
1833 CvC	27,000	30.00	45.00	100	175	240
1834 CvC	30,000	30.00	45.00	90.00	165	220

KM# 999 1/24 THALER (Groschen)
Billon **Obv:** Horse **Rev:** Value

Date	Mintage	F	VF	XF	Unc	BU
1802 MC	—	20.00	50.00	90.00	150	240

KM# 1061 1/24 THALER (Groschen)
1.9400 g., 0.3750 Silver .0233 oz. **Rev:** F. R. below date

Date	Mintage	F	VF	XF	Unc	BU
1814 FR	—	10.00	25.00	50.00	120	180
1815 FR	66,000	7.00	15.00	35.00	65.00	100

KM# 1089 1/24 THALER (Groschen)
1.9400 g., 0.3750 Silver .0233 oz. **Obv. Legend:** GEORG IV **Rev:** Value, M. C. below date

Date	Mintage	F	VF	XF	Unc	BU
1820 MC	—	10.00	25.00	50.00	90.00	120

KM# 1103 1/24 THALER (Groschen)
1.9400 g., 0.3750 Silver .0233 oz. **Rev:** C. v. C. below date

Date	Mintage	F	VF	XF	Unc	BU
1823 CvC	—	10.00	20.00	40.00	80.00	135

KM# 1112 1/24 THALER (Groschen)
1.9400 g., 0.3750 Silver .0233 oz. **Obv. Legend:** BRAUNSCHW. U. LUEN.

Date	Mintage	F	VF	XF	Unc	BU
1825 CvC	—	40.00	150	275	400	650

KM# 1000 1/12 THALER (2 Groschen)
Billon **Note:** Similar to KM#1051.3.

Date	Mintage	F	VF	XF	Unc	BU
1801 MC	—	5.00	15.00	60.00	75.00	120
1802 MC	—	5.00	15.00	60.00	75.00	120
1803 MC	—	5.00	15.00	60.00	75.00	120
1804 MC	—	5.00	15.00	60.00	75.00	120
1805 MC	—	5.00	10.00	50.00	60.00	90.00
1806 MC	—	5.00	10.00	30.00	50.00	80.00

KM# 1051.1 1/12 THALER (2 Groschen)
3.3400 g., 0.4370 Silver .0469 oz. **Obv:** Prancing horse left, Mc below **Rev:** Value

Date	Mintage	F	VF	XF	Unc	BU
1813 MC	—	35.00	65.00	120	125	240
1814 MC	—	35.00	65.00	120	200	270

KM# 1051.2 1/12 THALER (2 Groschen)
3.3400 g., 0.4370 Silver .0469 oz. **Obv:** FR below horse

Date	Mintage	F	VF	XF	Unc	BU
1815 FR	—	15.00	45.00	125	175	270

KM# 1051.3 1/12 THALER (2 Groschen)
3.3400 g., 0.4370 Silver .0469 oz. **Obv:** Without initials below horse **Rev:** FR below date

Date	Mintage	F	VF	XF	Unc	BU
1815 FR	—	15.00	45.00	130	200	300

KM# 1051.4 1/12 THALER (2 Groschen)
3.3400 g., 0.4370 Silver 0.0469 oz. **Obv:** Prancing horse with MC below **Rev:** Value with FR below

Date	Mintage	F	VF	XF	Unc	BU
1814 MC//FR	—	15.00	45.00	100	200	275
1815 MC//FR	—	10.00	25.00	75.00	175	250

KM# 1071 1/12 THALER (2 Groschen)
Billon **Obv. Legend:** GEORG D

Date	Mintage	F	VF	XF	Unc	BU
1816 FR	—	10.00	25.00	65.00	125	180
1817 FR	—	10.00	25.00	85.00	150	210
1818 FR	—	10.00	25.00	75.00	135	190
1819 FR	—	10.00	25.00	65.00	125	180

KM# 1090 1/12 THALER (2 Groschen)
Billon **Obv. Legend:** GEORG IV

Date	Mintage	F	VF	XF	Unc	BU
1820 MC	—	5.00	15.00	35.00	60.00	90.00

KM# 1092 1/12 THALER (2 Groschen)
Billon **Rev:** CvC below date

Date	Mintage	F	VF	XF	Unc	BU
1821 CvC	—	5.00	10.00	30.00	5.00	75.00
1822 CvC	—	5.00	10.00	40.00	60.00	100
1823 CvC	—	5.00	10.00	45.00	60.00	105

KM# 1104 1/12 THALER (2 Groschen)
Billon **Obv. Legend:** BRAUNSCHW. U. LUEN

Date	Mintage	F	VF	XF	Unc	BU
1823 CvC	—	5.00	10.00	40.00	100	150
1824 CvC	—	5.00	10.00	30.00	65.00	95.00
1825 CvC	—	5.00	10.00	25.00	60.00	90.00
1826 CvC	—	5.00	10.00	25.00	55.00	75.00
1827 CvC	—	5.00	10.00	25.00	55.00	75.00
1828 CvC	—	5.00	10.00	25.00	45.00	65.00
1829 CvC	—	5.00	10.00	25.00	45.00	65.00
1830 CvC	—	5.00	10.00	25.00	50.00	70.00

KM# 1105 1/12 THALER (2 Groschen)
Billon **Obv. Legend:** BRAUNSCHW. U. L.

Date	Mintage	F	VF	XF	Unc	BU
1823 CvC	—	5.00	15.00	45.00	120	170
1824 CvC	—	5.00	15.00	40.00	100	150
1825 CvC	—	5.00	15.00	35.00	80.00	135
1826 CvC	—	5.00	15.00	40.00	100	150

KM# 1106 1/12 THALER (2 Groschen)
Billon **Obv. Legend:** BRAUNS. U. LEUN.

Date	Mintage	F	VF	XF	Unc	BU
1823 CvC	—	5.00	10.00	30.00	60.00	95.00
1824 CvC	—	5.00	10.00	25.00	50.00	85.00
1828 CvC	—	5.00	10.00	20.00	40.00	80.00
1829 CvC	—	5.00	10.00	20.00	45.00	80.00

KM# 1001 1/6 THALER
Silver

Date	Mintage	F	VF	XF	Unc	BU
1801 MC	—	10.00	25.00	55.00	85.00	115
1802 MC	—	10.00	25.00	50.00	75.00	100
1803 MC	—	10.00	25.00	40.00	60.00	85.00
1804 MC	—	10.00	25.00	45.00	70.00	95.00

KM# 1052 1/6 THALER
5.2000 g., 0.5630 Silver .0941 oz. **Obv:** Prancing horse left, M. C. below

Date	Mintage	F	VF	XF	Unc	BU
1813 MC	—	75.00	125	350	525	720
1814 MC	—	75.00	200	400	575	780

KM# 1030 THALER
Silver **Obv:** Small arms **Rev:** Value, date **Note:** Dav.#2173.

Date	Mintage	F	VF	XF	Unc	BU
1801 Rare	—	—	—	—	—	—

KM# 1093 THALER
28.0600 g., 0.8330 Silver .7516 oz.

Date	Mintage	F	VF	XF	Unc	BU
1821 CvC	1,480	1,000	2,000	3,500	5,500	7,200

KM# 1129 THALER

22.2700 g., 0.7500 Silver .5371 oz. **Obv:** Head right, FRITZ. F. at truncation **Note:** Convention Thaler.

Date	Mintage	F	VF	XF	Unc	BU
1837 CvC	2,788	75.00	220	700	1,400	2,400
1838 CvC	33,000	45.00	100	450	900	1,700

KM# 1130 THALER

22.2700 g., 0.7500 Silver .5371 oz. **Obv:** Smaller head

Date	Mintage	F	VF	XF	Unc	BU
1839 CvC	41,000	55.00	95.00	650	2,000	4,200

KM# 1131 THALER

22.2700 g., 0.7500 Silver .5371 oz. **Obv:** Smaller head, without name at truncation

Date	Mintage	F	VF	XF	Unc	BU
1839 CvC	Inc. above	30.00	60.00	190	750	1,500
1840 CvC	86,000	15.00	35.00	175	400	840
1841 CvC	304,000	15.00	30.00	85.00	300	510
1842 CvC	117,000	20.00	45.00	150	350	720
1848 CvC	11,000	25.00	55.00	175	550	900
1850 CvC	5,671	30.00	80.00	180	700	1,325

KM# 1144 THALER

22.2700 g., 0.7500 Silver .5371 oz. **Obv. Legend:** Ends:. . . U. L. **Rev:** Similar to KM#1129

Date	Mintage	F	VF	XF	Unc	BU
1851 B	5,742	60.00	110	325	1,000	2,400

KM# 1146 THALER

22.2700 g., 0.7500 Silver .5371 oz. **Obv. Legend:** Ends:. . . LUN

Date	Mintage	F	VF	XF	Unc	BU
1853 B	24,000	45.00	75.00	200	450	775
1854 B	97,000	20.00	55.00	140	400	600
1855 B	10,000	50.00	95.00	300	825	1,125

KM# 1152 THALER

18.5200 g., 0.9000 Silver .5360 oz. **Note:** Vereins Thaler.

Date	Mintage	F	VF	XF	Unc	BU
1858 B	49,000	25.00	40.00	125	200	265
1859 B	30,000	35.00	65.00	150	275	330
1865 B	20,000	30.00	65.00	140	250	300
1866 B	107,000	25.00	40.00	100	200	240
1867 B	107,000	25.00	40.00	100	175	240
1870 B	107,000	25.00	40.00	120	225	275
1871 B	48,000	25.00	40.00	110	215	265

KM# 1136 2 THALER (3 1/2 Gulden)

37.1200 g., 0.9000 Silver 1.0743 oz. **Obv:** Wilhelm head right

Date	Mintage	F	VF	XF	Unc	BU
1842 CvC	52,000	95.00	200	350	700	1,400
1843 CvC	68,000	75.00	175	300	600	1,325
1844 CvC	15,000	100	185	375	750	1,800
1845 CvC	11,000	110	210	400	800	25,400
1846 CvC	15,000	100	185	365	725	1,550
1847 CvC	15,000	100	185	350	700	1,625
1848 CvC	11,000	100	185	375	750	1,800
1849 CvC	13,000	110	210	375	750	1,800
1850 CvC	77,000	110	210	375	750	1,800

KM# 1140 2 THALER (3 1/2 Gulden)

37.1200 g., 0.9000 Silver 1.0743 oz.

Date	Mintage	F	VF	XF	Unc	BU
1850	—	100	150	275	600	900
1850 B	Inc. above	75.00	125	375	800	1,200
1851 B	10,000	100	150	550	1,250	1,800
1852 B	11,000	80.00	125	625	1,250	1,140
1854 B	253,000	55.00	100	175	350	475
1855 B	620,000	35.00	90.00	150	325	450

KM# 1149 2 THALER (3 1/2 Gulden)

37.1200 g., 0.9000 Silver 1.0743 oz. **Subject:** 25th Anniversary of Reign

Date	Mintage	F	VF	XF	Unc	BU
1856 B	17,000	65.00	110	175	250	305

KM# 1032 2-1/2 THALER

3.3200 g., 0.9000 Gold .0961 oz. **Obv:** Arms change **Note:** Similar to KM#1072.

Date	Mintage	F	VF	XF	Unc	BU
1801 MC	—	375	750	1,350	2,000	—
1801 MC	—	375	750	1,350	2,000	—
1802 MC	—	300	625	1,150	1,750	—
1806 MC	—	300	625	1,150	2,000	—

KM# 1066 2-1/2 THALER

3.3200 g., 0.9000 Gold .0961 oz. **Obv:** Crowned many quartered arms with garlands **Rev:** Value, F.R. below

Date	Mintage	F	VF	XF	Unc	BU
1815 FR	—	600	1,000	1,650	2,500	—

KM# 1072 2-1/2 THALER

3.3200 g., 0.9000 Gold .0961 oz. **Rev. Legend:** BR. . .

Date	Mintage	F	VF	XF	Unc	BU
1816 FR	—	575	800	1,125	1,750	—
1818 FR	—	825	1,150	1,350	2,000	—
1819 FR	—	700	950	1,250	1,750	—

KM# 1095 2-1/2 THALER

3.3200 g., 0.9000 Gold .0961 oz.

Date	Mintage	F	VF	XF	Unc	BU
1822 CvC	—	550	900	1,500	2,000	—

KM# 1113 2-1/2 THALER

3.3200 g., 0.9000 Gold .0961 oz. **Rev:** Without legend around border

Date	Mintage	F	VF	XF	Unc	BU
1825 CvC	—	350	500	875	1,500	—
1828 CvC	—	425	625	1,000	1,650	—

KM# 1117 2-1/2 THALER

3.3200 g., 0.9000 Gold .0961 oz. **Obv:** Karl Ii bust left

Date	Mintage	F	VF	XF	Unc	BU
1829 CvC	—	400	600	900	1,500	—

KM# 1125 2-1/2 THALER

3.3200 g., 0.9000 Gold .0961 oz.

Date	Mintage	F	VF	XF	Unc	BU
1832 CvC	—	450	650	1,000	1,500	—

KM# 1145 2-1/2 THALER
3.3200 g., 0.9000 Gold .0961 oz. **Obv:** William head right

Date	Mintage	F	VF	XF	Unc	BU
1851 B	4,138	350	500	750	1,100	—

KM# 1025 5 THALER
6.6500 g., 0.9000 Gold .1924 oz. **Obv:** Similar to KM#1110; change in arms **Rev:** Similar to KM#1062

Date	Mintage	F	VF	XF	Unc	BU
1801 MC	—	475	875	1,250	2,000	—
1802 MC	—	325	625	1,000	1,800	—
1803 MC Rare	—	—	—	—	—	—
1804 MC	—	475	875	1,250	2,000	—
1805 MC	—	450	750	1,150	1,850	—
1806 MC	—	450	750	1,150	1,850	—

KM# 1062 5 THALER
6.6500 g., 0.9000 Gold .1924 oz.

Date	Mintage	F	VF	XF	Unc	BU
1814 FR	—	500	925	1,350	2,000	—
1815 FR	—	425	800	1,200	1,850	—

KM# 1073 5 THALER
6.6500 g., 0.9000 Gold .1924 oz. **Rev. Legend:** Ends:... BR. ET LVN

Date	Mintage	F	VF	XF	Unc	BU
1816 FR	—	575	1,000	1,650	2,250	—
1817 FR	—	475	875	1,500	2,150	—
1818 FR	—	575	1,000	1,650	2,250	—
1819 FR	—	575	1,000	1,650	2,250	—

KM# 1081 5 THALER
6.6500 g., 0.9000 Gold .1924 oz. **Obv. Legend:** FRIDERICVS...

Date	Mintage	F	VF	XF	Unc	BU
1814 FR	—	—	—	—	—	—

KM# 1096 5 THALER
6.6500 g., 0.9000 Gold .1924 oz.

Date	Mintage	F	VF	XF	Unc	BU
1822 CvC	—	575	1,000	1,650	2,250	—
1823 CvC	—	750	1,250	1,850	2,750	—

KM# 1110 5 THALER
6.6500 g., 0.9000 Gold .1924 oz.

Date	Mintage	F	VF	XF	Unc	BU
1824 CvC	—	325	625	950	1,500	—
1825 CvC	—	345	675	1,000	1,650	—
1828 CvC	—	345	675	1,000	1,650	—
1830 CvC	—	400	775	1,150	1,750	—

KM# 1126 5 THALER
6.6500 g., 0.9000 Gold .1924 oz.

Date	Mintage	F	VF	XF	Unc	BU
1832 CvC	—	425	800	1,250	1,850	—
1834 CvC	—	475	900	1,500	2,150	—

KM# 1041 10 THALER
13.3000 g., 0.9000 Gold .3848 oz. **Obv:** Change in arms **Note:** Similar to KM#1054.

Date	Mintage	F	VF	XF	Unc	BU
1801 MC	—	675	1,150	2,000	3,000	—
1804 MC	—	750	1,250	2,000	3,000	—
1805 MC	—	550	875	1,500	2,500	—
1806 MC	—	750	1,250	1,850	2,750	—

KM# 1054 10 THALER
13.3000 g., 0.9000 Gold .3848 oz.

Date	Mintage	F	VF	XF	Unc	BU
1813 MC	—	750	1,250	1,850	2,750	—
1814 MC	—	675	1,150	1,750	2,350	—

KM# 1055 10 THALER
13.3000 g., 0.9000 Gold .3848 oz.

Date	Mintage	F	VF	XF	Unc	BU
1814 FR	—	750	1,250	1,850	3,000	—

KM# 1074 10 THALER
13.3000 g., 0.9000 Gold .3848 oz.

Date	Mintage	F	VF	XF	Unc	BU
1817 FR	—	675	1,150	1,750	2,500	—
1818 FR	—	550	875	1,500	2,500	—
1819 FR	—	675	1,150	1,750	2,500	—

KM# 1097 10 THALER
13.3000 g., 0.9000 Gold .3848 oz.

Date	Mintage	F	VF	XF	Unc	BU
1822 CvC	—	750	1,250	1,850	3,000	—

KM# 1111 10 THALER
13.3000 g., 0.9000 Gold .3848 oz.

Date	Mintage	F	VF	XF	Unc	BU
1824 CvC	—	750	1,250	1,850	2,750	—
1825 CvC	—	600	1,000	1,650	2,500	—
1829 CvC	—	825	1,350	2,000	2,750	—
1830 CvC	—	750	1,250	1,850	2,500	—

KM# 1115 10 THALER
13.3000 g., 0.9000 Gold .3848 oz. **Obv:** Karl II bust left

Date	Mintage	F	VF	XF	Unc	BU
1827 CvC	—	900	1,500	2,500	3,750	—
1828 CvC	—	900	1,500	2,500	3,750	—
1829 CvC	—	825	1,350	2,000	3,000	—
1829 CvC Proof	—	Value: 5,500				

KM# 1121 10 THALER
13.3000 g., 0.9000 Gold .3848 oz.

Date	Mintage	F	VF	XF	Unc	BU
1831 CvC	—	750	1,250	1,850	2,500	—

KM# 1122 10 THALER
13.3000 g., 0.9000 Gold .3848 oz.

Date	Mintage	F	VF	XF	Unc	BU
1831 CvC	—	525	875	1,350	2,250	—
1832 CvC	—	525	875	1,350	2,250	—
1833 CvC	—	600	1,000	1,500	2,250	—
1834 CvC	—	450	750	1,250	2,250	—

KM# 1141 10 THALER
13.3000 g., 0.9000 Gold .3848 oz.

Date	Mintage	F	VF	XF	Unc	BU
1850 B	9,763	975	1,650	2,150	2,750	—

KM# 1147 10 THALER
13.3000 g., 0.9000 Gold .3848 oz. **Obv. Legend:** Ends:... LUN

Date	Mintage	F	VF	XF	Unc	BU
1853 B	150,000	400	650	1,000	2,000	—
1854 B	163,000	400	650	1,000	2,000	—
1855 B	20,000	750	1,250	1,750	2,500	—
1856 B	57,000	400	650	1,000	2,000	—
1857 B	54,000	400	650	1,100	2,250	—

KM# 1153 KRONE
11.1110 g., 0.9000 Gold .3215 oz. **Obv:** Wilhelm head right

Date	Mintage	F	VF	XF	Unc	BU
1858 B	32,000	500	950	1,450	2,500	—
1859 B	13,000	600	1,150	1,850	3,000	—

KM# 1160 20 MARK

7.9650 g., 0.9000 Gold .2304 oz. **Obv:** Wilhelm head left **Rev:** Type II

Date	Mintage	F	VF	XF	Unc	BU
1875A	100,000	300	600	1,000	1,750	2,250

TRADE COINAGE

KM# 1023 DUCAT

3.5000 g., 0.9860 Gold .1109 oz. **Note:** Similar to KM#1067.

Date	Mintage	F	VF	XF	Unc	BU
1801 MC	—	450	750	1,250	1,600	—

KM# 1063 DUCAT

3.5000 g., 0.9860 Gold .1109 oz. **Obv:** Crowned many quartered arms with garlands **Rev:** Value, EX AVRO HERCINIA

Date	Mintage	F	VF	XF	Unc	BU
ND1814 HC	376	575	1,000	1,750	2,350	—

KM# 1067 DUCAT

3.5000 g., 0.9860 Gold .1109 oz.

Date	Mintage	F	VF	XF	Unc	BU
ND1815 FR	220	725	1,250	2,000	2,750	—

KM# 1114 DUCAT

3.5000 g., 0.9860 Gold .1109 oz.

Date	Mintage	F	VF	XF	Unc	BU
ND1825 CvC	530	750	1,250	2,100	2,850	—

PATTERNS

Including off metal strikes

KM#	Date	Mintage	Identification	Mkt Val

Pn44	1813	—	5 Thaler.	—

Pn45	1814	—	4 Pfennige.	1,450

KM#	Date	Mintage	Identification	Mkt Val
Pn46	1827	—	10 Thaler. Copper.	—
Pn47	1827	—	10 Thaler. Silver.	—
Pn48	1827	—	10 Thaler. Silver. Uniface.	—

KM#	Date	Mintage	Identification	Mkt Val
Pn49	1837	—	Thaler.	15,000

Pn50	1846	—	Pfennig.	650

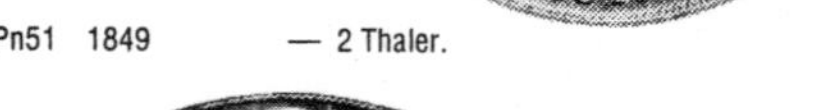

Pn51	1849	—	2 Thaler.	—

KM#	Date	Mintage	Identification	Mkt Val
Pn52	1850	—	2 Thaler. Rare.	—
Pn53	1857 B	—	Krone. 0.9000 Gold. KM#1153.	3,000

EAST FRIESLAND

The countship, and later principality, of East Friesland was located along the North Sea coast between the Rivers Ems and Weser. By the late 14th and early 15th centuries, several powerful families controlled various areas of what was to become the countship. The Cirksena family of Greetsyl managed to emerge during this period as a leading force in the region through astute marriages and sometimes by armed might. Ulrich I Cirksena was created the first count of East Friesland in 1454. This confirmed his line as the ruling dynasty with the capital at Aurich. In 1654, the count was raised to the rank of prince. In 1744, the Cirksenas became extinct and East Friesland passed to Prussia, which maintained the mint at Aurich for the new province. East Friesland became part of Hannover at the end of the Napoleonic Wars in 1815, but returned to Prussian control when Hannover itself was absorbed by Prussia in 1866.

RULERS

Friedrich Wilhelm III (of Prussia), 1797-1807
George IV (of Hannover and Great Britain), 1815-1820

MINT MARKS

A - Berlin
B - Breslau
D - Aurich
F - Magdeburg
Star - Dresden

MONETARY SYSTEM

Witte = 4 Hohlpfennig = 1/3 Schilling = 1/20 Schaf = 1/10 Stuber
Ciffert = 6 Witten
Stuber = 10 Witten = 1/30 Reichstaler
Schaf = 20 Witten = 2 Stuber
Flindrich = 3 Stuber
Schilling = 6 Stuber
288 Pfennige = 54 Stuber = 36 Mariengroschen = 1 Reichsthaler

COUNTSHIP

Principality from 1654

REGULAR COINAGE

KM# 272 1/4 STUBER (2-1/2 Witten)

Copper **Obv:** Crowned GW monogram **Rev:** Value, date

Date	Mintage	F	VF	XF	Unc	BU
1802A	1,296,000	4.00	12.50	25.00	75.00	—
1803A	Inc. above	4.00	12.50	25.00	75.00	—
1804A	216,000	4.00	12.50	25.00	75.00	—

KM# 290 1/4 STUBER (2-1/2 Witten)

Copper

Date	Mintage	F	VF	XF	Unc	BU
1823	710,000	5.00	12.00	25.00	70.00	—
1824	Inc. above	5.00	12.00	25.00	70.00	—
1825	Inc. above	5.00	12.00	25.00	70.00	—

KM# 280 STUBER

Billon

Date	Mintage	F	VF	XF	Unc	BU
1804A	378,000	30.00	50.00	85.00	175	—

KM# 291 STUBER

Billon

Date	Mintage	F	VF	XF	Unc	BU
1823B	161,000	12.00	20.00	45.00	100	—

KM# 281 2 STUBER

Billon **Obv:** Bust **Rev:** Value

Date	Mintage	F	VF	XF	Unc	BU
1804A	216,000	50.00	80.00	175	375	—

KM# 292 2 STUBER

Billon **Obv:** Crowned monogram GR **Rev:** Value

Date	Mintage	F	VF	XF	Unc	BU
1823B	81,000	15.00	30.00	70.00	150	—

ERFURT

The city of Erfurt is located in northern Thuringia (Thüringen), about 12.5 miles (21 kilometers) west of Weimar. It was a place of some importance as early as 741 when it became a branch bishopric of Mainz. The archbishops of the latter city remained very much involved in the affairs of Erfurt throughout the High Middle Ages and even located one of their mints there from the 11th through the 13th centuries. An imperial mint also produced coinage in Erfurt during the 12th century. By the mid-13th century, however, the town gained enough power to force the archbishop to grant it self-governing rights. Erfurt was given the right to mint its own coins in 1341 and 1354, and a long series of coins began which lasted until the beginning of the 19th century. Having joined the Hanseatic League during the early 15th century, Erfurt was at the height of its power and prestige, but events began to cause the decline of the city. Saxony managed to wrest control of Erfurt away from Mainz in 1483. During the Thirty Years' War, the city was seized and occupied by Swedish forces in 1631. The treaties which ended the war in 1648 gave control of Erfurt back to Mainz, but the good citizens refused to submit. The city held out until 1664 when it was captured by the archbishop's forces. It remained under Mainz until 1803, when the archbishopric was secularized, and then passed to Prussia.

RULERS

Friedrich Carl Josef, Freiherr von und zu Erthal, Archbishop, 1774-1802

MINT OFFICIALS' INITIALS

Initial	Date	Name
C	1779-1804	Julianus Eberhard Volkmar Claus, Mint director
S	1801-02	Johann Blasius Siegling, Mint director

CITY

REGULAR COINAGE

KM# 132 6 PFENNIG

Billon **Ruler:** Emerich Josef **Obv:** Wheel in crowned shield **Rev:** Value **Note:** Prev. KM#122.

Date	Mintage	F	VF	XF	Unc	BU
1801 S	—	20.00	40.00	100	350	—

KM# 133 GROSCHEN

Billon **Ruler:** Friedrich Carl Josef Archbishop **Note:** Prev. KM#123.

Date	Mintage	F	VF	XF	Unc	BU
1801 S	—	15.00	30.00	80.00	325	—

KM# 134 GROSCHEN

Billon **Ruler:** Friedrich Carl Josef Archbishop **Obv:** Shield within branches **Note:** Prev. KM#124.

Date	Mintage	F	VF	XF	Unc	BU
1802 S	—	12.00	25.00	65.00	300	—

PATTERNS

Including off metal strikes

KM#	Date	Mintage	Identification	Mkt Val
Pn8	1801	—	6 Pfennig. Copper. KM#122.	375

FRANKFURT AM MAIN

One of the largest cities of modern Germany, Frankfurt is located on the north bank of the Main River about 25 miles (42 kilometers) upstream from where it joins the Rhine at Mainz. It was the site of a Roman camp in the first century. Frankfurt was a commercial center from the early Middle Ages and became a favored location for imperial councils during the Carolingian period because of its central location. An imperial mint operated from early times and had a large production during the 12th to 14th centuries. Local issues were produced from at least the mid-14th century, but it was not until 1428 that the city was officially granted the right to coin its own money. In establishing the seven permanent electors of the Empire in 1356, the Golden Bull also made Frankfurt the site of those elections and increased the prestige of the city even further. Frankfurt remained a free city until 1806 and then was the capital of the Grand Duchy of Frankfurt from 1810 until 1814, only to regain its free status in 1815. The city chose the wrong side in the Austro-Prussian War of 1866 and thus was absorbed by victorious Prussia in the latter year.

RULERS

Carl Theodor v. Dalberg, 1810-15

MINT MARKS

F = Frankfurt

MINT OFFICIALS' INITIALS

Frankfurt Mint

Initial	Date	Name
A. V. NORDHEIM	1857-66	An engraver
G.B., I.G.B.	1790-1825	Johann Georg Bunsen
GH	1798-1816	Georg Hille, warden
S.T.	1836-37	Samuel Tomschutz
Z	1843-56	Johann Philipp Zollman

Wiesbaden Mint

Initial	Date	Name
ZOLLMANN	1818-43	Johann Philipp, engraver

NOTE: In some instances old dies were used with initials beyond the date range of the man that held the position.

FREE CITY

REGULAR COINAGE

KM# 300 HELLER

Copper **Note:** Prev. KM#300.1 and 300.2.

Date	Mintage	F	VF	XF	Unc	BU
1814 G.B.	332,000	70.00	125	300	700	—
1814 Without G.B.	Inc. above	90.00	200	400	800	—

KM# 301 HELLER

Copper **Note:** Varieties exist.

Date	Mintage	F	VF	XF	Unc	BU
1814F GB	Inc. above	5.00	10.00	35.00	50.00	—
1815F GB	166,000	5.00	10.00	30.00	45.00	—
1816F GB	—	5.00	10.00	30.00	45.00	—
1817F GB	—	4.00	8.00	22.00	40.00	—
1818F GB	—	4.00	7.00	20.00	40.00	—
1819F GB	—	3.00	5.00	15.00	25.00	—
1820F GB	—	3.00	5.00	15.00	25.00	—
1821F GB	—	3.00	5.00	15.00	25.00	—
1822F GB	—	4.00	8.00	22.00	40.00	—
1824F GB	—	4.00	8.00	22.00	40.00	—
1825F GB	—	4.00	8.00	22.00	40.00	—
1836F ST	120,000	8.00	20.00	60.00	100	—
1837F ST	144,000	8.00	20.00	60.00	100	—

KM# 311 HELLER

Copper **Obv:** Eagle with wide streched wings **Obv. Legend:** F. STADT FRANKFURT

Date	Mintage	F	VF	XF	Unc	BU
1838	—	5.00	15.00	40.00	90.00	—

KM# 327 HELLER

Copper **Obv:** Eagle with wide streched wings **Obv. Legend:** F. STADT FRANKFURT **Rev:** 1 / HELLER / date

Date	Mintage	F	VF	XF	Unc	BU
1841	173,000	4.00	8.00	18.00	35.00	—
1842	328,000	4.00	8.00	18.00	35.00	—
1843	38,400	20.00	30.00	50.00	80.00	—
1844	162,000	4.00	8.00	18.00	35.00	—
1845	169,000	4.00	8.00	18.00	35.00	—
1846	205,000	4.00	8.00	18.00	35.00	—
1847	453,000	4.00	8.00	18.00	35.00	—
1849	396,000	4.00	8.00	18.00	35.00	—
1850	669,000	4.00	8.00	18.00	35.00	—
1851	275,000	4.00	8.00	18.00	35.00	—
1852	325,000	4.00	8.00	18.00	35.00	—

KM# 332 HELLER

Copper **Obv. Legend:** FREIE STADT FRANKFURT

Date	Mintage	F	VF	XF	Unc	BU
1843	—	200	500	700	900	—

Note: Mintage included with KM#327.

KM# 351 HELLER

Copper **Obv:** Round eagle, legend at sides

Date	Mintage	F	VF	XF	Unc	BU
1853	411,000	4.00	8.00	18.00	32.00	—
1854	271,000	4.00	8.00	18.00	32.00	—
185/55	—	4.00	8.00	18.00	32.00	—
1855	430,000	4.00	8.00	18.00	32.00	—
1856	484,000	4.00	8.00	18.00	32.00	—
1857	723,000	4.00	8.00	18.00	32.00	—
1858	377,000	4.00	8.00	18.00	32.00	—

KM# 356 HELLER

Copper **Obv:** Small round eagle within legend **Obv. Legend:** SCHEIDEMÜNZE D. FR. ST. FRANKFURT

Date	Mintage	F	VF	XF	Unc	BU
1859	377,000	3.00	5.00	12.00	25.00	—
1860	353,000	3.00	5.00	12.00	25.00	—
1861	378,000	3.00	5.00	12.00	25.00	—
1862	391,000	3.00	5.00	12.00	25.00	—
1863	370,000	3.00	5.00	12.00	25.00	—
1864	390,000	3.00	5.00	12.00	25.00	—
1865	384,000	3.00	5.00	8.00	20.00	—

KM# 268 PFENNIG

Copper **Obv:** Eagle **Rev:** *1* / PFENNIG / date /* **Note:** Struck at Frankfurt Mint. Varieties exist.

Date	Mintage	F	VF	XF	Unc	BU
1801F GB	—	2.50	6.00	14.00	30.00	—
1801F GB	—	2.50	6.00	14.00	30.00	—
1802F GB	—	2.50	6.00	14.00	30.00	—
1803F PB	—	2.50	6.00	14.00	30.00	—
1803F GB	—	2.50	6.00	14.00	30.00	—
1804F GB	—	2.50	6.00	14.00	30.00	—
1805F GB	—	3.00	7.00	18.00	35.00	—
1806F GB	—	3.00	8.00	20.00	40.00	—

KM# 295 KREUZER

Billon **Obv:** STADT / FRANKFURT / date **Rev:** I / CONVENT KREUZER **Note:** Convention Kreuzer. Varieties exist with dots, rosettes, stars, and roses at sides of "1".

Date	Mintage	VG	F	VF	XF	Unc
1803 GB GH	—	5.00	15.00	40.00	90.00	—
1804 GB GH	—	6.00	20.00	50.00	120	—
1805 GB GH	—	5.00	15.00	40.00	90.00	—

KM# 298 KREUZER

Billon **Obv:** Rosette below date

Date	Mintage	VG	F	VF	XF	Unc
1805 GB GH	—	5.00	15.00	30.00	65.00	—

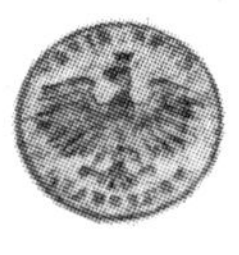

KM# 312 KREUZER

0.8350 g., 0.1670 Silver .0044 oz. **Obv:** Eagle with wide spread wings **Obv. Legend:** FREIE STADT FRANKFURT **Rev:** Value and date within oak wreath

Date	Mintage	F	VF	XF	Unc	BU
1838	78,000	3.00	6.00	12.00	25.00	—
1841	123,000	3.00	6.00	12.00	25.00	—
1842	402,000	3.00	6.00	12.00	25.00	—
1843	169,000	3.00	6.00	12.00	25.00	—
1844	215,000	3.00	6.00	12.00	25.00	—
1845	205,000	3.00	6.00	12.00	25.00	—
1846	101,000	3.00	6.00	12.00	25.00	—
1847	553,000	3.00	6.00	12.00	25.00	—
1848	482,000	3.00	6.00	12.00	25.00	—
1849	627,000	3.00	6.00	12.00	25.00	—
1850	612,000	3.00	6.00	12.00	25.00	—
1851	543,000	3.00	6.00	12.00	25.00	—
1852	889,000	3.00	6.00	12.00	25.00	—
1853	526,000	3.00	6.00	12.00	25.00	—
1854	589,000	3.00	6.00	12.00	25.00	—
1855	677,000	3.00	6.00	12.00	25.00	—
1856	1,227,000	3.00	6.00	12.00	25.00	—
1857	774,000	3.00	6.00	12.00	25.00	—

KM# 317 KREUZER
0.8350 g., 0.1670 Silver .0044 oz. **Obv:** Eagle with wide spread wings **Obv. Legend:** FREIE STADT FRANKFURT **Rev:** Value and date within oak wreath **Note:** Varieties exist.

Date	Mintage	F	VF	XF	Unc	BU
ND(1839)	—	3.00	8.00	16.00	40.00	—

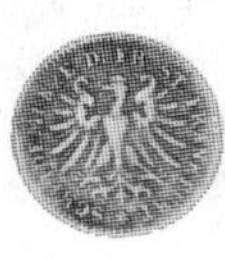

KM# 357 KREUZER
0.8350 g., 0.1670 Silver .0044 oz. **Obv:** Eagle with long body **Rev:** Value and date within oak wreath

Date	Mintage	F	VF	XF	Unc	BU
1859	358,000	3.00	6.00	12.00	25.00	—
1860	640,000	3.00	6.00	12.00	25.00	—
1861	313,000	3.00	6.00	12.00	25.00	—
1862	—	25.00	52.50	80.00	125	—

KM# 367 KREUZER
0.8350 g., 0.1670 Silver .0044 oz. **Obv:** Eagle with heart-shaped body **Rev:** Value and date within oak wreath

Date	Mintage	F	VF	XF	Unc	BU
1862	645,000	2.50	5.00	9.00	20.00	—
1863	611,000	2.50	5.00	9.00	20.00	—
1864	344,000	2.50	5.00	9.00	20.00	—
1865	366,000	2.50	5.00	9.00	20.00	—
1866	151,000	2.50	4.00	8.00	16.00	—

KM# 313 3 KREUZER
1.2990 g., 0.3330 Silver .0139 oz.

Date	Mintage	F	VF	XF	Unc	BU
1838	80,000	4.00	10.00	25.00	55.00	—
1841	85,000	—	—	—	—	—
Note: Reported, not confirmed						
1842	109,000	4.00	10.00	22.00	50.00	—
1843	89,000	4.00	10.00	22.00	50.00	—
1846	154,000	4.00	10.00	22.00	50.00	—

KM# 334 3 KREUZER
1.2990 g., 0.3330 Silver .0139 oz.

Date	Mintage	F	VF	XF	Unc	BU
1846	Inc. above	4.00	10.00	20.00	45.00	—
1848	38,000	4.00	10.00	20.00	45.00	—
1849	950,000	4.00	10.00	25.00	50.00	—
1850	182,000	4.00	10.00	25.00	50.00	—
1851	158,000	4.00	10.00	22.00	48.00	—
1852	129,000	4.00	10.00	22.00	48.00	—
1853	69,000	4.00	10.00	22.00	48.00	—
1854	154,000	4.00	10.00	22.00	48.00	—
1855	148,000	4.00	10.00	22.00	48.00	—
1856	84,000	4.00	10.00	20.00	40.00	—

KM# 373 3 KREUZER
1.2990 g., 0.3330 Silver .0139 oz.

Date	Mintage	F	VF	XF	Unc	BU
1866	96,000	2.00	4.00	9.00	20.00	—

KM# 314 6 KREUZER
2.5980 g., 0.3330 Silver .0277 oz.

Date	Mintage	F	VF	XF	Unc	BU
1838	110,000	6.00	16.00	30.00	65.00	—
1841	123,000	6.00	16.00	30.00	65.00	—
1842	161,000	6.00	16.00	30.00	65.00	—
1843	260,000	6.00	16.00	30.00	65.00	—
1844	370,000	4.00	12.00	25.00	45.00	—
1845	105,000	6.00	16.00	30.00	65.00	—
1846	211,000	8.00	20.00	35.00	70.00	—

KM# 335 6 KREUZER
2.5980 g., 0.3330 Silver .0277 oz.

Date	Mintage	F	VF	XF	Unc	BU
1846	Inc. above	8.00	18.00	30.00	55.00	—
1848	291,000	4.00	10.00	22.00	45.00	—
1849	171,000	6.00	12.00	25.00	50.00	—
1850	152,000	6.00	12.00	25.00	45.00	—
1851	159,000	6.00	12.00	25.00	45.00	—
1852	221,000	8.00	16.00	28.00	50.00	—
1853	106,000	8.00	16.00	28.00	50.00	—
1855	181,000	6.00	12.00	20.00	35.00	—
1856	166,000	6.00	12.00	20.00	35.00	—

KM# 350 6 KREUZER
2.5980 g., 0.3330 Silver .0277 oz.

Date	Mintage	F	VF	XF	Unc	BU
1852	Inc. above	4.00	12.00	30.00	70.00	—
1853	Inc. above	3.50	10.00	25.00	60.00	—
1854	212,000	3.50	10.00	25.00	60.00	—
1856	Inc. above	3.50	10.00	25.00	60.00	—

KM# 374 6 KREUZER
2.4630 g., 0.3500 Silver 0.0276 oz.

Date	Mintage	F	VF	XF	Unc	BU
1866	38,000	4.00	8.00	15.00	25.00	—

KM# 315 1/2 GULDEN
5.3030 g., 0.9000 Silver .1533 oz.

Date	Mintage	F	VF	XF	Unc	BU
1838	120,000	20.00	40.00	90.00	180	—
1838 Proof	—	Value: 225				
1840	96,400	—	—	—	—	—
Note: Reported, not confirmed						
1841	161,000	20.00	40.00	90.00	180	—

KM# 330 1/2 GULDEN
5.3030 g., 0.9000 Silver .1533 oz.

Date	Mintage	F	VF	XF	Unc	BU
1842	75,000	20.00	35.00	75.00	150	—
1843	56,000	20.00	35.00	75.00	150	—
1844	49,000	20.00	35.00	75.00	150	—
1845	72,000	20.00	35.00	75.00	150	—
1846	47,000	20.00	35.00	75.00	150	—
1847	51,000	20.00	35.00	75.00	150	—
1849	55,000	20.00	35.00	75.00	150	—

KM# 368 1/2 GULDEN
5.2910 g., 0.9000 Silver .1533 oz.

Date	Mintage	F	VF	XF	Unc	BU
1862	14,000	120	220	360	650	—

KM# 316 GULDEN
10.6060 g., 0.9000 Silver .3067 oz.

Date	Mintage	F	VF	XF	Unc	BU
1838	120,000	30.00	60.00	100	200	—
1838 Proof	—	Value: 1,000				
1840	391,000	30.00	60.00	170	220	—
1841	161,000	30.00	60.00	115	230	—

KM# 331 GULDEN
10.6060 g., 0.9000 Silver .3067 oz. **Obv:** Eagle with large arabesques

Date	Mintage	F	VF	XF	Unc	BU
1842	123,000	18.00	40.00	80.00	155	—
1843	172,000	18.00	40.00	80.00	155	—
1844	122,000	18.00	40.00	80.00	155	—
1845	101,000	18.00	40.00	80.00	155	—
1846	120,000	18.00	40.00	80.00	155	—
1847	121,000	18.00	40.00	80.00	155	—
1848	78,000	18.00	40.00	80.00	155	—
1849	90,000	18.00	40.00	80.00	155	—
1850	30,000	20.00	45.00	90.00	180	—
1851	64,000	20.00	45.00	90.00	180	—
1852	64,000	20.00	45.00	90.00	180	—
1853	29,000	20.00	45.00	90.00	180	—
1854	34,000	20.00	45.00	90.00	180	—
1855	38,000	20.00	45.00	90.00	180	—

KM# 358 GULDEN
10.5820 g., 0.9000 Silver .3069 oz. **Obv:** Eagle with small arabesques

Date	Mintage	F	VF	XF	Unc	BU
1859	59,000	20.00	55.00	125	260	—
1861	211,000	16.00	35.00	75.00	155	—

KM# 369 GULDEN
10.5820 g., 0.9000 Silver .3069 oz. **Obv:** Eagle without arabesques

Date	Mintage	F	VF	XF	Unc	BU
1862	11,000	150	270	500	800	—
1863	56,000	45.00	80.00	150	280	—

KM# 333 2 GULDEN
21.2110 g., 0.9000 Silver .6138 oz.

Date	Mintage	F	VF	XF	Unc	BU
1845	114,000	50.00	80.00	160	320	—
1846	281,000	40.00	70.00	140	260	—
1847	215,000	40.00	70.00	150	290	—
1848	147,000	40.00	70.00	150	290	—
1849	23,000	70.00	130	240	400	—
1850	31,000	70.00	130	240	400	—
1851	32,000	70.00	130	240	400	—
1852	26,000	70.00	130	240	400	—
1853	56,000	60.00	100	180	340	—
1854	6,028	70.00	130	240	400	—
1856	36,000	60.00	100	180	340	—

KM# 336 2 GULDEN
21.2110 g., 0.9000 Silver .6138 oz. **Subject:** Constitutional Convention, May 1, 1848

Date	Mintage	F	VF	XF	Unc	BU
1848 Rare	—	—	—	—	—	—

KM# 337 2 GULDEN
21.2110 g., 0.9000 Silver .6138 oz. **Subject:** Constitutional Convention, May 18, 1848

Date	Mintage	F	VF	XF	Unc	BU
1848	8,600	50.00	100	160	240	—

Note: Coins were struck in anticipation of the Constitutional Convention scheduled to take place May 1, 1848; When the convention was delayed until May 18, 1848 the coins were recalled and the dies were altered to reflect this new date

KM# 338 2 GULDEN
21.2110 g., 0.9000 Silver .6138 oz. **Subject:** Archduke Johann of Austria Elected as Vicar

Date	Mintage	F	VF	XF	Unc	BU
1848	36,000	30.00	55.00	85.00	160	—
1848 Proof	—	Value: 250				

KM# 339 2 GULDEN
21.2110 g., 0.9000 Silver .6138 oz. **Subject:** Archduke Johann of Austria Elected as Vicar **Note:** Mule.

Date	Mintage	F	VF	XF	Unc	BU
1848 Rare	—	—	—	—	—	—

KM# 340 2 GULDEN
21.2110 g., 0.9000 Silver .6138 oz. **Subject:** Opening of German Parliament **Obv:** KM#337 **Rev:** KM#333 **Note:** Mule.

Date	Mintage	F	VF	XF	Unc	BU
1848 Rare	—	—	—	—	—	—

KM# 341.1 2 GULDEN
21.2110 g., 0.9000 Silver .6138 oz. **Subject:** Friedrich Wilhelm IV of Prussia Elected as Emperor of Germany

Date	Mintage	F	VF	XF	Unc	BU
1849	200	—	2,800	4,000	5,500	—

KM# 341.2 2 GULDEN
21.2110 g., 0.9000 Silver .6138 oz. **Subject:** Friedrich Wilhelm IV of Prussia Elected as Emperor of Germany **Edge:** Plain

Date	Mintage	F	VF	XF	Unc	BU
1849 (1890) Restrike	—	—	—	—	—	—

KM# 342 2 GULDEN
21.2110 g., 0.9000 Silver .6138 oz. **Obv:** Similar to KM#333 **Note:** Mule.

Date	Mintage	F	VF	XF	Unc	BU
1849 Rare	—	—	—	—	—	—

KM# 343 2 GULDEN
21.2110 g., 0.9000 Silver .6138 oz. **Subject:** Centenary of Goethe's Birth

Date	Mintage	F	VF	XF	Unc	BU
1849	8,500	40.00	70.00	100	180	—
1849 Proof	—	Value: 250				

KM# 353 2 GULDEN
21.2110 g., 0.9000 Silver .6138 oz. **Subject:** 300th Anniversary of Religious Peace

Date	Mintage	F	VF	XF	Unc	BU
1855	32,000	40.00	60.00	90.00	160	—

KM# 354 THALER
18.5200 g., 0.9000 Silver .5360 oz. **Note:** Veriens Thaler.

Date	Mintage	F	VF	XF	Unc	BU
1857	1,350	160	300	700	1,500	—

KM# 355 THALER
18.5200 g., 0.9000 Silver .5360 oz. **Obv:** House roofs visible around tower at left

Date	Mintage	F	VF	XF	Unc	BU
1857	—	120	200	400	900	—
1858	12,000	30.00	80.00	180	400	—

KM# 359 THALER
18.5200 g., 0.9000 Silver .5360 oz. **Subject:** Schiller Centennial **Note:** Gedenk Thaler.

Date	Mintage	F	VF	XF	Unc	BU
1859	25,000	25.00	50.00	75.00	130	—
1859 Proof	—	Value: 175				

KM# 360 THALER
18.5200 g., 0.9000 Silver .5360 oz. **Note:** Vereins Thaler.

Date	Mintage	F	VF	XF	Unc	BU
1859	283,000	25.00	45.00	70.00	140	—
1860	1,700,000	20.00	35.00	60.00	100	—

KM# 366 THALER
18.5200 g., 0.9000 Silver .5360 oz. **Obv:** Different hair knot

Date	Mintage	F	VF	XF	Unc	BU
1861	16,000	120	200	280	700	—

KM# 370 THALER
18.5200 g., 0.9000 Silver .5360 oz. **Obv:** Different dress

Date	Mintage	F	VF	XF	Unc	BU
1862	312,000	25.00	45.00	70.00	140	—
1863	21,000	32.00	55.00	90.00	180	—
1864	105,000	30.00	45.00	70.00	150	—
1865	207,000	25.00	45.00	65.00	130	—

KM# 371 THALER
18.5200 g., 0.9000 Silver .5360 oz. **Subject:** German Shooting Festival **Obv:** Similar to KM#359 **Note:** Gedenk Thaler.

Date	Mintage	F	VF	XF	Unc	BU
1862	44,000	25.00	50.00	70.00	120	—
1862 Proof	—	Value: 225				

KM# 372 THALER
18.5200 g., 0.9000 Silver .5360 oz. **Subject:** Assembly of Princes

Date	Mintage	F	VF	XF	Unc	BU
1863	20,000	50.00	75.00	110	180	—
1863 Proof	—	Value: 250				

KM# 325 2 THALER (3-1/2 Gulden)
37.1000 g., 0.9000 Silver 1.0743 oz. **Subject:** New Mint Opening in 1840

Date	Mintage	F	VF	XF	Unc	BU
1840	649	450	700	130	2,500	—

KM# 326 2 THALER (3-1/2 Gulden)
37.1000 g., 0.9000 Silver 1.0743 oz. **Note:** Mintage included in KM#329.

Date	Mintage	F	VF	XF	Unc	BU
1840	—	80.00	130	250	450	—
1841	—	70.00	110	180	330	—
1842 Rare	—	—	—	—	—	—
1843	—	80.00	130	250	450	—
1844	—	90.00	160	280	500	—

KM# 328 2 THALER (3-1/2 Gulden)
37.1000 g., 0.9000 Silver 1.0743 oz. **Obv:** KM#326 **Rev:** Obverse of KM#329 **Note:** Mule.

Date	Mintage	F	VF	XF	Unc	BU
ND(1838) Rare	—	—	—	—	—	—

KM# 329 2 THALER (3-1/2 Gulden)
37.1000 g., 0.9000 Silver 1.0743 oz. **Rev:** Value

Date	Mintage	F	VF	XF	Unc	BU
1841	121,000	70.00	120	180	420	—
1841 Proof	—	Value: 800				
1842	287,000	60.00	110	170	360	—
1843	123,000	70.00	120	180	420	—
1844	196,000	60.00	110	180	420	—
1845	36,000	80.00	150	300	700	—
1846	72,000	70.00	120	220	580	—
1847	71,000	60.00	110	180	440	—
1851	8,354	80.00	150	300	700	—
1854	107,000	70.00	120	220	580	—
1855	72,000	70.00	120	200	500	—

KM# 365 2 THALER (3-1/2 Gulden)
37.0400 g., 0.9000 Silver 1.0717 oz.

Date	Mintage	F	VF	XF	Unc	BU
1860	341,000	30.00	55.00	90.00	160	—
1861	1,787,000	20.00	38.00	70.00	110	—
1862	344,000	30.00	50.00	80.00	140	—
1866	637,000	25.00	45.00	75.00	130	—

TOKEN COINAGE

KM# Tn1 THELER
Copper

Date	Mintage	F	VF	XF	Unc	BU
1807	—	5.00	12.00	25.00	45.00	—

KM# Tn2 ATRIBUO
Copper

Date	Mintage	F	VF	XF	Unc	BU
1809	—	7.00	15.00	28.00	55.00	—

KM# Tn3 1/4 HALBAG
Copper

Date	Mintage	F	VF	XF	Unc	BU
1818	—	7.00	15.00	28.00	55.00	—

KM# Tn4 HELLER
Copper **Obv:** Griffin **Rev:** Value

Date	Mintage	F	VF	XF	Unc	BU
1819	—	10.00	18.00	40.00	70.00	—

KM# Tn10 HELLER
Copper

Date	Mintage	F	VF	XF	Unc	BU
1820	—	4.00	8.00	16.00	35.00	—

KM# Tn11 HELLER
Copper **Rev:** Without asterisks on sides of "1"

Date	Mintage	F	VF	XF	Unc	BU
1820	—	10.00	18.00	40.00	70.00	—

KM# Tn12 HELLER
Copper

Date	Mintage	F	VF	XF	Unc	BU
1821	—	8.00	16.00	35.00	70.00	—

KM# Tn5 PFENNIG
Copper

Date	Mintage	F	VF	XF	Unc	BU
1819	—	3.00	6.00	14.00	28.00	—

KM# Tn6 PFENNIG
Copper

Date	Mintage	F	VF	XF	Unc	BU
1819	—	3.00	6.00	14.00	28.00	—

KM# Tn7 PFENNIG
Copper

Date	Mintage	F	VF	XF	Unc	BU
1819	—	3.00	6.00	14.00	28.00	—

KM# Tn8 PFENNIG
Copper **Obv:** Lion

Date	Mintage	F	VF	XF	Unc	BU
1819	—	5.00	10.00	18.00	30.00	—

KM# Tn9 PFENNIG
Copper **Obv:** Rose branch

Date	Mintage	F	VF	XF	Unc	BU
1819	—	5.00	10.00	18.00	30.00	—

KM# Tn13 PFENNIG
Copper

Date	Mintage	F	VF	XF	Unc	BU
1822	—	5.00	12.00	20.00	35.00	—

KM# Tn15 1/4 ROPELL
Copper

Date	Mintage	F	VF	XF	Unc	BU
1816	—	8.00	18.00	35.00	60.00	—

TRADE COINAGE

KM# 352 DUCAT
3.5000 g., 0.9860 Gold .1109 oz.

Date	Mintage	F	VF	XF	Unc	BU
1853	1,121	300	400	800	1,400	—
1856	665	325	550	950	1,600	—

PATTERNS

Including off metal strikes

KM#	Date	Mintage	Identification	Mkt Val
Pn48	1817	—	Heller. Silver. KM#301.	150
PnA48	1816	—	Heller. Silver. KM#301.	150
Pn51	1837	—	Heller. Silver. KM#310.	150
PnA51	1820	—	Heller. Silver. KM#301.	150
PnB51	1836	—	Heller. Silver.	150
Pn52	1838	—	Heller. Silver. KM#310.	150
Pn53	1839	—	1/2 Gulden.	—
Pn54	1839	—	Gulden. Silver. Proof	2,500
Pn55	1848	—	2 Gulden. Gold. KM#333.	—
PnA55	1847	—	1/2 Gulden. Gold. Proof. KM#330.	—
Pn56	1849	—	2 Gulden. Gold. KM#341.1.	—
Pn57	1852	—	Heller. Copper. KM#351.	—
PnA57	1852	—	Heller. Silver. KM#351.	—
Pn58	1852	—	6 Kreuzer. Silver. KM#350.	—
PnA58	1857	—	Heller. Silver. KM#351.	—

FRIEDBERG

The fortified town of Friedberg, located in Hesse about 14 miles north of Frankfurt am Main, dates from Roman times. It attained free status in 1211 and was the site of an imperial mint until the mid-13th century. In 1349 Friedberg passed to the countship of Schwarzburg, losing its free status shortly thereafter. Local nobles began electing one among themselves to the office of burgrave-for-life. The burgraves obtained the mint right in 1541 and recognized only the emperor as overlord. In 1802 Friedberg passed in fief to Hesse-Darmstadt and was mediatized in 1818.

RULERS
Johann Maria Rudolph von Waldbott Bassenheim, 1777-1805
Clemens August von Westphalen, 1805-1818

MINT OFFICIALS' INITIALS

Initial	Date	Name
GB (F) GH	1790-1833	Johann Georg Bunsen in Frankfurt
	1798-1816	Georg Hille, warden in Frankfurt

IMPERIAL CITY

REGULAR COINAGE

KM# 75 THALER
Silver **Ruler:** Johann Maria Rudolph **Obv:** Titles of Francis II
Note: Convention Thaler. Legend varieties exist.

Date	Mintage	F	VF	XF	Unc	BU
1804 GB(F)GH	—	200	350	700	1,450	—

FURSTENBERG

A noble family with holdings in Baden and Württemberg. The lord of Furstenberg assumed the title of Count in the 13th century, which was raised to the rank of Prince in 1664. The Furstenberg possessions were mediatized in 1806.

FURSTENBERG-STUHLINGEN

RULERS
Karl Joachim, 1796-1804
Carl Egon, 1804-1854

MINT MARKS
G - Gunzburg

MINT OFFICIALS' INITIALS

Initials	Date	Name
CH	1784-1808	Christian Heugelin, warden in Stüttgart
ILW, W	1798-1845	Johann Ludwig Wagner, die-cutter in Stüttgart

PRINCIPALITY

REGULAR COINAGE

KM# 35 KREUZER
Copper

Date	Mintage	F	VF	XF	Unc	BU
1804 W.	40,000	25.00	60.00	135	275	—

KM# 36 3 KREUZER
1.4200 g., 0.3120 Silver .0142 oz.

Date	Mintage	F	VF	XF	Unc	BU
1804 W.	12,000	60.00	125	260	485	—

KM# 37 6 KREUZER
2.3500 g., 0.3750 Silver .0283 oz.

Date	Mintage	F	VF	XF	Unc	BU
1804 W.	6,720	65.00	135	275	525	—

KM# 38 10 KREUZER
3.8900 g., 0.5000 Silver .0625 oz.

Date	Mintage	F	VF	XF	Unc	BU
1804 W.	6,075	100	175	300	550	—

KM# 39 20 KREUZER
6.6800 g., 0.5830 Silver .1252 oz. **Obv:** Bust right **Obv. Legend:** Ends: PRINC. IN FURSTENBERG **Rev:** Crowned arms

Date	Mintage	F	VF	XF	Unc	BU
1804 W.	3,011	150	250	425	750	—

KM# 40 20 KREUZER
6.6800 g., 0.5830 Silver .1252 oz. **Obv. Legend:** Ends: PRINC FURSTENBERG

Date	Mintage	F	VF	XF	Unc	BU
1804	Inc. above	135	225	375	650	—

KM# 41 THALER
28.0600 g., 0.8330 Silver .7515 oz. **Subject:** Karl Joachim **Note:** Convention Thaler.

Date	Mintage	F	VF	XF	Unc	BU
1804 ILW//CH	388	600	1,200	2,000	4,000	—

FURTHER AUSTRIA

(Vorderoesterreich)

Name given to imperial lands in South Swabia in the 18th century. In 1805 it was divided by Baden and Bavaria.

RULERS
Franz II (Austria), 1792-1805

MINT MARKS
A - Wien
F - Hall
G - Baia Mare (Nagybanya)
H - Gunzburg

PROVINCE

REGULAR COINAGE

KM# 21 HELLER
Copper **Note:** Varieties exist with and without period after date.

Date	Mintage	VG	F	VF	XF	Unc
1801H	—	—	8.00	20.00	30.00	125
1803H	—	—	8.00	20.00	30.00	125

KM# 25 1/4 KREUTZER
1.4000 g., Copper **Ruler:** Franz II (Austria) **Rev:** Smaller lettering **Note:** Reduced weight.

Date	Mintage	F	VF	XF	Unc	BU
1801H Rare	—	—	—	—	—	—
1802H	—	10.00	25.00	50.00	125	—
1803H	—	7.50	22.50	45.00	100	—

KM# 26 1/2 KREUTZER
2.8800 g., Copper **Ruler:** Franz II (Austria)

Date	Mintage	F	VF	XF	Unc	BU
1801H Rare	—	—	—	—	—	—
1802H	—	20.00	85.00	125	185	—
1803H	—	10.00	25.00	45.00	90.00	—
1804H Rare	—	—	—	—	—	—

KM# 31 1/2 KREUTZER
2.8800 g., Copper **Ruler:** Franz II (Austria)

Date	Mintage	F	VF	XF	Unc	BU
1805H Rare	—	—	—	—	—	—

KM# 27 KREUTZER
5.7000 g., Copper **Ruler:** Franz II (Austria) **Obv. Legend:** D. G. R. I. S. ...

Date	Mintage	F	VF	XF	Unc	BU
1801H	—	4.00	12.00	25.00	50.00	—
1802H	—	4.00	12.00	25.00	50.00	—
1803H	—	4.00	12.00	25.00	50.00	—
1804H	—	4.00	12.00	25.00	50.00	—

KM# 28 3 KREUTZER
1.4100 g., 0.3120 Silver .0141 oz. **Ruler:** Franz II (Austria)

Date	Mintage	F	VF	XF	Unc	BU
1802A Rare	—	—	—	—	—	—
1802G Rare	—	—	—	—	—	—
1802H	—	10.00	25.00	50.00	100	—
1803H Rare	—	—	—	—	—	—
1804H Rare	—	—	—	—	—	—
1805H Rare	—	—	—	—	—	—

KM# 29 6 KREUTZER
2.3500 g., 0.3750 Silver .0283 oz. **Ruler:** Franz II (Austria)

Date	Mintage	F	VF	XF	Unc	BU
1802A Rare	—	—	—	—	—	—
1802G Rare	—	—	—	—	—	—
1802H	—	4.50	12.50	30.00	75.00	—
1803H	—	4.50	12.50	30.00	75.00	—
1804H	—	4.50	12.50	30.00	75.00	—
1805A	—	4.50	12.50	30.00	75.00	—
1805H	—	4.50	12.50	30.00	75.00	—

KM# 30 KREUTZER
5.7000 g., Copper **Ruler:** Franz II (Austria) **Obv. Legend:** D. G. ROM. ET. ...

Date	Mintage	F	VF	XF	Unc	BU
1804H Rare	—	—	—	—	—	—
1805H	—	4.50	12.50	28.00	55.00	—

HAMBURG

The city of Hamburg is located on the Elbe River about 75 miles from the North Sea. It was founded by Charlemagne in the 9th century. In 1241 it joined Lubeck to form the Hanseatic League. The mint right was leased to the citizens in 1292. However, the first local halfpennies had been struck almost 50 years earlier. In 1510 Hamburg was formally made a Free City, though, in fact, it had been free for about 250 years. It was occupied by the French during the Napoleonic period. In 1866 it joined the North German Confederation and became a part of the German Empire in 1871. The Hamburg coinage is almost continuous up to the time of World War I.

MINT OFFICIALS' INITIALS

Initial	Date	Name
CAIG, CAJG	1813	C.A.J. Ginquembre, French director of mint
HSK	1805-42	Hans Schierven Knoph
OHK	1761-1805	Otto Heinrich Knorre

CITY ARMS

A triple-turreted gate

FREE CITY

REGULAR COINAGE

KM# 220 DREILING (3 Pfennig; 1/4 Schilling; 1/128 Thaler)
0.5100 g., 0.1870 Silver .0030 oz. **Obv:** Castle with O.H. K. below **Rev:** "1" between rosettes

Date	Mintage	F	VF	XF	Unc	BU
1803 OHK	355,000	2.00	4.00	10.00	30.00	—

KM# 235 DREILING (3 Pfennig; 1/4 Schilling; 1/128 Thaler)
0.5100 g., 0.1870 Silver .0030 oz. **Obv:** Castle with H. S. K. below

Date	Mintage	F	VF	XF	Unc	BU
1807 HSK	384,000	1.00	3.00	6.00	25.00	—
1809 HSK	768,000	1.00	3.00	6.00	25.00	—

KM# 250 DREILING (3 Pfennig; 1/4 Schilling; 1/128 Thaler)
0.5100 g., 0.1870 Silver .0030 oz. **Rev:** "I" between dots

Date	Mintage	F	VF	XF	Unc	BU
1823 HSK	21,000	1.00	3.00	6.00	25.00	—
1832 HSK	36,000	1.00	3.00	6.00	25.00	—
1833 HSK	303,000	1.00	3.00	6.00	25.00	—
1836 HSK	293,000	1.00	3.00	6.00	25.00	—
1839 HSK	299,000	1.00	3.00	6.00	25.00	—

KM# 260 DREILING (3 Pfennig; 1/4 Schilling; 1/128 Thaler)
0.5100 g., 0.1870 Silver .0030 oz. **Obv:** Redesigned castle **Rev:** "I" between rosettes

Date	Mintage	F	VF	XF	Unc	BU
1841 HSK	554,000	1.00	3.00	6.00	25.00	—

KM# 264 DREILING (3 Pfennig; 1/4 Schilling; 1/128 Thaler)
0.5100 g., 0.1870 Silver .0030 oz. **Obv:** Without initials below castle **Obv. Legend:** ` **Rev:** "I" between five-pointed stars

Date	Mintage	F	VF	XF	Unc	BU
1846	574,000	1.00	3.00	6.00	25.00	—

KM# 270 DREILING (3 Pfennig; 1/4 Schilling; 1/128 Thaler)
0.5100 g., 0.1870 Silver .0030 oz. **Rev:** "I" between six-pointed stars

Date	Mintage	F	VF	XF	Unc	BU
1851	578,000	1.00	3.00	6.00	25.00	—

KM# 275 DREILING (3 Pfennig; 1/4 Schilling; 1/128 Thaler)
0.5100 g., 0.1870 Silver .0030 oz. **Note:** Beaded borders.

Date	Mintage	F	VF	XF	Unc	BU
1855A	320,000	1.00	2.50	5.00	25.00	—
1855	2,613,000	1.00	2.00	4.00	25.00	—

KM# 213 SECHSLING (6 Pfennig; 1/2 Schilling; 1/64 Thaler)
0.7600 g., 0.2500 Silver .0061 oz. **Obv:** Castle with O. H. K. below **Rev:** "I" between rosettes

Date	Mintage	F	VF	XF	Unc	BU
1803 OHK	182,000	1.00	3.00	6.00	40.00	—

KM# 236.1 SECHSLING (6 Pfennig; 1/2 Schilling; 1/64 Thaler)
0.7600 g., 0.2500 Silver .0061 oz. **Obv:** Small castle with H. S. K. below

Date	Mintage	F	VF	XF	Unc	BU
1807 HSK	96,000	2.00	4.00	8.00	50.00	—
1809 HSK	192,000	1.00	3.00	6.00	40.00	—
1817 HSK	48,000	2.00	4.00	8.00	50.00	—

KM# 236.2 SECHSLING (6 Pfennig; 1/2 Schilling; 1/64 Thaler)
0.7600 g., 0.2500 Silver .0061 oz. **Obv:** Large castle

Date	Mintage	F	VF	XF	Unc	BU
1823 HSK	30,000	2.00	4.00	8.00	50.00	—
1833 HSK	135,000	1.00	3.00	6.00	40.00	—
1836 HSK	155,000	1.00	3.00	6.00	40.00	—
1839 HSK	354,000	1.00	3.00	6.00	40.00	—

KM# 255 SECHSLING (6 Pfennig; 1/2 Schilling; 1/64 Thaler)
0.7600 g., 0.2500 Silver .0061 oz. **Rev:** "I" between dots

Date	Mintage	F	VF	XF	Unc	BU
1832 HSK	66,000	2.00	4.00	8.00	45.00	—

KM# 261 SECHSLING (6 Pfennig; 1/2 Schilling; 1/64 Thaler)
0.7600 g., 0.2500 Silver .0061 oz. **Obv:** Redesigned castle **Rev:** "I" between rosettes

Date	Mintage	F	VF	XF	Unc	BU
1841 HSK	293,000	1.00	3.00	6.00	40.00	—

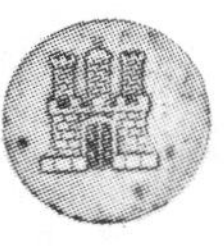

KM# 265 SECHSLING (6 Pfennig; 1/2 Schilling; 1/64 Thaler)
0.7600 g., 0.2500 Silver .0061 oz. **Obv:** Without initials below castle **Rev:** "I" between five-pointed stars

Date	Mintage	F	VF	XF	Unc	BU
1846	480,000	1.00	3.00	6.00	30.00	—

KM# 271 SECHSLING (6 Pfennig; 1/2 Schilling; 1/64 Thaler)
0.7600 g., 0.2500 Silver .0061 oz. **Rev:** "I" between six-pointed stars

Date	Mintage	F	VF	XF	Unc	BU
1851	480,000	1.00	3.00	6.00	30.00	—

KM# 276 SECHSLING (6 Pfennig; 1/2 Schilling; 1/64 Thaler)
0.7600 g., 0.2500 Silver .0061 oz. **Note:** Beaded borders

Date	Mintage	F	VF	XF	Unc	BU
1855A	98,000	2.00	4.00	8.00	35.00	—
1855	1,841,000	1.00	3.00	6.00	30.00	—

KM# 246 SCHILLING (12 Pfennig; 1/32 Thaler)
1.0800 g., 0.3750 Silver .0130 oz. **Obv:** Castle with H.S. K. below

Date	Mintage	F	VF	XF	Unc	BU
1817 HSK	19,000	2.00	6.00	12.00	60.00	—
1818 HSK	29,000	2.00	6.00	12.00	60.00	—
1819 HSK	149,000	2.00	6.00	12.00	60.00	—

KM# 251.1 SCHILLING
1.0800 g., 0.3750 Silver .0130 oz. **Rev:** "I" between dots **Rev. Legend:** HAMB. COVR.

Date	Mintage	F	VF	XF	Unc	BU
1823 HSK	138,000	1.50	3.50	8.00	35.00	—
1828 HSK	142,000	1.50	3.50	8.00	35.00	—
1832 HSK	142,000	1.50	3.50	8.00	35.00	—

KM# 251.2 SCHILLING
1.0800 g., 0.3750 Silver .0130 oz. **Rev:** "I" between rosettes

Date	Mintage	F	VF	XF	Unc	BU
1837 HSK	153,000	1.50	3.50	8.00	35.00	—
1840 HSK	144,000	1.50	3.50	8.00	35.00	—

KM# 262 SCHILLING
1.0800 g., 0.3750 Silver .0130 oz. **Obv:** Redesigned castle

Date	Mintage	F	VF	XF	Unc	BU
1841 HSK	149,000	1.50	3.50	8.00	35.00	—

KM# 266 SCHILLING
1.0800 g., 0.3750 Silver .0130 oz. **Rev:** "I" between five-pointed stars

Date	Mintage	F	VF	XF	Unc	BU
1846	240,000	1.50	3.50	8.00	35.00	—

KM# 272 SCHILLING
1.0800 g., 0.3750 Silver .0130 oz. **Rev:** "I" between six-pointed stars

Date	Mintage	F	VF	XF	Unc	BU
1851	240,000	1.50	3.50	8.00	35.00	—

KM# 277 SCHILLING
1.0800 g., 0.3750 Silver .0130 oz. **Note:** Beaded borders.

Date	Mintage	F	VF	XF	Unc	BU
1855A	112,000	1.50	2.50	7.00	25.00	—
1855	1,841,000	1.50	2.50	7.00	25.00	—

KM# 238 32 SCHILLING (2 Mark; 2/3 Thaler)
18.3200 g., 0.7500 Silver .4417 oz.

Date	Mintage	F	VF	XF	Unc	BU
1808 HSK	210,000	40.00	80.00	130	325	—

KM# 241 32 SCHILLING (2 Mark; 2/3 Thaler)
14.1700 g., 0.9680 Silver .4410 oz.

Date	Mintage	F	VF	XF	Unc	BU
1809 HSK	390,000	30.00	60.00	115	265	—

KM# 242 32 SCHILLING (2 Mark; 2/3 Thaler)
14.1700 g., 0.9680 Silver .4410 oz.

Date	Mintage	F	VF	XF	Unc	BU
1809 CAIG	3,058,000	25.00	50.00	90.00	245	—

REFORM COINAGE

KM# 290 2 MARK
11.1110 g., 0.9000 Silver .3215 oz.

Date	Mintage	F	VF	XF	Unc	BU
1876J	3,962,000	20.00	45.00	225	500	600
1877J	500,000	25.00	50.00	250	700	800
1878J	350,000	25.00	50.00	250	700	800
1880J	99,000	50.00	110	375	900	1,250
1883J	60,000	50.00	110	375	900	1,250
1888J	100,000	40.00	70.00	275	800	1,100

KM# 294 2 MARK
11.1110 g., 0.9000 Silver .3215 oz.

Date	Mintage	F	VF	XF	Unc	BU
1892J	141,000	15.00	30.00	85.00	500	600
1893J	146,000	15.00	30.00	85.00	500	600
1896J	286,000	15.00	25.00	60.00	300	400
1898J	118,000	25.00	70.00	160	600	700
1899J	286,000	15.00	25.00	70.00	250	300
1900J	577,000	15.00	25.00	60.00	200	300
Common date Proof	—	Value: 350				

KM# 287 5 MARK
27.7770 g., 0.9000 Silver .8038 oz. **Rev:** Type I

Date	Mintage	F	VF	XF	Unc	BU
1875J	286,000	30.00	60.00	400	1,250	1,750
1876J	930,000	30.00	50.00	350	1,250	1,750
1888J	40,000	45.00	125	475	1,500	2,000

KM# 291 5 MARK
1.9910 g., 0.9000 Gold .0576 oz.

Date	Mintage	F	VF	XF	Unc	BU
1877J	441,000	150	250	350	525	725
1877J Proof; Rare	—	—	—	—	—	—

KM# 293 5 MARK
27.7770 g., 0.9000 Silver .8038 oz.

Date	Mintage	F	VF	XF	Unc	BU
1891J	59,000	20.00	65.00	145	650	800
1893J	55,000	20.00	60.00	145	600	800
1894J	82,000	20.00	50.00	135	600	800
1895J	82,000	20.00	50.00	135	550	750
1896J	16,000	125	225	600	1,500	2,000

Date	Mintage	F	VF	XF	Unc	BU
1898J	176,000	20.00	50.00	125	500	600
1899J	82,000	20.00	50.00	125	600	800
1900J	172,000	20.00	40.00	90.00	500	600
Common date Proof	—	Value: 1,250				

KM# 285 10 MARK
3.9820 g., 0.9000 Gold .1152 oz. **Rev:** Type I

Date	Mintage	F	VF	XF	Unc	BU
1873B	25,000	600	1,000	1,600	3,000	4,000
1873B Proof; Rare	—	—	—	—	—	—

KM# 286 10 MARK
3.9820 g., 0.9000 Gold .1152 oz. **Rev:** Type II

Date	Mintage	F	VF	XF	Unc	BU
1874B	50,000	450	700	1,200	2,000	2,500

KM# 288 10 MARK
3.9820 g., 0.9000 Gold .1152 oz.

Date	Mintage	F	VF	XF	Unc	BU
1875J	608,000	80.00	125	200	350	450
1875J Proof	—	Value: 1,000				
1876J	6,321	550	850	1,350	1,750	2,000
1877J	221,000	80.00	125	200	350	450
1878J	316,000	80.00	125	200	350	450
1879J	255,000	80.00	125	200	350	450
1880J	139,000	80.00	125	200	350	450
1888J	163,000	80.00	125	200	350	450

KM# 292 10 MARK
3.9820 g., 0.9000 Gold .1152 oz. **Rev:** Type II

Date	Mintage	F	VF	XF	Unc	BU
1890J	245,000	80.00	150	225	350	400
1893J	246,000	80.00	150	225	350	400
1896J	164,000	80.00	150	225	350	400
1898J	344,000	80.00	150	225	350	400
1900J	82,000	80.00	150	225	350	450
1910J	—	Value: 1,200				

KM# 289 20 MARK
7.9650 g., 0.9000 Gold .2304 oz. **Rev:** Type II

Date	Mintage	F	VF	XF	Unc	BU
1875J	313,000	100	140	190	285	350
1876J	1,723,000	100	125	150	250	325
1877J	1,324,000	100	125	160	250	325
1878J	2,008,000	100	125	160	250	325
1879J	104,000	225	375	700	1,250	1,500
1880J	120,000	100	160	275	400	500
1881J	500	10,000	15,000	20,000	30,000	35,000
1883J	125,000	100	140	175	300	400
1884J	639,000	100	130	175	300	400
1887J	251,000	100	125	160	300	375
1889J	14,000	400	900	1,250	1,800	2,200

KM# 295 20 MARK
7.9650 g., 0.9000 Gold .2304 oz. **Rev:** Type III

Date	Mintage	F	VF	XF	Unc	BU
1893J	815,000	100	125	160	225	275
1894J	501,000	100	125	160	225	275
1895J	501,000	100	125	160	225	275
1897J	500,000	100	125	160	225	275
1899J	1,002,000	100	125	150	200	250
1900J	501,000	100	125	150	225	275

TRADE COINAGE

KM# 227.1 DUCAT
3.4900 g., 0.9790 Gold .1099 oz. **Obv:** Titles of Franz II

Date	Mintage	F	VF	XF	Unc	BU
1801	7,236	375	625	1,000	1,500	—
1802	9,199	375	625	1,000	1,500	—
1803	6,365	375	625	1,000	1,500	—
1804	7,284	375	625	1,000	1,500	—
1805	9,466	375	625	1,000	1,500	—

KM# 227.2 DUCAT
3.4900 g., 0.9790 Gold .1099 oz.

Date	Mintage	F	VF	XF	Unc	BU
1806	7,521	375	625	1,000	1,500	—

KM# 237 DUCAT
3.4900 g., 0.9790 Gold .1099 oz.

Date	Mintage	F	VF	XF	Unc	BU
1807	6,000	375	625	1,100	1,650	—

KM# 239 DUCAT
3.4900 g., 0.9790 Gold .1099 oz.

Date	Mintage	F	VF	XF	Unc	BU
1808	7,500	350	575	950	1,450	—
1809	7,500	300	500	875	1,400	—
1810	7,407	300	500	875	1,400	—

KM# 245 DUCAT
3.4900 g., 0.9790 Gold .1099 oz. **Obv:** Knight with lance

Date	Mintage	F	VF	XF	Unc	BU
1811	11,000	300	500	875	1,250	—
1815	9,965	300	500	875	1,250	—
1817	5,000	325	550	975	1,350	—
1818	7,000	325	550	975	1,350	—
1819	8,901	300	500	875	1,250	—
1820	7,000	300	500	875	1,250	—
1821	9,900	300	500	875	1,250	—
1822	13,000	300	500	875	1,250	—
1823	8,700	300	500	875	1,250	—
1824	6,970	300	500	875	1,250	—
1825	10,000	300	500	875	1,250	—
1826	12,000	300	500	875	1,250	—
1827	11,000	300	500	875	1,250	—
1828	8,601	300	500	875	1,250	—
1829	9,606	300	500	875	1,250	—
1830	12,000	300	500	875	1,250	—
1831	9,200	300	500	875	1,250	—
1832	9,500	300	500	875	1,250	—
1833	9,440	300	500	875	1,250	—
1834	10,000	250	400	750	1,000	—

KM# 256 DUCAT
3.4900 g., 0.9790 Gold .1099 oz. **Obv:** Knight with lance

Date	Mintage	F	VF	XF	Unc	BU
1835	10,000	250	425	750	1,150	—
1836	8,067	250	425	750	1,150	—

Date	Mintage	F	VF	XF	Unc	BU
1837	8,156	250	425	750	1,150	—
1838	9,000	250	425	750	1,150	—
1839	9,045	250	425	750	1,150	—
1840	9,882	250	425	750	1,150	—
1841	10,000	250	425	750	1,150	—
1842	12,000	225	375	625	1,000	—

KM# 263 DUCAT

3.4900 g., 0.9790 Gold .1099 oz. **Note:** Struck in a collar.

Date	Mintage	F	VF	XF	Unc	BU
1843	12,000	225	375	625	1,000	—
1844	9,768	250	425	750	1,150	—
1845	12,000	200	325	550	875	—
1846	11,000	200	325	550	875	—
1847	10,000	200	325	550	875	—
1848	13,000	200	325	550	875	—
1849	10,000	200	325	550	875	—
1850	11,000	200	325	550	875	—

KM# 273 DUCAT

3.4900 g., 0.9790 Gold .1099 oz. **Obv:** Knights shield redisigned

Date	Mintage	F	VF	XF	Unc	BU
1851	8,497	225	375	750	1,000	—
1852	9,476	225	375	750	1,000	—
1853	10,000	225	375	750	1,000	—

KM# 274 DUCAT

3.4900 g., 0.9790 Gold .1099 oz. **Rev. Legend:** Ends: ...979 MILLES

Date	Mintage	F	VF	XF	Unc	BU
1854	12,000	175	250	400	750	—
1855	11,000	175	250	400	750	—
1856	11,000	175	250	400	750	—
1857	12,000	175	250	400	750	—
1858	10,000	175	250	400	750	—
1859	14,000	175	250	400	750	—
1860	15,000	175	250	400	750	—
1861	15,000	175	250	400	750	—
1862	17,000	150	200	350	700	—
1863	20,000	150	200	350	700	—
1864	24,000	150	200	350	700	—
1865	17,000	150	200	350	700	—
1866	24,000	150	200	350	700	—
1867	26,000	150	200	350	700	—

KM# 280 DUCAT

3.4900 g., 0.9790 Gold .1099 oz. **Rev:** Mint mark B below shell

Date	Mintage	F	VF	XF	Unc	BU
1868B	25,000	135	175	300	600	—
1869B	26,000	135	175	300	600	—
1870B	30,000	135	175	300	600	—
1871B	30,000	135	175	300	600	—
1872B	30,000	135	175	300	600	—

KM# 228.1 2 DUCAT

6.9800 g., 0.9790 Gold .2197 oz. **Obv. Legend:** FRANCISVS II D. G. ROM. IMP...

Date	Mintage	F	VF	XF	Unc	BU
1801	1,273	650	1,250	1,750	2,450	—
1802	1,256	650	1,250	1,750	2,450	—
1803	837	650	1,350	2,350	3,000	—
1804	—	650	1,300	2,000	2,750	—
1805	—	650	1,250	1,750	2,450	—

Note: Mintage included in KM#227.1.

KM# 228.2 2 DUCAT

6.9800 g., 0.9790 Gold .2197 oz. **Obv. Legend:** ...D. G. R. IMP...

Date	Mintage	F	VF	XF	Unc	BU
1804	1,072	650	1,250	1,750	2,450	—
1806	1,201	650	1,250	1,750	2,450	—

KM# 240 2 DUCAT

6.9800 g., 0.9790 Gold .2197 oz.

Date	Mintage	F	VF	XF	Unc	BU
1808	1,250	500	1,000	1,500	2,150	—
1809	1,250	500	1,000	1,500	2,150	—
1810	1,050	500	1,000	1,500	2,150	—

PATTERNS

Including off metal strikes

KM#	Date	Mintage	Identification	Mkt Val
Pn15	1826 HSK	—	Schilling. Gold. KM#251.1	400
Pn16	1836 HSK	—	Sechsling. Gold. KM#236	175
Pn17	1877J	—	10 Mark. Silver. Plain edge. KM#288	—
Pn18	1877J	—	10 Mark. Copper. KM#288	—
Pn19	1882J	—	20 Mark. Silver. Plain edge. KM#288	—

HANNOVER

Located in North Central Germany, Hannover had its beginnings as early as the 12th century. The city obtained the mint right in 1331, but fell under the control of the dukes of Brunswick who later made it their residence. Hannover eventually became the capital of the Kingdom of the same name. The city coinage lasted until 1674.

MINT OFFICIALS' INITIALS

RULERS

George III, 1760-1820
Georg IV, 1820-1830
Wilhelm IV, 1830-1837
Ernst August, 1837-1851
Georg V, 1851-1866

MINT MARKS

A - Clausthal, 1832-1849
B - Hannover, 1866-1878
C - Clausthal, 1814-1833

MINT OFFICIALS' INITIALS

Initial	Date	Name
B	1817-38	Ludwig August Bruel
B	1844-68	Theodor Wilhelm Bruel
CHH, H	1802-17	Christian Heinrich Haase
LAB, LB	1817-38	Ludwig August Bruel
S	1839-44	Carl Schulter

ARMS

3-petaled flower or complex arms consisting of twin-towered city gate, 3-petaled flower in portal and rampant lion left between towers.

PROVINCIAL CITY

REGULAR COINAGE

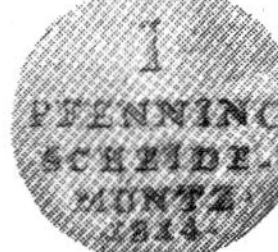

KM# 103.1 PFENNIG

Copper **Obv:** H below crowned GR monogram

Date	Mintage	F	VF	XF	Unc	BU
1814 H	—	4.00	8.00	22.00	65.00	—

KM# 103.2 PFENNIG

Copper **Obv:** C below crowned monogram

Date	Mintage	F	VF	XF	Unc	BU
1814C	—	5.00	10.00	25.00	75.00	—

KM# 104 PFENNIG

Copper

Date	Mintage	F	VF	XF	Unc	BU
1814C	—	2.50	5.00	15.00	45.00	—
1817C	—	2.50	5.00	15.00	45.00	—
1818C	—	2.50	5.00	15.00	45.00	—
1819C	—	2.50	5.00	15.00	45.00	—
1820C	—	2.50	5.00	15.00	45.00	—

KM# 125.1 PFENNIG

Copper

Date	Mintage	F	VF	XF	Unc	BU
1821C	—	3.50	6.00	18.00	50.00	—
1822C	—	2.00	4.00	10.00	30.00	—
1823C	—	2.00	4.00	10.00	30.00	—
1824C	—	2.00	4.00	10.00	30.00	—
1825C	—	2.00	4.00	10.00	30.00	—
1826C	—	2.00	4.00	10.00	30.00	—
1827	—	2.00	4.00	10.00	30.00	—
Note: Without mint mark						
1827C	—	2.00	4.00	10.00	30.00	—
1828C	—	2.00	4.00	10.00	30.00	—
1829C	—	2.00	4.00	10.00	30.00	—
1830C	—	2.00	4.00	10.00	30.00	—

KM# 125.2 PFENNIG

Copper **Rev:** B below value

Date	Mintage	F	VF	XF	Unc	BU
1826B	—	2.00	4.00	10.00	30.00	—
1828B	—	2.00	4.00	10.00	30.00	—
1829B	—	2.00	4.00	10.00	30.00	—
1830B	—	2.00	4.00	10.00	30.00	—

KM# 150.3 PFENNIG

Copper **Rev:** C below value

Date	Mintage	F	VF	XF	Unc	BU
1831/30C	—	2.00	4.50	12.00	35.00	—
1831C	—	2.00	4.00	10.00	30.00	—
1832C	—	2.00	4.00	10.00	30.00	—
1833C	—	2.00	4.00	10.00	30.00	—

KM# 150.2 PFENNIG

Copper **Rev:** B below value

Date	Mintage	F	VF	XF	Unc	BU
1832B	—	2.00	4.00	10.00	32.00	—
1833B	—	2.00	4.00	10.00	32.00	—
1834B	—	2.00	4.00	10.00	32.00	—
1835B	—	2.00	4.00	10.00	32.00	—

KM# 150.1 PFENNIG
Copper **Obv:** Date below crowned WR monogram **Rev:** A below value

Date	Mintage	F	VF	XF	Unc	BU
1832A	—	2.00	4.00	10.00	30.00	—
1833A	—	2.00	4.00	10.00	30.00	—
1834A	—	2.00	4.00	10.00	30.00	—

KM# 156 PFENNIG
Copper **Obv:** IV below WR monogram

Date	Mintage	F	VF	XF	Unc	BU
1834A	—	7.00	15.00	35.00	125	—

KM# 166.1 PFENNIG
Copper **Obv:** Crowned shield with prancing horse **Rev:** A below value

Date	Mintage	F	VF	XF	Unc	BU
1835A	—	2.00	4.00	10.00	30.00	—
1836A	—	2.00	4.00	10.00	30.00	—
1837A	—	2.00	4.00	10.00	30.00	—

KM# 166.2 PFENNIG
Copper **Rev:** B below value

Date	Mintage	F	VF	XF	Unc	BU
1835B	—	2.00	4.00	10.00	30.00	—
1836B	—	2.00	4.00	10.00	30.00	—
1837B	—	2.00	4.00	10.00	30.00	—

KM# 173.1 PFENNIG
Copper **Obv:** Crowned EAR monogram **Rev:** A below value

Date	Mintage	F	VF	XF	Unc	BU
1837A	—	2.00	4.00	10.00	30.00	—
1838A	—	2.00	4.00	10.00	30.00	—
1839A	—	2.00	4.00	10.00	30.00	—
1840A	—	2.00	4.00	10.00	30.00	—
1841A	—	2.00	4.00	10.00	30.00	—
1842A	—	2.00	4.00	10.00	30.00	—
1843A	—	2.00	4.00	10.00	30.00	—
1844A	—	2.00	4.00	10.00	30.00	—
1845A	—	2.00	4.00	10.00	30.00	—
1846A	—	2.00	4.00	10.00	30.00	—

KM# 173.2 PFENNIG
Copper **Rev:** B below value

Date	Mintage	F	VF	XF	Unc	BU
1838B	—	4.00	10.00	25.00	85.00	—

KM# 173.3 PFENNIG
Copper **Rev:** S below value

Date	Mintage	F	VF	XF	Unc	BU
1839 S	—	3.00	7.00	20.00	75.00	—
1841 S	—	3.00	7.00	20.00	75.00	—
1842 S	—	3.00	7.00	20.00	75.00	—

KM# 176 PFENNIG
Copper **Obv:** Date below monogram **Rev:** SCHEIDEMUNZE below value, B mint mark

Date	Mintage	F	VF	XF	Unc	BU
1838B	—	20.00	40.00	75.00	220	—

KM# 201.1 PFENNIG
Copper **Rev:** B below value

Date	Mintage	F	VF	XF	Unc	BU
1845B	—	1.50	3.00	7.00	25.00	—
1846B	—	1.50	3.00	7.00	25.00	—
1847B	—	1.50	3.00	7.00	25.00	—
1848B	—	1.50	3.00	7.00	25.00	—
1849B	—	1.50	3.00	7.00	25.00	—
1850B	—	1.50	3.00	7.00	25.00	—
1851B	—	1.50	3.00	7.00	25.00	—

KM# 201.2 PFENNIG
Copper **Rev:** A below value

Date	Mintage	F	VF	XF	Unc	BU
1846A	—	1.50	3.00	7.00	25.00	—
1847A	—	1.50	3.00	7.00	25.00	—
1848A	—	1.50	3.00	7.00	25.00	—
1849A	—	1.50	3.00	7.00	25.00	—

KM# 216 PFENNIG
Copper **Obv:** V below monogram

Date	Mintage	F	VF	XF	Unc	BU
1852B	—	15.00	30.00	60.00	185	—

KM# 221 PFENNIG
Copper

Date	Mintage	F	VF	XF	Unc	BU
1853B	—	2.00	4.00	10.00	30.00	—
1854B	—	2.00	4.00	10.00	30.00	—
1855B	—	2.00	4.00	10.00	30.00	—
1856B	—	2.00	4.00	10.00	30.00	—

KM# 233 PFENNIG
Copper

Date	Mintage	F	VF	XF	Unc	BU
1858B	—	1.50	3.00	7.00	25.00	—
1859B	—	1.50	3.00	7.00	25.00	—
1860B	—	1.50	3.00	7.00	25.00	—
1861B	—	1.50	3.00	7.00	25.00	—
1862B	—	1.50	3.00	7.00	25.00	—
1863B	2,324,000	1.50	3.00	7.00	25.00	—
1864B	—	1.50	3.00	7.00	25.00	—

KM# 115 2 PFENNIG
Copper **Obv:** Crowned GR monogram, date below **Rev:** Value

Date	Mintage	F	VF	XF	Unc	BU
1817C	—	5.00	10.00	25.00	100	—
1818C	—	5.00	10.00	25.00	100	—

KM# 126.1 2 PFENNIG
Copper

Date	Mintage	F	VF	XF	Unc	BU
1821C	—	3.00	6.00	18.00	55.00	—
1822C	—	3.00	6.00	18.00	55.00	—
1823C	—	3.00	6.00	18.00	55.00	—
1824C	—	3.00	6.00	18.00	55.00	—
1825C	—	3.00	6.00	18.00	55.00	—
1826C	—	3.00	6.00	18.00	55.00	—
1827C	—	3.00	6.00	18.00	55.00	—
1828C	—	3.00	6.00	18.00	55.00	—
1829C	—	3.00	6.00	18.00	55.00	—
1830C	—	3.00	6.00	18.00	55.00	—

KM# 126.2 2 PFENNIG
Copper **Rev:** B below value

Date	Mintage	F	VF	XF	Unc	BU
1826B	154,000	5.00	10.00	25.00	85.00	—

KM# 147.1 2 PFENNIG
Copper **Obv:** Crowned WR monogram above date **Rev:** C below value

Date	Mintage	F	VF	XF	Unc	BU
1831C	—	3.50	9.00	25.00	85.00	—
1833C	—	3.50	9.00	25.00	85.00	—
1834C	—	3.50	9.00	25.00	85.00	—

KM# 147.2 2 PFENNIG
Copper **Rev:** A below value

Date	Mintage	F	VF	XF	Unc	BU
1834A	—	12.00	25.00	50.00	175	—

KM# 157 2 PFENNIG
Copper **Obv:** IV below monogram **Rev:** Date

Date	Mintage	F	VF	XF	Unc	BU
1834A	—	15.00	30.00	60.00	200	—

KM# 167.1 2 PFENNIG
Copper **Obv:** Crowned shield with prancing horse

Date	Mintage	F	VF	XF	Unc	BU
1835A	—	3.00	7.00	20.00	70.00	—
1836A	—	3.00	7.00	20.00	70.00	—
1837A	—	3.00	7.00	20.00	70.00	—

KM# 167.2 2 PFENNIG
Copper **Note:** Pearl border.

Date	Mintage	F	VF	XF	Unc	BU
1837A	—	15.00	30.00	60.00	200	—

KM# 174.1 2 PFENNIG
Copper **Obv:** Crowned EAR monogram **Rev:** Value, A below date

Date	Mintage	F	VF	XF	Unc	BU
1837A	—	2.00	4.00	12.00	45.00	—
1838A	—	2.00	4.00	12.00	45.00	—
1839A	—	2.00	4.00	12.00	45.00	—
1840A	—	2.00	4.00	12.00	45.00	—
1841A	—	2.00	4.00	12.00	45.00	—
1842A	—	2.00	4.00	12.00	45.00	—
1843A	—	2.00	4.00	12.00	45.00	—
1844A	—	2.00	4.00	12.00	45.00	—
1845A	—	2.00	4.00	12.00	45.00	—
1846A	—	2.00	4.00	12.00	45.00	—

KM# 174.2 2 PFENNIG
Copper **Rev:** S below date

Date	Mintage	F	VF	XF	Unc	BU
1842 S	—	3.00	6.00	18.00	65.00	—
1844 S	—	3.00	6.00	18.00	65.00	—

KM# 202.1 2 PFENNIG
Copper **Rev:** B below date, struck in a ring

Date	Mintage	F	VF	XF	Unc	BU
1845B	—	1.50	3.00	10.00	32.00	—
1846B	—	1.50	3.00	10.00	32.00	—
1847B	—	1.50	3.00	10.00	32.00	—
1848B	—	1.50	3.00	10.00	32.00	—
1849B	—	1.50	3.00	10.00	32.00	—
1850B	—	1.50	3.00	10.00	32.00	—
1851B	—	1.50	3.00	10.00	32.00	—

KM# 202.2 2 PFENNIG
Copper **Rev:** A below date

Date	Mintage	F	VF	XF	Unc	BU
1846A	—	1.50	3.00	10.00	32.00	—
1847A	—	1.50	3.00	10.00	32.00	—
1848A	—	1.50	3.00	10.00	32.00	—
1849A	—	1.50	3.00	10.00	32.00	—

KM# 217 2 PFENNIG
Copper **Rev:** B below date

Date	Mintage	F	VF	XF	Unc	BU
1852B	—	1.25	2.50	8.00	30.00	—
1853B	—	1.25	2.50	8.00	30.00	—
1854B	—	1.25	2.50	8.00	30.00	—
1855B	—	1.25	2.50	8.00	30.00	—
1856B	—	1.25	2.50	8.00	30.00	—

KM# 234 2 PFENNIG
Copper

Date	Mintage	F	VF	XF	Unc	BU
1858B	—	1.25	2.50	7.00	28.00	—
1859B	—	1.25	2.50	7.00	28.00	—
1860B	—	1.25	2.50	7.00	28.00	—
1861B	—	1.25	2.50	7.00	28.00	—
1862B	—	1.25	2.50	7.00	28.00	—
1863B	607,000	1.25	2.50	7.00	28.00	—
1864B	—	1.25	2.50	7.00	28.00	—

KM# 105.1 4 PFENNIG (1/2 Mariengroschen)
1.2300 g., 0.1870 Silver .0073 oz. **Obv:** C below crowned GR monogram **Rev. Legend:** NACH DEM REICHS FUSS

Date	Mintage	F	VF	XF	Unc	BU
1814C	—	20.00	40.00	100	250	—
1815C	—	20.00	40.00	100	250	—

KM# 105.2 4 PFENNIG (1/2 Mariengroschen)
1.2300 g., 0.1870 Silver .0073 oz. **Obv:** H below monogram

Date	Mintage	F	VF	XF	Unc	BU
1815 H	—	15.00	30.00	80.00	225	—
1816 H	—	15.00	30.00	80.00	225	—

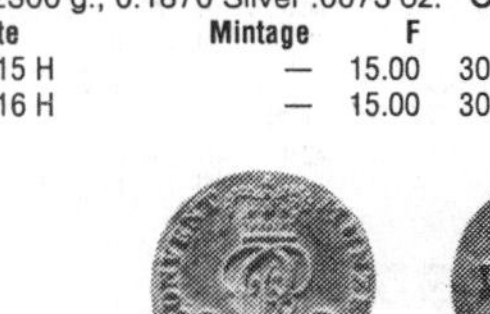

KM# 112 4 PFENNIG (1/2 Mariengroschen)
1.2300 g., 0.1870 Silver .0073 oz. **Obv. Legend:** CONVENT MUNZE

Date	Mintage	F	VF	XF	Unc	BU
1816 H	71,000	10.00	20.00	50.00	125	—
1817 H	Inc. above	10.00	20.00	50.00	125	—

KM# 135 4 PFENNIG (1/2 Mariengroschen)
1.2300 g., 0.1870 Silver .0073 oz. **Obv:** IV below monogram **Obv. Legend:** CONVENTIONS MUNZE.

Date	Mintage	F	VF	XF	Unc	BU
1822 B	—	6.00	12.00	25.00	65.00	—
1826 B	—	6.00	12.00	25.00	65.00	—
1828 B	—	6.00	12.00	25.00	65.00	—
1830 B	—	6.00	12.00	25.00	65.00	—

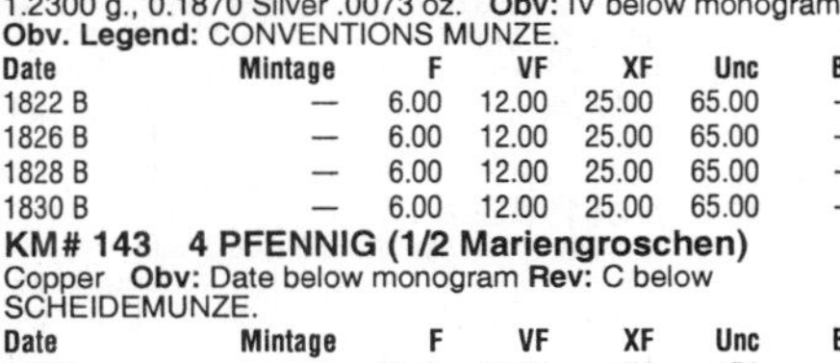

KM# 143 4 PFENNIG (1/2 Mariengroschen)
Copper **Obv:** Date below monogram **Rev:** C below SCHEIDEMUNZE.

Date	Mintage	F	VF	XF	Unc	BU
1827C	—	50.00	90.00	150	350	—

KM# 148 4 PFENNIG (1/2 Mariengroschen)
Copper

Date	Mintage	F	VF	XF	Unc	BU
1831C	—	30.00	60.00	120	300	—

KM# 168 4 PFENNIG (1/2 Mariengroschen)
0.9200 g., 0.2180 Silver .0064 oz. **Rev:** B below date

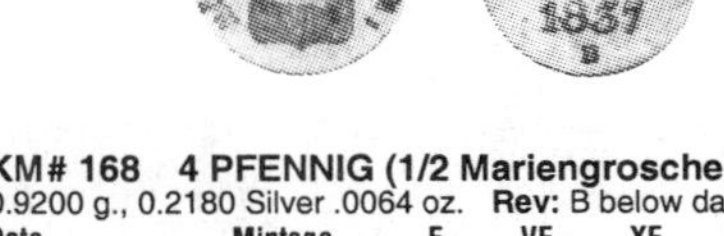

Date	Mintage	F	VF	XF	Unc	BU
1835B	—	2.00	4.00	12.00	35.00	—
1836B	—	2.00	4.00	12.00	35.00	—
1837B	—	2.00	4.00	12.00	35.00	—

KM# 177.1 4 PFENNIG (1/2 Mariengroschen)
0.9200 g., 0.2180 Silver .0064 oz.

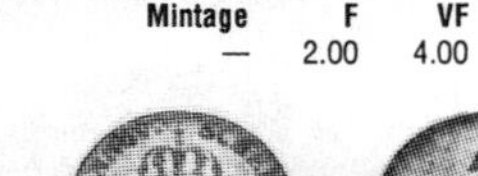

Date	Mintage	F	VF	XF	Unc	BU
1838B	—	2.00	4.00	10.00	32.00	—

KM# 177.2 4 PFENNIG (1/2 Mariengroschen)
0.9200 g., 0.2180 Silver .0064 oz. **Rev:** S below date

Date	Mintage	F	VF	XF	Unc	BU
1840 S	—	2.00	4.00	10.00	32.00	—
1841 S	—	2.00	4.00	10.00	32.00	—
1842 S	—	2.00	4.00	10.00	32.00	—

KM# 198.1 6 PFENNIG
1.3900 g., 0.2180 Silver .0097 oz. **Obv:** Crowned shield with prancing horse **Rev:** S below value

Date	Mintage	F	VF	XF	Unc	BU
1843 S	—	3.00	7.00	18.00	55.00	—
1844 S	—	3.00	7.00	18.00	55.00	—

KM# 198.2 6 PFENNIG
1.3900 g., 0.2180 Silver .0097 oz. **Rev:** B below value

Date	Mintage	F	VF	XF	Unc	BU
1844B	—	3.00	7.00	16.00	45.00	—
1845B	—	3.00	7.00	16.00	45.00	—
1846B	—	3.00	7.00	16.00	45.00	—

KM# 205 6 PFENNIG
1.3900 g., 0.2180 Silver .0097 oz.

Date	Mintage	F	VF	XF	Unc	BU
1846B	—	2.00	3.50	9.00	30.00	—
1847B	—	2.00	3.50	9.00	30.00	—
1848B	—	2.00	3.50	9.00	30.00	—
1849B	—	2.00	3.50	9.00	30.00	—
1850B	—	2.00	3.50	9.00	30.00	—
1851B	—	2.00	3.50	9.00	30.00	—

KM# 218 6 PFENNIG
1.3900 g., 0.2180 Silver .0097 oz.

Date	Mintage	F	VF	XF	Unc	BU
1852B	—	2.00	3.50	9.00	32.00	—
1853B	—	2.00	3.50	9.00	32.00	—
1854B	—	2.00	3.50	9.00	32.00	—
1855B	—	2.00	3.50	9.00	32.00	—

KM# 106 MARIENGROSCHEN (1/36 Thaler)
1.4800 g., 0.3120 Silver .0148 oz. **Obv:** C below crowned GR monogram **Rev:** Value **Rev. Legend:** NACH DEM REICHFUSS

Date	Mintage	F	VF	XF	Unc	BU
1814C	—	15.00	35.00	85.00	200	—

KM# 113 MARIENGROSCHEN (1/36 Thaler)
1.4800 g., 0.3120 Silver .0148 oz. **Rev:** H below date

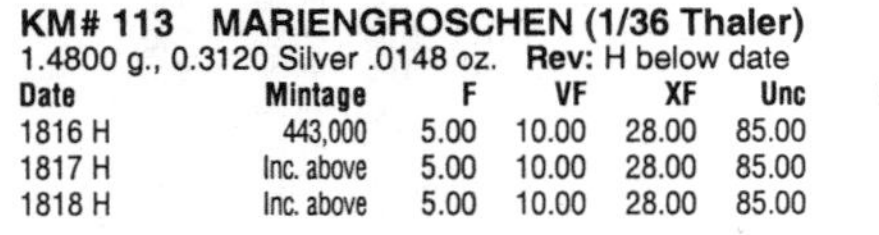

Date	Mintage	F	VF	XF	Unc	BU
1816 H	443,000	5.00	10.00	28.00	85.00	—
1817 H	Inc. above	5.00	10.00	28.00	85.00	—
1818 H	Inc. above	5.00	10.00	28.00	85.00	—

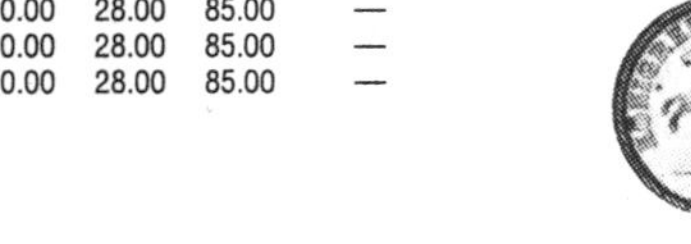

KM# 114.1 3 MARIENGROSCHEN
3.3400 g., 0.4370 Silver .0469 oz. **Obv. Legend:** CONVENTIONSMUNZE. **Rev:** C.H.H. below ledge

Date	Mintage	F	VF	XF	Unc	BU
1816 CHH	—	6.00	15.00	40.00	100	—
1817 CHH	—	6.00	15.00	40.00	100	—
1818 CHH	12,000,000	6.00	15.00	40.00	100	—

KM# 114.2 3 MARIENGROSCHEN
3.3400 g., 0.4370 Silver .0469 oz. **Rev:** L.A.B. below ledge

Date	Mintage	F	VF	XF	Unc	BU
1819 LAB	—	6.00	15.00	40.00	100	—
1820 LAB	Inc. above	6.00	15.00	40.00	100	—

KM# 114.3 3 MARIENGROSCHEN
3.3400 g., 0.4370 Silver .0469 oz. **Rev:** L.B. below ledge

Date	Mintage	F	VF	XF	Unc	BU
1819 LB	Inc. above	6.00	15.00	40.00	100	—
1820 LB	—	6.00	15.00	40.00	100	—

KM# 120 3 MARIENGROSCHEN
3.3400 g., 0.4370 Silver .0469 oz.

Date	Mintage	F	VF	XF	Unc	BU
1820 LB	—	6.00	15.00	40.00	100	—
1821 LB	Inc. above	6.00	15.00	40.00	100	—

KM# 107 1/24 THALER
1.9400 g., 0.3120 Silver .0194 oz. **Obv:** Date below prancing horse **Rev:** Value **Rev. Legend:** NACH DEM REICHFUSS

Date	Mintage	F	VF	XF	Unc	BU
1814C	—	7.00	15.00	40.00	150	—

KM# 116 1/24 THALER
1.9400 g., 0.3120 Silver .0194 oz.

Date	Mintage	F	VF	XF	Unc	BU
1817 H	946,000	5.00	10.00	30.00	120	—
1818	—	5.00	10.00	30.00	120	—

KM# 141 1/24 THALER
1.9400 g., 0.3120 Silver .0194 oz. **Obv:** IV below monogram

Date	Mintage	F	VF	XF	Unc	BU
1826B	139,000	4.00	7.00	15.00	60.00	—
1827B	328,000	4.00	7.00	15.00	60.00	—
1828B	904,000	4.00	7.00	15.00	60.00	—

KM# 235 1/2 GROSCHEN
1.0900 g., 0.2200 Silver .0077 oz.

Date	Mintage	F	VF	XF	Unc	BU
1858B	—	2.00	3.50	7.50	28.00	—
1859B	—	2.00	3.50	7.50	28.00	—
1861B	—	2.00	3.50	7.50	28.00	—
1862B	—	2.00	3.50	7.50	28.00	—
1863B	47,000	2.00	3.50	7.50	28.00	—
1864B	—	2.00	3.50	7.50	28.00	—
1865B	—	2.00	3.50	7.50	28.00	—

KM# 236 GROSCHEN
2.1900 g., 0.2200 Silver .0154 oz.

Date	Mintage	F	VF	XF	Unc	BU
1858B	—	2.00	3.50	7.50	28.00	—
1859B	—	2.00	3.50	7.50	28.00	—
1860B	—	2.00	3.50	7.50	28.00	—
1861B	—	2.00	3.50	7.50	28.00	—
1862B	—	2.00	3.50	7.50	28.00	—
1863B	69,000	2.00	3.50	7.50	28.00	—
1864B	—	2.00	3.50	7.50	28.00	—
1865B	—	2.00	3.50	7.50	28.00	—
1866B	76,000	2.00	3.50	7.50	28.00	—

KM# 121.1 16 GUTE GROSCHEN
11.7700 g., 0.9930 Silver .3758 oz. **Obv:** Prancing horse with M on ledge **Obv. Legend:** GEORGIUS. III. D. G. BRITAN. &. HANNOV. REX.

Date	Mintage	F	VF	XF	Unc	BU
1820	—	150	250	375	850	—

KM# 121.2 16 GUTE GROSCHEN
11.7700 g., 0.9930 Silver .3758 oz. **Obv. Legend:** GEORGIUS. III. D. G. BRITANNIARUM.

Date	Mintage	F	VF	XF	Unc	BU
1820	—	125	200	325	750	—

KM# 122 16 GUTE GROSCHEN
11.7700 g., 0.9930 Silver .3758 oz. **Obv:** Prancing horse, M on ledge, XX.EINE.F.MARK. below **Obv. Legend:** GEORGIUS. IV. D. G. BRITAN. & HANNOV. REX. **Rev:** Value, CONVENTIONS-MUNZE. below

Date	Mintage	F	VF	XF	Unc	BU
1820	—	30.00	60.00	120	185	—

KM# 123 16 GUTE GROSCHEN
11.7700 g., 0.9930 Silver .3758 oz. **Obv:** XX.E.F. MARK below ledge **Rev. Legend:** CONV-MUNZE FEIN SILBER.

Date	Mintage	F	VF	XF	Unc	BU
1820	—	30.00	55.00	100	175	—

KM# 124 16 GUTE GROSCHEN
11.7700 g., 0.9930 Silver .3758 oz. **Obv:** XX. EINE. F. MARK. below ledge

Date	Mintage	F	VF	XF	Unc	BU
1820	—	25.00	45.00	80.00	145	—

KM# 127 16 GUTE GROSCHEN
11.7700 g., 0.9930 Silver .3758 oz. **Obv:** XX. E. F. MARK. below ledge **Rev:** FEIN SILB.

Date	Mintage	F	VF	XF	Unc	BU
1821	—	25.00	45.00	75.00	135	—

KM# 128 16 GUTE GROSCHEN
11.7700 g., 0.9930 Silver .3758 oz. **Rev:** CONV MUNZE FEIN SILB around bottom **Note:** Seven obverse legend varieties exist.

Date	Mintage	F	VF	XF	Unc	BU
1821	—	30.00	60.00	125	200	—

KM# 136 16 GUTE GROSCHEN
11.7700 g., 0.9930 Silver .3758 oz. **Rev:** FEINES SILB below GROSCHEN **Note:** Two obverse legend varieties exist.

Date	Mintage	F	VF	XF	Unc	BU
1822	—	30.00	60.00	125	200	—

KM# 137 16 GUTE GROSCHEN
11.7700 g., 0.9930 Silver .3758 oz. **Note:** Two obverse legend varieties exist.

Date	Mintage	F	VF	XF	Unc	BU
1822	—	30.00	55.00	100	175	—

KM# 138 16 GUTE GROSCHEN
11.7700 g., 0.9930 Silver .3758 oz. **Note:** Two obverse legend varieties exist for 1822, 1823, and 1825.

Date	Mintage	F	VF	XF	Unc	BU
1822	—	20.00	30.00	65.00	140	—
1823	—	20.00	30.00	65.00	140	—
1824	—	20.00	30.00	65.00	140	—
1825	—	20.00	30.00	65.00	140	—
1826	—	20.00	30.00	65.00	140	—
1827	—	20.00	30.00	65.00	140	—
1828	—	20.00	30.00	65.00	140	—
1829	—	20.00	30.00	65.00	140	—
1830	—	20.00	30.00	65.00	140	—

KM# 145.1 16 GUTE GROSCHEN
11.7700 g., 0.9930 Silver .3758 oz.

Date	Mintage	F	VF	XF	Unc	BU
1830	—	20.00	30.00	65.00	140	—

KM# 145.2 16 GUTE GROSCHEN
11.7700 g., 0.9930 Silver .3758 oz.

Date	Mintage	F	VF	XF	Unc	BU
1831	—	20.00	30.00	65.00	140	—
1832	—	20.00	30.00	65.00	140	—
1832A	—	20.00	30.00	65.00	140	—

KM# 145.3 16 GUTE GROSCHEN
11.7700 g., 0.9930 Silver .3758 oz. **Obv:** With "L" on ledge

Date	Mintage	F	VF	XF	Unc	BU
1832A	—	20.00	30.00	65.00	140	—
1833A	—	20.00	30.00	65.00	140	—
1834A	—	20.00	30.00	65.00	140	—

KM# 145.4 16 GUTE GROSCHEN
11.7700 g., 0.9930 Silver .3758 oz. **Obv:** With "M" on ledge

Date	Mintage	F	VF	XF	Unc	BU
1832A	—	20.00	30.00	65.00	140	—

KM# 145.5 16 GUTE GROSCHEN
11.7700 g., 0.9930 Silver .3758 oz. **Obv:** With "W" on ledge

Date	Mintage	F	VF	XF	Unc	BU
1834A	—	20.00	30.00	65.00	140	—

KINGDOM

REGULAR COINAGE

KM# 158.1 1/24 THALER
1.9400 g., 0.3120 Silver .0194 oz. **Rev:** B below date

Date	Mintage	F	VF	XF	Unc	BU
1834B	—	3.00	6.00	12.50	50.00	—
1834.B.	—	—	—	—	—	—
1835B	—	3.00	6.00	12.50	50.00	—
1836B	—	3.00	6.00	12.50	50.00	—
1837B	—	3.00	6.00	12.50	50.00	—

KM# 158.2 1/24 THALER
1.9400 g., 0.3120 Silver .0194 oz. **Rev:** A below date

Date	Mintage	F	VF	XF	Unc	BU
1835A	—	4.50	9.00	20.00	70.00	—
1836A	—	4.50	9.00	20.00	70.00	—

KM# 178.1 1/24 THALER
1.9400 g., 0.3120 Silver .0194 oz. **Rev:** B below date

Date	Mintage	F	VF	XF	Unc	BU
1838B	—	2.50	6.00	12.00	40.00	—

KM# 178.2 1/24 THALER
1.9400 g., 0.3120 Silver .0194 oz. **Rev:** S below date

Date	Mintage	F	VF	XF	Unc	BU
1839 S	—	2.50	6.00	12.00	40.00	—
1841 S	—	2.50	6.00	12.00	40.00	—
1842 S	—	2.50	6.00	12.00	40.00	—

KM# 178.3 1/24 THALER
1.9400 g., 0.3120 Silver .0194 oz. **Rev:** A below date

Date	Mintage	F	VF	XF	Unc	BU
1839A	—	2.50	6.00	12.50	50.00	—
1840A	—	2.50	6.00	12.50	50.00	—
1841A	—	2.50	6.00	12.50	50.00	—
1842A	—	2.50	6.00	12.50	50.00	—
1843A	—	2.50	6.00	12.50	50.00	—
1844A	—	2.50	6.00	12.50	50.00	—
1845A	—	2.50	6.00	12.50	50.00	—
1846A	—	2.50	6.00	12.50	50.00	—

KM# 203 1/24 THALER
1.9400 g., 0.3120 Silver .0194 oz. **Obv:** B below prancing horse **Rev:** Value, SCHEIDEMUNZE

Date	Mintage	F	VF	XF	Unc	BU
1845B	—	2.50	6.00	12.50	50.00	—
1846B	—	2.50	6.00	12.50	50.00	—

KM# 227 1/24 THALER
1.9400 g., 0.3120 Silver .0194 oz. **Obv. Legend:** NEC ASPERA TERRENT

Date	Mintage	F	VF	XF	Unc	BU
1854B	—	2.50	6.00	12.00	40.00	—
1855B	—	2.50	6.00	12.00	40.00	—
1856B	—	2.50	6.00	12.00	40.00	—

KM# 108 1/12 THALER (3 Mariengroschen)
3.2400 g., 0.4370 Silver .0455 oz. **Obv:** Prancing horse, "S" on ledge **Rev:** Value **Rev. Legend:** NACH DEM REICHS FUSS

Date	Mintage	F	VF	XF	Unc	BU
1814C	—	7.00	18.00	55.00	150	—
1815C	—	7.00	18.00	55.00	150	—
1816C	—	7.00	18.00	55.00	150	—

KM# 139 1/12 THALER (3 Mariengroschen)
3.2400 g., 0.4370 Silver .0455 oz.

Date	Mintage	F	VF	XF	Unc	BU
1822 LB	1,908,000	5.00	15.00	40.00	100	—
1823 L.B.	1,900,000	5.00	15.00	40.00	100	—
1823 LB	Inc. above	5.00	15.00	40.00	100	—
1824 LB	502,000	5.00	15.00	40.00	100	—

KM# 159 1/12 THALER (3 Mariengroschen)
2.6700 g., 0.5200 Silver .0446 oz. **Obv:** B below head

Date	Mintage	F	VF	XF	Unc	BU
1834B	—	5.00	15.00	40.00	100	—
1835B	—	5.00	15.00	40.00	100	—
1836B	—	5.00	15.00	40.00	100	—
1837B	—	5.00	15.00	40.00	100	—

KM# 179.1 1/12 THALER (3 Mariengroschen)
2.6700 g., 0.5200 Silver .0446 oz. **Obv:** Ernst August, B behind head

Date	Mintage	F	VF	XF	Unc	BU
1838B	—	5.00	15.00	40.00	100	—

KM# 179.2 1/12 THALER (3 Mariengroschen)
2.6700 g., 0.5200 Silver .0446 oz. **Obv:** S below head

Date	Mintage	F	VF	XF	Unc	BU
1839 S	—	5.00	15.00	40.00	100	—
1840 S	—	5.00	15.00	40.00	100	—

KM# 194.1 1/12 THALER (3 Mariengroschen)
2.6700 g., 0.5200 Silver .0446 oz.

Date	Mintage	F	VF	XF	Unc	BU
1841 S	—	4.00	10.00	25.00	70.00	—
1842 S	—	4.00	10.00	25.00	70.00	—
1843 S	—	4.00	10.00	25.00	70.00	—
1844 S	—	4.00	10.00	25.00	70.00	—

KM# 194.2 1/12 THALER (3 Mariengroschen)
2.6700 g., 0.5200 Silver .0446 oz. **Obv:** B below head

Date	Mintage	F	VF	XF	Unc	BU
1844B	—	3.50	8.00	20.00	60.00	—
1845B	—	3.50	8.00	20.00	60.00	—
1846B	—	3.50	8.00	20.00	60.00	—
1847B	—	3.50	8.00	20.00	60.00	—

KM# 206 1/12 THALER (3 Mariengroschen)
2.6700 g., 0.5200 Silver .0446 oz. **Obv:** Larger head

Date	Mintage	F	VF	XF	Unc	BU
1848B	—	3.50	7.50	15.00	45.00	—
1849B	—	3.50	7.50	15.00	45.00	—
1850B	—	3.50	7.50	15.00	45.00	—
1851B	—	3.50	7.50	15.00	45.00	—

KM# 219 1/12 THALER (3 Mariengroschen)
2.6700 g., 0.5200 Silver .0446 oz. **Obv:** BREHMER F at truncation

Date	Mintage	F	VF	XF	Unc	BU
1852B	—	3.50	7.50	15.00	45.00	—
1853B	—	3.50	7.50	15.00	45.00	—

KM# 237 1/12 THALER (3 Mariengroschen)
3.2200 g., 0.3750 Silver .0388 oz. **Obv:** Without name at truncation **Rev:** Value: SCHEIDEMUNZE

Date	Mintage	F	VF	XF	Unc	BU
1859B	—	5.00	15.00	45.00	120	—
1860B	—	5.00	15.00	45.00	120	—
1862B	—	5.00	15.00	45.00	120	—

KM# 129 1/6 THALER
5.8500 g., 0.5000 Silver .0940 oz. **Obv:** B below ledge

Date	Mintage	F	VF	XF	Unc	BU
1821B	150,000	15.00	30.00	75.00	225	—

KM# 160 1/6 THALER
5.3500 g., 0.5200 Silver .0895 oz.

Date	Mintage	F	VF	XF	Unc	BU
1834	360,000	20.00	40.00	85.00	250	—

KM# 190 1/6 THALER
5.3500 g., 0.5200 Silver .0895 oz. **Obv:** S below larger head **Rev:** Crowned arms on cartouche

Date	Mintage	F	VF	XF	Unc	BU
1840 S	457,000	20.00	40.00	85.00	250	—

KM# 195 1/6 THALER
5.3500 g., 0.5200 Silver .0895 oz. **Rev:** Shield with square corners

Date	Mintage	F	VF	XF	Unc	BU
1841 S	Inc. above	20.00	40.00	85.00	250	—

KM# 199 1/6 THALER
5.3500 g., 0.5200 Silver .0895 oz.

Date	Mintage	F	VF	XF	Unc	BU
1844B	Inc. above	20.00	40.00	85.00	250	—
1845B	Inc. above	20.00	40.00	85.00	250	—
1847B	Inc. above	20.00	40.00	85.00	250	—

KM# 238 1/6 THALER
5.3400 g., 0.5200 Silver .0893 oz.

Date	Mintage	F	VF	XF	Unc	BU
1859B	—	12.00	20.00	35.00	85.00	—
1860B	—	12.00	20.00	35.00	85.00	—
1862B	—	12.00	20.00	35.00	85.00	—
1863B	87,000	12.00	20.00	35.00	85.00	—
1866B	5,904	30.00	50.00	90.00	165	—

KM# 100.1 2/3 THALER
13.0800 g., 0.9930 Silver .4176 oz.

Date	Mintage	F	VF	XF	Unc	BU
1813C	—	45.00	100	150	250	—
1814C	—	45.00	100	150	250	—

KM# 100.2 2/3 THALER
13.0800 g., 0.9930 Silver .4176 oz. **Obv:** M below truncation

Date	Mintage	F	VF	XF	Unc	BU
1814	—	50.00	110	175	275	—

KM# 140 2/3 THALER
13.0800 g., 0.9930 Silver .4176 oz. **Note:** Several varieties exist.

Date	Mintage	F	VF	XF	Unc	BU
1822C	—	40.00	80.00	125	250	—
1823C	—	40.00	80.00	125	250	—
1824C	—	40.00	80.00	125	250	—
1825C	—	40.00	80.00	125	250	—
1826C	—	40.00	80.00	125	250	—
1827C	—	40.00	80.00	125	250	—
1828C	—	40.00	80.00	125	250	—
1829C	—	40.00	80.00	125	250	—

KM# 142 2/3 THALER
17.3200 g., 0.7500 Silver .4177 oz. **Rev:** Value: 18 STUCK EINE MARK FEIN

Date	Mintage	F	VF	XF	Unc	BU
1826B	—	55.00	125	250	450	—
1827B	—	55.00	125	250	450	—
1828B	—	55.00	125	250	450	—

KM# 151 2/3 THALER
13.0800 g., 0.9930 Silver .4176 oz. **Obv:** Ribbon inscribed HONI SOIT QUI MAL Y PENSE

Date	Mintage	F	VF	XF	Unc	BU
1832	—	37.50	80.00	135	250	—
1833	—	37.50	80.00	135	250	—

KM# 154 2/3 THALER
13.0800 g., 0.9930 Silver .4176 oz. **Rev:** Similar to KM#151

Date	Mintage	F	VF	XF	Unc	BU
1833A	50,000	150	265	450	750	—

KM# 161.1 2/3 THALER
13.0800 g., 0.9930 Silver .4176 oz.

Date	Mintage	F	VF	XF	Unc	BU
1834A	Inc. above	135	250	385	650	—

KM# 161.2 2/3 THALER
13.0800 g., 0.9930 Silver .4176 oz. **Obv:** Raised edge and circle of dots around legend, struck in collar **Rev:** Raised edge and circle of dots around legend, struck in collar

Date	Mintage	F	VF	XF	Unc	BU
1834A	Inc. above	—	—	—	—	—

KM# 162 2/3 THALER
13.0800 g., 0.9930 Silver .4176 oz.

Date	Mintage	F	VF	XF	Unc	BU
1834A	Inc. above	550	750	1,250	1,750	—

KM# 163 2/3 THALER
13.0800 g., 0.9930 Silver .4176 oz. **Rev:** AUSBEUTE DER GRUBE

Date	Mintage	F	VF	XF	Unc	BU
1834A	Inc. above	1,350	2,000	3,000	4,500	—

KM# 180 2/3 THALER
13.0800 g., 0.9930 Silver .4176 oz. **Obv:** Different head right, A below

Date	Mintage	F	VF	XF	Unc	BU
1838A	—	50.00	110	250	375	—
1839A	—	50.00	110	250	375	—

KM# 146.1 THALER
23.5400 g., 0.9930 Silver .7516 oz. **Subject:** Silver Mines of Clausthal **Rev:** Large date

Date	Mintage	F	VF	XF	Unc	BU
1830	—	400	650	1,150	2,250	—

KM# 146.2 THALER
23.5400 g., 0.9930 Silver .7516 oz. **Rev:** Flat-topped 3 in small date

Date	Mintage	F	VF	XF	Unc	BU
1830	—	400	650	1,150	2,250	—

KM# 164 THALER
22.2700 g., 0.7500 Silver .5370 oz.

Date	Mintage	F	VF	XF	Unc	BU
1834B	44,000	40.00	115	350	1,000	—

KM# 165 THALER
16.8200 g., 0.9930 Silver .5370 oz.

Date	Mintage	F	VF	XF	Unc	BU
1834A	—	45.00	100	325	850	—
1835A	—	45.00	90.00	250	700	—

KM# 169 THALER
16.8200 g., 0.9930 Silver .5370 oz. **Subject:** Wilhelm IV

Date	Mintage	F	VF	XF	Unc	BU
1835A	—	70.00	100	375	900	—
1836A	—	30.00	50.00	150	450	—
1837A	—	30.00	50.00	150	450	—

KM# 172 THALER
22.2700 g., 0.7500 Silver .5370 oz.

Date	Mintage	F	VF	XF	Unc	BU
1836B	—	70.00	100	300	800	—

KM# 181 THALER

16.8200 g., 0.9930 Silver .5370 oz. **Subject:** Ernst August V

Date	Mintage	F	VF	XF	Unc	BU
1838A	—	35.00	75.00	185	500	—
1839A	—	35.00	75.00	185	500	—

KM# 182 THALER

16.8200 g., 0.9930 Silver .5370 oz.

Date	Mintage	F	VF	XF	Unc	BU
1838A	—	35.00	75.00	185	500	—
1839A	—	35.00	75.00	185	500	—
1840A	—	45.00	90.00	225	600	—

KM# 184 THALER

16.8200 g., 0.9930 Silver .5370 oz. **Subject:** King's Visit to Clausthal Mint

Date	Mintage	F	VF	XF	Unc	BU
1839A	—	150	250	450	700	—

KM# 191 THALER

16.8200 g., 0.9930 Silver .5370 oz. **Obv:** Similar to KM#182

Date	Mintage	F	VF	XF	Unc	BU
1840A Rare	—	—	—	—	—	—

KM# 192 THALER

16.8200 g., 0.9930 Silver .5370 oz.

Date	Mintage	F	VF	XF	Unc	BU
1840A	—	40.00	70.00	175	450	—
1841A	—	40.00	70.00	175	450	—

KM# 193 THALER

16.8200 g., 0.9930 Silver .5370 oz. **Obv:** S below truncation

Date	Mintage	F	VF	XF	Unc	BU
1840 S	—	75.00	150	500	1,300	—

KM# 196 THALER

16.8200 g., 0.9930 Silver .5370 oz. **Obv:** BRANDT F. at truncation

Date	Mintage	F	VF	XF	Unc	BU
1841 S	—	40.00	80.00	200	625	—

KM# 197.1 THALER

16.8200 g., 0.9930 Silver .5370 oz. **Obv:** A below head

Date	Mintage	F	VF	XF	Unc	BU
1842A	620,000	20.00	40.00	135	325	—
1843A	638,000	22.00	50.00	175	400	—
1844A	622,000	22.00	50.00	175	400	—
1845A	656,000	22.00	50.00	175	400	—
1846A	650,000	22.00	50.00	175	400	—
1847A	625,000	20.00	40.00	135	325	—
1848A	661,000	20.00	40.00	135	325	—
1849A	357,000	22.00	50.00	175	400	—

KM# 197.2 THALER

16.8200 g., 0.9930 Silver .5370 oz. **Obv:** B below head

Date	Mintage	F	VF	XF	Unc	BU
1844B	—	45.00	85.00	200	550	—
1845B	—	25.00	50.00	135	350	—
1846B	—	45.00	85.00	200	550	—
1847B	—	50.00	90.00	250	600	—

KM# 207 THALER

16.8200 g., 0.9930 Silver .5370 oz. **Subject:** Wedding of Crown Prince Georg of Hannover and Duchess Marie of Sachsen-Altenburg

Date	Mintage	F	VF	XF	Unc	BU
1843 S	1,010	175	350	600	1,000	—

KM# 208 THALER

16.8200 g., 0.9930 Silver .5370 oz. **Obv:** BREHMER F. at truncation

Date	Mintage	F	VF	XF	Unc	BU
1848B	—	22.00	50.00	150	400	—
1849B	—	22.00	50.00	150	400	—

KM# 209.1 THALER

16.8200 g., 0.9930 Silver .5370 oz. **Rev:** HARZ SEGEN above crown

Date	Mintage	F	VF	XF	Unc	BU
1849B	—	50.00	125	300	850	—

KM# 209.2 THALER

16.8200 g., 0.9930 Silver .5370 oz. **Rev:** BERGSEGEN DES HARZES above crown

Date	Mintage	F	VF	XF	Unc	BU
1850B	712,000	22.00	50.00	100	250	—
1851B	453,000	22.00	50.00	100	250	—

KM# 220 THALER
16.8200 g., 0.9930 Silver .5370 oz.

Date	Mintage	F	VF	XF	Unc	BU
1852B	170,000	22.00	50.00	100	250	—
1853B	180,000	22.00	50.00	100	250	—
1854/3B	—	—	—	—	—	—
1854B	951,000	22.00	50.00	100	250	—
1855B	974,000	22.00	50.00	100	250	—
1856B	77,000	22.00	50.00	100	250	—

KM# 230 THALER
18.5200 g., 0.9000 Silver .5360 oz.

Date	Mintage	F	VF	XF	Unc	BU
1857B	274,000	20.00	40.00	70.00	140	—
1858B	432,000	20.00	40.00	70.00	140	—
1859B	554,000	20.00	40.00	65.00	120	—
1860B	790,000	20.00	40.00	65.00	120	—
1861B	736,000	20.00	40.00	65.00	120	—
1862B	133,000	20.00	40.00	65.00	120	—
1863B	233,000	20.00	40.00	65.00	120	—
1864B	158,000	20.00	40.00	65.00	120	—
1865B	—	20.00	35.00	55.00	120	—
1866B	159,000	20.00	35.00	50.00	100	—

KM# 241 THALER
18.5200 g., 0.9000 Silver .5360 oz. **Subject:** 50th Anniversary - Battle of Waterloo

Date	Mintage	F	VF	XF	Unc	BU
1865 B	15,000	30.00	50.00	90.00	175	—

Note: This coin was given to veterans of the battle in pension payments

KM# 242 THALER
18.5200 g., 0.9000 Silver .5360 oz. **Subject:** 50th Anniversary Union East Friesia and Hannover

Date	Mintage	F	VF	XF	Unc	BU
1865B	1,000	175	300	500	850	—
1865B Proof	—	Value: 900				

KM# 243 THALER
18.5200 g., 0.9000 Silver .5360 oz. **Subject:** Frisian Oath Commemorative

Date	Mintage	F	VF	XF	Unc	BU
1865B	2,000	125	250	400	650	—

KM# 229 2 THALER (3-1/2 Gulden)
37.1200 g., 0.9000 Silver 1.0742 oz.

Date	Mintage	F	VF	XF	Unc	BU
1854B	102,000	100	150	200	350	—
1855B	842,000	90.00	125	175	325	—

KM# 240 2 THALER (3-1/2 Gulden)
37.0400 g., 0.9000 Silver 1.0719 oz.

Date	Mintage	F	VF	XF	Unc	BU
1862B	133,000	100	150	200	350	—
1866B	38,000	90.00	125	175	325	—

KM# 109 2-1/2 THALER
3.3400 g., 0.9030 Gold .0970 oz.

Date	Mintage	F	VF	XF	Unc	BU
1814 CHH	—	325	500	750	1,150	—

KM# 130 2-1/2 THALER
3.3400 g., 0.9030 Gold .0970 oz.

Date	Mintage	F	VF	XF	Unc	BU
1821B	—	225	450	675	1,100	—
1827B	—	225	450	675	1,100	—
1830B	—	225	450	675	1,100	—

KM# 152 2-1/2 THALER
3.3400 g., 0.9030 Gold .0970 oz.

Date	Mintage	F	VF	XF	Unc	BU
1832B	—	200	400	600	1,000	—
1833B	—	200	400	600	1,000	—
1835B	—	200	400	600	1,000	—

KM# 152a 2-1/2 THALER
3.3200 g., 0.8960 Gold .0956 oz.

Date	Mintage	F	VF	XF	Unc	BU
1836B	—	150	300	550	900	—
1837B	—	150	300	550	900	—

KM# 185.1 2-1/2 THALER
3.3200 g., 0.8960 Gold .0956 oz.

Date	Mintage	F	VF	XF	Unc	BU
1839 S	—	225	400	600	1,000	—
1840 S	—	225	400	600	1,000	—
1843 S	—	225	400	600	1,000	—

KM# 185.2 2-1/2 THALER
3.3200 g., 0.8960 Gold .0956 oz.

Date	Mintage	F	VF	XF	Unc	BU
1845B	—	225	400	600	1,000	—
1846B	—	225	400	600	1,000	—
1847B	—	225	400	600	1,000	—
1848B	—	225	400	600	1,000	—

KM# 215 2-1/2 THALER
3.3200 g., 0.8960 Gold .0956 oz.

Date	Mintage	F	VF	XF	Unc	BU
1850B	—	200	300	500	900	—

KM# 223 2-1/2 THALER
3.3200 g., 0.8960 Gold .0956 oz. **Obv:** BREHMER F. at truncation, B below

Date	Mintage	F	VF	XF	Unc	BU
1853B	—	250	500	1,000	1,500	—
1855B	—	175	350	700	1,000	—

KM# 101 5 THALER
6.6500 g., 0.8960 Gold .1916 oz.

Date	Mintage	F	VF	XF	Unc	BU
1813 TW	—	200	300	750	1,500	—
1814 TW	—	200	300	750	1,500	—
1815 TW	—	250	400	875	1,750	—

KM# 110 5 THALER
6.6800 g., 0.9030 Gold .1940 oz.

Date	Mintage	F	VF	XF	Unc	BU
1814C	—	825	1,200	2,000	3,250	—
1815C Rare	—	—	—	—	—	—

KM# 131 5 THALER
6.6800 g., 0.9030 Gold .1940 oz.

Date	Mintage	F	VF	XF	Unc	BU
1821C	185	1,500	2,000	3,000	7,500	—

KM# 132 5 THALER
6.6800 g., 0.9030 Gold .1940 oz.

Date	Mintage	F	VF	XF	Unc	BU
1821B	—	250	450	700	1,000	—
1825B	—	250	450	700	1,000	—
1828B	—	250	450	700	1,000	—
1829B	—	250	450	700	1,000	—
1830B	—	250	450	700	1,000	—

KM# 170 5 THALER
6.6500 g., 0.8960 Gold .1916 oz.

Date	Mintage	F	VF	XF	Unc	BU
1835B	—	350	500	750	1,500	—

KM# 186 5 THALER
6.6500 g., 0.8960 Gold .1916 oz.

Date	Mintage	F	VF	XF	Unc	BU
1839 S	—	400	700	1,000	1,800	—

KM# 204 5 THALER
6.6500 g., 0.8960 Gold .1916 oz. **Obv:** B below head

Date	Mintage	F	VF	XF	Unc	BU
1845B	—	300	500	800	1,350	—
1846B	—	375	650	1,000	1,600	—
1848B	—	375	650	1,000	1,600	—

KM# 210 5 THALER
6.6500 g., 0.8960 Gold .1916 oz.

Date	Mintage	F	VF	XF	Unc	BU
1849B	—	300	500	750	1,350	—
1851B	—	300	500	750	1,350	—

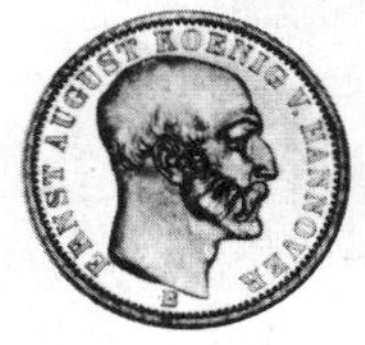

KM# 211 5 THALER
6.6500 g., 0.8960 Gold .1916 oz. **Rev:** HARZ GOLD added to legend

Date	Mintage	F	VF	XF	Unc	BU
1849B	—	350	550	800	1,400	—
1850B	—	300	500	750	1,300	—

KM# 224 5 THALER
6.6500 g., 0.8960 Gold .1916 oz. **Obv:** BREHMER F. at truncation, B below

Date	Mintage	F	VF	XF	Unc	BU
1853B	—	300	500	750	1,200	—
1855B	—	300	500	750	1,200	—
1856B	—	400	800	1,000	2,000	—

KM# 225 5 THALER
6.6500 g., 0.8960 Gold .1916 oz. **Rev:** HARZ GOLD added to legend

Date	Mintage	F	VF	XF	Unc	BU
1853B	—	500	875	1,200	2,250	—
1856B	—	550	1,150	1,500	2,650	—

KM# 102 10 THALER
13.3600 g., 0.9030 Gold .3879 oz.

Date	Mintage	F	VF	XF	Unc	BU
1813 CHH	—	1,000	1,500	2,000	3,250	—
1814 CHH	—	750	1,100	1,500	2,500	—

KM# 133 10 THALER
13.3600 g., 0.9030 Gold .3879 oz.

Date	Mintage	F	VF	XF	Unc	BU
1821B	—	600	1,000	1,500	2,200	—
1822B	—	475	800	1,300	1,800	—
1822B HAONV	—	—	—	—	—	—
1823B	—	475	800	1,300	1,800	—
1824B	—	475	800	1,300	1,800	—
1825B	—	325	550	1,100	1,600	—
1827B	—	325	550	1,100	1,600	—
1828B	—	325	550	1,100	1,600	—
1829B	—	325	550	1,100	1,600	—
1830B	—	325	550	1,100	1,600	—

KM# 153 10 THALER
13.3600 g., 0.9030 Gold .3879 oz.

Date	Mintage	F	VF	XF	Unc	BU
1832	—	550	900	1,250	2,500	—

KM# 155 10 THALER
13.3600 g., 0.9030 Gold .3879 oz.

Date	Mintage	F	VF	XF	Unc	BU
1833	—	550	900	1,250	2,500	—

KM# 171.1 10 THALER
13.3000 g., 0.8960 Gold .3832 oz. **Obv:** B below head **Obv. Legend:** Ends:... HANNOV

Date	Mintage	F	VF	XF	Unc	BU
1835B	—	675	1,150	1,900	2,650	—

KM# 171.2 10 THALER
13.3000 g., 0.8960 Gold .3832 oz. **Obv. Legend:** Ends:... HANNOVER

Date	Mintage	F	VF	XF	Unc	BU
1835B	—	675	1,150	1,900	2,650	—

KM# 171.3 10 THALER
13.3000 g., 0.8960 Gold .3832 oz. **Rev:** Date at bottom

Date	Mintage	F	VF	XF	Unc	BU
1836B	—	650	1,125	1,875	2,600	—
1837B	—	550	1,000	1,500	2,250	—

KM# 171.4 10 THALER
13.3000 g., 0.8960 Gold .3832 oz. **Obv. Legend:** KONIG

Date	Mintage	F	VF	XF	Unc	BU
1836B	—	650	1,125	1,875	2,600	—

KM# 175 10 THALER
13.3000 g., 0.8960 Gold .3832 oz.

Date	Mintage	F	VF	XF	Unc	BU
1837B	—	—	—	10,000	15,000	—
1838B	—	500	900	1,500	2,250	—

KM# 187 10 THALER
13.3000 g., 0.8960 Gold .3832 oz. **Obv:** S below head

Date	Mintage	F	VF	XF	Unc	BU
1839 S	—	400	600	1,200	2,000	—

KM# 200.1 10 THALER
13.3000 g., 0.8960 Gold .3832 oz. **Obv:** BRANDT F. on truncation

Date	Mintage	F	VF	XF	Unc	BU
1844 S	—	600	1,000	1,500	2,250	—

KM# 200.2 10 THALER
13.3000 g., 0.8960 Gold .3832 oz. **Obv:** B below head

Date	Mintage	F	VF	XF	Unc	BU
1844B	—	600	1,000	1,500	2,500	—

KM# 200.3 10 THALER
13.3000 g., 0.8960 Gold .3832 oz. **Obv:** Without markings on truncation **Obv. Legend:** Ends:...V. HANNOVER

Date	Mintage	F	VF	XF	Unc	BU
1846B	—	400	800	1,200	2,000	—
1847B	—	400	800	1,200	2,000	—
1848B	—	300	600	900	1,500	—

KM# 212 10 THALER
13.3000 g., 0.8960 Gold .3832 oz. **Obv. Legend:** Ends:...VON HANNOVER

Date	Mintage	F	VF	XF	Unc	BU
1849B	—	500	1,000	1,500	2,250	—
1850B	—	350	600	1,000	1,500	—
1851B	—	500	1,000	1,500	2,250	—

KM# 226 10 THALER
13.3000 g., 0.8960 Gold .3832 oz.

Date	Mintage	F	VF	XF	Unc	BU
1853B	—	450	750	1,250	1,750	—
1854B	—	300	500	900	1,250	—
1855B	—	450	750	1,250	1,750	—
1856B	—	500	900	1,500	2,150	—

TRADE COINAGE

KM# 111 DUCAT
3.5000 g., 0.8960 Gold .1109 oz.

Date	Mintage	F	VF	XF	Unc	BU
1815C	—	525	875	1,400	2,000	—
1818C	—	600	1,000	1,650	2,250	—

KM# 134 DUCAT
3.5000 g., 0.8960 Gold .1109 oz.

Date	Mintage	F	VF	XF	Unc	BU
1821C	252	975	1,650	2,400	3,250	—
1824C	749	900	1,500	2,250	3,000	—
1827C	1,300	825	1,400	2,000	2,750	—

KM# 149 DUCAT
3.5000 g., 0.8960 Gold .1109 oz.

Date	Mintage	F	VF	XF	Unc	BU
1831C	1,550	750	1,250	1,900	2,500	—

KM# 231 1/2 KRONE
5.5500 g., 0.9000 Gold .1606 oz.

Date	Mintage	F	VF	XF	Unc	BU
1857B	4,105	300	600	950	1,500	—
1858B	116	900	1,500	2,200	3,500	—
1859B	790	400	800	1,200	1,800	—
1862B	96	1,500	2,000	3,000	5,000	—
1864B	13,000	300	600	950	1,500	—
1866B	2,909	300	600	950	1,500	—

KM# 232 KRONE
11.1100 g., 0.9000 Gold .3215 oz.

Date	Mintage	F	VF	XF	Unc	BU
1857B	145,000	350	500	900	1,500	—
1858B	47,000	450	800	1,200	1,800	—
1859B	20,000	500	850	1,300	1,900	—
1860B	15,000	550	1,000	1,500	2,250	—
1861B	780	1,000	1,500	2,000	3,000	—
1862B	20,000	525	875	1,400	1,900	—
1863B	126,000	350	500	900	1,500	—
1864B	14,000	450	800	1,100	1,700	—
1866B	383,000	350	500	900	1,500	—

PATTERNS

Inlcuding off metal strikes

KM#	Date	Mintage	Identification	Mkt Val
Pn3	1813 T.W.	—	2/3 Thaler. Silver.	850
Pn4	1813	—	5 Thaler. Gold. Plain edge. KM#101.	1,500
Pn5	1834A	—	16 Gute Groschen. Silver. Plain edge. KM#122.	—
Pn6	1834.B	—	1/24 Thaler. Billon. KM#158.1.	—
Pn7	1834A	—	2/3 Thaler. 0.9930 Silver. KM#161.2.	1,150
Pn8	1840A	—	Thaler. Silver. KM#191.	30,000

HESSE-CASSEL

(Hessen-Kassel)

The Hesse principalities were located for the most part north of the Main River, bounded by Westphalia on the west, the Brunswick duchies on the north, the Saxon-Thuringian duchies on the east and Rhine Palatinate and the bishoprics of Mainz and Fulda on the south. The rule of the landgraves of Hesse began in the second half of the 13th century, the dignity of Prince of the Empire being acquired in 1292. In 1567 the patrimony was divided by four surviving sons, only those of Cassel and Darmstadt surviving for more than a generation in Hesse-Cassel the landgrave was raised to the rank of elector in 1803. The electorate formed part of the Kingdom of Westphalia from 1806 to 1813. In 1866 Hesse-Cassel was annexed by Prussia and became the province of Hesse-Nassau.

RULERS

Wilhelm IX, 1785-1803
Wilhelm I, as Elector, 1803-06, 1813-21
Wilhelm II, 1821-31
Wilhelm II and Friedrich Wilhelm, 1831-47
Friedrich Wilhelm, 1847-66

MINT MARKS
C – Cassel
C - Clausthal
(.L.) – Lippoldsberg

MINT OFFICIALS' INITIALS

Initials	Date	Name
CP	1820-61	Christoph Pfeuffer, die-cutter
D.F., F.	1774-1831	Dietrich Flalda
FH	1786-1821	Friedrich Heenwagen
D.F., F.	1774-1831	Dietrich Flalda
FH	1786-1821	Friedrich Heenwagen
H	1775-1820	Carl Ludwig Holzemer, die-cutter
K	1804-33	Wilhelm Korner

ARMS:
Hessian lion rampant left.
Diez – 2 leopards passant to left, one above the other.
Katzenelnbogen – Crowned lion springing to left.
Nidda – 2-fold divided horizontally, two 8-pointed stars in upper half, lower half shaded.
Ziegenhain – 2-fold divided horizontally, 6-pointed star in upper half, lower half shaded.

PRINCIPALITY

REGULAR COINAGE

KM# 543 HELLER
Copper **Ruler:** Wilhelm IX **Note:** Similar to KM#553 but 19 millimeters.

Date	Mintage	F	VF	XF	Unc	BU
1801	—	4.50	12.00	28.00	70.00	—
1802	—	5.00	13.00	30.00	75.00	—
1803	—	5.00	13.00	30.00	75.00	—

KM# 553.1 HELLER
Copper **Note:** Prev. KM#553.

Date	Mintage	F	VF	XF	Unc	BU
1803	—	5.00	12.00	40.00	110	—
1805	—	5.00	12.00	30.00	90.00	—
1806	—	5.00	12.00	40.00	110	—

KM# 553.2 HELLER
Copper **Note:** Smaller letters than 553.1. Prev. KM#553, part.

Date	Mintage	F	VF	XF	Unc	BU
1814	—	10.00	22.00	48.00	120	—

KM# 565 HELLER
Copper **Obv:** Crowned WK monogram with one ring at base of W

Date	Mintage	F	VF	XF	Unc	BU
1817	—	8.00	15.00	40.00	90.00	—
1818	—	5.00	10.00	35.00	70.00	—
1819	—	5.00	10.00	35.00	70.00	—
1820	—	5.00	10.00	35.00	70.00	—

KM# 576 HELLER
Copper **Obv:** Crowned WK monogram with two rings at base of W

Date	Mintage	F	VF	XF	Unc	BU
1822	—	4.00	9.00	28.00	45.00	—
1825	—	4.00	9.00	28.00	45.00	—
1827	—	4.00	9.00	28.00	45.00	—
1828	—	5.00	12.00	35.00	60.00	—
1829	—	4.00	9.00	28.00	45.00	—
1831	—	4.00	9.00	28.00	45.00	—

KM# 575 HELLER
Copper **Note:** Issued under Wilhelm II using king's crown.

Date	Mintage	F	VF	XF	Unc	BU
1822	—	5.00	10.00	32.00	70.00	—
1823	—	5.00	10.00	32.00	60.00	—
1824	—	5.00	10.00	32.00	60.00	—
1825	—	5.00	10.00	32.00	60.00	—
1827	—	5.00	10.00	32.00	70.00	—

KM# 602 HELLER
Copper **Obv:** Crowned arms **Obv. Legend:** KURHESSEN **Rev:** Value: SCHEIDE MUNZE

Date	Mintage	F	VF	XF	Unc	BU
1842	37,000	12.00	30.00	70.00	160	—

KM# 605 HELLER
Copper **Obv. Legend:** 360 EINEN THALER

Date	Mintage	F	VF	XF	Unc	BU
1843	—	4.00	8.00	16.00	35.00	—
1845	—	4.00	8.00	16.00	35.00	—
1847	—	4.00	8.00	16.00	35.00	—

KM# 613 HELLER
Copper **Note:** Issued under Friedrich Wilhelm.

Date	Mintage	F	VF	XF	Unc	BU
1849	—	4.00	8.00	16.00	35.00	—
1852	—	4.00	8.00	16.00	35.00	—
1854	—	4.00	8.00	16.00	35.00	—
1856	—	4.00	8.00	16.00	35.00	—
1858	—	4.00	8.00	16.00	35.00	—
1859	—	4.00	8.00	16.00	35.00	—
1860	—	4.00	8.00	16.00	35.00	—
1861	—	4.00	8.00	16.00	35.00	—
1862	—	4.00	8.00	16.00	35.00	—
1863	—	4.00	8.00	16.00	35.00	—
1864	—	4.00	8.00	16.00	35.00	—
1865	—	4.00	8.00	16.00	35.00	—
1866	—	4.00	8.00	15.00	30.00	—

KM# 561 2 HELLER
Copper **Obv:** Crowned WK monogram with one ring at base of W

Date	Mintage	F	VF	XF	Unc	BU
1814	—	10.00	22.00	48.00	120	—

KM# 564 2 HELLER
Copper **Obv:** Revised monogram with larger crown

Date	Mintage	F	VF	XF	Unc	BU
1816	—	8.00	18.00	40.00	90.00	—
1818	—	8.00	18.00	40.00	90.00	—
1820	—	8.00	18.00	40.00	90.00	—

KM# 606 2 HELLER
Copper **Obv:** Crowned WK monogram with two rings at base of W

Date	Mintage	F	VF	XF	Unc	BU
1843	—	5.00	16.00	35.00	80.00	—

KM# 607 3 HELLER
Copper

Date	Mintage	F	VF	XF	Unc	BU
1843	—	3.00	8.00	15.00	28.00	—
1844	—	3.00	8.00	15.00	28.00	—
1845	—	3.00	8.00	15.00	28.00	—
1846	—	3.00	8.00	15.00	28.00	—

KM# 612 3 HELLER
Copper **Note:** Issued under Friedrich Wilhelm.

Date	Mintage	F	VF	XF	Unc	BU
1848	—	2.50	8.00	12.00	25.00	—
1849	—	2.50	8.00	12.00	25.00	—
1850	—	2.50	8.00	12.00	25.00	—
1851	—	2.50	8.00	12.00	25.00	—
1852	—	2.50	6.00	10.00	22.00	—
1853	—	2.50	6.00	10.00	22.00	—
1854	—	2.50	6.00	10.00	22.00	—
1856	—	2.50	6.00	10.00	22.00	—
1858	—	2.50	6.00	10.00	22.00	—
1859	—	2.50	6.00	10.00	22.00	—
1860	—	2.50	6.00	10.00	22.00	—
1861	—	2.50	6.00	10.00	22.00	—
1862	—	2.50	6.00	10.00	22.00	—
1863	—	2.50	6.00	10.00	18.00	—
1864	—	2.50	6.00	10.00	18.00	—
1865	—	2.50	6.00	10.00	18.00	—
1866	—	2.50	6.00	10.00	18.00	—

KM# 562 4 HELLER (1/3 Albus; 1/96 Thaler)
Copper **Obv:** Crowned WK monogram with one ring at base of W

Date	Mintage	F	VF	XF	Unc	BU
1815	—	8.00	22.00	45.00	90.00	—
1816	—	8.00	22.00	45.00	90.00	—
1817	—	8.00	22.00	45.00	90.00	—
1818	—	8.00	22.00	45.00	90.00	—
1819	—	8.00	22.00	45.00	90.00	—
1820	—	8.00	22.00	45.00	90.00	—
1821	—	8.00	22.00	45.00	90.00	—

KM# 571.1 4 HELLER (1/3 Albus; 1/96 Thaler)
Copper, 26.5 mm. **Obv:** Crowned WK monogram with two rings at base of W

Date	Mintage	F	VF	XF	Unc	BU
1821	—	4.00	10.00	30.00	80.00	—
1822	—	4.00	10.00	30.00	80.00	—
1824	—	4.00	10.00	30.00	80.00	—

KM# 571.2 4 HELLER (1/3 Albus; 1/96 Thaler)
Copper, 26 mm. **Obv:** Crowned WK monogram with two rings at base of W

Date	Mintage	F	VF	XF	Unc	BU
1826	—	4.00	10.00	30.00	80.00	—
1827	—	4.00	12.00	35.00	90.00	—
1828	—	4.00	12.00	35.00	90.00	—
1829	—	4.00	12.00	35.00	90.00	—
1830	—	4.00	10.00	30.00	80.00	—
1831	—	4.00	10.00	30.00	80.00	—

KM# 603 1/2 SILBER GROSCHEN
0.9700 g., 0.2500 Silver .0077 oz. **Obv:** Crowned arms **Rev:** Value: SILBER GROSCHEN

Date	Mintage	F	VF	XF	Unc	BU
1842	1,491,000	5.00	16.00	32.00	80.00	—

KM# 601 SILBER GROSCHEN
1.5600 g., 0.3120 Silver .0156 oz.

Date	Mintage	F	VF	XF	Unc	BU
1841	5,925,000	4.00	10.00	20.00	50.00	—
1845	62,000	10.00	16.00	32.00	65.00	—
1847	456,000	10.00	16.00	32.00	65.00	—

KM# 615 SILBER GROSCHEN
2.0000 g., 0.3120 Silver .0156 oz.

Date	Mintage	F	VF	XF	Unc	BU
1851	262,000	10.00	20.00	30.00	70.00	—
1852	147,000	15.00	30.00	50.00	80.00	—
1853	125,000	12.00	20.00	30.00	70.00	—
1854	98,000	1,215	20.00	50.00	70.00	—
1855	54,000	10.00	30.00	50.00	80.00	—
1856	234,000	10.00	20.00	30.00	70.00	—
1857	119,000	10.00	20.00	30.00	70.00	—
1858	58,000	10.00	20.00	30.00	70.00	—
1859	235,000	10.00	20.00	30.00	70.00	—
1860	156,000	10.00	20.00	30.00	70.00	—
1861	165,000	8.00	16.00	26.00	52.00	—
1862	—	8.00	16.00	26.00	52.00	—
1863	—	8.00	16.00	26.00	52.00	—
1864	122,000	8.00	16.00	26.00	52.00	—
1865	192,000	8.00	16.00	26.00	52.00	—
1866	182,000	5.00	10.00	20.00	40.00	—

KM# 604 2 SILBER GROSCHEN
2.6000 g., 0.3750 Silver .0313 oz.

Date	Mintage	F	VF	XF	Unc	BU
1842	2,414,000	10.00	20.00	40.00	70.00	—

KM# 620 2-1/2 SILBER GROSCHEN
3.2500 g., 0.3750 Silver .0391 oz.

Date	Mintage	F	VF	XF	Unc	BU
1852 CP	34,000	8.00	16.00	32.00	65.00	—
1853 CP	49,000	8.00	16.00	32.00	65.00	—
1856 CP	39,000	6.00	12.00	25.00	55.00	—
1859 CP	69,000	6.00	12.00	25.00	55.00	—
1860 CP	42,000	6.00	12.00	25.00	55.00	—
1861 CP	34,000	6.00	12.00	25.00	55.00	—
1862 CP	31,000	6.00	12.00	25.00	55.00	—
1865 CP	23,000	6.00	12.00	20.00	40.00	—

KM# 529 1/24 THALER (Groschen)
Billon **Ruler:** Wilhelm IX **Obv:** Rampant lion left, garland below **Rev:** Value, date below, mintmasters initials in exergue

Date	Mintage	F	VF	XF	Unc	BU
1801 F	—	10.00	20.00	40.00	80.00	—
1802 F	—	8.00	16.00	32.00	65.00	—

KM# 554.1 1/24 THALER (Groschen)
Billon **Obv:** Lion on shorter line

Date	Mintage	F	VF	XF	Unc	BU
1803 F	526,000	8.00	18.00	40.00	80.00	—
1804 F	—	8.00	18.00	40.00	80.00	—
1805 F	—	8.00	18.00	40.00	80.00	—
1806 F	—	8.00	18.00	40.00	80.00	—
1807 F	997,000	5.00	12.00	30.00	60.00	—
1807 C	—	16.00	38.00	75.00	150	—

KM# 554.2 1/24 THALER (Groschen)
Billon **Obv:** Rampant lion left **Rev:** Value, without mark below date

Date	Mintage	F	VF	XF	Unc	BU
1814	—	8.00	22.00	50.00	100	—
1815	—	8.00	22.00	50.00	100	—
1816	—	10.00	25.00	60.00	110	—
1817	—	10.00	25.00	60.00	110	—
1818	—	15.00	30.00	65.00	125	—
1819	—	15.00	30.00	65.00	125	—
1820	—	8.00	22.00	50.00	100	—
1821	—	8.00	22.00	50.00	100	—

KM# 554.3 1/24 THALER (Groschen)
Billon **Obv:** With beaded border **Rev:** With beaded border

Date	Mintage	F	VF	XF	Unc	BU
1814	—	15.00	40.00	100	225	—
1819	—	15.00	40.00	100	225	—

KM# 577 1/24 THALER (Groschen)
Billon **Note:** Issued under Wilhelm II.

Date	Mintage	F	VF	XF	Unc	BU
1822	—	12.00	30.00	60.00	120	—

KM# 542 1/6 THALER
Silver **Ruler:** Wilhelm IX **Obv:** Arms **Rev:** Value above date

Date	Mintage	F	VF	XF	Unc	BU
1801 F	—	12.00	35.00	90.00	200	—
1802 F	—	16.00	40.00	100	240	—

KM# 555 1/6 THALER
0.6250 Silver **Obv:** Altered crown tops arms within laurel branches **Rev:** Value

Date	Mintage	F	VF	XF	Unc	BU
1803 F	—	12.00	25.00	55.00	185	—

KM# 556 1/6 THALER
0.6250 Silver

Date	Mintage	F	VF	XF	Unc	BU
1803 F	—	22.00	50.00	120	220	—
1804 F	—	22.00	50.00	120	220	—
1805 F	—	22.00	50.00	140	260	—
1806 F	—	22.00	50.00	140	260	—
1807 F	40,000	22.00	50.00	140	260	—
1807 C Rare	—	—	—	—	—	—

KM# 572 1/6 THALER
0.6250 Silver **Obv:** Lion in oval shield **Rev:** Value, date, without legend

Date	Mintage	F	VF	XF	Unc	BU
1821	38,000	25.00	45.00	150	300	—
1822	56,000	25.00	45.00	150	300	—

KM# 579.1 1/6 THALER
5.3200 g., 0.5000 Silver .0855 oz. **Obv. Legend:** ...KURF S. L. V. HESSEN...

Date	Mintage	F	VF	XF	Unc	BU
1823	182,000	15.00	35.00	70.00	150	—
1824	276,000	15.00	35.00	70.00	150	—
1825	306,000	15.00	35.00	70.00	150	—
1826	147,000	10.00	25.00	60.00	125	—
1827	280,000	10.00	25.00	60.00	125	—
1828	395,000	10.00	25.00	60.00	125	—
1828/7	—	—	—	—	—	—
1829	590,000	10.00	25.00	60.00	100	—
1830	524,000	10.00	25.00	60.00	150	—
1831	201,000	10.00	25.00	70.00	150	—

KM# 579.4 1/6 THALER
5.3200 g., 0.5000 Silver .0855 oz. **Obv. Legend:** ...KURF S. L. Z. HESSEN...

Date	Mintage	F	VF	XF	Unc	BU
1823	—	60.00	150	250	400	—

KM# 579.3 1/6 THALER
5.3200 g., 0.5000 Silver .0855 oz. **Rev:** Error: THAELR

Date	Mintage	F	VF	XF	Unc	BU
1828	—	50.00	115	200	350	—

KM# 579.2 1/6 THALER
5.3200 g., 0.5000 Silver .0855 oz. **Obv. Legend:** ...KURF V. HESSEN...

Date	Mintage	F	VF	XF	Unc	BU
1831	22,000	40.00	70.00	140	280	—

KM# 590 1/6 THALER
5.3200 g., 0.5000 Silver .0855 oz. **Obv. Legend:** Ends: ...KURPR. U. MITREG

Date	Mintage	F	VF	XF	Unc	BU
1833	46,000	5.00	17.00	50.00	120	—
1834	599,000	5.00	17.00	50.00	100	—
1835	810,000	5.00	17.00	50.00	100	—
1836	528,000	5.00	17.00	50.00	100	—
1837	624,000	5.00	17.00	50.00	100	—
1838	558,000	5.00	17.00	50.00	100	—
1839	228,000	5.00	17.00	60.00	120	—
1840	6,000	15.00	45.00	110	225	—
1841	192,000	5.00	17.00	50.00	100	—
1842	1,404,000	4.00	15.00	40.00	85.00	—
1843	138,000	15.00	50.00	110	220	—
1844	6,132	15.00	50.00	110	220	—
1845	95,000	4.00	15.00	40.00	85.00	—
1846	45,000	10.00	30.00	65.00	130	—

KM# 609 1/6 THALER

5.3200 g., 0.5000 Silver .0855 oz. **Obv. Legend:** Ends: ... KURPR. = MITREG

Date	Mintage	F	VF	XF	Unc	BU
1845 Rare	Inc. above	—	—	—	—	—
1846	Inc. above	40.00	75.00	160	350	—
1847	103,000	35.00	65.00	145	300	—

KM# 616 1/6 THALER

5.3500 g., 0.5200 Silver .0894 oz. **Obv:** C.P. at truncation

Date	Mintage	F	VF	XF	Unc	BU
1851 CP	30,000	15.00	30.00	70.00	140	—
1852 CP	33,000	15.00	30.00	70.00	140	—
1854 CP	13,000	15.00	30.00	70.00	140	—
1855 CP	22,000	15.00	30.00	80.00	200	—
1856 CP	—	15.00	30.00	70.00	140	—

KM# 578 1/3 THALER

8.5000 g., 0.6250 Silver .1708 oz.

Date	Mintage	F	VF	XF	Unc	BU
1822	105,000	20.00	50.00	130	250	—
1823	125,000	20.00	50.00	110	220	—
1824	99,000	20.00	50.00	110	220	—
1825	162,000	20.00	50.00	110	220	—
1826	280,000	20.00	50.00	110	220	—
1827	278,000	20.00	50.00	110	220	—
1828	—	20.00	50.00	110	220	—
1829	219,000	20.00	50.00	130	325	—

KM# 567 1/2 THALER

11.1200 g., 0.7500 Silver .2681 oz.

Date	Mintage	F	VF	XF	Unc	BU
1819	—	30.00	60.00	160	350	—
1820	—	40.00	70.00	200	450	—

KM# 532 THALER

Silver **Ruler:** Wilhelm IX **Note:** Dav. #2305. Many varieties exist.

Date	Mintage	F	VF	XF	Unc	BU
1802 FH Rare	—	—	—	—	—	—

KM# 560.1 THALER

Silver **Edge:** Inscription

Date	Mintage	F	VF	XF	Unc	BU
1813 K	—	—	3,000	6,000	10,000	—

KM# 560.2 THALER

Silver **Edge:** Plain **Note:** Some speculate that this is a later-day strike from the original dies.

Date	Mintage	F	VF	XF	Unc	BU
1813 K	—	—	—	—	—	—

KM# 568 THALER

22.2700 g., 0.7500 Silver .5371 oz. **Obv. Legend:** KURF. SOUV.

Date	Mintage	F	VF	XF	Unc	BU
1819	—	40.00	90.00	500	1,500	—
1820	—	50.00	120	600	1,700	—

KM# 573.1 THALER

22.2700 g., 0.7500 Silver .5371 oz. **Obv:** Bust right **Obv. Legend:** SOUV. LANDGR. Z. HESSEN...

Date	Mintage	F	VF	XF	Unc	BU
1821	2,385	100	220	700	1,500	—
1822	3,456	150	300	900	1,900	—

KM# 573.2 THALER

22.2700 g., 0.7500 Silver .5371 oz. **Obv:** Head right

Date	Mintage	F	VF	XF	Unc	BU
1821 Rare	Inc. above	—	—	—	—	—

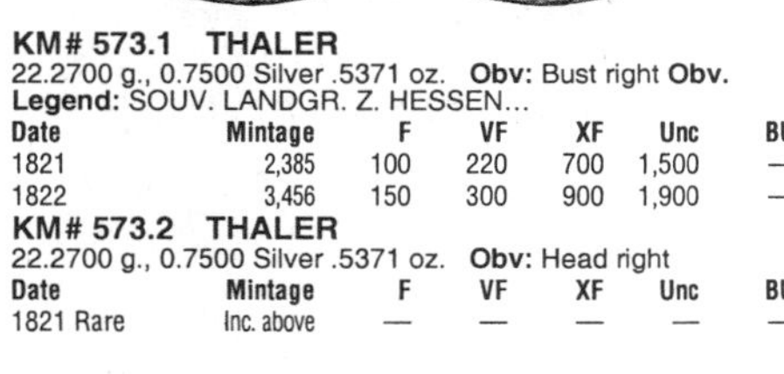

KM# 587 THALER

22.2700 g., 0.7500 Silver .5371 oz.

Date	Mintage	F	VF	XF	Unc	BU
1832	20,000	18.00	40.00	130	450	—
1833	17,000	18.00	40.00	130	450	—
1834	37,000	18.00	40.00	130	450	—
1835	14,000	18.00	40.00	130	450	—
1836	40,000	25.00	50.00	150	450	—
1837	26,000	25.00	50.00	150	450	—
1838	4,041	40.00	70.00	300	800	—
1839	2,574	25.00	50.00	150	450	—

Date	Mintage	F	VF	XF	Unc	BU
1841	25,000	18.00	40.00	150	450	—
1842	31,000	18.00	40.00	150	450	—

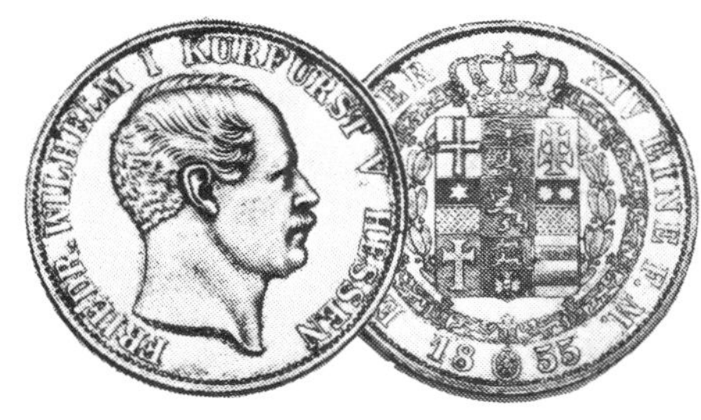

KM# 617 THALER

22.2700 g., 0.7500 Silver .5371 oz. **Obv:** C. PFEUFFER F. at truncation

Date	Mintage	F	VF	XF	Unc	BU
1851	3,963	75.00	160	500	1,500	—
1854	7,338	60.00	120	300	900	—
1855	28,000	35.00	80.00	200	600	—

KM# 621.1 THALER

18.5200 g., 0.9000 Silver .5360 oz. **Obv:** With C.P. at truncation

Date	Mintage	F	VF	XF	Unc	BU
1858 CP	62,000	30.00	55.00	150	300	—
1859 CP	37,000	35.00	60.00	160	350	—
1860 CP	31,000	35.00	60.00	160	350	—
1862 CP	32,000	35.00	60.00	160	350	—
1864 CP	32,000	35.00	60.00	160	350	—
1865 CP	31,000	30.00	55.00	150	275	—

KM# 621.2 THALER

18.5200 g., 0.9000 Silver .5360 oz. **Obv:** Without C.P. at truncation

Date	Mintage	F	VF	XF	Unc	BU
1858	Inc. above	40.00	65.00	160	300	—
1859	Inc. above	40.00	65.00	170	300	—
1860	Inc. above	40.00	65.00	170	300	—
1861	32,000	40.00	65.00	180	350	—
1862	—	40.00	65.00	170	300	—
1863	32,000	40.00	65.00	160	300	—
1864	Inc. above	40.00	65.00	160	300	—
1865	Inc. above	40.00	65.00	150	240	—

KM# 600 2 THALER (3-1/2 Gulden)

37.1200 g., 0.9000 Silver 1.0742 oz.

Date	Mintage	F	VF	XF	Unc	BU
1840	19,000	100	200	450	1,200	—
1841	19,000	100	200	450	1,350	—
1842	19,000	100	200	450	1,350	—
1843	18,000	115	250	500	1,500	—

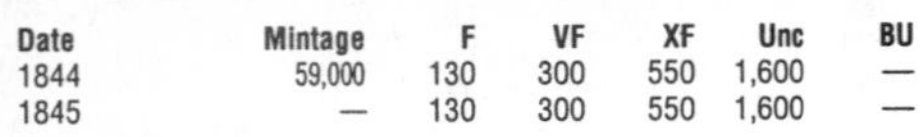

Date	Mintage	F	VF	XF	Unc	BU
1844	59,000	130	300	550	1,600	—
1845	—	130	300	550	1,600	—

KM# 608 2 THALER (3-1/2 Gulden)
37.1200 g., 0.9000 Silver 1.0742 oz. **Obv:** Larger letters

Date	Mintage	F	VF	XF	Unc	BU
1844	Inc. above	120	250	500	1,500	—
1845	—	150	300	550	1,600	—

KM# 610 2 THALER (3-1/2 Gulden)
37.1200 g., 0.9000 Silver 1.0742 oz. **Obv. Legend:** KURPRINZ-MITREGENT

Date	Mintage	F	VF	XF	Unc	BU
1847	10,000	400	750	1,700	3,800	—

KM# 618 2 THALER (3-1/2 Gulden)
37.1200 g., 0.9000 Silver 1.0742 oz. **Obv:** CP on truncation

Date	Mintage	F	VF	XF	Unc	BU
1851 CP	3,996	150	300	500	1,100	—
1854 CP	141,000	100	150	325	800	—
1855 CP	357,000	85.00	125	275	600	—

KM# 545 5 THALER (1 Pistole or Friedrich d'or)
6.6500 g., 0.9000 Gold .1924 oz. **Ruler:** Wilhelm IX **Obv:** Bust right **Rev:** Similar to KM#557

Date	Mintage	F	VF	XF	Unc	BU
1801 F	—	600	1,100	1,600	2,500	—

KM# 557 5 THALER (1 Pistole or Friedrich d'or)
6.6500 g., 0.9000 Gold .1924 oz.

Date	Mintage	F	VF	XF	Unc	BU
1803 F	1,659	2,000	3,300	5,000	7,000	—
1805 F	1,941	2,000	3,300	5,000	7,000	—
1806 F Rare, 3 known	875	—	—	—	—	—

KM# 563 5 THALER (1 Pistole or Friedrich d'or)
6.6500 g., 0.9000 Gold .1924 oz.

Date	Mintage	F	VF	XF	Unc	BU
1815	2,226	1,500	2,500	3,500	4,500	—

KM# 566 5 THALER (1 Pistole or Friedrich d'or)
6.6500 g., 0.9000 Gold .1924 oz. **Obv. Legend:** WILHELMUS I. ELECT. HASS

Date	Mintage	F	VF	XF	Unc	BU
1817	2,352	1,400	2,400	3,300	4,200	—
1819	1,548	1,600	2,600	3,700	4,800	—

KM# 570 5 THALER (1 Pistole or Friedrich d'or)
6.6500 g., 0.9000 Gold .1924 oz. **Obv. Legend:** WILHALM I KURF...

Date	Mintage	F	VF	XF	Unc	BU
1820	534	4,000	6,000	8,000	10,000	—

KM# 574.1 5 THALER (1 Pistole or Friedrich d'or)
6.6500 g., 0.9000 Gold .1924 oz. **Obv. Legend:** ...KURF. S. L. "Z". HESSEN...

Date	Mintage	F	VF	XF	Unc	BU
1821	1,142	1,000	1,800	3,000	5,000	—
1823	1,140	1,000	1,800	3,000	5,000	—

KM# 574.2 5 THALER (1 Pistole or Friedrich d'or)
6.6500 g., 0.9000 Gold .1924 oz. **Obv. Legend:** ...KURF. S. L. V. HESSEN...

Date	Mintage	F	VF	XF	Unc	BU
1823	518	1,600	3,000	4,400	6,000	—
1825	409	1,600	3,000	4,400	6,000	—
1828	952	1,600	3,000	4,400	6,000	—
1829	502	1,600	3,000	4,400	6,000	—

KM# 591 5 THALER (1 Pistole or Friedrich d'or)
6.6500 g., 0.9000 Gold .1924 oz.

Date	Mintage	F	VF	XF	Unc	BU
1834	1,025	450	750	1,500	2,000	—
1836	2,002	450	750	1,500	2,000	—
1837	256	650	1,200	1,800	2,500	—
1839	1,996	450	750	1,400	1,900	—
1840	17,000	425	700	1,250	1,750	—
1841	16,000	425	700	1,250	1,750	—
1842	6,909	450	750	1,400	1,900	—
1843	1,657	500	850	1,400	2,200	—
1844	1,495	500	850	1,400	2,200	—
1845	1,364	500	850	1,400	2,200	—

KM# 611 5 THALER (1 Pistole or Friedrich d'or)
6.6500 g., 0.9000 Gold .1924 oz. **Obv. Legend:** Ends: ...KURPR.-MITREG

Date	Mintage	F	VF	XF	Unc	BU
1847	1,438	800	1,300	2,400	4,000	—

KM# 619 5 THALER (1 Pistole or Friedrich d'or)
6.6500 g., 0.9000 Gold .1924 oz. **Obv:** CP on truncation

Date	Mintage	F	VF	XF	Unc	BU
1851 CP	596	1,000	1,250	1,900	2,700	—

KM# 594 10 THALER (2 Pistolen or 2 Friedrich d'or)
13.3000 g., 0.9000 Gold .3848 oz. **Note:** 1840 and 1841 mintage numbers included in KM#591.

Date	Mintage	F	VF	XF	Unc	BU
1838	126	1,400	2,000	3,000	5,000	—
1840	—	1,000	1,500	2,500	5,000	—
1841	—	1,000	1,500	2,500	5,000	—

REGIONAL COINAGE

Ober-Hessen

Under Wilhelm II

KM# 550 1/4 KREUZER
Copper **Obv:** Arms **Obv. Legend:** HESSSEN CASSEL **Rev:** Value

Date	Mintage	F	VF	XF	Unc	BU
1801	—	5.00	12.00	25.00	85.00	—
1802	—	5.00	9.00	18.00	75.00	—

KM# 580 1/4 KREUZER
Copper **Obv:** Crowned arms **Rev:** Value within rosettes

Date	Mintage	F	VF	XF	Unc	BU
1824	—	6.00	12.00	40.00	80.00	—
1825	—	6.00	12.00	40.00	80.00	—
1827	—	6.00	12.00	40.00	80.00	—
1829	—	10.00	20.00	60.00	100	—
1830	—	6.00	12.00	40.00	80.00	—

KM# 592 1/4 KREUZER
Copper **Note:** Similar to KM#580.

Date	Mintage	F	VF	XF	Unc	BU
1834	—	6.00	12.00	40.00	80.00	—
1835	—	10.00	20.00	60.00	100	—

KM# 551 1/2 KREUZER
Copper **Obv:** Arms **Obv. Legend:** HESSEN CASSEL **Rev:** Value

Date	Mintage	F	VF	XF	Unc	BU
1801	—	6.00	15.00	40.00	100	—

Date	Mintage	F	VF	XF	Unc	BU
1802	—	6.00	15.00	40.00	100	—
1803	—	6.00	15.00	40.00	100	—

KM# 558 1/2 KREUZER
Copper **Obv:** Elector's cap above arms **Rev:** Value

Date	Mintage	F	VF	XF	Unc	BU
1803 F	—	5.00	150	35.00	80.00	—
1804 F	—	5.00	150	35.00	80.00	—

KM# 581 1/2 KREUZER
Copper

Date	Mintage	F	VF	XF	Unc	BU
1824	—	3.00	8.00	25.00	60.00	—
1825	—	4.00	10.00	30.00	70.00	—
1826	—	4.00	10.00	30.00	70.00	—
1827	—	4.00	10.00	30.00	70.00	—
1828	—	4.00	10.00	30.00	70.00	—
1829	—	4.00	10.00	30.00	70.00	—
1830	—	4.00	10.00	30.00	70.00	—

KM# 593 1/2 KREUZER
Copper

Date	Mintage	F	VF	XF	Unc	BU
1834	—	3.00	8.00	25.00	60.00	—

KM# 582 KREUZER
Copper **Obv:** Crowned arms **Rev:** Value within rosettes

Date	Mintage	F	VF	XF	Unc	BU
1825	—	4.00	10.00	30.00	70.00	—
1828	—	5.00	11.00	33.00	80.00	—
1829	—	5.00	11.00	33.00	80.00	—

KM# 588 KREUZER
Copper **Note:** Similar to KM#582.

Date	Mintage	F	VF	XF	Unc	BU
1832	—	5.00	11.00	33.00	80.00	—
1833	—	5.00	11.00	33.00	80.00	—
1835	—	8.00	16.00	40.00	100	—

KM# 583 6 KREUZER
Billon **Obv:** Crowned arms **Rev:** Value within rosettes

Date	Mintage	F	VF	XF	Unc	BU
1826	—	9.00	24.00	60.00	150	—
1827	—	9.00	24.00	60.00	150	—
1828	—	9.00	24.00	60.00	150	—

KM# 586 6 KREUZER
Billon **Rev:** Without rosettes

Date	Mintage	F	VF	XF	Unc	BU
1831	—	9.00	24.00	55.00	150	—
1832	—	8.00	22.00	48.00	130	—
1833	—	6.00	16.00	40.00	100	—
1834	—	9.00	24.00	55.00	150	—

PATTERNS

Including off metal strikes

KM#	Date	Mintage	Identification	Mkt Val
Pn34	1814	3	5 Thaler. 0.9000 Gold.	—
Pn35	1821	—	Thaler. Silver.	—
Pn36	1842	—	2 Heller. Copper.	1,800
Pn37	1842	—	3 Heller. Copper.	1,800
Pn38	1835	—	1/2 Kreuzer. Billon. KM#593. Prev. KM#Pn1.	—

HESSE-DARMSTADT

Established by the division of the Landgraviate of Hesse in 1567, Hesse-Darmstadt was the territorially smaller of the two surviving branches of the family. The ruler was raised to the rank of Grand Duke in 1806. In 1815 the Congress of Vienna awarded Hesse-Darmstadt the cities of Mainz and Worms, which were relinquished along with the newly acquired Hesse-Homburg, to the Prussians in 1866. It became part of the German Empire in 1871.

RULERS

Ludwig X, 1790-1806
As Grand Duke Ludwig I, 1806-1830
Ludwig II, 1830-1848
Ludwig III, 1848-1877
Ludwig IV, 1877-1892
Ernst Ludwig, 1892-1918

MINT OFFICIALS' INITIALS

Initial	Date	Name
HR	1817-	Hector Roessler
RF	1772-1809	Remigius Fehr

GRAND DUCHY

REGULAR COINAGE

KM# 291 HELLER (Pfennig)
Copper **Ruler:** Ludwig X As Grand Duke Ludwig I **Obv:** Crowned pointed arms, G.H.-K.M **Rev:** Value

Date	Mintage	F	VF	XF	Unc	BU
1824	—	4.00	12.00	25.00	60.00	—

KM# 302 HELLER (Pfennig)
Copper **Ruler:** Ludwig II

Date	Mintage	F	VF	XF	Unc	BU
1837	—	3.00	8.00	18.00	50.00	—
1840	—	3.00	8.00	18.00	50.00	—
1841	—	3.00	8.00	18.00	50.00	—
1842	103,000	3.00	8.00	18.00	50.00	—
1843	175,000	3.00	8.00	18.00	50.00	—
1844	241,000	3.00	8.00	18.00	50.00	—
1845	—	3.00	8.00	18.00	50.00	—
1846	—	3.00	8.00	18.00	50.00	—
1847	—	3.00	8.00	18.00	50.00	—

KM# 322 HELLER (Pfennig)
Copper **Ruler:** Ludwig II **Obv:** Crowned square arms

Date	Mintage	F	VF	XF	Unc	BU
1847	—	2.50	7.00	12.00	40.00	—

KM# 323 HELLER (Pfennig)
Copper **Ruler:** Ludwig II

Date	Mintage	F	VF	XF	Unc	BU
1848	—	2.00	6.00	14.00	40.00	—
1849	—	2.00	6.00	14.00	40.00	—
1850	—	2.00	6.00	14.00	40.00	—
1851	—	2.00	6.00	14.00	40.00	—
1852	—	2.00	6.00	14.00	40.00	—
1853	—	2.00	6.00	14.00	40.00	—
1854	—	2.00	6.00	14.00	40.00	—
1855	—	2.00	6.00	14.00	40.00	—

KM# 251 PFENNIG
Copper **Ruler:** Ludwig X **Obv:** Crowned lion in oval **Rev:** Value above date, stars

Date	Mintage	F	VF	XF	Unc	BU
1801 RF	—	4.00	18.00	40.00	90.00	—
1802 RF	—	4.00	18.00	40.00	90.00	—
1803 RF	—	4.00	18.00	40.00	90.00	—
1804 RF	—	4.00	18.00	40.00	90.00	—
1805 RF	—	4.00	18.00	40.00	90.00	—
1805 Without RF	—	10.00	30.00	70.00	150	—

KM# 242 PFENNIG (Heller)
Copper **Ruler:** Ludwig X **Obv:** Lion in oval, H.D. and crown above, ornaments hanging from it **Rev:** Value above date **Note:** No stars on reverse.

Date	Mintage	VG	F	VF	XF	Unc
1806 RF	—	6.00	20.00	60.00	130	—

KM# 280 PFENNIG (Heller)
Ruler: Ludwig X As Grand Duke Ludwig I **Obv:** GH - SM

Date	Mintage	F	VF	XF	Unc	BU
1811	—	8.00	20.00	40.00	80.00	—
1819	—	6.00	15.00	30.00	60.00	—

KM# 283 PFENNIG (Heller)
0.3330 Silver **Ruler:** Ludwig X As Grand Duke Ludwig I **Obv:** GH-KM

Date	Mintage	F	VF	XF	Unc	BU
1819	—	6.00	15.00	35.00	70.00	—

KM# 337 PFENNIG (Heller)
Copper **Ruler:** Ludwig III

Date	Mintage	F	VF	XF	Unc	BU
1857	140,000	1.50	5.00	12.00	40.00	—
1858	202,000	1.50	5.00	12.00	40.00	—
1859	257,000	1.50	5.00	12.00	40.00	—
1860	268,000	1.50	5.00	12.00	40.00	—
1861	311,000	1.50	5.00	12.00	40.00	—
1862	324,000	1.50	5.00	12.00	40.00	—
1863	190,000	1.50	5.00	12.00	40.00	—
1864	—	1.50	5.00	12.00	40.00	—
1865	279,000	1.50	5.00	12.00	40.00	—
1866	317,000	1.50	5.00	12.00	40.00	—
1867	296,000	1.50	5.00	12.00	40.00	—
1868	332,000	1.50	5.00	12.00	40.00	—
1869	322,000	1.50	5.00	12.00	40.00	—
1870	526,000	1.50	5.00	12.00	40.00	—
1871	322,000	1.50	5.00	12.00	40.00	—
1872	338,000	1.50	5.00	12.00	40.00	—

KM# 258 1/4 STUBER
Copper **Ruler:** Ludwig X

Date	Mintage	F	VF	XF	Unc	BU
1805 RF	—	10.00	25.00	55.00	125	—

KM# 259 1/2 STUBER
Copper **Ruler:** Ludwig X **Obv:** Crowned LLX monogram **Rev:** Value

Date	Mintage	F	VF	XF	Unc	BU
1805	—	12.00	25.00	55.00	200	—

KM# 272 1/4 KREUZER
Copper **Ruler:** Ludwig X **Obv. Legend:** G. HESS. - SCHEID. M.

Date	Mintage	F	VF	XF	Unc	BU
1809	—	10.00	20.00	40.00	120	—
1816	—	20.00	40.00	80.00	150	—

KM# 273 1/4 KREUZER
Copper **Ruler:** Ludwig X As Grand Duke Ludwig I **Obv. Legend:** G.H.-S.M.

Date	Mintage	F	VF	XF	Unc	BU
1809	—	5.00	10.00	25.00	100	—
1816	—	5.00	10.00	25.00	100	—
1817	—	5.00	10.00	25.00	100	—

KM# 274 1/2 KREUZER
Copper **Ruler:** Ludwig X As Grand Duke Ludwig I

Date	Mintage	F	VF	XF	Unc	BU
1809	—	4.00	9.00	20.00	60.00	—
1817	—	4.00	9.00	20.00	60.00	—

KM# 281 1/2 KREUZER
Copper **Ruler:** Ludwig X As Grand Duke Ludwig I **Obv. Legend:** G.H.-S.M

Date	Mintage	F	VF	XF	Unc	BU
1817	—	3.00	8.00	18.00	50.00	—

KM# 257 KREUZER
0.7700 g., 0.1870 Silver .0046 oz. **Ruler:** Ludwig X **Obv:** Lion divides H.D **Rev:** Value **Rev. Legend:** LAND MUNZE

Date	Mintage	F	VF	XF	Unc	BU
1801	—	5.00	15.00	45.00	80.00	—
1802	—	5.00	15.00	45.00	80.00	—
1803	—	5.00	15.00	45.00	80.00	—
1804	—	5.00	15.00	45.00	80.00	—
1805	—	5.00	15.00	45.00	80.00	—

KM# 260 KREUZER
0.7700 g., 0.1870 Silver .0046 oz. **Ruler:** Ludwig X **Obv:** Crowned lion between H.D **Rev:** Value **Rev. Legend:** LAND MUNZ

Date	Mintage	F	VF	XF	Unc	BU
1806	—	20.00	60.00	120	250	—

KM# 261 KREUZER
0.7700 g., 0.1870 Silver .0046 oz. **Ruler:** Ludwig X **Obv:** Crowned lion with sword between H.D

Date	Mintage	F	VF	XF	Unc	BU
1806	—	15.00	40.00	80.00	160	—

KM# 262 KREUZER
0.7700 g., 0.1870 Silver .0046 oz. **Ruler:** Ludwig X As Grand Duke Ludwig I **Obv:** Crowned lion between H.D.-L.M **Rev:** Value

Date	Mintage	F	VF	XF	Unc	BU
1806	—	10.00	50.00	100	200	—
Note: Variety exists without dots						
1807	—	15.00	60.00	120	220	—

KM# 263 KREUZER
0.7700 g., 0.1870 Silver .0046 oz. **Ruler:** Ludwig X As Grand Duke Ludwig I **Obv:** Crowned lion with sword between H.D.-L.M

Date	Mintage	F	VF	XF	Unc	BU
1807	—	15.00	40.00	80.00	120	—

KM# 264 KREUZER
0.7700 g., 0.1870 Silver .0046 oz. **Ruler:** Ludwig X As Grand Duke Ludwig I **Obv:** Crowned lion with sword between G.H.-L.M **Rev:** Value

Date	Mintage	F	VF	XF	Unc	BU
1807	—	15.00	50.00	180	360	—
1808	—	15.00	40.00	160	320	—
1809	—	15.00	50.00	180	360	—

KM# 275 KREUZER
0.7700 g., 0.1870 Silver .0046 oz. **Ruler:** Ludwig X As Grand Duke Ludwig I **Obv:** Crowned arms between G.H.-L.M

Date	Mintage	F	VF	XF	Unc	BU
1809	—	8.00	20.00	60.00	140	—
1810	—	8.00	20.00	60.00	140	—
1817	—	8.00	20.00	60.00	140	—

KM# 284 KREUZER
0.7700 g., 0.1870 Silver .0046 oz. **Ruler:** Ludwig X As Grand Duke Ludwig I **Obv:** Crowned arms between G.H.-S.M

Date	Mintage	F	VF	XF	Unc	BU
1819	—	8.00	30.00	80.00	180	—

KM# 299 KREUZER
0.7700 g., 0.1870 Silver .0046 oz. **Ruler:** Ludwig II

Date	Mintage	F	VF	XF	Unc	BU
1834	—	3.00	9.00	20.00	45.00	—
1835	—	3.00	9.00	20.00	45.00	—
1836	—	3.00	9.00	20.00	45.00	—
1837	—	3.00	9.00	20.00	45.00	—
1838	—	3.00	9.00	20.00	45.00	—

KM# 303 KREUZER
0.8300 g., 0.1660 Silver .0044 oz. **Ruler:** Ludwig II

Date	Mintage	F	VF	XF	Unc	BU
1837	—	3.00	12.00	25.00	55.00	—
1838	—	3.00	12.00	25.00	55.00	—
1839	—	3.00	12.00	25.00	55.00	—
1840	—	3.00	12.00	25.00	55.00	—
1841	—	3.00	12.00	25.00	55.00	—
1842	438,000	3.00	12.00	25.00	55.00	—

KM# 316 KREUZER
0.8300 g., 0.1660 Silver .0044 oz. **Ruler:** Ludwig II

Date	Mintage	F	VF	XF	Unc	BU
1843	129,000	3.00	8.00	18.00	40.00	—
1844	—	3.00	8.00	18.00	40.00	—
1845	516,000	3.00	8.00	18.00	40.00	—
1847	—	3.00	8.00	18.00	40.00	—

KM# 324 KREUZER
0.8300 g., 0.1660 Silver .0044 oz. **Ruler:** Ludwig III

Date	Mintage	F	VF	XF	Unc	BU
1848	546,000	2.50	7.00	15.00	35.00	—
1849	—	2.50	7.00	15.00	35.00	—
1850	—	2.50	7.00	15.00	35.00	—
1852	—	2.50	7.00	15.00	35.00	—
1854	236,000	2.50	7.00	15.00	35.00	—
1855	162,000	2.50	7.00	15.00	35.00	—
1856	334,000	2.50	7.00	15.00	35.00	—

KM# 339 KREUZER
0.8300 g., 0.1660 Silver .0044 oz. **Ruler:** Ludwig III

Date	Mintage	F	VF	XF	Unc	BU
1858	271,000	2.00	6.00	13.00	30.00	—
1859	147,000	2.00	6.00	13.00	30.00	—
1860	268,000	2.00	6.00	13.00	30.00	—
1861	207,000	2.00	6.00	13.00	30.00	—
1862	211,000	2.00	6.00	13.00	30.00	—
1863	190,000	2.00	6.00	13.00	30.00	—
1864	376,000	2.00	6.00	13.00	30.00	—
1865	181,000	2.00	6.00	13.00	30.00	—
1866	247,000	2.00	6.00	13.00	30.00	—
1867	273,000	2.00	6.00	13.00	30.00	—
1868	199,000	2.00	6.00	13.00	30.00	—
1869	249,000	2.00	6.00	13.00	30.00	—
1870	349,000	2.00	6.00	13.00	30.00	—
1871	366,000	2.00	6.00	13.00	30.00	—
1872	128,000	2.00	6.00	13.00	30.00	—

KM# 256 3 KREUZER (Groschen)
Billon **Ruler:** Ludwig X **Obv:** Lion divides H.D **Rev:** Value **Rev. Legend:** LAND MUNZE

Date	Mintage	F	VF	XF	Unc	BU
1801	—	10.00	30.00	70.00	120	—
1801	—	10.00	30.00	70.00	120	—
1802	—	10.00	30.00	80.00	140	—
1803	—	10.00	30.00	80.00	140	—
1804	—	10.00	30.00	65.00	100	—
1805	—	10.00	30.00	65.00	100	—

KM# 269 3 KREUZER (Groschen)
1.3900 g., 0.2810 Silver .0125 oz. **Ruler:** Ludwig X As Grand Duke Ludwig I **Obv:** Crowned arms G.H.-L.H **Rev:** Value **Rev. Legend:** III KREUZER

Date	Mintage	F	VF	XF	Unc	BU
1808	—	12.00	40.00	90.00	250	—
1809	—	12.00	40.00	90.00	250	—
1810	—	12.00	40.00	90.00	250	—

KM# 282 3 KREUZER (Groschen)
1.3900 g., 0.2810 Silver .0125 oz. **Ruler:** Ludwig X As Grand Duke Ludwig I **Rev:** Value **Rev. Legend:** 3 KREUZER

Date	Mintage	F	VF	XF	Unc	BU
1817	—	20.00	60.00	120	250	—

KM# 285 3 KREUZER (Groschen)
1.3900 g., 0.2810 Silver .0125 oz. **Ruler:** Ludwig X As Grand Duke Ludwig I

Date	Mintage	F	VF	XF	Unc	BU
1819	—	10.00	35.00	80.00	180	—
1822	—	10.00	35.00	80.00	180	—

KM# 295 3 KREUZER (Groschen)
1.3900 g., 0.2810 Silver .0125 oz. **Ruler:** Ludwig II **Obv:** Crowned arms, GR HERZOGTH **Rev:** Value **Rev. Legend:** SCHEIDEMUNZE

Date	Mintage	F	VF	XF	Unc	BU
1833	—	15.00	45.00	85.00	180	—

KM# 296 3 KREUZER (Groschen)
1.3900 g., 0.2810 Silver .0125 oz. **Ruler:** Ludwig II

Date	Mintage	F	VF	XF	Unc	BU
1833	—	4.00	12.00	26.00	60.00	—
1834	—	4.00	12.00	26.00	60.00	—
1835	—	4.00	12.00	26.00	60.00	—
1836	—	4.00	12.00	26.00	60.00	—

KM# 305 3 KREUZER (Groschen)
1.3900 g., 0.2810 Silver .0125 oz. **Ruler:** Ludwig II

Date	Mintage	F	VF	XF	Unc	BU
1838	—	3.00	10.00	25.00	55.00	—
1839	—	3.00	10.00	25.00	55.00	—
1840	—	3.00	10.00	25.00	55.00	—
1841	—	3.00	10.00	25.00	55.00	—
1842	280,000	3.00	10.00	25.00	55.00	—

KM# 317 3 KREUZER (Groschen)
1.3900 g., 0.2810 Silver .0125 oz. **Ruler:** Ludwig II **Obv. Legend:** GROSHERZOGTHUM HESSEN

Date	Mintage	F	VF	XF	Unc	BU
1843	288,000	2.50	8.00	20.00	45.00	—
1844	—	2.50	8.00	20.00	45.00	—
1845	245,000	2.50	8.00	20.00	45.00	—
1846	—	2.50	8.00	20.00	45.00	—
1847	—	2.50	8.00	20.00	45.00	—

KM# 325 3 KREUZER (Groschen)
1.3900 g., 0.2810 Silver .0125 oz. **Ruler:** Ludwig III

Date	Mintage	F	VF	XF	Unc	BU
1848	82,000	2.50	8.00	20.00	45.00	—
1850	—	2.50	8.00	20.00	45.00	—
1851	—	2.50	8.00	20.00	45.00	—
1852	—	2.50	8.00	20.00	45.00	—
1853	—	2.50	8.00	20.00	45.00	—
1854	76,000	2.50	8.00	20.00	45.00	—
1855	148,000	2.50	8.00	20.00	45.00	—
1856	62,000	2.50	8.00	20.00	45.00	—

KM# 345 3 KREUZER (Groschen)
1.2300 g., 0.2500 Silver .0138 oz. **Ruler:** Ludwig III

Date	Mintage	F	VF	XF	Unc	BU
1864	95,000	3.00	12.00	25.00	55.00	—
1865	87,000	3.00	12.00	25.00	55.00	—
1866	90,000	3.00	12.00	25.00	55.00	—
1867	77,000	3.00	12.00	25.00	55.00	—

KM# 265 5 KREUZER
2.2300 g., 0.4370 Silver .0313 oz. **Ruler:** Ludwig X As Grand Duke Ludwig I **Obv:** Crowned L **Rev:** Value

Date	Mintage	F	VF	XF	Unc	BU
1807	—	30.00	80.00	220	400	—

KM# 266 5 KREUZER
2.2300 g., 0.4370 Silver .0313 oz. **Ruler:** Ludwig X As Grand Duke Ludwig I **Obv:** Curled edges on L

Date	Mintage	F	VF	XF	Unc	BU
1807	—	40.00	125	300	600	—

KM# 270 5 KREUZER
2.2300 g., 0.4370 Silver .0313 oz. **Ruler:** Ludwig X As Grand Duke Ludwig I **Obv:** L at truncation **Rev:** F. IUSTIRT F. below arms

Date	Mintage	F	VF	XF	Unc	BU
1808	—	50.00	150	450	900	—

KM# 286 6 KREUZER
2.4300 g., 0.3430 Silver .0267 oz. **Ruler:** Ludwig X As Grand Duke Ludwig I

Date	Mintage	F	VF	XF	Unc	BU
1819	—	6.00	12.00	35.00	150	—
1820	—	6.00	12.00	35.00	150	—

KM# 290 6 KREUZER
2.4300 g., 0.3430 Silver .0267 oz. **Ruler:** Ludwig X As Grand Duke Ludwig I

Date	Mintage	F	VF	XF	Unc	BU
1821	—	6.00	20.00	40.00	80.00	—
1824	—	6.00	20.00	40.00	80.00	—
1826	—	6.00	20.00	40.00	80.00	—
1827	—	6.00	20.00	40.00	80.00	—
1828	—	6.00	20.00	40.00	80.00	—
1833	—	6.00	20.00	40.00	80.00	—

KM# 297 6 KREUZER
2.4300 g., 0.3430 Silver .0267 oz. **Ruler:** Ludwig II

Date	Mintage	F	VF	XF	Unc	BU
1833	—	5.00	18.00	36.00	70.00	—
1834	—	5.00	18.00	36.00	70.00	—
1835	—	5.00	18.00	36.00	70.00	—
1836	—	5.00	18.00	36.00	70.00	—
1837	—	5.00	18.00	36.00	70.00	—

KM# 306 6 KREUZER
2.4600 g., 0.3500 Silver .0276 oz. **Ruler:** Ludwig II

Date	Mintage	F	VF	XF	Unc	BU
1838	—	6.00	24.00	48.00	95.00	—
1839	—	6.00	24.00	48.00	95.00	—
1840	—	6.00	24.00	48.00	95.00	—
1841	—	6.00	24.00	48.00	95.00	—
1842	816,000	6.00	24.00	48.00	95.00	—

KM# 318 6 KREUZER
2.4600 g., 0.3500 Silver .0276 oz. **Ruler:** Ludwig II

Date	Mintage	F	VF	XF	Unc	BU
1843	775,000	4.00	16.00	32.00	65.00	—
1844	331,000	4.00	16.00	32.00	65.00	—
1845	235,000	4.00	16.00	32.00	65.00	—
1846	897,000	4.00	16.00	32.00	65.00	—
1847	—	4.00	16.00	32.00	65.00	—

KM# 326 6 KREUZER
2.4600 g., 0.3500 Silver .0276 oz. **Ruler:** Ludwig III

Date	Mintage	F	VF	XF	Unc	BU
1848	243,000	5.00	18.00	36.00	70.00	—
1850	—	5.00	18.00	36.00	70.00	—
1851	—	5.00	18.00	36.00	70.00	—
1852	—	5.00	18.00	36.00	70.00	—
1853	—	5.00	18.00	36.00	70.00	—
1854	33,000	5.00	18.00	36.00	70.00	—
1855	72,000	5.00	18.00	36.00	70.00	—
1856	44,000	5.00	18.00	36.00	70.00	—

KM# 346 6 KREUZER
2.4600 g., 0.3500 Silver .0276 oz. **Ruler:** Ludwig III

Date	Mintage	F	VF	XF	Unc	BU
1864	52,000	5.00	18.00	36.00	70.00	—
1865	39,000	5.00	18.00	36.00	70.00	—
1866	43,000	5.00	18.00	36.00	70.00	—
1867	60,000	5.00	18.00	36.00	70.00	—

KM# 271 10 KREUZER
3.9000 g., 0.5000 Silver .0626 oz. **Ruler:** Ludwig X As Grand Duke Ludwig I

Date	Mintage	F	VF	XF	Unc	BU
1808 RF	—	32.00	90.00	220	500	—

KM# 267 20 KREUZER
6.6800 g., 0.5830 Silver .1252 oz. **Ruler:** Ludwig X As Grand Duke Ludwig I **Obv:** Head right, FRISCH F. at truncation **Rev:** Crowned arms dividing date, R.F. below

Date	Mintage	F	VF	XF	Unc	BU
1807 RF	—	28.00	70.00	180	500	—

KM# 268 20 KREUZER
6.6800 g., 0.5830 Silver .1252 oz. **Ruler:** Ludwig X As Grand Duke Ludwig I **Obv. Legend:** LUDEWIG

Date	Mintage	F	VF	XF	Unc	BU
1807 RF	—	30.00	80.00	200	500	—
1808 RF	—	30.00	80.00	200	500	—
1809 RF	—	30.00	80.00	200	500	—

KM# 276 20 KREUZER
6.6800 g., 0.5830 Silver .1252 oz. **Ruler:** Ludwig X As Grand Duke Ludwig I **Obv. Legend:** LUDWIG..

Date	Mintage	F	VF	XF	Unc	BU
1809 RF	—	35.00	90.00	250	700	—

KM# 307 1/2 GULDEN
5.3000 g., 0.9000 Silver .1533 oz. **Ruler:** Ludwig II **Obv:** VOIGHT below head

Date	Mintage	F	VF	XF	Unc	BU
1838	1,080,000	20.00	40.00	80.00	200	—
1839	Inc. above	20.00	40.00	80.00	200	—
1840	Inc. above	20.00	40.00	80.00	200	—
1841	Inc. above	20.00	40.00	80.00	200	—
1843	151,000	20.00	40.00	80.00	200	—
1844	81,000	20.00	40.00	80.00	250	—
1845	167,000	20.00	40.00	80.00	200	—
1846	33,000	22.00	45.00	100	250	—

KM# 336 1/2 GULDEN
5.3000 g., 0.9000 Silver .1533 oz. **Ruler:** Ludwig III **Obv:** VOIGHT below head

Date	Mintage	F	VF	XF	Unc	BU
1855	47,000	35.00	80.00	180	450	—

KM# 304 GULDEN (2/3 Thaler)
10.6000 g., 0.9000 Silver .3067 oz. **Ruler:** Ludwig II **Obv:** Small head left **Rev:** Value within wreath

Date	Mintage	F	VF	XF	Unc	BU
1837	1,122,000	35.00	90.00	180	400	—

KM# 308 GULDEN (2/3 Thaler)
10.6000 g., 0.9000 Silver .3067 oz. **Ruler:** Ludwig II **Obv:** Large letters in legend

Date	Mintage	F	VF	XF	Unc	BU
1838	Inc. above	35.00	100	200	450	—

KM# 309 GULDEN (2/3 Thaler)
10.6000 g., 0.9000 Silver .3067 oz. **Ruler:** Ludwig II **Obv:** VOIGT below head

Date	Mintage	F	VF	XF	Unc	BU
1839	Inc. above	20.00	45.00	100	250	—
1840	Inc. above	20.00	45.00	100	250	—
1841	Inc. above	20.00	45.00	100	250	—
1842	605,000	20.00	45.00	100	250	—
1843	314,000	20.00	45.00	100	250	—
1844	191,000	20.00	45.00	100	250	—
1845	176,000	20.00	45.00	100	250	—
1846	144,000	20.00	45.00	100	250	—
1847	251,000	20.00	45.00	100	250	—

KM# 319 GULDEN (2/3 Thaler)
10.6000 g., 0.9000 Silver .3067 oz. **Ruler:** Ludwig II **Subject:** Visit of Crown Prince of Russia **Obv:** VOIGT below head **Rev. Legend:** ZUR ERINNERUNG AN DEN 20 DECEMBER 1843

Date	Mintage	F	VF	XF	Unc	BU
1843	—	200	400	700	1,300	—

KM# 327 GULDEN (2/3 Thaler)
10.6000 g., 0.9000 Silver .3067 oz. **Ruler:** Ludwig II **Subject:** Public Freedom Through German Parliament **Rev. Legend:** PRESSEFREIHEIT...

Date	Mintage	F	VF	XF	Unc	BU
1848	—	125	200	400	650	—

KM# 328 GULDEN (2/3 Thaler)
10.5800 g., 0.9000 Silver .3061 oz. **Ruler:** Ludwig III

Date	Mintage	F	VF	XF	Unc	BU
1848	90,000	50.00	85.00	180	400	—
1854 VOIGT below head	44,000	40.00	75.00	150	350	—
1855 VOIGT below head	90,000	40.00	75.00	140	300	—
1856 VOIGT below head	153,000	30.00	50.00	130	260	—

KM# 321 2 GULDEN
21.2100 g., 0.9000 Silver .6138 oz. **Ruler:** Ludwig II **Obv:** VOIGHT below head

Date	Mintage	F	VF	XF	Unc	BU
1845	44,000	50.00	120	240	600	—
1846	270,000	45.00	100	200	500	—
1847	30,000	55.00	120	275	650	—

KM# 329 2 GULDEN
21.2100 g., 0.9000 Silver .6138 oz. **Ruler:** Ludwig III **Obv:** VOIGHT below head

Date	Mintage	F	VF	XF	Unc	BU
1848	252,000	60.00	130	280	800	—
1849	Inc. above	60.00	130	280	800	—
1853	Inc. above	60.00	130	280	800	—
1854	127,000	40.00	120	270	700	—
1855	149,000	40.00	120	270	700	—
1856	64,000	40.00	120	270	700	—

KM# 300 5 GULDEN
3.4250 g., 0.9040 Gold .0995 oz. **Ruler:** Ludwig II **Obv:** Head left, C.V. below **Rev:** Crowned draped arms, value 5G **Rev. Legend:** AUS HESS. RHEINGOLD

Date	Mintage	F	VF	XF	Unc	BU
1835 CV-HR	60	2,000	4,000	8,500	15,000	—

KM# 301 5 GULDEN
3.4250 g., 0.9040 Gold .0995 oz. **Ruler:** Ludwig II

Date	Mintage	F	VF	XF	Unc	BU
1835 CV-HR	22,000	700	1,500	2,000	3,250	—
1840 CV-HR	Inc. above	400	700	1,500	2,500	—
1841 CV-HR	Inc. above	400	700	1,500	2,500	—
1842 CV-HR	Inc. above	400	700	1,500	2,500	—

KM# 293 10 GULDEN
6.8500 g., 0.9040 Gold .1991 oz. **Ruler:** Ludwig X As Grand Duke Ludwig I

Date	Mintage	F	VF	XF	Unc	BU
1826 HR	1,700	1,000	2,000	3,500	4,500	—
1827 HR	1,705	1,000	2,000	3,500	4,500	—

KM# 315 10 GULDEN
6.8500 g., 0.9040 Gold .1991 oz. **Ruler:** Ludwig II

Date	Mintage	F	VF	XF	Unc	BU
1840 CV-HR	17,000	600	1,300	2,000	3,500	—
1841 CV-HR	Inc. above	600	1,300	2,000	3,500	—
1842 CV-HR	Inc. above	600	1,300	2,000	3,500	—

KM# 277 THALER
28.0600 g., 0.8330 Silver .7516 oz. **Ruler:** Ludwig X As Grand Duke Ludwig I

Date	Mintage	F	VF	XF	Unc	BU
1809 L	—	250	500	900	1,800	—

KM# 287 THALER
29.5100 g., 0.8710 Silver .8264 oz. **Ruler:** Ludwig X As Grand Duke Ludwig I **Note:** Krone Thaler.

Date	Mintage	F	VF	XF	Unc	BU
1819 HR	19,000	300	475	900	1,900	—

KM# 292 THALER
29.5100 g., 0.8710 Silver .8264 oz. **Ruler:** Ludwig X As Grand Duke Ludwig I

Date	Mintage	F	VF	XF	Unc	BU
1825 HR	171,000	90.00	150	320	750	—

KM# 298 THALER
29.5100 g., 0.8710 Silver .8264 oz. **Ruler:** Ludwig II **Obv:** VOIGHT below head

Date	Mintage	F	VF	XF	Unc	BU
1833 HR	124,000	90.00	175	350	800	—
1835 HR	558,000	90.00	175	350	800	—
1836 HR	Inc. above	90.00	175	350	800	—
1837 HR	Inc. above	100	200	380	1,000	—

KM# 338 THALER
18.5200 g., 0.9000 Silver .5360 oz. **Ruler:** Ludwig III **Note:** Vereins Thaler.

Date	Mintage	F	VF	XF	Unc	BU
1857	91,000	35.00	90.00	180	375	—
1858	537,000	35.00	70.00	160	330	—
1859	594,000	35.00	70.00	160	330	—
1860	608,000	35.00	70.00	160	330	—
1861	414,000	35.00	70.00	160	330	—
1862	242,000	35.00	70.00	160	330	—
1863	215,000	35.00	70.00	160	330	—
1864	73,000	35.00	70.00	200	450	—
1865	78,000	35.00	70.00	200	450	—
1866	59,000	35.00	70.00	200	450	—
1867	24,000	35.00	70.00	200	450	—
1868	48,000	35.00	70.00	200	450	—
1869	34,000	35.00	70.00	200	450	—
1870	39,000	35.00	70.00	200	450	—
1871	33,000	40.00	85.00	200	450	—

KM# 310 2 THALER (3-1/2 Gulden)
37.1200 g., 0.9000 Silver 1.0742 oz. **Ruler:** Ludwig II

Date	Mintage	F	VF	XF	Unc	BU
1839	24,000	120	220	400	850	—
1840	368,000	85.00	150	300	600	—
1841	688,000	80.00	150	300	600	—
1842	286,000	110	200	400	800	—

KM# 320 2 THALER (3-1/2 Gulden)
37.1200 g., 0.9000 Silver 1.0742 oz. **Ruler:** Ludwig II **Obv:** Similar to KM#310

Date	Mintage	F	VF	XF	Unc	BU
1844	377,000	90.00	175	350	900	—

KM# 335 2 THALER (3-1/2 Gulden)
37.1200 g., 0.9000 Silver 1.0742 oz. **Ruler:** Ludwig II **Rev:** Similar to KM#320

Date	Mintage	F	VF	XF	Unc	BU
1854	43,000	300	500	1,000	2,200	—

REFORM COINAGE

Grossherzogtum within the German Empire

KM# 355 2 MARK
11.1110 g., 0.9000 Silver .3215 oz. **Ruler:** Ludwig III

Date	Mintage	F	VF	XF	Unc	BU
1876H	202,000	130	290	2,700	7,500	12,000
1877H	338,000	100	275	2,500	6,500	10,000

KM# 359 2 MARK
11.1110 g., 0.9000 Silver .3215 oz. **Ruler:** Ludwig IV

Date	Mintage	F	VF	XF	Unc	BU
1888A	22,000	425	1,400	3,000	5,500	8,500
1888A Proof	500	Value: 10,000				

KM# 363 2 MARK
11.1110 g., 0.9000 Silver .3215 oz. **Ruler:** Ludwig IV **Rev:** Type III

Date	Mintage	F	VF	XF	Unc	BU
1891A	63,000	250	575	1,000	3,000	3,500
1891A Proof	—	Value: 4,500				

KM# 368 2 MARK
11.1110 g., 0.9000 Silver .3215 oz. **Ruler:** Ernst Ludwig

Date	Mintage	F	VF	XF	Unc	BU
1895A	54,000	165	350	750	1,500	2,250
1896A	8,950	320	700	1,250	1,750	4,200
1896A Proof	200	Value: 2,750				

Date	Mintage	F	VF	XF	Unc	BU
1898A	34,000	175	375	800	1,600	2,250
1898A Proof	360	Value: 2,500				
1899A	54,000	175	375	800	1,600	2,250
1899A Proof	128	Value: 2,750				
1900A	8,950	350	700	1,250	2,000	4,200
1900A Proof	200	Value: 3,500				

KM# 353 5 MARK
27.7770 g., 0.9000 Silver .8038 oz. **Ruler:** Ludwig III **Rev:** Type II

Date	Mintage	F	VF	XF	Unc	BU
1875H	148,000	75.00	730	2,500	6,500	10,000
1876H	290,000	60.00	120	2,200	5,500	9,000

KM# 356 5 MARK
1.9910 g., 0.9000 Gold .0576 oz. **Ruler:** Ludwig III

Date	Mintage	F	VF	XF	Unc	BU
1877H	103,000	400	700	1,250	1,450	2,000
1877H Proof; Rare	—	—	—	—	—	—

KM# 357 5 MARK
1.9910 g., 0.9000 Gold .0576 oz. **Ruler:** Ludwig IV **Rev:** Type II

Date	Mintage	F	VF	XF	Unc	BU
1877H	79,000	450	800	1,350	1,650	2,500
1877H Proof	—	Value: 3,500				

KM# 360 5 MARK
27.7770 g., 0.9000 Silver .8038 oz. **Ruler:** Ludwig IV **Rev:** Type II

Date	Mintage	F	VF	XF	Unc	BU
1888A	8,940	650	1,300	2,800	7,500	9,500
1888A Proof	400	Value: 10,000				

KM# 364 5 MARK
27.7770 g., 0.9000 Silver .8038 oz. **Ruler:** Ludwig IV **Rev:** Type III

Date	Mintage	F	VF	XF	Unc	BU
1891A	25,000	225	550	2,250	5,500	8,500
1891A Proof	—	Value: 10,000				

KM# 369 5 MARK
27.7770 g., 0.9000 Silver .8038 oz. **Ruler:** Ernst Ludwig

Date	Mintage	F	VF	XF	Unc	BU
1895A	39,000	90.00	200	800	2,250	2,500
1895A Proof	200	Value: 4,000				
1898A	37,000	90.00	200	850	2,250	2,500
1898A Proof	240	Value: 4,000				
1899A	18,000	120	260	1,150	2,500	3,000
1899A Proof	176	Value: 4,500				
1900A	18,000	120	260	1,150	2,500	3,000
1900A Proof	150	Value: 4,500				

KM# 350 10 MARK
3.9820 g., 0.9000 Gold .1152 oz. **Ruler:** Ludwig III

Date	Mintage	F	VF	XF	Unc	BU
1872H	30,000	120	250	500	1,000	1,700
1872H Proof	—	Value: 2,500				
1873H	432,000	110	220	450	900	1,500
1873H Proof	—	Value: 2,500				

KM# 354 10 MARK
3.9820 g., 0.9000 Gold .1152 oz. **Ruler:** Ludwig III **Rev:** Type II

Date	Mintage	F	VF	XF	Unc	BU
1875H	191,000	130	240	385	900	2,000
1876H	513,000	120	200	350	800	1,600
1877H	94,000	150	250	400	1,000	2,200

KM# 358 10 MARK
3.9820 g., 0.9000 Gold .1152 oz. **Ruler:** Ludwig IV

Date	Mintage	F	VF	XF	Unc	BU
1878H	132,000	220	420	650	1,000	1,500
1878H Proof	—	Value: 2,800				
1879H	56,000	250	450	700	1,150	1,600
1879H Proof	—	Value: 2,800				
1880H	109,000	280	500	750	1,200	1,800
1880H Proof	—	Value: 2,800				

KM# 361 10 MARK
3.9820 g., 0.9000 Gold .1152 oz. **Ruler:** Ludwig IV

Date	Mintage	F	VF	XF	Unc	BU
1888A	36,000	300	500	1,100	2,000	2,600
1888A Proof	500	Value: 4,000				

KM# 362 10 MARK
3.9820 g., 0.9000 Gold .1152 oz. **Ruler:** Ludwig IV **Edge:** Vines and stars

Date	Mintage	F	VF	XF	Unc	BU
1890A	54,000	350	600	900	1,600	2,200

KM# 366 10 MARK
3.9820 g., 0.9000 Gold .1152 oz. **Ruler:** Ernst Ludwig **Rev:** Type III

Date	Mintage	F	VF	XF	Unc	BU
1893A	54,000	400	650	950	1,600	2,500
1893A Proof	450	Value: 3,500				

KM# 370 10 MARK
3.9820 g., 0.9000 Gold .1152 oz. **Ruler:** Ernst Ludwig

Date	Mintage	F	VF	XF	Unc	BU
1896A	36,000	240	500	800	1,500	2,000
1896A Proof	230	Value: 2,800				
1898A	75,000	200	475	750	1,400	1,850
1898A Proof	500	Value: 2,800				

KM# 351 20 MARK
7.9650 g., 0.9000 Gold .2304 oz. **Ruler:** Ludwig III **Rev:** Type I

Date	Mintage	F	VF	XF	Unc	BU
1872H	183,000	130	250	480	850	1,400
1872H Proof	—	Value: 3,000				
1873H	521,000	120	220	450	800	1,300

KM# 352 20 MARK
7.9650 g., 0.9000 Gold .2304 oz. **Ruler:** Ludwig III **Rev:** Type II

Date	Mintage	F	VF	XF	Unc	BU
1874H	134,000	250	450	850	2,500	3,500

KM# 365 20 MARK
7.9650 g., 0.9000 Gold .2304 oz. **Ruler:** Ludwig IV

Date	Mintage	F	VF	XF	Unc	BU
1892A	25,000	500	900	1,500	2,600	3,600
1892A Proof	—	Value: 6,000				

KM# 367 20 MARK
7.9650 g., 0.9000 Gold .2304 oz. **Ruler:** Ernst Ludwig **Rev:** Type III

Date	Mintage	F	VF	XF	Unc	BU
1893A	25,000	550	850	1,250	1,850	2,500
1893A Proof	—	Value: 4,000				

KM# 371 20 MARK
7.9650 g., 0.9000 Gold .2304 oz. **Ruler:** Ernst Ludwig

Date	Mintage	F	VF	XF	Unc	BU
1896A	15,000	300	500	900	1,500	1,700
1896A Proof	230	Value: 2,500				
1897A	45,000	180	280	400	1,000	1,200
1897A Proof	400	Value: 2,000				
1898A	70,000	170	265	380	800	1,000
1898A Proof	500	Value: 2,000				
1899A	40,000	180	300	450	850	1,100
1899A Proof	600	Value: 2,000				
1900A	40,000	170	280	400	800	1,000
1900A Proof	500	Value: 2,000				

HESSE-HOMBURG

Located in west central Germany, Hesse-Homburg was created from part of Hesse-Darmstadt in 1622. It had six villages along with Homburg (today Bad Homburg) and is mostly known for its famous landgrave, Friedrich II. Commander of the Brandenburg cavalry, Friedrich II (with the silver leg) won the Battle of Fehrbellin in 1675. Hesse-Homburg was mediatized to Hesse-Darmstadt in 1806 and by 1816 had acquired full sovereignty and the lordship of Meisenheim. The Homburg line became extinct in 1866, and along with Hesse-Darmstadt, was annexed by Prussia.

RULERS
Friedrich V Ludwig, 1751-1820
Friedrich VI Josef, 1820-1829
Ludwig Wilhelm, 1829-1839
Philipp August, 1839-1846
Gustav Adolph, 1846-1848
Ferdinand Heinrich, 1848-1866

MINT OFFICIALS' INITIALS

Initial	Date	Name
RS	1817-45	Rudolph Stadelmann, die-cutter in Darmstadt and Homburg
C.SCHNITZSPAHN	(d. 1877)	Christian Schnitzspahn, chief die-cutter and medailleur in Darmstadt
C.VOIGT, VOIGT	1829-?	Carl F. Voigt, chief die-cutter and medailleur in Munich

PRINCIPALITY

REGULAR COINAGE

KM# 13 KREUZER
0.8300 g., 0.1660 Silver .0044 oz. **Ruler:** Philipp August

Date	Mintage	F	VF	XF	Unc	BU
1840	48,000	80.00	150	250	380	—

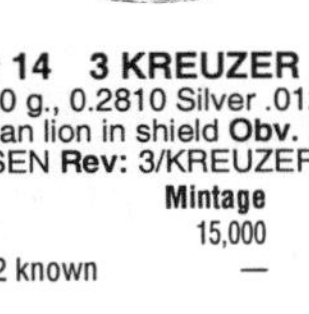

KM# 14 3 KREUZER
1.3800 g., 0.2810 Silver .0124 oz. **Ruler:** Philipp August **Obv:** Hessian lion in shield **Obv. Legend:** LANDGRAFTHUM HESSEN **Rev:** 3/KREUZER/date in oak wreath

Date	Mintage	F	VF	XF	Unc	BU
1840	15,000	600	1,200	1,500	2,000	—
1856 2 known	—	—	—	—	—	—

KM# 15 6 KREUZER
2.4300 g., 0.3430 Silver .0267 oz. **Ruler:** Philipp August

Date	Mintage	F	VF	XF	Unc	BU
1840	57,000	130	240	400	550	—

KM# 11 1/2 GULDEN
5.3000 g., 0.9000 Silver .1533 oz. **Ruler:** Philipp August

Date	Mintage	F	VF	XF	Unc	BU
1838 VOIGT	11,000	90.00	160	320	600	—
1839 Proof	—	Value: 800				

KM# 16 1/2 GULDEN
5.3000 g., 0.9000 Silver .1533 oz. **Ruler:** Philipp August **Obv:** RS at truncation

Date	Mintage	F	VF	XF	Unc	BU
1840 RS	10,000	90.00	180	360	700	—
1841 RS	6,560	90.00	180	360	700	—
1843 RS	6,900	90.00	180	360	700	—
1844 RS	18,000	90.00	180	360	700	—
1845	Inc. above	90.00	180	360	700	—
1846 RS	4,300	90.00	180	360	700	—

KM# 12 GULDEN
10.6000 g., 0.9000 Silver .3067 oz. **Ruler:** Philipp August

Date	Mintage	F	VF	XF	Unc	BU
1838 VOIGT	11,000	120	220	400	750	—
1839 Proof	—	Value: 875				

KM# 17 GULDEN
10.6000 g., 0.9000 Silver .3067 oz. **Ruler:** Philipp August

Date	Mintage	F	VF	XF	Unc	BU
1841 RS	14,000	110	220	450	850	—
1843 RS	6,800	112	230	480	900	—
1844 RS	14,000	110	220	450	850	—
1845 RS	8,100	110	220	450	850	—
1846 RS	8,100	110	220	450	850	—

KM# 18 2 GULDEN
21.2100 g., 0.9000 Silver .6317 oz. **Ruler:** Philipp August

Date	Mintage	F	VF	XF	Unc	BU
1846 VOIGT	11,000	400	700	1,400	3,000	—

KM# 20 THALER (Vereins)
18.5200 g., 0.9000 Silver .5358 oz. **Ruler:** Philipp August

Date	Mintage	F	VF	XF	Unc	BU
1858	5,000	70.00	130	220	500	—
1859	6,579	70.00	130	220	500	—

Date	Mintage	F	VF	XF	Unc	BU
1860	6,593	70.00	130	220	500	—
1861	6,588	70.00	130	220	500	—
1862	6,592	70.00	130	220	500	—
1863	6,575	70.00	130	220	500	—

HOHENLOHE

A countship located in the vicinity of Uffenheim in Franconia and originally centered on the village and castle of present-day Hohlach. The ruling family derived its name from the placename and has been traced back as far as the 10th century. The county gradually acquired various territories between Offenheim to Bad Mergentheim and beyond that became the basis for the many branches of the dynasty. The first of these was Weikersheim with its castle overlooking the confluence of the Vorbach with the Tauber River. In 1472, the surviving elder branch of counts was divided into Hohenlohe-Weikersheim and Hohenlohe Neuenstein. The former became extinct in 1545 and its lands reverted to Hohenlohe-Neuenstein, which itself was divided once again into Hohenlohe-Neuenstein-Neuenstein (Protestant) and Hohenlohe-Neuenstein-Waldenburg (Catholic) in 1551. Hohenlohe-Neuenstein-Neuenstein was further divided in 1610 and Hohenlohe-Neuenstein-Waldenburg underwent the same process in 1600 with the establishment of Hohenlohe-Waldenburg-Pfedelbach, Hohenlohe-Waldenburg-Schillingsfürst and Hohenlohe-Waldenburg-Waldenburg. See the sections under each of these branches for the subsequent history of each. The lands of all branches of Hohenlohe were mediatized in 1806 and passed to Bavaria and Württemberg.

MINT MARKS

S - Schwabach

MINT OFFICIALS' INITIALS

Initial	Date	Name
D	1800-06	Anton Paul Dallinger, die-cutter in Nüremberg
ICE	1803	Johann Christoph Eberhardt in Wertheim

HOHENLOHE-KIRCHBERG

This principality was located in southern Germany. The Kirchberg line was founded in 1701. The count was raised to the rank of prince of the empire in 1764 and the last prince died in 1819.

RULERS

Christian Friedrich Karl, 1767-1806

PRINCIPALITY

REGULAR COINAGE

KM# 15 1/2 THALER (Convention)
Silver **Ruler:** Christian Friedrich Karl

Date	Mintage	F	VF	XF	Unc	BU
1804 D	—	275	500	900	1550	—

HOHENLOHE-NEUENSTEIN-OEHRINGEN

This principality was located in southern Germany. The Neuenstein-Oehringen line was founded in 1610 and the first prince of the empire from this line was proclaimed in 1764. The line became extinct in 1805 and the lands passed to Ingelfingen.

RULERS

Ludwig Friedrich Karl, 1765-1805

PRINCIPALITY

REGULAR COINAGE

KM# 70 10 KREUZER
Silver **Ruler:** Ludwig Friedrich Karl

Date	Mintage	F	VF	XF	Unc	BU
1803 IC-E	—	20.00	40.00	90.00	185	—

TRADE COINAGE

KM# 71 DUCAT
3.5000 g., 0.9860 Gold .1109 oz. **Ruler:** Ludwig Friedrich Karl **Subject:** 81st Birthday - L.F. Karl

Date	Mintage	F	VF	XF	Unc	BU
1804 D	—	850	1,800	3,250	6,000	—

KM# 72 2 DUCAT
7.0000 g., 0.9860 Gold .2219 oz. **Ruler:** Ludwig Friedrich Karl **Subject:** 81st Birthday - L.F. Karl **Obv:** Bust right **Rev:** Crowned arms

Date	Mintage	F	VF	XF	Unc	BU
1804 D	—	1,000	2,500	4,500	8,500	—

PATTERNS

Including off metal strikes

KM#	Date	Mintage	Identification	Mkt Val
Pn1	1804 D	—	Ducat. Silver. 81st Birthday.	200

HOHENZOLLERN-HECHINGEN

The origins of this family, a branch of which produced the later rulers of Brandenburg-Prussia and the Kaisers of Imperial Germany, supposedly date from the 9th century. The castle of Zollern was first built in that time by Count Tassilo in Swabia, on a high hill just south of the town of Hechingen. The earliest historical member of the family was Burkhard, who died in 1040. His descendant, Count Friedrich I (III), obtained the burgraviate of Nürnberg by marriage and ruler there 1192-1200. The two sons of Friedrich I divided the family holdings, with Friedrich II succeeding in Swabia, while the younger Konrad III ruled in Nürnberg and the Franconian territories of the family. It was from the latter that the lines of Brandenburg-Prussia, Ansbach and Bayreuth descended. The elder line in Hohenzollern underwent several divisions in subsequent years, the most important having occurred in 1576, when Hohenzollern-Hechingen, Hohenzollern-Haigerloch and Hohenzollern-Sigmaringen were established. Haigerlock soon died out, but the other two continued into the 19th century.

RULERS

Hermann Friedrich Otto, 1798-1810
Friedrich Hermann Otto, 1810-1838
Friedrich Wilhelm Constantin, 1838-1849

MINT OFFICIALS' INITIALS

Initials	Date	Name
CH, ICH	1783-1808	Johann Christian Heuglin
C.VOIGT	1829-73	Carl Friedrich Voigt, medailleur in Munich
ILW, W	1798-1845	Johann Ludwig Wagner, die-cutter

ARMS

Hohenzollern: Quartered square, upper left and lower right dark, upper right and lower left light.

Office of hereditary chamberlain to the emperor: Crossed sceptres.

PRINCIPALITY

REGULAR COINAGE

KM# 47 3 KREUZER (Groschen)
1.2900 g., 0.3330 Silver .0138 oz. **Ruler:** Friedrich Wilhelm Constantin **Obv:** Crowned arms **Rev:** Value within wreath

Date	Mintage	F	VF	XF	Unc	BU
1845	30,000	10.00	25.00	50.00	160	—
1846	30,000	10.00	25.00	50.00	160	—
1847	8,000	15.00	30.00	60.00	200	—

KM# 45 6 KREUZER
2.5900 g., 0.3330 Silver .0277 oz. **Ruler:** Friedrich Wilhelm Constantin **Obv:** Crowned arms **Rev:** Value within wreath

Date	Mintage	F	VF	XF	Unc	BU
1841	24,000	15.00	35.00	60.00	175	—
1842	26,000	15.00	35.00	60.00	175	—
1845	25,000	15.00	35.00	60.00	175	—
1846	25,000	15.00	35.00	60.00	175	—
1847	26,000	15.00	35.00	60.00	175	—

KM# 40 1/2 GULDEN
5.3000 g., 0.9000 Silver .1533 oz. **Ruler:** Friedrich Wilhelm Constantin

Date	Mintage	F	VF	XF	Unc	BU
1839	15,000	35.00	60.00	150	300	—
1841	6,000	35.00	60.00	150	325	—
1842	5,540	35.00	60.00	150	325	—
1843	6,000	35.00	60.00	150	325	—
1844	6,000	35.00	60.00	150	325	—
1845	6,000	35.00	60.00	150	325	—
1846	6,000	35.00	60.00	150	325	—
1847	6,000	35.00	60.00	150	325	—

KM# 41 GULDEN
10.6000 g., 0.9000 Silver .3067 oz. **Ruler:** Friedrich Wilhelm Constantin

Date	Mintage	F	VF	XF	Unc	BU
1839	15,000	50.00	100	200	450	—
1841	6,000	50.00	100	200	500	—
1842	6,000	50.00	100	200	500	—
1843	8,280	50.00	100	200	500	—
1844	6,000	50.00	100	200	500	—
1845	5,465	50.00	100	200	500	—
1846	5,718	50.00	100	200	500	—
1847	6,324	50.00	100	200	500	—

KM# 48 2 GULDEN
21.2100 g., 0.9000 Silver .6138 oz. **Ruler:** Friedrich Wilhelm Constantin

Date	Mintage	F	VF	XF	Unc	BU
1846	4,300	175	450	1,000	1,500	—
1847	4,300	175	450	900	1,450	—

KM# 35 THALER
28.0600 g., 0.8330 Silver .7516 oz. **Ruler:** Hermann Friedrich Otto

Date	Mintage	F	VF	XF	Unc	BU
1804 W-CH	2,000	400	800	1,400	3,000	—

KM# 36 THALER
28.0600 g., 0.8330 Silver .7516 oz. **Ruler:** Hermann Friedrich Otto **Obv:** ILH below shoulder

Date	Mintage	F	VF	XF	Unc	BU
1804	—	400	800	1,400	3,000	—

KM# 46 2 THALER (3-1/2 Gulden)
37.1200 g., 0.9000 Silver 1.0742 oz. **Ruler:** Hermann Friedrich Otto

Date	Mintage	F	VF	XF	Unc	BU
1844	2,346	400	800	1,600	2,800	—
1845	1,000	425	925	1,800	3,200	—
1846	570	500	1,000	2,000	3,600	—

HOHENZOLLERN-SIGMARINGEN

Located in southern Germany, the Sigmaringen line was founded in 1576. The counts obtained the mint right in 1471 and were raised to the rank of Prince of the Empire in 1623. As a result of the 1848 revolutions the princes abdicated in favor of Prussia in 1849.

RULERS

Anton Aloys, 1785-1831
Carl, 1831-1848
Carl Anton, 1848-1849

MINT OFFICIALS' INITIALS

Initial	Date	Name
D	1828-48	Carl Wilhelm Doell in Karlsruhe
BALBACH	1848-56	Othemar Balbach, medailleur in Karlsruhe

ARMS

Hohenzollern - quartered black and silver
Sigmaringen - stag left

PRINCIPALITY

REGULAR COINAGE

KM# 21 KREUZER
Copper **Obv:** Cowned arms **Rev:** Value: EIN KRUEZER

Date	Mintage	F	VF	XF	Unc	BU
1842	180,000	3.00	8.00	25.00	100	—
1846	55,000	4.00	9.00	30.00	120	—

KM# 22 KREUZER
0.6200 g., 0.2500 Silver .0049 oz. **Rev:** Value: 1 KRUEZER

Date	Mintage	F	VF	XF	Unc	BU
1842	120,000	3.00	8.00	25.00	100	—
1846	60,000	4.00	9.00	30.00	120	—

KM# 17 3 KREUZER (Groschen)
1.2900 g., 0.3330 Silver .0138 oz.

Date	Mintage	F	VF	XF	Unc	BU
1839	52,000	6.00	12.00	35.00	145	—
1841	68,000	6.00	12.00	35.00	145	—
1842	72,000	6.00	12.00	35.00	145	—
1844	170,000	6.00	12.00	35.00	145	—
1845	126,000	6.00	12.00	35.00	145	—
1846	126,000	6.00	12.00	35.00	145	—
1847	60,000	6.00	12.00	35.00	145	—

KM# 18 6 KREUZER
2.5900 g., 0.3330 Silver .0277 oz. **Obv:** Crowned arms **Rev:** Value within wreath

Date	Mintage	F	VF	XF	Unc	BU
1839	75,000	9.00	18.00	45.00	160	—
1840	75,000	9.00	18.00	45.00	160	—
1841	75,000	9.00	18.00	45.00	160	—
1842	74,000	9.00	18.00	45.00	160	—
1844	140,000	9.00	18.00	45.00	160	—
1845	208,000	9.00	18.00	45.00	160	—
1846	208,000	9.00	18.00	45.00	160	—
1847	—	9.00	18.00	45.00	160	—

KM# 15 1/2 GULDEN
5.3000 g., 0.9000 Silver .1533 oz.

Date	Mintage	F	VF	XF	Unc	BU
1838	12,000	50.00	75.00	135	225	—
1839	12,000	50.00	75.00	135	225	—
1840	12,000	50.00	75.00	135	225	—
1841	12,000	50.00	75.00	135	225	—
1842	12,000	50.00	75.00	135	225	—
1843	12,000	50.00	75.00	135	225	—
1844	12,000	50.00	75.00	135	225	—
1845	12,000	50.00	75.00	135	225	—
1846	12,000	50.00	75.00	135	225	—
1847	3,068	70.00	110	150	300	—
1848	—	50.00	75.00	135	225	—

KM# 16.1 GULDEN
10.6000 g., 0.9000 Silver .3067 oz. **Obv:** Head left, D below **Rev:** Value within wreath

Date	Mintage	F	VF	XF	Unc	BU
1838 D	—	65.00	125	200	350	—

KM# 16.2 GULDEN
10.6000 g., 0.9000 Silver .3067 oz. **Obv:** DOELL below head

Date	Mintage	F	VF	XF	Unc	BU
1838	18,000	50.00	100	200	350	—
1839	12,000	50.00	100	200	350	—
1840	12,000	50.00	100	200	350	—
1841	12,000	50.00	100	200	350	—
1842	12,000	50.00	100	200	350	—
1843	12,000	50.00	100	200	350	—
1844	12,000	50.00	100	200	350	—
1845	12,000	50.00	100	200	350	—
1846	12,000	50.00	100	200	350	—
1847	12,000	50.00	100	200	350	—
1848	3,068	75.00	135	250	425	—

KM# 25 GULDEN
10.6000 g., 0.9000 Silver .3067 oz. **Obv:** BALBACH below head

Date	Mintage	F	VF	XF	Unc	BU
1849	5,000	150	250	450	675	—

KM# 24 2 GULDEN
21.2100 g., 0.9000 Silver .6138 oz.

Date	Mintage	F	VF	XF	Unc	BU
1845 D	9,206	125	250	650	1,200	—
1846 D	9,206	125	250	650	1,200	—
1847 D	9,206	125	250	650	1,200	—
1848 D	6,905	125	250	700	1,300	—

KM# 26 2 GULDEN
21.2100 g., 0.9000 Silver .6138 oz. **Obv:** BALBACH below bust

Date	Mintage	F	VF	XF	Unc	BU
1849	1,213	325	600	1,000	2,200	—

KM# 20 2 THALER (3-1/2 Gulden)
37.1200 g., 0.9000 Silver 1.0742 oz.

Date	Mintage	F	VF	XF	Unc	BU
1841	2,857	325	600	1,200	2,400	—
1842	2,857	325	600	1,200	2,400	—
1843	2,877	325	600	1,200	2,400	—

KM# 23 2 THALER (3-1/2 Gulden)
37.1200 g., 0.9000 Silver 1.0742 oz. **Obv:** Similar to KM#20

Date	Mintage	F	VF	XF	Unc	BU
1844	3,300	325	600	1,100	2,000	—
1846	6,600	300	550	1,100	2,200	—
1847	2,000	350	650	1,200	2,200	—

PIEFORTS

KM#	Date	Mintage	Identification	Mkt Val
P1	1840	3	Gulden. Silver. KM#16.2	—

HOHENZOLLERN (UNDER PRUSSIA)

In 1849, Prussia obtained the Hohenzollern lands due to the 1848 revolutions and political unrest. One series of coins was issued by Prussia for their Hohenzollern holdings.

RULERS
Friedrich Wilhelm IV (of Prussia), 1849-1861

PRINCIPALITY

REGULAR COINAGE

KM# 1 KREUZER
Copper **Ruler:** Friedrich Wilhelm IV (of Prussia)

Date	Mintage	F	VF	XF	Unc	BU
1852A	30,000	15.00	25.00	50.00	80.00	—

KM# 2 3 KREUZER
1.2900 g., 0.3330 Silver .0138 oz. **Ruler:** Friedrich Wilhelm IV (of Prussia)

Date	Mintage	F	VF	XF	Unc	BU
1852A	22,000	15.00	30.00	75.00	150	—
1852A Proof	—	Value: 200				

KM# 3 6 KREUZER
2.5900 g., 0.3330 Silver .0277 oz. **Ruler:** Friedrich Wilhelm IV (of Prussia)

Date	Mintage	F	VF	XF	Unc	BU
1852A	27,000	20.00	40.00	100	200	—
1852A Proof	—	Value: 200				

KM# 4 1/2 GULDEN
5.3000 g., 0.9000 Silver .1537 oz. **Ruler:** Friedrich Wilhelm IV (of Prussia)

Date	Mintage	F	VF	XF	Unc	BU
1852A	53,000	50.00	80.00	135	225	—

KM# 5 GULDEN
10.6000 g., 0.9000 Silver .3067 oz. **Ruler:** Friedrich Wilhelm IV (of Prussia)

Date	Mintage	F	VF	XF	Unc	BU
1852A	50,000	65.00	100	150	275	—
1852A Proof	—	Value: 350				

ISENBURG

The lands of the counts of Isenburg lay on both sides of the Main River to the east of Frankfurt. The dynasty traces its lineage back to the 10th century and began issuing coins in the mid-13th century. The county underwent many divisions in the Middle Ages, but by the early 17th century only one dominant branch was producing coins. This was Isenburg-Birstein, divided once again into Isenburg-Offenbach-Birstein and Isenburg-Budingen in 1635. The latter was further divided into four branches in 1673/1687 and two of the substrata became extinct in 1725 and 1780 respectively. Isenburg-Offenbach-Birstein was raised to the rank of prince in 1744 and all other branches had to relinquish their sovereignty to his descendant in 1806. The latter lost his sole leadership in 1813 because he sided with Napoleon and the lands of Isenburg-Offenbach-Birstein were mediatized to Hesse-Darmstadt in 1815. The subdivisions of Isenburg-Budigen did not issue a regular coinage, but struck the series of the quasi-official snipe hellers during the 19th century.

RULERS
Wolfgang Ernst II, 1754-1803
Karl I, 1803-1820
Wolfgang Ernst III, 1820-1866
Karl II, 1866--

Isenburg-Budingen

Ernst Kasimir II, 1775-1801
Ernst Kasimir III, 1801-1848
Adolf II (in Wachtersbach), 1805-1847
Ernst Kasimir IV, 1848-1861
Bruno, 1861-1906

COUNTY

REGULAR COINAGE

KM# 46 6 KREUZER
Billon

Date	Mintage	F	VF	XF	Unc	BU
1811	1,000	50.00	100	225	425	—

KM# 47 12 KREUZER
Silver **Obv:** J. LAROQUE F. at truncation

Date	Mintage	F	VF	XF	Unc	BU
1811	500	65.00	135	275	475	—

KM# 48 THALER
Silver **Note:** Reichs Thaler.

Date	Mintage	F	VF	XF	Unc	BU
1811	100	600	1,200	2,500	4,500	—

TRADE COINAGE

KM# 49 DUCAT
3.5000 g., 0.9860 Gold .1109 oz.

Date	Mintage	F	VF	XF	Unc	BU
1811	—	—	—	—	—	—

KM# 50 2 DUCAT
7.0000 g., 0.9860 Gold .2218 oz. **Note:** Struck with 1 Ducat dies, KM#49.

Date	Mintage	F	VF	XF	Unc	BU
1811	—	2,000	3,500	6,500	10,000	—

PATTERNS

Including off metal strikes

KM#	Date	Mintage	Identification	Mkt Val
Pn1	ND	—	Heller. Silver. KM#58.	—
Pn2	1805	—	Pfennig. Silver. KM#45.	—
Pn3	1811	—	12 Kreuzer. Copper. KM#47.	—
Pn4	1811	—	Thaler. Copper. KM#48.	—

KM#	Date	Mintage	Identification	Mkt Val
Pn5	1811	—	Ducat. Silver. KM#49.	250
Pn6	1811	—	2 Ducat. Silver. KM#50.	350

PIEFORTS

KM#	Date	Mintage	Identification	Mkt Val
P1	1811	—	Thaler. Silver. KM#48.	—

Note: Munzhandlung Moller Auction 10 10-92 XF++/VF realized $50,600

KNYPHAUSEN

The district of Knyphausen was located in northwestern Germany in East Friesland. Local nobility ruled from the 14th century until 1623 when it was sold to Olden- burg. It became autonomous in 1653 and was acquired through marriage to the Bentinck family in 1733. Coins were struck c. 1800. It was claimed by both Anhalt and Oldenburg, and the arms of Knyphausen appear on coins of both places.

RULERS
Wilhelm Gustav Friedrich, 1774-1835

COUNTY

REGULAR COINAGE

KM# 5 9 GROTE (1/8 Thaler)
Silver **Ruler:** Wilhelm Gustav Friedrich **Obv:** Arms **Rev:** Crowned double-headed eagle dividing value

Date	Mintage	F	VF	XF	Unc	BU
1807	—	350	650	1,400	2,000	—

KM# 6 9 GROTE (1/8 Thaler)
Silver **Ruler:** Wilhelm Gustav Friedrich

Date	Mintage	F	VF	XF	Unc	BU
1807	16,000	125	265	525	825	—

PATTERNS

Including off metal strikes

KM#	Date	Mintage	Identification	Mkt Val
Pn1	1806	10	2-1/2 Thaler. Gold.	—
Pn2	1806	—	5 Thaler. Gold.	—
Pn3	1806	—	10 Thaler. Gold.	—

LAUENBURG

The line of rulers of this Saxon duchy became extinct in 1689 and passed to Brunswick-Luneburg-Celle, then to Brunswick-Luneburg-Calenberg-Hannover in 1705. After the Napoleonic Wars, Lauenburg went to Prussia in 1813, to Denmark in 1814, and was regained by Prussia as part of the latter's annexation of Holstein in 1864. The Brunswick duchies struck special coins for Lauenburg. See Saxe-Lauenburg for coinage prior to 1689.

RULERS
Georg III von Brunswick-Luneburg-Calenberg-Hannover, 1760-1818
Frederick VI (of Denmark), 1816-1839

MINT OFFICIALS' INITIALS

Initial	Date	Name
FF	1830	Johann Friedrich Freund

DUCHY

REGULAR COINAGE

KM# 25 2/3 THALER
17.3200 g., 0.7500 Silver .4177 oz.

Date	Mintage	F	VF	XF	Unc	BU
1830 FF	4,000	150	300	550	900	—

LEININGEN-DAGSBURG-HARTENBURG

Established from an early division of Leiningen in 1317 and further divided in 1541, Leiningen-Dagsburg-Hartenburg was located some 30 miles west-southwest of Mannheim. The count was raised to the rank of prince in 1779 and was the only member of his line to issue any coins. His possessions were taken by France in 1801.

RULERS
Karl Friedrich Wilhelm, 1756-1807

PRINCIPALITY

STANDARD COINAGE

KM# 7 PFENNIG
Billon **Ruler:** Karl Friedrich Wilhelm **Obv:** Crown above three eagles within branches **Rev:** Denomination and date

Date	Mintage	VG	F	VF	XF	Unc
1805	—	18.00	35.00	75.00	165	300

KM# 8 2 PFENNIG
Billon **Ruler:** Karl Friedrich Wilhelm **Obv:** Crowned arms **Rev:** Denomination and date above branch

Date	Mintage	VG	F	VF	XF	Unc
1805	—	25.00	50.00	100	220	400

KM# 5 3 KREUZER
Billon **Ruler:** Karl Friedrich Wilhelm **Obv:** Crowned arms within branches **Rev:** Denomination and date above branch

Date	Mintage	VG	F	VF	XF	Unc
1804	—	20.00	40.00	90.00	220	400

KM# 9 3 KREUZER
Billon **Ruler:** Karl Friedrich Wilhelm **Obv:** Crown above three eagles within branches **Rev:** Denomination and date above branch

Date	Mintage	VG	F	VF	XF	Unc
1805	—	18.00	35.00	75.00	185	350

KM# 6 6 KREUZER
Billon **Ruler:** Karl Friedrich Wilhelm **Obv:** Crowned arms within branches **Rev:** Denomination and date above branch

Date	Mintage	VG	F	VF	XF	Unc
1804	—	25.00	50.00	125	325	600

KM# 10 6 KREUZER
Billon **Ruler:** Karl Friedrich Wilhelm **Obv:** Crown above three eagles within branches **Rev:** Denomination and date above branch

Date	Mintage	VG	F	VF	XF	Unc
1805	—	20.00	40.00	90.00	220	400

LIPPE-DETMOLD

The Counts of Lippe ruled over a small state in northwestern Germany. In 1528/9 they became counts; in 1720 they were raised to the rank of princes, but did not use the title until 1789. Another branch of the family ruled the even smaller Schaumburg-Lippe. Lippe joined North German Confederation in 1866, and became part of the German Empire in 1871. When the insane Prince Alexander succeeded to the throne in 1895, the main branch reached an end, and a ten-year testamentary dispute between the Biesterfeld and the Schaumburg-Lippe lines followed - a Wilhelmine cause celebre. The Biesterfeld line gained the principality in 1905, but abdicated in 1918. In 1947 Lippe was absorbed by the German Land of North Rhine-Westphalia.

RULERS
Friedrich Wilhelm Leopold
Alone, 1789-1802
Paul Alexander Leopold II
under Regency of Pauline of Anhalt-Bernburg, 1802-1820
As Independent Prince, 1820-1851
Paul Friedrich Emil Leopold III, 1851-1875
Woldemar, 1875 - 1895
Alexander, 1895 - 1905

MINT MARKS
A - Berlin, 1843-1918
ST - Strickling (Blomberg), 1820-1840
T - Trebbe (Lemgo), 1812-1820

MINT OFFICIALS' INITIALS

Initial	Date	Name
ST	1820-40	Strickling of Blomberg
T	1812-20	Trebbe of Lemgo
	1789-1803	Balthasar Reinhard
	1803	Siegmann

PRINCIPALITY

REGULAR COINAGE

KM# 225 HELLER
Copper **Ruler:** Paul Alexander Leopold II under Regency of Pauline of Anhalt-Bernburg

Date	Mintage	F	VF	XF	Unc	BU
1802 T	166,000	9.00	15.00	30.00	70.00	—
1802	Inc. above	3.00	7.00	18.00	60.00	—
1809 T	108,000	3.00	7.00	18.00	60.00	—

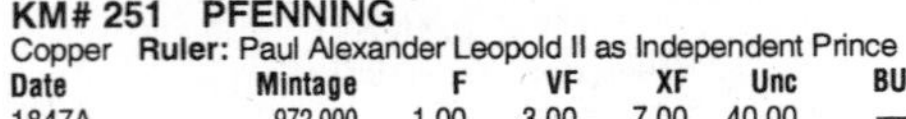

Date	Mintage	F	VF	XF	Unc	BU
1809	—	3.00	7.00	18.00	60.00	—
1812 T	—	3.00	7.00	18.00	60.00	—
1814 T	—	3.00	7.00	18.00	60.00	—
1816 T	—	3.00	7.00	18.00	60.00	—
1816	—	3.00	7.00	18.00	60.00	—

KM# 241 HELLER

Copper **Ruler:** Paul Alexander Leopold II as Independent Prince **Obv:** Blooming rose **Rev:** Value and date **Rev. Legend:** I HELLER

Date	Mintage	F	VF	XF	Unc	BU
1821ST	—	3.00	7.00	15.00	50.00	—
1822ST	—	3.00	7.00	15.00	50.00	—
1825ST	—	3.00	7.00	15.00	50.00	—
1826ST	—	3.00	7.00	15.00	50.00	—
1828ST	—	3.00	7.00	15.00	50.00	—
1835ST	—	3.00	7.00	15.00	50.00	—
1836ST	—	3.00	7.00	15.00	50.00	—
1840ST	—	3.00	7.00	15.00	50.00	—

KM# 244 HELLER

Copper **Ruler:** Paul Alexander Leopold II as Independent Prince **Rev:** Value and date **Rev. Legend:** 1 HELLER

Date	Mintage	F	VF	XF	Unc	BU
1826ST	—	3.00	7.00	15.00	50.00	—

KM# 226 PFENNING

Copper **Ruler:** Friedrich Wilhelm Leopold Alone

Date	Mintage	F	VF	XF	Unc	BU
1802	120,000	5.00	10.00	30.00	130	—

KM# 235 PFENNING

Copper **Ruler:** Paul Alexander Leopold II under Regency of Pauline of Anhalt-Bernburg **Rev:** T below date

Date	Mintage	F	VF	XF	Unc	BU
1818 T	—	4.00	8.00	20.00	120	—

KM# 236 PFENNING

Copper **Ruler:** Paul Alexander Leopold II under Regency of Pauline of Anhalt-Bernburg **Rev:** Without T

Date	Mintage	F	VF	XF	Unc	BU
1818	—	4.00	8.00	20.00	120	—

KM# 240 PFENNING

Copper **Ruler:** Paul Alexander Leopold II as Independent Prince **Rev:** ST below date

Date	Mintage	F	VF	XF	Unc	BU
1820 ST	—	3.00	7.00	18.00	80.00	—
1821 ST	—	3.00	7.00	18.00	80.00	—
1824 ST	—	3.00	7.00	18.00	80.00	—
1825 ST	—	3.00	7.00	18.00	80.00	—

KM# 242 PFENNING

Copper **Ruler:** Paul Alexander Leopold II as Independent Prince **Rev:** Value **Rev. Legend:** PFENNING

Date	Mintage	F	VF	XF	Unc	BU
1821 ST	—	—	—	—	—	—
1824 ST	—	3.00	7.00	20.00	85.00	—

KM# 245 PFENNING

Copper **Ruler:** Paul Alexander Leopold II as Independent Prince

Date	Mintage	F	VF	XF	Unc	BU
1828 ST	—	2.00	5.00	15.00	60.00	—
1829 ST	—	2.00	5.00	15.00	60.00	—
1830 ST	—	2.00	5.00	15.00	60.00	—
1836 ST	—	2.00	5.00	15.00	60.00	—
1840 ST	—	2.00	5.00	15.00	60.00	—

KM# 251 PFENNING

Copper **Ruler:** Paul Alexander Leopold II as Independent Prince

Date	Mintage	F	VF	XF	Unc	BU
1847A	972,000	1.00	3.00	7.00	40.00	—

KM# 260 PFENNING

Copper **Ruler:** Paul Friedrich Emil Leopold III

Date	Mintage	F	VF	XF	Unc	BU
1851A	1,080,000	1.00	3.00	7.00	35.00	—
1858A	900,000	1.00	3.00	7.00	35.00	—

KM# 243 1-1/2 PFENNING (1/192 Thaler)

Copper **Ruler:** Paul Alexander Leopold II as Independent Prince

Date	Mintage	F	VF	XF	Unc	BU
1821 T	—	4.00	8.00	30.00	140	—
1823 T	—	4.00	8.00	30.00	140	—
1824 T	—	4.00	8.00	30.00	140	—
1825 T	—	4.00	8.00	30.00	140	—

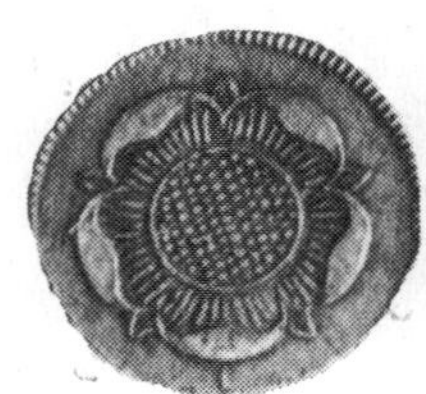

KM# 227 2 PFENNING

Copper **Ruler:** Friedrich Wilhelm Leopold Alone **Obv:** Blooming rose **Rev:** Value, rosette below date

Date	Mintage	F	VF	XF	Unc	BU
1802	127,000	6.00	12.00	35.00	120	—

KM# 252 3 PFENNINGE

Copper **Ruler:** Paul Alexander Leopold II as Independent Prince **Obv:** Crowned shield with blooming rose **Rev:** Value

Date	Mintage	F	VF	XF	Unc	BU
1847A	1,020,000	2.00	5.00	15.00	60.00	—

KM# 261 3 PFENNINGE

Copper **Ruler:** Paul Friedrich Emil Leopold III

Date	Mintage	F	VF	XF	Unc	BU
1858A	60,000	3.00	7.00	20.00	75.00	—

KM# 228 MARIENGROSCHEN (1/36 Thaler)

Billon **Ruler:** Paul Alexander Leopold II under Regency of Pauline of Anhalt-Bernburg **Obv:** Crowned mantled arms, small crown **Rev:** Value and date

Date	Mintage	VG	F	VF	XF	Unc
1802 BR	—	3.00	7.00	20.00	55.00	—
1803 BR	—	3.00	7.00	20.00	55.00	—

KM# 229 MARIENGROSCHEN (1/36 Thaler)

Billon **Ruler:** Paul Alexander Leopold II under Regency of Pauline of Anhalt-Bernburg **Obv:** Large crown

Date	Mintage	VG	F	VF	XF	Unc
1804 BR	—	3.00	7.00	20.00	55.00	—

KM# 253 1/2 SILBER GROSCHEN

0.9700 g., 0.2500 Silver .0077 oz. **Ruler:** Paul Alexander Leopold II as Independent Prince **Obv:** Head right **Rev:** Value

Date	Mintage	F	VF	XF	Unc	BU
1847A	321,000	6.00	12.00	35.00	100	—

KM# 254 SILBER GROSCHEN

1.5500 g., 0.3120 Silver .0155 oz. **Ruler:** Paul Alexander Leopold II as Independent Prince

Date	Mintage	F	VF	XF	Unc	BU
1847A	750,000	5.00	10.00	25.00	60.00	—

KM# 265 SILBER GROSCHEN

2.1900 g., 0.2200 Silver .0154 oz. **Ruler:** Paul Friedrich Emil Leopold III

Date	Mintage	F	VF	XF	Unc	BU
1860A	432,000	6.00	12.00	30.00	75.00	—

KM# 255 2-1/2 SILBER GROSCHEN

3.2400 g., 0.3750 Silver .0390 oz. **Ruler:** Paul Alexander Leopold II as Independent Prince **Obv:** Head right **Rev:** Value

Date	Mintage	F	VF	XF	Unc	BU
1847A	363,000	5.00	10.00	25.00	85.00	—

KM# 266 2-1/2 SILBER GROSCHEN

3.2200 g., 0.3750 Silver .0388 oz. **Ruler:** Paul Friedrich Emil Leopold III

Date	Mintage	F	VF	XF	Unc	BU
1860A	120,000	5.00	10.00	25.00	85.00	—

KM# 267 THALER

18.5200 g., 0.9000 Silver .5360 oz. **Ruler:** Paul Friedrich Emil Leopold III

Date	Mintage	F	VF	XF	Unc	BU
1860A	26,000	40.00	75.00	150	300	—
1866A	18,000	45.00	80.00	165	325	—

KM# 250 2 THALER (3-1/2 gulden)
37.1200 g., 0.9000 Silver 1.0742 oz. **Ruler:** Paul Alexander Leopold II as Independent Prince

Date	Mintage	F	VF	XF	Unc	BU
1843A	17,000	200	400	750	1,500	—

PATTERNS

Including off metal strikes

KM#	Date	Mintage	Identification	Mkt Val
Pn15	1809	—	Heller. Silver. KM#225.	320
Pn16	1847 A	—	3 Pfenninge. Silver. KM#252.	1,250
Pn17	1847 A	—	1/2 Silber Groschen. Copper. KM#253.	425

LOWENSTEIN-WERTHEIM-ROCHEFORT

Rochefort was the Catholic branch of Lowenstein-Wertheim, established in 1635. From 1622 until about 1650, coinage for Lowenstein-Wertheim-Rochefort was struck at the mint of Cugnon in Luxembourg. The ruler was made Prince of the Empire in 1711. All lands in his possession were mediatized in 1806.

RULERS
Dominik Constantin, 1789-1806

MINT
Cugnon Mint in Luxembourg

PRINCIPALITY

Catholic Branch

REGULAR COINAGE

KM# 100 PFENNING
Copper **Ruler:** Dominik Constantin **Obv:** Crowned C monogram **Rev:** Value and date

Date	Mintage	F	VF	XF	Unc	BU
1801	—	6.00	12.00	40.00	185	—
1802	—	6.00	12.00	40.00	185	—

LOWENSTEIN-WERTHEIM VIRNEBURG & ROCHEFORT

COUNTY

JOINT COINAGE

KM# 25 PFENNING
Copper **Note:** Uniface. Eagle above three roses, value: 1 PF above.

Date	Mintage	F	VF	XF	Unc	BU
1801	—	5.00	10.00	32.00	80.00	—
1802	—	5.00	10.00	32.00	80.00	—
1803	—	5.00	10.00	32.00	80.00	—
1804	—	5.00	10.00	32.00	80.00	—

KM# 28 PFENNING
Copper

Date	Mintage	F	VF	XF	Unc	BU
1802	—	3.00	6.00	15.00	50.00	—
1804	—	3.00	6.00	15.00	50.00	—

KM# 29 PFENNING
Copper **Note:** Tear-shaped arms.

Date	Mintage	F	VF	XF	Unc	BU
1802	—	6.00	12.00	35.00	90.00	—

KM# 31 PFENNING
Copper **Obv:** L.M. above shield (error)

Date	Mintage	F	VF	XF	Unc	BU
1804	—	7.00	15.00	40.00	100	—

KM# 30 PFENNING
Copper **Obv:** Spade shield

Date	Mintage	F	VF	XF	Unc	BU
1804	—	3.00	5.00	12.00	42.00	—

KM# 26 KREUZER
Billon **Note:** Varieties exist.

Date	Mintage	F	VF	XF	Unc	BU
1801	—	5.00	10.00	30.00	75.00	—
1802	—	5.00	10.00	30.00	75.00	—
1803	—	5.00	10.00	30.00	75.00	—
1804	—	5.00	10.00	30.00	75.00	—
1805	—	5.00	10.00	30.00	75.00	—
1806	—	5.00	10.00	30.00	75.00	—

KM# 27.1 3 KREUZER
Billon **Obv:** Arms **Rev:** Value

Date	Mintage	F	VF	XF	Unc	BU
1801	—	8.00	16.00	48.00	160	—

KM# 27.2 3 KREUZER
Billon

Date	Mintage	F	VF	XF	Unc	BU
1802	—	8.00	16.00	48.00	160	—
1803	—	8.00	16.00	48.00	160	—

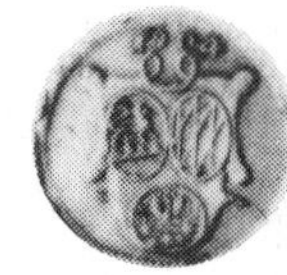

KM# 27.3 3 KREUZER
Billon

Date	Mintage	F	VF	XF	Unc	BU
1804	—	8.00	14.00	42.00	140	—
1805	—	8.00	14.00	42.00	140	—

KM# 32 3 KREUZER
Silver

Date	Mintage	F	VF	XF	Unc	BU
1805	—	—	—	225	—	—

LUBECK

Lübeck became a free city of the empire in 1188 and from c. 1190 into the 13th century an imperial mint existed in the town. It was granted the mint right in 1188, 1226 and 1340, but actually began its first civic coinage c.1350. Occupied by the French during the Napoleonic Wars, it was restored as a free city in 1813 and became part of the German Empire in 1871.

MINT OFFICIALS' INITIALS

Initials	Date	Name
HDF	1773-1801	Hermann David Friederichsen

FREE CITY

TRADE COINAGE

KM# 205 DUCAT
3.5000 g., 0.9860 Gold .1109 oz.

Date	Mintage	F	VF	XF	Unc	BU
1801 HDF	—	400	650	1,100	1,850	—

MECKLENBURG-SCHWERIN

The duchy of Mecklenburg was located along the Baltic coast between Holstein and Pomerania. Schwerin was annexed to Mecklenburg in 1357. During the Thirty Years' War, the dukes of Mecklenburg sided with the Protestant forces against the emperor. Albrecht von Wallenstein, the imperialist general, ousted the Mecklenburg dukes from their territories in 1628. They were restored to their lands in 1632. In 1658 the Mecklenburg dynasty was divided into two lines. No coinage was produced for Mecklenburg-Schwerin from 1708 until 1750. The 1815 Congress of Vienna elevated the duchy to the status of grand duchy and it became a part of the German Empire in 1871 until 1918 when the last grand duke abdicated.

RULERS
Friedrich Franz I, 1785-1837
Paul Friedrich, 1837-1842
Friedrich Franz II, 1842-1883
Friedrich Franz III, 1883-1897
Friedrich Franz IV, 1897-1918

MINT MARKS
A - Berlin
B - Hannover

GRAND DUCHY

REGULAR COINAGE

KM# 280 PFENNIG
Copper **Ruler:** Friedrich Franz I

Date	Mintage	F	VF	XF	Unc	BU
1831	514,000	3.00	6.00	12.00	45.00	—

KM# 315 PFENNIG
Copper **Ruler:** Friedrich Franz II

Date	Mintage	F	VF	XF	Unc	BU
1872B	2,335,000	1.50	3.00	6.00	20.00	—

KM# 281 2 PFENNIG (Zweier)
Copper **Ruler:** Friedrich Franz I

Date	Mintage	F	VF	XF	Unc	BU
1831	257,000	3.00	6.00	12.00	60.00	—

KM# 316 2 PFENNIG (Zweier)
Copper **Ruler:** Friedrich Franz II

Date	Mintage	F	VF	XF	Unc	BU
1872B	1,155,000	2.00	4.00	8.00	30.00	—

KM# 240 3 PFENNIG (Dreiling)
0.5000 g., 0.1870 Silver .0030 oz. **Ruler:** Friedrich Franz I **Rev:** Legend ends ...MECK.SCHWERIN:SCHEID

Date	Mintage	F	VF	XF	Unc	BU
1801	204,000	3.50	8.00	14.00	100	—
1803	117,000	3.50	8.00	14.00	100	—
1804	113,000	3.50	8.00	14.00	100	—
1805	414,000	3.50	8.00	14.00	100	—
1810	117,000	3.50	8.00	14.00	100	—
1811	273,000	3.50	8.00	14.00	100	—
1813	—	3.50	8.00	15.00	100	—
1814	60,000	3.50	8.00	15.00	100	—
1815	81,000	3.50	8.00	15.00	100	—

KM# 251 3 PFENNIG (Dreiling)
Billon **Ruler:** Friedrich Franz I **Obv:** Crowned FF monogram **Rev:** Value

Date	Mintage	F	VF	XF	Unc	BU
1816	199,000	3.00	8.00	15.00	100	—
1817	83,000	3.00	8.00	15.00	100	—
1818	77,000	3.00	8.00	15.00	100	—
1819	251,000	3.00	8.00	15.00	100	—

KM# 255 3 PFENNIG (Dreiling)
Billon **Ruler:** Friedrich Franz I **Rev:** Value: I DREILING, date

Date	Mintage	F	VF	XF	Unc	BU
1819	596,000	2.50	5.00	10.00	100	—
1820	845,000	2.50	5.00	10.00	100	—
1821	516,000	2.50	5.00	10.00	100	—
1822	1,021,000	2.50	5.00	10.00	100	—
1824	235,000	2.50	5.00	10.00	100	—

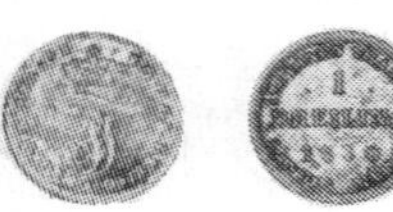

KM# 267 3 PFENNIG (Dreiling)
0.4500 g., 0.1250 Silver .0018 oz. **Ruler:** Friedrich Franz I

Date	Mintage	F	VF	XF	Unc	BU
1828	684,000	2.00	4.00	8.00	40.00	—
1829	207,000	2.00	4.00	8.00	40.00	—
1830	793,000	2.00	4.00	8.00	40.00	—

KM# 282 3 PFENNIG (Dreiling)
0.4500 g., 0.1250 Silver .0018 oz. **Ruler:** Friedrich Franz I

Date	Mintage	F	VF	XF	Unc	BU
1831	64,000	3.00	6.00	12.00	60.00	—
1832	308,000	3.00	5.00	8.00	40.00	—
1833	48,000	4.00	8.00	20.00	70.00	—
1836	452,000	3.00	5.00	8.00	40.00	—

KM# 285 3 PFENNIG (Dreiling)
0.4500 g., 0.1250 Silver .0018 oz. **Ruler:** Paul Friedrich

Date	Mintage	F	VF	XF	Unc	BU
1838	—	3.00	6.00	12.00	60.00	—
1839	172,000	3.00	6.00	12.00	60.00	—
1840	112,000	3.00	6.00	12.00	60.00	—
1841	100,000	3.00	6.00	12.00	60.00	—
1842	157,000	3.00	6.00	12.00	60.00	—

KM# 297 3 PFENNIG (Dreiling)
0.4500 g., 0.1250 Silver .0018 oz. **Ruler:** Friedrich Franz II

Date	Mintage	F	VF	XF	Unc	BU
1842	203,000	3.00	5.00	10.00	55.00	—
1843	230,000	3.00	5.00	10.00	55.00	—
1844	125,000	3.00	5.00	10.00	55.00	—
1845	170,000	3.00	5.00	10.00	55.00	—
1846	77,000	3.00	6.00	14.00	65.00	—

KM# 299 3 PFENNIG (Dreiling)
Copper **Ruler:** Friedrich Franz II

Date	Mintage	F	VF	XF	Unc	BU
1843	89,000	2.50	5.00	10.00	45.00	—
1845	151,000	2.50	5.00	10.00	45.00	—
1846	73,000	2.50	5.00	10.00	45.00	—
1848	—	2.50	5.00	10.00	45.00	—

KM# 310 3 PFENNIG (Dreiling)
Copper **Ruler:** Friedrich Franz II

Date	Mintage	F	VF	XF	Unc	BU
1852A	—	2.00	3.50	7.00	32.00	—
1853A	—	2.00	3.50	7.00	32.00	—
1854A	—	2.00	3.50	7.00	32.00	—
1855A	1,135,000	2.00	3.50	7.00	32.00	—
1858A	—	2.00	3.50	7.00	32.00	—
1859A	—	2.00	3.50	7.00	32.00	—
1860A	—	2.00	3.50	7.00	32.00	—
1861A	—	2.00	3.50	7.00	32.00	—
1863A	—	2.00	3.50	7.00	32.00	—
1864A	1,076,000	2.00	3.50	7.00	32.00	—

KM# 317 5 PFENNIG
Copper **Ruler:** Friedrich Franz II

Date	Mintage	F	VF	XF	Unc	BU
1872B	459,000	7.00	15.00	35.00	75.00	—

KM# 241 6 PFENNIG
0.7600 g., 0.2500 Silver .0061 oz. **Ruler:** Friedrich Franz I

Date	Mintage	F	VF	XF	Unc	BU
1801	80,000	4.00	7.00	20.00	65.00	—
1802	141,000	4.00	7.00	20.00	65.00	—
1803	60,000	4.00	7.00	20.00	65.00	—
1804	62,000	4.00	7.00	20.00	65.00	—
1805	321,000	4.00	7.00	20.00	65.00	—
1809	84,000	4.00	7.00	20.00	65.00	—
1810	81,000	4.00	7.00	20.00	65.00	—
1811	222,000	4.00	7.00	20.00	65.00	—
1813	254,000	4.00	7.00	20.00	65.00	—
1815	199,000	4.00	7.00	20.00	65.00	—

KM# 252 6 PFENNIG
0.7600 g., 0.2500 Silver .0061 oz. **Ruler:** Friedrich Franz I **Obv:** Crowned FF monogram **Rev:** Value 6 PFEN

Date	Mintage	F	VF	XF	Unc	BU
1816	255,000	4.00	7.00	20.00	65.00	—
1817	300,000	4.00	7.00	20.00	65.00	—

KM# 283 6 PFENNIG
0.9000 g., 0.1250 Silver .0036 oz. **Ruler:** Friedrich Franz I **Note:** Without legends.

Date	Mintage	F	VF	XF	Unc	BU
1831	128,000	4.00	8.00	22.00	75.00	—

KM# 260 SECHSLING (6 Pfennig - 1/96 Thaler)
0.7600 g., 0.2500 Silver .0061 oz. **Ruler:** Friedrich Franz I

Date	Mintage	F	VF	XF	Unc	BU
1820	150,000	3.00	6.00	12.00	60.00	—
1821	249,000	3.00	6.00	12.00	60.00	—
1822	272,000	3.00	6.00	12.00	60.00	—
1823	320,000	3.00	6.00	12.00	60.00	—
1824	419,000	3.00	6.00	12.00	60.00	—

KM# 268 SECHSLING (6 Pfennig - 1/96 Thaler)
0.9000 g., 0.1250 Silver .0036 oz. **Ruler:** Friedrich Franz I

Date	Mintage	F	VF	XF	Unc	BU
1828	—	3.00	6.00	12.00	60.00	—
1829	190,000	3.00	6.00	12.00	60.00	—

KM# 220 SCHILLING
1.0800 g., 0.3750 Silver .0130 oz. **Ruler:** Friedrich Franz I **Obv:** Crowned FF monogram **Rev:** Value, date **Rev. Legend:** 1/SCHILLING/COURANT/MECKLENB/SCHWERIN/MUNZE

Date	Mintage	F	VF	XF	Unc	BU
1801	1,301,000	4.00	8.00	20.00	65.00	—
1802	2,431,000	4.00	8.00	20.00	65.00	—
1803	2,348,000	4.00	8.00	20.00	65.00	—
1804	2,603,000	4.00	8.00	20.00	65.00	—
1805	2,501,000	4.00	8.00	20.00	65.00	—
1806	1,766,000	4.00	8.00	20.00	65.00	—
1807	585,000	4.00	8.00	20.00	65.00	—
1808	243,000	4.00	8.00	20.00	65.00	—
1809	342,000	4.00	8.00	20.00	65.00	—
1810	250,000	4.00	8.00	20.00	65.00	—

KM# 253 SCHILLING
1.0800 g., 0.3750 Silver .0130 oz. **Ruler:** Friedrich Franz I **Rev:** Value

Date	Mintage	F	VF	XF	Unc	BU
1817	31,000	10.00	20.00	50.00	250	—

KM# 263 SCHILLING
1.1100 g., 0.3120 Silver .0111 oz. **Ruler:** Friedrich Franz I **Obv. Legend:** GR. HZ. U. M. S

Date	Mintage	F	VF	XF	Unc	BU
1826	159,000	3.00	7.00	20.00	80.00	—
1827	342,000	3.00	7.00	20.00	80.00	—

KM# 273 SCHILLING
1.1100 g., 0.3120 Silver .0111 oz. **Ruler:** Friedrich Franz I **Obv. Legend:** GR. HERZOG V. **Rev:** Value, legend

Date	Mintage	F	VF	XF	Unc	BU
1829	54,000	5.00	10.00	25.00	90.00	—
1830	501,000	3.00	6.00	12.00	55.00	—
1831	528,000	3.00	6.00	12.00	55.00	—
1832	119,000	3.00	7.00	15.00	75.00	—
1833	91,000	3.00	7.00	15.00	75.00	—
1834	118,000	3.00	7.00	15.00	75.00	—
1835	109,000	3.00	7.00	15.00	75.00	—
1836	163,000	3.00	7.00	15.00	75.00	—
1837	82,000	3.00	7.00	15.00	75.00	—

KM# 286 SCHILLING
1.1100 g., 0.3120 Silver .0111 oz. **Ruler:** Paul Friedrich **Obv:** Crowned PF monogram

Date	Mintage	F	VF	XF	Unc	BU
1838	21,000	5.00	10.00	25.00	115	—
1839	125,000	4.00	7.00	15.00	65.00	—
1840	52,000	4.00	7.00	15.00	75.00	—

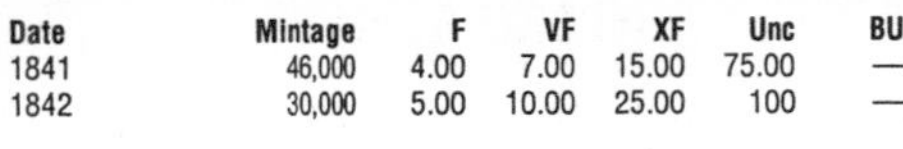

Date	Mintage	F	VF	XF	Unc	BU
1841	46,000	4.00	7.00	15.00	75.00	—
1842	30,000	5.00	10.00	25.00	100	—

KM# 298 SCHILLING
Billon **Ruler:** Friedrich Franz II

Date	Mintage	F	VF	XF	Unc	BU
1842	108,000	3.00	6.00	12.00	50.00	—
1843	139,000	3.00	6.00	12.00	50.00	—
1844	116,000	3.00	6.00	12.00	50.00	—
1845	246,000	3.00	6.00	12.00	50.00	—
1846	154,000	3.00	6.00	12.00	50.00	—

KM# 221 4 SCHILLING
3.0600 g., 0.5620 Silver .0553 oz. **Ruler:** Friedrich Franz I **Obv:** Crowned FF monogram on cartouche **Rev:** Value

Date	Mintage	F	VF	XF	Unc	BU
1809	1,408	60.00	100	200	450	—
1809	1,408	60.00	100	200	450	—

KM# 264 4 SCHILLING
3.3000 g., 0.4370 Silver .0464 oz. **Ruler:** Friedrich Franz I

Date	Mintage	F	VF	XF	Unc	BU
1826	621,000	12.00	20.00	50.00	175	—

KM# 269 4 SCHILLING
3.0600 g., 0.5000 Silver .0492 oz. **Ruler:** Friedrich Franz I **Obv:** Head left **Obv. Legend:** GR. HERZOG..

Date	Mintage	F	VF	XF	Unc	BU
1828	70,000	15.00	30.00	60.00	200	—

KM# 274 4 SCHILLING
3.0600 g., 0.5000 Silver .0492 oz. **Ruler:** Friedrich Franz I **Obv. Legend:** GROSSHERZOG..

Date	Mintage	F	VF	XF	Unc	BU
1829	200,000	10.00	15.00	35.00	125	—
1830	1,793,000	10.00	15.00	35.00	125	—
1831	476,000	10.00	15.00	35.00	125	—
1832	121,000	10.00	15.00	35.00	125	—
1833	49,000	10.00	20.00	40.00	140	—

KM# 287 4 SCHILLING
3.0600 g., 0.5000 Silver .0492 oz. **Ruler:** Paul Friedrich **Obv:** Crowned arms within 2 crossed branches

Date	Mintage	F	VF	XF	Unc	BU
1838	15,000	12.00	25.00	50.00	150	—
1839	39,000	10.00	20.00	40.00	140	—

KM# 266 8 SCHILLING
6.6000 g., 0.4370 Silver .0927 oz. **Ruler:** Friedrich Franz I

Date	Mintage	F	VF	XF	Unc	BU
1827	25,000	22.00	45.00	135	300	—

KM# 301 1/48 THALER (Schilling)
1.3000 g., 0.2080 Silver .0086 oz. **Ruler:** Friedrich Franz II

Date	Mintage	F	VF	XF	Unc	BU
1848	—	4.00	8.00	20.00	75.00	—

KM# 311 1/48 THALER (Schilling)
1.3000 g., 0.2080 Silver .0086 oz. **Ruler:** Friedrich Franz II

Date	Mintage	F	VF	XF	Unc	BU
1852A	—	3.00	6.00	15.00	65.00	—
1853A	—	3.00	6.00	15.00	65.00	—
1855A	2,819,000	3.00	6.00	15.00	65.00	—
1858A	—	3.00	6.00	15.00	65.00	—
1860A	—	3.00	6.00	15.00	65.00	—
1861A	—	3.00	6.00	15.00	65.00	—
1862A	—	3.00	6.00	15.00	65.00	—
1863A	—	3.00	6.00	15.00	65.00	—
1864A	—	3.00	6.00	15.00	65.00	—
1866A	2,033,999	3.00	6.00	15.00	65.00	—

KM# 302 1/12 THALER
2.4400 g., 0.5000 Silver .0392 oz. **Ruler:** Friedrich Franz II **Note:** Varieties exist.

Date	Mintage	F	VF	XF	Unc	BU
1848	2,047,000	6.00	12.00	35.00	90.00	—

KM# 303 1/6 THALER
5.3500 g., 0.5200 Silver .0894 oz. **Ruler:** Friedrich Franz II

Date	Mintage	F	VF	XF	Unc	BU
1848A	137,000	10.00	25.00	75.00	125	—

KM# 225 2/3 THALER (Gulden)
17.3200 g., 0.7500 Silver .4177 oz. **Ruler:** Friedrich Franz I

Date	Mintage	F	VF	XF	Unc	BU
1801	169,000	30.00	70.00	120	260	—
1808	655,000	30.00	70.00	120	260	—
1810	338,000	30.00	70.00	120	260	—

KM# 250 2/3 THALER (Gulden)
17.3200 g., 0.7500 Silver .4177 oz. **Ruler:** Friedrich Franz I

Date	Mintage	F	VF	XF	Unc	BU
1813	9,918	75.00	125	250	450	—

KM# 254 2/3 THALER (Gulden)
17.3200 g., 0.7500 Silver .4177 oz. **Ruler:** Friedrich Franz I **Obv. Legend:** ... G.G. HERZOG.. **Rev:** Date below value

Date	Mintage	F	VF	XF	Unc	BU
1817	6,783	275	450	800	1,250	—

KM# 261 2/3 THALER (Gulden)
17.3200 g., 0.7500 Silver .4177 oz. **Ruler:** Friedrich Franz I **Obv. Legend:** ...G.G. GR. HERZ..

Date	Mintage	F	VF	XF	Unc	BU
1825	35,000	85.00	175	325	625	—

KM# 262 2/3 THALER (Gulden)
17.3200 g., 0.7500 Silver .4177 oz. **Ruler:** Friedrich Franz I **Obv. Legend:** Ends ...SCHW

Date	Mintage	F	VF	XF	Unc	BU
1825	43,000	100	175	300	600	—
1826	—	100	175	300	600	—

KM# 265 2/3 THALER (Gulden)
17.3200 g., 0.7500 Silver .4177 oz. **Ruler:** Friedrich Franz I **Obv. Legend:** Ends ...SCHWERIN

Date	Mintage	F	VF	XF	Unc	BU
1826	103,000	100	175	300	600	—

KM# 270 2/3 THALER (Gulden)
17.3200 g., 0.7500 Silver .4177 oz. **Ruler:** Friedrich Franz I

Date	Mintage	F	VF	XF	Unc	BU
1828	57,000	110	185	325	650	—

KM# 275 2/3 THALER (Gulden)
17.3200 g., 0.7500 Silver .4177 oz. **Ruler:** Friedrich Franz I

Date	Mintage	F	VF	XF	Unc	BU
1829 Rare	—	—	—	—	—	—

KM# 288 2/3 THALER (Gulden)
13.1700 g., 0.9860 Silver .4175 oz. **Ruler:** Paul Friedrich

Date	Mintage	F	VF	XF	Unc	BU
1839	291,000	30.00	70.00	125	250	—
1840	856,000	25.00	50.00	100	200	—
1841	118,000	35.00	75.00	150	300	—

KM# 300 2/3 THALER (Gulden)
13.1700 g., 0.9860 Silver .4175 oz. **Ruler:** Friedrich Franz II

Date	Mintage	F	VF	XF	Unc	BU
1845	1,563	375	550	825	1,250	—

KM# 304 THALER
22.2700 g., 0.7500 Silver .5370 oz. **Ruler:** Christian Ludwig II

Date	Mintage	F	VF	XF	Unc	BU
1848A	528,000	30.00	60.00	120	225	—

KM# A310 THALER
18.5200 g., 0.9000 Silver .5360 oz. **Ruler:** Friedrich II **Note:** Previous KM#310.

Date	Mintage	F	VF	XF	Unc	BU
1864A	100,000	30.00	65.00	150	285	—

KM# A311 THALER
18.5200 g., 0.9000 Silver .5360 oz. **Ruler:** Friedrich II **Subject:** 25th Anniversary of Reign **Note:** Previous KM#311.

Date	Mintage	F	VF	XF	Unc	BU
1867A	10,000	35.00	75.00	175	325	—

KM# 284 2-1/2 THALER
3.3300 g., 0.8960 Gold .0959 oz. **Ruler:** Friedrich Franz I

Date	Mintage	F	VF	XF	Unc	BU
1831	7,755	375	750	1,250	2,500	—
1833	124	600	1,000	1,750	2,750	—
1835	195	600	1,000	1,750	2,750	—

KM# 295 2-1/2 THALER
3.3300 g., 0.8960 Gold .0959 oz. **Ruler:** Paul Friedrich

Date	Mintage	F	VF	XF	Unc	BU
1840	2,910	300	500	750	1,100	—

KM# 271 5 THALER
6.6600 g., 0.8960 Gold .1919 oz. **Ruler:** Friedrich Franz I

Date	Mintage	F	VF	XF	Unc	BU
1828	1,753	600	1,200	1,800	3,000	—
1831	3,878	600	1,200	1,800	3,000	—
1832	3,334	600	1,200	1,800	3,000	—
1833	125	1,000	2,000	4,000	6,000	—
1835	100	1,000	2,000	4,000	6,000	—

KM# 296 5 THALER
6.6600 g., 0.8960 Gold .1919 oz. **Ruler:** Paul Friedrich

Date	Mintage	F	VF	XF	Unc	BU
1840	1,454	650	1,250	1,750	3,000	—

KM# 272 10 THALER
13.3200 g., 0.8960 Gold .3837 oz. **Ruler:** Friedrich Franz I

Date	Mintage	F	VF	XF	Unc	BU
1828	876	1,250	2,500	3,750	5,000	—
1831	1,938	1,000	2,000	3,250	4,750	—
1832	1,667	1,000	2,000	3,250	4,750	—
1833	128	1,500	3,500	5,000	8,000	—

KM# 289 10 THALER
13.3200 g., 0.8960 Gold .3837 oz. **Ruler:** Paul Friedrich

Date	Mintage	F	VF	XF	Unc	BU
1839	92,000	500	1,100	1,500	2,200	—

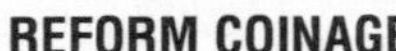

REFORM COINAGE

KM# 320 2 MARK
11.1110 g., 0.9000 Silver .3215 oz. **Ruler:** Friedrich Franz II

Date	Mintage	F	VF	XF	Unc	BU
1876A	300,000	110	250	775	2,750	3,500
1876A Proof	—	Value: 4,000				

KM# 318 10 MARK
3.9820 g., 0.9000 Gold .1152 oz. **Ruler:** Friedrich Franz II **Rev:** Type I

Date	Mintage	F	VF	XF	Unc	BU
1872A	16,000	1,000	1,500	2,500	5,000	8,000
1872A Proof	100	Value: 6,500				

KM# 321 10 MARK
3.9820 g., 0.9000 Gold .1152 oz. **Ruler:** Friedrich Franz II **Rev:** Type II

Date	Mintage	F	VF	XF	Unc	BU
1878A	50,000	400	700	1,000	1,500	2,000
1878A Proof	—	Value: 3,000				

KM# 325 10 MARK
3.9820 g., 0.9000 Gold .1152 oz. **Ruler:** Friedrich Franz III

Date	Mintage	F	VF	XF	Unc	BU
1890A	100,000	250	500	800	1,400	1,800
1890A Proof	—	Value: 2,500				

KM# 319 20 MARK
7.9650 g., 0.9000 Gold .2304 oz. **Ruler:** Friedrich Franz II **Rev:** Type I

Date	Mintage	F	VF	XF	Unc	BU
1872A	69,000	450	850	1,500	2,250	2,750
1872A Proof	200	Value: 5,000				

PATTERNS

Including off metal strikes

KM#	Date	Mintage	Identification	Mkt Val
Pn24	1828	—	5 Thaler. Gold. KM#271.	10,000
Pn25	1830	—	2 Thaler. 0.8750 Gold.	6,000

MECKLENBURG-STRELITZ

The duchy of Mecklenburg was located along the Baltic Coast between Holstein and Pomerania. The Strelitz line was founded in 1658 when the Mecklenburg line was divided into two lines. The 1815 Congress of Vienna elevated the duchy to the status of grand duchy. It became a part of the German Empire in 1871 until 1918 when the last grand duke died.

RULERS
Karl II, 1794-1816
Georg, 1816-1860
Friedrich Wilhelm, 1860-1904

MINT OFFICIALS' INITIALS

Initial	Date	Name
FN	1832-49	Franz Anton Nubell
IHL	1813	Johann Heinrich Lowe in Berlin

GRAND DUCHY

REGULAR COINAGE

KM# 81 PFENNIG
Copper **Obv:** Crowned G **Rev:** Value

Date	Mintage	F	VF	XF	Unc	BU
1838	60,000	6.00	12.00	35.00	145	—

KM# 101 PFENNIG
Copper **Note:** Prev. C#46.

Date	Mintage	F	VF	XF	Unc	BU
1872	626,000	2.00	4.00	9.00	35.00	—

KM# 82 1-1/2 PFENNIG
Copper

Date	Mintage	F	VF	XF	Unc	BU
1838	39,000	6.00	12.00	35.00	145	—

KM# 102 2 PFENNIG
Copper

Date	Mintage	F	VF	XF	Unc	BU
1872 B	203,000	2.50	5.00	14.00	40.00	—

KM# 80 3 PFENNIG
Copper

Date	Mintage	F	VF	XF	Unc	BU
1832 FN	466,000	3.50	7.00	20.00	50.00	—
1843	195,000	3.50	7.00	20.00	50.00	—
1845/3	193,000	3.50	7.00	20.00	50.00	—
1845	Inc. above	3.50	7.00	20.00	50.00	—
1847	204,000	3.50	7.00	20.00	50.00	—

KM# 90 3 PFENNIG
Copper

Date	Mintage	F	VF	XF	Unc	BU
1855A	305,000	3.50	7.00	20.00	50.00	—
1859A	192,000	3.50	7.00	20.00	50.00	—

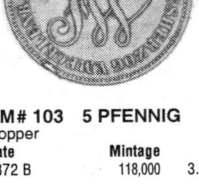

KM# 95 3 PFENNIG
Copper

Date	Mintage	F	VF	XF	Unc	BU
1862A	192,000	2.50	5.00	15.00	42.00	—
1864A	192,000	2.50	5.00	15.00	42.00	—

KM# 103 5 PFENNIG
Copper

Date	Mintage	F	VF	XF	Unc	BU
1872 B	118,000	3.50	7.00	20.00	55.00	—

KM# 85 4 SCHILLINGE
3.2500 g., 0.3750 Silver .0392 oz.

Date	Mintage	F	VF	XF	Unc	BU
1846	166,000	5.00	15.00	35.00	110	—
1847	273,000	5.00	15.00	35.00	110	—
1849	31,000	5.00	15.00	35.00	110	—

KM# 83 1/48 THALER (Schilling)
1.3300 g., 0.2080 Silver .0086 oz.

Date	Mintage	F	VF	XF	Unc	BU
1838	180,000	3.00	6.00	15.00	60.00	—
1841	138,000	4.00	7.00	20.00	65.00	—
1845	97,000	4.00	7.00	20.00	65.00	—
1847	231,000	3.00	6.00	15.00	60.00	—

KM# 91 1/48 THALER (Schilling)
1.3300 g., 0.2080 Silver .0086 oz.

Date	Mintage	F	VF	XF	Unc	BU
1855A	270,000	2.00	4.00	12.00	40.00	—
1859A	240,000	2.00	4.00	12.00	40.00	—

KM# 96 1/48 THALER (Schilling)
1.3300 g., 0.2080 Silver .0086 oz.

Date	Mintage	F	VF	XF	Unc	BU
1862A	240,000	2.00	4.00	12.00	40.00	—
1864A	240,000	2.00	4.00	12.00	40.00	—

KM# 100 THALER
18.5200 g., 0.9000 Gold .5360 oz.

Date	Mintage	F	VF	XF	Unc	BU
1870A	50,000	35.00	55.00	120	225	—

REFORM COINAGE

KM# 108 2 MARK
11.1110 g., 0.9000 Silver .3215 oz.

Date	Mintage	F	VF	XF	Unc	BU
1877A	100,000	175	300	1,600	3,000	4,000
1877A Proof	—	Value: 5,000				

KM# 104 10 MARK
3.9820 g., 0.9000 Gold .1152 oz. **Rev:** Type I

Date	Mintage	F	VF	XF	Unc	BU
1873A	1,500	5,000	8,500	12,500	17,500	28,000
1873A Proof	—	Value: 25,000				

KM# 106 10 MARK
3.9820 g., 0.9000 Gold .1152 oz.

Date	Mintage	F	VF	XF	Unc	BU
1874A	3,000	2,250	3,750	6,500	8,000	10,000
1880A	4,000	1,800	3,250	5,000	7,000	9,000

KM# 105 20 MARK
7.9650 g., 0.9000 Gold .2304 oz.

Date	Mintage	F	VF	XF	Unc	BU
1873A	6,750	1,750	3,000	5,000	8,000	10,000

KM# 107 20 MARK
7.9650 g., 0.9000 Gold .2304 oz. **Rev:** Type II

Date	Mintage	F	VF	XF	Unc	BU
1874A	6,000	1,750	3,000	4,750	7,000	9,000

MUNSTER

A Bishopric, located in Westphalia, was established c. 802. The first Munster coinage was struck c. 1228. In 1802 the bishopric was secularized and divided. From 1806-1810 most of Munster belonged to Berg, from 1810-1814 to France and from 1814 onward, to Prussia.

During the 16th and 17th centuries treasury tokens, mostly counterstamped with the arms or initials of the current treasurer were issued. These were replaced in the middle of the 17th century by Cathedral coins, showing St. Paul with a sword. They last appeared at the end of the 18th century.

RULERS
Maximilian Franz of Austria,
1784-1801
Sede Vacante, 1801
Anton Victor of Prussia, 1801-1802

BISHOPRIC

REGULAR COINAGE

KM# 210 1/24 THALER (Groschen)
Billon **Obv:** Value **Rev:** Date

Date	Mintage	F	VF	XF	Unc	BU
1801	—	20.00	40.00	80.00	150	—

KM# 211 1/3 THALER
Silver **Note:** Reichs 1/3 Thaler.

Date	Mintage	F	VF	XF	Unc	BU
1801	—	75.00	125	200	350	—

KM# 212 2/3 THALER (Gulden)
Silver **Obv:** Haloed St. Paul with sword on woven rampart **Rev:** Crowned Charlemagne with sword

Date	Mintage	F	VF	XF	Unc	BU
1801	—	150	250	400	650	—

KM# 213 THALER
Silver

Date	Mintage	F	VF	XF	Unc	BU
1801	200	850	1,350	2,350	4,600	—

NASSAU

The duchy of Nassau, located on both sides of the River Lahn in the Middle Rhineland was established in 1158. The lands were frequently divided and combined. The first coins were struck c. 1260. The Weilburg line was founded in 1355 and the Usingen line in 1642. In 1806 they united under a common administration. The Usingen line became extinct in 1816 leaving a fully united duchy under the Weilburg rulers. The house ended with the ouster of the duke in 1866 by Prus

DUCHY

Nassau-Weilburg and Nassau-Usingen

RULERS
Friedrich Wilhelm, 1788-1816
Friedrich August, 1803-1816

MINTMASTERS' INITIALS

Initial	Date	Name
CT		Christian Teichmann

JOINT COINAGE

C# A1 1/4 KREUZER
Copper **Obv:** Crowned arms **Obv. Legend:** HERZOGL NASS **Rev:** L below date

Date	Mintage	F	VF	XF	Unc	BU
1808	449,000	3.00	6.00	15.00	55.00	—

C# A1a 1/4 KREUZER
Copper **Note:** Several varieties exist.

Date	Mintage	F	VF	XF	Unc	BU
1808	Inc. above	2.00	4.00	8.00	45.00	—
1809	—	2.00	4.00	8.00	45.00	—
1810	—	2.00	4.00	8.00	45.00	—
1811	—	2.00	4.00	8.00	45.00	—
1812	11,470,000	2.00	4.00	8.00	45.00	—
1813	280,000	2.00	4.00	8.00	45.00	—
1814	278,000	2.00	4.00	8.00	45.00	—

C# A2 1/2 KREUZER
Copper

Date	Mintage	F	VF	XF	Unc	BU
1813	445,000	2.00	4.00	10.00	65.00	—

C# A3 KREUZER
Copper

Date	Mintage	F	VF	XF	Unc	BU
1808	779,000	15.00	40.00	80.00	275	—
1809	—	2.00	4.00	8.00	50.00	—

C# A3a KREUZER
Copper **Rev:** L below wreath **Note:** Previous #3a.

Date	Mintage	F	VF	XF	Unc	BU
1808	Inc. above	20.00	50.00	90.00	285	—

C# A3b KREUZER
Copper **Obv. Legend:** HERZ: **Note:** Previous #3b.

Date	Mintage	F	VF	XF	Unc	BU
1809	—	5.00	10.00	25.00	100	—
1810	—	3.00	6.00	18.00	60.00	—
1813	131,000	3.00	6.00	18.00	60.00	—

C# A4a 3 KREUZER (1 Groschen)
1.3800 g., 0.2810 Silver .0124 oz. **Obv. Legend:** HERZ. NASS. SCHEIDE. M. **Rev:** Value and date **Note:** Previous #4a.

Date	Mintage	F	VF	XF	Unc	BU
1809	10,000	25.00	60.00	120	300	—

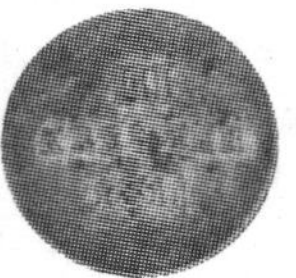

C# A4 3 KREUZER (1 Groschen)
1.3800 g., 0.2810 Silver .0124 oz. **Obv. Legend:** HERZ. NASSAU. SCHEIDEMUNZ.

Date	Mintage	F	VF	XF	Unc	BU
1810.	750,000	7.00	20.00	40.00	125	—
1811	—	10.00	30.00	60.00	150	—

C# A4c 3 KREUZER (1 Groschen)
1.3800 g., 0.2810 Silver .0124 oz. **Obv. Legend:** HERZ. NASS. SCH. M. **Note:** Previous #4c.

Date	Mintage	F	VF	XF	Unc	BU
1810	—	10.00	30.00	60.00	150	—

C# A4b 3 KREUZER (1 Groschen)
1.3800 g., 0.2810 Silver .0124 oz. **Obv. Legend:** HERZ. NASSAU. SCHEIDE. M. **Note:** Previous #4b.

Date	Mintage	F	VF	XF	Unc	BU
1811	270,000	7.00	15.00	25.00	125	—
1812	480,000	5.00	10.00	20.00	100	—
1813	506,000	5.00	10.00	20.00	90.00	—
1814	844,000	2.50	5.00	10.00	50.00	—
1815	675,000	2.50	5.00	10.00	50.00	—
1816	91,000	2.50	5.00	10.00	50.00	—
1817	259,000	2.50	5.00	10.00	50.00	—
1818	675,000	2.50	5.00	10.00	50.00	—
1819	928,000	2.50	5.00	10.00	50.00	—

C# 5 5 KREUZER
2.2200 g., 0.4370 Silver .0311 oz. **Obv. Legend:** HERZ. NASSAU...

Date	Mintage	F	VF	XF	Unc	BU
1808	4,000	175	350	700	1,250	—
1809	—	10.00	20.00	50.00	125	—

C# 5a 5 KREUZER
2.2200 g., 0.4370 Silver .0311 oz. **Obv. Legend:** HERZOGL. NASS...

Date	Mintage	F	VF	XF	Unc	BU
1808	Inc. above	10.00	20.00	50.00	140	—

C# 5b 5 KREUZER
2.2200 g., 0.4370 Silver .0311 oz. **Obv. Legend:** HERZ. NASSAUISCHE. **Rev:** Value, L below

Date	Mintage	F	VF	XF	Unc	BU
1808	—	10.00	20.00	50.00	140	—
1809	—	10.00	20.00	50.00	140	—

C# 6 10 KREUZER
3.8900 g., 0.5000 Silver .0625 oz. **Obv. Legend:** HERZ. NASSAUISCHE CONVENTIONS MUNZ. **Rev:** L below value

Date	Mintage	F	VF	XF	Unc	BU
1809	—	225	450	950	1,650	—

C# 6a 10 KREUZER
3.8900 g., 0.5000 Silver .0625 oz. **Obv. Legend:** HERZ. NASSA. CONVENT. MUNZ.

Date	Mintage	F	VF	XF	Unc	BU
1809	—	20.00	45.00	90.00	150	—

C# 6b 10 KREUZER
3.8900 g., 0.5000 Silver .0625 oz. **Obv. Legend:** HERZ. NASSAUISCHE...

Date	Mintage	F	VF	XF	Unc	BU
1809	—	20.00	45.00	90.00	150	—

C# 6c 10 KREUZER
3.8900 g., 0.5000 Silver .0625 oz. **Obv. Legend:** HERZ. NASSAU. **Rev:** Without L

Date	Mintage	F	VF	XF	Unc	BU
1809	—	20.00	45.00	90.00	150	—

C# 7 20 KREUZER
6.6800 g., 0.5830 Silver .1252 oz. **Obv. Legend:** HERZ. NASSAUISCHE CONVENTIONS MUNZ.

Date	Mintage	F	VF	XF	Unc	BU
1809	—	75.00	135	375	750	—

C# 7a 20 KREUZER
6.6800 g., 0.5830 Silver .1252 oz. **Obv. Legend:** HERZ. NASSAUISCHE CONVENT. MUNZ.

Date	Mintage	F	VF	XF	Unc	BU
1809	—	20.00	40.00	60.00	125	—

C# 7b 20 KREUZER
6.6800 g., 0.5830 Silver .1252 oz. **Rev:** Wreath without bow, running horse below

Date	Mintage	F	VF	XF	Unc	BU
1809	—	20.00	40.00	60.00	125	—

C# 7c 20 KREUZER
6.6800 g., 0.5830 Silver .1252 oz. **Rev:** 60 below rosettes

Date	Mintage	F	VF	XF	Unc	BU
1809	—	20.00	40.00	60.00	125	—

C# 7d 20 KREUZER
6.6800 g., 0.5830 Silver .1252 oz. **Obv. Legend:** ... CONVENTIONS **Rev:** Value within branches

Date	Mintage	F	VF	XF	Unc	BU
1809	—	20.00	40.00	60.00	125	—

C# 7e 20 KREUZER
6.6800 g., 0.5830 Silver .1252 oz. **Obv. Legend:** ... CONVENT. **Rev:** L below wreath

Date	Mintage	F	VF	XF	Unc	BU
1809	—	20.00	40.00	60.00	125	—

C# 7f 20 KREUZER
6.6800 g., 0.5830 Silver .1252 oz. **Rev:** Without bow on wreath, prancing horse below

Date	Mintage	F	VF	XF	Unc	BU
1809	—	20.00	40.00	60.00	125	—

C# 7g 20 KREUZER
6.6800 g., 0.5830 Silver .1252 oz. **Obv. Legend:** HERZ: NASS: CONV: MUNZ:

Date	Mintage	F	VF	XF	Unc	BU
1809	—	20.00	40.00	60.00	125	—

TRADE COINAGE

Separate coinage of Nassau-Weilburg

C# 8 DUCAT
3.5000 g., 0.9860 Gold .1109 oz.

Date	Mintage	F	VF	XF	Unc	BU
1809	3,543	500	1,000	1,600	3,000	—

DUCHY
Nassau-Usingen

RULER
Friedrich August, 1803-1816

STANDARD COINAGE

C# 9.1 10 KREUZER
3.8900 g., 0.5000 Silver .0625 oz.

Date	Mintage	F	VF	XF	Unc	BU
1809	—	200	375	700	1,200	—

C# 9.2 10 KREUZER
3.8900 g., 0.5000 Silver .0625 oz. **Obv:** L at truncation

Date	Mintage	F	VF	XF	Unc	BU
1809 L	—	200	375	700	1,200	—

C# 10 20 KREUZER
6.6800 g., 0.5830 Silver .1252 oz. **Obv:** Head right, L at truncation **Rev:** Crowned arms

Date	Mintage	F	VF	XF	Unc	BU
1809 L	—	20.00	45.00	90.00	250	—

C# 10a 20 KREUZER
6.6800 g., 0.5830 Silver .1252 oz.

Date	Mintage	F	VF	XF	Unc	BU
1809 L	—	20.00	60.00	120	350	—

C# 11 1/2 THALER
14.0300 g., 0.8330 Silver .3757 oz. **Note:** Convention 1/2 Thaler.

Date	Mintage	F	VF	XF	Unc	BU
1809 L	—	50.00	110	200	500	—

C# 12 THALER
28.0600 g., 0.0833 Silver .7515 oz. **Obv:** Head right, L at truncation **Rev:** Similar to C#12c **Note:** Convention Thaler.

Date	Mintage	F	VF	XF	Unc	BU
1809 L	—	400	850	1,650	3,500	—

C# 12c THALER
28.0600 g., 0.0833 Silver .7515 oz. **Rev:** Date dividing C.T.

Date	Mintage	F	VF	XF	Unc	BU
1810 CT	—	200	350	800	1,600	—
1811 CT	—	200	275	600	1,200	—
1812 CT	—	200	300	725	1,500	—
1813 CT	42,000	200	300	725	1,500	—
1815 CT	—	200	300	725	1,500	—

DUCHY
Nassau-Weilburg

RULER
Friedrich Wilhelm II, 1788-1816

STANDARD COINAGE

C# 30 10 KREUZER
3.8900 g., 0.5000 Silver .0625 oz.

Date	Mintage	F	VF	XF	Unc	BU
1809	—	25.00	50.00	150	250	—

C# 30a 10 KREUZER
3.8900 g., 0.5000 Silver .0625 oz. **Obv:** L at truncation

Date	Mintage	F	VF	XF	Unc	BU
1809	—	25.00	50.00	150	250	—

C# 31 20 KREUZER
6.6800 g., 0.5830 Silver .1252 oz.

Date	Mintage	F	VF	XF	Unc	BU
1809	—	25.00	50.00	150	250	—
1810	—	25.00	50.00	150	250	—

C# 32 1/2 THALER
14.0300 g., 0.8330 Silver .3757 oz. **Obv:** L on truncation **Note:** Convention 1/2 Thaler.

Date	Mintage	F	VF	XF	Unc	BU
1809 L	—	80.00	160	250	350	—

C# 33 THALER
28.0600 g., 0.8330 Silver .7515 oz. **Obv:** L on truncation

Date	Mintage	F	VF	XF	Unc	BU
1809 L	—	450	850	1,700	3,400	—

C# 33a THALER
28.0600 g., 0.8330 Silver .7515 oz. **Rev:** Arms between laurel and palm branches

Date	Mintage	F	VF	XF	Unc	BU
1809 L	—	450	850	1,700	3,400	—

C# 33b THALER
28.0600 g., 0.8330 Silver .7515 oz. **Obv:** L on truncation **Rev:** Date dividing C. T.

Date	Mintage	F	VF	XF	Unc	BU
1810 CT	—	175	375	900	1,900	—
1811 CT	—	175	275	700	1,500	—
1812 CT	—	175	375	900	1,900	—

C# 33c THALER
28.0600 g., 0.8330 Silver .7515 oz.

Date	Mintage	F	VF	XF	Unc	BU
1813	42,000	275	450	1,000	2,000	—
1815	—	300	560	1,150	2,400	—

C# 33d THALER
28.0600 g., 0.8330 Silver .7515 oz. **Obv:** Long bust

Date	Mintage	F	VF	XF	Unc	BU
1811	—	175	275	700	1,500	—

UNITED DUCHIES OF NASSAU

STANDARD COINAGE

C# 51 HELLER
Copper **Obv:** Crowned arms **Rev:** Value

Date	Mintage	F	VF	XF	Unc	BU
1842	182,000	2.00	4.00	8.00	35.00	—

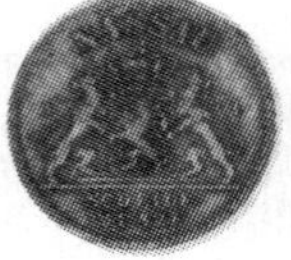

C# 52 PFENNIG
Copper

Date	Mintage	F	VF	XF	Unc	BU
1859	220,000	2.00	4.00	8.00	35.00	—
1860	580,000	2.00	4.00	8.00	35.00	—
1862	490,000	2.00	4.00	8.00	35.00	—

C# 35 1/4 KREUZER
Copper

Date	Mintage	F	VF	XF	Unc	BU
1817	433,000	1.50	2.50	5.00	20.00	—
1818	894,000	1.50	2.50	5.00	20.00	—
1819	4,932,000	1.50	2.50	5.00	20.00	—

C# 35a 1/4 KREUZER
Copper **Rev:** Without period after date **Note:** Several varieties exist.

Date	Mintage	F	VF	XF	Unc	BU
1817	Inc. above	1.50	2.50	5.00	20.00	—
1818	—	1.50	2.50	5.00	20.00	—
1819	Inc. above	1.50	2.50	5.00	20.00	—
1822	4,210,000	1.50	2.50	5.00	20.00	—

C# 36 KREUZER
Copper **Obv:** Crowned spade-shaped arms **Rev:** Value in wreath **Note:** Size varies: 22-24 millimeters.

Date	Mintage	F	VF	XF	Unc	BU
1817	203,000	1.75	3.50	7.00	30.00	—
1818	84,000	1.75	3.50	7.00	30.00	—

C# 37 KREUZER
Copper **Note:** Size varies: 22-24 millimeters.

Date	Mintage	F	VF	XF	Unc	BU
1830	265,000	1.75	3.50	7.00	30.00	—
1832	517,000	1.75	3.50	7.00	30.00	—
1834	326,000	1.75	3.50	7.00	30.00	—
1836	200,000	1.75	3.50	7.00	30.00	—
1838	269,000	1.75	3.50	7.00	30.00	—

C# 38 KREUZER
0.5300 g., 0.2290 Silver .0039 oz. **Rev:** Without wreath

Date	Mintage	F	VF	XF	Unc	BU
1817	79,000	1.75	3.50	7.00	30.00	—
1823	545,000	1.75	3.50	7.00	30.00	—
1824	564,000	1.75	3.50	7.00	30.00	—
1828	—	1.75	3.50	7.00	30.00	—

C# 39 KREUZER
0.5300 g., 0.2290 Silver .0039 oz.

Date	Mintage	F	VF	XF	Unc	BU
1832	144,000	1.75	3.50	7.00	30.00	—
1833	1,037,000	1.75	3.50	7.00	30.00	—
1835	408,000	1.75	3.50	7.00	30.00	—

C# 53 KREUZER
Copper

Date	Mintage	F	VF	XF	Unc	BU
1842	480,000	1.75	3.50	7.00	30.00	—
1844	188,000	1.75	3.50	7.00	30.00	—
1848	249,000	1.75	3.50	7.00	30.00	—
1854	274,000	1.75	3.50	7.00	30.00	—
1855	—	1.75	3.50	7.00	30.00	—
1856	357,000	1.75	3.50	7.00	30.00	—

C# 54 KREUZER
Copper

Date	Mintage	F	VF	XF	Unc	BU
1859	836,000	1.75	3.50	7.00	30.00	—
1860	610,000	1.75	3.50	7.00	30.00	—
1861	556,000	1.75	3.50	7.00	30.00	—
1862	610,000	1.75	3.50	7.00	30.00	—
1863	576,000	1.75	3.50	7.00	30.00	—

C# 55 KREUZER
0.5300 g., 0.2290 Silver .0039 oz.

Date	Mintage	F	VF	XF	Unc	BU
1861	664,000	1.75	3.50	7.00	30.00	—

C# 40 3 KREUZER
1.3800 g., 0.2810 Silver .0124 oz. **Obv:** Crowned spade-shaped arms, NASSAU **Rev:** Value

Date	Mintage	F	VF	XF	Unc	BU
1817	259,000	2.50	5.00	10.00	40.00	—
1818	675,000	2.50	5.00	10.00	40.00	—
1819	928,000	2.50	5.00	10.00	40.00	—

C# 40a 3 KREUZER
1.3800 g., 0.2810 Silver .0124 oz.

Date	Mintage	F	VF	XF	Unc	BU
1822	671,000	2.50	5.00	10.00	40.00	—
1823	671,000	2.50	5.00	10.00	40.00	—
1824	—	2.50	5.00	10.00	40.00	—
1825	192,000	2.50	5.00	10.00	40.00	—
1826	352,000	2.50	5.00	10.00	40.00	—
1827	308,000	2.50	5.00	10.00	40.00	—
1828	308,000	2.50	5.00	10.00	40.00	—

C# 41 3 KREUZER
1.2900 g., 0.2810 Silver .0116 oz.

Date	Mintage	F	VF	XF	Unc	BU
1831	509,000	2.50	5.00	10.00	40.00	—
1832	388,000	2.50	5.00	10.00	40.00	—
1833	42,000	2.50	5.00	10.00	40.00	—
1834	292,000	2.50	5.00	10.00	40.00	—
1836	340,000	2.50	5.00	10.00	40.00	—

C# 56 3 KREUZER
1.2900 g., 0.3330 Silver .0138 oz.

Date	Mintage	F	VF	XF	Unc	BU
1839 Rare	—	—	—	—	—	—
1841	—	60.00	100	150	225	—
1842	112,000	2.00	4.00	8.00	35.00	—
1844	56,000	2.00	4.00	8.00	35.00	—
1845	—	2.00	4.00	8.00	35.00	—
1847	210,000	2.00	4.00	8.00	35.00	—
1848	541,000	2.00	4.00	8.00	35.00	—
1853	91,000	2.00	4.00	8.00	35.00	—
1855	179,000	2.00	4.00	8.00	35.00	—

C# 42 6 KREUZER
2.2200 g., 0.3750 Silver .0267 oz. **Obv:** Crowned square arms **Obv. Legend:** NASSAUISCHE **Rev:** Value in wreath

Date	Mintage	F	VF	XF	Unc	BU
1817	109,000	3.00	6.00	12.00	40.00	—
1818	263,000	3.00	6.00	12.00	40.00	—
1819	378,000	3.00	6.00	12.00	40.00	—

C# 42a 6 KREUZER
2.2200 g., 0.3750 Silver .0267 oz. **Obv. Legend:** NASSAU

Date	Mintage	F	VF	XF	Unc	BU
1822	306,000	3.00	6.00	12.00	40.00	—
1823	306,000	3.00	6.00	12.00	40.00	—
1824	83,000	4.00	8.00	15.00	50.00	—
1825	176,000	3.00	6.00	12.00	40.00	—
1826	314,000	3.00	6.00	12.00	40.00	—
1827	302,000	3.00	6.00	12.00	40.00	—
1828	303,000	3.00	6.00	12.00	40.00	—

C# 43 6 KREUZER
2.2200 g., 0.3750 Silver .0267 oz.

Date	Mintage	F	VF	XF	Unc	BU
1831	1,100,000	3.00	6.00	12.00	40.00	—
1832	377,000	3.00	6.00	12.00	40.00	—
1833	641,000	3.00	6.00	12.00	40.00	—
1834	565,000	3.00	6.00	12.00	40.00	—
1835	832,000	3.00	6.00	12.00	40.00	—
1836	452,000	3.00	6.00	12.00	40.00	—
1837	314,000	3.00	6.00	12.00	40.00	—

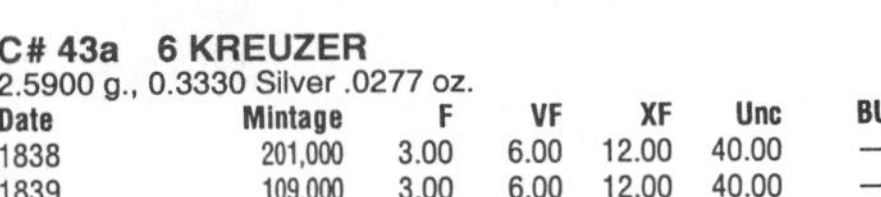

C# 43a 6 KREUZER
2.5900 g., 0.3330 Silver .0277 oz.

Date	Mintage	F	VF	XF	Unc	BU
1838	201,000	3.00	6.00	12.00	40.00	—
1839	109,000	3.00	6.00	12.00	40.00	—

C# 57 6 KREUZER
2.5900 g., 0.3330 Silver .0277 oz.

Date	Mintage	F	VF	XF	Unc	BU
1840	94,000	4.00	8.00	15.00	50.00	—
1841	321,000	3.00	6.00	12.00	40.00	—
1844	73,000	4.00	8.00	15.00	50.00	—
1846	—	3.00	6.00	12.00	40.00	—
1847	—	3.00	6.00	12.00	40.00	—
1848	198,000	3.00	6.00	12.00	40.00	—
1855	190,000	3.00	6.00	12.00	40.00	—

C# 44 1/2 GULDEN
5.3000 g., 0.9000 Silver .1533 oz.

Date	Mintage	F	VF	XF	Unc	BU
1838	108,000	20.00	40.00	75.00	150	—
1839	108,000	20.00	40.00	75.00	150	—

C# 58 1/2 GULDEN
5.3000 g., 0.9000 Silver .1533 oz.

Date	Mintage	F	VF	XF	Unc	BU
1840	95,000	20.00	40.00	75.00	150	—
1841	125,000	20.00	40.00	75.00	150	—
1842	31,000	20.00	40.00	75.00	150	—
1843	104,000	20.00	40.00	75.00	150	—
1844	117,000	20.00	40.00	75.00	150	—
1845	72,000	20.00	40.00	75.00	150	—

C# 59 1/2 GULDEN
5.3000 g., 0.9000 Silver .1533 oz. **Obv:** Head left

Date	Mintage	F	VF	XF	Unc	BU
1856	313,000	20.00	40.00	75.00	150	—
1860	104,000	20.00	40.00	75.00	150	—

C# 45 GULDEN
10.6000 g., 0.9000 Silver .3067 oz.

Date	Mintage	F	VF	XF	Unc	BU
1838	190,000	25.00	50.00	100	250	—
1839	108,000	25.00	50.00	100	250	—

C# 60 GULDEN
10.6000 g., 0.9000 Silver .3067 oz. **Obv:** ZOLLMANN on truncation

Date	Mintage	F	VF	XF	Unc	BU
1840	117,000	25.00	50.00	100	175	—
1841	124,000	25.00	50.00	100	175	—
1842	20,000	25.00	50.00	100	175	—
1843	236,000	25.00	50.00	100	175	—
1844	93,000	25.00	50.00	100	175	—
1845	138,000	25.00	50.00	100	175	—
1846	48,000	25.00	50.00	100	175	—
1847	231,000	25.00	50.00	100	175	—
1855	188,000	25.00	50.00	100	175	—

C# 61 GULDEN
10.6000 g., 0.9000 Silver .3067 oz.

Date	Mintage	F	VF	XF	Unc	BU
1855	Inc. above	25.00	50.00	100	200	—
1856	40,000	25.00	50.00	100	200	—

C# 65 2 GULDEN
21.2100 g., 0.9000 Silver .6138 oz. **Obv:** ZOLLMANN on truncation

Date	Mintage	F	VF	XF	Unc	BU
1846	177,000	50.00	125	300	800	—
1847	88,000	60.00	150	350	875	—

C# 46 THALER (Krone)
29.5300 g., 0.8710 Silver .8270 oz. **Obv:** Head right, L below **Rev:** Crowned draped arm, date below dividing C. T.

Date	Mintage	F	VF	XF	Unc	BU
1816 CT	—	—	—	—	8,000	—

C# 47 THALER (Krone)
29.5300 g., 0.8710 Silver .8270 oz.

Date	Mintage	F	VF	XF	Unc	BU
1817 CT-L	13,000	250	500	1,200	2,500	—

C# 48 THALER (Krone)
29.5300 g., 0.8710 Silver .8270 oz. **Obv:** Similar to C#49 with P.Z. on truncation

Date	Mintage	F	VF	XF	Unc	BU
1818	4,500	250	500	1,200	2,400	—
1825	2,000	300	600	1,400	2,800	—

C# 49 THALER (Krone)
29.5300 g., 0.8710 Silver .8270 oz. **Obv:** ZOLLMANN. F on truncation

Date	Mintage	F	VF	XF	Unc	BU
1831	9,385	200	350	500	1,400	—
1832	567	125	225	350	800	—
1833	—	125	225	350	800	—
1836	—	125	225	350	800	—
1837	2,683	125	225	350	800	—

C# 49a THALER (Krone)
29.5300 g., 0.8710 Silver .8270 oz. **Subject:** Duke's Visit to the Mint **Obv:** Similar to C#49

Date	Mintage	F	VF	XF	Unc	BU
1831	Inc. above	500	900	1,600	2,400	—

C# 62 THALER (Krone)
18.5200 g., 0.9000 Silver .5360 oz. **Obv:** Z on truncation **Note:** Vereins Thaler.

Date	Mintage	F	VF	XF	Unc	BU
1859 Z	50,000	45.00	80.00	175	400	—
1860 Z	30,000	45.00	80.00	175	400	—

C# 62a THALER (Krone)
18.5200 g., 0.9000 Silver .5360 oz. **Obv:** F. KORN on truncation

Date	Mintage	F	VF	XF	Unc	BU
1863	145,000	45.00	80.00	200	500	—

C# 63 THALER (Krone)
18.5200 g., 0.9000 Silver .5360 oz. **Subject:** Duke's Visit to the Mint

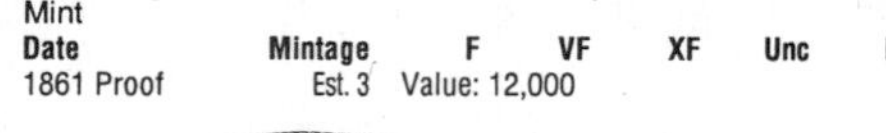

Date	Mintage	F	VF	XF	Unc	BU
1861 Proof	Est. 3	Value: 12,000				

C# 64 THALER (Krone)
18.5200 g., 0.9000 Silver .5360 oz. **Subject:** 25th Anniversary of Reign

Date	Mintage	F	VF	XF	Unc	BU
1864	6,162	35.00	55.00	115	190	—

C# 66 2 THALER (3-1/2 Gulden)
37.1200 g., 0.9000 Silver 1.0742 oz. **Obv:** Similar to C#67a, ZOLLMANN on truncation

Date	Mintage	F	VF	XF	Unc	BU
1840	56,000	250	450	1,000	2,000	—

C# 67a 2 THALER (3-1/2 Gulden)
37.1200 g., 0.9000 Silver 1.0742 oz.

Date	Mintage	F	VF	XF	Unc	BU
1844	21,000	175	300	650	1,400	—
1847	—	—	—	—	10,000	—

C# 67 2 THALER (3-1/2 Gulden)
37.1200 g., 0.9000 Silver 1.0742 oz. **Obv:** Truncation bare

Date	Mintage	F	VF	XF	Unc	BU
1844	Inc. above	175	300	650	1,400	—
1854	72,000	175	300	600	1,250	—

C# 68 2 THALER (3-1/2 Gulden)
37.0400 g., 0.9000 Silver 1.0719 oz. **Obv:** C ZOLLMANN on truncation

Date	Mintage	F	VF	XF	Unc	BU
1860	130,000	125	225	400	1,000	—

TRADE COINAGE

Separate coinage of Nassau-Weilburg

C# 50 DUCAT
3.5000 g., 0.9860 Gold .1109 oz. **Obv:** Head right **Rev:** Crowned draped arms

Date	Mintage	F	VF	XF	Unc	BU
1818 CT	501	650	1,150	2,000	3,500	—

PATTERNS

Including off metal strikes

KM#	Date	Mintage	Identification	Mkt Val
PnA1	1839	—	3 Kreuzer. C#56	—

NURNBERG

Nürnberg, (Nuremberg) in Franconia, was made a Free City in 1219. In that same year an Imperial mint was established there and continued throughout the rest of the century. The mint right was obtained in 1376 and again in 1422. City coins were struck from ca.1390 to 1806 when the city was made part of Bavaria. It was briefly occupied by Swedish forces until the death of Gustav II Adolfus in 1632.

MINT OFFICIALS' INITIALS

Initials	Date	Name
IER	1806-07	Johann Egydius Rosch

City Arms:

Divided vertically, eagle (or half eagle) on left, six diagonal bars downward to right on right side.

Paschal Lamb

The paschal lamb, Lamb of God or Agnes Dei was used in the gold Ducat series. It appears standing on a globe holding a banner with the word "PAX" (peace).

FREE CITY

REGULAR COINAGE

KM# 408 PFENNIG
Billon **Note:** Garland hanging from urn on pedestal above state shield, value and date below.

Date	Mintage	F	VF	XF	Unc	BU
1806	—	3.00	7.00	16.00	42.00	—
1807	—	5.00	10.00	30.00	90.00	—

KM# 406 PFENNIG
Billon **Note:** Oval state shield with garland draped above urn, value below date.

Date	Mintage	F	VF	XF	Unc	BU
1806	—	3.00	7.00	16.00	42.00	—

KM# 407 PFENNIG
Billon **Note:** Oval state shield, garland with loop above value and date.

Date	Mintage	F	VF	XF	Unc	BU
1806	—	3.00	8.00	17.00	45.00	—

KM# 409 PFENNIG
Billon **Note:** State shield in front of altar, value and date below.

Date	Mintage	F	VF	XF	Unc	BU
1806	—	3.00	7.00	15.00	40.00	—
1807	—	3.00	7.00	15.00	40.00	—

KM# 397 PFENNIG
Billon **Note:** Uniface. State shield between branches above value and date.

Date	Mintage	F	VF	XF	Unc	BU
1806	—	3.00	7.00	15.00	40.00	—

KM# 410 KREUZER (4 Pfennig)
Billon **Obv:** Pyramid with city arms, date below **Rev:** City view

Date	Mintage	VG	F	VF	XF	Unc
1806 IER	—	2.50	4.00	9.00	25.00	—

KM# 411 KREUZER (4 Pfennig)
Billon **Rev:** Rose bush

Date	Mintage	VG	F	VF	XF	Unc
1806	—	2.25	3.00	7.50	25.00	—

KM# 412 KREUZER (4 Pfennig)
Billon **Obv:** Spade arms with mural crown and garlands

Date	Mintage	VG	F	VF	XF	Unc
1806	—	4.50	9.00	18.00	40.00	—
1807	—	4.50	9.00	18.00	40.00	—

KM# 419 KREUZER (4 Pfennig)
Billon **Obv:** Pyramid with city arms, date below

Date	Mintage	VG	F	VF	XF	Unc
1807 IER	—	4.00	8.00	16.00	35.00	—

KM# 413 3 KREUZER
Billon **Obv:** Crowned shield with garland **Rev:** Value within wreath, date below

Date	Mintage	F	VF	XF	Unc	BU
1806	—	7.00	15.00	45.00	150	—

KM# 414 3 KREUZER
Billon **Rev. Legend:** NURNB: SCHEIDE MUNZ.

Date	Mintage	F	VF	XF	Unc	BU
1806	—	6.00	12.00	30.00	120	—
1807	—	6.00	12.00	30.00	120	—

KM# 415 6 KREUZER
Billon

Date	Mintage	F	VF	XF	Unc	BU
1806	—	6.00	12.00	35.00	125	—
1807	—	6.00	12.00	35.00	125	—

TRADE COINAGE

KM# 416 DUCAT
3.5000 g., 0.9860 Gold .1109 oz. **Obv:** City view **Rev:** Paschal lamb

Date	Mintage	F	VF	XF	Unc	BU
1806 KR	—	350	600	1,250	2,200	—

KM# 417 2 DUCAT
7.0000 g., 0.9860 Gold .2219 oz. **Obv:** City view **Rev:** Paschal lamb

Date	Mintage	F	VF	XF	Unc	BU
1806 KR	—	650	1,250	2,750	5,000	—

KM# 418 3 DUCAT
10.5000 g., 0.9860 Gold .3329 oz. **Obv:** City view, date below **Rev:** Paschal lamb

Date	Mintage	F	VF	XF	Unc	BU
1806 KR	—	1,200	2,500	4,500	7,500	—

OLDENBURG

The county of Oldenburg was situated on the North Seacoast, to the east of the principality of East Friesland. It was originally part of the old duchy of Saxony and the first recorded lord ruled from the beginning of the 11th century. The first count was named in 1091 and had already acquired the county of Delmenhorst prior to that time. The first identifiable Oldenburg coinage was struck in the first half of the 13thcentury. Oldenburg was divided into Oldenburg and Delmenhorst in 1270, but the two lines were reunited by marriage five generations later. Through another marriage to the heiress of the duchy of Schleswig and county of Holstein, the royal house of Denmark descended through the Oldenburg line beginning in 1448, while a junior branch continued as counts of Oldenburg. The lordship of Jever was added to the county's domains in 1575. In 1667, the last count died without a direct heir and Oldenburg reverted to Denmark until 1773. In the following year, Oldenburg was given to the bishop of Lübeck, of the Holstein-Gottorp line, and raised to the status of a duchy. Oldenburg was occupied several times during the Napoleonic Wars and became a grand duchy in 1829. In 1817, Oldenburg acquired the principality of Birkenfeld from Prussia and struck coins in denominations used there. World War I spelled the end of temporal power for the grand duke in 1918, but the title has continued up to the present time. Grand Duke Anton Gunther was born in 1923.

RULERS

Peter Friedrich Wilhelm, 1785-1823
Peter Friedrich Ludwig, as Administrator 1785-1823, as Duke, 1823-1829
Paul Friedrich August, 1829-1853
Nicolaus Friedrich Peter, 1853-1900
Friedrich August, 1900-1918

MINT OFFICIALS' INITIALS

Initial	Date	Name
B	1817-38	Ludwig August Bruel in Hannover
B	1844-68	Theodor Wilhelm Bruel in Hannover
S	1839-44	Karl Schluter in Hannover

ARMS

Oldenburg: Two bars on field.
Delmenhorst: Cross with pointed bottom bar.
Jever: Lion rampant to left.

NOTE:
Coins struck for lordship of Jever are listed under the latter.

DUCHY

REGULAR COINAGE

KM# 174 SCHWAREN (= 3 Light Pfennig)
Copper **Ruler:** Paul Friedrich August

Date	Mintage	F	VF	XF	Unc	BU
1846	126,000	2.50	5.00	12.00	48.00	—

KM# 185 SCHWAREN (= 3 Light Pfennig)
Copper **Ruler:** Paul Friedrich August **Rev:** B below date

Date	Mintage	F	VF	XF	Unc	BU
1852 B	144,000	2.50	5.00	12.00	48.00	—

KM# 188 SCHWAREN (= 3 Light Pfennig)
Copper **Ruler:** Nicolaus Friedrich Peter

Date	Mintage	F	VF	XF	Unc	BU
1854 B	72,000	2.00	4.00	10.00	45.00	—
1856 B	180,000	2.00	4.00	10.00	45.00	—

KM# 190 SCHWAREN (= 3 Light Pfennig)
Copper **Ruler:** Nicolaus Friedrich Peter

Date	Mintage	F	VF	XF	Unc	BU
1858 B	1,084,000	1.00	3.00	8.00	38.00	—
1859 B	108,000	1.00	3.00	8.00	38.00	—
1860 B	288,000	1.00	3.00	8.00	38.00	—
1862 B	180,000	1.00	3.00	8.00	38.00	—
1864 B	180,000	1.00	3.00	8.00	38.00	—
1865 B	108,000	1.00	3.00	8.00	38.00	—
1866 B	144,000	1.00	3.00	8.00	38.00	—
1869 B	180,000	1.00	3.00	8.00	38.00	—

KM# 191 3 SCHWAREN (3 Pfennig)
Copper **Ruler:** Nicolaus Friedrich Peter

Date	Mintage	F	VF	XF	Unc	BU
1858 B	372,000	2.50	5.00	12.00	42.00	—
1859 B	432,000	2.50	5.00	12.00	42.00	—
1860 B	60,000	4.00	8.00	20.00	55.00	—
1862 B	12,000	4.00	8.00	20.00	55.00	—
1864 B	60,000	4.00	8.00	20.00	55.00	—
1865 B	60,000	4.00	8.00	20.00	55.00	—
1866 B	36,000	4.00	8.00	20.00	55.00	—
1869 B	96,000	4.00	8.00	20.00	55.00	—

KM# 175 1/4 GROTEN (1 Pfennig)
Copper **Ruler:** Paul Friedrich August

Date	Mintage	F	VF	XF	Unc	BU
1846	90,000	4.00	8.00	25.00	65.00	—

KM# 150 1/2 GROTEN
Copper **Ruler:** Peter Friedrich Ludwig as Administrator

Date	Mintage	F	VF	XF	Unc	BU
1802	78,000	5.00	10.00	32.00	85.00	—
1816	149,000	3.00	7.00	20.00	65.00	—

KM# 165 1/2 GROTEN
Copper **Ruler:** Paul Friedrich August

Date	Mintage	F	VF	XF	Unc	BU
1831	72,000	4.00	8.00	25.00	75.00	—
1835	75,000	4.00	8.00	25.00	75.00	—

KM# 170 1/2 GROTEN
Copper **Ruler:** Paul Friedrich August

Date	Mintage	F	VF	XF	Unc	BU
1840	122,000	3.00	6.00	18.00	55.00	—

KM# 176 1/2 GROTEN
Copper **Ruler:** Paul Friedrich August

Date	Mintage	F	VF	XF	Unc	BU
1846	88,000	3.00	6.00	18.00	55.00	—

KM# 186 1/2 GROTEN
Copper **Ruler:** Nicolaus Friedrich Peter

Date	Mintage	F	VF	XF	Unc	BU
1853 B	72,000	2.00	4.00	10.00	45.00	—
1856 B	72,000	2.00	4.00	10.00	45.00	—

KM# 160 GROTEN (1/144 Thaler)
0.9700 g., 0.2080 Silver .0064 oz. **Ruler:** Peter Friedrich Wilhelm **Obv:** Crowned arms with garland, N.D.C.F

Date	Mintage	F	VF	XF	Unc	BU
1817	391,000	6.00	12.00	35.00	100	—

KM# 166 GROTEN (1/144 Thaler)
0.9200 g., 0.2180 Silver .0064 oz. **Ruler:** Peter Friedrich Wilhelm **Obv. Legend:** SCHEIDE-M

Date	Mintage	F	VF	XF	Unc	BU
1836 B	361,000	4.00	8.00	25.00	85.00	—

KM# 179 GROTEN (1/144 Thaler)
0.9200 g., 0.2180 Silver .0064 oz. **Ruler:** Peter Friedrich Wilhelm

Date	Mintage	F	VF	XF	Unc	BU
1849 B	43,000	5.00	10.00	30.00	75.00	—
1850 B	81,000	3.00	6.00	18.00	55.00	—

KM# 187 GROTEN (1/144 Thaler)
0.9200 g., 0.2180 Silver .0064 oz. **Ruler:** Peter Friedrich Wilhelm

Date	Mintage	F	VF	XF	Unc	BU
1853 B	57,000	3.00	6.00	18.00	55.00	—
1856 B	72,000	3.00	6.00	18.00	55.00	—
1857 B	27,000	4.00	8.00	25.00	65.00	—

KM# 155 2 GROTE (1/36 Thaler - 18 Witten)
1.3900 g., 0.2910 Silver .0130 oz. **Ruler:** Peter Friedrich Wilhelm
Obv. Legend: N.D.C.F

Date	Mintage	F	VF	XF	Unc	BU
1815	1,080,000	7.00	15.00	45.00	150	—

KM# 171 3 GROTE (1/24 Thaler)
1.9400 g., 0.3120 Silver .0194 oz. **Ruler:** Paul Friedrich August

Date	Mintage	F	VF	XF	Unc	BU
1840 S	486,000	4.00	8.00	25.00	85.00	—

KM# 189 3 GROTE (1/24 Thaler)
1.9400 g., 0.3120 Silver .0194 oz. **Ruler:** Nicolaus Friedrich Peter

Date	Mintage	F	VF	XF	Unc	BU
1856 B	156,000	4.00	8.00	25.00	85.00	—

KM# 156 4 GROTE (1/18 Thaler)
2.3900 g., 0.3400 Silver .0261 oz. **Ruler:** Peter Friedrich Wilhelm
Obv: Crowned arms with garlands, N.D.C.F **Rev:** Value

Date	Mintage	F	VF	XF	Unc	BU
1816	393,000	5.00	10.00	30.00	120	—
1818	126,000	6.00	12.00	35.00	125	—

KM# 172 4 GROTE (1/18 Thaler)
2.3900 g., 0.3400 Silver .0261 oz. **Ruler:** Paul Friedrich August

Date	Mintage	F	VF	XF	Unc	BU
1840 S	380,000	4.00	8.00	25.00	90.00	—

KM# 157 6 GROTE (1/12 Thaler)
3.5700 g., 0.3400 Silver .0390 oz. **Ruler:** Peter Friedrich Wilhelm

Date	Mintage	F	VF	XF	Unc	BU
1816	309,000	6.00	12.00	35.00	140	—
1818	60,000	10.00	20.00	50.00	175	—

KM# 158 12 GROTE (1/6 Thaler)
4.8700 g., 0.5200 Silver .0783 oz. **Ruler:** Peter Friedrich Wilhelm

Date	Mintage	VG	F	VF	XF	Unc
1816	36,000	10.00	20.00	70.00	220	—
1818	66,000	7.00	15.00	60.00	200	—

KM# 192 1/2 GROSCHEN
1.0900 g., 0.2200 Silver .0077 oz. **Ruler:** Nicolaus Friedrich Peter

Date	Mintage	F	VF	XF	Unc	BU
1858 B	1,020,000	2.00	4.00	12.00	40.00	—
1864 B	60,000	3.00	6.00	18.00	50.00	—
1865 B	48,000	3.00	6.00	18.00	50.00	—
1866 B	168,000	2.50	5.00	15.00	45.00	—
1869 B	120,000	2.50	5.00	15.00	45.00	—

KM# 193 GROSCHEN
2.1900 g., 0.2200 Silver .0154 oz. **Ruler:** Nicolaus Friedrich Peter

Date	Mintage	F	VF	XF	Unc	BU
1858 B	720,000	3.50	7.00	20.00	65.00	—

KM# 194 GROSCHEN
2.1900 g., 0.2200 Silver .0154 oz. **Ruler:** Nicolaus Friedrich Peter

Date	Mintage	F	VF	XF	Unc	BU
1858 B	1,080,000	3.50	7.00	20.00	60.00	—
1864 B	30,000	3.50	7.00	20.00	65.00	—
1865 B	30,000	3.50	7.00	20.00	65.00	—
1866 B	120,000	3.50	7.00	20.00	65.00	—
1869 B	90,000	3.50	7.00	20.00	65.00	—

KM# 195 2-1/2 GROSCHEN (1/12 Thaler)
3.2200 g., 0.3750 Silver .0388 oz. **Ruler:** Nicolaus Friedrich Peter

Date	Mintage	F	VF	XF	Unc	BU
1858 B	600,000	4.00	8.00	25.00	80.00	—

KM# 177 1/6 THALER
5.3500 g., 0.5200 Silver .0894 oz. **Ruler:** Paul Friedrich August

Date	Mintage	F	VF	XF	Unc	BU
1846 B	164,000	25.00	50.00	100	225	—

KM# 159 1/3 THALER
7.7900 g., 0.6250 Silver .1565 oz. **Ruler:** Peter Friedrich Ludwig as Administrator

Date	Mintage	F	VF	XF	Unc	BU
1816	18,000	60.00	120	350	550	—
1818	33,000	50.00	100	300	500	—

KM# 178 3/4 THALER
22.2700 g., 0.7500 Silver .5370 oz. **Ruler:** Paul Friedrich August

Date	Mintage	F	VF	XF	Unc	BU
1846 B	42,000	75.00	100	400	1,250	—

KM# 196 3/4 THALER
18.5200 g., 0.9000 Silver .5360 oz. **Ruler:** Nicolaus Friedrich Peter

Date	Mintage	F	VF	XF	Unc	BU
1858 B	17,000	70.00	140	250	450	—
1860 B	47,000	60.00	120	200	400	—
1866 B	72,000	50.00	100	175	350	—

KM# 173 2 THALER (3-1/2 Gulden)
37.1200 g., 0.9000 Silver 1.0742 oz. **Ruler:** Paul Friedrich August

Date	Mintage	F	VF	XF	Unc	BU
1840	10,000	700	1,250	2,500	4,750	—
1840 Proof	—	Value: 4,500				

REFORM COINAGE

KM# 201 2 MARK
11.1110 g., 0.9000 Silver .3215 oz. **Ruler:** Nicolaus Friedrich Peter

Date	Mintage	F	VF	XF	Unc	BU
1891A	100,000	150	250	400	750	900
1891A Proof	—	Value: 850				

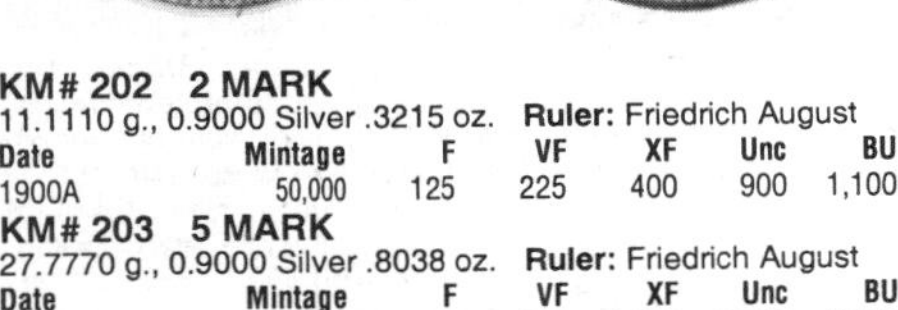

KM# 202 2 MARK
11.1110 g., 0.9000 Silver .3215 oz. **Ruler:** Friedrich August

Date	Mintage	F	VF	XF	Unc	BU
1900A	50,000	125	225	400	900	1,100

KM# 203 5 MARK
27.7770 g., 0.9000 Silver .8038 oz. **Ruler:** Friedrich August

Date	Mintage	F	VF	XF	Unc	BU
1900A	20,000	300	550	1,500	2,750	3,250
1900A Proof	—	Value: 4,000				

KM# 200 10 MARK
3.9820 g., 0.9000 Gold .1152 oz. **Ruler:** Nicolaus Friedrich Peter

Date	Mintage	F	VF	XF	Unc	BU
1874 B	15,000	1,000	2,000	4,000	6,000	8,000
1874 B Proof	—	Value: 12,500				

PATTERNS

Including off metal strikes

KM#	Date	Mintage	Identification	Mkt Val
Pn1	1816	—	6 Grote. Gold. KM#157.	—
Pn2	1816	—	1/3 Thaler. Gold. KM#159.	—

OSNABRUCK

The city of Osnabruck is located northeast of Munster. Although the city owed its original growth to the bishopric, it achieved considerable independence from the bishops and joined the Hanseatic League. It had its own local coinage from the early 16th century until 1805. It was absorbed by Hannover in 1803.

CITY

REGULAR COINAGE

C# 5 1-1/2 PFENNING
Copper

Date	Mintage	F	VF	XF	Unc	BU
1805	—	4.00	8.00	20.00	75.00	—

C# 7 2 PFENNING
Copper **Note:** Similar to 3 Pfennig, C#11.

Date	Mintage	F	VF	XF	Unc	BU
1805	—	5.00	9.00	25.00	100	—

C# 11 3 PFENNING
Copper

Date	Mintage	F	VF	XF	Unc	BU
1805	—	7.50	15.00	40.00	125	—

PFALZ

(Rhenish Palatinate, Rheinpfalz)

The Counts Palatine originally administered and exercised judicial functions over the imperial household of the Holy Roman Emperor, based at the center of Charlemagne's empire, Aachen. They gradually acquired territories in the middle Rhine. From1214 onwards the position was hereditary in the Wittelsbach family, who also controlled Bavaria. For a time the electoral dignity alternated between the Bavarian and Palatinate branches of the Wittelsbach family, until the Golden Bull in1356 settled it upon the Palatinate branch.

When the Protestant nobles in Prague elected Friedrich V, who was also a Protestant, as King of Bohemia in 1618, it precipitated a conflict which became known as the Thirty Years' War. Bohemia had been ruled by the Catholic Habsburg Emperors from Vienna since 1527 and Ferdinand II, was incensed at being rebuffed for the crown. Friedrich V lost his battles with Ferdinand II's armies and had to flee to the Hague and to the protection of his father-in-law, King James I of England. He would forever after be known as "The Winter King" in ridicule of his short reign. As punishment, the electoral dignity was taken from the Pfalz branch of the Wittelsbachs and given to the rival branch, the Catholic Duke of Bavaria. As one of the general conditions set forth in the Peace of Westphalia in 1648-50, an eighth electorship was created for Pfalz and thus the dignity was restored to the family.

The conversion of the electors to Roman Catholicism led to the expulsion of Huguenots and other Protestants from their territories, many of whom made their way to America, founding New Paltz, New York. In the course of the later seventeenth and eighteenth centuries, the various branches of the Palatinate were left without any legitimate heirs, so that Karl Theodor was able to combine the thrones of Julich-Berg, the Palatinate, and Bavaria after the War of the Bavarian Succession.

Karl Theodor was a great Maecenas, whose orchestra at Mannheim was one of the greatest in Europe. He was a patron of Mozart, who wrote *Idomeneo* for the opera house in Munich, and of the chemist Benjamin Thompson, later Count Rumford, who fled Massachusetts when the American Revolution broke out and sought refuge in Bavaria.

The Palatinate was administered as part of Bavaria from 1777, and did not mint any separate coins after 1802.The territories which composed the Palatinate were scattered over central Germany, and now form part of the West German states of Bavaria, Baden, Hesse, and Rheinland-Pfalz. The chief industry is bulk chemicals, from the great BASF factory at Ludwigshafen.

In 1753 Bavaria and Austria concluded a monetary convention, reducing the fineness of the thaler to the point that 20 gulden could be coined from a Mark of fine silver. The most important result was that henceforth the gulden, rather than being worth 2/3 of a thaler, was henceforth worth half a thaler. This Convention standard was soon afterwards adopted by most of the states of southwest Germany, including the Palatinate.

The Electors Palatine and the Saxon Elector acted as Vicars of the Empire after the death of a Holy Roman Emperor and before a new one was elected; the Elector Palatine in the areas of Franconian and Suevic law, the Saxon Elector in the areas where Saxon law applied. Both principalities issued coins commemorating the vicariates. Thus the Elector, Palatine Karl Theodor Actedas, Vicar of the Empire in 1790, after the death of Josef II, and again in 1792, after the early death of Leopold II, and issued coins in those two years. These coins are analogous to the "Sede Vacante" coins of ecclesiastical principalities.

ELECTORAL PFALZ

(Rhenish Pfalz, Rheinpfalz, Churpfalz, Kurpfalz)

Line of Succession in the Electoral Dignity

Once the electorship was vested in the Palatine line of the Wittelsbachs, it passed by right of succession through the senior male line until the death of Friedrich II in 1556. His nephew Otto Heinrich then received the dignity, but this failed at his death three years later. The branch of the family with the highest seniority aft this time was that of Pfalz-Simmern and it was to it that the electoral office passed. The electorship was lost, as stated above, in 1623 as a result of Friedrich V's actions and not restored until the end of the Thirty Years' War in 1648 as part of the peace settlement. The royal coinage of Friedrich V for Bohemia is listed under that entity. From 1622 until 1648, the Upper Palatinate and part of the Rhenish Palatinate were administered by Bavaria, which struck coins for use in those territories. See Bavaria for listings of those issues. The Simmern line died out in 1685 and the office of elector fell to Pfalz-Neuburg, the rulers of which were also dukes of Jülich-Berg. The coinage issued of these Pfalz-Neuburg rulers are often confused one with the other and it is sometimes difficult to separate issues for Electoral Pfalz from those of Jülich-Berg, particularly because some issues for one principality were produced or at least the dies were made in the mint of the other territory. The fate of extinction befell the Pfalz-Neuburg line in 1742 and all its lands and titles passed to Pfalz-Sulzbach for one generation. The Elector also became duke and elector in Bavaria when the Wittelsbach line in that principality became extinct and the two branches of the family were finally united after a breach of centuries. Once again the electoral dignity passed to another branch of the Palatine family, this time to Pfalz-Birkenfeld in 1799. With the abolition of the Holy Roman Empire by Napoleon in 1806, the electoral college was no longer needed and passed quietly away.

RULERS

Maximilian I Joseph von Birkenfeld, 1799-1805

MINT OFFICIALS' INITIALS

MANNHEIM MINT

Initials	Date	Name
	1789-1812	Heinrich Boltschauser, die-cutter
FE	1799-1805	Friedrich Christof Eberle, warden

ARMS:

Pfalz – rampant lion to left or right
Bavaria or old Wittelsbach – field of lozenges (diamond shapes)
Electorate – blank shield, sometimes shaded with closely spaced horizontal lines or ..arabesques.. - also, an imperial orb

PFALZ-SULZBACH

Chur Pfalz

Originally one of the four lines established in 1569, the first ruler died childless in 1604 and Sulzbach went to the eldest brother in Pfalz-Neuburg. The latter's younger son began a new line in 1614 upon the division of Pfalz-Neuburg. Early in the 18th century, the electoral dignity had passed to Pfalz-Neuburg, but that line also became extinct and all titles, including the electorate, reverted to Pfalz-Sulzbach in 1742 (see Electoral Pfalz for listings after this date).

RULERS

Christian August, 1632-1708
Theodor Eustach, 1708-32
Johann Christian, 1732-33
Karl IV Philipp Theodor, 1733-42 (died 1777)

MINT MARKS

D - Dusseldorf Mint
M - Mannheim Mint

MINT OFFICIALS' INITIALS

Initials	Date	Name
AK	1749-71	Andreas Kock
AS, S	1744-99	Anton Schäffer, die-cutter and mintmaster
CLS	1767-70	Karl Ludwig Selche
FO, O	1732-50	Franz Offner, in Heidelberg
	1743-50	In Mannheim
N	1746-47	C.Niesner
PM	1771-83	Paul Maasen
WS	1716-58	Wigand Schäffer, die-cutter

ELECTORATE

Rhein Pfalz

REGULAR COINAGE

KM# 185 1/2 KREUZER

Copper **Obv:** Crowned oval shield with lion, dividing RP **Rev:** Value and date within wreath

Date	Mintage	F	VF	XF	Unc	BU
1802	—	35.00	75.00	200	500	—

KM# 186 KREUZER

Copper **Obv:** Crowned oval shield with lion, dividing RP **Rev:** Value and date within wreath

Date	Mintage	F	VF	XF	Unc	BU
1802	—	45.00	100	300	700	—

KM# 187 THALER

Silver **Obv:** Head right **Rev:** Crowned shield within branches **Note:** Convention Thaler.

Date	Mintage	F	VF	XF	Unc	BU
1802	—	3,000	4,500	7,500	11,000	—

POMERANIA

The territory that became Pomerania, stretching along the Baltic coast from the Oder to the Vistula Rivers, was populated by Slavic peoples at least as early as the 5th century. A local ruler named Svantibor took the title of Duke of Pomerania in the late 11th century, thus announcing his claim of independence from Poland. Upon Svantibor's death in 1107, the duchy was divided by his four sons into Inner and Outer Pomerania. In 1181, Pomerania was admitted a constituent state of the Holy Roman Empire. Over the next several centuries, Pomerania underwent several divisions, although that entered on Wolgast emerged as the dominant branch by the early 15th century. Other family members ruled at Barth, Rügenwalde and most importantly, in Stettin, the eventural capital of united Pomerania. Several brothers of the dukes, as well as some dukes themselves, ruled as bishops of Cammin (see) some 20 miles (33km) north-northeast of Stettin.

The line at Wolgast became extinct in 1625 and its territories and titles passed to the Stettin branch, thus united all of Pomerania. The line at Stettin was established in 1569 and lost political power in 1637. The nephew of Bogislaw XIV, Ernst Bogislaw von Croy, was Bishop of Cammin from 1637 until 1650. Upon his death in 1684, the ducal line of almost 700 years came to an end.

Pomerania suffered severely during the Thirty Years' War and when the last duke succeeded to the bishopric of Cammin in 1637, as mentioned above, Sweden annexed the duchy. As part of the terms of the Treaty of Westphalia ending the war, Sweden was forced to pass the eastern part of Pomerania, called Hinter-Pommern, to Brandenburg-Prussia. Sweden did retain Stettin as the capital of its province of West Pomerania and struck a long series of coins specifically for that territory. Swedish control over its portion of Pomerania was continually challenged by the margraves of Brandenburg-Prussia, which succeeded in gaining part of the province in 1679, then all of West Pomerania to the River Peene in 1720. The remaining enclaves of Stralsund, Wolgast and Rügen were awarded to Prussia in 1815.

RULERS

Gustav IV Adolf of Sweden, 1792-1809

MINT

Stettin

SWEDISH OCCUPATION

REGULAR COINAGE

KM# 422 3 PFENNINGE

Copper **Obv:** Crowned griffin left holding sword **Obv. Legend:** K. S. P. L. M. **Rev:** Value above date

Date	Mintage	VG	F	VF	XF	Unc
1806	384,000	4.00	8.00	18.00	40.00	—
1808	258,000	4.00	8.00	18.00	40.00	—

KM# 424 3 PFENNINGE

Copper **Obv. Legend:** "K. SCHWED. POM. LANDES M

Date	Mintage	VG	F	VF	XF	Unc
1806	—	—	—	—	250	—

KM# 425 3 PFENNINGE

Copper **Obv. Legend:** "K. S. P. LANDESM"

Date	Mintage	VG	F	VF	XF	Unc
1808	—	—	—	—	250	—

PRUSSIA

The Duchy of Prussia, located along the eastern Baltic coast in what is now Poland and Lithuania, was created out of the remaining territory of the Knights of the Teutonic Order (see). Albrecht, the third son of Margrave Friedrich of Brandenburg-Ansbach (1486-1515), had been elected Grand Master of the Order in 1511. However, Albrecht converted to the Protestant faith in 1525 and, after declaring his vassalage to King Sigismund II of Poland, was created Duke of Prussia on 8 April of that year. The Teutonic Order removed from the Baltic region and set up its seat of operation in Mergentheim, Württemberg, remaining in that place until it was dissolved by Napoleon in 1809. Thus, Prussia became a hereditary domain of the House of Hohenzollern. The second duke, Albrecht Friedrich, only ruled effectively until 1578 and the duchy was administered by other members of the family for the rest of the 16th century. Albrecht Friedrich died in 1618 and the duchy was united with the Electorate/Margraviate of Brandenburg to become Brandenburg-Prussia (see). His widow was Maria Eleonore of Cleves and their marriage was the basis for the claims of Brandenburg on her family's domains in the Rhineland (see Cleves, Jülich-Berg, etc.). The former duchy of Prussia, with its capital of Königsberg, became the province of East Prussia (Ostpreussen).

NOTE:

For coins of Neuchatel previously listed here, see Switzerland.

RULERS

Friedrich Wilhelm III, 1797-1840
Friedrich Wilhelm IV, 1840-1861
Wilhelm I, 1861-1888
Friedrich III, March 1888-June 1888
Wilhelm II, 1888-1918

MINT MARKS

A - Berlin = Prussia, East Friesland, East Prussia, Posen
B - Bayreuth = Brandenburg-Ansbach-Bayreuth
B - Breslau = Silesia, Posen, South Prussia
C - Cleve
D - Aurich = East Friesland, Prussia
E - Konigsberg = East Prussia
F - Magdeburg
G - Stettin
G - Schwerin, Plon-Rethwisch Mint, 1763 only
S - Schwabach = Brandenburg--Ansbach-Bayreuth
Star - Dresden

KINGDOM

REGULAR COINAGE

KM# 372 PFENNIG

Copper **Ruler:** Friedrich Wilhelm III

Date	Mintage	VG	F	VF	XF	Unc
1801A	—	2.00	4.00	12.00	50.00	—
1804A	—	2.00	4.00	12.00	50.00	—
1806A	—	2.00	4.00	12.00	50.00	—

KM# 373 PFENNIG

Billon **Ruler:** Friedrich Wilhelm III **Obv:** Crowned FRW monogram

Date	Mintage	VG	F	VF	XF	Unc
1801A	—	2.00	4.00	12.00	50.00	—
1802A	—	2.00	4.00	12.00	50.00	—
1803A	—	2.00	4.00	12.00	50.00	—
1804A	—	2.00	4.00	12.00	50.00	—

KM# 383 PFENNIG

Billon **Ruler:** Friedrich Wilhelm III **Obv:** Smaller W in crowned FRW monogram

Date	Mintage	VG	F	VF	XF	Unc
1804A	—	4.00	8.00	25.00	75.00	—
1806A	—	4.00	8.00	25.00	75.00	—

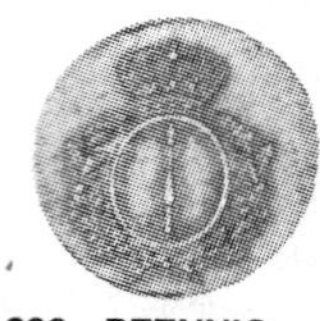

KM# 390 PFENNIG

Copper **Ruler:** Friedrich Wilhelm III **Note:** Brandenburg Provincial Issue.

Date	Mintage	F	VF	XF	Unc	BU
1810	—	2.50	5.00	15.00	55.00	—
1811	—	2.50	5.00	15.00	55.00	—
1814	—	2.50	5.00	15.00	55.00	—
1816	—	2.50	5.00	15.00	55.00	—

KM# 405 PFENNIG

Copper **Ruler:** Friedrich Wilhelm III

Date	Mintage	F	VF	XF	Unc	BU
1821A	—	2.00	3.50	7.00	35.00	—
1821B	—	2.00	3.50	7.00	35.00	—
1821D	—	2.00	3.50	7.00	35.00	—
1822A	—	2.00	3.50	7.00	35.00	—
1822B	—	2.00	3.50	7.00	35.00	—
1822D	—	2.00	3.50	7.00	35.00	—
1823D	—	2.00	3.50	7.00	35.00	—
1824D	—	2.00	3.50	7.00	35.00	—
1825A	—	2.00	3.50	7.00	35.00	—
1825D	—	2.00	3.50	7.00	35.00	—
1826A	—	2.00	3.50	7.00	35.00	—
1826C	—	2.00	3.50	7.00	35.00	—
1826D	—	2.00	3.50	7.00	35.00	—
1827A	—	2.00	3.50	7.00	35.00	—
1827D	—	2.00	3.50	7.00	35.00	—
1828A	—	2.00	3.50	7.00	35.00	—
1828D	—	2.00	3.50	7.00	35.00	—
1829D	—	2.00	3.50	7.00	35.00	—
1830D	—	2.00	3.50	7.00	35.00	—
1831D	—	2.00	3.50	7.00	35.00	—
1832A	—	2.00	3.50	7.00	35.00	—
1832D	—	2.00	3.50	7.00	35.00	—
1833A	—	2.00	3.50	7.00	35.00	—
1833D	—	2.00	3.50	7.00	35.00	—
1834D	—	2.00	3.50	7.00	35.00	—
1835A	—	2.00	3.50	7.00	35.00	—
1835D	—	2.00	3.50	7.00	35.00	—
1836A	—	2.00	3.50	7.00	35.00	—
1836D	—	2.00	3.50	7.00	35.00	—
1837A	—	2.00	3.50	7.00	35.00	—
1837D	—	2.00	3.50	7.00	35.00	—
1838A	—	2.00	3.50	7.00	35.00	—
1838D	—	2.00	3.50	7.00	35.00	—
1839A	—	2.00	3.50	7.00	35.00	—
1839D	—	2.00	3.50	7.00	35.00	—
1840A	—	2.00	3.50	7.00	35.00	—
1840D	—	2.00	3.50	7.00	35.00	—

KM# 430 PFENNIG

Copper **Ruler:** Friedrich Wilhelm IV

Date	Mintage	F	VF	XF	Unc	BU
1841A	—	1.50	2.00	5.00	32.00	—
1841D	—	1.50	2.00	5.00	32.00	—
1842A	—	1.50	2.00	5.00	32.00	—
1842D	—	1.50	2.00	5.00	32.00	—

KM# 447 PFENNIG

Copper **Ruler:** Friedrich Wilhelm IV

Date	Mintage	F	VF	XF	Unc	BU
1843A	—	1.50	2.00	5.00	32.00	—
1844A	—	1.50	2.00	5.00	32.00	—
1844D	—	1.50	2.00	5.00	32.00	—
1845A	—	1.50	2.00	5.00	32.00	—
1845D	—	1.50	2.00	5.00	32.00	—

KM# 451 PFENNIG

Copper **Ruler:** Friedrich Wilhelm IV

Date	Mintage	F	VF	XF	Unc	BU
1846A	—	0.75	1.50	5.00	32.00	—
1846D	—	0.75	1.50	5.00	32.00	—
1847A	—	0.75	1.50	5.00	32.00	—
1847D	—	0.75	1.50	5.00	32.00	—
1848A	—	0.75	1.50	5.00	32.00	—
1848D	—	0.75	1.50	5.00	32.00	—
1849A	—	0.75	1.50	5.00	32.00	—
1850A	—	0.75	1.50	5.00	32.00	—
1851A	—	0.75	1.50	5.00	32.00	—
1852A	—	0.75	1.50	5.00	32.00	—
1853A	—	0.75	1.50	5.00	32.00	—
1854A	—	0.75	1.50	5.00	32.00	—
1855A	—	0.75	1.50	5.00	32.00	—
1856A	—	0.75	1.50	5.00	32.00	—
1857A	—	0.75	1.50	5.00	32.00	—
1858A	—	0.75	1.50	5.00	32.00	—
1859A	—	0.75	1.50	5.00	32.00	—
1860A	—	0.75	1.50	5.00	32.00	—

KM# 480 PFENNIG

Copper **Ruler:** Wilhelm I

Date	Mintage	F	VF	XF	Unc	BU
1861A	—	0.50	1.00	2.50	20.00	—
1862A	—	0.50	1.00	2.50	20.00	—
1863A	—	0.50	1.00	2.50	20.00	—
1864A	—	0.50	1.00	2.50	20.00	—
1865A	—	0.50	1.00	2.50	20.00	—
1866A	—	0.50	1.00	2.50	20.00	—
1867A	—	0.50	1.00	2.50	20.00	—
1867B	—	0.50	1.00	2.50	20.00	—
1867C	—	0.50	1.00	2.50	20.00	—
1868A	—	0.50	1.00	2.50	20.00	—
1868B	—	0.50	1.00	2.50	20.00	—
1868C	—	0.50	1.00	2.50	20.00	—
1869A	—	0.50	1.00	2.50	20.00	—
1869B	—	0.50	1.00	2.50	20.00	—
1870A	—	0.50	1.00	2.50	20.00	—
1870B	—	0.50	1.00	2.50	20.00	—
1870C	—	0.50	1.00	2.50	20.00	—
1871A	—	0.50	1.00	2.50	20.00	—
1871B	—	0.50	1.00	2.50	20.00	—
1871C	—	0.50	1.00	2.50	20.00	—
1872A	—	0.50	1.00	2.50	20.00	—
1872B	—	0.50	1.00	2.50	20.00	—
1872C	—	0.50	1.00	2.50	20.00	—
1873A	—	0.50	1.00	2.50	20.00	—
1873B	—	0.50	1.00	2.50	20.00	—
1873C	—	0.50	1.00	2.50	20.00	—

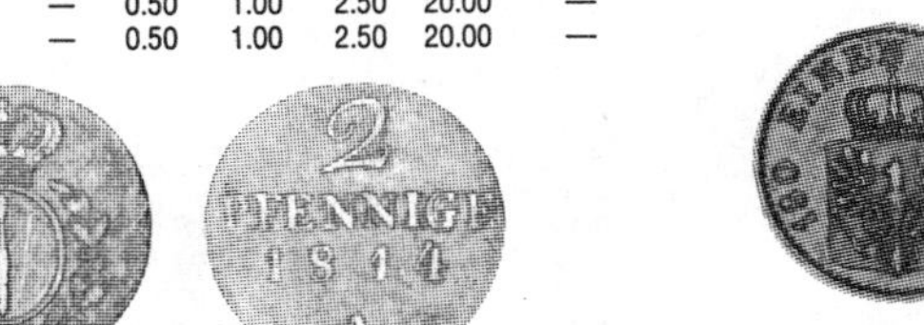

KM# 391 2 PFENNIG

Copper **Ruler:** Friedrich Wilhelm III **Note:** Brandenburg Provincial Issue.

Date	Mintage	F	VF	XF	Unc	BU
1810A	—	2.50	5.00	15.00	55.00	—
1814A	—	2.50	5.00	15.00	55.00	—
1816A	—	2.50	5.00	15.00	55.00	—

KM# 406 2 PFENNIG

Copper **Ruler:** Friedrich Wilhelm III

Date	Mintage	F	VF	XF	Unc	BU
1821A	—	2.00	4.00	8.00	40.00	—
1821B	—	2.00	4.00	8.00	40.00	—
1822A	—	2.00	4.00	8.00	40.00	—
1822B	—	2.00	4.00	8.00	40.00	—
1823D	—	2.00	4.00	8.00	40.00	—
1824D	—	2.00	4.00	8.00	40.00	—
1825A	—	2.00	4.00	8.00	40.00	—
1825D	—	2.00	4.00	8.00	40.00	—
1826A	—	2.00	4.00	8.00	40.00	—
1826D	—	2.00	4.00	8.00	40.00	—
1827A	—	2.00	4.00	8.00	40.00	—
1827D	—	2.00	4.00	8.00	40.00	—
1828A	—	2.00	4.00	8.00	40.00	—
1828D	—	2.00	4.00	8.00	40.00	—
1829D	—	2.00	4.00	8.00	40.00	—
1830A	—	2.00	4.00	8.00	40.00	—
1830D	—	2.00	4.00	8.00	40.00	—
1831D	—	2.00	4.00	8.00	40.00	—
1832A	—	2.00	4.00	8.00	40.00	—
1832D	—	2.00	4.00	8.00	40.00	—
1833A	—	2.00	4.00	8.00	40.00	—
1833D	—	2.00	4.00	8.00	40.00	—
1834D	—	2.00	4.00	8.00	40.00	—
1835A	—	2.00	4.00	8.00	40.00	—
1835D	—	2.00	4.00	8.00	40.00	—
1836A	—	2.00	4.00	8.00	40.00	—
1836D	—	2.00	4.00	8.00	40.00	—
1837A	—	2.00	4.00	8.00	40.00	—
1837D	—	2.00	4.00	8.00	40.00	—
1838A	—	2.00	4.00	8.00	40.00	—
1838D	—	2.00	4.00	8.00	40.00	—
1839A	—	2.00	4.00	8.00	40.00	—
1839D	—	2.00	4.00	8.00	40.00	—
1840A	—	2.00	4.00	8.00	40.00	—

KM# 431 2 PFENNIG

Copper **Ruler:** Friedrich Wilhelm IV

Date	Mintage	F	VF	XF	Unc	BU
1841A	—	1.00	2.00	5.00	35.00	—
1841D	—	1.00	2.00	5.00	35.00	—
1842A	—	1.00	2.00	5.00	35.00	—
1842D	—	1.00	2.00	5.00	35.00	—

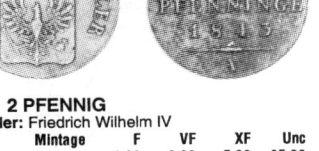

KM# 448 2 PFENNIG

Copper **Ruler:** Friedrich Wilhelm IV

Date	Mintage	F	VF	XF	Unc	BU
1843A	—	1.00	2.00	5.00	35.00	—
1844A	—	1.00	2.00	5.00	35.00	—
1844D	—	1.00	2.00	5.00	35.00	—
1845A	—	1.00	2.00	5.00	35.00	—
1845D	—	1.00	2.00	5.00	35.00	—

KM# 452 2 PFENNIG

Copper **Ruler:** Friedrich Wilhelm IV

Date	Mintage	F	VF	XF	Unc	BU
1846A	—	0.75	1.50	4.00	32.00	—
1846D	—	0.75	1.50	4.00	32.00	—
1847A	—	0.75	1.50	4.00	32.00	—
1847D	—	0.75	1.50	4.00	32.00	—
1848A	—	0.75	1.50	4.00	32.00	—
1848D	—	0.75	1.50	4.00	32.00	—
1849A	—	0.75	1.50	4.00	32.00	—
1850A	—	0.75	1.50	4.00	32.00	—
1851A	—	0.75	1.50	4.00	32.00	—
1852A	—	0.75	1.50	4.00	32.00	—
1853A	—	0.75	1.50	4.00	32.00	—
1854A	—	0.75	1.50	4.00	32.00	—
1855A	—	0.75	1.50	4.00	32.00	—
1856A	—	0.75	1.50	4.00	32.00	—
1857A	—	0.75	1.50	4.00	32.00	—
1858A	—	0.75	1.50	4.00	32.00	—
1859A	—	0.75	1.50	4.00	32.00	—
1860A	—	0.75	1.50	4.00	32.00	—

KM# 481 2 PFENNIG

Copper **Ruler:** Wilhelm I

Date	Mintage	F	VF	XF	Unc	BU
1861A	—	0.50	1.25	2.50	20.00	—
1862A	—	0.50	1.25	2.50	20.00	—
1863A	—	0.50	1.25	2.50	20.00	—
1864A	—	0.50	1.25	2.50	20.00	—
1865A	—	0.50	1.25	2.50	20.00	—
1866A	—	0.50	1.25	2.50	20.00	—
1867A	—	0.50	1.25	2.50	20.00	—
1867B	—	0.50	1.25	2.50	20.00	—
1867C	—	0.50	1.25	2.50	20.00	—
1868A	—	0.50	1.25	2.50	20.00	—
1868B	—	0.50	1.25	2.50	20.00	—
1868C	—	0.50	1.25	2.50	20.00	—
1869A	—	0.50	1.25	2.50	20.00	—
1869B	—	0.50	1.25	2.50	20.00	—
1870A	—	0.50	1.25	2.50	20.00	—
1870B	—	0.50	1.25	2.50	20.00	—
1871A	—	0.50	1.25	2.50	20.00	—
1871B	—	0.50	1.25	2.50	20.00	—
1871C	—	0.50	1.25	2.50	20.00	—
1872C	—	0.50	1.25	2.50	20.00	—
1873B	—	0.50	1.25	2.50	20.00	—
1873C	—	0.50	1.25	2.50	20.00	—

KM# 374 3 PFENNIG

0.7000 g., 0.2500 Silver .0056 oz. **Ruler:** Friedrich Wilhelm III

Date	Mintage	VG	F	VF	XF	Unc
1801A	—	2.00	4.00	12.00	50.00	—
1802A	—	2.00	4.00	12.00	50.00	—
1803A	—	2.00	4.00	12.00	50.00	—
1804A	—	2.00	4.00	12.00	50.00	—
1806A	—	2.00	4.00	12.00	50.00	—

KM# 384 3 PFENNIG

0.7000 g., 0.2500 Silver .0056 oz. **Ruler:** Friedrich Wilhelm III
Obv: Smaller crown

Date	Mintage	VG	F	VF	XF	Unc
1804	—	4.00	8.00	25.00	55.00	—

KM# 407 3 PFENNIG

Copper **Ruler:** Friedrich Wilhelm III

Date	Mintage	F	VF	XF	Unc	BU
1821A	—	2.00	4.00	9.00	45.00	—
1821B	—	2.00	4.00	9.00	45.00	—
1822A	—	2.00	4.00	9.00	45.00	—
1822B	—	2.00	4.00	9.00	45.00	—
1823D	—	2.00	4.00	9.00	45.00	—
1824D	—	2.00	4.00	9.00	45.00	—
1825A	—	2.00	4.00	9.00	45.00	—
1825D	—	2.00	4.00	9.00	45.00	—
1826A	—	2.00	4.00	9.00	45.00	—
1826D	—	2.00	4.00	9.00	45.00	—
1827A	—	2.00	4.00	9.00	45.00	—
1827D	—	2.00	4.00	9.00	45.00	—
1828A	—	2.00	4.00	9.00	45.00	—
1828D	—	2.00	4.00	9.00	45.00	—
1829A	—	2.00	4.00	9.00	45.00	—
1829D	—	2.00	4.00	9.00	45.00	—
1830A	—	2.00	4.00	9.00	45.00	—
1830D	—	2.00	4.00	9.00	45.00	—
1831A	—	2.00	4.00	9.00	45.00	—
1831D	—	2.00	4.00	9.00	45.00	—
1832A	—	2.00	4.00	9.00	45.00	—
1832D	—	2.00	4.00	9.00	45.00	—
1833A	—	2.00	4.00	9.00	45.00	—
1833D	—	2.00	4.00	9.00	45.00	—

Date	Mintage	F	VF	XF	Unc	BU
1834D	—	2.00	4.00	9.00	45.00	—
1835A	—	2.00	4.00	9.00	45.00	—
1835D	—	2.00	4.00	9.00	45.00	—
1836A	—	2.00	4.00	9.00	45.00	—
1836D	—	2.00	4.00	9.00	45.00	—
1837A	—	2.00	4.00	9.00	45.00	—
1837D	—	2.00	4.00	9.00	45.00	—
1838A	—	2.00	4.00	9.00	45.00	—
1838D	—	2.00	4.00	9.00	45.00	—
1839A	—	2.00	4.00	9.00	45.00	—
1839D	—	2.00	4.00	9.00	45.00	—
1840A	—	2.00	4.00	9.00	45.00	—
1840D	—	2.00	4.00	9.00	45.00	—

KM# 432 3 PFENNIG

Copper **Ruler:** Friedrich Wilhelm IV

Date	Mintage	F	VF	XF	Unc	BU
1841A	—	1.50	3.00	6.00	38.00	—
1841D	—	1.50	3.00	6.00	38.00	—
1842A	—	1.50	3.00	6.00	38.00	—
1842D	—	1.50	3.00	6.00	38.00	—

KM# 449 3 PFENNIG

Copper **Ruler:** Friedrich Wilhelm IV

Date	Mintage	F	VF	XF	Unc	BU
1843A	—	1.50	3.00	6.00	38.00	—
1843D	—	1.50	3.00	6.00	38.00	—
1844A	—	1.50	3.00	6.00	38.00	—
1844D	—	1.50	3.00	6.00	38.00	—
1845A	—	1.50	3.00	6.00	38.00	—

KM# 453 3 PFENNIG

Copper **Ruler:** Friedrich Wilhelm IV **Note:** Struck in collared dies.

Date	Mintage	F	VF	XF	Unc	BU
1846A	—	1.00	2.00	5.00	32.00	—
1846D	—	1.00	2.00	5.00	32.00	—
1847A	—	1.00	2.00	5.00	32.00	—
1847D	—	1.00	2.00	5.00	32.00	—
1848A	—	1.00	2.00	5.00	32.00	—
1848D	—	1.00	2.00	5.00	32.00	—
1849A	—	1.00	2.00	5.00	32.00	—
1850A	—	1.00	2.00	5.00	32.00	—
1851A	—	1.00	2.00	5.00	32.00	—
1852A	—	1.00	2.00	5.00	32.00	—
1853A	—	1.00	2.00	5.00	32.00	—
1854A	—	1.00	2.00	5.00	32.00	—
1855A	—	1.00	2.00	5.00	32.00	—
1856A	—	1.00	2.00	5.00	32.00	—
1857A	—	1.00	2.00	5.00	32.00	—
1858A	—	1.00	2.00	5.00	32.00	—
1859A	—	1.00	2.00	5.00	32.00	—
1860A	—	1.00	2.00	5.00	32.00	—

KM# 460 3 PFENNIG

Copper **Ruler:** Friedrich Wilhelm IV **Rev:** Reuss-Schleiz 3 PFENNIGE **Note:** Mule.

Date	Mintage	F	VF	XF	Unc	BU
1850A	—	15.00	40.00	75.00	150	—

KM# 482 3 PFENNIG

Copper **Ruler:** Wilhelm I

Date	Mintage	F	VF	XF	Unc	BU
1861A	—	0.75	1.50	3.00	20.00	—
1862A	—	0.75	1.50	3.00	20.00	—
1863A	—	0.75	1.50	3.00	20.00	—
1864A	—	0.75	1.50	3.00	20.00	—
1865A	—	0.75	1.50	3.00	20.00	—
1866A	—	0.75	1.50	3.00	20.00	—
1867A	—	0.75	1.50	3.00	20.00	—
1867B	—	0.75	1.50	3.00	20.00	—
1867C	—	0.75	1.50	3.00	20.00	—
1868A	—	0.75	1.50	3.00	20.00	—
1868B	—	0.75	1.50	3.00	20.00	—
1868C	—	0.75	1.50	3.00	20.00	—
1869A	—	0.75	1.50	3.00	20.00	—
1869B	—	0.75	1.50	3.00	20.00	—
1869C	—	0.75	1.50	3.00	20.00	—
1870A	—	0.75	1.50	3.00	20.00	—
1870B	—	0.75	1.50	3.00	20.00	—
1870C	—	0.75	1.50	3.00	20.00	—
1871A	—	0.75	1.50	3.00	20.00	—
1871B	—	0.75	1.50	3.00	20.00	—
1871C	—	0.75	1.50	3.00	20.00	—
1872A	—	0.75	1.50	3.00	20.00	—
1872B	—	0.75	1.50	3.00	20.00	—
1872C	—	0.75	1.50	3.00	20.00	—
1873A	—	0.75	1.50	3.00	20.00	—
1873B	—	0.75	1.50	3.00	20.00	—
1873C	—	0.75	1.50	3.00	20.00	—

KM# 408 4 PFENNIG

Copper **Ruler:** Friedrich Wilhelm III **Note:** Similar to KM#412.

Date	Mintage	F	VF	XF	Unc	BU
1821A	—	3.50	7.00	22.00	60.00	—
1821B	—	3.50	7.00	22.00	60.00	—
1822A	—	3.50	7.00	22.00	60.00	—
1822B	—	3.50	7.00	22.00	60.00	—
1825A	—	3.50	7.00	22.00	60.00	—
1825B	—	3.50	7.00	22.00	60.00	—
1826A	—	3.50	7.00	22.00	60.00	—
1827A	—	3.50	7.00	22.00	60.00	—
1829A	—	3.50	7.00	22.00	60.00	—
1830A	—	3.50	7.00	22.00	60.00	—
1832A	—	3.50	7.00	22.00	60.00	—
1836A	—	3.50	7.00	22.00	60.00	—
1837A	—	3.50	7.00	22.00	60.00	—
1838A	—	3.50	7.00	22.00	60.00	—
1839A	—	3.50	7.00	22.00	60.00	—
1840A	—	3.50	7.00	22.00	60.00	—

KM# 412 4 PFENNIG

Copper **Ruler:** Friedrich Wilhelm III

Date	Mintage	F	VF	XF	Unc	BU
1823D	—	3.50	7.00	22.00	60.00	—
1824D	—	3.50	7.00	22.00	60.00	—
1825D	—	3.50	7.00	22.00	60.00	—
1826D	—	3.50	7.00	22.00	60.00	—
1828D	—	3.50	7.00	22.00	60.00	—
1829D	—	3.50	7.00	22.00	60.00	—
1831D	—	3.50	7.00	22.00	60.00	—
1832D	—	3.50	7.00	22.00	60.00	—
1833D	—	3.50	7.00	22.00	60.00	—
1834D	—	3.50	7.00	22.00	60.00	—
1836D	—	3.50	7.00	22.00	60.00	—
1837D	—	3.50	7.00	22.00	60.00	—
1838D	—	3.50	7.00	22.00	60.00	—
1839D	—	3.50	7.00	22.00	60.00	—

KM# 433 4 PFENNIG

Copper **Ruler:** Friedrich Wilhelm IV

Date	Mintage	F	VF	XF	Unc	BU
1841A	—	3.00	6.00	18.00	50.00	—
1841D	—	3.00	6.00	18.00	50.00	—
1842A	—	3.00	6.00	18.00	50.00	—
1842D	—	3.00	6.00	18.00	50.00	—

KM# 450 4 PFENNIG

Copper **Ruler:** Friedrich Wilhelm IV

Date	Mintage	F	VF	XF	Unc	BU
1843A	—	3.00	6.00	18.00	50.00	—
1844A	—	3.00	6.00	18.00	50.00	—
1844D	—	3.00	6.00	18.00	50.00	—
1845A	—	3.00	6.00	18.00	50.00	—

KM# 454 4 PFENNIG

Copper **Ruler:** Friedrich Wilhelm IV **Note:** Struck in collared dies.

Date	Mintage	F	VF	XF	Unc	BU
1846A	—	3.00	6.00	18.00	50.00	—
1846D	—	3.00	6.00	18.00	50.00	—
1847A	—	3.00	6.00	18.00	50.00	—
1847D	—	3.00	6.00	18.00	50.00	—
1848A	—	3.00	6.00	18.00	50.00	—
1848D	—	3.00	6.00	18.00	50.00	—
1850A	—	3.00	6.00	18.00	50.00	—
1851A	—	3.00	6.00	18.00	50.00	—
1852A	—	3.00	6.00	18.00	50.00	—
1853A	—	3.00	6.00	18.00	50.00	—
1854A	—	3.00	6.00	18.00	50.00	—
1855A	—	3.00	6.00	18.00	50.00	—
1856A	—	3.00	6.00	18.00	50.00	—
1857A	—	3.00	6.00	18.00	50.00	—
1858A	—	3.00	6.00	18.00	50.00	—
1860A	—	3.00	6.00	18.00	50.00	—

KM# 483 4 PFENNIG

Copper **Ruler:** Wilhelm I

Date	Mintage	F	VF	XF	Unc	BU
1861A	—	2.00	4.00	10.00	40.00	—
1862A	—	2.00	4.00	10.00	40.00	—
1863A	—	2.00	4.00	10.00	40.00	—
1864A	—	2.00	4.00	10.00	40.00	—
1865A	—	2.00	4.00	10.00	40.00	—
1866A	—	2.00	4.00	10.00	40.00	—
1867A	—	2.00	4.00	10.00	40.00	—
1867C	—	2.00	4.00	10.00	40.00	—
1868A	—	2.00	4.00	10.00	40.00	—
1868C	—	2.00	4.00	10.00	40.00	—
1869A	—	2.00	4.00	10.00	40.00	—
1870A	—	2.00	4.00	10.00	40.00	—
1871A	—	2.00	4.00	10.00	40.00	—
1871C	—	2.00	4.00	10.00	40.00	—

KM# 409 1/2 SILBER GROSCHEN

1.0900 g., 0.2220 Silver .0077 oz. **Ruler:** Friedrich Wilhelm III

Date	Mintage	F	VF	XF	Unc	BU
1821A	—	3.00	6.00	15.00	50.00	—
1822A	—	3.00	6.00	15.00	50.00	—
1823A	—	3.00	6.00	15.00	50.00	—
1824A	—	3.00	6.00	15.00	50.00	—
1824D	—	3.00	6.00	15.00	50.00	—

Date	Mintage	F	VF	XF	Unc	BU
1825A	—	3.00	6.00	15.00	50.00	—
1825D	—	3.00	6.00	15.00	50.00	—
1826A	—	3.00	6.00	15.00	50.00	—
1826D	—	3.00	6.00	15.00	50.00	—
1827A	—	3.00	6.00	15.00	50.00	—
1828A	—	3.00	6.00	15.00	50.00	—
1828D	—	3.00	6.00	15.00	50.00	—
1829A	—	3.00	6.00	15.00	50.00	—
1830A	—	3.00	6.00	15.00	50.00	—
1831A	—	3.00	6.00	15.00	50.00	—
1832A	—	3.00	6.00	15.00	50.00	—
1833A	—	3.00	6.00	15.00	50.00	—
1834A	—	3.00	6.00	15.00	50.00	—
1835A	—	3.00	6.00	15.00	50.00	—
1836A	—	3.00	6.00	15.00	50.00	—
1837A	—	3.00	6.00	15.00	50.00	—
1838A	—	3.00	6.00	15.00	50.00	—
1839A	—	3.00	6.00	15.00	50.00	—
1840A	—	3.00	6.00	15.00	50.00	—

KM# 434 1/2 SILBER GROSCHEN

1.0900 g., 0.2220 Silver .0077 oz. **Ruler:** Friedrich Wilhelm IV

Date	Mintage	F	VF	XF	Unc	BU
1841A	—	2.50	5.00	12.00	45.00	—
1842A	—	2.50	5.00	12.00	45.00	—
1843A	—	2.50	5.00	12.00	45.00	—
1844A	—	2.50	5.00	12.00	45.00	—
1845A	—	2.50	5.00	12.00	45.00	—
1846A	—	2.50	5.00	12.00	45.00	—
1847A	—	2.50	5.00	12.00	45.00	—
1848A	—	2.50	5.00	12.00	45.00	—
1849A	—	2.50	5.00	12.00	45.00	—
1850A	—	2.50	5.00	12.00	45.00	—
1851A	—	2.50	5.00	12.00	45.00	—
1852A	—	2.50	5.00	12.00	45.00	—

KM# 461 1/2 SILBER GROSCHEN

1.0900 g., 0.2220 Silver .0077 oz. **Ruler:** Friedrich Wilhelm IV
Obv: Older head

Date	Mintage	F	VF	XF	Unc	BU
1853	—	4.00	8.00	20.00	65.00	—
1854	—	4.00	8.00	20.00	65.00	—
1855	—	4.00	8.00	20.00	65.00	—
1856	—	4.00	8.00	20.00	65.00	—
1858	—	4.00	8.00	20.00	65.00	—
1860	—	4.00	8.00	20.00	65.00	—

KM# 484 1/2 SILBER GROSCHEN

1.0900 g., 0.2220 Silver .0077 oz. **Ruler:** Wilhelm I

Date	Mintage	F	VF	XF	Unc	BU
1861A	—	1.00	2.00	5.00	22.00	—
1862A	—	1.00	2.00	5.00	22.00	—
1863A	—	1.00	2.00	5.00	22.00	—
1864A	—	1.00	2.00	5.00	22.00	—
1865A	—	1.00	2.00	5.00	22.00	—
1866A	—	1.00	2.00	5.00	22.00	—
1866B	—	1.00	2.00	5.00	22.00	—
1867A	—	1.00	2.00	5.00	22.00	—
1867B	—	1.00	2.00	5.00	22.00	—
1867C	—	1.25	2.50	5.00	22.00	—
1868A	—	1.00	2.00	5.00	22.00	—
1868B	—	1.00	2.00	5.00	22.00	—
1868C	—	1.25	2.50	5.00	22.00	—
1869A	—	1.00	2.00	5.00	22.00	—
1869B	—	1.00	2.00	5.00	22.00	—
1870A	—	1.00	2.00	5.00	22.00	—
1870B	—	1.00	2.00	5.00	22.00	—
1871A	—	1.00	2.00	5.00	22.00	—
1871B	—	1.00	2.00	5.00	22.00	—
1872A	—	1.00	2.00	5.00	22.00	—
1872B	—	1.00	2.00	5.00	22.00	—
1872C	—	1.25	2.50	5.00	22.00	—
1873B	—	1.00	2.00	5.00	22.00	—

KM# 410 GROSCHEN (Silber)

2.1900 g., 0.2220 Silver .0156 oz. **Ruler:** Friedrich Wilhelm III

Date	Mintage	F	VF	XF	Unc	BU
1821A	—	3.00	6.00	15.00	50.00	—
1821D	—	3.00	6.00	15.00	50.00	—
1822A	—	3.00	6.00	15.00	50.00	—
1822D	—	3.00	6.00	15.00	50.00	—
1823A	—	3.00	6.00	15.00	50.00	—
1823D	—	3.00	6.00	15.00	50.00	—
1824A	—	3.00	6.00	15.00	50.00	—
1824D	—	3.00	6.00	15.00	50.00	—
1825A	—	3.00	6.00	15.00	50.00	—
1825D	—	3.00	6.00	15.00	50.00	—
1826A	—	3.00	6.00	15.00	50.00	—
1826D	—	3.00	6.00	15.00	50.00	—
1827A	—	3.00	6.00	15.00	50.00	—
1827D	—	3.00	6.00	15.00	50.00	—
1828A	—	3.00	6.00	15.00	50.00	—
1828D	—	3.00	6.00	15.00	50.00	—
1829A	—	3.00	6.00	15.00	50.00	—
1830A	—	3.00	6.00	15.00	50.00	—
1830D	—	3.00	6.00	15.00	50.00	—
1831A	—	3.00	6.00	15.00	50.00	—
1832A	—	3.00	6.00	15.00	50.00	—
1832D	—	3.00	6.00	15.00	50.00	—
1833A	—	3.00	6.00	15.00	50.00	—
1833D	—	3.00	6.00	15.00	50.00	—
1834A	—	3.00	6.00	15.00	50.00	—
1834D	—	3.00	6.00	15.00	50.00	—
1835A	—	3.00	6.00	15.00	50.00	—
1836A	—	3.00	6.00	15.00	50.00	—
1837A	—	3.00	6.00	15.00	50.00	—
1837D	—	3.00	6.00	15.00	50.00	—
1838A	—	3.00	6.00	15.00	50.00	—
1839A	—	3.00	6.00	15.00	50.00	—
1839D	—	3.00	6.00	15.00	50.00	—
1840A	—	3.00	6.00	15.00	50.00	—
1840D	—	3.00	6.00	15.00	50.00	—

KM# 435 GROSCHEN (Silber)

2.1900 g., 0.2220 Silver .0156 oz. **Ruler:** Friedrich Wilhelm IV

Date	Mintage	F	VF	XF	Unc	BU
1841A	—	2.00	4.00	10.00	40.00	—
1841D	—	2.00	4.00	10.00	40.00	—
1842A	—	2.00	4.00	10.00	40.00	—
1842D	—	2.00	4.00	10.00	40.00	—
1843A	—	2.00	4.00	10.00	40.00	—
1843D	—	2.00	4.00	10.00	40.00	—
1844A	—	2.00	4.00	10.00	40.00	—
1844D	—	2.00	4.00	10.00	40.00	—
1845A	—	2.00	4.00	10.00	40.00	—
1845D	—	2.00	4.00	10.00	40.00	—
1846A	—	2.00	4.00	10.00	40.00	—
1847A	—	2.00	4.00	10.00	40.00	—
1847D	—	2.00	4.00	10.00	40.00	—
1848A	—	2.00	4.00	10.00	40.00	—
1848D	—	2.00	4.00	10.00	40.00	—
1849A	—	2.00	4.00	10.00	40.00	—
1850A	—	2.00	4.00	10.00	40.00	—
1851A	—	2.00	4.00	10.00	40.00	—
1852A	—	2.00	4.00	10.00	40.00	—

KM# 462 GROSCHEN (Silber)

2.1900 g., 0.2220 Silver .0156 oz. **Ruler:** Friedrich Wilhelm IV
Obv: Older head

Date	Mintage	F	VF	XF	Unc	BU
1853A	—	2.00	4.00	10.00	40.00	—
1854A	—	2.00	4.00	10.00	40.00	—
1855A	—	2.00	4.00	10.00	40.00	—
1856A	—	2.00	4.00	10.00	40.00	—
1857A	—	2.00	4.00	10.00	40.00	—
1858A	—	2.00	4.00	10.00	40.00	—
1859A	—	2.00	4.00	10.00	40.00	—
1860A	—	2.00	4.00	10.00	40.00	—

KM# 485 GROSCHEN (Silber)

2.1900 g., 0.2220 Silver .0156 oz. **Ruler:** Wilhelm I

Date	Mintage	F	VF	XF	Unc	BU
1861A	—	1.00	2.00	5.00	30.00	—
1862A	—	1.00	2.00	5.00	30.00	—
1863A	—	1.00	2.00	5.00	30.00	—
1864A	—	1.00	2.00	5.00	30.00	—
1865A	—	1.00	2.00	5.00	30.00	—
1866A	—	1.00	2.00	5.00	30.00	—
1866B	—	1.00	2.00	5.00	30.00	—
1867A	—	1.00	2.00	5.00	30.00	—
1867B	—	1.00	2.00	5.00	30.00	—
1867C	—	1.00	2.00	5.00	30.00	—
1868A	—	1.00	2.00	5.00	30.00	—
1868B	—	1.00	2.00	5.00	30.00	—
1868C	—	1.00	2.00	5.00	30.00	—
1869A	—	1.00	2.00	5.00	30.00	—
1869B	—	1.00	2.00	5.00	30.00	—
1869C	—	1.00	2.00	5.00	30.00	—
1870A	—	1.00	2.00	5.00	30.00	—
1870B	—	1.00	2.00	5.00	30.00	—
1870C	—	1.00	2.00	5.00	30.00	—
1871A	—	1.00	2.00	5.00	30.00	—
1871B	—	1.00	2.00	5.00	30.00	—
1871C	—	1.00	2.00	5.00	30.00	—
1872A	—	1.00	2.00	5.00	30.00	—
1872B	—	1.00	2.00	5.00	30.00	—
1872C	—	1.00	2.00	5.00	30.00	—
1873A	—	1.00	2.00	5.00	30.00	—
1873B	—	1.00	2.00	5.00	30.00	—
1873C	—	1.00	2.00	5.00	30.00	—

KM# 444 2-1/2 SILBER GROSCHEN

3.2400 g., 0.3750 Silver .0390 oz. **Ruler:** Friedrich Wilhelm IV

Date	Mintage	F	VF	XF	Unc	BU
1842A	—	3.00	6.00	15.00	55.00	—
1843A	—	3.00	6.00	15.00	55.00	—
1844A	—	3.00	6.00	15.00	55.00	—
1848A	—	3.00	6.00	15.00	55.00	—
1849A	—	3.00	6.00	15.00	55.00	—
1850A	—	3.00	6.00	15.00	55.00	—
1851A	—	3.00	6.00	15.00	55.00	—
1852A	—	3.00	6.00	15.00	55.00	—

KM# 463 2-1/2 SILBER GROSCHEN

3.2400 g., 0.3750 Silver .0390 oz. **Ruler:** Friedrich Wilhelm IV

Date	Mintage	F	VF	XF	Unc	BU
1853A	—	3.00	6.00	15.00	55.00	—
1854A	—	3.00	6.00	15.00	55.00	—
1855A	—	3.00	6.00	15.00	55.00	—
1856A	—	3.00	6.00	15.00	55.00	—
1857A	—	3.00	6.00	15.00	55.00	—
1858A	—	3.00	6.00	15.00	55.00	—
1859A	—	3.00	6.00	15.00	55.00	—
1860A	—	3.00	6.00	15.00	55.00	—

KM# 486 2-1/2 SILBER GROSCHEN

3.2400 g., 0.3750 Silver .0390 oz. **Ruler:** Wilhelm I

Date	Mintage	F	VF	XF	Unc	BU
1861A	—	2.00	4.00	10.00	40.00	—
1862A	—	2.00	4.00	10.00	40.00	—
1863A	—	2.00	4.00	10.00	40.00	—
1864A	—	2.00	4.00	10.00	40.00	—
1865A	—	2.00	4.00	10.00	40.00	—
1866A	—	2.00	4.00	10.00	40.00	—
1867A	—	2.00	4.00	10.00	40.00	—

Date	Mintage	F	VF	XF	Unc	BU
1867C	—	2.00	4.00	10.00	40.00	—
1868A	—	2.00	4.00	10.00	40.00	—
1868C	—	2.00	4.00	10.00	40.00	—
1869A	—	2.00	4.00	10.00	40.00	—
1869B	—	2.00	4.00	10.00	40.00	—
1869C	—	2.00	4.00	10.00	40.00	—
1870A	—	2.00	4.00	10.00	40.00	—
1870B	—	2.00	4.00	10.00	40.00	—
1870C	—	2.00	4.00	10.00	40.00	—
1871A	—	2.00	4.00	10.00	40.00	—
1871B	—	2.00	4.00	10.00	40.00	—
1871C	—	2.00	4.00	10.00	40.00	—
1872A	—	2.00	4.00	10.00	40.00	—
1872B	—	2.00	4.00	10.00	40.00	—
1872C	—	2.00	4.00	10.00	40.00	—
1873A	—	2.00	4.00	10.00	40.00	—
1873B	—	2.00	4.00	10.00	40.00	—
1873C	—	2.00	4.00	10.00	40.00	—

KM# 370 4 GROSCHEN (Marien)

5.3450 g., 0.5210 Silver .0895 oz. **Ruler:** Friedrich Wilhelm III

Date	Mintage	F	VF	XF	Unc	BU
1801A	—	10.00	20.00	70.00	185	—
1802A	—	10.00	20.00	70.00	185	—
1802B	—	10.00	20.00	70.00	185	—
1803A	—	10.00	20.00	70.00	185	—
1803B	—	10.00	20.00	70.00	185	—
1804A	—	10.00	20.00	70.00	185	—
1804B	—	10.00	20.00	70.00	185	—
1805A	—	10.00	20.00	70.00	185	—
1805B	—	10.00	20.00	70.00	185	—
1806A	—	12.00	25.00	100	225	—
1807A	—	12.00	25.00	100	225	—
1808A	—	12.00	25.00	100	225	—
1808G	—	12.00	25.00	100	225	—
1809A	—	12.00	25.00	100	225	—
1809G	—	12.00	25.00	100	225	—

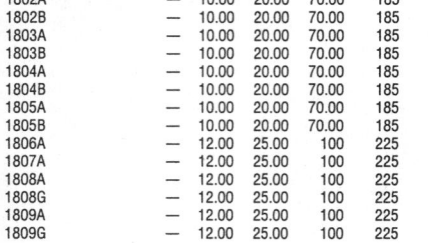

KM# 394 4 GROSCHEN (Marien)

5.3450 g., 0.5210 Silver .0895 oz. **Ruler:** Friedrich Wilhelm III

Date	Mintage	F	VF	XF	Unc	BU
1816A	11,652,000	12.00	25.00	100	250	—
1817A	14,484,000	12.00	25.00	100	250	—
1818A	—	12.00	25.00	100	250	—
1818D	—	25.00	50.00	175	300	—

KM# 385 1/6 THALER

5.3450 g., 0.5210 Silver .0895 oz. **Ruler:** Friedrich Wilhelm III

Date	Mintage	F	VF	XF	Unc	BU
1809A	—	10.00	20.00	75.00	200	—
1810A	—	10.00	20.00	75.00	200	—
1811A	—	10.00	20.00	75.00	200	—
1812A	—	10.00	20.00	75.00	200	—
1812B	—	10.00	20.00	75.00	200	—
1813A	—	10.00	20.00	75.00	200	—
1813B	—	10.00	20.00	75.00	200	—
1814A	—	10.00	20.00	75.00	200	—
1814B	—	10.00	20.00	75.00	200	—
1815A	—	10.00	20.00	75.00	200	—
1815B	—	10.00	20.00	75.00	200	—
1816A	—	10.00	20.00	75.00	200	—
1816B	—	10.00	20.00	75.00	200	—
1817B	—	10.00	20.00	75.00	200	—
1817D	—	15.00	30.00	100	225	—
1818D	—	15.00	30.00	100	225	—

KM# 411 1/6 THALER

5.3450 g., 0.5210 Silver .0895 oz. **Ruler:** Friedrich Wilhelm III

Date	Mintage	F	VF	XF	Unc	BU
1822A	3,264,000	4.00	10.00	40.00	100	—
1823A	8,550,000	4.00	10.00	40.00	100	—
1823D	66,000	7.00	15.00	50.00	150	—
1824A	3,504,000	4.00	10.00	40.00	100	—
1825A	4,662,000	4.00	10.00	40.00	100	—
1826A	3,300,000	4.00	10.00	40.00	100	—
1826D	636,000	4.00	10.00	45.00	125	—
1827A	972,000	4.00	10.00	40.00	100	—
1827D	924,000	4.00	10.00	45.00	125	—
1828D	—	4.00	10.00	45.00	125	—
1835A	60,000	7.00	15.00	50.00	150	—
1835D	—	4.00	10.00	45.00	125	—
1837A	42,000	7.00	15.00	50.00	150	—
1838A	48,000	7.00	15.00	50.00	150	—
1839A	576,000	4.00	10.00	40.00	100	—
1840A	954,000	4.00	10.00	40.00	100	—
1840D	762,000	4.00	10.00	45.00	125	—

KM# 436.1 1/6 THALER

5.3450 g., 0.5210 Silver .0895 oz. **Ruler:** Friedrich Wilhelm IV

Date	Mintage	F	VF	XF	Unc	BU
1841A	786,000	4.00	10.00	45.00	125	—
1841D	678,000	4.00	10.00	45.00	125	—
1842A	3,046,000	4.00	10.00	45.00	125	—
1842D	576,000	4.00	10.00	45.00	125	—
1843D	426,000	4.00	10.00	45.00	125	—
1844D	270,000	4.00	10.00	45.00	125	—
1845D	96,000	5.00	15.00	50.00	150	—

KM# 436.2 1/6 THALER

5.3450 g., 0.5210 Silver .0895 oz. **Ruler:** Friedrich Wilhelm IV
Rev: Different crown above shield

Date	Mintage	F	VF	XF	Unc	BU
1843A	1,566,000	4.00	10.00	45.00	125	—
1844A	948,000	4.00	10.00	45.00	125	—
1845A	312,000	4.00	10.00	45.00	125	—
1846A	270,000	4.00	10.00	45.00	125	—
1847A	240,000	4.00	10.00	45.00	125	—
1848A	912,000	4.00	10.00	45.00	125	—
1849A	2,556,000	4.00	10.00	45.00	125	—
1850A	78,000	5.00	15.00	50.00	150	—
1851A	—	4.00	10.00	45.00	125	—
1852A	372,000	4.00	10.00	45.00	125	—

KM# 464 1/6 THALER

5.3450 g., 0.5210 Silver .0895 oz. **Ruler:** Friedrich Wilhelm IV
Obv: Older head

Date	Mintage	F	VF	XF	Unc	BU
1853A	216,000	15.00	30.00	90.00	250	—
1854A	116,000	15.00	30.00	90.00	250	—
1855A	30,000	15.00	30.00	90.00	250	—
1856A	51,000	15.00	30.00	90.00	250	—

KM# 473 1/6 THALER

5.3450 g., 0.5210 Silver .0895 oz. **Ruler:** Friedrich Wilhelm IV
Rev: Crowned eagle with sceptre and orb

Date	Mintage	F	VF	XF	Unc	BU
1858	96,000	15.00	30.00	90.00	250	—
1859	32,000	15.00	30.00	90.00	250	—
1860	128,000	15.00	30.00	90.00	250	—

KM# 487 1/6 THALER

5.3450 g., 0.5210 Silver .0895 oz. **Ruler:** Friedrich Wilhelm IV

Date	Mintage	F	VF	XF	Unc	BU
1861	249,000	10.00	20.00	75.00	200	—
1862	1,180,000	10.00	20.00	75.00	200	—
1863	413,000	10.00	20.00	75.00	200	—
1864	441,000	10.00	20.00	75.00	200	—

KM# 495 1/6 THALER

5.3450 g., 0.5210 Silver .0895 oz. **Ruler:** Friedrich Wilhelm IV
Rev: Eagle with larger head

Date	Mintage	F	VF	XF	Unc	BU
1865	194,000	15.00	30.00	90.00	250	—
1867	148,000	15.00	30.00	90.00	250	—
1868	128,000	15.00	30.00	90.00	250	—

KM# 380 1/3 THALER (1/2 Gulden)

8.3520 g., 0.6660 Silver .1788 oz. **Ruler:** Friedrich Wilhelm III

Date	Mintage	F	VF	XF	Unc	BU
1800A	—	15.00	30.00	80.00	275	—
1801A	—	15.00	30.00	80.00	275	—
1802A	—	15.00	30.00	80.00	275	—
1804A	—	15.00	30.00	80.00	275	—
1807A	—	15.00	30.00	80.00	275	—
1809G	—	25.00	50.00	175	400	—

KM# 386 1/3 THALER (1/2 Gulden)

8.3520 g., 0.6660 Silver .1788 oz. **Ruler:** Friedrich Wilhelm III

Date	Mintage	F	VF	XF	Unc	BU
1809A	—	65.00	125	300	500	—
1809G	—	50.00	100	250	450	—

KM# 363 2/3 THALER (Gulden)

17.3230 g., 0.7500 Silver .4177 oz. **Ruler:** Friedrich Wilhelm II
Note: Gulden 2/3 Thaler.

Date	Mintage	F	VF	XF	Unc	BU
1801	—	25.00	50.00	90.00	225	—

KM# 392 2/3 THALER (Gulden)

17.3230 g., 0.7500 Silver .4177 oz. **Ruler:** Friedrich Wilhelm II
Note: Similar to KM#363, legend ends VON PREUSSEN.

Date	Mintage	F	VF	XF	Unc	BU
1810A	—	60.00	125	250	400	—

KM# 368 THALER

22.2720 g., 0.7500 Silver .5371 oz. **Ruler:** Friedrich Wilhelm III
Note: Reichs Thaler. Dav. #2603.

Date	Mintage	F	VF	XF	Unc	BU
1801A	—	30.00	80.00	200	700	—
1801B	—	35.00	120	300	800	—
1802A	—	30.00	80.00	200	700	—
1802B	—	35.00	120	300	800	—
1803A	—	30.00	80.00	200	700	—
1803A PRUSSEN (error)	—	—	—	—	—	—
1803B	—	40.00	180	400	1,000	—
1804A	—	30.00	80.00	275	750	—
1805A	—	30.00	80.00	275	750	—
1806A	—	30.00	80.00	275	750	—
1807A	—	30.00	80.00	275	750	—
1808G	33,000	200	350	1,400	3,200	—
1809A	—	50.00	80.00	275	750	—
1809G	—	200	350	7,500	13,000	—

KM# 387 THALER

22.2720 g., 0.7500 Silver .5371 oz. **Ruler:** Friedrich Wilhelm III

Date	Mintage	F	VF	XF	Unc	BU
1809A	—	25.00	50.00	175	500	—
1810A	—	25.00	50.00	175	500	—
1810A (error) THAELR	—	—	—	—	—	—
1811A	—	25.00	50.00	175	600	—
1812A	—	25.00	50.00	175	600	—
1812 B	—	35.00	75.00	300	800	—
1813A	—	25.00	50.00	150	325	—
1813 B	—	35.00	75.00	300	800	—
1814A	—	25.00	50.00	125	275	—
1814A (error) WILHELM	—	—	—	—	—	—
1815A	—	25.00	50.00	150	325	—
1815 B	—	50.00	100	400	1,000	—
1816A	—	25.00	50.00	150	325	—
1816 B	—	35.00	75.00	300	800	—

KM# 393 THALER

22.2720 g., 0.7500 Silver .5371 oz. **Ruler:** Friedrich Wilhelm III
Subject: Visit of Friedrich Wilhelm IV to Berlin Mint

Date	Mintage	F	VF	XF	Unc	BU
1812A	—	1,500	3,000	6,000	10,000	—

KM# 395 THALER

22.2720 g., 0.7500 Silver .5371 oz. **Ruler:** Friedrich Wilhelm III
Obv. Legend: FR. WILH..

Date	Mintage	F	VF	XF	Unc	BU
1816A	—	200	375	1,400	4,000	—
1817A	—	250	550	1,900	4,800	—

KM# 396 THALER

22.2720 g., 0.7500 Silver .5371 oz. **Ruler:** Friedrich Wilhelm III
Obv. Legend: FRIEDR. WILHELM..

Date	Mintage	F	VF	XF	Unc	BU
1816A	—	30.00	100	300	800	—
1817A	—	30.00	50.00	160	400	—
1818A	—	30.00	50.00	160	400	—
1818D	—	30.00	60.00	275	750	—
1819A	—	30.00	50.00	160	600	—
1819D	—	30.00	60.00	275	750	—
1820A	—	30.00	50.00	160	600	—
1820D	—	30.00	60.00	275	750	—
1821A	—	30.00	50.00	160	600	—
1821D Rare	—	—	—	—	—	—
1822A	—	30.00	100	300	800	—
1822D	—	30.00	65.00	300	850	—

KM# 413 THALER

22.2720 g., 0.7500 Silver .5371 oz. **Ruler:** Friedrich Wilhelm III

Date	Mintage	F	VF	XF	Unc	BU
1823A	761,000	25.00	50.00	120	400	—
1823D	13,000	75.00	125	500	1,200	—
1824A	1,144,000	25.00	50.00	120	400	—
1824D	16,000	40.00	100	300	850	—
1825A	405,000	25.00	50.00	120	400	—
1825D	36,000	50.00	120	350	950	—
1826A	687,000	25.00	50.00	120	400	—

KM# 417 THALER

22.2720 g., 0.7500 Silver .5371 oz. **Ruler:** Friedrich Wilhelm III
Note: Mining Thaler.

Date	Mintage	F	VF	XF	Unc	BU
1826A	50,000	35.00	80.00	200	600	—
1827A	50,000	35.00	80.00	200	600	—
1828A	50,000	35.00	80.00	200	600	—

KM# 418 THALER

22.2720 g., 0.7500 Silver .5371 oz. **Ruler:** Friedrich Wilhelm III
Rev: Arms of different design

Date	Mintage	F	VF	XF	Unc	BU
1827A	78,000	65.00	150	500	1,200	—
1828A	1,578,000	30.00	60.00	185	500	—
1828D	12,000	75.00	200	650	1,500	—

KM# 419 THALER

22.2720 g., 0.7500 Silver .5371 oz. **Ruler:** Friedrich Wilhelm III
Obv: Older head

Date	Mintage	F	VF	XF	Unc	BU
1828A Rare	1,578,000	—	—	—	—	—
1829A	4,002,000	20.00	50.00	90.00	200	—
1829	277,000	30.00	50.00	225	650	—
1830A	6,888,000	20.00	50.00	90.00	200	—
1830	651,000	30.00	50.00	175	550	—
1831A	4,595,000	20.00	50.00	90.00	200	—
1831	45,000	30.00	50.00	175	550	—
1832A	267,000	25.00	50.00	100	300	—
1832	29,000	30.00	60.00	225	700	—
1833A	448,000	25.00	50.00	100	300	—
1833	19,000	30.00	60.00	225	700	—
1834A	1,299,000	20.00	50.00	90.00	200	—
1834	21,000	30.00	60.00	225	700	—
1835A	449,000	25.00	50.00	100	300	—
1835 Proof	—	Value: 600				
1835	16,000	30.00	60.00	225	700	—
1836A	526,000	25.00	50.00	100	300	—
1836	21,000	30.00	60.00	225	700	—
1837A	466,000	25.00	50.00	100	300	—
1837	15,000	30.00	60.00	225	700	—
1838A	314,000	25.00	50.00	100	300	—
1838	25,000	30.00	60.00	225	700	—
1839A	247,000	25.00	50.00	100	300	—
1839	12,000	30.00	60.00	225	700	—
1840A	1,630,000	20.00	50.00	90.00	200	—
1840	11,000	30.00	60.00	225	700	—

KM# 420 THALER

22.2720 g., 0.7500 Silver .5371 oz. **Ruler:** Friedrich Wilhelm III
Obv: Older head

Date	Mintage	F	VF	XF	Unc	BU
1829A	50,000	25.00	60.00	110	250	—
1830A	50,000	25.00	60.00	110	250	—
1831A	50,000	25.00	60.00	110	250	—
1832A	50,000	25.00	60.00	110	325	—
1833A	50,000	25.00	60.00	110	325	—
1834A	50,000	25.00	60.00	110	300	—
1835A	50,000	25.00	60.00	110	325	—
1836A	50,000	25.00	60.00	110	325	—

Date	Mintage	F	VF	XF	Unc	BU
1837A	50,000	25.00	60.00	110	325	—
1838A	50,000	25.00	60.00	110	325	—
1839A	50,000	25.00	60.00	110	325	—
1840A	50,000	25.00	60.00	100	225	—

KM# 437 THALER
22.2720 g., 0.7500 Silver .5371 oz. **Ruler:** Friedrich Wilhelm IV

Date	Mintage	F	VF	XF	Unc	BU
1841A	2,280,000	35.00	85.00	275	800	—

KM# 438 THALER
22.2720 g., 0.7500 Silver .5371 oz. **Ruler:** Friedrich Wilhelm IV **Note:** Mining Thaler.

Date	Mintage	F	VF	XF	Unc	BU
1841A	50,000	50.00	110	300	950	—

KM# 445 THALER
22.2720 g., 0.7500 Silver .5371 oz. **Ruler:** Friedrich Wilhelm IV **Note:** Reichs Thaler.

Date	Mintage	F	VF	XF	Unc	BU
1842A	518,000	30.00	60.00	160	400	—
1843A	600,000	25.00	50.00	100	250	—
1844A	918,000	25.00	50.00	100	250	—
1845A	720,000	25.00	50.00	100	250	—
1846A	1,115,000	25.00	50.00	100	250	—
1847A	1,283,000	25.00	50.00	100	250	—
1848A	3,743,000	25.00	50.00	100	250	—
1849A	892,000	25.00	50.00	100	250	—
1850A	350,000	25.00	50.00	100	250	—
1851A	731,000	30.00	60.00	160	400	—
1852A	329,000	30.00	60.00	160	400	—

KM# 446 THALER
22.2720 g., 0.7500 Silver .5371 oz. **Ruler:** Friedrich Wilhelm IV **Obv:** Larger head **Rev:** Dot after THALER

Date	Mintage	F	VF	XF	Unc	BU
1842A	50,000	30.00	65.00	150	350	—
1843A	50,000	30.00	65.00	150	350	—
1844A	50,000	30.00	65.00	150	350	—
1845A	50,000	30.00	65.00	150	350	—
1846A	50,000	30.00	65.00	150	350	—

KM# 455 THALER
22.2720 g., 0.7500 Silver .5371 oz. **Ruler:** Friedrich Wilhelm IV **Rev:** Without dot after THALER

Date	Mintage	F	VF	XF	Unc	BU
1847A	50,000	30.00	65.00	150	350	—
1848A	50,000	30.00	65.00	150	350	—
1849A	50,000	30.00	65.00	150	350	—
1850A	50,000	30.00	65.00	150	350	—
1851A	50,000	30.00	65.00	150	350	—
1852A	50,000	30.00	65.00	150	350	—

KM# 466 THALER
22.2720 g., 0.7500 Silver .5371 oz. **Ruler:** Friedrich Wilhelm IV **Obv:** Older head

Date	Mintage	F	VF	XF	Unc	BU
1853A	50,000	30.00	65.00	150	350	—
1854A	50,000	30.00	65.00	150	350	—
1855A	50,000	30.00	65.00	150	350	—
1856A	50,000	30.00	65.00	150	350	—

KM# 465 THALER
22.2720 g., 0.7500 Silver .5371 oz. **Ruler:** Friedrich Wilhelm IV **Obv:** Older head

Date	Mintage	F	VF	XF	Unc	BU
1853A	300,000	30.00	60.00	125	250	—
1854A	3,500,000	25.00	50.00	100	225	—
1855A	7,300,000	25.00	50.00	100	225	—
1856A	940,000	25.00	50.00	100	225	—

KM# 471 THALER
18.5200 g., 0.9000 Silver .5360 oz. **Ruler:** Friedrich Wilhelm IV **Note:** Vereins Thaler.

Date	Mintage	F	VF	XF	Unc	BU
1857A	836,000	20.00	30.00	60.00	200	—
1858A	1,120,000	20.00	30.00	60.00	200	—
1859A	17,600,000	17.50	25.00	50.00	150	—
1860A	17,429,000	17.50	25.00	50.00	150	—
1861A	10,000	40.00	80.00	125	250	—
1861A Proof	—	Value: 250				

KM# 472 THALER
18.5200 g., 0.9000 Silver .5360 oz. **Ruler:** Friedrich Wilhelm IV **Obv:** Similar to KM#471 **Note:** Mining Thaler.

Date	Mintage	F	VF	XF	Unc	BU
1857A	47,000	30.00	65.00	150	350	—
1858A	95,000	30.00	65.00	150	350	—
1859A	94,000	30.00	65.00	150	350	—
1860A	298,000	30.00	65.00	150	350	—

KM# 488 THALER
18.5200 g., 0.9000 Silver .5360 oz. **Ruler:** Friedrich Wilhelm IV **Subject:** Coronation of Wilhelm and Augusta **Note:** Vereins Thaler.

Date	Mintage	F	VF	XF	Unc	BU
1861A	1,000,000	17.50	25.00	40.00	75.00	—
1861A Proof	—	—	—	—	—	—

KM# 490 THALER
18.5200 g., 0.9000 Silver .5360 oz. **Ruler:** Wilhelm I **Note:** Mining Thaler.

Date	Mintage	F	VF	XF	Unc	BU
1861A	70,000	35.00	55.00	100	300	—
1862A	145,000	30.00	50.00	90.00	250	—

KM# 489 THALER
18.5200 g., 0.9000 Silver .5360 oz. **Ruler:** Friedrich Wilhelm IV **Obv:** Similar to KM#494 **Rev:** Similar to KM#471

Date	Mintage	F	VF	XF	Unc	BU
1861A	13,716,000	20.00	35.00	65.00	150	—
1862A	6,057,000	20.00	35.00	75.00	160	—
1863A	1,668,000	20.00	45.00	90.00	200	—

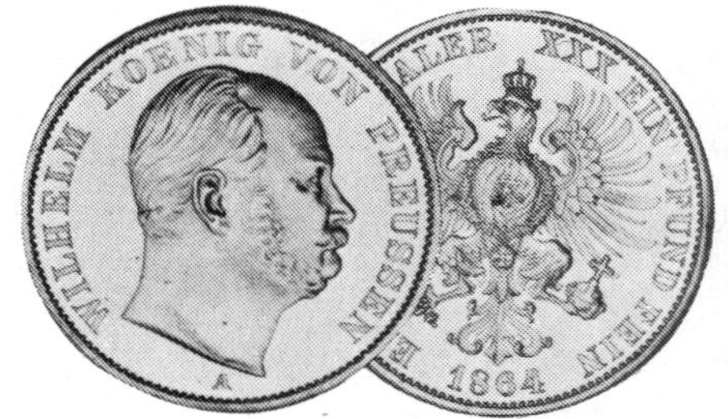

KM# 494 THALER
18.5200 g., 0.9000 Silver .5360 oz. **Ruler:** Wilhelm I

Date	Mintage	F	VF	XF	Unc	BU
1864A	1,379,000	25.00	35.00	75.00	160	—
1865A	2,584,000	20.00	35.00	65.00	150	—
1866A	24,409,000	20.00	35.00	65.00	150	—
1866B	34,000	25.00	55.00	150	350	—
1867A	31,390,000	20.00	35.00	65.00	150	—
1867B	593,000	25.00	55.00	150	350	—
1867C	179,000	35.00	100	250	600	—
1868A	6,286,000	20.00	35.00	65.00	150	—
1868B	48,000	30.00	75.00	175	450	—
1868C	5,139	75.00	165	600	1,250	—
1869A	3,630,000	20.00	35.00	65.00	150	—
1869B	370,000	30.00	75.00	175	450	—
1869C	44,000	50.00	125	300	700	—
1870A	3,140,000	20.00	35.00	65.00	150	—
1870B	611,000	25.00	55.00	150	350	—
1870C	190,000	35.00	100	250	600	—
1871A	7,600,000	20.00	35.00	65.00	150	—
1871B	245,000	25.00	55.00	150	350	—
1871C	28,000	50.00	125	300	700	—

KM# 497 THALER
18.5200 g., 0.9000 Silver .5360 oz. **Ruler:** Wilhelm I **Subject:** Victory of Austria **Note:** Vereins Thaler.

Date	Mintage	F	VF	XF	Unc	BU
1866A	500,000	30.00	55.00	80.00	125	—

KM# 500 THALER
18.5200 g., 0.9000 Silver .5360 oz. **Ruler:** Wilhelm I **Subject:** Victory of France

Date	Mintage	F	VF	XF	Unc	BU
1871A	880,000	17.50	25.00	40.00	75.00	—
1871A Proof	—	Value: 150				

KM# 425 2 THALER (3-1/2 Gulden)
37.1190 g., 2.9000 Silver 1.0742 oz. **Ruler:** Friedrich Wilhelm III

Date	Mintage	F	VF	XF	Unc	BU
1839A	172,000	100	150	300	800	—
1840A	789,000	75.00	125	225	600	—

KM# 439 2 THALER (3-1/2 Gulden)
37.1190 g., 2.9000 Silver 1.0742 oz. **Ruler:** Friedrich Wilhelm IV

Date	Mintage	F	VF	XF	Unc	BU
1841A Rare	—	—	—	—	—	—

KM# 440.1 2 THALER (3-1/2 Gulden)
37.1190 g., 2.9000 Silver 1.0742 oz. **Ruler:** Friedrich Wilhelm IV

Date	Mintage	F	VF	XF	Unc	BU
1841A	4,307,000	55.00	85.00	185	400	—
1842A	1,249,000	55.00	85.00	200	475	—

KM# 440.2 2 THALER (3-1/2 Gulden)
37.1190 g., 2.9000 Silver 1.0742 oz. **Ruler:** Friedrich Wilhelm IV **Rev:** Different crown above shield

Date	Mintage	F	VF	XF	Unc	BU
1843A	193,000	55.00	85.00	200	475	—
1844A	1,069,000	55.00	85.00	200	475	—
1845A	961,000	55.00	85.00	200	475	—
1846A	1,472,000	55.00	85.00	200	475	—
1847A Rare	232,000	—	—	—	—	—
1848A Rare	4,147	—	—	—	—	—
1850A	221,000	55.00	85.00	200	475	—
1851A	379,000	55.00	85.00	200	475	—

KM# 467 2 THALER (3-1/2 Gulden)
37.1190 g., 2.9000 Silver 1.0742 oz. **Ruler:** Friedrich Wilhelm IV

Date	Mintage	F	VF	XF	Unc	BU
1853A	2,500	200	450	1,200	2,000	—
1854A	147,000	90.00	125	275	500	—
1855A	100,000	75.00	110	225	425	—
1856A	627,000	60.00	90.00	160	375	—

KM# 474 2 THALER
37.0370 g., 2.9000 Silver 1.0718 oz. **Ruler:** Friedrich Wilhelm IV **Obv:** Similar to KM#467

Date	Mintage	F	VF	XF	Unc	BU
1858A	17,000	200	450	1,000	1,600	—
1859A	174,000	150	400	750	1,325	—

KM# 491 2 THALER
37.0370 g., 2.9000 Silver 1.0718 oz. **Ruler:** Friedrich Wilhelm IV **Rev:** Similar to KM#474

Date	Mintage	F	VF	XF	Unc	BU
1861A	9,490	500	1,000	1,800	3,200	—
1862A	58,000	250	460	1,200	2,000	—
1863A	337	—	—	—	5,000	—
1863A Proof	—	Value: 3,000				

KM# 496 2 THALER
37.0370 g., 2.9000 Silver 1.0718 oz. **Ruler:** Wilhelm I

Date	Mintage	F	VF	XF	Unc	BU
1865A	23,000	175	525	1,000	1,500	—
1866A	5,110	225	550	1,100	2,000	—
1866C	226,000	150	260	425	800	—
1867A	1,195	250	600	1,500	3,200	—
1867C	1,049,000	100	200	350	700	—
1868A	1,584	250	600	1,500	3,200	—
1869A	1,901	250	600	1,500	3,200	—
1870A	3,155	250	600	1,500	3,200	—
1871A	1,134	235	525	1,100	1,750	—

KM# 475 1/2 KRONE
5.5550 g., 0.9000 Gold .1607 oz. **Ruler:** Friedrich Wilhelm IV

Date	Mintage	F	VF	XF	Unc	BU
1858A	2,036	800	1,500	2,000	3,250	—

KM# 493 1/2 KRONE
5.5550 g., 0.9000 Gold .1607 oz. **Ruler:** Wilhelm I

Date	Mintage	F	VF	XF	Unc	BU
1862A	6,365	500	900	1,250	2,000	—
1863A	3,642	500	900	1,250	2,000	—
1864A	4,840	500	900	1,250	2,000	—
1866A	14,000	500	900	1,250	2,000	—
1867A	5,711	500	900	1,250	2,000	—
1868A	92,000	400	800	1,200	1,600	—
1868A	3,718	800	1,500	2,000	3,750	—
1869A	—	800	1,500	2,000	3,200	—

KM# 476 KRONE
11.1110 g., 0.9000 Gold .3272 oz. **Ruler:** Wilhelm I

Date	Mintage	F	VF	XF	Unc	BU
1858A	6,320	600	1,400	1,800	3,000	—
1859A	34,000	500	1,200	1,600	2,600	—
1860A	16,000	650	1,500	2,000	3,250	—

KM# 492 KRONE
11.1110 g., 0.9160 Gold .3272 oz. **Ruler:** Wilhelm I

Date	Mintage	F	VF	XF	Unc	BU
1861A	2,488	650	1,200	1,700	3,000	—
1862A	5,558	650	1,200	1,700	3,000	—
1863A	2,653	650	1,200	1,700	3,000	—
1864A	792	800	1,400	2,000	3,250	—
1866A	720	800	1,400	2,000	3,250	—
1867A	4,087	400	800	1,200	2,000	—
1867A Proof	—	Value: 2,500				
1867B	15,000	500	1,200	1,700	3,000	—
1868A	97,000	400	800	1,200	2,000	—
1868B	40,000	500	1,200	1,700	3,000	—
1869A	—	1,000	1,400	2,000	3,600	—
1870A	1,764	800	1,400	2,000	3,250	—

TRADE COINAGE

KM# 382 1/2 FREDERICK D'OR

3.3410 g., 0.9030 Gold .0970 oz. **Ruler:** Friedrich Wilhelm III
Obv: L at truncation

Date	Mintage	F	VF	XF	Unc	BU
1802A	—	275	350	800	1,500	—
1803A	—	550	800	1,200	2,000	—
1804A	—	300	500	900	1,625	—
1806A	—	275	400	800	1,500	—
1814A	—	300	500	900	1,625	—
1816A	—	350	600	1,000	1,750	—

KM# 397 1/2 FREDERICK D'OR

3.3410 g., 0.9030 Gold .0970 oz. **Ruler:** Friedrich Wilhelm III

Date	Mintage	F	VF	XF	Unc	BU
1817A	—	300	500	700	1,250	—

KM# 414 1/2 FREDERICK D'OR

3.3410 g., 0.9030 Gold .0970 oz. **Ruler:** Friedrich Wilhelm III

Date	Mintage	F	VF	XF	Unc	BU
1825A	—	300	500	750	1,000	—
1827A	—	375	650	875	1,125	—
1828A	—	600	1,000	1,250	1,500	—
1829A	—	500	875	1,125	1,375	—
1830A	—	350	625	875	1,125	—
1831A	—	350	625	875	1,125	—
1832A	—	350	625	875	1,125	—
1833A	—	350	625	875	1,125	—
1834A	—	350	625	875	1,125	—
1838A	—	350	625	875	1,125	—
1839A	—	400	750	1,000	1,250	—
1840A	—	500	875	1,125	1,375	—

KM# 441 1/2 FREDERICK D'OR

3.3410 g., 0.9030 Gold .0970 oz. **Ruler:** Friedrich Wilhelm IV

Date	Mintage	F	VF	XF	Unc	BU
1841A	—	300	500	750	1,000	—
1842A	—	300	500	750	1,000	—
1843A	—	400	750	1,000	1,250	—
1844A	—	400	750	1,000	1,250	—
1845A	—	400	750	1,000	1,250	—
1846A	—	400	750	1,000	1,250	—
1849A	—	400	750	1,000	1,250	—

KM# 468 1/2 FREDERICK D'OR

3.3410 g., 0.9030 Gold .0970 oz. **Ruler:** Friedrich Wilhelm IV

Date	Mintage	F	VF	XF	Unc	BU
1853A	—	500	900	1,250	1,600	—

KM# 371 FREDERICK D'OR

6.6820 g., 0.9030 Gold .1940 oz. **Ruler:** Friedrich Wilhelm III

Date	Mintage	F	VF	XF	Unc	BU
1801A	—	450	600	950	1,600	—
1801A	—	400	600	950	1,600	—
1801B	—	450	600	950	1,600	—
1802A	—	450	600	950	1,600	—
1802B	—	450	600	950	1,600	—
1803A	—	400	475	800	1,400	—
1803B	—	550	800	1,200	2,000	—
1804A	—	450	600	950	1,600	—
1804B	—	550	800	1,200	2,000	—
1805A	—	350	525	950	1,400	—
1805B	—	550	800	1,200	2,000	—
1806A	—	350	525	950	1,500	—
1807A	—	350	525	950	1,500	—
1808A	—	550	800	1,200	1,850	—
1809A	—	350	475	800	1,400	—
1810A	—	450	600	950	1,600	—
1811A	—	450	600	950	1,600	—
1812A	—	350	475	800	1,400	—
1813A	—	400	525	875	1,450	—
1816A	—	450	600	950	1,600	—

KM# 398 FREDERICK D'OR

6.6820 g., 0.9030 Gold .1940 oz. **Ruler:** Friedrich Wilhelm III

Date	Mintage	F	VF	XF	Unc	BU
1817A	—	500	800	1,200	2,000	—
1818A	—	400	550	1,000	1,800	—
1819A	—	650	1,000	1,500	2,250	—
1822A	—	400	550	1,100	1,850	—

KM# 415 FREDERICK D'OR

6.6820 g., 0.9030 Gold .1940 oz. **Ruler:** Friedrich Wilhelm III

Date	Mintage	F	VF	XF	Unc	BU
1825A	—	300	400	800	1,400	—
1827A	—	400	600	1,000	1,650	—
1828A	—	300	400	800	1,400	—
1829A	—	400	550	1,000	1,650	—
1830A	—	400	550	1,000	1,650	—
1831A	—	300	550	900	1,550	—
1832A	—	300	550	900	1,550	—
1833A	—	300	550	900	1,550	—
1834A	—	300	550	1,000	1,650	—
1836A	—	300	550	1,000	1,650	—
1837A	—	300	550	800	1,550	—
1838A	—	300	550	800	1,650	—
1839A	—	300	550	800	1,550	—
1840A	—	300	550	800	1,400	—

KM# 442 FREDERICK D'OR

6.6820 g., 0.9030 Gold .1940 oz. **Ruler:** Friedrich Wilhelm IV

Date	Mintage	F	VF	XF	Unc	BU
1841A	—	300	550	800	1,400	—
1842A	—	300	550	800	1,400	—
1843A	—	300	550	800	1,550	—
1844A	—	300	550	800	1,400	—
1845A	—	300	550	800	1,400	—
1846A	—	300	550	800	1,400	—
1847A	—	300	550	800	1,550	—
1848A	—	300	550	800	1,400	—
1849A	—	300	550	800	1,400	—
1850A	—	300	550	800	1,550	—
1851A	—	300	550	800	1,650	—
1852A	—	300	550	800	1,550	—

KM# 469 FREDERICK D'OR

6.6820 g., 0.9030 Gold .1940 oz. **Ruler:** Friedrich Wilhelm IV

Date	Mintage	F	VF	XF	Unc	BU
1853A	—	300	750	1,200	1,750	—
1854A	—	300	750	1,200	1,750	—
1855A	—	300	750	1,200	1,750	—

KM# 381 2 FREDERICK D'OR

13.3630 g., 0.9030 Gold .3880 oz. **Ruler:** Friedrich Wilhelm III
Obv: L at truncation

Date	Mintage	F	VF	XF	Unc	BU
1800A	—	600	875	1,600	2,400	—
1801A	—	700	975	1,800	2,600	—
1801A	—	700	975	1,800	2,600	—
1802A	—	800	1,250	2,200	3,000	—
1806A	—	800	1,250	2,200	3,000	—
1811A	—	700	975	1,800	2,600	—
1813A	—	725	1,000	2,000	2,800	—
1814A	—	800	1,250	2,200	3,000	—

KM# 416 2 FREDERICK D'OR

13.3630 g., 0.9030 Gold .3880 oz. **Ruler:** Friedrich Wilhelm III

Date	Mintage	F	VF	XF	Unc	BU
1825A	—	800	1,200	1,600	2,000	—
1826A	—	700	1,100	1,500	1,800	—
1827A	—	600	1,000	1,400	1,600	—
1828A	—	600	1,000	1,400	1,600	—
1829A	—	700	1,100	1,500	1,800	—
1830A	—	550	900	1,300	1,500	—
1831A	—	550	900	1,300	1,500	—
1832A	—	700	1,100	1,500	1,800	—
1836A	—	800	1,200	1,600	2,000	—
1837A	—	550	900	1,300	1,500	—
1838A	—	600	1,000	1,400	1,600	—
1839A	—	500	800	1,200	1,400	—
1840A	—	500	800	1,200	1,400	—

KM# 443 2 FREDERICK D'OR

13.3630 g., 0.9030 Gold .3880 oz. **Ruler:** Friedrich Wilhelm IV

Date	Mintage	F	VF	XF	Unc	BU
1841A	—	500	800	1,200	1,500	—
1842A	—	500	800	1,200	1,500	—
1843A	—	600	1,250	1,750	2,000	—
1844A	—	800	1,500	2,000	2,250	—
1845A	—	800	1,500	2,000	2,250	—
1846A	—	500	800	1,200	1,500	—
1848A	—	500	800	1,200	1,500	—
1849A	—	500	800	1,200	1,500	—
1852A	—	500	800	1,200	1,500	—

KM# 470 2 FREDERICK D'OR
13.3630 g., 0.9030 Gold .3880 oz. **Ruler:** Friedrich Wilhelm IV

Date	Mintage	F	VF	XF	Unc	BU
1853A	—	500	800	1,200	2,000	—
1854A	—	500	800	1,200	2,000	—
1855A	—	750	1,500	2,000	2,500	—

REFORM COINAGE

KM# 506 2 MARK
11.1110 g., 0.9000 Silver .3215 oz. **Ruler:** Wilhelm I

Date	Mintage	F	VF	XF	Unc	BU
1876A	13,368,000	10.00	30.00	180	450	600
1876B	3,985,000	10.00	30.00	180	500	700
1876C	5,233,000	10.00	30.00	200	500	700
1877A	3,634,000	10.00	30.00	190	500	700
1877B	1,301,000	15.00	35.00	225	650	800
1877C	1,307,000	15.00	35.00	225	650	850
1879A	29,000	100	200	850	2,250	3,000
1880A	665,000	30.00	85.00	400	1,200	1,500
1883A	164,000	35.00	90.00	300	800	1,000
1884A	140,000	40.00	120	350	900	1,200

KM# 510 2 MARK
11.1110 g., 0.9000 Silver .3215 oz. **Ruler:** Wilhelm I

Date	Mintage	F	VF	XF	Unc	BU
1888A	500,000	12.50	25.00	45.00	75.00	90.00
1888A Proof	—	Value: 500				

KM# 511 2 MARK
11.1110 g., 0.9000 Silver .3215 oz. **Ruler:** Wilhelm II

Date	Mintage	F	VF	XF	Unc	BU
1888A	141,000	120	250	400	500	600
1888A Proof	—	Value: 750				

KM# 522 2 MARK
11.1110 g., 0.9000 Silver .2215 oz. **Ruler:** Wilhelm II

Date	Mintage	F	VF	XF	Unc	BU
1891A	544,000	10.00	25.00	50.00	200	250
1891A Proof	—	Value: 500				
1892A	182,000	100	175	400	1,000	1,400
1892A Proof	—	Value: 2,500				

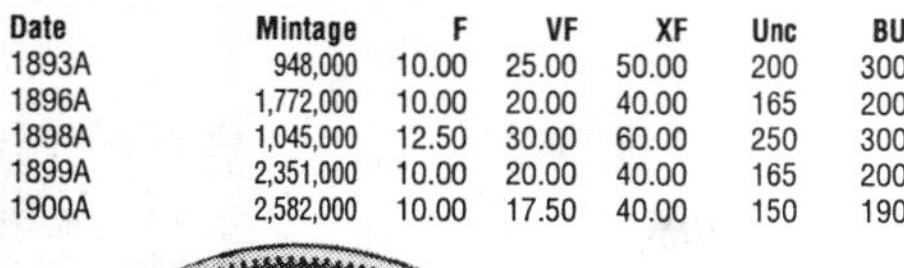

Date	Mintage	F	VF	XF	Unc	BU
1893A	948,000	10.00	25.00	50.00	200	300
1896A	1,772,000	10.00	20.00	40.00	165	200
1898A	1,045,000	12.50	30.00	60.00	250	300
1899A	2,351,000	10.00	20.00	40.00	165	200
1900A	2,582,000	10.00	17.50	40.00	150	190

KM# 503 5 MARK
27.7770 g., 0.9000 Silver .8038 oz. **Ruler:** Wilhelm I

Date	Mintage	F	VF	XF	Unc	BU
1874A	838,000	17.50	35.00	275	600	800
1875A	853,000	20.00	50.00	400	1,500	2,000
1875B	919,000	17.50	45.00	325	1,000	1,350
1876A	2,041,000	15.00	35.00	225	600	800
1876B	2,098,000	15.00	40.00	200	600	800
1876C	812,000	20.00	45.00	275	1,500	2,000

KM# 507 5 MARK
1.9910 g., 0.9000 Gold .0576 oz. **Ruler:** Wilhelm I

Date	Mintage	F	VF	XF	Unc	BU
1877A	1,217,000	125	175	250	400	600
1877A Proof	—	Value: 1,300				
1877B	517,000	125	175	250	400	600
1877B Proof	—	Value: 1,200				
1877C	688,000	125	175	250	400	600
1878A	502,000	125	175	250	400	600
1878A Proof	—	Value: 1,300				

KM# 512 5 MARK
27.7770 g., 0.9000 Silver .8038 oz. **Ruler:** Wilhelm I

Date	Mintage	F	VF	XF	Unc	BU
1888A	200,000	40.00	75.00	125	175	225
1888A Proof	—	Value: 500				

KM# 513 5 MARK
27.7770 g., 0.9000 Silver .8038 oz. **Ruler:** Wilhelm II **Rev:** Type II

Date	Mintage	F	VF	XF	Unc	BU
1888A	56,000	200	450	700	1,100	1,500
1888A Proof	—	Value: 2,000				

KM# 523 5 MARK
27.7770 g., 0.9000 Silver .8038 oz. **Ruler:** Wilhelm II **Rev:** Type III

Date	Mintage	F	VF	XF	Unc	BU
1891A	130,000	15.00	30.00	160	800	1,200
1892A	224,000	15.00	30.00	160	900	1,300
1893A	215,000	15.00	30.00	160	700	1,000
1894A	440,000	15.00	30.00	160	600	900
1895A	831,000	15.00	30.00	150	600	900
1896A	46,000	95.00	175	750	2,000	3,000
1898A	1,134,000	17.50	25.00	160	800	1,000
1899A	525,000	10.00	20.00	130	800	1,200
1900A	1,080,000	10.00	17.50	95.00	425	525
(1891-1908)A Proof	—	Value: 900				

KM# 502 10 MARK
3.9820 g., 0.9000 Gold .1152 oz. **Ruler:** Wilhelm I

Date	Mintage	F	VF	XF	Unc	BU
1872A	3,123,000	60.00	85.00	110	200	250
1872A Proof	—	Value: 1,600				
1872B	1,418,000	60.00	95.00	120	225	275
1872C	1,747,000	60.00	80.00	130	275	325
1873A	3,016,000	60.00	75.00	90.00	200	250
1873A Proof	—	Value: 1,600				
1873B	2,273,000	60.00	100	125	275	325
1873C	2,295,000	60.00	95.00	120	275	325

KM# 504 10 MARK
3.9820 g., 0.9000 Gold .1152 oz. **Ruler:** Wilhelm I **Rev:** Type II

Date	Mintage	F	VF	XF	Unc	BU
1874A	833,000	60.00	95.00	120	250	300
1874A Proof	—	Value: 1,100				
1874B	1,028,000	60.00	95.00	120	250	300
1874C	321,000	60.00	95.00	120	250	300
1874C Proof	—	Value: 1,300				
1875A	2,430,000	60.00	95.00	120	250	300
1875B	456,000	60.00	95.00	120	300	350
1875C	1,532,000	60.00	95.00	120	250	300
1876B	2,800	1,000	1,600	2,200	3,000	3,500
1876B Proof	—	Value: 10,000				
1876C	27,000	500	1,200	1,600	2,500	3,000
1877A	851,000	60.00	95.00	120	250	350
1877B	247,000	60.00	105	120	350	450
1877C	328,000	60.00	85.00	120	300	350
1878A	1,126,000	60.00	85.00	110	250	300
1878B	15,000	45,000	60,000	85,000	100,000	120,000
1878C	516,000	60.00	100	130	300	350
1879A	1,012,000	60.00	95.00	120	225	275
1879A Proof	—	Value: 800				
1879C	282,000	60.00	125	150	300	400
1880A	1,762,000	60.00	80.00	120	250	325
1882A	8,382	1,500	3,200	4,500	6,500	8,500
1883A	13,000	1,200	1,800	2,400	3,000	4,500
1883A Proof	—	Value: 10,000				
1886A	14,000	1,500	2,000	3,200	5,000	6,000

Date	Mintage	F	VF	XF	Unc	BU
1888A	189,000	60.00	95.00	130	275	325
1888A Proof	—	Value: 1,300				

KM# 514 10 MARK

3.9820 g., 0.9000 Gold .1152 oz. **Ruler:** Friedrich III March - June

Date	Mintage	F	VF	XF	Unc	BU
1888A	876,000	60.00	95.00	120	175	225
1888A Proof	—	Value: 700				

KM# 517 10 MARK

3.9820 g., 0.9000 Gold .1152 oz. **Ruler:** Wilhelm II **Rev:** Type II

Date	Mintage	F	VF	XF	Unc	BU
1889A	24,000	1,600	2,500	3,000	4,000	6,000
1889A Proof	—	Value: 6,000				

KM# 520 10 MARK

3.9820 g., 0.9000 Gold .1152 oz. **Ruler:** Wilhelm II **Rev:** Type III

Date	Mintage	F	VF	XF	Unc	BU
1890A	1,512,000	55.00	100	120	275	325
1890A Proof	—	Value: 1,000				
1892A	35,000	400	600	1,000	1,500	2,000
1893A	1,591,000	55.00	100	120	275	325
1894A	18,000	550	1,100	1,450	2,000	2,500
1895A	29,000	400	700	1,200	1,900	2,250
1896A	1,081,000	55.00	100	120	275	325
1897A	114,000	55.00	120	200	300	400
1898A	2,280,000	55.00	95.00	120	275	325
1899A	300,000	55.00	110	165	275	325
1900A	742,000	55.00	95.00	120	275	325
1900A Proof	—	Value: 900				

KM# 501 20 MARK

7.9650 g., 0.9000 Gold .2304 oz. **Ruler:** Wilhelm I

Date	Mintage	F	VF	XF	Unc	BU
1871A	502,000	125	200	275	500	750
1871A Proof	—	Value: 1,800				
1872A	7,717,000	BV	110	130	200	250
1872A Proof	2,491	Value: 1,800				
1872B	1,918,000	BV	110	130	225	275
1872C	3,056,000	BV	110	130	225	275
1873A	9,063,000	BV	110	130	225	275
1873A Proof	—	Value: 1,800				
1873B	3,441,000	BV	110	130	225	275
1873C	5,228,000	BV	110	130	225	275
1873C Proof	—	Value: 1,800				

KM# 505 20 MARK

7.9650 g., 0.9000 Gold .2304 oz. **Ruler:** Wilhelm I **Rev:** Type II

Date	Mintage	F	VF	XF	Unc	BU
1874A	762,000	BV	115	140	200	250
1874A Proof	—	Value: 1,300				
1874B	824,000	BV	120	150	225	275
1874C	88,000	BV	130	175	250	300
1875A	4,203,000	BV	105	140	200	250
1875B	Est. 1,500	180	350	600	1,200	1,500
1876A	2,673,000	BV	115	140	200	250

Date	Mintage	F	VF	XF	Unc	BU
1876C	423,000	150	250	400	600	900
1877A	1,250,000	BV	115	140	200	250
1877B	501,000	BV	125	200	300	350
1877C	6,384	1,000	1,700	2,400	3,000	4,000
1878A	2,175,000	BV	105	130	200	250
1878C	82,000	140	250	400	600	900
1879A	1,022,999	BV	115	140	200	250
1881A	428,000	BV	105	130	200	250
1882A	655,000	BV	115	140	200	250
1882A Proof	—	Value: 1,500				
1883A	4,283,000	BV	105	120	200	250
1884A	224,000	BV	115	140	200	250
1885A	407,000	BV	115	140	200	250
1886A	176,000	BV	115	140	200	250
1887A	5,645,000	BV	105	120	200	250
1887A Proof	—	Value: 1,500				
1888A	534,000	BV	115	150	200	250
1888A Proof	—	Value: 1,500				

KM# 515 20 MARK

7.9650 g., 0.9000 Gold .2304 oz. **Ruler:** Friedrich III March - June

Date	Mintage	F	VF	XF	Unc	BU
1888A	5,364,000	100	120	150	200	250
1888A Proof	—	Value: 900				

KM# 516 20 MARK

7.9650 g., 0.9000 Gold .2304 oz. **Ruler:** Wilhelm II

Date	Mintage	F	VF	XF	Unc	BU
1888A	756,000	BV	115	140	250	300
1888A Proof	—	Value: 1,250				
1889A	9,642,000	BV	100	130	200	275
1889A Proof	—	Value: 1,100				

KM# 521 20 MARK

7.9650 g., 0.9000 Gold .2304 oz. **Ruler:** Wilhelm II **Rev:** Type III

Date	Mintage	F	VF	XF	Unc	BU
1890A	3,695,000	—	BV	110	275	325
1891A	2,752,000	—	BV	110	275	325
1891A Proof	—	Value: 1,000				
1892A	1,815,000	—	BV	110	275	325
1893A	3,172,000	—	BV	110	275	325
1894A	5,815,000	—	BV	110	275	325
1895A	4,135,000	—	BV	110	275	325
1896A	4,239,000	—	BV	110	275	325
1896A Proof	—	Value: 1,000				
1897A	5,394,000	—	BV	110	275	325
1898A	6,542,000	—	BV	110	275	325
1899A	5,873,000	—	BV	110	275	325
1899A Proof	—	Value: 1,000				
1900A	5,163,000	—	BV	110	275	325

PATTERNS

Including off metal strikes

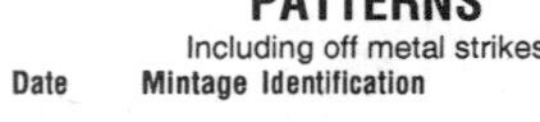

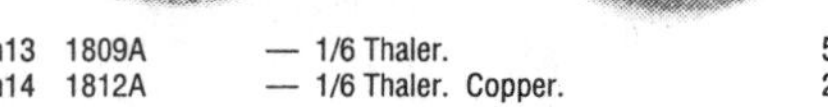

KM#	Date	Mintage	Identification	Mkt Val
Pn13	1809A	—	1/6 Thaler.	500
Pn14	1812A	—	1/6 Thaler. Copper.	200

KM#	Date	Mintage	Identification	Mkt Val
PnA14	1812A	—	5 Pfennig. Copper.	—

KM#	Date	Mintage	Identification	Mkt Val
PnB14	1812A	—	5 Pfennig. Copper.	—
Pn15	1817	—	1/6 Thaler.	800

KM#	Date	Mintage	Identification	Mkt Val
PnA16	1818A	—	Thaler. Silver.	—

KM#	Date	Mintage	Identification	Mkt Val
PnB16	1818A	—	Thaler. Silver.	—

KM#	Date	Mintage	Identification	Mkt Val
PnC16	1818A	—	Thaler. Silver.	—

KM#	Date	Mintage	Identification	Mkt Val

PnD16	1818A	—	Thaler. Silver.	—

Pn16	1819A	—	Thaler.	8,000

PnA17	1820A	—	5 Pfennig. Copper.	—

Pn17	1823	—	Thaler.	5,000
Pn18	1833	—	2 Pfenninge. Copper. KM#406.	70.00

KM#	Date	Mintage	Identification	Mkt Val

Pn19	1873A	—	5 Mark. Silver. Plain edge.	5,000
Pn20	1873A	—	5 Mark. Copper. Plain edge.	500

Pn21	1875A	—	2 Mark. Silver. Reeded edge.	1,500
Pn22	1875A	—	2 Mark. Copper. Plain edge.	300
Pn23	1878	—	20 Mark. Silver or Silvered. KM#505.	—

Pn24	1879A	—	5 Mark. Silver.	5,000
Pn25	1888	—	5 Mark. Tin.	—
Pn26	1888A	—	10 Mark. Silver. Weak edge, KM#517.	—
PnA27	1890A	—	10 Mark. Copper. 2.0300 g.	—
PnB27	1890A	—	20 Mark. Copper. 4.1300 g.	—
Pn27	1900	—	20 Mark. Silver. KM#521.	300

TRIAL STRIKES

KM#	Date	Mintage	Identification	Mkt Val

TS1	ND(1888)	—	5 Mark.	—

PYRMONT

A county southwest of Hannover, established c.1160, Pyrmont's first coins were struck in the 13th century. In 1625, it was incorporated with Waldeck. Occasional issues of special coins for Pyrmont were struck in the 18th and 19th centuries.

RULERS

Georg, Prince, 1805-1812

MINTMASTERS' INITIALS

Initial	Date	Name
FW	1807-29	Friedrich Welle

COUNTY

REGULAR COINAGE

C# 6 1/24 THALER

1.9900 g., 0.3680 Silver .0235 oz. **Ruler:** Georg as Prince **Obv:** Crowned and mantled 2 shields of arms **Rev:** Value above date

Date	Mintage	Good	VG	F	VF	XF
1806 FW	—	—	65.00	125	250	475
1807 FW	—	—	65.00	125	250	475

C# 7 THALER

28.0600 g., 0.8330 Silver .7515 oz. **Ruler:** Georg as Prince **Note:** Convention Thaler.

Date	Mintage	VG	F	VF	XF	Unc
1811 FW	—	—	850	1,500	3,250	6,000

REGENSBURG

The site of Regensburg was settled before the arrival of the Romans, who called the place Ratisbona. After the establishment of a bishopric there in the 5th century, the town was also the chief residence of the early dukes of Bavaria. From the 10th century through the early 13th century, Regensburg contained a mint which produced coins for the dukes and bishops. Regensburg was elevated to a free imperial city in 1180 and obtained the mint right in 1230. A long series of issues dating from 1508 and continuing into the early 19th century ensued.

Regensburg was the site of the Imperial Diet (Reichstag) or Parliament, which met continuously in the Reichssaal of the city hall from 1663 until 1806, when Napoleon dissolved the Holy Roman Empire. The opening of each year's session, attended by the emperor in person, all the secular princes and ecclesiastic rulers of the empire, was a source of great pride and prestige for the city. However, Regensburg lost its independence and was handed over to the bishop in 1803. It came into the possession of Bavaria, along with the bishopric, in 1810.

MINT OFFICIALS' INITIALS

Initial	Date	Name
B, BF, G.C.B.	1773-1803	Georg Christoph Busch
GZ, Z	1791-1802	Johann Leonhard Zollner
K, Korlein	1773-1802	Johann Nikolaus Kornlein

ARMS

2 crossed keys

FREE CITY

REGULAR COINAGE

KM# 470 HELLER

Copper **Ruler:** Josef Conrad **Note:** Uniface, crossed keys.

Date	Mintage	VG	F	VF	XF	Unc
1801	—	2.50	4.50	9.00	18.00	—
1802	192,000	2.50	4.50	9.00	18.00	—
1803	104,000	2.50	4.50	9.00	18.00	—

KM# 475 THALER
Silver

Date	Mintage	F	VF	XF	Unc	BU
1801 Z	—	1,000	2,000	3,000	5,000	—
1802 Z	—	1,000	2,000	3,000	5,000	—

TRADE COINAGE

KM# 467 DUCAT
3.5000 g., 0.9860 Gold .1109 oz. **Obv:** Crowned imperial eagle, titles of Franz II **Rev:** City view

Date	Mintage	VG	F	VF	XF	Unc
ND(1792-1803) GCB	—	250	500	900	1,500	—

KM# 468 10 DUCAT
35.0000 g., 0.9860 Gold 1.1096 oz. **Obv:** Bust of Franz II right **Rev:** Arms in sprays

Date	Mintage	VG	F	VF	XF	Unc
ND(1742-1806) GCB Rare	—	—	—	—	—	—

Note: Stack's International Sale 3-88, XF realized $14,300

REUSS

The Reuss family, whose lands were located in Thuringia, was founded c. 1035. By the end of the 12th century, the custom of naming all males in the ruling house Heinrich had been established. The Elder Line modified this strange practice in the late 17th century to numbering all males from 1 to 100, then beginning over again. The Younger Line, meanwhile, decided to start the numbering of Heinrichs with the first male born in each century. Greiz was founded in1303. Upper and Lower Greiz lines were founded in 1535 and the territories were divided until 1768. In 1778 the ruler was made a prince of the Holy Roman Empire. The principality endured until 1918.

MINT MARKS
A - Berlin
B – Hannover

MINT OFFICIALS' INITIALS

Initials	Date	Name
DF, DOELL	(d. 1835)	Johann Veit Doll, die-cutter
FA	1785-90	Facius, die-cutter
	1790-1835	In Eisenach
L	1803-33	Georg Christoph Lowel in Saalfeld
S, ST	1785-90	Johann Leonhard Stockmar, die-cutter
	1790-1835	In Eisenach

REUSS-EBERSDORF

The Reuss family, whose lands were located in Thuringia, was founded c. 1035. The Ebersdorf line was founded in 1671 from the Lobenstein branch. The county became a principality in 1806. They inherited Lobenstein in 1824and were forced to abdicate in 1849 and Lobenstein-Ebersdorf went to Schleiz.

RULERS
Heinrich LI, 1779-1822
Heinrich LXXII, 1822-1849

COUNTY

REGULAR COINAGE

KM# 25 PFENNIG
Copper **Obv:** Crowned shield with hound head **Rev:** Value

Date	Mintage	F	VF	XF	Unc	BU
1812	35,000	6.00	12.00	35.00	120	—

KM# 26 2 PFENNIG
Copper **Obv:** Crowned shield with hound head **Rev:** Value

Date	Mintage	F	VF	XF	Unc	BU
1812	29,000	10.00	20.00	60.00	150	—

KM# 27 3 PFENNIG
Copper **Obv:** Crowned shield with hound head **Rev:** Value

Date	Mintage	F	VF	XF	Unc	BU
1812	18,000	12.00	25.00	75.00	185	—

KM# 28 4 PFENNIG
Copper **Obv:** Crowned shield with hound head **Rev:** Value

Date	Mintage	F	VF	XF	Unc	BU
1812	23,000	12.00	25.00	65.00	160	—

KM# 29 6 PFENNIG
0.9500 g., 0.2500 Silver .0076 oz.

Date	Mintage	F	VF	XF	Unc	BU
1812	7,376	12.00	25.00	90.00	220	—

KM# 30 8 PFENNIG
1.3000 g., 0.2500 Silver .0104 oz.

Date	Mintage	F	VF	XF	Unc	BU
1812	11,000	15.00	30.00	100	240	—

KM# 31 GROSCHEN
1.7600 g., 0.3680 Silver .0208 oz.

Date	Mintage	F	VF	XF	Unc	BU
1812	8,962	12.00	25.00	75.00	210	—
1814	87,000	12.00	25.00	75.00	210	—

KM# 32 THALER
28.0600 g., 0.8330 Silver .7515 oz. **Note:** Species Thaler.

Date	Mintage	F	VF	XF	Unc	BU
1812 L	1,575	350	700	1,400	3,000	—

REUSS-LOBENSTEIN

The Reuss family, whose lands were located in Thuringia, was founded ca. 1035. The Lobenstein line was founded in 1635. The county became a principality in 1790. In 1824 Lobenstein was given to Ebersdorf.

RULERS
Heinrich XXXV, 1782-1805
Heinrich LIV, 1805-1824

COUNTY

REGULAR COINAGE

KM# 15 3 PFENNIG
Billon **Ruler:** Heinrich XXXV **Obv:** Crowned lion

Date	Mintage	VG	F	VF	XF	Unc
1804	110,000	—	10.00	20.00	45.00	150

KM# 16 1/48 THALER
0.9700 g., 0.2500 Silver .0077 oz. **Ruler:** Heinrich XXXV **Obv:** Crowned lion **Rev:** Value

Date	Mintage	VG	F	VF	XF	Unc
1805	33,000	—	12.00	25.00	55.00	170

KM# 17 3 PFENNIG
Billon **Ruler:** Heinrich LIV **Note:** Different ruler.

Date	Mintage	VG	F	VF	XF	Unc
1807	54,000	—	15.00	30.00	65.00	185

KM# 18 3 PFENNIG
Billon **Ruler:** Heinrich LIV **Obv:** Uncrowned lion

Date	Mintage	VG	F	VF	XF	Unc
1807	Inc. above	—	15.00	30.00	65.00	185

REUSS-LOBENSTEIN-EBERSDORF

This line was formed by the merger between Ebersdorf and Lobenstein in 1824. The prince abdicated during political troubles in 1848 and the lands went to Schleiz in1849.

RULERS
Heinrich LXXII (as Prince of Reuss-Ebersdorf) 1822-1824
(as Prince of Reuss-Lobenstein-Ebersdorf), 1824-1849

PRINCIPALITY

REGULAR COINAGE

KM# 1 PFENNIG
Copper

Date	Mintage	F	VF	XF	Unc	BU
1841A	316,000	5.00	10.00	20.00	50.00	—
1844A	381,000	5.00	10.00	20.00	50.00	—

KM# 2 3 PFENNIG
Copper

Date	Mintage	F	VF	XF	Unc	BU
1841A	107,000	6.00	12.00	25.00	60.00	—
1844A	180,000	6.00	12.00	25.00	60.00	—

KM# 3 1/2 SILBER GROSCHEN
1.0900 g., 0.2220 Silver .0077 oz. **Obv:** Crowned shield with crowned lion **Rev:** Value

Date	Mintage	F	VF	XF	Unc	BU
1841A	70,000	7.00	15.00	35.00	80.00	—

KM# 4 SILBER GROSCHEN
2.1900 g., 0.2220 Silver .0156 oz. **Obv:** Crowned shield with crowned lion **Rev:** Value

Date	Mintage	F	VF	XF	Unc	BU
1841A	59,000	7.00	15.00	35.00	80.00	—
1844A	87,000	7.00	15.00	35.00	80.00	—

KM# 5 2 THALER (3-1/2 gulden)
37.1200 g., 0.9000 Silver 1.0742 oz.

Date	Mintage	F	VF	XF	Unc	BU
1840A	2,750	225	450	800	1,800	—
1847A	5,500	200	400	750	1,700	—

KM# 6 2 THALER (3-1/2 gulden)
37.1200 g., 0.9000 Silver 1.0742 oz. **Subject:** 25th Anniversary of Reign **Obv:** Similar to KM#5

Date	Mintage	F	VF	XF	Unc	BU
1847A	500	400	700	1,500	2,850	—

REUSS-OBERGREIZ

The other branch of the division of 1635, Obergreiz went through a number of consolidations and further divisions. Upon the extinction of the Ruess-Untergreiz line in 1768, the latter passed to Reuss-Obergreiz and this line continued on into the 20th century, obtaining the rank of count back in 1673 and that of prince in 1778.

RULERS
Heinrich XIII, 1800-1817
Heinrich XIX, 1817-1836
Heinrich XX, 1836-1859
Heinrich XXII, 1859-1902

PRINCIPALITY

REGULAR COINAGE

KM# 100 HELLER
Copper **Obv:** Crowned lion on crowned oval shield **Rev:** Value

Date	Mintage	F	VF	XF	Unc	BU
1812	45,000	5.00	10.00	25.00	75.00	—
1815	45,000	5.00	10.00	25.00	75.00	—
1817	40,000	5.00	10.00	25.00	75.00	—
1819	48,000	5.00	10.00	25.00	75.00	—

KM# 92 PFENNIG
Copper **Ruler:** Heinrich XIII

Date	Mintage	F	VF	XF	Unc	BU
1806	187,000	4.00	8.00	20.00	65.00	—
1808	273,000	4.00	8.00	20.00	65.00	—

KM# 95 PFENNIG
Copper **Ruler:** Heinrich XIII **Obv:** Crowned lion on crowned oval shield

Date	Mintage	F	VF	XF	Unc	BU
1808	—	4.00	8.00	20.00	65.00	—
1810	443,000	4.00	8.00	20.00	65.00	—
1812	—	4.00	8.00	20.00	65.00	—
1813	—	4.00	8.00	20.00	65.00	—
1814	—	4.00	8.00	20.00	65.00	—
1815	—	4.00	8.00	20.00	65.00	—
1816	—	4.00	8.00	20.00	65.00	—

KM# 102 PFENNIG
Copper **Ruler:** Heinrich XIX

Date	Mintage	F	VF	XF	Unc	BU
1817	—	3.00	6.00	15.00	60.00	—
1819	—	3.00	6.00	15.00	60.00	—
1820	—	3.00	6.00	15.00	60.00	—
1821	—	3.00	6.00	15.00	60.00	—
1822	—	3.00	6.00	15.00	60.00	—
1823	—	3.00	6.00	15.00	60.00	—
1824	—	3.00	6.00	15.00	60.00	—
1825	—	3.00	6.00	15.00	60.00	—
1826	—	3.00	6.00	15.00	60.00	—
1827	—	3.00	6.00	15.00	60.00	—
1828	—	3.00	6.00	15.00	60.00	—
1829	—	3.00	6.00	15.00	60.00	—
1830	—	3.00	6.00	15.00	60.00	—
1831 L	—	3.00	6.00	15.00	60.00	—
1832 L	—	3.00	6.00	15.00	60.00	—

KM# 115 PFENNIG
Copper **Ruler:** Heinrich XXII **Obv:** King's crown

Date	Mintage	F	VF	XF	Unc	BU
1864A	360,000	2.00	4.00	8.00	40.00	—

KM# 117 PFENNIG
Copper **Ruler:** Heinrich XXII **Obv:** Prince's crown

Date	Mintage	F	VF	XF	Unc	BU
1868A	360,000	2.00	4.00	8.00	38.00	—

KM# 90 3 PFENNIG
Copper **Ruler:** Heinrich XIII

Date	Mintage	F	VF	XF	Unc	BU
1805	92,000	4.00	8.00	20.00	65.00	—
1806	—	4.00	8.00	20.00	65.00	—
1808	256,000	4.00	8.00	20.00	65.00	—
1810	415,000	4.00	8.00	20.00	65.00	—
1812	296,000	4.00	8.00	20.00	65.00	—
1813	—	4.00	8.00	20.00	65.00	—
1814	—	4.00	8.00	20.00	65.00	—
1815	—	4.00	8.00	20.00	65.00	—
1816	—	4.00	8.00	20.00	65.00	—

KM# 103 3 PFENNIG
Copper **Ruler:** Heinrich XIX **Note:** Varieties exist.

Date	Mintage	F	VF	XF	Unc	BU
1817	144,000	3.00	6.00	15.00	60.00	—
1819	—	3.00	6.00	15.00	60.00	—
1820	—	3.00	6.00	15.00	60.00	—
1821	—	3.00	6.00	15.00	60.00	—
1822	—	3.00	6.00	15.00	60.00	—
1823	—	3.00	6.00	15.00	60.00	—
1824	—	3.00	6.00	15.00	60.00	—
1825	—	3.00	6.00	15.00	60.00	—
1826	—	3.00	6.00	15.00	60.00	—
1827	—	3.00	6.00	15.00	60.00	—
1828	—	3.00	6.00	15.00	60.00	—
1829	—	3.00	6.00	15.00	60.00	—
1830	—	3.00	6.00	15.00	60.00	—
1831 L	—	3.00	6.00	15.00	60.00	—
1832 L	—	3.00	6.00	15.00	60.00	—
1833 L	—	3.00	6.00	15.00	60.00	—

KM# 116 3 PFENNIG
Copper **Ruler:** Heinrich XXII **Obv:** King's crown

Date	Mintage	F	VF	XF	Unc	BU
1864A	360,000	2.50	5.00	10.00	38.00	—

KM# 118 3 PFENNIG
Copper **Ruler:** Heinrich XXII **Obv:** Prince's crown

Date	Mintage	F	VF	XF	Unc	BU
1868A	240,000	2.50	5.00	10.00	38.00	—

KM# 91 GROSCHEN
1.7600 g., 0.3680 Silver .0208 oz. **Ruler:** Heinrich XIII

Date	Mintage	F	VF	XF	Unc	BU
1805	251,000	3.00	6.00	15.00	55.00	—
1812	110,000	3.00	6.00	15.00	55.00	—

KM# 119 GROSCHEN
2.1900 g., 0.2200 Silver .0154 oz. **Ruler:** Heinrich XXII

Date	Mintage	F	VF	XF	Unc	BU
1868A	90,000	4.00	8.00	20.00	70.00	—

KM# 96 1/6 THALER (1/4 Gulden)
5.3600 g., 0.5410 Silver .0932 oz. **Ruler:** Heinrich XIII

Date	Mintage	F	VF	XF	Unc	BU
1808 L	9,006	75.00	150	300	500	—

KM# 97 1/3 THALER (1/2 Gulden)
7.0100 g., 0.8330 Silver .1877 oz. **Ruler:** Heinrich XIII

Date	Mintage	F	VF	XF	Unc	BU
1809 L	1,500	125	300	600	1,100	—

KM# 93 THALER
28.0600 g., 0.8330 Silver .7515 oz. **Ruler:** Heinrich XIII **Obv. Legend:** D. G. HENR. XIII..

Date	Mintage	F	VF	XF	Unc	BU
1806 DOELL-L	345	750	1,400	3,200	7,500	—
1807 DOELL-L	200	750	1,400	3,200	7,500	—

KM# 94 THALER
28.0600 g., 0.8330 Silver .7515 oz. **Ruler:** Heinrich XIII **Obv. Legend:** V. G. G. HEINRICH.. **Rev:** Similar to KM#93

Date	Mintage	F	VF	XF	Unc	BU
1807 DF-L	300	1,000	1,600	3,500	7,500	—
1812 DF-L	2,275	900	1,500	2,750	6,500	—

KM# 101 THALER
28.0600 g., 0.8330 Silver .7515 oz. **Ruler:** Heinrich XIII

Date	Mintage	F	VF	XF	Unc	BU
1812 DF-L	Inc. above	350	700	1,250	3,000	—

KM# 110 THALER
18.5200 g., 0.9000 Silver .5360 oz. **Ruler:** Heinrich XX

Date	Mintage	F	VF	XF	Unc	BU
1858A	9,500	60.00	100	200	450	—

KM# 120 THALER
18.5200 g., 0.9000 Silver .5360 oz. **Ruler:** Heinrich XXII

Date	Mintage	F	VF	XF	Unc	BU
1868A	7,100	60.00	100	200	450	—

KM# 105 2 THALER (3-1/2 Gulden)
37.1200 g., 0.9000 Silver 1.0742 oz. **Ruler:** Heinrich XX

Date	Mintage	F	VF	XF	Unc	BU
1841A	2,400	200	375	750	1,500	—
1844A	2,400	200	375	750	1,500	—
1848A	2,400	200	375	750	1,500	—
1851A	2,400	200	375	750	1,500	—

REFORM COINAGE

KM# 126 2 MARK
11.1110 g., 0.9000 Silver .3215 oz. **Ruler:** Heinrich XXII **Rev:** Type II

Date	Mintage	F	VF	XF	Unc	BU
1877B	20,000	175	325	1,200	2,750	3,250
1877B Proof	—	Value: 3,500				

KM# 127 2 MARK
11.1110 g., 0.9000 Silver .3215 oz. **Ruler:** Heinrich XXII **Rev:** Type III

Date	Mintage	F	VF	XF	Unc	BU
1892A	10,000	150	350	650	950	1,250
1892A Proof	—	Value: 1,300				

KM# 128 2 MARK
11.1110 g., 0.9000 Silver .3215 oz. **Ruler:** Heinrich XXII

Date	Mintage	F	VF	XF	Unc	BU
1899A	10,000	125	225	375	625	750
1899A Proof	120	Value: 900				

KM# 125 20 MARK
7.9650 g., 0.9000 Gold .2304 oz. **Ruler:** Heinrich XXII **Rev:** Type II

Date	Mintage	F	VF	XF	Unc	BU
1875B	1,510	6,500	10,000	14,000	18,500	25,000
1875B Proof	—	Value: 27,500				

REUSS-SCHLEIZ

Originally part of the holdings of Reuss-Gera, Schleiz was ruled separately on and off during the first half of the 16th century. When the Gera line died out in 1550, Schleiz passed to Obergreiz. Schleiz was reintegrated into a new line of Gera and a separate countship at Schleiz was founded in 1635, only to last one generation. At its extinction in 1666, Schleiz passed to Reuss-Saalburg which thereafter took the name of Reuss-Schleiz.

RULERS
Heinrich XLII, 1784-1818
Heinrich LXII, 1818-1854
Heinrich LXVII, 1854-1867
Heinrich XIV, 1867-1913
Heinrich XXVII, 1913-1918

PRINCIPALITY

REGULAR COINAGE

KM# 56 1/2 PFENNIG (1 Heller)
Copper

Date	Mintage	F	VF	XF	Unc	BU
1841A	—	15.00	30.00	60.00	175	—

KM# 57 PFENNIG
Copper

Date	Mintage	F	VF	XF	Unc	BU
1841A	751,000	4.00	7.00	20.00	75.00	—
1847A	1,138,000	4.00	7.00	20.00	75.00	—

KM# 65 PFENNIG
Copper

Date	Mintage	F	VF	XF	Unc	BU
1850A	540,000	2.00	4.00	12.00	50.00	—

KM# 69 PFENNIG
Copper

Date	Mintage	F	VF	XF	Unc	BU
1855A	362,000	2.00	4.00	12.00	50.00	—
1858A	360,000	2.00	4.00	12.00	50.00	—
1862A	202,000	2.00	4.00	12.00	50.00	—
1864A	540,000	2.00	4.00	12.00	50.00	—

KM# 75 PFENNIG
Copper

Date	Mintage	F	VF	XF	Unc	BU
1868A	360,000	2.00	4.00	12.00	50.00	—

KM# 50 3 PFENNIG
Copper **Obv:** Oval crowned shield with crowned lion **Rev:** Value

Date	Mintage	F	VF	XF	Unc	BU
1815	76,000	6.00	12.00	25.00	120	—
1816	Inc. above	6.00	12.00	25.00	120	—

KM# 58 3 PFENNIG
Copper

Date	Mintage	F	VF	XF	Unc	BU
1841A	250,000	4.00	9.00	22.00	75.00	—
1844A	379,000	3.00	7.00	20.00	70.00	—

KM# 66 3 PFENNIG
Copper

Date	Mintage	F	VF	XF	Unc	BU
1850A	311,000	3.00	7.00	20.00	70.00	—

KM# 70 3 PFENNIG
Copper

Date	Mintage	F	VF	XF	Unc	BU
1855A	242,000	3.00	7.00	20.00	70.00	—
1858A	360,000	3.00	7.00	20.00	70.00	—
1862A	125,000	3.00	7.00	20.00	70.00	—
1864A	240,000	3.00	7.00	20.00	70.00	—

KM# 76 3 PFENNIG
Copper

Date	Mintage	F	VF	XF	Unc	BU
1868A	120,000	3.00	7.00	20.00	70.00	—

KM# 51 SILBER GROSCHEN
1.7600 g., 0.3680 Silver .0208 oz. **Obv:** Oval crowned arms, crowned lion with one tail **Rev:** Value

Date	Mintage	F	VF	XF	Unc	BU
1815	—	10.00	20.00	40.00	150	—

KM# 52 SILBER GROSCHEN
1.7600 g., 0.3680 Silver .0208 oz. **Obv:** Uncrowned lion with one tail

Date	Mintage	F	VF	XF	Unc	BU
1816S	33,000	10.00	20.00	40.00	150	—

KM# 53 SILBER GROSCHEN
1.7600 g., 0.3680 Silver .0208 oz. **Obv:** Crowned lion with two tails

Date	Mintage	F	VF	XF	Unc	BU
1816S	Inc. above	10.00	20.00	40.00	150	—

KM# 59 SILBER GROSCHEN
2.1900 g., 0.2220 Silver .0156 oz.

Date	Mintage	F	VF	XF	Unc	BU
1841A	64,000	5.00	10.00	25.00	100	—
1844A	92,000	5.00	10.00	25.00	100	—
1846A	62,000	5.00	10.00	25.00	100	—

KM# 67 SILBER GROSCHEN
2.1900 g., 0.2220 Silver .0156 oz. **Obv. Legend:** JUNGERER LINIE

Date	Mintage	F	VF	XF	Unc	BU
1850A	62,000	5.00	10.00	25.00	110	—

KM# 71 SILBER GROSCHEN
2.1900 g., 0.2220 Silver .0156 oz.

Date	Mintage	F	VF	XF	Unc	BU
1855A	31,000	6.00	12.00	30.00	125	—

KM# 68 2 SILBER GROSCHEN (1/12 Thaler)
3.1100 g., 0.3120 Silver .0311 oz. **Obv:** Crowned shield with crowned lion **Rev:** Value

Date	Mintage	F	VF	XF	Unc	BU
1850A	64,000	6.00	15.00	30.00	150	—

KM# 72 2 SILBER GROSCHEN (1/12 Thaler)
3.1100 g., 0.3120 Silver .0311 oz.

Date	Mintage	F	VF	XF	Unc	BU
1855A	31,000	10.00	20.00	40.00	150	—

KM# 73 THALER
18.5200 g., 0.9000 Silver .5360 oz.

Date	Mintage	F	VF	XF	Unc	BU
1858A	10,000	45.00	75.00	140	350	—
1862A	10,000	45.00	75.00	140	350	—

KM# 77 THALER
18.5200 g., 0.9000 Silver .5360 oz. **Rev:** Similar to KM#73

Date	Mintage	F	VF	XF	Unc	BU
1868A	14,000	40.00	65.00	125	325	—

KM# 55 2 THALER (3-1/2 Gulden)
37.1200 g., 0.9000 Silver 1.0742 oz.

Date	Mintage	F	VF	XF	Unc	BU
1840A	2,650	250	400	800	1,500	—
1844A	3,000	250	400	800	1,500	—
1846A	2,650	250	400	800	1,500	—
1853A	2,700	250	400	800	1,500	—
1854A	2,700	225	450	1,000	1,600	—

KM# 60 2 THALER (3-1/2 Gulden)
37.1200 g., 0.9000 Silver 1.0742 oz. **Subject:** 25th Anniversary of Reign **Obv:** Similar to KM#55

Date	Mintage	F	VF	XF	Unc	BU
1843A	500	350	700	1,500	3,000	—

REFORM COINAGE

KM# 82 2 MARK
11.1110 g., 0.9000 Silver .3215 oz.

Date	Mintage	F	VF	XF	Unc	BU
1884A	100,000	160	300	750	1,750	2,750
1884A Proof	—	Value: 3,500				

KM# 81 10 MARK
3.9820 g., 0.9000 Gold .1152 oz.

Date	Mintage	F	VF	XF	Unc	BU
1882A	4,800	1,500	3,000	5,000	6,500	8,000
1882A Proof	200	Value: 10,000				

KM# 80 20 MARK
7.9650 g., 0.9000 Gold .2304 oz.

Date	Mintage	F	VF	XF	Unc	BU
1881	12,000	1,250	2,000	3,000	4,000	6,000
1881 Proof	500	Value: 6,500				

RHENISH CONFEDERATION

Issues for Carl von Dahlberg, 1804-1817

MINT OFFICIALS' INITIALS

Initial	Date	Name
B, CB	1773-1811	Christoph Busch, Regensburg
BH	1790-1825	Johann Georg Bunsen, mintmaster in Frankfurt
	1798-1816	Johann Georg Hille, mint warden in Frankfurt

NAPOLEONIC PRINCIPALITY

REGULAR COINAGE

C# 1 HELLER
Copper **Obv. Legend:** FURST PRIM SCHEIDE MUNZ

Date	Mintage	F	VF	XF	Unc	BU
1808 BH	33,000	10.00	30.00	70.00	150	—
1810 BH	—	10.00	30.00	70.00	150	—
1812 BH	—	10.00	30.00	70.00	150	—

C# 2 HELLER
Copper **Obv. Legend:** GROSH FRANKF SCHEIDE MUNZ

Date	Mintage	F	VF	XF	Unc	BU
1810 BH	—	10.00	30.00	70.00	150	—
1812 BH	—	10.00	30.00	70.00	150	—

C# 3.1 KREUZER
Billon **Obv. Legend:** SCHEID. MUNZ.

Date	Mintage	F	VF	XF	Unc	BU
1808 BH	—	8.00	25.00	50.00	150	—
1809 BH	—	8.00	25.00	50.00	150	—
1810 BH	—	8.00	25.00	50.00	150	—

C# 3.2 KREUZER
Billon **Obv. Legend:** SCHEIDMUNZ

Date	Mintage	F	VF	XF	Unc	BU
1809 BH	—	8.00	25.00	60.00	150	—

C# 5 1/2 THALER
0.8330 Silver **Note:** Convention 1/2 Thaler.

Date	Mintage	F	VF	XF	Unc	BU
1809 B	—	65.00	120	200	350	—

C# 4 THALER
28.0600 g., 0.8330 Silver .7516 oz. **Note:** Convention Thaler.

Date	Mintage	F	VF	XF	Unc	BU
1808 BH	—	175	375	650	1,200	—

C# 6 THALER
28.0600 g., 0.8330 Silver .7516 oz.

Date	Mintage	F	VF	XF	Unc	BU
1809 B	—	150	325	1,100	2,500	—

C# 7 THALER
28.0600 g., 0.8330 Silver .7516 oz.

Date	Mintage	F	VF	XF	Unc	BU
1809 CB	—	150	325	800	2,200	—

TRADE COINAGE

C# 8 DUCAT
3.5000 g., 0.9860 Gold .1109 oz. **Obv:** Bust of Carl right **Rev:** Arms

Date	Mintage	F	VF	XF	Unc	BU
1809 BH	—	400	900	1,600	2,250	—

ROSTOCK

The town of Rostock is first mentioned in 1030 and was the seat of a lordship of the same name in the 13th century. It is located just a few miles inland from where the Warnow River enters the Baltic Sea and was an important trading center from earliest times. Although Rostock was usually under some control by the Mecklenburg dukes, it functioned somewhat as a free city, gaining a municipal charter as early as 1218. The city obtained control of its own coinage in 1323 and received the mint right unconditionally in 1361. From 1381, Rostock was a member of the Wendischen Münzverein (Wendish Monetary Union) and joined the Hanseatic League not long afterwards. The city coinage was struck from the 14th century until 1864.

ARMS:

Griffin, usually rampant to left. Also, shield divided by horizontal band above griffin walking left, below arabesques or sometimes an arrow.

MINT OFFICIALS' INITIALS

Initial	Date	Name
AIB	1805	Andreas Joachim Brand
AS	1815-24	Adam Schiller
BS	1843-59	Benjamin Steinhorst
FL	1796-1802	Friedrich Lautersack
HK	1862-64	Heinrich Kehr

FREE CITY

REGULAR COINAGE

C# 2a PFENNING
Copper **Obv:** Griffin shield within ring **Rev:** Value

Date	Mintage	VG	F	VF	XF	Unc
1801 FL	—	—	5.00	10.00	25.00	70.00
1802 FL	—	—	5.00	10.00	25.00	70.00

KM# 132 PFENNIG
Copper **Obv:** Griffin within ring **Rev:** Value

Date	Mintage	F	VF	XF	Unc	BU
1801 FL	—	5.00	10.00	25.00	100	—
1802 FL	—	5.00	10.00	25.00	100	—

C# 4 PFENNIG
Copper **Obv:** Legend begins at eight o'clock **Obv. Legend:** ROSTOCKER

Date	Mintage	F	VF	XF	Unc	BU
1802 FL	—	5.00	10.00	25.00	100	—
1805 AIB	—	5.00	10.00	25.00	100	—

C# 4a PFENNIG
Copper **Obv:** Without circle between griffin and legend

Date	Mintage	F	VF	XF	Unc	BU
1815 AS	—	4.00	8.00	22.00	100	—
1824 AS	—	4.00	8.00	22.00	100	—

C# 5 PFENNIG
Copper

Date	Mintage	VG	F	VF	XF	Unc
1848 BS	—	—	6.00	12.00	30.00	80.00

KM# 138 PFENNIG
Copper **Note:** Previous C#7a.

Date	Mintage	F	VF	XF	Unc	BU
1848 BS	—	6.00	12.00	30.00	100	—

C# 10 3 PFENNING
Copper

Date	Mintage	VG	F	VF	XF	Unc
1815 AS	—	—	5.00	10.00	25.00	75.00
1824 AS	—	—	5.00	10.00	25.00	75.00

C# 10a 3 PFENNING
Copper

Date	Mintage	VG	F	VF	XF	Unc
1843 BS	—	—	5.00	10.00	25.00	75.00

C# 11 3 PFENNINGE
Copper

Date	Mintage	VG	F	VF	XF	Unc
1855 BS	—	—	5.00	10.00	25.00	75.00

C# 12 3 PFENNINGE
Copper

Date	Mintage	VG	F	VF	XF	Unc
1855 BS	—	—	5.00	10.00	25.00	75.00

KM# 136 3 PFENNIG
Copper **Note:** Previous C#10.

Date	Mintage	F	VF	XF	Unc	BU
1815 AS	—	5.00	10.00	25.00	100	—
1824 AS	—	5.00	10.00	25.00	100	—

KM# 137 3 PFENNIG
Copper **Note:** Previous C#10a.

Date	Mintage	F	VF	XF	Unc	BU
1843 BS	192,000	5.00	10.00	25.00	100	—

KM# 139 3 PFENNIG
Copper **Note:** Previous C#11.

Date	Mintage	F	VF	XF	Unc	BU
1855 BS	—	5.00	10.00	27.00	100	—

KM# 140 3 PFENNIG
Copper **Note:** Previous C#12.

Date	Mintage	F	VF	XF	Unc	BU
1859 BS	—	5.00	10.00	27.00	100	—

KM# 141 3 PFENNIG
Copper **Note:** Previous C#12a.

Date	Mintage	F	VF	XF	Unc	BU
1862 HK	—	5.00	10.00	27.00	100	—
1864 HK	—	5.00	10.00	27.00	100	—

C# 12a 3 PFENNIG
Copper

Date	Mintage	VG	F	VF	XF	Unc
1862 HK	—	—	5.00	10.00	25.00	75.00
1864 HK	—	—	5.00	10.00	25.00	75.00

SAXE-ALTENBURG

A duchy, located in Thüringia in northwest Germany. It came into being in 1826 when Saxe-Gotha-Altenburg became extinct. The duke of Saxe-Hildburghausen ceded Hildburghausen to Meiningen in exchange for Saxe-Altenburg. The last duke abdicated in 1918.

RULERS
Joseph, 1834-1848
Georg, 1848-1853
Ernst I, 1853-1908
Ernst II, 1908-1918

MINT OFFICIALS' INITIALS

Initial	Date	Name
B		Gustav Julius Buschick
F		Gustav Theodor Fischer
G		Johann Georg Grohmann

DUCHY

REGULAR COINAGE

C# 1 PFENNIG
Copper **Ruler:** Joseph **Obv:** Crowned arms **Rev:** Value

Date	Mintage	F	VF	XF	Unc	BU
1841 G	220,000	1.50	3.00	6.00	40.00	—

C# 2 PFENNIG
Copper **Ruler:** Joseph **Obv:** Crowned heart-shaped arms

Date	Mintage	F	VF	XF	Unc	BU
1843	89,000	2.00	4.00	8.00	45.00	—

C# 11 PFENNIG
Copper **Ruler:** Joseph **Rev:** "F" below date

Date	Mintage	F	VF	XF	Unc	BU
1852 F	120,000	1.50	3.00	6.00	40.00	—

C# 14 PFENNIG
Copper **Ruler:** Joseph **Rev:** "F" below date

Date	Mintage	F	VF	XF	Unc	BU
1856 F	41,000	2.00	4.00	8.00	45.00	—
1858 F	129,000	1.50	3.00	6.00	40.00	—

C# 14a PFENNIG
Copper **Ruler:** Joseph **Rev:** Without initial

Date	Mintage	F	VF	XF	Unc	BU
1857	—	1.50	3.00	6.00	40.00	—

C# 14b PFENNIG
Copper **Ruler:** Joseph **Rev:** "B" below date

Date	Mintage	F	VF	XF	Unc	BU
1861 B	163,000	1.50	3.00	6.00	40.00	—
1863 B	302,000	1.50	3.00	6.00	40.00	—
1865 B	150,000	1.50	3.00	6.00	40.00	—

C# 3 2 PFENNIG
Copper **Ruler:** Joseph **Obv:** Crowned arms **Rev:** Value

Date	Mintage	F	VF	XF	Unc	BU
1841 G	150,000	2.00	4.00	8.00	45.00	—

C# 4 2 PFENNIG
Copper **Ruler:** Joseph **Obv:** Crowned heart-shaped arms

Date	Mintage	F	VF	XF	Unc	BU
1843 G	46,000	2.50	5.00	10.00	50.00	—

C# 12 2 PFENNIG
Copper **Ruler:** Joseph

Date	Mintage	F	VF	XF	Unc	BU
1852 F	60,000	2.50	5.00	10.00	50.00	—

C# 15 2 PFENNIG
Copper **Ruler:** Joseph

Date	Mintage	F	VF	XF	Unc	BU
1856 F	29,000	2.50	5.00	10.00	50.00	—

C# 5 5 PFENNIG (1/2 Neugroschen)
1.0600 g., 0.2990 Silver .0078 oz. **Ruler:** Joseph **Obv:** Crowned arms **Rev:** Value

Date	Mintage	F	VF	XF	Unc	BU
1841 G	97,000	4.00	8.00	20.00	75.00	—
1842 G	130,000	4.00	8.00	20.00	75.00	—

C# 6 10 PFENNIG (1 Neugroschen)
2.1200 g., 0.2990 Silver .0156 oz. **Ruler:** Joseph **Obv:** Crowned arms **Rev:** Value

Date	Mintage	F	VF	XF	Unc	BU
1841 G	146,000	4.00	8.00	20.00	75.00	—
1842 G	65,000	4.00	8.00	20.00	75.00	—

C# 7 20 PFENNIG (2 Neugroschen)
3.1100 g., 0.3120 Silver .0311 oz. **Ruler:** Joseph

Date	Mintage	F	VF	XF	Unc	BU
ND	—	5.00	10.00	20.00	60.00	—

C# 7a 20 PFENNIG (2 Neugroschen)
3.1100 g., 0.3120 Silver .0311 oz. **Ruler:** Joseph

Date	Mintage	F	VF	XF	Unc	BU
1841 G	231,000	6.00	12.00	25.00	80.00	—

C# 8 1/6 THALER
5.3450 g., 0.5200 Silver .0894 oz. **Ruler:** Joseph

Date	Mintage	F	VF	XF	Unc	BU
1841 G	60,000	12.00	28.00	80.00	220	—
1842 G	60,000	12.00	28.00	80.00	220	—

C# 9 THALER
22.2720 g., 0.7500 Silver .5371 oz. **Ruler:** Joseph

Date	Mintage	F	VF	XF	Unc	BU
1841 G	20,000	65.00	135	325	1,000	—

C# 16 THALER
18.5200 g., 0.9000 Silver .5360 oz. **Ruler:** Ernst I **Note:** Vereins Thaler.

Date	Mintage	F	VF	XF	Unc	BU
1858 F	32,000	40.00	70.00	145	400	—
1858 F Proof	—	Value: 500				
1864 B	22,000	30.00	60.00	125	400	—
1869 B	23,000	30.00	60.00	125	400	—

C# 10 2 THALER (3-1/2 Gulden)
37.1190 g., 0.9000 Silver 1.0742 oz. **Ruler:** Joseph

Date	Mintage	F	VF	XF	Unc	BU
1841 G	9,400	200	375	800	1,600	—
1842 G	4,700	250	500	1,000	2,000	—
1843 G	4,700	225	450	900	1,900	—
1847 F	9,400	200	375	850	1,800	—

C# 13 2 THALER (3-1/2 Gulden)
37.1190 g., 0.9000 Silver 1.0742 oz. **Ruler:** Georg **Rev:** Similar to 1 Thaler, C#16

Date	Mintage	F	VF	XF	Unc	BU
1852 F	9,400	250	450	900	1,900	—

REFORM COINAGE

Y# 146 20 MARK
7.9650 g., 0.9000 Gold .2304 oz. **Ruler:** Ernst I

Date	Mintage	F	VF	XF	Unc	BU
1887A	15,000	900	1,350	1,850	2,750	4,000
1887A Proof	—	Value: 4,250				

SAXE-COBURG-GOTHA

Upon the extinction of the ducal line in Saxe-Gotha-Altenburg in 1826, Gotha was assigned to Saxe-Coburg-Saalfeld and Saxe-Meiningen received Saalfeld. The resulting duchy became called Saxe-Coburg-Gotha. Albert, the son of Ernst I and younger brother of Ernst II, married Queen Victoria of Great Britain and the British royal dynastic name was that of Saxe-Coburg-Gotha. Their son, Alfred was made the Duke of Edinburgh and succeeded his uncle, Ernst II, as Duke of Saxe-Coburg-Gotha. Alfred's oldler brother, Eduard Albert, followed their mother as King Edward VII (1901-1910). The last duke of Saxe-Coburg-Gotha was Alfred's son, Karl Eduard, forced to abdicate in 1918 as a result of World War I, which was fought in part against his cousin, King George V.

RULERS
Ernst I, 1826-1844
Ernst II, 1844-1893
Alfred, 1893-1900
Karl Eduard, 1900-1918

MINT OFFICIALS' INITIALS

Initial	Date	Name
B	1860-87	Gustav Julius Buschick
EK	1828-38	Ernst Kleinsteuber
F	1845-60	Gustav Theodor Fischer
G	1826-28	Graupner
G	1838-44	Johann Georg Grohmann
ST	1826-28	Strebel

DUCHY

REGULAR COINAGE

C# 83 PFENNIG
Copper **Ruler:** Ernst I

Date	Mintage	F	VF	XF	Unc	BU
1833	—	2.00	4.00	8.00	50.00	—
1834	—	2.00	4.00	8.00	50.00	—
1835	—	2.00	4.00	8.00	50.00	—
1836	—	2.00	4.00	8.00	50.00	—
1837	—	2.00	4.00	8.00	50.00	—

C# 100 PFENNIG
Copper **Ruler:** Ernst I **Obv:** Crowned arms within branches

Date	Mintage	F	VF	XF	Unc	BU
1841 G	333,000	2.00	4.00	8.00	50.00	—

C# 109 PFENNIG
Copper **Ruler:** Ernst I **Obv:** "F" above crowned arms

Date	Mintage	F	VF	XF	Unc	BU
1847 F	207,000	1.50	3.00	6.00	50.00	—
1851 F	59,000	2.00	4.00	8.00	50.00	—
1852 F	201,000	1.50	3.00	6.00	50.00	—
1856 F	600,000	1.50	3.00	6.00	50.00	—

C# 109a PFENNIG
Copper **Ruler:** Ernst II **Obv:** "B" above arms

Date	Mintage	F	VF	XF	Unc	BU
1865 B	150,000	1.50	3.00	6.00	50.00	—

C# 109b PFENNIG
Copper **Ruler:** Ernst II

Date	Mintage	F	VF	XF	Unc	BU
1868 B	200,000	1.50	3.00	6.00	50.00	—
1870 B	96,000	2.00	4.00	8.00	50.00	—

C# 84 1-1/2 PFENNIG
Copper **Ruler:** Ernst I

Date	Mintage	F	VF	XF	Unc	BU
1834	—	2.00	4.00	8.00	50.00	—
1835	—	2.00	4.00	8.00	50.00	—

C# 85 2 PFENNIG
Copper **Ruler:** Ernst I

Date	Mintage	F	VF	XF	Unc	BU
1834	—	2.00	4.00	8.00	50.00	—
1835	—	2.00	4.00	8.00	50.00	—

C# 101 2 PFENNIG
Copper **Ruler:** Ernst I

Date	Mintage	F	VF	XF	Unc	BU
1841 G	333,000	2.00	4.00	8.00	50.00	—

C# 110 2 PFENNIG
Copper **Ruler:** Ernst II **Obv:** "F" and date below bow

Date	Mintage	F	VF	XF	Unc	BU
1847 F	130,000	1.50	3.00	6.00	50.00	—
1851 F	125,000	1.50	3.00	6.00	50.00	—
1852 F	146,000	1.50	3.00	6.00	50.00	—
1856 F	600,000	1.50	3.00	6.00	50.00	—

C# 110a 2 PFENNIG
Copper **Ruler:** Ernst II **Obv:** "B" and date below bow

Date	Mintage	F	VF	XF	Unc	BU
1868 B	136,000	1.50	3.00	6.00	50.00	—
1870 B	118,000	1.50	3.00	6.00	50.00	—

C# 86 3 PFENNIG
Copper **Ruler:** Ernst I

Date	Mintage	F	VF	XF	Unc	BU
1834	—	4.00	8.00	17.50	65.00	—

C# 86.5 KREUZER
0.7900 g., 0.1250 Silver .0031 oz. **Ruler:** Ernst I **Obv:** "ST" below crowned "E" **Rev:** Value in script

Date	Mintage	F	VF	XF	Unc	BU
1827 ST	—	5.00	12.00	30.00	120	—

C# 87 KREUZER
0.7900 g., 0.1250 Silver .0031 oz. **Ruler:** Ernst I

Date	Mintage	F	VF	XF	Unc	BU
1827 ST	—	5.00	12.00	30.00	120	—
1828 ST	—	5.00	12.00	30.00	120	—

C# 87a KREUZER
0.7900 g., 0.1250 Silver .0031 oz. **Ruler:** Ernst I **Obv:** "EK" below crowned "E"

Date	Mintage	F	VF	XF	Unc	BU
1829 EK	—	5.00	12.00	30.00	120	—
1830 EK	—	5.00	12.00	30.00	120	—

C# 88 KREUZER
0.7900 g., 0.1250 Silver .0031 oz. **Ruler:** Ernst I **Rev:** "KREUZER" along bottom rim

Date	Mintage	F	VF	XF	Unc	BU
1831	—	2.00	6.00	10.00	60.00	—
1832	—	2.00	6.00	10.00	60.00	—
1833	—	2.00	6.00	10.00	60.00	—
1834	—	2.00	6.00	10.00	60.00	—
1836	—	2.00	6.00	10.00	60.00	—
1837	—	2.00	6.00	10.00	60.00	—

C# 89.5 3 KREUZER
1.5000 g., 0.2430 Silver .0117 oz. **Ruler:** Ernst I **Obv:** Crowned "E" within branches, "ST" below **Rev:** Value in script

Date	Mintage	F	VF	XF	Unc	BU
1827 ST	—	50.00	150	300	650	—

C# 90 3 KREUZER
1.5000 g., 0.2430 Silver .0117 oz. **Ruler:** Ernst I

Date	Mintage	F	VF	XF	Unc	BU
1827 ST	—	8.00	20.00	40.00	175	—
1828 ST	—	8.00	20.00	40.00	175	—
1829 S	—	8.00	20.00	40.00	175	—
1829 ST	—	8.00	20.00	40.00	175	—

C# 90a 3 KREUZER
1.5000 g., 0.2430 Silver .0117 oz. **Ruler:** Ernst I **Obv:** "EK" below crowned "E"

Date	Mintage	F	VF	XF	Unc	BU
1828 EK	—	8.00	20.00	40.00	175	—
1830 EK	—	8.00	20.00	40.00	175	—
1831 EK	—	8.00	20.00	40.00	175	—

C# 91 3 KREUZER
1.5000 g., 0.2430 Silver .0117 oz. **Ruler:** Ernst I

Date	Mintage	F	VF	XF	Unc	BU
1831	—	2.00	6.00	20.00	80.00	—
1832	—	2.00	6.00	20.00	80.00	—
1833	—	2.00	6.00	20.00	80.00	—
1834	—	2.00	6.00	20.00	80.00	—
1835	—	2.00	6.00	20.00	80.00	—
1836	—	2.00	6.00	20.00	80.00	—
1837	—	2.00	6.00	20.00	80.00	—

C# 101.3 3 KREUZER
1.5000 g., 0.2430 Silver .0117 oz. **Ruler:** Ernst I **Obv:** Crowned arms **Rev:** Value within branches

Date	Mintage	F	VF	XF	Unc	BU
1838	358,000	2.00	6.00	20.00	80.00	—

C# 92 6 KREUZER
2.7300 g., 0.3050 Silver .0267 oz. **Ruler:** Ernst I

Date	Mintage	F	VF	XF	Unc	BU
1827 G	—	7.00	15.00	50.00	150	—
1827 ST	—	7.00	15.00	50.00	150	—
1828 ST	—	7.00	15.00	50.00	150	—
1828 EK	—	7.00	15.00	50.00	150	—
1829 EK	—	7.00	15.00	50.00	150	—
1830 EK	—	7.00	15.00	50.00	150	—

C# 93 6 KREUZER
2.7300 g., 0.3050 Silver 0.0268 oz. **Ruler:** Ernst I

Date	Mintage	F	VF	XF	Unc	BU
1831	—	3.00	5.00	20.00	100	—
1832	—	3.00	5.00	20.00	100	—
1833	—	3.00	5.00	20.00	100	—
1833/2	—	3.00	5.00	20.00	100	—
1834	—	3.00	5.00	20.00	100	—
1835	—	3.00	5.00	20.00	100	—
1836	—	3.00	5.00	20.00	100	—
1837	—	3.00	5.00	20.00	100	—

C# 101.6 6 KREUZER
2.7300 g., 0.3050 Silver .0267 oz. **Ruler:** Ernst I

Date	Mintage	F	VF	XF	Unc	BU
1838	209,000	3.00	5.00	20.00	100	—

C# 94 10 KREUZER
3.8900 g., 0.5000 Silver .0625 oz. **Ruler:** Ernst I **Note:** Similar to C#94b.

Date	Mintage	F	VF	XF	Unc	BU
1831	—	20.00	35.00	75.00	260	—
1832	—	20.00	35.00	75.00	260	—
1833	—	20.00	35.00	75.00	260	—
1834	—	20.00	35.00	75.00	260	—

C# 94b 10 KREUZER
3.8900 g., 0.5000 Silver .0625 oz. **Ruler:** Ernst I

Date	Mintage	F	VF	XF	Unc	BU
1835	—	15.00	30.00	60.00	200	—
1836	—	15.00	30.00	60.00	200	—
1837	—	18.00	35.00	70.00	250	—

C# 95 20 KREUZER
6.6800 g., 0.5830 Silver .1252 oz. **Ruler:** Ernst I **Obv:** Crowned arms **Obv. Legend:** ...COBURG & GOTHA... **Rev:** "ST" below value

Date	Mintage	F	VF	XF	Unc	BU
1827 ST	—	20.00	60.00	125	300	—

C# 95a 20 KREUZER
6.6800 g., 0.5830 Silver .1252 oz. **Ruler:** Ernst I **Obv. Legend:** ...COBURG UND GOTHA...

Date	Mintage	F	VF	XF	Unc	BU
1827 ST	—	20.00	60.00	125	300	—
1828 ST	—	20.00	60.00	125	300	—

C# 95b 20 KREUZER
6.6800 g., 0.5830 Silver .1252 oz. **Ruler:** Ernst I **Rev:** "E.K." below branches

Date	Mintage	F	VF	XF	Unc	BU
1828 EK	—	20.00	60.00	125	300	—
1830 EK	—	20.00	60.00	125	300	—

C# 96 20 KREUZER
6.6800 g., 0.5830 Silver .1252 oz. **Ruler:** Ernst I **Note:** Similar to C#96a.

Date	Mintage	F	VF	XF	Unc	BU
1831	—	20.00	60.00	125	300	—
1834	—	20.00	60.00	125	300	—

C# 96a 20 KREUZER
6.6800 g., 0.5830 Silver .1252 oz. **Ruler:** Ernst I **Obv. Legend:** Ends:...SACHSEN COBURG-GOTHA

Date	Mintage	F	VF	XF	Unc	BU
1835	—	15.00	35.00	50.00	250	—
1836	—	15.00	35.00	50.00	250	—

C# 102 1/2 GROSCHEN
1.0600 g., 0.2290 Silver .0078 oz. **Ruler:** Ernst I

Date	Mintage	F	VF	XF	Unc	BU
1841 G	247,000	5.00	10.00	25.00	125	—
1844 G	65,000	6.00	12.00	35.00	145	—

C# 111 1/2 GROSCHEN
1.0600 g., 0.2290 Silver .0078 oz. **Ruler:** Ernst II

Date	Mintage	F	VF	XF	Unc	BU
1851 F	32,000	3.00	6.00	12.00	65.00	—
1855 F	130,000	2.00	4.00	8.00	50.00	—
1858 F	60,000	2.00	4.00	8.00	50.00	—

C# 114 1/2 GROSCHEN
1.0600 g., 0.2290 Silver .0078 oz. **Ruler:** Ernst II **Obv:** "B" below arms

Date	Mintage	F	VF	XF	Unc	BU
1868 B	32,000	2.00	4.00	8.00	50.00	—
1870 B	52,000	2.00	4.00	8.00	50.00	—

C# 89 GROSCHEN
1.9800 g., 0.3680 Silver .0234 oz. **Ruler:** Ernst I

Date	Mintage	F	VF	XF	Unc	BU
1837	—	5.00	10.00	30.00	100	—

C# 103 GROSCHEN
2.1200 g., 0.2290 Silver .0156 oz. **Ruler:** Ernst I

Date	Mintage	F	VF	XF	Unc	BU
1841 G	355,000	8.00	15.00	40.00	150	—

C# 112 GROSCHEN
2.1200 g., 0.2290 Silver .0156 oz. **Ruler:** Ernst II

Date	Mintage	F	VF	XF	Unc	BU
1847 F	130,000	2.00	4.00	8.00	50.00	—
1851 F	49,000	2.00	4.00	8.00	50.00	—
1855 F	130,000	2.00	4.00	8.00	50.00	—
1858 F	33,000	2.00	4.00	8.00	50.00	—

C# 115 GROSCHEN
2.1200 g., 0.2290 Silver .0156 oz. **Ruler:** Ernst II

Date	Mintage	F	VF	XF	Unc	BU
1865 B	70,000	2.00	4.00	10.00	60.00	—
1868 B	31,000	2.00	4.00	10.00	60.00	—
1870 B	30,000	2.00	4.00	10.00	60.00	—

C# 104 2 GROSCHEN
3.1100 g., 0.3120 Silver .0311 oz. **Ruler:** Ernst I **Obv:** Crowned arms within branches **Rev:** Value

Date	Mintage	F	VF	XF	Unc	BU
1841 G	214,000	8.00	20.00	30.00	150	—
1844 G	32,000	8.00	20.00	30.00	150	—

C# 113 2 GROSCHEN
3.1100 g., 0.3120 Silver .0311 oz. **Ruler:** Ernst II

Date	Mintage	F	VF	XF	Unc	BU
1847 F	97,000	6.00	12.00	20.00	60.00	—
1851 F	32,000	6.00	12.00	20.00	60.00	—
1855 F	81,000	6.00	12.00	20.00	60.00	—
1858 F	55,000	6.00	12.00	20.00	60.00	—

C# 116 2 GROSCHEN
3.2200 g., 0.3000 Silver .0310 oz. **Ruler:** Ernst II

Date	Mintage	F	VF	XF	Unc	BU
1865 B	70,000	5.00	10.00	20.00	50.00	—
1868 B	30,000	5.00	10.00	20.00	50.00	—
1870 B	31,000	5.00	10.00	20.00	50.00	—

C# 105 1/6 THALER
5.3450 g., 0.5210 Silver .0895 oz. **Ruler:** Ernst I

Date	Mintage	F	VF	XF	Unc	BU
1841 G	48,000	15.00	40.00	75.00	225	—
1842 G	48,000	15.00	40.00	75.00	225	—
1843 G	48,000	15.00	40.00	75.00	225	—

C# 117 1/6 THALER
5.3450 g., 0.5210 Silver .0895 oz. **Ruler:** Ernst II **Obv:** Different head

Date	Mintage	F	VF	XF	Unc	BU
1845 F	123,000	15.00	35.00	75.00	250	—

C# 117a 1/6 THALER
5.3450 g., 0.5210 Silver .0895 oz. **Ruler:** Ernst II

Date	Mintage	F	VF	XF	Unc	BU
1848 F	130,000	10.00	30.00	60.00	200	—

C# 117b 1/6 THALER
5.3450 g., 0.5210 Silver .0895 oz. **Ruler:** Ernst II **Obv:** Head with beard

Date	Mintage	F	VF	XF	Unc	BU
1852 F	48,000	15.00	35.00	75.00	250	—
1855 F	60,000	15.00	35.00	75.00	250	—

C# 118 1/6 THALER
5.3400 g., 0.5200 Silver .0892 oz. **Ruler:** Ernst II

Date	Mintage	F	VF	XF	Unc	BU
1864 B	60,000	10.00	30.00	60.00	150	—

C# 119 1/6 THALER
5.3400 g., 0.5200 Silver .0892 oz. **Ruler:** Ernst II **Subject:** 25th Anniversary of Reign

Date	Mintage	F	VF	XF	Unc	BU
1869 B	12,000	10.00	30.00	50.00	125	—

C# 97 1/2 THALER (1 Gulden)
14.0300 g., 0.8330 Silver .3757 oz. **Ruler:** Ernst I **Note:** Convention Thaler.

Date	Mintage	F	VF	XF	Unc	BU
1830 EK	—	65.00	150	250	650	—
1831	—	65.00	150	250	650	—
1832	—	65.00	150	250	650	—
1834	—	65.00	150	250	650	—
1835 HF	—	65.00	150	250	650	—

C# 97a 1/2 THALER (1 Gulden)
14.0300 g., 0.8330 Silver .3757 oz. **Ruler:** Ernst I

Date	Mintage	F	VF	XF	Unc	BU
1834 HF	—	65.00	150	250	650	—

C# 98 THALER (Krone)
29.3800 g., 0.8710 Silver .8228 oz. **Ruler:** Ernst I

Date	Mintage	F	VF	XF	Unc	BU
1827	—	350	700	1,000	2,500	—

C# 99 THALER (Krone)
28.0600 g., 0.8330 Silver .7514 oz. **Ruler:** Ernst I **Note:** Convention Thaler.

Date	Mintage	F	VF	XF	Unc	BU
1828	31	—	—	—	8,000	—
1828 Proof	—	Value: 10,000				

C# 99a THALER (Krone)
28.0600 g., 0.8330 Silver .7514 oz. **Ruler:** Ernst I

Date	Mintage	F	VF	XF	Unc	BU
1829 E-K	1,095	400	1,000	1,500	2,500	—

C# 99b THALER (Krone)
28.0600 g., 0.8330 Silver .7514 oz. **Ruler:** Ernst I **Rev:** Without mintmaster's initials

Date	Mintage	F	VF	XF	Unc	BU
1832	304	—	—	—	6,500	—
1833	Inc. above	—	—	—	7,500	—

C# 99c THALER (Krone)
28.0600 g., 0.8330 Silver .7514 oz. **Ruler:** Ernst I

Date	Mintage	F	VF	XF	Unc	BU
1835	—	800	1,700	3,000	5,000	—

C# 106 THALER (Krone)
22.2700 g., 0.7500 Silver 0.537 oz. **Ruler:** Ernst I **Obv:** Bust of Ernst I facing left **Rev:** Crowned draped arms within wreath

Date	Mintage	F	VF	XF	Unc	BU
1841 G	16,000	75.00	150	300	1,000	—
1842 G	16,000	75.00	150	300	1,000	—

C# 120 THALER (Krone)
22.2700 g., 0.7500 Silver .5371 oz. **Ruler:** Ernst II **Rev:** Crowned draped arms within wreath

Date	Mintage	F	VF	XF	Unc	BU
1846 F	32,000	75.00	150	400	1,000	—

C# 120a THALER (Krone)
22.2700 g., 0.7500 Silver .5371 oz. **Ruler:** Ernst II

Date	Mintage	F	VF	XF	Unc	BU
1848 F	16,000	75.00	150	300	1,000	—

C# 120b THALER (Krone)
22.2700 g., 0.7500 Silver .5371 oz. **Ruler:** Ernst II

Date	Mintage	F	VF	XF	Unc	BU
1851 F	8,000	75.00	150	300	1,000	—
1852 F	8,000	75.00	150	300	1,000	—

C# 121 THALER (Krone)
18.5200 g., 0.9000 Silver .5360 oz. **Ruler:** Ernst II

Date	Mintage	F	VF	XF	Unc	BU
1862 B	40,000	45.00	90.00	150	400	—
1864 B	40,000	45.00	90.00	150	400	—
1870 B	22,000	60.00	100	175	350	—

C# 122 THALER (Krone)
18.5200 g., 0.9000 Silver .5360 oz. **Ruler:** Ernst II **Subject:** 25th Anniversary of Reign

Date	Mintage	F	VF	XF	Unc	BU
1869 B	6,000	45.00	85.00	150	250	—

C# 107 2 THALER (3-1/2 Gulden)
37.1200 g., 0.9000 Silver 1.0743 oz. **Ruler:** Ernst I

Date	Mintage	F	VF	XF	Unc	BU
1841 G	11,000	250	500	1,000	2,200	—
1842 G	5,350	300	600	1,100	2,400	—
1843 G	5,350	300	600	1,100	2,400	—

C# 123 2 THALER (3-1/2 Gulden)
37.1200 g., 0.9000 Silver 1.0743 oz. **Ruler:** Ernst II **Rev:** Similar to C#123a

Date	Mintage	F	VF	XF	Unc	BU
1847 F	11,000	350	625	1,400	2,800	—

C# 123a 2 THALER (3-1/2 Gulden)
37.1200 g., 0.9000 Silver 1.0743 oz. **Ruler:** Ernst II

Date	Mintage	F	VF	XF	Unc	BU
1854 F	16,000	225	425	1,000	2,000	—

REFORM COINAGE

Y# 149 2 MARK
11.1110 g., 0.9000 Silver .3215 oz. **Ruler:** Alfred

Date	Mintage	F	VF	XF	Unc	BU
1895A	15,000	250	650	900	1,500	1,800
1895A Proof	—	Value: 2,000				

Y# 150 5 MARK
27.7770 g., 0.9000 Silver .8038 oz. **Ruler:** Alfred

Date	Mintage	F	VF	XF	Unc	BU
1895A Proof	—	—	—	—	—	—
1895A	4,000	1,000	2,000	2,600	4,500	5,500

Y# 148 20 MARK
1.9650 g., 0.9000 Gold .2304 oz. **Ruler:** Ernst II **Rev:** Type I

Date	Mintage	F	VF	XF	Unc	BU
1872E Proof, rare	—	—	—	—	—	—
1872E	1,000	15,000	20,000	30,000	40,000	60,000

Y# 148a 20 MARK
1.9650 g., 0.9000 Gold .2304 oz. **Ruler:** Ernst II

Date	Mintage	F	VF	XF	Unc	BU
1886A	20,000	1,000	1,600	2,200	3,500	4,500
1886A Proof	—	Value: 5,000				

Y# 151 20 MARK
1.9650 g., 0.9000 Gold .2304 oz. **Ruler:** Alfred

Date	Mintage	F	VF	XF	Unc	BU
1895A	10,000	1,200	1,750	2,250	3,000	3,500
1895A Proof	—	Value: 4,500				

TRADE COINAGE

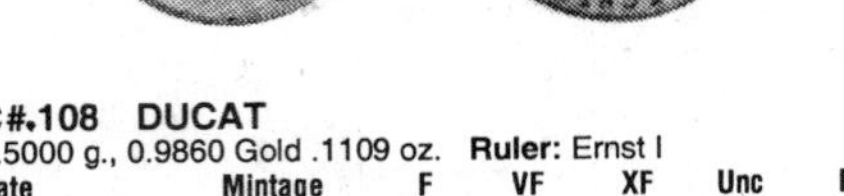

C# 108 DUCAT
3.5000 g., 0.9860 Gold .1109 oz. **Ruler:** Ernst I

Date	Mintage	F	VF	XF	Unc	BU
1831 E-K	600	1,000	2,500	3,500	5,000	—

C# 108a DUCAT
3.5000 g., 0.9860 Gold .1109 oz. **Ruler:** Ernst I

Date	Mintage	F	VF	XF	Unc	BU
1836	1,600	750	1,250	2,500	3,750	—
1842	508	750	1,500	3,000	4,000	—

SAXE-COBURG-SAALFELD

When Saxe-Saalfeld obtained Coburg in 1735, the duchy was henceforth called Saxe-Coburg-Saalfeld. In 1826, Saalfeld was transferred to Saxe-Meiningen and the duke was given Gotha. The new creation was then known as Saxe-Coburg-Gotha.

RULERS
Franz Friedrich Anton, 1800-1806
Ernst I, 1806-1826

MINT OFFICIALS' INITIALS

Initial	Date	Name
L	1803-16	Georg Christoph Loewel
S	1816-26	Laurentius Theodor Sommer, warden

DUCHY

REGULAR COINAGE

KM# 135 HELLER
Copper

Date	Mintage	F	VF	XF	Unc	BU
1808	—	2.00	6.00	12.00	50.00	—
1809	112,000	2.00	6.00	12.00	50.00	—
1810	71,000	2.00	6.00	12.00	50.00	—
1814	50,000	2.00	6.00	12.00	50.00	—
1815	Inc. above	2.00	6.00	12.00	50.00	—
1817	—	2.00	6.00	12.00	50.00	—
1818	—	2.00	6.00	12.00	50.00	—
1819	—	2.00	6.00	12.00	50.00	—
1824	—	2.00	6.00	12.00	50.00	—
1826	—	2.00	6.00	12.00	50.00	—

KM# 140 HELLER
Copper

Date	Mintage	F	VF	XF	Unc	BU
1809	—	3.00	6.00	12.00	50.00	—

KM# 119.1 PFENNIG
Copper

Date	Mintage	F	VF	XF	Unc	BU
1804	—	1.50	6.00	12.00	50.00	—
1805	—	1.50	6.00	12.00	50.00	—
1808	83,000	1.50	6.00	12.00	50.00	—
1809	55,000	1.50	6.00	12.00	50.00	—
1814	43,000	1.50	6.00	12.00	50.00	—
1815	Inc. above	1.50	6.00	12.00	50.00	—
1817	—	1.50	6.00	12.00	50.00	—
1819	—	1.50	6.00	12.00	50.00	—
1820	—	1.50	6.00	12.00	50.00	—
1821	—	1.50	6.00	12.00	50.00	—
1822	—	1.50	6.00	12.00	50.00	—
1823	—	1.50	6.00	12.00	50.00	—
1824	—	1.50	6.00	12.00	50.00	—
1826	—	1.50	6.00	12.00	50.00	—

KM# 119.2 PFENNIG
Copper **Rev:** Without rosettes on sides of "I"

Date	Mintage	F	VF	XF	Unc	BU
1805	—	1.50	6.00	12.00	50.00	—

KM# 120 PFENNIG
Billon

Date	Mintage	F	VF	XF	Unc	BU
1805	—	2.00	8.00	15.00	70.00	—

KM# 136 PFENNIG
Billon

Date	Mintage	F	VF	XF	Unc	BU
1808	962,000	4.00	9.00	18.00	75.00	—

KM# 141 PFENNIG
Copper

Date	Mintage	F	VF	XF	Unc	BU
1809	—	3.00	5.00	14.00	60.00	—

KM# 151.1 2 PFENNIG
Copper

Date	Mintage	F	VF	XF	Unc	BU
1810	124,000	5.00	15.00	30.00	70.00	—
1817	—	5.00	15.00	30.00	70.00	—
1818	—	5.00	15.00	30.00	70.00	—

KM# 151.2 2 PFENNIG
Copper **Rev:** Without rosettes on sides of "2"

Date	Mintage	F	VF	XF	Unc	BU
1810	Inc. above	5.00	15.00	30.00	70.00	—

KM# 121 3 PFENNIG
0.7900 g., 0.1250 Silver .0031 oz.

Date	Mintage	F	VF	XF	Unc	BU
1804	—	4.00	10.00	20.00	55.00	—
1805	—	4.00	10.00	20.00	55.00	—
1806	—	4.00	10.00	20.00	55.00	—

KM# 132 3 PFENNIG
Copper **Obv:** Arms on crowned cartouche with festoons

Date	Mintage	F	VF	XF	Unc	BU
1806	—	3.00	7.00	15.00	50.00	—

KM# 133.1 3 PFENNIG
Copper **Rev:** Value: III PFENNIG

Date	Mintage	F	VF	XF	Unc	BU
1807	—	5.00	10.00	25.00	70.00	—
1808	63,000	5.00	10.00	25.00	70.00	—

KM# 133.2 3 PFENNIG
Copper

Date	Mintage	F	VF	XF	Unc	BU
1821	—	3.00	8.00	20.00	60.00	—
1822	—	3.00	8.00	20.00	60.00	—
1823	—	3.00	8.00	20.00	60.00	—
1824	—	3.00	8.00	20.00	60.00	—
1825	—	3.00	8.00	20.00	60.00	—
1826	—	3.00	8.00	20.00	60.00	—

KM# 142 4 PFENNIG
Copper

Date	Mintage	F	VF	XF	Unc	BU
1809	27,000	5.00	10.00	30.00	85.00	—
1810	8,106	5.00	10.00	30.00	85.00	—
1818	—	5.00	10.00	30.00	85.00	—
1820	—	5.00	10.00	30.00	85.00	—

KM# A120 6 PFENNIG
1.2900 g., 0.2290 Silver .0094 oz.

Date	Mintage	F	VF	XF	Unc	BU
1808	47,000	5.00	10.00	25.00	80.00	—
1810	—	5.00	10.00	25.00	80.00	—
1818 S	—	5.00	10.00	25.00	80.00	—
1820 S	—	5.00	10.00	25.00	80.00	—

KM# 126 KREUZER
0.7900 g., 0.1250 Silver .0031 oz.

Date	Mintage	F	VF	XF	Unc	BU
1805	—	10.00	20.00	45.00	100	—

KM# 137 KREUZER
0.7900 g., 0.1250 Silver .0031 oz. **Obv:** Crowned "E" within two crossed branches **Rev:** Value **Rev. Legend:** H. S. C.

Date	Mintage	F	VF	XF	Unc	BU
1808	68,000	4.00	10.00	20.00	65.00	—
1812	18,000	4.00	10.00	20.00	65.00	—
1813	18,000	4.00	10.00	20.00	65.00	—

Date	Mintage	F	VF	XF	Unc	BU
1815	21,000	4.00	10.00	20.00	65.00	—
1817	—	4.00	10.00	20.00	65.00	—
1818	—	4.00	10.00	20.00	65.00	—
1820	—	4.00	10.00	20.00	65.00	—

KM# 163 KREUZER
0.7900 g., 0.1250 Silver .0031 oz. **Rev. Legend:** H. S. C. S.

Date	Mintage	F	VF	XF	Unc	BU
1824 S	—	3.00	10.00	20.00	70.00	—
1825 S	—	3.00	10.00	20.00	70.00	—
1826 S	—	3.00	10.00	20.00	70.00	—

KM# 122.1 3 KREUZER
1.5000 g., 0.2430 Silver .0117 oz. **Obv:** Crowned oval arms **Rev:** Value

Date	Mintage	F	VF	XF	Unc	BU
1804	—	10.00	20.00	40.00	90.00	—

KM# 122.2 3 KREUZER
1.5000 g., 0.2430 Silver .0117 oz. **Obv:** Pointed arms

Date	Mintage	F	VF	XF	Unc	BU
1805	—	8.00	16.00	35.00	85.00	—

KM# 127.1 3 KREUZER
1.5000 g., 0.2430 Silver .0117 oz. **Rev. Legend:** H. S. COBURG. L. M.

Date	Mintage	F	VF	XF	Unc	BU
1805	—	5.00	10.00	25.00	75.00	—

KM# 127.2 3 KREUZER
1.5000 g., 0.2430 Silver .0117 oz. **Rev. Legend:** H. S. COBURG. LAND. M.

Date	Mintage	F	VF	XF	Unc	BU
1805	—	10.00	20.00	40.00	90.00	—

KM# 128.1 3 KREUZER
1.5000 g., 0.2430 Silver .0117 oz. **Obv:** Crowned "E" within, "L" below crossed branches **Rev:** Value **Rev. Legend:** H. S. C.

Date	Mintage	F	VF	XF	Unc	BU
1808	—	4.00	10.00	20.00	65.00	—

KM# 128.2 3 KREUZER
1.5000 g., 0.2430 Silver .0117 oz.

Date	Mintage	F	VF	XF	Unc	BU
1808 L	137,000	4.00	10.00	20.00	65.00	—
1810 L	151,000	4.00	10.00	20.00	65.00	—
1812 L	196,000	4.00	10.00	20.00	65.00	—
1813 L	143,000	4.00	10.00	20.00	65.00	—
1814 L	116,000	4.00	10.00	20.00	65.00	—
1815 L	26,000	4.00	10.00	20.00	65.00	—

KM# 128.3 3 KREUZER
1.5000 g., 0.2430 Silver .0117 oz. **Obv:** "S" below crossed branches

Date	Mintage	F	VF	XF	Unc	BU
1816 S	—	4.00	10.00	20.00	65.00	—
1817 S	—	4.00	10.00	20.00	65.00	—
1818 S	—	4.00	10.00	20.00	65.00	—
1819 S	—	4.00	10.00	20.00	65.00	—
1820 S	—	4.00	10.00	20.00	65.00	—

KM# 128.4 3 KREUZER
1.5000 g., 0.2430 Silver .0117 oz. **Rev. Legend:** H. S. C. S.

Date	Mintage	F	VF	XF	Unc	BU
1821 S	—	5.00	10.00	22.00	70.00	—
1822 S	—	5.00	10.00	22.00	70.00	—
1823 S	—	5.00	10.00	22.00	70.00	—
1824 S	—	5.00	10.00	22.00	70.00	—
1825 S	—	5.00	10.00	22.00	70.00	—
1826 S	—	5.00	10.00	22.00	70.00	—

KM# 128.5 3 KREUZER
1.5000 g., 0.2430 Silver .0117 oz. **Obv:** "G" below crossed branches

Date	Mintage	F	VF	XF	Unc	BU
1826	—	5.00	10.00	22.00	70.00	—

KM# 123 6 KREUZER
2.7200 g., 0.3050 Silver .0266 oz. **Obv:** Crowned shield **Rev:** Value

Date	Mintage	F	VF	XF	Unc	BU
1804	—	6.00	12.00	30.00	100	—
1805	—	6.00	12.00	30.00	100	—

KM# 129 6 KREUZER
2.7200 g., 0.3050 Silver .0266 oz. **Rev. Legend:** H. S. COBURG. LAND. M.

Date	Mintage	F	VF	XF	Unc	BU
1805	—	6.00	12.00	30.00	100	—

KM# 138.1 6 KREUZER
2.7200 g., 0.3050 Silver .0266 oz. **Obv:** Crowned "E" within, "L" below crossed branches **Rev. Legend:** H. S. C.

Date	Mintage	F	VF	XF	Unc	BU
1808 L	75,000	4.00	10.00	20.00	70.00	—
1810 L	56,000	4.00	10.00	20.00	70.00	—
1812 L	89,000	4.00	10.00	20.00	70.00	—
1813 L	42,000	4.00	10.00	20.00	70.00	—
1814 L	50,000	4.00	10.00	20.00	70.00	—
1815 L	11,000	4.00	10.00	20.00	70.00	—

KM# 138.2 6 KREUZER
2.7200 g., 0.3050 Silver .0266 oz. **Obv:** "S" below crossed branches

Date	Mintage	F	VF	XF	Unc	BU
1816 S	—	4.00	10.00	20.00	70.00	—
1817 S	—	4.00	10.00	20.00	70.00	—
1818 S	—	4.00	10.00	20.00	70.00	—
1819 S	—	4.00	10.00	20.00	70.00	—
1820 S	—	4.00	10.00	20.00	70.00	—

KM# 138.3 6 KREUZER
2.7200 g., 0.3050 Silver .0266 oz. **Rev. Legend:** H. S. C. S.

Date	Mintage	F	VF	XF	Unc	BU
1821 S	—	5.00	10.00	25.00	100	—
1822 S	—	5.00	10.00	25.00	100	—
1823 S	—	5.00	10.00	25.00	100	—
1824 S	—	5.00	10.00	25.00	100	—
1825 S	—	5.00	10.00	25.00	100	—
1826 S	—	5.00	10.00	25.00	100	—

KM# 161.1 10 KREUZER
3.8900 g., 0.5000 Silver .0625 oz. **Obv:** Crowned arms **Obv. Legend:** ... SACHS. SOUV ... **Rev:** Value within bound branches

Date	Mintage	F	VF	XF	Unc	BU
1820 S	—	25.00	50.00	150	350	—

KM# 161.2 10 KREUZER
3.8900 g., 0.5000 Silver .0625 oz. **Obv. Legend:** ... SACHS. COBURG. ...

Date	Mintage	F	VF	XF	Unc	BU
1824 S	—	50.00	75.00	175	400	—

KM# 134.1 20 KREUZER
6.6800 g., 0.5830 Silver .1252 oz.

Date	Mintage	F	VF	XF	Unc	BU
1807 L	—	25.00	65.00	150	400	—

KM# 134.2 20 KREUZER
6.6800 g., 0.5830 Silver .1252 oz. **Rev:** Date below wreath

Date	Mintage	F	VF	XF	Unc	BU
1807	—	35.00	75.00	175	450	—

KM# 152 20 KREUZER
6.6800 g., 0.5830 Silver .1252 oz.

Date	Mintage	F	VF	XF	Unc	BU
1812 L	30,000	20.00	50.00	125	375	—
1813 L	46,000	20.00	50.00	125	375	—
1819 S	—	20.00	50.00	125	375	—
1820 S	—	20.00	50.00	125	375	—

KM# 162 20 KREUZER
6.6800 g., 0.5830 Silver .1252 oz.

Date	Mintage	F	VF	XF	Unc	BU
1823 S	—	20.00	50.00	125	375	—
1824 S	—	20.00	50.00	125	375	—
1825 S	—	20.00	50.00	125	375	—
1826 S	—	20.00	50.00	125	375	—

KM# 124 1/48 THALER
0.9700 g., 0.2500 Silver .0077 oz. **Obv:** Narrow crowned arms in cartouche

Date	Mintage	F	VF	XF	Unc	BU
1804	—	10.00	20.00	45.00	150	—

KM# 125 1/48 THALER
0.9700 g., 0.2500 Silver .0077 oz. **Obv:** Crowned oval arms in cartouche **Rev:** Legend not in cartouche

Date	Mintage	F	VF	XF	Unc	BU
1804	—	60.00	100	150	250	—
1805	—	8.00	16.00	40.00	150	—
1806	—	60.00	100	150	250	—

KM# 139 GROSCHEN (1/24 Thaler)
1.9800 g., 0.3680 Silver .0234 oz.

Date	Mintage	F	VF	XF	Unc	BU
1808	26,000	4.00	8.00	20.00	65.00	—
1810	—	4.00	8.00	20.00	65.00	—
1818 S	—	4.00	8.00	20.00	65.00	—

KM# 130 1/24 THALER (Groschen)
1.9800 g., 0.3680 Silver .0234 oz.

Date	Mintage	F	VF	XF	Unc	BU
1805	—	12.00	25.00	50.00	165	—

KM# 131 THALER
28.0600 g., 0.8330 Silver .7516 oz.

Date	Mintage	F	VF	XF	Unc	BU
1805 L	600	350	700	1,250	2,500	—

KM# 153.1 THALER
28.0600 g., 0.8330 Silver .7516 oz.

Date	Mintage	F	VF	XF	Unc	BU
1817	—	150	300	600	1,200	—

KM# 153.2 THALER
28.0600 g., 0.8330 Silver .7516 oz. **Edge Lettering:** EIN SPECIESTHALER

Date	Mintage	F	VF	XF	Unc	BU
1817	—	150	300	700	1,500	—

KM# 164 THALER (Krone)
29.3800 g., 0.8710 Silver .8228 oz.

Date	Mintage	F	VF	XF	Unc	BU
1825	—	1,000	2,000	3,500	6,000	—
1825 First strike	—	—	—	—	—	10,000

SAXE-HILDBURGHAUSEN

Saxe-Hildburghausen was founded from the division of Saxe-Gotha, by the sixth son of Ernst the Pious. In 1826, the last duke assigned Hildburghausen to Saxe-Meiningen in exchange for Altenburg.

RULERS
Friedrich I, 1780-1826

DUCHY

REGULAR COINAGE

KM# 130 HELLER
Copper

Date	Mintage	F	VF	XF	Unc	BU
1804	—	5.00	10.00	25.00	70.00	—
1805	—	5.00	10.00	25.00	70.00	—
1806	—	5.00	10.00	25.00	70.00	—

KM# 133 HELLER
Copper

Date	Mintage	F	VF	XF	Unc	BU
1808	—	2.50	6.00	20.00	60.00	—
1809	—	2.50	6.00	20.00	60.00	—
1811	—	2.50	6.00	20.00	60.00	—
1812	—	2.50	6.00	20.00	60.00	—
1816	—	2.50	6.00	20.00	60.00	—
1817	—	2.50	6.00	20.00	60.00	—
1818	—	2.50	6.00	20.00	60.00	—

KM# 140 HELLER
Copper

Date	Mintage	F	VF	XF	Unc	BU
1820	—	2.50	6.00	20.00	60.00	—
1821	—	2.50	6.00	20.00	60.00	—
1822	—	2.50	6.00	20.00	60.00	—
1823	—	2.50	6.00	20.00	60.00	—
1824	—	2.50	6.00	20.00	60.00	—
1825	—	2.50	6.00	20.00	60.00	—

KM# 142 PFENNIG
Copper

Date	Mintage	F	VF	XF	Unc	BU
1823	—	4.00	8.00	18.00	50.00	—
1825	—	4.00	8.00	18.00	50.00	—
1826	—	4.00	8.00	18.00	50.00	—

KM# 149 PFENNIG
Copper **Obv:** Crowned rectangular arms

Date	Mintage	F	VF	XF	Unc	BU
1826	—	5.00	10.00	25.00	80.00	—

KM# 146 1/8 KREUZER
Copper **Obv:** Crowned "F" within crossed branches **Rev:** Value **Rev. Legend:** KREUZER LANDMUNZE

Date	Mintage	F	VF	XF	Unc	BU
1825	—	10.00	20.00	40.00	100	—

KM# 147 1/4 KREUZER
Copper

Date	Mintage	F	VF	XF	Unc	BU
1825	—	10.00	20.00	45.00	110	—

KM# 148 1/4 KREUZER
Copper **Obv:** Crowned heart-shaped arms **Obv. Legend:** H.S.H.H.

Date	Mintage	F	VF	XF	Unc	BU
1825	—	12.00	25.00	50.00	125	—

KM# 134 1/2 KREUZER
Copper **Obv:** Crowned arms **Rev:** Value in script

Date	Mintage	F	VF	XF	Unc	BU
1809	—	5.00	10.00	25.00	80.00	—
1809	—	5.00	10.00	25.00	80.00	—

KM# 143 1/2 KREUZER
Copper **Obv:** Crowned heart-shaped arms **Obv. Legend:** HERZ. Z. S. **Rev:** Value

Date	Mintage	F	VF	XF	Unc	BU
1823	—	6.00	12.00	30.00	90.00	—

KM# 144 1/2 KREUZER
Copper **Obv. Legend:** HERSOGTHUM

Date	Mintage	F	VF	XF	Unc	BU
1823	—	6.00	12.00	30.00	90.00	—

KM# 145 1/2 KREUZER
Copper **Rev:** Value **Rev. Legend:** KREUZER LANDMUNZE

Date	Mintage	F	VF	XF	Unc	BU
1823	—	7.00	15.00	35.00	100	—

KM# 131 KREUZER
Billon

Date	Mintage	F	VF	XF	Unc	BU
1804	—	10.00	22.00	50.00	160	—
1805	—	10.00	22.00	50.00	160	—

KM# 132 KREUZER
Billon **Obv:** Crowned oval arms within branches **Rev:** Value

Date	Mintage	F	VF	XF	Unc	BU
1806	—	8.00	18.00	40.00	135	—
1811	—	8.00	18.00	40.00	135	—

KM# 135 3 KREUZER
Billon **Obv:** Crowned "F" within wreath **Rev:** Value within ring

Date	Mintage	F	VF	XF	Unc	BU
1808	—	6.00	12.00	30.00	120	—
1810	—	6.00	12.00	30.00	120	—
1811	—	6.00	12.00	30.00	120	—
1812	—	6.00	12.00	30.00	120	—
1815	—	6.00	12.00	30.00	120	—
1816	—	6.00	12.00	30.00	120	—
1817	—	6.00	12.00	30.00	120	—
1818	—	6.00	12.00	30.00	120	—
1820	—	6.00	12.00	30.00	120	—

KM# 136 6 KREUZER
Billon

Date	Mintage	F	VF	XF	Unc	BU
1805	—	8.00	20.00	45.00	150	—
1808	—	8.00	20.00	45.00	150	—
1811	—	8.00	20.00	45.00	150	—
1812	—	8.00	20.00	45.00	150	—
1815	—	8.00	20.00	45.00	150	—
1816	—	8.00	20.00	45.00	150	—
1817	—	8.00	20.00	45.00	150	—
1818	—	8.00	20.00	45.00	150	—

KM# 141 6 KREUZER
Billon **Obv:** Crowned "F" within crossed branches **Rev:** Value

Date	Mintage	F	VF	XF	Unc	BU
1820	—	8.00	18.00	40.00	135	—
1821	—	8.00	18.00	40.00	135	—
1823	—	8.00	18.00	40.00	135	—
1824	—	8.00	18.00	40.00	135	—
1825	—	8.00	18.00	40.00	135	—

SAXE-MEININGEN

(Sachsen-Meiningen)

The duchy of Saxe-Meiningen was located in Thuringia, sandwiched between Saxe-Weimar-Eisenach on the west and north and the enclave of Schmalkalden belonging to Hesse-Cassel on the east. It was founded upon the division of the Ernestine line in Saxe-Gotha in 1680. In 1735, due to an exchange of some territory, the duchy became known as Saxe-Coburg-Meiningen. In 1826, Saxe-Coburg-Gotha assigned Saalfeld to Saxe-Meiningen. The duchy came under the strong influence of Prussia from 1866, when Bernhard II was forced to abdicate because of his support of Austria. The monarchy ended with the defeat of Germany in 1918.

RULERS

Georg I, 1782-1803
Bernhard Erich Freund, under Regency of Louise Eleonore, 1803-1821
Bernhard II, 1821-1866
Georg II, 1866-1914

MINT OFFICIALS' INITIALS

Initial	Date	Name
F. HELFRICHT	d. 1892	Ferdinand Helfricht, die-cutter and chief medailleur
K	1835-37	Georg Krell, warden then mintmaster
L	1803-33	Georg Christoph Loewel
VOIGT		J.C. Voigt, die-cutter and medailleur

DUCHY

REGULAR COINAGE

KM# 106 HELLER
Copper **Ruler:** Bernhard Erich Freund under regency of Louise Eleonore **Obv:** Crowned heart-shaped arms **Obv. Legend:** H **Rev:** Value

Date	Mintage	F	VF	XF	Unc	BU
1814	—	2.50	5.00	10.00	60.00	—

KM# 107 HELLER
Copper **Ruler:** Bernhard Erich Freund under regency of Louise Eleonore **Obv. Legend:** HERZ

Date	Mintage	F	VF	XF	Unc	BU
1814	—	2.50	5.00	10.00	60.00	—

KM# 109 PFENNIG
Copper **Ruler:** Bernhard Erich Freund under regency of Louise Eleonore **Obv. Legend:** HERZ

Date	Mintage	F	VF	XF	Unc	BU
1818	90,000	4.00	8.00	20.00	80.00	—

KM# 135 PFENNIG
Copper **Ruler:** Bernhard II

Date	Mintage	F	VF	XF	Unc	BU
1832	275,000	2.50	5.00	10.00	50.00	—
1833	93,000	2.50	5.00	10.00	50.00	—
1835	34,000	2.50	5.00	10.00	50.00	—

KM# 143 PFENNIG
Copper **Ruler:** Bernhard II **Obv:** Crowned arms within branches

Date	Mintage	F	VF	XF	Unc	BU
1839	79,000	2.50	5.00	10.00	50.00	—
1842	132,000	2.50	5.00	10.00	50.00	—

KM# 170 PFENNIG
Copper **Ruler:** Bernhard II

Date	Mintage	F	VF	XF	Unc	BU
1860	240,000	2.00	4.00	8.00	50.00	—
1862	243,000	2.00	4.00	8.00	50.00	—
1863	240,000	2.00	4.00	8.00	50.00	—
1865	240,000	2.00	4.00	8.00	50.00	—
1866	480,000	2.00	4.00	8.00	50.00	—

KM# 173 PFENNIG
Copper **Ruler:** Georg II

Date	Mintage	F	VF	XF	Unc	BU
1867	240,000	2.00	4.00	8.00	50.00	—
1868	480,000	2.00	4.00	8.00	50.00	—

KM# 136 2 PFENNIG
Copper **Ruler:** Bernhard II

Date	Mintage	F	VF	XF	Unc	BU
1832	202,000	2.00	4.00	8.00	50.00	—
1833	101,000	2.00	4.00	8.00	50.00	—
1835	36,000	2.00	4.00	8.00	50.00	—

KM# 144 2 PFENNIG
Copper **Ruler:** Bernhard II

Date	Mintage	F	VF	XF	Unc	BU
1839	75,000	2.00	4.00	8.00	50.00	—
1842	184,000	2.00	4.00	8.00	50.00	—

KM# 171 2 PFENNIG
Copper **Ruler:** Bernhard II

Date	Mintage	F	VF	XF	Unc	BU
1860	361,000	2.00	4.00	8.00	50.00	—
1862	357,000	2.00	4.00	8.00	50.00	—
1863	120,000	2.00	4.00	8.00	50.00	—
1864	480,000	2.00	4.00	8.00	50.00	—
1865	240,000	2.00	4.00	8.00	50.00	—
1866	480,000	2.00	4.00	8.00	50.00	—

KM# 174 2 PFENNIG
Copper **Ruler:** Georg II

Date	Mintage	F	VF	XF	Unc	BU
1867	480,000	2.00	4.00	8.00	50.00	—
1868	240,000	2.00	4.00	8.00	50.00	—
1869	240,000	2.00	4.00	8.00	50.00	—
1870	720,000	2.00	4.00	8.00	50.00	—

KM# 118 1/8 KREUZER
Copper **Ruler:** Bernhard II

Date	Mintage	F	VF	XF	Unc	BU
1828	—	3.00	6.00	12.00	55.00	—

KM# 100 1/4 KREUZER
Copper **Ruler:** Bernhard Erich Freund under regency of Louise Eleonore **Obv:** Crowned heart-shaped arms **Obv. Legend:** HERZ

Date	Mintage	F	VF	XF	Unc	BU
1812	—	3.00	6.00	12.00	55.00	—
1814	—	3.00	6.00	12.00	55.00	—
1818	66,000	3.00	6.00	12.00	55.00	—

KM# 115 1/4 KREUZER
Copper **Ruler:** Bernhard II **Obv:** Crowned heart-shaped sarms **Obv. Legend:** HERZ **Rev:** Value **Rev. Legend:** LANDMUNZE

Date	Mintage	F	VF	XF	Unc	BU
1823	—	5.00	10.00	20.00	65.00	—

KM# 120 1/4 KREUZER
Copper **Ruler:** Bernhard II **Obv:** Legend below crowned arms

Date	Mintage	F	VF	XF	Unc	BU
1828	—	2.00	4.00	8.00	40.00	—

KM# 119 1/4 KREUZER
Copper **Ruler:** Bernhard II **Note:** Many varieties in legend size exist.

Date	Mintage	F	VF	XF	Unc	BU
1828	—	2.00	4.00	8.00	50.00	—
1829	168,000	2.00	4.00	8.00	40.00	—
1830	161,000	2.00	4.00	8.00	40.00	—
1831	321,000	2.00	4.00	8.00	40.00	—
1832	63,000	2.00	4.00	8.00	40.00	—

KM# 125 1/4 KREUZER
Copper **Ruler:** Bernhard II **Obv. Legend:** MEINIGEN

Date	Mintage	F	VF	XF	Unc	BU
1829	Inc. above	2.00	4.00	8.00	40.00	—

KM# 161 1/4 KREUZER
Copper **Ruler:** Bernhard II **Rev:** Value **Rev. Legend:** KREUZER

Date	Mintage	F	VF	XF	Unc	BU
1854	240,000	2.00	4.00	8.00	40.00	—

KM# 101 1/2 KREUZER
Copper **Ruler:** Bernhard Erich Freund under regency of Louise Eleonore

Date	Mintage	F	VF	XF	Unc	BU
1812	—	3.00	6.00	12.00	55.00	—
1814	—	3.00	6.00	12.00	55.00	—
1818	102,000	3.00	6.00	12.00	55.00	—

KM# 121 1/2 KREUZER
Copper **Ruler:** Bernhard II

Date	Mintage	F	VF	XF	Unc	BU
1828	—	2.50	5.00	10.00	50.00	—
1831	—	2.50	5.00	10.00	50.00	—

KM# 126 1/2 KREUZER
Copper **Ruler:** Bernhard II

Date	Mintage	F	VF	XF	Unc	BU
1829	121,000	2.00	4.00	8.00	40.00	—
1830 L	144,000	2.00	4.00	8.00	40.00	—
1831 L	341,000	2.00	4.00	8.00	40.00	—
1832 L	45,000	2.00	4.00	8.00	40.00	—

KM# 162 1/2 KREUZER
Copper **Ruler:** Bernhard II

Date	Mintage	F	VF	XF	Unc	BU
1854	240,000	2.00	4.00	8.00	40.00	—

KM# 96 KREUZER
0.7300 g., 0.1660 Silver .0038 oz. **Ruler:** Bernhard Erich Freund under regency of Louise Eleonore **Obv:** Crowned draped arms, H.S.C. M **Rev:** Value

Date	Mintage	F	VF	XF	Unc	BU
1808	—	3.00	6.00	12.00	60.00	—

KM# 102 KREUZER
0.7300 g., 0.1660 Silver .0038 oz. **Ruler:** Bernhard Erich Freund under regency of Louise Eleonore **Obv:** Drape extends beneath crown

Date	Mintage	F	VF	XF	Unc	BU
1812	307,000	5.00	10.00	20.00	80.00	—

KM# 108 KREUZER
Copper **Ruler:** Bernhard Erich Freund under regency of Louise Eleonore

Date	Mintage	F	VF	XF	Unc	BU
1814	—	5.00	10.00	20.00	70.00	—
1818	90,000	5.00	10.00	20.00	70.00	—

KM# 122 KREUZER
Copper **Ruler:** Bernhard II **Obv:** Crowned rectangular arms **Obv. Legend:** HERZ

Date	Mintage	F	VF	XF	Unc	BU
1828	—	3.00	6.00	12.00	55.00	—
1829	144,000	3.00	6.00	12.00	55.00	—
1830	118,000	3.00	6.00	12.00	55.00	—

KM# 123 KREUZER
0.7300 g., 0.1660 Silver .0038 oz. **Ruler:** Bernhard II **Obv:** Crowned arms dividing S. M

Date	Mintage	F	VF	XF	Unc	BU
1828	211,000	3.00	6.00	12.00	55.00	—
1829	—	3.00	6.00	12.00	55.00	—
1829 L	255,000	3.00	6.00	12.00	55.00	—
1830 L	92,000	3.00	6.00	12.00	55.00	—

KM# 131 KREUZER
Copper **Ruler:** Bernhard II

Date	Mintage	F	VF	XF	Unc	BU
1831	166,000	2.50	5.00	10.00	40.00	—
1832	32,000	2.50	5.00	10.00	40.00	—
1833	104,000	2.50	5.00	10.00	40.00	—
1834	177,000	2.50	5.00	10.00	40.00	—
1835	35,000	2.50	5.00	10.00	40.00	—

KM# 132 KREUZER
0.7300 g., 0.1660 Silver .0038 oz. **Ruler:** Bernhard II **Obv:** Crowned arms within bound branches, L initial

Date	Mintage	F	VF	XF	Unc	BU
1831 L	212,000	2.50	5.00	10.00	50.00	—
1832 L	348,000	2.50	5.00	10.00	50.00	—
1833 L	272,000	2.50	5.00	10.00	50.00	—
1834 L	162,000	2.50	5.00	10.00	50.00	—

KM# 137 KREUZER
0.7300 g., 0.1660 Silver .0038 oz. **Ruler:** Bernhard II **Obv:** K mintmasters initial

Date	Mintage	F	VF	XF	Unc	BU
1835 K	59,000	2.50	5.00	10.00	50.00	—
1836 K	55,000	2.50	5.00	10.00	50.00	—
1837 K	49,000	2.50	5.00	10.00	50.00	—

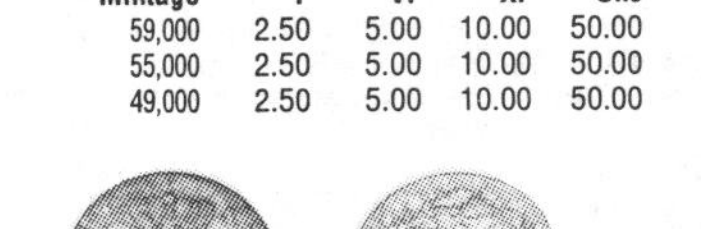

KM# 145 KREUZER
0.8300 g., 0.1660 Silver .0044 oz. **Ruler:** Bernhard II

Date	Mintage	F	VF	XF	Unc	BU
1839	348,000	2.50	5.00	10.00	45.00	—

KM# 153 KREUZER
Copper **Ruler:** Bernhard II **Obv:** Crowned arms within branches **Rev:** Value

Date	Mintage	F	VF	XF	Unc	BU
1842	180,000	2.50	5.00	10.00	40.00	—

KM# 163 KREUZER
Copper **Ruler:** Bernhard II **Obv:** Six-point star below crowned arms

Date	Mintage	F	VF	XF	Unc	BU
1854	202,000	2.50	5.00	10.00	40.00	—

KM# 172 KREUZER
0.8400 g., 0.1650 Silver .0044 oz. **Ruler:** Bernhard II

Date	Mintage	F	VF	XF	Unc	BU
1864	240,000	2.50	5.00	10.00	45.00	—
1866	240,000	2.50	5.00	10.00	45.00	—

KM# 97 3 KREUZER
1.3600 g., 0.3050 Silver .0133 oz. **Ruler:** Bernhard Erich Freund under regency of Louise Eleonore **Obv:** Crowned draped arms

Date	Mintage	F	VF	XF	Unc	BU
1808	—	7.00	12.00	35.00	125	—

KM# 103 3 KREUZER
1.3600 g., 0.3050 Silver .0133 oz. **Ruler:** Bernhard Erich Freund under regency of Louise Eleonore **Obv:** Drape extends beneath crown

Date	Mintage	F	VF	XF	Unc	BU
1812	263,000	4.00	8.00	25.00	100	—
1813	Inc. above	4.00	8.00	25.00	100	—

KM# 117 3 KREUZER
1.3600 g., 0.3050 Silver .0133 oz. **Ruler:** Bernhard II **Obv:** Crowned arms dividing S.M **Rev:** Value

Date	Mintage	F	VF	XF	Unc	BU
1827	171,000	2.50	5.00	10.00	50.00	—
1828	77,000	2.50	5.00	10.00	50.00	—
1829	—	2.50	5.00	10.00	50.00	—

KM# 127 3 KREUZER
1.3600 g., 0.3050 Silver .0133 oz. **Ruler:** Bernhard II **Obv:** L mintmasters initial

Date	Mintage	F	VF	XF	Unc	BU
1829 L	1,263,000	2.50	5.00	10.00	50.00	—
1830 L	533,000	2.50	5.00	10.00	50.00	—

KM# 133 3 KREUZER
1.3600 g., 0.3050 Silver .0133 oz. **Ruler:** Bernhard II

Date	Mintage	F	VF	XF	Unc	BU
1831 L	540,000	2.50	5.00	10.00	50.00	—
1832 L	918,000	2.50	5.00	10.00	50.00	—
1833 L	1,284,000	2.50	5.00	10.00	50.00	—
1834 L	187,000	2.50	5.00	10.00	50.00	—
1835 L	—	2.50	5.00	10.00	50.00	—

KM# 138 3 KREUZER
1.3600 g., 0.3050 Silver .0133 oz. **Ruler:** Bernhard II

Date	Mintage	F	VF	XF	Unc	BU
1835 K	800,000	2.50	5.00	10.00	50.00	—
1836 K	399,000	2.50	5.00	10.00	50.00	—
1837 K	246,000	2.50	5.00	10.00	50.00	—

KM# 150 3 KREUZER
1.2900 g., 0.3330 Silver .0138 oz. **Ruler:** Bernhard II **Obv:** Crowned arms **Obv. Legend:** HERZOGTHUM **Rev:** Value within branches

Date	Mintage	F	VF	XF	Unc	BU
1840	207,000	2.50	5.00	10.00	50.00	—

KM# 98 6 KREUZER
2.4300 g., 0.3330 Silver .0260 oz. **Ruler:** Bernhard Erich Freund under regency of Louise Eleonore **Obv:** Crowned, draped arms **Obv. Legend:** S. COB. MEIN **Rev:** Value within wreath

Date	Mintage	F	VF	XF	Unc	BU
1808	—	15.00	25.00	50.00	150	—
1812	—	15.00	25.00	50.00	150	—
1813	—	15.00	25.00	50.00	150	—

KM# 104 6 KREUZER
2.4300 g., 0.3330 Silver .0260 oz. **Ruler:** Bernhard Erich Freund under regency of Louise Eleonore **Obv:** Drape extends beneath crown

Date	Mintage	F	VF	XF	Unc	BU
1812	87,000	10.00	20.00	40.00	150	—
1813	Inc. above	10.00	20.00	40.00	150	—

KM# 116 6 KREUZER
2.4400 g., 0.3470 Silver .0272 oz. **Ruler:** Bernhard II

Date	Mintage	F	VF	XF	Unc	BU
1826	—	6.00	15.00	25.00	80.00	—
1827	486,000	6.00	15.00	25.00	80.00	—
1828	179,000	6.00	15.00	25.00	80.00	—
1829	—	6.00	15.00	25.00	80.00	—

KM# 124 6 KREUZER
2.4400 g., 0.3470 Silver .0272 oz. **Ruler:** Bernhard II **Obv:** With L mintmasters initial

Date	Mintage	F	VF	XF	Unc	BU
1828 L	—	6.00	15.00	25.00	80.00	—
1829 L	1,513,000	6.00	15.00	25.00	80.00	—
1830 L	747,000	6.00	15.00	25.00	80.00	—

KM# 134 6 KREUZER
2.4400 g., 0.3470 Silver .0272 oz. **Ruler:** Bernhard II

Date	Mintage	F	VF	XF	Unc	BU
1831 L	684,000	3.50	7.00	15.00	60.00	—
1832 L	658,000	3.50	7.00	15.00	60.00	—
1833 L	723,000	3.50	7.00	15.00	60.00	—
1834 L	409,000	3.50	7.00	15.00	60.00	—
1835 L	—	3.50	7.00	15.00	60.00	—

KM# 139 6 KREUZER
2.4400 g., 0.3470 Silver .0272 oz. **Ruler:** Bernhard II **Obv:** With K mintmaster initial

Date	Mintage	F	VF	XF	Unc	BU
1835 K	512,000	3.50	7.00	15.00	60.00	—
1836 K	432,000	3.50	7.00	15.00	60.00	—
1837 K	253,000	3.50	7.00	15.00	60.00	—

KM# 151 6 KREUZER
2.5900 g., 0.3330 Silver .0277 oz. **Ruler:** Bernhard II **Obv:** Crowned arms **Obv. Legend:** HERZOGTHUM **Rev:** Value within branches

Date	Mintage	F	VF	XF	Unc	BU
1840	97,000	5.00	10.00	20.00	75.00	—

KM# 105 20 KREUZER
0.5830 Silver **Ruler:** Bernhard Erich Freund under regency of Louise Eleonore

Date	Mintage	F	VF	XF	Unc	BU
1812	—	—	—	5,000	—	—

KM# 141 1/2 GULDEN
5.3000 g., 0.9000 Silver .1533 oz. **Ruler:** Bernhard II

Date	Mintage	F	VF	XF	Unc	BU
1838	71,000	25.00	55.00	120	265	—
1839	45,000	25.00	55.00	120	265	—
1840	32,000	25.00	55.00	120	265	—
1841	57,000	25.00	55.00	120	265	—

KM# 154 1/2 GULDEN
5.3000 g., 0.9000 Silver .1533 oz. **Ruler:** Bernhard II **Obv:** Different head with HELFRICHT below

Date	Mintage	F	VF	XF	Unc	BU
1843	133,000	22.00	55.00	120	250	—
1846	106,000	22.00	55.00	120	250	—

KM# 164 1/2 GULDEN
5.3000 g., 0.9000 Silver .1533 oz. **Ruler:** Bernhard II

Date	Mintage	F	VF	XF	Unc	BU
1854	108,000	22.00	55.00	120	265	—

KM# 128 GULDEN
11.8000 g., 0.9890 Silver .3752 oz. **Ruler:** Bernhard II

Date	Mintage	F	VF	XF	Unc	BU
1829	2,000	150	275	425	850	—

KM# 130 GULDEN
12.8300 g., 0.7500 Silver .3093 oz. **Ruler:** Bernhard II

Date	Mintage	F	VF	XF	Unc	BU
1830 L	9,118	75.00	150	220	385	—
1831 L	5,511	60.00	110	185	350	—
1832 L	4,688	60.00	110	185	350	—
1833 L	10,000	45.00	90.00	170	300	—

KM# 140 GULDEN
12.8300 g., 0.7500 Silver .3093 oz. **Ruler:** Bernhard II

Date	Mintage	F	VF	XF	Unc	BU
1835 K	2,015	85.00	165	220	450	—
1836 K	2,028	85.00	165	220	450	—
1837 K	2,148	85.00	165	220	450	—

KM# 142 GULDEN
10.6000 g., 0.9000 Silver .3067 oz. **Ruler:** Bernhard II

Date	Mintage	F	VF	XF	Unc	BU
1838	71,000	45.00	90.00	170	285	—
1839	71,000	45.00	90.00	170	285	—
1840	32,000	45.00	90.00	170	285	—
1841	31,000	45.00	90.00	170	285	—

KM# 155 GULDEN
10.6000 g., 0.9000 Silver .3067 oz. **Ruler:** Bernhard II **Obv:** HELFRICHT below bust

Date	Mintage	F	VF	XF	Unc	BU
1843	133,000	45.00	90.00	170	285	—
1846	149,000	45.00	90.00	170	285	—

KM# 165 GULDEN
10.6000 g., 0.9000 Silver .3067 oz. **Ruler:** Bernhard II

Date	Mintage	F	VF	XF	Unc	BU
1854	108,000	50.00	100	185	300	—

KM# 166 2 GULDEN
21.2100 g., 0.9000 Silver .6138 oz. **Ruler:** Bernhard II

Date	Mintage	F	VF	XF	Unc	BU
1854	167,000	65.00	145	285	485	—

KM# 95 THALER
28.0600 g., 0.8330 Silver .7514 oz. **Ruler:** Georg I **Subject:** Death of Georg I **Note:** Convention Thaler. Dav. #2734.

Date	Mintage	F	VF	XF	Unc	BU
ND(1803) L	—	300	600	1,200	2,000	—

KM# 167 THALER
18.5200 g., 0.9000 Silver .5360 oz. **Ruler:** Bernhard II **Obv:** HELFRICHT on truncation

Date	Mintage	F	VF	XF	Unc	BU
1859	40,000	45.00	85.00	175	350	—
1860	40,000	45.00	85.00	175	350	—
1861	40,000	45.00	85.00	175	350	—
1862	40,000	45.00	85.00	175	350	—
1863	40,000	45.00	85.00	175	350	—
1866	40,000	45.00	85.00	175	350	—

KM# 175 THALER
18.5200 g., 0.9000 Silver .5360 oz. **Ruler:** Georg II **Obv:** HELFRICHT on truncation

Date	Mintage	F	VF	XF	Unc	BU
1867	6,644	90.00	175	400	750	—

KM# 152 2 THALER (3-1/2 Gulden)
37.1200 g., 0.9000 Silver 1.0743 oz. **Ruler:** Bernhard II **Obv:** VOIGT below bust

Date	Mintage	F	VF	XF	Unc	BU
1841	12,000	300	600	1,500	2,750	—

KM# 156 2 THALER (3-1/2 Gulden)
37.1200 g., 0.9000 Silver 1.0743 oz. **Ruler:** Bernhard II **Obv:** Similar to KM#152

Date	Mintage	F	VF	XF	Unc	BU
1843	11,000	200	400	850	1,700	—
1846	15,000	200	350	750	1,600	—

KM# 160 2 THALER (3-1/2 Gulden)
37.1200 g., 0.9000 Silver 1.0743 oz. **Ruler:** Bernhard II **Obv:** HELFRICHT below bust **Rev:** Similar to KM#156

Date	Mintage	F	VF	XF	Unc	BU
1853	14,000	200	350	750	1,600	—
1854	14,000	200	350	750	1,600	—

REFORM COINAGE

KM# 190 10 MARK
3.9820 g., 0.9000 Gold .1152 oz. **Ruler:** Georg II

Date	Mintage	F	VF	XF	Unc	BU
1890D	2,000	1,500	2,500	3,000	4,000	5,000
1890D Proof	—	Value: 7,000				
1898D	2,000	1,500	2,500	3,000	4,000	5,000
1898D Proof	—	Value: 7,000				

KM# 180 20 MARK
7.9650 g., 0.9000 Gold .2304 oz. **Ruler:** Georg II **Rev:** Type I

Date	Mintage	F	VF	XF	Unc	BU
1872D	3,000	3,500	6,500	9,000	14,000	18,000
1872D Proof	—	Value: 17,500				

KM# 185 20 MARK
7.9650 g., 0.9000 Gold .2304 oz. **Ruler:** Georg II **Rev:** Type II

Date	Mintage	F	VF	XF	Unc	BU
1882D	3,061	2,500	4,000	5,000	9,000	14,000
1882D Proof	—	Value: 12,500				

KM# 186 20 MARK
7.9650 g., 0.9000 Gold .2304 oz. **Ruler:** Georg II

Date	Mintage	F	VF	XF	Unc	BU
1889D	4,032	2,000	3,500	5,000	7,500	10,000
1889D Proof	—	Value: 10,000				

KM# 195 20 MARK
7.9650 g., 0.9000 Gold .2304 oz. **Ruler:** Georg II **Rev:** Type III

Date	Mintage	F	VF	XF	Unc	BU
1900D	1,005	3,000	5,000	7,500	12,500	15,000
1900D Proof	—	Value: 12,500				

PATTERNS

Including off metal strikes

KM#	Date	Mintage	Identification	Mkt Val
Pn9	ND(1803) L	—	Thaler. Copper. KM#95.	—
Pn10	1881D	—	20 Mark. Copper. Plain edge. KM#185.	—
Pn11	1881D	—	20 Mark. Gold. KM#185.	25,000
Pn12	1900D	—	2 Mark. Silver. KM#196.	2,500
Pn13	1900D	—	5 Mark. Silver.	3,000
Pn14	1900D	—	5 Mark. Silver. KM#197.	3,000
Pn15	ND	—	5 Mark. Silver. KM#200.	—

TRIAL STRIKES

KM#	Date	Mintage	Identification	Mkt Val
TS1	ND	—	20 Mark. Gold. Uniface.	—

SAXE-WEIMAR-EISENACH

(Sachsen-Weimar-Eisenach)

When the death of the duke of Saxe-Eisenach in 1741 heralded the extinction of that line, its possessions reverted to Saxe-Weimar, which henceforth was known as Saxe-Weimar-Eisenach. Because of the strong role played by the duke during the Napoleonic Wars, Saxe-Weimar-Eisenach was raised to the rank of a grand duchy in 1814 and granted the territory of Neustadt, taken from Saxony. The last grand duke abdicated at the end of World War I.

RULERS

Karl Alexander, 1853-1901

MINT OFFICIALS' INITIALS

Initial	Date	Name
(a) lion or ILST or LS or LST or ST	1790-1835	Johann Leonhard Stockmar, mintmaster in Saalfeld
	1835-45	Georg Godecke, mintmaster in Saafeld

DUCHY

REGULAR COINAGE

C# 55c HELLER
Copper

Date	Mintage	F	VF	XF	Unc	BU
1801	—	2.50	7.00	20.00	65.00	—
1813	—	2.50	7.00	20.00	65.00	—

C# 56c PFENNIG
Copper **Rev:** Value and date; line below date

Date	Mintage	F	VF	XF	Unc	BU
1801	—	3.00	8.00	20.00	60.00	—
1801	—	3.00	8.00	20.00	60.00	—
1803	—	3.00	8.00	20.00	60.00	—
1807	30,000	3.00	8.00	20.00	60.00	—

C# 56d PFENNIG
Copper **Rev:** Value and date; 1's in date reveresed, line below date

Date	Mintage	F	VF	XF	Unc	BU
1810	80,000	3.00	8.00	20.00	60.00	—
1813	—	3.00	8.00	20.00	60.00	—

C# 61 PFENNIG
Copper **Rev:** Value and date; line below date

Date	Mintage	F	VF	XF	Unc	BU
1821	100,000	2.00	5.00	10.00	45.00	—
1824	—	2.00	5.00	10.00	45.00	—
1826	—	2.00	5.00	10.00	45.00	—

C# 77 PFENNIG
Copper

Date	Mintage	F	VF	XF	Unc	BU
1830	—	2.50	6.00	12.00	50.00	—

C# 81 PFENNIG
Copper

Date	Mintage	F	VF	XF	Unc	BU
1840A	760,000	2.00	5.00	10.00	45.00	—
1841A	760,000	2.00	5.00	10.00	45.00	—
1844A	361,000	2.00	5.00	10.00	45.00	—
1851A	360,000	2.00	5.00	10.00	45.00	—

C# 89 PFENNIG
Copper **Note:** Denticled border.

Date	Mintage	F	VF	XF	Unc	BU
1858A	720,000	2.00	4.00	8.00	40.00	—
1865A	720,000	2.00	4.00	8.00	40.00	—

C# 57 1-1/2 PFENNIG
Copper

Date	Mintage	F	VF	XF	Unc	BU
1807	34,000	10.00	20.00	35.00	125	—

C# 62 1-1/2 PFENNIG
Copper

Date	Mintage	F	VF	XF	Unc	BU
1824	—	4.00	9.00	20.00	60.00	—

C# 78 1-1/2 PFENNIG
Copper

Date	Mintage	F	VF	XF	Unc	BU
1830	—	4.00	9.00	20.00	60.00	—

C# 58c 2 PFENNIG
Copper

Date	Mintage	F	VF	XF	Unc	BU
1803	—	7.00	15.00	30.00	125	—
1807	36,000	4.00	8.00	22.00	80.00	—

C# 58d 2 PFENNIG
Copper **Edge:** Milled

Date	Mintage	F	VF	XF	Unc	BU
1803	—	7.00	15.00	30.00	125	—
1807	36,000	4.00	8.00	22.00	80.00	—

C# 58e 2 PFENNIG
Copper **Rev:** Similar to C#58c but with rosette below date

Date	Mintage	F	VF	XF	Unc	BU
1813	—	4.00	8.00	22.00	80.00	—

C# 63 2 PFENNIG
Copper **Obv:** Saxon arms; S.W.E. above **Rev:** Value above date; rosette below date

Date	Mintage	F	VF	XF	Unc	BU
1821	68,000	2.50	8.00	12.00	60.00	—
1826	—	2.50	8.00	12.00	60.00	—

C# 79 2 PFENNIG
Copper **Rev:** Line below date

Date	Mintage	F	VF	XF	Unc	BU
1830	—	2.50	8.00	12.00	60.00	—

C# 90 2 PFENNIG
Copper **Note:** Denticled border.

Date	Mintage	F	VF	XF	Unc	BU
1858	—	2.00	4.00	8.00	28.00	—
1865	—	2.00	4.00	8.00	28.00	—

C# 59e 3 PFENNIG
Copper **Rev:** Rosette below date

Date	Mintage	F	VF	XF	Unc	BU
1804	—	4.00	7.00	20.00	65.00	—

C# 59c 3 PFENNIG
Copper **Edge:** Leaf

Date	Mintage	F	VF	XF	Unc	BU
1807	49,000	5.00	10.00	30.00	100	—
1807	49,000	5.00	10.00	30.00	100	—

C# 59d 3 PFENNIG
Copper **Edge:** Reeded

Date	Mintage	F	VF	XF	Unc	BU
1807	Inc. above	4.00	7.00	20.00	65.00	—

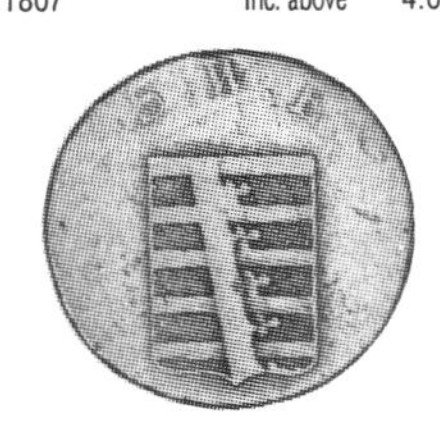

C# 64 3 PFENNIG
Copper **Edge:** Leaf

Date	Mintage	F	VF	XF	Unc	BU
1824	—	2.50	7.00	12.00	50.00	—

C# 64a 3 PFENNIG
Copper **Edge:** Reeded

Date	Mintage	F	VF	XF	Unc	BU
1824	—	2.50	7.00	12.00	50.00	—

C# 80 3 PFENNIG
Copper

Date	Mintage	F	VF	XF	Unc	BU
1830	—	2.50	6.00	12.00	50.00	—

C# 80.1 3 PFENNIG
Copper **Note:** Straight date.

Date	Mintage	F	VF	XF	Unc	BU
1830	—	2.50	5.00	10.00	45.00	—

C# 82 3 PFENNIG
Copper **Obv:** Crowned Saxon arms in circular legend **Rev:** Value above date; SCHEIDE MUNZE above

Date	Mintage	F	VF	XF	Unc	BU
1840A	—	2.50	5.00	10.00	45.00	—

C# 60 4 PFENNIG
Copper **Obv:** Saxon arms; S.W.u. E. above **Rev:** Value above date; without line below date

Date	Mintage	F	VF	XF	Unc	BU
1810	146,000	8.00	15.00	35.00	125	—

C# 60a 4 PFENNIG
Copper **Rev:** Line below date

Date	Mintage	F	VF	XF	Unc	BU
1810	Inc. above	6.00	12.00	30.00	125	—
1812	—	6.00	12.00	30.00	125	—

C# 60b 4 PFENNIG
Copper **Rev:** Rosette below date

Date	Mintage	F	VF	XF	Unc	BU
1813	—	6.00	12.00	30.00	125	—

C# 65 4 PFENNIG
Copper **Edge:** Reeded

Date	Mintage	F	VF	XF	Unc	BU
1821	92,000	5.00	10.00	25.00	110	—
1826	—	5.00	10.00	25.00	110	—

C# 65a 4 PFENNIG
Copper **Edge:** Leaf

Date	Mintage	F	VF	XF	Unc	BU
1821	Inc. above	5.00	10.00	25.00	110	—

C# 85 1/2 GROSCHEN
1.0900 g., 0.2220 Silver .0077 oz. **Obv:** Crowned arms **Rev:** Value

Date	Mintage	F	VF	XF	Unc	BU
1840A	2,400,000	2.00	4.00	8.00	45.00	—

C# 91 1/2 GROSCHEN
1.0900 g., 0.2220 Silver .0077 oz.

Date	Mintage	F	VF	XF	Unc	BU
1858A	300,000	2.50	50.00	10.00	50.00	—

C# 86 GROSCHEN
2.1900 g., 0.2220 Silver .0156 oz.

Date	Mintage	F	VF	XF	Unc	BU
1840A	2,408,000	2.00	4.00	8.00	45.00	—

C# 92 GROSCHEN
2.1900 g., 0.2220 Silver .0156 oz.

Date	Mintage	F	VF	XF	Unc	BU
1858A	300,000	2.50	5.00	10.00	50.00	—

C# 67 1/48 THALER
1.0600 g., 0.2290 Silver .0078 oz.

Date	Mintage	F	VF	XF	Unc	BU
1801	—	3.00	6.00	15.00	50.00	—
1801	—	3.00	6.00	15.00	50.00	—
1804	—	3.00	6.00	15.00	50.00	—
1808	286,000	3.00	6.00	15.00	50.00	—
1810	327,000	3.00	6.00	15.00	50.00	—
1813	—	3.00	6.00	15.00	50.00	—
1814	—	3.00	6.00	15.00	50.00	—

C# 68 1/48 THALER
1.0600 g., 0.2290 Silver .0078 oz. **Obv:** G.H.S.W.E. above arms

Date	Mintage	F	VF	XF	Unc	BU
1815	—	3.00	6.00	15.00	50.00	—

C# 69 1/48 THALER
1.0600 g., 0.2290 Silver .0078 oz. **Obv:** S.W.E. above arms

Date	Mintage	F	VF	XF	Unc	BU
1821	243,000	4.00	8.00	25.00	80.00	—
1824	—	4.00	8.00	25.00	80.00	—
1826	—	4.00	8.00	25.00	80.00	—

C# 83 1/48 THALER
1.0600 g., 0.2290 Silver .0078 oz. **Obv:** Saxon arms with S.W.E. above

Date	Mintage	F	VF	XF	Unc	BU
1831	—	3.00	7.00	20.00	70.00	—

C# 83a 1/48 THALER
1.0600 g., 0.2290 Silver .0078 oz. **Rev:** Reversed 1's in date

Date	Mintage	F	VF	XF	Unc	BU
1831	—	3.00	7.00	20.00	70.00	—

C# 70 1/24 THALER
2.1200 g., 0.2290 Silver .0156 oz. **Obv:** S.W.U.E. above arms **Rev:** Value

Date	Mintage	F	VF	XF	Unc	BU
1801	—	4.00	9.00	28.00	100	—
1801	—	4.00	9.00	28.00	100	—
1804	—	4.00	9.00	28.00	100	—
1808	199,000	4.00	9.00	28.00	100	—
1810	452,000	4.00	9.00	28.00	100	—
1813	—	4.00	9.00	28.00	100	—
1814 small letters	—	4.00	9.00	28.00	90.00	—

C# 71 1/24 THALER
2.1200 g., 0.2290 Silver .0156 oz. **Obv:** G.H.S.W.E. above arms

Date	Mintage	F	VF	XF	Unc	BU
1815	—	10.00	20.00	60.00	185	—

C# 72 1/24 THALER
2.1200 g., 0.2290 Silver .0156 oz. **Obv:** S.W.E. above arms

Date	Mintage	F	VF	XF	Unc	BU
1821	493,000	5.00	10.00	30.00	100	—
1824	—	5.00	10.00	30.00	100	—
1826	—	5.00	10.00	30.00	100	—

C# 72a 1/24 THALER
2.1200 g., 0.2290 Silver .0156 oz. **Rev:** Value: ENIEN

Date	Mintage	F	VF	XF	Unc	BU
1821	Inc. above	—	—	—	—	—

C# 84 1/24 THALER
2.1200 g., 0.2290 Silver .0156 oz. **Rev:** Value: EINEN

Date	Mintage	F	VF	XF	Unc	BU
1830	—	4.00	8.00	25.00	90.00	—

C# 74 1/2 THALER
14.0300 g., 0.8330 Silver .3757 oz. **Note:** Species 1/2 Thaler.

Date	Mintage	F	VF	XF	Unc	BU
1813 FS	—	35.00	75.00	125	300	—

C# 75 THALER
28.6000 g., 0.8330 Silver .7514 oz.

Date	Mintage	F	VF	XF	Unc	BU
1813 LS	—	125	275	600	1,000	—

C# 76 THALER
28.6000 g., 0.8330 Silver .7514 oz.

Date	Mintage	F	VF	XF	Unc	BU
1815	5,273	250	450	900	2,000	—

C# 87 THALER
22.2700 g., 0.7500 Silver .5370 oz.

Date	Mintage	F	VF	XF	Unc	BU
1841A	203,000	40.00	75.00	150	400	—

C# 93 THALER
22.2700 g., 0.7500 Silver .5370 oz. **Note:** Vereins Thaler.

Date	Mintage	F	VF	XF	Unc	BU
1858A	63,000	40.00	75.00	125	250	—
1866A	44,000	40.00	75.00	125	250	—
1870A	45,000	40.00	75.00	125	250	—

C# 88 2 THALER (3-1/2 Gulden)
37.1200 g., 0.9000 Silver 1.0742 oz.

Date	Mintage	F	VF	XF	Unc	BU
1840A	19,000	150	300	600	1,300	—
1842A	38,000	150	300	600	1,300	—
1843A	Inc. above	200	350	700	1,600	—
1848A	19,000	150	300	600	1,300	—

C# 94 2 THALER (3-1/2 Gulden)
37.1200 g., 0.9000 Silver 1.0742 oz. **Rev:** Similar to C#88

Date	Mintage	F	VF	XF	Unc	BU
1855A	19,000	225	400	900	1,750	—

REFORM COINAGE

Y# 168.1 2 MARK
11.1110 g., 0.9000 Silver .3215 oz. **Subject:** Golden Wedding of Carl Alexander

Date	Mintage	F	VF	XF	Unc	BU
1892A	50,000	100	200	350	575	700

Y# 168.2 2 MARK
11.1110 g., 0.9000 Silver .3215 oz. **Subject:** 80th Birthday of the Grand Duke

Date	Mintage	F	VF	XF	Unc	BU
1898A	100,000	75.00	150	325	575	700
1898A Proof	—	Value: 800				

Y# 169 20 MARK
7.9650 g., 0.9000 Gold .2304 oz. **Subject:** Golden Wedding of Carl Alexander

Date	Mintage	F	VF	XF	Unc	BU
1892A	5,000	600	1,000	1,400	2,750	3,250
1892A Proof	—	Value: 5,000				
1896A	15,000	700	1,150	1,600	2,450	2,750
1896A Proof	380	Value: 5,000				

SAXONY

Saxony, located in southeast Germany was founded in 850. The first coinage was struck c. 990. It was divided into two lines in 1464. The electoral right was obtained by the elder line in 1547. During the time of the Reformation, Saxony was one of the more powerful states in central Europe. It became a kingdom in 1806. At the Congress of Vienna in 1815, they were forced to cede half its territories to Prussia.

RULERS
Friedrich August III, 1763-1806
as Friedrich August I, 1806-1827
Anton, 1827-1836
Friedrich August II, 1836-1854
Johann, 1854-1873
Albert, 1873-1902

MINT MARKS
L - Leipzig

MINT OFFICIALS' INITIALS

Dresden Mint

Initial	Date	Name
B	1860-87	Gustav Julius Buschick
C, IC, IEC	1779-1804	Johann Ernst Croll
F	1845-60	Gustav Theodor Fischer
G	1833-44	Johann Georg Grohmann
GS, IGS, S	1812-32	Johann Gotthelf Studer
H, SGH	1804-13	Samuel Gottlieb Helbig

ROYAL DUCHY

Until 1806 when it became a Kingdom

REGULAR COINAGE

KM# 1002.1 HELLER
Copper **Ruler:** Friedrich August III **Obv:** Crowned arms **Rev:** Value above date

Date	Mintage	F	VF	XF	Unc	BU
1801 C	—	2.50	6.00	15.00	45.00	—
1805/705 large H	1,123,000	2.50	6.00	15.00	45.00	—
1805/705 small H	Inc. above	2.50	6.00	15.00	45.00	—
1805 H	—	2.50	6.00	15.00	45.00	—
1806 Rare	7,948	—	—	—	—	—

KM# 1000 PFENNIG
Copper **Ruler:** Friedrich August III **Obv:** Crowned arms **Rev:** Value above date

Date	Mintage	F	VF	XF	Unc	BU
1801 C	—	2.50	5.00	10.00	50.00	—
1804/799 C	—	2.50	5.00	10.00	50.00	—
1804 C	—	2.50	5.00	10.00	50.00	—
1805 H	—	—	—	—	—	—
1805 H/C	—	2.50	5.00	10.00	50.00	—
1806 H/795 C	—	2.50	5.00	10.00	50.00	—
1806 H	—	2.50	5.00	10.00	50.00	—

KM# 1037 3 PFENNIGE
Copper **Ruler:** Friedrich August III

Date	Mintage	F	VF	XF	Unc	BU
1801	—	3.00	6.00	18.00	55.00	—
1802 C	—	3.00	6.00	18.00	55.00	—
1802 C	—	3.00	6.00	18.00	55.00	—
1803 C	2,357,000	3.00	6.00	18.00	55.00	—
1804 SGH	—	3.00	6.00	18.00	55.00	—
1804 large H	—	3.00	6.00	18.00	55.00	—
1804 small H	—	3.00	6.00	18.00	55.00	—
1806 H	—	3.00	6.00	18.00	55.00	—

KM# 966 1/48 THALER (1/2 Groschen)
0.9700 g., 0.2500 Silver .0077 oz. **Ruler:** Friedrich August III **Obv:** Crowned shield within crossed laurel branches **Rev:** Value, date below

Date	Mintage	F	VF	XF	Unc	BU
1802/799	—	6.00	12.00	25.00	80.00	—
1802 C	—	6.00	12.00	25.00	80.00	—
1803 C	—	6.00	12.00	25.00	80.00	—
1803 C	—	6.00	12.00	25.00	80.00	—
1805 H	—	6.00	12.00	25.00	80.00	—
1805/3 H	—	6.00	12.00	25.00	80.00	—
1806/97	—	6.00	12.00	25.00	80.00	—
1806 H	—	6.00	12.00	25.00	80.00	—

KM# 968 1/24 THALER (Groschen)
1.9800 g., 0.3680 Silver .0234 oz. **Ruler:** Friedrich August III **Obv. Legend:** FRID. AVG. . .

Date	Mintage	F	VF	XF	Unc	BU
1801 EDC	—	5.00	12.00	25.00	60.00	—
1802 EDC	—	5.00	12.00	25.00	60.00	—
1806 SGH	—	—	—	—	—	—

KM# 956 1/12 THALER (Doppelgroschen)
3.3400 g., 0.4370 Silver .0469 oz. **Ruler:** Friedrich August III **Obv:** Crowned large oval arms **Rev:** Value above date

Date	Mintage	F	VF	XF	Unc	BU
1765 EDC	—	5.00	10.00	20.00	70.00	—
1800 EDC	—	5.00	10.00	20.00	70.00	—
1801 EDC	—	5.00	10.00	20.00	70.00	—
1802 EDC	—	5.00	10.00	20.00	70.00	—

KM# 1045 1/6 THALER (1/4 Gulden - 15 Kreuzer)
5.3900 g., 0.5410 Silver .0937 oz. **Ruler:** Friedrich August III

Date	Mintage	F	VF	XF	Unc	BU
1803 IEC	—	10.00	20.00	40.00	120	—
1804 IEC	—	10.00	20.00	40.00	120	—
1804 SGH	—	10.00	20.00	40.00	120	—
1805 SGH	—	10.00	20.00	40.00	120	—
1806 SGH	—	10.00	20.00	40.00	120	—

KM# 1024 1/3 THALER (1/2 Gulden - 30 Kreuzer - 8 Groschen)
7.0160 g., 0.8330 Silver .1880 oz. **Ruler:** Friedrich August III **Obv:** Head right **Rev:** Crowned oval arms within crossed branches

Date	Mintage	F	VF	XF	Unc	BU
1801 IEC	—	20.00	40.00	75.00	150	—
1802 IEC	—	20.00	40.00	75.00	150	—

KM# 1025 2/3 THALER (Cosel - Gulden)
14.0310 g., 0.8330 Silver .3760 oz. **Ruler:** Friedrich August III

Date	Mintage	F	VF	XF	Unc	BU
1801 IEC	—	35.00	75.00	150	275	—
1802	—	35.00	75.00	150	275	—
1805 SGH	—	35.00	75.00	150	275	—
1806 SGH	—	35.00	75.00	150	275	—

KM# 1027.2 THALER
28.0630 g., 0.8330 Silver .7520 oz. **Ruler:** Friedrich August III **Obv:** Similar to KM#1034, with date **Rev:** Similar to KM#1027 **Note:** Dav.#2701.

Date	Mintage	F	VF	XF	Unc	BU
1801 IEC	—	35.00	65.00	100	300	—
1802 IEC	—	35.00	65.00	100	300	—
1803 IEC	—	35.00	65.00	100	300	—
1804 IEC	—	35.00	65.00	100	300	—
1804 SGH	—	35.00	65.00	100	300	—
1805 SGH	—	35.00	65.00	100	300	—
1806 SGH	—	35.00	65.00	100	300	—

KM# 1036 THALER
28.0630 g., 0.8330 Silver .7520 oz. **Ruler:** Friedrich August III **Obv:** Head right **Rev:** Crowned oval arms **Rev. Legend:** Ends:. . . DES BERGBAVES **Note:** Dav.#2703.

Date	Mintage	F	VF	XF	Unc	BU
1801 IEC	—	75.00	150	300	600	—
1802 IEC	—	75.00	150	300	600	—
1803 IEC	—	75.00	150	300	600	—
1804 IEC	—	75.00	150	300	600	—
1804 SGH	—	75.00	150	300	600	—
1805 SGH	—	75.00	150	300	600	—
1806 SGH	—	75.00	150	300	600	—

KM# 1053 THALER
28.0630 g., 0.8330 Silver .7520 oz. **Ruler:** Friedrich August III

Date	Mintage	F	VF	XF	Unc	BU
1806 SGH	663,000	750	1,250	2,500	5,000	—

KM# 1028 5 THALER (August D'or)
6.6820 g., 0.9020 Gold .1940 oz. **Obv:** Bust right **Rev:** Crowned arms

Date	Mintage	F	VF	XF	Unc	BU
1801 IEC	—	400	900	1,500	3,000	—
1802 IEC	—	400	900	1,500	3,000	—

KM# 1047 5 THALER (August D'or)
6.6820 g., 0.9020 Gold .1940 oz. **Ruler:** Friedrich August III

Date	Mintage	F	VF	XF	Unc	BU
1805 SGH	—	500	1,000	1,500	3,500	—
1806 SGH	—	500	1,000	1,500	3,500	—

KM# 1029 10 THALER (2 August D'or)
13.3640 g., 0.9020 Gold .3880 oz. **Ruler:** Friedrich August III

Date	Mintage	F	VF	XF	Unc	BU
1801 IEC	—	800	2,000	3,000	5,000	—
1802 IEC	—	800	2,000	3,000	5,000	—
1803 IEC	—	800	2,000	3,000	5,000	—
1804 IEC	—	500	1,100	2,250	4,000	—
1805 IEC	—	600	1,500	2,750	4,000	—
1806 IEC	—	500	1,100	2,250	4,000	—

TRADE COINAGE

KM# 1030 DUCAT
3.5000 g., 0.9860 Gold .1109 oz. **Ruler:** Friedrich August III

Date	Mintage	F	VF	XF	Unc	BU
1801 IEC	—	300	600	1,250	3,000	—
1802 IEC	—	200	400	750	2,000	—
1803 IEC	—	300	600	1,250	3,000	—
1804 IEC	—	250	500	1,000	2,500	—

KM# 1046 DUCAT
3.5000 g., 0.9860 Gold .1109 oz. **Ruler:** Friedrich August III

Date	Mintage	F	VF	XF	Unc	BU
1804 SGH	—	300	700	1,250	2,500	—
1805 SGH	—	350	800	1,500	3,000	—
1806 SGH	—	300	700	1,250	2,500	—

KINGDOM

REGULAR COINAGE

KM# 1072 HELLER
Copper **Ruler:** Friedrich August III as Friedrich August I **Obv:** Crowned arms within branches **Rev:** Value, without legends

Date	Mintage	F	VF	XF	Unc	BU
1813 H	562,000	4.00	7.00	18.00	60.00	—
1813 S	Inc. above	4.00	7.00	18.00	60.00	—

Note: Varieties exist

KM# 1057 PFENNIG
Copper **Ruler:** Friedrich August III as Friedrich August I **Obv:** Crowned arms within branches **Rev:** Value, without legends, pearl borders both sides

Date	Mintage	F	VF	XF	Unc	BU
1807 H	691,000	3.00	7.00	20.00	75.00	—
1807 H/799 C	—	5.00	10.00	25.00	85.00	—
1807/86 H	—	5.00	10.00	25.00	85.00	—
1809/89 H	—	5.00	10.00	25.00	85.00	—

KM# 1062 PFENNIG
Copper **Ruler:** Friedrich August III as Friedrich August I **Obv:** Trefoil border

Date	Mintage	F	VF	XF	Unc	BU
1808 H	14,000	5.00	10.00	25.00	85.00	—

KM# 1070 PFENNIG
Copper **Ruler:** Friedrich August III as Friedrich August I

Date	Mintage	F	VF	XF	Unc	BU
1811 H	1,267,000	2.00	4.00	10.00	75.00	—
1815 S	—	2.00	4.00	10.00	75.00	—
1816 S	—	2.00	4.00	10.00	75.00	—
1822 S	—	2.00	4.00	10.00	75.00	—
1825 S	230,000	2.00	4.00	10.00	75.00	—

KM# 1132 PFENNIG
Copper **Ruler:** Anton

Date	Mintage	F	VF	XF	Unc	BU
1831 S	1,154,000	2.00	4.00	8.00	45.00	—
1832 S	527,000	2.00	4.00	8.00	45.00	—
1833 G	1,152,000	2.00	4.00	8.00	45.00	—

KM# 1135 PFENNIG
Copper **Ruler:** Friedrich August II

Date	Mintage	F	VF	XF	Unc	BU
1836 G	226,000	1.50	3.00	6.00	40.00	—
1837 G	940,000	1.50	3.00	6.00	40.00	—
1838 G	1,473,000	1.50	3.00	6.00	40.00	—

KM# 1155 PFENNIG
Copper **Ruler:** Friedrich August II

Date	Mintage	F	VF	XF	Unc	BU
1841 G	492,000	1.50	3.00	6.00	30.00	—
1842 G	323,000	1.50	3.00	6.00	30.00	—
1843 G	1,115,000	1.50	3.00	6.00	30.00	—
1846 F	450,000	1.50	3.00	6.00	30.00	—
1847 F	546,000	1.50	3.00	6.00	30.00	—
1848 F	1,447,000	1.50	3.00	6.00	30.00	—
1849 F	783,000	1.50	3.00	6.00	30.00	—
1850 F	815,000	1.50	3.00	6.00	30.00	—
1851 F	1,556,000	1.50	3.00	6.00	30.00	—
1852 F	918,000	1.50	3.00	6.00	30.00	—
1853 F	1,164,000	1.50	3.00	6.00	30.00	—
1854 F	548,000	1.50	3.00	6.00	30.00	—

KM# 1184 PFENNIG
Copper **Ruler:** Johann

Date	Mintage	F	VF	XF	Unc	BU
1855 F	657,000	1.50	3.00	6.00	30.00	—
1856 F	3,457,000	1.50	3.00	6.00	30.00	—
1859 F	2,341,000	1.50	3.00	6.00	30.00	—

KM# 1207 PFENNIG
Copper **Ruler:** Johann

Date	Mintage	F	VF	XF	Unc	BU
1861 B	338,000	1.50	3.00	6.00	30.00	—

KM# 1216 PFENNIG

Copper **Ruler:** Johann

Date	Mintage	F	VF	XF	Unc	BU
1862 B	1,094,000	1.50	3.00	6.00	30.00	—
1863 B	4,484,000	1.50	3.00	6.00	30.00	—
1865 B	3,877,000	1.50	3.00	6.00	30.00	—
1866 B	1,129,000	1.50	3.00	6.00	30.00	—
1868 B	2,084,000	1.50	3.00	6.00	30.00	—
1871 B	331,000	1.50	3.00	6.00	30.00	—
1872 B	591,000	1.50	3.00	6.00	30.00	—
1873 B	549,000	1.50	3.00	6.00	30.00	—

KM# 1156 2 PFENNIGE

Copper **Ruler:** Friedrich August II

Date	Mintage	F	VF	XF	Unc	BU
1841 G	1,263,000	2.00	4.00	8.00	40.00	—

KM# 1157 2 PFENNIGE

Copper **Ruler:** Friedrich August II

Date	Mintage	F	VF	XF	Unc	BU
1841 G	Inc. above	1.50	3.00	6.00	40.00	—
1843 G	112,000	1.50	3.00	6.00	40.00	—
1846 F	90,000	1.50	3.00	6.00	40.00	—
1847 F	401,000	1.50	3.00	6.00	40.00	—
1848 F	518,000	1.50	3.00	6.00	40.00	—
1849 F	365,000	1.50	3.00	6.00	40.00	—
1850 F	647,000	1.50	3.00	6.00	40.00	—
1851 F	271,000	1.50	3.00	6.00	40.00	—
1852 F	361,000	1.50	3.00	6.00	40.00	—
1853 F	576,000	1.50	3.00	6.00	40.00	—
1853 F	576,000	1.50	3.00	6.00	40.00	—
1854 F	56,000	2.00	4.00	8.00	45.00	—

KM# 1185 2 PFENNIGE

Copper **Ruler:** Johann

Date	Mintage	F	VF	XF	Unc	BU
1855 F	536,000	1.50	3.00	6.00	40.00	—
1856 F	2,182,000	1.50	3.00	6.00	40.00	—
1859 F	1,103,000	1.50	3.00	6.00	40.00	—

KM# 1208 2 PFENNIGE

Copper **Ruler:** Johann

Date	Mintage	F	VF	XF	Unc	BU
1861 B	163,000	2.00	4.00	8.00	45.00	—

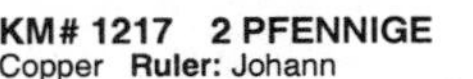

KM# 1217 2 PFENNIGE

Copper **Ruler:** Johann

Date	Mintage	F	VF	XF	Unc	BU
1862 B	739,000	1.25	2.50	5.00	30.00	—
1863 B	456,000	1.25	2.50	5.00	30.00	—
1864 B	3,139,000	1.25	2.50	5.00	30.00	—
1866 B	551,000	1.25	2.50	5.00	30.00	—
1869 B	2,220,000	1.25	2.50	5.00	30.00	—
1873 B	262,000	1.50	3.00	6.00	35.00	—

KM# 1058 3 PFENNIGE

Copper **Ruler:** Friedrich August III as Friedrich August I

Date	Mintage	F	VF	XF	Unc	BU
1807 H	317,000	4.00	8.00	22.00	70.00	—
1808 H	295,000	4.00	8.00	22.00	70.00	—
1809 H	4,800	15.00	30.00	60.00	125	—
1811 H	128,000	4.00	8.00	22.00	70.00	—
1812 H	96,000	4.00	8.00	22.00	70.00	—
1814 S	211,000	4.00	8.00	22.00	70.00	—
1815 S	432,000	4.00	8.00	22.00	70.00	—
1822 S	—	4.00	8.00	22.00	70.00	—
1823 S	19,000	4.00	8.00	22.00	70.00	—
1824 S	123,000	4.00	8.00	22.00	70.00	—

KM# 1100 3 PFENNIGE

Copper **Ruler:** Friedrich August III as Friedrich August I **Obv:** Crowned arched arms **Rev:** Value: 3 PFENNIGE

Date	Mintage	F	VF	XF	Unc	BU
1825 S	168,000	4.00	8.00	22.00	75.00	—
1826 S	31,000	5.00	10.00	25.00	80.00	—
1831 S	77,000	5.00	10.00	18.00	65.00	—
1832 S	226,000	3.00	6.00	12.00	50.00	—
1833 G	69,000	4.00	8.00	18.00	65.00	—

KM# 1134 3 PFENNIGE

Copper **Ruler:** Anton **Obv. Legend:** KOEN. SAECHS.

Date	Mintage	F	VF	XF	Unc	BU
1834 G	500,000	3.00	6.00	12.00	40.00	—

KM# 1136 3 PFENNIGE

Copper **Ruler:** Friedrich August II

Date	Mintage	F	VF	XF	Unc	BU
1836 G	39,000	5.00	10.00	20.00	70.00	—
1837 G	542,000	3.00	6.00	12.00	50.00	—

KM# 1064 4 PFENNIGE

Copper **Ruler:** Friedrich August III as Friedrich August I

Date	Mintage	F	VF	XF	Unc	BU
1808 H	1,548,000	6.00	12.50	30.00	100	—
1809/6 H	1,059,000	6.00	12.50	30.00	100	—
1809/8 H	Inc. above	6.00	12.50	30.00	100	—
1809 H	Inc. above	6.00	12.50	30.00	100	—
1810 H	886,000	6.00	12.50	30.00	100	—

KM# 1218 5 PFENNIGE

Copper **Ruler:** Johann

Date	Mintage	F	VF	XF	Unc	BU
1862 B	2,468,000	1.50	3.00	6.00	40.00	—
1863 B	693,000	1.50	3.00	6.00	40.00	—
1864 B	1,090,000	1.50	3.00	6.00	40.00	—
1864 B	1,090,000	1.50	3.00	6.00	40.00	—
1866 B	141,000	1.50	3.00	6.00	40.00	—
1867 B	444,000	1.50	3.00	6.00	40.00	—
1869 B	860,000	1.50	3.00	6.00	40.00	—
1869 B	860,000	1.50	3.00	6.00	40.00	—

KM# 1065 8 PFENNIGE

1.2900 g., 0.2500 Silver .0103 oz. **Ruler:** Friedrich August III as Friedrich August I

Date	Mintage	F	VF	XF	Unc	BU
1808 H	2,594,000	4.00	8.00	20.00	60.00	—
1809 H	4,722,000	4.00	8.00	20.00	60.00	—

KM# 1158 1/2 NEU-GROSCHEN (5 Pfennig)

1.0600 g., 0.2290 Silver .0078 oz. **Ruler:** Friedrich August II

Date	Mintage	F	VF	XF	Unc	BU
1841 G	2,248,000	1.50	3.00	5.00	25.00	—
1842 G	2,845,000	1.50	3.00	5.00	25.00	—
1843 G	3,552,000	1.50	3.00	5.00	25.00	—
1844 G	1,354,000	1.50	3.00	5.00	25.00	—
1848 F	500,000	1.50	3.00	5.00	25.00	—
1849 F	579,000	1.50	3.00	5.00	25.00	—
1851 F	506,000	1.50	3.00	5.00	25.00	—
1852 F	497,000	1.50	3.00	5.00	25.00	—
1853 F	256,000	2.00	4.00	6.00	35.00	—
1854 F	107,000	2.00	4.00	6.00	35.00	—
1855 F	444,000	2.00	3.00	5.00	45.00	—
1856 F	713,000	2.00	3.00	5.00	45.00	—

KM# 1159 NEU-GROSCHEN (10 Pfennig)

2.1200 g., 0.2290 Silver .0156 oz. **Ruler:** Friedrich August II

Date	Mintage	F	VF	XF	Unc	BU
1841 G	4,500,000	1.50	3.00	6.00	40.00	—
1842 G	2,463,000	1.50	3.00	6.00	40.00	—
1845 G	457,000	1.50	3.00	6.00	40.00	—
1846 F	1,656,000	1.50	3.00	6.00	40.00	—
1847 F	1,532,000	1.50	3.00	6.00	40.00	—
1848 F	105,000	1.50	3.00	6.00	40.00	—
1849 F	1,049,000	1.50	3.00	6.00	40.00	—
1850 F	505,000	1.50	3.00	6.00	40.00	—
1851 F	676,000	1.50	3.00	6.00	40.00	—
1852 F	949,000	1.50	3.00	6.00	40.00	—
1853 F	798,000	1.50	3.00	6.00	40.00	—
1854 F	443,000	1.50	3.00	6.00	40.00	—
1855 F	1,106,000	2.00	3.50	6.00	35.00	—
1856 F	1,188,000	2.00	3.50	6.00	35.00	—

KM# 1209 NEU-GROSCHEN (10 Pfennig)
2.1200 g., 0.2300 Silver .0156 oz. **Ruler:** Johann **Rev:** B below value

Date	Mintage	F	VF	XF	Unc	BU
1861 B	395,000	2.50	5.00	7.50	45.00	—

KM# 1219 NEU-GROSCHEN (10 Pfennig)
2.1200 g., 0.2300 Silver .0156 oz. **Ruler:** Johann

Date	Mintage	F	VF	XF	Unc	BU
1863 B	1,514,000	1.50	3.00	5.00	30.00	—
1865 B	557,000	2.00	4.00	6.00	35.00	—
1867 B	296,000	2.00	4.00	6.00	35.00	—

KM# 1221 NEU-GROSCHEN (10 Pfennig)
2.1200 g., 0.2300 Silver .0156 oz. **Ruler:** Johann

Date	Mintage	F	VF	XF	Unc	BU
1867 B	897,000	2.00	4.00	8.00	40.00	—
1868 B	608,000	2.00	4.00	8.00	40.00	—
1870 B	908,000	2.00	4.00	8.00	40.00	—
1871 B	293,000	2.00	4.00	8.00	40.00	—
1873 B	420,000	2.00	4.00	8.00	40.00	—

KM# 1160 2 NEU-GROSCHEN (20 Pfennig)
3.1100 g., 0.3120 Silver .0311 oz. **Ruler:** Friedrich August II

Date	Mintage	F	VF	XF	Unc	BU
1841 G	3,125,000	1.50	3.00	6.00	40.00	—
1842 G	1,413,000	1.50	3.00	6.00	40.00	—
1844 G	1,477,000	1.50	3.00	6.00	40.00	—
1846 F	516,000	1.50	3.00	6.00	40.00	—
1847 F	425,000	1.50	3.00	6.00	40.00	—
1848 F	1,062,000	1.50	3.00	6.00	40.00	—
1849 F	656,000	1.50	3.00	6.00	40.00	—
1850 F	380,000	1.50	3.00	6.00	40.00	—
1851 F	588,000	1.50	3.00	6.00	40.00	—
1852 F	974,000	1.50	3.00	6.00	40.00	—
1853 F	604,000	1.50	3.00	6.00	40.00	—
1854 F	790,000	1.50	3.00	6.00	40.00	—
1855 F	921,000	2.50	5.00	10.00	60.00	—
1856 F	2,207,000	2.50	5.00	10.00	60.00	—

KM# 1220 2 NEU-GROSCHEN (20 Pfennig)
3.2200 g., 0.3000 Silver .0310 oz. **Ruler:** Johann

Date	Mintage	F	VF	XF	Unc	BU
1863 B	557,000	2.50	5.00	10.00	50.00	—
1864 B	447,000	2.50	5.00	10.00	50.00	—
1865 B	371,000	2.50	5.00	10.00	50.00	—
1865 B	371,000	2.50	5.00	10.00	50.00	—
1866 B	448,000	2.50	5.00	10.00	50.00	—

KM# 1222 2 NEU-GROSCHEN (20 Pfennig)
3.2200 g., 0.3000 Silver .0310 oz. **Ruler:** Johann

Date	Mintage	F	VF	XF	Unc	BU
1868 B	419,000	4.00	8.00	15.00	55.00	—
1869 B	599,000	4.00	8.00	15.00	55.00	—
1871 B	245,000	4.00	8.00	15.00	55.00	—
1873 B	468,000	4.00	8.00	15.00	55.00	—

KM# 1048 1/48 THALER (1/2 Groschen)
0.9700 g., 0.2500 Silver .0077 oz. **Ruler:** Friedrich August III as Friedrich August I

Date	Mintage	F	VF	XF	Unc	BU
1806 H	—	4.00	9.00	20.00	75.00	—
1806/797 H	—	6.00	12.00	30.00	100	—
1807 H	2,990,000	4.00	9.00	20.00	75.00	—
1808 H	1,816,000	4.00	9.00	20.00	75.00	—
1811/01 H	4,242,000	6.00	12.00	30.00	100	—
1811 H	Inc. above	4.00	9.00	20.00	75.00	—
1812 H	5,382,000	4.00	9.00	20.00	75.00	—
1812 S	Inc. above	4.00	9.00	20.00	75.00	—
1813 H	730,000	4.00	9.00	20.00	75.00	—
1813 H	730,000	4.00	9.00	20.00	75.00	—
1813 S	Inc. above	4.00	9.00	20.00	75.00	—
1814 S	2,871,000	4.00	9.00	20.00	75.00	—
1815 S	1,059,000	4.00	9.00	20.00	75.00	—

KM# 1075 1/24 THALER (Groschen)
1.9800 g., 0.3680 Silver .0234 oz. **Ruler:** Friedrich August III as Friedrich August I

Date	Mintage	F	VF	XF	Unc	BU
1816 IGS	146,000	4.00	8.00	20.00	55.00	—
1817 IGS	252,000	4.00	8.00	20.00	55.00	—
1818 IGS	166,000	4.00	8.00	20.00	55.00	—

KM# 1082.1 1/24 THALER (Groschen)
1.9800 g., 0.3680 Silver .0234 oz. **Ruler:** Friedrich August III as Friedrich August I **Obv. Legend:** FRIED. . .

Date	Mintage	F	VF	XF	Unc	BU
1819 IGS	337,000	5.00	10.00	22.00	60.00	—
1820 IGS	268,000	5.00	10.00	22.00	60.00	—
1821 IGS	321,000	5.00	10.00	22.00	60.00	—
1822 IGS	439,000	5.00	10.00	22.00	60.00	—

KM# 1082.2 1/24 THALER (Groschen)
1.9800 g., 0.3680 Silver .0234 oz. **Ruler:** Friedrich August III as Friedrich August I **Obv. Legend:** FRIEDR. . .

Date	Mintage	F	VF	XF	Unc	BU
1823 IGS	368,000	5.00	10.00	22.00	60.00	—

KM# 1094 1/24 THALER (Groschen)
1.9800 g., 0.3680 Silver .0234 oz. **Ruler:** Friedrich August III as Friedrich August I **Obv:** Crowned arched arms

Date	Mintage	F	VF	XF	Unc	BU
1824 S	332,000	4.00	8.00	20.00	55.00	—
1825 S	262,000	4.00	8.00	20.00	55.00	—
1826 S	311,000	4.00	8.00	20.00	55.00	—
1827 S	67,000	5.00	10.00	22.00	60.00	—

KM# 1105 1/24 THALER (Groschen)
1.9800 g., 0.3680 Silver .0234 oz. **Ruler:** Anton **Obv:** Crowned arched arms within crossed branches

Date	Mintage	F	VF	XF	Unc	BU
1827 S	66,000	7.00	15.00	30.00	90.00	—
1828 S	100,000	7.00	15.00	30.00	90.00	—

KM# 1049.1 1/12 THALER (Doppelgroschen)
3.3400 g., 0.4370 Silver .0469 oz. **Ruler:** Friedrich August III as Friedrich August I

Date	Mintage	F	VF	XF	Unc	BU
1806 SGH	37,000	6.00	12.00	25.00	90.00	—
1807 SGH	38,000	6.00	12.00	25.00	90.00	—
1808 SGH	140,000	5.00	10.00	20.00	75.00	—
1809 SGH	1,071,000	5.00	10.00	20.00	75.00	—
1810 SGH	515,000	5.00	10.00	20.00	75.00	—
1811 SGH	—	5.00	10.00	20.00	75.00	—
1811 SGH	—	5.00	10.00	20.00	75.00	—
1812 IGS	5,172,000	5.00	10.00	20.00	75.00	—
1812 SGH	Inc. above	5.00	10.00	20.00	75.00	—
1813 IGS	2,055,000	5.00	10.00	20.00	75.00	—
1813 SGH	Inc. above	5.00	10.00	20.00	75.00	—
1814 IGS	63,000	6.00	12.00	25.00	90.00	—
1816 IGS	—	5.00	10.00	20.00	75.00	—
1817 IGS	—	5.00	10.00	20.00	75.00	—
1818 IGS	—	5.00	10.00	20.00	75.00	—

KM# 1049.2 1/12 THALER (Doppelgroschen)
3.3400 g., 0.4370 Silver .0469 oz. **Obv. Legend:** (error): FRID VGVST. . .

Date	Mintage	F	VF	XF	Unc	BU
1809 SGH	Inc. above	5.00	10.00	20.00	75.00	—

KM# 1083.1 1/12 THALER (Doppelgroschen)
3.3400 g., 0.4370 Silver .0469 oz. **Ruler:** Friedrich August III as Friedrich August I **Obv. Legend:** FRIED. . .

Date	Mintage	F	VF	XF	Unc	BU
1819 IGS	—	5.00	10.00	20.00	70.00	—
1820 IGS	—	5.00	10.00	20.00	70.00	—
1820 IGS	—	5.00	10.00	20.00	70.00	—
1821 IGS	—	5.00	10.00	20.00	70.00	—
1822 IGS	—	5.00	10.00	20.00	70.00	—
1823 IGS	1,624,000	5.00	10.00	20.00	70.00	—

KM# 1083.2 1/12 THALER (Doppelgroschen)
3.3400 g., 0.4370 Silver .0469 oz. **Ruler:** Friedrich August III as Friedrich August I **Obv. Legend:** FRIEDR. . .

Date	Mintage	F	VF	XF	Unc	BU
1823 IGS	Inc. above	5.00	10.00	20.00	70.00	—

KM# 1095 1/12 THALER (Doppelgroschen)
3.3400 g., 0.4370 Silver .0469 oz. **Ruler:** Friedrich August III as Friedrich August I **Obv:** Crowned arched arms

Date	Mintage	F	VF	XF	Unc	BU
1824 S	2,470,000	4.00	8.00	18.00	50.00	—
1825 S	1,721,000	4.00	8.00	18.00	50.00	—
1826 S	763,000	4.00	8.00	18.00	50.00	—
1826 S	—	4.00	8.00	18.00	50.00	—
1827 S	564,000	4.00	8.00	18.00	50.00	—

KM# 1106 1/12 THALER (Doppelgroschen)
3.3400 g., 0.4370 Silver .0469 oz. **Ruler:** Anton **Obv:** Crowned arched arms within crossed branches

Date	Mintage	F	VF	XF	Unc	BU
1827 S	60,000	5.00	10.00	20.00	70.00	—
1828 S	256,000	4.00	8.00	18.00	50.00	—

KM# 1117 1/12 THALER (Doppelgroschen)
3.3400 g., 0.4370 Silver .0469 oz. **Ruler:** Anton

Date	Mintage	F	VF	XF	Unc	BU
1829 S	1,431,000	4.00	8.00	18.00	50.00	—
1830 S	1,684,000	4.00	8.00	18.00	50.00	—
1831 S	206,000	4.00	8.00	18.00	50.00	—
1832 S	882,000	4.00	8.00	18.00	50.00	—

KM# 1137 1/12 THALER (Doppelgroschen)
3.3400 g., 0.4370 Silver .0469 oz. **Ruler:** Anton

Date	Mintage	F	VF	XF	Unc	BU
1836 G	690,000	5.00	10.00	20.00	65.00	—

KM# 1050 1/6 THALER (1/4 Gulden - 15 Kreuzer)
5.3900 g., 0.5410 Silver .0937 oz. **Ruler:** Friedrich August III as Friedrich August I

Date	Mintage	F	VF	XF	Unc	BU
1806 SGH	18,000	15.00	25.00	50.00	150	—
1807 SGH	317,000	8.00	16.00	35.00	115	—
1808 SGH	2,421,000	8.00	16.00	35.00	115	—
1809 SGH	3,608,000	8.00	16.00	35.00	115	—
1810 SGH	2,405,000	8.00	16.00	35.00	115	—
1813 SGH	229,000	8.00	16.00	35.00	115	—
1813 IGS	—	8.00	16.00	35.00	115	—
1817 IGS	119,000	8.00	16.00	35.00	115	—

KM# 1101 1/6 THALER (1/4 Gulden - 15 Kreuzer)
5.3400 g., 0.5210 Silver .0894 oz. **Ruler:** Friedrich August III as Friedrich August I

Date	Mintage	F	VF	XF	Unc	BU
1825 GS	68,000	15.00	30.00	60.00	150	—

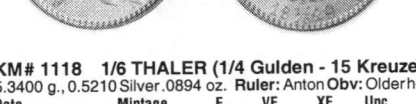

KM# 1107 1/6 THALER (1/4 Gulden - 15 Kreuzer)
5.3400 g., 0.5210 Silver .0894 oz. **Ruler:** Friedrich August III as Friedrich August I **Subject:** Death of King Friedrich August

Date	Mintage	F	VF	XF	Unc	BU
1827 S	48,000	7.00	15.00	30.00	60.00	—

KM# 1108 1/6 THALER (1/4 Gulden - 15 Kreuzer)
5.3400 g., 0.5210 Silver .0894 oz. **Ruler:** Anton **Rev:** Crowned arched arms within crossed branches

Date	Mintage	F	VF	XF	Unc	BU
1827 S	19,000	25.00	50.00	100	200	—
1828 S	18,000	25.00	50.00	100	200	—
1828 S	18,000	25.00	50.00	100	200	—

KM# 1118 1/6 THALER (1/4 Gulden - 15 Kreuzer)
5.3400 g., 0.5210 Silver .0894 oz. **Ruler:** Anton **Obv:** Older head

Date	Mintage	F	VF	XF	Unc	BU
1829 S	124,000	20.00	40.00	80.00	200	—

KM# 1138 1/6 THALER (1/4 Gulden - 15 Kreuzer)
5.3400 g., 0.5210 Silver .0894 oz. **Ruler:** Anton **Subject:** Death of King Anton

Date	Mintage	F	VF	XF	Unc	BU
1836 G	46,000	15.00	30.00	60.00	125	—

KM# 1161 1/6 THALER (1/4 Gulden - 15 Kreuzer)
5.3400 g., 0.5210 Silver .0894 oz. **Ruler:** Friedrich August II

Date	Mintage	F	VF	XF	Unc	BU
1841 G	450,000	6.00	12.00	30.00	90.00	—
1842 G	1,322,000	6.00	12.00	30.00	90.00	—
1843 G	655,000	6.00	12.00	30.00	90.00	—
1846 F	601,000	6.00	12.00	30.00	90.00	—
1847 F	366,000	6.00	12.00	30.00	90.00	—
1848 F	270,000	6.00	12.00	30.00	90.00	—
1849 F	449,000	6.00	12.00	30.00	90.00	—
1850 F	134,000	6.00	12.00	30.00	90.00	—

KM# 1176 1/6 THALER (1/4 Gulden - 15 Kreuzer)
5.3400 g., 0.5210 Silver .0894 oz. **Ruler:** Friedrich August II

Date	Mintage	F	VF	XF	Unc	BU
1851 F	228,000	6.00	12.00	30.00	90.00	—
1852 F	340,000	6.00	12.00	30.00	90.00	—

KM# 1178 1/6 THALER (1/4 Gulden - 15 Kreuzer)
5.3400 g., 0.5210 Silver .0894 oz. **Ruler:** Friedrich August II **Subject:** Death of King Kriedrich August II **Obv. Legend:** D.9.AUG. 1854 below head **Rev:** ER SAEETE. . . in sprays

Date	Mintage	F	VF	XF	Unc	BU
1854 F	521,000	5.00	10.00	25.00	85.00	—

KM# 1186 1/6 THALER (1/4 Gulden - 15 Kreuzer)
5.3400 g., 0.5210 Silver .0894 oz. **Ruler:** Johann

Date	Mintage	F	VF	XF	Unc	BU
1855 F	476,000	6.00	12.00	30.00	110	—
1856 F	1,529,000	5.00	10.00	25.00	100	—

KM# 1205 1/6 THALER (1/4 Gulden - 15 Kreuzer)
5.3420 g., 0.5200 Silver .0893 oz. **Ruler:** Johann

Date	Mintage	F	VF	XF	Unc	BU
1860 B	871,000	4.00	8.00	17.50	60.00	—
1860 F	52,000	6.00	12.50	25.00	100	—
1861 B	1,099,000	4.00	8.00	17.50	60.00	—
1863 B	589,000	4.00	8.00	17.50	60.00	—
1864 B	161,000	4.00	8.00	17.50	60.00	—
1865 B	683,000	4.00	8.00	17.50	60.00	—
1866/5 B	475,000	4.00	8.00	17.50	65.00	—
1866 B	Inc. above	4.00	8.00	15.00	60.00	—
1869 B	626,000	4.00	8.00	15.00	60.00	—
1870 B	280,000	4.00	8.00	15.00	60.00	—
1871 B	293,000	4.00	8.00	15.00	60.00	—
1871 B	293,000	4.00	8.00	15.00	60.00	—

KM# 1051.1 1/3 THALER (1/2 Gulden - 30 Kreuzer - 8 Groschen)
7.0160 g., 0.8330 Silver .1880 oz. **Ruler:** Friedrich August III as Friedrich August I **Rev. Legend:** VIERZIG EINE FEINE MARK

Date	Mintage	F	VF	XF	Unc	BU
1806 SGH	27,000	40.00	80.00	125	225	—
1808 SGH	277,000	20.00	45.00	80.00	160	—
1809 SGH	303,000	20.00	45.00	80.00	160	—
1810 SGH	295,000	20.00	45.00	80.00	160	—
1811 SGH	278,000	20.00	45.00	80.00	160	—
1812 SGH	80,000	30.00	60.00	100	175	—
1815 IGS	5,740,000	60.00	120	200	325	—
1816 IGS	9,049	50.00	100	160	275	—
1817 IGS	8,929	50.00	100	160	275	—

KM# 1051.2 1/3 THALER (1/2 Gulden - 30 Kreuzer - 8 Groschen)
7.0160 g., 0.8330 Silver .1880 oz. **Ruler:** Friedrich August III as Friedrich August I **Rev. Legend:** "FEIN"

Date	Mintage	F	VF	XF	Unc	BU
1808	Inc. above	30.00	60.00	90.00	175	—

KM# 1051.3 1/3 THALER (1/2 Gulden - 30 Kreuzer - 8 Groschen)
7.0160 g., 0.8330 Silver .1880 oz. **Ruler:** Friedrich August III as Friedrich August I **Rev. Legend:** "ACHTZIG"

Date	Mintage	F	VF	XF	Unc	BU
1808	Inc. above	40.00	85.00	135	225	—

KM# 1079 1/3 THALER (1/2 Gulden - 30 Kreuzer - 8 Groschen)
7.0160 g., 0.8330 Silver .1880 oz. **Ruler:** Friedrich August III as Friedrich August I

Date	Mintage	F	VF	XF	Unc	BU
1818 IGS	19,000	40.00	80.00	150	250	—
1821 IGS	—	40.00	80.00	150	250	—

KM# 1109 1/3 THALER (1/2 Gulden - 30 Kreuzer - 8 Groschen)
8.2540 g., 0.7080 Silver .1880 oz. **Ruler:** Anton **Obv:** Head right **Rev:** Crowned arched arms within crossed branches

Date	Mintage	F	VF	XF	Unc	BU
1827 S	8,700	50.00	100	200	350	—
1828 S	10,000	50.00	100	200	350	—
1829 S	21,000	35.00	70.00	150	300	—
1830 S	97,000	35.00	70.00	150	300	—

KM# 1177 1/3 THALER (1/2 Gulden - 30 Kreuzer - 8 Groschen)
8.3520 g., 0.6670 Silver .1790 oz. **Ruler:** Friedrich August II

Date	Mintage	F	VF	XF	Unc	BU
1852 F	194,000	15.00	30.00	60.00	125	—
1853 F	403,000	15.00	30.00	60.00	125	—
1853 F	403,000	15.00	30.00	60.00	125	—
1854 F	1,156,000	15.00	30.00	60.00	125	—

KM# 1179 1/3 THALER (1/2 Gulden - 30 Kreuzer - 8 Groschen)
8.3520 g., 0.6670 Silver .1790 oz. **Ruler:** Friedrich August II **Subject:** Death of King Friedrich August II

Date	Mintage	F	VF	XF	Unc	BU
1854 F	29,000	20.00	40.00	80.00	125	—

KM# 1191 1/3 THALER (1/2 Gulden - 30 Kreuzer - 8 Groschen)
8.3520 g., 0.6670 Silver .1790 oz. **Ruler:** Johann **Obv:** Head right **Rev:** Crowned draped rectangular arms

Date	Mintage	F	VF	XF	Unc	BU
1856 F	308,000	25.00	50.00	100	175	—

KM# 1198 1/3 THALER (1/2 Gulden - 30 Kreuzer - 8 Groschen)
8.3000 g., 0.6670 Silver .1784 oz. **Ruler:** Johann

Date	Mintage	F	VF	XF	Unc	BU
1858 F	326,000	20.00	40.00	80.00	150	—
1859 F	617,000	20.00	40.00	80.00	150	—

KM# 1206 1/3 THALER (1/2 Gulden - 30 Kreuzer - 8 Groschen)
8.3000 g., 0.6670 Silver .1784 oz. **Ruler:** Johann

Date	Mintage	F	VF	XF	Unc	BU
1860 B	345,000	17.50	35.00	70.00	125	—

KM# 1052 2/3 THALER (Cosel - Gulden)
14.0310 g., 0.8330 Silver .3760 oz. **Ruler:** Friedrich August III as Friedrich August I

Date	Mintage	F	VF	XF	Unc	BU
1806 SGH	84,000	35.00	70.00	140	275	—
1807 SGH	75,000	35.00	70.00	140	275	—
1808 SGH	171,000	35.00	70.00	140	275	—
1809 SGH	165,000	35.00	70.00	140	275	—
1810 SGH	165,000	35.00	70.00	140	275	—
1811 SGH	161,000	35.00	70.00	140	275	—
1812 SGH	86,000	35.00	70.00	140	275	—
1813 IGS	—	35.00	70.00	140	275	—
1814 IGS	25,000	35.00	70.00	140	275	—
1815 IGS	48,000	35.00	70.00	140	275	—
1816 IGS	55,000	35.00	70.00	140	275	—
1817 IGS	60,000	35.00	70.00	140	275	—

KM# 1090 2/3 THALER (Cosel - Gulden)
14.0310 g., 0.8330 Silver .3760 oz. **Ruler:** Friedrich August III as Friedrich August I

Date	Mintage	F	VF	XF	Unc	BU
1822 IGS	23,000	60.00	125	250	450	—

KM# 1110 2/3 THALER (Cosel - Gulden)
14.0310 g., 0.8330 Silver .3760 oz. **Ruler:** Anton

Date	Mintage	F	VF	XF	Unc	BU
1827 S	11,000	50.00	100	200	400	—
1828 S	12,000	50.00	100	200	400	—

KM# 1119 2/3 THALER (Cosel - Gulden)
14.0310 g., 0.8330 Silver .3760 oz. **Ruler:** Anton **Obv:** Different head right

Date	Mintage	F	VF	XF	Unc	BU
1829 S	13,000	60.00	125	250	450	—

KM# 1059.1 THALER
28.0630 g., 0.8330 Silver .7520 oz. **Ruler:** Friedrich August III as Friedrich August I **Obv:** Small bust

Date	Mintage	F	VF	XF	Unc	BU
1807 SGH	461,000	35.00	60.00	100	225	—
1808 SGH	1,534,000	35.00	60.00	100	225	—
1809 SGH	563,000	35.00	60.00	100	225	—
1810 SGH	368,000	35.00	60.00	100	225	—
1811 SGH	395,000	35.00	60.00	100	225	—
1812 SGH	134,000	35.00	60.00	100	225	—
1813 IGS	773,000	35.00	60.00	100	225	—
1813 (error)ENIE	—	100	130	200	300	—
1813 SGH	Inc. above	35.00	60.00	100	225	—
1815 IGS	510,000	35.00	60.00	150	225	—
1816 IGS	—	35.00	60.00	100	225	—
1817 IGS	—	35.00	60.00	125	250	—

KM# 1061 THALER
28.0630 g., 0.8330 Silver .7520 oz. **Ruler:** Friedrich August III as Friedrich August I

Date	Mintage	F	VF	XF	Unc	BU
1807 SGH	—	75.00	150	400	800	—
1808 SGH	—	75.00	150	400	800	—
1809 SGH	—	75.00	150	400	800	—
1810 SGH	—	75.00	150	400	800	—
1811 SGH	—	75.00	150	400	800	—
1812 SGH	—	75.00	150	400	800	—
1813 SGH	—	75.00	150	400	800	—
1813 IGS	—	40.00	80.00	150	300	—
CD1815 IGS	—	40.00	80.00	150	300	—
1816 IGS	—	40.00	80.00	150	300	—
1817 IGS	—	200	300	600	1,250	—

KM# 1060 THALER
28.0630 g., 0.8330 Silver .7520 oz. **Ruler:** Friedrich August III as Friedrich August I **Note:** Mining Thaler.

Date	Mintage	F	VF	XF	Unc	BU
1807 SGH	—	75.00	175	400	800	—

KM# 1071 THALER
28.0630 g., 0.8330 Silver .7520 oz. **Ruler:** Friedrich August III as Friedrich August I **Rev:** Legend right to left

Date	Mintage	F	VF	XF	Unc	BU
1811 SGH	—	75.00	150	400	800	—
1811 IGS	—	75.00	150	400	800	—
1813 SGH	—	75.00	150	400	800	—
1813 IGS	—	75.00	150	400	800	—
1815 IGS	—	75.00	150	400	800	—
1816 IGS	—	75.00	150	400	800	—

KM# 1074 THALER
28.0630 g., 0.8330 Silver .7520 oz. **Ruler:** Friedrich August III as Friedrich August I **Subject:** Mining Academy at Freiberg **Note:** Convention Thaler. Prize Thaler.

Date	Mintage	F	VF	XF	Unc	BU
1815	—	1,000	1,500	3,000	4,500	—

KM# 1059.2 THALER

28.0630 g., 0.8330 Silver .7520 oz. **Ruler:** Friedrich August III as Friedrich August I **Edge:** GOTT SEGNE SACHSEN

Date	Mintage	F	VF	XF	Unc	BU
1816 IGS	—	50.00	75.00	125	250	—

KM# 1076 THALER

28.0630 g., 0.8330 Silver .7520 oz. **Ruler:** Friedrich August III as Friedrich August I

Date	Mintage	F	VF	XF	Unc	BU
1816 IGS	—	600	800	1,500	2,500	—

KM# 1077 THALER

28.0630 g., 0.8330 Silver .7520 oz. **Ruler:** Friedrich August III as Friedrich August I

Date	Mintage	F	VF	XF	Unc	BU
1817 IGS	—	35.00	60.00	125	250	—
1818 IGS	—	35.00	60.00	125	250	—
1819 IGS	—	35.00	60.00	125	250	—
1820 IGS	—	35.00	60.00	125	250	—
1821 IGS	—	35.00	60.00	125	250	—

KM# 1078 THALER

28.0630 g., 0.8330 Silver .7520 oz. **Ruler:** Friedrich August III as Friedrich August I **Note:** Mining Thaler.

Date	Mintage	F	VF	XF	Unc	BU
1817 IGS	—	75.00	150	300	600	—
1818 IGS	—	75.00	150	300	600	—
1819 IGS	—	75.00	150	300	600	—
1820 IGS	—	75.00	150	300	600	—
1821 IGS	—	75.00	150	300	600	—

KM# 1092 THALER

28.0630 g., 0.8330 Silver .7520 oz. **Ruler:** Friedrich August III as Friedrich August I **Note:** Mining Thaler.

Date	Mintage	F	VF	XF	Unc	BU
1822 IGS	—	50.00	125	350	625	—
1823 IGS	—	50.00	125	350	625	—

KM# 1091 THALER

28.0630 g., 0.8330 Silver .7520 oz. **Ruler:** Friedrich August III as Friedrich August I **Note:** Convention Thaler.

Date	Mintage	F	VF	XF	Unc	BU
1822 IGS	—	40.00	60.00	150	300	—
1823 IGS	512,000	40.00	60.00	150	300	—

KM# 1098 THALER

28.0630 g., 0.8330 Silver .7520 oz. **Ruler:** Friedrich August III as Friedrich August I

Date	Mintage	F	VF	XF	Unc	BU
1824 GS	—	150	450	1,200	2,000	—

KM# 1097 THALER

28.0630 g., 0.8330 Silver .7520 oz. **Ruler:** Friedrich August III as Friedrich August I **Note:** Mining Thaler.

Date	Mintage	F	VF	XF	Unc	BU
1824 S	—	60.00	125	225	475	—
1825 S	—	60.00	125	225	475	—
1826 S	—	60.00	125	225	475	—
1827 S	18,000	60.00	125	225	475	—

KM# 1096 THALER

28.0630 g., 0.8330 Silver .7520 oz. **Ruler:** Friedrich August III as Friedrich August I **Note:** Convention Thaler.

Date	Mintage	F	VF	XF	Unc	BU
1824 S	546,000	35.00	60.00	125	275	—
1825 S	546,000	35.00	60.00	125	250	—
1826 S	546,000	35.00	60.00	125	250	—
1827 S	423,000	35.00	60.00	125	275	—

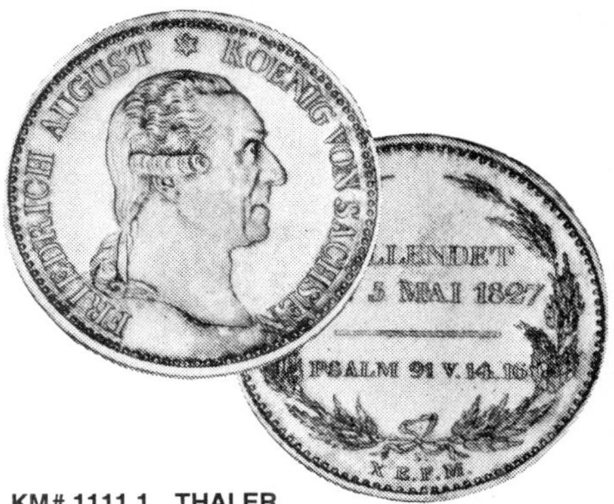

KM# 1111.1 THALER

28.0630 g., 0.8330 Silver .7520 oz. **Ruler:** Friedrich August III as Friedrich August I **Subject:** Death of King Friedrich August **Note:** Convention Thaler.

Date	Mintage	F	VF	XF	Unc	BU
1827 S	14,000	60.00	100	150	250	—

KM# 1111.2 THALER

28.0630 g., 0.8330 Silver .7520 oz. **Ruler:** Friedrich August III as Friedrich August I **Edge:** SEGEN DES BERGBAUS **Note:** Mining Thaler.

Date	Mintage	F	VF	XF	Unc	BU
1827 S	4,357	75.00	150	200	400	—

KM# 1112 THALER

28.0630 g., 0.8330 Silver .7520 oz. **Ruler:** Anton **Note:** Convention Thaler.

Date	Mintage	F	VF	XF	Unc	BU
1827 S	107,000	45.00	80.00	150	375	—
1828 S	609,000	40.00	60.00	125	300	—

KM# 1116 THALER

28.0630 g., 0.8330 Silver .7520 oz. **Ruler:** Anton **Rev. Legend:** SEGEN DES BERGBAUS **Note:** Mining Thaler.

Date	Mintage	F	VF	XF	Unc	BU
1828 S	18,000	150	300	750	1,900	—
1828 S	18,000	150	300	750	1,900	—

KM# 1122 THALER
28.0630 g., 0.8330 Silver .7520 oz. **Ruler:** Anton **Subject:** Mining Academy at Freiberg **Obv:** Similar to C#209 **Note:** Convention Thaler. Prize Thaler.

Date	Mintage	F	VF	XF	Unc	BU
1829	200	1,000	2,000	4,000	6,000	—

KM# 1120 THALER
28.0630 g., 0.8330 Silver .7520 oz. **Ruler:** Anton

Date	Mintage	F	VF	XF	Unc	BU
1829 S	534,000	30.00	60.00	100	200	—
1830 S	620,000	30.00	60.00	100	200	—
1831 S	697,000	30.00	60.00	100	200	—
1832 S	979,000	30.00	60.00	100	200	—
1833 G	190,000	30.00	60.00	100	200	—
1834 G	486,000	30.00	60.00	100	200	—
1835 G	458,000	30.00	60.00	100	200	—
1836 G	585,000	30.00	60.00	100	200	—

KM# 1121 THALER
28.0630 g., 0.8330 Silver .7520 oz. **Ruler:** Anton **Obv:** Older head

Date	Mintage	F	VF	XF	Unc	BU
1829 S	19,000	65.00	175	450	1,000	—
1830 S	19,000	65.00	200	500	1,200	—
1831 S	19,000	65.00	175	450	1,000	—
1832 S	13,000	65.00	175	450	1,000	—
1833 G	3,000	65.00	200	500	1,200	—
1834 G	5,500	65.00	175	450	1,000	—
1835 G	4,986	65.00	175	450	1,000	—
1836 G	4,836,000	65.00	175	450	1,000	—

KM# 1130 THALER
28.0630 g., 0.8330 Silver .7520 oz. **Ruler:** Anton **Subject:** Forestry Institute at Tharant **Note:** Prize Thaler.

Date	Mintage	F	VF	XF	Unc	BU
1830 Rare	25	—	—	—	—	—

KM# 1131 THALER
28.0630 g., 0.8330 Silver .7520 oz. **Ruler:** Anton **Subject:** Agriculture Educational Establishment at Tharant **Rev:** LANDWIRTSCHAFTL **Note:** Prize Thaler.

Date	Mintage	F	VF	XF	Unc	BU
1830	25	—	—	—	—	—

Note: Rare

KM# 1133 THALER
28.0630 g., 0.8330 Silver .7520 oz. **Ruler:** Anton **Subject:** New Constitution

Date	Mintage	F	VF	XF	Unc	BU
1831 S	14,000	40.00	80.00	125	250	—

KM# 1139 THALER
28.0630 g., 0.8330 Silver .7520 oz. **Ruler:** Anton **Subject:** Death of King Anton

Date	Mintage	F	VF	XF	Unc	BU
1836 G	12,000	40.00	80.00	125	250	—

KM# 1140 THALER
28.0630 g., 0.8330 Silver .7520 oz. **Ruler:** Anton **Edge:** SEGEN DES BERGBAUS **Note:** Mining Thaler.

Date	Mintage	F	VF	XF	Unc	BU
1836 G	2,500,000	100	250	500	1,000	—

KM# 1142 THALER
28.0630 g., 0.8330 Silver .7520 oz. **Ruler:** Friedrich August II **Obv:** Legend continous

Date	Mintage	F	VF	XF	Unc	BU
1836 G	3,260	450	1,000	2,200	4,000	—
1837 G	94,000	50.00	90.00	225	475	—
1838 G	139,000	40.00	75.00	200	400	—

KM# 1141 THALER
28.0630 g., 0.8330 Silver .7520 oz. **Ruler:** Friedrich August II **Note:** Convention Thaler.

Date	Mintage	F	VF	XF	Unc	BU
1836 G	34,000	100	200	600	1,200	—
1837 G	31,000	125	275	700	1,400	—

KM# 1143 THALER
28.0630 g., 0.8330 Silver .7520 oz. **Ruler:** Friedrich August II **Obv. Legend:** KOENIG **Rev. Legend:** SEGEN DES, etc **Note:** Mining Thaler.

Date	Mintage	F	VF	XF	Unc	BU
1836 G	3,262	450	1,000	2,200	4,000	—
1837 G	5,770,000	135	275	700	1,400	—
1838 G	36,000	90.00	175	475	875	—

KM# 1147.1 THALER
22.2720 g., 0.7500 Silver .5371 oz. **Ruler:** Friedrich August II **Subject:** Visit to Dresden Mint **Edge:** Lettered **Note:** Convention Thaler.

Date	Mintage	F	VF	XF	Unc	BU
1839 G	—	900	1,800	3,000	4,500	—

KM# 1148 THALER
22.2720 g., 0.7500 Silver .5371 oz. **Ruler:** Friedrich August II

Date	Mintage	F	VF	XF	Unc	BU
1839 G	643,000	25.00	50.00	100	250	—
1840 G	1,406,000	25.00	50.00	100	250	—
1841 G	2,505,000	25.00	50.00	100	250	—
1842 G	974,000	25.00	50.00	100	250	—
1843 G	1,251,000	25.00	50.00	100	250	—
1844 G	1,026,000	25.00	50.00	100	250	—
1845 F	973,000	25.00	50.00	100	250	—
1846 F	860,000	25.00	50.00	100	250	—
1847 F	677,000	25.00	50.00	100	250	—
1848 F	1,592,000	25.00	50.00	100	250	—
1849 F	1,368,000	25.00	50.00	100	250	—

KM# 1147.2 THALER
22.2720 g., 0.7500 Silver .5371 oz. **Ruler:** Friedrich August II **Edge:** Plain

Date	Mintage	F	VF	XF	Unc	BU
1839	—	—	—	—	—	—

Note: Rare

KM# 1162 THALER

22.2720 g., 0.7500 Silver .5371 oz. **Ruler:** Friedrich August II **Obv:** G below head **Note:** Mining Thaler.

Date	Mintage	F	VF	XF	Unc	BU
1841 G	11,000	75.00	150	450	1,000	—
1842 G	17,000	75.00	150	450	1,000	—
1843 G	17,000	75.00	150	450	1,000	—
1844 G	11,000	75.00	150	450	1,000	—
1845 F	19,000	60.00	150	300	600	—
1846 F	22,000	60.00	150	300	600	—
1847 F	40,000	60.00	125	250	500	—
1848 F	21,000	60.00	150	300	600	—
1849 F	38,000	60.00	150	300	600	—
1850 F	34,000	50.00	125	250	500	—
1851 F	33,000	50.00	100	200	400	—
1852 F	47,000	50.00	100	200	400	—
1853 F	55,000	50.00	100	200	400	—
1854 F	37,000	50.00	100	200	400	—

KM# 1175 THALER

22.2720 g., 0.7500 Silver .5371 oz. **Ruler:** Friedrich August II

Date	Mintage	F	VF	XF	Unc	BU
1850 F	1,074,000	25.00	50.00	125	325	—
1851 F	1,351,000	25.00	50.00	125	325	—
1852 F	1,105,000	25.00	50.00	125	325	—
1853 F	1,171,000	25.00	50.00	125	325	—
1854 F	1,075,000	25.00	50.00	125	325	—

KM# 1180.1 THALER

22.2720 g., 0.7500 Silver .5371 oz. **Ruler:** Friedrich August II **Subject:** Death of King Friedrich August II

Date	Mintage	F	VF	XF	Unc	BU
1854 F	16,000	30.00	60.00	100	200	—

KM# 1180.2 THALER

22.2720 g., 0.7500 Silver .5371 oz. **Ruler:** Friedrich August II **Edge:** SEGEN DES BERGBAUS **Note:** Edge inscripton with crossed hammers.

Date	Mintage	F	VF	XF	Unc	BU
1854 F	8,829	40.00	75.00	125	250	—

KM# 1182 THALER

22.2720 g., 0.7500 Silver .5371 oz. **Ruler:** Friedrich August II **Rev:** Similar to C#269 **Note:** Mining Thaler.

Date	Mintage	F	VF	XF	Unc	BU
1854 F	27,000	90.00	175	425	1,000	—

KM# 1181 THALER

22.2720 g., 0.7500 Silver .5371 oz. **Ruler:** Friedrich August II **Note:** Convention Thaler.

Date	Mintage	F	VF	XF	Unc	BU
1854 F	525,000	30.00	60.00	150	450	—

KM# 1188 THALER

22.2720 g., 0.7500 Silver .5371 oz. **Ruler:** Johann **Rev:** Similar to C#265

Date	Mintage	F	VF	XF	Unc	BU
1855 F	863,000	25.00	40.00	125	300	—
1856 F	1,089,000	25.00	40.00	100	250	—

KM# 1187 THALER

22.2720 g., 0.7500 Silver .5371 oz. **Ruler:** Johann **Subject:** Visit to Mint by King Johann **Note:** Convention Thaler.

Date	Mintage	F	VF	XF	Unc	BU
1855 F	5,250	35.00	65.00	125	300	—
1855 F Proof	—	Value: 400				

KM# 1189 THALER

22.2720 g., 0.7500 Silver .5371 oz. **Ruler:** Johann **Note:** Mining Thaler.

Date	Mintage	F	VF	XF	Unc	BU
1855 F	56,000	65.00	125	350	800	—
1856 F	56,000	65.00	125	350	800	—

KM# 1193 THALER

18.5200 g., 0.9000 Silver .5360 oz. **Ruler:** Johann **Obv:** Similar to C#269. **Note:** Mining Thaler.

Date	Mintage	F	VF	XF	Unc	BU
1857 F	35,000	75.00	150	400	800	—
1858 F	34,000	75.00	150	400	800	—

KM# 1192 THALER

18.5200 g., 0.9000 Silver .5360 oz. **Ruler:** Johann **Note:** Vereins Thaler.

Date	Mintage	F	VF	XF	Unc	BU
1857 F	969,000	25.00	45.00	100	250	—
1858 F	200,000	25.00	45.00	100	250	—
1859 F	2,490,000	20.00	35.00	90.00	225	—

KM# 1199 THALER

18.5200 g., 0.9000 Silver .5360 oz. **Ruler:** Johann **Obv. Legend:** Large Letters **Rev. Legend:** SEGEN DES BERGBAUS

Date	Mintage	F	VF	XF	Unc	BU
1858 F	61,000	35.00	65.00	135	325	—
1859 F	94,000	35.00	65.00	135	325	—
1860 B	298,000	25.00	50.00	100	250	—
1861 B	16,000	40.00	75.00	150	350	—

KM# 1210 THALER

18.5200 g., 0.9000 Silver .5360 oz. **Ruler:** Johann **Note:** Vereins Thaler.

Date	Mintage	F	VF	XF	Unc	BU
1860 B	2,669,000	25.00	50.00	90.00	200	—
1861 B	1,409,000	25.00	50.00	90.00	200	—

KM# 1214 THALER
18.5200 g., 0.9000 Silver .5360 oz. **Ruler:** Johann

Date	Mintage	F	VF	XF	Unc	BU
1861 B	1,070,000	20.00	35.00	70.00	150	—
1862 B	2,134,000	20.00	35.00	70.00	150	—
1863 B	1,471,000	20.00	35.00	70.00	150	—
1864 B	1,904,000	20.00	35.00	70.00	150	—
1865 B	1,335,000	20.00	35.00	70.00	150	—
1866 B	1,181,000	20.00	35.00	70.00	150	—
1867 B	2,020,000	20.00	35.00	70.00	150	—
1868 B	1,683,000	20.00	35.00	70.00	150	—
1869 B	1,622,000	20.00	35.00	70.00	150	—
1870 B	1,693,000	20.00	35.00	70.00	150	—
1871 B	1,687,000	20.00	35.00	70.00	150	—

KM# 1211 THALER
18.5200 g., 0.9000 Silver .5360 oz. **Ruler:** Johann **Obv. Legend:** Small letters

Date	Mintage	F	VF	XF	Unc	BU
1861 B	130,000	75.00	150	450	1,000	—

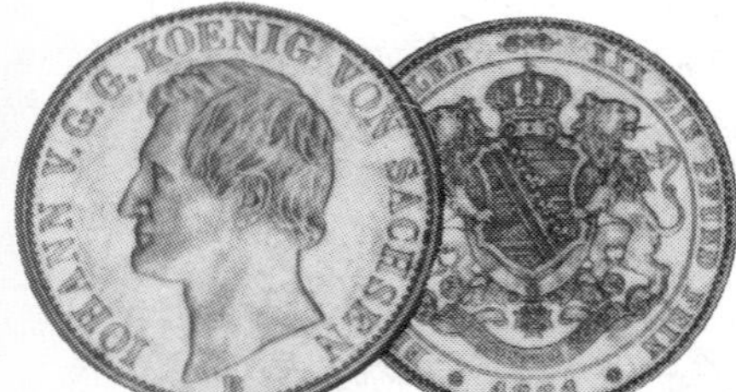

KM# 1212 THALER
18.5200 g., 0.9000 Silver .5360 oz. **Ruler:** Johann **Rev. Legend:** SEGEN DES BERGBAUSE

Date	Mintage	F	VF	XF	Unc	BU
1861 B	130,000	20.00	40.00	70.00	150	—
1862 B	145,000	20.00	40.00	70.00	150	—
1863 B	135,000	20.00	40.00	70.00	150	—
1864 B	120,000	20.00	40.00	70.00	150	—
1865 B	221,000	20.00	40.00	70.00	150	—
1866 B	185,000	20.00	40.00	70.00	150	—
1867 B	175,000	20.00	40.00	70.00	150	—

KM# 1213 THALER
18.5200 g., 0.9000 Silver .5360 oz. **Ruler:** Johann **Obv:** KM#1210 **Rev:** KM#1214

Date	Mintage	F	VF	XF	Unc	BU
1861	190,000	300	600	800	1,200	—

KM# 1223 THALER
18.5200 g., 0.9000 Silver .5360 oz. **Ruler:** Johann

Date	Mintage	F	VF	XF	Unc	BU
1868 B	181,000	20.00	40.00	70.00	150	—
1869 B	190,000	20.00	40.00	70.00	150	—
1870 B	236,000	20.00	40.00	70.00	150	—
1871 B	203,000	20.00	40.00	70.00	150	—

KM# 1230 THALER
18.5200 g., 0.9000 Silver .5360 oz. **Ruler:** Johann **Subject:** Victory Over France

Date	Mintage	F	VF	XF	Unc	BU
1871 B	45,000	30.00	50.00	80.00	175	—

KM# 1149 2 THALER (3-1/2 Gulden)
37.1200 g., 0.9000 Silver 1.0742 oz. **Ruler:** Friedrich August II

Date	Mintage	F	VF	XF	Unc	BU
1839 G	20,000	90.00	125	300	600	—
1840 G	68,000	90.00	125	300	600	—
1841 G	39,000	90.00	125	300	600	—
1841 G	39,000	90.00	125	300	600	—
1842 G	71,000	70.00	100	250	450	—
1843 G	59,000	70.00	100	250	450	—
1847 F	147,000	50.00	85.00	185	400	—
1848 F	78,000	65.00	125	225	550	—
1849 F	15,000	65.00	125	225	550	—
1850 F	113,000	50.00	85.00	185	400	—
1851 F	246,000	50.00	85.00	185	400	—
1852 F	209,000	50.00	85.00	185	400	—
1853 F	303,000	50.00	85.00	185	400	—
1854 F	886,000	50.00	85.00	185	400	—

KM# 1163 2 THALER (3-1/2 Gulden)
37.1200 g., 0.9000 Silver 1.0742 oz. **Ruler:** Friedrich August II **Subject:** Mining Academy at Freiberg **Obv:** Similar to KM#1149 **Note:** Prize Thaler.

Date	Mintage	F	VF	XF	Unc	BU
1841 G	200	750	1,500	3,000	4,500	—

KM# 1166 2 THALER (3-1/2 Gulden)
37.1200 g., 0.9000 Silver 1.0742 oz. **Ruler:** Friedrich August II **Subject:** Forest and Agriculture Academy **Obv:** Similar to KM#1149 **Note:** Prize Thaler.

Date	Mintage	F	VF	XF	Unc	BU
1847 F	50	3,000	5,000	7,500	10,000	—

KM# 1183 2 THALER (3-1/2 Gulden)
37.1200 g., 0.9000 Silver 1.0742 oz. **Ruler:** Friedrich August II **Subject:** Death of King Friedrich August II

Date	Mintage	F	VF	XF	Unc	BU
1854 F	6,148	100	200	300	500	—
1854 F Proof	—	Value: 800				

KM# 1190 2 THALER (3-1/2 Gulden)
37.1200 g., 0.9000 Silver 1.0742 oz. **Ruler:** Johann **Note:** Similar to KM#1149.

Date	Mintage	F	VF	XF	Unc	BU
1855 F	462,000	50.00	90.00	190	350	—
1856 F	91,000	75.00	110	210	400	—

KM# 1194 2 THALER (3-1/2 Gulden)
37.1200 g., 0.9000 Silver 1.0742 oz. **Ruler:** Johann **Subject:** Mining Academy at Freiberg **Obv:** Similar to KM#1190. **Note:** Prize Thaler.

Date	Mintage	F	VF	XF	Unc	BU
1857 F	100	750	1,500	3,000	4,500	—
1857 B	206	700	1,400	2,500	4,000	—

KM# 1195 2 THALER (3-1/2 Gulden)
37.0370 g., 0.9000 Silver 1.0718 oz. **Ruler:** Johann **Obv:** Similar to KM#1190.

Date	Mintage	F	VF	XF	Unc	BU
1857 F	351,000	50.00	80.00	180	325	—
1858 F	454,000	50.00	80.00	180	325	—
1859 F	323,000	50.00	80.00	180	325	—

KM# 1200 2 THALER (3-1/2 Gulden)
37.0370 g., 0.9000 Silver 1.0718 oz. **Ruler:** Johann **Obv:** Similar to KM#1190. **Rev:** Value: VEREINSTHAELR

Date	Mintage	F	VF	XF	Unc	BU
1858	Inc. above	35.00	90.00	175	375	—

KM# 1215 2 THALER (3-1/2 Gulden)
37.0370 g., 0.9000 Silver 1.0718 oz. **Ruler:** Johann **Obv:** Similar to KM#1190.

Date	Mintage	F	VF	XF	Unc	BU
1861 B	730,000	65.00	100	200	350	—
1861 B	730,000	65.00	100	200	350	—

KM# 1231.1 2 THALER (3-1/2 Gulden)
37.0370 g., 0.9000 Silver 1.0718 oz. **Ruler:** Johann **Subject:** Golden Wedding Anniversary

Date	Mintage	F	VF	XF	Unc	BU
1872 B	49,000	50.00	75.00	125	200	—

KM# 1231.2 2 THALER (3-1/2 Gulden)
37.0370 g., 0.9000 Silver 1.0718 oz. **Ruler:** Johann **Edge:** Plain

Date	Mintage	F	VF	XF	Unc	BU
1872 B	Inc. above	100	250	350	500	—

KM# 1164 2-1/2 THALER
3.3410 g., 0.9020 Gold .0970 oz. **Ruler:** Friedrich August II

Date	Mintage	F	VF	XF	Unc	BU
1842 G	560	300	600	1,000	2,250	—
1845 F	420	300	600	1,200	2,500	—
1848 F	2,445	250	500	1,000	2,000	—
1854 F	308	400	700	1,200	2,500	—

KM# 1054 5 THALER (August D'or)
6.6820 g., 0.9020 Gold .1940 oz. **Ruler:** Friedrich August III as Friedrich August I

Date	Mintage	F	VF	XF	Unc	BU
1806 SGH	44,000	750	1,500	3,500	6,000	—
1807 SGH	152,000	400	900	1,500	3,000	—
1808 SGH	135,000	300	600	1,250	2,750	—
1809 SGH	54,000	300	600	1,250	2,750	—
1810 SGH	235,000	300	600	1,250	2,750	—
1812 SGH	98,000	300	600	1,250	2,750	—
1813 SGH	118,000	300	600	1,250	2,750	—
1815 IGS	20,000	250	500	1,250	2,500	—
1816 IGS	—	400	900	1,500	3,250	—
1817 IGS	—	250	500	1,250	2,500	—

KM# 1080 5 THALER (August D'or)
6.6820 g., 0.9020 Gold .1940 oz. **Ruler:** Friedrich August III as Friedrich August I **Obv:** Uniformed bust left

Date	Mintage	F	VF	XF	Unc	BU
1818 igs	—	800	2,000	3,500	7,500	—

KM# 1102 5 THALER (August D'or)
6.6820 g., 0.9020 Gold .1940 oz. **Ruler:** Friedrich August III as Friedrich August I

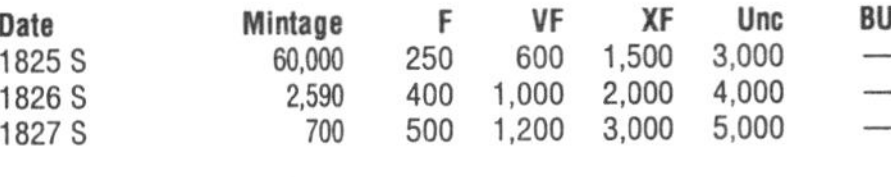

Date	Mintage	F	VF	XF	Unc	BU
1825 S	60,000	250	600	1,500	3,000	—
1826 S	2,590	400	1,000	2,000	4,000	—
1827 S	700	500	1,200	3,000	5,000	—

KM# 1113 5 THALER (August D'or)
6.6820 g., 0.9020 Gold .1940 oz. **Ruler:** Anton

Date	Mintage	F	VF	XF	Unc	BU
1827 S	405	500	1,000	2,000	4,000	—
1828 S	855	500	1,000	2,000	4,000	—

KM# 1123 5 THALER (August D'or)
6.6820 g., 0.9020 Gold .1940 oz. **Ruler:** Anton **Obv:** Older head

Date	Mintage	F	VF	XF	Unc	BU
1829 S	385	500	1,000	2,000	4,000	—
1830 S	2,800	550	1,100	2,000	4,250	—
1831 S	245	700	1,500	3,000	5,000	—
1832 S	175	700	1,250	3,000	6,000	—
1834 S	490	700	1,250	2,750	5,000	—
1835 S	380	700	1,250	3,000	6,000	—
1836 S	455	700	1,500	2,500	5,000	—

KM# 1146 5 THALER (August D'or)
6.6820 g., 0.9020 Gold .1940 oz. **Ruler:** Friedrich August II

Date	Mintage	F	VF	XF	Unc	BU
1837 G	490	400	750	2,000	3,250	—
1838 G	175	500	850	2,500	5,000	—
1839 G	210	500	850	2,150	4,000	—

KM# 1165 5 THALER (August D'or)
6.6820 g., 0.9020 Gold .1940 oz. **Ruler:** Friedrich August II

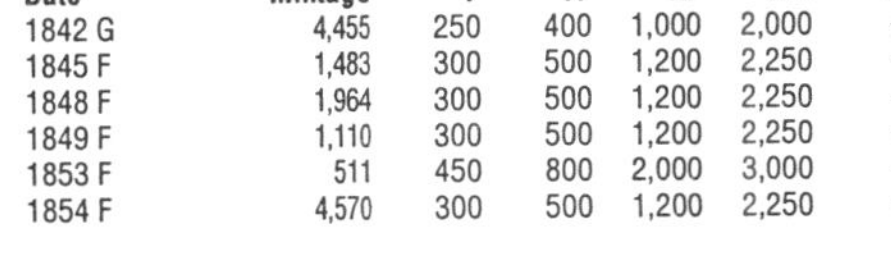

Date	Mintage	F	VF	XF	Unc	BU
1842 G	4,455	250	400	1,000	2,000	—
1845 F	1,483	300	500	1,200	2,250	—
1848 F	1,964	300	500	1,200	2,250	—
1849 F	1,110	300	500	1,200	2,250	—
1853 F	511	450	800	2,000	3,000	—
1854 F	4,570	300	500	1,200	2,250	—

KM# 1055 10 THALER (2 August D'or)
13.3640 g., 0.9020 Gold .3880 oz. **Ruler:** Friedrich August III as Friedrich August I

Date	Mintage	F	VF	XF	Unc	BU
1806 SGH	—	600	1,250	2,500	4,000	—
1807 SGH	—	600	1,250	2,500	4,000	—
1808 SGH	—	500	1,000	2,000	4,000	—
1809 SGH	—	600	1,250	2,500	4,000	—
1810 SGH	—	500	1,000	2,000	4,000	—
1811 SGH	—	500	1,000	2,000	3,500	—
1812 SGH	—	500	1,000	2,000	3,500	—
1813 SGH	—	450	850	1,750	2,500	—
1813 IGS	—	475	950	1,750	2,500	—
1815 IGS	—	450	850	1,750	3,000	—
1816 IGS	—	600	1,250	2,500	3,000	—
1817 IGS	—	450	850	1,750	2,500	—

KM# 1081 10 THALER (2 August D'or)

13.3640 g., 0.9020 Gold .3880 oz. **Ruler:** Friedrich August III as Friedrich August I

Date	Mintage	F	VF	XF	Unc	BU
1818 IGS	—	2,000	4,000	7,500	9,500	—

KM# 1103 10 THALER (2 August D'or)

13.3640 g., 0.9020 Gold .3880 oz. **Ruler:** Friedrich August III as Friedrich August I

Date	Mintage	F	VF	XF	Unc	BU
1825 S	—	800	2,000	4,000	5,500	—
1826 S	—	700	1,500	3,000	4,500	—
1827 S	9,250	700	1,500	3,000	4,500	—

KM# 1114 10 THALER (2 August D'or)

13.3640 g., 0.9020 Gold .3880 oz. **Ruler:** Anton **Obv:** Head right **Rev:** Crowned arched arms within corssed branches

Date	Mintage	F	VF	XF	Unc	BU
1827 S	875	1,200	3,000	6,000	9,000	—
1828 S	5,530	800	2,500	5,000	6,500	—

KM# 1124 10 THALER (2 August D'or)

13.3640 g., 0.9020 Gold .3880 oz. **Ruler:** Anton **Obv:** Older head

Date	Mintage	F	VF	XF	Unc	BU
1829 S	3,010	800	2,000	4,000	5,500	—
1830 S	18,000	650	1,600	3,000	4,500	—
1831	3,255	1,250	2,500	5,000	7,000	—
1832 S	2,625	800	2,000	4,000	5,500	—
1833 S	—	1,250	2,500	5,000	7,000	—
1834 S	3,080	1,250	2,500	5,000	7,000	—
1835 S	2,715	1,250	2,500	5,000	7,000	—
1836 S	4,655	1,250	2,500	5,000	7,000	—

KM# 1144 10 THALER (2 August D'or)

13.3640 g., 0.9020 Gold .3880 oz. **Ruler:** Friedrich August II **Obv:** Different head **Rev:** Crowned

Date	Mintage	F	VF	XF	Unc	BU
1836 G	1,110	600	1,250	2,500	3,500	—
1837 G	2,400	600	1,250	2,500	3,500	—
1838 G	1,750	700	1,500	3,000	4,000	—
1839 G	1,855	700	1,500	3,000	4,000	—

KM# 1150 10 THALER (2 August D'or)

13.3640 g., 0.9020 Gold .3880 oz. **Ruler:** Friedrich August II

Date	Mintage	F	VF	XF	Unc	BU
1839 G	1,855	800	2,000	4,000	5,500	—
1845 F	2,100	600	1,250	2,500	3,500	—
1848 F	4,761	700	1,500	3,000	4,500	—
1849 F	1,928	700	1,500	3,000	4,500	—
1853 F	1,038	700	1,500	3,000	4,500	—
1854 F	1,620	800	2,000	4,000	5,500	—

KM# 1196 1/2 KRONE

5.5560 g., 0.9000 Gold .1608 oz. **Ruler:** Johann

Date	Mintage	F	VF	XF	Unc	BU
1857 F	4,831	475	1,000	2,000	3,000	—
1858 F	2,455	475	1,000	2,000	3,000	—
1862 B	2,177	550	1,200	2,250	3,000	—
1866 B	1,559	550	1,200	2,250	3,200	—
1868 B	1,516	550	1,200	2,500	3,500	—
1870 B	1,740	550	1,200	2,500	3,500	—

KM# 1197 KRONE

11.1110 g., 0.9000 Gold .3215 oz. **Ruler:** Johann

Date	Mintage	F	VF	XF	Unc	BU
1857 F	3,580	525	1,350	2,500	3,200	—
1858 F	4,610	525	1,350	2,500	3,200	—
1859 F	9,040	525	1,350	2,500	3,200	—
1860 B	5,067	525	1,350	2,750	3,700	—
1861 B	3,908	525	1,350	2,500	3,200	—
1862 B	3,229	525	1,350	2,750	3,700	—
1863 B	3,538	525	1,350	2,750	3,700	—
1865 B	4,371	525	1,350	2,500	3,200	—
1867 B	2,155	525	1,350	2,750	3,700	—
1868 B	5,262	525	1,350	2,500	3,200	—
1870 B	2,700	525	1,350	2,500	3,200	—
1871 B	2,140	525	1,350	2,750	3,200	—

REFORM COINAGE

KM# 1238 2 MARK

11.1110 g., 0.9000 Silver .3215 oz. **Ruler:** Albert

Date	Mintage	F	VF	XF	Unc	BU
1876 E	1,613,000	30.00	80.00	525	1,200	1,400
1877 E	796,000	35.00	85.00	500	1,300	1,500
1877 E Proof	—	Value: 2,000				
1879 E	36,000	80.00	200	800	2,750	4,000
1880 E	58,000	80.00	150	650	2,500	3,000
1883 E	56,000	80.00	150	650	2,500	3,000
1888 E	91,000	40.00	90.00	550	1,750	2,250

KM# 1245 2 MARK

11.1110 g., 0.9000 Silver .3215 oz. **Ruler:** Albert **Note:** Similar to KM#185.

Date	Mintage	F	VF	XF	Unc	BU
1891E	130,000	25.00	65.00	125	350	500
1893E	130,000	25.00	75.00	160	375	500
1895E	117,000	30.00	90.00	180	475	575
1896E	144,000	25.00	75.00	160	400	500
1898E	107,000	25.00	75.00	175	475	700
1899E	401,000	15.00	60.00	110	350	450
1900E	384,000	15.00	60.00	110	300	400

KM# 1237 5 MARK

27.7770 g., 0.9000 Silver .8038 oz. **Ruler:** Albert

Date	Mintage	F	VF	XF	Unc	BU
1875E	494,000	35.00	60.00	750	2,200	2,600
1876E	635,000	30.00	60.00	650	1,900	2,200
1889E	36,000	50.00	100	900	2,750	3,250

KM# 1239 5 MARK

1.9910 g., 0.9000 Gold .0576 oz. **Ruler:** Albert **Rev:** Type I

Date	Mintage	F	VF	XF	Unc	BU
1877E	402,000	175	275	375	550	750
1877E Proof	—	Value: 1,000				

KM# 1249 5 MARK

Gold **Ruler:** Albert

Date	Mintage	F	VF	XF	Unc	BU
1889	—	—	—	2,600	3,500	—

KM# 1249a 5 MARK

Bronze **Ruler:** Albert

Date	Mintage	F	VF	XF	Unc	BU
1889	—	—	—	350	550	—

KM# 1246 5 MARK
27.7770 g., 0.9000 Silver .8038 oz. **Ruler:** Albert **Note:** Similar to KM#1256.

Date	Mintage	F	VF	XF	Unc	BU
1891E	52,000	30.00	65.00	450	1,200	1,600
1893E	52,000	30.00	65.00	450	1,200	1,600
1894E	75,000	30.00	65.00	450	1,200	1,600
1895E	89,000	30.00	65.00	400	1,200	1,600
1898E	160,000	25.00	55.00	350	1,000	1,400
1899E	74,000	25.00	55.00	350	1,000	1,400
1900E	157,000	25.00	55.00	300	800	1,200

KM# 1232 10 MARK
3.9820 g., 0.9000 Gold .1152 oz. **Ruler:** Johann

Date	Mintage	F	VF	XF	Unc	BU
1872E	339,000	90.00	175	285	500	800
1873E	822,000	90.00	175	285	500	800

KM# 1235 10 MARK
3.9820 g., 0.9000 Gold .1152 oz. **Ruler:** Albert **Rev:** Type II

Date	Mintage	F	VF	XF	Unc	BU
1874E	48,000	450	750	1,200	2,500	3,000
1875E	528,000	70.00	120	200	400	600
1877E	201,000	70.00	120	200	500	750
1878E	225,000	70.00	120	200	500	750
1879E	182,000	70.00	120	200	500	750
1881E	240,000	70.00	120	200	500	750
1888E	149,000	70.00	120	200	500	750

KM# 1247 10 MARK
3.9820 g., 0.9000 Gold .1152 oz. **Ruler:** Albert **Rev:** Type III

Date	Mintage	F	VF	XF	Unc	BU
1891 E	224,000	100	160	200	450	550
1893E	224,000	100	145	200	450	550
1896E	150,000	100	160	200	450	550
1898E	313,000	100	160	225	450	550
1900E	74,000	100	160	250	450	550
1900E Proof	—	Value: 1,500				

KM# 1233 20 MARK
7.9650 g., 0.9000 Gold .2304 oz. **Ruler:** Johann **Rev:** Type I

Date	Mintage	F	VF	XF	Unc	BU
1872E	890,000	120	150	200	400	650
1872E Proof	—	Value: 3,000				

KM# 1234 20 MARK
7.9650 g., 0.9000 Gold .2304 oz. **Ruler:** Johann **Obv:** Large letters in legend

Date	Mintage	F	VF	XF	Unc	BU
1873E	203,000	120	150	200	400	650

KM# 1236 20 MARK
7.9650 g., 0.9000 Gold .2304 oz. **Ruler:** Albert **Rev:** Type II

Date	Mintage	F	VF	XF	Unc	BU
1874E	153,000	120	150	180	425	650
1876E	482,000	120	150	180	425	650
1876E Proof	—	Value: 1,800				
1877E	1,181	8,000	15,000	20,000	30,000	40,000
1878E	1,564	9,500	17,500	27,500	35,000	45,000

KM# 1248 20 MARK
7.9650 g., 0.9000 Gold .2304 oz. **Ruler:** Albert **Rev:** Type III

Date	Mintage	F	VF	XF	Unc	BU
1894E	639,000	115	150	200	350	450
1895E	113,000	120	175	250	425	525

TRADE COINAGE

KM# 1056 DUCAT
3.5000 g., 0.9860 Gold .1109 oz. **Ruler:** Friedrich August III as Friedrich August I

Date	Mintage	F	VF	XF	Unc	BU
1806 SGH	3,207	200	400	1,000	2,000	—
1807 SGH	2,660	300	800	1,500	2,500	—
1808 SGH	2,010	300	800	1,500	2,500	—
1809 SGH	1,608	300	800	1,500	2,500	—
1810 SGH	1,072	300	800	1,500	2,500	—
1811 SGH	268	500	1,000	2,000	3,500	—
1812 SGH	67	500	1,000	2,000	4,000	—
1813 SGH	—	300	600	1,500	2,500	—

KM# 1063 DUCAT
3.5000 g., 0.9860 Gold .1109 oz. **Ruler:** Friedrich August III as Friedrich August I **Subject:** 400th Jubilee of Leipzig University **Obv:** Bust in coronet and cape right **Rev. Legend:** SALVA SIT

Date	Mintage	F	VF	XF	Unc	BU
1809	—	300	600	1,200	2,000	—

KM# 1073 DUCAT
3.5000 g., 0.9860 Gold .1109 oz. **Ruler:** Friedrich August III as Friedrich August I

Date	Mintage	F	VF	XF	Unc	BU
1813 IGS	—	300	600	1,500	2,500	—
1814 IGS	134	500	1,000	2,000	3,500	—
1815 IGS	804	350	800	1,750	3,000	—
1816 IGS	2,243	300	600	1,200	2,200	—
1817 IGS	1,812	300	600	1,200	2,200	—
1818 IGS	1,466	300	600	1,200	2,200	—
1819 IGS	1,466	300	600	1,200	2,200	—
1820 IGS	2,502	300	600	1,200	2,200	—
1821 IGS	1,948	300	600	1,200	2,200	—
1822 IGS	1,898	300	600	1,200	2,200	—

KM# 1093 DUCAT
3.5000 g., 0.9860 Gold .1109 oz. **Ruler:** Friedrich August III as Friedrich August I **Obv:** Uniformed bust left **Obv. Legend:** FRIEDR. AUGUST. . . **Rev:** Crowned oval arms within crossed branches

Date	Mintage	F	VF	XF	Unc	BU
1823 IGS	1,380,000	500	800	1,500	2,500	—

KM# 1099 DUCAT
3.5000 g., 0.9860 Gold .1109 oz. **Ruler:** Friedrich August III as Friedrich August I **Obv. Legend:** FRIEDR. AUG. KOEN...

Date	Mintage	F	VF	XF	Unc	BU
1824 IGS	2,847	300	600	1,000	1,500	—

KM# 1104 DUCAT
3.5000 g., 0.9860 Gold .1109 oz. **Ruler:** Friedrich August III as Friedrich August I

Date	Mintage	F	VF	XF	Unc	BU
1825 IGS	1,725	300	600	1,200	2,000	—
1826 IGS	2,415	300	600	1,200	2,000	—
1827 IGS	1,639	300	600	1,200	2,000	—

KM# 1115 DUCAT
3.5000 g., 0.9860 Gold .1109 oz. **Ruler:** Anton

Date	Mintage	F	VF	XF	Unc	BU
1827 S	587	400	900	1,500	2,500	—
1828 S	771	400	900	1,500	2,500	—

KM# 1125 DUCAT
3.5000 g., 0.9860 Gold .1109 oz. **Ruler:** Anton

Date	Mintage	F	VF	XF	Unc	BU
1829 S	2,070	300	600	1,200	2,000	—
1830 S	1,898	300	600	1,200	2,000	—
1831 S	862	400	900	1,500	2,500	—
1832 S	776	400	900	1,500	2,500	—
1833 S	2,156	400	900	1,500	2,500	—
1834 S	1,582	400	900	1,500	2,500	—
1835 S	119	600	1,300	2,500	4,000	—
1836 S	804	600	1,250	2,000	3,000	—

KM# 1145 DUCAT
3.5000 g., 0.9860 Gold .1109 oz. **Ruler:** Friedrich August II
Obv: Different head

Date	Mintage	F	VF	XF	Unc	BU
1836 G	100	600	1,250	2,250	3,250	—
1837 G	168	600	1,250	2,250	3,250	—
1838 G	637	400	1,100	2,250	3,250	—

PATTERNS

Including off metal strikes

KM#	Date	Mintage	Identification	Mkt Val
Pn60	1804	—	Heller. Gold. KM1002.	1,200
Pn61	1804	—	Pfennig. Gold. KM1000.	—
Pn62	1805	—	Pfennig. Gold. KM1000.	—
Pn63	1808 H	—	Pfennig. Gold. KM1057.	—

KM#	Date	Mintage	Identification	Mkt Val
Pn64	1808 SGH	—	Thaler. Silver.	3,000
Pn65	1813 H	—	Heller. Silver. KM1072.	500

KM#	Date	Mintage	Identification	Mkt Val
Pn66	1813 IGS	—	Thaler. Silver.	8,000

KM#	Date	Mintage	Identification	Mkt Val
Pn67	1814	—	Thaler.	10,000
Pn68	1814 IGS	134	Ducat. Gold.	6,000

KM#	Date	Mintage	Identification	Mkt Val
Pn69	1816	—	1/24 Thaler. Gold. KM1075.	—

KM#	Date	Mintage	Identification	Mkt Val
Pn70	1832 S	—	3 Pfennige. Silver.	1,200

KM#	Date	Mintage	Identification	Mkt Val
Pn71	183x G	—	3 Pfennige.	—

KM#	Date	Mintage	Identification	Mkt Val
Pn72	1857 F	—	5 Pfennige. Copper.	—

KM#	Date	Mintage	Identification	Mkt Val
Pn73	185x	—	1/6 Thaler.	—
Pn74	1873 E	—	10 Mark. Copper. KM1235. Plain edge, KM1232.	—
Pn75	1873 E	—	20 Mark. Copper. KM1233. Plain edge, KM1236.	—
Pn76	1875 E	—	5 Mark. Zinc. Plain edge, KM1237.	—
Pn77	1876 E	—	10 Mark. Silver. Plain edge, KM1235.	—

TRIAL STRIKES

KM#	Date	Mintage	Identification	Mkt Val
TS1	1871	—	Thaler. Uniface.	—

SCHAUMBURG-HESSEN

Located in northwest Germany, Schaumburg-Hessen was founded in 1640 when Schaumburg-Gehmen was divided between Hesse-Cassel and Lippe-Alverdissen. The two became known as Schaumburg-Hessen and Schaumburg--Lippe. Cassel struck coins for it half as late as 1832.

RULERS
Wilhelm (of Hesse-Cassel), 1785-1821
Wilhelm II, (of Hesse-Cassel), 1821-1847

MONETARY SYSTEM
12 Gute Pfennig = 1 Groschen

COUNTY

STANDARD COINAGE

C# 3 PFENNIG
Copper **Ruler:** Friedrich II **Obv:** Crowned shield separating WL **Rev:** Value

Date	Mintage	F	VF	XF	Unc	BU
1801	—	5.00	10.00	25.00	75.00	—
1802	—	5.00	10.00	25.00	75.00	—
1803	—	5.00	10.00	25.00	75.00	—

C# 4 PFENNIG
Copper **Ruler:** Friedrich II **Obv:** Elector's cap above arms dividing W.K. **Rev:** Value, F below

Date	Mintage	F	VF	XF	Unc	BU
1804	—	6.00	12.00	30.00	80.00	—
1805	—	6.00	12.00	30.00	80.00	—
1806	—	6.00	12.00	30.00	80.00	—
1807	—	6.00	12.00	30.00	80.00	—
1814	—	6.00	12.00	30.00	80.00	—

C# 4b PFENNIG
Copper **Ruler:** Friedrich II **Rev:** Rosette below value and date

Date	Mintage	F	VF	XF	Unc	BU
1815	—	8.00	16.00	35.00	90.00	—

C# 4a PFENNIG
Copper **Ruler:** Friedrich II

Date	Mintage	F	VF	XF	Unc	BU
1816	—	4.00	9.00	20.00	65.00	—
1818	—	4.00	9.00	20.00	65.00	—
1819	—	4.00	9.00	20.00	65.00	—
1820	—	4.00	9.00	20.00	65.00	—
1821	—	4.00	9.00	20.00	65.00	—

C# 5 PFENNIG
Copper **Ruler:** Friedrich II

Date	Mintage	F	VF	XF	Unc	BU
1824	—	4.00	9.00	20.00	65.00	—
1826	—	4.00	9.00	20.00	65.00	—
1827	—	4.00	9.00	20.00	65.00	—
1828	—	4.00	9.00	20.00	65.00	—
1829	—	4.00	9.00	20.00	65.00	—
1830	—	4.00	9.00	20.00	65.00	—

C# 6 PFENNIG
Copper **Ruler:** Friedrich II

Date	Mintage	F	VF	XF	Unc	BU
1832	—	4.00	9.00	20.00	65.00	—

SCHAUMBURG-LIPPE

Located in northwest Germany, Schaumburg-Lippe was founded in 1640 when Schaumburg-Gehmen was divided between Hesse-Cassel and Lippe-Alverdissen. The two became known as Schaumburg-Hessen and Schaumburg-Lippe. They were elevated into a county independent of Lippe. Schaumburg-Lippe minted currency into the 20th century. The last prince died in 1911.

RULERS
Georg Wilhelm, 1787-1860
Adolph Georg, 1860-1893
Albrecht Georg, 1893-1911

DUCHY

REGULAR COINAGE

C# 30 4 PFENNIG
Copper **Ruler:** Georg Wilhelm **Obv:** Crowned arms, garlands and roses **Rev:** Value

Date	Mintage	F	VF	XF	Unc	BU
1802	288,000	15.00	30.00	60.00	120	—

C# 32 MARIENGROSCHEN
1.5500 g., 0.3880 Silver .0193 oz. **Ruler:** Georg Wilhelm **Obv:** Crowned arms, garlands and roses **Rev:** Value

Date	Mintage	F	VF	XF	Unc	BU
1802	144,000	20.00	45.00	75.00	135	—

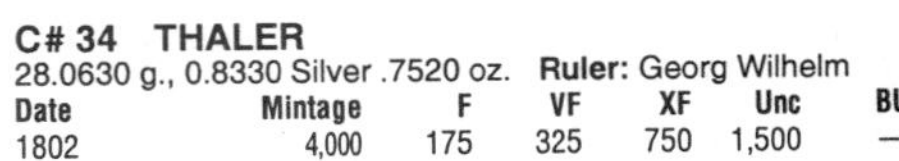

C# 34 THALER

28.0630 g., 0.8330 Silver .7520 oz. **Ruler:** Georg Wilhelm

Date	Mintage	F	VF	XF	Unc	BU
1802	4,000	175	325	750	1,500	—

PRINCIPALITY

REGULAR COINAGE

C# 36 PFENNIG

Copper **Ruler:** Georg Wilhelm **Obv:** Crowned arms **Rev:** Value **Note:** Guter-Pfennig.

Date	Mintage	F	VF	XF	Unc	BU
1824	—	4.00	8.00	25.00	70.00	—
1826	—	4.00	8.00	25.00	70.00	—

C# 37 PFENNIG

Copper **Ruler:** Georg Wilhelm

Date	Mintage	F	VF	XF	Unc	BU
1858A	1,440,000	4.00	8.00	25.00	70.00	—

C# 38 2 PFENNIG

Copper **Ruler:** Georg Wilhelm

Date	Mintage	F	VF	XF	Unc	BU
1858A	360,000	3.00	7.00	20.00	50.00	—

C# 39 3 PFENNIG

Copper **Ruler:** Georg Wilhelm

Date	Mintage	F	VF	XF	Unc	BU
1858A	360,000	3.50	8.00	25.00	55.00	—

C# 41 4 PFENNIG

0.7500 g., 0.1860 Silver .0044 oz. **Ruler:** Georg Wilhelm **Obv:** Crowned arms

Date	Mintage	F	VF	XF	Unc	BU
1821	491,000	7.50	17.50	35.00	75.00	—

C# 41a 4 PFENNIG

0.7500 g., 0.1860 Silver .0044 oz. **Ruler:** Georg Wilhelm

Date	Mintage	F	VF	XF	Unc	BU
1828	—	7.50	17.50	35.00	75.00	—

C# 40 4 PFENNIG

Copper **Ruler:** Georg Wilhelm

Date	Mintage	F	VF	XF	Unc	BU
1858	180,000	6.00	12.50	30.00	75.00	—

C# 45 1/2 SILBER GROSCHEN (1/60 Thaler)

1.0900 g., 0.2200 Silver .0077 oz. **Ruler:** Georg Wilhelm

Date	Mintage	F	VF	XF	Unc	BU
1858A	120,000	8.00	16.00	40.00	85.00	—

C# 42 MARIENGROSCHEN

1.5500 g., 0.3880 Silver .0193 oz. **Ruler:** Georg Wilhelm

Date	Mintage	F	VF	XF	Unc	BU
1821	143,000	10.00	20.00	50.00	90.00	—
1828	—	10.00	20.00	50.00	90.00	—

C# 46 SILBER GROSCHEN (1/50 Thaler)

2.1900 g., 0.2200 Silver .0154 oz. **Ruler:** Georg Wilhelm

Date	Mintage	F	VF	XF	Unc	BU
1858A	210,000	7.00	15.00	35.00	75.00	—

C# 47 2-1/2 SILBER GROSCHEN (1/12 Thaler)

3.2200 g., 0.3750 Silver .0388 oz. **Ruler:** Georg Wilhelm

Date	Mintage	F	VF	XF	Unc	BU
1858A	61,000	12.50	25.00	60.00	125	—

C# 43 1/24 THALER

1.9900 g., 0.3680 Silver .0235 oz. **Ruler:** Georg Wilhelm

Date	Mintage	F	VF	XF	Unc	BU
1821	195,000	12.00	25.00	50.00	100	—
1826	—	12.00	25.00	50.00	100	—

C# 44 1/2 THALER

14.0310 g., 0.8330 Silver .3760 oz. **Ruler:** Georg Wilhelm

Date	Mintage	F	VF	XF	Unc	BU
1821	5,400	75.00	150	300	450	—

C# 48 THALER

18.5200 g., 0.9000 Silver .5360 oz. **Ruler:** Adolph Georg

Date	Mintage	F	VF	XF	Unc	BU
1860B	8,356	60.00	100	250	500	—

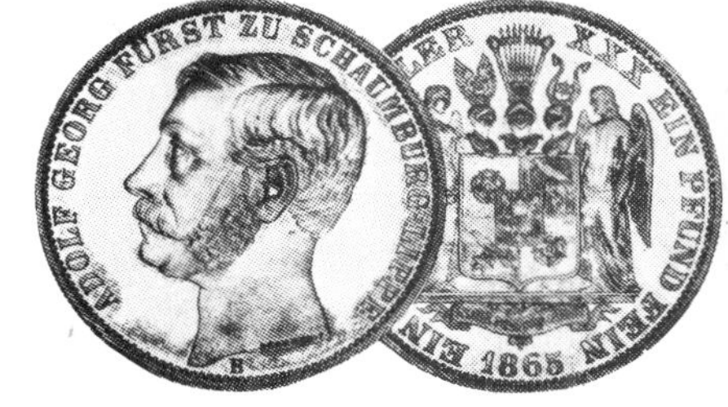

C# 51 THALER

18.5200 g., 0.9000 Silver .5360 oz. **Ruler:** Adolph Georg

Date	Mintage	F	VF	XF	Unc	BU
1865B	7,000	40.00	75.00	175	325	—

C# 49 2 THALER

37.0370 g., 0.9000 Silver 1.0718 oz. **Ruler:** Georg Wilhelm **Subject:** 50th Anniversary of Reign as Prince **Obv:** Similar to 1 Thaler, C#48.

Date	Mintage	F	VF	XF	Unc	BU
1857B	2,000	175	275	400	800	—

C# 50 10 THALER
13.2840 g., 0.9000 Gold .3826 oz. **Ruler:** Georg Wilhelm

Date	Mintage	F	VF	XF	Unc	BU
1829 FF	874	4,500	10,000	20,000	28,500	—
Note: Stack's Hammel sale 9/92 AU realized $20,000						
1829 w/o FF	179	5,500	12,500	25,000	35,000	—

REFORM COINAGE

Y# 203 2 MARK
11.1110 g., 0.9000 Silver 0.3215 oz. **Ruler:** Albrecht Georg
Subject: Death of Prince George

Date	Mintage	F	VF	XF	Unc	BU
1898A	5,000	250	450	750	1,250	1,400
1898A Proof	162	Value: 1,750				

Y# 204 5 MARK
27.7770 g., 0.9000 Silver 0.8038 oz. **Ruler:** Albrecht Georg
Subject: Death of Prince George

Date	Mintage	F	VF	XF	Unc	BU
1898A	3,000	400	825	1,350	2,250	2,600
1898A Proof	90	Value: 4,500				

Y# 202 20 MARK
7.9650 g., 0.9000 Gold .2304 oz. **Ruler:** Adolph Georg

Date	Mintage	F	VF	XF	Unc	BU
1874B	3,000	2,250	3,750	5,500	9,000	10,000
1874B Proof	—	Value: 15,000				

Y# 205 20 MARK
7.9650 g., 0.9000 Gold 0.2304 oz. **Ruler:** Albrecht Georg
Subject: Death of Prince George

Date	Mintage	F	VF	XF	Unc	BU
1898A	5,000	750	1,250	2,000	3,000	3,750
1898A Proof	250	Value: 4,700				

SCHLESWIG-HOLSTEIN

Schleswig-Holstein is the border area between Denmark and Germany. The duchy of Schleswig was Danish while Holstein was German. Christian I, son of Count Dietrich of Oldenburg (1423-40), was elected King of Denmark in 1448. By virtue of his marriage to Hedwig, the last surviving heir of the countship of Holstein-Rendsburg (see Holstein), Christian I became Duke of Schleswig and Count of Holstein in 1459. His status over Holstein was raised to that of duke in 1474 and from that year onwards, the dual duchies of Schleswig-Holstein were ruled by the Danish royal house. In 1533, a separate line for one of Friedrich I's sons was established in Gottorp. Similarly, a son of Christian III was given Sonderburg as his domain in 1559. The Danish kings continued to have coins struck for their remaining portions of Schleswig-Holstein during the next several centuries. Upon the dissolution of the Holy Roman Empire by Napoleon in 1806, Holstein was made a part of Denmark. However, Holstein, without Schleswig, joined the German Confederation following the final defeat of Napoleon in 1815. After Denmark tried to annex Schleswig and Holstein in 1846, she fought a war with Prussia for three years over control of the duchies, but it was inconclusive. In 1863, Denmark declared that Schleswig was part of that country although it had a German majority in the population. A second war was fought between Denmark against Prussia and Austria and Schleswig-Holstein was occupied by the victorious Prussians. The administration of Holstein was given to Austria, while that of Schleswig was obtained by Prussia in 1865. However, Austria was forced to give up Holstein after losing a war with Prussia in 1866. Schleswig-Holstein were controlled by Prussia and became part of the German Empire in 1871. Following World War I, a plebiscite was held in Schleswig and the northern part, with its majority Danish population, was ceded to Denmark in 1920.

RULERS
Christian VII (of Denmark), 1784-1808
Friedrich VI (of Denmark), 1808-1839
Christian VIII (of Denmark), 1839-1848

ALTONA MINT OFFICIALS' INITIALS
CB - Calus Branth
IFF, FF - Johann Friedrich Freund
MF, M.F, M.F. - Michael Flor
TA - Theodor C.W. Andersen

COPENHAGEN MINT OFFICIALS'
VS - Georg Vilhelm Svendsen

MONETARY SYSTEM
4 Dreiling = 2 Sechsling = 1 Schilling
60 Schilling = 1 Speciesdaler

N = Nypraeg = Restrike

DUCHY

JOINT COINAGE

C# 4 2-1/2 SCHILLING (1/24 Daler Specie)
2.8090 g., 0.3750 Silver .0339 oz. **Ruler:** Christian VII **Obv:** Crowned CR monogram **Rev:** Value above date

Date	Mintage	F	VF	XF	Unc	BU
1801 MF	211,000	9.00	25.00	50.00	100	—

C# 20 2-1/2 SCHILLING (1/24 Daler Specie)
2.8090 g., 0.0375 Silver .0339 oz. **Ruler:** Frederik VI

Date	Mintage	F	VF	XF	Unc	BU
1809 MF	960,000	10.00	20.00	50.00	175	—
1812	528,000	10.00	20.00	50.00	175	—

C# 5 5 SCHILLING (1/12 Daler Specie)
4.2140 g., 0.5000 Silver .0677 oz. **Ruler:** Christian VII **Obv:** Crowned CR monogram, VII within **Rev:** Value

Date	Mintage	F	VF	XF	Unc	BU
1801 MF	103,000	14.00	30.00	80.00	200	—

C# 21 8 REICHSBANK SCHILLING
Silver **Ruler:** Frederik VI

Date	Mintage	F	VF	XF	Unc	BU
1816 MF	56,000	60.00	180	300	575	—
1818 CB	243,000	30.00	70.00	110	200	—
1819 IFF	925,000	11.00	40.00	80.00	140	—

C# 22 16 REICHSBANK SCHILLING
4.2140 g., 0.5000 Silver .0677 oz. **Ruler:** Frederik VI

Date	Mintage	F	VF	XF	Unc	BU
1816 MF	31,000	65.00	220	300	575	—
1818 CB	125,000	35.00	85.00	160	265	—

C# 22a 16 REICHSBANK SCHILLING
4.2140 g., 0.5000 Silver .0677 oz. **Ruler:** Frederik VI **Rev:** 1/12 SP added

Date	Mintage	F	VF	XF	Unc	BU
1831 IFF	198,000	30.00	60.00	100	200	—
1839 IFF	63,000	40.00	70.00	140	200	—

C# 7 20 SCHILLING (1/3 Daler Specie)
9.6310 g., 0.8750 Silver .2709 oz. **Ruler:** Christian VII

Date	Mintage	F	VF	XF	Unc	BU
1808 MF	124,000	65.00	130	320	600	—

C# 8 40 SCHILLING (2/3 Daler Specie)
19.2630 g., 0.8750 Silver .5419 oz. **Ruler:** Christian VII **Obv:** "A" below head **Note:** Similar to 20 Schilling, C#7.

Date	Mintage	F	VF	XF	Unc	BU
1808 MF	—	150	320	525	1,000	—

C# 9 60 SCHILLING (Daler Specie)
28.8930 g., 0.8750 Silver .8128 oz. **Ruler:** Christian VII **Obv:** "B" below large head **Note:** Similar to 20 Schilling, C#7. Dav. #1311.

Date	Mintage	F	VF	XF	Unc	BU
1801 MF	312,000	110	300	450	900	—
1804 MF	106,000	90.00	200	300	500	—
1805 MF	—	—	—	—	2,000	—
1807 MF	102,000	85.00	180	280	500	—
1808 MF	1,304,000	75.00	160	275	500	—

PROVISIONAL GOVERNMENT

1848-1851

REGULAR COINAGE

C# 23 DREILING
Copper **Obv:** Arms of Schleswig-Holstein wihtin wreath **Rev:** Value and date within area name

Date	Mintage	F	VF	XF	Unc	BU
1850 TA	200,000	10.00	17.50	45.00	75.00	—

C# 24 SECHSLING
Copper **Obv:** Arms of Schleswig-Holstein within wreath **Rev:** Value and date within area name

Date	Mintage	F	VF	XF	Unc	BU
1850 TA	203,000	10.00	17.50	45.00	75.00	—
1851 TA	163,000	12.50	27.50	70.00	160	—

PATTERNS

Inlcuding off metal strikes

KM#	Date	Mintage	Identification	Mkt Val
Pn10	1801	—	2-1/2 Schilling. Gold. C#4.	—
Pn11	1805	—	60 Schilling. Tin. C#9.	—

SCHWARZBURG-RUDOLSTADT

The Schwarzburg family held territory in central and northern Thuringia. After many divisions, two lines, Sondershausen and Rudolstadt were founded in 1552. The count of Rudolstadt was raised to the rank of prince in 1710. The last prince abdicated in 1918.

RULERS
Ludwig Friedrich II, 1793-1807
Friedrich Gunther, 1807-1867
Albert, 1867-1869
Georg, 1869-1890
Gunther Viktor, 1890-1918

PRINCIPALITY

REGULAR COINAGE

C# 50 PFENNIG

Copper **Ruler:** Ludwig Friedrich II **Obv. Legend:** SCHWARZB/RUD-LM **Rev:** Value, 1 PF in script

Date	Mintage	F	VF	XF	Unc	BU
1801	—	4.00	8.00	20.00	65.00	—
1802	—	4.00	8.00	20.00	65.00	—

C# 63 PFENNIG

Copper **Ruler:** Friedrich Gunther

Date	Mintage	F	VF	XF	Unc	BU
1825	—	3.50	7.00	18.00	60.00	—

C# 65 PFENNIG

Copper **Ruler:** Friedrich Gunther **Obv:** Crowned arms **Rev:** Value **Rev. Legend:** SCHEIDE MUNZE

Date	Mintage	F	VF	XF	Unc	BU
1842A	—	2.50	5.50	15.00	45.00	—

C# 57 2 PFENNIG

Copper **Ruler:** Friedrich Gunther **Obv:** Crowned FG monogram within crossed branches **Rev:** Value

Date	Mintage	F	VF	XF	Unc	BU
1812	—	5.00	10.00	25.00	75.00	—

C# 66 2 PFENNIG

Copper **Ruler:** Friedrich Gunther **Obv:** Crowned arms

Date	Mintage	F	VF	XF	Unc	BU
1842A	—	4.00	8.00	20.00	65.00	—

C# 51 3 PFENNIG

Copper **Ruler:** Ludwig Friedrich II **Obv. Legend:** SCHWARZB/RUD-LM **Rev:** Value, 3 PF in script

Date	Mintage	F	VF	XF	Unc	BU
1804	—	6.00	12.00	30.00	80.00	—

C# 58 3 PFENNIG

Copper **Ruler:** Friedrich Gunther **Obv:** Monogram FG within crossed branches **Rev:** Value

Date	Mintage	F	VF	XF	Unc	BU
1813	—	6.00	12.00	30.00	80.00	—

C# 64 3 PFENNIG

Copper **Ruler:** Friedrich Gunther **Obv:** Crown above monogram

Date	Mintage	F	VF	XF	Unc	BU
1825	—	6.00	12.00	32.00	85.00	—

C# 67 3 PFENNIG

Copper **Ruler:** Friedrich Gunther **Obv:** Crowned arms **Rev. Legend:** SCHEIDEMUNZE

Date	Mintage	F	VF	XF	Unc	BU
1842A	—	3.00	6.00	18.00	55.00	—

C# 59 4 PFENNIG

Copper **Ruler:** Friedrich Gunther **Obv:** Monogram FG within crossed branches **Rev:** Value

Date	Mintage	F	VF	XF	Unc	BU
1812	—	7.00	15.00	40.00	100	—
1813	—	7.00	15.00	40.00	100	—

C# 53 6 PFENNIG

1.3300 g., 0.2500 Silver .0106 oz. **Ruler:** Ludwig Friedrich II

Date	Mintage	F	VF	XF	Unc	BU
1801	—	7.00	15.00	30.00	90.00	—

C# 60 6 PFENNIG

1.3300 g., 0.2500 Silver .0106 oz. **Ruler:** Friedrich Gunther

Date	Mintage	F	VF	XF	Unc	BU
1808	—	8.00	16.00	35.00	100	—

C# 60a 6 PFENNIG

1.3300 g., 0.2500 Silver .0106 oz. **Ruler:** Friedrich Gunther **Obv:** Rosette above and ledge below **Obv. Legend:** SCHWARZB/RUD-LM

Date	Mintage	F	VF	XF	Unc	BU
1812	—	7.00	15.00	30.00	90.00	—
1813	—	7.00	15.00	30.00	90.00	—

C# 73 1/8 KREUZER

Copper **Ruler:** Friedrich Gunther **Obv:** Crowned arms within branches **Rev:** Value

Date	Mintage	F	VF	XF	Unc	BU
1840	24,000	4.00	8.00	20.00	50.00	—
1855	—	4.00	8.00	20.00	50.00	—

C# 74 1/4 KREUZER

Copper **Ruler:** Friedrich Gunther

Date	Mintage	F	VF	XF	Unc	BU
1840	972,000	3.00	6.00	15.00	35.00	—
1852	—	3.00	6.00	15.00	35.00	—
1853	—	3.00	6.00	15.00	35.00	—
1855	—	3.00	6.00	15.00	35.00	—
1856	—	3.00	6.00	15.00	35.00	—

C# 74a 1/4 KREUZER

Copper **Ruler:** Friedrich Gunther

Date	Mintage	F	VF	XF	Unc	BU
1857	—	2.50	5.00	12.00	32.00	—
1859	—	2.50	5.00	12.00	32.00	—
1860	—	2.50	5.00	12.00	32.00	—
1861	—	2.50	5.00	12.00	32.00	—
1863	—	2.50	5.00	12.00	32.00	—
1865	—	2.50	5.00	12.00	32.00	—
1866	—	2.50	5.00	12.00	32.00	—

C# 82 1/4 KREUZER

Copper **Ruler:** Albert

Date	Mintage	F	VF	XF	Unc	BU
1868	96,000	3.00	6.00	15.00	45.00	—

C# 76 KREUZER

Copper **Ruler:** Friedrich Gunther

Date	Mintage	F	VF	XF	Unc	BU
1840	480,000	3.00	6.00	15.00	40.00	—

C# 76a KREUZER

Copper **Ruler:** Friedrich Gunther

Date	Mintage	F	VF	XF	Unc	BU
1864	—	2.00	4.00	10.00	30.00	—
1865	—	2.00	4.00	10.00	30.00	—
1866	—	2.00	4.00	10.00	30.00	—

C# 83 KREUZER

Copper **Ruler:** Albert

Date	Mintage	F	VF	XF	Unc	BU
1868	37,000	4.00	8.00	18.00	50.00	—

C# 77 3 KREUZER

1.2900 g., 0.3330 Silver .0138 oz. **Ruler:** Friedrich Gunther

Date	Mintage	F	VF	XF	Unc	BU
1839	155,000	5.00	10.00	30.00	100	—
1840	Inc. above	5.00	10.00	30.00	100	—
1841	Inc. above	5.00	10.00	30.00	100	—
1842	Inc. above	5.00	10.00	30.00	100	—
1846	Inc. above	5.00	10.00	30.00	100	—

C# 77a 3 KREUZER

1.2300 g., 0.3500 Silver .0138 oz. **Ruler:** Friedrich Gunther **Obv:** Legend added **Obv. Legend:** SCHEIDE MUZE

Date	Mintage	F	VF	XF	Unc	BU
1866	10,000	10.00	20.00	50.00	175	—

C# 78 6 KREUZER

2.5900 g., 0.3330 Silver .0277 oz. **Ruler:** Friedrich Gunther

Date	Mintage	F	VF	XF	Unc	BU
1840	165,000	6.00	12.00	35.00	125	—
1842	Inc. above	6.00	12.00	35.00	125	—
1846	Inc. above	6.00	12.00	35.00	125	—

C# 78a 6 KREUZER

2.4600 g., 0.3500 Silver .0276 oz. **Ruler:** Friedrich Gunther **Obv:** Legend added **Obv. Legend:** SCHEIDE MUNZE

Date	Mintage	F	VF	XF	Unc	BU
1866	10,000	12.00	25.00	55.00	165	—

C# 68 1/2 GROSCHEN

1.0900 g., 0.2220 Silver .0077 oz. **Ruler:** Friedrich Gunther **Obv:** Crowned arms **Rev:** Value

Date	Mintage	F	VF	XF	Unc	BU
1841A	—	4.00	8.00	25.00	100	—

C# 61 GROSCHEN

Billon **Ruler:** Ludwig Friedrich II **Obv. Legend:** SCHWARZB. RUD-LM **Rev:** Value

Date	Mintage	F	VF	XF	Unc	BU
1803	—	7.00	15.00	45.00	135	—
1808	—	5.00	10.00	30.00	110	—

C# 61a GROSCHEN

Billon **Ruler:** Friedrich Gunther **Obv:** Rosette above, legend below **Rev:** Value with rosettes

Date	Mintage	F	VF	XF	Unc	BU
1812	—	4.00	8.00	25.00	100	—

C# 69 GROSCHEN

2.1900 g., 0.2220 Silver .0156 oz. **Ruler:** Friedrich Gunther **Obv:** Crowned arms **Rev:** Value

Date	Mintage	F	VF	XF	Unc	BU
1841A	—	3.00	7.00	20.00	80.00	—

C# 79 1/2 GULDEN
5.3030 g., 0.9000 Silver .1535 oz. **Ruler:** Friedrich Gunther

Date	Mintage	F	VF	XF	Unc	BU
1841	157,000	15.00	30.00	75.00	200	—
1842	Inc. above	15.00	30.00	75.00	200	—
1843	Inc. above	15.00	30.00	75.00	200	—
1846	Inc. above	15.00	30.00	75.00	200	—

C# 80 GULDEN
10.6060 g., 0.9000 Silver .3069 oz. **Ruler:** Friedrich Gunther
Obv: Similar to 1/2 Gulden, C#79

Date	Mintage	F	VF	XF	Unc	BU
1841	163,000	25.00	50.00	100	250	—
1842	Inc. above	25.00	50.00	100	250	—
1843	Inc. above	25.00	50.00	100	250	—
1846	Inc. above	25.00	50.00	100	250	—

C# 81 2 GULDEN
21.2110 g., 0.9000 Silver .6138 oz. **Ruler:** Friedrich Gunther
Obv: Similar to 1/2 Gulden, C#79

Date	Mintage	F	VF	XF	Unc	BU
1846	500	300	500	1,000	2,000	—

C# 62 THALER
28.0630 g., 0.8330 Silver .7520 oz. **Ruler:** Friedrich Gunther
Note: Species Thaler.

Date	Mintage	F	VF	XF	Unc	BU
1812 L	—	90.00	175	300	800	—
1813 L	—	100	200	350	900	—

C# 70 THALER
18.5200 g., 0.9000 Silver .5360 oz. **Ruler:** Friedrich Gunther
Note: Vereins Thaler.

Date	Mintage	F	VF	XF	Unc	BU
1858	16,000	40.00	65.00	130	275	—
1859	6,000	50.00	75.00	150	300	—

C# 70a THALER
18.5200 g., 0.9000 Silver .5360 oz. **Ruler:** Friedrich Gunther

Date	Mintage	F	VF	XF	Unc	BU
1862	48,000	40.00	65.00	130	275	—
1863	17,000	40.00	65.00	130	275	—

C# 70b THALER
18.5200 g., 0.9000 Silver .5360 oz. **Ruler:** Friedrich Gunther

Date	Mintage	F	VF	XF	Unc	BU
1866	27,000	40.00	65.00	130	275	—

C# 71 THALER
18.5200 g., 0.9000 Silver .5360 oz. **Ruler:** Friedrich Gunther
Subject: 50th Anniversary of Reign

Date	Mintage	F	VF	XF	Unc	BU
1864	4,500	65.00	100	200	350	—
1864 Proof	—	Value: 600				

C# 84 THALER
18.5200 g., 0.9000 Silver .5360 oz. **Ruler:** Friedrich Gunther

Date	Mintage	F	VF	XF	Unc	BU
1867	13,000	50.00	80.00	175	450	—

C# 72 2 THALER (3-1/2 Gulden)
37.1200 g., 0.9000 Silver 1.0742 oz. **Ruler:** Friedrich Gunther

Date	Mintage	F	VF	XF	Unc	BU
1841A	10,000	100	200	450	1,000	—
1845A	5,100	100	200	450	1,000	—

REFORM COINAGE

Y# 207 2 MARK
11.1110 g., 0.9000 Silver .3215 oz. **Ruler:** Gunther Viktor

Date	Mintage	F	VF	XF	Unc	BU
1898A	100,000	150	250	450	650	800
1898A Proof	375	Value: 1,000				

Y# 208 10 MARK
3.9820 g., 0.9000 Gold .1152 oz. **Ruler:** Gunther Viktor

Date	Mintage	F	VF	XF	Unc	BU
1898A	10,000	700	1,250	1,800	2,750	3,250
1898A Proof	700	Value: 4,000				

TRADE COINAGE

C# 55 DUCAT
3.5000 g., 0.9860 Gold .1109 oz. **Ruler:** Ludwig Friedrich II

Date	Mintage	F	VF	XF	Unc	BU
1803	311	600	1,300	2,500	5,000	—

PATTERNS

Including off metal strikes

KM#	Date	Mintage	Identification	Mkt Val
Pn1	1803	—	Ducat. Copper. C#55.	300
Pn2	1803	—	Ducat. Silver. C#55.	500

TRIAL STRIKES

KM#	Date	Mintage	Identification	Mkt Val
TS1	1846	—	2 Groschen. C#81.	225

SCHWARZBURG-SONDERSHAUSEN

The Schwarzburg family held territory in central and northern Thuringia. After many divisions, two lines, Sondershausen and Rudolstadt were founded in 1552. The count of Sondershausen was raised to the rank of prince in 1709. The last prince died in 1909 and the lands passed to Rudolstadt.

RULERS
Gunther Friedrich Carl I, 1794-1835
Gunther Friedrich Carl II, 1835-1880
Karl Gunther, 1880-1909

PRINCIPALITY

REGULAR COINAGE

C# 18 PFENNIG
Copper **Ruler:** Gunther Friedrich Carl II **Note:** Struck at Arnstadt Mint.

Date	Mintage	F	VF	XF	Unc	BU
1846A	1,613,000	1.50	3.00	9.00	35.00	—
1858A	360,000	2.00	4.00	12.00	40.00	—

C# 19 3 PFENNIG
Copper **Ruler:** Gunther Friedrich Carl II **Note:** Struck at Arnstadt Mint.

Date	Mintage	F	VF	XF	Unc	BU
1846A	682,000	3.00	6.00	18.00	50.00	—
1858A	360,000	3.00	6.00	18.00	50.00	—
1870A	120,000	4.00	8.00	22.00	60.00	—

C# 20 1/2 SILBER GROSCHEN
1.0900 g., 0.2220 Silver .0077 oz. **Ruler:** Gunther Friedrich Carl II **Note:** Struck at Arnstadt Mint.

Date	Mintage	F	VF	XF	Unc	BU
1846A	657,000	3.00	6.00	18.00	50.00	—
1851A	Inc. above	3.00	6.00	18.00	50.00	—
1858A	180,000	4.00	8.00	22.00	60.00	—

C# 21 SILBER GROSCHEN
2.1900 g., 0.2220 Silver .0156 oz. **Ruler:** Gunther Friedrich Carl II **Note:** Struck at Arnstadt Mint.

Date	Mintage	F	VF	XF	Unc	BU
1846A	584,000	3.00	6.00	18.00	55.00	—
1851A	Inc. above	3.00	6.00	18.00	55.00	—
1858A	150,000	3.50	7.00	20.00	60.00	—
1870A	120,000	3.50	7.00	20.00	60.00	—

C# 22 THALER
18.5200 g., 0.9000 Silver .5360 oz. **Ruler:** Gunther Friedrich Carl II **Note:** Vereins Thaler. Struck at Arnstadt Mint.

Date	Mintage	F	VF	XF	Unc	BU
1859A	15,000	50.00	80.00	160	400	—
1865A	10,000	50.00	80.00	160	400	—
1870A	11,000	50.00	80.00	160	400	—

C# 23 2 THALER (3-1/2 Gulden)
37.1200 g., 0.9000 Silver 1.0741 oz. **Ruler:** Gunther Friedrich Carl II **Note:** Struck at Arnstadt Mint.

Date	Mintage	F	VF	XF	Unc	BU
1841A	4,300	150	250	550	1,200	—
1845A	8,600	100	200	450	1,000	—
1854A	8,600	100	200	450	1,000	—

REFORM COINAGE

Y# 209 2 MARK
11.1110 g., 0.9000 Silver .3215 oz. **Ruler:** Karl Gunther **Note:** Struck at Arnstadt Mint.

Date	Mintage	F	VF	XF	Unc	BU
1896A	50,000	125	250	425	675	850
1896A Proof	190	Value: 1,000				

Y# 210 20 MARK
7.9650 g., 0.9000 Gold .2304 oz. **Ruler:** Karl Gunther **Note:** Struck at Arnstadt Mint.

Date	Mintage	F	VF	XF	Unc	BU
1896A	5,000	850	1,500	2,500	3,000	4,000
1896A Proof	—	Value: 5,500				

SILESIA

A duchy, located in northeastern Germany, was separated into many segments. They were greatly influenced by Bohemia and Austria. The first coins were struck c. 1169. Special coins for Silesian possessions were struck by Bohemia from 1327. From 1526, when Bohemia and its Silesian possessions fell to Austria, a special series of coins were struck by Austria for the area. After the Prussian invasion in 1740, coins were minted from 1743 through 1797.

RULERS
Friedrich Wilhelm III, 1797-1840

MINT MARKS
A - Berlin
B - Breslau
G - Glatz, 1807-1809
W - Wratislawia (i.e. Breslau)

NOTE: For similar gold coins dated 1787-1805 refer to Prussian listings.

DUCHY

REGULAR COINAGE

C# 53 1/2 KREUZER
Copper **Obv:** Crowned FW monogram **Rev:** Value

Date	Mintage	F	VF	XF	Unc	BU
1806A	—	15.00	30.00	50.00	90.00	—

C# 57 KREUZER
Billon **Obv:** Uniformed bust left **Rev:** Crowned arms with eagle

Date	Mintage	F	VF	XF	Unc	BU
1806A	—	17.50	40.00	90.00	200	—
1808G	—	17.50	40.00	90.00	200	—

C# 54 KREUZER
Billon **Obv:** Crowned arms iwth eagle within crossed branches **Rev:** Value

Date	Mintage	F	VF	XF	Unc	BU
1810A	55,000	15.00	30.00	60.00	125	—

C# 60 9 KREUZER
Billon

Date	Mintage	F	VF	XF	Unc	BU
1808G	—	55.00	100	175	300	—

C# 61 18 KREUZER
0.5630 Silver **Obv:** Uniformed bust left **Rev:** Crowned eagle with scepter and orb

Date	Mintage	F	VF	XF	Unc	BU
1808G	—	100	200	375	750	—

C# 56 GROSCHEL
Billon **Ruler:** Friedrich Wilhelm III **Obv:** Crowned FWR monogram **Rev:** Value

Date	Mintage	F	VF	XF	Unc	BU
1805A	—	20.00	40.00	75.00	150	—
1806A	—	20.00	40.00	75.00	150	—
1808G	—	20.00	40.00	75.00	150	—
1809G	—	20.00	40.00	75.00	150	—

STOLBERG

The castle of Stolberg, located on the southern slopes of the Harz Mountains, 9 miles (15 km) northeast of Nordhausen, is the ancestral home of the counts of that name. The dynasty has a recognized line of succession from count Heinrich I (1210-1239), but the family claimed descent from Otto Colonna, an Italian noble of the 6th century. The column in the family arms signifies this supposed connection, whether historically accurate or not. Count Heinrich was the younger brother of the count of Hohnstein whose castle lay just 6 miles away. Whatever the origin of the earlier counts of Stolberg, they came to an end and the line founded by Heinrich I began in about 1222. The long series of coins, based on the rich Harz silver mine holdings of the family, began at this time. Various territories, some scattered a distance from the family home, were added to the Stolberg lands and two brothers established separate lines in 1538, Stolberg-Stolberg and Stolberg-Wernigerode. Another brother succeeded to the Dietz portion of Königstein in 1574.

ARMS

Stolberg - stag, usually to left, sometimes to right, antlers extend backwards
Wernigerode - one or two fish (trout) standing on tails
Königstein - lion left
Rochefort - eagle
Eppstein - three chevrons
Minzenberg - horizontal bar
Mark - checkerboard in horizontal bar
Agimont - five horizontal bars
Lohra - lion rampant left
Wertheim - top half of eagle above three roses
Breuberg - two horizontal bars
Hohnstein - checkerboard
Klettenberg - stag left, but antlers extend upwards

STOLBERG-ROSSLA

The small village of Rossla is situated on the main east-west road between Nordhausen and Sangerhausen, 9 miles (15 km) southeast of Stolberg castle. It became the seat of a cadet line of the junior branch of the dynasty upon the division of Stolberg in 1704. Although Stolberg-Rossla issued a few coins in the name of the individual counts, most of its extensive coinage during the 18th century was coined jointly with the rulers of Stolberg-Stolberg, under which the issues are listed.Although the Stolberg counts surrendered their sovereignty regarding military and foreign matters to Prussia during the latter half of the 18th century, the Stolberg-Rossla line continued well into the 20th century.

RULERS

Johann Wilhelm Christof, 1776-1826
August Friedrich Botho Christian, 1826-1846
Karl Martin, 1846-1870
Botho August Karl, 1870-1893
Jost Christian, 1893

COUNTY

REGULAR COINAGE

C# 47 PFENNIG
Copper **Ruler:** Johann Wilhelm Christof **Obv:** Stag left before column **Rev:** Value above date

Date	Mintage	VG	F	VF	XF	Unc
1801 Z	—	6.00	15.00	35.00	60.00	—

STOLBERG-WERNIGERODE

The castle of Wernigerode is situated across the Harz Mountains to the north of Stolberg castle, some 12 miles (20 km) west-southwest of Halberstadt. An early division of the old Stolberg line in 1538 resulted in a separate line in Wernigerode. A second division in 1572 established Stolberg-Ortenberg and Stolberg Schwarza (Wernigerode) and the latter was divided further into 1876 divided further into the senior branch of Stolberg-Wernigerode and the junior branch of Stolberg-Stolberg. Once again, Stolberg-Wernigerode was the foundation of three separate lines at Gedern, Schwarza and Wernigerodein 1710. The first two fell extinct within a century, but Stolberg-Wernigerode lasted into the 20th century.

RULERS

Christian Friedrich, 1778-1824
Heinrich XXIII, 1824-1854
Otto, 1854-1896
Christian Ernst II, 1896

DUCHY

TRADE COINAGE

C# 25 DUCAT
3.5000 g., 0.9860 Gold .1109 oz. **Subject:** Golden Wedding Anniversary

Date	Mintage	F	VF	XF	Unc	BU
1818	308	600	1,200	2,500	4,500	—

C# 26 DUCAT
3.5000 g., 0.9860 Gold .1109 oz. **Subject:** Henrich XII

Date	Mintage	F	VF	XF	Unc	BU
1824	—	450	900	1,800	3,500	—

PATTERNS

Including off metal strikes

KM#	Date	Mintage	Identification	Mkt Val
Pn9	1818	—	Ducat. Silver. C#25	250

TEUTONIC ORDER

(Deutschen Order)

The Order of Knights was founded during the Third Crusade in 1198. They acquired considerable territory by conquest from the heathen Prussians in the late 13th and early 14th centuries. The seat of the Grand Master moved from Acre to Venice and in 1309 to Marienburg, Prussia. The Teutonic Order began striking coins in the late 13th century. In 1355 permission was granted to strike hellersat Mergentheim. However, the bulk of the Order's coinage until 1525 was schillings and half schoters minted in and for Prussia. In 1809 the Order was suppressed and Mergentheim was annexed to Wurttemberg.

RULERS

Max Franz of Austria, 1780-1801
Karl Ludwig, 1801-1804
Anton Victor, 1804-1809

ARMS

Grand Master: Cross, shield w/eagle in ctr., shield is often w/double outline. Later versions include family and territorial arms in angles of cross.
Order Arms: Long cross superimposed, usually on empty shield, sometimes w/eagle in center.

ORDER OF KNIGHTS

REGULAR COINAGE

C# 22 10 KREUZER
Silver **Subject:** Death of Grand Master Max Franz

Date	Mintage	VG	F	VF	XF	Unc
1801	—	30.00	60.00	120	225	—

C# 26 1/4 THALER
Silver **Subject:** Death of Grand Master Max Franz

Date	Mintage	VG	F	VF	XF	Unc
1801	300	100	150	250	500	—

WALDECK

The county of Waldeck was located on the border of Hesse. Their first coinage appeared ca. 1250. Pyrmont was united with Waldeck in 1625 but was ruled separately for a while in the 19th century. They were reunited in 1812. The rulers gained the status of prince in 1712. The administration was turned over to Prussia in 1867 but the princes retained some sovereignty until 1918.

WALDECK-PYRMONT

RULERS

Friedrich Karl August in Waldeck, 1763-1812
Georg (in Pyrmont), 1805-1812 (Refer to Pyrmont for listings in Waldeck-Pyrmont), 1812-1813
Georg Heinrich, 1813-1845
Emma, Regent for Georg Victor, 1845-1852
Georg Victor, 1852-1893
Friedrich, 1893-1918

MINTMASTERS INITIALS

AW - Albert Welle
FW, F*w, W, .W. - Friedrich Welle

PRINCIPALITY

REGULAR COINAGE

C# 42b PFENNIG
Copper **Ruler:** Friedrich Karl August in Waldeck **Obv:** Crowned F monogram **Rev:** Value

Date	Mintage	F	VF	XF	Unc	BU
1809 FW	—	6.00	12.00	35.00	120	—
1810 FW	—	6.00	12.00	35.00	120	—

C# 43a PFENNIG
Copper **Ruler:** Friedrich Karl August in Waldeck **Obv:** Crowned arms

Date	Mintage	F	VF	XF	Unc	BU
1809 FW	—	6.00	12.00	35.00	125	—

C# 43b PFENNIG
Copper **Ruler:** Friedrich Karl August in Waldeck **Rev:** Value **Rev. Legend:** 1 PFENNIG

Date	Mintage	F	VF	XF	Unc	BU
1810 FW	—	6.00	12.00	35.00	125	—

C# 65 PFENNIG
Copper **Ruler:** Georg Heinrich **Obv:** Crowned GH monogram

Date	Mintage	F	VF	XF	Unc	BU
1816 FW	—	6.00	12.00	25.00	100	—
1817 FW	—	6.00	12.00	25.00	100	—

C# 66 PFENNIG
Copper **Ruler:** Georg Heinrich

Date	Mintage	F	VF	XF	Unc	BU
1816 FW	—	6.00	12.00	45.00	150	—
1817 W	—	6.00	12.00	45.00	150	—

C# 67 PFENNIG
Copper **Ruler:** Georg Heinrich **Obv:** Crowned Waldeck-Pyrmont arms

Date	Mintage	F	VF	XF	Unc	BU
1821 FW	—	5.00	10.00	20.00	80.00	—

C# 67a PFENNIG
Copper **Ruler:** Georg Heinrich **Obv:** Arms in beaded border

Date	Mintage	F	VF	XF	Unc	BU
1821 FW	—	5.00	10.00	20.00	80.00	—

C# 68 PFENNIG
Copper **Ruler:** Georg Heinrich **Obv:** Crowned draped arms

Date	Mintage	F	VF	XF	Unc	BU
1825 FW	—	6.00	12.00	35.00	125	—

C# 69 PFENNIG
Copper **Ruler:** Georg Heinrich **Note:** Struck at Hannover Mint.

Date	Mintage	F	VF	XF	Unc	BU
1842A	352,000	4.00	8.00	18.00	65.00	—
1843A	220,000	4.00	8.00	18.00	65.00	—
1845A	384,000	4.00	8.00	18.00	65.00	—

C# 85 PFENNIG
Copper **Ruler:** Georg Victor **Note:** Struck at Hannover Mint.

Date	Mintage	F	VF	XF	Unc	BU
1855A	366,000	3.00	6.00	12.00	45.00	—
1855A Proof	—	Value: 100				

C# 85a PFENNIG
Copper **Ruler:** Georg Victor **Note:** Struck at Prussia Mint.

Date	Mintage	F	VF	XF	Unc	BU
1867B	540,000	2.00	4.00	8.00	35.00	—

C# 44a 3 PFENNIG
Copper **Ruler:** Friedrich Karl August in Waldeck **Obv:** Crowned F monogram **Obv. Legend:** FURSTL. WALDECK SCH. MUNZ **Rev:** Value **Rev. Legend:** III PFENNIGE

Date	Mintage	F	VF	XF	Unc	BU
1809 FW	—	7.00	15.00	45.00	160	—
1809 FW	—	7.00	15.00	45.00	160	—
1810 FW	—	7.00	15.00	45.00	160	—

C# 45 3 PFENNIG
Copper **Ruler:** Friedrich Karl August in Waldeck **Obv:** Crowned star arms

Date	Mintage	F	VF	XF	Unc	BU
1809 FW	—	7.00	15.00	45.00	165	—

C# 45a 3 PFENNIG
Copper **Ruler:** Friedrich Karl August in Waldeck **Obv:** Arms within pearl circle

Date	Mintage	F	VF	XF	Unc	BU
1810 FW	—	8.00	16.00	50.00	175	—

C# 70 3 PFENNIG
Copper **Ruler:** Georg Heinrich

Date	Mintage	F	VF	XF	Unc	BU
1819 FW	—	6.00	12.00	35.00	145	—

C# 70b 3 PFENNIG
Copper **Ruler:** Georg Heinrich **Rev:** Value **Rev. Legend:** PFENNIG

Date	Mintage	F	VF	XF	Unc	BU
1819 FW	—	10.00	20.00	60.00	185	—

C# 70a 3 PFENNIG
Copper **Ruler:** Georg Heinrich

Date	Mintage	F	VF	XF	Unc	BU
1819 FW	—	7.00	15.00	45.00	160	—

C# 71 3 PFENNIG
Copper **Ruler:** Georg Heinrich

Date	Mintage	F	VF	XF	Unc	BU
1824 FW	—	6.00	12.00	35.00	145	—
1825 FW	—	6.00	12.00	35.00	145	—

C# 72 3 PFENNIG
Copper **Ruler:** Georg Heinrich **Note:** Struck at Hannover Mint.

Date	Mintage	F	VF	XF	Unc	BU
1842A	247,000	5.00	10.00	20.00	80.00	—
1843A	114,000	7.00	15.00	45.00	135	—
1845A	249,000	5.00	10.00	20.00	80.00	—

C# 86 3 PFENNIG
Copper **Ruler:** Georg Victor **Note:** Struck at Hannover Mint.

Date	Mintage	F	VF	XF	Unc	BU
1855A	243,000	4.00	8.00	16.00	60.00	—

C# 86.1 3 PFENNIG
Copper **Ruler:** Georg Victor **Note:** Struck at Prussia Mint.

Date	Mintage	F	VF	XF	Unc	BU
1867B	420,000	3.00	6.00	12.00	50.00	—

C# 46 1/2 GROSCHEN
Copper **Ruler:** Friedrich Karl August in Waldeck

Date	Mintage	F	VF	XF	Unc	BU
1809 FW	—	20.00	45.00	90.00	250	—

C# 73 1/2 GROSCHEN
Copper **Ruler:** Georg Heinrich **Obv:** Crowned draped arms

Date	Mintage	F	VF	XF	Unc	BU
1825 FW	—	20.00	40.00	80.00	235	—

C# 74 GROSCHEN
1.3900 g., 0.3120 Silver .0139 oz. **Ruler:** Georg Heinrich **Note:** Marien Groschen.

Date	Mintage	F	VF	XF	Unc	BU
1814 FW	—	15.00	30.00	75.00	220	—
1820 FW	—	15.00	30.00	75.00	220	—

C# 74a GROSCHEN
1.3900 g., 0.3120 Silver .0139 oz. **Ruler:** Georg Heinrich

Date	Mintage	F	VF	XF	Unc	BU
1820 FW	—	—	—	200	350	—

C# 74b GROSCHEN
1.3900 g., 0.3120 Silver .0139 oz. **Ruler:** Georg Heinrich **Obv:** Crowned draped arms

Date	Mintage	F	VF	XF	Unc	BU
1820 FW	—	12.00	25.00	60.00	190	—
1823 FW	—	12.00	25.00	60.00	190	—

C# 76 GROSCHEN
2.1900 g., 0.2220 Silver .0156 oz. **Ruler:** Georg Heinrich **Obv. Legend:** ... WALDECK U.P **Note:** Silber Groschen.

Date	Mintage	F	VF	XF	Unc	BU
1836 AW	164,000	10.00	20.00	45.00	160	—
1839 AW	46,000	12.00	25.00	50.00	170	—

C# 77 GROSCHEN
2.1900 g., 0.2220 Silver .0156 oz. **Ruler:** Georg Heinrich **Obv. Legend:** ... WALDECK U. PYRMONT **Note:** Struck at Hannover Mint.

Date	Mintage	F	VF	XF	Unc	BU
1842A	310,000	6.00	12.00	28.00	110	—
1843A	191,000	6.00	12.00	30.00	115	—
1845A	182,000	6.00	12.00	30.00	115	—

C# 87 GROSCHEN
2.1900 g., 0.2220 Silver .0156 oz. **Ruler:** Georg Victor **Rev:** A below value and date **Note:** Struck at Hannover Mint.

Date	Mintage	F	VF	XF	Unc	BU
1855A	156,000	7.00	15.00	30.00	125	—

C# 87a GROSCHEN
2.1900 g., 0.2220 Silver .0156 oz. **Ruler:** Georg Victor **Note:** Struck at Prussia Mint.

Date	Mintage	F	VF	XF	Unc	BU
1867B	180,000	6.00	12.00	20.00	90.00	—

C# 78 2 MARIENGROSCHEN
2.3900 g., 0.3750 Silver .0288 oz. **Ruler:** Georg Heinrich

Date	Mintage	F	VF	XF	Unc	BU
1820 FW	—	8.00	16.00	42.00	175	—
1822 FW	—	8.00	16.00	42.00	175	—

Date	Mintage	F	VF	XF	Unc	BU
1823 FW	—	8.00	16.00	42.00	175	—
1824 FW	—	8.00	16.00	42.00	175	—
1825 FW	—	8.00	16.00	42.00	175	—

C# 78a 2 MARIENGROSCHEN
2.3900 g., 0.3750 Silver .0288 oz. **Ruler:** Georg Heinrich **Rev:** A.W. below value

Date	Mintage	F	VF	XF	Unc	BU
1827 AW	—	10.00	20.00	50.00	185	—
1828 AW	—	10.00	20.00	50.00	185	—

C# 75 1/24 THALER
1.9800 g., 0.3680 Silver .0234 oz. **Ruler:** Georg Heinrich

Date	Mintage	F	VF	XF	Unc	BU
1818 FW	—	10.00	20.00	45.00	165	—
1819 FW	—	10.00	20.00	45.00	165	—

C# 79 1/6 THALER
5.3400 g., 0.5200 Silver .0892 oz. **Ruler:** Georg Heinrich

Date	Mintage	F	VF	XF	Unc	BU
1837 AW	34,000	22.00	45.00	90.00	225	—

C# 79a 1/6 THALER
5.3400 g., 0.5200 Silver .0892 oz. **Ruler:** Georg Heinrich **Note:** Struck at Hannover Mint.

Date	Mintage	F	VF	XF	Unc	BU
1843A	38,000	20.00	40.00	80.00	200	—
1845A	38,000	20.00	40.00	80.00	200	—

C# 53 1/4 THALER
7.0000 g., 0.6200 Silver .1395 oz. **Ruler:** Georg (in Pyrmont)

Date	Mintage	F	VF	XF	Unc	BU
1810 FW	—	100	200	375	700	—

C# 53a 1/4 THALER
7.0000 g., 0.6200 Silver .1395 oz. **Ruler:** Georg (in Pyrmont) **Rev:** Date and value in larger letters

Date	Mintage	F	VF	XF	Unc	BU
1810 FW	—	75.00	150	300	600	—

C# 62 1/4 THALER
7.0000 g., 0.6200 Silver .1395 oz. **Ruler:** Georg (in Pyrmont) **Obv. Legend:** ...PYRMONT &

Date	Mintage	F	VF	XF	Unc	BU
1812 FW	—	600	1,250	1,750	2,250	—

C# 62a 1/4 THALER
7.0000 g., 0.6200 Silver .1395 oz. **Ruler:** Georg Heinrich **Obv. Legend:** ...PYRMONT EC

Date	Mintage	F	VF	XF	Unc	BU
1813 FW	—	600	1,250	1,750	2,250	—

C# 80 1/3 THALER
8.8000 g., 0.6200 Silver .1754 oz. **Ruler:** Georg Heinrich

Date	Mintage	F	VF	XF	Unc	BU
1824 FW	—	55.00	110	220	375	—

C# 80a 1/3 THALER
8.8000 g., 0.6200 Silver .1754 oz. **Ruler:** Georg Heinrich

Date	Mintage	F	VF	XF	Unc	BU
1824 FW	—	50.00	100	200	350	—

C# 81 1/3 THALER
8.8000 g., 0.6200 Silver .1754 oz. **Ruler:** Georg Heinrich

Date	Mintage	F	VF	XF	Unc	BU
1824 FW	—	65.00	125	275	425	—

C# 59 THALER
28.0600 g., 0.8330 Silver .7515 oz. **Ruler:** Friedrich Karl August in Waldeck **Obv. Legend:** FRIDERICUS PR... **Note:** Dav. #922.

Date	Mintage	F	VF	XF	Unc	BU
1810 FW	—	400	700	1,500	3,500	—

C# 59a THALER
28.0600 g., 0.8330 Silver .7515 oz. **Ruler:** Friedrich Karl August in Waldeck **Obv. Legend:** FRIDERICUS D.G. PR...

Date	Mintage	F	VF	XF	Unc	BU
1810 FW	—	600	1,100	2,500	5,200	—

C# 90 THALER
18.5200 g., 0.9000 Silver .5358 oz. **Ruler:** Georg (in Pyrmont) **Obv:** Pyrmont C7 **Rev:** Waldeck-Pyrmont C59 **Note:** Mule.

Date	Mintage	F	VF	XF	Unc	BU
ND(1811-)	—	—	—	—	—	—

C# 92 THALER
18.5200 g., 0.9000 Silver .5358 oz. **Ruler:** Georg (in Pyrmont) **Obv:** Pyrmont C7 **Rev:** Waldeck-Pyrmont C59a **Note:** Mule.

Date	Mintage	F	VF	XF	Unc	BU
ND(1811-)	—	—	—	—	—	—

C# 63.1 THALER
28.0600 g., 0.8330 Silver .7515 oz. **Ruler:** Georg Heinrich **Edge Lettering:** X. EINE + + + + FEINE + + + + MARCK + + + +

Date	Mintage	F	VF	XF	Unc	BU
1813 FW	—	600	1,100	2,500	5,000	—

C# 63.2 THALER
28.0600 g., 0.8330 Silver .7515 oz. **Ruler:** Georg Heinrich **Edge Lettering:** X. EINE- FEINE - MARK

Date	Mintage	F	VF	XF	Unc	BU
1813 FW	—	600	1,100	2,500	5,000	—

C# 64.1 THALER
29.5170 g., 0.8680 Silver .8237 oz. **Ruler:** Georg Heinrich **Edge Lettering:** * K * R * O * N * T * H * A * L * E * R ** **Note:** Similar to C#63.

Date	Mintage	F	VF	XF	Unc	BU
1813 FW	—	600	1,100	2,500	5,000	—

C# 64.2 THALER
29.5170 g., 0.8680 Silver .8237 oz. **Ruler:** Georg Heinrich **Edge Lettering:** + K + R + O + N + T + H + A + L + E + R +

Date	Mintage	F	VF	XF	Unc	BU
1813 FW	—	600	1,100	2,500	5,000	—

C# 64.3 THALER
29.5170 g., 0.8680 Silver .8237 oz. **Ruler:** Georg Heinrich **Edge Lettering:** KRONTHALER + + + + + + + +

Date	Mintage	F	VF	XF	Unc	BU
1813 FW	—	600	1,100	2,500	5,000	—

C# 64.4 THALER
29.5170 g., 0.8680 Silver .8237 oz. **Ruler:** Georg Heinrich **Edge Lettering:** KRONTHALER and 38 rosettes

Date	Mintage	F	VF	XF	Unc	BU
1813 FW	—	600	1,100	2,500	5,000	—

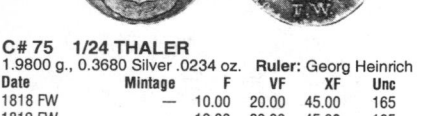

C# 64.5 THALER

29.5170 g., 0.8680 Silver .8237 oz. **Ruler:** Georg Heinrich **Edge Lettering:** KRONTHALER and 45 rosettes

Date	Mintage	F	VF	XF	Unc	BU
1813 FW	—	600	1,100	2,500	5,000	—

C# 64.6 THALER

29.5170 g., 0.8680 Silver .8237 oz. **Ruler:** Georg Heinrich **Edge Lettering:** KRONTHALER and 46 rosettes

Date	Mintage	F	VF	XF	Unc	BU
1813 FW	—	600	1,100	2,500	5,000	—

C# 64.7 THALER

29.5170 g., 0.8680 Silver .8237 oz. **Ruler:** Georg Heinrich **Edge Lettering:** + + WALDECKISCHER + + + KRONTHALER

Date	Mintage	F	VF	XF	Unc	BU
1813 FW	—	600	1,100	2,500	5,000	—

C# 64.9 THALER

29.5170 g., 0.8680 Silver .8237 oz. **Ruler:** Georg Heinrich **Edge Lettering:** + WALDEKISCHER + KRONTHALER + FEINSILBER

Date	Mintage	F	VF	XF	Unc	BU
1813 FW	—	600	1,100	2,500	5,000	—

C# 64.11 THALER

29.5170 g., 0.8680 Silver .8237 oz. **Ruler:** Georg Heinrich **Edge Lettering:** + WALDECKISCHER + KRONTHALER + F. + SILB

Date	Mintage	F	VF	XF	Unc	BU
1813 FW	—	600	1,100	2,500	5,000	—

C# 64.12 THALER

29.5170 g., 0.8680 Silver .8237 oz. **Ruler:** Georg Heinrich **Note:** Edge inscription appears 52 stars

Date	Mintage	F	VF	XF	Unc	BU
1813 FW	—	600	1,100	2,500	5,000	—

C# 64.8 THALER

29.5170 g., 0.8680 Silver .8237 oz. **Ruler:** Georg Heinrich **Note:** Edge inscription appears like KM#64.7 but with 4 stars instead of 5 crosses.

Date	Mintage	F	VF	XF	Unc	BU
1813 FW	—	600	1,100	2,500	5,000	—

C# 64.10 THALER

29.5170 g., 0.8680 Silver .8237 oz. **Ruler:** Georg Heinrich **Note:** Edge inscription appears like KM#64.9 but ends with a star.

Date	Mintage	F	VF	XF	Unc	BU
1813 FW	—	600	1,100	2,500	5,000	—

C# 82 THALER

29.4500 g., 0.8680 Silver .8218 oz. **Ruler:** Georg Heinrich

Date	Mintage	F	VF	XF	Unc	BU
1824 FW	—	200	350	700	1,400	—

C# 94 THALER

18.5200 g., 0.9000 Silver .5358 oz. **Ruler:** Georg (in Pyrmont) **Obv:** Pyrmont C7 **Rev:** Waldeck-Pyrmont C82 **Note:** Mule.

Date	Mintage	F	VF	XF	Unc	BU
ND(1824)	—	—	—	—	—	—

C# 88 THALER

18.5200 g., 0.9000 Silver .5358 oz. **Ruler:** Georg Victor

Date	Mintage	F	VF	XF	Unc	BU
1859A	14,000	40.00	85.00	165	325	—
1867A	19,000	40.00	85.00	165	325	—

C# 83 2 THALER (3-1/2 Gulden)

37.1200 g., 0.9000 Silver 1.0742 oz. **Ruler:** Georg Heinrich **Note:** Struck at Hannover Mint.

Date	Mintage	F	VF	XF	Unc	BU
1842A	4,500	350	700	1,200	2,000	—
1845A	4,500	350	700	1,200	2,000	—

C# 84 2 THALER (3-1/2 Gulden)

37.1200 g., 0.9000 Silver 1.0742 oz. **Ruler:** Emma, Regent for Georg Victor **Rev:** Similar to C#83 **Note:** Struck at Hannover Mint.

Date	Mintage	F	VF	XF	Unc	BU
1847A	1,000	650	1,100	1,900	3,250	—

C# 89 2 THALER (3-1/2 Gulden)

37.1200 g., 0.9000 Silver 1.0742 oz. **Ruler:** Georg Victor **Note:** Struck at Hannover Mint.

Date	Mintage	F	VF	XF	Unc	BU
1856A	11,000	200	400	800	1,600	—

WALLMODEN-GIMBORN

The town of Gimborn, located in Westphalia, was purchased from Schwarzenberg in 1782. The following year it was raised to the rank of county. In 1806, Wallmoden-Gimborn was annexed to Berg. In 1815, the land went to Prussia.

RULERS

Johann Ludwig, 1782-1806

TOWN

REGULAR COINAGE

C# 1 1/24 THALER

1.9900 g., 0.3680 Silver .0235 oz.

Date	Mintage	F	VF	XF	Unc	BU
1802	—	70.00	200	350	575	—

C# 2 1/2 THALER

14.0300 g., 0.8330 Silver .3757 oz.

Date	Mintage	F	VF	XF	Unc	BU
1802	—	350	500	950	—	—

TRADE COINAGE

C# 3 DUCAT

3.5000 g., 0.9860 Gold .1109 oz.

Date	Mintage	F	VF	XF	Unc	BU
1802	400	1,250	2,500	4,500	8,000	—

PATTERNS

Including off metal strikes

KM#	Date	Mintage	Identification	Mkt Val
Pn1	1802	—	Ducat. Silver. C#3.	650

WESTPHALIA

A kingdom, located in western Germany, created by Napoleon for his brother. It was comprised of parts of Hesse-Cassel, Brunswick, Hildesheim, Paderborn, Halberstadt, Osnabruck, Minden, etc. In 1813 and 1814,Westphalia was divided and returned to its former owners.

RULERS

Jerome (Hieronymus) Napoleon, 1807-1813

MINT MARKS

B - Brunswick
C,C. - Cassel, mm on rev.
C,C. - Clausthal, mm on obv.
F - Cassel

MINTMASTERS' MARKS

C & eagle head - Cassel
J & horse head - Cassel
J & horse head - Paris

MINT OFFICIALS' INITIALS

Initial	Date	Name
F	1783-1831	Dietrich Heinrich Fulda in Cassel

KINGDOM

GERMAN STANDARD COINAGE

C# 1 PFENNIG
Copper

Date	Mintage	F	VF	XF	Unc	BU
1808C	—	7.00	15.00	35.00	100	—

C# 2 2 PFENNIG
Copper **Obv:** Crowned HN monogram **Rev:** Value

Date	Mintage	F	VF	XF	Unc	BU
1808C	—	7.00	15.00	35.00	100	—
1810C	—	7.00	15.00	45.00	120	—

C# 3 4 PFENNIG
Billon Silver

Date	Mintage	F	VF	XF	Unc	BU
1808C	—	15.00	25.00	65.00	175	—

C# 3a 4 PFENNIG
Billon Silver

Date	Mintage	F	VF	XF	Unc	BU
1809C	—	10.00	20.00	50.00	150	—

C# 4 MARIENGROSCHEN
Billon Silver

Date	Mintage	F	VF	XF	Unc	BU
1808C	—	10.00	20.00	45.00	135	—
1810C	—	10.00	20.00	60.00	165	—

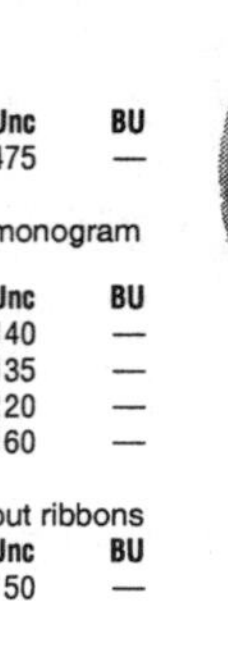

C# 12 24 MARIENGROSCHEN
17.3200 g., 0.7500 Silver .4177 oz.

Date	Mintage	F	VF	XF	Unc	BU
1810B	—	75.00	150	285	475	—

C# 17 1/24 THALER
1.9900 g., 0.3680 Silver .0235 oz. **Obv:** Crowned HN monogram with ribbons **Rev:** Value

Date	Mintage	F	VF	XF	Unc	BU
1807 F	—	12.00	25.00	50.00	140	—
1818/7 F	—	10.00	25.00	45.00	135	—
1808 F	—	10.00	20.00	40.00	120	—
1809 F	—	15.00	25.00	55.00	160	—

C# 17a 1/24 THALER
1.9900 g., 0.3680 Silver .0235 oz. **Obv:** Crown without ribbons

Date	Mintage	F	VF	XF	Unc	BU
1809C	—	10.00	20.00	45.00	150	—

C# 5 1/12 THALER
3.3400 g., 0.4370 Silver .0469 oz.

Date	Mintage	F	VF	XF	Unc	BU
1808C	—	12.50	25.00	65.00	175	—
1809C	—	12.50	25.00	65.00	175	—
1810C	—	12.50	25.00	65.00	175	—

C# 6 1/6 THALER (Reichs)
3.1800 g., 0.9940 Silver .1016 oz.

Date	Mintage	F	VF	XF	Unc	BU
1808C	—	15.00	30.00	65.00	125	—
1812C	—	15.00	30.00	65.00	125	—

C# 11 1/6 THALER (Reichs)
5.8500 g., 0.5000 Silver .0939 oz.

Date	Mintage	F	VF	XF	Unc	BU
1808B	—	12.50	25.00	55.00	100	—
1809B	—	12.50	25.00	55.00	100	—
1810B	—	12.50	25.00	55.00	100	—
1812B	—	12.50	25.00	55.00	100	—
1813B	—	12.50	25.00	55.00	100	—

C# 18 1/6 THALER (Reichs)
5.8500 g., 0.5000 Silver .0939 oz.

Date	Mintage	F	VF	XF	Unc	BU
1808 F	—	10.00	20.00	45.00	90.00	—
1809 C	—	10.00	20.00	45.00	90.00	—
1809 F	—	10.00	20.00	45.00	90.00	—
1810 C	—	10.00	20.00	45.00	90.00	—
1810 F	—	10.00	20.00	45.00	90.00	—
1813 C	—	10.00	20.00	45.00	90.00	—

C# 6a 1/6 THALER (Reichs)
3.1800 g., 0.9940 Silver .1016 oz.

Date	Mintage	F	VF	XF	Unc	BU
1810C	—	25.00	65.00	150	300	—

C# 7 2/3 THALER (Reichs)
13.0800 g., 0.9940 Silver .4180 oz.

Date	Mintage	F	VF	XF	Unc	BU
1808C	—	40.00	80.00	150	300	—
1810C	—	40.00	80.00	150	300	—

C# 7a 2/3 THALER (Reichs)
13.0800 g., 0.9940 Silver .4180 oz. **Rev:** Similar to C#7

Date	Mintage	F	VF	XF	Unc	BU
1809C	—	75.00	150	250	500	—
1810C	—	75.00	125	225	475	—

C# 8 2/3 THALER (Reichs)
13.0800 g., 0.9940 Silver .4180 oz.

Date	Mintage	F	VF	XF	Unc	BU
1811C	—	50.00	100	200	400	—

C# 9 2/3 THALER (Reichs)
13.0800 g., 0.9940 Silver .4180 oz.

Date	Mintage	F	VF	XF	Unc	BU
1811C	—	50.00	100	150	300	—
1812C	—	60.00	125	175	350	—
1813C	—	50.00	100	150	300	—

C# 19 THALER
28.0600 g., 0.8330 Silver .7515 oz.

Date	Mintage	F	VF	XF	Unc	BU
1810C	5	—	—	20,000	30,000	—

C# 20 THALER
28.0600 g., 0.8330 Silver .7515 oz.

Date	Mintage	F	VF	XF	Unc	BU
1810C	—	100	200	350	850	—
1811C	—	100	200	350	850	—
1812C	—	100	200	350	850	—

C# 20a THALER
28.0600 g., 0.8330 Silver .7515 oz.

Date	Mintage	F	VF	XF	Unc	BU
1811C	—	90.00	185	325	850	—
1812C	—	90.00	185	325	850	—
1813C	—	90.00	185	325	850	—

C# 10 THALER
28.0600 g., 0.8330 Silver .7515 oz. **Note:** Mining Thaler.

Date	Mintage	F	VF	XF	Unc	BU
1811C	—	225	450	1,000	2,250	—

C# 10a THALER
28.0600 g., 0.8330 Silver .7515 oz. **Obv:** Similar to C#10 but small bust

Date	Mintage	F	VF	XF	Unc	BU
1811C	—	225	450	1,000	2,250	—

C# 13 5 THALER
6.6500 g., 0.9000 Gold .1924 oz.

Date	Mintage	F	VF	XF	Unc	BU
1810B	—	1,100	2,250	3,500	6,500	—

C# 14 5 THALER
6.6500 g., 0.9000 Gold .1924 oz. **Obv:** Bust left without laurel wreath

Date	Mintage	F	VF	XF	Unc	BU
1811B Rare	—	—	—	—	—	—

C# 14a 5 THALER
6.6500 g., 0.9000 Gold .1924 oz.

Date	Mintage	F	VF	XF	Unc	BU
1811B	—	900	1,750	3,250	5,000	—
1812B	—	750	1,600	3,000	4,500	—
1813B	—	900	1,750	3,250	5,000	—

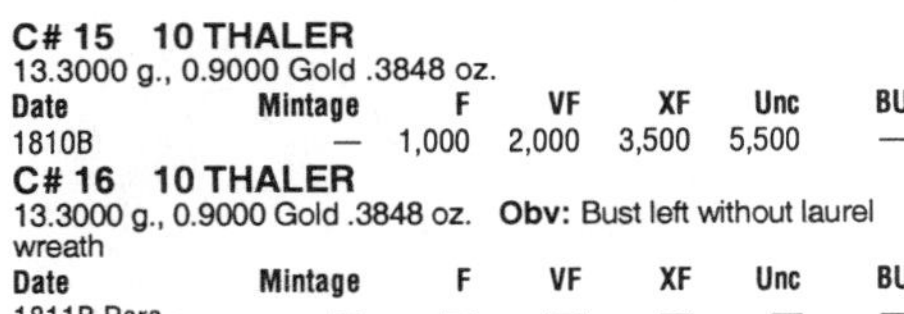

C# 15 10 THALER
13.3000 g., 0.9000 Gold .3848 oz.

Date	Mintage	F	VF	XF	Unc	BU
1810B	—	1,000	2,000	3,500	5,500	—

C# 16 10 THALER
13.3000 g., 0.9000 Gold .3848 oz. **Obv:** Bust left without laurel wreath

Date	Mintage	F	VF	XF	Unc	BU
1811B Rare	—	—	—	—	—	—

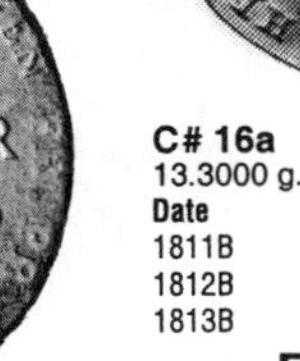

C# 16a 10 THALER
13.3000 g., 0.9000 Gold .3848 oz.

Date	Mintage	F	VF	XF	Unc	BU
1811B	—	725	1,650	3,000	4,850	—
1812B	—	650	1,550	2,750	4,500	—
1813B	—	725	1,650	2,500	4,250	—

FRENCH STANDARD COINAGE

C# 21 CENTIME
Copper

Date	Mintage	F	VF	XF	Unc	BU
1809C	—	2.50	7.50	20.00	50.00	—
1812C	—	2.50	7.50	20.00	50.00	—

C# 22 2 CENTIMES
Copper

Date	Mintage	F	VF	XF	Unc	BU
1808C	—	2.50	5.00	17.50	55.00	—
1809C	—	2.50	5.00	17.50	55.00	—
1810C	—	2.50	5.00	17.50	55.00	—
1812C	—	2.50	5.00	17.50	55.00	—

C# 22a 2 CENTIMES
Copper

Date	Mintage	F	VF	XF	Unc	BU
1808J	—	25.00	50.00	100	225	—

C# 23 3 CENTIMES
Copper

Date	Mintage	F	VF	XF	Unc	BU
1808C	—	2.50	5.00	20.00	55.00	—
1809C	—	2.50	5.00	20.00	55.00	—
1810C	—	2.50	5.00	20.00	55.00	—
1812C	—	2.50	5.00	20.00	55.00	—

C# 23a 3 CENTIMES
Copper

Date	Mintage	F	VF	XF	Unc	BU
1808J	—	25.00	50.00	100	225	—

C# 24 5 CENTIMES
Copper

Date	Mintage	F	VF	XF	Unc	BU
1808C	—	2.50	6.00	25.00	65.00	—
1809C	—	2.50	6.00	25.00	65.00	—
1812C	—	2.50	6.00	25.00	65.00	—

C# 24a 5 CENTIMES
Copper

Date	Mintage	F	VF	XF	Unc	BU
1808J	—	30.00	60.00	125	325	—
1809J Rare	—	—	—	—	—	—

C# 25 10 CENTIMES
1.9700 g., 0.2000 Silver 0.0126 oz.

Date	Mintage	F	VF	XF	Unc	BU
1808C	—	3.00	12.50	35.00	80.00	—
1809C	—	3.00	12.50	35.00	80.00	—
1810C	—	3.00	12.50	35.00	80.00	—
1812C	—	3.00	12.50	35.00	80.00	—

C# 26 20 CENTIMES
3.8700 g., 0.2000 Silver .0248 oz.

Date	Mintage	F	VF	XF	Unc	BU
1808C	—	4.00	17.50	45.00	110	—
1810C	—	4.00	17.50	45.00	110	—
1812C	—	4.00	17.50	45.00	110	—

C# 27a 1/2 FRANK
2.5000 g., 0.9000 Silver .0723 oz.

Date	Mintage	F	VF	XF	Unc	BU
1808J	—	100	175	350	500	—

C# 28 FRANK
5.0000 g., 0.9000 Silver .1447 oz.

Date	Mintage	F	VF	XF	Unc	BU
1808J	—	150	250	500	800	—

C# 29 2 FRANKEN
10.0000 g., 0.9000 Silver .2894 oz.

Date	Mintage	F	VF	XF	Unc	BU
1808J	—	200	350	600	1,000	—

C# 30 5 FRANKEN
25.0000 g., 0.9000 Silver .7235 oz.

Date	Mintage	F	VF	XF	Unc	BU
1808J	—	500	1,000	1,750	3,000	—

C# 30a 5 FRANKEN
25.0000 g., 0.9000 Silver .7235 oz.

Date	Mintage	F	VF	XF	Unc	BU
1809J	—	500	1,000	1,750	3,000	—

C# 31 5 FRANKEN
1.6200 g., 0.9000 Gold .0469 oz.

Date	Mintage	F	VF	XF	Unc	BU
1813C	1,045	225	350	500	1,200	—

C# 32.1 10 FRANKEN
3.2300 g., 0.9000 Gold .0936 oz.

Date	Mintage	F	VF	XF	Unc	BU
1813	1,000	350	600	900	1,500	—

C# 32.2 10 FRANKEN
3.2300 g., 0.9000 Gold .0936 oz. **Note:** Medal alignment.

Date	Mintage	F	VF	XF	Unc	BU
1813C Proof, rare	—	—	—	—	—	—

C# 33a 20 FRANKEN
6.4500 g., 0.9000 Gold .1868 oz. **Note:** Mintmaster's mark: Eagle head.

Date	Mintage	F	VF	XF	Unc	BU
1808C	13,000	225	300	600	1,500	—
1809C	9,104	225	300	600	1,500	—
1811C	19,000	225	300	600	1,500	—
1813C	—	500	1,000	1,500	3,000	—

C# 33 20 FRANKEN
6.4500 g., 0.9000 Gold .1868 oz. **Note:** Mintmaster's mark: Horse head.

Date	Mintage	F	VF	XF	Unc	BU
1808 J	—	250	400	700	1,600	—
1809 J	—	225	350	600	1,500	—

C# 33b 20 FRANKEN
6.4500 g., 0.9000 Gold .1868 oz. **Note:** Mintmaster's mark: Horse head.

Date	Mintage	F	VF	XF	Unc	BU
1809C	—	200	300	600	1,500	—

C# 33c 20 FRANKEN
6.4500 g., 0.9000 Gold .1868 oz. **Note:** Without edge inscription (restrikes ca.1867).

Date	Mintage	F	VF	XF	Unc	BU
1813C	—	—	—	—	4,000	—

C# 34 40 FRANKEN
12.9000 g., 0.9000 Gold .3733 oz.

Date	Mintage	F	VF	XF	Unc	BU
1813C	80	3,000	5,000	8,000	12,000	—

C# 34a 40 FRANKEN
12.9000 g., 0.9000 Gold .3733 oz. **Note:** Without edge inscription (restrikes ca.1867).

Date	Mintage	F	VF	XF	Unc	BU
1813C	5,465	—	—	2,500	5,000	—

PATTERNS

Including off metal strikes

KM#	Date	Mintage	Identification	Mkt Val
Pn1	1808J	—	10 Centimes. Billon. C#25a.	850
Pn2	1808J	—	20 Centimes. Billon. C#26a.	—

KM#	Date	Mintage	Identification	Mkt Val
Pn3	1808C	—	1/2 Frank. Silver. C#27.	—

KM#	Date	Mintage	Identification	Mkt Val
Pn4	18xx	—	2 Franken. Copper. C#29.	1,200
Pn5	1808S	—	20 Franken. Without edge inscription.	2,000
Pn6	1808C	—	20 Franken. Without edge inscription.	2,000
Pn7	1809C	—	20 Franken. Without edge inscription.	2,000
Pn8	1811C	22	2/3 Thaler. Gold. C#8.	20,000

KM#	Date	Mintage	Identification	Mkt Val
Pn9	1811C	—	Mining Thaler. Copper.	—

KM#	Date	Mintage	Identification	Mkt Val
Pn10	1812C	—	Convention Thaler. Copper.	—
Pn11	1813	1	5 Franken. C#31. Without mint mark.	—
Pn12	1813C	—	5 Franken. Copper. C#31.	450

WISMAR

A seaport on the Baltic, the city of Wismar is said to have obtained municipal rights from Mecklenburg in 1229. It was an important member of the Hanseatic League in the 13th and 14th centuries. Their coinage began at the end of the 13th century and terminated in 1854. They belonged to Sweden from 1648 to 1803. A special plate money was struck by the Swedes in 1715 when the town was under siege. In 1803, Sweden sold Wismar to Mecklenburg-Schwerin. The transaction was confirmed in 1815.

RULERS
Swedish, 1648-1803
Friedrich Franz I, 1785-1837
Paul Friedrich, 1837-1842
Friedrich Franz II, 1842-1883

ARMS

2-fold arms divided vertically, half of bull's head of Mecklenburg on left, four alternating light and dark horizontal bars on right. In coin designs, the darker bars are usually designated by cross-hatching or other filler. Some designs show only the four-bar arms in a shield and these are designated "single Wismar arms."

SWEDISH ADMINISTRATION

REGULAR COINAGE

C# 3 3 PFENNIG
Copper

Date	Mintage	F	VF	XF	Unc	BU
1824 IZ	—	5.00	10.00	30.00	80.00	—
1825 IZ	—	5.00	10.00	30.00	80.00	—

C# 3a 3 PFENNIG
Copper

Date	Mintage	F	VF	XF	Unc	BU
1829 HM	—	5.00	10.00	30.00	80.00	—
1830 HM	—	5.00	10.00	30.00	80.00	—

C# 3b 3 PFENNIG
Copper

Date	Mintage	F	VF	XF	Unc	BU
1835 ICM	—	5.00	10.00	30.00	80.00	—
1835 JCM	—	—	—	—	—	—

C# 3c 3 PFENNIG
Copper

Date	Mintage	F	VF	XF	Unc	BU
1840 FS	—	5.00	10.00	30.00	80.00	—

C# 3d 3 PFENNIG
Copper **Obv. Legend:** Ends: "MO J ETA"

Date	Mintage	F	VF	XF	Unc	BU
1840 FS	—	5.00	10.00	30.00	80.00	—

C# 3e 3 PFENNIG
Copper

Date	Mintage	F	VF	XF	Unc	BU
1845 S	—	5.00	10.00	30.00	80.00	—

C# 4 3 PFENNIG
Copper

Date	Mintage	F	VF	XF	Unc	BU
1854 S	—	6.00	12.00	35.00	75.00	—

WURTTEMBERG

Located in South Germany, between Baden and Bavaria, Württemberg obtained the mint right in 1374. In 1495 the rulers became dukes. In 1802 the duke exchanged some of his land on the Rhine with France for territories nearer his capital city. Napoleon elevated the duke to the status of elector in 1803 and made him a king in 1806. The kingdom joined the German Empire in 1871 and endured until the king abdicated in 1918.

RULERS
Friedrich, as Duke Friedrich II, 1797-1803
As Elector Friedrich I, 1803-1806
As King Friedrich I, 1806-1816
Wilhelm I, 1816-1864
Karl I, 1864-1891
Wilhelm II, 1891-1918

MINT MARKS
C, CT - Christophstal Mint
F - Freudenstadt Mint
S - Stuttgart Mint
T - Tubingen Mint

MINT OFFICIALS' INITIALS

Stuttgart Mint

Initial	Date	Name
AD/D	1837-70	Gottlob August Dietelbach, die-cutter
CH, ICH	1783-1813	Johann Christian Heuglin
CS, C, Sch F	d. 1877	Christian Schnitzspahn, die-cutter
C VOIGT	1838-?	Carl Friedrich Voigt, die-cutter in Berling 1425
ILW, LW, W	1798-1837	Johann Ludwig Wagner, die-cutter
PB	d. 1850	Peter Bruckman, die-cutter in Heilbronn, Augsburg in Karlsruhe
	d. 1850	Albert Wagner, die-cutter

ARMS
Wurttemberg: 3 stag antlers arranged vertically.
Teck (duchy): Field of lozenges, (diamond shapes).
Mompelgart (principality): 2 fish standing on tails.

DUCHY

REGULAR COINAGE

KM# 467 KREUZER
Billon **Obv:** Crowned FII **Rev:** Value, branches reach middle of coin

Date	Mintage	F	VF	XF	Unc	BU
1801	—	10.00	20.00	45.00	150	—
1802	—	10.00	20.00	55.00	165	—

KM# 478 KREUZER
Billon **Obv:** Legends **Rev:** Crowned arms

Date	Mintage	F	VF	XF	Unc	BU
1803	—	8.00	16.00	50.00	150	—
1804	—	8.00	16.00	50.00	150	—

KM# 487 KREUZER
Billon **Obv:** Crowned F II monogram, without legend **Rev:** Value above branches

Date	Mintage	F	VF	XF	Unc	BU
1805	—	12.00	25.00	75.00	225	—

KM# 477 3 KREUZER
1.3500 g., 0.3330 Silver .0144 oz. **Obv:** 3 in oval border **Rev:** Date divided by W

Date	Mintage	F	VF	XF	Unc	BU
1801	—	16.00	35.00	85.00	250	—
1802	—	16.00	35.00	85.00	250	—

KM# 479 3 KREUZER
1.3500 g., 0.3330 Silver .0144 oz. **Obv:** F. II. monogram, W below inscription **Rev:** Crowned oval arms

Date	Mintage	F	VF	XF	Unc	BU
1803	—	16.00	35.00	85.00	250	—

KM# 483 3 KREUZER
1.3500 g., 0.3330 Silver .0144 oz. **Rev:** Crowned rectangular arms

Date	Mintage	F	VF	XF	Unc	BU
1804	—	15.00	30.00	70.00	220	—
1805	—	15.00	30.00	70.00	220	—
1806	—	15.00	30.00	70.00	220	—
1086 (error)	—	16.00	35.00	80.00	240	—

KM# 491 3 KREUZER
1.3500 g., 0.3330 Silver .0144 oz. **Obv:** FR monogram **Rev:** Crowned electoral arms

Date	Mintage	F	VF	XF	Unc	BU
1806	—	20.00	45.00	120	300	—

KM# 480 6 KREUZER
2.7000 g., 0.3330 Silver .0289 oz.

Date	Mintage	F	VF	XF	Unc	BU
1803 W	—	18.00	45.00	150	350	—
1804 W	—	18.00	45.00	150	350	—

KM# 484 6 KREUZER
2.7000 g., 0.3330 Silver .0289 oz. **Obv:** Without W below monogram

Date	Mintage	F	VF	XF	Unc	BU
1804	—	18.00	45.00	150	350	—
1805	—	18.00	45.00	150	350	—

KM# 488 10 KREUZER
Billon

Date	Mintage	F	VF	XF	Unc	BU
1805 ILW	—	90.00	175	325	575	—

KM# 489 20 KREUZER
6.6800 g., 0.5830 Silver .1251 oz. **Obv:** Bust left **Obv. Legend:** ...ELECTOR **Rev:** Crowned oval arms

Date	Mintage	F	VF	XF	Unc	BU
1805 ILW	—	75.00	150	325	650	—

KM# 490 1/2 THALER
14.0300 g., 0.8330 Silver .3759 oz.

Date	Mintage	F	VF	XF	Unc	BU
1805 ILW	—	350	750	1,600	2,500	—

KM# 481 THALER
28.0600 g., 0.8330 Silver .7515 oz.

Date	Mintage	F	VF	XF	Unc	BU
1803	—	750	1,200	2,500	4,500	—

TRADE COINAGE

KM# 482 DUCAT
3.5000 g., 0.9860 Gold .1109 oz. **Subject:** Visit of Duke to Mint **Obv:** Bust right **Rev:** IN HOCHST... within wreath

Date	Mintage	F	VF	XF	Unc	BU
1803 ILW	—	—	—	25,000	35,000	—

KM# 485 DUCAT
3.5000 g., 0.9860 Gold .1109 oz. **Rev:** DEN 9. IAN 1804 added

Date	Mintage	F	VF	XF	Unc	BU
1804 ILW	—	—	—	25,000	35,000	—

KM# 486 DUCAT
3.5000 g., 0.9860 Gold .1109 oz. **Rev:** Crowned circular arms within branches

Date	Mintage	F	VF	XF	Unc	BU
1804 ILW	—	1,000	2,000	3,000	4,000	—

KINGDOM

REGULAR COINAGE

KM# 589 1/4 KREUZER
Copper **Ruler:** Wilhelm I

Date	Mintage	F	VF	XF	Unc	BU
1842	198,000	3.00	6.50	18.00	50.00	—
1843	118,000	3.00	6.50	18.00	50.00	—
1852	—	3.00	6.50	18.00	50.00	—
1853	—	3.00	6.50	18.00	50.00	—
1854	—	3.00	6.50	18.00	50.00	—
1855	—	3.00	6.50	18.00	50.00	—
1856	—	3.00	6.50	18.00	50.00	—

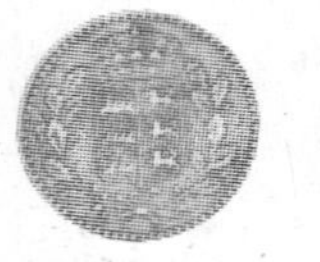

KM# 602 1/4 KREUZER
Copper **Ruler:** Wilhelm I

Date	Mintage	F	VF	XF	Unc	BU
1858	—	3.50	7.00	20.00	55.00	—
1860	—	3.50	7.00	20.00	55.00	—
1861	—	3.50	7.00	20.00	55.00	—
1862	—	3.50	7.00	20.00	55.00	—
1863	—	3.50	7.00	20.00	55.00	—
1864	—	3.50	7.00	20.00	55.00	—

KM# 610 1/4 KREUZER
Copper **Ruler:** Karl I

Date	Mintage	F	VF	XF	Unc	BU
1865	—	3.00	6.00	14.00	45.00	—
1866	—	3.00	6.00	14.00	45.00	—
1867	—	3.00	6.00	14.00	45.00	—
1868	—	3.00	6.00	14.00	45.00	—
1869	—	3.00	6.00	14.00	45.00	—
1871	—	3.00	6.00	14.00	45.00	—
1872	—	3.00	6.00	14.00	45.00	—

KM# 518 1/2 KREUZER
Billon

Date	Mintage	F	VF	XF	Unc	BU
1812	—	7.00	15.00	45.00	150	—
1813	470,000	7.00	15.00	45.00	150	—
1816	126,000	7.00	15.00	45.00	150	—
ND	—	7.00	15.00	45.00	150	—

KM# 527 1/2 KREUZER
Billon **Obv:** Crowned W

Date	Mintage	F	VF	XF	Unc	BU
ND	—	20.00	40.00	120	350	—

KM# 528 1/2 KREUZER
Billon **Obv:** Crowned W dividing date

Date	Mintage	F	VF	XF	Unc	BU
1818	—	15.00	30.00	90.00	260	—

KM# 547 1/2 KREUZER
Billon

Date	Mintage	F	VF	XF	Unc	BU
1824	840,000	4.00	8.00	25.00	70.00	—
1828	—	4.00	8.00	25.00	70.00	—
1829	780,000	4.00	8.00	25.00	70.00	—
1831	620,000	4.00	8.00	25.00	70.00	—
1833	Inc. above	4.00	8.00	25.00	70.00	—
1834	Inc. above	4.00	8.00	25.00	70.00	—
1835	Inc. above	4.00	8.00	25.00	70.00	—
1836	Inc. above	4.00	8.00	25.00	70.00	—
1837	Inc. above	4.00	8.00	25.00	70.00	—

KM# 585 1/2 KREUZER
Copper

Date	Mintage	F	VF	XF	Unc	BU
1840	—	3.00	6.00	14.00	45.00	—
1841	—	3.00	6.00	14.00	45.00	—
1842	452,000	3.00	6.00	14.00	45.00	—
1844	—	3.00	6.00	14.00	45.00	—
1845	—	3.00	6.00	14.00	45.00	—
1846	—	3.00	6.00	14.00	45.00	—
1847	—	3.00	6.00	14.00	45.00	—
1848	—	3.00	6.00	14.00	45.00	—
1849/7	—	—	—	—	—	—
1849	—	3.00	6.00	14.00	45.00	—
1850	—	3.00	6.00	14.00	45.00	—
1851	—	3.00	6.00	14.00	45.00	—
1852	—	3.00	6.00	14.00	45.00	—
1853	—	3.00	6.00	14.00	45.00	—
1854	—	3.00	6.00	14.00	45.00	—
1855	—	3.00	6.00	14.00	45.00	—
1856	—	3.00	6.00	14.00	45.00	—

KM# 603 1/2 KREUZER
Copper

Date	Mintage	F	VF	XF	Unc	BU
1858	—	2.50	5.00	12.00	40.00	—
1859	—	2.50	5.00	12.00	40.00	—
1860	—	2.50	5.00	12.00	40.00	—
1861	—	2.50	5.00	12.00	40.00	—
1862	—	2.50	5.00	12.00	40.00	—
1863	—	2.50	5.00	12.00	40.00	—
1864	—	2.50	5.00	12.00	40.00	—

KM# 611 1/2 KREUZER
Copper

Date	Mintage	F	VF	XF	Unc	BU
1865	—	2.50	5.00	12.00	40.00	—
1866	—	2.50	5.00	12.00	40.00	—
1867	—	2.50	5.00	12.00	40.00	—
1868	—	2.50	5.00	12.00	40.00	—
1869	—	2.50	5.00	12.00	40.00	—
1870	147,000	2.50	5.00	12.00	40.00	—
1871	290,000	2.50	5.00	12.00	40.00	—
1872	177,000	2.50	5.00	12.00	40.00	—

KM# 499 KREUZER
Billon **Obv:** Crowned FR monogram

Date	Mintage	F	VF	XF	Unc	BU
1807	—	8.00	16.00	45.00	140	—
1808	—	8.00	16.00	45.00	140	—
1809	—	8.00	16.00	45.00	140	—
1810	—	8.00	16.00	45.00	140	—
1811	—	8.00	16.00	45.00	140	—
1812	—	8.00	16.00	45.00	140	—
1813	530,000	8.00	16.00	45.00	140	—
1814	—	8.00	16.00	45.00	140	—
1816	630,000	8.00	16.00	45.00	140	—

KM# 529 KREUZER
Billon **Obv:** Crowned W within wreath

Date	Mintage	F	VF	XF	Unc	BU
1818	—	12.00	25.00	70.00	200	—

KM# 548 KREUZER
Billon

Date	Mintage	F	VF	XF	Unc	BU
1824 W	780,000	5.00	10.00	22.00	65.00	—
1825 W	300,000	5.00	10.00	22.00	65.00	—
1826 W	—	5.00	10.00	22.00	65.00	—
1827 W	—	5.00	10.00	22.00	65.00	—
1828 W	—	5.00	10.00	22.00	65.00	—
1829 W	—	5.00	10.00	22.00	65.00	—
1830 W	—	5.00	10.00	22.00	65.00	—
1831 W	—	5.00	10.00	22.00	65.00	—
1832 W	—	5.00	10.00	22.00	65.00	—
1833 W	—	5.00	10.00	22.00	65.00	—
1834 W	—	5.00	10.00	22.00	65.00	—
1835 W	—	5.00	10.00	22.00	65.00	—
1836 W	—	5.00	10.00	22.00	65.00	—
1837 W	—	5.00	10.00	22.00	65.00	—
1838 W	—	5.00	10.00	22.00	65.00	—

KM# 576 KREUZER
0.6200 g., 0.2500 Silver .0049 oz. **Obv:** Crowned arms **Obv. Legend:** WURTTEMBERG **Rev:** Value within wreath

Date	Mintage	F	VF	XF	Unc	BU
1839	—	6.00	12.00	30.00	80.00	—
1840	—	6.00	12.00	30.00	80.00	—
1841	—	6.00	12.00	30.00	80.00	—
1842	—	6.00	12.00	30.00	80.00	—

KM# 590 KREUZER
0.6200 g., 0.2500 Silver .0049 oz.

Date	Mintage	F	VF	XF	Unc	BU
1842	—	2.00	4.00	8.00	30.00	—
1843	—	2.00	4.00	8.00	30.00	—
1844	—	2.00	4.00	8.00	30.00	—
1845	—	2.00	4.00	8.00	30.00	—
1846	—	2.00	4.00	8.00	30.00	—
1847	—	2.00	4.00	8.00	30.00	—
1848	—	2.00	4.00	8.00	30.00	—
1849	—	2.00	4.00	8.00	30.00	—
1850	—	2.00	4.00	8.00	30.00	—
1851	—	2.00	4.00	8.00	30.00	—
1852	—	2.00	4.00	8.00	30.00	—
1853	—	2.00	4.00	8.00	30.00	—
1854	—	2.00	4.00	8.00	30.00	—
1855	—	2.00	4.00	8.00	30.00	—
1856/86	—	—	—	—	—	—
1856	—	2.00	4.00	8.00	30.00	—
1857	—	2.00	4.00	8.00	30.00	—

KM# 600 KREUZER
0.8300 g., 0.1660 Silver .0044 oz.

Date	Mintage	F	VF	XF	Unc	BU
1857	95,000	2.00	3.00	6.00	25.00	—
1858	72,000	2.00	3.00	6.00	25.00	—
1859	50,000	2.00	3.00	6.00	25.00	—
1860	49,000	2.00	3.00	6.00	25.00	—
1861	97,000	2.00	3.00	6.00	25.00	—
1862	56,000	2.00	3.00	6.00	25.00	—
1863	98,000	2.00	3.00	6.00	25.00	—
1864	151,000	2.00	3.00	6.00	25.00	—

KM# 612 KREUZER
0.8300 g., 0.1660 Silver .0044 oz.

Date	Mintage	F	VF	XF	Unc	BU
1865/3	86,000	2.00	4.00	7.00	25.00	—
1865	86,000	2.00	4.00	7.00	25.00	—
1866	78,000	2.00	4.00	7.00	25.00	—
1867	119,000	2.00	4.00	7.00	25.00	—
1868	119,000	2.00	4.00	7.00	25.00	—
1869	120,000	2.00	4.00	7.00	25.00	—
1870	126,000	2.00	4.00	7.00	25.00	—
1871	—	2.00	4.00	7.00	25.00	—
1872	100,000	2.00	4.00	7.00	25.00	—
1873	80,000	2.00	4.00	7.00	25.00	—

KM# 500 3 KREUZER
1.3500 g., 0.3330 Silver .0144 oz.

Date	Mintage	F	VF	XF	Unc	BU
1807	—	12.00	25.00	55.00	160	—
1808	—	12.00	25.00	55.00	160	—
1809	—	12.00	25.00	55.00	160	—
1810	—	12.00	25.00	55.00	160	—
1811	—	12.00	25.00	55.00	160	—
1812	—	12.00	25.00	55.00	160	—
1813	—	12.00	25.00	55.00	160	—
1814	160,000	12.00	25.00	55.00	160	—

KM# 530 3 KREUZER
1.3500 g., 0.3330 Silver .0144 oz. **Obv:** Crowned W within wreath **Rev:** Value

Date	Mintage	F	VF	XF	Unc	BU
1818	—	10.00	20.00	45.00	145	—

KM# 540 3 KREUZER
1.3500 g., 0.3330 Silver .0144 oz.

Date	Mintage	F	VF	XF	Unc	BU
1823	—	30.00	60.00	150	350	—
1824	—	—	—	—	—	—

KM# 541 3 KREUZER
1.3500 g., 0.3330 Silver .0144 oz. **Obv:** Date and W below head

Date	Mintage	F	VF	XF	Unc	BU
1823 W	—	15.00	30.00	65.00	180	—
1824 W	—	15.00	30.00	65.00	180	—
1825 w	380,000	15.00	30.00	65.00	180	—

KM# 565 3 KREUZER
1.3500 g., 0.3330 Silver .0144 oz.

Date	Mintage	F	VF	XF	Unc	BU
1826	—	7.00	15.00	35.00	125	—
1827	—	7.00	15.00	35.00	125	—
1828	—	7.00	15.00	35.00	125	—
1829	—	7.00	15.00	35.00	125	—
1830	—	7.00	15.00	35.00	125	—
1831	—	7.00	15.00	35.00	125	—
1832	—	7.00	15.00	35.00	125	—
1834	—	7.00	15.00	35.00	125	—
1835	—	7.00	15.00	35.00	125	—
1836	—	7.00	15.00	35.00	125	—
1837	—	7.00	15.00	35.00	125	—

KM# 577 3 KREUZER
1.2900 g., 0.3330 Silver .0138 oz. **Obv. Legend:** WURTTEMBERG

Date	Mintage	F	VF	XF	Unc	BU
1839	—	6.00	12.00	25.00	100	—
1840	—	6.00	12.00	25.00	100	—
1841	—	6.00	12.00	25.00	100	—
1842	—	6.00	12.00	25.00	100	—

KM# 591 3 KREUZER
1.2900 g., 0.3330 Silver .0138 oz.

Date	Mintage	F	VF	XF	Unc	BU
1842	—	2.00	4.00	10.00	40.00	—
1843	—	2.00	4.00	10.00	40.00	—
1844	—	2.00	4.00	10.00	40.00	—
1845	—	2.00	4.00	10.00	40.00	—
1846	—	2.00	4.00	10.00	40.00	—
1847	—	2.00	4.00	10.00	40.00	—
1848	—	2.00	4.00	10.00	40.00	—
1849	—	2.00	4.00	10.00	40.00	—
1850	—	2.00	4.00	10.00	40.00	—
1851	—	2.00	4.00	10.00	40.00	—
1852	—	2.00	4.00	10.00	40.00	—
1853	—	2.00	4.00	10.00	40.00	—
1854	—	2.00	4.00	10.00	40.00	—
1855	—	2.00	4.00	10.00	40.00	—
1856	—	2.00	4.00	10.00	40.00	—

KM# 492 6 KREUZER
2.7000 g., 0.3330 Silver .0289 oz. **Rev:** Electoral arms

Date	Mintage	F	VF	XF	Unc	BU
1806	—	18.00	45.00	150	350	—

KM# 493 6 KREUZER
2.7000 g., 0.3330 Silver .0289 oz. **Rev:** Crowned arms with flags in left half of shield

Date	Mintage	F	VF	XF	Unc	BU
1806	—	18.00	45.00	150	350	—

KM# 494 6 KREUZER
2.7000 g., 0.3330 Silver .0289 oz. **Rev:** Arms dividing date

Date	Mintage	F	VF	XF	Unc	BU
1806	—	100	200	350	600	—

KM# 495 6 KREUZER
2.7000 g., 0.3330 Silver .0289 oz.

Date	Mintage	F	VF	XF	Unc	BU
1806	—	7.00	15.00	50.00	150	—
1807	—	7.00	15.00	50.00	150	—
1808	—	7.00	15.00	50.00	150	—
1809	—	7.00	15.00	50.00	150	—
1810	—	7.00	15.00	50.00	150	—
1811	—	7.00	15.00	50.00	150	—
1812	—	7.00	15.00	50.00	150	—
1814	—	7.00	15.00	50.00	150	—

KM# 524 6 KREUZER
2.7000 g., 0.3330 Silver .0289 oz. **Obv:** Crowned W within wreath **Rev:** Value

Date	Mintage	F	VF	XF	Unc	BU
1817	—	15.00	30.00	65.00	185	—
1818	—	15.00	30.00	65.00	185	—

KM# 536 6 KREUZER
2.7000 g., 0.3330 Silver .0289 oz.

Date	Mintage	F	VF	XF	Unc	BU
1819	—	15.00	30.00	65.00	185	—
1821	—	18.00	40.00	75.00	200	—

KM# 542 6 KREUZER
2.7000 g., 0.3330 Silver .0289 oz. **Obv:** Head right, date below **Rev:** Crowned circular arms within wreath

Date	Mintage	F	VF	XF	Unc	BU
1823	—	20.00	40.00	120	300	—

KM# 543 6 KREUZER
2.7000 g., 0.3330 Silver .0289 oz. **Obv:** Narrower head

Date	Mintage	F	VF	XF	Unc	BU
1823	—	15.00	30.00	100	275	—

KM# 544 6 KREUZER
2.7000 g., 0.3330 Silver .0289 oz. **Obv. Legend:** WILHELM KON...

Date	Mintage	F	VF	XF	Unc	BU
1823	—	12.00	25.00	75.00	250	—
1825	—	12.00	25.00	75.00	250	—

KM# 556 6 KREUZER
2.7000 g., 0.3330 Silver .0289 oz. **Rev:** Crowned tapered arms within branches

Date	Mintage	F	VF	XF	Unc	BU
1825	—	8.00	15.00	55.00	185	—
1826	—	8.00	15.00	55.00	185	—
1827	—	8.00	15.00	55.00	185	—
1828	—	8.00	15.00	55.00	185	—
1829	—	8.00	15.00	55.00	185	—
1830	—	8.00	15.00	55.00	185	—
1831	—	8.00	15.00	55.00	185	—
1832	—	8.00	15.00	55.00	185	—
1833	—	8.00	15.00	55.00	185	—
1834	—	8.00	15.00	55.00	185	—
1835	—	8.00	15.00	55.00	185	—
1836	—	8.00	15.00	55.00	185	—
1837	—	8.00	15.00	55.00	185	—

KM# 572 6 KREUZER
2.5900 g., 0.3330 Silver .0277 oz.

Date	Mintage	F	VF	XF	Unc	BU
1838	—	6.00	12.00	20.00	85.00	—
1839	—	6.00	12.00	20.00	85.00	—
1840	—	6.00	12.00	20.00	85.00	—
1841	—	6.00	12.00	20.00	85.00	—
1842	—	6.00	12.00	20.00	85.00	—

KM# 592 6 KREUZER
2.5900 g., 0.3330 Silver .0277 oz.

Date	Mintage	F	VF	XF	Unc	BU
1842	—	3.00	6.00	15.00	55.00	—
1843	—	3.00	6.00	15.00	55.00	—
1844	—	3.00	6.00	15.00	55.00	—
1845	—	3.00	6.00	15.00	55.00	—
1846	—	3.00	6.00	15.00	55.00	—
1847	—	3.00	6.00	15.00	55.00	—
1848	—	3.00	6.00	15.00	55.00	—
1849	—	3.00	6.00	15.00	55.00	—
1850	—	3.00	6.00	15.00	55.00	—
1851	—	3.00	6.00	15.00	55.00	—
1852	—	3.00	6.00	15.00	55.00	—
1853	—	3.00	6.00	15.00	55.00	—
1854	—	3.00	6.00	15.00	55.00	—
1855	—	3.00	6.00	15.00	55.00	—
1856	—	3.00	6.00	15.00	55.00	—

KM# 502 10 KREUZER
Billon **Rev. Legend:** AD NORMAN

Date	Mintage	F	VF	XF	Unc	BU
1808 ILW	25,000	100	200	375	700	—
1809 ILW	10,000	110	225	400	750	—

KM# 519 10 KREUZER
Billon **Obv. Legend:** FRIEDRICH KOENIG... **Rev. Legend:** NACH DEM

Date	Mintage	F	VF	XF	Unc	BU
1812 ILW	26,000	100	200	375	700	—

KM# 520 10 KREUZER
Billon **Obv. Legend:** FRID. KOENIG...

Date	Mintage	F	VF	XF	Unc	BU
1812 ILW	—	100	200	375	700	—

KM# 531 10 KREUZER
Billon

Date	Mintage	F	VF	XF	Unc	BU
1818 W	152,000	80.00	150	300	600	—

KM# 545 10 KREUZER
Billon

Date	Mintage	F	VF	XF	Unc	BU
1823	11,000	110	225	400	750	—

KM# 549 12 KREUZER (Dreibatzner)
3.9000 g., 0.5000 Silver .0627 oz.

Date	Mintage	F	VF	XF	Unc	BU
1824 W	45,000	30.00	70.00	175	400	—

KM# 557 12 KREUZER (Dreibatzner)
3.9000 g., 0.5000 Silver .0627 oz.

Date	Mintage	F	VF	XF	Unc	BU
1825 W	25,000	35.00	85.00	200	500	—

KM# 501 20 KREUZER
6.6800 g., 0.5830 Silver .1251 oz. **Obv. Legend:** ...WURTTEMB

Date	Mintage	F	VF	XF	Unc	BU
1807 ILW	—	40.00	80.00	160	450	—
1808 ILW	—	40.00	80.00	160	450	—
1809 ILW	—	40.00	80.00	160	450	—
1810 ILW	—	40.00	80.00	160	450	—

KM# 510 20 KREUZER
6.6800 g., 0.5830 Silver .1251 oz.

Date	Mintage	F	VF	XF	Unc	BU
1810 ILW	—	50.00	100	200	500	—
1812 ILW	—	50.00	100	200	500	—

KM# 511 20 KREUZER
6.6800 g., 0.5830 Silver .1251 oz. **Obv:** Larger head

Date	Mintage	F	VF	XF	Unc	BU
1810 ILW	—	50.00	100	200	500	—

KM# 521 20 KREUZER
6.6800 g., 0.5830 Silver .1251 oz.

Date	Mintage	F	VF	XF	Unc	BU
1812 ILW	105,000	40.00	80.00	200	500	—

KM# 532 20 KREUZER
6.6800 g., 0.5830 Silver .1251 oz.

Date	Mintage	F	VF	XF	Unc	BU
1818 W	180,000	50.00	100	225	600	—

KM# 546 20 KREUZER
6.6800 g., 0.5830 Silver .1251 oz.

Date	Mintage	F	VF	XF	Unc	BU
1823 W	33,000	50.00	100	225	550	—

KM# 550 24 KREUZER (Sechsbatzner)
6.6800 g., 0.5830 Silver .1251 oz.

Date	Mintage	F	VF	XF	Unc	BU
1824 W	—	50.00	100	225	375	—
1825 W	—	50.00	100	225	375	—
1825	—	50.00	100	225	375	—

KM# 573 1/2 GULDEN
5.2900 g., 0.9000 Silver .1530 oz. **Obv:** VOIGT below head

Date	Mintage	F	VF	XF	Unc	BU
1838	824,000	15.00	50.00	100	200	—
1839	464,000	80.00	175	500	900	—
1840	516,000	12.00	25.00	75.00	150	—
1841	412,000	12.00	25.00	75.00	150	—
1844	154,000	100	200	400	800	—
1845	280,000	12.00	25.00	75.00	150	—
1846	338,000	12.00	25.00	75.00	150	—
1847	682,000	12.00	25.00	70.00	140	—
1848	498,000	12.00	25.00	70.00	140	—
1849	312,000	12.00	25.00	65.00	150	—
1850	286,000	12.00	25.00	65.00	150	—
1852	228,000	12.00	25.00	65.00	150	—
1853	192,000	12.00	25.00	65.00	150	—
1854	140,000	12.00	25.00	65.00	150	—
1855	112,000	12.00	25.00	65.00	150	—
1856	108,000	12.00	25.00	65.00	150	—
1858	—	12.00	25.00	65.00	150	—

KM# 604 1/2 GULDEN
5.2900 g., 0.9000 Silver .1530 oz. **Obv:** Without VOIGT below head

Date	Mintage	F	VF	XF	Unc	BU
1858	219,000	15.00	90.00	150	250	—
1859	72,000	15.00	90.00	150	250	—
1860	299,000	15.00	40.00	80.00	160	—
1861	693,000	15.00	40.00	80.00	160	—
1862	149,000	15.00	50.00	100	200	—
1863	—	15.00	50.00	100	200	—
1864	161,000	15.00	37.50	75.00	140	—

KM# 613 1/2 GULDEN
5.2900 g., 0.9000 Silver .1530 oz. **Obv:** Head right with C.S. on truncation

Date	Mintage	F	VF	XF	Unc	BU
1865 CS	166,000	15.00	50.00	100	250	—
1866 CS	276,000	15.00	50.00	100	250	—
1867 CS	71,000	15.00	50.00	100	250	—
1868 CS	105,000	15.00	50.00	100	250	—

KM# 616 1/2 GULDEN
5.2900 g., 0.9000 Silver .1530 oz. **Obv:** Without C.S. on truncation

Date	Mintage	F	VF	XF	Unc	BU
1868	Inc. above	15.00	50.00	100	200	—
1869	72,000	15.00	50.00	100	200	—
1870	44,000	15.00	60.00	100	200	—
1871	41,000	15.00	60.00	100	200	—

KM# 551 GULDEN
12.7200 g., 0.7500 Silver .3067 oz.

Date	Mintage	F	VF	XF	Unc	BU
1824 W	21,000	80.00	200	800	1,250	—

KM# 552 GULDEN
12.7200 g., 0.7500 Silver .3067 oz.

Date	Mintage	F	VF	XF	Unc	BU
1824	—	—	1,500	2,000	2,500	—

KM# 558 GULDEN
12.7200 g., 0.7500 Silver .3067 oz.

Date	Mintage	F	VF	XF	Unc	BU
1825 W	—	150	300	800	1,600	—

KM# 575 GULDEN
10.6000 g., 0.9000 Silver .3067 oz. **Obv:** A.D. below head

Date	Mintage	F	VF	XF	Unc	BU
1837 AD	443,000	25.00	100	150	400	—
1838 AD	Inc. above	25.00	100	150	400	—

KM# 574 GULDEN
10.6000 g., 0.9000 Silver .3067 oz. **Obv:** VOIGT below head

Date	Mintage	F	VF	XF	Unc	BU
1838	712,000	15.00	40.00	80.00	175	—
1839	365,000	15.00	40.00	80.00	175	—
1840	2,561,000	15.00	40.00	80.00	175	—
1841	—	25.00	100	200	400	—
1842	2,493,000	15.00	40.00	80.00	175	—
1843	1,983,000	15.00	40.00	80.00	175	—
1844	379,000	15.00	40.00	80.00	175	—
1845	44,000	15.00	40.00	80.00	175	—
1846	42,000	15.00	40.00	80.00	175	—
1847	56,000	15.00	40.00	80.00	175	—
1848/6	58,000	17.50	50.00	100	200	—
1848	Inc. above	15.00	40.00	80.00	175	—
1849	129,000	15.00	40.00	80.00	175	—
1850	114,000	15.00	40.00	80.00	175	—
1851	96,000	15.00	40.00	80.00	175	—
1852	32,000	15.00	40.00	80.00	175	—
1853	235,000	15.00	40.00	80.00	175	—
1854	90,000	15.00	40.00	80.00	175	—
1855	223,000	15.00	40.00	80.00	175	—
1856	—	15.00	40.00	80.00	175	—

KM# 578 GULDEN
10.6000 g., 0.9000 Silver .3067 oz. **Obv:** Without VOIGT below head

Date	Mintage	F	VF	XF	Unc	BU
1839	—	15.00	35.00	75.00	150	—
1840	—	15.00	35.00	75.00	150	—
1841	—	25.00	75.00	125	250	—

KM# 588 GULDEN
10.6000 g., 0.9000 Silver .3067 oz. **Subject:** 25th Anniversary of Reign

Date	Mintage	F	VF	XF	Unc	BU
1841	—	20.00	35.00	60.00	100	—

KM# 593 GULDEN
10.6000 g., 0.9000 Silver .3067 oz. **Subject:** Visit of King to New Mint

Date	Mintage	F	VF	XF	Unc	BU
1844	—	650	1,250	2,000	3,000	—

Note: Deceptive restrikes exist

KM# 594 GULDEN
10.6000 g., 0.9000 Silver .3067 oz. **Subject:** Visit of Queen to Mint

Date	Mintage	F	VF	XF	Unc	BU
1845	17	—	—	—	12,000	—

KM# 597 GULDEN
10.6000 g., 0.9000 Silver .3067 oz.

Date	Mintage	F	VF	XF	Unc	BU
1848	Inc. above	25.00	75.00	125	250	—

KM# 553 2 GULDEN
25.4500 g., 0.7500 Silver .6138 oz.

Date	Mintage	F	VF	XF	Unc	BU
1824 W	15,000	200	350	900	2,200	—

KM# 554 2 GULDEN
25.4500 g., 0.7500 Silver .6138 oz. **Obv:** Larger head right **Rev:** Legends ends with SC

Date	Mintage	F	VF	XF	Unc	BU
1824 ILW	Inc. above	—	—	—	3,500	—

KM# 559 2 GULDEN
25.4500 g., 0.7500 Silver .6138 oz. **Obv:** WAGNER F at truncation **Obv. Legend:** ...WURTTEMB **Rev:** Crowned pointed arms within branches

Date	Mintage	F	VF	XF	Unc	BU
1825 W	9,934	300	500	1,500	3,000	—

KM# 560 2 GULDEN
25.4500 g., 0.7500 Silver .6138 oz. **Obv:** Without name at bottom

Date	Mintage	F	VF	XF	Unc	BU
1825 W	Inc. above	—	—	—	3,500	—

KM# 595 2 GULDEN
21.2100 g., 900.0000 Silver .6138 oz.

Date	Mintage	F	VF	XF	Unc	BU
1845	562,000	40.00	60.00	150	350	—
1846	621,000	40.00	60.00	150	350	—
1847	1,160,000	40.00	60.00	150	350	—
1848	336,000	40.00	60.00	150	350	—
1849	486,000	40.00	60.00	150	350	—
1850	280,000	40.00	60.00	150	350	—
1851	140,000	40.00	60.00	150	350	—
1852	225,000	40.00	60.00	150	350	—
1853	175,000	40.00	60.00	150	350	—
1854	74,000	40.00	60.00	150	350	—
1855	133,000	40.00	60.00	150	350	—
1856	267,000	40.00	60.00	150	350	—

KM# 562 5 GULDEN
3.4250 g., 0.9040 Gold .0997 oz.

Date	Mintage	F	VF	XF	Unc	BU
1824 W	2,282	500	1,100	1,800	2,750	—
1835 W	1,443	600	1,400	2,750	4,500	—
1835 W	1,443	600	1,400	2,750	4,500	—

KM# 563 5 GULDEN
3.4250 g., 0.9040 Gold .0997 oz.

Date	Mintage	F	VF	XF	Unc	BU
1825 W	5,956	350	650	1,200	2,000	—

KM# 579 5 GULDEN
3.4250 g., 0.9040 Gold .0997 oz.

Date	Mintage	F	VF	XF	Unc	BU
1839 W	822	800	1,600	3,000	5,000	—

KM# 555 10 GULDEN
6.8500 g., 0.9040 Gold .1990 oz.

Date	Mintage	F	VF	XF	Unc	BU
1824 W	1,896	900	1,800	3,200	5,500	—
1825 W	1,240	1,000	2,000	4,000	7,500	—
1825 W	1,240	1,000	2,000	4,000	7,500	—

KM# 564 10 GULDEN
6.8500 g., 0.9040 Gold .1990 oz. **Subject:** Visit of King to Mint

Date	Mintage	F	VF	XF	Unc	BU
1825 W	8	—	—	18,500	22,500	—

KM# 496 THALER
28.0600 g., 0.8330 Silver .7515 oz. **Obv. Legend:** ... WURT. S. R.I. AR. VEXILL. ET ELECT

Date	Mintage	F	VF	XF	Unc	BU
1806	—	—	—	—	8,000	—

KM# 497 THALER
28.0600 g., 0.8330 Silver .7515 oz. **Obv. Legend:** ... WURTEMBERGIA

Date	Mintage	F	VF	XF	Unc	BU
1806	—	—	—	—	8,000	—

KM# 498 THALER
28.0600 g., 0.8330 Silver .7515 oz. **Obv:** I.L. WAGNER F. below bust **Rev:** Legend with larger letters

Date	Mintage	F	VF	XF	Unc	BU
1806	—	—	—	7,000	10,000	—

KM# 504 THALER
28.0600 g., 0.8330 Silver .7515 oz.

Date	Mintage	F	VF	XF	Unc	BU
1809	—	—	—	8,000	10,000	—

KM# 505 THALER
28.0600 g., 0.8330 Silver .7515 oz. **Obv:** I.L.W. below bust **Obv. Legend:** ...WURTTEMBERGIAE

Date	Mintage	F	VF	XF	Unc	BU
1809 ILW	—	—	—	—	8,000	—

KM# 513 THALER
29.4900 g., 0.8680 Silver .8230 oz. **Obv:** Bust **Obv. Legend:** FRIDERICH I KOENIG..

Date	Mintage	F	VF	XF	Unc	BU
1810 ILW	—	—	—	—	8,000	—

KM# 514 THALER
29.4900 g., 0.8680 Silver .8230 oz. **Obv:** Large head

Date	Mintage	F	VF	XF	Unc	BU
1810 ILW	—	300	800	2,000	4,500	—

KM# 515 THALER
29.4900 g., 0.8680 Silver .8230 oz. **Obv:** Small head, without period before legend

Date	Mintage	F	VF	XF	Unc	BU
1810 ILW	—	300	1,000	2,000	5,000	—

KM# 512 THALER
29.4900 g., 0.8680 Silver .8230 oz. **Obv:** Military bust **Obv. Legend:** ...D.G. REX.. **Rev:** Crowned arms between lion and stag **Note:** Kronen Thaler.

Date	Mintage	F	VF	XF	Unc	BU
1810 ILW	—	—	—	8,000	10,000	—

KM# 517 THALER
29.4900 g., 0.8680 Silver .8230 oz.

Date	Mintage	F	VF	XF	Unc	BU
1811 ILW	2,000	400	1,000	2,000	5,000	—

KM# 522 THALER
29.4900 g., 0.8680 Silver .8230 oz.

Date	Mintage	F	VF	XF	Unc	BU
1812 ILW	15,000	300	600	1,200	3,000	—

KM# 526 THALER
29.4900 g., 0.8680 Silver .8230 oz. **Note:** Kronen Thaler.

Date	Mintage	F	VF	XF	Unc	BU
1817	44,000	400	600	1,500	3,750	—

KM# 525 THALER
28.0600 g., 0.8330 Silver .7515 oz. **Obv:** Head left, WAGNER F below **Rev:** Value within wreath **Note:** Convention Thaler.

Date	Mintage	F	VF	XF	Unc	BU
1817	—	—	—	—	8,500	—

KM# 533 THALER
28.0600 g., 0.8330 Silver .7515 oz.

Date	Mintage	F	VF	XF	Unc	BU
1818	—	500	1,000	2,200	6,000	—

KM# 534 THALER
29.4900 g., 0.8680 Silver .8230 oz.

Date	Mintage	F	VF	XF	Unc	BU
1818	Inc. above	300	550	1,200	3,000	—
1818/7	Inc. above	400	750	1,500	3,500	—

KM# 561 THALER
29.4900 g., 0.8680 Silver .8230 oz.

Date	Mintage	F	VF	XF	Unc	BU
1825	226,000	85.00	135	300	600	—
1826	—	100	150	375	800	—
1827	—	100	150	375	800	—
1828	—	100	150	375	800	—
1829	—	100	150	375	800	—
1830 W below bust	6,695	100	150	375	800	—
1831	9,074	100	150	375	800	—
1832 W below bust	—	100	150	375	800	—
1833	—	100	150	375	800	—

KM# 570 THALER
29.4900 g., 0.8680 Silver .8230 oz. **Subject:** Free Trade

Date	Mintage	F	VF	XF	Unc	BU
1833 W	—	75.00	125	225	450	—
1833 LW	—	—	—	—	—	—

KM# 571 THALER
29.4900 g., 0.8680 Silver .8230 oz. **Obv:** W below truncation

Date	Mintage	F	VF	XF	Unc	BU
1834 W	—	100	150	375	800	—
1835 W	—	100	150	375	800	—
1837 W	170,000	85.00	135	300	600	—

KM# 601 THALER
18.5200 g., 0.9000 Silver .5360 oz. **Note:** Vereins Thaler.

Date	Mintage	F	VF	XF	Unc	BU
1857	452,000	20.00	40.00	135	275	—
1858	644,000	20.00	40.00	135	275	—
1859	1,333,000	20.00	40.00	135	275	—
1860	645,000	20.00	40.00	135	275	—
1861	754,000	20.00	40.00	135	275	—
1862	648,000	20.00	40.00	135	275	—
1863	621,000	20.00	40.00	135	275	—
1864	533,000	20.00	40.00	135	275	—

KM# 615 THALER
18.5200 g., 0.9000 Silver .5360 oz. **Rev:** Antlers extend into legend

Date	Mintage	F	VF	XF	Unc	BU
1865	Inc. above	40.00	75.00	200	475	—
1866	346,000	40.00	75.00	200	475	—
1867	165,000	40.00	75.00	200	475	—

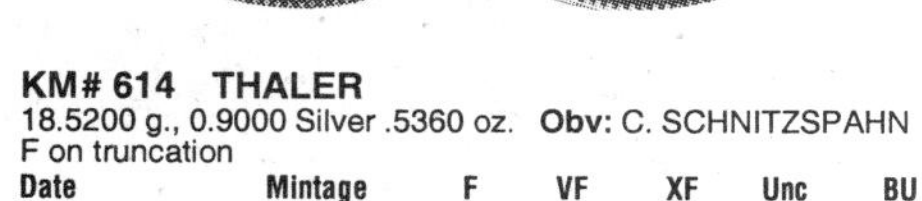

KM# 614 THALER
18.5200 g., 0.9000 Silver .5360 oz. **Obv:** C. SCHNITZSPAHN F on truncation

Date	Mintage	F	VF	XF	Unc	BU
1865	276,000	125	225	600	1,250	—

KM# 617 THALER
18.5200 g., 0.9000 Silver .5360 oz.

Date	Mintage	F	VF	XF	Unc	BU
1868	78,000	45.00	80.00	200	500	—
1869	31,000	50.00	85.00	210	520	—
1870	44,000	50.00	85.00	210	520	—

KM# 620 THALER
18.5200 g., 0.9000 Silver .5360 oz. **Subject:** Victorious Conclusion of Franco-Prussian War **Rev:** C. SCH. F at 7 o'clock

Date	Mintage	F	VF	XF	Unc	BU
1871	114,000	25.00	45.00	85.00	150	—
1871 First strike	—	—	—	—	—	—

KM# 586 2 THALER (3-1/2 Gulden)
37.1200 g., 0.9000 Silver 1.0742 oz.

Date	Mintage	F	VF	XF	Unc	BU
1840	162,000	125	225	450	1,000	—
1842	51,000	175	300	600	1,200	—
1843	245,000	125	225	450	1,000	—
1854	168,000	125	225	450	1,000	—
1855	Inc. above	125	225	450	1,000	—

KM# 596 2 THALER (3-1/2 Gulden)
37.1200 g., 0.9000 Silver 1.0742 oz. **Subject:** Marriage of Crown Prince Karl to Olga, Grand Duchess of Russia

Date	Mintage	F	VF	XF	Unc	BU
1846	5,808	100	200	375	750	—

KM# 618 2 THALER (3-1/2 Gulden)
37.0400 g., 0.9000 Silver 1.0717 oz. **Subject:** Restoration of Ulm Cathedral

Date	Mintage	F	VF	XF	Unc	BU
1869	—	125	200	350	700	—
1871	4,031	100	200	350	550	—

REFORM COINAGE

KM# 626 2 MARK
11.1110 g., 0.9000 Silver .3215 oz.

Date	Mintage	F	VF	XF	Unc	BU
1876F	1,550,000	30.00	60.00	475	1,100	1,400
1877F	1,107,000	30.00	125	550	1,800	2,200
1880F	129,000	70.00	175	750	2,750	3,250
1883F	74,000	75.00	175	750	4,000	4,500
1888F	123,000	40.00	130	575	1,500	1,750
1888F Proof	—	Value: 2,500				

KM# 631 2 MARK
11.1110 g., 0.9000 Silver .3215 oz. **Ruler:** Wilhelm II

Date	Mintage	F	VF	XF	Unc	BU
1892F	177,000	16.00	30.00	90.00	250	300
1893F	174,000	16.00	30.00	90.00	250	300
1896F	351,000	15.00	30.00	60.00	225	275
1898F	144,000	20.00	30.00	90.00	250	350
1899F	538,000	10.00	25.00	60.00	200	250
1900F	516,000	10.00	20.00	50.00	140	180
(1892-1900)F Proof	—	Value: 175				

KM# 623 5 MARK
27.7770 g., 0.9000 Silver .8038 oz.

Date	Mintage	F	VF	XF	Unc	BU
1874F	113,000	30.00	60.00	900	2,500	3,000
1875F	318,000	30.00	60.00	800	2,000	2,750
1876F	897,000	30.00	60.00	600	1,700	2,200
1888F	49,000	40.00	90.00	900	2,500	3,000

KM# 627 5 MARK
1.9910 g., 0.9000 Gold .0576 oz.

Date	Mintage	F	VF	XF	Unc	BU
1877F	488,000	150	275	300	500	600
1877F Proof	—	Value: 1,500				
1877F Proof	—	Value: 1,500				
1878F	50,000	400	650	1,000	1,500	1,750

KM# 632 5 MARK
27.7770 g., 0.9000 Silver .8038 oz. **Ruler:** Wilhelm II

Date	Mintage	F	VF	XF	Unc	BU
1892F	69,000	20.00	50.00	150	800	1,200
1893F	71,000	20.00	50.00	160	800	1,200
1894F	20,000	150	400	1,100	3,000	4,000
1895F	201,000	20.00	45.00	125	600	900
1898F	216,000	15.00	45.00	125	600	900
1899F	112,000	15.00	45.00	135	600	900
1900F	211,000	15.00	35.00	95.00	500	800
(1892-1900)F Proof	—	Value: 600				

KM# 621 10 MARK
3.9820 g., 0.9000 Gold .1152 oz. **Rev:** Type I

Date	Mintage	F	VF	XF	Unc	BU
1872F	271,000	100	150	200	500	600
1872F Proof	—	Value: 1,500				
1872F Proof	—	Value: 1,500				
1873F	675,000	100	150	200	500	600
1873F Proof	—	Value: 1,500				

KM# 624 10 MARK
3.9820 g., 0.9000 Gold .1152 oz. **Rev:** Type II

Date	Mintage	F	VF	XF	Unc	BU
1874F	205,000	75.00	130	180	350	450
1875F	532,000	75.00	130	160	350	400
1875F	532,000	75.00	130	160	350	450
1876F	933,000	75.00	130	170	350	450
1876F Proof	—	Value: 1,500				
1877F	271,000	75.00	130	180	350	450
1878F	337,000	75.00	130	170	350	450
1879F	211,000	75.00	130	170	400	600
1880F	245,000	90.00	140	170	400	650
1881F	79,000	100	160	225	450	700
1888F	200,000	75.00	130	170	300	350
1888F Proof	—	Value: 1,500				

KM# 630 10 MARK
3.9820 g., 0.9000 Gold .1152 oz. **Rev:** Type III

Date	Mintage	F	VF	XF	Unc	BU
1890F	220,000	150	225	300	500	600
1891F	80,000	150	250	300	600	800

KM# 633 10 MARK
3.9820 g., 0.9000 Gold .1152 oz. **Ruler:** Wilhelm II

Date	Mintage	F	VF	XF	Unc	BU
1893F	300,000	100	145	190	300	350
1896F	200,000	100	145	190	300	350
1898F	420,000	100	145	190	300	350
1900F	90,000	110	160	200	300	350

KM# 622 20 MARK
7.9650 g., 0.9000 Gold .2304 oz. **Rev:** Type I

Date	Mintage	F	VF	XF	Unc	BU
1872F	662,000	100	135	175	500	600
1872F Proof	—	Value: 1,900				
1872F Proof	—	Value: 1,900				
1873F	1,357,000	100	135	175	500	600
1873F Proof	—	Value: 1,900				

KM# 625 20 MARK
7.9650 g., 0.9000 Gold .2304 oz. **Rev:** Type II

Date	Mintage	F	VF	XF	Unc	BU
1874F	322,000	110	150	200	450	550
1876F	359,000	110	150	200	450	550

KM# 634 20 MARK
7.9650 g., 0.9000 Gold .2304 oz. **Ruler:** Wilhelm II

Date	Mintage	F	VF	XF	Unc	BU
1894F	501,000	100	140	170	250	300
1897F	400,000	100	140	170	250	300
1897F Proof	—	Value: 1,200				
1898F	106,000	100	140	170	275	325
1900F	500,000	100	140	170	250	300
1900F Proof	—	Value: 1,200				

TRADE COINAGE

KM# 503 DUCAT
3.5000 g., 0.9860 Gold .1109 oz.

Date	Mintage	F	VF	XF	Unc	BU
1808 CH	—	800	1,500	2,500	4,500	—

KM# 523 DUCAT
3.5000 g., 0.9860 Gold .1109 oz.

Date	Mintage	F	VF	XF	Unc	BU
1813 ILW	—	800	1,750	2,500	4,500	—

KM# 535 DUCAT
3.5000 g., 0.9860 Gold .1109 oz.

Date	Mintage	F	VF	XF	Unc	BU
1818 W	—	800	1,750	2,500	4,000	—

KM# 587 DUCAT
3.5000 g., 0.9860 Gold .1109 oz.

Date	Mintage	F	VF	XF	Unc	BU
1840 AD	81,000	200	350	525	850	—
1841	232,000	—	—	—	—	—
1841	232,000	—	—	—	—	—
1841/0 AD	Inc. above	200	300	425	750	—
1841 AD	Inc. above	200	300	425	750	—
1842 AD	25,000	200	350	525	850	—
1848 AD	62,000	200	350	525	850	—

KM# 516 FREDERICK D'OR (= 1 Karolin)
6.6500 g., 0.9000 Gold .1924 oz.

Date	Mintage	F	VF	XF	Unc	BU
1810 ILW	—	2,500	4,000	7,000	10,000	—

PATTERNS

Including off metal strikes

KM#	Date	Mintage	Identification	Mkt Val
Pn27	1804 ILW	—	Ducat. Silver. C#136a.	1,000
Pn28	1804 CH	—	Ducat. Silver. C#137.	1,000
Pn29	1808 CH	—	Ducat. Silver. C#155.	1,000
Pn30	1823	—	Gulden. Silver.	2,000

KM#	Date	Mintage	Identification	Mkt Val
Pn31	1823	—	2 Gulden. Silver.	3,000
Pn32	1824	—	2 Gulden.	—
Pn33	1824	—	10 Gulden. Tin.	—
Pn34	1825	—	10 Gulden. Tin.	—
Pn35	1825 W	—	10 Gulden. Silver. C#200.	1,000

KM#	Date	Mintage	Identification	Mkt Val
Pn36	1833	—	Thaler. Silver.	5,000
Pn37	1837	—	Gulden. Silver.	—
Pn38	1846	—	2 Thaler. Gold. Marriage of Crown Prince, C#195.	25,000
Pn41	ND(1894)	—	3 Mark. Silver Plated Copper.	—

TRIAL STRIKES

KM#	Date	Mintage	Identification	Mkt Val
TS1	1861	—	Thaler. Aluminum. Uniface.	—
TS2	1862	—	Thaler. Aluminum. Uniface.	—

WURZBURG

The Bishopric, located in Franconia, was established in 741. The mint right was obtained in the 11th century. The first coins were struck c. 1040. In 1441 the bishops were confirmed as dukes. In 1802 the area was secularized and granted to Bavaria. It was made a grand duchy in 1806 but the 1815 Congress of Vienna returned it to Bavaria.

RULERS

Georg Karl, Freiherr von Fechenbach, Bishop, 1795-1802
Ferdinand, Grand Duke, 1806-1814

MINT MARKS

F - Furth
N - Nurnberg
Wurzburg

MONETARY SYSTEM

3 Drier (Kortling) = 1 Shillinger
7 Shillinger = 15 Kreuzer
28 Shillinger = 1 Guter Gulden
44-4/5 Shillinger = 1 Convention Thaler

BISHOPRIC

REGULAR COINAGE

KM# 476 1/4 KREUZER
Copper

Date	Mintage	F	VF	XF	Unc	BU
1811	—	6.00	12.00	40.00	150	—

KM# 475 1/2 KREUZER
Copper

Date	Mintage	F	VF	XF	Unc	BU
1810	—	5.00	12.00	30.00	150	—
1811	—	5.00	12.00	30.00	150	—

KM# 468 KREUZER
Silver **Obv:** Crowned arms, dividing G. W. L. M. above **Rev:** Value

Date	Mintage	F	VF	XF	Unc	BU
1808	—	5.00	12.00	30.00	140	—

KM# 469 KREUZER
Silver **Obv:** Without legend

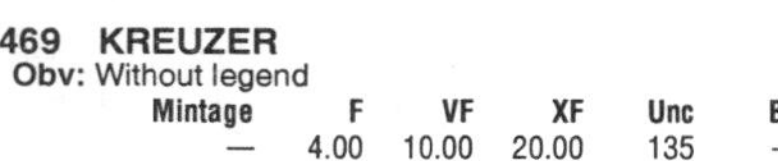

Date	Mintage	F	VF	XF	Unc	BU
1808	—	4.00	10.00	20.00	135	—

KM# 470 KREUZER
Silver **Rev:** G. W. L. M., value

Date	Mintage	F	VF	XF	Unc	BU
1808	—	4.50	10.00	25.00	140	—

KM# 465 3 KREUZER
Billon, 21 mm.

Date	Mintage	F	VF	XF	Unc	BU
1807	—	4.00	10.00	25.00	150	—
1808	—	4.00	10.00	25.00	150	—
1809	—	4.00	10.00	25.00	150	—

KM# 466 6 KREUZER
Silver **Obv:** Large crown

Date	Mintage	F	VF	XF	Unc	BU
1807	—	10.00	20.00	50.00	185	—
1808	—	10.00	20.00	50.00	185	—

KM# 471 6 KREUZER
Silver **Obv:** Small crown

Date	Mintage	F	VF	XF	Unc	BU
1809	—	10.00	20.00	50.00	185	—

TRADE COINAGE

KM# 467 GOLDGULDEN
3.2500 g., 0.7700 Gold .0805 oz. **Obv:** Head of Ferdinand right **Rev:** Palm tree, arms, value and date

Date	Mintage	F	VF	XF	Unc	BU
1807	—	1,000	1,800	2,800	3,500	—
1809	—	1,000	1,800	2,800	3,500	—

KM# 477 GOLDGULDEN
3.2500 g., 0.7700 Gold .0805 oz.

Date	Mintage	F	VF	XF	Unc	BU
1812 R	—	1,000	1,800	2,800	3,500	—

KM# 478 GOLDGULDEN
3.2500 g., 0.7700 Gold .0805 oz. **Rev:** Crowned battle flag, value and date

Date	Mintage	F	VF	XF	Unc	BU
1813 R	—	4,000	7,000	10,000	12,500	—

KM# 479 GOLDGULDEN
3.2500 g., 0.7700 Gold .0805 oz.

Date	Mintage	F	VF	XF	Unc	BU
1814 R	—	3,000	5,000	8,000	10,000	—

1871-1918

Germany, a nation of north-central Europe which from1871 to 1945 was, successively, an empire, a republic and a totalitarian state, attained its territorial peak as an empire when it comprised a 208,780 sq. mi. (540,740 sq. km.) homeland and an overseas colonial empire.

As the power of the Roman Empire waned, several war-like tribes residing in northern Germany moved south and west, invading France, Belgium, England, Italy and Spain. In 800 A.D. the Frankish king Charlemagne, who ruled most of France and Germany, was crowned Emperor of the Holy Roman Empire, a loose federation of an estimated 1,800 German States that lasted until 1806. Modern Germany was formed from the eastern part of Charlemagne's empire.

After 1812, the German States were reduced to a federation of 32, of which Prussia was the strongest. In 1871, Prussian chancellor Otto von Bismarck united the German States into an empire ruled by William I, the Prussian king. The empire initiated a colonial endeavor and became one of the world's greatest powers. Germany disintegrated as a result of World War I.

It was reestablished as the Weimar Republic. The humiliation of defeat, economic depression, poverty and discontent gave rise to Adolf Hitler, 1933, who reconstituted Germany as the Third Reich and after initial diplomatic and military triumphs, expanded his goals beyond Europe into Africa and USSR which led it into final disaster in World War II, ending on VE Day, May 7, 1945.

RULERS

Wilhelm I, 1871-1888
Friedrich III, 1888
Wilhelm II, 1888-1918

MINT MARKS

A - Berlin
B - Hannover (1866-1878)
C - Frankfurt (1866-1879)
D - Munich
E - Dresden (1872-1887)
E - Muldenhutten (1887-1953)
F - Stuttgart
G - Karlsruhe
H - Darmstadt (1872-1882)
J - Hamburg

MONETARY SYSTEM
(Until 1923)

100 Pfennig = 1 Mark
(Commencing 1945)
100 Pfennig = 1 Mark

EMPIRE

STANDARD COINAGE

KM# 1 PFENNIG

Copper

Date	Mintage	F	VF	XF	Unc	BU
1873A	184,000	125	250	450	1,000	—
1873B	95,000	225	525	900	1,450	—
1873D	52,000	200	500	750	1,250	—
1874A	26,760,000	0.75	2.50	15.00	40.00	—
1874B	8,743,000	2.00	9.00	20.00	65.00	—
1874C	15,744,000	2.00	9.00	20.00	65.00	—
1874D	7,074,000	5.00	15.00	25.00	65.00	—
1874E	4,522,000	10.00	15.00	35.00	90.00	—
1874F	3,985,000	2.50	7.50	17.50	65.00	—
1874G	4,768,000	12.00	40.00	60.00	125	—
1874H	2,013,000	40.00	65.00	125	350	—
1875A	64,669,000	0.75	1.50	7.50	20.00	—
1875B	27,618,000	1.00	2.50	15.00	40.00	—
1875C	22,654,000	1.00	2.50	15.00	40.00	—
1875D	13,342,000	1.00	2.50	10.00	30.00	—
1875E	7,779,000	5.00	15.00	30.00	60.00	—
1875F	15,271,000	1.00	3.00	12.50	35.00	—
1875G	12,021,000	5.00	10.00	20.00	60.00	—
1875H	3,516,000	30.00	60.00	100	250	—
1875J	7,242,000	2.50	8.00	20.00	50.00	—
1876A	34,542,000	0.75	1.50	6.50	20.00	—
1876B	5,995,000	3.00	5.00	10.00	32.00	—
1876C	11,044,000	3.00	5.00	10.00	32.00	—
1876D	12,651,000	3.00	5.00	10.00	32.00	—
1876E	6,532,000	2.50	7.50	20.00	50.00	—
1876F	11,404,000	3.00	6.00	10.00	32.00	—
1876G	3,331,000	10.00	30.00	50.00	100	—
1876H	2,998,000	20.00	50.00	100	200	—
1876J	1,165,000	50.00	100	275	475	—
1877A	472,000	70.00	185	475	800	—
1877B	88,000	350	650	1,400	2,150	—
1885A	5,448,000	1.50	6.00	15.00	30.00	—
1885E	430,000	40.00	60.00	100	300	—
1885G	1,100,000	20.00	50.00	80.00	200	—
1885J	1,696,000	10.00	20.00	45.00	90.00	—
1886A	14,114,000	1.00	2.50	10.00	25.00	—
1886D	2,873,000	1.00	2.50	12.50	40.00	—
1886E	2,060,000	5.00	10.00	30.00	75.00	—
1886F	1,726,000	6.00	12.00	35.00	80.00	—
1886G	814,000	40.00	90.00	130	250	—
1886J	1,593,000	7.50	15.00	30.00	50.00	—
1887A	15,923,000	1.00	1.50	10.00	25.00	—
1887D	5,177,000	2.50	4.00	10.00	25.00	—
1887E	2,315,000	3.00	6.00	20.00	50.00	—
1887E	25	—	—	7,000	10,000	—
Note: Dot after PFENNIG						
1887F	6,345,000	2.50	5.00	15.00	35.00	—
1887G	1,888,000	5.00	10.00	30.00	70.00	—
1887J	2,081,999	1.50	3.00	10.00	25.00	—
1888A	19,936,000	0.75	1.50	6.50	17.50	—
1888D	3,277,000	6.00	9.00	15.00	40.00	—
1888E	1,310,000	5.00	10.00	20.00	45.00	—
1888F	584,000	20.00	40.00	95.00	150	—
1888G	1,385,000	6.00	12.00	30.00	70.00	—
1888J	2,803,000	2.50	5.00	10.00	40.00	—
1889A	20,750,000	1.00	2.50	10.00	30.00	—
1889D	8,454,000	2.00	3.00	15.00	30.00	—
1889E	4,330,000	1.00	2.50	12.50	25.00	—
1889F	5,010,000	1.00	2.50	12.50	30.00	—
1889G	3,411,000	1.50	3.00	10.00	25.00	—
1889J	3,308,000	1.50	3.00	10.00	25.00	—
Common date Proof	—	Value: 200				

KM# 10 PFENNIG

Copper **Note:** Struck from 1890-1916.

Date	Mintage	F	VF	XF	Unc	BU
1890A	17,295,000	0.50	1.50	3.50	10.00	—
1890D	7,[illegible],000	1.00	2.50	5.00	12.50	—
1890E	3,730,000	0.50	2.00	6.50	12.50	—
1890F	4,189,000	0.50	2.00	6.50	15.00	—
1890G	3,050,000	1.50	3.00	6.50	15.00	—
1890J	2,247,000	1.50	3.00	6.50	15.00	—
1891A	12,040,000	1.50	3.00	5.00	10.00	—
1891D	876,000	10.00	25.00	75.00	135	—
1891E	528,000	20.00	40.00	85.00	140	—
1891F	1,263,000	5.00	10.00	25.00	65.00	—
1891G	360,000	40.00	75.00	145	300	—
1891J	1,837,000	7.50	25.00	75.00	135	—
1892A	22,341,000	0.25	0.50	1.50	20.00	—
1892D	6,139,000	2.00	4.00	9.00	40.00	—
1892E	3,195,000	2.00	4.00	9.00	35.00	—
1892F	5,013,000	1.00	2.00	5.00	30.00	—
1892G	2,689,000	5.00	10.00	25.00	65.00	—
1892J	3,980,000	0.50	1.50	4.00	20.00	—
1893A	18,966,000	0.25	0.50	2.00	12.00	—
1893D	7,027,000	0.25	1.00	4.00	20.00	—
1893E	1,218,000	10.00	20.00	30.00	60.00	—
1893F	1,460,000	5.00	10.00	20.00	40.00	—
1893G	700,000	12.50	25.00	40.00	120	—
1893J	1,825,000	2.00	7.00	25.00	80.00	—
1894A	17,592,000	0.25	0.50	2.00	7.50	—
1894D	5,530,000	0.25	1.00	4.00	12.50	—
1894E	5,040,000	0.50	1.50	5.00	15.00	—
1894F	4,206,000	0.20	1.00	4.00	15.00	—
1894G	2,351,000	3.00	9.00	20.00	40.00	—
1894J	2,619,000	0.50	2.00	6.00	12.50	—
1895A	20,152,000	0.25	1.00	2.50	8.50	—
1895D	1,496,000	10.00	25.00	35.00	100	—
1895E	1,191,000	5.00	10.00	25.00	35.00	—
1895F	4,366,000	0.25	2.50	6.50	12.50	—
1895G	3,051,000	1.00	3.00	7.50	25.00	—
1895J	3,839,000	2.00	4.00	10.00	20.00	—
1896A	27,094,000	0.10	0.25	1.50	6.50	—
1896D	7,025,000	0.10	0.25	1.50	6.50	—
1896E	3,725,000	0.25	2.50	5.00	10.00	—
1896F	3,450,000	0.10	0.20	1.50	6.50	—
1896G	3,028,000	0.25	4.00	7.50	15.00	—
1897A	8,534,000	0.25	1.00	3.50	8.50	—
1897D	2,600,000	1.00	2.50	6.00	15.00	—
1897E	1,294,000	3.50	7.50	15.00	45.00	—
1897F	2,390,000	5.00	10.00	30.00	70.00	—
1897G	1,122,000	10.00	20.00	50.00	100	—
1897J	4,941,000	1.00	2.00	5.00	10.00	—
1898A	18,564,000	0.10	0.25	1.50	6.50	—
1898D	4,430,000	0.25	2.00	5.00	15.00	—
1898E	2,432,000	0.50	5.00	10.00	20.00	—
1898F	4,193,000	0.20	1.00	2.50	7.50	—
1898G	1,951,000	0.25	5.00	15.00	30.00	—
1898J	3,231,000	0.25	2.50	5.00	10.00	—
1899A	22,009,000	0.10	0.25	2.00	6.00	—
1899D	4,590,000	0.10	0.25	2.00	6.00	—
1899E	3,725,000	0.25	2.50	5.00	12.50	—
1899F	4,300,000	0.10	0.20	1.50	5.50	—
1899G	2,550,000	0.20	1.50	5.00	15.00	—
1899J	2,416,000	0.20	1.00	4.00	10.00	—
1900A	51,804,000	0.10	0.25	1.50	5.50	—
1900D	14,635,000	0.10	0.25	1.50	5.50	—
1900E	7,887,000	0.20	1.00	3.50	8.50	—
1900F	10,312,000	0.10	0.50	1.50	6.00	—
1900G	6,138,000	0.20	1.00	3.50	8.50	—
1900J	9,917,000	0.20	1.00	3.50	8.50	—
1890-1900 Common date proof	—	Value: 70.00				

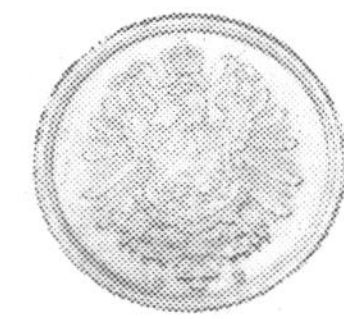

KM# 2 2 PFENNIG

Copper

Date	Mintage	VG	F	VF	XF	Unc
1873A	877,000	2.50	7.50	35.00	185	—
1873B	290,000	25.00	60.00	120	275	—
1873C	161,000	30.00	70.00	145	325	—
1873D	2,358,000	5.00	25.00	65.00	225	—
1873F	22,000	125	275	675	1,450	—
1873G	118,000	75.00	200	350	550	—
1874A	37,360,000	0.50	2.50	12.50	50.00	—
1874B	10,310,000	1.50	7.50	20.00	75.00	—
1874C	17,474,000	1.00	5.00	15.00	55.00	—
1874D	2,943,000	3.50	15.00	30.00	125	—
1874E	5,090,000	2.50	12.50	30.00	125	—
1874F	6,405,000	1.00	7.50	25.00	125	—
1874G	6,128,000	1.00	7.50	25.00	185	—
1874H	2,706,000	10.00	20.00	60.00	200	—
1875A	28,963,000	0.50	2.50	12.50	50.00	—
1875B	15,844,000	1.00	3.50	20.00	55.00	—
1875C	35,541,000	0.50	1.00	25.00	65.00	—
1875D	11,160,000	0.50	1.00	45.00	150	—
1875E	7,872,000	1.00	1.50	50.00	160	—
1875F	9,827,000	0.50	1.00	30.00	125	—
1875G	11,903,000	0.50	1.00	30.00	125	—
1875H	3,309,000	3.50	7.50	60.00	200	—
1875J	14,210,000	0.50	1.00	20.00	75.00	—
1876A	18,906,000	0.50	1.00	12.50	50.00	—
1876B	7,097,000	0.50	1.00	15.00	50.00	—
1876C	12,280,000	0.50	1.00	15.00	50.00	—
1876D	10,296,000	0.50	1.00	15.00	50.00	—
1876E	4,988,000	1.00	1.50	15.00	50.00	—
1876F	7,207,000	0.50	1.50	15.00	50.00	—
1876G	3,502,000	1.00	2.50	15.00	50.00	—
1876H	3,630,000	1.00	3.00	20.00	60.00	—
1876J	1,995,000	4.00	7.50	17.50	60.00	—
1877A	9,827,000	0.50	1.00	15.00	50.00	—
1877B	60,000	200	350	700	—	—
Common date Proof	—	Value: 220				

KM# 3 5 PFENNIG

Copper-Nickel

Date	Mintage	F	VF	XF	Unc	BU
1874A	10,003,000	0.25	1.00	12.50	90.00	—
1874B	5,054,000	0.50	2.50	15.00	120	—
1874C	3,707,000	0.50	2.50	15.00	120	—
1874D	2,447,000	0.50	2.50	15.00	120	—
1874E	5,465,000	0.50	2.50	15.00	135	—
1874F	3,562,000	1.50	4.00	17.50	135	—
1874G	2,721,000	1.50	4.00	17.50	140	—
1875A	30,844,000	0.25	1.00	12.50	65.00	—
1875B	11,658,000	0.50	2.50	14.00	90.00	—
1875C	18,082,000	0.50	2.50	14.00	90.00	—
1875D	12,380,000	0.50	2.50	14.00	90.00	—
1875E	6,745,000	0.50	2.50	16.00	100	—

Date	Mintage	F	VF	XF	Unc	BU
1875F	9,758,000	0.50	2.50	14.00	90.00	—
1875G	10,220,000	0.50	2.50	14.00	90.00	—
1875H	703,000	20.00	45.00	75.00	175	—
1875J	9,781,000	0.50	2.50	14.00	90.00	—
1876A	22,342,000	0.25	1.00	12.50	65.00	—
1876B	8,925,000	0.50	2.50	14.00	75.00	—
1876C	8,680,000	0.50	2.50	14.00	75.00	—
1876D	14,467,000	0.50	2.50	14.00	75.00	—
1876E	6,899,000	0.50	2.50	15.00	90.00	—
1876F	6,826,000	0.50	2.50	14.00	75.00	—
1876G	6,942,000	0.50	2.50	15.00	135	—
1876H	3,027,000	3.00	6.00	25.00	175	—
1876J	11,920,000	0.50	1.00	11.50	50.00	—
1888A	7,366,000	0.25	1.00	11.50	45.00	—
1888/83D	1,967,000	3.00	6.00	25.00	65.00	—
1888/78D	Inc. above	3.00	6.00	25.00	65.00	—
1888D	Inc. above	2.50	5.00	20.00	55.00	—
1888E	1,016,000	3.00	4.00	17.50	50.00	—
1888F	1,412,000	1.00	2.00	11.50	40.00	—
1888G	853,000	6.00	8.00	22.50	60.00	—
1888J	1,130,000	6.00	8.00	22.50	60.00	—
1889A	10,804,000	0.25	1.00	10.00	35.00	—
1889D	2,816,000	1.00	2.50	11.50	45.00	—
1889E	1,492,000	2.00	3.50	12.50	50.00	—
1889F	2,010,000	1.00	2.50	11.50	45.00	—
1889G	1,221,000	2.00	4.00	15.00	50.00	—
1889J	1,636,000	2.50	5.00	17.50	55.00	—
Common date Proof	—	Value: 225				

KM# 11 5 PFENNIG

Copper-Nickel **Note:** Struck from 1890-1915.

Date	Mintage	F	VF	XF	Unc	BU
1890A	4,548,000	0.10	0.50	4.00	12.50	—
1890D	2,813,000	0.25	1.00	5.00	15.00	—
1890E	1,318,000	0.25	1.00	6.00	17.50	—
1890F	1,068,000	0.25	1.00	5.00	15.00	—
1890G	948,000	0.25	1.00	6.00	17.50	—
1890J	1,629,000	0.20	1.00	5.00	15.00	—
1891A	6,313,000	0.10	0.50	4.00	12.50	—
1891E	173,000	12.50	35.00	50.00	80.00	—
1891F	942,000	0.25	1.00	5.00	15.00	—
1891G	271,000	5.00	17.50	30.00	55.00	—
1892A	2,279,000	0.10	1.00	4.00	12.50	—
1892D	920,000	0.25	1.00	5.00	15.00	—
1892E	346,000	2.50	12.50	20.00	35.00	—
1892F	464,000	4.00	15.00	25.00	45.00	—
1892G	800,000	3.00	15.00	22.50	35.00	—
1892J	93,000	50.00	90.00	150	225	—
1893A	8,572,000	0.10	0.50	4.00	15.00	—
1893D	1,892,000	0.25	1.00	5.00	16.50	—
1893E	1,149,000	0.25	1.00	6.00	17.50	—
1893F	1,546,000	0.15	1.00	5.00	15.00	—
1893G	422,000	4.00	15.00	20.00	40.00	—
1893J	1,544,000	0.20	1.00	5.00	15.00	—
1894A	10,830,000	0.10	0.50	4.00	12.50	—
1894D	2,812,000	0.25	1.00	5.00	15.00	—
1894E	802,000	0.25	1.50	6.00	17.50	—
1894F	300,000	1.00	4.00	10.00	30.00	—
1894G	280,000	1.00	5.00	12.50	35.00	—
1894J	1,634,000	0.20	1.00	5.00	15.00	—
1895E	686,000	0.25	2.50	7.50	22.50	—
1895F	1,705,000	0.15	1.50	5.00	15.00	—
1895G	940,000	0.25	2.00	6.00	17.50	—
1896A	1,459,000	0.25	1.00	5.00	15.00	—
1896E	658,000	0.25	2.50	7.50	17.50	—
1896F	2,009,000	0.10	1.00	5.00	15.00	—
1896G	—	1,500	2,500	—	—	—
Note: Mintage included under 1897G.						
1896J	1,634,000	0.20	1.00	5.00	15.00	—
1897A	9,390,000	0.10	0.50	3.00	11.50	—
1897D	2,812,000	0.25	1.00	3.00	11.50	—
1897E	833,000	0.25	2.00	5.00	15.00	—
1897/797G	1,221,000	1.00	4.00	10.00	30.00	—
1897G	Inc. above	0.10	1.00	4.50	15.00	—
1898A	10,836,000	0.10	0.30	2.25	10.00	—
1898D	2,812,000	0.10	0.50	2.25	11.50	—
1898E	1,492,000	0.10	0.50	2.75	14.00	—
1898F	2,007,000	0.10	0.50	2.75	14.00	—
1898G	1,220,000	0.10	0.50	2.25	17.50	—
1898J	1,635,000	0.20	1.00	2.25	12.00	—
1899A	10,884,000	0.10	0.30	2.00	11.50	—
1899D	2,812,000	0.10	0.50	2.75	14.00	—
1899E	1,488,000	0.10	0.50	3.00	17.50	—
1899F	2,006,000	0.10	0.50	2.75	14.00	—
1899G	1,222,000	0.10	0.50	2.25	12.00	—
1899J	1,634,000	0.10	0.50	2.25	12.00	—
1900A	18,941,000	0.10	0.30	2.00	10.00	—
1900D	4,254,000	0.10	0.50	2.25	12.00	—
1900E	2,236,000	0.10	0.50	2.75	14.00	—
1900F	3,209,000	0.10	0.25	2.25	12.00	—
1900G	2,136,000	0.10	0.50	2.25	12.00	—
1900J	2,859,000	0.10	0.50	2.25	12.00	—
1890-1900 Common date proof	—	Value: 80.00				

KM# 4 10 PFENNIG

Copper-Nickel

Date	Mintage	F	VF	XF	Unc	BU
1873A	931,000	4.00	8.00	22.50	120	—
1873B	333,000	17.50	25.00	90.00	250	—
1873C	522,000	15.00	20.00	70.00	225	—
1873D	472,000	5.00	10.00	40.00	185	—
1873F	476,000	25.00	35.00	70.00	200	—
1873G	519,000	25.00	35.00	80.00	235	—
1873H	44,000	125	250	500	1,100	—
1874A	7,664,000	0.25	2.00	15.00	75.00	—
1874B	2,669,000	2.50	5.00	20.00	90.00	—
1874C	12,029,000	0.25	2.00	15.00	70.00	—
1874D	3,586,000	8.00	17.50	65.00	165	—
1874E	3,157,000	8.00	17.50	40.00	150	—
1874F	7,309,000	1.00	2.50	17.50	80.00	—
1874G	5,552,000	1.00	2.50	20.00	100	—
1874H	3,323,000	12.50	20.00	50.00	150	—
1875A	15,523,000	0.25	2.00	12.50	70.00	—
1875B	4,120,000	3.00	12.00	40.00	120	—
1875C	8,304,000	1.00	2.50	15.00	70.00	—
1875D	13,365,000	1.00	2.50	15.00	70.00	—
1875E	9,833,000	1.00	2.50	15.00	70.00	—
1875F	7,975,000	1.00	2.50	15.00	70.00	—
1875G	5,390,000	2.50	5.00	17.50	75.00	—
1875H	4,268,000	12.50	20.00	50.00	165	—
1875J	9,407,000	1.00	2.50	15.00	70.00	—
1876A	34,175,000	0.25	2.00	12.50	45.00	—
1876B	10,120,000	1.00	2.50	14.00	50.00	—
1876C	13,214,000	0.25	2.00	12.50	45.00	—
1876D	16,787,000	0.25	2.00	12.50	45.00	—
1876E	6,161,000	1.00	2.50	14.00	50.00	—
1876F	7,034,000	1.00	2.50	14.00	50.00	—
1876G	6,222,000	1.00	2.50	14.00	50.00	—
1876H	3,227,000	17.50	30.00	40.00	75.00	—
1876J	11,315,000	1.00	2.50	14.00	45.00	—
1888A	8,519,000	1.00	2.50	16.00	50.00	—
1888D	2,493,000	0.50	2.50	14.00	40.00	—
1888E	1,268,000	1.00	7.50	20.00	55.00	—
1888F	1,340,000	1.00	7.50	20.00	55.00	—
1888G	1,081,000	1.00	7.50	20.00	50.00	—
1888J	1,436,000	0.50	2.50	14.00	45.00	—
1889A	11,542,000	0.25	2.00	12.00	35.00	—
1889D	2,813,000	0.50	2.00	12.00	40.00	—
1889E	1,493,000	0.50	2.50	14.00	40.00	—
1889F	2,432,000	0.50	2.50	14.00	40.00	—
1889G	1,223,000	0.50	5.00	20.00	50.00	—
1889J	1,638,000	0.50	2.50	14.00	40.00	—
Common date Proof	—	Value: 350				

KM# 12 10 PFENNIG

Copper-Nickel **Note:** Struck from 1890-1916.

Date	Mintage	F	VF	XF	Unc	BU
1890A	6,878,000	0.10	0.25	6.00	18.00	—
1890F	784,000	0.25	1.50	8.00	25.00	—
1890G	976,000	0.25	2.00	8.00	25.00	—
1890J	1,637,000	0.25	1.00	8.00	25.00	—
1891A	4,239,000	0.10	0.25	3.00	15.00	—
1891D	2,812,000	0.10	0.30	4.00	16.00	—
1891E	1,489,000	0.20	1.00	4.00	16.00	—
1891F	1,226,000	0.25	2.50	5.00	20.00	—
1891G	247,000	7.00	20.00	40.00	70.00	—
1892A	2,413,000	0.15	0.50	4.00	18.00	—
1892D	2,812,000	0.15	0.50	4.00	18.00	—
1892E	870,000	0.25	2.50	5.00	20.00	—
1892F	663,000	0.25	2.50	5.00	20.00	—
1892G	300,000	6.00	15.00	30.00	65.00	—
1892J	—	2,150	3,600	—	—	—
1893A	8,435,000	0.10	0.25	2.25	10.00	—
1893E	362,000	0.50	6.00	12.50	35.00	—
1893F	1,345,000	0.15	0.50	3.00	16.00	—
1893G	921,000	0.25	1.50	5.00	16.00	—
1893J	1,636,000	0.20	1.00	5.00	16.00	—
1894E	260,000	7.50	25.00	40.00	65.00	—
1896A	4,996,000	0.10	1.00	2.25	10.00	—
1896D	2,812,000	0.20	1.00	4.00	12.00	—
1896E	1,495,000	0.20	1.00	4.00	15.00	—
1896F	2,009,000	0.15	1.00	4.00	15.00	—
1896G	200,000	6.00	15.00	25.00	40.00	—
1896J	1,632,000	0.10	0.30	4.00	15.00	—
1897A	5,842,000	0.10	0.25	2.25	10.00	—
1897G	1,020,000	0.25	1.50	4.00	15.00	—
1898A	10,833,000	0.10	0.25	2.00	9.00	—
1898D	2,814,000	0.10	0.25	3.00	12.00	—

Date	Mintage	F	VF	XF	Unc	BU
1898E	805,000	0.20	0.50	3.00	14.00	—
1898F	2,007,000	0.15	0.50	2.25	14.00	—
1898G	480,000	0.50	3.00	6.00	22.50	—
1898J	1,635,000	0.10	0.30	2.25	14.00	—
1899A	10,838,000	0.10	0.25	2.00	9.00	—
1899D	3,813,000	0.10	0.25	3.00	12.00	—
1899E	2,175,000	0.10	0.30	3.00	14.00	—
1899F	2,008,000	0.10	0.25	3.00	12.00	—
1899G	1,382,000	0.10	0.25	3.00	12.00	—
1899J	1,635,000	0.10	0.25	3.00	12.00	—
1900A	34,559,000	0.10	0.25	1.75	8.00	—
1900D	8,694,000	0.10	0.25	1.75	12.00	—
1900E	4,490,000	0.10	0.30	2.00	12.00	—
1900F	5,933,000	0.10	0.25	1.75	12.00	—
1900G	4,239,000	0.10	0.25	2.00	14.00	—
1900J	5,720,000	2.00	14.00	60.00	280	—
1890-1900 Common date proof	—	Value: 95.00				

KM# 5 20 PFENNIG

1.1110 g., 0.9000 Silver .0321 oz.

Date	Mintage	F	VF	XF	Unc	BU
1873A	2,159,000	7.00	15.00	35.00	125	—
1873B	664,000	20.00	60.00	125	300	—
1873C	904,000	17.50	35.00	60.00	150	—
1873D	1,201,000	8.00	12.50	30.00	120	—
1873E	100	1,000	1,400	1,800	3,000	—
1873F	450,000	15.00	30.00	80.00	200	—
1873G	763,000	12.50	25.00	70.00	165	—
1873H	54,000	150	350	800	1,500	—
1874A	8,830,000	6.00	10.00	17.50	65.00	—
1874B	9,222,000	6.00	10.00	17.50	75.00	—
1874C	1,303,000	10.00	15.00	25.00	100	—
1874D	10,087,000	7.50	10.00	17.50	75.00	—
1874E	2,281,000	7.50	15.00	25.00	100	—
1874F	7,222,000	6.50	10.00	17.50	65.00	—
1874G	3,281,000	8.00	12.50	20.00	75.00	—
1874H	1,842,000	12.50	17.50	25.00	100	—
1875A	9,034,000	5.00	8.00	15.00	50.00	—
1875B	2,768,000	8.00	12.50	25.00	85.00	—
1875C	5,938,000	5.00	9.00	25.00	60.00	—
1875D	15,032,000	5.00	8.00	15.00	50.00	—
1875E	1,486,000	17.50	30.00	70.00	200	—
1875F	7,668,000	6.00	9.00	15.00	60.00	—
1875G	3,940,000	8.00	12.50	25.00	75.00	—
1875H	1,340,000	17.50	30.00	75.00	225	—
1875J	3,502,000	10.00	15.00	22.50	60.00	—
1876A	6,959,000	6.00	10.00	15.00	45.00	—
1876B	5,089,000	6.00	10.00	16.00	70.00	—
1876C	5,911,000	6.00	10.00	15.00	65.00	—
1876D	14,152,000	5.00	9.00	14.00	50.00	—
1876E	11,648,000	7.50	12.50	20.00	90.00	—
1876F	13,635,000	5.00	9.00	14.00	65.00	—
1876G	7,820,000	5.00	9.00	14.00	65.00	—
1876H	1,433,000	20.00	60.00	125	300	—
1876J	10,272,000	6.00	10.00	17.50	45.00	—
1877F	700,000	125	250	400	650	—
Common date Proot	—	Value: 350				

KM# 9.1 20 PFENNIG

Copper-Nickel

Date	Mintage	F	VF	XF	Unc	BU
1887A	2,712,000	7.50	20.00	30.00	55.00	—
1887D	704,000	7.50	25.00	45.00	90.00	—
1887E	373,000	15.00	35.00	55.00	125	—
1887F	503,000	15.00	30.00	45.00	100	—
1887G	306,000	15.00	30.00	55.00	135	—
1887J	408,000	15.00	30.00	55.00	125	—
1888A	5,426,000	6.50	18.50	27.50	50.00	—
1888/7D	1,406,000	12.00	27.50	40.00	90.00	—
1888D	Inc. above	10.00	25.00	35.00	85.00	—
1888E	744,000	10.00	25.00	35.00	100	—
1888F	1,005,000	10.00	25.00	35.00	90.00	—
1888G	611,000	10.00	25.00	45.00	135	—
1888/7J	818,000	25.00	45.00	60.00	150	—
1888J	Inc. above	10.00	25.00	35.00	85.00	—
Common date Proof	—	Value: 250				

KM# 9.2 20 PFENNIG

Copper-Nickel **Obv:** Star below value

Date	Mintage	F	VF	XF	Unc	BU
1887E	50	—	—	—	6,000	—

Note: Struck at the new mint facility at Muldenhutten

KM# 13 20 PFENNIG

Copper-Nickel

Date	Mintage	F	VF	XF	Unc	BU
1890A	2,716,000	20.00	37.50	65.00	185	—
1890/80D	703,000	20.00	47.50	90.00	200	—
1890D	Inc. above	20.00	47.50	90.00	200	—
1890E	373,000	22.50	60.00	165	345	—
1890F	503,000	20.00	40.00	95.00	275	—
1890G	306,000	22.50	55.00	150	345	—
1890J	410,000	20.00	47.50	90.00	345	—
1892A	2,712,000	12.50	35.00	55.00	175	—
1892D	703,000	20.00	47.50	65.00	250	—
1892E	372,000	20.00	55.00	100	400	—
1892F	502,000	20.00	47.50	90.00	275	—
1892G	304,000	27.50	67.50	180	450	—
1892J	409,000	20.00	55.00	165	445	—
Common date Proof	—	Value: 325				

KM# 6 50 PFENNIG

2.7770 g., 0.9000 Silver .0803 oz.

Date	Mintage	F	VF	XF	Unc	BU
1875A	7,095,000	7.50	15.00	30.00	100	—
1875B	2,799,000	8.00	16.00	50.00	135	—
1875C	2,047,000	8.00	16.00	50.00	145	—
1875D	4,668,000	8.00	16.00	32.50	125	—
1875E	353,000	150	325	650	1,800	—
1875F	874,000	22.50	50.00	100	200	—
1875G	2,034,000	15.00	17.50	50.00	155	—
1875H	175,000	150	300	700	2,000	—
1875J	2,411,000	12.50	20.00	50.00	165	—
1876A	34,475,000	6.00	12.00	25.00	85.00	—
1876B	11,016,000	6.00	12.00	25.00	90.00	—
1876C	10,945,000	6.00	12.00	25.00	90.00	—
1876D	3,641,000	12.50	25.00	45.00	125	—
1876E	4,127,000	12.50	25.00	50.00	135	—
1876F	4,448,000	12.50	25.00	55.00	145	—
1876G	1,797,000	10.00	18.00	40.00	125	—
1876H	1,877,000	20.00	40.00	100	300	—
1876J	3,589,000	8.00	16.00	35.00	100	—
1877A	3,249,000	8.00	16.00	35.00	100	—
1877B	3,691,000	10.00	18.00	40.00	100	—
1877C	2,388,000	15.00	32.50	55.00	150	—
1877D	3,004,000	12.50	25.00	55.00	150	—
1877E	1,121,000	30.00	50.00	160	265	—
1877F	1,311,000	25.00	40.00	100	200	—
1877H	622,000	75.00	120	200	400	—
1877J	1,526,000	40.00	65.00	155	285	—
Common date Proof	—	Value: 250				

KM# 8 50 PFENNIG

2.7770 g., 0.9000 Silver .0803 oz.

Date	Mintage	F	VF	XF	Unc	BU
1877A	6,746,000	20.00	40.00	90.00	220	—
1877B	3,097,000	22.50	45.00	100	250	—
1877C	2,820,000	20.00	45.00	100	260	—
1877D	5,315,000	18.00	35.00	90.00	220	—
1877E	2,296,000	20.00	40.00	110	255	—
1877F	2,145,000	20.00	40.00	110	255	—
1877G	2,061,000	22.50	50.00	125	280	—
1877H	1,510,000	30.00	75.00	165	325	—
1877J	1,337,000	22.50	45.00	110	260	—
1878E	364,000	250	400	600	1,150	—
Common date Proof	—	Value: 450				

KM# 15 50 PFENNIG

2.7770 g., 0.9000 Silver .0803 oz.

Date	Mintage	F	VF	XF	Unc	BU
1896A	389,000	125	300	400	600	—
1898A	387,000	100	220	360	600	—
1900J	192,000	110	250	400	720	—
1900J Proof	—	Value: 650				
1896-1900 Common date proof	—	Value: 525				

KM# 7 MARK

5.5500 g., 0.9000 Silver .1606 oz.

Date	Mintage	F	VF	XF	Unc	BU
1873A	930,000	2.50	5.00	45.00	175	—
1873B	89,000	12.50	22.50	100	350	—
1873C	18,000	65.00	125	375	800	—
1873D	244,000	5.00	12.50	80.00	185	—
1873F	109,000	10.00	20.00	100	285	—
1874A	6,310,000	2.50	6.00	40.00	90.00	—
1874B	2,672,000	6.00	15.00	65.00	185	—
1874C	840,000	6.00	15.00	80.00	200	—
1874D	7,079,000	2.50	6.00	30.00	100	—
1874E	3,240,000	5.00	20.00	60.00	150	—
1874F	6,155,000	2.50	8.00	40.00	125	—
1874G	4,210,000	2.50	8.00	40.00	135	—
1874H	1,893,000	4.00	15.00	85.00	300	—
1875A	30,340,000	2.50	4.00	22.00	100	—
1875B	7,690,000	2.50	7.50	50.00	150	—
1875C	6,209,000	2.50	7.50	50.00	140	—
1875D	7,538,000	2.50	5.00	30.00	100	—
1875E	4,646,000	2.50	7.50	50.00	165	—
1875F	7,074,000	2.50	4.00	22.00	120	—
1875G	6,072,000	2.50	4.00	22.00	100	—
1875H	2,300,000	3.50	10.00	65.00	200	—
1875J	7,728,000	2.50	7.50	40.00	125	—
1876A	17,297,000	2.50	4.00	22.00	90.00	—
1876C	4,790,000	2.50	7.50	45.00	110	—
1876D	2,956,000	2.50	10.00	65.00	200	—
1876F	4,161,000	2.50	7.50	45.00	100	—
1876G	2,333,000	2.50	10.00	65.00	200	—
1876H	2,481,000	2.50	10.00	70.00	285	—
1876J	1,109,000	2.50	10.00	75.00	300	—
1877A	697,000	10.00	20.00	120	600	—
1877B	48,000	150	250	600	1,600	—
1878A	1,527,000	2.50	7.50	65.00	200	—
1878B	582,000	10.00	20.00	200	750	—
1878C	600,000	15.00	30.00	200	650	—
1878E	318,000	15.00	30.00	250	1,100	—
1878F	1,039,000	5.00	12.50	65.00	220	—
1878G	525,000	7.50	20.00	125	375	—
1878J	895,000	6.50	18.00	100	275	—
1879A	156,000	45.00	90.00	500	1,400	—
1880A	1,071,000	5.00	12.50	75.00	250	—
1880D	338,000	10.00	20.00	100	450	—
1880E	173,000	15.00	30.00	200	750	—
1880F	223,000	15.00	30.00	200	700	—
1880G	146,000	50.00	75.00	275	1,250	—
1880H	164,000	30.00	60.00	250	1,150	—
1880J	197,000	10.00	22.50	120	750	—
1881A	6,386,000	2.50	4.00	25.00	125	—
1881D	2,040,000	2.50	4.00	25.00	115	—
1881E	1,081,000	5.00	10.00	75.00	175	—
1881F	1,455,000	3.00	6.50	45.00	150	—
1881G	426,000	10.00	22.50	135	600	—
1881H	387,000	10.00	22.50	135	600	—
1881J	790,000	5.00	10.00	65.00	150	—
1882A	1,474,000	2.50	8.00	60.00	225	—
1882G	459,000	10.00	25.00	90.00	450	—
1882H	109,000	50.00	100	450	1,550	—
1882J	98,000	10.00	30.00	115	525	—
1883A	809,000	5.00	10.00	55.00	150	—
1883D	208,000	22.00	50.00	115	400	—
1883E	112,000	50.00	100	475	1,650	—
1883F	148,000	30.00	75.00	275	1,250	—
1883G	91,000	75.00	150	400	1,450	—
1883J	121,000	30.00	75.00	250	1,100	—
1885A	1,467,000	2.50	5.00	30.00	120	—
1885G	468,000	5.00	15.00	80.00	325	—
1885J	413,000	7.50	20.00	100	260	—
1886A	1,101,000	3.00	7.50	40.00	125	—
1886D	1,445,000	3.00	7.50	30.00	100	—
1886E	764,000	7.50	15.00	65.00	190	—
1886F	1,031,000	2.50	6.00	45.00	155	—
1886G	161,000	15.00	45.00	165	335	—
1886J	427,000	7.50	15.00	70.00	200	—
1887A	3,006,000	2.50	7.50	30.00	120	—
Common date Proof	—	Value: 250				

KM# 14 MARK

5.5500 g., 0.9000 Silver .1606 oz. **Note:** Struck from 1890-1916.

Date	Mintage	F	VF	XF	Unc	BU
1891A	711,000	7.50	12.50	22.00	90.00	—
1891D	Inc. below	450	900	1,350	2,750	—
1892A	909,000	5.00	12.50	22.00	90.00	—
1892D	418,000	5.00	15.00	32.00	120	—
1892E	223,000	10.00	17.50	45.00	185	—
1892F	302,000	5.00	15.00	32.00	145	—
1892G	183,000	20.00	40.00	100	300	—
1892J	237,000	14.00	25.00	70.00	150	—
1893A	1,633,000	2.50	5.00	12.00	80.00	—
1893D	425,000	2.50	5.00	32.00	145	—
1893E	224,000	7.50	17.50	45.00	140	—
1893F	300,000	7.50	15.00	32.00	120	—
1893J	254,000	8.00	20.00	50.00	150	—
1894G	184,000	20.00	45.00	150	350	—
1896A	2,160,000	2.50	5.00	15.00	60.00	—
1896D	562,000	2.50	6.00	18.00	90.00	—
1896E	297,000	5.00	15.00	45.00	120	—
1896F	401,000	2.50	6.00	32.00	95.00	—
1896G	243,000	7.50	20.00	70.00	185	—
1896J	326,000	5.00	15.00	45.00	145	—
1898A	1,000,000	5.00	12.50	22.00	95.00	—
1899A	1,439,000	2.50	5.00	15.00	70.00	—
1899D	633,000	2.50	5.00	18.00	75.00	—
1899E	335,000	5.00	15.00	28.00	100	—
1899F	393,000	4.00	10.00	22.00	85.00	—
1899G	274,000	4.00	10.00	28.00	160	—
1899J	368,000	4.00	10.00	28.00	135	—
1900A	1,625,000	2.50	5.00	12.00	40.00	—
1900/800D	421,000	2.00	6.00	20.00	50.00	—
1900/801D	Inc. above	2.00	6.00	20.00	50.00	—
1900D	Inc. above	2.50	5.00	12.00	70.00	—
1900E	223,000	10.00	25.00	50.00	150	—
1900F	301,000	7.50	17.50	35.00	100	—
1900G	183,000	12.00	27.00	65.00	185	—
1900J	246,000	10.00	25.00	50.00	150	—
1891-1900 Common date Proof	—	Value: 150				

PATTERNS

Including off metal strikes

KM#	Date	Mintage	Identification	Mkt Val
Pn1	ND	—	Pfennig. Copper. With "PF".	100
Pn2	ND	—	Pfennig. Copper. Without "PF".	—

KM#	Date	Mintage	Identification	Mkt Val
Pn3	ND	—	2 Pfennig. Copper. Plain edge.	—
Pn4	1873G	—	2 Pfennig. Fine reeding.	—
Pn5	1873	—	10 Pfennig. Without mint mark.	—
Pn6	1873A	—	10 Pfennig. Fine reeding.	250
Pn7	1873A	—	10 Pfennig. Coarse reeding.	250
Pn8	1873C	—	10 Pfennig. Reeded edge.	225
Pn8a	1873C	—	10 Pfennig. Reeded edge.	225
PnA9	1874G	—	10 Pfennig. Gold. KM#4.	—
Pn9	1874G	—	Pfennig. Reeded edge.	—
Pn10	1874A	—	2 Pfennig. Coarse reeding.	—
Pn10a	1874C	—	2 Pfennig. Coarse reeding.	150
Pn11	1874F	—	2 Pfennig. Coarse reeding.	—
Pn12	1874G	—	2 Pfennig. Fine reeding.	—
Pn13	1874F	—	5 Pfennig. Reeded edge.	—
Pn14	1874	—	10 Pfennig. Reeded edge.	—
Pn15	1874A	—	10 Pfennig. Reeded edge.	—
Pn16	1874C	—	10 Pfennig. Reeded edge.	—
Pn17	1874D	—	10 Pfennig. Reeded edge.	—
Pn18	1874G	—	10 Pfennig. Diagonal reeding.	—
Pn19	1875G	—	Pfennig. Reeded edge.	—

KM#	Date	Mintage	Identification	Mkt Val
Pn20	1875G	—	2 Pfennig. Fine reeding.	—
Pn21	1875A	—	10 Pfennig. Diagonal reeding.	—
Pn22	1875G	—	10 Pfennig. Fine reeding.	—
Pn23	1875J	—	10 Pfennig. Reeded edge.	—
Pn24	1876G	—	Pfennig. Reeded edge.	—
Pn25	1876G	—	2 Pfennig. Fine reeding.	—
Pn26	1876A	—	5 Pfennig. Reeded edge.	—
Pn27	1876A	—	10 Pfennig. Reeded edge.	75.00
Pn28	1876C	—	10 Pfennig. Reeded edge.	—
Pn29	1876D	—	10 Pfennig. Reeded edge.	—
Pn30	1876G	—	10 Pfennig. Reeded edge.	—
Pn31	1876J	—	10 Pfennig. Fine reeding.	—
Pn32	1877A	—	50 Pfennig. Silver.	250
Pn33	1877A	—	50 Pfennig. Silver.	250
Pn34	1877D	—	1/2 Mark. Silver.	950
Pn35	1877A	—	1/2 Mark. Silver. Diagonal fraction bar.	—
Pn36	1877A	—	1/2 Mark. Silver. Larger eagle.	—
Pn37	1886A	—	20 Pfennig. Silver. KM#9.1.	—
Pn38	1886A	—	20 Pfennig. Silver. Scored fields.	—
Pn39	1886A	—	20 Pfennig. Copper-Nickel. Scored fields.	—
Pn40	1886A	—	20 Pfennig. Silver. Stars scored.	—
Pn41	1886A	—	20 Pfennig. Copper-Nickel. Stars scored.	—
Pn42	1886A	—	20 Pfennig. Silver. Stars plain.	—
Pn43	1886A	—	20 Pfennig. Copper-Nickel. Stars plain.	—
Pn44	1886A	—	20 Pfennig. Silver. Eagle plain.	250
Pn45	1886A	—	20 Pfennig. Silver. Eagle scored.	—
Pn46	1886A	—	20 Pfennig. Silver. Eagle looped.	—
Pn47	1886A	—	20 Pfennig. Nickel-Silver. Eagle looped.	—
Pn48	1888A	—	20 Pfennig. Eagle scored.	—
Pn49	1893A	—	10 Pfennig. Reeded edge. KM#12.	—

KM#	Date	Mintage	Identification	Mkt Val
Pn50	1898A	—	50 Pfennig. Silver. Plain edge. 24 denticles.	—
Pn51	1898A	—	50 Pfennig. Silver. Reeded edge.	—
Pn52	1898A	—	50 Pfennig. Silver. Wavy reeding.	—
Pn52a	ND	—	50 Pfennig. Silver. Reverse uniface.	150
Pn54	190xF	—	1/2 Mark. Iron. KM#17	200
Pn55	190xF	—	1/2 Mark. Copper-Nickel. KM#17	200
Pn56	190xF	—	1/2 Mark. Nickel. KM#17	200
Pn57	1900A	—	1/2 Mark. Silver. Fine reeded rim.	150
Pn58	1900A	—	1/2 Mark. Silver. Coarse reeded rim.	150
Pn59	1900A	—	1/2 Mark. 0.9600 Silver. Coarse wavy reeded rim.	—
Pn60	1900A	—	1/2 Mark. 0.9000 Silver. Coarse wavy reeded rim.	—
Pn61	1900A	—	1/2 Mark. Silver. Flat rims, fine reeding.	—
Pn62	1900A	—	1/2 Mark. 0.5850 Silver. Large eagle.	—
Pn63	1900A	—	1/2 Mark. 0.7500 Silver. Large eagle.	—
Pn64	1900	—	1/2 Mark. 0.9000 Silver. Large eagle.	—
Pn65	1900A	—	1/2 Mark. Silver. Deeper fields, weak reeding.	—

GIBRALTAR

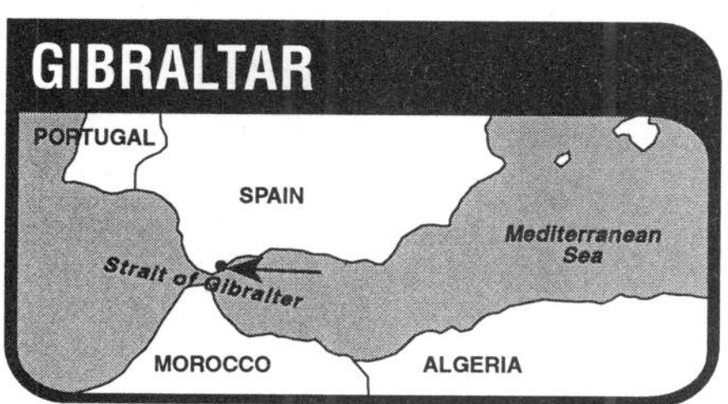

The British Colony of Gibraltar, located at the southernmost point of the Iberian Peninsula, has an area of 2.25sq. mi. (6.5 sq. km.). Capital (and only town): Gibraltar. Aside from its strategic importance as guardian of the western entrance to the Mediterranean Sea, Gibraltar is also a free port and a British naval base.

Gibraltar, rooted in Greek mythology as one of the Pillars of Hercules, has long been a coveted stronghold. Moslems took it from Spain and fortified it in 711. Spain retook it in 1309, lost it again to the Moors in 1333 and retook it in 1462. After 1540 Spain strengthened its defenses and held it until the War of the Spanish Succession when it was captured by a combined British and Dutch force in 1704. Britain held it against the Franco-Spanish attacks of 1704-05 and through the historic Great Siege of 1779-83. Recently Spain has attempted to discourage British occupancy by harassment and economic devices.

It may be of interest that Gibraltar's celebrated Barbary Ape is the last monkey to be found in a wild state in Europe; and a soldier from the local Regiment is appointed as Keeper of the Apes.

RULERS
British

MONETARY SYSTEM
24 Quarts (Quartos) = 1 Real

BRITISH COLONY

TOKEN COINAGE

KM# Tn1 QUART
Copper **Issuer:** Robert Keeling

Date	Mintage	F	VF	XF	Unc	BU
1802	—	10.00	25.00	50.00	160	—

KM# Tn3.1 QUARTO
Copper

Date	Mintage	F	VF	XF	Unc	BU
1810 Large date	—	10.00	17.50	50.00	135	—

KM# Tn3.2 QUARTO
Copper

Date	Mintage	F	VF	XF	Unc	BU
1810 Small date	—	10.00	17.50	50.00	135	—

KM# Tn5 QUARTO
Copper **Issuer:** Richard Cattons

Date	Mintage	F	VF	XF	Unc	BU
1813	—	17.50	30.00	60.00	175	—

KM# Tn8 QUARTO
Copper **Issuer:** James Spittles

Date	Mintage	F	VF	XF	Unc	BU
1820	—	10.00	18.50	55.00	145	—

KM# Tn2.1 2 QUARTS
Copper **Issuer:** Robert Keeling **Rev:** Horizontal and vertical lines in gate **Note:** Toothed border.

Date	Mintage	F	VF	XF	Unc	BU
1802	—	15.00	35.00	75.00	210	—

KM# Tn2.2 2 QUARTS
Copper **Rev:** Horizontal lines in gate **Note:** Plain border.

Date	Mintage	F	VF	XF	Unc	BU
1802	—	15.00	35.00	85.00	225	—

KM# Tn4.1 2 QUARTOS
Copper **Rev:** Large date 5mm tall

Date	Mintage	F	VF	XF	Unc	BU
1810	—	8.00	17.50	50.00	130	—

KM# Tn4.2 2 QUARTOS
Copper **Rev:** Small date 4mm tall

Date	Mintage	F	VF	XF	Unc	BU
1810	—	8.00	17.50	50.00	130	—

KM# Tn6 2 QUARTOS
Copper **Issuer:** Richard Cattons

Date	Mintage	F	VF	XF	Unc	BU
1813	—	17.50	35.00	75.00	185	—

KM# Tn7 2 QUARTOS
Copper **Issuer:** James Spittles

Date	Mintage	F	VF	XF	Unc	BU
1818	—	15.00	30.00	65.00	170	—

KM# Tn9 2 QUARTOS
Copper

Date	Mintage	F	VF	XF	Unc	BU
1820	—	10.00	20.00	50.00	130	—

REGULAR COINAGE

KM# 1 1/2 QUART
Copper

Date	Mintage	F	VF	XF	Unc	BU
ND(1841) Proof	—	Value: 760				
1842	387,000	5.00	15.00	40.00	100	—
1861 Proof	—	Value: 800				

KM# 2 QUART
Copper

Date	Mintage	F	VF	XF	Unc	BU
1841/0 Proof	—	Value: 850				
1842/0	97,000	10.00	30.00	65.00	175	—
1842/0 Proof	—	Value: 300				
1860 Proof; Rare	—	—	—	—	—	—
1861 Proof	—	Value: 725				

KM# 3 2 QUARTS
Copper

Date	Mintage	F	VF	XF	Unc	BU
1841 Proof; Rare	—	—	—	—	—	—
1842/1	48,000	15.00	45.00	100	275	—
1842/1 Proof	—	Value: 450				
1860 Proof; Rare	—	—	—	—	—	—
1861 Proof	—	Value: 850				

PATTERNS

Including off metal strikes

KM#	Date	Mintage	Identification	Mkt Val
Pn1	1802	—	2 Quarts. Copper. KM#2.	3,000
Pn2	1841/0	—	Quart. Bronzed Copper. KM#2.	850
Pn3	1842	—	1/2 Quart. Bronzed Copper. KM#1.	250

GOLD COAST

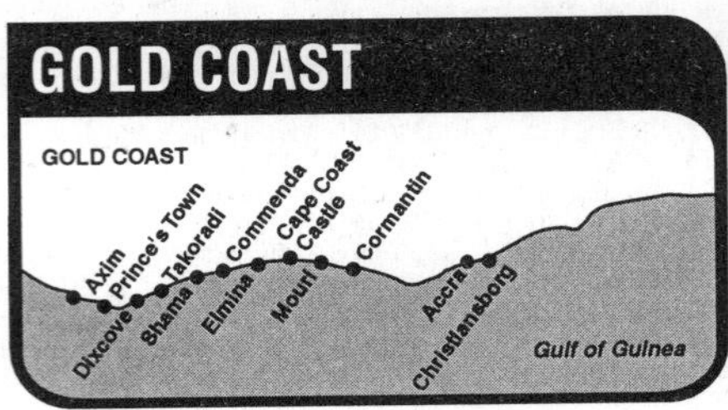

The Gold Coast, a region of Northwest Africa along the Gulf of Guinea, was first visited by Portuguese traders in 1470, and through the 17th century was used by various European powers -England, Denmark, Holland, Germany - as a center for their slave trade. Britain achieved control of the Gold Coast in 1821, and established the colony of Gold Coast in1874. In 1901 Britain annexed the neighboring Ashanti Kingdom in the same year a northern region known as the Northern Territories became a British protectorate. Part of the former German colony of Togoland was mandated to Britain by the League of Nations and administered as part of the Gold Coast.

RULERS
British

MONETARY SYSTEM
8 Tackow = 1 Ackey

BRITISH OUTPOST

STANDARD COINAGE

KM# 8 1/2 ACKEY
7.0900 g., 0.9250 Silver .2108 oz.

Date	Mintage	F	VF	XF	Unc	BU
1818	2,170	60.00	150	275	525	—
1818 Proof	—	Value: 650				

KM# 9 ACKEY
14.1300 g., 0.9250 Silver .4202 oz.

Date	Mintage	F	VF	XF	Unc	BU
1818	1,085	150	350	600	1,200	—
1818 Proof	—	Value: 1,400				

TOKEN COINAGE

KM# Tn1a TACKOE
0.8900 Silver **Note:** Prev. KM#1a.

Date	Mintage	F	VF	XF	Unc	BU
1796(1801)	6,400	110	225	300	600	—

KM# Tn2 1/4 ACKEY
3.8875 g., 0.9250 Silver .1156 oz. **Rev. Legend:** PARLIMENT (error) **Note:** Prev. KM#2.

Date	Mintage	F	VF	XF	Unc	BU
1796	2,880	125	250	375	750	—
1796 Proof	—	Value: 900				

KM# Tn3 1/4 ACKEY
0.8900 Silver **Rev. Legend:** PARLIAMENT **Note:** Prev. KM#3.

Date	Mintage	F	VF	XF	Unc	BU
1796(1801)	3,200	125	250	350	700	—
1796(1801) Proof	—	Value: 850				

KM# Tn5 1/2 ACKEY
7.0900 g., 0.8900 Silver **Rev. Legend:** PARLIAMENT **Note:** Prev. KM#5.

Date	Mintage	F	VF	XF	Unc	BU
1796(1801)	2,400	200	400	650	900	—
1796(1801) Proof	—	Value: 1,100				

KM# Tn7 ACKEY
0.8900 Silver **Rev. Legend:** PARLIAMENT **Note:** Prev. KM#7.

Date	Mintage	F	VF	XF	Unc	BU
1796(1801)	1,200,000	400	800	1,400	2,900	—
1796(1801) Proof	—	Value: 3,250				

PATTERNS

Including off metal strikes

KM#	Date	Mintage	Identification	Mkt Val
Pn9	1818	—	1/2 Ackey. Silver.	1,850
Pn10	1818	—	1/2 Ackey. Bronzed-Copper. KM8.	—
Pn11	1818	—	1/2 Ackey. Pewter. KM8.	500
Pn12	1818	—	Ackey. Bronzed-Copper. KM9	—
Pn13	1818	—	Ackey. Pewter. KM9	1,000

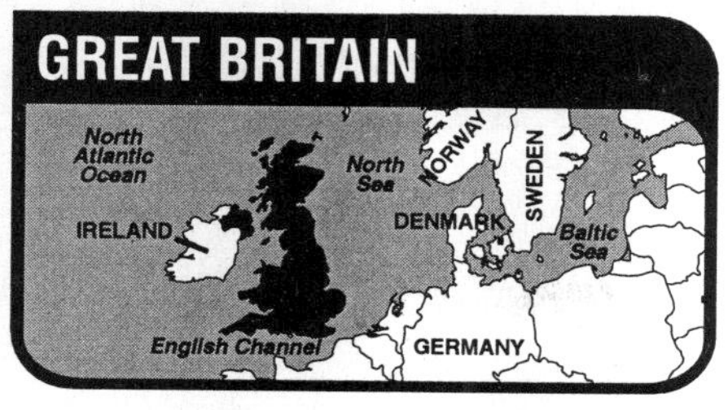

The United Kingdom of Great Britain and Northern Ireland, located off the northwest coast of the European continent, has an area of 94,227sq. mi. (244,820 sq. km.). Capital: London. The economy is based on industrial activity and trading. Machinery, motor vehicles, chemicals, and textile yarns and fabrics are exported.

After the departure of the Romans, who brought Britain into a more active relationship with Europe, it fell prey to invaders from Scandinavia and the Low Countries who drove the original Britons into Scotland and Wales, and established a profusion of kingdoms that finally united in the 11th century under the Danish King Canute. Norman rule, following the conquest of 1066, stimulated the development of those institutions, which have since distinguished British life. Henry VIII (1509-47) turned Britain from continental adventuring and faced it to the sea - a decision that made Britain a world power from the reign of Elizabeth I (1558-1603). Strengthened by the Industrial Revolution and the defeat of Napoleon, 19th century Britain turned to the remote parts of the world and established a colonial empire of such extent and prosperity that the world has never seen its like. World Wars I and II sealed the fate of the Empire and relegated Britain to a lesser role in world affairs by draining her resources and inaugurating a worldwide movement toward national self-determination in her former colonies.

RULERS

George III, 1760-1820
George IV, 1820-1830
William IV, 1830-1837
Victoria, 1837-1901

MINT MARKS

Commencing 1874
H - Heaton
KN - King's Norton

MONETARY SYSTEM

4 Farthings = 1 Penny
12 Pence = 1 Shilling
20 Shillings = 1 Pound (Sovereign)
21 Shillings = 1 Guinea

NOTE: Proofs exist for many dates of British coins in the 19th and early 20th centuries. Those not specifically listed here are extremely rare.

Frequently accepted speech colloquialisms:

"Ha'penny" = 1/2 Penny
(say: Hayp-ni)
"Tanner" = 6 Pence
"Bob" = 1 Shilling
"Half a Crown" = 2 Shillings 6 Pence
(Half a Dollar)
"Dollar" = 5 Shillings
"Half a Quid" = 10 Shillings
"Half a Guinea" = 10 Shillings 6 Pence
"Quid" = 1 Pound
"Tenner" = 10 Pounds
"Pony" = 20 Pounds

KINGDOM

Resumed

POUND COINAGE

KM# 737 1/4 FARTHING
Copper **Ruler:** Victoria

Date	Mintage	F	VF	XF	Unc	BU
1839	3,840,000	18.00	35.00	75.00	150	—
1839 Proof	—	Value: 375				
1851	2,215,000	18.00	35.00	80.00	175	—
1851 Proof	—	Value: 650				
1852	Inc. above	18.00	35.00	75.00	155	—
1853	Inc. above	18.00	35.00	80.00	170	—
1853 Proof	—	Value: 450				

KM# 737a 1/4 FARTHING
Bronzed Copper **Ruler:** Victoria

Date	Mintage	F	VF	XF	Unc	BU
1852 Proof	—	Value: 600				

KM# 703 1/3 FARTHING
Copper **Ruler:** George IV

Date	Mintage	F	VF	XF	Unc	BU
1827	—	10.00	17.00	75.00	175	—
1827 Proof	—	Value: 500				

KM# 721 1/3 FARTHING
Copper **Ruler:** William IV

Date	Mintage	F	VF	XF	Unc	BU
1835	—	7.00	20.00	85.00	175	—
1835 Proof	—	Value: 500				

KM# 743 1/3 FARTHING
Copper **Ruler:** Victoria

Date	Mintage	F	VF	XF	Unc	BU
1844 1	1,301,000	25.00	45.00	120	250	—
1844 2	Inc. above	35.00	60.00	300	700	—

Note: Error: RE for REG

KM# 750 1/3 FARTHING
Bronze **Ruler:** Victoria

Date	Mintage	F	VF	XF	Unc	BU
1866	576,000	2.50	7.00	18.00	45.00	—
1866 Proof	—	Value: 350				
1868	144,000	2.50	7.50	20.00	45.00	—
1868 Proof	—	Value: 300				
1876	162,000	5.00	10.00	20.00	60.00	—
1878	288,000	2.50	7.50	20.00	45.00	—
1878 Proof	—	—	—	—	—	—
1881	144,000	5.00	10.00	20.00	60.00	—
1881 Proof	—	Value: 300				
1884	144,000	2.50	7.50	20.00	50.00	—
1885	288,000	2.50	7.50	18.00	40.00	—

KM# 704.1 1/2 FARTHING
Copper **Ruler:** George IV **Rev:** Britannia's head breaks legend

Date	Mintage	F	VF	XF	Unc	BU
1828	7,680,000	10.00	25.00	100	300	—
1828 Proof	—	Value: 350				
1830 Proof	—	Value: 350				

KM# 704.2 1/2 FARTHING
Copper **Ruler:** George IV **Rev:** Britannia's head below legend

Date	Mintage	F	VF	XF	Unc	BU
1828	Inc. above	10.00	25.00	100	250	—
1830 Large date	8,776,000	10.00	25.00	100	300	—
1830 Small date	Inc. above	12.00	35.00	125	300	—
1830 Proof	—	Value: 350				

KM# 704.1a 1/2 FARTHING
Bronzed Copper **Ruler:** George IV

Date	Mintage	F	VF	XF	Unc	BU
1828 Proof	—	Value: 300				

KM# 724 1/2 FARTHING
Copper **Ruler:** William IV

Date	Mintage	F	VF	XF	Unc	BU
1837	1,935,000	60.00	150	325	550	—

KM# 738 1/2 FARTHING

Copper **Ruler:** Victoria **Note:** Although the design of the 1/2 Farthing is of the homeland type, the issues were originally struck for Ceylon; the issue was made legal tender in the United Kingdom by proclamation in 1842.

Date	Mintage	F	VF	XF	Unc	BU
1839	2,043,000	5.00	10.00	45.00	100	—
1842	—	6.00	12.00	45.00	100	—
1843	3,441,000	2.50	6.00	28.00	70.00	—
1844	6,451,000	2.50	5.00	22.00	65.00	—
1844	Inc. above	13.00	25.00	80.00	200	—
1847	3,011,000	5.00	8.00	30.00	70.00	—
1851/5851	—	11.00	25.00	80.00	175	—
1851	—	6.00	12.00	50.00	100	—
1852	989,000	5.00	12.00	50.00	100	—
1853	955,000	6.50	15.00	40.00	150	—
1853 Proof	—	Value: 450				
1854	677,000	10.00	30.00	90.00	175	—
1856 Small date	914,000	10.00	30.00	90.00	175	—
1856	Inc. above	50.00	100	250	525	—
1856 Small date	Inc. above	—	—	—	—	—
Note: Error: KRITANNIA						

KM# 661 FARTHING

Copper **Ruler:** George III

Date	Mintage	F	VF	XF	Unc	BU
1806	—	2.00	7.50	60.00	100	—
1806 Proof	—	Value: 225				
1807	—	3.00	7.50	55.00	125	—

KM# 661a FARTHING

Gilt Copper **Ruler:** George III

Date	Mintage	F	VF	XF	Unc	BU
1806 Proof	—	Value: 325				

KM# 661b FARTHING

Bronzed Copper **Ruler:** George III

Date	Mintage	F	VF	XF	Unc	BU
1806 Proof	—	Value: 225				

KM# 677 FARTHING

Copper **Ruler:** George IV

Date	Mintage	F	VF	XF	Unc	BU
1821	2,688,000	2.50	11.00	55.00	100	—
1821 Proof	—	Value: 375				
1821.	Inc. above	2.50	11.00	55.00	85.00	—
Note: Dot after date						
1822	5,924,000	2.50	11.00	45.00	70.00	—
1822 Proof	—	Value: 650				
1823	2,365,000	3.00	14.00	55.00	100	—
I823	Inc. above	25.00	80.00	200	300	—
Note: Letter I for 1 in date						
1825	4,300,000	4.00	16.00	55.00	125	—
1826	6,666,000	6.00	18.00	65.00	150	—

KM# 697 FARTHING

Copper **Ruler:** George IV

Date	Mintage	F	VF	XF	Unc	BU
1826	Inc. above	2.50	11.00	55.00	80.00	—
1826 Proof	—	Value: 200				
1827	2,365,000	3.00	12.00	65.00	125	—
1828	2,365,000	2.50	12.00	60.00	100	—
1829	1,505,000	4.00	17.00	75.00	175	—
1830	2,365,000	2.50	11.00	60.00	125	—
1831 Proof	—	Value: 300				

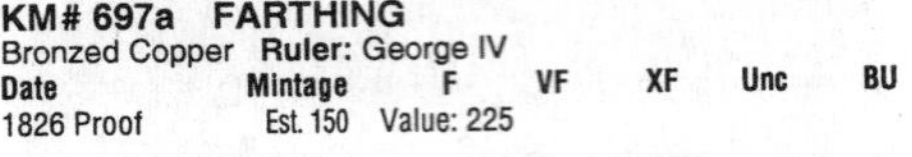

KM# 697a FARTHING

Bronzed Copper **Ruler:** George IV

Date	Mintage	F	VF	XF	Unc	BU
1826 Proof	Est. 150	Value: 225				

KM# 705 FARTHING

Copper **Ruler:** William IV

Date	Mintage	F	VF	XF	Unc	BU
1831	2,688,000	4.50	10.00	65.00	120	—
1831 Proof	—	Value: 250				
1834	1,935,000	4.50	10.00	65.00	120	—
1835	1,720,000	4.50	10.00	65.00	125	—
1836	1,290,000	5.00	12.00	65.00	135	—
1837	3,011,000	4.50	10.00	65.00	120	—

KM# 725 FARTHING

Copper **Ruler:** Victoria

Date	Mintage	F	VF	XF	Unc	BU
1838	591,000	6.00	12.00	40.00	100	—
1839	4,301,000	5.00	10.00	30.00	90.00	—
1839 Proof	—	Value: 200				
1840	3,011,000	5.00	10.00	35.00	90.00	—
1841	1,720,000	5.00	10.00	35.00	90.00	—
1841 Proof	—	Value: 175				
Note: Proofs dated 1841 were probably restruck at a later date						
1842	1,290,000	17.00	40.00	100	275	—
1842 Rare	—	—	—	—	—	—
1843	4,086,000	5.00	10.00	30.00	90.00	—
Note: 4 over inverted 4						
I843	Inc. above	45.00	200	350	500	—
Note: Letter I for 1 in date						
1844	430,000	55.00	125	450	700	—
1845	3,226,000	9.00	12.00	40.00	100	—
1846	2,580,000	10.00	15.00	60.00	150	—
1847	3,880,000	6.00	12.00	40.00	100	—
1848	1,290,000	6.00	12.00	40.00	100	—
1849	645,000	35.00	75.00	275	450	—
1850/70	430,000	10.00	30.00	95.00	275	—
1850	Inc. above	6.00	12.00	40.00	100	—
1851	1,935,000	12.00	25.00	65.00	175	—
1851	Inc. above	50.00	150	400	700	—
Note: D of DEI tipped						
1852	823,000	12.00	26.00	65.00	135	—
185./2	1,028,000	75.00	125	200	350	—
1853	Inc. above	6.00	12.00	40.00	95.00	—
Note: WW designer's initials raised						
1853 Proof	—	Value: 350				
1853	Inc. above	12.00	30.00	90.00	225	—
Note: WW designer's initials incuse						
1853 Proof	—	Value: 350				
1854	4,946,000	6.00	12.00	35.00	85.00	—
1855	3,441,000	9.00	15.00	50.00	125	—
Note: WW designer's initials raised						
1855	Inc. above	6.00	12.50	45.00	100	—
Note: WW designer's initials incuse						
1856	1,771,000	10.00	25.00	60.00	150	—
1856	Inc. above	25.00	60.00	150	300	—
Note: R of Victoria over E						
1857	1,075,000	6.00	12.00	40.00	95.00	—
1858	1,720,000	6.00	12.00	35.00	95.00	—
1859	1,290,000	10.00	20.00	60.00	175	—
1860/59	—	—	—	—	—	—
1860	—	800	2,200	4,500	7,000	—
1864 Rare	—	—	—	—	—	—

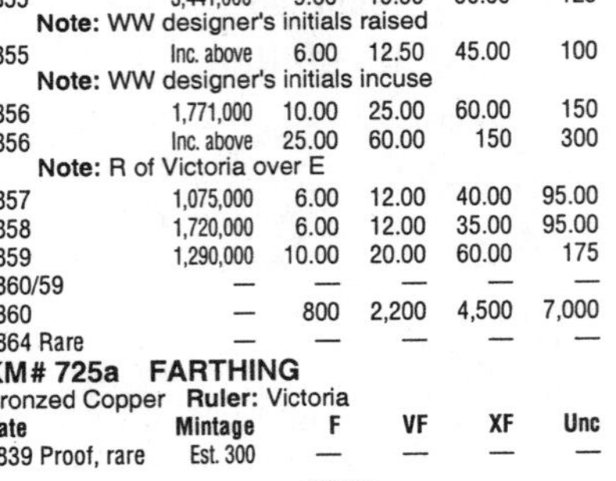

KM# 725a FARTHING

Bronzed Copper **Ruler:** Victoria

Date	Mintage	F	VF	XF	Unc	BU
1839 Proof, rare	Est. 300	—	—	—	—	—

KM# 747.1 FARTHING

Bronze **Ruler:** Victoria **Note:** Beaded border.

Date	Mintage	F	VF	XF	Unc	BU
1860	2,867,000	2.00	6.00	30.00	90.00	—
1860 Proof	—	Value: 300				

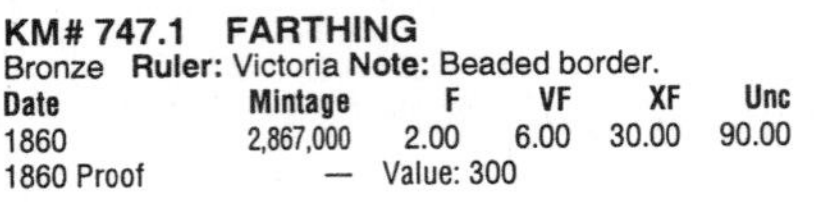

KM# 747.2 FARTHING

Bronze **Ruler:** Victoria **Note:** Toothed border.

Date	Mintage	F	VF	XF	Unc	BU
1860	Inc. above	2.00	5.00	30.00	85.00	—
1860	Inc. above	70.00	150	250	650	—
1861	8,602,000	1.00	2.75	28.00	80.00	—
1861 Proof	—	Value: 350				
1862 Small 8	14,336,000	1.00	2.75	28.00	80.00	—
1862 Large 8	Inc. above	3.00	5.00	35.00	100	—
1862 Proof	—	Value: 350				
1863	1,434,000	25.00	50.00	175	475	—
1863 Proof	—	Value: 700				
1864	2,509,000	2.00	6.00	35.00	100	—
1865/2	4,659,000	3.00	11.00	35.00	125	—
1865/3	Inc. above	4.00	8.00	25.00	100	—
1865	Inc. above	1.50	2.75	30.00	85.00	—
1866	3,584,000	1.00	2.75	22.00	75.00	—
1866 Proof	—	Value: 350				
1867	5,018,000	2.00	5.00	30.00	95.00	—
1867 Proof	—	Value: 350				
1868	4,851,000	1.50	5.00	30.00	95.00	—
1868 Proof	—	Value: 200				
1869	3,226,000	5.00	12.00	40.00	125	—
1872	2,150,000	1.50	3.50	30.00	85.00	—
1873	3,226,000	1.25	2.75	27.00	80.00	—

KM# 753 FARTHING

Bronze **Ruler:** Victoria **Obv:** Mature bust

Date	Mintage	F	VF	XF	Unc	BU
1874H	3,584,000	1.75	4.25	12.00	65.00	—
1874H Proof	—	Value: 200				
1874H	Inc. above	75.00	175	300	—	—
Note: Normal G's over horizontal G's						
1875	713,000	9.00	20.00	40.00	120	—
Note: Large date, five berries						
1875	Inc. above	15.00	25.00	100	325	—
Note: Small date, five berries						
1875	Inc. above	12.00	22.00	100	325	—
Note: Small date, four berries						
1875H	6,093,000	1.00	2.00	14.00	60.00	—
1875H Proof	—	Value: 200				
1876H	1,075,000	6.00	15.00	45.00	125	—
1877 Proof	—	Value: 3,900				
1878	4,009,000	1.00	2.00	17.00	65.00	—
1878	—	Value: 350				
1879	3,977,000	1.00	2.00	17.00	70.00	—
1879 Large 9	Inc. above	2.00	6.00	22.00	85.00	—
1880	1,843,000	3.75	7.50	30.00	100	—
Note: Three berries in wreath						
1880	Inc. above	1.25	2.75	30.00	90.00	—
Note: Four berries in wreath						
1881	3,495,000	1.50	3.00	17.00	70.00	—
Note: Three berries in wreath						
1881	Inc. above	3.50	7.50	20.00	85.00	—
Note: Four berries in wreath						
1881 Proof	—	Value: 800				
Note: Shield heraldically colored						
1881H	1,792,000	2.50	6.00	22.00	70.00	—
1882H	1,792,000	2.50	6.00	22.00	70.00	—
1882H Proof	—	Value: 400				
1883	1,129,000	2.00	12.00	40.00	100	—
1883 Proof	—	Value: 400				
1884	5,782,000	0.75	1.50	13.00	40.00	—
1884 Proof	—	Value: 400				
1885	5,442,000	1.00	2.00	13.00	40.00	—
1885 Proof	—	Value: 400				
1886	7,708,000	0.75	1.50	13.00	35.00	—
1886 Proof	—	Value: 400				
1887	1,341,000	2.00	4.00	22.00	70.00	—
1888	1,887,000	1.50	3.00	17.00	60.00	—
1890	2,133,000	1.50	2.50	16.00	60.00	—
1890 Proof	—	Value: 400				
1891	4,960,000	0.75	1.50	12.00	50.00	—
1891 Proof	—	Value: 350				
1892	887,000	3.00	12.00	40.00	100	—
1892 Proof	—	Value: 400				
1893	3,904,000	0.75	1.50	13.00	50.00	—
1894	2,397,000	0.75	2.50	17.00	60.00	—
1895	2,853,000	10.00	20.00	75.00	175	—

KM# 788.1 FARTHING

Bronze **Ruler:** Victoria

Date	Mintage	F	VF	XF	Unc	BU
1895	Inc. above	0.75	2.50	6.00	22.00	—
1896	3,669,000	0.50	2.50	6.00	22.00	—

Date	Mintage	F	VF	XF	Unc	BU
1896 Proof	—	Value: 300				
1897	4,580,000	0.75	2.00	5.00	30.00	—

KM# 788.2 FARTHING

2.8000 g., Bronze **Ruler:** Victoria **Note:** Blackened finish.

Date	Mintage	F	VF	XF	Unc	BU
1897	Inc. above	0.50	2.50	6.00	23.00	—
Note: Mintage included with KM#788.1						
1898	4,010,000	0.75	2.50	6.00	24.00	—
1899	3,865,000	0.50	2.50	6.00	22.00	—
1900	5,969,000	1.00	3.00	9.00	28.00	—
1901	8,016,000	0.30	0.50	2.00	17.00	—

KM# 662 1/2 PENNY

Copper **Ruler:** George III

Date	Mintage	F	VF	XF	Unc	BU
1806	—	3.00	7.00	40.00	150	—
Note: Without berries						
1806	—	5.00	11.00	65.00	175	—
Note: Three berries						
1806 Proof	—	Value: 250				
Note: Without berries						
1806 Proof	—	Value: 250				
Note: Two berries						
1806 Proof	—	Value: 250				
Note: Three berries						
1807	—	4.00	10.00	45.00	150	—

KM# 662a 1/2 PENNY

Bronzed Copper **Ruler:** George III

Date	Mintage	F	VF	XF	Unc	BU
1806 Proof	—	Value: 275				

KM# 692 1/2 PENNY

Copper **Ruler:** George IV

Date	Mintage	F	VF	XF	Unc	BU
1825	215,000	12.50	50.00	225	350	—
1825 Proof	—	Value: 275				
1826/5	9,032,000	10.00	25.00	100	200	—
1826	Inc. above	10.00	25.00	95.00	200	—
1826 Proof	—	Value: 300				
1827	5,376,000	10.00	26.00	100	225	—

KM# 692a 1/2 PENNY

Bronzed Copper **Ruler:** George IV

Date	Mintage	F	VF	XF	Unc	BU
1826 Proof	Est. 150	Value: 350				

KM# 706 1/2 PENNY

Copper **Ruler:** William IV

Date	Mintage	F	VF	XF	Unc	BU
1831	806,000	14.00	29.00	95.00	250	—
1834	538,000	15.00	30.00	100	250	—
1837	349,000	12.00	25.00	90.00	200	—

KM# 706a 1/2 PENNY

Bronzed Copper **Ruler:** William IV

Date	Mintage	F	VF	XF	Unc	BU
1831 Proof	—	Value: 300				

KM# 726 1/2 PENNY

Copper **Ruler:** Victoria

Date	Mintage	F	VF	XF	Unc	BU
1838	457,000	6.00	14.00	40.00	125	—
1841	1,075,000	4.00	12.00	30.00	95.00	—
1843	968,000	27.00	45.00	100	375	—
1844	1,075,000	7.00	18.00	50.00	125	—
1845	1,075,000	55.00	125	650	1,700	—
1846	860,000	10.00	23.00	50.00	150	—
1847	725,000	10.00	23.00	50.00	150	—
1848/7	323,000	9.00	22.00	50.00	150	—
1848	Inc. above	11.00	23.00	55.00	175	—
1851	215,000	6.00	18.00	45.00	125	—
1852	637,000	4.00	10.00	30.00	100	—
1853/2	1,559,000	16.00	35.00	100	275	—
1853	Inc. above	3.50	10.00	22.00	90.00	—
1853 Proof	—	Value: 175				
1854	12,257,000	3.50	10.00	23.00	90.00	—
1855	7,456,000	3.50	10.00	23.00	90.00	—
1856	1,942,000	6.00	19.00	45.00	125	—
1857	1,183,000	5.00	12.00	35.00	100	—
1857	Inc. above	5.00	12.00	35.00	100	—
Note: Dots on shield						
1858/6	2,473,000	6.00	12.00	40.00	125	—
1858/7	Inc. above	6.00	12.00	40.00	125	—
1858	Inc. above	6.00	12.00	40.00	125	—
1858 Small date	Inc. above	6.00	12.00	40.00	125	—
1859/8	1,290,000	11.00	23.00	75.00	200	—
1859	Inc. above	6.00	12.00	40.00	100	—
1860	—	600	1,700	4,200	7,000	—
1860 Proof	—	Value: 5,000				

KM# 726a 1/2 PENNY

Bronzed Copper **Ruler:** Victoria

Date	Mintage	F	VF	XF	Unc	BU
1839 Proof	Est. 300	Value: 350				
Note: Normal alignment						
1839 Proof	Inc. above	Value: 350				
Note: Coin alignment						
1841 Proof	—	—	—	—	—	—

KM# 748.2 1/2 PENNY

Bronze **Ruler:** Victoria **Note:** Toothed border.

Date	Mintage	F	VF	XF	Unc	BU
1860	Inc. above	2.50	12.00	45.00	175	—
1860	—	—	—	—	—	—
Note: Toothed and beaded border						
1860	Inc. above	2.50	12.00	45.00	175	—
Note: Seven berries in wreath						
1860 Proof	—	Value: 400				
Note: Seven berries in wreath						
1860	Inc. above	4.25	15.00	70.00	225	—
Note: Seven berries in wreath; round-top lighthouse						
1860	Inc. above	4.00	14.00	60.00	200	—
Note: Five berries in wreath						
1860	Inc. above	3.00	12.00	45.00	150	—
Note: Four berries in wreath						
1860	Inc. above	4.00	14.00	60.00	200	—
Note: Four berries in wreath; round-top lighthouse						
1861/81 Rare	54,118,000	—	—	—	—	—
1861	Inc. above	1.50	6.00	30.00	125	—
1861 Proof	—	Value: 300				
1861	Inc. above	10.00	6.00	100	300	—
Note: Five berries in wreath, L.C.W. on rock						
1861	Inc. above	2.00	6.00	30.00	125	—
Note: Four berries in wreath, L.C.W. on rock						
1861 Proof	—	Value: 550				
Note: Five berries in wreath, L.C.W. on rock						
1861	Inc. above	2.00	6.00	30.00	125	—
Note: Four berries in wreath						
1861	Inc. above	2.50	7.00	30.00	125	—
Note: L.C.W. on rock						
1861	Inc. above	20.00	60.00	175	450	—
Note: HALF over HALP						
1862	61,107,000	50.00	150	600	1,200	—
Note: L.C.W. on rock, B to left of lighthouse						
1862	Inc. above	50.00	150	600	1,200	—
Note: C to left of lighthouse						
1862	Inc. above	50.00	150	600	1,200	—
Note: A to left of lighthouse						
1862 Proof	—	Value: 300				
1862	Inc. above	1.25	5.00	28.00	100	—
1862 L.C.W.	Inc. above	7.00	15.00	40.00	90.00	—
1863 Small 3	15,949,000	2.50	7.00	50.00	175	—
1863 Large 3	Inc. above	2.50	7.00	50.00	175	—
1864	538,000	3.50	12.00	55.00	200	—
1865/3	8,064,000	50.00	125	270	600	—
1865	Inc. above	4.00	19.00	70.00	300	—
1866	2,509,000	2.50	12.00	55.00	200	—
1866 Proof	—	Value: 300				
1867	2,509,000	4.00	19.00	70.00	300	—
1867 Proof	—	Value: 300				
1868	3,046,000	2.50	12.00	65.00	225	—
1868 Proof	—	Value: 250				
1869	3,226,000	12.00	35.00	130	250	—
1870	4,351,000	2.50	7.50	50.00	65.00	—
1871	1,075,000	22.50	60.00	250	450	—
1872	4,659,000	3.00	7.50	45.00	150	—
1873	3,405,000	4.50	10.00	60.00	200	—
1874	Inc. above	5.00	30.00	125	400	—
Note: Five berries in wreath						

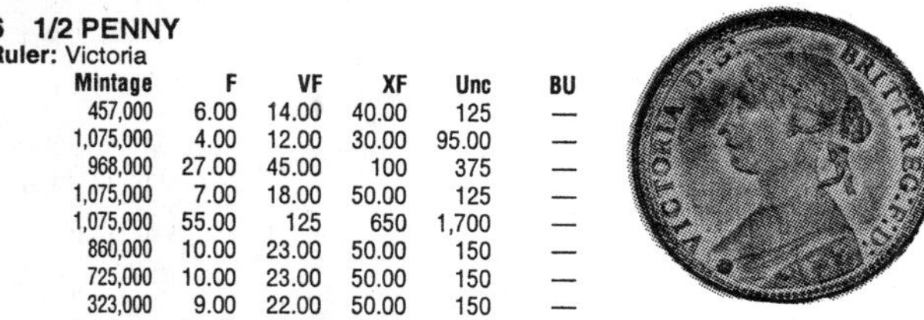

KM# 748.1 1/2 PENNY

Bronze **Ruler:** Victoria **Note:** Beaded border.

Date	Mintage	F	VF	XF	Unc	BU
1860	6,630,000	1.50	6.00	30.00	125	—
1860 Proof	—	Value: 400				

KM# 754 1/2 PENNY

Bronze **Ruler:** Victoria **Obv:** Mature bust

Date	Mintage	F	VF	XF	Unc	BU
1874	1,348,000	6.00	27.50	125	400	—
Note: Six berries in wreath; large date						
1874	Inc. above	—	27.50	125	400	—
Note: Six berries in wreath, small date						
1874	Inc. above	6.00	27.50	125	400	—
Note: Four berries in wreath; large date						
1874H	5,018,000	3.00	8.00	45.00	150	—
Note: Six berries in wreath; small date						
1874H Proof	—	Value: 300				
1874H	—	—	—	—	—	—
Note: Six berries in wreath; small date; heavy planchet						
1875	5,431,000	1.75	7.00	55.00	150	—
1875H	1,254,000	5.00	15.00	55.00	175	—
1875H Proof	—	Value: 350				
1876H Large date	6,810,000	3.00	7.50	45.00	150	—
1876H	Inc. above	2.00	5.00	45.00	150	—
1876H Proof, small date	—	Value: 350				
1876H	—	15.00	50.00	150	400	—
Note: Small date; heavy planchet						
1877	5,210,000	2.00	7.00	45.00	150	—
1877 Proof	—	Value: 300				
1878 Small date	1,426,000	8.00	24.00	75.00	325	—
1878 Proof, small date	—	Value: 400				
1878 Large date	Inc. above	55.00	125	275	800	—
1878 Proof, large date	—	Value: 850				
1879	3,583,000	1.50	4.00	35.00	125	—
1880	2,423,000	2.50	6.50	45.00	150	—
1880 Proof	—	Value: 400				
1881	2,008,000	2.50	7.50	45.00	150	—
1881 Proof	—	Value: 600				
Note: Shield heraldically colored						
1881 Proof, rare	—	Value: 1,250				
Note: Shield heraldically colored, broach on bust						
1881H	1,792,000	2.50	7.50	45.00	150	—
1882H	4,480,000	1.25	5.00	45.00	150	—
1882H Proof, different dies	—	Value: 700				
1883	3,001,000	5.00	10.00	45.00	150	—
Note: Rose on front of dress						
1883 Proof	—	Value: 400				
Note: Rose on front of dress						
1883	Inc. above	2.50	9.00	45.00	150	—
Note: Broach on front of dress						
1884	6,990,000	1.25	5.00	30.00	125	—
1884 Proof	—	Value: 350				
1885	8,601,000	1.25	5.00	30.00	125	—
1885 Proof	—	Value: 350				
1886	8,586,000	1.25	5.00	30.00	125	—
1886 Proof	—	Value: 175				
1887	10,701,000	1.25	5.00	27.00	100	—
1888	6,815,000	1.25	5.00	30.00	125	—
1889/8	7,748,000	25.00	45.00	120	275	—
1889/8 Proof, rare	—	—	—	30.00	—	—
1889	Inc. above	1.25	5.00	26.00	125	—
1890	11,254,000	1.25	5.00	26.00	100	—
1890 Proof	—	Value: 400				

Date	Mintage	F	VF	XF	Unc	BU
1891	13,192,000	1.25	5.00	45.00	100	—
1891 Proof	—	Value: 400				
1892	2,478,000	1.25	7.00	45.00	150	—
1892 Proof	—	Value: 400				
1893	7,229,000	1.25	5.00	30.00	125	—
1894	1,768,000	2.00	7.00	45.00	150	—

KM# 789 1/2 PENNY

5.7000 g., Bronze **Ruler:** Victoria

Date	Mintage	F	VF	XF	Unc	BU
1895	3,032,000	1.00	2.50	7.00	30.00	—
1895 Proof	—	Value: 400				
1896	9,143,000	1.25	2.50	6.00	25.00	—
1896 Proof	—	Value: 400				
1897	8,690,000	0.75	2.00	6.00	25.00	—
1897	Inc. above	2.00	5.00	10.00	30.00	—
Note: High sea level						
1898	8,595,000	1.00	3.00	7.50	25.00	—
1899	12,108,000	0.75	2.00	6.00	25.00	—
1900	13,805,000	1.50	3.00	8.00	26.00	—
1901	11,127,000	0.40	0.75	4.50	19.00	—
1901 Proof	—	Value: 500				

KM# 663 PENNY

Copper **Ruler:** George III

Date	Mintage	F	VF	XF	Unc	BU
1806	—	5.00	10.00	75.00	165	—
1806 Proof	—	Value: 285				
1807	—	6.00	12.00	85.00	180	—
1808 Unique	—	—	—	—	—	—

KM# 663a PENNY

Bronzed Copper **Ruler:** George III

Date	Mintage	F	VF	XF	Unc	BU
1806 Proof	—	Value: 300				

KM# 663b PENNY

Gilt Copper **Ruler:** George III

Date	Mintage	F	VF	XF	Unc	BU
1806 Proof	—	Value: 500				

KM# 668 PENNY

0.4713 g., 0.9250 Silver .0140 oz. **Ruler:** George III

Date	Mintage	F	VF	XF	Unc	BU
1817	—	5.00	8.00	15.00	30.00	—
1817 Prooflike	10,000	—	—	—	35.00	—
1818	—	5.00	8.00	15.00	30.00	—
1818 Prooflike	9,504	—	—	—	35.00	—
1820	—	5.00	8.00	15.00	30.00	—
1820 Prooflike	7,920	—	—	—	35.00	—

KM# 683 PENNY

0.4713 g., 0.9250 Silver .0140 oz. **Ruler:** George IV

Date	Mintage	F	VF	XF	Unc	BU
1822 Prooflike	12,000	—	—	—	25.00	—
1823 Prooflike	13,000	—	—	—	22.50	—
1824 Prooflike	9,504	—	—	—	25.00	—
1825 Prooflike	8,712	—	—	—	22.50	—
1826 Prooflike	8,712	—	—	—	22.50	—
1827 Prooflike	7,920	—	—	—	22.50	—
1828 Prooflike	7,920	—	—	—	22.50	—
1829 Prooflike	7,920	—	—	—	22.50	—
1830 Prooflike	7,920	—	—	—	22.50	—

KM# 693 PENNY

Copper **Ruler:** George IV

Date	Mintage	F	VF	XF	Unc	BU
1825	1,075,000	14.00	45.00	175	450	—
1825 Proof	—	Value: 1,100				
1826	5,914,000	12.00	45.00	150	450	—
1826 Proof	—	Value: 400				
1827	1,452,000	175	600	1,600	2,500	—

KM# 693a PENNY

Bronzed Copper **Ruler:** George IV

Date	Mintage	F	VF	XF	Unc	BU
1826 Proof	—	Value: 300				

KM# 707 PENNY

Copper **Ruler:** George IV

Date	Mintage	F	VF	XF	Unc	BU
1831	806,000	22.00	60.00	225	650	—
Note: .W.W incuse on truncation						
1831	Inc. above	23.00	65.00	225	700	—
Note: W.W incuse on truncation						
1831	Inc. above	20.00	55.00	175	500	—
1834	323,000	25.00	75.00	275	750	—
1837	175,000	45.00	12.00	450	1,100	—

KM# 707a PENNY

Bronzed Copper **Ruler:** William IV

Date	Mintage	F	VF	XF	Unc	BU
1831 Proof	—	Value: 400				

KM# 708 PENNY

0.4713 g., 0.9250 Silver .0140 oz. **Ruler:** William IV

Date	Mintage	F	VF	XF	Unc	BU
1831 Prooflike	10,000	—	—	—	22.50	—
1832 Prooflike	8,712	—	—	—	22.50	—
1833 Prooflike	8,712	—	—	—	22.50	—
1834 Prooflike	8,712	—	—	—	22.50	—
1835 Prooflike	8,712	—	—	—	22.50	—
1836 Prooflike	8,712	—	—	—	22.50	—
1837 Prooflike	8,712	—	—	—	22.50	—

KM# 727 PENNY

0.4713 g., 0.9250 Silver .0140 oz. **Ruler:** Victoria

Date	Mintage	F	VF	XF	Unc	BU
1838 Prooflike	8,976	—	—	—	15.00	—
1839 Prooflike	8,976	—	—	—	15.00	—
1840 Prooflike	8,976	—	—	—	15.00	—
1841 Prooflike	7,920	—	—	—	15.00	—
1842 Prooflike	8,896	—	—	—	15.00	—
1843 Prooflike	7,920	—	—	—	15.00	—
1844 Prooflike	7,920	—	—	—	15.00	—
1845 Prooflike	7,920	—	—	—	15.00	—
1846 Prooflike	7,920	—	—	—	15.00	—
1847 Prooflike	7,920	—	—	—	15.00	—
1848 Prooflike	7,920	—	—	—	15.00	—
1849 Prooflike	7,920	—	—	—	15.00	—
1850 Prooflike	7,920	—	—	—	15.00	—
1851 Prooflike	7,128	—	—	—	15.00	—
1852 Prooflike	7,920	—	—	—	15.00	—
1853 Prooflike	7,920	—	—	—	15.00	—

Date	Mintage	F	VF	XF	Unc	BU
1854 Prooflike	7,920	—	—	—	15.00	—
1855 Prooflike	7,920	—	—	—	15.00	—
1856 Prooflike	7,920	—	—	—	15.00	—
1857 Prooflike	7,920	—	—	—	15.00	—
1858 Prooflike	7,920	—	—	—	15.00	—
1859 Prooflike	7,920	—	—	—	15.00	—
1860 Prooflike	7,920	—	—	—	15.00	—
1861 Prooflike	7,920	—	—	—	15.00	—
1862 Prooflike	7,920	—	—	—	15.00	—
1863 Prooflike	7,920	—	—	—	15.00	—
1864 Prooflike	7,920	—	—	—	15.00	—
1865 Prooflike	7,920	—	—	—	15.00	—
1866 Prooflike	7,920	—	—	—	15.00	—
1867 Prooflike	7,920	—	—	—	15.00	—
1868 Prooflike	7,920	—	—	—	15.00	—
1869 Prooflike	7,920	—	—	—	15.00	—
1870 Prooflike	9,002	—	—	—	15.00	—
1871 Prooflike	9,286	—	—	—	15.00	—
1872 Prooflike	8,956	—	—	—	15.00	—
1873 Prooflike	7,932	—	—	—	15.00	—
1874 Prooflike	8,741	—	—	—	15.00	—
1875 Prooflike	8,459	—	—	—	15.00	—
1876 Prooflike	10,000	—	—	—	15.00	—
1877 Prooflike	8,936	—	—	—	15.00	—
1878 Prooflike	9,903	—	—	—	15.00	—
1879 Prooflike	11,000	—	—	—	15.00	—
1880 Prooflike	11,000	—	—	—	15.00	—
1881 Prooflike	9,017	—	—	—	15.00	—
1882 Prooflike	11,000	—	—	—	15.00	—
1883 Prooflike	12,000	—	—	—	15.00	—
1884 Prooflike	14,000	—	—	—	15.00	—
1885 Prooflike	12,000	—	—	—	15.00	—
1886 Prooflike	16,000	—	—	—	15.00	—
1887 Prooflike	18,000	—	—	—	20.00	—

KM# 739 PENNY

Copper **Ruler:** Victoria

Date	Mintage	F	VF	XF	Unc	BU
1841 REG:	914,000	9.00	25.00	90.00	285	—
1841 Proof	—	Value: 850				
1841	Inc. above	6.00	10.00	75.00	300	—
Note: Without colon after REG						
1843 REG:	484,000	40.00	150	900	1,800	—
1843	Inc. above	70.00	250	1,000	2,300	—
Note: Without colon after REG						
1844	215,000	11.00	18.00	85.00	145	—
1844 Proof	—	—	—	—	—	—
1845	323,000	17.00	30.00	125	300	—
1846 Near colon	484,000	16.00	30.00	100	325	—
1846 Far colon	Inc. above	12.00	25.00	100	275	—
1847 Far colon	Inc. above	10.00	20.00	85.00	165	—
1847 Near colon	430,000	10.00	20.00	85.00	160	—
1848/6	161,000	23.00	75.00	300	900	—
1848/7	Inc. above	5.00	20.00	75.00	145	—
1848	Inc. above	5.00	20.00	75.00	145	—
1849	269,000	50.00	135	950	1,900	—
1851 Far colon	269,000	12.00	25.00	100	300	—
1851 Near colon	Inc. above	12.00	25.00	100	300	—
1853	1,021,000	6.00	15.00	70.00	125	—
Note: Ornamental trident						
1853 Proof	—	Value: 600				
1853	Inc. above	10.00	22.00	90.00	250	—
Note: Plain trident						
1854/3	6,559,000	20.00	60.00	120	240	—
1854	Inc. above	8.00	17.00	70.00	150	—
Note: Ornamental trident						
1854	Inc. above	6.00	15.00	70.00	125	—
Note: Plain trident						
1855	5,274,000	6.00	15.00	70.00	125	—
Note: Ornamental trident						
1855	Inc. above	6.00	14.00	70.00	125	—
Note: Plain trident						
1856	1,212,000	25.00	60.00	175	1,100	—
Note: Ornamental trident						
1856 Proof	—	Value: 1,000				
1856	Inc. above	70.00	175	450	1,100	—
Note: Plain trident						
1857	753,000	8.00	17.00	75.00	175	—
Note: Large date						
1857	Inc. above	5.00	12.00	70.00	125	—
Note: Small date						
1858/3	Inc. above	8.00	75.00	275	700	—
1858/6	Inc. above	25.00	50.00	200	500	—
1858/7	Inc. above	20.00	12.00	70.00	125	—
1858	Inc. above	5.00	12.00	70.00	125	—
Note: Large date						
1858	Inc. above	5.00	17.00	75.00	175	—

Date	Mintage	F	VF	XF	Unc	BU
Note: Large date without w						
1858	—	5.00	12.00	70.00	125	—
Note: Small date						
1858	Inc. above	5.00	12.00	70.00	125	—
Note: Small date without w						
1859/8	1,075,000	15.00	22.50	90.00	160	—
1859	Inc. above	6.00	10.00	80.00	150	—
1859 Proof	—	—	—	—	—	—
1860/59	32,000	225	600	2,000	3,000	—

KM# 739a PENNY

Bronzed Copper **Ruler:** Victoria

Date	Mintage	F	VF	XF	Unc	BU
1839 Proof	Est. 300	Value: 900				
1841 Proof	—	Value: 1,000				

KM# 749.2 PENNY

Bronze **Ruler:** Victoria **Note:** Toothed border, wtihout die number.

Date	Mintage	F	VF	XF	Unc	BU
1860	Inc. above	55.00	145	630	2,700	—
Note: Beaded border/toothed border						
1860	Inc. above	50.00	120	550	—	—
Note: Toothed border/beaded border						
1860	Inc. above	70.00	150	400	900	—
Note: L.C.W. below foot, L.C.WYON on shoulder						
1860	Inc. above	3.00	12.00	50.00	250	—
Note: L.C.W. below shield, L.C. WYON below shoulder						
1860	Inc. above	3.00	12.00	50.00	200	—
Note: L.C.WYON on shoulder, L.C.W. below shield						
1860 Proof	—	Value: 400				
Note: L.C.WYON on shoulder, L.C.W. below shield						
1860	Inc. above	11.00	40.00	125	400	—
Note: Without obverse signature, 15 leaves						
1860	Inc. above	30.00	95.00	250	600	—
Note: Withouut obverse signature, 16 leaves						
1861	36,449,000	23.00	70.00	125	500	—
Note: L.C.WYON on truncation; L.C.W. below shield						
1861	Inc. above	23.00	65.00	225	700	—
Note: L.C.WYON on truncation, without signature on reverse						
1861	Inc. above	3.00	18.00	60.00	250	—
Note: L.C.WYON below truncation; L.C.W. below shield						
1861	Inc. above	35.00	100	275	800	—
Note: L.C.WYON below truncation, without signature on reverse						
1861	Inc. above	4.00	12.00	55.00	225	—
Note: Without obverse signature, 15 leaves, L.C.W. below shield						
1861	Inc. above	100	250	550	1,600	—
Note: Without obverse signature, 15 leaves without reverse signature						
1861	Inc. above	3.00	12.00	50.00	200	—
Note: Without obverse signature, 16 leaves, L.C.W. below shield						
1861 Proof	—	Value: 425				
Note: Without obverse signature, 16 leaves, L.C.W. below shield						
1861/81	Inc. above	50.00	150	300	1,000	—
Note: Without obverse signature, 16 leaves, L.C.W. below shield						
1861	Inc. above	2.50	9.00	50.00	225	—
Note: Without obverse signature, 16 leaves, without reverse signature						
1861 Proof	—	Value: 375				
Note: Without obverse signature, 16 leaves, without reverse signature						
1862/1662	50,534,000	22.50	75.00	175	600	—
1862 Proof	—	Value: 800				
1862	Inc. above	300	750	1,750	4,000	—
Note: L.C.WYON on shoulder without reverse signature						
1862	Inc. above	2.00	12.00	50.00	200	—
Note: Without signature on obverse						
1862	Inc. above	12.00	30.00	75.00	250	—
Note: Date numerals small, from 1/2 Penny die						
1863	28,063,000	2.00	12.00	50.00	200	—
1863 Proof	—	Value: 425				
1864	3,441,000	25.00	90.00	375	1,000	—
Note: Plain 4 in date						
1864	Inc. above	30.00	100	475	1,400	—
Note: Crosslet 4 in date						
1865/3	8,602,000	50.00	90.00	250	775	—
1865	Inc. above	9.00	25.00	90.00	375	—
1866	9,999,000	6.00	20.00	60.00	250	—
1867	5,484,000	9.00	30.00	90.00	425	—
1867 Proof	—	Value: 700				
1868	1,183,000	15.50	45.00	120	700	—
1868 Proof	—	Value: 500				
1869	2,580,000	50.00	200	500	1,350	—
1870	5,695,000	10.00	25.00	120	355	—
1871	1,290,000	25.00	75.00	400	700	—
1872	8,495,000	6.00	20.00	55.00	250	—
1872 Proof, unique	—	—	—	—	—	—
Note: Reverse upside down						
1873	8,494,000	6.00	20.00	55.00	250	—
1874	5,622,000	6.00	20.00	80.00	350	—
1874	Inc. above	7.50	20.00	80.00	350	—
Note: 16 leaves, small date						
1874H	6,666,000	6.00	25.00	75.00	275	—
1874H	Inc. above	6.00	25.00	75.00	275	—
Note: 16 leaves, large date						

KM# 749.1 PENNY

Bronze **Ruler:** Victoria **Note:** Beaded border.

Date	Mintage	F	VF	XF	Unc	BU
1860	5,053,000	35.00	80.00	175	550	—
Note: Raised lines on shield						
1860 Proof	—	Value: 400				
Note: Raised lines on shield						
1860 Proof	—	Value: 900				
Note: Raised lines on shidle, extra thick flan						
1860	Inc. above	10.00	27.00	75.00	375	—
Note: Incuse lines on shield						
1860 Proof	—	Value: 800				
Note: Incuse lines on shield						

KM# 749.3 PENNY

Bronze **Ruler:** Victoria **Note:** Toothed border, wtih die number.

Date	Mintage	F	VF	XF	Unc	BU
1863 Rare	Inc. above	—	—	—	—	—
Note: With small die number 5 below date						
1863	Inc. above	100	180	450	1,200	—
Note: With small die number 2, 3, or 4 below date						

KM# 755 PENNY

Bronze **Ruler:** Victoria **Obv:** Mature bust, without die number

Date	Mintage	F	VF	XF	Unc	BU
1874	Inc. above	10.00	30.00	90.00	350	—
Note: 17 leaves, thin ribbons						
1874	Inc. above	10.00	30.00	90.00	350	—
Note: 17 leaves, thin ribbons, small date						
1874	Inc. above	25.00	55.00	150	600	—
Note: 17 leaves, thick ribbons						
1874	Inc. above	19.00	45.00	100	500	—
Note: 17 leaves, thick ribbons, small date						
1874H	Inc. above	11.00	35.00	90.00	325	—
Note: 17 leaves, thin ribbons						
1874H	Inc. above	6.00	26.00	75.00	275	—
Note: 17 leaves, thin ribbons, small date						
1874H Proof	—	Value: 300				
Note: 17 leaves, thin ribbons, small date						
1874H	Inc. above	15.00	50.00	250	700	—
Note: 17 leaves, thin ribbons, large date						
1875	10,691,000	3.00	9.00	50.00	225	—
1875	Inc. above	3.00	9.00	45.00	125	—
Note: Small date						
1875	Inc. above	5.00	17.00	55.00	250	—
Note: Large date						
1875 Unique, proof	—	—	—	—	—	—
Note: Large date, heavy planchet						
1875H	753,000	45.00	90.00	650	1,500	—
Note: Large date						
1875H Proof	—	Value: 800				
Note: Large date						
1876H	11,075,000	10.00	30.00	100	350	—
Note: Large date						
1876H Proof	—	Value: 500				
Note: Large date						
1876H	Inc. above	3.00	19.00	50.00	200	—
Note: Small date						
1877	9,625,000	100	300	1,000	2,000	—
Note: Small date						
1877	Inc. above	3.25	9.50	50.00	225	—
Note: Large date						
1877 Proof	—	Value: 500				
Note: Large date						
1878	2,764,000	4.50	20.00	75.00	400	—
1878 Proof	—	Value: 500				
1879	7,666,000	15.00	40.00	125	500	—
Note: Large date, raised lines in wreath						
1879	Inc. above	2.50	8.50	40.00	175	—
Note: Large date, incuse lines in wreath						
1879 Unique, proof	—	—	—	—	—	—
Note: Large date, incuse lines in wreath						
1879	Inc. above	30.00	85.00	250	650	—
Note: Small date						
1880	3,001,000	5.00	13.50	100	325	—
1880 Proof	—	Value: 500				
1880	Inc. above	5.00	13.50	100	325	—
Note: Rock to left of lighthouse						
1880 Proof, rare	—	—	—	—	—	—
Note: Overse 15 leaves as 1881						
1881	2,302,000	4.00	20.00	80.00	400	—
1881 Proof	—	Value: 450				
1881	Inc. above	100	300	750	2,250	—
Note: Obverse as 1880; shield heraldically colored						
1881 Proof	Inc. above	—	—	—	—	—
Note: Obverse as 1880; shield heraldically colored						
1881 Proof	—	Value: 1,100				
Note: Shield heraldically colored						
1881	Inc. above	6.00	20.00	80.00	400	—
Note: Obverse and reverse as 1880						
1881H	3,763,000	3.50	20.00	50.00	250	—
Note: 15 leaves in wreath on obverse						
1881H Proof	Inc. above	Value: 600				
Note: 15 leaves in wreath on obverse						
1882H	7,526,000	2.75	12.00	50.00	175	—
Note: Convex shield						
1882H	Inc. above	2.75	12.00	40.00	175	—
Note: Flat shield						
1882H Proof	—	Value: 1,000				
1882	Inc. above	75.00	225	725	1,750	—
1883	6,237,000	3.50	12.00	50.00	200	—
1883 Proof	—	Value: 450				
1884	11,703,000	2.50	10.00	40.00	150	—
1884 Proof	—	Value: 500				
1885	7,146,000	2.50	10.00	40.00	150	—
1885 Proof	—	Value: 500				
1886	6,088,000	2.50	12.00	40.00	175	—
1886 Proof	—	Value: 700				
1887	5,315,000	2.50	10.00	35.00	150	—
1888	5,125,000	2.50	12.00	40.00	175	—
1889	12,560,000	2.50	16.00	65.00	375	—
1889	Inc. above	2.50	10.00	35.00	150	—
Note: 14 leaves in wreath						
1889 Proof	—	Value: 500				
Note: 14 leaves in wreath						
1890	15,331,000	2.50	10.00	35.00	150	—
1890 Proof	—	Value: 450				
1891	17,886,000	2.50	9.00	30.00	125	—
1891 Proof	—	Value: 450				
1892	10,502,000	2.50	10.00	3.50	150	—
1892 Proof	—	Value: 450				
1893	8,162,000	2.50	10.00	35.00	150	—
1893 Proof	—	Value: 500				
1894	3,883,000	3.00	20.00	55.00	200	—

KM# 770 PENNY

0.4713 g., 0.9250 Silver .0140 oz. **Ruler:** Victoria

Date	Mintage	F	VF	XF	Unc	BU
1888 Prooflike	14,000	—	—	—	15.00	—
1889 Prooflike	14,000	—	—	—	15.00	—
1890 Prooflike	13,000	—	—	—	15.00	—
1891 Prooflike	22,000	—	—	—	15.00	—
1892 Prooflike	16,000	—	—	—	15.00	—

KM# 775 PENNY

0.4713 g., 0.9250 Silver .0140 oz. **Ruler:** Victoria

Date	Mintage	F	VF	XF	Unc	BU
1893 Prooflike	22,000	—	—	—	19.00	—
1894 Prooflike	18,000	—	—	—	19.00	—
1895 Prooflike	17,000	—	—	—	19.00	—
1896 Prooflike	17,000	—	—	—	19.00	—
1897 Prooflike	16,000	—	—	—	19.00	—
1898 Prooflike	17,000	—	—	—	19.00	—
1899 Prooflike	17,000	—	—	—	19.00	—
1900 Prooflike	17,000	—	—	—	19.00	—
1901 Prooflike	18,000	—	—	—	19.00	—

KM# 790 PENNY

9.4500 g., Bronze **Ruler:** Victoria

Date	Mintage	F	VF	XF	Unc	BU
1895	5,396,000	20.00	60.00	225	475	—
Note: P 2mm from trident						
1895 Proof	Inc. above	Value: 450				

Date	Mintage	F	VF	XF	Unc	BU
Note: P 2mm from trident						
1895	Inc. above	0.50	2.00	12.00	55.00	—
Note: P 1mm from trident						
1895 Proof	—	Value: 350				
Note: P 1mm from trident						
1896	24,147,000	0.55	2.50	11.00	50.00	—
1896 Proof	—	Value: 325				
1897	20,757,000	0.65	2.50	10.00	50.00	—
Note: Normal sea level						
1897 Proof	—	Value: 375				
Note: Normal sea level						
1897	Inc. above	15.00	40.00	120	275	—
Note: High sea level						
1898	14,297,000	1.50	5.00	18.00	65.00	—
1899	26,441,000	0.55	2.50	11.00	55.00	—
1900	31,778,000	1.00	3.00	13.00	40.00	—
1901	22,206,000	0.30	1.00	10.00	25.00	—
1901 Proof	—	—	—	—	—	—

KM# 719 1-1/2 PENCE
0.7069 g., 0.9250 Silver .0210 oz. **Ruler:** William IV

Date	Mintage	F	VF	XF	Unc	BU
1834	800,000	5.00	12.00	40.00	80.00	—
1835/4	634,000	12.00	30.00	45.00	185	—
1835	Inc. above	10.00	30.00	75.00	200	—
1836	158,000	7.00	20.00	45.00	100	—
1837	31,000	20.00	45.00	125	325	—

KM# 728 1-1/2 PENCE
0.7069 g., 0.9250 Silver .0210 oz. **Ruler:** Victoria

Date	Mintage	F	VF	XF	Unc	BU
1838	539,000	6.00	15.00	35.00	80.00	—
1839	760,000	5.00	12.00	29.00	75.00	—
1840	95,000	10.00	27.00	80.00	150	—
1841	158,000	6.00	17.00	40.00	95.00	—
1842	1,869,000	6.00	17.00	40.00	95.00	—
1843/34	475,000	8.00	20.00	90.00	200	—
1843	Inc. above	3.50	7.00	25.00	50.00	—
1860	160,000	7.00	23.00	65.00	125	—
1862	256,000	7.00	23.00	65.00	125	—
1870 Proof	—	Value: 900				
Note: Although the design of the above series is of the homeland type, the issues were struck for Ceylon and Jamaica						

KM# 669 2 PENCE
0.9426 g., 0.9250 Silver .0280 oz. **Ruler:** George III

Date	Mintage	F	VF	XF	Unc	BU
1817	—	6.00	11.00	20.00	35.00	—
1817 Prooflike	2,376	—	—	—	30.00	—
1818	—	6.00	11.00	20.00	35.00	—
1818 Prooflike	2,376	—	—	—	30.00	—
1820	—	6.00	11.00	20.00	35.00	—
1820 Prooflike	1,584	—	—	—	30.00	—

KM# 684 2 PENCE
0.9426 g., 0.9250 Silver .0280 oz. **Ruler:** George IV

Date	Mintage	F	VF	XF	Unc	BU
1822 Prooflike	5,940	—	—	—	30.00	—
1823 Prooflike	3,960	—	—	—	30.00	—
1824 Prooflike	3,168	—	—	—	35.00	—
1825 Prooflike	3,960	—	—	—	30.00	—
1826 Prooflike	3,960	—	—	—	30.00	—
1827 Prooflike	3,960	—	—	—	30.00	—
1828 Prooflike	3,960	—	—	—	30.00	—
1829 Prooflike	3,960	—	—	—	30.00	—
1830 Prooflike	3,960	—	—	—	30.00	—

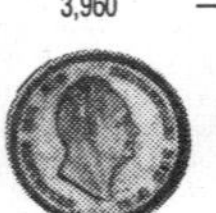

KM# 709 2 PENCE
0.9426 g., 0.9250 Silver .0280 oz. **Ruler:** William IV

Date	Mintage	F	VF	XF	Unc	BU
1831 Prooflike	4,752	—	—	—	22.50	—
1832 Prooflike	3,564	—	—	—	22.50	—
1833 Prooflike	3,564	—	—	—	22.50	—
1834 Prooflike	3,564	—	—	—	22.50	—
1835 Prooflike	3,564	—	—	—	22.50	—
1836 Prooflike	3,564	—	—	—	22.50	—
1837 Prooflike	3,564	—	—	—	22.50	—

KM# 729 2 PENCE
0.9426 g., 0.9250 Silver .0280 oz. **Ruler:** Victoria

Date	Mintage	F	VF	XF	Unc	BU
1838	Est. 1,045,000	2.00	4.00	8.00	15.00	—
1838 Prooflike	4,488	—	—	—	15.00	—
1839 Prooflike	4,488	—	—	—	15.00	—
1840 Prooflike	4,488	—	—	—	15.00	—
1841 Prooflike	3,960	—	—	—	15.00	—
1842 Prooflike	4,488	—	—	—	15.00	—
1843	Est. 903,000	2.00	4.00	8.00	15.00	—
1843 Prooflike	4,752	—	—	—	15.00	—
1844 Prooflike	4,752	—	—	—	15.00	—
1845 Prooflike	4,752	—	—	—	15.00	—
1846 Prooflike	4,752	—	—	—	15.00	—
1847 Prooflike	4,752	—	—	—	15.00	—
1848	Est. 261,000	2.00	4.00	8.00	15.00	—
Note: Struck for use in British Guyana and the West Indies. Other dates included in Maundy sets						
1848 Prooflike	4,752	—	—	—	15.00	—
1849 Prooflike	4,752	—	—	—	15.00	—
1850 Prooflike	4,752	—	—	—	15.00	—
1851 Prooflike	4,752	—	—	—	15.00	—
1852 Prooflike	4,752	—	—	—	15.00	—
1853 Prooflike	4,752	—	—	—	15.00	—
1854 Prooflike	4,752	—	—	—	15.00	—
1855 Prooflike	4,752	—	—	—	15.00	—
1856 Prooflike	4,752	—	—	—	15.00	—
1857 Prooflike	4,752	—	—	—	15.00	—
1858 Prooflike	4,752	—	—	—	15.00	—
1859 Prooflike	4,752	—	—	—	15.00	—
1860 Prooflike	4,752	—	—	—	15.00	—
1861 Prooflike	4,752	—	—	—	15.00	—
1862 Prooflike	4,752	—	—	—	15.00	—
1863 Prooflike	4,752	—	—	—	15.00	—
1864 Prooflike	4,752	—	—	—	15.00	—
1865 Prooflike	4,752	—	—	—	15.00	—
1866 Prooflike	4,752	—	—	—	15.00	—
1867 Prooflike	4,752	—	—	—	15.00	—
1868 Prooflike	4,752	—	—	—	15.00	—
1869 Prooflike	4,752	—	—	—	15.00	—
1870 Prooflike	5,347	—	—	—	15.00	—
1871 Prooflike	4,753	—	—	—	15.00	—
1872 Prooflike	4,719	—	—	—	15.00	—
1873 Prooflike	4,756	—	—	—	15.00	—
1874 Prooflike	5,578	—	—	—	15.00	—
1875 Prooflike	5,745	—	—	—	15.00	—
1876 Prooflike	6,655	—	—	—	15.00	—
1877 Prooflike	7,189	—	—	—	15.00	—
1878 Prooflike	6,709	—	—	—	15.00	—
1879 Prooflike	6,925	—	—	—	15.00	—
1880 Prooflike	6,247	—	—	—	15.00	—
1881 Prooflike	6,001	—	—	—	15.00	—
1882 Prooflike	7,264	—	—	—	15.00	—
1883 Prooflike	7,232	—	—	—	15.00	—
1884 Prooflike	6,042	—	—	—	15.00	—
1885 Prooflike	5,958	—	—	—	15.00	—
1886 Prooflike	9,167	—	—	—	15.00	—
1887 Prooflike	8,296	—	—	—	20.00	—

KM# 771 2 PENCE
0.9426 g., 0.9250 Silver .0280 oz. **Ruler:** Victoria

Date	Mintage	F	VF	XF	Unc	BU
1888 Prooflike	9,528	—	—	—	15.00	—
1889 Prooflike	6,727	—	—	—	15.00	—
1890 Prooflike	8,613	—	—	—	15.00	—
1891 Prooflike	10,000	—	—	—	15.00	—
1892 Prooflike	12,000	—	—	—	15.00	—

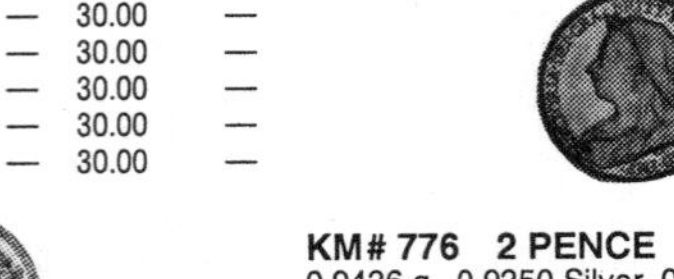

KM# 776 2 PENCE
0.9426 g., 0.9250 Silver .0280 oz. **Ruler:** Victoria

Date	Mintage	F	VF	XF	Unc	BU
1893 Prooflike	14,000	—	—	—	12.50	—
1894 Prooflike	12,000	—	—	—	12.50	—
1895 Prooflike	11,000	—	—	—	12.50	—
1896 Prooflike	11,000	—	—	—	12.50	—
1897 Prooflike	11,000	—	—	—	12.50	—
1898 Prooflike	12,000	—	—	—	12.50	—
1899 Prooflike	15,000	—	—	—	12.50	—
1900 Prooflike	11,000	—	—	—	12.50	—
1901 Prooflike	14,000	—	—	—	19.00	—

KM# 670 3 PENCE
1.4138 g., 0.9250 Silver .0420 oz. **Ruler:** George III **Obv:** George III bust right **Rev:** Value

Date	Mintage	F	VF	XF	Unc	BU
1817	—	7.00	15.00	30.00	70.00	—
1817 Prooflike	1,584	—	—	—	70.00	—
1818	—	7.00	15.00	30.00	70.00	—
1818 Prooflike	1,584	—	—	—	70.00	—
1820	—	7.00	15.00	30.00	70.00	—
1820 Prooflike	1,320	—	—	—	70.00	—

KM# 685.1 3 PENCE
1.4138 g., 0.9250 Silver .0420 oz. **Ruler:** George IV **Obv:** Small head

Date	Mintage	F	VF	XF	Unc	BU
1822 Prooflike	3,960	—	—	—	80.00	—
1822 Proof	—	—	—	—	—	—

KM# 685.2 3 PENCE
1.4138 g., 0.9250 Silver .0420 oz. **Ruler:** George IV **Obv:** Large head

Date	Mintage	F	VF	XF	Unc	BU
1823 Prooflike	2,640	—	—	—	45.00	—
1824 Prooflike	2,112	—	—	—	55.00	—
1825 Prooflike	3,432	—	—	—	45.00	—
1826 Prooflike	3,432	—	—	—	45.00	—
1827 Prooflike	3,168	—	—	—	45.00	—
1828 Prooflike	3,168	—	—	—	45.00	—
1829 Prooflike	3,168	—	—	—	45.00	—
1830 Prooflike	3,168	—	—	—	45.00	—

KM# 710 3 PENCE
1.4138 g., 0.9250 Silver .0420 oz. **Ruler:** William IV

Date	Mintage	F	VF	XF	Unc	BU
1831 Prooflike	3,960	—	—	—	80.00	—
1832 Prooflike	2,904	—	—	—	70.00	—
1833 Prooflike	2,904	—	—	—	70.00	—
1834	400,000	5.00	15.00	75.00	175	—
1834 Prooflike	2,904	—	—	—	70.00	—
1835	491,000	5.00	10.00	70.00	150	—
1835 Prooflike	2,904	—	—	—	70.00	—
1836	411,000	5.00	15.00	75.00	175	—
1836 Prooflike	2,904	—	—	—	70.00	—
1837	430,000	12.00	25.00	100	200	—
1837 Prooflike	2,904	—	—	—	70.00	—

KM# 730 3 PENCE
1.4138 g., 0.9250 Silver .0420 oz. **Ruler:** Victoria

Date	Mintage	F	VF	XF	Unc	BU
1838	1,200,000	6.00	12.00	70.00	125	—
1838 Prooflike	4,312	—	—	—	40.00	—
1839	570,000	6.00	23.00	95.00	200	—
1839 Prooflike	4,356	—	—	—	40.00	—
1840	630,000	6.00	17.00	85.00	150	—
1840 Prooflike	4,356	—	—	—	40.00	—
1841	440,000	4.50	22.00	95.00	200	—
1841 Prooflike	2,904	—	—	—	45.00	—
1842	—	6.00	23.00	90.00	200	—
1842 Prooflike	4,356	—	—	—	45.00	—
1843	2,029,999	6.00	15.00	75.00	125	—
1843 Prooflike	4,488	—	—	—	45.00	—
1844	1,050,000	6.00	23.00	90.00	175	—
1844 Prooflike	4,488	—	—	—	45.00	—
1845	1,319,000	3.50	10.00	50.00	100	—

Date	Mintage	F	VF	XF	Unc	BU
1845 Prooflike	4,488	—	—	—	45.00	—
1846	52,000	12.00	20.00	100	225	—
1846 Prooflike	4,488	—	—	—	45.00	—
1847 Prooflike	4,488	—	—	—	45.00	—
1848 Prooflike	4,488	—	—	—	45.00	—
1849	131,000	3.50	20.00	90.00	200	—
1849 Prooflike	4,488	—	—	—	45.00	—
1850	955,000	6.00	10.00	75.00	100	—
1850 Prooflike	4,488	—	—	—	45.00	—
1851	484,000	6.00	12.00	75.00	150	—
1851 Prooflike	4,488	—	—	—	45.00	—
1852 Prooflike	4,488	—	—	—	45.00	—
1853	36,000	10.00	30.00	100	250	—
1853 Prooflike	4,488	—	—	—	45.00	—
1854	1,472,000	5.00	12.00	70.00	150	—
1854 Prooflike	4,488	—	—	—	45.00	—
1855	388,000	6.00	23.00	90.00	200	—
1855 Prooflike	4,488	—	—	—	45.00	—
1856	1,018,000	5.00	12.00	70.00	125	—
1856 Prooflike	4,488	—	—	—	45.00	—
1857	1,767,000	6.00	20.00	85.00	200	—
1857 Prooflike	4,488	—	—	—	45.00	—
1858	1,446,000	5.00	12.00	65.00	125	—
1858 Prooflike	4,488	—	—	—	45.00	—
1859	3,584,000	5.00	12.00	60.00	125	—
1859 Prooflike	4,488	—	—	—	45.00	—
1860	3,410,000	5.00	20.00	80.00	175	—
1860 Prooflike	4,488	—	—	—	45.00	—
1861	3,299,000	5.00	12.00	60.00	125	—
1861 Prooflike	4,488	—	—	—	45.00	—
1862	1,161,000	5.00	12.00	65.00	125	—
1862 Prooflike	4,488	—	—	—	45.00	—
1863	954,000	5.00	22.00	85.00	175	—
1863 Prooflike	4,488	—	—	—	45.00	—
1864	1,335,000	5.00	12.00	65.00	125	—
1864 Prooflike	4,488	—	—	—	45.00	—
1865	1,747,000	5.00	22.00	85.00	175	—
1865 Prooflike	4,488	—	—	—	45.00	—
1866	1,905,000	5.00	12.00	65.00	125	—
1866 Prooflike	4,488	—	—	—	45.00	—
1867	717,000	6.00	13.00	70.00	125	—
1867 Prooflike	4,488	—	—	—	45.00	—
1868	1,462,000	5.00	12.00	65.00	125	—
1868 Prooflike	4,488	—	—	—	45.00	—
1868 Error: RRITANIAR	Inc. above	22.50	55.00	225	450	—
1869	—	30.00	75.00	150	325	—
1869 Prooflike	4,488	—	—	—	45.00	—
1870	1,288,000	5.00	13.00	70.00	125	—
1870 Prooflike	4,488	—	—	—	45.00	—
1871	1,004,000	5.00	16.00	75.00	125	—
1871 Prooflike	4,488	—	—	—	45.00	—
1872	1,298,000	5.00	15.00	70.00	125	—
1872 Prooflike	4,488	—	—	—	45.00	—
1873	4,059,999	3.50	9.00	50.00	85.00	—
1873 Prooflike	4,488	—	—	—	45.00	—
1874	4,432,000	3.50	9.00	50.00	85.00	—
1874 Prooflike	4,488	—	—	—	45.00	—
1875	3,311,000	3.50	9.00	45.00	85.00	—
1875 Prooflike	4,488	—	—	—	45.00	—
1876	1,839,000	2.25	9.00	45.00	85.00	—
1876 Prooflike	4,488	3.50	—	—	45.00	—
1877	2,627,000	4.50	11.00	55.00	95.00	—
1877 Prooflike	4,488	—	—	—	45.00	—
1878	2,424,000	4.50	11.00	55.00	95.00	—
1878 Prooflike	4,488	—	—	—	45.00	—
1879	3,145,000	4.50	11.00	55.00	95.00	—
1879 Prooflike	4,488	—	—	—	45.00	—
1879 Proof	—	Value: 150				
1880	1,615,000	4.50	11.00	50.00	90.00	—
1880 Prooflike	4,488	—	—	—	45.00	—
1881	3,253,000	3.50	6.00	35.00	75.00	—
1881 Prooflike	4,488	—	—	—	45.00	—
1882	447,000	6.00	12.00	65.00	125	—
1882 Prooflike	4,488	—	—	—	45.00	—
1883	4,374,000	3.00	7.00	35.00	75.00	—
1883 Prooflike	4,488	—	—	—	45.00	—
1884	3,327,000	3.00	7.00	40.00	75.00	—
1884 Prooflike	4,488	—	—	—	45.00	—
1885	5,188,000	3.00	7.00	35.00	75.00	—
1885 Prooflike	4,488	—	—	—	45.00	—
1886	6,157,000	3.00	7.00	35.00	75.00	—
1886 Prooflike	4,488	—	—	—	45.00	—
1887	2,785,000	5.00	13.00	50.00	90.00	—
1887 Prooflike	4,488	—	—	—	45.00	—
1887 Proof	—	Value: 100				

KM# 758 3 PENCE
1.4138 g., 0.9250 Silver .0420 oz. **Ruler:** Victoria

Date	Mintage	F	VF	XF	Unc	BU
1887	Inc. above	1.25	2.25	4.50	15.00	—
1887 Proof	Inc. above	Value: 70.00				
1888	523,000	3.00	6.00	15.00	30.00	—
1888 Prooflike	4,488	—	—	—	40.00	—
1889	4,591,000	1.50	2.75	12.50	25.00	—
1889 Prooflike	4,488	—	—	—	40.00	—
1890	4,470,000	1.50	2.75	12.50	25.00	—
1890 Prooflike	4,488	—	—	—	40.00	—
1891	6,328,000	1.50	2.75	12.50	25.00	—
1891 Prooflike	4,488	—	—	—	40.00	—
1892	2,583,000	2.00	6.00	20.00	35.00	—
1892 Prooflike	4,488	—	—	—	40.00	—
1893 Open 3	3,076,000	25.00	50.00	120	225	—
1893 Closed 3	Inc. above	20.00	40.00	100	200	—

KM# 777 3 PENCE
1.4138 g., 0.9250 Silver .0420 oz. **Ruler:** Victoria

Date	Mintage	F	VF	XF	Unc	BU
1893	Inc. above	1.00	2.00	5.00	25.00	—
1893 Prooflike	8,976	—	—	—	30.00	—
1893 Proof	1,312	Value: 75.00				
1894	1,618,000	1.00	2.75	8.00	28.00	—
1894 Prooflike	8,976	—	—	—	30.00	—
1895	4,798,000	1.25	2.75	8.00	28.00	—
1895 Prooflike	8,976	—	—	—	30.00	—
1896	4,607,000	1.25	2.50	7.00	20.00	—
1896 Prooflike	8,976	—	—	—	30.00	—
1897	4,550,000	1.25	2.50	7.00	18.00	—
1897 Prooflike	8,976	—	—	—	30.00	—
1898	4,576,000	1.25	2.50	7.00	18.00	—
1898 Prooflike	8,976	—	—	—	30.00	—
1899	6,253,000	1.25	2.50	5.00	18.00	—
1899 Prooflike	8,976	—	—	—	30.00	—
1900	10,661,000	1.50	3.00	6.00	18.00	—
1900 Prooflike	8,976	—	—	—	30.00	—
1901	6,100,000	1.00	2.00	6.50	20.00	—
1901 Prooflike	8,976	—	—	—	30.00	—

KM# 671 4 PENCE (Groat)
1.8851 g., 0.9250 Silver .0561 oz. **Ruler:** George III **Obv:** Old head of George III **Rev:** Value

Date	Mintage	F	VF	XF	Unc	BU
1817	—	10.00	22.50	40.00	70.00	—
1817 Prooflike	1,386	—	—	—	70.00	—
1818	—	10.00	22.50	40.00	70.00	—
1818 Prooflike	1,188	—	—	—	70.00	—
1820	—	10.00	22.50	40.00	70.00	—
1820 Prooflike	990	—	—	—	70.00	—

KM# 686 4 PENCE (Groat)
1.8851 g., 0.9250 Silver .0561 oz. **Ruler:** George IV

Date	Mintage	F	VF	XF	Unc	BU
1822	—	9.00	15.00	25.00	40.00	—
1822 Prooflike	2,970	—	—	—	50.00	—
1823	—	9.00	15.00	25.00	40.00	—
1823 Prooflike	1,980	—	—	—	45.00	—
1824	—	9.00	15.00	25.00	40.00	—
1824 Prooflike	1,584	—	—	—	50.00	—
1825	—	9.00	15.00	25.00	40.00	—
1825 Prooflike	2,376	—	—	—	45.00	—
1826	—	9.00	15.00	25.00	40.00	—
1826 Prooflike	2,376	—	—	—	45.00	—
1827	—	9.00	15.00	25.00	40.00	—
1827 Prooflike	2,772	—	—	—	45.00	—
1828	—	9.00	15.00	25.00	40.00	—
1828 Prooflike	2,772	—	—	—	45.00	—
1829	—	9.00	15.00	25.00	40.00	—
1829 Prooflike	2,772	—	—	—	45.00	—
1830	—	9.00	15.00	25.00	40.00	—
1830 Prooflike	2,772	—	—	—	45.00	—

KM# 711 4 PENCE (Groat)
1.8851 g., 0.9250 Silver .0561 oz. **Ruler:** William IV

Date	Mintage	F	VF	XF	Unc	BU
1831	—	5.00	12.00	22.50	45.00	—
1831 Prooflike	3,564	—	—	—	55.00	—
1832	—	5.00	12.00	22.50	45.00	—
1832 Prooflike	2,574	—	—	—	40.00	—
1833	—	5.00	12.00	22.50	45.00	—
1833 Prooflike	2,574	—	—	—	40.00	—
1834	—	5.00	12.00	22.50	45.00	—
1834 Prooflike	2,574	—	—	—	40.00	—
1835	—	5.00	12.00	22.50	45.00	—
1835 Prooflike	2,574	—	—	—	40.00	—
1836	—	5.00	12.00	22.50	45.00	—
1836 Prooflike	2,574	—	—	—	40.00	—
1837	—	6.00	12.00	22.50	45.00	—
1837 Prooflike	2,574	—	—	—	40.00	—

KM# 723 4 PENCE (Groat)
1.8851 g., 0.9250 Silver .0561 oz. **Ruler:** William IV **Note:** Although the design of this coin is of the homeland type, the issues were primarily used for circulation in British Guiana.

Date	Mintage	F	VF	XF	Unc	BU
1836	4,253,000	6.00	18.00	55.00	100	—
1836 Proof	—	—	—	—	—	—
Note: Reeded edge						
1836 Proof	—	—	—	—	—	—
Note: Plain edge						
1837	962,000	12.00	25.00	65.00	100	—
1837 Proof	—	Value: 750				

KM# 731.1 4 PENCE (Groat)
1.8851 g., 0.9250 Silver .0561 oz. **Ruler:** Victoria **Note:** This issue was produced for circulation in both Great Britain and British Guiana.

Date	Mintage	F	VF	XF	Unc	BU
1838	2,150,000	2.25	10.00	35.00	85.00	—
1838/8	Inc. above	6.00	20.00	45.00	150	—
1839	1,461,000	3.00	8.00	35.00	100	—
1840	1,497,000	2.75	11.00	35.00	95.00	—
1841	345,000	4.50	13.00	50.00	100	—
1842/1	725,000	6.00	15.00	37.50	150	—
1842	Inc. above	4.00	12.00	40.00	100	—
1842 Proof	—	Value: 500				
1843	1,818,000	5.00	12.00	40.00	100	—
1844	855,000	5.00	13.00	35.00	100	—
1845	915,000	5.00	12.00	40.00	100	—
1846	1,366,000	5.00	12.00	40.00	100	—
1847/6	226,000	30.00	90.00	350	500	—
1848/6	713,000	23.00	90.00	275	500	—
1848/7	Inc. above	10.00	27.00	85.00	200	—
1848	Inc. above	3.00	11.00	35.00	90.00	—
1849/8	380,000	6.00	15.00	55.00	125	—
1849	Inc. above	3.50	10.00	32.50	100	—
1851	31,000	25.00	85.00	200	500	—
1852	—	70.00	135	325	700	—
1853	12,000	65.00	125	300	650	—
1853 Proof	—	Value: 500				
1854	1,097,000	2.75	11.00	22.50	80.00	—
1855	646,000	4.00	8.00	22.50	80.00	—
1857 Proof, rare	—	Value: 1,400				
1862 Proof	—	Value: 800				

KM# 731.2 4 PENCE (Groat)
1.8851 g., 0.9250 Silver .0561 oz. **Ruler:** Victoria **Edge:** Plain

Date	Mintage	F	VF	XF	Unc	BU
1838 Proof	—	Value: 200				
1839 Proof	—	Value: 200				

KM# 732 4 PENCE (Groat)
1.8851 g., 0.9250 Silver .0561 oz. **Ruler:** Victoria

Date	Mintage	F	VF	XF	Unc	BU
1838 Prooflike	4,158	—	—	—	26.00	—
1839 Prooflike	4,125	—	—	—	26.00	—
1840 Prooflike	4,125	—	—	—	26.00	—
1841 Prooflike	2,574	—	—	—	26.00	—
1842 Prooflike	4,125	—	—	—	26.00	—
1843 Prooflike	4,158	—	—	—	26.00	—
1844 Prooflike	4,158	—	—	—	26.00	—
1845 Prooflike	4,158	—	—	—	26.00	—
1846 Prooflike	4,158	—	—	—	26.00	—
1847 Prooflike	4,158	—	—	—	26.00	—
1848 Prooflike	4,158	—	—	—	26.00	—
1849 Prooflike	4,158	—	—	—	26.00	—
1850 Prooflike	4,158	—	—	—	26.00	—
1851 Prooflike	4,158	—	—	—	26.00	—
1852 Prooflike	4,158	—	—	—	26.00	—
1853 Prooflike	4,158	—	—	—	26.00	—
1854 Prooflike	4,158	—	—	—	26.00	—
1855 Prooflike	4,158	—	—	—	26.00	—
1856 Prooflike	4,158	—	—	—	26.00	—
1857 Prooflike	4,158	—	—	—	26.00	—
1858 Prooflike	4,158	—	—	—	26.00	—
1859 Prooflike	4,158	—	—	—	26.00	—

Date	Mintage	F	VF	XF	Unc	BU
1860 Prooflike	4,158	—	—	—	26.00	—
1861 Prooflike	4,158	—	—	—	26.00	—
1862 Prooflike	4,158	—	—	—	26.00	—
1863 Prooflike	4,158	—	—	—	26.00	—
1864 Prooflike	4,158	—	—	—	26.00	—
1865 Prooflike	4,158	—	—	—	26.00	—
1866 Prooflike	4,158	—	—	—	26.00	—
1867 Prooflike	4,158	—	—	—	26.00	—
1868 Prooflike	4,158	—	—	—	26.00	—
1869 Prooflike	4,158	—	—	—	26.00	—
1870 Prooflike	4,569	—	—	—	26.00	—
1871 Prooflike	4,627	—	—	—	26.00	—
1872 Prooflike	4,328	—	—	—	26.00	—
1873 Prooflike	4,162	—	—	—	26.00	—
1874 Prooflike	5,937	—	—	—	26.00	—
1875 Prooflike	4,154	—	—	—	26.00	—
1876 Prooflike	4,862	—	—	—	26.00	—
1877 Prooflike	4,850	—	—	—	26.00	—
1878 Prooflike	5,735	—	—	—	26.00	—
1879 Prooflike	5,202	—	—	—	26.00	—
1880 Prooflike	5,199	—	—	—	26.00	—
1881 Prooflike	6,203	—	—	—	26.00	—
1882 Prooflike	4,146	—	—	—	26.00	—
1883 Prooflike	5,096	—	—	—	26.00	—
1884 Prooflike	5,353	—	—	—	26.00	—
1885 Prooflike	5,791	—	—	—	26.00	—
1886 Prooflike	6,785	—	—	—	26.00	—
1887 Prooflike	5,292	—	—	—	26.00	—

KM# 773 4 PENCE (Groat)

1.8851 g., 0.9250 Silver .0561 oz. **Ruler:** Victoria

Date	Mintage	F	VF	XF	Unc	BU
1888 Prooflike	9,583	—	—	—	20.00	—
1889 Prooflike	6,088	—	—	—	20.00	—
1890 Prooflike	9,087	—	—	—	20.00	—
1891 Prooflike	11,000	—	—	—	20.00	—
1892 Prooflike	8,524	—	—	—	20.00	—

KM# 772 4 PENCE (Groat)

1.8851 g., 0.9250 Silver .0561 oz. **Ruler:** Victoria **Note:** This piece was exclusively for use in British Guiana and the West Indies.

Date	Mintage	F	VF	XF	Unc	BU
1888	120,000	9.00	25.00	50.00	100	—
1888 Proof	—	Value: 700				

KM# 778 4 PENCE (Groat)

1.8851 g., 0.9250 Silver .0561 oz. **Ruler:** Victoria

Date	Mintage	F	VF	XF	Unc	BU
1893 Prooflike	11,000	—	—	—	15.00	—
1894 Prooflike	9,385	—	—	—	15.00	—
1895 Prooflike	8,877	—	—	—	15.00	—
1896 Prooflike	8,476	—	—	—	15.00	—
1897 Prooflike	9,388	—	—	—	15.00	—
1898 Prooflike	9,147	—	—	—	15.00	—
1899 Prooflike	14,000	—	—	—	15.00	—
1900 Prooflike	9,571	—	—	—	15.00	—
1901 Prooflike	12,000	—	—	—	15.00	—

KM# 665 6 PENCE

2.8276 g., 0.9250 Silver .0841 oz. **Ruler:** George III

Date	Mintage	F	VF	XF	Unc	BU
1816	—	7.00	15.00	35.00	65.00	—
1816 Proof	—	Value: 750				
1817	10,922,000	10.00	20.00	40.00	65.00	—
1817 Proof	—	Value: 1,000				
1817 Proof	—	Value: 500				
Note: Plain edge						
1818	4,285,000	12.00	26.00	60.00	140	—
1818 Proof	—	Value: 850				
1819/8	—	15.00	30.00	50.00	140	—
1819/8 Proof	—	Value: 1,000				
1819	4,712,000	12.00	25.00	50.00	70.00	—
1819 Proof	1,489,000	Value: 1,000				
1820	1,489,000	90.00	275	475	850	—
Note: Inverted I						
1820	Inc. above	11.00	22.00	50.00	85.00	—
1820 Proof	—	—	—	—	—	—

KM# 678 6 PENCE

2.8276 g., 0.9250 Silver .0841 oz. **Ruler:** George IV

Date	Mintage	F	VF	XF	Unc	BU
1821	863,000	12.00	30.00	95.00	200	—
1821 Proof	—	Value: 500				
1821	—	50.00	250	800	1,400	—
Note: Error: BBITANIAR						

KM# 691 6 PENCE

2.8276 g., 0.9250 Silver .0841 oz. **Ruler:** George IV

Date	Mintage	F	VF	XF	Unc	BU
1824	634,000	9.00	30.00	95.00	250	—
1824 Proof	—	Value: 1,200				
1825	483,000	12.00	30.00	90.00	250	—
1825 Proof	—	Value: 900				
1826	689,000	20.00	60.00	220	500	—
1826 Proof	—	Value: 1,300				

KM# 698 6 PENCE

2.8276 g., 0.9250 Silver .0841 oz. **Ruler:** George IV

Date	Mintage	F	VF	XF	Unc	BU
1826	Inc. above	12.00	30.00	90.00	225	—
1826 Proof	Inc. above	Value: 250				
1827	166,000	20.00	50.00	225	500	—
1828	16,000	12.00	35.00	125	225	—
1829	404,000	12.00	30.00	75.00	250	—
1829 Proof	—	—	—	—	—	—

KM# 712 6 PENCE

2.8276 g., 0.9250 Silver .0841 oz. **Ruler:** William IV

Date	Mintage	F	VF	XF	Unc	BU
1831	1,340,000	12.00	26.00	100	250	—
1831 Proof	Inc. above	Value: 250				
1831 Proof	—	Value: 250				
Note: Plain edge						
1834	5,892,000	12.00	25.00	100	225	—
1834 Proof	—	—	—	—	—	—
1834 Proof	Inc. above	—	—	—	—	—
Note: Round-topped 3						
1835	1,555,000	12.00	20.00	100	225	—
1835 Proof	Inc. above	—	—	—	—	—
Note: Round-topped 3						
1836	1,988,000	23.00	37.50	200	375	—
1836 Proof	Inc. above	—	—	—	—	—
1837	507,000	18.00	45.00	200	350	—
1837 Proof	—	—	—	—	—	—

KM# 712a 6 PENCE

Palladium **Ruler:** William IV

Date	Mintage	F	VF	XF	Unc	BU
1831 Proof	—	—	—	—	—	—

KM# 733.1 6 PENCE

3.0100 g., 0.9250 Silver .0895 oz. **Ruler:** Victoria **Rev:** Without die number

Date	Mintage	F	VF	XF	Unc	BU
1838	1,608,000	9.00	19.00	50.00	130	—
1838 Proof	—	Value: 850				
1839	3,311,000	9.00	19.00	50.00	130	—
1839 Proof	Inc. above	Value: 300				
1840	2,099,000	9.00	19.00	65.00	140	—
1841	1,386,000	9.00	23.00	70.00	225	—
1842	602,000	9.00	19.00	80.00	180	—
1843	3,160,000	9.00	19.00	65.00	150	—
1844 Small 44	3,976,000	7.00	18.00	50.00	125	—
1844 Large 44	Inc. above	11.00	29.00	60.00	225	—
1845	3,714,000	8.00	19.00	50.00	175	—
1846	4,267,000	7.00	18.00	50.00	125	—
1848/6	586,000	50.00	80.00	425	850	—
1848/7	Inc. above	50.00	80.00	425	850	—
1848	Inc. above	35.00	95.00	475	800	—
1849	210,000	—	—	—	—	—
Note: None reported						
1850/30	499,000	18.00	35.00	90.00	375	—
1850	Inc. above	8.00	20.00	75.00	180	—
1851	2,288,000	8.00	15.00	50.00	175	—
1852	905,000	5.50	15.00	50.00	135	—
1853	3,838,000	5.50	18.00	45.00	120	—
1853 Proof	Est. 40	Value: 450				
1854	840,000	60.00	150	550	1,000	—
1855	1,129,000	7.00	18.00	50.00	125	—
1855 Proof	—	—	—	—	—	—
1856	2,780,000	8.00	19.00	50.00	175	—
1857	2,233,000	8.00	19.00	65.00	175	—
1858	1,932,000	8.00	19.00	65.00	175	—
1858 Proof	—	Value: 600				
1859/8	4,689,000	11.00	25.00	60.00	175	—
1859	Inc. above	7.00	18.00	50.00	135	—
1860	1,101,000	8.00	19.00	60.00	175	—
1862	990,000	35.00	95.00	375	750	—
1863	491,000	23.00	60.00	250	650	—
1866	5,140,000	35.00	95.00	375	750	—

KM# 733.2 6 PENCE

3.0100 g., 0.9250 Silver .0895 oz. **Ruler:** Victoria **Rev:** With die number

Date	Mintage	F	VF	XF	Unc	BU
1864	4,253,000	8.00	19.00	50.00	175	—
1865	1,632,000	9.00	22.00	55.00	200	—
1866	Inc. above	8.00	19.00	50.00	175	—

KM# 751.1 6 PENCE

3.0100 g., 0.9250 Silver .0895 oz. **Ruler:** Victoria **Obv:** New portrait **Rev:** With die number

Date	Mintage	F	VF	XF	Unc	BU
1867	1,362,000	12.00	20.00	70.00	175	—
1867 Proof	—	Value: 1,000				
1868	1,069,000	12.00	20.00	70.00	175	—
1869	388,000	12.00	22.50	100	200	—
1869 Proof	—	Value: 1,000				
1870	480,000	12.00	23.00	100	225	—
1870 Proof	—	Value: 1,000				
1870	3,663,000	11.00	19.00	95.00	225	—
Note: Plain edge						
1871	3,663,000	9.00	19.00	60.00	150	—
1871 Proof	—	Value: 1,000				
1871	3,382,000	9.00	19.00	60.00	150	—
Note: Plain edge						
1872	3,382,000	9.00	15.00	60.00	150	—
1873	4,595,000	6.00	15.00	50.00	150	—
1874	4,226,000	6.00	15.00	50.00	150	—
1875	3,257,000	6.00	15.00	50.00	150	—
1876	841,000	12.00	20.00	65.00	250	—
1877	4,066,000	6.00	15.00	50.00	150	—
1878/7	2,625,000	45.00	125	400	700	—
1878	Inc. above	6.00	15.00	50.00	150	—
1878 Proof	—	Value: 1,000				
1878	Inc. above	35.00	75.00	350	900	—
Note: Error: DRITANNIAR						

KM# 751.2 6 PENCE

3.0100 g., 0.9250 Silver .0895 oz. **Ruler:** Victoria **Rev:** Without die number

Date	Mintage	F	VF	XF	Unc	BU
1871	Inc. above	9.00	20.00	75.00	200	—
1877	Inc. above	9.00	20.00	60.00	150	—
1878	Inc. above	—	—	—	—	—
1879	3,326,000	9.00	20.00	60.00	150	—
1879 Proof	—	Value: 1,000				
1880	3,892,000	10.00	20.00	75.00	175	—
Note: Obverse of 1879						

KM# 757 6 PENCE
3.0100 g., 0.9250 Silver .0895 oz. **Ruler:** Victoria **Obv:** New portrait, longer hair waves

Date	Mintage	F	VF	XF	Unc	BU
1880	Inc. above	6.00	12.00	50.00	100	—
1880 Proof	—	Value: 1,000				
1881 Proof	—	Value: 1,000				
Note: Plain edge						
1881	6,239,000	6.00	12.00	40.00	90.00	—
1881 Proof	—	Value: 1,000				
1882	760,000	12.00	30.00	90.00	200	—
1883	4,987,000	6.00	13.00	40.00	90.00	—
1884	3,423,000	6.00	13.00	40.00	90.00	—
1885	4,653,000	6.00	13.00	40.00	90.00	—
1885 Proof	—	Value: 800				
1886	2,728,000	6.00	13.00	40.00	90.00	—
1886 Proof	—	Value: 800				
1887	3,676,000	5.00	13.00	35.00	85.00	—
1887 Proof	—	Value: 800				

KM# 760 6 PENCE
3.0100 g., 0.9250 Silver .0895 oz. **Ruler:** Victoria

Date	Mintage	F	VF	XF	Unc	BU
1887	—	2.00	6.00	12.00	25.00	—
Note: Mintage included in KM#757						
1887 Proof	—	Value: 650				
Note: Mintage included in KM#757						
1888	4,198,000	5.00	7.50	17.50	40.00	—
1888 Proof	—	Value: 1,500				
1889	8,739,000	5.00	7.50	15.00	40.00	—
1890	9,387,000	5.00	7.50	17.50	60.00	—
1890 Proof	—	Value: 700				
1891	7,023,000	6.00	12.00	26.00	65.00	—
1892	6,246,000	6.00	12.00	26.00	95.00	—
1893	341,000	225	550	2,100	4,000	—

KM# 759 6 PENCE
3.0100 g., 0.9250 Silver .0895 oz. **Ruler:** Victoria

Date	Mintage	F	VF	XF	Unc	BU
1887	—	2.50	6.00	12.00	28.00	—
Note: Mintage included in KM#757						
1887 Proof	—	Value: 150				

KM# 779 6 PENCE
3.0100 g., 0.9250 Silver .0895 oz. **Ruler:** Victoria

Date	Mintage	F	VF	XF	Unc	BU
1893	7,010,000	6.00	7.00	19.00	50.00	—
1893 Proof	1,312	Value: 150				
1894	3,468,000	5.00	13.00	26.00	50.00	—
1895	7,025,000	5.00	10.00	19.00	50.00	—
1896	6,652,000	5.00	10.00	19.00	50.00	—
1897	5,031,000	5.00	10.00	19.00	45.00	—
1898	5,914,000	5.00	10.00	19.00	45.00	—
1899	7,997,000	5.00	10.00	19.00	45.00	—
1900	8,980,000	5.00	10.00	19.00	45.00	—
1901	5,109,000	4.00	8.00	15.00	50.00	—

KM# 666 SHILLING
5.6552 g., 0.9250 Silver .1682 oz. **Ruler:** George III

Date	Mintage	F	VF	XF	Unc	BU
1816	—	11.00	18.00	45.00	90.00	—
1816 Proof	—	Value: 750				
1816 Proof	—	Value: 1,000				
Note: Plain edge						
1817	23,031,000	11.00	23.00	50.00	100	—
1817 Proof	—	Value: 1,000				
Note: Plain edge						
1818	1,342,000	25.00	50.00	125	250	—
1818	Inc. above	—	—	—	—	—
Note: Error: GEOR/E						
1819/18	7,595,000	23.00	50.00	100	300	—
1819	Inc. above	11.00	23.00	45.00	135	—
1820	7,975,000	11.00	23.00	45.00	135	—
1820 Proof	—	Value: 1,000				

KM# 679 SHILLING
5.6552 g., 0.9250 Silver .1682 oz. **Ruler:** George IV

Date	Mintage	F	VF	XF	Unc	BU
1821	2,463,000	12.00	45.00	150	350	—
1821 Proof	—	Value: 650				

KM# 687 SHILLING
5.6552 g., 0.9250 Silver .1682 oz. **Ruler:** George IV

Date	Mintage	F	VF	XF	Unc	BU
1823	693,000	30.00	75.00	250	650	—
1823 Proof	—	Value: 2,300				
1824	4,158,000	12.00	45.00	125	350	—
1824 Proof	—	Value: 2,300				
1825/3	2,459,000	30.00	75.00	250	650	—
1825	Inc. above	20.00	55.00	150	400	—
1825 Proof	—	Value: 2,200				

KM# 694 SHILLING
5.6552 g., 0.9250 Silver .1682 oz. **Ruler:** George IV

Date	Mintage	F	VF	XF	Unc	BU
1825	Inc. above	12.00	40.00	125	325	—
1825 Proof	—	Value: 700				
1825 Proof	—	Value: 700				
Note: Plain edge						
1826/2	6,352,000	—	—	—	—	—
1826	Inc. above	7.50	35.00	100	220	—
1826 Proof	—	Value: 275				
1827	574,000	25.00	75.00	275	550	—
1829	879,000	19.00	60.00	175	475	—
1829 Proof	—	Value: 2,100				

KM# 713 SHILLING
5.6552 g., 0.9250 Silver .1682 oz. **Ruler:** William IV

Date	Mintage	F	VF	XF	Unc	BU
1831 Proof	—	Value: 450				
Note: Plain edge						
1831 Proof	—	Value: 2,100				
Note: Milled edge						
1834	3,223,000	18.00	45.00	150	375	—
1834 Proof	—	Value: 1,200				
1835	1,449,000	25.00	50.00	175	400	—
1835 Proof	—	Value: 2,100				
1836	3,568,000	25.00	50.00	150	375	—
1836 Proof	—	Value: 2,900				
1837	479,000	30.00	70.00	225	550	—
1837 Proof	—	Value: 2,200				

KM# 734.1 SHILLING
5.6552 g., 0.9250 Silver .1682 oz. **Ruler:** Victoria **Obv:** High relief **Note:** Without die number.

Date	Mintage	F	VF	XF	Unc	BU
1838 WW	1,956,000	12.00	30.00	150	300	—
1838 Proof	Inc. above	Value: 700				
1839 WW	5,667,000	12.00	30.00	150	300	—
1839 WW Proof	—	Value: 325				
1839	Inc. above	12.00	30.00	100	275	—
1839 Proof	Inc. above	Value: 325				
1840	1,639,000	15.00	50.00	150	350	—
1840 Proof	—	Value: 500				
1841	875,000	19.00	60.00	175	350	—
1842	2,095,000	12.00	26.00	100	250	—
1842 Proof	—	Value: 1,500				
1843	1,465,000	19.00	30.00	150	375	—
1844	4,467,000	12.00	26.00	100	250	—
1845	4,083,000	12.00	26.00	100	300	—
1846	4,031,000	12.00	26.00	100	250	—
1848/6	1,041,000	50.00	125	550	950	—
1849	645,000	19.00	30.00	100	350	—
1850/46	685,000	175	850	1,600	3,600	—
1850	Inc. above	175	850	1,600	3,600	—
1851	470,000	45.00	145	550	950	—
1851 Proof	—	Value: 3,200				
1852	1,307,000	12.00	26.00	90.00	200	—
1853	4,256,000	12.00	26.00	80.00	200	—
1853 Proof	—	Value: 600				
1854	552,000	60.00	150	450	1,600	—
1855	1,368,000	12.00	26.00	80.00	200	—
1856	3,168,000	12.00	26.00	80.00	200	—
1857	2,562,000	12.00	26.00	80.00	200	—
1858	3,109,000	12.00	26.00	80.00	200	—
1858 Proof	—	Value: 1,200				
1859/8	—	—	—	—	—	—
1859	4,562,000	12.00	26.00	80.00	200	—
1860	1,671,000	19.00	30.00	100	300	—
1861	1,382,000	19.00	30.00	100	300	—
1862	954,000	20.00	70.00	175	375	—
1863	859,000	30.00	75.00	300	650	—

KM# 734.2 SHILLING
5.6552 g., 0.9250 Silver .1682 oz. **Ruler:** Victoria **Obv:** Low relief **Note:** With die number.

Date	Mintage	F	VF	XF	Unc	BU
1867	—	55.00	125	650	850	—
1868	3,330,000	12.00	30.00	80.00	200	—
1869	737,000	22.00	40.00	100	250	—
1870	1,467,000	22.00	40.00	100	250	—
1871	4,910,000	12.00	26.00	80.00	200	—
1871 Proof	—	—	—	—	—	—
1871 Proof	—	Value: 2,200				
Note: Plain edge						
1872	8,898,000	12.00	26.00	80.00	200	—
1873	6,590,000	12.00	26.00	80.00	200	—
1874	5,504,000	12.00	26.00	80.00	200	—
1875	4,354,000	12.00	26.00	80.00	200	—
1876	1,057,000	17.00	35.00	95.00	200	—
1877	2,981,000	12.00	26.00	80.00	175	—
1878	3,127,000	12.00	26.00	80.00	175	—
1878 Proof	—	Value: 2,300				
1879	3,611,000	30.00	75.00	250	475	—

KM# 734.3 SHILLING
5.6552 g., 0.9250 Silver .1682 oz. **Ruler:** Victoria **Note:** With die number.

Date	Mintage	F	VF	XF	Unc	BU
1864	4,519,000	11.00	25.00	85.00	225	—
1865	5,619,000	11.00	25.00	85.00	225	—
1866	4,990,000	11.00	25.00	85.00	225	—
1867	2,166,000	11.00	25.00	95.00	225	—
1867	—	—	—	—	—	—
Note: Error: "BBITANNIAR"						
1867 Proof	—	Value: 1,000				
1867 Proof	—	—	—	—	—	—
Note: Plain edge						

KM# 734.4 SHILLING
5.6552 g., 0.9250 Silver .1682 oz. **Ruler:** Victoria **Note:** Without die number.

Date	Mintage	F	VF	XF	Unc	BU
1879	Inc. above	12.00	26.00	65.00	160	—
1880	4,843,000	11.00	23.00	60.00	150	—
1880 Proof	—	Value: 1,600				
1880 Proof	—	Value: 2,200				
Note: Plain edge						
1881	5,255,000	11.00	23.00	60.00	150	—
1881 Proof	—	Value: 1,900				
1881 Proof	—	Value: 2,900				
Note: Plain edge						
1882	1,612,000	19.00	50.00	100	190	—
1883	7,281,000	11.00	22.00	55.00	150	—
1884	3,924,000	11.00	22.00	55.00	150	—
1884 Proof	—	Value: 2,000				
1885	3,337,000	11.00	23.00	50.00	90.00	—
1885 Proof	—	Value: 2,000				
1886	2,087,000	11.00	23.00	50.00	90.00	—
1886 Proof	—	Value: 2,000				
1887	4,034,000	17.00	35.00	85.00	250	—
1887 Proof	—	Value: 1,800				

KM# 761 SHILLING

5.6552 g., 0.9250 Silver .1682 oz. **Ruler:** Victoria **Obv:** Small bust

Date	Mintage	F	VF	XF	Unc	BU
1887	Inc. above	3.50	6.00	12.00	35.00	—
1887 Proof	1,084	Value: 125				
1888/7	4,527,000	6.00	11.00	30.00	65.00	—
1888	Inc. above	5.00	10.00	20.00	55.00	—
1889	7,040,000	35.00	80.00	400	800	—
1889 Proof	—	Value: 2,000				

KM# 774 SHILLING

5.6552 g., 0.9250 Silver .1682 oz. **Ruler:** Victoria **Obv:** Large bust

Date	Mintage	F	VF	XF	Unc	BU
1889	—	6.00	10.00	30.00	60.00	—
1889 Proof	—	Value: 1,000				
1890	8,794,000	6.00	12.00	35.00	65.00	—
1891	5,665,000	6.00	12.00	40.00	75.00	—
1891 Proof	—	Value: 1,900				
1892	4,592,000	6.00	12.00	40.00	120	—

KM# 780 SHILLING

5.6552 g., 0.9250 Silver .1682 oz. **Ruler:** Victoria

Date	Mintage	F	VF	XF	Unc	BU
1893	7,039,000	4.00	7.50	20.00	45.00	—
1893 Proof	1,312	Value: 125				
1894	5,953,000	6.00	12.00	30.00	60.00	—
1895	8,800,000	5.00	12.00	22.00	55.00	—
1896	9,265,000	5.00	12.00	22.00	55.00	—
1897	6,270,000	5.00	12.00	22.00	55.00	—
1898	9,769,000	5.00	12.00	22.00	55.00	—
1899	10,965,000	5.00	12.00	30.00	55.00	—
1900	10,938,000	5.00	12.00	30.00	55.00	—
1901	3,426,000	4.00	10.00	25.00	75.00	—

KM# 745 FLORIN (Two Shillings)

11.3104 g., 0.9250 Silver .3364 oz. **Ruler:** Victoria

Date	Mintage	F	VF	XF	Unc	BU
1848 Proof	—	Value: 3,500				
1848 Proof	—	Value: 1,250				
Note: Plain edge						
1849	414,000	23.00	45.00	125	325	—

KM# 746.1 FLORIN (Two Shillings)

11.3104 g., 0.9250 Silver .3364 oz. **Ruler:** Victoria **Obv:** Without die number **Obv. Legend:** BRIT... **Note:** Gothic type.

Date	Mintage	F	VF	XF	Unc	BU
1851	1,540	—	—	—	—	—
1851 Proof	—	Value: 8,000				
1852	1,015,000	21.00	50.00	150	275	—
1852 Proof	—	Value: 2,200				
1853	3,920,000	21.00	50.00	150	325	—
1853 Proof	—	Value: 1,750				
1854	550,000	350	700	2,900	3,800	—
1855	831,000	28.00	85.00	200	475	—
1856	2,202,000	28.00	85.00	200	475	—
1857	1,671,000	23.00	50.00	150	325	—
1857 Proof	—	Value: 2,000				
1858	2,239,000	23.00	50.00	150	325	—
1858 Proof	—	Value: 3,000				
1859	2,568,000	23.00	50.00	150	325	—
1860	1,475,000	25.00	65.00	150	450	—
1862	594,000	55.00	175	650	1,500	—
1862 Proof	—	Value: 4,000				
Note: Plain edge						
1863	939,000	100	350	900	2,000	—
1863 Proof	—	Value: 3,000				
Note: Plain edge						

KM# 746.2 FLORIN (Two Shillings)

11.3104 g., 0.9250 Silver .3364 oz. **Ruler:** Victoria **Obv:** With die number **Obv. Legend:** BRITT...

Date	Mintage	F	VF	XF	Unc	BU
1868	870,000	35.00	95.00	250	600	—
1869	297,000	28.00	85.00	225	500	—
1869 Proof	—	Value: 2,000				
1870	1,081,000	23.00	50.00	150	350	—
1871	3,426,000	23.00	60.00	175	425	—
1871 Proof	—	Value: 2,250				
1871 Proof	—	Value: 2,250				
Note: Plain edge						
1872	7,200,000	22.00	50.00	90.00	250	—
1873	5,922,000	23.00	60.00	135	250	—
1873 Proof	—	Value: 2,500				
1874	1,643,000	28.00	65.00	200	450	—
1875	1,117,000	28.00	60.00	175	425	—
1876	580,000	23.00	50.00	150	350	—
1877	682,000	23.00	60.00	175	425	—
1878	1,787,000	23.00	50.00	150	350	—
1878 Proof	—	Value: 2,750				

KM# 746.3 FLORIN (Two Shillings)

11.3104 g., 0.9250 Silver .3364 oz. **Ruler:** Victoria **Obv:** With die number

Date	Mintage	F	VF	XF	Unc	BU
1863	—	—	—	—	—	—
Note: Reported, not confirmed						
1864	1,861,000	23.00	40.00	150	350	—
1864 Proof	—	Value: 3,000				
1865	1,580,000	40.00	100	275	550	—
1866	915,000	35.00	85.00	225	400	—
1867	424,000	35.00	90.00	250	700	—
1867 Proof	—	Value: 4,000				
Note: Plain edge						

KM# 746.4 FLORIN (Two Shillings)

11.3104 g., 0.9250 Silver .3364 oz. **Ruler:** Victoria **Obv:** Without die number **Note:** Varieties exist.

Date	Mintage	F	VF	XF	Unc	BU
1877	Inc. above	25.00	70.00	300	650	—
1878	Inc. above	23.00	50.00	150	350	—
1878 Proof	—	Value: 4,500				
1879	Inc. above	26.00	50.00	150	350	—
1879 Proof	—	Value: 2,250				
1880	2,161,000	19.00	50.00	150	275	—
1880 Proof	—	Value: 4,000				
1881	2,576,000	22.00	50.00	125	275	—
1881 Proof	—	Value: 2,250				
1881 Proof	—	Value: 2,500				
Note: Plain edge						
1881	Inc. above	35.00	95.00	200	450	—
Note: Error: MDCCCLXXRI						
1883	3,556,000	22.00	50.00	125	350	—
1884	1,447,000	22.00	50.00	125	350	—
1885	1,758,000	23.00	50.00	150	375	—
1885 Proof	—	Value: 2,000				
1886	592,000	19.00	32.00	125	300	—
1886 Proof	—	Value: 2,000				
1887	1,777,000	30.00	65.00	225	375	—
1887 Proof	—	Value: 2,000				

KM# 762 FLORIN (Two Shillings)

11.3104 g., 0.9250 Silver .3364 oz. **Ruler:** Victoria

Date	Mintage	F	VF	XF	Unc	BU
1887	Inc. above	6.00	10.00	16.00	40.00	—
1887 Proof	1,084	Value: 150				
1888	1,548,000	7.00	12.50	25.00	70.00	—
1889	2,974,000	9.00	19.00	35.00	70.00	—
1890	1,685,000	13.00	30.00	95.00	200	—
1891	836,000	25.00	55.00	165	500	—
1892	283,000	26.00	60.00	200	500	—
1892 Proof	—	Value: 2,500				

KM# 781 FLORIN (Two Shillings)

11.3104 g., 0.9250 Silver .3364 oz. **Ruler:** Victoria

Date	Mintage	F	VF	XF	Unc	BU
1893	1,666,000	6.00	12.50	40.00	70.00	—
1893 Proof	1,312	Value: 150				
1894	1,953,000	10.00	20.00	65.00	125	—
1895	2,183,000	9.00	22.00	50.00	100	—
1896	2,944,000	6.00	12.50	45.00	80.00	—
1897	1,700,000	6.00	12.50	45.00	75.00	—
1898	3,061,000	6.00	19.00	50.00	100	—
1899	3,970,000	6.00	12.50	45.00	75.00	—
1900	5,529,000	6.00	12.50	45.00	80.00	—
1901	2,649,000	6.00	12.50	45.00	75.00	—

KM# 667 1/2 CROWN

14.1380 g., 0.9250 Silver .4205 oz. **Ruler:** George III **Obv:** Large bust

Date	Mintage	F	VF	XF	Unc	BU
1816	—	25.00	70.00	225	550	—
1816 Proof	—	Value: 1,900				
Note: Reeded edge						
1816 Proof	—	Value: 1,900				
Note: Plain edge						
1817	8,093,000	23.00	70.00	200	375	—
1817 Proof	—	Value: 1,900				
Note: Reeded edge						
1817 Proof	—	Value: 2,100				
Note: Plain edge						

KM# 672 1/2 CROWN
14.1380 g., 0.9250 Silver .4205 oz. **Ruler:** George III **Obv:** Small head

Date	Mintage	F	VF	XF	Unc	BU
1817	Inc. above	23.00	70.00	225	350	—
1817 Proof	—	Value: 1,900				
1817 Proof	—	Value: 1,900				
Note: Plain edge						
1818	2,905,000	30.00	80.00	250	425	—
1818 Proof	—	Value: 2,500				
1819	4,790,000	23.00	70.00	225	400	—
1819 Proof	—	Value: 2,200				
1820	2,397,000	35.00	100	225	425	—
1820 Proof	—	Value: 2,500				
1820 Proof	—	Value: 1,750				
Note: Plain edge						

KM# 676 1/2 CROWN
14.1380 g., 0.9250 Silver .4205 oz. **Ruler:** George IV **Obv:** Small head

Date	Mintage	F	VF	XF	Unc	BU
1820	Inc. above	25.00	60.00	225	475	—
1820 Proof	—	Value: 900				
1820 Proof	—	Value: 1,200				
Note: Plain edge						
1821	1,435,000	26.00	60.00	250	500	—
1821 Proof	—	Value: 800				
1823	2,004,000	650	1,600	5,600	8,000	—

KM# 688 1/2 CROWN
14.1380 g., 0.9250 Silver .4205 oz. **Ruler:** George IV

Date	Mintage	F	VF	XF	Unc	BU
1823	Inc. above	26.00	60.00	250	400	—
1823 Proof	—	Value: 2,600				
1824	466,000	30.00	80.00	300	600	—
1824 Proof	—	Value: 3,000				

KM# 695 1/2 CROWN
14.1380 g., 0.9250 Silver .4205 oz. **Ruler:** George IV

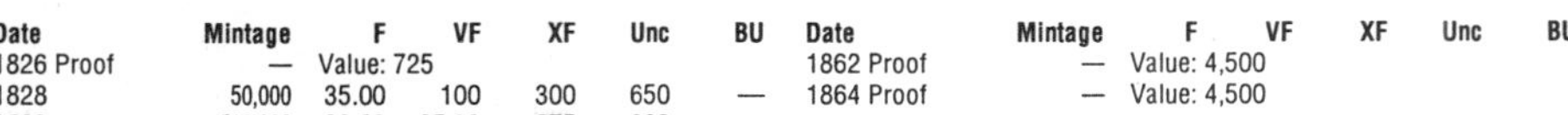

Date	Mintage	F	VF	XF	Unc	BU
1824 Proof	—	Value: 4,500				
1825	2,259,000	25.00	65.00	135	475	—
1825 Proof	—	Value: 1,000				
1825 Proof	—	Value: 1,200				
Note: Plain edge						
1826	2,189,000	23.00	50.00	115	425	—
1826 Proof	—	Value: 725				
1828	50,000	35.00	100	300	650	—
1829	508,000	30.00	95.00	275	600	—

KM# 714.1 1/2 CROWN
14.1380 g., 0.9250 Silver .4205 oz. **Ruler:** William IV

Date	Mintage	F	VF	XF	Unc	BU
1831 Proof	—	Value: 1,800				
1831 Proof	—	Value: 750				
Note: Plain edge						

KM# 714.2 1/2 CROWN
14.1380 g., 0.9250 Silver .4205 oz. **Ruler:** William IV **Obv:** Larger, modified bust

Date	Mintage	F	VF	XF	Unc	BU
1834	993,000	45.00	150	500	950	—
Note: W.W. in caps						
1834 Proof	—	Value: 1,500				
1834	Inc. above	25.00	70.00	200	500	—
Note: W.W. in script						
1834 Proof	—	Value: 1,500				
1834 Proof	—	Value: 3,400				
Note: Plain edge						
1835	282,000	35.00	125	350	750	—
1836/5	1,589,000	50.00	125	450	950	—
1836	Inc. above	25.00	70.00	200	500	—
1836 Proof	—	Value: 1,800				
Note: Plain edge						
1837	151,000	45.00	150	400	900	—

KM# 740 1/2 CROWN
14.1380 g., 0.9250 Silver .4205 oz. **Ruler:** Victoria

Date	Mintage	F	VF	XF	Unc	BU
1839	—	215	750	2,500	4,000	—
Note: W.W. in relief						
1839 Proof	—	Value: 1,100				
Note: Plain edge						
1840	386,000	35.00	75.00	475	850	—
Note: W.W. incuse						
1841	43,000	125	425	1,400	2,300	—
1842	486,000	30.00	95.00	450	800	—
1843	455,000	35.00	125	550	1,100	—
1844	1,999,000	25.00	60.00	400	700	—
1845/3	2,232,000	—	—	—	—	—
1845	Inc. above	26.00	60.00	375	650	—
1846	1,540,000	26.00	60.00	375	650	—
1848/6	367,000	70.00	175	750	1,700	—
1848	Inc. above	40.00	300	1,000	1,900	—
1848	261,000	35.00	100	500	1,100	—
Note: Large date						
1849	Inc. above	45.00	125	600	1,100	—
Note: Small date						
1850	485,000	30.00	65.00	500	1,100	—
1850 Proof	—	—	—	—	—	—
1851 Proof	—	—	—	—	—	—
1853 Proof	—	Value: 2,500				
1862 Proof	—	Value: 4,500				
1864 Proof	—	Value: 4,500				

KM# 756 1/2 CROWN
14.1380 g., 0.9250 Silver .4205 oz. **Ruler:** Victoria **Obv:** Second young head

Date	Mintage	F	VF	XF	Unc	BU
1874	2,189,000	18.00	40.00	150	375	—
1874 Proof	—	—	—	—	—	—
1875	1,113,000	18.00	45.00	150	375	—
1875 Proof	—	—	—	—	—	—
1875 Proof	—	—	—	—	—	—
Note: Plain edge						
1876/5	633,000	—	150	400	950	—
1876	Inc. above	19.00	50.00	175	425	—
1877	447,000	18.00	45.00	150	375	—
1878	1,466,000	18.00	45.00	150	375	—
1878 Proof	—	—	—	—	—	—
1879	901,000	19.00	50.00	200	425	—
1879 Proof	—	—	—	—	—	—
1880	1,346,000	18.00	40.00	150	375	—
1880 Proof	—	—	—	—	—	—
1881	2,301,000	17.00	40.00	125	375	—
1881 Proof	—	Value: 3,400				
1881 Proof	—	—	—	—	—	—
Note: Plain edge						
1882	808,000	19.00	50.00	175	400	—
1883	2,983,000	17.00	40.00	125	375	—
1884	1,569,000	17.00	40.00	125	375	—
1885	1,628,000	17.00	40.00	125	375	—
1885 Proof	—	—	—	—	—	—
1886	892,000	17.00	40.00	125	375	—
1886 Proof	—	—	—	—	—	—
1887	1,438,000	23.00	55.00	175	375	—
1887 Proof	—	—	—	—	—	—

KM# 764 1/2 CROWN
14.1380 g., 0.9250 Silver .4205 oz. **Ruler:** Victoria

Date	Mintage	F	VF	XF	Unc	BU
1887	Inc. above	9.00	15.00	26.00	80.00	—
1887 Proof	1,084	Value: 175				
1888	1,429,000	12.00	19.00	50.00	125	—
1889	4,812,000	12.00	22.00	60.00	125	—
1890	3,228,000	12.00	22.00	65.00	125	—
1891	2,285,000	12.00	22.00	65.00	125	—
1892	1,711,000	12.00	22.00	65.00	150	—

KM# 782 1/2 CROWN
14.1380 g., 0.9250 Silver .4205 oz. **Ruler:** Victoria

Date	Mintage	F	VF	XF	Unc	BU
1893	1,793,000	10.00	19.00	35.00	85.00	—
1893 Proof	1,312	Value: 150				
1894	1,525,000	12.00	22.00	70.00	150	—
1895	1,773,000	11.00	20.00	50.00	125	—
1896	2,149,000	11.00	20.00	50.00	125	—

Date	Mintage	F	VF	XF	Unc	BU
1897	1,679,000	10.00	17.50	40.00	70.00	—
1898	1,870,000	12.00	20.00	50.00	125	—
1899	2,866,000	12.00	20.00	50.00	125	—
1900	4,479,000	12.00	20.00	50.00	125	—
1901	1,577,000	12.00	20.00	50.00	125	—

KM# 763 DOUBLE FLORIN

22.6207 g., 0.9250 Silver 0.6727 oz. **Ruler:** Victoria

Date	Mintage	F	VF	XF	Unc	BU
1887 Roman I	483,000	16.00	24.00	50.00	95.00	—
1887 Roman I, Proof	1,084	Value: 650				
1887 Arabic 1	Inc. above	16.00	24.00	50.00	85.00	—
1887 Arabic 1, Proof	Est. 2,916	Value: 450				
1888	243,000	16.00	60.00	50.00	125	—
1888	Inc. above	30.00	40.00	175	325	—
Note: 2nd I in VICTORIA is an inverted 1						
1889	1,185,000	16.00	24.00	55.00	85.00	—
1889	Inc. above	30.00	60.00	150	500	—
Note: 2nd I in VICTORIA is an inverted 1						
1890	782,000	16.00	20.00	50.00	150	—

KM# 675 CROWN

28.2759 g., 0.9250 Silver .8409 oz. **Ruler:** George III

Date	Mintage	F	VF	XF	Unc	BU
1818 LVIII	155,000	25.00	75.00	300	600	—
1818 LIX	Inc. above	25.00	75.00	300	575	—
1819/8 LIX	683,000	60.00	200	300	1,500	—
1819 LIX	Inc. above	25.00	75.00	200	600	—
1819 LX	Inc. above	25.00	75.00	200	575	—
1819 Proof	—	—	—	—	—	—
Note: Plain edge						
1820/19 LX	—	50.00	125	350	850	—
1820 LX	448,000	75.00	225	500	1,600	—

KM# 680.2 CROWN

28.2759 g., 0.9250 Silver .8409 oz. **Ruler:** George IV **Edge Lettering:** TERTIO

Date	Mintage	F	VF	XF	Unc	BU
1821 Proof	—	Value: 5,200				
1822	—	30.00	150	900	2,200	—
1822 Proof	—	Value: 5,000				

KM# 680.1 CROWN

28.2759 g., 0.9250 Silver .8409 oz. **Ruler:** George IV **Edge Lettering:** SECUNDO

Date	Mintage	F	VF	XF	Unc	BU
1821	438,000	30.00	150	900	210	—
1821 Proof	—	Value: 3,900				
1822	125,000	55.00	200	1,100	2,500	—
1822 Proof	—	Value: 3,000				

KM# 699 CROWN

28.2759 g., 0.9250 Silver .8409 oz. **Ruler:** George IV

Date	Mintage	F	VF	XF	Unc	BU
1826	150	Value: 4,000				
Note: SEPTIMO on edge						
1826 Proof, rare	—	—	—	—	—	—
Note: LVIII on edge						

KM# 715 CROWN

28.2759 g., 0.9250 Silver .8409 oz. **Ruler:** William IV

Date	Mintage	F	VF	XF	Unc	BU
1831 Proof	100	Value: 8,000				

KM# 741 CROWN

28.2759 g., 0.9250 Silver .8409 oz. **Ruler:** Victoria

Date	Mintage	F	VF	XF	Unc	BU
1839 Proof	—	Value: 4,500				
1844	94,000	35.00	125	850	2,250	—
1844 Proof	—	Value: 12,000				
1845	159,000	35.00	125	850	2,250	—
1845 Proof	—	Value: 11,000				
1847	141,000	45.00	175	1,000	3,750	—
1847 Proof	—	—	—	—	—	—

KM# 744 CROWN

28.2759 g., 0.9250 Silver .8409 oz. **Ruler:** Victoria

Date	Mintage	F	VF	XF	Unc	BU
1847 Proof	8,000	Value: 2,500				
Note: UN DECIMO on edge						
1847 Impaired proof	—	500	850	1,400	—	—
1847 Proof	—	Value: 9,000				
Note: SEPTIMO on edge						
1847	—	Value: 3,800				
Note: Plain edge						
1847 Impaired proof	—	500	900	1,500	—	—
Note: Plain edge						
1853 Proof	—	Value: 7,000				
Note: SEPTIMO on edge						
1853 Proof	—	Value: 8,000				
Note: Plain edge						

KM# 765 CROWN

28.2759 g., 0.9250 Silver .8409 oz. **Ruler:** Victoria

Date	Mintage	F	VF	XF	Unc	BU
1887	173,000	13.50	27.50	75.00	125	—
1887 Proof	1,084	Value: 400				
1888	132,000	16.00	35.00	100	220	—
1889	1,807,000	13.50	27.50	80.00	160	—
189/80	—	—	—	—	—	—
1890	998,000	14.50	30.00	100	200	—
1891	566,000	16.00	35.00	100	210	—
1892	451,000	18.00	40.00	125	280	—

KM# 783 CROWN

28.2759 g., 0.9250 Silver .8409 oz. **Ruler:** Victoria **Obv:** Crowned and veiled bust left **Obv. Legend:** VICTORIA • DEI • GRA • BRITT • REGINA • FID • DEF • IND • IMP **Rev:** St. George on horseback right slaying dragon **Edge Lettering:** DECVS ET TVTAMEN ANNO REGNI

Date	Mintage	F	VF	XF	Unc	BU
1893-LVI	498,000	15.00	32.00	150	275	—
1893-LVI Proof	1,312	Value: 650				
1893-LVII	Inc. above	25.00	75.00	185	500	—
1894-LVII	145,000	15.00	50.00	175	475	—

Date	Mintage	F	VF	XF	Unc	BU
1894-LVIII	Inc. above	50.00	35.00	175	475	—
1895-LVIII	253,000	15.00	35.00	150	450	—
1895-LIX	Inc. above	15.00	32.00	150	450	—
1896-LIX	318,000	25.00	50.00	250	500	—
1896-LX	Inc. above	15.00	32.00	150	450	—
1897-LX	262,000	15.00	32.00	150	450	—
1897-LXI	Inc. above	15.00	32.00	150	450	—
1898-LXI	161,000	30.00	60.00	250	550	—
1898-LXII	Inc. above	15.00	50.00	175	475	—
1899-LXII	166,000	15.00	50.00	175	475	—
1899-LXIII	Inc. above	15.00	50.00	175	475	—
1900-LXIII	353,000	20.00	60.00	200	475	—
1900-LXIV	Inc. above	20.00	60.00	250	550	—

SOVEREIGN COINAGE

KM# 673 1/2 SOVEREIGN

3.9940 g., 0.9170 Gold .1177 oz. **Ruler:** George III

Date	Mintage	F	VF	XF	Unc	BU
1817	2,080,000	100	150	325	550	—
1817 Proof	—	Value: 3,500				
1818/7 Rare	1,030,000	—	—	—	—	—
1818	Inc. above	100	225	350	650	—
1818 Proof	—	Value: 5,000				
1820	35,000	90.00	175	400	700	—

KM# 681 1/2 SOVEREIGN

3.9940 g., 0.9170 Gold .1177 oz. **Ruler:** George IV

Date	Mintage	F	VF	XF	Unc	BU
1821	231,000	450	1,100	2,600	3,500	—
1821 Proof	—	Value: 5,000				

KM# 689 1/2 SOVEREIGN

3.9940 g., 0.9170 Gold .1177 oz. **Ruler:** George IV

Date	Mintage	F	VF	XF	Unc	BU
1823	224,000	100	225	525	800	—
1823	—	Value: 5,500				
1824	592,000	90.00	200	450	800	—
1825	761,000	90.00	200	450	800	—
1825 Proof	—	Value: 2,000				

KM# 700 1/2 SOVEREIGN

3.9940 g., 0.9170 Gold .1177 oz. **Ruler:** George IV **Obv:** Bare head

Date	Mintage	F	VF	XF	Unc	BU
1826	345,000	80.00	180	450	800	—
1826 Proof	—	Value: 1,750				
1827	492,000	85.00	200	475	1,000	—
1828	1,225,000	80.00	190	450	900	—

KM# 716 1/2 SOVEREIGN

3.9940 g., 0.9170 Gold .1177 oz. **Ruler:** William IV

Date	Mintage	F	VF	XF	Unc	BU
1831 Proof	—	Value: 2,000				

KM# 720 1/2 SOVEREIGN

3.9940 g., 0.9170 Gold .1177 oz., 18 mm. **Ruler:** Victoria

Date	Mintage	F	VF	XF	Unc	BU
1834	134,000	115	250	600	1,400	—

KM# 722 1/2 SOVEREIGN

3.9940 g., 0.9170 Gold .1177 oz., 19 mm. **Ruler:** William IV

Date	Mintage	F	VF	XF	Unc	BU
1835	773,000	150	225	600	1,200	—
1836	147,000	250	500	1,500	2,000	—
1837	160,000	150	250	550	1,000	—

KM# 735.1 1/2 SOVEREIGN

3.9940 g., 0.9170 Gold .1177 oz. **Ruler:** Victoria **Rev:** Without die number

Date	Mintage	F	VF	XF	Unc	BU
1838	273,000	75.00	90.00	225	625	—
1839 Proof	1,230	Value: 3,000				
1841	509,000	75.00	90.00	375	625	—
1842	2,223,000	75.00	90.00	225	550	—
1843	1,252,000	75.00	90.00	350	625	—
1844	1,127,000	75.00	90.00	300	550	—
1845	888,000	150	350	1,100	1,800	—
1846	1,064,000	75.00	100	300	625	—
1847	983,000	75.00	90.00	300	550	—
1848	411,000	75.00	150	300	800	—
1849	845,000	75.00	100	275	550	—
1850	180,000	180	275	900	1,625	—
1851	774,000	70.00	100	225	625	—
1852	1,378,000	70.00	100	250	550	—
1853	2,709,000	70.00	100	225	550	—
1853 Proof	—	Value: 5,000				
1854	1,125,000	225	350	650	1,500	—
1855	1,120,000	70.00	100	225	550	—
1856	2,392,000	70.00	100	225	550	—
1857	728,000	70.00	100	250	450	—
1858	856,000	70.00	100	225	495	—
1859	2,204,000	70.00	90.00	225	495	—
1860	1,132,000	70.00	90.00	225	495	—
1861	1,131,000	70.00	100	225	575	—
1862	—	350	950	2,700	6,500	—
1863	1,572,000	70.00	90.00	225	450	—
1880	1,008,999	60.00	75.00	250	325	—
1883	2,870,000	60.00	90.00	175	325	—
1884	1,114,000	60.00	90.00	175	325	—

Note: 1884 is much rarer than the mintage figure indicates

Date	Mintage	F	VF	XF	Unc	BU
1885/3	4,469,000	80.00	150	325	650	—
1885	Inc. above	60.00	90.00	175	290	—

KM# 735.2 1/2 SOVEREIGN

3.9940 g., 0.9170 Gold .1177 oz. **Ruler:** Victoria **Rev:** With die number

Date	Mintage	F	VF	XF	Unc	BU
1863	Inc. above	60.00	85.00	300	400	—
1864	1,758,000	60.00	85.00	225	400	—
1865	1,835,000	60.00	85.00	225	400	—
1866	2,059,000	60.00	85.00	225	400	—
1867	993,000	60.00	85.00	225	400	—
1869	1,862,000	60.00	85.00	225	400	—
1870	160,000	60.00	85.00	225	400	—
1871	2,063,000	60.00	85.00	225	400	—
1871 Proof	—	Value: 4,000				

Note: Plain edge

Date	Mintage	F	VF	XF	Unc	BU
1872	3,249,000	60.00	85.00	225	400	—
1873	1,927,000	60.00	85.00	225	400	—
1874	1,884,000	60.00	85.00	225	400	—
1875	516,000	60.00	85.00	225	400	—
1876	2,785,000	60.00	85.00	175	400	—
1877	2,197,000	60.00	75.00	175	325	—
1878	2,082,000	60.00	75.00	175	325	—
1879	35,000	75.00	125	350	600	—
1880	Inc. above	60.00	75.00	325	600	—

KM# 766 1/2 SOVEREIGN

3.9940 g., 0.9170 Gold .1177 oz. **Ruler:** Victoria **Rev:** Without die number

Date	Mintage	F	VF	XF	Unc	BU
1887	872,000	BV	65.00	100	125	—
1887 Proof	797	Value: 500				
1890	2,266,000	BV	50.00	100	150	—
1891	1,079,000	BV	50.00	100	150	—
1892	13,680,000	BV	50.00	100	150	—
1893	4,427,000	BV	50.00	100	150	—

KM# 784 1/2 SOVEREIGN

3.9940 g., 0.9170 Gold .1177 oz. **Ruler:** Victoria

Date	Mintage	F	VF	XF	Unc	BU
1893	Inc. above	BV	60.00	85.00	115	—
1893 Proof	773	Value: 500				
1894	3,795,000	BV	60.00	70.00	125	—
1895	2,869,000	BV	60.00	70.00	125	—
1896	2,947,000	BV	60.00	70.00	125	—
1897	3,568,000	BV	60.00	70.00	125	—
1898	2,869,000	BV	60.00	70.00	125	—
1899	3,362,000	BV	60.00	70.00	125	—
1900	4,307,000	BV	60.00	70.00	125	—
1901	2,037,999	BV	60.00	70.00	125	—

KM# 674 SOVEREIGN

7.9881 g., 0.9170 Gold .2354 oz. **Ruler:** George III

Date	Mintage	F	VF	XF	Unc	BU
1817	3,235,000	225	375	900	1,600	—
1817 Proof	—	Value: 8,000				
1818	2,347,000	250	425	1,100	1,900	—
1819 Rare	3,574	—	—	—	—	—
1820	932,000	250	400	1,000	1,600	—
1820 Proof	—	—	—	—	—	—

KM# 682 SOVEREIGN

7.9881 g., 0.9170 Gold .2354 oz. **Ruler:** George IV

Date	Mintage	F	VF	XF	Unc	BU
1821	9,405,000	225	375	1,000	1,250	—
1821 Proof	—	Value: 4,500				
1822	5,357,000	250	375	1,100	1,700	—
1823	617,000	375	1,200	3,500	7,000	—
1824	3,768,000	250	400	1,100	1,700	—
1825	4,200,000	350	1,000	2,800	5,000	—

KM# 696 SOVEREIGN

7.9881 g., 0.9170 Gold .2354 oz. **Ruler:** George IV

Date	Mintage	F	VF	XF	Unc	BU
1825	Inc. above	200	375	675	1,200	—
1825 Proof	—	Value: 3,500				
1825 Proof	—	Value: 5,000				

Note: Plain edge

Date	Mintage	F	VF	XF	Unc	BU
1826	5,724,000	200	350	675	1,100	—
1826 Proof	—	Value: 3,500				
1827	2,267,000	225	400	725	1,200	—
1828	386,000	1,200	2,500	6,500	—	—

Note: Only 6 or 7 known

Date	Mintage	F	VF	XF	Unc	BU
1829	2,445,000	250	425	1,000	1,200	—

Date	Mintage	F	VF	XF	Unc	BU
1830	2,388,000	250	425	1,000	1,200	—
1830 Proof	—	—	—	—	—	—
1830 Proof	—	Value: 10,000				

Note: Plain edge

KM# 717 SOVEREIGN

7.9881 g., 0.9170 Gold .2354 oz. **Ruler:** William IV

Date	Mintage	F	VF	XF	Unc	BU
1831	599,000	250	450	1,200	1,700	—
1831 Proof	—	Value: 5,500				
1832	3,737,000	225	350	1,000	1,500	—
1833	1,225,000	250	400	1,100	1,600	—
1835	723,000	250	400	1,200	1,700	—
1836	1,714,000	250	400	1,100	1,600	—
1837	1,173,000	275	400	1,200	1,700	—

KM# 736.1 SOVEREIGN

7.9881 g., 0.9170 Gold .2354 oz. **Ruler:** Victoria **Rev:** Without die number

Date	Mintage	F	VF	XF	Unc	BU
1838	2,719,000	150	350	750	1,600	—
1838 Proof	—	Value: 6,400				
1839	504,000	175	500	1,000	2,000	—
1839 Proof	—	Value: 5,000				
1841	124,000	1,100	1,800	5,500	—	—
1842	4,865,000	125	150	250	500	—
1843/2	5,982,000	500	—	—	—	—
1843	Inc. above	125	150	200	450	—
1843 Narrow shield	Inc. above	4,000	6,500	—	—	—
1844	3,000,000	125	150	225	450	—
1845	3,801,000	125	150	225	475	—
1846	3,803,000	125	150	200	475	—
1847	4,667,000	125	150	200	475	—
1848	2,247,000	BV	125	225	400	—
1849	1,755,000	BV	125	225	425	—
1850	1,402,000	BV	125	175	400	—
1851	4,014,000	BV	125	175	400	—
1852	8,053,000	BV	125	175	400	—
1853 Proof	—	Value: 7,200				
1853 WW raised	10,598,000	BV	125	175	400	—
1853 WW incuse	Inc. above	BV	125	175	475	—
1854 WW raised	3,590,000	125	150	325	800	—
1854 WW incuse	Inc. above	BV	125	175	400	—
1855 WW raised	8,448,000	150	200	250	600	—
1855	Inc. above	BV	125	175	400	—
1856	4,806,000	BV	125	175	400	—
1856 Small date	Inc. above	BV	125	175	400	—
1857	4,496,000	BV	125	175	400	—
1858	803,000	BV	125	200	625	—
1859	1,548,000	BV	125	175	400	—
1859 Small date	Inc. above	BV	125	175	400	—
1860	2,556,000	BV	125	225	500	—
1861	7,623,000	BV	125	200	400	—
1862/1	—	—	—	—	—	—
1862	7,836,000	BV	125	175	400	—
1863	5,922,000	BV	125	150	400	—
1872	13,487,000	BV	125	150	300	—

KM# 736.3 SOVEREIGN

7.9881 g., 0.9170 Gold .2354 oz. **Ruler:** Victoria **Obv:** Additional line on lower edge of ribbon **Rev:** Without die number **Note:** Ansell variety.

Date	Mintage	F	VF	XF	Unc	BU
1859	168,000	425	825	2,500	—	—

KM# 736.2 SOVEREIGN

7.9881 g., 0.9170 Gold .2354 oz. **Ruler:** Victoria **Rev:** Die number below wreath

Date	Mintage	F	VF	XF	Unc	BU
1863	Inc. above	BV	125	150	400	—
1864	8,656,000	BV	125	150	400	—
1865	1,450,000	BV	125	150	400	—
1866	4,047,000	BV	125	150	400	—

Date	Mintage	F	VF	XF	Unc	BU
1868	1,653,000	BV	125	150	400	—
1869	6,441,000	BV	125	150	400	—
1869 Proof	—	Value: 4,000				
1870	2,190,000	BV	125	150	400	—
1871	8,767,000	BV	125	150	275	—
1872	Inc. above	BV	125	150	300	—
1873	2,368,000	BV	125	150	300	—
1874	521,000	800	1,800	6,500	—	—

KM# 752 SOVEREIGN

7.9881 g., 0.9170 Gold .2354 oz. **Ruler:** Victoria

Date	Mintage	F	VF	XF	Unc	BU
1871	Inc. above	BV	125	150	275	—
1871 Proof	—	Value: 3,500				
1872	Inc. above	BV	125	150	290	—
1873	Inc. above	BV	125	160	275	—
1874	Inc. above	100	150	250	400	—
1876	3,319,000	BV	125	150	350	—
1876 Proof	Inc. above	Value: 6,500				
1878	1,091,000	BV	125	150	275	—
1879	20,000	180	325	1,350	4,000	—
1880	3,650,000	BV	125	150	275	—
1880	—	BV	125	150	275	—

Note: Without designer's initials on reverse

Date	Mintage	F	VF	XF	Unc	BU
1884	1,770,000	BV	125	150	275	—
1885	718,000	BV	125	150	300	—

KM# 767 SOVEREIGN

7.9881 g., 0.9170 Gold .2354 oz. **Ruler:** Victoria

Date	Mintage	F	VF	XF	Unc	BU
1887	1,111,000	—	BV	110	150	—
1887 Proof	797	Value: 750				
1888	2,777,000	—	BV	110	150	—
1889	7,257,000	—	BV	110	165	—
1890	6,530,000	—	BV	110	165	—
1891	6,329,000	—	BV	110	165	—
1892	7,105,000	—	BV	110	165	—

KM# 785 SOVEREIGN

7.9881 g., 0.9170 Gold .2354 oz. **Ruler:** Victoria

Date	Mintage	F	VF	XF	Unc	BU
1893	6,898,000	—	—	BV	115	—
1893 Proof	773	Value: 900				
1894	3,783,000	—	—	BV	130	—
1895	2,285,000	—	—	BV	130	—
1896	3,334,000	—	—	BV	130	—
1898	4,361,000	—	—	BV	130	—
1899	7,516,000	—	—	BV	115	—
1900	10,847,000	—	—	BV	115	—
1901	1,579,000	—	—	BV	115	—

KM# 690 2 POUNDS

15.9761 g., 0.9170 Gold .4708 oz. **Ruler:** George IV

Date	Mintage	F	VF	XF	Unc	BU
1823	—	300	500	1,000	1,800	—

KM# 701 2 POUNDS

15.9761 g., 0.9170 Gold .4708 oz. **Ruler:** George IV

Date	Mintage	F	VF	XF	Unc	BU
1826 Proof	450	Value: 6,000				

KM# 718 2 POUNDS

15.9761 g., 0.9170 Gold .4708 oz. **Ruler:** William IV

Date	Mintage	F	VF	XF	Unc	BU
1831 Proof	225	Value: 7,500				

KM# 768 2 POUNDS

15.9761 g., 0.9170 Gold .4708 oz. **Ruler:** Victoria

Date	Mintage	F	VF	XF	Unc	BU
1887	91,000	250	300	400	550	—
1887 Proof	797	Value: 1,200				

Note: Proof issues with mint mark S below right rear hoof of horse were struck at Sydney, refer to Australia listings

KM# 786 2 POUNDS

15.9761 g., 0.9170 Gold .4708 oz. **Ruler:** Victoria

Date	Mintage	F	VF	XF	Unc	BU
1893	52,000	250	325	675	900	—
1893 Proof	773	Value: 1,750				

KM# 702 5 POUNDS

39.9403 g., 0.9170 Gold 1.1773 oz. **Ruler:** George IV **Edge:** Lettered

Date	Mintage	F	VF	XF	Unc	BU
1826 Proof	150	Value: 12,500				

Note: Includes lettered edge patterns KM#Pn96

KM# 742 5 POUNDS
39.9403 g., 0.9170 Gold 1.1773 oz. **Ruler:** Victoria

Date	Mintage	F	VF	XF	Unc	BU
1839 Proof	400	Value: 28,000				

KM# 769 5 POUNDS
39.9403 g., 0.9170 Gold 1.1773 oz. **Ruler:** Victoria

Date	Mintage	F	VF	XF	Unc	BU
1887	54,000	625	725	1,000	1,500	—
1887 Proof	797	Value: 3,250				

Note: Proof issues with mint mark S below right rear hoof of horse were struck at Sydney, refer to Australia listings

KM# 787 5 POUNDS
39.9403 g., 0.9170 Gold 1.1773 oz. **Ruler:** Victoria

Date	Mintage	F	VF	XF	Unc	BU
1893	20,000	675	750	1,200	2,000	—
1893 Proof	773	Value: 3,750				

GUINEA COINAGE

KM# 648 1/3 GUINEA
2.7834 g., 0.9170 Gold .0820 oz. **Ruler:** George III

Date	Mintage	F	VF	XF	Unc	BU
1801	—	60.00	90.00	300	450	—
1802	—	60.00	90.00	300	450	—
1803	—	60.00	90.00	300	450	—

KM# 650 1/3 GUINEA
2.7834 g., 0.9170 Gold .0820 oz. **Ruler:** George III

Date	Mintage	F	VF	XF	Unc	BU
1804	—	60.00	90.00	300	450	—
1806	—	60.00	90.00	300	450	—
1808	—	60.00	90.00	300	450	—
1809	—	60.00	90.00	300	450	—
1810	—	60.00	90.00	300	450	—
1811	—	250	500	1,200	1,600	—
1813	—	125	325	700	1,400	—
1813 Proof	—	Value: 3,000				

KM# 649 1/2 GUINEA
4.1750 g., 0.9170 Gold .1230 oz. **Ruler:** George III

Date	Mintage	F	VF	XF	Unc	BU
1801	—	100	125	350	700	—
1802	—	100	175	375	800	—
1803	—	100	175	375	800	—

KM# 651 1/2 GUINEA
4.1750 g., 0.9170 Gold .1230 oz. **Ruler:** George III

Date	Mintage	F	VF	XF	Unc	BU
1804	—	100	125	350	700	—
1806	—	100	125	375	800	—
1808	—	100	125	375	800	—
1809	—	100	125	375	800	—
1810	—	100	125	375	800	—
1811	—	150	325	700	1,400	—
1813	—	100	275	500	1,000	—

KM# 664 GUINEA
8.3500 g., 0.9170 Gold .2461 oz. **Ruler:** George III

Date	Mintage	F	VF	XF	Unc	BU
1813	—	450	1,000	2,000	3,500	—
1813 Proof	—	Value: 5,000				

TRADE COINAGE

Britannia Series

Issued to facilitate British trade in the Orient, the reverse design incorporated the denomination in Chinese characters and Malay script.

This issue was struck at the Bombay (B) and Calcutta (C) Mints in India, except for 1925 and 1930 issues which were struck at London. Through error the mint marks did not appear on some early (1895-1900) issues as indicated.

KM# T5 DOLLAR
26.9568 g., 0.9000 Silver .7800 oz.

Date	Mintage	F	VF	XF	Unc	BU
1895B	3,316,000	20.00	80.00	125	350	—
1895B Proof	Inc. above	Value: 850				
1895(B)	Inc. above	40.00	75.00	100	300	—
1895(B) Proof	Inc. above	Value: 800				
1896B	6,136,000	60.00	90.00	150	500	—
1896B Proof	Inc. above	Value: 800				
1897/6B	21,286,000	40.00	60.00	100	150	—
1897B	Inc. above	15.00	20.00	25.00	60.00	—
1897B Proof	Inc. above	Value: 800				
1897(B)	Inc. above	15.00	20.00	25.00	60.00	—
1897(B) Proof	Inc. above	Value: 800				
1898B	21,546,000	15.00	20.00	25.00	60.00	—
1898B Proof	Inc. above	Value: 800				
1898(B)	Inc. above	15.00	20.00	25.00	60.00	—
1899B	30,743,000	15.00	20.00	25.00	60.00	—
1899B Proof	Inc. above	Value: 800				
1900/1000B	9,107,000	40.00	60.00	100	200	—
1900/890B	Inc. above	40.00	60.00	100	200	—
1900	—	100	175	250	600	—
1900B	Inc. above	15.00	20.00	25.00	60.00	—
1900B Proof	Inc. above	Value: 800				
1900B Restrike; Proof	—	Value: 1,000				
1900C	363,000	90.00	150	250	500	—

KM# T5a DOLLAR
Gold

Date	Mintage	F	VF	XF	Unc	BU
1895B Restrike; Proof	—	Value: 7,500				
1895 Restrike; Proof	—	Value: 7,500				
1896B Restrike; Proof	—	Value: 7,500				
1897B Restrike; Proof	—	Value: 7,500				
1897 Restrike; Proof	—	Value: 7,500				
1898B Restrike; Proof	—	Value: 7,500				
1899B Restrike; Proof	—	Value: 7,500				
1900B Restrike; Proof	—	Value: 7,500				

COUNTERMARKED COINAGE

Bank of England

Emergency issue consisting of foreign silver coins, usually Spanish Colonial, having a bust of George III within an oval (1797) or octagonal (1840) frame. Countermarked 8 Reales circulated at 4 Shillings 9 Pence in 1797 and 5 Shillings in 1804. The puncheons used for countermarking foreign coins for this series were available for many years afterward, especially the oval die and apparently a number of foreign coins other than Spanish or Spanish Colonial 8 Reales were countermarked for collectors.

KM# 652 DOLLAR
Silver **Countermark:** Type II **Note:** Countermark on Bolivia (Potosi) 8 Reales, KM#55.

CM Date	Host Date	Good	VG	F	VF	XF
ND	1773-89	—	300	500	1,000	1,700

KM# 653 DOLLAR
Silver **Countermark:** Type II **Note:** Countermark on Bolivia (Potosi) 8 Reales, KM#73.1.

CM Date	Host Date	Good	VG	F	VF	XF
ND	1791-1808	—	250	500	700	1,200

KM# 654 DOLLAR
Silver **Countermark:** Type II **Note:** Countermark on France 1 Ecu, C#78.

CM Date	Host Date	Good	VG	F	VF	XF
ND	1774-92 Rare	—	—	—	—	—

KM# 655 DOLLAR
Silver **Countermark:** Type II **Note:** Countermark on Mexico 8 Reales, KM#106.

CM Date	Host Date	Good	VG	F	VF	XF
ND	1772-89	—	125	250	600	1,000

KM# 656 DOLLAR
Silver **Countermark:** Type II **Note:** Countermark on Mexico 8 Reales, KM#109.

CM Date	Host Date	Good	VG	F	VF	XF
ND	1791-1808	—	125	250	600	1,000

KM# 657 DOLLAR
Silver **Countermark:** Type II **Note:** Countermark on Peru (Lima) 8 Reales, KM#78.

CM Date	Host Date	Good	VG	F	VF	XF
ND	1772-89	—	175	345	625	2,200

KM# 658 DOLLAR
Silver **Countermark:** Type II **Note:** Countermark on Peru (Lima) 8 Reales, KM#97.

CM Date	Host Date	Good	VG	F	VF	XF
ND	1791-1808	—	175	345	625	2,200

KM# 659 DOLLAR
Silver **Countermark:** Type II **Note:** Countermark on Spanish (Seville) 8 Reales, C#71.

CM Date	Host Date	Good	VG	F	VF	XF
ND	1788-1808 Rare	—	—	700	1,700	—

KM# 660a DOLLAR
Silver **Countermark:** Type II **Note:** Countermark on United States 1 Dollar, C#34a.

CM Date	Host Date	Good	VG	F	VF	XF
ND	1798-1803 Rare	—	—	—	—	—

KM# 660 DOLLAR
Silver **Countermark:** Type II **Note:** Countermark on United States 1 Dollar, C#43.

CM Date	Host Date	Good	VG	F	VF	XF
ND	1795-98 Rare	—	—	—	—	—

COUNTERMARKED COINAGE

English Tradesmen

During the last half of the 18th century and the early years of the 19th century, the gold coinage predominated in Great Britain and the limited issues of silver coins between the years 1758 and 1816 did little to relieve the shortage of smaller denominations. During the 1790s a partial solution to the problem began to be offered by private tradesmen through the countermarking of foreign dollars, chiefly Spanish Colonial issues from the Americas, with a punch validating them for local circulation and redemption. The majority of these tradesmens countermarked issues circulated in Scotland; in England two cotton mills, two colleries, and a merchant also countermarked foreign silver coins.

KM# 643 4 SHILLING 9 PENCE
0.9030 Silver **Countermark:** 4/9 CROMVORD • DERBYSHIRE
Note: Countermark on Spanish Colonial 8 Reales.

CM Date	Host Date	Good	VG	F	VF	XF
ND	18xx	—	200	300	500	—

KM# 644 4 SHILLING 9 PENCE
0.9030 Silver **Countermark:** 4/9 CROMFORD • DERBYSHIRE
Note: Countermark on French Ecu.

CM Date	Host Date	Good	VG	F	VF	XF
ND	18xx Rare	—	—	—	—	—

Note: False punches have been used on genuine host coins

KM# B645 5 SHILLING
0.9030 Silver **Countermark:** 5s. CROMFORD • DERBYSHIRE
Note: Countermark on Spanish Colonial 8 Reales.

CM Date	Host Date	Good	VG	F	VF	XF
ND	18xx	—	—	350	550	—

KM# C645 5 SHILLING
0.9030 Silver **Countermark:** 5/• DONALD & CO • BIRMINGHAM
Note: Countermark on Spanish Colonial 8 Reales.

CM Date	Host Date	Good	VG	F	VF	XF
ND	18XX Rare	—	—	—	—	—

KM# D645 5 SHILLING
0.9030 Silver **Countermark:** 5/- PERCY MAIN COLLIERY **Note:** Countermark on Spanish Colonial 8 Reales.

CM Date	Host Date	Good	VG	F	VF	XF
ND	18xx	—	—	800	1,100	—

TOKEN COINAGE

KM# Tn1 DOLLAR
0.9030 Silver **Issuer:** Bank of England

Date	Mintage	F	VF	XF	Unc	BU
1804	—	125	275	500	1,500	—
1804 Proof	—	Value: 1,250				

KM# Tn1a DOLLAR
Copper **Issuer:** Bank of England **Note:** The silver proofs were struck on specially prepared flans while circulation strikes were struck over Spanish and Spanish Colonial 8 Reales.

Date	Mintage	F	VF	XF	Unc	BU
1804 Proof	—	Value: 900				

KM# Tn2 1 SHILLING 6 PENCE (18 Pence)
0.9250 Silver **Issuer:** Bank of England

Date	Mintage	F	VF	XF	Unc	BU
1811	—	10.00	35.00	100	200	—
1811 Proof	—	Value: 600				
1812	—	10.00	35.00	100	200	—
1812 Proof	—	Value: 600				

KM# Tn3 1 SHILLING 6 PENCE (18 Pence)
0.9250 Silver **Issuer:** Bank of England

Date	Mintage	F	VF	XF	Unc	BU
1812	—	10.00	35.00	95.00	200	—
1813	—	10.00	40.00	100	200	—
1814	—	10.00	40.00	100	200	—
1815	—	10.00	40.00	100	200	—
1816	—	10.00	40.00	100	200	—

KM# Tn4 3 SHILLING
0.9250 Silver **Issuer:** Bank of England

Date	Mintage	F	VF	XF	Unc	BU
1811	—	20.00	60.00	100	200	—
1811 Proof	—	Value: 900				
1812	—	20.00	70.00	125	250	—

KM# Tn5 3 SHILLING
0.9250 Silver **Issuer:** Bank of England

Date	Mintage	F	VF	XF	Unc	BU
1812	—	20.00	60.00	100	200	—
1812 Proof	—	Value: 900				
1813	—	20.00	70.00	125	250	—
1814	—	20.00	70.00	125	250	—
1815	—	20.00	70.00	125	250	—
1816	—	225	500	1,100	2,000	—

19TH CENTURY ENGLISH

Penny

COPPER

Shilling

SILVER

2 Shillings

SILVER

4 Shillings

SILVER

40 Shillings

GOLD and SILVER

The early 1800's witnessed a severe shortage of both copper and silver. The last issue of shillings and sixpence was in 1787. The turn of the century brought into circulation the countermarked Spanish dollars in two issues, both being heavily counterfeited. The Bank of England introduced its dollar or 5 shillings but the rise in value of silver caused many to be melted down. Private traders' and town tokens appeared in 1811 and 1812 along with regular bank tokens of the Bank of England. Private tokens continued to circulate until 1813 when they were finally forbidden by an Act of Parliament. Various denominations were produced, the shilling being the commonest of the silver tokens and the penny of the copper tokens. These can be found listed in *'British Tokens and Their Values'* by P. Seaby and M. Bussell and *'The Silver Token Coinage, 1811-1812'* by R. Dalton.

PATTERNS

Including off metal strikes

KM#	Date	Mintage	Identification	Mkt Val
Pn66	1804	—	Dollar. Silver. C.H.K. on truncation.	5,000
Pn67	1804	—	Dollar. Silver. K on truncation.	5,000
PnA68	1806	—	Farthing. Silver. KM#661.	—
PnB68	1806	—	Farthing. Gold. KM#661.	—
PnC68	1811	—	5 Shilling 6 Pence. Silver. Britannia.	—

KM#	Date	Mintage	Identification	Mkt Val
PnE68	1811	—	5 Shilling 6 Pence. Bronzed Copper. Britannia.	—
PnF68	1811	—	5 Shilling 6 Pence. Copper Gilt. Britannia.	—
PnG68	1811	—	5 Shilling 6 Pence. White Metal. Britannia.	—

KM#	Date	Mintage	Identification	Mkt Val
PnH68	1811	—	5 Shilling 6 Pence. Silver. Wreath.	—
PnJ68	1811	—	5 Shilling 6 Pence. Copper. Wreath.	—
PnK68	1811	—	5 Shilling 6 Pence. Brass. Wreath.	—

KM#	Date	Mintage	Identification	Mkt Val
PnN68	1812	—	9 Pence. Silver. Token.	—

KM#	Date	Mintage	Identification	Mkt Val
Pn68	1813	—	Guinea. Gold. Plain edge. George III	10,500
Pn69	1813	—	Guinea. Gold. Reeded edge. George III	9,500
Pn70	1813	—	Guinea. Gold. Arms in wreath. Plain edge. George III.	—
Pn71	1813	—	Guinea. Gold. Arms in wreath. Reeded edge. George III.	9,500
Pn72	1813	—	Guinea. Gold. Banner. George III.	6,500
PnA73	1816	—	6 Pence. Gold. KM#665.	—
PnB73	1816	—	Shilling. Gold. KM#666.	—
Pn73	1816	—	Sovereign. Gold. George III.	17,500

KM#	Date	Mintage	Identification	Mkt Val
Pn74	1816	—	Sovereign. Gold. George III.	19,500

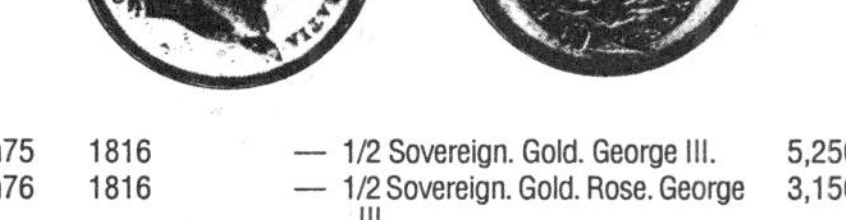

KM#	Date	Mintage	Identification	Mkt Val
Pn75	1816	—	1/2 Sovereign. Gold. George III.	5,250
Pn76	1816	—	1/2 Sovereign. Gold. Rose. George III.	3,150

KM#	Date	Mintage	Identification	Mkt Val
PnA77	1817	—	Crown. Silver. George III.	10,500
PnB77	1817	—	Crown. Silver. Plain edge. George III.	10,500
PnC77	1817	—	Crown. Gold. George III.	255,000
PnD77	1817	—	Crown. Copper. George III.	1,500
PnE77	1817	—	Crown. White Metal. George III.	5,000
PnF77	1817	—	Crown. Silver. ...GRATIA BRITANNUIARUM REX F: D:. Plain edge. George III.	—
PnG77	1817	—	Crown. Silver. ...GRATIA BRITANNUIAR: REX F: D.. George III.	—
PnH77	1817	—	Crown. Silver. ...D. G. BRITANNIARUM REX F: D. George III.	—
PnI77	1817	—	Crown. Silver. INCORRUPTA.... George IV.	8,500

KM#	Date	Mintage	Identification	Mkt Val
Pn77	1817	—	Crown. 0.9160 Gold. George III.	75,000

KM#	Date	Mintage	Identification	Mkt Val
PnA78	1818	—	Crown. 0.9160 Silver. Lettered edge. George III.	—
PnB78	1818	—	Crown. Silver. Plain edge. George III.	—
PnC78	1818	—	Crown. White Metal. Plain edge. George III.	—
Pn78	1820	—	6 Pence. Silver. George III.	1,500
Pn79	1820	—	Shilling. Silver. George III.	1,500
PnB80	ND(1820)	—	Crown. Silver. George III.	800
PnC80	ND(1820)	—	Crown. Lead. Plain edge. George III.	—
PnD80	1820	—	Crown. Silver. George III. St. George slaying the dragon.	—
PnE80	1820	—	Crown. Lead. George III. St. George slaying the dragon.	—
Pn80	1820	—	1/2 Sovereign. Gold. George III.	7,000
Pn81	1820	—	2 Pounds. Gold. Plain edge. George III.	31,500
Pn82	1820	60	2 Pounds. Gold. Lettered edge. George III.	12,200
Pn83	1820	—	5 Pounds. Gold. Plain edge. George III.	52,500
Pn84	1820	25	5 Pounds. Gold. Lettered edge. George III.	45,000
Pn85	1820 12	—	1/2 Sovereign. Gold. George IV.	—
PnA86	1821 1	—	Crown. Copper. KM#680.1.	1,100
Pn86	1821	—	1/2 Sovereign. Gold. George IV.	—
PnA87	1823	—	Crown. White Metal. KM#680.1.	9,500
PnB87	1823	—	1/2 Crown. Silver. George IV. Recut dies.	—
Pn87	1824	—	Sovereign. Gold. George IV.	—
Pn88	1824	—	2 Pounds. Gold. Lettered edge. George IV.	25,000
Pn89	1825	—	1/2 Sovereign. Gold. George V.	—
Pn90	1825	—	Crown. Silver. Plain edge.	—
Pn91	1825	—	2 Pounds. Gold. Plain edge. George IV.	11,500
Pn92	1825	—	2 Pounds. Gold. Lettered edge. George IV.	11,500
Pn93	1826	—	2 Pounds. Gold. Plain edge. George IV.	—
Pn94	1826	—	2 Pounds. Gold. Lettered edge. George IV.	—
Pn95	1826	—	5 Pounds. Gold. Plain edge. George IV.	—
Pn96	1826	—	5 Pounds. Gold. Lettered edge. George IV.	17,000

Note: Mintage included with KM#702

KM#	Date	Mintage	Identification	Mkt Val
PnA97	1829	—	5 Pounds. Gold. Plain edge. George IV.	—

Note: Stack's sale 12-92 BU realized $85,000.

KM#	Date	Mintage	Identification	Mkt Val
Pn97	1830	—	Sovereign. Gold. Plain edge. William IV.	—
PnA98	1831	—	Crown. Gold. Plain edge. William IV.	125,000
Pn98	1831	—	2 Pounds. Gold. Plain edge. William IV.	—
Pn99	1831	—	5 Pounds. Gold. Plain edge. William IV.	—
PnA100	1836	—	4 Pence. Silver. KM#723.	850
PnC100	1836	—	4 Pence. Gold. KM#723.	4,000
Pn100	1837	—	4 Pence. 0.9250 Silver.	450
Pn101	1837	—	Shilling. Copper. KM#713.	—
Pn102	1837	—	Sovereign. Gold. Victoria.	—
Pn103	1837	—	Sovereign. Gold. Victoria, large head.	—
Pn104	1837	—	Sovereign. Gold. Wide spaced letter. Victoria.	—
PnA105	1838	—	3 Pence. Gold. KM#730.	2,500
Pn105	1838	—	Sovereign. Gold. Victoria.	—
PnA106	1839	300	1/2 Farthing. Bronzed Copper. KM#738.	—
PnB106	1839	—	Farthing. Silver. KM#725.	—
Pn106	1839	—	5 Pounds. Gold. Victoria. Plain mantle.	92,500
Pn107	1839	—	5 Pounds. Gold. Victoria. Garter star on mantle.	—
Pn108	1839	—	5 Pounds. Gold. Plain edge. Victoria.	—
Pn109	1839	—	5 Pounds. Silver. Lettered edge. Victoria.	—
Pn110	1839	—	5 Pounds. Copper. Victoria.	—
PnA111	1841	—	1/2 Penny. Silver. KM#726.	—
PnB111	1841	—	Penny. Silver. KM#739.	—
PnC111	1843	—	Sovereign. Gold. Victoria. KM#736.	3,500
PnD111	1847	—	Crown. Gold. Plain edge. KM#741.	—
Pn111	1848	—	Florin. 0.9250 Silver.	1,000
PnA112	1848	—	Florin. Gold. KM#745.	10,000
PnB112	1853	—	1/2 Farthing. Bronzed Copper. KM#738.	—
Pn112	1853	—	5 Shilling. Gold. Victoria.	—
Pn113	1853	—	1/4 Sovereign. Gold. Victoria.	2,500
PnA114	1860	—	Penny. Copper. KM#749.2. L.C.W. on truncation.	300
PnB114	1860	—	Penny. Silver. KM#749.2.	2,500
PnC114	1860	—	Penny. Gold. KM#749.2.	—
PnD114	1861	—	Farthing. Silver. KM#747.2.	1,200
PnE114	1861	—	Farthing. Gold. KM#747.2.	—
PnF114	1861	—	1/2 Penny. Silver. KM#748.2.	1,250
PnG114	1861	—	1/2 Penny. Copper-Nickel. KM#748.2.	650
PnH114	1861	—	1/2 Penny. Aluminum-Bronze. KM#748.2.	750
PnJ114	1861	—	1/2 Penny. Gold. KM#748.2.	—
PnK114	1861	—	1/2 Penny. Brass. KM#748.2.	—
PnL114	1861	—	Penny. Copper. KM#749.2. L.C. WYON below truncation, .C.W. below shield.	375
PnM114	1861	—	Penny. Silver. KM#749.2.	3,000
PnN114	1861	—	Penny. Gold. KM#749.2.	—
Pn114	1864	—	Sovereign. Gold. Victoria.	—
PnA115	ND(1865)	—	Shilling. Silver. Victoria. Legend: REGINA.	—

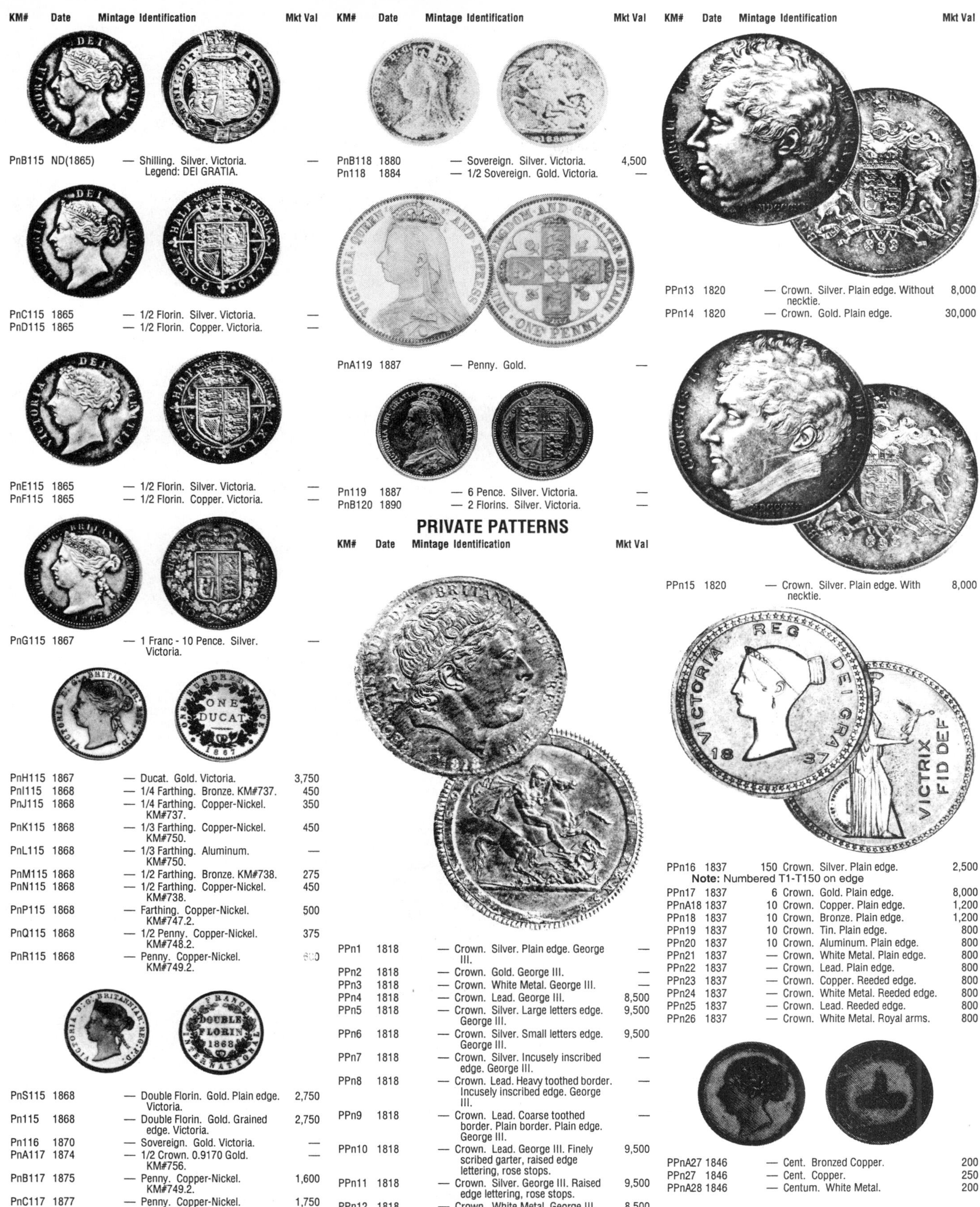

KM#	Date	Mintage	Identification	Mkt Val
PnB115	ND(1865)	—	Shilling. Silver. Victoria. Legend: DEI GRATIA.	—
PnC115	1865	—	1/2 Florin. Silver. Victoria.	—
PnD115	1865	—	1/2 Florin. Copper. Victoria.	—
PnE115	1865	—	1/2 Florin. Silver. Victoria.	—
PnF115	1865	—	1/2 Florin. Copper. Victoria.	—
PnG115	1867	—	1 Franc - 10 Pence. Silver. Victoria.	—
PnH115	1867	—	Ducat. Gold. Victoria.	3,750
PnI115	1868	—	1/4 Farthing. Bronze. KM#737.	450
PnJ115	1868	—	1/4 Farthing. Copper-Nickel. KM#737.	350
PnK115	1868	—	1/3 Farthing. Copper-Nickel. KM#750.	450
PnL115	1868	—	1/3 Farthing. Aluminum. KM#750.	—
PnM115	1868	—	1/2 Farthing. Bronze. KM#738.	275
PnN115	1868	—	1/2 Farthing. Copper-Nickel. KM#738.	450
PnP115	1868	—	Farthing. Copper-Nickel. KM#747.2.	500
PnQ115	1868	—	1/2 Penny. Copper-Nickel. KM#748.2.	375
PnR115	1868	—	Penny. Copper-Nickel. KM#749.2.	600
PnS115	1868	—	Double Florin. Gold. Plain edge. Victoria.	2,750
Pn115	1868	—	Double Florin. Gold. Grained edge. Victoria.	2,750
Pn116	1870	—	Sovereign. Gold. Victoria.	—
PnA117	1874	—	1/2 Crown. 0.9170 Gold. KM#756.	—
PnB117	1875	—	Penny. Copper-Nickel. KM#749.2.	1,600
PnC117	1877	—	Penny. Copper-Nickel. KM#749.2.	1,750
Pn117	1880	—	1/2 Sovereign. Gold. Victoria.	—
PnA118	1880	—	1/2 Sovereign. Silver. Victoria.	2,150
PnB118	1880	—	Sovereign. Silver. Victoria.	4,500
Pn118	1884	—	1/2 Sovereign. Gold. Victoria.	—
PnA119	1887	—	Penny. Gold.	—
Pn119	1887	—	6 Pence. Silver. Victoria.	—
PnB120	1890	—	2 Florins. Silver. Victoria.	—

PRIVATE PATTERNS

KM#	Date	Mintage	Identification	Mkt Val
PPn1	1818	—	Crown. Silver. Plain edge. George III.	—
PPn2	1818	—	Crown. Gold. George III.	—
PPn3	1818	—	Crown. White Metal. George III.	—
PPn4	1818	—	Crown. Lead. George III.	8,500
PPn5	1818	—	Crown. Silver. Large letters edge. George III.	9,500
PPn6	1818	—	Crown. Silver. Small letters edge. George III.	9,500
PPn7	1818	—	Crown. Silver. Incusely inscribed edge. George III.	—
PPn8	1818	—	Crown. Lead. Heavy toothed border. Incusely inscribed edge. George III.	—
PPn9	1818	—	Crown. Lead. Coarse toothed border. Plain border. Plain edge. George III.	—
PPn10	1818	—	Crown. Lead. George III. Finely scribed garter, raised edge lettering, rose stops.	9,500
PPn11	1818	—	Crown. Silver. George III. Raised edge lettering, rose stops.	9,500
PPn12	1818	—	Crown. White Metal. George III.	8,500
PPn13	1820	—	Crown. Silver. Plain edge. Without necktie.	8,000
PPn14	1820	—	Crown. Gold. Plain edge.	30,000
PPn15	1820	—	Crown. Silver. Plain edge. With necktie.	8,000
PPn16	1837	150	Crown. Silver. Plain edge. **Note:** Numbered T1-T150 on edge	2,500
PPn17	1837	6	Crown. Gold. Plain edge.	8,000
PPnA18	1837	10	Crown. Copper. Plain edge.	1,200
PPn18	1837	10	Crown. Bronze. Plain edge.	1,200
PPn19	1837	10	Crown. Tin. Plain edge.	800
PPn20	1837	10	Crown. Aluminum. Plain edge.	800
PPn21	1837	—	Crown. White Metal. Plain edge.	800
PPn22	1837	—	Crown. Lead. Plain edge.	800
PPn23	1837	—	Crown. Copper. Reeded edge.	800
PPn24	1837	—	Crown. White Metal. Reeded edge.	800
PPn25	1837	—	Crown. Lead. Reeded edge.	800
PPn26	1837	—	Crown. White Metal. Royal arms.	800
PPnA27	1846	—	Cent. Bronzed Copper.	200
PPn27	1846	—	Cent. Copper.	250
PPnA28	1846	—	Centum. White Metal.	200

KM#	Date	Mintage	Identification	Mkt Val
PPn28	1846	—	Centum. Copper.	250
PPn29	1846	—	2 Cents. Copper.	250
PPnA29	1846	—	2 Cents. Bronzed Copper.	200
PPn30	1846	—	2 Cents. White Metal.	200
PPn31	1846	—	2 Cents. Silver.	600
PPn32	1846	—	2 Cents. Gold.	2,000
PPn33	1846	—	5 Cents. Copper.	350
PPn34	1846	—	5 Cents. Bronzed Copper.	350
PPn35	1846	—	10 Cents. Copper.	550
PPn36	1846	—	10 Cents. White Metal.	550
PPn37	1846	—	10 Cents. Copper.	400
PPn38	1846	—	10 Cents. Bronzed Copper.	450
PPn39	1846	—	10 Cents. Silver.	1,000
PPn40	1860	—	Farthing. Copper. Milled edge.	350
PPn41	1860	—	Farthing. Bronzed Copper. Milled edge.	350
PPn42	1860	—	Farthing. Aluminum. Milled edge.	300
PPn43	1860	—	Farthing. Silver. Milled edge.	500
PPn44	1860	—	Farthing. Gold. Milled edge.	2,000
PPn45	1860	—	Farthing. Copper. Plain edge.	350
PPn46	1860	—	Farthing. Bronzed Copper. Plain edge.	350
PPn47	1860	—	Farthing. Aluminum. Plain edge.	300
PPn48	1860	—	Farthing. Silver. Plain edge.	600
PPn49	1860	—	Farthing. Gold. Plain edge.	2,000

KM#	Date	Mintage	Identification	Mkt Val
PPn50	1860	—	1/2 Penny. Copper. Milled edge.	400
PPn51	1860	—	1/2 Penny. Bronzed Copper. Milled edge.	—
PPn52	1860	—	1/2 Penny. Bronzed Copper. Milled edge.	300
PPn53	1860	—	1/2 Penny. Silver. Milled edge.	600
PPn54	1860	—	1/2 Penny. Gold. Milled edge.	2,200
PPn55	1860	—	1/2 Penny. Copper. Plain edge.	400
PPn56	1860	—	1/2 Penny. Bronzed Copper. Plain edge.	400
PPn57	1860	—	1/2 Penny. Aluminum. Plain edge.	300
PPn58	1860	—	1/2 Penny. Silver. Plain edge.	600
PPn59	1860	—	1/2 Penny. Gold. Plain edge.	2,200
PPn60	1860	—	Penny. Copper. Milled edge.	450
PPn61	1860	—	Penny. Bronzed Copper. Milled edge.	450
PPn62	1860	—	Penny. Aluminum. Milled edge.	350
PPn63	1860	—	Penny. Silver. Milled edge.	900
PPn64	1860	—	Penny. Gold. Milled edge.	3,500
PPn65	1860	—	Penny. Copper. Plain edge.	450
PPn66	1860	—	Penny. Bronzed Copper. Plain edge.	450
PPn67	1860	—	Penny. Aluminum. Plain edge.	350
PPn68	1860	—	Penny. Silver. Plain edge.	900
PPn69	1860	—	Penny. Gold. Plain edge.	3,500
PPn70	1887	—	Farthing. Copper. Milled edge.	350
PPn71	1887	—	Farthing. Bronzed Copper. Milled edge.	350
PPn72	1887	—	Farthing. Aluminum. Milled edge.	300
PPn73	1887	—	Farthing. Silver. Milled edge.	600
PPn74	1887	—	Farthing. Gold. Milled edge.	1,800
PPn75	1887	—	Farthing. Copper. Plain edge.	350
PPn76	1887	—	Farthing. Bronzed Copper. Plain edge.	350
PPn77	1887	—	Farthing. Aluminum. Plain edge.	300
PPn78	1887	—	Farthing. Silver. Plain edge.	600
PPn79	1887	—	Farthing. Gold. Plain edge.	1,800
PPn80	1887	—	1/2 Penny. Copper. Milled edge.	400
PPn81	1887	—	1/2 Penny. Bronzed Copper. Milled edge.	400
PPn82	1887	—	1/2 Penny. Aluminum. Milled edge.	300
PPn83	1887	—	1/2 Penny. Silver. Milled edge.	800
PPn84	1887	—	1/2 Penny. Gold. Milled edge.	3,000
PPn85	1887	—	1/2 Penny. Gold. Plain edge.	400
PPn86	1887	—	1/2 Penny. Bronzed Copper. Plain edge.	400
PPn87	1887	—	1/2 Penny. Aluminum. Plain edge.	300
PPn88	1887	—	1/2 Penny. Silver. Plain edge.	800
PPn89	1887	—	1/2 Penny. Gold. Plain edge.	3,000
PPn90	1887	—	Penny. Copper. Milled edge.	450
PPn91	1887	—	Penny. Bronzed Copper. Milled edge.	450
PPn92	1887	—	Penny. Aluminum. Milled edge.	350
PPn93	1887	—	Penny. Silver. Milled edge.	400
PPn94	1887	—	Penny. Gold. Milled edge.	3,500
PPn95	1887	—	Penny. Copper. Plain edge.	450
PPn96	1887	—	Penny. Bronzed Copper. Plain edge.	450
PPn97	1887	—	Penny. Aluminum. Plain edge.	350
PPn98	1887	—	Penny. Silver. Plain edge.	900
PPn99	1887	—	Penny. Gold. Plain edge.	3,500

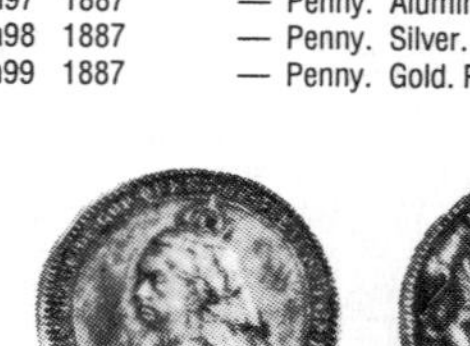

KM#	Date	Mintage	Identification	Mkt Val
PPn100	1887	64	6 Pence. Silver. Plain edge.	500
PPn101	1887	15	6 Pence. Gold.	1,600
PPn102	1887	10	6 Pence. Copper.	350
PPn103	1887	20	6 Pence. Aluminum.	250
PPn104	1887	9	6 Pence. Tin.	250
PPn105	1887	—	Crown. Silver. Plain edge. J.R.T. on truncation.	1,750
PPn106	1887	32	Crown. Silver. SPINK & SON on truncation.	1,750
PPn107	1887	—	Crown. Silver. Without signature.	1,750
PPn108	1887	—	Crown. Silver. SPINK & SON at bottom.	1,750
PPn109	1887	6	Crown. Gold. Plain edge.	6,000
PPn110	1887	5	Crown. Copper. Plain edge.	1,350
PPn111	1887	10	Crown. Aluminum. Plain edge.	1,250
PPn112	1887	—	Crown. Pewter. Plain edge.	1,250
PPn113	1887	—	Crown. Lead. Plain edge.	850
PPn114	1887	—	Crown. Silver. Reeded edge.	1,700
PPn115	1887	6	Crown. Gold. Reeded edge.	6,000
PPn116	1887	—	Crown. Copper.	1,300
PPn117	1887	—	Crown. Pewter.	1,200
PPn118	1887	—	Crown. Aluminum.	1,200

MAUNDY SETS

KM#	Date	Mintage	Identification	Issue Price	Mkt Val
MDS63	1817 (4)	1,584	KM#668-671	—	300
MDS64	1818 (4)	1,188	KM#668-671	—	300
MDS65	1820 (4)	1,584	KM#668-671	—	300
MDS66	1822 (4)	2,970	KM#683, 684, 685.1, 686	—	200
MDS67	1822 (4)	—	KM#683,684, 685.1, 686	—	345
MDS68	1823 (4)	1,980	KM#683,684, 685.2, 686	—	200
MDS69	1824 (4)	1,584	KM#683,684, 685.2, 686	—	200
MDS70	1825 (4)	2,376	KM#683,684, 685.2, 686	—	200
MDS71	1826 (4)	2,376	KM#683,684, 685.2, 686	—	200
MDS72	1826 (4)	—	KM#683,684, 685.2, 686	—	345
MDS73	1827 (4)	2,772	KM#683,684, 685.2, 686	—	200
MDS74	1828 (4)	2,772	KM#683, 684, 685.2, 686	—	200
MDS75	1828 (4)	—	KM#683, 684, 685.2, 686 Proof	—	345
MDS76	1829 (4)	2,772	KM#683, 684, 685.2, 686	—	200
MDS77	1830 (4)	2,772	KM#683, 684, 685.2, 686	—	200
MDS78	1831 (4)	3,564	KM#708-711	—	300
MDS79	1831 (4)	—	KM#708-711 Proof	—	500
MDS80	1832 (4)	2,574	KM#708-711	—	200
MDS81	1833 (4)	2,574	KM#708-711	—	200
MDS82	1834 (4)	2,574	KM#708-711	—	200
MDS83	1835 (4)	2,574	KM#708-711	—	200
MDS84	1836 (4)	2,574	KM#708-711	—	300
MDS85	1837 (4)	2,574	KM#708-711	—	300
MDS86	1838 (4)	4,158	KM#727, 729-730, 732	—	175
MDS87	1838 (4)	—	KM#727, 729-730, 732	—	700
MDS88	1839 (4)	4,125	KM#727, 729-730, 732	—	200
MDS89	1839 (4)	300	KM#727, 729-730, 732 Proof	—	400
MDS90	1840 (4)	4,125	KM#727, 729-730, 732	—	200
MDS91	1841 (4)	2,574	KM#727, 729-730, 732	—	225
MDS92	1842 (4)	4,125	KM#727, 729-730, 732	—	200
MDS93	1843 (4)	4,158	KM#727, 729-730, 732	—	200
MDS94	1844 (4)	4,158	KM#727, 729-730, 732	—	200
MDS95	1845 (4)	4,158	KM#727, 729-730, 732	—	175
MDS96	1846 (4)	4,158	KM#727, 729-730, 732	—	225
MDS97	1847 (4)	4,158	KM#727, 729-730, 732	—	200
MDS98	1848 (4)	4,158	KM#727, 729-730, 732	—	200

KM#	Date	Mintage	Identification	Issue Price	Mkt Val
MDS99	1849 (4)	4,158	KM#727, 729-730, 732	—	225
MDS100	1850 (4)	4,158	KM#727, 729-730, 732	—	150
MDS101	1851 (4)	4,158	KM#727, 729-730, 732	—	150
MDS102	1852 (4)	4,158	KM#727, 729-730, 732	—	175
MDS103	1853 (4)	4,158	KM#727, 729-730, 732	—	175
MDS104	1853 (4)	—	KM#727, 729-730, 732 Proof	—	750
MDS105	1854 (4)	4,158	KM#727, 729-730, 732	—	175
MDS106	1855 (4)	4,158	KM#727, 729-730, 732	—	175
MDS107	1856 (4)	4,158	KM#727, 729-730, 732	—	150
MDS108	1857 (4)	4,158	KM#727, 729-730, 732	—	150
MDS109	1858 (4)	4,158	KM#727, 729-730, 732	—	150
MDS110	1859 (4)	4,158	KM#727, 729-730, 732	—	150
MDS111	1860 (4)	4,158	KM#727, 729-730, 732	—	150
MDS112	1861 (4)	4,158	KM#727, 729-730, 732	—	150
MDS113	1862 (4)	4,158	KM#727, 729-730, 732	—	150
MDS114	1863 (4)	4,158	KM#727, 729-730, 732	—	150
MDS115	1864 (4)	4,158	KM#727, 729-730, 732	—	150
MDS116	1865 (4)	4,158	KM#727, 729-730, 732	—	150
MDS117	1866 (4)	4,158	KM#727, 729-730, 732	—	150
MDS118	1867 (4)	4,158	KM#727, 729-730, 732	—	150
MDS119	1867 (4)	—	KM#727, 729-730, 732 Proof	—	300
MDS120	1868 (4)	4,158	KM#727, 729-730, 732	—	150
MDS121	1869 (4)	4,158	KM#727, 729-730, 732	—	150
MDS122	1870 (4)	4,488	KM#727, 729-730, 732	—	150
MDS123	1871	4,488	KM#727, 729-730, 732	—	150
MDS124	1871 (4)	—	KM#727, 729-730, 732 Proof	—	300
MDS125	1872 (4)	4,328	KM#727, 729-730, 732	—	150
MDS126	1873 (4)	4,162	KM#727, 729-730, 732	—	150
MDS127	1874 (4)	4,488	KM#727, 729-730, 732	—	150
MDS128	1875 (4)	4,154	KM#727, 729-730, 732	—	150
MDS129	1876 (4)	4,488	KM#727, 729-730, 732	—	150
MDS130	1877 (4)	4,488	KM#727, 729-730, 732	—	150
MDS131	1878 (4)	4,488	KM#727, 729-730, 732	—	150
MDS132	1878 (4)	—	KM#727, 729-730, 732 Proof	—	300
MDS133	1879 (4)	4,488	KM#727, 729-730, 732	—	150
MDS134	1880 (4)	4,488	KM#727, 729-730, 732	—	150
MDS135	1881 (4)	4,488	KM#727, 729-730, 732	—	150
MDS136	1881 (4)	—	KM#727, 729-730, 732 Proof	—	350
MDS137	1882 (4)	4,488	KM#727, 729-730, 732	—	150
MDS138	1883 (4)	4,488	KM#727, 729-730, 732	—	150
MDS139	1884 (4)	4,488	KM#727, 729-730, 732	—	150
MDS140	1885 (4)	4,488	KM#727, 729-730, 732	—	150
MDS141	1886 (4)	4,488	KM#727, 729-730, 732	—	150
MDS142	1887 (4)	4,488	KM#727, 729-730, 732	—	150
MDS143	1888 (4)	4,488	KM#758, 770-771, 773	—	125
MDS144	1889 (4)	4,488	KM#758, 770-771, 773	—	125
MDS145	1889 (4)	—	KM#758, 770-771, 773 Proof	—	200
MDS146	1890 (4)	4,488	KM#758, 770-771, 773	—	125
MDS147	1891 (4)	4,488	KM#758, 770-771, 773	—	125
MDS148	1892 (4)	4,488	KM#758, 770-771, 773	—	125
MDS149	1893 (4)	8,976	KM#775-778	—	100
MDS150	1894 (4)	8,976	KM#775-778	—	100
MDS151	1895 (4)	8,877	KM#775-778	—	100
MDS152	1896 (4)	8,476	KM#775-778	—	100
MDS153	1897 (4)	9,388	KM#775-778	—	100
MDS154	1898 (4)	9,147	KM#775-778	—	100
MDS155	1899 (4)	8,976	KM#775-778	—	100
MDS156	1900 (4)	8,976	KM#775-778	—	100
MDS157	1901 (4)	8,976	KM#775-778	—	80.00

PROOF SETS

KM#	Date	Mintage	Identification	Issue Price	Mkt Val
PS1	1821 (6)	5	KM#677-680, 681.1, 682 Rare	—	—
PS2	1826 (15)	150	KM#683-684, 685.2, 686, 691, 692a, 693a, 694-695, 697a, 699-702	—	35,000
PS3	1826 (11)	Inc. Above	KM#691, 692a, 693a, 694-696, 697a, 700-702	—	30,000
PS4	1831 (14)	225	KM#705, 706a, 707a, 709-713, 714.1, 716-718, 720, 835	—	26,500
PS5	1839 (15)	300	KM#725a-726a, 727, 729-730, 731.2, 732-736, 739a, 740-742	—	47,000
PS6	1839/48 (16)	Inc. Above	KM#725a-726a, 727, 729, 730,731.2, 732-736, 739a, 740-742, 745	—	47,000
PS7	1853 (17)	—	KM#725a-726a, 727, 729-730, 731.2, 732-736, 737a, 739a, 740a, 744, 746	—	35,000
PS8	1853 (16)	Inc. Above	KM#725a, 726a, 727, 729-730, 731.2, 732-736, 737a, 739a, 740a, 744, 746	—	33,500
PS9	1887 (11)	797	KM#758-759, 761-769	—	10,000
PS10	1887 (11)	Inc. Above	KM#758-762, 764-769	—	10,000
PS11	1887 (7)	287	KM#758-759, 761-765	—	1,500
PS12	1887 (7)	Inc. Above	KM#758-762, 764-765	—	1,500
PS13	1893 (10)	773	KM#777, 779-787	—	10,000
PS14	1893 (6)	556	KM#777, 779-783	—	1,800

The Hellenic (Greek) Republic is situated in southeastern Europe on the southern tip of the Balkan Peninsula. The republic includes many islands, the most important of which are Crete and the Ionian Islands.

Greece, the Mother of Western civilization, attained the peak of its culture in the 5th century B.C., when it contributed more to government, drama, art and architecture than any other people to this time. Greece fell under Roman domination in the 2nd and 1st centuries B.C., becoming part of the Byzantine Empire until Constantinople fell to the Crusaders in 1202. With the fall of Constantinople to the Turks in 1453, Greece became part of the Ottoman Empire. Independence from Turkey was won with the revolution of 1821-27. In 1833, Greece was established as a monarchy, with sovereignty guaranteed by Britain, France and Russia. After a lengthy power struggle between the monarchist forces and democratic factions, Greece was proclaimed a republic in 1925.

RULERS

John Capodistrias, 1828-1831
Othon (Otto of Bavaria), 1832-1862
George I, 1863-1913

MINT MARKS

(a) - Paris, privy marks only
A - Paris
B - Vienna
BB - Strassburg
(c) - Aegina (1828-1832), Chain and anchor
H - Heaton, Birmingham
K - Bordeaux
KN - King's Norton
(o) - Athens (1838-1855), Owl
(p) - Poissy - Thunderbolt

MONETARY SYSTEM

Until 1831
100 Lepta = 1 Phoenix
Commencing 1831
100 Lepta = 1 Drachma

KINGDOM

DECIMAL COINAGE

KM# 1 LEPTON

Copper **Obv:** Phoenix in solid circle

Date	Mintage	F	VF	XF	Unc	BU
1828	480,000	50.00	100	250	500	—
1830	26,000	60.00	120	275	700	—

KM# 5 LEPTON

Copper **Obv:** Phoenix in pearl circle

Date	Mintage	F	VF	XF	Unc	BU
1830	400,000	50.00	100	250	600	—

KM# 9 LEPTON

Copper **Obv:** Without circle

Date	Mintage	F	VF	XF	Unc	BU
1831	612,000	50.00	100	250	600	—

KM# 13 LEPTON Type 1 — ΒΑΣΙΛΕΙΑ

Copper

Date	Mintage	F	VF	XF	Unc	BU
1832	2,200,000	50.00	100	250	600	—
1833	Inc. above	20.00	35.00	65.00	150	—
1834	Inc. above	50.00	100	300	950	—
1837	160,000	25.00	50.00	150	500	—
1838	270,000	25.00	50.00	150	500	—
1839	150,000	25.00	50.00	150	500	—
1840	700,000	25.00	50.00	150	500	—
1841	370,000	25.00	50.00	150	500	—
1842	120,000	25.00	50.00	150	500	—
1843	630,000	25.00	50.00	150	500	—

KM# 22 LEPTON Type 2 — ΒΑΣΙΛΕΙΟΝ

Copper

Date	Mintage	F	VF	XF	Unc	BU
1844	151,000	30.00	75.00	175	650	—
1845	160,000	30.00	75.00	175	650	—
1846	141,000	30.00	75.00	175	650	—

KM# 26 LEPTON

Copper **Obv:** Smaller crowned arms **Rev:** Redesigned wreath

Date	Mintage	F	VF	XF	Unc	BU
1847	273,000	70.00	120	300	950	—
1848	84,000	50.00	100	200	700	—
1849	90,000	50.00	100	200	700	—

KM# 30 LEPTON

Copper **Note:** Size reduced.

Date	Mintage	F	VF	XF	Unc	BU
1851	400,000	22.00	45.00	100	400	—
1857	243,000	22.00	45.00	100	400	—

KM# 40 LEPTON

Copper

Date	Mintage	F	VF	XF	Unc	BU
1869BB	14,976,000	4.00	10.00	25.00	75.00	—
1870BB	Inc. above	10.00	25.00	75.00	200	—

KM# 52 LEPTON

Copper

Date	Mintage	F	VF	XF	Unc	BU
1878K	7,132,000	4.00	10.00	25.00	75.00	—
1879A	398,000	5.00	12.00	50.00	150	—

KM# 14 2 LEPTA Type 1 — ΒΑΣΙΛΕΙΑ

Copper

Date	Mintage	F	VF	XF	Unc	BU
1832	2,475,000	35.00	75.00	200	600	—
1833	Inc. above	15.00	30.00	60.00	125	—
1834	Inc. above	50.00	100	250	650	—
1836	49,000	200	400	800	1,500	—
1837	222,000	25.00	50.00	125	450	—
1838	701,000	25.00	50.00	125	450	—
1839	661,000	25.00	50.00	125	450	—
1840	520,000	25.00	50.00	125	450	—
1842	470,000	25.00	50.00	125	450	—

KM# 23 2 LEPTA Type 2 — ΒΑΣΙΛΕΙΟΝ

Copper

Date	Mintage	F	VF	XF	Unc	BU
1844	206,000	45.00	85.00	225	650	—
1845	242,000	45.00	85.00	225	650	—

KM# 27 2 LEPTA

Copper **Obv:** Smaller crowned arms **Rev:** Redesigned wreath

Date	Mintage	F	VF	XF	Unc	BU
1847	82,000	50.00	150	300	850	—
1848	258,000	25.00	50.00	120	575	—
1849	146,000	35.00	75.00	200	600	—

KM# 31 2 LEPTA

Copper **Note:** Size reduced.

Date	Mintage	F	VF	XF	Unc	BU
1851	388,000	20.00	40.00	100	350	—
1857	544,000	20.00	40.00	100	350	—

KM# 41 2 LEPTA
Copper

Date	Mintage	F	VF	XF	Unc	BU
1869BB	7,482,000	3.00	6.00	18.00	65.00	—
1869BB Proof	—	Value: 220				

KM# 53 2 LEPTA
Copper

Date	Mintage	F	VF	XF	Unc	BU
1878K Large anchor	3,750,000	1.50	3.50	12.00	50.00	—
1878K Small anchor	Inc. above	10.00	25.00	40.00	85.00	—
1878K Proof	—	Value: 220				

KM# 2 5 LEPTA
Copper **Obv:** Phoenix in solid circle

Date	Mintage	F	VF	XF	Unc	BU
1828	400,000	50.00	100	200	600	—
1830	22,000	75.00	150	400	800	—

KM# 6 5 LEPTA
Copper **Obv:** Phoenix in pearl circle

Date	Mintage	F	VF	XF	Unc	BU
1830	150,000	65.00	125	225	600	—

KM# 10 5 LEPTA
Copper **Obv:** Without circle

Date	Mintage	F	VF	XF	Unc	BU
1831	230,000	45.00	100	225	600	—

KM# 16 5 LEPTA
Copper **Note:** Set specia Type 1 — ΒΑΣΙΛΕΙΑ

Date	Mintage	F	VF	XF	Unc	BU
1833	2,500,000	15.00	30.00	70.00	150	—
1834	Inc. above	50.00	100	250	650	—
1836	1,000	400	800	1,500	3,000	—
1837	116,000	50.00	100	225	500	—
1838/7	1,472,000	25.00	65.00	200	450	—
1838	Inc. above	25.00	50.00	175	400	—
1839	1,186,000	25.00	50.00	175	400	—
1840	417,000	25.00	50.00	175	400	—
1841	864,000	25.00	50.00	175	400	—
1842	682,000	25.00	50.00	175	400	—

KM# 24 5 LEPTA
Copper Type 2 — ΒΑΣΙΛΕΙΟΝ

Date	Mintage	F	VF	XF	Unc	BU
1844	89,000	50.00	100	200	600	—
1845	316,000	40.00	80.00	200	500	—
1846	190,000	40.00	60.00	175	450	—

KM# 28 5 LEPTA
Copper

Date	Mintage	F	VF	XF	Unc	BU
1847	270,000	50.00	100	200	500	—
1848	394,000	40.00	80.00	200	450	—
1849	374,000	40.00	60.00	175	400	—

KM# 32 5 LEPTA
Copper

Date	Mintage	F	VF	XF	Unc	BU
1851	620,000	25.00	50.00	100	350	—
1857	350,000	25.00	50.00	100	350	—

KM# 42 5 LEPTA
Copper

Date	Mintage	F	VF	XF	Unc	BU
1869BB	23,945,000	2.00	5.00	20.00	85.00	—
1870BB	Inc. above	18.00	35.00	90.00	275	—

KM# 54 5 LEPTA
Copper

Date	Mintage	F	VF	XF	Unc	BU
1878K	11,528,000	2.00	6.00	30.00	80.00	—
1879A	470,000	20.00	50.00	150	900	—
1882A	14,400,000	3.00	7.00	40.00	135	—

KM# 58 5 LEPTA
Copper-Nickel

Date	Mintage	F	VF	XF	Unc	BU
1894A	4,000,000	2.00	5.00	20.00	65.00	—
1895A	4,000,000	2.00	5.00	20.00	65.00	—

KM# 3 10 LEPTA
Copper **Obv:** Phoenix in solid circle

Date	Mintage	F	VF	XF	Unc	BU
1828	450,000	50.00	100	300	700	—
1830	34,000	70.00	150	400	900	—

KM# 8 10 LEPTA
Copper **Obv:** Phoenix in pearl circle

Date	Mintage	F	VF	XF	Unc	BU
1830	1,200,000	50.00	100	300	800	—

Note: Varieties exist

KM# 12 10 LEPTA
Copper **Obv:** Phoenix without circle

Date	Mintage	F	VF	XF	Unc	BU
1831	1,223,000	50.00	100	250	700	—

KM# 17 10 LEPTA
Copper

Date	Mintage	F	VF	XF	Unc	BU
1833	520,000	25.00	50.00	100	150	—
1836	919,000	40.00	100	200	600	—
1837	2,660,000	40.00	100	200	600	—
1838	918,000	40.00	100	200	600	—
1843	700,000	40.00	100	200	600	—
1844	1,064,000	100	175	400	800	—

KM# 25 10 LEPTA
Copper

Date	Mintage	F	VF	XF	Unc	BU
1844	Inc. above	30.00	60.00	200	750	—
1845	985,000	30.00	60.00	300	800	—
1846/45	1,275,000	30.00	60.00	200	900	—
1846	Inc. above	30.00	60.00	200	700	—

KM# 29 10 LEPTA
Copper

Date	Mintage	F	VF	XF	Unc	BU
1847	740,000	50.00	100	300	950	—
1848	1,174,000	40.00	80.00	175	550	—
1849/8 Small crown	1,160,000	40.00	80.00	175	550	—
1849 Small crown	Inc. above	40.00	80.00	175	550	—
1849 Large crown	Inc. above	200	400	700	1,500	—
1850	1,282,000	40.00	80.00	150	450	—
1851	587,000	40.00	80.00	150	450	—
1857	883,000	40.00	80.00	150	450	—

KM# 43 10 LEPTA
Center Composition: Copper

Date	Mintage	F	VF	XF	Unc	BU
1869BB	14,994,000	3.00	7.00	30.00	100	—
1869BB Proof	—	Value: 250				
1870BB	Inc. above	15.00	30.00	90.00	350	—

KM# 55 10 LEPTA
Copper

Date	Mintage	F	VF	XF	Unc	BU
1878K	7,140,000	2.00	6.00	28.00	100	—
1879A	358,000	20.00	60.00	175	950	—
1882A	16,000,000	2.00	6.00	35.00	275	—

KM# 59 10 LEPTA
Copper-Nickel

Date	Mintage	F	VF	XF	Unc	BU
1894A	3,000,000	2.00	5.00	20.00	65.00	—
1895A	3,000,000	2.00	5.00	20.00	65.00	—

KM# 11 20 LEPTA
Copper

Date	Mintage	F	VF	XF	Unc	BU
1831	2,273,000	50.00	100	350	950	—

KM# 44 20 LEPTA
1.0000 g., 0.8350 Silver .0268 oz.

Date	Mintage	F	VF	XF	Unc	BU
1874A	2,223,000	3.00	6.00	18.00	50.00	—
1874A Proof	—	Value: 400				
1883A	1,000,000	10.00	25.00	55.00	150	—

KM# 57 20 LEPTA
Copper-Nickel

Date	Mintage	F	VF	XF	Unc	BU
1893A	248,000	25.00	75.00	150	700	—
1894A	4,752,000	1.50	3.00	10.00	65.00	—
1895A	5,000,000	1.50	3.00	10.00	65.00	—

KM# 37 50 LEPTA
2.5000 g., 0.8350 Silver .0671 oz.

Date	Mintage	F	VF	XF	Unc	BU
1868A	60	—	—	—	6,000	—
1874A	4,501,000	3.00	7.00	20.00	50.00	—
1874A Proof	—	Value: 400				
1883A	600,000	5.00	12.00	35.00	120	—

KM# 4 PHOENIX
3.8700 g., 0.9430 Silver .1173 oz.

Date	Mintage	F	VF	XF	Unc	BU
1828(c)	12,000	250	400	1,000	2,000	—

KM# 18 1/4 DRACHMA
1.1190 g., 0.9000 Silver .0324 oz. **Obv:** Young head right

Date	Mintage	F	VF	XF	Unc	BU
1833	780,000	35.00	65.00	125	300	—
1834A	—	45.00	90.00	175	500	—
1845	—	300	500	1,500	4,000	—
1846	—	400	800	2,000	5,000	—

KM# 33 1/4 DRACHMA
1.1190 g., 0.9000 Silver .0324 oz. **Obv:** Old head left, 15mm

Date	Mintage	F	VF	XF	Unc	BU
1851	—	300	600	1,250	3,000	—
1855	—	100	200	500	1,000	—

KM# 19 1/2 DRACHMA
2.2380 g., 0.9000 Silver .0648 oz.

Date	Mintage	F	VF	XF	Unc	BU
1833	900,000	25.00	50.00	100	250	—
1834A	—	45.00	90.00	160	450	—
1842(o)	—	250	500	1,200	2,500	—
1843(o)	—	300	600	1,400	3,000	—
1846	—	250	500	1,200	2,500	—
1847	—	300	600	1,400	3,000	—

KM# 34 1/2 DRACHMA
2.2380 g., 0.9000 Silver .0648 oz. **Obv. Legend:** Old head left

Date	Mintage	F	VF	XF	Unc	BU
1851	—	250	550	1,150	3,000	—
1855	—	100	200	500	1,500	—

KM# 15 DRACHMA
4.0293 g., 0.9000 Silver .1295 oz. **Obv:** Young head right

Date	Mintage	F	VF	XF	Unc	BU
1832	1,125,000	50.00	100	200	650	—
1833	Inc. above	25.00	50.00	100	400	—
1833 Proof	—	Value: 1,000				
1833A	—	50.00	100	250	600	—
1833A Proof	—	Value: 1,000				
1834A	—	150	300	800	2,000	—
1845(o)	—	1,000	2,000	4,500	13,500	—
1846	—	200	500	1,000	3,000	—
1847	—	700	1,500	3,000	10,000	—

KM# 35 DRACHMA
4.0293 g., 0.9000 Silver .1295 oz. **Obv:** Old head left

Date	Mintage	F	VF	XF	Unc	BU
1851	—	350	750	1,500	3,500	—

KM# 38 DRACHMA
5.0000 g., 0.8350 Silver .1342 oz.

Date	Mintage	F	VF	XF	Unc	BU
1868A	480,000	20.00	45.00	100	350	—
1873A	1,802,000	20.00	40.00	80.00	300	—
1873A Proof	—	Value: 500				
1874A	2,249,000	20.00	45.00	120	400	—
1883A	800,000	20.00	50.00	300	850	—

KM# 39 2 DRACHMAI
10.0000 g., 0.8350 Silver .2684 oz.

Date	Mintage	F	VF	XF	Unc	BU
1868A	47,000	50.00	100	375	900	—
1873A	839,000	40.00	90.00	350	800	—
1873A Proof	—	Value: 1,000				
1883A	250,000	50.00	100	425	1,200	—

KM# 46 5 DRACHMAI
25.0000 g., 0.9000 Silver .7234 oz.

Date	Mintage	F	VF	XF	Unc	BU
1875A	1,000,000	25.00	60.00	225	600	—
1875A	—	150	200	600	2,550	—

Date	Mintage	F	VF	XF	Unc	BU
Note: Inverted anchor privy mark						
1875A Proof	—	Value: 2,000				
1876A	2,092,000	20.00	50.00	200	600	—
1876A Proof	—	Value: 2,000				

KM# 20 5 DRACHMAI

22.5000 g., 0.9000 Silver .6511 oz. **Obv:** Young head right

Date	Mintage	F	VF	XF	Unc	BU
1833	378,000	100	200	450	1,350	—
1833 Proof	—	Value: 3,000				
1833A	—	100	200	450	1,350	—
1833A Proof	—	Value: 3,000				
1833(o)	—	1,200	2,400	6,000	10,000	—
1844(o)	—	300	700	1,500	3,500	—
1845	—	3,000	4,500	6,500	12,000	—

KM# 36 5 DRACHMAI

22.5000 g., 0.9000 Silver .6511 oz. **Obv:** Old head left **Rev:** Similar to KM#20

Date	Mintage	F	VF	XF	Unc	BU
1851	—	500	850	2,500	6,000	—
1851 Proof	—	—	—	—	—	—

KM# 46 5 DRACHMAI

25.0000 g., 0.9000 Silver .7234 oz.

Date	Mintage	F	VF	XF	Unc	BU
1875A	1,000,000	25.00	75.00	350	1,000	1,500
1875A	—	200	400	1,250	2,750	4,000
Note: Inverted anchor privy mark						
1875A Proof	—	Value: 3,500				
1876A	2,092,000	20.00	50.00	300	1,000	1,500
1876A Proof	—	Value: 3,500				

KM# 47 5 DRACHMAI

1.6129 g., 0.9000 Gold .0467 oz.

Date	Mintage	F	VF	XF	Unc	BU
1876A	9,294	200	375	750	1,600	—

KM# 48 10 DRACHMAI

3.2258 g., 0.9000 Gold .0933 oz.

Date	Mintage	F	VF	XF	Unc	BU
1876A	19,000	165	285	500	1,400	—

KM# 21 20 DRACHMAI

5.7760 g., 0.9000 Gold .1672 oz.

Date	Mintage	F	VF	XF	Unc	BU
1833	18,000	175	375	700	1,500	—

KM# 49 20 DRACHMAI

6.4516 g., 0.9000 Gold .1867 oz.

Date	Mintage	F	VF	XF	Unc	BU
1876A	37,000	100	165	325	700	—
1876A Proof	—	Value: 12,000				
Note: Spink Coin Auction no. 109-80 Brilliant F.D.C. realized $12,000.						

KM# 56 20 DRACHMAI

6.4516 g., 0.9000 Gold .1867 oz.

Date	Mintage	F	VF	XF	Unc	BU
1884A	550,000	75.00	100	145	250	—
Note: Spink Coin Auction no. 109-80 Brilliant F.D.C. realized $12,000.						
1884A Proof	—	Value: 3,500				

KM# 50 50 DRACHMAI

16.1290 g., 0.9000 Gold .4667 oz.

Date	Mintage	F	VF	XF	Unc	BU
1876A	182	2,500	3,500	5,000	12,000	—

KM# 51 100 DRACHMAI

32.2580 g., 0.9000 Gold .9335 oz.

Date	Mintage	F	VF	XF	Unc	BU
1876A	76	4,500	7,000	12,000	20,000	—
1876A Proof	—	Value: 30,000				

ESSAIS

KM#	Date	Mintage	Identification	Mkt Val
E1	1868	4	50 Lepta. Silver. E on obverse.	3,500
E2	1868	—	Drachma. Silver. E to left of date.	3,500
E3	1868	3	Drachma. Plain edge. E to left of date.	—
E4	1869	—	Lepton. Copper. ESSAI.	800
E5	1869	—	2 Lepta. Copper. ESSAI.	800
E6	1869	—	5 Lepta. Copper. ESSAI.	1,000
E7	1869	—	10 Lepta. Copper. ESSAI.	1,200
E8	1869	—	20 Lepta. Silver. E (Essai) below date.	3,500
E9	1869	—	5 Drachmai. Gold. E (Essai)	8,250
E10	1869	—	10 Drachmai. Gold. E (Essai)	10,000

KM#	Date	Mintage	Identification	Mkt Val
E11	1869	—	20 Drachmai. Gold. E (Essai)	15,000
E12	1873	—	5 Drachmai. Silver. ESSAI, without mintmark.	8,500
E13	1875	—	5 Drachmai. Silver. ESSAI, without mintmark.	9,000
E14	1875	—	50 Drachmai. Gold. ESSAI	30,000
E15	1875	—	100 Drachmai. Gold. ESSAI	55,000
E16	1876	—	20 Lepta. Copper-Zinc. ESSAI.	800

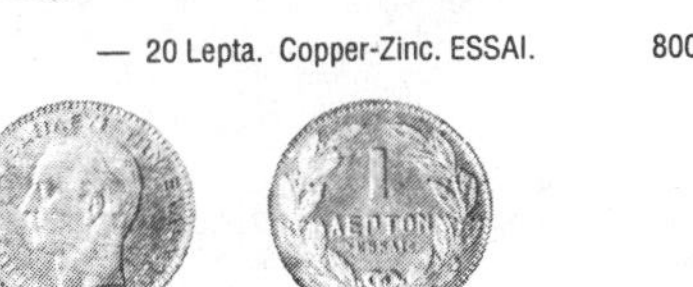

KM#	Date	Mintage	Identification	Mkt Val
E17	1877	—	Lepton. Copper. E. ESSAI. ESSAI.	1,000
E19	1877	—	2 Lepta. Copper. E. ESSAI. ESSAI.	1,000
E21	1877	—	5 Lepta. Copper. ESSAI.	1,600
E22	1877	—	10 Lepta. Copper. ESSAI.	600

PATTERNS

Including off metal strikes

KM#	Date	Mintage	Identification	Mkt Val
Pn1	1828	—	Lepton. Copper. 5 pointed stars, reeded edge.	800
Pn2	1828	—	5 Lepta. Copper. 5 pointed stars.	2,500
Pn3	1828	—	10 Lepta. Copper. 5 pointed stars.	2,500
Pn4	ND	—	Lepton. Copper. Legend in 5 lines.	300
Pn5	ND	—	Lepton. Copper. Legend in 4 lines.	200
Pn6	ND	—	2 Lepta. Copper.	400
Pn7	ND	—	5 Lepta. Copper.	500
Pn8	ND	—	10 Lepta. Copper.	500
Pn12	ND	—	5 Drachmai. Copper.	800
Pn13	1833A	—	5 Drachmai. Tin.	—
Pn19	1842	—	1/2 Drachma. Silver. X below bust.	2,500
Pn20	1845	—	5 Drachmai. Silver. Portrait by Lange.	10,000
Pn22	1847	—	10 Lepta. Copper. Large crown.	800
Pn24	1851	—	Drachma. Silver. Small head.	2,000
Pn25	1852	16	20 Drachmai. Gold. Moustached bust.	30,000

KM#	Date	Mintage	Identification	Mkt Val
Pn26	1852	8	40 Drachmai. Gold. Moustached bust.	40,000
Pn30	ND	—	Drachma. Nickel. Double reverse.	2,400
Pn31	1868	3	2 Drachmai. Silver. Without mintmark.	3,000
Pn32	1868A	—	2 Drachmai. Silver. Without mintmark on reverse.	—
Pn33	ND	—	2 Drachmai. Nickel. Double reverse.	2,000
Pn37	1875	—	20 Drachmai. Gold. Head right.	—
Pn38	1876	—	5 Drachmai. Gold. KM47.	—
PnA39	1876	—	100 Drachmai. Gold. Uniface.	—
Pn39	1889	—	50 Lepta. Nickel.	3,000

TRIAL STRIKES

KM#	Date	Mintage	Identification	Mkt Val
TS1	1832	—	Drachma. Tin. Uniface.	400
TS2	1832	—	Drachma. Tin. Uniface.	400
TS3	1833	—	5 Lepta. Tin. Uniface.	400
TS4	1833	—	1/2 Drachma. Tin. Uniface.	400
TS5	1833	—	1/2 Drachma. Tin. Uniface.	400
TS6	ND	—	20 Drachmai. Copper. Uniface.	500
TS7	1842	—	10 Lepta. Zinc. Uniface, octagonal.	—
TS8	1842	—	10 Lepta. Zinc. Uniface, octagonal.	—
TS9	1842	—	1/4 Drachma. Silver. Uniface.	—
TS10	1842	—	1/4 Drachma. Silver. Uniface.	—
TS11	ND	—	5 Drachmai. Silver. Uniface.	3,000
TS12	1851	—	Drachma. Copper.	600
TS13	ND	—	5 Drachmai. Bronze. Uniface. ESSAI.	3,000
TS14	1875	1	50 Drachmai. Gilt Copper. Uniface.	2,550

KM#	Date	Mintage	Identification	Mkt Val
TS15	ND	1	50 Drachmai. Gilt Copper. Uniface.	2,550

KM#	Date	Mintage	Identification	Mkt Val

TS16	1875	1	100 Drachmai. Gilt Copper. Uniface.	2,650

TS17	ND	1	100 Drachmai. Gilt Copper. Uniface. With Essai.	2,650

GREENLAND

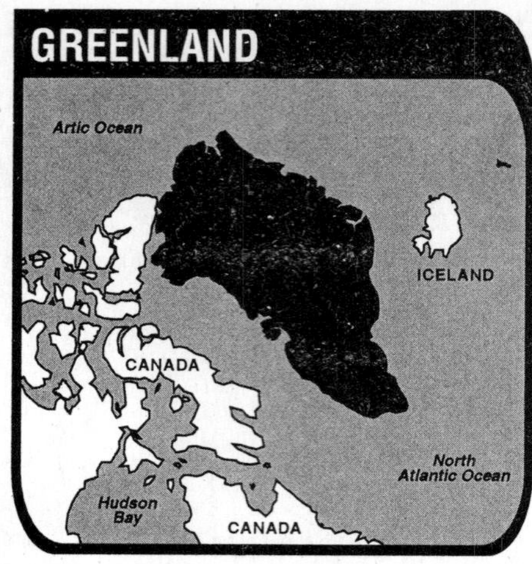

Greenland, an integral part of the Danish realm is situated between the North Atlantic Ocean and the Polar Sea, almost entirely within the Arctic Circle. An island nation, it has an area of 840,000 sq. mi. (2,175,600 sq. km.).

Eric the Red discovered Greenland in 982 and established the first settlement in 986. Greenland was a republic until 1261, when the sovereignty of Norway was extended to the island. The original colony was abandoned about 1400 when increasing cold interfered with the breeding of cattle. Successful recolonization was undertaken by Denmark in 1721. In 1921 Denmark extended its claim to include the entire island, and made it a colony of the crown in 1924. The island's colonial status was abolished by amendment to the Danish constitution on June 5, 1953, and Greenland became an integral part of the Kingdom of Denmark. It has been an autonomous state since May 1, 1979.

RULERS
Danish

MINT MARKS
Heart (h) Copenhagen (Kobenhavn)

MONETARY SYSTEM
100 Øre = 1 Krone

DANISH COLONY

TOKEN ISSUES

A. GIBBS & SONS

British trading and mining company located in eastern Greenland.

KM# Tn11 SKILLING
Brass **Obv. Legend:** ØST GRØNLAND above value **Rev. Legend:** A. GIBBS & SONS above date

Date	Mintage	VG	F	VF	XF	Unc
1863	—	450	850	1,400	—	—

KM# Tn12 6 SKILLING
Brass **Obv. Legend:** ØST GRØNLAND above value **Rev. Legend:** A. GIBBS & SONS above date

Date	Mintage	VG	F	VF	XF	Unc
1863	—	175	300	500	—	—

KM# Tn13 24 SKILLING
Brass **Obv. Legend:** ØST GRØNLAND above value **Rev. Legend:** A. GIBBS & SONS above date

Date	Mintage	VG	F	VF	XF	Unc
1863	—	225	400	650	—	—

KM# Tn14 DALER
Brass **Obv. Legend:** ØST GRØNLAND above value **Rev. Legend:** A. GIBBS & SONS above date

Date	Mintage	VG	F	VF	XF	Unc
1863	—	275	500	850	—	—

ORESUND

1859-1865

Danish company for mining cryolite located in Ivigtut, southwest Greenland.

KM# Tn51 SKILLING
Zinc **Obv. Legend:** ØRESUND above "1" **Note:** Uniface.

Date	Mintage	VG	F	VF	XF	Unc
ND	—	100	200	350	500	—

KM# Tn52 4 SKILLING
Zinc **Obv. Legend:** ØRESUND above "4"

Date	Mintage	VG	F	VF	XF	Unc
ND	—	135	275	450	650	—

KM# Tn53 16 SKILLING
Zinc **Obv. Legend:** ORESUND above "16" **Note:** Uniface.

Date	Mintage	VG	F	VF	XF	Unc
ND	—	165	325	550	750	—

KM# Tn54 48 SKILLING
Zinc **Obv. Legend:** ØRESUND above "48" **Note:** Uniface.

Date	Mintage	VG	F	VF	XF	Unc
ND	—	200	425	700	950	—

KM# Tn55 RIGSDALER
Zinc **Obv. Legend:** ØRESUND above "1 Rd" **Note:** Uniface.

Date	Mintage	VG	F	VF	XF	Unc
ND	—	275	500	900	1,200	—

IVIGTUT CRYOLITE MINING & TRADING CO.

Series I, 1875-1882

KM# Tn26 ORE
Zinc, 26 mm. **Obv. Legend:** IVIGTUT above "1" **Note:** Uniface. Currently unknown.

Date	Mintage	VG	F	VF	XF	Unc
ND	—	—	—	—	—	—

KM# Tn27 5 ORE
Zinc, 26.5 mm. **Obv. Legend:** IVIGTUT above "5" **Note:** Uniface.

Date	Mintage	VG	F	VF	XF	Unc
ND	—	—	—	450	—	—

KM# Tn28 10 ORE
Zinc, 26 mm. **Obv. Legend:** IVIGTUT above "10" **Note:** Uniface.

Date	Mintage	VG	F	VF	XF	Unc
ND	—	—	—	—	—	—

KM# Tn29 70 ORE
Zinc, 26 mm. **Obv. Legend:** IVIGTUT above "70" **Note:** Uniface.

Date	Mintage	VG	F	VF	XF	Unc
ND	—	—	—	—	—	—

KM# Tn30 85 ORE
Zinc, 30 mm. **Obv. Legend:** IVIGTUT above "85" **Note:** Uniface.

Date	Mintage	VG	F	VF	XF	Unc
ND	—	—	—	—	—	—

KM# Tn31 100 ORE
Zinc, 43.5 mm. **Obv. Legend:** IVIGTUT above "100" **Note:** Uniface.

Date	Mintage	VG	F	VF	XF	Unc
ND	—	—	—	600	900	—

Note: A unique strike of a 100 Øre struck on 70 Øre plancet exists

IVIGTUT CRYOLITE MINING & TRADING CO.

Series II, Pre-1882

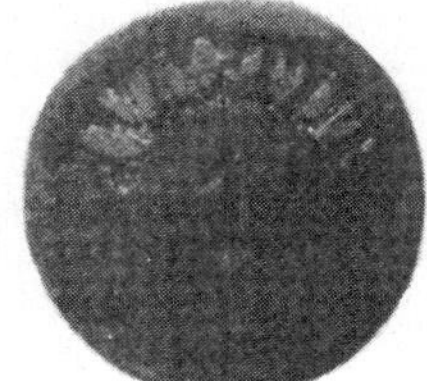

KM# Tn32 ORE
Zinc, 27.1 mm. **Obv. Legend:** IVIGTUT above "1" **Note:** 1.0mm thick, uniface

Date	Mintage	VG	F	VF	XF	Unc
ND Unique	—	—	—	—	—	—

KM# Tn33.2 5 ORE
Zinc **Obv. Legend:** IVIGTUT above "5" **Note:** 26.6-27.0mm, 1.4-1.5mm thick, uniface

Date	Mintage	VG	F	VF	XF	Unc
ND(1875-82)	—	—	—	125	200	—

KM# Tn33.1 5 ORE
Zinc, 27.3 mm. **Obv. Legend:** IVIGTUT above "5" **Note:** 1.0mm thick, uniface

Date	Mintage	VG	F	VF	XF	Unc
ND Unique	—	—	—	—	—	—

KM# Tn34 10 ORE
Zinc, 27.2 mm. **Obv. Legend:** IVIGTUT above "10" **Note:** 1.0mm thick, uniface

Date	Mintage	VG	F	VF	XF	Unc
ND Unique	—	—	—	—	—	—

KM# Tn35 50 ORE
Zinc, 30.8 mm. **Obv. Legend:** IVIGTUT above "50" **Note:** 1.0mm thick, uniface

Date	Mintage	VG	F	VF	XF	Unc
ND Unique	—	—	—	—	—	—

KM# Tn36 85 ORE
Zinc, 30.6 mm. **Obv. Legend:** IVIGTUT above "85" **Note:** 1.0mm thick, uniface

Date	Mintage	VG	F	VF	XF	Unc
ND Rare	—	—	—	3,500	—	—

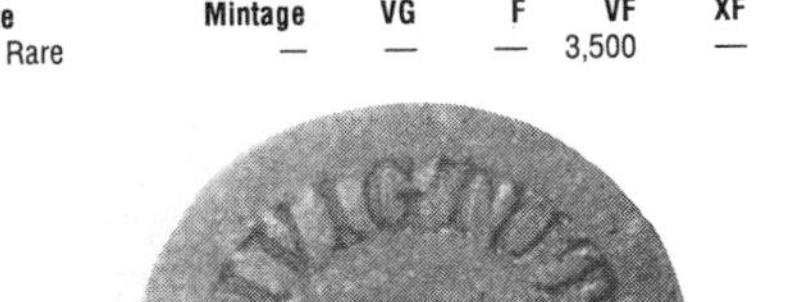

KM# Tn37 100 ORE
Zinc **Obv. Legend:** IVIGTUT above '100' **Note:** 38.3-39.8mm, 1.4-1.5mm thick, uniface

Date	Mintage	VG	F	VF	XF	Unc
ND	—	185	350	550	850	—

Note: A 100 Øre struck on 85 Øre planchet exists and is considered very rare

IVIGTUT CRYOLITE MINING & TRADING CO.

Series III, 1892-

KM# Tn38 ORE
Zinc, 27 mm. **Obv. Legend:** IVIGTUT above "1" **Note:** .75mm thick, uniface

Date	Mintage	VG	F	VF	XF	Unc
ND	—	—	225	375	550	—

KM# Tn39 5 ORE
Zinc, 26.6-27 mm. **Obv. Legend:** IVIGTUT above "5" **Note:** .75mm thick, uniface

Date	Mintage	VG	F	VF	XF	Unc
ND	—	—	65.00	110	160	—

KM# Tn40 10 ORE
Zinc, 30.5 mm. **Obv. Legend:** IVIGTUT above "10" **Note:** .75mm thick, uniface

Date	Mintage	VG	F	VF	XF	Unc
ND	—	—	60.00	100	150	—

KM# Tn41 50 ORE
Zinc, 38 mm. **Obv. Legend:** IVIGTUT above "50" **Note:** .75mm thick, uniface

Date	Mintage	VG	F	VF	XF	Unc
ND	—	—	200	350	500	—

KM# Tn42.1 100 ORE
Zinc, 44 mm. **Obv. Legend:** IVIGTUT above "100" **Note:** .75mm thick, uniface

Date	Mintage	VG	F	VF	XF	Unc
ND	—	—	250	400	575	—

KM# Tn42.2 100 ORE
Zinc **Obv. Legend:** IVIGTUT/IVIGTUT **Note:** Uniface

Date	Mintage	VG	F	VF	XF	Unc
ND Unique	—	—	—	—	—	—

KM# Tn43 500 ORE
Zinc **Note:** Uniface. Not seen since 1917.

Date	Mintage	VG	F	VF	XF	Unc
ND Unique	—	—	—	—	—	—

KM# Tn44 1000 ORE
Zinc **Obv. Legend:** IVIGTUT above "1000" **Note:** .9mm thick, uniface

Date	Mintage	VG	F	VF	XF	Unc
ND Unique	—	—	—	—	—	—

KM# Tn45 20 KRONER
Zinc **Obv. Legend:** IVIGTUT above "20 Kr" **Rev:** Inscription: 28 JULI 95

Date	Mintage	VG	F	VF	XF	Unc
ND Unique	—	—	—	—	—	—

ROYAL GREENLAND TRADE (COMPANY)

(Den Kongelige Grønlandske Handel)

Located on Angmagssalik Island off the east coast of Greenland just below the Arctic Circle.

KM# Tn15 ORE
Zinc, 26.8 mm. **Obv:** Crowned "1" **Obv. Legend:** ANGMAGSSALIK

Date	Mintage	VG	F	VF	XF	Unc
ND	155	120	200	350	650	—

KM# Tn16 5 ORE
Zinc, 30 mm. **Obv:** Crowned "5" **Obv. Legend:** ANGMAGSSALIK **Note:** Uniface

Date	Mintage	VG	F	VF	XF	Unc
ND	155	35.00	70.00	110	180	—

KM# Tn17 10 ORE
Zinc **Obv:** Crowned "10" **Obv. Legend:** ANGMAGSSALIK **Note:** Uniface

Date	Mintage	VG	F	VF	XF	Unc
ND	155	35.00	70.00	110	180	—

KM# Tn18 25 ORE
Zinc **Obv:** Crowned "25" **Obv. Legend:** ANGMAGSSALIK **Note:** Uniface

Date	Mintage	VG	F	VF	XF	Unc
ND	155	30.00	60.00	100	170	—

KM# Tn19.1 50 ORE
Zinc **Obv:** Crowned "50" **Obv. Legend:** ANGMAGSSALIK **Note:** Uniface, holed.

Date	Mintage	VG	F	VF	XF	Unc
ND	95	60.00	120	200	300	—

KM# Tn19.2 50 ORE
Zinc **Note:** Without hole

Date	Mintage	VG	F	VF	XF	Unc
ND	10	150	220	300	500	—

KM# Tn21.1 100 ORE
Zinc **Obv:** Crowned "100" **Obv. Legend:** ANGMAGSSALIK

Date	Mintage	VG	F	VF	XF	Unc
ND	205	30.00	60.00	100	175	—

KM# Tn21.2 100 ORE
Zinc **Rev:** Am.

Date	Mintage	VG	F	VF	XF	Unc
ND Unique	—	—	—	—	—	—

KM# Tn23.1 500 ORE
Zinc **Obv:** Crowned "500" **Obv. Legend:** ANGMAGSSALIK **Note:** Uniface

Date	Mintage	VG	F	VF	XF	Unc
ND Rare	3	—	—	—	—	—

KM# Tn23.2 500 ORE
Zinc **Rev:** Am.

Date	Mintage	VG	F	VF	XF	Unc
ND	99	75.00	150	250	400	—

KM# Tn25 500 ORE
Aluminum **Note:** Uniface

Date	Mintage	VG	F	VF	XF	Unc
ND	195	40.00	80.00	150	250	—

TRIAL STRIKES

ROYAL GREENLAND TRADE (COMPANY)

KM#	Date	Mintage	Identification	Mkt Val
TS1	ND	—	Ore. Aluminum. 27 mm.	—
TS2	ND	—	5 Ore. Aluminum. 30 mm.	—
TS3	ND	—	10 Ore. Aluminum. 34 mm.	—

KM#	Date	Mintage	Identification	Mkt Val

KM#	Date	Mintage	Identification	Mkt Val
TS4	ND	—	25 Ore. Aluminum. 34 mm.	—

KM#	Date	Mintage	Identification	Mkt Val
TS5	ND	—	50 Ore. Aluminum. 38 mm.	—
TS6	ND	—	100 Ore. Aluminum. 39 mm.	—

GRENADA

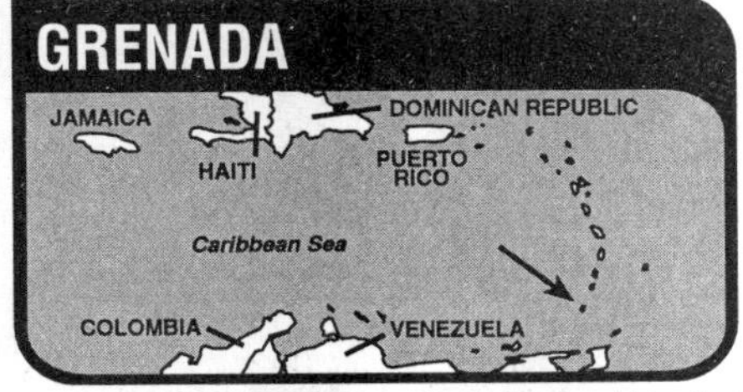

The island of Grenada, located in the Windward Islands of the Caribbean Sea 90 miles (145 km.) north of Trinidad, has (with Carriacou and Petit Martinique) an area of 133 sq. mi. (344 sq. km.). Capital: St.George's. Grenada is the smallest independent nation in the Western Hemisphere.

Columbus discovered Grenada in 1498 during his third voyage to the Americas. Spain failed to colonize the island, and in 1627 granted it to the British who sold it to the French who colonized it in 1650. Grenada was captured by the British in 1763, retaken by the French in 1779, and finally ceded to the British in 1783. The early coinage of Grenada consists of cut and countermarked pieces of Spanish or Spanish Colonial Reales, which were valued at 11 Bits. In 1787 8 Reales coins were cut into 11 triangular pieces and countermarked with an incuse G. Later in 1814 large denomination cut pieces were issued being 1/2, 1/3 or 1/6 cuts and countermarked with a TR, incuse G and a number 6, 4,2, or 1 indicating the value in bits.

RULERS

British

MONETARY SYSTEM

1798-1840

12 Bits = 9 Shillings = 1 Dollar

BRITISH COLONIAL

NECESSITY COINAGE

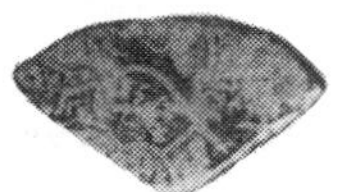

KM# 11 BIT (9 Pence)
Silver **Countermark:** "TR", "G", "1" **Note:** Countermark on 1/3 cut of Spanish or Spanish Colonial 2 Reales.

Date	Mintage	Good	VG	F	VF	XF
ND(c. 1818)	—	85.00	175	300	525	—

KM# 12 BIT (9 Pence)
Silver **Countermark:** "GS", "G", "1" **Note:** Countermark on 1/3 cut of Spanish or Spanish Colonial 2 Reales.

Date	Mintage	Good	VG	F	VF	XF
ND(c. 1818)	—	165	325	600	1,000	—

KM# 5 2 BITS (1 Shilling 6 Pence)
Silver **Countermark:** "TR", "G" "2" **Note:** Countermark on 1/6 cut of Spanish or Spanish Colonial 8 Reales.

Date	Mintage	Good	VG	F	VF	XF
ND(1814)	Est. 9,000	175	350	650	1,100	—

KM# 6 2 BITS (1 Shilling 6 Pence)
Silver **Countermark:** "GS", "G", "2" **Note:** Countermark on 1/6 cut of Spanish or Spanish Colonial 8 Reales.

Date	Mintage	Good	VG	F	VF	XF
ND(1814)	—	600	1,000	1,750	2,750	—

KM# 7 4 BITS (3 Shillings)
Silver **Countermark:** "TR", "G", "4" **Note:** Countermark on 1/3 cut of Spanish or Spanish Colonial 8 Reales.

Date	Mintage	Good	VG	F	VF	XF
ND(1814)	Est. 9,000	350	750	1,350	2,250	—

KM# 8 4 BITS (3 Shillings)
Silver **Countermark:** "GS", "G", "4" **Note:** Countermark on 1/3 cut of Spanish or Spanish Colonial 8 Reales.

Date	Mintage	Good	VG	F	VF	XF
ND(1814)	—	500	900	1,600	2,650	—

KM# 9 6 BITS (4 Shillings 6 Pence)
Silver **Countermark:** "TR", "G", "6" **Note:** Countermark on 1/2 cut of Spanish or Spanish Colonial 8 Reales.

Date	Mintage	Good	VG	F	VF	XF
ND(1814)	Est. 12,000	1,000	2,000	3,500	6,000	—

KM# 10 6 BITS (4 Shillings 6 Pence)
Silver **Countermark:** "GS", "G", "6" **Note:** Countermark on 1/2 cut of Spanish or Spanish Colonial 8 Reales.

Date	Mintage	Good	VG	F	VF	XF
ND(1814)	—	1,250	2,250	4,000	6,500	—

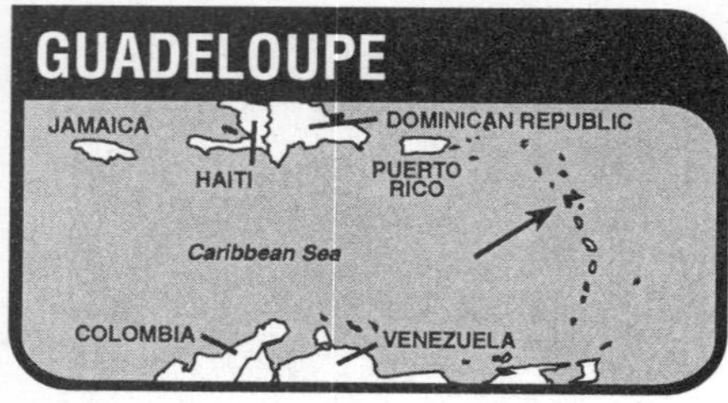

The French Overseas Department of Guadeloupe, located in the Leeward Islands of the West Indies about300 miles (493 km.) southeast of Puerto Rico, has an area of 687 sq. mi. (1,780 sq. km.) and a population of 306,000. Actually it is two islands separated by a narrow salt water stream: volcanic Basse-Terre to the west and the flatter limestone formation of Grande-Terre to the east. Capital: Basse-Terre, on the island of that name. The principal industries are agriculture, the distillation of liquors, and tourism. Sugar, bananas, and rum are exported.

Guadeloupe was discovered by Columbus in 1493 and settled in 1635 by two Frenchmen, L'Olive and Duplessis, who took possession in the name of the French Company of the Islands of America. When repeated efforts by private companies to colonize the island failed, it was relinquished to the French crown in 1674, and established as a dependency of Martinique. The British occupied the island on two occasions, 1759-63 and 1810-16, before it passed permanently to France. A colony until 1946 Guadeloupe was then made an overseas territory of the French Union. In 1958 it voted to become an Overseas Department within the new French Community.

The well-known R.F. in garland oval countermark of the French Government is only legitimate if on a French Colonies 12 deniers 1767 C#4. Two other similar but incuse RF countermarks are on cut pieces in the values of 1 and 4 escalins. Contemporary and modern counterfeits are known of both these types.

RULERS

French, until 1759, 1763-1810, 1816-
British, 1759-1763, 1810-1816

MONETARY SYSTEM

3 Deniers = 1 Liard
4 Liards = 1 Sol (Sous)
20 Sols = 1 Livre
6 Livres = 1 Ecu

NOTE: During the British Occupation period the Spanish and Spanish Colonial 8 Reales equaled 10 Livres.

FRENCH OCCUPATION

COUNTERMARKED COINAGE

KM# 2 ESCALIN
Silver **Countermark:** R.F **Note:** Countermark cut from outside ring of a center cut Spanish or Spanish Colonial 8 Reales.

CM Date	Host Date	Good	VG	F	VF	XF
ND(1802)	ND	200	375	675	1,200	—

KM# 3 4 ESCALINS
Silver **Countermark:** 4E RF **Note:** Countermark on center plug of Spanish or Spanish Colonial 8 Reales.

CM Date	Host Date	Good	VG	F	VF	XF
ND(1802)	ND	600	1,200	2,000	3,500	—

KM# 4.1 20 LIVRES
0.9170 Gold **Countermark:** 20 with small horse's head **Note:** Countermark on false Brazil 6400 Reis, type of KM#172.2.

CM Date	Host Date	Good	VG	F	VF	XF
ND(1803)	ND(1751-1777)	—	—	4,500	6,500	—

KM# 4.2 20 LIVRES
0.9170 Gold **Countermark:** 20 with small horse's head **Note:** Countermark on false Brazil 6400 Reis, type of KM#199.2.

CM Date	Host Date	Good	VG	F	VF	XF
ND(1803)	ND(1777-1786)	—	—	4,500	6,500	—

KM# 5 22 LIVRES
Gold **Countermark:** 22 with small bearded human face **Note:** Countermark on Brazil 6400 Reis, KM#199.2

CM Date	Host Date	Good	VG	F	VF	XF
ND(1803)	ND(1777-1786)	—	—	6,500	8,500	—

BRITISH OCCUPATION

COUNTERMARKED COINAGE

KM# 13 10 SOUS
Silver **Countermark:** Crowned G **Note:** Countermark on France 6 Sols, C#38.

CM Date	Host Date	Good	VG	F	VF	XF
ND(1811)	ND(1726-1740)	30.00	50.00	80.00	160	400

KM# 14 10 SOUS
Silver **Countermark:** Crowned G **Note:** Countermark on France 6 Sols, C#43.

CM Date	Host Date	Good	VG	F	VF	XF
ND(1811)	ND(1743-1770)	30.00	50.00	80.00	160	400

KM# 12 10 SOUS
Silver **Countermark:** Crowned G **Note:** Countermark on Great Britain 3 Pence, KM#591.

CM Date	Host Date	Good	VG	F	VF	XF
ND(1762-1786)	ND(1811)	30.00	50.00	80.00	160	400

KM# 11 10 SOUS
Silver **Countermark:** Crowned G **Note:** Countermark on Spanish or Spanish Colonial 1/4 Real.

CM Date	Host Date	Good	VG	F	VF	XF
ND(1811)	ND	30.00	50.00	80.00	160	400

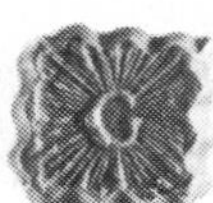

KM# 19 20 SOUS (Livre)
Silver **Countermark:** Radiant G **Note:** Countermark on center plug of Spanish or Spanish Colonial 8 Reales.

CM Date	Host Date	Good	VG	F	VF	XF
ND(1811)	ND	35.00	75.00	125	250	—

KM# 18 20 SOUS (Livre)
Silver **Countermark:** Crowned G **Note:** Countermark on France 12 Sols, C#39.

CM Date	Host Date	Good	VG	F	VF	XF
ND(1811)	ND(1726-1732)	40.00	70.00	100	185	—

KM# 16 20 SOUS (Livre)
Silver **Countermark:** Crowned G **Note:** Countermark on France 12 Sols, C#44.

CM Date	Host Date	Good	VG	F	VF	XF
ND(1811)	ND(1743-1770)	40.00	70.00	100	185	—

KM# 31 20 SOUS (Livre)
Silver **Countermark:** Crowned G **Note:** Countermark on France 12 Sols, C#75.

CM Date	Host Date	Good	VG	F	VF	XF
ND(1811)	ND(1775-1789)	40.00	70.00	100	185	—

KM# 17 20 SOUS (Livre)
Silver **Countermark:** Crowned G **Note:** Countermark on Great Britain 6 Pence, KM#582.

CM Date	Host Date	Good	VG	F	VF	XF
ND(1811)	ND(1743-1758)	40.00	70.00	100	185	—

KM# 15 20 SOUS (Livre)
Silver **Countermark:** Crowned G **Note:** Countermark on Spanish or Spanish Colonial 1 Real.

CM Date	Host Date	Good	VG	F	VF	XF
ND(1811)	ND	40.00	70.00	100	185	—

KM# 20 40 SOUS (2 Livres)
Silver **Countermark:** Crowned G **Note:** Countermark on France 1/3 Ecu, C#30.

CM Date	Host Date	Good	VG	F	VF	XF
ND(1811)	ND(1720-1723)	45.00	85.00	120	200	—

KM# 23 40 SOUS (2 Livres)
Silver **Countermark:** Crowned G **Note:** Countermark on France 24 Sols, C#40.

CM Date	Host Date	Good	VG	F	VF	XF
ND(1811)	ND(1726-1737)	45.50	85.00	120	200	—

KM# 32 40 SOUS (2 Livres)
Silver **Countermark:** Crowned G **Note:** Countermark on France 24 Sols, C#45.

CM Date	Host Date	Good	VG	F	VF	XF
ND(1811)	ND(1741-1770)	50.00	90.00	120	200	—

KM# 33 40 SOUS (2 Livres)
Silver **Countermark:** Crowned G **Note:** Countermark on France 24 Sols, C#45a.

CM Date	Host Date	Good	VG	F	VF	XF
ND(1811)	ND(1771-1774)	75.00	125	150	265	—

KM# 21 40 SOUS (2 Livres)
Silver **Countermark:** Crowned G **Note:** Countermark on France 24 Sols, C#76.

CM Date	Host Date	Good	VG	F	VF	XF
ND(1811)	ND(1774-1790)	45.00	85.00	120	210	—

KM# 22 40 SOUS (2 Livres)
Silver **Countermark:** Crowned G **Note:** Countermark on Great Britain 1 Shilling, KM#607.

CM Date	Host Date	Good	VG	F	VF	XF
ND(1811)	ND(1787)	40.00	80.00	110	190	—

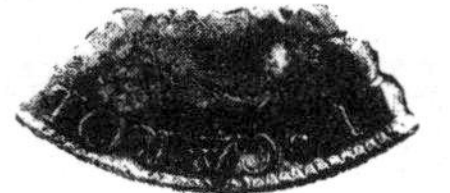

KM# 34 2 LIVRES
Silver **Countermark:** Crowned G **Note:** Countermark on quarter segment of 9 Livres, KM#24-26, 35-36.

CM Date	Host Date	Good	VG	F	VF	XF
ND(1811)	ND	—	—	—	—	—

Note: No official documentation for the issue of KM#34 exists. All known specimens are thought to be modern concoctions. At recent sales examples have sold for as little as $20 and as much as $400

KM# 30 2 LIVRES 5 SOUS
Silver **Countermark:** Crowned G **Note:** Countermark on quarter segment of Spanish or Spanish Colonial 8 Reales.

CM Date	Host Date	Good	VG	F	VF	XF
ND(1813)	ND	300	650	1,250	2,150	—

KM# 24 9 LIVRES
Silver **Countermark:** Crowned G **Note:** Countermark on obverse and reverse of Mexico 8 Reales, KM#106 with crenated square hole.

CM Date	Host Date	Good	VG	F	VF	XF
ND(1811)	ND(1772-1789)	200	250	350	500	1,000

KM# 25 9 LIVRES
Silver **Countermark:** Crowned G **Note:** Countermark on obverse and reverse of Mexico 8 Reales, KM#109 with crenated square hole.

CM Date	Host Date	Good	VG	F	VF	XF
ND(1811)	ND(1791-1808)	200	250	350	500	1,000

KM# 26 9 LIVRES
Silver **Countermark:** Crowned G **Note:** Countermark on obverse and reverse of Mexico 8 Reales, KM#110 with crenated square hole.

CM Date	Host Date	Good	VG	F	VF	XF
ND(1811)	ND(1808-1810)	200	250	350	500	1,000

KM# 35 9 LIVRES
Silver **Countermark:** Crowned G **Note:** Countermark on obverse and reverse of Peru (Lima) 8 Reales, KM#97 with crenated square hole.

CM Date	Host Date	Good	VG	F	VF	XF
ND(1811)	ND(1791-1808)	225	275	400	675	—

KM# 36 9 LIVRES
Silver **Countermark:** Crowned G **Note:** Countermark on obverse and reverse of Peru (Lima) 8 Reales, KM#106.2 with crenated square hole.

CM Date	Host Date	Good	VG	F	VF	XF
ND(1811)	ND(1809-1811)	250	350	650	900	2,000

Note: The square plug was used in making 20 Sous, KM#19

KM# 27 82 LIVRES 10 SOLS
0.9170 Gold **Countermark:** Crowned G and 82.10 **Note:** Countermark on Brazil 6400 Reis, KM#172.

CM Date	Host Date	Good	VG	F	VF	XF
ND(1811)	ND(1751-1777)	2,150	3,250	5,000	8,500	—

KM# 28 82 LIVRES 10 SOLS
0.9170 Gold **Countermark:** Crowned G and 82.10 **Note:** Countermark on Brazil 6400 Reis, KM#199.

CM Date	Host Date	Good	VG	F	VF	XF
ND(1811)	ND(1777-1786)	1,250	2,000	3,000	5,000	—

KM# 29 82 LIVRES 10 SOLS
0.9170 Gold **Countermark:** Crowned G and 82.10 **Note:** Countermark on Brazil 6400 Reis, KM#226. Spurious countermarks on KM#27-29 lack the raised decimal point between 82 and 10.

CM Date	Host Date	Good	VG	F	VF	XF
ND(1811)	ND(1789-1805)	2,000	3,000	4,500	7,500	—

GUATEMALA

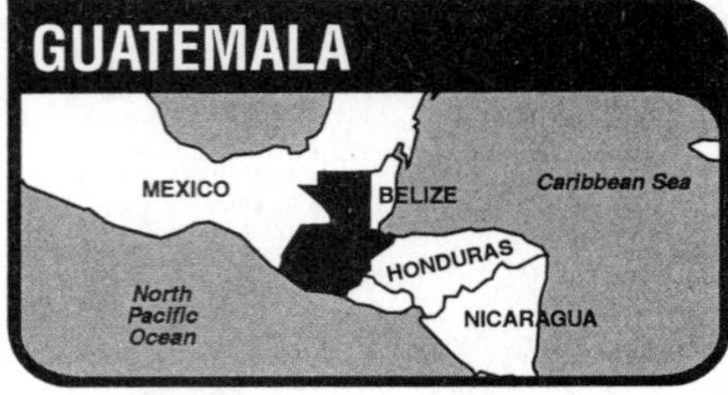

The Republic of Guatemala, the northernmost of the five Central American republics, has an area of 42,042 sq. mi. (108,890 sq. km.) and a population of 10.7 million. Capital: Guatemala City. The economy of Guatemala is heavily dependent on agriculture, however, the country is rich in nickel resources which are being developed. Coffee, cotton and bananas are exported.

Guatemala, once the site of an ancient Mayan civilization, was conquered by Pedro de Alvarado, the resourceful lieutenant of Cortes who undertook the conquest from Mexico. Cruel but strategically skillful, he progressed rapidly along the Pacific coastal lowlands to the highland plain of Quetzaltenango where the decisive battle for Guatemala was fought. After routing the Indian forces, he established the city of Guatemala in 1524. The Spanish Captaincy-General of Guatemala included all Central America but Panama. Guatemala declared its independence of Spain in 1821 and was absorbed into the Mexican empire of Augustin Iturbide (1822-23). From 1823 to 1839 Guatemala was a constituent state of the Central American Republic. Upon dissolution of that confederation, Guatemala proclaimed itself an independent republic. Like El Salvador, Guatemala suffered from internal strife between right-wing, US-backed military government and leftist indigenous peoples from ca. 1954 to ca. 1997.

RULERS

Spanish until 1821

MINT MARKS

Antigua, the old capital city of Santiago de los Caballeros, including the mint, was destroyed by a volcanic eruption and earthquake in 1773. A new mint and capital city was established in Nueva Guatemala City. Coin production recommenced in late 1776 using the NG mint mark.

G or G-G - Guatemala until 1776, 1878-1889
H - Heaton, Birmingham
NG - Nueva Guatemala, 1777-1829, 1992

ASSAYERS' INITIALS

Initial	Date	Name
M	1785-1822	Manuel Eusebio Sanchez

SPANISH COLONY

COLONIAL MILLED COINAGE

KM# 59 1/4 REAL
0.8458 g., 0.8960 Silver .0244 oz. **Ruler:** Charles IV **Obv:** Castle **Rev:** Lion

Date	Mintage	VG	F	VF	XF	Unc
1801G	—	20.00	35.00	50.00	70.00	—
1802G	—	20.00	35.00	50.00	70.00	—
1803G	—	20.00	35.00	50.00	70.00	—
1804G	—	20.00	35.00	50.00	70.00	—
1805G	—	30.00	50.00	70.00	100	—
1806G	—	30.00	50.00	70.00	100	—
1807G	—	20.00	35.00	50.00	70.00	—

KM# 72 1/4 REAL
0.8458 g., 0.8960 Silver .0244 oz. **Obv:** Castle **Rev:** Lion

Date	Mintage	VG	F	VF	XF	Unc
1808G	—	20.00	35.00	50.00	70.00	—
1809G	—	20.00	35.00	50.00	70.00	—
1810G	—	20.00	35.00	50.00	70.00	—
1811/09G	—	25.00	40.00	60.00	90.00	—
1812G	—	40.00	75.00	110	175	—
1813/2G	—	25.00	40.00	60.00	90.00	—
1813G	—	20.00	35.00	50.00	70.00	—
1814G	—	20.00	35.00	50.00	70.00	—
1815G	—	20.00	35.00	50.00	70.00	—
1816G	—	20.00	35.00	50.00	70.00	—
1817G	—	20.00	35.00	50.00	70.00	—
1818G	—	20.00	35.00	50.00	70.00	—
1819G	—	15.00	30.00	45.00	65.00	—
1820G	—	20.00	35.00	50.00	70.00	—
1821G	—	15.00	30.00	45.00	65.00	—
1822G	—	300	600	1,000	2,000	—

Note: The authenticity of the 1822 1/4 Real has been questioned by leading authorities of Latin American coinage

KM# 50 1/2 REAL
1.6921 g., 0.8960 Silver .0487 oz. **Ruler:** Charles IV **Obv:** Bust of Charles IV **Obv. Legend:** CAROLUS IIII... **Rev:** Arms, pillar

Date	Mintage	VG	F	VF	XF	Unc
1801NG M	—	15.00	30.00	75.00	120	—
1802NG M	—	15.00	30.00	75.00	120	—
1803NG M	—	15.00	30.00	75.00	120	—
1804NG M	—	15.00	30.00	75.00	120	—

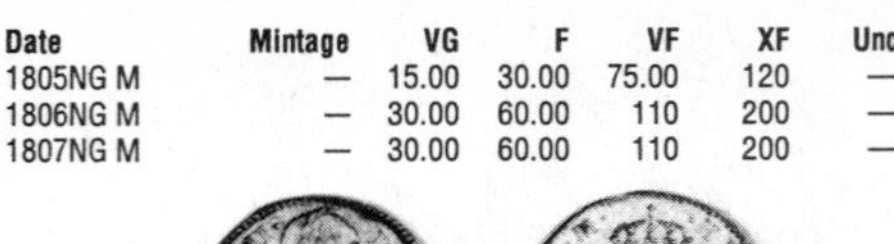

Date	Mintage	VG	F	VF	XF	Unc
1805NG M	—	15.00	30.00	75.00	120	—
1806NG M	—	30.00	60.00	110	200	—
1807NG M	—	30.00	60.00	110	200	—

KM# 60 1/2 REAL
1.6921 g., 0.8960 Silver .0487 oz. **Ruler:** Ferdinand VII **Obv:** Bust of Charles IV **Obv. Legend:** FERDIND VII...

Date	Mintage	VG	F	VF	XF	Unc
1808NG M	—	15.00	40.00	80.00	150	—
1809NG M	—	15.00	40.00	80.00	150	—
1810NG M	—	15.00	25.00	60.00	100	—

KM# 65 1/2 REAL
1.6921 g., 0.8960 Silver .0487 oz. **Ruler:** Ferdinand VII

Date	Mintage	VG	F	VF	XF	Unc
1808NG M	—	35.00	80.00	150	250	—
1811NG M	—	10.00	25.00	55.00	80.00	—
1812NG M	—	10.00	25.00	55.00	80.00	—
1813NG M	—	10.00	25.00	55.00	80.00	—
1814NG M	—	10.00	25.00	55.00	80.00	—
1815NG M	—	10.00	25.00	55.00	80.00	—
1816NG M	—	10.00	25.00	55.00	80.00	—
1817NG M	—	10.00	25.00	55.00	80.00	—
1818NG M	—	10.00	25.00	55.00	80.00	—
1819NG M	—	10.00	25.00	55.00	80.00	—
1820NG M	—	10.00	25.00	55.00	80.00	—
1821NG M	—	10.00	25.00	55.00	80.00	—

KM# 54 REAL
3.3834 g., 0.8960 Silver .0975 oz. **Ruler:** Charles IV **Obv:** Bust of Charles IIII **Rev:** Crowned hemispheres between pillars

Date	Mintage	VG	F	VF	XF	Unc
1801NG M	—	15.00	30.00	75.00	120	—
1802/1NG M	—	15.00	30.00	75.00	120	—
1802NG M	—	15.00	30.00	75.00	120	—
1803NG M	—	15.00	30.00	75.00	120	—
1804NG M	—	15.00	30.00	75.00	120	—
1805NG M	—	30.00	50.00	110	200	—
1806NG M	—	15.00	30.00	75.00	120	—
1807NG M	—	15.00	30.00	75.00	120	—
1808NG M	—	25.00	40.00	80.00	150	—

KM# 61 REAL
3.3834 g., 0.8960 Silver .0975 oz. **Ruler:** Ferdinand VII **Obv:** Bust of Charles IV **Obv. Legend:** FERDIND VII...

Date	Mintage	VG	F	VF	XF	Unc
1808NG M	—	20.00	40.00	80.00	150	—
1809NG M	—	20.00	40.00	80.00	150	—
1810NG M	—	20.00	40.00	80.00	150	—

KM# 66 REAL
3.3834 g., 0.8960 Silver .0975 oz. **Ruler:** Ferdinand VII

Date	Mintage	VG	F	VF	XF	Unc
1808NG M Rare	—	—	—	—	—	—
1811NG M	—	15.00	40.00	80.00	150	—
1812NG M	—	15.00	40.00	80.00	150	—
1813NG M	—	30.00	50.00	110	200	—
1814NG M	—	15.00	30.00	70.00	150	—
1815NG M	—	15.00	30.00	70.00	150	—
1816NG M	—	15.00	30.00	70.00	150	—
1817NG M	—	15.00	30.00	70.00	150	—
1818NG M	—	15.00	30.00	70.00	150	—
1819NG M	—	15.00	30.00	70.00	150	—
1820NG M	—	10.00	25.00	55.00	100	—
1821NG M	—	10.00	25.00	55.00	100	—

KM# 51 2 REALES
6.7668 g., 0.8960 Silver .1949 oz. **Ruler:** Charles IV **Obv:** Bust of Charles IIII **Rev:** Crowned hemispheres between pillars

Date	Mintage	VG	F	VF	XF	Unc
1801NG M	—	17.50	30.00	45.00	60.00	—
1802/1NG M	—	17.50	30.00	45.00	60.00	—
1802NG M	—	17.50	30.00	45.00	60.00	—
1803NG M	—	17.50	30.00	45.00	60.00	—
1804NG M	—	17.50	30.00	45.00	60.00	—
1805NG M	—	17.50	30.00	45.00	60.00	—
1806NG M	—	17.50	30.00	45.00	60.00	—
1807NG M	—	17.50	30.00	45.00	60.00	—

KM# 62 2 REALES
6.7668 g., 0.8960 Silver .1949 oz. **Ruler:** Ferdinand VII **Obv:** Bust of Charles IV **Obv. Legend:** FERDIND VII...

Date	Mintage	VG	F	VF	XF	Unc
1808NG M	—	20.00	40.00	80.00	150	—

Date	Mintage	VG	F	VF	XF	Unc
1809NG M	—	20.00	30.00	60.00	100	—
1810NG M	—	20.00	30.00	50.00	90.00	—

KM# 67 2 REALES
6.7668 g., 0.8960 Silver .1949 oz. **Ruler:** Ferdinand VII

Date	Mintage	VG	F	VF	XF	Unc
1808NG M	—	30.00	50.00	110	200	—
1811NG M	—	40.00	80.00	150	250	—
1812NG M	—	20.00	40.00	80.00	150	—
1813NG M	—	17.50	30.00	60.00	100	—
1814NG M	—	25.00	60.00	100	180	—
1815NG M	—	17.50	30.00	60.00	100	—
1816NG M	—	30.00	50.00	110	200	—
1817NG M	—	17.50	30.00	60.00	100	—
1818NG M	—	17.50	30.00	60.00	100	—
1819NG M	—	17.50	30.00	60.00	100	—
1820NG M	—	17.50	30.00	60.00	100	—
1821NG M	—	17.50	30.00	60.00	100	—

KM# 52 4 REALES
13.5337 g., 0.8960 Silver .3899 oz. **Ruler:** Charles IV

Date	Mintage	VG	F	VF	XF	Unc
1801NG M	—	50.00	100	200	350	—
1802NG M	—	75.00	150	250	400	—
1803NG M	—	75.00	150	250	400	—
1804NG M	—	75.00	150	250	400	—
1805NG M	—	75.00	150	250	400	—
1806/5NG M	—	50.00	100	200	350	—
1806NG M	—	50.00	100	200	350	—
1807NG M	—	50.00	100	200	350	—

KM# 63 4 REALES
13.5337 g., 0.8960 Silver .3899 oz. **Ruler:** Ferdinand VII **Obv:** Bust of Charles IV **Obv. Legend:** FERDIND VII...

Date	Mintage	VG	F	VF	XF	Unc
1808NG M	—	60.00	125	225	350	—
1809NG M	—	60.00	110	210	300	—
1810NG M	—	60.00	125	225	350	—

KM# 68 4 REALES
13.5337 g., 0.8960 Silver .3899 oz. **Ruler:** Ferdinand VII

Date	Mintage	VG	F	VF	XF	Unc
1808NG M	—	200	300	550	1,100	—
1811NG M	—	50.00	100	200	300	—
1812NG M	—	50.00	100	200	300	—
1813NG M	—	50.00	100	200	300	—
1814NG M	—	50.00	100	200	300	—

Date	Mintage	VG	F	VF	XF	Unc
1815/4NG M	—	50.00	100	200	300	—
1816NG M	—	50.00	100	200	300	—
1817NG M	—	50.00	100	200	300	—
1818NG M	—	50.00	100	200	300	—
1819NG M	—	50.00	100	200	300	—
1820NG M	—	50.00	100	200	300	—
1821NG M	—	50.00	100	200	300	—

KM# 53 8 REALES
27.0674 g., 0.8960 Silver .7797 oz. **Ruler:** Charles IV **Obv:** Bust of Charles IIII right **Rev:** Crowned shield between pillars

Date	Mintage	VG	F	VF	XF	Unc
1801NG M	—	55.00	100	200	350	—
1802NG M	—	60.00	150	225	375	—
1803NG M	—	55.00	100	200	350	—
1804NG M	—	55.00	100	200	350	—
1805NG M	—	55.00	100	200	350	—
1806/5NG M	—	75.00	200	325	425	—
1807NG M	—	55.00	100	200	350	—

KM# 64 8 REALES
27.0674 g., 0.8960 Silver .7797 oz. **Ruler:** Ferdinand VII **Obv:** Bust of Charles IIII **Obv. Legend:** FERDIND VII...

Date	Mintage	VG	F	VF	XF	Unc
1808NG M	—	70.00	150	225	375	—
1809/8NG M	—	150	300	450	750	—
1809NG M	—	70.00	150	225	375	—
1810NG M	—	70.00	150	225	375	—

KM# 69 8 REALES
27.0674 g., 0.8960 Silver .7797 oz. **Ruler:** Ferdinand VII

Date	Mintage	VG	F	VF	XF	Unc
1808NG M Rare	—	—	—	—	—	—
Note: Superior 12-90 sale choice VF realized $14,300.						
1811NG M	—	75.00	125	225	450	—
1812NG M	—	25.00	40.00	75.00	150	—
1813NG M	—	25.00	40.00	75.00	150	—
1814NG M	—	25.00	40.00	75.00	150	—
1815NG M	—	25.00	40.00	75.00	150	—
1816NG M	—	25.00	40.00	75.00	150	—
1817NG M	—	25.00	40.00	75.00	150	—
1818NG M	—	25.00	40.00	75.00	150	—
1819NG M	—	25.00	40.00	75.00	150	—
1820NG M	—	25.00	40.00	75.00	150	—
1821NG M	—	25.00	40.00	75.00	150	—

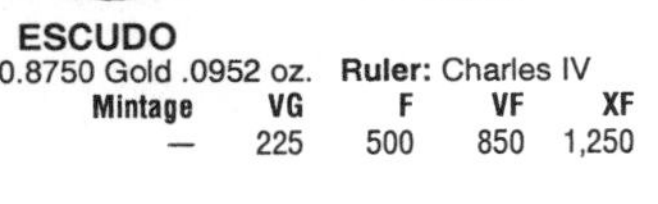

KM# 55 ESCUDO
3.3834 g., 0.8750 Gold .0952 oz. **Ruler:** Charles IV

Date	Mintage	VG	F	VF	XF	Unc
1801NG M	—	225	500	850	1,250	—

KM# 74 ESCUDO
3.3834 g., 0.8750 Gold .0952 oz. **Ruler:** Ferdinand VII

Date	Mintage	VG	F	VF	XF	Unc
1817NG M	—	250	450	850	1,350	—

KM# 56 2 ESCUDOS
6.7668 g., 0.8750 Gold .1904 oz. **Ruler:** Charles IV **Obv:** Bust of Charles IIII

Date	Mintage	VG	F	VF	XF	Unc
1794NG M	—	450	900	1,600	3,000	—
1797NG M	—	500	1,100	1,850	3,500	—
1801NG M	—	500	1,000	1,750	3,250	—

KM# 70 2 ESCUDOS
6.7668 g., 0.8750 Gold .1904 oz. **Ruler:** Ferdinand VII

Date	Mintage	VG	F	VF	XF	Unc
1808NG M	—	750	1,500	2,750	5,500	—
1811NG M Rare	—	—	—	—	—	—
1817NG M	—	400	750	1,400	2,500	—

KM# 57 4 ESCUDOS
13.5337 g., 0.8750 Gold .3807 oz. **Ruler:** Charles IV

Date	Mintage	VG	F	VF	XF	Unc
1801NG M	—	1,000	2,000	3,750	6,500	—
1801NG M	—	1,000	2,000	3,750	6,500	—

KM# 73 4 ESCUDOS
13.5337 g., 0.8750 Gold .3807 oz. **Ruler:** Ferdinand VII

Date	Mintage	VG	F	VF	XF	Unc
1817NG M	—	600	1,250	2,750	5,000	—

KM# 58 8 ESCUDOS
27.0674 g., 0.8750 Gold .7615 oz. **Ruler:** Charles IV

Date	Mintage	VG	F	VF	XF	Unc
1801NG M	—	—	1,850	5,000	9,500	—

KM# 71 8 ESCUDOS
27.0674 g., 0.8750 Gold .7615 oz. **Ruler:** Ferdinand VII

Date	Mintage	VG	F	VF	XF	Unc
1808NG M Rare	—	—	—	—	—	—
1811NG M Rare	—	—	—	—	—	—
1817NG M	—	—	1,500	3,500	5,000	—

CENTRAL AMERICAN REPUBLIC

PROVISIONAL COINAGE

Under Central American Republic

KM# 75 REAL

0.9030 Silver **Issuer:** Quetzaltenango **Obv. Legend:** ESTADO DE GUATEMALA

Date	Mintage	VG	F	VF	XF	Unc
1829NG M 4 known; Rare	—	—	—	—	—	—

REPUBLIC

REAL COINAGE

8 Reales = 1 Peso

KM# 175 1/4 REAL

Copper-Nickel **Note:** Medal rotation.

Date	Mintage	F	VF	XF	Unc	BU
1900H	2,944,000	0.15	0.35	1.00	2.50	—

KM# 176 1/2 REAL (Medio)

Copper-Nickel **Note:** Medal rotation.

Date	Mintage	F	VF	XF	Unc	BU
1900	5,348,000	0.35	0.65	1.00	2.50	—

KM# 177 REAL

Copper-Nickel **Note:** Medal rotation.

Date	Mintage	F	VF	XF	Unc	BU
1900	4,612,000	—	0.35	1.00	5.00	—

COUNTERMARKED COINAGE

1838 - Type I

Sun at left behind volcano under long cloud.

KM# 78 2 REALES

Silver **Countermark:** Type I **Note:** Countermark on Peru (Lima) "Cob" 2 Reales, KM#16.

CM Date	Host Date	Good	VG	F	VF	XF
ND(1838)	1659-1660 Rare	—	—	—	—	—

KM# 76.3 4 REALES

Silver **Countermark:** Type I **Note:** Countermark on Bolivia "Cob" 4 Reales, KM#30a.

CM Date	Host Date	Good	VG	F	VF	XF
ND(1838)	1729-1747	150	225	300	—	—

KM# 76.4 4 REALES

Silver **Countermark:** Type I **Note:** Countermark on Bolivia "cob" 4 Reales, KM#44.

CM Date	Host Date	Good	VG	F	VF	XF
ND(1838)	1760-1777	150	225	300	—	—

KM# 76.1 4 REALES

Silver **Countermark:** Type I **Note:** Countermark on Guatemala "Cob" 4 Reales, KM#11.

CM Date	Host Date	Good	VG	F	VF	XF
ND(1838)	1747-1753	225	325	450	—	—

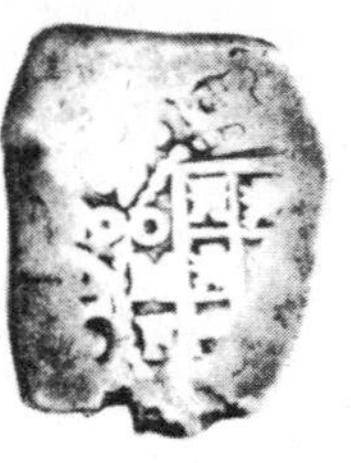

KM# 76.5 4 REALES

Silver **Countermark:** Type I **Note:** Countermark on Mexico "Cob" 4 Reales, KM#40a.

CM Date	Host Date	Good	VG	F	VF	XF
ND(1838)	1729-1734	500	700	1,000	—	—

KM# 76.2 4 REALES

Silver **Countermark:** Type I **Note:** Countermark on Mexico-Sombrerete 4 Reales, KM#175.

CM Date	Host Date	Good	VG	F	VF	XF
ND(1838)	1811-1812	500	—	—	—	—

KM# 77.1 8 REALES

Silver **Countermark:** Type I **Note:** Countermark on Guatemala "Cob" 8 Reales, KM#6.

CM Date	Host Date	Good	VG	F	VF	XF
ND(1838)	1733-1746	200	300	400	550	—

KM# 77.2 8 REALES

Silver **Countermark:** Type I **Note:** Countermark on Guatemala "Cob" 8 Reales, KM#12.

CM Date	Host Date	Good	VG	F	VF	XF
ND(1838)	1747-1753	200	300	400	550	—

KM# 77.3 8 REALES

Silver **Countermark:** Type I **Note:** Countermark on Peru (Lima) "Cob" 8 Reales of Philip V.

CM Date	Host Date	Good	VG	F	VF	XF
ND(1838)	1700-1746	200	300	400	550	—

KM# 77.4 8 REALES

Silver **Countermark:** Type I **Note:** Countermark on Peru 8 Reales, KM#142.3.

CM Date	Host Date	Good	VG	F	VF	XF
ND(1838)	1828-?	150	220	300	400	—

KM# 77.5 8 REALES

Silver **Countermark:** Type I **Note:** Countermark on Bolivia (Potosi) "Cob" 8 Reales, KM#45.

CM Date	Host Date	Good	VG	F	VF	XF
ND(1838)	1760-1773	225	325	450	—	—

KM# 77.6 8 REALES

Silver **Countermark:** Type I **Note:** Countermark on Mexico "Cob" 8 Reales, KM#46.

CM Date	Host Date	Good	VG	F	VF	XF
ND(1838)	1668-1701	225	325	450	—	—

KM# 77.7 8 REALES

Silver **Countermark:** Type I **Note:** Countermark on Mexico "Cob" 8 Reales, KM#47a.

CM Date	Host Date	Good	VG	F	VF	XF
ND(1838)	1729-1733	225	325	450	—	—

KM# 77.8 8 REALES

Silver **Countermark:** Type I **Note:** Countermark on Mexico "Klippe" 8 Reales, KM#48.

CM Date	Host Date	Good	VG	F	VF	XF
ND(1838)	1733-1734	225	325	450	—	—

KM# 77.9 8 REALES

Silver **Countermark:** Type I **Note:** Countermark on Peru 8 Reales, KM#130.

CM Date	Host Date	Good	VG	F	VF	XF
ND(1838)	1824	150	220	300	400	—

KM# 77.10 8 REALES

Silver **Countermark:** Type I **Note:** Countermark on Bolivia (Potosi) "Royal" 8 Reales, KM#R21.

CM Date	Host Date	Good	VG	F	VF	XF
ND(1838)	1621-1665	—	—	—	—	—

KM# 77.11 8 REALES

Silver **Countermark:** Type I **Note:** Countermark on Bolivia (Potosi) "Cob" 8 Reales, KM#31a.

CM Date	Host Date	Good	VG	F	VF	XF
ND(1838)	1729-1747	225	325	450	—	—

KM# 77.12 8 REALES
Silver **Countermark:** Type I **Note:** Countermark on Bolivia (Potosi) "Cob" 8 Reales, KM#40.

CM Date	Host Date	Good	VG	F	VF	XF
ND(1838)	1747-1760	225	325	450	—	—

KM# 77.13 8 REALES
Silver **Countermark:** Type I **Note:** Countermark on Peru (Lima) "Cob" 8 Reales, KM#24.

CM Date	Host Date	Good	VG	F	VF	XF
ND(1838)	1684-1701	200	300	400	550	—

KM# 77.14 8 REALES
Silver **Countermark:** Type I **Note:** Countermark on Peru 8 Reales, KM#142.1.

CM Date	Host Date	Good	VG	F	VF	XF
ND(1838)	1825-1828	150	220	300	400	—

KM# 77.15 8 REALES
Silver **Countermark:** Type I **Note:** Countermark on Bolivia (Potosi) "Cob" 8 Reales, KM#26.

CM Date	Host Date	Good	VG	F	VF	XF
ND(1838)	1679	—	—	—	—	—

KM# 77.16 8 REALES
Silver **Countermark:** Type I **Note:** Countermark on Bolivia (Potosi) "Cob" 8 Reales, KM#31a.

CM Date	Host Date	Good	VG	F	VF	XF
ND(1838)	1729	—	—	—	—	—

COUNTERMARKED COINAGE

1839 - Type II

Sun above a row of volcanos in 6.5mm circle.

KM# 81 2 REALES
Silver **Countermark:** Type II **Note:** Countermark on Bolivia 2 Soles, KM#95.

CM Date	Host Date	Good	VG	F	VF	XF
ND(1839)	1827-1830	55.00	85.00	110	150	—

KM# 82 2 REALES
Silver **Countermark:** Type II **Note:** Countermark on Peru 2 Reales, KM#141.1

CM Date	Host Date	Good	VG	F	VF	XF
ND(1839)	1825-1840	55.00	85.00	110	150	—

KM# 85.1 4 REALES
Silver **Countermark:** Type II **Note:** Countermark on Bolivia (Potosi) "Cob" 4 Reales of Philip II.

CM Date	Host Date	Good	VG	F	VF	XF
ND(1839)	1556-1598	125	185	260	350	—

KM# 85.4 4 REALES
Silver **Countermark:** Type II **Note:** Countermark on Bolivia (Potosi) "Cob" 4 Reales, KM#30.

CM Date	Host Date	Good	VG	F	VF	XF
ND(1839)	1712	—	—	—	—	—

KM# 85.5 4 REALES
Silver **Countermark:** Type II **Note:** Countermark on Bolivia (Potosi) "Cob" 4 Reales, KM#39.

CM Date	Host Date	Good	VG	F	VF	XF
ND(1839)	1746-1759	80.00	125	165	225	—

KM# 85.6 4 REALES
Silver **Countermark:** Type II **Note:** Countermark on Bolivia (Potosi) "Cob" 4 Reales, KM#44.

CM Date	Host Date	Good	VG	F	VF	XF
ND(1839)	1759-1788	80.00	125	165	225	—

KM# 87.2 4 REALES
Silver **Countermark:** Type II **Note:** Countermark on Guatemala "Cob" 4 Reales, KM#11.

CM Date	Host Date	Good	VG	F	VF	XF
ND(1839)	1747-1753	110	165	225	300	—

KM# 87.1 4 REALES
Silver **Countermark:** Type II **Note:** Countermark on Guatemala "Cob" 4 Reales, KM#5.

CM Date	Host Date	Good	VG	F	VF	XF
ND(1839)	1733-1746	110	165	225	300	—

KM# 88 4 REALES
Silver **Countermark:** Type II **Note:** Countermark on Honduras "Cob" 4 Reales, KM#16.1.

CM Date	Host Date	Good	VG	F	VF	XF
ND(1839)	1823-1824	—	—	—	—	—

KM# 89.2 4 REALES
Silver **Countermark:** Type II **Note:** Countermark on Mexico "Cob" 4 Reales of Philip II.

CM Date	Host Date	Good	VG	F	VF	XF
ND(1839)	ND(1556-1598)	125	185	260	350	—

KM# 89.5 4 REALES
Silver **Countermark:** Type II **Note:** Countermark on Mexico "Klippe" 4 Reales. KM#41.

CM Date	Host Date	Good	VG	F	VF	XF
ND(1839)	1733-1734	225	300	375	500	—

KM# 89.1 4 REALES
Silver **Countermark:** Type II **Note:** Countermark on Mexico 4 Reales of Carlos and Johanna, KM #0018.

CM Date	Host Date	Good	VG	F	VF	XF
ND(1839)	ND(1536-1542)	—	—	—	—	—

KM# 91 4 REALES
Silver **Countermark:** Type II **Note:** Countermark on Peru (Cuzco) 4 Reales, KM#151.1.

CM Date	Host Date	Good	VG	F	VF	XF
ND(1839)	1835-1836	60.00	110	175	250	—

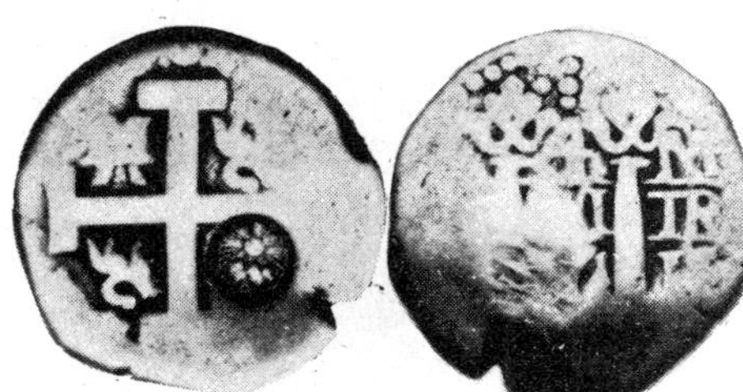

KM# 90.1 4 REALES
Silver **Countermark:** Type II **Note:** Countermark on Peru (Lima) "Cob" 4 Reales of Charles II.

CM Date	Host Date	Good	VG	F	VF	XF
ND(1839)	1665-1700	80.00	125	165	225	—

KM# 90.2 4 REALES
Silver **Countermark:** Type II **Note:** Countermark on Peru (Lima) "Cob" 4 Reales, KM#33.

CM Date	Host Date	Good	VG	F	VF	XF
ND(1839)	1700-1746	80.00	125	165	225	—

KM# 90.3 4 REALES
Silver **Countermark:** Type II **Note:** Countermark on Peru (Lima) "Royal" 4 Reales, KM#33.

CM Date	Host Date	Good	VG	F	VF	XF
ND(1839)	1700-1746	—	—	—	—	—

KM# 92 4 REALES
Silver **Countermark:** Type II **Note:** Countermark on Bolivia 4 Soles, KM#96.

CM Date	Host Date	Good	VG	F	VF	XF
ND(1839)	1827-1830	60.00	110	175	250	—

KM# 94.1 8 REALES
Silver **Countermark:** Type II **Note:** Countermark on Bolivia (Potosi) "Cob" 8 Reales, KM#5.

CM Date	Host Date	Good	VG	F	VF	XF
ND(1839)	1556-1598	80.00	125	165	225	—

KM# 94.2 8 REALES
Silver **Countermark:** Type II **Note:** Countermark on Bolivia (Potosi) "Royal" 8 Reales, KM#R5.

CM Date	Host Date	Good	VG	F	VF	XF
ND(1839)	1621-1665	750	1,100	1,500	2,000	—

KM# 95 8 REALES
Silver **Countermark:** Type II **Note:** Countermark on Bolivia (Potosi) "Cob" 8 Reales, KM#19.

CM Date	Host Date	Good	VG	F	VF	XF
ND(1839)	1621-1665	80.00	125	165	225	—

KM# 96.1 8 REALES
Silver **Countermark:** Type II **Note:** Countermark on Bolivia (Potosi) "Royal" 8 Reales, KM#R26.

CM Date	Host Date	Good	VG	F	VF	XF
ND(1839)	1665-1700	750	1,100	1,500	2,000	—

KM# 96.2 8 REALES

Silver **Countermark:** Type II **Note:** Countermark on Bolivia (Potosi) "Cob" 8 Reales, KM#26.

CM Date	Host Date	Good	VG	F	VF	XF
ND(1839)	1665-1700	125	185	250	350	—

KM# 97.1 8 REALES

Silver **Countermark:** Type II **Note:** Countermark on Bolivia (Potosi) 'cob' 8 Reales, KM#31.

CM Date	Host Date	Good	VG	F	VF	XF
ND(1839)	1701-1728	110	165	225	300	—

KM# 97.2 8 REALES

Silver **Countermark:** Type II **Note:** Countermark on Bolivia (Potosi) "Royal" 8 Reales, KM#R31.

CM Date	Host Date	Good	VG	F	VF	XF
ND1839	1702	—	—	—	—	—

KM# 97.3 8 REALES

Silver **Countermark:** Type II **Note:** Countermark on Bolivia (Potosi) "Cob" 8 Reales, KM#31a.

CM Date	Host Date	Good	VG	F	VF	XF
ND(1839)	1729-1746	110	165	225	300	—

KM# 98 8 REALES

Silver **Countermark:** Type II **Note:** Countermark on Bolivia (Potosi) "Cob" 8 Reales, KM#35.

CM Date	Host Date	Good	VG	F	VF	XF
ND(1839)	1725-1727	250	450	550	950	—

KM# 99 8 REALES

Silver **Countermark:** Type II **Note:** Countermark on Bolivia (Potosi) "Cob" 8 Reales, KM#40.

CM Date	Host Date	Good	VG	F	VF	XF
ND(1839)	1746-1759	80.00	125	165	225	—

KM# 100 8 REALES

Silver **Countermark:** Type II **Note:** Countermark on Bolivia (Potosi) "Cob" 8 Reales, KM#45.

CM Date	Host Date	Good	VG	F	VF	XF
ND(1839)	1759-1788	80.00	125	165	225	—

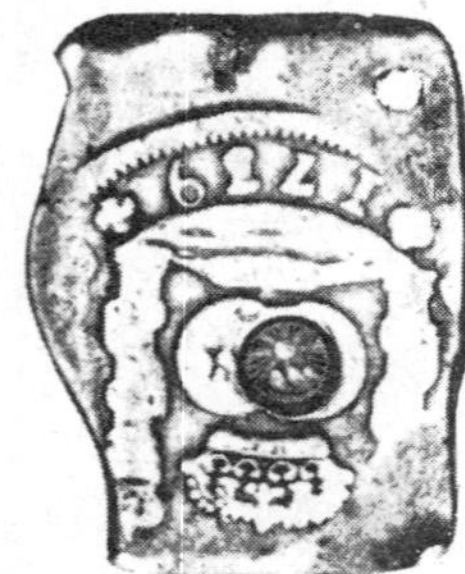

KM# 101 8 REALES

Silver **Countermark:** Type II **Note:** Countermark on Guatemala "Cob" 8 Reales, KM#6.

CM Date	Host Date	Good	VG	F	VF	XF
ND(1839)	1733-1746	125	185	250	350	—

KM# 102 8 REALES

Silver **Countermark:** Type II **Note:** Countermark on Guatemala "Cob" 8 Reales, KM#12.

CM Date	Host Date	Good	VG	F	VF	XF
ND(1839)	1747-1753	110	165	225	300	—

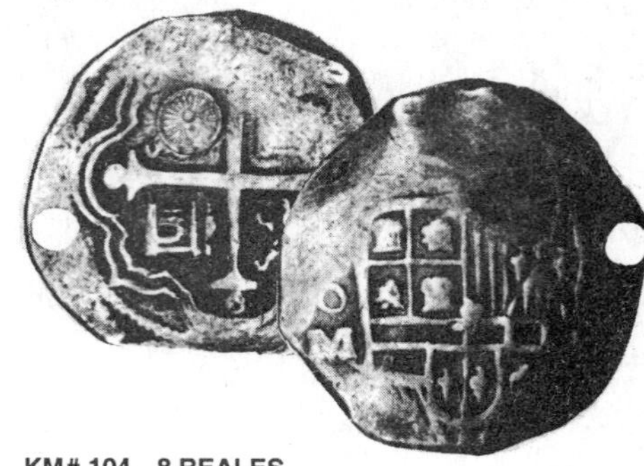

KM# 104 8 REALES

Silver **Countermark:** Type II **Note:** Countermark on Mexico "Cob" 8 Reales, KM#45.

CM Date	Host Date	Good	VG	F	VF	XF
ND(1839)	1621-1667	110	165	225	300	—

KM# 105.1 8 REALES

Silver **Countermark:** Type II **Note:** Countermark on Mexico "Royal" 8 Reales, KM#R47.

CM Date	Host Date	Good	VG	F	VF	XF
ND(1839)	1701-1728 Rare	—	—	—	—	—

KM# 105.2 8 REALES

Silver **Countermark:** Type II **Note:** Countermark on Mexico "Cob" 8 Reales, KM#47a.

CM Date	Host Date	Good	VG	F	VF	XF
ND(1839)	1729-1733	85.00	130	180	240	—

KM# 106 8 REALES

Silver **Countermark:** Type II **Note:** Countermark on Bolivia 8 Soles, KM#97.

CM Date	Host Date	Good	VG	F	VF	XF
ND(1839)	1827-1840	50.00	90.00	135	200	—

KM# 107 8 REALES

Silver **Countermark:** Type II **Note:** Countermark on Mexico "Klippe" 8 Reales, KM#48.

CM Date	Host Date	Good	VG	F	VF	XF
ND(1839)	1733-1734	185	275	375	500	—

KM# 108 8 REALES

Silver **Countermark:** Type II **Note:** Countermark on Peru (Lima) "Cob" 8 Reales of Philip II, KM#14.1.

CM Date	Host Date	Good	VG	F	VF	XF
ND(1839)	ND(1577-1588)P*	675	1,000	1,350	1,800	—

KM# 109 8 REALES

Silver **Countermark:** Type II **Note:** Countermark on Peru (Star of Lima) "Cob" 8 Reales of Philip IV, KM#18.

CM Date	Host Date	Good	VG	F	VF	XF
ND(1839)	1659-1660 Rare	—	—	—	—	—

KM# 110.1 8 REALES

Silver **Countermark:** Type II **Note:** Countermark on Peru (Lima) "Cob" 8 Reales, KM#24.

CM Date	Host Date	Good	VG	F	VF	XF
ND(1839)	1684-1701	85.00	130	180	240	—

KM# 110.2 8 REALES
Silver **Countermark:** Type II **Note:** Countermark on Peru (Lima) "Royal" 8 Reales, KM#R24.

CM Date	Host Date	Good	VG	F	VF	XF
ND(1839)	1684-1701	550	825	1,125	1,500	—

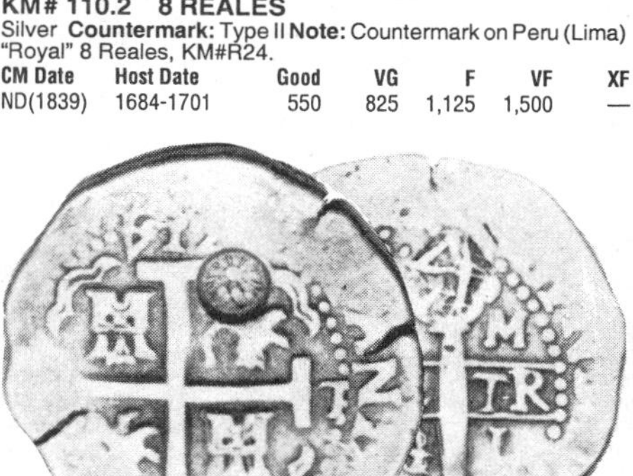

KM# 111.1 8 REALES
Silver **Countermark:** Type II **Note:** Countermark on Peru (Lima) "Cob" 8 Reales, KM#34.

CM Date	Host Date	Good	VG	F	VF	XF
ND(1839)	1701-1723	80.00	125	165	225	—

KM# 111.2 8 REALES
Silver **Countermark:** Type II **Note:** Countermark on Peru (Lima) "Cob" 8 Reales, KM#39.

CM Date	Host Date	Good	VG	F	VF	XF
ND(1839)	1725-1726	300	575	800	1,100	—

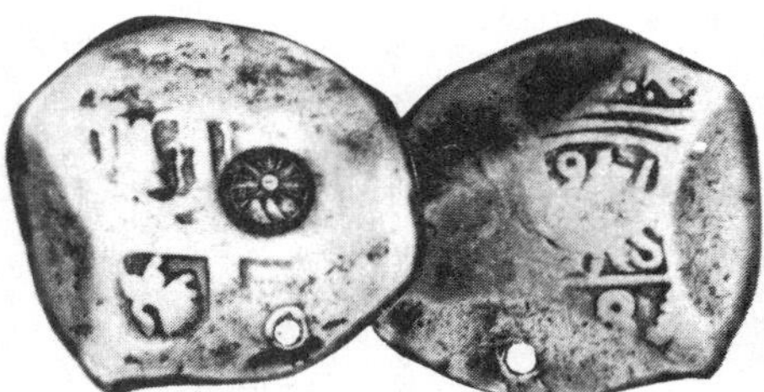

KM# 111.3 8 REALES
Silver **Countermark:** Type II **Note:** Countermark on Peru (Lima) "Cob" 8 Reales, KM#41.

CM Date	Host Date	Good	VG	F	VF	XF
ND(1839)	1727-1746	80.00	125	165	225	—

KM# 111.5 8 REALES
Silver **Countermark:** Type II **Note:** Countermark on Peru (Lima) 8 Reales, KM#142.3

CM Date	Host Date	Good	VG	F	VF	XF
ND(1839)	1828-?	80.00	125	165	225	—

KM# 111.6 8 REALES
Silver **Countermark:** Type II **Note:** Countermark on Spain (Segovia) 8 Reales, KM#191.3.

CM Date	Host Date	Good	VG	F	VF	XF
ND(1839)	1682-85	—	—	—	—	—

1840 - Type III

Obv: Sun above 3 volcanos in 6.5mm circle.

Rev: Sunface in star, bow and arrow in 7mm circle.

KM# 112.1 8 REALES
Silver **Countermark:** Type III **Note:** Countermark on Bolivia (Potosi) 8 Soles, KM#97.

CM Date	Host Date	Good	VG	F	VF	XF
ND(1840)	1827-1840	110	165	225	325	—

KM# 112.2 8 REALES
Silver **Countermark:** Type III **Note:** Countermark on Chile (Santiago) 8 Reales, KM#96.1.

CM Date	Host Date	Good	VG	F	VF	XF
ND(1840)	1837-1840	125	185	250	350	—

KM# 120.1 8 REALES
Silver **Countermark:** Type III **Note:** Countermark on Peru (Lima) 8 Reales, KM#136.

CM Date	Host Date	Good	VG	F	VF	XF
ND(1840)	1822-1823	150	225	300	400	—

KM# 120.2 8 REALES
Silver **Countermark:** Type III **Note:** Countermark on Peru (Lima) 8 Reales, KM#142.1.

CM Date	Host Date	Good	VG	F	VF	XF
ND(1840)	1825-1828	45.00	75.00	120	175	—

KM# 120.3 8 REALES
Silver **Countermark:** Type III **Note:** Countermark on Peru (Lima) 8 Reales, KM#142.3.

CM Date	Host Date	Good	VG	F	VF	XF
ND(1840)	1828-1840	40.00	65.00	100	150	—

KM# 120.4 8 REALES
Silver **Countermark:** Type III **Note:** Countermark on Peru (Cuzco) 8 Reales, KM#142.2.

CM Date	Host Date	Good	VG	F	VF	XF
ND(1840)	1826-1836	45.00	75.00	120	175	—

KM# 120.5 8 REALES
Silver **Countermark:** Type III **Note:** Countermark on Peru (North) 8 Reales, KM#155.

CM Date	Host Date	Good	VG	F	VF	XF
ND(1840)	1836-1839	45.00	75.00	120	175	—

KM# 120.6 8 REALES
Silver **Countermark:** Type III **Note:** Countermark on Peru (South) 8 Reales, KM#170.4.

CM Date	Host Date	Good	VG	F	VF	XF
ND(1840)	1837-1839	375	550	750	1,000	—

1841 - Type IV

Similar dies as used for Type III but instead of being applied as individual countermarks they were paired in hinged dies and counterstamped in one application. This was done without respect to the host coins obverse or reverse. Coins dated after 1841 with the Type IV counterstamp are believed to be counterfeit by some authorities.

KM# 113 8 REALES
Silver **Counterstamp:** Type IV **Note:** Counterstamp on Argentina (Potosi) 8 Reales, KM#14.

CS Date	Host Date	Good	VG	F	VF	XF
ND(1841)	1815	225	330	450	600	—

KM# 114 8 REALES
Silver **Counterstamp:** Type IV **Note:** Counterstamp on Bolivia 8 Soles, KM#97.

CS Date	Host Date	Good	VG	F	VF	XF
(1841)	1827-1840	45.00	75.00	120	175	—

KM# 115 8 REALES
Silver **Counterstamp:** Type IV **Note:** Counterstamp on Chile (Santiago) 8 Reales, KM#96.1.

CS Date	Host Date	Good	VG	F	VF	XF
ND(1841)	1837-1840	125	185	250	350	—

KM# 119 8 REALES
Silver **Counterstamp:** Type IV **Note:** Counterstamp on Peru (Cuzco) 8 Reales, KM#142.2.

CS Date	Host Date	Good	VG	F	VF	XF
ND(1841)	1826-1836	45.00	75.00	120	175	—

KM# 116 8 REALES
Silver **Counterstamp:** Type IV **Note:** Counterstamp on Peru (Lima) 8 Reales, KM#136.

CS Date	Host Date	Good	VG	F	VF	XF
ND(1841)	1822-1823	150	225	300	400	—

KM# 117 8 REALES
Silver **Counterstamp:** Type IV **Note:** Counterstamp on Peru (Lima) 8 Reales, KM#142.1.

CS Date	Host Date	Good	VG	F	VF	XF
ND(1841)	1825-1828	45.00	75.00	120	175	—

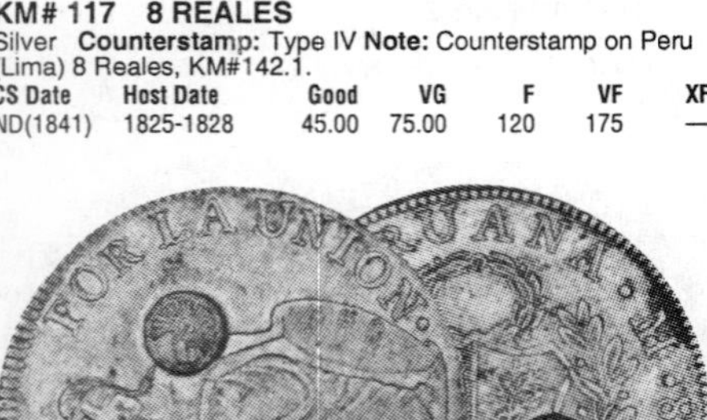

KM# 118.1 8 REALES
Silver **Counterstamp:** Type IV **Note:** Counterstamp on Peru (Lima) 8 Reales, KM#142.3.

CS Date	Host Date	Good	VG	F	VF	XF
ND(1841)	1828-1841	40.00	65.00	100	150	—

KM# 118.2 8 REALES
Silver **Counterstamp:** Type IV **Note:** Counterstamp on Peru (Lima) 8 Reales, KM#142.8.

CS Date	Host Date	Good	VG	F	VF	XF
ND(1841)	1828-1841	40.00	65.00	100	150	—

KM# 121 8 REALES
Silver **Counterstamp:** Type IV **Note:** Counterstamp on Peru (North) 8 Reales, KM#155.

CS Date	Host Date	Good	VG	F	VF	XF
ND(1841)	1836-1839	45.00	75.00	120	175	—

STANDARD COINAGE

8 Reales = 1 Peso

KM# 130 1/4 REAL
0.7600 g., 0.9030 Silver .0220 oz.

Date	Mintage	F	VF	XF	Unc	BU
1859	—	200	300	500	—	—
1860	116,000	6.00	10.00	20.00	35.00	—
1861	—	7.00	12.50	17.50	27.50	—
1862	—	6.50	10.00	15.00	25.00	—
1863	—	7.00	12.50	17.50	30.00	—
1864	—	7.00	12.50	17.50	30.00	—
1865	23,000	22.50	45.00	75.00	150	—
1866	205,000	5.00	8.50	12.50	22.50	—
1867	169,000	5.00	8.50	12.50	22.50	—
1868	148,000	5.00	8.50	12.50	22.50	—
1869	242,000	5.00	8.50	12.50	22.50	—

KM# 146 1/4 REAL
0.7700 g., 0.9000 Silver .0222 oz. **Rev:** 0.900 below wreath **Note:** Varieties exist.

Date	Mintage	F	VF	XF	Unc	BU
1872 P	—	2.00	3.50	5.50	9.00	—
1873/2 P	308,000	5.00	10.00	15.00	25.00	—
1873 P	Inc. above	1.00	1.75	3.00	5.00	—
1874 P	—	7.50	12.50	20.00	35.00	—
1875/3 P	—	10.00	20.00	35.00	75.00	—
1875 P	—	1.00	1.75	3.00	12.50	—
1876 P	—	10.00	15.00	25.00	40.00	—
1878 P 2 known	—	175	250	—	—	—
1878 F	680,000	1.00	1.75	3.00	8.00	—

KM# 146a.1 1/4 REAL
0.7700 g., 0.8350 Silver .0206 oz. **Rev:** 0.835 below small wreath **Note:** Mintage included above, in KM#146.

Date	Mintage	F	VF	XF	Unc	BU
1878	—	2.00	3.50	6.50	12.50	—

KM# 146a.2 1/4 REAL
0.7700 g., 0.8350 Silver .0206 oz. **Rev:** 0.835 below large wreath **Note:** 1878 mintage included above, in KM#146.

Date	Mintage	F	VF	XF	Unc	BU
1878	—	1.50	2.50	4.00	8.00	—
1879	171,000	1.50	2.50	4.00	8.00	—

KM# 146a.3 1/4 REAL
0.7700 g., 0.8350 Silver .0206 oz. **Rev:** Without fineness **Note:** 1878 mintages included above, in KM#146. 1879 mintage included above, in KM#146a.2.

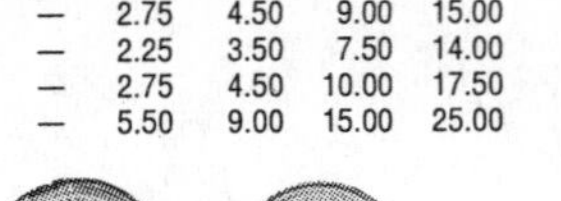

Date	Mintage	F	VF	XF	Unc	BU
1878 Large G/O	—	2.75	4.50	9.00	15.00	—
1878 Medium G	—	2.25	3.50	7.50	14.00	—
1878 Small G	—	2.75	4.50	10.00	17.50	—
1879 Large G	—	5.50	9.00	15.00	25.00	—

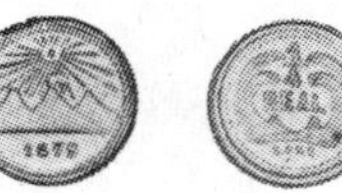

KM# 151 1/4 REAL
0.7700 g., 0.8350 Silver .0206 oz. **Obv:** Long-rayed sun **Rev:** 0.835 added **Note:** 1879 mintage included above, in KM#146a.2.

Date	Mintage	F	VF	XF	Unc	BU
1879	—	1.50	2.00	3.00	6.50	—
1880	115,000	1.00	1.75	3.00	6.50	—
1881/79	73,000	5.00	10.00	15.00	25.00	—
1881	Inc. above	3.00	4.50	8.00	13.50	—
1882	—	1.00	1.50	2.50	5.00	—
1883	195,000	15.00	25.00	40.00	70.00	—
1884	100,000	1.00	1.50	2.50	5.00	—
1885	—	7.50	12.50	20.00	35.00	—
1886/5	—	1.50	2.50	4.50	8.00	—
1886	—	1.50	2.50	4.50	8.00	—

KM# 156 1/4 REAL
0.7700 g., 0.8350 Silver .0206 oz. **Obv:** Mountain with short-rayed sun **Note:** Varieties exist.

Date	Mintage	F	VF	XF	Unc	BU
1887	—	1.50	2.50	4.00	8.00	—
1888	—	1.00	1.50	2.25	3.50	—

KM# 157 1/4 REAL
0.7700 g., 0.8350 Silver .0206 oz. **Obv:** G below mountains

Date	Mintage	F	VF	XF	Unc	BU
1889	870,000	2.00	3.00	5.00	15.00	—

KM# 158 1/4 REAL
0.7700 g., 0.8350 Silver .0206 oz. **Rev:** 5 stars below wreath **Note:** 1889 mintage included above, in KM#157. Varieties exist.

Date	Mintage	F	VF	XF	Unc	BU
1889	—	1.00	1.50	2.50	4.50	—
1890	—	1.00	1.50	2.50	4.50	—
1891	—	1.50	2.50	4.00	6.50	—

KM# 159 1/4 REAL
0.7700 g., 0.8350 Silver .0206 oz. **Obv:** Mountains with long-rayed sun

Date	Mintage	F	VF	XF	Unc	BU
1892	512,000	30.00	65.00	225	350	—
1893/2	749,000	2.00	4.00	8.00	15.00	—
1893 Large date	Inc. above	1.00	1.50	2.00	3.00	—
1893 Small date	Inc. above	1.00	1.50	2.00	3.00	—
1894	—	7.50	12.50	20.00	35.00	—

KM# 161 1/4 REAL
0.7700 g., 0.8350 Silver .0206 oz. **Rev:** 3 stars below thin wreath **Note:** 1893 mintage included above, in KM159.

Date	Mintage	F	VF	XF	Unc	BU
1893	—	1.00	1.50	2.00	3.00	—
1894	59,000	6.50	10.00	15.00	25.00	—

KM# 162 1/4 REAL
0.7700 g., 0.8350 Silver .0206 oz. **Rev:** 5 stars below full wreath

Date	Mintage	F	VF	XF	Unc	BU
1894	—	0.75	1.25	2.25	5.00	—
1894 H	800,000	0.50	0.75	1.50	2.50	—
1894 H Proof	—	Value: 100				
1895/8	—	—	—	—	—	—
1895	1,482,000	0.50	0.75	1.25	2.00	—

Date	Mintage	F	VF	XF	Unc	BU
1896	2,071,000	0.50	0.75	1.25	2.00	—
1897	989,000	0.50	0.75	1.50	2.25	—
1898	384,000	0.50	1.00	1.75	3.00	—
1899	80,000	1.50	2.50	4.50	8.00	—

KM# 131 1/2 REAL (Medio)
1.5500 g., 0.9030 Silver .0449 oz. **Rev:** MED: REAL

Date	Mintage	F	VF	XF	Unc	BU
1859	—	15.00	30.00	60.00	125	—
1859 Proof; Rare	—	—	—	—	—	—
1860 R	191,000	6.00	10.00	20.00	50.00	—
1861	—	15.00	30.00	60.00	125	—
1861 R	—	6.00	10.00	20.00	50.00	—

KM# 138 1/2 REAL (Medio)
1.5500 g., 0.9030 Silver .0449 oz. **Obv. Legend:** RAFAEL CARRERA PTE **Rev:** MED. RL

Date	Mintage	F	VF	XF	Unc	BU
1862 R	—	10.00	20.00	40.00	100	—
1863/2 R	—	6.00	10.00	20.00	50.00	—
1863 R	—	4.50	9.00	15.00	40.00	—
1865/3 R	57,000	4.50	9.00	15.00	40.00	—
1865 R	Inc. above	3.25	6.00	12.00	30.00	—

KM# 143 1/2 REAL (Medio)
1.5500 g., 0.9030 Silver .0449 oz. **Obv. Legend:** CARRERA FUNDADOR

Date	Mintage	F	VF	XF	Unc	BU
1867 R	92,000	4.00	8.50	15.00	40.00	—
1868 R	102,000	4.00	8.50	15.00	40.00	—
1869	117,000	4.00	8.50	15.00	40.00	—
1869 R	—	4.25	9.00	17.50	45.00	—

KM# 147 1/2 REAL (Medio)
1.5000 g., 0.9000 Silver .0435 oz.

Date	Mintage	F	VF	XF	Unc	BU
1872 P	—	8.00	13.50	25.00	55.00	—
1873 P	35,000	9.00	15.00	27.50	60.00	—

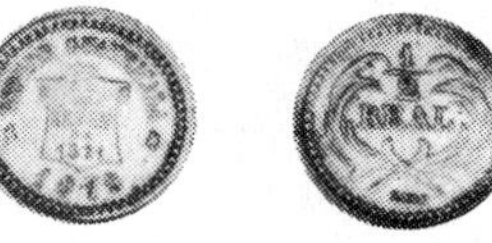

KM# 147a.1 1/2 REAL (Medio)
1.5000 g., 0.8350 Silver .0402 oz. **Note:** 1879 mintage included below, in KM#152.

Date	Mintage	F	VF	XF	Unc	BU
1878	—	2.75	4.50	8.50	25.00	—
Note: Large and small dates and letters exist for 1878						
1879	—	3.75	6.50	10.00	28.00	—
Note: Wide and narrow dates exist for 1879						

KM# 147a.2 1/2 REAL (Medio)
1.5000 g., 0.8350 Silver .0402 oz. **Rev:** Without fineness **Note:** 1893 mintage included below, in KM#163.

Date	Mintage	F	VF	XF	Unc	BU
1878 Large date	—	2.75	4.50	8.50	22.50	—
1878 Small date	—	2.75	4.50	8.50	22.50	—
1893	—	5.00	8.50	13.50	30.00	—

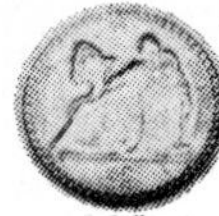

KM# 152 1/2 REAL (Medio)
1.5000 g., 0.8350 Silver .0402 oz. **Obv:** 1/2 RL **Note:** Varieties exist.

Date	Mintage	F	VF	XF	Unc	BU
1879 D	1,683,000	2.00	4.00	6.00	10.00	—
1879 D	—	2.50	5.00	8.00	15.00	—
1880/79 D	2,715,000	3.00	6.00	9.00	17.50	—
1880 D	Inc. above	0.75	1.25	2.50	5.00	—
1880/70 E	Inc. above	—	—	—	—	—
1880 E	Inc. above	6.00	10.00	15.00	22.50	—

KM# 155.1 1/2 REAL (Medio)
1.5000 g., 0.8350 Silver .0402 oz. **Obv:** MEDIO REAL **Note:** 1880 mintages included above, in KM#152. Varieties exist.

Date	Mintage	F	VF	XF	Unc	BU
1880/770 E	—	3.50	5.00	9.00	15.00	—
1880/777 E	—	3.00	4.50	7.50	12.50	—
1880/790 E	—	3.00	4.50	7.50	12.50	—
1880/79 E	—	3.00	4.50	7.50	12.50	—
1880 E	—	0.75	1.50	2.50	4.00	—
1881 E	—	0.75	2.00	3.00	4.50	—
1883/1 E	46,000	8.00	12.50	28.00	50.00	—
1883 E	Inc. above	4.50	8.50	15.00	22.50	—

KM# 155.2 1/2 REAL (Medio)
1.5000 g., 0.8350 Silver .0402 oz. **Rev:** Star between fineness and date

Date	Mintage	F	VF	XF	Unc	BU
1889/779	481,000	1.25	2.25	6.00	12.00	—
1889	Inc. above	1.25	2.25	6.00	12.00	—
1890/89	—	2.00	4.50	8.50	15.00	—
1890/9 With 8/7	—	9.00	18.00	35.00	60.00	—
1890	—	1.25	2.25	6.00	12.00	—

KM# 155.3 1/2 REAL (Medio)
1.5000 g., 0.8350 Silver .0402 oz. **Rev:** Without star between fineness and date

Date	Mintage	F	VF	XF	Unc	BU
1892 1 known	—	—	—	—	—	—

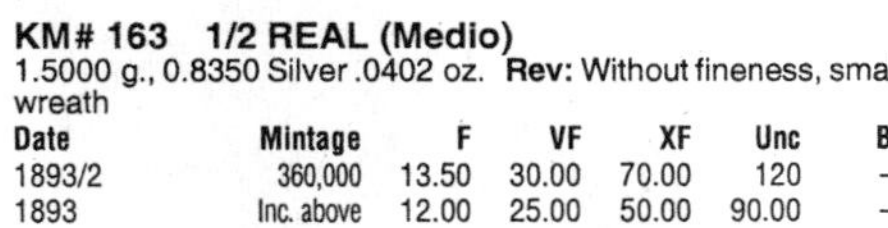

KM# 163 1/2 REAL (Medio)
1.5000 g., 0.8350 Silver .0402 oz. **Rev:** Without fineness, small wreath

Date	Mintage	F	VF	XF	Unc	BU
1893/2	360,000	13.50	30.00	70.00	120	—
1893	Inc. above	12.00	25.00	50.00	90.00	—

KM# 164 1/2 REAL (Medio)
1.5000 g., 0.8350 Silver .0402 oz. **Rev:** Large wreath **Note:** Mintages included above, in KM#163.

Date	Mintage	F	VF	XF	Unc	BU
1893 Large date, blundered flat top 3	—	7.00	15.00	30.00	55.00	—
1893 Small date, round top 3	—	7.00	15.00	30.00	55.00	—

KM# 165 1/2 REAL (Medio)
1.5000 g., 0.8350 Silver .0402 oz. **Note:** Varieties exist.

Date	Mintage	F	VF	XF	Unc	BU
1894	619,000	0.65	1.25	2.25	4.00	—
1894 H	900,000	0.65	1.25	2.00	3.00	—
1894 H Proof	—	Value: 100				
1895	819,000	0.65	1.25	2.00	3.00	—
1895 H	300,000	1.25	2.25	3.75	5.50	—
1896	1,062,000	0.65	1.25	2.00	3.00	—
1897	528,000	0.65	1.25	2.00	3.00	—

KM# 170 1/2 REAL (Medio)
1.5500 g., 0.6000 Silver .0299 oz.

Date	Mintage	F	VF	XF	Unc	BU
1899	486,000	0.75	1.25	2.50	3.50	—

KM# 132 REAL
3.0000 g., 0.9030 Silver .0870 oz. **Obv:** Frener F. below truncation **Obv. Legend:** RAFAEL CARRERA PTE... **Rev:** UN REAL

Date	Mintage	F	VF	XF	Unc	BU
1859	—	60.00	100	—	—	—
1859/95 R	—	—	—	—	—	—
1859 R	—	10.00	18.00	30.00	75.00	—
1860 R	177,000	5.00	9.00	18.00	40.00	—

KM# 137.1 REAL
3.0000 g., 0.9030 Silver .0870 oz. **Obv:** With FRENER F. below bust **Rev:** UN RL

Date	Mintage	F	VF	XF	Unc	BU
1861 R	—	4.00	7.50	15.00	35.00	—
1862 R	—	3.00	6.00	12.00	30.00	—
1863 R	—	5.00	9.00	18.00	40.00	—
1864 R	—	3.00	5.50	11.50	30.00	—
1865 R	—	5.50	10.00	20.00	45.00	—

KM# 137.2 REAL
3.0000 g., 0.9030 Silver .0870 oz. **Obv:** Without FRENER F below bust **Note:** Varieties exist.

Date	Mintage	F	VF	XF	Unc	BU
1865 R	—	3.00	6.00	12.00	30.00	—

KM# 141 REAL
3.0000 g., 0.9030 Silver .0870 oz. **Obv. Legend:** R. CARRERA FUNDADOR... **Rev:** 1 RL

Date	Mintage	F	VF	XF	Unc	BU
1866 R	385,000	4.00	9.00	18.00	40.00	—
1867 R	199,000	4.00	9.00	18.00	40.00	—

KM# 145 REAL
3.0000 g., 0.9030 Silver .0870 oz. **Rev:** UN REAL

Date	Mintage	F	VF	XF	Unc	BU
1868 R	335,000	4.00	9.00	18.00	40.00	—
1868/7 R	—	5.00	10.00	20.00	45.00	—
1869 R	131,000	4.00	9.00	18.00	40.00	—

KM# 148.1 REAL
3.1500 g., 0.9000 Silver .0911 oz.

Date	Mintage	F	VF	XF	Unc	BU
1872 P	3,816	10.00	22.50	55.00	100	—
1874 P	—	8.00	15.00	25.00	65.00	—
1878 F	159,000	9.00	18.00	32.50	75.00	—

KM# 148.2 REAL
3.1500 g., 0.9000 Silver .0911 oz. **Obv:** Without fineness

Date	Mintage	F	VF	XF	Unc	BU
1878	Inc. above	12.50	27.50	55.00	100	—

Note: Wide and narrow dates exist

KM# 153 REAL
3.1500 g., 0.9000 Silver .0911 oz.

Date	Mintage	F	VF	XF	Unc	BU
1879 D	37,000	10.00	22.50	37.50	60.00	—

KM# 153a.1 REAL
3.2500 g., 0.8350 Silver .0872 oz.

Date	Mintage	F	VF	XF	Unc	BU
1883	46,000	3.50	6.00	12.00	17.50	—

KM# 153a.2 REAL
3.2500 g., 0.8350 Silver .0872 oz. **Rev:** Star between fineness and date

Date	Mintage	F	VF	XF	Unc	BU
1889	332,000	1.50	2.75	3.50	6.00	—
1890/89	—	2.00	4.50	6.50	12.50	—
1890/8	—	2.00	4.50	6.50	12.50	—
1890	—	1.50	2.75	3.50	6.00	—
1891	—	1.50	2.75	3.50	6.00	—
1893	293,000	2.00	4.00	5.00	8.00	—

Note: Wide and narrow dates exist on 1893 dated coins

KM# 166 REAL
3.2500 g., 0.8350 Silver .0872 oz.

Date	Mintage	F	VF	XF	Unc	BU
1894	326,000	2.00	3.00	4.25	6.50	—
1894 H	600,000	2.00	3.00	4.00	5.50	—
1894 H Proof	—	Value: 100				
1895 H	200,000	3.00	6.00	9.00	15.00	—
1896	203,000	2.00	3.00	4.25	6.50	—
1897	701,000	2.00	3.00	4.00	5.50	—
1898	40,000	6.50	11.50	20.00	32.50	—

KM# 171 REAL
3.2500 g., 0.8350 Silver .0872 oz. **Rev:** Without fineness

Date	Mintage	F	VF	XF	Unc	BU
1899	—	6.50	10.00	20.00	32.50	—

KM# 172 REAL
3.1500 g., 0.7500 Silver .0759 oz.

Date	Mintage	F	VF	XF	Unc	BU
1899	—	85.00	135	250	—	—

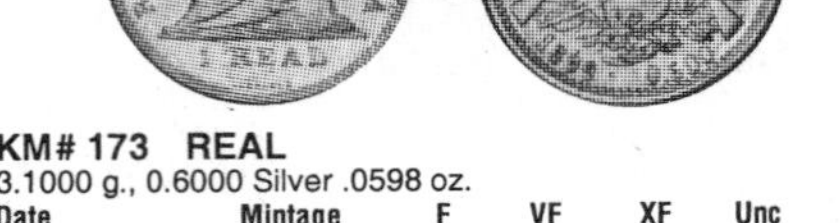

KM# 173 REAL
3.1000 g., 0.6000 Silver .0598 oz.

Date	Mintage	F	VF	XF	Unc	BU
1899	—	2.00	2.50	5.00	12.50	—

KM# 174 REAL
3.1500 g., 0.5000 Silver .0506 oz. **Note:** Varieties exist.

Date	Mintage	F	VF	XF	Unc	BU
1899/88	—	1.50	3.00	8.00	17.50	—
1899	—	1.25	2.75	6.00	12.50	—
1900	1,874,000	1.25	2.75	7.00	15.00	—

KM# 174a REAL
Silver **Note:** .500/.550 Silver

Date	Mintage	F	VF	XF	Unc	BU
1899/8	—	1.50	3.50	9.00	19.00	—
1899	—	1.25	3.00	6.50	14.00	—

KM# 133 2 REALES (Dos)
6.3000 g., 0.9030 Silver .1829 oz., 27.5 mm. **Obv:** Thick letters **Obv. Legend:** RAFAEL CARRERA PE

Date	Mintage	VG	F	VF	XF	Unc
1859	—	200	300	400	650	—

Note: Often holed; beware of repaired specimens

KM# 134 2 REALES (Dos)
6.2000 g., 0.9030 Silver .1800 oz., 26 mm. **Obv:** Thin letters

Date	Mintage	VG	F	VF	XF	Unc
1860 R	—	3.50	8.50	17.50	50.00	—
1861 R	—	4.50	11.50	22.50	55.00	—

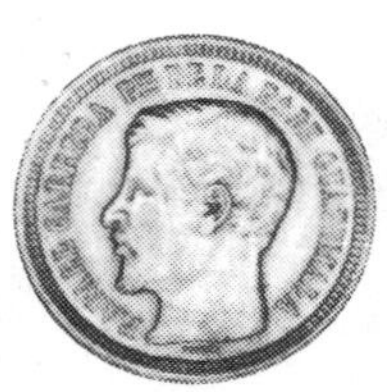

KM# 139 2 REALES (Dos)
6.1000 g., 0.9030 Silver .1770 oz., 24 mm. **Rev:** Narrower shield

Date	Mintage	F	VF	XF	Unc	BU
1862 R	—	6.00	12.00	25.00	50.00	—
1863 R	—	6.00	12.00	25.00	50.00	—

Note: Wide and narrow dates exist on 1863 dates coins

Date	Mintage	F	VF	XF	Unc	BU
1864 R	—	6.00	12.00	25.00	50.00	—
1865 R	410,000	6.00	12.00	25.00	50.00	—
1865 R Without period after date	Inc. above	12.00	25.00	60.00	100	—

KM# 142 2 REALES (Dos)
6.1000 g., 0.9030 Silver .1770 oz., 24 mm. **Obv. Legend:** R. CARRERA FUNDADOR...

Date	Mintage	F	VF	XF	Unc	BU
1866 R	334,000	4.00	8.50	16.00	40.00	—
1867 R	293,000	4.00	8.50	16.00	40.00	—
1868 R	267,000	4.50	8.50	16.00	40.00	—
1869 R	124,000	6.50	12.00	20.00	50.00	—

KM# 149 2 REALES (Dos)
6.1000 g., 0.9000 Silver .1765 oz., 24 mm.

Date	Mintage	F	VF	XF	Unc	BU
1872 P	—	6.00	12.50	25.00	55.00	—
1873 P	610,000	3.50	7.50	18.00	40.00	—

KM# 154 2 REALES (Dos)
6.1000 g., 0.9000 Silver .1765 oz., 24 mm.

Date	Mintage	F	VF	XF	Unc	BU
1879 D	101,000	7.50	12.00	18.00	50.00	—

KM# 154a 2 REALES (Dos)
Silver **Note:** .835/.900 Silver

Date	Mintage	F	VF	XF	Unc	BU
1881 E	2,975,000	7.50	10.00	12.50	25.00	—
1881 E (Error) G/R in Guatemala	—	10.00	15.00	20.00	35.00	—

KM# 154c 2 REALES (Dos)
0.8350 Silver **Note:** Without dot before fineness

Date	Mintage	F	VF	XF	Unc	BU
1881 E	—	10.00	15.00	20.00	35.00	—

KM# 154b.1 2 REALES (Dos)
6.2000 g., 0.8350 Silver .1664 oz. **Rev:** Star between fineness and date

Date	Mintage	VG	F	VF	XF	Unc
1892	—	60.00	120	280	400	—
1893 1 known	—	—	—	—	—	—

KM# 154b.2 2 REALES (Dos)
6.2000 g., 0.8350 Silver .1664 oz. **Rev:** Without star

Date	Mintage	VG	F	VF	XF	Unc
1892	—	70.00	170	280	400	—

KM# 167 2 REALES (Dos)
6.2000 g., 0.8350 Silver .1664 oz.

Date	Mintage	F	VF	XF	Unc	BU
1894	1,094,000	2.25	4.50	7.00	12.50	—
1894 H	900,000	2.25	4.50	7.00	12.50	—
1894 H Proof	—	Value: 300				
1895	2,783,000	2.25	4.50	7.00	12.50	—
1895 H	300,000	3.75	6.00	9.00	15.00	—
1896	605,000	2.25	4.50	7.00	12.50	—
1897	1,040,999	2.25	4.50	7.00	12.50	—
1898	5,172,000	1.75	3.25	6.50	12.00	—
1899	40,000	10.00	17.50	25.00	50.00	—

KM# 135 4 REALES (Cuatro)
0.8459 g., 0.8750 Gold .0238 oz.

Date	Mintage	F	VF	XF	Unc	BU
1860 R	—	20.00	35.00	50.00	90.00	—
1861 R	277,000	17.50	30.00	40.00	75.00	—
1864 R	—	25.00	55.00	85.00	150	—

KM# 136 4 REALES (Cuatro)
12.5000 g., 0.9030 Silver .3629 oz. **Obv. Legend:** RAFAEL CARRERA PTE...

Date	Mintage	VG	F	VF	XF	Unc
1860 R	4,760	7.50	22.00	40.00	80.00	—
1861 R	—	6.00	20.00	35.00	70.00	—

KM# 140 4 REALES (Cuatro)
12.5000 g., 0.9030 Silver .3629 oz. **Rev:** Shield narrowed

Date	Mintage	F	VF	XF	Unc	BU
1863 R	—	10.00	20.00	35.00	200	—
1865/55 R	82,000	—	—	—	—	—
1865/3 R	Inc. above	18.00	30.00	55.00	350	—
1865 R	Inc. above	10.00	20.00	35.00	200	—

KM# 144 4 REALES (Cuatro)
12.5000 g., 0.9030 Silver .3629 oz. **Obv. Legend:** R. CARRERA FUNDADOR...

Date	Mintage	VG	F	VF	XF	Unc
1867 R	54,000	5.00	15.00	20.00	35.00	—
1868 R	36,000	5.00	15.00	25.00	40.00	—
1869 R Rare	—	—	—	—	—	—

KM# 150 4 REALES (Cuatro)
12.5000 g., 0.9000 Silver .3617 oz.

Date	Mintage	F	VF	XF	Unc	BU
1873 P	24,000	18.50	40.00	100	200	—
1878 D	10,000	27.50	60.00	125	250	—
1879 D	7,664	27.50	60.00	125	250	—
1879 P	—	45.00	85.00	145	290	—
1892 R.G.	—	60.00	135	275	550	—
1893	—	100	225	550	875	—
1893 R.G.	—	100	225	550	875	—

KM# 160 4 REALES (Cuatro)
12.5000 g., 0.8350 Silver .3356 oz.

Date	Mintage	F	VF	XF	Unc	BU
1892	2,600	1,000	1,400	2,000	3,000	—

KM# 168.1 4 REALES (Cuatro)
12.5000 g., 0.9000 Silver .3617 oz.

Date	Mintage	F	VF	XF	Unc	BU
1894 H	500,000	6.00	12.50	20.00	37.50	—
1894 H Proof	—	Value: 400				

KM# 168.2 4 REALES (Cuatro)
12.5000 g., 0.9000 Silver .3617 oz. **Obv:** H mint mark **Rev:** H mint mark

Date	Mintage	F	VF	XF	Unc	BU
1894H	Inc. above	80.00	120	250	500	—

DECIMAL COINAGE

100 Centavos (Centimos) = 1 Peso

KM# 196 CENTAVO
Bronze

Date	Mintage	F	VF	XF	Unc	BU
1871	—	2.50	5.50	12.00	35.00	—

KM# 202.1 CENTAVO
Bronze

Date	Mintage	F	VF	XF	Unc	BU
1881	—	3.50	7.50	14.00	45.00	—

KM# 202.2 CENTAVO
Bronze **Note:** Die breaks in 1881 have the appearance of 1884.

Date	Mintage	F	VF	XF	Unc	BU
1881	—	5.00	10.00	18.00	50.00	—

Note: Some specimens overstruck on KM#196

KM# 203 5 CENTAVOS
1.2500 g., 0.8350 Silver .0335 oz.

Date	Mintage	F	VF	XF	Unc	BU
1881	118,000	10.00	25.00	40.00	110	—

KM# 204 10 CENTAVOS
2.5000 g., 0.8350 Silver .0671 oz.

Date	Mintage	F	VF	XF	Unc	BU
1881	56,000	16.50	32.50	55.00	130	—

KM# 189 25 CENTIMOS
6.2500 g., 0.9000 Silver .1808 oz.

Date	Mintage	F	VF	XF	Unc	BU
1869 R	181,000	6.00	13.50	25.00	70.00	—
1870 R	180,000	4.50	9.00	20.00	60.00	—

KM# 205.1 25 CENTAVOS
6.2500 g., 0.8350 Silver .1677 oz. **Note:** Varieties exist.

Date	Mintage	F	VF	XF	Unc	BU
1881 E	5,044,000	2.50	5.00	18.00	32.00	—
1882 E	—	2.50	5.00	18.00	32.00	—
1885 E	—	2.50	5.00	18.00	32.00	—
1888 E	—	12.00	25.00	45.00	75.00	—
1888	—	20.00	40.00	75.00	125	—
1888 G	—	2.50	5.00	18.00	32.00	—
1889 G	496,000	2.50	5.00	18.00	32.00	—
1889 G Medallic die alignment	Inc. above	—	—	—	—	—

KM# 206 25 CENTAVOS
6.2500 g., 0.8350 Silver .1677 oz.

Date	Mintage	VG	F	VF	XF	Unc
1882	—	125	225	325	450	—

KM# 205.2 25 CENTAVOS
6.2500 g., 0.8350 Silver .1677 oz. **Note:** Star replaces assayer's initial.

Date	Mintage	F	VF	XF	Unc	BU
1889	Inc. above	2.50	5.00	18.00	35.00	—
1890	—	3.00	6.00	20.00	35.00	—
1891	—	6.00	12.00	25.00	40.00	—

KM# 209.2 25 CENTAVOS
6.2500 g., 0.8350 Silver .1677 oz. **Rev:** Without star, "25 CENTS", large letters **Note:** Varieties exist.

Date	Mintage	F	VF	XF	Unc	BU
1890	—	6.00	12.00	22.50	35.00	—
1892	—	2.50	5.00	8.00	16.00	—
1893	—	2.25	4.50	7.00	14.00	—

KM# 209.1 25 CENTAVOS
6.2500 g., 0.8350 Silver .1677 oz. **Rev:** Without star. "25 cents" small letters

Date	Mintage	F	VF	XF	Unc	BU
1892	—	30.00	50.00	75.00	120	—

KM# 195 50 CENTAVOS
12.5000 g., 0.8350 Silver .3356 oz.

Date	Mintage	VG	F	VF	XF	Unc
1870 R	140,000	5.00	10.00	20.00	50.00	—

KM# 178 PESO
25.0000 g., 0.9030 Silver .7258 oz.

Date	Mintage	VG	F	VF	XF	Unc
1859	—	65.00	175	275	900	—
1859 R Rare	—	—	—	—	—	—

KM# 179 PESO
1.6917 g., 0.8750 Gold .0476 oz.

Date	Mintage	VG	F	VF	XF	Unc
1859 R	—	25.00	35.00	50.00	75.00	—
1860 R	37,000	25.00	35.00	50.00	75.00	—

KM# 182 PESO
27.0000 g., 0.9030 Silver .7839 oz.

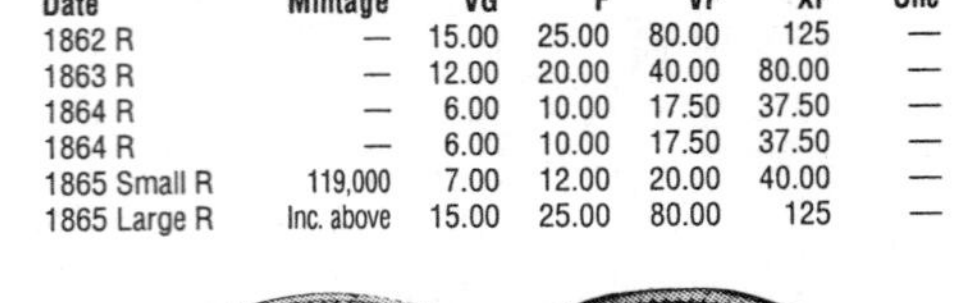

Date	Mintage	VG	F	VF	XF	Unc
1862 R	—	15.00	25.00	80.00	125	—
1863 R	—	12.00	20.00	40.00	80.00	—
1864 R	—	6.00	10.00	17.50	37.50	—
1864 R	—	6.00	10.00	17.50	37.50	—
1865 Small R	119,000	7.00	12.00	20.00	40.00	—
1865 Large R	Inc. above	15.00	25.00	80.00	125	—

KM# 186.1 PESO
27.0000 g., 0.9030 Silver .7839 oz. **Rev:** L.10D.20G

Date	Mintage	VG	F	VF	XF	Unc
1866 R	109,000	7.00	12.00	20.00	40.00	—
1867 R	173,000	6.00	10.00	17.50	37.50	—
1868 R	60,000	8.00	15.00	25.00	50.00	—

KM# 186.2 PESO
27.0000 g., 0.9030 Silver .7839 oz. **Rev:** Without "L" before 10Ds.20Gs

Date	Mintage	VG	F	VF	XF	Unc
1869	186,000	45.00	70.00	125	285	—
1869	Inc. above	40.00	60.00	100	250	—

KM# 190.1 PESO
25.0000 g., 0.9000 Silver .7234 oz. **Rev:** L.0,900 **Note:** 1869 mintages included above, in KM#186.

Date	Mintage	VG	F	VF	XF	Unc
1869/99 R	—	10.00	17.50	25.00	75.00	—
1869 R	—	6.00	10.00	17.50	37.50	—
1870 R	283,000	6.00	10.00	15.00	35.00	—
1871 R	—	6.00	10.00	15.00	30.00	—

KM# 190.2 PESO
25.0000 g., 0.9000 Silver .7234 oz. **Rev:** Without "L" before 0,900 **Note:** Mintage included above, in KM#186.

Date	Mintage	VG	F	VF	XF	Unc
1869 R	—	8.00	15.00	25.00	45.00	—

KM# 190.3 PESO
25.0000 g., 0.9000 Silver .7234 oz. **Rev:** Without "L" and 0,900 **Note:** Mintages included above, in KM#186.

Date	Mintage	VG	F	VF	XF	Unc
1869 R	—	30.00	50.00	80.00	120	—
1869	—	30.00	50.00	80.00	120	—

KM# 197.1 PESO
25.0000 g., 0.9000 Silver .7234 oz. **Rev:** Date and fineness at bottom

Date	Mintage	F	VF	XF	Unc	BU
1872 R Rare	—	—	—	—	—	—
1872 P	14,000	30.00	60.00	100	500	—
1873 P	78,000	20.00	40.00	80.00	300	—
1873 P (Error fineness 0900)	Inc. above	30.00	50.00	90.00	250	—

KM# 197.2 PESO
25.0000 g., 0.9000 Silver .7234 oz. **Rev:** Quetzal with short tail

Date	Mintage	F	VF	XF	Unc	BU
1873 P	—	30.00	50.00	90.00	250	—

KM# 200 PESO
25.0000 g., 0.9000 Silver .7234 oz. **Rev:** Date and fineness at top

Date	Mintage	VG	F	VF	XF	Unc
1878 D	1,076	300	600	1,200	2,000	—
1879 D	10,000	100	200	300	600	—

KM# 201 PESO
25.0000 g., 0.9000 Silver .7234 oz. **Rev:** Full spray design **Note:** 1879 mintage included above, in KM#200.

Date	Mintage	VG	F	VF	XF	Unc
1879 D	—	125	250	350	500	—
1893 G	—	800	—	—	—	—
1893 RG	1,119	550	1,000	1,700	2,750	—

KM# 207 PESO
25.0000 g., 0.9000 Silver .7234 oz. **Obv:** Modified Liberty design

Date	Mintage	F	VF	XF	Unc	BU
1882/1 E Rare	—	—	—	—	—	—
1888 G	—	350	600	1,100	2,000	—
1889 G	—	700	1,000	1,650	2,500	—

KM# 208 PESO
25.0000 g., 0.9000 Silver .7234 oz.

Date	Mintage	VG	F	VF	XF	Unc
1882 A.E.	—	20.00	35.00	80.00	240	—
1889 MG	6,794	125	200	350	600	—

KM# 210 PESO
25.0000 g., 0.9000 Silver .7234 oz.

Date	Mintage	F	VF	XF	Unc	BU
1894	1,696,000	7.00	12.50	17.50	45.00	—
1894 H	875,000	7.00	12.50	17.50	55.00	—
1894 H Proof	—	Value: 800				
1895	1,415,000	7.00	12.50	20.00	65.00	—
1895 H	375,000	8.00	15.00	22.00	75.00	—
1895 H Proof	—	—	—	—	—	—
1896/5	1,403,000	10.00	17.50	25.00	85.00	—
1896	Inc. above	7.00	12.50	17.50	50.00	—
1897	—	12.00	20.00	30.00	100	—

KM# 180 2 PESOS
3.3834 g., 0.8750 Gold .0952 oz.

Date	Mintage	VG	F	VF	XF	Unc
1859 R	—	50.00	65.00	125	200	—

KM# 181 4 PESOS
6.7669 g., 0.8750 Gold .1904 oz.

Date	Mintage	VG	F	VF	XF	Unc
1861 R	—	175	250	350	525	—
1862 R	—	175	250	350	525	—

KM# 187 4 PESOS
6.7669 g., 0.8750 Gold .1904 oz.

Date	Mintage	VG	F	VF	XF	Unc
1866 R Rare	561	—	—	—	—	—
1868 R	778	250	500	700	950	—
1869 R	20,000	100	175	250	375	—

KM# 191 5 PESOS
8.0645 g., 0.9000 Gold .2333 oz.

Date	Mintage	VG	F	VF	XF	Unc
1869 R	49,000	100	120	165	225	—

KM# 198 5 PESOS
8.0645 g., 0.9000 Gold .2333 oz.

Date	Mintage	VG	F	VF	XF	Unc
1872 P	—	120	200	300	500	—
1873 P Rare	—	—	—	—	—	—
1874 P	—	120	200	300	500	—
1875 P Rare	—	—	—	—	—	—
1876 F Rare	—	—	—	—	—	—
1877 F	—	120	200	300	500	—
1878 D	—	120	200	300	500	—

KM# 184 8 PESOS
13.5337 g., 0.8750 Gold .3807 oz.

Date	Mintage	VG	F	VF	XF	Unc
1864 R	—	300	450	750	1,200	—

KM# 192 8 PESOS
13.5337 g., 0.8750 Gold .3807 oz. **Note:** Similar to 4 Pesos, KM187.

Date	Mintage	VG	F	VF	XF	Unc
1869 R	—	500	650	2,000	3,000	—

KM# 193 10 PESOS
16.1290 g., 0.9000 Gold .4667 oz.

Date	Mintage	VG	F	VF	XF	Unc
1869 R	20,000	200	275	400	600	—

KM# 183 16 PESOS
27.0296 g., 0.8750 Gold .7604 oz.

Date	Mintage	VG	F	VF	XF	Unc
1863 R	—	—	—	3,500	5,500	—

Note: A few AU-Unc specimens of the 1863R were found in a box shook loose from its hiding place during the 1977 Guatemala earthquake

Date	Mintage	VG	F	VF	XF	Unc
1864 R Rare	—	—	—	—	—	—
1865 R Rare	—	—	—	—	—	—

KM# 185 16 PESOS
27.0296 g., 0.8750 Gold .7604 oz. **Note:** Reduced size.

Date	Mintage	VG	F	VF	XF	Unc
1865 R	190	1,000	2,000	4,000	6,000	—

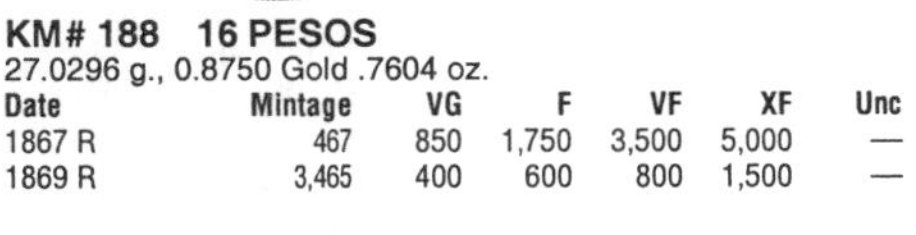

KM# 188 16 PESOS
27.0296 g., 0.8750 Gold .7604 oz.

Date	Mintage	VG	F	VF	XF	Unc
1867 R	467	850	1,750	3,500	5,000	—
1869 R	3,465	400	600	800	1,500	—

KM# 194 20 PESOS
32.2580 g., 0.9000 Gold .9334 oz.

Date	Mintage	VG	F	VF	XF	Unc
1869 R	16,000	450	550	700	950	—

KM# 199 20 PESOS
32.2580 g., 0.9000 Gold .9334 oz.

Date	Mintage	VG	F	VF	XF	Unc
1877 F	—	1,000	2,000	5,000	8,000	—
1878 F	—	1,000	2,000	5,000	8,000	—

COUNTERSTAMPED COINAGE

1894

By 1894, foreign coins had become so prevalent that on August 10, the government authorized their counter-stamping at the mint, with official 1/2 Real dies of 1894, to legitimize their circulation.

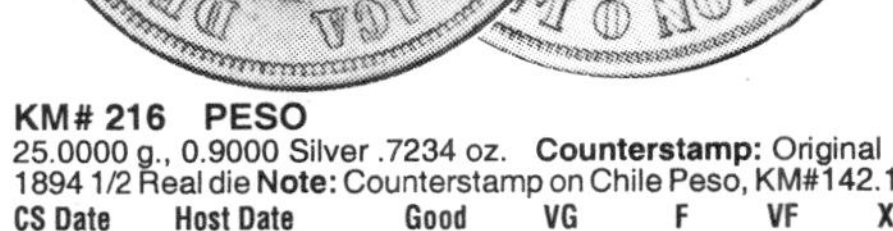

KM# 216 PESO
25.0000 g., 0.9000 Silver .7234 oz. **Counterstamp:** Original 1894 1/2 Real die **Note:** Counterstamp on Chile Peso, KM#142.1.

CS Date	Host Date	Good	VG	F	VF	XF
1894	1869	—	—	50.00	75.00	135
1894	1874	—	—	20.00	30.00	55.00
1894	1875	—	—	20.00	30.00	55.00
1894	1870/69	—	—	50.00	75.00	135
1894	1876	—	—	20.00	30.00	55.00
1894	1877	—	—	20.00	30.00	55.00
1894	1878	—	—	20.00	30.00	55.00
1894	1879	—	—	20.00	30.00	55.00
1894	1880	—	—	20.00	30.00	55.00
1894	1881	—	—	20.00	30.00	55.00
1894	1882/1	—	—	20.00	30.00	55.00
1894	1882	—	—	20.00	30.00	55.00
1894	1867	—	—	125	200	300
1894	1883	—	—	20.00	30.00	55.00
1894	1884	—	—	20.00	30.00	55.00
1894	1885/3	—	—	20.00	30.00	55.00
1894	1885	—	—	20.00	30.00	55.00
1894	1886	—	—	20.00	30.00	55.00
1894	1889	—	—	50.00	75.00	135
1894	1890/89	—	—	150	225	300
1894	1890	—	—	150	225	300
1894	1870	—	—	50.00	75.00	135
1894	1871	—	—	75.00	125	200
1894	1872	—	—	20.00	30.00	55.00
1894	1873/2	—	—	20.00	30.00	55.00
1894	1873	—	—	20.00	30.00	55.00
1894	1868	—	—	125	200	300

KM# 213 PESO
0.9170 Silver **Counterstamp:** Original 1894 1/2 Real die **Note:** Counterstamp on Brazil 2000 Reis, KM#475.

CS Date	Host Date	Good	VG	F	VF	XF
1894	1875 Rare	—	—	—	—	—

KM# 214 PESO
25.0000 g., 0.9000 Silver .7234 oz. **Counterstamp:** Original 1894 1/2 Real die **Note:** Counterstamp on Chile 8 Reales, KM#96.2.

CS Date	Host Date	Good	VG	F	VF	XF
1894	1848 JM Rare	—	—	—	—	—

KM# 215 PESO
25.0000 g., 0.9000 Silver .7234 oz. **Counterstamp:** Original 1894 1/2 Real stamp **Note:** Counterstamp on Chile Peso, KM129.

CS Date	Host Date	Good	VG	F	VF	XF
1894	1853	—	550	1,200	2,000	—
1894	1854	—	350	750	1,250	—
1894	1855	—	350	750	1,250	—

KM# 217 PESO
25.0000 g., 0.9000 Silver .7234 oz. **Counterstamp:** Original 1894 1/2 Real die **Note:** Counterstamp off center on Chile Peso, KM142.1

CS Date	Host Date	Good	VG	F	VF	XF
1894	1880	—	—	—	—	—

KM# 219 PESO
0.9030 Silver **Counterstamp:** Original 1894 1/2 Real die **Note:** Counterstamp on Guatemala Peso, KM190.1.

CS Date	Host Date	Good	VG	F	VF	XF
1894	1869 Rare	—	—	—	—	—

KM# 220 PESO
0.9030 Silver **Counterstamp:** Original 1894 1/2 Real die **Note:** Counterstamp on Guatemala Peso, KM#208.

CS Date	Host Date	Good	VG	F	VF	XF
1894	1882AE Rare	—	—	—	—	—

KM# 221 PESO
0.9030 Silver **Counterstamp:** Original 1894 1/2 Real die **Note:** Counterstamp on Guatemala Peso, KM#210.

CS Date	Host Date	Good	VG	F	VF	XF
1894	1894 H Rare	—	—	—	—	—

KM# 222 PESO
0.9000 Silver **Counterstamp:** Original 1894 1/2 Real die **Note:** Counterstamp on Honduras Peso, KM#47.

CS Date	Host Date	Good	VG	F	VF	XF
1894	1882 Rare	—	—	—	—	—

KM# 223 PESO
25.0000 g., 0.9000 Silver .7234 oz. **Counterstamp:** Original 1894 1/2 Real die **Note:** Counterstamp on Honduras Peso, KM#52.

CS Date	Host Date	Good	VG	F	VF	XF
1894	1890	—	—	850	1,350	—
1894	1890	—	—	850	1,350	—

KM# 224 PESO
25.0000 g., 0.9000 Silver .7234 oz. **Counterstamp:** Original 1894 1/2 Real die **Note:** Counterstamp on Peru Sol, KM#196.

CS Date	Host Date	Good	VG	F	VF	XF
1894	1864 Y.B.	—	—	15.00	25.00	35.00
1894	1864 Y.B. Deteano Rare	—	—	—	—	—
1894	1865 Y.B.	—	—	50.00	100	185
1894	1866 Y.B.	—	—	20.00	30.00	45.00
1894	1867 Y.B.	—	—	20.00	30.00	45.00
1894	1868 Y.B.	—	—	20.00	30.00	45.00
1894	1869 Y.B.	—	—	20.00	30.00	45.00
1894	1870 Y.J.	—	—	20.00	30.00	45.00
1894	1871 Y.J.	—	—	20.00	30.00	45.00
1894	1872 Y.J.	—	—	20.00	30.00	45.00
1894	1873 Y.J.	—	—	50.00	100	185
1894	1873 L.D.	—	—	50.00	100	185
1894	1874 Y.J.	—	—	20.00	30.00	45.00
1894	1875 Y.J.	—	—	20.00	30.00	45.00
1894	1879 Y.J.	—	—	25.00	45.00	65.00
1894	1880 Y.J.	—	—	40.00	60.00	100
1894	1881 B.F.	—	—	30.00	50.00	75.00
1894	1882 B.F.	—	—	40.00	60.00	100
1894	1882 F.N.	—	—	50.00	100	185
1894	1883 F.N.	—	—	100	165	250
1894	1884 B.D.	—	—	40.00	60.00	100
1894	1884 R.D.	—	—	20.00	30.00	45.00
1894	1885 R.D.	—	—	20.00	30.00	45.00
1894	1885 T.D.	—	—	20.00	30.00	45.00
1894	1886 R.D.	—	—	100	165	250
1894	1886 T.F.	—	—	25.00	45.00	65.00
1894	1887 T.F.	—	—	15.00	22.50	32.50
1894	1888 T.F.	—	—	15.00	22.50	32.50
1894	1889 T.F.	—	—	15.00	22.50	32.50
1894	1890/80 T.F.	—	—	30.00	50.00	75.00
1894	1890 T.F.	—	—	15.00	22.50	32.50
1894	1891 T.F.	—	—	15.00	22.50	32.50
1894	1892 T.F.	—	—	15.00	22.50	32.50
1894	1893 T.F.	—	—	15.00	22.50	32.80
1894	1393 T.F. (Error)	—	—	450	600	900
1894	1894 T.F.	—	—	20.00	30.00	45.00

KM# 225 PESO
25.0000 g., 0.9000 Silver .7234 oz. **Counterstamp:** Original 1894 1/2 Real die **Note:** Counterstamp on Peru 5 Pesetas, KM#201.1.

CS Date	Host Date	Good	VG	F	VF	XF
ND1894	1880	—	—	80.00	110	165
	Note: B.F. with B below wreath without dot					
ND1894	1880	—	—	80.00	110	165
	Note: B.F. with B. below wreath					

KM# 226 PESO
25.0000 g., 0.9000 Silver .7234 oz. **Counterstamp:** Original 1894 1/2 Real die **Note:** Counterstamp on Peru 5 Pesetas, KM#201.3.

CS Date	Host Date	Good	VG	F	VF	XF
ND1894	1882 LM	—	—	300	500	800

KM# 227 PESO
25.0000 g., 0.9000 Silver .7234 oz. **Counterstamp:** Original 1894 1/2 Real die **Note:** Counterstamp on El Salvador Peso, KM#115.1.

CS Date	Host Date	Good	VG	F	VF	XF
1894	1892	—	—	1,000	1,400	2,000
1894	1893	—	—	1,000	1,400	2,000

PATTERNS

Including off metal strikes

KM#	Date	Mintage	Identification	Mkt Val
Pn1	1854 AE	—	8 Reales. Silver. Columbus	18,500
Pn2	1854 AE	—	8 Reales. Copper.	6,500
PnA3	1860 R	—	Peso. Copper. 1.2290 g. 1/2 Real KM143. 1 Peso KM179.	—
Pn3	1876	—	10 Centavos. Silver Wash On Copper. Similar to 50 Centavos, KM195.	—
Pn4	1893	—	1/4 Real. Silver. with ESSAY.	—
Pn5	1893	—	1/2 Real. Silver. with ESSAY.	—
Pn6	1893	—	Real. Silver. with ESSAY	—
Pn7	1893	—	2 Reales. Silver. with ESSAY.	—
Pn8	1893	—	4 Reales. Silver. with ESSAY.	—
Pn9	1893	—	Peso. Silver. with ESSAY.	—
PnA10	1894	—	1/4 Real. Copper. 0.7320 g. KM162. KM159.	—
Pn10	1894(a)	10	5 Pesos. 0.9000 Gold. Small Liberty head left with ESSAI.	6,500
Pn11	1894 CB	17	5 Pesos. 0.9000 Gold. large Liberty head left.	5,000
Pn12	1894 CB	—	5 Pesos. Copper.	2,000

KM#	Date	Mintage	Identification	Mkt Val
Pn13	1894(a)	10	10 Pesos. 0.9000 Gold. small Liberty head left with ESSAI.	9,500

KM#	Date	Mintage	Identification	Mkt Val

KM#	Date	Mintage	Identification	Mkt Val
Pn14	1894 CB	17	10 Pesos. 0.9000 Gold. large Liberty head left	7,500
Pn15	1895 CB	—	4 Reales. 0.9000 Silver.	2,250

KM#	Date	Mintage	Identification	Mkt Val
Pn16	1895H	—	Peso. 0.9000 Silver.	5,000
Pn17	ND(ca.19 20-22)	—	2 Pesos. Porcelain. 25.26 mm. QUATEMALA/*PESOS*/large 2 in center. Arms of Quatemala wintin triangle; coffee tree leaf to each side; below: Meissen mintmark (crossed swords) separates two stars. Arms in triangle; made at state porcelain works, Meissen, Germany.	2,000

PROOF SETS

KM#	Date	Mintage	Identification	Issue Price	Mkt Val
PS2	1895/1896 (6)	—	Rare. KM#162, 165-167, 210, 4 Reales 1895 Pn9	—	—
PS1	1894 (6)	—	KM#162, 165-167, 168.1, 210	—	1,800

GUERNSEY

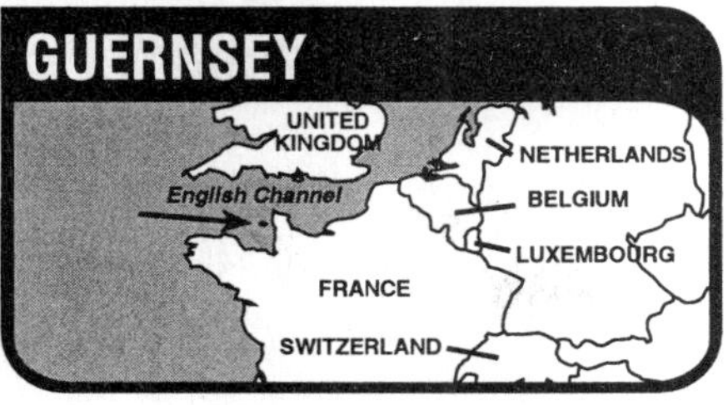

The Bailiwick of Guernsey, a British crown dependency located in the English Channel 30 miles (48 km.) west of Normandy, France, has an area of 30 sq. mi. (194 sq. km.)(including the isles of Alderney, Jethou, Herm, Brechou, and Sark), and a population of 54,000. Capital: St. Peter Port. Agriculture and cattle breeding are the main occupations.

Militant monks from the duchy of Normandy established the first permanent settlements on Guernsey prior to the Norman invasion of England, but the prevalence of prehistoric monuments suggests an earlier occupancy. The island, the only part of the duchy of Normandy belonging to the British crown, has been a possession of Britain since the Norman Conquest of 1066. During the Anglo-French wars, the harbors of Guernsey were employed in the building and out-fitting of ships for the English privateers preying on French shipping. Guernsey is administered by its own laws and customs. Unless the island is mentioned specifically, acts passed by the British Parliament are not applicable to Guernsey. During World War II, German troops occupied the island from June 30, 1940 till May 9,1945.

RULERS
British

MINT MARKS
H - Heaton, Birmingham

MONETARY SYSTEM
8 Doubles = 1 Penny
12 Pence = 1 Shilling
5 Shillings = 1 Crown
20 Shillings = 1 Pound

1 Stem

3 Stems

BRITISH DEPENDENCY

STANDARD COINAGE

KM# 1 DOUBLE
Copper

Date	Mintage	F	VF	XF	Unc	BU
1830	1,649,000	1.00	3.00	10.00	35.00	—
1830	Inc. above	5.00	15.00	30.00	45.00	—

KM# 1a DOUBLE
Bronzed Copper

Date	Mintage	F	VF	XF	Unc	BU
1830 Proof	—	Value: 250				

KM# 10 DOUBLE
Bronze

Date	Mintage	F	VF	XF	Unc	BU
1868/30	64,000	1.50	4.50	12.50	30.00	—
1868	Inc. above	2.00	6.00	18.00	37.50	—
1885H	56,000	0.50	1.50	4.50	12.50	—
1885H Proof	—	Value: 175				
1889H	112,000	0.30	0.85	3.00	7.50	—
1889H Proof	—	Value: 200				
1893H	56,000	0.50	1.50	4.50	12.50	—
1899H	56,000	0.25	0.75	3.00	8.50	—

KM# 10a DOUBLE
Bronzed Copper

Date	Mintage	F	VF	XF	Unc	BU
1885H Proof	—	Value: 275				

KM# 4 2 DOUBLES
Copper **Rev:** Leaves with 1 stem

Date	Mintage	F	VF	XF	Unc	BU
1858	56,000	6.00	18.00	55.00	125	—

KM# 9 2 DOUBLES
Bronze **Obv:** Leaves with 3 stems above shield

Date	Mintage	F	VF	XF	Unc	BU
1868	—	7.50	13.50	35.00	70.00	—
1874	45,000	4.50	9.00	25.00	50.00	—
1885H	71,000	1.25	2.75	6.00	12.00	—
1885H Proof	—	Value: 175				
1889H	36,000	0.85	3.00	8.00	15.00	—
1889H Proof	—	Value: 200				

KM# 9a 2 DOUBLES
Bronzed Copper

Date	Mintage	F	VF	XF	Unc	BU
1885H Proof	—	Value: 275				

KM# 2 4 DOUBLES
Copper **Note:** A rare mule restrike of the St. Helena obverse 1/2 Penny 1821 and reverse of Guernsey 4 Doubles dated 1830 exists. Market valuation $600.00 (VF).

Date	Mintage	F	VF	XF	Unc	BU
1830	655,000	2.25	7.50	30.00	75.00	—
1830 Proof	—	Value: 275				
1858	114,000	3.00	15.00	40.00	110	—

KM# 2a 4 DOUBLES
Bronzed Copper

Date	Mintage	F	VF	XF	Unc	BU
1830 Proof	—	Value: 325				

KM# 5 4 DOUBLES
Bronze **Obv:** Leaves with 3 stems above shield **Note:** Varieties exist.

Date	Mintage	F	VF	XF	Unc	BU
1864/54	213,000	0.85	1.75	9.00	18.50	—
1868	58,000	2.25	4.00	12.50	25.00	—
1874	69,000	1.50	3.00	11.50	22.50	—
1885H Proof	—	Value: 175				
1889H	104,000	0.75	1.25	6.00	15.00	—
1889H Proof	—	Value: 200				
1893H	52,000	1.50	3.00	7.50	20.00	—

KM# 6 4 DOUBLES
Bronze **Obv:** Leaves with one stem **Note:** Mintage included with KM#5.

Date	Mintage	F	VF	XF	Unc	BU
1864	—	1.25	2.25	9.00	18.50	—

KM# 5a 4 DOUBLES
Bronzed Copper **Obv:** Leaves with three stems

Date	Mintage	F	VF	XF	Unc	BU
1885 Proof	—	Value: 275				

KM# 3 8 DOUBLES
Copper

Date	Mintage	F	VF	XF	Unc	BU
1834	222,000	4.00	10.00	65.00	210	—
1834 Proof	—	Value: 400				

Date	Mintage	F	VF	XF	Unc	BU
1858	111,000	5.00	12.50	75.00	225	—
1858 Proof	—	Value: 450				

KM# 3a 8 DOUBLES
Bronzed Copper

Date	Mintage	F	VF	XF	Unc	BU
1834 Proof	—	Value: 600				

KM# 7 8 DOUBLES
Bronze

Date	Mintage	F	VF	XF	Unc	BU
1864	280,000	1.25	3.00	9.00	27.50	—
1864 Proof	—	Value: 175				
1868	60,000	4.00	9.00	27.50	55.00	—
1874	70,000	2.25	4.50	9.00	20.00	—
1885H	70,000	1.50	3.00	9.00	20.00	—
1885H Proof	—	Value: 200				
1889H	222,000	0.75	2.25	6.00	12.50	—
1889H Proof	—	Value: 175				
1893H	118,000	1.50	3.00	6.00	15.00	—
1893H	Inc. above	1.50	3.00	6.00	15.00	—

KM# 7a 8 DOUBLES
Bronzed Copper

Date	Mintage	F	VF	XF	Unc	BU
1885 Proof	—	Value: 325				

TOKEN COINAGE

KM# Tn1 5 SHILLING
0.8920 Silver **Issuer:** Bishop de Jersey & Co., Bank of Guernsey
Note: Struck over Spanish or Spanish Colonial 8 Reales. Forbidden by the Guernsey legislation to circulate in 1809.

Date	Mintage	VG	F	VF	XF	Unc
1809 Rare	—	—	—	—	—	—

Note: Spink R.J. Ford sale 10-90 good XF realized $19,380.

PROOF SETS

KM#	Date	Mintage	Identification	Issue Price	Mkt Val
PS2	1885H (4)	—	KM5a, 7a, 8a, 10a	—	1,150
PS1	1885H (4)	—	KM5, 7, 8, 10	—	725

GUYANA (British Guiana)

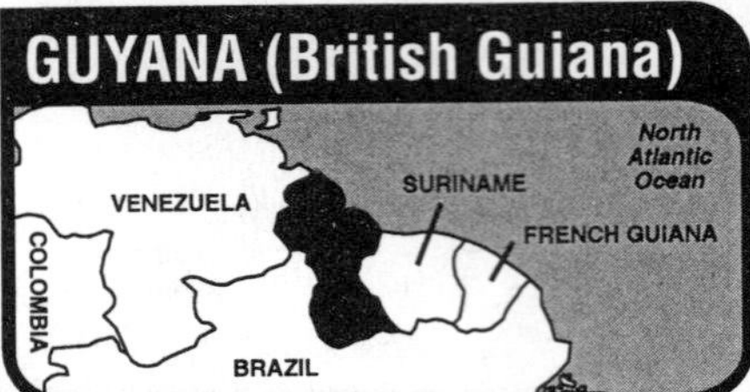

The Cooperative Republic of Guyana, is situated on the northeast coast of South America, has an area of 83,000sq. mi. (214,970 sq. km.) and a population of 729,000. Capital: Georgetown. The economy is basically agrarian. Sugar, rice and bauxite are exported.

The original area of Essequibo and Demerary, which included present-day Suriname, French Guiana, and parts of Brazil and Venezuela was sighted by Columbus in 1498.The first European settlement was made late in the 16th century by the Dutch, however, the region was claimed for the British by Sir Walter Raleigh during the reign of Elizabeth I. For the next 150 years, possession alternated between the Dutch and the British, with a short interval of French control. The British exercised de facto control after 1796, although the area, which included the Dutch colonies of Essequibo, Demerary and Berbice, was not ceded to them by the Dutch until 1814. From 1803 to1831, Essequibo and Demerary were administered separately from Berbice. The three colonies were united in the British Crown Colony of British Guiana in 1831. British Guiana won internal self-government in 1952 and full independence, under the traditional name of Guyana, on May 26,1966. Guyana became a republic on Feb. 23, 1970. It is a member of the Commonwealth of Nations. The president is the Chief of State. The prime minister is the Head of Government. Guyana is a member of the Caribbean Community and Common Market (CARICOM).

RULERS
British, until 1966

***NOTE:** From 1975-1985 the Franklin Mint produced coinage in up to 3 different qualities. Qualities of issue are designated in ( ) after each date and are defined as follows:

(M) MATTE - Normal circulation strike or a dull finish produced by sandblasting special uncirculated (polish finish) or proof quality dies.

(U) SPECIAL UNCIRCULATED - Polished or proof-like in appearance without any frosted features.

(P) PROOF - The highest quality obtainable having mirror-like fields and frosted features.

BRITISH GUIANA

COLONIAL COINAGE

KM# 22 1/8 GUILDER
0.9700 g., 0.8160 Silver .0255 oz.

Date	Mintage	F	VF	XF	Unc	BU
1836	180,000	10.00	20.00	40.00	90.00	—
1836 Proof	—	Value: 125				

KM# 23 1/4 GUILDER
1.9400 g., 0.8160 Silver .0509 oz.

Date	Mintage	F	VF	XF	Unc	BU
1836	216,000	15.00	30.00	60.00	125	—
1836 Proof	—	Value: 225				

KM# 24 1/2 GUILDER
3.8800 g., 0.8160 Silver .1018 oz.

Date	Mintage	F	VF	XF	Unc	BU
1836	118,000	15.00	40.00	90.00	250	—
1836 Proof	—	Value: 450				

KM# 25 GUILDER
7.7700 g., 0.8160 Silver .2039 oz.

Date	Mintage	F	VF	XF	Unc	BU
1836	57,000	25.00	75.00	150	350	—
1836 Proof; plain edge	—	Value: 550				
1836 Proof; reeded edge	—	Value: 1,250				

PRIVATE TOKEN COINAGE

KM# Tn1 STIVER
Copper **Obv:** Female seated on bale **Obv. Legend:** TRADE & NAVIGATION **Rev:** Legend around denomination **Rev. Legend:** PURE COPPER

Date	Mintage	VG	F	VF	XF	Unc
1838	—	9.00	18.00	35.00	75.00	250

KM# Tn2 STIVER
Copper **Obv:** Branch close to ampersand in legend **Rev:** Similar to Tn1

Date	Mintage	VG	F	VF	XF	Unc
1838	—	10.00	20.00	40.00	80.00	260

KM# Tn3 STIVER
Copper **Obv:** Similar to Tn1 **Rev:** Legend around laureate bust **Rev. Legend:** PURE COPPER

Date	Mintage	VG	F	VF	XF	Unc
1838	—	8.00	16.00	32.00	70.00	225

BRITISH GUIANA AND WEST INDIES

STERLING COINAGE

KM# 26 4 PENCE
1.8851 g., 0.9250 Silver .0560 oz.

Date	Mintage	F	VF	XF	Unc	BU
1891	336,000	3.00	10.00	20.00	45.00	—
1894	120,000	4.00	12.50	25.00	50.00	—
1900	45,000	5.00	20.00	40.00	80.00	—

HAITI

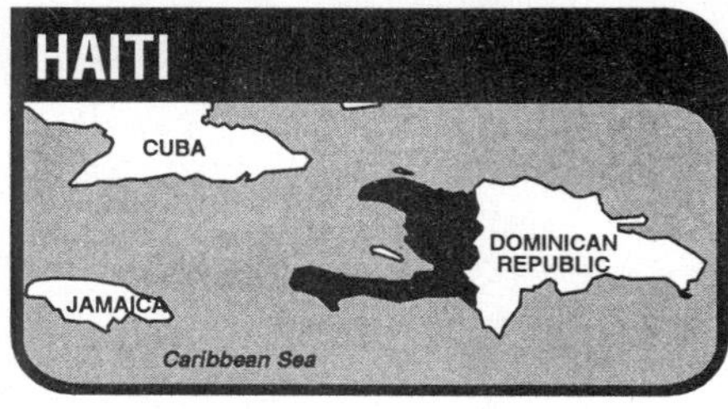

Haiti, which occupies the western one-third of the island of Hispaniola in the Caribbean Sea between Puerto Rico and Cuba, has an area of 10,714 sq. mi. (27,750 sq. km.). Capital: Port-au-Prince.

Columbus discovered Hispaniola in 1492. Spain colonized the island, making Santo Domingo the base for exploration of the Western Hemisphere. The area that is now Haiti was ceded to France by Spain in 1697. Slaves brought from Africa to work the coffee and sugar cane plantations made it one of the richest colonies of the French Empire. A slave revolt erupted in the French section in 1791. The Spanish section was ceded to France in 1795. A British Occupation force was ousted in 1798 by Toussaint l'Ouverture, who remained in control of the island until his capture by the French in 1802. After the French evacuation in 1803, The establishment of the Republic of Haiti in 1804, making it the oldest Black republic in the world and the second oldest republic (after the United States) in the Western Hemisphere. Internal dissension and conflicting ambitions of revolutionary generals resulted in separate Haitian governments from 1807 to 1820 under the name of the State of Haiti. Northern Haiti had Henri Christophe as president (til March 1811) and king (1811-1820). The remainder of the old French colony called itself Republic of Haiti with President Petion followed by President Boyer in 1818. Reunited by 1820, President Boyer brought Spanish Santo Domingo under the Haitian flag from 1822-44. That year a Dominican Republic gained independence in the chaos following Gen. Boyer's death in 1843. Note also a 2nd regal government: The Empire of Haiti (1849-59) under ex-president of the republic, Faustin Soulugue, as Emperor Faustin I. This aberration endured until a revolt led by subsequent President N.F. Geffrard overturned it. Since 1859, Haiti has continued as an ostensible Republic under a succession of strong-men presidents.

The French language is used on Haitian coins although it is spoken by only about 10% of the populace. A form of Creole is the language of the Haitians.

Two dating systems are used on Haiti's 19th century coins. One is Christian, the other Revolutionary – beginning in 1803 when the French were permanently ousted by a native revolt. Thus, a date of AN30, (i.e., year 30) is equivalent to 1833 A.D. Some coins carry both date forms. In the listings which follow, coins dated only in the Revolutionary system are listed by AN years in the date column.

RULERS

French, until 1804
Jacques I (Dessalines), 1804-1807
Henri Christophe as President of North Haiti, 1807-1811
Alexandre Petition President Western Republic, 1807-1818
Henri I (Christophe) as King of North Haiti, 1811-1820
Jean Pierre Boyer, President Western Republic, 1818-1843
Louis Pierrot, President Western Republic, 1845-1846
Jean Baptiste Riche, President Western Republic, 1846-1847
Faustin Soulougne, President Western Republic, 1847-1849
Faustin I (Soulouque), 1849-1858
Nicholas F. Geffrard, President,, 1859-1867

MINT MARKS

A - Paris
(a) - Paris, privy marks only
HEATON - Birmingham
R - Rome
(w) = Waterbury (Connecticut, USA) (Scoville Mfg. Co.)

MONETARY SYSTEM
12 Deniers = 1 Sol
20 Sols = 1 Livre
100 Centimes = 1 Gourde

REVOLUTIONARY GOVERNMENT
1798 - 1802

COLONIAL COINAGE

KM# 21 1/2 ESCALIN
Silver **Ruler:** Toussaint L'Ouverture

Date	Mintage	VG	F	VF	XF	Unc
ND(1802)	—	235	385	750	1,600	—

KM# 22 ESCALIN
Silver **Ruler:** Toussaint L'Ouverture

Date	Mintage	VG	F	VF	XF	Unc
ND(1802)	—	170	280	525	1,000	—

KM# 23 2 ESCALIN
Silver **Ruler:** Toussaint L'Ouverture

Date	Mintage	VG	F	VF	XF	Unc
ND(1802)	—	250	425	775	1,700	—

REPUBLIC OF NORTH HAITI
1807 - 1811

COLONIAL COINAGE

KM# 3 7 SOLS 6 DENIERS
Silver **Note:** Similar to 15 Sols, KM#6.

Date	Mintage	Good	VG	F	VF	XF
1807	—	50.00	120	250	550	—
Note: Average weight of 1.19g						
1808	—	35.00	75.00	130	375	—
Note: Sample weight range of 1.26-1.28g recorded						
1809	—	37.50	80.00	140	400	—
Note: Sample weight range of 1.03-1.48g recorded						

KM# 6 15 SOLS
Silver

Date	Mintage	Good	VG	F	VF	XF
1807	—	25.00	55.00	115	335	—
Note: Sample weight range of 2.28-2.46g recorded						
1808	—	27.50	65.00	145	400	—
Note: Sample weight range of 2.16-2.79g recorded						
1809	—	35.00	77.50	165	455	—
Note: Sample weight range of 1.03-1.48g recorded						

KM# 8 30 SOLS
Silver

Date	Mintage	Good	VG	F	VF	XF
1807 4 known	—	—	—	—	—	—

Note: Christie's Norweb sale 5-85 VF realized $7150. Bank Leu Bostonian sale 10-90 VF realized $4110. Sample weight range of 4.06-4.26g recorded

WESTERN REPUBLIC
1807 - 1818

DECIMAL COINAGE

100 Centimes = 1 Gourde

KM# 10 6 CENTIMES
0.8350 Silver **Obv:** Snake type

Date	Mintage	VG	F	VF	XF	Unc
1813 (AN 10)	—	115	220	400	675	—

KM# 17 6 CENTIMES
Silver **Rev:** Boyer bust

Date	Mintage	VG	F	VF	XF	Unc
1818 (AN 15)	—	10.00	18.50	32.50	50.00	—

KM# 11 12 CENTIMES
Silver **Obv:** Snake type

Date	Mintage	Good	VG	F	VF	XF
AN 10 (1813)	—	18.50	37.50	80.00	150	—
AN XI (1814)	—	4.50	12.50	23.50	37.50	85.00
AN 12 (1815)	—	6.50	15.00	30.00	60.00	—
AN 12 (1815)	—	7.50	18.00	35.00	70.00	—
Note: Error - 2 in AN 12 is upside down						

KM# 14 12 CENTIMES
Silver **Rev:** Petion type, small head

Date	Mintage	Good	VG	F	VF	XF
AN 14 (1817)	—	2.00	4.25	9.50	21.50	48.00

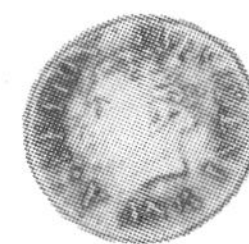

KM# 13 12 CENTIMES
Silver **Rev:** Petion type, large head **Note:** Varieties exist.

Date	Mintage	Good	VG	F	VF	XF
AN 14 (1817)	—	2.00	3.50	8.50	20.00	40.00

KM# 12.1 25 CENTIMES
Silver **Obv:** Snake type **Note:** Size varies 22-25 mm.

Date	Mintage	Good	VG	F	VF	XF
AN 10 (1813)	—	10.00	18.50	38.50	80.00	—
AN 10 (1813)P	—	12.00	20.00	40.00	85.00	—

KM# 12.2 25 CENTIMES
Silver **Obv:** Snake type **Note:** Size varies 20-21 mm. Diameter of snake circle, tree and cannon details vary by year.

Date	Mintage	VG	F	VF	XF	Unc
AN XI (1814)	—	5.50	10.00	18.50	30.00	—
Note: Brass and copper counterfeits, usually silver washed or plated, are occasionally seen.						
AN 12 (1815)	—	4.00	8.00	22.00	40.00	—
Note: Brass and copper counterfeits, usually silver washed or plated, are occasionally seen.						
AN 13 (1816)	—	5.00	8.00	18.50	30.00	—

KM# 15.1 25 CENTIMES
Silver **Rev:** Petion type **Note:** Bust sizes and design vary widely from smaller to larger, well to poorly engraved. Legends vary considerably in spacing and other details.

Date	Mintage	Good	VG	F	VF	XF
AN 14 (1817)	—	1.75	3.25	6.00	14.50	32.50
Note: Brass counterfeits, usually silver washed or plated, are known						

KM# 15.2 25 CENTIMES
Silver **Rev:** P below truncation of Petion bust **Note:** Varieties exist.

Date	Mintage	Good	VG	F	VF	XF
AN 14P (1817)	—	8.00	16.00	32.50	65.00	—

KM# 16 25 CENTIMES
2.3000 g., Silver **Obv:** Arms and denomination **Rev:** Bust of Boyer

Date	Mintage	Good	VG	F	VF	XF
AN 15 (1818)	—	6.00	15.00	32.50	65.00	—

REPUBLIC
1825 - 1849
DECIMAL COINAGE

100 Centimes = 1 Gourde

KM# A21 CENTIME
Copper **Note:** Previous KM#21; Die varieties exist with both diework and striking becoming progressively cruder over the life of this type.

Date	Mintage	VG	F	VF	XF	Unc
1828 // AN 25	—	7.50	20.00	42.50	90.00	—
1829 // AN 26	—	5.00	10.00	22.50	42.50	—
1830 // AN 27	—	3.25	8.50	15.00	35.00	—
1830 // AN 28	—	20.00	42.50	85.00	170	—
1830 // AN 29	—	75.00	150	250	—	—
1831 // AN 28	—	2.50	4.50	11.00	30.00	—
1832 // AN 28	—	20.00	42.50	85.00	170	—
1832 // AN 29	—	4.50	10.00	18.50	37.50	—
1834 // AN 31	—	2.75	6.00	12.00	32.50	—
1840 // AN 37	—	3.25	8.50	15.00	35.00	—
1841 // AN 38	—	3.25	8.50	15.00	35.00	—
1842 // AN 39	—	4.00	7.00	13.50	32.50	—

KM# 24 CENTIME
Copper, 22 mm.

Date	Mintage	VG	F	VF	XF	Unc
1846 // AN 43	—	.75	2.25	3.25	9.00	—

KM# 25.1 CENTIME
Copper, 21 mm. **Obv:** Leaves point inward **Rev:** With large star after legend **Note:** Reduced size.

Date	Mintage	VG	F	VF	XF	Unc
1846 // AN 43	—	0.75	2.00	4.50	12.50	35.00

KM# 25.2 CENTIME
Copper, 21 mm. **Obv:** Leaves point in and out **Rev:** Without star after legend **Note:** Varieties exist in style of wreath and legend.

Date	Mintage	VG	F	VF	XF	Unc
1846 // AN.43	—	0.75	2.00	5.00	15.00	35.00

KM# 30 CENTIME
Copper, 21 mm. **Obv:** Leaves point in and out **Rev:** Stop after legend

Date	Mintage	VG	F	VF	XF	Unc
1849 // AN 46	—	75.00	140	270	350	—

KM# A22 2 CENTIMES
Copper **Note:** Die varieties exist with both diework and striking becoming progressively cruder over the life of this type.

Date	Mintage	VG	F	VF	XF	Unc
1828 // AN 25	—	13.50	30.00	75.00	150	—
1828 // AN 26	—	12.00	28.00	65.00	135	—
1829 // AN 26	—	3.00	6.50	13.50	32.50	—
1830 // AN 26	—	15.00	35.00	72.50	145	—
1830 // AN 27	—	4.00	9.00	17.50	36.50	—
1831 // AN 28	—	3.50	7.00	15.00	35.00	—
1840 // AN 37	—	3.00	6.50	15.00	35.00	—
1840 // AN 37 Backwards 4	—	5.50	10.00	23.50	57.50	—
1841 // AN 38	—	3.00	6.50	15.00	35.00	—
1841 // AN 38 Backwards 4	—	15.00	36.50	75.00	135	—
1842 // AN 39	—	3.00	6.50	15.00	35.00	—

KM# 26 2 CENTIMES
Copper, 26 mm.

Date	Mintage	VG	F	VF	XF	Unc
1846 // AN 43	—	1.00	2.50	4.00	9.00	20.00
1846 // AN 43 Proof	—	Value: 300				
1846 // AN 43/2	—	2.25	5.00	7.50	18.50	33.50

KM# 27.1 2 CENTIMES
Copper, 24 mm. **Obv:** Leaves pointed inward **Rev:** With large star after legend **Note:** Reduced size.

Date	Mintage	VG	F	VF	XF	Unc
1846 // AN 43	—	2.00	3.50	6.25	20.00	—

KM# 27.2 2 CENTIMES
Copper **Obv:** Leaves pointed in and out **Note:** Varieties exist without accents on E's and with different size stars.

Date	Mintage	VG	F	VF	XF	Unc
1846 // AN 43	—	2.00	3.50	6.25	20.00	—

KM# 31 2 CENTIMES
Copper

Date	Mintage	VG	F	VF	XF	Unc
1849 // AN 46	—	30.00	55.00	100	215	—

KM# 28 6 CENTIMES
Copper

Date	Mintage	VG	F	VF	XF	Unc
1846 // AN 43	—	2.50	7.00	11.50	22.50	—

KM# 32 6 CENTIMES
Copper

Date	Mintage	Good	VG	F	VF	XF
1849 // AN 46	—	8.00	20.00	37.50	60.00	135

KM# 29 6-1/4 CENTIMES
Copper

Date	Mintage	VG	F	VF	XF	Unc
1846 // AN 43	—	3.75	8.50	14.00	27.50	50.00

KM# 19 12 CENTIMES
Silver **Rev:** Boyer type

Date	Mintage	VG	F	VF	XF	Unc
(1827) // AN 24	—	5.50	11.00	20.00	42.50	—
(1828) // AN 25	—	11.00	20.00	38.50	85.00	—
(1829) // AN 26	—	20.00	42.50	87.50	170	—

KM# 18.1 25 CENTIMES
Silver **Rev:** Boyer type, small head **Note:** Size varies 22-25 mm; varieties exist. Brass, mixed alloy and copper counterfeits, some with washed or silver plated surfaces, are common.

Date	Mintage	VG	F	VF	XF	Unc
(1827) // AN 24	—	1.75	3.75	7.00	16.50	—
(1828) // AN 25	—	4.50	11.00	22.50	45.00	—
Note: Formerly listed KM18.1a is now considered a copper counterfeit of this date						
(1829) // AN 26	—	7.00	13.50	25.00	50.00	—
(1831) // AN 28	—	3.25	6.00	13.50	35.00	—
(1834) // AN 31	—	2.25	4.50	11.50	27.50	—

KM# 18.1a 25 CENTIMES
Copper

Date	Mintage	VG	F	VF	XF	Unc
(1828) // AN 25	—	4.00	8.00	16.00	32.50	—

KM# 18.2 25 CENTIMES
Silver **Rev:** Large head with longer neck

Date	Mintage	VG	F	VF	XF	Unc
(1827) // AN 24	—	5.00	10.00	30.00	65.00	—

KM# 20 50 CENTIMES
Silver

Date	Mintage	VG	F	VF	XF	Unc
(1827) // AN 24	—	6.50	17.50	37.50	75.00	—
(1828) // AN 25	—	2.25	5.50	12.00	22.50	—
Note: Formerly listed KM20a is now considered a copper counterfeit of this date						
(1829) // AN 26	—	2.25	6.00	14.00	30.00	—
(1830) // AN 27	—	6.50	17.50	35.00	75.00	—
(1831) // AN 28	—	2.25	6.00	12.00	20.00	—

Date	Mintage	VG	F	VF	XF	Unc
(1832) // AN 29	—	2.25	6.00	12.00	20.00	—
(1833) // AN 30	—	5.50	13.50	30.00	60.00	—

KM# 20a 50 CENTIMES (0.50 Gourdes)
Copper

Date	Mintage	VG	F	VF	XF	Unc
(1828) // AN 25	—	—	—	—	—	—

KM# A23 100 CENTIMES
Silver

Date	Mintage	VG	F	VF	XF	Unc
(1829) // AN 26	—	5.00	11.00	20.00	45.00	—
Note: Formerly listed KMA23a is now considered a copper counterfeit of this date						
(1830) // AN 27	—	6.00	13.50	25.00	50.00	—
Note: Formerly listed KMA23a is now considered a copper counterfeit of this date						
(1833) // AN 30	—	8.00	16.50	33.50	70.00	—

EMPIRE
1849 - 1863
DECIMAL COINAGE

100 Centimes = 1 Gourde

KM# 33 CENTIME
Copper **Rev. Legend:** EMPIRE D'HAITI

Date	Mintage	VG	F	VF	XF	Unc
1850 // AN 47	—	45.00	100	175	250	—

KM# 34 CENTIME
Copper **Obv:** Leaves point in and out

Date	Mintage	VG	F	VF	XF	Unc
1850	—	2.50	5.00	8.00	20.00	—

KM# 35 2 CENTIMES
Copper **Obv. Legend:** EMPIRE D'HAITI

Date	Mintage	VG	F	VF	XF	Unc
1850 // AN 47	—	37.50	75.00	135	225	—

KM# 36 2 CENTIMES
Copper, 26 mm.

Date	Mintage	VG	F	VF	XF	Unc
1850	—	1.75	4.75	10.00	18.50	—

KM# 37 6 CENTIMES
Copper

Date	Mintage	VG	F	VF	XF	Unc
1850 // AN 47	—	160	285	450	1,000	—

KM# 38 6-1/4 CENTIMES
Copper

Date	Mintage	VG	F	VF	XF	Unc
1850	—	2.75	5.00	8.50	22.50	—

REPUBLIC
1863 -
DECIMAL COINAGE

100 Centimes = 1 Gourde

KM# 42 CENTIME
Bronze

Date	Mintage	F	VF	XF	Unc	BU
1881	830,000	2.00	3.50	5.50	20.00	—
1881 Proof	—	Value: 200				

KM# 48 CENTIME
Bronze

Date	Mintage	F	VF	XF	Unc	BU
1886A	2,500,000	1.75	3.00	5.00	15.00	—
1894A	2,070,000	1.75	3.00	5.00	20.00	—
1895A	5,420,000	1.75	3.00	5.00	30.00	—

KM# 43 2 CENTIMES
Bronze

Date	Mintage	F	VF	XF	Unc	BU
1881	830,000	2.75	4.50	8.00	20.00	—
1881 Proof	—	Value: 150				

KM# 49 2 CENTIMES
Bronze

Date	Mintage	F	VF	XF	Unc	BU
1886A	1,250,000	1.50	2.50	5.00	35.00	—
1894A	3,750,000	1.50	2.50	5.00	50.00	—

KM# 39 5 CENTIMES
Bronze **Note:** Coin and medal rotation varieties exist.

Date	Mintage	F	VF	XF	Unc	BU
1863HEATON	1,000,000	2.00	4.50	9.50	20.00	—
1863HEATON Proof	—	Value: 75.00				

KM# 50 5 CENTIMES
Copper-Nickel

Date	Mintage	F	VF	XF	Unc	BU
1889	120,000	15.00	32.50	62.50	115	—

KM# 40 10 CENTIMES
Bronze

Date	Mintage	F	VF	XF	Unc	BU
1863HEATON	1,000,000	2.25	4.50	7.50	22.50	—
1863HEATON Proof	—	Value: 80.00				

KM# 44 10 CENTIMES
2.5000 g., 0.8350 Silver 0.0671 oz.

Date	Mintage	F	VF	XF	Unc	BU
1881(a)	1,500,000	1.50	3.00	8.00	25.00	—
1881(a) Proof	—	Value: 575				
1882(a)	1,800,000	1.25	2.25	8.00	25.00	—
1882(a) Proof	—	Value: 550				
1886(a)	1,500,000	2.00	4.00	15.00	40.00	—
1886(a) Proof	—	Value: 550				
1887(a)	1,050,000	1.25	2.25	10.00	30.00	—
1887(a) Proof	—	Value: 500				
1890(a)	1,000,000	1.75	3.50	15.00	40.00	—
1890(a) Proof	—	Value: 550				
1894(a)	3,720,000	1.25	2.25	8.00	25.00	—
1894(a) Proof	—	Value: 500				

KM# 41 20 CENTIMES
Bronze

Date	Mintage	F	VF	XF	Unc	BU
1863HEATON	1,000,000	2.00	5.00	9.50	35.00	—
1863HEATON Proof	—	Value: 80.00				

KM# 45 20 CENTIMES
5.0000 g., 0.8350 Silver 0.1342 oz.

Date	Mintage	F	VF	XF	Unc	BU
1881(a)	1,250,000	2.50	4.50	8.00	40.00	—
1881(a) Proof	—	Value: 575				
1882(a)	1,250,000	2.50	4.50	8.00	40.00	—
1882(a) Proof	—	Value: 550				
1887(a)	350,000	3.00	5.00	10.00	50.00	—
1887(a) Proof	—	Value: 600				

Date	Mintage	F	VF	XF	Unc	BU
1890(a)	70,000	4.50	9.00	15.00	75.00	—
1890(a) Proof	—	Value: 800				
1894(a)	1,850,000	2.50	4.50	8.00	50.00	—
1894(a) Proof	—	Value: 550				
1895(a)	1,270,000	2.50	4.50	8.00	50.00	—
1895(a) Proof	—	Value: 550				

KM# 46 50 CENTIMES
25.0000 g., 0.9000 Silver 0.7234 oz.

Date	Mintage	F	VF	XF	Unc	BU
1881(a)	200,000	20.00	35.00	75.00	300	—
1881(a) Proof	—	Value: 2,000				
1882(a)	500,000	15.00	25.00	62.50	250	—
1882(a) Proof	—	Value: 2,000				
1887(a)	200,000	15.00	25.00	62.50	250	—
1887(a) Proof	—	Value: 2,500				
1895(a)	100,000	20.00	35.00	85.00	350	—
1895(a) Proof	—	Value: 2,750				

KM# 47 50 CENTIMES
12.5000 g., 0.8350 Silver 0.3356 oz.

Date	Mintage	F	VF	XF	Unc	BU
1882(a)	440,000	3.00	6.00	12.00	60.00	—
1882(a) Proof	—	Value: 600				
1883(a)	400,000	3.00	6.00	12.00	100	—
1883(a) Proof	—	Value: 600				
1887(a)	250,000	3.00	6.00	12.00	65.00	—
1887(a) Proof	—	Value: 750				
1890(a)	100,000	4.00	8.00	15.00	120	—
1890(a) Proof	—	Value: 1,000				
1895(a)	900,000	3.00	6.00	12.00	75.00	—
1895(a) Proof	—	Value: 600				

INSURRECTION COINAGE

Issued ca.1889 by General Florvil Hippolyte who became President from 1889-1896.

KM# 51 GOURDE
Bronze **Note:** Uniface; countermark: B.P.1G/GL.H.

Date	Mintage	F	VF	XF	Unc	BU
ND(1889)	100,000	50.00	100	300	500	—

Note: An 1881 dated 2 Centime coin with the same countermark was reported in the Medina collection. Also two examples; one on obverse, one on reverse, are listed in the Rudman collection exibit

PATTERNS

Including off metal strikes

KM#	Date	Mintage	Identification	Mkt Val
PnA1	ND(1802)	—	Escalin. Copper Plated White Metal.	—
Pn1	1807	—	Centime. Copper. Diagonal milling.	700
PnA2	ND(1802)	—	2 Escalin. Copper Plated White Metal.	—
Pn2	1807	—	Centime. Copper. Plain edge.	700
Pn3	1807	—	Centime. Copper. Piefort; diagonal milling.	800
Pn4	1807	—	Centime. Silver.	1,500
Pn5	1808	—	7-1/2 Sols. Silver.	450
Pn6	1808	—	15 Sols. Copper.	700
Pn7	1808	—	15 Sols. Silver.	750
Pn8	1808	—	30 Sols. Silver.	1,150
Pn13	1812	—	1/2 Crown. Copper. ESSAI; Diagonal milling.	1,000
Pn14	1812	—	1/2 Crown. Silver. ESSAI; Diagonal milling.	2,000
Pn15	1812	—	1/2 Crown. Silver. Plain edge. ESSAI.	—
Pn16	1812	—	Crown. Silver. Diagonal milling.	—
Pn17	1813	—	Crown. Silver.	3,000
Pn18	1814	—	1/2 Crown. White Metal. Diagonal milling.	600
Pn19	1814	—	1/2 Crown. Silver. 29 mm.	1,500
Pn20	1814	—	1/2 Crown. Silver. 33 mm.	—
Pn21	1814	—	Crown. Silver.	3,000
Pn22	1814	—	Crown. Base Metal. Crown. Crowned eagle.	500
Pn23	1814	—	Crown. Base Metal. Crown. Crowned eagle.	500
Pn24	AN 12 (1815)	—	25 Centimes. Copper.	—
Pn25	1815	—	Crown. Copper. Milled edge.	3,000
Pn26	1815	—	Crown. Silver. Milled edge.	3,000
Pn27	AN 13 (1816)	—	Centime. Copper. 'CENTIME' arched.	350
Pn28	AN 13 (1816)	—	Centime. Copper. 'CENTIME' straight.	350
Pn29	AN 13 (1816)	—	2 Centimes. Copper.	350
Pn30	AN 13 (1816)	—	2 Centimes. Copper.	350

KM#	Date	Mintage	Identification	Mkt Val
Pn31	1820	—	Crown. Aluminum.	—
Pn32	1820	—	Crown. Copper-Nickel.	—
Pn33	1820	—	Crown. Copper.	—
Pn33a	1820	—	Crown. Copper.	800
Pn34	1820	—	Crown. Plain edge.	2,750
Pn34a	1820	—	Crown. Silver. Plain edge.	1,150
Pn35	1820	—	Crown. Silver. Reeded edge.	1,000
Pn36	1820	—	Crown. White Metal. Crowned H-LM.	—
Pn37	1820	—	Crown. Silver. Crowned H-LM.	1,450
Pn38	AN 27 (1830)	—	100 Centimes. Copper.	—
Pn39	AN 44 (1846)	—	100 Centimes. Brass.	—
Pn40	AN 44 (1846)	—	100 Centimes. Copper.	—
Pn41	AN 44 (1846)	—	100 Centimes. Silver.	—
Pn42	1849	—	100 Centimes. Copper.	350
Pn43	1849	—	100 Centimes. Silver.	350
Pn44	1849	—	100 Centimes. Silver.	350
Pn45	1850	—	6 Centimes. Copper.	75.00
Pn46	1850	—	6 Centimes. Copper.	75.00
Pn47	1850	—	6 Centimes. Copper. KM#Pn46. KM#Pn48.	100
Pn48	1850	—	100 Centimes. Silver.	350
Pn49	1851	—	100 Centimes. Silvered-Bronze.	200
Pn50	1852	—	100 Centimes. Silver.	—
Pn51	1853	—	10 Centimes. Copper.	65.00
Pn52	1853	—	10 Centimes. Silver.	—
Pn53	1853	—	Gourde. Silver.	500
Pn54	1854	—	Gourde. Silver. ESSAI below bust.	950
Pn56	1854	—	Gourde. Copper.	800
Pn58	ND(1854)	—	Gourde. Copper.	—
Pn59	ND(1854)	—	Gourde. Bronze.	—
Pn60	ND(1854)	—	5 Gourdes. Silver. Small head. Plain edge.	1,100
Pn61	ND(1854)	—	5 Gourdes. Silver. Small head. Milled edge.	1,100
Pn62	ND(1854)	—	5 Gourdes. Bronze. Plain edge.	1,500
Pn63	ND(1854)	—	5 Gourdes. Bronze. Milled edge.	1,500
Pn64	ND(1854)	—	5 Gourdes. Silver. Large head. Plain edge.	950
Pn65	ND(1854)	—	5 Gourdes. Silver. Large head. Milled edge.	950
Pn66	ND(1854)	—	5 Gourdes. Silver. Thick planchet.	1,500
PnA67	1854	—	5 Gourdes. Silver.	2,000
PnB67	1854	—	5 Gourdes. Copper.	2,000
Pn67	1854	—	20 Gourdes. Gold.	20,000
Pn68	1854	—	20 Gourdes. Gold. ESSAI.	20,000
Pn69	1855	—	10 Centimes. Copper.	75.00
Pn69a	1855	—	10 Centimes. Brass.	75.00
Pn70	1856	—	Piastre. Silver.	—
Pn71	1857	—	Piastre. Base Silver. Milled edge.	—
Pn72	1857	—	Piastre. Copper. Plain edge.	—
Pn73	1857	—	Piastre. Silver. Milled edge.	—
Pn74	1858	—	Piastre. Silver.	—
PnA75	1863HEATON	—	20 Centimes. Nickel. KM#41.	—
PnB75	1877 IB CT	—	10 Centimes. Copper-Nickel.	75.00
PnC75	1877 IB CT	—	10 Centimes. Silver.	150
Pn75	1877 IB CT	—	20 Centimes. Copper. ESSAI.	100
Pn76	1877 IB CT	—	20 Centimes. Silver. ESSAI.	300
Pn77	1877 IB	—	20 Centimes. Copper. ESSAI.	100
Pn78	1877 IB	—	20 Centimes. Silver. ESSAI.	300

KM#	Date	Mintage	Identification	Mkt Val
Pn79	1877 IB CT	—	20 Centimes. Nickel.	220
Pn80	1877 IB CT	—	20 Centimes. Nickel. ESSAI.	220
Pn81	1877 IB CT	—	20 Centimes. Silver. 5.0000 g.	500
Pn82	1877 IB CT	—	20 Centimes. Silver. 5.0000 g. ESSAI.	500
Pn83	1881	—	Gourde. Copper.	—
Pn84	1881	—	Gourde. Silver.	—

KM#	Date	Mintage	Identification	Mkt Val
Pn85	1889	—	Centime. Copper.	60.00

KM#	Date	Mintage	Identification	Mkt Val
Pn86	1889	—	2 Centimes. Copper.	60.00

PIEFORTS WITH ESSAI

KM#	Date	Mintage	Identification	Mkt Val
PE1	1877 IB CT	—	20 Centimes. Silver. 11.4000 g. ESSAI.	550
PE2	1877 IB CT	—	20 Centimes. Silver. 22.2000 g.	700
PE3	1877 IB	—	20 Centimes. Silver. 11.4000 g. ESSAI.	550

KM#	Date	Mintage	Identification	Mkt Val
PE4	1877 IB CT	—	20 Centimes. Silver. 9.8000 g. ESSAI.	550
PE5	1877 IB CT	—	20 Centimes. Silver. 12.2000 g. ESSAI.	700

MECCA

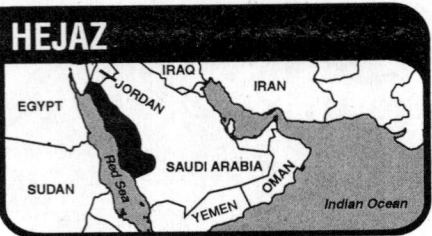

Mecca, the metropolis of Islam and the capital of Hejaz, is located inland from the Red Sea due east of the port of Jidda. A center of non-political commercial, cultural and religious activities, Mecca remained virtually independent until 1259. Two centuries of Egyptian rule were followed by four centuries of Turkish rule which lasted until the Arab revolts which extinguished pretensions to sovereignty over any part of the Arabian peninsula.

MINT NAME

Makkah, Mecca مكة

RULERS

Sharifs of Mecca

Ghalib b. Ma'sud, AH1219-1229
Yahya b. Surer, AH1230-1240
Abdul Muttalib and Ibn Awn, ...AH1240-1248

ANONYMOUS WAHHABI ISSUES

KINGDOM

ANONYMOUS HAMMERED COINAGE

Wahhabi Issues

KM# A5 1/2 MAHMUDI

Copper

Date	Mintage	Good	VG	F	VF	XF
AH1240	—	250	450	600	800	—

KM# A1 MAHMUDI

Copper

Date	Mintage	Good	VG	F	VF	XF
AH1219	—	100	175	300	400	—

KM# A2 MAHMUDI

Copper

Date	Mintage	Good	VG	F	VF	XF
AH1220	—	100	175	300	400	—
AH1221	—	100	175	300	400	—
AH1222	—	100	175	300	400	—

KM# B3 MAHMUDI

Copper **Obv:** Bird **Rev:** Fish

Date	Mintage	Good	VG	F	VF	XF
AH1223	—	125	200	325	450	—

KM# A4 MAHMUDI

Copper

Date	Mintage	Good	VG	F	VF	XF
AH1230	—	125	200	325	450	—

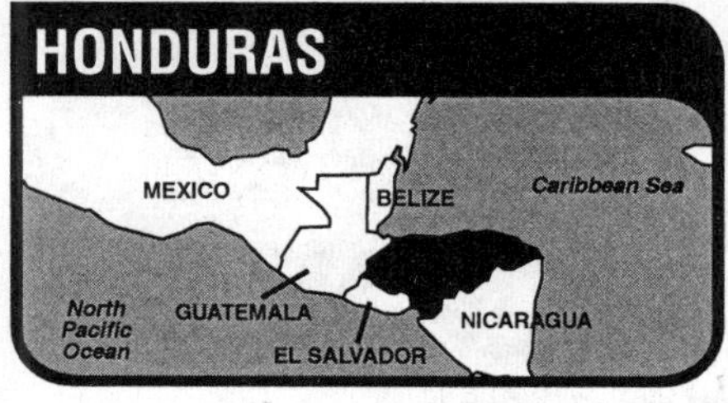

The Republic of Honduras, situated in Central America alongside El Salvador, between Nicaragua and Guatemala, has an area of 43,277sq. mi. (112,090 sq. km.). Capital: Tegucigalpa. Agriculture, mining (gold and silver), and logging are the major economic activities, with increasing tourism and emerging petroleum resource discoveries. Precious metals, bananas, timber and coffee are exported.

The eastern part of Honduras was part of the ancient Mayan Empire; however, the largest Indian community in Honduras was the not too well known Lencas. Honduras was claimed for Spain by Columbus in 1502, during his last voyage to the Americas. The first settlement was made by Cristobal de Olid under orders from Hernando Cortes., Regarded as one of the most promising sources of gold and silver in the New World, Honduras was a part of Spain's Captaincy General of Guatemala. After declaring its independence from Spain on September 15, 1821, Honduras fell under the Mexican empire of Augustin de Iturbide, and then joined the Central American Republic (1823-39). Upon the effective dissolution of that federation (ca. 1840), Honduras reclaimed its independence as a self-standing republic. Honduran forces played a major part in permanently ending the threat of William Walker to establish a slave holding empire in Central America based on his self engineered elections to the Presidency of Nicaragua. Thrice expelled from Central America, Walker was shot by a Honduran firing squad in 1860. 1876 to 1933 saw a period of instability and for some months U.S. Marine Corp military occupation. From 1933 to 1940 General Tiburcio Carias Andino was dictator president of the Republic. He was followed by a series of often strong-arm presidents, some elected by (more and some by less) democratic means. Cooperation w/U.S. backed Nicaraguan contra groups in the 1980's strained Honduras' political life for that time. Since 1990 democratic practices have become more consistent.

RULERS

Spanish, until 1821

Augustin Iturbide (Emperor of Mexico), 1822-1823

MINT MARKS

A - Paris, 1869-1871

P-Y - Provincia Yoro (?)

T - Tegucigalpa, 1825-1862

T.G. - Yoro

T.L. – Comayagua

NOTE: Extensive die varieties exist for coins struck in Honduras with almost endless date and over date varieties. Federation style coinage continued to be struck until 1861. (See Central American Republic listings.)

MONETARY SYSTEM

16 Reales = 1 Escudo

100 Centavos = 1 Peso

VICE ROYALTY OF NEW SPAIN

Truxillo (Trujillo)

COLONIAL COINAGE

KM# 2 2 REALES

Silver **Obv:** Ferdinand VII **Rev:** Crowned shield **Note:** A proclamation issue struck for Ferdinand VII as the new king of Spain while he was under Napoleonic French guard.

Date	Mintage	F	VF	XF	Unc	BU
1808	—	135	260	455	700	—

EMPIRE OF MEXICO

REAL COINAGE

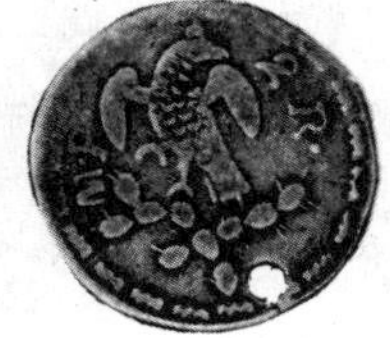

KM# 6 2 REALES

Silver **Obv:** Iturbide **Rev:** Eagle on cactus

Date	Mintage	Good	VG	F	VF	XF
1823 3 known	—	—	—	—	—	—

PROVISIONAL GOVERNMENT

1823

REAL COINAGE

KM# 9 1/2 REAL

Silver

Date	Mintage	Good	VG	F	VF	XF
1823T.L. Rare	—	—	—	—	—	—

KM# 10 1/2 REAL

Silver

Date	Mintage	Good	VG	F	VF	XF
1823 Rare	—	—	—	—	—	—

KM# 7.1 1/2 REAL

Silver

Date	Mintage	Good	VG	F	VF	XF
1823	—	150	250	350	—	—
(18)24	—	125	225	325	—	—

KM# 7.2 1/2 REAL

Silver **Rev:** Plain fields

Date	Mintage	Good	VG	F	VF	XF
(18)24	—	175	300	425	—	—

KM# 4 REAL

Silver

Date	Mintage	Good	VG	F	VF	XF
(18)23T.G.	—	60.00	85.00	150	—	—

KM# 8.1 REAL

Silver **Rev:** Lions facing left

Date	Mintage	Good	VG	F	VF	XF
(18)23P-Y	—	25.00	55.00	85.00	—	—

KM# 8.2 REAL

Silver **Rev:** Lions facing right **Note:** Varieties exist.

Date	Mintage	Good	VG	F	VF	XF
(18)24P-Y	—	30.00	55.00	115	—	—
(18)25P-Y Rare	—	—	—	—	—	—

KM# 5 2 REALES

Silver

Date	Mintage	Good	VG	F	VF	XF
(1)823T.G.	—	75.00	125	185	360	—

KM# 11.1 2 REALES

Silver

Date	Mintage	Good	VG	F	VF	XF
1823 Rare	—	—	—	—	—	—

KM# 11.2 2 REALES

Silver **Rev:** Lions and castles reversed

Date	Mintage	Good	VG	F	VF	XF
1823 Rare	—	—	—	—	—	—

KM# 12.1 2 REALES

Silver

Date	Mintage	Good	VG	F	VF	XF
1823 6-7 known	—	—	—	—	—	—

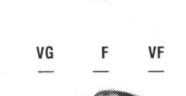

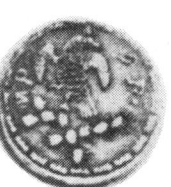

KM# 12.2 2 REALES

Silver **Rev:** Crowned arms

Date	Mintage	Good	VG	F	VF	XF
1823 Rare	—	—	—	—	—	—

KM# 14 2 REALES

Silver

Date	Mintage	Good	VG	F	VF	XF
1823 Rare	—	—	—	—	—	—

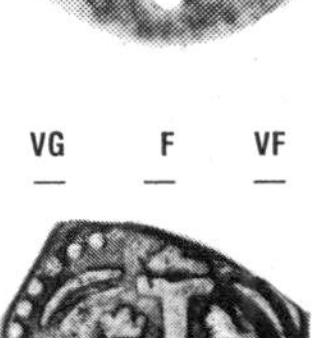

KM# 15.1 2 REALES
Silver

Date	Mintage	Good	VG	F	VF	XF
(18)23P-Y	—	75.00	125	175	310	—

KM# 15.2 2 REALES
Silver **Rev:** Lions and castles reversed **Note:** Varieties exist.

Date	Mintage	Good	VG	F	VF	XF
(18)24P-Y	—	55.00	110	160	300	—

KM# 16.1 4 REALES
Silver **Rev:** Lions facing left

Date	Mintage	Good	VG	F	VF	XF
(18)23P-Y	—	90.00	170	285	435	—

KM# 16.3 4 REALES
Silver **Rev:** Lions facing left and castles reversed

Date	Mintage	Good	VG	F	VF	XF
(18)23P-Y	—	85.00	165	285	450	—

KM# 16.2 4 REALES
Silver **Rev:** Lions facing right and castles reversed

Date	Mintage	Good	VG	F	VF	XF
(18)24P-Y	—	85.00	165	285	450	—
(18)24P-Y rev. retrograde 4	—	85.00	165	285	450	—

STATE OF HONDURAS

As A Constituent State of the Central American Federation

REAL COINAGE

Provisional Issues

KM# 17 1/2 REAL
0.3330 Silver

Date	Mintage	Good	VG	F	VF	XF
1832T F	—	27.50	40.00	75.00	175	—
1833T F	—	30.00	60.00	100	235	—

KM# 17a 1/2 REAL
0.2500 Silver

Date	Mintage	Good	VG	F	VF	XF
1844T F	—	65.00	125	250	485	—
1845T F	—	—	—	—	—	—

Note: Reported, not confirmed

Date	Mintage	Good	VG	F	VF	XF
1845T G	—	50.00	110	210	400	—

Note: Obverse legend: MON.PROV.DEL EST. DE HOND.

KM# 18 REAL
0.3330 Silver

Date	Mintage	Good	VG	F	VF	XF
1832T F	—	16.00	30.00	55.00	100	—
1839T F PROVISIONAL	—	25.00	45.00	85.00	185	—
1839T F PROVICIONAL	—	25.00	45.00	85.00	185	—

KM# 18a REAL
0.2000 Silver

Date	Mintage	Good	VG	F	VF	XF
1840T F PROVISIONAL	—	25.00	45.00	80.00	175	—
1840T F PROVICIONAL	—	25.00	45.00	80.00	175	—
1844T G CREZCA	—	15.00	30.00	60.00	125	—

KM# 18b REAL
0.1720 Silver

Date	Mintage	Good	VG	F	VF	XF
1845T G FECUNDO	—	16.50	30.00	55.00	110	—
1845T G FECNDO	—	20.00	35.00	60.00	120	—
1846T G	—	35.00	65.00	100	220	—
1849T G	—	25.00	45.00	85.00	175	—

KM# 18c REAL
0.1000 Silver

Date	Mintage	Good	VG	F	VF	XF
1851T G	—	12.50	25.00	45.00	75.00	—
1852T G	—	20.00	40.00	70.00	150	—

KM# 18d REAL
0.0400 Silver

Date	Mintage	Good	VG	F	VF	XF
1853T G	—	45.00	95.00	175	385	—

KM# 19 2 REALES
0.3330 Silver

Date	Mintage	Good	VG	F	VF	XF
1832T F	—	12.00	20.00	37.50	65.00	—
1833T F	—	—	—	—	—	—

Note: Coins dated 1833 struck in copper, with or without silvering, are common early counterfeits. A common variety contains a legend error...PROVISINAL...on the obverse. Legitimate examples are considered very scarce to rare.

Date	Mintage	Good	VG	F	VF	XF
1839T F	—	20.00	35.00	55.00	85.00	—

KM# 19a 2 REALES
0.2000 Silver

Date	Mintage	Good	VG	F	VF	XF
1840T F PROVICIONAL	—	22.50	40.00	75.00	140	—
1840T F PROVISIONAL	—	20.00	35.00	67.50	120	—
1842T G CRESCA	—	18.50	33.50	52.50	87.50	—
1842T G CREZCA	—	18.50	33.50	52.50	87.50	—
1844T F	—	18.50	32.50	50.00	80.00	—
1844T G CREZCA	—	18.50	32.50	50.00	80.00	—
1845T G	—	6.50	12.00	20.00	35.00	—
1846T G	—	25.00	45.00	85.00	160	—
1847/5T G	—	20.00	35.00	60.00	90.00	—
1847/6T G	—	20.00	35.00	60.00	90.00	—
1847T G	—	18.50	32.50	52.50	75.00	—

KM# 19b 2 REALES
0.1720 Silver

Date	Mintage	Good	VG	F	VF	XF
1848T G CREZCA	—	6.00	10.00	22.50	35.00	—
1848T G CREZUA	—	—	—	—	—	—

KM# 19c 2 REALES
0.1000 Silver

Date	Mintage	Good	VG	F	VF	XF
1851T G	—	15.00	27.50	47.50	100	—

KM# 19d 2 REALES
0.0625 Silver

Date	Mintage	Good	VG	F	VF	XF
1852T G	—	8.50	16.50	30.00	65.00	—

KM# 19e 2 REALES
0.0400 Silver

Date	Mintage	Good	VG	F	VF	XF
1853T G	—	7.50	15.00	28.50	52.50	—
1854T G	—	27.50	60.00	135	—	—

KM# 20 4 REALES
0.1720 Silver

Date	Mintage	Good	VG	F	VF	XF
1849T G	—	8.50	18.50	27.50	50.00	—
1850T G	—	6.50	15.00	23.50	42.50	—

KM# 20a 4 REALES
0.1000 Silver

Date	Mintage	Good	VG	F	VF	XF
1851T G	—	3.00	7.50	16.50	32.50	—

KM# 20b 4 REALES
0.0625 Silver

Date	Mintage	Good	VG	F	VF	XF
1852T G	—	3.00	7.00	13.50	25.00	—

KM# 20c 4 REALES
0.0400 Silver

Date	Mintage	Good	VG	F	VF	XF
1853T G	—	3.00	7.00	12.50	25.00	—
1854T G	—	3.00	7.00	12.50	25.00	—
1855T G HOND	—	3.00	7.50	15.00	28.50	—
1855T G HON	—	3.25	8.50	16.50	30.00	—

KM# 20d 4 REALES
Copper

Date	Mintage	Good	VG	F	VF	XF
1856T G	—	3.50	9.00	17.50	37.50	—
1856T F Rare	—	—	—	—	—	—
1857T F	—	—	—	—	—	—

KM# 20e 4 REALES
Copper-Lead Alloy

Date	Mintage	Good	VG	F	VF	XF
1857T F	—	7.00	13.00	25.00	50.00	—
1857/2T F/G	—	—	—	—	—	—

KM# 21 8 REALES
Copper

Date	Mintage	Good	VG	F	VF	XF
1856T G	—	6.50	12.50	30.00	60.00	—
1856T FL	—	50.00	100	200	—	—

KM# 21a 8 REALES
Copper-Lead Alloy

Date	Mintage	Good	VG	F	VF	XF
1857T FL	—	4.50	8.00	12.50	27.50	—
1858T FL with HON	—	5.50	12.50	22.00	37.50	—
1858T FL with HOND	—	6.00	12.50	22.00	37.50	—
1859T FL with PROVISIONAL	—	7.00	13.50	25.00	45.00	—
1859T FL with PROVISIONAL and retrograde N's	—	9.00	17.50	30.00	50.00	—
1859T FL with PROVICIONAL (error)	—	9.00	17.50	30.00	50.00	—
1860T FL 5 known	—	—	—	—	—	—
1861T FL	—	13.50	27.50	50.00	85.00	—

PROVISIONAL COINAGE

Similar coins, with rosettes instead of dots separating their legends, are patterns or trial strikes of the dies, which were made in England.

KM# 24 PESO
Copper **Rev:** Dots separate legends

Date	Mintage	VG	F	VF	XF	Unc
1862T A	—	2.75	7.50	15.00	27.50	100

KM# 25 2 PESOS
Copper **Rev:** Dots separate legends

Date	Mintage	VG	F	VF	XF	Unc
1862T A	—	2.75	7.50	17.50	37.50	150

KM# 26 4 PESOS
Copper **Rev:** Dots separate legends

Date	Mintage	VG	F	VF	XF	Unc
1862T A	—	4.00	12.50	30.00	60.00	200

KM# 27 8 PESOS
Copper **Rev:** Dots separate legends

Date	Mintage	VG	F	VF	XF	Unc
1862T A	—	8.50	22.50	47.50	100	300

REPUBLIC

REAL COINAGE

KM# 30 1/8 REAL
Copper Nickel

Date	Mintage	F	VF	XF	Unc	BU
1869A	—	3.50	10.00	15.00	35.00	—
1870A	—	3.00	7.00	10.00	17.50	—

KM# 31 1/4 REAL
Copper Nickel

Date	Mintage	F	VF	XF	Unc	BU
1869A	—	1.25	2.75	7.00	14.00	—
1870A	—	2.50	5.50	15.00	30.00	—

KM# 32 1/2 REAL
Copper Nickel

Date	Mintage	F	VF	XF	Unc	BU
1869A	—	1.25	3.00	7.00	17.50	—
1870A	—	10.00	22.50	40.00	100	—
1871A	—	—	—	90.00	175	—

KM# 33 REAL
Copper Nickel **Note:** Varieties exist.

Date	Mintage	F	VF	XF	Unc	BU
1869A	—	7.50	18.00	32.50	70.00	—
1870A	—	5.00	12.00	17.50	40.00	—

DECIMAL COINAGE

100 Centavos = 1 Peso

KM# 45 1/2 CENTAVO
Bronze

Date	Mintage	VG	F	VF	XF	Unc
1881	171,000	75.00	150	300	—	—
Note: Less than 10 examples known						
1883	—	17.50	35.00	62.50	135	—
1885	172,000	11.00	18.50	27.50	50.00	—
1886	97,000	10.00	20.00	28.50	55.00	—
1889	—	13.50	27.50	47.50	100	—
1891	—	125	250	400	—	—
Note: Between 5 and 10 examples known						

KM# 40 CENTAVO
Bronze

Date	Mintage	VG	F	VF	XF	Unc
1878	346,000	50.00	100	250	500	—
1879	Inc. above	20.00	40.00	100	250	—
1880	Inc. above	15.00	30.00	80.00	225	—

KM# 46 CENTAVO
Bronze **Edge:** Plain, reeded, and plain and reeded **Note:** Varieties exist.

Date	Mintage	VG	F	VF	XF	Unc
1881	132,000	3.75	10.00	27.00	55.00	—
1884	24,000	2.75	7.50	18.00	42.00	—
1885	86,000	2.50	6.00	12.00	28.00	—
1886	116,000	3.00	7.50	18.00	36.00	—
1889/5	—	6.50	15.00	32.00	60.00	—
1889 medal rotation	—	6.50	15.00	32.00	60.00	—
1890	—	3.00	7.50	18.00	40.00	—
1896	61,000	2.25	6.00	15.00	25.00	—
1897	9,362	—	—	—	—	—
1898/86	—	7.50	17.50	32.50	55.00	—
1898/88	54,000	7.00	15.00	35.00	52.50	—
1898	Inc. above	5.00	12.50	26.50	45.00	—
1899 small 99	180,000	5.50	13.50	30.00	57.00	—
1899 large 99	Inc. above	5.50	13.50	28.50	50.00	—
1900	29,000	5.00	12.50	26.50	48.50	—

KM# 59 CENTAVO
Bronze **Obv:** KM#46 **Rev:** Altered KM#49 **Note:** Varieties exist.

Date	Mintage	VG	F	VF	XF	Unc
1890	—	9.00	18.50	42.50	110	—
1893	—	12.50	27.50	50.00	140	—
1895	45,000	10.00	20.00	47.50	120	—

KM# 61 CENTAVO
Bronze **Obv:** KM#49 **Rev:** Altered KM#49 **Note:** The 1890, 1891 and 1908 dates are found with a die-cutting error or broken die that reads REPLBLICA. Other varieties exist.

Date	Mintage	VG	F	VF	XF	Unc
1890	—	12.00	25.00	45.00	90.00	—
1891	—	2.00	5.00	10.00	27.50	—
1892 Rare	—	—	—	—	—	—
1893/83	—	—	—	—	—	—
1893	—	2.00	5.00	10.00	27.50	—
1895	—	10.00	25.00	45.00	90.00	—

KM# 60 CENTAVO
Bronze **Obv:** KM#46 **Rev:** KM#40 **Note:** Mule.

Date	Mintage	VG	F	VF	XF	Unc
ND (c. 1895)	—	115	250	400	600	—

KM# 63 CENTAVO
Bronze **Obv:** KM#35 with altered date, 1895 engraved over 1871 **Rev:** KM#40

Date	Mintage	VG	F	VF	XF	Unc
1895	—	400	600	900	—	—

KM# 34 5 CENTAVOS
1.2500 g., 0.8350 Silver .0336 oz. **Obv:** Arms **Rev:** Tree

Date	Mintage	VG	F	VF	XF	Unc
1871	2,056	75.00	165	300	650	—
1871 Proof	—	—	—	—	—	—

Note: The 1871 proof reads "0.900" but is actually 0.835 fine and was not struck until 1879-1880

KM# 43 5 CENTAVOS
1.2500 g., 0.8350 Silver .0336 oz. **Obv:** Eagle **Rev:** Standing Liberty **Note:** Possible pattern. Similar to 50 Centavos, KM#44.

Date	Mintage	VG	F	VF	XF	Unc
1879 Rare	—	—	—	—	—	—

KM# 48 5 CENTAVOS
1.2500 g., 0.8350 Silver .0336 oz.

Date	Mintage	VG	F	VF	XF	Unc
1884	—	10.00	22.50	35.00	100	—
1885	—	12.50	20.00	30.00	90.00	—
1886	—	8.50	16.50	27.50	80.00	—

KM# 54 5 CENTAVOS
1.2500 g., 0.8350 Silver .0336 oz. **Note:** Varieties exist.

Date	Mintage	VG	F	VF	XF	Unc
1886	—	4.50	13.50	27.50	60.00	—
6188 Error; 2 known	—	—	—	—	—	—
1895/85 Rare	—	—	—	—	—	—
1895/85 Rare	—	—	—	—	—	—
1895 Rare	—	—	—	—	—	—
1896/85	35,000	5.00	8.50	15.00	40.00	—
1896/86	Inc. above	3.00	6.00	12.50	35.00	—
1896	Inc. above	5.00	15.00	30.00	70.00	—

KM# 35 10 CENTAVOS
2.5000 g., 0.8350 Silver 0.671 oz. **Note:** Coin reads "0.900" but is actually 0.835 fine. Not struck until 1879-1880.

Date	Mintage	VG	F	VF	XF	Unc
1871	17,000	16.50	28.50	47.50	100	—

KM# 42 10 CENTAVOS

2.5000 g., 0.8350 Silver 0.671 oz. **Obv:** KM#41 **Rev:** KM#35 **Note:** Mule.

Date	Mintage	VG	F	VF	XF	Unc
1878 Rare	—	—	—	—	—	—

KM# 41 10 CENTAVOS

2.5000 g., 0.8350 Silver 0.671 oz. **Obv:** Eagle **Rev:** Standing Liberty **Note:** Possible patterns. Similar to 50 Centavos, KM#44.

Date	Mintage	VG	F	VF	XF	Unc
1878 Rare	—	—	—	—	—	—
1879 Rare	—	—	—	—	—	—

KM# 49 10 CENTAVOS

2.5000 g., 0.8350 Silver 0.671 oz. **Note:** 1893, 1895 and 1900 are found with die-cutting error broken die that reads REPLBLICA.

Date	Mintage	VG	F	VF	XF	Unc
1884	—	8.50	22.50	45.00	85.00	—
1885	—	8.00	20.00	40.00	75.00	—
1886	—	7.00	16.50	30.00	60.00	—
1889	—	35.00	75.00	125	250	—
1893/83	—	—	—	—	—	—
1893	—	10.00	22.50	37.50	65.00	—
1895/85	53,000	—	—	—	—	—
1895	—	8.00	18.50	40.00	100	—
1897	16,000	—	—	—	—	—
1900 1 over inverted 1	—	—	—	—	—	—
1900	5,300	30.00	60.00	100	200	—

KM# 55.1 10 CENTAVOS

2.5000 g., 0.8350 Silver 0.671 oz. **Obv:** KM#35 **Rev:** KM#49, "P" **Note:** Mule.

Date	Mintage	VG	F	VF	XF	Unc
1886	—	16.50	30.00	60.00	—	—
1895/71	—	—	—	—	—	—
1895	—	25.00	45.00	85.00	—	—

KM# 55.2 10 CENTAVOS

2.5000 g., 0.8350 Silver 0.671 oz. **Rev:** 1 P replaced date

Date	Mintage	VG	F	VF	XF	Unc
ND	—	30.00	70.00	125	—	—

KM# 55.3 10 CENTAVOS

2.5000 g., 0.8350 Silver 0.671 oz. **Rev:** Without P

Date	Mintage	VG	F	VF	XF	Unc
1895 large date	—	—	—	—	—	—
1895/1 Reverse value over reverse of 1 centavo KM-61	—	—	—	—	—	—
1895 small date	—	—	—	—	—	—

KM# 36 25 CENTAVOS

6.2500 g., 0.9000 Silver .1808 oz.

Date	Mintage	VG	F	VF	XF	Unc
1871	177,000	—	4.50	10.00	30.00	67.50

KM# 50 25 CENTAVOS

6.2500 g., 0.9000 Silver .1808 oz. **Note:** Varieties exist.

Date	Mintage	VG	F	VF	XF	Unc
1883	—	2.25	6.00	10.00	18.50	—
1884	—	2.00	4.50	9.00	17.50	—
1885/4	—	—	—	—	—	—
1885	—	2.00	5.00	10.00	18.50	—
1886/1	—	2.25	6.00	11.00	20.00	—
1888/3	—	5.00	12.00	22.50	42.50	—
1888/7	—	3.75	8.50	17.50	32.50	—
1888	—	2.25	5.00	10.00	22.50	—
1890/85	—	3.50	7.50	15.00	27.50	—
1890/88	—	3.50	7.50	15.00	27.50	—
1890/89	—	3.50	7.50	15.00	27.50	—
1891/181	—	4.50	9.00	17.50	30.00	—
1891/81	—	3.50	7.50	15.00	27.50	—
1891	—	3.00	6.75	12.50	25.00	—
1892/81	—	2.25	5.00	10.00	20.00	—
1892/1	—	2.25	5.00	10.00	20.00	—
1893/83	—	2.75	6.00	11.00	22.50	—
1893/88	—	2.75	6.00	11.00	22.50	—
1895/83	12,000	3.50	7.50	15.00	27.50	—
1895	Inc. above	2.25	5.00	10.00	20.00	—
1896	274,000	3.50	7.00	12.50	22.50	—
1899/88	30,000	10.00	20.00	40.00	65.00	—

KM# 50a 25 CENTAVOS

6.2500 g., 0.8350 Silver .1678 oz. **Note:** Varieties exist.

Date	Mintage	VG	F	VF	XF	Unc
1899/88 .835/.900 **Note:** Medal rotation	Inc. above	6.00	13.50	25.00	32.50	—
1899	Inc. above	5.00	11.00	17.50	30.00	—
1900/1886	—	—	—	—	—	—
1900/800 .835/.900	39,000	2.75	5.00	11.00	22.50	—
1900/891	Inc. above	2.75	5.00	11.00	22.50	—
1900/1	Inc. above	2.75	5.00	11.00	22.50	—
1900	Inc. above	2.75	5.00	11.00	22.50	—

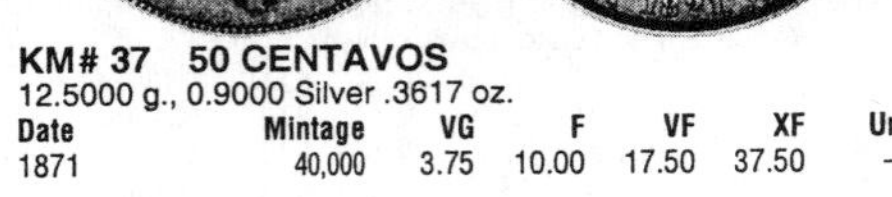

KM# 37 50 CENTAVOS

12.5000 g., 0.9000 Silver .3617 oz.

Date	Mintage	VG	F	VF	XF	Unc
1871	40,000	3.75	10.00	17.50	37.50	—

KM# 44 50 CENTAVOS

12.5000 g., 0.9000 Silver .3617 oz.

Date	Mintage	VG	F	VF	XF	Unc
1879	—	185	350	650	1,250	—

KM# 51 50 CENTAVOS

12.5000 g., 0.9000 Silver .3617 oz.

Date	Mintage	VG	F	VF	XF	Unc
1883	—	4.00	9.50	17.50	32.50	—
1883 P	—	7.00	15.00	27.50	55.00	—
1884	—	3.75	8.50	15.00	30.00	—
1885 medal rotation	—	4.25	9.00	16.50	32.50	—
1885 coin rotation	—	4.00	10.00	17.50	37.50	—
1886/5	—	5.00	12.50	27.50	55.00	—
1886	—	5.00	12.50	27.50	52.50	—
1887/5	—	7.00	15.00	30.00	60.00	—
1887	—	7.00	15.00	30.00	60.00	—
1896/86	—	135	260	535	—	—
1897	37,000	37.50	67.50	110	—	—

KM# 39 PESO

1.6120 g., 0.9000 Gold .0467 oz. **Obv:** KM#38 **Rev:** KM#56 **Note:** Mule.

Date	Mintage	F	VF	XF	Unc	BU
1871	—	325	550	825	1,700	—

KM# 38 PESO

1.6120 g., 0.9000 Gold .0467 oz. **Note:** Similar to 5 Centavos, KM#34.

Date	Mintage	F	VF	XF	Unc	BU
1871 Rare	—	—	—	—	—	—

KM# 47 PESO

25.0000 g., 0.9000 Silver .7234 oz. **Rev:** Small CENTRO-AMERICA

Date	Mintage	VG	F	VF	XF	Unc
1881	26,000	20.00	40.00	60.00	120	—
1882 medal rotation	76,000	20.00	35.00	50.00	100	—
1882 coin rotation	Inc. above	20.00	35.00	50.00	100	—
1883	—	20.00	37.50	55.00	110	—

KM# 52 PESO

25.0000 g., 0.9000 Silver .7234 oz. **Rev:** Large CENTRO-AMERICA **Note:** Overdates and recut dies are prevalent.

Date	Mintage	VG	F	VF	XF	Unc
1883/1	—	50.00	100	200	400	—
1884	—	18.00	32.50	50.00	90.00	—
1885	—	18.00	30.00	45.00	80.00	—
1886	—	18.00	32.50	50.00	90.00	—
1887	—	18.00	32.50	50.00	90.00	—
1888	—	18.00	30.00	45.00	80.00	—
1889/8	—	18.00	30.00	45.00	80.00	—
1889	—	18.00	30.00	45.00	80.00	—
1890	—	18.00	30.00	45.00	80.00	—
1891/88	—	18.00	30.00	45.00	80.00	—
1891/89	—	18.00	30.00	45.00	80.00	—
1892/0	—	18.00	30.00	45.00	80.00	—
1892/1	—	18.00	30.00	45.00	80.00	—
1893/1	—	200	500	950	1,600	—
1895/0	80,000	20.00	35.00	60.00	115	—
1895	Inc. above	20.00	35.00	60.00	115	—
1899/87 P	—	400	800	1,500	—	—

KM# 56 PESO

1.6120 g., 0.9000 Gold .0467 oz.

Date	Mintage	F	VF	XF	Unc	BU
1888	—	150	300	600	1,150	—
1895	43	150	300	600	1,150	—
1896	—	150	300	600	1,150	—

KM# 62 PESO
25.0000 g., 0.9000 Silver .7234 oz. **Obv:** KM#47 without 25 GMOS above UN PESO **Rev:** KM#52 **Note:** Mule.

Date	Mintage	VG	F	VF	XF	Unc
1894/82	—	20.00	35.00	60.00	115	—
1894/2 closed 4	—	25.00	40.00	70.00	135	—
1894/2 open 4	—	25.00	40.00	70.00	135	—
1895/85	Inc. above	20.00	35.00	60.00	115	—
1895/3	Inc. above	20.00	35.00	60.00	115	—
1895/4	Inc. above	20.00	35.00	60.00	115	—
1896/4	21,000	30.00	55.00	90.00	—	—

KM# 53 5 PESOS
8.0645 g., 0.9000 Gold .2333 oz.

Date	Mintage	F	VF	XF	Unc	BU
1883	—	450	650	1,000	2,500	—
1888/3	—	450	650	1,000	2,250	—
1890	—	600	750	1,100	2,250	—
1895	20	600	900	1,350	3,000	—
1896	55	600	900	1,350	3,000	—
1897	—	450	650	1,000	2,500	—
1900	—	450	650	1,000	2,500	—

KM# 58 10 PESOS
16.1290 g., 0.9000 Gold .4667 oz.

Date	Mintage	F	VF	XF	Unc	BU
1883 Rare	—	—	—	—	—	—
1889 Rare	25	—	—	—	—	—

KM# 57 20 PESOS
32.2580 g., 0.9000 Gold .9335 oz.

Date	Mintage	F	VF	XF	Unc	BU
1888	—	8,000	10,000	15,000	20,000	—
1895/88 Rare	—	—	—	—	—	—
1895 Rare	—	—	—	—	—	—

ESSAIS

KM#	Date	Mintage	Identification	Mkt Val
E1	1872	—	1/4 Real. Aluminum. Plain edge.	75.00
E2	1872	—	1/4 Real. Aluminum. Reeded edge.	75.00

PATTERNS

Including off metal strikes

Rosettes separate legends on Pn1-Pn5a.

KM#	Date	Mintage	Identification	Mkt Val
Pn1	1862T A	—	Peso. Bronze.	—
Pn1a	1862T A	—	Peso. Silver.	—

KM#	Date	Mintage	Identification	Mkt Val
Pn2	1862T A	—	2 Pesos. Bronze.	175
Pn2a	1862T A	—	2 Pesos. Silver.	—

KM#	Date	Mintage	Identification	Mkt Val
Pn3	1862T A	—	4 Pesos. Bronze.	175
Pn3a	1862T A	—	4 Pesos. Silver.	3,500

KM#	Date	Mintage	Identification	Mkt Val
Pn4	1862T A	—	8 Pesos. Bronze.	300
Pn4a	1862T A	—	8 Pesos. Silver.	—
Pn5	1862T A	—	16 Pesos. Bronze.	—
Pn5a	1862T A	—	16 Pesos. Silver.	—
Pn6	1869E	—	1/8 Real. Copper Nickel. KM#30.	100
Pn7	1869E	—	1/4 Real. Copper Nickel. KM#31.	100
Pn8	1869E	—	1/2 Real. Copper Nickel. KM#32.	175
Pn9	1869E	—	Real. Copper Nickel. KM#33.	175
Pn9a	1869E	—	Real. Copper. KM#33.	—

KM#	Date	Mintage	Identification	Mkt Val
Pn10	1870	—	Real. Copper Nickel. Medina.	150
Pn10a	1870	—	Real. Copper. Medina.	300

KM#	Date	Mintage	Identification	Mkt Val
Pn11	1870	—	2 Reales. Copper Nickel. Medina.	325

KM#	Date	Mintage	Identification	Mkt Val
Pn12	1870	—	5 Reales. Copper Nickel. Medina.	1,150
Pn13	1871	—	5 Centavos. Copper. KM#34.	500
Pn14	1871	—	10 Centavos. Copper. KM#35.	500
Pn15	1871	—	25 Centavos. Copper. KM#36.	500
Pn16	1871	—	50 Centavos. Copper. KM#37.	500
Pn16a	1871	—	50 Centavos. Nickel. KM#37.	—
Pn19	1872	—	1/4 Real.	—

KM#	Date	Mintage	Identification	Mkt Val
Pn20	1878	—	50 Centavos.	—

KM#	Date	Mintage	Identification	Mkt Val
PnA21	1878	—	Peso. 0.9000 Silver.	—
Pn21	1883	—	5 Pesos. Copper. KM#53.	250

TRIAL STRIKES

KM#	Date	Mintage	Identification	Mkt Val
TS1	1869	—	1/4 Real. Aluminum. Uniface obverse, Pn7.	75.00

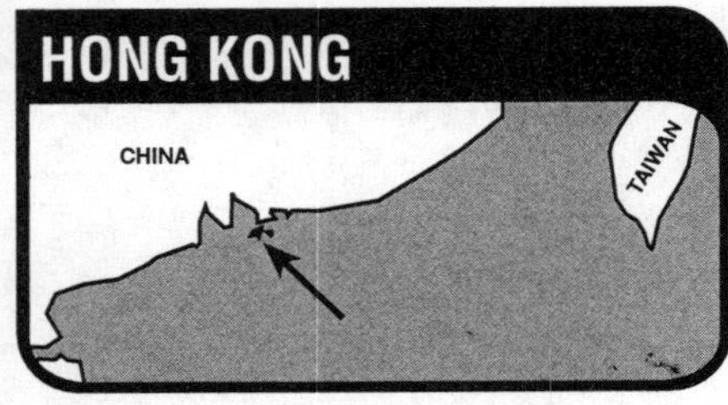

Hong Kong, a former British colony, is situated at the mouth of the Canton or Pearl River 90 miles (145 km.) southeast of Canton, has an area of 403 sq. mi. (1,040 sq. km.) and an estimated population of 6.3 million. Capital: Victoria. The free port of Hong Kong, the commercial center of the Far East, is a trans-shipment point for goods destined for China and the countries of the Pacific Rim. Light manufacturing and tourism are important components of the economy.

Long a haven for fishermen-pirates and opium smugglers, the island of Hong Kong was ceded to Britain at the conclusion of the first Opium War, 1839-1842. At the time, the acquisition of a 'barren rock' was ridiculed by both London and English merchants operating in the Far East. The Kowloon Peninsula and Stonecutter's Island were ceded in 1860, and the so-called New Territories, comprising most of the mainland of the colony, were leased to Britain for 99 years in 1898.

The legends on Hong Kong coinage are bilingual: English and Chinese. The rare 1941 cent was dispatched to Hong Kong in several shipments. One fell into Japanese hands while another was melted down by the British and a third was sunk during enemy action.

RULERS

British 1842-1997

MINT MARKS

H - Heaton

KN - King's Norton

MONETARY SYSTEM

10 Mils (Wen, Ch'ien) = 1 Cent (Hsien)

10 Cents = 1 Chiao

100 Cents = 10 Chiao = 1 Dollar (Yuan)

Shanghai Tael Series

The 1867 Tael and 2 Mace coins of 'Shanghai Tael' were minted at the Hong Kong mint as proposed trade coins for China. The Chinese expressed no interest in any form of struck coinage and the scheme was dropped. (KM#Pn123-Pn125)

Kwan Ping (Customs Tael) Series

Until recently these coins were a mystery, attributed by some to Taiwan and by others to Korea. Both attributions were wrong. It is now believed that they were struck at the Hong Kong mint as possible alternatives to the Hong Kong 'Shanghai Tael' patterns. The dies were presented to the Royal Mint, London in 1888 from the estate of the former Director of the Hong Kong mint. (KM#Pn126-PnA130).

BRITISH COLONY

DECIMAL COINAGE

KM# 1 MIL

Bronze **Obv:** Chinese value: "Wen"

Date	Mintage	F	VF	XF	Unc	BU
1863	19,000,000	6.00	12.00	25.00	110	—
1863 Proof	—	Value: 400				
1864	—	650	1,000	2,000	4,000	—
1864 Proof	—	Value: 6,000				
1865	40,000,000	—	—	2,150	4,250	—

KM# 2 MIL

Bronze **Rev:** Without hyphen between "HONG KONG"

Date	Mintage	F	VF	XF	Unc	BU
1865	Inc. above	6.00	12.00	25.00	110	—

KM# 3 MIL

Bronze **Obv:** Chinese value: "Ch'ien"

Date	Mintage	F	VF	XF	Unc	BU
1866	20,000,000	6.00	12.00	30.00	125	—

KM# 4.1 CENT

Bronze **Obv:** Fourteen pearls in left arch of crown

Date	Mintage	F	VF	XF	Unc	BU
1863	1,000,000	7.00	15.00	35.00	180	—
1863 Proof	—	Value: 500				
1863 Proof; Dot on reverse	—	Value: 600				
1865/3	1,000,000	20.00	30.00	60.00	500	—
1865	Inc. above	6.00	12.00	32.00	200	—
1865 Proof	—	Value: 550				
1866	1,000,000	5.00	10.00	28.00	200	—
1866 Proof	—	Value: 550				
1875	1,000,000	5.00	10.00	28.00	200	—
1875 Proof	—	Value: 550				
1876	1,000,000	5.00	10.00	28.00	250	—
1876 Proof	—	Value: 550				
1877	2,000,000	6.00	12.00	32.00	200	—
1877 Proof	—	Value: 750				

KM# 4.2 CENT

Bronze **Obv:** Fifteen pearls in left arch of crown

Date	Mintage	F	VF	XF	Unc	BU
1877	2,000,000	6.00	12.00	32.00	250	—
1877 Proof	—	Value: 550				
1879	Inc. below	6.00	12.00	32.00	250	—
1879 Proof	—	Value: 550				

KM# 4.3 CENT

Bronze **Obv:** Five pearls in center of crown

Date	Mintage	F	VF	XF	Unc	BU
1879	1,000,000	7.00	16.00	40.00	500	—
1879 Proof	—	Value: 500				
1880	1,000,000	6.00	12.00	35.00	220	—
1880 Proof	—	Value: 500				
1881	1,000,000	6.00	12.00	32.00	200	—
1881 Proof	—	Value: 500				
1899	1,000,000	5.00	10.00	25.00	170	—
1899 Proof	—	Value: 450				
1900H	1,000,000	3.00	7.50	18.00	100	—
1900H Proof	—	Value: 350				

KM# 5 5 CENTS

1.3577 g., 0.8000 Silver .0349 oz. **Obv:** Queen Victoria left **Note:** Coins dated 1866-1868 struck at the Hong Kong Mint; coins dated 1872-1901 struck at the British Royal Mint.

Date	Mintage	F	VF	XF	Unc	BU
1866	1,313,000	5.00	9.00	28.00	100	—
1866 Milled edge, proof	—	Value: 550				
1866 Plain edge, proof	—	Value: 750				
1867	Inc. above	6.00	10.00	28.00	100	—
1867 Proof	—	Value: 450				
1868	Inc. above	5.00	7.00	20.00	80.00	—
1872/68H	136,000	8.00	18.00	45.00	500	—
1872H Arabic 1	Inc. above	6.00	10.00	28.00	800	—
1872H Roman 1	Inc. above	9.00	20.00	45.00	800	—
1873/63	387,000	6.00	12.50	30.00	110	—
1873/63H	256,000	6.00	10.00	25.00	110	—
1873 Proof	—	Value: 450				
1874H	280,000	6.00	15.00	32.00	110	—
1875H	280,000	6.00	12.50	28.00	100	—
1875H Proof	—	Value: 500				
1876H	480,000	6.00	12.50	28.00	100	—
1877H	240,000	6.00	12.50	28.00	100	—
1879	288,000	6.00	12.50	28.00	100	—
1880H	300,000	6.00	12.50	25.00	80.00	—
1881	Inc. above	3.50	9.00	25.00	80.00	—
1881 Proof	—	Value: 450				
1882H	600,000	2.00	4.00	10.00	35.00	—
1883	550,000	2.00	4.00	10.00	40.00	—
1883 Proof	—	Value: 450				
1883H	250,000	4.00	12.50	25.00	65.00	—
1883H Proof	—	Value: 450				
1884	960,000	1.50	3.00	7.00	30.00	—
1884 Proof	—	Value: 450				

Date	Mintage	F	VF	XF	Unc	BU
1885	3,120,000	1.00	2.50	6.00	22.00	—
1885 Proof	—	Value: 475				
1886	2,100,000	1.00	2.50	6.00	22.00	—
1887	2,448,000	1.00	2.50	6.00	22.00	—
1888	Inc. above	1.00	2.50	6.00	22.00	—
1889	5,169,000	1.00	2.50	6.00	22.00	—
1889 Proof	—	Value: 300				
1889H	2,100,000	1.00	2.50	6.00	22.00	—
1890	1,500,000	1.00	2.50	6.00	22.00	—
1890 Proof	—	Value: 300				
1890H	5,400,000	1.00	2.50	6.00	20.00	—
1890H Proof	—	Value: 300				
1891	6,900,000	1.00	2.50	6.00	20.00	—
1891H	2,100,000	1.00	2.50	6.00	20.00	—
1892	4,200,000	1.00	2.50	6.00	20.00	—
1892H	1,200,000	1.50	3.00	6.50	25.00	—
1892 Proof	—	Value: 300				
1893	3,000,000	1.00	2.50	5.50	17.50	—
1894	4,600,000	1.00	2.50	5.50	17.50	—
1894 Proof	—	Value: 275				
1895	4,000,000	1.00	2.50	5.50	17.50	—
1897	4,000,000	1.00	2.50	5.50	17.50	—
1898	3,500,000	1.00	2.50	5.50	17.50	—
1899	9,377,000	1.00	2.50	5.00	15.00	—
1900	1,623,000	1.00	2.50	5.00	15.00	—
1900H	7,000,000	1.00	2.50	5.00	15.00	—

KM# 6.1 10 CENTS

2.7154 g., 0.8000 Silver .0698 oz.

Date	Mintage	F	VF	XF	Unc	BU
1863	100,000	10.00	22.00	45.00	160	—
1863 Proof, reeded edge	—	Value: 450				
1863 Proof, plain edge	—	Value: 550				
1864	200,000	300	550	850	1,500	—
1864 Proof	—	Value: 1,850				
1865	550,000	7.50	16.00	35.00	120	—
1865 Proof	—	Value: 400				

KM# 6.3 10 CENTS

2.7154 g., 0.8000 Silver .0698 oz. **Obv:** Queen Victoria left **Note:** Coins dated 1866-1868 struck at the Hong Kong Mint; coins dated 1869-1901 struck at the British Royal Mint.

Date	Mintage	F	VF	XF	Unc	BU
1866/5	—	60.00	120	200	—	—
1866	2,479,000	5.00	10.00	25.00	90.00	—
1866 Proof	—	Value: 350				
1867	Inc. above	7.50	15.00	35.00	125	—
1867 Proof	—	Value: 450				
1868	Inc. above	4.00	8.00	20.00	60.00	—
1869 Proof	—	Value: 650				
1872H	88,000	10.00	25.00	60.00	1,000	—
1872H Proof	—	Value: 500				
1873 Round top 3	197,000	5.00	10.00	25.00	80.00	—
1873 Proof	—	Value: 400				
1873 Plain edge, proof	—	Value: 1,200				
1873H Flat top 3	128,000	6.50	12.50	32.00	120	—
1874H	200,000	5.00	10.00	25.00	80.00	—
1875H	200,000	5.00	10.00	30.00	100	—
1875H Proof	—	Value: 450				
1876H	480,000	6.50	12.50	25.00	75.00	—
1877H	240,000	6.50	12.50	25.00	75.00	—
1877 Proof	—	Value: 450				
1879	288,000	5.00	10.00	25.00	75.00	—
1879	—	Value: 400				
1880H	300,000	5.00	10.00	25.00	75.00	—
1880H	—	Value: 400				
1881	300,000	4.00	8.00	22.00	70.00	—
1881 Proof	—	Value: 400				
1882H	500,000	4.00	8.00	20.00	65.00	—
1882H Proof	—	Value: 500				
1883	550,000	4.00	8.00	20.00	65.00	—
1883 Proof	—	Value: 400				
1883H Round top 3	250,000	5.00	9.00	30.00	80.00	—
1883H Proof	—	Value: 800				
1884	960,000	2.00	3.50	9.00	40.00	—
1884 Proof	—	Value: 250				
1885	3,120,000	1.50	3.00	7.00	32.00	—
1885 Proof	—	Value: 700				
1886	2,100,000	1.50	3.00	7.00	32.00	—
1886 Proof	—	Value: 250				
1887	2,441,000	1.50	3.00	7.00	32.00	—
1887 Proof	—	Value: 350				
1888	7,027,000	1.50	3.00	7.00	32.00	—

Date	Mintage	F	VF	XF	Unc	BU
1888 Proof	—	Value: 250				
1889	4,027,000	1.50	3.00	7.00	32.00	—
1889 Proof	—	Value: 250				
1889H	2,100,000	1.50	3.00	7.00	32.00	—
1890	1,500,000	1.50	3.00	9.00	32.00	—
1890 Proof	—	Value: 275				
1890H	5,400,000	1.50	3.00	6.00	22.00	—
1891	6,150,000	1.50	3.00	6.00	22.00	—
1891H	1,750,000	1.50	3.00	8.00	35.00	—
1892	5,500,000	1.50	3.00	6.00	22.00	—
1892 Proof	—	Value: 250				
1892	1,100,000	3.00	10.00	15.00	38.00	—
1892 Proof	—	Value: 250				
1893	11,250,000	1.50	3.00	6.00	22.00	—
1894	16,750,000	1.50	3.00	6.00	22.00	—
1894 Proof	—	Value: 250				
1895	19,000,000	1.50	3.00	6.00	22.00	—
1896	16,500,000	1.50	3.00	6.00	22.00	—
1897	23,500,000	1.50	3.00	6.00	18.50	—
1897	10,500,000	1.50	3.00	6.00	18.50	—
1897 Proof	—	Value: 400				
1898	29,500,000	1.50	3.00	6.00	18.50	—
1899	33,842,000	1.00	2.00	4.00	18.50	—
1900	7,758,000	1.00	2.00	4.00	18.50	—
1900	41,500,000	1.00	2.00	4.00	18.50	—

KM# 6.2 10 CENTS

2.7154 g., 0.8000 Silver .0698 oz. **Obv:** Ten pearls on right arch of crown **Note:** Struck at the Royal Mint.

Date	Mintage	F	VF	XF	Unc	BU
1866	300,000	5.00	10.00	25.00	100	—
1866 Proof	—	Value: 800				

KM# 7 20 CENTS

5.4308 g., 0.8000 Silver .1397 oz. **Note:** Coins dated 1866-68 struck at the Hong Kong Mint; 1872-98 at the Royal Mint.

Date	Mintage	F	VF	XF	Unc	BU
1866	445,000	12.00	30.00	75.00	335	—
1866 Proof, reeded edge	—	Value: 1,000				
1866 Proof, plain edge	—	Value: 1,500				
1867	Inc. above	16.00	35.00	85.00	400	—
1867 Proof	—	Value: 1,000				
1868	Inc. above	12.00	30.00	75.00	325	—
1868 Proof	—	Value: 1,000				
1872/68H	64,000	18.00	40.00	90.00	1,500	—
1872H	Inc. above	12.00	30.00	75.00	1,500	—
1872H Proof	—	Value: 1,600				
1873	96,000	12.00	30.00	80.00	350	—
1873 Proof, plain edge	—	Value: 2,500				
1873 Proof, reeded edge	—	Value: 3,450				
1873H	64,000	12.00	30.00	80.00	350	—
1874H	70,000	12.00	30.00	80.00	350	—
1875H	70,000	12.00	30.00	80.00	350	—
1875H Proof	—	Value: 1,500				
1876H	120,000	10.00	30.00	75.00	350	—
1877H	60,000	12.00	30.00	85.00	375	—
1879	20,000	250	550	950	2,200	—
1879 Proof	—	Value: 6,325				
1880H	25,000	75.00	125	265	650	—
1881	30,000	150	275	600	1,550	—
1881 Proof	—	Value: 2,650				
1882H	100,000	12.00	30.00	75.00	335	—
1882H Proof	—	Value: 1,600				
1883	138,000	12.00	30.00	75.00	335	—
1883 Proof	—	Value: 1,250				
1883H	63,000	16.00	35.00	85.00	375	—
1883H Proof	—	Value: 1,250				
1884	80,000	10.00	28.00	70.00	300	—
1884 Proof	—	Value: 1,250				
1885	260,000	10.00	20.00	50.00	225	—
1885 Proof	—	Value: 1,150				
1886	175,000	10.00	20.00	50.00	225	—
1886 Proof	—	Value: 1,150				
1887	200,000	10.00	20.00	50.00	225	—
1887 Proof	—	Value: 1,150				
1888	500,000	8.00	17.50	40.00	200	—
1888 Proof	—	Value: 1,150				
1889	440,000	8.00	17.50	40.00	200	—
1889 Proof	—	Value: 1,150				
1889H	175,000	10.00	20.00	50.00	225	—
1890	125,000	10.00	20.00	50.00	225	—
1890H	450,000	8.00	17.50	40.00	200	—
1891	575,000	8.00	17.50	40.00	200	—
1891 Proof	—	Value: 2,300				
1891H	175,000	10.00	20.00	50.00	240	—
1892	450,000	8.00	17.50	40.00	200	—
1892 Proof	—	Value: 1,725				
1892H	100,000	12.50	22.00	60.00	250	—
1892H Proof	—	Value: 1,625				
1893	750,000	8.00	16.50	35.00	160	—

Date	Mintage	F	VF	XF	Unc	BU
1894	650,000	8.00	16.50	35.00	160	—
1894 Proof	—	Value: 500				
1895	500,000	8.00	16.50	35.00	160	—
1896	250,000	8.00	16.50	35.00	160	—
1898	125,000	8.00	16.50	35.00	185	—

KM# 8 1/2 DOLLAR

0.9000 Silver .3900 oz. **Note:** Weight varies: 13.478-13.580 grams. Struck at the Hong Kong Mint.

Date	Mintage	F	VF	XF	Unc	BU
1866	59,000	300	550	950	2,500	—
1866 Proof, reeded edge	—	Value: 5,500				
1866 Proof, rare. plain edge	—	—	—	—	—	—

Note: Superior Goodman sale 5-95 choice brilliant proof realized, $14,375

Date	Mintage	F	VF	XF	Unc	BU
1867	Inc. above	500	1,000	1,500	8,000	—
1867 Proof, rare	—	—	—	—	—	—

Note: Superior Goodman sale 5-95 brilliant proof realized, $16,675

Date	Mintage	F	VF	XF	Unc	BU
1868 Proof, rare	—	—	—	—	—	—

Note: Superior Goodman sale 5-95 choice proof realized, $109,250

KM# 9.1 50 CENTS

13.5769 g., 0.8000 Silver .3492 oz. **Obv:** Without mint mark

Date	Mintage	F	VF	XF	Unc	BU
1890	50,000	30.00	50.00	120	600	—
1890 Proof	—	Value: 1,250				
1891	150,000	20.00	45.00	90.00	550	—
1891 Proof	—	Value: 1,450				
1892	90,000	30.00	60.00	120	600	—
1892 Proof	—	Value: 1,250				
1893	150,000	20.00	45.00	90.00	550	—
1894	130,000	20.00	45.00	90.00	550	—
1894 Proof	—	Value: 1,200				

KM# 9.2 50 CENTS

13.5769 g., 0.8000 Silver .3492 oz., 32 mm. **Obv:** Mint mark below bust

Date	Mintage	F	VF	XF	Unc	BU
1891H	70,000	35.00	60.00	100	550	—
1892H	20,000	65.00	125	250	750	—
1892H Proof	—	Value: 1,500				

KM# 10 DOLLAR

0.9000 Silver .7800 oz. **Note:** Struck at the Hong Kong Mint. Weight varies: 26.9568-27.2500 grams.

Date	Mintage	F	VF	XF	Unc	BU
1866	2,108,000	165	300	600	1,700	—
1866 Proof, reeded edge	—	Value: 3,500				
1866 Proof, plain edge	—	Value: 4,500				
1867/6	Inc. above	250	450	800	3,000	—
1867	Inc. above	165	300	600	1,650	—
1867 Proof	—	Value: 5,000				
1868	Inc. above	165	300	600	1,650	—
1868 Proof	—	Value: 4,500				

PATTERNS

Including off metal strikes

Obverse Types

Type A Type B

Type C Type D

KM#	Date	Mintage	Identification	Mkt Val
Pn1	ND	—	Cent. Copper. Type A. Similar to KM#Pn13. PR#254.	2,000
Pn2	ND	—	Cent. Copper. Type A. St. George and dragon in center, lion R. M. T. G. and anchors in angles. PR#255.	—
Pn3	1862	—	Cent. Copper. Type A. Wreath around center circle dividing value, HONG KONG at top, date at bottom. PR#256.	—
Pn4	1862	—	Cent. Copper. Type A. Similar to KM#Pn3 but with date between lions. PR#257.	—
Pn5	1862	—	Cent. Copper. Type A. Similar to KM#Pn3 but with T.G. and T.M. at sides. PR#258.	—
Pn6	1862	—	Cent. Copper. Type A. Similar to KM#Pn24. PR#259.	—
Pn7	1862	—	Cent. Copper. Type A. Similar to KM#Pn24 but with date between anchor and lion. PR#260.	—
Pn8	1862	—	Cent. Copper. Type A. Similar to KM#Pn24 but with date between crown and dragon. PR#261.	2,500
Pn9	1862	—	Cent. Copper. Type A. Similar to KM#Pn24 but with crown in center circle and anchor and lion between date. PR#262.	—
Pn10	1862	—	Cent. Copper. Type A. Similar to KM#Pn9 but with date between crown and dragon. PR#263.	—
Pn11	1862	—	Cent. Copper. PR#264.	—
Pn12	1862	—	Cent. Copper. Type A. Center dot value and date in outer circle. PR#265.	—

KM#	Date	Mintage	Identification	Mkt Val
Pn13	ND	—	Cent. Copper. PR#267.	1,250
Pn14	1862	—	Cent. Copper. Type B. Similar to KM#Pn3. PR#268.	—
Pn15	1862	—	Cent. Copper. Type B. Similar to KM#Pn4. PR#269.	—
Pn16	1862	—	Cent. Copper. Type B. Similar to KM#Pn6. PR#270.	—
Pn17	1862	—	Cent. Copper. Type B. Similar to KM#Pn7. PR#271.	—
Pn18	1862	—	Cent. Copper. Type B. Similar to KM#Pn11. PR#272.	1,750
Pn19	1862	—	Cent. Copper. Type B. Similar to KM#Pn12. PR#273.	—
Pn20	ND	—	Cent. Copper. Type C. Similar to KM#Pn13. PR#275.	—
Pn21	ND	—	Cent. Copper. Type C. Similar to KM#Pn2. PR#276.	—
Pn22	1862	—	Cent. Copper. Type C. Similar to KM#Pn3. PR#277.	—
Pn23	1862	—	Cent. Copper. Type C. Similar to KM#Pn4. PR#278.	—
Pn24	1862	—	Cent. Copper. PR#279.	—
Pn25	1862	—	Cent. Copper. Type C. Similar to KM#Pn7. PR#280.	—
Pn26	1862	—	Cent. Copper. Type C. Similar to KM#Pn8. PR#281.	1,650
Pn27	1862	—	Cent. Copper. Type C. Similar to KM#Pn4 but with crown in center circle. PR#282.	—
Pn28	1862	—	Cent. Copper. Type C. Similar to KM#Pn27 but with T.G. and R.M. at sides of wreath. PR#283.	—
Pn29	1862	—	Cent. Copper. Type C. Similar to KM#Pn28 but with T.G. and R.M. running vertically, date between anchor and lion. PR#284.	—
Pn30	1862	—	Cent. Copper. Type C. Similar to KM#Pn11. PR#285.	—
Pn31	1862	—	Cent. Copper. Type C. Similar to KM#Pn12. PR#286.	—
Pn32	1862	—	Cent. Copper. PR#288.	1,800
Pn33	1862	—	Cent. Copper. Similar to KM#Pn32. Similar to KM#Pn4. PR#289.	—
Pn34	1862	—	Cent. Copper. Similar to KM#Pn32. Similar to KM#Pn6. PR#290.	2,000
Pn35	1862	—	Cent. Copper. PR#291.	—
Pn36	1862	—	Cent. Copper. PR#292.	2,400
Pn37	1862	—	Cent. Copper. Similar to KM#Pn2. Similar to KM#Pn7. PR#293.	2,250
Pn38	1862	—	Cent. Copper. Similar to KM#Pn37. Similar to KM#Pn8. PR#294.	—
Pn39	1862	—	Cent. Copper. Similar to KM#Pn37. Similar to KM#Pn9. PR#295.	—
Pn40	1862	—	Cent. Copper. Similar to KM#Pn37. Similar to KM#Pn10. PR#296.	—
Pn41	1862	—	Cent. Copper. PR#297.	—
Pn42	1862	—	Cent. Copper. Similar to KM#Pn41. Similar to KM#Pn27. PR#298.	—
Pn43	1862	—	Cent. Copper. Similar to KM#Pn41. Similar to KM#Pn28. PR#299.	—
Pn44	1862	—	Cent. Copper. Similar to KM#Pn41. Similar to KM#Pn29. PR#300.	2,500
Pn45	1862	—	10 Cents. Silver. Type C. Similar to KM#Pn53. PR#238.	—
Pn46	1862	—	10 Cents. Bronze. Similar to KM#Pn45. PR#239.	—
Pn47	1862	—	10 Cents. Silver Gilt. Similar to KM#Pn45. Uniface. PR#240.	—
Pn48	1862	—	10 Cents. Silver. PR#241.	—
Pn49	1862	—	10 Cents. Bronze. Similar to KM#Pn48. PR#242.	—
Pn50	1862	—	10 Cents. Silver Gilt. Similar to KM#Pn48. Uniface. PR#243.	—
Pn51	ND	—	10 Cents. Silver. PR#244.	—
Pn52	ND	—	10 Cents. Bronze. Similar to KM#Pn51. PR#245.	—
Pn53	1862	—	10 Cents. Silver. PR#246.	2,400
Pn54	1862	—	10 Cents. Silver. Similar to reverse of KM#Pn45. Similar to reverse of KM#Pn51. Mule. PR#248.	—
Pn55	1862	—	10 Cents. Silver. Mule. PR#249.	—
Pn56	1862	—	10 Cents. Bronze. Similar to KM#Pn55. PR#250.	—

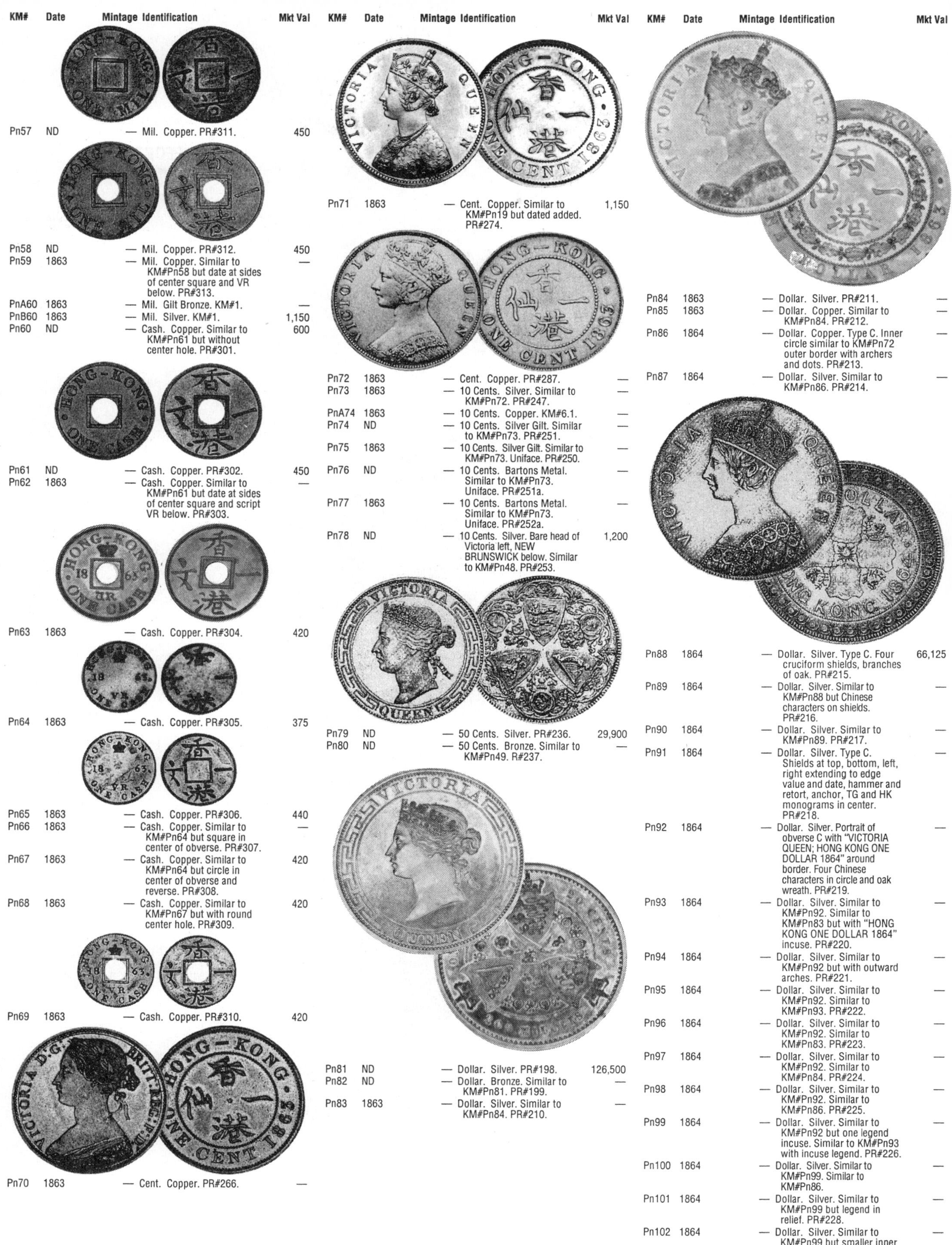

KM#	Date	Mintage Identification	Mkt Val
Pn57	ND	— Mil. Copper. PR#311.	450
Pn58	ND	— Mil. Copper. PR#312.	450
Pn59	1863	— Mil. Copper. Similar to KM#Pn58 but date at sides of center square and VR below. PR#313.	—
PnA60	1863	— Mil. Gilt Bronze. KM#1.	—
PnB60	1863	— Mil. Silver. KM#1.	1,150
Pn60	ND	— Cash. Copper. Similar to KM#Pn61 but without center hole. PR#301.	600
Pn61	ND	— Cash. Copper. PR#302.	450
Pn62	1863	— Cash. Copper. Similar to KM#Pn61 but date at sides of center square and script VR below. PR#303.	—
Pn63	1863	— Cash. Copper. PR#304.	420
Pn64	1863	— Cash. Copper. PR#305.	375
Pn65	1863	— Cash. Copper. PR#306.	440
Pn66	1863	— Cash. Copper. Similar to KM#Pn64 but square in center of obverse. PR#307.	—
Pn67	1863	— Cash. Copper. Similar to KM#Pn64 but circle in center of obverse and reverse. PR#308.	420
Pn68	1863	— Cash. Copper. Similar to KM#Pn67 but with round center hole. PR#309.	420
Pn69	1863	— Cash. Copper. PR#310.	420
Pn70	1863	— Cent. Copper. PR#266.	—
Pn71	1863	— Cent. Copper. Similar to KM#Pn19 but dated added. PR#274.	1,150
Pn72	1863	— Cent. Copper. PR#287.	—
Pn73	1863	— 10 Cents. Silver. Similar to KM#Pn72. PR#247.	—
PnA74	1863	— 10 Cents. Copper. KM#6.1.	—
Pn74	ND	— 10 Cents. Silver Gilt. Similar to KM#Pn73. PR#251.	—
Pn75	1863	— 10 Cents. Silver Gilt. Similar to KM#Pn73. Uniface. PR#250.	—
Pn76	ND	— 10 Cents. Bartons Metal. Similar to KM#Pn73. Uniface. PR#251a.	—
Pn77	1863	— 10 Cents. Bartons Metal. Similar to KM#Pn73. Uniface. PR#252a.	—
Pn78	ND	— 10 Cents. Silver. Bare head of Victoria left, NEW BRUNSWICK below. Similar to KM#Pn48. PR#253.	1,200
Pn79	ND	— 50 Cents. Silver. PR#236.	29,900
Pn80	ND	— 50 Cents. Bronze. Similar to KM#Pn49. R#237.	—
Pn81	ND	— Dollar. Silver. PR#198.	126,500
Pn82	ND	— Dollar. Bronze. Similar to KM#Pn81. PR#199.	—
Pn83	1863	— Dollar. Silver. Similar to KM#Pn84. PR#210.	—
Pn84	1863	— Dollar. Silver. PR#211.	—
Pn85	1863	— Dollar. Copper. Similar to KM#Pn84. PR#212.	—
Pn86	1864	— Dollar. Copper. Type C. Inner circle similar to KM#Pn72 outer border with archers and dots. PR#213.	—
Pn87	1864	— Dollar. Silver. Similar to KM#Pn86. PR#214.	—
Pn88	1864	— Dollar. Silver. Type C. Four cruciform shields, branches of oak. PR#215.	66,125
Pn89	1864	— Dollar. Silver. Similar to KM#Pn88 but Chinese characters on shields. PR#216.	—
Pn90	1864	— Dollar. Silver. Similar to KM#Pn89. PR#217.	—
Pn91	1864	— Dollar. Silver. Type C. Shields at top, bottom, left, right extending to edge value and date, hammer and retort, anchor, TG and HK monograms in center. PR#218.	—
Pn92	1864	— Dollar. Silver. Portrait of obverse C with "VICTORIA QUEEN; HONG KONG ONE DOLLAR 1864" around border. Four Chinese characters in circle and oak wreath. PR#219.	—
Pn93	1864	— Dollar. Silver. Similar to KM#Pn92. Similar to KM#Pn83 but with "HONG KONG ONE DOLLAR 1864" incuse. PR#220.	—
Pn94	1864	— Dollar. Silver. Similar to KM#Pn92 but with outward arches. PR#221.	—
Pn95	1864	— Dollar. Silver. Similar to KM#Pn92. Similar to KM#Pn93. PR#222.	—
Pn96	1864	— Dollar. Silver. Similar to KM#Pn92. Similar to KM#Pn83. PR#223.	—
Pn97	1864	— Dollar. Silver. Similar to KM#Pn92. Similar to KM#Pn84. PR#224.	—
Pn98	1864	— Dollar. Silver. Similar to KM#Pn92. Similar to KM#Pn86. PR#225.	—
Pn99	1864	— Dollar. Silver. Similar to KM#Pn92 but one legend incuse. Similar to KM#Pn93 with incuse legend. PR#226.	—
Pn100	1864	— Dollar. Silver. Similar to KM#Pn99. Similar to KM#Pn86.	—
Pn101	1864	— Dollar. Silver. Similar to KM#Pn99 but legend in relief. PR#228.	—
Pn102	1864	— Dollar. Silver. Similar to KM#Pn99 but smaller inner circle. PR#229.	—

KM#	Date	Mintage	Identification	Mkt Val
Pn103	1864	—	Dollar. Silver. Similar to KM#Pn102. Similar to KM#Pn92. PR#230.	—
Pn104	1864	—	Dollar. Silver. Similar to KM#Pn88. PR#231.	—
Pn105	1864	—	Dollar. Silver. PR#232.	71,875
Pn106	1864	—	Dollar. Pewter. Similar to KM#Pn105. PR#233.	—
Pn107	1864	—	Dollar. Silver. Similar to KM#Pn104. Similar to KM#Pn91. PR#234.	—
Pn108	1864	—	Dollar. Silver. Similar to KM#Pn91 but withou devices in angles. PR#235.	—
Pn109	1865	—	Dollar. Silver. Milled edge. PR#200.	25,300
Pn110	1865	—	Dollar. Silver. Plain edge. Similar to KM#Pn109. PR#201.	29,900
Pn111	1865	—	Dollar. Lead. Similar to KM#Pn109. Die defaced. PR#202.	—
Pn112	1865	—	Dollar. Lead. Plain edge. Similar to KM#Pn109 but "TRIAL" in relief behind Queen's head. PR#203.	—
Pn113	1865	—	Dollar. Silver. Milled edge. Similar to KM#Pn112. PR#204.	11,500
Pn114	1865	—	Dollar. Copper. Milled edge. Similar to KM#Pn112. PR#205.	4,500

KM#	Date	Mintage	Identification	Mkt Val
Pn115	1865	—	Dollar. Copper. With "TRIAL". Diagonal milled edge. Similar to KM#Pn112. PR#206.	—
Pn116	1865	—	Dollar. Silver. Type C with "TRIAL" incused behind Queen's head. Similar to KM#Pn109. Milled edge. PR#207.	—
Pn117	1865	—	Dollar. Silver. PR#208.	10,925
Pn118	ND(1865)	—	Dollar. Silver. Similar to KM#Pn94. PR#209.	—
Pn119	1866	—	5 Cents. Copper. KM#5.	—
Pn120	1866	—	10 Cents. Copper. KM#6.1.	500
Pn121	1866	—	Dollar. Copper. KM#10.	1,750
Pn122	1867	—	Tael. Silver. PR#314.	120,750
Pn123	1867	—	2 Mace. Silver. K913	—

Note: Superior Goodman sale 5-95 brilliant proof realized $39,100.

KM#	Date	Mintage	Identification	Mkt Val
Pn124	1867	—	Liang. Silver. Without rays from ring, K911a.	—

Note: Superior Goodman sale 5-95 choice brilliant proof realized $80,500.

KM#	Date	Mintage	Identification	Mkt Val
Pn125	1867	—	Liang. Silver. With rays from ring, K912.	—

Note: Superior Goodman sale 5-95 proof realized, $60,375.

KM#	Date	Mintage	Identification	Mkt Val
Pn126	ND(ca.1868)	—	5 Fen. Silver.	3,500
Pn127	ND(ca.1868)	—	Chien. Silver. K926-II	6,000
Pn128	ND(ca.1868)	—	2 Chien. Silver. K926-I	8,000
Pn129	ND(ca.1868)	—	5 Chien. Silver. Kwan Ping (Customs Tael). K926.	10,000
PnA130	ND(ca.1868)	—	Liang. Silver. K925.	—

Note: Superior Goodman sale 6-91 proof realized $50,600.

KM#	Date	Mintage	Identification	Mkt Val
Pn130	1869	—	10 Cents. Copper. KM#6.1.	1,350
Pn131	1873	—	10 Cents. Copper. KM#6.1.	—
Pn132	1877	—	Cent. Nickel. KM#4.2. Fifteen pearls.	—
Pn133	1894	—	10 Cents. Aluminum. KM#6.3	—
Pn134	1897	—	10 Cents. Aluminum. KM#6.1.	—

PIEFORTS

KM#	Date	Mintage	Identification	Mkt Val
P1	1886	—	10 Cents. Brass. KM#6.3.	200

PROOF SETS

KM#	Date	Mintage	Identification	Issue Price	Mkt Val
PS1	1866 (5)	—	KM#5, 6.2, 7-7, 10	—	11,500
PS2	1873 (3)	1	KM#5, 6.3, 7	—	7,000
PS3	1885 (3)	1	KM#5, 6.3, 7	—	5,000

The Republic of Hungary, located in central Europe, has an area of 35,929 sq. mi. (93,030 sq. km.) and a population of 10.7 million. Capital: Budapest. The economy is based on agriculture, bauxite and a rapidly expanding industrial sector. Machinery, chemicals, iron and steel, and fruits and vegetables are exported.

The ancient kingdom of Hungary, founded by the Magyars in the 9th century, achieved its greatest extension in the mid-14th century when its dominions touched the Baltic, Black and Mediterranean Seas. After suffering repeated Turkish invasions, Hungary accepted Habsburg rule to escape Turkish occupation, regaining independence in 1867 with the Emperor of Austria as king of a dual Austro-Hungarian monarchy.

RULERS

Franz Joseph I, 1848-1916

MINT MARKS

A, CA, WI - Vienna (Becs)
B, K, KB - Kremnitz (Kormoczbanya)
BP - Budapest
CH - Pressburg (Pozsony)
CM - Kaschau (Kassa)
(c) - castle - Pressburg
(d) - double trefoil - Pressburg
G, GN, NB - Nagybanya
(g) - GC script monogram - Pressburg
GYF - Karlsburg (Gyulafehervar)
HA - Hall
(L) - ICB monogram - Pressburg
(r) - rampant lion left - Pressburg
S - Schmollnitz (Szomolnok)

MONETARY SYSTEM

Until 1857
2 Poltura = 3 Krajczar
60 Krajczar = 1 Forint (Gulden)
2 Forint = 1 Convention Thaler

1857-1891
100 Krajczar = 1 Forint

1892-1925
100 Filler = 1 Korona

NOTE: Many coins of Hungary through 1948, especially 1925-1945, have been restruck in recent times. These may be identified by a rosette in the vicinity of the mintmark. Restrike mintages for KM#440-449, 451-458, 468-469,475-477, 480-483, 494, 496-498 are usually about 1000 pieces, later date mintages are not known.

KINGDOM

WAR OF INDEPENDENCE COINAGE

KM# 430.1 EGY (1) KRAJCZAR

Copper

Date	Mintage	F	VF	XF	Unc	BU
1848	—	2.00	6.00	12.50	25.00	—

KM# 430.2 EGY (1) KRAJCZAR

Copper

Date	Mintage	F	VF	XF	Unc	BU
1849NB	—	20.00	40.00	60.00	100	—

KM# 434 HAROM (3) KRAJCZAR

Copper **Note:** Varieties exist overstruck with figure of Madonna.

Date	Mintage	F	VF	XF	Unc	BU
1849NB	—	7.50	15.00	27.50	60.00	—

KM# 435 HAT (6) KRAJCZAR

0.2200 Silver

Date	Mintage	F	VF	XF	Unc	BU
1849NB	—	4.00	8.00	17.50	30.00	—

KM# 431 10 KRAJCZAR

3.8900 g., 0.5000 Silver .0625 oz. **Rev. Legend:** SZ. MARIA...

Date	Mintage	F	VF	XF	Unc	BU
1848KB	—	20.00	55.00	80.00	125	—

KM# 432 20 KRAJCZAR

6.6800 g., 0.5830 Silver .1252 oz. **Rev. Legend:** SZ. MARIA...

Date	Mintage	F	VF	XF	Unc	BU
1848KB	—	3.00	8.00	17.50	35.00	—

STANDARD COINAGE

KM# 468 5/10 KRAJCZAR

1.6700 g., Copper **Obv:** Arms of the Kingdom **Obv. Legend:** MAGYAR KIRALYI VALTO PENZ **Edge:** Plain

Date	Mintage	F	VF	XF	Unc	BU
1882KB	2,400,000	2.50	4.00	6.00	10.00	—
1882KB Restrike; proof	—	Value: 8.00				

KM# 441.1 KRAJCZAR

3.3300 g., Copper, 19 mm. **Obv:** Angels holding the crowned arms of the Kingdom

Date	Mintage	F	VF	XF	Unc	BU
1868KB	12,531,070	2.00	6.00	10.00	15.00	—
1868KB Restrike; proof	—	Value: 10.00				
1869KB	5,072,736	2.00	6.50	11.00	18.00	—
1872KB	—	2.00	6.50	11.00	18.00	—
1873KB	3,703,000	35.00	65.00	100	150	—

KM# 441.2 KRAJCZAR

Copper

Date	Mintage	F	VF	XF	Unc	BU
1868GYF Rare	—	—	—	—	—	—

KM# 459 KRAJCZAR

Copper **Obv:** KM#441 **Rev:** KM#458 **Note:** Mule.

Date	Mintage	F	VF	XF	Unc	BU
1878	—	25.00	35.00	60.00	85.00	—

KM# 458 KRAJCZAR

3.3300 g., Copper, 19 mm. **Obv:** Arms of the Kingdom **Note:** Wreath varieties exist for 1878 dated coins.

Date	Mintage	F	VF	XF	Unc	BU
1878KB	4,478,154	12.00	18.00	30.00	45.00	—
1879KB	10,100,984	3.00	7.50	12.00	17.50	—
1881KB	12,232,831	3.00	7.50	12.00	17.50	—
1882KB	19,799,904	5.00	11.00	17.50	27.50	—
1883KB	8,535,127	9.00	15.00	27.50	35.00	—
1885KB	26,605,955	1.25	3.50	7.50	12.00	—
1886KB	17,670,993	2.00	5.50	9.00	15.00	—
1887KB	11,988,907	2.50	6.00	12.00	18.00	—
1888KB	10,334,145	3.50	7.00	12.00	18.00	—

KM# 478 KRAJCZAR

3.3300 g., Copper, 19 mm.

Date	Mintage	F	VF	XF	Unc	BU
1891	16,271,659	2.50	5.00	8.00	14.50	—
Note: Variations in thickness of planchet exist						
1892	5,870,524	7.00	15.00	22.50	32.50	—

KM# 442 4 KRAJCZAR

13.3000 g., Copper, 27 mm. **Obv:** Arms of the Kingdom **Note:** Wreath varieties exist.

Date	Mintage	F	VF	XF	Unc	BU
1868KB	3,099,298	3.00	12.50	20.00	32.50	—
1868KB Restrike; proof	—	Value: 18.00				

KM# 421 10 KRAJCZAR

3.8900 g., 0.5000 Silver .0625 oz.

Date	Mintage	F	VF	XF	Unc	BU
1837	49,000	100	275	400	675	—
1838	49,000	50.00	90.00	140	240	—
1839	84,000	4.00	10.00	20.00	35.00	—
1840	44,000	5.00	12.00	24.00	50.00	—
1841	61,000	4.50	10.00	20.00	35.00	—
1842	71,000	4.50	10.00	20.00	35.00	—
1843	108,000	5.00	12.00	24.00	50.00	—
1844	52,000	5.00	9.00	17.50	32.50	—
1845	119,000	5.00	9.00	17.50	32.50	—
1846	150,000	4.00	8.00	15.00	27.00	—
1847	161,000	2.50	4.00	9.00	18.00	—
1848	406,000	2.50	4.00	9.00	18.00	—

KM# 440.3 10 KRAJCZAR

2.0000 g., 0.5000 Silver 0.0322 oz., 19 mm. **Ruler:** Franz J oseph I **Obv:** Large head **Rev:** Crown, denomination and mint mark **Edge:** Plain

Date	Mintage	F	VF	XF	Unc	BU
1867B Rare	1,000	—	—	—	—	—
1868B	—	80.00	160	475	800	—

KM# 440.1 10 KRAJCZAR

1.6600 g., 0.4000 Silver .0213 oz., 18 mm. **Obv. Legend:** ... AP. KIRALYA **Rev. Legend:** VALTO PENZ. **Edge:** Plain

Date	Mintage	F	VF	XF	Unc	BU
1868KB	—	50.00	110	200	320	—
1868KB Restrike; proof	—	Value: 20.00				

KM# 440.2 10 KRAJCZAR

1.6600 g., 0.4000 Silver .0213 oz., 18 mm. **Edge:** Plain

Date	Mintage	F	VF	XF	Unc	BU
1868GYF	1,011,508	70.00	150	450	750	—

KM# 443.1 10 KRAJCZAR
1.6600 g., 0.4000 Silver .0213 oz. **Rev. Legend:** MAGYAR KIRALYI VALTO PENZ

Date	Mintage	F	VF	XF	Unc	BU
1868KB	3,249,975	12.00	25.00	40.00	65.00	—
1868KB Restrike; proof	—	Value: 22.50				
1869KB	12,746,767	6.00	22.50	40.00	65.00	—

KM# 444 10 KRAJCZAR
1.6600 g., 0.4000 Silver .0213 oz. **Obv:** KM#451.1 **Rev:** KM#440.1 **Note:** Mule.

Date	Mintage	F	VF	XF	Unc	BU
1868KB Rare	—	—	—	—	—	—
1868KB Restrike	—	Value: 20.00				

KM# 443.2 10 KRAJCZAR
1.6600 g., 0.4000 Silver .0213 oz. **Note:** Varieties exist.

Date	Mintage	F	VF	XF	Unc	BU
1868GYF	Inc. above	35.00	90.00	140	200	—
1869GYF	2,747,272	17.50	35.00	60.00	90.00	—

KM# 451.1 10 KRAJCZAR
1.6600 g., 0.4000 Silver .0213 oz. **Obv. Legend:** AP. KIR. **Rev. Legend:** VALTO PENZ

Date	Mintage	F	VF	XF	Unc	BU
1870KB	21,933,353	5.50	20.00	35.00	60.00	—
1870KB Restrike; proof	—	Value: 17.50				
1871KB Restrike from 1885; rare	—	—	—	—	—	—
1872KB	1,153,922	12.50	35.00	60.00	85.00	—
1873KB	1,066,053	12.50	35.00	60.00	85.00	—
1874KB	1,323,713	12.50	35.00	60.00	85.00	—
1875KB	425,044	50.00	100	145	200	—
1876KB	518,486	50.00	100	145	200	—
1877KB	460,077	50.00	100	145	200	—
1887KB	25,369	60.00	200	325	450	—
1888KB	357,628	27.50	60.00	110	175	—
1889KB Reported, not confirmed	—	—	—	—	—	—

KM# 451.2 10 KRAJCZAR
1.6600 g., 0.4000 Silver .0213 oz.

Date	Mintage	F	VF	XF	Unc	BU
1870GYF	3,031,602	1,235	40.00	75.00	110	—
1871GYF	3,382,790	12.50	40.00	75.00	110	—

KM# 415.1 20 KRAJCZAR
Silver **Obv:** Ribbons on wreath forward across neck **Rev:** Madonna with child

Date	Mintage	F	VF	XF	Unc	BU
1830A	—	55.00	110	220	400	—

KM# 415.2 20 KRAJCZAR
Silver **Obv:** Left ribbon on wreath behind neck

Date	Mintage	F	VF	XF	Unc	BU
1830	—	125	225	400	650	—
1831	—	150	250	450	750	—

KM# 415.3 20 KRAJCZAR
Silver **Obv:** Both ribbons on wreath behind neck

Date	Mintage	F	VF	XF	Unc	BU
1832B	—	40.00	80.00	200	475	—
1833B	—	12.50	25.00	60.00	125	—
1834B	—	7.00	15.00	35.00	80.00	—
1835B	—	7.00	15.00	35.00	80.00	—

KM# 422 20 KRAJCZAR
6.6800 g., 0.5830 Silver .1252 oz. **Obv. Legend:** FERD. I **Rev. Legend:** 5. MARIA

Date	Mintage	F	VF	XF	Unc	BU
1837	—	4.00	10.00	15.00	40.00	—
1838	—	4.00	10.00	15.00	40.00	—
1839	—	3.50	5.00	7.50	20.00	—
1840	2,573,000	3.50	5.00	7.50	20.00	—
1841	3,105,000	3.50	5.00	7.50	20.00	—
1842	2,650,000	4.00	10.00	15.00	40.00	—
1843	2,709,000	3.50	5.00	7.50	20.00	—
1844	3,058,000	3.50	5.00	7.50	20.00	—
1845	3,144,000	3.50	5.00	7.50	20.00	—
1846	3,263,000	3.50	5.00	7.50	20.00	—
1847	3,183,000	3.50	5.00	7.50	20.00	—
1848	14,972,000	3.50	5.00	7.50	20.00	—

KM# 445.1 20 KRAJCZAR
2.6600 g., 0.5000 Silver .0427 oz. **Obv. Legend:** ... AP. KIRALYA **Rev. Legend:** VALTO PENZ

Date	Mintage	F	VF	XF	Unc	BU
1868KB	—	50.00	110	200	320	—
1868KB Restrike; proof	—	Value: 20.00				

KM# 445.2 20 KRAJCZAR
2.6600 g., 0.5000 Silver .0427 oz.

Date	Mintage	F	VF	XF	Unc	BU
1868 GY.F	—	60.00	160	300	400	—

KM# 446.1 20 KRAJCZAR
2.6600 g., 0.5000 Silver .0427 oz. **Rev. Legend:** MAGYAR KIRALYI VALTO PENZ

Date	Mintage	F	VF	XF	Unc	BU
1868KB	3,224,057	4.00	12.50	22.50	45.00	—
1868KB Restrike; proof	—	Value: 20.00				
1869KB	9,487,455	5.00	15.00	25.00	55.00	—

KM# 447 20 KRAJCZAR
2.6600 g., 0.5000 Silver .0427 oz. **Obv:** KM#452.1 **Rev:** KM#445.1 **Note:** Mule.

Date	Mintage	F	VF	XF	Unc	BU
1868KB Rare	—	—	—	—	—	—
1868KB Restrike; proof	—	Value: 20.00				

KM# 446.2 20 KRAJCZAR
2.6600 g., 0.5000 Silver .0427 oz. **Note:** Varieties exist.

Date	Mintage	F	VF	XF	Unc	BU
1868GYF	1,039,346	12.50	25.00	75.00	135	—
1869GYF	2,298,599	9.00	17.50	35.00	65.00	—

KM# 452.2 20 KRAJCZAR
2.6600 g., 0.5000 Silver .0427 oz.

Date	Mintage	F	VF	XF	Unc	BU
1870	7,213,000	30.00	65.00	110	150	—

KM# 452.1 20 KRAJCZAR
2.6600 g., 0.5000 Silver .0427 oz. **Rev. Legend:** VALTO PENZ

Date	Mintage	F	VF	XF	Unc	BU
1870KB	4,426,752	12.50	27.50	65.00	110	—
1870KB Restike	—	Value: 20.00				
1871KB Restrike from 1885	25	Value: 100				
1872KB	1,285,806	27.50	55.00	110	160	—

KM# 449.1 FORINT
12.3457 g., 0.9000 Silver .3572 oz.

Date	Mintage	F	VF	XF	Unc	BU
1868KB	573,584	11.00	25.00	55.00	100	—
1868KB Restrike; proof	—	Value: 40.00				
1869KB	493,698	10.00	20.00	27.50	45.00	—
1869KB Plain edge	—	—	—	—	—	—

KM# 449.2 FORINT
12.3457 g., 0.9000 Silver .3572 oz.

Date	Mintage	F	VF	XF	Unc	BU
1868GYF	266,486	11.00	22.50	32.50	70.00	—
1869GYF	362,175	10.00	20.00	45.00	60.00	—

KM# 453.1 FORINT
12.3457 g., 0.9000 Silver .3572 oz.

Date	Mintage	F	VF	XF	Unc	BU
1870KB	1,253,687	15.00	32.50	62.50	110	—
1871KB	2,444,984	12.00	25.00	45.00	90.00	—
1872KB	3,456,245	7.00	17.50	35.00	65.00	—
1873KB	2,338,364	12.00	25.00	50.00	90.00	—
1874KB	2,081,702	12.00	25.00	50.00	90.00	—
1875KB	2,073,958	8.00	17.50	37.50	65.00	—
1876KB	4,136,174	6.00	12.50	20.00	32.50	—
1877KB	2,241,286	6.00	12.50	20.00	32.50	—
1878KB	5,717,374	6.00	12.50	20.00	32.50	—
1879KB	25,755,927	6.00	12.50	20.00	32.50	—

KM# 453.2 FORINT
12.3457 g., 0.9000 Silver .3572 oz.

Date	Mintage	F	VF	XF	Unc	BU
1870GYF	567,922	80.00	150	225	500	—
1871GYF	242,750	300	425	625	1,100	—

KM# 465 FORINT
12.3457 g., 0.9000 Silver .3572 oz. **Obv:** Larger head and legends **Note:** Varieties exist.

Date	Mintage	F	VF	XF	Unc	BU
1880KB	3,814,618	5.00	8.00	12.00	22.50	—
1881KB	15,494,763	4.50	6.00	10.00	15.00	—

KM# 469 FORINT
12.3457 g., 0.9000 Silver .3572 oz. **Note:** Variety exists for 1882 date with larger mint mark.

Date	Mintage	F	VF	XF	Unc	BU
1882	1,897,441	10.00	20.00	50.00	85.00	—
1883	7,040,776	5.00	8.00	12.50	22.50	—
1884	1,721,725	5.00	10.00	20.00	40.00	—
1885	1,672,086	5.00	10.00	20.00	40.00	—
1886	1,565,967	7.00	12.50	25.00	50.00	—
1887	2,022,064	5.00	10.00	20.00	40.00	—
1888	1,841,360	5.00	10.00	18.00	35.00	—
1889	1,974,397	5.00	10.00	18.00	35.00	—
1890	2,021,792	8.00	17.50	32.50	60.00	—

KM# 475 FORINT
12.3457 g., 0.9000 Silver .3572 oz.

Date	Mintage	F	VF	XF	Unc	BU
1890	Inc. above	10.00	20.00	35.00	55.00	—
1891	1,469,863	7.50	15.00	22.50	45.00	—

Date	Mintage	F	VF	XF	Unc	BU
1892	1,606,566	7.00	15.00	22.50	45.00	—
1892 Restrike; proof	—	Value: 25.00				

KM# 416 1/2 THALER
14.0300 g., 0.8330 Silver .3757 oz.

Date	Mintage	F	VF	XF	Unc	BU
1830A	—	80.00	150	250	500	—

KM# 420 1/2 THALER
14.0300 g., 0.8330 Silver .3757 oz. **Note:** 1831 and 1833 dated coins are restrikes from 1841.

Date	Mintage	F	VF	XF	Unc	BU
1831B	—	100	200	400	600	—
1833B	—	85.00	175	325	500	—
1834B	—	250	400	575	875	—

KM# 423 1/2 THALER
14.0300 g., 0.8330 Silver .3757 oz.

Date	Mintage	F	VF	XF	Unc	BU
1837	—	250	400	550	850	—
1839	—	400	600	800	1,350	—

KM# 417.1 THALER
0.8330 Silver **Obv:** Head right, ribbons on wreath forward across neck **Rev:** Madonna with child

Date	Mintage	F	VF	XF	Unc	BU
1830A	—	60.00	125	275	550	—

KM# 417.2 THALER
0.8330 Silver

Date	Mintage	F	VF	XF	Unc	BU
1830B	—	275	550	1,000	1,500	—

KM# 418 THALER
0.8330 Silver **Obv:** Ribbons on wreath behind neck **Note:** 1831 and 1833 dated coins are restrikes from 1841.

Date	Mintage	F	VF	XF	Unc	BU
1830 Reported, not confirmed	—	—	—	—	—	—
1831	—	80.00	200	450	750	—
1833	—	70.00	140	300	600	—

KM# 424 THALER
0.8330 Silver **Obv:** Head right **Obv. Legend:** FERD. I. D. G...

Date	Mintage	F	VF	XF	Unc	BU
1837	—	300	550	700	1,350	—
1839	—	600	800	1,200	1,750	—

REFORM COINAGE

100 Filler = 1 Korona

KM# 480 FILLER
Bronze

Date	Mintage	F	VF	XF	Unc	BU
1892KB	8,153,000	17.50	32.50	60.00	95.00	—
1892KB Restrike with rosettes; proof	—	Value: 20.00				
1893KB	Inc. above	1.75	3.00	5.50	16.00	—
1894KB	8,642,000	0.50	1.00	1.75	6.00	—
1895KB	9,121,000	0.50	1.00	1.75	6.00	—
1896KB	5,397,000	1.25	3.00	6.00	15.00	—
1897KB	5,157,000	4.50	7.50	15.00	30.00	—
1898KB	1,419,000	5.00	10.00	20.00	40.00	—
1899KB	5,066,000	1.75	3.50	7.00	17.50	—
1900KB	10,461,000	1.00	2.00	4.00	11.50	—

KM# 481 2 FILLER
Bronze

Date	Mintage	F	VF	XF	Unc	BU
1892KB	17,176,000	40.00	60.00	95.00	150	—
1893KB	Inc. above	1.75	4.00	6.50	9.00	—
1894KB	39,150,000	0.50	1.00	2.50	5.00	—
1895KB	65,017,000	0.50	1.00	2.50	5.00	—
1896KB	53,716,000	0.50	1.00	2.50	5.00	—
1897KB	37,297,000	0.50	1.00	2.50	5.00	—
1898KB	14,073,000	2.25	4.50	8.50	12.50	—
1899KB	21,570,000	2.25	4.50	8.50	12.50	—
1900KB	584,000	100	150	220	280	—

KM# 482 10 FILLER
Nickel **Note:** Edge varieties exist.

Date	Mintage	F	VF	XF	Unc	BU
1892KB	15,753,000	3.00	6.00	17.50	27.50	—
1893KB	Inc. above	0.25	0.50	1.50	4.00	—
1894KB	39,463,000	0.25	0.50	1.50	4.00	—
1895KB	16,804,000	0.25	0.50	1.50	4.00	—
1896KB Reported, not confirmed	—	—	—	—	—	—

KM# 483 20 FILLER
Nickel **Note:** Edge varieties exist.

Date	Mintage	F	VF	XF	Unc	BU
1892KB	696,000	4.50	9.00	15.00	25.00	—
1893KB	27,187,000	0.50	1.25	2.50	6.00	—
1894KB	26,117,000	0.50	1.25	2.50	6.00	—

KM# 484 KORONA
5.0000 g., 0.8350 Silver .1342 oz. **Note:** Obverse varieties exist.

Date	Mintage	F	VF	XF	Unc	BU
1892KB	15,000	4.00	15.00	60.00	200	—
1893KB	24,385,000	BV	3.50	5.00	12.50	—
1894KB	12,077,000	BV	3.25	4.50	10.00	—
1895KB	18,544,000	BV	3.25	4.50	10.00	—
1896KB	3,983,000	3.50	6.00	8.50	13.50	—

KM# 487 KORONA
5.0000 g., 0.8350 Silver .1342 oz. **Subject:** Millennium Commemorative **Note:** This issue has been restruck in proof several times, both with and without edge inscriptions.

Date	Mintage	F	VF	XF	Unc	BU
1896	1,000,000	2.25	3.25	5.50	15.00	—
1896 Restrike; proof	—	Value: 17.50				

KM# 488 5 KORONA
24.0000 g., 0.9000 Silver .6944 oz.

Date	Mintage	F	VF	XF	Unc	BU
1900KB	3,840,000	10.00	18.00	40.00	80.00	—
1900KB Proof, restrike with rosette	—	Value: 40.00				
1900KB Proof, restrike without rosette	—	Value: 40.00				

KM# 485 10 KORONA
3.3875 g., 0.9000 Gold .0980 oz.

Date	Mintage	F	VF	XF	Unc	BU
1892KB	1,087,000	BV	45.00	55.00	85.00	—
1892KB Restrike; proof	—	Value: 45.00				
1893KB	Inc. above	BV	45.00	55.00	85.00	—
1894KB	986,000	BV	45.00	55.00	85.00	—
1895KB	—	1,500	2,500	3,500	4,500	—
1895KB Restrike; proof	—	Value: 50.00				
1896KB	32,000	60.00	85.00	100	125	—
1897KB	259,000	BV	45.00	55.00	85.00	—
1898KB	218,000	BV	45.00	55.00	85.00	—
1899KB	231,000	BV	45.00	55.00	85.00	—
1900KB	228,000	BV	45.00	55.00	85.00	—

KM# 486 20 KORONA
6.7750 g., 0.9000 Gold .1960 oz.

Date	Mintage	F	VF	XF	Unc	BU
1892KB	1,779,000	BV	85.00	95.00	135	—
1892KB Restrike; proof	—	Value: 100				
1893KB	5,089,000	BV	85.00	95.00	135	—

Date	Mintage	F	VF	XF	Unc	BU
1894KB	2,526,000	BV	85.00	95.00	135	—
1895KB	1,935,000	BV	85.00	95.00	135	—
1895KB Restrike; proof	—	Value: 100				
1896KB	1,023,000	BV	85.00	95.00	135	—
1897KB	1,819,000	BV	85.00	95.00	135	—
1898KB	1,281,000	BV	85.00	95.00	135	—
1899KB	712,000	BV	85.00	95.00	135	—
1900KB	435,000	BV	85.00	95.00	135	—

TRADE COINAGE

KM# 419 DUCAT

3.4900 g., 0.9860 Gold .1106 oz. **Obv. Legend:** FRANC. I. D. G...

Date	Mintage	F	VF	XF	Unc	BU
1830	—	175	250	325	500	—
1832	—	200	300	400	550	—
1833	—	115	175	250	350	—
1834	—	115	175	250	350	—
1835	—	115	175	250	350	—

KM# 425 DUCAT

3.4900 g., 0.9860 Gold .1106 oz. **Obv. Legend:** FERD. I. D. G...

Date	Mintage	F	VF	XF	Unc	BU
1837	—	175	350	500	750	—
1838	—	175	350	500	750	—
1839	—	115	175	250	375	—
1840	—	115	175	250	375	—
1841	—	115	175	250	375	—
1842	—	115	175	250	375	—
1843	—	175	350	450	650	—
1844	—	115	175	250	375	—
1845	—	175	300	450	650	—
1846	—	115	175	250	375	—
1847	—	115	175	250	375	—
1848	—	115	175	250	375	—

KM# 433 DUCAT

3.4900 g., 0.9860 Gold .1106 oz. **Obv. Legend:** SZ. MARIA...

Date	Mintage	F	VF	XF	Unc	BU
1848	—	100	175	250	350	—

KM# 448.1 DUCAT

3.4900 g., 0.9860 Gold .1106 oz.

Date	Mintage	F	VF	XF	Unc	BU
1868KB	127,531	100	200	275	400	—
1869KB	106,614	90.00	150	200	300	—

KM# 448.2 DUCAT

3.4900 g., 0.9860 Gold .1106 oz.

Date	Mintage	F	VF	XF	Unc	BU
1868GYF	399,914	85.00	140	200	300	—
1869GYF	270,425	90.00	150	200	300	—

KM# 457 DUCAT

3.4900 g., 0.9860 Gold .1106 oz.

Date	Mintage	F	VF	XF	Unc	BU
1870 Proof; restrike	—	Value: 95.00				
1877	452	800	1,250	1,500	2,500	—
1879	3,651	500	900	1,500	2,500	—
1880	5,075	600	1,000	1,500	2,000	—
1880 Proof; restrike	—	—	—	—	—	—
1881	Est. 43	1,250	2,000	2,500	4,000	—

KM# 454.1 4 FORINT 10 FRANCS

3.2258 g., 0.9000 Gold .0934 oz.

Date	Mintage	F	VF	XF	Unc	BU
1870GYF	48,672	50.00	60.00	90.00	125	—

KM# 454.2 4 FORINT 10 FRANCS

3.2258 g., 0.9000 Gold .0934 oz. **Note:** Semi-official restrikes have the letters UP below the bust.

Date	Mintage	F	VF	XF	Unc	BU
1870KB	80,733	50.00	60.00	90.00	125	—
1870KB UP Restrike; proof	—	Value: 70.00				
1871KB	111,142	50.00	75.00	100	130	—
1872KB	53,108	50.00	60.00	90.00	125	—
1873KB	13,284	80.00	115	175	200	—
1874KB	8,229	80.00	115	175	210	—
1875KB	10,682	85.00	125	175	225	—
1876KB	24,284	50.00	75.00	100	130	—
1877KB	24,240	50.00	70.00	100	125	—
1878KB	14,838	50.00	75.00	100	130	—
1879KB	12,367	50.00	75.00	100	130	—

KM# 466 4 FORINT 10 FRANCS

3.2258 g., 0.9000 Gold .0934 oz. **Note:** Older head.

Date	Mintage	F	VF	XF	Unc	BU
1880	12,546	50.00	75.00	100	130	—
1881	11,737	50.00	75.00	100	130	—
1882	13,350	50.00	75.00	100	125	—
1883	11,865	50.00	75.00	100	125	—
1884	53,533	50.00	60.00	90.00	125	—
1885	64,277	50.00	65.00	95.00	125	—
1886	39,066	50.00	60.00	90.00	125	—
1887	38,842	50.00	60.00	90.00	125	—
1888	48,682	50.00	60.00	90.00	125	—
1889	19,204	100	150	225	300	—
1890	28,989	95.00	140	200	275	—

KM# 476.1 4 FORINT 10 FRANCS

3.2258 g., 0.9000 Gold .0934 oz. **Rev:** Fiume arms

Date	Mintage	F	VF	XF	Unc	BU
1890	Inc. above	200	300	375	500	—
1891	32,001	55.00	75.00	100	150	—

KM# 476.2 4 FORINT 10 FRANCS

3.2258 g., 0.9000 Gold .0934 oz. **Note:** Mint unknown.

Date	Mintage	F	VF	XF	Unc	BU
1892	—	800	1,100	1,800	3,000	—

KM# 455.1 8 FORINT 20 FRANCS

6.4516 g., 0.9000 Gold .1867 oz.

Date	Mintage	F	VF	XF	Unc	BU
1870	45,890	BV	90.00	110	160	—
1871	75,575	BV	80.00	100	135	—
1872	273,161	BV	80.00	100	135	—
1873	244,505	BV	80.00	100	135	—
1874	240,359	BV	80.00	100	135	—
1875	260,537	BV	80.00	100	135	—
1876	303,920	BV	80.00	100	135	—
1877	312,959	BV	80.00	100	135	—
1878	307,755	BV	80.00	100	135	—
1879	305,621	BV	80.00	100	135	—
1880	301,422	90.00	120	150	200	—

KM# 455.2 8 FORINT 20 FRANCS

6.4516 g., 0.9000 Gold .1867 oz.

Date	Mintage	F	VF	XF	Unc	BU
1870GYF	125,308	BV	90.00	110	155	—
1871GYF	177,047	BV	90.00	110	145	—

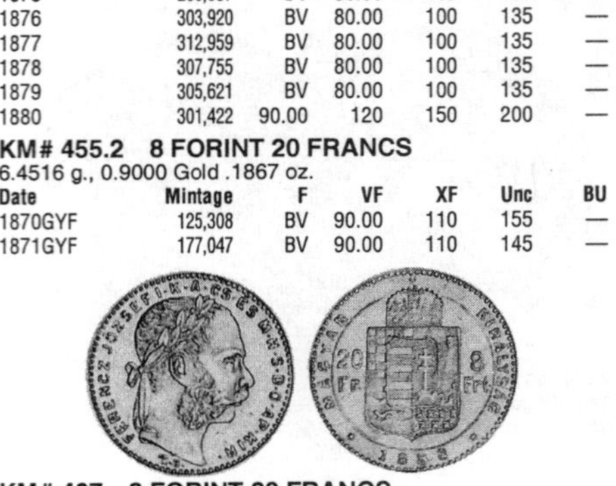

KM# 467 8 FORINT 20 FRANCS

6.4516 g., 0.9000 Gold .1867 oz. **Obv:** Larger head

Date	Mintage	F	VF	XF	Unc	BU
1880KB	Inc. above	BV	90.00	110	145	—
1881KB	308,789	BV	80.00	100	135	—
1882KB	304,152	BV	80.00	100	135	—
1883KB	300,429	BV	80.00	100	135	—
1884KB	284,185	BV	90.00	110	145	—
1885KB	266,928	BV	90.00	110	145	—
1886KB	312,611	BV	80.00	100	135	—
1887KB	294,112	BV	90.00	110	145	—
1888KB	296,147	BV	90.00	110	145	—
1889KB	351,370	BV	80.00	100	135	—
1890KB	329,221	BV	90.00	110	145	—

KM# 477 8 FORINT 20 FRANCS

6.4516 g., 0.9000 Gold .1867 oz. **Rev:** Fiume arms

Date	Mintage	F	VF	XF	Unc	BU
1890	Inc. above	BV	90.00	110	150	—
1891	378,201	BV	90.00	110	145	—
1892	232,194	BV	120	160	200	—

PATTERNS

Including off metal strikes

KM#	Date	Mintage	Identification	Mkt Val
Pn97	1835	—	1/2 Thaler.KM#420	—
Pn98	1848	—	3 Kreuzer. Without mint mark.	—
Pn100	1849KB	—	Krajczar. KM#430	—
Pn101	1849KB	—	3 Krajczar. Copper. KM#434	—
Pn102	1849	—	6 Kreuzer. Pewter. KM#435	—
Pn103	1849	—	20 Kreuzer. Pewter. Ferdinand I	—
Pn104	1849	—	Ducat. Pewter.	—
Pn99	1849Z	46	Krajczar. Copper. KM#430	2,200
Pn105	1857	—	1/4 Florin. Aluminum.	—
Pn106	1858	—	3 Kreuzer. Copper.	—
Pn107	1858B	—	3 Kreuzer. Lead. Arms. 3 in wreath.	—
Pn108	1858E	—	3 Kreuzer. Lead. Arms. 3 in wreath.	—
Pn109	1859	—	5 Kreuzer. Aluminum.	—
Pn111	1867	—	10 Kreuzer. Copper. KM#440.	—
Pn110	1867B	—	10 Krajczar. Silver. 2.0000 g. Larger bust. KM#440.	900
Pn114	1868GYF	—	10 Krajczar. Silver. KM#440.	900

KM#	Date	Mintage	Identification	Mkt Val
PnA113	1868KB	—	4 Kreuzer. Silver. KM#442.	—
Pn112	1868GYF	—	4 Krajczar. Copper. KM#442.	—
Pn113	1868B	—	10 Krajczar. Silver. KM#440.	—
Pn115	1869	—	20 Krajczar. Copper. KM#446.	—
Pn117	1878	—	Forint. Gold. KM#453.	—
Pn116	1878	3	Forint. Copper. KM#453.	250
Pn118	1882	—	5/10 Krajczar. Aluminum. KM#468.	—
Pn119	1883KB	—	Krajczar. Iron.	100
Pn120	1889	—	10 Krajczar. Aluminum. Three varieties.	—

KM#	Date	Mintage	Identification	Mkt Val
Pn121	1891	—	Krajczar. Aluminum. Bust right. Crown.	—
Pn124	1892	—	Krajczar. Aluminum. KM#458.	—
Pn122	1892	—	Filler. KM#480. With rosette.	—
Pn123	1892	—	Krajczar. Brass. KM#458.	—
Pn125	1896	—	Korona. Copper. KM#487.	360

TRIAL STRIKES

KM#	Date	Mintage	Identification	Mkt Val
TS10	1848	—	3 Krajczar. Copper. KM#434.	—
TS11	1849	—	6 Krajczar. Lead. KM#435.	—
TS12	1849	—	20 Krajczar. Lead. KM#422.	—
TS13	1849	—	Ducat. Lead. KM#425.	—
TS14	1867	—	10 Krajczar. Copper. KM#440.	—
TS15	1868KB	—	4 Krajczar. Silver. KM#442.	—
TS16	1868KB	—	4 Krajczar. Gold. KM#442.	—
TS17	1868	—	10 Krajczar. Copper. KM#440.	—
TS18	1868KB	—	20 Krajczar. Aluminum. KM#440.	—
TS19	1868	—	20 Krajczar. Aluminum. KM#445.	—
TS20	1869	—	20 Krajczar. Copper. KM#446.	—
TS21	1870KB	—	4 Forint 10 Francs. Copper. KM#454.	—
TS22	1870	—	4 Forint 10 Francs. Copper. KM#454.	—
TS23	1870KB	—	Ducat. Lead. KM#456.	—
TS24	1874KB	—	10 Krajczar. Gold. KM#451.	—
TS27	1882KB	—	5/10 Krajczar. Aluminum. KM#468.	—
TS28	1882KB	—	5/10 Krajczar. Nickel. KM#468.	—
TS29	1883KB	—	Krajczar. Nickel. KM#458.	175
TS30	1889	—	10 Krajczar. Aluminum. KM#451.	—
TS31	1891KB	—	Krajczar. KM#478. Thin planchet.	—
TS32	1891KB	—	Forint. Aluminum. KM#475.	—
TS33	1891KB	—	4 Forint 10 Francs. Nickel. KM#476.	—
TS34	1892KB	—	Krajczar. Aluminum. KM#478.	—
TS35	1892KB	—	Krajczar. Brass. KM#478.	—
TS36	1892KB	—	8 Forint 20 Francs. Nickel. KM#477.	—
TS37	1894KB	—	2 Filler. Nickel. KM#481.	—
TS38	1896	—	Korona. Lead. KM#487.	—

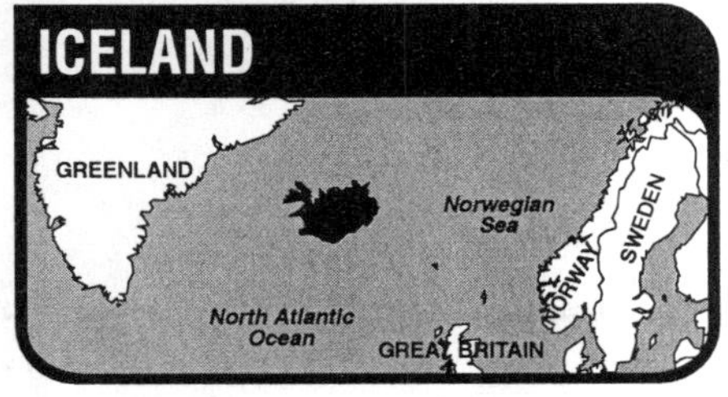

The Republic of Iceland, an island of recent volcanic origin in the North Atlantic east of Greenland and immediately south of the Arctic Circle, has an area of 39,768sq. mi. (103,000 sq. km.) and a population of 275,264. Capital: Reykjavik. Fishing is the chief industry and accounts for more than 70 percent of the exports.

Iceland was settled by Norwegians in the 9th century and established as an independent republic in 930. The Icelandic assembly called the Althingi', also established in 930, is the oldest parliament in the world. Iceland came under Norwegian sovereignty in 1262, and passed to Denmark when Norway and Denmark were united under the Danish crown in 1380. In 1918 it was established as a virtually independent kingdom in union with Denmark. On June 17, 1944, while Denmark was still under occupation by troops of the Third Reich, Iceland was established by plebiscite as an independent republic.

TOKEN ISSUES

Under the Scandinavian Monetary Convention of 1873, the coinage of Denmark, Norway and Sweden could circulate with validity in Iceland. Despite the various options for exchange, very few coins appear to have made their way to Iceland. As a result, Icelandic merchants resorted to manufacturing their own tokens. While some bare the crudeness of a homemade token, others had been elaborately struck by such well-known manufacturers as L. Chr. Lauer of Nurnberg, who most likely had N. Chr. Hansen & Co. Copenhagen as an agent.

Merchants posting inflated token prices alongside legal coinage prices on goods for sale led to the 1901 law which prohibited the manufacture and usage of private coinage, ending the token era which started in the mid 1800's.

NOTE: There are at least four different types of tokens for this time period. Only Type I tokens are cataloged here.

TYPES

I – Tokens with stated values; first in shillings, later in kronur and aurar.

II – Bread Tokens, used to barter for prearranged quantities of goods or labor.

III – Advertising or Address Tokens

IV – Miscellaneous Tokens

KINGDOM

TOKEN COINAGE

Olafur Arnason

Stokkseyri

KM# Tn1 10 AURAR

2.2000 g., Bronze **Issuer:** Olafur Arnason, Stokkseyri **Obv:** Merchant's name and shop location in legend, denomination **Rev:** GEGN VORUM (against goods) in wreath

Date	Mintage	VG	F	VF	XF	Unc
ND(1900)	—	10.00	25.00	50.00	120	—

KM# Tn2 25 AURAR

2.2000 g., Bronze **Issuer:** Olafur Arnason, Stokkseyri **Note:** Similar to KM#Tn1.

Date	Mintage	VG	F	VF	XF	Unc
ND(1900)	—	7.00	20.00	40.00	100	—

J.R.B. Lefolii

Eyrarbakka

KM# Tn5 10 AURAR

1.6000 g., Bronze **Issuer:** J.R.B. Lefolii, Eyrarbakka **Obv:** Merchant's name and shop location in legend, denomination **Rev:** GEGN VORUM (against goods) in wreath

Date	Mintage	VG	F	VF	XF	Unc
ND(1900)	—	12.00	25.00	60.00	125	—

KM# Tn6 25 AURAR

2.3000 g., Bronze **Issuer:** J.R.B. Lefolii, Eyrarbakka **Obv:** Merchant's name and shop location in legend, denomination **Rev:** GEGN VORUM (against goods) in wreath

Date	Mintage	VG	F	VF	XF	Unc
ND(1900)	—	12.00	25.00	60.00	125	—

KM# Tn7 100 AURAR

3.3000 g., Bronze **Issuer:** J.R.B. Lefolii, Eyrarbakka **Obv:** Merchant's name and shop location in legend, denomination **Rev:** GEGN VORUM (against goods) in wreath

Date	Mintage	VG	F	VF	XF	Unc
ND(1900)	—	15.00	30.00	75.00	145	—

C.F. Siemsen

Reykjavik

KM# Tn8 4 SKILDINGAR

1.5000 g., Bronze **Issuer:** C.F. Siemsen, Reykjavik **Obv:** Merchant's initials **Rev:** Denomination **Note:** Also valid at C. F. Siemsen's store on the Faeroe Islands

Date	Mintage	VG	F	VF	XF	Unc
ND(1846)	—	40.00	80.00	165	300	—

KM# Tn9 16 SKILDINGAR

2.5000 g., Bronze **Issuer:** C.F. Siemsen, Reykjavik **Obv:** Merchant's initials **Rev:** Denomination **Note:** Also valid at C. F. Siemsen's store on the Faeroe Islands

Date	Mintage	VG	F	VF	XF	Unc
ND(1846)	—	30.00	60.00	125	185	—

P.J. Thorsteinsson

Bildudal

KM# Tn10 5 AURAR

2.2000 g., Bronze **Issuer:** P.J. Thorsteinsson, Bildudal **Obv:** PT monogram **Rev:** Denomination

Date	Mintage	VG	F	VF	XF	Unc
ND(1880) Rare	—	—	—	—	—	—

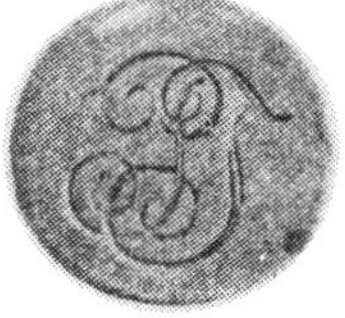

KM# Tn11 10 AURAR

3.0000 g., Bronze **Issuer:** P.J. Thorsteinsson, Bildudal **Obv:** PT monogram **Rev:** Denomination

Date	Mintage	VG	F	VF	XF	Unc
ND(1880) Rare	—	—	—	—	—	—

KM# Tn13 25 AURAR

3.7000 g., Bronze **Issuer:** P.J. Thorsteinsson, Bildudal **Obv:** PT monogram **Rev:** Denomination

Date	Mintage	VG	F	VF	XF	Unc
ND(1880)	—	20.00	40.00	80.00	150	—

KM# Tn14 25 AURAR

3.7000 g., Bronze **Issuer:** P.J. Thorsteinsson, Bildudal **Obv:** PT monogram above 97 **Rev:** Denomination

Date	Mintage	VG	F	VF	XF	Unc
xx97	—	15.00	30.00	60.00	135	—

KM# Tn16 50 AURAR

Bronze **Issuer:** P.J. Thorsteinsson, Bildudal **Obv:** PT monogram **Rev:** Denomination

Date	Mintage	VG	F	VF	XF	Unc
ND(1880)	—	20.00	40.00	80.00	150	—

KM# Tn17 50 AURAR

Bronze **Issuer:** P.J. Thorsteinsson, Bildudal **Obv:** PT monogram above 97 **Rev:** Denomination

Date	Mintage	VG	F	VF	XF	Unc
xx97	—	15.00	30.00	60.00	135	—

KM# Tn19 100 AURAR

Bronze **Issuer:** P.J. Thorsteinsson, Bildudal **Obv:** PT monogram **Rev:** Denomination

Date	Mintage	VG	F	VF	XF	Unc
ND(1880) Rare	—	—	—	—	—	—

KM# Tn20 100 AURAR

Bronze **Issuer:** P.J. Thorsteinsson, Bildudal **Obv:** PT monogram above 97 **Rev:** Denomination

Date	Mintage	VG	F	VF	XF	Unc
xx97 Rare	—	—	—	—	—	—

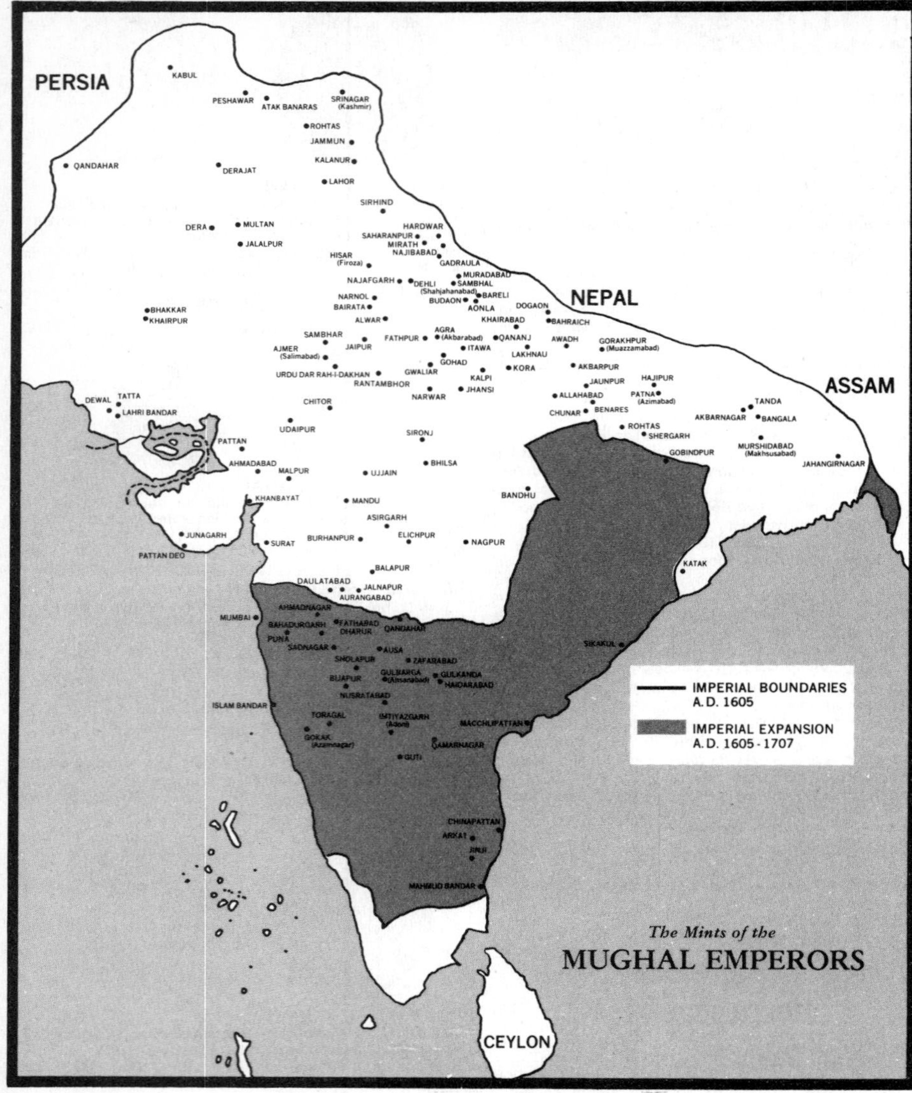

The Mints of the MUGHAL EMPERORS

The Lodi Sultanate of Delhi was conquered by Zahir-ud-din Muhammad Babur, a Chagatai Turk descended from Tamerlane, in 1525AD. His son, Nasir-ud-din Muham-mad Humayun, lost the new empire in a series of battles with the Bihari Afghan Sher Shah, who founded the short-lived Suri dynasty. Humayun, with the assistance of the Emperor of Persia, recovered his kingdom from Sher Shah's successors in 1555AD. He did not long enjoy the fruits of victory for his fatal fall down his library steps brought his teenage son Jalal-ud-din Muhammad Akbar to the throne in the following year. During Akbar's long reign of a half century, the Mughal Empire was firmly established throughout much of North India. Under Akbar's son and grandson, the emperors Nur-ud-din Muhammad Jahangir and Shihab-ud-din Muhammad Shah Jahan, the state reached its apogee and art, culture and commerce flourished.

One of the major achievements of the Mughal government was the establishment of a universal silver currency, based on the rupee, a coin of 11.6 grams and as close to pure silver content as the metallurgy of the time was capable of attaining. Supplementary coins were the copper dam and gold mohur. The values of these coin denominations were nominally fixed at 40 dams to 1 rupee, and 8 rupees to 1 mohur; however, market forces determined actual exchange rates.

The maximum expansion of the geographical area under direct Mughal rule was achieved during the reign of Aurangzeb Alamgir. By his death in 1707AD, the whole peninsula, with minor exceptions, the whole subcontinent of India owed fealty to the Mughal emperor.

Aurangzeb's wars, lasting decades, upset the stability and prosperity of the kingdom. The internal dissension and rebellion which resulted brought the eclipse of the empire in succeeding reigns. The Mughal monetary system, especially the silver rupee, supplanted most local currencies throughout India. The number of Mughal mints rose sharply and direct central control declined, so that by the time of the emperor Shah Alam II, many nominally Mughal mints served independent states. The common element in all these coinage issues was the presence of the Mughal emperor's name and titles on the obverse. In the following listings no attempt has been made to solve the problem of separating Mughal from Princely State coins by historical criteria: all Mughal-style coins are considered products of the Mughal empire until the death of Muhammad Shah in 1784AD; thereafter all coins are considered Princely State issues unless there is evidence of the mint being under ever-diminishing Imperial control.

EMPERORS

شاه عالم

Shah Alam II, AH1174-1202/1759-1788AD and AH1203-1221/1789-1806AD

محمد اکبر

Muhammad Akbar II
AH1221-1253/1806-1837AD

سراج الدین محمد بهادر شاه

Bahadur Shah II, Siraj-ud-din Muhammad
AH1253-1273/1837-1858AD

MINT NAMES

احمد آباد

Ahmadabad

اکبراباد

Akbarabad
(Agra)

The city and fort of Agra or Akbarabad fell to the Jats of Bharatpur after the battle of Panipat in 1761AD. For issues dated AH1175-1186/1761-1773AD see Indian Princely States, Bharatpur. A succession of governors from 1773AD controlled Agra nominally as officers of the Mughal emperor but actually for themselves and, after 1785, for the Maratha Peshwa.

الله اباد

Allahabad
(Ilahabad)

گوکل گره

Gokulgarh

Mint marks:

هاردوار

Hardwar
A mint of the Mughal governor of Saharanpur.

Muzaffargarh
NOTE: The placing of Muzaffargarh under Khetri has been discontinued as recent research has shown that no rupees had ever been struck there.

Mint marks:

سهارنپور

Saharanpur

Mint mark: stylized dagger

شاه جهان آباد

Shahjahanabad
(Dehli)

The mint of the walled city of Delhi (Shahjahanabad) produced a limited number of coins each year with which the East India Company's resident paid a pension to the Mughal Emperor. KM#777 was struck for this purpose until 1818, when the mint was closed for regular coinage. Thereafter, only a few presentation coins (KM#779.1) were struck annually on the occasion of the king's accession.

Mint marks:
(Silver and Gold)

Obv:

Rev.

NOTE: The size of the Shahjahanabad rupees of Shah Alam II was subject to a wide variance. The early issues tended to be normal size for the hammered coinage (about 22mm). As the power of the emperor waned, the flan size of the Shahjahanabad rupees waxed, reflecting the increasingly ceremonial role of the coinage. The later coins should not be confused with the Nazarana (presentation) coins, which always show a full border design around the legend.

Surat
The Nawab of Surat continued to issue coins in the name of his nominal Mughal suzerain Shah Alam II until the British took over Surat and its mint in 1800AD (AH1214/5), Shah Alam's 43rd regnal year. These coin types of the Nawab of Surat were replicated by the British East India Company in Surat using privy mark #1 and the frozen regnal year 46 of Shah Alam II, see Bombay Presidency types KM#209.1, 210.1, 211.1, 212.1 and 214.

DATING

The Mughal coins were dated both in the Hejira era and in the regnal era of each emperor. The four-digit Hejira year usually was shown on the obverse, with the one or two-digit regnal (jalus) year on the reverse. Since the regnal and calendar years did not coincide, it was common for two different regnal years to appear on the coins produced during any calendar year. The first jalus year of each reign was usually written as a word, ahd, rather than as a numeral.

EMPIRE

Shah Alam II

AH1174-1221 / 1759-1806AD

GOVERNORS' HAMMERED COINAGE

Mint: Akbarabad
KM# 549.1 PAISA
Copper **Issuer:** Daulat Rao Sindhia with John and George Hessing in charge. **Rev:** JWH

Date	Mintage	Good	VG	F	VF	XF
AH1215//43	—	12.50	25.00	42.00	60.00	—
AH1216//42 (sic)	—	12.50	25.00	42.00	60.00	—
AH12xx//43	—	12.50	25.00	42.00	60.00	—
AH1218//xx	—	12.50	25.00	42.00	60.00	—

Note: J.W.H. - John William Hessing, Governor of Agra.

Mint: Akbarabad
KM# 549.2 PAISA
Copper **Rev:** Spearhead

Date	Mintage	Good	VG	F	VF	XF
AH1217//x	—	5.00	10.00	15.00	20.00	—
AH1218//xx	—	5.00	10.00	15.00	20.00	—

Mint: Akbarabad
KM# 550 PAISA
Copper **Rev:** Pistol

Date	Mintage	Good	VG	F	VF	XF
AH1216//43	—	5.00	10.00	15.00	20.00	—
AH1217//44	—	5.00	10.00	15.00	20.00	—
AH1218//44 (sic)	—	5.00	10.00	15.00	20.00	—

Mint: Akbarabad
KM# 551 PAISA
Copper **Rev:** Pistol and fish

Date	Mintage	Good	VG	F	VF	XF
AH1216//43	—	5.50	11.00	17.50	25.00	—
AH1217//xx	—	5.50	11.00	17.50	25.00	—
AH1220//xx	—	5.50	11.00	17.50	25.00	—

Mint: Saharanpur
KM# 673 PAISA
Copper **Rev:** Additional symbols, chakra, and hexfoil; Mint epithet: Dar-us-Sarur

Date	Mintage	Good	VG	F	VF	XF
AH1215//42	—	4.00	6.50	10.00	15.00	—
AH12xx//43	—	4.00	6.50	10.00	15.00	—
AH1217//44	—	4.00	6.50	10.00	15.00	—
AH1218//45	—	4.00	6.50	10.00	15.00	—

Mint: Shahjahanabad
KM# 700 PAISA
Copper **Note:** Weight varies 11.00-11.60 grams.

Date	Mintage	Good	VG	F	VF	XF
AH1219//46	—	2.00	3.25	5.00	8.50	—
AH1219//47	—	2.00	3.25	5.00	8.50	—
AH1220//48	—	2.00	3.25	5.00	8.50	—

Mint: Akbarabad
KM# 554 RUPEE
11.4440 g., Silver **Issuer:** Daulat Rao Sindhia with John and George Hessing in charge. **Rev:** Fish

Date	Mintage	VG	F	VF	XF	Unc
AH12xx//38	—	7.50	15.00	25.00	35.00	—
AH12xx//42	—	7.50	15.00	25.00	35.00	—
AH1215//43 (sic)	—	7.50	15.00	25.00	35.00	—
AH1217//44	—	7.50	15.00	25.00	35.00	—
AH12xx//45	—	7.50	15.00	25.00	35.00	—

Mint: Akbarabad
KM# 560 RUPEE
11.4440 g., Silver **Issuer:** East India Company **Rev:** Fish

Date	Mintage	VG	F	VF	XF	Unc
AH1219//47	—	10.00	20.00	32.50	45.00	—
AH1220//47	—	10.00	20.00	32.50	45.00	—

Mint: Gokulgarh
KM# 624 RUPEE
11.4440 g., Silver **Issuer:** Sindhia Governor **Note:** Size varies: 21-23 millimeters.

Date	Mintage	VG	F	VF	XF	Unc
AH1215//42	—	6.50	13.50	22.50	35.00	—
AH1215//43	—	6.50	13.50	22.50	35.00	—
AH1216//4x	—	6.50	13.50	22.50	35.00	—
AH1217//44	—	6.50	13.50	22.50	35.00	—
AH1217//45	—	6.50	13.50	22.50	35.00	—
AH1218//45	—	6.50	13.50	22.50	35.00	—
AH1218//46	—	6.50	13.50	22.50	35.00	—

Mint: Hardwar
KM# 630 RUPEE
11.4440 g., Silver **Note:** Struck at a mint of the Mughal governor of Saharanpur.

Date	Mintage	VG	F	VF	XF	Unc
AH1219//46	—	35.00	70.00	100	150	—

Mint: Muzaffargarh
KM# 669 RUPEE
Silver **Obv. Legend:** SAHIB QIRAN **Note:** Prev. KM#2.

Date	Mintage	Good	VG	F	VF	XF
AH121x//43	—	4.50	11.50	20.00	28.50	—
AH12xx//44	—	4.50	11.50	20.00	28.50	—
AH12xx//45	—	4.50	11.50	20.00	28.50	—
AH1218//46	—	4.50	11.50	20.00	28.50	—
AH12xx//47	—	4.50	11.50	20.00	28.50	—

Mint: Saharanpur
KM# 675 RUPEE
11.4440 g., Silver **Note:** Mint epithet: "Dar-ul-Khilafat".

Date	Mintage	VG	F	VF	XF	Unc
AH1216//43	—	9.00	18.00	30.00	45.00	—
AH1217//44	—	9.00	18.00	30.00	45.00	—
AH1218/7//43 (sic)	—	9.00	18.00	30.00	45.00	—
AH1218//45	—	9.00	18.00	30.00	45.00	—

Mint: Surat
KM# 724 RUPEE
Silver **Obv:** Privy mark #1 **Note:** Weight varies 10.70-11.60 grams.

Date	Mintage	VG	F	VF	XF	Unc
AH1205	—	8.00	16.00	28.00	40.00	—
AHxxxx//44	—	8.00	16.00	28.00	40.00	—

Mint: Zebabad
KM# 725 NAZARANA MOHUR
Gold **Note:** Weight varies 10.65-11.1 grams. Struck at Sardhanah in the year of the Lord Lake's victory of Dehli by Begum Somru, Zebu-n-nisa Begam.

Date	Mintage	VG	F	VF	XF	Unc
AHxxxx//45 Rare	—	—	—	—	—	—

HAMMERED COINAGE

Mint: Saharanpur
KM# 670 1/2 PAISA
Copper **Note:** Local Governor Issue; mint mark is a symbol.

Date	Mintage	Good	VG	F	VF	XF
AH12xx//44	—	4.50	8.00	12.00	17.50	—

Mint: Khujista Bunyad
KM# 649 PAISA
Copper **Obv:** Emperor's titles, date **Rev:** Mint

Date	Mintage	Good	VG	F	VF	XF
AH1219	—	—	—	—	—	—

Mint: Saharanpur
KM# 690 PAISA
Copper **Issuer:** East India Company **Rev:** St. Stephen's cross **Note:** Weight varies 12.9 - 13.8 grams.

Date	Mintage	Good	VG	F	VF	XF
AH1218//45	—	15.00	25.00	35.00	50.00	—

Mint: Shahjahanabad
KM# 704 1/4 RUPEE
2.8610 g., Silver **Obv:** Additional cinquefoil symbol

Date	Mintage	VG	F	VF	XF	Unc
AH1220//48	—	45.00	70.00	100	140	—

Mint: Shahjahanabad
KM# 707 1/2 RUPEE
5.7220 g., Silver **Obv:** Additional cinquefoil symbol

Date	Mintage	VG	F	VF	XF	Unc
AH1220//47	—	60.00	100	150	200	—

Mint: Saharanpur
KM# 676 RUPEE
11.4440 g., Silver **Rev:** Circled dot additional symbol. Mint epithet, Dar-us-Sarur.

Date	Mintage	VG	F	VF	XF	Unc
AH1216//43	—	10.00	20.00	35.00	50.00	—
AH1217//44	—	10.00	20.00	35.00	50.00	—

Mint: Saharanpur
KM# 692 RUPEE
11.4440 g., Silver **Rev:** St. Stephen's cross

Date	Mintage	VG	F	VF	XF	Unc
AH1218//45	—	40.00	65.00	100	150	—

Mint: Saharanpur
KM# 693 RUPEE
11.4440 g., Silver **Rev:** Vertical spray

Date	Mintage	VG	F	VF	XF	Unc
AH1217//44	—	9.00	18.00	30.00	45.00	—
AH1218//45	—	9.00	18.00	30.00	45.00	—
AH1219//46	—	9.00	18.00	30.00	45.00	—

Mint: Saharanpur
KM# 694 RUPEE
11.4440 g., Silver **Rev:** Without symbol

Date	Mintage	VG	F	VF	XF	Unc
AH1220//47	—	9.00	18.00	30.00	45.00	—
AH1220//49 (sic)	—	9.00	18.00	30.00	45.00	—

Mint: Shahjahanabad
KM# 711 RUPEE
11.4440 g., Silver **Obv:** Additional bush symbol

Date	Mintage	VG	F	VF	XF	Unc
AH1216//44	—	30.00	50.00	80.00	120	—
AH1217//44	—	30.00	50.00	80.00	120	—
AH1217//45	—	30.00	50.00	80.00	120	—
AH1218//45	—	30.00	50.00	80.00	120	—

Mint: Shahjahanabad
KM# 712 RUPEE
11.4440 g., Silver **Obv:** Additional lion symbol

Date	Mintage	VG	F	VF	XF	Unc
AH1218//46	—	225	250	500	700	—

Mint: Shahjahanabad
KM# 713 RUPEE
11.4440 g., Silver **Obv:** Additional cinquefoil symbol

Date	Mintage	VG	F	VF	XF	Unc
AH1218//46	—	75.00	130	200	300	—
AH1219//46	—	75.00	130	200	300	—
AH1221//49	—	75.00	130	200	300	—

Mint: Shahjahanabad
KM# 714 RUPEE
11.4440 g., Silver **Obv:** Legend is within wreath of roses, thistles and shamrocks **Rev:** Legend is within wreath of roses, thistles and shamrocks

Date	Mintage	VG	F	VF	XF	Unc
AH1219//47	—	50.00	95.00	145	200	—
AH1220//47	—	50.00	95.00	145	200	—
AH1220//48	—	50.00	95.00	145	200	—
AH1221//48	—	50.00	95.00	145	200	—

Mint: Saharanpur
KM# 693a NAZARANA RUPEE
Silver, 28 mm. **Obv:** Emperor's titles, date **Rev:** Mint, regnal year

Date	Mintage	Good	VG	F	VF	XF
AH1218//45	—	—	—	—	—	—

Mint: Shahjahanabad
KM# 718 NAZARANA RUPEE
11.4440 g., Silver **Obv:** Additional bush symbol

Date	Mintage	VG	F	VF	XF	Unc
AH1218//46	—	250	400	600	850	—

Mint: Shahjahanabad
KM# B719 NAZARANA RUPEE
11.4440 g., Silver **Obv:** Additional cinquefoil symbol

Date	Mintage	VG	F	VF	XF	Unc
AH1218//46	—	300	525	800	1,150	—

Mint: Shahjahanabad
KM# 721 MOHUR
Gold **Obv:** Additional bush symbol

Date	Mintage	VG	F	VF	XF	Unc
AH1217//45	—	650	1,100	1,650	2,250	—
AH1218//46	—	650	1,100	1,650	2,250	—

Mint: Shahjahanabad
KM# 722 MOHUR
Gold **Obv:** Legend within wreath of roses, thistles and shamrocks **Rev:** Legend within wreath of roses, thistles and shamrocks

Date	Mintage	VG	F	VF	XF	Unc
AH1219//47	—	250	400	600	750	—
AH1220//48	—	250	400	600	750	—
AH1221//48	—	250	400	600	750	—

Muhammad Akbar II
AH1221-1253 / 1806-1837AD

HAMMERED COINAGE

Mint: Shahjahanabad
KM# 770 PAISA
Copper **Note:** Weight varies 12.9 - 13.8 grams.

Date	Mintage	Good	VG	F	VF	XF
AH1222//1	—	2.00	3.25	5.00	8.50	—
AH1222//2	—	2.00	3.25	5.00	8.50	—

Mint: Shahjahanabad
KM# 771 PAISA
Copper **Rev:** Letter "S" by regnal year **Note:** Weight varies 12.9-13.8 grams.

Date	Mintage	Good	VG	F	VF	XF
AH1225//4	—	2.00	3.25	5.00	8.50	—
AH1225//5	—	2.00	3.25	5.00	8.50	—
AH1226//5	—	2.00	3.25	5.00	8.50	—
AH1226//6	—	2.00	3.25	5.00	8.50	—
AH1230//9	—	2.00	3.25	5.00	8.50	—
AH1231//10	—	2.00	3.25	5.00	8.50	—
AH1232//12	—	—	—	—	—	—
AH1233//12	—	2.00	3.25	5.00	8.50	—

Mint: Shahjahanabad
KM# 773 1/4 RUPEE
2.8610 g., Silver

Date	Mintage	VG	F	VF	XF	Unc
AH-/1	—	12.50	25.00	42.00	60.00	—
AH122x//7	—	12.50	25.00	42.00	60.00	—

Mint: Shahjahanabad
KM# 775 1/2 RUPEE
5.7220 g., Silver

Date	Mintage	VG	F	VF	XF	Unc
AH1221//1	—	25.00	50.00	85.00	120	—
AH1225//4	—	25.00	50.00	85.00	120	—

Mint: Allahabad
KM# 764 RUPEE
Silver

Date	Mintage	Good	VG	F	VF	XF
AHxxx1//1	—	—	—	—	—	—

Mint: Muzaffargarh
KM# 766 RUPEE
Silver

Date	Mintage	Good	VG	F	VF	XF
AH1221//1	—	30.00	45.00	60.00	80.00	—
AH1222//2	—	30.00	45.00	60.00	80.00	—
AH1223//3	—	30.00	45.00	60.00	80.00	—

Mint: Shahjahanabad
KM# 777 RUPEE
11.4440 g., Silver **Obv:** Parasol symbol

Date	Mintage	VG	F	VF	XF	Unc
AH1221//1	—	20.00	40.00	65.00	95.00	—
AH1222//1	—	20.00	40.00	65.00	95.00	—
AH1222//2	—	20.00	40.00	65.00	95.00	—
AH1223//2	—	20.00	40.00	65.00	95.00	—
AH1223//3	—	20.00	40.00	65.00	95.00	—
AH1224//3	—	20.00	40.00	65.00	95.00	—
AH1224//4	—	20.00	40.00	65.00	95.00	—
AH1225//4	—	20.00	40.00	65.00	95.00	—
AH1226//5	—	20.00	40.00	65.00	95.00	—
AH1226//6	—	20.00	40.00	65.00	95.00	—
AH1227//6	—	20.00	40.00	65.00	95.00	—
AH1227//7	—	20.00	40.00	65.00	95.00	—
AH1228//7	—	20.00	40.00	65.00	95.00	—
AH1228//8	—	20.00	40.00	65.00	95.00	—
AH1229//9	—	20.00	40.00	65.00	95.00	—
AH12xx//11	—	20.00	40.00	65.00	95.00	—

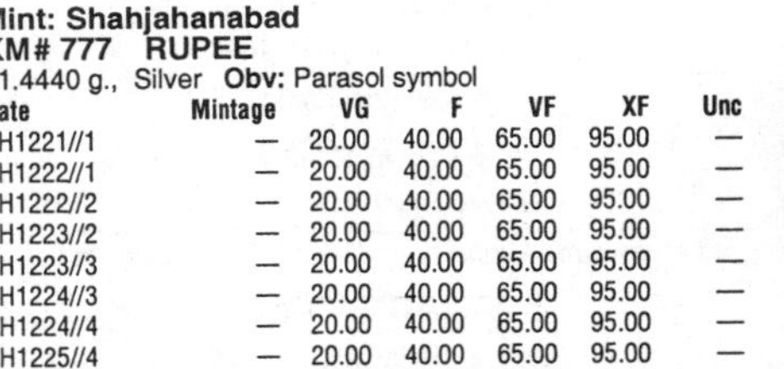
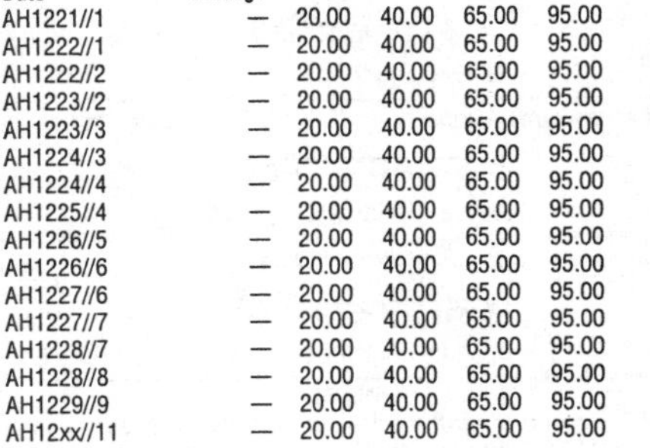

Mint: Shahjahanabad
KM# C719 NAZARANA RUPEE
11.4440 g., Silver **Obv:** Additional cinquefoil symbol

Date	Mintage	VG	F	VF	XF	Unc
AH1221//49	—	175	275	400	550	—

Mint: Shahjahanabad
KM# 779.1 NAZARANA RUPEE
11.4440 g., Silver

Date	Mintage	VG	F	VF	XF	Unc
AH1223//3	—	125	200	325	475	—
AH1224//3	—	125	200	325	475	—
AH1225//4	—	125	200	325	475	—
AH1226//5	—	125	200	325	475	—
AH1227//7	—	125	200	325	475	—
AH1235//15	—	125	200	325	475	—
AH1236//16 Rare	—	—	—	—	—	—
AH1237//17	—	135	225	350	600	—
AH1239//19	—	135	225	350	600	—
AH1240//20	—	135	225	350	600	—
AH1241//21	—	135	225	350	600	—
AH1242//22	—	135	225	350	600	—
AH1248//28	—	135	225	350	600	—
AH1249//29	—	135	225	350	600	—

Mint: Shahjahanabad
KM# 779.2 NAZARANA RUPEE
11.4440 g., Silver

Date	Mintage	VG	F	VF	XF	Unc
AH1251//31	—	275	450	750	1,250	—
AH1252//32	—	275	450	750	1,250	—

Mint: Shahjahanabad
KM# 781 MOHUR
Gold **Note:** Weight varies 10.70-11.40 grams.

Date	Mintage	VG	F	VF	XF	Unc
AH122x//2	—	200	350	500	700	—
AH1223//6 (sic)	—	200	350	500	700	—

Mint: Shahjahanabad
KM# 783 NAZARANA MOHUR
Gold **Note:** Weight varies 10.70-11.40 grams.

Date	Mintage	VG	F	VF	XF	Unc
AH1221//1 Rare	—	—	—	—	—	—
AH1234//12 (sic) Rare	—	—	—	—	—	—
AH1237//17 Rare	—	—	—	—	—	—

Siraj-ud-din Muhammad Bahadur Shah II

AH1253-1273 / 1837-1858AD

HAMMERED COINAGE

Mint: Shahjahanabad
KM# 790 NAZARANA RUPEE
11.4440 g., Silver

Date	Mintage	VG	F	VF	XF	Unc
AH1253//1	—	1,000	1,800	2,500	4,200	—
AH1254//2	—	1,000	1,800	2,500	4,200	—
AH1255//3	—	1,000	1,800	2,500	4,200	—
AH1256//4	—	1,000	1,800	2,500	4,200	—
AH1257//5	—	1,000	1,800	2,500	4,200	—
AH1258//6	—	1,000	1,800	2,500	4,200	—

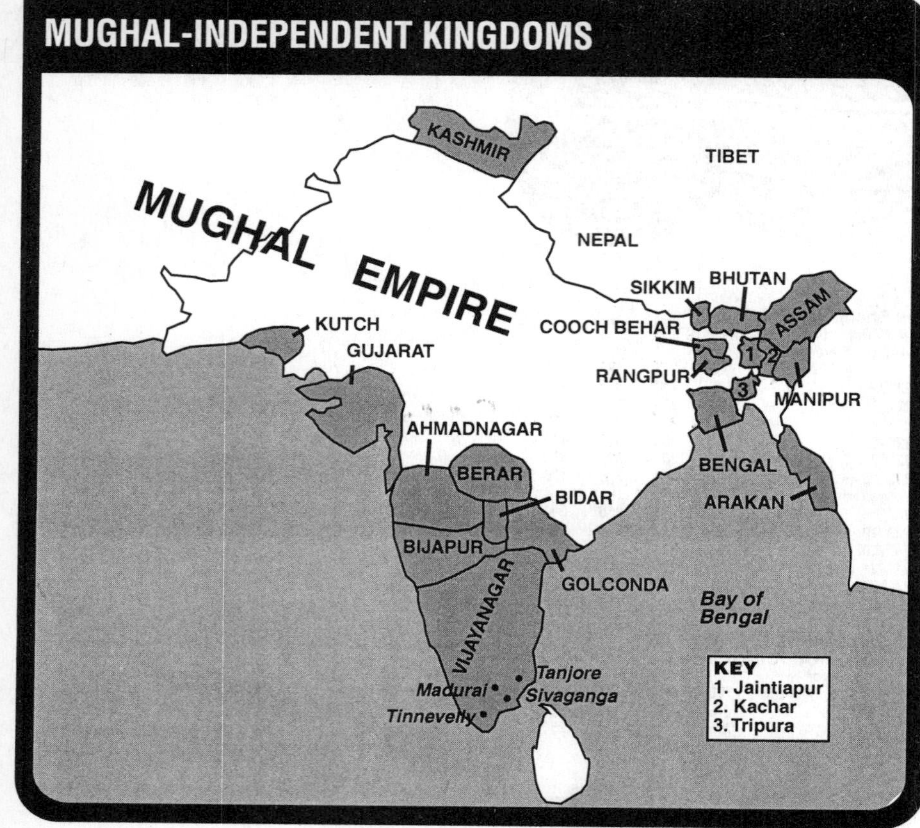

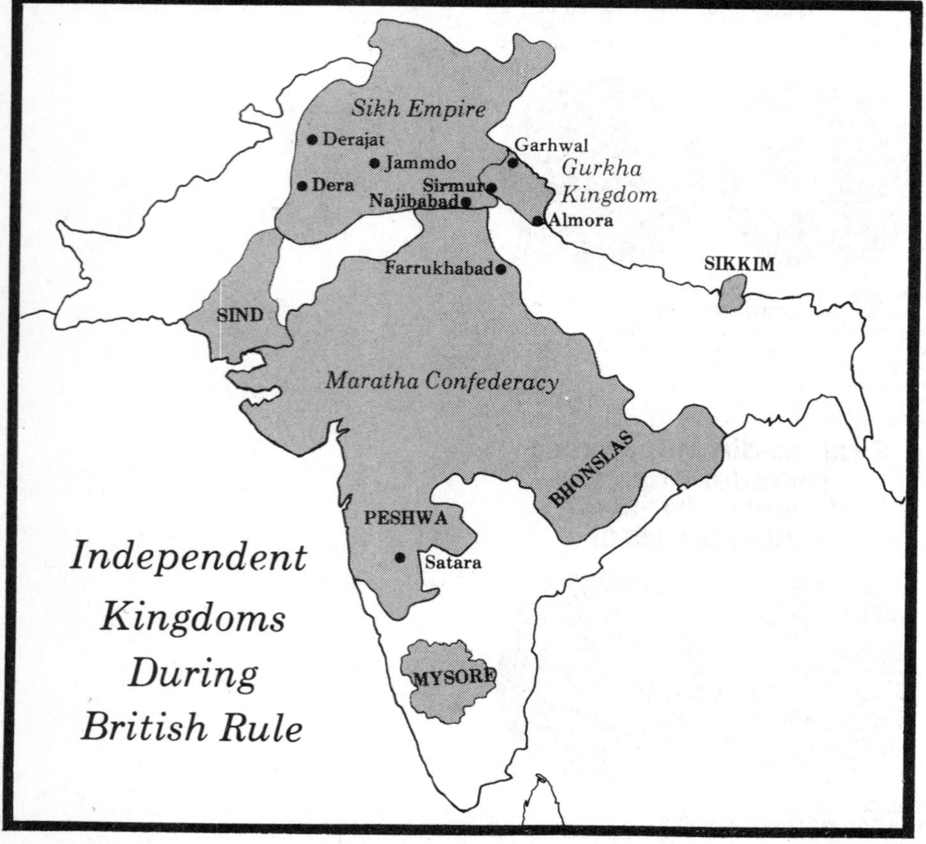

INDIA - INDEPENDENT KINGDOMS

ASSAM

AHOM KINGDOM

It was in the 13th century that a tribal leader called Sukapha, with about 9,000 followers, left their traditional home in the Shan States of Northern Burma, and carved out the Ahom Kingdom in upper Assam.

The Ahom Kingdom gradually increased in power and extent over the following centuries, particularly during the reign of King Suhungmung (1497-1539). This king also took on a Hindu title, Svarga Narayan, which shows the increasing influence of the Brahmins over the court. Although several of the other Hindu states in north-east India started a silver coinage during the 16th century, it was not until the mid-17th century that the Ahoms first struck coin.

From the time of Kusain Shah's invasion of Cooch Behar in 1494AD the Muslims had cast acquisitive eyes towards the valley of the Brahmaputra, but the Ahoms managed to preserve their independence. In 1661 Aurangzeb's governor in Bengal, Mir Jumla, made a determined effort to bring Assam under Mughal rule. Cooch Behar was annexed without difficulty, and in March 1662 Mir Jumla occupied Gargaon, the Ahom capital, without opposition. However, during the rainy season the Muslim forces suffered severely from disease, lack of food and from the occasional attacks from the Ahom forces, who had tactically withdrawn from the capital together with the king. After the end of the monsoon a supply line was opened with Bengal again, but morale in the Muslim army was low, so Mir Jumla was forced to agree to peach terms somewhat less onerous than the Mughals liked to impose on subjugated states. The Ahoms agreed to pay tribute, but the Ahom kingdom remained entirely independent of Mughal control, and never again did a Muslim army venture into upper Assam.

During the eighteenth century the kingdom became weakened with civil war, culminating in the expulsion of Gaurinatha Simha from his capital in 1787 by the Moamarias. The British helped Gaurinatha regain his kingdom in 1794, but otherwise took little interest in the affairs of Assam. The end of the Ahom Kingdom was not due to intervention from Bengal, but from Burma. After initial invasions commencing in 1816, the Burmese conquered the whole of Assam in 1821/2, and seemed bent on expanding their Kingdom even further. The British in Bengal were quick to retaliate and drove the Burmese from Assam in 1824, and from then on Assam became firmly under British control with no further independent coinage.

RULERS

Ruler's names, where present on the coins, usually appear on the obverse (dated) side, starting either at the end of the first line, after *Shri*, or in the second line. Most of the Ahom rulers after the adoption of Hinduism in about 1500AD had both an Ahom and a Hindu name.

HINDU NAME — **AHOM NAME**

Kamalesvara Simha — **Suklingpha**

কমলেশ্বৰসিংহ

SE1717-1733/1795-1811AD

Chandrakanta Simha — **Sudingpha**

চন্দ্ৰকান্তসিংহ

SE1733-1740/1811-1818AD

Brajanatha Simha

ব্ৰজনাথসিংহ

SE1740-1741/1818-1819AD

Chandrakanta Simha — **Sudingpha**

চন্দ্ৰকান্তসিংহ

SE1741-1743/1819-1821AD

Jogesvara Simha

জোগেশ্বৰসিংহ

SE1743-1746/1821-1824AD

COINAGE

It is frequently stated that coins were first struck in Assam during the reign of King Suklenmung (1539-1552), but this is merely due to a misreading of the Ahom legend on the coins of King Supungmung (1663-70). The earliest Ahom coins known, therefore, were struck during the reign of King Jayadhvaja Simha (1648-1663).

Although the inscription and general design of these first coins of the Ahom Kingdom were copied from the coins of Cooch Behar, the octagonal shape was entirely Ahom, and according to tradition was chosen because of the belief that the Ahom country was eight sided. Apart from the unique shape, the coins were of similar fabric and weight standard to the Mughul rupee.

The earliest coins had inscriptions in Sanskrit using the Bengali script, but the retreat of the Moghul army under Mir Jumla in 1663 seems to have led to a revival of Ahom nationalism that may account for the fact that most of the coins struck between 1663 and 1696 had inscriptions in the old Ahom script, with invocations to Ahom deities.

Up to this time all the coins, following normal practice in North-east India, were merely dated to the coronation year of the ruler, but Rudra Simha (1696-1714) instituted the practice of dating coins to the year of issue. This ruler was a fervent Hindu, and reinstated Sanskrit inscriptions on the coins. After this the Ahom script was used on a few rare ceremonial issues.

The majority of coins issued were of silver, with binary subdivions down to a fraction of 1/32nd rupee. Cowrie shells were used for small change. Gold coins were struck throughout the period, often using the same dies as were used for the silver coins. A few copper coins were struck during the reign of Brajanatha Simha (1818-19), but these are very rare.

MINT NAMES

رنگپور

Rangpur

Chandrakanta Simha (Sudingha)

SE1733-1740, 41- 43 / 1811-1818, 19 - 21AD

HAMMERED COINAGE

KM# 245 1/32 RUPEE
Silver **Shape:** Oval **Note:** Weight varies: 0.34-0.36 grams.

Date	Mintage	Good	VG	F	VF	XF
ND(1811-18)	—	5.00	12.50	25.00	40.00	60.00

KM# 246 1/16 RUPEE
Silver, 7 mm. **Shape:** Octagonal **Note:** Weight varies: 0.67-0.72 grams.

Date	Mintage	Good	VG	F	VF	XF
ND(1811-18)	—	5.00	12.50	25.00	40.00	60.00

KM# 247 1/8 RUPEE
Silver **Note:** Weight varies: 1.34-1.45 grams.

Date	Mintage	Good	VG	F	VF	XF
ND(1811-18)	—	6.00	15.00	25.00	40.00	60.00

KM# 248 1/4 RUPEE
Silver **Note:** Weight varies: 2.68-2.90 grams.

Date	Mintage	Good	VG	F	VF	XF
SE1741 (1819)	—	8.50	21.50	42.50	60.00	90.00
SE1742 (1820)	—	8.50	21.50	42.50	60.00	90.00

KM# 249 1/2 RUPEE
Silver **Note:** Weight varies: 5.35-5.80 grams.

Date	Mintage	Good	VG	F	VF	XF
ND(1811-18)	—	7.00	17.50	35.00	50.00	75.00

KM# 250 RUPEE
Silver **Note:** Weight varies: 10.70-11.60 grams.

Date	Mintage	Good	VG	F	VF	XF
SE1741 (1819)	—	11.00	27.50	55.00	80.00	120
SE1742 (1820)	—	11.00	27.50	55.00	80.00	120

KM# 251 RUPEE
Silver **Note:** Weight varies: 10.70-11.60 grams.

Date	Mintage	Good	VG	F	VF	XF
SE1742 (1820)	—	11.00	27.50	55.00	80.00	120

KM# 252 1/32 MOHUR
Gold **Note:** Weight varies: 0.34-0.36 grams.

Date	Mintage	Good	VG	F	VF	XF
ND(1811-18)	—	—	42.50	85.00	125	175

KM# 253 1/16 MOHUR
Gold **Note:** Weight varies: 0.67-0.72 grams.

Date	Mintage	Good	VG	F	VF	XF
ND(1811-18)	—	—	50.00	100	150	220

KM# 257 MOHUR
Gold **Note:** Weight varies: 10.70-11.40 grams.

Date	Mintage	Good	VG	F	VF	XF
SE1741 (1819)	—	—	210	420	600	875

Brajanatha Simha

SE1740-1741 / 1818-1819AD

HAMMERED COINAGE

KM# 260 1/32 RUPEE
Silver, 6 mm. **Shape:** Round **Note:** Weight varies: 0.34-0.36 grams.

Date	Mintage	Good	VG	F	VF	XF
ND(1818-19)	—	3.00	7.50	15.00	25.00	37.50

KM# 261 1/16 RUPEE
Silver **Note:** Weight varies: 0.67-0.72 grams.

Date	Mintage	Good	VG	F	VF	XF
ND(1818-19)	—	6.00	7.50	15.00	25.00	37.50

KM# 262 1/8 RUPEE
Silver **Note:** Weight varies: 1.34-1.45 grams.

Date	Mintage	Good	VG	F	VF	XF
ND(1818-19)	—	3.50	9.00	18.00	30.00	45.00

KM# 263 1/4 RUPEE
Silver **Note:** Weight varies: 2.68-2.90 grams.

Date	Mintage	Good	VG	F	VF	XF
SE1739 (1818)	—	5.00	12.50	25.00	40.00	60.00
SE1740 (1819)	—	5.00	15.50	25.00	40.00	60.00

KM# 264 1/2 RUPEE
Silver **Note:** Weight varies: 5.35-5.80 grams.

Date	Mintage	Good	VG	F	VF	XF
ND(1818-19)	—	5.00	12.50	25.00	40.00	60.00

KM# 265 RUPEE
Silver **Note:** Weight varies: 10.70-11.60 grams.

Date	Mintage	Good	VG	F	VF	XF
SE1739 (1818)	—	7.00	17.50	35.00	60.00	90.00
SE1740 (1819)	—	7.00	17.50	35.00	60.00	90.00

KM# 266 1/32 MOHUR
Gold **Note:** Weight varies: 0.34-0.36 grams.

Date	Mintage	Good	VG	F	VF	XF
ND(1818-19)	—	—	42.50	85.00	125	175

KM# 268 1/8 MOHUR
Gold **Shape:** Octagonal **Note:** Weight varies: 1.34-1.42 grams.

Date	Mintage	Good	VG	F	VF	XF
ND(1818-19)	—	—	70.00	140	200	285

KM# 269 1/4 MOHUR
Gold **Shape:** Octagonal **Note:** Weight varies: 2.68-2.85 grams.

Date	Mintage	Good	VG	F	VF	XF
SE1739 (1818)	—	—	100	200	300	425

KM# 271 MOHUR
Gold **Note:** Weight varies: 10.70-11.40 grams.

Date	Mintage	Good	VG	F	VF	XF
SE1739 (1818)	—	—	210	420	600	875
SE1740 (1819)	—	—	210	420	600	875

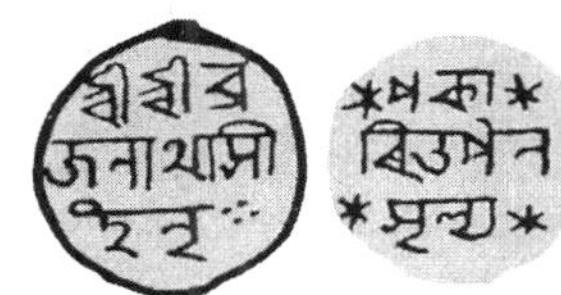

KM# 258 PANA
5.6000 g., Copper

Date	Mintage	Good	VG	F	VF	XF
ND(1818-19)	—	25.00	50.00	85.00	—	—

KM# 259 2 PANA
11.0000 g., Copper

Date	Mintage	Good	VG	F	VF	XF
SE1739 (1818)	—	30.00	60.00	100	—	—

Jogesvara Simha

SE1743-1746 / 1821-1824 AD

HAMMERED COINAGE

KM# 274 1/8 RUPEE
Silver **Note:** Weight varies: 1.34-1.45 grams.

Date	Mintage	Good	VG	F	VF	XF
ND(1824)	—	8.00	20.00	40.00	65.00	100

KM# 275 1/4 RUPEE
Silver **Shape:** Octagonal **Note:** Weight varies: 2.68-2.90 grams.

Date	Mintage	Good	VG	F	VF	XF
SE1743 (1821)	—	8.00	20.00	40.00	65.00	100

KM# 276 1/2 RUPEE
Silver **Note:** Weight varies: 5.35-5.80 grams.

Date	Mintage	Good	VG	F	VF	XF
ND(1824)	—	10.00	25.00	50.00	80.00	120

KM# 277 RUPEE
Silver **Note:** Weight varies: 10.70-11.60 grams.

Date	Mintage	Good	VG	F	VF	XF
SE1743 (1821)	—	18.00	45.00	90.00	150	225

KM# 281 1/2 MOHUR
Gold **Shape:** Octagonal **Note:** Weight varies: 2.68-2.85 grams.

Date	Mintage	Good	VG	F	VF	XF
SE1743 (1821)	—	—	150	300	450	650

FARRUKHABAD

Farrukhabad, a district in north India, was founded early in the eighteenth century by the Afghan, Mohammed Khan (d.1743), who was governor first of Allahabad and later of Malwa. The subsequent struggles of his sons with Awadh, with the Rohillas and with the Marathas, culminated in Farrukhabad becoming a tributary to Awadh, by which state Farrukhabad was entirely surrounded. In 1801 Farrukhabad was ceded to the British by the Nawab Vizier of Awadh.

BANGASH NAWABS

Amin-ud-Daula,
AH1210-1217/1796-1802AD

MINT NAME

Commencing AH1167/1753AD

احمدنگر فرخ اباد

Ahmadnagar-Farrukhabad

NOTE: Catalog numbers were in reference to Craig's basic Mughal listings.

HAMMERED COINAGE

KM# 28 RUPEE

Silver **Obv. Inscription:** "Shah Alam II" **Note:** Weight varies: 10.70-11.60 grams.

Date	Mintage	VG	F	VF	XF	Unc
AH1216//39 (1801)	—	8.50	13.50	20.00	35.00	—
AH1217//39 (1802)	—	8.50	13.50	20.00	35.00	—
AH1218//39 (1803)	—	8.50	13.50	20.00	35.00	—
AH1219//39 (1804)	—	8.50	13.50	20.00	35.00	—
AH1220//39 (1805)	—	8.50	13.50	20.00	35.00	—
AH1224//39 (1809)	—	8.50	13.50	20.00	35.00	—
AH1225//39 (1810)	—	8.50	13.50	20.00	35.00	—
AH1227//39 (1812)	—	8.50	13.50	20.00	35.00	—
AH1228//39 (1813)	—	8.50	13.50	20.00	35.00	—

KM# 20 FALUS

Copper **Obv. Inscription:** "Shah Alam II"

Date	Mintage	VG	F	VF	XF	Unc
AH1219//39 (1804)	—	4.50	8.50	13.50	20.00	—

KM# 24 1/2 ANNA

Copper **Obv. Inscription:** "Muhammad Akbar II"

Date	Mintage	VG	F	VF	XF	Unc
AH1226//6 (1811)	—	5.00	10.00	15.00	22.50	—
AH1233//12 (1818)	—	4.50	8.50	13.50	20.00	—

KM# 30 NAZARANA RUPEE

Silver **Note:** 10.70-11.60 grams. Issued after cession to the British.

Date	Mintage	VG	F	VF	XF	Unc
AH1218//39 (1813)	—	35.00	65.00	110	185	—

GURKHA KINGDOM

RULERS

Girvan Yuddha, of Nepal,
VS1860-1872/1803-1815AD

ALMORA

Chand Rajas

Until 1790AD

HAMMERED COINAGE

C# 5 PAISA

Copper **Note:** Struck in the name of local ruler Shah Alam II.

Date	Mintage	VG	F	VF	XF	Unc
ND//14 (1759)	—	8.50	13.50	20.00	—	—
ND//18 (1759)	—	8.50	13.50	20.00	—	—
ND//19 (1759)	—	8.50	13.50	20.00	—	—
ND//21 (1759)	—	8.50	13.50	20.00	—	—
ND//22 (1759)	—	8.50	13.50	20.00	—	—
ND//41 (1759)	—	8.50	13.50	20.00	—	—

KACHAR

The Kacharis are probably the original inhabitants of the Assam Valley, and in the 13th century ruled much of the south bank of the Brahmaputra from their capital at Dimapur.

Around 1530 the Ahoms inflicted several crushing defeats on the Kacharis, Dimapur was sacked, and the Kacharis were forced to retreat further south and set up a new capital at Maibong.

Very little is known about this obscure state, and the only time that coins were struck in any quantity was during the late 16th and early 17th centuries. One coin, indeed, proudly announces the conquest of Sylhet, but the military prowess seems to have been short lived, and the small kingdom was only saved from Muslim domination by its isolation and lack of economic worth.

A few coins were struck during the 18th and 19th centuries, but this was probably merely as a demonstration of independence, rather than for any economic reason.

In 1819, the last Kachari ruler, Govind Chandra was ousted by the Manipuri ruler Chaurajit Simha, and during the Burmese occupation of Manipur and Assam, the Manipuris remained in control of Kachar. In 1824, Govind Chandra was restored to his throne by the British, and ruled under British suzerainty. By all accounts his administration was not a success, and in 1832, soon after Govind Chandra had been murdered, the British took over the administration of the State in "compliance with the frequent and earnestly expressed wishes of the people.

The earliest coins of Kachar were clearly copied from the contemporary coins of Cooch Behar, with a weight standard also copied from the Bengali standard. The flans are, however, even broader than those of the Cooch Behar coins, making the coins very distinctive.

A number of spectacular gold and silver coins, purporting to come from Kachar, appeared in Calcutta during the 1960's, but as their authenticity has been doubted, they have been omitted from this listing.

RULERS

A list of the Kings of Kachar has been preserved in local traditions, but is rather unreliable. The following list has been compiled from this traditional list, together with names and dates obtained from other sources, but may not be completely accurate.

Krishna Chandra Narayan, SE1712-1735/
c.1790-1813AD

Govinda Chandra,
SE1735-1741/1814-1819AD

Chaurajit Singh, (of Manipur),
SE1741-1745/1819-1823AD

Gambhir Singh, (of Manipur),
SE1745-1746/1823-1824AD

Govinda Chandra,
SE1746-1752/1824-1830AD

Govinda Chandra

SE1735-1752 / 1814-1830AD

HAMMERED COINAGE

KM# 150 RUPEE

Silver, 25 mm. **Note:** Weight varies: 10.70-11.60 grams.

Date	Mintage	VG	F	VF	XF	Unc
SE1736 (1814)	—	100	150	225	325	—

KUMAON

Girvan Yuddha of Nepal

VS1860-73/1803-16AD

HAMMERED COINAGE

C# 10 PAISA

Copper

Date	Mintage	Good	VG	F	VF	XF
VS(18)66 (1809)	—	3.00	5.00	8.00	12.50	—

MANIPUR

Although the Manipuri traditions preserve a long list of kings which purports to go back to the early years of the Christian era, the first ruler whose existence can be verified from more tangible sources was a Naga called Panheiba, who adopted the Hindu religion and took the name of Gharib Niwaz about 1714AD.

Gharib Niwaz seems to have been a powerful ruler, who was successful in the frequent wars with Burma, and hence raised the country from obscurity. He was murdered in 1750, together with his eldest son, and it was during the reign of the latter's son, Gaura Singh, that the British first came into contact with Manipur. After the death of Gharib Niwaz the Burmese had more success with their incursions into Manipur, and by 1761 there was a danger that the capital would be captured, so the Manipuris appealed to the British for military assistance. This was granted, and in 1762 British troops helped the Manipuris drive out the Burmese, and a treaty of alliance was signed. On this occasion 500 meklee gold rupees were sent to the British as part payment for the expenses of this assistance.

Gaura Singh died in 1764 and from then until 1798 his brother Jai Singh heroically defended his country against the Burmese. In the early years of his reign he suffered many setbacks, but for the last ten years of his reign his position was fairly secure. In 1798 Jai Singh abdicated and died the following year. The next 35 years were to see five of his eight sons on the throne, plotting against each other and enlisting Burmese support for their internecine rivalry. After 1812 the Manipuri King was little more than a puppet in the hands of the Burmese, and when the Kings tried to assert their independence they were ousted to become Kings of Kachar.

In 1824, after the 1st Burma war, the Burmese were finally driven out of Manipur and Gambhir Singh, one of the younger sons of Jai Singh, asked for British assistance to regain control of his kingdom. This was granted, and from 1825 until his death in 1834 Gambhir Singh ruled well and restored an element of prosperity to his kingdom. A British resident was stationed in Manipur, but the king ruled his country independently. The British stayed aloof from several palace intrigues and revolutions, and it was only in 1891, after several British Officials had been killed, that the administration was brought under the control of a British political agent.

RULERS

Labanya Chandra, SE1720-1723/1798-1801AD
Madhu Chandra, SE1723-1728/1801-1806AD
Chaurajit Singh, SE1728-1734/1806-1812AD
Marjit Singh, under Burmese suzerainty, SE1734-1741/1812-1819AD
Huidromba Subol, SE1741-1742/1819-1820AD
Gambhir Singh, SE1742-1743/1820-1821AD
Jadu Singh, SE1743-1745/1821-1823AD
Raghab Singh, SE1745-1746/1823-1824AD
Bhadra Singh, SE1746-1747/1824-1825AD
Gambhir Singh, restored by the British, SE1747-1756/1825-1834AD
Chandra Kirti, SE1756-1765/1834-1843AD
Nar Singh, SE1765-1771/1843-1849AD
Chandra Kirti, SE1771-1808/1849-1886AD
Sura Chandra Singh, SE1808-1812/1886-1890AD
Kula Chandra Singh, SE1812-1813/1890-1891AD
Chura Chandra, SE1813-1862/1891-1941AD

COINAGE

The only coins struck in quantity for circulation in Manipur were small bell-metal (circa 74 percent copper, 23 percent tin, 3 percent zinc) coins called "sel". According to local tradition these coins were first struck in the 17th century, but this is doubtful, and it seems likely that the sels were first struck in the second half of the 18th century. Unfortunately few of the sels can be attributed to any particular ruler, as they merely bear a Nagari letter deemed auspicious for the particular reign, and it has not been recorded which letter was deemed auspicious for which ruler.

The value of the sel functioned relative to the rupees, which also circulated in Manipur for making large purchases, although Government accounts were kept in sel until 1891. Prior to 1838 the sel was valued at about 900 to the rupee, but after that date it rose in value to around 480 to the rupee, although there were occasional fluctuations. About 1878, speculative hoarding of sel forced the value up to 240 to the rupee, but large numbers of sel were struck at this time, and from then until 1891, when the sel were withdrawn from circulation, their value remained fairly stable at about 400 to the rupee.

During the years after 1714AD some square gold and silver coins were struck, but as few have survived, they were probably only struck in small quantities for ceremonial rather than monetary use.

Apart from the coins mentioned above, some larger bell-metal coins have been attributed to Manipur, but the attribution is still somewhat tentative. Also, several other gold coins, two with an image of Krishna playing the flute, have been discovered in Calcutta in recent years, but as their authenticity has been queried, they have not been included in the following listing.

DATING

Most of the silver and gold coins of Manipur are dated in the Saka era (Sake date + 78 = AD date), but at least one coin is dated in the Manipuri "Chandrabda" era, which may be converted to the AD year by adding 788 to the Chandrabda date.

MONETARY SYSTEM

(Until 1838AD)

880 to 960 Sel = 1 Rupee

(Commencing 1838AD)

420-480 Sel = 1 Rupee

ANONYMOUS COINAGE

These bear a single Bengali character, of uncertain significance, and cannot be assigned to particular rulers. All are uniface.

C# 1 SEL

Bronze Bell-Metal **Note:** "Sri"

Date	Mintage	Good	VG	F	VF	XF
ND	—	3.50	6.00	8.00	10.00	—

Note: Many variations in style exist, two varieties are illustrated above

C# 2 SEL

Bronze Bell-Metal **Note:** "Ma"

Date	Mintage	Good	VG	F	VF	XF
ND	—	5.00	8.00	11.50	15.00	—

C# 3 SEL

Bronze Bell-Metal **Note:** "Ra"

Date	Mintage	Good	VG	F	VF	XF
ND	—	6.00	10.00	15.00	20.00	—

Note: Said to be the issue of Nara Singh, 1843-50

C# 4 SEL

Bronze Bell-Metal **Note:** "Ka"

Date	Mintage	Good	VG	F	VF	XF
ND	—	6.00	10.00	15.00	20.00	—

Note: Struck before 1820

C# 5 SEL

Bronze Bell-Metal **Note:** "La"

Date	Mintage	Good	VG	F	VF	XF
ND	—	6.00	10.00	15.00	20.00	—

Note: Perhaps an issue of Sura Chandra, 1886-90

C# 6 SEL

Bronze Bell-Metal **Note:** "Ku"

Date	Mintage	Good	VG	F	VF	XF
ND	—	6.00	10.00	15.00	20.00	—

Note: Probably an issue of Kula Chandra Singh, 1890-91

C# 7 SEL

Bronze Bell-Metal **Note:** "Bha"

Date	Mintage	Good	VG	F	VF	XF
ND	—	6.00	10.00	15.00	20.00	—

C# 15 SEL

Bronze Bell-Metal **Note:** "L'L"

Date	Mintage	Good	VG	F	VF	XF
ND	—	6.00	10.00	15.00	20.00	—

Chaurajit Singh

SE1728-1734 / 1806-1812AD

HAMMERED COINAGE

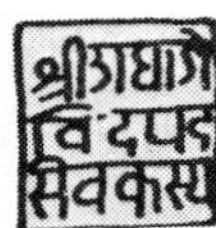

C# 55 1/4 RUPEE

Silver **Note:** Weight varies: 2.68-2.90 grams.

Date	Mintage	Good	VG	F	VF	XF
SE1726 (1804)	—	20.00	40.00	85.00	140	200
SE1729 (1807)	—	20.00	40.00	85.00	140	200

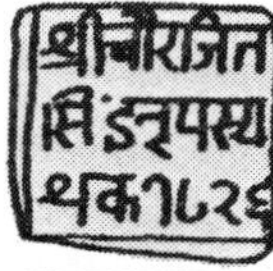

C# 56 1/2 RUPEE

Silver **Note:** Weight varies: 5.35-5.80 grams.

Date	Mintage	Good	VG	F	VF	XF
SE1726 (1804)	—	25.00	50.00	100	175	250

C# 57 RUPEE

Silver **Note:** Weight varies: 10.70-11.60 grams.

Date	Mintage	VG	F	VF	XF	Unc
SE1728 (1806)	—	90.00	180	300	450	—
SE1729 (1807)	—	90.00	180	300	450	—
SE1732 (1810)	—	90.00	180	300	450	—
SE1734 (1812)	—	60.00	120	200	300	—

C# 61 MOHUR

Gold **Note:** Weight varies: 11.20-12.50 grams.

Date	Mintage	VG	F	VF	XF	Unc
SE1731 (1809) Rare	—	—	—	—	—	—

Marjit Singh

SE1734-1741 / 1812-1819AD

HAMMERED COINAGE

C# 71 RUPEE

11.5000 g., Silver

Date	Mintage	VG	F	VF	XF	Unc
SE1736 (1814)	—	50.00	100	175	250	—

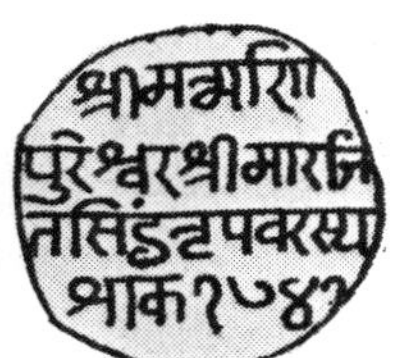

C# 75 MOHUR

Gold **Note:** Weight varies: 10.70-11.40 grams.

Date	Mintage	VG	F	VF	XF	Unc
SE1741 (1819) Rare	—	—	—	—	—	—

Gambhir Singh

SE1742-1743 / 1820-1821AD

HAMMERED COINAGE

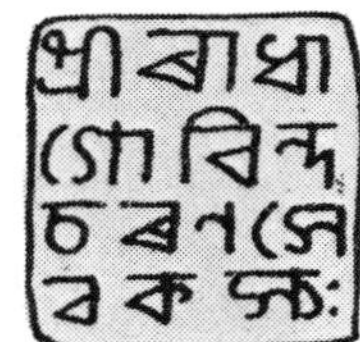
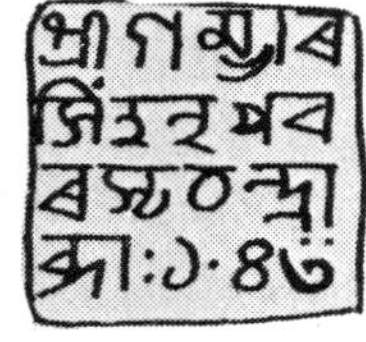

C# 85 MOHUR

Gold **Note:** Weight varies: 10.70-11.40 grams.

Date	Mintage	VG	F	VF	XF	Unc
CH1043 (1831) Rare	—	—	—	—	—	—

Note: Chandrabdah 1043 (a local dating system)

MARATHA CONFEDERACY

The origins of the Marathas are lost in the early history of the remote hill country of the Western Ghats in present-day Maharashtra. By the 15th century they had come into occasional prominence for their resistance to Muslim incursions into their homelands. They were a rugged wiry people who, by the 17th century, had accomodated themselves to the political realities of their times by becoming feudatories, or mercenaries, to the sultans of Bijapur. It is not clear exactly what happened to suddenly thrust the Marathas into the limelight of Indian history in the 17th century. The most likely explanation seems to be that the broad sweep of Aurangzeb's campaigns across the Deccan, his insensitivity towards Hindu sentiment, and the pre-eminence he gave to Islam, all served to politicize a hitherto politically quiescent people. And just as Aurangzeb supplied the occasion, the Marathas found in Sivaji the man

In the 17th century Shahji, the father of Sivaji, was holder of a small fiefdom under the Bijapur sultans. His son, taking advantage of the declining authority of his overlords, seized some of the surrounding territory. Bijapur proved incapable of quelling his insurrection. Drawing encouragement from this experience, Sivaji's forces sacked and plundered the Mughal port of Surat in1664. From this point until his death in 1680 Sivaji maintained a sort of running guerilla war with Aurangzeb. There were no decisive victories for either side but Sivaji left behind him a cohesive and well organized regional alliance in the Western Deccan, a small isolated kingdom in Tanjore and a few pockets of territory on the west coast.

After Sivaji's death the struggle was renewed as Aurangzeb advanced into the Deccan. It was the years after Aurangzeb's death in 1707, which really saw revival as the Maratha confederacy gained a new cohesiveness and its military successes began to make it look as if the Marathas might even become the new masters of India. The revenues of much of the Deccan now flowed into (finished up in) Maratha pockets. Baji Rao I, the Peshwa, pressed as far north as the gates of Delhi and in 1738 he gained control of Malwa. Parts of Gujarat also were in confederacy hands. Bengal was invaded, Orissa annexed (1751), and the territories of the Nizam of Hyderabad and the Carnatic appeared at risk. It was during this period that some of the great Maratha families gained prominence - the Holkars, the Sindhias, the Gaekwars and the Bhonslas - families who later, as the confederacy began to disintegrate and give way to rivalry, would assert their own regional interests at the expense of the alliance.

The turning point for Maratha fortunes was the battle of Panipat on January 14th 1761. Intending to stop the Afghan, Ahmad Shah Abdali (Durrani), in his tracks, the Marathas assembled the greatest army in their history and placed it under the unified command of the Peshwa of Poona. By nightfall the Peshwa's son and heir, Bhao Sahib, and all the leading chiefs, were dead. Maratha losses were said to have been in excess of a hundred thousand men. The Marathas would still remain a force to be reckoned with, they would again cross the Chambel (1767), and they would still give the Nizam's forces a thrashing (1795), but from 1761 onwards internal dissension grew rife and the Maratha Confederacy would never again exhibit sufficient cohesion to be considered a serious contender for the crown of India.

This powerful alliance of Marathi warriors owed nominal allegiance to the Rajas of Satara (descendents of Shivaji) and drew their unity from the leadership of the Peshwa, the hereditary prime minister of the confederation. In the mid-18th century the Marathas were at the apogee of their influence, having hastened the end of effective Mughal power in the Deccan and western India. They successfully checked the intrusions of the Durranis into north India, although the experience left them so militarily exhausted that the dominance in Hindustan passed to other hands.

The great families of the lieutenants of the Peshwa gradually carved out regional power bases and became progressively less responsive to the authority of their formal superiors. The Maratha power, as such, was broken in a series of wars with the East India Company, bitterly fought and very close contests which settled the fate of large sections of India. Broadly speaking, the Marathas may for convenience sake be listed in two categories, the lines which became extinct through British action and those which accommodated the English after defeat and survived to become Princely States. The latter will be found elsewhere in the catalogue; the non-surviving political units are catalogued below.

BHONSLAS

RULERS

Raghoji II, 1788-1816AD

MINTS

Cuttack (Katak) کتک

Rev. symbols

and "Zareepathka" flag. Additional symbol added after 1825.

Most coins are imitations of Mughal coins of Ahmad Shah (1748-54AD), more or less barbarized. The Bhonslas mints were closed when the state was abolished in 1854.

PESHWAS

RULERS

Baji Rao, 1796-1818AD

MINTS

احمد آباد

Ahmadabad

One of Maratha Mints from 1757-1800, it was leased to Baroda from 1800-1804, returned during 1804-1806, released to Baroda in 1806, and ceded to Baroda in 1817 (1232AH). In 1818, it was annexed by the East India Company and finally closed in 1835.

MINT MARKS

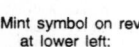

Obv: Ankus  Ankus w/pennant

Mint symbol on rev. at lower left: 

NOTE: Baroda coins of this mint have the Nagari initial of the ruler. British coins have the following mark on rev: 

بگلکوت

Bagalkot

گلشن اباد

Gulshanabad (Nasik)

Jalaun

Obv. symbols: 

Rev.: 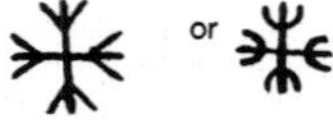

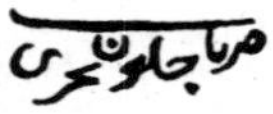

Zarb ba Jalaun Hijr

Zarb Ku(nch), Kuna(r), Jalaun

Jhansi

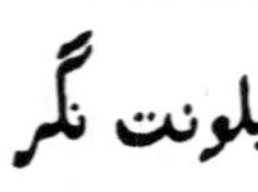

Balwantnagar

Mint mark: 

Kunch

Kunch

Kunch Hijr

Mint marks: 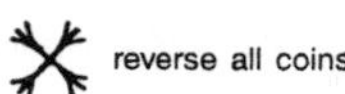 reverse all coins

#1 obv. #2 obv. 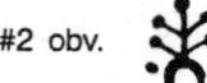

#3 obv.

#4 rev. #5 rev. 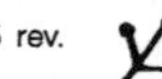

Miraj

Poona

"Muhiabad Poona" Mint opened in 1750 and closed between 1834-1835.

Poona

Mint marks:

Ankus  Scissors

Axe  *Sri* in Nagari 

Saugor

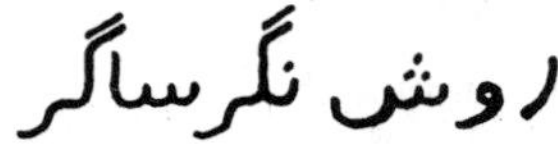

Ravishnagar Saugar

Ravishnagar Sagar

Mint marks:

Obverse: 

Reverse:

Pataka First type  Second type

Tristul First type  Second type

BHONSLAS

Anonymous Ruler

HAMMERED COINAGE

Mint: Katak

KM# A11 PAISA

Copper

Date	Mintage	VG	F	VF	XF	Unc
ND(1825-53)	—	3.00	4.00	7.00	—	—

Mint: Katak

KM# 11 1/16 RUPEE

Silver **Note:** Weight varies: 0.61-0.72 grams.

Date	Mintage	VG	F	VF	XF	Unc
ND(1825-53)	—	7.50	15.00	25.00	35.00	—

Mint: Katak

KM# 12 1/8 RUPEE

Silver **Note:** Weight varies: 1.33-1.45 grams.

Date	Mintage	VG	F	VF	XF	Unc
ND(1825-53)	—	7.50	15.00	25.00	35.00	—

Mint: Katak

KM# 13 1/4 RUPEE

Silver **Rev:** Flag only **Note:** Weight varies: 2.67-2.90 grams.

Date	Mintage	VG	F	VF	XF	Unc
ND(1825-53)	—	6.50	13.00	21.00	30.00	—

Mint: Katak

KM# 14 1/4 RUPEE

Silver **Rev:** Both symbols **Note:** Weight varies: 2.67-2.90 grams.

Date	Mintage	VG	F	VF	XF	Unc
ND(1825-53)	—	6.50	13.00	21.00	30.00	—

Mint: Katak

KM# 15 1/2 RUPEE

Silver **Rev:** Both symbols **Note:** Weight varies: 5.35-5.80 grams.

Date	Mintage	VG	F	VF	XF	Unc
ND(1825-53)	—	7.50	15.00	21.50	35.00	—

Mint: Katak

KM# 16 RUPEE

Silver **Rev:** Both symbols **Note:** Weight varies: 10.70-11.60 grams. Without mint marks. Pseudo regnal year.

Date	Mintage	VG	F	VF	XF	Unc
ND-//52 (1825)	—	12.50	22.50	42.50	55.00	—
ND-//57 (1825)	—	12.50	22.50	42.50	55.00	—
ND-//512 (1825)	—	12.50	22.50	42.50	55.00	—

Mint: Katak

KM# 17 RUPEE

Silver **Rev:** Flag only; psuedo regnal years **Note:** Weight varies: 10.70-11.60 grams.

Date	Mintage	VG	F	VF	XF	Unc
ND-//5 (1825)	—	10.00	20.00	35.00	50.00	—
ND-//51 (1825)	—	10.00	20.00	35.00	50.00	—
ND-//52 (1825)	—	10.00	20.00	35.00	50.00	—
ND-//511 (1825)	—	10.00	20.00	35.00	50.00	—
ND-//512 (1825)	—	10.00	20.00	35.00	50.00	—
ND-//521 (1825)	—	10.00	20.00	35.00	50.00	—

Mint: Katak

KM# 18 RUPEE

Silver **Rev:** Both symbols **Note:** Weight varies: 10.70-11.60 grams.

Date	Mintage	VG	F	VF	XF	Unc
ND-//5 (1825)	—	12.50	25.00	42.00	60.00	—

Mint: Katak
KM# 19 NAZARANA RUPEE
Silver

Date	Mintage	Good	VG	F	VF	XF
ND-//5 (1825)	—	—	12.50	25.00	42.00	60.00

PESHWAS

Anonymous Ruler

HAMMERED COINAGE

Mint: Kunch
KM# 180 PAISA
Silver **Obv. Inscription:** "Muhammad Akbar II" **Note:** Weight varies: 15.0-15.40 grams.

Date	Mintage	VG	F	VF	XF	Unc
ND(c.1805-06)	—	—	—	—	—	—

Symbol  on reverse

Mint: Sagar
KM# 236 PAISA
Copper **Obv:** Symbol () on obverse **Note:** Mint name: Ravishnagar Sagar.

Date	Mintage	Good	VG	F	VF	XF
AH-//55 (1802)	—	2.00	3.50	6.00	10.00	—

Mint: Satara
KM# 270 PAISA
Copper **Issuer:** East India Company **Obv. Inscription:** "Muhammad Akbar II" **Note:** Struck during East India Company administration.

Date	Mintage	Good	VG	F	VF	XF
FE1230 (1820)	—	3.50	5.00	7.00	10.00	—
FE1231 (1821)	—	3.50	5.00	7.00	10.00	—
FE1232 (1822)	—	3.50	5.00	7.00	10.00	—
FE1233 (1823)	—	3.50	5.00	7.00	10.00	—
FE1234 (1824)	—	3.50	5.00	7.00	10.00	—
FE1235 (1825)	—	3.50	5.00	7.00	10.00	—
FE1237 (1827)	—	3.50	5.00	7.00	10.00	—
FE1238 (1828)	—	3.50	5.00	7.00	10.00	—
FE1240 (1830)	—	3.50	5.00	7.00	10.00	—

Mint: Uncertain Mint
KM# 53 PAISA
8.0000 g., Copper **Obv. Inscription:** "Muhammad Akbar II"

Date	Mintage	VG	F	VF	XF	Unc
AHxxxx//9	—	3.00	4.00	6.50	9.00	—
AH1232//10	—	3.00	4.00	6.[illegible]	9.00	—

Mint: Poona

KM# 207 1/8 RUPEE
Silver **Obv. Inscription:** "Muhammad Akbar II" **Rev:** Mint mark #1 with regnal year in Persian numerals **Note:** Weight varies: 1.34-1.45 grams.

Date	Mintage	VG	F	VF	XF	Unc
ND(1820)	—	10.00	16.50	21.50	30.00	—

Note: This coin was copied by the local rulers at Alibagh Wai and Wadgaon

Mint: Gulshanabad
KM# 107 1/4 RUPEE
Silver **Obv. Inscription:** "Muhammad Akbar II" **Note:** Weight varies: 2.68-2.90 grams.

Date	Mintage	VG	F	VF	XF	Unc
AH1236	—	10.00	12.50	16.50	21.50	—

Mint: Poona
KM# 208 1/4 RUPEE
Silver **Obv:** Obverse inscription in the name of "Ali Gauhar" (Shah Alam II prior to his accession) **Rev:** Mint mark #1 with regnal year in Persian numerals **Note:** Weight varies: 2.68-2.90 grams.

Date	Mintage	VG	F	VF	XF	Unc
ND(1820)	—	—	—	—	—	—

Note: This coin was copied by the local rulers at Alibagh Wai and Wadgaon

Mint: Poona
KM# 209 1/4 RUPEE
Silver **Obv:** Obverse inscription in the name of "Ali Gauhar" (Shah Alam II prior to his accession) **Rev:** Mint mark #1 with Fasli date in Nagari numerals **Note:** Weight varies: 2.68-2.90 grams.

Date	Mintage	VG	F	VF	XF	Unc
FE1238 (1828)	—	8.50	13.50	20.00	28.50	—

Mint: Poona
KM# 210 1/4 RUPEE
Silver **Obv:** Obverse inscription in the name of "Ali Gauhar" (Shah Alam II prior to his accession) **Rev:** Mint mark #2 **Note:** Weight varies: 2.68-2.90 grams.

Date	Mintage	VG	F	VF	XF	Unc
FE1242 (1832)	—	16.00	22.50	35.00	50.00	—

Mint: Gulshanabad
KM# 108 1/2 RUPEE
Silver **Note:** Weight varies: 5.35-5.80 grams.

Date	Mintage	VG	F	VF	XF	Unc
AH1229 (1814)	—	10.00	16.50	21.50	30.00	—
AH1235 (1820)	—	10.00	16.50	21.50	30.00	—

Mint: Poona
KM# 211 1/2 RUPEE
Silver **Obv:** Obverse inscription in the name of "Ali Gauhar" (Shah Alam II prior to his accession) **Rev:** Mint mark #1 with regnal year in Persian numerals **Note:** Weight varies: 5.35-5.80 grams.

Date	Mintage	VG	F	VF	XF	Unc
ND (1820)	—	13.50	20.00	27.50	37.50	—

Note: This coin was copied by the local rulers at Alibagh Wai and Wadgaon

Mint: Poona
KM# 212 1/2 RUPEE
Silver **Obv:** Obverse inscription in the name of "Ali Gauhar" (Shah Alam II prior to his accession) **Rev:** Mint mark #1 with Fasli date in Nagari numerals **Note:** Weight varies: 5.35-5.80 grams.

Date	Mintage	VG	F	VF	XF	Unc
FE1233 (1823)	—	10.00	16.50	21.50	30.00	—
FE1236 (1826)	—	10.00	16.50	21.50	30.00	—
FE1240 (1830)	—	10.00	16.50	21.50	30.00	—

Mint: Sagar
KM# 237 1/2 RUPEE
Silver **Obv. Inscription:** "Shah Alam II" **Note:** Weight varies: 5.35-5.80 grams.

Date	Mintage	VG	F	VF	XF	Unc
AH-//51 (1809)	—	10.00	16.50	21.50	30.00	—

Mint: Sagar
KM# 241 1/2 RUPEE
Silver **Obv. Inscription:** "Shah Alam II" **Note:** Similar to KM#240 but very crude.

Date	Mintage	VG	F	VF	XF	Unc
AH-//52 (1810)	—	7.00	11.50	16.50	25.00	—
AH1230//55 (1813)	—	7.00	11.50	16.50	25.00	—

Mint: Uncertain Mint
KM# 54 1/2 RUPEE
Silver, 18 mm. **Obv. Inscription:** "Muhammad Akbar II" **Note:** Weight varies: 5.35-5.80 grams. Mint mark: Ankus.

Date	Mintage	VG	F	VF	XF	Unc
AH- (1816)	—	6.00	9.00	14.00	20.00	—

Mint: Uncertain Mint
KM# 55 1/2 RUPEE
Silver **Obv. Inscription:** "Muhammad Akbar II" **Note:** Mint mark: Ankus with pennant.

Date	Mintage	VG	F	VF	XF	Unc
AHxxxx//10 (1816)	—	6.00	9.00	14.00	20.00	—

Mint: Bagalkot
KM# 271 RUPEE
Silver **Issuer:** East India Company **Note:** Weight varies: 10.70-11.60 grams.

Date	Mintage	VG	F	VF	XF	Unc
FE1819 (1819)	—	25.00	33.50	50.00	70.00	—

Mint: Gulshanabad
KM# 109 RUPEE
Silver **Note:** Weight varies: 10.70-11.60 grams.

Date	Mintage	VG	F	VF	XF	Unc
AH1219 (1804)	—	12.50	18.50	25.00	35.00	—
AH1227 (1812)	—	12.50	18.50	25.00	35.00	—
AH1229 (1814)	—	12.50	18.50	25.00	35.00	—
AH1230 (1815)	—	12.50	18.50	25.00	35.00	—
AH1232 (1817)	—	12.50	18.50	25.00	35.00	—
AH1234 (1819)	—	12.50	18.50	25.00	35.00	—
AH1235 (1820)	—	12.50	18.50	25.00	35.00	—
AH1236 (1821)	—	12.50	18.50	25.00	35.00	—
AH1251 (1835)	—	12.50	18.50	25.00	35.00	—

Mint: Jalaun
KM# 124 RUPEE
Silver **Obv. Inscription:** "Shah Alam II" **Note:** Weight varies: 10.70-11.60 grams. Crude fabric, narrow flan. Mintname: Zarb ba Jalaun Hijri.

Date	Mintage	VG	F	VF	XF	Unc
AH-//46 (1803)	—	12.50	18.50	25.00	35.00	—
AH1222//49 (1807)	—	12.50	18.50	25.00	35.00	—
AH1226//4x (1808)	—	12.50	18.50	25.00	35.00	—
AH1224//55 (1809)	—	12.50	18.50	25.00	35.00	—

Mint: Jalaun
KM# 125 RUPEE
Silver **Obv. Inscription:** "Shah Alam II" **Note:** Weight varies: 10.70-11.60 grams. Fine fabric, normal flan. Mintname: Zarb Ku(nch), Kuna(r), Jalaun.

Date	Mintage	VG	F	VF	XF	Unc
AH-//49 (1807)	—	15.00	21.50	33.50	45.00	—
AH1222//5x (1810)	—	15.00	21.50	33.50	45.00	—

Mint: Jalaun
KM# 126 RUPEE
Silver **Obv. Inscription:** "Shah Alam II" **Note:** Weight varies: 10.70-11.60 grams. Crude fabric, narrow flan. Mintname: Zarb Ku(nch), Kuna(r), Jalaun.

Date	Mintage	VG	F	VF	XF	Unc
AH1222//17 (1807)	—	6.50	10.00	15.00	22.50	—
AH1222//21 (1807)	—	6.50	10.00	15.00	22.50	—
AH1223//17 (1807)	—	6.50	10.00	15.00	22.50	—
AH1235//17 (1808)	—	—	—	—	—	—
AH1222//51 (1809)	—	6.50	10.00	15.00	22.50	—
AH1222//52 (1810)	—	6.50	10.00	15.00	22.50	—
AH1222//53 (1811)	—	6.50	10.00	15.00	22.50	—
AH1223//53 (1811)	—	6.50	10.00	15.00	22.50	—
AH1222//55 (1811)	—	6.50	10.00	15.00	22.50	—
AH1223//55 (1813)	—	6.50	10.00	15.00	22.50	—
AH1224//55 (1813)	—	6.50	10.00	15.00	22.50	—
AH1222//57 (1814)	—	6.50	10.00	15.00	22.50	—

Mint: Jalaun
KM# 128 RUPEE
Silver **Obv. Inscription:** "Shah Alam II - Latif Khan" **Note:** Weight varies: 10.70-11.60 grams. Mintname: Zarb Ku(nch), Kuna(r), Jalaun.

Date	Mintage	VG	F	VF	XF	Unc
AH-//53 (1811)	—	30.00	40.00	55.00	75.00	—

Mint: Jhansi
KM# 144 RUPEE
Silver **Obv:** 99111 added **Obv. Inscription:** "Shah Alam II" **Note:** Weight varies: 10.70-11.60 grams.

Date	Mintage	VG	F	VF	XF	Unc
AH1220//47 (1805)	—	10.00	15.00	20.00	27.50	—
AH1221//48 (1806)	—	10.00	15.00	20.00	27.50	—
AH1223//50 (1808)	—	10.00	15.00	20.00	27.50	—
AH1224//52 (1809)	—	10.00	15.00	20.00	27.50	—
AH1234 (1819)	—	10.00	15.00	20.00	27.50	—

Mint: Kunch
KM# 178 RUPEE
Silver **Obv:** Symbols #1, #2, #3 **Rev:** Symbol #4 **Note:** Weight varies: 10.70-11.60 grams.

Date	Mintage	VG	F	VF	XF	Unc
AH1220//47 (1805)	—	16.00	22.50	35.00	50.00	—
AH1221//47 (1806)	—	16.00	22.50	35.00	50.00	—

Mint: Miraj
KM# 195 RUPEE
Silver **Obv:** Persian legend **Obv. Legend:** "Sri Gonapati" **Obv. Inscription:** "Shah Alam (Bahadur Shah) II" **Rev:** Persian legend **Rev. Legend:** "Sri Pant Pradhan"

Date	Mintage	VG	F	VF	XF	Unc
AH122x//27 (1805)	—	90.00	140	200	300	—

Mint: Poona
KM# 213 RUPEE
Silver **Obv. Inscription:** Obverse inscription in the name of "Ali Gauhar" (Shah Alam II prior to his accession) **Rev:** Mint mark #1 with regnal year in Persian numerals **Note:** Weight varies: 10.70-11.60 grams. Ankusi Rupee.

Date	Mintage	VG	F	VF	XF	Unc
AH1225 (1815)	—	7.50	12.50	18.50	27.50	—
AH1227 (1817)	—	7.50	12.50	18.00	27.50	—
AH1229 (1819)	—	7.50	12.50	18.50	27.50	—

Note: This coin was copied by the local rulers at Alibagh Wai and Wadgaon

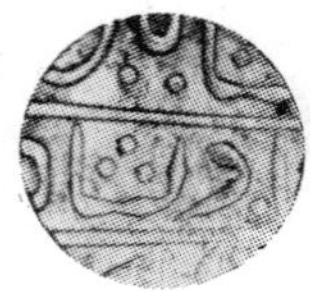

Mint: Poona
KM# 214 RUPEE
Silver **Obv:** Obverse inscription in the name of "Ali Gauhar" (Shah Alam II prior to his accession) **Rev:** Mint mark #1 with Fasli date in Nagari numerals **Note:** Weight varies: 10.70-11.60 grams.

Date	Mintage	VG	F	VF	XF	Unc
FE1232 (1822)	—	6.50	10.00	15.00	22.50	—
FE1233 (1823)	—	6.50	10.00	15.00	22.50	—
FE1234 (1824)	—	6.50	10.00	15.00	22.50	—
FE1235 (1825)	—	6.50	10.00	15.00	22.50	—
FE1236 (1826)	—	6.50	10.00	15.00	22.50	—
FE1237 (1827)	—	6.50	10.00	15.00	22.50	—
FE1238 (1828)	—	6.50	10.00	15.00	22.50	—
FE1239 (1829)	—	6.50	10.00	15.00	22.50	—
FE1240 (1830)	—	6.50	10.00	15.00	22.50	—
FE1241 (1831)	—	6.50	10.00	15.00	22.50	—
FE1242 (1832)	—	6.50	10.00	15.00	22.50	—
FE1243 (1833)	—	6.50	10.00	15.00	22.50	—
FE1244 (1834)	—	6.50	10.00	15.00	22.50	—

Mint: Poona
KM# 217 RUPEE
Silver **Obv:** Obverse inscription in the name of "Ali Gauhar" (Shah Alam II prior to his accession) **Rev:** Mint mark #3, Fasli date in Nagari numerals

Date	Mintage	VG	F	VF	XF	Unc
FE1230 (1815)	—	10.00	16.50	21.50	30.00	—
FE1231 (1816)	—	10.00	16.50	21.50	30.00	—
FE1232 (1817)	—	10.00	16.50	21.50	30.00	—
FE1234 (1819)	—	10.00	16.50	21.50	30.00	—
FE1236 (1821)	—	10.00	16.50	21.50	30.00	—
FE1238 (1823)	—	10.00	16.50	21.50	30.00	—
FE1239 (1824)	—	10.00	16.50	21.50	30.00	—
FE1240 (1825)	—	10.00	16.50	21.50	30.00	—
FE1241 (1826)	—	10.00	16.50	21.50	30.00	—
FE1242 (1827)	—	10.00	16.50	21.50	30.00	—
FE1243 (1828)	—	10.00	16.50	21.50	30.00	—
FE1244 (1829)	—	10.00	16.50	21.50	30.00	—
FE-//30 (1830-31)	—	11.50	17.50	23.50	33.50	—

Note: Earlier date (AH1207) exists for this type.

Mint: Sagar
KM# 240 RUPEE
Silver **Rev:** Pataka and trisul both second type **Note:** Weight varies: 10.70-11.60 grams. Mintname: Ravishnagar Sagar.

Date	Mintage	VG	F	VF	XF	Unc
AH1216//42 (1801)	—	7.00	11.50	16.50	25.00	—
AH1218//43 (1803)	—	7.00	11.50	16.50	25.00	—
AH1218//44 (1803)	—	7.00	11.50	16.50	25.00	—
AH1219//44 (1804)	—	7.00	11.50	16.50	25.00	—
AH1220//45 (1805)	—	7.00	11.50	16.50	25.00	—
AH1222//47 (1807)	—	7.00	11.50	16.50	25.00	—

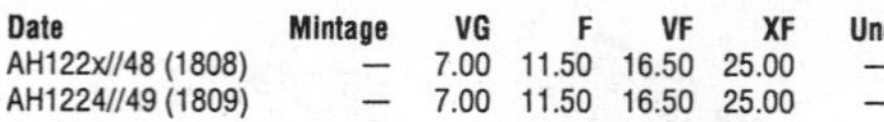

Date	Mintage	VG	F	VF	XF	Unc
AH122x//48 (1808)	—	7.00	11.50	16.50	25.00	—
AH1224//49 (1809)	—	7.00	11.50	16.50	25.00	—

Mint: Uncertain Mint
KM# 56 RUPEE
Silver **Obv. Inscription:** "Muhammad Akbar II" **Note:** Weight varies: 10.70-11.60 grams. Mint mark: Ankus and scissors.

Date	Mintage	VG	F	VF	XF	Unc
AH122x//8 (1813)	—	12.50	18.50	25.00	35.00	—
AH1230//8 (1815)	—	12.50	18.50	25.00	35.00	—

Mint: Uncertain Mint
KM# 57 RUPEE
Silver **Obv. Inscription:** "Muhammad Akbar II" **Note:** Weight varies: 10.70-11.60 grams. Mint mark: Ankus.

Date	Mintage	VG	F	VF	XF	Unc
AH122x//8 (1813)	—	7.50	12.50	18.50	27.50	—
AH-//9 (1814)	—	7.50	12.50	18.50	27.50	—

Mint: Uncertain Mint
KM# 58 RUPEE
Silver **Obv. Inscription:** "Muhammad Akbar II" **Note:** Weight varies: 10.70-11.60 grams. Mint mark: Ankus with pennant.

Date	Mintage	VG	F	VF	XF	Unc
AH1231//9 (1815)	—	8.50	13.50	20.00	30.00	—
AH1231//10 (1816)	—	8.50	13.50	20.00	30.00	—

Mint: Tanjore
KM# 275 CASH
3.4000 g., Copper **Issuer:** East India Company **Obv. Legend:** "Chatrapati" **Rev. Legend:** "Sri Siva"

Date	Mintage	VG	F	VF	XF	Unc
ND(c.1820-30)	—	10.00	14.00	21.50	30.00	—

Mint: Tanjore
KM# 276 CASH
3.4000 g., Copper **Issuer:** East India Company **Obv. Legend:** Similar to KM#275 but retrograde **Rev. Legend:** Similar to KM#275 but retrograde

Date	Mintage	VG	F	VF	XF	Unc
ND(c.1820-30)	—	10.00	14.00	21.50	30.00	—

Mint: Tanjore
KM# 277 CASH
3.4000 g., Copper **Issuer:** East India Company **Obv. Legend:** "Chatrapati" **Rev. Legend:** "Sri Siva"

Date	Mintage	VG	F	VF	XF	Unc
ND(c.1820-30)	—	10.00	14.00	21.50	30.00	—

Mint: Tanjore
KM# 278 CASH
3.4000 g., Copper **Issuer:** East India Company

Date	Mintage	VG	F	VF	XF	Unc
ND(c.1820-30)	—	10.00	14.00	21.50	30.00	—

Mint: Tanjore
KM# 279 CASH
3.4000 g., Copper **Issuer:** East India Company **Obv. Legend:** "Chatrapati" **Rev. Legend:** "Sri Siva"

Date	Mintage	VG	F	VF	XF	Unc
ND(c.1820-30)	—	10.00	14.00	21.50	30.00	—

Mint: Tanjore
KM# 280 FANAM
0.4000 g., Gold **Issuer:** East India Company

Date	Mintage	VG	F	VF	XF	Unc
ND(c.1820-30)	—	7.50	10.00	20.00	30.00	—

HAMMERED COINAGE

Shivrai

General issues used all over Maratha Country

Mint: Uncertain Mint
KM# 268 RUPEE
Silver **Obv:** Parasol design

Date	Mintage	Good	VG	F	VF	XF
AH121-//42 (1801) Rare	—	—	—	—	—	—

Note: Pseudo-Shahjahanabad Maratha issue struck 1801 AD

Mint: Jhansi
KM# 145 RUPEE
Silver **Obv. Inscription:** "Shah Alam II" **Rev:** Lily

Date	Mintage	Good	VG	F	VF	XF
AH-//3	—	—	11.50	17.50	23.50	33.50
AH-//4	—	—	11.50	17.50	23.50	33.50
AH-//6	—	—	11.50	17.50	23.50	33.50

PUDUKKOTTAI

Pudukota

Raghunatha Raya Tondaiman founded Pudukkottai in 1686 when he defeated the Pallavaraya chiefs of the area. The family came from Tondaimandalam, a small village near Tirupathi, and belonged to the Kallen (or robber) caste. In the late 18th century the Tondaimans aided the British in their struggles against the French in the Carnatic. With British ascendancy, the Pudukkottai rulers were confirmed in their control of the region. This was regularized in 1806 when, subject to a yearly tribute of one elephant, the rajas of Pudukkottai were guaranteed their position. In 1948 the State was merged into the Trichinopoly District.

RULERS

Martanda Bhairava, 1886-1928AD

Martanda Bhairava

HAMMERED COINAGE

KM# 3 AMMAN CASH
1.3000 g., Copper **Obv:** Goddess Brihadamba seated facing **Rev:** Telugu: "Vijaya"

Date	Mintage	VG	F	VF	XF	Unc
ND(1886)	—	0.90	1.50	2.50	4.00	—

KM# 4 HEAVY AMMAN CASH
1.6500 g., Copper

Date	Mintage	VG	F	VF	XF	Unc
ND(1886) Rare	—	—	—	—	—	—

MILLED COINAGE

KM# 6 AMMAN CASH
1.2500 g., Copper **Note:** Struck at Birmingham Mint. Later contracts were struck at the Calcutta Mint.

Date	Mintage	F	VF	XF	Unc
ND(1889-1906)	Est. 5,000,000	0.20	0.50	0.85	1.50

ROHILKHAND

The Nawabs of Rohilkhand were Rohillas who traced their origins to Sardar Daud Khan (d. 1749), an Afghan adventurer. Daud Khan's adopted son, Ali Muhammed, annexed a huge tract of land north of the Ganges between Itawa and the Himalayas, and received the Nawab title from the Mughal emperor.

In 1754 this territory was partitioned among his many sons, who thereafter formed a loose confederacy, alternately given to feuding internally and uniting to meet aggression by the Marathas, Awadh, and Imperial forces in turn. By the end of the century Rohilla power had been crushed by the combined forces of Awadh and the British, leaving only Rampur in Rohilla hands under the sovereignty of Nawab Faizullah Khan. In 1801 Rampur was ceded to the East India Company and in 1950 it was absorbed into Uttar Pradesh.

MINT

Bareli بریلی

HAMMERED COINAGE

KM# 46 RUPEE
Silver **Obv. Inscription:** "Shah Alam II" **Note:** Struck during the reign of local ruler, Hafiz Rahmat Khan, AH1167-88/1754-74AD at the Bareli Mint. 10.70-11.60 grams.

Date	Mintage	VG	F	VF	XF	Unc
AH1274/72	—	—	—	3,250	4,500	—

SIKH EMPIRE

The father of Sikhism, Guru Nanak (1469-1539), was distinguished from almost all others who founded states or empires in India by being a purely religious teacher. Deeply Indian in the basic premises, which underlay even those aspects of his theology which differed from the mainstream, he stressed the unity of God and the universal brotherhood of man. He was totally opposed to the divisions of the caste system and his teaching struggled to attain a practical balance between Hinduism and Islam. His message was a message of reconciliation, first with God, then with man. He exhibited no political ambition.

Guru Nanak was succeeded by nine other gurus of Sikhism. Together they laid the foundations of a religious community in the Punjab, which would, much later, transform itself into the Sikh Empire. Gradually this gentle religion of reconciliation became transformed into a formidable, aggressive military power. It was a metamorphosis, which was, at least partly, thrust upon the Sikh community by Mughal oppression. The fifth guru of Sikhism, Arjun, was executed in 1606 on the order of Jahangir. His successor, Hargobind, was to spend his years in constant struggle against the Mughals, first against Jahangir and later against Shah Jahan. The ninth guru, Tegh Bahadur, was executed by Aurangzeb for refusing to embrace Islam. The stage had been set for a full confrontation with Mughal authority. It was against such a background that Sikhism's tenth guru, Guru Govind Singh (1675-1708), set about organizing the Sikhs into a military power. He gave new discipline to Sikhism. Its adherents were forbidden wine and tobacco and they were required to conform to the 5 outward signs of allegiance - to keep their hair unshaven and to wear short drawers (kuchcha), a comb (kungha), an iron bangle (kara) and a dagger (kirpan).

With Govind Singh's death the Khalsa, the Sikh brotherhood, emerged as the controlling body of Sikhism and the Granth, the official compilation of Govind Singh's teaching, became the "Bible" of Sikhism. At this point the Sikhs took to the hills. It was here, constantly harassed by Mughal forces, that Sikh militarism was forged into an effective weapon and tempered by fire. Gradually the Sikhs emerged from their safe forts in the hills and made their presence felt in the plains of the Punjab. As Nadir Shah retired from Delhi laden with the prizes of war in 1739, the stragglers of his Persian army were cut down by the Sikhs. Similarly, Ahmad Shah Durrani's first intrusion into India (1747-1748) was made the more lively by Sikh sorties into his rear guard. Gradually the Sikhs became both more confident and more effective, and their quite frequent military reversals served only to strengthen their determination and to deepen their sense of identity. Their first notable success came about 1756 when the Sikhs temporarily occupied Lahore and used the Mughal mint to strike their own rupee bearing the inscription: *Coined by the grace of the Khalsa in the country of Ahmad, conquered by Jessa the Kalal.* But the Sikhs were, as yet, most effective as guerrilla bands operating out of the hill country. On Ahmad Shah's fifth expedition into India (1759-1761) the Sikhs reverted to their well-tried role of forming tight mobile units, which could choose both the time and the place of their attacks on the Durrani army. In spite of a serious reverse near Bernala in 1762 at the hands of Ahmad Shah, the Sikhs once again regrouped. In December 1763 they decisively defeated the Durrani governor of Sirhind and occupied the area.

The Sikhs now swept all before them, recapturing Lahore in 1765. The whole tract of land between the Jhelum and the Sutlej was now divided among the Sikh chieftains. At Lahore, and later at Amritsar, the Govind Shahi rupee proclaiming that Guru Govind Singh had received *Deg, Tegh and Fath* (Grace, Power and Victory) from Nanak was struck. The name of the Mughal emperor was pointedly omitted. The Sikhs now subdivided into twelve *misls* "equals", each responsible for its own fate and each conducting its own military adventures into surrounding areas. By 1792 the most prominent chief in the Punjab was Mahan Singh of the Sukerchakia *misl*. His death that same year left the boy destined to become Sikhism's best-known statesman, Ranjit Singh, as his successor. A year later Shah Zaman, King of Kabul, confirmed him as the possessor of Lahore.

For the next forty years Ranjit Singh dominated Sikh affairs. In 1802 he seized Amritsar and followed this by capturing Ludhiana (1806), Multan (1818), Kashmir (1819), Ladakh (1833) and Peshawar (1834). By the time of his death in June 1839 Ranjit was the only leader in India capable of offering a serious challenge to the East India Company.

By a treaty concluded in 1809 with the British, Ranjit had been confirmed as ruler of the tracts he had occupied south of the Sutlej, but the agreement had restricted him from seeking any further expansion to the north or west of the river. In spite of the terms of the treaty, the British remained suspicious of Ranjit's ultimate intentions. His steady policy of expansion frequently left apprehensions in the minds of the British - with whose interests Ranjit's own often clashed - that the Sikhs had secret ambitions against Company controlled territory. But it was to Ranjit's credit that he welded the Sikhs of the Punjab into an effective and unified fighting force, capable of resisting both the Afghans and the Marathas and able to stand up to British pressures. He inherited a loose alliance of fiercely independent chiefs, he left a disciplined and well equipped army of over fifty thousand men. He also left a well consolidated regional empire in the extreme northwest of India, roughly extending over the northern half of present-day Pakistan.

After the death of Ranjit the Sikh empire began to disintegrate as power passed from chief to chief in murderous rivalry. At the same time relationships with the British began to deteriorate. The treaty of 1809 no longer proved able to hold the peace, and the Sikh army attacked the British (1845-1846) only to be badly beaten in a series of confrontations. The Treaty of Lahore, which followed this first Anglo-Sikh war reduced the Sikh army to a maximum of twenty thousand men and twelve thousand cavalry. It obliged the Sikhs to cede the Jallandar Doab and Kashmir to the British, and required them to pay an indemnity of fifty thousand pounds and accept a British resident at their court. In 1848 the Sikhs again revolted, and were again crushed. In 1849 the Punjab was annexed and from that time onward they came under British rule.

RULERS

Ranjit Singh, VS1856-1896/1799-1839AD
Kharak Singh, VS1896-1897/1839-1840AD
Sher Singh, VS1897-1900/1840-1843AD
Dulip Singh, VS1900-1906/1843-1849AD

MINTS

Amritsar (Ambratsar) امرت سر

Dera دیره

Derajat دیراجات

Kashmir کشمیر

Lahore لاهور

Multan ملتان

Najibabad نجیب اباد or

Nimak (Pind Dadan Khan) نمك

Peshawar پشاور

NOTE: Most coins struck after the accession of Ranjit Singh bear a large leaf on one side, and have Persian or Gurmukhi (Punjabi) legends in the name of Gobind Singh, the tenth and last Guru of the Sikhs, 1675-1708AD. Earlier pieces are similar, but lack the leaf, except the Amritsar Mint where the leaf is present since VS1845.

There is a great variety of coppers, and only representative types are catalogued here; many crude pieces were struck at the official and at unofficial mints, and bear illegible or semi-literate inscriptions. None of the coins bear the name of the Sikh ruler.

There is a great variety of coppers, and only representative types are catalogued here; many crude pieces were struck at the official and at unofficial mints, and bear illegible or semi-literate inscriptions. None of the coins bear the name of the Sikh ruler.

HAMMERED COINAGE

Mint: Amritsar
KM# 3 1/2 PAISA
Copper **Note:** First copper series, Persian legends, various types.

Date	Mintage	Good	VG	F	VF	XF
VS1896 (1839)	—	3.50	7.00	12.00	18.00	—

Mint: Amritsar
KM# 4 HEAVY PAISA
Copper **Note:** Weight varies: 11.00-12.00 grams. First copper series, Persian legends, various types.

Date	Mintage	Good	VG	F	VF	XF
VS1880 (1823)	—	2.00	3.25	6.00	9.00	—
VS1881 (1824)	—	2.00	3.25	6.00	9.00	—
VS1882 (1825)	—	2.00	3.25	6.00	9.00	—

Mint: Amritsar
KM# 5 1/4 ANNA
Copper **Obv:** Date **Rev:** "Nanak Shahi", denomination and date **Note:** Weight varies: 8.00-9.00 grams. First copper series, Persian legends, various types.

Date	Mintage	Good	VG	F	VF	XF
VS1896 (1839)	—	3.00	5.00	9.00	14.00	—
VS1897 (1840)	—	3.00	5.00	9.00	14.00	—

Mint: Amritsar
KM# 7.1 PAISA
Copper **Obv:** Double leaf, date in bottom line **Note:** Weight varies: 7.00-12.00 grams. Second series, Gurmukhi legends.

Date	Mintage	Good	VG	F	VF	XF
VS1885 (1828)	—	1.50	3.00	5.00	7.00	—

Mint: Amritsar
KM# 7.2 PAISA
Copper **Obv:** Double leaf **Note:** Weight varies: 7.00-12.00 grams. Second series, Gurmukhi legends.

Date	Mintage	Good	VG	F	VF	XF
VS1885 (1828)	—	2.00	4.00	7.00	12.00	—

Mint: Amritsar
KM# 7.3 PAISA
Copper **Obv:** Double leaf **Rev:** Flower **Note:** Weight varies: 7.00-12.00 grams. Second series, Gurmukhi legends.

Date	Mintage	Good	VG	F	VF	XF
ND(1822-30)	—	1.50	3.00	5.00	9.00	—

Mint: Amritsar
KM# 7.4 PAISA
Copper **Obv:** Double leaf **Rev:** Cross **Note:** Weight varies: 7.00-12.00 grams. Second series, Gurmukhi legends.

Date	Mintage	Good	VG	F	VF	XF
VS188x (1822)	—	1.50	3.00	5.00	9.00	—

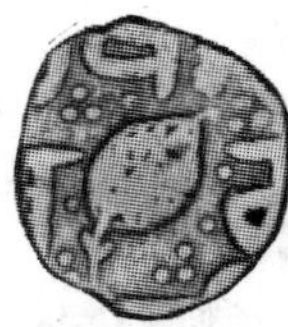

Mint: Amritsar
KM# 7.5 PAISA
Copper **Obv:** Double leaf **Rev:** Trident **Note:** Weight varies: 7.00-12.00 grams. Second series, Gurmukhi legends.

Date	Mintage	Good	VG	F	VF	XF
ND(1822-30)	—	1.50	3.00	5.00	9.00	—

Mint: Amritsar
KM# 7.6 PAISA
Copper **Obv:** Double leaf **Rev:** Katar right **Note:** Weight varies: 7.00-12.00 grams. Second series, Gurmukhi legends.

Date	Mintage	Good	VG	F	VF	XF
ND(1822-30)	—	1.75	3.50	6.00	12.00	—

Note: Variety exists with Katar facing up

Mint: Amritsar
KM# 7.7 PAISA
Copper **Obv:** Double leaf **Rev:** Tiger running right **Note:** Weight varies: 7.00-12.00 grams. Second series, Gurmukhi legends.

Date	Mintage	Good	VG	F	VF	XF
ND(1822-30)	—	3.50	8.00	15.00	25.00	—

Mint: Amritsar
KM# 7.8 PAISA
Copper **Obv:** Double leaf **Rev:** Leaf spray **Note:** Weight varies: 7.00-12.00 grams. Second series, Gurmukhi legends.

Date	Mintage	Good	VG	F	VF	XF
ND(1822-30)	—	2.25	4.50	7.50	12.50	—

Mint: Amritsar
KM# 7.9 PAISA
Copper **Obv:** Double leaf **Rev:** Banner with tail end up **Note:** Weight varies: 7.00-12.00 grams. Second series, Gurmukhi legends.

Date	Mintage	Good	VG	F	VF	XF
ND(1822-30)	—	2.25	4.50	7.50	12.50	—

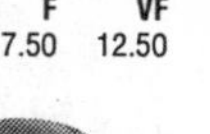

Mint: Amritsar
KM# 7.10 PAISA
Copper **Obv:** Double leaf, cross **Rev:** Double line **Note:** Weight varies: 7.00-12.00 grams. Second series, Gurmukhi legends.

Date	Mintage	Good	VG	F	VF	XF
ND(1822-30)	—	1.50	3.00	5.00	9.00	—

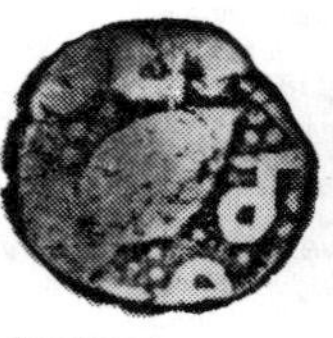

Mint: Amritsar
KM# 7.11 PAISA
Copper **Obv:** Double leaf, cross **Rev:** Katar left **Note:** Weight varies: 7.00-12.00 grams. Second series, Gurmukhi legends.

Date	Mintage	Good	VG	F	VF	XF
ND(1822-30)	—	1.75	3.50	6.00	12.00	—

Mint: Amritsar
KM# 7.12 PAISA
Copper **Obv:** Leaf spray, mint name **Rev:** Leaf **Note:** Weight varies: 7.00-12.00 grams. Second series, Gurmukhi legends.

Date	Mintage	Good	VG	F	VF	XF
ND(1822-30)	—	3.50	7.00	12.00	20.00	—

Mint: Amritsar
KM# 7.13 PAISA
Copper **Obv:** Leaf spray, mint name **Rev:** Quatrefoil **Note:** Weight varies: 7.00-12.00 grams. Second series, Gurmukhi legends.

Date	Mintage	Good	VG	F	VF	XF
ND(1822-30)	—	3.50	7.00	12.00	20.00	—

Mint: Amritsar
KM# 7.14 PAISA
Copper **Obv:** Leaf spray, mint name **Rev:** No control mark **Note:** Weight varies: 7.00-12.00 grams. Second series, Gurmukhi legends.

Date	Mintage	Good	VG	F	VF	XF
ND(1822-30)	—	3.50	7.00	12.00	20.00	—

Mint: Amritsar
KM# 7.15 PAISA
Copper **Obv:** Double leaf **Rev:** Four-petal flower **Note:** Weight varies: 7.00-12.00 grams.

Date	Mintage	Good	VG	F	VF	XF
ND(1822-30)	—	2.00	4.00	7.00	12.00	—

Mint: Amritsar
KM# 7.16 PAISA
Copper **Obv:** Double leaf, leaf facing opposite **Note:** Weight varies: 7.00-12.00 grams.

Date	Mintage	Good	VG	F	VF	XF
ND(1822-30)	—	2.00	4.00	7.00	12.00	—

Mint: Amritsar
KM# 7.17 PAISA
Copper **Obv:** Double leaf **Note:** Weight varies: 7.00-12.00 grams.

Date	Mintage	Good	VG	F	VF	XF
ND(1822-30)	—	1.00	3.00	6.00	10.00	—

Mint: Amritsar
KM# 7.18 PAISA
Copper **Obv:** Leaf facing right **Note:** Weight varies: 7.00-12.00 grams.

Date	Mintage	Good	VG	F	VF	XF
ND(1822-30)	—	1.00	3.00	6.00	10.00	—

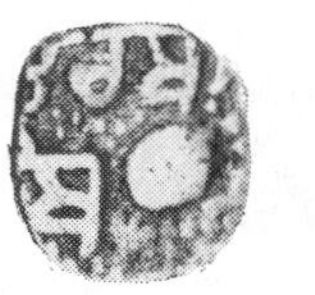

Mint: Amritsar
KM# 7.19 PAISA
Copper **Obv:** Double leaf **Rev:** Date without symbol **Note:** Weight varies: 7.00-12.00 grams.

Date	Mintage	Good	VG	F	VF	XF
VS1906 (1849)	—	5.00	10.00	16.50	30.00	—

Mint: Amritsar
KM# 7.20 PAISA
Copper **Obv:** Leaf facing left **Note:** Weight varies: 7.00-12.00 grams.

Date	Mintage	Good	VG	F	VF	XF
ND(1822-30)	—	2.00	4.00	7.00	12.00	—

Mint: Amritsar
KM# 7.21 PAISA
Copper **Obv:** Double leaf **Note:** Weight varies: 7.00-12.00 grams. Second series, Gurmukhi legends. Similar to KM#7.1 but cruder, undated.

Date	Mintage	Good	VG	F	VF	XF
ND(1822-30)	—	1.00	2.00	4.00	8.00	—

Mint: Amritsar
KM# 7.22 PAISA
Copper **Obv:** Double leaf **Rev:** Banner with tail end down **Note:** Weight varies: 7.00-12.00 grams. Second series, Gurmukhi legends.

Date	Mintage	Good	VG	F	VF	XF
ND(1822-30)	—	1.75	3.50	7.00	12.00	—

Mint: Amritsar
KM# 7.23 PAISA
Copper **Obv:** Double leaf **Note:** Weight varies: 7.00-12.00 grams. Second series, Gurmukhi legends.

Date	Mintage	Good	VG	F	VF	XF
VS1879 (1822)	—	5.00	10.00	18.00	30.00	—

Mint: Amritsar
KM# 7.24 PAISA
Copper **Obv:** Dotted leaf **Note:** Weight varies: 7.00-12.00 grams.

Date	Mintage	Good	VG	F	VF	XF
ND(1822-30)	—	3.50	7.00	12.00	20.00	—

Mint: Kashmir
KM# 40.1 PAISA
Copper **Note:** Gurmakhi and Persian legends.

Date	Mintage	Good	VG	F	VF	XF
VS1878 (1821)	—	6.50	11.50	18.50	30.00	—

Mint: Kashmir
KM# 40.2 PAISA
Copper **Note:** Persian and Gurmakhi legends.

Date	Mintage	Good	VG	F	VF	XF
VS188x (1823)	—	5.50	9.00	15.00	25.00	—

Mint: Kashmir
KM# 40.3 PAISA
Copper

Date	Mintage	Good	VG	F	VF	XF
VS188x (1823)	—	5.50	9.00	15.00	25.00	—

Mint: Kashmir
KM# 40.4 PAISA
Copper **Note:** Sword.

Date	Mintage	Good	VG	F	VF	XF
ND(1823-48)	—	5.50	9.00	15.00	25.00	—

Mint: Kashmir
KM# 41.1 PAISA
Copper **Note:** Persian legends, sword.

Date	Mintage	Good	VG	F	VF	XF
VS1894 (1837)	—	5.50	9.00	15.00	25.00	—

Mint: Kashmir
KM# 41.2 PAISA
Copper **Note:** Persian legends, rosette.

Date	Mintage	Good	VG	F	VF	XF
ND(1823-48)	—	4.50	7.50	12.50	20.00	—

Mint: Kashmir
KM# 41.3 PAISA
Copper

Date	Mintage	Good	VG	F	VF	XF
VS1895 (1838)	—	5.50	9.00	15.00	25.00	—

Mint: Kashmir
KM# 41.4 PAISA
Copper **Obv:** Nanak Shah **Rev:** Rosette

Date	Mintage	Good	VG	F	VF	XF
ND(1823-48)	—	5.50	9.00	15.00	25.00	—

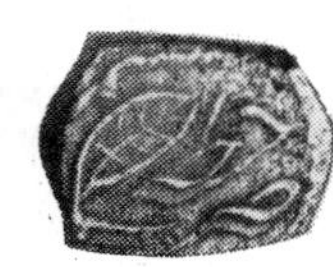
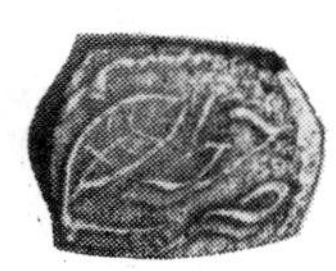

Mint: Kashmir
KM# 41.5 PAISA
Copper **Note:** Banner.

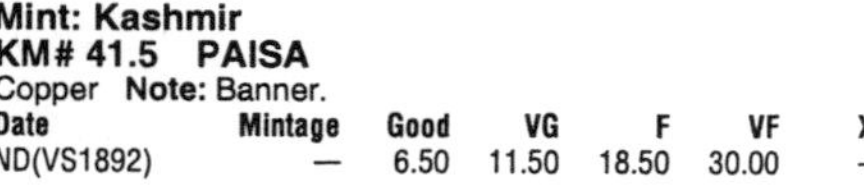

Date	Mintage	Good	VG	F	VF	XF
ND(VS1892)	—	6.50	11.50	18.50	30.00	—

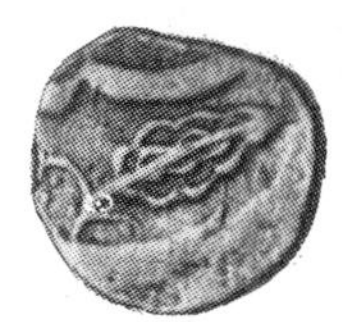

Mint: Kashmir
KM# 41.6 PAISA
Copper

Date	Mintage	Good	VG	F	VF	XF
ND(VS1897)	—	4.50	7.50	12.50	20.00	—

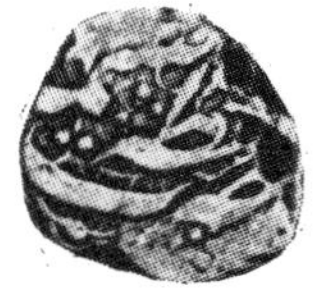

Mint: Kashmir
KM# 41.7 PAISA
Copper **Note:** Sikki Nanak Shahi

Date	Mintage	Good	VG	F	VF	XF
ND(1823-48)	—	4.50	7.50	12.50	20.00	—

Mint: Kashmir
KM# 42 PAISA
Copper

Date	Mintage	Good	VG	F	VF	XF
VS189x (1842)	—	5.50	9.00	15.00	25.00	—

Mint: Lahore
KM# 60 PAISA
Copper **Note:** Dar-us-Sultanat

Date	Mintage	Good	VG	F	VF	XF
VS1880 (1823)	—	4.50	7.50	12.50	20.00	—
VS1881 (1824)	—	4.50	7.50	12.50	20.00	—

Mint: Multan
KM# 77 PAISA
Copper

Date	Mintage	Good	VG	F	VF	XF
VS1875 (1818)	—	4.50	7.50	12.50	20.00	—
VS1878 (1821)	—	4.50	7.50	12.50	20.00	—

Note: Also found with botched or fictitious dates

Mint: Uncertain Mint
KM# A99 PAISA
Copper **Obv:** Leaf symbol overstruck on Afghanistan Durrani Falus

Date	Mintage	Good	VG	F	VF	XF
ND(1834-52)	—	4.00	6.00	10.00	18.00	—

Mint: Uncertain Mint
KM# B99 PAISA
Copper **Note:** Overstruck.

Date	Mintage	Good	VG	F	VF	XF
ND(1834-52)	—	2.00	4.00	8.00	12.00	—

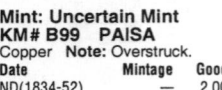

Mint: Amritsar
KM# 6 2 PAISE
Copper

Date	Mintage	Good	VG	F	VF	XF
VS1880 (1823)	—	5.00	8.00	15.00	25.00	—

Mint: Amritsar
KM# 8.1 2 PAISE
20.0000 g., Copper **Obv:** Leaf in center

Date	Mintage	Good	VG	F	VF	XF
VS1885 (1828)	—	18.00	35.00	55.00	85.00	—

Mint: Amritsar
KM# 8.2 2 PAISE
20.0000 g., Copper **Obv:** Leaf in center **Shape:** Octagon

Date	Mintage	Good	VG	F	VF	XF
ND(1822-30)	—	18.00	35.00	55.00	85.00	—

Mint: Amritsar
KM# 8.3 2 PAISE
20.0000 g., Copper **Obv:** Leaf in center **Shape:** Diamond

Date	Mintage	Good	VG	F	VF	XF
VS1885 (1828)	—	18.00	35.00	55.00	85.00	—

Mint: Amritsar
KM# 8.4 2 PAISE
20.0000 g., Copper **Obv:** Leaf in center

Date	Mintage	Good	VG	F	VF	XF
VS1885 (1828)	—	18.00	35.00	55.00	85.00	—

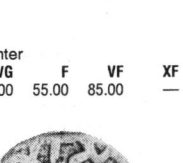

Mint: Amritsar
KM# 8.5 2 PAISE
20.0000 g., Copper **Obv:** Leaf in center **Rev:** Cross

Date	Mintage	Good	VG	F	VF	XF
ND(1822-30)	—	18.00	35.00	55.00	85.00	—

Mint: Multan
KM# 78 2 PAISE
Copper

Date	Mintage	Good	VG	F	VF	XF
VS1904 (1847)	—	40.00	65.00	100	150	—

Mint: Amritsar
KM# 9.1 MULTIPLE PAISE
Copper **Obv:** Leaf in center **Note:** Weight varies: 38.00-40.00 grams.

Date	Mintage	Good	VG	F	VF	XF
VS1885 (1828)	—	135	225	350	500	—

Mint: Amritsar
KM# 9.2 MULTIPLE PAISE
Copper **Obv:** Leaf in center **Rev:** Banner **Note:** Weight varies: 38.00-40.00 grams.

Date	Mintage	Good	VG	F	VF	XF
ND(1828)	—	135	225	350	500	—

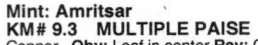

Mint: Amritsar
KM# 9.3 MULTIPLE PAISE
Copper **Obv:** Leaf in center **Rev:** Cross **Note:** Weight varies: 38.00-40.00 grams.

Date	Mintage	Good	VG	F	VF	XF
ND(1828)	—	135	225	350	500	—

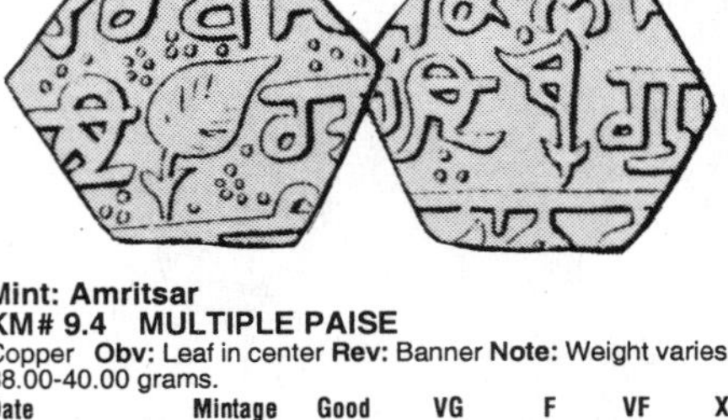

Mint: Amritsar
KM# 9.4 MULTIPLE PAISE
Copper **Obv:** Leaf in center **Rev:** Banner **Note:** Weight varies: 38.00-40.00 grams.

Date	Mintage	Good	VG	F	VF	XF
ND(1828)	—	135	225	350	500	—

Mint: Amritsar
KM# 9.5 MULTIPLE PAISE
Copper **Obv:** Leaf in center **Rev:** Trident

Date	Mintage	Good	VG	F	VF	XF
VS188(5) (1885)	—	135	225	350	500	—

Mint: Amritsar
KM# 10.1 FALUS
Copper **Note:** Third Copper Series. Persian and Gurmukhi legends.

Date	Mintage	Good	VG	F	VF	XF
ND(1843-44)	—	6.00	10.00	15.00	25.00	—

Note: Variety with "DEVKI" in Gurmukhi

Mint: Amritsar
KM# 10.2 FALUS
Copper **Note:** Third Copper Series. Persian and Gurmukhi legends.

Date	Mintage	Good	VG	F	VF	XF
VS1900 (1843)	—	2.75	5.00	7.50	12.50	—
VS1901 (1844)	—	2.75	5.00	7.50	12.50	—
ND(1843-44)	—	2.75	5.00	7.50	12.50	—

Mint: Amritsar
KM# 10.3 FALUS
Copper **Note:** Third Copper Series. Persian and Gurmukhi legends.

Date	Mintage	Good	VG	F	VF	XF
ND(1843-44)	—	7.00	12.00	20.00	35.00	—

Mint: Amritsar
KM# 10.4 FALUS
Copper **Note:** Third Copper Series. Persian and Gurmukhi legends.

Date	Mintage	Good	VG	F	VF	XF
ND(1843-44)	—	7.00	12.00	20.00	35.00	—

Mint: Amritsar
KM# 10.5 FALUS
Copper **Rev:** Four-petal flower **Note:** Third Copper Series. Persian and Gurmukhi legends.

Date	Mintage	Good	VG	F	VF	XF
ND(1843-44)	—	3.00	5.00	8.00	14.00	—

Mint: Peshawar
KM# 93.1 FALUS
Copper **Rev:** Persian legend

Date	Mintage	Good	VG	F	VF	XF
AH1248 (1832)	—	3.00	5.50	9.00	15.00	—
AH1249 (1833)	—	3.00	5.50	9.00	15.00	—

Mint: Peshawar
KM# 93.2 FALUS
Copper **Obv:** Leaf, mint name **Rev. Legend:** "Shah"

Date	Mintage	Good	VG	F	VF	XF
AH-//14 (1832)	—	3.50	6.00	10.00	16.50	—

Mint: Peshawar
KM# 94 FALUS
Copper **Rev:** Gurmukhi legend and Nagari date

Date	Mintage	Good	VG	F	VF	XF
VS1891 (1834)	—	5.50	9.00	15.00	25.00	—

Mint: Peshawar
KM# 94A FALUS
Copper **Obv:** Gurmukhi legend **Rev:** Leaf, Persian legend

Date	Mintage	Good	VG	F	VF	XF
ND(1834-35)	—	10.00	20.00	30.00	50.00	—

Mint: Peshawar
KM# 95 FALUS
Copper

Date	Mintage	Good	VG	F	VF	XF
ND(1834-35)	—	3.00	5.50	9.00	15.00	—

Note: No date or date off flan

Mint: Peshawar
KM# 96 FALUS
Copper

Date	Mintage	Good	VG	F	VF	XF
AH126x (1844)	—	3.00	5.50	9.00	15.00	—

Mint: Amritsar
KM# 17.1 1/8 RUPEE
Silver **Rev:** Dated VS1844 **Note:** Weight varies: 1.34-1.45 grams.

Date	Mintage	VG	F	VF	XF	Unc
VS(18)95 (1838)		28.00	50.00	80.00	120	—

Mint: Amritsar
KM# 17.2 1/8 RUPEE
Silver **Rev:** Dated VS1845 **Note:** Weight varies: 1.34-1.45 grams.

Date	Mintage	VG	F	VF	XF	Unc
VS(18)95 (1838)	—	28.00	50.00	80.00	120	—
VS(18)99 (1842)	—	28.00	50.00	80.00	120	—
VS1900 (1843)	—	28.00	50.00	80.00	120	—
VS1903 (1846)	—	28.00	50.00	80.00	120	—

Mint: Amritsar
KM# 18.1 1/4 RUPEE
Silver, 15 mm. **Note:** Weight varies: 2.68-2.90 grams.

Date	Mintage	VG	F	VF	XF	Unc
VS(18)71 (1814)	—	15.00	25.00	45.00	90.00	—
VS(18)79 (1822)	—	17.50	30.00	50.00	100	—
VS(18)80 (1823)	—	15.00	25.00	45.00	90.00	—
VS(18)83 (1826)	—	15.00	25.00	45.00	90.00	—

Mint: Amritsar
KM# 18.2 1/4 RUPEE
Silver, 15 mm. **Rev:** Dated: VS1884 **Note:** Weight varies: 2.68-2.90 grams.

Date	Mintage	VG	F	VF	XF	Unc
VS(18)85 (1828)	—	12.50	20.00	40.00	80.00	—
VS(18)86 (1829)	—	12.50	20.00	40.00	80.00	—
VS(18)89 (1832)	—	12.50	20.00	40.00	80.00	—
VS(18)92 (1835)	—	12.50	20.00	40.00	80.00	—
VS(18)95 (1838)	—	12.50	20.00	40.00	80.00	—
VS(18)97 (1840)	—	12.50	20.00	40.00	80.00	—

Mint: Amritsar
KM# 18.3 1/4 RUPEE
Silver, 15 mm. **Rev:** Dated: VS1885 **Note:** Weight varies: 2.68-2.90 grams.

Date	Mintage	VG	F	VF	XF	Unc
VS(18)93 (1836)	—	12.50	20.00	40.00	80.00	—
VS(18)94 (1837)	—	12.50	20.00	40.00	80.00	—
VS(18)95 (1838)	—	12.50	20.00	40.00	80.00	—
VS(18)97 (1840)	—	12.50	20.00	40.00	80.00	—
VS(18)98 (1841)	—	12.50	20.00	40.00	80.00	—
VS(18)99 (1842)	—	12.50	20.00	40.00	80.00	—
VS1900 (1843)	—	12.50	20.00	40.00	80.00	—
VS1901 (1844)	—	12.50	20.00	40.00	80.00	—
VS1902 (1845)	—	12.50	20.00	40.00	80.00	—
VS1903 (1846)	—	12.50	20.00	40.00	80.00	—
VS1904 (1847)	—	12.50	20.00	40.00	80.00	—

Mint: Kashmir
KM# 43 1/4 RUPEE
2.7500 g., Silver

Date	Mintage	Good	VG	F	VF	XF
VS1898 (1841) Rare		—	—	—	—	—
ND(1819-48)		—	—	—	—	—

Mint: Amritsar
KM# 19.1 1/2 RUPEE
Silver **Rev:** Actual date **Note:** Weight varies: 5.30-5.60 grams.

Date	Mintage	VG	F	VF	XF	Unc
VS1871 (1814)	—	55.00	90.00	150	225	—
VS1880 (1823)	—	55.00	90.00	150	225	—
VS1883 (1826)	—	55.00	90.00	150	225	—

Mint: Amritsar
KM# 19.2 1/2 RUPEE
Silver **Rev:** Dated: VS1884 **Note:** Weight varies: 5.30-5.60 grams.

Date	Mintage	VG	F	VF	XF	Unc
VS(18)85 (1828)		55.00	90.00	150	225	—
VS(18)86 (1829)		55.00	90.00	150	225	—
VS(18)89 (1832)		55.00	90.00	150	225	—
VS(18)92 (1835)		55.00	90.00	150	225	—
VS(18)93 (1836)		55.00	90.00	150	225	—
VS(18)95 (1838)		55.00	90.00	150	225	—
VS(18)98 (1841)		55.00	90.00	150	225	—
VS(18)99 (1842)		55.00	90.00	150	225	—

Mint: Amritsar
KM# 19.3a 1/2 RUPEE
Silver **Obv:** VS date and various symbols **Rev:** Dated: VS1885 **Note:** Weight varies: 5.30-5.60 grams.

Date	Mintage	VG	F	VF	XF	Unc
VS(18)93 (1836)	—	55.00	90.00	150	225	—
VS(18)94 (1837)	—	55.00	90.00	150	225	—
VS(18)95 (1838)	—	55.00	90.00	150	225	—
VS(18)96 (1839)	—	55.00	90.00	150	225	—
VS(18)97 (1840)	—	55.00	90.00	150	225	—

Mint: Amritsar
KM# 19.3b 1/2 RUPEE
Silver **Obv:** VS date and trident **Rev:** Dated: VS1885 **Note:** Weight varies: 5.30-5.60 grams.

Date	Mintage	VG	F	VF	XF	Unc
VS(18)98 (1841)	—	55.00	90.00	150	225	—
VS(18)99 (1842)	—	55.00	90.00	150	225	—

Mint: Amritsar
KM# 19.3c 1/2 RUPEE
Silver **Obv:** VS date and Chhatra (umbrella) **Rev:** Dated: VS1885 **Note:** Weight varies: 5.30-5.60 grams.

Date	Mintage	VG	F	VF	XF	Unc
VS1900 (1843)	—	55.00	90.00	150	225	—
VS1901 (1844)	—	55.00	90.00	150	225	—
VS1902 (1845)	—	55.00	90.00	150	225	—

Mint: Amritsar
KM# 19.3d 1/2 RUPEE
Silver **Obv:** VS date and Gurmukhi "State" **Rev:** Dated: VS1885 **Note:** Weight varies: 5.30-5.60 grams.

Date	Mintage	VG	F	VF	XF	Unc
VS1903 (1846)	—	55.00	90.00	150	225	—
VS1904 (1847)	—	55.00	90.00	150	225	—
VS1905 (1848)	—	55.00	90.00	150	225	—

Mint: Amritsar
KM# 19.4 1/2 RUPEE
Silver **Obv:** Gurmuki legend **Obv. Legend:** "Om" **Rev:** Dated: VS1885 **Note:** Weight varies: 5.30-5.60 grams.

Date	Mintage	VG	F	VF	XF	Unc
VS(18)85/96 (1839)	—	55.00	90.00	150	225	—
VS(18)99 (1840)	—	55.00	90.00	150	225	—

Mint: Amritsar
KM# 19.5 1/2 RUPEE
Silver **Obv:** Flowers **Note:** Weight varies: 5.30-5.60 grams.

Date	Mintage	VG	F	VF	XF	Unc
VS1902 (1845)	—	55.00	90.00	150	225	—

Mint: Kashmir
KM# 44 1/2 RUPEE
5.5000 g., Silver

Date	Mintage	Good	VG	F	VF	XF
VS1898 (1841)	—	10.00	25.00	45.00	75.00	125
ND(1819-48) Rare	—	—	—	—	—	—

Mint: Lahore
KM# 62 1/2 RUPEE
Silver, 18 mm. **Note:** Weight varies: 5.50-5.60 grams. Struck at Lahore Mint.

Date	Mintage	VG	F	VF	XF	Unc
VS1858 (1801)	—	18.50	30.00	50.00	85.00	—
VS1864 (1807)	—	18.50	30.00	50.00	85.00	—
VS1889 (1832)	—	18.50	30.00	50.00	85.00	—

Mint: Multan
KM# 81 1/2 RUPEE
Silver

Date	Mintage	VG	F	VF	XF	Unc
VS1876 (1819)	—	135	225	350	500	—
VS1877 (1820)	—	135	225	350	500	—
VS1885 (1828)	—	135	225	350	500	—

Mint: Peshawar
KM# 97 1/2 RUPEE
Silver **Note:** Weight varies: 4.10-4.25 grams.

Date	Mintage	Good	VG	F	VF	XF
VS1892 (1835) Rare	—	—	—	—	—	—

Mint: Amritsar
KM# 20.1 RUPEE
Silver **Rev:** Mint name and date **Note:** Double lines below dates exist for some 1869, 1870, and 1871 coins and are considered rare. Mint symbols seem to change frequently in this series.

Date	Mintage	VG	F	VF	XF	Unc
VS1858 (1801)	—	7.00	11.00	18.00	30.00	—
VS1859 (1802)	—	7.00	11.00	18.00	30.00	—
VS1860 (1803)	—	5.50	9.00	15.00	25.00	—
VS1806 (1803) Error for 1860	—	20.00	28.00	40.00	55.00	—
VS1861 (1804)	—	5.50	9.00	15.00	25.00	—
VS1862 (1805)	—	5.50	9.00	15.00	25.00	—
VS1863 (1806)	—	5.50	9.00	15.00	25.00	—
VS1864 (1807)	—	5.50	9.00	15.00	25.00	—
VS1865 (1808)	—	5.50	9.00	15.00	25.00	—
VS1866 (1809)	—	5.50	9.00	15.00	25.00	—
VS1867 (1810)	—	5.50	9.00	15.00	25.00	—
VS1868 (1811)	—	5.50	9.00	15.00	25.00	—
VS1869 (1812)	—	5.50	9.00	15.00	25.00	—
VS1870 (1813)	—	20.00	35.00	60.00	100	—
VS1871 (1814)	—	15.00	30.00	50.00	80.00	—
VS1872 (1815)	—	5.50	9.00	15.00	25.00	—
VS1873 (1816)	—	5.50	9.00	15.00	25.00	—
VS1874 (1817)	—	5.50	9.00	15.00	25.00	—
VS1875 (1818)	—	5.50	9.00	15.00	25.00	—
VS1876 (1819)	—	5.50	9.00	15.00	25.00	—
VS1877 (1820)	—	5.50	9.00	15.00	25.00	—
VS1878 (1821)	—	5.50	9.00	15.00	25.00	—
VS1879 (1822)	—	5.50	9.00	15.00	25.00	—
VS1880 (1823)	—	5.50	9.00	15.00	25.00	—
VS1881 (1824)	—	5.50	9.00	15.00	25.00	—
VS1882 (1825)	—	5.50	9.00	15.00	25.00	—
VS1883 (1826)		5.50	9.00	15.00	25.00	—
VS1884 (1827)	—	5.50	9.00	15.00	25.00	—
VS1885 (1828)	—	175	300	450	600	—
VS1886 (1829)	—	175	300	450	600	—
VS1888 (1831)	—	175	300	450	600	—
VS1889 (1832)	—	175	300	450	600	—

Mint: Amritsar
KM# 20.1a RUPEE
Silver **Rev:** "Dar Jhang" left of leaf **Note:** Weight varies: 11.20-12.00 grams.

Date	Mintage	VG	F	VF	XF	Unc
VS1873 (1816)	—	325	500	700	1,000	—
VS1874 (1817)	—	250	425	600	850	—

Note: Some rare varieties exist with either a trident below the leaf on reverse or a circular symbol

Mint: Amritsar
KM# A20.2 RUPEE
Silver **Obv:** Second legend arrangement **Rev:** Katar **Note:** Weight varies 10.60-11.20 grams.

Date	Mintage	VG	F	VF	XF	Unc
VS1859 (1802)	—	11.50	18.00	30.00	50.00	—
VS1860 (1803)	—	11.50	18.00	30.00	50.00	—
VS1862 (1805)	—	11.50	18.00	30.00	50.00	—
VS1863 (1806)	—	11.50	18.00	30.00	50.00	—
VS1864 (1807)	—	11.50	18.00	30.00	50.00	—
VS1865 (1808)	—	11.50	18.00	30.00	50.00	—

Mint: Amritsar
KM# 20.2a RUPEE
Silver **Obv:** Five-dot symbol, sprig at lower left **Rev:** Dotted leaf **Note:** Weight varies: 11.20-12.00 grams.

Date	Mintage	VG	F	VF	XF	Unc
VS1858 (1801)	—	13.00	19.00	25.00	35.00	—

Mint: Amritsar
KM# 20.2b RUPEE
Silver **Obv:** Double oval **Rev:** Dotted leaf **Note:** Weight varies: 11.20-12.00 grams.

Date	Mintage	VG	F	VF	XF	Unc
VS1858 (1801)	—	11.50	17.50	23.50	33.50	—
VS1859 (1802)	—	11.50	17.50	23.50	33.50	—

Note: Also exists without special mark on obverse

Mint: Amritsar
KM# 20.2c RUPEE
Silver **Obv:** Hand **Rev:** Dotted leaf **Note:** Weight varies: 11.20-12.00 grams.

Date	Mintage	VG	F	VF	XF	Unc
VS1859 (1802)	—	11.50	17.50	23.50	33.50	—

Mint: Amritsar
KM# 20.2d RUPEE
Silver **Obv:** Five-petal flower **Rev:** Dotted leaf **Note:** Weight varies: 11.20-12.00 grams.

Date	Mintage	VG	F	VF	XF	Unc
ND(1801-06)	—	15.00	25.00	40.00	60.00	—

Mint: Amritsar
KM# 20.3 RUPEE
Silver **Obv:** Fish at lower left **Rev:** Leaf **Note:** Weight varies: 11.20-12.00 grams.

Date	Mintage	VG	F	VF	XF	Unc
VS1861 (1804)	—	15.00	35.00	40.00	60.00	—

Mint: Amritsar
KM# 20.4 RUPEE
Silver **Rev:** Branches with berries **Note:** The "Mora" rupee. Weight varies: 11.20-12.00 grams.

Date	Mintage	VG	F	VF	XF	Unc
VS1858 (1801)	—	17.50	30.00	50.00	80.00	—
VS1859 (1802)	—	17.50	30.00	50.00	80.00	—
VS1860 (1803)	—	17.50	30.00	50.00	80.00	—
VS1861 (1804)	—	12.50	18.00	30.00	50.00	—
VS1862 (1805)	—	12.50	18.00	30.00	50.00	—
VS1863 (1806)	—	17.50	30.00	50.00	80.00	—

Mint: Amritsar
KM# 20.5 RUPEE
Silver **Rev:** Sprig with two leaves **Note:** Weight varies: 11.20-12.00 grams.

Date	Mintage	VG	F	VF	XF	Unc
VS1862 (1805)	—	25.00	45.00	75.00	120	—
VS1863 (1806)	—	25.00	45.00	75.00	120	—

Mint: Amritsar
KM# 20.6 RUPEE
Silver **Rev:** Symbol said to be a mirror **Note:** The "Arisi" rupee. Weight varies: 11.20-12.00 grams.

Date	Mintage	VG	F	VF	XF	Unc
VS1862 (1805)	—	35.00	60.00	100	150	—
VS1863 (1806)	—	35.00	60.00	100	150	—

Mint: Amritsar
KM# 21.1 RUPEE
Silver **Obv:** Partial or full actual dates **Rev:** VS1884 fixed

Date	Mintage	VG	F	VF	XF	Unc
VS(18)85 (1828)	—	5.50	9.00	15.00	25.00	—
VS(18)86 (1829)	—	5.50	9.00	15.00	25.00	—
VS(18)87 (1830)	—	5.50	9.00	15.00	25.00	—
VS(18)88 (1831)	—	5.50	9.00	15.00	25.00	—
VS(18)89 (1832)	—	5.50	9.00	15.00	25.00	—
VS(18)90 (1833)	—	5.50	9.00	15.00	25.00	—
VS(18)91 (1834)	—	5.5	9.00	15.00	25.00	—
VS(18)92 (1835)	—	5.50	9.00	15.00	25.00	—
VS(18)93 (1836)	—	5.50	9.00	15.00	25.00	—
VS(18)95 (1838)	—	5.50	9.00	15.00	25.00	—

Mint: Amritsar
KM# 21.2 RUPEE
Silver

Date	Mintage	VG	F	VF	XF	Unc
VS(18)95 (1838)	—	—	—	—	—	—
VS(18)96 (1839)	—	9.00	15.00	25.00	40.00	—
VS(18)97 (1840)	—	5.50	9.00	15.00	25.00	—
VS(18)98/7 (1841)	—	10.00	16.50	27.50	45.00	—
VS(18)98 (1841)	—	5.50	9.00	15.00	25.00	—
VS(18)99 (1842)	—	5.50	9.00	15.00	25.00	—
VS1900 (1843)	—	5.50	9.00	15.00	25.00	—
VS1901 (1844)	—	5.50	9.00	15.00	25.00	—
VS1902 (1845)	—	5.50	9.00	16.50	25.00	—
VS1903 (1846)	—	5.50	9.00	15.00	25.00	—
VS1904 (1847)	—	5.50	9.00	15.00	25.00	—
VS1905 (1848)	—	8.00	13.50	22.50	37.50	—

Mint: Amritsar
KM# 22A RUPEE
Silver **Rev:** Dated: VS1888

Date	Mintage	VG	F	VF	XF	Unc
VS1904 (1847)	—	100	165	275	400	—

Mint: Amritsar
KM# 22.1 RUPEE
Silver **Obv:** Partial actual dates **Rev:** VS1885 fixed

Date	Mintage	VG	F	VF	XF	Unc
VS(18)93 (1836)	—	7.50	12.50	20.00	32.50	—
VS(18)94 (1837)	—	7.50	12.50	20.00	32.50	—
VS(18)95 (1838)	—	5.50	9.00	15.00	25.00	—
VS(18)96 (1839)	—	5.50	9.00	15.00	25.00	—
VS(18)97 (1840)	—	5.50	9.00	15.00	25.00	—
VS(18)98 (1841)	—	5.50	9.00	15.00	25.00	—
VS1903 (1846)	—	5.50	9.00	15.00	25.00	—

Mint: Amritsar
KM# 22.2 RUPEE
Silver **Rev:** Katar

Date	Mintage	VG	F	VF	XF	Unc
VS(18)93 (1836)	—	7.50	12.50	21.50	35.00	—
VS(18)94 (1837)	—	7.50	12.50	21.50	35.00	—
VS(18)98 (1841)	—	5.50	9.00	15.00	25.00	—

Mint: Amritsar
KM# 22.4 RUPEE
Silver **Obv:** Nagari "Om"

Date	Mintage	VG	F	VF	XF	Unc
VS(18)97 (1840)	—	8.50	14.00	23.50	40.00	—

Mint: Amritsar
KM# 22.5 RUPEE
Silver **Obv:** Trisul (trident)

Date	Mintage	VG	F	VF	XF	Unc
VS(18)98 (1841)	—	8.00	13.50	21.50	35.00	—
VS(18)99 (1842)	—	8.00	13.50	21.50	35.00	—

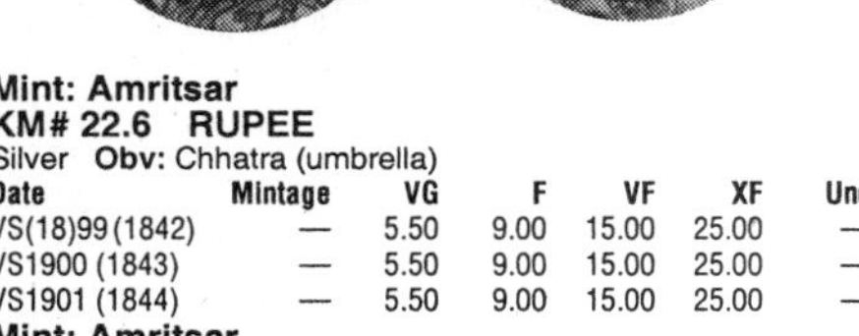

Mint: Amritsar
KM# 22.6 RUPEE
Silver **Obv:** Chhatra (umbrella)

Date	Mintage	VG	F	VF	XF	Unc
VS(18)99 (1842)	—	5.50	9.00	15.00	25.00	—
VS1900 (1843)	—	5.50	9.00	15.00	25.00	—
VS1901 (1844)	—	5.50	9.00	15.00	25.00	—

Mint: Amritsar
KM# 22.7 RUPEE
Silver **Obv:** Three-lobed leaf **Note:** Similar to 1/2 Rupee, KM#19.5.

Date	Mintage	VG	F	VF	XF	Unc
VS1902 (1845)	—	18.50	30.00	50.00	80.00	—

Mint: Amritsar
KM# 22.8 RUPEE
Silver **Obv:** Pataka (banner)

Date	Mintage	VG	F	VF	XF	Unc
VS1902 (1845)	—	7.50	12.00	20.00	35.00	—
VS1903 (1846)	—	7.50	12.00	20.00	35.00	—

Mint: Amritsar
KM# 22.9 RUPEE
Silver **Obv:** Gurmakhi "State" beneath chhatra

Date	Mintage	VG	F	VF	XF	Unc
VS1903 (1846)	—	7.50	12.00	20.00	35.00	—
VS1904 (1847)	—	7.50	12.00	20.00	35.00	—
VS1905 (1848)	—	7.50	12.00	20.00	35.00	—

Mint: Amritsar
KM# 22.10 RUPEE
Silver **Obv:** Lazy W beneath chhatra

Date	Mintage	VG	F	VF	XF	Unc
VS1905 (1848)	—	12.50	20.00	35.00	60.00	—
VS1906 (1849)	—	25.00	40.00	65.00	110	—

Mint: Amritsar
KM# 22.11 RUPEE
Silver **Obv:** Nagari "Shiva"

Date	Mintage	VG	F	VF	XF	Unc
VS1905 (1848)	—	12.50	20.00	32.50	55.00	—

Mint: Amritsar
KM# 22.12 RUPEE
Silver **Obv:** Dot cluster **Rev:** Dated: VS1884 **Note:** Mule.

Date	Mintage	VG	F	VF	XF	Unc
VS1905 (1848)	—	15.00	25.00	42.50	70.00	—

Mint: Kashmir
KM# 45 RUPEE
10.7000 g., Silver **Obv:** Gurmakhi legend **Rev:** Gurmakhi legend

Date	Mintage	VG	F	VF	XF	Unc
VS1892 (1835) Rare	—	—	—	—	—	—

Mint: Kashmir
KM# 45a RUPEE
7.6000 g., Silver **Obv:** "RAM" in Gurmakhi legend

Date	Mintage	VG	F	VF	XF	Unc
VS1892 (1835) Rare	—	—	—	—	—	—

Mint: Kashmir
KM# 46.1 RUPEE
Silver **Obv:** Flower spray **Rev:** Date to right of leaf **Note:** Weight varies: 11.00-11.30 grams.

Date	Mintage	VG	F	VF	XF	Unc
VS1876 (1819)	—	12.50	25.00	40.00	60.00	—

Mint: Kashmir
KM# 46.2 RUPEE
Silver **Obv:** Flower spray **Rev:** Date divided horizontally **Note:** Weight varies: 11.00-11.30 grams.

Date	Mintage	VG	F	VF	XF	Unc
VS1876 (1819)	—	12.50	25.00	40.00	60.00	—

Mint: Kashmir
KM# 46.3 RUPEE
Silver **Obv:** Flower spray **Rev:** Legend divided vertically, date at top **Note:** Weight varies: 11.00-11.30 grams.

Date	Mintage	VG	F	VF	XF	Unc
VS1877 (1820)	—	12.50	25.00	40.00	60.00	—
VS1878 (1821)	—	12.50	25.00	40.00	60.00	—

Mint: Kashmir
KM# 46.4 RUPEE
Silver **Obv:** Gurmakhi "Hara" **Note:** Weight varies: 11.00-11.30 grams.

Date	Mintage	VG	F	VF	XF	Unc
VS1878 (1821)	—	12.50	25.00	40.00	60.00	—
VS1879 (1822)	—	12.50	25.00	40.00	60.00	—

 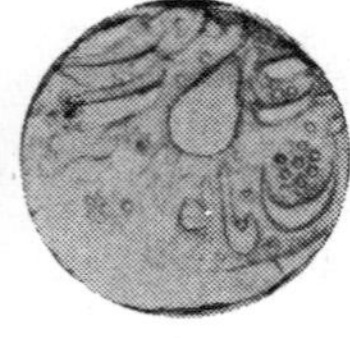

Mint: Kashmir
KM# 46.5 RUPEE
Silver **Obv:** Nagari "Om Sri" **Note:** Weight varies: 11.00-11.30 grams.

Date	Mintage	VG	F	VF	XF	Unc
VS1879 (1822)	—	12.50	25.00	40.00	60.00	—

Mint: Kashmir
KM# 46.6 RUPEE
Silver **Obv:** Nagari "Haraji" or "Hara" **Note:** Weight varies: 11.00-11.30 grams.

Date	Mintage	VG	F	VF	XF	Unc
VS1879 (1822)	—	12.50	25.00	40.00	60.00	—

Mint: Kashmir
KM# 46.7 RUPEE
Silver **Obv:** Floral symbol, four-pointed star **Note:** Weight varies: 11.00-11.30 grams.

Date	Mintage	VG	F	VF	XF	Unc
VS1881 (1824)	—	12.50	25.00	40.00	60.00	—

Mint: Kashmir
KM# 46.8 RUPEE
Silver **Obv:** Banner **Note:** Weight varies: 11.00-11.30 grams.

Date	Mintage	VG	F	VF	XF	Unc
VS1881 (1824)	—	12.50	25.00	40.00	60.00	—
VS1882 (1825)	—	12.50	25.00	40.00	60.00	—
VS1883 (1826)	—	12.50	25.00	40.00	60.00	—

Mint: Kashmir
KM# 46.9 RUPEE
Silver **Obv:** Flower **Note:** Weight varies: 11.00-11.30 grams.

Date	Mintage	VG	F	VF	XF	Unc
VS1883 (1826)	—	12.50	25.00	40.00	60.00	—

Mint: Kashmir
KM# 46.9A RUPEE
Silver **Obv:** Flower, Persian "Kaf" **Note:** Weight varies: 11.00-11.30 grams.

Date	Mintage	VG	F	VF	XF	Unc
VS1883 (1826)	—	12.50	25.00	40.00	60.00	—

Mint: Kashmir
KM# 46.10 RUPEE
Silver **Obv:** Persian "Ram" and "Kaf" **Note:** Weight varies: 11.00-11.30 grams.

Date	Mintage	Good	VG	F	VF	XF
ND(1819-35)	—	5.00	12.50	25.00	40.00	60.00

Mint: Kashmir
KM# 46.11 RUPEE
Silver **Obv:** Persian "Kaf" **Note:** Weight varies: 11.00-11.30 grams.

Date	Mintage	VG	F	VF	XF	Unc
VS1885 (1828)	—	12.50	25.00	40.00	60.00	—
VS1887 (1830)	—	12.50	25.00	40.00	60.00	—

Mint: Kashmir
KM# 46.12 RUPEE
Silver **Obv:** Persian "Kaf" **Rev:** Cross and letter form "I" **Note:** Weight varies: 11.00-11.30 grams.

Date	Mintage	VG	F	VF	XF	Unc
VS1886 (1829)	—	12.50	25.00	40.00	60.00	—

Mint: Kashmir
KM# 46.13 RUPEE
Silver **Rev:** Letter in field, "Bha" **Note:** Weight varies: 11.00-11.30 grams.

Date	Mintage	VG	F	VF	XF	Unc
VS1887 (1830)	—	12.50	25.00	40.00	60.00	—
VS1888 (1831)	—	12.50	25.00	40.00	60.00	—

Mint: Kashmir
KM# 46.14 RUPEE
Silver **Rev:** Sword across leaf stem, "Sri Ram" in Persian **Note:** Weight varies: 11.00-11.30 grams.

Date	Mintage	VG	F	VF	XF	Unc
VS1880 (1823)	—	35.00	55.00	85.00	120	—

Mint: Kashmir
KM# 46.15 RUPEE
Silver **Obv:** Sprig and "Kaf" **Note:** Weight varies: 11.00-11.30 grams.

Date	Mintage	VG	F	VF	XF	Unc
VS1886 (1829)	—	12.50	25.00	40.00	60.00	—
VS1887 (1830)	—	—	25.00	40.00	60.00	—

Mint: Kashmir
KM# 46.16 RUPEE
Silver **Obv:** Sprig and "Kaf" **Note:** Weight varies: 11.00-11.30 grams.

Date	Mintage	VG	F	VF	XF	Unc
VS1887 (1830)	—	12.50	25.00	40.00	60.00	—

Mint: Kashmir
KM# 46.17 RUPEE
Silver **Obv:** Face and "Kaf" **Rev:** Horizontal line on leaf **Note:** Weight varies: 11.00-11.30 grams.

Date	Mintage	VG	F	VF	XF	Unc
VS1884 (1827)	—	12.50	25.00	40.00	60.00	—

Mint: Kashmir
KM# 46.18 RUPEE
Silver **Obv:** Star and "Kaf" **Rev:** Horizontal line on leaf **Note:** Weight varies: 11.00-11.30 grams.

Date	Mintage	VG	F	VF	XF	Unc
VS1884 (1827)	—	12.50	25.00	40.00	60.00	—

Mint: Kashmir
KM# 46.19 RUPEE

Silver **Obv:** Trident and "Kaf" **Note:** Weight varies: 11.00-11.30 grams.

Date	Mintage	VG	F	VF	XF	Unc
VS1886 (1829)	—	12.50	25.00	40.00	60.00	—

Mint: Kashmir
KM# 48.1 RUPEE

Silver **Obv:** Face and "Kaf" **Rev:** Date in circle **Note:** Weight varies: 11.00-11.30 grams.

Date	Mintage	VG	F	VF	XF	Unc
VS1884 (1827)	—	55.00	90.00	140	200	—

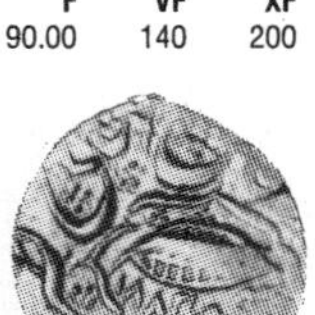

Mint: Kashmir
KM# 48.2 RUPEE

Silver **Rev:** Leaf and date within quatrefoil **Note:** Weight varies: 11.00-11.30 grams.

Date	Mintage	VG	F	VF	XF	Unc
VS1884 (1827)	—	55.00	90.00	140	200	—

Mint: Kashmir
KM# 49 RUPEE

Silver **Obv:** Date **Rev:** Katar **Note:** Weight varies: 11.00-11.30 grams.

Date	Mintage	VG	F	VF	XF	Unc
VS1889 (1832)	—	10.00	16.50	27.50	45.00	—
VS1890 (1833)	—	10.00	16.50	27.50	45.00	—

Mint: Kashmir
KM# A50 RUPEE

8.5000 g., Silver **Rev:** Lion right of leaf and Katar

Date	Mintage	VG	F	VF	XF	Unc
VS1890 (1833) Rare	—	—	—	—	—	—

Mint: Kashmir
KM# B50 RUPEE

Silver **Obv:** Sword through circle **Rev:** Date at top **Note:** Weight varies: 11.00-11.30 grams.

Date	Mintage	VG	F	VF	XF	Unc
VS1891 (1834)	—	21.50	35.00	60.00	100	—

Mint: Kashmir
KM# C50 RUPEE

8.5000 g., Silver **Rev:** Date divided by leaf, Katar at left

Date	Mintage	VG	F	VF	XF	Unc
VS1891 (1834)	—	15.00	25.00	42.50	70.00	—

Mint: Kashmir
KM# 50 RUPEE

Silver **Obv:** Sword through circle

Date	Mintage	VG	F	VF	XF	Unc
VS1892 (1835)	—	8.50	13.50	21.50	35.00	—
VS1893 (1836)	—	8.50	13.50	21.50	35.00	—

Mint: Kashmir
KM# 51 RUPEE

Silver **Rev:** Outlined leaf

Date	Mintage	VG	F	VF	XF	Unc
VS1893 (1836)	—	15.00	25.00	40.00	65.00	—
VS1894 (1837)	—	15.00	25.00	40.00	65.00	—
VS1895 (1838)	—	15.00	25.00	40.00	65.00	—
VS1896 (1839)	—	15.00	25.00	40.00	65.00	—
VS1897 (1840)	—	15.00	25.00	40.00	65.00	—
VS1898 (1841)	—	15.00	25.00	40.00	65.00	—

Mint: Kashmir
KM# 52.1 RUPEE

Silver **Obv:** Persian letter "Shin" in place of sword

Date	Mintage	VG	F	VF	XF	Unc
VS1898 (1841)	—	9.00	15.00	25.00	40.00	—
VS1899 (1842)	—	9.00	15.00	25.00	40.00	—

Mint: Kashmir
KM# 52.2 RUPEE

Silver **Rev:** Date of left side of leaf

Date	Mintage	VG	F	VF	XF	Unc
VS1900 (1843)	—	8.50	13.50	21.50	35.00	—
VS1901 (1844)	—	8.50	13.50	21.50	35.00	—
VS1902 (1845)	—	8.50	13.50	21.50	35.00	—
VS1903 (1846)	—	8.50	13.50	21.50	35.00	—

Mint: Lahore
KM# 66.1 RUPEE

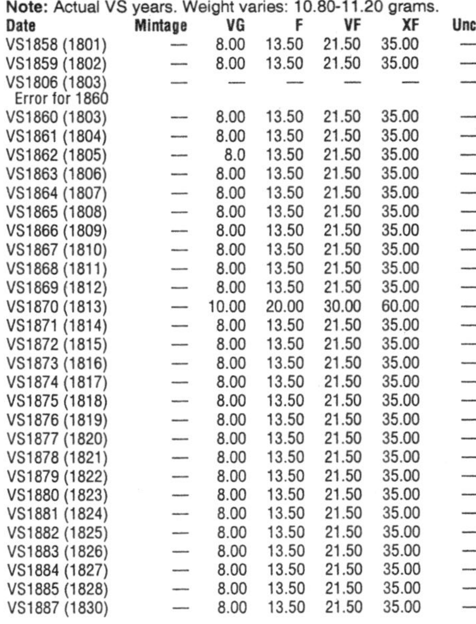

Silver **Obv. Inscription:** Guru Gobind Singh **Rev:** Leaf added **Note:** Actual VS years. Weight varies: 10.80-11.20 grams.

Date	Mintage	VG	F	VF	XF	Unc
VS1858 (1801)	—	8.00	13.50	21.50	35.00	—
VS1859 (1802)	—	8.00	13.50	21.50	35.00	—
VS1806 (1803) Error for 1860	—	—	—	—	—	—
VS1860 (1803)	—	8.00	13.50	21.50	35.00	—
VS1861 (1804)	—	8.00	13.50	21.50	35.00	—
VS1862 (1805)	—	8.0	13.50	21.50	35.00	—
VS1863 (1806)	—	8.00	13.50	21.50	35.00	—
VS1864 (1807)	—	8.00	13.50	21.50	35.00	—
VS1865 (1808)	—	8.00	13.50	21.50	35.00	—
VS1866 (1809)	—	8.00	13.50	21.50	35.00	—
VS1867 (1810)	—	8.00	13.50	21.50	35.00	—
VS1868 (1811)	—	8.00	13.50	21.50	35.00	—
VS1869 (1812)	—	8.00	13.50	21.50	35.00	—
VS1870 (1813)	—	10.00	20.00	30.00	60.00	—
VS1871 (1814)	—	8.00	13.50	21.50	35.00	—
VS1872 (1815)	—	8.00	13.50	21.50	35.00	—
VS1873 (1816)	—	8.00	13.50	21.50	35.00	—
VS1874 (1817)	—	8.00	13.50	21.50	35.00	—
VS1875 (1818)	—	8.00	13.50	21.50	35.00	—
VS1876 (1819)	—	8.00	13.50	21.50	35.00	—
VS1877 (1820)	—	8.00	13.50	21.50	35.00	—
VS1878 (1821)	—	8.00	13.50	21.50	35.00	—
VS1879 (1822)	—	8.00	13.50	21.50	35.00	—
VS1880 (1823)	—	8.00	13.50	21.50	35.00	—
VS1881 (1824)	—	8.00	13.50	21.50	35.00	—
VS1882 (1825)	—	8.00	13.50	21.50	35.00	—
VS1883 (1826)	—	8.00	13.50	21.50	35.00	—
VS1884 (1827)	—	8.00	13.50	21.50	35.00	—
VS1885 (1828)	—	8.00	13.50	21.50	35.00	—
VS1887 (1830)	—	8.00	13.50	21.50	35.00	—

Mint: Lahore
KM# 66.2 RUPEE

Silver **Obv:** Actual date **Rev:** VS1884 **Note:** Weight varies: 10.80-11.20 grams.

Date	Mintage	VG	F	VF	XF	Unc
VS(18)87 (1830)	—	9.00	18.00	30.00	45.00	—
VS(18)88 (1831)	—	9.00	18.00	30.00	45.00	—
VS(18)89 (1832)	—	9.00	18.00	30.00	45.00	—
VS(18)90 (1833)	—	9.00	18.00	30.00	45.00	—
VS(18)91 (1834)	—	9.00	18.00	30.00	45.00	—
VS(18)92 (1835)	—	9.00	18.00	30.00	45.00	—
VS(18)93 (1836)	—	9.00	18.00	30.00	45.00	—

Mint: Lahore
KM# 67 RUPEE

Silver **Rev:** VS1885 **Note:** Weight varies: 10.80-11.20 grams.

Date	Mintage	VG	F	VF	XF	Unc
VS(18)93 (1837)	—	9.00	18.00	30.00	45.00	—
VS(18)94 (1837)	—	9.00	18.00	30.00	45.00	—
VS(18)95 (1838)	—	9.00	18.00	30.00	45.00	—
VS(18)96 (1839)	—	9.00	18.00	30.00	45.00	—
VS(18)97 (1840)	—	9.00	18.00	30.00	45.00	—
VS1902 (1845)	—	9.00	18.00	30.00	45.00	—
VS1903 (1846)	—	9.00	18.00	30.00	45.00	—

Mint: Lahore
KM# 68.1 RUPEE

Silver **Rev:** Ranjit Singh, Guru Nanak **Note:** Weight varies: 10.80-11.40 grams.

Date	Mintage	VG	F	VF	XF	Unc
VS1885 (1828) Rare	—	—	—	—	—	—

Mint: Lahore
KM# 68.2 RUPEE
Silver **Rev:** With banner, fixed year VS1885 **Note:** Weight varies: 11.12-11.13 grams.

Date	Mintage	VG	F	VF	XF	Unc
VS(18)93 (1836) Rare	—	—	—	—	—	—

Mint: Malkarian
KM# 72 RUPEE
Silver **Rev:** "Sri Akalpur" **Note:** Weight varies: 10.70-11.60 grams.

Date	Mintage	VG	F	VF	XF	Unc
VS1879 (1822)	—	100	175	250	350	—
VS1880 (1823)	—	100	175	250	350	—

Mint: Multan
KM# 84 RUPEE
Silver **Obv:** Plain **Rev:** Leaf **Note:** Weight varies: 10.70-11.60 grams.

Date	Mintage	VG	F	VF	XF	Unc
VS1875 (1818)	—	11.00	18.50	30.00	50.00	—
VS1876 (1819)	—	11.00	18.50	30.00	50.00	—
VS1877 (1820)	—	11.00	18.50	30.00	50.00	—
VS1878 (1821)	—	11.00	18.50	30.00	50.00	—
VS1879 (1822)	—	11.00	18.50	30.00	50.00	—
VS1880 (1823)	—	11.00	18.50	30.00	50.00	—

Mint: Multan
KM# 85 RUPEE
Silver **Obv:** Trident **Rev:** Leaf **Note:** Weight varies: 10.70-11.60 grams.

Date	Mintage	VG	F	VF	XF	Unc
VS1880 (1823)	—	10.00	16.50	27.50	45.00	—
VS1881 (1824)	—	10.00	16.50	27.50	45.00	—
VS1882 (1825)	—	10.00	16.50	27.50	45.00	—
VS1883 (1826)	—	10.00	16.50	27.50	45.00	—
VS1884 (1827)	—	10.00	16.50	27.50	45.00	—

Mint: Multan
KM# 86.1 RUPEE
Silver **Obv:** Flower **Rev:** Leaf **Note:** Weight varies: 10.70-11.60 grams.

Date	Mintage	VG	F	VF	XF	Unc
VS1884 (1827)	—	8.00	13.50	21.50	35.00	—
VS1885 (1828)	—	8.00	13.50	21.50	35.00	—
VS1886 (1829)	—	8.00	13.50	21.50	35.00	—
VS1887 (1830)	—	8.00	13.50	21.50	35.00	—
VS1888 (1831)	—	8.00	13.50	21.50	35.00	—
VS1889 (1832)	—	8.00	13.50	21.50	35.00	—
VS1890 (1833)	—	8.00	13.50	21.50	35.00	—
VS1891 (1834)	—	8.00	13.50	21.50	35.00	—
VS1892 (1835)	—	8.00	13.50	21.50	35.00	—
VS1893 (1836)	—	8.00	13.50	21.50	35.00	—
VS1894 (1837)	—	8.00	13.50	21.50	35.00	—
VS1895 (1838)	—	8.00	13.50	21.50	35.00	—
VS1896 (1839)	—	8.00	13.50	21.50	35.00	—

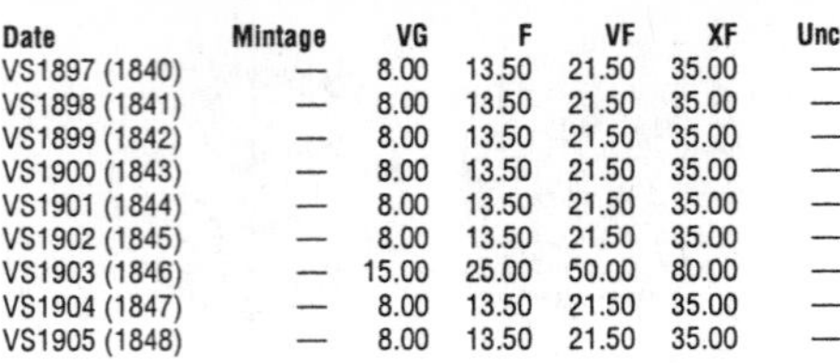

Date	Mintage	VG	F	VF	XF	Unc
VS1897 (1840)	—	8.00	13.50	21.50	35.00	—
VS1898 (1841)	—	8.00	13.50	21.50	35.00	—
VS1899 (1842)	—	8.00	13.50	21.50	35.00	—
VS1900 (1843)	—	8.00	13.50	21.50	35.00	—
VS1901 (1844)	—	8.00	13.50	21.50	35.00	—
VS1902 (1845)	—	8.00	13.50	21.50	35.00	—
VS1903 (1846)	—	15.00	25.00	50.00	80.00	—
VS1904 (1847)	—	8.00	13.50	21.50	35.00	—
VS1905 (1848)	—	8.00	13.50	21.50	35.00	—

Mint: Nimak
KM# 88 RUPEE
Silver **Note:** Pind Dadan Khan. Weight varies: 10.70-11.60 grams.

Date	Mintage	VG	F	VF	XF	Unc
VS1904 (1847)	—	75.00	125	200	325	—
VS1905 (1848)	—	75.00	125	200	325	—

Mint: Nimak
KM# 89 RUPEE
Silver **Obv:** Nagari "Ram Jim" **Note:** Weight varies: 10.70-11.60 grams.

Date	Mintage	VG	F	VF	XF	Unc
VS1905 (1848) Rare	—	—	—	—	—	—

Mint: Peshawar
KM# 98.1 RUPEE
8.5000 g., Silver **Obv:** Plain leaf

Date	Mintage	VG	F	VF	XF	Unc
VS1891 (1834)	—	12.50	20.00	40.00	75.00	—

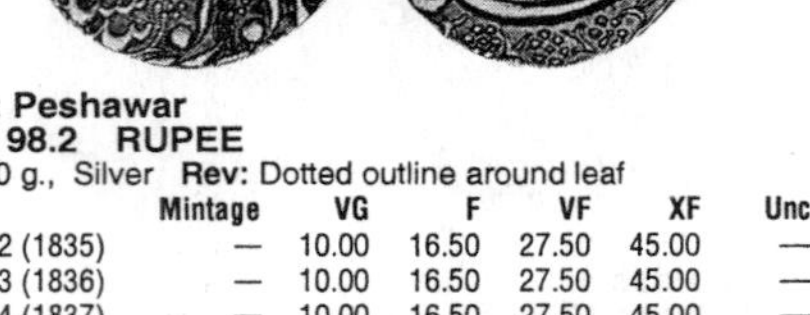

Mint: Peshawar
KM# 98.2 RUPEE
8.5000 g., Silver **Rev:** Dotted outline around leaf

Date	Mintage	VG	F	VF	XF	Unc
VS1892 (1835)	—	10.00	16.50	27.50	45.00	—
VS1893 (1836)	—	10.00	16.50	27.50	45.00	—
VS1894 (1837)	—	10.00	16.50	27.50	45.00	—

Note: Some specimens with oblique milled edges, dated VS1894 weigh 10.50-11.00 g

Mint: Uncertain Mint
KM# 99 RUPEE
11.2000 g., Silver **Obv:** Trident **Rev:** Lion **Note:** Bearing name f "Sarkar Ahluwalia". Issued by Fateh Singh Ahluwalia.

Date	Mintage	VG	F	VF	XF	Unc
VS1862 (1805)	—	4,500	7,000	10,000	13,500	—

Mint: Uncertain Mint
KM# C99 RUPEE
11.2000 g., Silver **Rev:** "Muzang" **Note:** This coin may have been struck at Gujarat.

Date	Mintage	VG	F	VF	XF	Unc
VS1889 (1832) Rare	—	—	—	—	—	—

Mint: Amritsar
KM# A21.1 NAZARANA RUPEE
10.4200 g., Silver **Rev:** "Dar jhang" left of leaf

Date	Mintage	VG	F	VF	XF	Unc
VS1873 (1816)	—	650	1,100	1,800	3,000	—
VS1882 (1825)	—	500	900	1,500	2,300	—

Mint: Multan
KM# 86.2 NAZARANA RUPEE
Silver **Note:** Weight varies: 10.70-11.60 grams.

Date	Mintage	VG	F	VF	XF	Unc
VS1896 (1839)	—	55.00	90.00	150	250	—

Mint: Multan
KM# 87 GOLD RUPEE
0.5700 g., Gold **Note:** Varieties with plain and reeded edge exist.

Date	Mintage	VG	F	VF	XF	Unc
VS1905 (1848)	—	50.00	75.00	150	200	—

Note: Struck by Diwan Mulraj (April 1848 - Jan. 1849/ VS1905)

Mint: Lahore
KM# A87 1/5 MOHUR
2.2100 g., Gold

Date	Mintage	VG	F	VF	XF	Unc
VS1896/85 (1839) Rare	—	—	—	—	—	—

Mint: Amritsar
KM# 23 1/4 MOHUR
Gold

Date	Mintage	VG	F	VF	XF	Unc
VS(18)95 (1838) Rare	—	—	—	—	—	—
VS(18)97 (1840) Rare	—	—	—	—	—	—

Mint: Amritsar
KM# 24 1/2 MOHUR
Gold

Date	Mintage	VG	F	VF	XF	Unc
VS1877 (1820) Rare	—	—	—	—	—	—

Mint: Amritsar
KM# 25.1 MOHUR
10.7600 g., Gold, 21 mm. **Obv:** Five dots **Rev:** Dotted leaf

Date	Mintage	VG	F	VF	XF	Unc
VS1858 (1801)	—	1,000	2,000	4,000	5,000	—

Mint: Amritsar
KM# 25.2 MOHUR
10.7400 g., Gold **Obv:** Fish at lower left **Rev:** Leaf

Date	Mintage	VG	F	VF	XF	Unc
VS1861 (1804) Rare	—	—	—	—	—	—

Mint: Amritsar
KM# 25.3 MOHUR
10.6900 g., Gold **Obv:** Rosette of seven dots **Rev:** Leaf

Date	Mintage	VG	F	VF	XF	Unc
VS1863 (1806) Rare	—	—	—	—	—	—
VS1864 (1807) Rare	—	—	—	—	—	—
VS1882 (1825) Rare	—	—	—	—	—	—

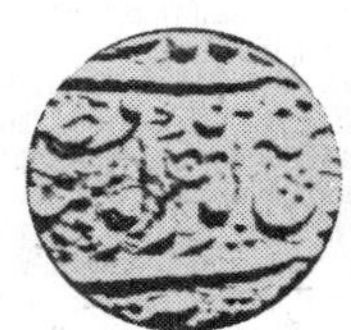

Mint: Amritsar
KM# 27 MOHUR
10.7300 g., Gold **Rev:** Without leaf symbol

Date	Mintage	VG	F	VF	XF	Unc
VS(18)88 (1831) Rare	—	—	—	—	—	—
VS1901 (1844) Rare	—	—	—	—	—	—

Mint: Amritsar
KM# 28A MOHUR
9.7200 g., Gold **Obv:** Gurmakhi legend, trident **Rev:** Gurmakhi legend, leaf

Date	Mintage	VG	F	VF	XF	Unc
ND (1828) Rare	—	—	—	—	—	—

Note: Struck from the dies for the copper 1 Paisa KM7.5; Similar Double Paise shows date VS1885 (1828)

Mint: Amritsar
KM# 26.1 MOHUR
Gold **Obv:** Branches with berries **Note:** "Mora" type. Similar to 1 Rupee, KM#20.

Date	Mintage	VG	F	VF	XF	Unc
VS1862 (1805) Rare	—	—	—	—	—	—

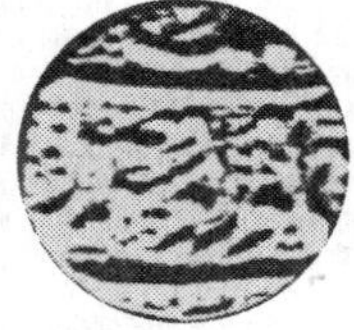

Mint: Amritsar
KM# 26.2 MOHUR
10.7500 g., Gold **Rev:** Symbol said to be mirror **Note:** The "Arisi" Mohur.

Date	Mintage	VG	F	VF	XF	Unc
VS1862 (1805) Rare	—	—	—	—	—	—
VS1863 (1806) Rare	—	—	—	—	—	—

Mint: Lahore
KM# 69 MOHUR
10.8500 g., Gold

Date	Mintage	VG	F	VF	XF	Unc
VS1884 (1827) Rare	—	—	—	—	—	—
VS1892/84 (1835) Rare	—	—	—	—	—	—

Mint: Multan
KM# 87A MOHUR
10.8500 g., Gold

Date	Mintage	VG	F	VF	XF	Unc
VS1876 (1815) Rare	—	—	—	—	—	—

Mint: Amritsar
KM# 29A DOUBLE MOHUR
21.1600 g., Gold

Date	Mintage	VG	F	VF	XF	Unc
VS1883 (1826) Rare	—	—	—	—	—	—

Mint: Amritsar
KM# 29B DOUBLE MOHUR
23.8900 g., Gold **Obv:** Partial actual date **Rev:** Dated: VS1884

Date	Mintage	VG	F	VF	XF	Unc
VS(18)85 (1828) Rare	—	—	—	—	—	—

TOKEN COINAGE

Mint: Uncertain Mint
KM# Tn1 MOHUR
Gold **Obv:** Gurmukhi legend **Rev:** Gurmukhi legend **Note:** Weight varies: 10.74-10.82 grams.

Date	Mintage	Good	VG	F	VF	XF
ND(1835-50) Rare	—	—	—	—	—	—

Ranjit Singh

VS1856-1896 / 1799-1839AD

HAMMERED COINAGE

Mint: Amritsar
KM# 7.25 HEAVY PAISA
Copper **Obv:** Double leaf

Date	Mintage	Good	VG	F	VF	XF
VS1879	—	—	—	—	—	—

Mint: Kashmir
KM# 41.8 PAISA
Copper **Obv:** Inscription with date **Rev:** Mint, leaf

Date	Mintage	Good	VG	F	VF	XF
VS186x	—	9.00	15.00	28.00	40.00	—

Mint: Peshawar
KM# 96a FALUS
Copper, 23 mm. **Obv:** Inscription, date **Rev:** Dotted leaf, mintname

Date	Mintage	Good	VG	F	VF	XF
VS1892	—	—	—	—	—	—

Sher Singh

VS1897-1900 / 1840-1843AD

HAMMERED COINAGE

Mint: Kashmir
KM# 52.1a RUPEE
Silver **Obv:** Persian letter "shin" with sprig **Rev:** Date divided by leaf

Date	Mintage	Good	VG	F	VF	XF
VS1898	—	15.00	20.00	28.00	40.00	—
VS1899	—	15.00	20.00	28.00	40.00	—

SIKH FEUDATORY DERA

PROTECTORATE

HAMMERED COINAGE

KM# 100 PAISA
Copper **Obv:** Flower and leaf, mint name, date above

Date	Mintage	Good	VG	F	VF	XF
VS1892	—	3.00	5.50	9.00	15.00	—

KM# 101.1 PAISA
Copper **Note:** Weight varies: 7-00-8.00 grams.

Date	Mintage	Good	VG	F	VF	XF
VS1898	—	3.00	5.50	9.00	15.00	—

KM# 101.2 PAISA
Copper **Obv:** Gumukhi legend, date **Note:** Weight varies: 7-00-8.00 grams.

Date	Mintage	Good	VG	F	VF	XF
VS1897	—	3.00	5.50	9.00	15.00	—
VS1898	—	3.00	5.50	9.00	15.00	—

KM# 101.3 PAISA
Copper **Note:** Weight varies: 7-00-8.00 grams.

Date	Mintage	Good	VG	F	VF	XF
ND(1835-41)	—	7.50	12.50	20.00	32.50	—

KM# 102 RUPEE
Silver **Obv:** "Ram" in Nagari; actual VS date of issue **Rev:** Dated VS1884 "Dera" **Note:** Weight varies: 11.00-11.10 grams.

Date	Mintage	Good	VG	F	VF	XF
VS(18)94	—	—	300	500	750	1,000
VS1884/VS Rare	—	—	—	—	—	—
VS1884/VS Rare	—	—	—	—	—	—

SIKH FEUDATORY DERAJAT

Sikh Protectorate, 1819-1847AD

Derajat was the region centered about Dera Ismail Khan where the mint was presumably located.

PROTECORATE

HAMMERED COINAGE

KM# A102 PAISA
Copper **Obv:** Crude lion right

Date	Mintage	Good	VG	F	VF	XF
ND(1830-60)	—	7.50	12.50	20.00	35.00	—

KM# B102 PAISA
Copper **Obv:** Funny lion right, AH date

Date	Mintage	Good	VG	F	VF	XF
AH1254	—	—	—	—	—	—

KM# C102 PAISA
Copper **Obv:** Lion left, AH date

Date	Mintage	Good	VG	F	VF	XF
AH1246	—	2.75	4.50	7.50	12.50	—
AH1247	—	2.75	4.50	7.50	12.50	—
AH1249	—	2.75	4.50	7.50	12.50	—
AH1254	—	2.75	4.50	7.50	12.50	—
AH1261	—	2.75	4.50	7.50	12.50	—
AH1262	—	2.75	4.50	7.50	12.50	—
AH1265	—	2.75	4.50	7.50	12.50	—
AH1267	—	2.75	4.50	7.50	12.50	—
AH1276	—	2.75	4.50	7.50	12.50	—

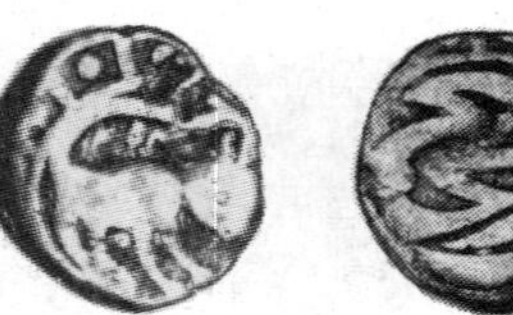

KM# D102 PAISA
Copper **Obv:** Lion right, AH date

Date	Mintage	Good	VG	F	VF	XF
AH1254	—	3.50	5.50	9.00	15.00	—

KM# E102 PAISA
Copper **Obv:** Horse, AH date

Date	Mintage	Good	VG	F	VF	XF
AH1252	—	4.50	7.50	12.50	20.00	—

KM# F102 PAISA
Copper **Obv:** "Fath" **Rev:** Leaf

Date	Mintage	Good	VG	F	VF	XF
ND(1825-60)	—	3.55	5.50	9.00	15.00	—

KM# G102 PAISA
Copper **Obv:** Lion right

Date	Mintage	Good	VG	F	VF	XF
VS1793	—	3.00	5.00	8.00	13.50	—

Note: Error for 1893

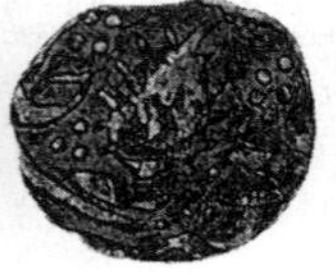

KM# 104 PAISA
Copper **Obv:** Leaf and "Gurmukhi" **Rev:** "DERAJAT"

Date	Mintage	Good	VG	F	VF	XF
ND(1825-60)	—	—	—	—	—	—

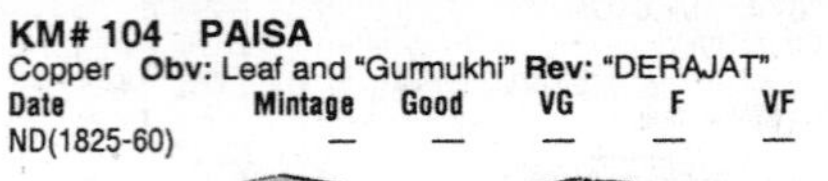

KM# 105 PAISA
Copper **Obv:** "Ra'ij"; mint name: "Derajat"

Date	Mintage	Good	VG	F	VF	XF
AH1241	—	3.00	5.50	9.00	15.00	—
AH1242	—	3.00	5.50	9.00	15.00	—

KM# 106 PAISA
Copper **Obv:** "Ra'ij" **Rev:** "Samadi" monogram

Date	Mintage	Good	VG	F	VF	XF
AH124x	—	4.50	7.50	12.50	20.00	—

KM# 108 PAISA
Copper **Obv:** "Sahih" **Rev:** Mint name and date

Date	Mintage	Good	VG	F	VF	XF
AH1252	—	3.50	6.00	10.00	16.50	—

KM# 114 PAISA
Copper **Note:** Similar to 1 Rupee, KM#120.

Date	Mintage	Good	VG	F	VF	XF
VS1896	—	17.50	30.00	45.00	60.00	—

KM# 119 RUPEE
Silver **Obv:** Date separated by Gurmukhi letter **Rev:** Neat leaf **Note:** Weight varies: 10.70-11.60 grams.

Date	Mintage	Good	VG	F	VF	XF
VS1892	—	7.50	18.50	30.00	50.00	85.00
VS1893	—	7.50	18.50	30.00	50.00	85.00
VS1894	—	7.50	18.50	30.00	50.00	85.00

KM# 120.1 RUPEE
Silver **Obv:** Date above Gurmukhi letter **Rev:** Normal leaf **Note:** Weight varies: 10.70-11.60 grams.

Date	Mintage	Good	VG	F	VF	XF
VS1893	—	7.50	18.50	27.00	45.00	75.00
VS1894	—	7.50	18.50	27.00	45.00	75.00

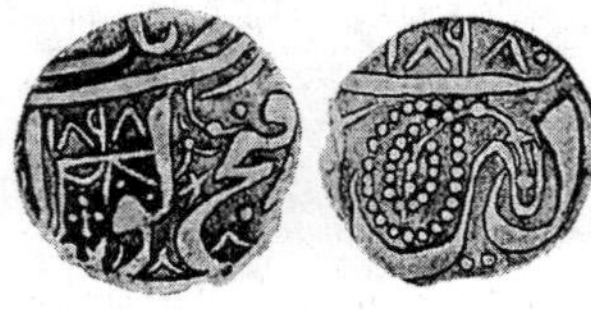

KM# 120.2 RUPEE
Silver **Rev:** Crude leaf **Note:** Weight varies: 10.70-11.60 grams.

Date	Mintage	Good	VG	F	VF	XF
VS1894	—	7.50	18.50	27.00	45.00	75.00
VS1895	—	7.50	18.50	27.00	45.00	75.00
VS1896	—	7.50	18.50	27.00	45.00	75.00
VS1897	—	7.50	18.50	27.00	45.00	75.00
VS1898	—	7.50	18.50	27.00	45.00	75.00
VS1899	—	7.50	18.50	27.00	45.00	75.00
VS1900	—	7.50	18.50	27.00	45.00	75.00
VS1901	—	7.50	18.50	27.00	45.00	75.00
VS1902	—	7.50	18.50	27.00	45.00	75.00
VS1903	—	7.50	18.50	27.00	45.00	75.00
VS1904	—	7.50	18.50	27.00	45.00	75.00
VS1905	—	7.50	18.50	27.00	45.00	75.00

SIKH FEUDATORY - NAJIBABAD

Symbol on obv:

PROTECTORATE

HAMMERED COINAGE

Mint: Najibabad
KM# 132 RUPEE
Silver **Obv:** Inscription, symbol, date **Obv. Inscription:** Shah Alam II **Rev:** Mintname, symbol, regnal year

Date	Mintage	Good	VG	F	VF	XF
AH1221//47	—	—	—	—	—	—

SIKKIM

A Kingdom located above northeast India between China, Bhutan and Nepal. In 1890 it became a British protectorate. In 1949 it became a protectorate of India and in 1975, a state.

The Kingdom of Sikkim covers an area of some 2,800sq. mi., and is situated on the southern slopes of the Himalayas, sandwiched between India to the south, Tibet to the north, Nepal to the west and Bhutan to the east. On its border with Nepal is the third highest mountain in the world, Kanchenjunga.

The Kingdom was founded in 1642 when Phuntsog Namgyal was proclaimed Chogyal or King. His ancestors had come to the Sikkim area about 150 years earlier from Eastern Tibet and over the years had gained the confidence and respect of the indigenous inhabitants, the Lapchas. The descendents of Phuntsog Namgyal have ruled Sikkim ever since.

In the latter part of the 18th century, Sikkim was subject to a number of Gurkha incursions, the impact of which was to place Sikkim on the British side in the Nepal War of 1815-1816. At the conclusion of this campaign, Sikkim received certain tracts of land relinquished by Nepal and in return, was obliged to accept British protection and control.

Initially, Sikkim covered an area at least twice as large as it is now, but annexations by neighboring powers reduced its size until in 1835, it reached its present area after the Chogyal "presented" the hills of Darjeeling to the British "out of friendship". In 1861, Sikkim became a protectorate of British India with the British exercising complete control over foreign affairs and defense and the Chogyal being in charge of all other internal matters.

India's independence brought little change to this situation until April 1973 when there was an uprising, during which the Chogyal asked for the assistance of the Indian Government. An agreement has now been reached under which the Chogyal's powers are to be greatly reduced and the administration of Sikkim is to be headed by a "chief nomination of the Government of India."

For practically the entire period of its history, Sikkim had no coinage of its own and until the last century, trade was carried out by barter with taxes paid in kind. On the few occasions when inhabitants needed money, Tibetan coins, silver or gold bullion, or later, Indian coins were used. For only three or four years in the 1800's, were coins struck in Sikkim and then Nepalese immigrants struck them. Since the beginning of the 20th century, Indian currency has circulated widely and exclusively.

Since the late 18th century, the Nepalese have exhibited a strong urge to leave the overcrowded hills of Nepal and seek their fortunes elsewhere. Sikkim, being so close, was an obvious target for settlement and in order to prevent this, the seventh ruler of Sikkim, Tsugphud Namgyal (1793-1864) prohibited the settlement of Nepalese in Sikkim. This ban was effective until the early years of the reign of Thutob Namgyal (1874-1914), when certain powerful landowners realized that it was profitable to allow Nepalese to settle and work the land. Foremost of these were the brothers Kangsa Dewan and Phodong Lama. These two brothers struck a deal with two rich Nepalese traders, the brothers Lachmidas and Chandrabir Pradhan, under which a large tract of land, which had recently been confiscated from a Sikkimese nobleman who had been convicted of embezzlement, was made over to the Nepalese brothers. This deal was strongly criticized by the Sikkimese people, but was supported by the British and finally the Kangsa brothers persuaded the Chogyal in 1878 to allow Nepalese settlement in "uninhabited and waste lands of Sikkim". Since then Nepalese immigrants have flooded into Sikkim and now comprise a majority of the population of the country.

It was the Pradhan brothers who were responsible for the Sikkim coinage. Soon after acquiring their lands, they obtained licenses to mine copper in a number of places, most important of which were Tuk Khani, Bhotan Khaninear Rangpo and Pachay Khani. Some of this copper was sold in Nepal and Darjeeling, but some remained unsold, so in 1882 the brothers sought and obtained the permission of the Chogyal to strike copper coins. The minting was done in two places near the mines of Tuk Khani and Pachay Khani. Unfortunately for the Pradhan brothers, the Deputy Commissioner of Darjeeling forbade circulation of the Sikkim coins in the Darjeeling district and this made the coins unpopular among the people. The minting was not profitable and was discontinued in 1885.

The coins themselves are, except for the inscription, exact copies of the Nepalese paisa of Surendra Vira Vikrama Shah. They are very poorly struck and very few specimens have all the details of the design visible. The date is only very rarely legible. Three major types are known, but there is no indication of the mint of origin and die-links exist between the types. The coins are all intended to be the same denomination, one paisa, although the weights of individual specimens vary within the range 6.00 g to 4.00 g around a mean of about 5.20 g.

RULERS

Thutab Namgyel, VS1931-1968/1874-1911AD

Thutab Namgyel
VS1931-1968 / 1874-1911AD
HAMMERED COINAGE

KM# 1 PAISA
Copper **Obv:** Three lines in square, date below **Rev:** Three line within square **Note:** Weight varies: 4.0-6.0 grams. Size varies: 20-22 mm.

Date	Mintage	Good	VG	F	VF	XF
VS1940 (1883)	—	10.00	17.50	25.00	35.00	—
VS1941 (1884)	—	5.00	8.50	12.50	17.50	—

KM# 2 PAISA
Copper **Obv:** Four lines within square, date below **Note:** Weight varies: 4.0-6.0 grams. Size varies: 20-22 mm.

Date	Mintage	Good	VG	F	VF	XF
VS1941 (1884)	—	10.00	17.50	25.00	35.00	—

KM# 3.1 PAISA
Copper **Obv:** Three lines within square, date below with "Ti" of "Sikimpati" on third line **Note:** Weight varies: 4.0-6.0 grams. Size varies: 20-22 mm.

Date	Mintage	Good	VG	F	VF	XF
VS1941 (1884)	—	5.00	8.50	12.50	17.50	—
VS1942 (1885)	—	5.00	8.50	12.50	17.50	—

KM# 3.2 PAISA
Copper **Rev:** "Sarkar" of legend spelled incorrectly "Sakar" **Note:** Weight varies: 4.0-6.0 grams. Size varies: 20-22 mm.

Date	Mintage	Good	VG	F	VF	XF
VS1941 (1884)	—	5.00	8.50	12.50	17.50	—
VS1942 (1885)	—	5.00	8.50	12.50	17.50	—

KM# 3.3 PAISA
Copper **Rev:** "Sarkar" of legend spelled incorrectly "Sikar" **Note:** Weight varies: 4.0-6.0 grams. Size varies: 20-22 mm.

Date	Mintage	Good	VG	F	VF	XF
VS1941 (1884)	—	5.00	8.50	12.50	17.50	—
VS1942 (1885)	—	5.00	8.50	12.50	17.50	—

Note: Varieties exist in spelling of "Maharaja"

SIND

Sind has an extremely ancient historical record having been successively occupied and governed by the Indus Valley civilization (ca. 1500 BC), Alexander the Great(325BC) Chandragupta Maurya (ca.305BC), Asoka (274-232BC) and others until the first Muslim inroads into Sind after 712AD. For almost the next three hundred years Sind was subject to Arab caliphs, after which it was conquered by Sultan Mahmud of Ghazni who conducted annual raids into India after 1000AD.Even then it remained semi-independent under local dynasties until, under Akbar (who was himself born at Umarkot in Sind), Sind became part of the Mughal empire.

The amirs of Hyderabad and Khairpur came into existence after the Mughal empire had started to disintegrate. Khairpur had been governed by the Kalhoras but in the 1780's they were overthrown by the Talpurs, a Baluchi family. Khairpur State was founded by Mir Sohrab Khan Talpur. In 1813 Khairpur ceased to pay tribute to Afghanistan and, in 1832 (1247/48AH), it was recognized by the British as a separate state within Sind. In 1843,when the rest of Sind was annexed by the British in the aftermath of the Anglo-Sikh War, Khairpur remained separate and was only merged into the neighboring territory by its accession in 1947 to Pakistan.

AMIRS of HYDERABAD

MINTS

Haidarabad Sind

AMIRS of KHAIRPUR

Bhakhar

شکارپور

Shikarpur
(Local issues)

Amirs of Hyderabad
HAMMERED COINAGE

Mint: Haidarabad Sind
KM# 17 RUPEE
Silver **Note:** Weight varies: 10.70-11.60 grams.

Date	Mintage	Good	VG	F	VF	XF
ND(1812-41)	—	6.00	15.00	30.00	50.00	75.00
ND(1813-14)	—	6.00	15.00	30.00	50.00	75.00

Mint: Sind
KM# 19.2 RUPEE
Silver **Rev:** Mint mark: Star below "Sana" **Note:** Weight varies: 10.70-11.60 grams.

Date	Mintage	Good	VG	F	VF	XF
ND(1812-48)	—	3.50	8.50	14.00	20.00	30.00

Mint: Sind
KM# 19.1 RUPEE
Silver **Rev:** Mint mark: Group of six dots **Note:** Weight varies: 10.70-11.60 grams.

Date	Mintage	Good	VG	F	VF	XF
ND(1812-48)	—	3.50	8.50	14.00	20.00	30.00

Mint: Sind
KM# 19.3 RUPEE
Silver **Rev:** Star in "S" of "Jalus" **Note:** Weight varies: 10.70-11.60 grams.

Date	Mintage	Good	VG	F	VF	XF
ND(1812-48)	—	3.50	8.50	14.00	20.00	30.00

Mint: Sind
KM# 19.4 RUPEE
Silver **Note:** Weight varies: 10.70-11.60 grams.

Date	Mintage	Good	VG	F	VF	XF
AH-//8	—	4.00	10.00	16.00	24.00	40.00

Mint: Sind
KM# 20.1 RUPEE
Silver **Rev:** Mint mark: Five-petal flowers **Note:** Weight varies: 7.50-7.80 grams.

Date	Mintage	Good	VG	F	VF	XF
ND(1812-48)	—	3.00	7.50	12.50	18.50	28.00

Mint: Sind
KM# 20.3 RUPEE
Silver **Rev:** Mint mark: Cross **Note:** Weight varies: 7.50-7.80 grams.

Date	Mintage	Good	VG	F	VF	XF
ND(1812-48)	—	3.50	8.50	14.00	20.00	30.00

Mint: Sind
KM# 20.4 RUPEE
Silver **Rev:** Mint mark: Sprig with three berries **Note:** Weight varies: 7.50-7.80 grams.

Date	Mintage	Good	VG	F	VF	XF
ND(1812-48)	—	3.50	8.50	14.00	20.00	30.00

Mint: Sind
KM# 21 RUPEE
Silver **Rev:** Without mint mark, with Fath (Victory) **Note:** Weight varies: 7.50-7.80 grams.

Date	Mintage	Good	VG	F	VF	XF
ND(1812-48)	—	5.00	12.50	20.00	28.00	42.50

Note: It is not known to which victory the reference is made

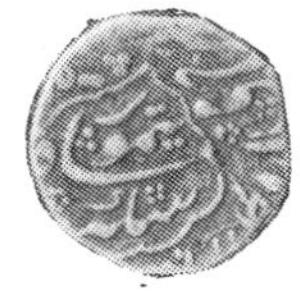

Mint: Sind
KM# 19 RUPEE
Silver **Note:** Weight varies: 10.70-11.60 grams.

Date	Mintage	VG	F	VF	XF	Unc
AH1239 (1824)		12.50	20.00	28.00	42.50	—
AH1240 (1825)		12.50	20.00	28.00	42.50	—
AH1241 (1826)		12.50	20.00	28.00	42.50	—
AH1242 (1827)		12.50	20.00	28.00	42.50	—
AH1244 (1828)		12.50	20.00	28.00	42.50	—
AH1245 (1829)		12.50	20.00	28.00	42.50	—

Mint: Sind
KM# 18 RUPEE
Silver **Rev:** Sind spelled "Sahind" **Note:** Weight varies: 10.70-11.60 grams. Several varieties exist with different symbols on reverse.

Date	Mintage	VG	F	VF	XF	Unc
AH1227 (1812)		13.50	25.00	40.00	65.00	—

Mint: Sind
KM# 20 RUPEE

Silver **Note:** Weight varies: 7.50-7.80 grams.

Date	Mintage	VG	F	VF	XF	Unc
AH1252 (1836)		8.50	14.00	20.00	30.00	—
AH1255 (1839)		8.50	14.00	20.00	30.00	—
AH1256 (1840)		8.50	14.00	20.00	30.00	—
AH1257 (1841)		8.50	14.00	20.00	30.00	—

Amirs of Khairpur
After AH1248 / 1832AD

HAMMERED COINAGE

Mint: Bakhar
C# 10.11 RUPEE
Silver **Obv:** Flower **Note:** Weight varies: 11.00-11.50 grams.

Date	Mintage	Good	VG	F	VF	XF
AH1256	—	4.00	10.00	17.50	25.00	37.50

Mint: Bakhar
C# 10 RUPEE
Silver **Obv:** Without mint mark **Rev:** Without mint mark **Note:** Weight varies: 11.00-11.50 grams.

Date	Mintage	VG	F	VF	XF	Unc
AH1240 (1825)	—	12.50	21.00	30.00	45.00	—
AH1245 (1829)	—	9.00	15.00	21.50	32.50	—
AH1246 (1830)	—	9.00	15.00	21.50	32.50	—
AH1252 (1836)	—	9.00	15.00	21.50	32.50	—
AH1254 (1838)	—	9.00	15.00	21.50	32.50	—

Mint: Bakhar
C# 10.1 RUPEE
Silver **Obv:** Star **Rev:** Star **Note:** Weight varies: 11.00-11.50 grams.

Date	Mintage	VG	F	VF	XF	Unc
AH1254 (1838)	—	9.00	15.00	21.50	32.50	—
AH1255 (1839)	—	9.00	15.00	21.50	32.50	—

Mint: Bakhar
C# 10.2 RUPEE
Silver **Obv:** Star **Rev:** Branch **Note:** Weight varies: 11.00-11.50 grams.

Date	Mintage	VG	F	VF	XF	Unc
AH1255 (1839)	—	9.00	15.00	21.50	32.50	—

Mint: Bakhar
C# 10.9 RUPEE
Silver **Obv:** Branch **Rev:** Star **Note:** Weight varies: 11.00-11.50 grams.

Date	Mintage	VG	F	VF	XF	Unc
AH1225 (1836)	—	10.00	16.00	22.50	35.00	—

Note: Error for 1252

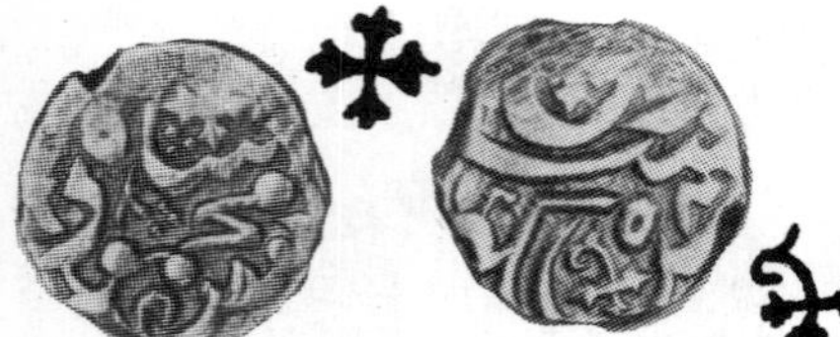

Mint: Bakhar
C# 10.10 RUPEE
Silver **Obv:** Ornate cross **Rev:** Ornate cross **Note:** Weight varies: 11.00-11.50 grams.

Date	Mintage	VG	F	VF	XF	Unc
AH1254 (1838)	—	12.50	20.00	32.00	50.00	—

Mint: Bakhar
C# 10.3 RUPEE
Silver **Obv:** Branch **Rev:** Branch **Note:** Weight varies: 11.00-11.50 grams.

Date	Mintage	VG	F	VF	XF	Unc
AH1256 (1840)	—	9.00	15.00	21.50	32.50	—
AH1258 (1842)	—	9.00	15.00	21.50	32.50	—

Mint: Bakhar
C# 10.4 RUPEE
Silver **Obv:** Pigeon **Rev:** Plume **Note:** Weight varies: 11.00-11.50 grams.

Date	Mintage	VG	F	VF	XF	Unc
AH1256 (1840)	—	9.00	15.00	21.50	32.50	—

Mint: Bakhar
C# 10.5 RUPEE
Silver **Obv:** Pigeon **Rev:** Peacock **Note:** Weight varies: 11.00-11.50 grams.

Date	Mintage	VG	F	VF	XF	Unc
AH1258 (1842)	—	10.00	17.50	25.00	37.50	—

Mint: Bakhar
C# 10.8 RUPEE
Silver **Obv:** Pigeon **Rev:** Leaf **Note:** Weight varies: 11.00-11.50 grams.

Date	Mintage	VG	F	VF	XF	Unc
AH1258 (1842)	—	10.00	17.50	25.00	37.50	—

Mint: Bakhar
C# 10.6 RUPEE
Silver **Obv:** Hare **Rev:** Peacock **Note:** Weight varies: 11.00-11.50 grams.

Date	Mintage	VG	F	VF	XF	Unc
AH1258 (1842)	—	10.00	17.50	25.00	37.50	—

Mint: Bakhar
C# 10.7 RUPEE
Silver **Rev:** Date in "S" of "Julus" **Note:** Weight varies: 11.00-11.50 grams.

Date	Mintage	VG	F	VF	XF	Unc
AH1259 (1843)	—	10.00	17.50	25.00	37.50	—

BRITISH OCCUPATION
From AH1259 / 1843AD

HAMMERED COINAGE

C# 11 RUPEE
Silver **Obv:** Hare **Rev:** British lion

Date	Mintage	VG	F	VF	XF	Unc
AH1259 (1843)	—	15.00	25.00	35.00	50.00	—
AH1261 (1845)	—	15.00	25.00	35.00	50.00	—

C# 12 RUPEE
Silver **Obv:** Floral mint marks of various kinds **Rev:** Floral mint marks of various kinds

Date	Mintage	VG	F	VF	XF	Unc
AH1262 (1846)	—	8.50	14.00	20.00	30.00	—
AH1263 (1847)	—	8.50	14.00	20.00	30.00	—
AH1264 (1848)	—	8.50	14.00	20.00	30.00	—
AH1265 (1849)	—	8.50	14.00	20.00	30.00	—
AH1266 (1850)	—	8.50	14.00	20.00	30.00	—
AH1267 (1851)	—	8.50	14.00	20.00	30.00	—
AH1268 (1852)	—	8.50	14.00	20.00	30.00	—
AH1269 (1853)	—	8.50	14.00	20.00	30.00	—

C# 13 RUPEE
Silver **Obv:** Hare **Rev:** Peacock

Date	Mintage	VG	F	VF	XF	Unc
AH1259 (1843)	—	16.50	23.50	32.50	48.00	—

Anonymous

HAMMERED COINAGE
Local Issues

Mint: Tatta
C# 45 RUPEE
Silver **Note:** Weight varies: 10.70-11.60 grams.

Date	Mintage	Good	VG	F	VF	XF
ND(1825)	—	3.50	8.50	13.50	20.00	30.00

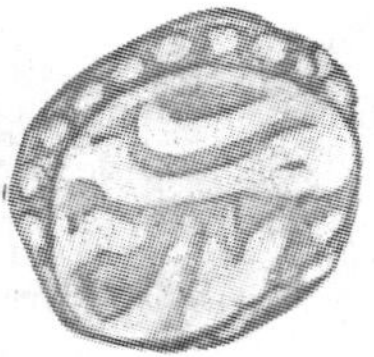

Mint: Shikarpur
C# 30.1 FALUS
Copper

Date	Mintage	Good	VG	F	VF	XF
AH1255 (1839)	—	3.00	5.00	7.50	12.50	—

Mint: Shikarpur
C# 30.2 FALUS
Copper **Rev:** Star at top

Date	Mintage	Good	VG	F	VF	XF
AH1255 (1839)	—	3.00	5.00	7.50	12.50	—

SIRMUR

Girvan Yuddha of Nepal
VS1860-73/1803-16AD

HAMMERED COINAGE

Mint: Nahan
C# 20 1/2 PAISA
Copper

Date	Mintage	Good	VG	F	VF	XF
AH1227 (1812)	—	12.50	22.50	35.00	50.00	—

Mint: Nahan
C# 21 PAISA
Copper

Date	Mintage	Good	VG	F	VF	XF
AH1227(VS(18) 68) (1812)	—	7.50	12.50	—	30.00	—

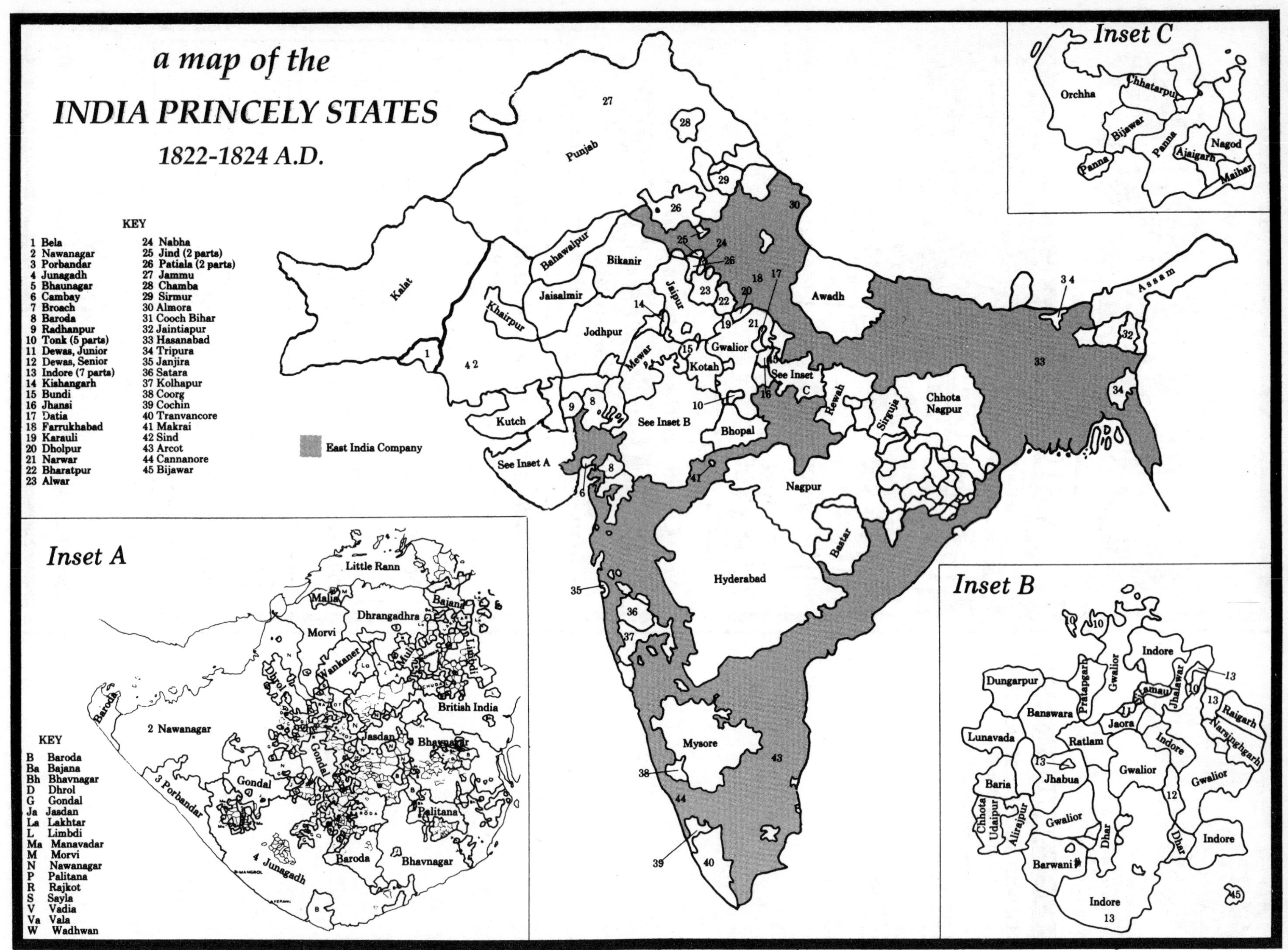

a map of the
INDIA PRINCELY STATES
1822-1824 A.D.
KEY
1 Bela
2 Nawanagar
3 Porbandar
4 Junagadh
5 Bhaunagar
6 Cambay
7 Broach
8 Baroda
9 Radhanpur
10 Tonk (5 parts)
11 Dewas, Junior
12 Dewas, Senior
13 Indore (7 parts)
14 Kishangarh
15 Bundi
16 Jhansi
17 Datia
18 Farrukhabad
19 Karauli
20 Dholpur
21 Narwar
22 Bharatpur
23 Alwar
24 Nabha
25 Jind (2 parts)
26 Patiala (2 parts)
27 Jammu
28 Chamba
29 Sirmur
30 Almora
31 Cooch Bihar
32 Jaintiapur
33 Hasanabad
34 Tripura
35 Janjira
36 Satara
37 Kolhapur
38 Coorg
39 Cochin
40 Tranvancore
41 Makrai
42 Sind
43 Arcot
44 Cannanore
45 Bijawar
East India Company
Kalat
Punjab
Bahawalpur
Bikanir
Khairpur
Jaisalmir
Jodhpur
Jaipur
Mewar
Kotah
Gwalior
Awadh
Assam
Kutch
See Inset A
See Inset B
See Inset C
Bhopal
Rewah
Sirguja
Chhota Nagpur
Nagpur
Bastar
Hyderabad
Mysore
Inset A
Little Rann
Malia
Morvi
Dhrangadhra
Bajana
Wankaner
Muli
Limbdi
Dhrol
British India
2 Nawanagar
Jasdan
Bhavnagar
Gondal
Palitana
3 Porbandar
4 Junagadh
Baroda
KEY
B Baroda
Ba Bajana
Bh Bhavnagar
D Dhrol
G Gondal
Ja Jasdan
La Lakhtar
L Limbdi
Ma Manavadar
M Morvi
N Nawanagar
P Palitana
R Rajkot
S Sayla
V Vadia
Va Vala
W Wadhwan
Inset B
Dungarpur
Pratapgarh
Gwalior
Indore
Jhalawar
Jamau
Banswara
Jaora
Raigarh
Narsinghgarh
Lunavada
Ratlam
Jhabua
Baria
Chhota Udaipur
Alirajpur
Dhar
Barwani
Inset C
Orchha
Chhatarpur
Bijawar
Panna
Ajaigarh
Nagod
Maihar

INDIA - PRINCELY STATES

MONETARY SYSTEMS

In each state, local rates of exchange prevailed. There was no fixed rate between copper, silver or gold coin, but the rates varied in accordance with the values of the metal and by the edict of the local authority.

Within the subcontinent, different regions used distinctive coinage standards. In North India and the Deccan, the silver rupee (11.6 g) and gold mohur (11.0 g) predominated. In Gujarat, the silver kori (4.7 g) and gold kori (6.4 g) were the main currency. In South India the silver fanam (0.7-1.0 g) and gold hun or Pagoda (3.4 g) were current. Copper coins in all parts of India were produced to a myriad of local metrologies with seemingly endless varieties.

NAZARANA ISSUES

Throughout the Indian Princely States listings are Nazarana designations for special full flan strikings of copper, silver and some gold coinage. The purpose of these issues was for presentation to the local monarch to gain favor. For example if one had an audience with one's ruler he would exchange goods, currency notes or the cruder struck circulating coinage for Nazarana pieces which he would present to the ruler as a gift. The borderline between true Nazarana pieces and well struck regular issues is often indistinct. The Nazaranas sometimes circulated alongside the cruder "dump" issues.

PRICING

As the demand for Indian Princely coinage develops, and more dealers handle the material, sale records and price lists enable a firmer basis for pricing most series. For scarcer types adequate sale records are often not available, and prices must be regarded as tentative. Inasmuch as date collectors of Princely States series are few, dates known to be scarce are usually worth little more than common ones. Coins of a dated type, which do not show the full date on their flans should be valued at about 70 per cent of the prices indicated.

DATING

Coins are dated in several eras. Arabic and Devanagari numerals are used in conjunction with the Hejira era (AH), the Vikrama Samvat (VS), Saka Samvat (Saka), Fasli era(FE) Mauludi era (AM), and Malabar era (ME), as well as the Christian era (AD).

GRADING

Copper coins are rarely found in high grade, as they were the workhorse of coinage circulation, and were everywhere used for day-to-day transactions. Moreover, they were carelessly struck and even when 'new', can often only be distinguished from VF coins with difficulty, if at all.

Silver coins were often hoarded and not infrequently, turn up in nearly as-struck condition. The silver coins of Hyderabad (dump coins) are common in high grades, and the rupees of some states are scarcer 'used' than 'new'. Great caution must be exercised in determining the value or scarcity of high grade dump coins.

Dump gold was rarely circulated, and usually occurs in high grades, or is found made into jewelry.

TREATY STATES ISSUES

The British Government issued a declaration in 1870 that any Princely State of India could strike coins in its mint or mints with the fineness and weight identical with that prescribed for the Government of India issues with obverse and reverse designs differing from coins already struck or issued in that Princely State with value inscribed in the English language; and that Princely State had to suppress its mint or mints for a period of not less than thirty years.

The States which had coins struck under the authority of this Act were ALWAR, BIKANIR, DEWAS (senior and junior branches) and DHAR.

After the closing of the Indian mints to private coinage in 1893 and the currency difficulties experienced at that period, other Princely States came to agreement with the Government for the substitution of the British for the local rupee, and many of the Princely States' mints were closed.

With the one exception of the SAILANA State, which obtained two bronze issues with their own reverse design, all agreements after 1893 with Princely States followed the principle of the Indian Government agreeing to take over all the coins circulating in the State, and giving the Government rupee in exchange at a fixed rate.

All States that were parties to these agreements introduced the Indian Government rupee as the sole legal tender.

INDEX

Ajmir – Gwalior and Jodhpur

Akbarabad – Bharatpur

Allahabad – Awadh

ALWAR
....Rajgarh

ARCOT
Arkat
Kadapa
Madras
Madurai
Nahtarnagar
Ramnad
Tanjore
Tinnevelly
Trichinopoly

Arkat – Arcot

Asafabad – Awadh

Asafnagar – Awadh

Aurangabad – Hyderabad

AWADH
Allahabad
Asafabad
Asafnagar
Awadh (Subah)
Banaras (Muhammadabad)
Bareli
Hathras
Itawa
Kanauj
Kora
Lucknow
Muradabad
Najibabad
Shahabad (Anupnagar)
Tanda (Muhammadnagar)

BAHAWALPUR
Bahawalpur
Khanpur

Banaras – Awadh

Bareli – Awadh

BARODA
Ahmadabad
Baroda

BHARATPUR
Akbarabad
Bharatpur
Dig
Kumber

BHAUNAGAR

Bhinda – Mewar

BHOPAL

BIKANIR

BINDRABAN (Vrindavan)
Bindraban
Gokul
Mathura

BROACH
See also Gwalior

BUNDI

Burhanpur – Gwalior

CANNANORE

Chanderi – Gwalior

Chandor – Indore

CHHATARPUR

Chitor – Mewar

COCHIN

COORG

Dalipnagar – Datia

DATIA
Dalipnagar

Daulatabad – Hyderabad

Deogarh – Partabgarh

DHOLPUR
Gohad

Dig – Bharatpur

DUNGARPUR

East India Company
See also Awadh, Bareli, Broach, Indore, Kunch and Satara

Gadwal – Hyderabad

Garhakota – Gwalior

GARHWAL (Srinagar)

Gohad – Dholpur

Gokul – Bindraban

GWALIOR
Ajmir
Broach
Burhanpur
Chanderi
Gwalior Fort
Jawad
Lashkar
Narwar
Sipri
Ujjain

HANSI

Hathras – Awadh

HYDERABAD
Aurangabad (Khujista Bunyad)
Daulatabad
Hyderabad (Farkhanda Bunyad)

HYDERABAD FEUDATORIES
Gadwal
Kalayani
Narayanpett

INDORE
Chandor
Maheshwar
Malharnagar

INDORE FEUDATORIES
Sironj

Itawa – Awadh

JAIPUR
Jaipur Sawai
Khetri
Muzaffargarh
Madhopur Sawai

JAISALMIR

Jambusar – Baroda

JANJIRA ISLAND

Jawad – Gwalior

JIND

JODHPUR (Marwar)
Ajmir
Jodhpur
Merta
Nagor

JODHPUR FEUDATORIES
Kuchawan

Kadapa – Arcot

KAITHAL

Kalayani – Hyderabad

Kanauj – Awadh

KARAULI

Khanpur – Bahawalpur

KISHANGARH

Kora – Awadh

KOTAH

Kuchawan – Jodhpur

Kumber – Bharatpur

KUTCH

LADAKH

Lashkar – Gwalior

Lucknow – Awadh

Madhopur – Jaipur

Madras – Arcot

Madurai – Arcot

Maheshwar – Indore

MALER KOTLA

Malharnagar – Indore

Mathura – Bindraban

Merta – Jodhpur

MEWAR
Chitor
Udaipur

MEWAR LOCAL ISSUES
Bhilwara
Chitor
Umarda

Muradabad – Awadh

MYSORE

Nagor – Jodhpur

Nahtarnagar – Arcot

Najibabad – Awadh
Awadh, Bharatpur (Pseudo)

Narayanpett – Hyderabad

NARWAR
See also Gwalior

NAWANAGAR

ORCHHA

PANNA

PARTABGARH (Pratapgarh)
Deogarh

PATIALA

Rajgarh – Alwar

Ramnad – Arcot

RATLAM

SELAM (Salem)

Shahabad – Awadh

Sironj – Indore
Srinagar – Garhwal
Tanda – Awadh
Tanjore – Arcot
Tinnevelly – Arcot
TRAVANCORE
Trichinopoly – Arcot
TRIPURA
Udaipur – Mewar
Ujjain – Gwalior
Umarda - Mewar

ALWAR

State located in Rajputana in northwestern India.

Alwar was founded about 1722 by a Rajput chieftain of the Naruka clan, Rao Pratap Singh of Macheri (1740-1791), a descendant of the family, which had ruled Jaipur in the 14th century. Alwar was distinguished by being the first of the Princely States to use coins struck at the Calcutta Mint. These, first issued in 1877, were of the same weight and assay as the Imperial Rupee, and carried the bust of Queen Victoria, Empress of India. Alwar State, having allied itself with East India Company interests in their struggles against the Marathas early in the 19th century, continued to maintain a good relationship with the British right up to Indian Independence in 1947. In May 1949, Alwar was merged into Rajasthan.

LOCAL RULERS

Bakhtawar Singh, AH1206-1230/1791-1815AD
Bani Singh, AH1231-1273/1815-1857AD
Sheodan Singh, AH1274-1291/1857-1874AD
Mangal Singh, AH1291-1310/1874-1892

MINT

راج گره

Rajgarh

Royal Mark

Parasol

Mint Marks

Jhar

Fish

HAMMERED COINAGE

KM# 15 TAKKA
Copper **Obv. Inscription:** "Muhammad Akbar II" **Mint:** Rajgarh **Note:** Weight varies 18.0-18.5 grams.

Date	Mintage	Good	VG	F	VF	XF
ND//4 (1809-10)	—	4.00	6.00	10.00	15.00	—
ND//6 (1811-12)	—	4.00	6.00	10.00	15.00	—
ND//10 (1815-16)	—	4.00	6.00	10.00	15.00	—
ND//11 (1816-17)	—	4.00	6.00	10.00	15.00	—
ND//12 (1817-18)	—	4.00	6.00	10.00	15.00	—
ND//13 (1818-19)	—	4.00	6.00	10.00	15.00	—
ND//14 (1819-20)	—	4.00	6.00	10.00	15.00	—
ND//16 (1821-22)	—	4.00	6.00	10.00	15.00	—
AH122x//17	—	4.00	6.00	10.00	15.00	—
ND//20 *1825-26)	—	4.00	6.00	10.00	15.00	—
AH12xx//21	—	4.00	6.00	10.00	15.00	—
ND//24 (1829-30)	—	4.00	6.00	10.00	15.00	—
ND//25 (1830-31)	—	4.00	6.00	10.00	15.00	—
ND//26 (1831-32)	—	4.00	6.00	10.00	15.00	—
ND//28 (1833-34)	—	4.00	6.00	10.00	15.00	—

KM# 17 1/8 RUPEE
Silver **Obv. Inscription:** "Muhammad Akbar II" **Mint:** Rajgarh **Note:** Weight varies 1.40-1.42 grams.

Date	Mintage	Good	VG	F	VF	XF
ND//6 (1811-12)	—	8.00	20.00	35.00	55.00	80.00

KM# 18 1/4 RUPEE
Silver, 13 mm. **Obv. Inscription:** Muhammad Akbar (II) **Mint:** Rajgarh **Note:** Weight varies 2.80-2.85 grams.

Date	Mintage	Good	VG	F	VF	XF
ND//22 (1827-28)	—	10.00	25.00	45.00	70.00	100

KM# 19 1/2 RUPEE
Silver, 18 mm. **Obv. Inscription:** "Muhammad Akbar II" **Mint:** Rajgarh **Note:** Weight varies 5.60-5.70 grams.

Date	Mintage	Good	VG	F	VF	XF
ND//19 (1824-25)	—	13.50	32.00	55.00	85.00	120
ND//20 (1825-26)	—	13.50	32.00	55.00	85.00	120
ND//21 (1826-27)	—	13.50	32.00	55.00	85.00	120
ND//22 (1827-28)	—	13.50	32.00	55.00	85.00	120

KM# 10 RUPEE
Silver **Obv. Inscription:** "Shah Alam II" **Note:** Weight varies 11.2 - 11.4 grams.

Date	Mintage	Good	VG	F	VF	XF
ND//42 (1800-01)	—	6.00	13.00	22.50	30.00	40.00
ND//44 (1802-03)	—	6.00	13.00	22.50	30.00	40.00
ND//46 (1803-04)	—	6.00	13.00	22.50	30.00	40.00

KM# 20 RUPEE
Silver **Obv. Inscription:** "Muhammad Akbar II" **Mint:** Rajgarh **Note:** Weight varies 11.20-11.40 grams.

Date	Mintage	Good	VG	F	VF	XF
ND//5 (1810-11)	—	6.00	11.00	17.50	25.00	37.50
ND//6 (1811-12)	—	6.00	11.00	17.50	25.00	37.50
ND//7 (1812-13)	—	6.00	11.00	17.50	25.00	37.50
ND//8 (1813)	—	6.00	11.00	17.50	25.00	37.50
AH1230//11 (sic)	—	6.00	11.00	17.50	25.00	37.50
ND//13 (1818-19)	—	6.00	11.00	17.50	25.00	37.50
ND//14 (1819-20)	—	6.00	11.00	17.50	25.00	37.50
AH1235//15	—	6.00	11.00	17.50	25.00	37.50
ND//17 (1822-23)	—	6.00	11.00	17.50	25.00	37.50
ND//18 (1823-24)	—	6.00	11.00	17.50	25.00	37.50
ND//19 (1824-25)	—	6.00	11.00	17.50	25.00	37.50
ND//20 (1825-26)	—	6.00	11.00	17.50	25.00	37.50
ND//22 (1827-28)	—	6.00	11.00	17.50	25.00	37.50
ND//23 (1828-29)	—	6.00	11.00	17.50	25.00	37.50
ND//24 (1829-30)	—	6.00	11.00	17.50	25.00	37.50
ND//25 (1830-31)	—	6.00	11.00	17.50	25.00	37.50
AH123x//26	—	6.00	11.00	17.50	25.00	37.50
AH123x//27	—	6.00	11.00	17.50	25.00	37.50
ND//30 (1835-36)	—	6.00	11.00	17.50	25.00	37.50
ND//31 (1836-37)	—	6.00	11.00	17.50	25.00	37.50

KM# 20a NAZARANA RUPEE
11.3000 g., Silver **Obv. Inscription:** "Muhammad Akbar II" **Mint:** Rajgarh

Date	Mintage	Good	VG	F	VF	XF
AH12xx//26	—	—	120	200	300	400

Bani Singh
AH1231-1273 / 1815-1857AD

HAMMERED COINAGE

KM# 25 TAKKA
Copper **Obv. Inscription:** "Bahadur Shah II" **Mint:** Rajgarh **Note:** Weight varies 18.0-18.5 grams.

Date	Mintage	Good	VG	F	VF	XF
ND//2 (1838-39)	—	2.50	3.50	5.00	8.00	—
ND//6 (1842-43)	—	2.50	3.50	5.00	8.00	—
ND//9 (1845)	—	2.50	3.50	5.00	8.00	—
ND//12 (1847-48)	—	2.50	3.50	5.00	8.00	—
ND//15 (1850-51)	—	2.50	3.50	5.00	8.00	—
ND//17 (1852-53)	—	2.50	3.50	5.00	8.00	—
ND//18 (1853-54)	—	2.50	3.50	5.00	8.00	—
ND//19 (1854-55)	—	2.50	3.50	5.00	8.00	—
ND//20 (1855-56)	—	2.50	3.50	5.00	8.00	—

KM# 28 1/4 RUPEE
Silver, 16 mm. **Obv. Inscription:** "Bahadur Shah II" **Mint:** Rajgarh **Note:** Weight varies 2.80-2.85 grams.

Date	Mintage	Good	VG	F	VF	XF
AH127x//1x	—	20.00	40.00	65.00	100	150
ND//20 (1855-56)	—	20.00	40.00	65.00	100	150

KM# 29 1/2 RUPEE
Silver, 18 mm. **Obv. Inscription:** "Bahadur Shah II" **Mint:** Rajgarh **Note:** Weight varies 5.60-5.70 grams.

Date	Mintage	Good	VG	F	VF	XF
ND//17 (1852-53)	—	22.50	45.00	80.00	120	175

KM# 30 RUPEE
Silver, 21 mm. **Obv. Inscription:** "Bahadur Shah II" **Mint:** Rajgarh **Note:** Weight varies 11.20-11.40 grams.

Date	Mintage	Good	VG	F	VF	XF
ND//1 (1837-38)	—	6.00	12.50	21.00	28.50	40.00
AH1255//2	—	7.00	15.00	25.00	35.00	50.00
AH1255//3	—	7.00	15.00	25.00	35.00	50.00
AH12xx//4	—	7.00	15.00	25.00	35.00	50.00
AH1262//9	—	7.00	15.00	25.00	35.00	50.00
AH1263//11	—	7.00	15.00	25.00	35.00	50.00
AH126x//12	—	7.00	15.00	25.00	35.00	50.00
AH1267//13 (sic)	—	7.00	15.00	25.00	35.00	50.00
AH12xx//15	—	7.00	15.00	25.00	35.00	50.00
ND//16 (1851-52)	—	7.00	15.00	25.00	35.00	50.00
AH(12)73//20	—	6.00	12.50	21.00	28.50	40.00

KM# 30a NAZARANA RUPEE
Silver **Obv. Inscription:** "Bahadur Shah II" **Mint:** Rajgarh **Note:** Weight varies 11.20-11.50 grams.

Date	Mintage	Good	VG	F	VF	XF
AH125x//1	—	—	120	200	300	425
AH1261//8	—	—	120	200	300	425
AH1262//9	—	—	120	200	300	425
AH1267//13	—	—	120	200	300	425

Sheodan Singh
AH1274-1291 / 1857-1874AD

HAMMERED COINAGE

KM# 35.1 TAKKA
Copper **Obv. Inscription:** "The Exalted Queen (Victoria) at the seat of the realm England" **Rev. Inscription:** "Maharao Raj" Sawai Sheodan Singh Bahadur **Mint:** Rajgarh **Note:** Weight varies 18.5-19.0 grams.

Date	Mintage	Good	VG	F	VF	XF
1859//2	—	1.50	2.50	3.50	5.00	—
1860//3	—	1.50	2.50	3.50	5.00	—
1861//4	—	1.50	2.50	3.50	5.00	—
1862//4	—	1.50	2.50	3.50	5.00	—
1864	—	1.50	2.50	3.50	5.00	—
1865//9	—	1.50	2.50	3.50	5.00	—

KM# 35.2 TAKKA
Copper **Obv. Inscription:** "The Exalted Queen (Victoria) at the seat of the realm England" **Rev. Inscription:** "Maharaja di-raj Maharao" Raja Shri Sawai Sheodan "Singh Bahadur" **Mint:** Rajgarh **Note:** Weight varies 18.5-19.0 grams.

Date	Mintage	Good	VG	F	VF	XF
1870//13	—	1.50	2.50	3.50	5.00	—
1871//15	—	1.50	2.50	3.50	5.00	—

KM# 35a.1 NAZARANA TAKKA
Copper **Obv. Inscription:** "The Exalted Queen (Victoria) at the seat of the realm England" **Rev. Inscription:** "Maharao Rajah Sawai" Sheodan Singh Bahadur **Mint:** Rajgarh **Note:** Weight varies 18.5-19.1 grams.

Date	Mintage	Good	VG	F	VF	XF
1865//9	—	—	120	200	300	425
1866//9	—	—	120	200	300	425

KM# 35a.2 NAZARANA TAKKA
Copper **Obverse:** Parasol at top **Obv. Inscription:** "The Exalted Queen (Victoria) at the seat of the realm England" **Reverse:** Parasol at top **Rev. Inscription:** "Maharaja di-raj Maharao" Rajah Shri Sawai Sheodan "Singh Bahadur" **Mint:** Rajgarh **Note:** Weight varies 18.5-19.1 grams.

Date	Mintage	Good	VG	F	VF	XF
1871//15	—	—	120	200	300	425

KM# 37 RUPEE
Silver **Obv. Inscription:** "The Exalted Queen (Victoria) at the seat of the realm England" **Rev. Inscription:** "Maharaja di-raj Maharao" Rajah Shri Sawai Sheodan "Singh Bahadur" **Mint:** Rajgarh **Note:** Weight varies 11.20-11.30 grams.

Date	Mintage	Good	VG	F	VF	XF
1859//2	—	5.00	12.50	21.50	30.00	40.00
1860//3	—	5.00	12.50	21.50	30.00	40.00
1860//4	—	5.00	12.50	21.50	30.00	40.00
1861//4	—	5.00	12.50	21.50	30.00	40.00
1863//6	—	5.00	12.50	21.50	30.00	40.00
1864//7	—	5.00	12.50	21.50	30.00	40.00
1865//8	—	6.00	15.00	21.50	30.00	40.00
1865//9	—	6.00	15.00	21.50	30.00	40.00
ND//10	—	6.00	15.00	21.50	30.00	40.00

KM# 37a.1 NAZARANA RUPEE
Silver **Obv. Inscription:** "The Exalted Queen (Victoria) at the seat of the realm England" **Rev. Inscription:** "Maharao Rajah Sawai" Sheodan Singh Bahadur **Mint:** Rajgarh **Note:** Weight varies 10.70-11.60 grams.

Date	Mintage	Good	VG	F	VF	XF
1865//9	—	—	120	200	300	425

KM# 37a.2 NAZARANA RUPEE
Silver **Obverse:** Parasol at top **Obv. Inscription:** "The Exalted Queen (Victoria) at the seat of the realm England" **Reverse:** Parasol at top **Rev. Inscription:** "Maharaja di-raj Maharao" Rajah Shri Sawai Sheodan "Singh Bahadur" **Mint:** Rajgarh **Note:** Weight varies 10.70-11.60 grams.

Date	Mintage	Good	VG	F	VF	XF
1867//10	—	—	120	200	300	425
1870//15	—	—	120	200	300	425
ND//18 (1874)	—	—	—	—	—	—

Mangal Singh
AH1291-1310 / 1874-1892AD

HAMMERED COINAGE

KM# 40 NAZARANA TAKKA
18.5000 g., Copper **Obv. Inscription:** Mangal Singh **Mint:** Rajgarh **Note:** Similar to Nazarana Rupe, KM#41. Only a few each of KM#40 and 41 were struck at the Rajgarh Mint each year for presentation purposes.

Date	Mintage	Good	VG	F	VF	XF
1874	—	16.50	40.00	65.00	100	145
1891	—	16.50	40.00	65.00	100	145

KM# 41 NAZARANA RUPEE
Silver **Obv. Inscription:** Mangal Singh **Mint:** Rajgarh **Note:** Weight varies 11.30-11.35 grams. Only a few each of KM#40 and 41 were struck at the Rajgarh Mint each year for presentation purposes.

Date	Mintage	Good	VG	F	VF	XF
ND//2 (1875)	—	60.00	150	250	350	500
1876//3	—	60.00	150	250	350	500
1877//4	—	60.00	150	250	350	500
188x	—	60.00	150	250	350	500

KM# 39 PAISA
Copper **Obv. Inscription:** Mangal Singh

Date	Mintage	Good	VG	F	VF	XF
VS1947	—	—	—	—	—	—

MILLED COINAGE

KM# 45 RUPEE
11.6600 g., 0.9170 Silver .3438 oz. ASW, 31.5 mm. **Obverse:** Crowned bust of Queen Victoria left **Obv. Legend:** VICTORIA EMPRESS **Rev. Inscription:** "Maharao Rajah Sawai Mangal Singh" **Mint:** Rajgarh

Date	Mintage	Good	VG	F	VF	XF
1788 (error)	200,000	—	2.75	7.00	12.00	20.00
1877	200,000	—	2.50	6.00	10.00	17.50
1877	—	Value: 250				
1878	206,000	—	2.75	7.00	12.00	20.00
1880	196,000	—	2.50	6.00	10.00	17.50
1882	206,000	—	2.50	6.00	10.00	17.50
1882	—	Value: 250				

KM# 46 RUPEE
11.6600 g., 0.9170 Silver .3438 oz. ASW, 31.5 mm. **Obverse:** Crowned bust of Queen Victoria left **Obv. Legend:** VICTORIA EMPRESS **Rev. Inscription:** "Maharaja Shri Sawai Mangal Singh" **Mint:** Rajgarh

Date	Mintage	Good	VG	F	VF	XF
1891	160,000	—	2.60	6.00	10.00	16.50
1891	—	Value: 250				

KM# 46a RUPEE
11.6600 g., 0.9170 Silver .3438 oz. ASW **Obverse:** Crowned bust of Quen Victoria left **Obv. Legend:** VICTORIA EMPRESS **Rev. Inscription:** "Maharaja Shri Sawai Mangal Singh" **Mint:** Rajgarh

Date	Mintage	Good	VG	F	VF	XF
1891	—	Value: 2,000				

AWADH

Oudh

Kingdom located in northeastern India. The Nawabs of Awadh traced their origins to Muhammed Amin, a Persian adventurer who had attached himself to the court of Muhammed Shah, the Mughal Emperor, early in the 18th century. In 1720 Muhammed Amin was appointed Mughal Subahdar of Awadh, in which capacity he soon exhibited a considerable measure of independence. Until 1819, after Ghazi-ud-din had been encouraged by the Governor-General, Lord Hastings, to accept the title of King, Muhammed Amim's successors were known simply as the Nawabs of Awadh. The British offer, and Ghazi-ud-din's acceptance of it provided a clear indication of just how far Mughal decline had proceeded. The Mughal Emperor was now little more than a pensioner of the East India Company. Yet the coinage of Ghazi-ud-din immediately after 1819 marks also the hesitation he felt in taking so dramatic, and in the eyes of some of the princes of India, so ungrateful a step.

In 1856 Awadh was annexed by the British on the grounds of internal misrule. The king makers were now also seen as the king breakers. In setting aside the royal house of Awadh, the Muslim princes of India were added to that growing list of those who had come to fear the outcome of British hegemony. And it was here, in Awadh, that the Great Revolt of 1857 found its most fertile soil.

In 1877, Awadh along with Agra was placed under one administrator. It was made part of the United Provinces in 1902.

RULERS

Sa'adat Ali, AH1213-1230/1798-1814AD
Ghazi-ud-Din Haidar,
as Nawab, AH1230-1234/1814-1819AD
as King, AH1234-1243/1819-1827AD
Nasir-ud-Din Haidar, AH1243-1253/1827-1837AD
Muhammad Ali Shah, AH1253-1258/1837-1842AD
Amjad Ali Shah, AH1258-1263/1842-1847AD
Wajid Ali Shah, AH1263-1272/1847-1856AD
Brijis Qadr, AH1273-1274/1857-1858AD

MINTS

الله اباد
Allahabad

آصف اباد بریلی
Asafabad (Bareli)

اصفنگر اصف نگر
Asafnagar

اوده
Awadh

بنارس
Banaras

بریلی
Bareli

هاتهر
Hathras

اتاوا
Itawa

قنوج
Kanauj

کورا
Kora

لکهنو
Lucknow

محمداباد بنارس
Muhammadabad Banaras

The issues of the Nawab-Wazir in this mintname are distinguished from East India Company issues on the basis of distinctive fabric and fixed regnal year: 26 for Awadh, 17 for East India Company.

معظم اباد

Muazzamabad
(Gorakhpur)

مراداباد

Muradabad

نجيب اباد

Najibabad

To Awadh in 1774AD (AH1188). For issues before AH1188/R.Y. 15, see Rohilkhand.

شاہاباد شاه اباد

Shahabad

تانده

Tanda

MINT EPITHETS
Awadh

دار الامارة لكهنو صوبه اوده

Variety I: *Dar al-Amaret Lakhnau Suba Awadh,* AH1234-1235.

دار السلطانة لكهنو صوبه اوده

Variety II: *Dar as-Sultanat Lakhnau Suba Awadh,* AH1236-1243.

صوبه اوده دار السلطانة لكهنو

Variety AIII: *Suba Awadh Dar-as-Sultanat Lakhnau,* Coins dated AH1253/Yr. 1.

صوبه اوده بيت السلطانة لكهنو

Variety III; *Suba Awadh Baitu-s-Sultanat Lakhnau,* All coins dated through AH1256/Yr. 3.

ملك اوده بيت السلطانة لكهنو

Variety IV; *Mulk Awadh Baitu-s-Sultanat Lakhnau,* All coins beginning with date AH1256/Yr. 3, Yr. 4.

ملك اوده اخترنگر

Variety V; *Mulk Awadh Akhtarnagar*

AH1267/Yr. 5 reported so far only for Rupees Dated 1267/Yr. 5. The same date/year combination Is also found in Variety VI.

بيت السلطانة لكهنو ملك اوده اخترنگر

Variety VI: *Baitus-s-Sultanat Lakhnau Mulk Awadh Akhtar-Nagar,* AH1267/Yr. 5-1272.

HAMMERED COINAGE

Mughal Style

KM# 98 FALUS
Copper **Obv. Inscription:** "Shah Alam II" **Mint:** Lucknow **Note:** Round flan.

Date	Mintage	Good	VG	F	VF	XF
AH1222	—	1.75	3.00	4.50	7.00	—
AH1223	—	1.75	3.00	4.50	7.00	—
AH1226//26	—	1.75	3.00	4.50	7.00	—
AH1228//26	—	1.75	3.00	4.50	7.00	—
AH1229//29	—	1.75	3.00	4.50	7.00	—
AH1233	—	1.75	3.00	4.50	7.00	—

KM# 113 PAISA (Various weight standards)
Copper **Obv. Inscription:** "Shah Alam II" **Reverse:** Horizontal fish **Mint:** Najibabad

Date	Mintage	Good	VG	F	VF	XF
AH1216//43	—	5.00	7.00	10.00	15.00	—
AH1217//44	—	5.00	7.00	10.00	15.00	—

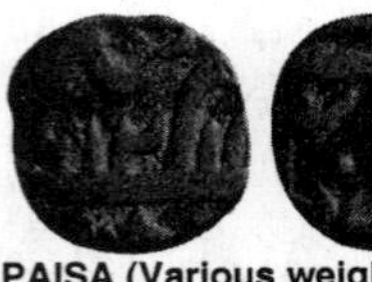

KM# 111 PAISA (Various weight standards)
Copper **Obverse:** Crescent **Obv. Inscription:** "Shah Alam II" **Reverse:** Vertical fish **Mint:** Najibabad **Note:** Various weight standards.

Date	Mintage	Good	VG	F	VF	XF
AH1216//43	—	3.00	4.00	6.00	8.50	—
AH1217//44	—	3.00	4.00	6.00	8.50	—
AH1218//47	—	3.00	4.00	6.00	8.50	—
AH1219	—	3.00	4.00	6.00	8.50	—

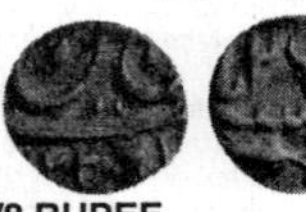

KM# 100.2 1/8 RUPEE
Silver **Obv. Inscription:** "Shah Alam II" **Reverse:** Frozen regnal year; mintmark: Flag and star **Mint:** Lucknow **Note:** Weight varies: 1.34-1.45 grams.

Date	Mintage	Good	VG	F	VF	XF
AH1207//26	—	10.00	25.00	50.00	80.00	120
AH1215//26	—	10.00	25.00	50.00	80.00	120
AH1218//26	—	10.00	25.00	50.00	80.00	120
AH1222//26	—	10.00	25.00	50.00	80.00	120
AH1226//26	—	10.00	25.00	50.00	80.00	120
AH1229//26	—	10.00	25.00	50.00	80.00	120
AH1232//26	—	10.00	25.00	50.00	80.00	120
AH1233//26	—	10.00	25.00	50.00	80.00	120

KM# 101.2 1/4 RUPEE
Silver **Obv. Inscription:** "Shah Alam II" **Reverse:** Frozen regnal year; mintmark: Flag and star **Mint:** Lucknow **Note:** Weight varies: 2.68-2.90 grams.

Date	Mintage	Good	VG	F	VF	XF
AH1218//26	—	16.00	40.00	75.00	120	170
AH1225//26	—	16.00	40.00	75.00	120	170
AH1231//26	—	16.00	40.00	75.00	120	170
AH1233//26	—	16.00	40.00	75.00	120	170

KM# 102.2 1/2 RUPEE
Silver **Obv. Inscription:** "Shah Alam II" **Reverse:** Frozen regnal year; mintmark: Flag and star **Mint:** Lucknow **Note:** Weight varies: 5.38-5.80 grams.

Date	Mintage	Good	VG	F	VF	XF
AH1207//26	—	25.00	60.00	100	150	200
AH1208//26	—	25.00	60.00	100	150	200
AH1223//26	—	25.00	60.00	100	150	200

KM# 103.3 RUPEE
Silver **Obverse:** Without AH date **Obv. Inscription:** "Shah Alam II" **Mint:** Lucknow **Note:** Weight varies: 10.70-11.60 grams.

Date	Mintage	Good	VG	F	VF	XF
AH-//26	—	5.00	10.00	20.00	35.00	50.00

KM# 103.2 RUPEE
Silver **Obv. Inscription:** "Shah Alam II" **Reverse:** Frozen regnal year; mintmark: Flag and star **Mint:** Lucknow **Note:** Weight varies: 10.70-11.60 grams.

Date	Mintage	Good	VG	F	VF	XF
AH1216//26	—	3.00	7.50	12.50	18.50	27.50
AH1217//26	—	3.00	7.50	12.50	18.50	27.50
AH1218//26	—	3.00	7.50	12.50	18.50	27.50
AH1219//26	—	3.00	7.50	12.50	18.50	27.50
AH1220//26	—	3.00	7.50	12.50	18.50	27.50
AH1221//26	—	2.75	7.00	11.00	16.50	25.00
AH1222//26	—	2.75	7.00	11.00	16.50	25.00
AH1223//26	—	2.75	7.00	11.00	16.50	25.00
AH1224//26	—	2.75	7.00	11.00	16.50	25.00
AH1225//26	—	2.75	7.00	11.00	16.50	25.00
AH1226//26	—	2.75	7.00	11.00	16.50	25.00
AH1227//26	—	2.75	7.00	11.00	16.50	25.00
AH1228//26	—	2.75	7.00	11.00	16.50	25.00
AH1229//26	—	2.75	7.00	11.00	16.50	25.00
AH1230//26	—	2.75	7.00	11.00	16.50	25.00
AH1231//26	—	2.75	7.00	11.00	16.50	25.00
AH1232//26	—	2.75	7.00	11.00	16.50	25.00
AH1233//26	—	2.75	7.00	11.00	16.50	25.00
AH1234//26	—	2.75	7.00	11.00	16.50	25.00

KM# 51.6 RUPEE
Silver **Obv. Inscription:** "Shah Alam II" **Reverse:** Fish, Persian letter "Mim", star-shaped flower, crescent **Mint:** Bareli **Note:** Weight varies: 10.70-11.60 grams.

Date	Mintage	Good	VG	F	VF	XF
AH1216//37 (sic)	—	4.00	10.00	16.50	22.50	32.50

KM# 116.7 RUPEE
Silver **Obv. Inscription:** "Shah Alam II" **Reverse:** Persian letter "Mim" written as word, bud, fish **Mint:** Najibabad **Note:** Weight varies: 10.70-11.60 grams.

Date	Mintage	Good	VG	F	VF	XF
AH1216//42	—	5.00	12.50	16.50	22.50	32.50

KM# 52.1 RUPEE
Silver **Obverse:** Cross **Obv. Legend:** "Shah Qirani" **Obv. Inscription:** "Shah Alam II" **Reverse:** Fish, star-shaped flower, Perisan letter "Alif" **Mint:** Bareli **Note:** Weight varies: 10.70-11.60 grams.

Date	Mintage	Good	VG	F	VF	XF
AH1216//37 (sic)	—	6.00	15.00	21.50	31.50	40.00

KM# 52.3 RUPEE
Silver **Obv. Inscription:** "Shah Alam II" **Reverse:** Fish, star-shaped flower, Persian letter "Wa" **Note:** Weight varies: 10.70-11.60 grams. The letter *Wa* on East India Company issues was reputedly the initial of the surname of the new settlement officer for Bareli, Henry Wellesley. The earlier issue, with letter *He,* may have been a less majestic initial of his personal name.

Date	Mintage	Good	VG	F	VF	XF
AH1216//37 (sic)	—	5.00	12.50	17.50	25.00	35.00
AH1217//37 (sic)	—	5.00	12.50	17.50	25.00	35.00
AH1218//37	—	5.00	12.50	17.50	25.00	35.00
AH1219//37	—	5.00	12.50	17.50	25.00	35.00
AH1220//37	—	5.00	12.50	17.50	25.00	35.00

KM# 52.2 RUPEE

Silver **Obv. Inscription:** "Shah Alam II" **Reverse:** Fish, star-shaped flower, Persian letter "He" **Note:** Weight varies: 10.70-11.60 grams.

Date	Mintage	Good	VG	F	VF	XF
AH1216//37 (sic)	—	6.00	15.00	21.50	31.50	40.00

KM# 116.8 RUPEE
Silver **Obv. Inscription:** "Shah Alam II" **Reverse:** Persian letter "Mim", Persian word "Ald", fish, Persian letter "He". **Mint:** Najibabad **Note:** Weight varies: 10.70-11.60 grams.

Date	Mintage	Good	VG	F	VF	XF
AH1216//43	—	5.00	12.50	16.50	22.50	32.50

KM# 116.11 RUPEE
Silver **Obv. Inscription:** "Shah Alam II" **Reverse:** Without horizontal fish **Mint:** Najibabad **Note:** Weight varies: 10.70-11.60 grams.

Date	Mintage	Good	VG	F	VF	XF
AHxxxx//47	—	5.00	12.50	16.50	22.50	32.50

KM# 115 RUPEE
Silver **Obv. Inscription:** "Shah Alam II" **Mint:** Najibabad

Date	Mintage	Good	VG	F	VF	XF
AH-//47	—	7.50	18.50	30.00	50.00	85.00

KM# 104 NAZARANA RUPEE
Silver, 28 mm. **Obv. Inscription:** "Shah Alam II" **Reverse:** Frozen regnal year **Mint:** Lucknow **Note:** Similar to 1 Rupee, KM#103, broad flan. Weight varies: 10.70-11.60 grams.

Date	Mintage	VG	F	VF	XF	Unc
AH1216//26	—	225	400	600	850	—

KM# B105 1/4 MOHUR
Gold **Obv. Inscription:** "Shah Alam II" **Mint:** Lucknow **Note:** Weight varies: 2.67-2.85 grams.

Date	Mintage	VG	F	VF	XF	Unc
AH-//26	—	325	550	850	1,200	—

KM# A105 1/2 MOHUR
Gold **Obv. Inscription:** "Shah Alam II" **Reverse:** Frozen regnal year **Mint:** Lucknow **Note:** Weight varies: 5.35-5.70 grams.

Date	Mintage	VG	F	VF	XF	Unc
AH1224//26	—	300	500	800	1,150	—

KM# 105 MOHUR
Gold **Obv. Inscription:** "Shah Alam II" **Reverse:** Frozen regnal year **Mint:** Lucknow **Note:** Weight varies: 10.70-11.40 grams.

Date	Mintage	VG	F	VF	XF	Unc
AH1218//26	—	185	225	265	350	—
AH1222/26	—	185	225	265	350	—
AH1230//26	—	185	225	265	350	—
AH1231//26	—	185	225	265	350	—

Ghazi-ud-Din Haidar, as King

AH1234-1243 / 1819-1827AD

HAMMERED COINAGE

KM# 140 FALUS
Copper **Obv. Inscription:** "Shah Alam II" **Mint:** Lucknow

Date	Mintage	Good	VG	F	VF	XF
AH1234//26	—	1.50	2.25	2.75	4.00	—
AH1235//26	—	1.50	2.25	2.75	4.00	—

KM# 155.1 FALUS
Copper **Obv. Inscription:** "Ghazi ud-din Haidar" **Mint:** Lucknow **Note:** Epithet: Variety I.

Date	Mintage	Good	VG	F	VF	XF
AH1234//5	—	1.35	2.75	4.50	7.50	—
AH1235//1	—	1.00	2.00	3.50	6.00	—

KM# 155.2 FALUS
Copper **Obv. Inscription:** "Ghazi ud-din Haidar" **Mint:** Lucknow **Note:** Epithet: Variety II.

Date	Mintage	Good	VG	F	VF	XF
AH1236//2	—	0.85	1.75	3.00	5.00	—
AH1237//3	—	0.85	1.75	3.00	5.00	—
AH1238//4	—	0.85	1.75	3.00	5.00	—
AH1239//5	—	0.85	1.75	3.00	5.00	—

KM# 155.3 FALUS
Copper **Obv. Inscription:** "Ghazi ud-din Haidar" **Mint:** Lucknow **Note:** Epithet: Variety II; size varies: 24-25 mm.

Date	Mintage	Good	VG	F	VF	XF
AH1240//6	—	7.50	12.00	20.00	35.00	—

KM# 157 1/16 RUPEE (Anna)
Silver **Obv. Inscription:** "Ghazi ud-din Haidar" **Mint:** Lucknow **Note:** Weight varies: 0.67-0.72 grams.

Date	Mintage	Good	VG	F	VF	XF
AH1235//1	—	8.00	20.00	32.00	50.00	70.00

KM# 142 1/8 RUPEE
Silver **Obv. Inscription:** "Ghazi ud-din Haidar" **Mint:** Lucknow **Note:** Weight varies: 1.34-2.45 grams.

Date	Mintage	Good	VG	F	VF	XF
AH1234//26	—	12.50	30.00	50.00	80.00	120

KM# 159 1/8 RUPEE (2 Annas)
Silver **Obv. Inscription:** "Ghazi ud-din Haidar" **Mint:** Lucknow **Note:** Weight varies: 1.34-1.45 grams; size varies: 14-16 mm.

Date	Mintage	Good	VG	F	VF	XF
AH1235//1	—	6.00	15.00	25.00	40.00	60.00
AH1236//2	—	6.00	15.00	25.00	40.00	60.00
AH-//5	—	6.00	15.00	25.00	40.00	60.00

KM# 144 1/4 RUPEE
Silver **Obv. Inscription:** "Ghazi ud-din Haidar" **Mint:** Lucknow **Note:** Weight varies: 2.68-2.90 grams.

Date	Mintage	Good	VG	F	VF	XF
AH1234//26	—	12.50	30.00	50.00	80.00	120

KM# 161 1/4 RUPEE
Silver **Obv. Inscription:** "Ghazi ud-din Haidar" **Mint:** Lucknow **Note:** Weight varies: 2.68-2.90 grams; size varies: 15-17 mm.

Date	Mintage	Good	VG	F	VF	XF
AH1236//2	—	5.00	12.50	20.00	30.00	45.00
AH-//4	—	5.00	12.50	20.00	30.00	45.00
AH-//6	—	5.00	12.50	20.00	30.00	45.00
AH124x//8	—	5.00	12.50	20.00	30.00	45.00

KM# 145 1/2 RUPEE
Silver **Obv. Inscription:** "Ghazi ud-din Haidar" **Mint:** Lucknow **Note:** Weight varies: 5.35-5.80 grams.

Date	Mintage	Good	VG	F	VF	XF
AH1234//26	—	18.50	45.00	75.00	120	170

KM# 163 1/2 RUPEE
Silver **Obv. Inscription:** "Ghazi ud-din Haidar" **Mint:** Lucknow **Note:** Weight varies: 5.35-5.80 grams.

Date	Mintage	Good	VG	F	VF	XF
AH1235//1	—	12.00	30.00	50.00	80.00	120
AH1236//2	—	12.00	30.00	50.00	80.00	120
AH1237//3	—	12.00	30.00	50.00	80.00	120
AH1238//4	—	12.00	30.00	50.00	80.00	120
AH1239//5	—	12.00	30.00	50.00	80.00	120
AH1240//6	—	12.00	30.00	50.00	80.00	120
AH1242//8	—	12.00	30.00	50.00	80.00	120

KM# 165.1 RUPEE
Silver **Obv. Inscription:** "Ghazi ud-din Haidar" **Mint:** Lucknow **Note:** Epithet: Variety I. Weight varies: 10.70-11.60 grams.

Date	Mintage	Good	VG	F	VF	XF
AH1234//1	—	3.00	7.50	12.50	18.50	27.50
AH1234//5	—	3.00	7.50	12.50	18.50	27.50
AH1235//1	—	3.00	7.50	12.50	18.50	27.50

KM# 146 RUPEE
Silver **Obv. Inscription:** "Ghazi ud-din Haidar" **Mint:** Lucknow **Note:** Weight varies: 10.70-11.60 grams.

Date	Mintage	Good	VG	F	VF	XF
AH1234//26	—	5.00	12.50	18.50	25.00	35.00

KM# 165.2 RUPEE
Silver **Obv. Inscription:** "Ghazi ud-din Haidar" **Mint:** Lucknow **Note:** Epithet: Variety II. Weight varies: 10.70-11.60 grams.

Date	Mintage	Good	VG	F	VF	XF
AH1236//2	—	3.00	7.50	12.50	18.50	27.50
AH1237//3	—	3.00	7.50	12.50	18.50	27.50
AH1238//4	—	3.00	7.50	12.50	18.50	27.50
AH1239//5	—	3.00	7.50	12.50	18.50	27.50
AH1240//6	—	3.00	7.50	12.50	18.50	27.50
AH1241//7	—	3.00	7.50	12.50	18.50	27.50
AH1242//8	—	3.00	7.50	12.50	18.50	27.50
AH1243//9	—	3.00	7.50	12.50	18.50	27.50

KM# 148 1/2 MOHUR
Gold **Obv. Inscription:** "Ghazi ud-din Haidar" **Mint:** Lucknow **Note:** Weight varies: 5.35-5.70 grams.

Date	Mintage	VG	F	VF	XF	Unc
AH1234//26	—	200	300	500	700	—

KM# 150 MOHUR
Gold **Obv. Inscription:** "Ghazi ud-din Haidar" **Mint:** Lucknow **Note:** Weight varies: 10.70-11.40 grams.

Date	Mintage	VG	F	VF	XF	Unc
AH1234//26	—	225	250	295	375	—

KM# 168 1/4 ASHRAFI
Gold **Obv. Inscription:** "Ghazi ud-din Haidar" **Mint:** Lucknow **Note:** Weight varies: 2.68-2.85 grams.

Date	Mintage	VG	F	VF	XF	Unc
AH1236//-	—	150	275	400	550	—
AH1243//-	—	150	275	400	550	—

KM# 170.1 ASHRAFI
Gold **Obv. Inscription:** "Ghazi ud-din Haidar" **Mint:** Lucknow **Note:** Epithet: Variety I. Weight varies: 10.70-11.40 grams.

Date	Mintage	VG	F	VF	XF	Unc
AH1234//5	—	250	285	325	425	—

KM# 170.2 ASHRAFI
Gold **Obv. Inscription:** "Ghazi ud-din Haidar" **Mint:** Lucknow **Note:** Epithet: II. Weight varies: 10.70-11.40 grams.

Date	Mintage	VG	F	VF	XF	Unc
AH1235//1	—	250	285	325	425	—
AH1236//1	—	250	285	325	425	—
AH1236//2	—	250	285	325	425	—
AH1238//4	—	250	285	325	425	—
AH1239//5	—	250	285	325	425	—
AH1240//6	—	250	285	325	425	—
AH1241//7	—	250	285	325	425	—
AH1242//8	—	250	285	325	425	—

Nasir-ud-Din Haidar
AH1243-1253 / 1827-1837AD
HAMMERED COINAGE

KM# 175 FALUS
Copper **Obv. Inscription:** Sulayman Jah **Mint:** Lucknow

Date	Mintage	Good	VG	F	VF	XF
AH1243//1	—	1.25	2.00	3.50	6.00	—
AH1244//1	—	1.25	2.00	3.50	6.00	—
AH1244//2	—	1.25	2.00	3.50	6.00	—

KM# 195.1 FALUS
Copper **Obv. Inscription:** Nasir al-Din Haidar **Mint:** Lucknow **Note:** Mint mark: Variety I.

Date	Mintage	Good	VG	F	VF	XF
AH1245//2	—	2.00	3.50	6.00	10.00	—
AH1245//3	—	2.00	3.50	6.00	10.00	—
AH1246//3	—	2.00	3.50	6.00	10.00	—
AH1246//4	—	2.00	3.50	6.00	10.00	—
AH1247//4	—	2.00	3.50	6.00	10.00	—
AH1247//5	—	2.00	3.50	6.00	10.00	—
AH1248//5	—	2.00	3.50	6.00	10.00	—
AH1249//6	—	2.00	3.50	6.00	10.00	—

KM# 195.2 FALUS
Copper **Obv. Inscription:** Nasir al-Din Haidar **Mint:** Lucknow **Note:** Mint mark: Variety II.

Date	Mintage	Good	VG	F	VF	XF
AH1249//6	—	2.00	3.50	6.00	10.00	—
AH1250//7	—	2.00	3.50	6.00	10.00	—

KM# 197 1/16 RUPEE (Anna)
Silver **Obv. Inscription:** Nasir al-Din Haidar **Mint:** Lucknow **Note:** Size varies: 9 - 13mm. Weight varies: 0.67-0.72 grams. Mint mark: Variety II.

Date	Mintage	Good	VG	F	VF	XF
AH1250	—	6.00	15.00	25.00	40.00	60.00
AH1252	—	6.00	15.00	25.00	40.00	60.00

KM# 180 1/8 RUPEE
Silver, 13 mm. **Obv. Inscription:** Sulayman Jah **Mint:** Lucknow **Note:** Weight varies: 1.34-1.45 grams.

Date	Mintage	Good	VG	F	VF	XF
AH1244//2	—	11.00	28.00	45.00	70.00	100
AH1245//3	—	11.00	28.00	45.00	70.00	100

KM# 199.1 1/8 RUPEE
Silver, 14 mm. **Obv. Inscription:** Nasir al-Din Haidar **Mint:** Lucknow **Note:** Weight varies: 1.34-1.45 grams. Mint mark: Variety I.

Date	Mintage	Good	VG	F	VF	XF
AH1246//3	—	4.00	10.00	20.00	30.00	45.00
AH1248//5	—	4.00	10.00	20.00	30.00	45.00

KM# 199.2 1/8 RUPEE
Silver, 14 mm. **Obv. Inscription:** Nasir al-Din Haidar **Mint:** Lucknow **Note:** Weight varies: 1.34-1.45 grams. Mint mark: Variety II.

Date	Mintage	Good	VG	F	VF	XF
AH1250	—	4.00	10.00	20.00	30.00	45.00

KM# 182 1/4 RUPEE
Silver **Obv. Inscription:** Sulayman Jah **Mint:** Lucknow **Note:** Weight varies: 2.68-2.90 grams.

Date	Mintage	Good	VG	F	VF	XF
AH1244//2	—	11.00	28.00	45.00	70.00	100
AH1251//8	—	11.00	28.00	45.00	700	100

KM# 201.1 1/4 RUPEE
Silver **Obv. Inscription:** Nasir al-Din Haidar **Mint:** Lucknow **Note:** Weight varies: 2.68-2.90 grams. Mint mark: Variety I.

Date	Mintage	Good	VG	F	VF	XF
AH1245//3	—	4.00	10.00	20.00	30.00	45.00
AH124x//4	—	4.00	10.00	20.00	30.00	45.00
AH1247//5	—	4.00	10.00	20.00	30.00	45.00
AH1248//5	—	4.00	10.00	20.00	30.00	45.00
AH-//6	—	4.00	10.00	20.00	30.00	45.00

KM# 201.2 1/4 RUPEE
Silver **Obv. Inscription:** Nasir al-Din Haidar **Mint:** Lucknow **Note:** Weight varies: 2.68-2.90 grams. Mint mark: Variety II.

Date	Mintage	Good	VG	F	VF	XF
AH1250	—	4.00	10.00	20.00	30.00	45.00
AH1251//8	—	4.00	10.00	20.00	30.00	45.00

KM# 184 1/2 RUPEE
Silver **Obv. Inscription:** Sulayman Jah **Mint:** Lucknow **Note:** Weight varies: 5.35-5.80 grams.

Date	Mintage	Good	VG	F	VF	XF
AH1243//1	—	11.00	28.00	45.00	70.00	100
AH1244//2	—	11.00	28.00	45.00	70.00	100

KM# 203 1/2 RUPEE
Silver **Obv. Inscription:** Nasir al-Din Haidar **Mint:** Lucknow **Note:** Weight varies: 5.35-5.80 grams. Mint mark: Variety I.

Date	Mintage	Good	VG	F	VF	XF
AH1243//1	—	8.00	20.00	32.00	50.00	70.00
AH1247//5	—	8.00	20.00	32.00	50.00	70.00
AH1248//5	—	8.00	20.00	32.00	50.00	70.00
AH1248//6	—	8.00	20.00	32.00	50.00	70.00
AH1250//7	—	8.00	20.00	32.00	50.00	70.00

KM# 186 RUPEE
Silver **Obv. Inscription:** Sulayman Jah **Mint:** Lucknow **Note:** Weight varies: 10.70-11.60 grams.

Date	Mintage	Good	VG	F	VF	XF
AH1243//1	—	3.00	7.50	12.50	18.50	27.50
AH1244//1	—	3.00	7.50	12.50	18.50	27.50
AH1244//2	—	3.00	7.50	12.50	18.50	27.50
AH1245//1	—	3.00	7.50	12.50	18.50	27.50
AH1245//2	—	3.00	7.50	12.50	18.50	27.50

KM# 205.1 RUPEE
Silver **Obv. Inscription:** Nasir al-Din Haidar **Mint:** Lucknow **Note:** Weight varies: 10.70-11.60 grams. Mint mark: Variety I.

Date	Mintage	Good	VG	F	VF	XF
AH1245//3	—	3.00	7.50	12.50	18.50	27.50
AH1246//3	—	3.00	7.50	12.50	18.50	27.50
AH1246//4	—	3.00	7.50	12.50	18.50	27.50
AH1247//4	—	3.00	7.50	12.50	18.50	27.50
AH1247//5	—	3.00	7.50	12.50	18.50	27.50
AH1248//5	—	3.00	7.50	12.50	18.50	27.50
AH1248//6	—	3.00	7.50	12.50	18.50	27.50
AH1249//6	—	3.00	7.50	12.50	18.50	27.50

KM# 205.2 RUPEE
Silver **Obv. Inscription:** Nasir al-Din Haidar **Mint:** Lucknow **Note:** Weight varies: 10.70-11.60 grams. Mint mark: Variety II.

Date	Mintage	Good	VG	F	VF	XF
AH1249//7	—	2.75	7.00	11.50	16.50	25.00
AH1250//7	—	2.75	7.00	11.50	16.50	25.00
AH1250//8	—	2.75	7.00	11.50	16.50	25.00
AH1251//7 (sic)	—	2.75	7.00	11.50	16.50	25.00
AH1251//8	—	2.75	7.00	11.50	16.50	25.00
AH1252//7 (sic)	—	2.75	7.00	11.50	16.50	25.00
AH1252//8 (sic)	—	2.75	7.00	11.50	16.50	25.00
AH1252//9	—	2.75	7.00	11.50	16.50	25.00
AH1253//9 (sic)	—	2.75	7.00	11.50	16.50	25.00
AH1253//10	—	2.75	7.00	11.50	16.50	25.00

KM# 205.3 RUPEE
Silver **Obv. Inscription:** Nasir al-Din Haidar **Mint:** Lucknow **Note:** Weight varies: 10.70-11.60 grams. Mint mark: Variety II. Reduced size. Struck with 1/4 Rupee dies.

Date	Mintage	VG	F	VF	XF	Unc
AH1250//7	—	20.00	31.50	42.50	60.00	—

KM# 189 1/2 ASHRAFI
Gold **Obv. Inscription:** Sulayman Jah **Mint:** Lucknow **Note:** Weight varies: 5.35 - 5.7 grams.

Date	Mintage	Good	VG	F	VF	XF
AH1243//1	—	—	—	—	—	—

KM# 235 1/2 ASHRAFI
Gold **Obv. Inscription:** Nasir al-Din Haidar **Mint:** Lucknow **Note:** Weight varies: 5.35-5.70 grams.

Date	Mintage	VG	F	VF	XF	Unc
AH1251//9	—	150	275	400	550	—

KM# 190 ASHRAFI
Gold **Obv. Inscription:** Sulayman Jah **Mint:** Lucknow **Note:** Weight varies: 10.70-11.40 grams.

Date	Mintage	Good	VG	F	VF	XF
AH1243//1	—	—	185	235	325	450
AH1244//2	—	—	185	235	325	450

KM# 240 ASHRAFI
Gold, 25 mm. **Obv. Inscription:** Nasir al-Din Haidar **Mint:** Lucknow **Note:** Weight varies: 10.70-11.40 grams. Mint mark: Variety I.

Date	Mintage	Good	VG	F	VF	XF
AH1245//3	—	—	185	235	300	400
AH1246//3	—	—	185	235	300	400
AH1252//9	—	—	185	235	300	400

Muhammad Ali Shah
AH1253-1258 / 1837-1842AD

HAMMERED COINAGE

KM# 305 FALUS
Copper **Obv. Inscription:** Muhammad Ali Shah **Mint:** Lucknow

Date	Mintage	Good	VG	F	VF	XF
AH1253//1	—	1.25	2.25	3.50	6.00	—
AH1254//2	—	1.25	2.25	3.50	6.00	—
AH1255//3	—	1.25	2.25	3.50	6.00	—

KM# 310 1/8 RUPEE
Silver, 10 mm. **Obv. Inscription:** Muhammad Ali Shah **Mint:** Lucknow **Note:** Weight varies: 1.34-1.45 grams.

Date	Mintage	Good	VG	F	VF	XF
AH1253//1	—	6.00	15.00	25.00	40.00	60.00
AH1256	—	6.00	15.00	25.00	40.00	60.00

KM# 312 1/4 RUPEE
Silver **Obv. Inscription:** Muhammad Ali Shah **Mint:** Lucknow **Note:** Weight varies: 2.68-2.90 grams.

Date	Mintage	Good	VG	F	VF	XF
AH1253	—	6.00	15.00	25.00	40.00	60.00
AH1254	—	6.00	15.00	25.00	40.00	60.00
AH1255	—	6.00	15.00	25.00	40.00	60.00
AH1256	—	6.00	15.00	25.00	40.00	60.00

KM# 314.1 1/2 RUPEE
Silver **Obv. Inscription:** "Muhammad Ali Shah" **Mint:** Lucknow **Note:** Epithet: Variety II.

Date	Mintage	Good	VG	F	VF	XF
AH1253/1	—	11.00	28.00	45.00	70.00	100

KM# 313 1/2 RUPEE
Silver **Obv. Inscription:** Muhammad Ali Shah **Mint:** Lucknow **Note:** Weight varies: 5.35-5.80 grams. Epithet: Variety AIII.

Date	Mintage	Good	VG	F	VF	XF
AH1253//1 Rare	—	—	—	—	—	—

KM# 314.2 1/2 RUPEE
Silver **Obv. Inscription:** Muhammad Ali Shah **Mint:** Lucknow **Note:** Weight varies: 5.35-5.80 grams. Epithet: Variety III.

Date	Mintage	Good	VG	F	VF	XF
AH1254	—	11.00	28.00	45.00	70.00	100
AH1254	—	11.00	28.00	45.00	70.00	100

KM# 314.3 1/2 RUPEE
Silver **Obv. Inscription:** Muhammad Ali Shah **Mint:** Lucknow **Note:** Weight varies: 5.35-5.80 grams. Epithet: Variety IV.

Date	Mintage	Good	VG	F	VF	XF
AH1256//3	—	11.00	28.00	45.00	70.00	100
AH1258	—	11.00	28.00	45.00	70.00	100

KM# 315 RUPEE
Silver **Obv. Inscription:** Muhammad Ali Shah **Mint:** Lucknow **Note:** Weight varies: 10.70-11.60 grams. Epithet: Variety AIII.

Date	Mintage	Good	VG	F	VF	XF
AH1253//1	—	4.00	10.00	20.00	35.00	55.00

KM# 316.3 RUPEE
Silver **Obv. Inscription:** Muhammad Ali Shah **Mint:** Lucknow **Note:** Weight varies: 10.70-11.60 grams. Epithet: Variety II.

Date	Mintage	Good	VG	F	VF	XF
AH1253//1	—	3.00	7.50	12.50	18.50	27.50

KM# 316.1 RUPEE
Silver **Obv. Inscription:** Muhammad Ali Shah **Mint:** Lucknow **Note:** Weight varies: 10.70-11.60 grams. Epithet: Variety III.

Date	Mintage	Good	VG	F	VF	XF
AH1254//1	—	3.00	7.50	12.50	18.50	27.50
AH1254//2	—	3.00	7.50	12.50	18.50	27.50
AH1255//2	—	3.00	7.50	12.50	18.50	27.50
AH1255//3	—	3.00	7.50	12.50	18.50	27.50
AH1256//3	—	3.00	7.50	12.50	18.50	27.50

KM# 316.2 RUPEE
Silver **Obv. Inscription:** Muhammad Ali Shah **Mint:** Lucknow **Note:** Weight varies: 10.70-11.60 grams. Epithet: Variety IV.

Date	Mintage	Good	VG	F	VF	XF
AH1254//1	—	3.00	7.50	12.50	18.50	27.50
AH1256//3	—	3.00	7.50	12.50	18.50	27.50
AH1256//4	—	3.00	7.50	12.50	18.50	27.50
AH1257//4	—	3.00	7.50	12.50	18.50	27.50
AH1257//5	—	3.00	7.50	12.50	18.50	27.50
AH1258//5	—	3.00	7.50	12.50	18.50	27.50

KM# 320 1/2 ASHRAFI
Gold **Obv. Inscription:** Muhammad Ali Shah **Mint:** Lucknow **Note:** Weight varies: 5.35-5.70 grams.

Date	Mintage	VG	F	VF	XF	Unc
AH1253//1	—	175	285	400	550	—

KM# 322.1 ASHRAFI
Gold **Obv. Inscription:** Muhammad Ali Shah **Mint:** Lucknow **Note:** Weight varies: 10.70-11.40 grams. Epithet: Variety III.

Date	Mintage	VG	F	VF	XF	Unc
AH1253//1	—	135	225	275	375	—
AH1255//3	—	135	225	275	375	—
AH1256//4	—	135	225	275	375	—

KM# 322.2 ASHRAFI
Gold **Obv. Inscription:** Muhammad Ali Shah **Mint:** Lucknow **Note:** Weight varies: 10.70-11.40 grams. Epithet: Variety IV.

Date	Mintage	VG	F	VF	XF	Unc
AH1258	—	135	225	275	375	—

Amjad Ali Shah
AH1258-1263 / 1842-1847AD

HAMMERED COINAGE

KM# 325 FALUS
Copper **Obv. Inscription:** Amjad Ali Shah **Mint:** Lucknow

Date	Mintage	Good	VG	F	VF	XF
AH1258//1(Ahad)	—	2.00	3.50	6.00	10.00	—
AH1259//1(Ahad)	—	2.00	3.50	6.00	10.00	—
AH1259//2	—	2.00	3.50	6.00	10.00	—
AH1260//2	—	2.00	3.50	6.00	10.00	—
AH1262	—	2.00	3.50	6.00	10.00	—

KM# 326 FALUS
Copper, 27 mm. **Obv. Inscription:** Amjad Ali Shah **Mint:** Lucknow **Note:** Finer style.

Date	Mintage	Good	VG	F	VF	XF
AH1258//1	—	5.00	10.00	15.00	21.50	—

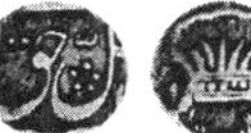

KM# 328 1/16 RUPEE
Silver **Obv. Inscription:** Amjad Ali Shah **Mint:** Lucknow **Note:** Weight varies: 0.67-0.72 grams.

Date	Mintage	Good	VG	F	VF	XF
AH1262	—	6.00	15.00	25.00	40.00	60.00

KM# 330 1/8 RUPEE
Silver **Obv. Inscription:** Amjad Ali Shah **Mint:** Lucknow **Note:** Weight varies: 1.34-1.45 grams.

Date	Mintage	Good	VG	F	VF	XF
AH1258	—	6.00	15.00	25.00	40.00	60.00

Date	Mintage	Good	VG	F	VF	XF
AH1259	—	6.00	15.00	25.00	40.00	60.00
AH1262	—	6.00	15.00	25.00	40.00	60.00

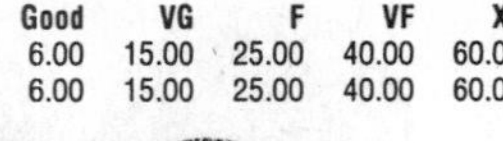

KM# 332 1/4 RUPEE
Silver **Obv. Inscription:** Amjad Ali Shah **Mint:** Lucknow **Note:** Weight varies: 2.68-2.90 grams.

Date	Mintage	Good	VG	F	VF	XF
AH1259//2	—	6.00	15.00	25.00	40.00	60.00
AH1260//3	—	6.00	15.00	25.00	40.00	60.00
AH1263	—	6.00	15.00	25.00	40.00	60.00

KM# 334 1/2 RUPEE
Silver **Obv. Inscription:** Ajmad Ali Shah **Mint:** Lucknow **Note:** Size varies: 18-20mm. Weight varies: 5.35-5.80 grams.

Date	Mintage	Good	VG	F	VF	XF
AH1259//2	—	11.00	28.00	45.00	70.00	100
AH1260//3	—	11.00	28.00	45.00	70.00	100
AH1261	—	11.00	28.00	45.00	70.00	100

KM# 336 RUPEE
Silver **Obv. Inscription:** Amjad Ali Shah **Mint:** Lucknow **Note:** Weight varies: 10.70-11.60 grams. Epithet: Variety IV.

Date	Mintage	Good	VG	F	VF	XF
AH1258//1	—	3.00	7.50	12.50	18.50	32.50
AH1259//1	—	3.00	7.50	12.50	18.50	32.50
AH1259//2	—	3.00	7.50	12.50	18.50	32.50
AH1260//2	—	3.00	7.50	12.50	18.50	32.50
AH1260//3	—	3.00	7.50	12.50	18.50	32.50
AH1261	—	3.00	7.50	12.50	18.50	32.50
AH1262//4	—	3.00	7.50	12.50	18.50	32.50
AH1261//4	—	3.00	7.50	12.50	18.50	32.50
AH1263//5	—	3.00	7.50	12.50	18.50	32.50
AH1262//5	—	3.00	7.50	12.50	18.50	32.50

KM# 339 1/4 ASHRAFI
Gold **Obv. Inscription:** Amjad Ali Shah **Mint:** Lucknow **Note:** Weight varies: 2.37-2.85 grams.

Date	Mintage	VG	F	VF	XF	Unc
AH1260	—	175	300	400	550	—

KM# 340 1/2 ASHRAFI
Gold **Obv. Inscription:** Amjad Ali Shah **Mint:** Lucknow **Note:** Weight varies: 5.35-5.70 grams.

Date	Mintage	VG	F	VF	XF	Unc
AH1258	—	200	325	500	650	—
AH1259//2	—	200	325	500	650	—
AH1263	—	200	325	500	650	—

KM# 342 ASHRAFI
Gold **Obv. Inscription:** Amjad Ali Shah **Mint:** Lucknow **Note:** Weight varies: 10.70-11.40 grams.

Date	Mintage	VG	F	VF	XF	Unc
AH1258	—	175	225	275	365	—
AH1259//2	—	175	225	275	365	—
AH1261//4	—	175	225	275	365	—
AH1262//5	—	175	225	275	365	—
AH1263	—	175	225	275	365	—

Wajid Ali Shah

AH1263-1272 / 1847-1856AD

HAMMERED COINAGE

KM# 345 1/8 FALUS
Copper **Obv. Inscription:** Wajid Ali Shah **Mint:** Lucknow

Date	Mintage	Good	VG	F	VF	XF
AH1270//7	—	7.00	15.00	25.00	40.00	—
AH1270//8	—	7.00	15.00	25.00	40.00	—
AH1271	—	7.00	15.00	25.00	40.00	—

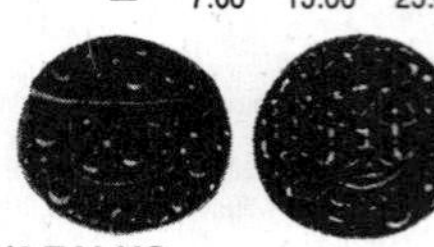

KM# 347 1/4 FALUS
Copper **Obv. Inscription:** Wajid Ali Shah **Mint:** Lucknow

Date	Mintage	Good	VG	F	VF	XF
AH1270//6	—	7.00	15.00	25.00	40.00	—
AH1270//7	—	7.00	15.00	25.00	40.00	—
AH1270//8	—	7.00	15.00	25.00	40.00	—
AH1272//9	—	7.00	15.00	25.00	40.00	—

KM# 349 1/2 FALUS
Copper **Obv. Inscription:** Wajid Ali Shah **Mint:** Lucknow

Date	Mintage	Good	VG	F	VF	XF
AH1269	—	2.75	4.50	6.00	8.50	—
AH1270//7	—	2.75	4.50	6.00	8.50	—
AH1270//8	—	2.75	4.50	6.00	8.50	—
AH1271	—	2.75	4.50	6.00	8.50	—
AH1272	—	2.75	4.50	6.00	8.50	—

KM# 351.1 FALUS
Copper **Obv. Inscription:** Wajid Ali Shah **Mint:** Lucknow **Note:** Epithet: Variety IV.

Date	Mintage	Good	VG	F	VF	XF
AH1263//1	—	2.00	3.50	5.00	7.00	—
AH1264//2	—	2.00	3.50	5.00	7.00	—

KM# 351.2 FALUS
Copper **Obv. Inscription:** Wajid Ali Shah **Mint:** Lucknow **Note:** Epithet: Variety V.

Date	Mintage	Good	VG	F	VF	XF
AH1267//4	—	10.00	15.00	25.00	40.00	—

KM# 351.3 FALUS
Copper **Obv. Inscription:** Wajid Ali Shah **Mint:** Lucknow **Note:** Epithet: Variety VI.

Date	Mintage	Good	VG	F	VF	XF
AH1270//8	—	2.00	3.50	5.00	7.00	—
AH1270//9 (sic)	—	2.00	3.50	5.00	7.00	—
AH1272	—	2.00	3.50	5.00	7.00	—

KM# 351.4 FALUS
Copper **Obv. Inscription:** Wajid Ali Shah **Mint:** Lucknow **Note:** Rectangular. 14x18mm.

Date	Mintage	Good	VG	F	VF	XF
AH1271	—	2.00	3.50	5.00	7.00	—

KM# 355 1/16 RUPEE
Silver **Obv. Inscription:** Wajid Ali Shah **Mint:** Lucknow **Note:** Weight varies: 0.67-0.72 grams.

Date	Mintage	Good	VG	F	VF	XF
AH126x	—	6.00	15.00	25.00	40.00	60.00
AH1270//8	—	6.00	15.00	25.00	40.00	60.00
AH1270//2 (sic)	—	6.00	15.00	25.00	40.00	60.00
AH1271	—	6.00	15.00	25.00	40.00	60.00
AH1272	—	6.00	15.00	25.00	40.00	60.00

KM# 357.1 1/8 RUPEE
Silver **Obv. Inscription:** Wajid Ali Shah **Mint:** Lucknow **Note:** Weight varies: 1.34-1.45 grams. Epithet: Variety IV.

Date	Mintage	Good	VG	F	VF	XF
AH1264//1	—	5.00	12.50	20.00	30.00	50.00
AH1264//2	—	5.00	12.50	20.00	30.00	50.00
AH1265//2	—	5.00	12.50	20.00	30.00	50.00
AH1266	—	5.00	12.50	20.00	30.00	50.00
AH126x//5	—	5.00	12.50	20.00	30.00	50.00
AH1268	—	5.00	12.50	20.00	30.00	50.00

KM# 357.2 1/8 RUPEE
Silver **Obv. Inscription:** Wajid Ali Shah **Mint:** Lucknow **Note:** Weight varies: 1.34-1.45 grams. Epithet: Variety VI.

Date	Mintage	Good	VG	F	VF	XF
AH1268	—	5.00	12.50	20.00	30.00	50.00
AH1269	—	5.00	12.50	20.00	30.00	50.00
AH1270//8	—	5.00	12.50	20.00	30.00	50.00
AH1271//9	—	5.00	12.50	20.00	30.00	50.00

KM# 361.1 1/4 RUPEE
Silver **Obv. Inscription:** Wajid Ali Shah **Mint:** Lucknow **Note:** Weight varies: 2.68-2.90 grams. Epithet: Variety IV.

Date	Mintage	Good	VG	F	VF	XF
AH1263//1	—	5.00	12.50	20.00	30.00	50.00
AH1265	—	5.00	12.50	20.00	30.00	50.00

KM# 361.2 1/4 RUPEE
Silver **Obv. Inscription:** Wajid Ali Shah **Mint:** Lucknow **Note:** Weight varies: 2.68-2.90 grams. Epithet: Variety VI.

Date	Mintage	Good	VG	F	VF	XF
AH1267//5	—	5.00	12.50	20.00	30.00	50.00
AH1268	—	5.00	12.50	20.00	30.00	50.00
AH1269//6	—	5.00	12.50	20.00	30.00	50.00
AH1271//9	—	5.00	12.50	20.00	30.00	50.00

KM# 363.1 1/2 RUPEE
Silver **Obv. Inscription:** Wajid Ali Shah **Mint:** Lucknow **Note:** Weight varies: 5.35-5.80 grams. Epithet: Variety IV.

Date	Mintage	Good	VG	F	VF	XF
AH1263//2 (sic)	—	9.00	22.50	40.00	60.00	85.00
AH1265//2	—	9.00	22.50	40.00	60.00	90.00
AH1266//3	—	9.00	22.50	40.00	60.00	85.00

KM# 363.2 1/2 RUPEE
Silver **Obv. Inscription:** Wajid Ali Shah **Mint:** Lucknow **Note:** Weight varies: 5.35-5.80 grams.

Date	Mintage	Good	VG	F	VF	XF
AH1268//5	—	9.00	22.50	40.00	60.00	85.00
AH1269//6	—	9.00	22.50	40.00	60.00	85.00
AH1271//8	—	9.00	22.50	40.00	60.00	85.00
AH1271//9	—	9.00	22.50	40.00	60.00	85.00

KM# 365.1 RUPEE
Silver **Obv. Inscription:** Wajid Ali Shah **Mint:** Lucknow **Note:** Weight varies: 10.70-11.60 grams. Epithet: Variety IV.

Date	Mintage	Good	VG	F	VF	XF
AH1263//1	—	3.00	7.50	11.00	16.50	25.00
AH1264//1	—	3.00	7.50	11.00	16.50	25.00
AH1264//2	—	3.00	7.50	11.00	16.50	25.00
AH1265//1	—	3.00	7.50	11.00	16.50	25.00
AH1265//2	—	3.00	7.50	11.00	16.50	25.00
AH1265//3	—	3.00	7.50	11.00	16.50	25.00
AH1266//3	—	3.00	7.50	11.00	16.50	25.00
AH1266//4	—	3.00	7.50	11.00	16.50	25.00
AH1267//3 (sic)	—	3.00	7.50	11.00	16.50	25.00
AH1267//4	—	3.00	7.50	11.00	16.50	25.00
AH1268//4 (sic)	—	3.00	7.50	11.00	16.50	25.00

KM# 365.2 RUPEE
Silver **Obv. Inscription:** Wajid Ali Shah **Mint:** Lucknow **Note:** Weight varies: 10.70-11.60 grams. Epithet: Variety V.

Date	Mintage	Good	VG	F	VF	XF
AH1267//5	—	7.00	17.50	25.00	35.00	50.00

KM# 365.3 RUPEE
Silver **Obv. Inscription:** Wajid Ali Shah **Mint:** Lucknow **Note:** Weight varies: 10.70-11.60 grams. Epithet: Variety VI.

Date	Mintage	Good	VG	F	VF	XF
AH1267//5	—	2.75	7.00	11.00	16.50	25.00
AH1268//5	—	2.75	7.00	11.00	16.50	25.00
AH1268//5	—	2.75	7.00	11.00	16.50	25.00
AH1269//6	—	2.75	7.00	11.00	16.50	25.00
AH1269//2 (sic)	—	2.75	7.00	11.00	16.50	25.00
Note: 2 is backwards 6						
AH1269//7	—	2.75	7.00	11.00	16.50	25.00
AH1270//7	—	2.75	7.00	11.00	16.50	25.00
AH1270//8	—	2.75	7.00	11.00	16.50	25.00
AH1271//8	—	2.75	7.00	11.00	16.50	25.00
AH1271//9	—	2.75	7.00	11.00	16.50	25.00
AH1272//9	—	2.75	7.00	11.00	16.50	25.00
AH1272//10	—	2.75	7.00	11.00	16.50	25.00

KM# 370 1/16 ASHRAFI
Gold, 10 mm. **Obv. Inscription:** Wajid Ali Shah **Mint:** Lucknow **Note:** Weight varies: 0.67-0.71 grams.

Date	Mintage	VG	F	VF	XF	Unc
AH1270	—	100	175	250	350	—

KM# 372 1/8 ASHRAFI
Gold **Obv. Inscription:** Wajid Ali Shah **Mint:** Lucknow **Note:** Weight varies: 1.34-1.42 grams.

Date	Mintage	VG	F	VF	XF	Unc
AH1263-72	—	120	200	300	450	—

KM# 374 1/4 ASHRAFI
Gold **Obv. Inscription:** Wajid Ali Shah **Mint:** Lucknow **Note:** Weight varies: 2.68-2.85 grams.

Date	Mintage	VG	F	VF	XF	Unc
AH1267//5	—	150	250	400	550	—
AH1268//5	—	150	250	400	550	—
AH1271	—	150	250	400	550	—

KM# 376 1/2 ASHRAFI
Gold **Obv. Inscription:** Wajid Ali Shah **Mint:** Lucknow **Note:** Weight varies: 5.35-5.70 grams. Epithet: Variety IV.

Date	Mintage	VG	F	VF	XF	Unc
AH1263//1	—	165	275	400	550	—
AH1264//2	—	165	275	400	550	—
AH1265//3	—	165	275	400	550	—
AH1266//4	—	165	275	400	550	—
AH1267//4	—	165	275	400	550	—
AH1267//5	—	165	275	400	550	—

KM# 378.1 ASHRAFI
Gold **Obv. Inscription:** Wajid Ali Shah **Mint:** Lucknow **Note:** Size varies: 23-24mm. Weight varies: 10.70-11.40 grams. Epithet: Variety IV. Struck with rupee dies.

Date	Mintage	VG	F	VF	XF	Unc
AH1263//1	—	165	200	250	300	—
AH1263//2 (sic)	—	165	200	250	300	—
AH1264/2	—	165	200	250	300	—
AH1265//2	—	165	200	250	300	—
AH1265//3	—	165	200	250	300	—
AH1266//3	—	165	200	250	300	—
AH1266//4	—	165	200	250	300	—
AH1267//4	—	165	200	250	300	—
AH1268//5	—	165	200	250	300	—

KM# 378.2 ASHRAFI
Gold, 21.5 mm. **Obv. Inscription:** Wajid Ali Shah **Mint:** Lucknow **Note:** Weight varies: 10.70-11.40 grams. Epithet: Variety IV. Struck with Asrafi dies.

Date	Mintage	VG	F	VF	XF	Unc
AH1264//2	—	165	200	250	300	—

KM# 378.3 ASHRAFI
Gold **Obv. Inscription:** Wajid Ali Shah **Mint:** Lucknow **Note:** Size varies: 23-24mm. Weight varies: 10.70-11.40 grams. Epithet: Variety VI.

Date	Mintage	VG	F	VF	XF	Unc
AH1272//9	—	165	200	250	300	—

Brijis Qadr
AH1273-1274 / 1857-1858AD

HAMMERED COINAGE
Nawab-Wazir during the Indian Mutiny

Ficticious dating in imitation of coinage before AH1234/1819. These are identifiable only by style and mint-name, "Awadh" appearing at top of reverse, and "Subah" at the bottom, dated only AH1229/yr.26.

KM# 380 FALUS
Copper **Obv. Inscription:** "Shah Alam II" **Mint:** Lucknow **Note:** Frozen date.

Date	Mintage	Good	VG	F	VF	XF
AH1229//26	—	12.50	22.50	32.50	50.00	—

KM# 382 1/8 RUPEE
Silver **Obv. Inscription:** "Shah Alam II" **Mint:** Lucknow **Note:** Frozen date. Size varies: 13-14mm. Weight varies: 1.34-1.45 grams.

Date	Mintage	Good	VG	F	VF	XF
AH1229//26	—	50.00	125	200	300	450

KM# 383 1/4 RUPEE
Silver **Obv. Inscription:** "Shah Alam II" **Mint:** Lucknow **Note:** Frozen date. Weight varies: 2.68-2.90 grams.

Date	Mintage	Good	VG	F	VF	XF
AH1229//26	—	60.00	150	225	300	450

KM# 384 1/2 RUPEE
Silver **Obv. Inscription:** "Shah Alam II" **Mint:** Lucknow **Note:** Frozen date. Weight varies: 5.35-5.80 grams.

Date	Mintage	Good	VG	F	VF	XF
AH1229//26	—	80.00	200	300	400	550

KM# 386 RUPEE
Silver **Obv. Inscription:** "Shah Alam II" **Mint:** Lucknow **Note:** Frozen date. Weight varies: 10.70-11.60 grams.

Date	Mintage	Good	VG	F	VF	XF
AH1229//26	—	10.00	25.00	45.00	70.00	100

KM# 390 ASHRAFI
Gold **Obv. Inscription:** "Shah Alam II" **Mint:** Lucknow **Note:** Frozen date. Weight varies: 10.70-11.40 grams.

Date	Mintage	VG	F	VF	XF	Unc
AH1229//26	—	350	500	700	1,100	—

BAHAWALPUR

The Amirs of Bahawalpur established their independence from Afghan control towards the close of the 18th century. In the 1830's the state's independence under British suzerainty became guaranteed by treaty. With the creation of Pakistan in 1947 Bahawalpur, with an area of almost 17,500 square miles, became its premier Princely State. Bahawalpur State, named after its capital, stretched for almost three hundred miles along the left bank of the Sutlej, Panjnad and Indus rivers.

For earlier issues in the names of the Durrani rulers, see Afghanistan.

RULERS

Amirs
Muhammad Bahawal Khan II, AH1186-1224/1772-1809AD
Sadiq Muhammad Khan II, AH1224-1241/1809-1825AD
Muhammad Bahawal Khan III, AH1241-1269/1825-1852AD
Sadiq Muhammad Khan III, AH1269-1270/1852-1853AD
Fateh Khan, AH1270-1275/1853-1858AD
Muhammad Bahawal Khan IV, AH1275-1283/1858-1866AD
Sir Sadiq Muhammad Khan IV, AH1283-1317/1866-1899AD
Alhaj Muhammad Bahawal Khan V, AH1317-1325/1899-1907AD

MINTS

احمدپور نمدپور
Ahmadpur

دار الاسلام
Dar al-Islam

بهاولپور
Bahawalpur

خانپور
Khanpur

The mint names at the bottom of the reverses of Bahawalpur State rupees are often off the flans. In most cases these rupees can be attributed to one of the three mints from other characteristics. Ahmadpur rupees weigh considerably less than those of the other two mints. Bahawalpur and Khanpur rupees can usually be differentiated by the location of their dates and other characteristics, as illustrated below (Y#4 and Y#5).

ANONYMOUS HAMMERED COINAGE

Y# 1 FALUS
Copper **Shape:** Square, irregular or round **Mint:** Bahawalpur **Note:** Contemporary ND imitations exist.

Date	Mintage	Good	VG	F	VF	XF
ND(1790-1864)	—	3.00	5.00	7.00	10.00	—
AH1205	—	3.00	5.00	7.00	10.00	—
AH1206	—	3.00	5.00	7.00	10.00	—
AH1214	—	3.00	5.00	7.00	10.00	—
AH1225	—	3.00	5.00	7.00	10.00	—
AH1237//13	—	3.00	5.00	7.00	10.00	—
AH1244	—	3.00	5.00	7.00	10.00	—
AH1248	—	3.00	5.00	7.00	10.00	—
AH1249	—	3.00	5.00	7.00	10.00	—
AH1254	—	3.00	5.00	7.00	10.00	—
AH1259	—	3.00	5.00	7.00	10.00	—
AH1261	—	3.00	5.00	7.00	10.00	—

Date	Mintage	Good	VG	F	VF	XF
AH1269	—	3.00	5.00	7.00	10.00	—
AH1270	—	3.00	5.00	7.00	10.00	—
AH1271	—	3.00	5.00	7.00	10.00	—
AH1273	—	3.00	5.00	7.00	10.00	—
AH1276	—	3.00	5.00	7.00	10.00	—
AH1277	—	3.00	5.00	7.00	10.00	—
AH1281	—	3.00	5.00	7.00	10.00	—

Muhammad Bahawal Khan II

AH1186-1224 / 1772-1809AD

ANONYMOUS HAMMERED COINAGE

C# 10 FALUS
Copper **Obverse:** Lion left looking right **Mint:** Ahmadpur

Date	Mintage	Good	VG	F	VF	XF
ND(1772-1809)	—	7.50	12.50	20.00	30.00	—

C# 18 RUPEE
Silver **Obv. Inscription:** Mahmud Shah **Mint:** Ahmadpur **Note:** Weight varies: 10.70-11.60 grams.

Date	Mintage	Good	VG	F	VF	XF
AH1217//48	—	5.50	13.50	20.00	27.50	37.50
ND//49	—	5.50	13.50	20.00	27.50	37.50

Y# 3.1 RUPEE
Silver **Obv. Inscription:** Mahmud Shah **Mint:** Ahmadpur **Note:** Reduced weight, 7.70-7.80 grams. Dated on obverse, sometimes also on reverse.

Date	Mintage	Good	VG	F	VF	XF
AH1246	—	3.50	9.00	18.00	28.00	40.00
AH1251	—	3.50	9.00	18.00	28.00	40.00
AH1252	—	3.50	9.00	18.00	28.00	40.00
AH1253	—	3.50	9.00	18.00	28.00	40.00
AH1254	—	3.50	9.00	18.00	28.00	40.00
AH1256	—	3.50	9.00	18.00	28.00	40.00
AH1257	—	3.50	9.00	18.00	28.00	40.00
AH1258	—	3.50	9.00	18.00	28.00	40.00
AH1259	—	3.50	9.00	18.00	28.00	40.00
AH1259//1260	—	6.00	15.00	30.00	50.00	65.00
AH1260	—	6.00	15.00	30.00	50.00	65.00
AH1261	—	3.50	9.00	18.00	28.00	40.00
AH1262	—	3.50	9.00	18.00	28.00	40.00
AH1263	—	3.50	9.00	18.00	28.00	40.00
AH1264	—	3.50	9.00	18.00	28.00	40.00
AH1265	—	3.50	9.00	18.00	28.00	40.00

Muhammad Bahawal Khan III

AH1241-1269 / 1825-1852AD

ANONYMOUS HAMMERED COINAGE

Y# 4.1 RUPEE
Silver **Obverse:** Lily, date in center **Mint:** Bahawalpur **Note:** Weight varies: 9.80-10.10 grams.

Date	Mintage	Good	VG	F	VF	XF
AH1254	—	3.50	9.00	18.00	28.00	40.00
AH1255	—	3.50	9.00	18.00	28.00	40.00
AH1256	—	3.50	9.00	18.00	28.00	40.00
AH1258	—	3.50	9.00	18.00	28.00	40.00
AH1259	—	3.50	9.00	18.00	28.00	40.00

Y# 5.1 RUPEE
Silver **Mint:** Khanpur **Note:** Weight varies: 9.80-10.10 grams. Dated on obverse and reverse.

Date	Mintage	Good	VG	F	VF	XF
AH1255	—	6.00	15.00	30.00	42.00	60.00
AH1256	—	6.00	15.00	30.00	42.00	60.00
AH1258	—	6.00	15.00	30.00	42.00	60.00
AH1259	—	6.00	15.00	30.00	42.00	60.00
AH1260	—	6.00	15.00	30.00	42.00	60.00
AH1261	—	6.00	15.00	30.00	42.00	60.00
AH1263	—	6.00	15.00	30.00	42.00	60.00
AH1264	—	6.00	15.00	30.00	42.00	60.00
AH1265	—	6.00	15.00	30.00	42.00	60.00
AH1266	—	6.00	15.00	30.00	42.00	60.00
AH1267	—	6.00	15.00	30.00	42.00	60.00
AH1268/7	—	6.00	15.00	30.00	42.00	60.00
AH1269	—	6.00	15.00	30.00	42.00	60.00

Y# 5.3 RUPEE
Silver **Shape:** Square **Mint:** Khanpur

Date	Mintage	VG	F	VF	XF	Unc
AH1280	—	400	500	625	750	—

Y# 5.2 RUPEE
Silver **Obverse:** Date in center **Mint:** Khanpur **Note:** Weight varies: 8.50-8.80 grams.

Date	Mintage	Good	VG	F	VF	XF
AH1280	—	4.00	10.00	20.00	35.00	50.00
AH1281	—	4.00	10.00	20.00	35.00	50.00
AH1282	—	4.00	10.00	20.00	35.00	50.00

Sadiq Muhammad Khan III

AH1269-1270 / 1852-1853AD

ANONYMOUS HAMMERED COINAGE

Y# 3.2 RUPEE
Silver **Obverse:** Date in oval **Mint:** Ahmadpur

Date	Mintage	VG	F	VF	XF	Unc
AH1270	—	25.00	37.50	50.00	70.00	—

Fateh Khan

AH1270-1275 / 1853-1858AD

ANONYMOUS HAMMERED COINAGE

Y# 4.2 RUPEE
Silver **Obverse:** Date in rectangle or cinqfoil **Reverse:** Date in rectangle or cinqfoil **Mint:** Bahawalpur **Note:** Weight varies: 10.40-10.50 grams.

Date	Mintage	Good	VG	F	VF	XF
AH1270	—	5.50	14.00	28.00	45.00	65.00
AH1272	—	5.50	14.00	28.00	45.00	65.00
AH1273	—	7.00	17.50	35.00	60.00	85.00
AH1274	—	5.50	14.00	28.00	45.00	65.00

Y# 4.3 RUPEE
Silver **Obverse:** Date in center **Mint:** Bahawalpur **Note:** Weight varies: 10.50-10.70 grams.

Date	Mintage	Good	VG	F	VF	XF
AH1272	—	3.50	9.00	18.00	28.00	40.00
AH1273	—	3.50	9.00	18.00	28.00	40.00
AH1274	—	3.50	9.00	18.00	28.00	40.00
AH1275	—	3.50	9.00	18.00	28.00	40.00

Muhammad Bahawal Khan IV

AH1275-1283 / 1858-1866AD

ANONYMOUS HAMMERED COINAGE

Y# 3.3 RUPEE
Silver **Obverse:** Date in center **Mint:** Ahmadpur **Note:** Weight varies: 7.00-7.60 grams.

Date	Mintage	VG	F	VF	XF	Unc
AH1275	—	12.50	18.50	25.00	35.00	—
AH1276	—	12.50	18.50	25.00	35.00	—
AH1277	—	12.50	18.50	25.00	35.00	—
AH1278	—	12.50	18.50	25.00	35.00	—
AH1279	—	12.50	18.50	25.00	35.00	—
AH1280	—	12.50	18.50	25.00	35.00	—
AH1281	—	12.50	18.50	25.00	35.00	—
AH1282	—	12.50	18.50	25.00	35.00	—
AH1283	—	12.50	18.50	25.00	35.00	—
AH1284	—	12.50	18.50	25.00	35.00	—

Y# 4.4 RUPEE
Silver **Obverse:** Date in center **Mint:** Bahawalpur **Note:** Weight varies: 8.50-8.80 grams.

Date	Mintage	Good	VG	F	VF	XF
AH1276	—	3.50	9.00	18.00	28.00	40.00
AH1278	—	3.50	9.00	18.00	28.00	40.00
AH1279	—	3.50	9.00	18.00	28.00	40.00
AH1280	—	3.50	9.00	18.00	28.00	40.00
AH1281	—	3.50	9.00	18.00	28.00	40.00
AH1282	—	3.50	9.00	18.00	28.00	40.00
AH1283	—	3.50	9.00	18.00	28.00	40.00
AH1283//1	—	3.50	9.00	18.00	28.00	40.00
AH1283//4	—	3.50	9.00	18.00	28.00	40.00

Sir Sadiq Muhammad Khan IV

AH1283-1317 / 1866-1899AD

ANONYMOUS HAMMERED COINAGE

Y# 3.4 RUPEE
Silver **Mint:** Ahmadpur **Note:** Dated on obverse and reverse. Weight varies: 7.90-8.10 grams.

Date	Mintage	VG	F	VF	XF	Unc
AH1285	—	20.00	30.00	45.00	65.00	—
AH1286	—	20.00	30.00	45.00	65.00	—

Anonymous

(Alhaj Muhammad Bahawal Khan V)

ANONYMOUS HAMMERED COINAGE

Y# 2.1 PAISA
Copper **Shape:** Irregular or square **Mint:** Bahawalpur

Date	Mintage	Good	VG	F	VF	XF
AH1301	—	3.50	6.00	8.50	12.50	20.00
AH1302	—	3.50	6.00	8.50	12.50	20.00
AH1304	—	3.50	6.00	8.50	12.50	20.00
AH1311	—	3.50	6.00	8.50	12.50	20.00
AH1312	—	3.50	6.00	8.50	12.50	20.00
AH1313	—	3.50	6.00	8.50	12.50	20.00

Date	Mintage	Good	VG	F	VF	XF
AH1315	—	3.50	6.00	8.50	12.50	20.00
AH1317	—	3.50	6.00	8.50	12.50	20.00

BAJRANGGARH

Bajranggarh was a small state in the district of Gwalior. The mint epithet of Bajranggarh was Jainagar. All the coins, irrespective of when they were minted, were struck in the name of Maharaja Jai Singh and bore similar legends in the Devanagri script.

RULERS

Jai Singh, 1797-1818AD

Jai Singh

AH1212-1234 / 1797-1818

HAMMERED COINAGE

KM# 2 PAISA

Copper

Date	Mintage	Good	VG	F	VF	XF
ND//11(1807)	—	7.50	15.00	25.00	40.00	—
ND //12(1808)	—	7.50	15.00	25.00	40.00	—

KM# 6 RUPEE

Silver **Note:** Weight varies: 10.70-11.60 grams. Without symbols, thin flan.

Date	Mintage	Good	VG	F	VF	XF
ND//12(1808)	—	4.00	10.00	20.00	35.00	55.00
ND//13(1809)	—	5.00	12.50	25.00	42.50	65.00
ND//15(1811)	—	4.00	10.00	20.00	35.00	55.00
ND//16(1812)	—	4.00	10.00	20.00	35.00	55.00
ND//17(1813)	—	4.00	10.00	20.00	35.00	55.00

KM# 7 RUPEE

Silver, 20 mm. **Note:** Weight varies: 10.70-11.60 grams. Thick flan.

Date	Mintage	Good	VG	F	VF	XF
ND//18(1814)	—	4.00	10.00	20.00	35.00	55.00
ND//19(1815)	—	4.00	10.00	20.00	35.00	55.00
ND//20(1816)	—	4.00	10.00	20.00	35.00	55.00

KM# 13 MOHUR

Gold **Note:** Weight varies: 10.70-11.40 grams. Small lettering, without symbols.

Date	Mintage	VG	F	VF	XF	Unc
ND//16(1812)	—	250	450	750	1,500	—

BANSWARA

This state in southern Rajputana was founded in 1538 when the state of Dungarpur was divided between 2 sons of the Maharawal, the younger receiving the territory of Banswara with the title also of Maharawal. The rulers of Banswara were Sissodia Rajputs who claimed descent from the powerful Maharanas of Mewar-Udaipur.

Constantly harassed by the Marathas during the 18th Century, Banswara concluded an alliance in 1818 with the British who provided protection from external enemies in exchange for a portion of the state's revenues. In 1935 the state comprised 1,606 square miles with a population of 225,000, a quarter of whom were aboriginal Bhil tribal people.

During most of the 19th Century, Banswara used the "Salim Shahi" coinage of neighboring Pratapgarh State. But around 1870 Maharawal Lakshman Singh, defying a British prohibiting order of that year, introduced a series of crude coins in copper, silver and gold for use within the state. The legends on these coins are in a secret script, said to have been invented by Lakshman Singh himself. The central word in these legends has been tentatively identified as "Samsatraba" (for "Samba Satra", a designation for the Hindu deity Shiva) in the longer form, or "Samba" for the shorter form. All the gold and silver coins, and a few rare copper ones, carry the longer form. The copper coins were made for circulation, but the gold and silver were produced mainly for presentation.

RULERS

Lakshman Singh, 1844-1905AD

LEGENDS

Samba

Samba is a name of Shiva

With *Ba* downwards is a common error of the die cutters.

Samsatraba

For Samba Satra

ANONYMOUS HAMMERED COINAGE

Samsatraba Series

KM# 1 1/4 PAISA

Copper **Obverse:** "Samba" in circle, ending downward **Reverse:** "Samba" in circle, ending downward **Note:** Weight varies: 2.40-2.60 grams.

Date	Mintage	Good	VG	F	VF	XF
ND(1870)	—	6.00	12.00	20.00	30.00	—

KM# 4 1/2 PAISA

Copper **Obverse:** "Samba" ends downward **Reverse:** "Samba" ends downward **Note:** Weight varies: 4.30-5.50 grams. Varieties in dots of circles exist.

Date	Mintage	Good	VG	F	VF	XF
ND(1807)	—	6.00	12.00	20.00	30.00	—

KM# 6 1/2 PAISA

Copper **Obverse:** "Samba" ends upward **Reverse:** "Samba" ends downward, all within a circular legend **Note:** Weight varies: 4.30-5.50 grams.

Date	Mintage	Good	VG	F	VF	XF
ND(1870)	—	1.75	3.00	6.50	10.00	—

KM# 3 1/2 PAISA

Copper **Obverse:** "Samba" ends upward **Reverse:** "Samba" ends upward **Note:** Weight varies: 4.30-5.50 grams.

Date	Mintage	Good	VG	F	VF	XF
ND(1870)	—	6.00	12.00	20.00	30.00	—

KM# 5 1/2 PAISA

Copper **Obverse:** "Samba" within legend ends upwards **Reverse:** "Samba" within legend ends upwards **Note:** Weight varies: 4.30-5.50 grams.

Date	Mintage	Good	VG	F	VF	XF
ND(1870)	—	1.00	1.75	4.00	6.50	—

KM# 7 PAISA

Copper **Obverse:** "Samba" ends down, in large circles **Reverse:** "Samba" ends down, in large circles **Note:** Weight varies: 10.20-11.70 grams.

Date	Mintage	Good	VG	F	VF	XF
ND(1870)	—	3.00	5.00	8.00	12.50	—

KM# 10 PAISA

Copper **Obverse:** "Samba" within legend ends upward **Reverse:** "Samba" within legend ends upward **Note:** Weight varies: 10.20-11.70 grams.

Date	Mintage	Good	VG	F	VF	XF
ND(1870)	—	1.00	1.75	4.00	6.50	—

KM# 11 PAISA

Copper **Obverse:** "Samba" ends downward **Reverse:** "Samba" ends downward, all within a circular legend and outer circle **Note:** Weight varies: 10.20-11.70 grams.

Date	Mintage	Good	VG	F	VF	XF
ND(1870)	—	1.00	1.75	4.00	6.50	—

KM# 12 PAISA

Copper **Obverse:** "Samba" ends upward **Reverse:** "Samba" ends downward **Note:** Weight varies: 10.20-11.70 grams.

Date	Mintage	Good	VG	F	VF	XF
ND(1870)	—	1.75	3.00	6.50	10.00	—

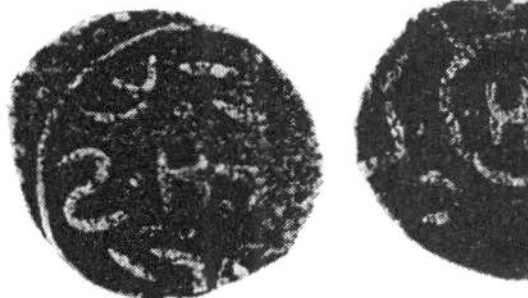

KM# 13 PAISA

Copper **Obverse:** "Samba" within legend ends downward **Reverse:** "Samba" within large circle ends downward **Note:** Weight varies: 10.20-11.70 grams.

Date	Mintage	Good	VG	F	VF	XF
ND(1870)	—	3.00	5.00	8.00	12.50	—

KM# 14 PAISA

Copper **Obv. Legend:** "Samsatraba" within circle **Rev. Legend:** "Samsatraba" within circle **Note:** Weight varies: 10.20-11.70 grams.

Date	Mintage	Good	VG	F	VF	XF
ND(1870)	—	3.00	5.00	8.00	12.50	—

KM# 9 PAISA

Copper **Obverse:** "Samba" within small circle ends downward **Reverse:** "Samba" within small circle ends downward, all within a circular legend within three circles, two solid and one dotted - the most ornate variety **Note:** Weight varies: 10.20-11.70 grams. Broad, thin flan.

Date	Mintage	Good	VG	F	VF	XF
ND(1870)	—	4.50	8.00	12.00	17.50	—

KM# 8 PAISA

Copper **Obverse:** "Samba" within small circle ends downward **Reverse:** "Samba" within small circle ends downward **Note:** Weight varies: 10.20-11.70 grams. Thick flan.

Date	Mintage	Good	VG	F	VF	XF
ND(1870)	—	3.00	5.00	8.00	12.00	—

KM# 20 NAZARANA 1/8 RUPEE

1.0000 g., Silver **Obverse:** "Samsatraba" **Reverse:** "Samsatraba"

Date	Mintage	Good	VG	F	VF	XF
ND(1870)	—	5.50	11.00	17.50	23.50	32.50

KM# 21 NAZARANA 1/4 RUPEE
2.0000 g., Silver **Obverse:** "Samsatraba" **Reverse:** "Samsatraba"

Date	Mintage	Good	VG	F	VF	XF
ND(1870)	—	5.75	11.50	18.50	25.00	35.00

KM# 22 NAZARANA 1/2 RUPEE
4.0000 g., Silver **Obverse:** "Samsatraba" **Reverse:** "Samsatraba"

Date	Mintage	Good	VG	F	VF	XF
ND(1870)	—	6.50	12.50	21.50	28.50	40.00

KM# 23 NAZARANA RUPEE
Silver **Obv. Legend:** "Samsatraba" **Rev. Legend:** "Samsatraba"
Note: Weight varies: 8.00-8.20 grams. Broad, thin flan.

Date	Mintage	Good	VG	F	VF	XF
ND(1870)	—	3.25	6.50	11.00	16.50	25.00

KM# 16 NAZARANA RUPEE
Silver **Obv. Legend:** "Samsatraba" **Rev. Legend:** "Samsatraba"
Note: Weight varies: 8.00-8.20 grams. Thick flan.

Date	Mintage	Good	VG	F	VF	XF
ND(1870)	—	4.50	9.00	15.00	21.50	30.00

KM# 17 HEAVY RUPEE
12.0000 g., Silver **Note:** Similar to Nazarana Rupee, KM#16.

Date	Mintage	Good	VG	F	VF	XF
ND(1870) Rare	—	—	—	—	—	—

KM# 24 HEAVY RUPEE
12.0000 g., Silver **Note:** Similar to Nazarana Rupee, KM#23.

Date	Mintage	Good	VG	F	VF	XF
ND(1870) Rare	—	—	—	—	—	—

KM# 25 NAZARANA MOHUR
12.0000 g., Gold **Obv. Legend:** "Samsatraba" **Rev. Legend:** "Samsatraba" **Note:** Broad, thin flan.

Date	Mintage	Good	VG	F	VF	XF
ND(1870)	—	200	325	500	700	—

KM# 18 NAZARANA MOHUR
12.0000 g., Gold **Obv. Legend:** "Samsatraba" **Rev. Legend:** "Samsatraba" **Note:** Thick flan.

Date	Mintage	Good	VG	F	VF	XF
ND(1870)	—	—	200	325	500	700

PATTERNS

Including off metal strikes

KM#	Date	Mintage	Identification	Mkt Val
			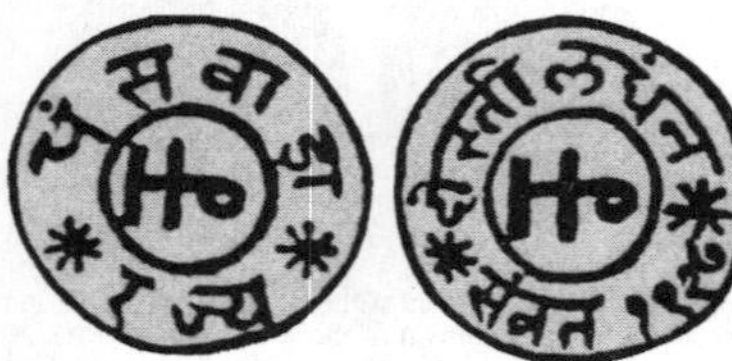	
Pn1	ND1927	—	Rupee. Silver.	—

BARODA

Maratha state located in western India. The ruling line was descended from Damaji, a Maratha soldier, who received the title of "Distinguished Swordsman" in 1721 (hence the scimitar on most Baroda coins). The Baroda title "Gaikwara" comes from "gaikwar" or cow herd, Damaji's father's occupation.

The Maratha rulers of Baroda, the Gaekwar family rose to prominence in the mid-18th century by carving out for themselves a dominion from territories, which were previously under the control of the Poona Marathas, and to a lesser extent, of the Raja of Jodhpur. Chronic internal disputes regarding the succession to the masnad culminated in the intervention of British troops in support of one candidate, Anand Rao Gaekwar, in 1800. Then, in 1802, an agreement with the East India Company released the Baroda princes from their fear of domination by the Maratha Peshwa of Poona but subordinated them to Company interests. Nevertheless, for almost the next century and a half Baroda maintained a good relationship with the British and continued as a major Princely State right up to 1947, when it acceded to the Indian Union.

RULERS

Gaekwars
Anand Rao, AH1215-1235/1800-1819AD
Sayaji Rao II, AH1235-1264/1819-1847AD
Ganpat Rao, AH1264-1273/1847-1856AD
Khande Rao, AH1273-1287/1856-1870AD
Malhar Rao, AH1287-1292/1870-1875AD
Sayaji Rao III, AH1292-1357/VS1932-1995/1875-1938AD

MINTS

احمد آباد

Ahmadabad

Ahmadabad was a Mughal city from 1572 to 1738 until it was divided between the Mughal governor and the emerging Marathas under the Peshwa. This arrangement ended in 1753 (AH1167) when the Marathas seized full control with the help of the Gaikwad of Baroda. The city was retaken by a Mughal governor in 1755 (AH1169) and held for two years, only to be reconquered by the Marathas who shared its revenues with the Gaikwad. However, these two forces frequently clashed and the Gaikwad turned to the British for help. The British then seized the city in 1780 (AH1194) and delivered it over to the Gaikwad who ruled it alone for three years. Then a treaty restored it to the Marathas in 1783 (AH1197). The Marathas leased it to Baroda for four years from 1800 (AH1215) to 1804 (AH1219), then renewed the lease for 10 years to 1814 (AH1230). Ahmadabad was ceded to Baroda and in private hands from 1814-1817. The following year it was annexed by the British East India Company. The mint of Ahmadabad was finally closed in 1835 (AH1251).
These frequent changes of political control are clearly reflected in Ahmadabad's coinage and account for gaps in production flowage throughout history. *Maratha Mints*, Maheshwari and Wiggins, Indian Institute of Research in Numismatic Studies, 1989.

Amreli

بروده

Baroda

Jambusar

Petlad

MINT MARKS

Ahmadabad Mint

Ankus, Maratha mark.

Nagari letters denoting Baroda ruler:

गा

Ga - Anand Rao's Shah Alam II coins, Ahmadabad Mint (with two vertical stems).

आ

A - Anand Rao's Shah Alam II coins, Petlad Mint.

सा गा

Sa Ga - Sayaji Rao III, Baroda Mint.

NOTE: The first 2 marks are found only on the coins of Ahmadabad Mint, and serve to identify it. The remaining 16 marks are used to indicate the ruler under whom the coin was struck; when no mint name is given after the ruler's name in the above list, that shows that the symbol was used at all his mints. Note the various forms of *'G'* and *'Ga'* used above.

Anand Rao

AH1215-1235 / 1800-1819AD

HAMMERED COINAGE

C# 20 1/2 PAISA
Copper, 14 mm. **Obv. Inscription:** Muhammad Akbar II **Mint:** Baroda

Date	Mintage	Good	VG	F	VF	XF
AH1232//11	—	2.00	3.00	4.00	5.00	—
AH123x//14	—	2.00	3.00	4.00	5.00	—

C# 10 PAISA
Copper, 20 mm. **Reverse:** Nagari A **Mint:** Petlad **Note:** Regnal years 1-7 of Anand Rao.

Date	Mintage	Good	VG	F	VF	XF
AH--//--	—	2.50	3.50	4.50	7.00	—

C# 21 PAISA
9.8000 g., Copper **Obv. Inscription:** Muhammad Akbar II **Mint:** Baroda

Date	Mintage	Good	VG	F	VF	XF
AH1226//6	—	1.25	2.50	3.50	5.00	—
AH1227//7	—	1.25	2.50	3.50	5.00	—
AH122x//8	—	1.25	2.50	3.50	5.00	—
AH122x//9	—	1.25	2.50	3.50	5.00	—
AH1231//11	—	1.25	2.50	3.50	5.00	—
ND(1817)//13	—	1.25	2.50	3.50	5.00	—
AH1234//14	—	1.25	2.50	3.50	5.00	—
AH1236//16	—	1.25	2.50	3.50	5.00	—

C# 24 1/8 RUPEE
Silver **Obv. Inscription:** Muhammad Akbar II **Mint:** Baroda
Note: Weight varies: 1.34-1.45 grams.

Date	Mintage	Good	VG	F	VF	XF
AH122x	—	6.00	15.00	25.00	40.00	60.00
AH1233	—	6.00	15.00	25.00	40.00	60.00
AH1234	—	6.00	15.00	25.00	40.00	60.00

C# 17 1/4 RUPEE
Silver **Obv. Inscription:** Shah Alam II **Mint:** Ahmadabad

Date	Mintage	Good	VG	F	VF	XF
ND(1759-1806)	—	6.00	15.00	25.00	40.00	60.00

C# 25 1/4 RUPEE
Silver **Obv. Inscription:** Muhammad Akbar II **Mint:** Baroda
Note: Weight varies: 2.68-2.90 grams.

Date	Mintage	Good	VG	F	VF	XF
AH1228	—	6.00	15.00	25.00	40.00	60.00

C# 18 1/2 RUPEE
Silver **Obv. Inscription:** "Shah Alam II" **Mint:** Ahmadabad **Note:** Weight varies: 5.35-5.80 grams.

Date	Mintage	Good	VG	F	VF	XF
ND//4x (1798-1806)	—	6.00	15.00	25.00	40.00	60.00

C# 12 1/2 RUPEE
Silver **Reverse:** Nagari A **Mint:** Petlad

Date	Mintage	Good	VG	F	VF	XF
ND(1800-19)	—	10.00	25.00	40.00	60.00	85.00

C# A28 1/2 RUPEE
Silver **Obv. Inscription:** Muhammad Akbar (II) **Mint:** Ahmadabad **Note:** Weight varies: 5.35-5.80 grams.

Date	Mintage	Good	VG	F	VF	XF
ND(1806-37)	—	5.00	12.50	20.00	30.00	50.00

C# 26 1/2 RUPEE
Silver **Obv. Inscription:** Muhammad Akbar II **Mint:** Baroda **Note:** Weight varies: 5.35-5.80 grams.

Date	Mintage	Good	VG	F	VF	XF
AH1222//2	—	6.00	15.00	25.00	40.00	60.00
AH1226//6	—	6.00	15.00	25.00	40.00	60.00
AH1228//8	—	6.00	15.00	25.00	40.00	60.00
AH1234//14	—	6.00	15.00	25.00	40.00	60.00

C# 19 RUPEE
Silver **Obv. Inscription:** Shah Alam (II) **Mint:** Ahmadabad **Note:** Weight varies: 10.70-11.60 grams.

Date	Mintage	Good	VG	F	VF	XF
ND//3x (1788-98)	—	2.25	5.50	11.00	18.00	28.00
ND//41(1799-1800)	—	2.25	5.50	11.00	18.00	28.00
ND//5x (1808)	—	2.25	5.50	11.00	18.00	28.00

C# 27 RUPEE
Silver **Obv. Inscription:** Muhammad Akbar II **Mint:** Baroda **Note:** Weight varies: 10.70-11.60 grams.

Date	Mintage	Good	VG	F	VF	XF
AH1222//2	—	3.00	7.50	12.50	18.50	27.50
AH1224//4	—	3.00	7.50	12.50	18.50	27.50
AH1225//5	—	3.00	7.50	12.50	18.50	27.50
AH1226//6	—	3.00	7.50	12.50	18.50	27.50
AH1227//7	—	3.00	7.50	12.50	18.50	27.50
AH1228//8	—	3.00	7.50	12.50	18.50	27.50
AH1229//9	—	3.00	7.50	12.50	18.50	27.50
AH1232//12	—	3.00	7.50	12.50	18.50	27.50
AH1233//13	—	3.00	7.50	12.50	18.50	27.50
AH1234//14	—	3.00	7.50	12.50	18.50	27.50

C# 28 RUPEE
Silver **Obv. Inscription:** Muhammad Akbar II **Mint:** Ahmadabad **Note:** Weight varies: 10.70-11.60 grams. The Ahmadabad Mint was acquired by the British in 1818AD (AH1233). Refer to British India, Bombay Presidency KM#257-260.

Date	Mintage	Good	VG	F	VF	XF
AH1225	—	2.25	5.50	11.00	18.00	28.00
AH1227//6	—	2.25	5.50	11.00	18.00	28.00
AH1229//7 (sic)	—	2.25	5.50	11.00	18.00	28.00
AH1229//8	—	2.25	5.50	11.00	18.00	28.00
AH1231//9 (sic)	—	2.25	5.50	11.00	18.00	28.00
AH1232//10	—	2.25	5.50	11.00	18.00	28.00
AH1232//11	—	2.25	5.50	11.00	18.00	28.00
AH1233//11	—	2.25	5.50	11.00	18.00	28.00

MILLED COINAGE

C# 13 RUPEE
Silver **Obv. Inscription:** "Shah Alam II" **Reverse:** Nagari A **Mint:** Petlad

Date	Mintage	Good	VG	F	VF	XF
AH-//3	—	4.00	10.00	15.00	21.50	30.00
AH-//4	—	4.00	10.00	15.00	21.50	30.00

Sayaji Rao II
AH1235-1264 / 1819-1847AD
HAMMERED COINAGE

C# A29.3 1/2 PAISA
3.2500 g., Copper **Obverse:** Elephant left, flag left. **Mint:** Amreli

Date	Mintage	Good	VG	F	VF	XF
AH12xx	—	2.50	4.50	7.00	11.00	—

C# A29.4 1/2 PAISA
3.2500 g., Copper **Obverse:** Flower at center **Mint:** Amreli

Date	Mintage	Good	VG	F	VF	XF
AH123x	—	3.00	5.50	8.50	13.50	—

C# A29.1 1/2 PAISA
Copper **Mint:** Amreli **Note:** Similar to 1 Paisa, C#30.

Date	Mintage	Good	VG	F	VF	XF
ND(1819-47)	—	2.50	4.50	7.00	11.00	—

C# 31.1 1/2 PAISA
4.3000 g., Copper **Obv. Inscription:** Muhammad Akbar II **Reverse:** Without symbols **Mint:** Baroda **Note:** Size varies: 14-15mm.

Date	Mintage	Good	VG	F	VF	XF
AH123x	—	1.25	2.50	4.00	6.00	—

C# 31.2 1/2 PAISA
4.3000 g., Copper **Obv. Inscription:** Muhammad Akbar II **Reverse:** Cross **Mint:** Baroda **Note:** Size varies: 14-15mm.

Date	Mintage	Good	VG	F	VF	XF
ND(1819-47)	—	1.25	2.50	4.00	6.00	—
AH1236//16	—	2.00	4.00	6.00	10.00	—

C# 31.4 1/2 PAISA
4.3000 g., Copper **Obv. Inscription:** Muhammad Akbar II **Reverse:** Sun **Mint:** Baroda **Note:** Size varies: 14-15mm.

Date	Mintage	Good	VG	F	VF	XF
ND(1819-47)	—	1.25	2.50	4.00	6.00	—

C# 31.5 1/2 PAISA
4.3000 g., Copper **Obv. Inscription:** Muhammad Akbar II **Reverse:** Flag **Mint:** Baroda

Date	Mintage	Good	VG	F	VF	XF
AH1251	—	2.00	4.00	6.00	10.00	—

C# A29.2 1/2 PAISA
Copper **Obverse:** Katar above scimitar **Mint:** Amreli

Date	Mintage	Good	VG	F	VF	XF
AH125x	—	2.50	4.50	7.00	11.00	—

C# 31.8 1/2 PAISA

4.3000 g., Copper **Obv. Inscription:** Muhammad Akbar Ii **Reverse:** Shaded ball **Mint:** Baroda **Note:** Size varies: 14-15mm.

Date	Mintage	Good	VG	F	VF	XF
AH1260//40	—	1.25	2.50	4.00	6.00	—

C# 33.11 PAISA
10.2000 g., Copper **Obv. Inscription:** Muhammad Akbar II **Reverse:** Flag and branch **Mint:** Baroda **Note:** Size varies: 18-24mm.

Date	Mintage	Good	VG	F	VF	XF
ND(1819-47)	—	2.00	3.50	6.00	10.00	—

C# 33.12 PAISA
10.2000 g., Copper **Obv. Inscription:** Muhammad Akbar II **Reverse:** Flower **Mint:** Baroda **Note:** Size varies: 18-24mm.

Date	Mintage	Good	VG	F	VF	XF
AH12xx	—	2.00	3.50	6.00	10.00	—

C# 29.5 PAISA
Copper **Obverse:** Elephant with flag right. **Reverse:** Similar to C#29.4 **Mint:** Amreli **Note:** Weight varies: 7.00-8.00 grams.

Date	Mintage	Good	VG	F	VF	XF
ND(1819-47)	—	5.00	6.50	10.00	16.50	—

C# 29.8 PAISA
Copper **Obverse:** Crescent **Reverse:** Trident **Mint:** Amreli **Note:** Weight varies: 7.00-8.00 grams.

Date	Mintage	Good	VG	F	VF	XF
ND(1819-47)	—	3.00	5.50	8.50	12.50	—

C# 30.1 PAISA
Copper **Obverse:** Large "Sa" **Mint:** Amreli **Note:** Weight varies: 7.00-8.00 grams.

Date	Mintage	Good	VG	F	VF	XF
ND(1819-47)	—	1.50	2.50	4.00	6.50	—

C# 30.2 PAISA
Copper **Obverse:** Large "Sa" **Mint:** Amreli **Note:** Weight varies: 7.00-8.00 grams.

Date	Mintage	Good	VG	F	VF	XF
ND(1819-47)	—	1.50	2.50	4.00	6.50	—

C# 33.1 PAISA
10.2000 g., Copper **Obv. Inscription:** Muhammad Akbar II **Reverse:** Without symbol **Mint:** Baroda **Note:** Size varies: 18-24mm.

Date	Mintage	Good	VG	F	VF	XF
AH1236//16	—	1.25	2.00	3.00	4.50	—

C# 33.2 PAISA

10.2000 g., Copper **Obv. Inscription:** Muhammad Akbar II **Reverse:** Accented outlined cross **Mint:** Baroda **Note:** Size varies: 18-24mm.

Date	Mintage	Good	VG	F	VF	XF
AH1241//20	—	1.25	2.25	3.50	5.00	—

C# 33.3 PAISA

10.2000 g., Copper **Obv. Inscription:** Muhammad Akbar II **Reverse:** Simple outlined cross **Mint:** Baroda **Note:** Size varies: 18-24mm.

Date	Mintage	Good	VG	F	VF	XF
AH1243//23	—	1.25	2.25	3.50	5.00	—
AH1244	—	1.25	2.25	3.50	5.00	—

C# 33.14 PAISA

10.2000 g., Copper **Obv. Inscription:** Muhammad Akbar Ii **Reverse:** Accented cross outline **Mint:** Baroda **Note:** Size varies: 18-24mm.

Date	Mintage	Good	VG	F	VF	XF
AH1243//23	—	1.25	2.25	3.50	5.00	—
AH1244	—	1.25	2.25	3.50	5.00	—

C# 33.4 PAISA

10.2000 g., Copper **Obv. Inscription:** Muhammad Akbar II **Reverse:** Rayed sun **Mint:** Baroda **Note:** Size varies: 18-24mm.

Date	Mintage	Good	VG	F	VF	XF
AH124x//23	—	1.25	2.25	3.50	5.00	—
AH1247//27	—	1.25	2.25	3.50	5.00	—

C# 33.16 PAISA

10.2000 g., Copper **Obverse:** "Fateh Singh" in Devanagari, Katar left **Obv. Inscription:** Gaekwar's brother Fateh Singh **Reverse:** Date **Mint:** Baroda **Note:** Size varies: 18-24mm. Fateh Singh was a brother of Maharao Sayaji Rao II.

Date	Mintage	Good	VG	F	VF	XF
AH1245	—	15.00	25.00	40.00	60.00	—

C# 29.4 PAISA

Copper **Obverse:** Katar above scimitar **Mint:** Amreli **Note:** Weight varies: 7.00-8.00 grams.

Date	Mintage	Good	VG	F	VF	XF
AH1245	—	2.50	4.50	7.00	11.00	—
AH1256	—	2.50	4.50	7.00	11.00	—
AH1257	—	2.50	4.50	7.00	11.00	—

C# 33.13 PAISA

10.2000 g., Copper **Obv. Inscription:** Muhammad Akbar II **Reverse:** Person **Mint:** Baroda **Note:** Size varies: 18-24mm.

Date	Mintage	Good	VG	F	VF	XF
AH1248//28	—	1.25	2.25	3.50	5.00	—
AH1249//29	—	1.25	2.25	3.50	5.00	—

C# 33.5 PAISA

10.2000 g., Copper **Obv. Inscription:** Muhammad Akbar II **Reverse:** Flag **Mint:** Baroda **Note:** Size varies: 18-24mm.

Date	Mintage	Good	VG	F	VF	XF
AH12xx//28	—	1.25	2.25	3.50	5.00	—
AH1249//29	—	1.25	2.25	3.50	5.00	—
AH1250//30	—	1.25	2.25	3.50	5.00	—
AH1250	—	1.25	2.25	3.50	5.00	—
AH1251	—	1.25	2.25	3.50	5.00	—
AH1253	—	1.25	2.25	3.50	5.00	—

C# 29.1 PAISA

Copper **Obverse:** Scimitar **Mint:** Amreli **Note:** Weight varies: 7.00-8.00 grams.

Date	Mintage	Good	VG	F	VF	XF
AH1253	—	2.50	4.50	7.00	11.00	—

C# 33.9 PAISA

10.2000 g., Copper **Obv. Inscription:** Muhammad Akbar II **Reverse:** Tulip **Mint:** Baroda **Note:** Size varies: 18-24mm.

Date	Mintage	Good	VG	F	VF	XF
AH1253//33	—	1.25	2.25	3.50	5.00	—
AH1254	—	1.25	2.25	3.50	5.00	—
AH1255//36	—	1.25	2.25	3.50	5.00	—

C# 33.7 PAISA

10.2000 g., Copper **Obv. Inscription:** Muhammad Akbar II **Reverse:** 5-petal flower **Mint:** Baroda **Note:** Size varies: 18-24mm.

Date	Mintage	Good	VG	F	VF	XF
ND(1838)//35	—	1.25	2.25	3.50	5.00	—
AH1255//36	—	1.25	2.25	3.50	5.00	—
AH1256//36	—	1.25	2.25	3.50	5.00	—
AH1263	—	1.25	2.25	3.50	5.00	—

C# 33.6 PAISA

10.2000 g., Copper **Obv. Inscription:** Muhammad Akbar II **Reverse:** Upright cross **Mint:** Baroda **Note:** Size varies: 18-24mm.

Date	Mintage	Good	VG	F	VF	XF
AH1255//35	—	1.25	2.50	3.50	5.00	—

C# 29.2 PAISA

Copper **Obverse:** Elephant left with flag right **Mint:** Amreli **Note:** Weight varies: 7.00-8.00 grams.

Date	Mintage	Good	VG	F	VF	XF
AH1256	—	3.00	5.50	8.50	13.00	—

C# 29.3 PAISA

Copper **Obverse:** Elephant and flag left **Mint:** Amreli **Note:** Weight varies: 7.00-8.00 grams.

Date	Mintage	Good	VG	F	VF	XF
AH1256	—	2.50	4.50	7.00	11.00	—

C# 29.6 PAISA

Copper **Obverse:** Scimitar **Mint:** Amreli **Note:** Weight varies: 7.00-8.00 grams.

Date	Mintage	Good	VG	F	VF	XF
AH1257	—	2.50	4.50	7.00	11.00	—

C# 33.8 PAISA

10.2000 g., Copper **Obv. Inscription:** Muhammad Akbar II **Reverse:** Shaded ball **Mint:** Baroda **Note:** Size varies: 18-24mm.

Date	Mintage	Good	VG	F	VF	XF
AH1260//40	—	1.00	2.00	3.00	4.00	—
AH1261//41	—	1.00	2.00	3.00	4.00	—
AH1262	—	1.00	2.00	3.00	4.00	—
AH1263//43	—	1.00	2.00	3.00	4.00	—
AH126x//44	—	1.00	2.00	3.00	4.00	—
AH1264	—	1.00	2.00	3.00	4.00	—

C# 33.10 PAISA

10.2000 g., Copper **Obv. Inscription:** Muhammad Akbar II **Reverse:** Hoof **Mint:** Baroda **Note:** Size varies: 18-24mm.

Date	Mintage	Good	VG	F	VF	XF
AH1260	—	2.50	4.00	7.50	12.00	—

C# 29.7 PAISA

Copper **Obverse:** Crescent **Mint:** Amreli **Note:** Weight varies: 7.00-8.00 grams.

Date	Mintage	Good	VG	F	VF	XF
AH1262	—	3.00	5.50	8.50	12.50	—

C# 35.3 1/8 RUPEE

Silver **Obv. Inscription:** Muhammad Akbar II **Reverse:** Scimitar to right of "Julus" **Mint:** Baroda **Note:** Size varies: 11-14mm. Weight varies: 1.34-1.45 grams.

Date	Mintage	Good	VG	F	VF	XF
AH12xx	—	2.00	5.00	7.00	10.00	15.00

C# 35.1 1/8 RUPEE

Silver **Obv. Inscription:** "Muhammad Akbar II" **Reverse:** Scimitar to left of "Julus" **Mint:** Baroda **Note:** Size varies: 11-14mm. Weight varies: 1.34-1.45 grams.

Date	Mintage	Good	VG	F	VF	XF
ND//17(1821)	—	2.00	5.00	7.00	10.00	15.00

C# 35.2 1/8 RUPEE

Silver **Obv. Inscription:** "Muhammad Akbar II" **Reverse:** Scimitar above "Julus" **Mint:** Baroda **Note:** Size varies: 11-14mm. Weight varies: 1.34-1.45 grams.

Date	Mintage	Good	VG	F	VF	XF
ND//26(1830)	—	2.00	5.00	7.00	10.00	15.00

C# 36.1 1/4 RUPEE

Silver **Obv. Inscription:** Muhammad Akbar II **Reverse:** Scimitar to left of "Julus" **Mint:** Baroda **Note:** Weight varies: 2.68-2.90 grams.

Date	Mintage	Good	VG	F	VF	XF
AH1238//18	—	2.25	5.50	8.00	12.50	18.50

C# 36.2 1/4 RUPEE

Silver **Obv. Inscription:** "Muhammad Akbar II" **Reverse:** Scimitar above "Julus" **Mint:** Baroda **Note:** Weight varies: 2.68-2.90 grams.

Date	Mintage	Good	VG	F	VF	XF
ND//24(1828)	—	2.25	5.50	8.00	12.50	18.50

C# 36.3 1/4 RUPEE

Silver **Obv. Inscription:** Muhammad Akbar II **Reverse:** Scimitar to right of "Julus" **Mint:** Baroda **Note:** Weight varies: 2.68-2.90 grams.

Date	Mintage	Good	VG	F	VF	XF
AH1249//29	—	2.25	5.50	8.00	12.50	18.50
AH1250//29	—	2.25	5.50	8.00	12.50	18.50
AH1257//37	—	2.25	5.50	8.00	12.50	18.50
AH1262	—	2.25	5.50	8.00	12.50	18.50

C# 37.1 1/2 RUPEE
Silver **Obv. Inscription:** Muhammad Akbar II **Reverse:** Scimitar to left of "Julus" **Mint:** Baroda **Note:** Weight varies: 5.35-5.80 grams.

Date	Mintage	Good	VG	F	VF	XF
AH1238//18	—	2.50	6.00	9.00	13.50	20.00
AH1239//19	—	2.50	6.00	9.00	13.50	20.00
AH12xx//20	—	2.50	6.00	9.00	13.50	20.00
AH1241//21	—	2.50	6.00	9.00	13.50	20.00
AH124x//27	—	2.50	6.00	9.00	13.50	20.00

C# 37.2 1/2 RUPEE
Silver **Obv. Inscription:** Muhammad Akbar II **Reverse:** Scimitar above "Julus" **Mint:** Baroda **Note:** Weight varies: 5.35-5.80 grams.

Date	Mintage	Good	VG	F	VF	XF
AH124x//24	—	2.50	6.00	9.00	13.50	20.00
AH124x//26	—	2.50	6.00	9.00	13.50	20.00
AH124x//27	—	2.50	6.00	9.00	13.50	20.00

C# 37.3 1/2 RUPEE
Silver **Obv. Inscription:** Muhammad Akbar II **Reverse:** Scimitar to right of "Julus" **Mint:** Baroda **Note:** Weight varies: 5.35-5.80 grams.

Date	Mintage	Good	VG	F	VF	XF
AH1254//33	—	2.50	6.00	9.00	13.50	20.00
AH125x//35	—	2.50	6.00	9.00	13.50	20.00
AH125x//37	—	2.50	6.00	9.00	13.50	20.00
AH125x//38	—	2.50	6.00	9.00	13.50	20.00
AH125x//39	—	2.50	6.00	9.00	13.50	20.00
AH1260//40	—	2.50	6.00	9.00	13.50	20.00
AH126x//42	—	2.50	6.00	9.00	13.50	20.00

C# 38.1 RUPEE
Silver **Obv. Inscription:** Muhammad Akbar II **Reverse:** Scimitar to left of "Julus" **Mint:** Baroda **Note:** Weight varies: 10.70-11.60 grams.

Date	Mintage	Good	VG	F	VF	XF
AH1237//17	—	3.00	7.50	12.50	18.50	27.50
AH1238//18	—	3.00	7.50	12.50	18.50	27.50
AH1239//19	—	3.00	7.50	12.50	18.50	27.50
AH1240//19	—	3.00	7.50	12.50	18.50	27.50
AH1240//20	—	3.00	7.50	12.50	18.50	27.50
AH1241//21	—	3.00	7.50	12.50	18.50	27.50
AH1242//22	—	3.00	7.50	12.50	18.50	27.50

C# 38.2 RUPEE
Silver **Obv. Inscription:** Muhammad Akbar II **Reverse:** Scimitar above "Julus" **Mint:** Baroda **Note:** Weight varies: 10.70-11.60 grams.

Date	Mintage	Good	VG	F	VF	XF
AH1244//24	—	3.00	7.50	12.50	18.50	27.50
AH124x//25	—	3.00	7.50	12.50	18.50	27.50
AH1248//27	—	3.00	7.50	12.50	18.50	27.50

C# 38.3 RUPEE
Obv. Inscription: Muhammad Akbar II **Reverse:** Scimitar to right of "Julus" **Mint:** Baroda **Note:** Weight varies: 10.70-11.60 grams.

Date	Mintage	Good	VG	F	VF	XF
AH1247	—	3.00	7.50	12.50	18.50	27.50
AH1249//29	—	3.00	7.50	12.50	18.50	27.50
AH1250//30	—	3.00	7.50	12.50	18.50	27.50
AH1251//32	—	3.00	7.50	12.50	18.50	27.50
AH1253//33	—	3.00	7.50	12.50	18.50	27.50
AH1254//33	—	3.00	7.50	12.50	18.50	27.50
AH1255//35	—	3.00	7.50	12.50	18.50	27.50
AH1256//36	—	3.00	7.50	12.50	18.50	27.50
AH1257//37	—	3.00	7.50	12.50	18.50	27.50

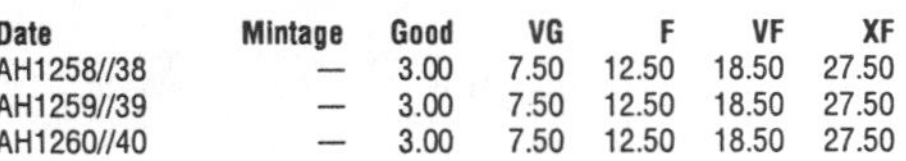

Date	Mintage	Good	VG	F	VF	XF
AH1258//38	—	3.00	7.50	12.50	18.50	27.50
AH1259//39	—	3.00	7.50	12.50	18.50	27.50
AH1260//40	—	3.00	7.50	12.50	18.50	27.50

MILLED COINAGE

Y# 37 1/6 MOHUR
Gold, 14.5 mm. **Obverse:** Bust of Sayaji Rao III right **Mint:** Baroda **Note:** 1.04-1.18 grams.

Date	Mintage	F	VF	XF	Unc
VS1951 (1894)	—	165	225	275	350
VS1951 (1894)	—	165	225	275	350
VS1953 (1896)	—	165	225	275	350

Y# 39 MOHUR
Gold, 21 mm. **Obverse:** Bust of Sayaji Rao III right **Mint:** Baroda **Note:** Weight varies: 6.20-6.40 grams.

Date	Mintage	F	VF	XF	Unc
VS1945 (1888)	—	250	325	450	650
VS1952 (1895)	—	250	325	450	650
VS1953 (1896)	—	250	325	450	650

Ganpat Rao
AH1264-1273 / 1847-1856AD

HAMMERED COINAGE

C# 41 1/2 PAISA
5.0000 g., Copper, 15 mm. **Obverse:** Shaded ball in center **Obv. Inscription:** Muhammad Akbar II **Mint:** Baroda

Date	Mintage	Good	VG	F	VF	XF
ND(1847-56)	—	1.00	2.00	3.00	4.50	—

C# A39 1/2 PAISA
Copper, 14 mm. **Mint:** Amreli

Date	Mintage	Good	VG	F	VF	XF
AH1266	—	2.50	4.50	6.00	9.00	—

C# 39.1 PAISA
Copper **Obverse:** Lotus at left, scimitar at right **Mint:** Amreli

Date	Mintage	Good	VG	F	VF	XF
ND(1847-56)	—	3.00	5.50	7.00	11.00	—
AH1266//3	—	3.00	5.50	7.00	11.00	—
AH1272	—	3.00	5.50	7.00	11.00	—

C# 42 PAISA
10.0000 g., Copper **Obv. Inscription:** Muhammad Akbar II **Mint:** Baroda

Date	Mintage	Good	VG	F	VF	XF
AH1263//43	—	2.00	3.00	4.00	5.50	—
AH1264//44	—	2.00	3.00	4.00	5.50	—
AH1265//45	—	2.00	3.00	4.00	5.50	—
AH1266//46	—	2.00	3.00	4.00	5.50	—
AH1272//52	—	2.00	3.00	4.00	5.50	—

C# 43 PAISA
10.0000 g., Copper **Obverse:** Shaded ball in center **Obv. Inscription:** Muhammad Akbar II **Mint:** Baroda

Date	Mintage	Good	VG	F	VF	XF
AH1264//4x	—	2.00	3.00	4.00	5.50	—
AH1266//4x	—	2.00	3.00	4.00	5.50	—
AH1268//4x	—	2.00	3.00	4.00	5.50	—

C# 39.2 PAISA
Copper **Obverse:** Scimitar at left, lotus at right **Mint:** Amreli

Date	Mintage	Good	VG	F	VF	XF
AH1266	—	3.00	5.50	7.00	11.00	—

C# 44 1/8 RUPEE
Silver, 11 mm. **Obv. Inscription:** Muhammad Akbar II **Mint:** Baroda **Note:** Weight varies: 1.34-1.45 grams.

Date	Mintage	Good	VG	F	VF	XF
AH1269	—	3.00	7.50	12.50	20.00	30.00

C# 45 1/4 RUPEE
Silver **Obv. Inscription:** Muhammad Akbar II **Mint:** Baroda **Note:** Weight varies: 2.68-2.90 grams.

Date	Mintage	Good	VG	F	VF	XF
AH126x	—	3.00	7.50	12.50	20.00	30.00
AH1272//52	—	3.00	7.50	12.50	20.00	30.00

C# 46 1/2 RUPEE
Silver **Obv. Inscription:** Muhammad Akbar II **Mint:** Baroda **Note:** Weight varies: 5.35-5.80 grams.

Date	Mintage	Good	VG	F	VF	XF
AH126x//43	—	3.00	7.50	12.50	20.00	30.00
AH1264//44	—	3.00	7.50	12.50	20.00	30.00
AH126x//45	—	3.00	7.50	12.50	20.00	30.00
AH1267//46	—	3.00	7.50	12.50	20.00	30.00
AH1268//47	—	3.00	7.50	12.50	20.00	30.00
AH12xx//49	—	3.00	7.50	12.50	20.00	30.00
AH1271	—	3.00	7.50	12.50	20.00	30.00
AH127x//51	—	3.00	7.50	12.50	20.00	30.00
AH1272//52	—	3.00	7.50	12.50	20.00	30.00

C# 47 RUPEE
Silver **Obv. Inscription:** Muhammad Akbar II **Mint:** Baroda **Note:** Weight varies: 10.70-11.60 grams.

Date	Mintage	Good	VG	F	VF	XF
AH1264//43	—	2.75	7.00	11.00	16.50	25.00
AH1265//43	—	2.75	7.00	11.00	16.50	25.00
AH1265//44	—	2.75	7.00	11.00	16.50	25.00
AH126x//45	—	2.75	7.00	11.00	16.50	25.00
AH126x//46	—	2.75	7.00	11.00	16.50	25.00
AH1268//47	—	2.75	7.00	11.00	16.50	25.00
AH1271//50	—	2.75	7.00	11.00	16.50	25.00
AH1272//51	—	2.75	7.00	11.00	16.50	25.00
AH1272//52	—	2.75	7.00	11.00	16.50	25.00

Khande Rao
AH 1273-1287 / 1856-1870AD

HAMMERED COINAGE

Y# 1.2 1/2 PAISA
4.2000 g., Copper, 15 mm. **Obv. Inscription:** "Muhammad Akbar II" **Reverse:** Pomegranate, Nagari "Kha" and scimitar **Mint:** Baroda **Note:** Prev. Y#1.

Date	Mintage	Good	VG	F	VF	XF
ND(1856-70)	—	1.25	2.00	3.00	4.00	—

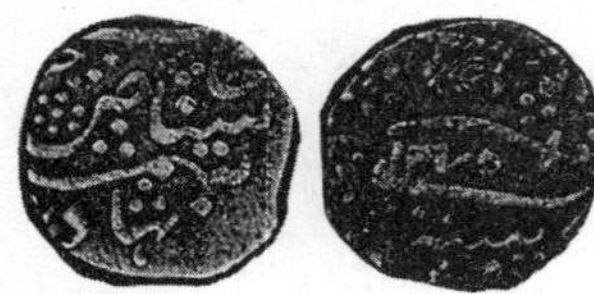

Y# 6 1/2 PAISA

3.4000 g., Copper **Obv. Inscription:** "Commander of the Sovereign Band" **Reverse:** Nagari "Kha Ga" and scimitar **Mint:** Baroda **Note:** Obverse inscription refers to a title of the Gaekwar, ruler of Baroda.

Date	Mintage	Good	VG	F	VF	XF
AH1275	—	2.50	4.00	6.00	9.00	15.00
AH1276	—	2.50	4.00	6.00	9.00	15.00
AH1277	—	2.50	4.00	6.00	9.00	15.00

Y# 1.1 1/2 PAISA

Copper **Obv. Inscription:** "Muhammad Akbar II" **Reverse:** Nagari "Kha" and scimitar **Mint:** Amreli **Note:** Prev. C#A1.

Date	Mintage	Good	VG	F	VF	XF
AH1277	—	3.00	5.00	8.00	12.00	20.00

Y# 6a 1/2 PAISA

3.4000 g., Copper **Obv. Inscription:** "Commander of the Sovereign Band" **Reverse:** Nagari "Kha Ga" and scimitar **Mint:** Baroda **Note:** Obverse inscription refers to a title of the Gaekwar, ruler of Baroda.

Date	Mintage	Good	VG	F	VF	XF
AH1281	—	5.00	7.50	10.00	15.00	—
AH1285	—	5.00	7.50	10.00	15.00	—

Y# 7.4 PAISA

7.0000 g., Copper **Obv. Inscription:** "Commander of the Sovereign Band" **Reverse:** Nagari "Kha Ga" and scimitar **Mint:** Amreli **Note:** Thin flan. Prev. Y#1.4; Obverse inscription refers to a title of the Gaekwar, ruler of Baroda.

Date	Mintage	Good	VG	F	VF	XF
AH1270	—	2.00	3.50	5.50	8.00	—

Y# 7.3 PAISA

7.0000 g., Copper **Obv. Inscription:** "Commander of the Sovereign Band" **Reverse:** Nagari "Kha Ga" and scimitar **Mint:** Amreli **Note:** Thin flan. Prev. Y#1.3; Obverse inscription refers to a title of the Gaekwar, ruler of Baroda.

Date	Mintage	Good	VG	F	VF	XF
ND(1856-70)	—	2.00	3.50	5.50	8.00	—

Y# 7.2 PAISA

7.0000 g., Copper **Obv. Inscription:** "Commander of the Sovereign Band" **Reverse:** Nagari "Kha Ga" and scimitar **Mint:** Amreli **Note:** Thin flan. Prev. Y#1.2; Obverse inscription refers to a title of the Gaekwar, ruler of Baroda.

Date	Mintage	Good	VG	F	VF	XF
ND(1856-70)	—	2.00	3.50	5.50	8.00	—

Y# 2 PAISA

8.4000 g., Silver **Obv. Inscription:** "Muhammad Akbar II" **Reverse:** Pomegranate, Nagari "Kha" and scimitar **Mint:** Baroda

Date	Mintage	Good	VG	F	VF	XF
AH1273//52	—	1.50	2.50	3.50	5.00	—

Y# 7.5 PAISA

7.0000 g., Copper **Obv. Inscription:** "Commander of the Sovereign Band" **Reverse:** Nagari "Kha Ga" and scimitar **Mint:** Amreli **Note:** Thick flan, cruder types. Prev. Y#1a; Obverse inscription refers to a title of the Gaekwar, ruler of Baroda.

Date	Mintage	Good	VG	F	VF	XF
ND(1856-70)	—	2.00	3.50	5.50	8.00	—

Y# 7.6 PAISA

7.0000 g., Copper **Obv. Inscription:** "Commander of the Sovereign Band" **Reverse:** Nagari "Kha Ga" and scimitar **Mint:** Amreli **Note:** Thick flan, cruder types. Prev. Y#1b; Obverse inscription refers to a title of the Gaekwar, ruler of Baroda.

Date	Mintage	Good	VG	F	VF	XF
ND(1856-70)	—	2.00	3.50	5.50	8.00	—

Y# 7.7 PAISA

Copper **Obv. Inscription:** "Commander of the Sovereign Band" **Reverse:** Nagari "Kha Ga" and scimitar **Mint:** Baroda **Note:** Prev. Y#7. Weight varies: 7.00-8.00 grams. Various die varieties exist; Obverse inscription refers to a title of the Gaekwar, ruler of Baroda.

Date	Mintage	Good	VG	F	VF	XF
AH1274	—	2.00	3.00	4.00	5.50	—
AH1275	—	1.25	2.25	3.25	4.00	—
AH1276	—	1.25	2.25	3.25	4.00	—
AH1277	—	2.00	3.00	4.00	5.50	—

Y# 7.1 PAISA

7.0000 g., Copper **Obv. Inscription:** "Commander of the Sovereign Band" **Reverse:** Nagari "Kha Ga" and scimitar **Mint:** Amreli **Note:** Thin flan. Prev. Y#1.1; Obverse inscription refers to a title of the Gaekwar, ruler of Baroda.

Date	Mintage	Good	VG	F	VF	XF
AH1277	—	2.00	3.50	5.50	8.00	—

Y# 7.8 PAISA

Copper **Obv. Inscription:** "Commander of the Sovereign Band" **Reverse:** Nagari "Kha Ga" and scimitar **Mint:** Baroda **Note:** Weight varies: 7.00-8.00 grams.

Date	Mintage	Good	VG	F	VF	XF
AH1281	—	3.50	4.50	6.00	8.00	—
AH1282	—	3.50	4.50	6.00	8.00	—
AH1283	—	3.50	4.50	6.00	8.00	—
AH1284	—	3.50	4.50	6.00	8.00	—
AH1285	—	3.50	4.50	6.00	8.00	—

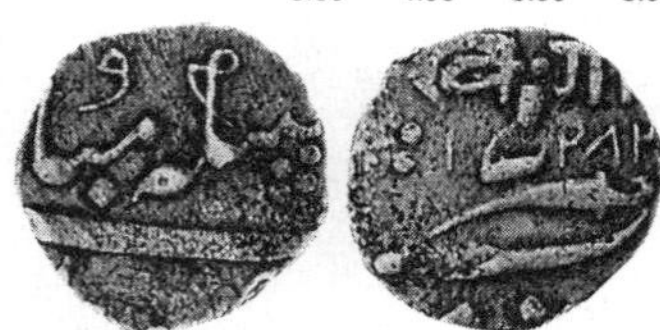

Y# 8 2 PAISA

15.0000 g., Copper **Obv. Inscription:** "Commander of the Sovereign Band" **Reverse:** Nagari "Kha Ga" and scimitar **Mint:** Baroda **Note:** Obverse inscription refers to a title of the Gaekwar, ruler of Baroda.

Date	Mintage	Good	VG	F	VF	XF
AH1281	—	3.50	6.00	10.00	15.00	—
AH1282	—	3.50	6.00	10.00	15.00	—
AH1284	—	3.50	6.00	10.00	15.00	—
AH1285	—	3.50	6.00	10.00	15.00	—

Y# 9 1/8 RUPEE

Silver **Obv. Inscription:** "Commander of the Sovereign Band" **Reverse:** Nagari "Kha Ga" and scimitar **Mint:** Baroda **Note:** Weight varies: 1.34-1.45 grams; Obverse inscription refers to a title of the Gaekwar, ruler of Baroda.

Date	Mintage	Good	VG	F	VF	XF
AH1282	—	2.00	5.00	7.00	10.00	15.00

Y# 3 1/4 RUPEE

Silver **Obv. Inscription:** "Muhammad Akbar II" **Reverse:** Nagari "Kha" and scimitar **Mint:** Baroda **Note:** Weight varies: 2.68-2.90 grams.

Date	Mintage	Good	VG	F	VF	XF
AH1273//52	—	2.00	5.00	8.00	12.50	18.50
AH1278	—	2.00	5.00	8.00	12.50	18.50

Y# 10 1/4 RUPEE

Silver **Obv. Inscription:** "Commander of the Sovereign Band" **Mint:** Baroda **Note:** Weight varies: 2.68-2.90 grams; Obverse inscription refers to a title of the Gaekwar, ruler of Baroda.

Date	Mintage	Good	VG	F	VF	XF
AH1274	—	1.75	4.50	6.50	9.00	18.50
AH1282	—	1.75	4.50	6.50	9.00	18.50
AH1283	—	1.75	4.50	6.50	9.00	18.50
AH1286	—	1.75	4.50	6.50	9.00	18.50

Y# 4 1/2 RUPEE

Silver **Obv. Inscription:** "Muhammad Akbar II" **Reverse:** Nagari "Kha" and scimitar **Mint:** Baroda **Note:** Weight varies: 5.35-5.80 grams.

Date	Mintage	Good	VG	F	VF	XF
AH1267	—	2.25	5.50	9.00	13.50	20.00
AH1272	—	2.25	5.50	9.00	13.50	20.00
AH127x//52	—	2.25	5.50	9.00	13.50	20.00
AH1274	—	2.25	5.50	9.00	13.50	20.00
AH1275	—	2.25	5.50	9.00	13.50	20.00
AH1282	—	2.25	5.50	9.00	13.50	20.00

Y# 11 1/2 RUPEE

Silver **Obv. Inscription:** "Commander of the Sovereign Band" **Mint:** Baroda **Note:** Weight varies: 5.35-5.80 grams; Obverse inscription refers to a title of the Gaekwar, ruler of Baroda.

Date	Mintage	Good	VG	F	VF	XF
AH1274	—	2.50	6.00	9.00	13.50	20.00
AH1275	—	2.50	6.00	9.00	13.50	20.00
AH1276	—	2.50	6.00	9.00	13.50	20.00
AH1277	—	2.50	6.00	9.00	13.50	20.00
AH1278	—	2.50	6.00	9.00	13.50	20.00
AH1279	—	2.50	6.00	9.00	13.50	20.00
AH1280	—	2.50	6.00	9.00	13.50	20.00
AH1282	—	2.50	6.00	9.00	13.50	20.00
AH1284	—	2.50	6.00	9.00	13.50	20.00
AH1285	—	2.50	6.00	9.00	13.50	20.00
AH1286	—	2.50	6.00	9.00	13.50	20.00

Y# A13 NAZARANA 1/2 RUPEE

18.1000 g., Silver **Obv. Inscription:** "Commander of the Sovereign Band" **Reverse:** Nagari "Kha Ga" and scimitar **Mint:** Baroda **Note:** Obverse inscription refers to a title of the Gaekwar, ruler of Baroda.

Date	Mintage	Good	VG	F	VF	XF
AH1275 Rare	—	—	—	—	—	—

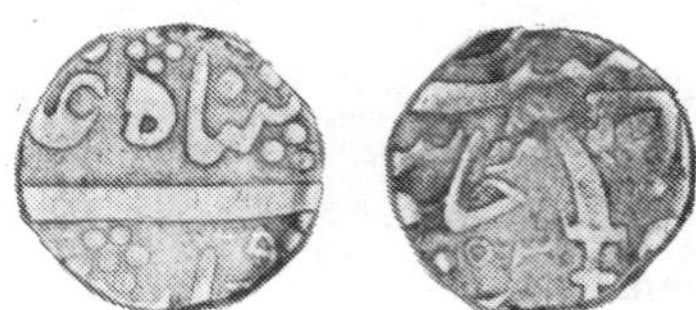

Y# 5 RUPEE

Silver **Obv. Inscription:** "Muhammad Akbar II" **Reverse:** Nagari "Kha" and scimitar **Mint:** Baroda **Note:** Weight varies: 10.70-11.60 grams.

Date	Mintage	Good	VG	F	VF	XF
AH1273//5x	—	2.75	6.50	11.00	16.50	25.00
AH1274//53	—	2.75	6.50	11.00	16.50	25.00
AH1275	—	2.75	6.50	11.00	16.50	25.00
AH128x	—	2.75	6.50	11.00	16.50	25.00

Y# 12 RUPEE
Silver **Obv. Inscription:** "Commander of the Sovereign Band" **Mint:** Baroda **Note:** Weight varies: 10.70-11.60 grams; Obverse inscription refers to a title of the Gaekwar, ruler of Baroda.

Date	Mintage	Good	VG	F	VF	XF
AH1274	—	2.75	6.50	10.00	15.00	22.50
AH1275	—	2.75	6.50	10.00	15.00	22.50
AH1276	—	2.75	6.50	10.00	15.00	22.50
AH1277	—	2.75	6.50	10.00	15.00	22.50
AH1278	—	2.75	6.50	10.00	15.00	22.50
AH1280	—	2.75	6.50	10.00	15.00	22.50
AH1281	—	2.75	6.50	10.00	15.00	22.50
AH1282	—	2.75	6.50	10.00	15.00	22.50
AH1283	—	2.75	6.50	10.00	15.00	22.50
AH1284	—	2.75	6.50	10.00	15.00	22.50
AH1285	—	2.75	6.50	10.00	15.00	22.50
AH1286	—	2.75	6.50	10.00	15.00	22.50
AH1287	—	2.75	6.50	10.00	15.00	22.50

Y# B13 1/4 MOHUR
2.8000 g., Gold, 15 mm. **Obv. Inscription:** "Commander of the Sovereign Band" **Reverse:** Nagari "Kha Ga" and scimitar **Mint:** Amreli **Note:** Obverse inscription refers to a title of the Gaekwar, ruler of Baroda.

Date	Mintage	Good	VG	F	VF	XF
AH127x Rare	—	—	—	—	—	—

MILLED COINAGE

Y# 13 NAZARANA 1/2 RUPEE
5.6500 g., Silver **Obv. Inscription:** "Commander of the Sovereign Band" **Mint:** Baroda

Date	Mintage	Good	VG	F	VF	XF
AH1287	—	25.00	50.00	85.00	120	175

Y# 14.1 NAZARANA RUPEE
11.3000 g., Silver **Obverse:** Persian leg: "Kahnde Rao" **Obv. Inscription:** "Commander of the Sovereign Band" **Mint:** Baroda

Date	Mintage	Good	VG	F	VF	XF
AH1287	—	20.00	40.00	70.00	100	140

Y# 14.2 NAZARANA RUPEE
11.3000 g., Silver **Obverse:** Persian leg: "Khande Rao" **Obv. Inscription:** "Commander of the Sovereign Band" **Mint:** Baroda

Date	Mintage	Good	VG	F	VF	XF
AH1287	—	30.00	60.00	100	140	200

Malhar Rao
AH1287-1292 / 1870-1875AD
HAMMERED COINAGE

Y# 16 1/2 PAISA
Copper **Reverse:** Nagari "Ma Ga" and scimitar **Mint:** Baroda **Note:** Weight varies: 7.60-7.80 grams.

Date	Mintage	Good	VG	F	VF	XF
ND(1870-75)	—	1.25	2.50	3.50	5.00	—
AH1288	—	1.25	2.50	3.50	5.00	—
AH1289	—	1.25	2.50	3.50	5.00	—
AH1290	—	1.25	2.50	3.50	5.00	—

Y# 15 1/2 PAISA
4.0000 g., Copper **Reverse:** Nagari "Ma Ga" and scimitar **Mint:** Baroda

Date	Mintage	Good	VG	F	VF	XF
AH1288	—	2.00	3.00	4.00	5.50	—
AH1290	—	2.00	3.00	4.00	5.50	—

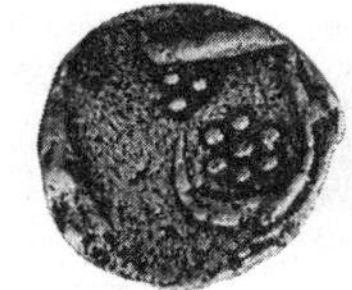

Y# 17 2 PAISA
16.1000 g., Copper **Reverse:** Nagari "Ma Ga" and scimitar **Mint:** Baroda

Date	Mintage	Good	VG	F	VF	XF
AH1288	—	2.00	3.00	4.00	5.50	—
AH1289	—	2.00	3.00	4.00	5.50	—
AH1290	—	2.00	3.00	4.00	5.50	—

Y# A17 NARAZANA 2 PAISA
Copper **Reverse:** Nagari "Ma Ga" and scimitar **Mint:** Baroda

Date	Mintage	Good	VG	F	VF	XF
AH1289 Rare	—	—	—	—	—	—

Y# 18 1/8 RUPEE
Silver, 11 mm. **Reverse:** Nagari "Ma Ga" and scimitar **Mint:** Baroda **Note:** Weight varies: 1.34-1.45 grams.

Date	Mintage	Good	VG	F	VF	XF
AH129x	—	1.75	4.00	6.00	9.00	13.50

Y# 19 1/4 RUPEE
Silver, 13 mm. **Reverse:** Nagari "Ma Ga" and scimitar **Mint:** Baroda **Note:** Weight varies: 2.68-2.90 grams.

Date	Mintage	Good	VG	F	VF	XF
AH1290	—	2.00	5.00	7.00	10.00	15.00

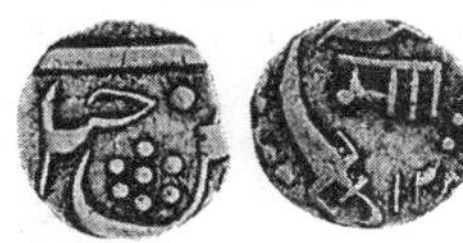

Y# 20 1/2 RUPEE
Silver **Reverse:** Nagari "Ma Ga" and scimitar **Mint:** Baroda **Note:** Weight varies: 5.35-5.80 grams.

Date	Mintage	Good	VG	F	VF	XF
AH1287	—	2.25	5.50	8.00	12.50	18.50
AH1288	—	2.25	5.50	8.00	12.50	18.50
AH1289	—	2.25	5.50	8.00	12.50	18.50
AH1290	—	2.25	5.50	8.00	12.50	18.50

Y# 21 RUPEE
Silver **Reverse:** Nagari "Ma Ga" and scimitar **Mint:** Baroda **Note:** Weight varies: 10.70-11.60 grams.

Date	Mintage	Good	VG	F	VF	XF
AH1287	—	2.50	6.00	9.00	13.50	20.00
AH1288	—	2.50	6.00	9.00	13.50	20.00
AH1289	—	2.50	6.00	9.00	13.50	20.00
AH1290	—	2.50	6.00	9.00	13.50	20.00
ND(ca.1875)//122	—	2.50	6.00	9.00	13.50	20.00

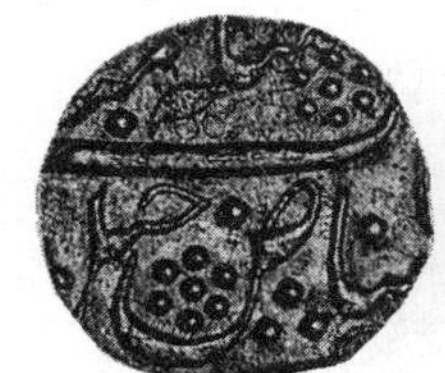

Y# 21a NAZARANA RUPEE
Silver **Reverse:** Nagari "Ma Ga" and scimitar **Mint:** Baroda **Note:** Weight varies: 10.70-11.60 grams.

Date	Mintage	Good	VG	F	VF	XF
AH1288	—	120	200	300	450	—

Y# 22 NAZARANA 2 RUPEES
Silver **Reverse:** Nagari "Ma Ga" and scimitar **Mint:** Baroda **Note:** Weight varies: 21.40-23.20 grams.

Date	Mintage	Good	VG	F	VF	XF
AH1288 Rare	—	—	—	—	—	—

Y# 22A NAZARANA 4 RUPEES
44.0000 g., Silver **Reverse:** Nagari "Ma Ga" and scimitar **Mint:** Baroda

Date	Mintage	Good	VG	F	VF	XF
AH1288 Rare	—	—	—	—	—	—

Sayaji Rao III
AH1292-1357 / VS1932-95 / 1875-1938AD
HAMMERED COINAGE

Y# A23 1/4 PAISA
Copper **Reverse:** Nagari "Sa Ga" and scimitar **Mint:** Baroda

Date	Mintage	Good	VG	F	VF	XF
VS194x (1883-92)	—	2.50	5.00	8.50	12.50	—

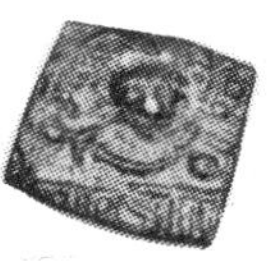

Y# A2 1/4 PAISA
Copper **Mint:** Amreli

Date	Mintage	Good	VG	F	VF	XF
AH1312 retrograde	—	5.00	8.00	12.00	18.00	—

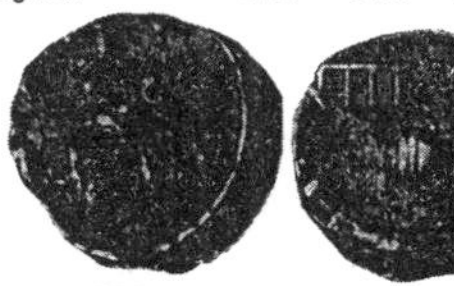

Y# 23 1/2 PAISA
Copper **Reverse:** Nagari "Sa Ga" and scimitar **Mint:** Baroda

Date	Mintage	Good	VG	F	VF	XF
VS1937 (1880)	—	1.50	2.50	4.00	5.50	—
VS1947 (1890)	—	1.50	2.50	4.00	5.50	—
VS1948 (1891)	—	1.50	2.50	4.00	5.50	—

Y# B23 1/2 PAISA
8.0000 g., Copper, 16 mm. **Mint:** Amreli **Note:** Prev. Y#2.

Date	Mintage	Good	VG	F	VF	XF
AH1312	—	1.75	3.25	4.50	6.00	—

C# 33.15 PAISA
10.2000 g., Copper **Obv. Inscription:** Muhammad Akbar II **Reverse:** 4-petal flower **Mint:** Baroda **Note:** Size varies: 18-24mm.

Date	Mintage	Good	VG	F	VF	XF
AH1255//35	—	2.00	3.50	5.00	7.00	—

Y# C23a PAISA
Copper **Reverse:** English "S" with serifs to left of "Sa Ga" and sword in "S" of "Julus" **Mint:** Amreli **Note:** Prev. Y#3a.

Date	Mintage	Good	VG	F	VF	XF
ND(1875-95)	—	6.00	10.00	14.00	18.50	—

Y# 24 PAISA
Copper **Reverse:** Nagari "Sa Ga" and scimitar **Mint:** Baroda

Date	Mintage	Good	VG	F	VF	XF
VS1937 (1880)	—	1.50	2.50	4.00	5.50	—
VS1947 (1890)	—	1.50	2.50	4.00	5.50	—
VS1948/7 (1891)	—	1.50	2.50	4.00	5.50	—
VS1948 (1891)	—	1.50	2.50	4.00	5.50	—

Y# 31.2a PAISA
Copper, 1.6 mm. **Obverse:** Similar inner circle **Reverse:** Similar inner circle **Mint:** Baroda **Note:** Weight varies: 6.50-6.80 grams. Thin planchet.

Date	Mintage	Good	VG	F	VF	XF
AH1948	—	0.10	0.30	0.60	1.00	1.50
AH1949	—	0.10	0.30	0.60	1.00	1.50
AH1950	—	0.10	0.30	0.60	1.00	1.50

Y# 24a PAISA
Copper **Reverse:** Nagari "Sa Ga" and scimitar **Mint:** Baroda **Note:** Machine-punched planchets. Generally struck off-center.

Date	Mintage	Good	VG	F	VF	XF
VS1949 (1892)	—	2.00	3.50	5.00	7.00	—

Y# C23 PAISA
Copper **Obverse:** Date **Reverse:** Date **Mint:** Amreli **Note:** Prev. Y#3.

Date	Mintage	Good	VG	F	VF	XF
AH1311 retrograde	—	3.00	5.00	7.50	10.00	—
AH1312 retrograde	—	3.00	5.00	7.50	10.00	—
AH1313 retrograde	—	3.00	5.00	7.50	10.00	—

Y# C23b PAISA
Copper **Reverse:** Sunface, sword and English "T" with serifs in right field **Mint:** Amreli **Note:** Prev. Y#3b. These coins may have been issued by Sayaji Rao II with blundered dates.

Date	Mintage	Good	VG	F	VF	XF
AH1312 retrograde	—	5.00	8.00	12.00	20.00	—

Y# 25 2 PAISE
Copper **Reverse:** Nagari "Sa Ga" and scimitar **Mint:** Baroda

Date	Mintage	Good	VG	F	VF	XF
VS1937 (1880)	—	3.50	5.00	6.50	8.50	—
VS1947 (1890)	—	3.50	5.00	6.50	8.50	—
VS1948 (1891)	—	3.50	5.00	6.50	8.50	—

Y# 25a 2 PAISE
17.0000 g., Copper **Reverse:** Nagari "Sa Ga" and scimitar **Mint:** Baroda **Note:** Machine-punched planchets. Generally struck off-center.

Date	Mintage	Good	VG	F	VF	XF
VS1949 (1892)	—	3.75	5.50	7.50	10.00	—

Y# 26 1/8 RUPEE
Silver **Reverse:** Nagari "Sa Ga" and scimitar **Mint:** Baroda **Note:** Weight varies: 1.34-1.45 grams.

Date	Mintage	Good	VG	F	VF	XF
AH1294	—	1.75	4.00	6.00	9.00	13.50
AH1295	—	1.75	4.00	6.00	9.00	13.50
AH1297	—	1.75	4.00	6.00	9.00	13.50
AH1299	—	1.75	4.00	6.00	9.00	13.50

Y# 27 1/4 RUPEE
Silver, 13 mm. **Reverse:** Nagari "Sa Ga" and scimitar **Mint:** Baroda **Note:** Weight varies: 2.68-2.90 grams.

Date	Mintage	Good	VG	F	VF	XF
AH1292	—	2.00	5.00	7.00	10.00	15.00
AH1299	—	2.00	5.00	7.00	10.00	15.00

Y# 28 1/2 RUPEE
Silver **Reverse:** Nagari "Sa Ga" and scimitar **Mint:** Baroda **Note:** Weight varies: 5.35-5.80 grams.

Date	Mintage	Good	VG	F	VF	XF
AH1292	—	2.25	5.50	8.00	12.50	18.50
AH1293	—	2.25	5.50	8.00	12.50	18.50
AH1294	—	2.25	5.50	8.00	12.50	18.50
AH1295	—	2.25	5.50	8.00	12.50	18.50
AH1297	—	2.25	5.50	8.00	12.50	18.50
AH1298	—	2.25	5.50	8.00	12.50	18.50
AH1299	—	2.25	5.50	8.00	12.50	18.50
AH1300	—	2.25	5.50	8.00	12.50	18.50
AH1301	—	2.25	5.50	8.00	12.50	18.50
AH1302	—	2.25	5.50	8.00	12.50	18.50

Y# 29 RUPEE
Silver **Reverse:** Nagari "Sa Ga" and scimitar **Mint:** Baroda **Note:** Weight varies: 10.70-11.60 grams.

Date	Mintage	Good	VG	F	VF	XF
AH1292	—	2.50	6.00	9.00	13.50	20.00
AH1293	—	2.50	6.00	9.00	13.50	20.00
AH1294	—	2.50	6.00	9.00	13.50	20.00
AH1295	—	2.50	6.00	9.00	13.50	20.00
AH1298	—	2.50	6.00	9.00	13.50	20.00
AH1299	—	2.50	6.00	9.00	13.50	20.00
AH1300	—	2.50	6.00	9.00	13.50	20.00
AH1301	—	2.50	6.00	9.00	13.50	20.00
AH1302	—	2.50	6.00	9.00	13.50	20.00

MILLED COINAGE

Y# 31.1 PAISA
Copper **Obverse:** Inner legend curved, long hoof **Mint:** Baroda

Date	Mintage	Good	VG	F	VF	XF
VS1940 (1883)	—	0.40	1.00	2.00	2.50	3.00
VS1941 (1884)	—	0.40	1.00	2.00	2.50	3.00
VS1942 (1885)	—	0.70	1.75	2.50	3.75	5.00

Y# 31.2 PAISA
Copper, 2 mm. **Obverse:** Inner legend straight, short hoof **Mint:** Baroda **Note:** Weight varies: 8.00-8.30 grams. Thick planchet.

Date	Mintage	Good	VG	F	VF	XF
VS1941 (1884)	—	0.30	0.75	1.50	2.00	2.75
VS1942 (1885)	—	0.15	0.35	0.75	1.25	1.75
VS1943 (1886)	—	0.15	0.35	0.75	1.25	1.75
VS1944 (1887)	—	0.15	0.35	0.75	1.25	1.75
VS1945 (1888)	—	0.20	0.50	1.00	1.50	2.00
VS1946/3 (1889)	—	0.40	1.00	2.00	3.00	4.50
VS1946/4 (1889)	—	0.40	1.00	2.00	3.00	4.50
VS1946 (1889)	—	0.20	0.50	1.00	1.50	2.00
VS1947 (1890)	—	0.15	0.35	0.75	1.25	1.75
VS1948 (1891)	—	0.30	0.75	1.50	2.00	2.75

Y# 30.3 PAI
Copper **Obverse:** Small legends **Mint:** Baroda **Note:** Varieties exist.

Date	Mintage	Good	VG	F	VF	XF
VS1949 (1892)	—	0.15	0.35	0.75	1.00	1.50
VS1950/49	—	0.15	0.35	0.75	1.00	1.50
VS1950 (1893)	—	0.15	0.35	0.75	1.00	1.50

Y# 30.1 PAI
Copper **Obverse:** Annulets between letters **Mint:** Baroda

Date	Mintage	Good	VG	F	VF	XF
VS1944 (1887)	—	0.20	0.50	1.00	1.50	2.00

Y# 30.1a PAI
Copper **Obverse:** Pellets between letters **Mint:** Baroda

Date	Mintage	Good	VG	F	VF	XF
VS1944 (1887)	—	1.00	2.50	5.00	8.00	12.00

Y# 30.2 PAI
Copper **Obverse:** Without annulets **Mint:** Baroda **Note:** Thick planchet.

Date	Mintage	Good	VG	F	VF	XF
VS1944 (1887)	—	0.30	0.75	1.50	2.00	2.50
VS1945 (1888)	—	0.15	0.35	0.75	1.00	1.50
VS1946 (1889)	—	0.30	0.75	1.50	2.00	2.50
VS1947 (1890)	—	0.30	0.75	1.50	2.00	2.50

Y# 30.2a PAI
Copper **Obverse:** Large legends **Mint:** Baroda **Note:** Thin planchets. Varieties exist.

Date	Mintage	Good	VG	F	VF	XF
VS1948 (1891)	—	0.30	0.75	1.50	2.00	2.50
VS1949 (1892)	—	0.15	0.35	0.75	1.00	1.50
VS1950 (1893)	—	0.30	0.75	1.25	1.75	2.25

Y# 32.1 2 PAISA
Copper **Obverse:** Inner legend curved, long hoof **Reverse:** Large inner legend and date. **Mint:** Baroda

Date	Mintage	Good	VG	F	VF	XF
VS1940 (1883)	—	0.80	2.00	3.50	5.50	9.00
VS1941 (1884)	—	0.80	2.00	3.50	5.50	9.00

Y# 32.2 2 PAISA
Copper, 2.9 mm. **Obverse:** Inner legend straight, short hoof **Reverse:** Small inner legend and date **Mint:** Baroda **Note:** Weight varies: 16.30-16.80 grams. Thick planchet.

Date	Mintage	Good	VG	F	VF	XF
VS1941 (1884)	—	0.40	1.00	2.00	3.00	5.00
VS1942 (1885)	—	0.40	1.00	2.00	3.00	5.00
VS1943 (1886)	—	0.30	0.75	1.50	2.25	3.50
VS1944/3 (1887)	—	0.30	0.75	1.50	2.25	3.50
VS1944 (1887)	—	0.30	0.75	1.50	2.25	3.50
VS1946 (1889)	—	0.50	1.25	2.50	4.00	7.50
VS1946/4 (1889)	—	0.80	2.00	4.00	7.00	11.00
VS1946/2 (1889)	—	0.40	1.00	2.00	3.00	5.00
VS1946/5 (1889)	—	0.80	2.00	4.00	7.00	11.00
VS1947 (1890)	—	0.30	0.75	1.50	2.25	3.50
VS1948 (1891)	—	1.00	2.50	4.00	6.00	10.00

Y# 32.2a 2 PAISA
Copper **Obverse:** Inner legend straight, short hoof **Reverse:** Small inner legend and date **Mint:** Baroda **Note:** Size varies: 2.4-2.5mm. Weight varies: 12.40-13.30 grams. Thin planchet.

Date	Mintage	Good	VG	F	VF	XF
VS1948 (1891)	—	0.20	0.50	1.00	1.50	2.50
VS1949/4 (1892)	—	0.20	0.50	1.00	1.50	2.50
VS1949/8 (1892)	—	0.30	0.75	1.50	2.25	3.50
VS1949 (1892)	—	0.30	0.75	1.50	2.25	3.50
VS1950 (1893)	—	0.25	0.65	1.25	1.75	3.00

Y# 33 2 ANNAS
Silver **Mint:** Baroda

Date	Mintage	VG	F	VF	XF	Unc
VS1949 (1892)	—	2.75	7.00	11.00	16.50	25.00

Y# 33a 2 ANNAS
Silver **Mint:** Baroda

Date	Mintage	VG	F	VF	XF	Unc
VS1951 (1894)	—	2.75	6.50	10.00	15.00	22.50
VS1952 (1895)	—	2.75	6.50	10.00	15.00	22.50

Y# 34 4 ANNAS
Silver **Mint:** Baroda

Date	Mintage	VG	F	VF	XF	Unc
VS1949 (1892)	—	2.75	7.00	11.00	16.00	25.00

Y# 35 1/2 RUPEE
Silver **Mint:** Baroda

Date	Mintage	VG	F	VF	XF	Unc
VS1948 (1891)	—	12.00	30.00	40.00	55.00	80.00
VS1949 (1892)	—	12.00	30.00	40.00	55.00	80.00

Y# 34a 4 ANNAS
Silver **Mint:** Baroda

Date	Mintage	VG	F	VF	XF	Unc
VS1951 (1894)	—	2.50	6.00	9.00	13.50	20.00
VS1952 (1895)	—	2.50	6.00	9.00	13.50	20.00

Y# 35a 1/2 RUPEE
Silver **Mint:** Baroda

Date	Mintage	VG	F	VF	XF	Unc
VS1951 (1894)	—	5.00	12.50	18.50	25.00	35.00
VS1952 (1895)	—	5.00	12.50	18.50	25.00	35.00

Y# 36 RUPEE
Silver **Mint:** Baroda

Date	Mintage	VG	F	VF	XF	Unc
VS1948 (1891)	—	5.50	13.50	20.00	27.50	37.50
VS1949 (1892)	—	5.50	13.50	20.00	27.50	37.50

Y# 36a RUPEE
Silver **Mint:** Baroda

Date	Mintage	VG	F	VF	XF	Unc
VS1951 (1894)	—	4.50	11.50	17.50	23.50	32.50
VS1952 (1895)	—	4.50	11.50	17.50	23.50	32.50
VS1953 (1896)	—	4.50	11.50	17.50	23.50	32.50
VS1954 (1897)	—	4.50	11.50	17.50	23.50	32.50
VS1955 (1898)	—	4.50	11.50	17.50	23.50	32.50
VS1956 (1899)	—	4.50	11.50	17.50	23.50	32.50

Y# A37 1/6 MOHUR
Gold, 14.5 mm. **Obverse:** Bust of Sayaji Rao III right **Mint:** Baroda **Note:** Weight varies: 1.04-1.18 grams

Date	Mintage	F	VF	XF	Unc
VS1943 (1886)	—	165	225	275	350

Y# A38 1/3 MOHUR
Gold, 16 mm. **Obverse:** Bust of Sayaji Rao III right **Mint:** Baroda **Note:** Weight varies: 2.07-2.39 grams.

Date	Mintage	F	VF	XF	Unc
VS1942 (1885)	—	185	250	325	400

Y# A39 MOHUR
Gold, 21 mm. **Obverse:** Bust of Sayaji Rao III right **Mint:** Baroda **Note:** Weight varies: 6.20-6.40 grams.

Date	Mintage	F	VF	XF	Unc
VS1942 (1885)	—	265	350	550	850

PATTERNS

Including off metal strikes

KM#	Date	Mintage	Identification	Mkt Val
Pn1	VS19xx (1893)	—	2 Annas. Silver. Y#33a.	200
Pn2	VS19xx (1893)	—	4 Annas. Silver. Y#34a.	250
Pn3	VS19xx (1893)	—	1/2 Rupee. Silver. Y#35a.	325
Pn4	VS19xx (1893)	—	Rupee. Silver.	475
PnA4	VS1943 (1886)	—	Rupee. Copper. 29 mm. Bust to right, name and titles in legend. 3-line inscription with date, sword above date, leafy border	—
Pn5	VS19xx (1893)	—	Rupee. White Metal.	300
Pn6	VS1995 (1938)	—	1/3 Mohur. Silver. Y#40.	—
Pn7	VS1995 (1938)	—	Mohur. Silver. Y#41.	—

TRIAL STRIKES

KM#	Date	Mintage	Identification	Mkt Val
TS1	VS1940 (1883)	—	2 Paisa. Tin. Uniface.	—

KM#	Date	Mintage	Identification	Mkt Val
TS2	VS- (ca.1883)	—	2 Paisa. Y#32.2.	—

BELA

Las Bela, Beylah

State located in Baluchistan.

Of very ancient origins, the later history of Las Bela was intimately associated with that of Kalat to which State it became subject in 1758. Thereafter, however, the Arab chieftains of Las Bela, known as Jams, proved capable of demonstrating a very considerable degree of independence. The State continued up to 1947, at which time it acceded to Pakistan.

RULERS

Mir Jamir Khan, AH1246-1287/1830-1869AD
Mir Ali Khan III, AH1287-1294/1869-1877AD
Mir Jamir Khan, restored, AH1294-1306/1877-1888AD

DENOMINATION:

فلوس

Falus

Mir Jamir Khan
AH1246-1287 / 1830-1869AD
HAMMERED COINAGE

C# 5 FALUS

Copper

Date	Mintage	Good	VG	F	VF	XF
AH1271	—	7.00	15.00	25.00	40.00	—
AH1276	—	7.00	15.00	25.00	40.00	—
AH1285	—	7.00	15.00	25.00	40.00	—
AH1286	—	7.00	15.00	25.00	40.00	—

Mir Ali Khan III
AH1287-1294 / 1869-1877AD
HAMMERED COINAGE

C# 10 FALUS

Copper **Obv. Inscription:** Mahmud Khan Durani **Note:** Struck by Khudadad Khan of Kalat in the name of his grandfather.

Date	Mintage	Good	VG	F	VF	XF
ND(1873-78)	—	6.00	12.50	21.50	35.00	—

BHARATPUR

State located in Rajputana in northwest India.

Bharatpur was founded by Balchand, a Jat chieftain who took advantage of Mughal confusion and weakness after the death of Aurangzeb to seize the area. In 1756 the ruler at that time, Suraj Mal, received the title of Raja. Bharatpur became increasingly associated with Maratha ambitions and, in spite of treaty ties to the East India Company, assisted the Maratha Confederacy in their struggles against the British. This gained them few friends in British circles, but the early attempts by the British to force the submission of Bharatpur fortress proved abortive. In 1826 however, the British took the opportunity offered by a bitter internal feud concerning the succession finally to reduce the stronghold. The rival claimant was exiled to Allahabad and Balwant Singh, then a child of seven, was placed on the throne under the supervision of a British Political Agent. From that time onwards Bharatpur came under British control until it acceded to the Indian Union at Independence.

RULERS

Ranjit Singh, AH1190-1220/1776-1805AD
Randhir Singh, AH1220-1239/1805-1823AD
Baldeo Singh, AH1239-1241/1823-1824AD
Durjan Singh, AH1241-1242/1825-1826AD
Balwant Singh, AH1242-1269/1826-1853AD
Jaswant Singh, AH1269-1311/1853-1893AD/VS1909-1950
Ram Singh, 1893-1900AD
Kishan Singh, 1900-1929AD

MINTS

Bharatpur

برج اندرپور or بهرت پور

Mint name: Bharatpur or Braj Indrapur

Mint marks:

Braj Indrapur

برج اندرپور

Mint name: Braj Indrapur

Katar Star

Mint marks:

Dig

مهه اندرپور

Mint name: Mahe Indrapur

Mint marks:

Kumber

مهه اندرپور

Mintname: Maha Indrapur

Mint marks:

Uncertain Mint

Mint marks:

HAMMERED COINAGE

KM# 143 1/8 RUPEE

Silver **Obv. Inscription:** Bahadur Shah (II) **Mint:** Braj Indrapur **Note:** Weight varies: 2.75-2.80 grams.

Date	Mintage	VG	F	VF	XF	Unc
AHxxxx//19	—	30.00	50.00	80.00	120	—

KM# 104 1/4 RUPEE

Silver, 15 mm. **Obv. Inscription:** Muhammad Akbar (II) **Mint:** Braj Indrapur **Note:** Weight varies: 2.75-2.80 grams.

Date	Mintage	Good	VG	F	VF	XF
AH-	—	16.00	40.00	65.00	100	150

KM# 174 1/4 RUPEE

Silver **Obverse:** Head of Victoria left **Obv. Inscription:** Queen Victoria **Mint:** Mahe Indrapur **Note:** Weight varies: 2.68-2.90 grams.

Date	Mintage	Good	VG	F	VF	XF
VS1910 (1858)	—	28.50	70.00	100	140	200

KM# 105 1/2 RUPEE

Silver **Obv. Inscription:** Muhammad Akbar (II) **Mint:** Braj Indrapur **Note:** Weight varies: 5.50-5.60 grams. The last two regnal years 34-35 are posthumous issues.

Date	Mintage	Good	VG	F	VF	XF
AH-//22	—	16.00	40.00	65.00	100	150
AH12xx//34	—	16.00	40.00	65.00	100	150
AH-//35	—	16.00	40.00	65.00	100	150

KM# 26 RUPEE

Silver **Mint:** Braj Indrapur **Note:** Weight varies: 11.00-11.10 grams.

Date	Mintage	Good	VG	F	VF	XF
AH1215//43	—	2.75	7.00	11.00	16.50	25.00
AH1216//44	—	2.75	7.00	11.00	16.50	25.00
AH1217//45	—	2.75	7.00	11.00	16.50	25.00
AH1218//46	—	2.75	7.00	11.00	16.50	25.00
AH1219//47	—	2.75	7.00	11.00	16.50	25.00

KM# 66 RUPEE

Silver **Obv. Inscription:** Shah Alam (II) **Mint:** Kumber **Note:** Weight varies: 11.00-11.10 grams.

Date	Mintage	Good	VG	F	VF	XF
AH121x//46	—	—	7.00	11.00	16.50	25.00

KM# 96 RUPEE

Silver **Obv. Inscription:** Shah Alam (II) **Mint:** Uncertain Mint **Note:** Weight varies: 11.00-11.10 grams. Possibly Mahe Indrapur Mint.

Date	Mintage	Good	VG	F	VF	XF
AH12xx//46	—	5.00	12.50	18.50	25.00	35.00

KM# 106 RUPEE

Silver **Mint:** Braj Indrapur **Note:** Weight varies: 11.00-11.20 grams. Size varies: 20-21mm. Thick flan. Regnal years 34-49 were posthumous, being struck during the reign of the Mughal emperor Bahadur Shah Zafar.

Date	Mintage	Good	VG	F	VF	XF
AH1221//(1)	—	2.75	7.00	11.00	16.50	25.00
AH1222//2	—	2.75	7.00	11.00	16.50	25.00
AH122x//3	—	2.75	7.00	11.00	16.50	25.00
AH1224//4	—	2.75	7.00	11.00	16.50	25.00
AH1225//4	—	2.75	7.00	11.00	16.50	25.00
AH1225//5	—	2.75	7.00	11.00	16.50	25.00
AH1226//6	—	2.75	7.00	11.00	16.50	25.00
AH1227//7	—	2.75	7.00	11.00	16.50	25.00
AH1228//8	—	2.75	7.00	11.00	16.50	25.00
AH1229//9	—	2.75	7.00	11.00	16.50	25.00
AH1230//10	—	2.75	7.00	11.00	16.50	25.00
AH1231//11	—	2.75	7.00	11.00	16.50	25.00
AH1232//12	—	2.75	7.00	11.00	16.50	25.00
AH1233//13	—	2.75	7.00	11.00	16.50	25.00
AH1234//14	—	2.75	7.00	11.00	16.50	25.00
AHxxxx//15	—	2.75	7.00	11.00	16.50	25.00
AH1236//16	—	2.75	7.00	11.00	16.50	25.00
AH1238//18	—	2.75	7.00	11.00	16.50	25.00
AH1239//19	—	2.75	7.00	11.00	16.50	25.00
AH12xx//21	—	2.75	7.00	11.00	16.50	25.00
AH1243//22	—	2.75	7.00	11.00	16.50	25.00
AH1244//23	—	2.75	7.00	11.00	16.50	25.00
AH124x//24	—	2.75	7.00	11.00	16.50	25.00
AH124x//25	—	2.75	7.00	11.00	16.50	25.00
AH12xx//26	—	2.75	7.00	11.00	16.50	25.00
AH1247//27	—	2.75	7.00	11.00	16.50	25.00
AH1248//28	—	2.75	7.00	11.00	16.50	25.00
AH1249//29	—	2.75	7.00	11.00	16.50	25.00
AH12xx//30	—	2.75	7.00	11.00	16.50	25.00

Date	Mintage	Good	VG	F	VF	XF
AH1251//31	—	2.75	7.00	11.00	16.50	25.00
AH1252//32	—	2.75	7.00	11.00	16.50	25.00
AH1253//34	—	2.75	7.00	11.00	16.50	25.00
AH1252//35 (sic)	—	2.75	7.00	11.00	16.50	25.00
AH1254//35 (sic)	—	2.75	7.00	11.00	16.50	25.00
AH12xx//36	—	2.75	7.00	11.00	16.50	25.00
AH1256//38 (sic)	—	2.75	7.00	11.00	16.50	25.00
AH12xx//39	—	2.75	7.00	11.00	16.50	25.00
AH1270//40 (sic)	—	2.75	7.00	11.00	16.50	25.00
AH1270//41 (sic)	—	2.75	7.00	11.00	16.50	25.00
AH1271//41 (sic)	—	2.75	7.00	11.00	16.50	25.00
AH-//42	—	2.75	7.00	11.00	16.50	25.00
AH-//45	—	2.75	7.00	11.00	16.50	25.00
AH-//46	—	2.75	7.00	11.00	16.50	25.00
AH12xx//47	—	2.75	7.00	11.00	16.50	25.00
AH-//48	—	2.75	7.00	11.00	16.50	25.00
AH12xx//49	—	2.75	7.00	11.00	16.50	25.00

KM# 126 RUPEE

Silver **Obv. Inscription:** Muhammad Akbar (II) **Mint:** Mahe Indrapur **Note:** Weight varies: 10.70-11.60 grams. Size varies: 20-21mm. Thick flan. Issues with regnal years 36-47 are posthumous. Struck during the time of Mughal Emperor Bahadur Shah Zafar.

Date	Mintage	Good	VG	F	VF	XF
AH-//1	—	2.75	7.00	11.00	16.50	25.00
AH-//3	—	2.75	7.00	11.00	16.50	25.00
AH12xx//7	—	2.75	7.00	11.00	16.50	25.00
AH1229//9	—	2.75	7.00	11.00	16.50	25.00
AH-//10	—	2.75	7.00	11.00	16.50	25.00
AH1231//11	—	2.75	7.00	11.00	16.50	25.00
AH1232//12	—	2.75	7.00	11.00	16.50	25.00
AH123x//13	—	2.75	7.00	11.00	16.50	25.00
AH1237//18 (sic)	—	2.75	7.00	11.00	16.50	25.00
AH12xx//19	—	2.75	7.00	11.00	16.50	25.00
AH12xx//21	—	2.75	7.00	11.00	16.50	25.00
AH12xx//24	—	2.75	7.00	11.00	16.50	25.00
AH12xx//26	—	2.75	7.00	11.00	16.50	25.00
AH1246//27 (sic)	—	2.75	7.00	11.00	16.50	25.00
AH12xx//28	—	2.75	7.00	11.00	16.50	25.00
AH12xx//29	—	2.75	7.00	11.00	16.50	25.00
AH12xx//31	—	2.75	7.00	11.00	16.50	25.00
AH-//32	—	2.75	7.00	11.00	16.50	25.00
AH1257//36	—	2.75	7.00	11.00	16.50	25.00
AH125x//40	—	2.75	7.00	11.00	16.50	25.00
AH1257//41 (sic)	—	2.75	7.00	11.00	16.50	25.00
AH-//42	—	2.75	7.00	11.00	16.50	25.00
AH12xx//44	—	2.75	7.00	11.00	16.50	25.00
AH-//47	—	2.75	7.00	11.00	16.50	25.00

KM# 116 RUPEE

Silver **Obv. Inscription:** Muhammad Akbar (II) **Mint:** Kumber **Note:** Weight varies: 11.05-11.10 grams. Size varies: 20-21mm. Thick flan. The issues with regnal years 46-48 are posthumous and were struck during the reign of Mughal emperor Bahadur Shah Zafar.

Date	Mintage	Good	VG	F	VF	XF
AH1222//3 (sic)	—	2.75	7.00	11.00	16.50	25.00
AH12xx//5	—	2.75	7.00	11.00	16.50	25.00
AH12xx//6	—	2.75	7.00	11.00	16.50	25.00
AH12xx//7	—	2.75	7.00	11.00	16.50	25.00
AH122x//8	—	2.75	7.00	11.00	16.50	25.00
AH1229//9	—	2.75	7.00	11.00	16.50	25.00
AH1229//10 (sic)	—	2.75	7.00	11.00	16.50	25.00
AH-//11	—	2.75	7.00	11.00	16.50	25.00
AH1233//13	—	2.75	7.00	11.00	16.50	25.00
AH12xx//21	—	2.75	7.00	11.00	16.50	25.00
AH1243//22	—	2.75	7.00	11.00	16.50	25.00
AH12XX//23	—	2.75	7.00	11.00	16.50	25.00
AH-//24	—	2.75	7.00	11.00	16.50	25.00
AH124X//25	—	2.75	7.00	11.00	16.50	25.00
AH124x//26	—	2.75	7.00	11.00	16.50	25.00
AH12xx//27	—	2.75	7.00	11.00	16.50	25.00
AH1248//28	—	2.75	7.00	11.00	16.50	25.00
AH1249//29	—	2.75	7.00	11.00	16.50	25.00
AH12xx//46	—	2.75	7.00	11.00	16.50	25.00
AH1261//47 (sic)	—	2.75	7.00	11.00	16.50	25.00
AH1262//48 (sic)	—	2.75	7.00	11.00	16.50	25.00

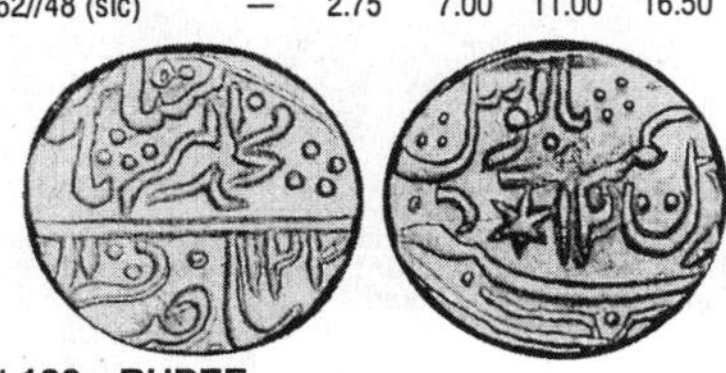

KM# 136 RUPEE

Silver **Obv. Inscription:** Muhammad Akbar (II) **Mint:** Uncertain Mint **Note:** Weight varies: 11.05-11.10 grams. The issues with regnal years 41 and 42 are posthumous and were struck during the reign of Mughal emperor Bahadur Shah Zafar.

Date	Mintage	Good	VG	F	VF	XF
AH12xx//3	—	—	7.00	11.00	16.50	25.00
AH12xx//5	—	—	7.00	11.00	16.50	25.00
AH12xx//6	—	—	7.00	11.00	16.50	25.00
AH122x//7	—	—	7.00	11.00	16.50	25.00
AH12xx//8	—	—	7.00	11.00	16.50	25.00
AH12xx//9	—	—	7.00	11.00	16.50	25.00
AH123x//11	—	—	7.00	11.00	16.50	25.00
AH123x//12	—	—	7.00	11.00	16.50	25.00
AH12xx//15	—	—	7.00	11.00	16.50	25.00
AH1238//16	—	—	7.00	11.00	16.50	25.00
AH-//19	—	—	7.00	11.00	16.50	25.00
AH124x//21	—	—	7.00	11.00	16.50	25.00
AH-//23	—	—	7.00	11.00	16.50	25.00
AH124x//25	—	—	7.00	11.00	16.50	25.00
AH12xx//26	—	—	7.00	11.00	16.50	25.00
AH124x//28	—	—	7.00	11.00	16.50	25.00
AH-//31	—	—	7.00	11.00	16.50	25.00
AH1252//32	—	—	7.00	11.00	16.50	25.00
AH12xx//41 (sic)	—	—	7.00	11.00	16.50	25.00
AH12xx//46	—	—	7.00	11.00	16.50	25.00
AH1261//47 (sic)	—	—	7.00	11.00	16.50	25.00

KM# 106a RUPEE

Silver **Obv. Inscription:** Muhammad Akbar (II) **Mint:** Braj Indrapur **Note:** Weight varies: 11.00-11.10 grams. Size varies: 27-28mm. Thin flan.

Date	Mintage	Good	VG	F	VF	XF
AH1213//13	—	7.50	18.50	26.50	37.50	55.00
AH1234//14	—	7.50	18.50	26.50	37.50	55.00
AH1235//14	—	7.50	18.50	26.50	37.50	55.00
AH1235//15	—	7.50	18.50	26.50	37.50	55.00
AH1236//16	—	7.50	18.50	26.50	37.50	55.00
AH1266//19 (sic)	—	7.50	18.50	26.50	37.50	55.00
AH1237//17	—	7.50	18.50	26.50	37.50	55.00
AH1238//18	—	7.50	18.50	26.50	37.50	55.00

KM# 126a RUPEE

Silver **Obv. Inscription:** Muhammad Akbar (II) **Mint:** Mahe Indrapur **Note:** Weight varies: 10.70-11.60 grams. Size varies: 25-26mm. Thin flan.

Date	Mintage	Good	VG	F	VF	XF
AH123x//13	—	9.00	22.50	35.00	47.50	65.00
AH1234//14	—	9.00	22.50	35.00	47.50	65.00
AH12xx//15	—	9.00	22.50	35.00	47.50	65.00
AH123x//16	—	9.00	22.50	35.00	47.50	65.00
AH-//17	—	9.00	22.50	35.00	47.50	65.00

KM# 116a RUPEE

Silver **Obv. Inscription:** Muhammad Akbar (II) **Mint:** Kumber **Note:** Weight varies: 11.05-11.10 grams. Size varies: 25-26mm. Thin flan.

Date	Mintage	VG	F	VF	XF	Unc
AH1234//14	—	20.00	31.50	42.50	60.00	—
AH1235//15	—	20.00	31.50	42.50	60.00	—
AH1238//16 (sic)	—	20.00	31.50	42.50	60.00	—

KM# 156 RUPEE

Silver **Obverse:** Head of Victoria left **Obv. Inscription:** Queen Victoria **Reverse:** Jaswant Singh **Note:** Struck at Bharatpur and Braj Indrapur. Weight varies: 11.00-11.20 grams.

Date	Mintage	Good	VG	F	VF	XF
VS1910 - 1858	—	20.00	50.00	70.00	100	150

KM# 157 RUPEE

Silver **Obverse:** Head of Victoria left **Obv. Inscription:** Queen Victoria **Reverse:** Star at left of katar and date **Rev. Inscription:** Jaswant Singh **Note:** Struck at Bharatpur and Braj Indrapur. Weight varies: 11.00-11.20 grams.

Date	Mintage	Good	VG	F	VF	XF
VS1910 - 1858	—	16.00	40.00	60.00	85.00	135

KM# 166.2 RUPEE

Silver **Obverse:** Head of Victoria left **Obv. Inscription:** Queen Victoria **Note:** Struck at Bharatpur and Braj Indrapur; Weight varies: 11.00-11.10 grams.

Date	Mintage	Good	VG	F	VF	XF
VS1914 - 1858	—	16.00	40.00	70.00	85.00	135
VS1915 - 1858	—	16.00	40.00	70.00	85.00	135
VS1916 - 1859	—	16.00	40.00	70.00	85.00	135
VS1917 - 1861	—	16.00	40.00	70.00	85.00	135
VS1917 - 1851 error	—	16.00	40.00	70.00	85.00	135
VS1922 - 1865	—	16.00	40.00	70.00	85.00	135

KM# 176 RUPEE

Silver **Obverse:** Head of Victoria left **Obv. Inscription:** Queen Victoria **Reverse:** Katar at left of star and date **Mint:** Mahe Indrapur **Note:** Weight varies: 10.70-11.60 grams.

Date	Mintage	Good	VG	F	VF	XF
VS1910 - 1858	—	18.00	45.00	75.00	110	175

KM# 146 RUPEE

Silver **Obv. Inscription:** "Bahadu Shah II" **Mint:** Braj Indrapur **Note:** Weight varies: 11.00-11.20 grams.

Date	Mintage	Good	VG	F	VF	XF
AH127x // VS1911 - 17	—	8.00	20.00	35.00	55.00	85.00
AH127x // VS1912 - 18	—	8.00	20.00	35.00	55.00	85.00
AH1273 // VS1913 - 19	—	8.00	20.00	35.00	55.00	85.00
AH- // VS1914 - 20	—	8.00	20.00	35.00	55.00	85.00

KM# 166.1 RUPEE

Silver **Note:** Weight varies 11 - 11.1 grams.

Date	Mintage	VG	F	VF	XF	Unc
VS1914 Rare	—	—	—	—	—	—

KM# 110 MOHUR

Gold **Obv. Inscription:** "Muhammad Akbar II" **Mint:** Braj Indrapur **Note:** Weight varies: 10.70-11.40 grams.

Date	Mintage	VG	F	VF	XF	Unc
AH12xx//1	—	275	450	650	950	—
AH12xx//3	—	275	450	650	950	—
AH123x//11	—	275	450	650	950	—
AH12xx//14	—	275	450	650	950	—
AH12xx//15	—	275	450	650	950	—
AH1248//28	—	275	450	650	950	—

KM# 170 MOHUR

Gold **Obverse:** Head of Victoria left **Obv. Inscription:** Queen Victoria **Note:** For similar coins with dagger at left and sword at right of Queen's bust, see Bindraban State. Struck at Bharatpur and Braj Indrapur. Weight varies: 10.70-11.40 grams.

Date	Mintage	VG	F	VF	XF	Unc
VS1915 - 1858	—	600	1,000	1,400	2,500	—
VS1916 - 1859	—	600	1,000	1,400	2,500	—
VS1918 - 1862	—	600	1,000	1,400	2,500	—
VS1919 - 1862	—	600	1,000	1,400	2,500	—

KM# 160 MOHUR

Gold **Obverse:** Head of Victoria left **Obv. Inscription:** Queen Victoria **Reverse:** Katar at left of star and date **Rev. Inscription:** Jaswant Singh **Note:** Struck at Bharatpur and Braj Indrapur. Weight varies: 10.70-11.40 grams.

Date	Mintage	VG	F	VF	XF	Unc
VS1910 - 1858	—	600	1,000	1,400	2,500	—
VS1910 - 1858	—	600	1,000	1,400	2,500	—

KM# 11 TAKKA

Copper **Obv. Inscription:** Shah Alam (II) **Mint:** Bharatpur **Note:** Weight varies: 17.50-18.50 grams.

Date	Mintage	Good	VG	F	VF	XF
AH-//44	—	1.25	2.50	4.00	5.50	—
AH-//44	—	1.25	2.50	4.00	5.50	—
AH-//45	—	1.25	2.50	4.00	5.50	—
AH-//48	—	1.25	2.50	4.00	5.50	—
AH1215//49 (sic)	—	1.00	2.00	3.00	4.50	—
AH1216//50 (sic)	—	1.25	2.50	4.00	5.50	—
AH-//54	—	1.25	2.50	4.00	5.50	—
AH-//56	—	1.25	2.50	4.00	5.50	—

KM# 101 TAKKA

Copper **Obv. Inscription:** Muhammad Akbar (II) **Mint:** Braj Indrapur **Note:** Weight varies: 17.50-18.50 grams. Regnal years 42, 48 and 49 were posthumous, struck during the reign of the Mughal emporor Bahadur Shah Zafar.

Date	Mintage	Good	VG	F	VF	XF
AH-//20	—	2.50	4.00	6.50	10.00	—
AH12xx//22	—	2.50	4.00	6.50	10.00	—
AH1276//42	—	2.50	4.00	6.50	10.00	—
AH1272//48	—	2.50	4.00	6.50	10.00	—
AH1279//49	—	2.50	4.00	6.50	10.00	—

KM# 107 NAZARANA RUPEE

Silver **Obv. Inscription:** Muhammad Akbar (II) **Mint:** Braj Indrapur **Note:** Weight varies: 11.00-11.20 grams.

Date	Mintage	Good	VG	F	VF	XF
AH1233//13	—	—	120	200	300	450
AH1235//15	—	—	120	200	300	450

BHAUNAGAR

State located in northwest India on the west shore of the Gulf of Cambay.

The Thakurs of Bhaunagar, as the rulers were titled, were Gohel Rajputs. They traced their control of the area back to the 13th century. Under the umbrella of British paramountcy, the Thakurs of Bhaunagar were regarded as relatively enlightened rulers. The State was absorbed into Saurashtra in February 1948.

Anonymous Types: Bearing the distinguishing Nagari legend *Bahadur* in addition to the Mughal legends.

MONETARY SYSTEM

2 Trambiyo = 1 Dokda

1-1/2 Dokda = 1 Dhingla

Thakurs of Bhaunagar

Gohel Rajputs

MUGHAL COINAGE

C# 15b DOKDO

Copper **Reverse:** 1825 incuse in panel **Note:** Actual date of striking unknown.

Date	Mintage	Good	VG	F	VF	XF
1825	—	3.00	5.00	8.00	12.00	—

C# 30 DHINGLO

Copper **Obv. Inscription:** Muhammad Akbar II

Date	Mintage	Good	VG	F	VF	XF
ND(1806-37)	—	3.00	5.00	8.00	12.00	—

C# 25 DOKDO

Copper **Obv. Inscription:** Shah Alam (II)

Date	Mintage	Good	VG	F	VF	XF
ND(1759-1806)	—	2.50	4.50	6.50	10.00	—

BHOPAL

Bhopal was the second largest Muslim state located in central India. It was founded in 1723 by Dost Muhammed Khan, an Afghan adventurer of the Mirazi Khel clan, who was in the service of Aurangzeb. After the Emperor's death in 1707 Dost Muhammed asserted his independence. Early in the following century his successors, threatened by the Marathas and subjected to Pindari raids into their territory, sought to cultivate a good relationship with the British. In 1817, at the time of the Maratha and Pindari War, Bhopal signed a treaty with the British East India Company, which placed them squarely under imperial protection and control. After 1897 the British rupee was recognized as the only legal tender.

RULERS

Kudsia Begam, AH1235-1253/1819-1837AD

Jahangir Muhammad Khan, AH1253-1261/1837-1844AD

Sikandar Begam, AH1261-1285/1844-1868AD

Shah Jahan Begam, AH1285-1319/1868-1901AD

Mints

بهوپال

Bhopal

دولت گره

Daulatgarh

Mint mark:

ANONYMOUS HAMMERED COINAGE

C# 20 PAISA

Copper **Obverse:** Year in circle **Reverse:** "Bhopal" **Mint:** Bhopal **Note:** Size varies: 21-22mm.

Date	Mintage	Good	VG	F	VF	XF
AH-//25	—	2.00	3.25	5.00	8.50	—
AH-//29	—	2.00	3.25	5.00	8.50	—

C# 20a PAISA

16.8500 g., Copper **Mint:** Bhopal **Note:** Uniface. Persian "Bhopal" in circular depressed area.

Date	Mintage	Good	VG	F	VF	XF
ND(c.1809)	—	3.00	5.00	8.00	12.50	—

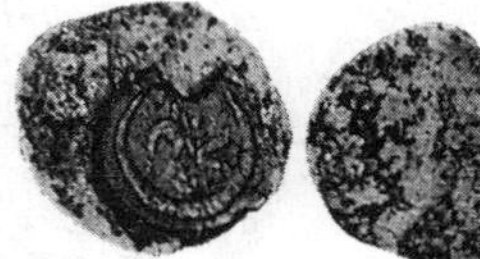

C# 21d PAISA

16.8500 g., Copper **Mint:** Bhopal **Note:** Uniface. Persian "Jim" and year. Regnal year 47 is a posthumous issue.

Date	Mintage	Good	VG	F	VF	XF
AH-//5	—	2.00	3.25	5.00	8.50	—
AH-//10	—	2.00	3.25	5.00	8.50	—
AH-//11	—	2.00	3.25	5.00	8.50	—
AH-//12	—	2.00	3.25	5.00	8.50	—
AH-//47	—	2.00	3.25	5.00	8.50	—

C# 21 PAISA

Copper **Obverse:** Whisk **Mint:** Bhopal **Note:** Size varies: 21-22mm.

Date	Mintage	Good	VG	F	VF	XF
AH-//28	—	4.00	6.50	10.00	17.50	—

C# 21a PAISA

16.8500 g., Copper **Mint:** Bhopal **Note:** Uniface. Persian "Sikka Bhopal" and date.

Date	Mintage	Good	VG	F	VF	XF
AH1255	—	3.00	5.00	8.00	12.50	—

C# 21b PAISA

16.8500 g., Copper **Mint:** Bhopal **Note:** Uniface. Fly whisk and scimitar.

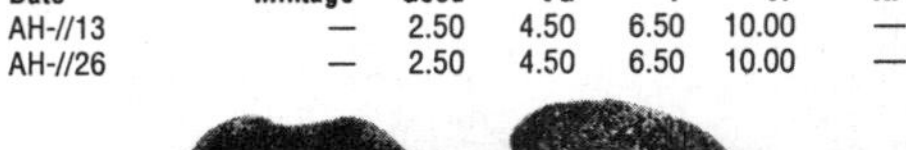

Date	Mintage	Good	VG	F	VF	XF
AH-//13	—	2.50	4.50	6.50	10.00	—
AH-//26	—	2.50	4.50	6.50	10.00	—

C# 21c PAISA

16.8500 g., Copper **Mint:** Bhopal **Note:** Uniface. Persian "Fateh" and scimitar.

Date	Mintage	Good	VG	F	VF	XF
AH-//8	—	2.50	4.50	6.50	10.00	—

C# 21e PAISA

16.8500 g., Copper **Mint:** Bhopal **Note:** Uniface. Persian "Fateh" without scimitar.

Date	Mintage	Good	VG	F	VF	XF
ND(1813-14)	—	—	—	—	—	—

Y# 1 1/4 ANNA

Copper **Obverse:** Denomination **Reverse:** Date above mintname **Mint:** Bhopal **Note:** Size varies: 7.00-8.00 grams.

Date	Mintage	Good	VG	F	VF	XF
AH1266	—	1.50	2.25	3.50	6.50	—
AH1269	—	1.50	2.25	3.50	6.50	—
AH1270	—	1.50	2.25	3.50	6.50	—
AH1272	—	1.50	2.25	3.50	6.50	—
AH1273	—	1.50	2.25	3.50	6.50	—
AH1276	—	1.50	2.25	3.50	6.50	—
AH1279	—	1.50	2.25	3.50	6.50	—
AH1282	—	1.50	2.25	3.50	6.50	—

Y# 4.1 1/4 ANNA

Copper **Obverse:** Date below denomination **Reverse:** Mintname **Mint:** Bhopal **Note:** Size varies: 7.00-8.00 grams.

Date	Mintage	Good	VG	F	VF	XF
AH1285	—	1.00	1.75	2.50	4.50	—

Y# 4.2 1/4 ANNA

Copper **Obverse:** Date above denomination **Reverse:** Sprays above mintname **Rev. Inscription:** Similar to Y#4.1 **Mint:** Bhopal **Note:** Size varies: 7.00-8.00 grams.

Date	Mintage	Good	VG	F	VF	XF
AH1285	—	1.00	1.75	2.50	4.50	—
AH1287	—	1.00	1.75	2.50	4.50	—
AH1288	—	1.00	1.75	2.50	4.50	—
AH1289	—	1.00	1.75	2.50	4.50	—
AH1292	—	1.00	1.75	2.50	4.50	—
AH1293	—	1.00	1.75	2.50	4.50	—
AH1296	—	1.00	1.75	2.50	4.50	—
AH1299	—	1.00	1.75	2.50	4.50	—
AH1300	—	1.00	1.75	2.50	4.50	—

Y# 4.3 1/4 ANNA

Copper **Rev. Inscription:** Denomination below date **Mint:** Bhopal **Note:** Size varies: 7.00-8.00 grams.

Date	Mintage	Good	VG	F	VF	XF
AH1285	—	1.00	1.75	2.50	4.50	—

Y# 4.4 1/4 ANNA

Copper **Rev. Inscription:** Without "hejira" above divided date **Mint:** Bhopal **Note:** Size varies: 7.00-8.00 grams.

Date	Mintage	Good	VG	F	VF	XF
AH1286	—	1.00	1.75	2.50	4.50	—

Y# 2 1/2 ANNA

Copper **Obv. Inscription:** Denomination **Reverse:** Mintname **Mint:** Bhopal **Note:** Weight varies: 15.00-15.50 grams. Size varies: 20-21mm.

Date	Mintage	Good	VG	F	VF	XF
AH1276	—	2.00	3.25	5.00	8.50	—
AH1278	—	2.00	3.25	5.00	8.50	—
AH1285	—	2.00	3.25	5.00	8.50	—

Y# 5 1/2 ANNA

Copper **Obverse:** Date and denomination **Reverse:** Mintname **Mint:** Bhopal **Note:** Weight varies: 15.00-15.50 grams. Size varies: 20-21mm.

Date	Mintage	Good	VG	F	VF	XF
AH1286	—	2.00	3.25	5.00	8.50	—
AH1289	—	2.00	3.25	5.00	8.50	—
AH1299	—	2.00	3.25	5.00	8.50	—
AH1300	—	2.00	3.25	5.00	8.50	—

Y# 3 ANNA

Copper **Obv. Inscription:** Denomination above sprays in wreath **Reverse:** Date above mintname in wreath **Mint:** Bhopal **Note:** Weight varies: 30.00-31.00 grams. Size varies: 25-30mm.

Date	Mintage	Good	VG	F	VF	XF
AH1272	—	25.00	40.00	60.00	85.00	—
AH1276	—	25.00	40.00	60.00	85.00	—

Y# 6 ANNA

Copper **Obverse:** Date and denomination **Reverse:** Mintname **Mint:** Bhopal **Note:** Weight varies: 30.00-31.00 grams. Size varies: 27-30mm.

Date	Mintage	Good	VG	F	VF	XF
AH1286	—	12.00	20.00	30.00	45.00	—
AH1288	—	12.00	20.00	30.00	45.00	—
AH1289	—	12.00	20.00	30.00	45.00	—
AH1300	—	12.00	20.00	30.00	45.00	—

Y# 7 1/8 RUPEE

Silver **Reverse:** "Zarb" above "Bhopal" **Mint:** Bhopal **Note:** Weight varies: 1.34-1.45 grams.

Date	Mintage	Good	VG	F	VF	XF
AH1271//5	—	1.85	4.50	9.00	15.00	22.00
AH1275	—	1.85	4.50	9.00	15.00	22.00
AH1288//7	—	1.85	4.50	9.00	15.00	22.00
AH1289//8	—	1.85	4.50	9.00	15.00	22.00
AH1291//8	—	1.85	4.50	9.00	15.00	22.00

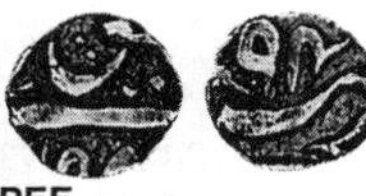

Y# 11 1/8 RUPEE

Silver **Reverse:** "Zarb" below "Bhopal" **Mint:** Bhopal **Note:** Weight varies: 1.34-1.45 grams.

Date	Mintage	Good	VG	F	VF	XF
AH129x//8	—	1.75	4.25	8.50	14.00	20.00
AH1294//9	—	1.75	4.25	8.50	14.00	20.00
AH1303//15	—	1.75	4.25	8.50	14.00	22.00
AH1306//17	—	1.75	4.25	8.50	14.00	22.00

Y# 8 1/4 RUPEE

Silver **Reverse:** "Zarb" above "Bhopal" **Mint:** Bhopal **Note:** Weight varies: 2.68-2.90 grams.

Date	Mintage	Good	VG	F	VF	XF
AH1275	—	1.75	4.25	8.50	14.00	20.00
AH1282//2	—	1.75	4.25	8.50	14.00	20.00
AH1283//2	—	1.75	4.25	8.50	14.00	20.00
AH1284//8	—	1.75	4.25	8.50	14.00	20.00
AH1285//8	—	1.75	4.25	8.50	14.00	20.00
AH1287//8	—	1.75	4.25	8.50	14.00	20.00
AH1288//8	—	1.75	4.25	8.50	14.00	20.00

Y# 12 1/4 RUPEE

Silver **Reverse:** "Zarb" below "Bhopal" **Mint:** Bhopal **Note:** Weight varies: 2.68-2.90 grams.

Date	Mintage	Good	VG	F	VF	XF
AH1293//8	—	1.50	3.75	7.50	12.50	18.50
AH1294//9	—	1.50	3.75	7.50	12.50	18.50
AH1295//10	—	1.50	3.75	7.50	12.50	18.50
AH1297//12	—	1.50	3.75	7.50	12.50	18.50
AH1298//13	—	1.50	3.75	7.50	12.50	18.50
AH1301	—	1.50	3.75	7.50	12.50	18.50
AH1303//15	—	1.50	3.75	7.50	12.50	18.50
AH1305//16	—	1.50	3.75	7.50	12.50	18.50

Y# 9 1/2 RUPEE

Silver **Reverse:** "Zarb" above "Bhopal" **Mint:** Bhopal **Note:** Weight varies: 5.35-5.80 grams.

Date	Mintage	Good	VG	F	VF	XF
AH1275	—	2.00	5.00	10.00	17.50	25.00
AH1278	—	2.00	5.00	10.00	17.50	25.00
AH1279//5	—	2.00	5.00	10.00	17.50	25.00
AH1280	—	2.00	5.00	10.00	17.50	25.00
AH1281	—	2.00	5.00	10.00	17.50	25.00
AH1282//2	—	2.00	5.00	10.00	17.50	25.00
AH1283//8	—	1.85	4.50	9.00	15.00	22.00
AH1285//5	—	1.85	4.50	9.00	15.00	22.00
AH1287//8	—	1.85	4.50	9.00	15.00	22.00
AH1288//7	—	1.85	4.50	9.00	15.00	22.00
AH1288//8	—	1.85	4.50	9.00	15.00	22.00
AH1289//8	—	1.85	4.50	9.00	15.00	22.00
AH1291//8	—	1.85	4.50	9.00	15.00	22.00
AH1292//8	—	1.85	4.50	9.00	15.00	22.00

Y# 13 1/2 RUPEE

Silver **Reverse:** "Zarb" below "Bhopal" **Mint:** Bhopal **Note:** Weight varies: 5.35-5.80 grams.

Date	Mintage	Good	VG	F	VF	XF
AH1294//4	—	1.75	4.25	8.50	14.00	20.00
AH1294//9	—	1.75	4.25	8.50	14.00	20.00
AH1295	—	1.75	4.25	8.50	14.00	20.00
AH1296//11	—	1.75	4.25	8.50	14.00	20.00
AH1298//13	—	1.75	4.25	8.50	14.00	20.00
AH130x//14	—	1.75	4.25	8.50	14.00	20.00
AH1303//15	—	1.75	4.25	8.50	14.00	20.00
AH130x//16	—	1.75	4.25	8.50	14.00	20.00
AH1306//17	—	1.75	4.25	8.50	14.00	20.00
AH1307//19	—	1.75	4.25	8.50	14.00	20.00
AH1308//20	—	1.75	4.25	8.50	14.00	20.00
AH130x//24	—	1.75	4.25	8.50	14.00	20.00

Y# 10 RUPEE

Silver **Reverse:** "Zarb" above "Bhopal" **Mint:** Bhopal **Note:** Weight varies: 10.70-11.60 grams.

Date	Mintage	Good	VG	F	VF	XF
AH1271//5	—	2.50	6.00	12.00	20.00	28.00
AH1272	—	2.50	6.00	12.00	20.00	28.00
AH1275	—	2.50	6.00	12.00	20.00	28.00
AH1276	—	2.50	6.00	12.00	20.00	28.00
AH1277	—	2.50	6.00	12.00	20.00	28.00
AH1278//2	—	2.50	6.00	12.00	20.00	28.00
AH1278//3	—	2.50	6.00	12.00	20.00	28.00
AH1279//3	—	2.50	6.00	12.00	20.00	28.00
AH1279//4	—	2.50	6.00	12.00	20.00	28.00
AH1279//5	—	2.50	6.00	12.00	20.00	28.00
AH1280//5	—	2.50	6.00	12.00	20.00	28.00
AH1281//8	—	2.50	6.00	12.00	20.00	28.00
AH1282//2	—	2.50	6.00	12.00	20.00	28.00
AH1282//6	—	2.50	6.00	12.00	20.00	28.00
AH1282//8	—	2.50	6.00	12.00	20.00	28.00
AH1283//7	—	2.50	6.00	12.00	20.00	28.00
AH1283//8	—	2.50	6.00	12.00	20.00	28.00
AH1284//8	—	2.50	6.00	12.00	20.00	28.00
AH1285//5	—	2.50	6.00	12.00	20.00	28.00
AH1285//8	—	2.50	6.00	12.00	20.00	28.00
AH1288//7	—	2.50	6.00	12.00	20.00	28.00
AH1288//8	—	2.50	6.00	12.00	20.00	28.00
AH1289//8	—	2.50	6.00	12.00	20.00	28.00
AH1289//9	—	2.50	6.00	12.00	20.00	28.00
AH1291//8	—	2.50	6.00	12.00	20.00	28.00
AH1292//8	—	2.50	6.00	12.00	20.00	28.00
AH1293//8	—	2.50	6.00	12.00	20.00	28.00

Y# 14 RUPEE

Silver **Reverse:** "Zarb" below "Bhopal" **Mint:** Bhopal **Note:** Weight varies: 10.70-11.60 grams.

Date	Mintage	Good	VG	F	VF	XF
AH1293//8	—	2.00	5.00	10.00	17.50	25.00
AH1294//8	—	2.00	5.00	10.00	17.50	25.00
AH1294//9	—	2.00	5.00	10.00	17.50	25.00
AH1295//10	—	2.00	5.00	10.00	17.50	25.00
AH1295//11	—	2.00	5.00	10.00	17.50	25.00
AH1296//11	—	2.00	5.00	10.00	17.50	25.00
AH1297//12	—	2.00	5.00	10.00	17.50	25.00
AH1298//9	—	2.00	5.00	10.00	17.50	25.00
AH1298//10	—	2.00	5.00	10.00	17.50	25.00
AH1298//13	—	2.00	5.00	10.00	17.50	25.00
AH1298//15	—	2.00	5.00	10.00	17.50	25.00
AH1302//14	—	2.00	5.00	10.00	17.50	25.00
AH1304//15	—	2.00	5.00	10.00	17.50	25.00
AH1305//16	—	2.00	5.00	10.00	17.50	25.00
AH1306//17	—	2.00	5.00	10.00	17.50	25.00
AH1308//14	—	2.00	5.00	10.00	17.50	25.00
AH1308//24	—	2.00	5.00	10.00	17.50	25.00

KM# A14 NAZARANA RUPEE

10.8500 g., Silver **Obverse:** Kalima **Reverse:** Kalima

Date	Mintage	F	VF	XF	Unc
AH1286//2	—	—	—	200	—

KM# B14 NAZARANA 1-1/2 RUPEES
16.4400 g., Silver

Date	Mintage	F	VF	XF	Unc
AH1286//2	—	—	—	250	400

KM# C14 NAZARANA 2 RUPEES
Silver **Note:** Weight varies: 21.40-23.20 grams.

Date	Mintage	F	VF	XF	Unc
AH1286//2	—	—	—	300	500

HAMMERED COINAGE

Mughal Series

C# 24 1/8 RUPEE
Silver, 12 mm. **Obv. Inscription:** Muhammad Akbar (II) **Mint:** Daulatgarh **Note:** Weight varies: 1.34-1.45 grams.

Date	Mintage	Good	VG	F	VF	XF
AH-//11	—	6.00	15.00	25.00	40.00	65.00
AH-//16	—	6.00	15.00	25.00	40.00	65.00
AH-//29	—	6.00	15.00	25.00	40.00	65.00

C# 25 1/4 RUPEE
Silver, 13 mm. **Obv. Inscription:** Muhammad Akbar (II) **Mint:** Daulatgarh **Note:** Weight varies: 2.68-2.90 grams.

Date	Mintage	Good	VG	F	VF	XF
AH-//16	—	6.00	15.00	25.00	40.00	65.00
AH-//18	—	6.00	15.00	25.00	40.00	65.00
AH-//26	—	6.00	15.00	25.00	40.00	65.00
AH-//29	—	6.00	15.00	25.00	40.00	65.00

C# 26 1/2 RUPEE
Silver, 15 mm. **Obv. Inscription:** Muhammad Akbar (II) **Mint:** Daulatgarh **Note:** Weight varies: 5.35-5.80 grams.

Date	Mintage	Good	VG	F	VF	XF
AH-//9	—	10.00	25.00	40.00	60.00	85.00
AH-//16	—	10.00	25.00	40.00	60.00	85.00
AH-//29	—	10.00	25.00	40.00	60.00	85.00

C# 12 RUPEE
Silver **Obv. Inscription:** Shah Alam (II) **Mint:** Bhopal **Note:** Weight varies: 10.70-11.60 grams.

Date	Mintage	Good	VG	F	VF	XF
AH-//17	—	4.50	11.50	17.50	23.50	32.50
AH-//44	—	4.50	11.50	17.50	23.50	32.50
AH12xx//49	—	4.50	11.50	17.50	23.50	32.50

C# 27 RUPEE
Silver **Obv. Inscription:** Muhammad Akbar (II) **Mint:** Daulatgarh **Note:** Weight varies: 10.70-11.60 grams. Issues with regnal years 33-35 are posthumous issues.

Date	Mintage	Good	VG	F	VF	XF
AH-//1	—	3.00	7.50	12.50	18.50	27.50
AH-//4	—	3.00	7.50	12.50	18.50	27.50
AH-//5	—	3.00	7.50	12.50	18.50	27.50
AH-//6	—	3.00	7.50	12.50	18.50	27.50
AH-//7	—	3.00	7.50	12.50	18.50	27.50
AH-//8	—	3.00	7.50	12.50	18.50	27.50
AH-//9	—	3.00	7.50	12.50	18.50	27.50
AH-//10	—	3.00	7.50	12.50	18.50	27.50
AH-//11	—	3.00	7.50	12.50	18.50	27.50
AH-//12	—	3.00	7.50	12.50	18.50	27.50
AH-//13	—	3.00	7.50	12.50	18.50	27.50
AH-//14	—	3.00	7.50	12.50	18.50	27.50
AH-//15	—	3.00	7.50	12.50	18.50	27.50
AH-//16	—	3.00	7.50	12.50	18.50	27.50
AH-//17	—	3.00	7.50	12.50	18.50	27.50
AH-//18	—	3.00	7.50	12.50	18.50	27.50
AH-//19	—	3.00	7.50	12.50	18.50	27.50
AH-//20	—	3.00	7.50	12.50	18.50	27.50
AH-//21	—	3.00	7.50	12.50	18.50	27.50
AH-//22	—	3.00	7.50	12.50	18.50	27.50
AH-//28	—	3.00	7.50	12.50	18.50	27.50
AH-//25	—	3.00	7.50	12.50	18.50	27.50
AH-//26	—	3.00	7.50	12.50	18.50	27.50
AH-//27	—	3.00	7.50	12.50	18.50	27.50
AH-//30	—	3.00	7.50	12.50	18.50	27.50
AH-//31	—	3.00	7.50	12.50	18.50	27.50
AH-//32	—	3.00	7.50	12.50	18.50	27.50
AH-//33	—	3.00	7.50	12.50	18.50	27.50
AH-//34	—	3.00	7.50	12.50	18.50	27.50
AH-//35	—	3.00	7.50	12.50	18.50	27.50

Shah Jahan Begam

AH1285-1319 / 1868-1901AD

ANONYMOUS HAMMERED COINAGE

Y# 15 PIE
Copper **Obv. Inscription:** Shah Jahan Begam

Date	Mintage	Good	VG	F	VF	XF
AH1305	—	1.50	2.25	3.50	6.50	—
AH1306	—	1.50	2.25	3.50	6.50	—

Y# 16 1/4 ANNA
Copper **Obv. Inscription:** Shah Jahan Begam **Note:** Weight varies: 7.50-7.75 grams.

Date	Mintage	Good	VG	F	VF	XF
AH1302	—	1.00	1.75	2.50	4.50	—
AH1303	—	1.00	1.75	2.50	4.50	—
AH1305	—	1.00	1.75	2.50	4.50	—
AH1306	—	1.00	1.75	2.50	4.50	—

Y# 17.1 1/2 ANNA
Copper **Obv. Inscription:** Shah Jahan Begam **Note:** Weight varies: 15.00-15.50 grams.

Date	Mintage	Good	VG	F	VF	XF
AH1302	—	1.25	2.00	3.00	5.50	—
AH1303	—	1.25	2.00	3.00	5.50	—
AH1304	—	1.25	2.00	3.00	5.50	—
AH1305	—	1.25	2.00	3.00	5.50	—
AH1306	—	1.25	2.00	3.00	5.50	—

Y# 17.2 1/2 ANNA
Copper **Obv. Inscription:** Shah Jahan Begam **Note:** Weight varies: 15.00-15.50 grams. Large flan.

Date	Mintage	Good	VG	F	VF	XF
AH1309	—	2.00	3.25	5.00	8.50	—

Y# 18 ANNA
Copper **Obv. Inscription:** Shah Jahan Begam **Note:** Weight varies: 30.00-31.00 grams.

Date	Mintage	Good	VG	F	VF	XF
AH1302	—	2.50	4.50	6.50	10.00	—
AH1303	—	2.50	4.50	6.50	10.00	—
AH1304	—	2.50	4.50	6.50	10.00	—
AH1305	—	2.50	4.50	6.50	10.00	—
AH1306	—	2.50	4.50	6.50	10.00	—

Y# 18a ANNA
Copper **Obv. Inscription:** Shah Jahan Begam **Note:** Weight varies: 30.00-31.00 grams. Struck from 1/2 Anna dies.

Date	Mintage	Good	VG	F	VF	XF
AH130x	—	2.50	4.50	6.50	10.00	—

Y# 18b NAZARANA ANNA
Copper **Obv. Inscription:** Shah Jahan Begam **Note:** Weight varies: 30.00-31.00 grams.

Date	Mintage	Good	VG	F	VF	XF
AH1303 Rare	—	—	—	—	—	—

BHOPAL FEUDATORY-NARSINGARH

The Rajput rulers of this feudatory traced their origins back into the fourteenth century when their ancestors migrated from Malwa through Sind before settling at Narsinghgarh.

HAMMERED COINAGE

KM# 1 PAISA
Copper **Shape:** Square

Date	Mintage	Good	VG	F	VF	XF
ND(c.1820)	—	2.50	4.50	6.50	10.00	—

BIJAWAR

State located in Bundelkhand District in north-central India. The rulers of Bijawar were Bundela Rajputs. They were descended from Maharaja Chhatarsal who, earlier, having ruled a much larger territory, became forebearer to a number of Rajput royal families in the region. As far as the British were concerned, the authority of the rulers of Bijawar stemmed from a mandate issued by the East India Company in 1811, which required, in return, a guarantee of allegiance. In 1866 the ruler became a maharaja.

RULERS
Lakshman Singh, 1833-1847AD
Bhau Pratap Singh, 1847-1900AD

HAMMERED COINAGE

KM# 15 RUPEE
Silver **Obv. Inscription:** Shah Alam (II) **Note:** Weight varies: 10.70-11.60 grams.

Date	Mintage	Good	VG	F	VF	XF
ND(1759-1806)	—	5.00	12.50	21.00	28.50	40.00

BIKANIR

Bikanir, located in Rajputana was established as a state sometime between 1465 and 1504 by Jodhpur Rathor Rajput named Rao Bikaji. During the period of the Great Mughals Bikanir was intimately linked to Delhi by ties of both loyalty and marriage. Both Akbar and Jahangir contracted marriages with princesses of the Bikanir Rajputs,and the Bikanir nobility rendered outstanding service in the Mughal armies. Bikanir came under British influence in 1817 and after 1947 was incorporated into Rajasthan.

RULERS

Surat Singh, AH1204-1244/1788-1828AD
Ratan Singh, AH1244-1268/1828-1851AD
Sardar Singh, AH1268-1289/1851-1872AD
Dungar Singh, AH1289-1305/1872-1887AD
Ganga Singhji, VS1944-1999/1887-1942AD

MINT

Bikanir

RULERS' SYMBOLS

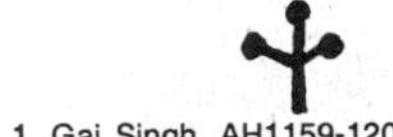

1. Gaj Singh, AH1159-1202

2. (")

3. Surat Singh, AH1202-1244

4. (")

5. (")

6. Ratan Singh, AH1244-1268 (2 Vars.)

7. Sardar Singh, AH1268-1289

8. Dungar Singh, AH1289-1305

9. Ganga Singh, VS1949-1999

NOTE: The above symbols normally occur in groups on the obverse or reverse of the coins; the various combinations are shown for each series.

Surat Singh

AH1204-1244 / 1788-1828AD

MUGHAL COINAGE

KM# 13 1/2 PAISA

Copper **Obv. Inscription:** Alamgir (II) **Note:** Regnal years 28-52 of Shah Alam II.

Date	Mintage	Good	VG	F	VF	XF
AH-//47	—	0.75	1.25	2.00	3.00	—

KM# 14 PAISA

Copper **Obv. Inscription:** Alamgir (II) **Reverse:** Mark #3 **Note:** Regnal years 28-52 of Shah Alam II. Year 47 is of much cruder fabric.

Date	Mintage	Good	VG	F	VF	XF
AH-//47 (1805)	—	1.50	2.25	3.00	4.00	—

KM# 17 RUPEE

Silver **Obverse:** Mark #1 **Obv. Inscription:** Alamgir (II) **Reverse:** Mark #3 **Note:** Regnal years 28-52 of Shah Alam II. Weight varies: 10.70-11.60 grams.

Date	Mintage	Good	VG	F	VF	XF
AH1204//28 (sic)	—	3.00	7.50	12.50	18.50	27.50
AH1205//35 (sic)	—	3.00	7.50	12.50	18.50	27.50
AH1205//37 (sic)	—	3.00	7.50	12.50	18.50	27.50
AH1209//42 (sic)	—	3.00	7.50	12.50	18.50	27.50
AH1217//41 (sic)	—	3.00	7.50	12.50	18.50	27.50
AH1217//42	—	3.00	7.50	12.50	18.50	27.50
AH1217//43 (sic)	—	3.00	7.50	12.50	18.50	27.50
AH1217//45	—	3.00	7.50	12.50	18.50	27.50
AH1227//47 (sic)	—	3.00	7.50	12.50	18.50	27.50
AH1229//47	—	3.00	7.50	12.50	18.50	27.50
AH1229//45	—	3.00	7.50	12.50	18.50	27.50
AH1229//51	—	3.00	7.50	12.50	18.50	27.50
AH1229//52	—	3.00	7.50	12.50	18.50	27.50

Ratan Singh

AH1244-1268 / 1828-1851AD

MUGHAL COINAGE

KM# 20 1/2 PAISA

Copper **Obv. Inscription:** Alamgir (II) **Note:** Regnal years of Shah Alam II.

Date	Mintage	Good	VG	F	VF	XF
ND(1828-51)	—	—	—	—	—	—

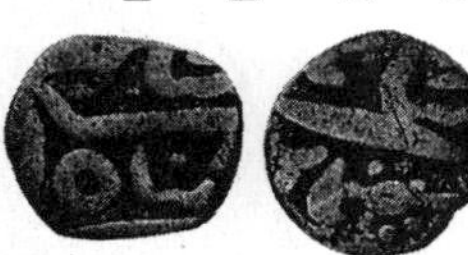

KM# 22 PAISA

Copper **Obv. Inscription:** Alamgir (II) **Reverse:** Mark #6 **Note:** Weight varies: 7.40-8.00 grams. Regnal years of Shah Alam.

Date	Mintage	Good	VG	F	VF	XF
AH-//25	—	0.75	1.25	2.00	3.00	—
AH-//41	—	0.75	1.25	2.00	3.00	—

KM# 32 RUPEE

Silver **Obverse:** Mark #1 **Obv. Inscription:** Alamgir (II) **Reverse:** Mark #3 and 6 **Note:** Weight varies: 10.70-11.60 grams. Regnal years 21-52 Muhammad Akbar II.

Date	Mintage	Good	VG	F	VF	XF
AH1229//25	—	2.75	7.00	11.00	16.50	25.00
AH1229//31	—	2.75	7.00	11.00	16.50	25.00
AH1229//32	—	2.75	7.00	11.00	16.50	25.00
AH1229//41	—	2.75	7.00	11.00	16.50	25.00
AH1229//47	—	2.75	7.00	11.00	16.50	25.00

KM# 32a NAZARANA RUPEE

Silver **Obv. Inscription:** Shah Alam (II) **Note:** Weight varies: 10.70-11.60 grams.

Date	Mintage	VG	F	VF	XF	Unc
AH1229//25	—	175	275	400	550	—

KM# 23 TAKKA

Copper **Reverse:** Mark #6 **Note:** Weight varies: 16.00-17.00 grams. Regnal years of Shah Alam. So called year 21 is debased copy of year 41.

Date	Mintage	Good	VG	F	VF	XF
AH-//41	—	0.75	1.25	2.00	3.00	—

KM# 33 1/4 MOHUR

Gold **Obv. Inscription:** Shah Alam (II) **Note:** Weight varies: 2.67-2.90 grams.

Date	Mintage	VG	F	VF	XF	Unc
AHxxxx	—	1,500	2,200	3,000	—	—

Sardar Singh

AH1268-1289 / 1851-1872AD

MUGHAL COINAGE

KM# 34 1/2 PAISA

Copper, 17 mm. **Obv. Inscription:** Alamgir (II) **Note:** Weight varies: 7.30-7.60 grams.

Date	Mintage	Good	VG	F	VF	XF
AH1229//18	—	2.00	3.00	4.50	6.50	—

KM# 35 1/4 RUPEE

Silver **Obv. Inscription:** Alamgir (II) **Note:** Regnal years 18-21 of Bahadur Shah II. Weight varies: 2.67-2.90 grams.

Date	Mintage	Good	VG	F	VF	XF
AHxxxx	—	5.00	12.50	18.50	28.50	42.50

KM# 37 RUPEE

Silver **Obv. Inscription:** Alamgir (II) **Reverse:** Marks #1, 4 (or 5), 6 and 7 **Note:** Weight varies: 10.70-11.60 grams. Years of Bahadur Shah II.

Date	Mintage	Good	VG	F	VF	XF
AH1229//18	—	2.50	6.00	9.00	13.50	20.00
AH1229//21	—	2.50	6.00	9.00	13.50	20.00

KM# 37a NAZARANA RUPEE

Silver, 29 mm. **Obv. Inscription:** Alamgir (II) **Note:** Weight varies: 10.70-11.60 grams.

Date	Mintage	Good	VG	F	VF	XF
AH1229//21	—	87.50	175	275	400	550

REGAL COINAGE

Beginning 1859AD

Reverse marks from left to right: #6, 7, 2, 5. All types in this series from KM#41 to KM#54a carry the frozen years VS1916/1859AD.

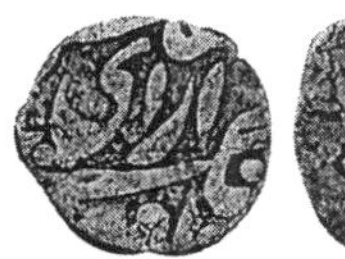

KM# 41 PAISA

Copper **Obv. Inscription:** Name of Victoria and Sardar Singh **Note:** Weight varies: 7.40-7.70 grams.

Date	Mintage	Good	VG	F	VF	XF
VS1916 (1859)	—	0.75	1.25	2.00	3.00	—

KM# 42 1/8 RUPEE

1.4000 g., Silver **Obv. Inscription:** Name of Victoria and Sardar Singh **Note:** Size varies: 11-12mm.

Date	Mintage	Good	VG	F	VF	XF
VS1916 (1859)	—	20.00	40.00	65.00	100	150

KM# 43 1/4 RUPEE
2.8000 g., Silver, 15 mm. **Obv. Inscription:** Name of Victoria and Sardar Singh

Date	Mintage	Good	VG	F	VF	XF
VS1916 (1859)	—	15.00	30.00	50.00	80.00	120

KM# 44 1/2 RUPEE
5.6000 g., Silver, 18 mm. **Obv. Inscription:** Name of Victoria and Sardar Singh

Date	Mintage	Good	VG	F	VF	XF
VS1916 (1859)	—	20.00	40.00	65.00	100	150

KM# 45 RUPEE
11.3000 g., Silver **Obv. Inscription:** Name of Victoria and Sardar Singh

Date	Mintage	Good	VG	F	VF	XF
VS1916 (1859)	—	2.75	7.00	11.00	16.50	25.00
VS1912 (1859) Error for 1916	—	—	—	—	—	—

KM# 46 NAZARANA RUPEE
11.3500 g., Silver, 30 mm. **Obv. Inscription:** Name of Victoria and Sardar Singh

Date	Mintage	Good	VG	F	VF	XF
VS1916 (1859)	—	87.50	175	275	400	550

Dungar Singh
AH1289-1305 / 1872-1887AD
LOCAL COINAGE

Reverse marks, left to right: #6, 7, 8, 2, 5. Frozen years VS1916/1859AD.

KM# 50 PAISA
Copper **Obv. Inscription:** Name of Victoria and Dungar Singh **Note:** Weight varies: 7.50-7.75 grams.

Date	Mintage	Good	VG	F	VF	XF
VS1916 (1859)	—	0.75	1.25	2.00	3.00	—

KM# 51 1/8 RUPEE
1.4000 g., Silver, 12 mm. **Obv. Inscription:** Name of Victoria and Dungar Singh

Date	Mintage	VG	F	VF	XF	Unc
VS1916 (1859)	—	40.00	65.00	100	150	—

KM# 52 1/4 RUPEE
2.8000 g., Silver, 14 mm. **Obv. Inscription:** Name of Victoria and Dungar Singh

Date	Mintage	Good	VG	F	VF	XF
VS1916 (1859)	—	15.00	30.00	50.00	80.00	120

KM# 53 1/2 RUPEE
5.6000 g., Silver, 17 mm. **Obv. Inscription:** Name of Victoria and Dungar Singh

Date	Mintage	Good	VG	F	VF	XF
VS1916 (1859)	—	20.00	40.00	65.00	100	150

KM# 54 RUPEE
Silver **Obv. Inscription:** Name of Victoria and Dungar Singh **Note:** Weight varies: 11.30-11.35 grams.

Date	Mintage	Good	VG	F	VF	XF
VS1916 (1859)	—	2.75	7.00	11.00	16.50	25.00

KM# 54a NAZARANA RUPEE
11.3500 g., Silver, 30 mm. **Obv. Inscription:** Victoria and Dungar Singh

Date	Mintage	Good	VG	F	VF	XF
VS1916 (1859)	—	87.50	175	275	400	550

Ganga Singh
VS1944-1999 / 1887-1942AD
MILLED COINAGE

KM# 72 RUPEE
11.6600 g., Silver **Obverse:** Bust of Victoria left

Date	Mintage	VG	F	VF	XF	Unc
1892	596,000	3.00	7.50	12.50	18.50	27.50
1892 Proof	—	Value: 200				
1897	111,000	8.00	20.00	31.50	42.50	60.00
1897 Proof	—	Value: 200				

KM# 70a 1/2 PICE
Silver **Obverse:** Bust of Victoria left

Date	Mintage	F	VF	XF	Unc
1894 Restrike; Proof	—	Value: 125			

KM# 70b 1/2 PICE
Gold **Obverse:** Bust of Victoria left

Date	Mintage	F	VF	XF	Unc
1894 Restrike; Proof	—	Value: 1,500			

KM# 70 1/2 PICE
Copper **Obverse:** Bust of Victoria left

Date	Mintage	VG	F	VF	XF	Unc
1894	500,000	2.00	5.00	12.00	20.00	35.00
1894 Proof	—	Value: 100				

KM# 71a 1/4 ANNA
Silver **Obverse:** Bust of Victoria left

Date	Mintage	F	VF	XF	Unc
VS1895 Restrike; Proof	—	Value: 125			

KM# 71b 1/4 ANNA
Gold **Obverse:** Bust of Victoria left

Date	Mintage	F	VF	XF	Unc
VS1895 Restrike; Proof	—	Value: 2,500			

KM# 71 1/4 ANNA
Copper **Obverse:** Bust of Victoria left

Date	Mintage	VG	F	VF	XF	Unc
1895	6,156,000	1.60	4.00	10.00	17.50	30.00
1895 Proof	—	Value: 125				

LOCAL COINAGE

Reverse marks, left to right: #6, 7, 9, 8, 2, 5. All dump coins with frozen date VS1916/1859AD and actual VS date.

KM# 61 PAISA
Copper, 18 mm. **Obverse:** 1859 date at bottom **Obv. Inscription:** Name of Victoria and Ganga Singh **Reverse:** 1916 date above, 1946 date below **Note:** Weight varies: 5.60-5.90 grams.

Date	Mintage	Good	VG	F	VF	XF
VS1946 (1889)	—	1.75	2.50	3.50	5.00	—

KM# 60 NAZARANA PAISA
Copper **Obverse:** 1859 date at bottom **Obv. Inscription:** Name of Victoria and Ganga Singh **Reverse:** 1916 date above, 1946 date below

Date	Mintage	Good	VG	F	VF	XF
VS1946 (1889)	—	85.00	135	200	300	—

KM# 62 1/8 RUPEE
1.4000 g., Silver, 12 mm. **Obverse:** 1859 date at bottom **Obv. Inscription:** Name of Victoria and Ganga Singh **Reverse:** 1916 date above, 1944 date below

Date	Mintage	Good	VG	F	VF	XF
VS1944 (1887)	—	20.00	40.00	65.00	100	150

KM# 63 1/4 RUPEE
2.8000 g., Silver **Obverse:** 1859 date at bottom **Obv. Inscription:** Name of Victoria and Ganga Singh **Reverse:** 1916 date above, actual VS date below

Date	Mintage	Good	VG	F	VF	XF
VS1944 (1887)	—	15.00	30.00	50.00	80.00	120
VS1946 (1889)	—	15.00	38.00	50.00	80.00	120

KM# 64 1/2 RUPEE
5.7000 g., Silver **Obverse:** 1859 date at bottom **Obv. Inscription:** Victoria and Ganga Singh **Reverse:** 1916 date above, 1944 date below

Date	Mintage	Good	VG	F	VF	XF
VS1944 (1887)	—	22.50	45.00	80.00	120	175

KM# 65 RUPEE
11.4000 g., Silver **Obverse:** 1859 date at bottom **Obv. Inscription:** Name of Victoria and Ganga Singh **Reverse:** 1916 date above, 1944 date below

Date	Mintage	Good	VG	F	VF	XF
VS1944 (1887)	—	2.75	7.00	11.00	16.50	25.00

KM# 65a NAZARANA RUPEE
11.4000 g., Silver, 30 mm. **Obverse:** 1859 date at bottom **Obv. Inscription:** Victoria and Ganga Singh **Reverse:** 1916 date above, 1944 date below **Note:** Weight varies: 10.70-11.60 grams.

Date	Mintage	Good	VG	F	VF	XF
VS1944 (1887)	—	87.50	175	275	400	550

KM# 65b NAZARANA RUPEE
Silver **Obverse:** 1859 date at bottom **Obv. Inscription:** Victoria and Ganga Singh **Reverse:** 1916 date above, 1944 date below **Note:** Size varies 22-23mm. Struck with 1 Paisa, KM#61 dies.

Date	Mintage	Good	VG	F	VF	XF
VS1946 (1889)	—	50.00	100	150	225	325

BINDRABAN

This city, the modern Vrindavan, was not a princely state. The area surrounding the city, including the neighboring city of Mathura, was under Jat control in the mid-18th century, although nominally subject to Awadh. After varying fortunes the area passed to the East India Company in 1803-05 (i.e. AH1217-1220; VS1860-1862). The coins below display symbols of Awadh, Mughals, Delhi and Bhartpur, although it is clear that they were not mints of any of those authorities, especially in the British period.

MINTS AND MINT NAMES

بندربن
Bindraban

مؤمن اباد
Muminabad

شاه جهان اباد
Shahjahanabad

گوکل
Gokul

اسلام اباد
Mathura
Islamabad

CITY

HAMMERED COINAGE

KM# 5 PAISA
Copper **Obverse:** Inscription: Shah Alam (II) **Mint:** Muminabad

Date	Mintage	Good	VG	F	VF	XF
AH121x//(4)3	—	1.75	2.50	4.00	7.50	—
AH1216//44	—	1.75	2.50	4.00	7.50	—

KM# 10.4 RUPEE
Silver **Obv. Inscription:** Shah Alam (II) **Reverse:** Scimitar, dagger, and trident **Note:** Weight varies: 10.70-11.60 grams.

Date	Mintage	Good	VG	F	VF	XF
AH12xx//44	—	2.75	7.00	11.00	16.50	25.00

KM# 10.5 RUPEE
Silver **Obv. Inscription:** Shah Alam (II) **Reverse:** Scimitar and dagger **Note:** Weight varies: 10.70-11.60 grams.

Date	Mintage	Good	VG	F	VF	XF
AH-//44	—	2.75	7.00	11.00	16.50	25.00

KM# 10.6 RUPEE
Silver **Obv. Inscription:** Shah Alam (II) **Reverse:** Trident and 5 trident figure **Note:** Weight varies: 10.70-11.60 grams.

Date	Mintage	Good	VG	F	VF	XF
AH1217//45	—	6.00	15.00	25.00	40.00	60.00

LOCAL COINAGE

KM# 51 1/2 PAISA
3.0000 g., Copper **Obv. Inscription:** Muhammad Akbar (II) **Mint:** Mathura **Note:** Similar to 1 Paisa, KM#35, but with royal legend.

Date	Mintage	Good	VG	F	VF	XF
ND(1806-38)	—	3.50	6.00	10.00	15.00	—

KM# 52 PAISA
6.0000 g., Copper **Obv. Inscription:** Muhammad Akbar (II) **Mint:** Mathura **Note:** Similar to 1/2 Paisa, KM#51.

Date	Mintage	Good	VG	F	VF	XF
ND(1806-38)	—	3.50	6.00	10.00	15.00	—

KM# 16 1/4 RUPEE
Silver **Obverse:** Head of Victoria left **Obv. Inscription:** Queen Victoria **Note:** Weight varies: 2.68-2.90 grams.

Date	Mintage	Good	VG	F	VF	XF
VS1915 (1858)	—	16.50	40.00	65.00	100	150
VS1916 (1859)	—	16.50	40.00	65.00	100	150
VS1924 (1867)	—	16.50	40.00	65.00	100	150

KM# 17 1/2 RUPEE
Silver **Obverse:** Head of Victoria left **Obv. Inscription:** Queen Victoria **Note:** Weight varies: 5.35-5.80 grams.

Date	Mintage	Good	VG	F	VF	XF
VS1915 (1858)	—	16.50	40.00	65.00	100	150
VS1916 (1859)	—	16.50	40.00	60.00	100	150
VS1924 (1867)	—	16.50	40.00	65.00	100	150

KM# 41 RUPEE
Silver **Obv. Inscription:** Shah Alam (II) **Reverse:** Cross, star, and dagger **Mint:** Mathura

Date	Mintage	Good	VG	F	VF	XF
AH-//43	—	3.50	9.00	15.00	21.50	30.00

KM# 18 RUPEE
Silver **Obverse:** Head of Victoria left **Obv. Inscription:** Queen Victoria **Note:** Weight varies: 10.70-11.60 grams.

Date	Mintage	Good	VG	F	VF	XF
VS1915 (1858)	—	12.00	30.00	50.00	75.00	110
VS1916 (1859)	—	12.00	30.00	50.00	75.00	110

KM# 19 RUPEE
Silver **Obverse:** Head of Victoria left **Obv. Inscription:** Queen Victoria **Reverse:** "Fazl Hami-din"

Date	Mintage	Good	VG	F	VF	XF
1867//12	—	25.00	60.00	100	150	225

BROACH

From very early times Broach, located on the north bank of the Narmada River 30 miles from the Gulf of Cambay, was an important port on the sea route to Europe. It was known as Barakacheva to early Chinese travellers, and as Barygaza to Ptolemy. After the Islamic invasions of India it was incorporated into the Muslim kingdom of Gujerat and remained so until 1572 when it was annexed by Akbar. During the reign of Aurangzeb, Broach first began to experience Maratha incursions. In 1772, it came briefly under British influence before being ceded to Sindhia in 1783. It was returned to the East India Company in 1803 and thereafter remained in British control.

RULERS
To British 1772-1783 and 1803 on
To Gwalior 1783-1803

MINT
Broach

Mint mark: Cross
(Gwalior and E.I.C.)

BRITISH ADMINISTRATION

Imtaya-ud-Daula
AH1182-1186 / 1768-1772AD

HAMMERED COINAGE

C# A36 1/2 RUPEE
Silver **Issuer:** East India Company **Obv. Inscription:** Shah Alam (II) **Reverse:** Mint mark cross of St. Stephan **Note:** Weight varies: 5.35-5.80 grams.

Date	Mintage	Good	VG	F	VF	XF
ND(1804)	—	7.00	17.50	25.00	35.00	50.00

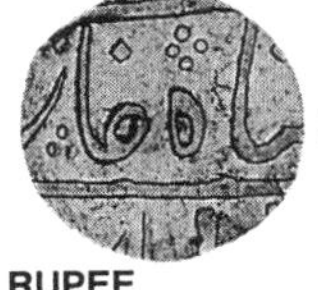 

C# 36 RUPEE
Silver **Note:** Weight varies: 10.70-11.60 grams.

Date	Mintage	Good	VG	F	VF	XF
ND(1805)	—	9.00	22.50	31.50	42.50	60.00

Note: Other coins with cross mint mark were probably also issued under the Sindhias. For other Broach issues see Gwalior.

BUNDI

State in Rajputana in northwest India.

Bundi was founded in 1342 by a Chauhan Rajput, Rao Dewa (Deoraj). Until the Maratha defeat early in the 19th century, Bundi was greatly harassed by the forces of Holkar and Sindhia. In 1818 it came under British protection and control and remained so until 1947.In 1948 the State was absorbed into Rajasthan.

RULERS
Bishen Singh, AH1187-1236/ VS1830-1878/1773-1821AD
Ram Singh, AH1236-1306/ VS1878-1946/1824-1889AD
Raghubir Singh VS1946-1984/1889-1927AD

MINT

بوندي or بنڈ

Bundi
Mint name: Bundi

All of the coins of Bundi struck prior to the Mutiny (1857) are in the name of the Mughal emperor and bear the following 2 marks on the reverse, to the left and right of the regnal year, respectively:

On all Mughal issues:

Only on Muhammad Akbar and Muhammad Bahadur issues:

The same symbols appear on the coins of Kotah, but the difference is that the Kotah pieces have the mintname *Kotahurf Nandgaon* and later issues only have *Nandgaon.*

HAMMERED COINAGE

Mughal Series

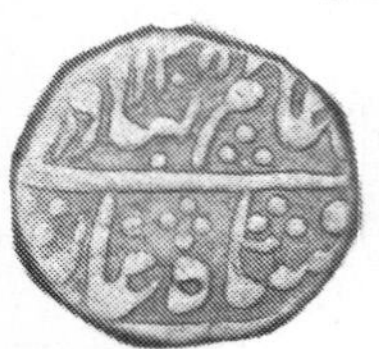

C# 5.1 TAKKA
Copper **Obv. Inscription:** Shah Alam (II) **Note:** Weight varies: 17.50-18.00 grams.

Date	Mintage	Good	VG	F	VF	XF
AH-//43	—	1.50	2.50	3.50	5.00	—
AH-//44	—	1.50	2.50	3.50	5.00	—

C# 5.2 TAKKA
Copper **Obv. Inscription:** Shah Alam (II) **Reverse:** Cross under leaf

Date	Mintage	Good	VG	F	VF	XF
AH-//45	—	1.50	2.50	3.50	5.00	—
AH-//46	—	1.50	2.50	3.50	5.00	—

C# 17a TAKKA
Copper **Obv. Inscription:** "Muhammad Akbar (II) and Sahib Qiran Sani" **Shape:** Square **Note:** Weight varies: 17.50-18.00 grams.

Date	Mintage	Good	VG	F	VF	XF
AH-//4	—	1.50	2.50	3.50	5.00	—
AH-//5	—	1.50	2.50	3.50	5.00	—
AH-//6	—	1.50	2.50	3.50	5.00	—
AH-//11	—	1.50	2.50	3.50	5.00	—
AH-//13	—	1.50	2.50	3.50	5.00	—
AH-//14	—	1.50	2.50	3.50	5.00	—
AH-//24	—	1.25	2.00	3.00	4.50	—
AH-//25	—	1.25	2.00	3.00	4.50	—
AH-//26	—	1.25	2.00	3.00	4.50	—

C# 35 TAKKA
Copper, 20 mm. **Obv. Inscription:** Bahadur Shah (II) **Shape:** Square **Note:** Weight varies: 17.60-17.70 grams.

Date	Mintage	Good	VG	F	VF	XF
AH-//9	—	4.50	6.50	8.50	12.50	—
AH-//11	—	4.50	6.50	8.50	12.50	—
AH-//14	—	4.50	6.50	8.50	12.50	—
AH-//19	—	4.50	6.50	8.50	12.50	—

C# 10.1 RUPEE
Silver **Obv. Inscription:** Shah Alam (II) **Note:** Weight varies: 10.90-11.15 grams.

Date	Mintage	Good	VG	F	VF	XF
AH-//43	—	4.00	10.00	15.00	22.50	35.00
AH-//44	—	4.00	10.00	15.00	22.50	35.00

C# 10.2 RUPEE
Silver **Obv. Inscription:** Shah Alam (II) **Reverse:** Cross under leaf

Date	Mintage	Good	VG	F	VF	XF
AH-//45	—	4.00	10.00	15.00	22.50	35.00
AH-//46	—	4.00	10.00	15.00	22.50	35.00
AH-//47	—	4.00	10.00	15.00	22.50	35.00

C# 30 RUPEE
5.5000 g., Silver **Obv. Inscription:** "Muhammad Akbar (II) and Sahib Qiran Sani"

Date	Mintage	Good	VG	F	VF	XF
AH-//3	—	3.25	8.00	13.50	20.00	32.50
AH-//5	—	3.25	8.00	13.50	20.00	32.50
AH-//6	—	3.25	8.00	13.50	20.00	32.50
AH-//9	—	3.25	8.00	13.50	20.00	32.50
AH-//10	—	3.25	8.00	13.50	20.00	32.50
AH-//11	—	3.25	8.00	13.50	20.00	32.50
AH-//12	—	3.25	8.00	13.50	20.00	32.50
AH-//13	—	3.25	8.00	13.50	20.00	32.50
AH-//15	—	3.25	8.00	13.50	20.00	32.50
AH-//16	—	3.25	8.00	13.50	20.00	32.50
AH-//17	—	3.25	8.00	13.50	20.00	32.50
AH-//18	—	3.25	8.00	13.50	20.00	32.50
AH-//19	—	3.25	8.00	13.50	20.00	32.50
AH-//20	—	3.25	8.00	13.50	20.00	32.50
AH-//21	—	3.25	8.00	13.50	20.00	32.50
AH-//22	—	3.25	8.00	13.50	20.00	32.50
AH-//24	—	3.25	8.00	13.50	20.00	32.50
AH-//27	—	3.25	8.00	13.50	20.00	32.50
AH-//30	—	3.25	8.00	13.50	20.00	32.50
AH-//31	—	3.25	8.00	13.50	20.00	32.50
AH-//32	—	3.25	8.00	13.50	20.00	32.50
AH-//33	—	3.25	8.00	13.50	20.00	32.50

C# 40 RUPEE
Silver, 19 mm. **Obv. Inscription:** "Bahadur Shah (II)" **Note:** Weight varies: 11.15-11.20 grams.

Date	Mintage	VG	F	VF	XF	Unc
AH-//Ahad (1) (1837)	—	8.00	13.50	20.00	32.50	—
AH-//2 (1838)	—	8.00	13.50	20.00	32.50	—
AH-//3 (1839)	—	8.00	13.50	20.00	32.50	—
AH-//4 (1840)	—	8.00	13.50	20.00	32.50	—
AH-//5 (1841)	—	8.00	13.50	20.00	32.50	—
AH-//6 (1842)	—	8.00	13.50	20.00	32.50	—
AH-//7 (1843)	—	8.00	13.50	20.00	32.50	—
AH-//8 (1844)	—	8.00	13.50	20.00	32.50	—
AH-//9 (1845)	—	8.00	13.50	20.00	32.50	—
AH-//10 (1845)	—	8.00	13.50	20.00	32.50	—
AH-//12 (1847)	—	8.00	13.50	20.00	32.50	—
AH-//13 (1848)	—	8.00	13.50	20.00	32.50	—
AH-//14 (1849)	—	8.00	13.50	20.00	32.50	—
AH-//15 (1850)	—	8.00	13.50	20.00	32.50	—
AH-//16 (1851)	—	8.00	13.50	20.00	32.50	—
AH-//18 (1853)	—	8.00	13.50	20.00	32.50	—
AH-//19 (1854)	—	8.00	13.50	20.00	32.50	—
AH-//21 (1856)	—	8.00	13.50	20.00	32.50	—

C# 40a NAZARANA RUPEE
Silver **Shape:** Square

Date	Mintage	VG	F	VF	XF	Unc
AH-//5	—	120	200	300	450	—
AH-//19	—	120	200	300	450	—

C# 33 MOHUR
10.7000 g., Gold

Date	Mintage	VG	F	VF	XF	Unc
AH-//15	—	225	325	500	700	—
AH-//17	—	225	325	500	700	—
AH-//19	—	225	325	500	700	—
AH-//33	—	225	325	500	700	—

Bishen Singh

AH1187-1236 / VS1830-1878 / 1773-1821AD

HAMMERED COINAGE

Mughal Series

C# 15 TAKKA
Copper **Obv. Inscription:** Shah Akbar Bahadur Badshah Ghazi **Shape:** Round **Note:** Weight varies: 17.50-18.00 grams.

Date	Mintage	Good	VG	F	VF	XF
AH-// Ahad (1) (1806)	—	2.50	3.50	4.50	6.00	—
AH-//2 (1807)	—	2.50	3.50	4.50	6.00	—
AH-//3 (1808)	—	2.50	3.50	4.50	6.00	—

C# 17 TAKKA
Copper **Obv. Inscription:** Sahib Qiran Sani

Date	Mintage	Good	VG	F	VF	XF
AH-//3	—	1.25	2.00	3.00	4.50	—
AH-//4	—	1.25	2.00	3.00	4.50	—
AH-//5	—	1.25	2.00	3.00	4.50	—
AH-//6	—	1.25	2.00	3.00	4.50	—
AH-//7	—	1.25	2.00	3.00	4.50	—
AH-//9	—	1.25	2.00	3.00	4.50	—
AH-//11	—	1.25	2.00	3.00	4.50	—
AH-//12	—	1.25	2.00	3.00	4.50	—
AH-//13	—	1.25	2.00	3.00	4.50	—
AH-//14	—	1.25	2.00	3.00	4.50	—
AH-//15	—	1.50	2.50	3.50	5.00	—
AH-//16	—	1.50	2.50	3.50	5.00	—

C# 25 1/2 RUPEE
5.5000 g., Silver, 15 mm. **Obv. Inscription:** Badshah Ghazi

Date	Mintage	Good	VG	F	VF	XF
AH-//Ahad (1)	—	25.00	50.00	75.00	125	175

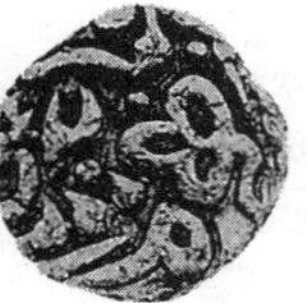

C# 29 RUPEE
5.5000 g., Silver **Obv. Inscription:** Badshah Ghazi **Note:** Weight varies: 11.10-11.15 grams.

Date	Mintage	Good	VG	F	VF	XF
AH-//Ahad (1)	—	6.00	15.00	25.00	40.00	65.00
AH1222//2	—	6.00	15.00	25.00	40.00	65.00
AH-//3	—	6.00	15.00	25.00	40.00	65.00

C# 31 NAZARANA RUPEE
11.1000 g., Silver **Shape:** Square

Date	Mintage	Good	VG	F	VF	XF
AH1246//25	—	37.50	75.00	120	185	275

Ram Singh
AH1236-1306 / VS1878-1946 / 1824-89AD

HAMMERED COINAGE
Mughal Series

C# 30a RUPEE
5.5000 g., Silver **Reverse:** Additional "Katar" above "Zarb"

Date	Mintage	Good	VG	F	VF	XF
AH-//20	—	6.50	16.50	27.50	40.00	65.00
AH-//21	—	6.50	16.50	27.50	40.00	65.00

Victoria
1837-1901AD

HAMMERED COINAGE
Regal Style

Y# 3 TAKKA
Copper **Obv. Inscription:** VIC/TORIA/QUEEN **Note:** Weight varies: 17.15-17.65 grams.

Date	Mintage	Good	VG	F	VF	XF
1858//VS1915	—	0.35	0.85	1.25	1.75	—
1862//VS1919	—	0.35	0.85	1.25	1.75	—
1864//VS1921	—	0.35	0.85	1.25	1.75	—
1864//VS1922	—	0.35	0.85	1.25	1.75	—
1865//VS1922	—	0.35	0.85	1.25	1.75	—
1866//VS1923	—	0.35	0.85	1.25	1.75	—
1867//VS1924	—	0.35	0.85	1.25	1.75	—
1868//VS1925	—	0.35	0.85	1.25	1.75	—
1869//VS1926	—	0.35	0.85	1.25	1.75	—
1871//VS1928	—	0.35	0.85	1.25	1.75	—
1872//VS1929	—	0.35	0.85	1.25	1.75	—
1875//VS1932	—	0.35	0.85	1.25	1.75	—
1877//VS1934	—	0.25	0.50	0.85	1.25	—
1878//VS1935	—	0.25	0.50	0.85	1.25	—
1879//VS1936	—	0.25	0.50	0.85	1.25	—
1882//VS1939	—	0.25	0.50	0.85	1.25	—
1883//VS1940	—	0.25	0.50	0.85	1.25	—
1885//VS1942	—	0.25	0.50	0.85	1.25	—
1886//VS1943	—	0.25	0.50	0.85	1.25	—
1887//VS1944	—	0.25	0.50	0.85	1.25	—
1888//VS1945	—	0.25	0.50	0.85	1.25	—
1889//VS1946	—	0.25	0.50	0.85	1.25	—
1898//VS1955	—	0.85	1.25	2.00	3.00	—
1894(sic)//VS1956	—	0.85	1.25	2.00	3.00	—
1898(sic)//VS1956	—	0.85	1.25	2.00	3.00	—
1899//VS1956	—	1.25	2.25	3.50	5.00	—
ND(1858-99)//VS(1915-56) Dates off flan	—	0.65	1.10	1.75	2.50	—

Y# 1 1/2 PAISA
5.5000 g., Copper **Obv. Inscription:** VIC/TORIA/QUEEN **Shape:** Square **Note:** Size varies: 9-11mm.

Date	Mintage	Good	VG	F	VF	XF
1867//VS1924	—	1.00	1.75	3.00	5.00	—

Y# 2 PAISA
Copper **Obverse:** Katar **Obv. Legend:** EMPEROR EDWARD **Obv. Inscription:** VIC/TORIA/QUEEN **Note:** Weight varies: 10.60-10.70 grams.

Date	Mintage	Good	VG	F	VF	XF
1858//VS1915	—	0.35	0.65	1.00	1.50	—
1867//VS1924	—	0.25	0.50	0.85	1.25	—
1877//VS1934	—	0.25	0.50	0.85	1.25	—
1878//VS1935	—	0.25	0.50	0.85	1.25	—
1879//VS1936	—	0.25	0.50	0.85	1.25	—
1883//VS1940	—	0.25	0.50	0.85	1.25	—
1885//VS1942	—	0.25	0.50	0.85	1.25	—
1886//VS1943	—	0.25	0.50	0.85	1.25	—
1887//VS1944	—	0.25	0.50	0.85	1.25	—
1888//VS1945	—	0.25	0.50	0.85	1.25	—
1889//VS1946	—	0.25	0.50	0.85	1.25	—
1890//VS1947	—	0.25	0.50	0.85	1.25	—
1898//VS1955	—	0.25	0.50	0.85	1.25	—

Y# 4 1/4 RUPEE
2.8000 g., Silver

Date	Mintage	Good	VG	F	VF	XF
1858//VS1915	—	4.00	10.00	16.50	25.00	35.00
1878//VS1935	—	4.00	10.00	16.50	25.00	35.00
1879//VS1936	—	4.00	10.00	16.50	25.00	35.00
ND(1858-79)//VS(1915-36) Dates off flan	—	4.00	5.00	8.50	12.50	17.50

Y# 7 1/4 RUPEE
2.8000 g., Silver **Obverse:** Katar **Obv. Legend:** VICTORIA QUEEN

Date	Mintage	Good	VG	F	VF	XF
1887//VS1944	—	4.00	10.00	16.50	25.00	35.00
1889//VS1946	—	4.00	10.00	16.50	25.00	35.00
1890//VS1947	—	4.00	10.00	16.50	25.00	35.00
1896//VS1953	—	4.00	10.00	16.50	25.00	35.00
1898//VS1955	—	4.00	10.00	16.50	25.00	35.00
ND (1887-98)//(VS1944-55) Dates off flan	—	4.00	5.00	8.50	12.50	17.50

Y# 5 1/2 RUPEE
Silver **Obv. Inscription:** VIC/TORIA/QUEEN **Note:** Weight varies: 5.50-5.60 grams.

Date	Mintage	Good	VG	F	VF	XF
1868//VS1915	—	8.00	20.00	30.00	50.00	70.00
1873//VS1930	—	8.00	20.00	30.00	50.00	70.00
1876//VS1933	—	8.00	20.00	30.00	50.00	70.00
1880//VS1937	—	8.00	20.00	30.00	50.00	70.00
1883//VS1940	—	8.00	20.00	30.00	50.00	70.00
1884//VS1941	—	8.00	20.00	30.00	50.00	70.00
1886//VS1943	—	8.00	20.00	30.00	50.00	70.00
ND(1858-86)//VS(1915-43) Dates off flan	—	8.00	10.00	15.00	25.00	35.00

Y# 8 1/2 RUPEE
Silver **Obverse:** Katar **Obv. Legend:** VICTORIA QUEEN

Date	Mintage	Good	VG	F	VF	XF
1888//VS1945	—	2.25	5.50	8.00	12.50	20.00
1889//VS1946	—	2.25	5.50	8.00	12.50	20.00
1891//VS1948	—	2.00	5.00	7.00	10.00	17.50
1892//VS1949	—	2.00	5.00	7.00	10.00	17.50
1896//VS1953	—	2.25	5.50	8.00	12.50	20.00
1897//VS1954	—	2.00	5.00	7.00	10.00	17.50
1898//VS1955	—	2.25	5.50	8.00	12.50	20.00
ND (1888-98)//(VS1945-55) Dates off flan	—	2.25	2.75	4.00	6.50	12.50

Y# 6 RUPEE
Silver **Obv. Inscription:** VIC/TORIA/QUEEN **Note:** Weight varies: 11.00-11.15 grams.

Date	Mintage	Good	VG	F	VF	XF
1858//VS1915	—	2.50	6.00	9.00	13.50	21.50
1859//VS1915	—	2.50	6.00	9.00	13.50	21.50
1859//VS1916	—	2.50	6.50	10.00	15.00	21.50
1860//VS1916	—	2.50	6.50	10.00	15.00	21.50
1860//VS1917	—	2.50	6.00	9.00	13.50	21.50
1861//VS1918	—	2.50	6.00	9.00	13.50	21.50
1862//VS1919	—	2.50	6.00	9.00	13.50	21.50
1863//VS1920	—	2.50	6.00	9.00	13.50	21.50
1864//VS1921	—	2.50	6.00	9.00	13.50	21.50
1865//VS1922	—	2.50	6.00	9.00	13.50	21.50
1866//VS1923	—	2.50	6.00	9.00	13.50	21.50
1867//VS1924	—	2.50	6.00	9.00	13.50	21.50
1868//VS1925	—	2.50	6.00	9.00	13.50	21.50
1864 (sic)//VS1925 (sic)	—	2.50	6.00	9.00	13.50	21.50
1869//VS1926	—	2.50	6.00	9.00	13.50	21.50
1870//VS1927	—	2.50	6.00	9.00	13.50	21.50
1871//VS1928	—	2.50	6.00	9.00	13.50	21.50
1872//VS1929	—	2.50	6.00	9.00	13.50	21.50
1873//VS1930	—	2.50	6.00	9.00	13.50	21.50
1874//VS1931	—	2.50	6.00	9.00	13.50	21.50
1875//VS1932	—	2.50	6.00	9.00	13.50	21.50
1876//VS1933	—	2.50	6.00	9.00	13.50	21.50
1877//VS1934	—	2.50	6.00	9.00	13.50	21.50
1878//VS1935	—	2.50	6.00	9.00	13.50	21.50
1879//VS1936	—	2.50	6.00	9.00	13.50	21.50
1880//VS1937	—	2.50	6.00	9.00	13.50	21.50
1881//VS1938	—	2.50	6.00	9.00	13.50	21.50
1882//VS1939	—	2.50	6.00	9.00	13.50	21.50
1883//VS1940	—	2.50	6.00	9.00	13.50	21.50
1884//VS1941	—	2.50	6.00	9.00	13.50	21.50
1885//VS1942	—	2.50	6.00	9.00	13.50	21.50
1886//VS1943	—	2.50	6.00	9.00	13.50	21.50
ND(1858-86)//VS(1915-43) Dates off flan	—	1.25	3.00	4.50	6.50	10.00

Y# 9 RUPEE
Silver **Obverse:** Katar **Obv. Legend:** VICTORIA QUEEN

Date	Mintage	Good	VG	F	VF	XF
1886//VS1943	—	2.50	6.00	9.00	13.50	21.50
1887//VS1944	—	2.50	6.00	9.00	13.50	21.50
1888//VS1945	—	2.50	6.00	9.00	13.50	21.50
1889//VS1946	—	2.50	6.00	9.00	13.50	21.50
1890//VS1947	—	2.50	6.00	9.00	13.50	21.50
1891//VS1948	—	2.50	6.00	9.00	13.50	21.50
1892//VS1949	—	2.50	6.00	9.00	13.50	21.50
1893//VS1950	—	2.50	6.00	9.00	13.50	21.50
1894//VS1951	—	2.50	6.00	9.00	13.50	21.50
1896//VS1953	—	2.50	6.00	9.00	13.50	21.50
1897//VS1954	—	2.50	6.00	9.00	13.50	21.50
1898//VS1955	—	2.50	6.00	9.00	13.50	21.50
1900//VS1957	—	2.50	6.00	9.00	13.50	21.50
ND(1886-1900)//(VS1943-1957) Dates off flan	—	1.25	3.00	4.50	6.50	10.00

Y# 6a NAZARANA RUPEE
Silver **Obv. Inscription:** VIC/TORIA/QUEEN **Shape:** Square **Note:** Weight varies: 10.60-11.00 grams.

Date	Mintage	Good	VG	F	VF	XF
1858//VS1915	—	18.50	37.50	60.00	90.00	140
1862//VS1919	—	18.50	37.50	60.00	90.00	140
1868//VS1925	—	18.50	37.50	60.00	90.00	140
1872//VS1929	—	18.50	37.50	60.00	90.00	140
1875//VS1932	—	18.50	37.50	60.00	90.00	140
1877//VS1934	—	18.50	37.50	60.00	90.00	140
1878//VS1935	—	18.50	37.50	60.00	90.00	140
1880//VS1937	—	18.50	37.50	60.00	90.00	140

Y# 9a NAZARANA RUPEE
Silver **Obverse:** Katar **Obv. Legend:** VICTORIA QUEEN

Date	Mintage	Good	VG	F	VF	XF
1886//VS1943	—	18.50	37.50	60.00	90.00	140
1888//VS1945	—	18.50	37.50	60.00	90.00	140
1889//VS1946	—	18.50	37.50	60.00	90.00	140
1890//VS1947	—	18.50	37.50	60.00	90.00	140
1891//VS1948	—	18.50	37.50	60.00	90.00	140
1892//VS1949	—	18.50	37.50	60.00	90.00	140
1893//VS1950	—	18.50	37.50	60.00	90.00	140

Date	Mintage	Good	VG	F	VF	XF
1894//VS1951	—	18.50	37.50	60.00	90.00	140
1895//VS1952	—	18.50	37.50	60.00	90.00	140
1896//VS1953	—	18.50	37.50	60.00	90.00	140

Y# A7 MOHUR
12.2500 g., Gold **Obv. Inscription:** VIC/TORIA/QUEEN/date. **Edge:** Plain. **Mint:** Bundi **Note:** All 5-6 known specimens exhibit traces of mounting.

Date	Mintage	F	VF	XF	Unc
VS1917(1860)	—	—	1,250	1,850	—

CAMBAY

Khanbayat

Although of very ancient origins as a port, located at the head of the Gulf of Cambay in West India, Cambay did not come into existence as a separate state until about 1730 after the break-down of Mughal authority in Delhi. The nawabs of Cambay traced their ancestry to Momin Khan II, the last of the Muslim governors of Gujerat. The State came under British control after two decades of Maratha rule.

RULERS
Hussain Yafar Khan, AH1257-1297/1841-1880AD
Ja'far Ali Khan, AH1297-1333/VS1937-1972/1880-1915AD

MINT

کنبایت

Khanbayat

Hussain Yafar Khan
1841-1880AD

ANONYMOUS HAMMERED COINAGE

Y# A1 FALUS
Copper **Countermark:** Persian "Shah" on irregular planchets **Obv. Inscription:** Shah Alam (II)

Date	Mintage	Good	VG	F	VF	XF
ND(ca. 1865-78)	—	4.00	5.00	6.50	9.00	—

Y# 1 RUPEE
Silver **Note:** Fractional denominations are reported to exist. Weight varies: 10.70-11.60 grams.

Date	Mintage	Good	VG	F	VF	XF
AH1282	—	5.00	12.50	20.00	30.00	45.00
AH1292	—	5.00	12.50	20.00	30.00	45.00
AH1293	—	5.00	12.50	20.00	30.00	45.00
AH1294	—	5.00	12.50	20.00	30.00	45.00

Jafar Ali Khan
1880-1915AD

ANONYMOUS HAMMERED COINAGE

Y# 3 1/2 PAISA
Copper **Countermark:** Persian "Shah" **Note:** Round flan. Varieties in countermark exist.

Date	Mintage	Good	VG	F	VF	XF
VS194x(1883-1892)	—	3.00	5.50	7.50	10.00	—
VS(19)62(1905)	—	3.00	5.50	7.50	10.00	—

Y# 3a 1/2 PAISA
Copper **Note:** Square flan.

Date	Mintage	Good	VG	F	VF	XF
VS194x(1883-92)	—	3.00	5.50	7.50	10.00	—
VS(19)62(1905)	—	3.00	5.50	7.50	10.00	—

Y# 7 1/8 RUPEE
Silver, 11 mm. **Obv. Inscription:** Persian-Ja'afar Ali Khan **Reverse:** Mint name **Mint:** Cambay **Note:** Weight varies 1.34-1.45 grams.

Date	Mintage	Good	VG	F	VF	XF
AH1313(1895-96)	—	20.00	40.00	65.00	100	150

Y# 8 1/4 RUPEE
Silver, 14 mm. **Reverse:** Mint name **Mint:** Cambay **Note:** Weight varies 2.68-2.90 grams.

Date	Mintage	Good	VG	F	VF	XF
AH1313//17(1895-96)	—	20.00	40.00	65.00	100	150

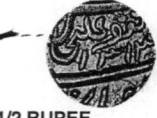

Y# 9 1/2 RUPEE
Silver **Reverse:** Mint name **Mint:** Cambay **Note:** Weight varies 5.35-5.80 grams.

Date	Mintage	Good	VG	F	VF	XF
AH1313(1895-96)	—	20.00	40.00	65.00	100	150
AH1317(1899-1900)	—	20.00	40.00	65.00	100	150

Y# 10 RUPEE
Silver **Obverse:** Persian legend **Obv. Legend:** Ja'afar Ali Khan **Reverse:** Mint name **Mint:** Cambay **Note:** Struck at Cambay. 10.70-11.60 grams.

Date	Mintage	Good	VG	F	VF	XF
AH1311(1893-1894)	—	15.00	30.00	50.00	80.00	120
AH1313(1895-1896)	—	15.00	30.00	50.00	80.00	120
AH1317(1899-1900)	—	15.00	30.00	50.00	80.00	120
AH1319(1901-1902)	—	15.00	30.00	50.00	80.00	120

CANNANORE

Cannanore, on the Malabar Coast in southwest India, was ruled by the Cherakal Rajas. Late in the 18th century it was overrun by Haider Ali, the Muslim ruler of Mysore. Then, in AH1198/1783, Cannanore was captured from Haider Ali's son, Tipu Sultan, by the East India Company. From that time onwards Cannanore was reduced to the status of a British tributary.

RULERS
Ali Rajas, Lord's of the deep,
AH1122-1231/1710-1815AD

KINGDOM

HAMMERED COINAGE

KM# 5 1/5 RUPEE
Silver **Note:** Varieties exist. Weight varies: 2.14-2.32 grams.

Date	Mintage	Good	VG	F	VF	XF
AH1220	—	1.50	4.00	7.00	10.00	15.00
AH1221	—	1.50	4.00	7.00	10.00	15.00
AH1231	—	1.50	4.00	7.00	10.00	15.00
AH1631(error)	—	1.50	4.00	7.00	10.00	15.00
AH1241	—	1.50	4.00	7.00	10.00	15.00
AH8711(error)	—	1.50	4.00	7.00	10.00	15.00

CHAMBA

The rulers of this mountainous state in north India, the origins of which go back as far as the 6th century, were Rajputs. Although Chamba was sometimes subject to the rulers of Kashmir, and later to the Mughals, even when nominally in subjection the remoteness of the region gave its rulers a considerable degree of autonomy. In 1846 the State came under British protection and in 1948 was merged into Himachal Pradesh.

RULERS
Charhat Singh, 1808-1844AD
Lakar Shah of Basoli, rebel, 1844AD
Sri Singh, 1844-1870AD
Sham Singh, 1870-1904AD

Mint mark:

Charhat Singh
1808-1844AD

HAMMERED COINAGE

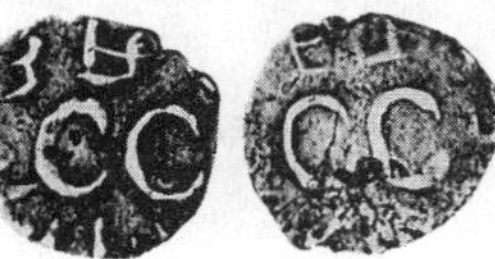

KM# 2 1/2 PAISA
Copper

Date	Mintage	Good	VG	F	VF	XF
ND(1808-44)	—	10.00	15.00	22.00	30.00	—

KM# 3 PAISA
Copper

Date	Mintage	Good	VG	F	VF	XF
ND(1808-44)	—	5.50	8.50	13.50	20.00	—
ND//15 (1822)	—	7.00	11.00	16.50	25.00	—
ND//16 (1823)	—	7.00	11.00	16.50	25.00	—
ND//17 (1824)	—	7.00	11.00	16.50	25.00	—

KM# 6 PAISA
Copper **Obverse:** Without trident below legend **Note:** Size varies 18-22mm.

Date	Mintage	Good	VG	F	VF	XF
ND(1844)	—	10.00	16.50	25.00	37.50	—

Sri Singh
1844-1870AD

HAMMERED COINAGE

KM# 10 PAISA
Copper **Note:** Crude, degenerate copy of KM#3.

Date	Mintage	Good	VG	F	VF	XF
1844	—	3.50	5.50	8.50	13.50	—

COUNTERMARKED COINAGE

KM# 9 PAISA
Copper **Countermark:** Trident on 1 Paisa, KM#6 **Obverse:** Without trident below legend

CM Date	Host Date	Good	VG	F	VF	XF
ND	(c.1844)	10.00	20.00	32.50	50.00	—

CHHOTA UDAIPUR

Formerly one of the non-Aryan-Chota Nagpur states located in Bengal, Chhota Udaipur originated in the late 15th century. Its founders were Chauhan Rajputs who, having been expelled from Ajmer, finally re-established themselves in Chhota Udaipur. The rulers were known as Maharawals, and by the 19th century became related to the British in India by the usual treaties.

RULERS
Guman Singhji, SE1744-1773/1822-1851AD
Jitsinghji, SE1773-1803/VS1908-1938/1851-1881AD
Motisinghji, VS1938-1952/1881-1905AD

Guman Singhji
SE1744-1773 / 1822-1851AD

HAMMERED COINAGE

KM# 10 PAISA
7.4000 g., Copper

Date	Mintage	Good	VG	F	VF	XF
ND(1843-75)	—	4.00	6.00	8.50	11.50	—

KM# 15.1 2 PAISA
Copper **Note:** Weight varies 13.40-14.00 grams.

Date	Mintage	Good	VG	F	VF	XF
SE(1)1765	—	3.50	5.50	7.50	10.00	—
SE1767	—	3.50	5.50	7.50	10.00	—

KM# 15.2 2 PAISA
Copper

Date	Mintage	Good	VG	F	VF	XF
SE1797 (1875)	—	3.50	5.50	7.50	10.00	—

KM# 15.3 2 PAISA
Copper **Note:** Weight varies: 13.4 - 14 grams.

Date	Mintage	Good	VG	F	VF	XF
ND(1875)	—	3.50	5.50	7.50	10.00	—

Jitsinghji
SE1773-1803 / VS1908-1938 / 1851-1881AD
HAMMERED COINAGE

Y# 1 PAISA
7.4000 g., Copper, 22 mm.

Date	Mintage	Good	VG	F	VF	XF
SE1787	—	2.50	4.50	6.50	9.00	—

Y# 3 2 PAISA
Copper **Note:** Weight varies 13.40-14.00 grams.

Date	Mintage	Good	VG	F	VF	XF
VS1919	—	7.00	9.00	12.00	16.50	—
VS1924	—	7.00	9.00	12.00	16.50	—

Y# 2.1 2 PAISA
Copper **Note:** Weight varies 13.40-14.00 grams.

Date	Mintage	Good	VG	F	VF	XF
SE1787	—	5.50	7.00	9.00	12.00	—

Y# 2.2 2 PAISA
Copper

Date	Mintage	Good	VG	F	VF	XF
SE1797	—	3.50	5.50	7.50	10.00	—

Motisinghji
VS1938-1952 / 1881-1905AD
HAMMERED COINAGE

Y# A4 1/2 PAISA
3.6000 g., Copper **Note:** Struck with one Paisa dies.

Date	Mintage	Good	VG	F	VF	XF
VS1948 Rare	—	—	—	—	—	—

Y# 4 PAISA
7.4000 g., Copper

Date	Mintage	Good	VG	F	VF	XF
VS1948	—	6.00	7.50	10.00	13.50	—

Y# 5 2 PAISA
Copper **Note:** Weight varies 13.40-14.00 grams.

Date	Mintage	Good	VG	F	VF	XF
VS1948	—	5.00	6.50	8.50	11.50	—

COCHIN

Located on the Malabar Coast, at the southern tip of India.

Although the name Cochin appears to have come into use only at the end of the 15th century, this was a very ancient state whose origins were lost in antiquity. In Roman times there was a steady trade between Cochin and the West, but from that time onward Cochin's history is largely conjecture until the arrival of the Portuguese under Vasco de Gama in the 15th century. In 1663 Cochin came under Dutch occupation and remained so for almost a hundred years until Haider Ali and Tipu Sultan of Mysore overran the region. In 1791, largely to escape the demands of Mysore, the Raja of Cochin placed himself under British protection. In 1809 a second treaty strengthened British control of the State.

In 1949 Cochin merged with Travancore forming the state of Travancore and Cochin which became part of the new state of Kerala in 1956.

See Netherlands possessions in India for similar coins prior to 1795AD.

HAMMERED COINAGE

KM# 1 PUTTUN
0.3240 g., Silver **Obverse:** Sun and moon above "lazy J" and dots **Reverse:** Conch shell

Date	Mintage	Good	VG	F	VF	XF
ND(1795-1850)	—	—	4.00	6.00	9.00	13.50

KM# 5 PUTTUN
0.5200 g., Silver **Obverse:** Siva seated **Reverse:** Conch shell

Date	Mintage	Good	VG	F	VF	XF
ND(1856-58)	—	—	5.50	8.00	10.00	15.00

KM# 6 2 PUTTUNS
1.0000 g., Silver **Obverse:** Siva seated **Reverse:** Conch shell

Date	Mintage	Good	VG	F	VF	XF
ND(1856-58)	—	—	6.00	9.00	13.50	20.00

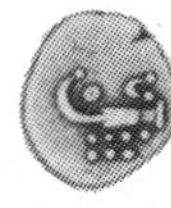

KM# 2 2 PUTTUNS
1.0000 g., Silver **Obverse:** Sun and moon above "lazy J" and dots **Reverse:** Conch shell

Date	Mintage	Good	VG	F	VF	XF
ND(1795-1850)	—	—	6.00	9.00	13.50	20.00

KM# 10 FANAM
Gold **Obverse:** Sun and moon above dots **Reverse:** Conch shell

Date	Mintage	Good	VG	F	VF	XF
ND(1795-1850)	—	—	7.00	11.00	16.50	25.00

COOCH BEHAR

During the 15th century, the area that was to become Cooch Behar was ruled by the powerful Hindu kings of Kamata, who were defeated by Sultan Ala al din Husain, Shah of Bengal in 1494AD. In 1511AD the kingdom of Cooch Behar was established by Chandan, a chieftain of the Koch tribe.

Chandan was succeeded about 1522 by Visvasimha, who consolidated the kingdom, and set up his capital at the present town of Cooch Behar. It was he who laid the foundations of the prosperity of the area by developing the Tibetan trade routes through Bhutan. Visvasimha is said to have abdicated about 1555AD to become an ascetic, and was succeeded by his son Nara Narayan, under whose reign the state reached the zenith of its power.

From the solid basis set up by his father, Nara Narayan set out, assisted by his brother Sukladhvaja, to extend the borders of his kingdom. Over the next quarter century he proceeded to subdue part of the Assam Valley, Kachar, Manipur, the Khasi and Jaintia Hills and part of Tripura and Sylhet. Nara Narayan was the first king of Cooch Behar to strike coins, and the varied style may indicate that he set up several mints over his empire. The style of one piece is very similar to that of later pieces struck by the Rajas of Jaintiapur, which suggests Jaintiapur as the mint for this variety, but no other varieties have been assigned to specific mints.

After the death of Sukladhvaja, who was a great general, the military strength of the kingdom waned. Nara Narayan quarrelled with Sukladhvaja's son Raghu Deva, and the latter set himself up as ruler of the eastern part of the kingdom in 1581, initially under the suzerainty of his uncle, but after Nara Narayan's death, as full independent ruler.

Nara Narayan's son, Lakshmi Narayan inherited the western part of the kingdom, but no attempt was made to consolidate the conquests made by his father, and Kachar, Tripura and other states reverted to their former fully independent state. Lakshmi Narayan was a weak, peace loving king who preferred to declare himself a vassal of the Mughal Emperor in 1596, rather than make any attempt to preserve his independence. In accepting any attempt to preserve his independence. In accepting Mughal suzerainty, he gravely offended his subjects, who rose in revolt. The Mughals assisted Lakshmi Narayan quell the rebellion, and in 1603 a treaty was signed under which Lakshmi Narayan agreed never again to strike full rupees and to abandon certain other royal prerogatives. The Eastern Kingdom under Raghu Deva and his son Parikshit refused to bow to Mughal domination in the same way, and in 1612 the Mughals invaded and destroyed their kingdom.

After Lakshmi Narayan's death in 1627, the new ruler Vira Narayan exhibited a certain degree of independence by striking full rupees and retaking the former Eastern Cooch Behar Kingdom from the Mughals. By this time, however, a powerful leader had emerged in Bhutan, and trade was disrupted by wars between Bhutan and Tibet, causing a reduction in the number of coins struck.

The Mughals soon recaptured the eastern territories, but the next ruler, Prana Narayan, was able to reopen trade links with Tibet through Bhutan. In 1661 Prana Narayan was expelled from his capital by the Mughal governor of Bengal, Mir Jumia, and sought refuge in Bhutan. At this time, Mir Jumia struck coins in Cooch Behar in the name of the Mughal Emperor Aurangzeb, but while Mir Jumia was stuck in Assam during the monsoon of 1663, Prana Narayan managed to regain control of his kingdom paying tribute to the Mughal Emperor.

For the next century Cooch Behar was relatively peaceful until there was a dispute over the succession in 1772. After a confusing period during which the Bhutanese installed their own nominated ruler and captured Dhairyendra Narandra, the Chief Minister appealed to the British for assistance. With an eye on the potentially lucrative Tibetan trade, which had increased somewhat in volume since Prithvi Narayan's rise to power in Nepal, the British agreed to support Darendra Narayan, so long as British suzerainty was acknowledged.

Bhutanese copies: Until the 1780's the Bhutanese used to periodically send surplus silver to the mint in Cooch Behar to strike into coin for local use, as Cooch Behar coins circulated widely in Bhutan. After the Cooch Behar mint was closed in 1788 the Bhutanese established their own mints, striking copies of the 1/2 rupees, initially of fine silver with slight differences in design from the original Cooch Behar coins, but later the silver content reduced until they were of pure copper or brass. For these issues see Bhutan listing.

RULERS

Harendra Narayan, CB273-329/SE1705-61/1783-1839AD

Shivendra Narayan, CB329-337/SE1761-1769/1839-1847AD
Narendra Narayan, CB337-353/SE1769-1785/1847-1863AD
Nripendra Narayan, CB353-401/SE1785-1833/1863-1911AD

DATING

The coins are dated in either the Saka era (Saka yr. + 78 = AD year) or the Cooch Behar era (CB yr. + 1510 = AD year) calculated from the year of the founding of the kingdom by Chandan in 1511AD.

Some coins have dates in both eras, but as the Saka always refers back to the accession year, and the Cooch Behar year seems to show the actual date of striking, the two years seems to show the actual date of striking, the two years do not necessarily correspond to the same AD year.

Unfortunately the dies for the half rupees were usually rather broader than the flans, so the year is only rarely visible.

Darendra Narayan // Narendra Narayan
SE1695-1761 / 1773-1839AD

HAMMERED COINAGE
Presentation Issues

KM# 141 1/2 RUPEE
4.7000 g., Silver **Note:** "Rendra" center left on obverse; ruler names cannot be differentiated.

Date	Mintage	Good	VG	F	VF	XF
ND(1773-1839)	—	2.00	5.00	8.00	11.00	16.50

Shivendra Narayan
SE1761-1769 / 1839-1847AD

HAMMERED COINAGE
Presentation Issues

KM# 151 NAZARANA 1/2 RUPEE
4.7000 g., Silver

Date	Mintage	Good	VG	F	VF	XF
ND(1839-47)	—	11.00	23.50	37.50	55.00	80.00

KM# 155 NAZARANA MOHUR
9.4000 g., Gold, 21 mm. **Note:** Similar to Nazarana 1/2 Rupee, KM#151.

Date	Mintage	Good	VG	F	VF	XF
ND39 (1839-47)	—	—	500	750	1,500	2,500

Narendra Narayan
SE1769-1785 / 1847-1863AD

HAMMERED COINAGE
Presentation Issues

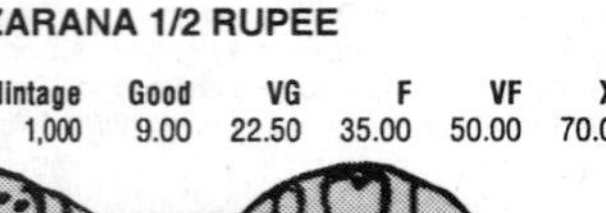

KM# 165 NAZARANA 1/2 RUPEE
4.7000 g., Silver

Date	Mintage	Good	VG	F	VF	XF
ND(1847-63)	1,000	9.00	22.50	35.00	50.00	70.00

KM# 170 NAZARANA MOHUR
9.4000 g., Gold, 21 mm. **Note:** Similar to Nazarana 1/2 Rupee, KM#165.

Date	Mintage	Good	VG	F	VF	XF
ND(1847-63)	—	—	350	600	1,200	2,000

Nripendra Narayan
SE1785-1833 / 1863-1911AD

HAMMERED COINAGE
Presentation Issues

KM# 180 NAZARANA 1/2 RUPEE
4.3000 g., Silver

Date	Mintage	Good	VG	F	VF	XF
CB354 (1864)	—	—	14.00	35.00	60.00	85.00

KM# 185 NAZARANA MOHUR
9.4000 g., Gold, 21 mm.

Date	Mintage	Good	VG	F	VF	XF
CB354 (1864)	—	—	—	300	500	1,200

DATIA

State located in north-central India, governed by Maharajas.

Datia was founded in 1735 by Bhagwan Das, son of Narsingh Dev of the Orchha royal house. In 1804 the State concluded its first treaty with the East India Company and thereafter came under British protection and control.

RULERS
Parachat, AH1217-1255/1802-1839AD
Vijaya Bahadur, AH1255-1274/1839-1857AD
Bhawani Singh, AH1274-1325/1857-1907AD

MINT

Dalipnagar

Gaja Shahi Series
Struck for more than 100 years, with the AH date on the obverse and the regnal year on the reverse bearing little relationship to each other. These are close copies of Orchha C#24-32 and can only be distinguished by the symbols, which are always different from those of Orchha, except for the Gaja (mace):

Gaja always on reverse

On obverse (Datia Mint Symbol)

On reverse

HAMMERED COINAGE
Gaja Shahi Series

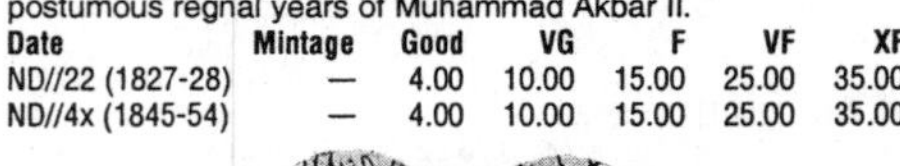

C# 35 1/8 RUPEE
Silver **Note:** Weight varies 1.34-1.45 grams. Regular and postumous regnal years of Muhammad Akbar II.

Date	Mintage	Good	VG	F	VF	XF
ND//22 (1827-28)	—	4.00	10.00	15.00	25.00	35.00
ND//4x (1845-54)	—	4.00	10.00	15.00	25.00	35.00

C# 36 1/4 RUPEE
Silver **Note:** Weight varies 2.68-2.90 grams.

Date	Mintage	Good	VG	F	VF	XF
AH1317//23	—	4.00	10.00	15.00	25.00	35.00
ND//36 (1900-01)	—	4.00	10.00	15.00	25.00	35.00

C# 37 1/2 RUPEE
Silver **Note:** Weight varies 5.35-5.80 grams.

Date	Mintage	VG	F	VF	XF
AH1311//19	—	5.00	12.50	20.00	30.00	45.00
ND//23 (1897-98)	—	5.00	12.50	20.00	30.00	45.00
ND//29 (1895-96)	—	5.00	12.50	20.00	30.00	45.00
ND//33 (1896-97)	—	5.00	12.50	20.00	30.00	45.00
ND//39 (1897)	—	5.00	12.50	20.00	30.00	45.00
AH1316//24	—	5.00	12.50	20.00	30.00	45.00
AH1317//25	—	5.00	12.50	20.00	30.00	45.00

C# 38 RUPEE
Silver **Note:** Weight varies 10.70-11.60 grams.

Date	Mintage	Good	VG	F	VF	XF
AH1221//43	—	2.00	5.00	8.00	12.00	20.00
AH1233//24	—	2.00	5.00	8.00	12.00	20.00
AH1233//28	—	2.00	5.00	8.00	12.00	20.00
AH1235//14	—	2.00	5.00	8.00	12.00	20.00
AH1240//19	—	2.00	5.00	8.00	12.00	20.00
AH1249//28	—	2.00	5.00	8.00	12.00	20.00
AH1250//28	—	2.00	5.00	8.00	12.00	20.00
AH1257//48	—	2.00	5.00	8.00	12.00	20.00
AH1258//38	—	2.00	5.00	8.00	12.00	20.00
AH1262//29	—	2.00	5.00	8.00	12.00	20.00
AH1270//36	—	2.00	5.00	8.00	12.00	20.00
AH1271//37	—	2.00	5.00	8.00	12.00	20.00
AH1272//38	—	2.00	5.00	8.00	12.00	20.00
AH1273//39	—	2.00	5.00	8.00	12.00	20.00
AH1273//42	—	2.00	5.00	8.00	12.00	20.00
AH1274//40	—	2.00	5.00	8.00	12.00	20.00
AH1274//41	—	2.00	5.00	8.00	12.00	20.00
AH1274//44	—	2.00	5.00	8.00	12.00	20.00
AH1275//41	—	2.00	5.00	8.00	12.00	20.00
AH1277//44	—	2.00	5.00	8.00	12.00	20.00
AH1278//45	—	2.00	5.00	8.00	12.00	20.00
AH1281//48	—	2.00	5.00	8.00	12.00	20.00
AH1282//46	—	2.00	5.00	8.00	12.00	20.00
AH1286//46	—	2.00	5.00	8.00	12.00	20.00
AH1287//46	—	2.00	5.00	8.00	12.00	20.00
AH1311//19	—	2.00	5.00	8.00	12.00	20.00
AH1312//24	—	2.00	5.00	8.00	12.00	20.00
AH1312//25	—	2.00	5.00	8.00	12.00	20.00
AH1312//29	—	2.00	5.00	8.00	12.00	20.00
AH1312//30	—	2.00	5.00	8.00	12.00	20.00
AH1313//24	—	2.00	5.00	8.00	12.00	20.00
AH1314//24	—	2.00	5.00	8.00	12.00	20.00
AH1314//40	—	2.00	5.00	8.00	12.00	20.00
AH1315//23	—	2.00	5.00	8.00	12.00	20.00
AH133x//27 (sic)	—	2.00	5.00	8.00	12.00	20.00
ND//35 (1898)	—	2.00	5.00	8.00	12.00	20.00

C# 45 RUPEE
Silver **Obv. Inscription:** "Muhammad Akbar II" **Note:** Weight varies 10.70-11.60 grams.

Date	Mintage	Good	VG	F	VF	XF
AH1270//33	—	—	15.00	25.00	35.00	50.00

Vijaha Bahadur
AH1255-1274 / 1839-1857AD

HAMMERED COINAGE
Gaja Shahi Series

KM# 50 NAZARANA 5 RUPEE
53.9200 g., Silver, 42 mm. **Obverse:** 6-line Sanskrit inscription with titles of maharaja **Reverse:** 6-line Sanskrit inscription with

date in chronogram **Rev. Inscription:** Friend of the Company **Mint:** Dalipnagar **Note:** The company referred to in inscription is the East India Co.

Date	Mintage	VG	F	VF	XF	Unc
VS1907 1 known	—	—	—	—	—	—

Bhawani Singh
AH1274-1325 / 1857-1907AD

HAMMERED COINAGE
Gaja Shahi Series

C# 22 1/2 PAISA
6.0000 g., Copper **Note:** Weight varies 6.00-6.50 grams. Postumous regal years of Muhammad Akbar II.

Date	Mintage	Good	VG	F	VF	XF
AH1233	—	3.50	5.00	8.00	15.00	—
ND//4x (1830-67)	—	2.50	3.50	5.00	7.50	—

C# 23 PAISA
Copper **Note:** Round or somewhat square shape, weight varies 12 - 13 grams. Regular and postumous regnal years of Muhammad Akbar II.

Date	Mintage	Good	VG	F	VF	XF
AH1246//24 (sic)	—	2.50	5.00	8.00	12.00	18.00
AH1246	—	2.50	5.00	8.00	12.00	18.00
AH1248	—	2.50	5.00	8.00	12.00	18.00
AH1258	—	2.50	5.00	8.00	12.00	18.00
ND//39 (1844-45)	—	2.50	5.00	8.00	12.00	18.00
ND//40 (1845)	—	2.50	5.00	8.00	12.00	18.00
AH1274//45 (sic)	—	2.50	5.00	8.00	12.00	18.00
AH1275//41	—	2.50	5.00	8.00	12.00	18.00
AH1278//45	—	2.50	5.00	8.00	12.00	18.00
AH1282//4x	—	2.50	5.00	8.00	12.00	18.00
AH1283	—	2.50	5.00	8.00	12.00	18.00
AH1320 /46 (sic)	—	2.50	5.00	8.00	12.00	18.00

DEWAS - JUNIOR BRANCH

A Maratha state located in west-central India. The raja, the brother of the raja of Dewas Senior Branch had a palace in Dewas City. They descended from two brothers, Tukoji and Jiwaji who were given Dewas City in 1726 by Peshwa Baji Rao as a reward for army services.

Largely due to its geographical location Dewas suffered much at the hands of the armies of Holkar and Sindhia,and from Pindari incursions. In 1818 the State came under British protection.

LOCAL RULERS
Narayan Rao, 1864-1892

Narayan Rao

MILLED COINAGE
Regal Style

KM# 1 1/12 ANNA
Copper **Obverse:** Crowned but of Victoria left

Date	Mintage	Good	VG	F	VF	XF
1888	112,000	—	4.00	10.00	20.00	35.00
1888 Proof	—	Value: 165				

KM# 3 1/4 ANNA
Copper **Obverse:** Crowned bust of Victoria left

Date	Mintage	Good	VG	F	VF	XF
1888	484,000	—	3.50	9.00	18.00	30.00
1888 Proof	—	Value: 165				

KM# 3a 1/4 ANNA
Silver **Obverse:** Crowned bust of Victoria left

Date	Mintage	Good	VG	F	VF	XF
1888 Proof, restrike	—	Value: 185				

DEWAS - SENIOR BRANCH

A Maratha state located in west-central India. The raja, the brother of the raja of Dewas Senior Branch had a palace in Dewas City. They descended from two brothers, Tukoji and Jiwaji who were given Dewas City in 1726 by Peshwa Baji Rao as a reward for army services.

Largely due to its geographical location Dewas suffered much at the hands of the armies of Holkar and Sindhia,and from Pindari incursions. In 1818 the State came under British protection.

LOCAL RULERS
Krishnaji Rao, 1860-1899AD
Vikrama Simha Rao, 1937-1948AD

Narayan Rao

HAMMERED COINAGE

KM# 10 PAISA
Copper **Mint:** Allote **Note:** Weight varies 10.50-12.77 grams; varieties exist; struck at the Allote Mint.

Date	Mintage	Good	VG	F	VF	XF
ND(c.1850-1904)	—	4.50	7.50	12.50	20.00	—

MILLED COINAGE
Regal Style

KM# 11 1/12 ANNA
Copper **Obverse:** Crowned bust of Victoria left **Mint:** Allote

Date	Mintage	Good	VG	F	VF	XF
1888	112,000	—	2.50	6.00	12.00	22.50
1888 Proof	—	Value: 135				

KM# 11a 1/12 ANNA
Silver **Obverse:** Crowned bust of Victoria left **Mint:** Allote

Date	Mintage	Good	VG	F	VF	XF
1888 Proof, restrike	—	Value: 135				

KM# 12 1/4 ANNA
Copper **Obverse:** Crowned bust of Victoria left **Mint:** Allote

Date	Mintage	Good	VG	F	VF	XF
1888	484,000	—	3.00	7.50	15.00	25.00
1888 Proof	—	Value: 160				

DHAR

The territory in central India in which Dhar was located had been controlled by the Paramara clan of Rajputs from the 9th century to the 13th century, after which it passed into Muslim hands. The modern Princely State of Dhar originated in the first half of the 18th century when the Maratha Peshwa, Baji Rao, handed over the region as a fief-dom to Anand Rao Ponwar. He was of the same stock as the rulers of Dewas and a descendant of the original Paramara Rajputs. Sometimes in conflict with Holkar, sometimes with Sindhia, in 1819 Dhar came under British protection. No silver or gold coinage was ever struck at Dhar. In 1895 the British silver rupee was adopted.

LOCAL RULERS
Jaswant Rao, AH1250-1274/1834-1857AD
Anand Rao III, AH1276-1316/1860-1898AD

Jaswant Rao
AH1250-1274 / 1834-1857AD

HAMMERED COINAGE

KM# 2 PAISA
Copper

Date	Mintage	Good	VG	F	VF	XF
ND(c.1840s)	—	2.50	4.00	6.50	12.50	—

KM# 1 PAISA
Copper **Obverse:** Banners

Date	Mintage	Good	VG	F	VF	XF
AH1266	—	2.50	4.00	6.50	12.50	—

Anand Rao III
AH1276-1316 / 1860-1898AD

HAMMERED COINAGE

KM# 5 1/2 PAISA
Copper, 16 mm. **Obverse:** Hanuman with banners

Date	Mintage	Good	VG	F	VF	XF
AH1289	—	3.00	5.00	10.00	20.00	—

KM# 6 PAISA
Copper **Obverse:** Hanuman with banners **Note:** Weight varies 7.19-7.52 grams.

Date	Mintage	Good	VG	F	VF	XF
AH1289	—	3.00	5.00	8.50	17.50	—

MILLED COINAGE
Regal Style

KM# 12 1/2 PICE
Copper **Obverse:** Crowned bust of Victoria left

Date	Mintage	Good	VG	F	VF	XF
1887	—	—	0.75	2.00	5.00	12.50
1887 Proof	—	Value: 175				

KM# 12a 1/2 PICE
Silver **Obverse:** Crowned bust of Victoria left

Date	Mintage	Good	VG	F	VF	XF
1887 Proof, restrike	—	Value: 200				

KM# 12b 1/2 PICE
Gold **Obverse:** Crowned bust of Victoria left

Date	Mintage	Good	VG	F	VF	XF
1887 Proof, restrike	—	Value: 2,200				

KM# 11 1/12 ANNA
Copper, 17.78mm mm. **Obverse:** Crowned bust of Victoria right

Date	Mintage	Good	VG	F	VF	XF
1887	—	—	0.50	1.35	3.50	10.00
1887 Proof	—	Value: 165				

KM# 11a 1/12 ANNA
Silver **Obverse:** Crowned bust of Victoria left

Date	Mintage	Good	VG	F	VF	XF
1887 Proof, restrike	—	Value: 185				

KM# 11b 1/12 ANNA
Gold **Obverse:** Crowned bust of Victoria left

Date	Mintage	Good	VG	F	VF	XF
1887 Proof, restrike	—	Value: 1,500				

KM# 13 1/4 ANNA
Copper, 25.40mm mm.

Date	Mintage	Good	VG	F	VF	XF
1887	—	—	—	3.00	7.50	17.50
1887 Proof	—	Value: 200				

KM# 13a 1/4 ANNA
Silver

Date	Mintage	Good	VG	F	VF	XF
1887 Proof, restrike	—	Value: 225				

KM# 13b 1/4 ANNA
Gold

Date	Mintage	Good	VG	F	VF	XF
1887 Proof, restrike	—	Value: 2,600				

DHOLPUR

State located in Rajputana, northwest India.

Dholpur had a varied and turbulent history. From the 8th until the 12th centuries it was ruled by Tonwar Rajputs. Early in the 16th century the entire region came under the Mughals. It was included by Akbar in Agra province. With Mughal decline after 1707, Dholpur experienced many masters until, in 1782, it fell into the hands of Sindhia. In 1803 the territory was captured by the British and in 1805 it was returned to the ranas of Gohad, Bamraolia Jats, from whom it had earlier been wrested by Sindhia. The ranas of Gohad opened the mint which operated until 1857.

RULER
Kirat Singh,
AH1203-1221/1788-1806AD, in Gohad

MINTS

دهولپور دهولپور

Dholpur

Mint marks:

On obverse:

On reverse: Type 1 or Type 2

Gohad

Mint marks:

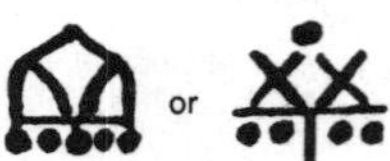

On obverse

On reverse

HAMMERED COINAGE

C# 5.1 RUPEE
11.0000 g., Silver **Obv. Inscription:** "Shah Alam II" **Reverse:** Pistol **Note:** Struck at Gohad Mint.

Date	Mintage	Good	VG	F	VF	XF
AH1218//46	—	10.00	25.00	40.00	60.00	85.00
AH1219//47	—	10.00	25.00	40.00	60.00	85.00
AH1221	—	8.00	20.00	35.00	55.00	80.00

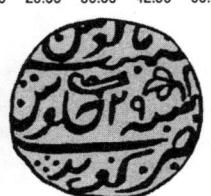

C# 12.1 RUPEE
11.0000 g., Silver **Obverse:** Parasol and inscription **Obv. Inscription:** "Muhammad Akbar II" **Reverse:** Pistol **Mint:** Dholpur **Note:** Struck at Dholpur Mint.

Date	Mintage	Good	VG	F	VF	XF
AH1225//4	—	15.00	35.00	50.00	70.00	100

C# 12.2 RUPEE
11.0000 g., Silver **Obverse:** Parasol and inscription **Reverse:** Pistol upside down **Mint:** Dholpur **Note:** Struck at Dholpur Mint.

Date	Mintage	Good	VG	F	VF	XF
AH1226//5	—	15.00	35.00	50.00	70.00	100
AH1228	—	7.00	17.50	25.00	35.00	50.00
AH1228//17 (sic)	—	7.00	17.50	25.00	35.00	50.00
ND//19	—	7.00	17.50	25.00	35.00	50.00
ND//21	—	7.00	17.50	25.00	35.00	50.00
AH1245//24	—	8.00	20.00	30.00	42.50	60.00
AH1251//30	—	8.00	20.00	30.00	42.50	60.00

C# 12a.1 RUPEE
11.0000 g., Silver **Obv. Inscription:** "Muhammad Akbar II" **Reverse:** Pistol upside down and leaf **Note:** Struck at Gohad Mint.

Date	Mintage	VG	F	VF	XF	Unc
AH1247//26 (1831)	—	25.00	40.00	60.00	85.00	—
AH1249//28 (1833)	—	25.00	40.00	60.00	85.00	—
AH1250//29 (1834)	—	25.00	40.00	60.00	85.00	—
AH1251//30 (1835)	—	25.00	40.00	60.00	85.00	—

C# 12a.2 RUPEE
Silver **Obv. Inscription:** "Muhammad Akbar II" **Reverse:** Pistol upside down and cross **Note:** Struck at Gohad Mint. 10.90-11.10 grams.

Date	Mintage	Good	VG	F	VF	XF
AH1251//30	—	10.00	25.00	40.00	60.00	85.00

C# 12c RUPEE
Silver **Obv. Inscription:** "Muhammad Akbar II" **Reverse:** Pistol **Note:** Struck at Gohad Mint.

Date	Mintage	Good	VG	F	VF	XF
AH1252//31	—	10.00	25.00	40.00	60.00	85.00

Note: Actually struck in AH1274/1857AD

C# 12b.2 NAZARANA RUPEE
Silver **Obv. Inscription:** "Muhammad Akbar II" **Reverse:** Pistol and leaf **Note:** Struck at Gohad Mint. 10.90-11.10 grams.

Date	Mintage	Good	VG	F	VF	XF
AH1252//30 (sic)	—	—	200	350	500	700

C# 15 MOHUR
10.7000 g., Gold **Obv. Inscription:** "Muhammad Akbar II" **Reverse:** Pistol **Note:** Struck at Gohad Mint.

Date	Mintage	Good	VG	F	VF	XF
AH1252//31 Rare	—	—	—	—	—	—

Note: Actually struck in AH1274/1857 AD

DUNGARPUR

A district in northwest India which became part of Rajasthan in 1948.

The maharawals of Dungarpur were descended from the Mewar chieftains of the 12th century. In 1527 the upper Mahi basin was bifurcated to form the Princely States of Dungarpur and Banswara. Thereafter Dungarpur came successively under Mughal and Maratha control until in 1818 it came under British protection.

RULERS
Udai Singh, VS1909-1955/1852-1898AD
Bijey Singh, VS1955-1975/1898-1918AD

INSCRIPTION:

सरकर डुंगरपुर

Sarkar Dungarpur

Udai Singh
VS1909-1955 / 1852-1898AD
HAMMERED COINAGE

KM# 1 1/4 PAISA
2.5000 g., Copper **Obv. Inscription:** Sarkar/Dungarpur **Reverse:** Sword and "jhar" to left

Date	Mintage	Good	VG	F	VF	XF
VS1916	—	12.50	25.00	40.00	60.00	—

KM# 4 1/2 PAISA
5.0000 g., Copper **Obv. Inscription:** Sarkar/Dungarpur **Reverse:** Sword and "jhar" to left

Date	Mintage	Good	VG	F	VF	XF
VS1916	—	8.50	16.50	27.50	40.00	—

KM# 2 PAISA
Copper **Obv. Inscription:** Sarkar/Dungarpur **Reverse:** Sword and "jhar" to **Note:** Weight varies 9.50-11.00 grams.

Date	Mintage	Good	VG	F	VF	XF
VS1916	—	4.50	7.50	12.50	20.00	—

KM# 3 PAISA
Copper **Obv. Inscription:** Sarkar/Dungarpur **Reverse:** Sword and "jhar" to **Note:** Weight varies 9.50-11.00 grams.

Date	Mintage	Good	VG	F	VF	XF
VS1916	—	4.50	7.50	12.50	20.00	—

KM# 6 MOHUR
11.0000 g., Gold **Obverse:** Sword and "jhar" to right **Rev. Inscription:** "Rajha Dungarpur" **Edge:** plain

Date	Mintage	Good	VG	F	VF	XF
VS1925 (1868)	—	—	—	—	—	850

KM# 5 NAZARANA MOHUR
11.0000 g., Gold **Obv. Inscription:** Sarkar/Dungarpur **Reverse:** Sword and "jhar" to right

Date	Mintage	Good	VG	F	VF	XF
VS1916 Rare	—	—	—	—	—	—

GARHWAL

Garhwal was a rugged tract embracing a number of peaks over twenty-three thousand feet in north India. The state dated from the 14th century when a number of local chieftains came under the sway of Ajai Pal. From that time onward his descendants ruled over this Himalayan kingdom until 1803, when the Gurkhas invaded both Garhwal and Kumaon. Shortly afterwards, in the Nepal War of 1814-1816, these States fell under British control and the State was then partially restored to its original ruler.

The Gurkhas captured Almora, the principal town of Kumaon, in 1790 and went on to seize Garhwal and Sirmur in 1803. From then until their definitive defeat at the hands of the East India Company, the Gurkhas issued coins from the Srinagar (Garhwal), Almora (Kumaon) and Nahan (Sirmur) mints.

MINT

Srinagar

KINGDOM

Sudarshan Shah

VS1872-1906 / 1815-1859AD

HAMMERED COINAGE

KM# A1 1/2 MOHUR
5.3500 g., Gold **Obverse:** Urdu legend on each side **Reverse:** Urdu legend on each side

Date	Mintage	Good	VG	F	VF	XF
VS1872	—	—	—	—	900	1,800

KM# A2 MOHUR
10.7000 g., Gold **Obverse:** Inscription **Reverse:** Urdu

Date	Mintage	Good	VG	F	VF	XF
VS1872	—	—	—	—	1,350	2,500

TOKEN COINAGE

KM# Tn1 RUPEE
Bronze **Obv. Legend:** F. WILSON, HURSIL

Date	Mintage	Good	VG	F	VF	XF
ND Rare	—	—	—	—	—	—

GWALIOR

Sindhia

State located in central India. Capital originally was Ujjain (= Daru-l-fath), but was later transferred to Gwalior in 1810. The Gwalior ruling family, the Sindhias, were descendants of the Maratha chief Ranoji Sindhia (d.1750). His youngest son, Mahadji Sindhia (d.1794) was anxious to establish his independence from the overlordship of the Peshwas of Poona. Unable to achieve this alone, it was the Peshwa's crushing defeat by Ahmad Shah Durrani at Panipat in 1761, which helped realize his ambitions. Largely in the interests of sustaining this autonomy, but partly as a result of a defeat at East India Company hands in 1781, Mahadji concluded an alliance with the British in 1782. In 1785, he reinstalled the fallen Mughal Emperor, Shah Alam, on the throne at Dehli. Very early in the 19th century, Gwalior's relationship with the British began to deteriorate, a situation which culminated in the Anglo-Maratha War of 1803. Gwalior's forces under Daulat Rao were defeated. In consequence, and by the terms of the peace treaty which followed, his territory was truncated. In 1818, Gwalior suffered a further loss of land at British hands. In the years that ensued, as the East India Company's possessions became transformed into empire and as the Pax Britannica swept across the subcontinent, the Sindhia family's relationship with their British overlords steadily improved.

RULERS

Daulat Rao, AH1209-1243/1794-1827AD
Baija Bai, Regent, (Widow of Daulat Rao) AH1243-1249/1827-1833AD
Jankoji Rao, AH1243-1259/1827-1843AD
Jayaji Rao, AH1259-1304/1843-1886AD
Madho Rao, VS1943-1982/1886-1925AD

MINTS

जयनगर

Bajranggarh
"Jaynagar"

Types of Jai Singh
with added mint marks:

Lotus Bow and arrow

بسوده

Basoda
In the name of Muhammad Akbar II

Mint marks:

In the name of Muhammad Akbar II
And Jankoji Rao

With additional mint mark:

عالم گیرپور

Bhilsa
"Alamgirpur"
In the name of Shah Alam II with
Additional initial of Jayaji Rao

NOTE: The bow & arrow and trident appear on nearly all coins of Bhilsa, Gwalior fort, and Lashkar Mints, and cannot be used to identify any one of them.

Broach

برهانپور

Burhanpur
In the name of Jayaji Rao

دار السرور

"Dar-as-Surar"
Abode of Happiness

Mint marks:

In the name of Alyjah Bahadur

Mint marks: To right of date

NOTE: Alyjah Bahadur was the hereditary title of the Sindhia rulers of Gwalior, and was used by all rulers of the dynasty.

Dohad

Mint mark:

روش نگر ساگر

Garhakota
"Ravishnagar Sagar"

Mint marks:

گواليار

Gwalior Fort
In the name of Muhammad Akbar II

Mint marks: On obverse On reverse

In the name of Muhammad Akar II
With additional initial of Jankoji Rao

Symbols:

On obverse

On rev. (points up or down)

In the name of Muhammad Shah

With initial *Ji*

Isagarh
In the name of Muhammad Akbar II

Mint marks:

In the name of Jankoji Rao

Mint marks: On reverse

Jawad

Jhansi
"Balwantnagar"
Regular Jhansi types (q.v.), Identifiable as Sindhia issues only by date, and by Persian *Ji* for *Jayaji*. Similar to coins struck by the Maratha Governors of the Peshwa until 1853AD.

Lashkar

NOTE: All the following coins of this mint are in the name of Shah Alam II, with initials and mint marks as shown.

With regnal years of Shah Alam II

Mint mark:

With regnal years of Muhammad Akbar II

Mint mark:

Struck by Jankoji Rao

Mint marks:

In name of Shah Alam II with initials
of Jayaji Rao

Copper coins have symbols

 or  on reverse

---

مند يسور

Mandasor

Narwar

Coins continued to be struck in the types of Narwar state with dates after AH1221/1806AD. The AH1230 date was retained for several years.

In the name of Shah Alam II

Katar 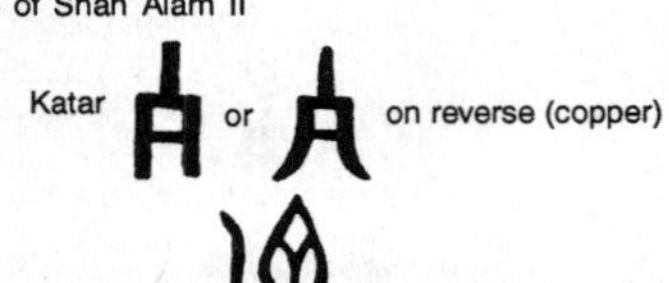 or on reverse (copper)

Bhilsa leaf on reverse (silver)

Mint marks:

राजोद

Rajod

دولت گره

Rathgarh
"Daulatgarh"

شادهوره

Shadorah
In the name of Muhammad Akbar II

KM#199 on rev.

Also has  on rev.

KM# 200 obv.

on rev.

Mint marks:

شيوپور

Sheopur
In the name of Muhammad Akbar II

Mint mark: On reverse

نروار

Sipri
"Narwar"

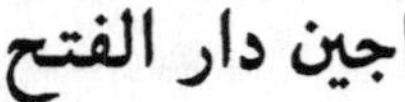

اجين دار الفتح

Ujjain, dar ul Fateh

On most issues

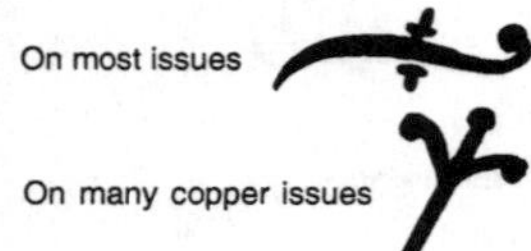

On many copper issues

Mint marks:

NOTE: None of the coins of Gwalior prior to the beginning of machine-struck coinage in 1889AD bears the name of the Sindhia (ruler of Gwalior), but beginning with the reign of Baija Bao, a Nagari letter is used to indicate the ruler under whom it was struck, as follows:

Letter		Ruler
श्री	*Sri*	Baija Bao
जे	*Jo*	Jankoji Rao
जी	*Ji*	Jayaji Rao
मा	*Ma*	Madho Rao

However, not all the coins bear the initial of the ruler, especially the copper.

The coinage of Gwalior is extremely complicated and not fully understood. Each mint, and there were probably more than twenty in all, maintained its own styles and types, and operated fully independently of every other mint. Hence it is most logical to list the issues of each mint together, rather than attempt to list the coins by reign or denomination. The mints are best identified by the presence of special symbols on the obverse or reverse of the coins, and those symbols are noted whenever possible. Types are listed with designation of reign only when the initial of the ruler appears on the coin; others are assigned a single number for the full duration of their issuance.

Most of the coins of Gwalior are undated, or issued overlong periods of time with frozen dates, in order to discourage the nefarious practice of devaluing coins of older dates (for example, one-year old coins might be devalued 1%, two-year olds 2%, and so forth). Many of the types were struck with frozen dates for several decades, and in many other cases, the dates remained frozen while the ruler's initial changed. The frozen dates may be either AH dates or regnal years, or both.

Regularly dated series often continued over long durations, such as the Ujjain rupees (C#259); the lists of such coins are probably very fragmentary, and many unlisted dates will be discovered. In general, unlisted dates are worth no more than listed dates of the same type.

HAMMERED COINAGE

KM# 144 1/2 PAISA
Copper **Obverse:** Trisul **Obv. Inscription:** "Shah Alam II" **Reverse:** Flywhisk, "Ji" for Jayaji and spear **Mint:** Lashkar **Note:** Weight varies 4.80-4.95 grams.

Date	Mintage	Good	VG	F	VF	XF
ND//23 (1865)	—	1.50	3.00	5.00	7.50	—

KM# 145 PAISA
Copper **Obverse:** Trisul **Obv. Inscription:** "Shah Alam II" **Reverse:** "Ji" for Jayaji **Mint:** Lashkar **Note:** Weight varies 9.60-9.90 grams.

Date	Mintage	Good	VG	F	VF	XF
ND//23 (1865)	—	1.00	1.75	3.00	5.00	—

KM# 146.1 2 PAISA
Copper **Obverse:** Trisul **Obv. Inscription:** "Shah Alam II" **Reverse:** "Ji" for Jayaji **Mint:** Lashkar **Note:** Weight varies 17.00-20.00 grams.

Date	Mintage	Good	VG	F	VF	XF
ND//23 (1865)	—	2.00	3.75	6.00	10.00	—

KM# 146.2 2 PAISA
Copper **Obv. Inscription:** "Shah Alam II" **Reverse:** Without "Ji" Jayaji **Mint:** Lashkar **Note:** Weight varies 17.00-20.00 grams.

Date	Mintage	Good	VG	F	VF	XF
ND//23 (1865)	—	3.00	5.00	8.00	12.50	—

KM# 147 1/16 RUPEE
Silver, 9 mm. **Obv. Inscription:** "Shah Alam II" **Reverse:** Bow and arrow points down, "Ji" for Jayaji **Mint:** Lashkar **Note:** Weight varies 0.67-0.72 grams.

Date	Mintage	Good	VG	F	VF	XF
ND//23 (1865)	—	1.00	2.50	4.50	6.50	10.00

KM# 116 1/8 RUPEE
Silver, 12 mm. **Obv. Inscription:** "Shah Alam II" **Mint:** Lashkar **Note:** Weight varies 1.34-1.45 grams.

Date	Mintage	Good	VG	F	VF	XF
ND(1759-1806)	—	2.35	6.00	9.00	13.50	20.00

KM# 148.2 1/8 RUPEE
Silver **Obv. Inscription:** "Shah Alam II" **Reverse:** ++ below "Ji" for Jayaji **Mint:** Lashkar **Note:** Weight varies 1.34-1.45 grams.

Date	Mintage	Good	VG	F	VF	XF
ND(1843-86)	—	1.50	4.00	6.00	9.00	14.00

KM# 148.1 1/8 RUPEE
Silver **Obv. Inscription:** "Shah Alam II" **Reverse:** Bow and arrow points down, "Ji" for Jayaji **Mint:** Lashkar **Note:** Weight varies 1.34-1.45 grams.

Date	Mintage	Good	VG	F	VF	XF
ND//23 (1865)	—	1.50	4.00	6.00	9.00	14.00
ND//25 (1867)	—	1.50	4.00	6.00	9.00	14.00

KM# 117 1/4 RUPEE
Silver **Obv. Inscription:** "Shah Alam II" **Mint:** Lashkar **Note:** Weight varies 2.68-2.90 grams.

Date	Mintage	Good	VG	F	VF	XF
ND(1759-1806)	—	2.35	6.00	9.00	13.50	20.00

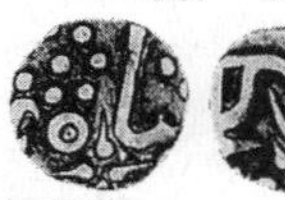

KM# 149 1/4 RUPEE
Silver **Obv. Inscription:** "Shah Alam II" **Reverse:** Bow and arrow points down, "Ji" for Jayaji **Mint:** Lashkar **Note:** Weight varies 2.68-2.90 grams.

Date	Mintage	Good	VG	F	VF	XF
ND//23 (1865)	—	1.50	4.00	6.00	9.00	14.00
ND//24 (1866)	—	1.50	4.00	6.00	9.00	14.00
ND//25 (1867)	—	1.50	4.00	6.00	9.00	14.00
ND//27 (1869)	—	1.50	4.00	6.00	9.00	14.00

KM# 118 1/2 RUPEE
Silver, 16 mm. **Obv. Inscription:** "Shah Alam II" **Mint:** Lashkar **Note:** Weight varies 5.35-5.80 grams.

Date	Mintage	Good	VG	F	VF	XF
ND(1759-1806)	—	2.75	7.00	11.00	16.50	25.00

KM# A34 1/2 RUPEE
Silver **Obv. Inscription:** "Shah Alam II" **Mint:** Broach **Note:** Weight varies 5.35-5.80 grams.

Date	Mintage	Good	VG	F	VF	XF
ND(1759-1806)	—	7.50	15.00	25.00	37.50	—

KM# A205 1/2 RUPEE
Silver **Obv. Inscription:** "Shah Alam II" **Mint:** Sipri **Note:** Weight varies 5.35-5.80 grams.

Date	Mintage	Good	VG	F	VF	XF
AH1106//47 (sic)	—	10.00	25.00	40.00	60.00	85.00

KM# 150 1/2 RUPEE
Silver **Obv. Inscription:** "Shah Alam II" **Reverse:** Bow and arrow points down, "Ji" for Jayaji **Mint:** Lashkar **Note:** Weight varies 5.35-5.80 grams.

Date	Mintage	Good	VG	F	VF	XF
ND//23 (1865)	—	2.00	5.00	7.00	10.00	15.00
ND//25 (1867)	—	2.00	5.00	7.00	10.00	15.00
ND//26 (1868)	—	2.00	5.00	7.00	10.00	15.00
ND//27 (1869)	—	2.00	5.00	7.00	10.00	15.00

KM# 151 1/2 RUPEE
Silver **Obv. Inscription:** "Shah Alam II" **Reverse:** Bow and arrow points up, "Ji" for Jayaji **Mint:** Lashkar **Note:** Weight varies 5.35-5.80 grams.

Date	Mintage	Good	VG	F	VF	XF
ND//2x (1865-71)	—	2.00	5.00	7.00	10.00	15.00

KM# 119 RUPEE
Silver **Obv. Inscription:** "Shah Alam II" **Mint:** Lashkar **Note:** Weight varies 10.70-11.60 grams.

Date	Mintage	Good	VG	F	VF	XF
ND(1759-1806)	—	4.00	10.00	15.00	21.50	30.00

KM# 57.2 RUPEE
Silver **Obv. Inscription:** "Shah Alam II" **Mint:** Gwalior Fort **Note:** Weight varies 10.70-11.60 grams.

Date	Mintage	Good	VG	F	VF	XF
AH1203//31	—	3.25	8.00	13.50	20.00	28.50
ND//43 (1801-02)	—	8.00	8.00	13.50	20.00	28.50
AH1216//44	—	3.25	8.00	13.50	20.00	28.50
AH1221//58	—	3.25	8.00	13.50	20.00	28.50

KM# 34 RUPEE
Silver **Obv. Inscription:** "Shah Alam II" **Mint:** Broach **Note:** Weight varies 10.70-11.60 grams.

Date	Mintage	Good	VG	F	VF	XF
ND//32 (1800-01)	—	2.00	5.00	10.00	17.50	25.00
ND//34 (1802-03)	—	2.00	5.00	10.00	17.50	25.00

KM# 205 RUPEE
Silver **Obv. Inscription:** "Shah Alam II" **Mint:** Sipri **Note:** Weight varies 10.70-11.60 grams.

Date	Mintage	Good	VG	F	VF	XF
AH1106//43 (sic)	—	2.75	7.00	14.00	24.00	35.00
AH1106//44 (sic)	—	2.75	7.00	14.00	24.00	35.00
AH1106//46 (sic)	—	2.75	7.00	14.00	24.00	35.00
AH1106//47 (sic)	—	2.75	7.00	14.00	24.00	35.00

KM# 206 RUPEE
Silver **Reverse:** Flower in outline **Mint:** Daulat Rao **Note:** Weight varies: 10.70-11.60 grams.

Date	Mintage	Good	VG	F	VF	XF
AH1106//47 (sic)	—	4.00	10.00	20.00	32.00	45.00

KM# 207 RUPEE
Silver **Reverse:** Solid flower **Mint:** Daulat Rao **Note:** Weight varies: 10.70-11.60 grams.

Date	Mintage	Good	VG	F	VF	XF
AH1106/47 (sic)	—	4.00	10.00	20.00	32.00	45.00

KM# 208 RUPEE
Silver **Mint:** Daulat Rao **Note:** Weight varies: 10.70-11.60 grams. With regnal years of Muhammad Akbar II, AH122-53/1806-37AD.

Date	Mintage	Good	VG	F	VF	XF
AH1106//9 (sic)	—	5.50	13.50	27.00	45.00	65.00

KM# 152 RUPEE
Silver **Obv. Inscription:** "Shah Alam II" **Reverse:** Bow and arrow points down, "Ji" for Jayaji **Mint:** Lashkar **Note:** Weight varies 10.70-11.60 grams.

Date	Mintage	Good	VG	F	VF	XF
ND//23 (1865)	—	2.35	6.00	9.00	13.50	20.00
ND//27 (1869)	—	2.35	6.00	9.00	13.50	20.00
ND//29 (1871)	—	2.35	6.00	9.00	13.50	20.00

KM# 153 RUPEE
Silver **Obv. Inscription:** "Shah Alam II" **Reverse:** Bow and arrow points up, "Ji" for Jayaji **Mint:** Lashkar **Note:** Weight varies 10.70-11.60 grams.

Date	Mintage	Good	VG	F	VF	XF
ND//2x (1865-71)	—	—	7.00	11.00	16.50	25.00

KM# 154 NAZARANA RUPEE
Silver **Obv. Inscription:** "Shah Alam II" **Reverse:** Bow and arrow points down, "Ji" for Jayaji, trisul **Mint:** Lashkar **Note:** Weight varies 10.70-11.60 grams.

Date	Mintage	Good	VG	F	VF	XF
ND//23 (1865)	—	—	150	275	400	575

KM# A155 1/5 MOHUR
2.2100 g., Gold **Obv. Inscription:** "Shah Alam II" **Reverse:** "Ji" for Jayaji **Mint:** Lashkar

Date	Mintage	Good	VG	F	VF	XF
ND(1843-86) Rare	—	—	—	—	—	—

KM# A59 MOHUR
Gold **Obv. Inscription:** "Shah Alam II" **Mint:** Gwalior Fort **Note:** Weight varies 10.70-11.40 grams.

Date	Mintage	Good	VG	F	VF	XF
AH1215//42	—	—	250	375	550	800

KM# 155 MOHUR
Gold **Obv. Inscription:** "Shah Alam II" **Reverse:** Bow and arrow points up, "Ji" for Jajaji **Mint:** Lashkar **Note:** Weight varies 10.70-11.40 grams.

Date	Mintage	Good	VG	F	VF	XF
AH1130//2 Frozen	—	—	250	325	500	800

Daulat Rao
AH1209-1243 / 1794-1827AD

HAMMERED COINAGE

KM# 184 1/2 PAISA
3.3700 g., Copper **Obv. Inscription:** "Shah Alam II" **Reverse:** Vertical katar **Mint:** Narwar **Note:** For previously listed earlier dates see Narwar.

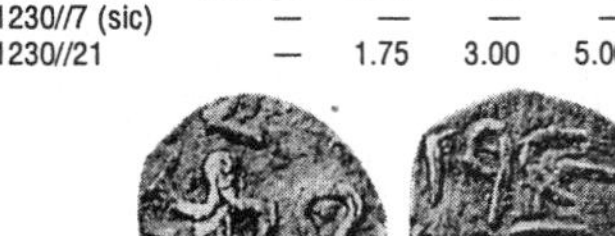

Date	Mintage	Good	VG	F	VF	XF
AH1230//7 (sic)	—	—	—	—	—	—
AH1230//21	—	1.75	3.00	5.00	8.00	—

KM# 191 1/2 PAISA
7.7100 g., Copper **Obverse:** Hanuman, lingam at right **Obv. Inscription:** "Shah Alam II" **Mint:** Rajod

Date	Mintage	Good	VG	F	VF	XF
VS1936	—	4.00	7.50	12.50	20.00	—

KM# 220 PAISA
Copper **Obv. Inscription:** "Shah Alam II" **Mint:** Ujjain

Date	Mintage	Good	VG	F	VF	XF
ND(1794-1827)	—	1.50	3.00	5.00	7.50	—

KM# 221 PAISA
Copper **Obv. Inscription:** "Shah Alam II" **Mint:** Ujjain **Note:** Square flan.

Date	Mintage	Good	VG	F	VF	XF
ND(1794-1827)	—	1.50	3.00	5.00	7.50	—

KM# 219 PAISA
Copper **Obv. Inscription:** "Shah Alam II" **Mint:** Ujjain **Note:** Weight varies 12.83-14.00 grams. With continued regnal years of Shah Alam II.

Date	Mintage	Good	VG	F	VF	XF
ND(1794-1827)	—	1.50	3.00	5.00	7.50	—

KM# 40.1 PAISA
18.1400 g., Copper **Obv. Inscription:** "Shah Alam II" **Mint:** Burhanpur **Note:** Square.

Date	Mintage	Good	VG	F	VF	XF
AH1218	—	2.50	4.00	6.50	10.00	—

KM# 222 PAISA
Copper **Obv. Inscription:** "Shah Alam II" **Mint:** Ujjain

Date	Mintage	Good	VG	F	VF	XF
AH1220	—	1.50	3.00	5.00	7.50	—

KM# 59 PAISA
Copper **Obv. Inscription:** "Muhammad Akbar II" **Mint:** Gwalior Fort

Date	Mintage	Good	VG	F	VF	XF
AH1224//3	—	1.00	1.65	2.50	4.50	—
AH122x//4	—	1.00	1.65	2.50	4.50	—
AH1232	—	1.00	1.65	2.50	4.50	—
AH1235//14	—	1.00	1.65	2.50	4.50	—
AH1236//15	—	1.00	1.65	2.50	4.50	—
AH1241	—	1.00	1.65	2.50	4.50	—

KM# 185 PAISA
Copper **Obv. Inscription:** "Shah Alam II" **Mint:** Narwar

Date	Mintage	Good	VG	F	VF	XF
AH1228//7 (sic)	—	2.00	3.50	5.00	7.50	—
AH1230//12 (sic)	—	2.00	3.50	5.00	7.50	—
AH1230//21	—	2.00	3.50	5.00	7.50	—

KM# 89 PAISA
Copper **Obverse:** Cannon right **Obv. Inscription:** "Muhammad Akbar II" **Reverse:** Snake **Mint:** Isagarh

Date	Mintage	Good	VG	F	VF	XF
ND//2x (1824-37)	—	11.50	17.50	27.50	40.00	—

KM# 64 PAISA
Copper **Obv. Inscription:** "Muhammad Akbar II" **Mint:** Gwalior Fort

Date	Mintage	Good	VG	F	VF	XF
AH1244//24	—	3.00	5.00	8.00	12.50	—
AH1245//25	—	3.00	5.00	8.00	12.50	—

KM# 192.1 PAISA
17.1000 g., Copper **Obverse:** Hanuman **Obv. Inscription:** "Shah Alam II" **Mint:** Rajod

Date	Mintage	Good	VG	F	VF	XF
VS1930	—	7.50	12.00	20.00	35.00	—

KM# 193 PAISA
Copper **Obverse:** Hanuman, flower above and at right **Obv. Inscription:** "Shah Alam II" **Reverse:** 9 of date in Gujarati **Mint:** Rajod

Date	Mintage	Good	VG	F	VF	XF
VS1930	—	7.50	12.00	20.00	35.00	—

KM# 192.2 PAISA
Copper **Obverse:** Hanuman **Obv. Inscription:** "Shah Alam II" **Reverse:** 9 of date in Sanskrit **Mint:** Rajod **Note:** Reduced weight, 11.50-12.30 grams.

Date	Mintage	Good	VG	F	VF	XF
VS1930	—	7.50	12.00	20.00	35.00	—

KM# 195 PAISA
Copper **Obverse:** Hanuman, lingam at right **Obv. Inscription:** "Shah Alam II" **Reverse:** 9 of date in Gujarati **Mint:** Rajod **Note:** Reduced weight, 11.50-12.30 grams.

Date	Mintage	Good	VG	F	VF	XF
VS1936	—	7.50	12.00	20.00	35.00	—

KM# 194 PAISA
Copper **Obverse:** Hanuman, lingam at right **Obv. Inscription:** "Shah Alam II" **Reverse:** 9 of date in sanskrit **Mint:** Rajod

Date	Mintage	Good	VG	F	VF	XF
VS1936	—	7.50	12.00	20.00	35.00	—

KM# 196 PAISA
Copper **Obverse:** Hanuman, cobra snake at right **Obv. Inscription:** "Shah Alam II" **Mint:** Rajod

Date	Mintage	Good	VG	F	VF	XF
VS1936	—	7.50	12.00	20.00	35.00	—
VS1940	—	7.50	12.00	20.00	35.00	—

KM# 186 1/16 RUPEE
Silver **Obv. Inscription:** "Shah Alam II" **Mint:** Narwar **Note:** Weight varies 0.67-0.72 grams.

Date	Mintage	Good	VG	F	VF	XF
AH1230	—	6.00	15.00	25.00	40.00	60.00

KM# A20 1/8 RUPEE
Silver **Obv. Inscription:** "Muhammad Akbar II" **Mint:** Bhilsa

Date	Mintage	Good	VG	F	VF	XF
ND//- (1794-1827)	—	10.00	25.00	40.00	60.00	85.00

KM# 187 1/8 RUPEE
Silver **Obv. Inscription:** "Shah Alam II" **Mint:** Narwar **Note:** Weight varies 1.34-1.45 grams.

Date	Mintage	Good	VG	F	VF	XF
AH1230	—	6.00	15.00	25.00	40.00	60.00

KM# A60 1/4 RUPEE
Silver **Obv. Inscription:** "Muhammad Akbar II" **Mint:** Gwalior Fort

Date	Mintage	Good	VG	F	VF	XF
AH1228	—	5.00	12.50	20.00	32.00	50.00

KM# 188 1/4 RUPEE
Silver **Obv. Inscription:** "Shah Alam II" **Mint:** Narwar **Note:** Weight varies 2.68-2.90 grams. For previously listed earlier date (AH1207) see Narwar.

Date	Mintage	Good	VG	F	VF	XF
AH1230//15 (sic)	—	7.00	12.00	20.00	30.00	45.00

KM# A223 1/4 RUPEE
Silver **Obverse:** AH date below **Obv. Inscription:** "Shah Alam II" **Mint:** Daulat Rao **Note:** Weight varies 2.67-2.90 grams.

Date	Mintage	Good	VG	F	VF	XF
ND//62 (1819-20)	—	2.00	5.00	7.00	10.00	15.00
ND//64 (1821-22)	—	5.00	7.00	10.00	15.00	—

KM# 20 1/4 RUPEE
Silver **Obv. Inscription:** "Muhammad Akbar II" **Mint:** Bhilsa **Note:** Weight varies 2.68-2.90 grams.

Date	Mintage	Good	VG	F	VF	XF
ND//16 (1821)	—	10.00	25.00	40.00	60.00	85.00

KM# A223 1/4 RUPEE
Silver **Obverse:** AH date below **Obv. Inscription:** "Shah Alam II" **Mint:** Daulat Rao **Note:** Weight varies 2.67-2.90 grams.

Date	Mintage	Good	VG	F	VF	XF
ND//62 (1819-20)	—	2.00	5.00	7.00	10.00	15.00
ND//64 (1821-22)	—	5.00	7.00	10.00	15.00	—

KM# 60 1/2 RUPEE
Silver **Obv. Inscription:** "Muhammad Akbar II" **Mint:** Gwalior Fort **Note:** Weight varies 5.35-5.80 grams. Similar to 1 Rupee, KM#61.

Date	Mintage	Good	VG	F	VF	XF
ND// (1806-37)	—	10.00	25.00	40.00	60.00	85.00

KM# 189 1/2 RUPEE
Silver **Obv. Inscription:** "Shah Alam II" **Mint:** Narwar **Note:** Weight varies 5.35-5.80 grams.

Date	Mintage	Good	VG	F	VF	XF
AH1230//12 (sic)	—	6.00	15.00	25.00	40.00	60.00
AH1230//21	—	6.00	15.00	25.00	40.00	60.00

KM# 21 1/2 RUPEE
Silver **Obv. Inscription:** "Muhammad Akbar II" **Mint:** Bhilsa **Note:** Weight varies 5.35-5.80 grams.

Date	Mintage	Good	VG	F	VF	XF
ND//15 (1820)	—	12.00	30.00	50.00	80.00	120

KM# B223 1/2 RUPEE
Silver **Obverse:** AH date below **Obv. Inscription:** "Shah Alam II" **Mint:** Daulat Rao **Note:** Weight varies 5.35-5.80 grams.

Date	Mintage	Good	VG	F	VF	XF
ND//64 (1821-22)	—	5.50	8.00	12.50	18.50	—

KM# B38 1/2 RUPEE
Silver, 17 mm. **Mint:** Burhanpur **Note:** Weight varies 5.35-5.70 grams.

Date	Mintage	Good	VG	F	VF	XF
AH1261	—	12.00	30.00	50.00	80.00	120
AH1274	—	12.00	30.00	50.00	80.00	120

KM# 44 RUPEE
Silver **Mint:** Burhanpur **Note:** Weight varies 10.70-11.60 grams.

Date	Mintage	Good	VG	F	VF	XF
AH1277	—	3.00	7.50	15.00	22.00	32.00
AH1259	—	3.00	7.50	15.00	22.00	32.00
AH1260	—	3.00	7.50	15.00	22.00	32.00
AH1261	—	3.00	7.50	15.00	22.00	32.00
AH1262	—	3.00	7.50	15.00	22.00	32.00
AH1266	—	3.00	7.50	15.00	22.00	32.00
AH1267	—	3.00	7.50	15.00	22.00	32.00
AH1268	—	3.00	7.50	15.00	22.00	32.00
AH1271	—	3.00	7.50	15.00	22.00	32.00
AH1272	—	3.00	7.50	15.00	22.00	32.00
AH1273	—	3.00	7.50	15.00	22.00	32.00
AH1274	—	3.00	7.50	15.00	22.00	32.00
AH1275	—	3.00	7.50	15.00	22.00	32.00
AH1276//3 (sic)	—	3.00	7.50	15.00	22.00	32.00

KM# 86 RUPEE
Silver **Obverse:** Cannon left **Obv. Inscription:** "Muhammad Akbar II" **Reverse:** Bhilsa leaf and battle axe **Mint:** Isagarh

Date	Mintage	Good	VG	F	VF	XF
ND-//(1794-1827)	—	5.50	13.50	20.00	27.50	38.00

KM# 88 RUPEE
Silver **Obverse:** Cannon right and snake **Obv. Inscription:** "Muhammad Akbar II" **Reverse:** Bhilsa leaf and battle axe **Mint:** Isagarh

Date	Mintage	Good	VG	F	VF	XF
AH-//(1794-1827)	—	5.50	13.50	20.00	27.50	40.00

KM# 223 RUPEE
Silver **Obverse:** AH date below **Obv. Inscription:** "Shah Alam II" **Mint:** Ujjain **Note:** Weight varies 10.70-11.60 grams.

Date	Mintage	Good	VG	F	VF	XF
AH1215//42	—	2.00	5.00	7.00	10.00	15.00
AH1216//44	—	2.00	5.00	7.00	10.00	15.00

KM# A184 RUPEE
Silver **Obverse:** Titles and date **Obv. Inscription:** "Shah Alam II" **Reverse:** Mint and regnal year **Mint:** Narwar

Date	Mintage	Good	VG	F	VF	XF
AH1216//44	—	—	—	—	—	—
AH1216//45	—	—	—	—	—	—
AH1217//44	—	—	—	—	—	—
AH1217//45	—	—	—	—	—	—

KM# 38.2 RUPEE
Silver **Obv. Inscription:** "Shah Alam II" **Mint:** Burhanpur **Note:** Weight varies 10.70-11.60 grams.

Date	Mintage	Good	VG	F	VF	XF
AH1216//4x	—	2.35	6.00	12.00	20.00	30.00
AH1217//45	—	2.35	6.00	12.00	20.00	30.00
AH1218	—	2.35	6.00	12.00	20.00	30.00
AH1219//4x	—	2.35	6.00	12.00	20.00	30.00
AH1220	—	2.35	6.00	12.00	20.00	30.00
AH1221//40	—	2.35	6.00	12.00	20.00	30.00
AH1222	—	2.35	6.00	12.00	20.00	30.00
AH1223//4x	—	2.35	6.00	12.00	20.00	30.00
AH1224//4x	—	2.35	6.00	12.00	20.00	30.00
AH1225	—	2.35	6.00	12.00	20.00	30.00
AH1227	—	2.35	6.00	12.00	20.00	30.00
AH1229	—	2.35	6.00	12.00	20.00	30.00
AH1230	—	2.35	6.00	12.00	20.00	30.00
AH1231	—	2.35	6.00	12.00	20.00	30.00
AH1232	—	2.35	6.00	12.00	20.00	30.00
AH1233	—	2.35	6.00	12.00	20.00	30.00
AH1234//3x	—	2.35	6.00	12.00	20.00	30.00
AH1235//39	—	2.35	6.00	12.00	20.00	30.00
AH1237	—	2.35	6.00	12.00	20.00	30.00
AH1238	—	2.35	6.00	12.00	20.00	30.00
AH1239	—	2.35	6.00	12.00	20.00	30.00
AH1240	—	2.35	6.00	12.00	20.00	30.00
AH1242	—	2.35	6.00	12.00	20.00	30.00
AH1243	—	2.35	6.00	12.00	20.00	30.00

KM# 224 RUPEE
Silver **Obverse:** AH date below **Obv. Inscription:** "Shah Alam II" **Mint:** Daulat Rao **Note:** Weight varies 10.70-11.60 grams.

Date	Mintage	Good	VG	F	VF	XF
ND//45 (1803-04)	—	2.00	5.00	7.00	10.00	15.00
ND//46 (1804-05)	—	2.00	5.00	7.00	10.00	15.00
ND//48 (1806-07)	—	2.00	5.00	7.00	10.00	15.00
ND//51 (1809-10)	—	2.00	5.00	7.00	10.00	15.00
ND//52 (1810-11)	—	2.00	5.00	7.00	10.00	15.00
AH1225//53	—	2.00	5.00	7.00	10.00	15.00
ND//55 (1813)	—	2.00	5.00	7.00	10.00	15.00
AH122x//57	—	2.00	5.00	7.00	10.00	15.00
ND//58 (1815-16)	—	2.00	5.00	7.00	10.00	15.00
ND//59 (1816-17)	—	2.00	5.00	7.00	10.00	15.00
ND//60 (1817-18)	—	2.00	5.00	7.00	10.00	15.00
ND//61 (1818-19)	—	2.00	5.00	7.00	10.00	15.00
ND//62 (1819-20)	—	2.00	5.00	7.00	10.00	15.00
ND//63 (1820-21)	—	2.00	5.00	7.00	10.00	15.00
AH123x//64	—	2.00	5.00	7.00	10.00	15.00
ND//67 (1824-25)	—	2.00	5.00	7.00	10.00	15.00
ND//68 (1825-26)	—	2.00	5.00	7.00	10.00	15.00
ND//69 (1826-27)	—	2.00	5.00	7.00	10.00	15.00

KM# 61 RUPEE
Silver **Obv. Inscription:** "Muhammad Akbar II" **Mint:** Gwalior Fort **Note:** Weight varies 10.70-11.60 grams.

Date	Mintage	VG	F	VF	XF	Unc
AH1222//1 (1807)	—	9.00	18.00	28.00	40.00	—

KM# 197 RUPEE
Silver **Obverse:** Snake **Obv. Inscription:** "Muhammad Akbar II" **Mint:** Rathgarh **Note:** Weight varies 10.70-11.60 grams.

Date	Mintage	Good	VG	F	VF	XF
AH1221//1	—	15.00	35.00	60.00	100	145
AH12xx//3	—	15.00	35.00	60.00	100	145
AH12xx//4	—	15.00	35.00	60.00	100	145
AH12xx//6	—	15.00	35.00	60.00	100	145
AH12xx//7	—	15.00	35.00	60.00	100	145
AH1232//8 (sic)	—	15.00	35.00	60.00	100	145
AH12xx//13	—	15.00	35.00	60.00	100	145
AH123x//15	—	15.00	35.00	60.00	100	145
AH12xx//18	—	15.00	35.00	60.00	100	145
AH12xx//22	—	15.00	35.00	60.00	100	145

KM# 62 RUPEE
Silver **Obv. Inscription:** "Muhammad Akbar II" **Mint:** Gwalior Fort **Note:** Weight varies 10.70-11.60 grams.

Date	Mintage	Good	VG	F	VF	XF
AH1227//6	—	2.75	6.50	13.00	22.00	32.00
AH1228//7	—	2.75	6.50	13.00	22.00	32.00
AH1229//8	—	2.75	6.50	13.00	22.00	32.00
AH1230//9	—	2.75	6.50	13.00	22.00	32.00
AH1231//10	—	2.75	6.50	13.00	22.00	32.00
AH1231//11	—	2.75	6.50	13.00	22.00	32.00
AH1232//12	—	2.75	6.50	13.00	22.00	32.00
AH1233//13	—	2.75	6.50	13.00	22.00	32.00
AH1234//14	—	2.75	6.50	13.00	22.00	32.00
AH1235//15	—	2.75	6.50	13.00	22.00	32.00
AH1236//19	—	2.75	6.50	13.00	22.00	32.00
AH1239//19	—	2.75	6.50	13.00	22.00	32.00
AH1240//19	—	2.75	6.50	13.00	22.00	32.00
AH1241//19 (sic)	—	2.75	6.50	13.00	22.00	32.00

KM# 22 RUPEE
Silver **Obverse:** 3 left symbol **Obv. Inscription:** "Muhammad Akbar II" **Reverse:** Regnal year **Mint:** Bhilsa

Date	Mintage	Good	VG	F	VF	XF
ND//7 (1812-13)	—	3.50	8.50	17.00	28.00	40.00
ND//9 (1814-15)	—	3.50	8.50	17.00	28.00	40.00
ND//11 (1816-17)	—	3.50	8.50	17.00	28.00	40.00
ND//13 (1818-19)	—	3.50	8.50	17.00	28.00	40.00
ND//14 (1819-20)	—	3.50	8.50	17.00	28.00	40.00
ND//15 (1820-21)	—	3.50	8.50	17.00	28.00	40.00
ND//16 (1821-22)	—	3.50	8.50	17.00	28.00	40.00
ND//17 (1822-23)	—	3.50	8.50	17.00	28.00	40.00
ND//19 (1824-25)	—	3.50	8.50	17.00	28.00	40.00
ND//20 (1825-26)	—	3.50	8.50	17.00	28.00	40.00
ND//26 (1831-32)	—	3.50	8.50	17.00	28.00	40.00
ND//51 (1884-85)	—	3.50	8.50	17.00	28.00	40.00

KM# 190 RUPEE
Silver **Obv. Inscription:** "Shah Alam II" **Mint:** Narwar **Note:** Weight varies 10.70-11.60 grams.

Date	Mintage	Good	VG	F	VF	XF
AH1228//7 (sic)	—	3.00	7.50	12.50	18.50	27.50
AH1230//9 (sic)	—	3.00	7.50	12.50	18.50	27.50
AH1230//11 (sic)	—	3.00	7.50	12.50	18.50	27.50
AH1230//12 (sic)	—	3.00	7.50	12.50	18.50	27.50
AH1230//15 (sic)	—	3.00	7.50	12.50	18.50	27.50
AH1230//21	—	3.00	7.50	12.50	18.50	27.50
ND//35 (1828)	—	3.00	7.50	12.50	18.50	27.50

KM# 199 RUPEE
Silver **Obv. Inscription:** "Muhammad Akbar II" **Reverse:** Cannon left, mintname at bottom **Mint:** Shadorah **Note:** Weight varies 10.70-11.60 grams.

Date	Mintage	Good	VG	F	VF	XF
AH1228	—	35.00	85.00	125	200	300

KM# 200 RUPEE
Silver **Obverse:** Cannon right, mintname at top **Obv. Inscription:** "Muhammad Akbar II" **Mint:** Shadorah **Note:** Weight varies 10.70-11.60 grams.

Date	Mintage	Good	VG	F	VF	XF
ND(ca.1813)	—	35.00	85.00	125	200	300

KM# 85 RUPEE
Silver **Obv. Inscription:** "Muhammad Akbar II" **Reverse:** Cannon left **Mint:** Isagarh **Note:** Weight varies 10.70-11.60 grams.

Date	Mintage	Good	VG	F	VF	XF
AH122x//8	—	5.50	13.50	20.00	27.50	38.00
AH1230//10	—	5.50	13.50	20.00	27.50	38.00
AH1230//11 (sic)	—	5.50	13.50	20.00	27.50	38.00

KM# 87 RUPEE
Silver **Obverse:** Cannon right **Obv. Inscription:** "Muhammad Akbar II" **Reverse:** Bhilsa leaf, battle axe and snake **Mint:** Isagarh **Note:** Weight varies 10.70-11.60 grams.

Date	Mintage	Good	VG	F	VF	XF
AH1229//8	—	5.50	13.50	20.00	27.50	38.00
AH1230//10	—	5.50	13.50	20.00	27.50	38.00
AH1231//11	—	5.50	13.50	20.00	27.50	38.00
AH123x//15	—	5.50	13.50	20.00	27.50	38.00
AH1234//17 (sic)	—	5.50	13.50	20.00	27.50	38.00

KM# 201 RUPEE
Silver **Obv. Inscription:** "Muhammad Akbar II" **Reverse:** Cannon left **Mint:** Sheopur **Note:** Weight varies 10.70-11.60 grams.

Date	Mintage	Good	VG	F	VF	XF
AH1228//7	—	2.65	6.50	13.00	22.00	32.00
AH1228//8	—	2.65	6.50	13.00	22.00	32.00
AH1228//9 (sic)	—	2.65	6.50	13.00	22.00	32.00
AH1228//10	—	2.65	6.50	13.00	22.00	32.00
AH1228//11	—	2.65	6.50	13.00	22.00	32.00
AH1228//12	—	2.65	6.50	13.00	22.00	32.00
AH1228//13	—	2.65	6.50	13.00	22.00	32.00
AH1228//15	—	2.65	6.50	13.00	22.00	32.00
AH1228//16	—	2.65	6.50	13.00	22.00	32.00
AH1228//17	—	2.65	6.50	13.00	22.00	32.00
AH1228//18	—	2.65	6.50	13.00	22.00	32.00
AH1228//19	—	2.65	6.50	13.00	22.00	32.00
AH1228//20	—	2.65	6.50	13.00	22.00	32.00
AH1228//21	—	2.65	6.50	13.00	22.00	32.00
AH1228//22	—	2.65	6.50	13.00	22.00	32.00
AH1228//27 (sic)	—	2.65	6.50	13.00	22.00	32.00

Date	Mintage	Good	VG	F	VF	XF
AH1228//28 (sic)	—	2.65	6.50	13.00	22.00	32.00
AH1230 (sic)	—	2.65	6.50	13.00	22.00	32.00

KM# 48 RUPEE

Billon **Obv. Inscription:** "Shah Alam II" **Mint:** Chanderi **Note:** KM#48 is an imitation of a Bajranggarh rupee reported struck ca. 1816AD.

Date	Mintage	Good	VG	F	VF	XF
ND//18 (ca. 1816)	—	4.00	10.00	13.50	20.00	30.00

KM# 18 RUPEE

Silver **Obv. Inscription:** "Muhammad Akbar II" **Mint:** Basoda **Note:** Weight varies 10.70-11.60 grams.

Date	Mintage	Good	VG	F	VF	XF
AH124x//18	—	10.00	25.00	37.50	50.00	70.00

KM# 65 RUPEE

Copper **Obverse:** Five-flowered symbol **Obv. Inscription:** "Muhammad Akbar II" **Reverse:** Nagari "Shri" for Baija Bao and five-flowered symbol **Mint:** Gwalior Fort **Note:** Weight varies 10.70-11.60 grams. The regnal year 23 becomes frozen with this issue on all size coins of this mint (identified by five-flowered symbol) and of Lashkar Mint.

Date	Mintage	Good	VG	F	VF	XF
ND//23 (1827)	—	4.75	11.50	22.50	35.00	50.00

Ajit Singh
AH1235-1274 / 1819-1857AD

HAMMERED COINAGE

KM# 12 1/8 RUPEE

Silver, 16 mm. **Obverse:** Bow and arrow **Reverse:** Lotus **Mint:** Bajranggarh **Note:** Weight varies 1.34-1.45 grams.

Date	Mintage	VG	F	VF	XF	Unc
ND(1827-61)	—	15.00	25.00	40.00	60.00	—

KM# 13 1/4 RUPEE

Silver **Obverse:** Bow and arrow **Reverse:** Lotus **Mint:** Bajranggarh **Note:** Weight varies 2.68-2.90 grams.

Date	Mintage	Good	VG	F	VF	XF
ND(1827-61) NRY	—	6.00	15.00	25.00	40.00	60.00

KM# 14 1/2 RUPEE

Silver **Obverse:** Bow and arrow **Reverse:** Lotus **Mint:** Bajranggarh **Note:** Weight varies 5.35-5.80 grams.

Date	Mintage	Good	VG	F	VF	XF
ND(1827-61)	—	8.00	20.00	35.00	50.00	70.00

KM# 15 RUPEE

Silver **Reverse:** Lotus **Mint:** Bajranggarh **Note:** Weight varies 10.70-11.60 grams.

Date	Mintage	Good	VG	F	VF	XF
ND(1819)//21	—	—	15.00	21.50	30.00	40.00
ND(1820)//22	—	—	15.00	21.50	30.00	40.00

KM# 16 RUPEE

Silver **Obverse:** Bow and arrow **Reverse:** Lotus **Mint:** Bajranggarh

Date	Mintage	Good	VG	F	VF	XF
ND(1821)//23	—	—	7.00	11.00	16.50	25.00
ND(1822)//24	—	—	7.00	11.00	16.50	25.00
ND(1823)//25	—	—	7.00	11.00	16.50	25.00
ND(1824)//26	—	—	7.00	11.00	16.50	25.00
ND(1825)//27	—	—	7.00	11.00	16.50	25.00
ND(1826)//28	—	—	7.00	11.00	16.50	25.00
ND(1827)//29	—	—	7.00	11.00	16.50	25.00

KM# 17 RUPEE

Silver **Mint:** Bajranggarh

Date	Mintage	Good	VG	F	VF	XF
ND(1827-61)//-	—	—	6.00	9.00	13.50	20.00

Baija Bai - Regent
AH1243-1249 / 1827-1833AD

HAMMERED COINAGE

KM# 127 1/4 RUPEE

Silver **Obv. Inscription:** "Shah Alam II" **Reverse:** "Shri" and trisul **Mint:** Lashkar **Note:** Weight varies 2.68-2.90 grams.

Date	Mintage	Good	VG	F	VF	XF
ND//23 (1827-33)	—	2.00	5.00	7.00	10.00	15.00

KM# 128 1/2 RUPEE

Silver **Obv. Inscription:** "Shah Alam II" **Reverse:** "Shri" and trisul **Mint:** Lashkar **Note:** Weight varies 5.35-5.80 grams.

Date	Mintage	Good	VG	F	VF	XF
ND//23 (1827-33)	—	2.00	5.00	8.00	12.50	18.50

KM# 226 1/2 RUPEE

Silver **Obv. Inscription:** "Shah Alam II" **Mint:** Daulat Rao **Note:** Weight varies 5.35-5.80 grams. With continued regnal years of Shah Alam II.

Date	Mintage	Good	VG	F	VF	XF
ND//73 (1830-31)	—	2.75	7.00	11.00	16.50	25.00

KM# 209 RUPEE

Silver **Reverse:** Shri **Mint:** Daulat Rao **Note:** Weight varies 10.70-11.60 grams.

Date	Mintage	Good	VG	F	VF	XF
AH1106//17 (sic)	—	15.00	35.00	60.00	100	150

KM# 129 RUPEE

Silver **Obv. Inscription:** "Shah Alam II" **Reverse:** "Shri" and trisul **Mint:** Lashkar **Note:** Weight varies 10.70-11.60 grams.

Date	Mintage	Good	VG	F	VF	XF
ND//23 (1827-33)	—	2.50	6.50	10.00	15.00	22.50

KM# 228 RUPEE

Silver **Obv. Inscription:** "Shah Alam II" **Reverse:** Shri **Mint:** Daulat Rao **Note:** Weight varies 10.70-11.60 grams. With continued regnal years of Mohammad Akbar.

Date	Mintage	Good	VG	F	VF	XF
ND//23 (1828)	—	26.50	65.00	100	150	220

KM# 227 RUPEE

Silver **Obv. Inscription:** "Shah Alam II" **Mint:** Daulat Rao **Note:** Weight varies 10.70-11.60 grams. With continued regnal years of Shah Alam II.

Date	Mintage	Good	VG	F	VF	XF
ND//71 (1828-29)	—	2.35	6.00	9.00	13.50	20.00
ND//73 (1830-31)	—	2.35	6.00	9.00	13.50	20.00

KM# 38.3 RUPEE

Silver **Obv. Inscription:** "Shah Alam II" **Mint:** Burhanpur **Note:** Weight varies 10.70-11.60 grams.

Date	Mintage	Good	VG	F	VF	XF
AH1247	—	3.00	7.50	15.00	25.00	36.00

KM# 202 RUPEE

Silver **Obv. Inscription:** "Muhammad Akbar II" **Reverse:** Cannon left **Mint:** Sheopur **Note:** Weight varies 10.70-11.60 grams.

Date	Mintage	Good	VG	F	VF	XF
AH1248//27	—	3.50	9.00	18.00	28.00	40.00
AH1248//28	—	3.50	9.00	18.00	28.00	40.00

KM# 63 NAZARANA 1/3 MOHUR

Gold, 18 mm. **Obv. Inscription:** "Muhammad Shah" **Reverse:** Nagari "Shri" for Baija Rao **Mint:** Gwalior Fort **Note:** Weight varies 3.57-3.80 grams.

Date	Mintage	Good	VG	F	VF	XF
AH1130//2 Frozen	—	—	175	275	400	575

Note: Struck ca. 1827AD

KM# 126 MOHUR

Gold **Obv. Inscription:** "Muhammad Shah" **Reverse:** Shri **Mint:** Lashkar **Note:** Weight varies 10.70-11.60 grams.

Date	Mintage	Good	VG	F	VF	XF
AH1130//2 Frozen	—	—	175	225	350	500

Jankoji Rao
AH1243-1259 / 1827-1843AD

HAMMERED COINAGE

KM# 130 1/2 PAISA

Copper **Obverse:** Trisul **Reverse:** Flywhisk and spear **Mint:** Lashkar **Note:** Weight varies 5.60-6.20 grams.

Date	Mintage	Good	VG	F	VF	XF
ND//23 (1827-43)	—	2.50	5.00	8.00	12.50	—

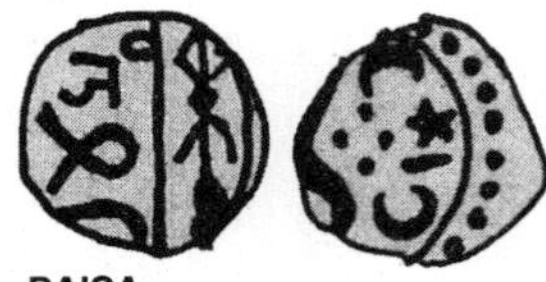

KM# 103 PAISA

Copper **Obverse:** Letter "Ja" and spear **Mint:** Jawad

Date	Mintage	Good	VG	F	VF	XF
ND(1827-43)	—	2.50	4.50	6.50	10.00	—

KM# 104 PAISA

Copper **Obverse:** Letter "Ja" (retrograde) and spear **Mint:** Jawad

Date	Mintage	Good	VG	F	VF	XF
ND(1827-43)	—	2.50	4.50	6.50	10.00	—

KM# 105 PAISA

Copper **Obverse:** Scimitar, banner and letter "Ji" **Reverse:** Trisul **Mint:** Jawad

Date	Mintage	Good	VG	F	VF	XF
ND(1827-43)	—	3.00	5.00	8.00	12.50	—

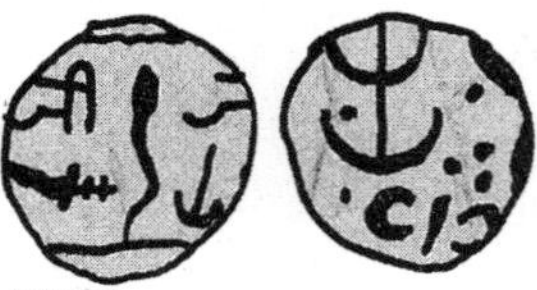

KM# 106 PAISA

Copper **Obverse:** Letter "Ji" scimitar and snake **Mint:** Jawad

Date	Mintage	Good	VG	F	VF	XF
ND(1827-43)	—	2.50	4.50	6.50	10.00	—

KM# 107 PAISA

Copper **Obverse:** Letters "Ja, Ja, Ja?" and snake **Mint:** Jawad

Date	Mintage	Good	VG	F	VF	XF
ND(1827-43)	—	2.50	4.50	6.50	10.00	—

KM# 108 PAISA

Copper **Obverse:** Snake between letters "S" and "Ra" scimitar **Mint:** Jawad

Date	Mintage	Good	VG	F	VF	XF
ND(1827-43)	—	2.50	4.50	6.50	7.50	—

KM# 131.1 PAISA

13.3500 g., Copper **Obverse:** Trisul **Reverse:** Flywhisk and spear **Mint:** Lashkar

Date	Mintage	Good	VG	F	VF	XF
ND//12 (1827-43)	—	1.25	2.50	3.50	5.50	—

KM# 131.2 PAISA

13.3500 g., Copper **Obverse:** Trisul **Reverse:** Spear, r.y. off flan **Mint:** Lashkar

Date	Mintage	Good	VG	F	VF	XF
ND//22 (1827-43)	—	1.25	2.50	3.50	5.50	—

KM# 131.3 PAISA

13.3500 g., Copper **Obverse:** Flower **Reverse:** Whisk and trident **Mint:** Lashkar

Date	Mintage	Good	VG	F	VF	XF
ND//23 (1827-43)	—	1.25	2.50	3.50	5.50	—

KM# 131.5 PAISA

13.3500 g., Copper **Obverse:** Winged sun burst **Reverse:** Spear, trident and whisk **Mint:** Lashkar

Date	Mintage	Good	VG	F	VF	XF
ND(1827-43)	—	1.25	2.50	3.50	5.50	—

KM# 131.6 PAISA

13.3500 g., Copper **Obverse:** Double pennant **Reverse:** Whisk, trident and spear **Mint:** Lashkar

Date	Mintage	Good	VG	F	VF	XF
ND(1827-43)	—	1.25	2.50	3.50	5.50	—

KM# 131.7 PAISA

13.3500 g., Copper **Obverse:** Trident **Reverse:** Spear and standard **Mint:** Lashkar

Date	Mintage	Good	VG	F	VF	XF
ND(1827-43)	—	1.25	2.50	3.50	5.50	—

KM# 131.4 PAISA

13.3500 g., Copper **Obverse:** Flower **Reverse:** Spear, trisul and whisk **Mint:** Lashkar

Date	Mintage	Good	VG	F	VF	XF
ND//31 (1835)	—	1.25	2.50	3.50	5.50	—

KM# A132 2 PAISA

Bronze **Mint:** Lashkar

Date	Mintage	Good	VG	F	VF	XF
ND//22 (1827-43)	—	—	—	—	—	—
ND//23 (1827-43)	—	—	—	—	—	—

KM# 67 1/8 RUPEE

Silver **Obv. Inscription:** "Muhammad Akbar II" **Reverse:** Nagari "Ja" for Jankoji **Mint:** Gwalior Fort **Note:** Weight varies 1.34-1.45 grams. Similar to Rupee, KM#72.

Date	Mintage	Good	VG	F	VF	XF
AH1244//23	—	2.00	5.00	7.00	10.00	15.00

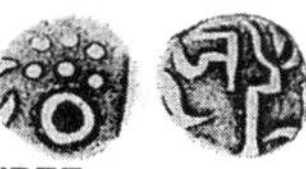

KM# 134 1/8 RUPEE

Silver **Obv. Inscription:** "Shah Alam II" **Reverse:** Bow and arrow points up, "Ja" and trisul **Mint:** Lashkar **Note:** Weight varies 1.34-1.45 grams.

Date	Mintage	Good	VG	F	VF	XF
ND//23 (1827-43)	—	1.25	3.00	4.50	6.50	10.00

KM# 135 1/8 RUPEE

Silver **Obv. Inscription:** "Shah Alam II" **Reverse:** Bow and arrow points down, "Ja" and trisul **Mint:** Lashkar **Note:** Weight varies 1.34-1.45 grams.

Date	Mintage	Good	VG	F	VF	XF
ND//23 (1827-43)	—	1.25	3.00	4.50	6.50	10.00

KM# A19 1/4 RUPEE

Silver **Obv. Inscription:** "Muhammad Akbar II" and "Jankoji Rao" **Mint:** Basoda

Date	Mintage	Good	VG	F	VF	XF
ND(1794-1827)	—	16.00	40.00	65.00	100	150

KM# 68 1/4 RUPEE

Silver **Obv. Inscription:** "Muhammad Akbar II" **Reverse:** Nagari "Ja" for Jankoji **Mint:** Gwalior Fort **Note:** Weight varies 2.68-2.90 grams. Similar to Rupee, KM#72.

Date	Mintage	Good	VG	F	VF	XF
AH1244//23	—	2.35	6.00	10.00	14.00	20.00

KM# 69 1/4 RUPEE

Silver **Obv. Inscription:** "Muhammad Akbar II" **Reverse:** Nagari "Ja" for Jankoji **Mint:** Gwalior Fort **Note:** Weight varies 2.68-2.90 grams. Similar to Rupee, KM#73.

Date	Mintage	VG	F	VF	XF	Unc
AH1244//23 (1806)	—	6.00	10.00	14.00	20.00	—

KM# 90 1/4 RUPEE

Silver **Mint:** Isagarh **Note:** Weight varies 5.35-5.80 grams. Similar to 1 Rupee, KM#92.

Date	Mintage	Good	VG	F	VF	XF
AH1243//23	—	10.00	25.00	40.00	60.00	85.00

KM# 137 1/4 RUPEE

Silver, 12 mm. **Obv. Inscription:** "Shah Alam II" **Reverse:** Bow and arrow points down, "Ja" and trisul **Mint:** Lashkar **Note:** Weight varies 2.68-2.90 grams.

Date	Mintage	Good	VG	F	VF	XF
ND//23 (1827-43)	—	1.50	4.00	6.00	9.00	14.00

KM# A90 1/4 RUPEE

Silver **Mint:** Isagarh **Note:** Weight varies 2.67-2.90 grams. Similar to 1 Rupee, KM#92.

Date	Mintage	Good	VG	F	VF	XF
AH12xx//10	—	10.00	25.00	40.00	60.00	85.00

KM# 136 1/4 RUPEE

Silver, 12 mm. **Obv. Inscription:** "Shah Alam II" **Reverse:** Bow and arrow points up, "Ja" and trisul **Mint:** Lashkar **Note:** Weight varies 2.68-2.90 grams.

Date	Mintage	Good	VG	F	VF	XF
ND//23 (1827-43)	—	1.50	4.00	6.00	9.00	14.00

KM# A229 1/4 RUPEE

Silver **Obv. Inscription:** "Shah Alam II" **Mint:** Daulat Rao **Note:** Weight varies 2.67-2.90 grams. With continued regnal years of Shah Alam II.

Date	Mintage	Good	VG	F	VF	XF
ND//80 (1837-38)	—	2.00	5.00	7.00	10.00	15.00

KM# B19 1/2 RUPEE

Silver **Obv. Inscription:** "Muhammad Akbar II" and "Jankoji Rao" **Mint:** Basoda **Note:** Weight varies 5.35-5.80 grams.

Date	Mintage	Good	VG	F	VF	XF
ND(1794-1827)	—	18.00	45.00	80.00	120	175

KM# 70 1/2 RUPEE

Silver **Obv. Inscription:** "Muhammad Akbar II" **Reverse:** Nagari "Ja" for Jankoji **Mint:** Gwalior Fort **Note:** Weight varies 5.35-5.70 grams.

Date	Mintage	Good	VG	F	VF	XF
AH1244//33	—	3.00	7.50	12.50	17.50	25.00

KM# 71 1/2 RUPEE

Silver **Obv. Inscription:** "Muhammad Akbar II" **Reverse:** Nagari "Ja" for Jankoji **Mint:** Gwalior Fort **Note:** Weight varies 5.35-5.70 grams.

Date	Mintage	Good	VG	F	VF	XF
AH1244//23	—	3.00	7.50	12.50	17.50	25.00

KM# 138 1/2 RUPEE

Silver, 16 mm. **Obv. Inscription:** "Shah Alam II" **Reverse:** Bow and arrow points up, "Ja" and trisul **Mint:** Lashkar **Note:** Weight varies 5.35-5.80 grams.

Date	Mintage	Good	VG	F	VF	XF
ND//23 (1827-43)	—	2.00	5.00	7.00	10.00	15.00

KM# 139 1/2 RUPEE

Silver, 16 mm. **Obv. Inscription:** "Shah Alam II" **Reverse:** Bow and arrow points down, "Ja" and trisul **Mint:** Lashkar **Note:** Weight varies 5.35-5.80 grams.

Date	Mintage	Good	VG	F	VF	XF
ND//23 (1827-43)	—	2.00	5.00	7.00	10.00	15.00

KM# 91 1/2 RUPEE

Silver **Mint:** Isagarh **Note:** Weight varies 5.35-5.80 grams. Similar to 1 Rupee, KM#93.

Date	Mintage	Good	VG	F	VF	XF
AH1223/23 (Error 1243)	—	10.00	25.00	40.00	60.00	85.00

KM# 229 1/2 RUPEE

Silver **Obv. Inscription:** "Shah Alam II" **Mint:** Daulat Rao **Note:** Weight varies 5.35-5.80 grams. With continued regnal years of Shah Alam II.

Date	Mintage	Good	VG	F	VF	XF
ND//77 (1834-35)	—	2.35	6.00	9.00	12.50	18.50
ND//78 (1835-36)	—	2.35	6.00	9.00	12.50	18.50
ND//80 (1837-38)	—	2.35	6.00	9.00	12.50	18.50

KM# 72 RUPEE

Silver **Obv. Inscription:** "Muhammad Akbar II" **Reverse:** Bow and arrow points down; Nagori "Ja" for Jankoji **Mint:** Gwalior Fort **Note:** Weight varies 10.70-11.60 grams.

Date	Mintage	Good	VG	F	VF	XF
AH1244//23	—	3.50	8.50	14.00	20.00	28.00

KM# 73 RUPEE
Silver **Obv. Inscription:** "Muhammad Akbar II" **Reverse:** Bow and arrow points up; Nagori "Ja" for Jankoji **Mint:** Gwalior Fort **Note:** Weight varies 10.70-11.60 grams.

Date	Mintage	Good	VG	F	VF	XF
AH1244//23	—	3.50	8.50	14.00	20.00	28.00

KM# 210 RUPEE
Silver **Reverse:** Ja **Mint:** Daulat Rao **Note:** Weight varies 10.70-11.60 grams. With regnal years of Muhammad Akbar II AH1221-1253/1806-1837AD.

Date	Mintage	Good	VG	F	VF	XF
ND//9 (1814-15)	—	10.00	25.00	40.00	60.00	85.00

KM# 93 RUPEE
Silver **Obverse:** Lotus bud **Mint:** Isagarh **Note:** Weight varies 10.70-11.60 grams.

Date	Mintage	Good	VG	F	VF	XF
ND(1827-43)	—	2.75	7.00	11.00	16.50	25.00
AH1252	—	2.75	7.00	11.00	16.50	25.00

KM# 140 RUPEE
Silver **Obv. Inscription:** "Shah Alam II" **Reverse:** Bow and arrow points up, "Ja" and trisul **Mint:** Lashkar **Note:** Weight varies 10.70-11.60 grams.

Date	Mintage	Good	VG	F	VF	XF
ND//23 (1827-43)	—	2.75	7.00	11.00	16.50	25.00

KM# 141 RUPEE
Silver **Obv. Inscription:** "Shah Alam II" **Reverse:** Bow and arrow points down, "Ja" and trisul **Mint:** Lashkar **Note:** Weight varies 10.70-11.60 grams.

Date	Mintage	Good	VG	F	VF	XF
ND//23 (1827-43)	—	2.75	7.00	11.00	16.50	25.00

KM# 92 RUPEE
Silver **Mint:** Isagarh **Note:** Weight varies 10.70-11.60 grams.

Date	Mintage	Good	VG	F	VF	XF
AH1223//23 (Error/243)	—	4.50	11.50	16.50	25.00	37.50
AH1243//23	—	4.50	11.50	16.50	25.00	37.50

KM# 230 RUPEE
Silver **Obv. Inscription:** "Shah Alam II" **Mint:** Daulat Rao **Note:** Weight varies 10.70-11.60 grams.

Date	Mintage	Good	VG	F	VF	XF
ND//77 (1834-35)	—	2.35	6.00	9.00	13.50	20.00
ND//78 (1835-36)	—	2.35	6.00	9.00	13.50	20.00
ND//79 (1836-37)	—	2.35	6.00	9.00	13.50	20.00
ND//80 (1837-38)	—	2.35	6.00	9.00	13.50	20.00
ND//83 (1840-41)	—	2.35	6.00	9.00	13.50	20.00
ND//84 (1841-42)	—	2.35	6.00	9.00	13.50	20.00
ND//85 (1842-43)	—	2.35	6.00	9.00	13.50	20.00

KM# 19.1 RUPEE
Silver **Obv. Inscription:** "Muhammad Akbar II" and "Jankoji Rao" **Mint:** Basoda **Note:** Weight varies 10.70-11.60 grams.

Date	Mintage	Good	VG	F	VF	XF
AH1252//32	—	10.00	25.00	37.50	50.00	70.00
AH1254//32	—	10.00	25.00	37.50	50.00	70.00

KM# 38.4 RUPEE
Silver **Obv. Inscription:** "Shah Alam II" **Mint:** Burhanpur **Note:** Weight varies 10.70-11.60 grams.

Date	Mintage	Good	VG	F	VF	XF
AH1255	—	5.00	12.50	20.00	30.00	45.00

KM# 66 NAZARANA 1/3 MOHUR
Gold **Obv. Inscription:** "Muhammad Shah" **Reverse:** Nagari "Ja" for Jankoji **Mint:** Gwalior Fort **Note:** Weight varies 3.57-3.80 grams.

Date	Mintage	Good	VG	F	VF	XF
AH1130//2 Frozen	—	—	175	275	400	575

Note: Struck ca.1834AD.

KM# 132 MOHUR
Gold **Obv. Inscription:** "Muhammad Shah" **Reverse:** Bow and arrow points up, "Ja" **Mint:** Lashkar **Note:** Weight varies 10.70-11.40 grams.

Date	Mintage	Good	VG	F	VF	XF
AH1130//2 Frozen	—	—	175	225	350	500

KM# 133 MOHUR
Gold **Obv. Inscription:** "Muhammad Shah" **Reverse:** Bow and arrow points down, "Ja" **Mint:** Lashkar **Note:** Weight varies 10.70-11.40 grams.

Date	Mintage	Good	VG	F	VF	XF
AH1130//2 Frozen	—	—	175	225	350	500

Jayaji Rao
AH1259-1304 / 1843-1886AD
HAMMERED COINAGE

KM# 49 1/3 PAISA
Copper **Mint:** Dohad **Note:** Weight varies 1.69-1.88 grams.

Date	Mintage	Good	VG	F	VF	XF
VS1912	—	6.00	12.00	20.00	30.00	—

KM# 142 1/2 PAISA
3.0000 g., Copper, 12 mm. **Mint:** Lashkar

Date	Mintage	Good	VG	F	VF	XF
VS1926	—	5.00	7.00	10.00	15.00	—

KM# 41 PAISA
15.2300 g., Copper **Mint:** Burhanpur

Date	Mintage	Good	VG	F	VF	XF
ND(1827-33)	—	2.50	4.50	6.50	10.00	—

KM# 76 PAISA
Copper **Obverse:** Trisul **Obv. Inscription:** "Muhammad Akbar II" **Reverse:** Nagari "Ji" for Jayagi **Mint:** Gwalior Fort

Date	Mintage	Good	VG	F	VF	XF
ND(1843-86)	—	1.25	2.00	3.00	5.00	—

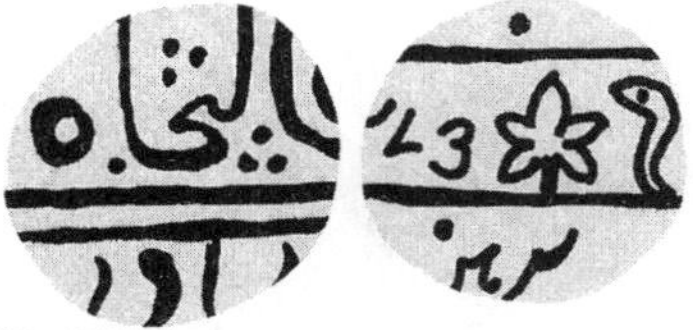

KM# 45 PAISA
Copper **Obv. Inscription:** "Alyjah Bahadur" **Reverse:** Leaf and snake **Mint:** Burhanpur **Note:** Weight varies 12.44-15.29 grams.

Date	Mintage	Good	VG	F	VF	XF
AH1260	—	4.50	8.00	12.00	18.50	—
AH1273	—	4.50	8.00	12.00	18.50	—
AH1274	—	4.50	8.00	12.00	18.50	—
AH1275	—	4.50	8.00	12.00	18.50	—

KM# 231 PAISA
Copper **Obv. Inscription:** "Shah Alam II" **Mint:** Daulat Rao **Note:** Round or square.

Date	Mintage	Good	VG	F	VF	XF
AH1262 (1845)	—	2.00	3.25	5.00	8.50	—
AH1263 (1846)	—	2.00	3.25	5.00	8.50	—
AH1266 (1849)	—	2.00	3.25	5.00	8.50	—
AH1267 (1850)	—	2.00	3.25	5.00	8.50	—

KM# 75 PAISA
Copper **Obv. Inscription:** "Muhammad Akbar II" **Reverse:** Nagari "Ji" for Jayagi **Mint:** Gwalior Fort

Date	Mintage	Good	VG	F	VF	XF
AH1269	—	1.25	2.00	3.00	5.00	—
AH127x//42	—	1.25	2.00	3.00	5.00	—
AH127x//45	—	1.25	2.00	3.00	5.00	—
AH127x//46	—	1.25	2.00	3.00	5.00	—
AH127x//47	—	1.25	2.00	3.00	5.00	—
AH1277//48	—	1.25	2.00	3.00	5.00	—
AH1278//49	—	1.25	2.00	3.00	5.00	—
AH1279//49	—	1.25	2.00	3.00	5.00	—
ND//54 (1867)	—	1.25	2.00	3.00	5.00	—
ND//56 (1869)	—	1.25	2.00	3.00	5.00	—

KM# 233 PAISA
Copper **Obverse:** Shri **Obv. Inscription:** "Shah Alam II" **Mint:** Daulat Rao

Date	Mintage	Good	VG	F	VF	XF
AH1272 (1855)	—	2.00	3.25	5.00	8.50	—
AH1278 (1861)	—	2.00	3.25	5.00	8.50	—
AH1287 (1870)	—	2.00	3.25	5.00	8.50	—

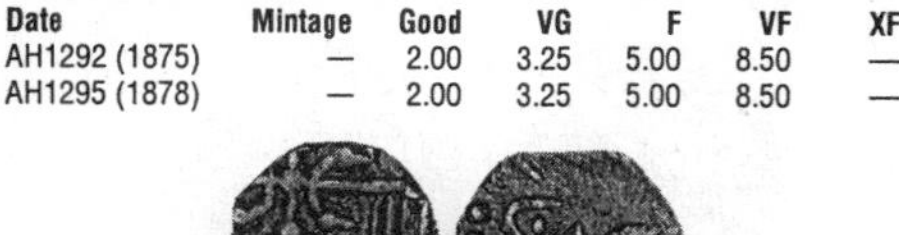

Date	Mintage	Good	VG	F	VF	XF
AH1292 (1875)	—	2.00	3.25	5.00	8.50	—
AH1295 (1878)	—	2.00	3.25	5.00	8.50	—

KM# 50.1 PAISA
Copper **Mint:** Dohad **Note:** Thick flan, weight varies 6.00-6.20 grams.

Date	Mintage	Good	VG	F	VF	XF
VS1912	—	5.00	9.00	13.00	20.00	—

KM# 50.2 PAISA
Copper **Mint:** Dohad **Note:** Thin flan, weight varies 6.00-6.20 grams.

Date	Mintage	Good	VG	F	VF	XF
VS1912	—	5.00	9.00	13.00	20.00	—

KM# 232 PAISA
Copper **Obverse:** Arrow added **Obv. Inscription:** "Shah Alam II" **Mint:** Daulat Rao

Date	Mintage	Good	VG	F	VF	XF
AH1278 (1861)	—	2.00	3.25	5.00	8.50	—
AH1281 (1864)	—	2.00	3.25	5.00	8.50	—
AH1292 (1875)	—	2.00	3.25	5.00	8.50	—
AH1295 (1878)	—	2.00	3.25	5.00	8.50	—

KM# 111 PAISA
Copper **Obverse:** Trisul **Reverse:** Persian "Ji" above leaf, flywhisk **Mint:** Jhansi **Note:** Weight varies 11.15-15.55 grams.

Date	Mintage	Good	VG	F	VF	XF
ND(1865-86)	—	3.00	5.00	8.00	12.50	—

KM# 143 PAISA
6.0000 g., Copper **Mint:** Lashkar

Date	Mintage	Good	VG	F	VF	XF
VS1926	—	0.35	0.75	1.25	2.25	—

KM# 180 PAISA
Copper **Obv. Legend:** "Sa Ma Sa" **Reverse:** Trisul divides date **Rev. Legend:** A(lijah) Ba(hadur) **Mint:** Mandasor

Date	Mintage	Good	VG	F	VF	XF
VS1937	—	1.25	2.75	4.00	6.00	—
VS3791 Error 1937	—	1.25	2.75	4.00	6.00	—
VS3711 Error 1937	—	1.25	2.75	4.00	6.00	—

KM# 181 PAISA
Copper **Reverse:** Date to left of trisul **Mint:** Mandasor

Date	Mintage	Good	VG	F	VF	XF
VS1937	—	1.25	2.75	4.00	6.00	—

KM# 182 PAISA
Copper **Reverse:** Legend is retrograde **Mint:** Mandasor

Date	Mintage	Good	VG	F	VF	XF
VS1937	—	1.25	2.75	4.00	6.00	—

KM# 183 PAISA
Copper **Obverse:** Retrograde legend **Reverse:** Retrograde legend **Mint:** Mandasor

Date	Mintage	Good	VG	F	VF	XF
VS1937	—	1.25	2.75	4.00	6.00	—

KM# A42 2 PAISA
30.0000 g., Copper **Mint:** Burhanpur

Date	Mintage	Good	VG	F	VF	XF
ND(1827-33)	—	5.00	9.00	13.50	20.00	—

KM# 77 1/16 RUPEE
Silver, 9 mm. **Obv. Inscription:** "Muhammad Akbar II" **Reverse:** Nagari "Ji" for Jayagi **Mint:** Gwalior Fort **Note:** Weight varies 0.67-0.72 grams.

Date	Mintage	Good	VG	F	VF	XF
ND//23 (1843-86)	—	1.50	4.00	6.00	9.00	14.00

KM# 120 1/8 RUPEE
Silver **Obv. Inscription:** "Shah Alam II" **Reverse:** Regnal years of Muhammad Akbar II **Mint:** Lashkar **Note:** Weight varies 1.34-1.45 grams.

Date	Mintage	Good	VG	F	VF	XF
ND(1806-37)	—	1.50	4.00	6.00	9.00	14.00

KM# A203 1/8 RUPEE
Silver **Obv. Inscription:** "Muhammad Akbar II" **Reverse:** Cannon left "Ji" **Mint:** Sheopur **Note:** Weight varies 1.34-1.45 grams.

Date	Mintage	Good	VG	F	VF	XF
AH12xx//1	—	10.00	25.00	40.00	60.00	85.00

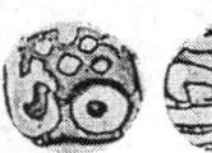

KM# 29 1/8 RUPEE
Silver **Obv. Inscription:** "Shah Alam II" **Mint:** Bhilsa **Note:** Weight varies 1.34-1.45 grams. Size varies 9-10 millimeters.

Date	Mintage	Good	VG	F	VF	XF
AH(12)25	—	2.35	6.00	9.00	13.50	20.00

KM# 234 1/8 RUPEE
Silver **Obv. Inscription:** "Shah Alam II" **Mint:** Daulat Rao **Note:** With continued postumous regnal years of Shah Alam II. Weight varies 1.34-1.45 grams.

Date	Mintage	Good	VG	F	VF	XF
ND(1843-86)	—	1.65	4.00	6.00	9.00	13.50

KM# 23.2 1/8 RUPEE
Silver **Obverse:** With sword **Obv. Inscription:** "Shah Alam II" **Mint:** Bhilsa

Date	Mintage	Good	VG	F	VF	XF
AH(12)25	—	2.75	7.00	11.00	16.50	25.00

KM# 23.1 1/8 RUPEE
Silver **Obverse:** Without sword **Obv. Inscription:** "Shah Alam II" **Mint:** Bhilsa **Note:** Weight varies 1.34-1.45 grams.

Date	Mintage	Good	VG	F	VF	XF
AH(12)25	—	2.75	7.00	11.00	16.50	25.00

KM# 78 1/8 RUPEE
Silver, 11 mm. **Obv. Inscription:** "Muhammad Akbar II" **Reverse:** Nagari "Ji" for Jayagi **Mint:** Gwalior Fort **Note:** Weight varies 1.34-1.45 grams.

Date	Mintage	Good	VG	F	VF	XF
ND//23 (1843-86)	—	2.00	5.00	7.00	10.00	15.00

KM# 112 1/8 RUPEE
Silver **Reverse:** Persian "Ji" **Mint:** Jhansi **Note:** Weight varies 1.34-1.45 grams.

Date	Mintage	Good	VG	F	VF	XF
ND//5x (1865-86)	—	8.00	20.00	30.00	50.00	70.00

KM# A238 1/8 RUPEE
Silver **Mint:** Daulat Rao **Note:** With continued regnal years of the British "Raj". Weight varies 1.34-1.45 grams.

Date	Mintage	Good	VG	F	VF	XF
ND//23 (1883)	—	2.00	5.00	7.00	10.00	15.00
ND//26 (1886)	—	2.00	5.00	7.00	10.00	15.00

KM# 121.1 1/4 RUPEE
Silver **Obv. Inscription:** "Shah Alam II" **Reverse:** With dot in "J" of Julus **Mint:** Lashkar **Note:** Weight varies 2.68-2.90 grams.

Date	Mintage	Good	VG	F	VF	XF
ND(1806-37)	—	2.00	5.00	7.00	10.00	15.00

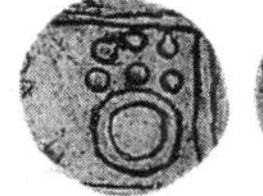

KM# 122 1/4 RUPEE
Silver **Obv. Inscription:** "Shah Alam II" **Reverse:** Lily in "J" of Julus **Mint:** Lashkar **Note:** Weight varies 2.68-2.90 grams.

Date	Mintage	Good	VG	F	VF	XF
ND//17 (1822)	—	2.00	5.00	7.00	10.00	15.00

KM# 121.2 1/4 RUPEE
Silver **Obv. Inscription:** "Shah Alam II" **Reverse:** Without dot in "J" of Julus **Mint:** Lashkar **Note:** Weight varies 2.68-2.90 grams.

Date	Mintage	Good	VG	F	VF	XF
ND//18 (1823)	—	2.00	5.00	7.00	10.00	15.00

KM# 24.2 1/4 RUPEE
Silver **Obverse:** With sword **Obv. Inscription:** "Shah Alam II" **Mint:** Bhilsa

Date	Mintage	Good	VG	F	VF	XF
AH(12)25	—	2.75	7.00	11.00	16.50	25.00

KM# 79 1/4 RUPEE
Silver, 13 mm. **Obv. Inscription:** "Muhammad Akbar II" **Reverse:** Nagari "Ji" for Jayagi **Mint:** Gwalior Fort **Note:** Weight varies 2.68-2.90 grams.

Date	Mintage	Good	VG	F	VF	XF
ND//23 (1843-86)	—	2.35	6.00	10.00	14.00	20.00

KM# 24.1 1/4 RUPEE
Silver **Obverse:** Without sword **Obv. Inscription:** "Shah Alam II" **Mint:** Bhilsa **Note:** Weight varies 2.68-2.90 grams. Size varies 12-14 millimeters.

Date	Mintage	Good	VG	F	VF	XF
AH(12)25	—	2.75	7.00	11.00	16.50	25.00

KM# 30 1/4 RUPEE
Silver **Obv. Inscription:** "Shah Alam II" **Mint:** Bhilsa **Note:** Weight varies 2.68-2.90 grams.

Date	Mintage	VG	F	VF	XF	Unc
AH(12)25 (1843)	—	6.00	9.00	13.50	20.00	—

KM# 235 1/4 RUPEE
Silver **Obv. Inscription:** "Shah Alam II" **Mint:** Daulat Rao **Note:** With continued postumous regnal years of Shah Alam II. Weight varies 2.68-2.90 grams.

Date	Mintage	Good	VG	F	VF	XF
ND//92 (1848-49)	—	2.00	5.00	7.00	10.00	15.00

KM# 43 1/2 RUPEE
Silver, 17 mm. **Mint:** Burhanpur **Note:** Weight varies: 5.35 - 5.7 grams.

Date	Mintage	Good	VG	F	VF	XF
AH1214	—	—	30.00	50.00	80.00	120
AH1261	—	—	30.00	50.00	80.00	120
AH1274	—	—	30.00	50.00	80.00	120

KM# 123.1 1/2 RUPEE
Silver **Obv. Inscription:** "Shah Alam II" **Reverse:** With dot in "J" of Julus **Mint:** Lashkar **Note:** Weight varies 5.35-5.80 grams.

Date	Mintage	Good	VG	F	VF	XF
ND(1806-37)	—	2.35	6.00	9.00	13.50	20.00

KM# 123.2 1/2 RUPEE
Silver **Obv. Inscription:** "Shah Alam II" **Reverse:** Without dot in "J" of Julus **Mint:** Lashkar **Note:** Weight varies 5.35-5.80 grams.

Date	Mintage	Good	VG	F	VF	XF
ND(1806-37)	—	2.35	6.00	9.00	13.50	20.00

KM# A124 1/2 RUPEE
Silver **Obv. Inscription:** "Shah Alam II" **Reverse:** Lily blossom in "J" in Julus **Mint:** Lashkar **Note:** Weight varies 5.35-5.80 grams.

Date	Mintage	Good	VG	F	VF	XF
ND//17 (1822)	—	2.35	6.00	9.00	13.50	20.00

KM# 26 1/2 RUPEE
Silver **Obverse:** Sword **Obv. Inscription:** "Shah Alam II" **Mint:** Bhilsa

Date	Mintage	Good	VG	F	VF	XF
AH(12)25	—	4.00	10.00	15.00	21.50	30.00

KM# 80 1/2 RUPEE

Silver, 15 mm. **Obv. Inscription:** "Muhammad Akbar II" **Reverse:** Nagari "Ji" for Jayagi; Bow and arrow points down **Mint:** Gwalior Fort **Note:** Weight varies 5.35-5.70 grams.

Date	Mintage	Good	VG	F	VF	XF
ND//23 (1843-86)	—	2.35	6.00	10.00	17.50	25.00

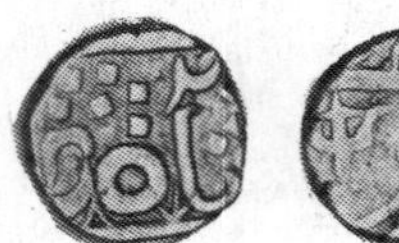

KM# 25 1/2 RUPEE
Silver **Obverse:** Without sword **Obv. Inscription:** "Shah Alam II" **Mint:** Bhilsa **Note:** Weight varies 5.35-5.80 grams.

Date	Mintage	Good	VG	F	VF	XF
AH(12)25	—	4.00	10.00	15.00	21.50	30.00

KM# 31 1/2 RUPEE
Silver **Obv. Inscription:** "Shah Alam II" **Mint:** Bhilsa **Note:** Weight varies 5.35-5.80 grams.

Date	Mintage	Good	VG	F	VF	XF
AH(12)25	—	2.75	7.00	11.00	16.50	25.00

KM# 236 1/2 RUPEE
Silver **Obv. Inscription:** "Shah Alam II" **Mint:** Daulat Rao **Note:** With continued postumous regnal years of Shah Alam II. Weight varies 5.35-5.80 grams.

Date	Mintage	Good	VG	F	VF	XF
ND//98 (1854-55)	—	2.25	5.50	8.00	12.50	18.50

KM# 51 1/2 RUPEE
Silver **Mint:** Garhakota **Note:** Weight varies 5.35-5.80 grams. Similar to 1 Rupee, KM#53.

Date	Mintage	Good	VG	F	VF	XF
ND//55 (1886)	—	10.00	25.00	40.00	60.00	85.00

KM# C238 1/2 RUPEE
Silver **Mint:** Daulat Rao **Note:** With continued regnal years of the British "Raj". Weight varies 5.35-5.80 grams.

Date	Mintage	Good	VG	F	VF	XF
ND//28 (1888)	—	2.75	7.00	11.00	16.50	25.00

KM# 124 RUPEE
Silver **Obv. Inscription:** "Shah Alam II" **Reverse:** With and without dot in "J" of Julus **Mint:** Lashkar **Note:** Weight varies 10.70-11.60 grams.

Date	Mintage	Good	VG	F	VF	XF
ND//16 (1821)	—	2.35	6.00	10.00	15.00	22.50
ND//17 (1822)	—	2.35	6.00	10.00	15.00	22.50
ND//18 (1823)	—	2.35	6.00	10.00	15.00	22.50
ND//19 (1824)	—	2.35	6.00	10.00	15.00	22.50
ND//21 (1826)	—	2.35	6.00	10.00	15.00	22.50
ND//22 (1827)	—	2.35	6.00	10.00	15.00	22.50

KM# 125 RUPEE
Silver **Obv. Inscription:** "Shah Alam II" **Reverse:** Lily in "J" of Julus **Mint:** Lashkar **Note:** Weight varies 10.70-11.60 grams.

Date	Mintage	Good	VG	F	VF	XF
ND//17 (1822)	—	2.35	6.00	10.00	15.00	22.50
ND//19 (1824)	—	2.35	6.00	10.00	15.00	22.50

KM# 32 RUPEE
Silver **Obv. Inscription:** "Shah Alam II" **Mint:** Bhilsa **Note:** Weight varies 10.70-11.60 grams.

Date	Mintage	Good	VG	F	VF	XF
AH(12)25	—	2.75	7.00	11.00	16.50	25.00

KM# 81 RUPEE
Silver **Obv. Inscription:** "Muhammad Akbar II" **Reverse:** Nagari "Ji" for Jayagi; Bow and arrow points up **Mint:** Gwalior Fort **Note:** Weight varies 5.35-5.70 grams. Size varies 17-19mm.

Date	Mintage	Good	VG	F	VF	XF
ND//23 (1843-86)	—	2.25	5.50	9.00	14.00	20.00

KM# 82 RUPEE
Silver **Obv. Inscription:** "Muhammad Akbar II" **Reverse:** Nagari "Ji" for Jayagi; Bow and arrow points down **Mint:** Gwalior Fort **Note:** Weight varies 5.35-5.70 grams. Size varies 17-19mm.

Date	Mintage	Good	VG	F	VF	XF
ND//23 (1843-86)	—	2.25	5.50	9.00	14.00	20.00

KM# 28 RUPEE
Silver **Obverse:** Sword **Obv. Inscription:** "Shah Alam II" **Reverse:** Bow and arrow **Mint:** Bhilsa **Note:** With additional initials of Madho Rao II.

Date	Mintage	Good	VG	F	VF	XF
AH(12)25	—	2.25	5.50	8.00	12.50	18.50

KM# 237 RUPEE
Silver **Obv. Inscription:** "Shah Alam II" **Mint:** Daulat Rao **Note:** With continued postumous regnal years of Shah Alam II. Weight varies 10.70-11.60 grams.

Date	Mintage	Good	VG	F	VF	XF
ND//89 (1845)	—	2.35	6.00	9.00	13.50	20.00
ND//92 (1848-49)	—	2.35	6.00	9.00	13.50	20.00
ND//93 (1849-50)	—	2.35	6.00	9.00	13.50	20.00
ND//94 (1850-51)	—	2.35	6.00	9.00	13.50	20.00
ND//95 (1851-52)	—	2.35	6.00	9.00	13.50	20.00
ND//98 (1854-55)	—	2.35	6.00	9.00	13.50	20.00
ND//99 (1855-56)	—	2.35	6.00	9.00	13.50	20.00
ND//100 (1856)	—	2.35	6.00	9.00	13.50	20.00

KM# 203 RUPEE
Silver **Obv. Inscription:** "Muhammad Akbar II" **Reverse:** Cannon left "Ji" **Mint:** Sheopur **Note:** Weight varies 10.70-11.60 grams.

Date	Mintage	Good	VG	F	VF	XF
AH1270//1 (sic)	—	3.50	9.00	18.00	28.00	40.00
AH1271//1 (sic)	—	3.50	9.00	18.00	28.00	40.00
AH1272//1 (sic)	—	3.50	9.00	18.00	28.00	40.00
AH1273//1 (sic)	—	3.50	9.00	18.00	28.00	40.00
AH1274//1 (sic)	—	3.50	9.00	18.00	28.00	40.00
AH1276//1 (sic)	—	3.50	9.00	18.00	28.00	40.00

KM# 204 RUPEE
Silver **Obverse:** KM#113 **Obv. Inscription:** "Muhammad Akbar II" **Reverse:** KM#113 and "Ji" **Mint:** Sheopur

Date	Mintage	Good	VG	F	VF	XF
ND//13 (1855-56)	—	3.50	9.00	18.00	27.00	38.00
ND//15 (1857-58)	—	3.50	9.00	18.00	27.00	38.00

KM# 19.2 RUPEE
Silver **Obv. Inscription:** "Muhammad Akbar II" and "Jankoji Rao" **Mint:** Basoda **Note:** Weight varies 10.70-11.60 grams.

Date	Mintage	Good	VG	F	VF	XF
AH1274//3x	—	10.00	25.00	37.50	50.00	70.00
AH1274//46	—	10.00	25.00	37.50	50.00	70.00

KM# 238 RUPEE
Silver **Mint:** Daulat Rao **Note:** With continued regnal years of the British "Raj". Weight varies 10.70-11.60 grams.

Date	Mintage	Good	VG	F	VF	XF
ND//3 (1861)	—	2.35	6.00	10.00	15.00	22.50
ND//4 (1862)	—	2.35	6.00	10.00	15.00	22.50
ND//8 (1866)	—	2.35	6.00	10.00	15.00	22.50
ND//9 (1867)	—	2.35	6.00	10.00	15.00	22.50
ND//20 (1878)	—	2.35	6.00	10.00	15.00	22.50
ND//22 (1880)	—	2.35	6.00	10.00	15.00	22.50
ND//25 (1883)	—	2.35	6.00	10.00	15.00	22.50
ND//26 (1884)	—	2.35	6.00	10.00	15.00	22.50
ND//28 (1886)	—	2.35	6.00	10.00	15.00	22.50

KM# 27 RUPEE
Silver **Obverse:** Without sword **Obv. Inscription:** "Shah Alam II" **Reverse:** Bow and arrow **Mint:** Bhilsa **Note:** Weight varies 10.70-11.60 grams.

Date	Mintage	Good	VG	F	VF	XF
AH(12)25//23	—	2.35	6.00	9.00	13.50	20.00

KM# 113 RUPEE
Silver **Reverse:** Persian "Ji" **Mint:** Jhansi **Note:** Weight varies 10.70-11.60 grams.

Date	Mintage	Good	VG	F	VF	XF
ND//48 (1865)	—	2.75	7.00	11.00	16.50	25.00
AH1282//5x	—	2.75	7.00	11.00	16.50	25.00
AH1284//5x	—	2.75	7.00	11.00	16.50	25.00

KM# 53 RUPEE
Silver **Mint:** Garhakota **Note:** Weight varies 10.70-11.60 grams.

Date	Mintage	Good	VG	F	VF	XF
ND//55 (1886)	—	2.75	7.00	11.50	18.50	30.00

KM# 83 NAZARANA RUPEE
Silver **Obv. Inscription:** "Muhammad Akbar II" **Reverse:** Nagari "Ji" for Jayagi **Mint:** Gwalior Fort **Note:** Weight varies 10.70-11.60 grams.

Date	Mintage	Good	VG	F	VF	XF
AH125x//23	—	—	175	275	400	550

KM# 74 NAZARANA 1/3 MOHUR
Gold **Obv. Inscription:** "Muhammad Shah" **Reverse:** Nagari "Ji" for Jayaji **Mint:** Gwalior Fort **Note:** Weight varies 3.57-3.80 grams.

Date	Mintage	Good	VG	F	VF	XF
AH1130//2 Frozen	—	—	175	275	400	575

Note: Struck ca.1843AD

KM# A75 MOHUR
Gold **Obv. Inscription:** "Muhammad Shah" **Reverse:** Nagari "Ji" for Jayaji **Mint:** Gwalior Fort

Date	Mintage	Good	VG	F	VF	XF
AH1130//2	—	—	400	475	550	700

Madho Rao
VS1943-1982 / 1886-1925AD
HAMMERED COINAGE

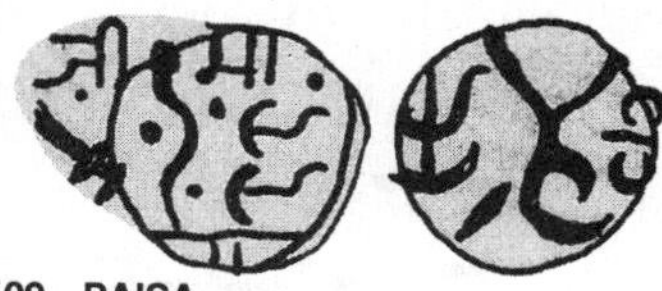

KM# 109 PAISA
Copper **Obverse:** Snake between letters "Ji" and "Ma" for Madho, scimitar **Reverse:** Trisul **Mint:** Jawad

Date	Mintage	Good	VG	F	VF	XF
ND(1886)	—	3.00	5.00	8.00	12.50	—

KM# 110 PAISA
Copper **Obverse:** Letters "Ji" and "Ma" for Madho, snake **Reverse:** Trisul **Mint:** Jawad

Date	Mintage	Good	VG	F	VF	XF
ND(1886)	—	3.00	5.00	8.00	12.50	—

KM# 246 PAISA
Copper **Obverse:** Horse **Reverse:** Retrograde legend **Mint:** Uncertain Mint

Date	Mintage	Good	VG	F	VF	XF
ND//32 (1890)	—	10.00	20.00	32.00	50.00	—

KM# 247 PAISA
Copper **Obverse:** Hand **Mint:** Uncertain Mint

Date	Mintage	Good	VG	F	VF	XF
ND(ca.1890)	—	5.00	10.00	16.50	25.00	—

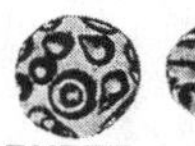 

KM# A156 1/16 RUPEE
Silver **Reverse:** Bow and arrow points down, "Ma" trisul **Mint:** Lashkar **Note:** With initial of Madho Rao II. Weight varies 0.67-0.72 grams.

Date	Mintage	Good	VG	F	VF	XF
ND//23 (1886)	—	1.25	3.00	4.50	6.50	10.00

KM# 239 1/16 RUPEE
Silver **Mint:** Daulat Rao **Note:** With continued regnal years of the British "Raj". Weight varies 0.67-0.72 grams.

Date	Mintage	Good	VG	F	VF	XF
AH1312	—	1.50	4.00	6.00	9.00	13.50
AH1313//37	—	1.50	4.00	6.00	9.00	13.50

KM# 156 1/8 RUPEE
Silver **Reverse:** Bow and arrow points down, "Ma" trisul **Mint:** Lashkar **Note:** Weight varies 1.34-1.45 grams.

Date	Mintage	Good	VG	F	VF	XF
ND//23 (1886)	—	1.50	4.00	6.00	9.00	14.00

KM# A240 1/8 RUPEE
Silver **Mint:** Daulat Rao **Note:** With continued regnal years of the British "Raj". Weight varies 1.34-1.45 grams.

Date	Mintage	Good	VG	F	VF	XF
ND//31 (1889)	—	2.00	5.00	7.00	10.00	15.00

KM# 240 1/8 RUPEE
Silver **Mint:** Daulat Rao **Note:** With continued regnal years of the British "Raj". Weight varies 1.34-1.45 grams.

Date	Mintage	Good	VG	F	VF	XF
AH13xx//33	—	2.00	5.00	7.00	10.00	15.00
AH1310//34	—	2.00	5.00	7.00	10.00	15.00
AH1311//35	—	2.00	5.00	7.00	10.00	15.00
AH1312//36	—	2.00	5.00	7.00	10.00	15.00
AH1313//37	—	2.00	5.00	7.00	10.00	15.00

KM# 157 1/4 RUPEE
Silver **Reverse:** Bow and arrow points down, "Ma" trisul **Mint:** Lashkar **Note:** Weight varies 2.68-2.90 grams.

Date	Mintage	Good	VG	F	VF	XF
ND//23 (1886)	—	2.00	5.00	7.00	10.00	15.50

KM# 241 1/4 RUPEE
Silver **Mint:** Daulat Rao **Note:** With continued regnal years of the British "Raj". Weight varies 2.68-2.90 grams.

Date	Mintage	Good	VG	F	VF	XF
AH1310//34	—	2.25	5.50	8.00	12.50	18.50
AH1311//35	—	2.25	5.50	8.00	12.50	18.50
AH1312//36	—	2.25	5.50	8.00	12.50	18.50
AH1313//37	—	2.25	5.50	8.00	12.50	18.50
AH1314//38	—	2.25	5.50	8.00	12.50	18.50

KM# 158 1/2 RUPEE
Silver **Reverse:** Bow and arrow points down, "Ma" trisul **Mint:** Lashkar **Note:** Weight varies 5.35-5.80 grams.

Date	Mintage	Good	VG	F	VF	XF
ND//23 (1886)	—	2.35	6.00	9.00	13.50	20.00

KM# A242 1/2 RUPEE
Silver **Mint:** Daulat Rao **Note:** With continued regnal years of the British "Raj". Weight varies 5.35-5.80 grams. Size varies 14-15mm.

Date	Mintage	Good	VG	F	VF	XF
ND//29 (1887)	—	2.35	6.00	9.00	13.50	20.00
ND//31 (1889)	—	2.35	6.00	9.00	13.50	20.00

KM# 242 1/2 RUPEE
Silver **Mint:** Daulat Rao **Note:** With continued regnal years of the British "Raj". Weight varies 5.35-5.80 grams. Size varies 14-15mm.

Date	Mintage	Good	VG	F	VF	XF
AH1310//34	—	2.35	6.00	9.00	13.50	20.00
AH1311//35	—	2.35	6.00	9.00	13.50	20.00
AH1312//36	—	2.35	6.00	9.00	13.50	20.00
AH1313//37	—	2.35	6.00	9.00	13.50	20.00
AH1314//38	—	2.35	6.00	9.00	13.50	20.00

KM# 159 RUPEE
Silver **Reverse:** Bow and arrow points down, "Ma" trisul **Mint:** Lashkar **Note:** Weight varies 10.70-11.60 grams.

Date	Mintage	Good	VG	F	VF	XF
ND//23 (1886)	—	2.25	5.50	8.00	12.50	18.50

KM# 243 RUPEE
Silver **Mint:** Daulat Rao **Note:** With continued regnal years of the British "Raj". Weight varies 10.70-11.60 grams.

Date	Mintage	Good	VG	F	VF	XF
ND//29 (1887)	—	2.50	6.50	10.00	15.00	22.50
ND//31 (1889)	—	2.50	6.50	10.00	15.00	22.50
ND//32 (1890)	—	2.50	6.50	10.00	15.00	22.50

KM# 244 RUPEE
Silver **Obverse:** AH date below **Mint:** Daulat Rao **Note:** With continued regnal years of the British "Raj". Weight varies 10.70-11.60 grams.

Date	Mintage	Good	VG	F	VF	XF
AH130x//33	—	2.50	6.50	10.00	15.00	22.50
AH13xx//34	—	2.50	6.50	10.00	15.00	22.50

KM# 245 RUPEE
Silver **Obverse:** AH date in center **Mint:** Daulat Rao **Note:** With continued regnal years of the British "Raj". Weight varies 10.70-11.60 grams.

Date	Mintage	Good	VG	F	VF	XF
AH1310//34	—	2.25	5.50	8.00	12.50	18.50
AH1310//35	—	2.25	5.50	8.00	12.50	18.50
AH1311//34	—	2.25	5.50	8.00	12.50	18.50
AH1311//35	—	2.25	5.50	8.00	12.50	18.50
AH1311//36	—	2.25	5.50	8.00	12.50	18.50
AH1312//34 (sic)	—	2.50	6.50	10.00	15.00	22.50
AH1312//36	—	2.25	5.50	8.00	12.50	18.50
AH1313//37	—	2.25	5.50	8.00	12.50	18.50
AH1314//38	—	2.25	5.50	8.00	12.50	18.50

KM# A160 1/4 MOHUR
Gold **Mint:** Lashkar

Date	Mintage	Good	VG	F	VF	XF
ND(1886) Rare	—	—	—	—	—	—

KM# 84 1/3 MOHUR
Gold, 21 mm. **Obv. Inscription:** "Muhammad Shah" **Reverse:** Nagari "Ma" for Madho Rao II **Mint:** Gwalior Fort **Note:** Weight varies 3.57-3.80 grams.

Date	Mintage	Good	VG	F	VF	XF
AH1130//2 Frozen	—	—	125	165	225	275

Note: Struck ca.1886AD

KM# 160 MOHUR
Gold **Reverse:** Bow and arrow points up, "Ma" trisul **Mint:** Lashkar **Note:** Weight varies 10.70-11.40 grams.

Date	Mintage	Good	VG	F	VF	XF
AH1130//2 Frozen	—	—	250	325	400	500

MILLED COINAGE

KM# 162 1/2 PICE
Copper, 20 mm. **Mint:** Gwalior Fort

Date	Mintage	Good	VG	F	VF	XF
VS1946	—	30.00	75.00	125	200	300

KM# 163 1/2 PICE
Copper, 20 mm. **Mint:** Gwalior Fort **Note:** Punched from 1/4 Anna, KM#168.

Date	Mintage	Good	VG	F	VF	XF
VS1946	—	30.00	75.00	125	200	—

KM# 164 1/2 PICE
Copper, 20 mm. **Obverse:** Plumes above crossed spear and trident **Mint:** Gwalior Fort

Date	Mintage	Good	VG	F	VF	XF
VS1956	—	—	0.25	0.65	2.00	4.00
VS1957	—	—	0.25	0.65	2.00	4.00

KM# A161 PIE
Copper **Mint:** Gwalior Fort

Date	Mintage	Good	VG	F	VF	XF
VS1946	—	30.00	75.00	125	200	300

KM# 161 PIE
Copper **Mint:** Gwalior Fort

Date	Mintage	Good	VG	F	VF	XF
VS(19)55	—	40.00	100	150	200	—

KM# 165 1/4 ANNA
Copper **Obverse:** 16 point star, wide nose on sun **Mint:** Gwalior Fort

Date	Mintage	Good	VG	F	VF	XF
VS1944	—	40.00	100	175	250	375

KM# 166 1/4 ANNA
Copper **Obverse:** 18 point star, wide nose on sun **Mint:** Gwalior Fort

Date	Mintage	Good	VG	F	VF	XF
VS1944	—	40.00	100	175	250	375

KM# 167 1/4 ANNA
Copper **Obverse:** 17 point star, wide nose on sun **Mint:** Gwalior Fort

Date	Mintage	Good	VG	F	VF	XF
VS1945	—	40.00	100	150	225	375

KM# 168 1/4 ANNA
Copper **Obverse:** 16 point star, narrow nose on sun **Mint:** Gwalior Fort

Date	Mintage	Good	VG	F	VF	XF
VS1946	—	25.00	60.00	80.00	130	200

KM# 169 1/4 ANNA
Copper **Obverse:** Plumes above crossed spear and trident

Date	Mintage	VG	F	VF	XF	Unc
VS1953	—	0.30	0.75	2.25	4.50	11.00
VS1954	—	0.30	0.75	2.25	4.50	11.00
VS1956	—	0.30	0.75	2.25	4.50	11.00
VS1957	—	0.30	0.75	2.25	4.50	11.00

KM# 173 1/2 ANNA
Copper

Date	Mintage	VG	F	VF	XF	Unc
VS1946	—	80.00	200	300	450	650

KM# 174 RUPEE
Silver, 32 mm.

Date	Mintage	VG	F	VF	XF	Unc
VS1954 Rare	—	—	—	—	—	—

HANSI

A Cis-Sutlej state until the first Sikh war (1845-46) and then their independence became restricted until 1849 when the Punjab was annexed and the states were melded into the new province of British India. Most of the Cis-Sutlej states distinguished themselves on the side of the British during the great revolt of 1857.

RULER
Raja George Thomas

MINT

صاحب اباد هنسي

Sahibabad

Raja George Thomas

HAMMERED COINAGE

KM# 1 RUPEE
Silver **Obverse:** Parasol **Obv. Inscription:** "Muhammad Shah Alam II" **Reverse:** Sun face **Mint:** Sahibabad

Date	Mintage	VG	F	VF	XF	Unc
AH1214/42 (1825)	—	350	525	750	1,000	—

HYDERABAD

Haidarabad

Hyderabad State, the largest Indian State and the last remnant of Mughal suzerainty in South or Central India, traced its foundation to Nizam-ul Mulk, the Mughal viceroy in the Deccan. From about 1724 the first nizam, as the rulers of Hyderabad came to be called, took advantage of Mughal decline in the North to assert an all but ceremonial independence of the emperor. The East India Company defeated Hyderabad's natural enemies, the Muslim rulers of Mysore and the Marathas, with the help of troops furnished under alliances between them and the Nizam. This formed the beginning of a relationship, which persisted for a century and a half until India's Independence. Hyderabad City is located beside Golkonda, the citadel of the Qutb Shahi sultans until they were overthrown by Aurangzeb in 1687. A beautifully located city on the bank of the Musi river, the mint epithet was appropriately Farkhanda Bunyad, "of happy foundation".

Hyderabad exercised authority over a number of feudatories or samasthans. Some of these, such as Gadwal and Shorapur, paid tribute to both the Nizam and the Marathas. These feudatories were generally in the hands of local rajas whose ancestry predated the establishment of Hyderabad State. There were also many mints in the State, both private and government. There was little or no standardization of the purity of silver coinage until the 20th century. At least one banker, Pestonji Meherji by name, was distinguished by minting his own coins.

RULERS

Nizam Ali Khan, AH1175-1218/1761-1803AD
Sikandar Jah, AH1218-1244/1803-1829AD
Nasir-ad-Daula, AH1244-1273/1829-1857AD

Mint mark:

ن

Rev: Persian letter "N".

Afzal-ad-Daula, AH1273-1285/1857-1869AD

Mint marks:

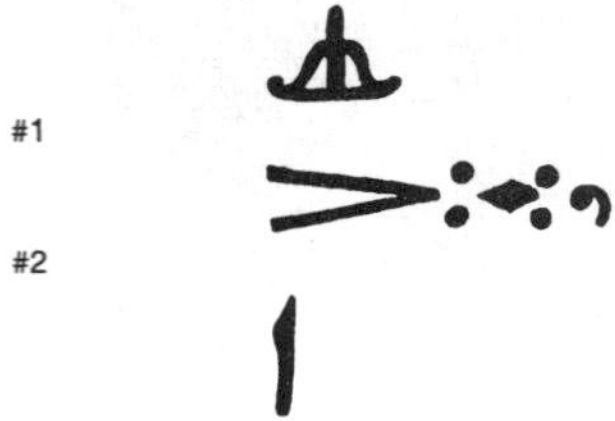

#1

#2

#3

For his last two years, AH1274-75, regnal year 18 w/Persian letter "A" (symbol 3) above Padishah on obv. Copper coins have symbol #1, while silver and gold have #2.

Mir Mahbub Ali Khan II, AH1285-1329/1869-1911AD

Persian letter "M" for Mahbub above "k" of Mulk on obverse.

MINTS

امراوتي

Amaravati

اورنگ اباد

Aurangabad

خجسته بنیاد

Mint name: Khujista Bunyad

Mint marks:

دولت اباد

Daulatabad

حیدراباد

Haidarabad

Mint mark:

س

Persian letter "S".

فرخنده بنیاد

Hyderabad
Mint name: Farkhanda Bunyad

Mint mark:

ن

Rev: Persian letter "N".

Nizam Ali Khan

AH1175-1218 / 1761-1803AD

HAMMERED COINAGE

KM# 2 PAISA
Copper **Obv. Inscription:** "Shah Alam II" **Mint:** Aurangabad

Date	Mintage	Good	VG	F	VF	XF
ND(1798-1805)	—	2.00	2.50	3.50	5.00	—
AH1219	—	2.50	3.25	4.50	6.00	—

KM# 5 RUPEE
Silver **Obv. Inscription:** "Shah Alam II" **Mint:** Aurangabad **Note:** Weight varies 10.7 - 11.6 grams.

Date	Mintage	Good	VG	F	VF	XF
AH1218	—	4.00	10.00	17.50	30.00	45.00

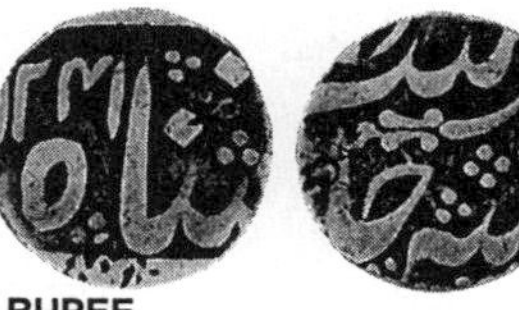

KM# 45 RUPEE
Silver **Obverse:** Without Persian letter "S" **Obv. Inscription:** "Muhammad Akbar II" **Mint:** Aurangabad **Note:** Weight varies 10.70-11.60 grams.

Date	Mintage	Good	VG	F	VF	XF
AH1227//6	—	3.00	7.50	12.50	18.50	27.50
AH1228//6 (sic)	—	3.00	7.50	12.50	18.50	27.50
AH1230//9	—	3.00	7.50	12.50	18.50	27.50
AH(12)32//11	—	3.00	7.50	12.50	18.50	27.50
AH1234//17 (sic)	—	3.00	7.50	12.50	18.50	27.50
ND//16 (1821-22)	—	3.00	7.50	12.50	18.50	27.50
AH1239//17 (sic)	—	3.00	7.50	12.50	18.50	27.50
AH1240//20	—	3.00	7.50	12.50	18.50	27.50
AH1241//2x	—	3.00	7.50	12.50	18.50	27.50
AH1242//21	—	3.00	7.50	12.50	18.50	27.50

Sikandar Jah
AH1218-1244 / 1803-1829AD

HAMMERED COINAGE

C# 40 PAISA
Copper **Obv. Inscription:** "Shah Alam II" **Mint:** Haidarabad (Farkhanda Bunyad)

Date	Mintage	Good	VG	F	VF	XF
AH1217//44	—	1.25	2.00	3.00	4.50	—
AH1218	—	1.25	2.00	3.00	4.50	—

C# 44 PAISA
Copper **Obv. Inscription:** "Muhammad Akbar II" **Mint:** Haidarabad **Note:** Size varies 17-20mm.

Date	Mintage	Good	VG	F	VF	XF
AH1221	—	1.25	2.00	2.75	3.50	—
AH1229	—	1.25	2.00	2.75	3.50	—
AH1237	—	1.25	2.00	2.75	3.50	—

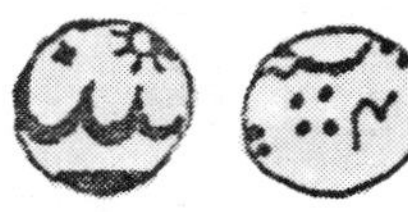

C# 63.2 1/8 RUPEE
Silver **Obv. Inscription:** Bahadur Shah **Mint:** Aurangabad **Note:** Weight varies 1.34-1.45 grams.

Date	Mintage	Good	VG	F	VF	XF
AH1256//4	—	16.00	40.00	65.00	100	150

C# 46 1/4 RUPEE
Silver **Obv. Inscription:** "Muhammad Akbar II" **Mint:** Haidarabad **Note:** Weight varies 2.68-2.90 grams.

Date	Mintage	Good	VG	F	VF	XF
AH1238	—	2.35	6.00	10.00	15.00	25.00
AH1239	—	2.35	6.00	10.00	15.00	25.00
AH1241	—	2.35	6.00	10.00	15.00	25.00
AH1242//23	—	2.35	6.00	10.00	15.00	25.00

C# 64.1 1/4 RUPEE
Silver **Obv. Inscription:** "Bahadur Shah" **Mint:** Aurangabad **Note:** Weight varies 2.68-2.90 grams.

Date	Mintage	Good	VG	F	VF	XF
AH1256//4	—	16.00	40.00	65.00	100	150

C# 47 1/2 RUPEE
Silver **Obv. Inscription:** "Muhammad Akbar II" **Mint:** Haidarabad **Note:** Weight varies 5.35-5.80 grams.

Date	Mintage	Good	VG	F	VF	XF
AH1235//14	—	2.35	6.00	10.00	15.00	25.00
AH1237	—	2.35	6.00	10.00	15.00	25.00
AH1238	—	2.35	6.00	10.00	15.00	25.00
AH1241	—	2.35	6.00	10.00	15.00	25.00
AH1242//23 (sic)	—	2.35	6.00	10.00	15.00	25.00

C# 65.2 1/2 RUPEE
Silver **Obv. Inscription:** "Bahadur Shah" **Mint:** Aurangabad **Note:** Weight varies 5.35-5.80 grams.

Date	Mintage	Good	VG	F	VF	XF
AH1256//4	—	16.00	40.00	65.00	100	150

C# 41 RUPEE
Silver **Obv. Inscription:** "Shah Alam II" **Mint:** Haidarabad (Farkhanda Bunyad) **Note:** Weight varies 10.70-11.60 grams. Size varies 20-22mm.

Date	Mintage	Good	VG	F	VF	XF
AH1218	—	16.00	40.00	65.00	100	150
AH1220	—	16.00	40.00	65.00	100	150

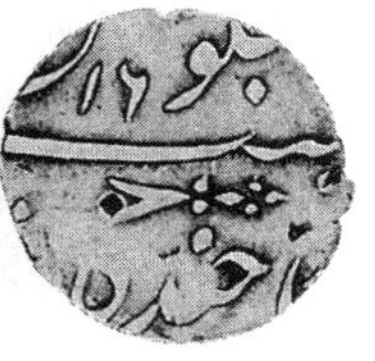

C# 48.1 RUPEE
Silver **Obv. Inscription:** "Muhammad Akbar II" **Mint:** Haidarabad **Note:** Weight varies 10.70-11.60 grams.

Date	Mintage	Good	VG	F	VF	XF
AH1222	—	2.35	6.00	9.00	13.50	20.00
AH1224	—	2.35	6.00	9.00	13.50	20.00
AH1225//4	—	2.35	6.00	9.00	13.50	20.00
AH1226//4 (sic)	—	2.35	6.00	9.00	13.50	20.00
AH1227//6	—	2.35	6.00	9.00	13.50	20.00
AH1227//7	—	2.35	6.00	9.00	13.50	20.00
AH1228//7	—	2.35	6.00	9.00	13.50	20.00
AH1229//8	—	2.35	6.00	9.00	13.50	20.00
AH1230//9	—	2.35	6.00	9.00	13.50	20.00
AH1231//10	—	2.35	6.00	9.00	13.50	20.00
AH1232//11	—	2.35	6.00	9.00	13.50	20.00
AH1233//12	—	2.35	6.00	9.00	13.50	20.00
AH1234//13	—	2.35	6.00	9.00	13.50	20.00
AH1235//15	—	2.35	6.00	9.00	13.50	20.00
AH1236//15	—	2.35	6.00	9.00	13.50	20.00
AH1237//16	—	2.35	6.00	9.00	13.50	20.00
AH1238//12 (sic)	—	2.35	6.00	9.00	13.50	20.00
AH1239//21 (sic)	—	2.35	6.00	9.00	13.50	20.00
AH1240//21 (sic)	—	2.35	6.00	9.00	13.50	20.00
AH1240//22 (sic)	—	2.35	6.00	9.00	13.50	20.00
AH1241//22 (sic)	—	2.35	6.00	9.00	13.50	20.00
AH1242//23 (sic)	—	2.35	6.00	9.00	13.50	20.00
AH1243//24 (sic)	—	2.35	6.00	9.00	13.50	20.00
AH1244//25 (sic)	—	2.35	6.00	9.00	13.50	20.00

C# 48.2 RUPEE
Silver **Obv. Inscription:** "Muhammad Akbar II" **Reverse:** "Maharaja" above mintname **Mint:** Haidarabad **Note:** Weight varies 10.70-11.60 grams.

Date	Mintage	Good	VG	F	VF	XF
AH1238	—	25.00	60.00	100	150	220

C# 48.3 RUPEE
Silver **Obv. Inscription:** "Muhammad Akbar II" **Reverse:** "Sikandar" **Mint:** Haidarabad **Note:** Weight varies 10.70-11.60 grams.

Date	Mintage	Good	VG	F	VF	XF
AH1239	—	25.00	60.00	100	150	220

KM# 1 RUPEE
Silver **Mint:** Amaravati

Date	Mintage	Good	VG	F	VF	XF
AH1240	—	15.00	40.00	65.00	100	150
AH1241	—	15.00	40.00	65.00	100	150

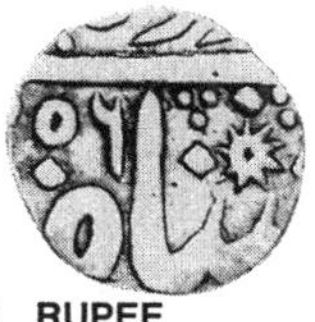

C# 66.2 RUPEE
Silver **Obv. Inscription:** "Bahadur Shah" **Mint:** Aurangabad **Note:** Weight varies 10.70-11.60 grams.

Date	Mintage	Good	VG	F	VF	XF
AH1254//1	—	3.00	7.50	12.50	18.50	27.50
AH1254//2	—	3.00	7.50	12.50	18.50	27.50
AH1256//4	—	3.00	7.50	12.50	18.50	27.50
AH1264	—	3.00	7.50	12.50	18.50	27.50

C# 48a NAZARANA RUPEE
Silver **Obv. Inscription:** "Muhammad Akbar II" **Mint:** Haidarabad **Note:** Weight varies 10.70-11.60 grams.

Date	Mintage	Good	VG	F	VF	XF
AH1237//16	—	40.00	100	175	250	350
AH1238//17	—	40.00	100	175	250	350

C# 56 1/16 MOHUR
Gold **Obv. Inscription:** "Muhammad Akbar II" **Mint:** Haidarabad **Note:** Weight varies 0.67-0.70 grams.

Date	Mintage	Good	VG	F	VF	XF
AH123x	—	—	50.00	70.00	125	200

C# 57 1/8 MOHUR
Gold **Obv. Inscription:** "Muhammad Akbar II" **Mint:** Haidarabad **Note:** Weight varies 1.34-1.42 grams.

Date	Mintage	Good	VG	F	VF	XF
AH123x	—	—	60.00	85.00	150	225

C# 58 1/4 MOHUR
Gold **Obv. Inscription:** "Muhammad Akbar II" **Mint:** Haidarabad **Note:** Weight varies 2.68-2.85 grams.

Date	Mintage	Good	VG	F	VF	XF
AH1236//15	—	—	75.00	110	175	250

C# A58 NAZARANA 1/4 MOHUR
Gold **Mint:** Haidarabad **Note:** Weight varies 2.68-2.85 grams.

Date	Mintage	Good	VG	F	VF	XF
AH1236//15 Rare	—	—	—	—	—	—

C# 59 1/2 MOHUR
Gold **Obv. Inscription:** "Muhammad Akbar II" **Mint:** Haidarabad **Note:** Weight varies 5.35-5.70 grams.

Date	Mintage	Good	VG	F	VF	XF
AH123x	—	—	100	150	250	350

C# 60 MOHUR
Gold **Obv. Inscription:** "Muhammad Akbar II" **Mint:** Haidarabad **Note:** Weight varies 10.70-11.40 grams.

Date	Mintage	Good	VG	F	VF	XF
AH1226	—	—	185	235	285	400
AH1227	—	—	185	235	285	400
AH1228//7	—	—	185	235	285	400
AH1231	—	—	185	235	285	400
AH1234	—	—	185	235	285	400
AH1235	—	—	185	235	285	400
AH1236//15	—	—	185	235	285	400

Date	Mintage	Good	VG	F	VF	XF
AH1237//16	—	—	185	235	285	400
AH1238	—	—	185	235	285	400
AH1241	—	—	185	235	285	400
AH1242	—	—	185	235	285	400
AH1243//24 (sic)	—	—	185	235	285	400
AH1244	—	—	185	235	285	400

C# 60a NAZARANA MOHUR
Gold **Obv. Inscription:** "Muhammad Akbar II" **Mint:** Haidarabad **Note:** Weight varies 10.70-11.40 grams.

Date	Mintage	Good	VG	F	VF	XF
AH1236//15 Rare	—	—	—	—	—	—

Nasir-ad-Daula
AH1244-1273 / 1829-1857AD
HAMMERED COINAGE

C# 61.3 PAISA
Copper **Obv. Inscription:** "Muhammad Akbar II" **Mint:** Haidarabad

Date	Mintage	Good	VG	F	VF	XF
ND(1806-37) Date off flan	—	1.00	2.00	3.50	5.00	—
AH1247	—	2.00	3.00	4.50	7.50	—
AH1250	—	2.00	3.00	4.50	7.50	—

C# 73 PAISA
Copper **Obv. Inscription:** "Bahadur Shah" **Mint:** Haidarabad **Note:** Round or square.

Date	Mintage	Good	VG	F	VF	XF
ND(1837-58) Date off flan	—	1.00	2.00	3.00	4.50	—
AH1257//4	—	2.00	3.00	4.00	7.00	—
AH1258	—	2.00	3.00	4.00	7.00	—
AH1262//7 (sic)	—	2.00	3.00	4.00	7.00	—
AH1272	—	2.00	3.00	4.00	7.00	—
AH1273	—	2.00	3.00	4.00	7.00	—

KM# 63 PAISA
Copper **Obv. Inscription:** "Muhammad Akbar II" **Mint:** Aurangabad

Date	Mintage	Good	VG	F	VF	XF
AH1257	—	—	2.50	4.00	6.50	10.00

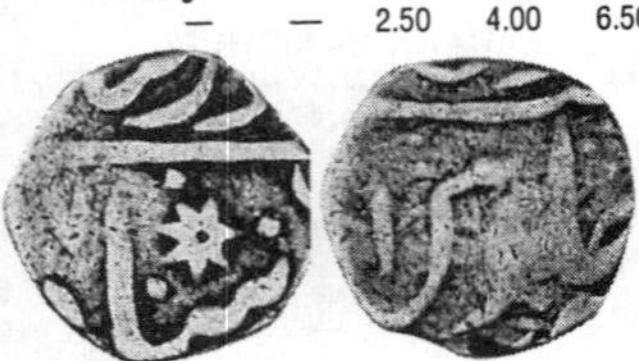

KM# 62 PAISA
11.7000 g., Copper **Obverse:** Star and date **Obv. Inscription:** "Bahadur Shah" **Mint:** Aurangabad

Date	Mintage	Good	VG	F	VF	XF
AH(12)57	—	—	4.50	7.50	12.00	—

C# 75 1/16 RUPEE
Silver **Obv. Inscription:** "Bahadur Shah" **Mint:** Haidarabad **Note:** Size varies 9-11mm. Weight varies 0.67-0.72 grams.

Date	Mintage	Good	VG	F	VF	XF
AH1272	—	3.00	7.50	12.50	20.00	30.00

C# 76 1/8 RUPEE
Silver **Obv. Inscription:** "Bahadur Shah" **Mint:** Haidarabad **Note:** Size varies 11-13mm. Weight varies 1.34-1.45 grams.

Date	Mintage	Good	VG	F	VF	XF
AH1272	—	3.00	7.50	12.50	20.00	30.00

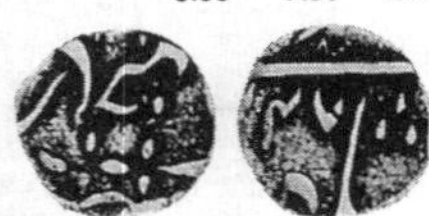

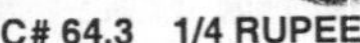

C# 64.3 1/4 RUPEE
Silver **Obv. Inscription:** "Muhammad Akbar II" **Mint:** Haidarabad **Note:** Weight varies 2.68-2.90 grams.

Date	Mintage	Good	VG	F	VF	XF
AH1246	—	1.35	3.50	5.00	7.50	12.50
AH1247	—	1.35	3.50	5.00	7.50	12.50
AH1249	—	1.35	3.50	5.00	7.50	12.50
AH1251	—	1.35	3.50	5.00	7.50	12.50

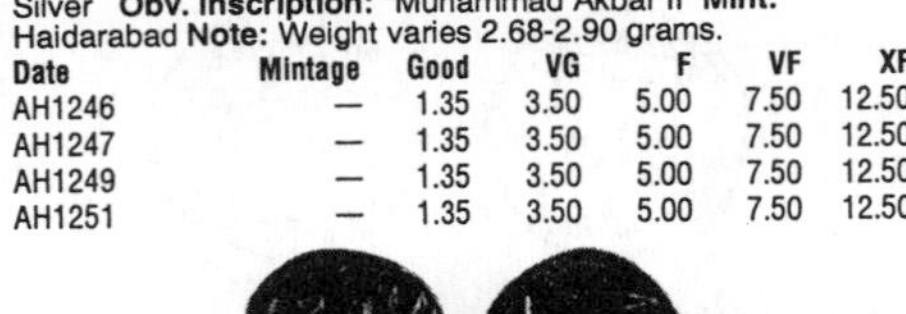

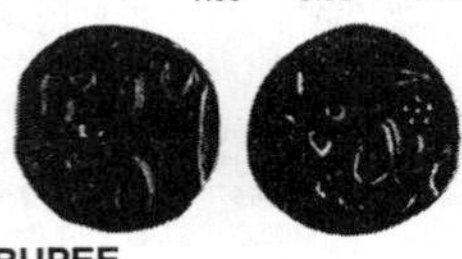

C# 77 1/4 RUPEE
Silver **Obv. Inscription:** "Bahadur Shah" **Mint:** Haidarabad **Note:** Size varies 14-15mm. Weight varies 2.68-2.90 grams.

Date	Mintage	Good	VG	F	VF	XF
AH1257	—	2.75	7.00	11.00	16.50	25.00
AH1268	—	2.75	7.00	11.00	16.50	25.00
AH1272//17 (sic)	—	2.75	7.00	11.00	16.50	25.00
AH1273//18 (sic)	—	2.75	7.00	11.00	16.50	25.00

C# 65.3 1/2 RUPEE
Silver, 18 mm. **Obv. Inscription:** "Muhammad Akbar II" **Mint:** Haidarabad **Note:** Weight varies 5.35-5.80 grams.

Date	Mintage	Good	VG	F	VF	XF
AH1249	—	2.25	5.50	8.00	12.50	18.50
AH1250	—	2.25	5.50	8.00	12.50	18.50
AH1251//33	—	2.25	5.50	8.00	12.50	18.50

C# 78 1/2 RUPEE
Silver **Obv. Inscription:** "Bahadur Shah" **Mint:** Haidarabad **Note:** Size varies 16-19mm. Weight varies 5.35-5.80 grams.

Date	Mintage	Good	VG	F	VF	XF
AH1257//5	—	2.50	6.50	10.00	15.00	22.50
AH1260	—	2.50	6.50	10.00	15.00	22.50

C# 66.3 RUPEE
Silver **Obv. Inscription:** "Muhammad Akbar II" **Mint:** Haidarabad **Note:** Weight varies 0.70-11.60 grams.

Date	Mintage	Good	VG	F	VF	XF
AH1245//26 (sic)	—	3.00	7.50	10.00	16.50	25.00
AH1246	—	3.00	7.50	10.00	16.50	25.00
AH1248//29 (sic)	—	3.00	7.50	10.00	16.50	25.00
AH1249	—	3.00	7.50	10.00	16.50	25.00
AH1250//31 (sic)	—	3.00	7.50	10.00	16.50	25.00
AH1251//33 (sic)	—	3.00	7.50	10.00	16.50	25.00
AH1252//34 (sic)	—	3.00	7.50	10.00	16.50	25.00
AH1253//35 (sic)	—	3.00	7.50	10.00	16.50	25.00

KM# 66.1 RUPEE
Silver **Obv. Inscription:** "Muhammad Akbar II" **Mint:** Aurangabad **Note:** Weight varies 11.70-11.60 grams.

Date	Mintage	VG	F	VF	XF	Unc
AH1251 (1835)	—	7.50	12.50	18.50	27.50	—

C# 79 RUPEE
Silver **Obv. Inscription:** "Bahadur Shah" **Mint:** Haidarabad **Note:** Weight varies 10.70-11.60 grams.

Date	Mintage	Good	VG	F	VF	XF
AH1253//1	—	2.35	6.00	9.00	13.50	20.00
AH1258//6	—	2.35	6.00	9.00	13.50	20.00
AH1261//8	—	2.35	6.00	9.00	13.50	20.00
AH1262//9	—	2.35	6.00	9.00	13.50	20.00
AH1266//11 (sic)	—	2.35	6.00	9.00	13.50	30.00
AH1267//12 (sic)	—	2.35	6.00	9.00	13.50	20.00
AH1268//12 (sic)	—	2.35	6.00	9.00	13.50	20.00
AH1268//13 (sic)	—	2.35	6.00	9.00	13.50	20.00
AH1270//15 (sic)	—	2.35	6.00	9.00	13.50	20.00
AH1270//16 (sic)	—	2.35	6.00	9.00	13.50	20.00
AH1271//16 (sic)	—	2.35	6.00	9.00	13.50	20.00
AH1271//17 (sic)	—	2.35	6.00	9.00	13.50	20.00
AH1272//17 (sic)	—	2.35	6.00	9.00	13.50	20.00
AH1273//18 (sic)	—	2.35	6.00	9.00	13.50	20.00

C# 68 1/16 MOHUR
Gold **Obv. Inscription:** "Muhammad Akbar II" **Mint:** Haidarabad **Note:** Weight varies 0.67-.0.71 grams.

Date	Mintage	Good	VG	F	VF	XF
ND(1806-37)	—	—	25.00	35.00	60.00	100

C# 80 1/16 MOHUR
Gold **Obv. Inscription:** "Bahadur Shah" **Mint:** Haidarabad **Note:** Weight varies 0.67-0.71 grams.

Date	Mintage	Good	VG	F	VF	XF
ND(1837-58)	—	—	35.00	50.00	80.00	120

C# 69 1/8 MOHUR
Gold **Obv. Inscription:** "Muhammad Akbar II" **Mint:** Haidarabad **Note:** Weight varies 1.34-1.42 grams.

Date	Mintage	Good	VG	F	VF	XF
ND(1806-37)	—	—	35.00	50.00	90.00	125

C# 81 1/8 MOHUR
Gold **Obv. Inscription:** "Bahadur Shah" **Mint:** Haidarabad **Note:** Weight varies 1.34-1.42 grams.

Date	Mintage	Good	VG	F	VF	XF
ND(1837-58)	—	—	40.00	65.00	100	140

C# 70 1/4 MOHUR
Gold **Obv. Inscription:** "Muhammad Akbar II" **Mint:** Haidarabad **Note:** Weight varies 2.68-2.85 grams.

Date	Mintage	Good	VG	F	VF	XF
ND(1806-37)	—	—	50.00	85.00	130	175

C# 82 1/4 MOHUR
Gold **Obv. Inscription:** "Bahadur Shah" **Mint:** Haidarabad **Note:** Weight varies 2.68-2.85 grams.

Date	Mintage	Good	VG	F	VF	XF
ND(1837-58)	—	—	50.00	85.00	120	200

C# 71 1/2 MOHUR
Gold **Obv. Inscription:** "Muhammad Akbar II" **Mint:** Haidarabad **Note:** Weight varies 5.35-5.70 grams.

Date	Mintage	Good	VG	F	VF	XF
ND(1806-37)	—	—	90.00	125	175	250

C# 83 1/2 MOHUR
Gold **Obv. Inscription:** "Bahadur Shah" **Mint:** Haidarabad **Note:** Weight varies 5.35-5.70 grams.

Date	Mintage	Good	VG	F	VF	XF
ND(1837-58)	—	—	80.00	130	200	275

C# 72 MOHUR
Gold **Obv. Inscription:** "Muhammad Akbar II" **Mint:** Haidarabad **Note:** Size varies 22-23mm.

Date	Mintage	Good	VG	F	VF	XF
AH1244	—	—	185	235	285	375
AH1246	—	—	185	235	285	375
AH1248	—	—	185	235	285	375
AH1249	—	—	185	235	285	375
AH1251	—	—	185	235	285	375

C# 84 MOHUR
Gold, 22 mm. **Obv. Inscription:** "Bahadur Shah" **Mint:** Haidarabad **Note:** Weight varies 10.70-11.40 grams.

Date	Mintage	Good	VG	F	VF	XF
AH1258//6	—	—	175	215	265	325
AH1260	—	—	175	215	265	325
AH1261//8	—	—	175	215	265	325
AH1263//9 (sic)	—	—	175	215	265	325
AH1264	—	—	175	215	265	325
AH1265	—	—	175	215	265	325
AH1266//11 (sic)	—	—	175	215	265	325
AH1267//12 (sic)	—	—	175	215	265	325
AH1268	—	—	175	215	265	325
AH1269	—	—	175	215	265	325
AH1270//15 (sic)	—	—	175	215	265	325
AH1271	—	—	175	215	265	325
AH1273//17 (sic)	—	—	175	215	265	325

Afzal-ad-Daula
AH1273-1285 / 1857-1869AD
HAMMERED COINAGE

C# 85 1/2 PAISA
Copper **Obv. Inscription:** "Bahadur Shah II" **Mint:** Haidarabad

Date	Mintage	Good	VG	F	VF	XF
AH1275	—	1.50	2.50	3.50	6.00	—
ND//19 (1859-60)	—	1.50	2.50	3.50	6.00	—

C# 86 PAISA

Copper **Obv. Inscription:** "Bahadur Shah II" **Mint:** Haidarabad

Date	Mintage	Good	VG	F	VF	XF
AH1275//18	—	1.50	2.50	3.50	6.00	—
ND(1858-60) Date off flan	—	1.25	2.25	3.00	4.50	—
AH1276//19	—	1.50	2.50	3.50	6.00	—
AH1277//19	—	1.50	2.50	3.50	6.00	—

Y# 1 PAISA (Dub)

Copper **Series:** Second **Obv. Inscription:** "Asaf Jah, Nizam al-Mulk" **Mint:** Haidarabad **Note:** Irregular and regular shapes, size varies 16-30mm.

Date	Mintage	Good	VG	F	VF	XF
AH1282	—	1.75	2.50	3.50	5.00	—
ND(1865-67)	—	1.00	2.00	3.00	4.00	—
AH1283	—	1.75	2.50	3.50	5.00	—

Y# 2 1/16 RUPEE (Anna)

Silver, 9 mm. **Obv. Inscription:** "Asaf Jah, Nizam al-Mulk" **Mint:** Haidarabad **Note:** Weight varies 0.67-0.72 grams.

Date	Mintage	Good	VG	F	VF	XF
AH1275	—	5.00	12.50	20.00	30.00	45.00

C# 88 1/8 RUPEE

Silver, 13 mm. **Obv. Inscription:** "Bahadur Shah II" **Mint:** Haidarabad **Note:** Weight varies 1.34-1.45 grams.

Date	Mintage	Good	VG	F	VF	XF
AH1275	—	3.00	7.50	12.50	20.00	30.00

Y# 3 1/8 RUPEE

Silver **Obv. Inscription:** "Asaf Jah, Nizam al-Mulk" **Mint:** Haidarabad **Note:** Size varies 11.13mm. Weight varies 1.34-1.45 grams.

Date	Mintage	Good	VG	F	VF	XF
AH1278	—	2.35	6.00	10.00	15.00	22.00
AH1279	—	2.35	6.00	10.00	15.00	22.00

C# 89 1/4 RUPEE

Silver, 14 mm. **Obv. Inscription:** "Bahadur Shah II" **Mint:** Haidarabad **Note:** Weight varies 2.68-2.90 grams.

Date	Mintage	Good	VG	F	VF	XF
AH1274	—	1.65	4.00	7.50	10.00	16.50

Y# 4 1/4 RUPEE

Silver **Obv. Inscription:** "Asaf Jah, Nizam al-Mulk" **Mint:** Haidarabad **Note:** Weight varies 2.68-2.90 grams.

Date	Mintage	Good	VG	F	VF	XF
AH1276	—	1.25	3.00	5.00	7.50	12.00
AH1278	—	1.25	3.00	5.00	7.50	12.00
AH1283//10	—	1.25	3.00	5.00	7.50	12.00

C# 90 1/2 RUPEE

Silver, 17 mm. **Obv. Inscription:** "Bahadur Shah II" **Mint:** Haidarabad **Note:** Weight varies 5.35-5.80 grams.

Date	Mintage	Good	VG	F	VF	XF
AH1274	—	2.65	6.50	10.00	15.00	22.50

Y# 5 1/2 RUPEE

Silver **Obv. Inscription:** "Asaf Jah, Nizam al-Mulk" **Mint:** Haidarabad **Note:** Weight varies 5.35-5.80 grams.

Date	Mintage	Good	VG	F	VF	XF
AH1276	—	1.50	3.50	6.50	9.00	15.00
AH1277	—	1.50	3.50	6.50	9.00	15.00
AH128(4)//11	—	1.50	3.50	6.50	9.00	15.00

C# 91 RUPEE

Silver **Obv. Inscription:** "Bahadur Shah II" **Mint:** Haidarabad **Note:** Weight varies 10.70-11.60 grams.

Date	Mintage	Good	VG	F	VF	XF
AH1273//18	—	3.00	7.50	10.00	13.50	20.00
AH1274//18	—	3.00	7.50	10.00	13.50	20.00
AH1275//18	—	3.00	7.50	10.00	13.50	20.00

Y# 6 RUPEE

Silver **Obv. Inscription:** "Asaf Jah, Nizam al-Mulk" **Mint:** Haidarabad **Note:** Weight varies 10.70-11.60 grams.

Date	Mintage	Good	VG	F	VF	XF
AH1275//2	—	2.00	3.00	6.00	8.00	12.50
AH1276//3	—	2.00	3.00	6.00	8.00	12.50
AH1276//4	—	2.00	3.00	6.00	8.00	12.50
AH1277//4	—	2.00	3.00	6.00	8.00	12.50
AH1278//5	—	2.00	3.00	6.00	8.00	12.50
AH1279//6	—	2.00	3.00	6.00	8.00	12.50
AH1280//7	—	2.00	3.00	6.00	8.00	12.50
AH1281//7 (sic)	—	2.00	3.00	6.00	8.00	12.50
AH1281//8	—	2.00	3.00	6.00	8.00	12.50
AH1282//9	—	2.00	3.00	6.00	8.00	12.50
AH1283//10	—	2.00	3.00	6.00	8.00	12.50
AH1284//11	—	2.00	3.00	6.00	8.00	12.50
AH1285//12	—	2.00	3.00	6.00	8.00	12.50

Y# 8 1/8 MOHUR

Gold, 11 mm. **Obv. Inscription:** "Asaf Jah, Nizam al-Mulk" **Mint:** Haidarabad **Note:** Weight varies 1.34-1.42 grams.

Date	Mintage	Good	VG	F	VF	XF
AH1279	—	—	40.00	55.00	90.00	125
AH1280	—	—	40.00	55.00	90.00	125
AH1281	—	—	40.00	55.00	90.00	125

Y# 9 1/4 MOHUR

Gold, 14 mm. **Obv. Inscription:** "Asaf Jah, Nizam al-Mulk" **Mint:** Haidarabad **Note:** Weight varies 2.68-2.85 grams.

Date	Mintage	Good	VG	F	VF	XF
AH1281	—	—	50.00	75.00	125	175

Y# 10 1/2 MOHUR

Gold, 16 mm. **Obv. Inscription:** "Asaf Jah, Nizam al-Mulk" **Mint:** Haidarabad **Note:** Weight varies 5.35-5.70 grams.

Date	Mintage	Good	VG	F	VF	XF
AH1281	—	—	90.00	120	175	250

C# 96 MOHUR

Gold, 23 mm. **Obv. Inscription:** "Bahadur Shah II" **Mint:** Haidarabad

Date	Mintage	Good	VG	F	VF	XF
AH1274	—	—	185	225	275	325
AH1275	—	—	185	225	275	325

Y# 11 MOHUR

Gold **Obv. Inscription:** "Asaf Jah, Nizam al-Mulk" **Mint:** Haidarabad **Note:** Weight varies 10.70-11.40 grams.

Date	Mintage	Good	VG	F	VF	XF
AH1275//2	—	—	160	185	220	280
AH1276	—	—	160	185	220	280
AH1277	—	—	160	185	220	280
AH1278	—	—	160	185	220	280
AH1279	—	—	160	185	220	280
AH1280	—	—	160	185	220	280
AH1281//8	—	—	160	185	220	280
AH1282	—	—	160	185	220	280
AH1283	—	—	160	185	220	280
AH1284	—	—	160	185	220	280
AH1285	—	—	160	185	220	280

Mir Mahbub Ali Khan II

AH1285-1329 / 1869-1911AD

HAMMERED COINAGE

Y# A12 1/2 PAISA

Copper **Obverse:** Persian letter "M" for Mahbub above "k" of "Mulk" **Obv. Inscription:** "Asaf Jah, NIzam al-Mulk" **Mint:** Haidarabad (Farkhanda Bunyad)

Date	Mintage	Good	VG	F	VF	XF
ND(1868-1900)	—	—	—	—	—	—

Y# 12 PAISA (Dub)

Copper **Obv. Inscription:** "Asaf Jah, Nizam al-Mulk" **Mint:** Haidarabad (Farkhanda Bunyad) **Note:** Round, rectangular, irregular shape. Many sizes and weights.

Date	Mintage	Good	VG	F	VF	XF
AH1290	—	1.00	2.00	3.50	6.00	—
AH1291	—	1.00	2.00	3.50	6.00	—
AH1292	—	1.00	2.00	3.50	6.00	—
AH1296	—	1.00	2.00	3.50	6.00	—
AH1297	—	1.00	2.00	3.50	6.00	—
AH1298//14	—	1.00	2.00	3.50	6.00	—
AH1300	—	1.00	2.00	3.50	6.00	—
AH1301	—	1.00	2.00	3.50	6.00	—
AH1302//18	—	1.00	2.00	3.50	6.00	—
AH1303	—	1.00	2.00	3.50	6.00	—
AH1308	—	1.00	2.00	3.50	6.00	—
AH1313	—	1.00	2.00	3.50	6.00	—

Y# A13 1/2 ANNA

Copper **Obv. Inscription:** "Asaf Jah, NIzam al-Mulk" **Mint:** Haidarabad (Farkhanda Bunyad)

Date	Mintage	Good	VG	F	VF	XF
AH1311//27	—	—	—	—	—	—

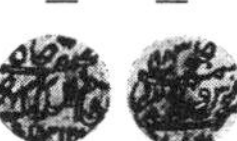

Y# 13 1/16 RUPEE

0.6980 g., 0.8180 Silver .0183 oz. ASW **Obverse:** Persian letter "M' for Mahbub above "k" of "Mulk" **Obv. Inscription:** "Asaf Jah, Nizam al-Mulk" **Mint:** Haidarabad (Farkhanda Bunyad)

Date	Mintage	Good	VG	F	VF	XF
AH1299//15	—	0.40	1.00	1.75	2.50	4.00
AH1300	—	0.40	1.00	1.75	2.50	4.00
AH1303	—	0.40	1.00	1.75	2.50	4.00
AH1304	—	0.40	1.00	1.75	2.50	4.00
AH1305	—	0.40	1.00	1.75	2.50	4.00
AH1307	—	0.40	1.00	1.75	2.50	4.00
AH1313//28	—	0.40	1.00	1.75	2.50	4.00
AH1314//30	—	0.40	1.00	1.75	2.50	4.00

Y# 14 1/8 RUPEE

1.3970 g., 0.8180 Silver .0367 oz. ASW **Obverse:** Persian letter "M' for Mahbub above "k" of "Mulk" **Obv. Inscription:** "Asaf Jah, Nizam al-Mulk" **Mint:** Haidarabad (Farkhanda Bunyad)

Date	Mintage	Good	VG	F	VF	XF
AH1286	—	0.75	1.75	2.25	3.00	4.50
AH1287//2	—	0.75	1.75	2.25	3.00	4.50
AH1289	—	0.75	1.75	2.25	3.00	4.50
AH1290	—	0.75	1.75	2.25	3.00	4.50
AH1295//11	—	0.75	1.75	2.25	3.00	4.50
AH1297	—	0.75	1.75	2.25	3.00	4.50
AH1298//14	—	0.75	1.75	2.25	3.00	4.50
AH1299//15	—	0.75	1.75	2.25	3.00	4.50
AH1300	—	0.75	1.75	2.25	3.00	4.50
AH1301//17	—	0.75	1.75	2.25	3.00	4.50
AH1302//17	—	0.75	1.75	2.25	3.00	4.50
AH1302//18	—	0.75	1.75	2.25	3.00	4.50
AH1304//20	—	0.75	1.75	2.25	3.00	4.50
AH1305	—	0.75	1.75	2.25	3.00	4.50
AH1306	—	0.75	1.75	2.25	3.00	4.50
AH1307	—	0.75	1.75	2.25	3.00	4.50
AH1308//24	—	0.75	1.75	2.25	3.00	4.50
AH1309	—	0.75	1.75	2.25	3.00	4.50
AH1310	—	0.75	1.75	2.25	3.00	4.50
AH1311	—	0.75	1.75	2.25	3.00	4.50
AH1316//33 (sic)	—	0.75	1.75	2.25	3.00	4.50
AH1317//33	—	0.75	1.75	2.25	3.00	4.50
AH1318	—	0.75	1.75	2.25	3.00	4.50

Y# 15 1/4 RUPEE

2.7940 g., 0.8180 Silver .0735 oz. ASW **Obverse:** Persian letter "M' for Mahbub above "k" of "Mulk" **Obv. Inscription:** "Asaf Jah, Nizam al-Mulk" **Mint:** Haidarabad (Farkhanda Bunyad)

Date	Mintage	Good	VG	F	VF	XF
AH1286	—	0.80	2.00	2.75	4.50	7.00
AH1287	—	0.80	2.00	2.75	4.50	7.00
AH1288	—	0.80	2.00	2.75	4.50	7.00
AH1289	—	0.80	2.00	2.75	4.50	7.00
AH1290	—	0.80	2.00	2.75	4.50	7.00

Date	Mintage	Good	VG	F	VF	XF
AH1291//7	—	0.80	2.00	2.75	4.50	7.00
AH1294	—	0.80	2.00	2.75	4.50	7.00
AH1295	—	0.80	2.00	2.75	4.50	7.00
AH1297	—	0.80	2.00	2.75	4.50	7.00
AH1298//14	—	0.80	2.00	2.75	4.50	7.00
AH1299//15	—	0.80	2.00	2.75	4.50	7.00
AH1300//16	—	0.80	2.00	2.75	4.50	7.00
AH1301//17	—	0.80	2.00	2.75	4.50	7.00
AH1302	—	0.80	2.00	2.75	4.50	7.00
AH1304	—	0.80	2.00	2.75	4.50	7.00
AH1305//22 (sic)	—	0.80	2.00	2.75	4.50	7.00
AH1306//22	—	0.80	2.00	2.75	4.50	7.00
AH1307//23	—	0.80	2.00	2.75	4.50	7.00
AH1307//24 (sic)	—	0.80	2.00	2.75	4.50	7.00
AH1308	—	0.80	2.00	2.75	4.50	7.00
AH1309	—	0.80	2.00	2.75	4.50	7.00
AH1310	—	0.80	2.00	2.75	4.50	7.00
AH1313//29	—	0.80	2.00	2.75	4.50	7.00
AH1314	—	0.80	2.00	2.75	4.50	7.00
AH1315//31	—	0.80	2.00	2.75	4.50	7.00
AH1316//32	—	0.80	2.00	2.75	4.50	7.00
AH1316//33	—	0.80	2.00	2.75	4.50	7.00
AH1317//33 (sic)	—	0.80	2.00	2.75	4.50	7.00

Y# 16 1/2 RUPEE
5.5890 g., 0.8180 Silver .1470 oz. ASW **Mint:** Haidarabad (Farkhanda Bunyad)

Date	Mintage	Good	VG	F	VF	XF
AH1286//1	—	1.25	3.00	4.00	6.00	12.00
AH1289	—	1.25	3.00	4.00	6.00	12.00
AH1290//5	—	1.25	3.00	4.00	6.00	12.00
AH1291//7	—	1.25	3.00	4.00	6.00	12.00
AH1292	—	1.25	3.00	4.00	6.00	12.00
AH1294//10	—	1.25	3.00	4.00	6.00	12.00
AH1295	—	1.25	3.00	4.00	6.00	12.00
AH1299//15	—	1.25	3.00	4.00	6.00	12.00
AH1301//17	—	1.25	3.00	4.00	6.00	12.00
AH1302//18	—	1.25	3.00	4.00	6.00	12.00
AH1304	—	1.25	3.00	4.00	6.00	12.00
AH1305//22 (sic)	—	1.25	3.00	4.00	6.00	12.00
AH1306//22	—	1.25	3.00	4.00	6.00	12.00
AH1307//23	—	1.25	3.00	4.00	6.00	12.00
AH1308	—	1.25	3.00	4.00	6.00	12.00
AH1310	—	1.25	3.00	4.00	6.00	12.00
AH1316//32	—	1.25	3.00	4.00	6.00	12.00
AH1317	—	1.25	3.00	4.00	6.00	12.00

Y# 17 RUPEE
11.1780 g., 0.8180 Silver .2940 oz. ASW **Obverse:** Persian letter "M" for Mahbub above "k" of "Mulk" **Obv. Inscription:** "Asaf Jah, Nizam al-Mulk" **Mint:** Haidarabad (Farkhanda Bunyad)

Date	Mintage	Good	VG	F	VF	XF
AH1286//1	—	1.75	4.50	5.50	7.00	14.00
AH1287	—	1.75	4.50	5.50	7.00	14.00
AH1288//3	—	1.75	4.50	5.50	7.00	14.00
AH1289//4	—	1.75	4.50	5.50	7.00	14.00
AH1293	—	1.75	4.50	5.50	7.00	14.00
AH1294//10	—	1.75	4.50	5.50	7.00	14.00
AH1295//10	—	1.75	4.50	5.50	7.00	14.00
AH1295//11	—	1.75	4.50	5.50	7.00	14.00
AH1298	—	1.75	4.50	5.50	7.00	14.00
AH1299//15	—	1.75	4.50	5.50	7.00	14.00
AH1299//16 (sic)	—	1.75	4.50	5.50	7.00	14.00
AH1300//16	—	1.75	4.50	5.50	7.00	14.00
AH1301	—	1.75	4.50	5.50	7.00	14.00
AH1302//18	—	1.75	4.50	5.50	7.00	14.00
AH1305	—	1.75	4.50	5.50	7.00	14.00
AH1306//22	—	1.75	4.50	5.50	7.00	14.00
AH1307//23	—	1.75	4.50	5.50	7.00	14.00
AH1308//24	—	1.75	4.50	5.50	7.00	14.00
AH1308//25 (sic)	—	1.75	4.50	5.50	7.00	14.00
AH1309//25	—	1.75	4.50	5.50	7.00	14.00
AH1310//26	—	1.75	4.50	5.50	7.00	14.00
AH1315//32 (sic)	—	1.75	4.50	5.50	7.00	14.00
AH1316//32	—	1.75	4.50	5.50	7.00	14.00
AH1317//33	—	1.75	4.50	5.50	7.00	14.00
AH1317//34 (sic)	—	1.75	4.50	5.50	7.00	14.00
AH1318//34	—	1.75	4.50	5.50	7.00	14.00

Y# 18 1/16 ASHRAFI
0.6980 g., 0.9100 Gold **Obverse:** Persian letter "M" for Mahbub above "k" of "Mulk" **Obv. Inscription:** "Asaf Jah, Nizam al-Mulk" **Mint:** Haidarabad (Farkhanda Bunyad)

Date	Mintage	Good	VG	F	VF	XF
AH1305	—	1.75	20.00	30.00	40.00	60.00
AH1314	—	1.75	20.00	30.00	40.00	60.00
AH1315	—	1.75	20.00	30.00	40.00	60.00

Y# 19 1/8 ASHRAFI
1.3970 g., 0.9100 Gold .0408 oz. AGW **Obverse:** Persian letter "M" for Mahbub above "k" of "Mulk" **Obv. Inscription:** "Asaf Jah, Nizam al-Mulk" **Mint:** Haidarabad (Farkhanda Bunyad)

Date	Mintage	Good	VG	F	VF	XF
AH1293	—	—	25.00	40.00	60.00	75.00
AH1302	—	—	25.00	40.00	60.00	75.00
AH1306	—	—	25.00	40.00	60.00	75.00
AH1309	—	—	25.00	40.00	60.00	75.00
AH1313	—	—	25.00	40.00	60.00	75.00
AH1316	—	—	25.00	40.00	60.00	75.00
AH1317//33	—	—	25.00	40.00	60.00	75.00
AH1318	—	—	25.00	40.00	60.00	75.00

Y# 20 1/4 ASHRAFI
2.7940 g., 0.9100 Gold .0817 oz. AGW **Obverse:** Persian letter "M" for Mahbub above "k" of "Mulk" **Obv. Inscription:** "Asaf Jah, Nizam al-Mulk" **Mint:** Haidarabad (Farkhanda Bunyad)

Date	Mintage	Good	VG	F	VF	XF
AH1301	—	—	45.00	60.00	80.00	100
AH1304	—	—	45.00	60.00	80.00	100
AH1306	—	—	45.00	60.00	80.00	100
AH1309	—	—	45.00	60.00	80.00	100
AH1314//30	—	—	45.00	60.00	80.00	100
AH1315	—	—	45.00	60.00	80.00	100
AH1316	—	—	45.00	60.00	80.00	100

Y# 21 1/2 ASHRAFI
5.5890 g., 0.9100 Gold .1635 oz. AGW **Obverse:** Persian letter "M" for Mahbub above "k" of "Mulk" **Obv. Inscription:** "Asaf Jah, Nizam al-Mulk" **Mint:** Haidarabad (Farkhanda Bunyad)

Date	Mintage	Good	VG	F	VF	XF
AH1301//17	—	—	—	—	—	—
AH1316	—	—	75.00	90.00	110	140
AH1317	—	—	75.00	90.00	110	140

Y# 22 ASHRAFI
11.1780 g., 0.9100 Gold .3270 oz. AGW **Obverse:** Persian letter "M" for Mahbub above "k" of "Mulk" **Obv. Inscription:** "Asaf Jah, Nizam al-Mulk" **Mint:** Haidarabad (Farkhanda Bunyad)

Date	Mintage	Good	VG	F	VF	XF
AH1286//1	—	—	150	170	200	250
AH1287	—	—	150	170	200	250
AH1288	—	—	150	170	200	250
AH1289	—	—	150	170	200	250
AH1290	—	—	150	170	200	250
AH1292	—	—	150	170	200	250
AH1293	—	—	150	170	200	250
AH1294	—	—	150	170	200	250
AH1295	—	—	150	170	200	250
AH1296	—	—	150	170	200	250
AH1297	—	—	150	170	200	250
AH1298//14	—	—	150	170	200	250
AH1299	—	—	150	170	200	250
AH1300//16	—	—	150	170	200	250
AH1301	—	—	150	170	200	250
AH1302	—	—	150	170	200	250
AH1303	—	—	150	170	200	250
AH1304	—	—	150	170	200	250
AH1305	—	—	150	170	200	250
AH1306	—	—	150	170	200	250
AH1307	—	—	150	170	200	250
AH1308	—	—	150	170	200	250
AH1309//25	—	—	150	170	200	250
AH1310	—	—	150	170	200	250
AH1311	—	—	150	170	200	250
AH1312//28	—	—	150	170	200	250
AH1313	—	—	150	170	200	250
AH1314//30	—	—	150	170	200	250
AH1314//31	—	—	150	170	200	250
AH1315	—	—	150	170	200	250
AH1316	—	—	150	170	200	250
AH1317	—	—	150	170	200	250
AH1318	—	—	150	170	200	250

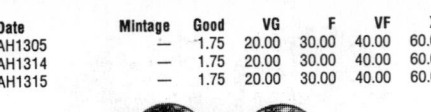

MILLED COINAGE

Provisional Series

Y# 30 4 ANNAS
2.7940 g., 0.8180 Silver **Obverse:** Persian letter "M" for Mahbub above "k" of "Mulk" **Obv. Inscription:** "Asaf Jah, Nizam al-Mulk" **Mint:** Haidarabad (Farkhanda Bunyad)

Date	Mintage	Good	VG	F	VF	XF
AH1318//32 (sic)	—	3.50	27.50	37.50	50.00	60.00
AH1318//34	—	3.50	8.50	16.50	25.00	33.50

Y# 31 8 ANNAS
5.5890 g., 0.8180 Silver **Obverse:** Persian letter "M" for Mahbub above "k" of "Mulk" **Obv. Inscription:** "Asaf Jah, Nizam al-Mulk" **Mint:** Haidarabad (Farkhanda Bunyad)

Date	Mintage	Good	VG	F	VF	XF
AH1312//28	—	4.00	10.00	20.00	30.00	40.00
AH1318//34	—	4.00	10.00	20.00	30.00	40.00

Y# 32 RUPEE
11.1780 g., 0.8180 Silver **Obverse:** Inscription with Persian letter "M" for Mahbub above "k" of "Mulk" **Obv. Inscription:** "Asaf Jah, Nizam al-Mulk" **Mint:** Haidarabad (Farkhanda Bunyad)

Date	Mintage	Good	VG	F	VF	XF
AH1312//28	—	4.00	10.00	15.00	20.00	30.00
AH1313//29	—	4.00	10.00	15.00	20.00	30.00
AH1314//30	—	4.00	10.00	15.00	20.00	30.00
AH1318//34	—	4.00	10.00	15.00	20.00	30.00

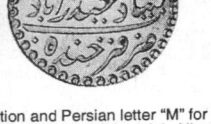

Y# 33 ASHRAFI
0.9100 Gold **Obverse:** Inscription and Persian letter "M" for Mahbub above "k" of "Mulk" **Obv. Inscription:** "Asaf Jah, Nizam al-Mulk" **Mint:** Haidarabad (Farkhanda Bunyad) **Note:** Weight varies 11.05-11.20 g.

Date	Mintage	Good	VG	F	VF	XF
AH1311//27	—	—	600	800	1,000	1,250

PATTERNS

Including off metal strikes

KM#	Date	Mintage	Identification	Mkt Val
Pn1	AH1305//21	—	Rupee. Copper.	—
Pn2	AH1307//22	—	Rupee. Silver.	—
Pn3	AH1311	—	Ashrafi. Gold. Y33a	—

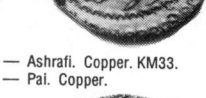

KM#	Date	Mintage	Identification	Mkt Val
Pn4	AH1311//27	—	Ashrafi. Copper. KM33.	—
Pn5	AH1312	—	Pai. Copper.	—
Pn6	AH1312//28	—	1/4 Anna. Copper. KM27.	—
Pn7	AH1312//28	—	8 Annas. Copper. Y31.	—
Pn8	AH1312//29 (sic)	—	2 Pai. Copper.	—
Pn9	AH1312//29 (sic)	—	1/2 Anna. Copper.	—

TRIAL STRIKES

KM#	Date	Mintage	Identification	Mkt Val
TS1	AH(1869)	—	8 Annas. Copper. Uniface.	—

KM#	Date	Mintage	Identification	Mkt Val
TS2	AH131x	—	8 Annas. Tin. Uniface, yr. 2x.	—

KM#	Date	Mintage	Identification	Mkt Val
TS3	AH131x	—	8 Annas. Tin. Uniface, yr. 2x.	—

KM#	Date	Mintage	Identification	Mkt Val
TS4	AH131x	—	Rupee. Tin. Uniface, obverse.	—

KM#	Date	Mintage	Identification	Mkt Val
TS5	AH1311	—	Rupee. Tin. Uniface, obverse, yr.27.	—

KM#	Date	Mintage	Identification	Mkt Val
TS6	AH1311	—	Rupee. Tin. Uniface, reverse, yr. 27.	—

HYDERABAD FEUDATORIES - AURANGABAD

MILLED COINAGE

C# 28 TOKA CASH

Copper **Reverse:** Battle-axe in canopy, date below **Note:** Date in Nagari numerals.

Date	Mintage	Good	VG	F	VF	XF
FE1241	—	5.00	10.00	16.50	25.00	—

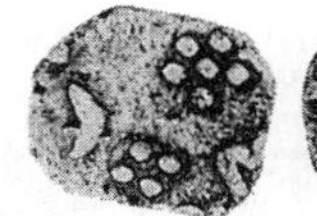

C# 29 TOKA CASH

Copper **Reverse:** Sword at right

Date	Mintage	Good	VG	F	VF	XF
AH1255	—	2.00	4.00	6.50	10.00	—

C# 30 TOKA CASH

Copper **Note:** C#28 and #30 were named after Toka Raj who operated the Aurangabad Mint under a state license from about 1830.

Date	Mintage	Good	VG	F	VF	XF
AH1273	—	2.00	4.00	6.50	10.00	—
AH1276	—	2.00	4.00	6.50	10.00	—

HYDERABAD FEUDATORIES - ELICHPUR

ANONYMOUS HAMMERED COINAGE

C# 10 PAISA

11.5000 g., Copper **Obverse:** Tiger left **Note:** Size varies 18-20mm.

Date	Mintage	Good	VG	F	VF	XF
AH1250	—	4.00	6.50	10.00	16.50	—
AH1263	—	4.00	6.50	10.00	16.50	—

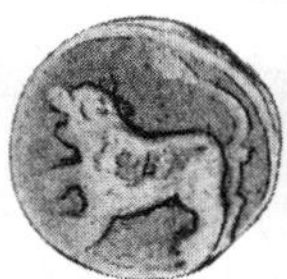

C# 10a PAISA

11.5000 g., Copper **Obverse:** Tiger left **Note:** Size varies 18-20mm.

Date	Mintage	Good	VG	F	VF	XF
AH1250	—	4.00	6.50	10.00	16.50	—
AH1263	—	4.00	6.50	10.00	16.50	—
AH1285	—	4.00	6.50	10.00	16.50	—

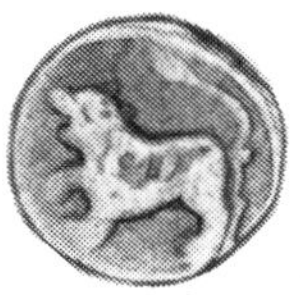

C# 15 2 PAISA

15.5000 g., Copper **Obverse:** Tiger left

Date	Mintage	Good	VG	F	VF	XF
AH1250	—	5.00	9.00	15.00	22.50	—

C# 15a 2 PAISA

15.5000 g., Copper **Obverse:** Tiger right

Date	Mintage	Good	VG	F	VF	XF
AH1250	—	5.00	9.00	15.00	22.50	—

HYDERABAD FEUDATORIES - KALAYANI

Kallian

A town located in north Mysore.

Nawab

Mohammad Shah Khair al-Din

Mint mark: 

TOWN

Mohammad Shah Khair al-Din

HAMMERED COINAGE

KM# 2 1/8 RUPEE

Silver **Note:** Weight varies 1.34-1.45 grams.

Date	Mintage	Good	VG	F	VF	XF
AH1226	—	—	60.00	100	150	220

KM# 6 RUPEE

Silver **Reverse:** Persian 'Ha' to right of tiger

Date	Mintage	Good	VG	F	VF	XF
ND(1797-1812)	—	—	60.00	100	150	220
AH1215	—	—	60.00	100	160	230
AH1226	—	—	60.00	100	150	220

KM# 5 RUPEE

Silver **Reverse:** Without Persian 'Ha' to right of tiger **Note:** Weight varies 10.7 - 11.6 grams.

Date	Mintage	Good	VG	F	VF	XF
AH1215	—	—	55.00	90.00	150	220

KM# 9 MOHUR

10.9400 g., Gold **Note:** Similar to 1 Rupee, KM#6.

Date	Mintage	Good	VG	F	VF	XF
AH12xx Rare	—	—	—	—	—	—

HYDERABAD FEUDATORIES - NARAYANPETT

Local Rajas

Dilshadabad on coins.

Mint Marks:

ती

Ti obv. dated AH1186/1186, C#40

क

K rev. dated AH1186/1186, C#40

गो

Go obv. dated AH1186/1252, C#37-40

ल

L rev. dated AH1186/1252, C#37-40

HAMMERED COINAGE

C# 37 1/8 RUPEE
Silver **Obv. Inscription:** Shah Alam (II) **Mint:** Dilshadabad **Note:** Weight varies 1.34 - 1.45 grams.

Date	Mintage	Good	VG	F	VF	XF
AH1186//1252	—	—	12.00	20.00	30.00	45.00

C# 38 1/4 RUPEE
Silver, 13 mm. **Obv. Inscription:** Shah Alam (II) **Mint:** Dilshadabad **Note:** Weight varies 2.68 - 2.9 grams.

Date	Mintage	Good	VG	F	VF	XF
AH1186//1252	—	—	12.00	20.00	30.00	45.00

C# 39 1/2 RUPEE
Silver, 16 mm. **Obv. Inscription:** Shah Alam (II) **Mint:** Dilshadabad **Note:** Weight varies 5.35-5.8 grams.

Date	Mintage	Good	VG	F	VF	XF
AH1186//1252	—	—	20.00	32.00	50.00	70.00

C# 40 RUPEE
Silver **Obv. Inscription:** Shah Alam (II) **Mint:** Dilshadabad **Note:** Weight varies 10.7 - 11.6 grams.

Date	Mintage	Good	VG	F	VF	XF
AH1186//1239	—	—	9.00	15.00	21.50	30.00
AH1186//1245	—	—	9.00	15.00	21.50	30.00
AH1186//1246	—	—	9.00	15.00	21.50	30.00
AH1186//1251	—	—	9.00	15.00	21.50	30.00
AH1186//1252	—	—	9.00	15.00	21.50	30.00
AH1186//1254	—	—	9.00	15.00	21.50	30.00

HYDERABAD FEUDATORIES - SHORAPUR

BAHIRI FEUDATORY

HAMMERED COINAGE

C# 62 1/2 PAISA
Copper, 14 mm.

Date	Mintage	Good	VG	F	VF	XF
ND(1845-46)	—	3.50	5.50	8.00	12.00	—

C# 65 1/2 PAISA
Copper, 13 mm. **Note:** Similar to 1 Paisa, C#66.

Date	Mintage	Good	VG	F	VF	XF
AH1262	—	2.50	4.00	6.50	10.00	—

 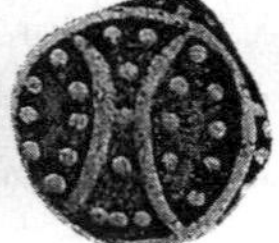

C# 63 PAISA
Copper

Date	Mintage	Good	VG	F	VF	XF
ND(1845-46)	—	2.00	3.25	5.00	8.50	—

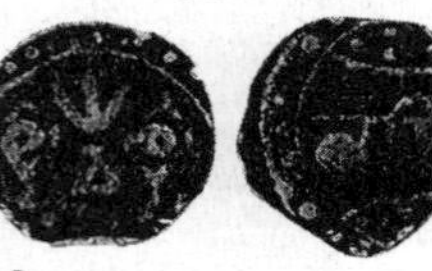

C# 64 PAISA
Copper **Reverse:** Inscribed "Bahiri"

Date	Mintage	Good	VG	F	VF	XF
ND(1845-46)	—	2.50	4.00	6.50	10.00	—

C# 66 PAISA
Copper **Reverse:** "Bahiri" date

Date	Mintage	Good	VG	F	VF	XF
AH1261	—	6.00	10.00	16.50	25.00	—
AH1262	—	6.00	10.00	16.50	25.00	—

C# 67 PAISA
Copper **Obverse:** Different from C#66

Date	Mintage	Good	VG	F	VF	XF
AH1262	—	6.00	10.00	16.50	25.00	—

HYDERABAD FEUDATORIES - WANPARTI

Sagur mintname on coins is Nasirabad. The latter is honorific for the Sagur Mint copied from the rupees of Dharwar.

MINT

نصرت آباد

Nusratabad
(Fathpur)

In the name of Muhammad Akbar II
AH1221-1253/1806-1837AD

BAHIRI RAJAS

HAMMERED COINAGE

C# 78 1/4 RUPEE
Silver **Obv. Inscription:** Muhammad Akbar (II) **Mint:** Nusratabad **Note:** Weight varies 2.67-2.90 grams.

Date	Mintage	Good	VG	F	VF	XF
AH1235//14	—	8.00	20.00	32.00	50.00	75.00

C# 80 RUPEE
Silver **Obverse:** "J" **Obv. Inscription:** Muhammad Akbar (II) **Reverse:** "A" in Nagari **Mint:** Nusratabad **Note:** Weight varies 10.70-11.60 grams.

Date	Mintage	Good	VG	F	VF	XF
AH1235//14	—	3.00	7.50	12.50	20.00	35.00
AH1235//15	—	3.00	7.50	12.50	20.00	35.00

INDORE

The Holkars were one of the three dominant Maratha powers (with the Peshwas and Sindhias), with major landholdings in Central India.

Indore State originated in 1728 with a grant of land north of the Narbada river by the Maratha Peshwa of Poona to Malhar Rao Holkar, a cavalry commander in his service. After Holkar's death (ca.1765) his daughter-in-law, Ahalya Bai, assumed the position of Queen Regent. Together with Tukoji Rao she effectively ruled the State until her death thirty years later. But it was left to Tukoji's son, Jaswant Rao, to challenge the dominance of the Poona Marathas in the Maratha Confederacy, eventually defeating the Peshwa's army in 1802. But at this point the fortunes of the Holkars suffered a serious reverse. Although Jaswant Rao had initially defeated a small British force under Col. William Monson, he was badly beaten by a contingent under Lord Lake. As a result Holkar was forced to cede a considerable portion of his territory and from this time until India's independence in 1947, the residual State of Indore was obliged to accept British protection.

For more detailed data on the Indore series, see *A Study of Holkar State Coinage*, by P.K. Sethi, S.K. Bhatt and R. Holkar (1976).

HOLKAR RULERS

Jaswant Rao, SE1719-1734/AH1213-1226/1798-1811AD
Mulhar Rao II, AH1226-1248/1811-1833AD
Martand Rao, AH1249/1834AD
Hari Rao, AH1250-1260/1834-1843AD
Khande Rao, AH1260-1261/1843-1844AD
Tukoji Rao II, VS1891-1943/SE1766-1808/AH1261-1304/1844-1886AD
Shivaji Rao, VS1943-1960/FE1296-1313/1886-1903AD

HONORIFIC TITLE

Bahadur

REGNAL YEARS

In reference to:
Muhammad Akbar II, Year 1/AH1221-1222

MINTS

اندور or इंदोर

Indore

Maheshwar
In operation from 1767 to 1803.

Distinctive marks:

 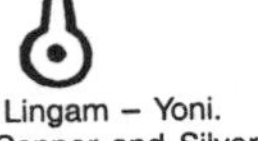

Bilva Leaf
Silver

Lingam – Yoni.
Copper and Silver

ملهارنگر

Malharnagar

Located in capital, Indore City. In operation regularly from 1768 to 1878.

Bilva Leaf
Copper

Sunface
Copper and Silver

NOTE: According to Sethi, Bhatt and Holkar, the coins of both the Maheshwar and Malharnagar mints bear the mintname "Malharnagar" in honor of Malhar Rao I, founder of the state. They can only be distinguished by their distinctive mint marks, as noted above.

MUGHAL ISSUES

In the name of Shah Alam II
AH1173-1221/1759-1806AD

Until AH1296/1880AD all coinage of Indore was struck in the name of Shah Alam II, with the exception of a few rare special or nazarana issues. The coinage of the individual rulers, until 1880AD, cannot be told apart except by the date, as no change of type was made for more than a century.

HAMMERED COINAGE

KM# 61 1/4 ANNA
Copper **Obverse:** Bilva leaf **Obv. Inscription:** "Shah Alam II" **Reverse:** Bull reclining left **Mint:** Malharnagar **Note:** Weight varies 9.60-9.70 grams.

Date	Mintage	Good	VG	F	VF	XF
AH1244	—	3.00	4.00	5.50	7.50	—
AH12xx//88	—	3.00	4.00	5.50	7.50	—

KM# 62 1/4 ANNA
Copper **Obverse:** Bilva leaf **Obv. Inscription:** "Shah Alam II" **Reverse:** Bull reclining left **Mint:** Malharnagar **Note:** Weight varies 12.20-12.40 grams.

Date	Mintage	Good	VG	F	VF	XF
AH1267//97 (sic)	—	5.00	6.50	8.50	11.50	—

 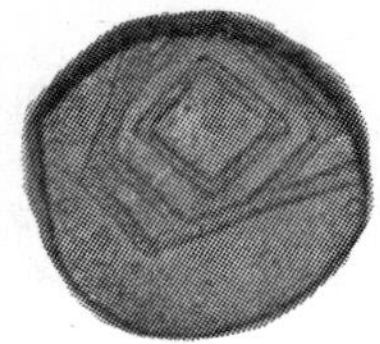

KM# 96 1/2 ANNA

Copper **Obverse:** Pinwheel **Reverse:** Geometric design **Mint:** Uncertain Mint

Date	Mintage	Good	VG	F	VF	XF
ND(1804)	—	3.50	4.50	5.50	7.50	—

KM# 97 1/2 ANNA

Copper **Obverse:** Trisul and double pennant flags **Reverse:** Broad axe **Mint:** Uncertain Mint

Date	Mintage	Good	VG	F	VF	XF
AH1220	—	3.50	4.50	5.50	7.50	—

KM# 90.3 1/2 ANNA

Copper **Reverse:** Jhar **Mint:** Uncertain Mint

Date	Mintage	Good	VG	F	VF	XF
AH1225	—	3.50	4.50	5.50	7.50	—

KM# 91 1/2 ANNA

Copper **Obverse:** Mace **Reverse:** Branch with 3 leaves **Mint:** Uncertain Mint

Date	Mintage	Good	VG	F	VF	XF
AH1228	—	3.50	4.50	5.50	7.50	—

KM# 92.1 1/2 ANNA

Copper **Obverse:** Katar **Reverse:** Bilva leaf and pennant **Mint:** Uncertain Mint

Date	Mintage	Good	VG	F	VF	XF
AH1230	—	3.50	4.50	5.50	7.50	—

KM# 92.2 1/2 ANNA

Copper **Obverse:** Katar **Reverse:** Axe and whisk **Mint:** Uncertain Mint

Date	Mintage	Good	VG	F	VF	XF
AH1230//27	—	3.50	4.50	5.50	7.50	—

KM# 93.1 1/2 ANNA

Copper **Reverse:** Jhar and mace **Mint:** Uncertain Mint

Date	Mintage	Good	VG	F	VF	XF
AH1230	—	3.50	4.50	5.50	7.50	—

KM# 93.2 1/2 ANNA

Copper **Reverse:** Bilva leaf **Mint:** Uncertain Mint

Date	Mintage	Good	VG	F	VF	XF
AH1230	—	3.50	4.50	5.50	7.50	—

KM# 93.3 1/2 ANNA

Copper **Reverse:** Flower and flag **Mint:** Uncertain Mint

Date	Mintage	Good	VG	F	VF	XF
AH1230	—	3.50	4.50	5.50	7.50	—

KM# 93.4 1/2 ANNA

Copper **Reverse:** 6-petal flower and sword **Mint:** Uncertain Mint

Date	Mintage	Good	VG	F	VF	XF
AH1230	—	3.50	4.50	5.50	7.50	—

KM# 94 1/2 ANNA

Copper **Obverse:** Katar **Reverse:** Broad axe **Mint:** Uncertain Mint

Date	Mintage	Good	VG	F	VF	XF
AH1230	—	3.50	4.50	5.50	7.50	—

KM# 98 1/2 ANNA

Copper **Obverse:** 1230 **Reverse:** 6-petal flower and sword **Mint:** Uncertain Mint **Note:** These coins were struck AH1202-1244 with many minor varieties of symbols of which the above are only a sample.

Date	Mintage	Good	VG	F	VF	XF
AH1230	—	3.50	4.50	5.50	7.50	—

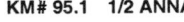

KM# 95.1 1/2 ANNA

Copper **Obverse:** Broad axe **Reverse:** Dagger **Mint:** Uncertain Mint

Date	Mintage	Good	VG	F	VF	XF
AH1233//66	—	3.50	4.50	5.50	7.50	—
AH1241	—	3.50	4.50	5.50	7.50	—

KM# 95.2 1/2 ANNA

Copper **Obverse:** Broad axe **Reverse:** Sword **Mint:** Uncertain Mint

Date	Mintage	Good	VG	F	VF	XF
AH1233	—	3.50	4.50	5.50	7.50	—

KM# 95.5 1/2 ANNA

Copper **Obverse:** Leaf **Reverse:** Pennant and cannon **Mint:** Uncertain Mint

Date	Mintage	Good	VG	F	VF	XF
AH128x/1261	—	3.50	4.50	5.50	7.50	—

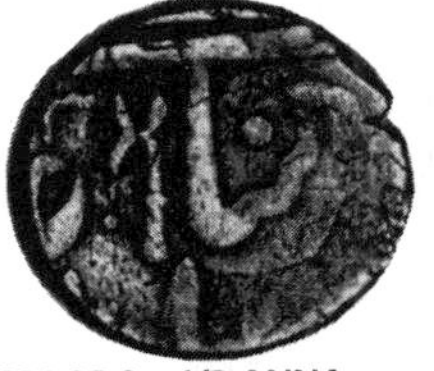 

KM# 95.3 1/2 ANNA

Copper **Obverse:** Halberd and date **Reverse:** Double pennant **Mint:** Uncertain Mint

Date	Mintage	Good	VG	F	VF	XF
AH(123)3	—	3.50	4.50	6.00	8.00	—

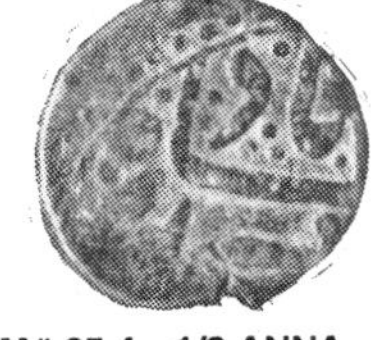 

KM# 95.4 1/2 ANNA

Copper **Reverse:** Triple banner **Mint:** Uncertain Mint

Date	Mintage	Good	VG	F	VF	XF
ND(1818)	—	3.50	4.50	5.50	7.50	—

 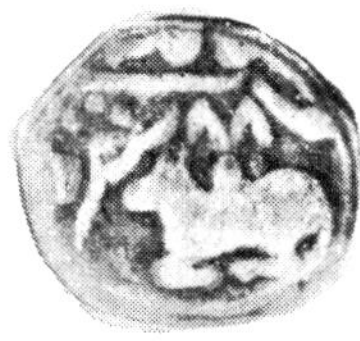

KM# 63.2 1/2 ANNA

Copper **Obverse:** Bilva leaf **Obv. Inscription:** "Shah Alam II" **Reverse:** Without alter before bull reclining left **Mint:** Malharnagar **Note:** Weight varies 18.70-20.00 grams.

Date	Mintage	Good	VG	F	VF	XF
AH1243//1251	—	3.00	4.00	5.50	7.50	—
AH1244	—	3.00	4.00	5.50	7.50	—
AH12xx//88	—	3.00	4.00	5.50	7.50	—

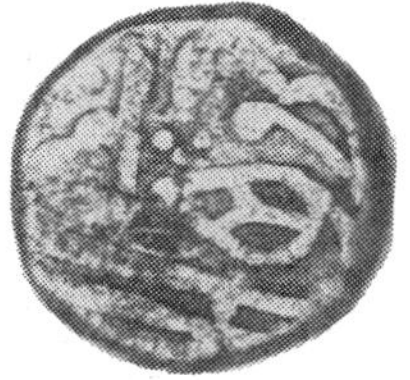 

KM# 63.1 1/2 ANNA

Copper **Obverse:** Leaf **Obv. Inscription:** "Shah Alam II" **Reverse:** Altar before bull reclining left **Mint:** Malharnagar **Note:** Weight varies 18.70-20.00 grams.

Date	Mintage	Good	VG	F	VF	XF
AH1244	—	5.00	6.50	9.00	12.00	—

KM# 64 1/2 ANNA

Copper **Obverse:** Leaf **Obv. Legend:** Hindi "Adha Anna" **Obv. Inscription:** "Shah Alam II" **Reverse:** Bull reclining left **Mint:** Malharnagar **Note:** Weight varies 12.00-17.30 grams.

Date	Mintage	Good	VG	F	VF	XF
AH1261	—	2.50	3.25	4.00	6.00	—
AH1266	—	2.50	3.25	4.00	6.00	—
AH1267//97	—	2.75	3.50	4.50	6.50	—
AH1268	—	2.50	3.25	4.00	6.00	—
AH1269//99	—	3.00	3.50	4.50	6.50	—
AH1271	—	2.50	3.25	4.00	6.00	—
AH1285	—	1.75	2.50	3.50	5.50	—
AH1286//113	—	2.25	3.00	4.00	6.00	—
AH1286//1286	—	3.00	3.50	4.00	6.00	—

KM# 68 1/2 ANNA

Copper **Obverse:** Bilva leaf **Obv. Inscription:** "Shah Alam II" **Reverse:** Alter before bull reclining left **Mint:** Malharnagar

Date	Mintage	Good	VG	F	VF	XF
AH1286	—	3.00	4.00	5.00	6.50	—

KM# 65 NAZARANA 1/2 ANNA

Copper **Obverse:** Bilva leaf **Obv. Inscription:** "Shah Alam II" **Reverse:** Bull reclining left **Mint:** Malharnagar **Note:** Weight varies 12-17.30 grams.

Date	Mintage	Good	VG	F	VF	XF
AH12xx//99	—	—	—	—	—	—

KM# 70 1/16 RUPEE

Silver **Obv. Inscription:** "Shah Alam II" **Reverse:** Sunface **Mint:** Malharnagar **Note:** Weight varies 0.67-0.72 grams.

Date	Mintage	Good	VG	F	VF	XF
AH1248 Rare	—	—	—	—	—	—
AH1266 Rare	—	—	—	—	—	—

KM# 71 1/8 RUPEE

Silver **Obv. Inscription:** "Shah Alam II" **Reverse:** Sunface **Mint:** Malharnagar **Note:** Weight varies 1.34-1.45 grams.

Date	Mintage	Good	VG	F	VF	XF
AH1227	—	1.40	3.50	6.00	8.50	15.00
AH1236	—	1.40	3.50	6.00	8.50	15.00
AH1237	—	1.40	3.50	6.00	8.50	15.00
AH1248	—	1.00	2.50	4.00	6.00	10.00
AH(12)55	—	1.00	2.50	4.00	6.00	10.00
AH1257	—	1.00	2.50	4.00	6.00	10.00
AH1262	—	1.00	2.50	4.00	6.00	10.00
AH1268	—	1.00	2.50	4.00	6.00	10.00
AH1269	—	1.00	2.50	4.00	6.00	10.00
AH1270	—	1.00	2.50	4.00	6.00	10.00
AH1271	—	1.00	2.50	4.00	6.00	10.00
AH1272	—	1.00	2.50	4.00	6.00	10.00
AH1278	—	1.00	2.50	4.00	6.00	10.00
AH1279	—	1.00	2.50	4.00	6.00	10.00
AH1282	—	1.00	2.00	4.00	6.00	10.00
AH1287	—	1.00	2.50	4.00	6.00	10.00
AH1289	—	1.00	2.50	4.00	6.00	10.00
AH1291	—	1.00	2.50	4.00	6.00	10.00
AH1292	—	1.00	2.50	4.00	6.00	10.00
AH1293	—	1.00	2.50	4.00	6.00	10.00
AH1294	—	1.00	2.50	4.00	6.00	10.00
AH1295	—	1.00	2.50	4.00	6.00	10.00

KM# 56.2 1/4 RUPEE

Silver **Obv. Inscription:** "Shah Alam II" **Reverse:** Bilva leaf and lingam **Mint:** Maheshwar **Note:** 2.68-2.90 grams.

Date	Mintage	Good	VG	F	VF	XF
AH1215	—	5.00	12.50	20.00	30.00	50.00
AH1216	—	5.00	12.50	20.00	30.00	50.00
AH1217	—	5.00	12.50	20.00	30.00	50.00

KM# 72 1/4 RUPEE

Silver **Obv. Inscription:** "Shah Alam II" **Reverse:** Sunface **Mint:** Malharnagar **Note:** Weight varies 2.68-2.90 grams.

Date	Mintage	Good	VG	F	VF	XF
AH1231	—	1.20	3.00	5.00	7.00	12.00
AH1232	—	1.20	3.00	5.00	7.00	12.00
AH1233	—	1.20	3.00	5.00	7.00	12.00
AH1234	—	1.20	3.00	5.00	7.00	12.00
AH1235	—	1.20	3.00	5.00	7.00	12.00
AH1236	—	1.20	3.00	5.00	7.00	12.00
AH1237	—	1.20	3.00	5.00	7.00	12.00
AH1240	—	1.20	3.00	5.00	7.00	12.00
AH1241	—	1.20	3.00	5.00	7.00	12.00
AH1243	—	1.20	3.00	5.00	7.00	12.00
AH1244	—	1.20	3.00	5.00	7.00	12.00
AH1246	—	1.20	3.00	5.00	7.00	12.00
AH1249	—	1.20	3.00	5.00	7.00	12.00
AH1250	—	1.20	3.00	5.00	7.00	12.00
AH1251	—	1.20	3.00	5.00	7.00	12.00
AH1252	—	1.20	3.00	5.00	7.00	12.00
AH1253	—	1.20	3.00	5.00	7.00	12.00
AH1255	—	1.20	3.00	5.00	7.00	12.00
AH1256	—	1.20	3.00	5.00	7.00	12.00
AH1261	—	1.20	3.00	5.00	7.00	12.00
AH1263	—	1.20	3.00	5.00	7.00	12.00
AH1264	—	1.20	3.00	5.00	7.00	12.00
AH1265	—	1.20	3.00	5.00	7.00	12.00
AH1266	—	1.20	3.00	5.00	7.00	12.00
AH1267	—	1.20	3.00	5.00	7.00	12.00
AH1268	—	1.20	3.00	5.00	7.00	12.00
AH1269	—	1.20	3.00	5.00	7.00	12.00
AH1270	—	1.20	3.00	5.00	7.00	12.00
AH1272	—	1.20	3.00	5.00	7.00	12.00
AH1273	—	1.20	3.00	5.00	7.00	12.00
AH1275	—	1.20	3.00	5.00	7.00	12.00
AH1277	—	1.20	3.00	5.00	7.00	12.00
AH1278	—	1.20	3.00	5.00	7.00	12.00
AH1279	—	1.20	3.00	5.00	7.00	12.00
AH1282	—	1.20	3.00	5.00	7.00	12.00
AH1285	—	1.20	3.00	5.00	7.00	12.00
AH1286	—	1.20	3.00	5.00	7.00	12.00
AH1288	—	1.20	3.00	5.00	7.00	12.00
AH1289	—	1.20	3.00	5.00	7.00	12.00
AH1290	—	1.20	3.00	5.00	7.00	12.00
AH1291	—	1.20	3.00	5.00	7.00	12.00
AH1292	—	1.20	3.00	5.00	7.00	12.00
AH1293	—	1.20	3.00	5.00	7.00	12.00
AH1294	—	1.20	3.00	5.00	7.00	12.00
AH1295	—	1.20	3.00	5.00	7.00	12.00

KM# 57.2 1/2 RUPEE

Silver **Obv. Inscription:** "Shah Alam II" **Reverse:** Bilva leaf and lingam **Mint:** Maheshwar **Note:** 5.35-5.80 grams.

Date	Mintage	Good	VG	F	VF	XF
AH1216//44	—	6.00	15.00	25.00	40.00	60.00
AH1217	—	6.00	15.00	25.00	40.00	60.00

KM# 73 1/2 RUPEE

Silver **Obv. Inscription:** "Shah Alam II" **Reverse:** Sunface **Mint:** Malharnagar **Note:** Weight varies 5.35-5.80 grams.

Date	Mintage	Good	VG	F	VF	XF
AH1227	—	1.60	4.00	6.50	10.00	16.50
AH1228	—	1.60	4.00	6.50	10.00	16.50
AH1230//62	—	1.60	4.00	6.50	10.00	16.50
AH1231	—	1.60	4.00	6.50	10.00	16.50
AH1233	—	1.60	4.00	6.50	10.00	16.50
AH1234//6x	—	1.60	4.00	6.50	10.00	16.50
AH1237	—	1.60	4.00	6.50	10.00	16.50
AH1238	—	1.60	4.00	6.50	10.00	16.50
AH1240	—	1.60	4.00	6.50	10.00	16.50
AH1242	—	1.60	4.00	6.50	10.00	16.50
AH1244//72	—	1.60	4.00	6.50	10.00	16.50
AH1245	—	1.60	4.00	6.50	10.00	16.50
AH1246	—	1.60	4.00	6.50	10.00	16.50
AH1247	—	1.60	4.00	6.50	10.00	16.50
AH1248	—	1.60	4.00	6.50	10.00	16.50
AH1250	—	1.60	4.00	6.50	10.00	16.50
AH1251	—	1.60	4.00	6.50	10.00	16.50
AH1253	—	1.60	4.00	6.50	10.00	16.50
AH1255	—	1.60	4.00	6.50	10.00	16.50
AH1258	—	1.60	4.00	6.50	10.00	16.50
AH1260	—	1.60	4.00	6.50	10.00	16.50
AH1262	—	1.60	4.00	6.50	10.00	16.50
AH1263	—	1.60	4.00	6.50	10.00	16.50
AH1264	—	1.60	4.00	6.50	10.00	16.50
AH1265	—	1.60	4.00	6.50	10.00	16.50
AH1266	—	1.60	4.00	6.50	10.00	16.50
AH1267	—	1.60	4.00	6.50	10.00	16.50
AH1268	—	1.60	4.00	6.50	10.00	16.50
AH1270	—	1.60	4.00	6.50	10.00	16.50
AH1272	—	1.60	4.00	6.50	10.00	16.50
AH1273	—	1.60	4.00	6.50	10.00	16.50
AH1274	—	1.60	4.00	6.50	10.00	16.50
AH1275	—	1.60	4.00	6.50	10.00	16.50
AH1276	—	1.60	4.00	6.50	10.00	16.50
AH1277	—	1.60	4.00	6.50	10.00	16.50
AH1278	—	1.60	4.00	6.50	10.00	16.50
AH1279	—	1.60	4.00	6.50	10.00	16.50
AH1280	—	1.60	4.00	6.50	10.00	16.50
AH1281	—	1.60	4.00	6.50	10.00	16.50
AH1283	—	1.60	4.00	6.50	10.00	16.50
AH1286	—	1.60	4.00	6.50	10.00	16.50
AH1285//121	—	1.60	4.00	6.50	10.00	16.50
AH1288	—	1.60	4.00	6.50	10.00	16.50
AH1289	—	1.60	4.00	6.50	10.00	16.50
AH1291	—	1.60	4.00	6.50	10.00	16.50
AH1292	—	1.60	4.00	6.50	10.00	16.50
AH1293	—	1.60	4.00	6.50	10.00	16.50
AH1294//120	—	1.60	4.00	6.50	10.00	16.50
AH1295	—	1.60	4.00	6.50	10.00	16.50
AH1296	—	1.60	4.00	6.50	10.00	16.50

KM# 72a NAZARANA 1/4 RUPEE

Silver **Obv. Inscription:** "Shah Alam II" **Reverse:** Sunface **Mint:** Malharnagar **Note:** Weight varies 2.68-2.90 grams; broad, thin planchet.

Date	Mintage	Good	VG	F	VF	XF
AH1280//110	—	—	17.50	25.00	35.00	50.00

KM# 74 NAZARANA 1/2 RUPEE

Silver, 27.5 mm. **Obv. Inscription:** "Shah Alam II" **Reverse:** Sunface **Mint:** Malharnagar **Note:** Weight varies 5.35-5.80 grams; broad, think planchet.

Date	Mintage	Good	VG	F	VF	XF
AH1236//69	—	37.50	75.00	125	200	300
AH1280//110	—	37.50	75.00	125	200	300

KM# 58.2 RUPEE

Silver **Obv. Inscription:** "Shah Alam II" **Reverse:** Bilva leaf and lingam **Mint:** Maheshwar **Note:** 10.70-11.60 grams.

Date	Mintage	Good	VG	F	VF	XF
AH1215//42	—	3.50	6.00	10.00	14.00	20.00
AH1216//44	—	3.50	6.00	10.00	15.00	22.00
AH1217//46	—	3.50	6.00	10.00	15.00	22.00

KM# 76 RUPEE

Silver **Obv. Inscription:** "Shah Alam II" **Reverse:** Sunface **Mint:** Malharnagar **Note:** 10.70-11.60 grams.

Date	Mintage	Good	VG	F	VF	XF
AH1215//42	—	2.00	5.00	7.50	11.50	18.50
AH1216	—	2.00	5.00	7.50	11.50	18.50
AH1217//44 (sic)	—	2.00	5.00	7.50	11.50	18.50

Date	Mintage	Good	VG	F	VF	XF
AH1224	—	2.00	5.00	7.50	11.50	18.50
AH1225//59	—	2.00	5.00	7.50	11.50	18.50
AH1226//60	—	2.00	5.00	7.50	11.50	18.50
AH1228//62	—	2.00	5.00	7.50	11.50	18.50
AH1230//61	—	2.00	5.00	7.50	11.50	18.50
AH1230//62	—	2.00	5.00	7.50	11.50	18.50
AH1231//63	—	2.00	5.00	7.50	11.50	18.50
AH1231//64	—	2.00	5.00	7.50	11.50	18.50
AH1232//65	—	2.00	5.00	7.50	11.50	18.50
AH1233//66	—	2.00	5.00	7.50	11.50	18.50
AH1234//67	—	2.00	5.00	7.50	11.50	18.50
AH1235//68	—	2.00	5.00	7.50	11.50	18.50
AH1237//67	—	2.00	5.00	7.50	11.50	18.50
AH1237//70	—	2.00	5.00	7.50	11.50	18.50
AH1238//70	—	2.00	5.00	7.50	11.50	18.50
AH1240	—	2.00	5.00	7.50	11.50	18.50
AH1241	—	2.00	5.00	7.50	11.50	18.50
AH1242//75	—	2.00	5.00	7.50	11.50	18.50
AH1243//76	—	2.00	5.00	7.50	11.50	18.50
AH1244//72	—	2.00	5.00	7.50	11.50	18.50
AH(12)44//74	—	2.00	5.00	7.50	11.50	18.50
AH1246//76	—	2.00	5.00	7.50	11.50	18.50
AH1248//77	—	2.00	5.00	7.50	11.50	18.50
AH1249	—	2.00	5.00	7.50	11.50	18.50
AH1250//79	—	2.00	5.00	7.50	11.50	18.50
AH1251//81	—	2.00	5.00	7.50	11.50	18.50
AH1255//85	—	2.00	5.00	7.50	11.50	18.50
AH1257//87	—	2.00	5.00	7.50	11.50	18.50
AH1258//88	—	2.00	5.00	7.50	11.50	18.50
AH1260//9x	—	2.00	5.00	7.50	11.50	18.50
AH1264//94	—	2.00	5.00	7.50	11.50	18.50
AH1262	—	2.00	5.00	7.50	11.50	18.50
AH1263	—	2.00	5.00	7.50	11.50	18.50
AH1265//95	—	2.00	5.00	7.50	11.50	18.50
AH1266//96	—	2.00	5.00	7.50	11.50	18.50
AH1267//97	—	2.00	5.00	7.50	11.50	18.50
AH1268//97	—	2.00	5.00	7.50	11.50	18.50
AH1268//98	—	2.00	5.00	7.50	11.50	18.50
AH1269//9x	—	2.00	5.00	7.50	11.50	18.50
AH1270	—	2.00	5.00	7.50	11.50	18.50
AH1272//102	—	2.00	5.00	7.50	11.50	18.50
AH1273	—	2.00	5.00	7.50	11.50	18.50
AH1275//105	—	2.00	5.00	7.50	11.50	18.50
AH1276//105	—	2.00	5.00	7.50	11.50	18.50
AH1277	—	2.00	5.00	7.50	11.50	18.50
AH1278	—	2.00	5.00	7.50	11.50	18.50
AH1279	—	2.00	5.00	7.50	11.50	18.50
AH1280	—	2.00	5.00	7.50	11.50	18.50
AH1282//111	—	2.00	5.00	7.50	11.50	18.50
AH1285//112	—	2.00	5.00	7.50	11.50	18.50
AH1286//113	—	2.00	5.00	7.50	11.50	18.50
AH1288//115	—	2.00	5.00	7.50	11.50	18.50
AH1289//115	—	2.00	5.00	7.50	11.50	18.50
AH1292//118	—	2.00	5.00	7.50	11.50	18.50
AH1292//120	—	2.00	5.00	7.50	11.50	18.50
AH1293//111	—	2.00	5.00	7.50	11.50	18.50
AH1293//119	—	2.00	5.00	7.50	11.50	18.50
AH1294//120	—	2.00	5.00	7.50	11.50	18.50
AH1295//121	—	2.00	5.00	7.50	11.50	18.50
AH1296//122	—	2.00	5.00	7.50	11.50	18.50
AH1295//122	—	2.00	5.00	7.50	11.50	18.50

KM# 5 RUPEE
Silver **Obv. Inscription:** "Muhammad Akbar II" **Mint:** Chandor **Note:** Weight varies 10.70-11.60 grams; previous KM#3.2.

Date	Mintage	Good	VG	F	VF	XF
AH12(22)//2	—	5.50	13.50	20.00	32.50	50.00

KM# 77 NAZARANA RUPEE
Silver, 30 mm. **Obv. Inscription:** "Shah Alam II" **Reverse:** Sunface **Mint:** Malharnagar **Note:** Weight varies 10.70-11.60 grams.

Date	Mintage	Good	VG	F	VF	XF
AH1225//59	—	100	200	325	500	700
AH1280//110	—	100	200	325	500	700

KM# 59 NAZARANA RUPEE
Silver **Obv. Inscription:** "Shah Alam II" **Mint:** Maheshwar

Date	Mintage	Good	VG	F	VF	XF
AH1267//97	—	—	—	—	—	—

Note: Brief revival of this type under Tukoji Rao II for presentation

Jaswant Rao
SE1719-1734 / AH1213-1226 / 1798-1811AD

HAMMERED COINAGE

KM# 6 NAZARANA RUPEE
Silver **Obv. Inscription:** Mughal King of Delhi and Jaswant Rao **Mint:** Indore **Note:** Weight varies 10.70-11.60 grams.

Date	Mintage	Good	VG	F	VF	XF
SE1728 (1806)	—	27.50	65.00	100	150	225

KM# 7 NAZARANA RUPEE
Silver **Obv. Inscription:** "Muhammad Akbar II" **Mint:** Indore **Note:** Weight varies 10.70-11.60 grams.

Date	Mintage	Good	VG	F	VF	XF
SE1728 (1806) Rare	—	—	—	—	—	—

KM# 8 NAZARANA RUPEE
Silver **Obv. Inscription:** "Muhammad Akbar II" **Mint:** Indore **Note:** Weight varies 10.70-11.60 grams.

Date	Mintage	Good	VG	F	VF	XF
AH1222	—	12.50	25.00	40.00	65.00	100

Tukoji Rao II
VS1891-1943 / SE1766-1808 / AH1261-1304 / 1844-1886AD

HAMMERED COINAGE

KM# 12 1/2 ANNA
16.6000 g., Copper, 25 mm. **Obverse:** Sunface **Reverse:** Reclining bull left **Mint:** Indore

Date	Mintage	Good	VG	F	VF	XF
VS1942 (1885)	—	45.00	90.00	180	300	425

KM# 13 1/2 ANNA
13.4000 g., Copper, 31 mm. **Reverse:** Reclining bull right **Mint:** Indore

Date	Mintage	Good	VG	F	VF	XF
VS1942 (1885)	—	—	—	600	1,000	1,350

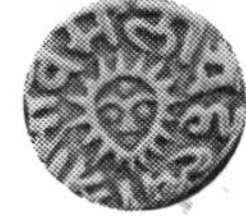

KM# 21 1/2 RUPEE
5.5000 g., Silver, 15 mm. **Obverse:** Crossed swords **Reverse:** Sunface **Mint:** Indore

Date	Mintage	Good	VG	F	VF	XF
AH1289	—	22.50	55.00	70.00	85.00	110

KM# 22 1/2 RUPEE
5.5000 g., Silver, 14.5 mm. **Obverse:** Crossed swords **Reverse:** Sunface **Mint:** Indore

Date	Mintage	Good	VG	F	VF	XF
ND(c.1873)	—	22.50	55.00	70.00	85.00	110

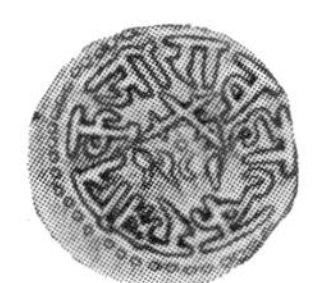

KM# 24 RUPEE
11.2000 g., Silver, 18 mm. **Obverse:** Crossed swords **Reverse:** Sunface **Mint:** Indore

Date	Mintage	Good	VG	F	VF	XF
AH1289	—	16.50	40.00	55.00	70.00	90.00

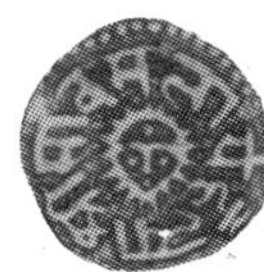

KM# 23 RUPEE
11.2000 g., Silver, 17 mm. **Obverse:** Crossed swords **Reverse:** Sunface **Mint:** Indore

Date	Mintage	Good	VG	F	VF	XF
ND(c.1873)	—	10.00	25.00	35.00	45.00	60.00

KM# 25 RUPEE
11.2000 g., Silver, 17.5 mm. **Obverse:** Crossed swords **Reverse:** Sunface **Mint:** Indore

Date	Mintage	Good	VG	F	VF	XF
AH1295	—	16.50	40.00	55.00	70.00	90.00

KM# 10 COPPER 1/2 MUDRA
Copper, 17 mm. **Reverse:** Sunface **Mint:** Indore **Note:** Weight varies 4.35-5.10 grams.

Date	Mintage	Good	VG	F	VF	XF
SE1780 (1858)	—	30.00	60.00	120	200	285
SE1788 (1866)	—	30.00	60.00	120	200	285

KM# 11.1 COPPER MUDRA
Copper, 25 mm. **Reverse:** Sunface **Mint:** Indore **Note:** Weight varies 7.80-11.00 grams.

Date	Mintage	Good	VG	F	VF	XF
SE1780 (1858)	—	22.50	45.00	90.00	150	220
SE1788 (1866)	—	22.50	45.00	90.00	150	220

KM# 11.2 COPPER MUDRA

Copper, 21 mm. **Reverse:** Sunface **Mint:** Indore **Note:** Weight varies 7.80-11.00 grams. Reduced size.

Date	Mintage	Good	VG	F	VF	XF
AH1288 (1871)	—	22.50	45.00	90.00	150	220

KM# 15 SILVER MUDRA
11.2000 g., Silver, 25 mm. **Reverse:** Sunface **Mint:** Indore

Date	Mintage	Good	VG	F	VF	XF
SE1780 (1858)	—	20.00	40.00	60.00	90.00	125

KM# 16 SILVER MUDRA
11.2000 g., Silver, 24.5 mm. **Obverse:** Without inscription within wreath **Reverse:** Sunface **Mint:** Indore

Date	Mintage	Good	VG	F	VF	XF
SE1780 (1858)	—	30.00	60.00	100	150	220

KM# 17 SILVER MUDRA
11.2000 g., Silver, 21 mm. **Obverse:** 2 varieties of swirls **Reverse:** Sunface **Mint:** Indore

Date	Mintage	Good	VG	F	VF	XF
SE1780 (1858)	—	30.00	60.00	100	140	175

KM# 18 SILVER MUDRA
11.2000 g., Silver, 24 mm. **Reverse:** Sunface **Mint:** Indore

Date	Mintage	Good	VG	F	VF	XF
SE1788 (1866)	—	37.50	75.00	110	150	200

KM# 19 SILVER MUDRA
11.2000 g., Silver, 20 mm. **Reverse:** Sunface above cross swords and sprays **Mint:** Indore

Date	Mintage	Good	VG	F	VF	XF
VS1934 (1877)	—	37.50	75.00	110	150	200

KM# 20 SILVER MUDRA
11.2000 g., Silver, 20 mm. **Obverse:** Inscription in ornate plaque **Reverse:** Sunface above cross swords and sprays **Mint:** Indore

Date	Mintage	Good	VG	F	VF	XF
VS1934 (1877)	—	50.00	100	150	200	250

KM# 27 MOHUR
10.8300 g., Gold **Mint:** Indore

Date	Mintage	Good	VG	F	VF	XF
VS1941 (1883) Rare	—	—	—	—	—	—

Shivaji Rao
VS1943-1960 / FE1296-1313 / 1886-1903AD
MILLED COINAGE

KM# 30.1 1/2 PAISA
3.1250 g., Copper, 21 mm. **Obverse:** Reclining bull left **Reverse:** Denomination in 2 lines "1/2 Adhela Paisa" **Mint:** Indore

Date	Mintage	Good	VG	F	VF	XF
VS1944 (1887)	—	10.00	15.00	21.50	30.00	—

KM# 30.2 1/2 PAISA
3.1250 g., Copper, 21 mm. **Obverse:** Reclining bull left **Reverse:** Denomination in 3 lines "1/2 Dhaleka Paisa" **Mint:** Indore

Date	Mintage	Good	VG	F	VF	XF
VS1944 (1887)	—	10.00	15.00	21.50	30.00	—

KM# 31 1/2 PAISA
3.1250 g., Copper, 21 mm. **Obverse:** Reclining bull left **Obv. Legend:** "Shivaji Rao" **Reverse:** Denomination in 2 lines "Adha Paisa" **Mint:** Indore

Date	Mintage	Good	VG	F	VF	XF
VS1946 (1889)	—	11.50	16.50	23.50	32.50	—

KM# 32.1 1/4 ANNA
Copper, 25.5 mm. **Obverse:** Date below bull reclining left **Reverse:** Inscription "Indore" below denomination **Mint:** Indore **Note:** Weight varies 6.026-6.675 grams.

Date	Mintage	Good	VG	F	VF	XF
VS1943 (1886)	—	1.50	3.00	5.00	7.50	—

KM# 32.2 1/4 ANNA
Copper, 25 mm. **Obverse:** Date below bull reclining left **Reverse:** Inscription retrograde **Mint:** Indore **Note:** Weight varies 6.026-6.675 grams.

Date	Mintage	Good	VG	F	VF	XF
VS1943 (1886)	—	—	—	—	—	—

KM# 32.3 1/4 ANNA
Copper, 25 mm. **Obverse:** Continuous legend, "Indore" below bull reclining left **Reverse:** Date below denomination **Mint:** Indore **Note:** Weight varies 6.026-6.675 grams.

Date	Mintage	Good	VG	F	VF	XF
VS1943 (1886)	—	0.35	0.75	1.25	2.50	—
VS1944 (1887)	—	0.50	1.00	1.50	3.00	—
VS1945 (1888)	—	0.75	1.25	2.00	4.00	—

KM# 32.4 1/4 ANNA
Copper, 25 mm. **Obverse:** Broken legend with "Indore" below bull reclining left **Mint:** Indore **Note:** Weight varies 6.026-6.675 grams.

Date	Mintage	Good	VG	F	VF	XF
VS1943 (1886)	—	2.00	4.00	6.50	8.50	—
VS1944 (1887)	—	2.00	4.00	6.50	8.50	—

KM# 32.5 1/4 ANNA
Copper, 25 mm. **Obverse:** Cross with dot in each quadrant flanking "Indore" below bull reclining left **Mint:** Indore **Note:** Weight varies 6.026-6.675 grams.

Date	Mintage	Good	VG	F	VF	XF
VS1943 (1886)	—	1.00	2.00	3.00	6.00	—

KM# 33.1 1/4 ANNA
Copper, 26 mm. **Obverse:** Bull reclining left **Obv. Legend:** Continuous with ruler's name and "Indore" **Obv. Inscription:** Sivaji Rao **Reverse:** Date below denomination **Mint:** Indore **Note:** Weight varies 6.026-6.675 grams.

Date	Mintage	Good	VG	F	VF	XF
VS1944 (1887)	—	0.85	1.75	2.50	5.00	—
VS1945 (1888)	—	0.75	1.50	2.00	4.00	—
VS1946 (1889)	—	0.85	1.75	2.50	5.00	—
VS1947 (1890)	—	0.75	1.50	2.00	4.00	—

KM# 33.2 1/4 ANNA
Copper, 27 mm. **Obverse:** Bull reclining left **Obv. Legend:** Ruler's name spelled "Sayaji Rao" **Mint:** Indore **Note:** Weight varies 6.026-6.675 grams.

Date	Mintage	Good	VG	F	VF	XF
VS1944 (1887)	—	1.00	2.00	4.00	8.00	—

KM# 33.3 1/4 ANNA
Copper, 27 mm. **Obverse:** Continuous legend around reclining bull **Obv. Legend:** Shivaji Rao...Bahadur **Reverse:** "Indore" above denomination and date **Note:** Floral border varieties exist. Struck at the Indore Mint. Weight varies 6.026-6.674 grams.

Date	Mintage	Good	VG	F	VF	XF
VS1947 (1890)	—	0.75	1.50	2.25	4.50	9.00
VS1948 (1891)	—	0.50	1.00	1.50	3.00	6.00

Date	Mintage	Good	VG	F	VF	XF
VS1956 (1899)	—	0.35	0.75	1.25	2.50	5.00
VS1957 (1900)	—	0.65	1.25	1.75	2.50	5.00
VS1958 (1901)	—	0.65	1.25	1.75	3.50	7.00
VS1959 (1902)	—	0.65	1.25	1.75	3.50	7.00

KM# 33.4 1/4 ANNA
Copper, 25 mm. **Obverse:** Bull reclining left **Rev. Inscription:** Date below denomination **Mint:** Indore **Note:** Weight varies 6.026-6.675 grams.

Date	Mintage	Good	VG	F	VF	XF
VS1948 (1891)	—	1.00	2.00	4.00	6.00	—

KM# 34.1 1/2 ANNA
Copper, 30 mm. **Obverse:** Date below bull reclining left **Mint:** Indore **Note:** Weight varies 12.182-12.960 grams.

Date	Mintage	Good	VG	F	VF	XF
VS1943 (1886)	—	3.00	5.00	8.50	14.00	—

KM# 34.3 1/2 ANNA
Copper, 30 mm. **Obv. Legend:** "Indore" behind bull reclining left **Reverse:** "Indore" above denomination and date **Mint:** Indore **Note:** Weight varies 12.182-12.960 grams.

Date	Mintage	Good	VG	F	VF	XF
VS1943 (1886)	—	4.00	6.00	8.50	12.50	—

KM# 34.4 1/2 ANNA
Copper, 30 mm. **Obverse:** Legend broken with "Indore" upright below bull reclining left **Mint:** Indore **Note:** Weight varies 12.182-12.960 grams.

Date	Mintage	Good	VG	F	VF	XF
VS1943 (1886)	—	3.00	5.00	7.00	10.00	—

KM# 35.2 1/2 ANNA
Copper, 30 mm. **Obverse:** Legend broken with "Bahadur" upright below bull reclining left **Reverse:** "Indore" above denomination and date **Mint:** Indore **Note:** Weight varies 12.182-12.960 grams.

Date	Mintage	Good	VG	F	VF	XF
VS1943 (1886)	—	3.50	5.50	8.50	11.50	—

KM# 34.2 1/2 ANNA
Copper, 30 mm. **Obverse:** Legend continuous with "Indore" below bull reclining left **Mint:** Indore **Note:** Weight varies 12.182-12.960 grams. Strikes with local countermark exist.

Date	Mintage	Good	VG	F	VF	XF
VS1943 (1886)	—	3.00	5.00	7.00	10.00	—
VS1944 (1887)	—	3.00	5.00	7.00	10.00	—

KM# 35.1 1/2 ANNA
Copper, 30 mm. **Obverse:** Bull reclining left **Obv. Legend:** "Sivaji Rao" and "Indore" **Mint:** Indore **Note:** Weight varies 12.182-12.960 grams. Floral border varieties exist.

Date	Mintage	Good	VG	F	VF	XF
VS1944 (1887)	—	3.00	5.00	7.00	10.00	—
VS1945 (1888)	—	3.00	5.00	7.00	10.00	—
VS1947 (1890)	—	7.50	13.50	20.00	30.00	—

KM# 35.3 1/2 ANNA
Copper, 31 mm. **Obverse:** Continuous legend around reclining bull **Obv. Legend:** Shivaji Rao **Reverse:** "Indore" above denomination and date **Note:** Struck at the Indore Mint.

Date	Mintage	Good	VG	F	VF	XF
VS1945 (1888)	—	1.00	1.50	2.25	4.50	9.00
VS1947 (1890)	—	1.00	1.50	2.00	4.00	8.00
VS1948 (1891)	—	1.00	1.50	2.00	3.00	6.00
VS1956 (1899)	—	1.00	1.50	2.00	3.00	6.00
VS1957 (1900)	—	1.00	1.50	2.00	3.00	6.00
VS1958 (1901)	—	1.00	1.50	2.00	4.00	8.00
VS1959 (1902)	—	1.00	1.50	2.00	4.00	8.00

Tukoji Rao III
VS1960-1983 / 1903-1926AD

HAMMERED COINAGE

KM# 40 PAISA
Copper **Obverse:** Sunface with "U" on forehead **Rev. Inscription:** Shah Alam (II) in sprays **Mint:** Indore

Date	Mintage	Good	VG	F	VF	XF
VS1947 (1890) Rare	—	—	—	—	—	—

KM# 41 1/8 RUPEE
Silver **Obverse:** Sunface **Rev. Inscription:** Shah Alam (II) in sprays **Mint:** Indore **Note:** Weight varies 1.34-1.45 grams.

Date	Mintage	Good	VG	F	VF	XF
VS1947 (1890)	—	1.50	3.50	5.50	7.00	10.00

Date	Mintage	Good	VG	F	VF	XF
VS1950 (1893)	—	1.50	3.50	5.50	7.00	10.00
VS1951 (1894)	—	1.50	3.50	5.50	7.00	10.00

KM# 37 1/4 RUPEE
Silver **Obverse:** Sunface above crossed swords **Rev. Inscription:** Shah Alam (II) **Mint:** Indore **Note:** Weight varies 2.68-2.90 grams.

Date	Mintage	Good	VG	F	VF	XF
FE1295 (1885)	—	7.00	17.50	25.00	35.00	50.00

KM# 42 1/4 RUPEE
Silver **Obverse:** Sunface **Rev. Inscription:** Shah Alam (II) in sprays **Mint:** Indore **Note:** Weight varies 2.68-2.90 grams.

Date	Mintage	Good	VG	F	VF	XF
VS1947 (1890)	—	1.50	3.50	6.00	8.50	12.50
VS1948 (1891)	—	1.60	4.00	7.50	11.00	18.00
VS1951 (1894)	—	1.50	3.50	6.00	8.50	12.50
VS1954 (1897)	—	1.50	3.50	6.00	8.50	12.50

KM# 38 1/2 RUPEE
Silver **Obverse:** Sunface above crossed swords **Rev. Inscription:** Shah Alam (II) **Mint:** Indore **Note:** Weight varies 5.35-5.80 grams.

Date	Mintage	Good	VG	F	VF	XF
FE1295 (1885)	—	7.00	17.50	25.00	35.00	50.00
FE1296 (1886)	—	7.00	17.50	25.00	35.00	50.00

KM# 43 1/2 RUPEE
Silver **Obverse:** Sunface **Rev. Inscription:** Shah Alam (II) in sprays **Mint:** Indore **Note:** Weight varies 5.35-5.80 grams.

Date	Mintage	Good	VG	F	VF	XF
VS1947 (1890)	—	1.60	4.00	7.00	10.00	15.00
VS1948 (1891)	—	1.60	4.00	7.00	10.00	15.00
VS1949 (1892)	—	1.60	4.00	7.00	10.00	15.00
VS1950 (1893)	—	1.60	4.00	7.00	10.00	15.00
VS1951 (1894)	—	1.60	4.00	7.00	10.00	15.00
VS1952 (1895)	—	1.60	4.00	7.00	10.00	15.00
VS1953 (1896)	—	1.60	4.00	7.00	10.00	15.00
VS1954 (1897)	—	1.60	4.00	7.00	10.00	15.00

KM# 39.1 RUPEE
Silver **Obverse:** Sunface above crossed swords and long flames **Rev. Inscription:** Shah Alam (II) **Mint:** Indore **Note:** Weight varies 10.70-11.60 grams.

Date	Mintage	Good	VG	F	VF	XF
FE1294 (1884)	—	6.50	16.50	23.50	32.50	45.00
FE1295 (1885)	—	6.50	16.50	23.50	32.50	45.00
FE1296 (1886)	—	6.50	16.50	23.50	32.50	45.00

KM# 39.2 RUPEE
Silver **Obverse:** Sunface above crossed swords and long flames **Rev. Inscription:** Shah Alam (II) **Mint:** Indore **Note:** Weight varies 10.70-11.60 grams.

Date	Mintage	Good	VG	F	VF	XF
FE1295 (1885)	—	6.00	15.00	21.50	30.00	40.00
FE1296 (1886)	—	6.00	15.00	21.50	30.00	40.00

KM# 39.3 RUPEE
Silver **Obverse:** Sunface above crossed swords, without flames **Rev. Inscription:** Shah Alam (II) **Mint:** Indore **Note:** Weight varies 10.70-11.60 grams. There are 2 minor sub-varieties, one with U-shaped mark on forehead of sunface and the other with dot.

Date	Mintage	Good	VG	F	VF	XF
FE1295 (1885)	—	6.50	16.50	23.50	32.50	45.00
FE1296 (1886)	—	6.50	16.50	23.50	32.50	45.00
FE1297 (1887)	—	6.50	16.50	23.50	32.50	45.00

KM# 44 RUPEE
Silver **Obverse:** Sunface **Rev. Inscription:** Shah Alam (II) in sprays **Mint:** Indore **Note:** Weight varies 10.70-11.60 grams.

Date	Mintage	Good	VG	F	VF	XF
VS1947 (1890)	—	2.25	5.50	8.50	12.50	18.50
VS1948 (1891)	—	2.25	5.50	8.50	12.50	18.50
VS1949 (1892)	—	2.25	5.50	8.50	12.50	18.50
VS1950 (1893)	—	2.25	5.50	8.50	12.50	18.50
VS1951 (1894)	—	2.25	5.50	8.50	12.50	18.50
VS1952 (1895)	—	2.25	5.50	8.50	12.50	18.50
VS1953 (1896)	—	2.25	5.50	8.50	12.50	18.50
VS1954 (1897)	—	2.25	5.50	8.50	12.50	18.50
VS1955 (1898)	—	2.25	5.50	8.50	12.50	18.50

KM# 45 NAZARANA RUPEE
Silver, 25 mm. **Obverse:** Sunface **Rev. Inscription:** Shah Alam (II) in sprays **Mint:** Indore **Note:** Weight varies 11.13-11.21 grams.

Date	Mintage	Good	VG	F	VF	XF
VS1947 (1890)	—	35.00	75.00	125	200	300

MILLED COINAGE

KM# 46 1/2 ANNA
10.0300 g., Copper **Mint:** Indore

Date	Mintage	Good	VG	F	VF	XF
VS1955 (1898) Rare	—	—	—	—	—	—

KM# 47.1 RUPEE
11.2000 g., Silver **Obverse:** Bust of Shivaji Rao facing slightly left, turban separates legend **Reverse:** Arms **Mint:** Indore

Date	Mintage	VG	F	VF	XF	Unc
VS1956 (1899)	—	45.00	90.00	140	200	350

PATTERNS

KM#	Date	Mintage	Identification	Mkt Val
Pn1	VS1955	—	Rupee. 0.9000 Silver. 12 pieces.	650

TRIAL STRIKES

KM#	Date	Mintage	Identification	Mkt Val
TS1	VS1955	—	Rupee. Copper. Obverse, Pn1.	400

JAIPUR

Tradition has it that the region of Jaipur, located in northwest India, once belonged to an ancient Kachwaha Rajput dynasty which claimed descent from Kush, one of the sons of Rama, King of Ayodhya. But the Princely State of Jaipur originated in the 12th century. Comparatively small in size, the State remained largely unnoticed until after the 16th century when the Jaipur royal house became famous for its military skills and thereafter supplied the Mughals with some of their more distinguished generals. The city of Jaipur was founded about 1728 by Maharaja Jai Singh II who was well known for his knowledge of mathematics and astronomy. The late 18th and early 19th centuries were difficult times for Jaipur. They were marked by internal rivalry, exacerbated by Maratha or Pindari incursions. In 1818 this culminated with a treaty whereby Jaipur came under British protection and oversight.

RULERS
Pratap Singh, AH1192-1218/1778-1803AD
Jagat Singh II, AH1218-1234/1803-1818AD
Mohan Singh, AH1234-1235/1818-1819AD
Jai Singh III, AH1235-1251/1819-1835AD
Ram Singh, AH1251-1298/1835-1880AD
Madho Singh II, 1880-1922AD

All coins struck prior to AH1274/1857AD are in the name of the Mughal emperor. The corresponding AH date is listed in ( ) with each regnal year. Some overlapping of AH dates with regnal years will be found. Partial dates and recorded full dates are represented by partial ( ) or without ( ).

Beginning in 1857AD, coins were struck jointly in the names and corresponding AD dates of the British sovereign and the names and regnal years of the Maharajas of Jaipur.

The coins ordinarily bear both the AH date before 1857 or the AD date after 1857, as well as the regnal year, but as it is found only at the extreme right of the obverse die, it is almost never visible on the regular coinage but generally legible on the Nazarana coins which were struck utilizing the entire dies.

The listing of regnal years is very incomplete and many more years will turn up. In general, unlisted years are usually worth no more than years listed.

MINT NAMES

Coins were struck at two mints, which bear the following characteristic marks on the reverse:

سواي جيپور

Sawai Jaipur

سواي مادهوپور

Sawai Madhopur

NOTE: *Sawai* is merely an honorific title accorded each of the two cities.

Mint marks:

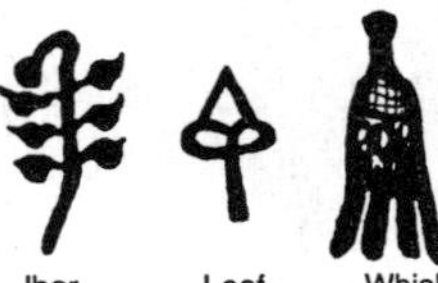

Jhar Leaf Whisk

REGAL ISSUES

To distinguish coins between Ram Singh and his son/successor Madho Singh II, note that the coins of Ram Singh have a small slanting cross or dagger between the Ram and Singh symbols whereas the coins of Singh II do not.

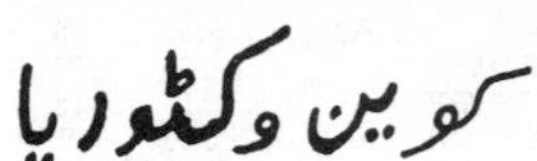

In the names of Queen Victoria

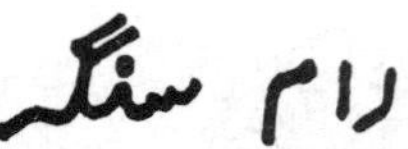

And Ram Singh
Years 22-45/1857-1880AD

كوين وكٹوريا

In the names of Queen Victoria

And Madho Singh II

HAMMERED COINAGE

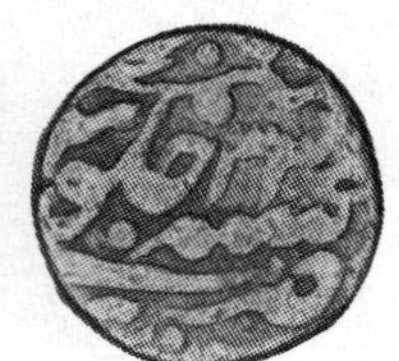

KM# 58 PAISA
Copper **Obv. Inscription:** "Shah Alam II" **Mint:** Sawai Madhopur

Date	Mintage	Good	VG	F	VF	XF
ND//42 (1800-01)	—	2.50	4.00	6.00	9.00	—

KM# A61 PAISA
Copper **Obv. Inscription:** "Muhammad Akbar II" **Mint:** Sawai Jaipur **Note:** Size varies 18-20mm. Similar to Nazarana Paisa, C#47a.

Date	Mintage	Good	VG	F	VF	XF
ND//12 (1817-18)	—	2.00	3.25	5.00	7.50	—
ND//13 (1818-19)	—	2.00	3.25	5.00	7.50	—
ND//17 (1822-23)	—	2.00	3.25	5.00	7.50	—
ND//22 (1827-28)	—	2.00	3.25	5.00	7.50	—
ND//26 (1831-32)	—	2.00	3.25	5.00	7.50	—
ND//33 (1832-33)	—	2.00	3.25	5.00	7.50	—
ND//29 (1834-35)	—	2.00	3.25	5.00	7.50	—

KM# A66 1/4 RUPEE
Silver **Obv. Inscription:** "Muhammad Akbar II" **Mint:** Sawai Jaipur **Note:** Size varies 18-19mm, weight varies 2.68-2.90 grams.

Date	Mintage	Good	VG	F	VF	XF
ND//17 (1822-23)	—	10.00	25.00	40.00	60.00	85.00
ND//16 (1823) (sic)	—	10.00	25.00	40.00	60.00	85.00
ND//20 (1825-26)	—	10.00	25.00	40.00	60.00	85.00
ND//24 (1829-30)	—	10.00	25.00	40.00	60.00	85.00
ND//28 (1833-34)	—	10.00	25.00	40.00	60.00	85.00

KM# 63 RUPEE
Silver **Obv. Inscription:** "Shah Alam II" **Mint:** Sawai Madhopur **Note:** Weight varies: 10.70-11.60 grams.

Date	Mintage	Good	VG	F	VF	XF
ND//43 (1810-02)	—	2.75	6.50	10.00	15.00	22.50

KM# A76 RUPEE
Silver **Obv. Inscription:** "Bahadur Shah II" **Mint:** Sawai Madhopur **Note:** Weight varies 10.70-11.60 grams.

Date	Mintage	Good	VG	F	VF	XF
AH1255//2	—	2.25	5.50	8.00	12.50	18.50
AH125(x)//3	—	2.25	5.50	8.00	12.50	18.50
ND//4 (1840-41)	—	2.25	5.50	8.00	12.50	18.50
ND//5 (1841-42)	—	2.25	5.50	8.00	12.50	18.50
ND//6 (1842-43)	—	2.25	5.50	8.00	12.50	18.50
ND//7 (1843-44)	—	2.25	5.50	8.00	12.50	18.50
ND//8 (1844-45)	—	2.25	5.50	8.00	12.50	18.50
ND//10 (1845-46)	—	2.25	5.50	8.00	12.50	18.50
ND//12 (1847-48)	—	2.25	5.50	8.00	12.50	18.50
ND//15 (1850-51)	—	2.25	5.50	8.00	12.50	18.50
ND//17 (1852-53)	—	2.25	5.50	8.00	12.50	18.50
ND//18 (1853-54)	—	2.25	5.50	8.00	12.50	18.50

KM# A73 1/2 NAZARANA RUPEE
5.3000 g., Silver **Obv. Inscription:** "Muhammad Akbar II" **Mint:** Sawai Madhopur

Date	Mintage	Good	VG	F	VF	XF
AH12(xx)//1	—	—	—	—	—	—

KM# A62 NAZARANA RUPEE
Copper, 34 mm. **Obv. Inscription:** "Muhammad Akbar II" **Reverse:** Jhar **Mint:** Sawai Jaipur

Date	Mintage	Good	VG	F	VF	XF
ND//4 (1809-10)	—	15.00	25.00	40.00	60.00	—
ND//7 (1812-13)	—	15.00	25.00	40.00	60.00	—
ND//9 (1814-15)	—	15.00	25.00	40.00	60.00	—
ND//10 (1815-16)	—	15.00	25.00	40.00	60.00	—
ND//11 (1816-17)	—	15.00	25.00	40.00	60.00	—
ND//12 (1817-18)	—	15.00	25.00	40.00	60.00	—
ND//15 (1820-21)	—	15.00	25.00	40.00	60.00	—
ND//16 (1821-22)	—	15.00	25.00	40.00	60.00	—
ND//22 (1827-28)	—	15.00	25.00	40.00	60.00	—
ND//28 (1833-34)	—	15.00	25.00	40.00	60.00	—

KM# 55 MOHUR
Gold **Obv. Inscription:** "Shah Alam II" **Mint:** Sawai Jaipur **Note:** Weight varies: 10.70-11.40 grams.

Date	Mintage	Good	VG	F	VF	XF
ND//43 (1802-03)	—	—	135	160	225	325
AH121x//44	—	—	135	160	225	325

HAMMERED COINAGE

Mughal Style

KM# 70 PAISA
Copper **Obv. Inscription:** "Muhammad Akbar II" **Mint:** Sawai Madhopur

Date	Mintage	Good	VG	F	VF	XF
ND//13	—	3.00	5.00	7.50	11.50	—
ND//14	—	3.00	5.00	7.50	11.50	—

KM# 39 PAISA
Copper **Obv. Inscription:** "Shah Alam II" **Reverse:** Large Jhar **Mint:** Sawai Jaipur

Date	Mintage	Good	VG	F	VF	XF
ND//44 (1802-03)	—	2.50	4.50	6.50	10.00	—
ND//45 (1803-04)	—	2.50	4.50	6.50	10.00	—

KM# 80 PAISA
Copper **Obv. Inscription:** "Bahadur Shah II" **Mint:** Sawai Jaipur

Date	Mintage	Good	VG	F	VF	XF
ND//13 (1848-49)	—	3.00	5.00	8.00	12.50	—

KM# 40 NAZARANA PAISA
Copper **Obv. Inscription:** "Shah Alam II" **Reverse:** Large Jhar **Mint:** Sawai Jaipur

Date	Mintage	Good	VG	F	VF	XF
ND//45 (1803-04)	—	15.00	27.50	40.00	60.00	—
ND//46 (1804-05)	—	15.00	27.50	40.00	60.00	—

KM# 60 NAZARANA PAISA
Copper, 31 mm. **Obv. Inscription:** "Muhammad Akbar II" **Reverse:** Whisk **Mint:** Sawai Jaipur

Date	Mintage	Good	VG	F	VF	XF
ND//3 (1808-09)	—	25.00	42.50	65.00	100	—
ND//8 (1813)	—	25.00	42.50	65.00	100	—
ND//11 (1816-17)	—	25.00	42.50	65.00	100	—

KM# 81.1 NAZARANA PAISA
Copper **Obv. Inscription:** "Bahadur Shah II" **Mint:** Sawai Jaipur

Date	Mintage	Good	VG	F	VF	XF
ND//1 (1837-38)	—	16.00	26.50	40.00	60.00	—
ND//2 (1838-39)	—	16.00	26.50	40.00	60.00	—
ND//6 (1842-43)	—	16.00	26.50	40.00	60.00	—
ND//10 (1845-46)	—	16.00	26.50	40.00	60.00	—
ND//11 (1846-47)	—	16.00	26.50	40.00	60.00	—
ND//12 (1847-48)	—	16.00	26.50	40.00	60.00	—
ND//13 (1848-49)	—	16.00	26.50	40.00	60.00	—
ND//14 (1849-50)	—	16.00	26.50	40.00	60.00	—
ND//17 (1852-53)	—	16.00	26.50	40.00	60.00	—

KM# 81.2 NAZARANA PAISA
Copper **Obv. Inscription:** "Bahadur Shah II" **Mint:** Sawai Jaipur **Note:** Shape: square.

Date	Mintage	Good	VG	F	VF	XF
ND//13 (1848-49) Rare	—	—	—	—	—	—

KM# 83 1/16 RUPEE
Silver **Obv. Inscription:** "Bahadur Shah II" **Mint:** Sawai Jaipur **Note:** Weight varies 0.67-0.72 grams.

Date	Mintage	Good	VG	F	VF	XF
ND//7 (1843-44)	—	6.00	15.00	25.00	40.00	60.00
ND//9 (1845)	—	6.00	15.00	25.00	40.00	60.00
ND//18 (1853-54)	—	6.00	15.00	25.00	40.00	60.00

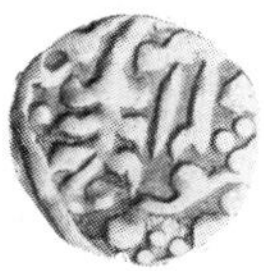

KM# 65 1/8 RUPEE
Silver **Obv. Inscription:** "Muhammad Akbar II" **Mint:** Sawai Jaipur **Note:** Size varies 17-18mm, weight varies 1.34-1.45 grams.

Date	Mintage	Good	VG	F	VF	XF
ND//21 (1826-27)	—	8.00	20.00	32.00	50.00	70.00
ND//22 (1827-28)	—	8.00	20.00	32.00	50.00	70.00

KM# 85 1/8 RUPEE
Silver, 15 mm. **Obv. Inscription:** "Bahadur Shah II" **Mint:** Sawai Jaipur **Note:** Weight varies 1.34-1.45 grams.

Date	Mintage	Good	VG	F	VF	XF
ND//18 (1853-54)	—	5.00	12.50	20.00	30.00	50.00

KM# 87 1/4 RUPEE
Silver **Obv. Inscription:** "Bahadur Shah II" **Reverse:** Jhar **Mint:** Sawai Jaipur **Note:** Size varies 16-18mm, weight varies 2.68-2.90 grams.

Date	Mintage	Good	VG	F	VF	XF
ND//7 (1843-44)	—	5.00	12.50	20.00	30.00	45.00
ND//19 (1854-55)	—	5.00	12.50	20.00	30.00	45.00
ND//20 (1855-56)	—	5.00	12.50	20.00	30.00	45.00

KM# 67 1/2 RUPEE
Silver **Obv. Inscription:** "Muhammad Akbar II" **Mint:** Sawai Jaipur **Note:** Size varies 18-20mm, weight varies 5.35-5.80 grams.

Date	Mintage	Good	VG	F	VF	XF
ND//16 (1821-22)	—	10.00	25.00	40.00	60.00	85.00
ND//23 (1828-29)	—	10.00	25.00	40.00	60.00	85.00
ND//31 (1836-37)	—	10.00	25.00	40.00	60.00	85.00

KM# 90 1/2 RUPEE
Silver **Obv. Inscription:** "Bahadur Shah II" **Mint:** Sawai Jaipur **Note:** Size varies 18-19mm, weight varies 5.35-5.80 grams.

Date	Mintage	Good	VG	F	VF	XF
ND//5 (1841-42)	—	8.00	20.00	32.00	50.00	70.00
ND//11 (1846-47)	—	8.00	20.00	32.00	50.00	70.00
ND//18 (1853-54)	—	8.00	20.00	32.00	50.00	70.00

KM# 50 RUPEE
Silver **Obv. Inscription:** "Shah Alam II" **Mint:** Sawai Jaipur **Note:** Mintmark: Jhar. Weight varies: 10.70-11.60 grams.

Date	Mintage	Good	VG	F	VF	XF
AH1218//44 (sic)	—	2.25	5.50	8.00	12.50	18.50
AH1218//45	—	2.25	5.50	8.00	12.50	18.50
ND//46 (1804-05)	—	2.25	5.50	8.00	12.50	18.50
ND//47 (1805-06)	—	2.25	5.50	8.00	12.50	18.50

KM# 72 RUPEE
Silver **Mint:** Sawai Jaipur **Note:** Weight varies 10.70-11.60 grams.

Date	Mintage	Good	VG	F	VF	XF
AH1221//1	—	2.50	6.00	9.00	13.50	20.00
AH1222//2	—	2.50	6.00	9.00	13.50	20.00
AH1226//4 (sic)	—	2.50	6.00	9.00	13.50	20.00
ND//7 (1812-13)	—	2.50	6.00	9.00	13.50	20.00
AH1228//6 (sic)	—	2.50	6.00	9.00	13.50	20.00
AH1229//9	—	2.50	6.00	9.00	13.50	20.00
AH1230//10	—	2.50	6.00	9.00	13.50	20.00
AH1233//11 (sic)	—	2.50	6.00	9.00	13.50	20.00
AH123x//12	—	2.50	6.00	9.00	13.50	20.00
AH1233//13	—	2.50	6.00	9.00	13.50	20.00
AH1234//13	—	2.50	6.00	9.00	13.50	20.00
AH122(x)//3	—	2.50	6.00	9.00	13.50	20.00
AH1234//14	—	2.50	6.00	9.00	13.50	20.00
AH1235//15	—	2.50	6.00	9.00	13.50	20.00
AH1238//18	—	2.50	6.00	9.00	13.50	20.00
AH1240//20	—	2.50	6.00	9.00	13.50	20.00
AH1243//22	—	2.50	6.00	9.00	13.50	20.00
ND//23 (1828-29)	—	2.50	6.00	9.00	13.50	20.00
ND//24 (1829-30)	—	2.50	6.00	9.00	13.50	20.00
AH1246//25	—	2.50	6.00	9.00	13.50	20.00
AH124x//26	—	2.50	6.00	9.00	13.50	20.00
AH1249//27 (sic)	—	2.50	6.00	9.00	13.50	20.00
ND//28 (1833-34)	—	2.50	6.00	9.00	13.50	20.00
AH1250//30	—	2.50	6.00	9.00	13.50	20.00
AH125x//31	—	2.50	6.00	9.00	13.50	20.00

KM# 75 RUPEE
Silver **Obv. Inscription:** "Muhammad Akbar II" **Mint:** Sawai Madhopur **Note:** Weight varies 10.70-11.60 grams.

Date	Mintage	Good	VG	F	VF	XF
AH1221//1	—	2.50	6.00	9.00	13.00	20.00
ND//2 (1807-08)	—	2.50	6.00	9.00	13.00	20.00
ND//4 (1809-10)	—	2.50	6.00	9.00	13.00	20.00
ND//5 (1810-11)	—	2.50	6.00	9.00	13.00	20.00
ND//6 (1811-12)	—	2.50	6.00	9.00	13.00	20.00
ND//7 (1812-13)	—	2.50	6.00	9.00	13.00	20.00
ND//8 (1813-14)	—	2.50	6.00	9.00	13.00	20.00
ND//9 (1814-15)	—	2.50	6.00	9.00	13.00	20.00
ND//10 (1815-16)	—	2.50	6.00	9.00	13.00	20.00
ND//11 (1816-17)	—	2.50	6.00	9.00	13.00	20.00
ND//12 (1817-18)	—	2.50	6.00	9.00	13.00	20.00
ND//13 (1818-19)	—	2.50	6.00	9.00	13.00	20.00
ND//14 (1819-20)	—	2.50	6.00	9.00	13.00	20.00
ND//15 (1820-21)	—	2.50	6.00	9.00	13.00	20.00
ND//16 (1821-22)	—	2.50	6.00	9.00	13.00	20.00
ND//17 (1822-23)	—	2.50	6.00	9.00	13.00	20.00
ND//18 (1823-24)	—	2.50	6.00	9.00	13.00	20.00
ND//20 (1825-26)	—	2.50	6.00	9.00	13.00	20.00
ND//21 (1826-27)	—	2.50	6.00	9.00	13.00	20.00
ND//22 (1827-28)	—	2.50	6.00	9.00	13.00	20.00
ND//23 (1828-29)	—	2.50	6.00	9.00	13.00	20.00
ND//24 (1829-30)	—	2.50	6.00	9.00	13.00	20.00
ND//26 (1831-32)	—	2.50	6.00	9.00	13.00	20.00
ND//29 (1834-35)	—	2.50	6.00	9.00	13.00	20.00
ND//30 (1835-36)	—	2.50	6.00	9.00	13.00	20.00
ND//31 (1836-37)	—	2.50	6.00	9.00	13.00	20.00

KM# 74 RUPEE

Silver **Obv. Inscription:** "Muhammad Akbar II" **Mint:** Sawai Jaipur **Note:** Weight varies 10.70-11.60 grams. Shape: square.

Date	Mintage	Good	VG	F	VF	XF
AH123x//10 Rare	—	—	—	—	—	—

KM# 93 RUPEE

Silver **Obv. Inscription:** "Bahadur Shah II" **Mint:** Sawai Jaipur **Note:** Weight varies 10.70-11.60 grams.

Date	Mintage	Good	VG	F	VF	XF
AH1253//1	—	2.00	5.00	7.00	10.00	15.00
AH1256//3	—	2.00	5.00	7.00	10.00	15.00
AH1257//4	—	2.00	5.00	7.00	10.00	15.00
AH1258//5	—	2.00	5.00	7.00	10.00	15.00
AH1261//8	—	2.00	5.00	7.00	10.00	15.00
AH1262//9	—	2.00	5.00	7.00	10.00	15.00
AH1263//10	—	2.00	5.00	7.00	10.00	15.00
ND//11 (1846-47)	—	2.00	5.00	7.00	10.00	15.00
AH1265//12	—	2.00	5.00	7.00	10.00	15.00
AH1268//14 (sic)	—	2.00	5.00	7.00	10.00	15.00
ND//15 (1850-51)	—	2.00	5.00	7.00	10.00	15.00
AH1270//17	—	2.00	5.00	7.00	10.00	15.00
AH1271//17 (sic)	—	2.00	5.00	7.00	10.00	15.00
ND//19 (1854-55)	—	2.00	5.00	7.00	10.00	15.00
AH1273//20	—	2.00	5.00	7.00	10.00	15.00

KM# 46 NAZARANA 1/4 RUPEE

Silver **Obv. Inscription:** "Shah Alam II" **Mint:** Sawai Jaipur **Note:** Weight varies 2.67-2.90 grams.

Date	Mintage	Good	VG	F	VF	XF
ND//44 (1802-03)	—	22.50	45.00	75.00	120	175

KM# 68 NAZARANA 1/2 RUPEE

Silver **Obv. Inscription:** "Muhammad Akbar II" **Mint:** Sawai Jaipur **Note:** Weight varies 5.35-5.70 grams.

Date	Mintage	Good	VG	F	VF	XF
ND//20 (1825-26)	—	22.50	55.00	90.00	140	200

KM# 51 NAZARANA RUPEE

Silver, 35 mm. **Obv. Inscription:** "Shah Alam II" **Mint:** Sawai Jaipur **Note:** Large flan. Weight varies: 10.70-11.60 grams.

Date	Mintage	Good	VG	F	VF	XF
AH1217//43 (sic)	—	21.50	60.00	100	140	200

KM# 73 NAZARANA RUPEE

Silver **Obv. Inscription:** "Muhammad Akbar II" **Mint:** Sawai Jaipur **Note:** Weight varies 10.70-11.60 grams.

Date	Mintage	Good	VG	F	VF	XF
AH1221//1	—	15.00	30.00	50.00	70.00	100
AH1230//9	—	15.00	30.00	50.00	70.00	100
AH1232//11	—	15.00	30.00	50.00	70.00	100
AH1237//16	—	15.00	30.00	50.00	70.00	100
AH1240//20	—	15.00	30.00	50.00	70.00	100
AH1240//21 (sic)	—	15.00	30.00	50.00	70.00	100
AH1242//22	—	15.00	30.00	50.00	70.00	100
AH1243//23	—	15.00	30.00	50.00	70.00	100
AH1246//25	—	15.00	30.00	50.00	70.00	100
AH1248//27	—	15.00	30.00	50.00	70.00	100
AH1249//27 (sic)	—	15.00	30.00	50.00	70.00	100
AH1249//29	—	15.00	30.00	50.00	70.00	100
AH1250//28 (sic)	—	15.00	30.00	50.00	70.00	100
AH1251//29	—	15.00	30.00	50.00	70.00	100
AH125x//30	—	15.00	30.00	50.00	70.00	100

KM# 95 NAZARANA RUPEE

Silver **Obv. Inscription:** "Bahadur Shah II" **Mint:** Sawai Jaipur **Note:** Size varies 32-36mm, weight varies 10.70-11.60 grams.

Date	Mintage	Good	VG	F	VF	XF
AH1256//3	—	13.50	33.50	47.50	65.00	90.00
AH1258//4 (sic)	—	13.50	33.50	47.50	65.00	90.00
AH1258//5	—	13.50	33.50	47.50	65.00	90.00
AH1262//9	—	13.50	33.50	47.50	65.00	90.00
AH1263//10	—	13.50	33.50	47.50	65.00	90.00
AH1264//11	—	13.50	33.50	47.50	65.00	90.00
AH1266//13	—	13.50	33.50	47.50	65.00	90.00
AH1268//8 (sic)	—	13.50	33.50	47.50	65.00	90.00
AH1269//15 (sic)	—	13.50	33.50	47.50	65.00	90.00
AH1271//19	—	13.50	33.50	47.50	65.00	90.00
AH1273//20	—	13.50	33.50	47.50	65.00	90.00

KM# 98 1/4 MOHUR

Gold **Obv. Inscription:** "Bahadur Shah II" **Mint:** Sawai Jaipur **Note:** Weight varies 2.68-2.85 grams.

Date	Mintage	Good	VG	F	VF	XF
ND//12 (1847-48)	—	—	80.00	125	150	225

KM# 76 1/2 MOHUR

Gold **Obv. Inscription:** "Muhammad Akbar II" **Mint:** Sawai Jaipur **Note:** Weight varies 5.35-5.80 grams.

Date	Mintage	Good	VG	F	VF	XF
AH124x//25	—	—	100	150	225	325

KM# 100 1/2 MOHUR

Gold **Obv. Inscription:** "Bahadur Shah II" **Mint:** Sawai Jaipur **Note:** Weight varies 5.35-5.70 grams.

Date	Mintage	Good	VG	F	VF	XF
ND//12 (1847-48)	—	—	100	150	200	275

KM# 77 MOHUR

Gold **Obv. Inscription:** "Muhammad Akbar II" **Mint:** Sawai Jaipur **Note:** Weight varies 10.70-11.60 grams.

Date	Mintage	Good	VG	F	VF	XF
AH122(x)//1	—	—	BV	160	225	300
ND//2 (1807-08)	—	—	BV	160	225	300
ND//7 (1812-13)	—	—	BV	160	225	300
ND//8 (1813-14)	—	—	BV	160	225	300
ND//9 (1814-15)	—	—	BV	160	225	300
ND//11 (1816-17)	—	—	BV	160	225	300
ND//12 (1817-18)	—	—	BV	160	225	300
ND//16 (1821-22)	—	—	BV	160	225	300
ND//19 (1824-25)	—	—	BV	160	225	300
AH12(xx)//24	—	—	BV	160	225	300
ND//29 (1834-35)	—	—	BV	160	225	300
ND//30 (1835-36)	—	—	BV	160	225	300

KM# 102 MOHUR

Gold **Obv. Inscription:** "Bahadur Shah II" **Mint:** Sawai Jaipur **Note:** Weight varies 10.70-11.40 grams.

Date	Mintage	Good	VG	F	VF	XF
AH1253//1	—	—	160	200	250	325
ND//5 (1841-42)	—	—	160	200	250	325
AH12(xx)//7	—	—	160	200	250	325
AH1262//9	—	—	160	200	250	325
ND//10 (1845-46)	—	—	160	200	250	325
ND//11 (1846-47)	—	—	160	200	250	325
ND//12 (1847-48)	—	—	160	200	250	325
ND//13 (1848-49)	—	—	160	200	250	325
ND//14 (1849-50)	—	—	160	200	250	325
AH//15 (1850-51)	—	—	160	200	250	325
AH1272//18 (sic)	—	—	160	200	250	325
AH1272//19	—	—	160	200	250	325
ND//20 (1855-56)	—	—	160	200	250	325

HAMMERED COINAGE

Regal Style

To distinguish coins betweenRam Singh and his son/successor Madho Singh II, note that the coins of Ram Singh have a small slanting cross or dagger between the Ram and Singh symbols, whereas the coins of Singh II do not.

KM# 129 1/2 NEW PAISA

2.9800 g., Copper **Obv. Inscription:** Victoria **Rev. Inscription:** Ram Singh **Mint:** Sawai Jaipur

Date	Mintage	Good	VG	F	VF	XF
ND//22 (1857)	—	1.00	2.00	3.50	5.50	—

KM# 105 NEW PAISA

Copper **Obv. Inscription:** Victoria **Rev. Inscription:** Ram Singh **Mint:** Sawai Jaipur **Note:** Weight varies 6.09-6.22 grams. Years 36 and 37 are struck on broader flans.

Date	Mintage	Good	VG	F	VF	XF
ND//36 (1871)	—	1.00	2.00	2.75	5.00	—
ND//37 (1872)	—	1.00	2.00	2.75	5.00	—
ND//38 (1873)	—	1.00	2.00	2.75	5.00	—
ND//39 (1874)	—	1.00	2.00	2.75	5.00	—
ND//40 (1875)	—	1.00	2.00	2.75	5.00	—
ND//41 (1876)	—	1.00	2.00	2.75	5.00	—
ND//42 (1877)	—	1.00	2.00	2.75	5.00	—
ND//45 (1880)	—	1.25	2.25	3.25	6.00	—

KM# 107 NAZARANA NEW PAISA

Copper, 28 mm. **Obv. Inscription:** Victoria **Rev. Inscription:** Ram Singh **Mint:** Sawai Jaipur **Note:** Weight varies 6.20-6.50 grams.

Date	Mintage	Good	VG	F	VF	XF
1862//27	—	12.00	18.50	30.00	45.00	—
1864//29	—	12.00	18.50	30.00	45.00	—

Date	Mintage	Good	VG	F	VF	XF
1865//30	—	12.00	18.50	30.00	45.00	—
1872//37	—	12.00	18.50	30.00	45.00	—
1873//38	—	12.00	18.50	30.00	45.00	—
1875//40	—	12.00	18.50	30.00	45.00	—
1876//41	—	12.00	18.50	30.00	45.00	—
1877//42	—	12.00	18.50	30.00	45.00	—
1879//44	—	12.00	18.50	30.00	45.00	—
1880//45	—	12.00	18.50	30.00	45.00	—

KM# 106 NAZARANA OLD PAISA
Copper **Obv. Inscription:** Victoria **Rev. Inscription:** Ram Singh **Mint:** Sawai Jaipur **Note:** Weight varies 16.00-18.50 grams, size varies 27-31mm.

Date	Mintage	Good	VG	F	VF	XF
1858//23	—	25.00	45.00	65.00	100	—
1859//24	—	25.00	45.00	65.00	100	—
1862//27	—	25.00	45.00	65.00	100	—
1870//35	—	25.00	45.00	65.00	100	—

KM# 110 1/8 RUPEE
Silver, 14 mm. **Obv. Inscription:** Victoria **Rev. Inscription:** Ram Singh **Mint:** Sawai Jaipur **Note:** Weight varies 1.34-1.45 grams.

Date	Mintage	Good	VG	F	VF	XF
ND//23 (1857)	—	3.00	7.50	12.50	20.00	30.00
ND//26 (1861)	—	3.00	7.50	12.50	20.00	30.00
ND//27 (1862)	—	3.00	7.50	12.50	20.00	30.00
ND//42 (1877)	—	3.00	7.50	12.50	20.00	30.00

KM# 111 1/4 RUPEE
Silver **Obv. Inscription:** Victoria **Rev. Inscription:** Ram Singh **Mint:** Sawai Jaipur **Note:** Weight varies 2.68-2.90 grams.

Date	Mintage	Good	VG	F	VF	XF
ND//26 (1861)	—	3.00	7.50	12.50	20.00	30.00
ND//27 (1862)	—	3.00	7.50	12.50	20.00	30.00
ND//28 (1863)	—	3.00	7.50	12.50	20.00	30.00
ND//29 (1864)	—	3.00	7.50	12.50	20.00	30.00
ND//32 (1867)	—	3.00	7.50	12.50	20.00	30.00
ND//33 (1868)	—	3.00	7.50	12.50	20.00	30.00
ND//41 (1876)	—	3.00	7.50	12.50	20.00	30.00
ND//43 (1878)	—	3.00	7.50	12.50	20.00	30.00
ND//44 (1879)	—	3.00	7.50	12.50	20.00	30.00
ND//45 (1880)	—	3.00	7.50	12.50	20.00	30.00

KM# 115 1/2 RUPEE
Silver **Obv. Inscription:** Victoria **Rev. Inscription:** Ram Singh **Mint:** Sawai Jaipur **Note:** Size varies 18-21mm, weight varies 5.35-5.80 grams.

Date	Mintage	Good	VG	F	VF	XF
ND//22 (1857)	—	5.00	12.50	20.00	30.00	45.00
ND//27 (1862)	—	5.00	12.50	20.00	30.00	45.00
ND//28 (1863)	—	5.00	12.50	20.00	30.00	45.00
ND//33 (1868)	—	5.00	12.50	20.00	30.00	45.00
ND//35 (1869)	—	5.00	12.50	20.00	30.00	45.00
ND//36 (1871)	—	5.00	12.50	20.00	30.00	45.00
ND//42 (1877)	—	5.00	12.50	20.00	30.00	45.00
ND//44 (1879)	—	5.00	12.50	20.00	30.00	45.00
ND//45 (1880)	—	5.00	12.50	20.00	30.00	45.00

KM# 119 RUPEE
Silver **Obv. Inscription:** Victoria **Rev. Inscription:** Ram Singh **Mint:** Sawai Jaipur **Note:** Weight varies 10.70-11.60 grams.

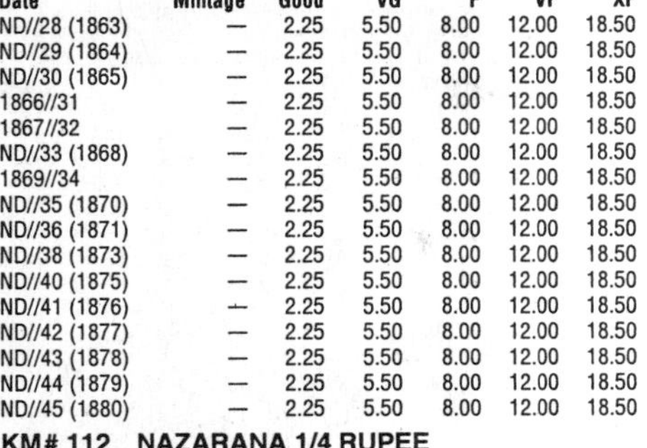

Date	Mintage	Good	VG	F	VF	XF
1858//23	—	2.25	5.50	8.00	12.00	18.50
ND//25 (1860)	—	2.25	5.50	8.00	12.00	18.50
ND//26 (1861)	—	2.25	5.50	8.00	12.00	18.50
ND//27 (1862)	—	2.25	5.50	8.00	12.00	18.50
ND//28 (1863)	—	2.25	5.50	8.00	12.00	18.50
ND//29 (1864)	—	2.25	5.50	8.00	12.00	18.50
ND//30 (1865)	—	2.25	5.50	8.00	12.00	18.50
1866//31	—	2.25	5.50	8.00	12.00	18.50
1867//32	—	2.25	5.50	8.00	12.00	18.50
ND//33 (1868)	—	2.25	5.50	8.00	12.00	18.50
1869//34	—	2.25	5.50	8.00	12.00	18.50
ND//35 (1870)	—	2.25	5.50	8.00	12.00	18.50
ND//36 (1871)	—	2.25	5.50	8.00	12.00	18.50
ND//38 (1873)	—	2.25	5.50	8.00	12.00	18.50
ND//40 (1875)	—	2.25	5.50	8.00	12.00	18.50
ND//41 (1876)	—	2.25	5.50	8.00	12.00	18.50
ND//42 (1877)	—	2.25	5.50	8.00	12.00	18.50
ND//43 (1878)	—	2.25	5.50	8.00	12.00	18.50
ND//44 (1879)	—	2.25	5.50	8.00	12.00	18.50
ND//45 (1880)	—	2.25	5.50	8.00	12.00	18.50

KM# 112 NAZARANA 1/4 RUPEE
Silver **Mint:** Sawai Jaipur

Date	Mintage	Good	VG	F	VF	XF
ND//44 (1879)	—	12.50	25.00	40.00	60.00	85.00

KM# 116 NAZARANA 1/2 RUPEE
Silver **Obv. Inscription:** Victoria **Rev. Inscription:** Ram Singh **Mint:** Sawai Jaipur

Date	Mintage	Good	VG	F	VF	XF
1865//30	—	15.00	30.00	50.00	80.00	120

KM# 120 NAZARANA RUPEE
Silver **Obv. Inscription:** Victoria **Rev. Inscription:** Ram Singh **Mint:** Sawai Jaipur **Note:** Weight varies 10.70-11.60 grams.

Date	Mintage	Good	VG	F	VF	XF
1858//23	—	13.50	27.00	40.00	55.00	85.00
1859//24	—	13.50	27.00	40.00	55.00	85.00
1861//26	—	13.50	27.00	40.00	55.00	85.00
1864//29	—	13.50	27.00	40.00	55.00	85.00
1865//30	—	13.50	27.00	40.00	55.00	85.00
1866//31	—	13.50	27.00	40.00	55.00	85.00
1867//32	—	13.50	27.00	40.00	55.00	85.00
1870//35	—	13.50	27.00	40.00	55.00	85.00
1871//36	—	13.50	27.00	40.00	55.00	85.00
1875//40	—	13.50	27.00	40.00	55.00	85.00

KM# 121 NAZARANA RUPEE
Silver **Obv. Inscription:** Victoria **Rev. Inscription:** Ram Singh **Mint:** Sawai Jaipur **Note:** Weight varies 10.70-11.60 grams. Shape: square.

Date	Mintage	Good	VG	F	VF	XF
1858//23	—	37.50	75.00	100	150	250

KM# 125 MOHUR
Gold **Obv. Inscription:** Victoria **Rev. Inscription:** Ram Singh **Mint:** Sawai Jaipur **Note:** Weight varies 10.70-11.40 grams.

Date	Mintage	VG	F	VF	XF	Unc
ND//21 (1856)	—	140	160	185	225	—
ND//22 (1857)	—	140	160	185	225	—
ND//23 (1858)	—	140	160	185	225	—
ND//24 (1859)	—	140	160	185	225	—
ND//25 (1860)	—	140	160	185	225	—
18(60)//25	—	140	160	185	225	—
1861//26 (1861)	—	140	160	185	225	—
ND//27 (1862)	—	140	160	185	225	—
ND//29 (1864))	—	140	160	185	225	—
ND//31 (1866)	—	140	160	185	225	—
187(0)//35	—	140	160	185	225	—
ND//36 (1871)	—	140	160	185	225	—
ND//37 (1872)	—	140	160	185	225	—
ND//41 (1876)	—	140	160	185	225	—
ND//42 (1877)	—	140	160	185	225	—
ND//43 (1878)	—	140	160	185	225	—
ND//45 (1880)	—	140	160	185	225	—

Madho Singh
1880-1922AD

HAMMERED COINAGE
Regal Style

To distinguish coins betweenRam Singh and his son/successor Madho Singh II, note that the coins of Ram Singh have a small slanting cross or dagger between the Ram and Singh symbols, whereas the coins of Singh II do not.

KM# 130 PAISA
Copper **Obverse:** Inscription: Queen Victoria... **Reverse:** Jhar, inscription **Rev. Inscription:** "Madho Singh II" **Mint:** Sawai Jaipur **Note:** Weight varies 6.15-6.30g .

Date	Mintage	Good	VG	F	VF	XF
ND(1882)//3	—	0.60	1.00	2.00	4.00	—
ND(1883)//4	—	0.60	1.00	2.00	4.00	—
ND(1884)//5	—	0.60	1.00	2.00	4.00	—
ND(1887)//8	—	0.60	1.00	2.00	4.00	—
ND(1898)//19	—	0.30	0.65	1.35	2.00	—
ND(1899)//20	—	0.30	0.65	1.35	2.00	—
ND(1900)//21	—	0.30	0.65	1.35	2.00	—

KM# 135 1/16 RUPEE
Silver **Obv. Inscription:** Victoria... **Reverse:** Jhar **Rev. Inscription:** "Madho Singh II" **Mint:** Sawai Jaipur **Note:** Weight varies 0.67-0.72g.

Date	Mintage	Good	VG	F	VF	XF
ND//2 (1881)	—	2.00	5.00	7.00	10.00	15.00
ND//3 (1882)	—	2.00	5.00	7.00	10.00	15.00
ND//10 (1889)	—	2.00	5.00	7.00	10.00	15.00

KM# 137 1/8 RUPEE
Silver **Obv. Inscription:** Victoria... **Reverse:** Jhar **Rev. Inscription:** "Madho Singh II" **Mint:** Sawai Jaipur **Note:** Weight varies 1.34-1.45g.

Date	Mintage	Good	VG	F	VF	XF
ND//4 (1883)	—	1.00	2.50	3.50	5.00	8.00
ND//6 (1885)	—	1.00	2.50	3.50	5.00	8.00
ND//7 (1886)	—	1.00	2.50	3.50	5.00	8.00
ND//9 (1888)	—	1.00	2.50	3.50	5.00	8.00
ND//11 (1890)	—	1.00	2.50	3.50	5.00	8.00
ND//12 (1891)	—	1.00	2.50	3.50	5.00	8.00
ND//18 (1897)	—	1.00	2.50	3.50	5.00	8.00
ND//19 (1898)	—	1.00	2.50	3.50	5.00	8.00
ND//21 (1900)	—	1.00	2.50	3.50	5.00	8.00

KM# 139 1/4 RUPEE
Silver **Obv. Inscription:** Victoria... **Reverse:** Jhar **Rev. Inscription:** "Madho Singh II" **Mint:** Sawai Jaipur **Note:** Weight varies 2.68-2.90g.

Date	Mintage	Good	VG	F	VF	XF
ND//1 (1880)	—	1.25	3.00	4.50	6.50	10.00
ND//2 (1881)	—	1.25	3.00	4.50	6.50	10.00
ND//4 (1883)	—	1.25	3.00	4.50	6.50	10.00
ND//6 (1885)	—	1.25	3.00	4.50	6.50	10.00
ND//7 (1886)	—	1.25	3.00	4.50	6.50	10.00
ND//8 (1887)	—	1.25	3.00	4.50	6.50	10.00
ND//10 (1889)	—	1.25	3.00	4.50	6.50	10.00
ND//11 (1890)	—	1.25	3.00	4.50	6.50	10.00
ND//12 (1891)	—	1.25	3.00	4.50	6.50	10.00
ND//14 (1893)	—	1.25	3.00	4.50	6.50	10.00
ND//15 (1894)	—	1.25	3.00	4.50	6.50	10.00
ND//16 (1895)	—	1.25	3.00	4.50	6.50	10.00
ND//17 (1896)	—	1.25	3.00	4.50	6.50	10.00
ND//18 (1897)	—	1.25	3.00	4.50	6.50	10.00
ND//19 (1898)	—	1.25	3.00	4.50	6.50	10.00
ND//20 (1899)	—	1.25	3.00	4.50	6.50	10.00
ND//22 (1900)	—	1.25	3.00	4.50	6.50	10.00

KM# 142 1/2 RUPEE
Silver **Obv. Inscription:** Victoria... **Reverse:** Jhar **Rev. Inscription:** "Madho Singh II" **Mint:** Sawai Jaipur **Note:** Weight varies 5.35-5.80g.

Date	Mintage	Good	VG	F	VF	XF
ND//1 (1880)	—	1.35	3.50	5.00	7.50	12.50
ND//3 (1882)	—	1.35	3.50	5.00	7.50	12.50
ND//4 (1883)	—	1.35	3.50	5.00	7.50	12.50
ND//5 (1884)	—	1.35	3.50	5.00	7.50	12.50
ND//7 (1886)	—	1.35	3.50	5.00	7.50	12.50
ND//8 (1887)	—	1.35	3.50	5.00	7.50	12.50
ND//9 (1888)	—	1.35	3.50	5.00	7.50	12.50
ND//10 (1889)	—	1.35	3.50	5.00	7.50	12.50
ND//11 (1890)	—	1.35	3.50	5.00	7.50	12.50
ND//12 (1891)	—	1.35	3.50	5.00	7.50	12.50

Date	Mintage	Good	VG	F	VF	XF
ND//13 (1892)	—	1.35	3.50	5.00	7.50	12.50
ND//14 (1893)	—	1.35	3.50	5.00	7.50	12.50
ND//15 (1894)	—	1.35	3.50	5.00	7.50	12.50
ND//17 (1896)	—	1.35	3.50	5.00	7.50	12.50
ND//18 (1897)	—	1.35	3.50	5.00	7.50	12.50
ND//19 (1898)	—	1.35	3.50	5.00	7.50	12.50
ND//20 (1899)	—	1.35	3.50	5.00	7.50	12.50
190(0)//21	—	1.35	3.50	5.00	7.50	12.50

KM# 145 RUPEE
Silver **Obv. Inscription:** Victoria... **Reverse:** Jhar **Rev. Inscription:** "Madho Singh II" **Mint:** Sawai Jaipur **Note:** Weight varies 10.70-11.60g.

Date	Mintage	Good	VG	F	VF	XF
ND//1 (1880)	—	1.50	4.00	6.00	9.00	14.00
ND//2 (1881)	—	1.50	4.00	6.00	9.00	14.00
ND//3 (1882)	—	1.50	4.00	6.00	9.00	14.00
ND//4 (1883)	—	1.50	4.00	6.00	9.00	14.00
ND//5 (1884)	—	1.50	4.00	6.00	9.00	14.00
ND//6 (1885)	—	1.50	4.00	6.00	9.00	14.00
ND//7 (1886)	—	1.50	4.00	6.00	9.00	14.00
1886//8	—	1.50	4.00	6.00	9.00	14.00
1887//8	—	1.50	4.00	6.00	9.00	14.00
1888//9	—	1.50	4.00	6.00	9.00	14.00
ND//19 (1888)	—	1.50	4.00	6.00	9.00	14.00
ND//10 (1889)	—	1.50	4.00	6.00	9.00	14.00
ND//11 (1890)	—	1.50	4.00	6.00	9.00	14.00
ND//12 (1891)	—	1.50	4.00	6.00	9.00	14.00
ND//13 (1892)	—	1.50	4.00	6.00	9.00	14.00
ND//14 (1893)	—	1.50	4.00	6.00	9.00	14.00
ND//15 (1894)	—	1.50	4.00	6.00	9.00	14.00
ND//16 (1895)	—	1.50	4.00	6.00	9.00	14.00
ND//18 (1896)	—	1.50	4.00	6.00	9.00	14.00
ND//18 (1897)	—	1.50	4.00	6.00	9.00	14.00
ND//20 (1899)	—	1.50	4.00	6.00	8.50	14.00
ND//21 (1900)	—	1.50	4.00	6.00	9.00	14.00

KM# 150 MOHUR
Gold **Obv. Inscription:** Victoria.... **Reverse:** Jhar **Rev. Inscription:** "Madho Singh II" **Mint:** Sawai Jaipur **Note:** Weight varies 10.70-11.40 g.

Date	Mintage	Good	VG	F	VF	XF
ND//2 (1881)	—	—	135	155	185	225
ND//5 (1884)	—	—	135	155	185	225
ND//16 (1895)	—	—	135	155	185	225
ND//17 (1896)	—	—	135	155	185	225
189(8)//19	—	—	135	155	185	225
ND//20 (1899)	—	—	135	155	185	225

KM# 131 MOHUR
Copper **Obv. Inscription:** Victoria **Reverse:** Jhar **Rev. Inscription:** "Madho Singh II" **Mint:** Sawai Jaipur **Note:** Weight varies 13.50-16.50 grams.

Date	Mintage	Good	VG	F	VF	XF
1897//18	—	12.50	22.50	32.50	50.00	—

MILLED COINAGE

KM# 132 NAZARANA NEW PAISA
Copper **Obv. Inscription:** Victoria... **Reverse:** Jhar **Rev. Inscription:** "Madho Singh II" **Mint:** Sawai Jaipur **Note:** Well-centered issues on thin planchets may be restrikes.

Date	Mintage	Good	VG	F	VF	XF
1880//1	—	5.00	12.50	17.50	25.00	40.00
1886//7	—	5.00	12.50	17.50	25.00	40.00
1891//12	—	5.00	12.50	17.50	25.00	40.00
1895//16	—	5.00	12.50	17.50	25.00	40.00
1897//17	—	5.00	12.50	17.50	25.00	40.00
1897//18	—	5.00	12.50	17.50	25.00	40.00
1899//20	—	5.00	12.50	17.50	25.00	40.00
1900//21	—	5.00	12.50	17.50	25.00	40.00

KM# 151 NAZARANA RUPEE
Gold **Obv. Inscription:** Victoria... **Reverse:** Jhar **Rev. Inscription:** "Madho Singh II" **Mint:** Sawai Jaipur **Note:** Size varies 29-36mm, weight varies 10.70-11.40 grams.

Date	Mintage	Good	VG	F	VF	XF
1880//1	—	—	425	700	2,000	3,500
1887//8	—	—	425	700	2,000	3,500
1888//9	—	—	425	700	2,000	3,500

KM# 146 NAZARANA RUPEE
Silver **Obv. Inscription:** Victoria... **Reverse:** Jhar **Rev. Inscription:** "Madho Singh II" **Mint:** Sawai Jaipur **Note:** Size varies 30-31mm, weight varies 10.70-11.60 grams.

Date	Mintage	Good	VG	F	VF	XF
1880//1	—	17.50	35.00	50.00	70.00	100
1881//2	—	17.50	35.00	50.00	70.00	100
1882//3	—	17.50	35.00	50.00	70.00	100
1883//4	—	17.50	35.00	50.00	70.00	100
1884//5	—	17.50	35.00	50.00	70.00	100

KM# 147 NAZARANA RUPEE
Silver **Obv. Inscription:** Victoria... **Reverse:** Jhar **Rev. Inscription:** "Madho Singh II" **Mint:** Sawai Jaipur **Note:** Size varies 36-37mm.

Date	Mintage	Good	VG	F	VF	XF
1882//3	—	13.50	27.50	40.00	52.50	75.00
1884//5	—	13.50	27.50	40.00	52.50	75.00
1886//7	—	13.50	27.50	40.00	52.50	75.00
1887//8	—	13.50	27.50	40.00	52.50	75.00
1888//9	—	13.50	27.50	40.00	52.50	75.00
1889//10	—	13.50	27.50	40.00	52.50	75.00
1890//11	—	13.50	27.50	40.00	52.50	75.00
1891//12	—	13.50	27.50	40.00	52.50	75.00
1895//16	—	13.50	27.50	40.00	52.50	75.00
1896//13	—	13.50	27.50	40.00	52.50	75.00
1897//18	—	13.50	27.50	40.00	52.50	75.00
1899//20	—	13.50	27.50	40.00	52.50	75.00

JAISALMIR

Although the ruling Rajputs (or rawals) of this desert territory, located in northwest India traced their ancestry back to pre-Asokan times, the State of Jaisalmir was founded by Deoraj, the first rawal, only in the 10th century. Jaisalmir city was established by Rawal Jaisal, after whom both the city and the State were named. Like Jaipur, Jaisalmir reached its zenith in Mughal times, after being forced to acknowledge the supremacy of Delhi in the time of the Emperor Shah Jahan. With Mughal disintegration, Jaisalmir also fell upon hard times and most of its outlying provinces were lost. The state came under British protection in 1818, and on March 30th, 1949 it was merged into Rajasthan.

RULERS
Mulraj Singh, AH1176-1235/1762-1819AD
Gaj Singh, AH1235-1263/1819-1846AD
Ranjit Singh, AH1263-1281/1846-1864AD
Bairi Sal, 1865-1891AD

MINT

Jaisalmir

REGAL ISSUES

In the name of Queen Victoria

First Series:
Frozen regnal year 22 without mint marks.

Bird

Umbrella

Second Series:
Frozen regnal year 22 with mint marks on reverse.

Anonymous

ANONYMOUS HAMMERED COINAGE
Mughal Style

KM# 7 1/8 RUPEE
1.3655 g., Silver **Series:** Akhey Shahi **Obv. Inscription:** "Muhammad Shah" **Note:** Struck 1756-1860AD; previous C#7.

Date	Mintage	Good	VG	F	VF	XF
AH1153//22 Frozen	—	—	5.50	8.00	10.00	15.00

KM# 8 1/4 RUPEE
2.4310 g., Silver **Series:** Akhey Shahi **Obverse:** Gujarati "105" (inverted) above "n" in "qiran" **Obv. Inscription:** "Muhammad Shah" **Note:** Struck 1756-1860AD; previous C#8.

Date	Mintage	Good	VG	F	VF	XF
AH1153//22 Frozen	—	—	4.00	6.00	9.00	14.00

KM# 9 1/2 RUPEE
5.4620 g., Silver **Series:** Akhey Shahi **Obverse:** Gujarati "106" above "n" in "qiran" **Obv. Inscription:** "Muhammad Shah" **Note:** Struck 1756-1860AD; previous C#9.

Date	Mintage	Good	VG	F	VF	XF
AH1153//22 Frozen	—	—	5.50	8.00	10.00	15.00

KM# 5.1 RUPEE
10.9240 g., Silver **Series:** Akhey Shahi **Obv. Inscription:** "Muhammad Shah" **Note:** Struck 1756-1860AD.

Date	Mintage	Good	VG	F	VF	XF
AH1152//22 Frozen	—	—	12.00	20.00	30.00	45.00
AH1153//22 Frozen	—	—	9.00	15.00	21.50	30.00
AH1155//25	—	—	—	—	—	—

KM# 5.2 RUPEE
10.9240 g., Silver **Series:** Ahkey Shahi **Obv. Inscription:** "Muhammad Shah" **Reverse:** Swastika at lower right

Date	Mintage	Good	VG	F	VF	XF
AH1153//22 Frozen	—	8.00	12.00	20.00	30.00	40.00

KM# 10.1 RUPEE
10.9240 g., Silver **Series:** Akhey Shahi **Obverse:** Gujarati "l" (inverted) above "n" in "giran" **Obv. Inscription:** "Muhammad Shah" **Note:** Struck 1756-1860AD.

Date	Mintage	Good	VG	F	VF	XF
AH1153// Frozen	—	—	—	—	—	—

KM# 10.2 RUPEE
10.9240 g., Silver **Series:** Akhey Shahi **Obverse:** Gujarati "15" (inverted) above "n" in "giran" **Obv. Inscription:** "Muhammad Shah" **Note:** Struck 1756-1860AD.

Date	Mintage	Good	VG	F	VF	XF
AH1153//22 Frozen	—	—	—	—	—	—

KM# 10.3 RUPEE
10.9240 g., Silver **Obverse:** Gujarati "106" above "n" in "giran" **Obv. Inscription:** "Muhammad Shah" **Note:** Struck 1756-1860AD.

Date	Mintage	Good	VG	F	VF	XF
AH1150//22 Frozen	—	—	—	—	—	—

KM# 10.4 RUPEE
10.9240 g., Silver **Series:** Ahkey Shahi **Obverse:** Gujarati "601" above "n" in "giran" **Obv. Inscription:** "Muhammad Shah" **Note:** Struck 1756-1860AD.

Date	Mintage	Good	VG	F	VF	XF
AH115-//22 Frozen	—	10.00	15.00	25.00	35.00	50.00

KM# 11 RUPEE
10.9240 g., Silver **Series:** Akhey Shahi **Obverse:** Gujarati "11" above "n" in "giran" **Obv. Inscription:** "Muhammad Shah" **Reverse:** Trisul at left **Note:** Struck 1756-1860AD.

Date	Mintage	Good	VG	F	VF	XF
AH1153//22 Frozen, Rare	—	—	—	—	—	—

KM# 14.1 RUPEE
10.9240 g., Silver **Series:** Akhey Shahi **Obverse:** Gujarati "1" above "n" in "giran" **Obv. Inscription:** "Muhammad Shah" **Reverse:** Swastika at bottom right **Note:** Struck 1756-1860AD.

Date	Mintage	Good	VG	F	VF	XF
AH1153//22 Frozen	—	—	—	—	—	—

KM# 14.2 RUPEE
10.9240 g., Silver **Series:** Akhey Shahi **Obverse:** Gujarati "107" above "n" in "giran" **Obv. Inscription:** "Muhammad Shah" **Reverse:** Swastika at bottom right

Date	Mintage	Good	VG	F	VF	XF
AH1153//22 Frozen	—	—	—	—	—	—

KM# 14.3 RUPEE
10.9240 g., Silver **Series:** Akhey Shahi **Obverse:** Persian "801" (108 retrograde) above "n" in "giran" **Obv. Inscription:** "Muhammad Shah" **Reverse:** Swastika at lower right **Note:** Struck 1756-1860AD.

Date	Mintage	Good	VG	F	VF	XF
AH1153/22 Frozen	—	—	—	—	—	—

KM# 14.4 RUPEE
10.9240 g., Silver **Series:** Akhey Shahi **Obverse:** Gujarati "106" above "n" in "giran" **Obv. Inscription:** "Muhammad Shah" **Reverse:** Swastika at lower left **Note:** Struck 1756-1860AD.

Date	Mintage	Good	VG	F	VF	XF
AH1153//22 Frozen	—	—	—	—	—	—

KM# 5a NAZARANA RUPEE
10.9240 g., Silver **Series:** Akhey Shahi **Obv. Inscription:** "Muhammad Shah" **Shape:** Square **Note:** Struck 1756-1860AD.

Date	Mintage	Good	VG	F	VF	XF
AH1153//22 Frozen	—	—	—	—	—	—

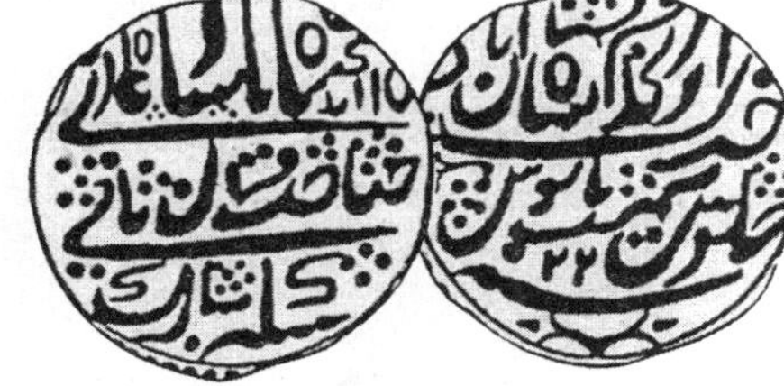

KM# 5aa NAZARANA RUPEE
10.9240 g., Silver, 29 mm. **Series:** Akhey Shahi **Obv. Inscription:** Muhammad Shah **Note:** C#10a; Struck 1756-1860AD.

Date	Mintage	Good	VG	F	VF	XF
AH1153//22 Frozen	—	—	45.00	75.00	110	150

KM# 10a NAZARANA RUPEE
10.9240 g., Silver, 31 mm. **Series:** Akhey Shahi **Obverse:** Gujarati "1" above "n" in "giran" **Obv. Inscription:** Muhammad Shah **Reverse:** Swastika at bottom right **Note:** Struck 1756-1860AD.

Date	Mintage	Good	VG	F	VF	XF
AH1153//22 Frozen	—	—	—	—	—	—

KM# 4 1/2 NAZARANA RUPEE
5.4620 g., Silver **Series:** Akhey Shahi **Obv. Inscription:** Muhammad Shah **Shape:** Square **Note:** Struck 1756-1860AD.

Date	Mintage	Good	VG	F	VF	XF
AH1153//22 Frozen	—	20.00	40.00	65.00	100	—

KM# 15 NAZARANA 2-1/2 RUPEE
28.0000 g., Silver **Series:** Akhey Shahi **Obverse:** Persian "801" (108 retrograde) above "n" in "giran" **Obv. Inscription:** Muhammad Shah **Reverse:** Swastika at bottom right **Shape:** Square

Date	Mintage	Good	VG	F	VF	XF
AH1153//22 Frozen; Rare	—	—	—	—	—	—

Ranjit Singh
AH1263-1281 / 1846-1864AD

HAMMERED COINAGE
Regal Style

KM# 17 1/8 RUPEE
Silver **Obv. Inscription:** "...Victoria farman rawai Inglistan..." Gujarati "17" in "n" of "farman" **Note:** Weight varies 1.3125-1.3187 grams.

Date	Mintage	Good	VG	F	VF	XF
ND//22 (1860)	—	—	2.50	3.50	5.00	8.00

KM# 31 1/8 RUPEE
1.3300 g., Silver **Obv. Inscription:** "... Victoria farmen rawai Inglistan...", Gujarati "17" in "n" of farmen" **Note:** Mint mark: bird and umbrella on reverse.

Date	Mintage	Good	VG	F	VF	XF
ND//22 (1860)	—	—	2.00	3.00	4.00	7.00

KM# 18 1/4 RUPEE
Silver **Obv. Inscription:** "...Victoria farman rawai Inglistan...", Gujarati "17" in "n" of "farman" **Note:** Weight varies 2.6250-2.6375 grams.

Date	Mintage	Good	VG	F	VF	XF
ND//22 (1860)	—	—	—	—	—	—

KM# 32 1/4 RUPEE
2.6500 g., Silver **Obv. Inscription:** "... Victoria farmen rawai Inglistan..." Gujarati "17" in "n" of "farmen" **Note:** Mint mark: bird and umbrella on reverse.

Date	Mintage	Good	VG	F	VF	XF
ND//22 (1860)	—	—	2.50	3.50	5.00	8.00

KM# 19 1/2 RUPEE

Silver **Obv. Inscription:** "... Victoria farman rawai Inglistan...", Gujarati "17" in "n" of "farman" **Note:** Weight varies 5.2500-5.2750 grams.

Date	Mintage	Good	VG	F	VF	XF
ND//22 (1860)	—	—	5.50	8.00	10.00	15.00

KM# 33 1/2 RUPEE

5.3000 g., Silver **Obv. Inscription:** "... Victoria farmen rawai Inglistan...", Gujarati "17" in "n" of "farmen" **Note:** Mint mark: bird and umbrella on reverse.

Date	Mintage	Good	VG	F	VF	XF
ND//22 (1860)	—	—	3.00	4.50	6.50	10.00

KM# 20 RUPEE

Silver **Obv. Inscription:** "... Victoria farman rawai Inglistan..." Gujarati "17" in "n" of "farman" **Reverse:** Trisul at left **Note:** Weight varies 10.5000-10.5500 grams.

Date	Mintage	Good	VG	F	VF	XF
ND//22 (1860) Rare	—	—	—	—	—	—

KM# 21 RUPEE

Silver **Obv. Inscription:** "... Victoria farman rawai Inglistan..." Gujarati "17" in "n" of "farman" **Note:** Weight varies 10.5000-10.5500 grams.

Date	Mintage	Good	VG	F	VF	XF
ND//22 (1860)	—	—	8.50	13.50	20.00	28.50

KM# 21a RUPEE

Silver **Obv. Inscription:** "... Victoria farman rawai Inglistan...", Gujarati "17" in "n" of "farman" **Note:** Shape: octagonal. Weight varies 10.5000-10.5500 grams.

Date	Mintage	Good	VG	F	VF	XF
ND//22 (1860)	—	—	—	—	—	—

KM# 21b RUPEE

Silver **Obv. Inscription:** "... Victoria farmen rawai Inglistan...", Gujarati "17" in "n" in "farmen" **Note:** Weight varies 10.5000-10.5500 grams. Flan cut from sheet metal. Shape: square.

Date	Mintage	Good	VG	F	VF	XF
ND//22 (1860)	—	—	—	—	—	—

KM# 21c RUPEE

Silver **Obv. Inscription:** "... Victoria farmen rawai Inglistan..." Gujarati "17" in "n" of "farmen" **Note:** Weight varies 10.5000-10.5500 grams. Flan cut from sheet metal. Shape: hexagonal.

Date	Mintage	Good	VG	F	VF	XF
ND//22 (1860)	—	—	—	—	—	—

KM# 21d RUPEE

Silver **Obv. Inscription:** "... Victoria farmen rawai Inglistan...", Gujarati "17" in "n" of "farmen" **Note:** Weight varies 10.5000-10.5500 grams. Flan cut from sheet metal. Shape: octagonal.

Date	Mintage	Good	VG	F	VF	XF
ND//22 (1860)	—	—	—	—	—	—

KM# 34 RUPEE

10.6000 g., Silver **Obv. Inscription:** "... Victoria farmen rawai Inglistan...", Gujarati "17" in "n" of "farmen" **Note:** Mint mark: bird and umbrella on reverse.

Date	Mintage	Good	VG	F	VF	XF
ND//22 (1860)	—	—	5.00	7.00	10.00	15.00

KM# 34a RUPEE

10.5500 g., Silver **Obv. Inscription:** "... Victoria farmen rawai Inglistan...", Gujarati "17" in "n" of "farmen" **Note:** Mint mark: bird and umbrella on reverse. Shape: hexagonal.

Date	Mintage	Good	VG	F	VF	XF
ND//22 (1860)	—	—	—	—	—	—

KM# 21e NAZARANA RUPEE

Silver **Obv. Inscription:** "... Victoria farmen rawai Inglistan...", Gujarati "17" in "n" of "farmen" **Note:** Weight varies 10.5000-10.5500 grams. Shape: square.

Date	Mintage	Good	VG	F	VF	XF
ND//22 (1860)	—	—	55.00	100	150	220

KM# 21f NAZARANA RUPEE

10.6000 g., Silver, 39 mm. **Obv. Inscription:** "... Victoria farmen rawai Inglistan...", Gujarati "17" in "n" of "farmen"

Date	Mintage	Good	VG	F	VF	XF
ND//22 (1860)	—	—	90.00	150	220	300

KM# 34b NAZARANA RUPEE

10.6000 g., Silver **Obv. Inscription:** "... Victoria farmen rawai Inglistan...", Gujarati "17" in "n" of "farmen" **Note:** Mint mark: bird and umbrella on reverse. Shape: square.

Date	Mintage	Good	VG	F	VF	XF
ND//22 (1860)	—	—	85.00	145	220	320

KM# 34c NAZARANA RUPEE

10.6000 g., Silver **Obv. Inscription:** "... Victoria farmen rawai Inglistan...", Gujarati "17" in "n" of "farmen" **Note:** Mint mark: bird and umbrella on reverse. Shape: round.

Date	Mintage	Good	VG	F	VF	XF
ND//22 (1860)	—	—	150	265	400	575

KM# 22 NAZARANA 1-1/2 RUPEE

15.9500 g., Silver **Obv. Inscription:** "... Victoria farmen rawai Inglistan...", Gujarati "17" in "n" of "farmen" **Note:** Shape: round.

Date	Mintage	Good	VG	F	VF	XF
ND//22 (1860)	—	—	150	265	400	575

KM# 23 NAZARANA 2 RUPEE

21.3000 g., Silver **Obv. Inscription:** "... Victoria farmen rawai Inglistan...", Gujarati "17" in "n" of "farmen"

Date	Mintage	Good	VG	F	VF	XF
ND//22 (1860)	—	—	150	250	350	500

KM# 35 NAZARANA 2 RUPEE
21.3000 g., Silver **Obv. Inscription:** "... Victoria farmen rawai Inglistan...", Gujarati "17" in "n" of "farmen" **Note:** Mint mark: bird and umbrella on reverse.

Date	Mintage	Good	VG	F	VF	XF
ND//22 (1860)	—	—	150	250	350	500

KM# 24 NAZARANA 5 RUPEE
52.5000 g., Silver **Obv. Inscription:** "... Victoria farmen rawai Inglistan...", Gujarati "17" in "n" of "farmen" **Note:** Shape: hexagonal.

Date	Mintage	Good	VG	F	VF	XF
ND//22 (1860)	—	—	325	525	800	1,100

KM# 28 NAZARANA 5 MOHURS
54.0000 g., Gold **Obv. Inscription:** "... Victoria farmen rawai Inglistan,,,", Gujarati "17" in "n' of "farmen" **Note:** Shape: Hexagonal.

Date	Mintage	Good	VG	F	VF	XF
ND//22 (1860) Rare	—	—	—	—	—	—

KM# 37 1/8 MOHUR
1.3500 g., Gold, 12 mm. **Obv. Inscription:** "... Victoria farmen rawai Inglistan...", Gujarati "17" in "n" of "farmen" **Note:** Mint mark: bird and umbrella on reverse.

Date	Mintage	Good	VG	F	VF	XF
ND//22 (1860) Rare	—	—	—	—	—	—

KM# 38 1/4 MOHUR
2.7000 g., Gold, 15 mm. **Obv. Inscription:** "... Victoria farmen rawai Inglistan...", Gujarati "17" in "n" of "farmen" **Note:** Mint mark: bird and umrella on reverse.

Date	Mintage	Good	VG	F	VF	XF
ND//22 (1860) Rare	—	—	—	—	—	—

KM# 39 1/2 MOHUR
5.4000 g., Gold, 18 mm. **Obv. Inscription:** "... Victoria farmen rawai Inglistan...", Gujarati "17" in "n" of "farmen" **Note:** Mint mark: bird and umbrella on reverse.

Date	Mintage	Good	VG	F	VF	XF
ND//22 (1860) Rare	—	—	—	—	—	—

KM# 40 MOHUR
10.8000 g., Gold **Obv. Inscription:** "... Victoria farmen rawai Inglistan...", Gujarati "17" in "n" of "farmen" **Note:** Mint mark: bird and umbrella on reverse. Fr. #1202.

Date	Mintage	Good	VG	F	VF	XF
ND//22 (1860)	—	—	165	265	400	600

JANJIRA ISLAND

Island near Bombay. Dynasty of Nawabs dates from 1489AD.

The origin of the nawabs of Janjira is obscure. They were Sidi or Abyssinian Muslims whose ancestors, serving as admirals to the Muslim rulers of the Deccan, had been granted jagirs (revenue-producing land tenures) under the Adil Shahi sultans of Bijapur. In 1870, Janjira came under direct British rule. Until 1924 the nawabs of Janjira also exercised suzerainty over Jafarabad on the Kathiawar peninsular.

RULERS
Sidi Ibrahim Khan II, First Reign: AH1204-06 / 1789-92
Sidi Ibrahim Khan II, Second Reign: AH1219-42 / 1804-26AD
Sidi Muhammad Khan, AH1242-1265 / 1826-1848AD
Sidi Ibrahim Khan III, AH1265-1297 / 1848-1879AD

Sidi Muhammad Khan
AH1242-1265 / 1826-1848AD
HAMMERED COINAGE

KM# 10 PAISA
Copper

Date	Mintage	Good	VG	F	VF	XF
ND(1826-48)	—	4.50	8.50	12.50	18.50	—

Sidi Ibrahim Khan III
AH1265-1297 / 1848-1879AD
HAMMERED COINAGE

KM# 15 PAISA
Copper **Note:** Weight varies 2.60-3.20 grams.

Date	Mintage	Good	VG	F	VF	XF
ND(1848-79)	—	6.00	12.00	22.50	40.00	—

KM# 18 PAISA
Copper **Obverse:** Date **Note:** Weight varies 6.0-7.0 grams.

Date	Mintage	Good	VG	F	VF	XF
AH1272	—	6.00	12.00	20.00	32.50	—

KM# 25 PAISA
Copper **Obverse:** Date **Note:** Weight varies 6.0-7.0 grams.

Date	Mintage	Good	VG	F	VF	XF
AH1284	—	3.00	5.00	8.00	12.50	—

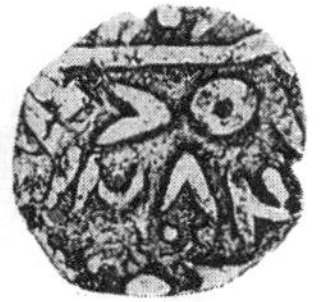

KM# 26 PAISA
Copper **Reverse:** Date **Note:** Weight varies 6.0-7.0 grams.

Date	Mintage	Good	VG	F	VF	XF
AH1284	—	2.50	4.00	6.50	10.00	—

KM# 28 PAISA
Copper **Reverse:** Date **Note:** Weight varies 6.0-7.0 grams.

Date	Mintage	Good	VG	F	VF	XF
AH1288	—	4.00	6.50	10.00	15.00	—

KM# 35 MOHUR
Gold, 23 mm.

Date	Mintage	Good	VG	F	VF	XF
AH1283	—	—	650	1,100	1,500	2,000

JAORA

Ghafar Khan (d. 1825), the first Nawab of Jaora, was brother-in-law to Amir Khan, the Pindari leader. Jaora was subordinate to Indore, having been granted control of the territory in central India in return for the maintenance of a body of cavalry and, later, of foot soldiers which were to be made available to Indore when required. The nawabs of Jaora maintained a good relationship with the British which, after 1818, left them in control of the area independently of Indore. In August 1948 Jaora was absorbed into Madhya Pradesh.

RULERS
Muhammad Ismail, AH1282-1313/1865-1895AD

MINT

جاوره

Jaora

Muhammad Ismail
AH1282-1313 / 1865-1895AD
HAMMERED COINAGE

KM# 2 PAISA
Copper **Reverse:** Flag left **Mint:** Jaora

Date	Mintage	Good	VG	F	VF	XF
ND	—	—	—	—	—	—

KM# 3 PAISA
Copper **Reverse:** Wheel right of flag **Mint:** Jaora

Date	Mintage	Good	VG	F	VF	XF
ND	—	—	—	—	—	—

KM# 4 PAISA
Copper **Reverse:** Wheel right of flag **Mint:** Jaora

Date	Mintage	Good	VG	F	VF	XF
ND(c.1865)	—	5.00	9.00	13.00	20.00	—

KM# 5 PAISA
Copper **Reverse:** Wheel left of flag **Mint:** Jaora

Date	Mintage	Good	VG	F	VF	XF
AH1282	—	5.00	9.00	13.00	20.00	—

KM# 6 PAISA
Copper **Reverse:** Flag and inscription **Mint:** Jaora

Date	Mintage	Good	VG	F	VF	XF
AH1284	—	12.00	20.00	30.00	45.00	—
AH1285	—	12.00	20.00	30.00	45.00	—

KM# 7 PAISA

Copper **Reverse:** Flag and inscription, finer style **Mint:** Jaora

Date	Mintage	Good	VG	F	VF	XF
AH1295	—	2.50	4.00	6.50	10.00	—

MILLED COINAGE

KM# 10 PAISA

Copper **Obverse:** AH date, flag and value in inner circle **Rev. Legend:** H.H. THE NAWAB OF JAORA **Mint:** Jaora **Note:** This type contains all 3 dating systems.

Date	Mintage	Good	VG	F	VF	XF
AH1310-VS1950//1893	—	1.00	2.50	4.00	6.50	10.00
AH1311-VS1950//1893	—	1.25	3.00	5.00	10.00	16.50
AH1310-VS1950//1894	—	1.00	2.50	4.00	7.50	12.50
AH1311-VS1950//1894	—	1.00	2.50	4.00	7.50	12.50
AH1311-VS1951//1894	—	1.00	2.50	4.00	7.50	12.50
AH1311-VS1951//1895	—	1.00	2.50	4.00	7.50	12.50
AH1311-VS1952//1895	—	1.00	2.50	4.00	7.50	12.50
AH1312-VS1952//1895	—	1.25	3.00	5.00	10.00	16.50
AH1313-VS1952//1895	—	1.00	2.50	4.00	7.50	12.50
AH1313-VS1953//1895	—	1.25	3.00	5.00	10.00	16.50
AH1313-VS1953//1896	—	1.00	2.50	4.00	7.50	12.50
AH1331-VS1953//1896	—	1.25	3.00	5.00	10.00	16.50
Note: Error for 1313 with second 3 in retrograde						
AH1331-VS1953//1896	—	1.50	4.00	6.25	12.50	20.00
Note: Error for 1313						

KM# 12 2 PAISA

19.3750 g., Copper **Obverse:** AH date, flag and value in inner circle **Rev. Legend:** H.H. THE NAWAB OF JAORA **Mint:** Jaora

Date	Mintage	Good	VG	F	VF	XF
AH1310-VS1950//1893	—	1.75	4.50	7.50	15.00	25.00
AH1310-VS1950//1894	—	2.00	4.75	8.00	16.50	27.50

JHABUA

A state located in northwest India, west of Indore.

Prior to 1818 the Raja of Jhabua was responsible for paying an annual tribute to Indore. The rajas were Rathor Rajputs who had been established in the area since the 17th century. They were descended from the rajas of Jodhpur. In 1818 Jhabua came under British protection and control.

RULERS

Gopal Singh, VS1897-1952/1840-1895AD

MINT

Jhabua

Gopal Singh
VS1897-1952 / 1840-1895AD

HAMMERED COINAGE

In addition to the types listed here, there are other symbols occurring in different combinations. The crude fabric of these coins and uncommon variety of dies indicate that they were struck locally, with or without official sanction. They are commonly found overstruck on earlier types or on coins of other states.

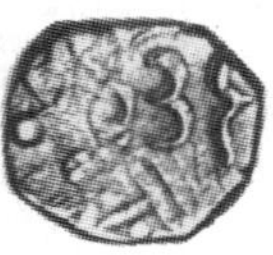

C# A1.1 1/2 PAISA

Copper **Obverse:** Leaf **Reverse:** Date **Mint:** Jhabua **Note:** Weight varies 5.60-12.0 grams.

Date	Mintage	Good	VG	F	VF	XF
VS(19)36	—	6.00	10.00	15.00	22.50	—

C# A1.2 1/2 PAISA

Copper **Obverse:** Flower **Reverse:** Circle within circle of dots **Mint:** Jhabua **Note:** Weight varies 5.60-12.0 grams.

Date	Mintage	Good	VG	F	VF	XF
ND	—	7.50	12.00	18.00	27.50	—

C# A1.3 1/2 PAISA

Copper **Obverse:** 5-petalled flower **Reverse:** 5-petalled flower **Mint:** Jhabua **Note:** Weight varies 5.60-12.0 grams.

Date	Mintage	Good	VG	F	VF	XF
ND	—	7.50	12.00	18.00	27.50	—

KM# 1 PAISA

Copper **Obv. Legend:** Devanagari "Jabuva" **Rev. Legend:** Arabic "Jabua" **Mint:** Jhabua

Date	Mintage	Good	VG	F	VF	XF
VS(19)29	—	8.50	11.50	15.00	22.50	—
VS(19)35	—	8.50	11.50	15.00	22.50	—

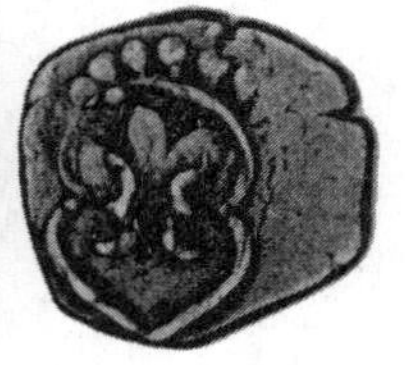

KM# 2 PAISA

Copper **Obv. Legend:** Devanagari "Sa-bu-va" **Reverse:** Date **Mint:** Jhabua

Date	Mintage	Good	VG	F	VF	XF
VS(19)36	—	8.50	11.50	15.00	22.50	—

KM# 3 PAISA

Copper **Obverse:** Devanagari date: Sa(mvat) 21 **Mint:** Jhabua

Date	Mintage	Good	VG	F	VF	XF
VS(19)21	—	7.00	10.00	13.50	18.50	—
VS(19)22	—	7.00	10.00	13.50	18.50	—

KM# 4 PAISA

Copper **Obverse:** Trident **Reverse:** Date **Mint:** Jhabua

Date	Mintage	Good	VG	F	VF	XF
VS(19)31	—	3.50	5.00	6.50	8.50	—
ND//(1874)	—	3.50	5.00	6.50	8.50	—

KM# 5 PAISA

Copper **Obverse:** 4 lobed flower **Reverse:** Date **Mint:** Jhabua

Date	Mintage	Good	VG	F	VF	XF
VS(19)34	—	3.50	5.00	6.50	8.50	—

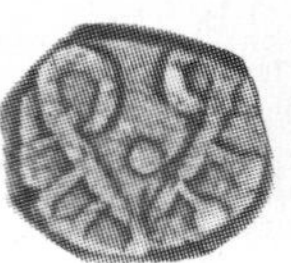

KM# 6.1 PAISA

Copper **Obverse:** Stylized leaf **Mint:** Jhabua **Note:** Thick and thin planchets exist.

Date	Mintage	Good	VG	F	VF	XF
VS(19)22	—	7.50	10.00	12.50	16.50	—
VS(19)23	—	5.00	7.00	10.00	14.00	—
VS(19)24	—	5.00	7.00	10.00	14.00	—
VS(19)25	—	5.00	7.00	10.00	14.00	—
VS(19)26	—	5.00	7.00	10.00	14.00	—
VS(19)28	—	5.00	7.00	10.00	14.00	—
VS(19)32	—	3.00	5.00	7.00	10.00	—
VS(19)33	—	3.00	5.00	7.00	10.00	—
VS(19)34	—	5.00	7.00	10.00	14.00	—
VS(19)35	—	5.00	7.00	10.00	14.00	—

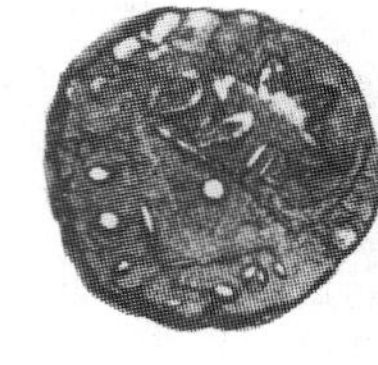

KM# 6.2 PAISA

Copper **Obverse:** 6-petalled flower in heart-shape **Reverse:** Date VS (19)21 **Mint:** Jhabua

Date	Mintage	Good	VG	F	VF	XF
VS(19)21	—	5.00	7.00	10.00	14.00	—

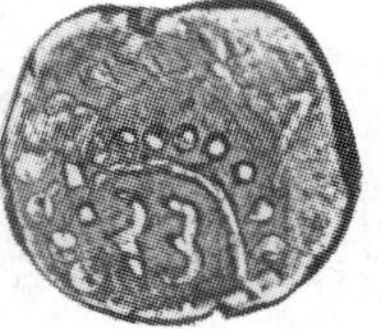

KM# 6.3 PAISA

Copper **Obverse:** Oval in heart-shape **Reverse:** Date VS (19)23 **Mint:** Jhabua

Date	Mintage	Good	VG	F	VF	XF
VS(19)23	—	5.00	7.00	10.00	14.00	—

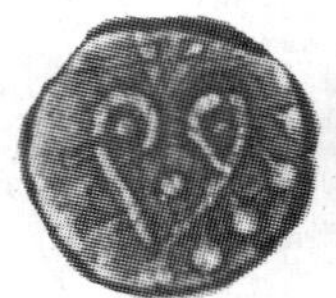
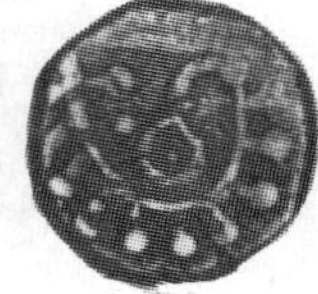

KM# 7 PAISA

Copper **Reverse:** Curled branch with berry **Mint:** Jhabua

Date	Mintage	Good	VG	F	VF	XF
ND	—	5.00	7.00	10.00	14.00	—

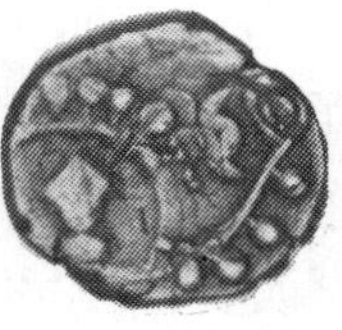

KM# 8 PAISA

Copper **Reverse:** Spear point **Mint:** Jhabua

Date	Mintage	Good	VG	F	VF	XF
ND	—	3.00	5.00	7.00	10.00	—

KM# 9 PAISA

Copper **Reverse:** Curved daggar **Mint:** Jhabua

Date	Mintage	Good	VG	F	VF	XF
ND	—	5.00	7.00	10.00	14.00	—

 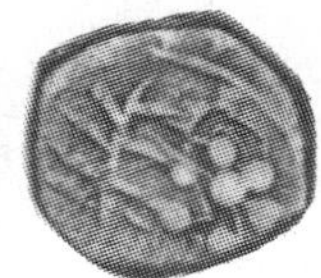

KM# 10 PAISA

Copper **Reverse:** Jhar and blosom **Mint:** Jhabua

Date	Mintage	Good	VG	F	VF	XF
ND	—	4.50	6.50	9.00	13.00	—

 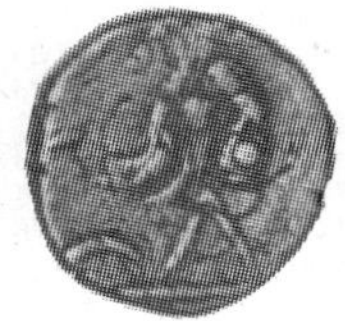

KM# 11 PAISA

Copper **Reverse:** 6 lobed flower **Mint:** Jhabua

Date	Mintage	Good	VG	F	VF	XF
ND	—	5.00	7.00	10.00	14.00	—

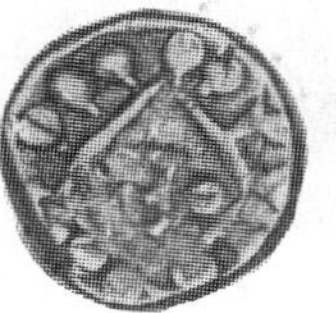 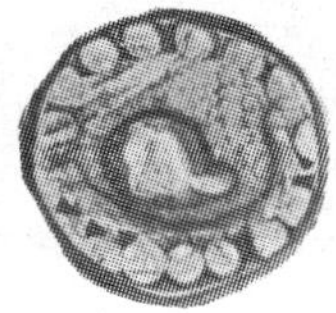

KM# 12 PAISA

Copper **Reverse:** Tailed ball **Mint:** Jhabua

Date	Mintage	Good	VG	F	VF	XF
NDYr. 30	—	4.00	6.00	8.00	12.00	—

KM# 13 PAISA

Copper **Obverse:** Cross **Reverse:** Tailed ball **Mint:** Jhabua

Date	Mintage	Good	VG	F	VF	XF
ND	—	3.00	5.00	7.00	11.00	—

KM# 14 PAISA

Copper **Obverse:** Square **Reverse:** Indistinct **Mint:** Jhabua

Date	Mintage	Good	VG	F	VF	XF
ND	—	4.00	6.00	8.00	12.00	—

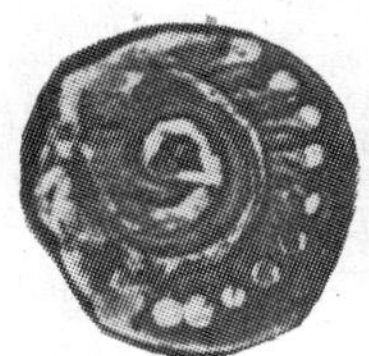 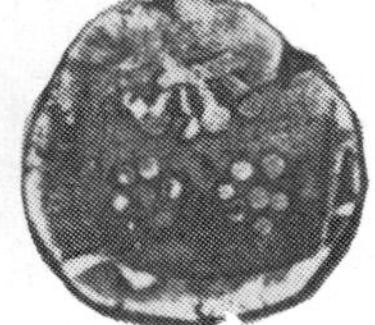

KM# 15 PAISA

Copper **Obverse:** Arabic "Wa" **Reverse:** Groups of dots **Mint:** Jhabua

Date	Mintage	Good	VG	F	VF	XF
ND	—	7.00	9.00	12.00	16.00	—

KM# 16 PAISA

Copper **Obverse:** Cross and dots **Mint:** Jhabua

Date	Mintage	Good	VG	F	VF	XF
ND	—	7.00	9.00	12.00	16.00	—

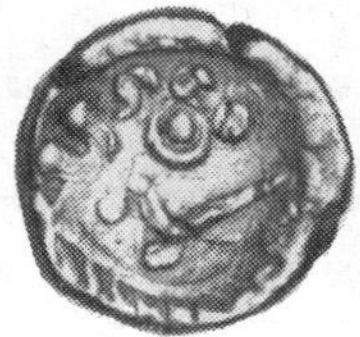 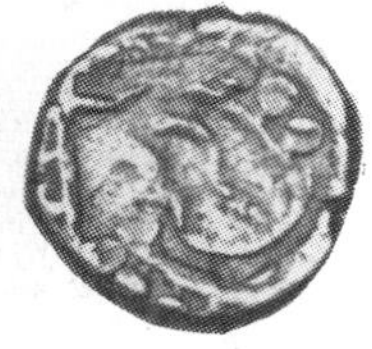

KM# 17 PAISA

Copper **Obverse:** Floral design **Reverse:** Date **Mint:** Jhabua

Date	Mintage	Good	VG	F	VF	XF
VS(19)32	—	3.50	5.00	6.50	8.50	—
VS(19)35	—	3.50	5.00	6.50	8.50	—

KM# 18.1 PAISA

Copper **Obverse:** Date **Reverse:** Swastika within segmented circle **Mint:** Jhabua

Date	Mintage	Good	VG	F	VF	XF
VS(19)29	—	8.00	12.00	20.00	30.00	—

KM# 18.2 PAISA

Copper **Obverse:** Date **Reverse:** Swastika within dotted wreath **Mint:** Jhabua

Date	Mintage	Good	VG	F	VF	XF
VS(19)2x	—	8.00	12.50	20.00	30.00	—

KM# 18.3 PAISA

Copper **Obverse:** Stylized leaf **Reverse:** Swastika **Mint:** Jhabua

Date	Mintage	Good	VG	F	VF	XF
ND	—	8.00	12.50	20.00	30.00	—

 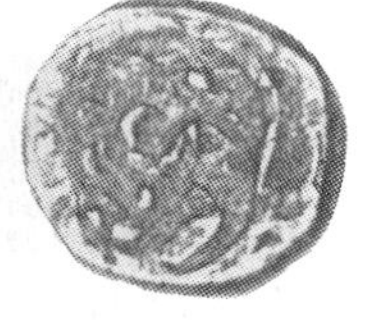

KM# 19 PAISA

Copper **Obverse:** Trefoil **Reverse:** Swastika **Mint:** Jhabua
Note: Obverse varieties exist.

Date	Mintage	Good	VG	F	VF	XF
ND	—	8.00	12.50	20.00	30.00	—

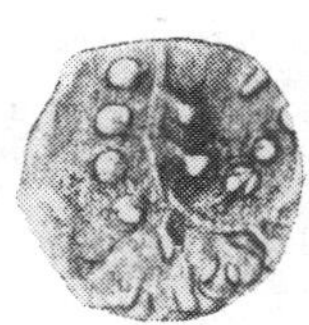 

KM# 20 PAISA

Copper **Obverse:** Stylized leaf **Reverse:** Larger leaf **Mint:** Jhabua

Date	Mintage	Good	VG	F	VF	XF
ND	—	8.00	12.50	20.00	30.00	—

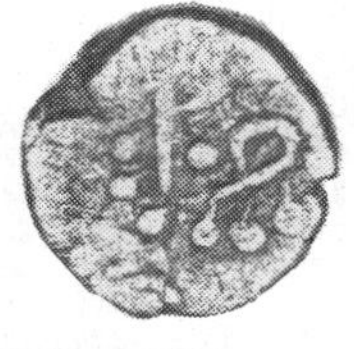 

KM# 21 PAISA

Copper **Obverse:** Stylized leaf **Reverse:** Bow and arrow **Mint:** Jhabua

Date	Mintage	Good	VG	F	VF	XF
ND	—	8.00	12.50	20.00	30.00	—

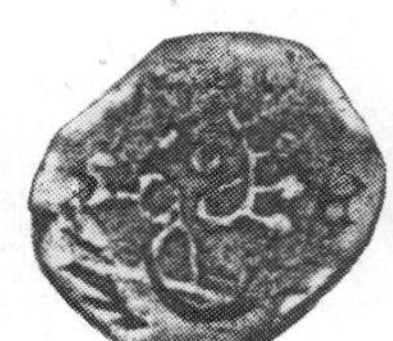 

KM# 22 PAISA

Copper **Obverse:** Stylized leaf **Reverse:** 4-petal flower **Mint:** Jhabua

Date	Mintage	Good	VG	F	VF	XF
ND	—	8.00	12.50	20.00	30.00	—

 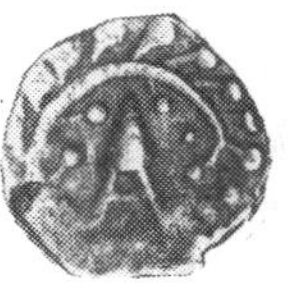

KM# 23 PAISA

Copper **Obverse:** Stylized leaf **Reverse:** Katar **Mint:** Jhabua

Date	Mintage	Good	VG	F	VF	XF
ND	—	8.00	12.50	20.00	30.00	—

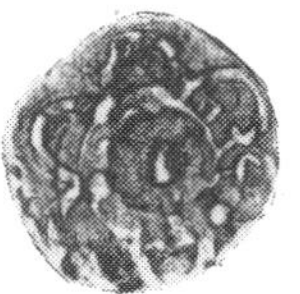 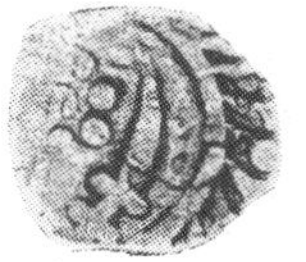

KM# 24 PAISA

Copper **Obverse:** 6-petal flower **Reverse:** Dotted circle, sword **Mint:** Jhabua

Date	Mintage	Good	VG	F	VF	XF
ND	—	8.00	12.50	20.00	30.00	—

KM# 25 PAISA

Copper **Reverse:** Bird walking left **Mint:** Jhabua

Date	Mintage	Good	VG	F	VF	XF
ND	—	8.00	12.50	20.00	30.00	—

KM# 26 PAISA

Copper **Obverse:** Tree **Reverse:** Date in circle **Mint:** Jhabua

Date	Mintage	Good	VG	F	VF	XF
VS(19)3x	—	8.00	12.50	20.00	30.00	—

KM# 27 PAISA

Copper **Obverse:** 3 dots in heart shape **Reverse:** 4 lobed flower **Mint:** Jhabua

Date	Mintage	Good	VG	F	VF	XF
ND	—	8.00	12.50	20.00	30.00	—

KM# 28 PAISA

Copper **Obverse:** 7-leaf plant left of spoke wheel **Mint:** Jhabua

Date	Mintage	Good	VG	F	VF	XF
ND	—	8.00	12.50	20.00	30.00	—

KM# 29 PAISA

Copper **Obverse:** Stylized flower **Mint:** Jhabua

Date	Mintage	Good	VG	F	VF	XF
ND	—	8.00	12.50	20.00	30.00	—

KM# 30 PAISA

Copper **Obverse:** Circle of dots **Reverse:** Leaf and arcs **Mint:** Jhabua

Date	Mintage	Good	VG	F	VF	XF
ND	—	8.00	12.50	20.00	30.00	—

KM# 31 PAISA

Copper **Obverse:** Solar symbol in leaf **Mint:** Jhabua

Date	Mintage	Good	VG	F	VF	XF
ND	—	8.00	12.50	20.00	30.00	—

KM# 32 PAISA

Copper **Obverse:** 16-square grid **Reverse:** Flower in circle **Mint:** Jhabua

Date	Mintage	Good	VG	F	VF	XF
ND	—	10.00	15.00	25.00	37.50	—

KM# 33 PAISA

Copper **Obverse:** 9-square grid **Reverse:** Plant **Mint:** Jhabua

Date	Mintage	Good	VG	F	VF	XF
ND	—	10.00	15.00	25.00	37.50	—

JHALAWAR

State located in Rajputana, northwest India, which was originally part of Kotah. Established in memory of services to Kotah of Zalim Singh, long-time administrator of that state. His grandson was given Jhalawar in 1837AD with the title of Raj Rana.

In 1838, at a time of great internal dissention, certain districts were removed from the territory of the Princely State of Kotah to form a principality for Madan Singh, one of the contestants for power. The new state was named Jhalawar. In 1896 the ruling maharaj-rana, Zalim Singh, was deposed by the Government of India for maladministration, and much of the area that had once been ceded to Jhalawar was returned to the sovereignty of the rulers of Kotah. Madan Singh and his successors were Jhala Rajputs from Kathiawar. The residual State of Jhalawar was incorporated into Rajasthan in 1948.

RULERS

Madan Singh, AH1253-1261/1837-1845AD
Prithvi Singh, AH1261-1292/1845-1875AD
Zalim Singh, AH1294-1314/1876-1896AD
British Administration, 1896-1899

MINT NAMES

جهالاوار

Jhalawar

MINT MARKS

Both marks on reverse

HAMMERED COINAGE

Mughal Style

C# 25 1/8 RUPEE

1.4000 g., Silver **Series:** Old "Madan Shahi" **Obv. Inscription:** "Bahadur Shah II" **Mint:** Jhalawar

Date	Mintage	Good	VG	F	VF	XF
ND//11 (1846-47)	—	8.00	20.00	32.00	50.00	70.00

C# 8 RUPEE

Silver **Obv. Inscription:** "Muhammad Akbar II - Sahib Qiran" **Mint:** Jhalawar **Note:** Weight varies 11.15-11.25 grams.

Date	Mintage	Good	VG	F	VF	XF
ND//32 (1837-38)	—	16.00	40.00	62.50	85.00	135

C# 28 RUPEE

Silver **Series:** Old "Madan Shahi" **Obv. Inscription:** "Bahadur Shah II" **Mint:** Jhalawar **Note:** Weight varies 11.15-11.25 grams.

Date	Mintage	Good	VG	F	VF	XF
ND//1 (1837-38)	—	2.75	6.50	10.00	15.00	22.50
ND//3 (1839-40)	—	2.75	6.50	10.00	15.00	22.50
AH1259//6	—	2.75	6.50	10.00	15.00	22.50
AH1259//13 (sic)	—	2.75	6.50	10.00	15.00	22.50
ND//15 (1850-51)	—	2.75	6.50	10.00	15.00	22.50
ND//17 (1852-53)	—	2.75	6.50	10.00	15.00	22.50
ND//18 (1853-54)	—	2.75	6.50	10.00	15.00	22.50
AH1259//19 (sic)	—	2.75	6.50	10.00	15.00	22.50
AH1259//20 (sic)	—	2.75	6.50	10.00	15.00	22.50
AH125x//22 (sic)	—	2.75	6.50	10.00	15.00	22.50

C# 29 NAZARANA RUPEE

Silver **Series:** Old "Madan Shahi" **Obv. Inscription:** "Bahadur Shah II" **Mint:** Jhalawar **Note:** Weight varies 11.00-11.20 grams.

Date	Mintage	Good	VG	F	VF	XF
AH1259//6	—	37.50	75.00	125	200	300
ND//8 (1844-45)	—	37.50	75.00	125	200	300
AH1263//10	—	37.50	75.00	125	200	300
ND//21 (1856-57)	—	37.50	75.00	125	200	300

C# 21 TAKKA

Copper **Series:** Old "Madan Shahi" **Obv. Inscription:** "Bahadur Shah II" **Mint:** Jhalawar **Note:** Weight varies 17.70-17.80 grams, square.

Date	Mintage	Good	VG	F	VF	XF
ND//5 (1841-42)	—	4.00	6.50	10.00	15.00	—
ND//6 (1842-43)	—	4.00	6.50	10.00	15.00	—
ND//9 (1844-45)	—	4.00	6.50	10.00	15.00	—
ND//12 (1847-48)	—	4.00	6.50	10.00	15.00	—
ND//21 (1856-57)	—	4.00	6.50	10.00	15.00	—

HAMMERED COINAGE

Regal Style

Y# 3.1 1/8 RUPEE

1.4000 g., Silver, 13 mm. **Series:** New "Madan Shahi" **Obv. Inscription:** "...Victoria Badsah Inglistan" **Mint:** Jhalawar

Date	Mintage	Good	VG	F	VF	XF
VS1915//5	—	4.00	10.00	16.50	25.00	37.50
VS1915//17	—	4.00	10.00	16.50	25.00	37.50
VS1915//25	—	4.00	10.00	16.50	25.00	37.50
VS1915//27	—	4.00	10.00	16.50	25.00	37.50
VS1915//28	—	4.00	10.00	16.50	25.00	37.50

Y# 3.2 1/8 RUPEE

1.4000 g., Silver, 13 mm. **Series:** New "Madan Shahi" **Obv. Inscription:** "...Victoria Badsah Inglistan" **Mint:** Jhalawar

Date	Mintage	Good	VG	F	VF	XF
ND//37 (1894)	—	4.00	10.00	16.50	25.00	37.50
ND//38 (1895)	—	4.00	10.00	16.50	25.00	37.50

Y# 6.1 RUPEE

Silver **Series:** New "Madan Shahi" **Obv. Inscription:** "...Victoria Badsah Inglistan" **Mint:** Jhalawar **Note:** Weight varies 11.20-11.30 grams.

Date	Mintage	Good	VG	F	VF	XF
VS1915//1	—	2.25	5.50	8.50	13.50	22.50
VS1915//2	—	2.25	5.50	8.50	13.50	22.50
VS1915//3	—	2.25	5.50	8.50	13.50	22.50
VS1915//4	—	2.25	5.50	8.50	13.50	22.50
VS1915//5	—	2.25	5.50	8.50	13.50	22.50
VS1915//7	—	2.25	5.50	8.50	13.50	22.50
VS1915//9	—	2.25	5.50	8.50	13.50	22.50
VS1915//10	—	2.25	5.50	8.50	13.50	22.50
VS1915//11	—	2.25	5.50	8.50	13.50	22.50
VS1915//12	—	2.25	5.50	8.50	13.50	22.50
VS1915//13	—	2.25	5.50	8.50	13.50	22.50
VS1915//14	—	2.25	5.50	8.50	13.50	22.50
VS1915//15	—	2.25	5.50	8.50	13.50	22.50
VS1915//16	—	2.25	5.50	8.50	13.50	22.50
VS1915//17	—	2.25	5.50	8.50	13.50	22.50
VS1915//18	—	2.25	5.50	8.50	13.50	22.50
VS1915//19	—	2.25	5.50	8.50	13.50	22.50
VS1915//20	—	2.25	5.50	8.50	13.50	22.50
VS1915//21	—	2.25	5.50	8.50	13.50	22.50
VS1915//22	—	2.25	5.50	8.50	13.50	22.50
VS1915//24	—	2.25	5.50	8.50	13.50	22.50
VS1915//25	—	2.25	5.50	8.50	13.50	22.50
VS1915//26	—	2.25	5.50	8.50	13.50	22.50
VS1915//27	—	2.25	5.50	8.50	13.50	22.50
VS1915//28	—	2.25	5.50	8.50	13.50	22.50
VS1915//29	—	2.25	5.50	8.50	13.50	22.50
VS1915//30	—	2.25	5.50	8.50	13.50	22.50

Y# 6.2 RUPEE

Silver **Series:** New "Madan Shahi" **Obv. Inscription:** "...Victoria Badsah Inglistan" **Mint:** Jhalawar **Note:** Weight varies 11.20-11.30 grams.

Date	Mintage	Good	VG	F	VF	XF
ND//30 (1887)	—	2.25	5.50	8.50	13.50	22.50
ND//31 (1888)	—	2.25	5.50	8.50	13.50	22.50
ND//33 (1890)	—	2.25	5.50	8.50	13.50	22.50
ND//34 (1891)	—	2.25	5.50	8.50	13.50	22.50
ND//35 (1892)	—	2.25	5.50	8.50	13.50	22.50
ND//36 (1893)	—	2.25	5.50	8.50	13.50	22.50
ND//37 (1894)	—	2.25	5.50	8.50	13.50	22.50
ND//38 (1895)	—	2.25	5.50	8.50	13.50	22.50
ND//39 (1896)	—	2.25	5.50	8.50	13.50	22.50
ND//41 (1898)	—	2.25	5.50	8.50	13.50	22.50

Y# 6a NAZARANA RUPEE

Silver, 27 mm. **Series:** New "Madan Shahi" **Mint:** Jhalawar **Note:** Weight varies 11.20-11.25 grams.

Date	Mintage	Good	VG	F	VF	XF
VS1915//2	—	17.50	35.00	60.00	85.00	125
VS1915//4	—	17.50	35.00	60.00	85.00	125
VS1915//5	—	17.50	35.00	60.00	85.00	125
VS1915//7	—	17.50	35.00	60.00	85.00	125
VS1915//9	—	17.50	35.00	60.00	85.00	125
VS1915//12	—	17.50	35.00	60.00	85.00	125
VS1915//13	—	17.50	35.00	60.00	85.00	125
VS1915//15	—	17.50	35.00	60.00	85.00	125
VS1915//21	—	17.50	35.00	60.00	85.00	125
VS1915//22	—	17.50	35.00	60.00	85.00	125
VS1915//23	—	17.50	35.00	60.00	85.00	125
VS1915//24	—	17.50	35.00	60.00	85.00	125
VS1915//25	—	17.50	35.00	60.00	85.00	125
VS1915//27	—	17.50	35.00	60.00	85.00	125
VS1915//28	—	17.50	35.00	60.00	85.00	125

Y# 6b NAZARANA RUPEE

Silver, 38 mm. **Series:** New "Madan Shahi" **Obv. Inscription:** "...Victoria fadsah Inglistan" **Mint:** Jhalawar **Note:** Weight varies 11.20-11.25 grams.

Date	Mintage	Good	VG	F	VF	XF
VS1915//3	—	50.00	100	175	250	350
VS1915//15	—	50.00	100	175	250	350

Y# 6c NAZARANA RUPEE

Silver **Series:** New "Madan Shahi" **Mint:** Jhalawar **Note:** Weight varies 11.20-11.25 grams.

Date	Mintage	Good	VG	F	VF	XF
ND//30 (1887)	—	22.50	45.00	75.00	110	150
ND//31 (1888)	—	22.50	45.00	75.00	110	150
ND//33 (1890)	—	22.50	45.00	75.00	110	150
ND//34 (1891)	—	22.50	45.00	75.00	110	150
ND//35 (1892)	—	22.50	45.00	75.00	110	150
ND//36 (1893)	—	22.50	45.00	75.00	110	150
ND//37 (1894)	—	22.50	45.00	75.00	110	150
ND//38 (1895)	—	22.50	45.00	75.00	110	150
ND//39 (1896)	—	22.50	45.00	75.00	110	150
ND//40 (1897)	—	22.50	45.00	75.00	110	150

Y# 1 PAISA

9.0000 g., Copper **Series:** New "Madan Shahi" **Obv. Inscription:** "...Victoria fadsah Inglistan" **Mint:** Jhalawar **Shape:** Rectangular.

Date	Mintage	Good	VG	F	VF	XF
ND//2 (1859)	—	2.50	4.50	7.50	12.50	—
ND//5 (1862)	—	2.50	4.50	7.50	12.50	—

Y# 2 DOUBLE PAISA

18.0000 g., Copper **Series:** New "Madan Shahi" **Obv. Inscription:** "...Victoria fadsah Inglistan" **Mint:** Jhalawar **Note:** Size varies 19-21mm. Shape: squarish.

Date	Mintage	Good	VG	F	VF	XF
VS1915//27	—	1.25	2.25	4.00	7.50	—
VS1915//1	—	1.25	2.25	4.00	7.50	—
VS1915//4	—	1.25	2.25	4.00	7.50	—
VS1915//5	—	1.25	2.25	4.00	7.50	—
VS1915//6	—	1.25	2.25	4.00	7.50	—
VS1915//7	—	1.25	2.25	4.00	7.50	—
VS1915//8	—	1.25	2.25	4.00	7.50	—
VS1915//9	—	1.25	2.25	4.00	7.50	—
VS1915//10	—	1.25	2.25	4.00	7.50	—
VS1915//11	—	1.25	2.25	4.00	7.50	—
VS1915//12	—	1.25	2.25	4.00	7.50	—
VS1915//13	—	1.25	2.25	4.00	7.50	—
VS1915//16	—	1.25	2.25	4.00	7.50	—
VS1915//18	—	1.25	2.25	4.00	7.50	—
VS1915//21	—	1.25	2.25	4.00	7.50	—
VS1915//22	—	1.25	2.25	4.00	7.50	—
VS1915//23	—	1.25	2.25	4.00	7.50	—
VS1915//24	—	1.25	2.25	4.00	7.50	—
VS1915//28	—	1.25	2.25	4.00	7.50	—
ND//29 (1886)	—	1.25	2.25	4.00	7.50	—

Y# 4.1 1/4 RUPEE

2.8000 g., Silver **Series:** New "Madan Shahi" **Obv. Inscription:** "...Victoria fadsah Inglistan" **Mint:** Jhalawar

Date	Mintage	Good	VG	F	VF	XF
VS1915//7	—	4.00	10.00	16.50	25.00	37.50
VS1915//9	—	4.00	10.00	16.50	25.00	37.50
VS1915//17	—	4.00	10.00	16.50	25.00	37.50
VS1915//25	—	4.00	10.00	16.50	25.00	37.50
VS1915//28	—	4.00	10.00	16.50	25.00	37.50

Y# 4.2 1/4 RUPEE

2.8000 g., Silver **Series:** New "Madan Shahi" **Obv. Inscription:** "...Victoria fadsah Inglistan" **Mint:** Jhalawar

Date	Mintage	Good	VG	F	VF	XF
ND//30 (1887)	—	4.00	10.00	16.50	25.00	37.50
ND//33 (1890)	—	4.00	10.00	16.50	25.00	37.50
ND//36 (1893)	—	4.00	10.00	16.50	25.00	37.50
ND//37 (1894)	—	4.00	10.00	16.50	25.00	37.50
ND//38 (1895)	—	4.00	10.00	16.50	25.00	37.50

Y# 5.1 1/2 RUPEE

Silver **Series:** New "Madan Shahi" **Obv. Inscription:** "...Victoria Badsah Inglistan" **Mint:** Jhalawar **Note:** Weight varies 5.60-5.65 grams.

Date	Mintage	Good	VG	F	VF	XF
VS1915//1	—	4.75	11.50	20.00	32.50	50.00
VS1915//11	—	4.75	11.50	20.00	32.50	50.00
VS1915//15	—	4.75	11.50	20.00	32.50	50.00
VS1915//22	—	4.75	11.50	20.00	32.50	50.00
VS1915//25	—	4.75	11.50	20.00	32.50	50.00

Y# 5.2 1/2 RUPEE

Silver **Series:** New "Madan Shahi" **Obv. Inscription:** "...Victoria Badsah Inglistan" **Mint:** Jhalawar **Note:** Weight varies 5.60-5.65 grams.

Date	Mintage	Good	VG	F	VF	XF
ND//30 (1887)	—	4.75	11.50	20.00	32.50	50.00
ND//31 (1888)	—	4.75	11.50	20.00	32.50	50.00
ND//35 (1892)	—	4.75	11.50	20.00	32.50	50.00
ND//36 (1893)	—	4.75	11.50	20.00	32.50	50.00

Y# 5a NAZARANA 1/2 RUPEE

Silver **Series:** New "Madan Shahi" **Obv. Inscription:** "...Victoria fadsah Inglistan" **Mint:** Jhalawar **Note:** Weight varies 5.60-5.65 grams, size varies 21-22mm.

Date	Mintage	Good	VG	F	VF	XF
ND//38 (1895)	—	17.50	35.00	55.00	90.00	130

JIND

A Cis-Sutlej State located in the southern Punjab and north Haryana States.

The ruling princes belonged to the same Jat family as the maharajas of Patiala. Like them, they traced their ancestry back to Baryam, a revenue collector under Babur (1526). Gajpat Singh founded the state after he took part in the Sikh uprising against the Afghan governor of Sarhind in 1763. One of Gajpat Singh's daughters became the mother of Ranjit Singh.

Their independence remained intact until the first Sikh war (1845-46) and then their independence faltered until 1849, when the Punjab was annexed and the states were melded into the new province of British India. Most of the states distinguished themselves on the side of the British during the great revolt of 1857.

RULERS:

Bhag Singh, 1786-1819AD
Fateh Singh, 1819-1922AD
Sangat Singh, 1822-1834AD
Sarup Singh, 1834-1864AD
Raghbir Singh, 1864-1887AD
Ranbir Singh, VS1943-2004 / 1887-1948AD

Bhag Singh
VS1843-1892 / 1786-1819AD

HAMMERED COINAGE

KM# 3 RUPEE

Silver **Note:** 10.70-11.60 grams. 16-18 milimeters. Uniface.

Date	Mintage	Good	VG	F	VF	XF
ND(1786-1819)	—	10.00	25.00	37.50	50.00	70.00

Raghbir Singh

HAMMERED COINAGE

KM# 5 RUPEE

Silver, 18 mm. **Reverse:** Similar to 1 Rupee, KM#1 but finer style **Note:** 10.70-11.60 grams.

Date	Mintage	Good	VG	F	VF	XF
ND/4(1864-87) Frozen	—	8.00	20.00	31.50	42.50	60.00

JODHPUR

Jodhpur, also known as Marwar, located in northwest India, was the largest Princely State in the Rajputana Agency. Its population in 1941 exceeded two and a half million. The "Maharajadhirajas" ("Great Kings of Kings") of Jodhpur were Rathor Rajputs who claimed an extremely ancient ancestry from Rama, king of Ayodhya. With the collapse of the Rathor rulers of Kanauj in 1194 the family entered Marwar where they laid the foundation of the new state. The city of Jodhpur was built by Rao Jodha in 1459, and the city and the state were named after him. In 1561 the Mughal Emperor Akbar invaded Jodhpur, forcing its submission. In 1679 Emperor Aurangzeb sacked the city, an experience which stimulated the Rajput royal house to forge a new unity among themselves in order to extricate themselves from Mughal hegemony. Internal dissension once again asserted itself and Rajput unity, which had both benefited from and accelerated Mughal decline, fell apart before the Marathas. In 1818 Jodhpur came under British protection and control and after Indian independence in 1947 the State was merged into Rajasthan. Jodhpur is best known for its particular style of riding breeches (jodpurs) which became very popular in the West in the late 19th century.

RULERS

The issues of the first four rulers before 1858AD bearing both the AH and VS dates as well as the regnal years, are rarely actual dates and years, but were "frozen" and used for many years without change, and were often quite indiscriminately applied. Mismatched regnal years and dates are frequently encountered, as well as blundered dates of all sorts. Dates lying outside the reigns of the rulers named on coins (after 1858AD) were often used. Thus the date or regnal year may not represent the actual dating of the coin.

Coinage of the first four rulers (until 1858AD) is not distinguished by reign, but by type of inscription, mint, and pseudo-date.

Bhim Singh, AH1207-1218/1792-1803AD
Man Singh, AH1218-1259/1803-1843AD
Takhat Singh, AH1259-1290/VS1900-1930/1843-1873AD
Jaswant Singh, AH1290-1313/VS1930-1952/1873-1895AD
Sardar Singh, VS1952-1968/1895-1911AD

MINTS

جودهپور
Jodhpur

جودلاپور
Jodhpur

دار المنصور جودهپور
Dar-al-Mansur

ناگور
Nagor

دار البركات
Dar-al-Barkat

پالي
Pali

سوجت or سجت
Sojat

MINT MARKS
Before 1858AD

Sojat, always on reverse. (KM#226)

Sojat, sometimes on obverse. (KM#226)

Pali, (KM#227)

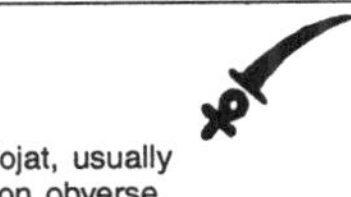

Pali, Sojat, usually on obverse

Jodhpur, on obverse. (KM#47)

Issues of 1858-1873AD

After 1858AD, the mint marks vary, and are given for each listing, wherever there is a difference.

All gold coins struck at Jodhpur Mint. All mints except Jodhpur closed by or before 1893AD. All copper coins were probably struck at the Jodhpur Mint, but if struck elsewhere, they bear no distinguishing marks.

In addition to the mint marks indicating the mint cities, there are also the marks of the Darogas (mint overseers), which are very useful in identifying the mints, especially when the city marks are missing or off the flan. These are given by cat.# and mint: (Only one of the marks appears on any one coin, always on the obverse.)

Jodhpur (KM#46)

Sojat (KM#237)

गं न श्री
Jodhpur (KM#66)

Jodhpur (KM#76)

कै

Pali (KM#197)

على

Sojat (KM#246)

Issues of Jaswant Singh

उ ज रू

Jodhpur (KM#76 & 81)

卐 卐 ᴧ. मा मा

Jodhpur (KM#76)

ज जँ बा ब्रा ग पँ

Pali (KM#206)

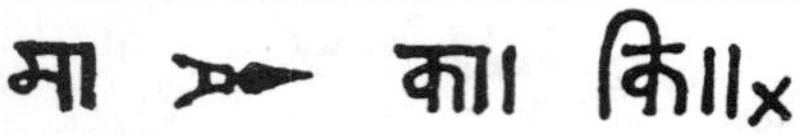

मा ➤ का। कि॥x

Pali (KM#240)

ट॥ कि कि॥

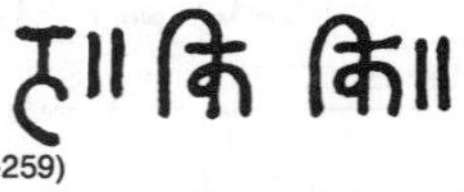

Sojat (KM#258-259)

Issues of Victoria and Sardar Singh

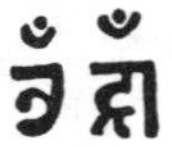

जँ ह्रँ

Jodhpur all

Issues of Edward VII and George V and Sardar Singh and Sumer Singh

म

Jodhpur (KM#91-95, 98-100, 109, 113-115)

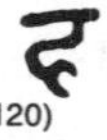

ट

Jodhpur (KM#120)

Issues of George V and Sumer Singh

द

Jodhpur (KM#111-112)

Issues of George V and Umaid Singh

अँ

Jodhpur (KM#128 & 129)

श्री

Jodhpur (KM#129)

Issues of Edward VIII and Umaid Singh

रं

Jodhpur all

Issues of George VI and Umaid Singh

रं

Jodhpur (KM#141-143)

गो

Jodhpur (KM#144-147, 150-151)

Issues of George VI and Hanwant Singh

Jodhpur all

The Daroga's marks generally consist of a symbol or a single Nagari letter, sometimes inverted, and even lying on its side. Some letters are found on more than one series, so that the mark is not a positive identification, but taken together with the city mark and the style of the coin, will provide a correct attribution.

HAMMERED COINAGE

KM# 14.2 TAKKA (2 Paisas)

Copper **Series:** Bhim Shahi **Obverse:** Trident at top **Mint:** Jodhpur **Note:** Weight varies 20.00-21.00 grams. Some specimens portray a wide, floral border.

Date	Mintage	Good	VG	F	VF	XF
AH1215//45 (sic)	—	1.25	2.00	3.50	6.00	—
AH1267 Error for 1227	—	6.00	9.00	13.50	22.50	—
AH1227	—	2.00	3.00	4.50	7.50	—

KM# 32 TAKKA (2 Paisas)

Copper **Obverse:** Sword **Obv. Inscription:** "Muhammad Akbar II" **Mint:** Jodhpur **Note:** Weight varies 22.50-23.00 grams.

Date	Mintage	Good	VG	F	VF	XF
ND(1221) 31//22	—	4.00	6.00	10.00	15.00	—

KM# 240 TAKKA (2 Paisas)

Copper **Obverse:** Frozen date AH1205 and Nagari "MA" **Obv. Inscription:** Victoria and Takhat Singh **Reverse:** Katar **Mint:** Sojat **Note:** Weight varies 20.80-21.10 grams.

Date	Mintage	Good	VG	F	VF	XF
AH1267	—	—	3.50	8.50	14.00	20.00
AH1227 Error for 1267; Rare	—	—	—	—	—	—

KM# 34 1/4 RUPEE

Copper **Obv. Inscription:** "Muhammad Akbar II" **Mint:** Jodhpur

Date	Mintage	Good	VG	F	VF	XF
ND(1221) 31//22 (1806)	—	15.00	25.00	40.00	60.00	—

KM# 204 1/4 RUPEE

2.8000 g., Silver **Obv. Inscription:** Victoria and Jaswant Singh **Mint:** Pali

Date	Mintage	Good	VG	F	VF	XF
ND(1882-98)	—	6.00	15.00	25.00	40.00	60.00

KM# 205 1/2 RUPEE

5.6000 g., Silver **Obv. Inscription:** Victoria and Jaswant Singh **Mint:** Pali

Date	Mintage	Good	VG	F	VF	XF
VS1945	—	8.00	20.00	32.00	50.00	70.00

KM# 35 RUPEE

Silver **Obv. Inscription:** "Muhammad Akbar II" **Mint:** Jodhpur **Note:** Weight varies 11.20-11.30 grams.

Date	Mintage	Good	VG	F	VF	XF
AH1121 Error for 1221	—	—	—	—	—	—

KM# 226 RUPEE

Silver **Obv. Inscription:** "Shah Alam II" **Mint:** Sojat **Note:** Weight varies 11.2-11.30 grams. Fictitious mintname: Jodhpur.

Date	Mintage	Good	VG	F	VF	XF
AH1204//23	—	3.00	7.50	12.50	18.50	27.50
AH12064//23 (sic)	—	3.00	7.50	12.50	18.50	27.50
AH12x4//23	—	3.00	7.50	12.50	18.50	27.50

KM# 177.1 RUPEE

Silver **Obv. Inscription:** "Shah Alam II" **Reverse:** "Nagore" at top **Mint:** Nagor **Note:** Weight varies 11.20-11.30 grams.

Date	Mintage	Good	VG	F	VF	XF
AH1215	—	6.00	15.00	25.00	40.00	60.00
AH1217//44	—	6.00	15.00	25.00	40.00	60.00
AH1218	—	6.00	15.00	25.00	40.00	60.00

KM# 18 RUPEE

11.3000 g., Silver **Series:** Bijai Shahi **Obverse:** Various styles of swords **Obv. Inscription:** "Shah Alam II" **Mint:** Jodhpur

Date	Mintage	Good	VG	F	VF	XF
AH1215//42	—	2.75	6.50	10.00	15.00	22.50
AH1218//45	—	2.75	6.50	10.00	15.00	22.50
AH1220	—	2.75	6.50	10.00	15.00	22.50

KM# 183 RUPEE

11.3000 g., Silver **Obverse:** Dagger **Obv. Inscription:** "Shah ALam II" **Mint:** Pali

Date	Mintage	Good	VG	F	VF	XF
AH1218//45	—	2.75	6.50	10.00	15.00	22.50
AH1128//45 Error for 1218	—	2.75	6.50	10.00	15.00	22.50

KM# 184 RUPEE

11.3000 g., Silver **Obverse:** Sword **Obv. Inscription:** "Shah Alam II" **Mint:** Pali

Date	Mintage	Good	VG	F	VF	XF
AH1228//45 Error for 1218	—	2.75	6.50	10.00	15.00	22.50

KM# 185 RUPEE

11.3000 g., Silver **Obv. Inscription:** "Shah Alam II" **Mint:** Pali

Date	Mintage	Good	VG	F	VF	XF
AH12x8//45	—	2.75	6.50	10.00	15.00	22.50

KM# 179 RUPEE

Silver **Obv. Inscription:** "Muhammad Akbar II" **Mint:** Nagor **Note:** Weight varies 11.20-11.30 grams.

Date	Mintage	Good	VG	F	VF	XF
AH1222//1	—	11.00	27.50	45.00	70.00	100
AH1223//2	—	11.00	27.50	45.00	70.00	100
AH1232	—	11.00	27.50	45.00	70.00	100
AH1234	—	11.00	27.50	45.00	70.00	100

KM# 36.3 RUPEE

Silver **Obverse:** Small sword **Obv. Inscription:** "Muhammad Akbar II" **Mint:** Jodhpur **Note:** Weight varies 11.20-11.30 grams.

Date	Mintage	Good	VG	F	VF	XF
ND(1221)	—	4.00	10.00	16.00	25.00	40.00

KM# 36.1 RUPEE
Silver **Obverse:** Jhar and sword **Obv. Inscription:** "Muhammad Akbar II" **Mint:** Jodhpur **Note:** Weight varies 11.20-11.30 grams. Struck ca.1816-1859AD.

Date	Mintage	Good	VG	F	VF	XF
ND(1221) 31//22	—	3.50	9.00	15.00	22.50	35.00

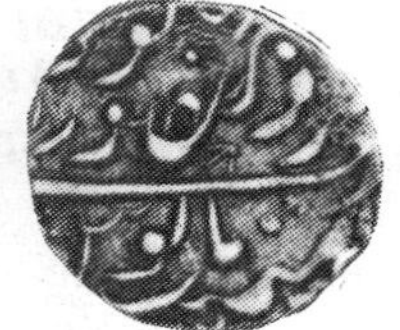

KM# 36.2 RUPEE
Silver **Obverse:** Sword right **Obv. Inscription:** "Muhammad Akbar II" **Mint:** Jodhpur **Note:** Weight varies 11.20-11.30 grams.

Date	Mintage	Good	VG	F	VF	XF
ND(1221) 31//22	—	2.50	6.00	10.00	14.00	20.00

KM# 237 RUPEE
Silver **Obverse:** Jhar **Obv. Inscription:** Victoria and Takhat Singh **Reverse:** Katar and 13 **Mint:** Sojat **Note:** Weight varies 11.20-11.30 grams.

Date	Mintage	Good	VG	F	VF	XF
ND//16 (ca.1869)	—	—	8.50	13.50	20.00	28.50

KM# 246 RUPEE
Silver **Obverse:** Persian S **Obv. Inscription:** Victoria and Takhat Singh **Reverse:** Jhar, sword and "SRI MATAJI" **Mint:** Sojat **Note:** Weight varies 11.20-11.30 grams.

Date	Mintage	Good	VG	F	VF	XF
VS1926	—	3.50	9.00	15.00	21.50	30.00
VS1927	—	3.50	9.00	15.00	21.50	30.00

KM# 186 RUPEE
Silver **Obverse:** 2 Jhars **Obv. Inscription:** "Shah Alam II" **Reverse:** Sword and 54 **Mint:** Pali **Note:** Weight varies 11.20-11.30 grams.

Date	Mintage	Good	VG	F	VF	XF
ND//16 (1872)	—	4.50	11.50	17.50	23.50	32.50

KM# 187 RUPEE
Silver **Obverse:** Jhar and swastika or Hindu letters **Obv. Inscription:** "Shah Alam II" **Reverse:** Sword and 52 **Mint:** Pali **Note:** Weight varies 11.20-11.30 grams.

Date	Mintage	Good	VG	F	VF	XF
ND//16 (1872)	—	4.50	11.50	17.50	23.50	32.50

KM# 259 RUPEE
Silver **Obverse:** Devanagari "Sri Ragunathji" **Obv. Inscription:** Victoria and Jaswant Singh **Mint:** Sojat **Note:** Weight varies 11.30-11.40 grams.

Date	Mintage	Good	VG	F	VF	XF
ND(1873-95)	—	5.50	13.50	20.00	27.50	37.50

KM# 258.1 RUPEE
Silver **Obverse:** Devanagari "Sri Madevaji" and Jhar **Obv. Inscription:** Victoria and Jaswant Singh **Reverse:** "SRI MATAJI", sword and 22 **Mint:** Sojat **Note:** Weight varies 11.30-11.40 grams.

Date	Mintage	Good	VG	F	VF	XF
VS193x (1873)	—	—	11.50	17.50	23.50	32.50

KM# 258.2 RUPEE
Silver **Obverse:** MADEVAJI and Jhar **Obv. Inscription:** Victoria and Jaswant Singh **Mint:** Sojat **Note:** Weight varies 11.30-11.40 grams.

Date	Mintage	Good	VG	F	VF	XF
ND(1874)	—	—	—	—	—	—

KM# 196.2 RUPEE
Silver **Obv. Inscription:** "Shah Alam II" **Reverse:** Symbol added **Mint:** Pali **Note:** Weight varies 11.20-11.30 grams.

Date	Mintage	Good	VG	F	VF	XF
VS1926 (1879)	—	3.50	8.50	13.50	20.00	28.50

KM# 196.1 RUPEE
Silver **Obverse:** 54 in Nagari **Obv. Inscription:** "Shah Alam II" **Reverse:** Jhar and sword, "SRI MATAJI" **Mint:** Pali **Note:** Weight varies 11.20-11.30 grams.

Date	Mintage	VG	F	VF	XF	Unc
VS1926 (1879)	—	8.50	13.50	20.00	28.50	—

KM# 206 RUPEE
Silver **Obverse:** Swastika, Persian 4 and Nagari letters **Obv. Inscription:** Victoria and Jaswant Singh **Reverse:** Jhar and sword, "SRI MATAJI" **Mint:** Pali **Note:** Size varies 19-21mm, weight varies 11.20-11.30 grams.

Date	Mintage	Good	VG	F	VF	XF
VS1929 (1882)	—	3.50	6.00	10.00	15.00	22.50
VS1930 (1883)	—	3.50	6.00	10.00	15.00	22.50
VS1931 (1884)	—	3.50	6.00	10.00	15.00	22.50
VS1932 (1885)	—	3.50	6.00	10.00	15.00	22.50
VS1933 (1886)	—	3.50	6.00	10.00	15.00	22.50
VS1934 (1887)	—	3.50	6.00	10.00	15.00	22.50
VS1935 (1888)	—	3.50	6.00	10.00	15.00	22.50
VS1936 (1889)	—	2.50	6.00	10.00	15.00	22.50
VS1939 (1892)	—	2.50	6.00	10.00	15.00	22.50
VS1940 (1893)	—	2.50	6.00	10.00	15.00	22.50
VS1950 (1893)	—	2.50	6.00	10.00	15.00	22.50
VS1941 (1894)	—	2.50	6.00	10.00	15.00	22.50
VS1942 (1895)	—	2.50	6.00	10.00	15.00	22.50
VS1943 (1896)	—	2.50	6.00	10.00	15.00	22.50
VS1953 (1896)	—	2.50	6.00	10.00	15.00	22.50
NDDate off flan (1896)	—	2.00	3.50	5.50	9.00	15.00
VS1944 (1897)	—	2.50	6.00	10.00	15.00	22.50
VS1945 (1898)	—	2.50	6.00	10.00	15.00	22.50

KM# 216 RUPEE
11.2000 g., Silver **Obv. Inscription:** Victoria and Sardar Singh **Reverse:** Straight sword and jhar **Mint:** Pali

Date	Mintage	Good	VG	F	VF	XF
VS1956 (1899)	—	6.00	15.00	25.00	35.00	50.00

KM# 23 NAZARANA RUPEE
11.3000 g., Silver **Obv. Inscription:** "Shah Alam II" **Mint:** Jodhpur **Note:** Similar to 1 Rupee, KM#19, shape: square.

Date	Mintage	Good	VG	F	VF	XF
AH1218//45	—	—	60.00	100	150	220

KM# 210 NAZARANA RUPEE
Silver **Obverse:** Swastika **Obv. Inscription:** Victoria and Jaswant Singh **Reverse:** Jhar and sword **Mint:** Pali **Note:** Shape: square.

Date	Mintage	VG	F	VF	XF	Unc
VS1929-31 (1872)	—	55.00	90.00	140	200	—

KM# 26 MOHUR
11.0000 g., Gold, 19 mm. **Obv. Inscription:** "Shah Alam II" **Mint:** Jodhpur

Date	Mintage	Good	VG	F	VF	XF
AH1218//45	—	—	200	300	425	600

KM# 40 MOHUR
11.0000 g., Gold, 20 mm. **Obverse:** Sword **Obv. Inscription:** "Muhammad Akbar II" **Mint:** Jodhpur

Date	Mintage	Good	VG	F	VF	XF
ND(1221)//22	—	—	200	300	425	600

Takhat Singh
AH1259-1290 / VS1900-1930 / 1843-1873AD

HAMMERED COINAGE

KM# 71 TAKKA (2 Paisas)
21.0000 g., Copper **Obv. Inscription:** Takhat Singh **Rev. Inscription:** Sri Mataji **Mint:** Jodhpur **Note:** Size varies 20-25mm.

Date	Mintage	Good	VG	F	VF	XF
ND//30 (1859)	—	0.50	1.00	1.50	2.25	—
VS1923//61	—	1.00	2.00	2.75	3.75	—
ND//61 (1866)	—	0.50	1.00	1.50	2.25	—

KM# 72 TAKKA (2 Paisas)
21.0000 g., Copper **Obv. Inscription:** Victoria **Mint:** Jodhpur

Date	Mintage	Good	VG	F	VF	XF
VS1940 (1883)	—	1.25	2.25	3.00	4.00	—
VS1940 (1883) Inverted	—	2.50	4.00	6.50	9.00	—
VS1941 (1884)	—	1.00	2.00	2.75	3.75	—
VS1942 (1885)	—	1.25	2.25	3.00	4.00	—
VS1943 (1886)	—	1.25	2.25	3.00	4.00	—
VS1944 (1887)	—	1.25	2.25	3.00	4.00	—
VS1945 (1888)	—	1.25	2.25	3.00	4.00	—
VS1946 (1889)	—	1.25	2.25	3.00	4.00	—
VS1947 (1890)	—	1.25	2.25	3.00	4.00	—
VS1948 (1891)	—	2.00	3.50	5.50	7.00	—

KM# A72 NAZARANA TAKKA
21.0000 g., Copper, 27 mm. **Obv. Inscription:** Takhat Singh **Rev. Inscription:** Sri Mataji **Mint:** Jodhpur

Date	Mintage	Good	VG	F	VF	XF
VS1923 (1866)	—	—	—	—	—	—

KM# 46 RUPEE
Silver **Obverse:** Jhar and Nagari letter **Obv. Inscription:** Victoria and Takhat Singh **Reverse:** Sword, jhar and 22 **Mint:** Jodhpur **Note:** Weight varies 11.20-11.30 grams.

Date	Mintage	Good	VG	F	VF	XF
ND//16 (1858-59)	—	3.00	7.50	12.50	18.50	27.50

KM# 56 RUPEE
Silver, 21 mm. **Obverse:** Jhar and Nagari letter **Obv. Inscription:** Victoria & Takhat Singh **Reverse:** Sword, "Jodhpur" in Persian and 22 **Mint:** Jodhpur **Note:** Weight varies 11.20-11.30 grams.

Date	Mintage	Good	VG	F	VF	XF
ND//16 (1860-69)	—	2.75	7.00	11.00	16.50	25.00
ND//52 & 16 (1860-69)	—	2.75	7.00	11.00	16.50	25.00

KM# 66 RUPEE
Silver, 21 mm. **Obverse:** Jhar and Magari GA **Obv. Inscription:** Takhat Singh **Reverse:** Sword **Rev. Legend:** Sri Mataji **Rev. Inscription:** Sri Mataji **Mint:** Jodhpur **Note:** Weight varies 11.20-11.30 grams. Struck ca.1849-1862AD.

Date	Mintage	Good	VG	F	VF	XF
ND//22 (1865)	—	3.00	7.50	12.50	18.50	27.50
ND//22 & 61 (1866)	—	3.00	7.50	12.50	18.50	27.50
ND//61 (1867)	—	3.00	7.50	12.50	18.50	27.50

KM# 67 RUPEE
Silver **Reverse:** Jhar, sword and 22 **Mint:** Jodhpur **Note:** Weight varies 11.20-11.45 grams. Queen Victoria referred to in title only as "Queen Ruler of India and Europe".

Date	Mintage	Good	VG	F	VF	XF
VS1926 (1869)	—	2.75	7.00	11.00	16.50	25.00

KM# 68 RUPEE
Silver **Obverse:** Legend differently arranged **Reverse:** Sword, Persian "Ha" **Mint:** Jodhpur **Note:** Reduced size, weight varies 11.20-11.30 grams.

Date	Mintage	Good	VG	F	VF	XF
VS1927//22 (1870)	—	—	20.00	31.50	42.50	60.00
VS1928//22 (1871)	—	—	20.00	31.50	42.50	60.00

KM# 50 MOHUR
11.0000 g., Gold, 20 mm. **Obv. Inscription:** Victoria and Takhat Singh **Mint:** Jodhpur

Date	Mintage	Good	VG	F	VF	XF
ND//16 (1858-59)	—	—	175	250	350	500

KM# 70 MOHUR
10.9000 g., Gold **Mint:** Jodhpur **Note:** Struck with rupee dies.

Date	Mintage	Good	VG	F	VF	XF
VS1926 (1869) Rare	—	—	—	—	—	—

Jaswant Singh
AH1290-1313 / VS1930-1952 / 1873-1895AD
HAMMERED COINAGE

KM# 73 1/8 RUPEE
1.4000 g., Silver **Obv. Inscription:** Victoria and Jaswant Singh **Mint:** Jodhpur

Date	Mintage	Good	VG	F	VF	XF
ND(1885-93)	—	—	12.50	20.00	30.00	50.00

KM# 74 1/4 RUPEE
2.8000 g., Silver **Obv. Inscription:** Victoria & Jaswant Singh **Mint:** Jodhpur

Date	Mintage	Good	VG	F	VF	XF
ND(1885-93)	—	5.00	12.50	20.00	30.00	50.00

KM# 75 1/2 RUPEE
5.6000 g., Silver, 17 mm. **Obv. Inscription:** Victoria & Jaswant Singh **Mint:** Jodhpur

Date	Mintage	Good	VG	F	VF	XF
VS1944 (1887)	—	8.00	20.00	32.00	50.00	70.00
VS1945 (1888)	—	8.00	20.00	32.00	50.00	70.00

KM# 76 RUPEE
Silver **Obverse:** Jhar, Nagari letter and Persian word **Obv. Inscription:** Victoria & Jaswant Singh **Reverse:** Sword and 22 **Mint:** Jodhpur **Note:** Weight varies 11.20-11.30 grams.

Date	Mintage	Good	VG	F	VF	XF
AH1291	—	2.75	6.50	10.00	16.50	25.00
ND(1874-77)	—	2.00	5.00	7.00	10.00	15.00
AH1923 Error for 1293	—	2.75	6.50	11.00	16.50	25.00
AH1293	—	2.75	6.50	10.00	16.50	25.00

KM# 77 RUPEE
Silver **Obv. Inscription:** Victoria & Jaswant Singh **Mint:** Jodhpur **Note:** Weight varies 11.20-11.30 grams.

Date	Mintage	Good	VG	F	VF	XF
ND(1885-93)	—	2.00	5.00	7.00	10.00	15.00
AH1924 Error for 1942	—	2.75	6.50	10.00	16.50	25.00
AH2491 Error for 1942	—	2.75	6.50	10.00	16.50	25.00
VS1942	—	2.75	6.50	10.00	16.50	25.00
VS1943	—	2.75	6.50	10.00	16.50	25.00
VS1947	—	2.75	6.50	10.00	16.50	25.00
AH8941 Error for 1948	—	2.75	6.50	10.00	16.50	25.00
VS1948	—	2.75	6.50	10.00	16.50	25.00
VS1950	—	2.75	6.50	10.00	16.50	25.00

KM# 78 1/4 MOHUR
Gold **Obv. Inscription:** Victoria & Jaswant Singh **Mint:** Jodhpur

Date	Mintage	Good	VG	F	VF	XF
AH1293	—	—	—	—	—	—

KM# 79 1/2 MOHUR
5.5000 g., Gold **Obv. Inscription:** Victoria & Jaswant Singh **Mint:** Jodhpur

Date	Mintage	Good	VG	F	VF	XF
AH1293	—	—	—	—	—	—

KM# 80 MOHUR
10.1000 g., Gold **Obv. Inscription:** Victoria & Jaswant Singh **Mint:** Jodhpur

Date	Mintage	Good	VG	F	VF	XF
AH1293	—	—	—	—	—	—

KM# 81 MOHUR
11.0000 g., Gold, 20 mm. **Obv. Inscription:** Victoria & Jaswant Singh **Mint:** Jodhpur

Date	Mintage	Good	VG	F	VF	XF
VS1942 (1885)	—	—	175	250	350	550
VS1943 (1886)	—	—	175	250	350	550
VS1944 (1887)	—	—	175	250	350	550

Sardar Singh
VS1952-1968 / 1895-1911AD
HAMMERED COINAGE

KM# 83 1/8 RUPEE
1.4000 g., Silver **Obv. Inscription:** Victoria and Sardar Singh **Mint:** Jodhpur

Date	Mintage	Good	VG	F	VF	XF
VS1955 (1898)	—	5.00	12.50	20.00	30.00	50.00

KM# 84 1/4 RUPEE
2.8000 g., Silver **Obv. Inscription:** Victoria and Sardar Singh **Mint:** Jodhpur

Date	Mintage	Good	VG	F	VF	XF
VS1955 (1898)	—	5.00	12.50	20.00	30.00	50.00

KM# 85 1/2 RUPEE
5.6000 g., Silver **Obv. Inscription:** Victoria and Sardar Singh **Mint:** Jodhpur

Date	Mintage	Good	VG	F	VF	XF
VS1955 (1898)	—	8.00	20.00	32.50	50.00	70.00

KM# 86 RUPEE
11.2000 g., Silver **Obv. Inscription:** Victoria and Sardar Singh **Mint:** Jodhpur

Date	Mintage	Good	VG	F	VF	XF
VS1955 (1898)	—	5.50	13.50	22.50	32.50	45.00
VS1956 (1899)	—	5.50	13.50	22.50	32.50	45.00

KM# 88 1/4 MOHUR
2.7500 g., Gold, 15 mm. **Obv. Inscription:** Victoria and Sardar Singh **Mint:** Jodhpur

Date	Mintage	Good	VG	F	VF	XF
VS1952 (1895)	—	—	75.00	125	200	300

KM# 89 1/2 MOHUR
5.5000 g., Gold, 18 mm. **Obv. Inscription:** Victoria and Sardar Singh **Mint:** Jodhpur

Date	Mintage	Good	VG	F	VF	XF
VS1952 (1895)	—	—	100	150	210	325

KM# 90 MOHUR
11.0000 g., Gold, 21 mm. **Obv. Inscription:** Victoria and Sardar Singh **Mint:** Jodhpur

Date	Mintage	Good	VG	F	VF	XF
VS1952 (1895)	—	—	175	250	350	550

JODHPUR FEUDATORY - KUCHAWAN

Kuchaman was a semi-independent feudatory. The Thakur of Kuchaman, an Udawat Rajput, was the only feudatory of Jodhpur permitted to strike his own coinage.

Refer also to Gwalior-Ajmir Mint and Maratha Confederacy-Ajmir Mint.

FEUDATORY STATE

HAMMERED COINAGE

KM# 284 1/4 RUPEE
2.7000 g., 0.7500 Silver, 13 mm. **Obv. Inscription:** "Victoria Inglistan..."

Date	Mintage	Good	VG	F	VF	XF
1863	—	6.00	15.00	25.00	40.00	60.00

KM# 285 1/2 RUPEE
5.7000 g., 0.7500 Silver **Obv. Inscription:** "Victoria Inglistan..." **Note:** Size varies 15-16mm.

Date	Mintage	Good	VG	F	VF	XF
1863	—	6.00	15.00	25.00	40.00	60.00

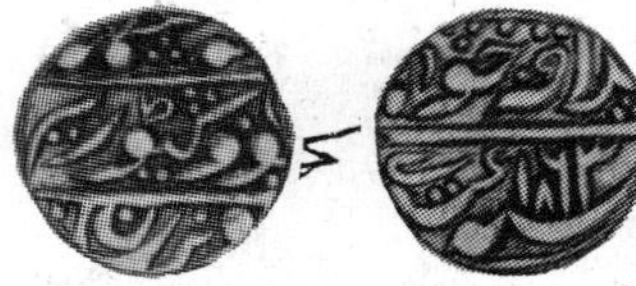

KM# 286 RUPEE
0.7500 Silver **Obv. Inscription:** "Victoria Inglistan..." **Note:** Weight varies 10.60-10.80 grams.

Date	Mintage	Good	VG	F	VF	XF
1863	—	2.25	5.50	9.00	13.50	20.00

KM# 287 NAZARANA RUPEE
10.9000 g., 0.7500 Silver, 25 mm. **Obv. Inscription:** "Victoria Inglistan..."

Date	Mintage	Good	VG	F	VF	XF
1863	—	75.00	150	250	400	575

JUNAGADH

A state located in the Kathiawar peninsula of Western India was originally a petty Rajput kingdom until conquered by the Sultan of Ahmadabad in 1472. It became a Mughal dependency under the Emperor Akbar, administered by the Ahmadabad Subah. In 1735, when the empire began to disintegrate, a Mughal officer and military adventurer, Sher Khan Babi, expelled the Mughal governor and asserted his independence. From that time until Indian independence his descendents ruled the state as nawabs. In 1947 the Nawab of Junagadh tried to accede to the new nation of Pakistan but the Hindu majority in the state objected and Junagadh was absorbed by the Republic of India.

Junagadh first entered into treaty relations with the British in 1807 and maintained a close and friendly association with the Raj. In 1924 this relationship was formalized when Junagadh was placed under an Agent to the Governor General in the western India States. In 1935 the state comprised 3,337 square miles with a population of 545,152, four-fifths of whom were Hindus.

RULERS

Bahadur Khan,
AH1226-1256/VS1868-1897/1811-1840AD
Hamid Khan II,
AH1256-1268/VS1897-1908/1840-1851AD
Mahabat Khan II,
AH1268-1300/VS1908-1939/1851-1882AD
Bahadur Khan III,
AH1300-1309/VS1939-1948/1882-1891AD
Rasul Muhammad Khan,
AH1309-1329/VS1948-1968/1891-1911AD

Bahadur Khan
AH1226-1256 / VS1868-1897 / 1811-1840AD

HAMMERED COINAGE

KM# 11 DOKDO
Copper **Obv. Inscription:** Muhammad Akbar II **Mint:** Junagadh

Date	Mintage	Good	VG	F	VF	XF
AH1239	—	5.00	10.00	16.00	25.00	—
AH-//VS1885	—	5.00	10.00	16.00	25.00	—
AH1245//VS1886	—	5.00	10.00	16.00	25.00	—
AH1(2)47//VS1888	—	5.00	10.00	16.00	25.00	—
ND(1823-32)	—	2.50	5.00	8.00	12.50	—
AH-//VS1889	—	5.00	10.00	16.00	25.00	—

KM# 13 1/2 KORI
2.3000 g., Silver **Obv. Inscription:** Muhammad Akbar II **Mint:** Junagadh

Date	Mintage	Good	VG	F	VF	XF
AH1236//VS1877	—	1.25	3.00	4.50	6.50	10.00
AH1245//VS1886	—	1.25	3.00	4.50	6.50	10.00
AH1247//VS1889	—	1.25	3.00	4.50	6.50	10.00
AH1251//VS1892	—	1.25	3.00	4.50	6.50	10.00
AH1267//VS1877	—	1.25	3.00	4.50	6.50	10.00
AH1268//VS1909	—	1.25	3.00	4.50	6.50	10.00
AH1270//VS1910	—	1.25	3.00	4.50	6.50	10.00
AH1271//VS1911	—	1.25	3.00	4.50	6.50	10.00
AH1272//VS1912	—	1.25	3.00	4.50	6.50	10.00
AH1273//VS1913	—	1.25	3.00	4.50	6.50	10.00
AH1274//VS1914	—	1.25	3.00	4.50	6.50	10.00
AH1275//VS1915	—	1.25	3.00	4.50	6.50	10.00
AH1276//VS1916	—	1.25	3.00	4.50	6.50	10.00
AH1277//VS1917	—	1.25	3.00	4.50	6.50	10.00
AH1278//VS1918	—	1.25	3.00	4.50	6.50	10.00
AH1279//VS1919	—	1.25	3.00	4.50	6.50	10.00
AH1280//VS1920	—	1.25	3.00	4.50	6.50	10.00

KM# 15 KORI
4.6000 g., Silver **Obv. Inscription:** Muhammad Akbar II **Mint:** Junagadh

Date	Mintage	Good	VG	F	VF	XF
AH1235//VS1875	—	1.00	2.50	3.50	5.00	8.50
AH1235//VS1876	—	1.00	2.50	3.50	5.00	8.50
AH1236//VS1877	—	1.00	2.50	3.50	5.00	8.50
AH1245//VS1885	—	1.00	2.50	3.50	5.00	8.50
ND//40 (c.1828)	—	8.00	20.00	32.50	55.00	90.00
AH1245//VS1886	—	1.00	2.50	3.50	5.00	8.50
AH1246//VS1886	—	1.00	2.50	3.50	5.00	8.50
AH1246//VS1887	—	1.00	2.50	3.50	5.00	8.50
AH1247//VS1887	—	1.00	2.50	3.50	5.00	8.50
AH1247//VS1888	—	1.00	2.50	3.50	5.00	8.50
AH1249//VS1889	—	1.00	2.50	3.50	5.00	8.50
AH1249//VS1890	—	1.00	2.50	3.50	5.00	8.50
AH1251//VS1892	—	1.00	2.50	3.50	5.00	8.50
AH1561//VS1892 Error	—	1.00	1.00	2.50	3.50	8.50
AH1252//VS1892	—	1.00	2.50	3.50	5.00	8.50

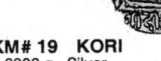

KM# 19 KORI
4.6000 g., Silver

Date	Mintage	Good	VG	F	VF	XF
AH1263//VS190x	—	1.00	2.50	3.50	5.00	8.50
AH1267//VS1907	—	1.00	2.50	3.50	5.00	8.50
AH1268//VS1908	—	1.00	2.50	3.50	5.00	8.50

KM# 23 KORI
4.6000 g., Silver **Obv. Inscription:** Muhammad Akbar II **Mint:** Junagadh **Note:** After the death of the Mughal Emperor Muhammad Akbar II in AH1353/1837AD, Junagadh continued to issue its coins in his name posthumously until at least AH1280/VS1920 (1863AD0, well into the reign of Nawab Mahabat Khan II.

Date	Mintage	Good	VG	F	VF	XF
AH1270//VS1910	—	1.00	2.50	3.50	5.00	8.50
AH1272//VS1912	—	1.00	2.50	3.50	5.00	8.50
AH1273//VS1913	—	1.00	2.50	3.50	5.00	8.50
AH1273//VS1914	—	1.00	2.50	3.50	5.00	8.50
AH1274//VS1914	—	1.00	2.50	3.50	5.00	8.50
AH1275//VS1915	—	1.00	2.50	3.50	5.00	8.50
AH1276//VS1915	—	1.00	2.50	3.50	5.00	8.50
AH1277//VS1917	—	1.00	2.50	3.50	5.00	8.50
AH1278//VS1918	—	1.00	2.50	3.50	5.00	8.50
AH1279//VS1919	—	1.00	2.50	3.50	5.00	8.50
AH1280//VS1920	—	1.00	2.50	3.50	5.00	8.50

Bahadur Khan III
AH1300-1309 / VS1939-1948 / 1882-1891AD

MILLED COINAGE

KM# 39 1/2 GOLD KORI
Gold

Date	Mintage	Good	VG	F	VF	XF
AH1309//VS1947	—	—	—	150	300	500

KM# 41 GOLD KORI
4.6100 g., Gold

Date	Mintage	Good	VG	F	VF	XF
AH1309//VS1947	—	—	—	225	450	750

Rasul Muhammad Khan
AH1309-1329 / VS1948-1968 / 1891-1911AD

MILLED COINAGE

KM# 56 GOLD KORI
Gold **Obv. Inscription:** Perso-Arabic Nawab Bahadur Muhammad Khanji **Reverse:** Date, mintname **Mint:** Junagadh **Note:** Weight varies 4.02-4.77 grams.

Date	Mintage	VG	F	VF	XF	Unc
AH1309//VS1948	—	—	—	550	900	1,300

KM# 57 GOLD KORI
Gold **Obv. Inscription:** Perso-Arabic Nawab Bahadur Muhammad Khanji **Reverse:** Date, mintname **Mint:** Junagadh **Note:** Weight varies 4.02-4.77 grams.

Date	Mintage	VG	F	VF	XF	Unc
AH1318//VS956	—	—	—	650	1,100	1,600

Mahabat Khan III
AH1329-1368 / VS1968-2005 / 1911-1948AD

HAMMERED COINAGE

KM# 27 DOKDO
Copper

Date	Mintage	Good	VG	F	VF	XF
VS1931(1874)	—	15.00	25.00	40.00	60.00	—
VS1935(1878)	—	13.50	22.50	35.00	50.00	—

KM# 29 1/2 KORI
2.3000 g., Silver

Date	Mintage	Good	VG	F	VF	XF
AH1293//VS1934	—	3.50	6.00	9.00	13.50	20.00
AH1299//VS1938	—	3.50	6.00	9.00	13.50	20.00

KM# 30 KORI
4.6000 g., Silver

Date	Mintage	Good	VG	F	VF	XF
AH1292//VS1932	—	0.75	2.00	3.00	4.00	7.50
AH1293//VS1933	—	0.75	2.00	3.00	4.00	7.50
AH1293//VS1934	—	0.75	2.00	3.00	4.00	7.50
AH1297//VS1935	—	0.75	2.00	3.00	4.00	7.50
AH1297//VS1936	—	0.75	2.00	3.00	4.00	7.50
AH1298//VS1937	—	0.75	2.00	3.00	4.00	7.50
AH1299//VS1938	—	0.75	2.00	3.00	4.00	7.50

KM# 31 NAZARANA KORI
4.6000 g., Silver

Date	Mintage	Good	VG	F	VF	XF
AH1297//VS1936	—	10.00	20.00	32.50	45.00	65.00

MILLED COINAGE

KM# 34 GOLD KORI
Gold **Note:** Size varies 15-16mm.

Date	Mintage	Good	VG	F	VF	XF
AH1292//VS1932	—	—	—	225	450	750

KAITHAL

HAMMERED COINAGE

KM# 10 RUPEE
Silver **Obv. Inscription:** Shah Alam (II) **Note:** 10.70-11.60 grams.

Date	Mintage	Good	VG	F	VF	XF
ND(1767-1819)	—	4.00	10.00	15.00	21.50	30.00

KM# 11 MOHUR
10.7000 g., Gold, 14 mm. **Obv. Inscription:** Shah Alam (II)

Date	Mintage	Good	VG	F	VF	XF
ND(1767-1819)	—	—	600	900	1,400	2,000

KALAT

Khelat or Kelat

A state located in Baluchistan, Pakistan.

The Khanate of Kalat had originally been a feudatory of Kabul. Its ruler, the wali, later became a trusted leader in the army of Ahmad Shah Durrani, who in 1761 invaded India and crushed both Mughal and Maratha forces at the battle of Panipat. In 1839 Kalat was taken by the British, and the wali, Mehrab Khan, was killed. The victors then installed his son, Nasir Khan, as ruler and in 1854 a formal treaty was executed. From that time Kalat came under British control, with the Government of India frequently acting as referees in disputes between the wali and his chiefs. In 1893 the wali was deposed for misrule and Kalat's mint was closed.

RULERS

Mehrab Khan, AH1232-1255/1816-1839AD
Nasir Khan, AH1256-1274/1841-1856AD
Khudadad Khan, AH1274-1311/1856-1893AD

MINT

كلات

Kalat

Mehrab Khan
AH1232-1255 / 1816-1839AD

HAMMERED COINAGE

KM# 11 FALUS
Copper **Obverse:** Scimitar between flowers **Rev. Inscription:** Kalat, falus **Mint:** Kalat

Date	Mintage	Good	VG	F	VF	XF
AH1237	—	10.00	20.00	32.00	50.00	—
AH1238	—	10.00	20.00	32.00	50.00	—
AH1240	—	10.00	20.00	32.00	50.00	—

Khudadad Khan
AH1274-1311 / 1856-1893AD

HAMMERED COINAGE

KM# 21 FALUS
Copper **Obv. Inscription:** Mahud Khan Durrani **Rev. Inscription:** Kalat, falus **Mint:** Kalat **Note:** Round, irregular, or rough-cut octagonal

Date	Mintage	Good	VG	F	VF	XF
AH1281	—	3.50	6.00	10.00	15.00	—
ND(1864-79)	—	2.00	3.25	5.00	8.50	—
AH1282	—	3.50	6.00	10.00	15.00	—
AH10786 (error)	—	3.50	6.00	10.00	15.00	—
AH1186 (error)	—	3.50	6.00	10.00	15.00	—
AH1290	—	3.50	6.00	10.00	15.00	—
AH1293	—	3.50	6.00	10.00	15.00	—
1294//1293	—	3.50	6.00	10.00	15.00	—
AH1294	—	3.50	6.00	10.00	15.00	—
AH1295	—	2.50	4.00	7.00	10.00	—
AH1296	—	3.50	6.00	10.00	15.00	—

KALSIA

A Cis-Sutlej (Sikh) state, (located in the Punjab), until 1849 when the Punjab was annexed and the states were merged into the new province of British India. Most of the Cis-Sutlej states distinguished themselves on the side of the British during the great revolt of 1857.

MINT

چحچرولي

Chhachrauli

HAMMERED COINAGE

KM# 32 PAISA
Copper **Obverse:** Dagger mint mark **Reverse:** Quatrefoil and sword

Date	Mintage	Good	VG	F	VF	XF
AH1216//41 (sic) (1801) Error	—	15.00	25.00	40.00	60.00	—
AH1218//44 (sic) (1803)	—	15.00	25.00	40.00	60.00	—

KARAULI

State located in Rajputana, northwest India.

Karauli was established in the 11th century by Jadon Rajputs, of the same stock as the royal house of Jaisalmir. They are thought to have migrated to Rajasthan from the Mathura region some years earlier. The state passed successively under Mughal and Maratha suzerainty before coming under British authority in 1817.

The Maharajas of Karauli first struck coins in the reign of Manak Pal.

RULERS

Manak Pal, AH1186-1233/1772-1817AD
Harbaksh Pal, AH1233-1254/1817-1838AD
Pratap Pal, AH1255-1264/1838-1848AD
Nar Singh Pal, AH1264-1268/1848-1852AD
Bharat Pal, AH1268-1270/1852-1854AD
Madan Pal, AH1270-1286/1854-1869AD

म
Mark of Madan Pal

Jai Singh Pal, 1869-1875AD
Arjun Pal, 1876-1886AD

अ
Mark of Arjun Pal

Bhanwar Pal, 1886-1927

भ
Mark of Bhanwar Pal

MINT

كرولي and करौली

Karauli

MINT NAME

سواي جيپور

Sawai Jaipur

MINT MARKS

Katar

Jhar on reverse

HAMMERED COINAGE

Mughal Style

KM# 21 TAKKA
Copper **Obv. Inscription:** "Muhammad Akbar II" **Note:** Weight varies 17.80-17.90 grams.

Date	Mintage	Good	VG	F	VF	XF
AH122x//4	—	6.00	12.00	20.00	30.00	—
ND//10 (1815-16)	—	6.00	12.00	20.00	30.00	—
ND//28 (1833-34)	—	6.00	12.00	20.00	30.00	—

KM# 33 RUPEE
Silver **Obv. Inscription:** "Bahadur Shah II" **Reverse:** With character "Ma" for Madan Pal, without legible AH year **Note:** Weight varies 10.90-11.05 grams.

Date	Mintage	Good	VG	F	VF	XF
ND//13	—	7.00	17.50	25.00	35.00	50.00
ND//15	—	7.00	17.50	25.00	35.00	50.00

KM# 16 RUPEE
Silver **Obv. Inscription:** "Shah Alam II" **Note:** Weight varies 10.8 - 11.2 grams.

Date	Mintage	Good	VG	F	VF	XF
ND//42 (1800-01)	—	8.00	20.00	31.50	42.50	60.00
AH1216//43	—	8.00	20.00	31.50	42.50	60.00
ND//44 (1802-03)	—	8.00	20.00	31.50	42.50	60.00

KM# 26 RUPEE
Silver **Obv. Inscription:** "Muhammad Akbar II" **Note:** Weight varies 10.90-11.10 grams.

Date	Mintage	Good	VG	F	VF	XF
AH1223//2	—	8.00	20.00	31.50	42.50	60.00
AH1227//6	—	8.00	20.00	31.50	42.50	60.00
AH1228//7	—	8.00	20.00	31.50	42.50	60.00
AH122x//9	—	8.00	20.00	31.50	42.50	60.00
AH1231//10	—	8.00	20.00	31.50	42.50	60.00
AH1232//11	—	8.00	20.00	31.50	42.50	60.00
AH1233//12	—	8.00	20.00	31.50	42.50	60.00
AH1233//14	—	8.00	20.00	31.50	42.50	60.00
AH1233//15	—	8.00	20.00	31.50	42.50	60.00
AH1237//16	—	8.00	20.00	31.50	42.50	60.00
AH1238//16 (sic)	—	8.00	20.00	31.50	42.50	60.00
AH1239//17 (sic) (Retrograde 9)	—	8.00	20.00	31.50	42.50	60.00
AH1240//19	—	8.00	20.00	31.50	42.50	60.00
AH1254//23 Error for 1244	—	8.00	20.00	31.50	42.50	60.00
AH1244//25	—	8.00	20.00	31.50	42.50	60.00

KM# 31 RUPEE
Silver **Obv. Inscription:** "Bahadur Shah II" **Note:** Weight varies 10.60-11.00 grams.

Date	Mintage	Good	VG	F	VF	XF
AH12xx//9	—	7.00	17.50	25.00	35.00	50.00
ND//11 (1846-47)	—	7.00	17.50	25.00	35.00	50.00
ND//12 (1847-48)	—	7.00	17.50	25.00	35.00	50.00

HAMMERED COINAGE

Regal Style

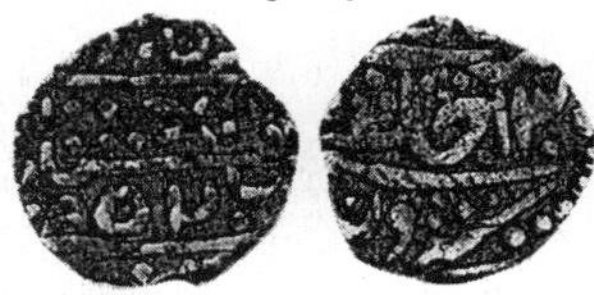

KM# 36 TAKKA
Copper **Obv. Inscription:** "... farman rawai Inglistan" (for Queen Victoria)

Date	Mintage	Good	VG	F	VF	XF
1852//12	—	2.50	5.00	7.50	12.00	—
1852//13	—	2.50	5.00	7.50	12.00	—

KM# 51 TAKKA
18.0000 g., Copper **Obv. Inscription:** The exalted Queen, the Emperor for Queen Victoria **Reverse:** Katar upper right

Date	Mintage	Good	VG	F	VF	XF
1881	—	1.75	2.75	4.50	8.00	—
1882//11 Error for 1886	—	1.75	2.75	4.50	8.00	—
1883	—	1.75	2.75	4.50	8.00	—
1885//9	—	1.75	2.75	4.50	8.00	—
1885//10	—	1.75	2.75	4.50	8.00	—
1886//11	—	1.75	2.75	4.50	8.00	—

KM# 62 TAKKA
Copper **Obv. Inscription:** The exalted Queen, the Emperor of India Years and mark of Bhanwar Pal **Note:** Weight varies 17.80-18.30 grams.

Date	Mintage	Good	VG	F	VF	XF
1886//1	—	1.75	2.75	4.50	8.00	—
1887//2	—	1.75	2.75	4.50	8.00	—
1891//5	—	1.75	2.75	4.50	8.00	—
1891//6	—	1.75	2.75	4.50	8.00	—
1893//8	—	1.75	2.75	4.50	8.00	—

KM# 44.1 RUPEE
Silver **Obv. Inscription:** "... farman rawai Inglistan" (for Queen Victoria) **Note:** Weight varies 10.90-11.00 grams.

Date	Mintage	Good	VG	F	VF	XF
1859//7	—	—	15.00	21.50	30.00	40.00
1859//9	—	—	15.00	21.50	30.00	40.00

KM# 44.2 RUPEE
Silver **Obv. Inscription:** "... farman rawai Inglistan" (for Queen Victoria) **Note:** Weight varies 10.90-11.00 grams.

Date	Mintage	Good	VG	F	VF	XF
1852//9	—	6.00	15.00	21.50	30.00	40.00
1852//10	—	6.00	15.00	21.50	30.00	40.00
1852//11	—	6.00	15.00	21.50	30.00	40.00
1852//12	—	6.00	15.00	21.50	30.00	40.00
1852//13	—	6.00	15.00	21.50	30.00	40.00
1852//14	—	6.00	15.00	21.50	30.00	40.00
AH1856//14 Error for 1852	—	6.00	15.00	21.50	30.00	40.00

KM# 56 RUPEE
Silver **Obv. Inscription:** The exalted Queen, the Emperor for Queen Victoria **Note:** Weight varies 10.90-11.10 grams.

Date	Mintage	Good	VG	F	VF	XF
1882//7	—	6.00	15.00	21.50	30.00	40.00
1883//8	—	6.00	15.00	21.50	30.00	40.00
1884//9	—	6.00	15.00	21.50	30.00	40.00
1885//10	—	6.00	15.00	21.50	30.00	40.00
1886//11	—	6.00	15.00	21.50	30.00	40.00

KM# 70 RUPEE
Silver **Obv. Inscription:** The exalted Queen, the Emperor of India Years and mark of Bhanwar Pal **Note:** Weight varies 10.90-11.15 grams.

Date	Mintage	Good	VG	F	VF	XF
1886//1	—	4.00	10.00	15.00	21.50	30.00
1882//2 Error for 1886	—	4.00	10.00	15.00	21.50	30.00
1886//2	—	4.00	10.00	15.00	21.50	30.00
1887//2	—	4.00	10.00	15.00	21.50	30.00
1888//2	—	4.00	10.00	15.00	21.50	30.00
1888//3	—	4.00	10.00	15.00	21.50	30.00
1889//4	—	4.00	10.00	15.00	21.50	30.00
1890//4	—	4.00	10.00	15.00	21.50	30.00
1890	—	4.00	10.00	15.00	21.50	30.00
1891//5	—	4.00	10.00	15.00	21.50	30.00
1891//6	—	4.00	10.00	15.00	21.50	30.00
1892//8	—	4.00	10.00	15.00	21.50	30.00
1893//8	—	4.00	10.00	15.00	21.50	30.00
1894//8	—	4.00	10.00	15.00	21.50	30.00
1894//9	—	4.00	10.00	15.00	21.50	30.00
1895//10	—	4.00	10.00	15.00	21.50	30.00
1896//11	—	4.00	10.00	15.00	21.50	30.00
1897//11	—	4.00	10.00	15.00	21.50	30.00

KM# 42.1 1/4 RUPEE
Silver, 13 mm. **Obv. Inscription:** "... farman rawai Inglistan" (for Queen Victoria) **Note:** Weight varies 2.68-2.90 grams.

Date	Mintage	Good	VG	F	VF	XF
1859//7	—	—	25.00	40.00	60.00	85.00

KM# 42.2 1/4 RUPEE
Silver, 13 mm. **Obv. Inscription:** "... farman rawai Inglistan" (for Queen Victoria) **Note:** Weight varies 2.68-2.90 grams.

Date	Mintage	Good	VG	F	VF	XF
1852//13	—	—	25.00	40.00	60.00	85.00
1852//14	—	—	25.00	40.00	60.00	85.00

KM# 68 1/4 RUPEE
2.7500 g., Silver **Obv. Inscription:** The exalted Queen, the Emperor of India Years and mark of Bhanwar Pal

Date	Mintage	Good	VG	F	VF	XF
1891//5	—	10.00	25.00	40.00	60.00	85.00
1892//6	—	10.00	25.00	40.00	60.00	85.00
1893//8	—	10.00	25.00	40.00	60.00	85.00
1896//11	—	10.00	25.00	40.00	60.00	85.00

KM# 43.1 1/2 RUPEE
Silver, 18 mm. **Obv. Inscription:** "... farman rawai Inglistan" (for Queen Victoria) **Note:** Weight varies 5.35-5.80 grams.

Date	Mintage	Good	VG	F	VF	XF
1859	—	—	30.00	50.00	80.00	120

KM# 43.2 1/2 RUPEE
Silver, 18 mm. **Obv. Inscription:** "... farman rawai Inglistan" (for Queen Victoria) **Note:** Weight varies 5.35-5.80 grams.

Date	Mintage	Good	VG	F	VF	XF
1852	—	—	30.00	50.00	80.00	120

KM# 69 1/2 RUPEE
Silver, 18 mm. **Obv. Inscription:** The exalted Queen, the Emperor of India Years and mark of Bhanwar Pal **Note:** Weight varies 5.45-5.60 grams.

Date	Mintage	Good	VG	F	VF	XF
ND//4 (1891)	—	12.00	30.00	50.00	80.00	120
1891//5	—	12.00	30.00	50.00	80.00	120
1893//8	—	12.00	30.00	50.00	80.00	120
1896//10	—	12.00	30.00	50.00	80.00	120

KM# 66 1/8 RUPEE
1.3500 g., Silver **Obv. Inscription:** The exalted Queen, the Emperor of India Years and mark of Bhanwar Pal

Date	Mintage	Good	VG	F	VF	XF
ND//5 (1891)	—	10.00	25.00	40.00	60.00	90.00

KM# 49 1/2 PAISA
4.5000 g., Copper **Obv. Inscription:** The exalted Queen, the Emperor for Queen Victoria

Date	Mintage	Good	VG	F	VF	XF
1886//11	—	4.50	6.00	10.00	15.00	—

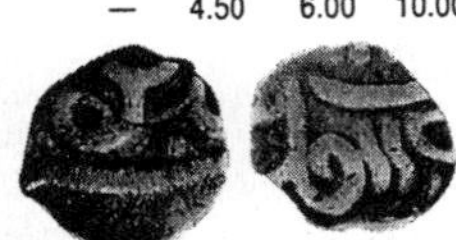

KM# 50 1/2 PAISA
9.0000 g., Copper **Obv. Inscription:** The exalted Queen, the Emperor for Queen Victoria

Date	Mintage	Good	VG	F	VF	XF
1886//11	—	1.75	2.75	4.50	8.00	—

KM# 61 PAISA
9.0000 g., Copper **Obv. Inscription:** The exalted Queen, the Emperor of India Years and mark of Bhanwar Pal

Date	Mintage	Good	VG	F	VF	XF
1886//1	—	1.75	3.00	5.00	9.00	—
1887//2	—	1.75	3.00	5.00	9.00	—
1891//5	—	1.75	3.00	5.00	9.00	—

KM# 57 MOHUR
Gold **Obv. Inscription:** The exalted Queen, the Emperor for Queen Victoria **Note:** Similar to 1 Rupee, KM#56.

Date	Mintage	Good	VG	F	VF	XF
ND//3 (1878)	—	—	225	350	500	700

KASHMIR

State located in extreme northern India. Part of Afghanistan, Durrani Empire 1752-1819AD, under Sikhs of Punjab 1819-1846AD, locally ruled by Dogra Rajas thereafter. For earlier coinage refer to Afghanistan and Sikh Empire.

RULERS

Dogra Rajas

Gulab Singh, VS1903-1913/1846-1856AD

Ranbir Singh, VS1914-1942/1857-1885AD

Pertab Singh, VS1942-1979/1885-1925AD

MINTS

Jammu جمون

Ladakh لداخ لداکه

Srinagar سرینگر

HAMMERED COINAGE

Y# 21a RUPEE
6.6500 g., Silver **Series:** Fourt Silver (Chilki) **Obverse:** Persian date in second line **Reverse:** Davanagari date in second line **Mint:** Srinagar

Date	Mintage	Good	VG	F	VF	XF
VS1934	—	2.25	5.50	8.00	12.50	22.50
VS1935	—	2.25	5.50	8.00	12.50	22.50
VS1936	—	2.25	5.50	8.00	12.50	22.50
VS1937	—	2.25	5.50	8.00	12.50	22.50
VS1938	—	2.25	5.50	8.00	12.50	22.50
VS1939	—	2.25	5.50	8.00	12.50	22.50
VS1940	—	2.25	5.50	8.00	12.50	22.50
VS1941	—	2.25	5.50	8.00	12.50	22.50
VS1942	—	2.25	5.50	8.00	12.50	22.50
VS1943	—	2.25	5.50	8.00	12.50	22.50
VS1944	—	2.25	5.50	8.00	12.50	22.50
VS1945	—	2.25	5.50	8.00	12.50	22.50
VS1946	—	2.25	5.50	8.00	12.50	22.50
VS1947	—	2.25	5.50	8.00	12.50	22.50
VS1948	—	2.25	5.50	8.00	12.50	22.50
VS1949	—	2.25	5.50	8.00	12.50	22.50
VS1950	—	2.25	5.50	8.00	12.50	22.50
VS1951	—	2.25	5.50	8.00	12.50	22.50
VS1952	—	2.25	5.50	8.00	12.50	22.50

Gulab Singh

VS1903-1913 / 1846-1856AD

HAMMERED COINAGE

Y# 1.1 PAISA
Copper **Series:** First Copper **Obverse:** Fancy leaf **Mint:** Srinagar **Note:** Many varieties exist.

Date	Mintage	Good	VG	F	VF	XF
VS1904	—	3.00	7.00	12.00	20.00	—

Y# 1.2 PAISA
Copper **Series:** First Copper **Obverse:** Trident **Reverse:** Scimitar through circle **Mint:** Srinagar

Date	Mintage	Good	VG	F	VF	XF
VS1908	—	3.00	7.00	12.00	20.00	—

Y# 1.3 PAISA
Copper **Series:** First Copper **Reverse:** Fancy leaf **Mint:** Srinagar

Date	Mintage	Good	VG	F	VF	XF
ND	—	3.00	7.00	12.00	20.00	—

Y# 9.1 1/16 RUPEE
Silver **Series:** Second Silver **Obv. Inscription:** Persian initials "JHS" **Rev. Inscription:** Persian initials "JHS" **Mint:** Srinagar **Note:** Weight varies 0.64-0.67 grams.

Date	Mintage	Good	VG	F	VF	XF
ND	—	5.00	12.50	20.00	30.00	45.00

Y# 2 1/8 RUPEE
Silver **Series:** First Silver **Reverse:** Leaf and date, without initials "JHS" **Mint:** Srinagar **Note:** Weight varies 1.28-1.35 grams. The dot for "0" in 1903, 1904, 1905 is sometimes omitted.

Date	Mintage	Good	VG	F	VF	XF
VS1903	—	5.00	12.50	20.00	30.00	45.00
VS1904	—	5.00	12.50	20.00	30.00	45.00
VS1905	—	5.00	12.50	20.00	30.00	45.00

Y# 3 1/4 RUPEE
Silver **Series:** First Silver **Reverse:** Leaf and date, without initials "JHS" **Mint:** Srinagar **Note:** Weight varies 2.57-2.70 grams.

Date	Mintage	Good	VG	F	VF	XF
VS1903	—	4.00	10.00	16.50	25.00	35.00
VS1904	—	4.00	10.00	16.50	25.00	35.00

Y# 4 1/2 RUPEE
Silver **Series:** First Silver **Reverse:** Leaf and date, without initials "JHS" **Mint:** Srinagar **Note:** Weight varies 5.15-5.40 grams.

Date	Mintage	Good	VG	F	VF	XF
VS1903	—	5.00	12.50	20.00	30.00	45.00
VS1904	—	5.00	12.50	20.00	30.00	45.00
VS1905	—	5.00	12.50	20.00	30.00	45.00
VS1906	—	5.00	12.50	20.00	30.00	45.00

Y# 5 RUPEE
Silver **Series:** First Silver **Reverse:** Leaf and date, without initials "JHS" **Mint:** Srinagar **Note:** Weight varies 10.30-10.80 grams.

Date	Mintage	Good	VG	F	VF	XF
VS1903	—	2.75	6.50	11.00	16.50	30.00
VS1904	—	2.75	6.50	11.00	16.50	30.00
VS1905	—	3.00	7.50	12.50	18.50	32.50
VS1906	—	3.00	7.50	12.50	18.50	32.50

Y# 13 KHAM RUPEE
Silver **Series:** Second Silver **Obv. Inscription:** Persian initials "JHS" **Rev. Inscription:** Persian initials "JHS" **Mint:** Srinagar **Note:** Weight varies 10.30-10.80 grams.

Date	Mintage	Good	VG	F	VF	XF
VS1906	—	3.00	7.50	11.00	16.50	30.00
VS1907	—	3.00	7.50	11.00	16.50	30.00
VS1908	—	3.00	7.50	11.00	16.50	30.00
VS1909	—	3.00	7.50	11.00	16.50	30.00
VS1910	—	3.00	7.50	11.00	16.50	30.00
VS1911	—	3.00	7.50	11.00	16.50	30.00
VS1912	—	2.75	7.00	11.00	16.50	30.00
VS1913	—	2.75	7.00	11.00	16.50	30.00
VS1914	—	2.75	7.00	11.00	16.50	30.00
VS1915	—	2.75	7.00	11.00	16.50	30.00
VS1916	—	2.75	7.00	11.00	16.50	30.00
VS1917	—	2.75	7.00	11.00	16.50	30.00
VS1918	—	2.75	7.00	11.00	16.50	30.00
VS1919	—	2.75	7.00	11.00	16.50	30.00
VS1920	—	2.75	7.00	11.00	16.50	30.00
VS1921	—	2.75	7.00	11.00	16.50	30.00
VS1922	—	2.75	7.00	11.00	16.50	30.00
VS1923	—	2.75	7.00	11.00	16.50	30.00
VS1924	—	2.75	7.00	11.00	16.50	30.00
VS1925	—	2.75	7.00	11.00	16.50	30.00
VS1926	—	2.75	7.00	11.00	16.50	30.00
VS1927	—	2.75	7.00	11.00	16.50	30.00

Ranbir Singh

VS1914-1942 / 1857-1885AD

HAMMERED COINAGE

Y# 17 1/4 PAISA
1.5000 g., Copper **Series:** Fourth Copper **Obverse:** Initials "JHS" **Rev. Inscription:** "Takari" **Mint:** Srinagar

Date	Mintage	Good	VG	F	VF	XF
VS1935	—	3.00	5.00	8.00	12.50	—
VS1941	—	3.00	5.00	8.00	12.50	—

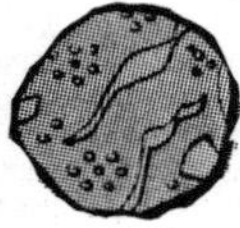

Y# 6 1/2 PAISA
Copper **Series:** Third Copper **Obverse:** Date in cartouche **Mint:** Srinagar **Note:** Weight varies 2.50-3.00 grams.

Date	Mintage	Good	VG	F	VF	XF
VS1922	—	2.00	3.25	5.00	8.50	—
VS1924	—	2.00	3.25	5.00	8.50	—

Y# 18 1/2 PAISA
3.0000 g., Copper **Series:** Fourth Copper **Mint:** Srinagar

Date	Mintage	Good	VG	F	VF	XF
VS1927	—	1.50	2.50	4.00	6.00	—
VS1928	—	1.50	2.50	4.00	6.00	—
VS1929	—	1.50	2.50	4.00	6.00	—
VS1932	—	1.00	1.75	2.50	4.00	—
VS1933//1934	—	1.25	2.25	3.50	5.50	—
VS1933	—	1.00	1.75	2.50	4.00	—
VS1934	—	1.00	1.75	2.50	4.00	—
VS1936	—	1.00	1.75	2.50	4.00	—
VS1937	—	1.00	1.75	2.50	4.00	—
VS1938	—	1.00	1.75	2.50	4.00	—
VS1939	—	1.00	1.75	2.50	4.00	—
VS1940	—	1.00	1.75	2.50	4.00	—
VS1941	—	1.00	1.75	2.50	4.00	—

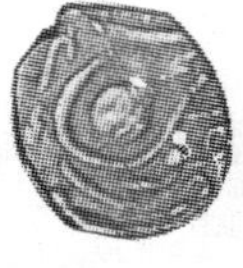

KM# 2a 1/2 PAISA
Copper **Mint:** Jammu **Note:** Shape: Dump style, uneven planchets.

Date	Mintage	Good	VG	F	VF	XF
VS1935	—	1.00	1.75	2.50	4.00	—
VS1936	—	1.00	1.75	2.50	4.00	—
VS1937	—	1.00	1.75	2.50	4.00	—
VS1938	—	1.00	1.75	2.50	4.00	—
VS1939	—	1.00	1.75	2.50	4.00	—
VS1940	—	1.00	1.75	2.50	4.00	—
VS1941	—	1.00	1.75	2.50	4.00	—
VS1942	—	1.00	1.75	2.50	4.00	—
VS1943	—	1.00	1.75	2.50	4.00	—
VS1946	—	1.00	1.75	2.50	4.00	—
VS1947	—	1.00	1.75	2.50	4.00	—
VS1948	—	1.00	1.75	2.50	4.00	—
VS1949	—	1.00	1.75	2.50	4.00	—

KM# 2 1/2 PAISA
Copper **Reverse:** Takari legend **Mint:** Jammu **Note:** Weight varies 3.40-3.50 grams. Shape: Machine-punched planchets.

Date	Mintage	Good	VG	F	VF	XF
VS1935	—	5.00	9.00	12.00	20.00	—
VS1936	—	5.00	9.00	12.00	20.00	—

KM# 1.1 PAISA
Copper **Obv. Legend:** Persian **Reverse:** Sword below top line **Rev. Legend:** Gurmukhi **Mint:** Jammu **Note:** Weight varies 6.80-7.00 grams.

Date	Mintage	Good	VG	F	VF	XF
VS1914	—	1.00	1.75	2.50	4.00	—
VS1915	—	1.00	1.75	2.50	4.00	—
VS1917	—	1.00	1.75	2.50	4.00	—
VS1918	—	1.00	1.75	2.50	4.00	—
VS1919	—	1.00	1.75	2.50	4.00	—

Y# 7 PAISA
Copper **Series:** Third Copper **Obverse:** Date in cartouche **Mint:** Srinagar **Note:** Weight varies 5.50-6.00 grams.

Date	Mintage	Good	VG	F	VF	XF
VS1920	—	0.85	1.35	2.00	3.50	—
VS1921	—	0.85	1.35	2.00	3.50	—
VS1922	—	0.85	1.35	2.00	3.50	—
VS1923	—	1.00	1.75	2.50	4.00	—
VS1926	—	1.00	1.75	2.50	4.00	—
VS1927	—	0.85	1.35	2.00	3.50	—
VS1928	—	0.85	1.35	2.00	3.50	—
VS1930	—	1.00	1.75	2.50	4.00	—
VS1931	—	1.00	1.75	2.50	4.00	—

KM# 1.2 PAISA
Copper **Reverse:** Sword below middle line **Mint:** Jammu

Date	Mintage	Good	VG	F	VF	XF
VS1921	—	1.00	1.75	2.50	4.00	—
VS1922	—	1.00	1.75	2.50	4.00	—

Y# 19 PAISA

6.0000 g., Copper **Series:** Fourth Copper **Mint:** Srinagar

Date	Mintage	Good	VG	F	VF	XF
VS1937	—	2.00	3.25	5.00	8.50	—
VS1938	—	2.00	3.25	5.00	8.50	—
VS1939	—	2.00	3.25	5.00	8.50	—
VS1940	—	2.00	3.25	5.00	8.50	—

KM# 3 1/3 MOHUR

Gold **Mint:** Jammu **Note:** Weight varies 3.57-3.80 grams.

Date	Mintage	Good	VG	F	VF	XF
VS1921	—	185	300	1,000	2,000	—

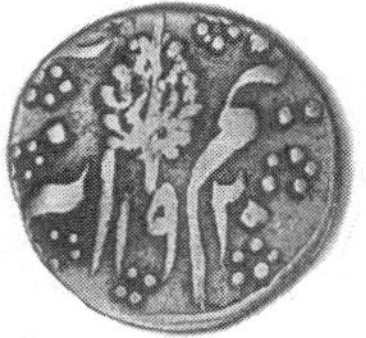

Y# 8 1/2 ANNA

Copper **Series:** Second Copper **Obverse:** Fancy leaf **Reverse:** Scimitar through circle **Mint:** Srinagar

Date	Mintage	Good	VG	F	VF	XF
VS1920	—	5.00	9.00	13.00	20.00	—

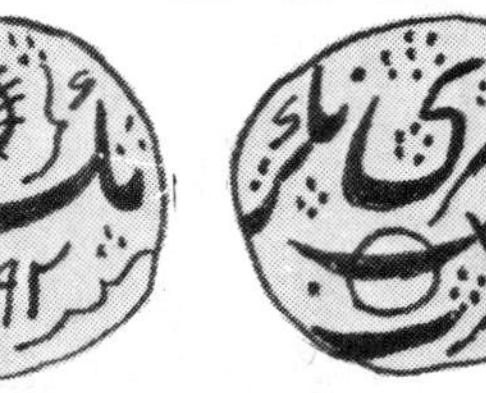

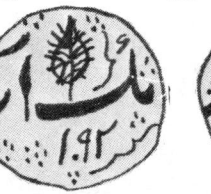

Y# 9 ANNA

Copper **Series:** Second Copper **Obverse:** Fancy leaf **Reverse:** Scimitar through circle **Mint:** Srinagar

Date	Mintage	Good	VG	F	VF	XF
VS1920	—	12.00	20.00	32.00	50.00	—
VS1092 Error for 1920	—	12.00	20.00	32.00	50.00	—
VS1924	—	12.00	20.00	32.00	50.00	—

Y# 10 1/8 RUPEE

Silver **Series:** Second Silver **Obv. Inscription:** Persian initials "JHS" **Rev. Inscription:** Persian initials "JHS" **Mint:** Srinagar **Note:** Weight varies 1.28-1.35 grams.

Date	Mintage	Good	VG	F	VF	XF
VS1914	—	5.00	12.50	20.00	30.00	45.00
VS1925	—	5.00	12.50	20.00	30.00	45.00

Y# 11 1/4 RUPEE

Silver **Series:** Second Silver **Obv. Inscription:** Persian initials "JHS" **Rev. Inscription:** Persian initials "JHS" **Mint:** Srinagar **Note:** Weight varies 2.57-2.69 grams.

Date	Mintage	Good	VG	F	VF	XF
VS1914	—	4.00	10.00	16.50	25.00	35.00
VS1922	—	4.00	10.00	16.50	25.00	35.00
VS1925	—	4.00	10.00	16.50	25.00	35.00

Y# 16 1/4 RUPEE

Silver **Series:** Third Silver **Obv. Inscription:** Persian initials "JHS" **Rev. Inscription:** Takari **Mint:** Srinagar **Note:** Reduced weight, weight varies 6.60-6.80 grams. Machine struck in collar.

Date	Mintage	Good	VG	F	VF	XF
VS1927	—	11.00	27.50	45.00	62.50	95.00
VS1928	—	11.00	27.50	45.00	62.50	95.00

Y# 14 1/4 RUPEE

Silver, 15 mm. **Series:** Third Silver **Obv. Inscription:** Persian initials "JHS" **Rev. Inscription:** Takari **Mint:** Srinagar **Note:** Reduced weight, weight varies 1.65-1.70 grams.

Date	Mintage	Good	VG	F	VF	XF
VS1928	—	27.50	65.00	100	150	250

Y# 12 1/2 RUPEE

Silver **Series:** Second Silver **Obv. Inscription:** Persian initials "JHS" **Rev. Inscription:** Persian initials "JHS" **Mint:** Srinagar **Note:** Weight varies 5.15-5.40 grams.

Date	Mintage	Good	VG	F	VF	XF
VS1914	—	5.00	12.50	20.00	30.00	45.00
VS1922	—	5.00	12.50	20.00	30.00	45.00

Y# 15 1/2 RUPEE

Silver, 17 mm. **Series:** Third Silver **Obv. Inscription:** Persian initials "JHS" **Rev. Inscription:** Takari **Mint:** Srinagar **Note:** Reduced weight, weight varies 3.30-3.40 grams.

Date	Mintage	Good	VG	F	VF	XF
VS1928	—	27.50	65.00	100	150	250

Y# 16a RUPEE

Silver **Series:** Third Silver **Obv. Inscription:** Persian initials "JHS" **Rev. Inscription:** Takari **Mint:** Srinagar **Note:** Struck on machine punched planchets. Reduced weight, weight varies 6.60-6.80 grams.

Date	Mintage	Good	VG	F	VF	XF
VS1927	—	2.75	7.00	11.00	16.50	30.00
VS1928	—	2.75	7.00	11.00	16.50	30.00
VS1929	—	3.50	9.00	15.00	21.50	35.00

Y# 16b RUPEE

Silver **Series:** Third Silver **Obv. Inscription:** Persian initials "JHS" **Rev. Inscription:** Takari **Mint:** Srinagar **Note:** Struck on dump planchets. Weight varies 6.60-6.80 grams.

Date	Mintage	Good	VG	F	VF	XF
VS1929	—	3.00	7.50	12.50	18.50	32.50
VS1930	—	3.00	7.50	12.50	18.50	32.50
VS1931	—	3.00	7.50	12.50	18.50	32.50
VS1932	—	3.00	7.50	12.50	18.50	32.50

Y# 22 NAZARANA 1/4 MOHUR

2.3000 g., Gold **Series:** Fourth Silver (Chilki) **Mint:** Srinagar **Note:** Size varies 14-15mm.

Date	Mintage	Good	VG	F	VF	XF
VS193x	—	—	300	500	900	1,500

Pertab Singh
VS1942-1979 / 1885-1925AD

HAMMERED COINAGE

Y# 20 1/2 RUPEE

3.3000 g., Silver **Series:** Fourth Silver (Chilki) **Obverse:** Persian date in second line **Reverse:** Davanagari date in second line **Mint:** Srinagar

Date	Mintage	Good	VG	F	VF	XF
VS1946	—	16.00	40.00	65.00	100	150
VS1948	—	16.00	40.00	65.00	100	150
VS1950	—	16.00	40.00	65.00	100	150
VS1951	—	16.00	40.00	65.00	100	150

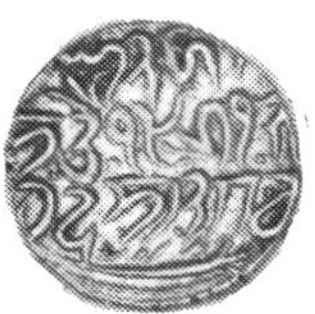

Y# 21 RUPEE

6.8000 g., Silver **Series:** Fourth Silver (Chilki) **Obverse:** Persian date in second line **Reverse:** Davanagari date in second line **Mint:** Srinagar

Date	Mintage	Good	VG	F	VF	XF
VS1931	—	5.00	12.50	18.50	25.00	40.00
VS1932	—	5.00	12.50	18.50	25.00	40.00
VS1933	—	5.00	12.50	18.50	25.00	40.00

KISHANGARH

The maharajas of Kishangarh, a small state in northwest India, in the vicinity of Ajmer, belonged to the Rathor Rajputs. The town of Kishangarh, which gave its name to the state, was founded in 1611 and was itself named after Kishen Singh, the first ruler. The maharajas succeeded in reaching terms with Akbar in the late 16th century, and again in 1818 with the British. In 1949 the state was merged into Rajasthan.

RULERS

Kalyan Singh, VS1854-1889/1797-1832AD
Mokham Singh, VS1889-1898/1832-1841AD
Prithvi Singh, VS1898-1936/1841-1879AD
Sardul Singh, VS1936-1957/1879-1900AD

MINT

Kishangarh

MINT MARK:

Symbol on reverse: Jhar

HAMMERED COINAGE

Mughal Style

C# 24 1/2 PAISA

Copper **Obv. Inscription:** "Muhammad Akbar II" **Mint:** Kishangarh

Date	Mintage	Good	VG	F	VF	XF
ND(1806-37)	—	1.50	2.25	3.50	6.50	—

C# 5 TAKKA

Copper **Obv. Inscription:** "Muhammad Akbar II" **Mint:** Kishangarh **Note:** Crude copy of Jaipur 1 Paisa, KM#39. Weight varies 17.25-17.50 grams.

Date	Mintage	Good	VG	F	VF	XF
ND(1806-37)	—	1.25	1.75	2.50	5.00	—
ND//7 (1812-13)	—	1.25	1.75	2.50	5.00	—

C# 25 TAKKA

Copper **Obv. Inscription:** "Muhammad Akbar II" **Mint:** Kishangarh **Note:** Crude copy of Jaipur, C#47. Weight vaires 17.25-17.50 grams.

Date	Mintage	Good	VG	F	VF	XF
ND(1806-37)	—	1.00	1.50	2.50	5.00	—

HAMMERED COINAGE

Regal Style

1858-1879

Y# 1.1 RUPEE

Silver **Obv. Inscription:** "Victoria Inglistan..." **Rev. Inscription:** "Prithvi Singh" **Mint:** Kishangarh **Note:** Weight varies 10.70-10.85 grams.

Date	Mintage	Good	VG	F	VF	XF
1858//24	—	4.00	10.00	17.50	23.50	32.50

Y# 1.2 RUPEE

Silver **Obv. Inscription:** "Victoria Luglistan..." **Rev. Inscription:** "Prithvi Singh" **Mint:** Kishangarh **Note:** Weight varies 10.70-10.85 grams.

Date	Mintage	VG	F	VF	XF	Unc
1859//24 (1859)	—	10.00	17.50	23.50	32.50	—

Y# B2 NAZARANA 2-1/4 RUPEE

24.3300 g., Silver **Obv. Inscription:** "Victoria Inglistan..." **Rev. Inscription:** "Prithvi Singh" **Mint:** Kishangarh

Date	Mintage	Good	VG	F	VF	XF
1859//24 Rare	—	—	—	—	—	—

Y# A1 MOHUR

10.9000 g., Gold **Obv. Inscription:** "Victoria Inglistan..." **Rev. Inscription:** "Prithvi Singh" **Mint:** Kishangarh

Date	Mintage	Good	VG	F	VF	XF
1858//24	—	—	—	—	—	—

HAMMERED COINAGE

Regal Style

1879-1900

Y# A2 1/2 RUPEE

5.4000 g., Silver **Obv. Inscription:** "Qaisar-i-Hind" **Rev. Inscription:** "Sardul Singh/Bahadur..." **Mint:** Kishangarh

Date	Mintage	Good	VG	F	VF	XF
1880	—	16.00	40.00	65.00	100	145

Y# 2 RUPEE

10.8000 g., Silver **Obv. Inscription:** "Qaisar-i-Hind" **Rev. Inscription:** "Sardul Singh/Bahadur..." **Mint:** Kishangarh

Date	Mintage	Good	VG	F	VF	XF
1880//24	—	6.00	15.00	25.00	35.00	50.00

HAMMERED COINAGE

Regal Style

1900-1926

Y# A3 1/2 RUPEE

5.4000 g., Silver **Obv. Inscription:** Empress Victoria... **Reverse:** Jhar **Rev. Inscription:** Madan Singh...

Date	Mintage	Good	VG	F	VF	XF
ND(1900-01)	—	20.00	40.00	65.00	100	145

Y# C3 RUPEE

10.8000 g., Silver **Obv. Inscription:** Empress Victoria... **Reverse:** Jhar **Rev. Inscription:** Madan Singh...

Date	Mintage	Good	VG	F	VF	XF
ND(1900-01)	—	—	—	—	—	—

Y# D3 MOHUR

10.9000 g., Gold **Obv. Inscription:** Empress Victoria... **Reverse:** Jhar **Rev. Inscription:** Madan Singh...

Date	Mintage	Good	VG	F	VF	XF
ND(1900-01)	—	100	200	300	550	900

KOLHAPUR

Maratha state in southwest India between Goa and Bombay.

The maharajas of Kolhapur traced their origins and ancestry to Raja Ram, son of Shivaji, the founder of the Maratha kingdom, and to his courageous wife Tarabai who officiated as regent on behalf of her son after Raja Ram's death in 1698. Kolhapur's existence as a separate state dates from about 1730 when a family quarrel left Sambaji, the great-grandson of Sivaji, as the first raja of Kolhapur. In recognition of their special eminence among the Maratha chieftains the rulers of Kolhapur bore the honorific title of "Chhatrapati Maharaja". Between 1811 and 1862 Kolhapur concluded a series of treaties and agreements with the British whereby the state came increasingly under British protection and control.

The mint closed ca. 1850AD.

MINT

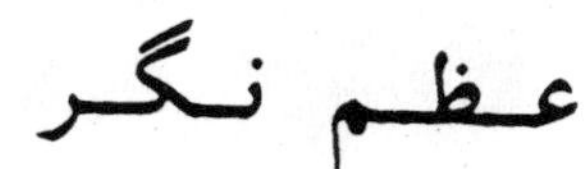

Mintname: A'zamnagar Gokak, Pseudo

HAMMERED COINAGE

Mughal Style

C# 14 1/4 RUPEE

Silver, 12 mm. **Obv. Inscription:** "Muhammad Shah" **Note:** Weight varies 2.68-2.90 grams.

Date	Mintage	Good	VG	F	VF	XF
ND(1759-1839)	—	5.00	12.50	20.00	30.00	50.00

C# 15 1/2 RUPEE

Silver, 15 mm. **Obv. Inscription:** "Muhammad Shah" **Note:** Weight varies 5.35-5.80 grams.

Date	Mintage	Good	VG	F	VF	XF
ND(1759-1839)	—	5.00	12.50	20.00	30.00	50.00

C# 24 1/2 RUPEE

Silver **Obv. Inscription:** "Muhammad Shah" **Note:** Weight varies 5.35-5.80 grams.

Date	Mintage	Good	VG	F	VF	XF
1821	—	18.00	45.00	75.00	120	175

C# 16 RUPEE

Silver **Obv. Inscription:** "Muhammad Shah" **Note:** Weight varies 10.70-11.60 grams.

Date	Mintage	Good	VG	F	VF	XF
ND(1759-1839)	—	3.50	9.00	15.00	25.00	42.50

C# 25 RUPEE

Silver **Obv. Inscription:** "Muhammad Shah" **Note:** Weight varies 10.70-11.60 grams.

Date	Mintage	Good	VG	F	VF	XF
1821	—	6.00	15.00	25.00	40.00	65.00

HAMMERED COINAGE

Regal Style

C# 29 1/2 RUPEE

Silver **Issuer:** East India Company **Note:** Local issue from Shahupur; weight varies: 5.35 - 5.8 grams.

Date	Mintage	VG	F	VF	XF	Unc
1821	—	45.00	75.00	120	175	—

C# 30 RUPEE

Silver **Note:** Local issue from Shahupur; weight varies: 10.7 - 11.6 grams.

Date	Mintage	VG	F	VF	XF	Unc
1821	—	16.50	26.50	37.50	55.00	—

KOTAH

Kotah State, located in northwest India was subdivided out of Bundi early in the 17th century when it was given to a younger son of the Bundi raja by the Mughal emperor. The ruler, or maharao, was a Chauhan Rajput. During the years of Maratha ascendancy Kotah fell on hard times, especially from the depredations of Holkar. In 1817 the State came under treaty with the British.

RULERS

Ram Singh II,
VS1885-1923/1828-1866AD
Chattar Singh,
VS1923-1946/1866-1889AD
Umed Singh II,
VS1946-1992/1889-1935AD

MINT

نندگانو

Mint name: *Nandgaon*

نندگانو عرف کوته

Kotah urf Nandgaon
or Nandgaon urf Kotah on earliest issues.

MINT MARKS

1.

2.

3.

4.

5.

Mint mark #1 appears beneath #4 on most Kotah coins, and serves to distinguish coins of Kotah from similar issues of Bundi in the pre-Victoria period.

C#28 has mint mark #2 on obv., #1, 3 and 4 on rev. All later issues have #1 on obv., #1, 5 and 4 on rev.

HAMMERED COINAGE

Mughal Style

C# 20 TAKKA

Copper **Obv. Inscription:** "Shah Alam II" **Note:** Weight varies 17.5-18.5 grams.

Date	Mintage	Good	VG	F	VF	XF
ND//46 (1801)	—	3.00	4.00	5.50	8.00	—

C# 29 TAKKA

Copper **Obv. Inscription:** "Muhammad Akbar (II)" **Reverse:** With mintmark #4 and #5 **Note:** Weight varies 17.00-18.00 grams, shape: square.

Date	Mintage	Good	VG	F	VF	XF
ND//4 (1809-10)	—	1.50	2.50	4.50	7.00	—
ND//5 (1810-11)	—	1.50	2.50	4.50	7.00	—
ND//6 (1811-12)	—	1.50	2.50	4.50	7.00	—
ND//7 (1812-13)	—	1.50	2.50	4.50	7.00	—
ND//8 (1813-14)	—	1.50	2.50	4.50	7.00	—
ND//10 (1815-16)	—	1.50	2.50	4.50	7.00	—
ND//11 (1816-17)	—	1.50	2.50	4.50	7.00	—
ND//12 (1817-18)	—	1.50	2.50	4.50	7.00	—
ND//13 (1818-19)	—	1.50	2.50	4.50	7.00	—
ND//14 (1819-20)	—	1.50	2.50	4.50	7.00	—
ND//15 (1820-21)	—	1.50	2.50	4.50	7.00	—
ND//16 (1821-22)	—	1.50	2.50	4.50	7.00	—
ND//17 (1822-23)	—	1.50	2.50	4.50	7.00	—
ND//18 (1823-24)	—	1.50	2.50	4.50	7.00	—
ND//24 (1829-30)	—	1.50	2.50	4.50	7.00	—
ND//25 (1830-31)	—	1.50	2.50	4.50	7.00	—
ND//26 (1831-32)	—	1.50	2.50	4.50	7.00	—
ND//27 (1832-33)	—	1.50	2.50	4.50	7.00	—
ND//28 (1833-34)	—	1.50	2.50	4.50	7.00	—
ND//29 (1834-35)	—	1.50	2.50	4.50	7.00	—
ND//30 (1835-36)	—	1.50	2.50	4.50	7.00	—
ND//33 (1838)	—	1.50	2.50	4.50	7.00	—

C# 29c 1/4 RUPEE

2.8000 g., Silver **Obverse:** With #1 mint mark **Obv. Inscription:** "Muhammad Ahbar II"

Date	Mintage	Good	VG	F	VF	XF
ND//23 (1828-29)	—	6.00	15.00	25.00	40.00	60.00

C# A31 1/4 RUPEE

2.8000 g., Silver, 12 mm. **Obv. Inscription:** "Muhammad Akbar II"

Date	Mintage	Good	VG	F	VF	XF
ND//4 (1840-41)	—	10.00	25.00	40.00	60.00	85.00
ND//16 (1852-53)	—	10.00	25.00	40.00	60.00	85.00

C# 30 RUPEE

Silver **Obverse:** Without mint mark #1 **Obv. Inscription:** "Muhammad Ahbar II" **Note:** Weight varies 11.20-11.25 grams.

Date	Mintage	Good	VG	F	VF	XF
ND//1	—	2.50	6.50	10.00	15.00	22.50
ND//3 (1808-09)	—	2.50	6.50	10.00	15.00	22.50

C# 28.3 RUPEE

Silver **Obv. Inscription:** "Shah Alam II" **Reverse:** Flower mint mark in front of regnal year **Mint:** Nandgaon **Note:** Weight varies 11.05-11.20 grams.

Date	Mintage	Good	VG	F	VF	XF
ND//42 (1800-01)	—	3.50	8.50	13.50	20.00	28.50
ND//43 (1801-02)	—	3.50	8.50	13.50	20.00	28.50
ND//44 (1802-03)	—	3.50	8.50	13.50	20.00	28.50
ND//45 (1803-04)	—	3.50	8.50	13.50	20.00	28.50
ND//46 (1804-05)	—	3.50	8.50	13.50	20.00	28.50
ND//47 (1805)	—	3.50	8.50	13.50	20.00	28.50

C# 30c RUPEE

Silver **Obverse:** Without mint mark #1 **Obv. Inscription:** "Muhammad Akbar II" **Note:** Weight varies 11.20-11.25 grams.

Date	Mintage	Good	VG	F	VF	XF
ND//9 (1814-15)	—	2.50	6.50	10.00	15.00	22.50
ND//12 (1817-18)	—	2.50	6.50	10.00	15.00	22.50
ND//13 (1818-19)	—	2.50	6.50	10.00	15.00	22.50
ND//15 (1820-21)	—	2.50	6.50	10.00	15.00	22.50
ND//16 (1821-22)	—	2.50	6.50	10.00	15.00	22.50
ND//18 (1823-24)	—	2.50	6.50	10.00	15.00	22.50
ND//20 (1825-26)	—	2.50	6.50	10.00	15.00	22.50
ND//22 (1827-28)	—	2.50	6.50	10.00	15.00	22.50
ND//23 (1828-29)	—	2.50	6.50	10.00	15.00	22.50
ND//24 (1829-30)	—	2.50	6.50	10.00	15.00	22.50
ND//28 (1833-34)	—	2.50	6.50	10.00	15.00	22.50
ND//30 (1835-36)	—	2.50	6.50	10.00	15.00	22.50
ND//31 (1836-37)	—	2.50	6.50	10.00	15.00	22.50
ND//32 (1837-38)	—	2.50	6.50	10.00	15.00	22.50
AH1252//29 (sic)	—	2.50	6.50	10.00	15.00	22.50

C# 32 RUPEE

Silver **Obv. Inscription:** "Muhammad Akbar II" **Note:** Weight varies 11.00-11.25 grams.

Date	Mintage	Good	VG	F	VF	XF
ND//1 (1837-38)	—	2.25	5.50	9.00	13.50	20.00
ND//3 (1839-40)	—	2.25	5.50	9.00	13.50	20.00
ND//4 (1840-41)	—	2.25	5.50	9.00	13.50	20.00
ND//5 (1841-42)	—	2.25	5.50	9.00	13.50	20.00
ND//6 (1842-43)	—	2.25	5.50	9.00	13.50	20.00
ND//7 (1843-44)	—	2.25	5.50	9.00	13.50	20.00
ND//8 (1844-45)	—	2.25	5.50	9.00	13.50	20.00
ND//9 (1845-46)	—	2.25	5.50	9.00	13.50	20.00
ND//11 (1847-48)	—	2.25	5.50	9.00	13.50	20.00
ND//12 (1848-49)	—	2.25	5.50	9.00	13.50	20.00
ND//13 (1849-50)	—	2.25	5.50	9.00	13.50	20.00
ND//15 (1851-52)	—	2.25	5.50	9.00	13.50	20.00
ND//16 (1852-53)	—	2.25	5.50	9.00	13.50	20.00
ND//17 (1853-54)	—	2.25	5.50	9.00	13.50	20.00
ND//18 (1854-55)	—	2.25	5.50	9.00	13.50	20.00
ND//19 (1855-56)	—	2.25	5.50	9.00	13.50	20.00
ND//20 (1856-57)	—	2.25	5.50	9.00	13.50	20.00
ND//21 (1857)	—	2.25	5.50	9.00	13.50	20.00

C# 30a NAZARANA RUPEE

Silver **Obverse:** Without mint mark #1 **Obv. Inscription:** "Muhammad Akbar (II)" **Shape:** Square **Note:** Weight varies 11.20-11.30 grams.

Date	Mintage	Good	VG	F	VF	XF
ND//5 (1810-11)	—	30.00	60.00	10.00	150	220

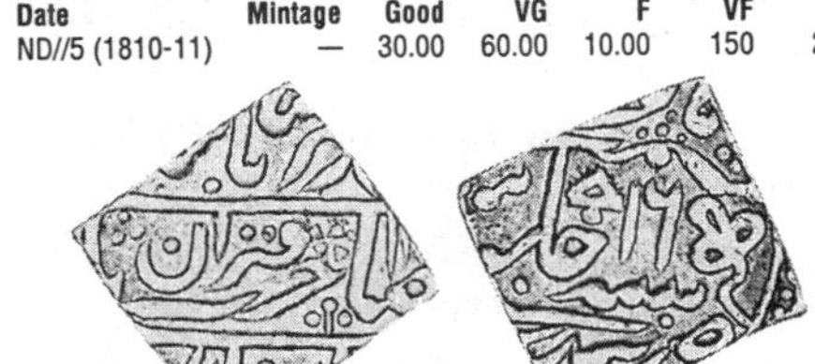

C# 30d NAZARANA RUPEE

Silver **Obverse:** Without mint mark #1 **Obv. Inscription:** "Muhammad Akbar II" **Shape:** Square **Note:** Weight varies 11.20-11.30 grams.

Date	Mintage	Good	VG	F	VF	XF
ND//11 (1816-17)	—	30.00	30.00	100	150	220
ND//16 (1821-22)	—	30.00	30.00	100	150	220
ND//18 (1823-24)	—	32.50	65.00	100	150	220
ND//19 (1824-25)	—	32.50	65.00	100	150	220
ND//22 (1827-28)	—	32.50	65.00	100	150	220
ND//23 (1828-29)	—	32.50	65.00	100	150	220
ND//24 (1829-30)	—	32.50	65.00	100	150	220
ND//27 (1832-33)	—	32.50	65.00	100	150	220

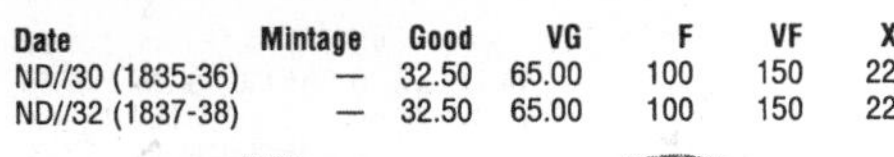

Date	Mintage	Good	VG	F	VF	XF
ND//30 (1835-36)	—	32.50	65.00	100	150	220
ND//32 (1837-38)	—	32.50	65.00	100	150	220

C# 30b NAZARANA RUPEE

Silver **Obverse:** Without mint mark #1 **Obv. Inscription:** "Muhammad Akbar II" **Shape:** Round **Note:** Size varies 27-33mm. Listed under Bundi State.

Date	Mintage	Good	VG	F	VF	XF
AH1237//16	—	32.50	65.00	100	150	220
AH1239//18	—	32.50	65.00	100	150	220
AH1240//19	—	32.50	65.00	100	150	220
AH1242//22	—	32.50	65.00	100	150	220
AH1245//24	—	32.50	65.00	100	150	220
AH124x//30	—	32.50	65.00	100	150	220
AH125x//32	—	32.50	65.00	100	150	220

C# 32a NAZARANA RUPEE

11.2000 g., Silver **Obv. Inscription:** "Muhammad Akbar II" **Shape:** Round.

Date	Mintage	Good	VG	F	VF	XF
ND//1	—	13.50	27.50	45.00	62.50	85.00
ND//2 (1838-39)	—	13.50	27.50	45.00	62.50	85.00
ND//3 (1839-40)	—	13.50	27.50	45.00	62.50	85.00
ND//4 (1840-41)	—	13.50	27.50	45.00	62.50	85.00
ND//5 (1841-42)	—	13.50	27.50	45.00	62.50	85.00
ND//6 (1842-43)	—	13.50	27.50	45.00	62.50	85.00
ND//7 (1843-44)	—	13.50	27.50	45.00	62.50	85.00
ND//8 (1844-45)	—	13.50	27.50	45.00	62.50	85.00
ND//9 (1945-46)	—	13.50	27.50	45.00	62.50	85.00
ND//10 (1846-47)	—	13.50	27.50	45.00	62.50	85.00
ND//11 (1847-48)	—	13.50	27.50	45.00	62.50	85.00
ND//12 (1848-49)	—	13.50	27.50	45.00	62.50	85.00
ND//13 (1849-50)	—	13.50	27.50	45.00	62.50	85.00
ND//14 (1850-51)	—	13.50	27.50	45.00	62.50	85.00
ND//15 (1851-52)	—	13.50	27.50	45.00	62.50	85.00
ND//16 (1852-53)	—	13.50	27.50	45.00	62.50	85.00
ND//17 (1853-54)	—	13.50	27.50	45.00	62.50	85.00
ND//18 (1854-55)	—	13.50	27.50	45.00	62.50	85.00
ND//19 (1855-56)	—	13.50	27.50	45.00	62.50	85.00
ND//20 (1856-57)	—	13.50	27.50	45.00	62.50	85.00
ND//21 (1857-58)	—	13.50	27.50	45.00	62.50	85.00
ND//22 (1858)	—	13.50	27.50	45.00	62.50	85.00

C# 32b NAZARANA RUPEE

11.2000 g., Silver **Obv. Inscription:** "Muhammad Akbar II" **Shape:** Square **Note:** All specimens show rudimentary traces of AH dates on obverse.

Date	Mintage	Good	VG	F	VF	XF
ND//11 (1847-48)	—	20.00	40.00	70.00	100	145

C# 30e MOHUR

10.7000 g., Gold **Obverse:** Without mint mark #1 **Obv. Inscription:** "Muhammad Akbar II"

Date	Mintage	Good	VG	F	VF	XF
ND//2 (1807-08)	—	—	200	350	500	700

C# 30f MOHUR

10.7000 g., Gold **Obverse:** Without mint mark #1 **Obv. Inscription:** "Muhammad Akbar II"

Date	Mintage	Good	VG	F	VF	XF
ND//19 (1824-25)	—	—	200	350	500	700

C# 33 MOHUR

11.2000 g., Gold, 19 mm. **Obv. Inscription:** "Muhammad Akbar II" **Note:** Weight varies 10.70-11.40 grams.

Date	Mintage	Good	VG	F	VF	XF
ND//1 (1837-38)	—	—	185	300	550	850
ND//19 (1855-56)	—	—	185	300	550	850
ND//20 (1856-57)	—	—	185	300	550	850
ND//21 (1857)	—	—	185	300	550	850

HAMMERED COINAGE

Regal Style

Y# 1 PAISA

Copper **Obv. Inscription:** "Badshah Zaman Inglistan...(Victoria)" **Note:** Weight varies 9.00-12.00 grams, size varies 12-16mm.

Date	Mintage	Good	VG	F	VF	XF
ND//37 (1894)	—	1.50	2.50	3.75	6.00	—
ND//38 (1895)	—	1.50	2.50	3.75	6.00	—
ND//39 (1896)	—	1.50	2.50	3.75	6.00	—
ND//40 (1897)	—	1.50	2.50	3.75	6.00	—

Y# 2 TAKKA

Copper **Obv. Inscription:** "Badshah Zaman Inglistan... (Victoria)" **Note:** Weight varies 16.80-18.00 grams, size varies 15-20mm.

Date	Mintage	Good	VG	F	VF	XF
ND//1 (1858)	—	1.25	2.00	3.25	5.00	—
ND//2 (1859)	—	1.25	2.00	3.25	5.00	—
ND//6 (1863)	—	1.25	2.00	3.25	5.00	—
ND//8 (1865)	—	1.25	2.00	3.25	5.00	—
ND//24 (1881)	—	1.25	2.00	3.25	5.00	—
ND//27 (1884)	—	1.25	2.00	3.25	5.00	—
ND//28 (1885)	—	1.25	2.00	3.25	5.00	—
ND//29 (1886)	—	1.25	2.00	3.25	5.00	—
ND//30 (1887)	—	1.25	2.00	3.25	5.00	—
ND//31 (1888)	—	1.25	2.00	3.25	5.00	—
ND//32 (1889)	—	1.25	2.00	3.25	5.00	—
ND//35 (1892)	—	1.25	2.00	3.25	5.00	—
ND//37 (1894)	—	1.25	2.00	3.25	5.00	—
ND//38 (1895)	—	1.25	2.00	3.25	5.00	—
ND//39 (1896)	—	1.25	2.00	3.25	5.00	—
ND//40 (1897)	—	1.25	2.00	3.25	5.00	—
ND//41 (1898)	—	1.25	2.00	3.25	5.00	—

Y# 2a NAZARANA TAKKA

18.0000 g., Copper **Obv. Inscription:** "Badshah Zaman Inglistan... (Victoria)" **Shape:** Square

Date	Mintage	Good	VG	F	VF	XF
ND//15 (1872)	—	—	—	—	—	—

Y# 3 1/8 RUPEE

1.4000 g., Silver **Obv. Inscription:** "Badshah Zaman Inglistan... (Victoria)"

Date	Mintage	Good	VG	F	VF	XF
ND//22 (1879)	—	2.00	5.00	7.00	10.00	15.00
ND//27 (1884)	—	2.00	5.00	7.00	10.00	15.00
ND//29 (1886)	—	2.00	5.00	7.00	10.00	15.00
ND//30 (1887)	—	2.00	5.00	7.00	10.00	15.00
ND//31 (1888)	—	2.00	5.00	7.00	10.00	15.00
ND//32 (1889)	—	2.00	5.00	7.00	10.00	15.00
ND//33 (1890)	—	2.00	5.00	7.00	10.00	15.00
ND//34 (1891)	—	2.00	5.00	7.00	10.00	15.00
ND//36 (1893)	—	2.00	5.00	7.00	10.00	15.00
ND//37 (1894)	—	2.00	5.00	7.00	10.00	15.00
ND//38 (1895)	—	2.00	5.00	7.00	10.00	15.00

Y# 4 1/4 RUPEE

2.8000 g., Silver **Obv. Inscription:** "Badshah Zaman Inglistan... (Victoria)"

Date	Mintage	Good	VG	F	VF	XF
ND//1 (1858)	—	1.65	4.00	6.00	9.00	14.00
ND//2 (1859)	—	1.65	4.00	6.00	9.00	14.00
ND//5 (1862)	—	1.65	4.00	6.00	9.00	14.00
ND//8 (1865)	—	1.65	4.00	6.00	9.00	14.00
ND//10 (1867)	—	1.65	4.00	6.00	9.00	14.00
ND//22 (1879)	—	1.65	4.00	6.00	9.00	14.00
ND//23 (1880)	—	1.65	4.00	6.00	9.00	14.00
ND//26 (1883)	—	1.65	4.00	6.00	9.00	14.00
ND//27 (1884)	—	1.65	4.00	6.00	9.00	14.00
ND//29 (1886)	—	1.65	4.00	6.00	9.00	14.00
ND//30 (1887)	—	1.65	4.00	6.00	9.00	14.00
ND//31 (1888)	—	1.65	4.00	6.00	9.00	14.00
ND//32 (1889)	—	1.65	4.00	6.00	9.00	14.00
ND//33 (1890)	—	1.65	4.00	6.00	9.00	14.00
ND//35 (1891)	—	1.65	4.00	6.00	9.00	14.00
ND//37 (1894)	—	1.65	4.00	6.00	9.00	14.00
ND//38 (1895)	—	1.65	4.00	6.00	9.00	14.00

Y# 5 1/2 RUPEE

5.6000 g., Silver

Date	Mintage	Good	VG	F	VF	XF
ND//1 (1858)	—	2.25	5.50	8.00	12.50	18.50
ND//4 (1861)	—	2.25	5.50	8.00	12.50	18.50
ND//8 (1865)	—	2.25	5.50	8.00	12.50	18.50
ND//18 (1875)	—	2.25	5.50	8.00	12.50	18.50

Date	Mintage	Good	VG	F	VF	XF
ND//22 (1879)	—	2.25	5.50	8.00	12.50	18.50
ND//24 (1881)	—	2.25	5.50	8.00	12.50	18.50
ND//25 (1882)	—	2.25	5.50	8.00	12.50	18.50
ND//27 (1884)	—	2.25	5.50	8.00	12.50	18.50
ND//28 (1885)	—	2.25	5.50	8.00	12.50	18.50
ND//29 (1886)	—	2.25	5.50	8.00	12.50	18.50
ND//30 (1887)	—	2.25	5.50	8.00	12.50	18.50
ND//31 (1888)	—	2.25	5.50	8.00	12.50	18.50
ND//32 (1889)	—	2.25	5.50	8.00	12.50	18.50
ND//33 (1890)	—	2.25	5.50	8.00	12.50	18.50
ND//34 (1891)	—	2.25	5.50	8.00	12.50	18.50
ND//35 (1892)	—	2.25	5.50	8.00	12.50	18.50
ND//36 (1893)	—	2.25	5.50	8.00	12.50	18.50
ND//37 (1894)	—	2.25	5.50	8.00	12.50	18.50
ND//38 (1895)	—	2.25	5.50	8.00	12.50	18.50

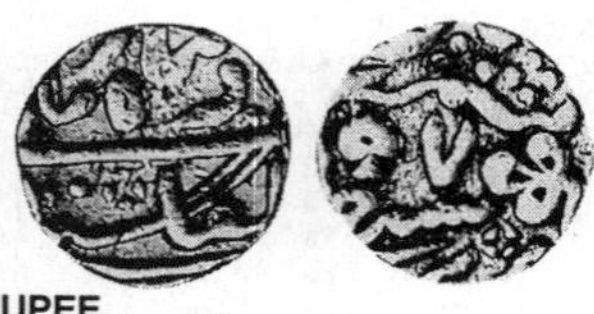

Y# 6 RUPEE

11.2000 g., Silver **Obv. Inscription:** "Badshah Zaman Inglistan... (Victoria)"

Date	Mintage	Good	VG	F	VF	XF
ND//1 (1858)	—	2.25	5.50	8.00	10.00	15.00
ND//2 (1859)	—	2.25	5.50	8.00	10.00	15.00
ND//4 (1861)	—	2.25	5.50	8.00	10.00	15.00
ND//5 (1862)	—	2.25	5.50	8.00	10.00	15.00
ND//6 (1863)	—	2.25	5.50	8.00	10.00	15.00
ND//7 (1864)	—	2.25	5.50	8.00	10.00	15.00
ND//8 (1865)	—	2.25	5.50	8.00	10.00	15.00
ND//9 (1866)	—	2.25	5.50	8.00	10.00	15.00
ND//10 (1867)	—	2.25	5.50	8.00	10.00	15.00
ND//11 (1868)	—	2.25	5.50	8.00	10.00	15.00
ND//12 (1869)	—	2.25	5.50	8.00	10.00	15.00
ND//13 (1870)	—	2.25	5.50	8.00	10.00	15.00
ND//14 (1871)	—	2.25	5.50	8.00	10.00	15.00
ND//15 (1872)	—	2.25	5.50	8.00	10.00	15.00
ND//16 (1873)	—	2.25	5.50	8.00	10.00	15.00
ND//17 (1874)	—	2.25	5.50	8.00	10.00	15.00
ND//18 (1875)	—	2.25	5.50	8.00	10.00	15.00
ND//19 (1876)	—	2.25	5.50	8.00	10.00	15.00
ND//20 (1877)	—	2.25	5.50	8.00	10.00	15.00
ND//21 (1878)	—	2.25	5.50	8.00	10.00	15.00
ND//22 (1879)	—	2.25	5.50	8.00	10.00	15.00
ND//24 (1881)	—	2.25	5.50	8.00	10.00	15.00
ND//25 (1882)	—	2.25	5.50	8.00	10.00	15.00
ND//26 (1883)	—	2.25	5.50	8.00	10.00	15.00
ND//27 (1884)	—	2.25	5.50	8.00	10.00	15.00
ND//28 (1885)	—	2.25	5.50	8.00	10.00	15.00
ND//29 (1886)	—	2.25	5.50	8.00	10.00	15.00
ND//31 (1888)	—	2.25	5.50	8.00	10.00	15.00
ND//32 (1889)	—	2.25	5.50	8.00	10.00	15.00
ND//33 (1890)	—	2.25	5.50	8.00	10.00	15.00
ND//34 (1891)	—	2.25	5.50	8.00	10.00	15.00
ND//35 (1892)	—	2.25	5.50	8.00	10.00	15.00
ND//37 (1894)	—	2.25	5.50	8.00	10.00	15.00
ND//38 (1895)	—	2.25	5.50	8.00	10.00	15.00
ND//39 (1896)	—	2.25	5.50	8.00	10.00	15.00
ND//40 (1897)	—	2.25	5.50	8.00	10.00	15.00
ND//41 (1898)	—	2.25	5.50	8.00	10.00	15.00
ND//43 (1900)	—	2.25	—	—	—	—

Y# 7 RUPEE

11.2000 g., Silver **Subject:** 10th Anniversary of Reign of Umed Singh II and 80th Birthday of Queen Victoria **Obv. Inscription:** "Badshah Zaman Inglistan... (Victoria)"

Date	Mintage	Good	VG	F	VF	XF
VS1956	—	—	17.50	25.00	35.00	50.00

Y# 6a NAZARANA RUPEE

11.2000 g., Silver **Obv. Inscription:** "Badshah Zaman Inglistan... (Victoria)"

Date	Mintage	Good	VG	F	VF	XF
ND//1 (1858)	—	16.50	32.50	45.00	62.50	85.00
ND//2 (1859)	—	16.50	32.50	45.00	62.50	85.00
ND//3 (1860)	—	16.50	32.50	45.00	62.50	85.00
ND//4 (1861)	—	16.50	32.50	45.00	62.50	85.00
ND//5 (1862)	—	16.50	32.50	45.00	62.50	85.00
ND//6 (1863)	—	16.50	32.50	45.00	62.50	85.00
ND//7 (1864)	—	16.50	32.50	45.00	62.50	85.00
ND//8 (1865)	—	16.50	32.50	45.00	62.50	85.00
ND//9 (1866)	—	16.50	32.50	45.00	62.50	85.00
ND//10 (1867)	—	16.50	32.50	45.00	62.50	85.00
ND//11 (1868)	—	16.50	32.50	45.00	62.50	85.00
ND//12 (1869)	—	16.50	32.50	45.00	62.50	85.00
ND//13 (1870)	—	16.50	32.50	45.00	62.50	85.00
ND//14 (1871)	—	16.50	32.50	45.00	62.50	85.00
ND//15 (1872)	—	16.50	32.50	45.00	62.50	85.00
ND//16 (1873)	—	16.50	32.50	45.00	62.50	85.00
ND//17 (1874)	—	16.50	32.50	45.00	62.50	85.00
ND//18 (1875)	—	16.50	32.50	45.00	62.50	85.00
ND//19 (1876)	—	16.50	32.50	45.00	62.50	85.00
ND//20 (1877)	—	16.50	32.50	45.00	62.50	85.00
ND//21 (1878)	—	16.50	32.50	45.00	62.50	85.00
ND//22 (1879)	—	16.50	32.50	45.00	62.50	85.00
ND//23 (1880)	—	16.50	32.50	45.00	62.50	85.00
ND//24 (1881)	—	16.50	32.50	45.00	62.50	85.00
ND//25 (1882)	—	16.50	32.50	45.00	62.50	85.00
ND//26 (1883)	—	16.50	32.50	45.00	62.50	85.00
ND//27 (1884)	—	16.50	32.50	45.00	62.50	85.00
ND//28 (1885)	—	16.50	32.50	45.00	62.50	85.00
ND//29 (1886)	—	16.50	32.50	45.00	62.50	85.00
ND//30 (1887)	—	16.50	32.50	45.00	62.50	85.00
ND//31 (1888)	—	16.50	32.50	45.00	62.50	85.00
ND//32 (1889)	—	16.50	32.50	45.00	62.50	85.00
ND//39 (1896)	—	16.50	32.50	45.00	62.50	85.00
ND//43 (1900)	—	16.50	32.50	45.00	62.50	85.00

Y# 6b NAZARANA RUPEE

11.2000 g., Silver **Obv. Inscription:** "Badshah Zaman Inglistan... (Victoria)" **Note:** Shape: square.

Date	Mintage	Good	VG	F	VF	XF
ND//15 (1872)	—	—	—	—	—	—
ND//16 (1873)	—	—	—	—	—	—

Y# 7a NAZARANA RUPEE

11.2000 g., Silver **Subject:** 10th Anniversary of Reign of Umed Singh II and 80th Birthday of Queen Victoria **Obv. Inscription:** "Badshah Zaman Inglistan... (Victoria)"

Date	Mintage	Good	VG	F	VF	XF
VS1956	—	—	100	175	250	350

Y# A8a 1/8 MOHUR

1.3400 g., Gold **Subject:** 10th Anniversary of Reign of Umed Singh II and 80th Birthday of Queen Victoria **Obv. Inscription:** "Badshah Zaman Inglistan... (Victoria)"

Date	Mintage	Good	VG	F	VF	XF
VS(19)56	—	—	185	300	500	800

Y# C8 1/2 MOHUR

5.3500 g., Gold **Obv. Inscription:** "Badshah Zaman Inglistan... (Victoria)"

Date	Mintage	Good	VG	F	VF	XF
ND//42 (1899)	—	—	150	275	400	650

Y# 8 MOHUR

10.7000 g., Gold **Obv. Inscription:** "Badshah Zaman Inglistan... (Victoria)"

Date	Mintage	Good	VG	F	VF	XF
ND//1 (1858)	—	—	175	250	400	600
ND//6 (1863)	—	—	175	250	400	600
ND//8 (1865)	—	—	175	250	400	600
ND//9 (1866)	—	—	175	250	400	600
ND//15 (1872)	—	—	175	250	400	600
ND//31 (1888)	—	—	175	250	400	600
ND//32 (1889)	—	—	175	250	400	600

KUTCH

State located in northwest India, consisting of a peninsula north of the Gulf of Kutch.

The rulers of Kutch were Jareja Rajputs who, coming from Tatta in Sind, conquered Kutch in the 14th or 15th centuries. The capital city of Bhuj is thought to date from the mid-16th century. In 1617, after Akbar's conquest of Gujerat and the fall of the Gujerat sultans, the Kutch ruler, Rao Bharmal I (1586-1632) visited Jahangir and established a relationship which was sufficiently warm as to leave Kutch virtually independent throughout the Mughal period. Early in the 19th century internal disorder and the existence of rival claimants to the throne resulted in British intrusion into the state's affairs. Rao Bharmalji II was deposed in favor of Rao Desalji II who proved much more amenable to the Government of India's wishes. He and his successors continued to rule in a manner considered by the British to be most enlightened and, as a result, Maharao Khengarji III was created a Knight Grand Commander of the Indian Empire. In view of its geographical isolation Kutch came under the direct control of the Central Government at India's independence.

First coinage was struck in 1617AD.

RULERS

Rayadhanji II, AH1192-1230/1778-1814AD

राउ श्री रायधणजी

Ra-o Sri Ra-y(a)-dh(a)-n-ji

Bharmalji II, AH1230-1235/1814-1819AD

राउ श्री भारमलजी

Ra-o Sri Bha-r-m(a)-l-ji

Desalji II, AH1235-1277/VS1876-1917/1819-1860AD

राउ श्री देसलजी

Ra-o Sri De-sa-l-ji

Pragmalji II, VS1917-1932/1860-1875AD

राउ श्री प्रागमलजी

Ra-o Sri Pra-g-m(a)-l-ji

राउ श्री प्रागमलजी

M(a)-ha-ra-o Sri Pra-g-m(a)-l-ji

मदाराउ श्री प्रागमलजी

Ma-ha-ra-ja Dhi-ra-j Mi-r-ja M(a)-ha-ra-o Sri

मादाराजाधिराजमिरजा मदाराउ श्री

Pra-g-m(a)-l-ji B(a)-ha-du-r

Khengarji III, VS1932-1999/1875-1942AD

मदाराओ श्री खेंगारजी

M(a)-ha-ra-o Sri Khen-ga-r-ji

मादाराउ खेंगारजी

Ma-ha-ra-o Khen-ga-r-ji

मादाराजाधिराज मिरजा मदाराओ श्री

Ma-ha-ra-ja Dhi-ra-j Mi-r-ja M(a)-ha-ra-o Sri

खेंगारजी बहादुर कछभुज

Khen-ga-r-ji B(a)-ha-du-r K(a)-chh-bhu-j

मिरजा महाराओ श्री खेंगारजी

Mi-r-jan M(a)-ha-ra-o Sri Khen-ga-r-ji

मदाराओं श्री खेंगारजी

M(a)-ha-ra-o Sri Khen-ga-r-ji

मदाराजाधिराज मिरजा मदाराउ

M(a)-ha-ra-ja Dhi-ra-j Mi-r-jan M(a)-ha-ra-o

श्री खेंगारजी बहादुर

Sri-Khen-ga-r-ji B(a)-ha-du-r

श्री खेंगारजी सवाई बहादुर

Sri Khen-ga-r-ji Sa-va-i B(a)-ha-du-r

मदाराउ श्री खेंगारजी कछभुज

M(a)-ha-ra-o Sri Khen-ga-r-ji K(a)-chchh-bhu-j

MINT

Bhuj (Devanagari) (Persian)

MONETARY SYSTEM

1/2 Trambiyo = 1 Babukiya
2 Tramiyo = 1 Dokda
3 Trambiyo = 1 Dhinglo
2 Dhinglo = 1 Dhabu
2 Dhabu = 1 Payalo

2 Payalo = 1 Adlinao
2 Adlina = 1 Kori

NOTE: All coins through Bharmalji II bear a common type, derived from the Gujarati coinage of Muzaffar III (late 16th century AD), and bear a stylized form of the date AH978 (1570AD). The silver issues of Bharmalji II also have the fictitious date AH1165. The rulers name appears in the Devanagri script on the obverse.

NOTE: Br#'s are in reference to *Coinage of Kutch* by Richard K. Bright.

KINGDOM

HAMMERED COINAGE

Third Series

C# 45 TRAMBIYO

4.1000 g., Copper **Obv:** Persian legend **Obv. Inscription:** "Muhammad Akbar II" **Rev:** Devanagari legend below Persian mint-name on copper, date below Devanagari legend on silver

Date	Good	VG	F	VF	XF
ND(1806-37)	1.00	1.50	2.50	4.50	—

Bharmalji II

AH1230-1235 / 1814-1819AD

HAMMERED COINAGE

C# 31 TRAMBIYO

4.0000 g., Copper

Date	Good	VG	F	VF	XF
ND(1814-19)	2.50	4.00	5.50	8.00	—

C# 33 DHINGLO

12.5000 g., Copper, 17 mm.

Date	Good	VG	F	VF	XF
ND(1814-19)	3.00	4.50	6.00	9.00	—

C# 32 DOKDA

7.5000 g., Copper, 16 mm.

Date	Good	VG	F	VF	XF
ND(1814-19)	2.50	4.00	5.50	8.00	—

C# 35 1/2 KORI

2.1000 g., Silver

Date	Good	VG	F	VF	XF
AH1165	1.35	3.50	5.00	7.50	12.50

C# 36 KORI

4.4000 g., Silver

Date	Good	VG	F	VF	XF
AH1165	1.25	3.00	4.50	6.50	10.00

Desalji II

AH1234-1277 / VS1875-1917 / 1818-1860AD

The coins of Desalji II may be divided into four basic series, which may be differentiated as follows:

FIRST SERIES: Similar to coins of Bharmalji, but w/Desalji's name in Devanagari on reverse.

SECOND SERIES: In the name of the Mughal Emperor Akbar II and of Desalji in Devanagari on obverse, mint and both dates in Persian leg. On reverse but actual SE date in Devangari numerals. AH date is frozen (12)34, SE dates 1875-1887.

THIRD SERIES: Obv: Persian legend, rev: in Devanagari script. Dates: AH1250-1266, VS1892-1904. Many sub-varieties of type, some w/only AH dates, some w/only SE dates, some w/both. In the name of Muhammad Akbar II.

FOURTH SERIES: Same as third series, but in the name of Bahadur II. VS1909-1916 on silver and gold issues and AH1267-1274 on copper.

NOTE: Although Muhammad Akbar II was succeeded by Bahadur II on the Mughal throne in AH1253, the change is not acknowledged on Kutch coinage until AH1263 and Bahadur Shah is honored until VS1916/1859AD, the year after he was deposed by the British following the mutiny.

HAMMERED COINAGE

C# 38 TRAMBIYO

Copper **Note:** Weight varies: 3.80-4.20 grams.

Date	Good	VG	F	VF	XF
ND(1818-60)	1.00	1.50	2.50	4.50	—

C# 40 DHINGLO

Copper, 18 mm. **Note:** Weight varies: 12.00-12.60 grams.

Date	Good	VG	F	VF	XF
ND(1818-60)	1.25	2.00	3.00	5.00	—

C# 39 DOKDA

Copper **Note:** Weight varies: 8.00-8.30 grams.

Date	Good	VG	F	VF	XF
ND(1818-60)	1.00	1.50	2.50	4.50	—

C# 52 1/2 KORI

Silver **Obv:** Persian legend with Devanagari name below **Obv. Inscription:** "Muhammad Akbar II" **Rev:** Persian legend **Note:** Weight varies: 2.10-2.2 grams. The frozen date AH1234 on this series is the accession date of Desalji II. Varieties exist.

Date	Good	VG	F	VF	XF
AH1234//VS1877	1.50	4.00	6.00	9.00	14.00

HAMMERED COINAGE

Second Series

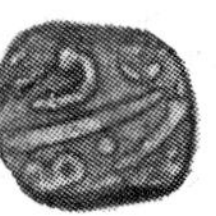

C# 41 TRAMBIYO

4.0000 g., Copper **Obv:** AH1234 (frozen); Persian legend with Devanagari name below **Obv. Inscription:** "Muhammad Akbar (II)" **Rev:** Persian legend **Note:** The frozen date AH1234 on this series is the accession date of Desalji II.

Date	Good	VG	F	VF	XF
AH1234//VS1880	2.50	3.50	5.00	7.50	—

C# 42 DOKDO

Copper **Obv:** AH1234 (frozen); Persian legend with Devanagari name below **Obv. Inscription:** "Muhammad Akbar (II)" **Rev:** Persian legend **Note:** Weight varies 7.90-8.20 grams. The frozen date AH1234 on this series is the accession date of Desalji II.

Date	Good	VG	F	VF	XF
AH1234//VS1880	2.50	3.50	5.00	7.50	—

C# 43 DHINGLO

Copper **Obv:** AH1234 (frozen); Persian legend with Devanagari name below **Obv. Inscription:** "Muhammad Akbar (II)" **Rev:** Persian legend **Note:** Weight varies: 12.10-12.40 grams. The frozen date AH1234 on this series is the accession date of Desalji II.

Date	Good	VG	F	VF	XF
AH1234//VS1880	2.75	4.00	5.50	8.00	—

C# 53 KORI

Silver **Obv:** Persian legend with Devanagari name below **Obv. Inscription:** "Muhammad Akbar II" **Rev:** Persian legend **Note:** Weight varies: 4.60-4.70 grams. The frozen date AH1234 on this series is the accession date of Desalji II.

Date	Good	VG	F	VF	XF
AH1234//VS1875	1.25	3.00	4.50	6.50	10.00
AH1234//VS1876	1.25	3.00	4.50	6.50	10.00
AH1234//VS1877	1.25	3.00	4.50	6.50	10.00
AH1234//VS1879	1.25	3.00	4.50	6.50	10.00
AH1234//VS1880	1.25	3.00	4.50	6.50	10.00
AH1234//VS1881	1.25	3.00	4.50	6.50	10.00
AH1234//VS1882	1.25	3.00	4.50	6.50	10.00
AH1234//VS1884	1.25	3.00	4.50	6.50	10.00
AH1234//VS1885	1.25	3.00	4.50	6.50	10.00
AH1234//VS1887	1.25	3.00	4.50	6.50	10.00

HAMMERED COINAGE

Third Series

C# 46 DOKDO

8.1000 g., Copper **Obv:** Persian legend **Obv. Inscription:** "Muhammad Akbar II" **Rev:** Devanagari legend below Persian mint-name on copper, date below Devanagari legend on silver

Date	Good	VG	F	VF	XF
AH1259	1.00	1.50	2.50	4.50	—
AH1261	1.00	1.50	2.50	4.50	—
AH1262	1.00	1.50	2.50	4.50	—

C# 47 DHINGLO

Copper **Obv:** Persian legend **Obv. Inscription:** "Muhammad Akbar II" **Rev:** Devanagari legend below Persian mint-name on copper, date below Devanagari legend on silver **Note:** Weight varies: 12.00-12.50 grams.

Date	Good	VG	F	VF	XF
AH1255	1.75	3.00	4.00	6.00	—
AH1257	1.25	2.00	3.00	5.00	—
AH1258	1.25	2.00	3.00	5.00	—
AH1259	1.25	2.00	3.00	5.00	—
AH1261	1.25	2.00	3.00	5.00	—
AH1262	1.25	2.00	3.00	5.00	—
AH1263	1.25	2.00	3.00	5.00	—
AH1266	1.50	2.50	3.50	5.50	—

C# 55 1/2 KORI

Silver **Obv. Inscription:** "Muhammad Akbar II" **Rev:** Katar below Devanagari date with Kutch "9" **Note:** Weight varies: 2.10-2.20 grams.

Date	Good	VG	F	VF	XF
VS1891	1.60	4.00	6.00	9.00	14.00
VS1892	1.40	3.50	5.00	7.50	12.00

C# 55a 1/2 KORI

Silver **Obv. Inscription:** "Muhammad Akbar II" **Rev:** Katar below date **Note:** Weight varies: 2.10-2.20 grams.

Date	Good	VG	F	VF	XF
AH1252//VS1893	1.60	4.00	6.00	9.00	14.00

C# 55b 1/2 KORI

Silver **Obv. Inscription:** "Muhammad Akbar (II)" **Rev:** Katar at right of Devanagari date **Note:** Weight varies: 2.10-2.20 grams.

Date	Good	VG	F	VF	XF
AH1252/VS1894	1.60	4.00	6.00	9.00	14.00
AH1253/VS1895	1.60	4.00	6.00	9.00	14.00
AH1258/VS1899	1.60	4.00	6.00	9.00	14.00
AH1259/VS1900	1.60	4.00	6.00	9.00	14.00
AH1260/VS1901	1.60	4.00	6.00	9.00	14.00
AH1261/VS1902	1.60	4.00	6.00	9.00	14.00

C# 58 1/2 KORI

Silver **Obv. Inscription:** "Muhammad Akbar II" **Rev:** Katar below Kutch date **Note:** Weight varies: 2.10-2.20 grams.

Date	Good	VG	F	VF	XF
VS1895	1.20	3.00	4.50	6.50	10.00

C# 58a 1/2 KORI

Silver **Obv:** AH date at left in middle legend **Obv. Inscription:** "Muhammad Akbar II" **Note:** Weight varies: 2.10-2.20 grams.

Date	Good	VG	F	VF	XF
AH1260//VS1901	1.40	3.50	5.00	7.50	12.00
AH1263//VS1904	1.40	3.50	5.00	7.50	12.00

C# 56 KORI

Silver **Obv. Inscription:** "Muhammad Akbar II" **Rev:** Katar below Devanagari date with Kutch "9" **Note:** Weight varies: 4.40-4.50 grams.

Date	Good	VG	F	VF	XF
AH1250//VS1892	1.60	4.00	6.00	9.00	14.00
AH1251//VS1892	1.20	3.00	4.50	6.50	10.00
AH1252//VS1893	1.20	3.00	4.50	6.50	10.00

C# 56a KORI

Silver **Obv. Inscription:** "Muhammad Akbar II" **Rev:** Katar at right of Devanagari date **Note:** Weight varies: 4.40-4.50 grams.

Date	Good	VG	F	VF	XF
AH1252//VS1894	1.40	3.50	5.00	7.50	12.00

C# 59 KORI

Silver **Obv. Inscription:** "Muhammad Akbar II" **Rev:** Katar at right of Devanagari date **Note:** Weight varies: 4.40-4.50 grams.

Date	Good	VG	F	VF	XF
VS1895	1.40	3.50	5.00	7.50	12.00

C# 59b KORI

Silver **Obv. Inscription:** "Muhammad Akbar II" **Rev:** Katar at right of Devanagari date **Note:** Weight varies: 4.40-4.50 grams.

Date	Good	VG	F	VF	XF
VS1899	1.20	3.00	4.50	6.50	10.00
VS1901	1.20	3.00	4.50	6.50	10.00
VS1902	1.20	3.00	4.50	6.50	10.00

C# 59a KORI

Silver **Obv:** AH date at left in middle legend **Obv. Inscription:** "Muhammad Akbar II" **Note:** Weight varies: 4.40-4.50 grams.

Date	Good	VG	F	VF	XF
AH1262//VS1903	1.00	2.50	3.50	5.00	8.00

HAMMERED COINAGE

Fourth Series

C# 61 TRAMBIYO

Copper, 14 mm. **Obv. Inscription:** "Bahadur Shah II" **Rev:** Katar upper left **Note:** Weight varies: 3.80-4.20 grams.

Date	Good	VG	F	VF	XF
AH1261	2.00	3.50	5.50	8.00	—
ND(1845-50)	1.75	2.75	4.00	5.50	—
AH1263	1.75	2.75	4.00	5.50	—
AH1266	1.75	2.75	4.00	5.50	—

C# 61a TRAMBIYO

Copper **Obv. Inscription:** "Bahadur Shah II" **Rev:** Indent upper left **Note:** Weight varies: 3.80-4.20 grams.

Date	Good	VG	F	VF	XF
AH1267	1.00	1.50	2.00	3.50	—
AH1269	1.00	1.50	2.00	3.50	—
AH1274	1.00	1.50	2.00	3.50	—

C# 62 DOKDO

8.1000 g., Copper **Obv. Inscription:** "Bahadur Shah II" **Note:** Size varies: 17-19mm.

Date	Good	VG	F	VF	XF
AH1263	1.50	2.50	4.00	5.50	—
AH1266	1.50	2.50	4.00	5.50	—

C# 62a DOKDO

8.1000 g., Copper **Obv. Inscription:** "Bahadur Shah II" **Note:** Size varies: 17-19mm.

Date	Good	VG	F	VF	XF
AH1267	1.50	2.50	4.00	5.50	—
AH1269	1.00	1.50	2.00	3.00	—
AH1274	1.00	1.50	2.00	3.00	—

C# 63 DHINGLO

Copper **Obv. Inscription:** "Bahadur Shah (II)" **Note:** Size varies: 18-21mm, weight varies: 12.00-12.50 grams.

Date	Good	VG	F	VF	XF
AH1263	2.50	4.00	5.25	7.00	—
AH1266	2.00	3.50	4.50	6.00	—

C# 63a DHINGLO

Copper **Obv. Inscription:** "Bahadur Shah II" **Note:** Size varies: 18-21mm, weight varies: 12.00-12.50 grams.

Date	Good	VG	F	VF	XF
AH1267	1.25	2.00	2.50	3.50	—
AH1268	1.25	2.00	2.50	3.50	—
AH1269	1.25	2.00	2.50	3.50	—
AH1270	1.50	2.75	3.25	4.50	—
AH1271	1.50	2.75	3.25	4.50	—
AH1272	1.25	2.00	2.50	3.50	—
AH1273	1.50	2.75	3.25	4.50	—
AH1274	1.50	2.75	3.25	4.50	—

C# 65 1/2 KORI

2.2000 g., Silver **Obv. Inscription:** "Bahadur Shah II"

Date	Good	VG	F	VF	XF
VS1909	1.00	2.50	3.50	5.00	8.00
VS1910	1.00	2.50	3.50	5.00	8.00
VS1911	1.00	3.00	4.50	6.50	10.00
VS1912	1.00	2.50	3.50	5.00	8.00
VS1913	1.00	2.50	3.50	5.00	8.00
VS1914	1.00	2.50	3.50	5.00	8.00

C# 66 KORI

Silver **Obv. Inscription:** "Bahadur Shah II" **Note:** Weight varies: 4.40-4.50 grams.

Date	Good	VG	F	VF	XF
VS1909	1.00	2.50	3.50	5.00	8.00
VS1910	1.00	2.50	3.50	5.00	8.00
VS1911	1.20	3.00	4.50	6.50	10.00
VS1912	1.00	2.50	3.50	5.00	8.00
VS1913	1.00	2.50	3.50	5.00	8.00
VS1914	1.00	2.50	3.50	5.00	8.00
VS1915	2.00	5.00	7.00	10.00	15.00
VS1916	2.25	5.50	8.00	12.50	18.50

C# 67 25 KORI

4.6800 g., 0.9990 Gold **Obv. Inscription:** "Bahadur Shah II"

Date	Good	VG	F	VF	XF
VS1911	—	—	70.00	110	135
VS1912	—	—	70.00	110	135
VS1913	—	—	70.00	110	135
VS1914	—	—	70.00	110	135
VS1915	—	—	70.00	110	135

Pragmalji II

VS1917-1932 / 1860-1875AD

Pragmalji II is the first ruler of Kutch to pay homage to Queen Victoria. He experimented with a joint formulation his first year, VS1917/1860AD, see the rare coin type Y#A14. In VS1919/1862AD he settled on standard type acknowledging "Queen Victoria, Mighty Queen" and himself as "Rao" or "Maharao", see types Y#13, 14 and 17.

MILLED COINAGE

Regal Series

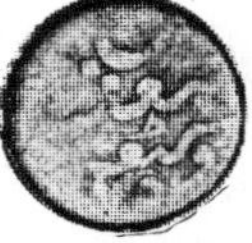

Y# 1 TRAMBIYO

Copper **Note:** Weight varies: 3.00-3.40 grams.

Date	Good	VG	F	VF	XF
1865	1.25	2.00	3.00	4.50	—

Y# 5 TRAMBIYO

Copper **Rev:** 2 characters right of trident **Note:** Weight varies: 3.00-3.40 grams.

Date	Good	VG	F	VF	XF
1865	0.50	0.85	1.50	2.50	—
1866	1.50	2.50	3.50	5.00	—

Y# 5.1 TRAMBIYO

Copper **Rev:** Trident above legend **Note:** Weight varies: 3.00-3.40 grams.

Date	Good	VG	F	VF	XF
1865	0.75	1.25	1.75	2.50	—
1866	0.50	0.85	1.50	2.50	—
1867	1.25	2.00	3.00	4.50	—
1767 Error for 1867	0.50	0.85	1.50	2.50	—
1868	0.50	0.85	1.50	2.50	—

Y# 9 TRAMBIYO

Copper **Obv:** Persian legend with "Victoria" at bottom **Note:** Weight varies: 3.00-3.40 grams.

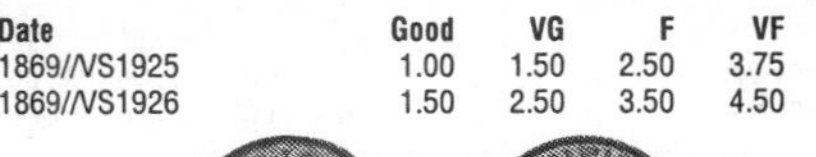

Date	Good	VG	F	VF	XF
1869//VS1925	1.00	1.50	2.50	3.75	—
1869//VS1926	1.50	2.50	3.50	4.50	—

Y# 9.1 TRAMBIYO

Copper **Obv:** Persian lgend with "Victoria" at top **Note:** Weight varies: 3.00-3.40 grams.

Date	Good	VG	F	VF	XF
1869//VS1926	0.50	1.00	2.00	3.00	—
1873//VS1930	0.50	1.00	2.00	3.00	—
1874//VS1930	0.50	1.00	2.00	3.00	—

Y# 6 DOKDO

Copper **Note:** Weight varies: 6.30-6.60 grams.

Date	Good	VG	F	VF	XF
1865	1.25	2.00	2.50	3.50	—
1866	1.00	1.75	2.25	3.00	—
1867	0.90	1.50	1.75	2.50	—
1868	0.60	1.00	1.50	2.75	—
1869 Retrograde 9	1.50	2.50	3.75	5.00	—
1869	1.00	1.75	2.25	3.00	—

Y# 10 DOKDO

Copper **Obv:** Persian legend with "Victoria" at top **Note:** Weight varies: 6.30-6.60 grams.

Date	Good	VG	F	VF	XF
1869//VS1925	1.25	2.00	3.00	4.50	—

Y# 10.1 DOKDO

Copper **Obv:** Persian legend with "Victoria" at bottom **Note:** Weight varies: 6.30-6.60 grams.

Date	Good	VG	F	VF	XF
1869//VS1925	0.60	1.00	1.50	2.50	—
1869//VS1926	1.00	1.50	2.00	3.00	—
1869//VS1927	1.50	2.50	3.50	5.00	—

Y# 10.2 DOKDO

Copper **Obv:** Persian legend with "Victoria" right **Note:** Weight varies: 6.30-6.60 grams.

Date	Good	VG	F	VF	XF
1873//VS1930	1.00	1.50	2.00	3.00	—
1874//VS1930	0.60	1.00	1.50	2.50	—

Y# 11 1-1/2 DOKDA

Copper **Obv:** Persian legend with "Victoria" at top **Note:** Weight varies: 9.00-10.00 grams.

Date	Good	VG	F	VF	XF
1869//VS1926	0.75	1.25	1.75	2.25	—
1780//VS1925 Error for 1870	1.75	3.00	3.50	4.25	—
1780//VS1926 Error for 1870	0.90	1.50	2.00	2.50	—
1870//VS1927	0.60	1.00	1.50	2.00	—
1870//VS1928	0.60	1.00	1.50	2.00	—
1780//VS1928 Error	0.75	1.25	1.75	2.25	—
1871//VS1928	0.60	1.00	1.50	2.00	—
1872//VS1928	0.75	1.25	1.75	2.25	—

Y# 11.1 1-1/2 DOKDA

Copper **Obv:** Persian legend with "Victoria" at right **Note:** Weight varies: 9.00-10.00 grams.

Date	Good	VG	F	VF	XF
1871//VS1928	0.90	1.50	2.00	2.50	—
1872//VS1928	0.90	1.50	2.00	2.50	—
1872//VS1929	0.75	1.25	1.75	2.25	—
1873//VS1929	0.60	1.00	1.50	2.25	—
1873//VS1930	0.60	1.00	1.50	2.25	—
1783//VS1930 (sic)	0.75	1.25	1.75	2.50	—
1874//VS1930	0.60	1.00	1.50	2.00	—
1874//VS1931	0.60	1.00	1.50	2.00	—
1874//VS1932 (sic)	2.25	5.50	9.00	14.00	—
1875//VS1931	1.25	2.00	2.75	3.50	—
1875//VS1932	1.00	1.75	2.50	3.50	—
1879//VS1929 (sic)	0.75	1.25	1.75	2.25	—

Y# 11.3 1-1/2 DOKDA

Copper **Obv:** Persian legend on top written differently, with "Victoria" at right **Note:** Weight varies: 9.00-10.00 grams.

Date	Good	VG	F	VF	XF
1872//VS1928	1.50	2.50	3.75	5.00	—
1872//VS1929	1.50	2.50	3.75	5.00	—

Y# 11.2 1-1/2 DOKDA

Copper **Obv:** Persian legend on top written differently with "Victoria" at right **Note:** Weight varies: 9.00-10.00 grams.

Date	Good	VG	F	VF	XF
1875//VS1932	0.75	1.25	1.75	2.25	—
1876//VS1933	0.75	1.25	1.75	2.25	—

Y# 8 3 DOKDA

Copper **Rev:** "Sa(m)vat" at upper left, date at right **Note:** Weight varies: 18.80-19.60 grams.

Date	Good	VG	F	VF	XF
1868//VS1925	2.50	4.00	6.00	8.00	—

Y# 8.1 3 DOKDA

Copper **Obv:** Similar to Y#8.2 **Rev:** "Sa(m)vat" and date at top **Note:** Weight varies: 18.80-19.60 grams.

Date	Good	VG	F	VF	XF
1868//VS1925	2.50	4.00	6.00	8.00	—

Y# 8.2 3 DOKDA

Copper **Rev:** "Sa(m)vat" at top, date at right **Note:** Weight varies: 18.80-19.60 grams.

Date	Good	VG	F	VF	XF
1868//VS1925	2.50	4.00	6.00	8.00	—

Y# 12 3 DOKDA

Copper **Note:** Weight varies: 18.80-19.60 grams.

Date	Good	VG	F	VF	XF
1868//VS1925	2.50	4.00	6.00	8.00	—
1869//VS1925	2.00	3.50	5.00	7.50	—
1869//VS1926	2.00	3.50	5.00	7.50	—

Y# 13 1/2 KORI

2.3500 g., 0.6100 Silver .0460 oz. ASW

Date	Good	VG	F	VF	XF
1862//VS1919	1.00	2.50	3.50	5.00	9.00
1862//VS1920	0.75	2.00	3.00	4.00	8.00
1863//VS1920	1.00	2.50	3.50	5.00	9.00
1763//VS1920 Error for 1863	1.00	2.50	3.50	5.00	9.00
1863//VS1921	0.75	2.00	3.00	4.00	8.00

Y# A14 KORI

4.7000 g., 0.6100 Silver .0921 oz. ASW **Rev:** Rosette at end of third line, Katar after date

Date	Good	VG	F	VF	XF
1860//VS1917 Rare	—	—	—	—	—

Y# 14.1 KORI

4.7000 g., 0.6100 Silver .0921 oz. ASW **Rev:** Closed crescent

Date	Good	VG	F	VF	XF
1862//VS1918	0.75	2.00	3.00	4.00	8.00
1862//VS1919	1.00	2.50	3.50	5.00	9.00

Y# 14.2 KORI

4.7000 g., 0.6100 Silver .0921 oz. ASW **Rev:** Open crescent **Note:** Error strike dated 1862, VS1919 with dies of 1 Kori, Y14.1 on 1/2 Kori planchet exists.

Date	Good	VG	F	VF	XF
1862//VS1920	0.75	2.00	3.00	4.00	8.00
1863//VS1920	0.75	2.00	3.00	4.00	8.00
1863//VS1921	0.75	2.00	3.00	4.00	8.00

Y# 15 2-1/2 KORI

6.9350 g., 0.9370 Silver .2089 oz. ASW

Date	Good	VG	F	VF	XF
1875//VS1931	1.60	4.00	6.00	9.00	13.50
1785//VS1931	2.25	5.50	8.50	13.50	20.00
1875//VS1932	1.60	4.00	6.00	9.00	13.50

Y# 16 5 KORI

13.8700 g., 0.9370 Silver .4178 oz. ASW

Date	Good	VG	F	VF	XF
1863//VS1921	8.00	20.00	31.50	42.50	60.00

Y# 16.1 5 KORI

13.8700 g., 0.9370 Silver .4178 oz. ASW **Obv:** Legend rearranged

Date	Good	VG	F	VF	XF
1865//VS1921	3.50	8.50	13.50	20.00	28.50
1865//VS1922	2.75	7.00	11.00	16.50	25.00
1866//VS1922	2.50	6.50	10.00	15.00	22.50
1866//VS1923	2.50	6.50	10.00	15.00	22.50
1870//VS1927	2.75	7.00	11.00	16.50	25.00
1874//VS1931	2.35	6.00	9.00	13.50	20.00
1875//VS1931	2.35	6.00	9.00	13.50	20.00
1875//VS1932	2.35	6.00	9.00	13.50	20.00

Y# 17.1 25 KORI

4.6750 g., 0.9990 Gold .1501 oz. AGW **Rev:** Closed crescent

Date	Good	VG	F	VF	XF
1862//VS1919	—	—	70.00	110	135
1863//VS1920	—	—	70.00	110	135

Y# 17.2 25 KORI

4.6750 g., 0.9990 Gold .1501 oz. AGW **Rev:** Open crescent

Date	Good	VG	F	VF	XF
1863//VS1921	—	—	70.00	110	135

Y# 17a 25 KORI

4.6750 g., 0.9990 Gold .1501 oz. AGW

Date	Good	VG	F	VF	XF
1870//VS1926	—	—	70.00	110	135
1870//VS1927	—	—	70.00	110	135

Y# 18 50 KORI

9.3500 g., 0.9060 Gold .2723 oz. AGW

Date	Good	VG	F	VF	XF
1668//VS1923 (Sic, error for 1866)	—	—	130	185	275
1866//VS1923	—	—	110	150	220
1873//VS1930	—	—	110	150	220
1874//VS1930	—	—	110	150	220
1874//VS1931	—	—	110	150	220

Y# 19 100 KORI

18.7000 g., 0.9060 Gold .5446 oz. AGW

Date	Good	VG	F	VF	XF
1866//VS1922	—	—	225	300	425
1866//VS1923	—	—	225	300	425

Khengarji III
VS1932-98 / 1875-1942AD

MILLED COINAGE

Regal Series

Y# 35 KORI

4.7000 g., 0.6100 Silver .0921 oz. ASW **Obv. Inscription:** "Victoria, Empress of India" **Rev:** Closed crescent

Date	Good	VG	F	VF	XF
1881//VS1938	1.00	2.50	3.50	5.00	8.00
1882//VS1938	1.00	2.50	3.50	5.00	8.00
1882//VS1939	0.75	2.00	3.00	4.00	7.00
1883//VS1939	0.75	2.00	3.00	4.00	7.00
1883//VS1940	0.75	2.00	3.00	4.00	7.00
1884//VS1941	1.00	2.50	3.50	5.00	8.00
1885//VS1941	0.75	2.00	3.00	4.00	7.00

Y# 36 2-1/2 KORI

6.9350 g., 0.9370 Silver .2089 oz. ASW **Obv. Inscription:** "Victoria, Empress of India" **Rev:** Closed crescent

Date	Good	VG	F	VF	XF
1881//VS1938	2.00	5.00	7.00	10.00	15.00
1882//VS1938	1.60	4.00	6.00	9.00	13.50

Y# 36.1 2-1/2 KORI

6.9350 g., 0.9370 Silver .2089 oz. ASW **Obv. Inscription:** "Victoria, Empress of India" **Rev:** Open crescent

Date	Good	VG	F	VF	XF
1894//VS1951	1.60	4.00	6.00	9.00	13.50
1895//VS1951	1.35	3.50	5.00	7.00	12.00
1897//VS1953	1.35	3.50	5.00	7.00	12.00
1897//VS1954	1.35	3.50	5.00	7.00	12.00
1898//VS1954	1.60	4.00	6.00	9.00	13.50
1898//VS1955	1.60	4.00	6.00	9.00	13.50
1899//VS1955	1.60	4.00	6.00	9.00	13.50

Y# 36.2 2-1/2 KORI

6.9350 g., 0.9370 Silver .2089 oz. ASW **Obv. Inscription:** "Victoria, Empress of India"

Date	Good	VG	F	VF	XF
1899//VS1955	1.60	4.00	6.00	9.00	13.50
1899//VS1956	1.35	3.50	5.00	7.50	12.00

Y# 37.2 5 KORI

13.8700 g., 0.9370 Silver .4178 oz. ASW **Obv:** Similar to Y#37 **Obv. Inscription:** "Victoria, Empress of India" **Rev:** Bars to left and right of center legend

Date	Good	VG	F	VF	XF
1880//VS1937	2.75	7.00	11.00	16.50	25.00
1881//VS1937	2.50	6.50	10.00	15.00	22.50

Y# 37.3 5 KORI

13.8700 g., 0.9370 Silver .4178 oz. ASW **Obv:** Similar to Y#37.1 **Obv. Inscription:** "Victoria, Empress of India" **Rev:** Similar to Y#37.2

Date	Good	VG	F	VF	XF
1880//VS1937	2.50	6.50	10.00	15.00	22.50

Y# 37.4 5 KORI

13.8700 g., 0.9370 Silver .4178 oz. ASW **Obv:** Changed wreath **Obv. Inscription:** "Victoria, Empress of India" **Rev:** Closed crescent

Date	Good	VG	F	VF	XF
1881//VS1938	2.50	6.50	10.00	15.00	22.50
1882//VS1938	2.50	6.50	10.00	15.00	22.50
1882//VS1939	2.50	6.50	10.00	15.00	22.50
1883//VS1939	2.50	6.50	10.00	15.00	22.50
1883//VS1940	2.50	6.50	10.00	15.00	22.50
1884//VS1940	2.50	6.50	10.00	15.00	22.50
1884//VS1941	2.50	6.50	10.00	15.00	22.50
1884//VS1939 (sic)	—	—	—	—	—
1885//VS1941	2.50	6.50	10.00	15.00	22.50
1885//VS1942	6.00	15.00	21.50	30.00	40.00
1886//VS1943	6.00	15.00	21.50	30.00	40.00

Y# 37.1 5 KORI

13.8700 g., 0.9370 Silver .4178 oz. ASW **Obv:** Leaves of wreath point clockwise **Obv. Inscription:** "Victoria, Empress of India" **Rev:** Without bars

Date	Good	VG	F	VF	XF
1881//VS1937	2.50	6.50	10.00	15.00	22.50
1881//VS938	2.50	6.50	10.00	15.00	22.50

Y# 37 5 KORI

13.8700 g., 0.9370 Silver .4178 oz. ASW **Obv:** Leaves of wreath point counter-clockwise **Obv. Inscription:** "Victoria, Empress of India" **Rev:** Without bars

Date	Good	VG	F	VF	XF
1881//VS1937	2.50	6.50	10.00	15.00	22.50
1881//VS1938	2.50	6.50	10.00	15.00	22.50

Y# 37.7 5 KORI

13.8700 g., 0.9370 Silver .4178 oz. ASW **Obv:** Similar to Y#37 **Obv. Inscription:** "Victoria, Empress of India" **Rev:** Similar to Y#37.1

Date	Good	VG	F	VF	XF
1881//VS1938	3.00	7.50	12.00	20.00	30.00

Y# 37.5 5 KORI

13.8700 g., 0.9370 Silver .4178 oz. ASW **Obv. Inscription:** "Victoria, Empress of India" **Rev:** Open crescent

Date	Good	VG	F	VF	XF
1890//VS1947	5.50	13.50	20.00	27.50	37.50
1893//VS1950	4.00	10.00	15.00	21.50	30.00
1894//VS1951	2.50	6.50	10.00	15.00	22.50
1894//VS1950	2.50	6.50	10.00	15.00	22.50
1895//VS1951	2.50	6.50	10.00	15.00	22.50
1895//VS1952	2.50	6.50	10.00	15.00	22.50
1896//VS1952	2.50	6.50	10.00	15.00	22.50
1896//VS1953	2.50	6.50	10.00	15.00	22.50
1896//VS1954 (sic)	5.50	13.50	20.00	27.50	37.50
1897//VS1951 (sic)	2.75	7.00	11.00	16.50	25.00
1897//VS1953	2.50	6.50	10.00	15.00	22.50
1897//VS1954	2.50	6.50	10.00	15.00	22.50
1898//VS1951 (sic)	5.00	12.50	18.50	25.00	35.00
1898//VS1953	2.50	6.50	10.00	15.00	22.50
1898//VS1954	2.50	6.50	10.00	15.00	22.50
1898//VS1955	2.50	6.50	10.00	15.00	22.50
1899//VS1955	2.75	7.00	11.00	16.50	25.00

MILLED COINAGE

Regal Issues - First Series

Y# 22 DOKDO

8.0000 g., Copper **Obv. Inscription:** "Queen Victoria, Mighty Queen"

Date	Good	VG	F	VF	XF
1878//VS1934	10.00	17.50	20.00	25.00	—
1878//VS1935	13.50	22.50	25.00	30.00	—
(1)878//VS1935	15.00	25.00	27.50	32.50	—

Y# 23 1-1/2 DOKDA

12.0000 g., Copper **Obv. Inscription:** "Queen Victoria, Mighty Queen"

Date	Good	VG	F	VF	XF
1876//VS1933	0.90	1.50	2.00	2.75	—
1877//VS1933	0.90	1.50	2.00	2.75	—
1877//VS1934	0.90	1.50	2.00	2.75	—
1877//VS1922 Error	0.90	1.50	2.00	2.75	—
1878//VS1934	0.90	1.50	2.00	2.75	—
1878//VS1935	1.25	2.00	2.50	3.25	—

Y# 23.1 1-1/2 DOKDA

12.0000 g., Copper **Obv:** Similar to 1-1/2 Dokda, Y#11 **Obv. Inscription:** "Queen Victoria, Mighty Queen"

Date	Good	VG	F	VF	XF
1876//VS1933	1.25	2.00	2.50	3.50	—

Y# 26 KORI

4.7000 g., 0.6100 Silver .921 oz. ASW **Obv. Inscription:** "Queen Victoria, Mighty Queen"

Date	Good	VG	F	VF	XF
1876//VS1932	25.00	50.00	75.00	110	150
1876//VS1933	25.00	50.00	75.00	110	150

Y# 28 5 KORI

13.8700 g., 0.9370 Silver .4178 oz. ASW **Obv. Inscription:** "Queen Victoria, Mighty Queen" **Note:** Edge varieties exist.

Date	Good	VG	F	VF	XF
1876//VS1933	8.00	20.00	31.50	42.50	60.00

MILLED COINAGE

Regal Issues - Second Series

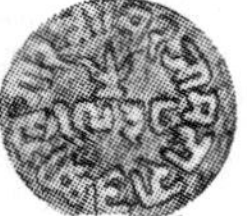

Y# 30 TRAMBIYO

4.0000 g., Copper **Obv. Inscription:** "Victoria, Empress of India"

Date	Good	VG	F	VF	XF
1881//VS1938	0.50	0.75	1.00	1.50	—
1882//VS1938	0.30	0.50	0.75	1.25	—
1883//VS1939	0.30	0.50	0.75	1.25	—
1883//VS1940	0.50	0.75	1.00	1.50	—

Y# 30.1 TRAMBIYO

4.0000 g., Copper **Obv. Inscription:** "Victoria, Empress of India" **Rev:** "Kutch" added below date

Date	Good	VG	F	VF	XF
1883//VS1940	0.50	0.75	1.00	1.50	—

Y# 31 DOKDO

8.0000 g., Copper **Obv. Inscription:** "Victoria, Empress of India"

Date	Good	VG	F	VF	XF
1882//VS1938	0.50	0.75	1.00	1.50	—
1882//VS1939	0.90	1.50	2.00	2.50	—
1883//VS1939	0.50	0.75	1.00	1.50	—

Y# 31.1 DOKDO

8.0000 g., Copper **Obv. Inscription:** "Victoria, Empress of India" **Rev:** "Kutch" added below date

Date	Good	VG	F	VF	XF
1883//VS1940	0.50	0.75	1.00	1.50	—
1884//VS1940	0.50	0.75	1.00	1.50	—

Y# 31.2 DOKDO

8.0000 g., Copper **Obv:** Legend similar to Y#31.1 but spcaced similar to Y#31.3 **Obv. Inscription:** "Victoria, Empress of India"

Date	Good	VG	F	VF	XF
1892//VS1948	2.50	4.00	6.00	9.00	—

Y# 31.3 DOKDO

8.0000 g., Copper **Obv:** Urdu legend "Victoria" written differently **Obv. Inscription:** "Victoria, Empress of India"

Date	Good	VG	F	VF	XF
1899//VS1956	0.90	1.50	2.00	3.00	—

Y# 32 1-1/2 DOKDA

12.0000 g., Copper **Obv. Inscription:** "Victoria, Empress of India"

Date	Good	VG	F	VF	XF
1882//VS1938	0.60	1.00	1.25	1.75	—
1882//VS1939	0.60	1.00	1.25	1.75	—
1883//VS1939	0.60	1.00	1.25	1.75	—
1883//VS1940	0.60	1.00	1.25	1.75	—

Y# 32.1 1-1/2 DOKDA

12.0000 g., Copper **Obv. Inscription:** "Victoria, Empress of India" **Rev:** "Kutch" added below date

Date	Good	VG	F	VF	XF
1883//VS1940	0.60	1.00	1.25	1.75	—
1884//VS1940	0.60	1.00	1.25	1.75	—
1884//VS1941	0.60	1.00	1.25	1.75	—

Y# 32.2 1-1/2 DOKDA

12.0000 g., Copper **Obv. Inscription:** "Victoria, Empress of India" **Note:** Finer style.

Date	Good	VG	F	VF	XF
1885//VS1943	0.75	1.25	1.50	2.00	—
1887//VS1944	0.75	1.25	1.50	2.00	—
1888//VS1944	0.75	1.25	1.50	2.00	—

Y# 32.3 1-1/2 DOKDA

12.0000 g., Copper **Obv. Inscription:** "Victoria, Empress of India"

Date	Good	VG	F	VF	XF
1892//VS1948	0.75	1.25	1.50	2.00	—
1894//VS1950	0.75	1.25	1.50	2.00	—

Y# 32.4 1-1/2 DOKDA

12.0000 g., Copper **Obv. Inscription:** "Victoria, Empress of India"

Date	Good	VG	F	VF	XF
1899//VS1955	1.25	2.00	2.50	3.00	—
1899//VS1956	1.25	2.00	2.75	3.50	—

Y# 33 3 DOKDA

24.0000 g., Copper **Obv. Inscription:** "Victoria, Empress of India"

Date	Good	VG	F	VF	XF
1883//VS1940	1.25	2.00	2.50	3.25	—
1885//VS1942	0.90	1.50	2.00	2.75	—
1886//VS1942	1.35	2.25	3.00	4.25	—
1887//VS1944	0.90	1.50	2.00	2.75	—
1888//VS1944	1.25	2.00	2.50	3.25	—

Y# 33.1 3 DOKDA

24.0000 g., Copper **Obv. Inscription:** "Victoria, Empress of India"

Date	Good	VG	F	VF	XF
1894//VS1951	1.50	2.50	3.00	3.75	—
1899//VS1955	1.50	2.50	3.00	3.75	—

Y# 34 1/2 KORI

2.3500 g., 0.6100 Silver .0460 oz. ASW **Obv. Inscription:** "Victoria, Empress of India"

Date	Good	VG	F	VF	XF
1898//VS1954	1.00	2.50	3.50	5.00	8.00
1899//VS1955	1.00	2.50	3.50	5.00	8.00
1899//VS1956	1.00	2.50	3.50	5.00	8.00
1900//VS1956	1.00	2.50	3.50	5.00	8.00
1900//VS1957	1.25	3.00	4.50	6.50	10.00

Y# 35.1 KORI

4.7000 g., 0.6100 Silver .0921 oz. ASW **Obv. Inscription:** "Victoria, Empress of India" **Rev:** Open crescent

Date	Good	VG	F	VF	XF
1894//VS1950	—	2.50	3.50	5.00	8.00
1896//VS1952	—	2.50	3.50	5.00	8.00
1897//VS1953	—	2.00	3.00	4.00	7.00
1897//VS1954	—	2.00	3.00	4.00	7.00
1898//VS1954	—	2.00	3.00	4.00	7.00
1898//VS1955	—	2.00	3.00	4.00	7.00
1899//VS1955	—	2.00	3.00	4.00	7.00
1899//VS1956	—	2.00	3.00	4.00	7.00
1900//VS1956	—	2.00	3.00	4.00	7.00
1900//VS1957	—	2.00	3.00	4.00	7.00

Y# 37.6 5 KORI

13.8700 g., 0.9370 Silver .4178 oz. ASW **Obv. Inscription:** "Victoria, Empress of India"

Date	Good	VG	F	VF	XF
1899//VS1955	2.50	6.50	10.00	15.00	22.50
1899//VS1956	2.50	6.50	10.00	15.00	22.50
1901//VS1957	7.00	17.50	25.00	35.00	50.00

LADAKH

Ladakh, a district in northern India, contained the western Himalayas and the valley of the upper Indus River. Area: 45,762 sq. mi. Capital: Leh.

In 1639, the Moghuls marched on Ladakh and defeated them near Karpu. King Sen-ge-mam-rgyal promised to pay tribute if allowed to return home, but never did. In1665, the Moghul governor of Kashmir demanded the acceptance of Moghul suzerainty under threat of invasion. Knowing the strength of Aurangzeb, King Deb-ldan-mam-rgyal sent a tribute of gold ashraphis, rupees and other precious objects. It is probable that coins were struck for this occasion in the name of Aurangzeb, but no such coins have yet been discovered.

For the next century, no further mention is made of coins until in 1781, it is recorded that a Muslim goldsmith from Leh was hired to strike Ladakhi coins called ja'u.

The obverse of the first Ladakhi timashas or ja'u is a close copy of the Farrukhsiyar inscription of the early Garhwali timashas even including the regnal year at the bottom. The reverse has a clearly written "Zarb Tibet" at the bottom and dots at the top. At the center are crescents and an illegible inscription.

On some of the early Ladakh coins Hejira dates appear which coincide with the period when the Garhwal mint was closed and trade was diverted from Garhwal to Ladakh. No other Ladakh coins of this first issue have been discovered with a literate date. Between 1781 and 1803 it is likely that a considerable number of ja'u were struck. Most specimens were of good silver, but later issues were very debased because of the scarcity of silver.

The next type of coin has a different obverse with the Muslim title of the King of Ladakh clearly inscribed, as well as the number 14 at the lower left. This issue may have been prompted to demonstrate Ladakhi independence and is the only ja'u to bear a date.

The most remarkable of all Ladakhi coins has a fully legible inscription on the obverse in smaller writing and is enclosed in a circle with no regnal year. The reverse legend refers to the prime minister as well as the title of the king. It is the only Ladakhi coin to do so and is very rare.

The appearance of Mahmud Shah on the obverse of the next type coin is thought to acknowledge suzerainty of the ruler of Kashmir. There is a plain circle surrounded by a border of dots. The reverse reverts to the earlier designs, but has a finer style with thicker writing.

The next change in type took place after the conquest of Ladakh by Gulab Singh and the Dogra army in 1835. After a crushing defeat of the Dogra army in Tibet, the Ladakhis tried to shake off the Dogra supremacy, but the rebellion was crushed. Ladakh was now firmly incorporated within the Empire of Jammu and the monarchy was abolished. Until 1845, Gulab Singh acknowledged Sikh suzerainty but ruled Ladakh as a part of Jammu.

After the defeat of the Sikhs by the British, Gulab Singh offered to pay the war indemnities to the British in exchange for being made independent ruler of Jammu and Kashmir.

Two types of ja'u were struck during the period of the Dogra domination. One combined the tiger knife and Mahmud Shah design and the other the tiger knife and Raja Gulab Singh in Nagari script.

Between 1867 and 1870 an issue of copper coins was made for Ladakh for local use and in 1871, a small issue of ja'u was made. Neither of these coins seemed to have much commercial impact in Ladakh and their issue was suspended after 1871. No special currency was struck in or for Ladakh after this.

RULERS

Tshe Pal Namgyal, 1802-1830AD
Tshe Wan Rabtan Namgyal, 1830-1837AD
Tshe Pal Namgyal, restored, 1839-1840AD
Kunda Namgyal, 1840-1842AD,

HAMMERED COINAGE

KM# 2 JA'U

Silver **Obverse:** Square around "Siyar" of Farrukhsiyar

Date	Mintage	Good	VG	F	VF	XF
ND(1771-1815)	—	20.00	32.00	50.00	75.00	—

KM# 3 JA'U

Silver **Obv. Legend:** "Aqibat Mahmud Khan" **Obv. Inscription:** "Mahmud Khan"

Date	Mintage	Good	VG	F	VF	XF
ND(1815-16)	—	8.50	15.00	25.00	35.00	—

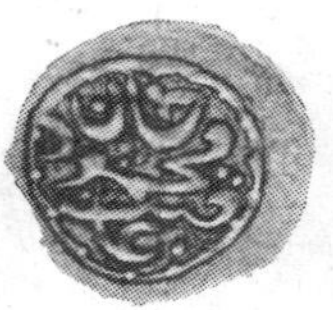

KM# 4 JA'U

Silver **Obv. Legend:** "Aqibat Mahmud Khan" within circle **Obv. Inscription:** "Mahmud Khan" **Rev. Legend:** "Qalon Seban Tondub, Tibet"

Date	Mintage	Good	VG	F	VF	XF
ND(1815-16)	—	50.00	75.00	100	150	—

KM# 5.1 JA'U

Silver **Obverse:** Plain border **Obv. Legend:** "Mahmud Shah" **Obv. Inscription:** "Mahmud Shah" **Reverse:** Plain border

Date	Mintage	Good	VG	F	VF	XF
ND(1816-42)	—	10.00	14.00	18.50	25.00	—

KM# 5.2 JA'U

Silver **Obverse:** Dotted border **Obv. Inscription:** "Mahmud Shah" **Reverse:** Dotted border

Date	Mintage	Good	VG	F	VF	XF
ND(1816-42)	—	10.00	14.00	18.50	25.00	—

KM# 5.3 JA'U

Silver **Obverse:** Dotted border **Obv. Inscription:** "Mahmud Shah" **Reverse:** Plain border

Date	Mintage	Good	VG	F	VF	XF
ND(1816-42)	—	10.00	14.00	18.50	25.00	—

KM# 5.4 JA'U

Silver **Obv. Inscription:** "Mahmud Shah"

Date	Mintage	Good	VG	F	VF	XF
ND(1816-42)	—	10.00	14.00	18.50	25.00	—

KM# 5.5 JA'U
Silver **Obverse:** Retrograde **Obv. Inscription:** "Mahmud Shah"

Date	Mintage	Good	VG	F	VF	XF
ND(1816-42)	—	10.00	14.00	18.50	25.00	—

KM# 5.6 JA'U
Silver **Obv. Inscription:** "Mahmud Shah"

Date	Mintage	Good	VG	F	VF	XF
ND(1816-42)	—	10.00	14.00	18.50	25.00	—

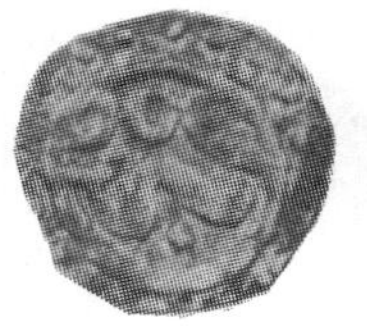

KM# 6 JA'U
Silver **Obverse:** Dotted border **Obv. Inscription:** "Mahmud Shah" within circle **Reverse:** Katar pointing right, "Zarb Butan" above and below

Date	Mintage	Good	VG	F	VF	XF
ND(1841)	—	10.00	14.00	18.50	25.00	—

KM# 7.1 JA'U
Silver **Obv. Inscription:** "Raja Gulab Singh" in Nagari in 3 lines

Date	Mintage	Good	VG	F	VF	XF
ND(1842-50)	—	6.00	10.00	12.50	15.00	—

KM# 7.2 JA'U
Silver **Obv. Inscription:** "Raja Gulab Singh" in Nagari in 3 lines **Reverse:** Dot on blade of Katar

Date	Mintage	Good	VG	F	VF	XF
ND(1842-50)	—	6.00	10.00	12.50	15.00	—

KM# 7.3 JA'U
Silver **Obv. Inscription:** "Raja Gulab Singh" in Nagari in 3 lines **Reverse:** Figure 8 on its side of blade of Katar

Date	Mintage	Good	VG	F	VF	XF
ND(1842-50)	—	6.00	10.00	12.50	15.00	—

KM# 7.4 JA'U
Silver **Obv. Inscription:** Error "Raja Galab Bing" **Reverse:** Figure 8 on its side of blade of Katar

Date	Mintage	Good	VG	F	VF	XF
ND(1842-50)	—	6.00	10.00	12.50	15.00	—

KM# 7.5 JA'U
Silver **Reverse:** Legend blundered

Date	Mintage	Good	VG	F	VF	XF
ND(1842-50)	—	6.00	10.00	12.50	15.00	—

KM# 8 JA'U
Silver **Obv. Inscription:** "1928 Jam-bu'i Par" in Tibetan script **Rev. Inscription:** "Zarb Ladakh, Qilimrao Jamun, Sanah 1928" in Arabic script

Date	Mintage	Good	VG	F	VF	XF
ND(1871)	—	15.00	25.00	32.50	40.00	—

OCCUPATION COINAGE

Issued Under the Dogras of Jammu

KM# 9 PAISA
Copper

Date	Mintage	Good	VG	F	VF	XF
VS1923 (1866)	—	4.50	8.50	13.50	20.00	—
VS1924 (1867)	—	4.50	8.50	13.50	20.00	—
VS1925 (1868)	—	4.50	8.50	13.50	20.00	—
VS1926 (1869)	—	4.50	8.50	13.50	20.00	—
VS1927 (1870)	—	4.50	8.50	13.50	20.00	—

LUNAVADA

This small state in the Panch Mahal district of western India was ruled by Solanki Rajputs who claimed descent from Sidraj Jaisingh, the ruler of Anhalwara Patan and Gujerat. The rulers, or maharanas, traced their sovereignty to the early decades of the 15th century. At different times the State was feudatory to either Baroda or Sindhia.

Wakhat Singhji
VS1924-1986/1867-1929AD
HAMMERED COINAGE

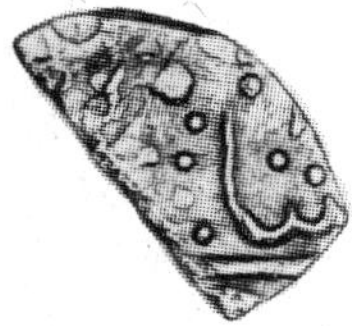

KM# 2.2 1/2 PAISA
Copper **Obverse:** Crescent left and star right of hand **Note:** Weight varies: 3.50-4.00 grams.

Date	Mintage	Good	VG	F	VF	XF
ND(ca.1885-92)	—	3.00	6.00	8.50	12.50	—

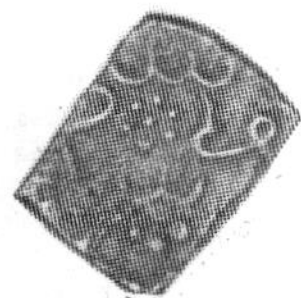

KM# 3 1/2 PAISA
Copper **Obverse:** Open hand in square, "Lunavada" around clockwise **Reverse:** Date and Devanagari legend **Note:** Weight varies: 3.50-4.00 grams.

Date	Mintage	Good	VG	F	VF	XF
VS1942	—	3.00	5.00	7.50	10.00	—

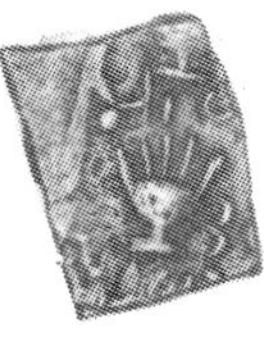
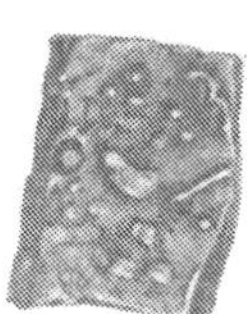

KM# 2.1 1/2 PAISA
Copper **Obverse:** Open hand **Reverse:** Mughal style **Rev. Legend:** Persian **Note:** Weight varies: 3.50-4.00 grams. Struck with paisa dies, either on small planchets, or paisas cut in half.

Date	Mintage	Good	VG	F	VF	XF
ND(ca.1885-92)	—	2.75	4.50	6.00	9.00	—

KM# 4 1/2 PAISA
Copper **Obverse:** Lion right "Lunavada" and date **Reverse:** Devanagari legend with ruler's name **Note:** Weight varies: 3.50-4.00 grams.

Date	Mintage	Good	VG	F	VF	XF
VS1949	—	2.75	4.50	6.00	9.00	—

KM# 11 PAISA
Copper **Obverse:** Katar

Date	Mintage	Good	VG	F	VF	XF
ND(ca.1885-92)	—	6.00	12.00	17.50	25.00	—

KM# 9.1 PAISA
Copper **Obverse:** Open hand in square, copper square

Date	Mintage	Good	VG	F	VF	XF
VS1942	—	2.50	4.00	5.50	8.50	—
VS1249 (1885) Error	—	2.50	4.00	5.50	8.50	—

KM# 8.2 PAISA
Copper **Obverse:** Legend between open hands above and below **Note:** Shape: square.

Date	Mintage	Good	VG	F	VF	XF
ND(ca.1885)	—	3.50	6.00	8.50	12.50	—

KM# 9.2 PAISA
Copper **Note:** Similar to KM9.1, copper, round.

Date	Mintage	Good	VG	F	VF	XF
VS1942	—	2.50	4.00	5.50	8.50	—

KM# 8.1 PAISA
Copper **Obverse:** Open hand above legend **Note:** Weight varies 6.50-8.30 grams. Shape: rectangular.

Date	Mintage	Good	VG	F	VF	XF
ND(ca.1885)	—	2.50	4.00	5.50	8.50	—

KM# 5 PAISA
Copper **Obverse:** 2 sabres **Note:** Weight varies: 6.50-8.30 grams. Shape: round or rectangular.

Date	Mintage	Good	VG	F	VF	XF
ND(ca.1885-92)	—	3.50	6.00	8.50	12.50	—

KM# 6 PAISA
Copper **Obverse:** Cannon barrel **Note:** Weight varies: 6.50-8.30 grams. Shape: round or rectangular.

Date	Mintage	Good	VG	F	VF	XF
ND(ca.1885-92)	—	3.50	6.00	8.50	12.50	—

KM# 10 PAISA
Copper **Obverse:** Lion, "Lunavada" and date **Note:** Coins of Lunavada are frequently found overstruck over earlier types, and over other coins of Rampura.

Date	Mintage	Good	VG	F	VF	XF
VS1949	—	2.50	4.00	5.50	8.50	—

MAKRAI

The rajas of Makrai belong to a very ancient Gond family whose title, Raja Hatiyarai, had been conferred upon them by the emperors of Delhi. This small state of some forty-five villages struggled with varying degrees of success against the Poona Peshwa, Sindhia and the Pindaris before passing under British protection in the 19th century.

RULER
Raja Bharat Shah, 1886-1920AD

Raja Bharat Shah
1886-1920AD

HAMMERED COINAGE

KM# 1 PAISA
Copper **Obverse:** Katar **Rev. Legend:** SHRI/MAK/RAI **Rev. Inscription:** Hindi **Note:** Weight varies: 9.00-11.00 grams.

Date	Mintage	Good	VG	F	VF	XF
ND(1886-1920)	—	2.50	4.00	6.00	9.00	—

KM# 2 PAISA
Copper **Obverse:** Katar **Rev. Legend:** SHRI/MAK/RAI **Rev. Inscription:** Hindi **Note:** Shape: square. Weight varies: 9.00-11.00 grams.

Date	Mintage	Good	VG	F	VF	XF
ND(1886-1920)	—	3.50	6.00	9.00	13.50	—

MALER KOTLA

Cis-Sutlej state located in the Punjab in northwest India, founded by the Maler Kotla family who were Sherwani Afghans who had travelled to India from Kabul in 1467 as officials of the Delhi emperors.

Coins are rupees of Ahmad Shah Durrani, and except for the last ruler, contain the chief's initial on the reverse. The chiefs were called Ra'is until 1821, Nawabs thereafter.

In 1849 the Punjab was annexed and the Cis-Sutlej states were merged into the new province of British India. Most of the Cis-Sutlej states distinguished themselves on the side of the British during the great revolt of 1857.

For similar issues see Jind, Nabha and Patiala.

RULERS:
Amir Khan, AH1237-1261/1821-1845AD
Identifying Marks:

On reverse

Sube (Mah bub) Khan, AH1261-1276/1845-1859AD
Identifying Marks:

On reverse

Sikandar Ali Khan, AH1276-1288/1859-1871AD
Identifying Marks:

On reverse

Ibrahim Ali Khan, AH1288-1326/1871-1908AD
Identifying Marks:

On reverse

Amir Khan
AH1237-1261 / 1821-1845AD

HAMMERED COINAGE

C# 13 1/4 RUPEE
Silver **Note:** 2.68-2.90 grams.

Date	Mintage	Good	VG	F	VF	XF
ND/4 (1821-45) Frozen	—	20.00	40.00	65.00	100	150

C# 14 1/2 RUPEE
Silver, 16 mm. **Note:** 5.35-5.80 grams.

Date	Mintage	Good	VG	F	VF	XF
ND/4 (1821-45) Frozen	—	18.00	45.00	75.00	120	170

C# 15 RUPEE
Silver, 17 mm. **Note:** 10.70-11.60 grams.

Date	Mintage	Good	VG	F	VF	XF
ND/4 (1821-45) Frozen	—	2.25	5.50	9.00	13.50	20.00

Sube (Mah bub) Khan
AH1261-1276 / 1845-1859AD

HAMMERED COINAGE

C# 18 1/4 RUPEE
Silver **Note:** 2.68-2.90 grams.

Date	Mintage	Good	VG	F	VF	XF
ND/4 (1845-59) Frozen	—	16.00	40.00	65.00	100	150

C# 19 1/2 RUPEE
Silver, 15 mm. **Note:** 5.35-5.80 grams.

Date	Mintage	Good	VG	F	VF	XF
ND/4 (1845-59) Frozen	—	18.00	45.00	75.00	120	170

C# 20 RUPEE
Silver **Note:** 10.70-11.60 grams.

Date	Mintage	Good	VG	F	VF	XF
ND(1845-59)	—	2.25	5.50	9.00	13.50	20.00

Sikandar Ali Khan
AH1276-1288 / 1859-1871AD

HAMMERED COINAGE

Y# 1 1/4 RUPEE
Silver **Note:** 2.68-2.90 grams.

Date	Mintage	Good	VG	F	VF	XF
ND(1859-71)	—	16.00	40.00	65.00	100	150

Y# 2 1/2 RUPEE
Silver **Note:** 5.35-5.80 grams.

Date	Mintage	Good	VG	F	VF	XF
ND(1859-71)	—	18.00	45.00	75.00	120	170

Y# 3.1 RUPEE
Silver **Note:** 10.70-11.60 grams.

Date	Mintage	Good	VG	F	VF	XF
ND(1859-71)	—	2.75	7.00	11.00	16.50	25.00
AH1281	—	20.00	50.00	60.00	85.00	110

Y# 3.2 RUPEE
Silver **Reverse:** 11-pointed star beneath small "s" within large "S" of "Falus" **Note:** 10.70-11.60 grams.

Date	Mintage	Good	VG	F	VF	XF
ND(1859-71)	—	6.00	15.00	22.00	30.00	42.50

Ibrahim Ali Khan
AH1288-1326 / 1871-1908AD

HAMMERED COINAGE

Y# 4 1/4 RUPEE
Silver **Note:** 2.68-2.90 grams.

Date	Mintage	Good	VG	F	VF	XF
ND(1871-1908)	—	16.00	40.00	65.00	100	150

Y# 5 1/2 RUPEE
Silver, 16 mm. **Note:** 5.35-5.80 grams.

Date	Mintage	Good	VG	F	VF	XF
ND(1871-1908)	—	18.00	45.00	75.00	120	170

Y# 6 RUPEE
Silver **Note:** 10-70.11.60 grams.

Date	Mintage	Good	VG	F	VF	XF
ND(1871-1908)	—	2.50	6.00	9.00	13.50	20.00
AH1292	—	5.00	12.50	15.00	20.00	35.00
AH1311	—	5.00	12.50	15.00	20.00	35.00

MEWAR

State located in Rajputana, northwest India. Capital:Udaipur.

The rulers of Mewar were universally regarded as the highest ranking Rajput house in India. The maharana of Mewar was looked upon as the representative of Rama, the ancient king of Ayodhya - and the family who were Sesodia Rajputs of the Gehlot clan, traced its descent through Rama to Kanak Sen who ruled in the 2nd century. The clan is believed to have migrated to Chitor from Gujarat sometime in the 8th century.

None of the indigenous rulers of India resisted the Muslim invasions into India with greater tenacity than the Rajputs of Mewar. It was their proud boast that they had never permitted a daughter to go into the Mughal harem. Three times the fortress and town of Chitor had fallen to Muslim invaders, to Alauddin Khilji (1303), to Bahadur Shah of Gujarat (1534) and to Akbar (1568). Each time Chitor gradually recovered but the last was the most traumatic experience of all. Rather than to submit to the Mughal onslaught, the women burned themselves on funeral pyres in a fearful rite called jauhar, and the men fell on the swords of the invaders.

After the sacking of Chitor the rana, Udai Singh, retired to the Aravali hills where he founded Udaipur, the capital after 1570. Udai Singh's son, Partab, refused to submit to the Mughal and recovered most of the territory lost in 1568. In the early 19th century Mewar suffered much at the hands of Marathas - Holkar, Sindhia and the Pindaris - until, in 1818, the State came under British supervision. In April 1948 Mewar was merged into Rajasthan and the maharana became governor Maharaj pramukh of the new province.

RULERS
Bhim Singh, AH1192-1244/1777-1828AD
Jawan Singh, AH1244-1254/1828-1838AD
Sirdar Singh, AH1254-1258/1838-1842AD
Swarup Singh, AH1258-1278/1842-1861AD
Shambhu Singh, AH1278-1291/1861-1874AD
Sajjan Singh, AH1291-1302/1874-1884AD
Fatteh Singh, VS1941-1986/1884-1929AD

MINTS

بهيلوارا

Bhilwara

Coins struck at Bhilwara Mint between ca. 1760 to the middle of the 19th century w/fictitious mint epithet: *Dar al-Khilafat Shahjahanabad.*

Mint mark: jhar

Symbol on obverse: (local issues)

चितोड़

Chitor

Coins struck at Chitor Mint between ca. 1760 to the middle of the 19th century w/fictitious mint epithet: *Dar al-Khilafat 'Shahjahanabad.*

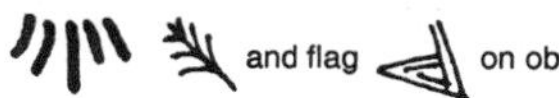

Mint marks:

चित्रकूट

Chitarkot

उदयपुर

Udaipur

Struck at the Udaipur mint between ca. 1780 to the middle of the 19th century w/fictitious mint epithet*: Dar al-Khilafat Shshjahanabad.*

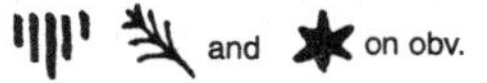

Mint marks:

Ordered y Bhim Singh, and struck at the Udaipur Mint until 1842AD. Recalled by Swarup Shah.

Mint marks:

Struck at the Udaipur Mint between 1842-1890AD. Many die varieties exist.

NOTE: All Mewar coinage is struck without ruler's name, and is largely undated. Certain types were generally struck over several reigns.

HAMMERED COINAGE

 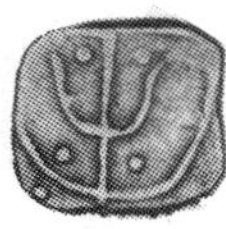

Y# 23 1/2 PAISA

Copper **Mint:** Umarda **Note:** Varieties exist.

Date	Mintage	Good	VG	F	VF	XF
ND//6 (1810)	—	0.45	0.75	1.00	1.50	—

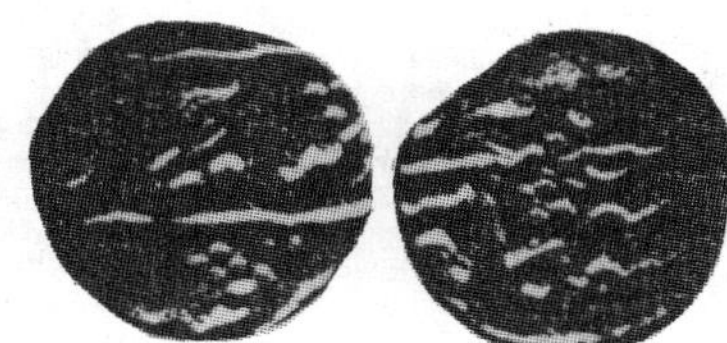

C# 2.5 PAISA

Copper **Obverse:** Symbol vertical **Obv. Inscription:** "Shah Alam (II)" **Mint:** Bhilwara

Date	Mintage	Good	VG	F	VF	XF
ND//4 (1760-1806)	—	3.00	5.00	7.50	11.50	—

Note: Known as the old Bhilwari Paisa, struck between 1780 and 1800AD

 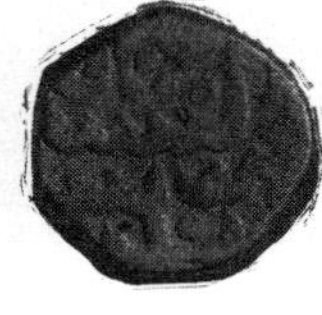

C# 3.1 PAISA

Copper **Obverse:** Leaf **Obv. Inscription:** "Shah Alam (II)" **Mint:** Bhilwara

Date	Mintage	Good	VG	F	VF	XF
ND(1760-1806)	—	1.50	2.50	4.00	6.50	—

C# 3.2 PAISA

Copper **Obverse:** Symbol oblique **Obv. Inscription:** "Shah Alam II" **Mint:** Bhilwara

Date	Mintage	Good	VG	F	VF	XF
ND//5 (1760-1806)	—	1.50	2.50	4.00	6.50	—
ND//12 (1760-1806)	—	1.50	2.50	4.00	6.50	—

Note: Known as the new Bhilwari Paisa, struck between about 1795 and 1845

C# 5 PAISA

Copper **Obverse:** Symbol **Obv. Inscription:** "Shah Alam II" **Reverse:** Legend **Mint:** Bhilwara

Date	Mintage	Good	VG	F	VF	XF
ND(1760-1806)	—	1.50	2.50	4.00	6.50	—

C# 1.1 PAISA

Copper **Obverse:** Pennant **Obv. Inscription:** "Shah Alam II" **Reverse:** Trident **Mint:** Chitor

Date	Mintage	Good	VG	F	VF	XF
ND(1760-1806)	—	1.50	2.50	4.00	6.50	—

C# 1.2 PAISA

Copper **Obverse:** Palm frond **Obv. Inscription:** "Shah Alam II" **Mint:** Chitor

Date	Mintage	Good	VG	F	VF	XF
ND(1760-1806)	—	1.50	2.50	4.00	6.50	—

C# 27 PAISA

Copper **Obv. Inscription:** "Alamgir II" **Mint:** Udaipur **Note:** Weight varies 10.00-10.20 grams.

Date	Mintage	Good	VG	F	VF	XF
ND(1780-1850)	—	—	—	—	—	—

C# 4 PAISA

Copper **Mint:** Jawad **Note:** For later issues, see Gwalior.

Date	Mintage	Good	VG	F	VF	XF
ND(1810)	—	3.50	6.00	7.50	10.00	—

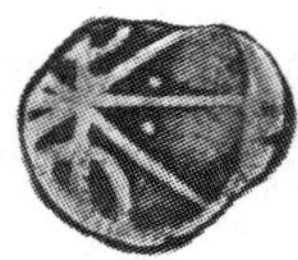 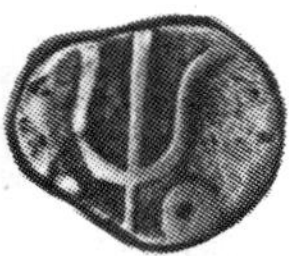

C# 2.1 2 PIES

Copper **Obv. Inscription:** "Shah Alam II" **Mint:** Chitor

Date	Mintage	Good	VG	F	VF	XF
ND(1760-1806)	—	0.45	0.75	1.25	1.75	—

C# 2.2 2 PIES

Copper **Obv. Inscription:** "Shah Alam II" **Mint:** Chitor

Date	Mintage	Good	VG	F	VF	XF
ND(1760-1806)	—	0.60	1.00	1.40	2.00	—

C# 2.3 2 PIES

Copper **Obverse:** Pennant **Obv. Inscription:** "Shah Alam II" **Reverse:** Trident **Mint:** Chitor

Date	Mintage	Good	VG	F	VF	XF
ND(1760-1806)	—	1.50	2.50	4.00	6.50	—

Note: Struck by local coppersmiths

C# 22 1/16 RUPEE

0.7000 g., Silver **Obv. Inscription:** "Alamgir II" **Mint:** Chitor

Date	Mintage	Good	VG	F	VF	XF
ND(1760-1850)	—	3.00	7.50	12.50	20.00	30.00

Y# 1 1/16 RUPEE

0.6500 g., Silver, 9 mm. **Mint:** Udaipur

Date	Mintage	Good	VG	F	VF	XF
ND(1842-90)	—	1.25	3.00	4.50	6.50	10.00

Y# 7.1 1/16 RUPEE

0.6500 g., Silver **Series:** Swarupshahi **Obv. Inscription:** Chitarkot/Udaipur **Rev. Inscription:** "Dosti Lundhun - Friendship With London" **Shape:** Round **Mint:** Udaipur

Date	Mintage	Good	VG	F	VF	XF
ND(1858-1920)	—	1.00	2.50	3.50	5.00	8.00

Y# 7.2 1/16 RUPEE

0.6500 g., Silver, 8-10 mm. **Obv. Inscription:** Chitarkot/Udaipur **Rev. Inscription:** "Dosti Lundhun - Friendship With London" **Shape:** Irregular **Mint:** Udaipur

Date	Mintage	Good	VG	F	VF	XF
ND(1858-1920)	—	1.25	3.00	4.50	6.50	10.00

C# 23 1/8 RUPEE

1.3000 g., Silver **Obv. Inscription:** "Alamgir II" **Mint:** Chitor

Date	Mintage	Good	VG	F	VF	XF
ND(1760-1850)	—	3.00	7.50	12.50	20.00	30.00

Y# 2 1/8 RUPEE

1.3500 g., Silver **Mint:** Udaipur

Date	Mintage	Good	VG	F	VF	XF
ND(1842-90)	—	1.00	2.50	3.50	5.00	8.00

Y# 8 1/8 RUPEE

1.3000 g., Silver, 11-12 mm. **Series:** Swarupshahi **Obv. Inscription:** Chitarkot/Udaipur **Rev. Inscription:** "Dosti Lundhun - Friendship With London" **Mint:** Udaipur

Date	Mintage	Good	VG	F	VF	XF
ND(1858-1920)	—	1.25	3.00	4.50	6.50	10.00

C# 24 1/4 RUPEE

Silver **Obv. Inscription:** "Alamgir II" **Mint:** Chitor **Note:** Weight varies 2.60-2.70 grams.

Date	Mintage	Good	VG	F	VF	XF
ND(1760-1850)	—	2.50	6.00	10.00	15.00	25.00

C# 30 1/4 RUPEE

2.7000 g., Silver **Obv. Inscription:** "Alamgir II" **Mint:** Udaipur

Date	Mintage	Good	VG	F	VF	XF
ND(1780-1850)	-	3.00	7.50	12.50	20.00	30.00

 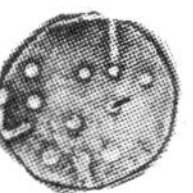

Y# 3 1/4 RUPEE

2.7000 g., Silver **Mint:** Udaipur **Note:** Struck at Udaipur Mint.

Date	Mintage	Good	VG	F	VF	XF
ND(1842-90)	—	1.00	2.50	3.50	5.00	8.00

Y# 9 1/4 RUPEE
2.6000 g., Silver **Series:** Swarupshahi **Obv. Inscription:** Chitarkot/Udaipur **Rev. Inscription:** "Dosti Lundhun - Friendship With London" **Mint:** Udaipur

Date	Mintage	Good	VG	F	VF	XF
ND(1858-1920)	—	1.00	2.50	3.50	5.00	8.00

C# 25 1/2 RUPEE
Silver **Obv. Inscription:** "Alamgir II" **Mint:** Chitor **Note:** Weight varies 5.30-5.40 grams.

Date	Mintage	Good	VG	F	VF	XF
ND(1760-1850)	—	2.50	6.00	10.00	15.00	25.00

C# 43 1/2 RUPEE
Silver **Obv. Inscription:** "Alamgir II" **Mint:** Udaipur **Note:** Weight varies 5.35-5.80 grams.

Date	Mintage	Good	VG	F	VF	XF
ND(1777-1842)	—	2.75	7.00	11.00	16.50	25.00

C# 31 1/2 RUPEE
5.4000 g., Silver **Obv. Inscription:** "Alamgir II" **Mint:** Udaipur

Date	Mintage	Good	VG	F	VF	XF
ND(1780-1850)	—	3.00	7.50	12.50	20.00	30.00

Y# 4 1/2 RUPEE
5.4000 g., Silver **Mint:** Udaipur

Date	Mintage	Good	VG	F	VF	XF
ND(1842-90)	—	1.25	3.00	4.50	6.50	10.00

Y# 10 1/2 RUPEE
Silver **Series:** Swarupshahi **Obv. Inscription:** Chitarkot / Udaipur **Rev. Inscription:** "Dosti Lundhun - Friendship With London" **Mint:** Udaipur **Note:** Weight varies: 5.20-5.40 grams.

Date	Mintage	Good	VG	F	VF	XF
ND(1858-1920)	—	1.25	3.00	4.50	6.50	10.00

C# 26 RUPEE
Silver **Obv. Inscription:** "Alamgir II" **Mint:** Chitor **Note:** Weight varies 10.70-11.10 grams.

Date	Mintage	Good	VG	F	VF	XF
ND(1760-1850)	—	1.35	3.50	7.00	10.00	15.00

C# 44 RUPEE
Silver **Obv. Inscription:** "Alamgir II" **Mint:** Udaipur **Note:** Weight varies 10.90-11.00 grams.

Date	Mintage	Good	VG	F	VF	XF
ND(1777-1842)	—	2.75	7.00	11.00	16.50	25.00

C# 32 RUPEE
11.8000 g., Silver **Obv. Inscription:** "Alamgir II" **Mint:** Udaipur

Date	Mintage	Good	VG	F	VF	XF
ND(1780-1850)	—	1.60	4.00	8.00	12.50	18.50

Y# 5 RUPEE
Silver **Mint:** Udaipur **Note:** Weight varies 10.80-10.90 grams.

Date	Mintage	Good	VG	F	VF	XF
ND(1842-90)	—	2.00	5.00	7.00	10.00	15.00

Y# 11 RUPEE
Silver **Series:** Swarupshahi **Obv. Inscription:** Chitarkot / Udaipur **Rev. Inscription:** "Dosti Lundhun - Friendship With London" **Mint:** Udaipur **Note:** Weight varies: 10.75-10.85 grams.

Date	Mintage	Good	VG	F	VF	XF
ND(1858-1920)	—	1.65	4.00	6.00	9.00	14.00

Y# B12 1/8 MOHUR
1.3500 g., Gold **Series:** Swarupshahi **Obv. Inscription:** Chitarkot/ Udaipur **Mint:** Udaipur

Date	Mintage	Good	VG	F	VF	XF
ND(1858-1920)	—	—	—	150	225	400

Y# A12 1/4 MOHUR
Gold **Series:** Swarupshahi **Obv. Inscription:** Chitarkot/Udaipur **Mint:** Udaipur **Note:** Weight varies: 2.70-2.75 grams.

Date	Mintage	Good	VG	F	VF	XF
ND(1858-1920)	—	—	—	150	300	500

Y# C12 1/2 MOHUR
5.4000 g., Gold **Series:** Swarupshahi **Obv. Inscription:** Chitarkot/ Udaipur **Mint:** Udaipur

Date	Mintage	Good	VG	F	VF	XF
ND(1858-1920)	—	—	—	150	300	500

Y# 6 2/3 MOHUR
7.5200 g., Gold **Mint:** Udaipur **Note:** Weight varies 10.80-10.90 grams.

Date	Mintage	Good	VG	F	VF	XF
ND(1842-90)	—	—	150	225	400	500

Y# 12 MOHUR
10.9500 g., Gold **Series:** Swarupshahi **Obv. Inscription:** Chitarkot/Udaipur **Mint:** Udaipur

Date	Mintage	Good	VG	F	VF	XF
ND(1858-1920)	—	—	—	165	225	350

Fatteh Singh
VS1941-1986 / 1884-1929AD
HAMMERED COINAGE

C# 38 RUPEE
Silver **Mint:** Bhilwara **Note:** Weight varies: 10.70-11.10 grams.

Date	Mintage	Good	VG	F	VF	XF
AH-//1	—	4.00	10.00	20.00	30.00	45.00
ND//1 (1760-1850)	—	4.00	10.00	20.00	30.00	45.00
ND//2 (1760-1850)	—	4.00	10.00	20.00	30.00	45.00
ND//3 (1760-1850)	—	4.00	10.00	20.00	30.00	45.00
ND//4 (1760-1850)	—	4.00	10.00	20.00	30.00	45.00
ND//5 (1760-1850)	—	4.00	10.00	20.00	30.00	45.00
ND//6 (1760-1850)	—	4.00	10.00	20.00	30.00	45.00
ND//7 (1760-1850)	—	4.00	10.00	20.00	30.00	45.00
ND//8 (1760-1850)	—	4.00	10.00	20.00	30.00	45.00

MEWAR FEUDATORIES - BHINDA

Zurawar Singh
AH1214-1243 / 1799-1827AD
HAMMERED COINAGE

C# 1 PAISA
Copper

Date	Mintage	Good	VG	F	VF	XF
ND(1815)	—	3.00	5.00	7.50	12.50	—

MEWAR FEUDATORIES - SALUMBA

HAMMERED COINAGE

C# 1 2 PIES
Copper

Date	Mintage	Good	VG	F	VF	XF
ND(1815-34)	—	3.00	5.00	7.50	12.50	—
ND(1835-70)	—	3.00	5.00	7.50	12.50	—

MEWAR FEUDATORIES - SHAHPUR

HAMMERED COINAGE

C# 20 1/4 RUPEE
2.6000 g., Silver, 14 mm. **Obv. Inscription:** "Alamgir II"

Date	Mintage	Good	VG	F	VF	XF
AHxxx8//12	—	—	20.00	32.00	50.00	70.00

C# 10 PAISA
Copper

Date	Mintage	Good	VG	F	VF	XF
ND(1827-70)	—	20.00	30.00	45.00	65.00	—

C# 21 1/2 RUPEE
5.3100 g., Silver, 17 mm.

Date	Mintage	Good	VG	F	VF	XF
AHxxx8/12	—	8.00	20.00	32.00	50.00	70.00

C# 22 RUPEE
10.6000 g., Silver

Date	Mintage	Good	VG	F	VF	XF
AHxxx8//12	—	5.00	12.50	18.50	25.00	35.00

C# 29 MOHUR
Gold, 18 mm. **Note:** Weight varies 10.30-10.50 grams.

Date	Mintage	Good	VG	F	VF	XF
AHxxx8//12	—	—	150	275	400	600

MYSORE

Large state in Southern India. Governed until 1761AD by various Hindu dynasties, then by Haider Ali and Tipu Sultan.

In 1831, Krishnaraja being deposed for mal-administration and pensioned off, the administration of Mysore State then came directly under the British. The coinage of Mysore ceased in 1843. After the Great Revolt of 1857, the policy of eliminating Indian princes was discontinued and as a result, Mysore was returned in 1881 to the control of an adopted son of Krishnaraja Wodeyar. The Wodeyars continued to hold the State until 1947 although they did not issue coins. In November 1956 modern Mysore was inaugurated as a linguistic state within the Indian Union.

NOTE: For earlier issues see Mysore, Independent Kingdoms during British rule.

RULERS
Dewan Purnaiya, regent AH1214-1225/1799-1810AD
Krishna Raja Wodeyar, AH1225-1285/1810-1868AD

MINTS

مهي سور

Mysore

نكر or نگر

Nagar

MONETARY SYSTEM
2 Fanams = 1 Anna
4 Annas = 1 Pavali
4 Pavalis = 1 Rupee

ANONYMOUS HAMMERED COINAGE

C# 199 1/6 PAVALI
Silver **Obv. Inscription:** "Shah Alam II" **Mint:** Mysore **Note:** Weight varies 0.45-0.48 grams.

Date	Mintage	Good	VG	F	VF	XF
ND(1799-1810)	—	2.25	5.50	11.00	18.00	25.00

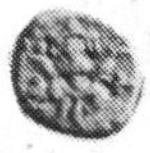

C# 200 1/3 PAVALI
Silver **Obverse:** Dancing figure (Chamundi) **Obv. Inscription:** "Shah Alam II" **Mint:** Mysore **Note:** Weight varies 0.89-0.96 grams.

Date	Mintage	VG	F	VF	XF	Unc
ND(1799-1810)	—	12.50	25.00	42.00	70.00	—

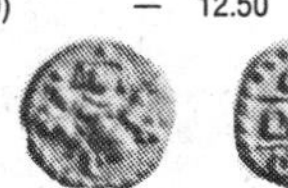

C# 201 2/3 PAVALI
Silver **Obverse:** Dancing figure (Chamundi) **Obv. Inscription:** "Shah Alam II" **Mint:** Mysore **Note:** Weight varies: 1.78-1.92 grams.

Date	Mintage	Good	VG	F	VF	XF
ND(1799-1810)	—	5.00	12.50	25.00	42.00	70.00

C# 202 1/4 RUPEE (Pavali)
Silver **Obverse:** Dancing figure (Chamundi) **Obv. Inscription:** "Shah Alam II" **Mint:** Mysore **Note:** Weight varies: 2.68-2.90 grams.

Date	Mintage	Good	VG	F	VF	XF
AH1220	—	3.00	7.50	15.00	25.00	35.00
AH1221	—	3.00	7.50	15.00	25.00	35.00
AH1223	—	3.00	7.50	15.00	25.00	35.00
AH1226	—	3.00	7.50	15.00	25.00	35.00
AH1229	—	3.00	7.50	15.00	25.00	35.00
AH1243	—	3.00	7.50	15.00	25.00	35.00
AH3421	—	3.00	7.50	15.00	25.00	35.00
AH4421	—	3.00	7.50	15.00	25.00	35.00
AH1244	—	3.00	7.50	15.00	25.00	35.00
AH1245	—	3.00	7.50	15.00	25.00	35.00
AH1246	—	3.00	7.50	15.00	25.00	35.00
AH1247	—	3.00	7.50	15.00	25.00	35.00
AH1248	—	3.00	7.50	15.00	25.00	35.00

C# 205 1/4 RUPEE (Pavali)
Silver **Obverse:** Dancing figure (Chamundi) **Obv. Inscription:** "Shah Alam II" **Mint:** Mysore **Note:** Weight varies: 2.68-2.90 grams. Similar coins were issued by the Arcot Mint of French India.

Date	Mintage	Good	VG	F	VF	XF
AH1220//44 (sic)	—	5.00	12.50	20.00	30.00	45.00
AH1220//45 (sic)	—	5.00	12.50	20.00	30.00	45.00
AH1221//45 (sic)	—	5.00	12.50	20.00	30.00	45.00
ND//76 (1807-08)	—	5.00	12.50	20.00	30.00	45.00
ND//84 (1808-09)	—	5.00	12.50	20.00	30.00	45.00

C# 206 1/2 RUPEE
Silver **Obv. Inscription:** "Shah Alam II" **Mint:** Mysore **Note:** Weight varies 5.35-5.80 grams.

Date	Mintage	Good	VG	F	VF	XF
ND//76 (1808-09)	—	6.00	15.00	25.00	40.00	60.00

C# 207 RUPEE
Silver **Obv. Inscription:** "Shah Alam II" **Mint:** Mysore **Note:** Weight varies 10.70-11.60 grams.

Date	Mintage	Good	VG	F	VF	XF
AH1219//44 (sic)	—	3.00	7.50	12.50	20.00	30.00
AH1221//25 (sic)	—	3.00	7.50	12.50	20.00	30.00
AH1221//45 (sic)	—	3.00	7.50	12.50	20.00	30.00
AH1221//47 (sic)	—	3.00	7.50	12.50	20.00	30.00
AH1221//48 (sic)	—	3.00	7.50	12.50	20.00	30.00
AH12xx//48 (sic)	—	3.00	7.50	12.50	20.00	30.00
AH1222//46 (sic)	—	3.00	7.50	12.50	20.00	30.00
AH1222//64 (sic)	—	3.00	7.50	12.50	20.00	30.00
AH1223//64 (sic)	—	3.00	7.50	12.50	20.00	30.00
AH1224//64 (sic)	—	3.00	7.50	12.50	20.00	30.00
AH1224//74 (sic)	—	3.00	7.50	12.50	20.00	30.00
AH1225//74 (sic)	—	3.00	7.50	12.50	20.00	30.00
AH1225//94 (sic)	—	3.00	7.50	12.50	20.00	30.00
AH1226//94 (sic)	—	3.00	7.50	12.50	20.00	30.00
AH1227//95 (sic)	—	3.00	7.50	12.50	20.00	30.00
AH1228//95 (sic)	—	3.00	7.50	12.50	20.00	30.00
AH1229//96 (sic)	—	3.00	7.50	12.50	20.00	30.00
AH1230//97 (sic)	—	3.00	7.50	12.50	20.00	30.00
AH1231//98 (sic)	—	3.00	7.50	12.50	20.00	30.00
AH1232//99 (sic)	—	3.00	7.50	12.50	20.00	30.00
AH1234//98 (sic)	—	3.00	7.50	12.50	20.00	30.00
AH1234//99 (sic)	—	3.00	7.50	12.50	20.00	30.00
AH1235//98 (sic)	—	3.00	7.50	12.50	20.00	30.00
AH1236//98 (sic)	—	3.00	7.50	12.50	20.00	30.00
AH1237//37 (sic)	—	3.00	7.50	12.50	20.00	30.00
AH1238//37 (sic)	—	3.00	7.50	12.50	20.00	30.00
AH1239//3x (sic)	—	3.00	7.50	12.50	20.00	30.00
AH1240//98 (sic)	—	3.00	7.50	12.50	20.00	30.00
AH1242//37 (sic)	—	3.00	7.50	12.50	20.00	30.00
AH1243//98 (sic)	—	3.00	7.50	12.50	20.00	30.00
AH1247//47 (sic)	—	3.00	7.50	12.50	20.00	30.00
AHx421//47 (sic)	—	3.00	7.50	12.50	20.00	30.00
AH1248//48 (sic)	—	3.00	7.50	12.50	20.00	30.00
AHx421//45 (sic)	—	3.00	7.50	12.50	20.00	30.00

C# 212 FANAM
Gold **Subject:** Narasimha **Obv. Inscription:** "Shah Alam II" **Mint:** Mysore **Note:** Weight varies: 0.33-0.40 grams.

Date	Mintage	Good	VG	F	VF	XF
ND(1799-1810)	—	—	7.50	10.00	20.00	30.00

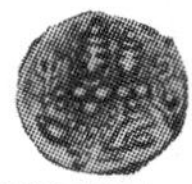

C# 210 PAGODA
3.4000 g., Gold **Subject:** Shiva and Parvati **Obv. Inscription:** "Shah Alam II" **Mint:** Mysore **Note:** Fanams and 1/2 Pagodas of this type are recent fabrications.

Date	Mintage	Good	VG	F	VF	XF
ND(1799-1806)	—	—	45.00	60.00	75.00	100

C# 215 1/4 MOHUR
Gold **Obv. Inscription:** "Shah Alam II" **Mint:** Mysore **Note:** Weight varies 2.68-2.85 grams.

Date	Mintage	Good	VG	F	VF	XF
ND//45 (1803-04) Rare	—	—	—	—	—	—

Dewan Purnaiya
AH1214-1225 / 1799-1810AD

A Sardula (mythical tiger) is illustrated on all of Dewan Purnaiya's coins.

HAMMERED COINAGE

C# 185 6-1/4 CASH
Copper **Obverse:** Sardula (mythical tiger) **Reverse:** Without value, with Mysore **Mint:** Mysore

Date	Mintage	Good	VG	F	VF	XF
ND(1799-1810)	—	4.00	6.50	10.00	16.00	—

C# 185a 6-1/4 CASH
Copper **Obverse:** Sardula (mythical tiger) **Reverse:** Without value or Mysore **Mint:** Mysore

Date	Mintage	Good	VG	F	VF	XF
ND(1799-1810)	—	2.50	4.50	7.00	12.00	—

C# 185b 6-1/4 CASH
Copper **Obverse:** Sardula (mythical tiger) **Reverse:** Value in English, with Mysore **Mint:** Mysore

Date	Mintage	Good	VG	F	VF	XF
ND(1799-1810)	—	3.00	5.50	9.00	14.00	—
ND(1799-1810) CASH retrograde	—	4.00	6.50	10.00	16.00	—

C# 186 12-1/2 CASH
Copper **Obverse:** Sardula (mythical tiger) **Mint:** Mysore

Date	Mintage	Good	VG	F	VF	XF
ND(1799-1810)	—	7.00	12.00	18.00	28.00	—

C# 187 25 CASH
Copper **Obverse:** Sardula (mythical tiger) **Reverse:** English legend often blundered **Mint:** Mysore

Date	Mintage	Good	VG	F	VF	XF
ND(1799-1810)	—	3.50	6.00	9.50	15.00	—

C# 189 75 CASH
23.5900 g., Copper **Obverse:** Sardula (mythical tiger) **Mint:** Mysore

Date	Mintage	Good	VG	F	VF	XF
ND(1799-1810)	—	—	—	—	—	—

Note: Silver coinage of Dewan Purnaiya is identical to that of Krishna Raja Wodeyar and they are all listed together following these copper issues

Krishna Raja Wodeyar
AH1225-1285 / 1810-1868AD

British control after 1831
(Types I-IV struck 1811-1833)
SRI VARIETIES

Variety I:

Variety II:

Type I, ca. 1811
Obv: Elephant left below sun and moon. Rev: 3-line Nagari legend.

Type II
Obv: Elephant below Kanarese, *Sri* between sun and moon. Rev: 2 lines of Kanarese, denomination in English at the top on the 5 and 10 Cash, at the bottom on the 20 and 40 Cash. The English denomination is often encountered blundered.

Type III
Obv: Elephant below Kanarese, *Sri* between sun and moon. Rev: 3 line Kanarese legend, denomination in English at the bottom. The English denomination is often encountered blundered or retrograde.

Type IV
Obv: Elephant below Kanarese leg. *Sri* between sun and moon/*Chamuni*. Rev: Similar to Type III.

Type V
Obv: Sardula (mythical lion) below Kanarese legend *Sri* between sun and moon/*Chamundi*. Rev. Kanarese legend *Krishna* in center surrounded by mintname and denomination.
NOTE: The 1833 has 2 varieties: W/palm frond before Sardula and w/frond before and above.

Type VI
Obv: Lion, date below. Struck at the Bangalore subsidary mint facility.

HAMMERED COINAGE

C# 206a 1/2 RUPEE
Silver **Mint:** Nagar **Note:** Weight varies 5.35-5.80 grams.

Date	Mintage	Good	VG	F	VF	XF
ND//74 (1810)	—	17.50	35.00	60.00	100	145
ND//84 (1810)	—	17.50	35.00	60.00	100	145

C# 207a RUPEE
Silver **Mint:** Nagar **Note:** Weight varies 10.70-11.60 grams.

Date	Mintage	Good	VG	F	VF	XF
ND//46 (1810)	—	13.50	27.50	45.00	62.50	85.00
AH1225/84	—	13.50	27.50	45.00	62.50	85.00

C# 190.1 2-1/2 CASH
Copper **Series:** Type V **Obverse:** Sardula (mythical lion) below Kanarese legend "Sri" between sun and moon, "Chamund" **Reverse:** Kanarese legend, "Krishna" in center surrounded by mintname and denomination **Mint:** Mysore

Date	Mintage	Good	VG	F	VF	XF
1833	—	4.00	6.00	9.00	13.50	—

C# 190.2 2-1/2 CASH
Copper **Series:** Type VI **Obverse:** Lion, date below **Mint:** Mysore **Note:** Struck at the Bangalore subsidary mint facility.

Date	Mintage	Good	VG	F	VF	XF
1834	—	3.00	5.00	8.00	12.50	—
1836	—	3.00	5.00	8.00	12.50	—
1839	—	2.50	4.00	6.50	10.00	—
1840	—	2.50	4.00	6.50	10.00	—
1841	—	2.50	4.00	6.50	10.00	—
1842	—	2.00	3.25	5.00	8.50	—
1843	—	2.00	3.25	5.00	8.50	—

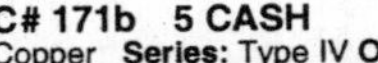

C# 171b 5 CASH
Copper **Series:** Type IV **Obverse:** Elephant below Kanarese, "Sri" between sun and moon, "Chamuni" **Obv. Legend:** "Sri" var. I **Reverse:** Similar to Type III **Mint:** Mysore

Date	Mintage	Good	VG	F	VF	XF
ND(1811-33)	—	2.50	4.00	6.50	10.00	—

C# 171a.1 5 CASH
Copper **Series:** Type III **Obverse:** Elephant below Kanarese, "Sri" between sun and moon **Obv. Legend:** "Sri" var. I **Reverse:** 3 line Kanarese legend, denomination in English at the bottom **Mint:** Mysore **Note:** The English denomination is often encountered blundered or retrograde.

Date	Mintage	Good	VG	F	VF	XF
ND(1811-33)	—	4.00	6.50	10.00	15.00	—

C# 171a.2 5 CASH
Copper **Series:** Type III **Obverse:** Elephant below Kanarese, "Sri" between sun and moon **Obv. Legend:** "Sri" var. II **Reverse:** 3 line Kanarese legend, denomination in English at the bottom **Mint:** Mysore **Note:** The English denomination is often encountered blundered or retrograde.

Date	Mintage	Good	VG	F	VF	XF
ND(1811-33)	—	4.00	6.50	10.00	15.00	—

C# 171 5 CASH
Copper **Series:** Type II **Obverse:** Elephant below Kanarese, "Sri" between sun and moon **Reverse:** 2 lines of Kanarese, denomination in English at the top on the 5 and 10 Cash, at the bottom on the 20 and 40 Cash **Mint:** Mysore **Note:** The English denomination is often encountered blundered.

Date	Mintage	Good	VG	F	VF	XF
ND(1811-33)	—	2.00	3.25	5.00	8.50	—
ND(1811-33) (X CASH in error)	—	2.50	4.50	7.00	11.50	—
ND(1811) Yr. 2	—	9.00	16.00	24.00	35.00	—

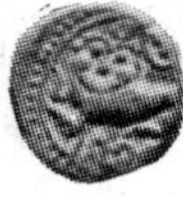 

C# 191.1 5 CASH
Copper **Series:** Type V **Obverse:** Sardula (mythical lion) below Kanarese legend "Sri" between sun and moon, "Chamund" **Reverse:** Kanarese legend, "Krishna" in center surrounded by mintname and denomination **Mint:** Mysore

Date	Mintage	Good	VG	F	VF	XF
1833	—	2.00	3.25	5.00	8.50	—
1834	—	2.00	3.25	5.00	8.50	—
1838	—	2.00	3.25	5.00	8.50	—

C# 191.2 5 CASH
Copper **Series:** Type VI **Obverse:** Lion, date below **Mint:** Mysore **Note:** Struck at the Bangalore subsidary mint facility.

Date	Mintage	Good	VG	F	VF	XF
1834	—	1.75	2.75	4.00	7.00	—
1835	—	1.75	2.75	4.00	7.00	—
1836	—	1.75	2.75	4.00	7.00	—
1837	—	1.75	2.75	4.00	7.00	—
1838	—	1.75	2.75	4.00	7.00	—
1839	—	1.75	2.75	4.00	7.00	—
1840	—	1.75	2.75	4.00	7.00	—
1841	—	1.75	2.75	4.00	7.00	—
1842	—	1.75	2.75	4.00	7.00	—
1843	—	1.75	2.75	4.00	7.00	—

C# 170 6-1/4 CASH
Copper **Series:** Type I, ca.1811 **Obverse:** Elephant left below sun and moon **Reverse:** 3 line Nagari legend **Mint:** Mysore

Date	Mintage	Good	VG	F	VF	XF
ND(1811)	—	5.00	9.00	13.00	20.00	—

C# 174b 10 CASH
Copper **Series:** Type IV **Obverse:** Elephant below Kanarese, "Sri" between sun and moon, "Chamuni" **Obv. Legend:** "Sri" var. I **Reverse:** Similar to Type III **Mint:** Mysore

Date	Mintage	Good	VG	F	VF	XF
ND(1811-33)	—	4.00	6.50	10.00	15.00	—

C# 174a 10 CASH
Copper **Series:** Type III **Obverse:** Elephant below Kanarese, "Sri" between sun and moon **Obv. Legend:** "Sri" var. II **Reverse:** 3 line Kanarese legend, denomination in English at the bottom **Mint:** Mysore **Note:** The English denomination is often encountered blundered or retrograde.

Date	Mintage	Good	VG	F	VF	XF
ND(1811-33)	—	3.00	5.00	8.00	12.50	—
ND(1811-33) (X CASH retrograde)	—	4.00	6.50	10.00	15.00	—

C# 174 10 CASH
Copper **Series:** Type II **Obverse:** Elephant below Kanarese, "Sri" between sun and moon **Obv. Legend:** "Sri" var. I **Reverse:** 2 lines of Kanarese, denomination in English at the top on the 5 and 10 Cash, at the bottom on the 20 and 40 Cash **Mint:** Mysore **Note:** The English denomination is often encountered blundered.

Date	Mintage	Good	VG	F	VF	XF
ND(1811-33)	—	4.50	8.00	12.00	18.00	—

C# 192.1 10 CASH
Copper **Series:** Type V **Obverse:** Sardula (mythical lion) below Kanarese legend "Sri" between sun and moon, "Chamund" **Reverse:** Kanarese legend, "Krishna" in center surrounded by mintname and denomination **Mint:** Mysore

Date	Mintage	Good	VG	F	VF	XF
1833	—	2.50	4.00	6.50	10.00	—
1834/3	—	2.50	4.00	6.50	10.00	—
1834	—	2.50	4.00	6.50	10.00	—

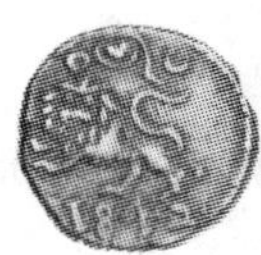 

C# 192.2 10 CASH
Copper **Series:** Type VI **Obverse:** Lion, date below **Mint:** Mysore **Note:** Struck at the Bangalore subsidary mint facility.

Date	Mintage	Good	VG	F	VF	XF
1834/3	—	4.00	6.50	11.00	17.00	—
1834	—	4.00	6.50	10.00	15.00	—
1835	—	3.00	5.00	8.00	12.50	—
1836	—	3.00	5.00	8.00	12.50	—
1837	—	3.00	5.00	8.00	12.50	—
1838	—	3.00	5.00	8.00	12.50	—
1839	—	3.00	5.00	8.00	12.50	—
1840	—	3.00	5.00	8.00	12.50	—
1841	—	3.00	5.00	8.00	12.50	—
1842	—	3.00	5.00	8.00	12.50	—
1843	—	3.00	5.00	8.00	12.50	—
1848 (sic)	—	2.00	3.25	5.50	8.50	—
1848 (sic) Reverse legend MEILLEE XX CASH... retrograde	—	2.00	3.25	5.50	8.50	—

C# 177b 20 CASH
Copper **Series:** Type IV **Obverse:** Elephant below Kanarese, "Sri" between sun and moon, "Chamuni" **Obv. Legend:** "Sri" var. I **Reverse:** Similar to Type III **Mint:** Mysore

Date	Mintage	Good	VG	F	VF	XF
ND(1811-33)	—	3.00	5.00	8.00	12.50	—

C# 177a 20 CASH
Copper **Series:** Type III **Obverse:** Elephant below Kanarese, "Sri" between sun and moon **Obv. Legend:** "Sri" var. II **Reverse:** 3 line Kanarese legend, denomination in English at the bottom **Mint:** Mysore **Note:** The English denomination is often encountered blundered or retrograde.

Date	Mintage	Good	VG	F	VF	XF
ND(1811-33)	—	1.00	1.75	2.50	4.00	—

C# 177 20 CASH
Copper **Series:** Type II **Obverse:** Elephant below Kanarese, "Sri" between sun and moon **Obv. Legend:** "Sri" var. I **Reverse:** 2 lines of Kanarese, denomination in English at the top on the 5 and 10 Cash, at the bottom on the 20 and 40 Cash **Mint:** Mysore **Note:** The English denomination is often encountered blundered.

Date	Mintage	Good	VG	F	VF	XF
ND(1811-33)	—	1.25	2.25	3.50	5.50	—

C# 193.1 20 CASH
Copper **Series:** Type V **Obverse:** Sardula (mythical lion) below Kanarese legend "Sri" between sun and moon, "Chamund" **Reverse:** Kanarese legend, "Krishna" in center surrounded by mintname and denomination **Mint:** Mysore **Note:** The 1833 has 2 varieties: with palm frond before Sardula and with frond before and above.

Date	Mintage	Good	VG	F	VF	XF
1833	—	2.00	3.25	5.00	8.50	—
1834	—	2.00	3.25	5.00	8.50	—
1835	—	2.00	3.25	5.00	8.50	—
1836	—	2.00	3.25	5.00	8.50	—
1837	—	2.00	3.25	5.00	8.50	—
1838	—	2.00	3.25	5.00	8.50	—

C# 193.2 20 CASH
Copper **Series:** Type VI **Obverse:** Lion, date below **Mint:** Mysore **Note:** Struck at the Bangalore subsidary mint facility. All dates have MEILEE on reverse; some 1834 have MILAY, and some 1837 have MILEE. Some numerals are distored.

Date	Mintage	Good	VG	F	VF	XF
1833	—	3.00	5.00	8.00	12.50	—
1834	—	3.00	5.00	8.00	12.50	—
1835	—	2.50	4.00	6.50	10.00	—
1836	—	2.50	4.00	6.50	10.00	—
1837/5	—	2.00	3.25	5.50	8.50	—
1837	—	2.00	3.25	5.50	8.50	—
1838	—	2.00	3.25	5.50	8.50	—
1839	—	2.00	3.25	5.50	8.50	—
1840	—	2.00	3.25	5.50	8.50	—
1841	—	2.00	3.25	5.50	8.50	—
1843	—	2.00	3.25	5.50	8.50	—

C# 179 25 CASH
Copper **Series:** Type IV **Obverse:** Elephant below Kanarese, "Sri" between sun and moon, "Chamuni" **Obv. Legend:** "Sri" var. I **Reverse:** Similar to Type III **Mint:** Mysore **Note:** Weight varies: 11.20-11.40 grams.

Date	Mintage	Good	VG	F	VF	XF
ND(1811-33)	—	100	175	275	400	—

C# 180 40 CASH
Copper **Series:** Type II **Obverse:** Elephant below Kanarese, "Sri" between sun and moon **Obv. Legend:** "Sri" var. I **Reverse:** 2 lines of Kanarese, denomination in English at the top on the 5 and 10 Cash, at the bottom on the 20 and 40 Cash **Mint:** Mysore **Note:** The English denomination is often encountered blundered.

Date	Mintage	VG	F	VF	XF	Unc
ND(1811-33)	—	60.00	100	150	—	—

NABHA

Cis-Sutlej state located in the Punjab in northwest India and founded in the 18th century.

The ancestry of these rulers was identical to that of Jind. Until 1845 Nabha's history closely paralleled that of Patiala. At this point, however, the raja sided with the Sikhs. It was left to his son to make amends to the British in 1847 after the first Sikh war (1845-46). Their independence became somewhat circumscribed and in 1849 the Punjab was annexed and the states were merged into the new province of British India.

RULERS

Jaswant Singh, VS1840-1897/1783-1840AD
Identifying Marks:

On rev. C#20.1-20.3 On rev. C#20.4

Bharpur Singh, VS1903-1920/1846-1863AD
Identifying Marks:

On reverse

Hira Singh, VS1928-1968/1871-1911AD
Identifying Marks:

On reverse

MINT

سرکار نابهه

Sarkar Nabha

Jaswant Singh
VS1840-1897 / 1783-1840AD
HAMMERED COINAGE

C# 20.1 RUPEE
Silver **Obv. Inscription:** Ahmad Shah Durrani **Reverse:** Cross-like symbol below "Sin"

Date	Mintage	Good	VG	F	VF	XF
ND(1782-1840)	—	11.00	—	—	70.00	100

C# 20.2 RUPEE
Silver **Obv. Inscription:** Ahmad Shah Durrani **Reverse:** Star below "Sin"

Date	Mintage	Good	VG	F	VF	XF
VS(18)77 (1820)	—	11.00	28.00	45.00	70.00	100

C# 20.3 RUPEE
Silver **Obv. Inscription:** Ahmad Shah Durrani **Reverse:** Branch symbol

Date	Mintage	Good	VG	F	VF	XF
VS(18)82 (1825)	—	11.00	28.00	45.00	70.00	100
VS(18)83 (1826)	—	11.00	28.00	45.00	70.00	100
VS(18)85 (1828)	—	11.00	28.00	45.00	70.00	100
VS(18)93 (1836)	—	11.00	28.00	45.00	70.00	100

C# 20.4 RUPEE
Silver **Obv. Inscription:** Guru Govind Singh **Reverse:** Leaf to left of stylized "4"

Date	Mintage	Good	VG	F	VF	XF
VS1892 (1835)	—	25.00	60.00	100	150	225
VS1893 (1836)	—	25.00	60.00	100	150	225
VS1895 (1838)	—	25.00	60.00	100	150	225

Bharpur Singh
VS1903-1920 / 1846-1863AD
HAMMERED COINAGE

Y# 1.1 RUPEE
Silver **Obv. Inscription:** Guru Govind Singh **Reverse:** Leaf to left of stylized "4", star to right **Note:** 11.00-11.10 grams.

Date	Mintage	Good	VG	F	VF	XF
VS1903 (1849)	—	18.00	45.00	75.00	120	170
VS1907 (1850)	—	18.00	45.00	75.00	120	170
VS1908 (1851)	—	18.00	45.00	75.00	120	170
VS1909 (1852)	—	18.00	45.00	75.00	120	170
VS1911 (1854)	—	18.00	45.00	75.00	120	170
VS1912 (1855)	—	18.00	45.00	75.00	120	170
VS1913 (1856)	—	18.00	45.00	75.00	120	170
VS1916 (1859)	—	18.00	45.00	75.00	120	170
VS1917 (1860)	—	18.00	45.00	75.00	120	170
VS1920 (1863)	—	18.00	45.00	75.00	120	170

Y# 1.2 RUPEE
Silver **Obv. Inscription:** Guru Govind Singh **Note:** 11.00-11.10 grams. Struck from Y-A2 mohur dies, possibly for presentation.

Date	Mintage	Good	VG	F	VF	XF
VS1907 (1850)	—	20.00	50.00	100	175	250

Y# A2 MOHUR
Gold **Obv. Inscription:** Guru Govind Singh **Note:** 9.50-9.60 grams.

Date	Mintage	Good	VG	F	VF	XF
VS1907 (1850)	—	—	275	400	600	800
VS1911 (1854)	—	—	275	400	600	800

Hira Singh
VS1928-1968 / 1871-1911AD
HAMMERED COINAGE

Y# 2 RUPEE
Silver **Obverse:** Date **Obv. Inscription:** Guru Govind Singh **Reverse:** Branch and katar to left of stylized "4", date **Note:** 10.70-11.60 grams.

Date	Mintage	Good	VG	F	VF	XF
VS1927 (1870)	—	18.00	45.00	75.00	120	170
VS1928 (1871)	—	18.00	45.00	75.00	120	170
VS1929 (1872)	—	18.00	45.00	75.00	120	170

Y# 3 MOHUR
10.1500 g., Gold **Obverse:** Date **Obv. Inscription:** Guru Govind Singh **Reverse:** Branch and katar to left of stylized "4", date

Date	Mintage	Good	VG	F	VF	XF
VS192x (1873)	—	—	250	400	650	800

NARWAR

Narwar was a tiny state in western Malwa with a population of about four thousand (ca.1900). The ruling chiefs were Jhala Rajputs. In AH1220/1805AD it came under Gwalior.

For later issues see Gwalior - Narwar Mint listings.

RULERS
Daulat Rao, AH1209-1243/1794-1827AD

MINT MARKS:

Katar 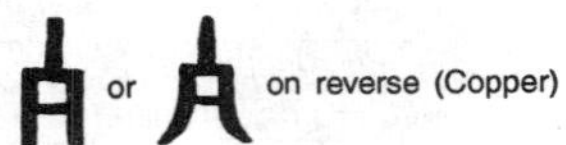 or on reverse (Copper)

Bhilsa leaf on reverse (Silver)

HAMMERED COINAGE

KM# 22 1/2 PAISA
3.3700 g., Copper **Obv. Inscription:** "Shah Alam II" **Reverse:** Vertical katar **Note:** Struck during the reign of local ruler Daulat Rao, AH1209-43/1794-1827AD.

Date	Mintage	Good	VG	F	VF	XF
AH1216//43	—	1.75	3.00	5.00	8.00	—
AH1216//44	—	1.75	3.00	5.00	8.00	—
AH1216//45	—	1.75	3.00	5.00	8.00	—
AH1217//44	—	1.75	3.00	5.00	8.00	—
AH1217//45	—	1.75	3.00	5.00	8.00	—
AH1217//46	—	1.75	3.00	5.00	8.00	—
AH1219//46	—	1.75	3.00	5.00	8.00	—

KM# 26 RUPEE
Silver **Obv. Inscription:** "Shah Alam II" **Reverse:** Katar and floral spray **Note:** 10.70-11.60 grams. Struck during the reign of local ruler Daulat Rao, AH1209-43/1794-1827AD.

Date	Mintage	VG	F	VF	XF	Unc
AH1216//44	—	15.00	25.00	35.00	50.00	—
AH1216//45	—	15.00	25.00	35.00	50.00	—
AH1217//44	—	15.00	25.00	35.00	50.00	—
AH1217//45	—	15.00	25.00	35.00	50.00	—
AH1217//48	—	15.00	25.00	35.00	50.00	—

NAWANAGAR

(Navanagar)

State located on the Kathiawar peninsula, west-central India.

The rulers, or jams, of Kutch were Jareja Rajputs who had entered the Kathiawar peninsular from Kutch and dispossessed the ancient family of Jathwas. Jam Raval, who was possibly the elder brother of the Jam of Kutch, founded Nawanagar about 1535. The great fort of Nawanagar was built by Jam Jasaji (d. 1814). The state became tributary to the Gaekwar family and, in the 19th century, also to the British. In 1948, the state was merged into Saurashtra.

RULERS
Vibhaji, VS1909-1951/1852-1894AD
Jaswant Singh, VS1951-1964/1894-1907AD

MONETARY SYSTEM
2 Trambiyo = 1 Dokda
3 Trambiyo = 1 Dhinglo
8 Dokda = 1 Kori

Early Types: Stylized imitations of the coins of Muzaffar III of Gujarat (1561-1573AD), dated AH978 (= 1570AD), were struck from the end of the 16th century until the early part of the reign of Vibhaji. These show a steady degradation of style over the nearly 300 years of issue, but no types can be dated to specific rulers. The former attribution of these coins to Ranmalji II (1820-1852AD) is incorrect. All are inscribed Sri Jamji, title of all rulers of Nawanagar.

Varieties in this series are the rule, not the exception. These include legend style, small marks in the field such as a crescent, Katar (dagger), etc., and weight ranges.

HAMMERED COINAGE
Crude Style; ca. 1570 - 1850AD

KM# 1 TRAMBIYO
Copper **Note:** Weight varies 3.2 - 4 grams.

Date	Mintage	Good	VG	F	VF	XF
AH(9)78 frozen	—	1.25	2.00	3.00	4.50	—

KM# 2 DOKDO
Copper **Note:** Weight varies 7 - 8 grams, but earlier issues weigh up to 9.3 grams.

Date	Mintage	Good	VG	F	VF	XF
AH(9)78 frozen	—	0.40	0.75	1.00	1.50	—

KM# 3 DHINGLO (1-1/2 Dokda)
Copper **Note:** Weight varies 10.5 - 12.5 grams.

Date	Mintage	Good	VG	F	VF	XF
AH(9)78 frozen	—	1.25	2.00	3.00	4.00	—

KM# 4 1/2 KORI
Silver **Note:** Weight varies 2.3 - 2.4 grams.

Date	Mintage	Good	VG	F	VF	XF
AH(9)78 frozen	—	1.75	3.00	4.50	6.00	—

KM# 5 KORI
Silver **Note:** Weight varies 4.6 - 4.8 grams.

Date	Mintage	Good	VG	F	VF	XF
AH(9)78 frozen	—	1.50	2.50	3.50	5.00	—

HAMMERED COINAGE
Finer Style; ca.1850

KM# 6 TRAMBIYO
Copper **Note:** Weight varies: 3.10-3.30 grams.

Date	Mintage	Good	VG	F	VF	XF
AH(9)78	—	1.00	2.00	3.25	4.50	—

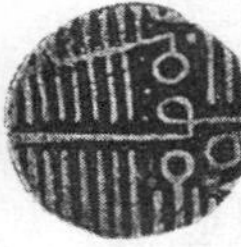

KM# 7 DOKDO
Copper **Note:** Weight varies: 6.20-6.60 grams.

Date	Mintage	Good	VG	F	VF	XF
AH(9)78 Frozen	—	0.65	1.15	1.75	2.50	—

KM# 8 DHINGLO (1-1/2 Dokda)
Copper **Note:** Weight varies: 9.30-9.90 grams.

Date	Mintage	Good	VG	F	VF	XF
AH(9)78 Frozen	—	1.00	1.75	2.50	3.50	—

KM# 9 1/2 KORI
Silver **Note:** Weight varies: 2.30-2.40 grams.

Date	Mintage	Good	VG	F	VF	XF
AH(9)78 Frozen	—	2.50	3.50	5.00	8.00	—

KM# 10 KORI
Silver **Note:** Weight varies: 4.60-4.80 grams.

Date	Mintage	Good	VG	F	VF	XF
AH(9)78 Frozen	—	2.00	3.00	4.00	7.00	—

Vibhaji
VS1909-1951 / 1852-1894AD
HAMMERED COINAGE

KM# 13 TRAMBIYO
Copper **Note:** Weight varies: 3.10-3.20 grams.

Date	Mintage	Good	VG	F	VF	XF
AH(9)78 Frozen	—	1.00	1.75	3.00	4.00	—

KM# 15 TRAMBIYO
Copper **Note:** Weight varies: 3.30-3.50 grams. Similar to Dokdo, KM#16.

Date	Mintage	Good	VG	F	VF	XF
VS1919	—	3.50	6.00	7.50	10.00	—

KM# 16 DOKDO
Copper **Note:** Weight varies: 6.70-7.00 grams.

Date	Mintage	Good	VG	F	VF	XF
VS1909	—	1.35	3.50	6.00	7.50	—
VS1917	—	1.35	3.50	6.00	7.50	—
VS1919	—	1.35	3.50	6.00	7.50	—

KM# 14 DOKDO
Copper **Note:** Weight varies: 6.20-6.40 grams.

Date	Mintage	Good	VG	F	VF	XF
AH(9)78 Frozen	—	0.60	1.50	2.50	4.00	—

KM# 18 2 DOKDA
Copper **Note:** Weight varies: 12.40-12.80 grams.

Date	Mintage	Good	VG	F	VF	XF
VS1943	—	1.50	4.00	7.00	10.00	—

KM# 17 3 DOKDA
Copper **Note:** Weight varies: 18.00-19.60 grams.

Date	Mintage	Good	VG	F	VF	XF
VS1928	—	1.35	3.50	5.50	7.00	—

KM# 19 3 DOKDA
Copper **Note:** Weight varies: 18.00-19.60 grams.

Date	Mintage	Good	VG	F	VF	XF
VS1942	—	1.25	3.00	4.50	6.50	—

KM# 20 KORI
Silver **Edge:** Plain **Note:** Weight varies: 4.60-4.80 grams.

Date	Mintage	VG	F	VF	XF	Unc
VS1934 (1877)	—	5.00	7.00	12.00	20.00	—
VS1935 (1878)	—	5.00	7.00	12.00	20.00	—
VS1936 (1879)	—	3.00	5.00	9.00	18.00	—

KM# 21 2-1/2 KORI
Silver **Edge:** Milled **Note:** Weight varies: 6.80-7.20 grams. Reduced weight.

Date	Mintage	VG	F	VF	XF	Unc
VS1948 (1891)	—	6.50	10.00	15.00	22.50	—
VS1949 (1892)	—	6.50	10.00	15.00	22.50	—
VS1950 (1893)	—	6.50	10.00	15.00	22.50	—

KM# 22 5 KORI
Silver **Obverse:** Large inner circle **Reverse:** Large inner circle **Edge:** Milled **Note:** Weight varies: 13.60-14.40 grams. Reduced weight.

Date	Mintage	F	VF	XF	Unc
VS1945 (1888)	—	7.50	12.50	18.50	30.00
VS1946 (1889)	—	7.50	12.50	18.50	30.00
VS1947 (1890)	—	7.50	12.50	18.50	30.00

KM# 23 5 KORI
Silver **Obverse:** Smaller characters **Reverse:** Smaller characters **Note:** Weight varies: 13.60-14.40 grams.

Date	Mintage	F	VF	XF	Unc
VS1948 (1891)	—	7.50	12.50	18.50	30.00
VS1949 (1892)	—	7.50	12.50	18.50	30.00
VS1950 (1893)	—	7.50	12.50	18.50	30.00

KM# 11 1/2 GOLD KORI
Gold **Note:** Weight varies: 3.20-3.30 grams.

Date	Mintage	VG	F	VF	XF	Unc
AH978 Frozen	—	135	225	350	500	—

KM# 12 GOLD KORI
Gold **Note:** Weight varies: 6.40-6.60 grams.

Date	Mintage	VG	F	VF	XF	Unc
AH(9)78 Frozen	—	135	225	350	500	—

Jaswant Singh
VS1951-1964 / 1894-1907AD
HAMMERED COINAGE

KM# 24 TRAMBIYO
Copper **Note:** Weight varies: 3.10-3.20 grams.

Date	Mintage	Good	VG	F	VF	XF
VS1956 (1899)	—	10.00	16.50	25.00	40.00	—

KM# 25 DOKDO
Copper **Note:** Weight varies: 6.20-6.40 grams.

Date	Mintage	Good	VG	F	VF	XF
VS1956 (1899)	—	9.00	15.00	22.50	36.50	—

KM# 27 2 DOKDA
Copper **Note:** Weight varies: 12.40-13.20 grams.

Date	Mintage	Good	VG	F	VF	XF
VS1956 (1899)	—	12.50	20.00	33.50	45.00	—

KM# 28 3 DOKDA
Copper **Note:** Weight varies: 18.60-19.80 grams.

Date	Mintage	Good	VG	F	VF	XF
VS1956 (1899)	—	12.50	22.50	35.00	50.00	—

KM# 26 DHINGLO (1-1/2 Dokda)
Copper **Note:** Weight varies: 9.30-9.60 grams.

Date	Mintage	Good	VG	F	VF	XF
VS1956 (1899)	—	7.50	12.50	20.00	30.00	—

ORCHHA

State located in north-central India.

Orchha, the oldest and highest ranking of all the Bundela States, was founded by Rudra Pratap, a Garhwar Rajput, early in the 16th century. During the years of Mughal expansion, Orchha came under the supervision of Delhi. A few years later Jujhar Singh (1626-1635) rebelled but was defeated and dispossessed. Shah Jahan installed his brother as ruler in 1641. In the 18th century, as the Marathas took control of the region, only Orchha from among the Bundela States was not totally subjugated by the Peshwa. In the 19th century Orchha came under British protection.

The Orchha coinage was called Gaja Shahi because of the gaja or mace which was its symbol.

RULERS

Vikramajit Mahendra, AH1211-1233/1796-1817AD
Dharam Pal, AH1233-1250/1817-1834AD
Taj Singh, AH1250-1258/1834-1842AD
Surjain Singh, AH1258-1265/1842-1848AD
Hamir Singh, AH1265-1291/1848-1874AD
Pratap Singh, AH1291-1349/1874-1930AD

MINT MARKS

1. Reverse.
(This is the symbol mostcharacteristic of Orchha's coinage and is copied on the Datia imitations).

2. Obverse, most common.

3. Obverse, less common.

4. Reverse

5. Reverse

6. Reverse

7. Reverse

8. Reverse

9. Reverse

10. Reverse

Marks #4 through #10 are found in addition to Mark#1.

The Datia copies can only be distinguished by the mintmarks, other than #1, which is common to both series for the list of Datia marks, see listings under that state.

There seems to be no correspondence between AH dates on the obverse and regnal years on the reverse.

Vikramajit Mahendra
AH1211-1233 / 1796-1817AD
HAMMERED COINAGE

C# 24 1/2 PAISA
Silver, 16 mm. **Obv. Inscription:** "Shah Alam II"

Date	Mintage	Good	VG	F	VF	XF
AH(12)32 (1816-17)	—	1.75	3.00	5.00	8.00	—
AH(12)33 (1817-18)	—	1.75	3.00	5.00	8.00	—

C# 37 1/2 PAISA
Copper **Obv. Inscription:** "Muhammad Akbar II"

Date	Mintage	Good	VG	F	VF	XF
ND//33 (1838)	—	4.50	7.50	12.50	20.00	—

C# 25 PAISA
Copper **Obv. Inscription:** "Shah Alam II"

Date	Mintage	Good	VG	F	VF	XF
AH1216//4x	—	1.00	2.00	3.25	4.50	—
AH1232//46	—	1.00	2.00	3.25	4.50	—
AH1237//16	—	1.00	2.00	3.25	4.50	—
AH1278//45	—	1.00	2.00	3.25	4.50	—
AH1282//42	—	1.00	2.00	3.25	4.50	—

C# 38 PAISA
Copper **Obv. Inscription:** "Muhammad Akbar II"

Date	Mintage	Good	VG	F	VF	XF
AH12xx/3x	—	2.00	4.00	6.00	9.00	—
AH1231/4x	—	—	—	—	—	—

C# 29 1/8 RUPEE
Silver **Note:** Weight varies 1.34 - 1.45 grams.

Date	Mintage	Good	VG	F	VF	XF
ND//45 (1233)	—	—	10.00	16.50	25.00	35.00

C# 30 1/4 RUPEE
Silver, 12 mm. **Note:** Weight varies 2.68 - 2.90 grams.

Date	Mintage	Good	VG	F	VF	XF
AH1228//40	—	10.00	16.50	25.00	35.00	—
AH1233//45	—	10.00	16.50	25.00	35.00	—
AH1232//46	—	10.00	16.50	25.00	35.00	—
AH1233//5x	—	10.00	16.50	25.00	35.00	—
AH1251//3x	—	10.00	16.50	25.00	35.00	—

C# 32 RUPEE
Silver **Note:** Similar to 1/2 Rupee, C#31; weight varies 10.7 - 11.6 grams.

Date	Mintage	Good	VG	F	VF	XF
AH1216//44	—	6.00	10.00	14.00	20.00	—
AH1216//46	—	6.00	10.00	14.00	20.00	—
AH1217//45	—	6.00	10.00	14.00	20.00	—
AH1218//46	—	6.00	10.00	14.00	20.00	—
AH1218//47	—	6.00	10.00	14.00	20.00	—
AH121x//47	—	6.00	10.00	14.00	20.00	—
AH1219//48	—	6.00	10.00	14.00	20.00	—
AH1221//40	—	6.00	10.00	14.00	20.00	—
AH1232//30	—	6.00	10.00	14.00	20.00	—
AH1232//40	—	6.00	10.00	14.00	20.00	—
AH1233//40	—	6.00	10.00	14.00	20.00	—
AH1233//42	—	6.00	10.00	14.00	20.00	—
AH1234	—	6.00	10.00	14.00	20.00	—
AH1235//11	—	6.00	10.00	14.00	20.00	—
AH1236//15	—	6.00	10.00	14.00	20.00	—
AH1238//17	—	6.00	10.00	14.00	20.00	—
AH1240	—	6.00	10.00	14.00	20.00	—
AH1245//43	—	6.00	10.00	14.00	20.00	—
AH1251//31	—	6.00	10.00	14.00	20.00	—
AH1252//32	—	6.00	10.00	14.00	20.00	—
AH1253//35	—	6.00	10.00	14.00	20.00	—
AH1257//39	—	6.00	10.00	14.00	20.00	—
AH1258//38	—	6.00	10.00	14.00	20.00	—

C# 42 RUPEE
Silver

Date	Mintage	Good	VG	F	VF	XF
AH1219/2	—	2.50	6.00	10.00	14.00	20.00
AH1321/9	—	2.50	7.00	11.00	16.50	25.00
Note: Error for 1231						
AH1257/48	—	2.50	6.00	10.00	14.00	20.00
AH1232/10	—	2.50	6.00	10.00	14.00	20.00
AH1258/38	—	2.50	6.00	10.00	14.00	20.00
AH1270/33	—	2.50	6.00	10.00	14.00	20.00
AH1271	—	2.50	6.00	10.00	14.00	20.00
AH1273/39	—	2.50	6.00	10.00	14.00	20.00
AH127x/41	—	2.50	6.00	10.00	14.00	20.00
AH1275/4x	—	2.50	6.00	10.00	14.00	20.00
AH1278/45	—	2.50	6.00	10.00	14.00	20.00

PATIALA

A Cis-Sutlej State, located in the Punjab in northwest India. In the mid-18th century the Raja was given his title and mint right by Ahmad Shah Durrani of Afghanistan, whose coin he copied.

The maharaja of Patiala was also recognized as the leader of the Phulkean tribe. Unlike others, Patiala's Sikh rulers had never hesitated to seek British assistance at those times when they felt threatened by their co-religionist neighbors. It remained a state until the first Sikh war (1845-46) and then their independence became restricted until 1849 when the Punjab was annexed and the states were melded into the new province of British India.

In 1857, Patiala's forces were immediately made available on the side of the British.

RULERS:
Sahib Singh, AH1196-1229/1781-1813AD
Karm Singh, AH1229-1261/1813-1845AD
Identifying Marks:

On reverse

Narinder Singh, VS1902-1919/1845-1862AD
Identifying Marks:

On reverse

Mahindar Singh, VS19191933/1862-1876AD
Identifying Marks:

On reverse

Rajindar Singh, VS1933-1957/1876-1900AD
Identifying Marks:

On reverse

Bhupindar Singh, VS1958-1994/1900-1937AD

MINT

Sirhind (Sahrind)

Sahib Singh
AH1196-1229 / 1781-1813AD

HAMMERED COINAGE

C# 20 RUPEE
Silver **Obverse:** Similar to 1 Rupee, C#10 **Obv. Inscription:** Ahmad Shah Durrani **Note:** 11.10-11.20 grams.

Date	Mintage	Good	VG	F	VF	XF
ND(1781-1813)	—	7.00	17.50	25.00	35.00	50.00

Karm Singh
AH1229-1261 / 1813-1845AD

HAMMERED COINAGE

C# 28 1/4 RUPEE
2.8000 g., Silver

Date	Mintage	Good	VG	F	VF	XF
ND(1813-45)	—	4.00	10.00	15.00	21.50	30.00

C# 30.1 RUPEE
Silver **Reverse:** Without symbols around **Note:** Weight varies 11.10-11.20 grams.

Date	Mintage	Good	VG	F	VF	XF
ND(1813-45)	—	4.75	11.50	17.50	25.00	35.00

C# 30.2 RUPEE
Silver **Reverse:** Alif to left of **Note:** Weight varies 11.10-11.20 grams.

Date	Mintage	Good	VG	F	VF	XF
ND(1813-45)	—	4.75	11.50	17.50	25.00	35.00

C# 30.3 RUPEE
Silver **Reverse:** Crescent to right of **Note:** Weight varies 11.10-11.20 grams.

Date	Mintage	Good	VG	F	VF	XF
ND(1813-45)	—	4.75	11.50	17.50	25.00	35.00

C# 30.4 RUPEE
Silver **Reverse:** 3-pointed leaf to right of **Note:** Weight varies 11.10-11.20 grams.

Date	Mintage	Good	VG	F	VF	XF
ND(1813-45)	—	4.75	11.50	17.50	25.00	35.00

C# 30.5 RUPEE
Silver **Reverse:** Crescent to right, branch to left of **Note:** Weight varies 11.10-11.20 grams.

Date	Mintage	Good	VG	F	VF	XF
ND(1813-45)	—	4.75	11.50	17.50	25.00	35.00

C# 30.6 RUPEE
Silver **Reverse:** Branch to right of **Note:** Weight varies 11.10-11.20 grams.

Date	Mintage	Good	VG	F	VF	XF
ND(1813-45)	—	4.75	11.50	17.50	25.00	35.00

C# 30.7 RUPEE
Silver **Reverse:** Branches both sides of **Note:** Weight varies 11.10-11.20 grams.

Date	Mintage	Good	VG	F	VF	XF
ND(1813-45)	—	4.75	11.50	17.50	25.00	35.00

C# 31 RUPEE
Silver **Reverse:** Scimitar to left of **Note:** Weight varies 11.10-11.20 grams.

Date	Mintage	Good	VG	F	VF	XF
ND(1813-45)	—	6.50	16.50	23.50	32.50	45.00

C# 30a NAZARANA RUPEE
Silver, 24 mm. **Note:** Weight varies 11.10-11.20 grams.

Date	Mintage	Good	VG	F	VF	XF
VS1893 (1836) Rare	—	—	—	—	—	—
VS(18)98 (1841) Rare	—	—	—	—	—	—

C# 35 MOHUR
10.5000 g., Gold **Reverse:** 3-pointed leaf to right of

Date	Mintage	Good	VG	F	VF	XF
ND(1813-45)	—	—	200	250	300	375
VS(18)96 (1896)	—	—	—	—	—	—

Narindar Singh
VS1902-1919 / 1845-1862AD

HAMMERED COINAGE

Y# B1 1/4 RUPEE
Silver **Reverse:** + **Note:** Weight varies: 2.75-2.80 grams.

Date	Mintage	Good	VG	F	VF	XF
ND(1845-62)	—	12.00	30.00	50.00	80.00	120

Y# 1 RUPEE
Silver **Obv. Inscription:** Ahmad Shah Durrani **Note:** Weight varies 11.10-11.20 grams.

Date	Mintage	Good	VG	F	VF	XF
VS1902 (1845)	—	6.00	15.00	27.50	40.00	55.00

Y# A2 RUPEE
Silver **Obv. Inscription:** Guru Govind Singh **Note:** Weight varies 11.10-11.20 grams. Sikh legend.

Date	Mintage	Good	VG	F	VF	XF
VS1906 (1849)	—	40.00	100	165	250	350

Y# 2 MOHUR
10.5000 g., Gold **Obv. Inscription:** Guru Govind Singh **Note:** 17-18mm.

Date	Mintage	Good	VG	F	VF	XF
VS190(6) (1849)	—	—	200	250	300	375

Mahindar Singh
VS1919-1933 / 1862-1876AD

HAMMERED COINAGE

Y# 4 1/4 RUPEE
Silver, 13 mm. **Note:** Weight varies 2.75-2.80 grams.

Date	Mintage	Good	VG	F	VF	XF
ND(1876-1900)	—	16.00	40.00	65.00	100	150

Y# 5 1/2 RUPEE
Silver, 16 mm. **Note:** Weight varies 5.50-5.60 grams.

Date	Mintage	Good	VG	F	VF	XF
ND(1876-1900)	—	18.00	45.00	75.00	120	170

Y# 3 RUPEE
Silver **Obv. Inscription:** Ahmad Shah Durrani **Note:** Weight varies 11.10-11.20 grams. 16-17mm.

Date	Mintage	Good	VG	F	VF	XF
ND(1862-76)	—	14.00	35.00	50.00	70.00	100

Y# 6 RUPEE
Silver **Note:** Weight varies 11.10-11.20 grams.

Date	Mintage	Good	VG	F	VF	XF
VS(19)42 (1885)	—	7.00	17.50	25.00	35.00	50.00
VS(19)43 (1886)	—	7.00	17.50	25.00	35.00	50.00
VS(19)44 (1887)	—	7.00	17.50	25.00	35.00	50.00
VS(19)45 (1888)	—	7.00	17.50	25.00	35.00	50.00
VS(19)46 (1889)	—	7.00	17.50	25.00	35.00	50.00
VS(19)47 (1890)	—	7.00	17.50	25.00	35.00	50.00
VS(19)48 (1891)	—	8.00	20.00	31.50	42.50	60.00

Y# 6a NAZARANA RUPEE
Silver **Note:** Weight varies 11.10-11.20 grams.

Date	Mintage	Good	VG	F	VF	XF
ND(1876-1900) Rare	—	—	—	—	—	—

Y# 9 MOHUR
10.5000 g., Gold, 18 mm.

Date	Mintage	Good	VG	F	VF	XF
ND(1876-1900)	—	—	200	250	300	375
VS(19)48 (1891)	—	—	200	250	300	375

PORBANDAR

State located on the Kathiawar peninsula in western India. The rulers, or ranas, of Porbandar were Jethwa Rajputs of ancient Rajput lineage. They are believed to have arrived from the north and settled the area as early as the 10th century. Their seat of government was transferred to Porbandar from Chaya, the ancient capital, in 1785. The Rana of Porbandar paid an annual tribute of 30,000 rupees to the Gaekwar of Baroda. In 1807 Porbandar acceded to British control, and in February 1948 became part of Saurashtra State. The coins of Porbandar are similar to the coins of Kutch and Navanagar and derive from a prototype struck in AH978/1570AD by Muzaffar Shah III of Gujarat. They have, in Nagari, the additional inscription, *Sri Rana*.

All are dated AH(9)78. They were struck until about 1890AD, and cannot be assigned to any specific ruler.

MONETARY SYSTEM
2 Trambiyo = 1 Dokda
3 Trambiyo = 1 Dhingla
8 Dokda = 1 Kori

HAMMERED COINAGE

C# 30 1/2 TRAMBIYO
Copper

Date	Mintage	Good	VG	F	VF	XF
AH(9)78 Frozen	—	2.00	4.00	7.50	11.50	—

C# 31 TRAMBIYO
Copper

Date	Mintage	Good	VG	F	VF	XF
AH(9)78 Frozen	—	2.00	3.25	5.00	8.50	—

C# 32 DOKDO
Copper

Date	Mintage	Good	VG	F	VF	XF
AH(9)78 Frozen	—	1.00	1.75	2.50	4.50	—

C# 34 DHINGLA
Copper, 20x15 mm. **Shape:** Rectangular **Note:** Cruder calligraphy.

Date	Mintage	Good	VG	F	VF	XF
AH(9)78 Frozen	—	4.50	8.50	12.50	17.50	—

Note: Said to have been struck by Khimji (1813-31AD)

C# 33 DHINGLA
Copper **Note:** Size varies: 18-19mm.

Date	Mintage	Good	VG	F	VF	XF
AH(9)78 Frozen	—	3.00	5.00	8.00	12.50	—

C# 36 1/4 KORI
Silver **Note:** Size varies: 8-9mm.

Date	Mintage	Good	VG	F	VF	XF
AH(9)78 Frozen	—	2.50	6.50	10.00	15.00	22.50

C# 37 1/2 KORI
Silver

Date	Mintage	Good	VG	F	VF	XF
AH(9)78 Frozen	—	1.60	4.00	6.50	10.00	15.00

C# 38 KORI
Silver

Date	Mintage	Good	VG	F	VF	XF
AH(9)78 Frozen	—	1.00	2.50	4.00	6.50	10.00

PRATABGARH

Pratapgarh

The rulers of Pratabgarh, a state located in northwest India, the maharawals, were Sesodia Rajputs who are believed to have migrated in 1553 from Mewar, where their ancestors once ruled. Arriving in the area they seized control from the local Bhil chieftains but it was not until the early 18th century that Pratabgarh town was founded by Maharawal Partab Singh. Pratabgarh was tributary to Holkar until 1818 when, with the collapse of the Maratha states, the state came under British protection. The state was then managed through the Rajputana Agency until, in April 1948, it was merged into Rajasthan.

RULERS
Sawant Singh, AH1189-1241/1775-1825AD
Dulep Singh, AH1241-1281/1825-1864AD
Udaya Singh, VS1921-1947/1864-1890AD
Raganath Singh, VS1947-1986/1890-1929AD

MINT

ديوگره

Deogarh
Devgadh

Kanthal

Pratabgarh

Sawant Singh
AH1189-1241 / 1775-1825AD

HAMMERED COINAGE

KM# 10 1/8 RUPEE
1.3000 g., Silver, 11 mm.

Date	Mintage	Good	VG	F	VF	XF
AH1199/29	—	—	3.50	6.00	9.00	14.00

KM# 11 1/4 RUPEE
2.6500 g., Silver

Date	Mintage	Good	VG	F	VF	XF
AH1199/29	—	2.00	5.00	7.00	10.00	16.00

KM# 12 1/2 RUPEE
5.3000 g., Silver

Date	Mintage	Good	VG	F	VF	XF
AH1199/29	—	1.50	3.50	6.00	9.00	14.00

KM# 13 RUPEE
10.7000 g., Silver **Note:** Size varies: 19-20mm.

Date	Mintage	Good	VG	F	VF	XF
AH1199/29	—	2.00	5.00	7.00	10.00	16.00

KM# 14 NAZARANA RUPEE
10.8500 g., Silver **Shape:** Square

Date	Mintage	Good	VG	F	VF	XF
AH1199/29	—	17.50	35.00	60.00	85.00	125

Dulep Singh
AH1241-1281 / 1825-1864AD
HAMMERED COINAGE

KM# 20 1/8 RUPEE
1.3500 g., Silver **Obv. Inscription:** "Shah Alam (II)"

Date	Mintage	Good	VG	F	VF	XF
AH1236/45(c.1823-5)	—	1.35	3.50	5.50	8.00	12.50

KM# 21 1/4 RUPEE
2.7000 g., Silver **Obv. Inscription:** "Shah Alam II"

Date	Mintage	Good	VG	F	VF	XF
AH1236/45(c.1823-58)	—	1.35	3.50	6.00	9.00	14.00

KM# 22 1/2 RUPEE
5.4000 g., Silver **Obv. Inscription:** "Shah Alam II"

Date	Mintage	Good	VG	F	VF	XF
AH1236/45(c.1823-58)	—	1.35	3.50	5.50	8.50	12.50

KM# 23 RUPEE
10.9000 g., Silver **Obv. Inscription:** "Shah Alam II"

Date	Mintage	Good	VG	F	VF	XF
AH1236/45(c.1823-58)	—	1.50	4.00	6.00	9.00	14.00

KM# 25 NAZARANA RUPEE
Silver **Obv. Inscription:** "Shah Alam II" **Shape:** Square **Note:** Weight varies: 10.70-10.90 grams.

Date	Mintage	Good	VG	F	VF	XF
AH1236/45(c.1823-58)	—	17.50	35.00	60.00	85.00	125

KM# 26 NAZARANA 2-1/2 RUPEE
Silver **Obv. Inscription:** "Shah Alam II" **Note:** Weight varies: 27.20-27.45 grams.

Date	Mintage	Good	VG	F	VF	XF
AH1236/45(c.1823-58)	—	—	—	—	850	1,200

Udaya Singh
VS1921-1947 / 1864-1890AD
HAMMERED COINAGE

KM# 33 1/8 RUPEE
1.3600 g., Silver **Obv. Inscription:** "Shah - i - London"

Date	Mintage	Good	VG	F	VF	XF
AH1236/45	—	1.25	3.00	4.50	6.50	10.00

KM# 34 1/4 RUPEE
2.6800 g., Silver **Obv. Inscription:** "Shah - i - London"

Date	Mintage	Good	VG	F	VF	XF
AH1236/45	—	1.35	3.50	5.50	8.50	12.50

KM# 35 1/2 RUPEE
5.4500 g., Silver **Obv. Inscription:** "Shah - i - London"

Date	Mintage	Good	VG	F	VF	XF
AH1236/45	—	1.25	3.00	4.50	6.50	10.00

KM# 37 RUPEE
10.9000 g., Silver **Obv. Inscription:** "Shah - i - London" **Shape:** Square

Date	Mintage	Good	VG	F	VF	XF
AH1236/45	—	18.50	37.50	62.50	85.00	120

KM# 36 RUPEE
10.9000 g., Silver **Obv. Inscription:** "Shah - i - London"

Date	Mintage	Good	VG	F	VF	XF
AH1236/45	—	1.60	4.00	6.00	9.00	14.00

KM# 38 RUPEE
11.0000 g., Silver, 37 mm. **Obv. Inscription:** "Shah - i - London" **Note:** Large flan.

Date	Mintage	Good	VG	F	VF	XF
AH1236/45	—	—	—	—	500	700

KM# 30.1 PAISA
8.0000 g., Copper **Obverse:** Ornate face of God Mahadev (Shiva) has two eyes **Rev. Inscription:** "Shri/Riyasat Kan-/thal Samat" **Note:** Varieties exist.

Date	Mintage	Good	VG	F	VF	XF
VS1935	—	1.25	2.25	3.25	5.00	—

KM# 30.2 PAISA
Copper **Obverse:** Ornate face of God Mahadev (Shiva) has one eye **Rev. Inscription:** "Shri/Riyasat Kan-/thal Samat" **Note:** Weight varies: 7.50-8.00 grams.

Date	Mintage	Good	VG	F	VF	XF
VS1942	—	1.25	2.25	3.50	—	6.00

KM# 31.1 PAISA
Copper **Obverse:** Rayed oval face of sun god Surya, dot on forehead **Rev. Legend:** "Riyasat Pratapgarh" **Note:** Weight varies: 7.50-8.00 grams. Varieties exist.

Date	Mintage	Good	VG	F	VF	XF
VS1942	—	1.00	1.75	2.50	4.00	—
VS1943	—	1.00	1.75	2.50	4.00	—
VS1947	—	0.50	1.00	1.50	2.50	—

KM# 31.2 PAISA
Copper **Obverse:** Rayed oval face of sun god Surya without dot on forehead **Rev. Legend:** "Riyasat Pratapgarh" **Note:** Weight varies: 7.50-8.00 grams.

Date	Mintage	Good	VG	F	VF	XF
VS1943	—	1.00	1.75	2.50	4.00	—

KM# 32 PAISA
Copper **Obverse:** Round face of sun god Surya without dot on forehead **Rev. Legend:** "Pratapgarh Riyasat" **Note:** Weight varies: 7.50-8.00 grams. Prev. KM#31.2.

Date	Mintage	Good	VG	F	VF	XF
VS1943 (1886)	—	2.50	5.00	16.00	20.00	—

KM# 39a NAZARANA 1/2 RUPEE
5.4000 g., Silver **Obv. Inscription:** "Shah - i - London" **Shape:** Square

Date	Mintage	Good	VG	F	VF	XF
AH1236/45	—	22.50	45.00	75.00	120	175

Raganath Singh
VS1947-1986 / 1890-1929AD
HAMMERED COINAGE

KM# 40 PAISA
Copper **Obverse:** Legend, date **Obv. Legend:** "Samat" **Rev. Inscription:** "Shri/Raj Dev-/gadh Prata-/pgadh" **Note:** Weight varies: 7.50-8.40 grams.

Date	Mintage	Good	VG	F	VF	XF
VS1953	—	1.50	2.50	3.50	5.00	—

RADHANPUR

State located on the Kathiawar peninsula.

The nawabs of Radhanpur were Pathans of the Babi family who rose to high office in the service of Shah Jahan and Murad Bakhsh in Gujarat. Sometime in the late 17th or early 18th centuries one of the family was appointed faujdar of Radhanpur and the surrounding area. After Aurangzeb's death, Kamal-ud-din Khan Babi seized the governorship of Ahmadabad, but this was relinquished in 1753 to the forces of the Peshwa of Poona and the Gaekwar of Baroda. Radhanpur, however, remained in Babi control as a Maratha Jagir until 1820 when the State came under British protection.

All silver coins of Radhanpur appear to be nazarana issues.

RULERS

Zorawar Khan, AH1241-1291/1825-1874AD

In the name of Queen Victoria and Zorawar Khan

Bismilla Khan, AH1291-1313/1874-1895AD

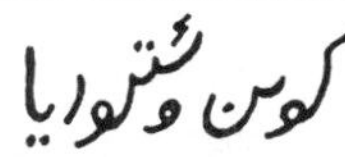

In the name of Queen Victoria

MINT

رادھنپور

Radhanpur

Zorawar Khan
AH1241-1291 / 1825-1874AD
HAMMERED COINAGE

KM# 3 PAISA
Copper Or Bronze **Obverse:** Character "Jo" **Note:** Uniface.

Date	Mintage	Good	VG	F	VF	XF
ND(1825-74)	—	1.35	2.75	4.50	7.50	—

KM# 8 2 ANNAS
Silver **Obv. Inscription:** "...Zorawar Khan" **Rev. Inscription:** "...Queen Victoria" **Note:** Weight varies: 1.34-1.45 grams.

Date	Mintage	Good	VG	F	VF	XF
AH1288	—	13.50	32.50	65.00	110	165

KM# 9 4 ANNAS
Silver **Obv. Inscription:** "...Zorawar Khan"" **Rev. Inscription:** "...Queen Victoria" **Note:** Weight varies: 2.68-2.90 grams.

Date	Mintage	Good	VG	F	VF	XF
AH1286//1869	—	12.00	30.00	60.00	100	150
AH1287//1869	—	12.00	30.00	60.00	100	150
AH1287//1871	—	12.00	30.00	60.00	100	150
AH1288//1871	—	12.00	30.00	60.00	100	150
AH1288//1872	—	12.00	30.00	60.00	100	150

KM# 10 8 ANNAS
Silver **Obv. Inscription:** "...Zorawar Khan"" **Rev. Inscription:** "...Queen Victoria" **Note:** Weight varies: 5.35-5.80 grams.

Date	Mintage	Good	VG	F	VF	XF
AH1286	—	10.00	25.00	50.00	85.00	125
AH1284	—	10.00	25.00	50.00	85.00	125
AH1286	—	10.00	25.00	50.00	85.00	125
AH1287	—	10.00	25.00	50.00	85.00	125
AH1287	—	10.00	25.00	50.00	85.00	125
AH1288	—	10.00	25.00	50.00	85.00	125
AH1289	—	10.00	25.00	50.00	85.00	125

KM# 5 50 FALUS
Silver **Obv. Inscription:** "...Zorawar Khan"" **Rev. Inscription:** "...Queen Victoria"

Date	Mintage	Good	VG	F	VF	XF
AH1284	—	12.50	30.00	60.00	100	150

KM# 11 RUPEE
Silver **Obv. Inscription:** "...Zorawar Khan" **Rev. Inscription:** "...Queen Victoria" **Note:** Weight varies: 10.70-11.60 grams.

Date	Mintage	Good	VG	F	VF	XF
AH1286	—	10.00	25.00	50.00	80.00	120
AH1287	—	10.00	25.00	50.00	80.00	120
AH1288	—	10.00	25.00	50.00	80.00	120
AH1289	—	10.00	25.00	50.00	80.00	120

KM# 6 100 FALUS
Silver **Obv. Inscription:** "...Zorawar Khan" **Rev. Inscription:** "...Queen Victoria"

Date	Mintage	Good	VG	F	VF	XF
AH1284//1867	—	11.00	27.50	55.00	90.00	135
AH1285//1867	—	11.00	27.50	55.00	90.00	135
AH1286//1868	—	11.00	27.50	55.00	90.00	135
AH1286//1869	—	11.00	27.50	55.00	90.00	135
AH1287//1870	—	11.00	27.50	55.00	90.00	135
AH1287//1877	—	11.00	27.50	55.00	90.00	135

Note: 18771 Error for 1871

KM# 15 MOHUR
Gold, 27 mm. **Obv. Inscription:** "...Zorawar Khan" **Rev. Inscription:** "...Queen Victoria" **Note:** Weight varies: 10.70-11.40 grams.

Date	Mintage	Good	VG	F	VF	XF
AH1277	—	—	—	—	650	1,000

Bismilla Khan
AH1291-1313 / 1874-1895AD
HAMMERED COINAGE

KM# 16 PAISA
8.3900 g., Copper Or Bronze **Obverse:** Character "Ji" **Shape:** Rectangular **Note:** Uniface.

Date	Mintage	Good	VG	F	VF	XF
ND(1874-95)	—	1.35	2.75	4.50	7.50	—

KM# 18 2 ANNAS
Silver, 15 mm. **Obv. Inscription:** "...Queen Victoria" **Rev. Inscription:** "...Bismillah Khan" **Note:** Weight varies: 1.34-1.45 grams.

Date	Mintage	Good	VG	F	VF	XF
ND(1880)	—	12.50	32.50	65.00	110	165

KM# 19 4 ANNAS
Silver **Obv. Inscription:** "...Bismillah Khan" **Rev. Inscription:** "...Victoria Queen" **Note:** Weight varies: 2.68-2.90 grams.

Date	Mintage	Good	VG	F	VF	XF
ND(1880)	—	12.00	30.00	60.00	100	150

KM# 21 8 ANNAS
Silver **Obv. Inscription:** "... Bismillah Khan" **Rev. Inscription:** "...Empress Victoria" **Note:** Weight varies: 5.35-5.80 grams.

Date	Mintage	Good	VG	F	VF	XF
AH1291	—	12.00	30.00	60.00	100	150

KM# 22 8 ANNAS
Silver **Obverse:** Field divided twice, Nawab's name at top **Obv. Inscription:** "Bismillah Khan" **Reverse:** Two field dividers, Queen's name center left, center line three words **Rev. Inscription:** "Queen Victoria" **Note:** Weight varies: 5.35-5.80 grams.

Date	Mintage	Good	VG	F	VF	XF
AH1297	—	8.50	21.50	42.50	75.00	110

KM# 23 8 ANNAS
Silver **Obv. Inscription:** "Bismillah Khan" **Reverse:** Without field dividers, Queen's name lower left **Rev. Inscription:** "Queen Victoria" **Note:** Weight varies: 5.35-5.80 grams.

Date	Mintage	Good	VG	F	VF	XF
AH1297	—	8.50	21.50	42.50	75.00	110

KM# 24 8 ANNAS
Silver **Obverse:** Two field dividers, center line three words **Obv. Inscription:** "Bismillah Khan" **Rev. Inscription:** "Queen Victoria" **Note:** Weight varies: 5.35-5.80 grams.

Date	Mintage	Good	VG	F	VF	XF
AH1299	—	8.50	21.50	42.50	75.00	110

KM# 25 8 ANNAS
Silver **Obverse:** Two field dividers, Nawab's name center in one line **Obv. Inscription:** "Bismillah Khan" **Reverse:** Without field dividers, Queen's name lower left **Rev. Inscription:** "Queen Victoria" **Note:** Weight varies: 5.35-5.80 grams.

Date	Mintage	Good	VG	F	VF	XF
AH1299	—	8.50	21.50	42.50	75.00	110

KM# 27 RUPEE
Silver **Obverse:** Two field dividers, Nawab's name center in one line **Obv. Inscription:** "Bismillah Khan" **Reverse:** Field divided once above "Dak" **Rev. Inscription:** "Queen Victoria" **Note:** Weight varies: 10.70-11.60 grams.

Date	Mintage	Good	VG	F	VF	XF
AH1297	—	11.00	27.50	55.00	90.00	135
AH1298	—	11.00	27.50	55.00	90.00	135

KM# 29 RUPEE
Silver **Obverse:** Two field dividers, Nawab's name center in one line **Reverse:** Field divided once with Queen's titles in different order **Rev. Inscription:** "Queen Victoria" **Note:** Weight varies: 10.70-11.60 grams.

Date	Mintage	Good	VG	F	VF	XF
AH1297	—	10.00	25.00	50.00	80.00	120
AH1298	—	10.00	25.00	50.00	80.00	120

KM# 28 RUPEE
Silver **Obverse:** Field divided twice, Nawab's name at top **Obv. Inscription:** "Bismillah Khan" **Reverse:** Two field dividers, Queen's name center left, center line three words **Rev. Inscription:** "Queen Victoria" **Note:** Weight varies: 10.70-11.60 grams.

Date	Mintage	Good	VG	F	VF	XF
AH1299	—	10.00	25.00	50.00	80.00	120

KM# 30 RUPEE
Silver **Reverse:** One field divider, without Queen's name, mint name above **Note:** Weight varies: 10.70-11.60 grams.

Date	Mintage	Good	VG	F	VF	XF
AH1311	—	12.00	30.00	60.00	100	150

KM# 31 RUPEE
Silver **Obverse:** One field divider, Nawab's name above **Reverse:** Without Queen's name, mint name below **Note:** Weight varies: 10.70-11.60 grams.

Date	Mintage	Good	VG	F	VF	XF
AH1311	—	12.50	32.50	65.00	110	165

RAMPURA

This tiny estate of four and a half square miles was held by Chauda Rajputs in the old Gujerat States Agency Area. It was feudatory to Lunavada and the estate was controlled by a thakur or latterly by four shareholders.

HAMMERED COINAGE

The following listings may be from Lunavada or from Rampur. They are often found overstruck on coins of Lunavada, and over other states, including Sailana.

KM# 1 1/2 PAISA
Copper **Obverse:** Open hand in square **Rev. Legend:** RAMPAR **Note:** Weight varies: 3-4g.

Date	Mintage	Good	VG	F	VF	XF
ND(1880-1920)	—	4.00	6.50	10.00	15.00	—

KM# 2 1/2 PAISA
Copper **Obverse:** Sunbursts **Rev. Legend:** RAMPAR **Note:** Weight varies: 3-4g.

Date	Mintage	Good	VG	F	VF	XF
ND(1880-1920)	—	5.00	9.00	13.00	20.00	—

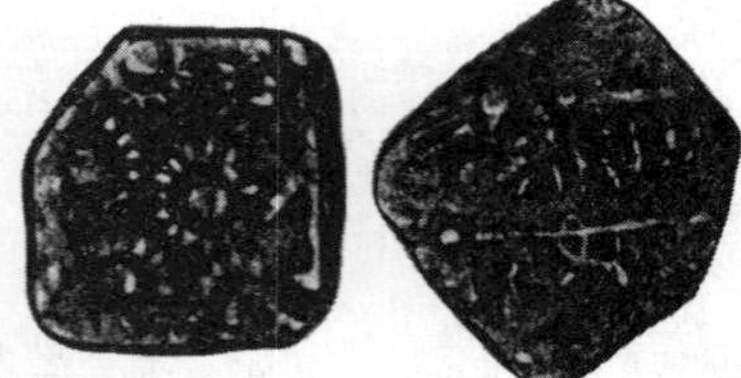

KM# 6.2 PAISA
Copper **Obverse:** Solar symbols with serrated rays **Rev. Legend:** RAMPURA

Date	Mintage	Good	VG	F	VF	XF
ND(1880-1920)	—	2.00	3.25	5.00	8.50	—

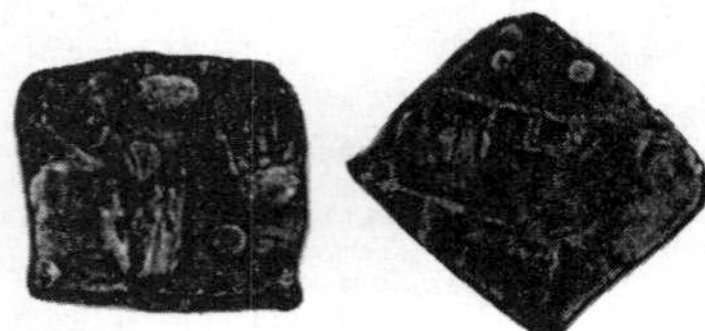

KM# 9 PAISA
Copper **Obverse:** Open hands **Rev. Legend:** RAMPUR **Shape:** Square

Date	Mintage	Good	VG	F	VF	XF
ND(1880-1920)	—	—	—	—	—	—

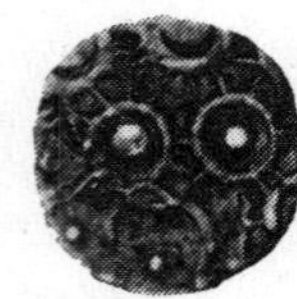 

KM# 6.1 PAISA
Copper **Obverse:** Sunbursts **Rev. Legend:** RAMPAR **Shape:** Round

Date	Mintage	Good	VG	F	VF	XF
ND(1880-1920)	—	2.00	3.25	5.00	8.50	—

KM# 5 PAISA
8.5000 g., Copper **Obverse:** Spears **Rev. Legend:** RAMPAR **Shape:** Round or square

Date	Mintage	Good	VG	F	VF	XF
ND(1880-1920)	—	2.00	3.25	5.00	8.50	—

KM# 8 PAISA
Copper **Obverse:** Spears **Reverse:** Persian legend

Date	Mintage	Good	VG	F	VF	XF
ND(1880-1920)	—	2.00	3.25	5.00	8.50	—

KM# 3 PAISA
Copper **Obverse:** Sunbursts **Rev. Legend:** RAMPAR **Shape:** Square **Note:** Weight varies: 1.90-4.30g.

Date	Mintage	Good	VG	F	VF	XF
ND(1880-1920)	—	2.00	3.25	5.00	8.50	—

KM# 4 PAISA
Copper **Obverse:** Spears **Reverse:** Spears **Shape:** Square **Note:** Weight varies: 1.90-4.30g.

Date	Mintage	Good	VG	F	VF	XF
ND(1880-1920)	—	2.00	3.25	5.00	8.50	—

KM# 7 PAISA
Copper **Obverse:** Solar symbol **Rev. Legend:** RAMPAR **Shape:** Square **Note:** Weight varies: 7.50-8.30g.

Date	Mintage	Good	VG	F	VF	XF
ND(1880-1920)	—	4.00	6.00	9.00	13.50	—

KM# 12 PIE
2.3000 g., Copper

Date	Mintage	Good	VG	F	VF	XF
ND(1880-1920)	—	—	—	—	—	—

RATLAM

State located northwest of Indore in Madhya Pradesh.

The rajas of Ratlam were Rathor Rajputs, descendants of the younger branch of the Jodhpur ruling family. Ratlam became the premier Rajput state in western Malwa. The founder, Ratan Singh, received the territory as a grant from Shah Jahan in 1631. Before Maratha collapse some 15% of the state's annual revenue went to Sindhia as tribute. Under British protection it was supervised by the Central India Agency and in 1948 Ratlam became a district of Madhya Bharat.

RULERS
Ranjit Singh,
VS1921-1950/1864-1893AD

NOTE: For 1 Paisa previously listed here refer to Banswara-IPS.

Uncertain Ruler

HAMMERED COINAGE

KM# 15 PAISA
Copper **Obverse:** Katar **Reverse:** Sword

Date	Mintage	Good	VG	F	VF	XF
ND(c.1780-1806)	—	5.00	10.00	18.00	25.00	—

KM# 21 PAISA
Copper **Obverse:** "Ra'ej" retrograde in dotted circle **Reverse:** Spade symbol

Date	Mintage	Good	VG	F	VF	XF
ND(1785-89)	—	6.50	12.00	20.00	30.00	—

KM# 20 PAISA
Copper **Obverse:** "Ra'ej" in dotted circle right of "jalus"

Date	Mintage	Good	VG	F	VF	XF
ND//25 (1783-84)	—	5.00	10.00	18.00	25.00	—

Ranjit Singh
VS1921-1950 / 1864-1893AD

HAMMERED COINAGE

KM# A21 PAISA
Copper, 22 mm.

Date	Mintage	Good	VG	F	VF	XF
VS1921	—	6.00	9.00	12.50	18.50	—

KM# 22.1 PAISA
Copper **Obverse:** Katar and spray **Reverse:** Sword

Date	Mintage	Good	VG	F	VF	XF
VS1927 (1870)	—	3.00	5.00	8.00	12.50	—

KM# 22.2 PAISA
Copper **Obverse:** Katar **Reverse:** Flower and spray

Date	Mintage	Good	VG	F	VF	XF
VS1928 (1871)	—	2.00	3.25	5.00	8.50	—

KM# 23 PAISA

Copper **Obverse:** Arms **Rev. Legend:** RVTLAM

Date	Mintage	Good	VG	F	VF	XF
1885	—	3.00	5.00	8.00	12.50	—

MILLED COINAGE

KM# 24 PAISA
Copper, 23.5 mm. **Obverse:** Hanuman **Note:** Weight varies: 5.70-5.80 grams. Thick planchet.

Date	Mintage	VG	F	VF	XF	Unc
VS1947	—	—	3.50	6.00	10.00	17.50

REWA

State located in eastern north-central India.

The rulers of Rewa were Baghela Rajputs of the Solanki clan who probably migrated from Anhilwara Patan in Gujarat about the 11th century. Arriving in Bundelkhand, they carved out for themselves a substantial kingdom, which remained independent until 1597, when they were obliged to become Mughal tributaries under Akbar. With Mughal decline, Rewa began to move once more towards independence, this time under the nominal suzerainty of the Peshwa. In 1812, the raja of Rewa, Jai Singh Deo was coerced into a treaty with the British and, failing to observe its conditions, was forced to yield to British control in 1813-1814. In 1948 Rewa was merged into Vindhya Pradesh.

RULERS
Jai Singh Deo, VS1866-1892/1809-1835AD
Vishvanath Singh, VS1892-1900/1835-1843AD
Raghuraj Singh, VS1900-1937/1843-1880AD
Venkat Raman Singh, VS1937-1975/1880-1918AD

Jai Singh Deo
VS1866-1892 / 1809-1835AD

HAMMERED COINAGE

KM# 12 PAISA
Copper **Note:** Weight varies: 8.80-12.60 grams.

Date	Mintage	Good	VG	F	VF	XF
ND(1809-35)	—	1.75	2.75	4.00	6.00	—

KM# 11 PAISA
6.8000 g., Copper

Date	Mintage	Good	VG	F	VF	XF
VS1890	—	2.00	3.00	4.50	7.00	—

KM# 14 2 PAISA
Copper **Obverse:** "Sikka Rewa" in center

Date	Mintage	Good	VG	F	VF	XF
ND(1809-35)	—	6.00	12.00	20.00	30.00	—

Vishvanath Singh
VS1892-1900 / 1835-1843AD

HAMMERED COINAGE

KM# 16 PAISA
7.8000 g., Copper

Date	Mintage	Good	VG	F	VF	XF
ND(1835-43)	—	2.50	3.50	5.00	8.50	—

KM# 17 PAISA
Copper **Obverse:** "Sikka Rewa" in center **Note:** Weight varies: 7.40-7.60 grams.

Date	Mintage	Good	VG	F	VF	XF
ND(1835-43)	—	4.00	7.00	12.50	20.00	—

KM# 18 2 PAISA
16.8000 g., Copper

Date	Mintage	Good	VG	F	VF	XF
ND(1835-43)	—	4.00	7.00	12.50	20.00	—

KM# 22 MOHUR
9.7500 g., Gold **Note:** Fr. #1370.

Date	Mintage	Good	VG	F	VF	XF
ND(1835-43)	—	—	250	500	800	1,100

Raghuraj Singh
VS1900-1937 / 1843-1880AD

HAMMERED COINAGE

KM# 24 PAISA
Copper **Reverse:** "...Agent Bushby Saheb"

Date	Mintage	Good	VG	F	VF	XF
VS1906 (1849)	—	8.00	15.00	25.00	40.00	—

KM# 26 2 PAISE
Copper **Obverse:** Lion left

Date	Mintage	Good	VG	F	VF	XF
VS1906 (1849)	—	12.00	20.00	32.00	50.00	—

KM# 27 2 PAISE
Copper **Obverse:** Lion right

Date	Mintage	Good	VG	F	VF	XF
VS1906 (1849)	—	15.00	25.00	40.00	60.00	—

SAILANA

This small state in west-central India, of slightly over one hundred square miles, had once been part of Ratlam, but about 1709 it asserted its independence under the leadership of Pratab Singh, the second son of Chhatrasal. The town of Sailana was founded in 1730 by Jai Singh's successor and from that date the state was named after him. Due to its small size and vulnerability, Sailana was obliged to become tributary to Sindhia to ensure its survival. In 1819, this payment was limited to one-third of the state's revenues. Later, under agreements of 1840 and 1860, the tribute went to the British for the support of British Indian troops in the region. Barmawal was feudatory to Sailana.

LOCAL RULERS
Dule Singh, VS1907-1952/1850-1895AD
Jaswant Singh, 1895-1919AD

HAMMERED COINAGE

KM# 10 1/2 PAISA
5.2000 g., Copper **Obverse:** Pennant points up or down

Date	Mintage	Good	VG	F	VF	XF
VS1944 (1887)	—	2.00	3.25	5.00	8.00	—

Dule Singh
VS1907-1952 / 1850-1895AD

ANONYMOUS HAMMERED COINAGE

KM# 4 1/2 PAISA
Copper **Obverse:** Pennant points either up or down **Note:** Weight varies: 4.80-5.80 grams.

Date	Mintage	Good	VG	F	VF	XF
ND(c.1880)	—	1.50	2.25	3.50	5.00	—

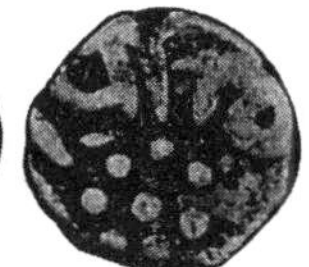

KM# 5 PAISA
Copper **Obverse:** Pennant points either up or down **Note:** Weight varies: 7.50-9.70 grams.

Date	Mintage	Good	VG	F	VF	XF
ND(c.1880)	—	0.50	0.85	1.25	2.00	—

Note: KM#5 is known struck over an Egyptian 20 Para KM#244 or #246, cut down to an irregular shape; Other combinations could exist

KM# 6 2 PAISA
Copper **Note:** Weight varies: 11.60-12.30 grams.

Date	Mintage	Good	VG	F	VF	XF
ND(c.1880)	—	2.00	3.25	5.00	8.50	—

HAMMERED COINAGE

KM# 11 1/2 PAISA
5.2000 g., Copper

Date	Mintage	Good	VG	F	VF	XF
VS1937 (1880)	—	1.25	2.25	3.50	5.50	—
VS7391 (1880) Retrograde	—	1.25	2.25	3.50	5.50	—

KM# 12 1/2 PAISA
11.8000 g., Copper **Reverse:** Sprig, Nagari date

Date	Mintage	Good	VG	F	VF	XF
VS1940 (1883)	—	1.75	2.75	4.00	7.00	—

KM# 13 1/2 PAISA

10.9000 g., Copper **Reverse:** Arabic numerals in Samvat date

Date	Mintage	Good	VG	F	VF	XF
VS1941 (1884)	—	1.75	2.75	4.00	7.00	—

KM# 14 PAISA
Copper **Obverse:** Pennant points right **Reverse:** Trident **Note:** Weight varies: 10.80-11.00 grams.

Date	Mintage	Good	VG	F	VF	XF
VS1944 (1887)	—	1.75	2.75	4.00	7.00	—

SAILANA FEUDATORY - BARMAWAL

Raja Handa Singh

HAMMERED COINAGE

KM# 1 PAISA
Copper **Obverse:** Hanuman running left

Date	Mintage	Good	VG	F	VF	XF
ND(c.1870)	—	8.00	15.00	25.00	40.00	—

SIRMUR

Sirmur Nahan

The ruling Rajput family of this Himalayan principality claimed descent from the Jaisalmir royal house and had ruled the region, located in north India, since the end of the 11th century. From 1803 to 1815, Sirmur came under Gurkha control but on their expulsion by the British during the Nepal War, the original Rajput family was restored to their ancestral dominions as a British feudatory.

NOTE: For earlier issues, see Gurkhas Kingdom.

RULERS
Gurkha Control from Nepal,
AH1218-1232/1803-1815AD
Fath Prakash, restored,
VS1872-1890/1815-1833AD

MINTS
Nahan

MINT MARK

Bow and arrow

HAMMERED COINAGE

KM# 11 PAISA
Copper **Note:** Weight varies: 17.00-18.00 grams. Mint mark: Bow and arrow.

Date	Mintage	Good	VG	F	VF	XF
VS1877 (1820)	—	12.00	20.00	32.00	50.00	—

SIROHI

Formerly Rajputana States Agency; merged in Rajasthan State, except for the tehsils (districts) of Abu Road and Dilawara which were merged with Bombay. Bordered on the north, north-east and west by Jodhpur, on the south by Palanpur, Danta and Idar; and on the east by Mewar.

While the ruling family claims descent from Prithwiraj, the Chauhan King of Delhi, the actual founder of the Sirohi house was one Deoraj, a 13th century figure who was the progenitor of the Deora clan of Rajputs. The present capital, Sirohi, was founded in 1425, about which time the Rana of Chitor is said to have taken refuge at Mount Abu from the army of Kutb-ud-din of Gujarat. The British entered by treaty in 1823, disallowed the claims of Jodhpur to Sirohi lands, ultimately bringing the Minas to submission and the straying thakurs back into line.

RULER
Sheo Singh, VS1873-1919/1816-1862AD

Sheo singh

VS1873-1919/1816-62AD

HAMMERED COINAGE

KM# 11 1/4 ANNA
Copper **Rev. Legend:** "Zarb Raj Sirohi," Scimitar **Note:** Weight varies: 9.75-10.90 grams.

Date	Mintage	Good	VG	F	VF	XF
VS1910 (1853)	—	3.50	5.50	8.50	13.50	—

Note: Previously listed under Jodhpur State; May be of Shapura according to a leading authority

SITAMAU

Sitamau, in western Malwa, was founded in 1695 by Raja Kesho Das, a scion of the Rathor rulers of Ratlam. Sitamau was tributary to Sindhia before passing under British protection and control in the 19th century.

RULERS
Fateh Singh, VS1859-1924/1802-1867AD
Bhawani Singh, VS1924-1942/1867-1885AD
Bahadur Singh, VS1942-1956/1885-1899AD
Shadul Singh, VS1956-1957/1899-1900AD

Bahadur Singh

VS1942-1956 / 1885-1899AD

HAMMERED COINAGE

KM# 5 1/4 PAISA
2.2000 g., Copper **Obverse:** Trident **Reverse:** Mint name in Devanagari and Persian

Date	Mintage	Good	VG	F	VF	XF
VS1944 (1887)	—	5.00	10.00	18.00	30.00	—

KM# 10 PAISA
10.7000 g., Copper **Obverse:** Trident, VS date **Reverse:** Mint name in Devanagari, six-pointed star and sword

Date	Mintage	Good	VG	F	VF	XF
VS1944 (1887)	—	5.00	10.00	18.00	30.00	—

KM# 12 PAISA
9.8000 g., Copper **Obverse:** Trident, VS date **Reverse:** Ruler's name, mint name in Devanagari and Persian

Date	Mintage	Good	VG	F	VF	XF
VS1948 (1891)	—	4.00	8.00	15.00	25.00	—

KM# 15 PAISA
Copper **Obverse:** Trident, two stars above, AD date **Reverse:** Similar to KM#12 **Note:** Weight varies: 9.60-9.80 grams.

Date	Mintage	Good	VG	F	VF	XF
1892	—	7.00	15.00	25.00	40.00	—

Note: The date is expressed by the word "San" followed by Devanagari numerals and "I", the abbreviation for "Isvi" denoting the Christian calendar, and "Samvat"

KM# 18 PAISA
10.3500 g., Copper **Obverse:** Trident, two stars below, AD date **Reverse:** Similar to KM#12

Date	Mintage	Good	VG	F	VF	XF
1896	—	10.00	20.00	35.00	55.00	—

Note: The date is expressed by the word "San" followed by Devanagari numerals and "I", the abbreviation for "Isvi" denoting the Christian calendar, and "Samvat"

Shadul Singh

VS1956-1957 / 1899-1900AD

HAMMERED COINAGE

KM# 25 1/2 PAISA
4.7500 g., Copper **Obverse:** Trident, VS date **Reverse:** Ruler's name, mint name in Persian

Date	Mintage	Good	VG	F	VF	XF
VS1956 (1899)	—	5.00	10.00	20.00	35.00	—

SUNTH

Located 15 miles east of Lunawada with an area of 394 sq. miles, (1,020 sq. km.). This state was ruled by a Maharana who was a member of the Pramara Rajput clan. The state capital was Rampur.

RULERS
Shivsinghji, 1774-1819
Kalyan Singhji, 1819-1835
Bhawan Singhji, 1835-1871
Pratap Singhji, 1871-1896
Jarawar Singhji, 1896-?

HAMMERED COINAGE

KM# 1 1/2 PAISA
Copper **Obverse:** Open hand in square **Rev. Legend:** "Rampura" **Note:** Weight varies: 3.00-4.00 grams.

Date	Mintage	Good	VG	F	VF	XF
ND(c.1870-1920)	—	2.50	6.50	10.00	15.00	—

KM# 2 1/2 PAISA
Copper **Obverse:** Sunbursts **Rev. Legend:** "Rampura" **Note:** Weight varies: 3.00-4.00 grams.

Date	Mintage	Good	VG	F	VF	XF
ND(c.1870-1920)	—	3.50	9.00	13.00	20.00	—

KM# 5 PAISA
8.5000 g., Copper **Obverse:** Spears **Rev. Legend:** "Rampura" **Shape:** Round, rectangular, or square

Date	Mintage	Good	VG	F	VF	XF
ND(c.1870-1920)	—	1.25	3.25	5.00	8.50	—

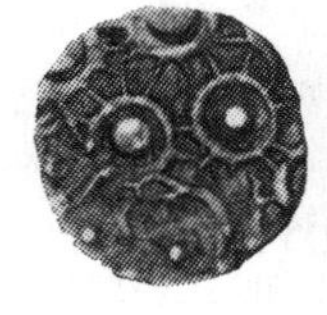

KM# 6.1 PAISA
Copper **Obverse:** Sunbursts **Rev. Legend:** "Rampura"

Date	Mintage	Good	VG	F	VF	XF
ND(c.1870-1920)	—	1.25	3.25	5.00	8.50	—

KM# 6.2 PAISA

Copper **Obverse:** Sunburst with serrated rays **Rev. Legend:** "Rampura" **Shape:** Odd, rectangular, or square

Date	Mintage	Good	VG	F	VF	XF
ND(c.1870-1920)	—	2.50	6.00	9.00	14.00	—

 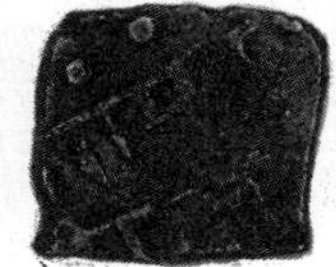

KM# 9 PAISA

Copper **Obverse:** Open hands **Reverse:** "Rampur" **Shape:** Rectangular or square

Date	Mintage	Good	VG	F	VF	XF
ND(c.1870-1920)	—	2.50	6.00	9.00	14.00	—

KM# 8 PAISA

Copper **Obverse:** Spears **Reverse:** Persian legend **Shape:** Odd **Note:** Attribution uncertain.

Date	Mintage	Good	VG	F	VF	XF
ND(c.1870-1920)	—	1.25	3.25	5.00	8.50	—

KM# 3 PAISA

Copper **Obverse:** Sunbursts **Rev. Legend:** "Rampura" **Shape:** Rectangular or square **Note:** Weight varies: 1.90-4.30 grams.

Date	Mintage	Good	VG	F	VF	XF
ND(c.1870-1920)	—	1.25	3.25	5.00	8.50	—

KM# 4 PAISA

Copper **Obverse:** Spears **Reverse:** Spears **Shape:** Rectangular or square **Note:** Weight varies: 1.90-4.30 grams. Attribution uncertain.

Date	Mintage	Good	VG	F	VF	XF
ND(c.1870-1920)	—	1.25	3.25	5.00	8.50	—

KM# 7 PAISA

Copper **Obverse:** Solar symbol **Rev. Legend:** "Rampura" **Shape:** Odd or square **Note:** Weight varies: 7.50-8.30 grams.

Date	Mintage	Good	VG	F	VF	XF
ND(c.1870-1920)	—	2.50	6.00	9.00	14.00	—

TONK

Tunk

State located partially in Rajputana and in central India. Tonk was founded in 1806 by Amir Khan (d. 1834), the Pathan Pindari leader who received the territory from Holkar. Amir Khan caused great havoc in Central India by his lightning raids into neighboring states. In 1817 he was forced into submission by the East India Company and remained under British control until India's independence. In March 1948 Tonk was incorporated into Rajasthan.

RULERS

Amir Khan, AH1213-1250/1798-1834AD
Wazir Muhammad Khan, AH1250-1281/1834-1864AD
Muhammad Ali Khan, AH1280-1284/1864-1867AD
Muhammad Ibrahim Ali Khan, AH1284-1349/1868-1930AD

MINT MARKS

سيرونج

Sironj

تونك

Tonk

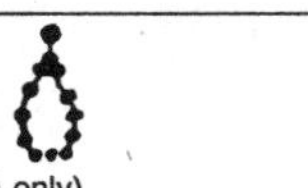

Necklace (on C#50 only)

Flower (on all)

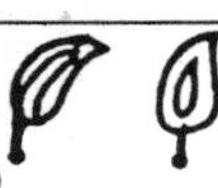

Leaf (several forms)

Beginning with the reign of Muhammad Ibrahim Ali Khan, most coins have both AD and AH dates. Coins with both dates fully legible are worth about 20% more than listed prices. Coins with one date fully legible are worth prices shown. Coins with both dates off are of little value.

There are many minor and major variations of type, varying with location of date, orientation of leaf, arrangement of legend. Although these fall into easily distinguished patterns, they are strictly for the specialist and are omitted here.

The Tonk rupee was known as the "Chanwarshahi".

HAMMERED COINAGE

Mughal Series

C# 45 PAISA

Copper, 23 mm. **Obv. Inscription:** "Muhammad Akbar II" **Reverse:** Jhar **Mint:** Sironj

Date	Mintage	Good	VG	F	VF	XF
AH1225	—	4.00	10.00	15.00	25.00	—

C# 45a PAISA

Copper **Obv. Inscription:** "Muhammad Akbar II" **Reverse:** Horse **Mint:** Sironj

Date	Mintage	Good	VG	F	VF	XF
AH1226	—	5.00	12.50	20.00	30.00	—

C# 45c PAISA

Copper **Obv. Inscription:** "Muhammad Akbar II" **Reverse:** Uncertain symbols **Mint:** Sironj

Date	Mintage	Good	VG	F	VF	XF
AH1247	—	3.50	7.00	12.00	20.00	—

C# 45d PAISA

Copper **Obv. Inscription:** "Muhammad Akbar II" **Reverse:** Rosette and katar **Mint:** Sironj

Date	Mintage	Good	VG	F	VF	XF
AH1250	—	4.00	10.00	15.00	25.00	—

C# 50 PAISA

Copper **Obv. Inscription:** "Muhammad Akbar II" **Reverse:** Rosette and necklace **Mint:** Sironj **Note:** Size varies: 20-21mm.

Date	Mintage	Good	VG	F	VF	XF
AH1252	—	3.00	7.00	12.00	20.00	—
AH1253	—	3.00	7.00	12.00	20.00	—
AH1254	—	3.00	7.00	12.00	20.00	—
AH1269	—	3.00	7.00	12.00	20.00	—

C# 58 1/4 RUPEE

Silver, 13 mm. **Obv. Inscription:** "Muhammad Akbar II" **Mint:** Sironj **Note:** Weight varies: 2.68-2.90 grams.

Date	Mintage	Good	VG	F	VF	XF
AH1253	—	10.00	25.00	40.00	60.00	85.00

C# 59 1/2 RUPEE

Silver **Obv. Inscription:** "Muhammad Akbar II" **Mint:** Sironj **Note:** Weight varies: 5.35-5.80 grams.

Date	Mintage	Good	VG	F	VF	XF
AH1253	—	10.00	25.00	40.00	60.00	85.00
AH1256	—	10.00	25.00	40.00	60.00	85.00
AH1267	—	10.00	25.00	40.00	60.00	85.00

HAMMERED COINAGE

Regal Series

 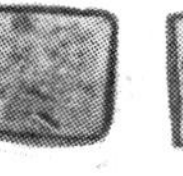  

C# 15 1/4 PAISA

Copper **Obv. Inscription:** "Muhammad Ibrahim Ali Khan" **Rev. Inscription:** "Queen Victoria" **Mint:** Tonk **Note:** Weight varies: 2.00-3.00 grams. Uniface. Mint name "Tonk".

Date	Mintage	Good	VG	F	VF	XF
ND(1873-77)	—	10.00	15.00	22.50	32.00	—

Y# 1 PAISA

Copper **Obv. Inscription:** "Wazir Muhammad Khan" **Rev. Inscription:** "Victoria" **Mint:** Sironj **Note:** Size varies: 18-20mm.

Date	Mintage	Good	VG	F	VF	XF
AH1278	—	4.00	6.25	10.00	16.50	—

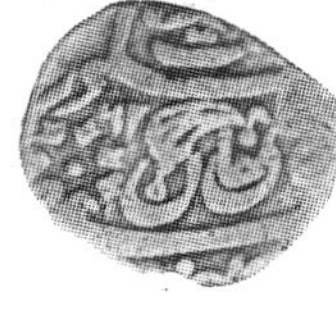 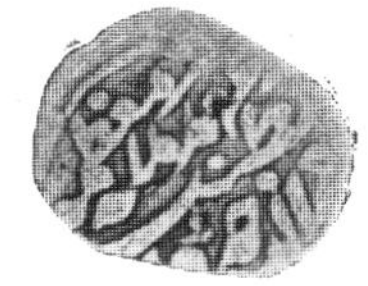

Y# 3 PAISA

Copper **Obv. Inscription:** "Muhammad Ali Khan" **Rev. Inscription:** "Victoria" **Mint:** Sironj **Note:** Size varies: 23-24mm.

Date	Mintage	Good	VG	F	VF	XF
AH1283	—	3.00	5.00	7.50	12.50	—
AH1285	—	3.00	5.00	7.50	12.50	—
AH1286	—	3.00	5.00	7.50	12.50	—
AH1288	—	3.00	5.00	7.50	12.50	—
AH1289	—	3.00	5.00	7.50	12.50	—

Y# 16 PAISA

Copper **Obverse:** AH date in exergue **Obv. Inscription:** "Muhammad Ibrahim Ali Khan" **Rev. Inscription:** "Victoria, Empress" **Mint:** Tonk **Note:** Four varieties are known.

Date	Mintage	Good	VG	F	VF	XF
AH1290	—	1.75	3.25	5.00	8.00	—
AH1292	—	1.75	3.25	5.00	8.00	—
AH1294	—	1.75	3.25	5.00	8.00	—
AH1295	—	1.50	3.00	4.00	6.50	—
AH1298	—	1.50	3.00	4.00	6.50	—
AH1298	—	1.50	3.00	4.00	6.50	—
AH1302	—	1.00	2.50	3.50	5.50	—
AH1303	—	1.00	2.50	3.50	5.50	—
AH1303	—	1.00	2.50	3.50	5.50	—

Y# 8 PAISA

Copper **Obv. Inscription:** "Muhammad Ibrahim Ali Khan" **Rev. Inscription:** "Queen Victoria" **Mint:** Tonk

Date	Mintage	Good	VG	F	VF	XF
AH1290	—	3.50	6.00	10.00	17.50	—

Y# 12 PAISA

Copper, 23 mm. **Obv. Inscription:** "Muhammad Ibrahim Ali Khan" **Rev. Inscription:** "Victoria Empress" **Mint:** Sironj

Date	Mintage	Good	VG	F	VF	XF
AH1298	—	5.00	99.00	15.00	25.00	—
AH1299	—	5.00	9.00	15.00	25.00	—
AH1302	—	5.00	9.00	15.00	25.00	—
AH1308	—	5.00	9.00	15.00	25.00	—

Y# 4 1/8 RUPEE

Silver, 12 mm. **Obv. Inscription:** "Muhammad Ali Khan" **Rev. Inscription:** "Victoria" **Mint:** Sironj **Note:** Weight varies: 1.34-1.45 grams.

Date	Mintage	Good	VG	F	VF	XF
AH(12)8x	—	6.00	15.00	25.00	40.00	60.00
ND(1865-78) Date off flan	—	3.50	8.50	12.50	20.00	35.00

Y# 9 1/8 RUPEE

Silver **Obv. Inscription:** "Muhammad Ibrahim Ali Khan" **Rev. Inscription:** "Queen Victoria" **Mint:** Tonk **Note:** Weight varies: 1.34-1.45 grams.

Date	Mintage	Good	VG	F	VF	XF
ND(1873-77)	—	10.00	25.00	40.00	60.00	85.00

Y# 17 1/8 RUPEE

Silver **Obv. Inscription:** "Muhammad Ibrahim Ali Khan" **Rev. Inscription:** "Victoria, Empress" **Mint:** Tonk **Note:** Weight varies: 1.34-1.45 grams.

Date	Mintage	Good	VG	F	VF	XF
AH1309	—	4.00	10.00	16.50	25.00	35.00
AH1317	—	4.00	10.00	16.50	25.00	35.00

Y# A13 1/8 RUPEE

Silver **Obv. Inscription:** "Muhammad Ibrahim Ali Khan" **Rev. Inscription:** "Victoria Empress" **Mint:** Sironj **Note:** Weight varies: 1.34-1.45 grams.

Date	Mintage	Good	VG	F	VF	XF
AH(13)10	—	10.00	25.00	40.00	60.00	85.00

Y# 5 1/4 RUPEE

Silver, 15 mm. **Obv. Inscription:** "Muhammad Ali Khan" **Rev. Inscription:** "Victoria" **Mint:** Sironj **Note:** Weight varies: 2.68-2.90 grams.

Date	Mintage	Good	VG	F	VF	XF
AH1289	—	6.00	15.00	25.00	40.00	60.00

Y# 18 1/4 RUPEE

Silver **Obv. Inscription:** "Muhammad Ibrahim Ali Khan" **Rev. Inscription:** "Victoria, Empress" **Mint:** Tonk **Note:** Weight varies: 2.68-2.90 grams. Size varies: 14-15mm.

Date	Mintage	Good	VG	F	VF	XF
AH1305	—	4.00	10.00	16.50	25.00	35.00
AH1309	—	4.00	10.00	16.50	25.00	35.00
AH1316	—	4.00	10.00	16.50	25.00	35.00
AH1317	—	4.00	10.00	16.50	25.00	35.00
AH1318	—	4.00	10.00	16.50	25.00	35.00

Y# 13 1/4 RUPEE

Silver **Obv. Inscription:** "Muhammad Ibrahim Ali Khan" **Rev. Inscription:** "Victoria Empress" **Mint:** Sironj **Note:** Weight varies: 2.68-2.90 grams. Approx. 12mm.

Date	Mintage	Good	VG	F	VF	XF
AH(13)10	—	10.00	25.00	40.00	60.00	85.00
AH(13)14	—	10.00	25.00	40.00	60.00	85.00

Y# 19 1/2 RUPEE

Silver **Obv. Inscription:** "Muhammad Ibrahim Ali Khan" **Rev. Inscription:** "Victoria, Empress" **Mint:** Tonk **Note:** Weight varies: 5.35-5.80 grams.

Date	Mintage	Good	VG	F	VF	XF
AH1209	—	4.00	10.00	16.50	25.00	35.00
AH129x	—	4.00	10.00	16.50	25.00	35.00
AH1305	—	4.00	10.00	16.50	25.00	35.00
AH1309	—	4.00	10.00	16.50	25.00	35.00
AH1317	—	4.00	10.00	16.50	25.00	35.00

Y# 6 1/2 RUPEE

Silver **Obv. Inscription:** "Muhammad Ali Khan" **Rev. Inscription:** "Victoria" **Mint:** Sironj **Note:** Weight varies: 5.35-5.80 grams. Size varies: 16-17mm.

Date	Mintage	Good	VG	F	VF	XF
AH1289	—	10.00	25.00	40.00	60.00	85.00

Y# 14 1/2 RUPEE

Silver **Obv. Inscription:** "Muhammad Ibrahim Ali Khan" **Rev. Inscription:** "Victoria Empress" **Mint:** Sironj **Note:** Weight varies: 5.35-5.80 grams.

Date	Mintage	Good	VG	F	VF	XF
AH1306	—	3.00	7.50	15.00	25.00	37.50
AH1310	—	3.00	7.50	15.00	25.00	37.50
AH1314	—	3.00	7.50	15.00	25.00	37.50

Y# 2 RUPEE

Silver **Obv. Inscription:** "Wazir Muhammad Khan" **Rev. Inscription:** "Victoria" **Mint:** Sironj **Note:** Weight varies: 10.70-11.60 grams.

Date	Mintage	Good	VG	F	VF	XF
AH1276	—	5.00	12.50	18.50	25.00	37.50
AH1277	—	5.00	12.50	18.50	25.00	37.50
AH1280	—	5.00	12.50	18.50	25.00	37.50

Y# 7 RUPEE

Silver **Obv. Inscription:** "Muhammad Ali Khan" **Rev. Inscription:** "Victoria" **Mint:** Sironj **Note:** Weight varies: 10.70-11.60 grams.

Date	Mintage	Good	VG	F	VF	XF
AH1282	—	3.50	9.00	18.00	28.00	40.00
AH1286	—	3.50	9.00	18.00	28.00	40.00
AH1288	—	3.50	9.00	18.00	28.00	40.00
AH1289	—	3.50	9.00	18.00	28.00	40.00
AH1292	—	3.50	9.00	18.00	28.00	40.00
AH1296	—	3.50	9.00	18.00	28.00	40.00
ND(1891)	—	3.50	9.00	18.00	28.00	40.00

Y# 10 RUPEE

Silver **Obv. Inscription:** "Muhammad Ibrahim Ali Khan" **Rev. Inscription:** "Queen Victoria" **Mint:** Tonk **Note:** Weight varies: 10.70-11.60 grams.

Date	Mintage	Good	VG	F	VF	XF
AH1290	—	4.00	10.00	15.00	21.50	30.00
AH1291	—	4.00	10.00	15.00	21.50	30.00
AH1292	—	4.00	10.00	15.00	21.50	30.00
AH1293	—	4.00	10.00	15.00	21.50	30.00
AH1294	—	4.00	10.00	15.00	21.50	30.00

Note: Var. 1, illustrated above, has no leaf, but a branch on obverse; All others have the leaf, as on the 1 Paisa, Y#8; Six varieties are known

Y# 20 RUPEE

Silver **Obv. Inscription:** "Muhammad Ibrahim Ali Khan" **Rev. Inscription:** "Victoria, Empress" **Mint:** Tonk **Note:** Weight varies: 10.70-11.60 grams.

Date	Mintage	Good	VG	F	VF	XF
AH1292	—	2.50	6.50	10.00	15.00	22.50
AH1293	—	2.50	6.50	10.00	15.00	22.50
AH1294	—	2.50	6.50	10.00	15.00	22.50
AH1295	—	2.50	6.50	10.00	15.00	22.50
AH1296	—	2.50	6.50	10.00	15.00	22.50
AH1296	—	2.50	6.50	10.00	15.00	22.50
AH1297	—	2.50	6.50	10.00	15.00	22.50
AH1297	—	2.50	6.50	10.00	15.00	22.50
AH1298	—	2.50	6.50	10.00	15.00	22.50
AH1299	—	2.50	6.50	10.00	15.00	22.50
AH1301	—	2.50	6.50	10.00	15.00	22.50
AH1302	—	2.50	6.50	10.00	15.00	22.50
AH1304	—	2.50	6.50	10.00	15.00	22.50
AH1305	—	2.50	6.50	10.00	15.00	22.50

Date	Mintage	Good	VG	F	VF	XF
AH1307	—	2.50	6.50	10.00	15.00	22.50
AH1308	—	2.50	6.50	10.00	15.00	22.50
AH1308	—	2.50	6.50	10.00	15.00	22.50
AH1309	—	2.50	6.50	10.00	15.00	22.50
AH1309	—	2.50	6.50	10.00	15.00	22.50
AH1310	—	2.50	6.50	10.00	15.00	22.50
AH1311	—	2.50	6.50	10.00	15.00	22.50
AH1312	—	2.50	6.50	10.00	15.00	22.50
AH1313	—	2.50	6.50	10.00	15.00	22.50
AH1315	—	2.50	6.50	10.00	15.00	22.50

Y# 15 RUPEE

Silver **Obv. Inscription:** "Muhammad Ibrahim Ali Khan" **Rev. Inscription:** "Victoria Empress" **Mint:** Sironj **Note:** Weight varies: 10.70-11.60 grams.

Date	Mintage	Good	VG	F	VF	XF
AH1299	—	3.50	9.00	18.00	28.00	40.00
AH1303	—	3.50	9.00	18.00	28.00	40.00
AH1304//23 (Sic)	—	3.50	9.00	18.00	28.00	40.00
AH1306	—	3.50	9.00	18.00	28.00	40.00
AH1309//1892	—	3.50	9.00	18.00	28.00	40.00
AH1310	—	3.50	9.00	18.00	28.00	40.00

Y# 11 PIE

Copper, 16 mm. **Obv. Inscription:** "Muhammad Ibrahim Ali Khan" **Rev. Inscription:** "Victoria Empress" **Mint:** Sironj

Date	Mintage	Good	VG	F	VF	XF
AH1314	—	5.00	9.00	15.00	25.00	—

Y# 20a NAZARANA RUPEE

Silver **Obv. Inscription:** "Muhammad Ibrahim Ali Khan" **Rev. Inscription:** "Victoria, Empress" **Mint:** Tonk **Note:** Weight varies: 10.70-11.60 grams.

Date	Mintage	Good	VG	F	VF	XF
AH1297	—	—	—	350	600	850

Y# 21 NAZARANA 2 RUPEE

Silver, 32 mm. **Obv. Inscription:** "Muhammad Ibrahim Ali Khan" **Rev. Inscription:** "Victoria, Empress" **Mint:** Tonk **Note:** Weight varies: 21.40-23.20 grams.

Date	Mintage	Good	VG	F	VF	XF
AH1297	—	—	—	—	1,500	2,000
AH1298	—	—	—	—	1,500	2,000

Y# 22 MOHUR

Gold **Obv. Inscription:** "Muhammad Ibrahim Ali Khan" **Rev. Inscription:** "Victoria, Empress" **Mint:** Tonk **Note:** Weight varies: 10.70-11.40 grams. Fr#1397.

Date	Mintage	Good	VG	F	VF	XF
AH1297	—	—	220	350	500	850
AH1298	—	—	220	350	500	850

Y# 23 NAZARANA 2 MOHURS
Gold **Obv. Inscription:** "Muhammad Ibrahim Ali Khan" **Rev. Inscription:** "Victoria, Empress" **Mint:** Tonk **Note:** Weight varies: 21.40-22.80 grams. Fr#1396.

Date	Mintage	Good	VG	F	VF	XF
AH1297	—	—	—	—	2,250	3,200

TRAVANCORE

State located in extreme southwest India. A mint was established in ME965/1789-1790AD.

The region of Travancore had a lengthy history before being annexed by the Vijayanagar kingdom. With Vijayanagar's defeat at the battle of Talikota in 1565, Travancore passed under Muslim control until the late 18th century, when it emerged as a state in its own right under Raja Martanda Varma. At this time, the raja allied himself with British interests as a protection against the Muslim dynasty of Mysore. In 1795 the raja of Travancore officially accepted a subsidiary alliance with the East India Company and remained within the orbit of British influence from then until India's independence.

RULERS

Bala Rama Varma I, ME973-986/1798-1810AD
Rani Parvathi Bai, regent, ME990-1004/1815-1829AD
Rama Varma III, ME1004-1022/1829-1847AD
Martanda Varma II, ME1022-1035/1847-1860AD
Rama Varma IV, ME1035-1055/1860-1880AD
Rama Varma V, ME1057-1062/1880-1885AD
Rama Varma VI, ME1062-1101/1885-1924AD

MONETARY SYSTEM

16 Cash (Kasu) = 1 Chuckram
4 Chuckram = 1 Fanam
2 Fanams = 1 Anantaraya
7 Fanams = 1 Rupee
52-1/2 Fanam = 1 Pagoda

DATING

ME dates are of the Malabar Era. Add 824 or 825 to the ME date for the AD date. (i.e., ME1112 plus 824-825 =1936-1937AD).

ANONYMOUS HAMMERED COINAGE

KM# 5 1/2 CHUCKRAM
Copper **Obverse:** Six-pointed star, flower center **Reverse:** Sankha (conch shell)

Date	Mintage	Good	VG	F	VF	XF
ND(1809-10)	—	1.50	4.00	7.50	12.00	20.00

KM# 7 1/2 CHUCKRAM
Silver

Date	Mintage	Good	VG	F	VF	XF
ND(1809-10)	—	0.75	2.00	3.75	5.50	9.00

KM# 2 1/2 ANANTARAYA (Fanam)
Gold

Date	Mintage	Good	VG	F	VF	XF
ND(1790-1830)	—	—	6.00	9.00	14.00	25.00

KM# 3 ANANTARAYA (2 Fanam)
Gold

Date	Mintage	Good	VG	F	VF	XF
ND(1790-1860)	—	—	10.00	15.00	21.50	40.00

Note: For similar coins with leaf sprays on the obverse, see KM#23 in the 19th century listings

HAMMERED COINAGE

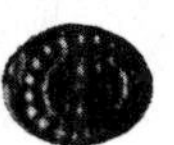

KM# A1 KASU
Copper

Date	Mintage	Good	VG	F	VF	XF
ND	—	—	—	—	—	—

KM# 1 CHUCKRAM
Silver **Obverse:** Left and right angles with dots at bottom

Date	Mintage	Good	VG	F	VF	XF
ND(1600-1847)	—	1.00	2.50	5.00	8.00	12.00

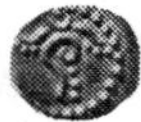

KM# 8 2 CHUCKRAMS
Silver **Obverse:** "Sankha" (conch shell) **Reverse:** Six-pointed star

Date	Mintage	VG	F	VF	XF	Unc
ND(1809-10)	—	4.00	8.00	13.50	22.50	—

Rani Parvathi Bai
ME990-1004 / 1815-1829AD
HAMMERED COINAGE

KM# 9 CASH
Copper

Date	Mintage	Good	VG	F	VF	XF
ME991 (1815)	—	—	—	—	—	—
ME991-7(1815-21)	—	1.25	3.00	5.00	8.50	12.50

KM# 10 2 CASH
Copper

Date	Mintage	Good	VG	F	VF	XF
ME991(1815)	—	1.50	4.00	7.00	10.00	15.00
ME997(1821)	—	1.50	4.00	7.00	10.00	15.00

KM# 11 4 CASH
Copper

Date	Mintage	Good	VG	F	VF	XF
ME991(1815)	—	2.50	6.00	10.00	14.00	20.00

KM# 12 8 CASH
Copper

Date	Mintage	Good	VG	F	VF	XF
ME991(1815)	—	4.00	10.00	17.50	25.00	35.00

Rama Varma III
ME1004-1022 / 1829-1847AD
HAMMERED COINAGE

KM# 14 CASH
Copper

Date	Mintage	Good	VG	F	VF	XF
ME1005(1830)	—	0.90	2.25	3.50	5.00	7.50

KM# 15 CASH
Copper **Reverse:** Diety seated

Date	Mintage	Good	VG	F	VF	XF
ND(1830-39)	—	0.60	1.50	2.25	3.50	5.00

KM# 16 CASH
Copper **Obverse:** Full bodied Kasu **Reverse:** Six-pointed star **Note:** Size varies 8 - 10 mm.

Date	Mintage	Good	VG	F	VF	XF
ND(1848-60)	—	0.30	0.75	1.50	2.50	4.00

KM# 17 2 CASH
Copper **Obverse:** Full bodied Kasu **Reverse:** Six-pointed star

Date	Mintage	Good	VG	F	VF	XF
ND(1848-49)	—	0.85	2.25	4.50	7.50	12.50

KM# 18 4 CASH
Copper **Obverse:** Full bodied Kasu **Reverse:** Six-pointed star

Date	Mintage	Good	VG	F	VF	XF
ND(1848-49)	—	1.25	3.00	6.00	10.00	17.50

KM# 19 8 CASH
Copper **Obverse:** Full bodied Kasu **Reverse:** Six-pointed star

Date	Mintage	Good	VG	F	VF	XF
ND(1848-49)	—	2.25	5.50	11.00	18.00	30.00

Martanda Varma II
ME1022-1035 / 1847-1860AD
HAMMERED COINAGE

KM# A20 CHUCKRAM
Silver **Reverse:** Dot at center above leaf spray over left angel and dot/1 at right near bottom

Date	Mintage	Good	VG	F	VF	XF
ND(1860-85)	—	0.75	1.75	3.50	6.00	10.00

Rama Varma IV
ME1035-1055 / 1860-1880AD
HAMMERED COINAGE

KM# 20 CASH
Copper **Obverse:** Stick bodied Kasu **Reverse:** Six-pointed star in circle **Note:** Size varies: 5 - 7 mm.

Date	Mintage	Good	VG	F	VF	XF
ND(1860-85)	—	0.15	0.45	0.90	1.50	2.50

KM# 21 CHUCKRAM

Silver **Reverse:** Without dot at center, over leaf spray

Date	Mintage	Good	VG	F	VF	XF
ND(1860-1901)	—	—	0.85	1.40	2.00	3.00

KM# 23 ANATARAYA (Fanam)

Gold

Date	Mintage	Good	VG	F	VF	XF
ND(1860-90)	—	—	—	7.50	12.50	18.50

KM# 22 VELLI FANAM

Dump Silver

Date	Mintage	Good	VG	F	VF	XF
ND(1860-61)	—	1.25	3.00	5.00	7.00	10.00

MILLED COINAGE

KM# 24.1 VELLI FANAM

Dump Silver **Obverse:** Large "R.V." in wreath

Date	Mintage	VG	F	VF	XF	Unc
ND(1864)	—	1.00	1.75	2.75	4.00	—

KM# 24.2 VELLI FANAM

Dump Silver **Obverse:** Large "R.V." in wreath **Reverse:** Without two upper dots

Date	Mintage	VG	F	VF	XF	Unc
ND(1864)	—	1.00	1.75	2.75	4.00	—

KM# 25 1/2 PAGODA

1.2800 g., Gold **Obverse:** Sankha (conch shell) in sprays **Reverse:** Large "R.V." in sprays

Date	Mintage	VG	F	VF	XF	Unc
1877	—	—	65.00	100	150	250

KM# 26 PAGODA

2.5500 g., Gold **Obverse:** Sanckha (conch shell) in sprays **Reverse:** Large inscription "R.V." in sprays **Note:** Fr.#1402.

Date	Mintage	VG	F	VF	XF	Unc
1877	—	—	110	175	275	400

KM# 27 2 PAGODA

5.1000 g., Gold **Obverse:** Sanckha (conch shell) in sprays **Reverse:** Large inscription "R.V." in sprays **Note:** Fr.#1401.

Date	Mintage	VG	F	VF	XF	Unc
1877	—	—	160	265	400	600

Rama Varma V

ME1057-1062 / 1880-1885AD

HAMMERED COINAGE

KM# 29 VIRARAYA FANAM

Silver

Date	Mintage	Good	VG	F	VF	XF
ND(1881)	—	—	0.40	1.00	1.75	2.50

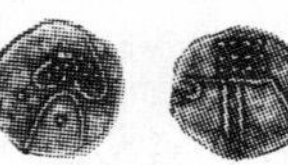 

KM# 30 VIRARAYA FANAM

Gold

Date	Mintage	Good	VG	F	VF	XF
ND(1881)	—	—	—	6.00	10.00	15.00

MILLED COINAGE

KM# 31 1/2 SOVEREIGN

3.9940 g., 0.9170 Gold .1177 oz. AGW **Obverse:** Bust of Rama Varma IV 3/4 right **Reverse:** Arms

Date	Mintage	F	VF	XF	Unc
ME1057//1881	2,000	300	550	900	1,250

KM# 32 SOVEREIGN

7.9881 g., 0.9170 Gold .2354 oz. AGW **Obverse:** Bust of Rama Varma IV 3/4 right **Reverse:** Arms

Date	Mintage	F	VF	XF	Unc
ME1057//1881	1,000	200	600	1,200	1,600

Rama Varma VI

ME1062-1101 / 1885-1924AD

HAMMERED COINAGE

KM# 34 CASH

Copper **Obverse:** Kasu with dot body **Note:** KM#34 is a rather degenerated copy of KM#16.

Date	Mintage	Good	VG	F	VF	XF
ND(1885-95)	—	0.25	0.60	1.00	1.50	2.25

KM# 34.1 CASH

Copper **Obverse:** Two dot bodied Kasu **Reverse:** 6-pointed star **Note:** Size varies 5 - 7 mm.

Date	Mintage	Good	VG	F	VF	XF
ND(1885-95)	—	0.15	0.35	0.75	1.75	3.00

KM# 34.2 CASH

Copper **Obverse:** One dot bodied Kasu **Reverse:** 6-pointed star **Note:** Size varies 5 - 7 mm.

Date	Mintage	Good	VG	F	VF	XF
ND(1885-95)	—	0.15	0.35	0.75	1.75	3.00

 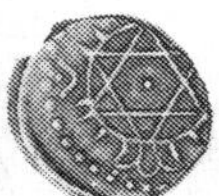

KM# 35 1/4 CHUCKRAM

Copper **Obverse:** 6-pointed star in circle with flames

Date	Mintage	VG	F	VF	XF	Unc
ND(1888-89)	—	3.00	5.00	7.00	10.00	—

KM# 36 1/2 CHUCKRAM

Copper **Reverse:** Six-pointed star in circle

Date	Mintage	Good	VG	F	VF	XF
ND(1888-89)	—	1.50	4.00	6.50	9.00	15.00

KM# 39 KALI FANAM

Gold **Note:** Fr.#1405.

Date	Mintage	Good	VG	F	VF	XF
ND(1890-95)	—	—	—	5.00	8.50	12.50

MILLED COINAGE

KM# 37 1/4 RUPEE

2.7200 g., Silver

Date	Mintage	VG	F	VF	XF	Unc
1889	—	—	7.50	12.50	17.50	25.00

KM# 38 1/2 RUPEE

5.4400 g., Silver

Date	Mintage	VG	F	VF	XF	Unc
1889	—	—	12.00	20.00	28.00	40.00

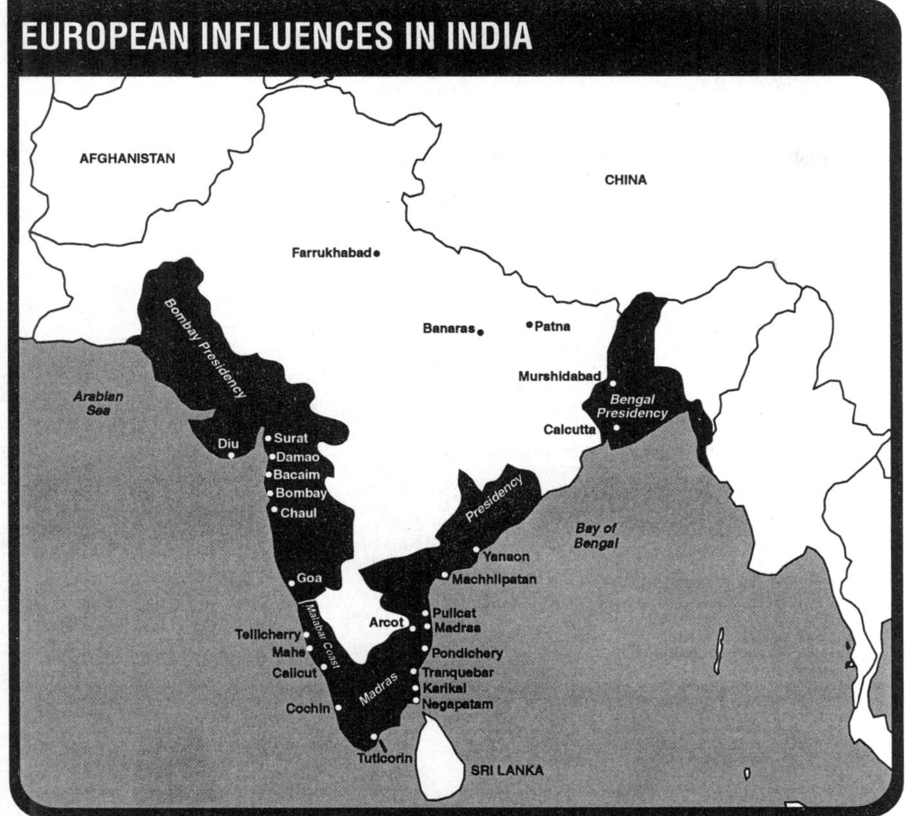

INDIA-DANISH, TRANQUEBAR

Danish India or Tranquebar is a town and former Danish colony on the southeast coast of India. In Danish times, 1620-1845, it was a factory site and seaport operated by the Danish Asiatic Company. Tranquebar and the other Danish settlements in India were sold to the British East India Company in 1845.

RULERS
Danish, until 1845

ADMINISTRATION OF TRANQUEBAR
Danish Crown
1777-Oct. 1845
British Occupation May, 1801-Aug., 1802
British Occupation Feb., 1808-Sept., 1815

MONETARY SYSTEM
80 Kas (Cash) = Royaliner (Fano or
8 Royaliner = 1 Rupee
18 Royaliner = 1 Speciesdaler

COLONY

HAMMERED COINAGE

KM# 151 CASH
0.6000 g., Copper **Ruler:** Frederik VI **Obverse:** Crowned FVIR monogram **Reverse:** Value, date below

Date	Good	VG	F	VF	XF
1816 Unique	—	—	—	—	—
1819	15.00	25.00	60.00	130	—

Note: The 1819 date exists in several die varieties

KM# 155 4 CASH
2.4000 g., Copper **Ruler:** Christian VII **Issuer:** Danish Royal Colony **Obverse:** Crowned C7 monogram

Date	Good	VG	F	VF	XF
1807	7.00	10.00	25.00	50.00	—

KM# 158 4 CASH
2.4000 g., Copper **Ruler:** Frederik VI **Obverse:** Crowned FR, VI below

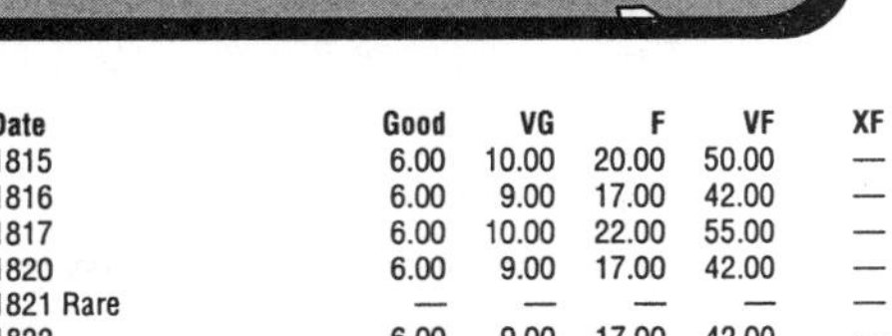

Date	Good	VG	F	VF	XF
1815	6.00	10.00	20.00	50.00	—
1816	6.00	9.00	17.00	42.00	—
1817	6.00	10.00	22.00	55.00	—
1820	6.00	9.00	17.00	42.00	—
1821 Rare	—	—	—	—	—
1822	6.00	9.00	17.00	42.00	—
1823	6.00	9.00	18.00	46.00	—
1824	6.00	9.00	15.00	38.00	—

KM# 159.1 4 CASH
2.4000 g., Copper **Ruler:** Frederik VI **Obverse:** Crown design standardized

Date	Good	VG	F	VF	XF
1824	6.00	9.00	18.00	45.00	—
1825	20.00	30.00	60.00	150	—
1830	6.00	10.00	20.00	50.00	—
1831	4.50	7.00	15.00	35.00	—
1832	4.50	7.00	15.00	35.00	—
1833	6.00	9.00	17.00	42.00	—
1834	6.00	10.00	20.00	50.00	—
1837	6.00	10.00	20.00	50.00	—
1838	6.00	10.00	18.00	45.00	—
1839	4.00	6.00	14.00	35.00	—

KM# 159.2 4 CASH
2.4000 g., Copper **Ruler:** Frederik VI **Reverse:** Retrograde S in KAS

Date	Good	VG	F	VF	XF
1817	8.00	10.00	20.00	50.00	—
1831	100	175	285	450	—

KM# 160 4 CASH
2.4000 g., Copper **Ruler:** Frederik VI **Obverse:** Value VI (error) for IV

Date	Good	VG	F	VF	XF
1824 Rare	—	—	—	—	—

KM# 161 4 CASH
2.4000 g., Copper **Ruler:** Christian VIII **Obverse:** Crowned C VIII R monogram **Note:** Varieties exist.

Date	Good	VG	F	VF	XF
1840	7.00	11.00	22.00	55.00	—
1841	6.00	9.00	20.00	48.00	—
1841 Error	20.00	30.00	50.00	100	—
Note: Crowned C VIIII R monogram					
1842	6.00	9.00	20.00	48.00	—
1843	6.00	9.00	20.00	48.00	—
1844	6.00	11.00	22.00	50.00	—
1844	7.00	12.00	25.00	60.00	—
Note: Without VIII					
1845	7.00	11.00	22.00	55.00	—
Note: Without VIII					
1845	7.00	11.00	22.00	55.00	—

KM# 166 10 CASH
Copper **Ruler:** Frederik VI **Obverse:** Crowned FR, VI between and below

Date	Good	VG	F	VF	XF
1816	10.00	16.00	50.00	130	—
1822	17.00	28.00	80.00	160	—
1838	12.00	18.00	65.00	130	—
1839	10.00	16.00	50.00	100	—

KM# 167 10 CASH
Copper **Ruler:** Christian VIII **Obverse:** Crowned CR, VIII between and below

Date	Good	VG	F	VF	XF
1842	60.00	100	200	375	—

KM# 168 ROYALIN
Silver **Ruler:** Christian VII **Issuer:** Danish Royal Colony **Obverse:** Crowned C7 monogram **Reverse:** Value, arms with lion between date

Date	VG	F	VF	XF	Unc
1807	20.00	30.00	80.00	155	—

KM# 171 2 ROYALINER (2 Fano, 2 Fanams)
Silver **Ruler:** Christian VII **Issuer:** Danish Royal Colony **Obverse:** Crowned C7 monogram

Date	VG	F	VF	XF	Unc
1807	27.00	38.00	105	190	—

KM# 170 FANO (Royalin, Fanam)
Copper **Ruler:** Frederik VI **Obverse:** Crowned FR, VI between and below

Date	Good	VG	F	VF	XF
1816	—	75.00	115	250	450
1818	—	100	150	325	600

KM# 173 2 FANO (2 Royaliner, 2 Fanams)

Copper **Ruler:** Frederik VI **Obverse:** Crowned FR, VI between and below

Date	Good	VG	F	VF	XF
1816	—	85.00	135	310	550
1818	—	125	200	450	800

INDIA-FRENCH

It was not until 1664, during the reign of Louis XIV, that the Compagnie des Indes Orientales was formed for the purpose of obtaining holdings on the subcontinent of India. Between 1666 and 1721, French settlements were established at Arcot, Mahe, Surat, Pondichery, Masulipatam, Karikal, Yanam, Murshidabad, Chandernagore, Balasore and Calicut. War with Britain reduced the French holdings to Chandernagore, Pondichery, Karikal, Yanam and Mahe. Chandernagore voted in 1949 to join India and became part of the Republic of India in 1950. Pondichery, Karikal, Yanam and Mahe formed the Pondichery union territory and joined the republic of India in 1954.

RULERS

French, until 1945

MINTS

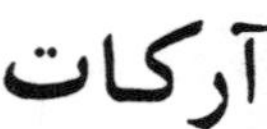

Arcot (Arkat)

Mint mark:

Crescent

A crescent moon mint mark is found to left of the regnal year for those struck at the Pondichery Mint. For listings of similar coins with lotus mint mark refer to India-British-Madras Presidency.

Pondichery

A city south of Madras on the southeast coast which became the site of the French Mint from 1700 to 1841. Pondichery was settled by the French in 1683. It became their main Indian possession even though it was occupied by the Dutch in 1693-1698 and several times by the British from 1761-1816.

صورت

Surat

The French silver coins struck similar to late Mughal issues in two different periods. See also India-British, Bombay Presidency.

MONETARY SYSTEM

Cache Kas or Cash
Doudou = 4 Caches
Biche = 1 Pice
2 Royalins = 1 Fanon Pondichery
5 Heavy Fanons = 1 Rupee Mahe
64 Biches = 1 Rupee

NOTE: The undated coinage was struck ca. 1720 well into the early 19th century.

ARCOT

HAMMERED COINAGE

KM# 13 1/4 RUPEE

2.8000 g., Silver **Ruler:** Shah Alam II **Mint:** *Arkat* **Obverse:** Persian - Shah Alam II couplet **Reverse:** Persian - Julus (formula), mint name **Note:** Similar coins with crescent mint mark were also issued by Mysore Sate, using the latter mint name. Struck at Arcot Mint.

Date	Good	VG	F	VF	XF
AH1221//49	—	21.50	42.00	85.00	120
AH1222//49	—	35.00	70.00	100	160

KM# 14 1/2 RUPEE

5.7000 g., Silver **Ruler:** Shah Alam II **Mint:** Arcot **Obverse:** Persian - Shah Alam II couplet **Reverse:** Persian - Julus (formula), mint name

Date	Good	VG	F	VF	XF
AH1221//49	12.50	25.00	45.00	90.00	130

KM# 15 RUPEE

11.4000 g., Silver **Ruler:** Shah Alam II **Mint:** Arcot **Obv. Inscription:** "Shah Alam II"

Date	Good	VG	F	VF	XF
AH1177//4	—	12.50	20.00	30.00	50.00
AH1178//5	—	12.50	20.00	30.00	50.00
AH1181//7	—	12.50	20.00	30.00	50.00
AH1182//8	—	12.50	20.00	30.00	50.00
AH1183//8	—	12.50	20.00	30.00	50.00
AH1183//9	—	12.50	20.00	30.00	50.00
AH1184//10	—	12.50	20.00	30.00	50.00
AH1185//10	—	12.50	20.00	30.00	50.00
AH1186//11	—	12.50	20.00	30.00	50.00
AH1187//12	—	12.50	20.00	30.00	50.00
AH1188//13	—	12.50	20.00	30.00	50.00
AH1189//14	—	12.50	20.00	30.00	50.00
AH(11)89//15	—	12.50	20.00	30.00	50.00
AH1190//15	—	12.50	20.00	30.00	50.00
AH1191//16	—	12.50	20.00	30.00	50.00
AH1191//17	—	12.50	20.00	30.00	50.00
AH1197//22	—	12.50	20.00	30.00	50.00
AH1198//32(sic)	—	12.50	20.00	30.00	50.00
AH1199//24	—	12.50	20.00	30.00	50.00
AH1200//25	—	12.50	20.00	30.00	50.00
AH1201//26	—	12.50	20.00	30.00	50.00
AH1202//27	—	12.50	20.00	30.00	50.00
AH1203//27	—	12.50	20.00	30.00	50.00
AH1204//29	—	12.50	20.00	30.00	50.00
AH1205//30	—	12.50	20.00	30.00	50.00
AH1206//31	—	12.50	20.00	30.00	50.00
AH1207//32	—	12.50	20.00	30.00	50.00
AH1208//34	—	12.50	20.00	30.00	50.00
AH1218//43	—	12.50	20.00	30.00	50.00
AH1218//44	—	12.50	20.00	30.00	50.00
AH1219/8//44	—	12.50	20.00	30.00	50.00
AH1219//44	—	12.50	20.00	30.00	50.00
AH1219//45	—	12.50	20.00	30.00	50.00
AH1220//43(sic)	—	12.50	20.00	30.00	50.00
AH1220//45	—	12.50	20.00	30.00	50.00
AH1221//43(sic)	—	12.50	20.00	30.00	50.00
AH1221//45	—	12.50	20.00	30.00	50.00
AH1222//43(sic)	—	12.50	20.00	30.00	50.00

KM# 16 NAZARANA RUPEE

11.4000 g., Silver **Ruler:** Shah Alam II **Mint:** Arcot **Obverse:** Persian - Shah Alam II couplet **Reverse:** Persian - Julius (formula), mint name **Note:** Size varies: 32-33 mm.

Date	VG	F	VF	XF	Unc
AH1218//43(sic)	150	250	450	750	—
AH1218//58	150	250	450	750	—
AH1233//58(sic)	150	250	450	750	—

PONDICHERY

Dutch Occupation

HAMMERED COINAGE

KM# 33 CACHE

1.6000 g., Bronze **Mint:** Tamil - *Pudu/tche/ri*

Date	Good	VG	F	VF	XF
ND(1720-1835)	3.50	6.50	13.50	25.00	—

KM# 34 1/2 DOUDOU

Bronze **Mint:** Tamil - *Pudu/tche/ri* **Obverse:** Lis **Note:** Weight varies 2.00-2.50 grams. Size varies 13-15 mm.

Date	Good	VG	F	VF	XF
ND(1720-1835)	2.00	3.00	6.00	15.00	—

KM# 35 DOUDOU

4.2000 g., Copper **Mint:** Tamil - *Pudu/tche/ri* **Obverse:** Lis

Date	Good	VG	F	VF	XF
ND(1720-1835)	2.00	3.00	5.00	12.00	—

KM# 52 DOUDOU

4.0000 g., Bronze **Mint:** Tamil - *Pudu/tche/ri* **Obverse:** Rooster

Date	Good	VG	F	VF	XF
1836	3.50	6.50	13.50	25.00	—
1837	3.50	6.50	13.50	25.00	—

KM# 39 1/2 FANON

Silver **Obverse:** Large pearley crown **Reverse:** 5 Fleur-de-lis **Note:** Weight varies 0.50-0.70 grams.

Date	Good	VG	F	VF	XF
ND(1720-1837)	5.00	10.00	15.00	25.00	40.00

KM# 53 1/2 FANON

0.7500 g., Silver **Obverse:** Crown **Reverse:** Rooster **Note:** Size varies 8-9 mm.

Date	Good	VG	F	VF	XF
1837	8.50	16.50	28.50	45.00	75.00

KM# 45 FANON

Silver **Obverse:** Large ornamented crown **Reverse:** 5 fleur-de-lis **Note:** Weight varies 1.50-1.59 grams.

Date	Good	VG	F	VF	XF
ND(1835)	6.50	12.50	20.00	35.00	60.00

KM# 54 FANON

Silver **Obverse:** Large pearled crown **Reverse:** Rooster

Date	Good	VG	F	VF	XF
1837	8.50	16.50	28.50	45.00	75.00

KM# 49 2 FANON

3.0000 g., Silver **Obverse:** Ornamented crown **Reverse:** 5 fleur-de-lis **Note:** Size varies 14-15 mm.

Date	Good	VG	F	VF	XF
ND(1720-1837)	8.50	16.50	28.50	45.00	75.00

KM# 55 2 FANON

3.0000 g., Silver **Obverse:** Large ornamented crown **Reverse:** Rooster **Note:** Size varies 13-15 mm.

Date	Good	VG	F	VF	XF
1837	10.00	20.00	32.50	55.00	90.00

KM# 48 2 FANON

3.0000 g., Silver **Obverse:** Pearled crown **Reverse:** 5 fleur-de-lis **Note:** Size varies 15-16 mm.

Date	Good	VG	F	VF	XF
ND(1720-1837)	8.50	16.50	28.50	45.00	75.00

KM# 51 PAGODA

3.4000 g., Gold **Obverse:** Large ornamented crown **Reverse:** 5 fleur-de-lis **Note:** Size varies 10-12 mm.

Date	Good	VG	F	VF	XF
ND(1830-48)	600	1,000	2,000	3,500	4,200

SURAT

HAMMERED COINAGE

KM# 73 1/8 RUPEE

1.4200 g., Silver **Mint:** Surat **Obverse:** Persian - Shah Alam II couplet **Obv. Inscription:** "Shah Alam II..." **Reverse:** Persian - Julus (formula), mint name **Note:** Shah Alam II (posthumous) issue.

Date	Good	VG	F	VF	XF
ND//4x (1807)	20.00	40.00	70.00	100	150

KM# 75 1/2 RUPEE

5.7000 g., Silver **Mint:** Surat **Obverse:** Persian - Shah Alam II couplet **Reverse:** Persian - Julus (formula), mint name **Note:** For listings with regnal year 46 see India-British, Bombay Presidency.

Date	Good	VG	F	VF	XF
ND//49 (1806)	12.50	25.00	50.00	100	150
AH122(5)//52	12.50	25.00	50.00	100	150

KM# 76 RUPEE

11.4000 g., Silver **Ruler:** Shah Alam II **Mint:** Surat **Obverse:** Persian - Shah Alam II couplet **Obv. Inscription:** "Shan Alam II" **Reverse:** Persian - Julus (formula), mint name **Note:** Shah Alam II (posthumous) issue.

Date	Good	VG	F	VF	XF
NDxxxx//49	—	20.00	35.00	60.00	100
AH122(4)//51	—	20.00	35.00	60.00	100
AH122(5)//52	—	20.00	35.00	60.00	100
AH122(6)//53	—	20.00	35.00	60.00	100
AH1227//54	—	20.00	35.00	60.00	100
NDxxxx//6x	—	20.00	35.00	60.00	100

KM# 78 2/3 MOHUR

7.8000 g., Gold **Ruler:** Shah Alam II **Mint:** Surat **Obverse:** Persian - Shah Alam II couplet **Reverse:** Persian - Julus (formula), mint name

Date	Good	VG	F	VF	XF
NDxxxx//5x Rare	—	—	—	—	—

PATTERNS

Including off metal strikes

KM#	Date	Mintage	Identification	Mkt Val
Pn1	ND(1720-1835)	—	Doudou. Bronze. 4.4000 g.	—

INDIA-PORTUGUESE

Vasco da Gama, the Portuguese explorer, first visited India in 1498. Portugal seized control of a number of islands and small enclaves on the west coast of India, and for the next hundred years enjoyed a monopoly on trade. With the arrival of powerful Dutch and English fleets in the first half of the 17th century, Portuguese power in the area declined until virtually all of India that remained under Portuguese control were the west coast enclaves of Goa, Damao and Diu. They were forcibly annexed by India in 1962.

RULERS

Portuguese, until 1961

IDENTIFICATION

The undated coppers are best identified by the shape of the coat of arms.

Maria I – Somewhat triangular shield (Baroque style)
Joao VI, as Regent: oval shield
Joao VI, as King: square shield

DENOMINATION

The denomination of most copper coins appears in numerals on the reverse, though 30 Reis is often given as "1/2 T", and 60 Reis as "T" (T = Tanga). The silver coins have the denomination in words, usually on the obverse until 1850, then on the reverse.

DAMAO

(Daman)

A city located 100 miles north of Bombay. It was captured by the Portuguese in 1559. A mint was opened in Damao in 1611. This mint continued in operation until 1854. While important to early Portuguese trade, Damao dwindled as time passed. It was annexed to India in 1962.

MONETARY SYSTEM

375 Bazacucos = 300 Reis
300 Reis = 1 Pardao
60 Reis = 1 Tanga
2 Pardao (Xerafins) = 1 Rupia

COLONY

HAMMERED COINAGE

KM# 25 15 REIS

Copper **Subject:** Maria II

Date	Good	VG	F	VF	XF
1843	8.50	16.50	30.00	60.00	—

KM# 26 15 REIS

Copper **Subject:** Pedro V

Date	Good	VG	F	VF	XF
1854	7.00	15.00	25.00	50.00	—

KM# 23 30 REIS

Copper **Subject:** Maria II

Date	Good	VG	F	VF	XF
1840	10.00	20.00	35.00	70.00	—
1845	15.00	30.00	50.00	100	—

KM# 27 30 REIS

Copper **Subject:** Pedro V **Note:** Similar to KM#23.

Date	Good	VG	F	VF	XF
1854	9.00	18.00	32.00	65.00	—

KM# 24 60 REIS

Copper **Subject:** Maria II

Date	Good	VG	F	VF	XF
1840	15.00	30.00	50.00	100	—

KM# 28 60 REIS

Copper **Subject:** Pedro V **Note:** Similar to KM#24.

Date	Good	VG	F	VF	XF
1854	—	—	—	—	—

DIU

A district in Western India formerly belonging to Portugal. It is 170 miles northwest of Bombay on the Kathiawar peninsula. The Portuguese settled here and built a fort in 1535. A mint was opened in 1685 and was closed in 1859. As with Damao, the importance of Diu diminished with the passage of time. It was annexed to India in 1962.

MONETARY SYSTEM

750 Bazarucos = 600 Reis
40 Atia = 10 Tanga = 1 Rupia

COLONY

CAST COINAGE

KM# 44 5 BAZARUCOS

Lead Or Tin **Subject:** Joao **Obverse:** Crude crowned arms **Reverse:** Date in angles of cross

Date	Good	VG	F	VF	XF
1801	6.00	12.00	25.00	45.00	—

KM# 47 20 BAZARUCOS

Tin **Subject:** Joao **Note:** 14.00-16.50 grams.

Date	Good	VG	F	VF	XF
1801	10.00	20.00	40.00	70.00	—

HAMMERED COINAGE

KM# 52 5 BAZARUCOS

Zinc, 21 mm. **Note:** Similar to 20 Bazarucos, KM#47.

Date	Good	VG	F	VF	XF
1807	7.00	15.00	30.00	55.00	—

KM# 56 5 BAZARUCOS

Zinc **Subject:** Pedro IV **Note:** Size varies 20-22mm.

Date	Good	VG	F	VF	XF
1827	8.00	16.00	35.00	60.00	—
1828	8.00	16.00	35.00	60.00	—

KM# 57 10 BAZARUCOS

Zinc, 27 mm.

Date	Good	VG	F	VF	XF
1827	16.00	30.00	45.00	75.00	—
1828	20.00	35.00	50.00	90.00	—

KM# 53 20 BAZARUCOS

Zinc **Note:** Size varies 33-36mm. Similar to KM#47.

Date	Good	VG	F	VF	XF
1807	—	—	—	—	—

Note: Reported, not confirmed

KM# 58 20 BAZARUCOS

Zinc **Subject:** Pedro IV

Date	Good	VG	F	VF	XF
1827	7.00	14.00	27.50	50.00	—
1828	7.00	14.00	27.50	50.00	—

KM# 54 30 REIS

Copper **Subject:** Joao

Date	Good	VG	F	VF	XF
1818	7.00	13.50	27.50	50.00	—

KM# 55 60 REIS

Copper **Subject:** Joao **Note:** Similar to 30 Reis, KM#54.

Date	Good	VG	F	VF	XF
1818	15.00	25.00	45.00	95.00	—

KM# 50 150 REIS

Silver **Subject:** Joao **Obverse:** Crowned arms **Reverse:** Date in angles of cross

Date	Good	VG	F	VF	XF
1806	30.00	50.00	110	225	—

KM# 60 150 REIS

Silver **Subject:** Pedro V

Date	Good	VG	F	VF	XF
1859	20.00	35.00	70.00	150	—

KM# 51 300 REIS

Silver **Subject:** Joao

Date	Good	VG	F	VF	XF
1806	25.00	40.00	100	200	—

KM# 61 300 REIS

Silver **Subject:** Pedro V

Date	Good	VG	F	VF	XF
1859	25.00	40.00	100	200	—

KM# 59 RUPIA (600 Reis)

10.6300 g., Silver **Subject:** Maria II

Date	Good	VG	F	VF	XF
1841	100	150	300	600	—

KM# 49 RUPIA

10.6300 g., Silver **Subject:** Joao **Obverse:** Crowned arms **Reverse:** Date in angles of cross

Date	Good	VG	F	VF	XF
1804	75.00	125	250	—	500
1805	75.00	125	250	—	500
1806	75.00	125	250	—	500

PATTERNS

Including off metal strikes

KM#D	Date	Mintage	Identification	Mkt Val
Pn1	1851	—	1/4 Atia. Copper. 2.1300 g.	—

KM#D	Date	Mintage	Identification	Mkt Val
Pn2	1851	—	1/2 Atia. Copper. 3.8000 g.	—
Pn3	1851	—	Atia. Copper. 7.6000 g.	—

GOA

Goa was the capitol of Portuguese India and is located 250 miles south of Bombay on the west coast of India. It was taken by Albuquerque in 1510. A mint was established immediately and operated until closed by the British in 1869. Later coins were struck at Calcutta and Bombay. Goa was annexed by India in 1962.

MONETARY SYSTEM

375 Bazarucos = 300 Reis
240 Reis = 1 Pardao
2 Xerafim = 1 Rupia

NOTE: The silver Xerafim was equal to the silver Pardao, but the gold Xerafim varied according to fluctuations in the gold/silver ratio.

COLONY

HAMMERED COINAGE

KM# 209 3 REIS

Copper **Subject:** Joao **Note:** Similar to 6 Reis, KM#211.

Date	Good	VG	F	VF	XF
ND	6.00	12.00	25.00	45.00	—

KM# 224 3 REIS

Copper **Note:** Similar to 4-1/2 Reis, KM#225.

Date	Good	VG	F	VF	XF
ND	6.50	12.50	26.50	50.00	—

KM# 210 4-1/2 REIS

Copper **Subject:** Joao **Note:** Similar to 6 Reis, KM#211.

Date	Good	VG	F	VF	XF
ND	6.00	12.00	25.00	45.00	—

KM# 225 4-1/2 REIS

Copper

Date	Good	VG	F	VF	XF
ND	7.00	13.50	27.50	55.00	—

KM# 258 4-1/2 REIS

Copper **Subject:** Maria II

Date	Good	VG	F	VF	XF
ND	20.00	45.00	90.00	200	—
1843 Unique	—	—	—	—	—
1845	5.00	8.00	15.00	28.00	—
1846	5.00	8.00	15.00	28.00	—
1847	5.00	8.00	15.00	28.00	—
1848	5.00	8.00	15.00	28.00	—

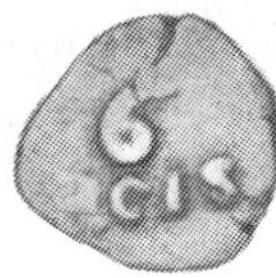

KM# 226 6 REIS

Copper

Date	Good	VG	F	VF	XF
ND	6.00	12.00	25.00	55.00	—

KM# 259 6 REIS

Copper

Date	Good	VG	F	VF	XF
ND	5.00	8.00	15.00	30.00	—
1845	5.00	8.00	15.00	30.00	—
1846	5.00	8.00	15.00	30.00	—
1847 Rare	—	—	—	—	—
1848	5.00	8.00	—	30.00	—

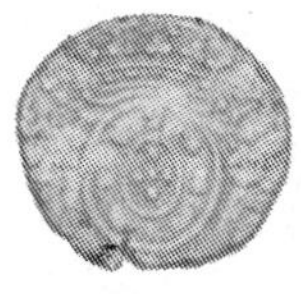

KM# 211 6 REIS

Copper **Subject:** Joao **Note:** Weight varies 3.70-4.30 grams.

Date	Good	VG	F	VF	XF
ND	6.00	12.00	25.00	45.00	—

KM# 212 7-1/2 REIS

4.8000 g., Copper **Subject:** Joao **Obverse:** Similar to 6 Reis, KM#211 **Reverse:** Denomination 7-1/2 Reis.

Date	Good	VG	F	VF	XF
ND	8.00	16.00	35.00	65.00	—

KM# 213 7-1/2 REIS

4.8000 g., Copper **Reverse:** Denomination: 7-2/4 Reis

Date	Good	VG	F	VF	XF
ND	12.50	25.00	40.00	85.00	—

KM# 227 7-1/2 REIS

4.8000 g., Copper **Obverse:** Similar to 6 Reis, KM#226 **Reverse:** Denomination: 7-1/2 Reis

Date	Good	VG	F	VF	XF
ND	10.00	17.50	37.50	70.00	—

KM# 260 7-1/2 REIS

4.8000 g., Copper **Subject:** Maria II

Date	Good	VG	F	VF	XF
ND	5.00	8.00	17.50	35.00	—
1845	4.00	7.00	14.00	30.00	—
1846	4.00	7.00	14.00	30.00	—
1847	4.50	7.50	15.00	32.00	—
1848	4.50	7.50	15.00	32.00	—
1849	4.50	7.50	15.00	32.00	—

KM# 228 9 REIS

Copper **Subject:** Joao **Obverse:** Similar to 6 Reis, KM#226 **Reverse:** Denomination : 9 Reis

Date	Good	VG	F	VF	XF
ND	11.50	17.50	32.00	60.00	—

KM# 229 9 REIS

Copper **Reverse:** Denomination: Nove Reis

Date	Good	VG	F	VF	XF
ND	7.50	13.50	30.00	55.00	—

KM# 214 10 REIS

Copper **Subject:** Joao **Reverse:** Retrograde S

Date	Good	VG	F	VF	XF
ND	7.00	15.00	30.00	60.00	—

KM# 230 10 REIS

Copper **Note:** Similar to 6 Reis, KM#226.

Date	Good	VG	F	VF	XF
ND	10.00	17.50	37.50	70.00	—

KM# 261 10 REIS

Copper **Subject:** Maria II

Date	Good	VG	F	VF	XF
ND	5.00	8.00	17.50	35.00	—
1845	4.00	7.00	14.00	30.00	—

KM# 215 12 REIS

Copper **Subject:** Joao

Date	Good	VG	F	VF	XF
ND	7.00	12.50	25.00	45.00	—

KM# 231 12 REIS

Copper **Note:** Similar to 6 Reis, KM#226.

Date	Good	VG	F	VF	XF
ND	11.50	17.50	30.00	60.00	—

KM# 262 12 REIS

Copper **Subject:** Maria II

Date	Good	VG	F	VF	XF
ND	7.00	13.50	27.50	55.00	—
1848	7.00	13.50	27.50	55.00	—

KM# 216 15 REIS

9.3000 g., Copper **Subject:** Joao

Date	Good	VG	F	VF	XF
ND	6.00	12.00	20.00	40.00	—

KM# 232 15 REIS

9.3000 g., Copper

Date	Good	VG	F	VF	XF
ND	10.00	17.50	37.50	70.00	—

KM# 263 15 REIS

9.3000 g., Copper

Date	Good	VG	F	VF	XF
ND	3.50	7.00	15.00	30.00	—

KM# 217 1/2 TANGA

Copper **Subject:** Joao **Note:** Similar to 15 Reis, KM#216.

Date	Good	VG	F	VF	XF
ND	7.50	15.00	27.50	50.00	—

KM# 233 1/2 TANGA

Copper

Date	Good	VG	F	VF	XF
ND	12.00	20.00	40.00	75.00	—

KM# 249 1/2 TANGA

Copper **Subject:** Miguel

Date	Good	VG	F	VF	XF
ND	6.50	12.00	22.00	45.00	—

KM# 265 1/2 TANGA

Copper **Subject:** Maria II

Date	Good	VG	F	VF	XF
ND	6.50	12.00	20.00	42.00	—

KM# 208 TANGA (60 Reis)

Silver **Obverse:** Head right **Reverse:** Crowned arms

Date	Good	VG	F	VF	XF
1802	45.00	100	175	475	—
1803	45.00	100	175	475	—

KM# 218 TANGA (60 Reis)

Copper **Obverse:** Crowned arms **Reverse:** Value

Date	Good	VG	F	VF	XF
ND	10.00	20.00	35.00	60.00	—

KM# 234 TANGA (60 Reis)

Copper

Date	Good	VG	F	VF	XF
ND	12.50	25.00	45.00	95.00	—

KM# 240 TANGA (60 Reis)

1.1000 g., Silver

Date	Good	VG	F	VF	XF
1819	35.00	60.00	120	325	—
1823	35.00	60.00	120	325	—

KM# 251 TANGA (60 Reis)

Copper **Subject:** Miguel

Date	Good	VG	F	VF	XF
ND	8.50	16.50	30.00	55.00	—

KM# 266 TANGA (60 Reis)

Copper **Subject:** Maria II

Date	Good	VG	F	VF	XF
ND	7.50	15.00	28.00	50.00	—

KM# 277 TANGA (60 Reis)

Silver **Subject:** Pedro V **Note:** Weight varies 1.03-1.25 grams.

Date	Good	VG	F	VF	XF
1856	25.00	35.00	50.00	90.00	—
1858	25.00	35.00	50.00	90.00	—
1859	25.00	35.00	50.00	90.00	—

KM# 235 1/2 XERAFIM (150 Reis)

Silver **Subject:** Joao **Note:** Weight varies 2.67-2.71 grams.

Date	Good	VG	F	VF	XF
1818	35.00	45.00	60.00	95.00	—
1819	35.00	45.00	60.00	95.00	—

KM# 236 1/2 XERAFIM (150 Reis)

Silver

Date	Good	VG	F	VF	XF
1818	25.00	35.00	45.00	75.00	—
1819/8	35.00	45.00	60.00	90.00	—
1819	25.00	35.00	45.00	75.00	—
1820	25.00	35.00	45.00	75.00	—
1823	25.00	35.00	45.00	75.00	—

KM# 255 1/2 XERAFIM (150 Reis)

Silver **Subject:** Miguel

Date	Good	VG	F	VF	XF
1831 Rare	—	—	—	—	—

KM# 206 1/2 PARDAO (150 Reis)

Silver **Subject:** Maria I **Obverse:** Head right, value: 150 RES. **Reverse:** Crowned arms **Note:** 2.80-2.95 grams.

Date	Good	VG	F	VF	XF
1802	20.00	40.00	85.00	175	—
1803	20.00	40.00	85.00	175	—
1804	20.00	40.00	85.00	175	—
1806	20.00	40.00	85.00	175	—

KM# 271 1/2 PARDAO (150 Reis)

Silver **Subject:** Maria II **Note:** Weight varies 2.80-2.95 grams.

Date	Good	VG	F	VF	XF
1843 Unique	—	—	—	—	—
1845	20.00	30.00	40.00	70.00	—
1846	20.00	30.00	40.00	70.00	—
1846/5	25.00	35.00	50.00	90.00	—
1849	30.00	50.00	85.00	175	—

KM# 280 1/2 PARDAO (150 Reis)

Silver **Subject:** Pedro V **Note:** Weight varies 2.80-2.95 grams.

Date	Good	VG	F	VF	XF
1857	22.00	32.00	45.00	85.00	—
1860	25.00	35.00	50.00	90.00	—
1861	25.00	40.00	55.00	100	—

KM# 221 PARDAO

Silver **Subject:** Joao **Note:** Weight varies 5.84-5.95 grams.

Date	Good	VG	F	VF	XF
1808	17.50	27.50	40.00	85.00	—
1809	17.50	27.50	40.00	85.00	—
1810	17.50	27.50	40.00	85.00	—
1811	17.50	27.50	40.00	85.00	—
1812/09	35.00	60.00	100	225	—
1815/09	35.00	60.00	100	225	—
1815	17.50	27.50	40.00	85.00	—
1816	17.50	27.50	40.00	85.00	—
1817	17.50	27.50	40.00	85.00	—
1818	17.50	27.50	40.00	85.00	—

KM# 238 PARDAO

Silver **Obverse:** Diademed head

Date	Good	VG	F	VF	XF
ND	20.00	30.00	40.00	80.00	—

KM# 247 PARDAO

Silver **Subject:** Pedro IV

Date	Good	VG	F	VF	XF
ND	40.00	55.00	75.00	200	—
1827	40.00	55.00	75.00	200	—

KM# 237 PARDAO

Silver **Note:** Weight varies 5.84-5.95 grams.

Date	Good	VG	F	VF	XF
1818	20.00	30.00	50.00	85.00	—
1819	20.00	30.00	50.00	85.00	—
1820	20.00	30.00	50.00	85.00	—
1821	20.00	30.00	50.00	85.00	—
1822	20.00	30.00	50.00	85.00	—
1823	20.00	30.00	50.00	85.00	—
1824	20.00	30.00	50.00	85.00	—
1825	20.00	30.00	50.00	85.00	—

KM# 256 PARDAO

Silver **Subject:** Miguel

Date	Good	VG	F	VF	XF
1831	40.00	55.00	85.00	235	—
1833	40.00	55.00	85.00	235	—

KM# 268 PARDAO

Silver **Subject:** Maria II

Date	Good	VG	F	VF	XF
1839	32.50	45.00	60.00	125	—
1840	32.50	45.00	60.00	125	—
1841	35.00	50.00	75.00	150	—

KM# 272 PARDAO

Silver

Date	Good	VG	F	VF	XF
1845	20.00	30.00	50.00	95.00	—
1846	20.00	30.00	45.00	85.00	—
1847	30.00	40.00	65.00	135	—
1848	20.00	30.00	50.00	95.00	—

KM# 276 PARDAO

Silver **Reverse:** Vaue and arms

Date	Good	VG	F	VF	XF
1851	30.00	40.00	60.00	120	—

KM# 278 PARDAO

Silver **Subject:** Pedro V

Date	Good	VG	F	VF	XF
1856	25.00	35.00	55.00	110	—
1857	25.00	35.00	55.00	110	—
1860	25.00	35.00	55.00	110	—
1861	25.00	35.00	55.00	110	—

KM# 281 PARDAO

Silver

Date	Good	VG	F	VF	XF
1866	30.00	40.00	65.00	135	—
1868	30.00	40.00	65.00	135	—
1869	—	—	—	—	—

KM# 204 PARDAO (300 Reis)

Silver **Obverse:** Head right **Reverse:** Crowned arms **Note:** Weight varies 5.84-5.95 grams.

Date	Good	VG	F	VF	XF
1801	10.00	20.00	55.00	135	—
1802	10.00	20.00	55.00	135	—
1803	10.00	20.00	55.00	135	—
1804	10.00	20.00	55.00	135	—
1805	10.00	20.00	55.00	135	—
1806	10.00	20.00	55.00	135	—

KM# 241 XERAFIM

Gold **Subject:** Joao **Obverse:** Arms on crowned globe **Reverse:** Value and date in angles of cross **Note:** Weight varies 0.40-0.41 grams.

Date	Good	VG	F	VF	XF
1819	450	800	1,350	2,000	—

KM# 205 RUPIA

11.8000 g., Silver **Note:** Several varieties exist.

Date	Good	VG	F	VF	XF
1801	11.50	18.50	30.00	50.00	—
1802	11.50	18.50	30.00	50.00	—
1803	11.50	18.50	30.00	50.00	—
1804	11.50	18.50	30.00	50.00	—
1805	11.50	18.50	30.00	50.00	—
1806	11.50	18.50	30.00	50.00	—
1807	11.50	18.50	30.00	50.00	—

KM# 220 RUPIA

Silver **Obverse:** KM#219 **Reverse:** KM#205 **Note:** Mule.

Date	Good	VG	F	VF	XF
1807	40.00	55.00	70.00	145	—

KM# 219 RUPIA

Silver **Subject:** Joao

Date	Good	VG	F	VF	XF
1807 Inverted "A" for "V" in "Rupia"	40.00	55.00	75.00	150	—
1808	35.00	45.00	65.00	125	—
1809	35.00	45.00	65.00	125	—
1810	35.00	45.00	65.00	125	—
1811	35.00	45.00	65.00	125	—
1812	35.00	45.00	65.00	125	—
1813	40.00	55.00	75.00	150	—
1814	40.00	55.00	75.00	150	—
1815	40.00	55.00	75.00	150	—
1816	35.00	45.00	65.00	125	—
1817	35.00	45.00	65.00	125	—

KM# 239 RUPIA

Silver

Date	Good	VG	F	VF	XF
1818	40.00	55.00	70.00	145	—
1819	40.00	55.00	70.00	145	—
1820	40.00	55.00	70.00	145	—
1821	40.00	55.00	70.00	145	—
1822	40.00	55.00	70.00	145	—
1823	40.00	55.00	70.00	145	—
1824	40.00	55.00	70.00	145	—
1825	40.00	55.00	70.00	145	—
1826	40.00	55.00	70.00	145	—

KM# 248 RUPIA

11.8000 g., Silver **Subject:** Pedro IV

Date	Good	VG	F	VF	XF
1827	80.00	100	125	250	—
1828	80.00	100	125	250	—

KM# 254 RUPIA

11.8000 g., Silver **Subject:** Miguel

Date	Good	VG	F	VF	XF
1829	70.00	85.00	110	225	—
1830	60.00	75.00	90.00	180	—
1831	55.00	65.00	80.00	160	—
1832	55.00	65.00	80.00	160	—
1833	55.00	65.00	80.00	160	—

KM# 269 RUPIA

11.8000 g., Silver **Subject:** Maria II

Date	Good	VG	F	VF	XF
1839	22.50	45.00	60.00	85.00	—
1840	25.00	50.00	70.00	120	—
1841	25.00	50.00	75.00	130	—

KM# 273 RUPIA

11.8000 g., Silver

Date	Good	VG	F	VF	XF
1845	20.00	40.00	55.00	80.00	—
1846	20.00	40.00	55.00	80.00	—
1847	20.00	40.00	55.00	80.00	—
1848	20.00	40.00	55.00	80.00	—
1849	20.00	40.00	55.00	80.00	—

KM# 275 RUPIA

11.8000 g., Silver

Date	Good	VG	F	VF	XF
1850	25.00	50.00	70.00	100	—
1851	28.00	55.00	90.00	175	—
1852	28.00	55.00	90.00	175	—

KM# 279 RUPIA

11.8000 g., Silver **Subject:** Pedro V

Date	Good	VG	F	VF	XF
1856	20.00	40.00	55.00	80.00	—
1857	20.00	40.00	55.00	80.00	—
1858	20.00	40.00	55.00	80.00	—
1859	20.00	40.00	55.00	80.00	—
1860	20.00	40.00	55.00	80.00	—
1861	20.00	40.00	55.00	80.00	—

KM# 282 RUPIA

11.8000 g., Silver **Subject:** Luiz I

Date	Good	VG	F	VF	XF
1866	25.00	50.00	70.00	100	—
1867	—	—	—	—	—
1868	25.00	50.00	65.00	90.00	—
1869	25.00	50.00	65.00	90.00	—

KM# 223 2 XERAFINS

0.8100 g., Gold

Date	Good	VG	F	VF	XF
1815	—	—	—	—	—

Note: Reported, not confirmed

KM# 242 2 XERAFINS

0.8100 g., Gold **Obverse:** Crowned round arms **Reverse:** Cross divides value and date

Date	Good	VG	F	VF	XF
1819	500	950	1,550	2,250	—

KM# 202 4 XERAFINS

1.6300 g., Gold **Subject:** Maria I

Date	Good	VG	F	VF	XF
1803	275	500	850	1,400	—

KM# 243 4 XERAFINS

1.6300 g., Gold **Subject:** Joao

Date	Good	VG	F	VF	XF
1819	550	1,000	1,650	2,500	—

KM# 192.2 8 XERAFINS

3.2500 g., Gold **Subject:** Maria I

Date	Good	VG	F	VF	XF
1804	450	800	1,250	1,850	—
1805	450	800	1,250	1,850	—

KM# 244 8 XERAFINS

3.2500 g., Gold **Subject:** Joao **Obverse:** Crowned oval arms

Date	Good	VG	F	VF	XF
1819	500	800	1,500	2,500	—

KM# 245 8 XERAFINS

3.2500 g., Gold **Obverse:** Similar to 1 Rupia, KM#239

Date	Good	VG	F	VF	XF
1819	—	—	—	—	—

Note: Reported, not confirmed

KM# 187 12 XERAFINS

4.8700 g., Gold **Subject:** Maria I

Date	Good	VG	F	VF	XF
1801	250	450	750	1,300	—
1802	250	450	750	1,300	—
1803	250	400	650	1,100	—
1804	250	400	650	1,100	—
1806	250	400	650	1,100	—
1809	250	400	650	1,100	—

KM# 222 12 XERAFINS

4.8700 g., Gold **Subject:** Joao

Date	Good	VG	F	VF	XF
1808	450	650	1,150	1,700	—
1811	450	650	1,150	1,700	—
1812	450	650	1,150	1,700	—
1813	450	650	1,150	1,700	—
1814	450	650	1,150	1,700	—
1815	450	650	1,150	1,700	—
1816	450	650	1,150	1,700	—

KM# 246 12 XERAFINS

4.8700 g., Gold

Date	Good	VG	F	VF	XF
1819	500	800	1,400	1,850	—
1820	500	800	1,400	1,850	—
1822	500	800	1,400	1,850	—
1824	500	800	1,400	1,850	—
1825	500	800	1,400	1,850	—

KM# 270 12 XERAFINS

4.8700 g., Gold **Subject:** Maria II

Date	Good	VG	F	VF	XF
1840	550	1,000	1,650	2,350	—
1841	550	1,000	1,650	2,350	—

COUNTERMARKED COINAGE

KM# 264 15 REIS

Copper **Series:** 1846 **Countermark:** 15 in circle

CM Date	Host Date	Good	VG	F	VF	XF
ND(1846)	(1846)	10.00	15.00	25.00	50.00	—

KM# 267 30 REIS

Copper **Series:** 1846 **Countermark:** 60 in circle on earlier

CM Date	Host Date	Good	VG	F	VF	XF
ND(1846)	(1846)	12.00	20.00	35.00	70.00	—

KM# 274 30 REIS

Copper **Series:** 1846 **Countermark:** 30 in circle on earlier **Note:** 30 Reis (1/2 Tanga) coins.

CM Date	Host Date	Good	VG	F	VF	XF
ND(1846)	(1846)	10.00	15.00	25.00	50.00	—

KM# 250.1 1/2 TANGA

Copper **Countermark:** PR809 in dentilated circle

CM Date	Host Date	Good	VG	F	VF	XF
ND(1831)	(1750-1826)	6.50	12.00	20.00	45.00	—

KM# 250.2 1/2 TANGA

Copper **Countermark:** PR809 in dentilated circle **Note:** Countermark on 1/2 Tanga KM#249.

CM Date	Host Date	Good	VG	F	VF	XF
ND(1828-34)	(1831)	12.00	25.00	40.00	85.00	—

KM# 253.1 TANGA

Copper **Countermark:** PR809 in dentilated circle

CM Date	Host Date	Good	VG	F	VF	XF
ND(1831)	(1750-1826)	7.50	15.00	28.00	50.00	—

KM# 253.2 TANGA

Copper **Countermark:** PR809 in dentilated circle **Note:** Countermark on Tanga KM#251.

CM Date	Host Date	Good	VG	F	VF	XF
ND(1831)	(1828-1834)	15.00	30.00	55.00	100	—

COLONIAL COINAGE

KM# 301 3 REIS

Copper **Note:** Prev. KM#1.

Date	Mintage	Good	VG	F	VF	XF
1871	52,000	—	—	6.00	12.00	28.00

KM# 302 5 REIS

Copper **Note:** Prev. KM#2.

Date	Mintage	Good	VG	F	VF	XF
1871	51,000	—	—	7.00	15.00	32.00

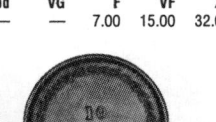

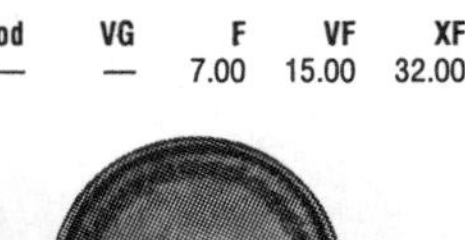

KM# 303 10 REIS

Copper **Note:** Prev. KM#3.

Date	Mintage	Good	VG	F	VF	XF
1871	51,000	—	—	8.00	16.00	38.00

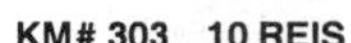
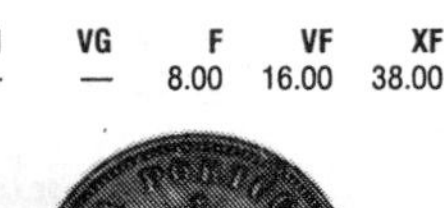

KM# 307 1/8 TANGA

Copper **Subject:** Luiz I **Note:** Prev. KM#7.

Date	Mintage	Good	VG	F	VF	XF
1881	12,397	—	—	2.50	5.00	15.00
1884	Inc. above	—	—	2.50	5.00	16.00
1886	Inc. above	—	—	3.00	6.00	18.00

KM# 309 1/8 TANGA (Oitavo)

1.4600 g., 0.9170 Silver .430 oz. ASW **Subject:** Luiz I **Note:** Prev. KM#9.

Date	Mintage	Good	VG	F	VF	XF
1881	902,000	—	—	6.00	12.00	30.00

KM# 304 1/4 TANGA (15 Reis)

Copper **Note:** Prev. KM#4.

Date	Mintage	Good	VG	F	VF	XF
1871	51,000	—	—	15.00	25.00	50.00

KM# 308 1/4 TANGA (15 Reis)

Copper **Subject:** Luiz I **Note:** Prev. KM#8.

Date	Mintage	Good	VG	F	VF	XF
1881	7,242,000	—	—	7.00	15.00	30.00
1884	Inc. above	—	—	7.50	16.00	35.00
1886	Inc. above	—	—	7.00	15.00	30.00
1888 Rare	Inc. above	—	—	—	—	—

KM# 305 1/2 TANGA (30 Reis)

Copper **Note:** Prev. KM#5.

Date	Mintage	Good	VG	F	VF	XF
1871	50,000	—	—	18.00	28.00	55.00

KM# 306 TANGA (60 Reis)

Copper

Date	Mintage	Good	VG	F	VF	XF
1871	50,000	—	—	25.00	40.00	85.00

KM# 310 1/4 RUPIA

2.9200 g., 0.9170 Silver .0860 oz. ASW **Subject:** Luiz I

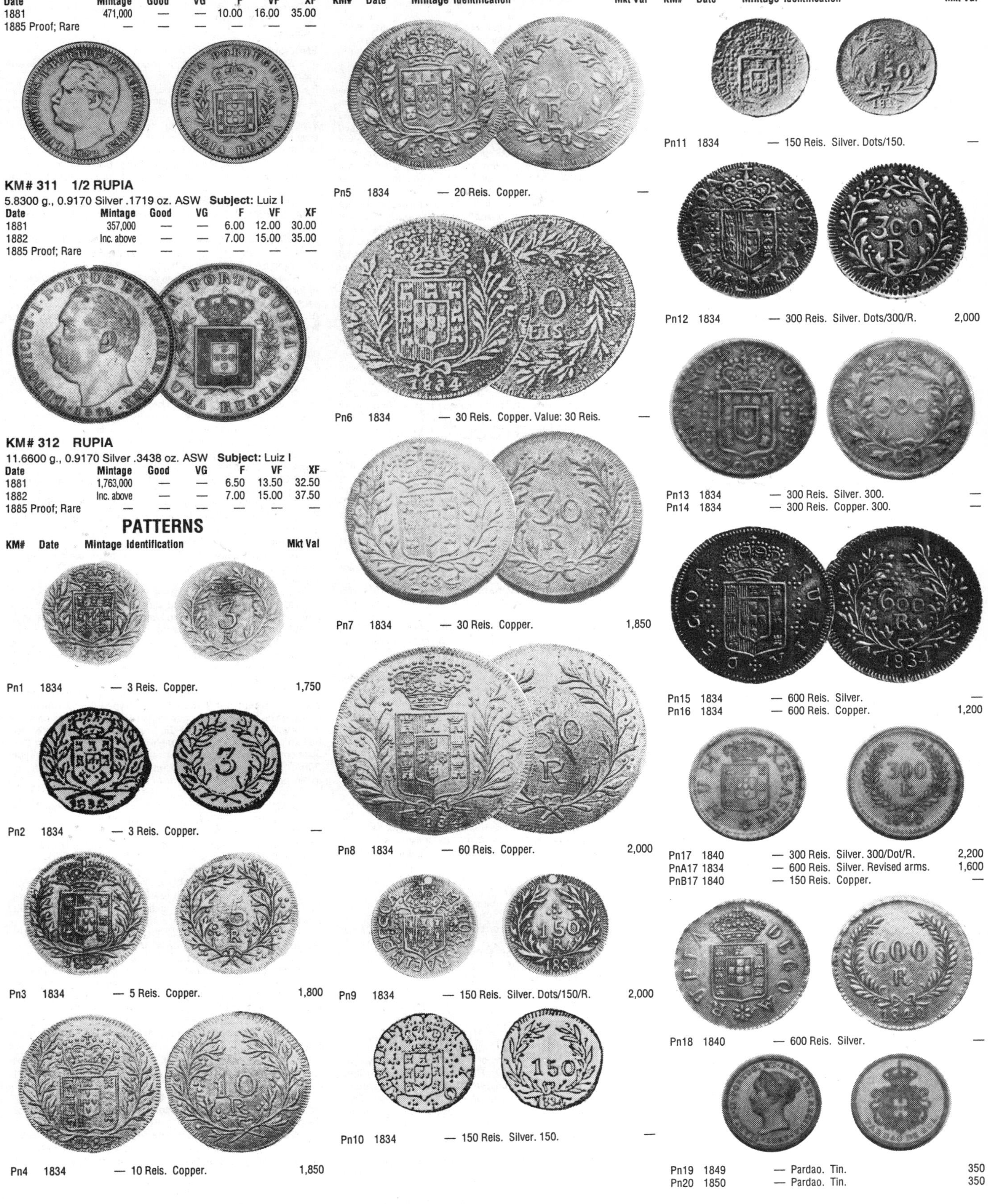

Date	Mintage	Good	VG	F	VF	XF
1881	471,000	—	—	10.00	16.00	35.00
1885 Proof; Rare	—	—	—	—	—	—

KM# 311 1/2 RUPIA

5.8300 g., 0.9170 Silver .1719 oz. ASW **Subject:** Luiz I

Date	Mintage	Good	VG	F	VF	XF
1881	357,000	—	—	6.00	12.00	30.00
1882	Inc. above	—	—	7.00	15.00	35.00
1885 Proof; Rare	—	—	—	—	—	—

KM# 312 RUPIA

11.6600 g., 0.9170 Silver .3438 oz. ASW **Subject:** Luiz I

Date	Mintage	Good	VG	F	VF	XF
1881	1,763,000	—	—	6.50	13.50	32.50
1882	Inc. above	—	—	7.00	15.00	37.50
1885 Proof; Rare	—	—	—	—	—	—

PATTERNS

KM#	Date	Mintage	Identification	Mkt Val
Pn1	1834	—	3 Reis. Copper.	1,750
Pn2	1834	—	3 Reis. Copper.	—
Pn3	1834	—	5 Reis. Copper.	1,800
Pn4	1834	—	10 Reis. Copper.	1,850
Pn5	1834	—	20 Reis. Copper.	—
Pn6	1834	—	30 Reis. Copper. Value: 30 Reis.	—
Pn7	1834	—	30 Reis. Copper.	1,850
Pn8	1834	—	60 Reis. Copper.	2,000
Pn9	1834	—	150 Reis. Silver. Dots/150/R.	2,000
Pn10	1834	—	150 Reis. Silver. 150.	—
Pn11	1834	—	150 Reis. Silver. Dots/150.	—
Pn12	1834	—	300 Reis. Silver. Dots/300/R.	2,000
Pn13	1834	—	300 Reis. Silver. 300.	—
Pn14	1834	—	300 Reis. Copper. 300.	—
Pn15	1834	—	600 Reis. Silver.	—
Pn16	1834	—	600 Reis. Copper.	1,200
Pn17	1840	—	300 Reis. Silver. 300/Dot/R.	2,200
PnA17	1834	—	600 Reis. Silver. Revised arms.	1,600
PnB17	1840	—	150 Reis. Copper.	—
Pn18	1840	—	600 Reis. Silver.	—
Pn19	1849	—	Pardao. Tin.	350
Pn20	1850	—	Pardao. Tin.	350

KM#	Date	Mintage	Identification	Mkt Val

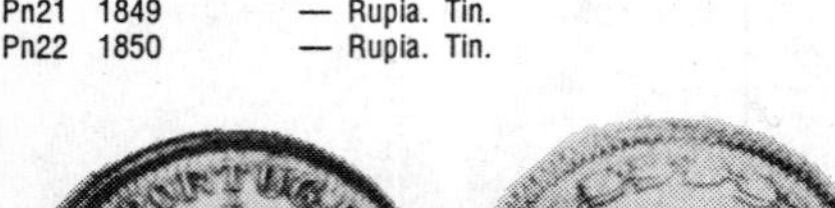

KM#	Date	Mintage	Identification	Mkt Val
Pn21	1849	—	Rupia. Tin.	425
Pn22	1850	—	Rupia. Tin.	425

KM#	Date	Mintage	Identification	Mkt Val
Pn23	1862	—	Rupia. Silver.	—
Pn24	1862	—	Rupia. Lead.	—
Pn25	1868	—	30 Reis. Copper.	250
Pn26	1871	—	3 Reis. Gold. KM#1.	—
Pn27	1871	—	3 Reis. Silver. KM#1.	1,350

TRIAL STRIKES

KM#	Date	Mintage	Identification	Mkt Val
TS1	1881	—	1/8 Tanga. KM7, uniface obverse.	400
TS2	(1881)	—	1/8 Tanga. KM7, uniface reverse.	400
TS3	1881	—	1/4 Tanga. KM8, uniface obverse.	400
TS4	(1881)	—	1/4 Tanga. KM8, uniface reverse.	400
TS5	1881	—	1/8 Rupia. KM9, uniface obverse.	250
TS6	(1881)	—	1/8 Rupia. KM9, uniface reverse.	250
TS7	(1881)	—	1/8 Rupia. KM9, copper, uniface reverse.	200
TS8	1881	—	1/4 Rupia. KM10, uniface obverse.	250
TS9	(1881)	—	1/4 Rupia. KM10, uniface reverse.	250
TS10	(1881)	—	1/4 Rupia. KM10, Copper, uniface reverse.	200
TS11	1881	—	1/2 Rupia. KM11, uniface obverse.	325
TS12	(1881)	—	1/2 Rupia. KM11, uniface reverse.	325
TS13	1881	—	1/2 Rupia. KM11, Copper, uniface obverse.	300
TS14	(1881)	—	1/2 Rupia. KM11, Copper, uniface reverse.	300
TS15	1881	—	Rupia. KM12, uniface obverse.	350
TS16	(1881)	—	Rupia. KM12, uniface reverse.	350
TS17	1881	—	Rupia. KM12, Copper, uniface obverse.	350

INDIA-BRITISH

The civilization of India, which began about 2500 B.C., flourished under a succession of empires - notably those of the Mauryas, the Kushans, the Guptas, the Delhi Sultans and the Mughals – until undermined in the 18th and 19th centuries by European colonial powers.

The Portuguese were the first to arrive, off Calicut in May 1498. It wasn't until 1612, after the Portuguese and Spanish power had begun to wane, that the British East India Company established its initial settlement at Surat. Britain could not have chosen a more propitious time as the central girdle of petty states, and the southern Vijayanagar Empire were crumbling and ripe for foreign exploitation. By the end of the century, English traders were firmly established in Bombay, Madras, Calcutta and lesser places elsewhere, and Britain was implementing its announced policy to create such civil and military institutions as may be the foundation of secure English domination for all time'. By 1757, following the successful conclusion of a war of colonial rivalry with France during which the military victories of Robert Clive, a young officer with the British East India Company, made him a powerful man in India, the British were firmly settled in India not only as traders but as conquerors. During the next 60 years, the British East India Company acquired dominion over most of India by bribery and force, and governed it directly or through puppet princelings.

As a result of the Sepoy Mutiny of 1857-58, a large scale mutiny among Indian soldiers of the Bengal army, control of the government of India was transferred from the East India Company to the British Crown. At this point in world history, India was the brightest jewel in the British imperial diadem, but even then a movement for greater Indian representation in government presaged the Indian Empire's twilight hour less than a century later - it would pass into history on Aug. 15, 1947.

BRITISH COLONIAL

This section lists the coins of British India from the reign of William IV (1835) to the reign of George VI (1947). The issues are divided into two main parts:

1. Coins struck under the authority of the East India Company (E.I.C.) from 1835 until the trading monopoly of the E.I.C. was abolished in 1853. From August 2, 1858 the property and powers of the Company were transferred to the British Crown. From November 1, 1858 to November 1, 1862 the coins continued to bear the design and inscription of the Company.

2. Coins struck under the authority of the Crown (Regal issues) from 1862 until 1947.

The first regal issues bear the date 1862 and were struck with the date 1862 unchanged until 1874. From then onward all coins bear the year date.

The copper coins dated 1862 have been tentatively attributed by their size to the mint of issue. The silver coins dated 1862 have been attributed to various years of issue by their characteristic marks according to mint records.

In 1877 Queen Victoria was proclaimed Empress of India and the title of the obverse legend was changed accordingly.

For a detailed account of the work of the various mints and the numerous die varieties the general collector and specialist should refer to *"The Coins of the British Commonwealth of Nations to the End of the Reign of King George VI - 1952"*, Part 4, India, Vol. 1 and 2, by F. Pridmore, Spink, 1980.

RULERS

British until 1947

MINT MARKS

The coins of British India were struck at the following mints, indicated in the catalogue by either capital letters after the date when the actual letter appears on the coins or small letters in ( ) designating the mint of issue. Plain dates indicate Royal Mint strikes.

B-Bombay, 1835-1947
C or CM-Calcutta, 1835-1947
H - Ralph Heaton & Sons, Birmingham (1857-1858)
I-Bombay, 1918-1919
L-Lahore, 1943-1945
M-Madras, 1869 (closed Sept. 1869)
P-Pretoria, South Africa, 1943-1944
W - J. Watt & Sons, Birmingham (1860)

MONETARY SYSTEM

3 Pies = 1 Pice (Paisa)
4 Pice = 1 Anna
16 Annas = 1 Rupee
15 Rupees = 1 Mohur

The transition from the coins of the Moslem monetary system began with the silver pattern Rupees of William IV, 1834, issued by the East India Company, with the value on the reverse, given in English, Bengali, Persian and Nagari characters. This coinage was struck for several years, as dated, except for the currency Rupee which was struck from 1835 to 1840, all dated 1835.

The portrait coins issued by the East India Company for Victoria show two different head designs on the obverse, which are called Type I and Type II. The coins with Type I head have a continuous obverse legend and were struck from 1840 to 1851. The coins with the Type II head have a divided obverse legend and were struck from 1850 (Calcutta) until 1862. The date on the coins remained unchanged: the Rupee, 1/2 Rupee and 1/4 Rupee are dated 1840, the 2 Annas and the Mohur are dated 1841. Both issues were struck at the Calcutta, Mumbai (Bombay) and Madras Mints. Numerous varieties exist in the rupee series of 1840. Noticable differences in the ribbon designs of the English vs. Indian obverses exist.

Type I coins have on the reverse a dot after the date, those of Type II have no dot, except for some rare 1/4 Rupees and 2 Annas. The latter are mules, struck from reverse dies of the preceding issue.

ENGRAVER INITIALS

The following initials appear on the obverse on the truncation:

F - William N. Forbes, Calcutta, 1836-1855
R.S. - Robert Saunders, Calcutta, 1826-1836
S Incuse (Type I)
WW raised or incuse (Type II)
WWS or SWW (Type II)
WWB raised (Type II)

On both issues, the "S" is the initial of Major, later Lt. Col. J. T. Smith, mintmaster at Madras from February 1840 to September 1855.

The B' which occurs only on Rupees of Type II, is the initial of Major, later Lt. Col. J. H. Bell (mintmaster at Madras, 1855-1859).

The initials WW which appear on all coins of Type II, are those of William Wyon, Chief Engraver of the Royal Mint, London, who prepared this obverse design in 1849.

The major reverse varieties occur on the Type I Rupees of all three mints. The first reverse has 19 berries in the wreath, the second reverse has 34 and 35 berries (Calcutta) and 35 berries (Bombay and Madras). There are several minor varieties of the first reverse, but these are not listed. Madras specimens of Type I with the 1st reverse also have a small, raised "V" on the lower part of the right ribbon bow.

REGAL COINAGE

1/12 ANNA

NOTE: 1/12 Anna dated 1862 were minted at Calcutta, Bombay, and Madres using Bust A. They may be attributed according to size Bust A was used on all issues except 1877 and subsequent Calcutta issues which used Bust B.

Distinguishing Features

BUST A - Front of dress has 4-1/3 panels with a flower at center on bottom panel.

BUST B - Front of dress has 4 panels with a flower at right on bottom panel.

CALCUTTA - Issues of 1874-76 are 17.5mm in diameter. From 1877 Bust B was used and the legend at lower right is distant from the bust. 1882-86 issues have a tiny incuse "C" on a bead of the inner circle below the date.

BOMBAY - Issues of 1874-76 are 18.0mm in diameter. From 1877 Bust A was used and the legend at lower right is close to the bust.

1/2 PICE

NOTE: The 1/2 Pice dated 1862 was struck at Indian Govemment Mints i.e. Calcutta and Madras. Tentative attribution to the mint of issue has been determined by their size.

Proofs and restrikes dated 1862 were struck from pattern dies with 4-3/4 panels, a different floral dress design on obverse and counter clockwise leaves on reverse.

1/4 ANNA

NOTE: The initial 1862 dated Calcutta 1/4 Annas were struck with a diameter of 26.2-26.3mm (Type A/I). With the opening of the new Calcutta copper mint in 1865 the 1/4 Annas were struck with a diameter of 25.3-25.4mm and a tiny raised v on the bottom center of the bust. Probably only a month or so later Calcutta began to strike coins with a new obverse and reverse (Type B/II). This type was used by Calcutta for the remainder of the Victorian period.

Distinguishing Features

BUST A - Front of dress has 4 panels with a single flower at right on bottom panel.

BUST B - Front of dress has 4 panels with flowers at left and right on bottom panel. Tiny raised v on bottom center of bust. Floral design of dress differs.

REVERSE I - Leaf below first and last digit of date.

REVERSE II - Leaf below center of date.

CALCUTTA - Issues from 1874 onward are Type B/II. Most 1879-1887 issues have a tiny incuse "C" on a bead of the inner circle below the center of the date.

BOMBAY - Issues of 1875-76 have Bust A and Rev. I (A/I) and from 1877 onward are Type B/I.

1/2 ANNA

NOTE: 1862 dated issues were struck at all three mints using Obverse A and Reverse I (A/I). They may be attributed according to size. Later 1862 dated Calcutta issues use Bust B and Reverse II (B/II).

Distinguishing Features

BUST A - Front of dress has 4-1/2 panels with no flowers on bottom incomplete panel.

BUST B - Front of dress has 4 panels with a small flower at upper left and large flower at right on bottom panel. Floral design of dress differs from Bust A. Tiny raised v on bottom left of bust.

BUST C - Front of dress has 4-3/4 panels with a single flower in center of bottom incomplete panel. An enlarged bust with floral design similar to Bust B.

REVERSE I - Slant top 1 in date and narrow spaced "ANNA".

REVERSE II - Flat top 1 in date and wide spaced "ANNA".

CALCUTTA - Issues from 1877 onward are Type C/II. 1877 Calcutta isues also have short, wide 7's in date. 1879 Calcutta issues have a tiny incuse "C" on a bead of the inner circle below the center of the date.

BOMBAY - Issues from 1877 onward are Type B/II. 1877 Bombay issues also have tall, narrow 7's in date. This type 7 appears on most Bombay issues but not on any denomination of the Calcutta Mint.

NOTE: The designations of Bust A, B and C have been changed to correspond with designations in *"Coins of the British Commonwealth of Nations Part 4, Vol. 2"* by F. Pridmore.

2 ANNAS

Distinguishing Features

BUST A - Front of dress has 4 panels. The bottom panel has 3 leaves at left and a small flower at upper right.

BUST B - Front of dress has 3-1/2 panels. The bottom incomplete panel has only 3 leaf tops.

REVERSE I - Large top flower; 2 large petals above the base of the top flower are long and curved downward.

REVERSE II - Small top flower; 2 large petals above the base of the top flower are short and horizontal.

CALCUTTA - Issues dated 1862-1878 are 15.3-15.4mm in diameter and have no mint mark. From 1879 the mint mark is a tiny incuse "C" on the whorl below the center of the bottom flower. The 1877 issue with a bead in the tip of the top flower is attributed to Calcutta based on its diameter of 15.4 mm.

BOMBAY - Issues dated 1862-1876 are 15.7-15.9mm in diameter and until 1876 have no mint mark. From 1876-1884 the mint mark is a raised dot above the bottom flower. From 1884 the mint mark is a small "B" incuse or raised on the stem of the top flower.

MADRAS - Issues dated 1862 are 16mm in diameter.

1/4 RUPEE

Distinguishing Features

Differences of the 3 busts and 2 reverses:

BUST A - The front of dress has 4 panels w/flower at right on bottom panel.

BUST B - Front of dress has 3-3/4 panels w/flower at center on incomplete bottom panel.

BUST C - Front of dress has 3 panels w/flower at left on bottom panel.

REVERSE I - The 2 large petals above the base of the top flower are long and curved downward; long stroke between "1/4".

Small Rupee, "ana" in Hindi.

REVERSE II - The 2 large petals above the base of the top flower are short and horizontal; short stroke between "1/4".

Small Rupee, "ana" in Persian

Reverse III: Large Rupee, "ana" in Persian.

CALCUTTA - Issues dated 1862-1878 have no mint mark. The diameter of the coins is 19.3-19.4mm and the milling is coarse. From 1879 the mint mark is a tiny incuse "C" on the whorl below the center of the bottom flower.

BOMBAY - Issues dated 1862, 1875 and 1876 have no mint mark. These have a diameter of 19.7-19.8mm and the milling is narrow. The coins dated 1874, 1877-1883 have as mint mark a small bead directly above the bottom flower. From 1884 the mint mark is a small "B" raised or incuse on the stem of the top flower.

MADRAS - Issues dated 1862 have a diameter of 19.9-20.0mm and coarse milling.

1/2 RUPEE

Distinguishing Features

BUST A - Front of dress has 4 panels w/a flower at left and right on bottom panel. Tiny raised v on bottom center of bust.

BUST B - Front of dress has 4-1/2 or 4-2/3 panels. The incomplete bottom panel has a flower at left of center.

BUST C - Front of dress similar to Bust B but with 4-3/4 panels floral design of dress differs.

Bust B Bust C

REVERSE I - The top flower is open and the 2 large petals above the base of the top flower are short and horizontal, flat top 1 in date.

REVERSE II - The top flower is closed and the 2 large petals above the base of the top flower are long and curved downward, slant top 1 in date.

CALCUTTA - Issues have Bust A/Reverse I and Bust C/Reverse II, dated 1862-1878, and have no mint mark. From 1879 the mint mark is a small incuse "C" below the center of the bottom flower.

BOMBAY - Issues dated 1862 have no mint mark. From 1874-1884 the mint mark is a small dot above the center of the bottom flower. From 1885 the mint mark is a small "B" raised or incuse, on the stem of the top flower.

MADRAS - Issues dated 1862 have no mint mark and cannot be distinguished from the Bombay issues.

RUPEE

Distinguishing Features

NOTE: The Rupees dated 1862 were struck with the date unchanged until 1874. However, in 1863 Bombay Mint adopted a method of adding dots or beads to its dies to indicate the exact year of minting.

The beads occur in the following positions:

1. Below the base or whorl of the top flower.
2. Above or around the top of the bottom flower.
3. In both positions together.

The different busts are identified as follows:

BUST A - Front of dress has 3-3/4 panels with a small flower at left on bottom incomplete panel.

BUST B - Front of dress has 4-1/4 panels with a small flower right on bottom panel, floral design of dress differs.

BUST C - Similar to Bust A, but shorter at the bottom. Front of dress has 3-1/3 or 3-1/2 panels.

REVERSE I - The top of flower is open, flat top 1 in date.

REVERSE II - The top flower is closed, slant top 1 in date.

REVERSE IIa - Similar to Reverse II but flower buds above "E" of "ONE" and above right of second "E" of "RUPEE" have a "pineapple-like" pattern.

REVERSE III - The top flower is half open, flat 1 in date.

NOTE: The top flowers on reverse vary as illustrated below.

I

II

III

NOTE: In the listing of 1862 Rupees, the date column indicates the year in which the coins are believed to have been struck. The variety column lists the Obverse/reverse combination and the bead position. For example, A/I 0/0 means Bust A, Reverse I and no beads. A/II 1/2 means Bust A, Reverse II, and 1 bead at the top and 2 beads at the bottom.

Mintage for 1862 Rupees

CALCUTTA 269,427,222
Mumbai (Bombay) 408,003,034
Madras 29,481,923

NOTE: The B/II 0/0 coins are attributed to the mint of issues as follows:

CALCUTTA - 30.7mm or smaller, round pearls in crown arch.

BOMBAY -30.7-30.9mm, elongated pearls in crown arch. The scroll-like floral design of the dress is in flat relief and is retouched with incuse lines.

MADRAS - 30.9-31.0mm, elongated pearls in crown arch. The floral design is in high relief and is not retouched.

From 1874 onward the coins show the year date. The designs are similar to those on the 1862 Rupees but only Busts "A" and "C" and Reverse I and II were used.

CALCUTTA - Mint issues dated 1874-78 have no mint mark. From 1879 the mint mark is a small incuse "C" on the whorl below the center of the bottom lotus flower on the reverse. All Calcutta issues have Reverse I.

BOMBAY - Mint issues dated 1874-83 usually have as mint mark a small dot directly above the bottom lotus flower. From 1883 the mint mark is a small "B" raised or incuse on the stem of the top flower. Some issues dated 1874-84 have no mint mark but except for an 1883 issue have Reverse II. Issues dated 1874-76 have Reverse II only, those dated 1877-85 have both Reverses I and II, and from 1886 only Reverse I.

NOTE: There are reverse varieties in most of the following Rupees. Reverse II flowers are found in various sizes. Two bottom rosettes are found rotated, i.e., 1 petal up or down.

COLONIAL

MILLED COINAGE

KM# 445 1/12 ANNA (1 Pie)

Copper **Issuer:** East India Company **Note:** Mints: Calcutta: 17.5mm; Mumbai (Bombay): 18.0mm; Madras: 17.7-17.9mm.

Date	Mintage	F	VF	XF	Unc
1835(b)	72,313,000	1.00	2.50	4.00	8.00
1835(m)	133,788,000	0.75	2.00	3.00	6.00
1835(c) Proof	—	Value: 75.00			
1848(c)	14,380,000	1.25	3.00	5.00	10.00

KM# 464 1/2 PICE

Copper **Issuer:** East India Company **Mint:** Calcutta

Date	Mintage	F	VF	XF	Unc
1853(c)	62,408,000	1.75	3.50	8.00	20.00
1853(c) Proof	—	Value: 100			
1853(c) Prooflike; Restrike	—	—	—	—	25.00

KM# 446.1 1/4 ANNA

Copper **Issuer:** East India Company **Obverse:** Small shield **Rev. Legend:** large ONE QUARTER ANNA **Note:** The 1835 dated coins exist in both medal and coin rotations.

Date	Mintage	F	VF	XF	Unc
1833(b) Proof	—	Value: 175			
1835(b)	36,767,000	1.00	2.00	4.00	10.00
1835(m)	186,530,000	1.00	2.00	4.00	10.00

KM# 446.2 1/4 ANNA

Copper **Issuer:** East India Company **Obverse:** Small shield **Rev. Legend:** Small ONE QUARTER ANA **Note:** Mints: Calcutta: 26.2mm; Mubai (Bombay): 25.2mm; Madras: 25.5mm. 6 varieties for Madras, 2 varieties for Calcutta.

Date	Mintage	F	VF	XF	Unc
1835(b)	Inc. above	1.00	2.00	4.00	10.00
1835(c)	755,059,000	1.00	2.00	4.00	10.00
1835(c) Proof	—	Value: 75.00			
1835(m)	Inc. above	1.00	2.00	4.00	10.00
1849 Proof	—	Value: 250			

KM# 463.1 1/4 ANNA

Copper **Issuer:** East India Company **Obverse:** Large shield **Reverse:** Wreath tips are single leaves

Date	Mintage	F	VF	XF	Unc
1857(h)	47,040,000	1.00	2.00	10.00	45.00
1858(w)	62,720,000	0.85	1.50	2.50	10.00
1858(w) Proof	—	Value: 125			

KM# 463.2 1/4 ANNA

Copper **Issuer:** East India Company **Mint:** Ralph Heaton & Sons **Reverse:** Wreath tips are double leaves

Date	Mintage	F	VF	XF	Unc
1857(h)	Inc. above	0.85	2.00	10.00	45.00
1857(h) Proof	—	Value: 125			
1858(h)	172,480,000	1.00	2.00	4.00	10.00
1858(h) Proof	—	Value: 125			

KM# A447 1/2 ANNA

Copper **Issuer:** East India Company **Obverse:** Mumbai (Bombay) KM#251 **Reverse:** KM#447 **Note:** Mule.

Date	Mintage	F	VF	XF	Unc
1834	—	—	—	275	450

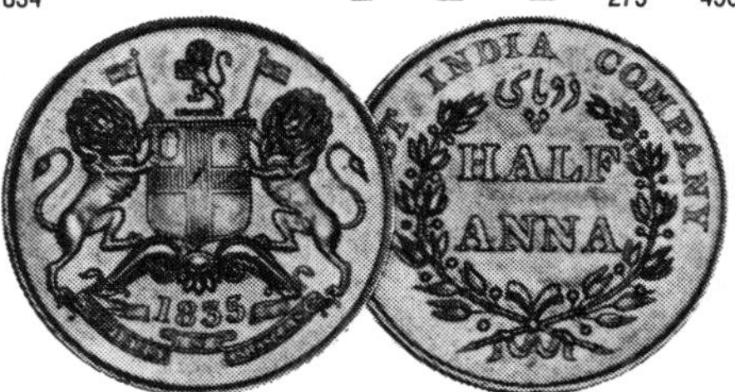

KM# 447.1 1/2 ANNA

Copper **Issuer:** East India Company **Note:** Mumbai (Bombay): 29.7mm; Nadras: 30.8mm.

Date	Mintage	F	VF	XF	Unc
1835(b)	8,658,000	2.00	4.00	10.00	50.00'
1835(b) Proof	—	Value: 100			
1835(b) Prooflike; restrike	—	—	—	—	35.00
1835(m)	95,203,000	2.00	4.00	10.00	50.00
1835(m) Proof	—	Value: 100			
1845C	17,160,000	2.00	4.00	12.50	65.00

KM# 447.2 1/2 ANNA

Copper **Issuer:** East India Company **Mint:** Calcutta **Edge:** Beaded rim with milled edge

Date	Mintage	F	VF	XF	Unc
1835(c) Proof	—	Value: 300			

KM# 447.2a 1/2 ANNA

Silver **Issuer:** East India Company **Mint:** Calcutta

Date	Mintage	F	VF	XF	Unc
1835(c) Proof	—	Value: 550			

KM# 459.2 2 ANNAS

1.4600 g., 0.9170 Silver 0.043 oz. ASW, 15.3 mm. **Issuer:** East India Company **Mint:** Calcutta **Reverse:** With crescent on left ribbon bow

Date	Mintage	F	VF	XF	Unc
1841.(c)	8,385,000	2.00	4.00	8.50	20.00
1841.(c) Prooflike; Restrike	—	—	—	—	25.00
1841.(c) Proof	—	Value: 50.00			

KM# 460.2 2 ANNAS

1.4600 g., 0.9170 Silver 0.043 oz. ASW **Issuer:** East India Company **Mint:** Calcutta **Obverse:** W.W. raised on truncation

Date	Mintage	F	VF	XF	Unc
1841(c)	—	1.50	3.00	7.50	15.00
1841(c) Proof	—	Value: 150			

KM# 460.3 2 ANNAS

1.4600 g., 0.9170 Silver 0.043 oz. ASW, 15.7 mm. **Issuer:** East India Company **Mint:** Bombay **Obverse:** W. W. raised on truncation

Date	Mintage	F	VF	XF	Unc
1841(b)	8,427,000	1.50	3.00	7.50	15.00

KM# 460.4 2 ANNAS

1.4600 g., 0.9170 Silver 0.043 oz. ASW, 15.7 mm **Issuer:** East India Company **Mint:** Madras **Obverse:** S incuse, W. W raised

Date	Mintage	F	VF	XF	Unc
1841(m)	26,930,000	2.00	4.00	8.50	17.50
1841(m) Proof	—	Value: 150			

KM# 459.1 2 ANNAS

1.4600 g., 0.9170 Silver 0.043 oz. ASW, 15.8 mm. **Issuer:** East India Company **Mint:** Bombay **Obverse:** Legend continuous **Note:** Type I.

Date	Mintage	F	VF	XF	Unc
1841.(b)	11,431,000	2.00	4.00	8.50	20.00

KM# 460.1 2 ANNAS

1.4600 g., 0.9170 Silver 0.043 oz. ASW, 15.3 mm. **Issuer:** East India Company **Mint:** Calcutta **Obverse:** Legend divided **Reverse:** KM#459.2, dot after date **Note:** Type II.

Date	Mintage	F	VF	XF	Unc
1841.(c)	43,002,000	7.50	12.50	25.00	50.00
1841.(c) Proof; Early restrike	—	Value: 150			

KM# 460.5 2 ANNAS

1.4600 g., 0.9170 Silver 0.043 oz. ASW **Issuer:** East India Company **Obverse:** WW raised

Date	Mintage	F	VF	XF	Unc
1849 Proof; Early restrike	—	Value: 250			
1849 Prooflike; Restrike	—	—	—	—	25.00

KM# 448.3 1/4 RUPEE

2.9200 g., 0.9170 Silver 0.0861 oz. ASW **Issuer:** East India Company **Mint:** Bombay **Obverse:** Without initials on truncation **Reverse:** Small Rupee, "ana" in Persian with 20 berries

Date	Mintage	F	VF	XF	Unc
1835(b)	5,760,000	5.00	10.00	20.00	40.00
1835(b) Proof	—	Value: 500			
1835(b) Prooflike; Restrike	—	—	—	—	30.00

KM# 448a 1/4 RUPEE

Gold **Issuer:** East India Company **Mint:** Calcutta

Date	Mintage	F	VF	XF	Unc
1835(c)	—	—	—	—	—

KM# 448.6 1/4 RUPEE

2.9200 g., 0.9170 Silver 0.0861 oz. ASW **Issuer:** East India Company **Mint:** Calcutta **Obverse:** F in relief in truncation **Reverse:** Large Rupee, "ana" in Persian with 18 berries **Note:** Prev. KM#448.1.

Date	Mintage	F	VF	XF	Unc
1835.(c)	—	4.50	7.50	15.00	40.00
1835.(c) Proof	—	Value: 500			
1835.(c) Prooflike; Restrike	—	—	—	—	30.00

KM# 448.4 1/4 RUPEE

2.9200 g., 0.9170 Silver 0.0861 oz. ASW **Issuer:** East India Company **Mint:** Calcutta **Obverse:** F incuse on truncation **Reverse:** Small Rupee, "ana" in Persian with 20 berries **Note:** Prev. KM#448.2.

Date	Mintage	F	VF	XF	Unc
1835(c)	9,842,000	4.50	7.50	15.00	40.00

KM# 448.5 1/4 RUPEE

2.9200 g., 0.9170 Silver 0.0861 oz. ASW **Issuer:** East India Company **Mint:** Calcutta **Obverse:** F incuse on truncation Rev. Designer: Large Rupee, "ana" in Persian **Note:** Prev. KM#448.2.

Date	Mintage	F	VF	XF	Unc
1835(c) with 19 berries	—	4.50	7.50	15.00	40.00
1835.(c) with 18 berries	—	4.50	7.50	15.00	40.00

KM# 448.2 1/4 RUPEE

2.9200 g., 0.9170 Silver 0.0861 oz. ASW **Issuer:** East India Company **Mint:** Calcutta **Obverse:** RS incuse on truncation **Reverse:** Small Rupee, "ana" in Persian with 20 berries **Note:** Prev. KM#448.4. Robert Saunders was Calcutta Mint Director from 1826-Jan. 1836.

Date	Mintage	F	VF	XF	Unc
1835(c)	—	5.00	10.00	20.00	40.00

2.9200 g, .917 SILVER, .0860 oz ASW

Rev. I: Small Rupee, "ana" in Hindi.

Rev II: Small Rupee, "ana" in Persian.

Rev. III: Large Rupee, "ana" in Persian.

Rev. I w/20 berries.

KM# 448.1 1/4 RUPEE

2.9200 g., 0.9170 Silver 0.0861 oz. ASW **Issuer:** East India Company **Mint:** Calcutta **Reverse:** Small Rupee, "ana" in Hindi with 20 berries **Note:** Prev. KM#448.5.

Date	Mintage	F	VF	XF	Unc
1835(c)	922,000	11.50	22.50	45.00	90.00
1835(c) Proof	—	Value: 500			

KM# 453.1 1/4 RUPEE

2.9200 g., 0.9170 Silver 0.0861 oz. ASW, 19.5 mm. **Issuer:** East India Company **Mint:** Bombay **Obverse:** Legend continuous. English head **Note:** Type I.

Date	Mintage	F	VF	XF	Unc
1840.(b)	10,617,000	2.50	5.00	10.00	25.00
1840.(b) Prooflike; Restrike	—	—	—	—	30.00

KM# 454.1 1/4 RUPEE

2.9200 g., 0.9170 Silver 0.0861 oz. ASW **Issuer:** East India Company **Obverse:** Legend divided **Reverse:** Mule. KM#453.4 **Note:** Type II.

Date	Mintage	F	VF	XF	Unc
1840.(b & c)	40,532	10.00	20.00	40.00	80.00
1840.(c) Proof	—	Value: 200			

KM# 453.2 1/4 RUPEE

2.9200 g., 0.9170 Silver 0.0861 oz. ASW, 19.3 mm. **Issuer:** East India Company **Mint:** Calcutta **Reverse:** With crescent on left ribbon bow, 20 berries

Date	Mintage	F	VF	XF	Unc
1840.(c)	12,994,000	2.50	5.00	10.00	20.00
1840.(c) Proof	—	Value: 200			

KM# 453.3 1/4 RUPEE

2.9200 g., 0.9170 Silver 0.0861 oz. ASW, 19.6 mm. **Issuer:** East India Company **Mint:** Madras **Obverse:** S incuse on truncation **Reverse:** With "v" on right ribbon bow, 20 berries

Date	Mintage	F	VF	XF	Unc
1840.(m)	6,450,000	3.75	7.50	15.00	30.00

KM# 453.4 1/4 RUPEE

2.9200 g., 0.9170 Silver 0.0861 oz. ASW **Issuer:** East India Company **Mint:** Calcutta **Obverse:** "Indian" head with thinner features **Reverse:** 34 berries

Date	Mintage	F	VF	XF	Unc
1840.(c)		2.50	5.00	10.00	20.00
1840.(c) Proof	—	Value: 200			

KM# 454.2 1/4 RUPEE

2.9200 g., 0.9170 Silver 0.0861 oz. ASW **Issuer:** East India Company **Obverse:** W.W. raised on truncation

Date	F	VF	XF	Unc
1840(b & c) Plain 4	2.50	5.00	10.00	20.00
1840(b & c) Crosslet 4	3.00	6.00	12.00	25.00
1840(c) Proof —	Value: 200			

KM# 454.3 1/4 RUPEE

2.9200 g., 0.9170 Silver 0.0861 oz. ASW **Issuer:** East India Company **Mint:** Madras **Obverse:** W.W. and B raised on truncation

Date	Mintage	F	VF	XF	Unc
1840(m)	13,664,000	4.00	6.00	12.00	30.00

KM# 454.5 1/4 RUPEE

2.9200 g., 0.9170 Silver 0.0861 oz. ASW **Issuer:** East India Company **Obverse:** W.W. on truncation **Edge:** Plain

Date	Mintage	F	VF	XF	Unc
1849 Proof; Early restrike	—	Value: 300			
1849 Prooflike; Restrike	—	—	—	—	45.00

KM# 454.6 1/4 RUPEE

2.9200 g., 0.9170 Silver 0.0861 oz. ASW **Issuer:** East India Company **Edge:** Milled

Date	Mintage	F	VF	XF	Unc
1849 Proof; Early restrike	—	Value: 300			
1849 Prooflike; Restrike	—	—	—	—	45.00

KM# 449.1 1/2 RUPEE

5.8300 g., 0.9170 Silver 0.1719 oz. ASW **Issuer:** East India Company **Mint:** Bombay **Obverse:** Without initial on truncation

Date	Mintage	F	VF	XF	Unc
1835.(b)	3,573,000	7.50	15.00	30.00	60.00
1835.(b) Prooflike; Restrike	—	—	—	—	60.00

KM# 449.2 1/2 RUPEE

5.8300 g., 0.9170 Silver 0.1719 oz. ASW **Mint:** Calcutta **Obverse:** F raised on truncation

Date	Mintage	F	VF	XF	Unc
1835.(c)	6,700,000	7.50	15.00	30.00	60.00
1835(c) Prooflike; Restrike	—	—	—	—	60.00

KM# 449.3 1/2 RUPEE

5.8300 g., 0.9170 Silver 0.1719 oz. ASW **Mint:** Calcutta **Obverse:** F incuse

Date	Mintage	F	VF	XF	Unc
1835.(c)	—	7.50	15.00	30.00	60.00
1835.(c) Proof; Early restrike	—	—	—	—	250

KM# 449a 1/2 RUPEE

Gold **Mint:** Calcutta

Date	Mintage	F	VF	XF	Unc
1835(c)	—	—	—	—	—

KM# 455.3 1/2 RUPEE

5.8300 g., 0.9170 Silver 0.1719 oz. ASW **Mint:** Madras **Obverse:** S incuse on truncation

Date	Mintage	F	VF	XF	Unc
1840.(m) Rare	1,874,000	—	—	—	—

KM# 455.4 1/2 RUPEE

5.8300 g., 0.9170 Silver 0.1719 oz. ASW **Mint:** Calcutta **Obverse:** "Indian" head with thinner features **Reverse:** With millimeters, crescent, on left ribbon bow

Date	Mintage	F	VF	XF	Unc
1840.(c)	—	5.00	10.00	20.00	45.00
1840.(c) Proof	Inc. above	Value: 250			
1840.(c) Prooflike; Restrike	—	—	—	—	35.00

KM# A455 1/2 RUPEE

5.8300 g., 0.9170 Silver 0.1719 oz. ASW **Mint:** Calcutta **Obverse:** Mule. KM#455.1 **Reverse:** KM#456.1

Date	Mintage	F	VF	XF	Unc
1840(c)	—	4.50	8.50	17.50	40.00

KM# 456.2 1/2 RUPEE

5.8300 g., 0.9170 Silver 0.1719 oz. ASW **Mint:** Madras **Obverse:** W.W. incuse and raised S

Date	Mintage	F	VF	XF	Unc
1840(m)	2,507,000	5.00	10.00	20.00	40.00

KM# 456.3 1/2 RUPEE

5.8300 g., 0.9170 Silver 0.1719 oz. ASW **Mint:** Madras **Obverse:** W.W. incuse, B raised

Date	Mintage	F	VF	XF	Unc
1840(m)	—	7.50	15.00	30.00	80.00

KM# B455 1/2 RUPEE

5.8300 g., 0.9170 Silver 0.1719 oz. ASW **Obverse:** Mule. KM#456.1 **Reverse:** KM#455.4 **Note:** Prev. KM#A456.

Date	Mintage	F	VF	XF	Unc
1840.	—	4.50	8.50	17.50	40.00

KM# 455.2 1/2 RUPEE

5.8300 g., 0.9170 Silver 0.1719 oz. ASW **Mint:** Calcutta **Reverse:** With crescent on left ribbon bow **Note:** Size varies: 24.2-24.4 millimeters.

Date	Mintage	F	VF	XF	Unc
1840.(c)	8,049,000	5.00	10.00	20.00	45.00
1840.(c) Proof	—	Value: 250			
1840.(c) Prooflike; Restrike	—	—	—	—	35.00

KM# 455.1 1/2 RUPEE

5.8300 g., 0.9170 Silver 0.1719 oz. ASW **Mint:** Bombay **Obverse:** "Plump" head **Obv. Legend:** Continuous **Note:** Type I. Size varies: 24.5-24.6 millimeters.

Date	Mintage	F	VF	XF	Unc
1840.(b)	9,844,000	5.00	10.00	20.00	45.00
1840.(b) Prooflike; Restrike	—	—	—	—	35.00

KM# 456.1 1/2 RUPEE

5.8300 g., 0.9170 Silver 0.1719 oz. ASW **Obverse:** W. W. incuse **Obv. Legend:** Divided **Note:** Type II.

Date	Mintage	F	VF	XF	Unc
1840(b & c)	18,551,000	4.00	8.00	15.00	35.00

KM# 456.5 1/2 RUPEE

5.8300 g., 0.9170 Silver 0.1719 oz. ASW **Edge:** Plain **Note:** Prev. KM#456.4.

Date	Mintage	F	VF	XF	Unc
1849 Proof; Early restrike	—	Value: 400			
1849 Prooflike; Restrike	—	—	—	—	50.00

KM# 456.4 1/2 RUPEE

5.8300 g., 0.9170 Silver 0.1719 oz. ASW **Obverse:** W.W. incuse **Edge:** Milled **Note:** Prev. KM#456.3

Date	Mintage	F	VF	XF	Unc
1849 Proof; Early restrike	—	Value: 400			
1849 Prooflike; Restrike	—	—	—	—	50.00

KM# 450.1 RUPEE

11.6600 g., 0.9170 Silver 0.3438 oz. ASW **Mint:** Bombay **Obv. Legend:** Thick lettering. Without initial on truncation

Date	Mintage	F	VF	XF	Unc
1835.(b)	53,713,000	8.50	12.50	25.00	50.00
1835.(b) Proof	—	Value: 500			
1835.(b) Prooflike; Restrike	—	—	—	—	40.00

KM# 450.2 RUPEE

11.6600 g., 0.9170 Silver 0.3438 oz. ASW **Mint:** Calcutta **Obverse:** F raised on truncation

Date	Mintage	F	VF	XF	Unc
1835.(c)	—	8.50	15.00	30.00	60.00
1835.(c) Proof	—	Value: 500			
1835.(c) Prooflike	—	—	—	—	60.00

KM# 450.3 RUPEE

11.6600 g., 0.9170 Silver 0.3438 oz. ASW **Mint:** Calcutta **Obverse:** F incuse on truncation

Date	Mintage	F	VF	XF	Unc
1835.(c)	—	8.50	15.00	30.00	60.00
1835.(c) Proof	—	Value: 750			
1835.(c) Prooflike; Restrike	—	—	—	—	60.00

KM# 450.4 RUPEE

11.6600 g., 0.9170 Silver 0.3438 oz. ASW **Mint:** Calcutta **Obverse:** RS incuse on truncation

Date	Mintage	F	VF	XF	Unc
1835.(c)	15,759,000	10.00	204	40.00	85.00
1835.(c) Proof	—	Value: 750			

KM# 450a RUPEE

Gold **Mint:** Calcutta

Date	Mintage	F	VF	XF	Unc
1835.(c)	—	—	—	—	—

KM# 457.3 RUPEE

11.6600 g., 0.9170 Silver 0.3438 oz. ASW **Mint:** Bombay **Reverse:** 19 berries, small diamonds

Date	Mintage	F	VF	XF	Unc
1840.(b)	—	7.00	10.00	17.50	40.00

KM# 450.5 RUPEE

11.6600 g., 0.9170 Silver 0.3438 oz. ASW **Mint:** Calcutta

Date	Mintage	F	VF	XF	Unc
1840/35.(c)	—	90.00	175	300	600

KM# 450.6 RUPEE

11.6600 g., 0.9170 Silver 0.3438 oz. ASW **Mint:** Calcutta

Date	Mintage	F	VF	XF	Unc
1840.(c) Rare	—	—	—	—	—

KM# 450.7 RUPEE

11.6600 g., 0.9170 Silver 0.3438 oz. ASW **Mint:** Calcutta **Obverse:** RS incuse on truncation **Reverse:** Thin lettering

Date	Mintage	F	VF	XF	Unc
1835.(c)	—	35.00	60.00	100	250

KM# 457.4 RUPEE

11.6600 g., 0.9170 Silver 0.3438 oz. ASW **Mint:** Bombay **Reverse:** 19 berries, large diamonds

Date	Mintage	F	VF	XF	Unc
1840.(b)	—	7.00	10.00	17.50	40.00

KM# 457.6 RUPEE

11.6600 g., 0.9170 Silver 0.3438 oz. ASW **Mint:** Madras **Reverse:** 19 berries, large diamonds

Date	Mintage	F	VF	XF	Unc
1840.(m)	—	9.00	18.50	37.50	75.00

KM# 457.7 RUPEE

11.6600 g., 0.9170 Silver 0.3438 oz. ASW **Mint:** Madras **Obverse:** Without S **Reverse:** 19 berries, with v on right ribbon bow

Date	Mintage	F	VF	XF	Unc
1840.(m)	—	9.00	18.50	37.50	75.00

KM# 457.8 RUPEE

11.6600 g., 0.9170 Silver 0.3438 oz. ASW **Mint:** Madras **Obverse:** S incuse **Reverse:** 20 berries, without small v

Date	Mintage	F	VF	XF	Unc
1840.(m)	—	8.00	12.50	20.00	40.00

KM# 457.9 RUPEE

11.6600 g., 0.9170 Silver 0.3438 oz. ASW **Mint:** Madras **Obverse:** S incuse **Reverse:** 35 berries, without small v

Date	Mintage	F	VF	XF	Unc
1840.(m)	—	10.00	15.00	30.00	60.00

KM# 457.10 RUPEE

11.6600 g., 0.9170 Silver 0.3438 oz. ASW **Mint:** Calcutta **Obverse:** "Indian" head with thinner features **Reverse:** 35 berries with crescent on left ribbon bow

Date	Mintage	F	VF	XF	Unc
1840.(c)	—	9.00	18.50	37.50	75.00
1840.(c) Proof	—	Value: 350			

KM# 457.11 RUPEE

11.6600 g., 0.9170 Silver 0.3438 oz. ASW **Mint:** Calcutta **Reverse:** 34 berries, small "m" on left ribbon end, dot after date

Date	Mintage	F	VF	XF	Unc
1840.(c) Proof	—	Value: 350			

KM# 457.12 RUPEE

11.6600 g., 0.9170 Silver 0.3438 oz. ASW **Mint:** Madras **Reverse:** 34 berries, small "m" on left ribbon end, dot after date

Date	Mintage	F	VF	XF	Unc
1840.(m)	—	—	—	225	350

KM# 458.2 RUPEE

11.6600 g., 0.9170 Silver 0.3438 oz. ASW **Mint:** Calcutta **Obverse:** W.W. raised **Reverse:** 28 berries, large diamonds

Date	Mintage	F	VF	XF	Unc
1840(c)	—	3.00	6.00	12.00	25.00

KM# 458.3 RUPEE

11.6600 g., 0.9170 Silver 0.3438 oz. ASW, 30.8 mm. **Mint:** Bombay **Obverse:** W.W. raised **Reverse:** 27 berries

Date	Mintage	F	VF	XF	Unc
1840(b)	312,598,000	3.00	6.00	12.00	25.00
1840(b) Proof	—	Value: 325			

KM# 458.4 RUPEE

11.6600 g., 0.9170 Silver 0.3438 oz. ASW **Mint:** Madras **Obverse:** W.W.B raised, small B **Reverse:** 28 berries

Date	Mintage	F	VF	XF	Unc
1840(m)	55,049,000	3.00	6.00	12.00	25.00

KM# 458.5 RUPEE

11.6600 g., 0.9170 Silver 0.3438 oz. ASW **Mint:** Madras **Obverse:** W.W. B raised, large B **Reverse:** 28 berries

Date	Mintage	F	VF	XF	Unc
1840(m)	—	3.00	6.00	12.00	25.00

KM# 458.6 RUPEE

11.6600 g., 0.9170 Silver 0.3438 oz. ASW **Mint:** Madras **Obverse:** W.W.B raised, small letters **Reverse:** 28 berries

Date	Mintage	F	VF	XF	Unc
1840(m)	—	3.00	6.00	12.00	25.00

KM# 458.7 RUPEE

11.6600 g., 0.9170 Silver 0.3438 oz. ASW **Mint:** Madras **Obverse:** W.W.S raised **Reverse:** 28 berries

Date	Mintage	F	VF	XF	Unc
1840(m)	—	3.00	6.00	12.00	25.00

KM# 458.10 RUPEE

11.6600 g., 0.9170 Silver 0.3438 oz. ASW **Obverse:** Mule. KM#458.1 **Reverse:** 25 berries

Date	Mintage	F	VF	XF	Unc
1840 Rare	—	—	—	—	—

KM# 458a RUPEE

Copper **Mint:** Madras **Obverse:** W.W.B

Date	Mintage	F	VF	XF	Unc
1840(m) Rare	—	—	—	—	—

KM# 457.2 RUPEE

11.6600 g., 0.9170 Silver 0.3438 oz. ASW **Mint:** Bombay **Reverse:** 35 berries **Note:** Size varies: 31.6-31.8 millimeters.

Date	Mintage	F	VF	XF	Unc
1840.(b)	109,838,000	7.00	10.00	17.50	40.00

KM# 457.5 RUPEE

11.6600 g., 0.9170 Silver 0.3438 oz. ASW **Mint:** Madras **Obverse:** S incuse on truncation **Reverse:** 19 berries, small diamonds, with V on right ribbon bow **Note:** Size varies: 31.9-32.2 millimeters.

Date	Mintage	F	VF	XF	Unc
1840.(m)	21,898,000	9.00	18.50	37.50	75.00

KM# 457.1 RUPEE

11.6600 g., 0.9170 Silver 0.3438 oz. ASW **Mint:** Calcutta **Obverse:** "Plump" head **Reverse:** 19 berries with crescent on left ribbon bow **Note:** Type I: Obv. legend continuous. 1st rev. 31.5 mm, 2nd rev. 31.1-31.4 mm.

Date	Mintage	F	VF	XF	Unc
1840.(c)	179,935,000	6.00	10.00	17.50	40.00
1840.(c) Proof	—	Value: 325			

KM# 458.1 RUPEE

11.6600 g., 0.9170 Silver 0.3438 oz. ASW, 30.5 mm. **Mint:** Calcutta **Obverse:** W.W. raised **Reverse:** 28 berries, small diamonds **Note:** Type II: Obv. legend divided.

Date	Mintage	F	VF	XF	Unc
1840(c)	398,554,000	3.00	6.00	12.00	25.00

KM# 458.8 RUPEE

11.6600 g., 0.9170 Silver 0.3438 oz. ASW **Obverse:** W.W. **Reverse:** 25 berries **Edge:** Milled

Date	Mintage	F	VF	XF	Unc
1849 Proof; Early restrike	—	Value: 500			
1849 Prooflike; Restrike	—	—	—	—	100

KM# 458.9 RUPEE

11.6600 g., 0.9170 Silver 0.3438 oz. ASW **Obverse:** W.W. **Reverse:** 25 berries **Edge:** Plain

Date	Mintage	F	VF	XF	Unc
1849 Proof; Early restrike	—	Value: 500			
1849 Prooflike; Restrike	—	—	—	—	100

KM# 451.1 MOHUR

11.6600 g., 0.9170 Gold 0.3438 oz. AGW **Mint:** Bombay **Obverse:** Without initials **Edge:** Milled

Date	Mintage	F	VF	XF	Unc
1835(b)	—	300	500	800	1,100
1835(b) Prooflike; Restrike	—	—	—	—	550

KM# 451.2 MOHUR

11.6600 g., 0.9170 Gold 0.3438 oz. AGW **Mint:** Calcutta **Obverse:** RS incuse on truncation **Edge:** Milled

Date	Mintage	F	VF	XF	Unc
1835.(c)	29,000	350	600	850	1,250
1835.(c) Proof	—	—	—	—	—
1835.(c) Prooflike; Restrike	—	—	—	—	700

KM# 451.3 MOHUR

11.6600 g., 0.9170 Gold 0.3438 oz. AGW **Mint:** Calcutta **Obverse:** F incuse on truncation **Edge:** Milled

Date	Mintage	F	VF	XF	Unc
1835.(c)	111,000	300	500	800	1,100
1835.(c) Prooflike; Restrike	—	—	—	—	550

KM# 451.4 MOHUR

11.6600 g., 0.9170 Gold 0.3438 oz. AGW **Mint:** Calcutta **Obverse:** RS incuse on truncation **Edge:** Plain

Date	Mintage	F	VF	XF	Unc
1835.(c) Proof; Rare	—	—	—	—	—

KM# 451.5 MOHUR

11.6600 g., 0.9170 Gold 0.3438 oz. AGW **Mint:** Calcutta **Obverse:** F incuse on truncation **Edge:** Plain

Date	Mintage	F	VF	XF	Unc
1835.(c) Proof; Rare	—	—	—	—	—

KM# 451a MOHUR

Silver **Mint:** Calcutta

Date	Mintage	F	VF	XF	Unc
1835.(c) Proof; Rare	—	—	—	—	—

KM# 451b MOHUR

Copper **Mint:** Calcutta

Date	Mintage	F	VF	XF	Unc
1835.(c) Proof	—	Value: 650			

KM# 461.2 MOHUR

11.6600 g., 0.9170 Gold 0.3438 oz. AGW **Mint:** Calcutta **Obverse:** Dot on truncation

Date	Mintage	F	VF	XF	Unc
1841.(c)	601,000	225	275	350	475
1841.(c) Proof	—	Value: 2,000			

KM# 461.3 MOHUR

11.6600 g., 0.9170 Gold 0.3438 oz. AGW **Mint:** Madras **Obverse:** S incuse on truncation

Date	Mintage	F	VF	XF	Unc
1841.(m)	32,000	350	425	550	700
1841.(m) Proof	—	Value: 2,000			

KM# 462.2 MOHUR

11.6600 g., 0.9170 Gold 0.3438 oz. AGW **Mint:** Calcutta **Obverse:** W.W. incuse, large legend and large date with crosslet 4

Date	Mintage	F	VF	XF	Unc
1841.(c)	—	225	275	350	475

KM# A462 MOHUR

11.6600 g., 0.9170 Gold 0.3438 oz. AGW **Mint:** Calcutta **Obverse:** Mule. KM#462 **Reverse:** KM#451

Date	Mintage	F	VF	XF	Unc
1841.(c) Prooflike; Restrike	—	—	—	—	600

KM# 462.3 MOHUR

11.6600 g., 0.9170 Gold 0.3438 oz. AGW **Obverse:** W.W. incuse, small legend and small date with normal 4 **Note:** Small date.

Date	Mintage	F	VF	XF	Unc
1841	—	200	325	450	600

KM# 461.1 MOHUR

11.6600 g., 0.9170 Gold 0.3438 oz. AGW **Mint:** Bombay **Obverse:** Dot on truncation **Note:** Type I: Obv. legend continuous.

Date	Mintage	F	VF	XF	Unc
1841.(b)	5,960	—	—	650	1,000

Large date, normal 4

Large date, crosslet 4

KM# 462.1 MOHUR

11.6600 g., 0.9170 Gold 0.3438 oz. AGW **Mint:** Calcutta **Obverse:** W.W. incuse, large legend and large date with normal 4 **Note:** Type II: Obv. legend divided.

Date	Mintage	F	VF	XF	Unc
1841.(c)	442,000	225	275	350	475
1841. (c) Prooflike; Restrike	—	—	—	—	550

KM# 452.2 2 MOHURS

23.3200 g., 0.9170 Gold 0.6875 oz. AGW **Mint:** Calcutta **Obverse:** RS incuse on truncation **Edge:** Plain

Date	Mintage	F	VF	XF	Unc
1835.(c) Rare	—	—	—	—	—

KM# 452a 2 MOHURS

Silver **Mint:** Calcutta **Obverse:** RS incuse on truncation

Date	Mintage	F	VF	XF	Unc
1835.(c) Proof	—	Value: 1,500			

KM# 452b 2 MOHURS

Copper **Mint:** Calcutta

Date	Mintage	F	VF	XF	Unc
1835. (c) Proof	—	Value: 750			

KM# 452.1 2 MOHURS

23.3200 g., 0.9170 Gold 0.6875 oz. AGW **Mint:** Calcutta **Obverse:** RS incuse on truncation **Edge:** Milled **Note:** Restrikes have fewer leaves on reverse palm tree.

Date	Mintage	F	VF	XF	Unc
1835.(c) Rare	1,170	—	—	—	—
1835.(c) Proof	—	Value: 5,000			
1835.(c) Prooflike; Restrike	—	—	—	—	1,500

MILLED COINAGE

Regal Style

KM# 465b 1/12 ANNA (1 Pie)

Gold **Mint:** Calcutta

Date	Mintage	F	VF	XF	Unc
1862(c) Prooflike; Restrike	—	—	—	—	400

KM# 465 1/12 ANNA (1 Pie)

Copper **Obv. Legend:** VICTORIA QUEEN **Note:** Size varies: 17.4-18.0 mm.

Date	Mintage	F	VF	XF	Unc
1862(c)	2,502,000	1.25	2.50	5.00	10.00
1862(b)	2,999,000	1.25	2.50	5.00	10.00
1862(m)	40,487,000	0.75	1.25	2.50	7.50
1862(c) Proof	—	Value: 50.00			
1862(c) Prooflike; Restrike	—	—	—	—	35.00
1874(c)	4,819,000	1.25	2.50	5.00	10.00
1874(b)	2,960,000	1.25	2.50	5.00	10.00
1875(c)	4,646,000	1.25	2.50	5.00	10.00
1875(c) Proof	3,068,000	Value: 65.00			
1876(c)	3,068,000	1.25	2.50	5.00	10.00
1876(c)	20,318,000	1.00	1.50	2.50	7.50
1876(b) Inc. 1875 (b)	—	1.25	2.50	5.00	10.00

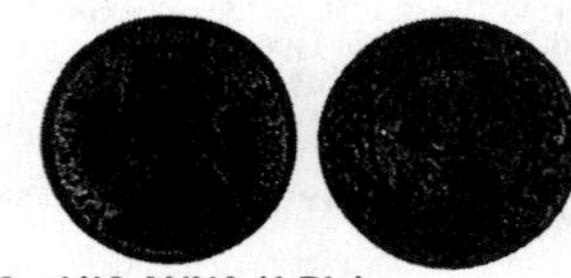

KM# 483 1/12 ANNA (1 Pie)

Copper **Obv. Legend:** VICTORIA EMPRESS

Date	Mintage	F	VF	XF	Unc
1877(c)	5,880,000	0.50	1.00	2.50	6.00
1877(c) Proof	—	Value: 50.00			
1877(c) Prooflike; Restrike	—	—	—	—	25.00
1877(b)	1,551,000	0.50	1.00	2.50	6.00
1877(b) Proof	—	Value: 50.00			
1878(c)	5,525,000	0.50	1.00	2.50	6.00
1878(c) Proof	—	Value: 50.00			
1881(b)	2,954,000	0.50	1.00	2.50	6.00
1882(c)	4,344,000	0.50	1.00	2.00	5.00
1883(c)	9,840,000	0.50	1.00	2.00	5.00
1883(b)	4,794,000	0.35	0.75	1.75	4.00
1883(b) Proof	—	Value: 50.00			
1884(b)	8,074,000	0.50	1.00	2.50	6.00
1884(b) Proof	—	Value: 50.00			
1885(c)	4,783,000	0.50	1.00	2.00	5.00
1886(c)	18,663,000	0.35	0.75	1.75	4.00
1886(b)	5,783,000	0.50	1.00	2.50	6.00
1886(b) Proof	—	Value: 50.00			
1887(c)	8,724,000	0.50	1.00	2.00	5.00
1887(b)	8,242,000	0.50	1.00	2.50	6.00
1888(c)	4,662,000	0.50	1.00	2.00	5.00
1888(b)	2,143,000	0.50	1.00	2.50	6.00
1889(c)	7,602,000	0.50	1.00	2.00	5.00
1889(b)	5,660,000	0.50	1.00	2.50	6.00
1890(c)	21,732,000	0.35	0.75	1.75	4.00
1890(b) Proof	—	Value: 50.00			
1890 Prooflike; Restrike	—	—	—	—	20.00
1891(c)	17,306,000	0.35	0.75	1.75	4.00
1891(c) Proof	—	Value: 50.00			
1891(c) Prooflike; Restrike	—	—	—	—	20.00
1892(c)	13,793,000	0.35	0.75	1.75	4.00
1892(c) Proof	—	Value: 50.00			
1892(c) Prooflike; Restrike	—	—	—	—	20.00
1893(c)	10,034,000	0.35	0.75	1.75	4.00
1893(c) Proof	—	Value: 50.00			
1893(c) Prooflike; Restrike	—	—	—	—	20.00
1894(c)	18,392,000	0.35	0.75	1.75	4.00
1894(c) Proof	—	Value: 50.00			
1894(c) Prooflike; Restrike	—	—	—	—	20.00
1895(c)	15,208,000	0.35	0.75	1.75	4.00
1895(c) Proof	—	Value: 50.00			
1896(c)	922,000	0.50	1.25	2.50	6.00
1896(c) Proof	—	Value: 50.00			
1896(c) Prooflike; Restrike	—	—	—	—	20.00
1897(c)	20,822,000	0.35	0.75	1.75	4.00
1897(c) Proof	—	Value: 50.00			
1897(c) Prooflike; Restrike	—	—	—	—	20.00
1898(c)	13,882,000	0.35	0.75	1.75	4.00
1898(c) Proof	—	Value: 50.00			
1898(c) Prooflike; Restrike	—	—	—	—	20.00
1899(c)	10,056,000	0.35	0.75	1.75	4.50
1899(c) Proof	—	Value: 50.00			
1899(c) Prooflike; Restrike	—	—	—	—	20.00

KM# 483a 1/12 ANNA (1 Pie)

Aluminum **Mint:** Bombay

Date	Mintage	F	VF	XF	Unc
1891(b) Proof	—	Value: 100			

KM# 483b 1/12 ANNA (1 Pie)

Silver **Mint:** Calcutta

Date	Mintage	F	VF	XF	Unc
1892(c) Prooflike; Restrike	—	—	—	—	75.00
1893(c) Prooflike; Restrike	—	—	—	—	75.00
1894(c) Prooflike; Restrike	—	—	—	—	75.00
1895(c) Prooflike; Restrike	—	—	—	—	75.00
1896(c) Prooflike; Restrike	—	—	—	—	75.00
1897(c) Prooflike; Restrike	—	—	—	—	75.00
1898(c) Prooflike; Restrike	—	—	—	—	75.00
1899(c) Prooflike; Restrike	—	—	—	—	75.00

KM# 483c 1/12 ANNA (1 Pie)

Gold **Mint:** Calcutta

Date	Mintage	F	VF	XF	Unc
1891(c) Prooflike; Restrike	—	—	—	—	400
1892(c) Prooflike; Restrike	—	—	—	—	400
1893(c) Prooflike; Restrike	—	—	—	—	400
1895(c) Prooflike; Restrike	—	—	—	—	400
1896(c) Prooflike; Restrike	—	—	—	—	400
1897(c) Prooflike; Restrike	—	—	—	—	400

Date	Mintage	F	VF	XF	Unc
1898(c) Prooflike; Restrike	—	—	—	—	400
1899(c) Prooflike; Restrike	—	—	—	—	400

KM# 466b 1/2 PICE

Gold **Mint:** Calcutta

Date	Mintage	F	VF	XF	Unc
1862(c) Proof	—	Value: 1,000			

KM# 466 1/2 PICE

Copper **Obv. Legend:** VICTORIA QUEEN **Note:** Size varies: 21.20-21.4 mm.

Date	Mintage	F	VF	XF	Unc
1862(c)	96,843,000	1.25	2.50	5.00	15.00
1862(m)	6,400,000	1.50	3.50	6.50	20.00
1862(c) Proof	—	Value: 50.00			
1862(c) Prooflike; Restrike	—	—	—	—	25.00
1875(c) Proof	—	Value: 75.00			
1875(c) Prooflike; Restrike	—	—	—	—	25.00

KM# 484 1/2 PICE

Copper **Mint:** Calcutta **Obv. Legend:** VICTORIA EMPRESS

Date	Mintage	F	VF	XF	Unc
1877(c) Proof	—	Value: 75.00			
1877(c) Prooflike; Restrike	—	—	—	—	25.00
1878(c) Proof	—	Value: 75.00			
1885(c)	6,206,000	1.25	2.50	4.00	10.00
1886(c)	7,733,000	1.25	2.50	4.00	10.00
1887(c)	6,464,000	1.25	2.50	4.00	10.00
1888(c)	3,190,000	1.25	2.50	4.00	10.00
1889(c)	7,587,000	1.25	2.50	4.00	10.00
1890(c)	3,504,000	1.25	2.50	4.00	10.00
1890(c) Proof	—	Value: 50.00			
1890(c) Prooflike; Restrike	—	—	—	—	20.00
1891(c)	5,139,000	1.25	2.50	4.00	10.00
1891(c) Proof	—	Value: 50.00			
1891(c) Prooflike; Restrike	—	—	—	—	20.00
1892(c)	4,774,000	1.25	2.50	4.00	10.00
1892(c) Proof	—	Value: 50.00			
1892(c) Prooflike; Restrike	—	—	—	—	20.00
1893(c)	7,005,000	1.25	2.50	4.00	10.00
1893(c) Proof	—	Value: 50.00			
1893(c) Prooflike; Restrike	—	—	—	—	20.00
1894(c)	7,777,000	1.25	2.50	4.00	10.00
1894(c) Proof	—	Value: 50.00			
1894(c) Prooflike; Restrike	—	—	—	—	20.00
1895(c)	9,874,000	1.00	1.75	3.50	8.50
1895(c) Proof	—	Value: 50.00			
1896(c)	6,113,000	1.25	2.50	4.00	10.00
1896(c) Proof	—	Value: 50.00			
1897(c)	8,484,000	1.25	2.50	4.00	10.00
1897(c) Proof	—	Value: 35.00			
1897(c) Prooflike; Restrike	—	—	—	—	20.00
1898(c)	12,940,000	1.00	1.75	3.50	8.50
1898(c) Proof	—	Value: 50.00			
1898(c) Prooflike; Restrike	—	—	—	—	20.00
1899(c)	7,936,000	1.25	2.50	4.00	10.00
1899(c) Proof	—	Value: 50.00			
1899(c) Prooflike; Restrike	—	—	—	—	20.00
1900(c)	5,219,000	1.25	2.50	4.00	10.00
1900(c) Prooflike; Restrike	—	—	—	—	20.00

KM# 484a 1/2 PICE

Aluminum **Mint:** Bombay

Date	Mintage	F	VF	XF	Unc
1891(b) Proof	—	Value: 85.00			

KM# 484c 1/2 PICE

Gold **Mint:** Calcutta

Date	Mintage	F	VF	XF	Unc
1891(c) Prooflike; Restrike	—	—	—	—	700
1892(c) Prooflike; Restrike	—	—	—	—	700
1893(c) Prooflike; Restrike	—	—	—	—	700
1895(c) Prooflike; Restrike	—	—	—	—	700
1896(c) Prooflike; Restrike	—	—	—	—	700
1897(c) Prooflike; Restrike	—	—	—	—	700
1898(c) Prooflike; Restrike	—	—	—	—	700
1899(c) Prooflike; Restrike	—	—	—	—	700
1901(c) Prooflike; Restrike	—	—	—	—	700

KM# 484b 1/2 PICE

Silver **Mint:** Calcutta

Date	Mintage	F	VF	XF	Unc
1892(c) Prooflike; Restrike	—	—	—	—	75.00
1893(c) Prooflike; Restrike	—	—	—	—	75.00
1894(c) Prooflike; Restrike	—	—	—	—	75.00
1895(c) Prooflike; Restrike	—	—	—	—	75.00
1896(c) Prooflike; Restrike	—	—	—	—	75.00
1897(c) Prooflike; Restrike	—	—	—	—	75.00
1898(c) Prooflike; Restrike	—	—	—	—	75.00
1899(c) Prooflike; Restrike	—	—	—	—	75.00
1900(c) Prooflike; Restrike	—	—	—	—	75.00

KM# 467 1/4 ANNA

Copper **Obv. Legend:** VICTORIA QUEEN

Date	Mintage	F	VF	XF	Unc
1862(c)	99,504,000	0.75	1.50	3.00	9.00
Note: Type A Bust, Type I Reverse					
1862(c) V raised on bottom center of bust	10,654,000	1.25	2.50	5.00	15.00
Note: Type A Bust, Type I Reverse					
1862(c)	178,731,000	0.75	1.50	3.00	9.00
Note: Type B Bust, Type II Reverse					
1862(c) Proof	—	Value: 90.00			
Note: Type B Bust, Type II Reverse					
1862(c) Prooflike; Restrike	—	—	—	—	30.00
1862(b) V incuse on point of shoulder	32,149,000	1.00	2.00	4.00	12.00
Note: Type A Bust, Type I Reverse					
1862(b) Dot below date	2,366,000	2.50	5.00	10.00	25.00
Note: Type A Bust, Type I Reverse					
1862(b) Prooflike; Restrike	—	—	—	—	30.00
1862(m)	186,227,000	0.75	1.50	3.00	9.00
Note: Type A Bust, Type I Reverse					
1874(c)	44,678,000	2.00	4.00	8.00	20.00
1875(c)	36,237,000	2.50	5.00	10.00	25.00
1875(c) Proof	—	Value: 65.00			
1875(b)	14,494,000	3.00	6.00	12.00	35.00
1876(b)	3,360,000	3.00	6.00	12.00	35.00
1876(c)	43,581,000	2.50	5.00	10.00	25.00
1876 Proof	—	Value: 65.00			

KM# 467b 1/4 ANNA

12.8500 g., Gold **Mint:** Calcutta

Date	Mintage	F	VF	XF	Unc
1862(c) Prooflike; Restrike	—	—	—	—	750

KM# 485 1/4 ANNA

Copper **Mint:** Calcutta **Obverse:** Mule. KM#467 **Obv. Legend:** VICTORIA QUEEN **Reverse:** KM#486

Date	Mintage	F	VF	XF	Unc
1875(c) Prooflike; Restrike	—	—	—	—	40.00

KM# 486 1/4 ANNA

Copper **Obv. Legend:** VICTORIA EMPRESS

Date	Mintage	F	VF	XF	Unc
1877(c)	65,210,000	0.75	1.50	3.00	9.00
1877(c) Proof	—	Value: 65.00			
1877(c) Prooflike; Restrike	—	—	—	—	25.00
1877(b)	9,320,000	0.75	1.50	3.00	9.00
1877(b) Prooflike; Restrike	—	—	—	—	25.00
1878(c)	40,813,000	0.75	1.50	3.00	9.00
1878(c) Proof	—	Value: 65.00			
1878(c) Restrike; prooflike	—	—	—	—	25.00
1879(c)	43,072,000	0.50	1.00	2.00	6.00
1879(c) Proof	—	Value: 65.00			
1880(c)	10,278,000	0.35	0.75	1.50	4.50
1882(c)	52,291,000	0.40	1.00	2.00	6.00
1882(b)	12,409,000	0.75	1.50	2.50	7.50
1883(c)	57,571,000	0.75	1.50	2.50	7.50
1883(b)	12,443,000	0.75	1.50	2.50	7.50
1884(c)	43,196,000	0.50	1.00	2.00	6.00
1884(c) Proof	—	Value: 65.00			
1884(b)	16,845,000	0.75	1.50	2.50	7.50
1885(c)	36,699,000	0.50	1.00	2.00	6.00
1886(c)	36,121,000	0.50	1.00	2.00	6.00
1886(b)	14,390,000	0.75	1.50	2.50	7.50
1887(c)	59,060,000	0.50	1.00	2.00	6.00
1887(b)	26,205,000	0.75	1.50	2.50	7.50
1888(c)	34,531,000	0.75	1.50	2.50	7.50
1888(b)	8,293,000	1.50	2.50	3.50	10.00
1889(c)	88,559,000	0.35	0.75	1.50	4.50
1889(b)	19,110,000	0.50	1.00	2.00	6.00
1890(c)	82,909,000	0.35	0.75	1.50	4.50
1890(c) Proof	—	Value: 65.00			
1891(c)	86,076,000	0.35	0.75	1.50	4.50
1891(c) Proof	—	Value: 65.00			
1891(c) Prooflike; Restrike	—	—	—	—	25.00
1892(c)	68,131,000	0.35	0.75	1.50	4.50
1892(c) Proof	—	Value: 65.00			
1892(c) Prooflike; Restrike	—	—	—	—	25.00
1893(c)	76,039,000	0.35	0.75	1.50	4.50
1893(c) Proof	—	Value: 65.00			
1893(c) Prooflike; Restrike	—	—	—	—	25.00
1894(c)	45,744,000	0.35	0.75	1.50	4.50
1894(c) Proof	—	Value: 65.00			
1894(c) Prooflike; Restrike	—	—	—	—	25.00
1895(c)	35,744,000	0.35	0.75	1.50	4.50
1895(c) Proof	—	Value: 65.00			
1896(c)	109,853,000	0.35	0.75	1.50	4.50
1896(c) Proof	—	Value: 65.00			
1897(c)	82,288,000	0.35	0.75	1.50	4.50
1897(c) Proof	—	Value: 65.00			
1897(c) Prooflike; Restrike	—	—	—	—	25.00
1898(c)	12,118,000	0.35	0.75	1.50	4.50
1898(c) Proof	—	Value: 65.00			
1898(c) Prooflike; Restrike	—	—	—	—	25.00
1899(c)	36,896,000	0.35	0.75	1.50	4.50
1899(c) Proof	Inc. above	Value: 65.00			
1899(c) Prooflike; Restrike	—	—	—	—	25.00
1900(c)	30,534,000	0.35	0.75	1.50	4.50
1900(c) Proof	—	Value: 65.00			
1900(c) Prooflike; Restrike	—	—	—	—	25.00
1901(c)	136,091,000	0.35	0.75	1.50	4.50
1901(c) Proof	—	Value: 65.00			
1901(c) Prooflike; Restrike	—	—	—	—	25.00

KM# 486b 1/4 ANNA

Silver

Date	Mintage	F	VF	XF	Unc
1891(c) Prooflike; Restrike	—	—	—	—	75.00
1892(c) Prooflike; Restrike	—	—	—	—	75.00
1893(c) Prooflike; Restrike	—	—	—	—	75.00
1894(c) Prooflike; Restrike	—	—	—	—	75.00
1895(c) Prooflike; Restrike	—	—	—	—	75.00
1896(c) Prooflike; Restrike	—	—	—	—	75.00
1897(c) Prooflike; Restrike	—	—	—	—	75.00
1898(c) Prooflike; Restrike	—	—	—	—	75.00
1899(c) Prooflike; Restrike	—	—	—	—	75.00
1900(c) Prooflike; Restrike	—	—	—	—	75.00

KM# 486c 1/4 ANNA

Gold **Mint:** Calcutta

Date	Mintage	F	VF	XF	Unc
1891(c) Prooflike; Restrike	—	—	—	—	750
1892(c) Prooflike; Restrike	—	—	—	—	750
1893(c) Prooflike; Restrike	—	—	—	—	750
1895(c) Prooflike; Restrike	—	—	—	—	750
1896(c) Prooflike; Restrike	—	—	—	—	750
1897(c) Prooflike; Restrike	—	—	—	—	750
1898(c) Prooflike; Restrike	—	—	—	—	750
1899(c) Prooflike; Restrike	—	—	—	—	750
1900(c) Prooflike; Restrike	—	—	—	—	750

KM# 486a 1/4 ANNA

Aluminum **Mint:** Bombay

Date	Mintage	F	VF	XF	Unc
1891(b) Proof	—	Value: 150			

KM# 468 1/2 ANNA

Copper **Obv. Legend:** VICTORIA QUEEN

Date	Mintage	F	VF	XF	Unc
1862(c)	7,236,000	10.00	20.00	30.00	75.00
Note: Type A Bust, Type 1 Reverse					
1862(c)	7,399,000	10.00	20.00	30.00	75.00
Note: Type C Bust, Type II Reverse					
1862(c) Proof	—	Value: 125			
Note: Type B Bust, Type II Reverse					
1862(b)	4,802,000	10.00	20.00	30.00	75.00
Note: Type A Bust, Type I Reverse					
1862(m)	66,515,000	5.00	10.00	18.50	60.00
Note: Type A Bust, Type I Reverse					
1862(b) Prooflike; Restrike	—	—	—	—	35.00
1875(c)	1,146,000	12.50	25.00	50.00	100
Note: Type B Bust, Type II Reverse					
1875(c) Proof	—	Value: 150			
1875(c) Prooflike; Restrike	—	—	—	—	50.00

Date	Mintage	F	VF	XF	Unc
1876(c)	2,291,000	12.50	25.00	50.00	100
Note: Type B Bust, Type II Reverse					

KM# 468b 1/2 ANNA

Gold **Mint:** Calcutta

Date	Mintage	F	VF	XF	Unc
1862(c) Proof	—	Value: 2,000			

KM# 487 1/2 ANNA

Copper **Obv. Legend:** VICTORIA QUEEN

Date	Mintage	F	VF	XF	Unc
1877(c)	—	10.00	20.00	40.00	100
Note: Type C Bust, Type II Reverse					
1877(c) Proof	Inc. above	Value: 100			
1877(c) Prooflike; Restrike	—	—	—	—	90.00
1877(b)	—	12.00	20.00	40.00	100
Note: Type B Bust, Type II Reverse					
1878(c) Proof	1	Value: 100			
1878(c) Prooflike; Restrike	—	—	—	—	90.00
1879(c) Proof	—	Value: 100			
1879(c) Prooflike; Restrike	—	—	—	—	90.00
1884(b) Proof	—	Value: 100			
1884(b) Prooflike; Restrike	—	—	—	—	90.00
1890(c) Proof	—	Value: 100			
1890(c) Prooflike; Restrike	—	—	—	—	90.00
1891(c) Proof	—	Value: 100			
1891(c) Prooflike; Restrike	—	—	—	—	90.00
1892(c) Proof	—	Value: 100			
1892(c) Prooflike; Restrike	—	—	—	—	90.00
1893(c) Proof	—	Value: 100			
1893(c) Prooflike; Restrike	—	—	—	—	90.00

KM# 487c 1/2 ANNA

Gold

Date	Mintage	F	VF	XF	Unc
1877(b) Prooflike; Restrike	—	—	—	—	900
1890(b) Prooflike; Restrike	—	—	—	—	900
1890(b) Prooflike; Restrike	—	—	—	—	900
1892(c) Prooflike; Restrike	—	—	—	—	900
1893(c) Prooflike; Restrike	—	—	—	—	900

KM# 487a 1/2 ANNA

Aluminum **Mint:** Bombay

Date	Mintage	F	VF	XF	Unc
1891(b) Proof	—	Value: 100			

KM# 487b 1/2 ANNA

Silver **Mint:** Calcutta

Date	Mintage	F	VF	XF	Unc
1892(c) Prooflike; Restrike	—	—	—	—	150
1893(c) Prooflike; Restrike	—	—	—	—	150

KM# 469 2 ANNAS

1.4600 g., 0.9170 Silver 0.043 oz. ASW **Obverse:** Bust "A" **Obv. Legend:** VICTORIA QUEEN

Date	Mintage	F	VF	XF	Unc
1862(c)	29,653,000	1.75	3.50	7.50	15.00
1862(c) Proof	—	Value: 100			
1862(b)	21,037,000	2.50	5.00	10.00	20.00
1862(b) Prooflike; Restrike	—	—	—	—	35.00
1862(m)	4,202,000	2.75	5.50	11.00	22.00
1874(c)	5,690,000	1.75	3.50	7.50	15.00
1874(b)	9,508,000	1.50	3.00	6.00	12.00
1874(b) dot	Inc. above	2.50	5.00	10.00	20.00
1875(c)	6,512,000	1.50	3.00	6.00	12.00
1875(c) Proof	—	Value: 100			
1875(b)	1,712,000	2.50	5.00	10.00	20.00
1876(c)	10,504,000	1.00	2.00	4.00	8.00
1876(b)	3,911,000	2.00	4.00	8.00	16.00

KM# 469a 2 ANNAS

Gold

Date	Mintage	F	VF	XF	Unc
1862 Proof	—	Value: 600			

KM# 488 2 ANNAS

1.4600 g., 0.9170 Silver .0430 oz. ASW **Obv. Legend:** VICTORIA EMPRESS

Date	Mintage	F	VF	XF	Unc
1877(c) Without mm	3,575,000	1.25	2.50	5.00	10.00
Note: Type C Bust, Type I Reverse					
1877(c) Proof	—	Value: 100			
1877(c) Without mm	Inc. above	1.75	3.50	7.00	14.00
Note: Type B Bust, Type II Reverse					
1877(c) Prooflike; Restrike	—	—	—	—	30.00
1877(c) Dot in top flower	Inc. above	1.25	2.50	5.00	10.00
Note: Type B Bust, Type II Reverse					
1877(b) Dot above lower flower	2,215,000	1.25	2.50	5.00	10.00
Note: Type A Bust, Type I Reverse					
1878B A.I. Dot	2,215	1.25	2.50	5.00	10.00
1878B Proof	—	Value: 100			
1878B Prooflike; Restrike	—	—	—	—	30.00
1878(c) Without mm	3,994,000	1.25	2.50	5.00	10.00
Note: Type B Bust, Type II Reverse					
1878C Incuse	3,541,000	1.25	2.50	5.00	10.00
Note: Type B Bust, Type II Reverse					
1880C Incuse	2,539,000	1.25	2.50	5.00	10.00
Note: Type B Bust, Type II Reverse					
1881C Incuse	4,400,000	1.25	2.50	5.00	10.00
Note: Type B Bust, Type II Reverse					
1881C Proof	—	Value: 100			
1881(b) Dot	2,449,000	1.25	2.50	5.00	10.00
Note: Type A Bust, Type I Reverse					
1881(b) Dot	Inc. above	1.75	3.50	7.00	14.00
Note: Type A Bust, Type II Reverse					
1881(b) Dot	Inc. above	1.25	2.50	5.00	10.00
Note: Type B Bust, Type II Reverse					
1882C Incuse	14,360,000	1.25	2.50	5.00	10.00
Note: Type B Bust, Type II Reverse					
1882(b) Dot	2,629,000	1.25	2.50	5.00	10.00
Note: Type A Bust, Type I Reverse					
1882(b) Dot	Inc. above	1.25	2.50	5.00	10.00
Note: Type B Bust, Type II Reverse					
1882 Proof	—	Value: 100			
1883C Incuse	2,736,000	1.25	2.50	5.00	10.00
Note: Type B Bust, Type II Reverse					
1883(b) Without mm	Inc. above	1.25	2.50	5.00	10.00
Note: Type A Bust, Type I Reverse					
1883(b) Dot	4,416,000	1.25	2.50	5.00	10.00
Note: Type A Bust, Type I Reverse					
1883(b) Dot	Inc. above	1.25	2.50	5.00	10.00
Note: Type B Bust, Type II Reverse					
1884C Incuse	7,200,000	1.25	2.50	5.00	10.00
Note: Type B Bust, Type II Reverse					
1884(b) Without mm	1,638,000	1.25	2.50	5.00	10.00
Note: Type A Bust, Type I Reverse					
1884(b) Dot	Inc. above	1.25	2.50	5.00	10.00
Note: Type A Bust, Type I Reverse					
1884B Raised	Inc. above	1.25	2.50	5.00	10.00
Note: Type A Bust, Type I Reverse					
1884B Dot; Raised	Inc. above	1.25	2.50	5.00	10.00
Note: Type A Bust, Type I Reverse					
1884B Incuse	Inc. above	1.25	2.50	5.00	10.00
Note: Type B Bust, Type II Reverse					
1885C Incuse	1,335,000	1.75	3.50	7.00	14.00
Note: Type B Bust, Type II Reverse					
1885B Without mm	2,262,000	1.75	3.50	7.00	14.00
Note: Type A Bust, Type I Reverse					
1885B Raised	Inc. above	1.75	3.50	7.00	14.00
Note: Type A Bust, Type I Reverse					
1885B Raised	Inc. above	1.25	2.50	5.00	10.00
Note: Type B Bust, Type II Reverse					
1886C Incuse	10,346,000	1.25	2.50	5.00	10.00
Note: Type B Bust, Type II Reverse					
1886B Incuse	3,155,000	1.25	2.50	5.00	10.00
Note: Type B Bust, Type II Reverse					
1887C Incuse	13,927,000	1.25	2.50	5.00	10.00
Note: Type B Bust, Type II Reverse					
1887B Incuse	3,283,000	1.25	2.50	5.00	10.00
Note: Type B Bust, Type II Reverse					
1888(c) Without mm	9,307,000	1.25	2.50	5.00	10.00
Note: Type B Bust, Type II Reverse					
1888B Incuse	8,039,000	1.25	2.50	5.00	10.00
Note: Type B Bust, Type II Reverse					
1888B Proof	—	Value: 100			
1889C Incuse	135,000	1.75	3.50	7.00	14.00
Note: Type B Bust, Type II Reverse					
1889B Incuse	5,895,000	1.25	2.50	5.00	10.00
Note: Type B Bust, Type II Reverse					
1890C Incuse	9,836,000	1.25	2.50	5.00	10.00
Note: Type B Bust, Type II Reverse					
1890C Proof	—	Value: 100			
1890B Incuse	Inc. above	1.25	2.50	5.00	10.00
Note: Type B Bust, Type II Reverse					
1890B Raised	7,790,000	1.25	2.50	5.00	10.00
Note: Type B Bust, Type II Reverse					
1890B Prooflike; Restrike	—	—	—	—	30.00
1891C Incuse	8,621,000	1.25	2.50	5.00	10.00
Note: Type B Bust, Type II Reverse					
1891C Proof	—	Value: 100			
1891B Incuse	4,230,000	1.25	2.50	5.00	10.00
Note: Type B Bust, Type II Reverse					
1891B Prooflike; Restrike	—	—	—	—	30.00
1892C Incuse	6,971,000	1.25	2.50	5.00	10.00
Note: Type B Bust, Type II Reverse					
1892C Proof	—	Value: 100			
1892B Incuse	9,347,000	1.25	2.50	5.00	10.00
Note: Type B Bust, Type II Reverse					
1892B Prooflike; Restrike	—	—	—	—	30.00
1893C Incuse	8,003,000	1.25	2.50	5.00	10.00
Note: Type B Bust, Type II Reverse					
1893/2(b) Incuse	—	20.00	40.00	85.00	100
Note: Type B Bust, Type II Reverse					
1893C Proof	—	Value: 100			
1894B Incuse	Inc. above	1.25	2.50	5.00	10.00
Note: Type B Bust, Type II Reverse					
1894B Prooflike; Restrike	—	—	—	—	30.00
1895C Incuse	9,668,000	1.25	2.50	5.00	10.00
Note: Type B Bust, Type II Reverse					
1896C Incuse	6,616,000	1.25	2.50	5.00	10.00
Note: Type B Bust, Type II Reverse					
1896C Proof	—	Value: 100			
1896B Incuse	8,235,000	1.25	2.50	5.00	10.00
Note: Type B Bust, Type II Reverse					
1897C Incuse	12,103,000	1.25	2.50	5.00	10.00
Note: Type B Bust, Type II Reverse					
1897B Incuse	8,041,000	1.25	2.50	5.00	10.00
Note: Type B Bust, Type II Reverse					
1897B Proof	—	Value: 100			
1897B Prooflike; Restrike	—	—	—	—	30.00
1897C Proof	—	Value: 100			
1898C Incuse	4,011,000	1.25	2.50	5.00	10.00
Note: Type B Bust, Type II Reverse					
1898B Incuse	3,250,000	1.25	2.50	5.00	10.00
Note: Type B Bust, Type II Reverse					
1898B Proof	—	Value: 100			
1898B Prooflike; Restrike	—	—	—	—	30.00
1899 Proof	—	Value: 100			
1900C Incuse	1,705,000	1.25	2.50	5.00	10.00
Note: Type B Bust, Type II Reverse					
1900	—	—	—	—	—
1900B Raised	—	2.50	5.00	10.00	20.00
Note: Type B Bust, Type I Reverse					
1900B Raised	4,439,000	1.25	2.50	5.00	10.00
Note: Type B Bust, Type II Reverse					
1900B Proof	—	Value: 100			
1900B Prooflike; Restrike	—	—	—	—	30.00

KM# 489 2 ANNAS

1.4600 g., 0.9170 Silver 0.043 oz. ASW **Obverse:** Mule. KM#469 **Obv. Legend:** VICTORIA QUEEN

Date	Mintage	F	VF	XF	Unc
1877 Prooflike; Restrike	—	—	—	—	20.00

KM# 488b 2 ANNAS

Copper Or Bronze **Obv. Legend:** VICTORIA EMPRESS

Date	Mintage	F	VF	XF	Unc
1884 Proof	—	Value: 75.00			
1891 Proof	—	Value: 75.00			
1892 Proof	—	Value: 75.00			

KM# 488c 2 ANNAS

Gold **Obv. Legend:** VICTORIA EMPRESS

Date	Mintage	F	VF	XF	Unc
1891 Prooflike; Restrike	—	—	—	—	450
1892 Prooflike; Restrike	—	—	—	—	450
1893 Prooflike; Restrike	—	—	—	—	450
1896 Prooflike; Restrike	—	—	—	—	450
1897 Prooflike; Restrike	—	—	—	—	450
1898 Prooflike; Restrike	—	—	—	—	450
1900 Prooflike; Restrike	—	—	—	—	450

KM# 470 1/4 RUPEE

2.9200 g., 0.9170 Silver 0.0861 oz. ASW **Obverse:** Bust A **Obv. Legend:** VICTORIA QUEEN **Reverse:** I **Note:** Size varies: 19.3-20.0mm.

Date	Mintage	F	VF	XF	Unc
1862(c)	19,412,000	2.50	5.00	10.00	20.00
1862(c) Proof	—	Value: 125			
1862(b)	11,390,000	2.50	5.00	10.00	20.00
1862(b) Prooflike; restrike	—	—	—	—	35.00
1862(m)	5,049,000	5.00	10.00	20.00	40.00
1862(m) V1(i)CTORIA (error)	Inc. Above	5.00	10.00	20.00	40.00
1874(c)	5,444,000	3.00	6.00	12.00	24.00
1874(b)	1,612,000	3.50	7.50	15.00	30.00
1875(c)	2,797,000	3.00	6.00	12.00	24.00
1875(c) Proof	—	Value: 125			
1875(b)	5,239,000	3.00	6.00	12.00	24.00
1876(c)	6,457,000	3.00	6.00	12.00	24.00
1876(b)	1,427,000	3.50	7.50	15.00	30.00

KM# 470a 1/4 RUPEE

Gold **Obverse:** Bust A **Obv. Legend:** VICTORIA QUEEN **Reverse:** I

Date	Mintage	F	VF	XF	Unc
1862(c) Prooflike; Restrike	—	—	—	—	500

KM# 471 1/4 RUPEE

2.9200 g., 0.9170 Silver 0.0861 oz. ASW **Obverse:** Mule. 5 Rupee, KM#476 **Reverse:** 1/4 Rupee, KM#470

Date	Mintage	F	VF	XF	Unc
1862(c) Prooflike; Restrike	—	—	—	—	50.00

KM# 490 1/4 RUPEE

2.9200 g., 0.9170 Silver .0860 oz. ASW **Obverse:** Mule. 5 Rupee, KM#476 **Obv. Legend:** VICTORIA EMPRESS **Reverse:** 1/4 Rupee, KM#470

Date	Mintage	F	VF	XF	Unc
1877(c) Without mint mark		2.50	5.00	10.00	20.00
Note: Type B Bust, Type I Reverse					
1877(c) Proof	44,000	Value: 125			
1877(b) Dot	—	3.50	7.50	15.00	30.00
Note: Type A Bust, Type I Reverse					
1877(b) Dot	—	3.50	7.50	15.00	30.00
Note: Type B Bust, Type I Reverse					
1877(b) Proof	—	Value: 125			
1877(b) Prooflike; Restrike	—	—	—	—	30.00
1878C	—	2.00	3.50	7.50	15.00
1878(c) Without mint mark	—	2.00	3.50	8.00	20.00
Note: Type C Bust, Type II Reverse					
1878(c) Proof	—	Value: 125			
1878(c) Prooflike; Restrike	—	—	—	—	30.00
1879C Incuse	—	2.00	3.50	8.00	20.00
Note: Type C Bust, Type II Reverse					
1879(b) Proof	—	—	—	—	125
1880C Incuse		2.00	3.50	8.00	20.00
Note: Type C Bust, Type II Reverse					
1881C Incuse	—	2.00	3.75	8.00	20.00
Note: Type C Bust, Type II Reverse					
1881C Proof	—	—	—	—	125
1881(b) Dot	—	2.00	3.75	8.00	20.00
Note: Type A Bust, Type II Reverse					
1881(b) Dot	—	4.00	7.50	15.00	30.00
Note: Type B Bust, Type I Reverse					
1881(b) Dot	—	4.00	7.50	15.00	30.00
Note: Type C Bust, Type II Reverse					
1882C Incuse	—	2.00	3.50	8.00	20.00
Note: Type C Bust, Type II Reverse					
1882C Proof	—	Value: 125			
1882(b) Dot	—	2.00	3.75	8.00	20.00
Note: Type A Bust, Type II Reverse					
1882(b) Dot	—	3.00	6.00	12.00	25.00
Note: Type B Bust, Type I Reverse					
1882(b) Dot	—	2.25	4.00	8.00	20.00
Note: Type C Bust, Type II Reverse					
1883C Incuse	—	4.00	7.50	15.00	30.00
Note: Type C Bust, Type II Reverse					
1883(b) Dot	—	5.00	10.00	20.00	35.00
Note: Type B Bust, Type I Reverse					
1884C Incuse	—	3.75	7.50	15.00	30.00
Note: Type C Bust, Type II Reverse					
1884B Raised	—	3.75	7.50	15.00	30.00
Note: Type B Bust, Type I Reverse					
1884B Raised	—	3.75	7.50	15.00	30.00
Note: Type C Bust, Type I Reverse					
1884B Proof	—	Value: 125			
1885C Incuse	—	3.75	7.50	15.00	30.00
Note: Type C Bust, Type II Reverse					
1885B Raised	—	3.75	7.50	15.00	30.00
Note: Type B Bust, Type I Reverse					
1886C Incuse	—	2.25	4.00	8.00	20.00
Note: Type C Bust, Type II Reverse					
1886B Raised	—	3.75	7.50	15.00	30.00
Note: Type C Bust, Type II Reverse					
1886B Without mm	—	5.00	10.00	20.00	40.00
Note: Type C Bust, Type II Reverse					
1887C Incuse	—	2.25	4.00	8.00	20.00
Note: Type C Bust, Type II Reverse					
1897C Incuse	—	—	—	—	—
Note: Type C Bust, Type II Reverse					
1887B Raised	—	2.50	5.00	10.00	20.00
Note: Type C Bust, Type II Reverse					
1888(c) Without mm	—	2.50	5.00	10.00	20.00
Note: Type C Bust, Type II Reverse					
1888B Raised	—	3.00	6.00	12.00	25.00
Note: Type C Bust, Type II Reverse					
1888B Incuse	—	3.75	7.50	15.00	30.00
Note: Type C Bust, Type II Reverse					
1889C Incuse	—	2.25	4.00	8.00	20.00
Note: Type C Bust, Type II Reverse					
1889B Incuse	—	2.50	5.00	10.00	20.00
Note: Type C Bust, Type II Reverse					
1889 Proof	—	Value: 125			
1890C Incuse	—	2.50	5.00	10.00	20.00
Note: Type C Bust, Type II Reverse					
1890C Proof	—	Value: 125			
1890B Incuse	—	4.00	7.50	15.00	30.00
Note: Type C Bust, Type I Reverse					
1890B Incuse	—	4.50	8.50	16.50	32.50
Note: Type C Bust, Type II Reverse					
1890B Prooflike; Restrike	—	—	—	—	30.00
1891C Incuse	—	2.25	4.00	8.00	20.00
Note: Type C Bust, Type II Reverse					
1891B Incuse	—	3.75	7.50	15.00	30.00
Note: Type C Bust, Type I Reverse					
1892(c) Incuse	—	2.50	5.00	10.00	20.00
Note: Type C Bust, Type II Reverse					
1892(c) Proof	—	Value: 125			
Note: Type C Bust, Type II Reverse					
1892B Incuse	—	2.00	3.00	6.00	15.00
Note: Type C Bust, Type I Reverse					
1892B Proof	—	Value: 125			
1893C Incuse	—	2.00	3.00	6.00	15.00
Note: Type C Bust, Type II Reverse					
1893C Proof	—	Value: 125			
1893B Incuse	—	2.00	3.00	6.00	15.00
Note: Type C Bust, Type I Reverse					
1893B Prooflike; Restrike	—	—	—	—	30.00
1894C Incuse	—	2.00	3.00	6.00	15.00
Note: Type C Bust, Type II Reverse					
1894C Proof	—	Value: 125			
1894B Incuse	—	2.00	3.00	6.00	15.00
Note: Type C Bust, Type I Reverse					
1894B Proof	—	Value: 125			
1894B Prooflike; Restrike	—	—	—	—	30.00
1896C Incuse	—	2.00	3.00	6.00	15.00
Note: Type C Bust, Type II Reverse					
1896C Proof	—	Value: 125			
1897C Incuse	—	2.00	3.00	6.00	15.00
Note: Type C Bust, Type II Reverse					
1897C Proof	—	Value: 125			
1897B Incuse	—	2.00	3.00	6.00	15.00
Note: Type C Bust, Type I Reverse					
1897B Proof	—	Value: 125			
1897B Prooflike; Restrike	—	—	—	—	30.00
1898C Incuse	—	2.00	3.00	6.00	15.00
Note: Type C Bust, Type II Reverse					
1898C Proof	—	Value: 125			
1898B Incuse	—	2.00	3.00	6.00	15.00
Note: Type C Bust, Type I Reverse					
1898B Proof	—	Value: 125			
1898B Prooflike; Restrike	—	—	—	—	30.00
1900C Incuse	—	2.00	3.00	6.00	15.00
Note: Type C Bust, Type II Reverse					
1900C Proof	—	Value: 125			
1900C Prooflike; Restrike	—	—	—	—	30.00

KM# 490b 1/4 RUPEE

Copper **Note:** Bronze plated examples may exist.

Date	Mintage	F	VF	XF	Unc
1884 Proof	—	Value: 100			
1891 Proof	—	Value: 100			
1892 Proof	—	Value: 100			

KM# 490c 1/4 RUPEE

Gold

Date	Mintage	F	VF	XF	Unc
1891 Prooflike; Restrike	—	—	—	—	500
1892 Prooflike; Restrike	—	—	—	—	500
1893 Prooflike; Restrike	—	—	—	—	500
1896 Prooflike; Restrike	—	—	—	—	500
1897 Prooflike; Restrike	—	—	—	—	500
1898 Prooflike; Restrike	—	—	—	—	500
1900 Prooflike; Restrike	—	—	—	—	500

KM# 472 1/2 RUPEE

5.8300 g., 0.9170 Silver 0.1719 oz. ASW **Obv. Legend:** VICTORIA QUEEN

Date	Mintage	F	VF	XF	Unc
1862(c)	1,623,000	5.00	10.00	20.00	40.00
Note: Type C Bust, Type II Reverse					
1862(b) Prooflike; Restrike	—	—	—	—	35.00
1862(c)	7,649,000	5.00	10.00	20.00	50.00
Note: Type A Bust, Type I Reverse					
1862(c) Proof	—	Value: 175			
1862(c)	736,000	7.50	15.00	30.00	60.00
Note: Type A Bust, Type II Reverse					
1862(c) Proof	—	Value: 175			
1862(b & m)	7,122,000	5.00	10.00	20.00	40.00
Note: Type B Bust, Type II Reverse					
1862(b) Prooflike; Restrike	—	—	—	—	35.00
1874(b) Dot	1,654,000	7.50	15.00	30.00	65.00
Note: Type B Bust, Type II Reverse					
1875(c)	2,257,000	5.00	10.00	20.00	50.00
Note: Type A Bust, Type I Reverse					
1875(c) Proof	—	Value: 175			
1875(b) Dot	1,023,000	7.50	15.00	30.00	65.00
Note: Type B Bust, Type II Reverse					
1876(b) Dot	966,000	7.50	15.00	30.00	65.00
Note: Type B Bust, Type II Reverse					

KM# 472a 1/2 RUPEE

Gold

Date	Mintage	F	VF	XF	Unc
1862(c) Prooflike; Restrike	—	—	—	—	1,000

KM# 491 1/2 RUPEE

5.8300 g., 0.9170 Silver 0.1719 oz. ASW **Obv. Legend:** VICTORIA EMPRESS

Date	Mintage	F	VF	XF	Unc
1877(c)	858,000	5.00	10.00	20.00	45.00
Note: Type A Bust, Type I Reverse					
1877(b) Prooflike; Restrike	—	—	—	—	30.00
1877(c) Proof	—	Value: 175			
1877(b) Dot	214,000	7.50	15.00	30.00	60.00
Note: Type B Bust, Type II Reverse					
1878(c)	1,390,000	5.00	10.00	20.00	45.00
Note: Type A Bust, Type I Reverse					
1878(c) Proof	—	Value: 175			
1878(c) Prooflike; Restrike	—	—	—	—	30.00
1879C Incuse	1,008,000	5.00	10.00	20.00	45.00
Note: Type A Bust, Type I Reverse					
1879(b) Proof	—	Value: 175			
1880C Incuse	180,000	7.50	15.00	30.00	60.00
Note: Type A Bust, Type I Reverse					
1881C Incuse	921,000	5.00	10.00	20.00	45.00
Note: Type A Bust, Type I Reverse					
1881C Proof	—	Value: 175			
1881(b) Dot	1,591,000	5.00	10.00	20.00	45.00
Note: Type B Bust, Type II Reverse					
1882C Incuse	1,161,000	5.00	10.00	20.00	45.00
Note: Type A Bust, Type I Reverse					
1882C Proof	—	Value: 175			
1882(b) Dot	308,000	8.00	17.50	35.00	70.00
Note: Type B Bust, Type II Reverse					
1882(b) Dot	Inc. above	8.00	17.50	35.00	70.00
Note: Type A Bust, Type II Reverse					
1883C Incuse	1,036,000	5.00	10.00	20.00	45.00
Note: Type A Bust, Type I Reverse					
1884C Incuse	—	5.00	10.00	20.00	45.00
Note: Type A Bust, Type I Reverse					
1884(b) Dot	1,110,000	5.00	10.00	20.00	45.00
Note: Type A Bust, Type II Reverse					
1884(b) Without mm	Inc. above	5.00	10.00	20.00	45.00
Note: Type A Bust, Type II Reverse					
1884 Proof	—	Value: 175			
1885C Incuse	1,408,000	3.75	7.50	15.00	40.00
Note: Type A Bust, Type I Reverse					
1885B Raised	390,000	5.00	10.00	20.00	45.00
Note: Type A Bust, Type II Reverse					
1886C Incuse	2,645,000	3.75	7.50	15.00	40.00
Note: Type A Bust, Type I Reverse					
1886B Raised	1,116,000	3.75	7.50	15.00	40.00
Note: Type A Bust, Type II Reverse					
1887C Incuse	2,275,000	3.75	7.50	15.00	40.00
Note: Type A Bust, Type I Reverse					
1887B Raised	407,000	5.00	10.00	20.00	45.00
Note: Type A Bust, Type II Reverse					
1888C Incuse	1,100,000	3.75	7.50	15.00	40.00
Note: Type A Bust, Type I Reverse					
1888B Raised	1,748,000	5.00	10.00	20.00	45.00
Note: Type A Bust, Type II Reverse					
1888(b) Without mm	Inc. above	5.00	10.00	20.00	45.00
Note: Type A Bust, Type II Reverse					
1889C Incuse	2,331,000	3.75	7.50	15.00	40.00
Note: Type A Bust, Type I Reverse					
1889B Raised	1,083,000	3.75	7.50	15.00	40.00
Note: Type A Bust, Type II Reverse					
1889B Incuse	Inc. above	3.75	7.50	15.00	40.00
Note: Type A Bust, Type I Reverse					
1890C Proof	—	Value: 175			
1890C Prooflike; Restrike	—	—	—	—	30.00
1891C Proof	—	Value: 175			
1891B Incuse	—	Value: 175			
Note: Type A Bust, Type I Reverse					
1891B Proof	—	Value: 175			
1891 Prooflike; Restrike	—	—	—	—	30.00
1892C Incuse	1,761,000	3.75	7.50	15.00	40.00
Note: Type A Bust, Type I Reverse					
1892C Proof	—	Value: 175			
1892B Incuse	1,104,000	3.75	7.50	15.00	40.00
Note: Type A Bust, Type I Reverse					
1892B Proof	—	Value: 175			
1893C Incuse	—	3.75	7.50	15.00	40.00
Note: Type A Bust, Type I Reverse					
1893C Proof	—	Value: 175			
1893B Incuse	2,462,000	3.75	7.50	15.00	40.00
Note: Type A Bust, Type I Reverse					
1893B Prooflike; Restrike	—	—	—	—	40.00
1894C Incuse	1,277,000	3.75	7.50	15.00	40.00
Note: Type A Bust, Type I Reverse					
1894C Proof	—	Value: 175			
1894B Incuse	—	4.00	10.00	20.00	50.00
Note: Type A Bust, Type I Reverse					
1894B Prooflike; Restrike	—	—	—	—	40.00
1896C Incuse	2,114,000	3.75	7.50	15.00	40.00

Date	Mintage	F	VF	XF	Unc
Note: Type A Bust, Type I Reverse					
1896C Proof	—	Value: 175			
1897C Incuse	—	3.75	7.50	15.00	40.00
Note: Type A Bust, Type I Reverse					
1897B Prooflike; Restrike	—	—	—	—	35.00
1897C Proof	—	Value: 175			
1897B Incuse	560	3.75	7.50	15.00	40.00
Note: Type A Bust, Type I Reverse					
1897B Proof	—	Value: 175			
1898C Incuse	2,057,000	3.75	7.50	15.00	40.00
Note: Type A Bust, Type I Reverse					
1898C Proof	—	Value: 175			
1898B Incuse	458,000	5.00	10.00	20.00	45.00
Note: Type A Bust, Type I Reverse					
1898B Proof	—	Value: 175			
1898B Prooflike; Restrike	—	—	—	—	35.00
1899C	6,893,000	3.75	7.50	15.00	40.00
1899C Proof	—	Value: 175			
1899B Incuse, inverted B	11,174,000	2.50	5.00	10.00	30.00
Note: Type A Bust, Type I Reverse					
1899B Proof	—	Value: 175			
1899B Prooflike; Restrike	—	—	—	—	35.00
1900C Prooflike; Restrike	—	—	—	—	35.00

KM# 491b 1/2 RUPEE

Copper **Obv. Legend:** VICTORIA EMPRESS **Note:** Bronze plated examples may exist.

Date	Mintage	F	VF	XF	Unc
1884 Proof	—	Value: 100			
1891 Proof	—	Value: 100			
1892 Proof	—	Value: 100			

KM# 491c 1/2 RUPEE

Gold **Obv. Legend:** VICTORIA EMPRESS

Date	Mintage	F	VF	XF	Unc
1891 Prooflike; Restrike	—	—	—	—	750
1892 Prooflike; Restrike	—	—	—	—	750
1893 Prooflike; Restrike	—	—	—	—	750
1896 Prooflike; Restrike	—	—	—	—	750
1897 Prooflike; Restrike	—	—	—	—	750
1898 Prooflike; Restrike	—	—	—	—	750
1899 Prooflike; Restrike	—	—	—	—	750

KM# 491a 1/2 RUPEE

Aluminum **Obv. Legend:** VICTORIA EMPRESS

Date	Mintage	F	VF	XF	Unc
1891	—	—	—	—	—

KM# 473.1 RUPEE

11.6600 g., 0.9170 Silver 0.3438 oz. ASW **Obv. Legend:** VICTORIA QUEEN

Date	Mintage	F	VF	XF	Unc
1862(m)	—	5.00	7.50	12.50	25.00
Note: Type A Bust, Type I Reverse, 0/0					
1862(b) 30.7mm	—	12.50	20.00	32.50	60.00
Note: Type A Bust, Type II Reverse, 0/0					
1862(c)	—	7.50	12.50	16.50	35.00
Note: Type A Bust, Type IIa Reverse, 0/0					
1862(c)	—	6.50	11.50	15.00	30.00
Note: Type B Bust, Type II Reverse, 0/0					
1862(b)	—	5.00	7.50	12.50	25.00
Note: Type B Bust, Type II Reverse, 0/0					
1862(m)	—	5.00	7.50	12.50	25.00
Note: Type B Bust, Type II Reverse, 0/0					
1862(b)	—	12.50	20.00	30.00	60.00
Note: Type B Bust, Type IIa Reverse, 0/0					
1862(c)	—	12.50	20.00	30.00	60.00
Note: Type A Bust, Type III Reverse, 0/0					
1862(c)	—	12.50	20.00	30.00	60.00
Note: Type B Bust, Type III Reverse, 0/0					
1862(c) Proof	—	Value: 200			
1862(c) Prooflike; Restrike	—	—	—	—	60.00
1862(b)	—	7.50	12.50	16.50	32.00
Note: Type B Bust, Type II Reverse, 1/0					
1862(b)	—	12.50	20.00	40.00	80.00
Note: Type A Bust, Type II Reverse, 0/2					
1862(b)	—	12.50	20.00	40.00	80.00
Note: Type B Bust, Type II Reverse, 2/0					
1862(b)	—	12.50	20.00	40.00	80.00
Note: Type B Bust, Type II Reverse, 3/0					
1862(b) Rare	—	—	—	—	—
Note: Type A Bust, Type II Reverse, 2/0					
1862(b)	—	5.00	7.50	12.50	30.00
Note: Type B Bust, Type II Reverse, 0/3					
1862(c)	—	12.50	20.00	40.00	80.00
Note: Type B Bust, Type II Reverse, 2/3					
1862(b)	—	12.50	20.00	40.00	80.00
Note: Type A Bust, Type I Reverse, 0/4					
1862(b)	—	12.50	20.00	40.00	80.00
Note: Type B Bust, Type I Reverse, 0/4					
1862(b)	—	8.00	15.00	30.00	60.00
Note: Type A Bust, Type II Reverse, 0/4					
1862(b)	—	15.00	30.00	50.00	90.00
Note: Type A Bust, Type II Reverse, 2/4					
1862(b)	—	8.00	15.00	30.00	60.00
Note: Type B Bust, Type II Reverse, 0/4					
1862(b)	—	5.00	7.50	13.50	30.00
Note: Type A Bust, Type II Reverse, 0/5					
1862(b)	—	5.00	7.50	13.50	30.00
Note: Type A Bust, Type II Reverse, 0/6					
1862(b)	—	5.00	7.50	13.50	30.00
Note: Type A Bust, Type II Reverse, 0/7					
1862(b)	—	12.50	20.00	32.50	60.00
Note: Type B Bust, Type II Reverse, 0/7					
1862(b) Rare	—	—	—	—	—
Note: Type B Bust, Type II Reverse, 0/6					
1862(b) Rare; Top dot in top flower	—	—	—	—	—
Note: Type A Bust, Type II Reverse, 1/7					
1862(b)	—	12.50	20.00	40.00	80.00
Note: Type A Bust, Type II Reverse, 0/8					
1862(b)	—	12.50	20.00	40.00	80.00
Note: Type A Bust, Type II Reverse, 0/9					
1862(b)	—	7.50	12.50	16.50	35.00
Note: Type A Bust, Type II Reverse, 0/10					
1862(b) Top dot in top flower	—	12.50	20.00	40.00	80.00
Note: Type A Bust, Type II Reverse, 1/10					
1862(b) Top dot in normal position	—	12.50	20.00	40.00	80.00
Note: Type A Bust, Type II Reverse, 1/7					
1862(b) Top dot in normal position	—	12.50	20.00	40.00	80.00
Note: Type A Bust, Type II Reverse, 1/10					
1862(b)	—	7.50	12.50	16.50	35.00
Note: Type A Bust, Type I Reverse, 1/11					
1862(b)	—	12.50	20.00	40.00	80.00
Note: Type A Bust, Type II Reverse, 0/1					
1862(b)	—	12.50	20.00	40.00	80.00
Note: Type A Bust, Type II Reverse, 1/1					
1862(b)	—	12.50	20.00	40.00	80.00
Note: Type A Bust, Type II Reverse, 0/12					
1862(b)	—	10.00	17.50	27.50	50.00
Note: Type A Bust, Type II Reverse, 1/2					
1862(b)	—	12.50	20.00	40.00	80.00
Note: Type A Bust, Type I Reverse, 1/2					
1862(b)	—	12.50	20.00	40.00	80.00
Note: Type C Bust, Type I Reverse, 1/2					
1862(b)	—	10.00	17.50	27.50	50.00
Note: Type C Bust, Type II Reverse, 1/2					

KM# 473.1a RUPEE

Gold **Obv. Legend:** VICTORIA QUEEN

Date	Mintage	F	VF	XF	Unc
1862(c) Prooflike; Restrike	—	—	—	—	—

KM# 473.2 RUPEE

11.6600 g., 0.9170 Silver 0.3438 oz. ASW

Date	Mintage	F	VF	XF	Unc
1874(c)	15,014,000	5.00	8.00	12.00	25.00
1874(b) Without mm	28,509,000	5.00	8.00	12.00	25.00
Note: Type A Bust, Type II Reverse					
1874(b) Dot	Inc. above	7.00	10.00	15.00	30.00
Note: Type A Bust, Type II Reverse					
1874(b) Proof	—	Value: 175			
1874(b) Prooflike; Restrike	—	—	—	—	35.00
1875(c)	11,632,000	5.00	8.00	12.00	25.00
Note: Type A Bust, Type I Reverse					
1875(b) Dot below	Inc. above	—	—	—	—
Note: Type C Bust, Type II Reverse					
1875(c) Proof	—	Value: 175			
1875(b) Without mm	19,360,000	5.00	8.00	12.00	25.00
Note: Type A Bust, Type II Reverse					
1875(b) Dot below	Inc. above	5.00	8.00	12.00	25.00
Note: Type A Bust, Type II Reverse					
1875(b) Proof	—	Value: 175			
1875(b) Prooflike; Restrike	—	—	—	—	35.00
1876(c)	12,001,000	5.00	8.00	12.00	25.00
Note: Type A Bust, Type I Reverse					
1876(b) Dot	28,950,000	5.00	8.00	12.00	25.00
Note: Type A Bust, Type II Reverse					
1876(b) Proof	—	Value: 175			
1876(c) Proof	—	—	—	—	—
Note: Type A Bust, Type I Reverse					
1876(b) Prooflike; Restrike	—	—	—	—	35.00
1876(c) Proof	—	Value: 75.00			

KM# 492 RUPEE

11.6600 g., 0.9170 Silver .3438 oz. ASW **Obv. Legend:** VICTORIA EMPRESS

Date	Mintage	F	VF	XF	Unc
1877(c)	39,252,000	5.00	8.00	12.00	25.00
Note: Type A Bust, Type I Reverse					
1877(c) Proof	—	Value: 175			
1877(b) Dot	95,554,000	5.00	8.00	12.00	25.00
Note: Type A Bust, Type I Reverse					
1877(b) Dot	Inc. above	5.00	8.00	12.00	25.00
Note: Type A Bust, Type II Reverse					
1877(b) Proof	—	Value: 175			
1877(b) Prooflike; Restrike	—	—	—	—	75.00
1878(c)	32,658,000	5.00	8.00	12.00	25.00
Note: Type A Bust, Type I Reverse					
1878(b) Proof	—	Value: 175			
1878(b) Prooflike; Restrike	—	—	—	—	35.00
1878(c) Proof	—	Value: 175			
1878(b) Dot	63,927,000	5.00	8.00	12.00	25.00
Note: Type A Bust, Type I Reverse					
1878(b) Dot	Inc. above	5.00	8.00	12.00	25.00
Note: Type A Bust, Type II Reverse					
1879C Incuse	15,928,000	5.00	8.00	12.00	25.00
Note: Type A Bust, Type I Reverse					
1879(b) Dot	72,800,000	9.00	17.50	27.50	50.00
Note: Type A Bust, Type I Reverse					
1879(b) Dot	Inc. above	5.00	8.00	12.00	25.00
Note: Type A Bust, Type II Reverse					
1879(b) Dot (rosette var.)	Inc. above	5.00	8.00	12.00	25.00
Note: Type A Bust, Type II Reverse					
1879(b) Proof	—	Value: 175			
1879(b) Prooflike; Restrike	—	—	—	—	35.00
1880C Incuse	18,400,000	7.00	10.00	15.00	30.00
Note: Type A Bust, Type I Reverse					
1880(b) Dot	53,786,000	5.00	8.00	12.00	25.00
Note: Type A Bust, Type I Reverse					
1880(b) Dot	Inc. above	5.00	8.00	12.00	25.00
Note: Type A Bust, Type II Reverse					
1880(b) Prooflike; Restrike	—	—	—	—	35.00
1881C Incuse	2,436,000	7.00	10.00	15.00	35.00
Note: Type A Bust, Type I Reverse					
1881C Proof	—	Value: 175			
1881(b) Dot	3,162,000	9.00	17.50	27.50	50.00
Note: Type A Bust, Type I Reverse					
1881(b) Dot	Inc. above	9.00	17.50	27.50	50.00
Note: Type A Bust, Type II Reverse					
1881(b) Prooflike; Restrike	—	—	—	—	35.00
1882C Incuse	15,090,000	5.00	8.00	12.00	25.00
Note: Type A Bust, Type I Reverse					
1882C Proof	—	—	—	—	175
1882(b) Dot	56,397,000	5.00	8.00	12.00	25.00
Note: Type A Bust, Type I Reverse					
1882(b) Prooflike; Restrike	—	—	—	—	35.00
1882(b) Dot	Inc. above	5.00	8.00	12.00	25.00
Note: Type A Bust, Type II Reverse					
1883C Incuse	5,123,000	7.00	10.00	15.00	30.00
Note: Type A Bust, Type I Reverse					
1883(b) Without mm	18,023,000	10.00	20.00	37.50	70.00
Note: Type A Bust, Type I Reverse					
1883(b) Dot	Inc. above	9.00	17.50	27.50	50.00
Note: Type A Bust, Type I Reverse					
1883B Raised	Inc. above	9.00	17.50	27.50	50.00
Note: Type A Bust, Type I Reverse					
1883B Raised	Inc. above	10.00	20.00	37.50	70.00
Note: Type A Bust, Type I Reverse					
1883B Prooflike; Restrike	—	—	—	—	35.00
1884C Incuse	11,642,000	5.00	8.00	12.00	25.00
Note: Type A Bust, Type I Reverse					
1884B Raised	36,847,000	7.00	10.00	17.50	35.00
Note: Type A Bust, Type I Reverse					
1884B Raised on whorl below bottom flower	Inc. above	9.00	17.50	27.50	50.00
Note: Type A Bust, Type II Reverse					
1884B Prooflike; Restrike	—	—	—	—	35.00
1885C Incuse	34,152,000	5.00	8.00	12.00	25.00
Note: Type A Bust, Type I Reverse					
1885C Proof	—	Value: 175			
1885B Raised	64,878,000	5.00	8.00	12.00	25.00
Note: Type A Bust, Type I Reverse					
1885B Raised	Inc. above	5.00	8.00	12.00	25.00
Note: Type A Bust, Type II Reverse					
1885B Raised	Inc. above	7.00	10.00	15.00	30.00
Note: Type C Bust, Type I Reverse					
1885B Incuse	Inc. above	5.00	8.00	12.00	25.00
Note: Type C Bust, Type I Reverse					
1885B Incuse	Inc. above	9.00	17.50	27.50	50.00
Note: Type A Bust, Type II Reverse					
1885B Prooflike; Restrike	—	—	—	—	35.00

Date	Mintage	F	VF	XF	Unc
1886C Incuse	10,878,000	5.00	8.00	12.00	25.00
Note: Type A Bust, Type I Reverse					
1886C Proof	—	Value: 175			
1886B Incuse	41,146,000	5.00	8.00	12.00	25.00
Note: Type C Bust, Type I Reverse					
1886B Prooflike; Restrike	—	—	—	—	35.00
1887B Incuse, inverted B	Inc. above	5.00	8.00	12.00	25.00
Note: Type A Bust, Type I Reverse					
1887C Incuse	40,200,000	5.00	8.00	12.00	25.00
Note: Type C Bust, Type I Reverse					
1887B Raised	48,400,000	5.00	8.00	12.00	25.00
Note: Type C Bust, Type I Reverse					
1887B Incuse	Inc. above	5.00	8.00	12.00	25.00
Note: Type C Bust, Type I Reverse					
1887B Incuse, inverted B	Inc. above	5.00	8.00	12.00	25.00
Note: Type C Bust, Type I Reverse					
1887B Prooflike; Restrike	—	—	—	—	35.00
1888C Incuse	7,568,000	5.00	8.00	12.00	25.00
Note: Type C Bust, Type I Reverse					
1888B Raised	63,200,000	5.00	8.00	12.00	25.00
Note: Type C Bust, Type I Reverse					
1888B Incuse	Inc. above	7.00	10.00	17.50	35.00
Note: Type C Bust, Type I Reverse					
1888B Incuse, inverted B	Inc. above	7.00	10.00	17.50	35.00
Note: Type C Bust, Type I Reverse					
1888B Prooflike; Restrike	—	—	—	—	35.00
1889C Incuse	9,368,000	5.00	8.00	12.00	25.00
Note: Type C Bust, Type I Reverse					
1889B Raised	65,300,000	5.00	8.00	12.00	30.00
Note: Type C Bust, Type I Reverse					
1889B Incuse	Inc. above	5.00	8.00	12.00	25.00
Note: Type C Bust, Type I Reverse					
1889B Prooflike; Restrike	—	—	—	—	35.00
1890C Incuse	24,742,000	5.00	8.00	12.00	25.00
Note: Type C Bust, Type I Reverse					
1890C Proof	—	Value: 175			
1890B Incuse	92,900,000	5.00	8.00	12.00	25.00
Note: Type C Bust, Type I Reverse					
1890B Prooflike; Restrike	—	—	—	—	35.00
1891C Incuse	14,670	5.00	8.00	12.00	25.00
Note: Type C Bust, Type I Reverse					
1891C Proof	—	Value: 175			
1891B Incuse	49,500,000	5.00	8.00	12.00	25.00
Note: Type C Bust, Type I Reverse					
1891B Proof	—	Value: 175			
1892C Incuse	32,455	5.00	8.00	12.00	25.00
Note: Type C Bust, Type I Reverse					
1892C Proof	—	Value: 175			
1892B Raised	72,200,000	5.00	8.00	12.00	25.00
Note: Type C Bust, Type I Reverse					
1892B Incuse	Inc. above	5.00	8.00	12.00	25.00
Note: Type C Bust, Type I Reverse					
1892B Proof	—	Value: 175			
1892B Prooflike; Restrike	—	—	—	—	35.00
1893C Incuse	9,140,000	5.00	8.00	12.00	25.00
Note: Type C Bust, Type I Reverse					
1893C Proof	—	Value: 175			
1893B Incuse	69,590,000	5.00	8.00	12.00	25.00
Note: Type C Bust, Type I Reverse					
1893B Proof	—	Value: 175			
1893B Prooflike; Restrike	—	—	—	—	35.00
1894C Proof	—	Value: 200			
Note: Type C Bust, Type I Reverse					
1897C Incuse	470,000	20.00	35.00	70.00	175
Note: Type C Bust, Type I Reverse					
1897C Proof	—	Value: 225			
1897B Incuse	1,055,000	9.00	17.50	27.50	50.00
Note: Type C Bust, Type I Reverse					
1897B Proof	—	Value: 175			
1897B Prooflike; Restrike	—	—	—	—	35.00
1898C Incuse	1,251,000	8.00	12.50	22.50	40.00
Note: Type C Bust, Type I Reverse					
1898C Proof	—	Value: 175			
1898B Incuse	6,268,000	5.00	8.00	12.00	25.00
Note: Type C Bust, Type I Reverse					
1898B Proof	—	Value: 175			
1898B Prooflike; Restrike	—	—	—	—	35.00
1900C Incuse	5,291,000	5.00	8.00	12.00	25.00
Note: Type C Bust, Type I Reverse					
1900C Proof	—	Value: 175			
1900B Incuse	65,237,000	5.00	8.00	12.00	25.00
Note: Type A Bust, Type I Reverse					
1900B Proof	—	Value: 175			
1900B Prooflike; Restrike	—	—	—	—	35.00

KM# 492b RUPEE

Copper Or Bronze **Obv. Legend:** VICTORIA EMPRESS

Date	Mintage	F	VF	XF	Unc
1884 Proof	—	Value: 100			
1885 Proof	—	Value: 100			
1887 Proof	—	Value: 100			
1891 Proof	—	Value: 100			
1892 Proof	—	Value: 100			

KM# 492a RUPEE

Aluminum **Obv. Legend:** VICTORIA EMPRESS

Date	Mintage	F	VF	XF	Unc
1891B Proof	—	—	—	—	—

KM# 492c RUPEE

Gold **Obv. Legend:** VICTORIA EMPRESS

Date	Mintage	F	VF	XF	Unc
1891 Prooflike; Restrike	—	—	—	—	850
1892 Prooflike; Restrike	—	—	—	—	850
1893 Prooflike; Restrike	—	—	—	—	850
1898 Prooflike; Restrike	—	—	—	—	850
1900B Prooflike; Restrike	—	—	—	—	850

KM# 474 5 RUPEES

3.8870 g., 0.9170 Gold 0.1146 oz. AGW **Obverse:** Young bust **Obv. Legend:** VICTORIA QUEEN **Edge:** Reeded

Date	Mintage	F	VF	XF	Unc
1870CM	—	225	325	500	700
1875 Proof	—	Value: 1,500			

KM# 475 5 RUPEES

3.8870 g., 0.9170 Gold 0.1146 oz. AGW **Obverse:** Young bust **Obv. Legend:** VICTORIA QUEEN **Edge:** Plain

Date	Mintage	F	VF	XF	Unc
1870 Proof	—	Value: 1,500			

KM# 475a 5 RUPEES

Silver **Obverse:** Young bust **Obv. Legend:** VICTORIA QUEEN

Date	Mintage	F	VF	XF	Unc
1870 Proof	—	—	—	—	—

KM# 476 5 RUPEES

3.8870 g., 0.9170 Gold 0.1146 oz. AGW **Obverse:** Mature bust **Obv. Legend:** VICTORIA QUEEN **Edge:** Reeded

Date	Mintage	F	VF	XF	Unc
1870(c)	13,000	225	325	500	700
1870(c) Proof	—	Value: 800			
1870(c) Prooflike; Restrike	—	—	—	—	550

KM# 494 5 RUPEES

3.8870 g., 0.9170 Gold 0.1146 oz. AGW **Obverse:** Mature bust **Obv. Legend:** VICTORIA EMPRESS

Date	Mintage	F	VF	XF	Unc
1879(b) Prooflike; Restrike	—	—	—	—	400

KM# 493.1 5 RUPEES

3.8870 g., 0.9170 Gold 0.1146 oz. AGW **Obverse:** Young bust **Obv. Legend:** VICTORIA EMPRESS **Reverse:** KM#476 **Note:** Mule. Obv: 1/4 Rupee, Bust A, KM#490.

Date	Mintage	F	VF	XF	Unc
1879(b) Prooflike; Restrike	—	—	—	—	550

KM# 493.2 5 RUPEES

3.8870 g., 0.9170 Gold 0.1146 oz. AGW **Reverse:** KM#476 **Note:** Mule. Obv: 1/4 Rupee, Bust B.

Date	Mintage	F	VF	XF	Unc
1879(b) Prooflike; Restrike	—	—	—	—	550

KM# 493.3 5 RUPEES

3.8870 g., 0.9170 Gold 0.1146 oz. AGW **Reverse:** KM#476 **Note:** Mule. Obv: 1/4 Rupee, Bust C.

Date	Mintage	F	VF	XF	Unc
1879(b) Prooflike; Restrike	—	—	—	—	550

KM# 477 10 RUPEES

7.7740 g., 0.9170 Gold 0.2292 oz. AGW **Obverse:** Young bust **Obv. Legend:** VICTORIA QUEEN **Edge:** Reeded

Date	Mintage	F	VF	XF	Unc
1870CM Proof	—	Value: 1,000			
1870CM Prooflike, restrike	—	—	—	—	700
1875 Proof	—	Value: 1,850			

KM# 478 10 RUPEES

7.7740 g., 0.9170 Gold 0.2292 oz. AGW **Obverse:** Young bust **Obv. Legend:** VICTORIA QUEEN **Edge:** Plain

Date	Mintage	F	VF	XF	Unc
1870 Proof	—	Value: 2,000			

KM# 478a 10 RUPEES

Silver **Obverse:** Young bust **Obv. Legend:** VICTORIA QUEEN

Date	Mintage	F	VF	XF	Unc
1870 Proof	—	—	—	—	—

KM# 479 10 RUPEES

7.7740 g., 0.9170 Gold 0.2292 oz. AGW **Obverse:** Mature bust **Obv. Legend:** VICTORIA QUEEN **Edge:** Reeded

Date	Mintage	F	VF	XF	Unc
1870(c)	7,932	250	350	550	750
1870(c) Proof	—	Value: 1,000			
1870(c) Prooflike; Restrike	—	—	—	—	650

KM# 495 10 RUPEES

7.7740 g., 0.9170 Gold 0.2292 oz. AGW **Obverse:** Mature bust **Obv. Legend:** VICTORIA EMPRESS **Edge:** Reeded

Date	Mintage	F	VF	XF	Unc
1878(b) Proof	—	Value: 2,000			
1878(b) Prooflike; Restrike	—	—	—	—	750
1879(b) Proof	—	Value: 2,000			
1879(b) Prooflike; Restrike	—	—	—	—	650

KM# 480 MOHUR

11.6600 g., 0.9170 Gold 0.3438 oz. AGW **Obverse:** Young bust **Obv. Legend:** VICTORIA QUEEN

Date	Mintage	F	VF	XF	Unc
1862(c)	153,000	220	320	425	500
1862(c) Proof	Inc. above	Value: 1,250			
1862(c) Prooflike; Restrike	—	—	—	—	450
1862(c) With V on bust	Inc. above	220	320	425	500
1862(c) With V on rev. in design below date	Inc. above	220	320	425	500
1862(c) With V on bust and on rev.	—	220	320	425	500
1862(c) With V on bust and 2 flowers in bottom panel	Inc. above	220	320	425	500
1870(c) Proof	—	Value: 1,500			
1870(c) Prooflike; Restrike	—	—	—	—	550
1875(c) With V on bust	11,000	350	500	750	1,000
1875(c) Proof	—	Value: 4,500			
1875(c) Prooflike; Restrike	—	—	—	—	600

KM# 480a MOHUR

Copper **Obverse:** Young bust **Obv. Legend:** VICTORIA QUEEN

Date	Mintage	F	VF	XF	Unc
1862(c)	—	—	—	350	—

KM# A481 MOHUR

Copper **Obverse:** Mule. KM#481 **Reverse:** KM#480

Date	Mintage	F	VF	XF	Unc
1862(c) Prooflike; Restrike	—	—	—	—	400

KM# 481 MOHUR

11.6600 g., 0.9170 Gold 0.3438 oz. AGW **Obverse:** Mature bust **Obv. Legend:** VICTORIA QUEEN

Date	Mintage	F	VF	XF	Unc
1870(c) Proof	—	Value: 3,500			
1870(c) Prooflike; Restrike	—	—	—	—	650

KM# 482 MOHUR

11.6600 g., 0.9170 Gold 0.3438 oz. AGW **Obverse:** Mule. KM#496 **Reverse:** KM#481

Date	Mintage	F	VF	XF	Unc
1870(c) Prooflike; Restrike	—	—	—	—	800

KM# 496 MOHUR

11.6600 g., 0.9170 Gold 0.3438 oz. AGW **Obverse:** Young bust **Obv. Legend:** VICTORIA EMPRESS

Date	Mintage	F	VF	XF	Unc
1877(c)	10,000	175	225	300	500
1878(c) Prooflike; Restrike	—	—	—	—	600
1879C	19,000	175	225	300	500
1879(b) Proof	—	Value: 3,500			
Note: Modified rev.					
1879(b) Prooflike; Restrike	—	—	—	—	550
1881	23,000	175	225	300	500
1882C	12,000	175	225	300	500
1882(b) Without C mm; Prooflike; Restrike	—	—	—	—	550
1884(c)	8,643	185	275	375	600
1885(c)	15,000	175	225	300	500
1888(c)	15,000	175	225	300	500
1889(c)	15,000	175	225	300	500
1889(c) Prooflike; Restrike	—	—	—	—	550
1891(c)	17,000	175	225	300	500

KM# 496a MOHUR

Copper Or Bronze

Date	Mintage	F	VF	XF	Unc
1878(b)	—	—	—	350	—

TOKEN ISSUES

The British Indian Government introduced a special series of tokens for use by Famine Relief Officials as part of a policy to deal with great famine disasters in Bengal in 1874 and in Southern India in 1876.

KM# Tn1 1/2 RUPEE

Copper **Subject:** Famine Relief

Date	Mintage	F	VF	XF	Unc
ND	—	50.00	75.00	120	175

KM# Tn2 RUPEE

Brass **Subject:** Famine Relief

Date	Mintage	F	VF	XF	Unc
1874(c)	—	50.00	75.00	120	175
1874(c) Proof	—	Value: 400			

KM# Tn2a RUPEE

Gold

Date	Mintage	F	VF	XF	Unc
1874(c) 1 known; Rare	—	—	—	—	—

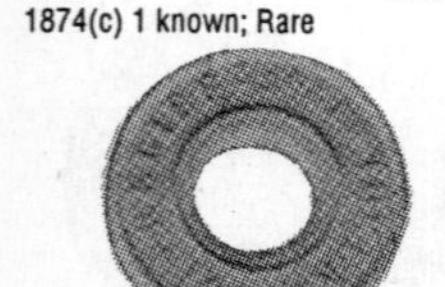

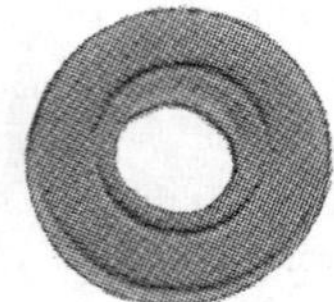

KM# Tn3 1/2 SEER

Brass **Subject:** Famine Relief **Note:** 1/2 Seer = 1.028 lbs.

Date	Mintage	F	VF	XF	Unc
1876	—	125	200	275	—

PATTERNS

Including off metal strikes

P# are in reference to The Coins of the British Commonwealth of Nations Part 4, India, Vol. 1 and 2 by F. Pridmore (Spink and Son Ltd., London 1980).

KM#	Date	Mintage	Identification	Mkt Val
Pn1	1834(c)	—	Rupee. Silver. 26.5 mm. Plain edge. Prid.#168.	1,750

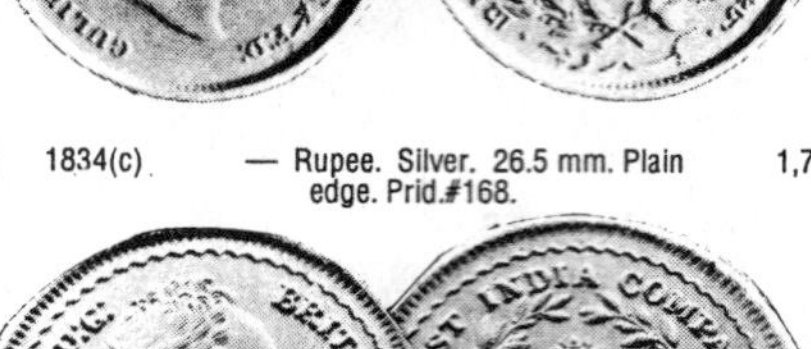

KM#	Date	Mintage	Identification	Mkt Val
Pn2	1834(c)	—	Rupee. Silver. 32 mm. Prid.#170.	1,000

KM#	Date	Mintage	Identification	Mkt Val
Pn3	1834(c)	—	Rupee. Silver. Prid.#171.	1,250

KM#	Date	Mintage	Identification	Mkt Val
Pn4	1834(c)	—	Rupee. Silver. Milled edge. Prid.#172.	500
Pn5	1834(c)	—	Rupee. Silver. Plain edge. Prid.#173.	500

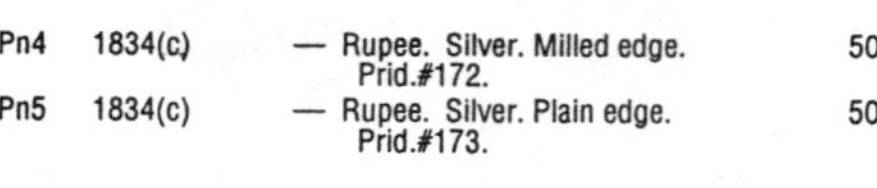

KM#	Date	Mintage	Identification	Mkt Val
Pn6	1834(c)	—	Rupee. Silver. 31.7 mm. Prid.#174.	1,500
Pn7	1834(c)	—	Rupee.	450
Pn8	1835(b)	—	1/2 Rupee. Silver. Prid.#180.	1,000

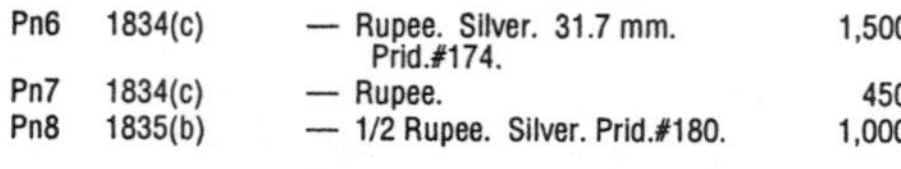

KM#	Date	Mintage	Identification	Mkt Val
Pn9	(1835)(c)	—	Rupee. Silver. Prid.#176.	1,000
Pn10	(1835)(c)	—	Rupee. Gold. Prid.#177.	—

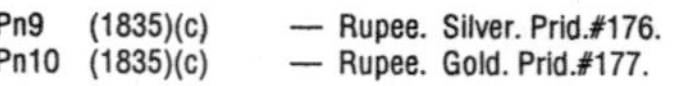

KM#	Date	Mintage	Identification	Mkt Val
Pn11	1835(c)	—	Rupee. Silver. Prid.#178.	1,000

KM#	Date	Mintage	Identification	Mkt Val
Pn12	1835(b)	—	Rupee. Silver. Prid.#179.	1,250
Pn13	1839(b)	—	Rupee. Silver. Prid.#181.	—

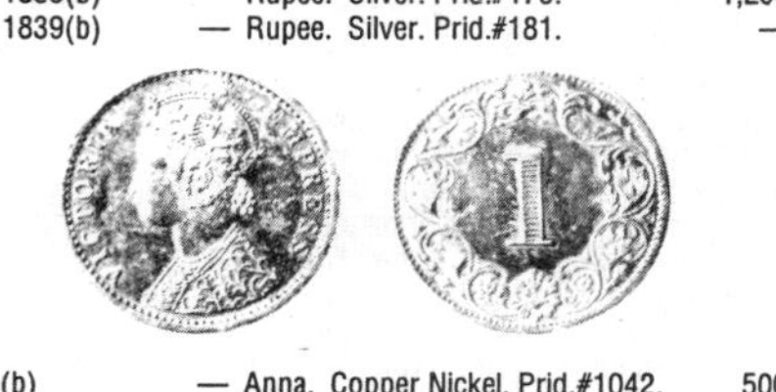

KM#	Date	Mintage	Identification	Mkt Val
Pn14	(b)	—	Anna. Copper Nickel. Prid.#1042.	500

KM#	Date	Mintage	Identification	Mkt Val
Pn15	(b)	—	2 Annas. Copper Nickel. Prid.#1041.	500

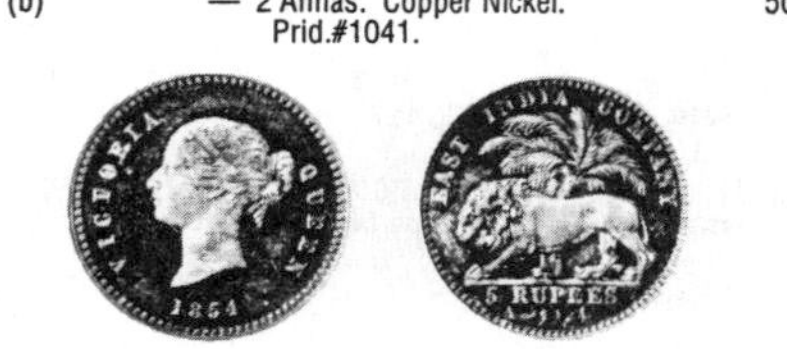

KM#	Date	Mintage	Identification	Mkt Val
Pn16	1854	—	5 Rupees. Silver. Plain edge. Prid.#31.	1,250
Pn17	1854	—	5 Rupees. Gold. Plain edge. Prid.#30.	3,000

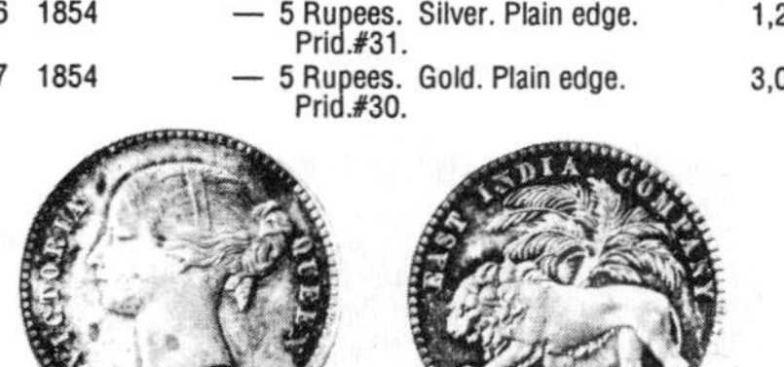

KM#	Date	Mintage	Identification	Mkt Val
Pn18	1854	—	10 Rupees. Silver. Plain edge. Prid.#28.	2,000
Pn19	1854	—	10 Rupees. Gold. Plain edge. Prid.#27.	4,000

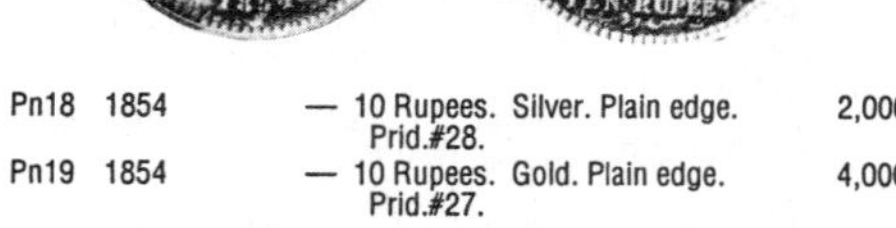

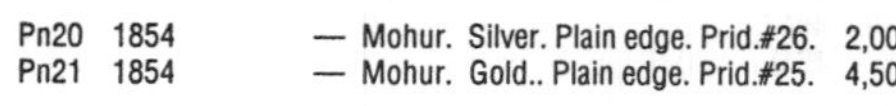

KM#	Date	Mintage	Identification	Mkt Val
Pn20	1854	—	Mohur. Silver. Plain edge. Prid.#26.	2,000
Pn21	1854	—	Mohur. Gold.. Plain edge. Prid.#25.	4,500

KM#	Date	Mintage	Identification	Mkt Val
Pn22	1854	—	2 Mohurs. Silver. Plain edge. Prid.#7.	4,500
Pn23	1854	—	2 Mohurs. Gold. Plain. edge. Prid.#6.	7,500
Pn24	1854	—	2 Mohurs. Gold. Plain edge	—
Pn25	186-	—	Rupee. Copper. Prid.#46.	—
Pn26	1860	—	Rupee. Silver. Prid.#47.	700
Pn27	1860	—	Rupee. Silver. Piefort. Prid.#48.	800
Pn28	1861(c)	—	1/12 Anna. Copper. Prid.#775.	—

KM#	Date	Mintage	Identification	Mkt Val
Pn29	1861	—	1/2 Pice. Copper. Piefort. Prid.#707.	—
Pn30	1861	—	1/4 Anna. Copper. Prid.#596.	—

KM#	Date	Mintage	Identification	Mkt Val
Pn31	1861	—	1/4 Anna. Copper. Last digit Roman numeral I. Prid.#597.	—
Pn32	1861	—	1/2 Pice. Copper. Prid.#708.	50.00
Pn33	1861	—	1/2 Anna. Copper. Prid.#575.	—
Pn34	1861	—	2 Annas. Silver. Prid.#480.	125
Pn35	1861(c)	—	2 Annas. Silver. Prid.#481.	100
Pn36	1861(c)	—	2 Annas. Silver.	35.00
Pn37	1861	—	1/4 Rupee. Silver. Prid.#371.	125
Pn38	1861	—	1/4 Rupee. Silver. Piefort. Prid.#370.	—
Pn39	1861(c)	—	1/2 Rupee. Silver. Pearled center jewel on crown. Prid.#251.	175
Pn40	1861	—	1/2 Rupee. Silver. Far "6-1". Prid.#250.	—
Pn41	1861	—	1/2 Rupee. Silver. Piefort. Close "6-1". Prid.#249.	200
Pn42	1861	—	Rupee. Silver. Royal Mint. Prid.#49.	200
Pn43	1861	—	Rupee. Copper. Prid.#53.	250
Pn44	1861(c)	—	Rupee. Silver. With L. C. Wyon. Prid.#51.	200
Pn45	1861(c)	—	Rupee. Silver. Prid.#52.	200
Pn46	1862(c)	—	1/12 Anna. Copper. Prid.#776.	60.00
Pn47	1862(c)	—	1/12 Anna. Copper.	—
Pn48	1862(c)	—	1/12 Anna. Silver. Prid.#777.	125
Pn49	1862	—	1/2 Pice. Copper. Prid.#709.	50.00
Pn50	1862	—	1/2 Pice. Silver. Prid.#709A.	125
Pn51	1862(c)	—	1/2 Pice. Copper. Prid.#710.	50.00
Pn52	1862(c)	—	1/4 Anna. Copper. Prid.#598.	—
Pn53	1862(c)	—	1/4 Anna. Copper.	—
Pn54	1862(c)	—	1/4 Anna. Silver. Prid.#599.	150
Pn55	1862	—	1/2 Anna. Copper. Prid.#575A.	100
Pn56	1862(c)	—	1/2 Anna. Copper. With V in bottom of bust. Prid.#579.	100
Pn57	1862(c)	—	1/2 Anna. Silver. Prid.#580.	200
Pn58	1862(c)	—	2 Annas. Silver. Prid.#482.	100
Pn59	1862(c)	—	1/4 Rupee. Silver. With inverted V on bust. Prid.#372.	125
Pn60	1863	—	Rupee. Silver. Prid.#106.	1,000
Pn61	1864	—	Rupee. Silver. Prid.#107.	1,000
Pn62	1867	—	Rupee. Silver. Plain edge. Prid.#108.	1,000
Pn63	1867	—	Rupee. Silver. Plain edge. Without L. C. W. Prid.#109.	1,000
Pn64	1867(c)	—	Rupee. Silver. Milled edge. Prid.#110.	1,000
Pn65	1870	—	Rupee. Silver. Prid.#9.	—
PnA66	1891(b)	—	2 Annas. Aluminum. KM#488a.	—
PnB66	1891B	—	1/4 Rupee. Aluminum. KM#490a.	100

TRIAL STRIKES

KM#	Date	Mintage	Identification	Mkt Val
TS1	ND(1840)	—	1/4 Rupee. Pewter. KM#453. Prid.#184.	225
TS2	ND(1840)	—	1/2 Rupee. Pewter. KM#455. Prid.#183.	275
TS3	ND(1840)	—	Rupee. KM#457.	300
TS4	1858	—	1/4 Anna. Copper. With "J.W./& Co.". Prid.#158.	—

KM#	Date	Mintage	Identification	Mkt Val
TS5	ND(1854)	—	10 Rupees. Copper. Reverse. Prid.#29.	—
TS6	ND(1854)	—	2 Mohurs. Copper. Reverse. Prid.#8.	—
TS7	ND(1867)	—	Rupee. Tin. Obverse. Prid.#111A.	—
TS8	1867	—	Rupee. Tin. Reverse. Prid.#111B.	—
TS9	1891	—	Rupee. Copper. Obverse. KM#492.	250
TS10	1891	—	Rupee. Copper. Reverse. KM#492.	250

PROOF SETS

KM#	Date	Mintage	Identification	Issue Price	Mkt Val
PS1	1835(c) (3)	—	KM#445, 446.2, 447.2	—	500
PS2	1875 (3)	—	KM#474, 477, 480	—	4,500

BENGAL PRESIDENCY

East India Company

(Until 1835)

In 1633 a group of 8 Englishmen obtained a permit to trade in Bengal from the Nawab of Orissa. Shortly thereafter trading factories were established at Balasore and Hariharpur. Although greater trading privileges were granted to the East India Company by the Emperor Shah Jahan in 1634, by 1642 the 2 original factories were abandoned.

In 1651, through an English surgeon named Broughton, a permit was acquired to trade at Bengal. Hugli was the first location, followed by Kasimbazar, Balasore and Patna (the last 3 in 1653). Calcutta became of increasing importance in this area and on December 20, 1699 Calcutta was declared a presidency and renamed Fort William. During these times there were many conflicts with the Nawab, both diplomatic and military, and the ultimate outcome was the intervention of Clive and the restoration of Calcutta as an important trading center.

During the earlier trading times in Bengal most of the monies used were imported rupees from the Madras factory. These were primarily of the Arcot type. After Clive's victory one of the concessions in the peace treaty was the right to make Mughal type coinage. The Nawab gave specific details as to what form the coinage should take.

In 1765 Emperor Shah Alam gave the East India Company possessions in Bengal, Orissa and Bihar. This made the company nominally responsible only to the Emperor.

In 1777 the "Frozen Year 19" (of Shah Alam) rupees were made at Calcutta and were continued until 1835. The Arcot rupees were discontinued at Calcutta about 1777.

MINTS

علي نگر كلكته

Alinagar Kalkatah (Calcutta)

بنارس

Banaras

NOTE: Coins of similar dates with different legends are listed in Indian Princely States, Awadh under Lucknow Mint, with fixed regnal year 26.

كلكته

Calcutta (Kalkatah)

فرخ اباد

Farrukhabad

مرشد اباد

Murshidabad

ساكر

Sagar

BRITISH COLONIAL

HAMMERED COINAGE

KM# A63 1/2 PICE

2.4500 g., Copper **Mint:** Farrukhabad **Obverse:** Persian inscription, julus **Obv. Inscription:** "Shah Alam II Badshah" **Reverse:** Value in Persian, Bengali and Hindi **Note:** Size varies 19-20mm.

Date	Mintage	Good	VG	F	VF	XF
ND(1816)	—	15.00	40.00	100	200	325

KM# 16 PICE

10.0600 g., Copper **Issuer:** East India Company **Mint:** Muhammadabad Banaras **Obverse:** Trisul (trident) symbol **Obv. Inscription:** "falus..Shah Alam II" **Reverse:** Trisul (trident) symbol, Persian mintname

Date	Mintage	Good	VG	F	VF	XF
ND-//45	—	2.00	5.00	10.00	20.00	—
ND-//49	—	2.00	5.00	10.00	20.00	—

KM# 27 PICE

6.2300 g., Copper **Mint:** Murshidabad **Obverse:** Trisul (trident) symbol, Persian inscription **Obv. Inscription:** "Falus, Shah Alam II" **Reverse:** Inscription with value in Persian and Hindi, Persian mint name **Edge:** Plain **Note:** Size varies 22-26mm, thick letters. Varieties exist.

Date	Mintage	Good	VG	F	VF	XF
ND-//37	—	0.75	2.00	3.00	6.00	10.00

KM# 28 PICE

6.1500 g., Copper **Mint:** Murshidabad **Obverse:** Inscription in plain circles **Obv. Inscription:** "Falus..Shah Alam II" **Reverse:** Persian mint name in plain circles **Edge:** Plain **Note:** Size varies 19-23mm.

Date	Mintage	Good	VG	F	VF	XF
ND-//37	—	0.65	1.75	3.75	7.50	12.50

KM# 32 1/16 RUPEE

Silver **Issuer:** East India Company **Mint:** Muhammadabad Banaras **Obverse:** Darogah's marks of stylized fish within Persian inscription, couplet **Obv. Inscription:** "Shah Alam II Badshah" **Reverse:** Darogah's mark of flower, Persian-julus (formula), mintname **Note:** Weight varies 0.67-0.73 grams.

Date	Mintage	Good	VG	F	VF	XF
AH1226//17-49	—	10.00	25.00	60.00	100	175

KM# 33 1/8 RUPEE

Silver **Issuer:** East India Company **Mint:** Muhammadabad Banaras **Obverse:** Darogah's marks of stylized fish within Persian inscription, couplet **Obv. Inscription:** "Shah Alam (II) Badshah" **Reverse:** Darogah's mark of flower, Persian-julus (formula), mintname

Date	Mintage	Good	VG	F	VF	XF
ND-//17-47	—	—	—	—	—	—
AH1221//17-48	—	15.00	40.00	100	200	300
AH1225//17-49	—	15.00	40.00	100	200	300
AH1226//17-49	—	15.00	40.00	100	200	300

KM# 34 1/4 RUPEE

Silver **Issuer:** East India Company **Mint:** Banaras **Obverse:** Darogah's marks of stylized fish within Persian inscription, couplet **Obv. Inscription:** "Shah Alam II Badshah" **Reverse:** Darogah's mark of flower, Persian-julus (formula), mintname **Note:** Weight varies 2.68-2.91 grams.

Date	Mintage	Good	VG	F	VF	XF
AH119x//17-26	—	20.00	50.00	150	300	400
AH120x//17-30	—	20.00	50.00	150	300	400
AH121x//17-42	—	20.00	50.00	150	300	400
AH122x//17-46	—	20.00	50.00	150	300	400
AH1225//17-49	—	20.00	50.00	150	300	400
AH1226//17-49	—	20.00	50.00	150	300	400

KM# 35 1/4 RUPEE

Silver **Mint:** Banaras **Obverse:** Without Darogah's marks of stylized fish within Persian inscription, couplet **Obv. Inscription:** "Shah Alam II Badshah" **Reverse:** Darogah's mark of flower, Persian-julus (formula), mint name **Note:** Weight varies 2.68-2.91 grams.

Date	Mintage	Good	VG	F	VF	XF
AH1229//17-49	—	40.00	100	200	400	650

KM# 37 1/2 RUPEE

Silver **Issuer:** East India Company **Mint:** Banaras **Obverse:** Darogah's marks of stylized fish within Persian inscription, couplet **Obv. Inscription:** "Shah Alam II Badshah" **Reverse:** Darogah's mark of flower, Persian-julus (formula), mintname **Note:** Weight varies 5.35-5.82 grams.

Date	Mintage	Good	VG	F	VF	XF
AH1225//17-49	—	50.00	125	250	500	800
AH1226//17-49	—	50.00	125	250	500	800

KM# 38 1/2 RUPEE

Silver **Mint:** Banaras **Obverse:** Without Darogah's marks of stylized fish within Persian inscription, couplet **Obv. Inscription:** "Shah Alam II Badshah" **Reverse:** Darogah's mark of flower, Persian-julus (formula), mint name **Note:** Weight varies: 5.35 - 5.82 grams.

Date	Mintage	VG	F	VF	XF	Unc
AH1229//17-49(1813)	—	125	250	500	800	—

KM# 40 RUPEE

11.3300 g., Silver **Issuer:** East India Company **Mint:** Muhammadabad Banaras **Obverse:** Darogah's marks of stylized fish within Persian inscription, couplet **Obv. Inscription:** "Shah Alam II Badshah" **Reverse:** Darogah's mark of flower, Persian-julus (formula), mintname

Date	Mintage	Good	VG	F	VF	XF
AH1215//17-42	—	5.50	14.00	23.50	25.00	45.00
AH1215//17-43	—	5.50	14.00	23.50	25.00	45.00
AH1216//17-43	—	5.50	14.00	23.50	25.00	45.00
AH1216//17-44	—	5.50	14.00	23.50	25.00	45.00
AH1217//17-44	—	5.50	14.00	23.50	25.00	45.00
AH1217//17-45	—	5.50	14.00	23.50	25.00	45.00
AH1218//17-45	—	5.50	14.00	23.50	25.00	45.00
AH1218//17-46	—	5.50	14.00	23.50	25.00	45.00
AH1219//17-46	—	5.50	14.00	23.50	25.00	45.00
AH1219//17-47	—	5.50	14.00	23.50	25.00	45.00
AH1220//17-47	—	5.50	14.00	23.50	25.00	45.00
AH1220//17-48	—	5.50	14.00	23.50	25.00	45.00
AH1221//17-48	—	5.50	14.00	23.50	25.00	45.00
AH1221//17-49	—	5.50	14.00	23.50	25.00	45.00
AH1222//17-49	—	5.50	14.00	23.50	25.00	45.00
AH1223//17-49	—	5.50	14.00	23.50	25.00	45.00
AH1224//17-49	—	5.50	14.00	23.50	25.00	45.00
AH1225//17-49	—	5.50	14.00	23.50	25.00	45.00
AH1226//17-49	—	5.50	14.00	23.50	25.00	45.00
AH1227//17-49	—	10.00	25.00	40.00	52.50	75.00

KM# 41 RUPEE

11.3300 g., Silver **Mint:** Muhammadabad Banaras **Obverse:** Without Darogah's marks of stylized fish within Persian inscription, couplet **Obv. Inscription:** "Shah Alam II Badshah" **Reverse:** Darogah's mark of flower, Persian-julus (formula), mint name

Date	Mintage	VG	F	VF	XF	Unc
AH1227//17-49(1812)	—	40.00	60.00	80.00	125	—
AH1228//17-49(1813)	—	40.00	60.00	80.00	125	—
AH1229//17-49(1813)	—	25.00	40.00	52.50	75.00	—

KM# 44 NAZARANA RUPEE

11.6400 g., Silver **Mint:** Muhammadabad Banaras **Obverse:** Persian inscription, couplet **Obv. Inscription:** "Shah Alam II Badshah" **Reverse:** Persian-julus (formula), mint name **Note:** Large flan.

Date	Mintage	Good	VG	F	VF	XF
AH1217//17-45	—	—	—	—	600	950

KM# 45 NAZARANA RUPEE

11.6400 g., Silver **Mint:** Muhammadabad Banaras **Obverse:** Persian inscription, couplet **Obv. Inscription:** "Shah Alam II Badshah" **Reverse:** Persian-julus (formula), mint name **Note:** Large full flan.

Date	Mintage	Good	VG	F	VF	XF
AH1219//17-47	—	—	—	—	2,000	3,250

MILLED COINAGE

KM# A54 1/2 PICE

3.1100 g., Copper, 17.5 mm. **Mint:** Calcutta **Obverse:** Persian inscription **Obv. Inscription:** "Shah Alam II Badshah" **Reverse:** Inscription with value in Persian and Nagari **Edge:** Plain

Date	Mintage	Good	VG	F	VF	XF
ND-//37	—	1.00	2.50	5.00	10.00	15.00
ND-//37 Restrike; Proof	—	Value: 65.00				

KM# A64 1/2 PICE (Trisul)

2.4500 g., Copper **Obverse:** Persian inscription **Obv. Inscription:** "Shah Alam II Badshah" **Reverse:** Inscription with value in Bengali, Persian and Hindi

Date	Mintage	Good	VG	F	VF	XF
ND(ca.1805) Rare	—	—	—	—	—	—

KM# 54 PICE

6.2300 g., Copper, 24.7 mm. **Mint:** Calcutta **Obverse:** Persian inscription **Obv. Inscription:** "Shah Alam II Badshah" **Reverse:** Inscription with value in Bengali, Persian and Hindi **Edge:** Plain

Date	Mintage	Good	VG	F	VF	XF
ND-//37	—	0.15	0.40	1.00	8.00	45.00
ND-//37 Restrike; Proof	—	Value: 80.00				

KM# 64 PICE

6.4800 g., Copper, 24.5 mm. **Obverse:** Persian inscription, julus **Obv. Inscription:** "Shah Alam II Badshah" **Reverse:** Inscription with value in Bengali, Persian and Hindi

Date	Mintage	Good	VG	F	VF	XF
ND-//45(1816)	—	35.00	75.00	120	200	—

KM# 55 PICE

6.4600 g., Copper, 27.2 mm. **Mint:** Calcutta **Obverse:** Persian inscription, julus **Obv. Inscription:** "Shah Alam II Badshah" **Reverse:** Inscription with value in Bengali, Persian and Hindi

Date	Mintage	Good	VG	F	VF	XF
ND-//37	—	0.15	0.40	1.00	8.00	45.00

KM# 29 PICE

5.8000 g., Copper **Mint:** Murshidabad **Obverse:** Persian inscription **Obv. Inscription:** "Falus..Shah Alam II" **Reverse:** Inscription with Persian mint name **Note:** Large flan, size varies 24.5-26.5mm.

Date	Mintage	Good	VG	F	VF	XF
ND-//37	—	1.25	3.00	6.00	10.00	16.00

KM# 30 PICE

5.8000 g., Copper **Mint:** Murshidabad **Obv. Inscription:** "Falus..Shah Alam II" **Reverse:** Crossbar on trisul, Persian mint name **Edge:** Plain **Note:** Size varies 23-24mm.

Date	Mintage	VG	F	VF	XF	Unc
ND-//37(1827)	—	2.50	4.50	8.50	13.50	—
ND-//37 Proof	—	Value: 80.00				

KM# 56 PICE

Copper, 26 mm. **Mint:** Calcutta **Obverse:** Persian inscription, julus **Obv. Inscription:** "Shah Alam II Badshah" **Reverse:** Value in Bengali, Persian and Hindi

Date	Mintage	Good	VG	F	VF	XF
ND-//37	—	0.50	1.25	3.00	6.00	35.00
ND-//37 Proof	—	Value: 200				

KM# 57 PICE

6.1300 g., Copper, 23 mm. **Mint:** Calcutta **Obverse:** Persian inscription, julus **Obv. Inscription:** "Shah Alam II Badshah" **Reverse:** Value in Bengali, Persian and Hindi

Date	Mintage	Good	VG	F	VF	XF
ND-//37	—	0.20	0.50	1.50	3.00	25.00
ND-//37 Proof	—	Value: 200				

KM# 65 PICE (Trisul)

2.4500 g., Copper **Obverse:** Persian inscription, julus **Obv. Inscription:** "Shah ALam II Badshah" **Reverse:** Value in Bengali, Persian and Hindi **Note:** Mint mark: TrisuL (trident).

Date	Mintage	Good	VG	F	VF	XF
ND-//45	—	0.60	1.50	3.00	10.00	45.00

KM# 71 PICE (Trisul)

2.4500 g., Copper **Mint:** Sagar **Obverse:** Persian inscription, julus, trisul (trident) **Obv. Inscription:** "Shah Alam II Badshah" **Reverse:** Value in Bengali, Persian and Hindi

Date	Mintage	Good	VG	F	VF	XF
ND-//45	—	0.60	1.50	3.00	10.00	45.00

KM# 72 PICE (Trisul)

2.4500 g., Copper **Mint:** Sagar **Obverse:** Persian inscription, trisul (trident), julus **Obv. Inscription:** "Shah Alam II Badshah" **Reverse:** Value in Bengali, Persian and Hindi, trisul (trident) **Note:** Mint mark: 6-petalled rosette

Date	Mintage	Good	VG	F	VF	XF
ND-//45	—	0.60	1.50	3.00	10.00	45.00

KM# A65 PICE (Trisul)

6.2000 g., Copper **Mint:** Sagar **Obverse:** Persian inscription, Trisul (trident), julus **Obv. Inscription:** "Shah Alam II Badshah" **Reverse:** Value in Bengali, Persian and Hindi, trisul (trident) **Note:** Weight varies 22-24mm. Mint mark: 6-pointed star.

Date	Mintage	Good	VG	F	VF	XF
ND-//45	—	—	—	—	—	—

KM# A55 2 PICE

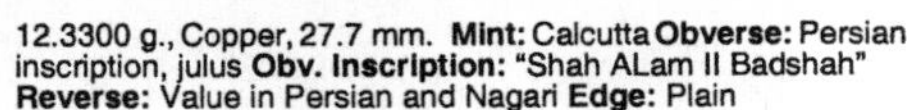

12.3300 g., Copper, 27.7 mm. **Mint:** Calcutta **Obverse:** Persian inscription, julus **Obv. Inscription:** "Shah ALam II Badshah" **Reverse:** Value in Persian and Nagari **Edge:** Plain

Date	Mintage	Good	VG	F	VF	XF
ND-//37	—	4.00	10.00	20.00	35.00	50.00
ND-//37 Restrike; Proof	—	Value: 100				

KM# 63 2 PICE

12.9600 g., Copper, 29 mm. **Mint:** Farrukhabad **Obverse:** Persian inscription, julus **Obv. Inscription:** "Shah Alam II Badshah" **Reverse:** Value in Bengali, Persian and Hindi

Date	Mintage	Good	VG	F	VF	XF
ND-//45	—	27.50	62.50	125	200	—

KM# 58 PIE

2.1600 g., Copper, 16.5 mm. **Mint:** Calcutta **Obverse:** Value in English and Bengali **Reverse:** Value in Bengali, Persian and Hindi

Date	Mintage	VG	F	VF	XF	Unc
ND(1831-35)	—	0.15	0.35	1.00	8.00	20.00
ND(1831-35) Proof	—	Value: 85.00				

KM# 59 1/2 ANNA

12.9500 g., Copper, 27.7 mm. **Obverse:** Value in English and Bengali **Reverse:** Value in Persian and Nagari **Edge:** Plain

Date	Mintage	Good	VG	F	VF	XF
ND(1831-35)	—	0.15	0.40	1.00	3.00	15.00
ND(1831-35) Proof	—	Value: 150				

KM# 66 1/4 RUPEE

2.8000 g., 0.9550 Silver **Mint:** Farrukhabad **Obverse:** Persian inscription, rosette at top **Obv. Inscription:** "Shah Alam II Badshah" **Reverse:** Inscription with Persian mint name **Edge:** Oblique milling

Date	Mintage	Good	VG	F	VF	XF
ND-//45	—	0.60	1.50	4.00	8.00	20.00

KM# 73 1/4 RUPEE

2.9200 g., 0.9090 Silver **Mint:** Calcutta and Banaras **Obv. Inscription:** "Shah Alam II Badshah" **Reverse:** Persian mint name **Note:** Mint name: Farrukhabad.

Date	Mintage	Good	VG	F	VF	XF
AH1204//45 Frozen	—	0.60	1.50	4.00	8.00	20.00

KM# ~~104 1/4 RUPEE~~

3.1000 g., Silver **Mint:** Calcutta **Obverse:** Persian inscription, couplet **Obv. Inscription:** "Shah Alam II Badshah" **Reverse:** Persian-sanat (year, mint name) **Edge:** Vertical milling **Note:** Mint name: Murshidabad.

Date	Mintage	Good	VG	F	VF	XF
AH1204//19 Frozen	—	0.25	0.60	1.50	5.00	15.00

KM# 67 1/4 RUPEE

2.9200 g., 0.9090 Silver **Mint:** Farrukhabad **Obv. Inscription:** "Shah Alam II Badshah" **Reverse:** Persian mint name **Edge:** Vertical milling **Note:** Mint name: Farrukhabad.

Date	Mintage	Good	VG	F	VF	XF
ND-//45	—	0.60	1.50	4.00	8.00	20.00

KM# 115 1/4 RUPEE

2.9000 g., Silver **Mint:** New Calcutta **Obv. Inscription:** "Shah Alam II Badshah" **Reverse:** Persian-sanat (year, mint name) **Edge:** Plain **Note:** Mint name: Murshidabad.

Date	Mintage	Good	VG	F	VF	XF
AH1204//19 Frozen	—	0.25	0.60	1.50	5.00	15.00

KM# 75 1/4 RUPEE

2.9200 g., 0.9090 Silver **Mint:** Calcutta **Obv. Inscription:** "Shah Alam II Badshah" **Reverse:** Persian mint name **Edge:** Plain **Note:** Mint name: Farrukhabad.

Date	Mintage	Good	VG	F	VF	XF
AH1204//45 Frozen	—	0.50	1.25	3.00	6.00	15.00
AH1204//45 Frozen; Proof	—	Value: 250				

KM# 97.2 1/2 RUPEE

5.8000 g., Silver **Mint:** Dacca **Obverse:** Persian inscription, couplet **Obv. Inscription:** "Shah Alam II Badshah" **Reverse:** Persian-julus (formula), mintname **Note:** Mint name: Murshidabad; Privy mark - center of first circle.

Date	Good	VG	F	VF	XF
ND-//19 Frozen	1.25	3.00	7.50	25.00	75.00

KM# 97.3 1/2 RUPEE

5.8000 g., Silver **Mint:** Murshidabad **Obverse:** Persian inscription, couplet **Obv. Inscription:** "Shah Alam II Badshah" **Reverse:** Persian-julus (formula), mintname **Note:** Privy mark - center of second circle.

Date	Mintage	Good	VG	F	VF	XF
ND-//19 Frozen	—	1.25	3.00	7.50	25.00	75.00

KM# 97.1 1/2 RUPEE

5.8000 g., Silver **Mint:** Calcutta **Obverse:** Persian inscription, couplet **Obv. Inscription:** "Shah Alam II Badshah" **Reverse:** Milling: Persian-julus (formula), mintname **Edge:** Oblique **Note:** Struck at Calcutta Darra, Murshidabad, Patna Mint. Mintname: Murshidabad. Privy mark - top line; mintmark: 6 petalled rosette.

Date	Mintage	Good	VG	F	VF	XF
AH-//19 Frozen	—	0.40	1.00	2.50	8.50	25.00

KM# 97.4 1/2 RUPEE

5.8000 g., Silver **Mint:** Patna **Obverse:** Persian inscription, couplet **Obv. Inscription:** "Shah Alam II Badshah" **Reverse:** Persian - julus (formula), mintname **Rev. Inscription:** "Murshidabad" **Note:** Struck at Patna Mint. Privy mark - center of third dot group.

Date	Mintage	Good	VG	F	VF	XF
ND-//19 Frozen	—	1.25	3.00	7.50	25.00	75.00
ND-//19 Proof; Frozen	—	Value: 400				

KM# 68 1/2 RUPEE

5.6000 g., 0.9550 Silver **Mint:** Farrukhabad **Obverse:** Persian inscription, couplet **Obv. Inscription:** "Shah Alam II Badshah" **Reverse:** Persian - julus (formula), mintname **Rev. Inscription:** "Zarb" **Edge:** Oblique milling

Date	Mintage	Good	VG	F	VF	XF
ND-//45	—	1.25	3.00	7.50	15.00	35.00

KM# 39 1/2 RUPEE

Silver **Mint:** Banaras **Obverse:** Daragah's marks within Persian inscription, stylized fish, couplet **Obv. Inscription:** "Shah Alam II Badshah" **Reverse:** Flower, Persian-julus (formula), mintname **Edge:** Oblique milling **Note:** Broad flan.

Date	Mintage	VG	F	VF	XF	Unc
AH1229//17-49	—	40.00	100	200	325	550

KM# 105 1/2 RUPEE

2.8000 g., Silver **Mint:** Murshidabad **Obverse:** Persian inscription, couplet **Obv. Inscription:** "Shah Alam II" **Reverse:** Persian-julus (formula), mintname Murshidabad **Edge:** Vertical milling

Date	Mintage	F	VF	XF	Unc
ND-//19(1819) Frozen	—	3.50	10.00	30.00	50.00
ND-//19(1819) Frozen; Proof	—	Value: 300			

KM# 74 1/2 RUPEE

5.8000 g., 0.9090 Silver **Obverse:** Persian inscription, couplet **Obv. Inscription:** "Shah Alam II Badshah" **Reverse:** Persian - julus (formula), Zarb Farrukhabad **Edge:** Vertical milling **Note:** Struck at Calcutta and Banaras.

Date	Mintage	Good	VG	F	VF	XF
ND-//45	—	1.25	3.00	7.50	15.00	35.00

KM# 116 1/2 RUPEE

2.8000 g., Silver **Obverse:** Persian inscription, couplet **Obv. Inscription:** "Shah Alam II Badshah" **Reverse:** Crescent at upper left, Persian-julus (formula), Murshidabad **Edge:** Plain **Note:** Struck at New Calcutta.

Date	Mintage	Good	VG	F	VF	XF
ND-//19 Frozen	—	0.50	1.35	3.50	10.00	30.00
ND-//19 Frozen; Proof	—	Value: 300				

KM# 76 1/2 RUPEE

5.8000 g., 0.9090 Silver **Obverse:** Persian inscription, couplet **Obv. Inscription:** "Shah Alam II Badshah" **Reverse:** Persian-julus (formula), Farrukhabad **Edge:** Plain **Note:** Struck at Calcutta.

Date	Mintage	Good	VG	F	VF	XF
ND-//45	—	0.75	2.00	5.00	10.00	25.00
ND-//45 Proof	—	Value: 300				

KM# 69 RUPEE

11.2100 g., 0.9550 Silver **Obverse:** Persian inscription, couplet **Obv. Inscription:** "Shah Alam II Badshah" **Reverse:** Persian - julus (formula), Zarb Farrukhabad **Edge:** Oblique milling **Note:** Struck at Farrukhabad and Calcutta.

Date	Mintage	Good	VG	F	VF	XF
ND-//45	—	0.75	2.00	5.00	10.00	30.00

KM# 42 RUPEE

Silver **Mint:** Muhammadabad Banaras **Obverse:** Darogah's marks within Persian inscription, stylized fish, couplet **Obv. Inscription:** "Shah Alam II Badshah" **Reverse:** Flower, Persian-julus (formula), mintname **Edge:** Oblique milling **Note:** Broad flan.

Date	Mintage	Good	VG	F	VF	XF
AH1229//17-49	—	25.00	—	60.00	120	200

KM# 108 RUPEE

11.6000 g., Silver **Obverse:** Star added, Persian inscription, couplet **Obv. Inscription:** "Shah Alam II Badshah" **Reverse:** Persian-julus (formula), mintname Murshidabad **Edge:** Vertical milling

Date	Mintage	VG	F	VF	XF	Unc
ND-//19	—	2.00	5.00	8.50	15.00	50.00

KM# 109 RUPEE

11.6000 g., Silver **Obverse:** Persian inscription, couplet **Obv. Inscription:** "Shah Alam II Badshah" **Reverse:** Privy mark "S" at upper left, Persian-julus (formula), mintname Murshidabad

Date	Mintage	VG	F	VF	XF	Unc
ND-//19	—	6.00	15.00	25.00	60.00	100

KM# 70 RUPEE

11.6800 g., 0.9090 Silver **Mint:** Farrukhabad, Calcutta, Banaras, Sagar **Obverse:** Persian inscription, couplet **Obv. Inscription:** "Shah Alam II Badshah" **Reverse:** Persian - julus (formula), Zarb Farrukhabad **Edge:** Vertical milling **Note:** Struck at Farrukhabad, Calcutta, Banaras, and Sagar

Date	Mintage	VG	F	VF	XF	Unc
ND-//45	—	2.00	5.00	10.00	30.00	75.00

KM# 117 RUPEE

11.6000 g., Silver **Mint:** New Calcutta **Obverse:** Persian inscription, couplet **Obv. Inscription:** "Shah Alam II Badshah" **Reverse:** Crescent at upper left, Persian-julus (formula), mintname Murshidabad

Date	Mintage	Good	VG	F	VF	XF
ND-//19	—	0.85	2.25	5.50	11.50	22.50
ND-//19 Proof	—	Value: 350				

KM# 77 RUPEE

11.6800 g., 0.9090 Silver **Mint:** Calcutta **Obverse:** Persian inscription, couplet, thin rim **Obv. Inscription:** "Shah Alam II Badshah" **Reverse:** Persian - julus (formula), Zarb, mintname Farrukhabad, thin rim **Edge:** Plain **Note:** Mintmark: Crescent.

Date	Mintage	Good	VG	F	VF	XF
ND-//45	—	0.60	1.50	4.00	8.00	25.00
ND-//45 Proof	—	Value: 400				

KM# 78 RUPEE

11.6800 g., 0.9090 Silver **Mint:** Farrukhabad **Obverse:** Persian inscription, couplet, broad rims **Obv. Inscription:** "Shah Alam II Badshah" **Reverse:** Persian - julus (formula), Zarb, mintname Farrukhabad, broad rims **Edge:** Plain **Note:** Without mint mark.

Date	Mintage	Good	VG	F	VF	XF
ND-//45	—	—	2.00	5.00	12.00	30.00
ND-//45 Proof	—	Value: 400				

KM# 100 1/4 MOHUR

3.0900 g., 0.9960 Gold **Mint:** Murshidabad **Obv. Inscription:** "Shah Alam II Badshah" **Reverse:** Sanat, mintname **Edge:** Oblique milling

Date	Mintage	Good	VG	F	VF	XF
AH1204//19 Frozen	—	30.00	BV	45.00	75.00	150

KM# 110 1/4 MOHUR

3.3100 g., 0.9170 Gold **Mint:** Murshidabad **Obv. Inscription:** "Shah Alam II Badshah" **Reverse:** Sanat, mintname Murshidabad **Edge:** Vertical milling

Date	Mintage	Good	VG	F	VF	XF
AH1204//19 Frozen	—	BV	30.00	50.00	90.00	175
AH1204//19 Frozen; Proof	—	Value: 1,250				

KM# 111 1/2 MOHUR

6.6300 g., 0.9170 Gold **Mint:** Murshidabad **Obverse:** Persian inscription, couplet **Obv. Inscription:** "Shah Alam II Badshah" **Reverse:** Persian-julus (formula), mintname Murshidabad **Edge:** Vertical milling

Date	Mintage	Good	VG	F	VF	XF
AH1202//19	—	BV	60.00	100	200	350
AH1202//19 Proof	—	Value: 1,500				

KM# 101 1/2 MOHUR

6.1800 g., 0.9960 Gold **Mint:** Calcutta **Obverse:** Persian inscription, couplet **Obv. Inscription:** "Shah Alam II Badshah" **Reverse:** Persian-julus (formula), mintname Murshidabad **Edge:** Oblique milling

Date	Mintage	VG	F	VF	XF	Unc
AH1202//19	—	60.00	100	200	350	—

KM# 103 MOHUR

12.3600 g., 0.9960 Gold **Obverse:** Persian inscription, couplet **Obv. Inscription:** "Shah Alam II Badshah" **Reverse:** Persian-julus (formula), mintname Murshidabad **Edge:** Oblique milling **Note:** Struck at Calcutta and Murshidabad Mints.

Date	Mintage	VG	F	VF	XF	Unc
AH1202//19	—	BV	150	250	350	—

KM# 112 MOHUR

13.2600 g., 0.9170 Gold **Mint:** Calcutta **Obverse:** Persian inscription, couplet **Obv. Inscription:** "Shah Alam II Badshah" **Reverse:** Persian-julus (formula), mintname Murshidabad **Edge:** Vertical milling

Date	Mintage	Good	VG	F	VF	XF
AH1202//19	—	BV	110	175	250	400
AH1202//19 Proof	—	Value: 1,650				

KM# 113 MOHUR

12.3600 g., 0.9170 Gold **Mint:** Murshidabad **Obverse:** Persian inscription, couplet, low relief **Obv. Inscription:** "Shah Alam II Badshah" **Reverse:** Persian-julus (formula), mintname Murshidabad, low relief **Edge:** Oblique milling

Date	Mintage	Good	VG	F	VF	XF
AH1202//19	—	BV	BV	150	200	350

KM# 114 MOHUR

12.3600 g., 0.9170 Gold **Obverse:** Persian inscription, couplet **Obv. Inscription:** "Shah Alam II Badshah" **Reverse:** Persian-julus (formula), mintname Murshidabad **Note:** Mint mark: crescent.

Date	Mintage	Good	VG	F	VF	XF
AH1202//19	—	BV	BV	175	300	450
AH1202//19 Proof	—	Value: 1,750				

PATTERNS

Including off metal strikes

Due to extensive revisions and new information, the following section in part is listed by Pridmore(P#) numbers. These are in reference to The Coins of the Commonwealth of Nations, Part 4, India - Volume I: East India Company Presidency Series ca. 1642-1835, by F. Pridmore (Spink and Son, Ltd.).

KM#	Date	Mintage	Identification	Mkt Val
Pn1.1	AH1229//49	—	1/4 Rupee. Silver. Oblique milling edge. P293.	—
Pn2.1	AH1229//17-49	—	1/2 Rupee. Silver. Oblique milling edge. P292.	—
Pn3.1	AH1229//17-49	—	Rupee. Silver. Oblique milling edge. P291.	600

KM#	Date	Mintage	Identification	Mkt Val
Pn20	AH-//48	—	1/4 Pice. Copper. Prid.#302.	—

KM#	Date	Mintage	Identification	Mkt Val
Pn21	AH1221//48	—	2 Pice. Copper. Prid.#303.	600

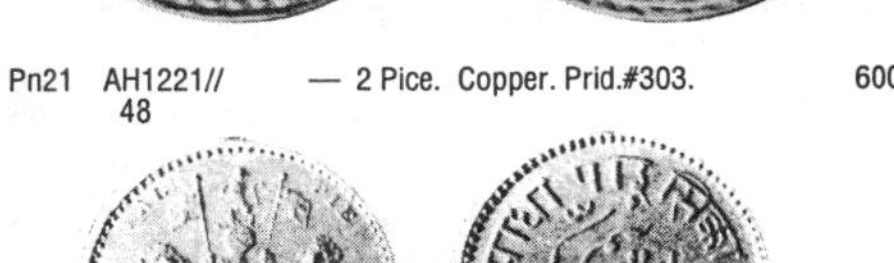

KM#	Date	Mintage	Identification	Mkt Val
Pn22	AH1809	—	1/2 Pie. Copper. Prid.#395.	200
Pn22a	AH1809	—	1/2 Pie. Copper Gilt. Prid.#394.	—
Pn22b	AH1809	—	1/2 Pie. Silver. Prid.#393.	—
Pn22c	AH1809	—	1/2 Pie. Gold. Prid.#392.	—

KM#	Date	Mintage	Identification	Mkt Val
Pn23	AH1809	—	Pice. Copper. Prid.#384.	300

KM#	Date	Mintage	Identification	Mkt Val
Pn24	AH1809	—	Pie. Pewter. No motto on scroll, Prid.#390.	—
Pn24a	AH1809	—	Pie. Copper. Thick planchet, Prid.#389.	300
Pn24b	AH1809	—	Pie. Copper. Thin planchet, Prid.#389a.	—
Pn24c	AH1809	—	Pie. Copper Gilt. Prid.#388.	—
Pn24d	AH1809	—	Pie. Silver. Prid.#387.	—
Pn24e	AH1809	—	Pie. Gold. Prid.#386.	—

KM#	Date	Mintage	Identification	Mkt Val
Pn25	AH1228//49	—	Pie. Copper. Prid.#380A.	—

KM#	Date	Mintage	Identification	Mkt Val
Pn26	AH(1818)	—	Rupee. Silver. Prid.#361.	3,000

TRIAL STRIKES

KM#	Date	Mintage	Identification	Mkt Val
TS3	AH1809	—	1/2 Pie. Copper. 1.7800 g. 21.5 mm. U.E.I. Co. crest lion. Uniface, P#396.	—

KM#	Date	Mintage	Identification	Mkt Val
TS4	AH1809	—	Pie. Copper. 7.8500 g. 27.5 mm. U.E.I. Co. arms. Prid.#385.	—

BOMBAY PRESIDENCY

Following a naval victory over the Portuguese on December 24, 1612 negotiations were started that developed into the opening of the first East India Company factory in Surat in 1613. Silver coins for the New World as well as various other foreign coins were used in early trade. Within the decade the Mughal mint at Surat was melting all of these foreign coins and re-minting them as various denominations of Mughal coinage.

Bombay became an English holding as part of the dowry of Catherine of Braganza, Princess of Portugal when she was betrothed to Charles II of England. Also included in the dowry was Tangier and $500,000. With this acquisition the trading center of the Indian West Coast moved from Surat to Bombay.

Possession of Bombay Island took place on February 8, 1665 and by 1672 the East India Company had a mint in Bombay to serve their trading interests. European designed coins were struck here until 1717. Experimental issues of Mughal style rupees with regnal years pertaining to the reigns of James II and William and Mary were made in 1693-94.

From 1717 to 1778 the Mughal style Bombay rupee was the principal coin of the West India trade, although bulk foreign coins were used for striking rupees at Surat.

After the East India Company took over the city of Surat in 1800 they slowed the mint production and finally transferred all activity to Bombay in 1815.

MINTS

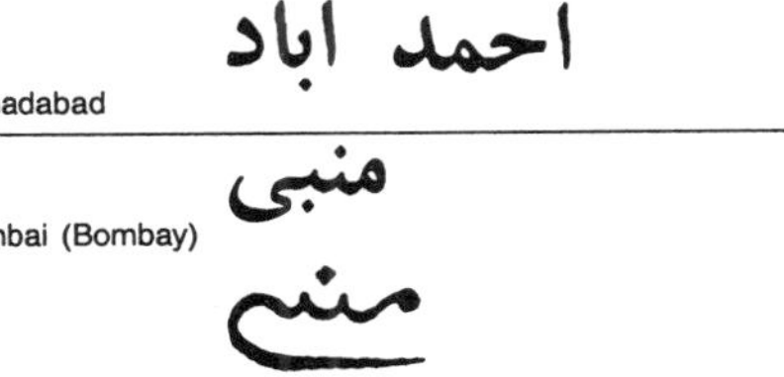

Ahmadabad

Mumbai (Bombay)

Mint name:

SILVER COINAGE

Privy Marks

Mint privy marks on dump issues often were intended to be "secret" (=privy marks), indicating changes in standards as well as mint of origin. The following chart is derived from IV Pridmore.

Privy marks involve the 3 diamonds and 4 dots in center line of obverse.

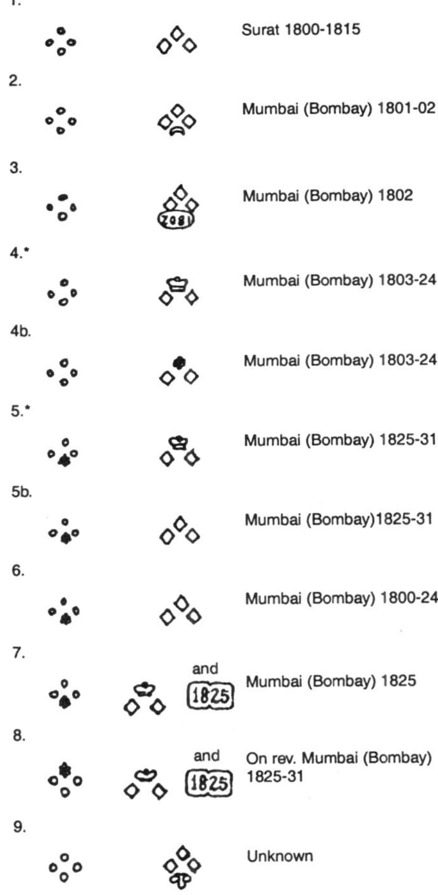

***NOTE:** Crown also may be inverted.

COLONIAL

HAMMERED COINAGE

KM# 219 1/4 PICE

2.6500 g., Copper **Obverse:** U.E.I. Co. bale mark **Reverse:** Scales, Persian "Adil" (just)

Date	Mintage	Good	VG	F	VF	XF
1816	—	6.00	15.00	45.00	75.00	—
1821	—	6.00	15.00	45.00	75.00	—
1825	—	6.00	15.00	45.00	75.00	—

KM# 197 1/2 PICE

5.3100 g., Copper **Obverse:** U.E.I. Co bale mark **Reverse:** Scales, Persian "Adil" (just)

Date	Mintage	Good	VG	F	VF	XF
1802	—	3.00	10.00	30.00	75.00	—
1808	—	3.00	10.00	30.00	75.00	—
1810	—	3.00	10.00	30.00	75.00	—
1813	—	3.00	10.00	30.00	75.00	—
1815	—	3.00	10.00	30.00	75.00	—
1816	—	3.00	10.00	30.00	75.00	—
1818	—	3.00	10.00	30.00	75.00	—
1819	—	3.00	10.00	30.00	75.00	—
1825	—	3.00	10.00	30.00	75.00	—
1826	—	3.00	10.00	30.00	75.00	—
1827	—	3.00	10.00	30.00	75.00	—
1829	—	3.00	10.00	30.00	75.00	—

KM# 202 1/2 PICE

Copper, 9 mm. **Obverse:** U.E.I.Co. bale mark **Reverse:** Date **Note:** Weight varies 0.90-1.20 grams.

Date	Mintage	Good	VG	F	VF	XF
1803	—	3.00	10.00	30.00	75.00	—

KM# 225 1/2 PICE

3.7600 g., Copper **Obverse:** U.E.I. Co. bale mark **Reverse:** Scales, value in Hindi, date in Devanagari script **Note:** Size varies 17-18mm. Struck at local Southern Concan.

Date	Mintage	Good	VG	F	VF	XF
1820	—	3.00	10.00	35.00	100	—
1821	—	3.00	10.00	35.00	100	—

KM# 198 PICE

10.6200 g., Copper **Obverse:** U.E.I. Co. bale mark **Reverse:** Scales, Persian "Adil" (just)

Date	Mintage	Good	VG	F	VF	XF
1802	—	0.75	2.00	5.00	12.00	40.00
1803	—	0.75	2.00	5.00	12.00	40.00
1804	—	0.75	2.00	5.00	12.00	40.00
1808	—	0.75	2.00	5.00	12.00	40.00
1809	—	0.75	2.00	5.00	12.00	40.00
1810	—	0.75	2.00	5.00	12.00	40.00
1813	—	0.75	2.00	5.00	12.00	40.00
1815	—	0.75	2.00	5.00	12.00	40.00
1816	—	0.75	2.00	5.00	12.00	40.00
1818	—	0.75	2.00	5.00	12.00	40.00
1819	—	0.75	2.00	5.00	12.00	40.00
1825	—	0.75	2.00	5.00	12.00	40.00
1826	—	0.75	2.00	5.00	12.00	40.00
1827	—	0.75	2.00	5.00	12.00	40.00
1828	—	0.75	2.00	5.00	12.00	40.00
1829	—	0.75	2.00	5.00	12.00	40.00

KM# 203 PICE

Copper **Mint:** Calicut **Obverse:** Center of U.E.I. Co. bale mark **Reverse:** Date **Note:** Weight varies 2.20-2.85 grams.

Date	Mintage	Good	VG	F	VF	XF
1803	—	1.25	3.00	10.00	30.00	75.00
1807	—	1.25	3.00	10.00	30.00	75.00

KM# 226 PICE

Copper **Obverse:** U.E.I. Co. bale mark **Reverse:** Scales, value in Hindi, date in Devanagari script **Note:** Struck at local Southern Concan. Size varies 20-22mm, weight varies 7.00-7.55 grams.

Date	Mintage	Good	VG	F	VF	XF
1820	—	5.00	20.00	60.00	125	—
1821	—	5.00	20.00	60.00	125	—

KM# 227 PICE

6.7000 g., Copper, 20 mm. **Obverse:** U.E.I. Co. bale mark **Reverse:** Date

Date	Mintage	Good	VG	F	VF	XF
1829	—	5.00	15.00	45.00	125	—

KM# 199 2 PICE (8 Reas = Nim (1/2) Anna)

21.2500 g., Copper **Obverse:** U.E.I. Co. bale mark **Reverse:** Scales, value 2 above Persian "Adil" (just)

Date	Mintage	Good	VG	F	VF	XF
1802	—	2.50	6.00	11.00	30.00	—
1803	—	2.50	6.00	11.00	30.00	—
1804	—	2.50	6.00	11.00	30.00	—
1808	—	3.50	8.00	15.00	35.00	—

KM# 206 2 PICE (8 Reas = Nim (1/2) Anna)

12.9500 g., Copper, 30.5 mm. **Obverse:** E.I. Co. arms **Reverse:** Scales, Persian "Adil" (just)

Date	Mintage	Good	VG	F	VF	XF
1804//AH1219	—	0.15	0.40	1.00	10.00	50.00
1804//AH1219 Proof	—	Value: 120				

KM# 206a 2 PICE (8 Reas = Nim (1/2) Anna)

Copper Gilt **Obverse:** E.I. Co. arms **Reverse:** Scales, Persian "Adil" (just)

Date	Mintage	Good	VG	F	VF	XF
1804//AH1219 Proof	—	Value: 175				

KM# 207 2 PICE (8 Reas = Nim (1/2) Anna)

Copper **Obverse:** KM#206 **Reverse:** Madras 20 Cash, KM#321 **Note:** Mule.

Date	Mintage	Good	VG	F	VF	XF
ND(1804) Proof	—	Value: 175				

KM# 200 2 PICE (8 Reas = Nim (1/2) Anna)

21.2500 g., Copper **Obverse:** U.E.I. Co. bale mark **Reverse:** Without value "2" above Persian "Adil"

Date	Mintage	Good	VG	F	VF	XF
1808	—	1.00	3.00	15.00	45.00	—
1809	—	1.00	3.00	15.00	45.00	—
1810	—	1.00	3.00	15.00	45.00	—
1813	—	1.00	3.00	15.00	45.00	—
1816	—	1.00	3.00	15.00	45.00	—
1818	—	1.00	3.00	15.00	45.00	—
1819	—	1.00	3.00	15.00	45.00	—
1825	—	1.00	3.00	15.00	45.00	—
1826	—	1.00	3.00	15.00	45.00	—
1827	—	—	—	—	—	—
Note: Reported, not confirmed						
1828	—	1.00	3.00	15.00	45.00	—
1829	—	1.00	3.00	15.00	45.00	—

KM# 201 4 PICE

42.5100 g., Copper **Obverse:** U.E.I. Co. bale mark **Reverse:** Scales, value "4" above Persian-Adil (just)

Date	Mintage	Good	VG	F	VF	XF
1802	—	20.00	50.00	100	200	350
1803	—	20.00	50.00	100	200	350
1804	—	20.00	50.00	100	200	350
1816	—	22.50	55.00	110	220	375

KM# 228 1/2 ANNA

15.6000 g., Copper **Obverse:** U.E.I. Co bale mark **Reverse:** Scales, value in Hindi, date in Devanagari script **Note:** Struck at local Southern Concan. Size varies 23-24mm.

Date	Mintage	Good	VG	F	VF	XF
1820	—	2.00	5.00	10.00	35.00	100
1821	—	2.00	5.00	10.00	35.00	100

KM# 229 1/2 ANNA

13.6000 g., Copper, 22.5 mm. **Obverse:** U.E.I. Col. bale mark **Reverse:** Scales, Western date

Date	Mintage	Good	VG	F	VF	XF
1828	—	3.00	7.50	15.00	45.00	125
1829	—	3.00	7.50	15.00	45.00	125

KM# 208 1/16 RUPEE

0.7200 g., Silver **Mint:** Surat **Obverse:** Persian inscription, couplet **Obv. Inscription:** "Shah Alam II Badshah" **Reverse:** Persian-julus (formula), mint name

Date	Mintage	Good	VG	F	VF	XF
ND-//46	—	3.50	8.50	20.00	50.00	100

KM# 256 1/16 RUPEE

0.7200 g., Silver **Mint:** Ahmadabad **Obverse:** Persian inscription, couplet **Obv. Inscription:** "Muhammad Akbar II" **Reverse:** Persian-julus (formula), mint name

Date	Mintage	Good	VG	F	VF	XF
AH1234//12 Frozen	—	2.50	6.00	18.00	30.00	50.00

KM# 209.1 1/8 RUPEE

1.4400 g., Silver **Mint:** Surat **Obverse:** Persian inscription, couplet **Obv. Inscription:** "Shah Alam II Badshah" **Reverse:** Persian-julus (formula), mintname **Note:** Privy mark #1.

Date	Mintage	Good	VG	F	VF	XF
ND-//46	—	3.00	7.50	13.50	25.00	42.00

KM# 209.2 1/8 RUPEE

1.4400 g., Silver **Mint:** Mumbai **Obverse:** Persian inscription, couplet **Obv. Inscription:** "Shah Alam II Badshah" **Reverse:** Persian-julus (formula), mintname **Note:** Privy mark #6.

Date	Mintage	Good	VG	F	VF	XF
ND-//46	—	3.00	7.50	13.50	25.00	42.00

KM# 257 1/8 RUPEE

11.4400 g., Silver **Mint:** Ahmadabad **Obverse:** Persian inscription, couplet **Obv. Inscription:** "Muhammad Akbar II" **Reverse:** Persian-julus (formula), mint name **Note:** See note after Rupee KM#260. Size varies 11-14mm.

Date	Mintage	Good	VG	F	VF	XF
AH1234//12 Frozen	—	3.00	7.50	13.50	25.00	42.00
AH1248	—	3.00	7.50	13.50	25.00	42.00

KM# 215 1/8 RUPEE

1.4400 g., Silver **Mint:** Mumbai **Obverse:** Persian inscription, couplet **Obv. Inscription:** "Shah Alam II Badshah" **Reverse:** Persian-Julus (formula), mint name **Note:** Privy mark #8.

Date	Mintage	Good	VG	F	VF	XF
1825//46	—	3.00	7.50	13.50	25.00	42.00

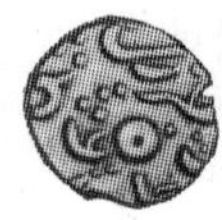

KM# 277 1/5 RUPEE

2.3200 g., Silver **Mint:** Mumbai **Obverse:** Persian-Zarb, mint name, Shah Alam (II) julus **Reverse:** "T" between scales **Note:** Mint name: Mumbai, struck at Calicut for Tellicherry.

Date	Mintage	VG	F	VF	XF	Unc
1805(1805)	—	1.00	2.00	5.00	15.00	—

KM# 210.1 1/4 RUPEE

2.8800 g., Silver **Mint:** Surat **Obverse:** Persian inscription, couplet **Obv. Inscription:** "Shah Alam II Badshah" **Reverse:** Persian-julus (formula), mintname **Note:** Privy mark #1.

Date	Mintage	Good	VG	F	VF	XF
ND-//46	—	0.60	1.50	5.00	10.00	15.00

KM# 210.2 1/4 RUPEE

2.8800 g., Silver **Mint:** Mumbai **Obverse:** Persian inscription, couplet **Obv. Inscription:** "Shah Alam II Badshah" **Reverse:** Persian-julus (formula), mintname **Note:** Privy mark #7.

Date	Mintage	Good	VG	F	VF	XF
ND-//46	—	0.60	1.50	5.00	10.00	15.00

KM# 210.3 1/4 RUPEE

2.8800 g., Silver **Mint:** Mumbai **Obverse:** Persian inscription, couplet **Obv. Inscription:** "Shah Alam II Badshah" **Reverse:** Persian-julus (formula), mint name **Note:** Privy mark #7.

Date	Mintage	Good	VG	F	VF	XF
ND-//46	—	—	—	—	—	—

KM# 216 1/4 RUPEE

2.9100 g., Silver **Mint:** Mumbai **Obverse:** Persian inscription, couplet **Obv. Inscription:** "Shah Alam II Badshah" **Reverse:** Persian-julus (formula), mint name **Note:** Privy mark #8.

Date	Mintage	Good	VG	F	VF	XF
1825//46	—	3.00	7.50	13.50	25.00	42.00

KM# 211.1 1/2 RUPEE (1/2 Angelina)

5.7600 g., Silver **Mint:** Surat **Obverse:** Persian inscription, couplet **Obv. Inscription:** "Shah Alam II Badshah" **Reverse:** Persian-julus (formula), mintname **Note:** Privy mark #1.

Date	Mintage	Good	VG	F	VF	XF
ND-//46	—	1.35	3.50	7.50	15.00	25.00

KM# 211.2 1/2 RUPEE (1/2 Angelina)

5.7600 g., Silver **Mint:** Mumbai **Obverse:** Persian inscription, couplet **Obv. Inscription:** "Shah Alam II Badshah" **Reverse:** Persian-julus (formula), mintname **Note:** Privy mark #6. For listings of coins with regnal year 52 see India-French.

Date	Mintage	Good	VG	F	VF	XF
ND-//46	—	1.35	3.50	7.50	15.00	25.00

KM# 259.1 1/2 RUPEE (1/2 Angelina)

5.8300 g., Silver **Mint:** Ahmadabad **Obverse:** Date at upper right above line, Persian inscription, couplet **Obv. Inscription:** "Muhammad Akbar II" **Reverse:** Persian-julus (formula), mint name

Date	Mintage	Good	VG	F	VF	XF
AH1239//15 Frozen	—	2.00	5.00	10.00	20.00	38.00

KM# 217.1 1/2 RUPEE (1/2 Angelina)

5.8300 g., Silver **Mint:** Mumbai **Obverse:** Persian inscription, couplet **Obv. Inscription:** "Shah Alam II Badshah" **Reverse:** Persian-julus (formula), mint name **Note:** Privy mark #7.

Date	Mintage	Good	VG	F	VF	XF
1825//46	—	2.75	6.50	12.50	25.00	42.00

KM# 217.2 1/2 RUPEE (1/2 Angelina)

5.8300 g., Silver **Mint:** Mumbai **Obverse:** Persian inscription, couplet **Obv. Inscription:** "Shah Alam II Badshah" **Reverse:** Persian-julus (formula), mint name **Note:** Privy mark #8.

Date	Mintage	Good	VG	F	VF	XF
1825-31//46	—	2.00	5.00	10.00	20.00	35.00

KM# 217.3 1/2 RUPEE (1/2 Angelina)

5.8300 g., Silver **Mint:** Mumbai **Note:** Privy mark #9.

Date	Mintage	Good	VG	F	VF	XF
ND-//46	—	4.00	10.00	20.00	45.00	—

KM# 259.2 1/2 RUPEE (1/2 Angelina)

5.8300 g., Silver **Mint:** Ahmadabad **Obverse:** Date at left below line **Note:** See note after Rupee, KM#260.

Date	Mintage	Good	VG	F	VF	XF
AH1242	—	2.00	5.00	10.00	20.00	38.00
AH1243	—	2.00	5.00	10.00	20.00	38.00
AH1248	—	2.00	5.00	10.00	20.00	38.00

KM# 212.1 RUPEE

11.5900 g., Silver **Mint:** Surat **Note:** Privy mark #1.

Date	Mintage	Good	VG	F	VF	XF
ND-//46	—	2.75	7.00	10.00	15.00	25.00

KM# 212.2 RUPEE

11.5900 g., Silver **Mint:** Mumbai **Note:** Privy mark #6. For coins with regnal years 51-54 see India-French listings.

Date	Mintage	Good	VG	F	VF	XF
ND-//46	—	2.75	7.00	10.00	15.00	25.00

KM# 260.1 RUPEE

11.5900 g., Silver **Mint:** Ahmadabad **Obverse:** Date at upper right above line, Persian inscription, couplet **Obv. Inscription:** "Muhammad Akbar II" **Reverse:** Persian-julus (formula), mint name

Date	Mintage	Good	VG	F	VF	XF
AH1233//11	—	2.50	6.00	10.00	15.00	25.00
AH1233//12	—	2.50	6.00	10.00	15.00	25.00
AH1234//12	—	2.50	6.00	10.00	15.00	25.00
AH1234//13	—	2.50	6.00	10.00	15.00	25.00
AH1235//13	—	2.50	6.00	10.00	15.00	25.00
AH1235//14	—	2.50	6.00	10.00	15.00	25.00
AH1236//13 Frozen	—	2.50	6.00	10.00	15.00	25.00
AH1236//14 Frozen	—	2.50	6.00	10.00	15.00	25.00
AH1239//15 Frozen	—	2.50	6.00	10.00	15.00	25.00
AH1241//16 Frozen	—	2.50	6.00	10.00	15.00	25.00

KM# 218.1 RUPEE

11.6600 g., Silver **Obverse:** Persian inscription, couplet **Obv. Inscription:** "Shah Alam II Badshah" **Reverse:** Persian-julus (formula), mint name **Note:** Mint name: Surat, struck at Mumbai. Privy mark #7.

Date	Mintage	Good	VG	F	VF	XF
1825//46	—	3.00	7.50	12.50	20.00	35.00

KM# 218.2 RUPEE

11.6600 g., Silver **Obverse:** Persian inscription, couplet **Obv. Inscription:** "Shah Alam II Badshah" **Reverse:** Persian-julus (formula), mint name **Note:** Mint name: Surat, struck at Mumbai. Privy mark #8.

Date	Mintage	Good	VG	F	VF	XF
1825-31//46	—	3.00	7.50	12.50	20.00	35.00

KM# 218.3 RUPEE

11.6600 g., Silver **Obverse:** Persian inscription, couplet **Obv. Inscription:** "Shah Alam II" **Reverse:** Persian-julus (formula), mint name **Note:** Mint name: Surat, struck at Mumbai. Privy mark #9.

Date	Mintage	Good	VG	F	VF	XF
ND-//46 Rare	—	—	—	—	—	—

KM# 260.2 RUPEE

11.5900 g., Silver **Mint:** Ahmadabad **Obverse:** Date at left below line **Note:** Ahmadabad Mint was acquired by the British in 1818AD/AH1233 and finally closed in 1835AD. For other issues, see Mughals, Baroda, and Ahmadabad. Symbols as on Ahmadabad State Issues (q.v.), struck in the name of Muhammad Akbar II.

Date	Mintage	Good	VG	F	VF	XF
AH1242	—	2.50	6.00	10.00	15.00	25.00
AH1243	—	2.50	6.00	10.00	15.00	25.00
AH1244	—	2.50	6.00	10.00	15.00	25.00
AH1248	—	2.50	6.00	10.00	15.00	25.00
AH1249	—	2.50	6.00	10.00	15.00	25.00
AH1250	—	2.50	6.00	10.00	15.00	25.00
AH1251	—	2.50	6.00	10.00	15.00	25.00

KM# 213 1/15 MOHUR (Gold Rupee)

0.7700 g., Gold **Mint:** Surat **Obverse:** Persian inscription, couplet **Obv. Inscription:** "Shah Alam II Badshah" **Reverse:** Persian-julus (formula), mintname **Note:** Size varies 7-8mm.

Date	Mintage	Good	VG	F	VF	XF
AH-//46	—	—	27.50	45.00	75.00	135

KM# 236 1/15 MOHUR (Gold Rupee)

0.7700 g., Gold **Mint:** Mumbai **Obverse:** Persian inscription, couplet **Obv. Inscription:** "Shah Alam II Badshah" **Reverse:** Persian-julus (formula), mint name **Note:** Size varies 7-8mm. Privy mark: Crescent.

Date	Mintage	Good	VG	F	VF	XF
ND-//46	—	35.00	60.00	100	250	350

KM# 237.1 1/15 MOHUR (Gold Rupee)

0.7700 g., Gold **Mint:** Mumbai **Obverse:** Persian inscription, couplet **Obv. Inscription:** "Shah Alam II Badshah" **Reverse:** Persian-julus (formula), mint name **Note:** Size varies 7-8mm. Privy mark #4b.

Date	Mintage	Good	VG	F	VF	XF
ND-//46	—	21.50	35.00	75.00	140	250

KM# 237.2 1/15 MOHUR (Gold Rupee)

0.7700 g., Gold **Mint:** Mumbai **Obverse:** Persian inscription, couplet **Obv. Inscription:** "Shah Alam II Badshah" **Reverse:** Persian-julus (formula), mint name **Note:** Size varies 7-8mm. Privy mark #5b.

Date	Mintage	Good	VG	F	VF	XF
ND-//46	—	—	27.50	45.00	75.00	135

KM# 239 PANCHIA (1/3 Mohur)

3.8600 g., Gold **Mint:** Surat **Obverse:** Persian inscription, couplet **Obv. Inscription:** "Shah Alam II Badshah" **Reverse:** Persian-julus (formula), mint name

Date	Mintage	Good	VG	F	VF	XF
ND-//46	—	27.50	45.00	75.00	125	250

KM# 240 PANCHIA (1/3 Mohur)

3.8600 g., Gold **Mint:** Mumbai **Obverse:** Persian inscription, couplet **Obv. Inscription:** "Shah Alam II Badshah" **Reverse:** Persian-julus (formula), mint name **Note:** Privy mark: crescent.

Date	Mintage	Good	VG	F	VF	XF
ND-//46	—	55.00	90.00	150	250	375

KM# 241 PANCHIA (1/3 Mohur)

3.8600 g., Gold **Mint:** Mumbai **Note:** Privy mark: inverted date.

Date	Mintage	VG	F	VF	XF	Unc
1802//46(1802)	—	120	200	350	500	—

KM# 243 PANCHIA (1/3 Mohur)

3.8600 g., Gold **Mint:** Mumbai **Obverse:** Persian inscription, couplet **Obv. Inscription:** "Shah Alam II Badshah" **Reverse:** Persian-julus (formula), mint name **Note:** Privy mark: normal crown.

Date	Mintage	Good	VG	F	VF	XF
ND-//46	—	27.50	45.00	75.00	125	250

KM# 245 PANCHIA (1/3 Mohur)

3.8600 g., Gold **Mint:** Mumbai **Obverse:** Persian inscription, couplet **Obv. Inscription:** "Shah Alam II Badshah" **Reverse:** Persian-julus (formula), mint name **Note:** Privy mark: inverted crown.

Date	Mintage	Good	VG	F	VF	XF
ND-//46	—	27.50	45.00	75.00	125	250

KM# 247 PANCHIA (1/3 Mohur)

3.8800 g., Gold **Mint:** Mumbai **Obverse:** Persian inscription, couplet **Obv. Inscription:** "Shah Alam II Badshah" **Reverse:** Persian-julus (formula), mint name **Note:** Privy mark: Normal crown and 6 petal rosette

Date	Mintage	Good	VG	F	VF	XF
ND-//46	—	27.50	45.00	75.00	125	250

KM# 249 PANCHIA (1/3 Mohur)

3.8800 g., Gold **Mint:** Mumbai **Obverse:** Persian inscription, couplet **Obv. Inscription:** "Shah Alam II Badshah" **Reverse:** Persian-julus (formula), mint name **Note:** Privy mark: Inverted crown and 6 petal rosette.

Date	Mintage	Good	VG	F	VF	XF
ND-//46	—	27.50	45.00	75.00	125	250

KM# 242 MOHUR (15 Rupees)

11.5900 g., Gold **Mint:** Mumbai **Obverse:** Persian inscription, couplet **Obv. Inscription:** "Shah Alam II Badshah" **Reverse:** Persian-julus (formula), mint name **Note:** Privy mark: crescent.

Date	Mintage	Good	VG	F	VF	XF
ND-//46	—	200	350	650	1,200	2,000

KM# 214 MOHUR (15 Rupees)

11.5900 g., Gold **Mint:** Surat **Obverse:** Persian inscription, couplet **Obv. Inscription:** "Shah Alam II Badshah" **Reverse:** Persian-julus (formula), mint name **Note:** Size varies 16-19mm.

Date	Mintage	Good	VG	F	VF	XF
ND-//46	—	BV	100	175	250	350

KM# 246 MOHUR (15 Rupees)

11.5900 g., Gold **Mint:** Mumbai **Obverse:** Persian inscription, couplet **Obv. Inscription:** "Shah Alam II Badshah" **Reverse:** Persian-julus (formula), mint name **Note:** Privy mark: inverted crown

Date	Mintage	Good	VG	F	VF	XF
ND-//46	—	BV	100	175	250	350

KM# 244 MOHUR (15 Rupees)

11.5900 g., Gold **Mint:** Mumbai **Obverse:** Persian inscription, couplet **Obv. Inscription:** "Shah Alam II Badshah" **Reverse:** Persian-julus (formula), mint name **Note:** Privy mark: normal crown.

Date	Mintage	Good	VG	F	VF	XF
ND-//46	—	BV	110	185	300	450

KM# 248 MOHUR (15 Rupees)

11.5900 g., Gold **Mint:** Mumbai **Obverse:** Persian inscription, couplet **Obv. Inscription:** "Shah Alam II Badshah" **Reverse:** Persian-julus (formula), mint name **Note:** Privy marks: normal crown and 6 petal rosette.

Date	Mintage	Good	VG	F	VF	XF
ND-//46	—	BV	100	175	250	350

KM# 278 PAGODA

3.0000 g., Gold **Mint:** Tellicherry **Obverse:** T-99, Persian Sikkanishini (government coin), date **Reverse:** Persian "Zarb", mint name, julus

Date	Mintage	Good	VG	F	VF	XF
1809	—	30.00	75.00	100	250	400

MILLED COINAGE

KM# 230 PIE

2.1600 g., Copper, 18 mm. **Mint:** Mumbai **Obverse:** E.I. Co. arms **Reverse:** Scales, Persian-Adil (just) **Edge:** Plain

Date	Mintage	Good	VG	F	VF	XF
1830//AH1246 Proof	—	Value: 300				
1831//AH1246	—	0.10	0.30	0.75	2.00	25.00
1831//AH1246 Proof	—	Value: 175				

KM# 261 PIE

2.1600 g., Copper, 18 mm. **Mint:** Calcutta **Obverse:** E.I. Co. arms **Reverse:** Large PIE in 1.2mm letters, tall Persial "L" in "Adil"

Date	Mintage	Good	VG	F	VF	XF
1833//AH1248	—	0.10	0.15	0.40	1.00	12.00
1833//AH1248 Proof	—	Value: 100				

KM# 262 PIE

2.1600 g., Copper **Obverse:** E.I. Co. arms **Reverse:** Short Persian "L" in "Adil"

Date	Mintage	Good	VG	F	VF	XF
1833//AH1248	—	0.10	0.15	0.40	1.00	12.00

KM# 263 PIE

2.1600 g., Copper **Obverse:** KM#261 **Reverse:** KM#230 **Note:** Mule.

Date	Mintage	Good	VG	F	VF	XF
1833//AH1246	—	—	—	—	—	—

KM# 264 PIE

2.1600 g., Copper **Obverse:** KM#230 **Reverse:** KM#261 **Note:** Mule.

Date	Mintage	Good	VG	F	VF	XF
1831//AH1248	—	—	—	—	—	—

KM# 204 1/2 PICE

3.2300 g., Copper, 21.2 mm. **Obverse:** E.I.Co. arms **Reverse:** Scales, Persian-Adil (just) **Edge:** Plain

Date	Mintage	Good	VG	F	VF	XF
1804//AH1219	—	0.15	0.40	1.00	8.00	40.00
1804//AH1219 Proof	—	Value: 50.00				

KM# 204a 1/2 PICE

3.8300 g., Copper Gilt **Edge:** Plain

Date	Mintage	Good	VG	F	VF	XF
1804//AH1219 Proof	—	Value: 85.00				

KM# 255 1/2 PICE

3.8300 g., Copper **Mint:** Ahmadabad **Edge:** Plain

Date	Mintage	Good	VG	F	VF	XF
AH1234//13	—	—	—	—	—	—

KM# 205 PICE

6.4700 g., Copper, 25.8 mm. **Obverse:** E.I. Co. arms **Reverse:** Scales, Persian-Adil (just) **Edge:** Plain

Date	Mintage	Good	VG	F	VF	XF
1804//AH1219	—	0.15	0.40	1.00	10.00	50.00
1804//AH1219 Proof	—	Value: 65.00				

KM# 205a PICE

6.4700 g., Copper Gilt

Date	Mintage	Good	VG	F	VF	XF
1804//AH1219 Proof	—	Value: 90.00				

KM# A256 PICE

7.5300 g., Copper **Mint:** Ahmadabad **Edge:** Plain **Note:** Size varies 19-20mm.

Date	Mintage	Good	VG	F	VF	XF
AH1232	—	—	—	—	—	—
AH1233//12	—	—	—	—	—	—
AH1234//12 Rare	—	—	—	—	—	—
AH1236	—	3.00	10.00	18.00	30.00	—

KM# 231.1 1/4 ANNA (Paisa)

6.9700 g., Copper, 25 mm. **Mint:** Mumbai **Obverse:** E.I. Co. arms **Obv. Legend:** EAST INDIA COMPANY **Reverse:** Scales, Persian "Adil" (just) **Edge:** Plain

Date	Mintage	Good	VG	F	VF	XF
1830//AH1246	—	0.20	0.50	1.25	3.00	35.00
1830//AH1246 Proof	—	Value: 250				
1832//AH1246	—	0.20	0.50	1.25	3.00	35.00

KM# 231.2 1/4 ANNA (Paisa)

6.9700 g., Copper **Mint:** Mumbai **Obv. Legend:** Persian-Adil in different style, medium English letters **Edge:** Plain

Date	Mintage	Good	VG	F	VF	XF
1832//AH1247	—	0.20	0.50	1.25	3.00	35.00

KM# 233 1/4 ANNA (Paisa)

6.9700 g., Copper **Mint:** Calcutta **Obverse:** KM#232 **Reverse:** KM#231.2 **Edge:** Plain **Note:** Mule.

Date	Mintage	Good	VG	F	VF	XF
1833//AH1247	—	2.50	6.00	15.00	50.00	150

KM# 235 1/4 ANNA (Paisa)

6.9700 g., Copper **Mint:** Calcutta **Obverse:** KM#231 **Reverse:** KM#232 **Edge:** Plain **Note:** Mule.

Date	Mintage	Good	VG	F	VF	XF
1832//AH1249	—	—	—	9.00	27.50	80.00

KM# 232 1/4 ANNA (Paisa)

6.9700 g., Copper **Mint:** Calcutta **Obverse:** Flat shield, without E.I. Co. legend **Reverse:** Large English letters **Edge:** Plain

Date	Mintage	Good	VG	F	VF	XF
1833//AH1249	—	0.10	0.30	0.75	2.00	30.00
1833//AH1249 Proof	—	Value: 200				

KM# 234 1/4 ANNA (Paisa)

6.9700 g., Copper **Mint:** Calcutta **Obverse:** Convex shield without E.I. Co. legend **Reverse:** Small English letters **Edge:** Plain

Date	Mintage	Good	VG	F	VF	XF
1833//AH1249	—	0.10	0.30	0.75	2.00	30.00
1833//AH1249 Proof	—	Value: 200				

KM# 251 1/2 ANNA

12.9500 g., Copper, 30.5 mm. **Obverse:** E.I. Co. arms **Reverse:** Scale, Persian "Adil" (just), English letters, 2mm

Date	Mintage	Good	VG	F	VF	XF
1834//AH1249	—	0.30	0.75	2.00	5.00	65.00
1834//AH1249 Proof	—	Value: 350				

KM# 252 1/2 ANNA

12.9500 g., Copper **Obverse:** E.I. Co. arms **Reverse:** Scale, Persian "Adil" (just), English letters, 2.5mm

Date	Mintage	Good	VG	F	VF	XF
1834//AH1249	—	0.30	0.75	2.00	5.00	65.00

KM# 253 1/2 ANNA

12.9500 g., Copper **Obverse:** E.I. Co. arms **Reverse:** Scale, Persian "Adil" (just), English letters, 1mm

Date	Mintage	Good	VG	F	VF	XF
1834//AH1249	—	0.30	0.75	2.00	5.00	65.00

KM# 251a 1/2 ANNA

Silver **Obverse:** E.I. Co. arms **Reverse:** Scale, Persian "Adil" (just)

Date	Mintage	Good	VG	F	VF	XF
1834//AH1249 Proof	—	—	—	—	—	—

KM# 258 1/4 RUPEE

2.9100 g., Silver **Mint:** Surat **Obverse:** Persian inscription, couplet **Obv. Inscription:** "Muhammad Akbar II" **Reverse:** Persian-julus (formula), mint name **Note:** Mint name: Ahmadabad. See note after Rupee, KM#260.

Date	Mintage	Good	VG	F	VF	XF
AH1234//12	—	2.00	5.00	10.00	20.00	35.00

KM# 222 1/4 RUPEE

2.9100 g., Silver **Mint:** New Mumbai **Edge:** Plain

Date	Mintage	Good	VG	F	VF	XF
AH1215//46	—	0.20	0.50	1.25	3.00	15.00
AH1215//46 Proof	—	Value: 275				

KM# 223 1/2 RUPEE (1/2 Angelina)

5.8300 g., Silver **Mint:** New Mumbai **Obverse:** Persian inscription, couplet **Obv. Inscription:** "Shah Alam II" **Reverse:** Persian-julus (formula), mint name **Edge:** Plain **Note:** Mint name: Surat.

Date	Mintage	Good	VG	F	VF	XF
AH1215//46	—	0.40	1.00	2.50	7.50	20.00
AH1215//46 Proof	—	Value: 350				

KM# 220 RUPEE

11.6000 g., Silver **Mint:** Calcutta **Obverse:** Persian inscription, couplet, Inverted crescent privy mark **Obv. Inscription:** "Shah Alam II Badshah" **Reverse:** Persian-julus (formula), mint name **Edge:** Plain **Note:** Mint name: Surat.

Date	Mintage	Good	VG	F	VF	XF
ND(1810-13)	2,037,000	6.00	15.00	35.00	75.00	125

KM# 221 RUPEE

11.5900 g., Silver **Mint:** Calcutta **Obverse:** Persian inscription, couplet **Obv. Inscription:** "Shah Alam II" **Reverse:** Persian-julus (formula), mint name **Edge:** Vertical milling **Note:** Mint name: Surat.

Date	Mintage	Good	VG	F	VF	XF
AH1215//46	—	1.50	4.00	10.00	25.00	60.00
AH1215//46 Proof	—	Value: 400				

KM# 224 RUPEE

11.5900 g., Silver **Mint:** New Mumbai **Obverse:** Persian inscription, couplet **Obv. Inscription:** "Shah Alam II", couplet **Reverse:** Persian-julus (formula), mint name **Edge:** Plain **Note:** Mint name: Surat.

Date	Mintage	Good	VG	F	VF	XF
AH1215//46	—	BV	1.25	3.25	8.00	20.00
AH1215//46 Proof	—	Value: 400				

PATTERNS

Including off metal strikes

KM#	Date	Mintage	Identification	Mkt Val
Pn6	AH1804	—	2 Pice. Copper. Mule, KM#206 obverse and reverse, Prid.#197.	225
Pn7	AH1804	—	2 Pice. Copper. Mule. Obverse: Bombay KM#206. Reverse: Madras 20 Cash, KM#321. Prid.#192a.	175

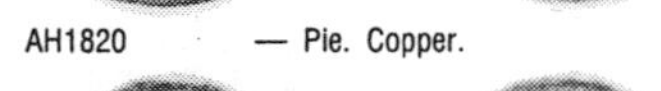

KM#	Date	Mintage	Identification	Mkt Val
Pn8	AH1820	—	Pie. Copper.	850

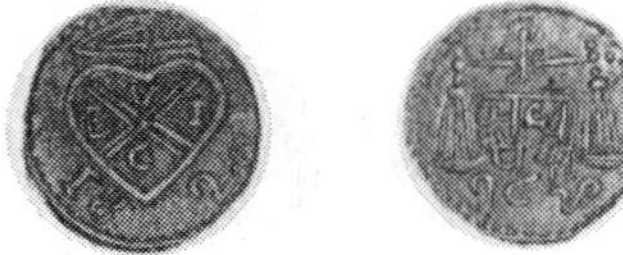
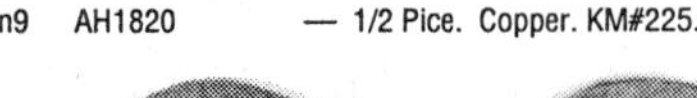

KM#	Date	Mintage	Identification	Mkt Val
Pn9	AH1820	—	1/2 Pice. Copper. KM#225.	350

KM#	Date	Mintage	Identification	Mkt Val
Pn10	AH1820	—	Pice. Copper. KM#226.	600

KM#	Date	Mintage	Identification	Mkt Val
Pn11	AH1820	—	1/4 Anna. Copper. KM#205.	500

KM#	Date	Mintage	Identification	Mkt Val
Pn12	AH1820	—	1/2 Anna. Copper. KM#228.	950

KM#	Date	Mintage	Identification	Mkt Val
Pn13	AH1821	—	Pie. Copper.	850

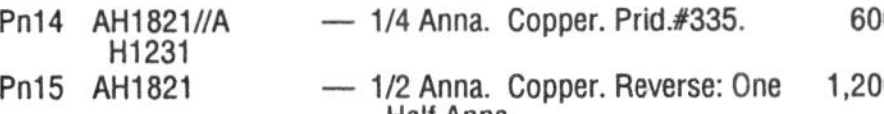

KM#	Date	Mintage	Identification	Mkt Val
Pn14	AH1821//AH1231	—	1/4 Anna. Copper. Prid.#335.	600
Pn15	AH1821	—	1/2 Anna. Copper. Reverse: One Half Anna.	1,200

KM#	Date	Mintage	Identification	Mkt Val
Pn16	AH1821//AH1231	—	1/2 Anna. Copper. Prid.#334.	750

KM#	Date	Mintage	Identification	Mkt Val
Pn17	AH1821	—	Anna. Copper.	2,250

KM#	Date	Mintage	Identification	Mkt Val
Pn18	AH1828	—	Mohur. Copper. Prid.#336.	500

KM#	Date	Mintage	Identification	Mkt Val

Pn19	AH1828//46	—	Mohur. Copper. Prid.#337.	—

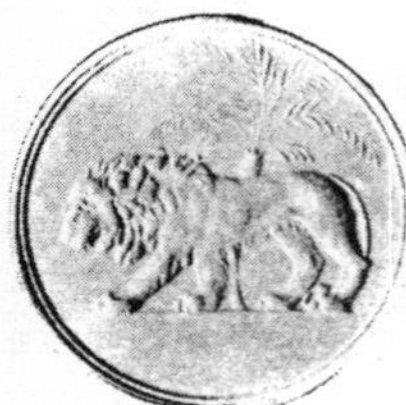

Pn20	AH(1828)	—	Mohur. Copper. Prid.#338.	600

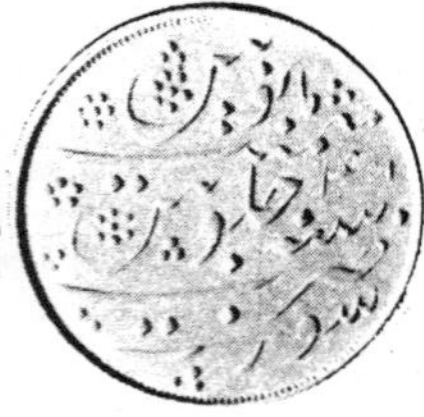

Pn21	AH1215//46	—	Rupee. Silver. Prid.#332.	—

KM#	Date	Mintage	Identification	Mkt Val
Pn22	AH1215//46	—	Mohur. Silver. Prid.#333.	—
Pn23	AH1832//A H1246	—	1/2 Anna. Copper. 12.9500 g. 30.5 mm. Prid.#204.	500
Pn24	AH1249	—	1/2 Anna. Silver. Prid.#253.	1,000

MADRAS PRESIDENCY

English trade was begun on the east coast of India in 1611. The first factory was at Mazulipatam and was maintained intermittently until modern times.

Madras was founded in 1639 and Fort St. George was made the chief factory on the east coast in 1641. A mint was established at Fort St. George where coins of the style of Vijayanagar were struck.

The Madras mint began minting copper coins after the renovation. In 1689 silver fanams were authorized to be struck by the new Board of Directors.

In 1692 the Mughal Emperor Aurangzeb gave permission for Mughal type rupees to be struck at Madras. These circulated locally and were also sent to Bengal. The chief competition for the Madras coins were the Arcot rupees. Some of the bulk coins from Madras were sent to the Nawabs mint to be made into Arcot rupees. In 1742 the East India Company applied for and received permission to make their own Arcot rupees. Coining operations ceased in Madras in 1869.

MONETARY SYSTEM

1 Dudu = 10 Cash
8 Dudu = 1 Fanam
36 Fanam = 1 Pagoda (1688-1802)
42 Fanam = 1 Pagoda (1802-1817)
45 Fanam = 1 Pagoda (1817-1835)
3-1/2 Rupees = 1 Pagoda

MINTS

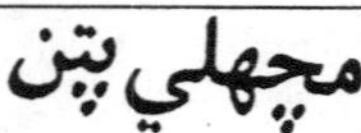

اركات

Arcot

مچهلي پٹن

Masulipatnam (Machilipatnam)

BRITISH COLONIAL

HAMMERED COINAGE

KM# 314 CASH

1.1000 g., Copper **Obverse:** Bale mark **Reverse:** Date

Date	Mintage	Good	VG	F	VF	XF
1803	—	1.75	3.00	12.00	50.00	—

KM# 306 DUDU (10 Cash)

Copper **Obverse:** Bale mark with CC/E **Reverse:** Date with wavy lines above and below **Note:** Weight varies 8.21-8.35 grams.

Date	Mintage	Good	VG	F	VF	XF
1801	—	2.00	5.00	15.00	70.00	—
1805	—	2.00	5.00	15.00	70.00	—

KM# 385 1/2 DUB

Copper, 16 mm. **Mint:** Machhlipatan **Rev. Inscription:** Sanat julus mubarak **Note:** Wight varies 6.60-6.90 grams. Prid#302.

Date	Mintage	Good	VG	F	VF	XF
AH1175-1222	—	5.00	9.00	13.50	20.00	—

KM# 321a 20 CASH

Silver **Mint:** Soho

Date	Mintage	Good	VG	F	VF	XF
1808 Proof	—	Value: 150				

KM# 321c 20 CASH

Gold **Mint:** Soho

Date	Mintage	Good	VG	F	VF	XF
1808 Proof; Rare	—	—	—	—	—	—

KM# 322 20 CASH

9.3300 g., Copper, 30.7 mm. **Mint:** Soho **Note:** Nice salvaged (and cleaned) examples from the Admiral Gardner exist, trading near XF.

Date	Mintage	Good	VG	F	VF	XF
1808	—	0.30	0.75	2.00	8.00	60.00
1808 Proof	—	Value: 120				

KM# 386 DUB

Copper, 20 mm. **Mint:** Machhlipatan **Rev. Inscription:** Sanat julus mubarak **Note:** Prid#301. Weight varies 13.00-14.00 grams.

Date	Mintage	Good	VG	F	VF	XF
AH1175-1222	—	5.50	11.50	21.50	35.00	—

KM# 387 DUB

Copper, 20 mm. **Mint:** Machhlipatan **Reverse:** Similar to KM#386 but with English "M" **Note:** Weight varies 13.00-14.00 grams.

Date	Mintage	Good	VG	F	VF	XF
AH1218	—	7.50	15.00	22.50	40.00	—

KM# 307 FANAM

0.9100 g., Silver **Obverse:** Large deity Vishnu **Note:** Prid#19.

Date	Mintage	Good	VG	F	VF	XF
ND(1764-1807)	—	1.50	3.00	7.00	17.50	40.00

KM# 337 FANAM

0.9200 g., Silver **Obverse:** Without branches below star

Date	Mintage	Good	VG	F	VF	XF
ND(1807)	—	1.50	4.00	10.00	25.00	45.00

KM# 335 FANAM

0.9200 g., Silver, 10 mm. **Obverse:** Star in center circle, value above, branches below **Reverse:** Star in center circle, value above and below in Telugu and Tamil

Date	Mintage	Good	VG	F	VF	XF
ND(1807)	386,000	1.50	4.00	10.00	25.00	45.00

KM# 336 FANAM

0.9200 g., Silver **Obverse:** Star in center, value above, branches below

Date	Mintage	Good	VG	F	VF	XF
ND(1807)	—	1.50	4.00	10.00	25.00	45.00

KM# 308 2 FANAM

1.8300 g., Silver

Date	Mintage	Good	VG	F	VF	XF
ND(1764-1807)	—	1.50	4.00	10.00	25.00	50.00

KM# 303 PAGODA

Gold **Obverse:** "Star Pagoda" diety Vishnu **Reverse:** Star in center, granulations around **Note:** Size varies 10-11 mm. Prid#9, Prid#10.

Date	Mintage	Good	VG	F	VF	XF
ND(1740-1807)	—	BV	50.00	125	175	275

KM# 304 PAGODA

3.4300 g., Gold **Obverse:** Three 1/2 figure deities (3 Swami Pagoda) **Note:** Size varies 12-14 mm. Prid#3B.

Date	Mintage	Good	VG	F	VF	XF
ND(1740-1807)	—	BV	50.00	125	175	275

KM# 380 1/16 RUPEE

0.7300 g., Silver, 8.8 mm. **Mint:** Arcot **Obverse:** Couplet **Obv. Inscription:** "Alamgir II" **Reverse:** Julus (formula), mintname **Note:** Struck at Calcutta, Dacca, Madras, Murshidabad Mint. Mintname: Arkat (Arcot). The regnal year 6 was a frozen date struck unitl 1809. Prid#145.

Date	Mintage	Good	VG	F	VF	XF
ND-//6 Frozen	—	4.00	10.00	15.00	35.00	75.00

KM# 381 1/8 RUPEE

1.4200 g., Silver, 11 mm. **Obverse:** Inscription and couplet **Obv. Inscription:** "Alamgir II" **Reverse:** Julus (formula), mintname **Note:** Struck at Calcutta, Dacca, Madras, Murshidabad Mint. Mintname: Arcot. The regnal year 6 was a frozen date struck until 1809. Prid#144.

Date	Mintage	Good	VG	F	VF	XF
ND-//6 Frozen	—	4.00	10.00	15.00	35.00	75.00

KM# 382 1/4 RUPEE

Silver, 15.5 mm. **Obverse:** Inscription, couplet **Obv. Inscription:** "Alamgir II" **Reverse:** Julus (formula) mintname **Note:** Weight varies 2.81-2.86 grams. Struck at Calcutta, Dacca, Madras, Murshidabad Mint. Mintname: Arcot. Prid#143.

Date	Mintage	Good	VG	F	VF	XF
ND-//6 Frozen	—	5.00	10.00	25.00	50.00	100

MILLED COINAGE

KM# 315a CASH

Silver **Mint:** Soho **Obverse:** E.I. Co. crest, lion rampant left **Reverse:** Value in Persian and English

Date	Mintage	Good	VG	F	VF	XF
1803 Proof	—	Value: 75.00				

KM# 315b CASH

Copper **Mint:** Soho **Obverse:** E.I. Co. crest, lion rampant left **Reverse:** Value in Persian and English

Date	Mintage	Good	VG	F	VF	XF
1803 Proof	—	Value: 350				

KM# 315c CASH

Gold **Mint:** Soho **Obverse:** E.I. Co. crest, lion rampant left **Reverse:** Value in Persian and English

Date	Mintage	Good	VG	F	VF	XF
1803 Proof	—	—	—	—	—	—

KM# 315 CASH

0.6400 g., Copper **Mint:** Soho **Obverse:** E.I. Co. crest, lion rampant left **Reverse:** Value in Persian and English **Note:** Similar pieces weighing 1.27g are modern fantasies. Refer to "Unusual World Coins" 4th edition.

Date	Mintage	Good	VG	F	VF	XF
1803	—	0.50	1.25	3.00	5.00	10.00
1803 Proof	—	Value: 35.00				

KM# 309 2-1/2 CASH

1.2100 g., Copper **Mint:** Madras **Obverse:** Value in Persian and English **Reverse:** Value in Tamil and Telegu **Note:** The above exists struck on a V Cash planchet.

Date	Mintage	Good	VG	F	VF	XF
ND(1807)	—	2.50	5.00	10.00	20.00	—

KM# 316 5 CASH (1 Falus)

3.2300 g., Copper, 21 mm. **Mint:** Soho **Obverse:** Large letters, E.I. Co. arms **Reverse:** Value in Persian and English

Date	Mintage	Good	VG	F	VF	XF
1803	—	0.30	0.75	2.00	4.00	35.00

KM# 317 5 CASH (1 Falus)

2.4100 g., Copper, 21 mm. **Mint:** Soho **Obverse:** E.I. Co. arms **Obv. Legend:** Small lettering, 0.8mm

Date	Mintage	Good	VG	F	VF	XF
1803	—	0.30	0.75	2.00	4.00	35.00

KM# 318a 5 CASH (1 Falus)

Silver **Mint:** Soho **Obverse:** E.I. Co. arms

Date	Mintage	Good	VG	F	VF	XF
1803 Proof	—	Value: 125				

KM# 318c 5 CASH (1 Falus)

Gold **Mint:** Soho **Obverse:** E.I. Co. arms

Date	Mintage	Good	VG	F	VF	XF
1803 Proof	—	—	—	—	—	—

KM# 318 5 CASH (1 Falus)

2.4100 g., Copper **Mint:** Soho **Obverse:** E.I. Co. arms **Note:** Modified design.

Date	Mintage	Good	VG	F	VF	XF
1803 Proof	—	Value: 70.00				

KM# 318b 5 CASH (1 Falus)

Copper **Mint:** Soho **Obverse:** E.I. Co. arms **Note:** Similar to 10 Cash, KM#319.

Date	Mintage	Good	VG	F	VF	XF
1803 Proof	—	—	—	—	—	—

KM# 324 5 CASH (1 Falus)

2.4100 g., Copper, 21 mm. **Mint:** Madras **Obverse:** Dotted line seperates value in Persian and English **Reverse:** Value in Tamil and Teluga **Note:** Varieties exist with line or without dotted line above English value.

Date	Mintage	Good	VG	F	VF	XF
ND(1807)	—	1.50	4.00	15.00	50.00	175

KM# 325 1/4 DUB (5 Cash)

2.5700 g., Copper **Mint:** Soho **Obverse:** Value in Tamil and Teluga **Obv. Inscription:** "Honorable Company" **Reverse:** Tamil inscription, value **Rev. Inscription:** "Honorable Company"

Date	Mintage	Good	VG	F	VF	XF
ND(1807)	—	4.00	10.00	25.00	75.00	—

KM# 319 10 CASH

6.4700 g., Copper, 25.8 mm. **Mint:** Soho **Obverse:** E.I. Co. arms **Reverse:** Value in Persian and English **Note:** Heavy issue.

Date	Mintage	Good	VG	F	VF	XF
1803	—	0.30	0.75	1.75	6.00	45.00
1803 Proof	—	Value: 90.00				
1808	—	0.30	0.75	1.75	6.00	45.00
1808 Proof	—	Value: 90.00				

KM# 326 10 CASH

4.8300 g., Copper, 23.5 mm. **Mint:** Madras **Obverse:** Value in Persian and English **Reverse:** Value in Tamil and Teluga **Note:** Seven varieties exist: i.e. dividing lines, dots and star, etc above English value. Also exists struck on a XX Cash planchet.

Date	Mintage	Good	VG	F	VF	XF
ND(1807)	—	1.50	4.00	18.00	50.00	—

KM# 320 10 CASH

4.6600 g., Copper, 25.8 mm. **Mint:** Soho **Obverse:** E.I. Co. arms **Reverse:** Value in Persian and English **Note:** Nice salvaged (and cleaned) examples from the ship Admiral Gardner are very common.

Date	Mintage	Good	VG	F	VF	XF
1808	—	0.30	0.75	1.75	6.00	45.00
1808 Proof	—	Value: 90.00				

KM# 319c 10 CASH

Gold **Mint:** Soho **Obverse:** E.I. Co. arms **Reverse:** Value in Persian and English

Date	Mintage	Good	VG	F	VF	XF
1808 Proof; Rare	—	—	—	—	—	—

KM# 319a 10 CASH

Silver **Mint:** Soho **Obverse:** E.I. Co. arms **Reverse:** Value in Persian and English

Date	Mintage	Good	VG	F	VF	XF
1808 Proof	—	Value: 150				

KM# 319b 10 CASH

Copper **Mint:** Soho **Obverse:** E.I. Co. arms **Reverse:** Value in Persian and English

Date	Mintage	Good	VG	F	VF	XF
1808 Proof	—	Value: 600				

KM# 327 1/2 DUB (10 Cash, 1/2 Falus)

5.1500 g., Copper, 22.7 mm. **Obverse:** Value in Teluga and Tamil **Reverse:** Value in Persian

Date	Mintage	Good	VG	F	VF	XF
1807	—	6.00	15.00	35.00	100	175

KM# 345 1/2 DUB (10 Cash, 1/2 Falus)

4.7500 g., Copper, 26 mm. **Obverse:** Value in Persian **Reverse:** Value in Telugu

Date	Mintage	Good	VG	F	VF	XF
1808	—	5.00	10.00	20.00	50.00	—

KM# 323 20 CASH

9.3300 g., Copper **Mint:** Soho **Obverse:** KM#321 **Reverse:** 1/48 Rupee, KM#394 **Note:** Mule.

Date	Mintage	Good	VG	F	VF	XF
180x	—	—	—	—	—	—

KM# 321 20 CASH

12.9500 g., Copper, 30.7 mm. **Mint:** Soho **Obverse:** E.I. Co. arms **Reverse:** Value in Persian and English **Note:** Heavy issue. For 1804 date see Bombay 2 Pice Mule, KM#207.

Date	Mintage	Good	VG	F	VF	XF
1803	—	0.40	1.00	2.50	8.00	60.00
1803 Proof	—	Value: 120				
1808	—	0.40	1.00	2.50	8.00	60.00
1808 Proof	—	Value: 120				

KM# 321b 20 CASH

Gilt Gold **Mint:** Soho **Obverse:** E.I. Co. arms **Reverse:** Value in Persian and English

Date	Mintage	Good	VG	F	VF	XF
1803 Proof	—	Value: 750				
1808 Proof	—	Value: 750				

KM# 328 20 CASH

9.6500 g., Copper, 26.5 mm. **Mint:** Madras **Obverse:** Value in Persian and English **Reverse:** Value in Tamil and Teluga **Note:** Five varieties exist; i.e. dividing lines, dots and star above English value.

Date	Mintage	Good	VG	F	VF	XF
ND(1807)	—	1.50	4.00	18.00	50.00	—

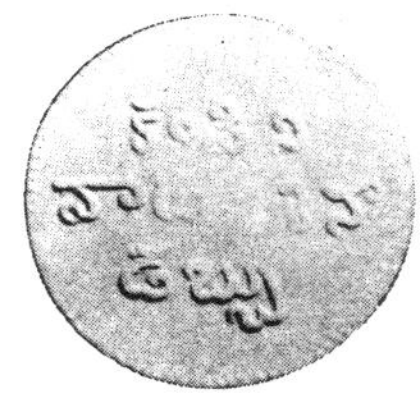

KM# 330 DUB (20 Cash)

10.3100 g., Copper, 26.5 mm. **Mint:** Madras **Obverse:** Value in Persian **Reverse:** Value in Telugu

Date	Mintage	Good	VG	F	VF	XF
ND(1807)	—	5.50	16.50	50.00	125	—

KM# 329 DUB (20 Cash)

7.5600 g., Copper, 27.2 mm. **Mint:** Madras **Obverse:** Persian inscription, value **Obv. Inscription:** "Honorable Company" **Reverse:** Telugu and Tamil - This and three new dubs are one small fanam **Note:** An unusual issue referred to as a "Regulating Dub".

Date	Mintage	VG	F	VF	XF	Unc
1807	—	15.00	75.00	150	200	—
1808	—	15.00	75.00	150	200	—

KM# 347 DUB (20 Cash)

9.9000 g., Copper, 24.3 mm. **Mint:** Madras **Obverse:** Persian inscription, value **Obv. Inscription:** "Honorable Company" **Reverse:** Telugu inscription, value **Rev. Inscription:** "Honorable Company"

Date	Mintage	Good	VG	F	VF	XF
1808	—	7.50	15.00	35.00	75.00	—

KM# 346 DUB (20 Cash)

10.0000 g., Copper, 26.8 mm. **Mint:** Madras **Obverse:** Persian inscription, value **Obv. Inscription:** "Honorable Company" **Reverse:** Telugu inscription, value **Rev. Inscription:** "Honorable Company"

Date	Mintage	Good	VG	F	VF	XF
1808	—	7.50	15.00	35.00	75.00	—

KM# 331.1 40 CASH

19.3100 g., Copper, 36 mm. **Mint:** Madras **Obverse:** Dots and star above XL CASH, value in Persian and English **Reverse:** Value in Tamil and Telugu

Date	Mintage	Good	VG	F	VF	XF
ND(1807)	—	5.00	12.50	50.00	200	—

KM# 331.2 40 CASH

19.3100 g., Copper **Mint:** Madras **Obverse:** Lines above XL CASH

Date	Mintage	Good	VG	F	VF	XF
ND(1807)	—	5.00	12.50	50.00	200	—

KM# 331.3 40 CASH

19.3100 g., Copper **Mint:** Madras **Obverse:** Dots and star above, dots below XL CASH

Date	Mintage	Good	VG	F	VF	XF
ND(1807)	—	5.00	12.50	50.00	400	—

KM# 334 2 DUBS (2 Falus)

20.6100 g., Copper, 39.2 mm. **Mint:** Madras **Obverse:** Persian-Value **Reverse:** Telugu and Tamil-Value

Date	Mintage	Good	VG	F	VF	XF
ND(1807)	—	450	1,150	1,850	3,150	4,500

KM# 348 2 DUBS (2 Falus)

19.6900 g., Copper, 36 mm. **Mint:** Madras **Obverse:** Persian inscription, value **Obv. Inscription:** "Honorable Company" **Reverse:** Value in Telugu and English **Rev. Inscription:** "Honorable Company"

Date	Mintage	Good	VG	F	VF	XF
ND(1808)	—	8.00	20.00	75.00	150	—

KM# 349 FANAM

0.9200 g., Silver **Obverse:** Buckled garer, value in Persian and English **Reverse:** Ribbon, star, value in Telugu and Tamil **Note:** Size varies 11-11.5mm. Two varieties exist, shaped or circular buckle.

Date	Mintage	Good	VG	F	VF	XF
ND(1808)	1,545,000	0.40	1.00	2.00	5.00	12.00

KM# 338 2 FANAM

1.8500 g., Silver, 12.5 mm. **Obverse:** Value in English around center circle **Reverse:** Value in Telugu and Tamil, without center circle **Edge:** Verticle

Date	Mintage	Good	VG	F	VF	XF
ND(1807)	1,511,000	0.75	2.00	5.00	15.00	35.00

KM# 339 2 FANAM

1.8500 g., Silver **Obverse:** Without center circle, value in English **Reverse:** Without center circle, value in Telugu and Tamil

Date	Mintage	Good	VG	F	VF	XF
ND(1807)	—	0.75	2.00	5.00	15.00	35.00

KM# 340 2 FANAM

1.8500 g., Silver **Obverse:** Center circles **Reverse:** Center circles

Date	Mintage	Good	VG	F	VF	XF
ND(1807)	—	0.75	2.00	5.00	15.00	35.00

KM# 341 2 FANAM

1.8500 g., Silver **Obverse:** Without center circle, value in English **Reverse:** With center circle, value in Telugu and Tamil **Edge:** Vertical

Date	Mintage	Good	VG	F	VF	XF
ND(1807)	—	0.75	2.00	5.00	15.00	35.00

KM# 350 2 FANAM

1.8500 g., Silver **Obverse:** Buckled garter, value in Persian and English **Reverse:** Ribbon, star, value in Telugu and Tamil **Note:** Four varieties exist of the buckle at the bottom of the obverse.

Date	Mintage	Good	VG	F	VF	XF
ND(1808)	6,044,000	0.60	1.50	3.00	9.00	15.00

KM# 342 5 FANAMS

4.6500 g., Silver, 17.3 mm. **Obverse:** Value in English around value in Persian **Reverse:** Value in Tamil around value in Telugu **Edge:** Vertical

Date	Mintage	Good	VG	F	VF	XF
ND(1807)	988,000	3.25	8.00	20.00	50.00	85.00

KM# 351 5 FANAMS

4.6500 g., Silver **Obverse:** Buckled garter, value in Persian and English **Reverse:** Ribbon, star, value in Telugu and Tamil **Note:** Size varies 21-22mm. Eight varieties exist of the buckle at lower left of the obverse.

Date	Mintage	Good	VG	F	VF	XF
ND(1808)	3,954,000	2.00	5.00	12.50	40.00	75.00

KM# 343 1/4 PAGODA

10.5800 g., Silver, 27.2 mm. **Obverse:** Value in English and Persian on ribbon around Gopuram **Reverse:** Value in Tamil and Telugu around deity Vishnu **Edge:** Vertical milling **Note:** Two varieties exist, one with 9 stars to each side of the Gopuram, the other having 13 stars.

Date	Mintage	Good	VG	F	VF	XF
ND(1807)	1,773,000	5.50	13.50	35.00	125	300

KM# 352 1/4 PAGODA

10.5800 g., Silver, 25.5 mm. **Obverse:** Value in English and Persian on buckled garter **Reverse:** Value in Tamil and Telugu around deity Vishnu **Edge:** Vertical milling

Date	Mintage	Good	VG	F	VF	XF
ND(1808)	7,092,000	6.50	16.00	32.00	60.00	100

KM# 344 1/2 PAGODA

21.1700 g., Silver, 36.5 mm. **Obverse:** Value in English and Persian on ribbon around Gopuram **Reverse:** Value in Tamil and Telugu around deity Vishnu **Edge:** Vertical **Note:** Dav. #246. Four varieties exist; 12, 14, 15 or 18 stars in the field at left and right of the Gopuram. KM#344 can be found overstruck on large plugs made from Spanish or Spanish Colonial 8 Reales.

Date	Mintage	Good	VG	F	VF	XF
ND(1807)	501,000	100	250	500	1,000	1,500

KM# 353 1/2 PAGODA

21.1700 g., Silver, 35.5 mm. **Obverse:** Value in large English lettering and Persian on buckled garter around Gopuram **Reverse:** Value in Tamil and Telegu around deity Vishnu **Edge:** Vertical milling **Note:** Dav. #247. KM#353 can be found overstruck on large plugs made from Spanish or Spanish Colonial 8 reales. Varieties exist and can vary in value considerably.

Date	Mintage	Good	VG	F	VF	XF
ND(1808-11)	2,000,000	13.50	35.00	85.00	225	400

KM# 354 1/2 PAGODA

21.1700 g., Silver **Obverse:** Value in small English lettering **Edge:** Vertical milling **Note:** Dav. #247. KM#354 can be found overstruck on large plugs made from Spanish or Spanish Colonial 8 reales. Varieties exist and can vary in value considerably.

Date	Good	VG	F	VF	XF
ND(1808-11)	13.50	35.00	85.00	225	400

KM# 355 1/2 PAGODA

21.1700 g., Silver, 36.5 mm. **Obverse:** Value "HALF PGODA" (error) **Edge:** Vertical **Note:** Dav.#247. KM#355 can be found overstruck on large plugs made from Spanish or Spanish Colonial 8 reales.

Date	Mintage	Good	VG	F	VF	XF
ND(1808-11)	—	13.50	35.00	85.00	225	400

KM# 356 PAGODA

2.9700 g., Gold, 17.4 mm. **Obverse:** Value in English and Persian on buckled garter around Gopuram **Reverse:** Value in Tamil and Telugu on ribbon around deity Vishnu **Edge:** Vertical milling

Date	Mintage	Good	VG	F	VF	XF
ND(1808-15)	1,382,000	BV	—	50.00	125	175

KM# 357 2 PAGODAS

5.9700 g., Gold **Obverse:** Value in English and Persian on buckled garter around Gopuram with 14 stars in field **Reverse:** Value in Tamil and Telugu on ribbon around deity Vishnu **Edge:** Vertical milling **Note:** Size varies 20.5-22.0mm.

Date	Mintage	Good	VG	F	VF	XF
ND(1808-15)	1,064,000	BV	60.00	100	250	400

KM# 358 2 PAGODAS

5.9700 g., Gold **Obverse:** 18 stars in field, varieties in size of English lettering exist **Edge:** Vertical milling **Note:** Size varies 21.0-22.2mm.

Date	Mintage	Good	VG	F	VF	XF
ND(1808-15)	—	BV	60.00	100	250	400

KM# 428 PIE

2.1300 g., Copper, 17.7 mm. **Mint:** London **Obverse:** E.I. Co. arms **Rev. Inscription:** Value in Persian **Edge:** Plain

Date	Mintage	Good	VG	F	VF	XF
1825//AH1240	4,741,000	0.10	0.20	0.50	1.00	4.00
1825//AH1240	Inc. above	Value: 80.00				
1833//AH1248	—	0.75	2.00	5.00	10.00	20.00

KM# 429 2 PIES

4.2700 g., Copper, 22.0 mm. **Mint:** London **Obverse:** E.I. Co. arms **Rev. Inscription:** Value in Persian **Edge:** Plain

Date	Mintage	Good	VG	F	VF	XF
1825//AH1240	7,126,000	0.15	0.40	1.00	2.00	6.00
1825..AH1240 Proof	Inc. above	Value: 100				

KM# 431 4 PIES

8.5500 g., Copper **Mint:** London **Obverse:** E.I. Co. arms **Reverse:** Value in sprays

Date	Mintage	Good	VG	F	VF	XF
1825//AH1240	—	0.25	0.60	1.50	3.00	8.00
1825//AH1240 Proof	Inc. above	Value: 150				

KM# 432 4 PIES

8.5500 g., Copper **Mint:** London **Obverse:** E.I. Co. arms **Reverse:** Value in sprays, right tip points up

Date	Mintage	Good	VG	F	VF	XF
1825//AH1240	—	0.25	0.60	1.50	3.00	8.00

KM# 433 4 PIES

8.5500 g., Copper **Mint:** London **Obverse:** E.I. Co. arms **Reverse:** Value in sprays, right spray tip in straight line

Date	Mintage	Good	VG	F	VF	XF
1825//AH1240	—	0.25	0.60	1.50	3.00	8.00

KM# 430 4 PIES

8.5500 g., Copper, 27.0 mm. **Mint:** London **Obverse:** E.I. Co. arms **Reverse:** Persian value in sprays, right spray tip points down

Date	Mintage	F	VF	XF	Unc
1824//AH1240(1825)	7,136,000	1.50	3.00	8.00	25.00
1824//AH1240(1825) Proof	Inc. above	Value: 150			

KM# 411 1/16 RUPEE

0.7300 g., Silver, 10.5 mm. **Mint:** Madras **Obv. Inscription:** "Sikkah Badshah Alamgir II" **Reverse:** Persian-Sanat, Zarb, mint name **Edge:** Olbique milling **Note:** Mint mark: Lotus.

Date	Mintage	Good	VG	F	VF	XF
AH1172//6 Frozen	8,684,254	0.15	0.40	1.00	2.00	10.00

KM# 423 1/16 RUPEE

0.7300 g., Silver, 10.5 mm. **Mint:** Calcutta **Obv. Inscription:** "Sikkah Badshah Alamgir II" **Reverse:** Sanat, Zarb, mint name **Edge:** Oblique milling **Note:** Mint mark: Rose.

Date	Mintage	Good	VG	F	VF	XF
AH1172//6 Frozen	—	0.15	0.40	1.00	2.00	8.00

KM# 405 2 ANNAS

1.4800 g., Silver, 16.4 mm. **Mint:** Madras **Obverse:** Two Annas on a garter around value in Persian **Reverse:** Value in Tamil on a ribbon around value in Telugu **Edge:** Vertical milling

Date	Mintage	Good	VG	F	VF	XF
ND(1808)	64,558	40.00	100	250	500	650

KM# 406 2 ANNAS

1.4800 g., Silver **Mint:** Madras **Obverse:** Two Annas on a garter around value in Persian **Reverse:** Value in Tamil on a ribbon around value in Telugu **Edge:** Vertical milling

Date	Mintage	Good	VG	F	VF	XF
ND(1808)	—	40.00	100	250	500	650

KM# 399 1/8 RUPEE

1.5100 g., Silver, 16.5 mm. **Mint:** Madras **Obv. Inscription:** "Sikkah Badshah Alamgir II" **Reverse:** Sanat, Zarb, mint name **Edge:** Oblique milling **Note:** Mint mark: Lotus. Dies and machinery were in Calcutta.

Date	Mintage	Good	VG	F	VF	XF
AH1172//6 Frozen	20,046	2.25	6.00	15.00	45.00	100

KM# 408 1/8 RUPEE

1.5100 g., Silver **Mint:** Madras **Obv. Inscription:** "Sikkah Badshah Alamgir II" **Reverse:** Sanat, Zarb, Arkat **Edge:** Oblique milling **Note:** Mint mark: Lotus.

Date	Mintage	Good	VG	F	VF	XF
AH1172//6 Frozen	104,020	0.20	0.50	1.25	2.00	8.00

KM# 412 1/8 RUPEE

1.5100 g., Silver **Mint:** Madras **Obv. Inscription:** "Sikkah Badshah Alamgir II" **Reverse:** Sanat, Zarb, Arkat **Edge:** Oblique milling **Note:** Mint mark: Closed form lotus.

Date	Mintage	Good	VG	F	VF	XF
AH1172//6	10,789,655	0.20	0.50	1.25	2.00	8.00

KM# 424 1/8 RUPEE

1.5100 g., Silver **Mint:** Calcutta **Obv. Inscription:** "Sikkah Badshah Alamgir II" **Reverse:** Sanat, Zarb, Arcot **Edge:** Oblique milling **Note:** Mint mark: Rose.

Date	Mintage	Good	VG	F	VF	XF
AH1172//6 Frozen	—	0.20	0.50	1.25	2.00	10.00

KM# 407 4 ANNAS

2.9700 g., Silver, 17 mm. **Mint:** Madras **Obverse:** Four Annas on a garter around value in Persian **Reverse:** Value in Tamil on a ribbon around value in Telugu **Edge:** Vertical milling

Date	Mintage	Good	VG	F	VF	XF
ND(1808)	44,225	50.00	125	300	600	750

KM# 400 1/4 RUPEE

3.0200 g., Silver, 16.5 mm. **Mint:** Madras **Obv. Inscription:** "Sikkah Badshah Alamgir II" **Reverse:** Sanat, Zarb, Arkat **Edge:** Oblique milling **Note:** Struck at Madras. Dies and machinery were produced in Calcutta.

Date	Mintage	Good	VG	F	VF	XF
AH1172//6 Frozen	18,216	2.00	5.00	12.50	25.00	100

KM# 409 1/4 RUPEE

2.9100 g., Silver, 17.4 mm. **Mint:** Madras **Obv. Inscription:** "Sikkah Badshah Alamgir II" **Reverse:** Sanat, Zarb, Arkat **Edge:** Indented cord milling **Note:** Mint mark: Lotus.

Date	Mintage	Good	VG	F	VF	XF
AH1172//6 Frozen	784,021	0.30	0.75	1.75	3.00	10.00
AH1176//6 (sic) Frozen	Inc. above	0.30	0.75	1.75	3.00	10.00

KM# 413 1/4 RUPEE

2.9100 g., Silver **Mint:** Madras **Obv. Inscription:** "Sikkah Badshah Alamgir II" **Reverse:** Sanat, Zarb, Arkat **Edge:** Indented cord milling **Note:** Mint mark: Closed form lotus. Struck at Madras.

Date	Mintage	Good	VG	F	VF	XF
AH1172//6 Frozen	5,227,322	0.50	1.25	3.00	5.00	15.00

KM# 425 1/4 RUPEE

2.9100 g., Silver, 17.4 mm. **Obv. Inscription:** "Sikkah Badshah Alamgir II" **Reverse:** Sanat, Zarb, Arkat **Edge:** Vertical milling **Note:** Mint mark: Rose. Struck at Calcutta.

Date	Mintage	Good	VG	F	VF	XF
AH1172//6 Frozen	—	0.40	1.00	2.50	4.00	10.00

KM# 434 1/4 RUPEE

2.9100 g., Silver **Obv. Inscription:** "Sikkah Badshah Alamgir II" **Reverse:** Sanat, Zarb, Arkat **Edge:** Vertical milling **Note:** Mint mark: Rose, crescent. Struck at Calcutta.

Date	Mintage	Good	VG	F	VF	XF
AH1172//6 Frozen	—	0.50	1.25	3.00	5.00	25.00
AH1172//6 Frozen; Proof	—	Value: 300				

KM# 401 1/2 RUPEE

6.0500 g., Silver, 22 mm. **Obverse:** Inscription, couplet **Obv. Inscription:** "Alamgir II" **Reverse:** Julus (formula), Arkat **Edge:** Oblique milling **Note:** Mint mark: Struck at Madras, Prid#248. Dies and machinery were produced in Calcutta.

Date	Mintage	Good	VG	F	VF	XF
AH1172//6	108,180	3.00	7.50	17.50	30.00	75.00

KM# 402 1/2 RUPEE

5.8300 g., Silver, 21.7 mm. **Obverse:** Inscription, couplet **Obv. Inscription:** "Alamgir II" **Reverse:** Julus (formula), Arkat **Edge:** Indented cord milling **Note:** Mint mark: Lotus, struck at Madras. Prid#253, Prid#254.

Date	Mintage	Good	VG	F	VF	XF
AH1172//6	3,392,021	0.50	1.25	3.00	5.00	18.00
AH1176//6 (sic)	Inc. above	0.50	1.25	3.00	5.00	18.00

KM# 414 1/2 RUPEE

5.8300 g., Silver, 21.7 mm. **Obverse:** Inscription, couplet **Obv. Inscription:** "Alamgir II" **Reverse:** Julus (formula), Arkat **Edge:** Indented cord milling **Note:** Mint mark: closed formed lotus. Struck at Madras. Prid#259.

Date	Mintage	F	VF	XF	Unc
AH1172//6	10,674,396	1.75	3.00	15.00	25.00

KM# 426 1/2 RUPEE

5.8300 g., Silver **Mint:** Calcutta **Obverse:** Inscription, couplet **Obv. Inscription:** "Alamgir II" **Reverse:** Julus (formula), Arkat **Edge:** Vertical milling **Note:** Mint mark: Rose. Struck at Calcutta. Prid#264.

Date	Mintage	Good	VG	F	VF	XF
AH1172//6 Proof	—	—	—	—	—	—
AH1172//6	—	0.50	1.25	3.00	5.00	25.00

KM# 435 1/2 RUPEE

5.8300 g., Silver, 21.7 mm. **Obverse:** Inscription, couplet **Obv. Inscription:** "Alamgir II" **Reverse:** Julus (formula), Arkat **Edge:** Vertical milling **Note:** Mint mark: Rose, crescent. Struck at Calcutta. Prid#270.

Date	Mintage	Good	VG	F	VF	XF
AH1172//6	—	1.00	2.50	6.00	10.00	35.00
AH1172//6	—	Value: 350				

KM# 403 RUPEE

12.1000 g., Silver, 28 mm. **Mint:** Madras **Obverse:** Inscription, regal title **Obv. Inscription:** "Alamgir II" **Reverse:** Julus (formula), Arkat **Edge:** Oblique milling **Note:** Mint mark: Lotus. Struck at Madras. Prid#247. Dies and machinery were produced in Calcutta.

Date	Mintage	Good	VG	F	VF	XF
AH1172//6 Frozen	2,144,806	2.00	3.50	9.00	15.00	50.00

KM# 410 RUPEE

11.6600 g., Silver, 27.8 mm. **Mint:** Madras **Obverse:** Inscription, regal title **Obv. Inscription:** "Alamgir II" **Reverse:** Julus (formula), Arkat **Edge:** Indented cord milling **Note:** Mint mark: Lotus, struck at Madras. Prid.#251, Prid.#252.

Date	Mintage	Good	VG	F	VF	XF
AH1172//6 Frozen	10,939,021	1.25	2.25	3.75	7.50	15.00
AH1176(sic)//6 Frozen	Inc. above	1.25	2.25	3.75	7.50	15.00

KM# 415.1 RUPEE

11.6600 g., Silver, 27.8 mm. **Obverse:** Inscription, regal title **Obv. Inscription:** "Alamgir II" **Reverse:** Julus (formula), Arkat **Edge:** Indented cord milling **Note:** Mint mark: Closed form lotus. Struck at Madras. Prid#258.

Date	Mintage	Good	VG	F	VF	XF
AH1172//6 Frozen	63,116,258	1.25	2.25	3.75	7.50	15.00

KM# 415.2 RUPEE

11.6600 g., Silver, 28.8 mm. **Obverse:** Inscription, couplet **Obv. Inscription:** "Alamgir II" **Reverse:** Julus (formula), Arkat **Edge:** Center graining left **Note:** Mint mark: Open lotus. Struck at Madras.

Date	Mintage	Good	VG	F	VF	XF
AH1172//6 Frozen	—	1.25	2.25	3.75	7.50	15.00

KM# 427 RUPEE

Silver, 26 mm. **Obverse:** Inscription, regal title **Obv. Inscription:** "Alamgir II" **Reverse:** Julus (formula), Arkat **Edge:** Vertical milling **Note:** Mint mark: Rose. Struck at Calcutta. Prid.#263.

Date	Mintage	Good	VG	F	VF	XF
AH1172//6 Frozen	—	1.25	2.25	3.75	7.50	20.00

KM# 436 RUPEE

Silver, 26 mm. **Mint:** Calcutta **Obverse:** Inscription, regal title **Obv. Inscription:** "Alamgir II" **Reverse:** Julus (formula), Arkat **Edge:** Vertical milling **Note:** Mint mark: Rose, crescent added. Struck at Calcutta. Prid#268. Dump rupees in the name of Alamgir, with a small crescent to left of regnal year and mint name "Arkat (Arcot)", were struck by the French (see India-French) as were Arcot rupees in the names of other Mughal emperors, dated AH1149-1233.

Date	Mintage	Good	VG	F	VF	XF
AH1172//6 Frozen	—	1.25	2.25	3.75	7.50	20.00
AH1172//6 Frozen; Proof	—	Value: 400				

KM# 404.1 2 RUPEES

24.1900 g., Silver, 39.5 mm. **Mint:** Madras **Obverse:** Inscription, regal title **Obv. Inscription:** "Alamgir II" **Reverse:** Julus (formula), Arkat **Edge:** Oblique milling **Note:** Mint mark: Lotus. Struck at Madras. Prid.#245. Dav.# 248.

Date	Mintage	Good	VG	F	VF	XF
AH1172//2(sic)	165,000	87.50	175	300	500	1,500

KM# 404.2 2 RUPEES

24.1900 g., Silver, 39.5 mm. **Mint:** Madras **Obverse:** Inscription, regal title **Obv. Inscription:** "Alamgir II" **Reverse:** Julus (formula), Arkat **Note:** Mint mark: Lotus. Struck at Madras. Prid.#245. Usually found struck over Spanish or Spanish Colonial 8 Reales.

Date	Mintage	Good	VG	F	VF	XF
AH1172//6 Frozen	—	100	200	350	600	1,600

KM# 416 1/4 MOHUR

2.9100 g., Gold, 17.4 mm. **Mint:** Madras **Obverse:** Inscription, couplet **Obv. Inscription:** "Alamgir II" **Reverse:** Julus (formula), Arkat **Note:** Mint mark: Lotus. Struck at Madras. Prid.#240.

Date	Mintage	Good	VG	F	VF	XF
AH1172//6 Frozen	2,000	175	300	500	850	1,350

KM# 419 1/4 MOHUR

2.9100 g., Gold, 17 mm. **Mint:** Madras **Obverse:** Company crest **Obv. Legend:** BRITISH EAST INDIA COMPANY **Reverse:** Value in Persian **Rev. Inscription:** "of the Honorable English Company" **Edge:** Vertical milling **Note:** Prid.#243.

Date	Mintage	Good	VG	F	VF	XF
ND(1819)	91,834	75.00	125	250	350	600

KM# 422 5 RUPEES

3.8800 g., Gold, 19.5 mm. **Mint:** Madras **Obverse:** Company arms without supporters **Obv. Legend:** BRITISH EAST INDIA COMPANY **Reverse:** Value in Persian **Edge:** Vertical milling **Note:** Prid.#244.

Date	Mintage	Good	VG	F	VF	XF
ND(1820)	2,179,573	BV	BV	45.00	75.00	125

KM# 417 1/2 MOHUR

5.8300 g., Gold, 21.7 mm. **Obverse:** Inscription, regal title **Obv. Inscription:** "Alamgir II" **Reverse:** Julus (formula), Arkat **Rev. Inscription:** Julus (formula), mint name **Edge:** Indented cord milling **Note:** Mint mark: Lotus. Struck at Madras. Prid.#239.

Date	Mintage	Good	VG	F	VF	XF
AH1172//6 Frozen	7,500	165	275	450	750	1,250

KM# 420 1/2 MOHUR

5.8300 g., Gold, 21.2 mm. **Mint:** Madras **Obverse:** Company crest **Obv. Legend:** BRITISH EAST INDIA COMPANY **Reverse:** Value in Persian **Rev. Inscription:** "of the Honorable English Company" **Edge:** Vertical milling **Note:** Prid.#242.

Date	Mintage	Good	VG	F	VF	XF
ND(1819)	212,690	55.00	90.00	150	350	550

KM# 421.1 MOHUR

11.6600 g., Gold, 28 mm. **Mint:** Madras **Obverse:** E.I. Company arms, Small letters **Obv. Legend:** BRITISH EAST INDIA COMPANY **Reverse:** Value in Persian **Rev. Inscription:** "of the Honorable English Company" **Edge:** Vertical milling **Note:** Prid.#241.

Date	Mintage	Good	VG	F	VF	XF
ND(1819)	117,800	BV	100	175	225	425

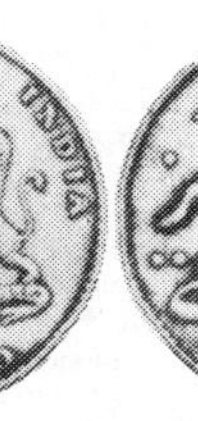 

KM# 421.2 MOHUR

11.6600 g., Gold, 28 mm. **Mint:** Madras **Obverse:** Large letters in legend, E.I. Co. arms **Edge:** Vertical milling **Note:** Prid.#241.

Date	Good	VG	F	VF	XF
ND(1819)	BV	100	175	225	425

KM# 418 MOHUR

11.6600 g., Gold, 27.8 mm. **Obverse:** Inscription, regal title **Obv. Inscription:** "Alamgir II" **Reverse:** Julus (formula), Arkat **Edge:** Indented cord milling **Note:** Mint mark: Lotus. Struck at Madras. Prid.#238.

Date	Mintage	Good	VG	F	VF	XF
AH1172//6 Frozen	—	125	200	350	650	1,000

PATTERNS

Including off metal strikes

KM#	Date	Mintage	Identification	Mkt Val
Pn2	AH1807	—	20 Cash. Copper. Prid.#342.	—
Pn3	AH1824	—	4 Pice. Copper. Prid.#343.	—
Pn4	AH1172//6	—	Rupee. Silver. Prid.#339.	—

The Ionian Islands, situated in the Ionian Sea to the west of Greece, is the collective name for the islands of Corfu, Cephalonia, Zante, Santa Maura, Ithaca, Cythera and Paxo, with their minor dependencies. Before Britain acquired the islands, 1809-14, they were at various times subject to the authority of Venice, France, Russia and Turkey. They remained under British control until their cession to Greece on March 29, 1864.

(1799-1807)

MONETARY SYSTEM
2 Soldi = 1 Gazetta

VENETIAN AUTHORITY

VENETIAN COINAGE

KM# 1 GAZETTA
Copper **Note:** Similar to 5 Gazettae, KM#2.

Date	Mintage	VG	F	VF	XF	Unc
1801	—	75.00	175	450	1,000	—

KM# 2 5 GAZETTAE
Copper **Rev:** Denomination in Greek

Date	Mintage	VG	F	VF	XF	Unc
1801	—	100	250	500	1,100	—

KM# 3 5 GAZETTAE
Copper **Rev:** Denomination in Italian

Date	Mintage	VG	F	VF	XF	Unc
1801	—	100	250	500	1,100	—

KM# 4 10 GAZETTAE
Copper **Obv. Legend:** **Rev:** Denomination in Greek

Date	Mintage	VG	F	VF	XF	Unc
1801	—	150	350	750	1,600	—

KM# 5 10 GAZETTAE
Copper **Obv. Legend:** ΣΠΤΑΝΗΣΟΣ ΠΟΛΙΤΣΙΑ **Rev:** Denomination in Italian

Date	Mintage	VG	F	VF	XF	Unc
1801 Rare	—	—	—	—	—	—

BRITISH ADMINISTRATION

COUNTERMARKED COINAGE

(1809-1863)

The British military forces under General Campbell were headquartered on the island of Zacynthos (Zante). A shortage of small silver coinage resulted in the countermarking of circulated coins of the Two Sicilies of 10 and 20 Grani denominations and worn Spanish and Spanish Colonial silver 1 and 2 reales coinage.

The Type I countermarks of 1813 were raised numerals 25, 30, 50 and 60 in rectangular indent. These being easily counterfeited lead to the 1814 Type II oval indent with a crudely executed bust of King George III over raised numerals. The Type II countermark was applied to existing Type I countermarked coinage and other coins found in circulation. No single countermarked Type I pieces are known to have survived.

MONETARY SYSTEM
40 Paras = 1 Piastre
220 Paras = 1 Spanish Dollar (8 Reales)

Type I
Raised 25, 30, 50, or 60 in rectangular indent.

Type II
Poretrait of King George III over 25, 30, 50, or 60 in oval indent.

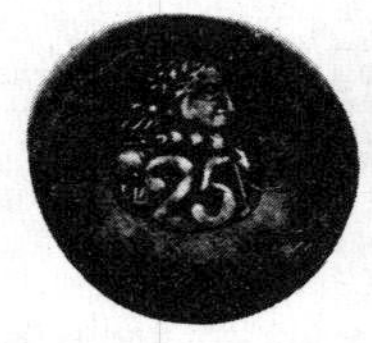

KM# 18 25 PARAS
Silver **Countermark:** Type I and II **Note:** Countermark on Naples and Sicily 10 Grani of Charles II.

CM Date	Host Date	Good	VG	F	VF	XF
ND(1814)	ND	150	250	425	800	—

KM# 19 25 PARAS
Silver **Countermark:** Type II **Note:** Countermark on Spanish or Spanish Colonial 1 Real.

CM Date	Host Date	Good	VG	F	VF	XF
ND(1814)	ND	150	200	325	600	—

KM# 20 30 PARAS
Silver **Countermark:** Type II **Note:** Countermark on Naples and Sicily 10 Grani.

CM Date	Host Date	Good	VG	F	VF	XF
ND(1814)	ND Rare	—	—	—	—	—

KM# 21 30 PARAS
Silver **Countermark:** Type II **Note:** Countermark on Spanish Colonial 1 Real.

CM Date	Host Date	Good	VG	F	VF	XF
ND(1814)	ND Rare	—	—	—	—	—

Note: One unusual piece exists with only one countermark on a French coin of Louis XIV. It is considered by some experts to be a contemporary counterfeit, since the authorization for these coins mentions only Spanish and Two Sicilies coinage. However, it may be that the islanders were permitted to present any silver coins in their possession for countermarking.

KM# 22.1 50 PARAS
Silver **Countermark:** Type II **Note:** Countermark on Naples and Sicily 20 Grani of Charles II.

CM Date	Host Date	Good	VG	F	VF	XF
ND(1814)	ND	150	225	400	750	—

KM# 23.1 50 PARAS
Silver **Countermark:** Type I and II **Note:** Countermark on Spanish or Spanish Colonial 2 Reales.

CM Date	Host Date	Good	VG	F	VF	XF
ND(1814)	ND	150	225	400	750	—

KM# 23.2 50 PARAS
Silver **Countermark:** Type I and II **Note:** Countermark on worn disc.

CM Date	Host Date	Good	VG	F	VF	XF
ND(1814)	ND	125	200	300	600	—

KM# 22.2 50 PARAS
Silver **Countermark:** Type II **Note:** Countermark on Naples and Sicily 20 Grani of Ferdinando IV.

CM Date	Host Date	Good	VG	F	VF	XF
ND(1814)	ND	150	225	400	750	—

KM# 24 60 PARAS
Silver **Countermark:** Type II **Note:** Countermark on Naples and Sicily 20 Grani.

CM Date	Host Date	Good	VG	F	VF	XF
ND(1814)	ND	275	400	650	1,100	—

KM# 25 60 PARAS
Silver **Countermark:** Type I and II **Note:** Countermark on Spanish 2 Reales of Philip V.

CM Date	Host Date	Good	VG	F	VF	XF
ND(1814)	ND	275	400	650	1,100	—

DECIMAL COINAGE

KM# 30 LEPTON
Copper **Obv:** Winged lion above date **Rev:** Seated Britannia above 4 (= 1/4 Obol) **Note:** Most of these coins are overstruck on Venetian coins by native craftsmen, and are very crude.

Date	Mintage	F	VF	XF	Unc	BU
1821	—	100	250	500	1,000	—

KM# 34 LEPTON
Copper **Obv:** Winged lion above date

Date	Mintage	F	VF	XF	Unc	BU
1834.	—	2.00	7.00	20.00	65.00	—
1834. Proof	—	Value: 300				
1835.	—	2.00	7.00	20.00	65.00	—
1835	—	2.00	7.00	20.00	65.00	—
1848.	13,483,000	3.00	10.00	30.00	75.00	—
1848	Inc. above	4.00	12.00	35.00	90.00	—
1849.	Inc. above	2.00	7.00	20.00	65.00	—
1849 Proof	—	Value: 300				
1851.	Inc. above	2.00	7.00	20.00	65.00	—
1851. Proof	—	Value: 300				
1853.	1,344,000	2.00	7.00	20.00	65.00	—
1853 Proof	—	Value: 300				
1857.	Inc. above	2.00	7.00	20.00	65.00	—
1857	Inc. above	2.00	7.00	20.00	65.00	—
1862.	Inc. above	2.00	7.00	20.00	65.00	—
1862 Proof	—	Value: 300				

KM# 31 2 LEPTA
Copper

Date	Mintage	F	VF	XF	Unc	BU
1819.	9,462,000	10.00	25.00	55.00	125	—
1819 Proof	—	Value: 250				
1820.	Inc. above	10.00	25.00	55.00	125	—
1820 Proof	—	Value: 250				

KM# 32 OBOL
Copper

Date	Mintage	F	VF	XF	Unc	BU
1819.	8,279,000	25.00	50.00	85.00	245	—
1819 Proof	—	Value: 450				
1819 Proof; medal strike	—	Value: 500				

KM# 33 2 OBOLI
Copper

Date	Mintage	F	VF	XF	Unc	BU
1819	4,140,000	25.00	50.00	100	265	—
1819 Proof	—	Value: 550				
1819 Proof	—	Value: 600				

KM# 35 30 LEPTA
1.4100 g., 0.9250 Silver .0419 oz.

Date	Mintage	F	VF	XF	Unc	BU
1834	—	25.00	50.00	75.00	225	—
1834 Proof	—	Value: 500				
1834.	—	25.00	50.00	75.00	250	—
1848.	331,000	65.00	125	325	750	—
1849	Inc. above	25.00	50.00	75.00	250	—
1849 Proof	—	Value: 550				
1849.	Inc. above	25.00	50.00	75.00	250	—
1851	Inc. above	25.00	50.00	75.00	250	—
1851 Proof	—	Value: 550				
1852	Inc. above	25.00	50.00	75.00	250	—
1852 Proof	—	Value: 550				
1857	Inc. above	25.00	50.00	75.00	250	—
1857.	Inc. above	25.00	50.00	75.00	250	—
1862	Inc. above	10.00	25.00	60.00	200	—

PATTERNS

Including off metal strikes

KM#	Date	Mintage	Identification	Mkt Val
Pn1	ND(1819)	—	Obol. Copper. Ceylon 1 Stiver, C29. 1 Obol, W on ground line, KM32. Mule. Obv: Ceylon 1 Stiver, C29. Rev: 1 Obol, W on ground line, KM32.	2,200

KM#	Date	Mintage	Identification	Mkt Val
Pn2	ND(1819)	—	2 Oboli. Copper. Ireland 1 Penny, C12. 2 Oboli, W WYON on ground line, KM33. Mule. Obv: Ireland 1 Penny, C12. Rev: 2 Oboli, W WYON on ground line, KM33	3,500
Pn3	1819	—	Obol. Silver. KM#32	1,750

KM#	Date	Mintage	Identification	Mkt Val
Pn4	1819	—	Obol. W.W. in exergue	1,650

IRAN

The Islamic Republic of Iran is located between the Caspian Sea and the Persian Gulf in southwestern Asia. Iran (historically known as Persia until 1931 AD) is one of the world's most ancient and resilient nations. Strategically astride the lower land gate to Asia, it has been conqueror and conquered, sovereign nation and vassal state, ever emerging from its periods of glory or travail with its culture and political individuality intact. Iran (Persia) was a powerful empire under Cyrus the Great (600-529 B.C.), its borders extending from the Indus to the Nile. It has also been conquered by the predatory empires of antique and recent times - Assyrian, Medean, Macedonian, Seljuq, Turk, Mongol - and more recently been coveted by Russia, the Third Reich and Great Britain. Revolts against the absolute power of the Persian shahs resulted in the establishment of a constitutional monarchy in1906.

TITLES

دار الخلافة
Dar al-Khilafat

RULERS

Husain Quli Khan, rebel in Isfahan, AH1216/1801AD

سلطان علی
Sultan 'Ali Shah, AH1250/1834AD

حسین علی
Husayn 'Ali Shah, AH1250/1834AD

شاهنشه انبیا محمد
Muhammad Shah, AH1250-64/1834-48AD

ناصرالدین
Nasir al-Din Shah, AH1264-1313/1848-96AD

مظفرالدین
Muzaffar Al-Din Shah, AH1313-24/1896-1907AD

MINT NAMES

ابو شهر
Abu Shahr (Bushire)

اردبیل
Ardebil

استراباد
Astarabad (located in Iran)

بندر عباس
Bandar Abbas

بندر ابو شهر
Bandar Abu Shahr

البصره
Basra (al-Basrah, Iraq)

بهبهان

Behbahan

بهکر

Bahkar
(see Afghanistan map)

بروجرد

Borujerd

دربند

Darband

دزفول

Dezful

ایروان

Eravan (Iravan, Armenia)

فومان

Fouman

گنجه

Ganjeh (Ganja, Azerbaijan)

گیلان

Gilan

همدان

Hamadan

هرات

Herat, (Afghanistan)

حویزه

Huwayza

اصفهان

Isfahan (Esfahan)

جلو

Jelou (Army Mint)

کاشان

Kashan

کرمان

Kirman (Kerman)

کرمانشاهان

Kirmanshahan (Kermanshah)

خوی

Khoy (Khoi)

لاهیجان

Lahijan

لاهور

Lahore
(Pakistan, see Afghanistan map)

مراغه

Maragheh

مشهد

Mashhad

مازندران

Mazandaran

نهاوند

Nahawand

نخجوان

Nakhjawan (Azerbaijan)

ناصری

Naseri

نخوی

Nukhwi

پناه آباد

Panahabad

پشاور

Peshawar
(Pakistan, see Afghanistan map)

قندهار

Qandahar (Kandahar, Afghanistan)

قزوین

Qazvin

قم

Qomm (Kumm)

رعنش

Ra'nash

رشت

Rasht

رکاب

Rekab (Rikab)

رضائیه

Reza'iyeh (Army Mint)

سرخس

Sarakhs

ساری

Sari

ساوج بلاق

Sawuj Balagh

شماخه

Shamakha (Shemakhi, Azerbaijan)

شیراز

Shiraz

شروان

Shirwan (Azerbaijan)

شوشتر

Shushtar

سمنان

Simnan (Semnan)

سند

Sind
(see Afghanistan map)

سلطان آباد

Sultanabad

طبرستان

Tabaristan
(also Tabarestan, region N.W. of Iran)

تبریز

Tabriz

طهران

Tehran

تفلیس

Tiflis (Georgia)

توی سرکان

Tuyserkan

ارومی

Urumi (Reza'iyeh)

یزد

Yazd

زنجان

Zanjan

COIN DATING

Iranian coins were dated according to the Moslem lunar calendar until March 21, 1925 (AD), when dating was switched to a new calendar based on the solar year, indicated by the notation SH. The monarchial calender system was adopted in 1976 = MS2535 and was abandoned in 1978 = MS2537. The previously used solar year calendar was restored at that time.

MONETARY SYSTEM

1798-1825 (AH 1212-1241)

1250 Dinars = 1 Riyal
8 Riyals = 1 Toman

1825-1931
(AH1241-1344, SH1304-09)

50 Dinars = 1 Shahi
20 Shahis = 1 Kran (Qiran)
10 Krans = 1 Toman

NOTE: From AD1830-34 (AH1245-50) the gold Toman was known as a 'Keshwarsetan.'

Copper Hammered Coinage

During the nineteenth century, copper coins (falus, flus) were issued at some 40 or more local mints, each of which coined falus for local use only. Copper coins did not circulate generally, but were restricted to the city of their origin and its immediate environs. The local mintmaster, often in collaboration with the local governor, determined the type, design, and weight of the coinage, and regulated its circulation.

In theory, copper coins were recalled and changed about every year, with a substantial fee payable to the mintmaster for the exchange of old coin for new. To discourage further use the old coin was either demonetized or tariffed at a lower value, usually about half its original.

In order to facilitate the recognition of new and old coin, the type was changed annually, the type being the obverse pictorial design, so that illiterate shopkeepers could tell the difference and not be deceived by obsolete coins. However, after a number of years, the same types would be reinstated for another year. In practice, the system worked more informally, and surviving coins show that at some mints, identical types were struck for several years running and were not recalled annually.

The metrology of the copper Falus is uncertain. While it seems that Falus were intended to follow an assigned weight standard, great tolerance was permitted. The weight standard was frequently changed (or the mintmaster issued lighter coins and pocketed the difference), and each mint city maintained its own standard and copper currency policies.

As a result of the frequent recoinage of copper and its frequent demonetization, copper coins were not hoarded or saved, and are consequently quite scarce today. Annual change meant that each mint had a multiplicity of types and varieties, most of which are uncommon today. The following listings are not an attempt at completeness, but give a representative selection of the products of each mint.

IMPORTANT: Most types were used at many different mints. The type can therefore not be used to attribute a coin to the mint of its issue. The ONLY certain way of attributing the coin is to read the mint name on the reverse. Well struck copper falus with clear mint-name and date are worth a premium.

Silver and Gold Hammered Coinage

The precious metal monetary system of Qajar Persia prior to the reforms of 1878 was the direct descendant of the Mongol system introduced by Ghazan Mahmud in 1297AD, and was the last example of a medieval Islamic coinage. It is not a modern system, and cannot be understood as such. It is not possible to list types, dates, and mints as for other countries, both because of the nature of the coinage, and because very little research has been done on the series. The following comments should help elucidate its nature.

STANDARDS: The weight of the primary silver and gold coins was set by law and was expressed in terms of the Mesqal (about 4.61 g) and the Nokhod (24 Nokhod = 1 Mesqal). The primary silver coin was the Rupee from AH1211-1212, the Riyal from AH1212-1241, and the Gheran from AH1241-1344. The standard gold coin was the Toman. Currently the price of gold is quoted in Mesqals.

DENOMINATIONS: In addition to the primary denominations, noted in the last paragraph, fractional pieces were coined, valued at one-eighth, one-fourth, and one-half the primary denomination, usually in much smaller quantities. These were ordinarily struck from the same dies as the larger pieces, sometimes on broad, thin flans, sometimes on thick, dumpy flans. On the smaller coins, the denomination can best be determined only by weighing the coin. The denomination is almost never expressed on the coin!

DEVALUATIONS: From time to time, the standard for silver and gold was reduced, and the old coin recalled and replaced with lighter coin, the difference going to the government coffers. The effect was that of a devaluation of the primary silver and gold coins, or inversely regarded, an increase in the price of silver and gold. The durations of each standard varied from about 2 to 20 years. The standards are given for each ruler, as the denomination can only be determined when the standard is known.

LIGHTWEIGHT AND ALLOYED PIECES: Most of the smaller denomination coins were issued at lighter weights than those prescribed by law, with the difference going to the pockets of the mint-masters. Other mints, notably Hamadan, added excessive amounts of alloy to the coins, and some mintmasters lost their heads as a result. Discrepancies in weight of as much as 15 percent and more are observed, with the result that it is often quite impossible to determine the denomination of a coin!

OVERSIZE COINS: Occasionally multiples of the primary denominations were produced, usually on special occasions, for presentation by the Shah to his favorites. These coins' did not circulate (except as bullion), and were usually worn as ornaments. They were the NCLT's' of their day.

MINTS & EPITHETS: Qajar coinage was struck at 34 mints (plus at least a dozen others striking only copper Falus), which are listed previously, with drawings of the mintnames in Persian, as they appear on the coins. However, the Persian script admits of infinite variation and stylistic whimsy, so the forms given are only guides, and not absolute. Only a knowledge of the script will assure correct reading. In addition to the city name, most mintnames were given identifying epithets, which occasionally appear in lieu of the mint name, particularly at Iravan and Mashhad.

TYPES: There were no types in the modern sense, but the arrangement of the legends and the ornamental borders were frequently changed. These changes do not coincide with changes in standards, and cannot be used to determine the mint, which must be found by actually reading the reverse inscriptions.

ARRANGEMENT: The following listings are arranged first by ruler, with various standards explained. Then, the coins are listed by denomination within each reign. For each denomination, one or more pieces, when available, are illustrated, with the mint and date noted beneath each photo. For each type, a date range is given, but this range indicates the years during which the particular type was current, and does not imply that every year of the interval is known on actual coins. Because dates were carelessly engraved, and old dies were used until they wore out or broke, we occasionally find coins of a particular type dated before or after the indicated interval. Such coins command no premium. No attempt has been made to determine which mints actually exist for which types.

KINGDOM

Anonymous

HAMMERED COINAGE

Mint: Abu Shahr
KM# A57 FALUS

Copper **Obv:** Bird to right **Rev:** Inscription with mint and date

Date	Mintage	Good	VG	F	VF	XF
AH124x	—	—	—	—	—	—

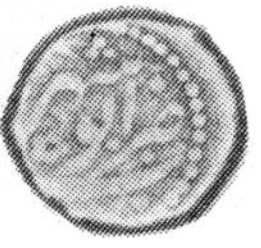

Mint: Abu Shahr
KM# 2 FALUS

Copper **Obv:** Lion

Date	Mintage	Good	VG	F	VF	XF
AH1270	—	9.00	15.00	25.00	40.00	—

Mint: Abu Shahr
KM# 56 FALUS

Copper **Obv:** Two lions facing

Date	Mintage	Good	VG	F	VF	XF
AHxxxx	—	7.50	12.50	20.00	32.50	—

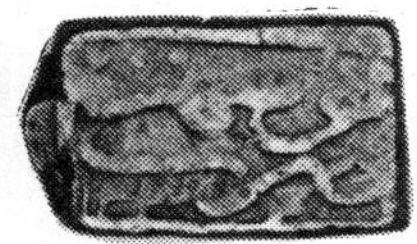

Mint: Abu Shahr
KM# 3 FALUS

Copper **Obv:** Bale mark

Date	Mintage	Good	VG	F	VF	XF
AH1234	—	11.50	18.50	30.00	50.00	—

Mint: Abu Shahr
KM# 4 FALUS

Copper **Obv:** Peacock

Date	Mintage	Good	VG	F	VF	XF
AH1239	—	9.00	15.00	25.00	40.00	—

Mint: Abu Shahr
KM# 57 FALUS

Copper **Obv:** Two peacocks facing left and right

Date	Mintage	Good	VG	F	VF	XF
AH1257	—	11.50	18.50	30.00	50.00	—

Mint: Abu Shahr
KM# 5 FALUS

Copper **Obv:** Fish

Date	Mintage	Good	VG	F	VF	XF
AH1221	—	9.00	15.00	25.00	40.00	—
AH1231	—	9.00	15.00	25.00	40.00	—

Mint: Ardebil
KM# 6 FALUS

Copper **Obv:** Peacock holding snake in beak

Date	Mintage	Good	VG	F	VF	XF
AH1232	—	9.00	15.00	25.00	40.00	—

Mint: Astarabad
KM# A7 FALUS

Copper **Obv:** Man on horseback

Date	Mintage	Good	VG	F	VF	XF
AH1259	—	9.00	15.00	25.00	40.00	—

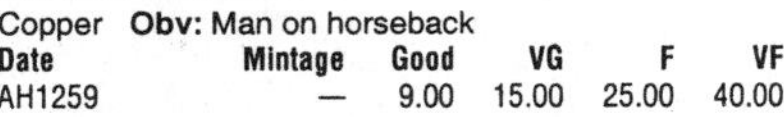

Mint: Astarabad
KM# 7 FALUS

Copper **Obv:** Two ibexes

Date	Mintage	Good	VG	F	VF	XF
ND	—	9.00	15.00	25.00	40.00	—

Mint: Astarabad
KM# 58 FALUS

Copper **Obv:** Sun above lion facing right

Date	Mintage	Good	VG	F	VF	XF
ND	—	9.00	15.00	25.00	40.00	—

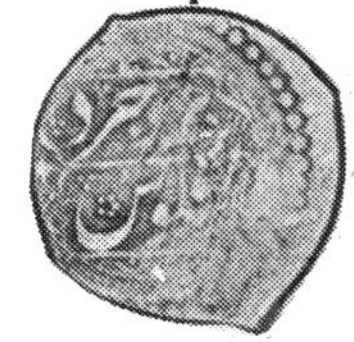

Mint: Borujerd
KM# 10 FALUS

Copper **Obv:** Soldier leaning on his rifle

Date	Mintage	Good	VG	F	VF	XF
AH124x	—	11.50	18.50	30.00	50.00	—
AH1261	—	—	—	—	—	—

Mint: Borujerd
KM# 11 FALUS

Copper **Obv:** Small bird

Date	Mintage	Good	VG	F	VF	XF
ND	—	9.00	15.00	25.00	40.00	—

Mint: Darband
KM# 59 FALUS

Copper **Obv:** Peacock right

Date	Mintage	Good	VG	F	VF	XF
AH1228	—	11.50	18.50	30.00	50.00	—

Mint: Eravan
KM# 19 FALUS

Copper **Obv:** Camel

Date	Mintage	Good	VG	F	VF	XF
AH1223	—	11.50	18.50	30.00	50.00	—

Mint: Ganjeh
KM# 15 FALUS

Copper **Obv:** Goose

Date	Mintage	Good	VG	F	VF	XF
AH1257	—	11.50	18.50	30.00	50.00	—

Mint: Ganjeh
KM# 60 FALUS

Copper **Obv:** Horse

Date	Mintage	Good	VG	F	VF	XF
AH1220	—	—	—	—	—	—

Mint: Hamadan
KM# 18 FALUS
Copper

Date	Mintage	Good	VG	F	VF	XF
AH1254	—	9.00	15.00	25.00	40.00	—

Mint: Isfahan
KM# 21 FALUS
Copper **Obv:** Scales

Date	Mintage	Good	VG	F	VF	XF
AH1242	—	9.00	15.00	25.00	40.00	—

Mint: Kashan
KM# 24 FALUS
Copper **Obv:** Lion and sun in wreath **Rev:** Denomination: 50 dinars

Date	Mintage	Good	VG	F	VF	XF
AH1293	—	11.50	18.50	30.00	50.00	—

Note: This type was an attempt to reform the copper coinage by Nasir al-Din Shah.

Mint: Khoy
KM# 26 FALUS
Copper **Obv:** Gazelle

Date	Mintage	Good	VG	F	VF	XF
AH1230	—	9.00	15.00	25.00	40.00	—

Mint: Khoy
KM# B26 FALUS
Copper **Obv:** Peacock (?) **Rev:** Mintname inverted

Date	Mintage	Good	VG	F	VF	XF
AH1241	—	11.50	18.50	30.00	50.00	—

Mint: Kirman
KM# 27 FALUS
Copper **Obv:** Lion in wreath

Date	Mintage	Good	VG	F	VF	XF
AH1287	—	6.50	11.50	18.50	30.00	—

Mint: Kirmanshahan
KM# 28 FALUS
Copper **Obv:** Sun face

Date	Mintage	Good	VG	F	VF	XF
AH1245	—	6.50	11.50	18.50	30.00	—

Mint: Kirmanshahan
KM# 62 FALUS
Copper **Obv:** Horseman riding left **Rev:** Lion and sun

Date	Mintage	Good	VG	F	VF	XF
AH1231	—	—	—	—	—	—

Mint: Kirmanshahan
KM# A63 FALUS
Copper **Obv:** Rider on elephant standing to left, date backwards in field in front and in back of rider **Rev:** Legend and mintname

Date	Mintage	Good	VG	F	VF	XF
AH1258	—	15.00	25.00	40.00	65.00	—

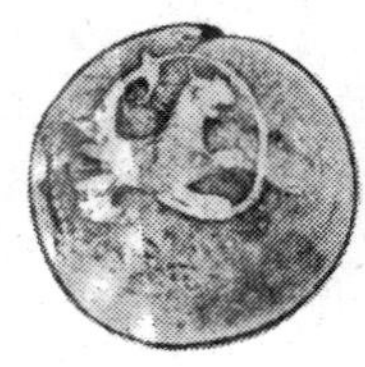 

Mint: Kirmanshahan
KM# 29 FALUS
Copper **Obv:** Lion lying right

Date	Mintage	Good	VG	F	VF	XF
ND	—	9.00	15.00	25.00	40.00	—

Mint: Lenjeh - Bandar Lengeh
KM# B30 FALUS
Copper

Date	Mintage	Good	VG	F	VF	XF
AH1247	—	27.50	45.00	75.00	125	—
AH1259	—	32.50	55.00	90.00	150	—

 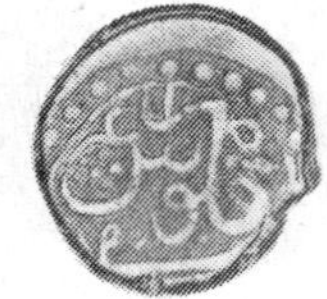

Mint: Maragheh
KM# 31 FALUS
Copper **Obv:** Peacock

Date	Mintage	Good	VG	F	VF	XF
AH1270	—	11.50	18.50	30.00	50.00	—

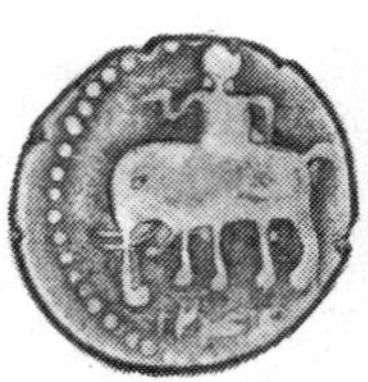  

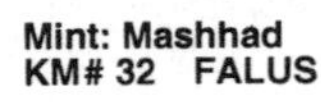

Mint: Mashhad
KM# 32 FALUS
Copper **Obv:** Elephant and rider

Date	Mintage	Good	VG	F	VF	XF
AH1246	—	11.50	18.50	30.00	50.00	—

Mint: Mashhad
KM# 63 FALUS
Copper **Obv:** Sunface

Date	Mintage	Good	VG	F	VF	XF
AH1237	—	7.50	12.50	20.00	35.00	—

Mint: Mashhad
KM# 64 FALUS
Copper **Obv:** Lion and sun

Date	Mintage	Good	VG	F	VF	XF
AH1258	—	6.50	11.50	18.50	30.00	—
AH1261	—	6.50	11.50	18.50	30.00	—

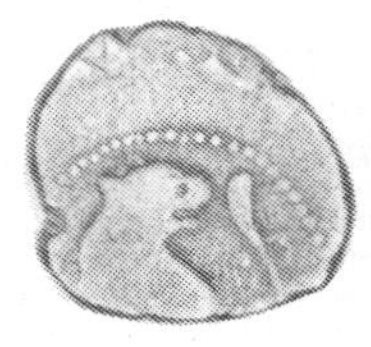 

Mint: Nihavand
KM# 34 FALUS
Copper **Obv:** Lion sitting

Date	Mintage	Good	VG	F	VF	XF
AH1240	—	9.00	15.00	25.00	40.00	—

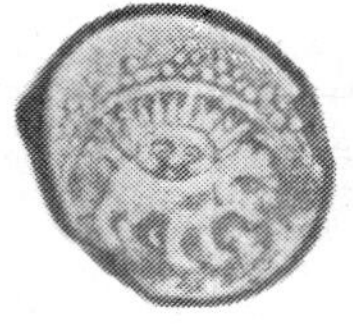 

Mint: Qazvín
KM# A35 FALUS
Copper **Obv:** Lion right and sun **Note:** Struck at Qazvín.

Date	Mintage	Good	VG	F	VF	XF
ND	—	7.50	12.50	20.00	35.00	—

Mint: Qazvín
KM# 35 FALUS
Copper **Obv:** Lion left facing with sword and sun in wreath **Note:** Struck at Qazvín.

Date	Mintage	Good	VG	F	VF	XF
AH1293	—	7.50	12.50	20.00	35.00	—
AH1294	—	7.50	12.50	20.00	35.00	—

Mint: Rasht
KM# B37 FALUS
Copper **Obv:** Religious invocation **Rev:** Inscription with mint name

Date	Mintage	Good	VG	F	VF	XF
ND	—	—	—	—	—	—

Mint: Rasht
KM# 36 FALUS
Copper **Obv:** Lion and sun

Date	Mintage	Good	VG	F	VF	XF
AH1246	—	7.50	12.50	20.00	35.00	—

Mint: Rasht
KM# A37 FALUS

Copper **Obv:** Sun face

Date	Mintage	Good	VG	F	VF	XF
AH1247	—	7.50	12.50	20.00	35.00	—

Mint: Sa'ujbulagh
KM# A40 FALUS

Copper **Obv:** Antelope (?) to left **Rev:** Inscription with mint and date

Date	Mintage	Good	VG	F	VF	XF
AH1234	—	—	—	—	—	—

Mint: Sawuj Balagh
KM# 70 FALUS

8.3000 g., Copper **Obv:** Sunface in ornamental border **Rev:** Mintname in ornamental border

Date	Mintage	Good	VG	F	VF	XF
AH1230	—	9.00	22.50	45.00	75.00	125

Mint: Sawuj Balagh
KM# 40 FALUS

Copper **Obv:** Lion and sun stylized

Date	Mintage	Good	VG	F	VF	XF
AH1230	—	6.50	11.50	18.50	30.00	—

Mint: Sawuj Balagh
KM# 39 FALUS

Copper

Date	Mintage	Good	VG	F	VF	XF
ND	—	11.50	18.50	30.00	50.00	—

Mint: Shiraz
KM# B41 FALUS

Copper **Obv:** Lion reclining to right **Rev:** Inscription with mintname

Date	Mintage	Good	VG	F	VF	XF
ND	—	—	—	—	—	—

Mint: Shiraz
KM# C41 FALUS

Copper **Obv:** Lion (?) to right **Rev:** Inscription with mint and date

Date	Mintage	Good	VG	F	VF	XF
AHxx13	—	—	—	—	—	—

Mint: Shiraz
KM# 41 FALUS

Copper **Obv:** Scales

Date	Mintage	Good	VG	F	VF	XF
AH126x	—	7.50	12.50	20.00	35.00	—

Mint: Shiraz
KM# A41 FALUS

Copper **Obv:** Lion right, sun face behind **Rev:** Mintname, date **Rev. Inscription:** Falus **Edge:** Plain

Date	Mintage	Good	VG	F	VF	XF
AH1227 (1812)	—	7.50	12.50	20.00	35.00	—

Mint: Tabriz
KM# 122 FALUS

Copper **Obv:** Passant lion left with radiant sun behind **Rev:** Legend

Date	Mintage	Good	VG	F	VF	XF
AH1220	—	—	—	—	—	—

Mint: Tabriz
KM# 114 FALUS

Copper **Obv:** Lion left and sun

Date	Mintage	Good	VG	F	VF	XF
AH1224	—	9.00	15.00	25.00	40.00	—

Mint: Tabriz
KM# 115 FALUS

Copper **Obv:** Radiant sun face within wreath **Edge:** Oblique milling

Date	Mintage	Good	VG	F	VF	XF
AH1229	—	11.50	18.50	30.00	50.00	—
AH1230	—	11.50	18.50	30.00	50.00	—
AH1238	—	11.50	18.50	30.00	50.00	—
AH1239	—	11.50	18.50	30.00	50.00	—
AH1240	—	11.50	18.50	30.00	50.00	—
AH124x	—	11.50	18.50	30.00	50.00	—

Mint: Tabriz
KM# A116 FALUS

Copper **Obv:** LIon right and sun

Date	Mintage	Good	VG	F	VF	XF
AH1235	—	3.50	6.00	10.00	16.50	—
AH1236	—	3.50	6.00	10.00	16.50	—

Mint: Tabriz
KM# 116 FALUS

Copper **Obv:** Lion recumbent left and sun **Rev:** Arabesque border

Date	Mintage	Good	VG	F	VF	XF
AH1235	—	9.00	15.00	25.00	40.00	—

Mint: Tabriz
KM# 117 FALUS

Copper **Rev:** Quatrefoil border

Date	Mintage	Good	VG	F	VF	XF
AH1236	—	9.00	15.00	25.00	40.00	—

Mint: Tabriz
KM# 119 FALUS

Copper **Rev:** Two leaves added

Date	Mintage	Good	VG	F	VF	XF
AH124x	—	9.00	15.00	25.00	40.00	—

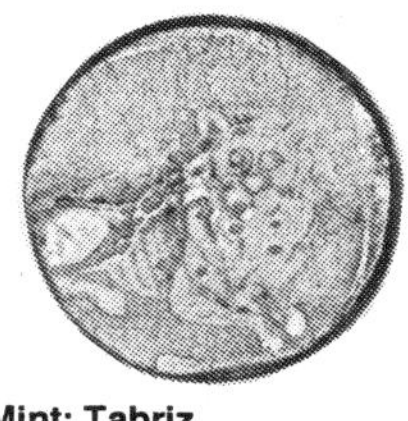

Mint: Tabriz
KM# 120 FALUS

Copper **Obv:** Lion passant right, facing

Date	Mintage	Good	VG	F	VF	XF
AH1255	—	9.00	15.00	25.00	40.00	—
AH1256	—	9.00	15.00	25.00	40.00	—

Mint: Tabriz
KM# 112 FALUS

Copper **Obv:** Sun **Note:** Struck at Tabriz Mint.

Date	Mintage	Good	VG	F	VF	XF
AH(1)24x	—	11.50	18.50	30.00	50.00	—

Mint: Tabriz
KM# 118 FALUS

Copper **Obv:** Rayed sun within wreath border **Rev:** Ornament, flower above, branches below **Note:** Varieties exist.

Date	Mintage	Good	VG	F	VF	XF
AH1239	—	9.00	15.00	25.00	40.00	—

Mint: Tehran
KM# 48 FALUS

Copper **Obv:** Peacock

Date	Mintage	Good	VG	F	VF	XF
AH1222	—	7.50	12.50	20.00	35.00	—

Mint: Tehran
KM# B49 FALUS

Copper **Obv:** Lion **Rev:** "Minted in Iran"

Date	Mintage	Good	VG	F	VF	XF
AH1255	—	5.00	8.00	15.00	25.00	—

Mint: Tehran
KM# 49 FALUS

Copper **Obv:** Russian eagle

Date	Mintage	Good	VG	F	VF	XF
ND	—	7.50	12.50	20.00	35.00	—

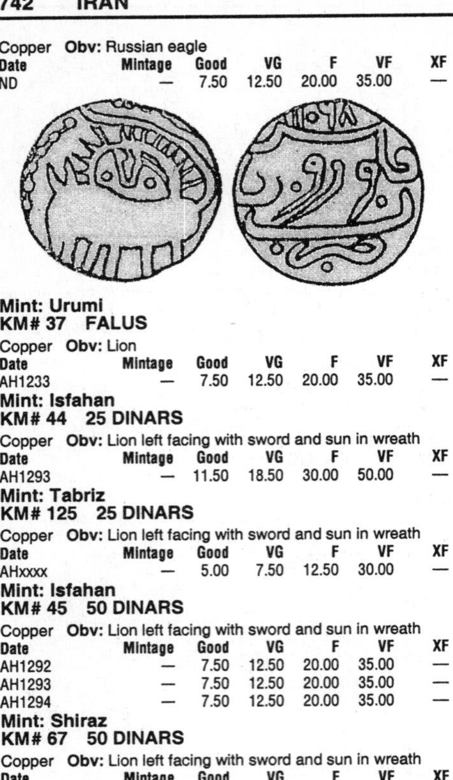

Mint: Urumi
KM# 37 FALUS

Copper **Obv:** Lion

Date	Mintage	Good	VG	F	VF	XF
AH1233	—	7.50	12.50	20.00	35.00	—

Mint: Isfahan
KM# 44 25 DINARS

Copper **Obv:** Lion left facing with sword and sun in wreath

Date	Mintage	Good	VG	F	VF	XF
AH1293	—	11.50	18.50	30.00	50.00	—

Mint: Tabriz
KM# 125 25 DINARS

Copper **Obv:** Lion left facing with sword and sun in wreath

Date	Mintage	Good	VG	F	VF	XF
AHxxxx	—	5.00	7.50	12.50	30.00	—

Mint: Isfahan
KM# 45 50 DINARS

Copper **Obv:** Lion left facing with sword and sun in wreath

Date	Mintage	Good	VG	F	VF	XF
AH1292	—	7.50	12.50	20.00	35.00	—
AH1293	—	7.50	12.50	20.00	35.00	—
AH1294	—	7.50	12.50	20.00	35.00	—

Mint: Shiraz
KM# 67 50 DINARS

Copper **Obv:** Lion left facing with sword and sun in wreath

Date	Mintage	Good	VG	F	VF	XF
AHxxxx	—	11.50	18.50	30.00	50.00	—

Mint: Tabriz
KM# 135 50 DINARS

Copper **Obv:** Lion left facing with sword and sun in wreath

Date	Mintage	Good	VG	F	VF	XF
AH1293	—	4.00	6.00	10.00	25.00	—

Fath Ali Shah

AH1212-1250 / 1797-1834AD

Fath Ali Khan succeeded his uncle, Agha Muhammad Shah, upon the latter's death on 16 June 1797, striking coins with the nickname Baba Khan. His formal enthronement took place three months later, on 15 or 16 September 1797, at which time he received the name Fath Ali Shah. His coin types are distinguished both by inscription, calligraphy, and weight standard. As the silver and gold weight standards were not altered simultaneously, the type sequences for silver and gold differ.

Note: All coins of this and succeeding reigns for hammered coinage bear the mint & date on the reverse, the mint usually with its distinguishing epithet. Only the obverse is noted in the type descriptions.

Coinage Standards of Fath Ali Shah

NOTE: Prices for silver coins are for average strikes, with some weakness or unevenness. Poorly struck coins are worth less, well-struck and well-centered coins can be worth from 25-100% more, depending on eye appeal and ornateness of design. Gold coins are generally better struck, but really attractive strikes or fancy designs also command a premium.

NOTE: Coins without legible date are worth about half the price of the cheapest date of the mint & type. Coins without legible mint are of little value. This and the previous note apply to coins of the later rulers Muhammad Shah and Nasir al-Din Shah as well as those of Fath Ali Shah.

Silver Types:

CO (Coronation Type). Obverse, double legend: *Amadeh az Fath-e 'Ali sekke be-zar-e shahi,* "From Fath Ali came the die to the royal precious metals." Standard for the rial (=1250 dinars) was 11.52 g.

A. Obverse, name of ruler with title *al-sultan.* Standard for the rial was 10.36 g.

B. Obverse, name of ruler with the expanded title *al-sultan, ibn al-sulan,* "Sultan, son of the sultan." Plain backgrounds with rather thick calligraphy. Same standard as Type A.

C. Obverse, as Type B, but with floriated backgrounds and finer calligraphy. Same standard as Types A and B.

D. Obverse, as Type C, similar backgrounds & calligraphy, but standard reduced to 9.21 g for the rial.

E. Obverse, new form of the royal protocol, *Fath 'Ali Shah Qajar Khusro-ve Sahebqeran,* "Fath Ali Shah Qajar, Caesar, Sahebqeran (i.e., possessor of an auspicious conjunction)." The rial was abandoned except at Mashhad and replaced by a qiran (kran) of 1000 dinars weighing 6.91 g.

F. Obverse, as Type E but the final portion of the protocol is *Khosro-ve Keshvarsetan,* "World-conquering Caesar." Same standard as type, with which it is contemporary (1246-1250). All Type F silver coins are probably mules with obverse dies intended for the gold.There are also a number of local types, which have not been assigned type letters and are listed following the regular imperial types.

Gold Types:

R. Same as silver Type CO (Coronation Type). Standard for the toman (=10,000 dinars) is 6.14 g.

S. Inscriptions as Type A (Type S.1) or as Type B (Type S.2) same standard as Type R.

T. Inscriptions as Type B (Type T.1) or as Type C (Type T.2), based on a toman of 5.76 g. (No examples of Type T.2 with mint & date are confirmed at the present time.)

U. Inscriptions as Type C, based on a toman of 5.37 g.

V. Inscriptions as Type C, based on a toman of 4.80 g.

W. Inscriptions as Type C or D, based on a toman of 4.61 g (one mithqal weight).

X. Inscriptions as Type E (*sahebqeran* type), based on a toman of 4.61 g.

Y. Inscriptions as Type F (*keshvarsetan* type), based on a toman of 3.45 g.

HAMMERED COINAGE

Riyal Standard

Mint: Tabriz
KM# 710.21 KRAN

6.9100 g., Silver **Note:** Type E.

Date	Mintage	F	VF	XF	Unc
AH1241	—	8.00	12.50	18.50	—
AH1242	—	8.00	12.50	18.50	—
AH1245	—	12.50	18.50	27.50	—
AH1246	—	12.50	18.50	27.50	—

Mint: Without Mint Name
KM# 681 1/12 RIAL

Silver **Note:** Type C.

Date	Mintage	F	VF	XF	Unc
AH1230 Isfahan	—	40.00	60.00	80.00	—

Mint: Borujerd
KM# 682.1 1/8 RIAL

Silver

Date	Mintage	F	VF	XF	Unc
AH1227	—	50.00	65.00	90.00	—

Mint: Eravan
KM# 682.2 1/8 RIAL

Silver

Date	Mintage	F	VF	XF	Unc
AH1227	—	50.00	65.00	90.00	—

Mint: Isfahan
KM# 669 1/8 RIAL

1.3000 g., Silver

Date	Mintage	F	VF	XF	Unc
AH1217	—	40.00	55.00	75.00	—

Mint: Isfahan
KM# 682.3 1/8 RIAL

Silver

Date	Mintage	F	VF	XF	Unc
AH1223	—	17.50	25.00	35.00	—
AH1225	—	17.50	25.00	35.00	—
AH1226	—	17.50	25.00	35.00	—
AH1227	—	17.50	25.00	35.00	—
AH1228	—	17.50	25.00	35.00	—

Mint: Isfahan
KM# 692 1/8 RIAL

1.1500 g., Silver

Date	Mintage	F	VF	XF	Unc
AH1239	—	30.00	40.00	50.00	—

Mint: Khoy
KM# 682.4 1/8 RIAL

Silver

Date	Mintage	F	VF	XF	Unc
AH1226	—	50.00	65.00	90.00	—

Mint: Qazvin
KM# 682.5 1/8 RIAL

Silver

Date	Mintage	F	VF	XF	Unc
AH1226	—	30.00	45.00	65.00	—

Mint: Shiraz
KM# 682.6 1/8 RIAL

Silver

Date	Mintage	F	VF	XF	Unc
AH1227	—	30.00	45.00	65.00	—

Mint: Tabriz
KM# 682.7 1/8 RIAL

Silver

Date	Mintage	F	VF	XF	Unc
AH1223	—	25.00	35.00	55.00	—

Mint: Eravan
KM# 683.1 1/5 RIAL

2.0700 g., Silver **Note:** Type C.

Date	Mintage	F	VF	XF	Unc
AH1225	—	—	—	—	—

Note: Reported, not confirmed.

Mint: Isfahan
KM# 683.2 1/5 RIAL

2.0700 g., Silver **Note:** Type C.

Date	Mintage	F	VF	XF	Unc
AH1224	—	20.00	27.50	40.00	—
AH1228	—	20.00	27.50	40.00	—

Mint: Yazd
KM# 683.3 1/5 RIAL

2.0700 g., Silver **Note:** Type C.

Date	Mintage	F	VF	XF	Unc
AH1225	—	20.00	27.50	40.00	—
AH1228	—	17.50	25.00	35.00	—
AH1229	—	17.50	25.00	35.00	—
AH1230	—	17.50	25.00	35.00	—
AH1231	—	17.50	25.00	35.00	—

Mint: Yazd
KM# 693 1/5 RIAL

1.8400 g., Silver **Note:** Type D.

Date	Mintage	F	VF	XF	Unc
AH1232	—	17.50	25.00	35.00	—
AH1233	—	17.50	25.00	35.00	—
AH1234	—	17.50	25.00	35.00	—
AH1235	—	17.50	25.00	35.00	—

Mint: Borujerd
KM# 684.1 1/4 RIAL

2.5900 g., Silver **Note:** Type C.

Date	Mintage	F	VF	XF	Unc
AH1229	—	30.00	45.00	60.00	—

Mint: Borujerd
KM# 694.1 1/4 RIAL

2.3000 g., Silver **Note:** Type D.

Date	Mintage	F	VF	XF	Unc
AH1236	—	25.00	33.50	42.50	—

Mint: Eravan
KM# 694.2 1/4 RIAL

2.3000 g., Silver **Note:** Type C.

Date	Mintage	F	VF	XF	Unc
AH1232	—	50.00	70.00	95.00	—

Mint: Isfahan
KM# A684.2 1/4 RIAL

2.5900 g., Silver **Note:** Type C.

Date	Mintage	VG	F	VF	XF	Unc
AH1226	—	—	30.00	45.00	60.00	—

Mint: Kirman
KM# 684.2 1/4 RIAL

2.5900 g., Silver **Note:** Type C.

Date	Mintage	F	VF	XF	Unc
AH1224	—	30.00	45.00	60.00	—
AH1229	—	30.00	45.00	60.00	—

Mint: Kirmanshahan
KM# 684.3 1/4 RIAL

2.5900 g., Silver **Note:** Type C.

Date	Mintage	F	VF	XF	Unc
AH1225	—	20.00	30.00	45.00	—

Mint: Mazandaran
KM# 684.4 1/4 RIAL

2.5900 g., Silver **Note:** Type C.

Date	Mintage	F	VF	XF	Unc
AH1231	—	25.00	35.00	50.00	—

Mint: Shiraz
KM# 694.3 1/4 RIAL

2.3000 g., Silver **Note:** Type D.

Date	Mintage	F	VF	XF	Unc
AH1232	—	20.00	30.00	40.00	—

Mint: Tabriz
KM# 684.5 1/4 RIAL

2.5900 g., Silver **Note:** Type C.

Date	Mintage	F	VF	XF	Unc
AH1227	—	15.00	22.50	32.50	—
AH1228	—	15.00	22.50	32.50	—
AH1229	—	15.00	22.50	32.50	—

Mint: Tabriz
KM# 685 1/4 RIAL

2.5900 g., Silver **Edge:** Milled **Note:** Type C. Struck on specially prepared flan.

Date	Mintage	F	VF	XF	Unc
AH1224	—	25.00	45.00	70.00	—
AH1225	—	25.00	45.00	70.00	—

Mint: Tabriz
KM# 694.4 1/4 RIAL

2.3000 g., Silver **Note:** Type D.

Date	Mintage	F	VF	XF	Unc
AH1232	—	15.00	22.50	30.00	—

Mint: Without Mint Name
KM# 686 1/3 RIAL

3.4500 g., Silver **Note:** Type C. Struck on rectangular flan.

Date	Mintage	F	VF	XF	Unc
AHxxxx Isfahan	—	60.00	75.00	100	—

Mint: Isfahan
KM# 695 1/3 RIAL

3.0700 g., Silver **Note:** Type D.

Date	Mintage	F	VF	XF	Unc
AH1236	—	25.00	40.00	60.00	—

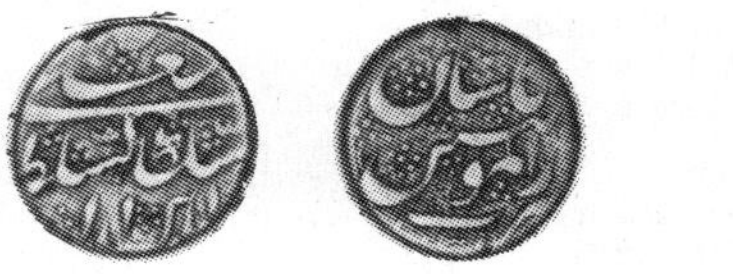

Mint: Astarabad
KM# 696.1 1/2 RIAL

4.6100 g., Silver

Date	Mintage	F	VF	XF	Unc
AH1232	—	25.00	35.00	47.50	—
AH1234	—	25.00	35.00	47.50	—

Mint: Borujerd
KM# 696.2 1/2 RIAL

4.6100 g., Silver

Date	Mintage	F	VF	XF	Unc
AH1233	—	25.00	37.50	50.00	—

Mint: Isfahan
KM# 677.1 1/2 RIAL

5.7600 g., Silver

Date	Mintage	F	VF	XF	Unc
AH1220	—	25.00	37.50	55.00	—

Mint: Isfahan
KM# 687.1 1/2 RIAL

5.7600 g., Silver

Date	Mintage	F	VF	XF	Unc
AH1224	—	17.50	27.50	40.00	—

Mint: Kashan
KM# 687.2 1/2 RIAL

5.7600 g., Silver

Date	Mintage	F	VF	XF	Unc
AH1225	—	20.00	30.00	45.00	—
AH1230	—	20.00	30.00	45.00	—

Mint: Kashan
KM# 696.3 1/2 RIAL

4.6100 g., Silver

Date	Mintage	F	VF	XF	Unc
AH1239	—	25.00	35.00	47.50	—

Mint: Kashan
KM# 673.1 1/2 RIAL

5.1800 g., Silver **Note:** Type A.

Date	Mintage	F	VF	XF	Unc
AH1216	—	30.00	40.00	55.00	—

Mint: Kirman
KM# 673.2 1/2 RIAL

5.1800 g., Silver **Note:** Type A.

Date	Mintage	F	VF	XF	Unc
AH1214	—	35.00	47.50	65.00	—

Mint: Kirmanshahan
KM# 677.2 1/2 RIAL

5.7600 g., Silver

Date	Mintage	F	VF	XF	Unc
AH1219	—	30.00	42.50	65.00	—

Mint: Kirmanshahan
KM# 687.3 1/2 RIAL

5.7600 g., Silver

Date	Mintage	F	VF	XF	Unc
AH1230	—	20.00	30.00	45.00	—

Mint: Kirmanshahan
KM# 696.4 1/2 RIAL

4.6100 g., Silver

Date	Mintage	F	VF	XF	Unc
AH1232	—	15.00	22.50	32.50	—
AH1234	—	15.00	22.50	32.50	—
AH1235	—	15.00	22.50	32.50	—

Mint: Kirmanshahan
KM# 673.3 1/2 RIAL

5.1800 g., Silver **Note:** Type A.

Date	Mintage	F	VF	XF	Unc
ND	—	50.00	70.00	90.00	—

Mint: Lahijan
KM# 673.4 1/2 RIAL

5.1800 g., Silver **Note:** Type A.

Date	Mintage	F	VF	XF	Unc
ND	—	30.00	40.00	55.00	—
AH1217	—	30.00	40.00	55.00	—

Mint: Mashhad
KM# 711 1/2 RIAL

4.6100 g., Silver **Note:** Type E.

Date	Mintage	Good	VG	F	VF	XF
AH1242	—	—	22.50	50.00	70.00	90.00

Mint: Mashhad
KM# 687.4 1/2 RIAL

5.7600 g., Silver

Date	Mintage	F	VF	XF	Unc
AH1228	—	22.50	35.00	50.00	—

Mint: Mazandaran
KM# 696.5 1/2 RIAL

4.6100 g., Silver

Date	Mintage	F	VF	XF	Unc
AH1233	—	20.00	30.00	40.00	—
AH1232	—	20.00	30.00	40.00	—

Mint: Qazvin
KM# 687.5 1/2 RIAL

5.7600 g., Silver

Date	Mintage	F	VF	XF	Unc
AH1228	—	20.00	30.00	45.00	—
AH1229	—	20.00	30.00	45.00	—
AH1230	—	20.00	30.00	45.00	—

Mint: Qazvin
KM# 696.6 1/2 RIAL

4.6100 g., Silver

Date	Mintage	F	VF	XF	Unc
AH1232	—	30.00	40.00	55.00	—

Mint: Rasht
KM# 696.7 1/2 RIAL

4.6100 g., Silver

Date	Mintage	VG	F	VF	XF	Unc
AH1233	—	8.00	20.00	30.00	42.50	—

Mint: Rasht
KM# 677.3 1/2 RIAL

5.7600 g., Silver

Date	Mintage	F	VF	XF	Unc
AH1217	—	25.00	37.50	55.00	—

Mint: Rasht
KM# 673.5 1/2 RIAL

5.1800 g., Silver **Note:** Type A.

Date	Mintage	F	VF	XF	Unc
AH1213	—	25.00	35.00	50.00	—

Mint: Shiraz
KM# 677.4 1/2 RIAL

5.7600 g., Silver

Date	Mintage	F	VF	XF	Unc
AH1220	—	25.00	37.50	55.00	—
AH1222	—	25.00	37.50	55.00	—

Mint: Simnan
KM# 677.5 1/2 RIAL

5.7600 g., Silver

Date	Mintage	F	VF	XF	Unc
AH1217	—	50.00	75.00	100	—

Mint: Tabriz
KM# 677.6 1/2 RIAL

5.7600 g., Silver

Date	Mintage	F	VF	XF	Unc
AH1219	—	25.00	37.50	55.00	—
AH1221	—	25.00	37.50	55.00	—

Mint: Tabriz
KM# 687.6 1/2 RIAL

5.7600 g., Silver

Date	Mintage	F	VF	XF	Unc
AH1222	—	17.50	27.50	40.00	—
AH1224	—	17.50	27.50	40.00	—

Mint: Tehran
KM# 677.7 1/2 RIAL

5.7600 g., Silver

Date	Mintage	F	VF	XF	Unc
AH1219	—	25.00	37.50	55.00	—

Mint: Urumi
KM# 696.8 1/2 RIAL

4.6100 g., Silver

Date	Mintage	VG	F	VF	XF	Unc
AH1232	—	12.00	30.00	40.00	55.00	—

Mint: Urumi
KM# 677.8 1/2 RIAL

5.7600 g., Silver

Date	Mintage	F	VF	XF	Unc
AH1222	—	45.00	65.00	85.00	—

Mint: Ardebil
KM# 697.1 RIAL

9.2100 g., Silver **Note:** Type D.

Date	Mintage	F	VF	XF	Unc
AH1233	—	50.00	75.00	100	—
AH1235	—	50.00	75.00	100	—

Mint: Astarabad
KM# 674.1 RIAL

10.3600 g., Silver **Note:** Type A.

Date	Mintage	F	VF	XF	Unc
AH1215	—	12.50	20.00	30.00	—
AH1216	—	12.50	20.00	30.00	—

Mint: Astarabad
KM# 688.1 RIAL

10.3600 g., Silver **Note:** Type C.

Date	Mintage	F	VF	XF	Unc
AH1223	—	17.50	26.00	37.50	—
AH1225	—	17.50	26.00	37.50	—
AH1230	—	15.00	22.50	35.00	—

Mint: Astarabad
KM# 697.2 RIAL

9.2100 g., Silver **Note:** Type D.

Date	Mintage	F	VF	XF	Unc
AH1232	—	8.00	12.50	18.50	—
AH1235	—	14.00	20.00	30.00	—
AH1236	—	14.00	20.00	30.00	—
AH1238	—	14.00	20.00	30.00	—

Mint: Borujerd
KM# 697.3 RIAL

9.2100 g., Silver **Note:** Type D.

Date	Mintage	F	VF	XF	Unc
AH1232	—	20.00	32.50	45.00	—
AH1233	—	20.00	32.50	45.00	—
AH1234	—	20.00	32.50	45.00	—

Mint: Eravan
KM# 678.1 RIAL

10.3600 g., Silver **Note:** Type B.

Date	Mintage	F	VF	XF	Unc
AH1218	—	30.00	45.00	65.00	—

Mint: Eravan
KM# 688.2 RIAL

10.3600 g., Silver **Note:** Type C.

Date	Mintage	F	VF	XF	Unc
AH1223	—	30.00	45.00	70.00	—
AH1225	—	30.00	45.00	70.00	—
AH1226	—	30.00	45.00	70.00	—

Mint: Eravan
KM# 697.4 RIAL

9.2100 g., Silver **Note:** Type D.

Date	Mintage	F	VF	XF	Unc
AH1237	—	60.00	85.00	115	—

Mint: Iravan
KM# 674.2 RIAL

11.5200 g., Silver

Date	Mintage	VG	F	VF	XF	Unc
AH1216	—	—	25.00	45.00	65.00	—
AH1217	—	—	20.00	45.00	65.00	—

Mint: Isfahan
KM# 674.3 RIAL

10.3600 g., Silver **Note:** Type A.

Date	Mintage	F	VF	XF	Unc
AH1215	—	10.00	15.00	25.00	—
AH1216	—	10.00	15.00	25.00	—

Mint: Isfahan
KM# 678.2 RIAL

10.3600 g., Silver **Note:** Type B.

Date	Mintage	F	VF	XF	Unc
AH1217	—	9.00	14.00	25.00	—
AH1222	—	11.50	16.50	27.50	—

Mint: Isfahan
KM# 688.3 RIAL

10.3600 g., Silver **Note:** Type C.

Date	Mintage	F	VF	XF	Unc
AH1223	—	9.00	14.00	20.00	—
AH1224	—	9.00	14.00	20.00	—
AH1225	—	9.00	14.00	20.00	—
AH1226	—	9.00	14.00	20.00	—
AH1227	—	9.00	14.00	20.00	—

Mint: Isfahan
KM# 697.5 RIAL

9.2100 g., Silver **Note:** Type D.

Date	Mintage	F	VF	XF	Unc
AH1232	—	8.00	12.50	18.50	—
AH1233	—	8.00	12.50	18.50	—
AH1234	—	9.00	14.00	20.00	—
AH1236	—	10.00	16.00	22.50	—
AH1238	—	10.00	16.00	22.50	—
AH1239	—	10.00	16.00	22.50	—

Mint: Kashan
KM# 674.4 RIAL

10.3600 g., Silver **Note:** Type A.

Date	Mintage	F	VF	XF	Unc
AH1215	—	12.50	20.00	30.00	—
AH1216	—	12.50	20.00	30.00	—

Mint: Kashan
KM# 678.3 RIAL

10.3600 g., Silver **Note:** Type B.

Date	Mintage	F	VF	XF	Unc
AH1218	—	9.00	14.00	25.00	—
AH1219	—	9.00	14.00	25.00	—
AH1220	—	9.00	14.00	25.00	—
AH1221	—	9.00	14.00	25.00	—

Mint: Kashan
KM# 688.4 RIAL

10.3600 g., Silver **Note:** Type C.

Date	Mintage	F	VF	XF	Unc
AH1222	—	9.00	14.00	20.00	—
AH1223	—	9.00	14.00	20.00	—
AH1224	—	9.00	14.00	20.00	—
AH1225	—	9.00	14.00	20.00	—
AH1226	—	9.00	14.00	20.00	—
AH1227	—	9.00	14.00	20.00	—
AH1228	—	9.00	14.00	20.00	—
AH1229	—	9.00	14.00	20.00	—

Mint: Kashan
KM# 697.6 RIAL

9.2100 g., Silver **Note:** Type D.

Date	Mintage	F	VF	XF	Unc
AH1232	—	8.00	12.50	18.50	—
AH1233	—	8.00	12.50	18.50	—
AH1234	—	9.00	14.00	20.00	—
AH1236	—	10.00	16.00	22.50	—
AH1238	—	10.00	16.00	22.50	—

Mint: Khoy
KM# 674.5 RIAL

10.3600 g., Silver **Note:** Type A.

Date	Mintage	F	VF	XF	Unc
AH1215	—	17.50	27.50	40.00	—
AH1216	—	17.50	27.50	40.00	—
AH1217	—	17.50	27.50	40.00	—

Mint: Khoy
KM# 678.4 RIAL

10.3600 g., Silver **Note:** Type B.

Date	Mintage	F	VF	XF	Unc
AH1217	—	17.50	27.50	40.00	—
AH1219	—	17.50	27.50	40.00	—
AH1220	—	17.50	27.50	40.00	—

Mint: Khoy
KM# 688.5 RIAL

10.3600 g., Silver **Note:** Type C.

Date	Mintage	F	VF	XF	Unc
AH1224	—	16.50	25.00	40.00	—
AH1225	—	16.50	25.00	40.00	—
AH1227	—	16.50	25.00	40.00	—
AH1229	—	16.50	25.00	40.00	—
AH1230	—	16.50	25.00	40.00	—
AH1231	—	16.50	25.00	40.00	—

Mint: Khoy
KM# 697.7 RIAL

9.2100 g., Silver **Note:** Type D.

Date	Mintage	F	VF	XF	Unc
AH1233	—	15.00	22.50	32.50	—
AH1234	—	15.00	22.50	32.50	—
AH1235	—	15.00	22.50	32.50	—
AH1238	—	16.50	25.00	35.00	—
AH1239	—	20.00	30.00	45.00	—
AH1240	—	20.00	30.00	45.00	—

Mint: Kirman
KM# 674.6 RIAL

10.3600 g., Silver **Note:** Type A.

Date	Mintage	F	VF	XF	Unc
AH1216	—	22.50	35.00	50.00	—

Mint: Kirman
KM# 688.6 RIAL

10.3600 g., Silver **Note:** Type C.

Date	Mintage	F	VF	XF	Unc
AH1222	—	20.00	30.00	45.00	—
AH1224	—	20.00	30.00	45.00	—
AH1226	—	25.00	37.50	55.00	—
AH1227	—	25.00	37.50	55.00	—

Mint: Kirmanshahan
KM# 674.7 RIAL

10.3600 g., Silver **Note:** Type A.

Date	Mintage	F	VF	XF	Unc
AH1216	—	15.00	25.00	35.00	—

Mint: Kirmanshahan
KM# 678.6 RIAL

10.3600 g., Silver **Note:** Type B.

Date	Mintage	F	VF	XF	Unc
AH1218	—	9.00	14.00	25.00	—
AH1219	—	9.00	14.00	25.00	—
AH1220	—	9.00	14.00	25.00	—
AH1221	—	9.00	14.00	25.00	—

Mint: Kirmanshahan
KM# 688.7 RIAL

10.3600 g., Silver **Note:** Type C.

Date	Mintage	F	VF	XF	Unc
AH1222	—	9.00	14.00	20.00	—
AH1224	—	9.00	14.00	20.00	—
AH1225	—	9.00	14.00	20.00	—
AH1227	—	9.00	14.00	20.00	—
AH1228	—	9.00	14.00	20.00	—

Mint: Kirmanshahan
KM# 697.8 RIAL

9.2100 g., Silver **Note:** Type D.

Date	Mintage	F	VF	XF	Unc
AH1232	—	8.00	12.50	18.50	—
AH1233	—	8.00	12.50	18.50	—
AH1234	—	9.00	14.00	20.00	—
AH1235	—	9.00	14.00	20.00	—
AH1236	—	9.00	14.00	20.00	—
AH1238	—	9.00	14.00	20.00	—
AH1239	—	10.00	16.00	22.50	—
AH1240	—	14.00	20.00	30.00	—

Mint: Lahijan
KM# 674.8 RIAL

10.3600 g., Silver **Note:** Type A.

Date	Mintage	F	VF	XF	Unc
AH1215	—	40.00	60.00	90.00	—
AH1216	—	40.00	60.00	90.00	—

Mint: Lahijan
KM# 678.7 RIAL

10.3600 g., Silver **Note:** Type B.

Date	Mintage	F	VF	XF	Unc
AH1219	—	35.00	55.00	85.00	—
AH1222	—	40.00	60.00	90.00	—

Mint: Lahijan
KM# 688.8 RIAL

10.3600 g., Silver **Note:** Type C.

Date	Mintage	F	VF	XF	Unc
AH1224	—	40.00	65.00	100	—

Mint: Maragheh
KM# 674.9 RIAL

10.3600 g., Silver **Note:** Type A.

Date	Mintage	F	VF	XF	Unc
AH1215	—	50.00	75.00	110	—

Mint: Mashhad
KM# 712 RIAL

9.2100 g., Silver **Note:** Type E.

Date	Mintage	Good	VG	F	VF	XF
AH1242	—	—	10.00	25.00	35.00	50.00
AH1243	—	—	10.00	25.00	35.00	50.00
AH1244	—	—	10.00	25.00	35.00	50.00
AH1246	—	—	10.00	25.00	35.00	50.00

Mint: Mashhad
KM# 678.8 RIAL

10.3600 g., Silver **Note:** Type B.

Date	Mintage	F	VF	XF	Unc
AH1218	—	25.00	40.00	60.00	—
AH1220	—	13.50	20.00	30.00	—
AH1222	—	13.50	20.00	30.00	—

Mint: Mashhad
KM# 688.9 RIAL

10.3600 g., Silver **Note:** Type C.

Date	Mintage	F	VF	XF	Unc
AH1223	—	12.50	18.50	27.50	—
AH1224	—	12.50	18.50	27.50	—
AH1225	—	12.50	18.50	27.50	—
AH1226	—	12.50	18.50	27.50	—
AH1227	—	12.50	18.50	27.50	—
AH1228	—	12.50	18.50	27.50	—
AH1229	—	12.50	18.50	27.50	—
AH1230	—	12.50	18.50	27.50	—
AH1231	—	14.00	20.00	30.00	—

Mint: Mashhad
KM# 697.9 RIAL

9.2100 g., Silver **Note:** Type D.

Date	Mintage	F	VF	XF	Unc
AH1232	—	10.00	16.50	25.00	—
AH1233	—	10.00	16.50	25.00	—
AH1234	—	15.00	22.50	32.50	—
AH1235	—	17.50	25.00	37.50	—
AH1237	—	20.00	32.50	40.00	—
AH1239	—	14.00	20.00	30.00	—
AH1241	—	20.00	30.00	45.00	—

Mint: Mazandaran
KM# 674.10 RIAL

10.3600 g., Silver **Note:** Type A.

Date	Mintage	F	VF	XF	Unc
AH1215	—	12.50	20.00	30.00	—
AH1216	—	12.50	20.00	30.00	—

Mint: Mazandaran
KM# 678.9 RIAL

10.3600 g., Silver **Note:** Type B.

Date	Mintage	F	VF	XF	Unc
AH1218	—	12.50	20.00	30.00	—

Mint: Mazandaran
KM# 688.10 RIAL

10.3600 g., Silver **Note:** Type C.

Date	Mintage	F	VF	XF	Unc
AH1227	—	11.50	17.50	25.00	—
AH1228	—	12.50	18.50	27.50	—
AH1229	—	11.50	16.50	25.00	—

Mint: Mazandaran
KM# 697.10 RIAL

9.2100 g., Silver **Note:** Type D.

Date	Mintage	F	VF	XF	Unc
AH1232	—	8.00	12.50	18.50	—
AH1233	—	8.00	12.50	18.50	—

Mint: Qazvin
KM# 674.11 RIAL

10.3600 g., Silver **Note:** Type A.

Date	Mintage	F	VF	XF	Unc
AH1216	—	10.00	15.00	25.00	—

Mint: Qazvin
KM# 678.10 RIAL

10.3600 g., Silver **Note:** Type B.

Date	Mintage	F	VF	XF	Unc
AH1217	—	11.00	16.50	27.50	—

Mint: Qazvin
KM# 688.11 RIAL

10.3600 g., Silver **Note:** Type C.

Date	Mintage	F	VF	XF	Unc
AH1222	—	9.00	14.00	20.00	—
AH1223	—	9.00	14.00	20.00	—
AH1224	—	9.00	14.00	20.00	—
AH1225	—	9.00	14.00	20.00	—
AH1226	—	9.00	14.00	20.00	—
AH1227	—	9.00	14.00	20.00	—
AH1228	—	9.00	14.00	20.00	—
AH1229	—	9.00	14.00	20.00	—

Mint: Qazvin
KM# 697.11 RIAL

9.2100 g., Silver **Note:** Type D.

Date	Mintage	F	VF	XF	Unc
AH1232	—	8.00	12.50	18.50	—
AH1233	—	8.00	12.50	18.50	—
AH1235	—	9.00	14.00	20.00	—
AH1236	—	10.00	16.00	22.50	—
AH1239	—	10.00	16.00	22.50	—

Mint: Rasht
KM# 674.12 RIAL

10.3600 g., Silver **Note:** Type A.

Date	Mintage	F	VF	XF	Unc
AH1216	—	10.00	15.00	25.00	—
AH1217	—	12.50	18.50	26.50	—

Mint: Rasht
KM# 678.11 RIAL

10.3600 g., Silver **Note:** Type B.

Date	Mintage	F	VF	XF	Unc
AH1218	—	9.00	14.00	25.00	—
AH1218	—	20.00	28.00	40.00	—
Note: With month of "Rajab"					
AH1219	—	9.00	14.00	25.00	—
AH1220	—	9.00	14.00	25.00	—
AH1221	—	9.00	14.00	25.00	—
AH1222	—	9.00	14.00	25.00	—

Mint: Rasht
KM# 688.12 RIAL

10.3600 g., Silver **Note:** Type C.

Date	Mintage	F	VF	XF	Unc
AH1222	—	9.00	14.00	20.00	—
AH1223	—	9.00	14.00	20.00	—

Date	Mintage	F	VF	XF	Unc
AH1224	—	9.00	14.00	20.00	—
AH1225	—	9.00	14.00	20.00	—
AH1226	—	9.00	14.00	20.00	—
AH1227	—	9.00	14.00	20.00	—
AH1228	—	9.00	14.00	20.00	—
AH1230	—	9.00	14.00	20.00	—

Mint: Rasht
KM# 697.12 RIAL

9.2100 g., Silver **Note:** Type D.

Date	Mintage	F	VF	XF	Unc
AH1232	—	8.00	12.50	18.50	—
AH1233	—	8.00	12.50	18.50	—
AH1234	—	9.00	14.00	20.00	—
AH1239	—	10.00	16.00	22.50	—
AH1240	—	10.00	16.00	22.50	—

Mint: Shiraz
KM# 674.14 RIAL

10.3600 g., Silver **Note:** Type A.

Date	Mintage	F	VF	XF	Unc
AH1215	—	10.00	15.00	25.00	—
AH1216	—	10.00	15.00	25.00	—

Mint: Shiraz
KM# 678.12 RIAL

10.3600 g., Silver **Note:** Type B.

Date	Mintage	F	VF	XF	Unc
AH1218	—	9.00	14.00	25.00	—
AH1220	—	9.00	14.00	25.00	—

Mint: Shiraz
KM# 688.13 RIAL

10.3600 g., Silver **Note:** Type C.

Date	Mintage	F	VF	XF	Unc
AH1222	—	9.00	14.00	20.00	—
AH1223	—	9.00	14.00	20.00	—
AH1225	—	9.00	14.00	20.00	—
AH1226	—	9.00	14.00	20.00	—
AH1227	—	9.00	14.00	20.00	—
AH1228	—	9.00	14.00	20.00	—
AH1229	—	9.00	14.00	20.00	—

Mint: Shiraz
KM# 697.13 RIAL

9.2100 g., Silver **Note:** Type D.

Date	Mintage	F	VF	XF	Unc
AH1232	—	8.00	12.50	18.50	—
AH1232	—	8.00	12.50	18.50	—
AH1233	—	8.00	12.50	18.50	—
AH1234	—	9.00	14.00	20.00	—
AH1236	—	10.00	16.00	22.50	—

Mint: Shushtar
KM# 697.14 RIAL

9.2100 g., Silver **Note:** Type D.

Date	Mintage	F	VF	XF	Unc
AH1233	—	40.00	60.00	80.00	—

Mint: Tabaristan
KM# 697.15 RIAL

9.2100 g., Silver **Note:** Type D.

Date	Mintage	F	VF	XF	Unc
AH1236	—	30.00	40.00	55.00	—
AH1238	—	14.00	20.00	30.00	—
AH1240	—	14.00	20.00	30.00	—

Mint: Tabriz
KM# 689 RIAL

10.3600 g., Silver **Edge:** Milled **Note:** Special strike on full even flan.

Date	Mintage	F	VF	XF	Unc
AH1221 (sic)	—	65.00	100	175	—
AH1222	—	65.00	100	175	—

Mint: Tabriz
KM# 674.16 RIAL

10.3600 g., Silver **Note:** Type A.

Date	Mintage	F	VF	XF	Unc
AH1215	—	10.00	15.00	25.00	—
AH1216	—	10.00	15.00	25.00	—
AH1217	—	10.00	15.00	25.00	—
AH1218	—	12.50	20.00	30.00	—
AH1219	—	12.50	20.00	30.00	—

Mint: Tabriz
KM# 678.13 RIAL

10.3600 g., Silver **Note:** Type B.

Date	Mintage	F	VF	XF	Unc
AH1219	—	10.00	15.00	25.00	—
AH1220	—	9.00	14.00	25.00	—
AH1221	—	9.00	14.00	25.00	—
AH1222	—	9.00	14.00	25.00	—

Mint: Tabriz
KM# 688.14 RIAL

10.3600 g., Silver **Note:** Type C.

Date	Mintage	F	VF	XF	Unc
AH1222	—	10.00	15.00	22.50	—
AH1223	—	10.00	15.00	22.50	—
AH1224	—	10.00	15.00	22.50	—
AH1225	—	10.00	15.00	22.50	—
AH1226	—	10.00	15.00	22.50	—
AH1228	—	9.00	14.00	20.00	—

Mint: Tabriz
KM# 697.16 RIAL

9.2100 g., Silver **Note:** Type D.

Date	Mintage	F	VF	XF	Unc
AH1233	—	8.00	12.50	18.50	—
AH1238	—	10.00	16.00	22.50	—
AH1239	—	10.00	16.00	22.50	—
AH1240	—	14.00	20.00	30.00	—

Mint: Tehran
KM# 674.17 RIAL

10.3600 g., Silver **Note:** Type A.

Date	Mintage	F	VF	XF	Unc
AH1215	—	10.00	15.00	25.00	—
AH1216	—	10.00	15.00	25.00	—

Mint: Tehran
KM# 678.14 RIAL

10.3600 g., Silver **Note:** Type B.

Date	Mintage	F	VF	XF	Unc
AH1217	—	9.00	14.00	25.00	—

Mint: Tehran
KM# 688.15 RIAL

10.3600 g., Silver **Note:** Type C.

Date	Mintage	F	VF	XF	Unc
AH1222	—	9.00	14.00	20.00	—
AH1224	—	9.00	14.00	20.00	—
AH1226	—	10.00	15.00	22.50	—
AH1229	—	10.00	15.00	22.50	—
AH1231	—	11.50	16.50	25.00	—

Mint: Tehran
KM# 697.17 RIAL

9.2100 g., Silver **Note:** Type D.

Date	Mintage	F	VF	XF	Unc
AH1232	—	8.00	12.50	18.50	—
AH1233	—	8.00	12.50	18.50	—
AH1234	—	10.00	16.00	22.50	—
AH1238	—	10.00	16.00	22.50	—
AH1239	—	10.00	16.00	22.50	—

Mint: Urumi
KM# 678.15 RIAL

10.3600 g., Silver **Note:** Type B.

Date	Mintage	F	VF	XF	Unc
AH1221	—	20.00	30.00	45.00	—
AH1222	—	20.00	30.00	45.00	—

Mint: Urumi
KM# 688.16 RIAL

10.3600 g., Silver **Note:** Type C.

Date	Mintage	F	VF	XF	Unc
AH1223	—	20.00	30.00	45.00	—
AH1224	—	20.00	30.00	45.00	—
AH1225	—	20.00	30.00	45.00	—
AH1228	—	20.00	30.00	45.00	—
AH1229	—	20.00	30.00	45.00	—

Mint: Urumi
KM# 688.18 RIAL

10.3600 g., Silver **Note:** Type C.

Date	Mintage	F	VF	XF	Unc
AH1226	—	25.00	37.50	55.00	—
AH1228	—	25.00	37.50	55.00	—
AH1229	—	25.00	37.50	55.00	—

Mint: Urumi
KM# 697.18 RIAL

9.2100 g., Silver **Note:** Type D.

Date	Mintage	F	VF	XF	Unc
AH1233	—	25.00	35.00	55.00	—

Mint: Yazd
KM# 674.18 RIAL

10.3600 g., Silver **Note:** Type A.

Date	Mintage	F	VF	XF	Unc
AH1216	—	10.00	15.00	25.00	—

Mint: Yazd
KM# 678.16 RIAL

10.3600 g., Silver **Note:** Type B.

Date	Mintage	F	VF	XF	Unc
AH1218	—	9.00	14.00	25.00	—
AH1219	—	9.00	14.00	25.00	—
AH1220	—	9.00	14.00	25.00	—
AH1221	—	9.00	14.00	25.00	—
AH1222	—	9.00	14.00	25.00	—

Mint: Yazd
KM# 688.17 RIAL

10.3600 g., Silver **Note:** Type C.

Date	Mintage	F	VF	XF	Unc
AH1222	—	10.00	15.00	22.50	—
AH1224	—	9.00	14.00	20.00	—
AH1225	—	9.00	14.00	20.00	—
AH1230	—	11.50	16.50	25.00	—
AH1231	—	11.50	16.50	25.00	—
AH1232	—	12.50	18.50	30.00	—

Note: Coins of AH1232 of types C and D can only be distinguished by weight

Mint: Yazd
KM# 697.19 RIAL

9.2100 g., Silver **Note:** Type D.

Date	Mintage	F	VF	XF	Unc
AH1232	—	8.00	12.50	18.50	—
AH1233	—	8.00	12.50	18.50	—
AH1238	—	10.00	16.00	22.50	—
AH1239	—	10.00	16.00	22.50	—

Mint: Zanjan
KM# 697.20 RIAL

9.2100 g., Silver **Note:** Type D.

Date	Mintage	F	VF	XF	Unc
AH1232	—	20.00	32.50	45.00	—
AH1233	—	20.00	32.50	45.00	—
AH1234	—	20.00	32.50	45.00	—

Mint: Tabriz
KM# 690 2 RIALS

20.7200 g., Silver **Note:** Type C.

Date	Mintage	F	VF	XF	Unc
AH1226	—	125	175	250	—

Mint: Zanjan
KM# 699 2 RIALS

18.4200 g., Silver **Note:** Type D.

Date	Mintage	F	VF	XF	Unc
AH1234 Rare	—	—	—	—	—

Mint: Zanjan
KM# 698 NAZARANA RIAL

9.2100 g., Silver **Edge:** Milled **Note:** Type D. Special strike on full even flan.

Date	Mintage	F	VF	XF	Unc
AH1238	—	100	135	185	—

HAMMERED COINAGE

Kran Standard

Mint: Isfahan
KM# A705 1/8 KRAN

Silver **Note:** Type E obverse muled with reverse of KM#682.

Date	Mintage	Good	VG	F	VF	XF
AH1230	—	—	—	—	—	—

Mint: Khoy
KM# 705 1/8 KRAN

0.8600 g., Silver **Note:** Kran standard. Type E.

Date	Mintage	F	VF	XF	Unc
AH1243	—	35.00	50.00	70.00	—

Mint: Isfahan
KM# 719 1/4 KRAN

1.7200 g., Silver **Obv:** Shah seated on throne **Note:** Special type.

Date	Mintage	F	VF	XF	Unc
AH1247	—	100	150	200	—

Mint: Tabriz
KM# 700.1 1/4 KRAN

1.7200 g., Silver **Note:** Type D.

Date	Mintage	F	VF	XF	Unc
AH1237	—	22.50	30.00	40.00	—
AH1238	—	22.50	30.00	40.00	—

Mint: Tabriz
KM# 706 1/4 KRAN

1.7200 g., Silver **Note:** Type E.

Date	Mintage	F	VF	XF	Unc
AH1242	—	20.00	30.00	40.00	—

Mint: Tehran
KM# 700.2 1/4 KRAN

1.7200 g., Silver **Note:** Type D.

Date	Mintage	F	VF	XF	Unc
AH1236	—	25.00	35.00	45.00	—

Mint: Astarabad
KM# 709.1 1/2 KRAN

3.4500 g., Silver **Note:** Type E.

Date	Mintage	F	VF	XF	Unc
AH1246	—	30.00	42.50	55.00	—

Mint: Hamadan
KM# 709.2 1/2 KRAN

3.4500 g., Silver **Note:** Type E.

Date	Mintage	F	VF	XF	Unc
AH1241	—	20.00	30.00	40.00	—

Mint: Isfahan
KM# 702.1 1/2 KRAN

3.4500 g., Silver **Note:** Type D.

Date	Mintage	F	VF	XF	Unc
AH1245	—	15.00	22.50	32.50	—
AH1246	—	15.00	22.50	32.50	—

Note: Dates after AH1240 are presumed struck with old obverse dies

Mint: Kashan
KM# 709.3 1/2 KRAN

3.4500 g., Silver **Note:** Type E.

Date	Mintage	F	VF	XF	Unc
AH1241	—	18.50	27.50	37.50	—
AH1243	—	18.50	27.50	37.50	—

Mint: Kirman
KM# 702.2 1/2 KRAN

3.4500 g., Silver **Note:** Type D.

Date	Mintage	F	VF	XF	Unc
AH1238	—	30.00	40.00	55.00	—

Mint: Mashhad
KM# 709.4 1/2 KRAN

3.4500 g., Silver **Note:** Type E.

Date	Mintage	F	VF	XF	Unc
AH1248	—	20.00	30.00	40.00	—

Mint: Qazvin
KM# 702.3 1/2 KRAN

3.4500 g., Silver **Note:** Type D.

Date	Mintage	F	VF	XF	Unc
AH1237	—	25.00	35.00	45.00	—

Mint: Qomm
KM# 709.5 1/2 KRAN

3.4500 g., Silver **Note:** Type E.

Date	Mintage	F	VF	XF	Unc
AH1241	—	50.00	70.00	100	—

Mint: Rasht
KM# 709.6 1/2 KRAN

3.4500 g., Silver **Note:** Type E.

Date	Mintage	F	VF	XF	Unc
AH1241	—	17.50	25.00	35.00	—
AH1244	—	18.50	27.50	37.50	—

Mint: Shiraz
KM# 702.4 1/2 KRAN

3.4500 g., Silver **Note:** Type D.

Date	Mintage	F	VF	XF	Unc
AH1238	—	12.50	18.50	27.50	—
AH1239	—	12.50	18.50	27.50	—

Mint: Shiraz
KM# 709.7 1/2 KRAN

3.4500 g., Silver **Note:** Type E.

Date	Mintage	F	VF	XF	Unc
AH1246	—	10.00	16.50	25.00	—
AH1247	—	10.00	16.50	25.00	—
AH1248	—	10.00	16.50	25.00	—

Mint: Tabaristan
KM# 709.8 1/2 KRAN

3.4500 g., Silver **Note:** Type E.

Date	Mintage	F	VF	XF	Unc
AH1241	—	20.00	30.00	40.00	—

Mint: Tehran
KM# 702.5 1/2 KRAN

3.4500 g., Silver **Note:** Type D.

Date	Mintage	F	VF	XF	Unc
AH1237	—	20.00	30.00	40.00	—
AH1238	—	20.00	30.00	40.00	—
AH1240	—	20.00	30.00	40.00	—

Note: Dates after AH1240 are presumed struck with old obverse dies

Mint: Kirman
KM# 701.1 2/5 KRAN

2.7600 g., Silver **Note:** Type D.

Date	Mintage	F	VF	XF	Unc
AH1249	—	25.00	35.00	45.00	—

Mint: Kirman
KM# 707 2/5 KRAN

2.7600 g., Silver **Note:** Type E.

Date	Mintage	F	VF	XF	Unc
AH1242	—	25.00	35.00	45.00	—
AH1244	—	25.00	35.00	45.00	—

Mint: Kirman
KM# 716 2/5 KRAN

2.7600 g., Silver **Note:** Type F.

Date	Mintage	F	VF	XF	Unc
AH1247	—	30.00	40.00	55.00	—
AH1250	—	30.00	40.00	55.00	—

Mint: Kirmanshahan
KM# 701.2 2/5 KRAN

2.7600 g., Silver **Note:** Type D.

Date	Mintage	F	VF	XF	Unc
AH1245	—	25.00	35.00	45.00	—
AH1246	—	25.00	35.00	45.00	—

Note: All 2/5 Kran coins were struck during the Type E period, but with obverse dies with Type D inscriptions (probably old dies)

Mint: Ardebil
KM# 710.1 KRAN

6.9100 g., Silver **Note:** Type E.

Date	Mintage	F	VF	XF	Unc
AH1240	—	40.00	60.00	85.00	—
AH1243	—	40.00	60.00	85.00	—
AH1244	—	40.00	60.00	85.00	—
AH1245	—	40.00	60.00	85.00	—

Mint: Astarabad
KM# 710.2 KRAN

6.9100 g., Silver **Note:** Type E.

Date	Mintage	F	VF	XF	Unc
AH1241	—	10.00	16.00	25.00	—
AH1242	—	10.00	16.00	25.00	—
AH1244	—	10.00	16.00	25.00	—
AH1245	—	10.00	16.00	25.00	—
AH1246	—	9.00	13.50	20.00	—

Mint: Borujerd
KM# 710.3 KRAN

6.9100 g., Silver **Note:** Type E.

Date	Mintage	F	VF	XF	Unc
AH1241	—	15.00	22.50	30.00	—
AH1242	—	15.00	22.50	30.00	—
AH1243	—	15.00	22.50	30.00	—
AH1244	—	15.00	22.50	30.00	—
AH1245	—	15.00	22.50	30.00	—
AH1246	—	15.00	22.50	30.00	—
AH1247	—	15.00	22.50	30.00	—
AH1248	—	15.00	22.50	30.00	—

Mint: Eravan
KM# 710.4 KRAN

6.9100 g., Silver **Note:** Type E.

Date	Mintage	F	VF	XF	Unc
AH1241	—	35.00	50.00	75.00	—

Mint: Hamadan
KM# 710.5 KRAN

6.9100 g., Silver **Note:** Type E.

Date	Mintage	F	VF	XF	Unc
AH1240	—	15.00	22.50	32.50	—
AH1241	—	8.00	12.50	18.50	—
AH1242	—	8.00	12.50	18.50	—
AH1243	—	8.00	12.50	18.50	—
AH1244	—	8.00	12.50	18.50	—
AH1245	—	9.00	13.50	20.00	—
AH1246	—	9.00	13.50	20.00	—
AH1247	—	9.00	13.50	20.00	—
AH1248	—	9.00	13.50	20.00	—
AH1250	—	20.00	30.00	45.00	—

Mint: Isfahan
KM# 710.6 KRAN

6.9100 g., Silver **Note:** Type E.

Date	Mintage	F	VF	XF	Unc
AH1241	—	8.00	12.50	18.50	—
AH1242	—	8.00	12.50	18.50	—
AH1243	—	8.00	12.50	18.50	—
AH1244	—	8.00	12.50	18.50	—
AH1245	—	9.00	13.50	20.00	—
AH1246	—	10.00	16.00	25.00	—
AH1247	—	10.00	16.00	25.00	—
AH1248	—	10.00	16.00	25.00	—
AH1249	—	12.50	20.00	30.00	—

Mint: Kashan
KM# 710.7 KRAN

6.9100 g., Silver **Note:** Type E.

Date	Mintage	F	VF	XF	Unc
AH1240	—	15.00	22.50	32.50	—
AH1241	—	8.00	12.50	18.50	—
AH1242	—	8.00	12.50	18.50	—

Mint: Khoy
KM# 710.8 KRAN

6.9100 g., Silver **Note:** Type E.

Date	Mintage	F	VF	XF	Unc
AH1241	—	10.00	16.00	25.00	—
AH1242	—	10.00	16.00	25.00	—
AH1243	—	10.00	16.00	25.00	—
AH1246	—	15.00	22.50	30.00	—
AH1249	—	20.00	30.00	45.00	—

Mint: Kirman
KM# 710.9 KRAN

6.9100 g., Silver **Note:** Type E.

Date	Mintage	F	VF	XF	Unc
AH1241	—	25.00	37.50	55.00	—
AH1245	—	25.00	37.50	55.00	—

Mint: Kirmanshahan
KM# 710.10 KRAN

6.9100 g., Silver **Note:** Type E.

Date	Mintage	F	VF	XF	Unc
AH1241	—	8.00	12.50	18.50	—
AH1242	—	8.00	12.50	18.50	—
AH1243	—	8.00	12.50	18.50	—
AH1244	—	8.00	12.50	18.50	—
AH1246	—	9.00	13.50	20.00	—
AH1247	—	10.00	16.00	25.00	—
AH1248	—	10.00	16.00	25.00	—

Mint: Mashhad
KM# 710.11 KRAN

6.9100 g., Silver **Note:** Type E.

Date	Mintage	F	VF	XF	Unc
AH1247	—	12.50	18.50	27.50	—
AH1248	—	12.50	18.50	27.50	—
AH1249	—	12.50	20.00	30.00	—
AH1250	—	20.00	30.00	45.00	—

Mint: Nihavand
KM# 710.12 KRAN

6.9100 g., Silver **Note:** Type E.

Date	Mintage	F	VF	XF	Unc
AH1242	—	50.00	75.00	100	—
AH1248	—	50.00	75.00	100	—

Mint: Qazvin
KM# 710.13 KRAN

6.9100 g., Silver **Note:** Type E.

Date	Mintage	F	VF	XF	Unc
AH1241	—	8.00	12.50	18.50	—
AH1242	—	8.00	12.50	18.50	—
AH1243	—	8.00	12.50	18.50	—
AH1244	—	8.00	12.50	18.50	—
AH1245	—	9.00	13.50	20.00	—
AH1246	—	11.50	17.50	25.00	—

Mint: Qomm
KM# 710.14 KRAN

6.9100 g., Silver **Note:** Type E.

Date	Mintage	F	VF	XF	Unc
AH1241	—	25.00	37.50	55.00	—
AH1242	—	25.00	37.50	55.00	—
AH1243	—	25.00	37.50	55.00	—
AH1244	—	25.00	37.50	55.00	—
AH1246	—	25.00	37.50	55.00	—
AH1247	—	25.00	37.50	55.00	—
AH1248	—	25.00	37.50	55.00	—

Mint: Rasht
KM# 710.15 KRAN

6.9100 g., Silver **Note:** Type E.

Date	Mintage	F	VF	XF	Unc
AH1235	—	25.00	35.00	47.50	—
AH1240	—	12.50	18.50	27.50	—
AH1241	—	8.00	12.50	18.50	—
AH1242	—	8.00	12.50	18.50	—
AH1243	—	8.00	12.50	18.50	—
AH1244	—	8.00	12.50	18.50	—
AH1245	—	8.00	12.50	18.50	—
AH1246	—	9.00	13.50	20.00	—

Mint: Rekab
KM# 710.16 KRAN

6.9100 g., Silver **Note:** Type E.

Date	Mintage	F	VF	XF	Unc
AH1241	—	25.00	37.50	55.00	—
AH1242	—	25.00	37.50	55.00	—

Mint: Shiraz
KM# 710.17 KRAN

6.9100 g., Silver **Note:** Type E.

Date	Mintage	F	VF	XF	Unc
AH1241	—	8.00	12.50	18.50	—
AH1242	—	8.00	12.50	18.50	—
AH1243	—	8.00	12.50	18.50	—
AH1244	—	8.00	12.50	18.50	—
AH1245	—	9.00	13.50	20.00	—
AH1246	—	10.00	16.00	25.00	—

Mint: Shushtar
KM# 710.18 KRAN

6.9100 g., Silver **Note:** Type E.

Date	Mintage	F	VF	XF	Unc
AH1243	—	40.00	55.00	75.00	—

Mint: Simnan
KM# 710.19 KRAN

6.9100 g., Silver **Note:** Type E.

Date	Mintage	F	VF	XF	Unc
AH1242	—	40.00	60.00	85.00	—
AH1245	—	40.00	60.00	85.00	—
AH1246	—	40.00	60.00	85.00	—

Mint: Tabaristan
KM# 710.20 KRAN

6.9100 g., Silver **Note:** Type E.

Date	Mintage	F	VF	XF	Unc
AH1241	—	10.00	16.00	25.00	—
AH1242	—	10.00	16.00	25.00	—
AH1243	—	10.00	16.00	25.00	—
AH1244	—	10.00	16.00	25.00	—
AH1246	—	12.50	18.50	27.50	—

Mint: Tabaristan
KM# 717 KRAN

6.9100 g., Silver **Note:** Type F.

Date	Mintage	F	VF	XF	Unc
AH1246	—	40.00	55.00	75.00	—

Mint: Tehran
KM# 710.22 KRAN

6.9100 g., Silver **Note:** Type E.

Date	Mintage	F	VF	XF	Unc
AH1241	—	8.00	12.50	18.50	—
AH1242	—	8.00	12.50	18.50	—
AH1243	—	8.00	12.50	18.50	—
AH1244	—	8.00	12.50	18.50	—
AH1246	—	9.00	13.50	20.00	—
AH1248	—	15.00	24.00	32.50	—

Mint: Tuyserkan
KM# 710.23 KRAN

6.9100 g., Silver **Note:** Type E.

Date	Mintage	F	VF	XF	Unc
AH1241	—	30.00	45.00	65.00	—
AH1242	—	30.00	45.00	65.00	—
AH1243	—	30.00	45.00	65.00	—

Mint: Urumi
KM# 710.24 KRAN

6.9100 g., Silver **Note:** Type E.

Date	Mintage	F	VF	XF	Unc
AH1241	—	25.00	37.50	55.00	—

Mint: Yazd
KM# 710.25 KRAN

6.9100 g., Silver **Note:** Type E.

Date	Mintage	F	VF	XF	Unc
AH1241	—	8.00	12.50	18.50	—
AH1242	—	8.00	12.50	18.50	—
AH1243	—	8.00	12.50	18.50	—
AH1244	—	8.00	12.50	18.50	—
AH1245	—	9.00	13.50	20.00	—
AH1247	—	10.00	16.00	25.00	—
AH1248	—	10.00	16.00	25.00	—
AH1250	—	20.00	30.00	45.00	—

Mint: Zanjan
KM# 710.26 KRAN

6.9100 g., Silver **Note:** Type E.

Date	Mintage	F	VF	XF	Unc
AH1241	—	16.50	25.00	35.00	—
AH1242	—	16.50	25.00	35.00	—
AH1243	—	16.50	25.00	35.00	—
AH1244	—	16.50	25.00	35.00	—
AH1246	—	20.00	30.00	42.50	—

HAMMERED COINAGE

Gold Toman Issues

Mint: Borujerd
KM# 751.1 1/4 TOMAN

1.1500 g., Gold **Note:** Type W.

Date	Mintage	F	VF	XF	Unc
AH1236	—	125	160	200	—

Mint: Isfahan
KM# 747 1/4 TOMAN

1.2000 g., Gold **Note:** Type V.

Date	Mintage	F	VF	XF	Unc
AH1228	—	150	200	260	—

Mint: Isfahan
KM# 751.2 1/4 TOMAN

1.1500 g., Gold **Note:** Type W.

Date	Mintage	F	VF	XF	Unc
AH1234	—	150	180	225	—

Mint: Isfahan
KM# 748.1 1/2 TOMAN

2.4000 g., Gold **Note:** Type V.

Date	Mintage	F	VF	XF	Unc
AH1228	—	150	200	250	—

Mint: Tabriz
KM# 744 1/2 TOMAN

2.6800 g., Gold **Note:** Type U.

Date	Mintage	F	VF	XF	Unc
AH1224	—	175	240	300	—

Mint: Tabriz
KM# 748.2 1/2 TOMAN

2.4000 g., Gold **Note:** Type V.

Date	Mintage	F	VF	XF	Unc
AH1228	—	150	200	250	—
AH1231	—	150	200	250	—

Mint: Tabriz
KM# 752.2 1/2 TOMAN

2.3000 g., Gold **Note:** Type W.

Date	Mintage	F	VF	XF	Unc
AH1232	—	120	145	180	—
AH1238	—	120	145	180	—

Mint: Tabriz
KM# 756 1/2 TOMAN

2.3000 g., Gold **Note:** Type X.

Date	Mintage	F	VF	XF	Unc
AH1242	—	120	145	180	—

Mint: Tehran
KM# 740 1/2 TOMAN

2.8800 g., Gold **Note:** Type T.

Date	Mintage	F	VF	XF	Unc
AH1220	—	200	275	350	—

Mint: Ardebil
KM# 759.1 TOMAN

3.4500 g., Gold **Obv:** "Keshvarsetan" **Note:** Type Y.

Date	Mintage	F	VF	XF	Unc
AH1246	—	250	300	375	—

Mint: Astarabad
KM# 745.1 TOMAN

5.3700 g., Gold **Note:** Type U.

Date	Mintage	F	VF	XF	Unc
AH1225	—	135	175	250	—

Mint: Borujerd
KM# 753.1 TOMAN

4.6100 g., Gold **Note:** Type W.

Date	Mintage	F	VF	XF	Unc
AH1233	—	140	180	225	—
AH1236	—	120	150	200	—
AH1239	—	120	150	225	—

Mint: Eravan
KM# 753.2 TOMAN

4.6100 g., Gold **Note:** Type W.

Date	Mintage	F	VF	XF	Unc
AH1233	—	140	180	225	—
AH1235	—	140	180	225	—
AH1236	—	150	200	250	—

Mint: Hamadan
KM# 753.3 TOMAN

4.6100 g., Gold **Note:** Type W.

Date	Mintage	F	VF	XF	Unc
AH1240	—	100	125	175	—

Mint: Hamadan
KM# 757.1 TOMAN

4.6100 g., Gold **Obv:** "Sahebqeran" **Note:** Type X.

Date	Mintage	F	VF	XF	Unc
AH1242	—	100	125	175	—

Mint: Hamadan
KM# 759.2 TOMAN

3.4500 g., Gold **Obv:** "Keshvarsetan" **Note:** Type Y.

Date	Mintage	F	VF	XF	Unc
AH1246	—	100	125	175	—
AH1248	—	90.00	115	160	—
AH1249	—	90.00	115	160	—
AH1250	—	100	125	175	—

Mint: Iravan
KM# 753.15 TOMAN

4.6100 g., Gold

Date	Mintage	VG	F	VF	XF	Unc
AH1233	—	—	140	180	225	—
AH1235	—	—	140	180	225	—

Mint: Isfahan
KM# 763 TOMAN

3.4500 g., Gold **Obv:** Shah seated on throne, facing right **Rev:** Mintname and date in central circle **Note:** Special Type.

Date	Mintage	F	VF	XF	Unc
AH1245	—	650	1,100	1,600	—

Mint: Isfahan
KM# 764 TOMAN

3.4500 g., Gold **Obv:** Shah seated on throne, facing left **Rev:** Mint and date in central square **Note:** Special Type.

Date	Mintage	F	VF	XF	Unc
AH1245	—	650	1,100	1,600	—

Mint: Isfahan
KM# 765 TOMAN

3.4500 g., Gold **Rev:** Mint and date in 8-pointed star **Note:** Special Type.

Date	Mintage	F	VF	XF	Unc
AH1248//1250	—	600	1,000	1,400	—

Note: All known pieces are dated 1248 on obverse, 1250 on reverse

Mint: Isfahan
KM# 766 TOMAN

3.4500 g., Gold **Rev:** Mint and date in elongated lozenge **Note:** Special Type.

Date	Mintage	F	VF	XF	Unc
AH1249	—	600	1,000	1,600	—

Mint: Isfahan
KM# 739.1 TOMAN

6.1400 g., Gold **Note:** Type S.

Date	Mintage	F	VF	XF	Unc
AH1217	—	200	250	325	—

Mint: Isfahan
KM# 745.2 TOMAN

5.3700 g., Gold **Note:** Type U.

Date	Mintage	F	VF	XF	Unc
AH1225	—	125	160	225	—

Mint: Isfahan
KM# 749.1 TOMAN

4.8000 g., Gold **Note:** Type V.

Date	Mintage	F	VF	XF	Unc
AH1228	—	90.00	110	150	—
AH1229	—	110	140	200	—

Mint: Isfahan
KM# 753.4 TOMAN

4.6100 g., Gold **Note:** Type W.

Date	Mintage	F	VF	XF	Unc
AH1232	—	80.00	100	145	—
AH1233	—	80.00	100	145	—
AH1234	—	90.00	115	150	—
AH1238	—	90.00	115	150	—
AH1240	—	100	125	175	—

Mint: Isfahan
KM# 757.2 TOMAN

4.6100 g., Gold **Obv:** "Sahebqeran" **Note:** Type X.

Date	Mintage	F	VF	XF	Unc
AH1242	—	100	125	175	—

Mint: Isfahan
KM# 759.3 TOMAN

3.4500 g., Gold **Obv:** "Keshvarsetan" **Note:** Type Y.

Date	Mintage	F	VF	XF	Unc
AH1249	—	100	125	175	—

Mint: Kashan
KM# 741.1 TOMAN

5.7600 g., Gold **Note:** Type T.

Date	Mintage	F	VF	XF	Unc
AH1221	—	200	275	350	—

Mint: Kashan
KM# 749.2 TOMAN

4.8000 g., Gold **Note:** Type V.

Date	Mintage	F	VF	XF	Unc
AH1227	—	100	125	175	—
AH1228	—	100	125	175	—
AH1231	—	110	140	200	—

Mint: Kashan
KM# 753.5 TOMAN

4.6100 g., Gold **Note:** Type W.

Date	Mintage	F	VF	XF	Unc
AH1232	—	80.00	100	145	—
AH1233	—	80.00	100	145	—
AH1235	—	90.00	115	150	—
AH1236	—	90.00	115	150	—
AH1239	—	100	125	175	—

Mint: Kashan
KM# 759.4 TOMAN

3.4500 g., Gold **Obv:** "Keshvarsetan" **Note:** Type Y.

Date	Mintage	F	VF	XF	Unc
AH1246	—	100	125	175	—

Mint: Khoy
KM# 739.2 TOMAN

6.1400 g., Gold **Note:** Type S.

Date	Mintage	F	VF	XF	Unc
AH1215	—	200	250	325	—
AHxxxx	—	150	185	225	—

Mint: Khoy
KM# 753.6 TOMAN

4.6100 g., Gold **Note:** Type W.

Date	Mintage	F	VF	XF	Unc
AH1232	—	130	175	225	—
AH1233	—	120	160	200	—
AH1234	—	120	160	200	—
AH1235	—	120	160	200	—
AH1236	—	120	160	200	—
AH1238	—	125	165	215	—

Mint: Khoy
KM# 759.5 TOMAN

3.4500 g., Gold **Obv:** "Keshvarsetan" **Note:** Type Y.

Date	Mintage	F	VF	XF	Unc
AH1246	—	100	125	175	—

Mint: Kirman
KM# 759.6 TOMAN

3.4500 g., Gold **Obv:** "Keshvarsetan" **Note:** Type Y.

Date	Mintage	F	VF	XF	Unc
AH1248	—	150	215	275	—
AH1249	—	150	215	275	—

Mint: Kirmanshahan
KM# 753.7 TOMAN

4.6100 g., Gold **Note:** Type W.

Date	Mintage	F	VF	XF	Unc
AH1234	—	90.00	115	150	—

Mint: Kirmanshahan
KM# 757.3 TOMAN

4.6100 g., Gold **Obv:** "Sahebqeran" **Note:** Type X.

Date	Mintage	F	VF	XF	Unc
AH1241	—	100	125	175	—

Mint: Kirmanshahan
KM# 759.7 TOMAN

3.4500 g., Gold **Obv:** "Keshvarsetan" **Note:** Type Y.

Date	Mintage	F	VF	XF	Unc
AH1246	—	100	125	175	—
AH1248	—	100	125	175	—

Mint: Mashhad
KM# 749.3 TOMAN

4.8000 g., Gold **Note:** Type V.

Date	Mintage	F	VF	XF	Unc
AH1232	—	125	150	200	—

Mint: Mazandaran
KM# 749.4 TOMAN

4.8000 g., Gold **Note:** Type V.

Date	Mintage	F	VF	XF	Unc
AH1228	—	100	125	175	—

Mint: Qazvin
KM# 753.8 TOMAN

4.6100 g., Gold **Note:** Type W.

Date	Mintage	F	VF	XF	Unc
AH1231	—	80.00	100	145	—
AH1232	—	80.00	100	145	—
AH1234	—	80.00	100	145	—
AH1235	—	80.00	100	145	—
AH1236	—	90.00	115	150	—
AH1240	—	100	125	175	—

Mint: Qazvin
KM# 759.8 TOMAN

3.4500 g., Gold **Obv:** "Keshvarsetan" **Note:** Type Y.

Date	Mintage	F	VF	XF	Unc
AH1246	—	100	125	175	—
AH1248	—	100	125	175	—
AH1249	—	100	125	175	—

Mint: Rasht
KM# 749.5 TOMAN

4.8000 g., Gold **Note:** Type V.

Date	Mintage	F	VF	XF	Unc
AH1231	—	110	140	200	—

Mint: Rasht
KM# 753.9 TOMAN

4.6100 g., Gold **Note:** Type W.

Date	Mintage	F	VF	XF	Unc
AH1230	—	100	125	165	—
AH1231	—	80.00	100	145	—
AH1232	—	80.00	100	145	—
AH1235	—	90.00	115	150	—

Mint: Rasht
KM# 757.4 TOMAN

4.6100 g., Gold **Obv:** "Sahebqeran" **Note:** Type X.

Date	Mintage	F	VF	XF	Unc
AH1243	—	100	125	175	—

Mint: Rasht
KM# 759.9 TOMAN

3.4500 g., Gold **Obv:** "Keshvarsetan" **Note:** Type Y.

Date	Mintage	F	VF	XF	Unc
AH1246	—	90.00	115	160	—
AH1249	—	100	125	175	—
AH1250	—	100	125	175	—

Mint: Shiraz
KM# 749.6 TOMAN

4.8000 g., Gold **Note:** Type V.

Date	Mintage	F	VF	XF	Unc
AH1228	—	90.00	110	150	—
AH1229	—	110	140	200	—

Mint: Shiraz
KM# 753.10 TOMAN

4.6100 g., Gold **Note:** Type W.

Date	Mintage	F	VF	XF	Unc
AH1232	—	80.00	100	145	—
AH1233	—	80.00	100	145	—
AH1234	—	80.00	100	145	—
AH1239	—	100	125	175	—
AH1240	—	100	125	175	—

Mint: Shiraz
KM# 759.10 TOMAN

3.4500 g., Gold **Obv:** "Keshvarsetan" **Note:** Type Y.

Date	Mintage	F	VF	XF	Unc
AH1248	—	100	125	175	—
AH1249	—	100	125	175	—

Mint: Simnan
KM# 759.11 TOMAN

3.4500 g., Gold **Obv:** "Keshvarsetan" **Note:** Type Y.

Date	Mintage	F	VF	XF	Unc
AH1246	—	250	300	375	—

Mint: Tabriz
KM# 745.3 TOMAN

5.3700 g., Gold **Note:** Type U.

Date	Mintage	F	VF	XF	Unc
AH1224	—	125	160	225	—

Mint: Tabriz
KM# 753.11 TOMAN

4.6100 g., Gold **Note:** Type W.

Date	Mintage	F	VF	XF	Unc
AH1233	—	90.00	115	150	—
AH1236	—	90.00	115	150	—
AH1238	—	90.00	115	150	—

Mint: Tabriz
KM# 757.5 TOMAN

4.6100 g., Gold **Obv:** "Sahebqeran" **Note:** Type X.

Date	Mintage	F	VF	XF	Unc
AH1242	—	100	125	175	—
AH1243	—	100	125	175	—
AH1244	—	100	125	175	—

Mint: Tabriz
KM# 759.12 TOMAN

3.4500 g., Gold **Obv:** "Keshvarsetan" **Note:** Type Y.

Date	Mintage	F	VF	XF	Unc
AH1246	—	90.00	115	160	—

Mint: Tehran
KM# 745.4 TOMAN

5.3700 g., Gold **Note:** Type U.

Date	Mintage	F	VF	XF	Unc
AH1224	—	125	160	225	—

Mint: Tehran
KM# 749.7 TOMAN

4.8000 g., Gold **Note:** Type V.

Date	Mintage	F	VF	XF	Unc
AH1228	—	90.00	110	150	—
AH1229	—	110	140	200	—
AH1234 (sic)	—	125	150	200	—

Mint: Tehran
KM# 753.12 TOMAN

4.6100 g., Gold **Note:** Type W.

Date	Mintage	F	VF	XF	Unc
AH1232	—	80.00	100	145	—
AH1234	—	80.00	100	145	—
AH1235	—	90.00	115	150	—
AH1239	—	90.00	115	150	—

Mint: Tehran
KM# 757.6 TOMAN

4.6100 g., Gold **Obv:** "Sahebqeran" **Note:** Type X.

Date	Mintage	F	VF	XF	Unc
AH1242	—	100	125	175	—

Mint: Tehran
KM# 759.13 TOMAN

3.4500 g., Gold **Obv:** "Keshvarsetan" **Note:** Type Y.

Date	Mintage	F	VF	XF	Unc
AH1248	—	100	125	175	—
AH1249	—	100	125	175	—

Mint: Urumi
KM# 757.7 TOMAN

4.6100 g., Gold **Obv:** "Sahebqeran" **Note:** Type X.

Date	Mintage	F	VF	XF	Unc
AH1241	—	125	175	250	—

Mint: Yazd
KM# 739.10 TOMAN

6.1400 g., Gold **Note:** Type S.

Date	Mintage	F	VF	XF	Unc
AH1219	—	200	250	325	—

Mint: Yazd
KM# 741.2 TOMAN

5.7600 g., Gold **Note:** Type T.

Date	Mintage	F	VF	XF	Unc
AH1221	—	200	275	350	—

Mint: Yazd
KM# 745.5 TOMAN

5.3700 g., Gold **Note:** Type U.

Date	Mintage	F	VF	XF	Unc
AH1225	—	125	160	225	—

Mint: Yazd
KM# 749.8 TOMAN

4.8000 g., Gold **Note:** Type V.

Date	Mintage	F	VF	XF	Unc
AH1228	—	100	125	175	—
AH1230	—	110	140	200	—
AH1231	—	110	140	200	—

Mint: Yazd
KM# 753.13 TOMAN

4.6100 g., Gold **Note:** Type W.

Date	Mintage	F	VF	XF	Unc
AH1231	—	80.00	100	145	—
AH1232	—	80.00	100	145	—
AH1233	—	80.00	100	145	—
AH1234	—	80.00	100	145	—
AH1236	—	90.00	115	150	—

Mint: Zanjan
KM# 761 TOMAN

4.6100 g., Gold **Obv:** Shah on horseback **Note:** Special Type.

Date	Mintage	F	VF	XF	Unc
AH1236	—	750	1,250	2,000	—

Mint: Zanjan
KM# 753.14 TOMAN

4.6100 g., Gold **Note:** Type W.

Date	Mintage	F	VF	XF	Unc
AH1233	—	140	180	225	—

Mint: Kirmanshahan
KM# 754.1 3 TOMAN

13.8200 g., Gold **Note:** Type W.

Date	Mintage	F	VF	XF	Unc
AH1233	—	1,500	2,500	4,000	—

Mint: Yazd
KM# 754.2 3 TOMAN

13.8200 g., Gold

Date	Mintage	VG	F	VF	XF	Unc
AH1221	—	—	—	—	—	—

Mint: Zanjan
KM# 762 3 TOMAN

13.8200 g., Gold **Obv:** Shah on horseback **Note:** Special Type.

Date	Mintage	F	VF	XF	Unc
AH1239 Rare	—	—	—	—	—

Mint: Tabriz
KM# 746.1 5 TOMAN

26.8500 g., Gold **Note:** Type U.

Date	Mintage	F	VF	XF	Unc
AH1226	—	—	3,000	5,000	—
AH1227	—	—	3,000	5,000	—

Mint: Tehran
KM# 742 5 TOMAN

28.8000 g., Gold **Note:** Type T.

Date	Mintage	F	VF	XF	Unc
AH1221 Rare	—	—	—	—	—

Mint: Tehran
KM# 746.2 5 TOMAN

26.8500 g., Gold **Note:** Type U.

Date	Mintage	F	VF	XF	Unc
AH1227	—	—	3,000	5,000	—

COUNTERMARKED COINAGE

Mint: Tehran
KM# 730.2 RIAL

10.3600 g., Silver **Countermark:** Zarb Tehran 1229 **Note:** Countermark on KM#678.

CM Date	Host Date	Good	VG	F	VF	XF
ND(AH1229)	AH1216-22	—	15.00	30.00	40.00	55.00

Mint: Tehran
KM# 730.3 RIAL

10.3600 g., Silver **Countermark:** Zarb Tehran 1229 **Note:** Countermark on KM#688.

CM Date	Host Date	Good	VG	F	VF	XF
ND(AH1229)	AH1222-28	—	15.00	30.00	40.00	55.00

Mint: Tehran
KM# 730.1 RIAL

10.3600 g., Silver **Countermark:** Zarb Tehran 1229 **Note:** Countermark on KM#674.

CM Date	Host Date	Good	VG	F	VF	XF
ND(AH1229)	AH1213-15	—	15.00	30.00	40.00	55.00

Nadir Mirza Afshar
AH1210-1218 / 1796-1803AD

Ruler in Mashad

Type A Coinage

Name of ruler within central cartouche with blank margins around, *al-Sultan Nadir*. Reverse, mint and date below, benediction above, *Edama Allah Daulatahu*, "may God prolong his reign."

HAMMERED COINAGE

Mint: Mashhad
KM# 768 SHAHI

1.1500 g., Silver **Note:** Type A.

Date	Mintage	F	VF	XF	Unc
AH1216	—	75.00	125	200	—

Mint: Mashhad
KM# 769 RUPI

11.5000 g., Silver **Note:** Type A.

Date	Mintage	F	VF	XF	Unc
AH1216	—	100	160	250	—

Husain Quli Khan Qajar
AH1216 / 1801AD

Rebel in Isfahan

HAMMERED COINAGE

Mint: Isfahan
KM# 770 RIYAL

10.4000 g., Silver **Note:** Rebel issue.

Date	Mintage	F	VF	XF	Unc
AH1216	—	125	200	300	—

Sultan Ali Shah
AH1250 / 1834AD

HAMMERED COINAGE

Mint: Tehran
KM# 771 KRAN

6.9000 g., Silver **Note:** Pretender issue; holed or mounted coins are worth about half the listed price.

Date	Mintage	F	VF	XF	Unc
AH1250	—	250	300	400	—

Mint: Tehran
KM# 772 TOMAN

3.5000 g., Gold **Note:** Pretender issue.

Date	Mintage	F	VF	XF	Unc
AH1250	—	400	650	850	—

Husain Ali Shah
AH1250 / 1834AD

Ruler for six months in southern Iran

There is only one type for this reign. Obverse: *al-sultan ibn al-sultan Husayn Ali Shah Qajar*. Reverse: Mint and date.

HAMMERED COINAGE

Mint: Shiraz
KM# 774 KRAN

6.9000 g., Silver **Note:** Pretender issue.

Date	Mintage	F	VF	XF	Unc
AH1250	—	350	425	500	—

Mint: Shiraz
KM# 775 TOMAN

3.4500 g., Gold **Note:** Pretender issue.

Date	Mintage	F	VF	XF	Unc
AH1250	—	—	—	—	—

Note: Reported, not confirmed

Muhammad Shah
AH1250-1264 / 1834-1848AD

Silver Types:

All purely inscriptional coins of Muhammad Shah share a common obverse legend, *Mohammad Shahansha-e Anbiyja*, "Muhammad, King of the Prophets," a word-play on the name of the ruler. All have mint & date on reverse, as in previous reigns. The types differ only in their weight standards:

A. Based on a kran of 6.91 g.
B. Based on a kran of 6.33 g.
C. Based on a kran of 5.76 g.
D. Based on a kran of 5.37 g.
E. Obverse: Lion & sun within wreath.

Reverse: The normal Muhammad Shah legend, together with mint & date, all within a square. Same standards as type D, with which it was contemporary.

Gold Types:

R. Based on a toman of 3.84 g.
S. Based on a toman of 3.45 g.

HAMMERED COINAGE

Mint: Kirmanshahan
KM# 788.1 1/8 KRAN

0.6700 g., Silver **Note:** Type C.

Date	Mintage	Good	VG	F	VF	XF
AH1253	—	—	15.00	30.00	40.00	60.00

Mint: Mashhad
KM# 792.1 1/8 KRAN

0.6700 g., Silver **Note:** Type D. Sometimes uniface, obverse or reverse.

Date	Mintage	Good	VG	F	VF	XF
AH1260	—	—	7.50	15.00	20.00	27.50

Mint: Rasht
KM# 788.2 1/8 KRAN

0.6700 g., Silver

Date	Mintage	Good	VG	F	VF	XF
ND	—	—	—	30.00	40.00	60.00

Mint: Rasht
KM# 792.2 1/8 KRAN

0.6700 g., Silver **Note:** Type D.

Date	Mintage	Good	VG	F	VF	XF
ND(AH1255-63)	—	—	7.50	15.00	20.00	27.50

Mint: Shiraz
KM# 788.3 1/8 KRAN

0.6700 g., Silver **Note:** Type C.

Date	Mintage	Good	VG	F	VF	XF
AH1252	—	—	15.00	30.00	40.00	60.50
AH1253	—	—	15.00	30.00	40.00	60.50

Mint: Shiraz
KM# 792.3 1/8 KRAN

0.6700 g., Silver **Note:** Type D.

Date	Mintage	Good	VG	F	VF	XF
AH1255	—	—	7.50	15.00	20.00	27.50

Mint: Yazd
KM# 793 1/5 KRAN

1.0700 g., Silver **Note:** Type D.

Date	Mintage	Good	VG	F	VF	XF
AH1260	—	—	12.50	25.00	35.00	50.00

Mint: Tabriz
KM# 781 1/4 KRAN

1.7200 g., Silver **Note:** Type A.

Date	Mintage	Good	VG	F	VF	XF
AH1250	—	—	15.00	30.00	40.00	60.00

Mint: Tabriz
KM# 789 1/4 KRAN

1.4400 g., Silver **Note:** Type C.

Date	Mintage	Good	VG	F	VF	XF
AH1252	—	—	20.00	40.00	55.00	75.00

Mint: Kirman
KM# 795 1/3 KRAN

1.7900 g., Silver **Note:** Type D.

Date	Mintage	Good	VG	F	VF	XF
AH1255	—	—	15.00	30.00	40.00	55.00

Mint: Isfahan
KM# 790.1 1/2 KRAN

2.8800 g., Silver **Note:** Type C.

Date	Mintage	Good	VG	F	VF	XF
AH1254	—	—	10.00	20.00	30.00	47.50

Note: Coins of Isfahan dated AH1254 may belong to the following standard, KM#796

Mint: Isfahan
KM# 796.1 1/2 KRAN

2.6800 g., Silver **Note:** Type D.

Date	Mintage	Good	VG	F	VF	XF
AH1257	—	—	5.00	10.00	15.00	22.50
AH1258	—	—	5.00	10.00	15.00	22.50
AH1260	—	—	5.00	10.00	15.00	22.50
AH1261	—	—	5.00	10.00	15.00	22.50
AH1263	—	—	5.00	10.00	15.00	22.50

Mint: Mashhad
KM# 796.2 1/2 KRAN

2.6800 g., Silver **Note:** Type D.

Date	Mintage	Good	VG	F	VF	XF
AH1264	—	—	7.50	15.00	20.00	27.50

Mint: Shiraz
KM# 782 1/2 KRAN

3.4500 g., Silver **Note:** Type A.

Date	Mintage	Good	VG	F	VF	XF
AH1250	—	—	12.50	25.00	35.00	55.00
AH1251	—	—	12.50	25.00	35.00	55.00

Mint: Shiraz
KM# 796.3 1/2 KRAN

2.6800 g., Silver **Note:** Type D.

Date	Mintage	Good	VG	F	VF	XF
AH1259	—	—	6.25	12.50	18.50	27.50
AH1261	—	—	6.25	12.50	18.50	27.50
AH1262	—	—	6.25	12.50	18.50	27.50

Mint: Tabaristan
KM# 796.4 1/2 KRAN

2.6800 g., Silver **Note:** Type D.

Date	Mintage	Good	VG	F	VF	XF
AH1255	—	—	6.25	12.50	18.50	27.50
AH1258	—	—	6.25	12.50	18.50	27.50
AH1261	—	—	6.25	12.50	18.50	27.50
AH1264	—	—	7.50	15.00	20.00	27.50

Mint: Tabriz
KM# 790.2 1/2 KRAN

2.8800 g., Silver **Note:** Type C.

Date	Mintage	Good	VG	F	VF	XF
AH1251	—	—	10.00	20.00	30.00	47.50
AH1252	—	—	10.00	20.00	30.00	47.50

Mint: Tabriz
KM# 796.5 1/2 KRAN

2.6800 g., Silver **Note:** Type D.

Date	Mintage	Good	VG	F	VF	XF
ND(AH1839-48)	—	—	6.25	12.50	18.50	27.50

Mint: Tehran
KM# 798 1/2 KRAN

2.6800 g., Silver **Note:** Type E.

Date	Mintage	Good	VG	F	VF	XF
AH1263	—	—	15.00	30.00	40.00	55.00
AH1264	—	—	15.00	30.00	40.00	55.00

Mint: Tehran
KM# 790.3 1/2 KRAN

2.8800 g., Silver **Note:** Type C.

Date	Mintage	F	VF	XF	Unc
AH1251	—	20.00	30.00	47.50	—

Mint: Kirman
KM# 785 2/5 KRAN

2.5300 g., Silver **Note:** Type B.

Date	Mintage	Good	VG	F	VF	XF
AH1252	—	—	20.00	40.00	50.00	65.00
AH1255	—	—	20.00	40.00	50.00	65.00

Mint: Astarabad
KM# 797.1 KRAN

5.3700 g., Silver **Note:** Type D.

Date	Mintage	Good	VG	F	VF	XF
AH1255	—	—	2.50	6.00	10.00	17.50
AH1256	—	—	2.75	7.00	11.50	20.00

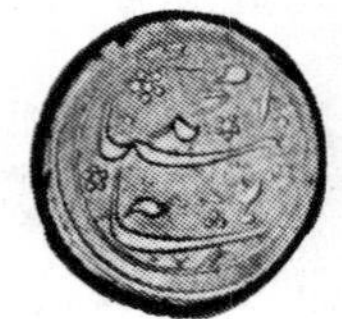

Mint: Hamadan
KM# 787.1 KRAN

6.3300 g., Silver **Note:** Type B.

Date	Mintage	Good	VG	F	VF	XF
AH1251	—	—	6.25	12.50	20.00	30.00

Mint: Isfahan
KM# 787.2 KRAN

6.3300 g., Silver **Note:** Type B.

Date	Mintage	Good	VG	F	VF	XF
AH1251	—	—	6.25	12.50	20.00	30.00

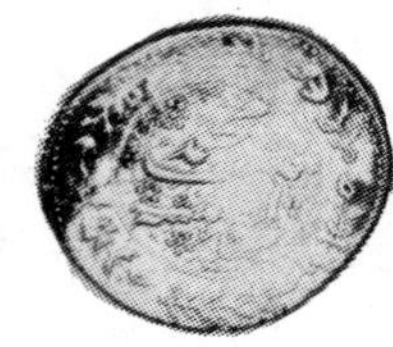

Mint: Isfahan
KM# 791.1 KRAN

5.7600 g., Silver **Note:** Type C.

Date	Mintage	Good	VG	F	VF	XF
AH1252	—	—	2.75	7.00	11.00	17.50
AH1253	—	—	2.75	7.00	11.00	17.50
AH1254	—	—	4.00	10.00	15.00	22.50

Mint: Isfahan
KM# 797.2 KRAN

5.3700 g., Silver **Note:** Type D.

Date	Mintage	Good	VG	F	VF	XF
AH1255	—	—	2.50	6.00	10.00	17.50
AH1256	—	—	2.50	6.00	10.00	17.50
AH1257	—	—	2.50	6.00	10.00	17.50
AH1258	—	—	2.50	6.00	10.00	17.50
AH1259	—	—	2.50	6.00	10.00	17.50
AH1260	—	—	2.50	6.00	10.00	17.50
AH1261	—	—	2.50	6.00	10.00	17.50
AH1263	—	—	2.75	7.00	11.50	18.50

Mint: Kirmanshahan
KM# 791.2 KRAN

5.7600 g., Silver **Note:** Type C.

Date	Mintage	Good	VG	F	VF	XF
AH1251	—	—	4.00	10.00	15.00	22.50
AH1252	—	—	2.75	7.00	11.00	17.50
AH1253	—	—	2.75	7.00	11.00	17.50
AH1254	—	—	4.00	10.00	15.00	22.50

Mint: Kirmanshahan
KM# 797.3 KRAN

5.3700 g., Silver **Note:** Type D.

Date	Mintage	Good	VG	F	VF	XF
AH1256	—	—	7.50	15.00	22.50	35.00
AH1258	—	—	7.50	15.00	22.50	35.00
AH1260	—	—	7.50	15.00	22.50	35.00

Mint: Kirmanshahan
KM# 797.4 KRAN

5.3700 g., Silver **Note:** Type D.

Date	Mintage	Good	VG	F	VF	XF
AH1255	—	—	2.50	6.00	10.00	17.50
AH1256	—	—	2.50	6.00	10.00	17.50
AH1257	—	—	2.50	6.00	10.00	17.50
AH1258	—	—	2.50	6.00	10.00	17.50
AH1259	—	—	2.50	6.00	10.00	17.50
AH1260	—	—	2.50	6.00	10.00	17.50
AH1261	—	—	2.75	7.00	11.50	18.50
AH1262	—	—	3.25	8.00	12.50	20.00
AH1263	—	—	3.25	8.00	12.50	20.00
AH1264	—	—	2.75	7.00	11.50	18.50

Mint: Mashhad
KM# 783 KRAN

6.9100 g., Silver **Note:** Type A.

Date	Mintage	Good	VG	F	VF	XF
AH1250	—	—	22.50	45.00	70.00	100
AH1251	—	—	22.50	45.00	70.00	100

Mint: Mashhad
KM# 791.3 KRAN

5.7600 g., Silver **Note:** Type C.

Date	Mintage	Good	VG	F	VF	XF
AH1252	—	—	2.75	7.00	11.00	17.50
AH1253	—	—	2.75	7.00	11.00	17.50
AH1254	—	—	4.00	10.00	15.00	22.50

Mint: Mashhad
KM# 797.5 KRAN

5.3700 g., Silver **Note:** Type D.

Date	Mintage	Good	VG	F	VF	XF
AH1255	—	—	2.50	6.00	10.00	17.50
AH1256	—	—	2.50	6.00	10.00	17.50
AH1257	—	—	2.50	6.00	10.00	17.50
AH1258	—	—	2.50	6.00	10.00	17.50
AH1259	—	—	2.50	6.00	10.00	17.50
AH1260	—	—	2.50	6.00	10.00	17.50
AH1261	—	—	2.50	6.00	10.00	17.50
AH1262	—	—	2.50	6.00	10.00	17.50
AH1264	—	—	2.75	7.00	11.50	18.50
AH1265 (sic)	—	—	20.00	40.00	55.00	75.00
AH1265//1266 (sic)	—	—	—	50.00	65.00	90.00

Note: Coins of AH1265 and AH1266 are issues of the rebellion of Hasan Khan Salar in Mashhad (AH1264-1266)

Mint: Rasht
KM# 787.3 KRAN

6.3300 g., Silver **Note:** Type B.

Date	Mintage	Good	VG	F	VF	XF
AH1251	—	—	6.25	12.50	20.00	30.00

Mint: Rasht
KM# 791.4 KRAN

5.7600 g., Silver **Note:** Type C.

Date	Mintage	Good	VG	F	VF	XF
AH1251	—	—	4.00	10.00	15.00	22.50
AH1252	—	—	2.75	7.00	11.00	17.50
AH1253	—	—	2.75	7.00	11.00	17.50

Mint: Rasht
KM# 797.6 KRAN

5.3700 g., Silver **Note:** Type D.

Date	Mintage	Good	VG	F	VF	XF
AH1255	—	—	2.50	6.00	10.00	17.50
AH1256	—	—	2.50	6.00	10.00	17.50
AH1257	—	—	2.50	6.00	10.00	17.50
AH1258	—	—	2.50	6.00	10.00	17.50
AH1259	—	—	2.50	6.00	10.00	17.50
AH1260	—	—	2.50	6.00	10.00	17.50
AH1261	—	—	2.50	6.00	10.00	17.50
AH1262	—	—	2.50	6.00	10.00	17.50
AH1263	—	—	2.75	7.00	11.50	18.50

Mint: Shiraz
KM# 787.4 KRAN

6.3300 g., Silver **Note:** Type B.

Date	Mintage	Good	VG	F	VF	XF
AH1251	—	—	6.25	12.50	20.00	30.00

Mint: Shiraz
KM# 791.5 KRAN

5.7600 g., Silver **Note:** Type C.

Date	Mintage	Good	VG	F	VF	XF
AH1252	—	—	3.25	8.00	12.50	20.00
AH1254	—	—	4.00	10.00	15.00	22.50

Mint: Shiraz
KM# 797.7 KRAN

5.3700 g., Silver **Note:** Type D.

Date	Mintage	Good	VG	F	VF	XF
AH1255	—	—	2.50	6.00	10.00	17.50
AH1256	—	—	2.50	6.00	10.00	17.50
AH1258	—	—	2.50	6.00	10.00	17.50
AH1259	—	—	3.25	8.00	12.50	20.00
AH1260	—	—	3.25	8.00	12.50	20.00
AH1263	—	—	3.25	8.00	12.50	20.00

Mint: Tabaristan
KM# 797.8 KRAN

5.3700 g., Silver **Note:** Type D.

Date	Mintage	Good	VG	F	VF	XF
AH1256	—	—	2.50	6.00	10.00	17.50
AH1257	—	—	2.50	6.00	10.00	17.50
AH1258	—	—	2.50	6.00	10.00	17.50
AH1260	—	—	2.50	6.00	10.00	17.50
AH1259/8	—	—	2.50	6.00	10.00	17.50
AH1261	—	—	2.50	6.00	10.00	17.50
AH1262	—	—	2.50	6.00	10.00	17.50
AH1263	—	—	2.75	7.00	11.50	18.50
AH1264	—	—	2.75	7.00	11.50	18.50

Mint: Tabriz
KM# 787.5 KRAN

6.3300 g., Silver **Note:** Type B.

Date	Mintage	Good	VG	F	VF	XF
AH1251	—	—	6.25	12.50	20.00	30.00

Mint: Tabriz
KM# 791.6 KRAN

5.7600 g., Silver **Note:** Type C.

Date	Mintage	Good	VG	F	VF	XF
AH1252	—	—	2.75	7.00	11.00	17.50
AH1253	—	—	2.75	7.00	11.00	17.50
AH1254	—	—	4.00	10.00	15.00	22.50

Note: Coins of Isfahan dated AH1254 may belong to the following standard, KM#797

Mint: Tabriz
KM# 797.9 KRAN

5.3700 g., Silver **Note:** Type D.

Date	Mintage	Good	VG	F	VF	XF
AH1254 (sic)	—	—	10.00	20.00	27.50	37.50
AH1255	—	—	2.50	6.00	10.00	17.50
AH1256	—	—	2.50	6.00	10.00	17.50
AH1257	—	—	2.50	6.00	10.00	17.50
AH1260	—	—	2.75	7.00	11.50	18.50
AH1261	—	—	2.75	7.00	11.50	18.50

Mint: Tehran
KM# 787.6 KRAN

6.3300 g., Silver **Note:** Type B.

Date	Mintage	Good	VG	F	VF	XF
AH1251	—	—	6.25	12.50	20.00	30.00

Mint: Tehran
KM# 791.7 KRAN

5.7600 g., Silver **Note:** Type C.

Date	Mintage	Good	VG	F	VF	XF
AH1251	—	—	4.00	10.00	15.00	22.50
AH1252	—	—	2.75	7.00	11.00	17.50
AH1253	—	—	2.75	7.00	11.00	17.50
AH1254	—	—	2.75	7.00	11.00	17.50

Mint: Tehran
KM# 797.10 KRAN

5.3700 g., Silver **Note:** Type D.

Date	Mintage	Good	VG	F	VF	XF
AH1255	—	—	2.50	6.00	10.00	17.50
AH1257	—	—	2.50	6.00	10.00	17.50
AH1258	—	—	2.75	7.00	11.50	20.00

Mint: Tehran
KM# 799 KRAN

5.3700 g., Silver **Note:** Type E.

Date	Mintage	Good	VG	F	VF	XF
AH1258	—	—	10.00	20.00	30.00	50.00
AH1259	—	—	12.50	25.00	37.50	60.00
AH1260	—	—	12.50	25.00	37.50	60.00
AH1261	—	—	10.00	20.00	30.00	50.00
AH1262	—	—	10.00	20.00	30.00	50.00
AH1263	—	—	10.00	20.00	30.00	50.00

Mint: Yazd
KM# 787.7 KRAN

6.3300 g., Silver **Note:** Type B.

Date	Mintage	Good	VG	F	VF	XF
AH1251	—	—	6.25	12.50	20.00	30.00

Mint: Yazd
KM# 791.8 KRAN

5.7600 g., Silver **Note:** Type C.

Date	Mintage	Good	VG	F	VF	XF
AH1252	—	—	3.25	8.00	12.50	20.00
AH1253	—	—	3.25	8.00	12.50	20.00

Mint: Yazd
KM# 797.11 KRAN

5.3700 g., Silver **Note:** Type D.

Date	Mintage	Good	VG	F	VF	XF
AH1255	—	—	2.50	6.00	10.00	17.50
AH1256	—	—	2.50	6.00	10.00	17.50
AH1257	—	—	2.50	6.00	10.00	17.50
AH1258	—	—	2.50	6.00	10.00	17.50
AH1259	—	—	2.50	6.00	10.00	17.50
AH1260	—	—	2.50	6.00	10.00	17.50
AH1261	—	—	2.50	6.00	10.00	17.50
AH1262	—	—	2.50	6.00	10.00	17.50
AH1264	—	—	2.75	7.00	11.50	18.50

Mint: Tehran
KM# 784 2 KRANS

13.8200 g., Silver **Note:** Type A.

Date	Mintage	Good	VG	F	VF	XF
AH1251	—	—	65.00	125	150	200

Mint: Tehran
KM# 800 2 KRANS

13.8200 g., Silver **Note:** Type E.

Date	Mintage	Good	VG	F	VF	XF
AH1263	—	—	30.00	60.00	85.00	125

Mint: Tabriz
KM# 805 1/2 TOMAN

1.9200 g., Gold **Note:** Type R.

Date	Mintage	Good	VG	F	VF	XF
AH1252	—	—	65.00	125	160	200

Mint: Tehran
KM# 811 1/2 TOMAN

1.7200 g., Gold **Note:** Lion and sun type. Similar to 1 Kran, KM#799.

Date	Mintage	Good	VG	F	VF	XF
AH1258	—	—	125	200	250	350

Mint: Hamadan
KM# 806.1 TOMAN

3.8400 g., Gold **Note:** Type R.

Date	Mintage	Good	VG	F	VF	XF
AH1250	—	—	42.50	60.00	80.00	100

Mint: Isfahan
KM# 806.2 TOMAN

3.8400 g., Gold **Note:** Type R.

Date	Mintage	Good	VG	F	VF	XF
AH1250	—	—	35.00	50.00	70.00	90.00
AH1252	—	—	35.00	50.00	70.00	90.00
AH1253	—	—	35.00	50.00	70.00	90.00

Mint: Isfahan
KM# 809.1 TOMAN

3.8400 g., Gold **Note:** Type S.

Date	Mintage	Good	VG	F	VF	XF
AH1259	—	—	35.00	50.00	70.00	90.00
AH1260	—	—	—	—	—	—
AH1265 (sic)	—	—	35.00	50.00	70.00	90.00

Mint: Kirmanshahan
KM# 806.3 TOMAN

3.8400 g., Gold **Note:** Type R.

Date	Mintage	Good	VG	F	VF	XF
AH1250	—	—	42.50	60.00	80.00	100

Mint: Mashhad
KM# 806.4 TOMAN

3.8400 g., Gold **Note:** Type R.

Date	Mintage	Good	VG	F	VF	XF
AH1254	—	—	50.00	70.00	90.00	125

Mint: Mashhad
KM# 809.2 TOMAN

3.8400 g., Gold **Note:** Type S.

Date	Mintage	Good	VG	F	VF	XF
AH1256	—	—	35.00	50.00	70.00	90.00
AH1257	—	—	35.00	50.00	70.00	90.00
AH1259	—	—	35.00	50.00	70.00	90.00
AH1260	—	—	35.00	50.00	70.00	90.00
AH1261	—	—	35.00	50.00	70.00	90.00
AH1263	—	—	35.00	50.00	70.00	90.00
AH1264	—	—	35.00	50.00	70.00	90.00
AH1265//1265 (sic)	—	—	125	200	275	375

Note: Coins of Mashhad struck in AH1265 (and dated on both sides) are issues of the rebel Hasan Khan Salar after Muhammad Shah's death.

Mint: Rasht
KM# 806.5 TOMAN

3.8400 g., Gold **Note:** Type R.

Date	Mintage	Good	VG	F	VF	XF
AH1251	—	—	35.00	50.00	70.00	90.00
AH1252	—	—	35.00	50.00	70.00	90.00

Mint: Rasht
KM# 809.3 TOMAN

3.8400 g., Gold **Note:** Type S.

Date	Mintage	Good	VG	F	VF	XF
AH1255	—	—	35.00	50.00	70.00	90.00
AH1257	—	—	35.00	50.00	70.00	90.00
AH1258	—	—	35.00	50.00	70.00	90.00
AH1259	—	—	35.00	50.00	70.00	90.00
AH1262	—	—	35.00	50.00	70.00	90.00

Mint: Shiraz
KM# 806.6 TOMAN

3.8400 g., Gold **Note:** Type R.

Date	Mintage	Good	VG	F	VF	XF
AH1252	—	—	35.00	50.00	70.00	90.00
AH1253	—	—	35.00	50.00	70.00	90.00

Mint: Shiraz
KM# 809.4 TOMAN

3.8400 g., Gold **Note:** Type S.

Date	Mintage	Good	VG	F	VF	XF
AH1255	—	—	35.00	50.00	70.00	90.00

Mint: Tabriz
KM# 806.7 TOMAN

3.8400 g., Gold **Note:** Type R.

Date	Mintage	Good	VG	F	VF	XF
AH1250	—	—	35.00	50.00	70.00	90.00
AH1254	—	—	35.00	50.00	70.00	90.00

Mint: Tabriz
KM# 809.5 TOMAN

3.8400 g., Gold **Note:** Type S.

Date	Mintage	Good	VG	F	VF	XF
AH1255	—	—	35.00	50.00	70.00	90.00
AH1256	—	—	35.00	50.00	70.00	90.00
AH1257	—	—	35.00	50.00	70.00	90.00
AH1259	—	—	35.00	50.00	70.00	90.00
AH1261	—	—	35.00	50.00	70.00	90.00

Mint: Tehran
KM# 812 TOMAN

3.8400 g., Gold **Note:** Lion and sun type. Similar to 1 Kran, KM#799.

Date	Mintage	Good	VG	F	VF	XF
AH1258	—	—	125	200	300	400
AH1260	—	—	125	200	300	400
AH1261	—	—	125	200	300	400
AH1262	—	—	125	200	300	400
AH1263	—	—	125	200	300	400

Mint: Tehran
KM# 806.8 TOMAN

3.8400 g., Gold **Note:** Type R.

Date	Mintage	Good	VG	F	VF	XF
AH1251	—	—	35.00	50.00	70.00	90.00
AH1252	—	—	35.00	50.00	70.00	90.00

Mint: Tehran
KM# 809.6 TOMAN

3.8400 g., Gold **Note:** Type S.

Date	Mintage	Good	VG	F	VF	XF
AH1255	—	—	35.00	50.00	70.00	90.00
AH1256	—	—	35.00	50.00	70.00	90.00
AH1257	—	—	35.00	50.00	70.00	90.00

Mint: Isfahan
KM# 814 2 TOMAN

6.9000 g., Gold **Obv:** Crowned ruler on throne **Note:** Special type.

Date	Mintage	Good	VG	F	VF	XF
AH1254	—	—	—	—	—	3,000

Mint: Tehran
KM# 807 6 TOMAN

Gold **Obv:** Crowned ruler on throne **Note:** Type R; weight approximately 23 grams.

Date	Mintage	Good	VG	F	VF	XF
AH1251	—	—	—	—	—	5,000

COUNTERMARKED COINAGE

Mint: Tehran
KM# 816 TOMAN

3.4500 g., Gold **Countermark:** Duribe Tehran (12)50 **Note:** Countermark on Fath Ali Shah, KM#759.

CM Date	Host Date	Good	VG	F	VF	XF
AH12(50)	AH1246-49	—	200	300	375	475

Note: Countermarks appear on these coins ranging from AH1246-1249; Anonymous type, could be an issue of either Sultan Ali Shah or Muhammad Shah

Nasir al-Din Shah

AH1264-1313 / 1848-1896AD

The hammered silver coinage of this reign comprises two standards, one based on a kran of 5.37 g, the second based on a kran of 4.99 g. The first was inherited from the previous reign and maintained for the kran until AH1273 or 1274 (AH1276 at Tabriz). The second standard was introduced for the half kran as early as AH1269 or 1270, and seems to have been in general use for the half kran as early as AH1269 or 1270, and seems to have been in general use for the half kran by AH1271. Unfortunately, not enough information is currently available to separate all issues. For that reason, the two standards are lumped together as a single type, but will be separated in a future edition of this catalog. The 5.37 g standard will be types KM#821-824, those on the 4.99 g standard will be KM#821a-824a.

The eighth kran was intended largely for ceremonial purposes, and varies considerably in weight. It is the ancestor of the Shahi Sefid of the machine-struck period.

Machine-struck coinage was introduced in AH1293 and became general by AH1296. The latest known hammered coins are dated AH1297. All of the provincial markets were closed when hammered coinage ceased.

All of Nasir al-Din's hammered gold was struck to the 3.45 g toman standard.

All normal hammered silver and gold coinage of this reign bears on the obverse the inscription *al-sultan ibn al-sultan Nasir al-Din Shah Qajar*, occasionally somewhat shortened. The reverse bears the mint & the date, though the date occasionally appears on the obverse or on both sides.

There is great variety of design for both obverse and reverse during this reign, with many attractive and elegant cartouches and calligraphic styles. The more attractive and ornate designs command a significant premium over listed prices, from 25% to at least 200%, depending on attractiveness and rarity.

KRAN STANDARD

AH1293-1344, SH1304-1309,
1876-1931AD

50 Dinars = 1 Shahi
1000 Dinars = 20 Shahis = 1 Kran (Qiron)
10 Krans = 1 Toman

NOTE: Dated reverse dies lacking the ruler's name were not discarded at the end of a reign (especially from Nasir al-Din to Muzaffar al-Din), but remained in use until broken or worn out. Sometimes the old date was scratched out or changed, but often the die was used with the old date unaltered. Some dies with date below wreath retained the old date but had the new date engraved among the lion's legs.

HAMMERED COINAGE

Mint: Without Mint Name
KM# 123 FALUS

Copper **Obv:** Radiant sun behind lion left with sword in sprays

Date	Mintage	Good	VG	F	VF	XF
AH1283	—	7.50	12.50	20.00	35.00	—

Mint: Without Mint Name
KM# A135 12-1/2 DINAR

Copper **Obv:** Lion right, radiant sun behind

Date	Mintage	Good	VG	F	VF	XF
AH1284	—	7.50	12.50	30.00	35.00	—

Mint: Without Mint Name
KM# 136 25 DINARS

Copper **Obv:** Passant lion left, radiant sun behind

Date	Mintage	Good	VG	F	VF	XF
AH1270	—	5.00	7.50	12.50	20.00	—
AH1272	—	5.00	7.50	12.50	20.00	—

Mint: Without Mint Name
KM# 818 25 DINARS

Copper **Obv:** Sun behind reclining lion left **Note:** This and KM#819 bear no mintname. Several variations of type.

Date	Mintage	Good	VG	F	VF	XF
AH1271	—	0.80	2.00	3.00	6.00	17.00
AH1272	—	0.80	2.00	3.00	6.00	17.00
AH1273	—	0.80	2.00	3.00	6.00	17.00

Mint: Tehran
KM# A67 25 DINARS

Copper **Obv:** Lion left facing with sword and sun in wreath

Date	Mintage	Good	VG	F	VF	XF
AH1294	—	7.50	12.50	20.00	35.00	—

Mint: Tehran
KM# A49 50 DINARS

Copper **Obv:** Lion left facing with sword and sun in wreath

Date	Mintage	Good	VG	F	VF	XF
AH1293	—	4.50	7.50	12.50	20.00	—
AH1294	—	4.50	7.50	12.50	20.00	—

Mint: Without Mint Name
KM# 819 50 DINARS

Copper **Obv:** Sun behind reclining lion left

Date	Mintage	Good	VG	F	VF	XF
AH1270-86	—	0.80	2.00	3.00	6.00	20.00

Mint: Without Mint Name
KM# 137 50 DINARS

Copper

Date	Mintage	Good	VG	F	VF	XF
AH1270-86	—	5.00	7.50	12.50	20.00	—

Mint: Hamadan
KM# 821.1 1/8 KRAN

Silver **Note:** Uniface. Weight varies: 0.62 - 0.67 grams.

Date	Mintage	Good	VG	F	VF	XF
AH1281	—	—	7.50	15.00	22.50	32.50

Mint: Isfahan
KM# 821.2 1/8 KRAN

Silver **Note:** Uniface. Weight varies: 0.62 - 0.67 grams.

Date	Mintage	Good	VG	F	VF	XF
AH1271	—	—	3.00	7.50	12.50	17.50
AH1273	—	—	3.00	7.50	12.50	17.50
AH1286	—	—	4.00	10.00	16.00	25.00

Mint: Mashhad
KM# 821.3 1/8 KRAN

Silver **Note:** Uniface. Weight varies: 0.62 - 0.67 grams.

Date	Mintage	Good	VG	F	VF	XF
AH1276	—	—	7.50	15.00	22.50	32.50

Mint: Qazvin
KM# 821.4 1/8 KRAN

Silver **Note:** Uniface. Weight varies: 0.62 - 0.67 grams.

Date	Mintage	Good	VG	F	VF	XF
AH1267	—	—	6.00	12.50	20.00	30.00

Mint: Rasht
KM# 821.5 1/8 KRAN

Silver **Note:** Uniface. Weight varies: 0.62 - 0.67 grams.

Date	Mintage	Good	VG	F	VF	XF
AH1272	—	—	6.00	12.50	20.00	30.00
AH1274	—	—	6.00	12.50	20.00	30.00

Mint: Shiraz
KM# 821.6 1/8 KRAN

Silver **Note:** Uniface. Weight varies: 0.62 - 0.67 grams.

Date	Mintage	Good	VG	F	VF	XF
AH1284	—	—	7.50	15.00	22.50	32.50
AH1288	—	—	7.50	15.00	22.50	32.50

Mint: Sistan
KM# 821.7 1/8 KRAN

Silver **Note:** Uniface. Weight varies: 0.62 - 0.67 grams.

Date	Mintage	Good	VG	F	VF	XF
AH1274	—	—	45.00	75.00	115	175

Mint: Tabriz
KM# 821.8 1/8 KRAN

Silver **Note:** Uniface. Weight varies: 0.62 - 0.67 grams.

Date	Mintage	Good	VG	F	VF	XF
AH1275	—	—	4.00	10.00	16.00	25.00

Mint: Tehran
KM# 821.9 1/8 KRAN

Silver **Note:** Uniface. Weight varies: 0.62 - 0.67 grams.

Date	Mintage	Good	VG	F	VF	XF
AH1293	—	—	7.50	15.00	22.50	32.50

Mint: Isfahan
KM# 838 1/4 KRAN

1.2500 g., Silver **Obv:** Shah seated facing, holding sabre **Note:** Special type.

Date	Mintage	Good	VG	F	VF	XF
AH1274	—	—	125	200	250	300

Mint: Mashhad
KM# 831 1/4 KRAN

1.2500 g., Silver **Obv:** Ruler's name in toughra form **Note:** Toughra type.

Date	Mintage	Good	VG	F	VF	XF
AH1284	—	—	25.00	50.00	75.00	100

Mint: Mashhad
KM# 822.1 1/4 KRAN

Silver **Note:** Weight varies: 1.25 - 1.34 grams.

Date	Mintage	Good	VG	F	VF	XF
AH1284	—	—	6.00	12.50	17.50	26.00

Mint: Tabriz
KM# 822.2 1/4 KRAN

Silver **Note:** Weight varies: 1.25 - 1.34 grams.

Date	Mintage	Good	VG	F	VF	XF
AH1294	—	—	7.50	15.00	25.00	40.00

Mint: Tehran
KM# 827 1/4 KRAN

1.2500 g., Silver **Obv:** Portrait left, name and accession date AH1264 in field **Note:** Portrait type.

Date	Mintage	Good	VG	F	VF	XF
AH1274	—	—	25.00	50.00	75.00	115

Mint: Tehran
KM# 822.3 1/4 KRAN

Silver **Note:** Weight varies: 1.25 - 1.34 grams.

Date	Mintage	Good	VG	F	VF	XF
AH1274	—	—	4.00	10.00	14.00	22.50
AH1276	—	—	4.00	10.00	14.00	22.50
AH1280	—	—	4.00	10.00	14.00	22.50
AH1288	—	—	4.00	10.00	14.00	22.50
AH1289	—	—	4.00	10.00	14.00	22.50
AH1292	—	—	4.00	10.00	14.00	22.50
AH1293	—	—	4.00	10.00	14.00	22.50
AH1294	—	—	7.50	15.00	25.00	40.00

Mint: Astarabad
KM# 823.1 1/2 KRAN

Silver **Note:** Weight varies: 2.49 - 2.68 grams.

Date	Mintage	Good	VG	F	VF	XF
AH1265	—	—	5.00	12.50	16.50	25.00
AH1269	—	—	4.00	10.00	14.00	22.50
AH1275	—	—	2.50	6.00	9.50	15.00
AH1276	—	—	2.50	6.00	9.50	15.00
AH1277	—	—	2.50	6.00	9.50	15.00

Mint: Hamadan
KM# 823.2 1/2 KRAN

Silver **Note:** Weight varies: 2.49 - 2.68 grams.

Date	Mintage	Good	VG	F	VF	XF
AH1266	—	—	3.25	8.00	12.50	17.50
AH1267	—	—	3.25	8.00	12.50	17.50
AH1269	—	—	3.25	8.00	12.50	17.50
AH1271	—	—	3.25	8.00	12.50	17.50
AH1274	—	—	2.50	6.00	9.50	15.00
AH1275	—	—	2.00	5.00	8.00	13.50

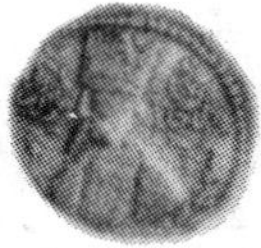

Mint: Isfahan
KM# 828.1 1/2 KRAN

2.5000 g., Silver **Note:** Portrait type. Prices are for well-struck examples. Weak or flat strikes are worth about half as much as shown.

Date	Mintage	Good	VG	F	VF	XF
AH1272	—	—	6.00	15.00	22.50	35.00
AH1273	—	—	6.00	15.00	22.50	35.00
AH1274	—	—	6.00	15.00	22.50	35.00

Mint: Isfahan
KM# 823.3 1/2 KRAN

Silver **Note:** Weight varies: 2.49 - 2.68 grams.

Date	Mintage	Good	VG	F	VF	XF
ND (date missing)	—	—	3.25	8.00	12.50	17.50
AH1265	—	—	3.25	8.00	12.50	17.50
AH1267	—	—	3.25	8.00	12.50	17.50
AH1271	—	—	3.25	8.00	12.50	17.50
AH1275	—	—	2.00	5.00	8.00	13.50
AH1276	—	—	2.00	5.00	8.00	13.50
AH1277	—	—	3.25	8.00	12.50	17.50

Mint: Kashan
KM# 823.4 1/2 KRAN

Silver **Note:** Weight varies: 2.49 - 2.68 grams.

Date	Mintage	Good	VG	F	VF	XF
AH1264	—	—	4.00	10.00	14.00	22.50
AH1265	—	—	3.25	8.00	12.50	17.50
AH1272	—	—	2.50	6.00	9.50	15.00
AH1273	—	—	2.50	6.00	9.50	15.00
AH1274	—	—	2.00	5.00	8.00	13.50
AH1275	—	—	2.00	5.00	8.00	13.50
AH1276	—	—	2.50	6.00	12.50	17.50
AH1279	—	—	2.75	7.00	11.00	17.50

Mint: Khoy
KM# 823.5 1/2 KRAN

Silver **Note:** Weight varies: 2.49 - 2.68 grams.

Date	Mintage	Good	VG	F	VF	XF
AH1266	—	—	8.00	20.00	27.50	40.00
AH1271	—	—	8.00	20.00	27.50	40.00

Mint: Kirman
KM# 823.6 1/2 KRAN

Silver **Note:** Weight varies: 2.49 - 2.68 grams.

Date	Mintage	Good	VG	F	VF	XF
AH1276	—	—	4.00	10.00	17.50	27.50
AH1277	—	—	4.00	10.00	17.50	27.50
AH1282	—	—	4.00	10.00	17.50	27.50

Mint: Kirmanshahan
KM# 823.7 1/2 KRAN

Silver **Note:** Weight varies: 2.49 - 2.68 grams.

Date	Mintage	Good	VG	F	VF	XF
AH1268	—	—	2.50	6.00	10.00	15.00
AH1274	—	—	2.50	6.00	9.50	15.00
AH1275	—	—	2.00	5.00	8.00	13.50

Mint: Qazvin
KM# 828.2 1/2 KRAN

2.5000 g., Silver **Note:** Portrait type. Prices are for well-struck examples. Weak or flat strikes are worth about half as much as shown.

Date	Mintage	Good	VG	F	VF	XF
AH1274	—	—	6.50	16.50	24.00	37.50
AH1275	—	—	6.50	16.50	24.00	37.50

Mint: Qazvin
KM# 823.8 1/2 KRAN

Silver **Note:** Weight varies: 2.49 - 2.68 grams.

Date	Mintage	Good	VG	F	VF	XF
AH1266	—	—	2.50	6.00	10.00	15.00
AH1273	—	—	2.50	6.00	9.50	15.00
AH1274	—	—	2.00	5.00	8.00	13.50
AH1275	—	—	2.00	5.00	8.00	13.50
AH1276	—	—	2.00	5.00	8.00	13.50
AH1280	—	—	2.75	7.00	11.00	17.50
AH1283	—	—	2.75	7.00	11.00	17.50

Mint: Rasht
KM# 823.9 1/2 KRAN

Silver **Note:** Weight varies: 2.49 - 2.68 grams.

Date	Mintage	Good	VG	F	VF	XF
AH1265	—	—	3.25	8.00	12.50	17.50

Mint: Shiraz
KM# 823.10 1/2 KRAN

Silver **Note:** Weight varies: 2.49 - 2.68 grams.

Date	Mintage	Good	VG	F	VF	XF
AH1267	—	—	5.50	13.50	20.00	27.50
AH1275	—	—	2.50	6.00	9.50	15.00
AH1276	—	—	2.50	6.00	9.50	15.00

Mint: Tabaristan
KM# 823.11 1/2 KRAN

Silver **Note:** Weight varies: 2.49 - 2.68 grams.

Date	Mintage	Good	VG	F	VF	XF
AH1264	—	—	4.00	10.00	14.00	22.50
AH1266	—	—	2.50	6.00	10.00	15.00
AH1268	—	—	3.25	8.00	12.50	17.50
AH1269	—	—	3.25	8.00	12.50	17.50
AH1272	—	—	2.50	6.00	9.50	15.00
AH1274	—	—	2.50	6.00	9.50	15.00
AH1275	—	—	2.00	5.00	8.00	13.50
AH1276	—	—	2.00	5.00	8.00	13.50

Mint: Tabriz
KM# 823.12 1/2 KRAN

Silver **Note:** Weight varies: 2.49 - 2.68 grams.

Date	Mintage	Good	VG	F	VF	XF
AH1266	—	—	3.25	8.00	12.50	17.50
AH1271	—	—	2.50	6.00	9.50	15.00
AH1275	—	—	1.50	4.00	7.50	13.50
AH1276	—	—	1.50	4.00	7.50	13.50
AH1277	—	—	2.50	6.00	9.50	15.00
AH1278	—	—	2.50	6.00	9.50	15.00

Mint: Tehran
KM# 828.3 1/2 KRAN

2.5000 g., Silver **Note:** Portrait type. Prices are for well-struck examples. Weak or flat strikes are worth about half as much as shown.

Date	Mintage	Good	VG	F	VF	XF
AH1271	—	—	4.00	10.00	16.00	25.00
AH1272	—	—	4.00	10.00	16.00	25.00
AH1273	—	—	4.00	10.00	16.00	25.00
AH1274	—	—	4.00	10.00	16.00	25.00
AH1275	—	—	4.00	10.00	16.00	25.00

Mint: Tehran
KM# 823.13 1/2 KRAN

Silver **Note:** Weight varies: 2.49 - 2.68 grams.

Date	Mintage	Good	VG	F	VF	XF
AH1270	—	—	3.25	8.00	12.50	17.50
AH1271	—	—	2.50	6.00	9.50	15.00
AH1275	—	—	2.00	5.00	8.00	13.50
AH1276	—	—	2.00	5.00	8.00	13.50
AH1277	—	—	2.50	6.00	9.50	15.00
AH1278	—	—	2.50	6.00	9.50	15.00

Mint: Yazd
KM# 823.14 1/2 KRAN

Silver **Note:** Weight varies: 2.49 - 2.68 grams.

Date	Mintage	Good	VG	F	VF	XF
AH1272	—	—	3.25	8.00	12.50	17.50
AH1274	—	—	2.00	5.00	8.00	13.50
AH1275	—	—	2.00	5.00	8.00	13.50
AH1276	—	—	2.00	5.00	8.00	13.50
AH1278	—	—	2.75	7.00	11.00	17.50

Mint: Arz-e-Muqadda's
KM# 824.1 KRAN

Silver **Note:** Weight varies: 5.37 and 4.99 grams. Prev. KM#824.2.

Date	Mintage	Good	VG	F	VF	XF
AH1281	—	—	4.00	10.00	17.50	27.50
AH1282	—	—	4.00	10.00	17.50	27.50
AH1284	—	—	5.00	12.50	20.00	35.00

Mint: Astarabad
KM# 836 KRAN

4.9900 g., Silver **Rev:** Mint and date inscribed upon breast of a double-headed (Russian style) eagle

Date	Mintage	Good	VG	F	VF	XF
AH1277	—	—	22.50	45.00	60.00	90.00
AH1278	—	—	22.50	45.00	60.00	90.00

Mint: Astarabad
KM# 829.1 KRAN

5.3700 g., Silver **Obv:** Portrait left, name and accession date (1264) in field **Note:** Portrait type.

Date	Mintage	Good	VG	F	VF	XF
AH1279	—	—	—	100	175	250

Mint: Astarabad
KM# 824.2 KRAN

Silver **Note:** Weight varies: 5.37 - 4.99 grams. Prev. KM#824.1.

Date	Mintage	Good	VG	F	VF	XF
AH1265	—	—	5.00	12.50	18.50	30.00
AH1266	—	—	3.50	9.00	14.00	22.50
AH1267	—	—	3.50	9.00	14.00	22.50
AH1269	—	—	5.00	12.50	18.50	30.00
AH1270	—	—	4.00	10.00	16.00	25.00
AH1271	—	—	4.00	10.00	16.00	25.00
AH1272	—	—	3.25	8.50	12.50	20.00
AH1273	—	—	4.00	10.00	16.00	25.00
AH1276	—	—	4.00	10.00	16.00	25.00
AH1277	—	—	3.25	8.50	12.50	20.00
AH1278	—	—	—	—	—	—
Note: See KM#836						
AH1279	—	—	3.50	8.50	12.50	20.00
AH1280	—	—	2.50	6.50	10.00	16.00
AH1281	—	—	2.50	6.50	10.00	16.00
AH1282	—	—	2.50	6.50	10.00	16.00
AH1283	—	—	3.00	7.50	11.50	18.50
AH1284	—	—	3.00	7.50	11.50	18.50
AH1287	—	—	3.00	7.50	11.50	18.50
AH1290	—	—	3.00	7.50	11.50	18.50
AH1291	—	—	4.00	10.00	16.00	25.00
AH1292	—	—	4.00	10.00	16.00	25.00

Mint: Hamadan
KM# 824.3 KRAN

Silver **Note:** Weight varies: 5.37 - 4.99 grams. Prev. KM#824.2.

Date	Mintage	Good	VG	F	VF	XF
AH1268	—	—	4.00	10.00	17.50	27.50
AH1271	—	—	3.25	8.00	12.50	20.00
AH1274	—	—	3.25	8.00	12.50	20.00
AH1275	—	—	3.25	8.00	12.50	20.00
AH1276	—	—	3.25	8.00	12.50	20.00
AH1277	—	—	2.50	6.50	10.00	16.00
AH1278	—	—	2.50	6.50	10.00	16.00
AH1279	—	—	2.50	6.50	10.00	16.00
AH1280	—	—	2.50	6.50	10.00	16.00
AH1281	—	—	2.50	6.50	10.00	16.00
AH1282	—	—	2.50	6.50	10.00	16.00
AH1284	—	—	2.50	6.50	10.00	16.00
AH1285	—	—	2.50	6.50	10.00	16.00
AH1286	—	—	2.50	6.50	10.00	16.00
AH1287	—	—	2.50	6.50	10.00	16.00
AH1288	—	—	2.50	6.50	10.00	16.00
AH1289	—	—	2.50	6.50	10.00	16.50
AH1290	—	—	2.50	6.50	10.00	16.50
AH1292	—	—	3.25	8.00	12.50	20.00
AH1293	—	—	3.25	8.00	12.50	20.00
AH1294	—	—	3.25	8.00	12.50	20.00

Mint: Herat
KM# 824.4 KRAN

Silver **Note:** Weight varies: 5.37 - 4.99 grams. Prev. KM#824.3.

Date	Mintage	Good	VG	F	VF	XF
AH1269	—	—	22.50	50.00	75.00	100
AH1273	—	—	8.00	20.00	30.00	45.00
AH1274	—	—	8.00	20.00	30.00	45.00
AH1275	—	—	8.00	20.00	30.00	45.00
AH1277	—	—	8.00	20.00	30.00	45.00
AH1278	—	—	8.00	20.00	30.00	45.00
AH1287	—	—	9.00	22.50	35.00	55.00
Note: Error for 1278						
AH1279	—	—	8.00	20.00	30.00	45.00

Mint: Isfahan
KM# 824.5 KRAN

Silver **Note:** Weight varies: 5.37 - 4.99 grams. Prev. KM#824.4.

Date	Mintage	Good	VG	F	VF	XF
AH1265	—	—	2.50	6.50	10.00	16.00
AH1267	—	—	4.00	10.00	17.50	27.50
AH1273	—	—	2.50	6.50	10.00	16.00
AH1278	—	—	2.50	6.50	10.00	16.00
AH1279	—	—	2.50	6.50	10.00	16.00
AH1280	—	—	2.50	6.50	10.00	16.00
AH1281	—	—	2.50	6.50	10.00	16.00
AH1282	—	—	2.50	6.50	10.00	16.00
AH1284	—	—	2.50	6.50	10.00	16.00
AH1286	—	—	3.00	7.50	11.50	18.50
AH1287	—	—	2.50	6.50	10.00	16.00
AH1288	—	—	3.00	7.50	11.50	18.50
AH1289	—	—	2.50	6.50	10.00	16.50
AH1291	—	—	3.00	7.50	11.50	18.50
AH1293	—	—	3.25	8.00	12.50	20.00

Mint: Kashan
KM# 824.6 KRAN

Silver **Note:** Weight varies: 5.37 - 4.99 grams. Prev. KM#824.5.

Date	Mintage	Good	VG	F	VF	XF
AH1273	—	—	2.50	6.50	10.00	16.00
AH1277	—	—	2.50	6.50	10.00	16.00
AH1278	—	—	2.50	6.50	10.00	16.00
AH1280	—	—	3.00	7.50	11.50	18.50
AH1281	—	—	3.00	7.50	11.50	18.50
AH1282	—	—	2.50	6.50	10.00	16.00
AH1283	—	—	3.00	7.50	11.50	18.50
AH1287	—	—	3.25	8.00	12.50	20.00
AH1292	—	—	5.00	12.50	18.50	27.50

Mint: Khoy
KM# 824.7 KRAN

Silver **Note:** Weight varies: 5.37 - 4.99 grams. Prev. KM#824.6.

Date	Mintage	Good	VG	F	VF	XF
AH1266	—	—	6.00	15.00	23.50	32.50
AH1269	—	—	6.00	15.00	23.50	32.50
AH1270	—	—	6.00	15.00	23.50	32.50
AH1271	—	—	6.00	15.00	23.50	32.50

Mint: Kirman
KM# 824.8 KRAN

Silver **Note:** Weight varies: 5.37 - 4.99 grams. Prev. KM#824.7.

Date	Mintage	Good	VG	F	VF	XF
AH1265	—	—	5.00	12.50	18.50	30.00
AH1266	—	—	5.00	12.50	18.50	30.00
AH1269	—	—	4.00	10.00	16.00	25.00
AH1270	—	—	4.00	10.00	16.00	25.00
AH1271	—	—	4.00	10.00	16.00	25.00
AH1272	—	—	4.00	10.00	16.00	25.00
AH1277	—	—	4.00	10.00	16.00	25.00
AH1280	—	—	3.00	7.50	11.50	18.50
AH1281	—	—	3.00	7.50	11.50	18.50
AH1282	—	—	2.50	6.50	10.00	16.00
AH1283	—	—	3.00	7.50	11.50	18.50
AH1284	—	—	3.25	8.00	12.50	20.00
AH1286	—	—	3.00	7.50	11.50	18.50
AH1287	—	—	3.25	8.00	12.50	20.00
AH1288	—	—	5.00	12.50	18.50	30.00
AH1290	—	—	3.25	8.00	12.50	20.00
AH1292	—	—	4.00	10.00	16.00	25.00
AH1293	—	—	4.00	10.00	16.00	25.00

Mint: Kirmanshahan
KM# 825.1 KRAN

Silver **Note:** Struck on machine-punched planchet.

Date	Mintage	Good	VG	F	VF	XF
AH1294	—	—	25.00	50.00	80.00	115

Mint: Kirmanshahan
KM# 824.9 KRAN

Silver **Note:** Weight varies: 5.37 - 4.99 grams. Prev. KM#824.8.

Date	Mintage	Good	VG	F	VF	XF
AH1264	—	—	8.00	20.00	27.50	35.00
AH1269	—	—	4.00	10.00	16.00	25.00
AH1271	—	—	4.00	10.00	16.00	25.00
AH1272	—	—	4.00	10.00	16.00	25.00
AH1277	—	—	4.00	10.00	16.00	25.00
AH1279	—	—	2.50	6.50	10.00	16.00

Date	Mintage	Good	VG	F	VF	XF
AH1280	—	—	4.00	10.00	16.00	25.00
AH1281	—	—	3.50	8.50	13.50	20.00
AH1282	—	—	2.50	6.50	10.00	16.00
AH1284	—	—	3.25	8.00	12.50	20.00
AH1287	—	—	4.00	10.00	16.00	25.00
AH1289	—	—	3.25	8.00	12.50	20.00

Mint: Mashhad
KM# 832 KRAN

5.3700 g., Silver **Obv:** Ruler's name in toughra form **Note:** Toughra type.

Date	Mintage	Good	VG	F	VF	XF
AH1286	—	—	15.00	30.00	50.00	75.00
AH1287	—	—	15.00	30.00	50.00	75.00
AH1295	—	—	22.50	42.50	65.00	100

Mint: Mashhad
KM# 834.1 KRAN

5.3700 g., Silver **Rev:** Mint and date in toughra form **Note:** Toughra type.

Date	Mintage	Good	VG	F	VF	XF
AH1291	—	—	17.50	35.00	55.00	85.00

Mint: Mashhad
KM# 824.10 KRAN

Silver **Note:** Weight varies: 4.99 - 5.37 grams. Prev. KM#824.9.

Date	Mintage	Good	VG	F	VF	XF
AH1266	—	—	2.50	6.50	10.00	16.00
AH1267	—	—	2.50	6.50	10.00	16.00
AH1268	—	—	2.50	6.50	10.00	16.00
AH1269	—	—	2.50	6.50	10.00	16.00
AH1270	—	—	2.50	6.50	10.00	16.00
AH1271	—	—	2.50	6.50	10.00	16.00
AH1272	—	—	2.50	6.50	10.00	16.00
AH1273	—	—	2.50	6.50	10.00	16.00
AH1274	—	—	2.50	6.50	10.00	16.00
AH1276	—	—	2.50	6.50	10.00	16.00
AH1277	—	—	2.50	6.50	10.00	16.00
AH1278	—	—	2.25	5.50	8.50	14.50
AH1279	—	—	2.25	5.50	8.50	14.50
AH1280	—	—	2.50	6.50	10.00	16.00
AH1281	—	—	2.50	6.50	10.00	16.00
AH1282	—	—	2.50	6.50	10.00	16.00
AH1283	—	—	2.50	6.50	10.00	16.00
AH1285	—	—	2.50	6.50	10.00	16.00
AH1287	—	—	2.50	6.50	10.00	16.00
AH1288	—	—	3.00	7.50	11.50	18.50
AH1289	—	—	3.00	7.50	11.50	18.50
AH1290	—	—	3.00	7.50	11.50	18.50
AH1292	—	—	3.00	7.50	11.50	18.50
AH1293	—	—	3.25	8.00	12.50	20.00
AH1294	—	—	4.00	10.00	16.00	25.00
AH1295	—	—	4.00	10.00	16.00	25.00

Mint: Naseri
KM# 843 KRAN

4.9900 g., Silver **Obv:** Name and titles in legend, mint epithet and date in central wreath **Rev:** Persian lion in crowned wreath

Date	Mintage	Good	VG	F	VF	XF
AH1292	—	—	37.50	75.00	125	200

Note: This type and types KM#844, 845, 846 are regarded as transitional types between the hammered and machine-struck coinage; All four types are struck on machine-punched planchets

Mint: Qazvin
KM# 824.11 KRAN

Silver **Note:** Weight varies: 4.99 - 5.37 grams. Prev. KM#824.10.

Date	Mintage	Good	VG	F	VF	XF
AH1272	—	—	2.50	6.50	10.00	16.00
AH1273	—	—	2.50	6.50	10.00	16.00
AH1280	—	—	2.50	6.50	10.00	16.00
AH1281	—	—	2.50	6.50	10.00	16.00
AH1282	—	—	3.00	7.50	11.50	18.50

Mint: Rasht
KM# 846 KRAN

4.9900 g., Silver **Obv:** Toughra **Rev:** Legend

Date	Mintage	Good	VG	F	VF	XF
AH1292	—	—	—	75.00	125	200

Mint: Rasht
KM# 839 KRAN

5.3700 g., Silver **Obv:** Kalima **Rev:** Mint and date **Note:** Special type.

Date	Mintage	Good	VG	F	VF	XF
AH1269	—	—	12.50	25.00	40.00	70.00

Note: Possibly a privately produced souvenir or jewelry piece

Mint: Rasht
KM# 834.2 KRAN

5.3700 g., Silver **Rev:** Mint and date in toughra form **Note:** Toughra type.

Date	Mintage	Good	VG	F	VF	XF
AH1291	—	—	22.50	45.00	70.00	115
AH1292 (sic)	—	—	—	—	—	—

Mint: Rasht
KM# 824.12 KRAN

Silver **Note:** Weight varies: 4.99 - 5.37 grams. Prev. KM#824.11.

Date	Mintage	Good	VG	F	VF	XF
AH1265	—	—	2.50	6.50	10.00	16.00
AH1266	—	—	2.50	6.50	10.00	16.00
AH1268	—	—	2.50	6.50	10.00	16.00
AH1270	—	—	3.00	7.50	11.50	18.50
AH1280	—	—	2.50	6.50	10.00	16.00
AH1281	—	—	2.50	6.50	10.00	16.00
AH1282	—	—	2.50	6.50	10.00	16.00
AH1288	—	—	3.00	7.50	11.50	18.50
AH1289	—	—	3.00	7.50	11.50	18.50
AH1290	—	—	3.00	7.50	11.50	18.50
AH1291	—	—	—	—	—	—

Note: See KM#834

Mint: Sarakhs
KM# 824.13 KRAN

Silver **Note:** Weight varies: 4.99 - 5.37 grams. Prev. KM#824.12.

Date	Mintage	Good	VG	F	VF	XF
AH1276	—	—	32.50	65.00	100	150

Mint: Shiraz
KM# 824.14 KRAN

Silver **Note:** Weight varies: 4.99 - 5.37 grams. Prev. KM#824.13.

Date	Mintage	Good	VG	F	VF	XF
AH1265	—	—	2.50	6.50	10.00	16.00
AH1267	—	—	2.50	6.50	10.00	16.00
AH1277	—	—	2.50	6.50	10.00	16.00
AH1278	—	—	2.50	6.50	10.00	16.00
AH1279	—	—	2.50	6.50	10.00	16.00
AH1280	—	—	2.50	6.50	10.00	16.00
AH1281	—	—	2.50	6.50	10.00	16.00
AH1285	—	—	3.50	9.00	14.00	22.50
AH1287	—	—	2.50	6.50	10.00	16.00
AH1289	—	—	3.00	7.50	11.50	18.50
AH1293	—	—	4.00	10.00	16.00	25.00

Mint: Tabaristan
KM# 824.15 KRAN

Silver **Note:** Weight varies: 4.99 - 5.37 grams. Prev. KM#824.14.

Date	Mintage	Good	VG	F	VF	XF
AH1264	—	—	4.00	10.00	17.50	27.50
AH1265	—	—	2.50	6.50	10.00	16.00
AH1266	—	—	2.50	6.50	10.00	16.00
AH1269	—	—	2.50	6.50	10.00	16.00
AH1270	—	—	2.50	6.50	10.00	16.00
AH1271	—	—	2.50	6.50	10.00	16.00
AH1272	—	—	2.50	6.50	10.00	16.00
AH1273	—	—	2.50	6.50	10.00	16.00
AH1274	—	—	2.50	6.50	10.00	16.00
AH1277	—	—	2.50	6.50	10.00	16.00
AH1278	—	—	2.50	6.50	10.00	16.00
AH1280	—	—	2.50	6.50	10.00	16.00
AH1281	—	—	2.50	6.50	10.00	16.00
AH1282	—	—	2.50	6.50	10.00	16.00
AH1283	—	—	2.50	6.50	10.00	16.00
AH1287	—	—	3.00	7.50	11.50	18.50
AH1288	—	—	3.00	7.50	11.50	18.50

Mint: Tabriz
KM# 840 KRAN

4.9900 g., Silver **Obv:** Royal title "khosrov-e sahebqeran-e ghazi"

Date	Mintage	Good	VG	F	VF	XF
AH1293	—	—	40.00	80.00	125	200

Mint: Tabriz
KM# 824.16 KRAN

Silver **Note:** Weight varies: 4.99 - 5.37 grams. Prev. KM#824.15.

Date	Mintage	Good	VG	F	VF	XF
AH1265	—	—	2.50	6.50	10.00	16.00
AH1266	—	—	2.50	6.50	10.00	16.00
AH1267	—	—	2.50	6.50	10.00	16.00
AH1268	—	—	2.50	6.50	10.00	16.00
AH1269	—	—	2.50	6.50	10.00	16.00
AH1270	—	—	2.50	6.50	10.00	16.00
AH1271	—	—	2.50	6.50	10.00	16.00
AH1272	—	—	2.50	6.50	10.00	16.00
AH1273	—	—	2.50	6.50	10.00	16.00

Date	Mintage	Good	VG	F	VF	XF
AH1274	—	—	3.00	7.50	11.50	18.50
AH1275	—	—	3.00	7.50	11.50	18.50
AH1276	—	—	3.00	7.50	11.50	18.50
AH1277	—	—	2.50	6.50	10.00	16.00
AH1278	—	—	2.50	6.50	10.00	16.00
AH1279	—	—	2.50	6.50	10.00	16.00
AH1280	—	—	2.50	6.50	10.00	16.00
AH1281	—	—	2.50	6.50	10.00	16.00
AH1282	—	—	2.50	6.50	10.00	16.00
AH1283	—	—	2.50	6.50	10.00	16.00
AH1288	—	—	3.00	7.50	11.50	18.50
AH1290	—	—	3.00	7.50	11.50	18.50
AH1291	—	—	3.00	7.50	11.50	18.50
AH1293	—	—	3.25	8.00	12.50	20.00
AH1294	—	—	4.00	10.00	16.00	25.00

Mint: Tabriz
KM# 825.2 KRAN

Silver **Note:** Struck on broad-rimmed planchets, possibly machine punched.

Date	Mintage	F	VF	XF	Unc
AH1279	—	40.00	65.00	100	—
AH1280	—	40.00	65.00	100	—

Mint: Tehran
KM# 844 KRAN

4.9900 g., Silver **Obv:** Ruler's name in crowned wreath **Rev:** Mint, epithet and date in crowned wreath

Date	Mintage	Good	VG	F	VF	XF
AH1295	—	—	17.50	35.00	50.00	70.00

Mint: Tehran
KM# 845.1 KRAN

4.9900 g., Silver **Obv:** Date within wreath **Rev:** Persian lion in crowned wreath

Date	Mintage	Good	VG	F	VF	XF
AH1295	—	—	15.00	30.00	45.00	65.00

Mint: Tehran
KM# 845.2 KRAN

4.9900 g., Silver **Rev:** Date below lion

Date	Mintage	Good	VG	F	VF	XF
AH1295	—	—	15.00	30.00	45.00	65.00

Mint: Tehran
KM# 845.3 KRAN

4.9900 g., Silver **Rev:** Date below wreath

Date	Mintage	Good	VG	F	VF	XF
AH1295	—	—	17.50	35.00	50.00	75.00
AH1296	—	—	17.50	35.00	50.00	75.00

Mint: Tehran
KM# 845.4 KRAN

4.9900 g., Silver **Obv:** Shortened titles of ruler in circle **Rev:** Mint and date in crowned wreath

Date	Mintage	Good	VG	F	VF	XF
AH1296	—	—	17.50	35.00	50.00	75.00

Mint: Tehran
KM# 829.2 KRAN

5.3700 g., Silver **Obv:** Portrait left, name and accession date (1264) in field **Note:** Portrait type.

Date	Mintage	Good	VG	F	VF	XF
AH1271	—	—	45.00	85.00	140	200
AH1272	—	—	45.00	85.00	140	200

Mint: Tehran
KM# 824.17 KRAN

Silver **Note:** Weight varies: 4.99 - 5.37 grams. Prev. KM#824.16.

Date	Mintage	Good	VG	F	VF	XF
AH1264	—	—	4.00	10.00	17.50	27.50
AH1265	—	—	2.50	6.50	10.00	16.00
AH1266	—	—	2.50	6.50	10.00	16.00
AH1268	—	—	2.50	6.50	10.00	16.00
AH1270	—	—	2.50	6.50	10.00	16.00
AH1271	—	—	2.50	6.50	10.00	16.00
AH1277	—	—	2.50	6.50	10.00	16.00
AH1278	—	—	2.50	6.50	10.00	16.00
AH1279	—	—	2.50	6.50	10.00	16.00
AH1280	—	—	2.50	6.50	10.00	16.00
AH1281	—	—	2.50	6.50	10.00	16.00
AH1282	—	—	2.50	6.50	10.00	16.00
AH1285	—	—	2.50	6.50	10.00	16.00
AH1286	—	—	3.00	7.50	11.50	18.50
AH1288	—	—	3.00	7.50	11.50	18.50
AH1289	—	—	3.00	7.50	11.50	18.50
AH1291	—	—	3.00	7.50	11.50	18.50
AH1292	—	—	3.00	7.50	11.50	18.50
AH1295	—	—	4.00	10.00	16.00	25.00

Mint: Yazd
KM# 841 KRAN

4.9900 g., Silver **Obv:** Royal title "sahebqeran" only **Rev:** Dated 1289

Date	Mintage	Good	VG	F	VF	XF
AH1294//1289	—	—	40.00	80.00	125	200

Note: Reverse dated 1289 (muling with old die).

Mint: Yazd
KM# 824.18 KRAN

Silver **Note:** Weight varies: 4.99 - 5.37 grams. Prev. KM#824.17.

Date	Mintage	Good	VG	F	VF	XF
AH1264	—	—	4.00	10.00	17.50	27.50
AH1265	—	—	2.50	6.50	10.00	16.00
AH1266	—	—	2.50	6.50	10.00	16.00
AH1270	—	—	2.50	6.50	10.00	16.00
AH1274	—	—	3.00	7.50	11.50	18.50
AH1276	—	—	3.00	7.50	11.50	18.50
AH1278	—	—	2.75	7.00	11.50	17.50
AH1280	—	—	3.50	9.00	15.00	22.50
AH1288	—	—	2.50	6.50	10.00	16.00
AH1292	—	—	4.00	10.00	16.00	25.00

Mint: Tabriz
KM# 842 2 KRANS

9.9800 g., Silver **Obv:** Royal title "khosrov-e sahebqeran-e ghazi"

Date	Mintage	Good	VG	F	VF	XF
AH1294	—	—	135	225	275	325

Note: A number of broad copper, silver and gold medals exist with lion and sun on obverse (usually in crowned wreath), mint, date, and a couplet on reverse; The couplet states that the coin is a medal for service to the Shah; These are decorations and not coins, even though most of them conform to weights of 2, 3, 4, or 5 krans. Refer to "Unusual World Coins"

Mint: Rasht
KM# 851.1 1/5 TOMAN

0.6900 g., Gold

Date	Mintage	Good	VG	F	VF	XF
AH1283	—	—	72.50	120	150	200

Mint: Shiraz
KM# 851.2 1/5 TOMAN

0.6900 g., Gold

Date	Mintage	Good	VG	F	VF	XF
ND	—	—	60.00	120	150	200

Mint: Tehran
KM# 851.3 1/5 TOMAN

0.6900 g., Gold

Date	Mintage	Good	VG	F	VF	XF
AH1270	—	—	60.00	100	125	160
AH1277	—	—	60.00	100	125	160
AH1294	—	—	60.00	100	125	160

Mint: Arz-e Aqdas
KM# 862 1/2 TOMAN

1.7200 g., Gold **Obv:** Inscription in form of toughra

Date	Mintage	Good	VG	F	VF	XF
AH1283	—	—	100	175	215	260

Mint: Herat
KM# 852.1 1/2 TOMAN

1.7200 g., Gold

Date	Mintage	Good	VG	F	VF	XF
AH1276	—	—	175	300	375	475

Mint: Isfahan
KM# 852.2 1/2 TOMAN

1.7200 g., Gold

Date	Mintage	Good	VG	F	VF	XF
AH1271	—	—	50.00	85.00	100	140
AH1273	—	—	50.00	85.00	100	140

Mint: Mashhad
KM# 852.3 1/2 TOMAN

1.7200 g., Gold

Date	Mintage	Good	VG	F	VF	XF
AH1274	—	—	72.50	120	150	200
AH1279	—	—	72.50	120	150	200
AH1280	—	—	72.50	120	150	200
AH1288	—	—	72.50	120	150	200

Mint: Qazvin
KM# 852.4 1/2 TOMAN

1.7200 g., Gold

Date	Mintage	Good	VG	F	VF	XF
AH1271	—	—	60.00	100	125	160

Mint: Sarakhs
KM# 852.5 1/2 TOMAN

1.7200 g., Gold

Date	Mintage	Good	VG	F	VF	XF
AH1276	—	—	200	350	425	525

Mint: Tabriz
KM# 852.6 1/2 TOMAN

1.7200 g., Gold

Date	Mintage	Good	VG	F	VF	XF
AH1275	—	—	50.00	85.00	100	140
AH1282	—	—	50.00	85.00	100	140
AH1294	—	—	90.00	150	185	240

Mint: Tehran
KM# 852.7 1/2 TOMAN

1.7200 g., Gold

Date	Mintage	Good	VG	F	VF	XF
AH1265	—	—	50.00	85.00	100	140
AH1268	—	—	50.00	85.00	100	140
AH1276	—	—	50.00	85.00	100	140
AH1280	—	—	50.00	85.00	100	140
AH1282	—	—	50.00	85.00	100	140
AH1285	—	—	50.00	85.00	100	140

Mint: Tehran
KM# A862 1/2 TOMAN

1.6800 g., Gold

Date	Mintage	Good	VG	F	VF	XF
AH1295 Rare	—	—	—	—	—	—

Mint: Tehran
KM# 860 1/2 TOMAN

1.7200 g., Gold **Obv:** Profile bust of shah **Note:** Special types.

Date	Mintage	Good	VG	F	VF	XF
AH1272	—	—	150	250	325	400

Mint: Astarabad
KM# 861.1 TOMAN

3.4500 g., Gold **Obv:** Profile portrait of the shah

Date	Mintage	Good	VG	F	VF	XF
AH1279	—	—	175	300	400	500

Mint: Astarabad
KM# 853.1 TOMAN

3.4500 g., Gold

Date	Mintage	F	VF	XF	Unc
AH1274	—	100	140	175	—
AH1277	—	100	140	175	—
AH1279	—	100	140	175	—

Mint: Hamadan
KM# 853.2 TOMAN

3.4500 g., Gold

Date	Mintage	Good	VG	F	VF	XF
AH1267	—	—	35.00	60.00	75.00	100
AH1268	—	—	35.00	60.00	75.00	100
AH1269	—	—	35.00	60.00	75.00	100
AH1272	—	—	35.00	60.00	75.00	100
AH1272	—	—	35.00	60.00	75.00	100
AH1278	—	—	42.50	70.00	90.00	115
AH1280	—	—	42.50	70.00	90.00	115
AH1288	—	—	35.00	60.00	75.00	100

Mint: Isfahan
KM# 853.3 TOMAN

3.4500 g., Gold

Date	Mintage	Good	VG	F	VF	XF
AH1288	—	—	35.00	60.00	75.00	100

Mint: Isfahan
KM# 861.4 TOMAN

3.4500 g., Gold **Obv:** Profile portrait of the Shah

Date	Mintage	VG	F	VF	XF	Unc
AH1274	—	—	250	275	350	—

Mint: Khoy
KM# 853.4 TOMAN

3.4500 g., Gold

Date	Mintage	Good	VG	F	VF	XF
AH1266	—	—	90.00	150	200	250
AH1267	—	—	90.00	150	200	250

Mint: Kirmanshahan
KM# 853.5 TOMAN

3.4500 g., Gold

Date	Mintage	Good	VG	F	VF	XF
AH1273	—	—	47.50	80.00	100	140
AH1274	—	—	47.50	80.00	100	140

Mint: Mashhad
KM# 853.6 TOMAN

3.4500 g., Gold

Date	Mintage	Good	VG	F	VF	XF
AH1266	—	—	35.00	60.00	75.00	100
AH1267	—	—	35.00	60.00	75.00	100
AH1268	—	—	35.00	60.00	75.00	100
AH1273	—	—	35.00	60.00	75.00	100
AH1274	—	—	35.00	60.00	75.00	100
AH1276	—	—	40.00	65.00	85.00	115
AH1280	—	—	35.00	60.00	75.00	100
AH1286	—	—	42.50	70.00	90.00	115
AH1287	—	—	42.50	70.00	90.00	115
AH1288	—	—	42.50	70.00	90.00	115

Mint: Mashhad
KM# 863 TOMAN

3.4500 g., Gold **Obv:** Inscription in toughra form **Note:** Similar to 1 Kran, KM#832.

Date	Mintage	Good	VG	F	VF	XF
AH1286	—	—	125	200	250	325

Mint: Qazvin
KM# 853.7 TOMAN

3.4500 g., Gold

Date	Mintage	Good	VG	F	VF	XF
AH1265	—	—	35.00	60.00	75.00	100
AH1267	—	—	35.00	60.00	75.00	100
AH1268	—	—	35.00	60.00	75.00	100
AH1269	—	—	35.00	60.00	75.00	100
AH1271	—	—	35.00	60.00	75.00	100
AH1273	—	—	35.00	60.00	75.00	100
AH1280	—	—	35.00	60.00	75.00	100
AH1281	—	—	32.50	55.00	70.00	90.00

Mint: Rasht
KM# 853.8 TOMAN

3.4500 g., Gold

Date	Mintage	Good	VG	F	VF	XF
AH1266	—	—	35.00	60.00	75.00	100
AH1267	—	—	35.00	60.00	75.00	100
AH1268	—	—	35.00	60.00	75.00	100
AH1269	—	—	35.00	60.00	75.00	100
AH1271	—	—	32.50	55.00	70.00	90.00
AH1272	—	—	32.50	55.00	70.00	90.00
AH1273	—	—	32.50	55.00	70.00	90.00
AH1274	—	—	35.00	60.00	75.00	100
AH1275	—	—	35.00	60.00	75.00	100
AH1276	—	—	35.00	60.00	75.00	100
AH1277	—	—	35.00	60.00	75.00	100
AH1278	—	—	35.00	60.00	75.00	100
AH1280	—	—	32.50	55.00	70.00	90.00

Mint: Rasht
KM# 861.2 TOMAN

3.4500 g., Gold **Obv:** Profile portrait of the shah

Date	Mintage	Good	VG	F	VF	XF
AH1272	—	—	150	250	325	425

Mint: Sarakhs
KM# 853.9 TOMAN

3.4500 g., Gold

Date	Mintage	Good	VG	F	VF	XF
AH1276	—	—	200	350	450	550

Mint: Tabaristan
KM# 853.10 TOMAN

3.4500 g., Gold

Date	Mintage	Good	VG	F	VF	XF
AH1271	—	—	35.00	60.00	75.00	100
AH1272	—	—	35.00	60.00	75.00	100
AH1273	—	—	35.00	60.00	75.00	100
AH1274	—	—	35.00	60.00	75.00	100
AH1275	—	—	35.00	60.00	75.00	100
AH1276	—	—	35.00	60.00	75.00	100
AH1277	—	—	35.00	60.00	75.00	100
AH1280	—	—	35.00	60.00	75.00	100
AH1288	—	—	42.50	70.00	90.00	115

Mint: Tabriz
KM# 853.11 TOMAN

3.4500 g., Gold

Date	Mintage	Good	VG	F	VF	XF
AH1265	—	—	35.00	60.00	75.00	100
AH1268	—	—	42.50	70.00	85.00	115
AH1271	—	—	35.00	60.00	75.00	100
AH1272	—	—	35.00	60.00	75.00	100
AH1274	—	—	35.00	60.00	75.00	100
AH1278	—	—	35.00	60.00	75.00	100
AH1280	—	—	35.00	60.00	75.00	100
AH1284	—	—	35.00	60.00	75.00	100

Mint: Tehran
KM# 853.12 TOMAN

3.4500 g., Gold

Date	Mintage	Good	VG	F	VF	XF
AH1265	—	—	35.00	60.00	75.00	100
AH1275	—	—	35.00	60.00	75.00	100
AH1277	—	—	35.00	60.00	75.00	100
AH1281	—	—	35.00	60.00	75.00	100

Mint: Tehran
KM# 861.3 TOMAN

3.4500 g., Gold **Obv:** Profile portrait of the shah

Date	Mintage	Good	VG	F	VF	XF
AH1273	—	—	135	225	275	350
AH1274	—	—	135	225	275	350
AH1291	—	—	175	300	400	500

Mint: Tehran
KM# 858 TOMAN

3.4500 g., Gold **Obv:** Facing portrait of the shah **Note:** Special types.

Date	Mintage	Good	VG	F	VF	XF
AH1271	—	—	300	500	700	900

Mint: Kirmanshahan
KM# 859 2 TOMAN

6.9000 g., Gold **Obv:** Facing portrait of the shah **Note:** Special types.

Date	Mintage	Good	VG	F	VF	XF
AH1271	—	—	200	350	550	750

Mint: Mashhad
KM# 864 2 TOMAN

6.9000 g., Gold **Obv:** Inscriptions in toughra form

Date	Mintage	Good	VG	F	VF	XF
AH1281	—	—	135	225	350	500

Mint: Tabriz
KM# 854 2 TOMAN

6.9000 g., Gold

Date	Mintage	Good	VG	F	VF	XF
AH1280	—	—	350	600	750	950

Mint: Tabriz
KM# 855 3 TOMAN

10.3500 g., Gold

Date	Mintage	Good	VG	F	VF	XF
AH1280	—	—	—	—	1,250	1,500
AH1292	—	—	—	—	1,250	1,500

Mint: Tehran
KM# 754.3 3 TOMAN

13.8200 g., Gold

Date	Mintage	VG	F	VF	XF	Unc
AH1227	—	—	—	—	—	—

MILLED COINAGE

Silver Kran Standard

Mint: Tehran
KM# 881.1 12 DINARS

Copper

Date	Mintage	Good	VG	F	VF	XF
AH128x	—	30.00	45.00	75.00	100	—
AH1301	—	20.00	30.00	65.00	85.00	—
AH1303	—	30.00	40.00	75.00	100	—
AH130x	—	15.00	25.00	35.00	60.00	—
ND	—	15.00	25.00	35.00	60.00	—

 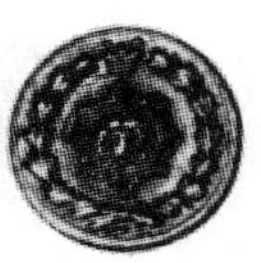

Mint: Tehran
KM# 881.2 12 DINARS

Copper **Obv:** Beaded circle **Rev:** Beaded circle

Date	Mintage	Good	VG	F	VF	XF
AH1310	—	25.00	35.00	75.00	100	—

Note: Error for 1301

 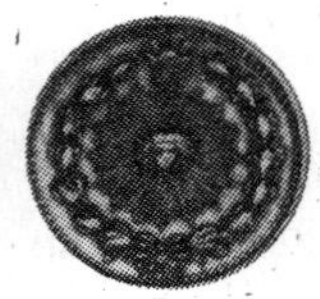

Mint: Tehran
KM# 882 25 DINARS

Copper **Note:** FP are the initials of the Austrian Mint official, F. Pechan.

Date	Mintage	Good	VG	F	VF	XF
AH128x	—	—	10.00	17.50	30.00	50.00
AH1294 FP	—	—	10.00	15.00	30.00	50.00
AH1294	—	—	—	25.00	40.00	75.00
AH1295 FP	—	—	4.00	7.50	20.00	42.00
AH1296	—	—	5.00	10.00	25.00	50.00
AH1296 FP	—	—	4.00	7.50	20.00	42.00
AH1297	—	—	7.50	15.00	30.00	60.00
AH1298	—	—	7.50	15.00	30.00	60.00
AH1299	—	—	5.00	10.00	25.00	50.00
AH129x	—	—	3.00	7.00	18.00	40.00
AH1300	—	—	5.00	10.00	25.00	50.00
AH1303	—	—	10.00	20.00	35.00	75.00
ND	—	—	3.00	7.00	18.00	40.00

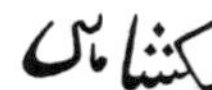

Mint: Tehran
KM# 884 SHAHI

Copper

Date	Mintage	Good	VG	F	VF	XF
AH1305	—	40.00	60.00	75.00	145	—
ND	—	30.00	45.00	60.00	100	—

شاهی

Mint: Tehran
KM# 888 SHAHI SEFID

0.6908 g., Silver .0200 oz. ASW

Date	Mintage	Good	VG	F	VF	XF
AH1296	—	—	25.00	40.00	75.00	160

Note: Date below lion instead of denomination, which is omitted

Mint: Tehran
KM# 889 SHAHI SEFID

0.6908 g., Silver .0200 oz. ASW

Date	Mintage	VG	F	VF	XF	Unc
AH1297	—	3.00	7.50	15.00	28.00	—
AH1298	—	3.00	6.00	12.50	25.00	—
AH1299	—	4.00	8.00	15.00	35.00	—
AH1300	—	3.00	6.00	12.50	25.00	—
AH13--	—	10.00	20.00	40.00	90.00	—
AH1301	—	2.00	4.50	9.00	15.00	—
AH1302	—	7.50	12.50	25.00	50.00	—
AH1303	—	2.00	4.50	9.00	15.00	—
AH1304	—	10.00	15.00	30.00	65.00	—
AH1305	—	3.00	6.00	15.00	30.00	—
AH1307/1	—	7.50	15.00	30.00	60.00	—
AH1307	—	7.50	15.00	30.00	60.00	—
AH1308	—	10.00	15.00	30.00	60.00	—
AH1309/01	—	6.00	15.00	30.00	60.00	—
AH1309	—	6.00	15.00	30.00	60.00	—
ND	—	2.00	5.00	10.00	30.00	—

Mint: Tehran
KM# 890 SHAHI SEFID

0.6908 g., Silver .0200 oz. ASW **Obv:** Date amidst lion's legs **Note:** Variations exist.

Date	Mintage	VG	F	VF	XF	Unc
AH1313	—	20.00	35.00	60.00	100	—
AH1--3	—	20.00	35.00	60.00	100	—

Note: Error for 1313

Mint: Tehran
KM# 883 50 DINARS

Copper

Date	Mintage	Good	VG	F	VF	XF
AH1293	—	—	30.00	45.00	70.00	125
Note: AH1293 is probably a mispunched date						
AH1294 FP	—	—	4.00	15.00	25.00	75.00
AH1295 FP	—	—	2.00	6.00	15.00	40.00
AH1296	—	—	2.00	6.00	15.00	40.00
AH1296/9	—	—	2.00	6.00	—	50.00
AH1297	—	—	2.00	6.00	18.00	50.00
AH1792	—	—	15.00	25.00	50.00	100
Note: Error for 1297						
AH1298	—	—	8.00	15.00	35.00	75.00
AH1299	—	—	7.00	12.00	30.00	65.00
AH129x	—	—	2.00	6.00	15.00	40.00
AH1300	—	—	2.00	6.00	15.00	40.00
AH1301	—	—	2.00	6.00	15.00	40.00
AH1302	—	—	8.00	15.00	35.00	75.00
AH1303	—	—	2.00	6.00	15.00	40.00
AH3301	—	—	6.00	10.00	25.00	65.00
Note: Error for 1303						
AH1330	—	—	10.00	20.00	35.00	75.00
Note: Error for 1303						
AH1304	—	—	8.00	15.00	35.00	75.00
AH1305	—	—	6.00	10.00	25.00	65.00
ND	—	—	4.00	10.00	25.00	50.00

صد دینار

Mint: Tehran
KM# 885 100 DINARS

Copper

Date	Mintage	Good	VG	F	VF	XF
AH1297	—	—	10.00	20.00	40.00	85.00
AH1298	—	—	15.00	30.00	50.00	100
AH1299	—	—	15.00	30.00	50.00	100
AH1300	—	—	10.00	20.00	40.00	80.00

Date	Mintage	Good	VG	F	VF	XF
AH3100	—	—	—	—	—	—
Note: Error for 1300						
AH1301	—	—	10.00	20.00	40.00	80.00
AH1302	—	—	20.00	40.00	60.00	125
AH1303	—	—	7.50	15.00	40.00	70.00
AH1330	—	—	20.00	40.00	60.00	125
Note: Error for 1303						
AH1304	—	—	20.00	40.00	60.00	125
AH1305	—	—	10.00	20.00	35.00	75.00
AH1307	—	—	30.00	50.00	75.00	150
AH1308	—	—	30.00	50.00	75.00	150
AH1313	—	—	50.00	100	200	300
ND	—	—	7.50	15.00	30.00	60.00

دو شاهی

Mint: Tehran
KM# 886 100 DINARS

Copper

Date	Mintage	Good	VG	F	VF	XF
AH1305	—	40.00	80.00	150	300	—
ND	—	20.00	35.00	75.00	150	—

۲۰۰ دینار

Mint: Tehran
KM# 887 200 DINARS

Copper

Date	Mintage	Good	VG	F	VF	XF
AH1300	—	—	50.00	125	200	350
AH1301	—	—	20.00	35.00	90.00	140

Mint: Tehran
KM# 894.1 500 DINARS

2.3025 g., 0.9000 Silver .0666 oz. ASW **Rev:** First legend: 500 Dinars

Date	Mintage	VG	F	VF	XF	Unc
AH1297	—	8.00	15.00	30.00	70.00	—
AH1298	—	8.00	15.00	30.00	70.00	—
AH1301	—	7.00	25.00	55.00	120	—
AH1306	—	7.00	15.00	35.00	100	—
AH1307	—	50.00	85.00	175	350	—
AH1311	—	25.00	40.00	75.00	140	—
ND	—	4.00	7.50	15.00	30.00	—

Note: The undated issue is often found in higher grades than dated coins

Mint: Tehran
KM# 894.2 500 DINARS

2.3025 g., 0.9000 Silver .0666 oz. ASW **Obv:** Second legend

Date	Mintage	VG	F	VF	XF	Unc
AH1301 Rare	—	—	—	—	—	—

Mint: Tehran
KM# 895 500 DINARS

2.3025 g., 0.9000 Silver .0666 oz. ASW **Subject:** Nasir al-din's Return From Europe

Date	Mintage	VG	F	VF	XF	Unc
AH1307	—	50.00	100	215	325	—
AH1307//1306	—	100	200	300	525	—

Mint: Tehran
KM# 896 500 DINARS

2.3025 g., 0.9000 Silver .0666 oz. ASW **Obv:** First legend; no crown **Rev:** "10 Shahis"; date amidst legs

Date	Mintage	VG	F	VF	XF	Unc
AH1310	—	40.00	75.00	150	275	—

Mint: Tehran
KM# 897 500 DINARS

2.3025 g., 0.9000 Silver .0666 oz. ASW **Obv:** Second legend; crown added above legend **Rev:** "10 Shahis"; date amidst legs

Date	Mintage	VG	F	VF	XF	Unc
AH1310	—	30.00	60.00	125	200	—
AH1311	—	30.00	60.00	125	200	—

Mint: Tehran
KM# 898 500 DINARS

2.3025 g., 0.9000 Silver .0666 oz. ASW **Obv:** First legend; no crown **Rev:** "500 Dinars"; date amidst legs

Date	Mintage	VG	F	VF	XF	Unc
AH1311	—	25.00	50.00	80.00	160	—
AH1312	—	20.00	40.00	65.00	110	—
AH1313	—	25.00	50.00	80.00	160	—

Mint: Tehran
KM# 899 1000 DINARS

4.6050 g., 0.9000 Silver .1332 oz. ASW **Obv. Legend:** "Nasir al-din Shah" **Rev:** First legend; "1000 Dinars"

Date	Mintage	VG	F	VF	XF	Unc
AH1294	—	—	—	—	300	400
AH1295	—	—	—	—	300	400
AH1296	—	—	4.00	8.00	20.00	55.00
AH1297	—	—	5.00	10.00	25.00	60.00
AH1298/7	—	—	10.00	20.00	40.00	80.00
AH1298	—	—	10.00	20.00	40.00	80.00
ND	—	—	4.00	10.00	25.00	60.00

Mint: Tehran
KM# 900 1000 DINARS

4.6050 g., 0.9000 Silver .1332 oz. ASW **Obv:** Second legend **Rev:** "1000 Dinars"

Date	Mintage	VG	F	VF	XF	Unc
AH1298	—	—	5.00	10.00	25.00	60.00
AH1299	—	—	10.00	20.00	50.00	90.00
AH1301	—	—	—	—	—	—
AH1303	—	—	150	250	500	600
ND	—	—	5.00	10.00	25.00	45.00

Mint: Tehran
KM# 901 1000 DINARS

4.6050 g., 0.9000 Silver .1332 oz. ASW **Obv:** Second legend, crown above **Rev:** Yek (=1) Kran

Date	Mintage	VG	F	VF	XF	Unc
AH1310	—	—	100	150	250	425
AH1311	—	—	60.00	125	225	375

Mint: Tehran
KM# 902 1000 DINARS

4.6050 g., 0.9000 Silver .1332 oz. ASW **Obv:** Second legend, without crown **Rev:** Yek (=1) Kran

Date	Mintage	VG	F	VF	XF	Unc
AH1311	—	—	100	150	250	—

Mint: Tehran
KM# 903 1000 DINARS

4.6050 g., 0.9000 Silver .1332 oz. ASW **Obv:** Second legend, without crown **Rev:** "1000 Dinars"

Date	Mintage	VG	F	VF	XF	Unc
AH1311	—	—	90.00	135	225	—
AH1312	—	—	100	150	250	—

Mint: Tehran
KM# 970 1000 DINARS

4.6050 g., 0.9000 Silver .1332 oz. ASW **Obv:** Without crown **Obv. Legend:** "Muzaffar al-Din Shah"

Date	Mintage	VG	F	VF	XF	Unc
AH1314	—	—	125	200	400	—

Mint: Tehran
KM# A972 1000 DINARS

4.6050 g., 0.9000 Silver .1332 oz. ASW **Obv:** KM#972 **Rev:** KM#903 **Note:** Mule.

Date	Mintage	F	VF	XF	Unc
AH1312	—	200	300	400	—

Mint: Tehran
KM# 971 1000 DINARS

4.6050 g., 0.9000 Silver .1332 oz. ASW **Obv:** KM#972 **Rev:** Date below wreath, KM#900 **Note:** Mule.

Date	Mintage	F	VF	XF	Unc
AH1303	—	200	300	400	—

Mint: Tehran
KM# 893 1/4 KRAN

1.1513 g., 0.9000 Silver .0333 oz. ASW **Obv:** Date amidst legs

Date	Mintage	VG	F	VF	XF	Unc
AH1311	—	20.00	40.00	75.00	160	—
AH1312	—	20.00	40.00	75.00	160	—
AH1313	—	25.00	50.00	100	185	—

ربعی

Mint: Tehran
KM# 892 1/4 KRAN

1.1513 g., 0.9000 Silver .0333 oz. ASW **Obv:** Date below wreath **Note:** Many examples of KM#892 bear broken or partial dates. These command no premium.

Date	Mintage	VG	F	VF	XF	Unc
AH1294	—	30.00	50.00	100	175	—
AH1296	—	4.00	7.00	15.00	30.00	—
AH1297	—	10.00	20.00	40.00	75.00	—
AH1298	—	10.00	20.00	30.00	50.00	—
AH1299	—	5.00	8.00	20.00	40.00	—
AH1300	—	4.00	7.00	15.00	30.00	—
AH1301	—	3.00	6.00	14.00	30.00	—
AH1303	—	3.00	6.00	14.00	30.00	—
AH1304	—	20.00	40.00	60.00	125	—
AH1305	—	8.00	15.00	25.00	50.00	—
AH1306	—	7.00	12.50	20.00	50.00	—
AH1307	—	20.00	40.00	60.00	135	—
AH1308	—	20.00	40.00	60.00	135	—
AH1309	—	15.00	25.00	50.00	100	—
AH1311	—	20.00	40.00	60.00	135	—
ND	—	3.00	6.00	15.00	25.00	—

Mint: Tehran
KM# 904 2000 DINARS

9.2100 g., 0.9000 Silver .2665 oz. ASW **Obv:** First legend **Obv. Legend:** "Nasir al-din Shah **Rev:** "2000 Dinars"

Date	Mintage	VG	F	VF	XF	Unc
AH1296	—	—	8.00	12.00	30.00	80.00
AH1297	—	—	7.50	11.00	25.00	70.00
AH1298/7	—	—	12.50	20.00	45.00	100
AH1298	—	—	12.50	20.00	45.00	100
ND	—	—	6.00	11.00	25.00	80.00

Mint: Tehran
KM# 905 2000 DINARS

9.2100 g., 0.9000 Silver .2665 oz. ASW **Obv:** Second legend **Rev:** "2000 Dinars"

Date	Mintage	VG	F	VF	XF	Unc
AH1298	—	—	10.00	15.00	35.00	80.00
AH1299	—	—	10.00	15.00	35.00	80.00
AH1299 B	—	—	25.00	50.00	100	175
Note: B on reverse						
AH1300	—	—	10.00	15.00	35.00	90.00
AH1301	—	—	10.00	15.00	35.00	100
ND	—	—	10.00	15.00	35.00	90.00

Note: All dates after AH1301 were struck from worn dies and hence incomplete even in high grades. Coins dated AH1300-1305 show a "B" to the lower left obverse, often missing on poorly struck specimens or specimens from filled dies.

Date	Mintage	VG	F	VF	XF	Unc
AH1302	—	—	22.50	35.00	75.00	140
AH1303	—	—	20.00	30.00	75.00	140
AH1304	—	—	22.50	35.00	75.00	140
AH1305	—	—	10.00	15.00	35.00	100
AH1306	—	—	22.50	35.00	75.00	140
AH1307	—	—	22.50	35.00	75.00	140
AH1308	—	—	20.00	30.00	65.00	140

Mint: Tehran
KM# 908 2000 DINARS

9.2100 g., 0.9000 Silver .2665 oz. ASW **Rev:** Crown above date below wreath

Date	Mintage	VG	F	VF	XF	Unc
AH1310	—	—	100	150	300	—

Note: In blundered form as 13010

Mint: Tehran
KM# 910 2000 DINARS

9.2100 g., 0.9000 Silver .2665 oz. ASW **Obv:** Second legend, without crown

Date	Mintage	VG	F	VF	XF	Unc
AH1311	—	—	100	150	300	—

Mint: Tehran
KM# 909 2000 DINARS

9.2100 g., 0.9000 Silver .2665 oz. ASW **Obv:** Second legend, crown above wreath **Rev:** "Krans", date amidst legs

Date	Mintage	VG	F	VF	XF	Unc
AH1310	—	—	40.00	75.00	125	—
AH1311	—	—	30.00	60.00	100	—

Mint: Tehran
KM# 907 2000 DINARS

9.2100 g., 0.9000 Silver .2665 oz. ASW **Obv:** Second legend, without crown above **Rev:** "Krans", date below wreath

Date	Mintage	VG	F	VF	XF	Unc
AH1310	—	—	100	150	300	—

Note: Date in blundered form as 13010

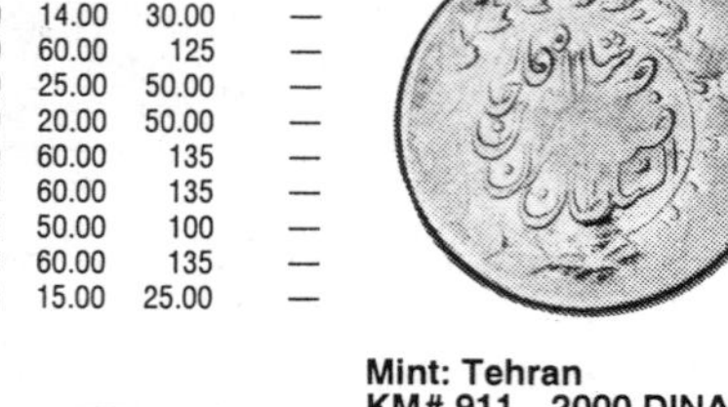

Mint: Tehran
KM# 911 2000 DINARS

9.2100 g., 0.9000 Silver .2665 oz. ASW **Obv:** Second legend, without crown **Rev:** "2000 Dinars"

Date	Mintage	VG	F	VF	XF	Unc
AH1311	—	—	40.00	75.00	150	—
AH1312	—	—	40.00	75.00	150	—

Mint: Tehran
KM# 913 2000 DINARS

9.2100 g., 0.9000 Silver .2665 oz. ASW

Date	Mintage	VG	F	VF	XF	Unc
AH1313	—	—	1,150	2,250	5,000	—

Note: Struck from reverse die of KM#904 with date effaced from die

Mint: Tehran
KM# 912 2000 DINARS

9.2100 g., 0.9000 Silver .2665 oz. ASW **Subject:** 50th Year of Reign **Obv:** Y#C15 **Obv. Legend:** "Dhu'l-Qarneyn" **Rev:** Y#12d **Note:** Mule.

Date	Mintage	VG	F	VF	XF	Unc
AH1313//1312	—	—	—	2,500	—	—

Note: This coin was struck in quantity and was due to be released at Nasir's 50th anniversary as a largesse piece; A number of specimens were passed out to persons close to the royal court before the celebration which accounts for the few known today; Nasir al-din was assassinated just before the fiftieth year of his reign began and the balance of the issue was probably melted

Mint: Tehran
KM# A914 5000 DINARS

23.0251 g., 0.9000 Silver .6662 oz. ASW **Subject:** 100th Anniversary - Qajar Regime

Date	Mintage	VG	F	VF	XF	Unc
AH1293	—	—	175	275	450	700

Mint: Tehran
KM# 915 5000 DINARS

23.0251 g., 0.9000 Silver .6662 oz. ASW **Obv:** Crown above legend, value: "Krans" below

Date	Mintage	VG	F	VF	XF	Unc
AH1311	—	—	1,300	2,000	3,500	—

Mint: Tehran
KM# 914 5000 DINARS

23.0251 g., 0.9000 Silver .6662 oz. ASW **Obv. Legend:** "Nasar al-Din Shah" **Note:** Dav. #285.

Date	Mintage	VG	F	VF	XF	Unc
AH1296	—	—	100	150	275	450
AH1297	—	—	75.00	100	200	375

Mint: Tehran
KM# 917 TOMAN

46.0501 g., 0.9000 Silver, 50.3 mm. **Note:** Dav. #286.

Date	Mintage	VG	F	VF	XF	Unc
AH1301	—	—	500	700	1,000	—

Mint: Tehran
KM# 918 TOMAN

46.1700 g., 0.9000 Silver 1.3325 oz. ASW, 50.3 mm. **Subject:** Shah's Return From Europe **Note:** Similar to 25 Tomans, KM#952.

Date	Mintage	VG	F	VF	XF	Unc
AH1307 Rare	—	—	—	—	—	—

Mint: Tehran
KM# 919 TOMAN

45.4500 g., 0.9000 Silver **Subject:** 50th Anniversary - Reign of Nasir al-Din

Date	Mintage	VG	F	VF	XF	Unc
AH1313	—	—	400	500	700	1,000

Mint: Tehran
KM# 920 TOMAN

46.8000 g., 0.9000 Silver 1.3542 oz. ASW, 51.4 mm. **Obv:** Similar to KM#917 **Rev:** Similar to KM#919 **Note:** Mule; possible restrike.

Date	Mintage	VG	F	VF	XF	Unc
AH1313	—	—	250	500	800	1,450

MILLED COINAGE

Gold Toman Standard

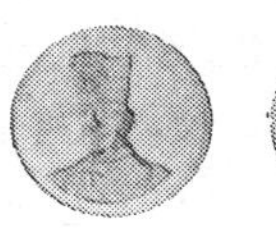
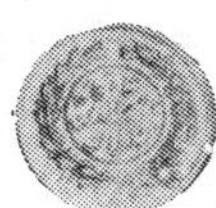

Mint: Tehran
KM# 924 2000 DINARS

0.5749 g., 0.9000 Gold .0166 oz. AGW **Obv:** Bust of Nasir al-Din Shah

Date	Mintage	VG	F	VF	XF	Unc
AH1297	—	—	20.00	40.00	75.00	125
AH1298	—	—	22.50	45.00	100	150
AH1299	—	—	20.00	40.00	75.00	125
AH1300	—	—	20.00	40.00	75.00	135
AH1301	—	—	20.00	40.00	75.00	135

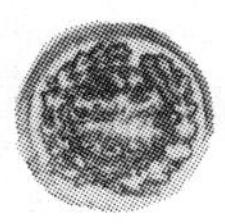
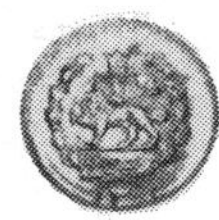

Mint: Tehran
KM# 925 2000 DINARS

0.5749 g., 0.9000 Gold .0166 oz. AGW **Obv:** Legend in sprays **Rev:** Lion and sun

Date	Mintage	VG	F	VF	XF	Unc
AH1309 Rare	—	—	—	—	—	—

Mint: Tehran
KM# 923 2000 DINARS

0.6520 g., 0.9000 Gold .0188 oz. AGW **Obv:** First Nasir-type legend **Rev:** Lion and sun

Date	Mintage	F	VF	XF	Unc
AH1295	—	125	175	350	425

Mint: Tehran
KM# 926 5000 DINARS

1.6300 g., 0.9000 Gold .0472 oz. AGW **Obv. Legend:** "Nasir al-Din Shah" **Rev:** Lion and sun

Date	Mintage	VG	F	VF	XF	Unc
AH1294	—	—	200	400	750	1,250

Mint: Tehran
KM# 921 5000 DINARS

1.4372 g., 0.9000 Gold .0416 oz. AGW

Date	Mintage	VG	F	VF	XF	Unc
AH1296	—	—	100	200	300	400
AH1309	—	—	200	400	750	1,250

Mint: Tehran
KM# 927 5000 DINARS

1.4372 g., 0.9000 Gold .0416 oz. AGW **Obv:** First Nasir bust

Date	Mintage	VG	F	VF	XF	Unc
AH1297	—	—	50.00	70.00	120	200
AH1299	—	—	50.00	70.00	120	200
AH1300	—	—	50.00	70.00	120	200
AH1301	—	—	65.00	120	200	350
AH1303	—	—	65.00	120	200	350
AH1305	—	—	65.00	120	200	350
AH13(0)5	—	—	65.00	120	200	350
AH1307	—	—	125	275	400	600
AH1213	—	—	100	150	275	350
Note: Error for 1312						
AH1313	—	—	150	275	400	600

Mint: Tehran
KM# 928 5000 DINARS

1.4372 g., 0.9000 Gold .0416 oz. AGW **Obv. Legend:** "Nasir Dhu'l Qarnayn"

Date	Mintage	VG	F	VF	XF	Unc
AH1313 Rare	—	—	—	—	—	—

Mint: Tehran
KM# 930 TOMAN

3.4525 g., 0.9000 Gold .0988 oz. AGW **Subject:** 30th Year of Reign **Obv:** Legend **Rev:** Lion and sun

Date	Mintage	VG	F	VF	XF	Unc
AH1293	—	—	400	500	700	1,000

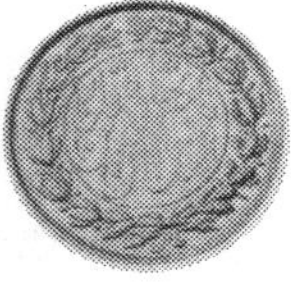

Mint: Tehran
KM# 932 TOMAN

3.1900 g., 0.9000 Gold .0923 oz. AGW **Obv:** First Nasir bust without legend **Rev:** First Nasir-type legend

Date	Mintage	VG	F	VF	XF	Unc
ND(1294-95)	—	—	100	185	250	350

Mint: Tehran
KM# 934 TOMAN

3.4525 g., 0.9000 Gold .0988 oz. AGW **Subject:** Shah's Return From Europe

Date	Mintage	VG	F	VF	XF	Unc
AH1307	—	—	400	750	1,250	1,750

Mint: Tehran
KM# 936 TOMAN

3.4525 g., 0.9000 Gold .0988 oz. AGW **Obv:** Second Nasir bust, actual date right **Rev:** First Nasir-type legend, date added

Date	Mintage	VG	F	VF	XF	Unc
AH1310	—	—	250	400	600	1,000

Mint: Tehran
KM# 937 TOMAN

3.4525 g., 0.9000 Gold .0988 oz. AGW **Rev:** Second Nasir-type legend

Date	Mintage	VG	F	VF	XF	Unc
AH1311	—	—	100	150	250	375

Mint: Tehran
KM# 989 TOMAN

2.8744 g., 0.9000 Gold .0832 oz. AGW **Obv. Legend:** "Nasir al-Din Shah" **Rev:** Lion and sun

Date	Mintage	VG	F	VF	XF	Unc
AH1311	—	—	550	900	1,500	2,500
Note: Although inscribed "Two Tomans", this type is known only on 1 Toman planchets						

Mint: Tehran
KM# A932 TOMAN

2.8700 g., 0.9000 Gold 0.083 oz. AGW **Obv:** First Nasir bust without legend **Rev:** First Nasir-type legend

Date	Mintage	VG	F	VF	XF	Unc
AH1297	—	—	110	200	300	450

Mint: Tehran
KM# 933 TOMAN

3.4525 g., 0.9000 Gold .0988 oz. AGW **Rev:** First Nasir-type legend **Note:** Accession date: AH1264. Many of these coins have carelessly engraved dates, especially 1303 onward. Nasir al-Din Shah coins have two dates surrounding the Shah's head. The date to the left is the date of the coin, the date to the right is the accession date.

Date	Mintage	VG	F	VF	XF	Unc
AH1297	—	—	150	300	500	750
Note: Error with accession date AH1294						
AH1297	—	—	40.00	70.00	100	200
AH1298	—	—	100	200	300	500
AH1299	—	—	40.00	60.00	100	175
AH1300	—	—	80.00	165	250	425
AH1301	—	—	45.00	80.00	140	200
AH1303	—	—	50.00	100	150	225
AH1304	—	—	85.00	150	225	400
AH1305	—	—	45.00	80.00	140	200
AH1306	—	—	100	150	250	425
AH1307	—	—	80.00	125	200	325
AH1309	—	—	85.00	125	200	325
AH1311	—	—	100	150	250	375
AH1312	—	—	150	200	275	500

Mint: Tehran
KM# 931 TOMAN

3.4525 g., 0.9000 Gold .0988 oz. AGW **Obv:** First Nasir-type legend **Rev:** Lion and sun **Note:** Coins of this type dated AH1296 and of reduced weight, 2.87 grams, .900 gold, have been reported to exist.

Date	Mintage	VG	F	VF	XF	Unc
AH1294	—	—	500	800	1,150	1,750

Mint: Tehran
KM# 938 TOMAN

3.4525 g., 0.9000 Gold .0988 oz. AGW **Obv:** KM#933 **Rev:** KM#936 **Note:** Mule.

Date	Mintage	VG	F	VF	XF	Unc
AH1313//1310	—	—	225	350	525	750

Mint: Tehran
KM# 940 2 TOMAN

6.5150 g., 0.9000 Gold .1885 oz. AGW **Subject:** Discovery of Gold in Khurason **Obv:** Legend within wreath, crown above **Rev:** Legend within wreath

Date	Mintage	VG	F	VF	XF	Unc
AH1295 Rare	—	—	—	—	—	—

Mint: Tehran
KM# 941 2 TOMAN

6.5150 g., 0.9000 Gold .1885 oz. AGW **Subject:** 8th Emam Commemorative **Obv:** First Nasir bust **Rev:** Legend within wreath, crown above

Date	Mintage	VG	F	VF	XF	Unc
AH1295 Rare	—	—	—	—	—	—

Mint: Tehran
KM# 942 2 TOMAN

5.7488 g., 0.9000 Gold .1663 oz. AGW **Obv:** First Nasir bust **Rev:** First Nasir-type legend **Note:** Accession date: AH1264.

Date	Mintage	VG	F	VF	XF	Unc
AH1297	—	—	125	200	275	450
AH1298	—	—	250	400	750	1,250
AH1299	—	—	100	150	200	375

Mint: Tehran
KM# 943 2 TOMAN

5.7488 g., 0.9000 Gold .1663 oz. AGW **Subject:** Shah's Return From Europe **Rev:** Legend in wreath , star above

Date	Mintage	VG	F	VF	XF	Unc
AH1299//1307	—	—	525	850	1,400	2,350

Mint: Tehran
KM# 944 2 TOMAN

5.7488 g., 0.9000 Gold .1663 oz. AGW **Subject:** Shah's Visit to Tehran Mint **Rev:** Legend in wreath

Date	Mintage	VG	F	VF	XF	Unc
AH1308 Rare	—	—	—	—	—	—

Mint: Tehran
KM# 945 10 TOMAN

28.7440 g., 0.9000 Gold .8317 oz. AGW **Obv:** First bust of Nasir **Rev. Legend:** "Nasir al-Din Shah"

Date	Mintage	VG	F	VF	XF	Unc
AH1297 H	—	—	1,250	1,500	2,250	3,500
AH1311 H	—	—	—	—	7,000	10,000

Mint: Tehran
KM# 946 10 TOMAN

28.7440 g., 0.9000 Gold .8317 oz. AGW **Obv:** Second bust of Nasir with medals on chest

Date	Mintage	VG	F	VF	XF	Unc
AH1311	—	—	2,000	3,000	5,000	7,500

Mint: Tehran
KM# 947 10 TOMAN

28.7440 g., 0.9000 Gold .8317 oz. AGW **Obv. Legend:** "Nasir al-Din Shah" **Rev:** Lion and sun

Date	Mintage	VG	F	VF	XF	Unc
AH1311	—	—	1,500	2,500	3,500	6,000

Mint: Tehran
KM# 951 25 TOMAN

0.9000 Gold, 50 mm. **Obv:** Bust of Nasir **Rev. Legend:** "Nasir al-Din Shah"

Date	Mintage	F	VF	XF	Unc
AH1301 B	—	—	—	15,000	—

Mint: Tehran
KM# 952 25 TOMAN

0.9000 Gold **Subject:** Shah's Return From Europe **Obv:** First Nasir bust circled with laurel leaves **Rev:** Legend with crown above and date below

Date	Mintage	F	VF	XF	Unc
AH1307 Rare	—	—	—	—	—

Note: Stack's Hammel sale 9-82 AU realized $17,000

Muzaffar al-Din Shah
AH1313-1324 / 1896-1907AD

MILLED COINAGE

Mint: Tehran
KM# 965 SHAHI SEFID

0.0691 g., 0.9000 Silver .0200 oz. ASW **Obv. Legend:** "Muzaffar al-Din Shah"

Date	Mintage	F	VF	XF	Unc
ND	—	8.00	20.00	40.00	—

Note: Some undated issues show traces of an old date (usually AH1301 or AH1303) below wreath on reverse; these are worth slightly more than other undated issues

Date	Mintage	F	VF	XF	Unc
AH1313 Rare	—	—	—	—	—
AH1314	—	20.00	40.00	75.00	—
AH1315	—	20.00	40.00	75.00	—
AH1316	—	20.00	40.00	75.00	—
AH1317	—	25.00	50.00	100	—
AH1318	—	15.00	30.00	60.00	—
AH8310	—	15.00	30.00	60.00	—

Note: Error for 1318

Mint: Tehran
KM# 969 500 DINARS

2.3025 g., 0.9000 Silver .0666 oz. ASW **Obv. Legend:** "Muzaffar al-din", 500 Dinars **Rev:** Date amidst legs, arranged variously **Note:** Some reverse dies were previously used under Nasir al-Din and show traces of old date beneath wreath on reverse.

Date	Mintage	F	VF	XF	Unc
ND	—	10.00	20.00	35.00	—
AH1298 (sic)	—	100	150	250	—

Note: The 1298 is an "undated" variety showing 1298 of the dies previous user

Date	Mintage	F	VF	XF	Unc
AH1313	—	40.00	75.00	150	—
AH1314	—	20.00	40.00	100	—
AH1315	—	40.00	75.00	150	—
AH1316	—	40.00	75.00	150	—
AH1318	—	30.00	50.00	125	—
AH1319	—	20.00	40.00	100	—
AH1322	—	20.00	30.00	50.00	—

Mint: Tehran
KM# 972 1000 DINARS

4.6050 g., 0.9000 Silver .1332 oz. ASW **Obv:** Crown added above legend **Rev:** Date amidst lion's legs

Date	Mintage	F	VF	XF	Unc
AH1317	—	100	175	250	—
AH1318	—	100	175	250	—

Mint: Tehran
KM# 968 1/4 KRAN

1.1513 g., 0.9000 Silver .0333 oz. ASW **Obv. Legend:** "Muzaffar al-din Shah" **Note:** 300 specimens reportedly struck in AH1322, but none known to exist.

Date	Mintage	F	VF	XF	Unc
ND	—	8.00	15.00	28.00	—
AH1314	—	50.00	100	200	—
AH1316	—	12.50	20.00	35.00	—
AH1318	—	25.00	50.00	85.00	—

Mint: Without Mint Name
KM# 922 2000 DINARS

0.6520 g., 0.9000 Gold .0188 oz. AGW **Note:** Mule. Reverse: KM#923, reverse: KM#991.

Date	Mintage	VG	F	VF	XF	Unc
AH1295 (sic)	—	—	—	—	—	—

Mint: Without Mint Name
KM# 922 2000 DINARS

0.6520 g., 0.9000 Gold .0188 oz. AGW **Note:** Mule. Reverse: KM#923, reverse: KM#991.

Date	Mintage	VG	F	VF	XF	Unc
AH1295 (sic)	—	—	—	—	—	—

Mint: Tehran
KM# 974 2000 DINARS

9.2100 g., 0.9000 Silver .2665 oz. ASW **Obv:** Crown added **Rev:** Position of date amidst legs varies **Rev. Legend:** "2000 Dinars" **Note:** Blundered dates exist.

Date	Mintage	F	VF	XF	Unc
AH1312	—	75.00	100	200	—
AH1314	—	25.00	40.00	100	200
AH1315	—	18.50	27.50	65.00	150
AH1316	—	15.00	25.00	50.00	110
AH1317	—	15.00	25.00	50.00	110
AH1318	—	10.00	20.00	35.00	90.00

Mint: Tehran
KM# 973 2000 DINARS

9.2100 g., 0.9000 Silver .2665 oz. ASW **Obv:** Legend without crown **Obv. Legend:** "Muzaffar al-din Shah" **Rev. Legend:** "2000 Dinars"

Date	Mintage	F	VF	XF	Unc
AH1313	—	100	150	250	—
AH1314	—	75.00	125	225	—

Mint: Without Mint Name
KM# 986 2000 DINARS

0.6520 g., 0.9000 Gold .0188 oz. AGW **Obv. Legend:** "Mazaffar-al-Din Shah" **Rev:** Lion and sun

Date	Mintage	F	VF	XF	Unc
AH9301 Error for 1319	—	125	175	275	400

Mint: Without Mint Name
KM# 994.1 5000 DINARS

1.4372 g., 0.9000 Gold .0416 oz. AGW **Obv:** Portrait of Muzaffar al-Din Shah 3/4 right **Rev:** Large legend **Note:** Prev. KM#994.

Date	Mintage	F	VF	XF	Unc
AH1316	—	25.00	50.00	70.00	135
AH1318	—	25.00	50.00	75.00	150

Mint: Tehran
KM# 987 5000 DINARS

1.4372 g., 0.9000 Gold .0416 oz. AGW **Obv. Legend:** "Muzaffar al-Din Shah"

Date	Mintage	F	VF	XF	Unc
AH1314	—	115	225	325	450
Note: AH1314 has 13 left of front legs and 14 between front and back legs					
AH1315	—	135	275	450	675

Mint: Tehran
KM# 993 5000 DINARS

1.4372 g., 0.9000 Gold .0416 oz. AGW **Obv:** Bust of Muzaffer left

Date	Mintage	F	VF	XF	Unc
ND	—	175	275	400	550

Mint: Without Mint Name
KM# 995 TOMAN

2.8744 g., 0.9000 Gold .0832 oz. AGW **Obv:** Bust of Muzaffer 1/2 right, accession date, AH1314 above left

Date	Mintage	F	VF	XF	Unc
AH1316	—	50.00	90.00	140	225
AH1318	—	45.00	75.00	125	200

Mint: Tehran
KM# 988 TOMAN

2.8744 g., 0.9000 Gold .0832 oz. AGW **Obv. Legend:** "Muzaffar al-Din Shah, AH1313-1314" **Rev:** Lion and sun

Date	Mintage	F	VF	XF	Unc
AH1314	—	150	200	300	550

Mint: Tehran
KM# 1000 10 TOMAN

28.7440 g., 0.9000 Gold .8317 oz. AGW **Obv:** Date stamped **Rev:** With denomination

Date	Mintage	F	VF	XF	Unc
AH1314	—	2,500	3,250	5,000	7,000

Mint: Tehran
KM# 998 10 TOMAN

28.7440 g., 0.9000 Gold .8317 oz. AGW **Obv:** Bust of Muzaffar half left **Rev:** Denomination below legend **Rev. Legend:** "Muzaffar al-Din Shah"

Date	Mintage	F	VF	XF	Unc
AH1314	—	2,500	3,500	5,500	8,000

Mint: Tehran
KM# 999 10 TOMAN

28.7440 g., 0.9000 Gold .8317 oz. AGW **Rev:** Second date replaces denomination

Date	Mintage	F	VF	XF	Unc
AH1314	—	2,500	3,250	5,000	7,000

PATTERNS

Including off metal strikes

KM#	Date	Mintage	Identification	Mkt Val
Pn1	AH(ca.1830)B	—	Kran. Silver.	1,000
PnA2	AH(ca.1830)B	—	Kran. Bronze.	600
Pn2	AH1281	—	25 Dinars. Bronze.	650

KM#	Date	Mintage	Identification	Mkt Val
Pn3	AH1281	—	50 Dinars. Bronze.	1,000
Pn4	AH1281	—	1/4 Kran. Copper.	550
Pn5	AH1281	—	1/4 Kran. Silver.	550
Pn6	AH1281	—	500 Dinars. Copper.	525
Pn7	AH1281	—	500 Dinars. Silver.	575

KM#	Date	Mintage	Identification	Mkt Val
Pn8	AH1281	—	1000 Dinars. Copper.	450
Pn9	AH1281	—	1000 Dinars. Silver. 11.0200g.	550

KM#	Date	Mintage	Identification	Mkt Val
Pn10	AH1281	—	2000 Dinars. Copper.	450
Pn11	AH1281	—	2000 Dinars. Silver.	700

KM#	Date	Mintage	Identification	Mkt Val

Pn12	AH1281	—	2 Toman. Gold.	1,850

Pn14	AH1293	—	500 Dinars. Silver.	500
PnA15	AH1316	—	1/2 Toman. Gilt Bronze. KM#994. Prev. KM#Pn22.	600

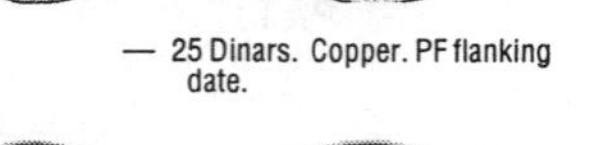

Pn15	AH1294	—	25 Dinars. Copper. PF flanking date.	225

Pn16	AH1294	—	1/2 Toman. Gold. 1.6000 g. First Nasir type legend. KM#926.	500
Pn17	AH1295	—	1/4 Toman. First Nasir type legend. KM#931.	500

Pn18	AH1297	—	5000 Dinars. Silver. 22.8500 g. Plain edge. KM#914.	550
Pn19	AH1297	—	1/4 Toman. First Nasir type legend. KM#931.	500
Pn20	AH1297	—	1/4 Toman. First bust of Nasir	500
Pn21	AH	—	1000 Dinars. KM#899.	—

Pn23	AH1316	—	Toman. Gilt Bronze. KM#995.	800

KM#	Date	Mintage	Identification	Mkt Val
Pn24	AH	—	5 Krans. Silver.	1,000

TRIAL STRIKES

KM#	Date	Mintage	Identification	Mkt Val
TS1	AH	—	Toman. Copper. First portrait. KM#932	350

GANJA KHANATE

HAMMERED COINAGE

Mint: Without Mint Name
KM# 722 1/2 ABBASI

1.5000 g., Silver **Obv. Inscription:** "Fath Ali Shah" **Note:** Rectangular flan.

Date	Mintage	VG	F	VF	XF	Unc
AH1216 Rare	—	—	—	—	—	—

Mint: Without Mint Name
KM# 723 ABBASI

3.0000 g., Silver **Obv. Inscription:** "Fath Ali Shah" **Note:** Round flan.

Date	Mintage	VG	F	VF	XF	Unc
AH1217 Rare	—	—	—	—	—	—

Mint: Panahabad
KM# 728 ABBASI

Silver **Obv. Inscription:** "Fath Ali Shah" **Note:** Generally found looped or holed; about 4.5 grams.

Date	Mintage	VG	F	VF	XF	Unc
AH1216	—	—	50.00	75.00	120	—

KANGUN KHANATE

Anonymous Ruler

HAMMERED COINAGE

Mint: Kangun
KM# 680 FALUS

5.1800 g., Copper, 20 mm. **Obv. Inscription:** "Kangu/n" **Rev. Inscription:** "Ra'ij / 1228"

Date	Mintage	Good	VG	F	VF	XF
AH1228	—	—	—	—	—	—

Mint: Kangun
KM# 802 FALUS

Copper, 18 mm. **Obv. Inscription:** "Kangun / 1255 / Sana"

Date	Mintage	Good	VG	F	VF	XF
AH1255	—	—	—	—	—	—

Mint: Kangun
KM# 803 FALUS

Copper, 15 mm. **Obv. Inscription:** "Kangun / duriba" **Rev. Inscription:** "1266"

Date	Mintage	Good	VG	F	VF	XF
AH1266	—	—	—	—	—	—

Mint: Kangun
KM# 837 FALUS

Copper, 15 mm. **Obv. Inscription:** "Kangun / duriba / 1271" **Rev. Inscription:** "711"

Date	Mintage	Good	VG	F	VF	XF
AH1271	—	—	—	—	—	—

Mint: Kangun
KM# 838 FALUS

Copper, 16 mm. **Obv. Inscription:** "Kangun / duriba / 1274"

Date	Mintage	Good	VG	F	VF	XF
AH1274	—	—	—	—	—	—

Madhkur
AH1283-1297 / 1866-1880AD

HAMMERED COINAGE

Mint: Kangun
KM# 875 FALUS

Copper, 15 mm. **Obv:** Two leaves **Obv. Inscription:** "Kangun" **Rev. Inscription:** "12 / duriba / 88"

Date	Mintage	Good	VG	F	VF	XF
AH1288	—	—	—	—	—	—

KARABAKH KHANATE

COUNTERMARKED COINAGE

Mint: Without Mint Name
KM# 730 ABBASI

Silver **Obv. Legend:** "Fath Ali Shah" **Note:** Countermark: "Zarb Tehran 1229" On various Rials of the same ruler.

CM Date	Host Date	Good	VG	F	VF	XF
	AH1229	—	—	30.00	40.00	55.00

SHEKI KHANATE

HAMMERED COINAGE

Mint: Without Mint Name
KM# 726 ABBASI

Silver **Obv. Inscription:** "Fath Ali Shah" **Note:** Weight about 1.8 grams.

Date	Mintage	VG	F	VF	XF	Unc
AH1241	—	—	50.00	75.00	100	—
AH1242	—	—	50.00	75.00	100	—

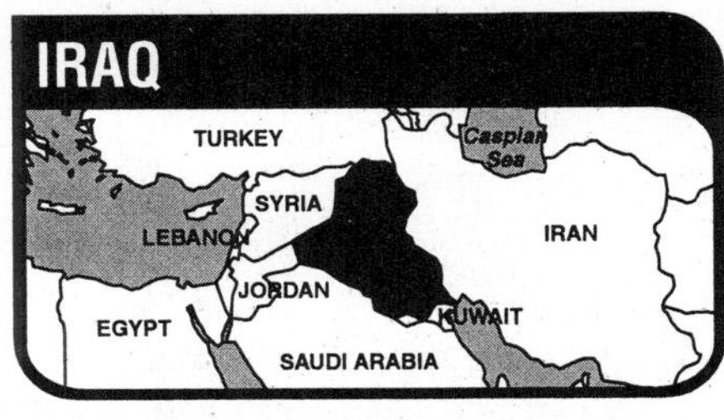

The Republic of Iraq, historically known as Mesopotamia, is located in the Near East and is bordered by Kuwait, Iran, Turkey, Syria, Jordan and Saudi Arabia. Capital: Baghdad.

Mesopotamia was thes te of a number of flourishing civilizations of antiquity - Sumeria, Assyria, Babylonia, Parthia, Persia and the Biblical cities of Ur, Ninevehand and Babylon. Desired because of its favored location, which embraced the fertile alluvial plains of the Tigris and Euphrates Rivers, Mesopotamia - 'land between the rivers'- was conquered by Cyrus the Great of Persia, Alexander of Macedonia and by Arabs who made the legendary city of Baghdad the capital of the ruling caliphate. Suleiman the Magnificent conquered Mesopotamia for Turkey in1534, and it formed part of the Ottoman Empire until 1623, and from 1638 to 1917. Great Britain, given a League of Nations mandate over the territory in 1920, recognized Iraq as a kingdom in 1922. Iraq became an independent constitutional monarchy presided over by the Hashemite family, direct descendants of the prophet Mohammed, in 1932. In 1958, the army-led revolution of July 14 overthrew the monarchy and proclaimed a republic.

RULERS
Ottoman, until 1917

MESOPOTAMIA

MONETARY SYSTEM
40 Para = 1 Piastre (Kurus)

MINTS

الحله
Baghdad

البصره
al-Basrah (Basra)

الحله
al-Hille

OTTOMAN EMPIRE

Mahmud II
1808-1839AD

HAMMERED COINAGE

KM# A75 PARA
Copper **Obv:** Toughra **Rev:** Mint name, date

Date	Mintage	Good	VG	F	VF	XF
AH1223 (1808)	—	15.00	30.00	50.00	—	—

KM# 74 HAYRIYE ALTIN
1.4000 g., Gold **Note:** 20-21mm.

Date	Mintage	Good	VG	F	VF	XF
AH1223//25 (1831)	—	—	175	350	600	1,000

KM# 63 2 PARA
Copper **Rev:** Year above mintname **Note:** 4.7-5.7 g.

Date	Mintage	Good	VG	F	VF	XF
ND(1808-09) (1808)	—	25.00	40.00	60.00	100	—
AH1223//18 (1824)	—	25.00	40.00	60.00	100	—
AH1223//26 (1832)	—	25.00	40.00	60.00	100	—

KM# 50 2 PARA
Billon **Obv:** Toughra **Rev:** Regnal year, mint name and date

Date	Mintage	Good	VG	F	VF	XF
AH1223//12 (1818)	—	22.50	45.00	75.00	—	—

KM# 54 2 PARA
Copper **Obv:** Flower to right of toughra **Rev:** Mint name, date **Note:** Weight varies: 4.7-5.7 g.

Date	Mintage	Good	VG	F	VF	XF
AH1238 (1822)	—	22.50	45.00	75.00	—	—
AH1240 (1824)	—	22.50	45.00	75.00	—	—
AH1241 (1825)	—	22.50	45.00	75.00	—	—
AH1244 (1828)	—	22.50	45.00	75.00	—	—

KM# 59 2 PARA
0.8000 g., Billon, 18 mm.

Date	Mintage	Good	VG	F	VF	XF
AH1223//17 (1823)	—	25.00	50.00	80.00	—	—

KM# 80 2 PARA
Copper **Obv:** Ornament to right of toughra **Rev:** Mint name, date **Note:** 16-19mm.

Date	Mintage	Good	VG	F	VF	XF
AH1239 (1823)	—	25.00	50.00	85.00	—	—
AH1240 (1824)	—	15.00	30.00	50.00	—	—
AH1241//16 (1825)	—	—	—	—	—	—

Note: Reported, not confirmed

KM# 58 2 PARA
Copper **Obv:** Flower to right of toughra **Rev:** Mint name, date **Note:** Weight varies: 4.7-5.7 g.

Date	Mintage	Good	VG	F	VF	XF
AH1240 (1824)	—	17.50	35.00	60.00	—	—

KM# 69 2 PARA
Copper **Obv:** Star and crescent inside Star of David **Rev:** Mint name, date **Note:** 17-25mm.

Date	Mintage	Good	VG	F	VF	XF
AH1223//23 (1829)	—	22.50	45.00	75.00	—	—
AH1223//25 (1831)	—	22.50	45.00	75.00	—	—

KM# 70 2 PARA
Copper **Obv:** Star and crescent in Star of David **Rev:** Regnal year above mintname **Note:** 17-25mm.

Date	Mintage	Good	VG	F	VF	XF
AH1223//25 (1831)	—	22.50	45.00	75.00	—	—

KM# 71 2 PARA
Copper **Obv:** Star of David **Rev:** Mint name and date **Note:** 17-25mm.

Date	Mintage	Good	VG	F	VF	XF
AH1223//25 (1831)	—	—	—	—	—	—

KM# 72 2 PARA
Copper **Obv:** Star of David **Rev:** Mint name, date

Date	Mintage	Good	VG	F	VF	XF
AH1248 (1832)	—	25.00	50.00	85.00	—	—

KM# A70 2 PARA
Copper **Obv:** Similar to KM#69 **Rev:** Mint name and date "1249" in dotted circle **Note:** 17-25mm.

Date	Mintage	Good	VG	F	VF	XF
AH1249//2 (1833)	—	30.00	60.00	100	—	—

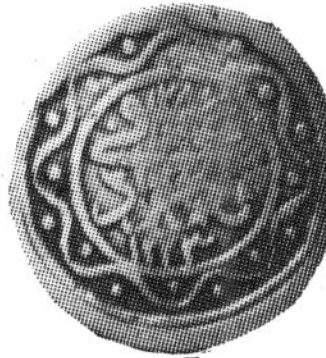

KM# 79 2 PARA
Copper **Obv:** Toughra in inner circle **Rev:** Mint name, date in inner circle **Note:** 20-22mm.

Date	Mintage	Good	VG	F	VF	XF
AH1223//28 (1834)	—	18.00	36.00	60.00	—	—

KM# 51 10 PARA
2.1000 g., Billon **Obv:** Flower to right of toughra **Rev:** Mint name and date within beaded inner circle

Date	Mintage	Good	VG	F	VF	XF
AH1223//13 (1819)	—	60.00	120	200	—	—
AH1223//15 (1821)	—	60.00	120	200	—	—

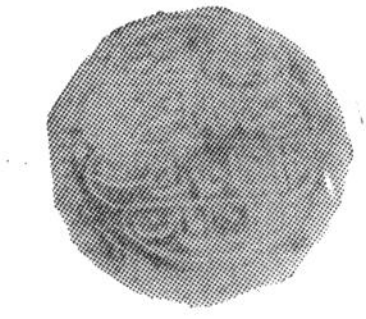

KM# 55 10 PARA
Billon **Obv:** Toughra, mint name and date **Rev. Legend:** 4-line inscription **Note:** Weight varies: 1.60-1.80 g.

Date	Mintage	Good	VG	F	VF	XF
AH1223//15 (1821)	—	60.00	120	200	—	—
AH1223//17 (1823)	—	60.00	120	200	—	—

KM# 60 10 PARA
Billon **Obv:** Ornamental border around toughra, mint name in inner circle **Rev:** Ornamental border around 4-line inscription in inner circle **Note:** Weight varies: 1.60-1.80 g.

Date	Mintage	Good	VG	F	VF	XF
AH1223//17 (1823)	—	50.00	100	175	—	—

KM# 61 10 PARA
1.4000 g., Billon **Obv:** Floral border arounf toughra in inner circle **Rev:** Floral border around mint name, date in inner circle

Date	Mintage	Good	VG	F	VF	XF
AH1223//17 (1823)	—	50.00	100	175	—	—

KM# A63 20 PARA

Billon **Obv:** Legend in margin **Rev:** Legend in margin **Note:** Weight varies: 2.933-3.00 g.

Date	Mintage	Good	VG	F	VF	XF
AH1223//21 (1223)	—	—	—	—	—	—

KM# 52 20 PARA

Billon **Obv:** Flower to right of toughra **Note:** Weight varies: 3.50-4.20 g.

Date	Mintage	Good	VG	F	VF	XF
AH1223//13 (1819)	—	62.50	135	225	—	—

KM# 56 20 PARA

3.2000 g., Billon **Obv:** Toughra, mint name and date **Rev. Legend:** 4-line

Date	Mintage	Good	VG	F	VF	XF
AH1223//15 (1821)	—	60.00	120	200	—	—
AH1223//17 (1823)	—	60.00	120	200	—	—

KM# 68 20 PARA

2.0000 g., Billon **Obv:** Toughra, mint name and date **Rev:** 4-line inscription

Date	Mintage	Good	VG	F	VF	XF
AH1223//17 (1823)	—	37.50	75.00	125	—	—
AH1223//22 (1828)	—	37.50	75.00	125	—	—

KM# 62 20 PARA

Billon **Obv:** Flower to right of toughra, ornamental design in margin **Rev:** Ornamental design in margin **Note:** Weight varies: 2.933-3.00 g.

Date	Mintage	Good	VG	F	VF	XF
AH1223//17 (1823)	—	62.50	135	225	—	—
AH1223//21 (1827) Rare	—	—	—	—	—	—

KM# 64 20 PARA

Billon **Obv:** Legend in margin **Rev:** Legend in margin **Note:** Reduced weight; 22mm, weight varies: 1.20-1.60 g.

Date	Mintage	Good	VG	F	VF	XF
AH1223//21 (1827)	—	50.00	100	175	—	—

KM# 65 20 PARA

Billon, 22 mm. **Obv:** Legend around toughra in inner circle **Rev:** Legend around regnal year, mint name and date in inner cicle **Note:** Weight varies: 1.80-2.00 grams.

Date	Mintage	Good	VG	F	VF	XF
AH1223//21 (1827)	—	60.00	120	200	—	—

KM# 75 20 PARA

Billon **Note:** 22-24mm; similar to 5 Para, KM#59.

Date	Mintage	Good	VG	F	VF	XF
AH1223//26 (1832)	—	30.00	60.00	100	—	—
AH1223//28 (1834)	—	30.00	60.00	100	—	—
AH1223//29 (1835)	—	30.00	60.00	100	—	—

KM# 57 30 PARA (Zolata)

4.5000 g., Billon **Obv:** 4-line inscription **Rev:** 4-line inscription

Date	Mintage	Good	VG	F	VF	XF
AH1223//15 (1821)	—	75.00	150	250	400	—

KM# A54 50 PARA

4.6200 g., Billon, 30.2 mm. **Obv:** Ornamental design to right of toughra **Rev:** Inscription with regnal year, mint name and date

Date	Mintage	Good	VG	F	VF	XF
AH1223//13	—	80.00	200	400	650	1,000

KM# 76 100 PARA

Billon **Obv:** Flower to right of toughra in fancy ornamented inner circle **Rev:** Regnal year, mint name and date in ornamented inner circle **Note:** Weight varies: 3.00-3.20 g.

Date	Mintage	Good	VG	F	VF	XF
AH1223//26 (1832)	—	60.00	120	200	325	—

KM# 77 100 PARA

Billon **Obv:** Flower to right of toughra **Rev:** 4-line inscription **Note:** Weight varies: 3.00-3.20 g.

Date	Mintage	Good	VG	F	VF	XF
AH1223//26 (1832)	—	75.00	150	250	400	—
AH1223//27 (1833)	—	75.00	150	250	400	—

KM# 53 PIASTRE (40 Para)

Billon **Obv:** Ornament to right of toughra **Rev:** Regnal year, mint name and date **Note:** Weight varies: 3.20-4.00 g.

Date	Mintage	Good	VG	F	VF	XF
AH1223//13 (1819)	—	75.00	135	250	400	—

KM# 66 PIASTRE (40 Para)

Billon **Obv:** Flower to right of toughra **Rev:** 4-line inscription **Note:** Weight varies: 3.20-4.00 g.

Date	Mintage	Good	VG	F	VF	XF
AH1223//21 (1827)	—	55.00	110	180	300	—

KM# 67 PIASTRE (40 Para)

3.6900 g., Billon **Obv:** Flower to right of tooughra **Note:** Extra legend added around central device.

Date	Mintage	Good	VG	F	VF	XF
AH1223//21 (1827)	—	75.00	150	250	400	—

KM# B78 5 PIASTRES

Silver, 36.6 mm. **Obv:** "el-ghazi" to right of toughra in inner circle **Rev:** Mint name and date in inner rope circle

Date	Mintage	Good	VG	F	VF	XF
AH1123//25	—	—	—	—	—	—

KM# 78 5 PIASTRES

8.6500 g., Billon, 36.6 mm. **Obv:** Toughra, "Ghazi" to right, wavy border **Rev:** Mint, date and regnal year in 4 lines **Edge:** Diagonally reeded

Date	Mintage	Good	VG	F	VF	XF
AH1223//25	—	—	—	—	—	—

KM# A78 5 PIASTRES

Billon **Obv:** Flower to the right of toughra in roped inner circle **Rev:** Regnal year, mint name and date in roped inner circle **Note:** weight varies 5.50-6.90 grams; previous KM#78.

Date	Mintage	Good	VG	F	VF	XF
AH1223//21 (1832)	—	37.50	75.00	125	200	—
AH1223//26 (1832)	—	27.50	55.00	90.00	150	—
AH1223//27 (1833)	—	27.50	55.00	90.00	150	—

Governor Sait Pasa

AH1231 / 1815AD

HAMMERED COINAGE

KM# 82 2 PARA

Copper **Obv:** Lion walking left **Rev:** Dariba fi Baghdad, date **Note:** 15-18mm.

Date	Mintage	Good	VG	F	VF	XF
AH1230 (1814)	—	37.50	75.00	125	200	—

KM# 85 5 PARA

Copper **Obv:** Inscription within octagram **Obv. Inscription:** "Sait Pasa" **Rev:** Mint name and date

Date	Mintage	Good	VG	F	VF	XF
AH1231 (1815)	—	35.00	60.00	100	160	—

Note: This is the only Ottoman coin ever struck with a governor's name. Sait Pasa was beheaded for this infringement of tradition

KM# 88 5 PARA

Copper **Obv:** Inscription within octagram **Obv. Inscription:** "Tamgha" **Rev:** Mint name and date

Date	Mintage	Good	VG	F	VF	XF
AH1231 (1815)	—	25.00	50.00	85.00	140	—

Note: The Tamgha was originally a sheep and cattle brand, later seal or brand. Each Turkish clan formerly kept its own Tamgha, to use both as a brand and as a seal doucuments

Abdul Mejid
1839-1861AD

HAMMERED COINAGE

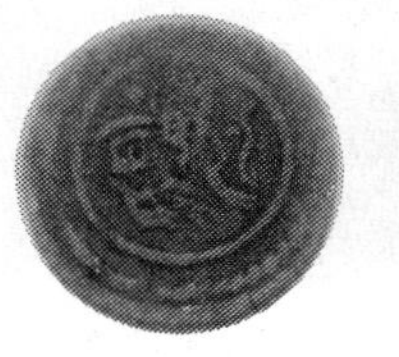

KM# 91 5 PARA

Billon **Obv:** Flower to right of toughra in inner circle **Rev:** Mint name and date in inner circle **Note:** 19-21mm.

Date	Mintage	Good	VG	F	VF	XF
AH1255 //1 (1839)	—	75.00	150	250	375	—

IRELAND

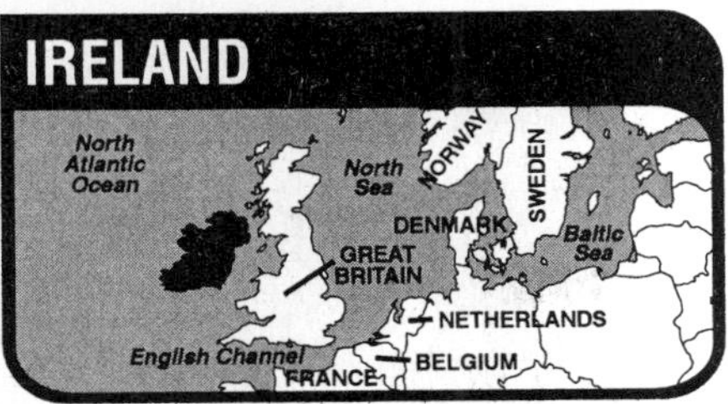

Ireland, the island located in the Atlantic Ocean west of Great Britain, was settled by a race of tall, red-haired Celts from Gaul about 400 BC. They assimilated the native Erainn and Picts and established a Gaelic civilization. After the arrival of St. Patrick in 432 AD, Ireland evolved into a center of Latin learning, which sent missionaries to Europe and possibly North America. In 1154, Pope Adrian IV gave all of Ireland to English King Henry II to administer as a Papal fief. Because of the enactment of anti-Catholic laws and the awarding of vast tracts of Irish land to Protestant absentee landowners, English control did not become reasonably absolute until 1800 when England and Ireland became the "United Kingdom of Great Britain and Ireland". Religious freedom was restored to the Irish in 1829, but agitation for political autonomy continued until the Irish Free State was established as a Dominion on Dec. 6, 1921 while Northern Ireland remained under the British rule.

RULERS

British to 1921

MONETARY SYSTEM

4 Farthings = 1 Penny
12 Pence = 1 Shilling
5 Shillings = 1 Crown
20 Shillings = 1 Pound

BRITISH INFLUENCE - COLONIAL

STANDARD COINAGE

KM# 146.2 FARTHING

Copper **Edge:** Engrailed

Date	Mintage	F	VF	XF	Unc	BU
1806 Proof, restrike	—	Value: 150				

KM# 146.1 FARTHING

Copper **Edge:** Plain

Date	Mintage	F	VF	XF	Unc	BU
1806	—	4.00	9.00	35.00	120	—
1806 Proof	—	Value: 150				

KM# 146a FARTHING

Copper Gilt

Date	Mintage	F	VF	XF	Unc	BU
1806 Proof, restrike	—	Value: 250				

KM# 146b FARTHING

Copper Bronzed

Date	Mintage	F	VF	XF	Unc	BU
1806 Proof, restrike	—	Value: 175				

KM# 146c FARTHING

Silver **Edge:** Plain

Date	Mintage	F	VF	XF	Unc	BU
1806 Proof, restrike	—	Value: 1,500				

KM# 146d FARTHING

Gold **Edge:** Plain

Date	Mintage	F	VF	XF	Unc	BU
1806 Proof, restrike	—	—	—	—	—	—

KM# 147.2 1/2 PENNY

Copper **Edge:** Plain

Date	Mintage	F	VF	XF	Unc	BU
1805 Proof, restrike	—	Value: 225				

KM# 147.1 1/2 PENNY

Copper **Edge:** Engrailed

Date	Mintage	F	VF	XF	Unc	BU
1805	—	6.00	12.00	50.00	150	—
1805 Proof	—	Value: 225				

KM# 147a 1/2 PENNY

Copper Gilt

Date	Mintage	F	VF	XF	Unc	BU
1805 Proof, restrike	—	Value: 285				

KM# 147b 1/2 PENNY

Copper Bronzed **Edge:** Plain

Date	Mintage	F	VF	XF	Unc	BU
1805 Proof, restrike	—	Value: 185				

KM# 147c 1/2 PENNY

Silver

Date	Mintage	F	VF	XF	Unc	BU
1805 Proof, restrike	—	Value: 1,500				

KM# 147d 1/2 PENNY

Gold **Edge:** Plain

Date	Mintage	F	VF	XF	Unc	BU
1805 Proof, Rare, restrike	—	—	—	—	—	—

KM# 150 1/2 PENNY

Copper

Date	Mintage	F	VF	XF	Unc	BU
1822	—	8.00	20.00	65.00	225	—
1822 Proof	—	Value: 350				
1823	—	8.00	20.00	65.00	225	—
1823 Proof	—	Value: 350				

KM# 148.2 PENNY

Copper **Edge:** Plain

Date	Mintage	F	VF	XF	Unc	BU
1805 Proof	—	Value: 300				

KM# 148.1 PENNY

Copper **Edge:** Engrailed

Date	Mintage	F	VF	XF	Unc	BU
1805	—	10.00	20.00	65.00	200	—
1805 Proof	—	Value: 300				

KM# 148a PENNY

Copper Gilt **Edge:** Plain

Date	Mintage	F	VF	XF	Unc	BU
1805 Proof, restrike	—	Value: 450				

KM# 148b PENNY

Copper Bronzed **Edge:** Plain

Date	Mintage	F	VF	XF	Unc	BU
1805 Proof, restrike	—	Value: 285				

KM# 148c PENNY

Silver **Edge:** Plain

Date	Mintage	F	VF	XF	Unc	BU
1805 Proof, restrike	—	Value: 1,650				

KM# 148d PENNY

Gold **Edge:** Plain

Date	Mintage	F	VF	XF	Unc	BU
1805 Proof, restrike	—	Value: 4,000				

KM# 151 PENNY

Copper

Date	Mintage	F	VF	XF	Unc	BU
1822	—	10.00	25.00	80.00	250	—
1822 Proof	—	Value: 450				
1823	—	10.00	25.00	80.00	250	—
1823 Proof	—	Value: 450				

Note: For mule obv. KM#151 and rev. Ionian Islands 2 Oboli, KM#33 refer to Ionian Islands' pattern listings

COUNTERMARKED COINAGE

Merchant Issues

KM# 145 5 SHILLING 5 PENCE

0.9030 Silver **Countermark:** PAYABLE AT CASTLE COMER COLLIERY, 5s. 5d. countermarked on Spanish or Spanish Colonial 8 Reales

CM Date	Host Date	Good	VG	F	VF	XF
ND	1804 16 known	225	450	800	1,500	—

Note: 3 false punches have been applied to genuine Spanish Colonial coins.

TOKEN COINAGE

KM# Tn2 5 PENCE TOKEN

Silver **Issuer:** Bank of Ireland

Date	Mintage	F	VF	XF	Unc	BU
1805	—	7.50	25.00	50.00	150	—
1806	—	15.00	50.00	125	225	—
1806/5 5 known	—	50.00	150	350	750	—

KM# Tn3 10 PENCE TOKEN

Silver **Issuer:** Bank of Ireland

Date	Mintage	F	VF	XF	Unc	BU
1805	—	12.00	35.00	125	385	—
1806	—	10.00	25.00	85.00	275	—

KM# Tn5 10 PENCE TOKEN

Silver **Issuer:** Bank of Ireland

Date	Mintage	F	VF	XF	Unc	BU
1813	—	7.50	25.00	50.00	165	—
1813 Proof	—	Value: 450				

KM# Tn4 30 PENCE TOKEN

Silver **Issuer:** Bank of Ireland

Date	Mintage	F	VF	XF	Unc	BU
1808	—	17.50	85.00	275	575	—

Note: Harp top points to O in TOKEN

Date	Mintage	F	VF	XF	Unc	BU
1808	—	17.50	85.00	275	575	—

Note: Harp top points between O and K in TOKEN.

KM# Tn1 6 SHILLING TOKEN

Silver **Issuer:** Bank of Ireland **Note:** Many minor varieties exist.

Date	Mintage	F	VF	XF	Unc	BU
1804	—	125	250	600	1,200	—
1804 Proof	—	Value: 1,550				

Note: The silver proofs were struck on specially prepared plain edge polished planchets while circulation strikes were struck over Spanish and Spanish Colonial 8 Reales, that had been planed (removing 15 grains)

TRADESMEN'S TOKEN COINAGE

Various token issues exist which include the following: "VOCE POPULI"; with HIBERNIA reverse of the 1760s, many varieties of imitation regal harp Halfpennies of the 18th Century, genuine trade tokens issued by various merchants between 1789-1804, lead tokens ca. 1780-1820, silver issues including countermarked foreign coins ca. 1804, copper tokens ca. 1805-1830 followed by the Farthing tokens of 1830-1856. These are found listed in Seabys "Coins and Tokens of Ireland", 1970 edition.

KM# TTN2 1/2 PENNY

Copper **Note:** Dublin 1/2 Penny token of 1795.

Date	Mintage	F	VF	XF	Unc	BU
1795	—	—	—	—	—	—

KM# TTN3 PENNY

Copper **Note:** Stephen's Dublin Penny token of 1816.

Date	Mintage	F	VF	XF	Unc	BU
1816	—	—	—	—	—	—

PATTERNS

Including off metal strikes

KM#	Date	Mintage	Identification	Mkt Val
Pn33	1804	—	6 Shilling. Copper. KM-Tn1.	850

KM#	Date	Mintage	Identification	Mkt Val
PnA34	1804	—	6 Shilling. Bronzed Copper. KM-Tn1.	1,150
Pn34	1804	—	6 Shilling. Copper Gilt. KM-Tn1.	1,650

KM#	Date	Mintage	Identification	Mkt Val
Pn35	1804	—	6 Shilling. Copper. Head left, short hair.	1,900
Pn37	1805	—	1/2 Penny. Copper. Laureate, draped bust right. Crowned harp.	—
Pn38	1806	—	Farthing. Copper. Large lettering. Large lettering. KM#18.	500
Pn39	1806	—	Farthing. Copper. Small lettering. Large lettering. KM#18.	500
Pn40	1813	—	Penny. Copper. Large laureated, draped bust right. Small crowned harp.	—
Pn41	1813	—	Penny. Copper. GEORGIUS III. D. G. BRITANNIARUM REX.	—

KM#	Date	Mintage	Identification	Mkt Val
Pn42	1822	—	Farthing. Copper. Thick and thin planchets, KM#152.	1,750

KM#	Date	Mintage	Identification	Mkt Val
Pn43	1822	—	Penny. Copper. KM#22.	1,500

ISLE de BOURBON

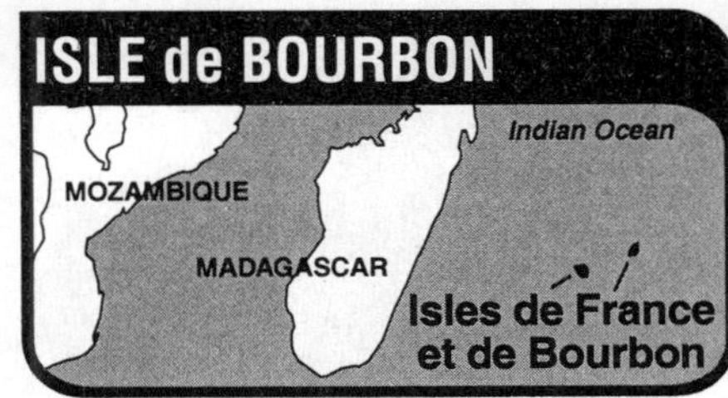

Isles de France et de Bourbon, (later called Mauritius and Reunion) are located in the Indian Ocean about 500 miles east of Madagascar, were administered by France as a single colony. They utilized a common currency issue. Ownership of the isle passed to Great Britain in 1814.Isle de Bourbon, renamed Reunion in 1793, remained a French possession and is now an Overseas Department.

RULERS
French, until 1810

MONETARY SYSTEM
20 Sols (Sous) = 1 Livre

FRENCH COLONIAL

STANDARD COINAGE

KM# A1 10 CENTIMES
Billon **Obv:** Crowned double L monogram

Date	Mintage	VG	F	VF	XF	Unc
1816	150,000	20.00	40.00	90.00	275	500

ISLE DE FRANCE ET BONAPART

Reunion had become the official name in 1792 but after the French Revolution and the beginning of the Napoleonic era (1801-1814) the name was changed to Isle de Bonaparte.

FRENCH ADMINISTRATION

STANDARD COINAGE

KM# 1 10 LIVRES (Dix)
Silver

Date	Mintage	VG	F	VF	XF	Unc
1810	—	225	375	650	1,000	—

Note: This coin was weakly struck on the obverse and reverse centers; Well struck examples command a premium

ISLE OF MAN

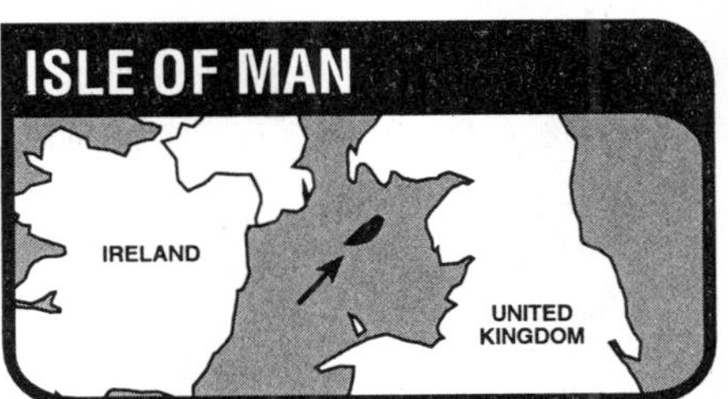

The Isle of Man, a dependency of the British Crown located in the Irish Sea equidistant from Ireland, Scotland and England. Capital: Douglas. Agriculture, dairy farming, fishing and tourism are the chief industries.

The prevalence of prehistoric artifacts and monuments on the island give evidence that its' mild, almost sub-tropical climate was enjoyed by mankind before the dawn of history. Vikings came to the Isle of Man during the 9th century and remained until ejected by the Scottish in 1266. The island came under the protection of the British Crown in 1288, and in 1406 was granted, in perpetuity, to the earls of Derby, from whom it was inherited, 1736, by the Duke of Atholl. The British Crown purchased the rights and title in 1765; the remaining privileges of the Atholl family were transferred to the crown in 1829. The Isle of Man is ruled by its own legislative council and the House of Keys, one of the oldest legislative assemblies in the world. Acts of Parliament passed in London do not affect the island unless it is specifically mentioned.

RULERS
British Commencing 1765

MONETARY SYSTEM
14 Pence (Manx) = 1 Shilling (Br.)
5 Shillings = 1 Crown
20 Shillings = 1 Pound

CROWN COLONY

STANDARD COINAGE

KM# 12 FARTHING
Copper

Date	Mintage	F	VF	XF	Unc	BU
1839	213,000	3.00	9.00	35.00	110	—
1839 Proof	—	Value: 225				
1841 Proof; Rare	—	—	—	—	—	—
1860 Proof	—	Value: 2,000				
1864 Proof; Rare	—	—	—	—	—	—

KM# 12a FARTHING
Copper-Gilt

Date	Mintage	F	VF	XF	Unc	BU
1839 Proof; Rare	—	—	—	—	—	—
1860 Proof; Rare	—	—	—	—	—	—

KM# 10 1/2 PENNY
Copper

Date	Mintage	F	VF	XF	Unc	BU
1798	—	5.00	30.00	100	220	—
1798 Proof	—	Value: 300				
1813	—	10.00	35.00	80.00	200	—
1813 Proof	—	Value: 300				

KM# 10a 1/2 PENNY
Copper-Gilt

Date	Mintage	F	VF	XF	Unc	BU
1798 Proof; Rare	—	—	—	—	—	—
1813 Proof; Rare	—	—	—	—	—	—

KM# 10b 1/2 PENNY
Bronze

Date	Mintage	F	VF	XF	Unc	BU
1798 Proof	—	Value: 350				
1813 Proof	—	Value: 350				

KM# 13 1/2 PENNY
Copper

Date	Mintage	F	VF	XF	Unc	BU
1839 Proof	—	—	—	—	—	—
1839	214,000	5.00	15.00	50.00	160	—
1841 Proof	—	—	—	—	—	—
1860 Proof	—	Value: 2,500				

KM# 11 PENNY
Copper

Date	Mintage	F	VF	XF	Unc	BU
1798	—	8.00	35.00	100	225	—
1798 Proof	—	Value: 350				
1813	—	8.00	35.00	100	225	—
1813 Proof	—	Value: 350				

KM# 11a PENNY
Bronze

Date	Mintage	F	VF	XF	Unc	BU
1798 Proof	—	Value: 1,250				
1813 Proof; Rare	—	—	—	—	—	—

KM# 14 PENNY
Copper

Date	Mintage	F	VF	XF	Unc	BU
1839	81,000	20.00	35.00	85.00	275	—
1839 Proof; Rare	—	—	—	—	—	—
1841 Proof; Rare	—	—	—	—	—	—
1859 Proof	—	Value: 1,850				

BANK TOKEN COINAGE

KM# Tn1 1/2 PENNY
Copper **Obv:** Peel Castle **Rev. Legend:** Large: DOUGLAS BANK TOKEN

Date	Mintage	F	VF	XF	Unc	BU
1811	—	25.00	75.00	200	400	—

KM# Tn2 1/2 PENNY
Copper **Obv:** Peel Castle **Rev. Legend:** Small: DOUGLAS BANK TOKEN

Date	Mintage	F	VF	XF	Unc	BU
1811	—	30.00	100	325	500	—
1811 Proof	—	Value: 650				

KM# Tn3 1/2 PENNY
Copper

Date	Mintage	F	VF	XF	Unc	BU
1811	—	4.00	10.00	40.00	75.00	—

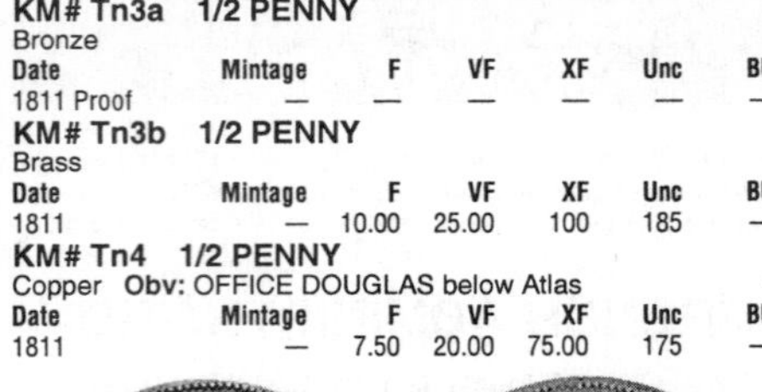

KM# Tn3a 1/2 PENNY
Bronze

Date	Mintage	F	VF	XF	Unc	BU
1811 Proof	—	—	—	—	—	—

KM# Tn3b 1/2 PENNY
Brass

Date	Mintage	F	VF	XF	Unc	BU
1811	—	10.00	25.00	100	185	—

KM# Tn4 1/2 PENNY
Copper **Obv:** OFFICE DOUGLAS below Atlas

Date	Mintage	F	VF	XF	Unc	BU
1811	—	7.50	20.00	75.00	175	—

KM# Tn5 1/2 PENNY
Copper **Obv:** DOUGLAS below Atlas

Date	Mintage	F	VF	XF	Unc	BU
1811	—	350	600	—	—	—

KM# Tn15 1/2 PENNY
Brass **Note:** A mule with obverse of Canadian token.

Date	Mintage	F	VF	XF	Unc	BU
1815	—	200	325	—	—	—

KM# Tn16 1/2 PENNY
Copper **Obv:** Roman numeral I and flat top 3 in date

Date	Mintage	F	VF	XF	Unc	BU
1830	—	12.00	35.00	90.00	—	—
1830 Proof	—	—	—	—	—	—

Note: Issued by John Caine, a miller and baker of Castletown

KM# Tn17 1/2 PENNY
Copper **Obv:** Arabic numeral 1 and round 3 in date

Date	Mintage	F	VF	XF	Unc	BU
1830	—	10.00	25.00	65.00	—	—

KM# Tn21 1/2 PENNY
Copper **Obv:** Knee points to "B" in "STABIT"

Date	Mintage	F	VF	XF	Unc	BU
1831	—	10.00	25.00	80.00	—	—

KM# Tn21a 1/2 PENNY
Copper **Obv:** Knee points between "A" and "B" in "STABIT"

Date	Mintage	F	VF	XF	Unc	BU
1831	—	12.50	30.00	95.00	—	—

KM# Tn21b 1/2 PENNY
Copper **Obv:** Knee points to "A" in "STABIT"

Date	Mintage	F	VF	XF	Unc	BU
1831	—	12.50	30.00	95.00	—	—

KM# Tn10 PENNY
Copper

Date	Mintage	F	VF	XF	Unc	BU
1811	—	6.00	15.00	65.00	120	—
1811 Proof	—	—	—	—	—	—

KM# Tn11 PENNY
Copper

Date	Mintage	F	VF	XF	Unc	BU
1811	—	5.00	10.00	35.00	200	—
1811 Proof	—	—	—	—	—	—

KM# Tn6 PENNY
Copper **Rev. Legend:** DOUGLAS BANK TOKEN... **Note:** Normal flan.

Date	Mintage	F	VF	XF	Unc	BU
1811	—	20.00	65.00	200	450	—
1811 Proof	—	Value: 650				

KM# Tn8 PENNY
Copper **Obv:** Similar to KM#Tn6 **Rev. Legend:** DOUGLAS TOKEN... **Note:** Normal flan.

Date	Mintage	F	VF	XF	Unc	BU
1811	—	20.00	60.00	200	400	—
1811 Proof	—	Value: 600				

KM# Tn7 PENNY
Copper **Note:** Thin flan.

Date	Mintage	F	VF	XF	Unc	BU
1811 Proof	—	Value: 850				

KM# Tn9 PENNY
Copper **Note:** Thin flan.

Date	Mintage	F	VF	XF	Unc	BU
1811 Proof	—	—	—	—	—	—

KM# Tn20 PENNY
Copper **Rev:** With pellet in quatrefoils

Date	Mintage	F	VF	XF	Unc	BU
1830	—	15.00	35.00	125	—	—

KM# Tn18 PENNY
Copper **Obv:** Arabic 1 and round top 3 in date

Date	Mintage	F	VF	XF	Unc	BU
1830	—	8.00	22.00	75.00	—	—

KM# Tn19 PENNY
Copper **Obv:** Similar to KMTN18 with I and flat top 3 in date
Rev: With quatrefoils

Date	Mintage	F	VF	XF	Unc	BU
1830	—	8.00	22.00	65.00	—	—

Note: KM#Tn18 and 19 were issued by John Caine, a miller and baker of Castletown

KM# Tn12 SHILLING
Silver

Date	Mintage	F	VF	XF	Unc	BU
1811	—	175	375	750	1,200	—
1811 Proof	—	Value: 1,500				

KM# Tn13 2 SHILLING 6 PENCE
Silver

Date	Mintage	F	VF	XF	Unc	BU
1811	—	300	600	1,200	2,000	—

KM# Tn13a 2 SHILLING 6 PENCE
Copper

Date	Mintage	F	VF	XF	Unc	BU
1811 Proof, Rare	—	—	—	—	—	—

KM# Tn14 5 SHILLING
Silver

Date	Mintage	F	VF	XF	Unc	BU
1811	—	350	700	1,500	2,500	—
1811 Proof	—	Value: 3,000				

TRIAL STRIKES

KM#	Date	Mintage	Identification	Mkt Val
TS1	1813	—	Penny. Tin. Uniface. KM11.	115

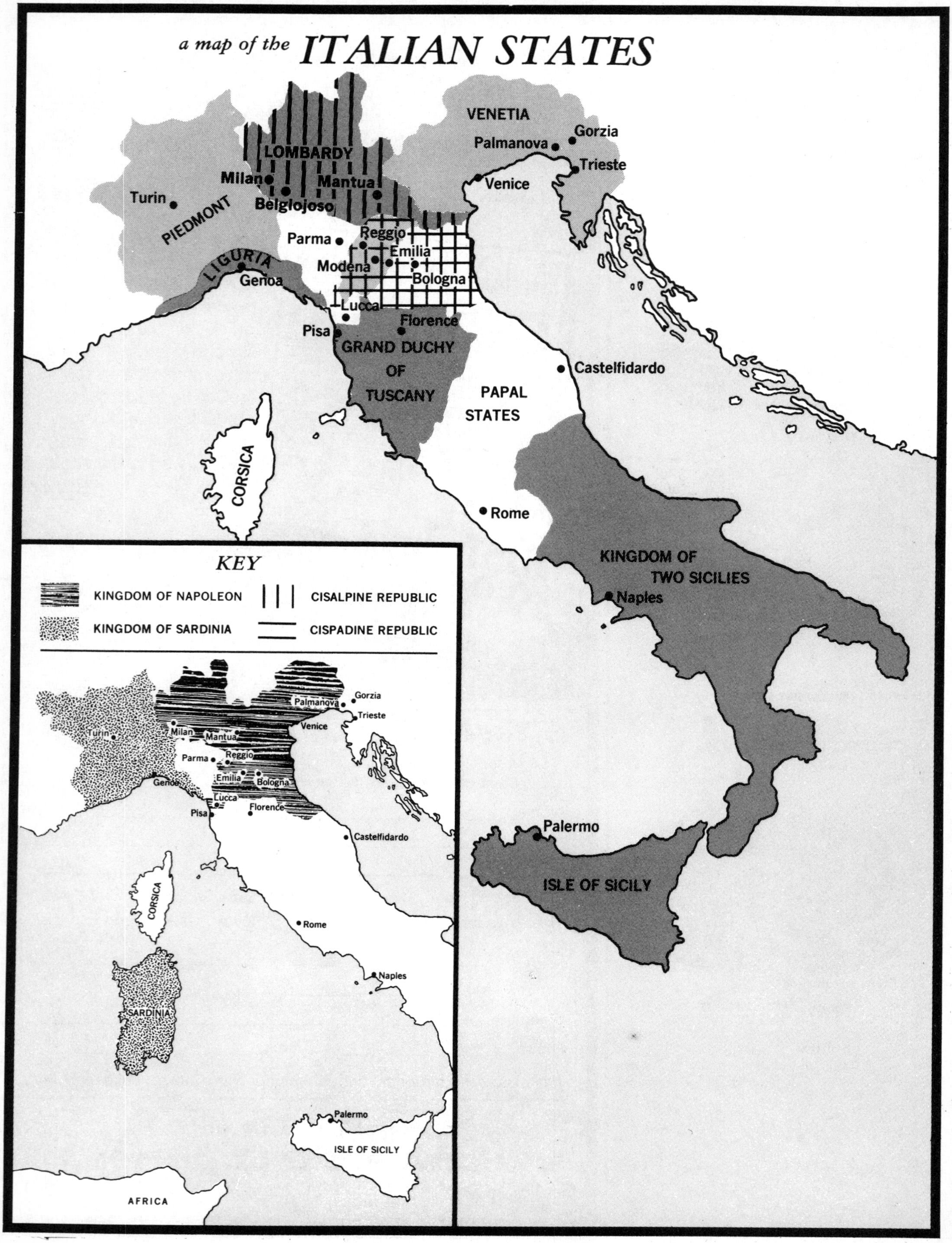

a map of the ITALIAN STATES

VENETIA
Gorzia
Palmanova
Trieste
Venice
LOMBARDY
Milan
Mantua
Turin
Belglojoso
PIEDMONT
Parma
Reggio
Emilia
Modena
Bologna
LIGURIA
Genoa
Lucca
Florence
Pisa
GRAND DUCHY OF TUSCANY
Castelfidardo
PAPAL STATES
CORSICA
Rome
KINGDOM OF TWO SICILIES
Naples
Palermo
ISLE OF SICILY

KEY

KINGDOM OF NAPOLEON
CISALPINE REPUBLIC
KINGDOM OF SARDINIA
CISPADINE REPUBLIC

Gorzia
Palmanova
Trieste
Venice
Turin
Milan
Mantua
Parma
Reggio
Genoa
Emilia
Bologna
Lucca
Pisa
Florence
Castelfidardo
CORSICA
Rome
Naples
SARDINIA
Palermo
ISLE OF SICILY
AFRICA

CISALPINE REPUBLIC

A short-lived revolutionary state comprising the northern Italian districts of Reggio nell'Emilia, Modena and Bologna, was formed in Oct. 1796. In July 1797 it merged into the Cisalpine Republic.

REVOLUTIONARY STATE

STANDARD COINAGE

KM# 1 30 SOLDI
7.3300 g., 0.6840 Silver 0.1612 oz.

Date	Mintage	F	VF	XF	Unc	BU
(1801)IX	300,000	50.00	100	200	400	—

EMILIA

Emilia-Romagna

A northern division of Italy, came under nominal control of the papacy in 755. From 1796-1814 it was incorporated into the Italian Republic and the Kingdom of Napoleon. It returned to the papacy in 1815.

MONETARY SYSTEM
100 Centesimi = 1 Lira

MINT MARKS
B - Bologna
(none) - Birmingham

KINGDOM

STANDARD COINAGE

KM# 1 CENTESIMO
Copper **Obv:** Crowned arms in branches **Rev:** Value and date in wreath

Date	F	VF	XF	Unc	BU
1826 (1860)	4.00	7.00	15.00	30.00	—

KM# 2 3 CENTESIMI
Copper **Obv:** Crowned arms in branches **Rev:** Value and date in wreath

Date	F	VF	XF	Unc	BU
1826 (1860)	4.00	7.00	18.00	35.00	—

KM# 3 5 CENTESIMI
Copper **Obv:** Crowned arms in branches **Rev:** Value and date in wreath

Date	F	VF	XF	Unc	BU
1826 (1860)	4.00	7.00	20.00	40.00	—

Note: For KM#1, 2, and 3 with anchor and eagle head mint marks see Sardinia C#98, 99, and 100

C# 1 50 CENTESIMI
2.5000 g., 0.9000 Silver .0723 oz. **Note:** Similar to 1 Lira, C#2.

Date	Mintage	F	VF	XF	Unc	BU
1859B	179,012	25.00	50.00	100	275	—

C# 2 LIRA
5.0000 g., 0.9000 Silver .1446 oz.

Date	Mintage	F	VF	XF	Unc	BU
1859B	213,751	30.00	65.00	150	550	—

C# 3 2 LIRE
10.0000 g., 0.9000 Silver .2892 oz. **Note:** Similar to 1 Lira, C#2.

Date	Mintage	F	VF	XF	Unc	BU
1859B	—	300	500	800	2,500	—
1860B	13,000	200	400	700	2,000	—

C# 4 5 LIRE
25.0000 g., 0.9000 Silver .7320 oz. **Rev:** Similar to 1 Lira, C#2

Date	Mintage	F	VF	XF	Unc	BU
1859	6,566	500	1,000	2,000	5,000	—
1860	—	400	800	1,500	4,000	—

C# 5 10 LIRE
3.2200 g., 0.9000 Gold .0931 oz.

Date	Mintage	F	VF	XF	Unc	BU
1860B	1,145	600	1,500	3,000	6,000	—

C# 6 20 LIRE
6.4500 g., 0.9000 Gold .1866 oz.

Date	Mintage	F	VF	XF	Unc	BU
1860B Rare	159	—	—	—	—	—

Note: Stack's Hammel sale 9-82 XF realized $24,000; Stack's International sale 3-88 Gem BU realized $16,500

GENOA

A seaport in Liguria, Genoa was a dominant republic and colonial power in the Middle Ages. In 1798 Napoleon remodeled it into the Ligurian Republic, and in 1805 it was incorporated in the Kingdom of Napoleon. Following a brief restoration of the republic, it was absorbed by the Kingdom of Sardinia in 1815.

MINT MARKS

During the occupation by the French forces regular French coins, 1/2, 1, 2, 5, 20 and 40 Francs were struck between1813 and 1814 with the mint mark C.L.

After Sardinia absorbed Genoa in 1815, regular Sardinian coins were struck until 1860 with a fouled anchor mint mark.

MONETARY SYSTEM
12 Denari = 1 Soldo
20 Soldi = 10 Parpagliola =
5 Cavallotti = 1 Lira (Madonnina)

LIGURIAN REPUBLIC

1798-1805

STANDARD COINAGE

KM# 276 3 DENARI
Copper **Obv:** R. L. A. V 1802 around D. 3, **Rev:** Cross

Date	VG	F	VF	XF	Unc
ND(1802)/V (1802)	10.00	20.00	35.00	70.00	—

KM# 265 4 LIRE
16.6400 g., 0.8890 Silver .4756 oz.

Date	VG	F	VF	XF	Unc
1804/VII (1804)	25.00	50.00	125	225	—

KM# 266.2 8 LIRE
33.2700 g., 0.8890 Silver 0.9509 oz.

Date	VG	F	VF	XF	Unc
1804//VII	70.00	120	220	400	—

KM# 270 96 LIRE
25.2140 g., 0.9170 Gold .7435 oz.

Date	F	VF	XF	Unc	BU
1801//IV	450	750	1,400	3,500	—
1803//VI	450	750	1,400	3,500	—
1804//VII	450	750	1,400	3,500	—
1805//VIII	450	750	1,400	3,500	—

REPUBLIC

1814

STANDARD COINAGE

KM# 278 QUATTRO (4) DENARI
Copper

Date	VG	F	VF	XF	Unc
1814	2.50	5.00	9.00	20.00	—

KM# 282.1 2 SOLDI
Billon **Rev. Legend:** ...PRESIDIUM

Date	VG	F	VF	XF	Unc
1814	3.50	7.50	12.00	28.00	—

KM# 282.2 2 SOLDI
Billon **Rev. Legend:** ...PRAESIDIUM

Date	VG	F	VF	XF	Unc
1814	4.00	8.00	15.00	32.00	—

KM# 284 4 SOLDI
Billon

Date	VG	F	VF	XF	Unc
1814	5.00	10.00	16.50	35.00	—

KM# 286 10 SOLDI
2.1000 g., 0.8890 Silver .0600 oz. **Obv:** Crowned shield **Obv. Legend:** GENUENSIS **Rev:** John the Baptist standing

Date	VG	F	VF	XF	Unc
1814	5.50	11.50	18.50	40.00	—

KM# 286a 10 SOLDI
2.1000 g., 0.8890 Silver .0600 oz. **Obv. Legend:** JANUENSIS

Date	VG	F	VF	XF	Unc
1814	5.50	11.50	18.50	40.00	—

GORIZIA

Goricia, Gorz

A city in Venetia, passed to Maximilian I of Austria in 1500, and became the holding of Charles, son of Austrian emperor Ferdinand I in 1564.

RULERS
Franz II (Austria) 1792-1835

MINT MARKS
A, W - Wien - Vienna
F, H, HA - Hall
G - Graz
G - Nagybanya
H - Gunzburg
K - Kremnitz
O - Oravitza
S - Schmollnitz

MONETARY SYSTEM
20 Soldi = 1 Lira

AUSTRIAN ADMINISTRATION

STANDARD COINAGE

C# 8.1 SOLDO
Copper **Ruler:** Leopold II **Obv:** Crowned arms **Rev:** Value, date

Date	VG	F	VF	XF	Unc
1801F	4.00	8.00	16.00	35.00	—

C# 8.4 SOLDO
Copper **Ruler:** Franz II

Date	VG	F	VF	XF	Unc
1801H	3.00	6.00	12.50	30.00	—
1802H	4.00	8.00	16.00	35.00	—

C# 9.2 2 SOLDI
Copper **Ruler:** Franz II **Obv:** Crowned arms **Rev:** Value, date

Date	VG	F	VF	XF	Unc
1801F	5.00	10.00	20.00	45.00	—

C# 9.3 2 SOLDI
Copper **Ruler:** Franz II

Date	VG	F	VF	XF	Unc
1801H	2.50	5.00	15.00	35.00	—
1802H	2.50	5.00	15.00	35.00	—

C# 10.1 15 SOLDI (8-1/2 Kreuzer)
Billon **Ruler:** Franz II

Date	VG	F	VF	XF	Unc
1802A	4.00	8.00	16.00	45.00	—

C# 10.2 15 SOLDI (8-1/2 Kreuzer)
Billon **Ruler:** Franz II

Date	VG	F	VF	XF	Unc
1802F	5.00	10.00	20.00	50.00	—

C# 10.3 15 SOLDI (8-1/2 Kreuzer)
Billon **Ruler:** Franz II

Date	VG	F	VF	XF	Unc
1802H	8.00	16.00	35.00	85.00	—

ITALIAN REPUBLIC

Repubblica Italiana

Created in 1802 out of the Cisalpine Republic (q.v.) with some additions. Converted into the Kingdom of Italy in 1805. Capital: Milan. Years 1-4 of the republic = 1802-1805.

RULERS
Napoleon, 1802-1805

MONETARY SYSTEM
(1803)
10 Denari = 1 Soldo
20 Soldi = 1 Lira

PATTERNS

Including off metal strikes

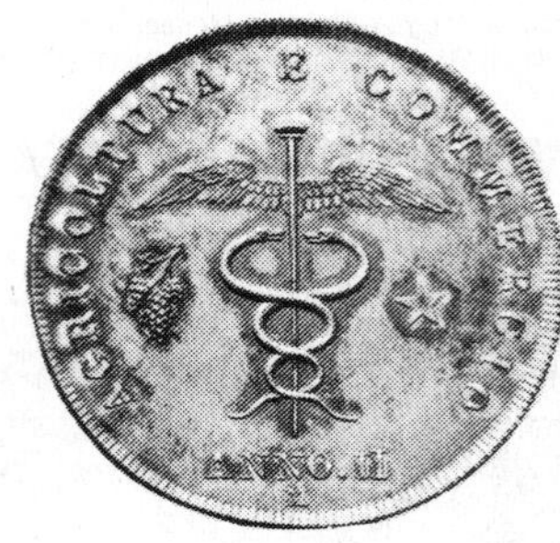

KM#	Date	Mintage	Identification	Mkt Val
Pn1	A.II (1803)M	—	Denaro. Copper.	250
Pn2	A.II (1803)M	—	2 Denari. Copper.	350
Pn3	A.II (1803)M	—	Soldo Da 5 Denari. Copper.	550
Pn4	A.II (1803)M	—	5 Soldi. 0.9000 Silver.	1,800
Pn5	A.II (1803)M	—	10 Soldi. 0.9000 Silver.	2,350
Pn6	A.II (1803)M	—	Lira Da 20 Soldi. 0.9000 Silver.	3,350
Pn7	A.II (1803)M	—	30 Soldi. 0.9000 Silver.	4,500
Pn8	A.II (1803)M	—	Scudo Da 5 Lire. 0.9000 Silver.	12,500
Pn9	A.II (1803)M	—	Mezzo (1/2) Doppia. 0.9000 Gold.	—
Pn10	A.II (1803)M	—	Mezzo (1/2) Doppia. 0.9000 Gold. In wreath.	40,000
Pn11	A.II (1803)M	—	Doppia. 0.9000 Gold.	—
Pn12	A.II (1803)M	—	Doppia. 0.9000 Gold. In wreath.	50,000

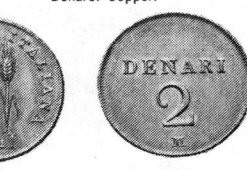

KM#	Date	Mintage	Identification	Mkt Val
Pn13	1804M	—	1/100 Centesimo. Copper.	275

KM#	Date	Mintage	Identification	Mkt Val
Pn14	1804M	—	Centesimo. Copper.	350

KM#	Date	Mintage	Identification	Mkt Val
Pn15	1804M	—	1/2 Soldo. Copper.	350

KM#	Date	Mintage	Identification	Mkt Val
Pn16	1804M	—	Mezzo (1/2) Soldo. Copper.	500

KM#	Date	Mintage	Identification	Mkt Val
Pn17	1804M	—	Soldo. Copper.	550

KM#	Date	Mintage	Identification	Mkt Val
Pn18	1804M	—	5 Soldi. 0.9000 Silver.	1,150

KM#	Date	Mintage	Identification	Mkt Val
Pn19	1804M	—	10 Soldi. 0.9000 Silver.	1,750

KM#	Date	Mintage	Identification	Mkt Val
Pn20	1804M	—	Lira. 0.9000 Silver.	3,250

KM#	Date	Mintage	Identification	Mkt Val
Pn21	1804M	—	2 Lire. 0.9000 Silver. 8.0000 g.	4,750
Pn21a	1804M	—	2 Lire. 0.9000 Silver. 8.2100 g.	4,750

KM#	Date	Mintage	Identification	Mkt Val
Pn22	1804M	—	5 Lire. 0.9000 Silver.	16,000

KM#	Date	Mintage	Identification	Mkt Val
Pn23	1804M	—	(Venti-20 Lire) Denari 8. 0.9000 Gold.	32,000
Pn24	1804M	—	(Venti-20 Lire) Denari 8. Copper.	1,350

KINGDOM OF NAPOLEON

Came into being shortly after the first French empire was proclaimed on May 18, 1804; Napoleon's Italian coronation took place at Naples on May 26, 1805.

French rule

RULER
Napoleon I, 1804-1814

MINT MARKS
B - Bologna
M - Milan
V - Venice

MONETARY SYSTEM
100 Centesimi = 20 Soldi
20 Soldi = 1 Lira

KINGDOM

STANDARD COINAGE

C# 1.1 CENTESIMO
Copper **Ruler:** Napoleon I

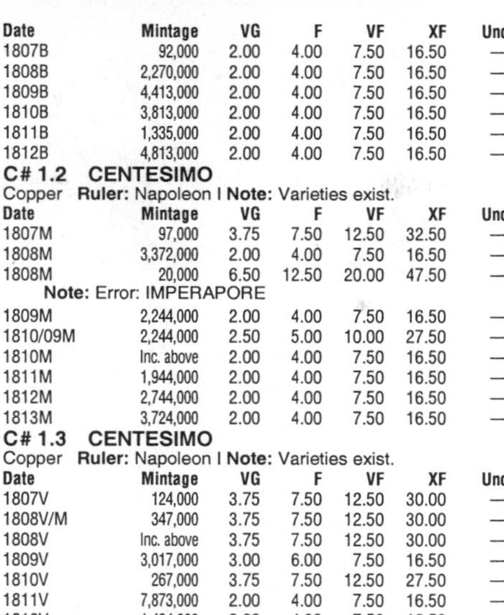

Date	Mintage	VG	F	VF	XF	Unc
1807B	92,000	2.00	4.00	7.50	16.50	—
1808B	2,270,000	2.00	4.00	7.50	16.50	—
1809B	4,413,000	2.00	4.00	7.50	16.50	—
1810B	3,813,000	2.00	4.00	7.50	16.50	—
1811B	1,335,000	2.00	4.00	7.50	16.50	—
1812B	4,813,000	2.00	4.00	7.50	16.50	—

C# 1.2 CENTESIMO
Copper **Ruler:** Napoleon I **Note:** Varieties exist.

Date	Mintage	VG	F	VF	XF	Unc
1807M	97,000	3.75	7.50	12.50	32.50	—
1808M	3,372,000	2.00	4.00	7.50	16.50	—
1808M	20,000	6.50	12.50	20.00	47.50	—
Note: Error: IMPERAPORE						
1809M	2,244,000	2.00	4.00	7.50	16.50	—
1810/09M	2,244,000	2.50	5.00	10.00	27.50	—
1810M	Inc. above	2.00	4.00	7.50	16.50	—
1811M	1,944,000	2.00	4.00	7.50	16.50	—
1812M	2,744,000	2.00	4.00	7.50	16.50	—
1813M	3,724,000	2.00	4.00	7.50	16.50	—

C# 1.3 CENTESIMO
Copper **Ruler:** Napoleon I **Note:** Varieties exist.

Date	Mintage	VG	F	VF	XF	Unc
1807V	124,000	3.75	7.50	12.50	30.00	—
1808V/M	347,000	3.75	7.50	12.50	30.00	—
1808V	Inc. above	3.75	7.50	12.50	30.00	—
1809V	3,017,000	3.00	6.00	7.50	16.50	—
1810V	267,000	3.75	7.50	12.50	27.50	—
1811V	7,873,000	2.00	4.00	7.50	16.50	—
1812V	1,424,000	2.00	4.00	7.50	16.50	—
1813V	4,424,000	2.00	4.00	7.50	16.50	—

C# 2.1 3 CENTESIMI
Copper **Ruler:** Napoleon I

Date	Mintage	VG	F	VF	XF	Unc
1807B	63,000	3.00	8.00	15.00	27.50	—
1808B	215,000	2.00	4.00	7.50	16.50	—
1810/9B	1,845,000	4.00	8.00	15.00	32.50	—
1810B	Inc. above	2.00	4.00	7.50	16.50	—
1813/08B	845,000	2.50	5.00	10.00	22.00	—
1813B	Inc. above	2.00	4.00	7.50	16.50	—

C# 2.3 3 CENTESIMI
Copper **Ruler:** Napoleon I

Date	Mintage	VG	F	VF	XF	Unc
1807V	117,000	7.50	12.50	20.00	32.50	—
1808V	527,000	2.00	4.00	8.00	17.50	—
1809V	127,000	2.00	4.00	8.00	17.50	—
1810/00V	—	2.50	5.00	10.00	22.00	—
1810V	—	2.00	4.00	8.00	17.50	—

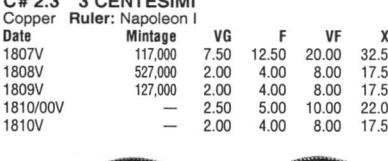

C# 2.2 3 CENTESIMI
Copper **Ruler:** Napoleon I **Note:** Varieties exist.

Date	Mintage	VG	F	VF	XF	Unc
1807M	212,000	2.00	4.00	7.50	16.50	—
1808M	1,878,000	2.00	4.00	7.50	16.50	—
1809M	2,098,000	2.00	4.00	7.50	16.50	—
1810/09M	2,798,000	2.50	5.00	10.00	20.00	—
1810M	Inc. above	2.00	4.00	7.50	16.50	—
1811M	2,798,000	2.00	4.00	7.50	16.50	—
1812M	3,012,000	2.00	4.00	7.50	16.50	—
1813M	2,598,000	2.00	4.00	7.50	16.50	—

C# 3.1 SOLDO
Copper **Ruler:** Napoleon I

Date	Mintage	VG	F	VF	XF	Unc
1807B	345,000	5.00	10.00	20.00	40.00	—
1808B	300,000	2.00	4.00	7.50	16.50	—
1809B	1,340,000	2.00	4.00	7.50	16.50	—

C# 3.3 SOLDO
Copper **Ruler:** Napoleon I

Date	Mintage	VG	F	VF	XF	Unc
1807V	265,000	2.50	5.00	15.00	37.50	—
1808V	300,000	2.50	5.00	10.00	22.00	—
1812V	1,196,000	2.50	5.00	15.00	27.50	—

C# 3.2 SOLDO
Copper **Ruler:** Napoleon I **Note:** Varieties exist.

Date	Mintage	VG	F	VF	XF	Unc
1807M	105,000	2.50	6.00	12.50	22.00	—
1808M	1,454,000	2.00	4.00	7.50	16.50	—
1809M	1,350,000	2.00	4.00	7.50	16.50	—
1810M	1,450,000	2.00	4.00	7.50	16.50	—
1811M	2,390,000	2.00	4.00	7.50	16.50	—
1812M	2,260,000	2.00	4.00	7.50	16.50	—
1813M	2,897,000	2.00	4.00	7.50	16.50	—

C# 4 10 CENTESIMI
2.0000 g., 0.2000 Silver .0128 oz. **Ruler:** Napoleon I

Date	Mintage	VG	F	VF	XF	Unc
1808M	12,000	10.00	20.00	30.00	65.00	—
1809M	875,000	2.00	4.00	7.50	16.50	—
1810M	760,000	2.00	4.00	7.50	16.50	—
1811M	1,540,000	2.00	4.00	7.50	16.50	—
1812M	740,000	2.00	4.00	7.50	16.50	—
1813M	2,670,000	2.00	4.00	7.50	16.50	—

C# 5.1 5 SOLDI
1.2500 g., 0.9000 Silver .0361 oz. **Ruler:** Napoleon I **Note:** Varieties exist.

Date	Mintage	VG	F	VF	XF	Unc
1808M Edge stars raised	130,000	15.00	30.00	60.00	100	—
1808M Edge stars incuse	Inc. above	4.00	6.00	10.00	22.50	—
1809M	600,000	4.00	6.00	10.00	22.50	—
1810M	1,050,000	4.00	6.00	10.00	22.50	—
1811/0M	3,000,000	4.50	7.00	13.00	27.50	—
1811M	Inc. above	4.00	6.00	10.00	22.50	—
1812M	1,700,000	4.00	6.00	10.00	22.50	—
1813M	2,800,000	4.00	6.00	10.00	22.50	—
1814M	700,000	4.00	6.00	10.00	22.50	—
1814M	Inc. above	17.50	35.00	65.00	100	—
Note: Error: IMPERARORE						

C# 5.2 5 SOLDI
1.2500 g., 0.9000 Silver .0361 oz. **Ruler:** Napoleon I **Note:** Varieties exist.

Date	Mintage	VG	F	VF	XF	Unc
1812V	110,000	5.00	10.00	20.00	45.00	—

C# 5.3 5 SOLDI
1.2500 g., 0.9000 Silver .0361 oz. **Ruler:** Napoleon I

Date	Mintage	VG	F	VF	XF	Unc
1812B	330,000	4.50	7.00	11.00	25.00	—
1812B/M	390,000	4.50	7.00	11.00	25.00	—
1813B	2,800,000	4.00	6.50	10.00	22.50	—
1813B/M	320,000	4.50	7.00	11.00	25.00	—

C# 6.1 10 SOLDI

2.5000 g., 0.9000 Silver .0722 oz. **Ruler:** Napoleon I

Date	Mintage	VG	F	VF	XF	Unc
1808M Edge stars raised	175,000	10.00	20.00	40.00	80.00	—
1808M Edge stars incuse	Inc. above	4.50	6.50	10.00	22.50	—
1809M	430,000	4.50	6.50	10.00	22.50	—
1810M	550,000	4.50	6.50	10.00	22.50	—
1811M	2,050,000	4.50	6.50	10.00	22.50	—
1812M	600,000	4.50	6.50 ·	10.00	22.50	—
1813M	490,000	4.50	6.50	10.00	22.50	—
1814M	450,000	4.50	6.50	10.00	22.50	—

C# 6.2 10 SOLDI

2.5000 g., 0.9000 Silver .0722 oz. **Ruler:** Napoleon I **Note:** Varieties exist.

Date	Mintage	VG	F	VF	XF	Unc
1811V	310,000	10.00	15.00	25.00	55.00	—
1812V	160,000	4.50	7.00	12.50	27.50	—
1813V	332,000	4.50	6.50	10.00	22.50	—

C# 6.3 10 SOLDI

2.5000 g., 0.9000 Silver .0722 oz. **Ruler:** Napoleon I

Date	Mintage	VG	F	VF	XF	Unc
1812B	18,000	5.00	10.00	15.00	32.50	—
1812B/M	15,000	5.00	10.00	15.00	32.50	—
1813B	350,000	4.00	6.00	10.00	22.50	—

C# 7 15 SOLDI

3.7500 g., 0.9000 Silver .1083 oz. **Ruler:** Napoleon I

Date	Mintage	VG	F	VF	XF	Unc
1808M	38,000	22.50	40.00	65.00	150	—
1809M	15,000	22.50	50.00	100	220	—
1810M	9,000	45.00	80.00	200	450	—
1814M	370	45.00	80.00	150	350	—

C# 8.1 LIRA

5.0000 g., 0.9000 Silver .1444 oz. **Ruler:** Napoleon I

Date	Mintage	VG	F	VF	XF	Unc
1808M Edge stars raised	495,000	10.00	20.00	30.00	75.00	—
1808M Edge stars incuse	Inc. above	10.00	20.00	30.00	75.00	—
1809M	25,000	5.00	10.00	20.00	45.00	—
1810M	495,000	5.00	10.00	20.00	45.00	—
1810M	Inc. above	20.00	45.00	70.00	150	—
Note: Error: NATOLEON						
1811M	1,185,000	5.00	10.00	20.00	45.00	—
1811/08M	Inc. above	25.00	50.00	85.00	175	—
1812M	340,000	5.00	10.00	20.00	45.00	—
1813M	230,000	5.00	10.00	20.00	45.00	—
1814M	275,000	5.00	10.00	20.00	45.00	—
1814M/V	Inc. above	10.00	25.00	50.00	100	—

C# 8.2 LIRA

5.0000 g., 0.9000 Silver .1444 oz. **Ruler:** Napoleon I

Date	Mintage	VG	F	VF	XF	Unc
1808B	103,000	6.50	12.50	30.00	60.00	—
1810B Edge stars raised	336,000	6.50	12.50	30.00	60.00	—
1810B Edge stars incuse	310,000	6.50	12.50	30.00	60.00	—
1811B	310,000	6.50	12.50	30.00	60.00	—
1812B	310,000	6.50	12.50	30.00	60.00	—
1813B	220,000	6.50	12.50	30.00	60.00	—

C# 8.3 LIRA

5.0000 g., 0.9000 Silver .1444 oz. **Ruler:** Napoleon I **Note:** Varieties exist.

Date	Mintage	VG	F	VF	XF	Unc
1811V	45,000	13.50	22.50	35.00	80.00	—
1812V	90,000	13.50	22.50	35.00	80.00	—
1813V	310,000	12.50	20.00	32.50	75.00	—

C# 9.1 2 LIRE

10.0000 g., 0.9000 Silver .2888 oz. **Ruler:** Napoleon I **Note:** Varieties exist.

Date	Mintage	VG	F	VF	XF	Unc
1807M	10,000	20.00	40.00	125	250	—
1808M Edge lettering raised	Inc. above	125	250	300	450	—
1808M Edge lettering incuse	311,000	17.50	35.00	70.00	125	—
1809M	332,000	15.00	30.00	50.00	90.00	—
1810M	370,000	15.00	30.00	50.00	90.00	—
1811M	513,000	15.00	30.00	50.00	90.00	—
1812M	334,000	15.00	30.00	50.00	90.00	—
1813M	223,000	15.00	30.00	50.00	90.00	—
1814M	3,100	35.00	60.00	75.00	150	—

C# 9.2 2 LIRE

10.0000 g., 0.9000 Silver .2888 oz. **Ruler:** Napoleon I

Date	Mintage	VG	F	VF	XF	Unc
1808B	2,200	25.00	50.00	200	400	—
1812B	44,000	10.00	15.00	35.00	60.00	—
1813B	348,000	10.00	15.00	30.00	55.00	—

C# 9.3 2 LIRE

10.0000 g., 0.9000 Silver .2888 oz. **Ruler:** Napoleon I **Note:** Varieties exist.

Date	Mintage	VG	F	VF	XF	Unc
1811V	10,000	15.00	30.00	60.00	125	—
1812V	239,000	10.00	20.00	40.00	80.00	—
1813V	213,000	10.00	20.00	40.00	80.00	—

KM# 10.1 5 LIRE

25.0000 g., 0.9000 Silver .7234 oz. **Ruler:** Napoleon I **Edge:** Large lettering in relief **Edge Lettering:** DIO PROTEGGE L'ITALIA **Note:** Varieties exist.

Date	Mintage	F	VF	XF	Unc	BU
1807M	39,000	125	275	550	1,250	—
1808M	3,278,000	75.00	175	375	800	—
1809M	2,480,000	75.00	175	375	800	—
1810M	263,000	85.00	200	500	1,000	—

KM# 10.2 5 LIRE

25.0000 g., 0.9000 Silver .7234 oz. **Ruler:** Napoleon I **Note:** Varieties exist.

Date	Mintage	F	VF	XF	Unc	BU
1807V Rare	610	—	—	—	—	—
1808V Rare	204	—	—	—	—	—

KM# 10.3 5 LIRE

25.0000 g., 0.9000 Silver .7234 oz. **Ruler:** Napoleon I

Date	Mintage	F	VF	XF	Unc	BU
1808B	23,000	50.00	125	250	1,250	—
1809B	221,000	50.00	125	250	1,000	—
1810B	317,000	50.00	125	250	1,000	—
1811B	—	50.00	125	250	1,000	—

KM# 10.4 5 LIRE

25.0000 g., 0.9000 Silver .7234 oz. **Ruler:** Napoleon I **Edge:** Large, incuse inscription **Note:** Varieties exist.

Date	Mintage	F	VF	XF	Unc	BU
1809M	—	50.00	125	300	1,000	—
1810M	—	50.00	125	300	1,000	—
1811M	—	50.00	125	300	1,000	—
1812M	1,848,000	50.00	125	300	1,000	—
1813M	772,000	50.00	125	300	1,000	—
1814M	102,000	75.00	150	375	1,000	—

KM# 10.5 5 LIRE

25.0000 g., 0.9000 Silver .7234 oz. **Ruler:** Napoleon I

Date	F	VF	XF	Unc	BU
1810B	50.00	125	300	1,000	—

KM# 10.6 5 LIRE

25.0000 g., 0.9000 Silver .7234 oz. **Ruler:** Napoleon I **Note:** Varieties exist.

Date	Mintage	F	VF	XF	Unc	BU
1810V	—	—	—	—	—	—
1811V	367,000	110	200	550	1,650	—
1812V	207,000	110	200	550	1,500	—
1813V	71,000	110	200	550	1,500	—

KM# 10.7 5 LIRE

25.0000 g., 0.9000 Silver .7234 oz. **Ruler:** Napoleon I **Note:** Letters in legend smaller, edge inscription incuse, small.

Date	Mintage	F	VF	XF	Unc	BU
1808M	—	110	200	550	1,000	—
1811M	2,820,000	110	200	550	1,000	—
1812M	—	110	200	550	1,000	—

KM# 10.8 5 LIRE

25.0000 g., 0.9000 Silver .7234 oz. **Ruler:** Napoleon I

Date	Mintage	F	VF	XF	Unc	BU
1810V	14,000	110	200	550	1,000	—
1811V	—	110	200	550	1,000	—

KM# 10.9 5 LIRE

25.0000 g., 0.9000 Silver .7234 oz. **Ruler:** Napoleon I

Date	Mintage	F	VF	XF	Unc	BU
1811B	451,000	110	200	550	1,000	—
1812B	210,000	110	200	550	1,000	—
1813B	110,000	110	200	550	1,000	—

KM# 11 20 LIRE

6.4510 g., 0.9000 Gold .1866 oz. **Ruler:** Napoleon I

Date	Mintage	F	VF	XF	Unc	BU
1808M	87,000	150	250	475	1,200	—
1809M	53,000	150	250	475	1,200	—
1810M	114,000	150	250	475	1,200	—
1811M	55,000	150	250	475	1,200	—
1812M	45,000	150	250	475	1,200	—
1813M	39,000	150	275	500	1,250	—
1814M	57,000	150	250	475	1,200	—

KM# 12 40 LIRE

12.9030 g., 0.9000 Gold .3733 oz. **Ruler:** Napoleon I **Note:** Varieties exist.

Date	Mintage	F	VF	XF	Unc	BU
1807M	3,430	500	800	1,750	2,800	—
1808	352,000	200	350	800	1,350	—
Note: Without mint mark						
1808M	Inc. above	200	225	500	1,200	—
Note: Edge lettering raised						
1808M	213,000	200	225	500	1,200	—
Note: Edge lettering incuse						
1809M	38,000	200	275	650	1,275	—
1810M	158,000	200	225	500	1,200	—
1811M	106,000	200	225	500	12,100	—
1812M	56,000	200	250	600	1,250	—
1813M	41,000	200	275	650	1,275	—
1814M	264,000	200	225	500	1,200	—

PATTERNS

Including off metal strikes

KM#	Date	Mintage	Identification	Mkt Val
Pn1	1806M	—	Centesimo. Copper.	100
Pn2	1806M	—	2 Centesimi. Copper.	200
Pn3	1806M	—	3 Centesimi. Copper.	200

KM#	Date	Mintage	Identification	Mkt Val
Pn4	1806M	—	Soldo. Copper.	100
Pn5	1806M	—	5 Soldi. Silver.	150
Pn6	1806M	—	10 Soldi. Silver.	150
Pn7	1806M	—	15 Soldi. Silver.	150
Pn8	1806M	—	Lira. Silver.	200
Pn9	1806M	—	2 Lire. Silver.	200
Pn10	1806M	—	5 Lire. Silver.	500
Pn11	1806M	—	20 Lire. Gold.	—
Pn12	1806M	—	40 Lire. Gold.	—
Pn13	1812M	—	5 Lire. Lead.	220

LOMBARDY-VENETIA

Comprised the northern Italian duchies of Milan and Mantua and the Venetian Republic; all these were absorbed into the Kingdom of Napoleon in 1805. After Napoleon's fall they were awarded to Austria and incorporated into the Hapsburg monarchy as the Kingdom of Lombardy-Venetia.

The Lombard campaign of 1859 restored rule under the Kingdom of Italy for Lombard in 1859 and Venetia in1866.

RULERS

French, until 1814
Austrian, until 1814-48, 1849-59
Italian, until 1946

MINT MARKS

A, W - Vienna
B - Kremnitz
M - Milan
S - Schmollnitz
V - Venice

MONETARY SYSTEM

(Until 1857)
100 Centesimi = 20 Soldi = 1 Lira
6 Lire = 1 Scudo
14 Lire = 1 Ducato
40 Lire = 1 Sovrano

AUSTRIAN ADMINISTRATION

STANDARD COINAGE

C# 1.1 CENTESIMO
Copper

Date	F	VF	XF	Unc	BU
1822A	—	—	—	250	—

C# 1.2 CENTESIMO
Copper **Note:** Varieties exist.

Date	F	VF	XF	Unc	BU
1822M	4.00	7.50	25.00	50.00	—
1834M	4.00	7.50	22.50	45.00	—

C# 1.3 CENTESIMO
Copper **Note:** Varieties exist.

Date	F	VF	XF	Unc	BU
1822V	4.00	7.50	25.00	50.00	—
1834V	3.00	7.50	15.00	27.50	—

C# 12.1 CENTESIMO
Copper

Date	F	VF	XF	Unc	BU
1839M	3.00	7.50	15.00	27.50	—
1843M	5.00	8.00	16.00	30.00	—
1846M	3.00	5.00	15.00	27.50	—

C# 12.2 CENTESIMO
Copper

Date	F	VF	XF	Unc	BU
1839V	3.00	7.50	15.00	27.50	—
1843V	3.00	7.50	15.00	27.50	—
1846V	3.00	7.50	15.00	27.50	—

C# 25 CENTESIMO
Copper

Date	F	VF	XF	Unc	BU
1849M	5.00	8.00	16.00	30.00	—
1850M	5.00	8.00	16.00	30.00	—
1852M	6.00	9.00	16.00	32.50	—

C# 29.1 CENTESIMO
Copper

Date	F	VF	XF	Unc	BU
1852	7.00	12.50	20.00	37.50	—

C# 29.2 CENTESIMO
Copper

Date	F	VF	XF	Unc	BU
1852V	3.00	7.50	25.00	45.00	—

C# 34.1 5/10 SOLDO
Copper

Date	Mintage	F	VF	XF	Unc	BU
1862A	12,495,000	2.00	3.50	6.00	15.00	—

C# 34.2 5/10 SOLDO
Copper

Date	Mintage	F	VF	XF	Unc	BU
1862B	5,970,000	3.50	6.00	8.00	17.50	—

C# 34.3 5/10 SOLDO
Copper

Date	Mintage	F	VF	XF	Unc	BU
1862V	1,915,000	3.50	6.00	12.50	27.50	—

C# 2.1 3 CENTESIMI
Copper

Date	F	VF	XF	Unc	BU
1822A Rare	—	—	—	—	—

C# 2.2 3 CENTESIMI
Copper **Note:** Varieties exist.

Date	F	VF	XF	Unc	BU
1822M	4.00	10.00	25.00	45.00	—
1834M	6.00	14.00	30.00	50.00	—

C# 2.3 3 CENTESIMI
Copper

Date	F	VF	XF	Unc	BU
1822V	4.00	8.00	25.00	50.00	—
1834V	4.00	9.00	27.50	55.00	—

C# 13.1 3 CENTESIMI
Copper

Date	F	VF	XF	Unc	BU
1839M	4.00	7.00	15.00	30.00	—
1843M	5.00	8.00	16.50	35.00	—
1846M	3.00	5.00	12.50	25.00	—

C# 13.2 3 CENTESIMI
Copper

Date	F	VF	XF	Unc	BU
1839V	3.00	6.00	15.00	32.50	—
1843V	3.00	6.00	15.00	32.50	—
1846V	3.00	6.00	15.00	32.50	—

C# 26 3 CENTESIMI
Copper

Date	F	VF	XF	Unc	BU
1849M	3.50	10.00	40.00	75.00	—
1850M	3.50	10.00	40.00	75.00	—
1852M	4.00	12.00	45.00	80.00	—

C# 30.1 3 CENTESIMI
Copper

Date	F	VF	XF	Unc	BU
1852M	4.00	8.00	25.00	50.00	—

C# 30.2 3 CENTESIMI
Copper

Date	F	VF	XF	Unc	BU
1852V	3.00	8.00	20.00	40.00	—

C# 3.1 5 CENTESIMI
Copper

Date	F	VF	XF	Unc	BU
1822A	75.00	125	200	350	—

C# 3.2 5 CENTESIMI
Copper

Date	F	VF	XF	Unc	BU
1822M	5.00	10.00	40.00	80.00	—
1834M	8.00	14.00	45.00	85.00	—

C# 3.3 5 CENTESIMI
Copper

Date	F	VF	XF	Unc	BU
1822V	5.00	10.00	40.00	75.00	—
1834V	5.00	10.00	40.00	75.00	—

C# 14.1 5 CENTESIMI
Copper

Date	F	VF	XF	Unc	BU
1839M	4.50	9.00	20.00	45.00	—
1843M	4.00	8.00	17.50	40.00	—
1846M	4.00	8.00	17.50	40.00	—

C# 14.2 5 CENTESIMI
Copper

Date	F	VF	XF	Unc	BU
1839V	4.50	9.00	20.00	50.00	—
1843V	10.00	20.00	80.00	160	—
1846V	4.00	10.00	20.00	40.00	—

C# 27 5 CENTESIMI
Copper

Date	F	VF	XF	Unc	BU
1849M	6.00	12.00	50.00	90.00	—
1850M	6.00	12.00	50.00	90.00	—

C# 31.1 5 CENTESIMI
Copper

Date	F	VF	XF	Unc	BU
1852	4.00	10.00	40.00	80.00	—

C# 31.2 5 CENTESIMI
Copper

Date	F	VF	XF	Unc	BU
1852	3.00	7.00	45.00	90.00	—

C# 35.1 SOLDO
Copper

Date	Mintage	F	VF	XF	Unc	BU
1862A	22,275,000	1.50	4.50	9.00	20.00	—

C# 35.2 SOLDO
Copper

Date	Mintage	F	VF	XF	Unc	BU
1862B	8,971,000	2.00	4.50	9.00	20.00	—

C# 35.3 SOLDO
Copper

Date	Mintage	F	VF	XF	Unc	BU
1862V	9,395,000	2.50	5.00	10.00	22.50	—

C# 28 10 CENTESIMI
Copper **Note:** Similar to 5 Centesimi, C#3.

Date	F	VF	XF	Unc	BU
1849M	100	300	625	1,250	—

C# 32 10 CENTESIMI
Copper

Date	F	VF	XF	Unc	BU
1852V	8.00	15.00	35.00	80.00	—

C# 33 15 CENTESIMI
Copper **Note:** Similar to 10 Centesimi, C#32.

Date	F	VF	XF	Unc	BU
1852V	75.00	250	450	900	—

C# 4.1 1/4 LIRA
1.6200 g., 0.6000 Silver .0312 oz.

Date	F	VF	XF	Unc	BU
1822A	35.00	50.00	90.00	225	—
1823A	150	225	325	750	—

C# 4.2 1/4 LIRA
1.6200 g., 0.6000 Silver .0312 oz.

Date	F	VF	XF	Unc	BU
1822M	15.00	25.00	40.00	120	—
1823/2M	15.00	25.00	40.00	120	—
1823M	15.00	25.00	40.00	120	—
1824M	25.00	75.00	175	350	—

C# 4.3 1/4 LIRA
1.6200 g., 0.6000 Silver .0312 oz.

Date	F	VF	XF	Unc	BU
1822	15.00	25.00	40.00	120	—
1823	60.00	150	300	625	—
1824	10.00	20.00	40.00	120	—

C# 15.1 1/4 LIRA
1.6200 g., 0.6000 Silver .0312 oz.

Date	F	VF	XF	Unc	BU
1835A	—	—	—	—	—

Note: Reported, not confirmed

C# 15.2 1/4 LIRA
1.6200 g., 0.6000 Silver .0312 oz.

Date	F	VF	XF	Unc	BU
1837V	75.00	100	150	300	—
1838V	75.00	100	150	300	—
1839V	75.00	100	150	300	—
1840V	75.00	100	150	250	—
1841V	75.00	100	150	300	—
1842V	75.00	100	150	300	—
1843V	75.00	100	150	250	—
1844V	75.00	100	150	300	—

C# 5.1 1/2 LIRA
2.1650 g., 0.9000 Silver .0626 oz.

Date	F	VF	XF	Unc	BU
1822A	60.00	100	180	350	—
1823A	50.00	90.00	175	300	—

C# 5.2 1/2 LIRA
2.1650 g., 0.9000 Silver .0626 oz.

Date	F	VF	XF	Unc	BU
1822M	12.50	25.00	50.00	125	—
1823M	12.50	25.00	50.00	125	—
1824/2M	12.50	25.00	50.00	125	—
1824M	12.50	25.00	50.00	125	—

C# 5.3 1/2 LIRA
2.1650 g., 0.9000 Silver .0626 oz.

Date	F	VF	XF	Unc	BU
1822V	10.00	25.00	40.00	100	—
1823/2V	10.00	25.00	40.00	100	—
1823V	10.00	25.00	40.00	100	—

C# 16.1 1/2 LIRA
2.1650 g., 0.9000 Silver .0626 oz.

Date	F	VF	XF	Unc	BU
1835A	—	—	—	—	—

Note: Reported, not confirmed

C# 16.2 1/2 LIRA
2.1650 g., 0.9000 Silver .0626 oz.

Date	F	VF	XF	Unc	BU
1837V	50.00	100	225	450	—
1838V	50.00	100	225	450	—
1839V	60.00	125	250	500	—
1840V	60.00	125	250	500	—
1841V	60.00	125	250	500	—
1842V	60.00	125	250	500	—
1843V	60.00	125	250	500	—
1844V	60.00	125	250	500	—

C# 36 1/2 LIRA
2.1650 g., 0.9000 Silver .0626 oz.

Date	F	VF	XF	Unc	BU
1854	30.00	50.00	100	200	—
1855	35.00	75.00	150	300	—

C# 6.1 LIRA
4.3300 g., 0.9000 Silver .1253 oz.

Date	F	VF	XF	Unc	BU
1822A	100	200	425	800	—
1823A	17.50	35.00	50.00	100	—
1835A	—	—	—	—	—

Note: Reported, not confirmed

C# 6.2 LIRA
4.3300 g., 0.9000 Silver .1253 oz.

Date	F	VF	XF	Unc	BU
1822M	17.50	35.00	50.00	100	—
1823M	17.50	35.00	50.00	100	—
1824/3M	17.50	35.00	50.00	100	—
1824M	17.50	35.00	50.00	100	—
1825M	17.50	35.00	50.00	100	—

C# 6.3 LIRA
4.3300 g., 0.9000 Silver .1253 oz.

Date	F	VF	XF	Unc	BU
1822V	17.50	30.00	50.00	100	—
1823V	50.00	175	425	800	—

C# 17.1 LIRA
4.3300 g., 0.9000 Silver .1253 oz.

Date	F	VF	XF	Unc	BU
1835A	—	—	—	—	—

Note: Reported, not confirmed

C# 17.2 LIRA
4.3300 g., 0.9000 Silver .1253 oz.

Date	F	VF	XF	Unc	BU
1837V	60.00	125	275	500	—
1838V	60.00	125	275	500	—
1839V	60.00	125	275	500	—
1840V	100	200	425	800	—
1841V	100	200	425	800	—
1842V	100	200	425	800	—
1843V	100	200	425	800	—
1844V	100	200	425	800	—

C# 37.1 LIRA
4.3300 g., 0.9000 Silver .1253 oz.

Date	F	VF	XF	Unc	BU
1852	60.00	100	200	350	—

C# 37.2 LIRA
4.3300 g., 0.9000 Silver .1253 oz.

Date	F	VF	XF	Unc	BU
1853M	60.00	100	200	350	—
1854M	125	225	450	850	—
1855M	125	225	450	850	—
1856M	100	200	400	800	—
1858M	150	300	650	1,300	—

C# 7.1 1/2 SCUDO
12.3450 g., 0.9000 Silver .3527 oz.

Date	F	VF	XF	Unc	BU
1822A	35.00	65.00	125	350	—
1823A	30.00	55.00	110	225	—

C# 7.2 1/2 SCUDO
12.3450 g., 0.9000 Silver .3527 oz.

Date	F	VF	XF	Unc	BU
1822M	25.00	40.00	80.00	150	—
1823M	25.00	40.00	90.00	175	—
1824M	25.00	40.00	80.00	160	—
1825M	90.00	145	250	450	—
1827M	90.00	145	250	450	—

C# 7.3 1/2 SCUDO
12.3450 g., 0.9000 Silver .3527 oz.

Date	F	VF	XF	Unc	BU
1822V	25.00	35.00	80.00	175	—
1823V	60.00	100	250	500	—
1824V	25.00	35.00	80.00	200	—
1825V	25.00	35.00	80.00	200	—
1826V	25.00	35.00	80.00	200	—
1827V	30.00	55.00	100	225	—

C# 18.1 1/2 SCUDO
12.3450 g., 0.9000 Silver .3527 oz.

Date	F	VF	XF	Unc	BU
1835A	—	—	—	—	—

Note: Reported, not confirmed

C# 18.2 1/2 SCUDO
12.3450 g., 0.9000 Silver .3527 oz.

Date	F	VF	XF	Unc	BU
1837V	100	200	400	750	—
1838V	100	200	550	900	—
1839V	100	200	550	900	—
1840V	100	200	400	750	—
1841V	100	200	550	900	—
1842V	100	200	400	750	—
1843V	100	200	400	750	—
1844V	100	200	400	750	—
1845V	100	200	550	900	—
1846V	100	200	550	900	—

C# 38 1/2 SCUDO
12.3450 g., 0.9000 Silver .3527 oz. **Note:** Without value.

Date	F	VF	XF	Unc	BU
1853	200	350	600	1,500	—

C# A1 6 LIRE
26.0000 g., 0.9000 Silver .7524 oz.

Date	F	VF	XF	Unc	BU
1816M Rare	—	—	—	—	—

Note: Swiss Bank sale No.19 1-88 XF-FDC realized $10,500

C# 8.2 SCUDO
26.0000 g., 0.9000 Silver .7524 oz.

Date	F	VF	XF	Unc	BU
1821A Proof	—	—	—	—	—
1822A	50.00	80.00	125	275	—
1823A	50.00	70.00	100	225	—
1824A	65.00	90.00	150	300	—
1825A	—	—	—	—	—

Note: Reported, not confirmed

Date	F	VF	XF	Unc	BU
1835A	—	—	—	—	—

Note: Reported, not confirmed

C# 8.3 SCUDO
26.0000 g., 0.9000 Silver .7524 oz.

Date	F	VF	XF	Unc	BU
1822V	35.00	75.00	125	250	—
1823V	100	300	750	1,300	—
1824V	30.00	50.00	125	325	—
1825V	30.00	65.00	115	225	—
1826V	30.00	50.00	110	200	—
1827V	50.00	80.00	140	350	—
1828V	90.00	140	450	800	—
1829V	90.00	140	450	800	—
1830V	50.00	75.00	125	325	—
1831V	35.00	65.00	115	300	—
1832V	35.00	65.00	115	300	—

C# 8.1 SCUDO
26.0000 g., 0.9000 Silver .7524 oz.

Date	F	VF	XF	Unc	BU
1822	25.00	45.00	125	350	—
1823	35.00	65.00	125	350	—
1824	35.00	65.00	125	350	—
1825	30.00	50.00	125	350	—
1826	30.00	50.00	125	350	—
1827	50.00	90.00	200	450	—
1828	125	200	450	900	—
1829	45.00	80.00	125	350	—
1830	45.00	80.00	125	350	—
1831	30.00	55.00	125	350	—

C# 19.1 SCUDO
26.0000 g., 0.9000 Silver .7524 oz.

Date	F	VF	XF	Unc	BU
1835A	—	—	—	—	—

Note: Reported, not confirmed

C# 19.2 SCUDO
26.0000 g., 0.9000 Silver .7524 oz.

Date	F	VF	XF	Unc	BU
1837M	250	400	900	1,750	—

C# 19.3 SCUDO
26.0000 g., 0.9000 Silver .7524 oz.

Date	F	VF	XF	Unc	BU
1837V	110	200	400	800	—
1838V	125	225	450	950	—
1839V	100	180	400	800	—
1840V	100	180	400	800	—
1841V	125	200	900	1,750	—
1842V	125	200	450	900	—
1843V	100	180	900	1,750	—
1844V	100	180	900	1,750	—
1845V	90.00	175	900	1,750	—
1846V	100	180	400	900	—

C# 39 SCUDO
26.0000 g., 0.9000 Silver .7524 oz. **Note:** Without value.

Date	F	VF	XF	Unc	BU
1853	200	400	750	1,600	—

TRADE COINAGE

C# 9 ZECCHINO
3.5000 g., 0.9000 Gold .1012 oz. **Obv:** Doge kneeling before St. Mark **Obv. Legend:** FRANC. I... **Rev:** Christ standing **Note:** Varieties exist.

Date	F	VF	XF	Unc	BU
ND(1815)	750	1,500	2,000	2,500	—

C# 10.1 1/2 SOVRANO
5.6700 g., 0.9000 Gold .1640 oz.

Date	F	VF	XF	Unc	BU
1820M	400	900	2,000	3,500	—
1822M	350	700	1,250	2,000	—
1831M	150	300	500	1,000	—

C# 10.2 1/2 SOVRANO
5.6700 g., 0.9000 Gold .1640 oz.

Date	F	VF	XF	Unc	BU
1822A	200	400	1,250	2,400	—
1823A	200	500	1,500	3,000	—
1831A	200	400	1,250	2,400	—

C# 10.3 1/2 SOVRANO
5.6700 g., 0.9000 Gold .1640 oz.

Date	F	VF	XF	Unc	BU
1822V	300	800	1,500	3,300	—
1823V	150	250	550	1,200	—

C# 10a.1 1/2 SOVRANO
5.6700 g., 0.9000 Gold .1640 oz.

Date	F	VF	XF	Unc	BU
1835A	—	—	—	—	—

Note: Reported, not confirmed

C# 10a.2 1/2 SOVRANO
5.6700 g., 0.9000 Gold .1640 oz. **Note:** Varieties exist.

Date	F	VF	XF	Unc	BU
1835M	150	225	550	1,100	—
1835M	—	—	—	—	—

Note: Error: AVSIRIAE

C# 20.2 1/2 SOVRANO
5.6700 g., 0.9000 Gold .1640 oz.

Date	F	VF	XF	Unc	BU
1837M	750	1,600	3,250	5,000	—
1838M	300	600	1,400	2,250	—
1839M	300	600	1,400	2,250	—
1841M	300	600	1,400	2,250	—
1842M	350	700	1,600	2,500	—
1843M	600	1,250	3,250	5,000	—
1844M	350	700	1,600	2,500	—
1845M	350	700	1,600	2,500	—
1846M	350	700	1,600	2,500	—
1847M	350	700	1,600	2,500	—
1848M	300	700	1,600	2,500	—

C# 20.3 1/2 SOVRANO
5.6700 g., 0.9000 Gold .1640 oz.

Date	F	VF	XF	Unc	BU
1837V	300	650	1,500	2,400	—
1838V	300	650	1,500	2,400	—
1839V	300	650	1,500	2,400	—
1840V	300	650	1,500	2,400	—
1841V	300	650	1,500	2,400	—
1842V	650	1,100	1,800	3,000	—
1843V	350	700	1,500	2,750	—
1844V	350	700	1,500	2,750	—
1845V	350	700	1,500	2,750	—
1846V	600	1,250	2,000	3,500	—
1847V	750	2,000	4,000	6,500	—

C# 20.1 1/2 SOVRANO
5.6700 g., 0.9000 Gold .1640 oz.

Date	F	VF	XF	Unc	BU
1839A	200	400	900	1,800	—

C# 20a 1/2 SOVRANO
5.6700 g., 0.9000 Gold .1640 oz.

Date	F	VF	XF	Unc	BU
1849M	250	400	800	1,650	—

C# 40.1 1/2 SOVRANO
5.6700 g., 0.9000 Gold .1640 oz.

Date	F	VF	XF	Unc	BU
1854M	600	1,750	3,500	6,500	—
1855M	600	1,750	3,500	6,500	—
1856M	600	1,750	3,500	6,500	—

C# 40.2 1/2 SOVRANO
5.6700 g., 0.9000 Gold .1640 oz.

Date	F	VF	XF	Unc	BU
1854V	600	1,750	3,500	6,500	—
1855V	600	1,750	3,500	6,500	—
1856V	600	1,750	3,500	6,500	—

C# 11.1 SOVRANO
11.3300 g., 0.9000 Gold .3278 oz.

Date	F	VF	XF	Unc	BU
1820M	700	1,500	3,750	7,500	—
1822M	350	700	1,400	3,000	—
1823M	350	700	1,400	3,000	—
1824M	350	1,500	3,750	7,500	—
1826M	500	1,000	2,500	5,000	—
1827M	500	1,000	2,500	5,000	—
1828M	500	1,000	2,500	5,000	—
1829M	350	700	1,400	3,000	—
1830/20M	—	—	—	—	—

Date	F	VF	XF	Unc	BU
1830M	350	700	1,400	3,000	—
1831/21M	350	700	1,400	3,000	—
1831M	325	650	1,250	2,200	—

C# 11.2 SOVRANO

11.3300 g., 0.9000 Gold .3278 oz.

Date	F	VF	XF	Unc	BU
1822A	625	1,250	2,500	5,000	—
1823A	625	1,250	2,500	5,000	—
1831A	350	700	1,400	2,800	—

C# 11.3 SOVRANO

11.3300 g., 0.9000 Gold .3278 oz.

Date	F	VF	XF	Unc	BU
1822V	550	1,000	2,000	3,500	—

C# 11a.1 SOVRANO

11.3300 g., 0.9000 Gold .3278 oz.

Date	F	VF	XF	Unc	BU
1835A	—	—	—	—	—

Note: Reported, not confirmed

C# 11a.2 SOVRANO

11.3300 g., 0.9000 Gold .3278 oz.

Date	F	VF	XF	Unc	BU
1835M	600	1,250	2,500	5,500	—

C# 21.1 SOVRANO

11.3300 g., 0.9000 Gold .3278 oz.

Date	F	VF	XF	Unc	BU
1837A	500	800	1,600	3,000	—
1838A Rare	—	—	—	—	—
1839A	500	800	1,600	3,000	—
1840A Rare	—	—	—	—	—
1841A	550	900	1,750	3,250	—
1842A Rare	—	—	—	—	—
1843A Rare	—	—	—	—	—
1845A Rare	—	—	—	—	—
1847A	850	2,000	4,000	8,500	—

C# 21.2 SOVRANO

11.3300 g., 0.9000 Gold .3278 oz.

Date	F	VF	XF	Unc	BU
1837M	800	2,000	4,000	8,500	—
1838M	400	800	1,600	3,000	—
1840M	400	800	1,600	3,000	—
1841M	850	2,000	4,000	8,500	—
1848M	850	2,000	4,000	8,500	—

C# 21.3 SOVRANO

11.3300 g., 0.9000 Gold .3278 oz.

Date	F	VF	XF	Unc	BU
1837V	350	750	1,500	3,000	—
1838V	350	750	1,500	3,000	—
1839V	400	800	1,600	3,200	—
1840V	350	750	1,500	3,000	—
1841V	350	750	1,500	3,000	—
1842V	350	750	1,500	3,000	—
1843V	400	800	1,600	3,200	—
1844V	400	800	1,600	3,200	—
1845V	400	800	1,600	3,200	—
1846V	350	750	1,500	3,000	—
1847V	350	750	1,500	3,000	—

C# 41.1 SOVRANO

11.3300 g., 0.9000 Gold .3278 oz.

Date	F	VF	XF	Unc	BU
1853M	850	2,000	4,500	8,000	—
1855M	850	2,000	4,500	8,000	—
1856M	850	2,000	4,500	8,000	—

C# 41.2 SOVRANO

11.3300 g., 0.9000 Gold .3278 oz.

Date	F	VF	XF	Unc	BU
1854V	1,250	2,500	5,000	9,000	—
1855V	1,000	2,000	4,750	8,000	—
1856V	1,000	2,000	4,500	8,000	—

REVOLUTIONARY PROVISIONAL GOVERNMENT

PROVISIONAL COINAGE

C# 22.1 5 LIRE

25.0000 g., 0.9000 Silver .7234 oz. **Obv:** Short stems above date

Date	Mintage	F	VF	XF	Unc	BU
1848M	120,000	50.00	95.00	225	400	—

C# 22.2 5 LIRE

25.0000 g., 0.9000 Silver .7234 oz. **Obv:** Long stems extend beyond date

Date	F	VF	XF	Unc	BU
1848M	150	300	700	1,250	—

C# 22.3 5 LIRE

25.0000 g., 0.9000 Silver .7234 oz. **Obv:** Short stems end above date **Rev:** Star near crown

Date	F	VF	XF	Unc	BU
1848M	50.00	95.00	225	400	—

C# 23 20 LIRE

6.4500 g., 0.9000 Gold .1866 oz.

Date	Mintage	F	VF	XF	Unc	BU
1848M	4,593	400	700	1,000	2,200	—

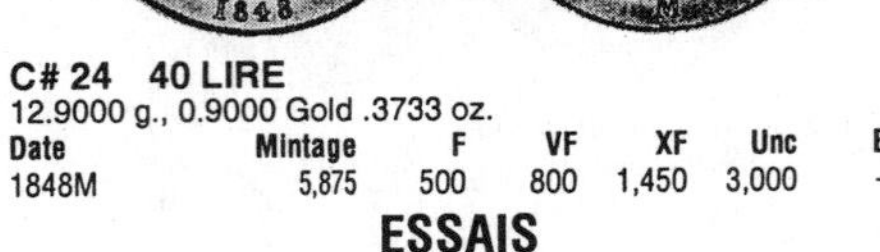

C# 24 40 LIRE

12.9000 g., 0.9000 Gold .3733 oz.

Date	Mintage	F	VF	XF	Unc	BU
1848M	5,875	500	800	1,450	3,000	—

ESSAIS

KM#	Date	Mintage	Identification	Mkt Val
E1	1816	—	Scudo. Lead. C#8.1.	—

PATTERNS

Including off metal strikes

KM#	Date	Mintage	Identification	Mkt Val
Pn1	1821V	—	1/2 Lira. Silver. C#5.	—

KM#	Date	Mintage	Identification	Mkt Val
Pn2	1848M	—	Lira. Silver. 4.9600 g.	450
Pn3	1848M	—	Lira. Bronze. 5.0600 g.	800
Pn4	1848M	—	Lira. Tin. 5.0600 g.	500
Pn5	1848M	—	Lira. Tin. 4.2800 g.	400
Pn6	1848M	—	Lira. Tin. 2.9200 g.	400
Pn7	1848M	—	2 Lira. Silver. 10.0000 g.	600
Pn8	1848M	—	2 Lira. Bronze. 9.8100 g.	800
Pn9	1848M	—	2 Lira. Tin. 9.1500 g.	450
Pn10	1848M	—	2 Lira. Tin. 6.9800 g.	400

KM#	Date	Mintage	Identification	Mkt Val
Pn11	1848M	—	5 Lira. Copper. 24.1000 g. C#22.1.	800
Pn12	1848M	—	5 Lira. Tin. 18.4200 g. C#22.1.	1,000

KM#	Date	Mintage	Identification	Mkt Val
Pn13	1852M	—	10 Centesimi. Copper. C#32.	1,500
Pn14	1852M	—	15 Centesimi. Copper. C#33.	1,600

TRIAL STRIKES

KM#	Date	Mintage	Identification	Mkt Val
TS1	ND(1835M)	—	Soldo. Tin. Uniface obverse.	175
TS2	ND(1835M)	—	1/4 Lira. Tin. Uniface obverse.	175
TS3	ND(1835M)	—	1/2 Lira. Tin. Uniface obverse.	175
TS4	1835(M)	—	1/2 Lira. Tin. Uniface reverse.	175
TS5	ND(1835M)	—	Lira. Tin. Uniface obverse.	175
TS6	1835(M)	—	Lira. Tin. Uniface reverse.	175
TS7	ND(1835M)	—	1/4 Scudo. Tin. Uniface obverse.	175
TS8	1835(M)	—	1/4 Scudo. Tin. Uniface reverse.	175
TS9	ND(1835M)	—	1/2 Scudo. Tin. Uniface obverse.	175
TS10	1835(M)	—	1/2 Scudo. Tin. Uniface reverse.	175

KM#	Date	Mintage	Identification	Mkt Val
TS11	ND(1835)M	—	Scudo. Tin. Uniface obverse.	175

KM#	Date	Mintage	Identification	Mkt Val

KM#	Date	Mintage	Identification	Mkt Val
TS12	1835(M)	—	Scudo. Tin. Uniface reverse.	175
TS13	ND(1835)M	—	Scudo. Tin.	550
TS14	1848(M)	—	Lira. Tin. Uniface obverse. Klippe.	900
TS15	ND1848(M)	—	Lira. Tin. Uniface reverse. Klippe.	900
TS16	1848(M)	—	5 Lira. Tin. Uniface obverse. C#22.1.	375
TS17	ND(1848)M	—	5 Lira. Tin. Uniface reverse. C#22.1.	375

LUCCA

Luca, Lucensis
Lucca and Piombino

A town in Tuscany and the residence of a marquis, was nominally a fief but managed to maintain a *de facto* independence until awarded by Napoleon to his sister Elisa in 1805. In 1814 it was occupied by the Neapolitans, from 1817 to 1847 it was a duchy of the queen of Etruria, after which it became a division of Tuscany.

Principality, 1805-1814
Lucca, Duchy, 1817-1847

RULERS

Felix and Elisa (Bonaparte), 1805-1814
Maria Luisa di Borbone, Duchess, 1817-1824
Carlo Lodovico di Borbone, Duke, 1824-1847

MONETARY SYSTEM

100 Centesimi = 1 Franco

REPUBLIC

REFORM COINAGE

100 Centesimi = 1 Franco

KM# 21 3 CENTESIMI
Copper

Date	VG	F	VF	XF	Unc
1806	6.00	15.00	35.00	100	—

KM# 22 5 CENTESIMI
Copper

Date	VG	F	VF	XF	Unc
1806	10.00	20.00	50.00	150	—

KM# 23 FRANCO
5.0000 g., 0.9000 Silver .1446 oz.

Date	VG	F	VF	XF	Unc
1805 Rare	—	—	—	—	—
1806	25.00	50.00	100	200	—
1807	25.00	50.00	100	200	—
1808	25.00	50.00	100	200	—

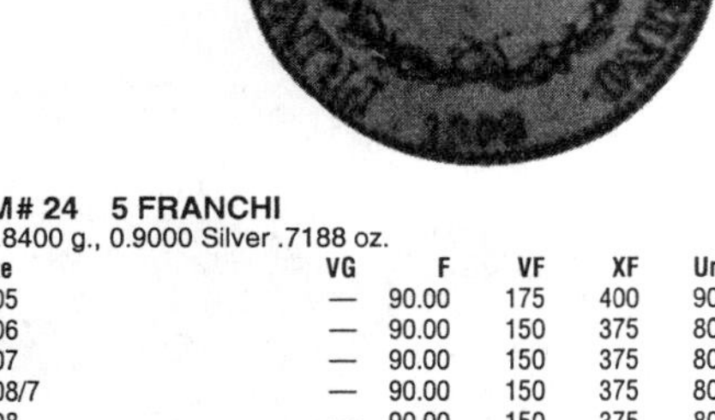

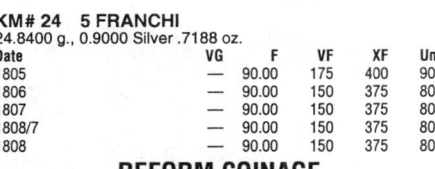

KM# 24 5 FRANCHI
24.8400 g., 0.9000 Silver .7188 oz.

Date	VG	F	VF	XF	Unc
1805	—	90.00	175	400	900
1806	—	90.00	150	375	800
1807	—	90.00	150	375	800
1808/7	—	90.00	150	375	800
1808	—	90.00	150	375	800

REFORM COINAGE

4 Denari = 1 Quattrino; 3 Quattrini = 1 Soldo; 20 Soldi = 1 Lira

KM# A34 SOLDO
Copper **Obv. Legend:** CARLO L. D. B. I. D. S. DUCA DI LUCCA

Date	VG	F	VF	XF	Unc
1826	3.50	7.00	25.00	90.00	—

KM# 34a SOLDO
Copper

Date	VG	F	VF	XF	Unc
1841	7.50	15.00	25.00	50.00	—

C# 4a BOLOGNINO (2 Soldi)
3.0700 g., 0.2000 Silver .0197 oz. **Obv:** Branch with six leaves

Date	F	VF	XF	Unc	BU
1790(1835) Restrike	20.00	32.00	70.00	—	—

KM# A33 2 QUATTRINI
Copper

Date	VG	F	VF	XF	Unc
1826	4.00	8.00	16.00	50.00	—

KM# A35 5 QUATTRINI
Copper **Obv:** Crowned arms **Rev:** Value, date **Note:** Varieties exist.

Date	VG	F	VF	XF	Unc
1826	15.00	35.00	55.00	100	—

KM# 36 2 SOLDI
1.4000 g., 0.2000 Silver .0090 oz. **Obv:** Crowned arms **Rev:** Value, date

Date	Mintage	VG	F	VF	XF	Unc
1835	50,157	7.50	14.00	30.00	60.00	—

KM# 37 3 SOLDI
1.6000 g., 0.2000 Silver .0102 oz. **Obv:** Crowned CL monogram

Date	VG	F	VF	XF	Unc
1835 Rare	—	—	—	—	—

KM# 38 5 SOLDI
3.0000 g., 0.2000 Silver .0192 oz.

Date	VG	F	VF	XF	Unc
1833 Flat-top 3's	7.50	14.00	22.00	50.00	—
1833 Round-top 3's	7.50	14.00	22.00	50.00	—
1838	7.50	14.00	22.00	50.00	—

C# 39 10 SOLDI
2.3600 g., 0.6660 Silver .0505 oz.

Date	F	VF	XF	Unc	BU
1833	10.00	20.00	40.00	100	—
1838	10.00	20.00	40.00	100	—

C# 40 LIRA
4.7200 g., 0.6660 Silver .1010 oz.

Date	F	VF	XF	Unc	BU
1834	25.00	50.00	100	200	—
1837	20.00	40.00	100	225	—
1838	15.00	30.00	65.00	150	—

C# 41 2 LIRE
9.4300 g., 0.6660 Silver .2019 oz.

Date	F	VF	XF	Unc	BU
1837	50.00	100	250	450	—

NAPLES & SICILY

Two Sicilies

Consisting of Sicily and the south of Italy, Naples & Sicily came into being in 1130. It passed under Spanish control in 1502; Naples was conquered by Austria in 1707. In 1733 Don Carlos of Spain was recognized as king. From then until becoming part of the United Kingdom of Italy, Naples and Sicily, together and separately, were contested for by Spain, Austria, France, and the republican and monarchial factions of Italy.

RULERS

Bourbon

Ferdinando IV, 1799-1805 (2nd reign)
1815-1816 (restored in Naples)
1816-1825 (as King of the Two Sicilies)
Joseph Napoleon, 1806-1808
Joachim Murat, (Gioacchino Napoleone) 1808-1815

Two Sicilies

Francesco I, 1825-1830
Ferdinand II, 1830-1859
Francesco II, 1859-1869

MONETARY SYSTEM

(Until 1813)

6 Cavalli = 1 Tornese
240 Tornese = 120 Grana = 12 Carlini= 6 Tari = 1 Piastra
5 Grana = 1 Cinquina
100 Grana = 1 Ducato (Tallero)

KINGDOM OF NAPLES

STANDARD COINAGE

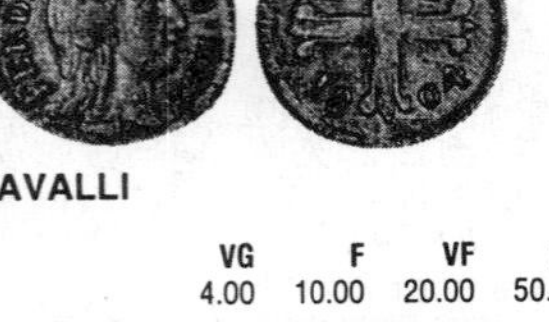

C# 91 3 CAVALLI
Copper

Date	VG	F	VF	XF	Unc
1804	4.00	10.00	20.00	50.00	—

C# 92 4 CAVALLI
Copper

Date	VG	F	VF	XF	Unc
1804 LD	4.00	10.00	20.00	50.00	—

C# 93 TORNESE (6 Cavalli)
Copper **Obv:** Head right **Rev:** Value within wreath

Date	VG	F	VF	XF	Unc
1804 LD	6.00	12.00	25.00	55.00	—

C# 94 9 CAVALLI
Copper **Obv:** Head right **Rev:** Castle

Date	VG	F	VF	XF	Unc
1801	15.00	35.00	65.00	120	—
1804	6.00	12.00	25.00	60.00	—
1804 LD	6.00	12.00	25.00	60.00	—

C# 96 6 TORNESI
Copper **Ruler:** Ferdinando IV 2nd reign

Date	VG	F	VF	XF	Unc
1801 A P	6.00	12.00	25.00	55.00	—
1802 A P	6.00	12.00	28.00	60.00	—
1803 A P	6.00	12.00	28.00	60.00	—
1803 R C	7.50	15.00	30.00	65.00	—

C# 101 2 GRANA
Copper

Date	VG	F	VF	XF	Unc
1810	20.00	40.00	100	300	—

C# 102 3 GRANA
Copper

Date	VG	F	VF	XF	Unc
1810	20.00	40.00	100	350	—

C# 102a 3 GRANA
Copper **Rev:** Date below wreath

Date	VG	F	VF	XF	Unc
1810	20.00	40.00	100	350	—

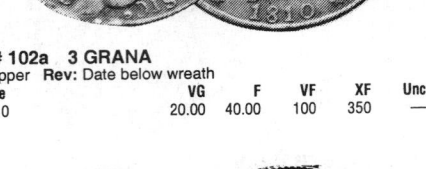

C# 97 60 GRANA
13.7500 g., 0.8330 Silver .3682 oz.

Date	VG	F	VF	XF	Unc
1805 LD	35.00	75.00	175	350	—

C# 98 120 GRANA
27.5000 g., 0.8330 Silver .7365 oz. **Ruler:** Ferdinando IV 2nd reign **Note:** Dav. #1409.

Date	VG	F	VF	XF	Unc
1802 AP	25.00	45.00	100	225	—
1802 P-AP	25.00	45.00	100	225	—

C# 99.1 120 GRANA
27.5000 g., 0.8330 Silver .7365 oz. **Obv:** Head right with smooth hair **Rev:** Crown above small shield

Date	VG	F	VF	XF	Unc
1805 LD	30.00	60.00	125	275	—

C# 99.2 120 GRANA
27.5000 g., 0.8330 Silver .7365 oz. **Edge:** Plain

Date	VG	F	VF	XF	Unc
1805 LD	30.00	60.00	125	275	—

C# 99.3 120 GRANA
27.5000 g., 0.8330 Silver .7365 oz. **Obv:** Head right with curly hair **Note:** Varieties exist.

Date	VG	F	VF	XF	Unc
1805 LD	25.00	50.00	120	265	—

C# 100 120 GRANA
27.5000 g., 0.8330 Silver .7365 oz.

Date	VG	F	VF	XF	Unc
1806	100	175	350	600	—
1807/6	100	175	350	700	—
1807	80.00	150	275	450	—
1808	80.00	150	275	450	—

C# 103 DODICI (12) CARLINI
27.5300 g., 0.8330 Silver .7373 oz. **Note:** Many varieties including mulings exist.

Date	VG	F	VF	XF	Unc
1809	80.00	150	300	650	—
1810	80.00	150	325	700	—

REFORM COINAGE

100 Centesimi = 1 Franco = 1 Lira

C# 105 3 CENTESIMI
Bronze **Obv:** Head left **Rev:** Value

Date	Mintage	F	VF	XF	Unc	BU
1813	1,350,000	500	1,100	1,500	3,750	—

C# 106 5 CENTESIMI
Bronze

Date	Mintage	F	VF	XF	Unc	BU
1813	1,280,000	750	1,250	1,750	5,250	—

C# 107 10 CENTESIMI
Bronze **Obv:** Head left **Rev:** Value

Date	Mintage	F	VF	XF	Unc	BU
1813	450,000	850	1,350	2,000	6,000	—

C# 108 MEZZA (1/2) LIRA
2.5000 g., 0.9000 Silver .0723 oz.

Date	Mintage	F	VF	XF	Unc	BU
1813	166,000	50.00	75.00	175	475	—

C# 109 LIRA
5.0000 g., 0.9000 Silver .1446 oz.

Date	Mintage	F	VF	XF	Unc	BU
1812	27,000	50.00	125	250	500	—
1813	199,000	30.00	75.00	150	250	—

C# 110 2 LIRE
10.0000 g., 0.9000 Silver .2892 oz.

Date	Mintage	F	VF	XF	Unc	BU
1812	28,000	100	200	350	700	—
1813	220,000	50.00	75.00	175	400	—

C# 111 5 LIRE
25.0000 g., 0.9000 Silver .7234 oz.

Date	Mintage	F	VF	XF	Unc	BU
1812	2,921	600	1,200	2,500	5,250	—
1813	37,000	100	275	550	1,200	—

C# 112 20 LIRE
6.4500 g., 0.9000 Gold .1866 oz.

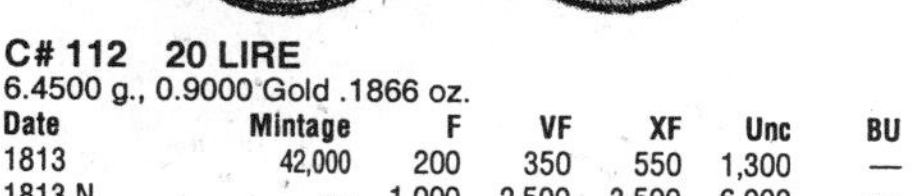

Date	Mintage	F	VF	XF	Unc	BU
1813	42,000	200	350	550	1,300	—
1813 N	—	1,000	2,500	3,500	6,000	—

C# 104 40 FRANCHI
12.9000 g., 0.9000 Gold .3732 oz.

Date	Mintage	F	VF	XF	Unc	BU
1810 Rare	18	—	—	—	—	—

Note: Bowers and Merena Guia sale 3-88 VF realized $19,800; Superior Pipito sale 12-87 about XF realized $30,250

C# 113 40 LIRE
12.9000 g., 0.9000 Gold .3732 oz.

Date	Mintage	F	VF	XF	Unc	BU
1813	24,000	300	500	1,000	2,200	—

TWO SICILIES

REFORM COINAGE

100 Centesimi = 1 Franco = 1 Lira

C# 142 MEZZO (1/2) TORNESE
Copper

Date	F	VF	XF	Unc	BU
1832	2.00	4.00	10.00	27.50	—
1833	2.00	4.00	10.00	27.50	—
1835	2.00	4.00	10.00	27.50	—
1836	2.00	4.00	10.00	27.50	—
1838	2.00	4.00	10.00	27.50	—
1839	2.00	4.00	10.00	27.50	—
1840	4.00	7.00	15.00	32.50	—
1844	2.00	4.00	8.50	22.50	—
1845	2.00	4.00	8.50	22.50	—
1846	2.00	4.00	8.50	22.50	—
1847	2.00	4.00	8.50	22.50	—

C# 142a MEZZO (1/2) TORNESE
Copper

Date	F	VF	XF	Unc	BU
1848	2.00	4.00	8.50	22.50	—
1849	2.00	4.00	8.50	22.50	—
1850	2.00	4.00	8.50	22.50	—
1851	2.00	4.00	8.50	22.50	—
1852	2.00	4.00	8.50	22.50	—
1853	2.00	4.00	8.50	22.50	—
1854	2.00	4.00	8.50	22.50	—

C# 119 UNO (1) TORNESE
Copper

Date	VG	F	VF	XF	Unc
1817	7.50	15.00	25.00	50.00	—

C# 130 UNO (1) TORNESE
Copper

Date	VG	F	VF	XF	Unc
1827	4.00	8.00	15.00	30.00	—

C# 143 UNO (1) TORNESE
Copper **Obv:** Young head without beard, large letters

Date	F	VF	XF	Unc	BU
1832	3.00	6.00	15.00	35.00	—
1833	3.00	6.00	15.00	35.00	—
1835	3.50	6.00	15.00	35.00	—
1836	10.00	17.50	25.00	45.00	—

C# 143a UNO (1) TORNESE
Copper **Obv:** Legend with small letters

Date	F	VF	XF	Unc	BU
1838	3.00	6.00	15.00	35.00	—
1839	3.00	6.00	15.00	35.00	—
1840	3.00	6.00	15.00	35.00	—
1843	10.00	15.00	20.00	45.00	—
1844	3.00	6.00	12.00	30.00	—
1845	3.00	6.00	12.50	30.00	—
1846	3.00	6.00	12.50	30.00	—
1847	3.00	6.00	12.50	30.00	—
1848	10.00	15.00	20.00	45.00	—

C# 143b UNO (1) TORNESE
Copper **Obv:** Older head with beard

Date	F	VF	XF	Unc	BU
1845	2.00	4.00	10.00	25.00	—
1849	2.00	4.00	10.00	25.00	—
1851	2.00	4.00	10.00	25.00	—
1852	2.00	4.00	10.00	25.00	—
1853	2.00	4.00	10.00	25.00	—
1854	2.00	4.00	10.00	25.00	—
1855	8.00	12.50	17.50	38.00	—
1857	2.00	4.00	10.00	25.00	—
1858	2.00	4.00	10.00	25.00	—
1859	2.00	4.00	10.00	25.00	—

C# 144 UNO E MEZZO (1-1/2) TORNESE

Copper **Obv:** Young head without beard

Date	F	VF	XF	Unc	BU
1832	7.50	15.00	30.00	75.00	—
1835	7.50	15.00	30.00	75.00	—
1836	7.50	15.00	30.00	75.00	—
1838	5.00	12.50	40.00	75.00	—
1839	7.50	15.00	30.00	75.00	—
1840	7.50	15.00	30.00	75.00	—

C# 144a UNO E MEZZO (1-1/2) TORNESE

Copper **Obv:** Young head with beard

Date	F	VF	XF	Unc	BU
1844	5.00	12.50	25.00	65.00	—
1847	5.00	12.50	25.00	65.00	—
1848	5.00	12.50	25.00	65.00	—

C# 144b UNO E MEZZO (1-1/2) TORNESE

Copper **Obv:** Older head with beard

Date	F	VF	XF	Unc	BU
1849	5.00	12.50	25.00	60.00	—
1850	5.00	12.50	25.00	60.00	—
1851	5.00	12.50	25.00	60.00	—
1853	5.00	12.50	25.00	60.00	—
1854	5.00	12.50	25.00	60.00	—

C# 131 DUE (2) TORNESI

Copper

Date	VG	F	VF	XF	Unc
1825	3.00	6.50	12.50	25.00	—
1826	3.00	6.50	12.50	25.00	—

C# 145 DUE (2) TORNESI

Copper **Obv:** Young head without beard

Date	F	VF	XF	Unc	BU
1832	12.00	30.00	75.00	125	—
1835	12.00	30.00	75.00	125	—

C# 145a DUE (2) TORNESI

Copper **Obv:** Young head with beard

Date	F	VF	XF	Unc	BU
1838	4.00	13.50	20.00	45.00	—
1839	3.00	7.50	18.00	40.00	—
1842	3.00	7.50	18.00	40.00	—
1843	3.00	7.50	18.00	40.00	—
1847	3.00	7.50	18.00	40.00	—
1848	3.00	7.50	18.00	40.00	—
1849	3.00	7.50	18.00	40.00	—
1851	3.00	7.50	18.00	40.00	—
1852	3.00	7.50	18.00	40.00	—
1853	3.00	7.50	18.00	40.00	—
1854	3.00	7.50	18.00	40.00	—
1855	3.00	7.50	18.00	40.00	—
1856	3.00	7.50	18.00	40.00	—

C# 145b DUE (2) TORNESI

Copper **Note:** Many minor varieties exist such as position of the obverse legend, placement of dots in the legend, large and small dates, etc.

Date	F	VF	XF	Unc	BU
1857	2.50	6.00	18.00	40.00	—
1858	2.50	6.00	18.00	40.00	—
1859	2.50	6.00	18.00	40.00	—

C# 158 DUE (2) TORNESI

Copper

Date	F	VF	XF	Unc	BU
1859	3.50	8.50	20.00	45.00	—

C# 146 TRE (3) TORNESI

Copper **Obv:** Young head without beard

Date	F	VF	XF	Unc	BU
1833	5.00	15.00	30.00	75.00	—
1835	5.00	15.00	30.00	75.00	—
1837	5.00	15.00	30.00	75.00	—
1838	5.00	15.00	30.00	75.00	—

C# 146a TRE (3) TORNESI

Copper **Obv:** Young head with beard

Date	F	VF	XF	Unc	BU
1839	4.00	12.50	25.00	65.00	—
1842	4.00	12.50	25.00	65.00	—
1847	4.00	12.50	25.00	65.00	—
1848	4.00	12.50	25.00	50.00	—
1849	4.00	12.50	25.00	50.00	—
1851	4.00	12.50	25.00	50.00	—
1852	4.00	12.50	25.00	50.00	—
1854	4.00	12.50	25.00	50.00	—
1858	4.00	12.50	25.00	50.00	—

C# 120 QUATTRO (4) TORNESI

Copper

Date	VG	F	VF	XF	Unc
1817	15.00	30.00	45.00	90.00	—

C# 114 CINQUE (5) TORNESI

Copper **Obv. Legend:** FERDINANDVS IV. D. G...

Date	VG	F	VF	XF	Unc
1816	10.00	25.00	35.00	70.00	—

C# 121 CINQUE (5) TORNESI

Copper **Obv. Legend:** FERD. I. D. G...

Date	VG	F	VF	XF	Unc
1816	9.00	25.00	45.00	80.00	—
1817	5.00	10.00	20.00	45.00	—
1818	5.00	10.00	20.00	45.00	—

C# 121a CINQUE (5) TORNESI

Copper

Date	VG	F	VF	XF	Unc
1819	7.50	15.00	30.00	55.00	—

C# 132 CINQUE (5) TORNESI

Copper

Date	VG	F	VF	XF	Unc
1826 Rare	—	—	—	—	—
1827	7.50	15.00	30.00	55.00	—

Note: Many varieties exist of 1827

C# 147 CINQUE (5) TORNESI

Copper **Obv:** Young head without beard

Date	F	VF	XF	Unc	BU
1831	6.00	12.50	25.00	75.00	—
1832	6.00	12.50	25.00	75.00	—
1833	6.00	12.50	25.00	75.00	—
1838	6.00	12.50	25.00	75.00	—
1839	6.00	12.50	25.00	75.00	—
1840	6.00	12.50	25.00	75.00	—
1841	6.00	12.50	25.00	75.00	—

C# 147a CINQUE (5) TORNESI

Copper **Obv:** Young head with beard

Date	F	VF	XF	Unc	BU
1841	5.00	10.00	25.00	75.00	—
1842	5.00	10.00	25.00	75.00	—
1843	5.00	10.00	25.00	75.00	—
1845	5.00	10.00	25.00	75.00	—

C# 147b CINQUE (5) TORNESI

Copper **Obv:** Older head with beard

Date	F	VF	XF	Unc	BU
1846	4.00	8.00	22.00	65.00	—
1847	4.00	8.00	22.00	65.00	—
1848	8.50	17.50	42.00	150	—
1849	4.00	8.00	22.00	65.00	—
1851	4.00	8.00	22.00	65.00	—
1853	4.00	8.00	22.00	65.00	—
1854	4.00	8.00	22.00	65.00	—
1857	4.00	8.00	22.00	65.00	—
1858	6.50	12.50	25.00	70.00	—
1859	4.00	8.00	22.00	65.00	—

Note: Overstruck on 10 Centesimi, 1813, C#107

C# 107a 6 TORNESI

Bronze **Note:** Overstruck on 1813 10 Centesimi, C#107.

Date	F	VF	XF	Unc	BU
ND	650	900	1,500	2,500	—

C# 115 OTTO (8) TORNESI

Copper **Obv:** FERDINANDUS IV D. G. ... **Rev:** Similar to C#122

Date	VG	F	VF	XF	Unc
1816	10.00	20.00	40.00	100	—

C# 122 OTTO (8) TORNESI
Copper **Obv:** FERD. I. D. G. ...

Date	VG	F	VF	XF	Unc
1816	10.00	20.00	35.00	75.00	—
1817	10.00	20.00	35.00	75.00	—
1818	10.00	20.00	35.00	75.00	—

C# 123 DIECI (10) TORNESI
Copper **Rev:** Similar to 5 Tornesi, C#121a

Date	VG	F	VF	XF	Unc
1819	5.00	10.00	30.00	85.00	—

C# 133 DIECI (10) TORNESI
Copper **Rev:** Similar to C#148

Date	VG	F	VF	XF	Unc
1825	5.00	10.00	30.00	75.00	—

C# 148 DIECI (10) TORNESI
Copper **Obv:** Large head without beard

Date	F	VF	XF	Unc	BU
1831	15.00	35.00	75.00	175	—
1832	7.50	17.50	30.00	150	—
1833	7.50	17.50	30.00	150	—
1834	25.00	50.00	100	250	—
1835	7.50	17.50	30.00	90.00	—
1836	16.00	35.00	60.00	160	—
1837	10.00	20.00	40.00	150	—
1838	10.00	20.00	40.00	150	—
1839	10.00	20.00	40.00	100	—

C# 148a DIECI (10) TORNESI
Copper **Obv:** Medium head with beard

Date	F	VF	XF	Unc	BU
1839	7.50	17.50	30.00	90.00	—
1840	12.50	25.00	40.00	95.00	—
1841	7.50	17.50	30.00	90.00	—
1844	7.50	17.50	30.00	90.00	—
1846	7.50	17.50	30.00	90.00	—
1847	10.00	25.00	50.00	150	—
1848	7.50	17.50	30.00	90.00	—
1849	7.50	17.50	30.00	90.00	—
1851	16.00	35.00	60.00	160	—

C# 148b DIECI (10) TORNESI
Copper **Obv:** Older head with beard **Note:** Minor varieties exist, i.e. legend size, location.

Date	F	VF	XF	Unc	BU
1851	6.00	12.50	27.50	75.00	—
1852	6.00	12.50	27.50	75.00	—
1853	6.00	12.50	27.50	75.00	—
1854	6.00	12.50	27.50	75.00	—
1855	6.00	12.50	27.50	75.00	—
1856	6.00	12.50	27.50	75.00	—
1857	9.00	18.00	45.00	135	—
1858	6.00	12.50	27.50	75.00	—
1859	6.00	12.50	27.50	75.00	—

C# 159 DIECI (10) TORNESI
Copper

Date	F	VF	XF	Unc	BU
1859	12.50	25.00	50.00	125	—

C# 149 CINQUE (5) GRANA
1.1500 g., 0.8330 Silver .0308 oz. **Obv:** Young head right without beard

Date	F	VF	XF	Unc	BU
1836	3.50	6.00	15.00	50.00	—
1838	3.50	6.00	15.00	50.00	—
1844	3.50	6.00	15.00	50.00	—
1845	3.50	6.00	15.00	50.00	—
1846	3.50	6.00	15.00	50.00	—
1847	3.50	6.00	15.00	50.00	—

C# 149a CINQUE (5) GRANA
1.1500 g., 0.8330 Silver .0308 oz. **Obv:** Young head with beard

Date	F	VF	XF	Unc	BU
1848	7.50	12.50	20.00	50.00	—
1851	3.50	6.00	15.00	50.00	—
1853	3.50	6.00	15.00	50.00	—

C# 116 10 GRANA
2.2900 g., 0.8330 Silver .0613 oz. **Obv:** Head right **Rev:** Arms

Date	VG	F	VF	XF	Unc
1815	7.50	15.00	35.00	65.00	—
1816	7.50	15.00	35.00	65.00	—

C# 124 10 GRANA
2.2900 g., 0.8330 Silver .0613 oz.

Date	VG	F	VF	XF	Unc
1818	5.00	10.00	20.00	50.00	—

C# 134 10 GRANA
2.2900 g., 0.8330 Silver .0613 oz. **Obv:** Head right

Date	VG	F	VF	XF	Unc
1826	5.00	10.00	15.00	35.00	—

C# 150 10 GRANA
2.2900 g., 0.8330 Silver .0613 oz. **Obv:** Young head without beard, continuous legend

Date	F	VF	XF	Unc	BU
1832	7.50	15.00	30.00	60.00	—
1833	7.50	12.50	25.00	45.00	—
1834	7.50	15.00	30.00	60.00	—
1835	7.50	15.00	30.00	60.00	—

C# 150a 10 GRANA
2.2900 g., 0.8330 Silver .0613 oz. **Obv:** Legend divided over young head without beard

Date	F	VF	XF	Unc	BU
1835	6.00	12.50	20.00	50.00	—
1836	6.00	12.50	20.00	50.00	—
1837	6.00	12.50	20.00	50.00	—
1838	6.00	12.50	20.00	50.00	—
1839	6.00	12.50	20.00	50.00	—

C# 150b 10 GRANA
2.2900 g., 0.8330 Silver .0613 oz. **Obv:** Young head with beard

Date	F	VF	XF	Unc	BU
1838	10.00	18.00	25.00	60.00	—
1839	6.00	12.50	20.00	50.00	—
1840	6.00	12.50	20.00	50.00	—
1841	6.00	12.50	20.00	50.00	—
1842	6.00	12.50	20.00	50.00	—
1843	15.00	25.00	40.00	70.00	—
1844	6.00	12.50	20.00	50.00	—
1845	6.00	12.50	20.00	50.00	—
1846	6.00	12.50	20.00	50.00	—

C# 150c 10 GRANA
2.2900 g., 0.8330 Silver .0613 oz. **Obv:** Older head with beard

Date	F	VF	XF	Unc	BU
1847	5.00	7.50	15.00	40.00	—
1848	5.00	7.50	15.00	40.00	—
1849	10.00	20.00	40.00	100	—
1850	6.00	12.50	20.00	50.00	—
1851	6.00	12.50	20.00	50.00	—
1853	5.00	7.50	15.00	40.00	—
1854	5.00	7.50	15.00	40.00	—
1855	5.00	7.50	15.00	40.00	—
1856	5.00	7.50	15.00	40.00	—
1859	5.00	7.50	15.00	40.00	—

C# 135 20 GRANA
4.5900 g., 0.8330 Silver .1229 oz.

Date	VG	F	VF	XF	Unc
1826	10.00	20.00	40.00	80.00	—

C# 151 20 GRANA
4.5900 g., 0.8330 Silver .1229 oz. **Obv:** Young head without beard

Date	F	VF	XF	Unc	BU
1831	8.50	17.50	35.00	130	—
1832	8.50	17.50	35.00	130	—
1833	8.50	17.50	35.00	130	—
1834	8.50	17.50	35.00	130	—
1835	8.50	17.50	35.00	130	—
1836	8.50	17.50	35.00	130	—
1837	8.50	17.50	35.00	130	—
1838	8.50	17.50	35.00	130	—
1839	8.50	17.50	35.00	130	—

C# 151a 20 GRANA
4.5900 g., 0.8330 Silver .1229 oz. **Obv:** Young head with beard

Date	F	VF	XF	Unc	BU
1839	8.50	17.50	35.00	130	—
1840	8.50	17.50	35.00	130	—
1841	8.50	17.50	35.00	130	—
1842	8.50	17.50	30.00	125	—
1843	8.50	17.50	35.00	130	—
1844	8.50	17.50	35.00	130	—
1845	8.50	17.50	35.00	130	—
1846	12.50	25.00	45.00	150	—
1847	8.50	17.50	35.00	130	—
1848	8.50	17.50	35.00	130	—
1850	8.50	17.50	35.00	130	—
1851	8.50	17.50	35.00	130	—
1852	8.50	17.50	35.00	130	—
1853	8.50	17.50	35.00	130	—
1854	8.50	17.50	35.00	130	—
1855	8.50	17.50	35.00	130	—
1856	8.50	17.50	35.00	130	—
1857	8.50	17.50	35.00	130	—
1858	8.50	17.50	35.00	130	—
1859/8	10.00	22.50	45.00	150	—
1859	8.50	17.50	35.00	130	—

C# 160 20 GRANA
4.5900 g., 0.8330 Silver .1229 oz.

Date	F	VF	XF	Unc	BU
1859	12.50	25.00	65.00	185	—

C# 117 60 GRANA
13.7500 g., 0.8330 Silver .3682 oz. **Obv:** Head right, FERD IV. D. G., etc.

Date	VG	F	VF	XF	Unc
1816	15.00	25.00	75.00	175	—

C# 125 60 GRANA
13.7500 g., 0.8330 Silver .3682 oz. **Obv:** Crowned head right, FERD I D. G., etc.

Date	VG	F	VF	XF	Unc
1818	20.00	35.00	65.00	150	—

C# 136 60 GRANA
13.7500 g., 0.8330 Silver .3682 oz. **Obv:** Head right **Rev:** Arms within wreath

Date	VG	F	VF	XF	Unc
1826	25.00	45.00	90.00	250	—

C# 152 60 GRANA
13.7500 g., 0.8330 Silver .3682 oz. **Obv:** Young head without beard, legend continuous

Date	F	VF	XF	Unc	BU
1831	20.00	35.00	75.00	300	—
1832	20.00	35.00	75.00	300	—
1833	20.00	35.00	75.00	300	—
1834	20.00	35.00	75.00	300	—

C# 152a 60 GRANA
13.7500 g., 0.8330 Silver .3682 oz. **Obv:** Legend divided

Date	F	VF	XF	Unc	BU
1835	20.00	40.00	80.00	350	—
1836	20.00	35.00	75.00	300	—
1837	50.00	90.00	125	600	—
1838	20.00	35.00	75.00	300	—
1839	35.00	60.00	100	350	—

C# 152b 60 GRANA
13.7500 g., 0.8330 Silver .3682 oz. **Obv:** Young head with beard

Date	F	VF	XF	Unc	BU
1841	35.00	65.00	115	300	—
1842	35.00	65.00	115	300	—
1845	35.00	65.00	115	300	—

C# 152c 60 GRANA
13.7500 g., 0.8330 Silver .3682 oz. **Obv:** Older head with beard

Date	F	VF	XF	Unc	BU
1846	35.00	60.00	100	300	—
1847	35.00	60.00	100	300	—
1848	35.00	60.00	100	300	—
1850	35.00	60.00	100	300	—
1851	35.00	60.00	100	300	—
1852	35.00	60.00	100	300	—
1854	35.00	60.00	100	300	—
1855	35.00	60.00	75.00	250	—
1856	35.00	60.00	100	300	—
1857	35.00	60.00	100	300	—
1858	35.00	60.00	100	300	—
1859	35.00	60.00	100	300	—

C# 118 120 GRANA
27.5300 g., 0.8330 Silver .7373 oz.

Date	VG	F	VF	XF	Unc
1815	45.00	70.00	100	200	—
1816	50.00	80.00	125	225	—
1816R	55.00	90.00	140	275	—

Note: The R(istampato) issues were struck over the coins of Joseph Napoleon and Joachim Murat

C# 126 120 GRANA
27.5300 g., 0.8330 Silver .7373 oz. **Obv:** Large crowned head

Date	VG	F	VF	XF	Unc
1817	30.00	50.00	90.00	165	—
1818	20.00	30.00	50.00	145	—

C# 126a 120 GRANA
27.5300 g., 0.8330 Silver .7373 oz. **Obv:** Small crowned head

Date	VG	F	VF	XF	Unc
1818	25.00	35.00	75.00	200	—

C# 137 120 GRANA
27.5300 g., 0.8330 Silver .7373 oz.

Date	F	VF	XF	Unc	BU
1825R	35.00	75.00	200	600	—
1825	45.00	90.00	250	800	—
1826	35.00	75.00	200	600	—
1826 R	45.00	90.00	250	800	—
1828	55.00	100	275	900	—

C# 153 120 GRANA
27.5300 g., 0.8330 Silver .7373 oz. **Rev:** Similar to C#153a

Date	F	VF	XF	Unc	BU
1831	22.50	30.00	75.00	200	—
1832	22.50	30.00	75.00	200	—
1833	30.00	50.00	90.00	225	—
1834	30.00	50.00	90.00	225	—
1835	22.50	30.00	75.00	200	—

C# 153a 120 GRANA
27.5300 g., 0.8330 Silver .7373 oz.

Date	F	VF	XF	Unc	BU
1835	27.50	40.00	90.00	225	—
1836	22.50	30.00	75.00	200	—
1837	30.00	60.00	100	300	—
1838	22.50	30.00	75.00	200	—
1839	30.00	60.00	100	300	—

C# 153b 120 GRANA
27.5300 g., 0.8330 Silver .7373 oz. **Rev:** Similar to C#153a
Note: Many varieties exist.

Date	F	VF	XF	Unc	BU
1840	22.50	30.00	70.00	175	—
1841	22.50	30.00	70.00	175	—
1842	22.50	30.00	70.00	175	—
1843	22.50	30.00	70.00	175	—
1844	22.50	30.00	70.00	175	—
1845	22.50	30.00	70.00	175	—
1846	22.50	30.00	70.00	175	—
1847	25.00	50.00	100	200	—
1848	25.00	50.00	100	200	—
1849	100	150	500	1,000	—

Date	F	VF	XF	Unc	BU
1850	22.50	30.00	50.00	175	—
1851	22.50	30.00	70.00	175	—

C# 153c 120 GRANA

27.5300 g., 0.8330 Silver .7373 oz. **Rev:** Similar to C#153a

Date	F	VF	XF	Unc	BU
1851	22.50	30.00	60.00	125	—
1852	22.50	30.00	60.00	125	—
1853	22.50	30.00	60.00	125	—
1854	22.50	30.00	60.00	125	—
1855	22.50	30.00	60.00	125	—
1856	22.50	30.00	60.00	125	—
1857	22.50	30.00	60.00	125	—
1858	22.50	30.00	60.00	125	—
1859	22.50	30.00	60.00	125	—

C# 161 120 GRANA

27.5300 g., 0.8330 Silver .7373 oz. **Rev:** Similar to C#153a

Date	F	VF	XF	Unc	BU
1859	30.00	50.00	125	250	—

C# 127 3 DUCATI

3.7900 g., 0.9960 Gold .1213 oz.

Date	VG	F	VF	XF	Unc
1818	150	225	350	700	—

C# 138 3 DUCATI

3.7900 g., 0.9960 Gold .1213 oz. **Obv:** Head right **Rev:** Winged Genius

Date	VG	F	VF	XF	Unc
1826	300	450	1,200	2,500	—

C# 154 3 DUCATI

3.7900 g., 0.9960 Gold .1213 oz. **Obv:** Young head without beard

Date	F	VF	XF	Unc	BU
1831	200	250	350	800	—
1832	200	250	350	800	—
1835	200	250	350	800	—

C# 154a 3 DUCATI

3.7900 g., 0.9960 Gold .1213 oz.

Date	F	VF	XF	Unc	BU
1837	200	250	450	1,000	—

C# 154b 3 DUCATI

3.7900 g., 0.9960 Gold .1213 oz. **Obv:** Young head with beard

Date	F	VF	XF	Unc	BU
1839	200	250	325	700	—
1840	200	250	350	750	—

C# 154c 3 DUCATI

3.7900 g., 0.9960 Gold .1213 oz.

Date	F	VF	XF	Unc	BU
1842	200	250	325	700	—
1845	200	250	325	700	—
1846	200	250	350	750	—
1848	200	250	325	700	—

C# 154d 3 DUCATI

3.7900 g., 0.9960 Gold .1213 oz. **Obv:** Older head with beard

Date	F	VF	XF	Unc	BU
1850	175	225	300	500	—
1851	175	225	300	500	—
1852	175	225	300	500	—
1854	125	175	250	450	—
1856	175	225	300	500	—

C# 139 6 DUCATI

7.5700 g., 0.9960 Gold .2424 oz.

Date	VG	F	VF	XF	Unc
1826	200	400	1,500	3,850	—

C# 155 6 DUCATI

7.5700 g., 0.9960 Gold .2424 oz. **Obv:** Young head without beard **Rev:** Winged Genius

Date	F	VF	XF	Unc	BU
1831	200	350	525	1,300	—
1833	200	350	525	1,300	—
1835	250	450	600	1,650	—

C# 155b 6 DUCATI

7.5700 g., 0.9960 Gold .2424 oz. **Obv:** Young head with beard

Date	F	VF	XF	Unc	BU
1840	200	350	525	1,300	—

C# 155c 6 DUCATI

7.5700 g., 0.9960 Gold .2424 oz. **Obv:** Older head with beard

Date	F	VF	XF	Unc	BU
1842	200	350	525	1,300	—
1845	200	350	525	1,300	—
1847	200	350	525	1,300	—
1848	200	350	525	1,300	—
1850	200	350	525	1,300	—
1851	200	350	525	1,300	—
1852	200	350	600	1,300	—
1854	200	350	600	1,300	—
1856	200	350	600	1,300	—

C# 128 15 DUCATI

18.9300 g., 0.9960 Gold .6062 oz.

Date	VG	F	VF	XF	Unc
1818	300	550	750	1,400	—

C# 140 15 DUCATI

18.9300 g., 0.9960 Gold .6062 oz.

Date	F	VF	XF	Unc	BU
1825 Rare	—	—	—	—	—

Note: Bowers and Merena Guia sale 3-88 XF realized $26,400

C# 156 15 DUCATI

18.9300 g., 0.9960 Gold .6062 oz.

Date	F	VF	XF	Unc	BU
1831	500	800	1,250	2,750	—

C# 156c 15 DUCATI

18.9300 g., 0.9960 Gold .6062 oz. **Obv:** Young head with beard **Rev:** Winged Genius

Date	F	VF	XF	Unc	BU
1842	500	800	1,250	2,750	—
1844	450	700	1,000	2,000	—
1845	450	700	1,000	2,000	—
1847	450	700	1,000	2,000	—

C# 156d 15 DUCATI

18.9300 g., 0.9960 Gold .6062 oz. **Obv:** Older head with beard

Date	F	VF	XF	Unc	BU
1848	500	800	1,250	2,750	—
1850	400	675	800	1,750	—
1851	400	675	800	1,750	—
1852	400	675	800	1,750	—
1854	400	675	800	1,750	—
1856	400	675	800	1,750	—

C# 129 30 DUCATI
37.8700 g., 0.9960 Gold 1.2128 oz.

Date	VG	F	VF	XF	Unc
1818	600	750	1,400	2,200	—

C# 141 30 DUCATI
37.8700 g., 0.9960 Gold 1.2128 oz.

Date	VG	F	VF	XF	Unc
1825	600	750	1,500	3,500	—
1826	600	750	1,500	3,500	—

C# 157 30 DUCATI
37.8700 g., 0.9960 Gold 1.2128 oz.

Date	F	VF	XF	Unc	BU
1831	500	800	1,500	2,500	—
1833	550	850	1,600	3,000	—
1835	550	850	1,600	3,000	—

C# 157b 30 DUCATI
37.8700 g., 0.9960 Gold 1.2128 oz.

Date	F	VF	XF	Unc	BU
1839	550	850	1,600	3,000	—
1840	550	850	1,600	3,000	—

C# 157c 30 DUCATI
37.8700 g., 0.9960 Gold 1.2128 oz.

Date	F	VF	XF	Unc	BU
1842 Rare	—	—	—	—	—
1844	550	850	1,600	3,000	—
1845	550	850	1,600	3,000	—
1847	550	850	1,600	3,000	—
1848	550	850	1,600	3,000	—
1851	550	850	1,600	3,000	—
1854	550	850	1,600	3,000	—

C# 157e 30 DUCATI
37.8700 g., 0.9960 Gold 1.2128 oz.

Date	F	VF	XF	Unc	BU
1850	500	800	1,500	2,500	—
1851	550	850	1,600	3,000	—
1852	550	850	1,600	3,000	—

C# 157d 30 DUCATI
37.8700 g., 0.9960 Gold 1.2128 oz. **Obv:** Small older head with beard

Date	F	VF	XF	Unc	BU
1854	550	850	1,600	3,000	—
1856	550	850	1,600	3,000	—

PATTERNS

Including off metal strikes

KM#	Date	Mintage	Identification	Mkt Val
Pn1	1856	—	60 Grana. Gold. C#152.	4,400

PAPAL STATES

During many centuries prior to the formation of the unified Kingdom of Italy, when Italy was divided into numerous independent papal and ducal states, the Popes held temporal sovereignty over an area in central Italy comprising some 17,000 sq. mi. (44,030 sq. km.) including the city of Rome. At the time of the general unification of Italy under the Kingdom of Sardinia, 1861, the papal dominions beyond Rome were acquired by that kingdom diminishing the Pope's sovereignty to Rome and its environs. In 1870, while France's opposition to papal dispossession was neutralized by its war with Prussia, the Italian army seized weakly defended Rome and made it the capital of Italy, thereby abrogating the last vestige of papal temporal power. In 1871, the Italian Parliament enacted the Law of Guarantees, which guaranteed a special status for the Vatican area, and spiritual freedom and a generous income for the Pope. Pope Pius IX and his successors adamantly refused to acknowledge the validity of these laws and voluntarily "imprisoned" themselves in the Vatican. The impasse between State and Church lasted until the signing of the Lateran Treaty, Feb. 11, 1929, by which Italy recognized the sovereignty and independence of the new Vatican City state.

PONTIFFS

Pius VII, 1800-1823
Sede Vacante, Aug. 20-Sept. 28, 1823
Leo XII, 1823-1829
Sede Vacante, Feb. 10-Mar. 31, 1829
Pius VIII, 1829-1830
Sede Vacante, Nov. 30, 1830-Feb. 2, 1831
Gregory XVI, 1831-1846
Sede Vacante, June 1-16, 1846
Pius IX, 1846-1878
Leo XIII, 1878-1903

MINT MARKS

B - Bologna
R – Rome

MONETARY SYSTEM

(Until 1860)

5 Quattrini = 1 Baiocco
5 Baiocchi = 1 Grosso
6 Grossi = 4 Carlini = 3 Giulio =
3 Paoli = 1 Testone.
14 Carlini = 1 Piastre
100 Baiocchi = 1 Scudo
10 Testone = Doppia

PAPACY

STANDARD COINAGE

KM# 1260 QUATTRINO
Copper **Ruler:** Pius VII **Note:** SAEROSAN.

Date	VG	F	VF	XF	Unc
MDCCCI (1801)R	5.00	10.00	25.00	45.00	—

KM# 1264 QUATTRINO
Copper **Ruler:** Pius VII

Date	VG	F	VF	XF	Unc
MDCCCII (1802)-IIR	4.00	7.50	12.50	25.00	—

KM# 1276.1 QUATTRINO
Copper **Ruler:** Pius VII **Obv:** Value: QVATTRINO

Date	VG	F	VF	XF	Unc
MDCCCXVI (1816)-XVIR	4.00	7.50	12.50	25.00	—
MDCCCXVI (1816)-XVIIR	6.00	10.00	15.00	35.00	—
MDCCCXXI (1821)-XXIIR	8.00	10.00	15.00	35.00	—

KM# 1276.3 QUATTRINO
Copper **Ruler:** Pius VII

Date	VG	F	VF	XF	Unc
MDCCCXVI (1816)-XVIB	4.00	7.50	12.50	25.00	—
MDCCCXXI (1821)-XXIIB	8.00	10.00	17.50	35.00	—
MDCCCXXII (1822)-XXIIB	4.00	7.50	12.50	25.00	—

KM# 1276.2 QUATTRINO
Copper **Ruler:** Pius VII **Obv:** Value: VN QVATTRINO

Date	VG	F	VF	XF	Unc
MDCCCXVI (1816)-XVIB	20.00	35.00	50.00	90.00	—

KM# 1294.1 QUATTRINO
Copper **Ruler:** Leo XII

Date	VG	F	VF	XF	Unc
1824-I (B)	4.00	8.00	15.00	30.00	—

KM# 1294.2 QUATTRINO
Copper **Ruler:** Leo XII

Date	VG	F	VF	XF	Unc
1824-IR	3.00	7.00	15.00	30.00	—
1825-IIR	3.00	7.00	15.00	30.00	—

KM# 1298 QUATTRINO
Copper **Ruler:** Leo XII

Date	VG	F	VF	XF	Unc
1826-IVR	3.00	7.00	15.00	30.00	—

KM# 1299 QUATTRINO
Copper **Ruler:** Pius VIII

Date	VG	F	VF	XF	Unc
1829-IR	4.00	10.00	20.00	40.00	—

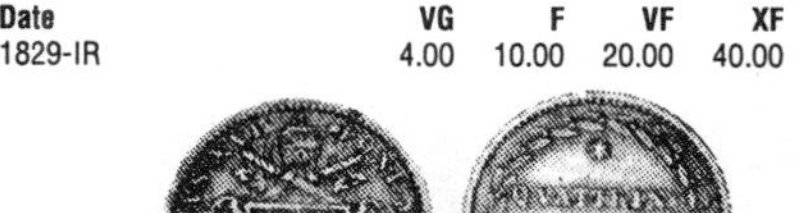

KM# 1312 QUATTRINO

Copper **Ruler:** Gregory XVI **Note:** Retrograde 1s in date.

Date	VG	F	VF	XF	Unc
1831-IR	2.00	4.00	7.50	15.00	—

KM# 1318 QUATTRINO

Copper **Ruler:** Gregory XVI

Date	VG	F	VF	XF	Unc
1835-VR	2.00	4.00	7.50	20.00	—
1836-VIB	2.00	4.00	7.50	20.00	—
1838-VIIIR	2.00	4.00	7.50	20.00	—
1839-IXB	4.00	7.50	12.50	25.00	—
1839-IXR	2.00	4.00	7.50	20.00	—
1840-XB	4.00	7.50	12.50	25.00	—
1841-XR	3.00	5.00	8.50	20.00	—
1841-XIR	2.00	7.50	12.50	25.00	—
1843-XIIIB	2.00	4.00	7.50	20.00	—
1843-XIIIR	2.00	4.00	7.50	20.00	—
1844-XIVB	2.00	4.00	7.50	20.00	—
1844-XIVR	2.00	4.00	7.50	20.00	—

KM# 1359 QUATTRINO

Copper **Ruler:** Pius IX

Date	Mintage	VG	F	VF	XF	Unc
1851-VIR	90,000	3.00	5.00	8.50	18.00	—
1854-IXB	173,000	3.00	5.00	8.50	18.00	—

KM# 1261 MEZZO (1/2) BAIOCCO

Copper **Ruler:** Pius VII **Note:** Varieties exist. SACROSAN.

Date	VG	F	VF	XF	Unc
MDCCCI (1801)R	4.00	7.50	15.00	30.00	—

KM# 1265 MEZZO (1/2) BAIOCCO

Copper **Ruler:** Pius VII

Date	VG	F	VF	XF	Unc
MDCCCII (1802)-IIR	3.00	5.00	12.00	25.00	—

KM# 1277 MEZZO (1/2) BAIOCCO

Copper **Ruler:** Pius VII

Date	VG	F	VF	XF	Unc
MDCCCXVI (1816)-XVIR	6.00	10.00	15.00	35.00	—
MDCCCXVI (1816)-XVIIR	6.00	10.00	15.00	35.00	—

KM# 1278 MEZZO (1/2) BAIOCCO

Copper **Ruler:** Pius VII

Date	VG	F	VF	XF	Unc
MDCCCXVI (1816)-XVIB	3.00	5.00	8.50	15.00	—
MDCCCXVI (1816)-XVIIB	3.00	5.00	8.50	15.00	—
MDCCCXXII (1822)-XXIIB	4.00	7.50	14.00	25.00	—
MDCCCXXII (1822)-XXIIR	4.00	7.50	14.00	25.00	—

KM# 1290 MEZZO (1/2) BAIOCCO

Copper **Ruler:** Pius VII

Date	VG	F	VF	XF	Unc
MDCCCXXII (1822)-XXIIR	10.00	20.00	35.00	50.00	—

KM# 1295 MEZZO (1/2) BAIOCCO

Copper **Ruler:** Leo XII

Date	VG	F	VF	XF	Unc
1824-IB	6.00	12.50	20.00	35.00	—

KM# 1296 MEZZO (1/2) BAIOCCO

Copper **Ruler:** Leo XII

Date	VG	F	VF	XF	Unc
1825-IIR	4.00	9.00	18.00	35.00	—
1826-IIIR	4.00	9.00	18.00	35.00	—

KM# 1300 MEZZO (1/2) BAIOCCO

Copper **Ruler:** Pius VIII

Date	VG	F	VF	XF	Unc
1829-IB	6.00	15.00	30.00	55.00	—
1829-IR	6.00	15.00	30.00	55.00	—

KM# 1313 MEZZO (1/2) BAIOCCO

Copper **Ruler:** Gregory XVI

Date	VG	F	VF	XF	Unc
1831-IR	2.00	4.00	7.50	20.00	—
1832-IIB	3.00	6.00	10.00	25.00	—
1832-IIIB	2.00	5.00	9.00	22.00	—
1833-IIIB	2.00	4.00	7.50	20.00	—
1834-IVB	2.00	4.00	7.50	20.00	—

KM# 1319 MEZZO (1/2) BAIOCCO

Copper **Ruler:** Gregory XVI

Date	VG	F	VF	XF	Unc
1835-VB	2.00	4.00	7.50	15.00	—
1835-VR	2.00	4.00	7.50	15.00	—
1836-VIB	2.00	4.00	7.50	15.00	—
1836/5-VIR	2.00	4.00	7.50	15.00	—
1836-VIR	2.00	4.00	7.50	15.00	—
1837-VIIB	2.00	4.00	7.50	15.00	—
1837-VIIR	3.50	6.50	12.50	17.50	—
1838-VIIIB	2.00	4.00	7.50	15.00	—
1838-VIIIR	3.50	6.50	12.50	17.50	—
1839-IXB	2.00	4.00	7.50	15.00	—
1839-IXR	3.50	6.50	12.50	17.50	—
1840-IXR	3.50	6.50	12.50	17.50	—
1840-XB	3.00	5.00	8.50	15.00	—
1840-XR	2.00	4.00	7.50	15.00	—
1841-XB	3.00	6.00	9.00	17.50	—
1841-XIR	2.00	4.00	7.50	15.00	—
1842-XIB	2.00	4.00	7.50	15.00	—
1842-XIIB	2.00	4.00	7.50	15.00	—
1842-XIIR	2.00	4.00	7.50	15.00	—
1843-XIIB	2.00	4.00	7.50	15.00	—
1843-XIIIB	2.00	4.00	7.50	15.00	—
1843-XIIIR	2.00	4.00	7.50	15.00	—
1844-XIIIB	2.00	4.00	7.50	15.00	—
1844-XIVB	2.00	4.00	7.50	15.00	—
1844-XIVR	2.00	4.00	7.50	15.00	—
1845-XVB	2.00	4.00	7.50	15.00	—
1845-XVR	2.00	4.00	7.50	15.00	—

KM# 1340 MEZZO (1/2) BAIOCCO

Copper **Ruler:** Pius IX

Date	Mintage	VG	F	VF	XF	Unc
1847-IIB	74,000	2.00	4.00	7.50	22.50	—
1847-IIR	9,000	3.50	6.50	12.50	25.00	—
1848/7-IIB	49,000	2.50	4.50	7.50	22.50	—
1848-IIB	Inc. above	3.50	6.50	12.50	25.00	—
1848-IIR	644,000	2.00	4.00	7.50	22.50	—
1848-IIIR	Inc. above	2.00	4.00	7.50	22.50	—
1848-IIIIR	Inc. above	3.50	6.50	12.50	25.00	—
1849-IIIB	104,000	2.00	4.00	7.50	22.50	—
1849-IVB	Inc. above	2.00	4.00	7.50	22.50	—
1849-IIIIR	1,921,000	2.00	4.00	7.50	22.50	—
1849-IVR	Inc. above	2.00	4.00	7.00	22.50	—

KM# 1355 MEZZO (1/2) BAIOCCO

Copper **Ruler:** Pius IX

Date	Mintage	VG	F	VF	XF	Unc
1850-IVB	176,000	2.00	4.00	7.50	15.00	—
1850-IVR	5,552,000	2.00	4.00	7.50	15.00	—
1850-VB	Inc. above	2.00	4.00	7.50	15.00	—
1850-VR	Inc. above	2.00	4.00	7.50	15.00	—
1851-VB	1,257,000	2.00	4.00	7.50	15.00	—
1851-VR	4,001,000	2.00	4.00	7.50	15.00	—
1851-VIB	Inc. above	2.00	4.00	7.50	15.00	—
1851-VIR	Inc. above	2.00	4.00	7.50	15.00	—
1852-VIB	706,000	2.00	4.00	7.50	15.00	—

KM# 1246 BAIOCCO

Copper **Ruler:** Pius VII

Date	VG	F	VF	XF	Unc
MDCCCI (1801)-IR	12.00	25.00	45.00	75.00	—

KM# 1263 BAIOCCO
Copper **Ruler:** Pius VII

Date	VG	F	VF	XF	Unc
MDCCCI (1801)R	5.00	12.00	20.00	38.00	—

KM# 1266 BAIOCCO
Copper **Ruler:** Pius VII **Rev:** G. PASINATES S. C. below date

Date	VG	F	VF	XF	Unc
MDCCCI (1801)R	25.00	50.00	75.00	125	—

KM# 1262 BAIOCCO
Copper **Ruler:** Pius VII **Note:** SACROSAN.

Date	VG	F	VF	XF	Unc
MDCCCI (1801)R	5.00	12.00	20.00	38.00	—

KM# 1267 BAIOCCO
Copper **Ruler:** Pius VII

Date	VG	F	VF	XF	Unc
MDCCCII (1802)-IIR	5.00	12.00	20.00	32.00	—
MDCCCXV (1815)-XVIB	5.00	12.00	20.00	32.00	—

KM# 1279 BAIOCCO
Copper **Ruler:** Pius VII

Date	VG	F	VF	XF	Unc
MDCCCXVI (1816)-XVIB	5.00	12.00	20.00	32.00	—
MDCCCXVI (1816)-XVIR	5.00	12.00	20.00	32.00	—
MDCCCXVI (1816)-XVIIB	5.00	12.00	20.00	32.00	—
MDCCCXVI (1816)-XVIIR	15.00	30.00	50.00	90.00	—

KM# 1301 BAIOCCO
Copper **Ruler:** Pius VIII **Note:** Two varieties of inscription exist.

Date	VG	F	VF	XF	Unc
1829-IR	7.50	20.00	35.00	50.00	—

KM# 1314 BAIOCCO
Copper **Ruler:** Gregory XVI

Date	VG	F	VF	XF	Unc
1831-IR	5.00	10.00	15.00	25.00	—
1832-IR	15.00	25.00	45.00	70.00	—
1832-IIR	7.50	12.50	25.00	45.00	—

KM# 1320 BAIOCCO
Copper **Ruler:** Gregory XVI

Date	VG	F	VF	XF	Unc
1835-VB	2.00	5.00	8.00	22.00	—
1835-VR	2.00	5.00	8.00	22.00	—
1836-VIB	2.00	5.00	8.00	22.00	—
1836-VIR	2.00	5.00	8.00	22.00	—
1837-VIIB	2.00	5.00	8.00	22.00	—
1837-VIIR	2.00	5.00	8.00	22.00	—
1838-VIIIB	15.00	25.00	45.00	75.00	—
1838-VIIIR	5.00	10.00	15.00	25.00	—
1839-VIIIR	7.50	12.50	20.00	30.00	—
1839-IXB	2.00	5.00	8.00	22.00	—
1839-IXR	5.00	10.00	15.00	25.00	—
1840-XB	2.00	5.00	8.00	22.00	—
1840-XR	2.00	5.00	8.00	22.00	—
1841-XB	5.00	10.00	15.00	25.00	—
1841-XIB	10.00	20.00	35.00	50.00	—
1841-XIR	3.50	6.50	12.50	17.50	—
1842-XIR	3.50	6.50	12.50	17.50	—
1842-XIIB	2.00	5.00	8.00	22.00	—
1842-XIIR	3.50	6.50	12.50	17.50	—
1843-XIIR	3.50	6.50	12.50	17.50	—
1843-XIIIB	3.50	6.50	12.50	17.50	—
1843-XIIIR	3.50	6.50	12.50	17.50	—
1844-XIIIB	2.00	5.00	10.00	25.00	—
1844-XIVB	2.00	5.00	10.00	25.00	—
1844-XIVR	2.00	5.00	10.00	25.00	—
1845-XVB	2.00	5.00	10.00	25.00	—
1845-XVR	3.50	6.50	12.50	17.50	—

KM# 1339.1 BAIOCCO
Copper **Ruler:** Pius IX **Note:** Varieties of date wording exist.

Date	Mintage	VG	F	VF	XF	Unc
1846-IB	—	6.00	10.00	17.50	30.00	—
1846-IR	7,500	4.00	7.50	12.50	25.00	—
1847-IB	58,000	4.00	7.50	12.50	25.00	—
1847-IR	14,000	7.50	12.50	20.00	35.00	—
1847-IIR	Inc. above	4.00	7.50	12.50	25.00	—
1848-IIR	494,000	3.50	6.50	12.50	17.50	—
1848-IIIR	Inc. above	2.00	4.00	7.50	15.00	—
1848-IVR	Inc. above	2.00	4.00	7.50	15.00	—
1849-IIIB Rare	—	—	—	—	—	—
1849-IVB Rare	—	—	—	—	—	—
1849-IVR Rare	—	—	—	—	—	—

KM# 1345 BAIOCCO
Copper **Ruler:** Pius IX

Date	Mintage	VG	F	VF	XF	Unc
1850-IVB	402,000	2.00	7.00	12.50	25.00	—
1850-IVR	4,681,000	2.00	6.00	9.00	17.50	—
1850-VB	Inc. above	2.00	7.00	12.50	25.00	—
1850-VR	Inc. above	2.00	6.00	9.00	17.50	—
1851-VB	899,000	2.00	6.00	9.00	17.50	—
1851-VR	5,706,000	2.00	7.00	12.50	25.00	—
1851-VIB	Inc. above	2.00	4.00	7.50	15.00	—
1851-VIR	Inc. above	2.00	7.00	12.50	25.00	—
1852-VIB	655,000	2.00	4.00	7.50	15.00	—
1852-VIR	1,211,000	7.50	15.00	20.00	35.00	—
1853-VIIR	35,000	7.50	15.00	20.00	35.00	—

KM# 1343 2 BAIOCCHI (Muraiola)
Copper **Ruler:** Pius IX

Date	Mintage	VG	F	VF	XF	Unc
1848-IIIB	644,000	3.00	8.00	14.00	22.00	—
1848-IIIR	227,000	3.00	8.00	14.00	22.00	—
1849-IVR	1,117,000	3.00	8.00	14.00	22.00	—
1849-IIIB	—	3.00	8.00	14.00	22.00	—
1849-IVB	—	3.00	8.00	14.00	22.00	—

KM# 1344 2 BAIOCCHI (Muraiola)
Copper **Ruler:** Pius IX

Date	Mintage	VG	F	VF	XF	Unc
1850-IVB	—	3.00	8.00	14.00	22.00	—
1850-IVR	3,784,000	3.00	8.00	14.00	22.00	—
1850-VB	—	7.50	12.50	20.00	35.00	—
1850-VR	Inc. above	2.00	7.00	12.00	20.00	—
1851-VB	—	2.00	7.00	12.00	20.00	—
1851-VR	2,557,000	2.00	7.00	12.00	20.00	—
1851-VIB	—	2.00	7.00	12.00	20.00	—
1851-VIR	Inc. above	2.00	7.00	12.00	20.00	—
1852-VB	—	5.00	10.00	17.50	30.00	—
1852-VR	1,727,000	4.00	9.00	15.00	25.00	—
1852-VIB	—	2.00	7.00	12.00	20.00	—
1852-VIR	Inc. above	2.00	7.00	12.00	20.00	—
1852-VIIR	Inc. above	4.00	9.00	15.00	30.00	—
1853-VIR	1,460,000	4.00	9.00	15.00	30.00	—
1853-VIIB	—	3.50	8.00	12.50	22.50	—
1853-VIIR	Inc. above	2.00	7.00	12.00	20.00	—
1853-VIIIR	Inc. above	2.00	7.00	12.00	20.00	—
1854-VIIIR	5,000	35.00	75.00	100	140	—

KM# 1075 GROSSO
1.3210 g., 0.9170 Silver 0.0389 oz. **Ruler:** Pius VII

Date	VG	F	VF	XF	Unc
MDCCCXV (1815) XVIR	7.50	15.00	22.50	40.00	—
MDCCCXVI (1816) XVIB	15.00	25.00	40.00	70.00	—
MDCCCXVI (1816) XVIIB	7.50	15.00	22.50	40.00	—
MDCCCXVII (1817) XVIIB	7.50	15.00	22.50	40.00	—

KM# 1321 5 BAIOCCHI
1.3430 g., 0.9000 Silver .0388 oz. **Ruler:** Gregory XVI

Date	VG	F	VF	XF	Unc
1835-VR	3.00	7.50	15.00	25.00	—
1836-VIB	3.00	7.50	15.00	25.00	—
1839-IXR	5.00	10.00	17.50	30.00	—
1840-XB	3.00	7.50	15.00	25.00	—
1841-XR	10.00	20.00	35.00	50.00	—
1841-XIB	3.00	7.50	15.00	25.00	—
1841-XIR	15.00	25.00	40.00	70.00	—
1842-XIB	3.00	7.50	15.00	25.00	—
1842-XIR	15.00	25.00	40.00	70.00	—
1842-XIIB	3.00	7.50	15.00	25.00	—
1842-XIIR	3.00	7.50	15.00	25.00	—
1843-XIIIB	3.00	7.50	15.00	25.00	—
1843-XIIIR	3.00	7.50	15.00	25.00	—
1844-XIIIB	3.00	7.50	15.00	25.00	—
1844-XIVB	3.00	7.50	15.00	25.00	—
1844/3R	3.50	8.00	17.50	32.50	—
1844-XIVR	3.00	7.50	15.00	25.00	—
1845-XVB	3.00	7.50	15.00	25.00	—
1845-XVR	3.00	7.50	15.00	25.00	—
1846-XVIR	3.00	7.50	15.00	25.00	—

KM# 1341a 5 BAIOCCHI
1.3430 g., 0.9000 Silver .0388 oz. **Ruler:** Pius IX

Date	Mintage	VG	F	VF	XF	Unc
1847-IB	2,387,000	3.00	7.50	15.00	25.00	—
1847-IIR	1,191,000	3.00	7.50	15.00	25.00	—
1848-IIR	2,122	18.00	40.00	75.00	125	—
1849-IVR	21,000	3.00	7.50	15.00	25.00	—
1850-VR	10,000	3.00	7.50	15.00	25.00	—
1851-VR	11,000	3.00	7.50	15.00	25.00	—
1851-VIR	Inc. above	3.00	7.50	15.00	25.00	—
1852-VIIR	20,000	3.00	7.50	15.00	25.00	—
1853-VIIR	14,000	3.00	7.50	15.00	25.00	—
1855-IXR	9,200	18.00	40.00	75.00	120	—
1855-XR	Inc. above	18.00	40.00	75.00	120	—

KM# 1346 5 BAIOCCHI
Copper **Ruler:** Pius IX

Date	Mintage	VG	F	VF	XF	Unc
1849-IVB	—	5.00	12.00	25.00	40.00	—
1849-IVR	938,000	5.00	12.00	25.00	40.00	—
1850-IVB	—	5.00	12.00	25.00	40.00	—
1850-IVR	10,164,000	5.00	12.00	25.00	40.00	—
1850-VB	—	5.00	12.00	25.00	40.00	—
1850-VR	Inc. above	5.00	12.00	25.00	40.00	—

KM# 1356 5 BAIOCCHI
Copper **Ruler:** Pius IX **Rev:** Similar to KM#1346

Date	Mintage	VG	F	VF	XF	Unc
1850-VB	—	5.00	12.00	22.50	37.50	—
1850-VR	Inc. above	5.00	12.00	22.50	37.50	—
1851-VB	—	5.00	12.00	22.50	37.50	—
1851-VR	7,949,000	5.00	12.00	22.50	37.50	—
1851-VIB	—	4.00	12.00	22.50	37.50	—
1851-VIR	Inc. above	4.00	12.00	22.50	37.50	—
1852-VIB	—	4.00	12.00	22.50	37.50	—
1852-VIR	9,746,000	4.00	12.00	22.50	37.50	—
1852-VIIB	—	4.00	12.00	22.50	37.50	—
1853-VIIB	Inc. above	4.00	12.00	22.50	37.50	—
1853-VIIB	—	4.00	12.00	22.50	37.50	—
1853-VIIR	8,428,000	4.00	12.00	22.50	37.50	—
1853-VIIIB	—	4.00	12.00	22.50	37.50	—
1853-VIIIR	Inc. above	4.00	12.00	22.50	37.50	—
1854-VIIIB	—	—	—	—	—	—
1854-VIIIR	1,977,000	9.00	17.50	25.00	45.00	—
1854-IXB	—	4.00	12.00	22.50	37.50	—
1854-IXR	Inc. above	9.00	17.50	25.00	45.00	—

KM# 1341b 5 BAIOCCHI
1.4280 g., 0.8000 Silver .0367 oz. **Ruler:** Pius IX

Date	Mintage	VG	F	VF	XF	Unc
1856-XR	3,440	18.00	40.00	75.00	120	—
1857-XIR	23,000	3.00	7.50	15.00	30.00	—
1858-XIIR	1,573,000	3.00	7.50	15.00	25.00	—
1858-XIIIB	224,000	10.00	25.00	40.00	75.00	—
1858-XIIIR	Inc. above	3.00	7.50	15.00	30.00	—
1859-XIIIB	173,000	10.00	25.00	40.00	75.00	—
1859-XIIIR	83,000	3.00	7.50	15.00	30.00	—
1860-XVR	169,000	3.00	7.50	15.00	25.00	—
1861-XVIR	147,000	3.00	7.50	15.00	25.00	—
1862-XVIIR	135,000	3.00	7.50	15.00	25.00	—
1863-XVIIIR	44,000	3.00	7.50	15.00	30.00	—
1864-XIXR	101,000	3.00	7.50	15.00	30.00	—

KM# 1341c 5 BAIOCCHI
1.3330 g., 0.8350 Silver .0357 oz. **Ruler:** Pius IX

Date	Mintage	VG	F	VF	XF	Unc
1865-XIXR	106,000	9.00	15.00	25.00	45.00	—
1865-XXR	Inc. above	3.00	7.50	15.00	30.00	—
1866-XXR	40,000	5.00	10.00	17.50	35.00	—

KM# 1079 GIULIO
2.6420 g., 0.9170 Silver .0779 oz. **Ruler:** Pius VII

Date	VG	F	VF	XF	Unc
1817/6-XVIIIB	18.00	38.00	55.00	100	—
1817-XVIIIB	15.00	35.00	45.00	100	—

KM# 1325 10 BAIOCCHI
2.6870 g., 0.9000 Silver .0777 oz. **Ruler:** Gregory XVI

Date	Good	VG	F	VF	XF
1836-VIB	12.50	25.00	40.00	75.00	—
1836-VIR	5.00	10.00	15.00	35.00	—
1839-IXB	5.00	10.00	15.00	35.00	—
1839-IXR	5.00	10.00	15.00	35.00	—
1841-XIB	5.00	8.00	15.00	30.00	—
1841-XIR	10.00	20.00	35.00	50.00	—
1842-XIB	5.00	10.00	15.00	35.00	—
1842-XIIB	5.00	8.00	15.00	30.00	—
1842-XIIR	12.50	25.00	40.00	75.00	—
1843-XIIIB	5.00	10.00	15.00	35.00	—
1844-XIVB	5.00	10.00	15.00	35.00	—
1846-XVIR	10.00	20.00	35.00	50.00	—

KM# 1342a 10 BAIOCCHI
2.6870 g., 0.9000 Silver .0777 oz. **Ruler:** Pius IX

Date	Mintage	VG	F	VF	XF	Unc
1847-IB	11,000	12.50	25.00	40.00	75.00	—
1847-IIB	Inc. above	12.50	25.00	40.00	75.00	—
1847-IIR	12,000	5.00	10.00	15.00	35.00	—
1848/7-IIIR	33,000	5.00	10.00	15.00	35.00	—
1848-IIB	17,000	12.50	25.00	40.00	75.00	—
1848-IIR	Inc. above	5.00	10.00	15.00	35.00	—
1848-IIIB	Inc. above	12.50	25.00	40.00	75.00	—
1848-IIIR	Inc. above	5.00	10.00	15.00	35.00	—
1849-IIIIR	1,274	25.00	45.00	75.00	125	—
1850-IIIIR	89,000	5.00	10.00	15.00	35.00	—
1850-VR	Inc. above	5.00	10.00	15.00	35.00	—
1852-VIIR	33,000	5.00	10.00	15.00	35.00	—
1853-VIIR	41,000	5.00	10.00	15.00	35.00	—
1854-VIIIR	5,570	35.00	75.00	100	175	—
1855-IXR	4,400	35.00	75.00	100	175	—
1856-XR	1,140	45.00	80.00	100	175	—

KM# 1342b 10 BAIOCCHI
2.8570 g., 0.8000 Silver .0734 oz. **Ruler:** Pius IX

Date	Mintage	VG	F	VF	XF	Unc
1858-XIIR	2,548,000	3.50	7.50	15.00	25.00	—
1858-XIIIR	—	4.00	7.50	15.00	25.00	—
1858-XIIIB	Inc. above	10.00	25.00	40.00	75.00	—
1859-XIIIR	88,000	10.00	20.00	35.00	50.00	—
1860-XIVR	150,000	10.00	20.00	35.00	50.00	—
1861-XVIR	327,000	3.00	7.50	15.00	25.00	—
1862-XVIR	7,417,000	3.00	7.50	15.00	25.00	—
1862-XVIIR	Inc. above	3.00	7.50	15.00	25.00	—
1863-XVIR	—	65.00	125	175	225	—
1863-XVIIR	1,084,000	3.00	7.50	15.00	25.00	—
1863-XVIIIR	Inc. above	3.00	7.50	15.00	25.00	—
1864-XVIIIR	1,147,000	8.00	20.00	35.00	50.00	—
1864-XIXR	Inc. above	8.00	20.00	35.00	50.00	—

KM# 1342c 10 BAIOCCHI
2.6660 g., 0.8350 Silver .0715 oz. **Ruler:** Pius IX

Date	Mintage	VG	F	VF	XF	Unc
1865-XIXR	409,000	7.00	15.00	22.50	40.00	—
1865-XXR	Inc. above	7.00	15.00	22.50	40.00	—

KM# 1816 DOPPIO (2) GIULIO (1/5 Scudo)
5.2850 g., 0.9170 Silver .1558 oz. **Ruler:** Pius VII

Date	VG	F	VF	XF	Unc
1816-XVIIB	25.00	50.00	90.00	135	—
1816-XVIIIB	35.00	75.00	110	150	—
1818-XVIIB	10.00	20.00	38.00	65.00	—
1818-XVIIIB	10.00	20.00	38.00	65.00	—

KM# 1823 DOPPIO (2) GIULIO (1/5 Scudo)
5.2850 g., 0.9170 Silver .1558 oz. **Obv:** Arms of Cardinal Bartolomeo Pacca **Note:** Sede Vacante issue.

Date	VG	F	VF	XF	Unc
1823B	35.00	75.00	110	175	—

KM# 1317 20 BAIOCCHI
5.2850 g., 0.9170 Silver .1558 oz. **Ruler:** Gregory XVI

Date	VG	F	VF	XF	Unc
1834-IVR	15.00	25.00	45.00	70.00	—

KM# 1322 20 BAIOCCHI
5.3740 g., 0.9000 Silver .1555 oz. **Ruler:** Gregory XVI

Date	VG	F	VF	XF	Unc
1835-VB	8.00	15.00	18.00	30.00	—
1835-VR	10.00	20.00	30.00	40.00	—
1836-VR	80.00	125	200	350	—
1836-VIB	8.00	15.00	18.00	30.00	—
1836-VIR	40.00	75.00	100	175	—
1837-VIIR	20.00	40.00	75.00	120	—
1838-VIIIB	8.00	15.00	18.00	30.00	—
1838-VIIIR	10.00	20.00	30.00	40.00	—
1839-IXR	10.00	20.00	30.00	40.00	—
1840-XB	8.00	15.00	18.00	30.00	—
1841-XIB	8.00	15.00	18.00	30.00	—
1841-XIR	10.00	20.00	30.00	40.00	—
1842-XIIB	25.00	45.00	75.00	125	—
1842-XIIR	10.00	20.00	30.00	40.00	—
1844-XIIIB	8.00	15.00	18.00	30.00	—
1844-XIIIR	100	200	350	650	—
1844-XIVB	8.00	15.00	18.00	30.00	—
1845-XVB	8.00	15.00	18.00	30.00	—
1846XVIR	10.00	20.00	30.00	40.00	—

KM# 1337 20 BAIOCCHI
5.3740 g., 0.9000 Silver .1555 oz. **Ruler:** Pius IX **Note:** Two varieties of ANNO III exist.

Date	Mintage	VG	F	VF	XF	Unc
1848-IIR	—	8.00	20.00	35.00	50.00	—
1848-IIIR	—	8.00	20.00	35.00	50.00	—
1849-IIIB	—	10.00	25.00	40.00	75.00	—
1849-IVB	—	15.00	25.00	40.00	75.00	—
1849-IVR	—	8.00	20.00	35.00	50.00	—
1850-IVB	—	15.00	25.00	40.00	75.00	—
1850-IVR	—	8.00	15.00	22.50	40.00	—
1850-VR	—	8.00	15.00	22.50	40.00	—
1851-VB	—	15.00	25.00	40.00	75.00	—
1852-VIIB	—	30.00	60.00	90.00	125	—
1852-VIIR	10,000	15.00	25.00	40.00	75.00	—
1853-VIIR	126,000	10.00	25.00	40.00	75.00	—
1854-VIIIR	—	8.00	20.00	35.00	50.00	—
1856-XR	—	10.00	25.00	40.00	75.00	—

KM# 1360 20 BAIOCCHI
5.7140 g., 0.8000 Silver .1469 oz. **Ruler:** Pius IX

Date	Mintage	VG	F	VF	XF	Unc
1858-XIIB	—	10.00	25.00	40.00	75.00	—
1858-XIIR	—	6.00	15.00	22.50	40.00	—
1858-XIIIB	—	10.00	20.00	35.00	60.00	—
1858-XIIIR	—	4.00	10.00	15.00	25.00	—
1859-XIIIB	604,000	8.00	20.00	35.00	60.00	—
1859-XIIIR	1,104,000	4.00	12.00	20.00	28.00	—
1859-XIVR	Inc. above	4.00	12.00	20.00	28.00	—
1860/50R	—	4.00	10.00	15.00	25.00	—
1860-XIVR	3,656,000	4.00	10.00	15.00	25.00	—
1860-XVR	Inc. above	4.00	10.00	15.00	25.00	—
1861-XVR	2,987,000	4.00	12.00	20.00	28.00	—
1861-XVIR	Inc. above	4.00	12.00	20.00	28.00	—
1862-XVIR	1,150,000	4.00	12.00	20.00	28.00	—
1862-XVIIR	Inc. above	4.00	12.00	20.00	28.00	—

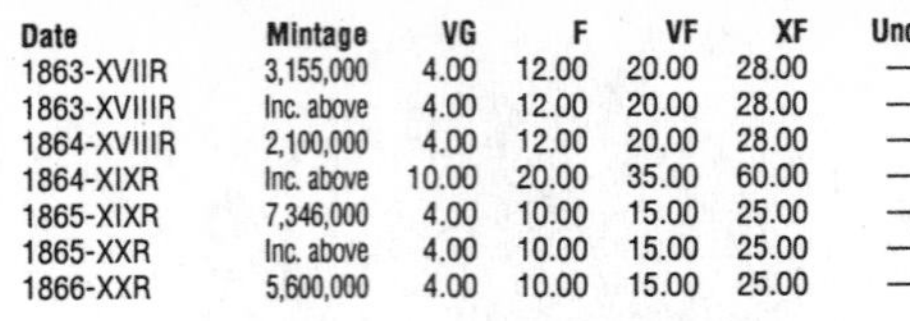

Date	Mintage	VG	F	VF	XF	Unc
1863-XVIIR	3,155,000	4.00	12.00	20.00	28.00	—
1863-XVIIIR	Inc. above	4.00	12.00	20.00	28.00	—
1864-XVIIIR	2,100,000	4.00	12.00	20.00	28.00	—
1864-XIXR	Inc. above	10.00	20.00	35.00	60.00	—
1865-XIXR	7,346,000	4.00	10.00	15.00	25.00	—
1865-XXR	Inc. above	4.00	10.00	15.00	25.00	—
1866-XXR	5,600,000	4.00	10.00	15.00	25.00	—

KM# 1071 TESTONE (30 Baiocchi)
7.9280 g., 0.9170 Silver .2337 oz. **Ruler:** Pius VII

Date	VG	F	VF	XF	Unc
MDCCCII (1802)-IIIR	25.00	40.00	75.00	120	—
MDCCCIII (1803)-IIIR	25.00	40.00	75.00	120	—

KM# 1100 30 BAIOCCHI
7.9280 g., 0.9170 Silver .2337 oz. **Ruler:** Pius VIII

Date	VG	F	VF	XF	Unc
1830-IIR	25.00	45.00	85.00	150	—

KM# 1101 30 BAIOCCHI
7.9280 g., 0.9170 Silver .2337 oz. **Obv:** Arms of Cardinal Francesco Galeffi **Note:** Sede Vacante issue.

Date	VG	F	VF	XF	Unc
1830B	25.00	45.00	85.00	150	—
1830R	25.00	45.00	85.00	150	—

KM# 1104 30 BAIOCCHI
7.9280 g., 0.9170 Silver .2337 oz. **Ruler:** Gregory XVI

Date	VG	F	VF	XF	Unc
1834-IVR	20.00	40.00	80.00	120	—

KM# 1109 30 BAIOCCHI
8.0610 g., 0.9000 Silver .2332 oz. **Ruler:** Gregory XVI

Date	VG	F	VF	XF	Unc
1836-VIB	25.00	40.00	70.00	100	—
1836-VIR	25.00	65.00	125	200	—
1837-VIIB	25.00	40.00	70.00	100	—
1837-IIR	25.00	65.00	125	200	—
1838-VIIIR	25.00	40.00	70.00	100	—
1846-XVIR	25.00	40.00	70.00	100	—

KM# 1316 50 BAIOCCHI
13.2140 g., 0.9170 Silver .3896 oz. **Ruler:** Gregory XVI

Date	VG	F	VF	XF	Unc
1832-IIB	25.00	40.00	90.00	160	—
Note: Two varieties of 1832B exist					
1832-IIR	28.00	45.00	90.00	160	—
1834-IVR	28.00	45.00	90.00	160	—

KM# 1323 50 BAIOCCHI
13.4350 g., 0.9000 Silver .3887 oz. **Ruler:** Gregory XVI

Date	VG	F	VF	XF	Unc
1835-VR	20.00	35.00	65.00	90.00	—
1836-VIB	20.00	35.00	65.00	90.00	—
1836-VIR	45.00	65.00	110	175	—
1837-VIIB	20.00	35.00	65.00	90.00	—
1840-XB	45.00	65.00	110	175	—
1841-XIB	20.00	35.00	65.00	90.00	—
1842-XIIR	45.00	65.00	110	175	—
1843-XIIIR	20.00	35.00	65.00	110	—
1845-XVR	20.00	35.00	65.00	110	—
1846-XVIR	20.00	35.00	65.00	110	—

KM# 1357 50 BAIOCCHI
13.4350 g., 0.9000 Silver .3887 oz. **Ruler:** Pius IX

Date	Mintage	VG	F	VF	XF	Unc
1850-IVR	104,000	25.00	45.00	75.00	100	—
1850-VR	Inc. above	25.00	45.00	75.00	100	—
1853-VIIR	684,000	50.00	75.00	110	175	—
1853-VIIIR	Inc. above	25.00	45.00	75.00	100	—
1854-IXB	2,718	25.00	45.00	75.00	100	—
1856-XB	4,226	25.00	45.00	75.00	100	—
1857-XIIB	8,711	50.00	75.00	110	175	—

KM# 1247 1/2 SCUDO
13.2500 g., 0.9170 Silver .3907 oz. **Ruler:** Pius VII

Date	VG	F	VF	XF	Unc
1802-IIR	30.00	70.00	100	150	—
1802-IIIR	30.00	70.00	100	150	—
1803-IIIR	30.00	70.00	100	150	—
1816-XVIIR	30.00	70.00	100	150	—

KM# 1291 1/2 SCUDO
13.2500 g., 0.9170 Silver .3907 oz. **Obv:** Arms of Cardinal Bartolomeo Pacca **Note:** Sede Vacante issue.

Date	VG	F	VF	XF	Unc
MDCCCXXIII (1823)-IIB	40.00	75.00	140	200	—

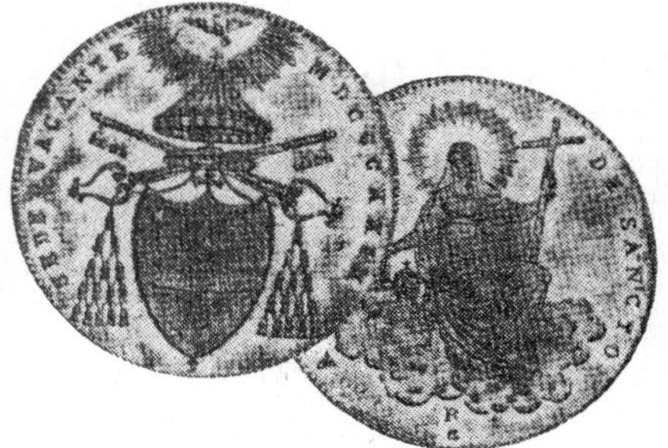

KM# 1302 1/2 SCUDO
13.2500 g., 0.9170 Silver .3907 oz. **Obv:** Arms of Cardinal Francesco Galeffi **Note:** Sede Vacante issue.

Date	VG	F	VF	XF	Unc
MDCCCXIX (1829)B	35.00	70.00	135	185	—
MDCCCXIX (1829)R	35.00	70.00	135	185	—

KM# 1249 SCUDO
26.2500 g., 0.9170 Silver .7739 oz. **Ruler:** Pius VII

Date	VG	F	VF	XF	Unc
1802-IIR	38.00	80.00	125	225	—
1802-IIIR	40.00	100	140	250	—
1802-IVR	38.00	80.00	125	225	—
1803-IVR	60.00	125	175	300	—
1805-VIR	38.00	80.00	125	225	—
1807-VIIIR	38.00	80.00	125	235	—

KM# 1275 SCUDO
26.4280 g., 0.9170 Silver .7792 oz. **Ruler:** Pius VII **Rev:** Similar to KM#1280

Date	VG	F	VF	XF	Unc
1815-XVIR	35.00	80.00	110	200	—
1816-XVIIB	35.00	75.00	110	200	—

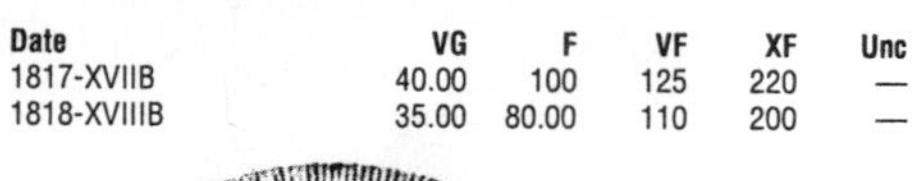

Date	VG	F	VF	XF	Unc
1817-XVIIB	40.00	100	125	220	—
1818-XVIIIB	35.00	80.00	110	200	—

KM# 1280 SCUDO
26.4280 g., 0.9170 Silver .7792 oz. **Ruler:** Pius VII

Date	VG	F	VF	XF	Unc
1816-XVIIR Rare	—	—	—	—	—

KM# 1292 SCUDO
26.4280 g., 0.9170 Silver .7792 oz. **Obv:** Arms of Cardinal Bartolomeo Pacca **Note:** Sede Vacante issue.

Date	VG	F	VF	XF	Unc
1823B	100	150	300	500	—

KM# 1293 SCUDO
26.4280 g., 0.9170 Silver .7792 oz. **Obv:** Arms of Cardinal Francesco Galeffi **Note:** Sede Vacante issue.

Date	VG	F	VF	XF	Unc
MDCCCXXIII (1823)R	300	450	750	1,800	—

KM# 1297.1 SCUDO
26.4280 g., 0.9170 Silver .7792 oz. **Ruler:** Leo XII **Obv:** Large bust

Date	VG	F	VF	XF	Unc
1825-IIIB	75.00	125	200	325	—
1826-IIIB	75.00	125	200	325	—

KM# 1297.2 SCUDO
26.4280 g., 0.9170 Silver .7792 oz. **Ruler:** Leo XII **Obv:** Small bust

Date	VG	F	VF	XF	Unc
1825-IIR	90.00	150	225	325	—
1826-IIIR	90.00	150	225	325	—

KM# 1297.3 SCUDO
26.4280 g., 0.9170 Silver .7792 oz. **Ruler:** Leo XII **Obv:** Large thick rays above

Date	VG	F	VF	XF	Unc
1826-IIIR	90.00	160	235	335	—

KM# 1303 SCUDO
26.4280 g., 0.9170 Silver .7792 oz. **Note:** Sede Vacante issue.

Date	VG	F	VF	XF	Unc
MDCCCXIX (1829)B	75.00	150	250	325	—
MDCCCXIX (1829)R	125	200	275	400	—

KM# 1310 SCUDO
26.4280 g., 0.9170 Silver .7792 oz. **Ruler:** Pius VIII

Date	VG	F	VF	XF	Unc
1830-IB	85.00	150	185	300	—
1830-IROMA	65.00	125	175	250	—

KM# 1311 SCUDO
26.4280 g., 0.9170 Silver .7792 oz. **Obv:** Arms of Cardinal Francesco Galeffi **Note:** Sede Vacante issue.

Date	VG	F	VF	XF	Unc
MDCCCXXX (1830)B	65.00	125	185	265	—
MDCCCXXX (1830)ROMA	85.00	150	200	300	—

KM# 1315.1 SCUDO
26.4280 g., 0.9170 Silver .7792 oz. **Ruler:** Gregory XVI **Obv:** Legend dates as AN

Date	VG	F	VF	XF	Unc
1831-IB	50.00	85.00	135	185	—
1831-IR	50.00	75.00	125	185	—
1833-IIIB	90.00	150	225	325	—
1833-IIIR	50.00	85.00	135	185	—
1834-IVR	50.00	75.00	125	185	—

KM# 1324 SCUDO
26.8710 g., 0.9000 Silver .7776 oz. **Ruler:** Pius IX

Date	VG	F	VF	XF	Unc
1835-VB	45.00	75.00	110	175	—
1835-VR	60.00	110	165	225	—
1836-VIR	60.00	110	165	225	—
1837-VIIR	45.00	75.00	110	175	—
1838-VIIIB	60.00	110	165	225	—
1838-VIIIR	60.00	110	165	225	—
1839-VIIIR	60.00	110	165	225	—
1839-IXR	60.00	110	165	225	—
1840-XR	55.00	100	150	200	—
1841-XIR	60.00	110	165	225	—
1842-XIR	75.00	175	250	350	—
1842-XIIR	110	300	500	1,000	—
1843-XIIIR	45.00	75.00	110	175	—
1844-XIVR	60.00	110	165	225	—
1845-XVR	45.00	75.00	100	175	—
1846-XVIR	45.00	75.00	100	175	—

KM# 1335 SCUDO
26.8710 g., 0.9000 Silver 0.7775 oz. **Obv:** Arms of Cardinal Tomasso Riario-Sforza **Note:** Sede Vacante issue.

Date	VG	F	VF	XF	Unc
MDCCCXXXXVI (1846)R	90.00	175	250	350	—

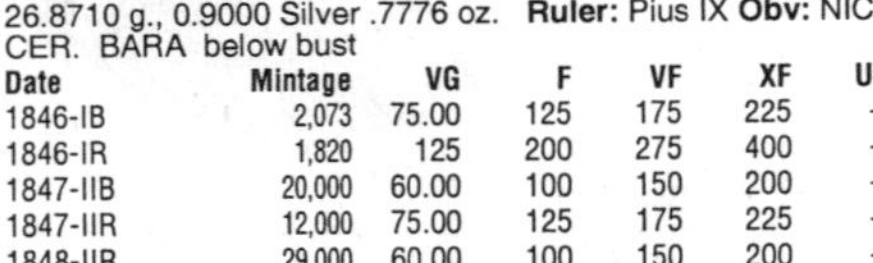

KM# 1336.1 SCUDO
26.8710 g., 0.9000 Silver .7776 oz. **Ruler:** Pius IX **Obv:** NIC. CER. BARA below bust

Date	Mintage	VG	F	VF	XF	Unc
1846-IB	2,073	75.00	125	175	225	—
1846-IR	1,820	125	200	275	400	—
1847-IIB	20,000	60.00	100	150	200	—
1847-IIR	12,000	75.00	125	175	225	—
1848-IIR	29,000	60.00	100	150	200	—
1848-IIIR	Inc. above	75.00	125	175	225	—

KM# 1336.2 SCUDO
26.8710 g., 0.9000 Silver .7776 oz. **Ruler:** Pius IX **Obv:** Without NIC. CER. BARA below bust

Date	Mintage	VG	F	VF	XF	Unc
1850-IVR	9,222	35.00	65.00	125	155	—
1853-VIIIB	2,310	100	200	300	500	—
1853-VIIR	527,000	35.00	65.00	125	155	—
1853-VIIIR	Inc. above	35.00	65.00	125	155	—
1854-IXB	3,715	100	200	300	500	—
1854-IXR	146,000	35.00	65.00	125	155	—
1856-XIR	1,050	125	250	450	750	—

KM# 1358 SCUDO
1.7330 g., 0.9000 Gold .0501 oz., 14.4 mm. **Ruler:** Pius IX

Date	Mintage	F	VF	XF	Unc	BU
1853-VIIIB	3,306	70.00	150	200	500	—
1853-VIIIR	209,000	50.00	120	150	200	—
1854-VIIIB	5,539	65.00	150	200	500	—
1854-VIIIR	97,000	50.00	120	150	200	—
1854-IXR	Inc. above	50.00	120	150	200	—
1857-XIIR	16,000	75.00	150	225	500	—

KM# 1361 SCUDO
1.7330 g., 0.9000 Gold .0501 oz., 16.3 mm. **Ruler:** Pius IX

Date	Mintage	F	VF	XF	Unc	BU
1858-XIIR	359,000	50.00	110	150	200	—
1858-XIIR	Inc. above	50.00	110	150	200	—
1859-XIIIR	103,000	50.00	110	150	200	—
1861-XVR	84,000	50.00	110	150	200	—
1861-XVIR	Inc. above	50.00	110	150	200	—
1862-XVIR	226,000	50.00	110	150	200	—
1862-XVIIR	Inc. above	50.00	110	150	200	—
1863-XVIIR	149,000	50.00	110	150	200	—
1863-XVIIIR	Inc. above	50.00	110	150	200	—
1864-XIXR	5,735	75.00	150	225	500	—
1865-XIXR	21,000	50.00	110	150	200	—

KM# 1088 2 ZECCHINI
6.9040 g., 0.9980 Gold .2215 oz. **Ruler:** Leo XII

Date	F	VF	XF	Unc	BU
1825-IIIR	500	900	1,500	3,000	—

KM# 1089 2 ZECCHINI
6.9040 g., 0.9980 Gold .2215 oz. **Ruler:** Leo XII

Date	F	VF	XF	Unc	BU
1828-VR	500	900	1,500	3,000	—

KM# 1106 2-1/2 SCUDI
4.3340 g., 0.9000 Gold .1254 oz. **Ruler:** Gregory XVI

Date	F	VF	XF	Unc	BU
1835-VB	150	250	350	450	—
1835-VR	150	250	350	450	—
1836-VB	150	250	350	450	—
1836-VIB	100	200	250	325	—
1836-VIR	150	250	350	450	—
1837-VIIR	150	250	350	450	—
1839-IXR	150	250	350	450	—
1840-XB	100	200	250	325	—
1841-XIR	150	250	350	500	—
1842-XIIB	100	200	250	325	—
1842-XIIR	175	275	400	600	—
1843-XIIIB	100	200	250	325	—
1844-XIIIB	150	250	350	450	—
1845-XVB	250	500	750	1,000	—
1845-XVR	150	250	350	500	—
1846-XVIB	100	200	250	325	—

KM# 1117 2-1/2 SCUDI
4.3340 g., 0.9000 Gold .1254 oz. **Ruler:** Pius IX

Date	Mintage	F	VF	XF	Unc	BU
1848-IIR	3,197	175	275	375	500	—
1853-VIIR	117,000	100	175	250	325	—
1853-VIIIR	Inc. above	100	160	225	325	—
1854-VIIIR	276,000	80.00	135	175	300	—
1854-IXB	32,000	80.00	135	175	300	—
1854-IXR	Inc. above	80.00	135	175	300	—
1855-IXR	59,000	80.00	135	175	300	—
1855-XR	Inc. above	80.00	135	175	300	—
1856-XB	8,040	100	175	250	350	—
1856-XR	104,000	80.00	135	175	300	—
1856-XIR	Inc. above	80.00	135	175	300	—
1857-XR	—	100	160	225	325	—
1857-XIR	—	175	275	375	500	—
1857-XIIB	6,284	175	275	375	500	—
1857-XIIR	—	90.00	135	175	300	—
1858-XIIR	—	90.00	135	200	325	—
1858-XIIIB	2,787	175	275	375	500	—
1858-XIIIR	—	90.00	135	175	300	—
1859-XIIIB	66,000	100	160	225	325	—
1859-XIIIR	—	80.00	135	175	300	—
1859-XIVR	—	80.00	135	175	300	—
1860-XIVR	—	80.00	135	175	300	—
1860-XVR	—	80.00	135	175	300	—
1861-XVR	—	80.00	135	175	300	—
1861-XVIR	—	80.00	135	175	300	—
1862-XVIR	—	80.00	135	175	300	—
1862-XVIIR	—	80.00	135	175	300	—
1863-XVIIR	—	80.00	135	175	300	—

KM# 1105 5 SCUDI
8.6680 g., 0.9000 Gold .2508 oz. **Ruler:** Gregory XVI

Date	F	VF	XF	Unc	BU
1834-IVR Rare	—	—	—	—	—

Note: Bowers and Merena Guia sale 3-88 XF (cleaned) realized $12,650

KM# 1107 5 SCUDI
8.6680 g., 0.9000 Gold .2508 oz. **Ruler:** Gregory XVI

Date	F	VF	XF	Unc	BU
1835-VB	225	450	650	800	—
1835-VR	225	450	650	800	—
1836-VIR	225	450	650	800	—
1837-VIR	350	700	900	1,500	—
1837-VIIR	225	450	650	800	—
1838-VIIR	225	450	650	800	—

Date	F	VF	XF	Unc	BU
1838-VIIIR	225	450	650	800	—
1839-VIIIR	300	600	800	1,200	—
1839-IXR	300	600	800	1,200	—
1840-IXR	350	700	900	1,500	—
1841-XIB	350	550	750	1,500	—
1841-XIR	225	450	650	800	—
1842-XIIB	225	450	650	800	—
1842-XIIR	225	450	650	800	—
1843-XIIIB	350	550	750	1,500	—
1843-XIIIR	225	450	650	800	—
1845-XVR	225	450	650	800	—
1846-XVIR	225	450	650	800	—

KM# 1116 5 SCUDI
8.6680 g., 0.9000 Gold .2508 oz. **Ruler:** Pius IX

Date	Mintage	F	VF	XF	Unc	BU
1846-IB	11,000	225	450	600	800	—
1846-IR	5,755	300	500	750	1,000	—
1847-IIR	1,399	400	700	900	1,250	—
1848-IIIR	1,633	325	575	800	1,200	—
1850-IVR	6,473	300	700	850	1,100	—
1854-IXR	104,000	225	375	500	750	—

KM# 1115 5 SCUDI
8.6680 g., 0.9000 Gold .2508 oz. **Obv:** Arms of Cardinal Tommaso Riario-Sforza **Note:** Sede Vacante issue.

Date	F	VF	XF	Unc	BU
1846R	800	1,300	1,800	2,500	—

KM# 1108 10 SCUDI
17.3360 g., 0.9000 Gold .5016 oz. **Ruler:** Gregory XVI

Date	F	VF	XF	Unc	BU
1835-VB	350	675	950	1,350	—
1835-VR	275	550	750	1,100	—
1836-VR	275	550	750	1,100	—
1836-VB	275	550	750	1,100	—
1836-VIR	300	675	950	1,400	—
1837-VIR	300	675	950	1,400	—
1837-VIIR	275	550	750	1,100	—
1838-VIIR	275	550	750	1,250	—
1838-VIIIR	275	550	750	1,250	—
1839-VIIIR	275	550	750	1,250	—
1839-IXR	300	675	950	1,400	—
1840-XB	300	675	950	1,400	—
1840-XR	275	550	750	1,250	—
1841-XR	275	550	750	1,250	—
1841-XIB	275	550	750	1,250	—
1841-XIR	275	550	750	1,250	—
1842-XIR	275	550	750	1,250	—
1842-XIIB	275	550	750	1,250	—
1842-XIIR	275	550	750	1,250	—
1843-XIIIR	300	675	950	1,400	—
1844-XIVR	300	675	950	1,400	—
1845-XVB	275	550	750	1,250	—
1845-XVR	350	675	950	1,450	—

KM# 1125 10 SCUDI
17.3360 g., 0.9000 Gold .5016 oz. **Ruler:** Pius IX

Date	Mintage	F	VF	XF	Unc	BU
1850-IVR	5,875	650	1,250	1,750	2,750	—
1850-VR	Inc. above	450	1,000	1,500	2,000	—
1856-XIR	2,483	650	1,000	1,500	2,500	—

KM# 1070 DOPPIA
5.4690 g., 0.9170 Gold .1612 oz. **Ruler:** Pius VII

Date	F	VF	XF	Unc	BU
ND(1801) IR	125	200	275	475	—
ND(1801) IIR	125	200	275	475	—
ND(1802) IIIR	125	200	275	475	—
ND(1803) IVR	125	200	275	475	—
ND(1804) VR	125	200	275	475	—
ND(1807) VIIIR	125	200	275	475	—
ND(1809) XR	150	225	300	550	—

KM# 1077 DOPPIA
5.4690 g., 0.9170 Gold .1612 oz. **Ruler:** Pius VII

Date	F	VF	XF	Unc	BU
ND(1815) XVIB	200	300	500	900	—
ND(1816) XVIIB	175	275	450	800	—
ND(1820) XXIB	200	300	500	1,000	—
ND(1821) XXIIB	175	275	450	800	—

KM# 1076 DOPPIA
5.4690 g., 0.9170 Gold .1612 oz. **Ruler:** Pius VII **Note:** Modified design.

Date	F	VF	XF	Unc	BU
ND(1815) XVIR	125	200	275	475	—
ND(1817) XVIIIR	150	200	300	500	—
ND(1823) XXIVR	150	200	300	500	—

KM# 1087 DOPPIA
5.4690 g., 0.9170 Gold .1612 oz. **Ruler:** Leo XII

Date	F	VF	XF	Unc	BU
ND(1823) IR	150	250	400	800	—
ND(1824) IIB	150	250	400	800	—
ND(1824) IIR	150	250	400	800	—

KM# 1086 DOPPIA
5.4690 g., 0.9170 Gold .1612 oz. **Obv:** Arms of Cardinal Bartolomeo Pacca **Note:** Sede Vacante isuse.

Date	F	VF	XF	Unc	BU
1823B	225	350	550	1,250	—
1823R	225	350	550	1,250	—

KM# 1090 DOPPIA

5.4690 g., 0.9170 Gold .1612 oz. **Obv:** Arms of Cardinal Francesco Galeffi **Note:** Sede Vacante isuse.

Date	F	VF	XF	Unc	BU
1829B	275	400	750	1,500	—
1829R	275	400	750	1,500	—

KM# 1102 DOPPIA

5.4690 g., 0.9170 Gold .1612 oz. **Obv:** Arms of Cardinal Francesco Galeffi **Note:** Sede Vacante isuse.

Date	F	VF	XF	Unc	BU
1830R	325	650	1,000	1,800	—

KM# 1103 DOPPIA

5.4500 g., 0.9170 Gold .1606 oz. **Ruler:** Gregory XVI

Date	F	VF	XF	Unc	BU
1833-IIIR	300	500	900	1,500	—
1834-IIIB	275	450	700	1,200	—

DECIMAL COINAGE

5 Centesimi = 1 Soldi; 20 Soldi = 1 Lira

KM# 1370 CENTESIMO

Copper **Ruler:** Pius IX

Date	Mintage	F	VF	XF	Unc	BU
1866-XXIR	500,000	5.00	10.00	15.00	55.00	—
1867-XXIIR	2,900,000	5.00	10.00	15.00	55.00	—
1868-XXIIR	1,950,000	6.00	18.00	25.00	75.00	—

KM# 1371 1/2 SOLDO (2-1/2 Centesimi)

Copper **Ruler:** Pius IX

Date	Mintage	F	VF	XF	Unc	BU
1866-XIIR	200,000	3.50	10.00	20.00	35.00	—
1867-XXIR	2,890,000	2.50	6.50	12.00	25.00	—
1867-XXIIR	2,890,000	2.50	6.50	12.00	25.00	—

KM# 1372.1 SOLDO (5 Centesimi)

Copper **Ruler:** Pius IX **Obv:** Small bust

Date	Mintage	F	VF	XF	Unc	BU
1866-XXIR	1,300,000	2.50	6.00	15.00	35.00	—

KM# 1372.2 SOLDO (5 Centesimi)

Copper **Ruler:** Pius IX **Obv:** Large bust

Date	Mintage	F	VF	XF	Unc	BU
1866-XXIR	2,850,000	6.00	18.00	40.00	100	—
Note: Large date						
1866-XXIR	Inc. above	1.75	4.00	8.00	20.00	—
Note: Small date						
1867-XXIR	6,500,000	3.50	10.00	20.00	50.00	—

Date	Mintage	F	VF	XF	Unc	BU
Note: Large date						
1867-XXIR	Inc. above	1.75	4.00	8.00	25.00	—
Note: Small date						

KM# 1373 2 SOLDI (10 Centesimi)

Copper **Ruler:** Pius IX

Date	Mintage	F	VF	XF	Unc	BU
1866-XXIR	3,500,000	3.50	10.00	20.00	50.00	—
1867-XXIR	3,500,000	3.50	10.00	20.00	50.00	—

KM# 1374 4 SOLDI (20 Centesimi)

Copper **Ruler:** Pius IX

Date	Mintage	F	VF	XF	Unc	BU
1866-XXOR	2,470,000	6.00	12.00	20.00	50.00	—
1867-XXIR	2,100,000	6.00	12.00	20.00	50.00	—
1867-XXIIR	2,876,000	6.00	12.00	20.00	50.00	—
1868-XXIIR	4,987,000	6.00	12.00	20.00	40.00	—
1868-XXIIIR	4,876,000	6.00	12.00	20.00	40.00	—
1869-XXIIIR	2,767,000	6.00	12.00	20.00	50.00	—
1869-XXIIIR	3,150,000	6.00	12.00	20.00	40.00	—

KM# 1375 5 SOLDI (25 Centesimi)

1.2500 g., 0.8350 Silver .0335 oz. **Ruler:** Pius IX

Date	Mintage	F	VF	XF	Unc	BU
1866-XXIR	100,000	4.00	10.00	20.00	30.00	—
1867-XXIR	915,000	3.00	8.00	12.00	20.00	—
1867-XXIIR	1,124,000	3.00	8.00	12.00	20.00	—

KM# 1376 10 SOLDI (50 Centesimi)

2.5000 g., 0.8350 Silver .0671 oz. **Ruler:** Pius IX **Obv. Legend:** PIVS IX PON. MAX. A....

Date	Mintage	F	VF	XF	Unc	BU
1866-XXIR	290,000	15.00	22.50	40.00	60.00	—
1867-XXIR	3,950,000	2.50	5.00	9.00	20.00	—
1867-XXIIR	3,950,000	2.50	5.00	9.00	20.00	—
1868-XXIIR	8,200,000	2.50	5.00	9.00	18.00	—

KM# 1386.1 10 SOLDI (50 Centesimi)

2.5000 g., 0.8350 Silver .0671 oz. **Ruler:** Pius IX **Obv. Legend:** PIVS IX P. M. A... **Rev:** Large R at wreath bottom

Date	Mintage	F	VF	XF	Unc	BU
1867-XXIIIR	4,765,000	2.50	5.00	9.00	20.00	—
1869-XXIIIR	4,435,000	2.50	5.00	9.00	20.00	—
1869-XXIVR	2,765,000	3.00	7.00	12.50	25.00	—

KM# 1386.2 10 SOLDI (50 Centesimi)

2.5000 g., 0.8350 Silver .0671 oz. **Ruler:** Pius IX **Rev:** Wreath nearly closed at top, small R below

Date	F	VF	XF	Unc	BU
1868-XXIIIR	2.50	5.00	9.00	20.00	—

KM# 1377.1 LIRA

5.0000 g., 0.8350 Silver .1342 oz. **Ruler:** Pius IX **Obv:** Small bust without ornament below

Date	Mintage	F	VF	XF	Unc	BU
1866-XXR	100	300	500	800	1,400	—

KM# 1377.2 LIRA

5.0000 g., 0.8350 Silver .1342 oz. **Ruler:** Pius IX **Obv:** Ornament below bust

Date	Mintage	F	VF	XF	Unc	BU
1866-XXIR	1,765,000	15.00	25.00	30.00	75.00	—

KM# 1377.3 LIRA

5.0000 g., 0.8350 Silver .1342 oz. **Ruler:** Pius IX **Obv:** Medium bust

Date	Mintage	F	VF	XF	Unc	BU
1866-XXIR	275,000	30.00	100	135	200	—

KM# 1378 LIRA

5.0000 g., 0.8350 Silver .1342 oz. **Ruler:** Pius IX **Obv:** Large bust **Obv. Legend:** PIUS IX PON. MAX. AN...

Date	Mintage	F	VF	XF	Unc	BU
1866-XXIR	1,675,000	4.00	10.00	20.00	40.00	—
1867-XXIR	3,876,000	4.00	8.00	15.00	30.00	—
1867-XXIIR	3,987,000	4.00	8.00	15.00	30.00	—
1868-XXIIR	2,050,000	4.00	10.00	20.00	40.00	—

KM# 1387 LIRA

5.0000 g., 0.8350 Silver .1342 oz. **Ruler:** Pius IX **Obv:** Large bust **Obv. Legend:** PIUS IX PON. M. A...

Date	Mintage	F	VF	XF	Unc	BU
1868-XXIIIR	3,877,000	4.00	8.00	20.00	40.00	—
1869-XXIIIR	1,145,000	7.50	12.50	27.50	55.00	—
1869-XXIVR	346,000	30.00	65.00	100	200	—

KM# 1379.1 2 LIRE

10.0000 g., 0.8350 Silver .2684 oz. **Ruler:** Pius IX **Obv:** Small bust without ornament **Obv. Legend:** PIUS IX PON. MAX. A...

Date	Mintage	F	VF	XF	Unc	BU
1866-XXR	610	700	1,250	2,500	4,000	—

KM# 1379.2 2 LIRE
10.0000 g., 0.8350 Silver .2684 oz. **Ruler:** Pius IX **Obv:** Ornament below large bust

Date	Mintage	F	VF	XF	Unc	BU
1866-XXIR	987,000	12.50	20.00	40.00	85.00	—
1867-XXIR	224,000	75.00	150	250	500	—
1867-XXIIR	1,220,000	12.50	20.00	35.00	80.00	—
1868-XXIIR	530,000	50.00	120	175	350	—

KM# 1379.3 2 LIRE
10.0000 g., 0.8350 Silver .2684 oz. **Ruler:** Pius IX **Obv. Legend:** PIUS IX PON. M. A...

Date	Mintage	F	VF	XF	Unc	BU
1868-XXIIIR	978,000	12.50	20.00	40.00	85.00	—
1869-XXIVR	810,000	12.50	20.00	40.00	85.00	—
1870-XXIVR	179,000	40.00	100	150	275	—

KM# 1384 2-1/2 LIRE
12.5000 g., 0.9000 Silver .3617 oz. **Ruler:** Pius IX

Date	Mintage	F	VF	XF	Unc	BU
1867-XXIR	257,000	45.00	125	200	325	—

KM# 1380 5 LIRE
1.6120 g., 0.9000 Gold .0466 oz. **Ruler:** Pius IX

Date	Mintage	F	VF	XF	Unc	BU
1866-XXIR	3,230	225	375	550	900	—
1867-XXIIR	3,787	250	400	700	1,200	—

KM# 1385 5 LIRE
25.0000 g., 0.9000 Silver .7234 oz. **Ruler:** Pius IX

Date	Mintage	F	VF	XF	Unc	BU
1867-XXIR	5,800	100	200	350	550	—
1870-XX!VR	99,000	60.00	90.00	200	350	—
1870-XXVR	115,000	50.00	80.00	175	325	—

KM# 1381.1 10 LIRE
3.2250 g., 0.9000 Gold .0933 oz. **Ruler:** Pius IX **Obv. Legend:** PIUS IX PONT. MAX. A...

Date	Mintage	F	VF	XF	Unc	BU
1866-XXIR	8,579	150	285	375	550	—

KM# 1381.2 10 LIRE
3.2250 g., 0.9000 Gold .0933 oz. **Ruler:** Pius IX **Obv. Legend:** PIUS IX PON. MAX. A...

Date	Mintage	F	VF	XF	Unc	BU
1867-XXIR	8,580	150	285	375	550	—
1867-XXIIR	9,176	150	250	350	500	—

KM# 1381.3 10 LIRE
3.2250 g., 0.9000 Gold .0933 oz. **Ruler:** Pius IX **Obv. Legend:** PIUS IX P. M. A...

Date	Mintage	F	VF	XF	Unc	BU
1869-XXIVR	5,944	175	350	550	850	—

KM# 1382.1 20 LIRE
6.4510 g., 0.9000 Gold .1866 oz. **Ruler:** Pius IX **Obv:** Small bust **Edge:** Plain

Date	Mintage	F	VF	XF	Unc	BU
1866-XXR	945	900	1,500	2,500	5,500	—

KM# 1382.2 20 LIRE
6.4510 g., 0.9000 Gold .1866 oz. **Ruler:** Pius IX **Edge:** Reeded

Date	Mintage	F	VF	XF	Unc	BU
1866-XXR	22,000	350	600	900	1,350	—
1866-XXIR	102,000	125	175	275	350	—
1867-XXIR	44,000	150	225	350	550	—

KM# 1382.3 20 LIRE
6.4510 g., 0.9000 Gold .1866 oz. **Ruler:** Pius IX **Obv:** Medium bust

Date	Mintage	F	VF	XF	Unc	BU
1867-XXIIR	57,000	125	175	275	350	—
1868-XXIIR	38,000	150	225	350	550	—
1868-XXIIIR	Inc. above	350	600	900	1,350	—

KM# 1382.4 20 LIRE
6.4510 g., 0.9000 Gold .1866 oz. **Ruler:** Pius IX **Obv:** Large bust

Date	Mintage	F	VF	XF	Unc	BU
1868-XXIIIR	112,000	125	175	250	300	—
1869-XXIIIR	54,000	125	175	275	350	—
1869-XXIVR	76,000	125	175	250	300	—
1870-XXIVR	24,000	200	275	350	500	—
1870-XXVR	27,000	150	225	300	425	—

KM# 1388 50 LIRE
16.1290 g., 0.9000 Gold .4667 oz. **Ruler:** Pius IX

Date	Mintage	F	VF	XF	Unc	BU
1868-XXIIR	1,172	750	850	2,000	4,000	—
1868-XXIIIR	257	2,300	4,000	6,000	8,000	—
1870-XXIVR	1,460	750	850	2,000	4,000	—

KM# 1383 100 LIRE
32.2580 g., 0.9000 Gold .9335 oz. **Ruler:** Pius IX

Date	Mintage	F	VF	XF	Unc	BU
1866-XXIR	1,117	900	1,000	2,500	4,750	—
1868-XXIIIR	545	2,000	2,750	4,500	6,500	—
1869-XXIIIR	625	2,000	2,750	4,500	6,500	—
1869-XXIVR	450	2,500	7,500	10,000	8,500	—

PATTERNS

Including off metal strikes

KM#	Date	Mintage	Identification	Mkt Val
Pn2	1834R	—	5 Scudi. Silver. 17.6000 g. Klippe.	800
Pn3	MDCCCX XXXV (1845)	—	Scudo. Silver. 41.0000 g. KM#1335.	1,500
Pn4	1868-XXII	—	4 Soldi. 0.8350 Silver. Reeded edge.	7,250
Pn5	1868-XXII	—	4 Soldi. 0.8350 Silver. Plain edge.	6,000

KM#	Date	Mintage	Identification	Mkt Val
Pn6	1878	—	5 Lire. Leo XIII (fantasy).	—

PARMA

A town in Emillia, which was a papal possession from 1512 to 1545, was seized by France in 1796, and was attached to the Napoleonic Empire in 1808. In 1814, Parma was assigned to Marie Louise, empress of Napoleon I. It was annexed to Sardinia in 1860.

RULERS

Ferdinando di Borbone, 1765-1802
Maria Luigia, Duchess, 1815-1847
Carlo II di Borbone, 1847-1849
Carlo III di Borbone, 1849-1854
Roberto di Borbone, 1854-1858

MONETARY SYSTEM

Until 1802

12 Denari = 2 Sesini = 1 Soldo
20 Soldi = 1 Lira
7 Lire = 1 Ducato

TOWN

REFORM COINAGE

100 Centesimi = 20 Soldi = 1 Lira

C# 23 CENTESIMO
Copper **Ruler:** Maria Luigia **Note:** Similar to 5 Centesimi, C#25.

Date	Mintage	F	VF	XF	Unc	BU
1830	2,029,000	4.00	7.50	12.50	40.00	—

C# 33 CENTESIMO
Copper **Ruler:** Carlo III di Borbone **Obv:** Head of Carlo III left **Rev:** Oval arms

Date	F	VF	XF	Unc	BU
1854	300	500	700	1,200	—

C# 24 3 CENTESIMI
Copper **Ruler:** Maria Luigia **Note:** Similar to 5 Centesimi, C#25.

Date	Mintage	F	VF	XF	Unc	BU
1830	511,000	20.00	30.00	50.00	100	—

C# 34 3 CENTESIMI
Copper **Ruler:** Carlo III di Borbone **Obv:** Head of Carlo III left **Rev:** Oval arms

Date	F	VF	XF	Unc	BU
1854	450	650	900	1,500	—

C# 25 5 CENTESIMI
Copper **Ruler:** Maria Luigia

Date	Mintage	F	VF	XF	Unc	BU
1830	1,506,000	5.00	10.00	20.00	60.00	—

C# 35 5 CENTESIMI
Copper **Ruler:** Carlo III di Borbone **Obv:** Head of Carlo III left **Rev:** Oval arms

Date	F	VF	XF	Unc	BU
1854	700	1,000	1,500	2,200	—

C# 26 5 SOLDI
1.2500 g., 0.9000 Silver .0361 oz. **Ruler:** Maria Luigia

Date	Mintage	F	VF	XF	Unc	BU
1815/3	360,000	9.00	15.00	25.00	75.00	—
1815	Inc. above	7.50	12.50	20.00	50.00	—
1830	320,000	10.00	15.00	25.00	50.00	—

C# 27 10 SOLDI
2.5000 g., 0.9000 Silver .0722 oz. **Ruler:** Maria Luigia

Date	Mintage	F	VF	XF	Unc	BU
1815	530,000	12.00	20.00	30.00	85.00	—
1830	80,000	25.00	50.00	100	200	—

C# 28 LIRA
5.0000 g., 0.9000 Silver .1444 oz. **Ruler:** Maria Luigia

Date	Mintage	F	VF	XF	Unc	BU
1815	66,000	20.00	40.00	65.00	175	—

C# 29 2 LIRE
10.0000 g., 0.9000 Silver .2888 oz. **Ruler:** Maria Luigia

Date	Mintage	F	VF	XF	Unc	BU
1815	22,000	50.00	100	185	450	—

C# 30 5 LIRE
25.0000 g., 0.9000 Silver .7234 oz. **Ruler:** Maria Luigia

Date	Mintage	F	VF	XF	Unc	BU
1815	93,000	150	300	550	1,250	—
1821 Rare	—	—	—	—	—	—
1832	44,000	200	400	700	1,800	—

C# 36 5 LIRE
25.0000 g., 0.9000 Silver .7234 oz. **Ruler:** Roberto di Borbone

Date	Mintage	F	VF	XF	Unc	BU
1858	1,000	500	800	1,200	2,500	—

C# 31 20 LIRE
6.4500 g., 0.9000 Gold .1866 oz. **Ruler:** Maria Luigia

Date	Mintage	F	VF	XF	Unc	BU
1815	12,000	400	700	1,200	2,000	—
1832	1,000	1,800	3,000	4,500	7,000	—

C# 32 40 LIRE
12.9000 g., 0.9000 Gold .3733 oz. **Ruler:** Maria Luigia

Date	Mintage	F	VF	XF	Unc	BU
1815	220,000	175	275	375	700	—
1821	37,000	250	400	600	1,400	—

PATTERNS

Including off metal strikes

KM#	Date	Mintage	Identification	Mkt Val
Pn1	1815	—	Ducato. (No Composition).	5,500

KM#	Date	Mintage	Identification	Mkt Val
Pn2	1842	—	5 Centesimi. (No Composition).	—

PIEDMONT REPUBLIC

Established by Napoleon in 1798 in the Piedmont area of northwest Italy. It was the mainland possession of the kingdom of Sardinia. The republic was overthrown by Austro-Russian forces in 1799.

SUBALPINE REPUBLIC

STANDARD COINAGE

C# 4 5 FRANCS
25.0000 g., 0.9000 Silver .7234 oz.

Date	Mintage	Good	VG	F	VF	XF
L'AN 10 (1801)	33,000	—	40.00	60.00	125	300

C# 5 20 FRANCS
6.4500 g., 0.9000 Gold .1866 oz.

Date	Mintage	Good	VG	F	VF	XF
L'AN 10 (1801)	1,492	—	300	550	1,000	1,500

ROMAN REPUBLIC

Repubblica Romana

A short-lived Republican movement fostered by the French Revolution, submerged the Papal States in 1798-99. They reappeared in 1814, and except for the Republican movement of 1848-49, maintained their authority until 1860.

MINT MARKS

B - Bologna
R - Rome

SECOND REPUBLIC
1848-1849

STANDARD COINAGE

KM# 21 1/2 BAIOCCO
Copper **Rev:** Eagle in wreath, standing on fasces

Date	F	VF	XF	Unc	BU
1849R	6.00	12.00	25.00	50.00	—

KM# 22 BAIOCCO
Copper **Rev:** Eagle in wreath, standing on fasces

Date	F	VF	XF	Unc	BU
1849R	8.50	16.00	32.00	65.00	—

KM# 23.2 3 BAIOCCHI
Copper **Obv:** Flat topped 3 **Rev:** Eagle in wreath, standing on fasces

Date	F	VF	XF	Unc	BU
1849R	12.00	25.00	50.00	80.00	—
1849B	18.00	35.00	70.00	120	—

KM# 23.1 3 BAIOCCHI
Copper **Obv:** Round 3 **Rev:** Eagle in wreath, standing on fasces

Date	F	VF	XF	Unc	BU
1849R	12.00	25.00	50.00	80.00	—

KM# 23.3 3 BAIOCCHI
Copper **Obv:** Small round 3 **Rev:** Eagle in wreath, standing on fasces

Date	F	VF	XF	Unc	BU
1849R	15.00	30.00	60.00	110	—

KM# 24 4 BAIOCCHI
1.9500 g., 0.2000 Silver 0.0125 oz. **Rev:** Eagle within wreath, standing on fasces

Date	F	VF	XF	Unc	BU
1849B	7.00	14.00	35.00	80.00	—
1849R	6.00	12.00	25.00	55.00	—

KM# 25 8 BAIOCCHI
3.9000 g., 0.2000 Silver 0.0251 oz. **Rev:** Eagle in wreath, standing on fasces

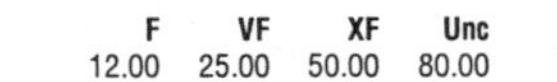

Date	F	VF	XF	Unc	BU
1849R	12.00	25.00	50.00	80.00	—

KM# 26 16 BAIOCCHI
7.8000 g., 0.2000 Silver 0.0502 oz. **Rev:** Eagle within wreath, standing on fasces

Date	F	VF	XF	Unc	BU
1849R	20.00	35.00	70.00	120	—

KM# 27 40 BAIOCCHI
20.0000 g., 0.2000 Silver 0.1286 oz. **Rev:** Eagle within wreath, standing on fasces

Date	F	VF	XF	Unc	BU
1849R	30.00	60.00	150	250	—

ROMAN REPUBLIC - ANCONA

Anconna

A city in the Marches, was founded by Syracusan refugees about 390 B.C. It became a semi-independent republic under papal protection in the 14th century, and a papal state in 1532. From 1797 until the formation of the United Kingdom of Italy it was part of the Roman Republic (1798-99), a papal state (1799-1808), part of the Italian Kingdom of Napoleon (1808-14), a papal state (1814-48),a part of the Roman Republic (1848-49), and a papal state(1849-60).

MINT MARKS
A – Ancona

SECOND REPUBLIC
1848-1849
STANDARD COINAGE

KM# 12 BAIOCCO
Cast Copper **Rev:** A below date

Date	VG	F	VF	XF	Unc
1849A	10.00	20.00	40.00	85.00	—

KM# 13 3 BAIOCCHI
Cast Copper **Obv:** Legend around fasces **Obv. Legend:** REPUBBLICA ROMANA **Rev:** Value, date, milimeters

Date	VG	F	VF	XF	Unc
1849 Rare	—	—	—	—	—

Note: Some authorities consider this a contemporary counterfeit

SARDINIA

Sardinia is an island located in the Mediterranean Sea, west of the southern Italian peninsula. Along with some minor islands, it constitutes an autonomous region of Italy separated on the north from Corsica, France by the Strait of Bonifacio.

Settled by Phoenician's and Greeks before it came under control of Carthage during 600 BC; taken by the Romans in 238 BC; in the Vandal Kingdom during the5th century; re-conquered by the Byzantine Empire in533 AD. From the 8th century it was frequently raided by Muslims whose threat was eliminated by Pisa in 1016 as an object of a rivalrous bet. The Genoese and Pisans were driven out by the Aragonese during the 14th-15th centuries, remaining under Spanish rule until 1708; held by Austria 1708-17, regained by the Spanish in 1717 until it was finally ceded to Savoy in 1720 in exchange for Sicily, after which the ruler of Savoy and Piedmont took the title as King of Sardinia.

RULERS
Carlo Emanuele IV 1796-1802
Vittorio Emanuele I 1802-1821
Carlo Felice 1821-1831
Carlo Alberto 1831-1849
Vittorio Emanuele II 1849-1878

MINT MARKS
None Before 1802 = Turin (Torino)
M = Milan
(t) after 1802 - Eagles head = Turin (Torino)

MONETARY SYSTEM
12 Denari = 6 Cagliarese = 1 Soldo
50 Soldi = 10 Reales = 2 1/2 Lire = 1 Scudo Sardo
2 Scudi Sardi = 1 Doppietta
Commencing 1816
100 Centesimi = 1 Lira

KINGDOM
ISLAND COINAGE

C# A88 CAGLIARESE
Copper, 17 mm. **Obv:** Cross on arms **Rev:** Value

Date	F	VF	XF	Unc	BU
ND(1813) Rare	—	—	—	—	—

C# 88 TRE (3) CAGLIARESE
Copper **Obv:** Cross on arms **Rev:** Value

Date	F	VF	XF	Unc	BU
ND(1813)	65.00	100	185	350	—

C# 89.1 REALE
3.1800 g., 0.5000 Silver .0551 oz. **Obv:** Head right, legend around, date **Obv. Legend:** VIC. EM. D. G. REX. SAR. CYP. ET. IER **Rev:** Eagle on shield with head to right, crown above

Date	F	VF	XF	Unc	BU
1812	60.00	90.00	145	285	—

C# 89.2 REALE
3.1800 g., 0.5000 Silver .0551 oz. **Obv:** Head right, legend around, date **Obv. Legend:** VIC.EM.D.G.REX.SAR.CYP.ET.IER **Rev:** Eagle on shield with head to left, crown above

Date	F	VF	XF	Unc	BU
1812	60.00	90.00	145	285	—

ISLAND REFORM COINAGE

C# 118 CENTESIMO
Copper **Note:** Mint mark: Eagle head.

Date	Mintage	F	VF	XF	Unc	BU
1842	1,933,000	40.00	60.00	75.00	140	—

C# 119 3 CENTESIMI
Copper **Obv:** Arms **Rev:** Value and date **Note:** Mint mark: Eagle head.

Date	Mintage	F	VF	XF	Unc	BU
1842	2,169,000	10.00	20.00	40.00	75.00	—

C# 120 5 CENTESIMI
Copper **Obv:** Arms **Rev:** Value and date **Note:** Mint mark: Eagle head.

Date	Mintage	F	VF	XF	Unc	BU
1842	1,845,000	10.00	25.00	50.00	90.00	—

MAINLAND COINAGE

C# 90 2.6 SOLDI
Billon **Ruler:** Vittorio Emanuele I **Obv:** Head right, VICTORIVS EMANVEL around, date **Rev:** Crowned displayed eagle with arms of Savoy on breast

Date	F	VF	XF	Unc	BU
1814	4.00	8.00	20.00	50.00	—
1815	4.00	8.00	20.00	50.00	—

C# 91 1/2 SCUDO
17.5820 g., 0.9050 Silver .5116 oz. **Ruler:** Vittorio Emanuele I

Date	F	VF	XF	Unc	BU
1814	400	600	700	1,500	—
1815	600	900	1,250	2,500	—

C# 94 DOPPIA
9.1160 g., 0.9050 Gold .2652 oz. **Ruler:** Vittorio Emanuele I **Obv. Legend:** VICTORIVS EMANVEL. **Rev. Legend:** D. G. REX. SAR...

Date	VG	F	VF	XF	Unc
1814	2,000	4,000	8,500	12,000	—

C# 94a DOPPIA
9.1160 g., 0.9050 Gold .2652 oz. **Ruler:** Vittorio Emanuele I **Obv. Legend:** VIC. EM. D. G. REX. SAR... **Rev. Legend:** MONTISF. PR. PED. & ...

Date	VG	F	VF	XF	Unc
1815	—	—	13,000	15,000	—

Note: Superior Pipito sale 12-87 choice VF realized $13,750;Stack's International sale 3-88 XF realized $11,550

MAINLAND REFORM COINAGE

C# 98.1 CENTESIMO
Copper **Note:** Mint mark: Anchor.

Date	Mintage	F	VF	XF	Unc	BU
1826 P	11,485,000	5.00	10.00	25.00	50.00	—

C# 98.2 CENTESIMO
Copper **Note:** Mint mark: Eagle head.

Date	Mintage	F	VF	XF	Unc	BU
1826 L	—	3.50	6.00	15.00	45.00	—
1826 P	4,812,000	3.50	6.00	15.00	45.00	—

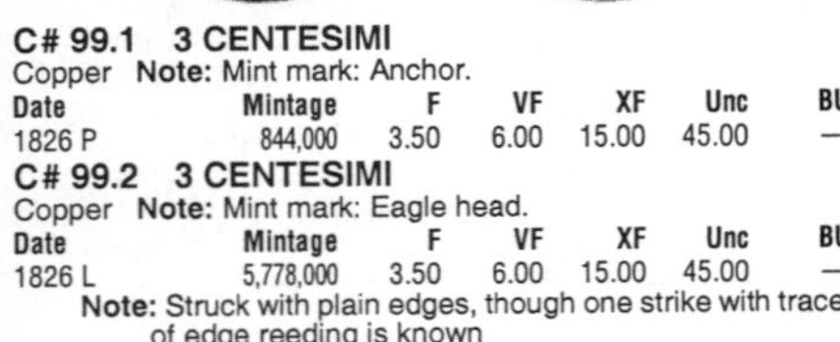

C# 99.1 3 CENTESIMI
Copper **Note:** Mint mark: Anchor.

Date	Mintage	F	VF	XF	Unc	BU
1826 P	844,000	3.50	6.00	15.00	45.00	—

C# 99.2 3 CENTESIMI
Copper **Note:** Mint mark: Eagle head.

Date	Mintage	F	VF	XF	Unc	BU
1826 L	5,778,000	3.50	6.00	15.00	45.00	—

Note: Struck with plain edges, though one strike with trace of edge reeding is known

C# 100.1 5 CENTESIMI
Copper **Note:** Mint mark: Anchor.

Date	Mintage	F	VF	XF	Unc	BU
1826 P	10,514,000	3.50	7.00	18.00	50.00	—

C# 100.2 5 CENTESIMI
Copper **Note:** Mint mark: Eagle head.

Date	Mintage	F	VF	XF	Unc	BU
1826 L	32,177,000	3.50	7.00	18.00	50.00	—
1826 P	Inc. above	3.50	7.00	18.00	50.00	—

Note: C#98, 99, 100 were struck without mint mark at Bologna in 1860; See Emilia KM#1, 2 and 3

C# 101.1 25 CENTESIMI
1.2500 g., 0.9000 Silver .0361 oz. **Obv:** Head right **Rev:** Arms **Note:** Mint mark: Anchor.

Date	Mintage	F	VF	XF	Unc	BU
1829 P	450,000	15.00	25.00	40.00	90.00	—
1830 P	135,000	17.50	30.00	50.00	100	—

C# 101.2 25 CENTESIMI
1.2500 g., 0.9000 Silver .0361 oz. **Note:** Mint mark: Eagle head.

Date	Mintage	F	VF	XF	Unc	BU
1829 L	110,000	17.50	30.00	50.00	100	—
1830 L	234,000	15.00	25.00	40.00	90.00	—
1830 P	Inc. above	20.00	35.00	60.00	150	—

C# 109.1 25 CENTESIMI
1.2500 g., 0.9000 Silver .0361 oz.

Date	Mintage	F	VF	XF	Unc	BU
1832 P	120,000	75.00	150	300	600	—
1833 P	—	20.00	35.00	60.00	150	—
1837 P	230,000	75.00	150	300	600	—

C# 109.2 25 CENTESIMI
1.2500 g., 0.9000 Silver .0361 oz. **Note:** Mint mark: Anchor.

Date	Mintage	F	VF	XF	Unc	BU
1833 P	7,921	25.00	40.00	60.00	120	—

C# 102.1 50 CENTESIMI
2.5000 g., 0.9000 Silver .0722 oz. **Note:** Mint mark: Eagle head.

Date	Mintage	F	VF	XF	Unc	BU
1823 L Rare	—	—	—	—	—	—
1824 L Rare	—	—	—	—	—	—
1825 L	492,000	12.50	25.00	50.00	150	—
1826 L	640,000	12.50	25.00	50.00	150	—
1827 L	401,000	12.50	25.00	50.00	150	—
1828 L	611,000	12.50	25.00	50.00	150	—
1828 P	Inc. above	12.50	25.00	50.00	150	—
1829 P	255,000	35.00	75.00	125	200	—
1830 L	456,000	12.50	25.00	50.00	150	—
1830 P	Inc. above	100	150	200	300	—
1831 L	143,000	12.50	25.00	50.00	150	—
1831 P	Inc. above	50.00	80.00	150	400	—

C# 102.2 50 CENTESIMI
2.5000 g., 0.9000 Silver .0722 oz. **Note:** Mint mark: Anchor.

Date	Mintage	F	VF	XF	Unc	BU
1826 P	79,000	20.00	40.00	75.00	150	—
1827 P	143,000	15.00	30.00	60.00	125	—
1828 P	194,000	35.00	75.00	100	175	—
1829 P	107,000	15.00	30.00	60.00	125	—

C# 110.1 50 CENTESIMI
2.5000 g., 0.9000 Silver .0722 oz. **Obv:** Head right **Rev:** Arms **Note:** Mint mark: Eagle head.

Date	Mintage	F	VF	XF	Unc	BU
1832 P Rare	—	—	—	—	—	—
1833 P	62,000	20.00	40.00	75.00	200	—
1834 P	61,000	40.00	80.00	200	600	—
1835 P	—	40.00	80.00	200	400	—
1836 P	22,000	40.00	80.00	200	600	—
1837 P	12,000	40.00	80.00	200	600	—
1841 P	6,600	40.00	80.00	200	600	—
1842 P	10,000	20.00	35.00	75.00	200	—
1843 P	14,000	20.00	35.00	75.00	200	—
1844 P	9,100	50.00	100	300	800	—
1845 P	16,000	40.00	75.00	125	250	—
1846 P	23,000	50.00	100	300	800	—
1847 P	11,000	50.00	100	200	400	—

C# 110.2 50 CENTESIMI
2.5000 g., 0.9000 Silver .0722 oz. **Note:** Mint mark: Anchor.

Date	Mintage	F	VF	XF	Unc	BU
1833 P	136	50.00	100	200	400	—
1844 P	23,000	50.00	100	300	800	—

C# 121.1 50 CENTESIMI
2.5000 g., 0.9000 Silver .0722 oz. **Obv:** Head with beard

Date	Mintage	F	VF	XF	Unc	BU
1850 P	9,268	30.00	60.00	100	200	—
1860 P Rare	15	—	—	—	—	—

C# 121.2 50 CENTESIMI
2.5000 g., 0.9000 Silver .0722 oz. **Note:** Mint mark: Eagle head.

Date	Mintage	F	VF	XF	Unc	BU
1850 B	—	12.50	25.00	50.00	150	—
1852 B	55,000	12.50	25.00	50.00	150	—
1853 B	21,000	12.50	25.00	50.00	150	—
1855 B	—	30.00	60.00	150	300	—
1856 B	9,754	12.50	25.00	50.00	150	—
1857 B	15,000	12.50	25.00	50.00	150	—
1858 B	8,114	12.50	25.00	50.00	150	—
1860 B	6,484	12.50	25.00	50.00	150	—

C# 121.3 50 CENTESIMI
2.5000 g., 0.9000 Silver .0722 oz.

Date	Mintage	F	VF	XF	Unc	BU
1860M	982,000	15.00	30.00	65.00	175	—
1861M	—	50.00	100	200	500	—

C# 103.1 LIRA
5.0000 g., 0.9000 Silver .1444 oz. **Note:** Mint mark: Eagle head.

Date	Mintage	F	VF	XF	Unc	BU
1823 L	—	—	—	—	—	—
1824 L	92,000	25.00	50.00	100	300	—
1825 L	—	50.00	100	200	600	—
1826 L	547,000	20.00	40.00	75.00	200	—
1827 L	836,000	20.00	40.00	75.00	200	—
1828 L	345,000	20.00	40.00	75.00	200	—
1828 P	Inc. above	20.00	40.00	75.00	200	—
1829 L	111,000	20.00	50.00	100	400	—
1830 P	313,000	20.00	40.00	75.00	200	—

C# 103.2 LIRA
5.0000 g., 0.9000 Silver .1444 oz. **Note:** Mint mark: Anchor.

Date	Mintage	F	VF	XF	Unc	BU
1824 P	5,670	25.00	50.00	100	400	—
1825 P	—	20.00	40.00	75.00	200	—
1826 P	154,000	20.00	40.00	75.00	200	—
1827 P	251,000	20.00	40.00	75.00	200	—
1828 P	388,000	20.00	40.00	75.00	200	—
1829 P	159,000	20.00	40.00	75.00	200	—
1830 P	60,000	20.00	40.00	75.00	400	—

C# 111.1 LIRA
5.0000 g., 0.9000 Silver .1444 oz. **Obv:** Head right **Rev:** Arms

Date	Mintage	F	VF	XF	Unc	BU
1831 P	19,000	50.00	100	200	700	—
1832 P	35,000	35.00	75.00	200	600	—
1833 P	7,620	50.00	100	200	700	—
1834 P Rare	40,000	—	—	—	—	—
1835 P	23,000	25.00	50.00	100	300	—
1837 P Rare	18,000	—	—	—	—	—
1838 P	—	25.00	50.00	100	250	—
1841 P Rare	11,000	—	—	—	—	—
1844 P Rare	33,000	—	—	—	—	—

C# 111.2 LIRA
5.0000 g., 0.9000 Silver .1444 oz. **Note:** Mint mark: Eagle head.

Date	Mintage	F	VF	XF	Unc	BU
1831 P	5,000	50.00	100	200	600	—
1832 P	30,000	50.00	100	200	600	—
1833 P	85	50.00	100	200	750	—
1835 P	—	50.00	100	200	750	—
1837 P	28,000	50.00	100	200	600	—
1838 P	11,000	50.00	100	200	600	—
1839 P Rare	8,558	—	—	—	—	—
1841 P Rare	20,000	—	—	—	—	—
1842 P Rare	5,184	—	—	—	—	—
1843 P	15,000	20.00	40.00	100	300	—
1844 P Rare	15,000	—	—	—	—	—
1845 P	10,000	20.00	40.00	100	300	—
1846 P Rare	19,000	—	—	—	—	—
1847 P	11,000	20.00	40.00	100	300	—
1848 P	8,110	175	300	500	1,000	—
1849 P Rare	3,037	—	—	—	—	—

C# 122.2 LIRA
5.0000 g., 0.9000 Silver .1444 oz. **Note:** Mint mark: Eagle head.

Date	Mintage	F	VF	XF	Unc	BU
1850 B	92,000	25.00	50.00	150	400	—
1851 B Rare	—	—	—	—	—	—
1852 B Rare	—	—	—	—	—	—
1853 B	22,000	25.00	50.00	150	400	—
1854 B Rare	—	—	—	—	—	—
1855 B	16,000	25.00	50.00	150	400	—
1856 B	58,000	20.00	40.00	100	300	—
1857 B	31,000	20.00	40.00	100	300	—
1858 B Rare	—	—	—	—	—	—
1859 B	5,150	20.00	40.00	100	250	—
1860 B	4,752	40.00	80.00	100	300	—

C# 122.1 LIRA

5.0000 g., 0.9000 Silver .1444 oz. **Note:** Mint mark: Anchor.

Date	Mintage	F	VF	XF	Unc	BU
1850 P	—	50.00	75.00	125	400	—
1853 P	7,051	50.00	75.00	150	600	—
1859 P	12,000	40.00	75.00	125	400	—
1860 P Rare	—	—	—	—	—	—

C# 122.3 LIRA

5.0000 g., 0.9000 Silver .1444 oz.

Date	Mintage	F	VF	XF	Unc	BU
1859M	—	50.00	100	200	600	—
1860M	603,000	50.00	100	200	600	—

C# 104.1 2 LIRE

10.0000 g., 0.9000 Silver .2888 oz. **Note:** Mint mark: Eagle head.

Date	Mintage	F	VF	XF	Unc	BU
1823 L Rare	—	—	—	—	—	—
1825 L	261,000	25.00	50.00	100	300	—
1826 L	235,000	25.00	50.00	100	350	—
1827 L	170,000	25.00	50.00	100	350	—
1828 L	102,000	25.00	50.00	200	400	—
1829 L Rare	—	—	—	—	—	—
1830 L	49,000	25.00	50.00	100	350	—
1830 P	Inc. above	25.00	50.00	150	400	—

C# 104.2 2 LIRE

10.0000 g., 0.9000 Silver .2888 oz. **Note:** Mint mark: Anchor.

Date	Mintage	F	VF	XF	Unc	BU
1825 P	—	25.00	50.00	100	400	—
1826 P	157,000	25.00	50.00	100	350	—
1827 P	366,000	25.00	50.00	100	350	—
1830 P	115,000	25.00	50.00	100	350	—
1831 P	72,000	25.00	50.00	100	350	—

C# 112.1 2 LIRE

10.0000 g., 0.9000 Silver .2888 oz. **Obv:** Younger head right

Date	Mintage	F	VF	XF	Unc	BU
1832 P	35,000	25.00	50.00	150	600	—
1833 P	187	50.00	100	200	1,000	—
1835 P	5,142	50.00	100	200	1,000	—
1836 P	30,000	50.00	100	200	1,000	—
1844 P	30,000	25.00	50.00	100	500	—
1845 P	52,000	50.00	100	200	750	—
1847 P	—	50.00	100	200	750	—

C# 112.2 2 LIRE

10.0000 g., 0.9000 Silver .2888 oz. **Obv:** Younger head right **Note:** Mint mark: Eagle head.

Date	Mintage	F	VF	XF	Unc	BU
1833 P	287	250	500	1,000	2,000	—
1834 P	—	250	500	750	1,000	—
1835 P	24,000	35.00	75.00	150	500	—
1836 P	—	35.00	75.00	150	500	—
1838 P Rare	20,000	—	—	—	—	—
1839 P Rare	14,000	—	—	—	—	—
1841 P	4,259	150	250	350	800	—
1842 P	10,000	35.00	75.00	150	500	—
1843 P	12,000	35.00	75.00	150	500	—
1844 P	12,000	35.00	75.00	150	500	—
1845 P	15,000	35.00	75.00	150	500	—
1846 P	15,000	35.00	75.00	150	500	—
1847 P Rare	15,000	—	—	—	—	—
1848 P Rare	13,000	—	—	—	—	—
1849 P Rare	3,159	—	—	—	—	—

C# 123.2 2 LIRE

10.0000 g., 0.9000 Silver .2888 oz. **Obv:** Head with beard right **Note:** Mint mark: Eagle head.

Date	Mintage	F	VF	XF	Unc	BU
1850 B	18,000	60.00	125	300	900	—
1852 B	23,000	60.00	125	300	900	—
1853 B	4,859	60.00	125	300	900	—
1854 B	18,000	60.00	125	300	900	—
1855 B	9,414	60.00	125	300	900	—
1856 B	11,000	60.00	125	300	900	—
1860 B	8,963	60.00	125	300	900	—

C# 123.1 2 LIRE

10.0000 g., 0.9000 Silver .2888 oz. **Obv:** Head with beard right **Note:** Mint mark: Anchor.

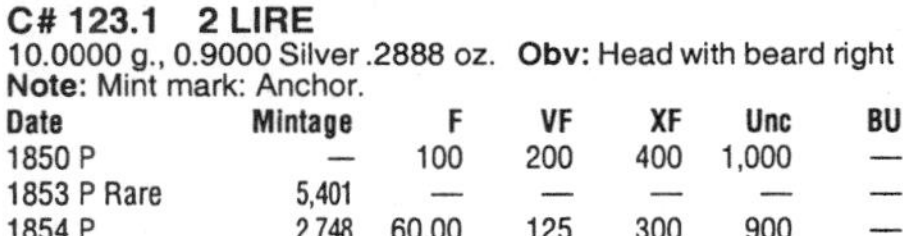

Date	Mintage	F	VF	XF	Unc	BU
1850 P	—	100	200	400	1,000	—
1853 P Rare	5,401	—	—	—	—	—
1854 P	2,748	60.00	125	300	900	—

C# 92 5 LIRE

25.0000 g., 0.9000 Silver .7234 oz. **Obv:** Similar to C#93 **Note:** Mint mark: Eagle head.

Date	Mintage	F	VF	XF	Unc	BU
1816 L	23,000	150	300	600	1,700	—
1817 L	44,000	100	200	500	1,450	—
1818 L	55,000	100	200	500	1,450	—
1819 L	35,000	100	200	500	1,450	—
1820 L	101,000	100	200	500	1,450	—

C# 93 5 LIRE

25.0000 g., 0.9000 Silver .7234 oz.

Date	F	VF	XF	Unc	BU
1821	850	1,500	3,200	7,000	—

C# 105.1 5 LIRE

25.0000 g., 0.9000 Silver .7234 oz.

Date	Mintage	F	VF	XF	Unc	BU
1821 L	35,000	150	300	750	2,500	—
1822 L	37,000	100	200	450	1,400	—
1823 L	35,000	85.00	175	350	1,000	—
1824 L	162,000	70.00	150	385	750	—
1825 L	395,000	35.00	65.00	200	550	—
1826 L	907,000	35.00	65.00	200	550	—
1827 L	724,000	35.00	65.00	200	550	—
1828 L	253,000	35.00	65.00	200	550	—
1829 L	312,000	35.00	65.00	200	550	—
1830 L	913,000	35.00	65.00	200	550	—
1830 P	Inc. above	35.00	65.00	200	550	—
1831 P	49,000	80.00	165	325	750	—

C# 105.2 5 LIRE

25.0000 g., 0.9000 Silver .7234 oz. **Note:** Mint mark: Anchor.

Date	Mintage	F	VF	XF	Unc	BU
1824 P	16,000	90.00	185	400	1,300	—
1825 P	17,000	100	200	450	1,450	—
1826 P	489,000	35.00	65.00	200	550	—
1827 P	2,137,000	35.00	65.00	200	550	—
1828 P	1,149,000	35.00	65.00	200	550	—
1829 P	597,000	35.00	65.00	200	550	—
1830 P	1,122,000	35.00	65.00	200	550	—
1831 P	451,000	100	200	450	1,450	—

C# 113.3 5 LIRE

25.0000 g., 0.9000 Silver .7234 oz. **Obv:** FERRARIS on truncation **Note:** Mint mark: Anchor.

Date	Mintage	F	VF	XF	Unc	BU
1831 P	—	30.00	60.00	200	600	—
Note: Mintage included with C#113.1						
1832 P	317,000	30.00	60.00	200	600	—
1833 P	275,000	30.00	60.00	200	600	—
1834 P	154,000	30.00	60.00	200	600	—
1835 P	336,000	30.00	60.00	200	600	—
1836 P	595,000	30.00	60.00	200	600	—
1837 P	359,000	30.00	60.00	200	600	—
1838 P	307,000	30.00	60.00	200	600	—
1839 P	141,000	30.00	60.00	200	600	—
1840 P	193,000	30.00	60.00	200	600	—
1841 P	313,000	30.00	60.00	200	600	—
1842 P	396,000	30.00	60.00	200	600	—
1843 P	787,000	30.00	60.00	200	600	—
1844 P	1,043,000	30.00	60.00	200	600	—
1845 P	302,000	30.00	60.00	200	600	—
1846 P	264,000	30.00	60.00	200	600	—
1847 P	142,000	30.00	60.00	200	600	—
1848 P	778,000	30.00	60.00	200	600	—
1849 P	739,000	30.00	60.00	200	600	—

C# 113.1 5 LIRE

25.0000 g., 0.9000 Silver .7234 oz. **Obv:** F on truncation **Rev:** Arms

Date	Mintage	F	VF	XF	Unc	BU
1831 P	451,000	50.00	100	300	750	—

C# 113.2 5 LIRE

25.0000 g., 0.9000 Silver .7234 oz. **Obv:** F on truncation **Rev:** Arms **Note:** Mint mark: Eagle head.

Date	Mintage	F	VF	XF	Unc	BU
1831 P	49,000	65.00	125	325	900	—

C# 113.4 5 LIRE

25.0000 g., 0.9000 Silver .7234 oz. **Obv:** FERRARIS on truncation **Note:** Mint mark: Eagle head.

Date	Mintage	F	VF	XF	Unc	BU
1831 P	—	65.00	125	325	1,000	—
Note: Mintage included with C#113.2						
1832 P	95,000	30.00	60.00	200	600	—
1833 P	60,000	30.00	60.00	200	600	—
1834 P	37,000	30.00	60.00	200	600	—
1835 P	69,000	30.00	60.00	200	600	—
1836 P	51,000	30.00	60.00	200	600	—
1837 P	36,000	30.00	60.00	200	600	—
1838 P	42,000	30.00	60.00	200	600	—
1839 P	205,000	30.00	60.00	200	600	—
1840 P	50,000	30.00	60.00	200	600	—
1841 P	15,000	75.00	150	350	450	—
1842 P	42,000	30.00	60.00	200	1,100	—
1843 P	37,000	30.00	60.00	200	600	—
1844 P	171,000	30.00	60.00	200	600	—
1845 P	42,000	30.00	60.00	200	600	—
1846 P	46,000	30.00	60.00	200	600	—
1847 P	37,000	30.00	60.00	200	600	—
1848 P	79,000	30.00	60.00	200	600	—
1849 P	104,000	125	300	550	725	—

C# 124.2 5 LIRE

25.0000 g., 0.9000 Silver .7234 oz. **Note:** Mint mark: Eagle head.

Date	Mintage	F	VF	XF	Unc	BU
1850 B	58,000	55.00	125	350	1,350	—
1851 B	49,000	55.00	125	350	1,350	—
1852 B	97,000	55.00	125	350	1,350	—
1854 B	74,000	55.00	125	350	1,350	—
1855 B	52,000	55.00	125	350	1,350	—
1856 B	37,000	55.00	125	350	1,350	—
1857 B	19,000	55.00	125	350	1,350	—
1858 B	11,000	55.00	125	350	1,350	—
1859 B	12,000	55.00	125	350	1,350	—
1860 B	5,044	55.00	125	350	1,350	—
1861 B	12,000	55.00	125	350	1,350	—

C# 124.1 5 LIRE

25.0000 g., 0.9000 Silver .7234 oz. **Note:** Mint mark: Anchor.

Date	Mintage	F	VF	XF	Unc	BU
1850 P	721,000	55.00	125	350	450	—
1851 P	316,000	55.00	125	350	450	—
1852 P	391,000	55.00	125	350	450	—
1853 P	167,000	55.00	125	350	450	—
1854 P	284,000	55.00	125	350	450	—
1855 P	84,000	55.00	125	350	450	—
1856 P	58,000	55.00	125	350	450	—
1857 P	35,000	55.00	125	350	450	—
1858 P	30,000	55.00	125	350	450	—
1859 P	49,000	55.00	125	350	450	—

C# 114.1 10 LIRE

3.2200 g., 0.9000 Gold .0931 oz. **Note:** Mint mark: Eagle head.

Date	Mintage	F	VF	XF	Unc	BU
1832 P Rare	—	—	—	—	—	—
1833 P	5,004	125	300	450	1,000	—
1835 P	5,118	225	375	550	1,200	—
1838 P	2,826	250	400	575	1,250	—
1839 P	2,237	175	350	500	1,100	—
1841 P	1,583	175	350	500	1,100	—
1842 P	759	250	475	650	1,800	—
1843 P	950	250	475	650	1,800	—
1845 P	3,009	225	450	600	1,500	—
1846 P	970	250	475	650	1,800	—
1847 P	405	250	500	750	2,100	—

C# 114.2 10 LIRE

3.2200 g., 0.9000 Gold .0931 oz. **Note:** Mint mark: Anchor.

Date	Mintage	F	VF	XF	Unc	BU
1833 P	1,550	225	425	850	1,350	—
1835 P Rare	—	—	—	—	—	—
1841 P	2,809	225	425	850	1,250	—
1843 P	4,566	225	425	850	1,250	—
1844 P	11,000	175	325	450	1,000	—
1845 P	1,535	225	425	850	1,250	—
1846 P	3,373	225	425	850	1,250	—
1847 P Rare	—	—	—	—	—	—

C# 125.1 10 LIRE

3.2200 g., 0.9000 Gold .0931 oz.

Date	Mintage	F	VF	XF	Unc	BU
1850 P	4,141	300	750	1,250	1,800	—
1853 P	600	—	—	—	—	—

C# 125.2 10 LIRE

3.2200 g., 0.9000 Gold .0931 oz. **Note:** Mint mark: Eagle head.

Date	Mintage	F	VF	XF	Unc	BU
1850 B	2,326	225	400	600	1,000	—
1852 B	—	500	1,000	1,500	2,000	—
1853 B	—	225	400	600	1,000	—
1854 B	1,833	225	400	600	1,000	—
1855 B	2,566	225	400	600	1,000	—
1856 B	2,526	225	400	600	1,000	—
1857 B	7,193	225	400	600	1,000	—
1858 B	2,931	225	400	600	1,000	—
1859 B 1 known	—	—	—	7,040	—	—
1860 B	6,036	225	400	600	1,000	—

C# 95 20 LIRE

6.4500 g., 0.9000 Gold .1866 oz. **Note:** Mint mark: Eagle head.

Date	Mintage	F	VF	XF	Unc	BU
1816	19,000	225	350	450	750	—
1817	40,000	125	225	350	600	—
1818	35,000	125	225	350	600	—
1819	22,000	125	225	350	600	—
1820	33,000	125	225	350	600	—

C# 96 20 LIRE

6.4500 g., 0.9000 Gold .1866 oz.

Date	F	VF	XF	Unc	BU
1821	1,500	2,500	3,750	6,000	—

C# 106.1 20 LIRE

6.4500 g., 0.9000 Gold .1866 oz.

Date	Mintage	F	VF	XF	Unc	BU
1821 L	18,000	125	200	275	475	—
1822 L	7,460	125	200	325	500	—
1823 L	22,000	125	200	275	475	—
1824 L	2,381	200	275	375	650	—
1825 L	28,000	125	200	275	475	—
1826 L	144,000	125	185	250	475	—
1827 L	150,000	125	185	250	475	—
1828 L	95,000	125	185	250	475	—
1828 P	—	225	300	400	650	—
1829 L	61,000	225	300	400	650	—
1829 P	—	225	300	400	650	—
1830 L	—	225	300	400	650	—
1830 P	35,000	200	275	375	600	—
1831 P	42,000	125	200	275	475	—

C# 106.2 20 LIRE

6.4500 g., 0.9000 Gold .1866 oz. **Note:** Mint mark: Anchor.

Date	Mintage	F	VF	XF	Unc	BU
1824 P	2,394	375	500	600	850	—
1825 P	313	375	500	1,000	2,200	—
1827 P	1,766	225	300	400	500	—
1828 P Rare	—	—	—	—	—	—
1829 P	—	225	300	400	500	—
1830 P	3,270	375	500	600	800	—
1831 P Rare	16,189	—	—	—	—	—

C# 115.2 20 LIRE

6.4500 g., 0.9000 Gold .1866 oz. **Note:** Mint mark: Eagle head.

Date	Mintage	F	VF	XF	Unc	BU
1831 P	—	BV	90.00	120	265	—
1832 P	53,000	BV	90.00	120	265	—
1833 P	16,000	BV	90.00	120	265	—
1834 P	261,000	BV	90.00	120	265	—
1836 P Rare	14,000	—	—	—	—	—
1837 P Rare	15,000	—	—	—	—	—
1838 P	31,000	BV	90.00	120	265	—
1839 P	70,000	BV	90.00	120	265	—
1840/30 P	28,000	100	200	300	550	—
1840 P	Inc. above	BV	90.00	120	265	—
1841 P Rare	31,000	—	—	—	—	—
1842 P	26,000	BV	90.00	120	265	—
1843 P Rare	24,000	—	—	—	—	—
1844 P	30,000	BV	90.00	120	265	—
1845 P	35,000	BV	90.00	120	265	—
1846 P	30,000	BV	90.00	120	265	—
1847 P	33,000	BV	90.00	120	265	—
1848 P Rare	59,000	BV	—	—	—	—
1849 P	58,000	BV	90.00	120	265	—

C# 115.1 20 LIRE

6.4500 g., 0.9000 Gold .1866 oz.

Date	Mintage	F	VF	XF	Unc	BU
1831 P	—	BV	90.00	120	265	—
1832 P	74,000	BV	90.00	120	265	—
1833 P Rare	80,000	—	—	—	—	—
1834 P	133,000	BV	90.00	120	265	—
1835 P	52,000	BV	90.00	120	265	—
1836 P	90,000	BV	90.00	120	265	—
1837 P Rare	56,000	—	—	—	—	—
1838 P	120,000	BV	90.00	120	265	—
1839 P Rare	74,000	—	—	—	—	—
1840 P	176,000	BV	90.00	120	265	—
1841 P	206,000	125	175	250	375	—
1842 P	66,000	BV	90.00	120	265	—
1843 P Rare	45,000	—	—	—	—	—
1844 P Rare	34,000	—	—	—	—	—
1845 P	43,000	BV	90.00	120	265	—
1846 P Rare	43,000	—	—	—	—	—
1847 P	52,000	BV	90.00	120	265	—
1848 P	59,000	125	150	175	265	—
1849 P	111,000	BV	90.00	120	250	—

C# 115.3 20 LIRE

6.4500 g., 0.9000 Gold .1866 oz. **Note:** Unknown mint.

Date	F	VF	XF	Unc	BU
1834	BV	90.00	120	265	—
1847	BV	90.00	120	265	—

C# 126.2 20 LIRE

6.4500 g., 0.9000 Gold .1866 oz. **Note:** Mint mark: Eagle head.

Date	Mintage	F	VF	XF	Unc	BU
1850 B	66,000	BV	80.00	110	245	—
1851 B	163,000	BV	80.00	110	245	—
1852 B	46,000	BV	80.00	110	245	—
1853 B	41,000	—	—	—	—	—
1855 B	41,000	BV	80.00	110	245	—
1855 B	—	BV	80.00	110	245	—
Note: Error: EMMANVEL H for II						
1856 B	61,000	375	500	750	1,200	—
1857 B	67,000	BV	80.00	110	245	—
1858 B	103,000	150	250	400	600	—
1859 B	187,000	BV	80.00	110	245	—
1860 B	111,000	BV	150	175	375	—
1861 B	156,000	BV	150	175	375	—

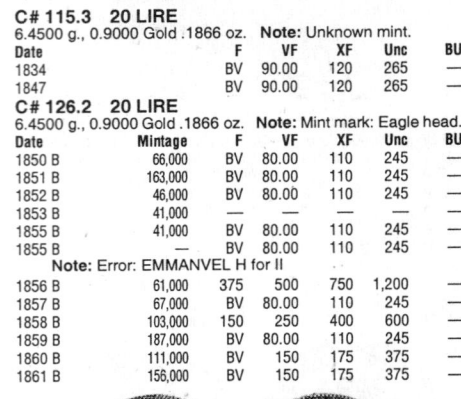

C# 126.1 20 LIRE

6.4500 g., 0.9000 Gold .1866 oz. **Note:** Mint mark: Anchor.

Date	Mintage	F	VF	XF	Unc	BU
1850 P	139,000	BV	80.00	110	245	—
1851 P	296,000	BV	80.00	110	245	—
1852 P	103,000	BV	80.00	110	245	—
1853 P	137,000	BV	80.00	110	245	—
1854 P	142,000	BV	80.00	110	245	—
1855 P	148,000	BV	80.00	110	245	—
1856 P	113,000	BV	80.00	110	245	—
1857 P	59,000	BV	80.00	110	245	—
1858 P	176,000	BV	80.00	110	245	—
1859 P	436,000	BV	80.00	110	245	—
1860 P	163,000	BV	80.00	110	245	—

C# 126.3 20 LIRE

6.4500 g., 0.9000 Gold .1866 oz.

Date	Mintage	F	VF	XF	Unc	BU
1860M	23,000	125	200	300	500	—

C# 107.1 40 LIRE

12.9000 g., 0.9000 Gold .3733 oz. **Note:** Mint mark: Eagle head.

Date	Mintage	F	VF	XF	Unc	BU
1822 L	5,011	300	400	600	1,350	—
1823 L Rare	—	—	—	—	—	—
1825 L	39,000	125	200	300	750	—
1831 L	—	300	400	500	1,150	—
1831 P	7,711	300	400	500	1,150	—

C# 107.2 40 LIRE

12.9000 g., 0.9000 Gold .3733 oz. **Note:** Mint mark: Anchor.

Date	Mintage	F	VF	XF	Unc	BU
1825 P	3,994	300	400	600	1,400	—
1826 P	2,844	300	400	750	1,500	—

C# 116.1 50 LIRE

16.1200 g., 0.9000 Gold .4664 oz. **Note:** Mint mark: Eagle head.

Date	Mintage	F	VF	XF	Unc	BU
1832 P Rare	93	—	—	—	—	—
1833 P	1,773	750	1,000	1,500	2,500	—
1834 P Rare	657	—	—	—	—	—
1835 P Rare	1,296	—	—	—	—	—
1836 P	385	900	1,250	1,750	2,750	—
1838 P Rare	992	—	—	—	—	—
1839 P Rare	553	—	—	—	—	—
1840 P Rare	1,402	—	—	—	—	—
1841 P Rare	2,753	—	—	—	—	—
1843 P Rare	586	—	—	—	—	—

C# 116.2 50 LIRE

16.1200 g., 0.9000 Gold .4664 oz. **Note:** Mint mark: Anchor.

Date	Mintage	F	VF	XF	Unc	BU
1833 P	92	4,000	5,000	6,000	8,000	—
1835 P Rare	—	—	—	—	—	—
1841 P Rare	562	—	—	—	—	—

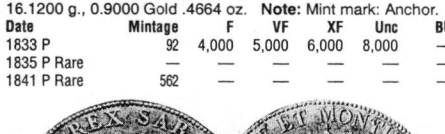

C# 97 80 LIRE

25.8000 g., 0.9000 Gold .7466 oz. **Note:** Mint mark: Eagle head.

Date	Mintage	F	VF	XF	Unc	BU
1821	965	4,000	7,000	10,000	20,000	—

C# 108.1 80 LIRE

25.8000 g., 0.9000 Gold .7466 oz.

Date	Mintage	F	VF	XF	Unc	BU
1823 L Rare	—	—	—	—	—	—
1824 L	5,919	450	550	650	1,000	—
1825 L	14,000	400	500	600	900	—
1826 L	76,000	400	500	600	900	—
1827 L	38,000	400	500	600	900	—
1828 L	23,000	400	500	600	900	—
1828 P	Inc. above	600	750	1,000	1,500	—
1829 P	8,181	400	500	600	900	—
1830 P	5,972	400	500	600	900	—
1831 P	740	800	1,000	1,250	2,000	—

C# 108.2 80 LIRE

25.8000 g., 0.9000 Gold .7466 oz. **Note:** Mint mark: Anchor.

Date	Mintage	F	VF	XF	Unc	BU
1824 P	3,904	500	700	900	1,500	—
1825 P	8,465	425	550	725	1,200	—
1826 P	2,305	700	900	1,100	1,750	—
1827 P	15,000	400	500	600	1,100	—
1828 P	8,961	400	500	600	1,100	—
1829 P	7,436	400	500	600	1,100	—
1830 P	26,000	425	550	725	1,200	—
1831 P	21,000	600	800	1,250	2,000	—

C# 117.1 100 LIRE

32.2500 g., 0.9000 Gold .9332 oz. **Note:** Mint mark: Anchor.

Date	Mintage	F	VF	XF	Unc	BU
1832 P	—	500	600	850	1,800	—
1833 P	2,587	600	700	800	1,750	—
1834 P	12,000	500	575	700	1,400	—
1835 P	8,513	500	600	850	1,500	—
1836 P	703	700	900	1,100	2,250	—
1837 P	250	900	1,100	1,350	2,750	—
1838 P Rare	4,774	—	—	—	—	—
1839 P Rare	2,922	—	—	—	—	—
1840 P	1,003	700	900	1,100	2,250	—
1841 P	8,889	475	600	850	1,750	—
1842 P	3,606	700	900	1,100	2,250	—
1843 P	424	1,500	2,000	2,500	4,000	—
1844 P	2,213	1,000	1,500	2,000	3,500	—
1845 P	646	1,000	1,500	2,000	3,500	—

C# 117.2 100 LIRE

32.2500 g., 0.9000 Gold .9332 oz. **Note:** Mint mark: Eagle head.

Date	Mintage	F	VF	XF	Unc	BU
1832 P	—	475	550	750	1,600	—
1833 P	6,769	475	550	750	1,600	—
1834 P	37,000	475	525	700	1,400	—
1835 P	26,000	475	525	700	1,400	—
1836 P	6,236	475	525	700	1,400	—
1837 P	3,885	475	550	750	1,600	—
1838 P Rare	3,916	—	—	—	—	—
1840 P	2,898	475	550	750	1,600	—
1841 P	1,207	700	1,000	1,300	2,000	—
1842 P	864	700	1,000	1,300	2,000	—
1843 P	827	700	900	1,100	2,250	—
1844 P Rare	91	—	—	—	—	—

PATTERNS

Including off metal strikes

KM#	Date	Mintage	Identification	Mkt Val
Pn4	1832	—	2 Lire. 0.9000 Silver. C#112.2.	—

SICILY

Has a history of occupation extending back to the ancient Phoenicians. In more recent times it was part of the Kingdom of Naples and Sicily.

RULERS

Ferdinando III, 1759-1825
(became Ferdinando I in 1816 as King of Two Sicilies)
Ferdinando II, 1830-1859

MINT OFFICIALS' INITIALS

Palermo Mint

Initial	Date	Name
JVI	1798-1807	Guiseppe Ugo
VB	1810-1816	Vicenzo Beninati

MONETARY SYSTEM

6 Cavalli = 1 Grano
20 Grani = 2 Carlini = 1 Tari
12 Tari = 1 Piastra
15 Tari = 1 Scudo
2 Scudi = 1 Oncia

KINGDOM

STANDARD COINAGE

C# 52 MEZZO (1/2) GRANO

Copper **Ruler:** Ferdinando II **Obv:** Head right **Rev:** Value, SICILIANO, date

Date	VG	F	VF	XF	Unc
1836	40.00	90.00	180	325	—

C# 41 UN (1) GRANO

Copper **Ruler:** Ferdinando III

Date	VG	F	VF	XF	Unc
1801 JVI	6.00	10.00	20.00	45.00	—
1802 JVI	25.00	40.00	75.00	150	—
1803 JVI	20.00	30.00	50.00	100	—

C# 42 UN (1) GRANO

Copper **Ruler:** Ferdinando III **Note:** Varieties exist.

Date	VG	F	VF	XF	Unc
ND(1814) VB	20.00	30.00	50.00	100	—
1814 VB	5.00	10.00	20.00	45.00	—
1815 VB	5.00	10.00	20.00	45.00	—

C# 53 UN (1) GRANO

Copper **Ruler:** Ferdinando II **Obv:** Head right **Rev:** SICILIANO, value, date

Date	VG	F	VF	XF	Unc
1836	50.00	100	200	350	—

C# 43 DUE (2) GRANI

Copper **Ruler:** Ferdinando III **Obv:** Eagle, legend **Rev:** Value, date within wreath

Date	VG	F	VF	XF	Unc
1801 JVI	20.00	30.00	50.00	100	—
1802 JVI	6.00	10.00	20.00	45.00	—
1803 JVI	6.00	10.00	20.00	45.00	—
1804 JVI	6.00	10.00	20.00	45.00	—

C# 45 DUE (2) GRANI

Copper **Ruler:** Ferdinando III **Obv:** Eagle, legend **Rev:** Value, date within wreath

Date	VG	F	VF	XF	Unc
1801 JVI	30.00	45.00	75.00	150	—
1802 JVI	15.00	22.50	50.00	125	—
1803 JVI	15.00	22.50	50.00	125	—
1804 JVI	15.00	22.50	50.00	125	—

C# 44 DUE (2) GRANI

Copper **Ruler:** Ferdinando III

Date	VG	F	VF	XF	Unc
1814 VB	10.00	15.00	25.00	50.00	—

Note: 1814 exists with large and small G.2

Date	VG	F	VF	XF	Unc
1815 VB	8.00	12.00	22.00	50.00	—

C# 54 DUE (2) GRANI

Copper **Ruler:** Ferdinando II **Obv:** Head right **Rev:** SICILIANI, value, date

Date	VG	F	VF	XF	Unc
1836	50.00	100	200	350	—

C# 46 CINQUE (5) GRANI

Copper **Ruler:** Ferdinando III **Obv:** Large head

Date	VG	F	VF	XF	Unc
ND(1814) VB	30.00	45.00	75.00	150	—
1814 VB	12.00	20.00	40.00	90.00	—
1815 VB	12.00	20.00	40.00	90.00	—

Note: Varieties exist of 1815

C# 46a CINQUE (5) GRANI

Copper **Ruler:** Ferdinando III **Obv:** Small head

Date	VG	F	VF	XF	Unc
1815 VB	12.00	20.00	40.00	90.00	—
1816 VB	20.00	30.00	50.00	100	—

C# 55 CINQUE (5) GRANI

Copper **Ruler:** Ferdinando III **Obv:** Head right **Rev:** SICILIANI, crown, value, date

Date	VG	F	VF	XF	Unc
1836	100	200	300	500	—

C# 47 DIECI (10) GRANI

Copper **Ruler:** Ferdinando III **Obv:** Eagle, legend **Rev:** Value, date within wreath

Date	VG	F	VF	XF	Unc
1801 JVI	20.00	30.00	65.00	185	—
1802 JVI	20.00	30.00	65.00	185	—
1803 JVI	20.00	30.00	65.00	185	—
1804 JVI	20.00	30.00	65.00	185	—

C# 48 DIECI (10) GRANI

Copper **Ruler:** Ferdinando III

Date	VG	F	VF	XF	Unc
ND(1814) VB	30.00	50.00	100	200	—
1814 VB	20.00	30.00	50.00	150	—
1815 VB	20.00	30.00	60.00	180	—

Note: 1815 exists with G.10. and G.10, and with lower right tip of bust pointing to E in REX ; also tip of bust pointing to X in REX

C# 56 DIECI (10) GRANI

Copper **Ruler:** Ferdinando II **Obv:** Head right **Rev:** SICILIANI, crown, value, date

Date	VG	F	VF	XF	Unc
1835	400	500	750	1,000	—
1836	150	250	400	650	—

C# 49 12 TARI

27.5330 g., 0.8330 Silver .7817 oz. **Ruler:** Ferdinando III **Obv:** Bust right **Obv. Legend:** FERDINAN • D • G • SICIL... **Rev:** Eagle, date **Note:** Dav. #1425.

Date	VG	F	VF	XF	Unc
1801 JVI	40.00	75.00	125	200	—

Note: 1801 exists with REX • and REX

Date	VG	F	VF	XF	Unc
1803 JVI	40.00	75.00	125	200	—

C# 49a 12 TARI

27.5330 g., 0.8330 Silver .7817 oz. **Ruler:** Ferdinando III **Obv. Legend:** FERDINAN • III • D • G • SICIL...

Date	VG	F	VF	XF	Unc
1801 JVI	40.00	75.00	125	200	—
1802 JVI	40.00	75.00	125	200	—
1803 JVI	40.00	75.00	125	200	—
1804 JVI	40.00	75.00	125	200	—

C# 50 12 TARI

27.5330 g., 0.8830 Silver .7817 oz. **Ruler:** Ferdinando III **Rev:** J.V.I. above eagle within wreath

Date	VG	F	VF	XF	Unc
1805 JVI	50.00	100	200	400	—
1806 JVI	50.00	100	200	400	—
1807 JVI	50.00	100	200	400	—

C# 50a 12 TARI

27.5330 g., 0.8830 Silver .7817 oz. **Ruler:** Ferdinando III **Rev:** Eagle between V. and B. within wreath **Note:** Seven varieties exist.

Date	VG	F	VF	XF	Unc
1810 VB	50.00	100	150	350	—

C# 51 2 ONCIE

8.8150 g., 0.9060 Gold .2567 oz. **Ruler:** Ferdinando III

Date	F	VF	XF	Unc	BU
1814 VB	3,000	5,000	8,000	15,000	—

TUSCANY

Etruria

An Italian territorial division on the west-central peninsula, belonged to the Medici from 1530 to 1737,when it was given to Francis, duke of Lorraine. In 1800 the French established it as part of the Spanish dominions; from 1807 to 1809 it was a French department. After the fall of Napoleon it reverted to its pre-Napoleonic owner, Ferdinand III.

RULERS

Ferdinando III, 1791-1801
Louis I, 1801-1803
Charles Louis, under regency of his mother Maria Louisa, 1803-1807
Annexed To France, 1807-1814
Ferdinando III, Restored, 1814-1824
Leopold II, 1824-1848, 1849-1859
Provisional Government, 1859
United to Italian Provisional Government, 1859-1861

MINT MARKS

FIRENZE - Florence
LEGHORN - Livorno
PISIS – Pisa

MONETARY SYSTEM

Until 1826

12 Denari = 3 Quattrini = 1 Soldo
20 Soldi = 1 Lira
10 Lire = 1 Dena
40 Quattrini = 1 Paolo
1-1/2 Paoli = 1 Lira
10 Paoli = 1 Francescone, Scudo, Tallero
3 Zecchini = 1 Ruspone = 40 Lire

1826-1859

100 Quattrini = 1 Fiorino
4 Fiorini = 10 Paoli

1859

100 Centesimi = 1 Lira

DUCHY

STANDARD COINAGE

C# 30 QUATTRINO

Copper **Obv:** Square arms **Rev:** Value and date

Date	VG	F	VF	XF	Unc
1801	3.00	5.00	10.00	25.00	—

C# 40 QUATTRINO

Copper **Obv:** Crowned arms **Rev:** Value

Date	VG	F	VF	XF	Unc
1802	12.00	20.00	80.00	125	—
1803	4.50	8.00	35.00	60.00	—
1805 Error date	5.00	8.50	36.50	65.00	—

C# 44 QUATTRINO

Copper

Date	VG	F	VF	XF	Unc
1803	4.50	8.00	40.00	80.00	—
1804	4.50	8.00	40.00	80.00	—
1805	4.50	8.00	40.00	80.00	—
1806	4.50	8.00	40.00	80.00	—
1807	4.50	8.00	40.00	80.00	—

C# 53 QUATTRINO

Copper **Obv:** Arms **Obv. Legend:** FERD. III... **Rev:** Value

Date	VG	F	VF	XF	Unc
1819	2.50	4.00	12.00	30.00	—
1820	2.50	4.00	12.00	30.00	—
1821	2.50	4.00	12.00	30.00	—
1822	2.50	4.00	12.00	30.00	—
1824	2.50	4.00	12.00	30.00	—

C# 62 QUATTRINO

Copper **Obv. Legend:** LEOP. II A. D. 'A. GRAND. DI TOSC.

Date	VG	F	VF	XF	Unc
1827	2.50	4.00	10.00	22.00	—
1828	2.50	4.00	10.00	22.00	—
1829	2.50	4.00	10.00	22.00	—
1830	2.50	4.00	10.00	22.00	—
1831	2.50	4.00	10.00	22.00	—
1832	2.50	4.00	10.00	22.00	—
1833	2.50	4.00	10.00	22.00	—
1834	2.50	4.00	10.00	22.00	—
1835	2.50	4.00	10.00	22.00	—
1836	2.50	4.00	10.00	22.00	—
1837	2.50	4.00	10.00	22.00	—
1838	2.50	4.00	10.00	22.00	—
1840	2.50	4.00	10.00	22.00	—
1841	5.00	7.50	35.00	60.00	—
1843	5.00	7.50	35.00	60.00	—

C# 62a QUATTRINO

Copper **Obv. Legend:** LEOP. II A. D. 'A. G-D. DI TOSC.

Date	VG	F	VF	XF	Unc
1842	5.00	7.50	35.00	60.00	—
1843	2.50	4.00	10.00	22.00	—
1844	2.50	4.00	10.00	22.00	—
1845	2.50	4.00	10.00	22.00	—
1846	2.50	4.00	10.00	22.00	—
1847	2.50	4.00	10.00	22.00	—
1848	2.50	4.00	10.00	22.00	—
1849	2.50	4.00	10.00	22.00	—
1850	2.50	4.00	10.00	22.00	—
1851	2.50	4.00	10.00	22.00	—
1852	2.50	4.00	10.00	22.00	—
1853	2.50	4.00	10.00	22.00	—
1854	2.50	4.00	10.00	22.00	—
1856	2.50	4.00	10.00	22.00	—
1857	2.50	4.00	10.00	22.00	—

C# 45 MEZZO (1/2) SOLDO

Copper

Date	VG	F	VF	XF	Unc
ND(1804)	3.50	5.00	40.00	65.00	—

C# 64 3 QUATTRINI

Copper **Obv:** Crowned arms **Rev:** Patriarch's cross

Date	VG	F	VF	XF	Unc
1826	2.50	4.00	10.00	30.00	—
1827	2.50	4.00	10.00	30.00	—
1828	2.50	4.00	10.00	30.00	—
1829	4.50	9.00	35.00	60.00	—
1830	2.50	4.00	10.00	30.00	—
1832	2.50	4.00	10.00	30.00	—
1833	2.50	4.00	10.00	30.00	—
1834	2.50	4.00	10.00	30.00	—
1835	2.50	4.00	10.00	30.00	—
1836	2.50	4.00	10.00	30.00	—
1838	2.50	4.00	10.00	30.00	—
1839	2.50	4.00	10.00	30.00	—
1840	2.50	4.00	10.00	30.00	—
1843	2.50	4.00	10.00	30.00	—
1845	2.50	4.00	10.00	30.00	—
1846	2.50	4.00	10.00	30.00	—
1851	2.50	4.00	10.00	30.00	—
1853	2.50	4.00	10.00	30.00	—
1854	4.50	9.00	35.00	60.00	—

C# 54 SOLDO

Copper **Obv:** Arms **Obv. Legend:** FERD. III... **Rev:** Value

Date	VG	F	VF	XF	Unc
1822	2.00	4.00	10.00	30.00	—
1823	2.00	4.00	10.00	30.00	—

C# 63 SOLDO

Copper **Obv:** Arms **Obv. Legend:** LEOP. II... **Rev:** Value

Date	VG	F	VF	XF	Unc
1824	15.00	30.00	50.00	100	—

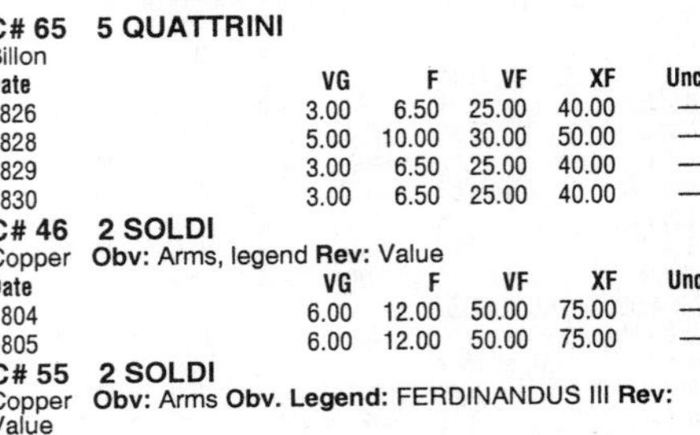

C# 65 5 QUATTRINI

Billon

Date	VG	F	VF	XF	Unc
1826	3.00	6.50	25.00	40.00	—
1828	5.00	10.00	30.00	50.00	—
1829	3.00	6.50	25.00	40.00	—
1830	3.00	6.50	25.00	40.00	—

C# 46 2 SOLDI

Copper **Obv:** Arms, legend **Rev:** Value

Date	VG	F	VF	XF	Unc
1804	6.00	12.00	50.00	75.00	—
1805	6.00	12.00	50.00	75.00	—

C# 55 2 SOLDI

Copper **Obv:** Arms **Obv. Legend:** FERDINANDUS III **Rev:** Value

Date	VG	F	VF	XF	Unc
1818	2.00	4.00	10.00	30.00	—
1822	2.00	4.00	10.00	30.00	—

C# 32 DIECI (10) QUATTRINI

Billon **Ruler:** Ferdinando III **Obv:** Crowned shield

Date	VG	F	VF	XF	Unc
1801	4.50	6.50	15.00	40.00	—

C# 41 DIECI (10) QUATTRINI

Billon **Obv:** Squarish arms **Rev:** Value

Date	VG	F	VF	XF	Unc
1801	6.00	10.00	35.00	75.00	—
1802	6.00	10.00	35.00	75.00	—

C# 41a DIECI (10) QUATTRINI

Billon **Obv:** Arms and date **Rev:** Value in value

Date	VG	F	VF	XF	Unc
1802	12.00	20.00	50.00	100	—

C# 41b DIECI (10) QUATTRINI

Billon **Obv:** Arms **Rev:** Value and date

Date	VG	F	VF	XF	Unc
1802	6.00	10.00	20.00	50.00	—

C# 66 DIECI (10) QUATTRINI

Billon **Obv:** Round arms **Rev:** 10 QUATTRINI

Date	VG	F	VF	XF	Unc
1826	6.00	10.00	15.00	25.00	—
1827	6.00	10.00	15.00	25.00	—

Date	VG	F	VF	XF	Unc
1853	6.00	10.00	15.00	25.00	—
1854	6.00	10.00	15.00	25.00	—

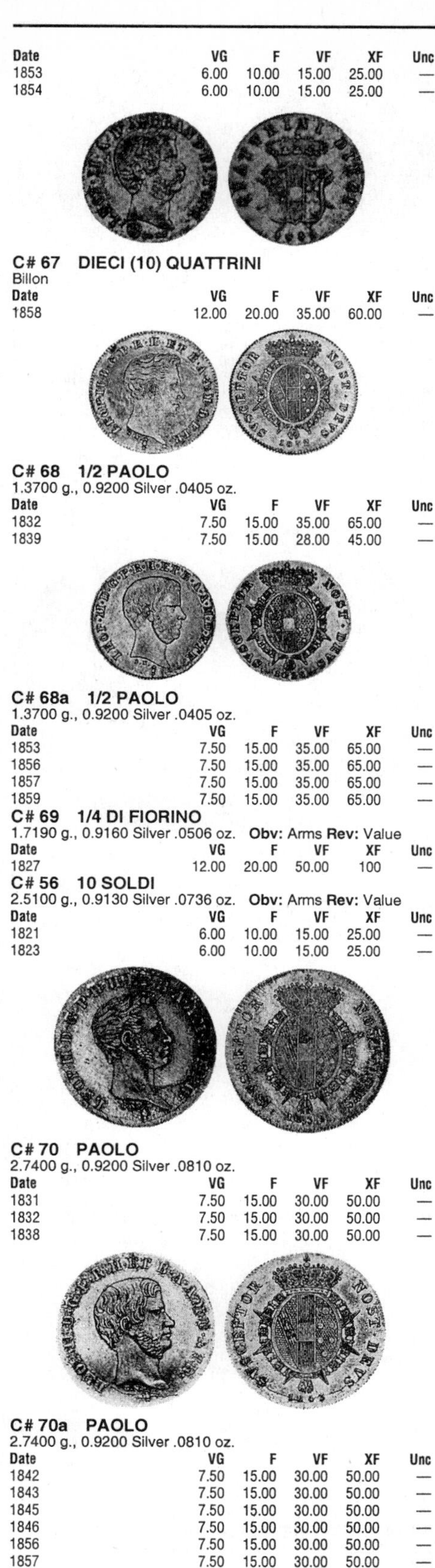

C# 67 DIECI (10) QUATTRINI
Billon

Date	VG	F	VF	XF	Unc
1858	12.00	20.00	35.00	60.00	—

C# 68 1/2 PAOLO
1.3700 g., 0.9200 Silver .0405 oz.

Date	VG	F	VF	XF	Unc
1832	7.50	15.00	35.00	65.00	—
1839	7.50	15.00	28.00	45.00	—

C# 68a 1/2 PAOLO
1.3700 g., 0.9200 Silver .0405 oz.

Date	VG	F	VF	XF	Unc
1853	7.50	15.00	35.00	65.00	—
1856	7.50	15.00	35.00	65.00	—
1857	7.50	15.00	35.00	65.00	—
1859	7.50	15.00	35.00	65.00	—

C# 69 1/4 DI FIORINO
1.7190 g., 0.9160 Silver .0506 oz. **Obv:** Arms **Rev:** Value

Date	VG	F	VF	XF	Unc
1827	12.00	20.00	50.00	100	—

C# 56 10 SOLDI
2.5100 g., 0.9130 Silver .0736 oz. **Obv:** Arms **Rev:** Value

Date	VG	F	VF	XF	Unc
1821	6.00	10.00	15.00	25.00	—
1823	6.00	10.00	15.00	25.00	—

C# 70 PAOLO
2.7400 g., 0.9200 Silver .0810 oz.

Date	VG	F	VF	XF	Unc
1831	7.50	15.00	30.00	50.00	—
1832	7.50	15.00	30.00	50.00	—
1838	7.50	15.00	30.00	50.00	—

C# 70a PAOLO
2.7400 g., 0.9200 Silver .0810 oz.

Date	VG	F	VF	XF	Unc
1842	7.50	15.00	30.00	50.00	—
1843	7.50	15.00	30.00	50.00	—
1845	7.50	15.00	30.00	50.00	—
1846	7.50	15.00	30.00	50.00	—
1856	7.50	15.00	30.00	50.00	—
1857	7.50	15.00	30.00	50.00	—
1858	7.50	15.00	30.00	50.00	—

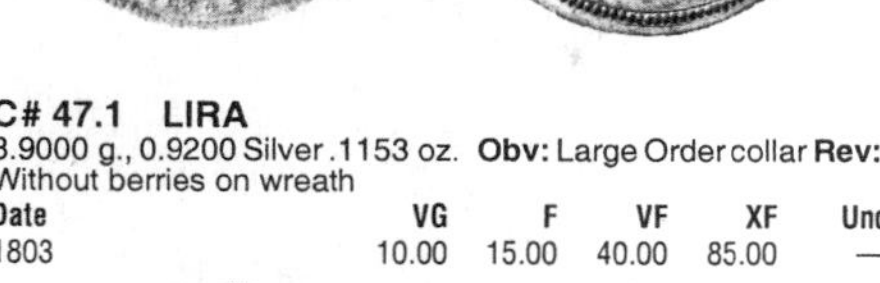

C# 47.1 LIRA
3.9000 g., 0.9200 Silver .1153 oz. **Obv:** Large Order collar **Rev:** Without berries on wreath

Date	VG	F	VF	XF	Unc
1803	10.00	15.00	40.00	85.00	—

C# 47.2 LIRA
3.9000 g., 0.9200 Silver .1153 oz. **Obv:** Small Order collar **Rev:** Berries on wreath

Date	VG	F	VF	XF	Unc
1806	10.00	15.00	40.00	85.00	—

C# 57 LIRA
4.1030 g., 0.9130 Silver .1204 oz. **Obv:** Head right **Rev:** Value

Date	VG	F	VF	XF	Unc
1821	12.00	20.00	50.00	100	—
1822	12.00	20.00	50.00	100	—
1823	12.00	20.00	50.00	100	—

C# 71 1/2 FIORINO
3.4380 g., 0.9160 Silver .1012 oz. **Obv:** Arms **Rev:** Value

Date	VG	F	VF	XF	Unc
1827	10.00	17.50	35.00	75.00	—

C# 72 FIORINO
6.8760 g., 0.9160 Silver .2025 oz.

Date	VG	F	VF	XF	Unc
1826	10.00	15.00	25.00	75.00	—
1828	10.00	15.00	25.00	75.00	—
1830	10.00	15.00	25.00	75.00	—
1840	10.00	15.00	25.00	75.00	—
1842	10.00	15.00	25.00	75.00	—

C# 72a FIORINO
6.8760 g., 0.9160 Silver .2025 oz.

Date	VG	F	VF	XF	Unc
1843	10.00	15.00	25.00	50.00	—
1844	10.00	15.00	25.00	50.00	—
1847	10.00	15.00	25.00	50.00	—
1848	10.00	15.00	25.00	50.00	—
1856	10.00	15.00	25.00	50.00	—
1857	10.00	15.00	25.00	50.00	—
1858	10.00	15.00	25.00	50.00	—

C# 58 5 PAOLI
13.7500 g., 0.9130 Silver .4036 oz.

Date	VG	F	VF	XF	Unc
1819	30.00	50.00	200	350	—
1820	30.00	50.00	100	200	—

C# 58a 5 PAOLI
13.7500 g., 0.9130 Silver .4036 oz. **Obv:** Longer hair

Date	VG	F	VF	XF	Unc
1823	60.00	100	250	500	—

C# 73 5 PAOLI
13.7500 g., 0.9160 Silver .4049 oz.

Date	VG	F	VF	XF	Unc
1827	25.00	40.00	80.00	200	—
1828	25.00	40.00	80.00	200	—
1829 PC	25.00	40.00	80.00	200	—

C# 73a 5 PAOLI
13.7500 g., 0.9160 Silver .4049 oz.

Date	VG	F	VF	XF	Unc
1834	125	150	250	600	—

C# 42.1 FRANCESCONE (10 Paoli)
27.5000 g., 0.9340 Silver .8258 oz.

Date	VG	F	VF	XF	Unc
1801	200	400	800	1,500	—
1802	200	400	800	1,500	—

C# 37 FRANCESCONE (10 Paoli)
27.5000 g., 0.9170 Silver .8108 oz. **Ruler:** Ferdinando III **Obv:** Bust right **Rev:** Crowned arms **Note:** Dav. #1521.

Date	VG	F	VF	XF	Unc
1801	25.00	50.00	100	200	—

C# 42.2 FRANCESCONE (10 Paoli)
27.5000 g., 0.9340 Silver .8258 oz. **Obv:** Small legend **Rev:** Small legend

Date	VG	F	VF	XF	Unc
1803	65.00	100	150	300	—

C# 42.3 FRANCESCONE (10 Paoli)
27.5000 g., 0.9340 Silver .8258 oz. **Rev:** Modified Order chain

Date	VG	F	VF	XF	Unc
1803	65.00	100	150	300	—

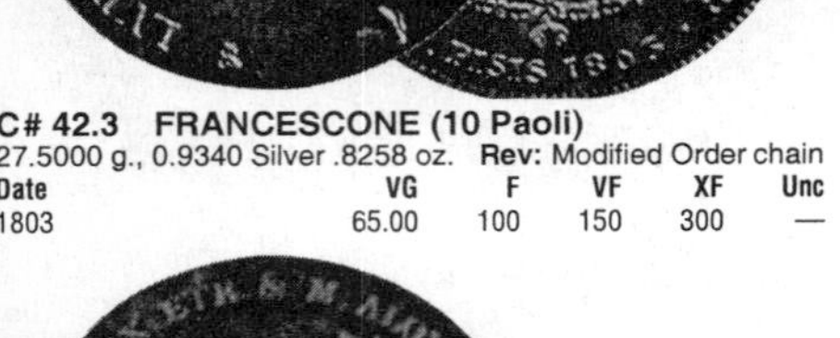

C# 50.1 FRANCESCONE (10 Paoli)
27.5000 g., 0.9130 Silver .8073 oz. **Obv. Legend:** CAROLVS LVD...

Date	VG	F	VF	XF	Unc
1803	45.00	65.00	110	250	—
1806	45.00	65.00	110	250	—
1807	40.00	60.00	85.00	225	—

C# 50.2 FRANCESCONE (10 Paoli)
27.5000 g., 0.9130 Silver .8073 oz. **Obv. Legend:** CAROLUS LUD...

Date	VG	F	VF	XF	Unc
1806	45.00	65.00	110	250	—

C# 59 FRANCESCONE (10 Paoli)
27.5000 g., 0.9130 Silver .8073 oz.

Date	VG	F	VF	XF	Unc
1814	50.00	75.00	125	275	—
1815	50.00	75.00	125	250	—
1819	50.00	75.00	125	250	—
1820	50.00	75.00	125	250	—
1824	50.00	75.00	125	250	—

C# 74 QUATTRO (4) FIORINI
27.5000 g., 0.9160 Silver .8099 oz.

Date	VG	F	VF	XF	Unc
1826	50.00	100	200	500	—

C# 75 QUATTRO (4) FIORINI
27.5000 g., 0.9160 Silver .8099 oz.

Date	VG	F	VF	XF	Unc
1830	100	300	500	1,450	—

C# 75a QUATTRO (4) FIORINI
27.5000 g., 0.9160 Silver .8099 oz.

Date	VG	F	VF	XF	Unc
1833	35.00	80.00	125	200	—
1834	35.00	80.00	125	200	—
1836	35.00	80.00	125	200	—
1839	50.00	100	250	635	—
1840	35.00	80.00	125	200	—
1841	35.00	80.00	125	200	—

C# 75b QUATTRO (4) FIORINI
27.5000 g., 0.9160 Silver .8099 oz.

Date	VG	F	VF	XF	Unc
1845	35.00	70.00	100	200	—
1846	35.00	70.00	100	200	—
1856	35.00	70.00	100	200	—
1858	35.00	70.00	100	200	—
1859	35.00	70.00	100	200	—

C# 48 5 LIRE
19.7230 g., 0.9580 Silver .6075 oz.

Date	VG	F	VF	XF	Unc
1803	25.00	40.00	125	250	—
1804	25.00	40.00	100	200	—

C# 49.1 10 LIRE
39.4470 g., 0.9580 Silver 1.2151 oz. **Rev. Legend:** FLORENTIAE - date **Note:** Legend varieties exist.

Date	VG	F	VF	XF	Unc
1803	50.00	90.00	150	350	—
1804	50.00	90.00	150	350	—
1805	50.00	90.00	150	350	—
1806	60.00	100	175	400	—

C# 49.2 10 LIRE
39.4470 g., 0.9580 Silver 1.2151 oz. **Rev. Legend:** FLOR - date

Date	VG	F	VF	XF	Unc
1807	40.00	75.00	135	300	—

C# 51 ZECCHINO
3.4900 g., 0.9980 Gold .1119 oz. **Obv:** St. Zenobio kneeling before Christ **Rev:** St. John **Note:** For Levant Trade.

Date	VG	F	VF	XF	Unc
ND(1805)	4,000	7,500	12,000	20,000	—

C# 60 ZECCHINO
3.4900 g., 0.9980 Gold .1119 oz.

Date	VG	F	VF	XF	Unc
1816	200	300	500	1,100	—
1821	200	300	500	1,100	—

C# 76 ZECCHINO
3.4520 g., 0.9980 Gold .1107 oz.

Date	VG	F	VF	XF	Unc
1824	150	250	400	850	—
1826	150	250	400	850	—
1829	150	250	400	850	—
1832	150	250	400	850	—
1853	150	250	400	850	—

C# 39 RUSPONE (3 Zecchini)
10.4610 g., 0.9990 Gold .3360 oz. **Obv. Legend:** FERDINANDUS III...

Date	VG	F	VF	XF	Unc
1801	400	800	1,250	2,000	—

C# 43 RUSPONE (3 Zecchini)
10.4110 g., 0.9980 Gold .3340 oz. **Obv. Legend:** LUD. D. G...

Date	VG	F	VF	XF	Unc
1801	500	800	1,600	3,000	—
1803	400	650	1,200	2,000	—

C# 52 RUSPONE (3 Zecchini)
10.4110 g., 0.9980 Gold .3340 oz.

Date	VG	F	VF	XF	Unc
1803	375	600	800	1,250	—
1804	375	600	800	1,250	—
1805	300	400	650	1,000	—
1806	300	400	650	1,000	—
1807	300	400	650	1,000	—

C# 61 RUSPONE (3 Zecchini)
10.4110 g., 0.9980 Gold .3340 oz.

Date	VG	F	VF	XF	Unc
1815	350	550	800	1,250	—
1816	350	550	800	1,250	—
1818	350	550	800	1,250	—
1820	350	550	800	1,250	—
1823	350	550	800	1,250	—

C# 77 RUSPONE (3 Zecchini)
10.4110 g., 0.9980 Gold .3340 oz.

Date	VG	F	VF	XF	Unc
1824	250	400	650	1,000	—
1825	250	400	650	1,000	—
1829	250	400	650	1,000	—
1834	250	400	650	1,000	—
1836	250	400	650	1,000	—

C# 78 OTTANTA (80) FIORINI
32.6500 g., 0.9990 Gold 1.0487 oz.

Date	VG	F	VF	XF	Unc
1827	400	550	1,000	2,250	—
1828	400	550	1,000	2,250	—

1ST PROVISIONAL GOVERNMENT
1859

STANDARD COINAGE

C# 79 FIORINO
6.8800 g., 0.9170 Silver .2028 oz.

Date	VG	F	VF	XF	Unc
1859	12.50	25.00	50.00	100	—

C# 80 RUSPONE (3 Zecchini)
10.4700 g., 0.9980 Gold .3359 oz.

Date	F	VF	XF	Unc	BU
1859	3,000	4,000	6,000	10,000	—

2ND PROVISIONAL GOVERNMENT
Italian 1859-61

STANDARD COINAGE

C# 81 CENTESIMO
Copper

Date	Mintage	F	VF	XF	Unc	BU
1859	25,000,000	4.00	8.00	17.50	40.00	—

C# 82 2 CENTESIMI
Copper

Date	Mintage	F	VF	XF	Unc	BU
1859	12,500,000	4.00	9.00	20.00	45.00	—

C# 83 5 CENTESIMI
Copper

Date	Mintage	F	VF	XF	Unc	BU
1859	10,000,000	5.00	10.00	22.00	50.00	—

C# 84 CINQUANTA (50) CENTESIMI
2.5000 g., 0.9000 Silver .0723 oz. **Note:** Mint mark: FIRENZE.

Date	Mintage	F	VF	XF	Unc	BU
1860	2,430,000	5.00	10.00	25.00	75.00	—
1861	1,222,000	100	200	400	1,000	—

C# 85.1 LIRA
5.0000 g., 0.9000 Silver .1446 oz. **Rev:** Without dash between FIRENZE and date **Note:** Mint mark: FIRENZE.

Date	Mintage	F	VF	XF	Unc	BU
1859	61,000	15.00	30.00	75.00	200	—
1860/59	1,655,000	12.50	22.50	55.00	110	—
1860	Inc. above	10.00	20.00	50.00	100	—

C# 85.2 LIRA
5.0000 g., 0.9000 Silver .1446 oz. **Rev:** FIRENZE - 1860

Date	F	VF	XF	Unc	BU
1860	7.50	15.00	30.00	80.00	—

C# 86 2 LIRE
10.0000 g., 0.9000 Silver .2892 oz. **Note:** Mint mark: FIRENZE.

Date	Mintage	F	VF	XF	Unc	BU
1860	559,000	30.00	60.00	100	300	—
1861	164,000	200	400	1,000	3,000	—

VENICE

Venezia

A seaport of Venetia was founded by refugees from the Hun invasions. From that time until the arrival of Napoleon in 1797, it maintained an enormous foreign trade involving the possession of many islands in the Mediterranean while keeping a state of quasi-independence despite the antagonism of jealous Italian states and the Ottoman Turks. During the French Occupation Napoleon handed it over to Austria. Later, upon the defeat of the Austrians by Prussia in 1860, Venice then became a part of the United Kingdom of Italy.

RULERS
Franz II (of Austria) 1798-1806

MINT MARKS
A - Vienna
F - Hall
V - Venice
ZV - Zecca Venezia - Venice
None - Venice

AUSTRIAN OCCUPATION

OCCUPATION COINAGE

C# 163.1 MEZZA (1/2) LIRA
4.5000 g., 0.2500 Silver .0361 oz. **Obv:** Similar to 1 Lira, KM#164.1 **Rev:** Value, date within ornate border

Date	VG	F	VF	XF	Unc
1802V	15.00	25.00	75.00	185	—

C# 163.2 MEZZA (1/2) LIRA
4.5000 g., 0.2500 Silver .0361 oz.

Date	VG	F	VF	XF	Unc
1802A	—	—	—	—	—

C# 163.3 MEZZA (1/2) LIRA
4.5000 g., 0.2500 Silver .0361 oz.

Date	VG	F	VF	XF	Unc
1802F	—	—	—	—	—

C# 164.1 UNA (1) LIRA
11.3600 g., 0.2500 Silver .0913 oz.

Date	VG	F	VF	XF	Unc
1802	15.00	25.00	75.00	185	—

C# 164.2 UNA (1) LIRA
11.3600 g., 0.2500 Silver .0913 oz.

Date	VG	F	VF	XF	Unc
1802A	—	—	—	—	—

C# 164.3 UNA (1) LIRA
11.3600 g., 0.2500 Silver .0913 oz.

Date	VG	F	VF	XF	Unc
1802F	—	—	—	—	—

C# 165.1 1-1/2 LIRE
8.4900 g., 0.2500 Silver .0682 oz. **Obv:** Imperial eagle **Rev:** Value, date within ornate border

Date	VG	F	VF	XF	Unc
1802A	10.00	15.00	35.00	75.00	—

C# 165.2 1-1/2 LIRE
8.4900 g., 0.2500 Silver .0682 oz.

Date	VG	F	VF	XF	Unc
1802F	15.00	30.00	60.00	150	—

C# 162a DUE (2) LIRE
0.2500 Silver .0682 oz. **Obv:** Smaller imperial eagle, uncollared strike **Note:** Overstrikes exist. Weight varies: 7.95-9.46 grams.

Date	VG	F	VF	XF	Unc
1801	20.00	50.00	100	265	—

C# 162 DUE (2) LIRE
0.2500 Silver .0682 oz. **Obv:** Large imperial eagle **Rev:** Value, date within wreath **Note:** Three varieties exist. Weight varies: 7.95-9.46 grams.

Date	VG	F	VF	XF	Unc
1801	25.00	40.00	80.00	210	—

C# 166 ZECCHINO
3.4900 g., 0.9870 Gold .1107 oz. **Obv:** St. Mark , Doge **Obv. Legend:** FRANC. II. S. M. VENET **Rev:** Imperial eagle **Rev. Legend:** SIT. T. XPE. DAT. Q. TV-REGIS. ISTE. DVCA

Date	VG	F	VF	XF	Unc
ND(1798-1806)	200	500	1,500	2,800	—

C# 166a ZECCHINO
3.4900 g., 0.9870 Gold .1107 oz. **Obv. Legend:** Christ holding orb

Date	VG	F	VF	XF	Unc
ND(1798-1806)	200	500	1,500	2,800	—

REVOLUTION
1848-1849

REVOLUTIONARY COINAGE

C# 181 CENTESIMO
Copper

Date	Mintage	F	VF	XF	Unc	BU
1849ZV	2,761,000	3.00	7.00	15.00	35.00	—

C# 182 3 CENTESIMI
Copper

Date	Mintage	F	VF	XF	Unc	BU
1849ZV	1,044,000	3.00	6.00	12.00	28.00	—

C# 183 5 CENTESIMI
Copper

Date	Mintage	F	VF	XF	Unc	BU
1849ZV	1,187,000	3.00	7.00	15.00	35.00	—

C# 184 15 CENTESIMI
1.2600 g., 0.2290 Silver .0092 oz.

Date	Mintage	F	VF	XF	Unc	BU
1848ZV	155,000	7.50	12.50	25.00	55.00	—

C# A184 25 CENTESIMI
1.2500 g., 0.9000 Silver .0361 oz.

Date	F	VF	XF	Unc	BU
1848V	75.00	150	400	1,000	—

C# 185 5 LIRE
25.0000 g., 0.9000 Silver .7234 oz.

Date	Mintage	F	VF	XF	Unc	BU
1848	6,011	75.00	125	200	385	—

C# 186 5 LIRE
25.0000 g., 0.9000 Silver .7234 oz. **Edge Lettering:** DIO BENEDITE L'ITALIA

Date	Mintage	F	VF	XF	Unc	BU
1848V	11,000	75.00	125	225	460	—

C# 186a 5 LIRE
25.0000 g., 0.9000 Silver .7234 oz. **Edge Lettering:** Error: DIO BENEDETE L'ITALIA

Date	F	VF	XF	Unc	BU
1848	100	200	325	665	—

C# 187 20 LIRE
6.4500 g., 0.9000 Gold .1866 oz.

Date	Mintage	F	VF	XF	Unc	BU
1848	5,210	350	700	1,650	2,700	—

PATTERNS
Including off metal strikes

KM#	Date	Mintage	Identification	Mkt Val
Pn66	1802	—	1-1/2 Lire. 0.2500 Silver. C#165.	—

VENICE - PALMA NOVA

(In Venetia)

Was ceded to France by Austria in 1806 and was returned to Austria in 1814. In 1860 it was incorporated in the united Kingdom of Italy.

FRENCH OCCUPATION
SEIGE COINAGE

C# 2 50 CENTESIMI
Billon

Date	VG	F	VF	XF	Unc
1814	150	200	350	650	—

Note: Presentation pieces struck in a collar exhibit a raised rim and carry a premium

PATTERNS
Including off metal strikes

KM#	Date	Mintage	Identification	Mkt Val
Pn1	1814	—	25 Centesimi. Billon. C#1.	—

Italy, a 700-mile-long peninsula extending into the heart of the Mediterranean Sea, has an area of 116,304 sq. mi. (301,230 sq. km.). Capital: Rome

From the fall of Rome until modern times, 'Italy' was little more than a geographical expression. Although nominally included in the Empire of Charlemagne and the Holy Roman Empire, it was in reality divided into a number of independent states and kingdoms presided over by wealthy families, soldiers of fortune or hereditary rulers. The 19th century unification movement fostered by Mazzini, Garibaldi and Cavour attained fruition in 1860-70 with the creation of the Kingdom of Italy and the installation of Victor Emmanuel, king of Sardinia, as king of Italy

RULERS

Vittorio Emanuele II, 1861-1878
Umberto I, 1878-1900
Vittorio Emanuele III, 1900-1946

MINT MARKS

B – Bologna (1861)
B/I – Birmingham (1893-94)
FIRENZE – Florence (1861)
H – Birmingham (1866-67)
KB – Berlin (1894)
M – Milan (1861-87)
N – Naples (1861-67)
OM – Strasbourg (1866-67)
R – Rome (All coins from 1878 have R except where noted.)
T – Turin (1861-67)
No MM – Paris (1862-66)

MONETARY SYSTEM

100 Centesimi = 1 Lira

KINGDOM

DECIMAL COINAGE

KM# 1.1 CENTESIMO

Copper **Ruler:** Vittorio Emanuele II

Date	Mintage	F	VF	XF	Unc	BU
1861M	75,000,000	0.75	1.50	3.00	12.00	20.00
1861M Inverted M	Inc. above	25.00	45.00	90.00	275	—
1867M	72,759,000	0.75	1.50	3.00	12.00	20.00

KM# 1.2 CENTESIMO

Copper **Ruler:** Vittorio Emanuele II

Date	Mintage	F	VF	XF	Unc	BU
1861N	48,280,000	3.75	8.00	15.00	32.00	65.00
1862/1N	37,500,000	6.00	12.00	20.00	40.00	80.00
1862N	Inc. above	1.25	2.00	4.00	18.00	40.00

KM# 1.3 CENTESIMO

Copper **Ruler:** Vittorio Emanuele II

Date	Mintage	F	VF	XF	Unc	BU
1867	5,000,000	5.00	12.50	22.50	50.00	90.00

KM# 29 CENTESIMO

Copper **Ruler:** Umberto I

Date	Mintage	F	VF	XF	Unc	BU
1895/8R	13,860,000	1.50	3.00	7.00	25.00	35.00
1895R	Inc. above	1.00	2.00	4.00	10.00	20.00
1896R	3,730,000	1.00	2.00	4.00	10.00	20.00
1897R	1,845,000	12.00	20.00	40.00	75.00	150
1899R	1,287,000	1.25	2.00	4.00	10.00	20.00
1900R	10,000,000	1.00	2.00	4.00	10.00	20.00

KM# 2.1 2 CENTESIMI

Copper **Ruler:** Vittorio Emanuele II

Date	Mintage	F	VF	XF	Unc	BU
1861M	37,500,000	0.60	1.50	4.00	18.00	32.00
1867M	54,212,000	0.60	1.50	4.00	22.00	45.00

KM# 2.2 2 CENTESIMI

Copper **Ruler:** Vittorio Emanuele II

Date	Mintage	F	VF	XF	Unc	BU
1861N	23,055,000	2.00	5.00	20.00	60.00	150
1862N	33,195,000	1.00	3.00	18.00	50.00	135

KM# 2.3 2 CENTESIMI

Copper **Ruler:** Vittorio Emanuele II

Date	Mintage	F	VF	XF	Unc	BU
1867T	5,000,000	2.00	4.50	15.00	35.00	100

KM# 30 2 CENTESIMI

Copper **Ruler:** Umberto I

Date	Mintage	F	VF	XF	Unc	BU
1895R	305,000	10.00	17.50	35.00	65.00	145
1896R	282,000	25.00	50.00	100	175	325
1897R	4,415,000	0.60	1.50	4.00	15.00	30.00
1898R	4,161,000	0.60	1.50	4.00	15.00	30.00
1900R	2,735,000	0.60	1.50	4.00	15.00	30.00

KM# 3.1 5 CENTESIMI

Copper **Ruler:** Vittorio Emanuele II

Date	Mintage	F	VF	XF	Unc	BU
1861B	3,809,000	25.00	45.00	90.00	175	375

KM# 3.2 5 CENTESIMI

Copper **Ruler:** Vittorio Emanuele II

Date	Mintage	F	VF	XF	Unc	BU
1861M	210,000,000	0.60	1.50	6.00	45.00	85.00
1867M	24,000,000	0.60	1.50	6.50	48.00	100

KM# 3.3 5 CENTESIMI

Copper **Ruler:** Vittorio Emanuele II

Date	Mintage	F	VF	XF	Unc	BU
1861N	103,707,000	0.60	1.50	9.00	70.00	180
1862N	106,293,000	0.60	1.50	8.00	60.00	170
1867N	46,000,000	0.60	1.50	7.50	50.00	160

KM# 31 5 CENTESIMI

Copper **Ruler:** Umberto I

Date	Mintage	F	VF	XF	Unc	BU
1895R	508,000	12.50	25.00	35.00	90.00	200
1896R	380,000	12.50	27.50	45.00	110	275
1900R Rare	2,000	—	—	—	—	—

Note: 2,000 of the 1900 dated coins were struck, but most were remelted and not issued.

KM# 11.1 10 CENTESIMI

Copper **Ruler:** Vittorio Emanuele II

Date	Mintage	F	VF	XF	Unc	BU
1862M	40,000,000	1.50	3.50	8.00	55.00	145
1866M	36,000,000	1.50	3.50	8.00	55.00	145

KM# 11.2 10 CENTESIMI

Copper **Ruler:** Vittorio Emanuele II

Date	Mintage	F	VF	XF	Unc	BU
1862	—	2.50	5.00	20.00	100	350
1863	80,000,000	1.50	3.50	8.00	55.00	145
1866	—	—	—	—	—	—

KM# 11.3 10 CENTESIMI

Copper **Ruler:** Vittorio Emanuele II

Date	Mintage	F	VF	XF	Unc	BU
1866H	40,000,000	1.50	3.50	8.00	55.00	145
1867H	50,000,000	1.50	3.50	8.00	55.00	145

KM# 11.4 10 CENTESIMI

Copper **Ruler:** Vittorio Emanuele II

Date	Mintage	F	VF	XF	Unc	BU
1866N	67,650,000	1.50	3.50	8.00	55.00	145
1867N	31,360,000	1.50	3.50	8.00	55.00	145

KM# 11.5 10 CENTESIMI

Copper **Ruler:** Vittorio Emanuele II

Date	Mintage	F	VF	XF	Unc	BU
1866OM	20,000,000	1.50	3.50	8.00	55.00	145
1866OM	Inc. above	1.50	3.50	8.00	55.00	145
1867OM	—	3.00	5.00	14.50	65.00	165
1867OM	—	2.50	4.50	12.50	60.00	150

KM# 11.6 10 CENTESIMI

Copper **Ruler:** Vittorio Emanuele II

Date	Mintage	F	VF	XF	Unc	BU
1866T	16,350,000	1.50	3.50	8.00	55.00	145
1867T	18,640,000	1.50	3.50	8.00	55.00	145

KM# 27.1 10 CENTESIMI

Copper **Ruler:** Umberto I

Date	Mintage	F	VF	XF	Unc	BU
1893B/I	28,900,000	1.50	3.50	7.00	35.00	75.00
1894B/I	32,000,000	1.50	3.50	7.00	40.00	85.00

KM# 27.2 10 CENTESIMI

Copper **Ruler:** Umberto I

Date	Mintage	F	VF	XF	Unc	BU
1893R	8,547,000	5.00	10.00	20.00	65.00	175
1894R	5,910,000	10.00	20.00	40.00	100	225

KM# 12 20 CENTESIMI

1.0000 g., 0.8350 Silver .0268 oz. **Ruler:** Vittorio Emanuele II

Date	Mintage	F	VF	XF	Unc	BU
1863T NB Rare	461	—	—	—	—	—

KM# 13.1 20 CENTESIMI

1.0000 g., 0.8350 Silver .0268 oz. **Ruler:** Vittorio Emanuele II

Date	Mintage	F	VF	XF	Unc	BU
1863M BN	27,845,000	3.00	6.00	12.50	45.00	125

KM# 13.2 20 CENTESIMI
1.0000 g., 0.8350 Silver .0268 oz. **Ruler:** Vittorio Emanuele II

Date	Mintage	F	VF	XF	Unc	BU
1863T BN	6,289,000	4.00	9.00	25.00	65.00	140
1863T BN Inverted BN	Inc. above	15.00	35.00	75.00	250	—
1867T BN	866,000	20.00	50.00	100	300	450

KM# 28.1 20 CENTESIMI
Copper Nickel **Ruler:** Umberto I

Date	Mintage	F	VF	XF	Unc	BU
1894KB	75,000,000	0.50	1.25	5.00	20.00	60.00

KM# 28.2 20 CENTESIMI
Copper Nickel **Ruler:** Umberto I

Date	Mintage	F	VF	XF	Unc	BU
1894R	13,901,000	0.75	2.00	7.00	28.00	100
1895R	11,099,000	1.00	2.50	8.00	35.00	120

KM# A4 50 CENTESIMI
2.5000 g., 0.9000 Silver .0723 oz. **Ruler:** Vittorio Emanuele II

Date	Mintage	F	VF	XF	Unc	BU
1861 F	1,222,000	50.00	100	225	600	1,850

KM# 4.1 50 CENTESIMI
2.5000 g., 0.9000 Silver .0723 oz. **Ruler:** Vittorio Emanuele II

Date	F	VF	XF	Unc	BU
1861M BN Rare	—	—	—	—	—

KM# 4.2 50 CENTESIMI
2.5000 g., 0.9000 Silver .0723 oz. **Ruler:** Vittorio Emanuele II

Date	Mintage	F	VF	XF	Unc	BU
1861T B in shield	45,000	4,500	8,500	—	—	—
1862T BN	185,000	45.00	90.00	200	550	1,500

KM# 4.3 50 CENTESIMI
2.5000 g., 0.9000 Silver .0723 oz. **Ruler:** Vittorio Emanuele II

Date	Mintage	F	VF	XF	Unc	BU
1862N	630,000	25.00	60.00	135	320	950

KM# 4a.1 50 CENTESIMI
2.5000 g., 0.8350 Silver .0671 oz. **Ruler:** Vittorio Emanuele II

Date	Mintage	F	VF	XF	Unc	BU
1863M BN	4,706,000	8.00	16.00	35.00	100	300

KM# 14.1 50 CENTESIMI
2.5000 g., 0.8350 Silver .0671 oz. **Ruler:** Vittorio Emanuele II

Date	Mintage	F	VF	XF	Unc	BU
1863M BN	33,760,000	5.00	9.00	18.00	50.00	165
1866M BN	19,199,000	15.00	30.00	60.00	150	425
1867M BN	10,984,000	5.00	9.00	18.00	50.00	165

KM# 14.2 50 CENTESIMI
2.5000 g., 0.8350 Silver .0671 oz. **Ruler:** Vittorio Emanuele II

Date	Mintage	F	VF	XF	Unc	BU
1863N BN	16,062,000	6.00	12.00	25.00	65.00	200
1867N BN	7,838,000	7.00	15.00	30.00	75.00	220

KM# 14.3 50 CENTESIMI
2.5000 g., 0.8350 Silver .0671 oz. **Ruler:** Vittorio Emanuele II

Date	Mintage	F	VF	XF	Unc	BU
1863T BN	6,301,000	6.00	12.00	25.00	65.00	200
1867T BN	396,000	60.00	120	250	750	2,200

KM# 4a.2 50 CENTESIMI
2.5000 g., 0.8350 Silver .0671 oz. **Ruler:** Vittorio Emanuele II

Date	Mintage	F	VF	XF	Unc	BU
1863T BN	2,753,000	15.00	30.00	75.00	200	600

KM# 26 50 CENTESIMI
2.5000 g., 0.8350 Silver .0671 oz. **Ruler:** Vittorio Emanuele II

Date	Mintage	F	VF	XF	Unc	BU
1889R	635,000	35.00	65.00	125	375	1,150
1892R	148,000	50.00	90.00	175	475	1,450

KM# A5 LIRA
5.0000 g., 0.9000 Silver .1147 oz. **Ruler:** Vittorio Emanuele II

Date	Mintage	F	VF	XF	Unc	BU
1861 F	432,000	50.00	100	200	600	1,700

KM# 5.1 LIRA
5.0000 g., 0.9000 Silver .1147 oz. **Ruler:** Vittorio Emanuele II

Date	Mintage	F	VF	XF	Unc	BU
1861T B in shield	19,000	850	1,750	—	—	—
1862T BN	105,000	60.00	120	350	850	2,250

KM# 5.2 LIRA
5.0000 g., 0.9000 Silver .1147 oz. **Ruler:** Vittorio Emanuele II

Date	Mintage	F	VF	XF	Unc	BU
1862N	497,000	30.00	70.00	200	600	1,700

KM# 5a.1 LIRA
5.0000 g., 0.8350 Silver .1342 oz. **Ruler:** Vittorio Emanuele II

Date	Mintage	F	VF	XF	Unc	BU
1863M BN	24,054,000	3.00	6.00	18.00	50.00	150
1867/3M BN	7,665,000	7.00	15.00	40.00	120	320
1867M BN	Inc. above	5.00	10.00	30.00	80.00	225

KM# 5a.2 LIRA
5.0000 g., 0.8350 Silver .1342 oz. **Ruler:** Vittorio Emanuele II

Date	Mintage	F	VF	XF	Unc	BU
1863T BN	2,270,000	7.00	15.00	40.00	120	320
1867T BN	335,000	50.00	100	300	800	2,200

KM# 15.1 LIRA
5.0000 g., 0.8350 Silver .1342 oz. **Ruler:** Vittorio Emanuele II

Date	Mintage	F	VF	XF	Unc	BU
1863M BN	29,837,000	3.00	6.00	20.00	60.00	175

KM# 15.2 LIRA
5.0000 g., 0.8350 Silver .1342 oz. **Ruler:** Vittorio Emanuele II

Date	Mintage	F	VF	XF	Unc	BU
1863T BN	3,839,000	75.00	150	400	950	2,500

KM# 24.1 LIRA
5.0000 g., 0.8350 Silver .1342 oz. **Ruler:** Umberto I

Date	Mintage	F	VF	XF	Unc	BU
1883R	5,420	3,500	6,500	10,000	—	—
1884R	1,995,000	5.00	12.00	35.00	150	375
1886R	6,095,000	2.50	6.00	20.00	100	220
1892R	32,000	500	950	1,850	4,500	—
1899R	1,818,000	3.00	7.50	25.00	110	240
1900R	318,000	5.00	12.50	35.00	165	400

KM# 24.2 LIRA
5.0000 g., 0.8350 Silver .1342 oz. **Ruler:** Umberto I

Date	Mintage	F	VF	XF	Unc	BU
1887M	16,305,000	2.50	7.50	20.00	90.00	200

KM# 6.1 2 LIRE
10.0000 g., 0.9000 Silver .2893 oz. **Ruler:** Vittorio Emanuele II

Date	Mintage	F	VF	XF	Unc	BU
1861T B in shield	9,871	3,000	5,500	—	—	—

KM# 6.2 2 LIRE
10.0000 g., 0.9000 Silver .2893 oz. **Ruler:** Vittorio Emanuele II

Date	Mintage	F	VF	XF	Unc	BU
1862N	62,000	250	400	750	1,850	3,750

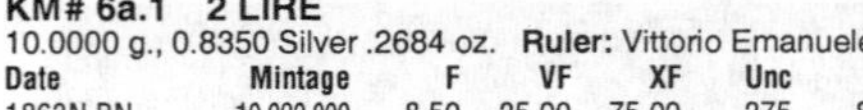

KM# 6a.1 2 LIRE
10.0000 g., 0.8350 Silver .2684 oz. **Ruler:** Vittorio Emanuele II

Date	Mintage	F	VF	XF	Unc	BU
1863N BN	10,090,000	8.50	25.00	75.00	275	800

KM# 6a.2 2 LIRE
10.0000 g., 0.8350 Silver .2684 oz. **Ruler:** Vittorio Emanuele II

Date	Mintage	F	VF	XF	Unc	BU
1863T BN	4,910,000	20.00	40.00	125	375	950

KM# 16.1 2 LIRE
10.0000 g., 0.8350 Silver .2684 oz. **Ruler:** Vittorio Emanuele II

Date	F	VF	XF	Unc	BU
1863N BN	12.50	30.00	100	300	850

KM# 16.2 2 LIRE
10.0000 g., 0.8350 Silver .2684 oz. **Ruler:** Vittorio Emanuele II

Date	F	VF	XF	Unc	BU
1863T BN	22.00	45.00	150	450	1,100

KM# 23 2 LIRE
10.0000 g., 0.8350 Silver .2684 oz. **Ruler:** Umberto I

Date	Mintage	F	VF	XF	Unc	BU
1881R	4,141,000	6.00	14.00	50.00	180	525
1882R	2,859,000	5.00	12.00	45.00	170	500
1883R	3,500,000	5.00	12.00	45.00	170	500
1884R	4,500,000	5.00	12.00	45.00	170	500
1885R	598,000	35.00	65.00	125	500	1,650
1886R	1,902,000	6.00	14.00	50.00	180	525
1887R	7,500,000	5.00	10.00	40.00	160	475
1897R	848,000	7.50	12.50	45.00	170	500
1898R	1,320,000	35.00	60.00	100	450	1,500
1899R	610,000	7.50	12.50	55.00	190	545

KM# 7 5 LIRE
25.0000 g., 0.9000 Silver .7234 oz. **Ruler:** Vittorio Emanuele II
Subject: Accession to throne of unified Italy

Date	Mintage	F	VF	XF	Unc	BU
1861FIRENZE	21,000	650	1,400	2,750	5,750	—

KM# 8.1 5 LIRE

25.0000 g., 0.9000 Silver .7234 oz. **Ruler:** Vittorio Emanuele II

Date	Mintage	F	VF	XF	Unc	BU
1861T B in shield	160,000	225	475	975	2,450	4,000
1862T BN	51,000	100	200	450	1,150	2,250
1865T BN	491,000	20.00	45.00	120	400	650

KM# 8.2 5 LIRE

25.0000 g., 0.9000 Silver .7234 oz. **Ruler:** Vittorio Emanuele II

Date	Mintage	F	VF	XF	Unc	BU
1862N BN	142,000	35.00	80.00	200	700	1,000
1864N BN	120,000	25.00	50.00	135	450	700
1865N BN	312,000	20.00	45.00	120	400	650
1866N BN	460,000	2,500	5,500	—	—	—

KM# 17 5 LIRE

1.6129 g., 0.9000 Gold .0466 oz. **Ruler:** Vittorio Emanuele II

Date	Mintage	F	VF	XF	Unc	BU
1863T BN	197,000	75.00	100	175	275	—
1865T BN	408,000	100	175	250	400	—

KM# 8.3 5 LIRE

25.0000 g., 0.9000 Silver .7234 oz. **Ruler:** Vittorio Emanuele II

Date	Mintage	F	VF	XF	Unc	BU
1869M BN	3,995,000	12.00	20.00	70.00	350	525
1870M BN	5,969,000	12.00	20.00	65.00	300	450
1871M BN	6,697,000	12.00	20.00	65.00	300	450
1872M BN	7,093,000	12.00	20.00	65.00	300	450
1873M BN	8,438,000	12.00	20.00	65.00	300	450
1874M BN	12,000,000	12.00	20.00	65.00	300	450
1875M BN	8,982,000	12.00	20.00	65.00	300	450

KM# 8.4 5 LIRE

25.0000 g., 0.9000 Silver .7234 oz. **Ruler:** Vittorio Emanuele II

Date	Mintage	F	VF	XF	Unc	BU
1870R	—	60.00	125	300	625	950
1871R	404,000	75.00	165	375	800	1,250
1872R	29,000	350	700	1,650	5,000	7,500
1873R	17,000	450	1,000	3,000	7,000	—
1875R	1,018,000	17.50	45.00	150	600	900
1876R	6,390,000	12.00	25.00	65.00	300	450
1877R	4,410,000	12.00	25.00	65.00	300	450
1878R	1,700,000	15.00	30.00	85.00	450	650

KM# 20 5 LIRE

25.0000 g., 0.9000 Silver .7234 oz. **Ruler:** Umberto I

Date	Mintage	F	VF	XF	Unc	BU
1878R	100,000	225	450	900	2,750	—
1879R	4,000,000	35.00	65.00	200	1,000	2,200

KM# 9.1 10 LIRE

3.2258 g., 0.9000 Gold .0933 oz., 18 mm. **Ruler:** Vittorio Emanuele II

Date	Mintage	F	VF	XF	Unc	BU
1861T B in shield	1,916	1,500	3,000	4,500	7,500	—

KM# 9.2 10 LIRE

3.2258 g., 0.9000 Gold .0933 oz., 18.5 mm. **Ruler:** Vittorio Emanuele II

Date	Mintage	F	VF	XF	Unc	BU
1863T BN	543,000	75.00	100	150	250	—
1865T BN	444,000	100	175	225	350	—

KM# 9.3 10 LIRE

3.2258 g., 0.9000 Gold .0933 oz. **Ruler:** Vittorio Emanuele II

Date	F	VF	XF	Unc	BU
1863T BN	70.00	95.00	125	185	—

KM# 9.4 10 LIRE

3.2258 g., 0.9000 Gold .0933 oz., 19.5 mm. **Ruler:** Vittorio Emanuele II

Date	F	VF	XF	Unc	BU
1863T BN	75.00	100	135	220	—

KM# 10.1 20 LIRE

6.4516 g., 0.9000 Gold .1867 oz. **Ruler:** Vittorio Emanuele II

Date	Mintage	F	VF	XF	Unc	BU
1861T B in shield	3,267	125	200	300	500	—
1861T T/F	Inc. above	—	BV	110	165	—
1862T BN	1,955,000	—	BV	85.00	115	—
1863T BN	2,981,000	—	BV	85.00	115	—
1864T BN	609,000	—	BV	85.00	115	—
1865T BN	3,109,000	—	BV	85.00	115	—
1866T BN	196,000	125	150	200	425	—
1867T BN	276,000	—	BV	85.00	160	—
1868T BN	340,000	—	85.00	85.00	160	—
1869T BN	185,000	—	BV	85.00	160	—
1870T bn	55,000	125	200	400	850	—

KM# 10.2 20 LIRE

6.4516 g., 0.9000 Gold .1867 oz. **Ruler:** Vittorio Emanuele II

Date	Mintage	F	VF	XF	Unc	BU
1870R	—	150	300	600	1,450	—
1871R	—	BV	125	200	450	—
1873R	2,174	400	800	1,600	3,500	—
1874R	41,000	—	BV	85.00	170	—
1875R	51,000	—	BV	85.00	170	—
1876R	108,000	—	BV	85.00	115	—
1877R	247,000	—	BV	85.00	115	—
1878R	316,000	—	BV	85.00	100	—

KM# 10.3 20 LIRE

6.4516 g., 0.9000 Gold .1867 oz. **Ruler:** Vittorio Emanuele II

Date	Mintage	F	VF	XF	Unc	BU
1872M BN	—	100	150	250	500	—
1873M BN	1,018,000	—	BV	85.00	145	—
1874M BN	255,000	—	BV	85.00	155	—

KM# 21 20 LIRE

6.4516 g., 0.9000 Gold .1867 oz. **Ruler:** Umberto I

Date	Mintage	F	VF	XF	Unc	BU
1880R	129,000	—	BV	80.00	110	—
1881R	843,000	—	BV	80.00	110	—
1882R	6,970,000	—	BV	70.00	100	—
1/1882	—	BV	75.00	110	150	—
1883/2	183,000	BV	75.00	110	150	—
1883R	182,000	—	BV	80.00	110	—
1884R	9,775	175	300	500	1,200	—
1885R	165,000	—	BV	80.00	110	—
1886R	59,000	—	BV	80.00	110	—
1888R	111,000	—	BV	80.00	110	—
1889R	—	150	250	400	600	—
1890R	68,000	—	BV	80.00	110	—
1891R	32,000	—	BV	120	160	—
1893R	41,000	—	BV	80.00	145	—
1897R	38,000	—	BV	80.00	155	—

KM# 21a 20 LIRE

Red Gold **Ruler:** Umberto I

Date	F	VF	XF	Unc	BU
1882R	—	—	120	175	—

KM# 18 50 LIRE

16.1290 g., 0.9000 Gold .4667 oz. **Ruler:** Vittorio Emanuele II

Date	Mintage	F	VF	XF	Unc	BU
1864T BN	103	10,000	15,000	27,500	35,000	—

KM# 25 50 LIRE

16.1290 g., 0.9000 Gold .4667 oz. **Ruler:** Umberto I

Date	Mintage	F	VF	XF	Unc	BU
1884R	2,532	900	1,500	2,000	3,250	—
1888R	2,125	1,000	2,000	2,750	3,750	—
1891R	414	1,500	2,500	4,000	7,500	—

KM# 19.1 100 LIRE

32.2580 g., 0.9000 Gold .9334 oz. **Ruler:** Vittorio Emanuele II

Date	Mintage	F	VF	XF	Unc	BU
1864T BN	579	2,000	4,500	8,500	16,000	—

KM# 19.2 100 LIRE

32.2580 g., 0.9000 Gold .9334 oz. **Ruler:** Vittorio Emanuele II

Date	Mintage	F	VF	XF	Unc	BU
1872R	661	2,000	4,500	8,000	14,000	—
1878R	294	3,500	7,000	12,000	20,000	—

KM# 22 100 LIRE

32.2580 g., 0.9000 Gold .9334 oz. **Ruler:** Umberto I

Date	Mintage	F	VF	XF	Unc	BU
1880R	145	6,000	12,000	16,000	25,000	—
1882R	1,229	900	1,500	2,500	3,750	—
1883R	4,219	800	1,250	2,250	3,500	—
1888R	1,169	900	1,500	3,000	4,500	—
1891R	209	2,000	4,000	9,000	18,000	—

JAMAICA

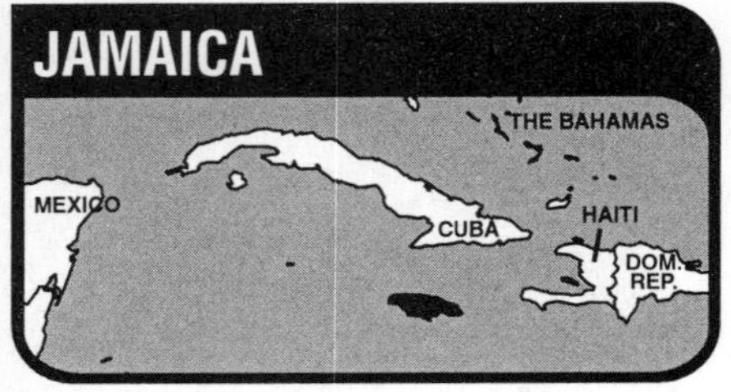

Jamaica, situated in the Caribbean Sea 90 miles south of Cuba Jamaica was discovered by Columbus on May 3, 1494, and settled by Spain in 1509. The island was captured in 1655 by a British naval force under the command of Admiral William Penn, sent by Oliver Cromwell and ceded to Britain by the Treaty of Madrid, 1670. For more than 150 years, the Jamaican economy of sugar, slaves and piracy was one of the most prosperous in the new world. Dissension between the property-oriented island legislature and the home government prompted parliament to establish a crown colony government for Jamaica in 1866.

In 1758, the Jamaican Assembly authorized stamping a certain amount of Spanish milled coinage. Token coinage by merchants aided the island's monetary supply in the early 19th century. Sterling coinage was introduced in Jamaica in 1825, with the additional silver three halfpence under William IV and Victoria. Certain issues of three pence of William IV and Victoria were intended for colonial use, including Jamaica.

There was an extensive token and work tally coinage for Jamaica in the late 19th and early 20th centuries.

RULERS

British, until 1962

MINT MARKS

H - Heaton

no mint mark - Royal Mint, London

MONETARY SYSTEM

4 Farthings = 1 Penny

12 Pence = 1 Shilling

8 Reales = 6 Shillings, 8 Pence

BRITISH ADMINISTRATION

REGULAR COINAGE

KM# 15 FARTHING

Copper-Nickel

Date	Mintage	F	VF	XF	Unc	BU
1880	192,000	1.50	2.50	12.00	35.00	—
1880 Proof	—	Value: 225				
1882H	384,000	1.00	1.75	10.00	30.00	—
1882H Proof	—	Value: 200				
1884	96,000	2.00	4.00	20.00	50.00	—
1884 Proof	—	Value: 350				
1885	96,000	2.00	4.00	20.00	50.00	—
1885 Proof	—	Value: 200				
1887	192,000	1.50	2.50	12.00	35.00	—
1887 Proof	—	Value: 200				
1888	192,000	1.50	2.50	12.00	30.00	—
1888 Proof	—	Value: 200				
1889	192,000	1.50	2.50	12.00	35.00	—
1890H	96,000	2.00	4.00	20.00	50.00	—
1891	96,000	2.00	4.00	20.00	90.00	—
1893	96,000	2.00	4.00	20.00	70.00	—
1894	144,000	1.75	3.25	15.00	40.00	—
1894 Proof	—	Value: 200				
1895	144,000	1.75	3.25	15.00	40.00	—
1897	144,000	1.75	3.25	15.00	40.00	—
1899	144,000	1.75	3.25	15.00	40.00	—
1900	144,000	1.75	3.25	15.00	40.00	—

KM# 16 1/2 PENNY

Copper-Nickel

Date	Mintage	F	VF	XF	Unc	BU
1869	192,000	1.25	2.50	15.00	40.00	—
1869 Proof	—	Value: 300				
1870	240,000	1.25	2.50	15.00	45.00	—
1870 Proof	—	Value: 500				
1871	240,000	1.25	2.50	15.00	45.00	—
1871 Proof	—	Value: 375				
1880	192,000	2.00	4.00	20.00	55.00	—
1880 Proof	—	Value: 475				
1882H	96,000	2.00	5.00	20.00	80.00	—
1882H Proof	—	Value: 400				
1884	96,000	2.00	5.00	20.00	55.00	—
1884 Proof	—	Value: 550				
1885	96,000	2.00	5.00	20.00	55.00	—
1885 Proof	—	Value: 400				
1887	72,000	4.00	8.00	40.00	90.00	—
1888	96,000	1.75	5.00	20.00	50.00	—
1888 Proof	—	Value: 350				
1889	96,000	2.00	5.00	25.00	65.00	—
1890H	120,000	1.75	3.25	20.00	50.00	—
1891	120,000	1.75	3.25	20.00	70.00	—
1893	144,000	1.75	3.25	20.00	50.00	—
1894	96,000	2.00	5.00	25.00	65.00	—
1895	96,000	2.00	5.00	25.00	65.00	—
1897	120,000	1.75	3.25	20.00	50.00	—
1899	120,000	1.75	3.25	20.00	50.00	—
1900	120,000	1.75	3.25	20.00	60.00	—

KM# 17 PENNY

Copper-Nickel

Date	Mintage	F	VF	XF	Unc	BU
1869	144,000	2.00	6.50	25.00	65.00	—
1869 Proof	—	Value: 225				
1870	120,000	2.00	5.00	25.00	70.00	—
1870 Proof	—	Value: 775				
1871	120,000	2.00	5.00	25.00	70.00	—
1871 Proof	—	Value: 600				
1880	96,000	4.00	12.00	50.00	110	—
1880 Proof	—	Value: 600				
1882H	48,000	5.00	15.00	60.00	170	—
1882H Proof	—	Value: 500				
1882	Inc. above	15.00	40.00	120	250	—
1882 Proof	—	Value: 1,000				
1884	48,000	4.00	12.00	50.00	110	—
1884 Proof	—	Value: 850				
1885	48,000	4.00	12.00	50.00	110	—
1885 Proof	—	Value: 400				
1887	24,000	4.50	15.00	60.00	185	—
1888	24,000	4.50	15.00	60.00	185	—
1888 Proof	—	Value: 400				
1889	24,000	5.00	15.00	60.00	180	—
1890	36,000	4.00	12.00	50.00	125	—
1891	36,000	4.00	12.00	50.00	125	—
1893	24,000	5.00	15.00	60.00	185	—
1894	36,000	4.00	12.00	50.00	125	—
1895	36,000	4.00	12.00	50.00	125	—
1897	24,000	5.00	15.00	60.00	185	—
1899	24,000	5.00	15.00	60.00	185	—
1900	24,000	5.00	15.00	60.00	185	—

PATTERNS

Including off metal strikes

KM#	Date	Mintage	Identification	Mkt Val
Pn1	1869	—	1/2 Penny. Brass. KM#16	400
Pn2	1869	—	Penny. Bronze. KM#17	400
Pn3	1870	—	Penny. Copper. KM#17	400

JAPAN

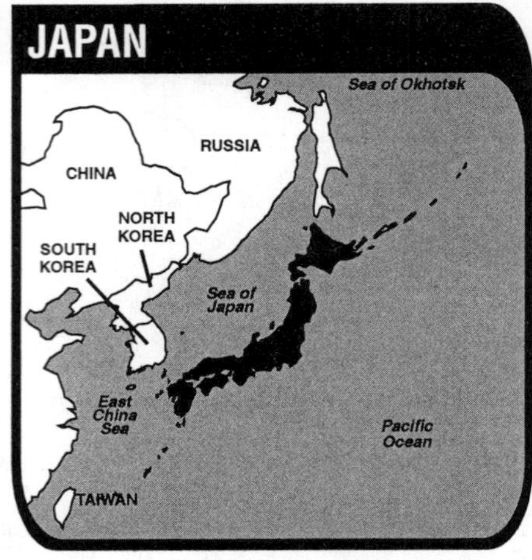

Japan is situated off the east coast of Asia. Japan, founded (so legend holds) in 660 B.C. by a direct descendant of the Sun Goddess, was first brought into contact with the west by a storm-blown Portuguese ship in 1542. European traders and missionaries proceeded to enlarge the contact until the Shogunate, sensing a military threat in the foreign presence, expelled all foreigners and restricted relations with the outside world in the 17th century. After Commodore Perry's U.S. flotilla visited in 1854, Japan rapidly industrialized, abolished the Shogunate and established a parliamentary form of government, and by the end of the 19th century achieved the status of a modern economic and military power. A series of wars with China and Russia, and participation with the allies in World War I, enlarged Japan territorially but brought its interests into conflict with the Far Eastern interests of the United States, Britain and the Netherlands, causing it to align with the Axis Powers for the pursuit of World War II. After its defeat in World War II, General Douglas MacArthur forced Japan to renounce military aggression as a political instrument, and he instituted constitutional democratic self-government. Japan quickly gained a position as an economic world power.

Japanese coinage of concern to this catalog includes those issued for the Ryukyu Islands (also called Liuchu), a chain of islands extending southwest from Japan toward Taiwan (Formosa), before the Japanese government converted the islands into a prefecture under the name Okinawa. Many of the provinces of Japan issued their own definitive coinage under the Shogunate.

RULERS

Shoguns

Iyenari, 1787-1837

Iyeoshi, 1837-1853

Iyesada, 1853-1858

Iyemochi, 1858-1866

Yoshinobu, 1866-1867

Emperors

Komei, 1847-1866

Mutsuhito (Meiji), 1867-1912

NOTE: The personal name of the emperor is followed by the name that he chose for his regnal era.

MONETARY SYSTEM

Until 1870

Prior to the Meiji currency reform, there was no fixed exchange rate between the various silver, gold and copper "cash" coins (which previously included Chinese "cash") in circulation. Each coin exchanged on the basis of its own merits and the prevailing market conditions. The size and weight of the copper coins and the weight and fineness of the silver and gold coins varied widely. From time to time the government would declare an official exchange rate, but this was usually ignored. For gold and silver, nominal equivalents were:

16 Shu = 4 Bu = 1 Ryo

Commencing 1870

10 Rin = 1 Sen

100 Sen = 1 Yen

MONETARY UNITS

Momme	匁
Ryo	両
Bu	分
Shu	朱
Rin	厘
Sen	銭

円 or 圓 or 圓

Yen

MINT MARKS ON MON

A - Edo (Tokyo)	文
B -Sado	佐佐佐
C -Jiuman Tsubo	十
D -Koume Mura	小
E -Ichi-no-se	一
F -Onagi-gawa	川
G -Osaka	元
H -Nagasaki	長
I -Ashio	足
J -Sendai	仙
K -Sendai	千
L -Kuji (Hitachi Ohta)	久
M -Mito	ト,ト
N -Aizu	ノ
O - Ise	イ
P - Morioka	盛
Q - Hiroshima	了
R - Yamanouchi	山

DATING

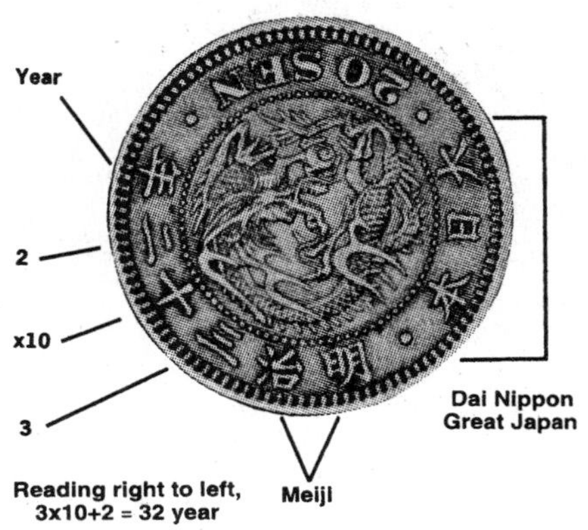

LEGENDS

Reading top-bottom, right-left.

Kanei Tsuho

Bunkyu-Eiho

KEY TO DATING MODERN MAMEITA GIN

'BUN'
GENBUN PERIOD
1736-1741
(Used 1736-1818)

'BUN'
UNSEI PERIOD
1818-1830
(Used 1820-1837)

'HO'
TEMPO PERIOD
1830-1844
(Used 1837-1858)

'ISEI'
ANSEI PERIOD
1854-1860
(Used 1859-1865)

One of the above characters is usually found on the obverse of C#8 or both sides of C#8a and C#8b. The same characters are found at both ends of chogin pieces C#9. Era designators were used continuously until the next one was introduced, regardless of intervening eras.

NOTE: Values are for pieces weighing 5-8 grams. Pieces over 10 grams may command up to twice the values shown; pieces under 5 grams somewhat less.

KEY TO DATING MODERN CHO GIN (SILVER)

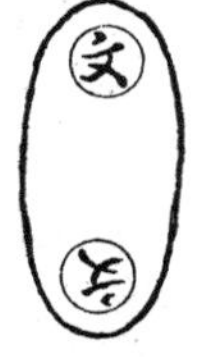

BUNSEIERA, 1818-1830

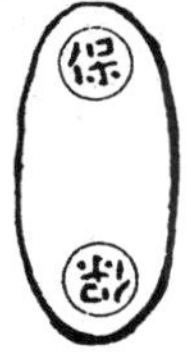

TEMPO ERA, 1830-1844

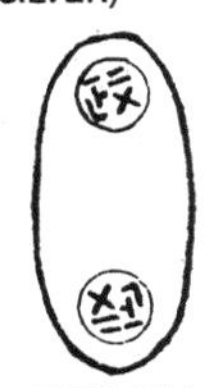

ANSEI ERA, 1854-1860

KEY TO DATING 1 SHU

KAEI ERA, 1848-1854
(Used 1853-1865)

MEIJI ERA, 1868-1912
(Used 1868-1869)

NOTE: C#12 type 1 Shu are dated according to how the character illustrated is written on the reverse. Meiji 1 Shu are also known as Kaheishi 1 Shu.

KEY TO DATING 1 BU

TEMPO ERA, 1830-1844 (Used 1837-1854)

常是

ANSEI ERA, 1854-1860 (Used 1859-1868)

常是

MEIJI ERA, 1868-1912 (Used 1868-1869)

NOTE: 1 Bu are dated according to how the two characters above are written on the reverse of the piece. There are other variations as well. Meiji Bu also are known as Kaheishi Bu.

KEY TO DATING 1 AND 2 BU

GENBUN PERIOD 1 BU
(Used 1736-1818)

TEMPO PERIOD
1830-1844 (Used 1837-1858)

BUNSEI PERIOD 2 BU
TYPE A DATE MARK
1818-1830 (Used 1818-1828)

BUNSEI PERIOD 1 BU and 2 BU
TYPE B DATE MARK
1818-1830
(Used 1819-1829 on 1 Bu)
(Used 1828-1832 on 2 Bu)

ANSEI PERIOD
1854-1859 (Used 1859)

MANEN PERIOD
1859-1860
(Without era designator)

C#2b is dated according to its wieght. C#21c and C#21d can be distinguished by the character to the left on the obverse.

KEY TO DATING C#21c and C#21d

MANEN PERIOD
1860-1861 (Used 1860)

MEIJI PERIOD
1868-1912 (Used 1868-1869)

'GIN' COUNTERMARKS

Countermark: Gin right on 1 Yen Meiji Year 3, (1870), Y#5.

Countermark: *Gin* left on 1 Yen, Meiji Years 7-30, (1874-1897), Y#A25.

In 1897 Japan demonetized the silver one Yen and Trade Dollar coins, and many were melted to provide bullion from which to produce subsidiary coins. However, some 20 million Trade Dollars and one Yen coins were countermarked with the character *Gin* (meaning silver) and shipped to Taiwan, Korea and Southern Manchuria for use in circulation there. The countermark was applied to indicate that the coin was to be treated simply as bullion and to prevent the coins from returning to Japan where they could be sold to the government for gold.

The actual countermarking was done by the Tokyo and Osaka Mints; the Osaka Mint putting its *Gin* on the left side, the Tokyo Mint putting its *Gin* on the right side. Only 2,100,000 coins were countermarked at the Tokyo Mint Mint as opposed to 18,350,000 countermarked at Osaka, making the Tokyo pieces scarcer than the Osaka pieces.

Formerly *Gin* marked coins were regarded as damaged and sold for about 80 per cent of the price of the same coin without countermark. Now, however, the *Gin* coins are being collected by date and placement of the mark, and some sell for more than a non-countermarked piece. Any additional chop marks are still considered defacement and reduce the value of a coin substantially.

SHOGUNATE

CAST COINAGE

C# 1.1a MON

Cast Iron **Rev:** Plain

Date	VG	F	VF	XF	Unc
ND(1739-1867)	2.00	5.00	7.50	15.00	—

C# 1.12 MON
Cast Iron

Date	VG	F	VF	XF	Unc
ND(1838)(K)	3.00	5.00	8.00	15.00	—

C# 1.14s MON
Cast Copper

Date	VG	F	VF	XF	Unc
ND(1844) Bosen	—	—	—	500	—

Note: C#1.14a is known only as "bosen" - seed or mother coins

C# 4.2 4 MON
Cast Copper or Brass **Rev:** 11 waves

Date	VG	F	VF	XF	Unc
ND(1769-1860)	1.00	2.50	5.00	10.00	—

C# 6 4 MON
Cast Copper or Brass **Obv. Inscription:** "Bun-Kyu Ei-Ho"

Date	VG	F	VF	XF	Unc
ND(1863-67)	2.00	5.00	8.00	15.00	—

C# 6a 4 MON
Cast Copper or Brass **Obv. Inscription:** "Bun" in different style **Rev:** Eleven waves

Date	VG	F	VF	XF	Unc
ND(1863-67)	2.00	5.00	8.00	15.00	—

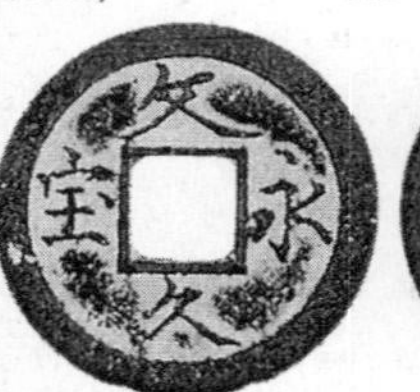

C# 6b 4 MON
Cast Copper or Brass **Obv. Inscription:** "Bun" in different style and "Ho" at left abbreviated **Rev:** Eleven waves

Date	VG	F	VF	XF	Unc
ND(1863-67)	3.00	5.00	8.00	15.00	—

C# 4.2a 4 MON
Iron **Obv. Inscription:** "Kwan-Ei (kanei) Tsu-Ho" **Rev:** Eleven waves; without mint mark

Date	VG	F	VF	XF	Unc
ND(1866)	5.00	9.00	15.00	25.00	—

C# 4.12 4 MON
Iron **Rev:** Eleven waves; various mint marks

Date	VG	F	VF	XF	Unc
ND(1866)(K)	5.00	9.00	15.00	25.00	—

C# 4.14 4 MON
Iron **Rev:** Eleven waves; various mint marks

Date	VG	F	VF	XF	Unc
ND(1866)(M)	15.00	20.00	25.00	35.00	—

C# 4.15 4 MON
Iron **Rev:** Eleven waves; various mint marks

Date	VG	F	VF	XF	Unc
ND(1866)(N)	5.00	12.00	20.00	25.00	—

C# 4.16 4 MON
Iron **Rev:** Eleven waves; various mint marks

Date	VG	F	VF	XF	Unc
ND(1866)(O)	5.00	12.50	20.00	25.00	—

C# 4.17 4 MON
Iron **Rev:** Eleven waves; various mint marks

Date	VG	F	VF	XF	Unc
ND(1866)(P)	5.00	12.50	20.00	25.00	—

C# 4.18 4 MON
Iron **Rev:** Eleven waves; various mint marks

Date	VG	F	VF	XF	Unc
ND(1866)(Q)	300	500	750	900	—

C# 4.19 4 MON
Iron **Rev:** Eleven waves; various mint marks

Date	VG	F	VF	XF	Unc
ND(1866)(R) Rare	—	—	—	—	—

Note: Copper 4 Mon pieces similar to those listed only under iron issues are "bosen" - seed or mother coins

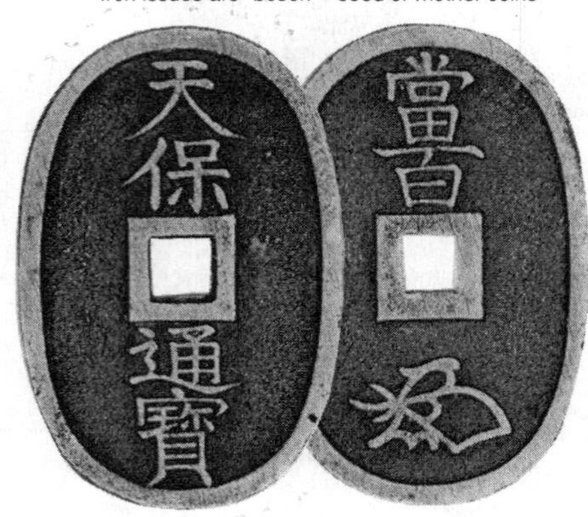

C# 7 100 MON (Tempo Tsuho)
Cast Bronze **Obv. Inscription:** Ten-Ho (Tempo) Tsu-Ho **Rev. Inscription:** To Hyacku (100) **Edge:** Smooth rim with validation mark at left and right **Note:** Cast at Edo (Tokyo) and Osaka. Large center hole. Varieties exist.

Date	VG	F	VF	XF	Unc
ND(1835-70)	5.00	8.00	12.00	17.50	—

BULLION COINAGE

C# 8.1a MAMEITA GIN
0.4600 Silver **Obv:** One or more large characters, without "God of Plenty"; Era designator between characters **Rev:** Blank or with chop marks

Date	VG	F	VF	XF	Unc
ND(1736-1818)	15.00	20.00	35.00	45.00	—

C# 8.1b MAMEITA GIN
0.4600 Silver **Obv:** "God of Plenty" with other large characters; Era designator between characters and on God's belly

Date	VG	F	VF	XF	Unc
ND(1736-1818)	25.00	35.00	50.00	65.00	—

C# 8a.1 MAMEITA GIN
0.4600 Silver **Obv:** "God of Plenty" design, era designator on belly

Date	VG	F	VF	XF	Unc
ND(1736-1818)	50.00	85.00	150	250	—

C# 8b.1 MAMEITA GIN
0.4600 Silver **Obv:** "God of Plenty" design **Rev:** Single large "Bun" or multiple small era designator

Date	VG	F	VF	XF	Unc
ND(1736-1818)	800	1,000	1,300	1,600	—

C# 8.2a MAMEITA GIN
0.3600 Silver **Subject:** Tempo **Obv:** One or more large characters, without "God of Plenty", era designator between characters

Date	VG	F	VF	XF	Unc
ND(1820-37)	20.00	35.00	45.00	60.00	—

C# 8.2b MAMEITA GIN
0.3600 Silver **Obv:** "God of Plenty" with other large characters, era designator between charactes and on God's belly

Date	VG	F	VF	XF	Unc
ND(1820)	25.00	45.00	60.00	80.00	—

C# 8a.2 MAMEITA GIN
0.3600 Silver **Subject:** Bunsei **Obv:** "God of Plenty" design, era designator on belly **Rev:** "God of Plenty" design

Date	VG	F	VF	XF	Unc
ND(1820-37)	90.00	150	225	375	—

C# 8b.2 MAMEITA GIN
0.3600 Silver **Subject:** Bunsei **Obv:** "God of Plenty" design **Rev:** Single large "Bun" or multiple small era designators

Date	VG	F	VF	XF	Unc
ND(1820-37)	1,000	1,250	1,600	2,000	—

C# 8.3a MAMEITA GIN
0.2610 Silver **Obv:** One or more large characters, without "God of Plenty", era designator between characters

Date	VG	F	VF	XF	Unc
ND(1837-58)	20.00	29.00	35.00	45.00	—

C# 8.3b MAMEITA GIN
0.2610 Silver **Obv:** "God of Plenty" with other large characters, era designator between characters and on God's belly

Date	VG	F	VF	XF	Unc
ND(1837-58)	25.00	40.00	60.00	70.00	—

C# 8a.3a MAMEITA GIN
0.2610 Silver **Subject:** Tempo **Obv:** "God of Plenty" design, era designator on belly **Rev:** "God of Plenty" design

Date	VG	F	VF	XF	Unc
ND(1837-58)	50.00	100	150	250	—

C# 8a.3b MAMEITA GIN
0.2610 Silver **Obv:** "God of Plenty" design, era designator on belly **Rev:** Character "Ho" (treasure) on belly of "God of Plenty"

Date	VG	F	VF	XF	Unc
ND(1837-58)	150	250	375	525	—

C# 8b.3a MAMEITA GIN
0.2610 Silver **Subject:** Tempo **Obv:** "God of Plenty" design **Rev:** Single or multiple era designator

Date	VG	F	VF	XF	Unc
ND(1837-58)	1,000	1,500	2,000	2,500	—

C# 8b.3b MAMEITA GIN
0.2610 Silver **Obv:** "God of Plenty" **Rev:** Large single character "Ho" (treasure)

Date	VG	F	VF	XF	Unc
ND(1837-58)	1,000	1,500	2,000	2,500	—

C# 8.4a MAMEITA GIN
0.1350 Silver **Subject:** Ansei **Obv:** One or more large characters, without "God of Plenty", era designator between characters

Date	VG	F	VF	XF	Unc
ND(1859-65)	13.00	21.00	27.00	35.00	—

C# 8.4b MAMEITA GIN
0.1350 Silver **Obv:** "God of Plemty" with other large characters, era designator between characters and on God's belly

Date	VG	F	VF	XF	Unc
ND(1859-65)	125	175	275	375	—

C# 8a.4 MAMEITA GIN
0.1350 Silver **Subject:** Ansei **Obv:** "God of Plenty" design **Rev:** "God of Plenty" design

Date	VG	F	VF	XF	Unc
ND(1859-65)	65.00	80.00	125	175	—

C# 8b.4a MAMEITA GIN
0.1350 Silver **Subject:** Ansei **Obv:** "God of Plenty" design **Rev:** Single or multiple era designator

Date	VG	F	VF	XF	Unc
ND(1859-65)	1,900	2,600	3,400	4,100	—

C# 8b.4b MAMEITA GIN
0.1350 Silver **Obv:** "God of Plenty" design **Rev:** Large single character "Ho" (treasure)

Date	VG	F	VF	XF	Unc
ND(1859-65)	1,000	1,250	1,650	2,000	—

HAMMERED COINAGE

C# 9 CHO GIN
0.4600 Silver **Obv:** Era marks at each end; Miscellaneous marks elsewhere **Rev:** Blank except for occasional chop marks

Date	VG	F	VF	XF	Unc
ND(1736-1818)	300	400	500	600	—

C# 9a CHO GIN
0.3600 Silver **Note:** Bunsei era.

Date	VG	F	VF	XF	Unc
ND(1820-37)	350	500	600	800	—

C# 9b CHO GIN
0.2610 Silver **Note:** Illustration full size. Tempo era.

Date	VG	F	VF	XF	Unc
ND(1837-58)	250	325	400	500	—

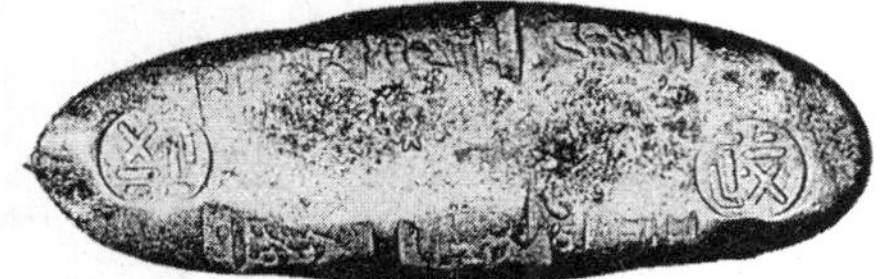

C# 9c CHO GIN
0.1350 Silver **Note:** Illustration reduced. Ansei era.

Date	VG	F	VF	XF	Unc
ND(1859-65)	200	275	350	450	—

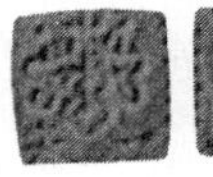

C# 17 SHU (Isshu Gin)
1.3900 g., Gold And Silver .123 gold and .877 silver **Note:** Bunsei era.

Date	Mintage	VG	F	VF	XF	Unc
ND(1824-32)	46,723,000	200	350	450	600	—

C# 11 SHU (Isshu Gin)
2.6300 g., 0.9890 Silver **Note:** Bunsei era.

Date	Mintage	VG	F	VF	XF	Unc
ND(1829-37)	139,915,000	60.00	100	125	175	—

C# 12 SHU (Isshu Gin)
1.8900 g., 0.9680 Silver **Note:** Kaei era.

Date	Mintage	VG	F	VF	XF	Unc
ND(1853-65)	159,245,000	7.50	12.00	15.00	20.00	—

C# 12a SHU (Isshu Gin)
1.8800 g., 0.8800 Silver **Ruler:** Mutsuhito (Meiji) **Rev:** Three top stokes are straight without curves or hooks

Date	Mintage	VG	F	VF	XF	Unc
ND(1868-69)	18,742,000	15.00	22.50	30.00	40.00	—

Note: C#12 type 1 Shu are dated according to how the character illustrated is written on the reverse; Meiji 1 Shu are also known as Kaheishi 1 Shu

C# 13 2 SHU (Nishu Gin)
10.1900 g., 0.9780 Silver **Note:** Meiwa-Ko-Nanryo

Date	Mintage	VG	F	VF	XF	Unc
ND(1772-1824)	47,464,000	150	225	275	325	—

C# 13a 2 SHU (Nishu Gin)
7.5300 g., 0.9780 Silver **Note:** Brunsei-Shin-Nanryo

Date	Mintage	VG	F	VF	XF	Unc
ND(1824-30)	60,624,000	70.00	100	125	175	—

C# 18 2 SHU (Nishu Gin)
1.6200 g., Gold And Silver .298 gold and .702 silver **Note:** Tempo era.

Date	Mintage	VG	F	VF	XF	Unc
ND(1832-58)	103,070,000	20.00	25.00	30.00	40.00	—

C# 15 2 SHU (Nishu Gin)
13.6200 g., 0.8450 Silver **Note:** Ansei era.

Date	Mintage	VG	F	VF	XF	Unc
ND(1859)	706,000	400	800	1,200	1,600	—

C# 18a 2 SHU (Nishu Gin)
0.7500 g., Gold And Silver .229 gold and .771 silver **Note:** Manen.

Date	Mintage	VG	F	VF	XF	Unc
ND(1860-69)	25,120,000	25.00	35.00	45.00	60.00	—

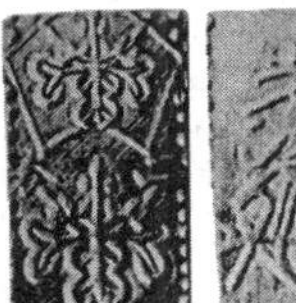
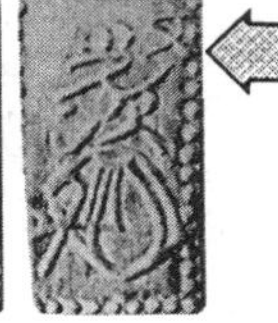

C# 19 BU (Ichibu)
3.2500 g., Gold And Silver **Note:** .653 Gold and .347 Silver. Kyoho era.

Date	VG	F	VF	XF	Unc
ND(1736-1818)	150	250	300	350	—

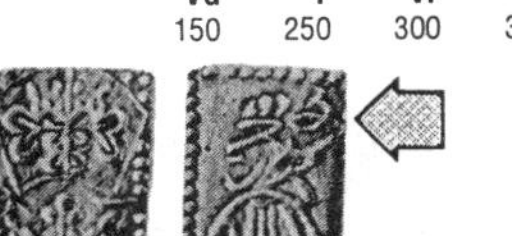

C# 20 BU (Ichibu)
3.2700 g., Gold And Silver .560 gold and .440 silver **Rev:** Type B mint mark **Note:** Bunsei era.

Date	VG	F	VF	XF	Unc
ND(1819-29)	125	175	225	275	—

C# 20a BU (Ichibu)
2.8000 g., Gold And Silver .568 gold and .432 silver **Note:** Tempo era.

Date	VG	F	VF	XF	Unc
ND(1837-58)	150	200	250	350	—

C# 16 BU (Ichibu)
8.6600 g., 0.9910 Silver **Note:** Varieties of countermark. Tempo era.

Date	Mintage	VG	F	VF	XF	Unc
ND(1837-54)	78,917,000	20.00	26.00	30.00	40.00	—

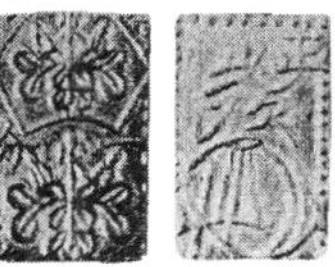

C# 20b BU (Ichibu)
2.2400 g., Gold And Silver .570 gold and .430 silver **Note:** Ansei era.

Date	VG	F	VF	XF	Unc
ND(1859)	1,250	1,750	2,250	3,250	—

C# 16a BU (Ichibu)
8.6300 g., 0.8730 Silver **Note:** Ansei era.

Date	Mintage	VG	F	VF	XF	Unc
ND(1859-68)	11,399,000	18.00	24.00	28.00	35.00	—

C# 20c BU (Ichibu)
0.8200 g., Gold And Silver .574 gold and .426 silver **Rev:** Without dating mark **Note:** Manen era.

Date	VG	F	VF	XF	Unc
ND(1860-67)	500	650	800	1,000	—

Note: Similar pieces without dating mark but weighing about 4 grams were made during the Kyoho era, 1716-34

C# 16b BU (Ichibu)
8.6600 g., 0.8070 Silver **Ruler:** Mutsuhito (Meiji)

Date	Mintage	VG	F	VF	XF	Unc
ND(1868-69)	4,267,000	150	200	275	365	—

C# 21 2 BU (Ni Bu)
6.5200 g., Gold And Silver .563 gold and .437 silver **Rev:** Type A mark **Note:** Bunsei era.

Date	Mintage	VG	F	VF	XF	Unc
ND(1818-28)	5,972,000	300	400	600	850	—

C# 21a 2 BU (Ni Bu)
6.5600 g., Gold And Silver .490 gold and .510 silver **Rev:** Type B mark **Note:** Bunsei era.

Date	Mintage	VG	F	VF	XF	Unc
ND(1828-32)	4,066,000	250	375	500	750	—

C# 21b 2 BU (Ni Bu)
5.6200 g., Gold And Silver .209 gold and .791 silver **Rev:** Without mint mark **Note:** Ansei era.

Date	Mintage	VG	F	VF	XF	Unc
ND(1856-60)	7,103,000	75.00	100	150	200	—

A.

B.

C# 21c.1 2 BU (Ni Bu)
3.0000 g., Gold And Silver .229 gold and .771 silver **Obv:** Paulownia leaf type A **Rev:** Without mint mark **Note:** Manen era.

Date	Mintage	VG	F	VF	XF	Unc
ND(1860)	100,201,000	350	550	750	1,100	—

C# 21c.2 2 BU (Ni Bu)
3.0000 g., Gold And Silver .229 gold and .771 silver **Obv:** Paulownia leaf type B **Note:** Manen era.

Date	VG	F	VF	XF	Unc
ND(1860)	250	450	600	850	—

C# 21d 2 BU (Ni Bu)
3.0000 g., Gold And Silver .223 gold and .777 silver **Ruler:** Mutsuhito (Meiji)

Date	VG	F	VF	XF	Unc
ND(1868-69)	40.00	50.00	65.00	90.00	—

C# 22 KOBAN (1 Ryo)
13.1300 g., Gold And Silver **Note:** .653 Gold and .347 Silver. Genbun era.

Date	Mintage	VG	F	VF	XF	Unc
ND(1736-1818)	17,436,000	600	800	1,200	1,600	—

C# 22a KOBAN (1 Ryo)
13.1300 g., Gold And Silver .559 gold and .441 silver **Rev:** Mark B **Note:** Brunsei era.

Date	VG	F	VF	XF	Unc
ND(1819-28)	700	1,100	1,600	2,200	—

C# 22b KOBAN (1 Ryo)
11.2500 g., Gold And Silver .568 gold and .432 silver **Note:** Tempo era.

Date	VG	F	VF	XF	Unc
ND(1837-58)	750	1,000	1,250	1,750	—

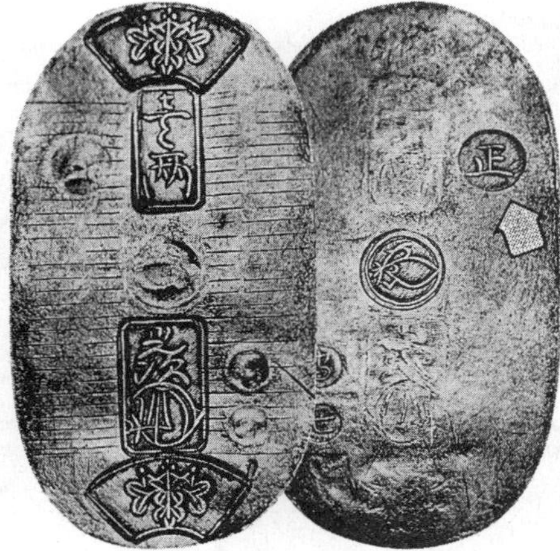

C# 22c KOBAN (1 Ryo)
8.9700 g., Gold And Silver .570 gold and .430 silver **Note:** Ansei era.

Date	Mintage	VG	F	VF	XF	Unc
ND(1859)	351,000	3,000	3,500	5,500	7,500	—

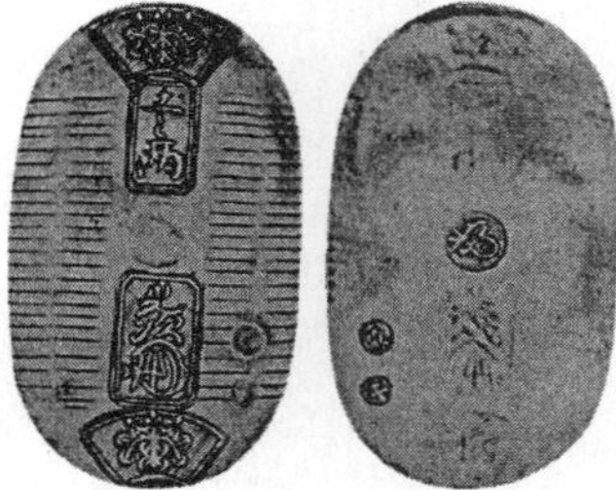

C# 22d KOBAN (1 Ryo)
3.3000 g., Gold And Silver .574 gold and .426 silver **Rev:** Without mint mark **Note:** Manen era.

Date	Mintage	VG	F	VF	XF	Unc
ND(1860-67)	625,000	500	800	1,000	1,250	—

Note: Koban mintage figures are in Ryo and also include Ichibu Kin

C# 23 GORYOBAN (5 Ryo)
33.7500 g., Gold And Silver .842 gold and .158 silver, 51x89 mm.
Note: Tempo era.

Date	Mintage	VG	F	VF	XF	Unc
ND(1837-43)	34,000	7.50	12,000	14,000	16,500	—

C# 24.1 OBAN
165.3800 g., Gold And Silver, 94x153 mm. **Subject:** Kyoho
Note: .676 Gold and .324 Silver. Kyoho era.

Date	Mintage	VG	F	VF	XF	Unc
ND(1725-1837)	8,515	—	—	25,000	35,000	—
Note: Original inking						
ND(1725-1837)	Inc. above	—	—	20,000	27,500	—
Note: Re-inked during Tempo period						

C# 24.2 GORYOBAN (5 Ryo)
165.3800 g., Gold And Silver .674 gold and .326 silver, 95x157 mm. **Note:** Tempo era.

Date	Mintage	VG	F	VF	XF	Unc
ND(1838-60)	1,887	—	—	50,000	60,000	—

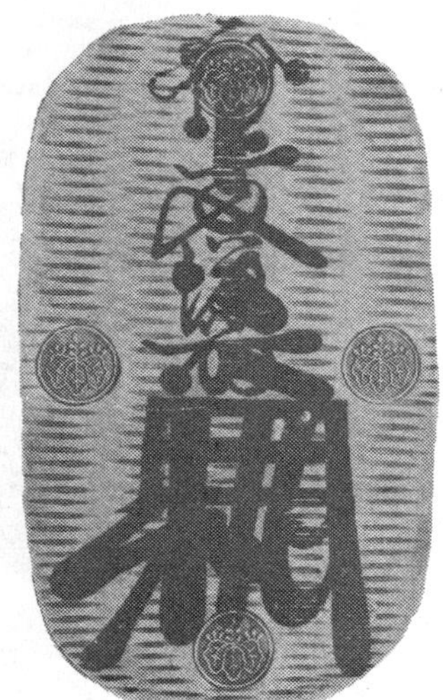

C# 24a.1 GORYOBAN (5 Ryo)
112.4000 g., Gold And Silver .344 gold and .639 silver **Note:** Handmade horizontal crenulations. Manen era.

Date	Mintage	VG	F	VF	XF	Unc
ND(1860-62)	17,000	—	—	18,000	25,000	—

C# 24a.2 GORYOBAN (5 Ryo)
112.4000 g., Gold And Silver .344 gold and .639 silver **Note:** Machine-made horizontal crenulations. Manen era.

Date	VG	F	VF	XF	Unc
ND(1860-62)	—	—	16,000	20,000	—

COUNTERMARKED COINAGE

1859

At the time the treaty ports were opened in 1859, Mexican 8 Reales pieces were counterstamped ""guaranteed 3 bu"" so that they could circulate without having to be weighed at each transaction. In fact, the coins were about 3 percent over the weight of three one-bu pieces, but about 10 percent below the actual silver content of three one-bu pieces (because of the lower fineness of the Mexican coins).

KM# 101.1 3 BU (Sanbu)
0.9030 Silver **Countermark:** Four characters **Note:** Countermark on Culiacan 8 Reales, KM#377.3. Dav. #272. Ansei Trade Dollar.

CM Date	Host Date	Good	VG	F	VF	XF
ND(1859)	ND(1846-58)	—	3,000	4,500	5,500	6,500

KM# 101.2 3 BU (Sanbu)
0.9030 Silver **Countermark:** Four characters **Note:** Countermark on Guanajuato 8 Reales, KM#377.8.

CM Date	Host Date	Good	VG	F	VF	XF
ND(1859)	ND(1825-58)	—	3,000	4,500	5,500	6,500

KM# 101.3 3 BU (Sanbu)
0.9030 Silver **Countermark:** Four characters **Note:** Countermark on Mexico City 8 Reales, KM#377.10.

CM Date	Host Date	Good	VG	F	VF	XF
ND(1859)	ND(1824-58)	—	3,000	4,500	5,500	6,500

KM# 101.4 3 BU (Sanbu)
0.9030 Silver **Countermark:** Four characters **Note:** Countermark on Zacatecas 8 Reales, KM#377.13.

CM Date	Host Date	Good	VG	F	VF	XF
ND(1859)	ND(1825-58)	—	3,000	4,500	5,500	6,500

EMPIRE

DECIMAL COINAGE

Y# 15 RIN
Copper **Ruler:** Mutsuhito (Meiji)

Date	Mintage	F	VF	XF	Unc	BU
Yr.6(1873)	6,979,260	4.50	10.00	20.00	50.00	—
Yr.7(1874)	Inc. above	2.00	5.00	10.00	30.00	—
Yr.8(1875)	3,718,840	4.50	10.00	25.00	60.00	—

Note: Two varieites of year 8 exist: one with characters separate and a second with characters connected

Date	Mintage	F	VF	XF	Unc	BU
Yr.9(1876)	23,000	1,000	2,000	3,500	5,500	—
Yr.10(1877)	Inc. above	350	750	1,100	1,400	—
Yr.13(1880)	810	1,500	2,500	4,500	7,000	—
Yr.15(1882)	3,632,360	2.00	5.00	8.00	25.00	—
Yr.16(1883)	14,128,150	1.50	3.50	6.50	22.00	—
Yr.17(1884)	16,009,130	1.50	3.50	6.50	22.00	—
Yr.25(1892)	—	—	—	—	—	—

Note: None struck for circulation

Y# 16.1 1/2 SEN

Copper **Ruler:** Mutsuhito (Meiji) **Obv:** Square scales on dragon's body

Date	Mintage	F	VF	XF	Unc	BU
Yr.6(1873)	16,804,440	3.50	15.00	65.00	300	—
Yr.7(1874)	Inc. above	3.50	15.00	65.00	350	—

Note: Varieties exist for year 7

Date	Mintage	F	VF	XF	Unc	BU
Yr.8(1875)	17,037,928	2.00	5.00	45.00	300	—
Yr.9(1876)	24,292,478	1.00	4.00	35.00	275	—
Yr.10(1877)	29,278,520	75.00	150	275	2,500	—

Y# 16.2 1/2 SEN

Copper **Ruler:** Mutsuhito (Meiji) **Obv:** V-scales on dragon's body

Date	Mintage	F	VF	XF	Unc	BU
Yr.10(1877)	Inc. above	1.00	3.00	12.00	50.00	—
Yr.12(1879)	29,963,706	7.50	30.00	50.00	800	—
Yr.13(1880)	14,090,894	1.00	3.00	12.00	50.00	—
Yr.14(1881)	17,929,026	1.00	3.00	12.00	50.00	—
Yr.15(1882)	26,458,976	1.00	3.00	14.00	55.00	—
Yr.16(1883)	38,202,062	1.00	3.00	14.00	55.00	—
Yr.17(1884)	38,480,248	1.00	3.00	5.00	35.00	—
Yr.18(1885)	31,166,240	1.00	3.00	17.50	60.00	—
Yr.19(1886)	31,831,244	1.00	3.00	17.50	60.00	—
Yr.20(1887)	35,651,564	1.00	3.00	17.50	60.00	—
Yr.21(1888)	25,744,686	5.00	8.00	16.00	120	—
Yr.25(1892)	—	—	—	—	—	—

Note: None struck for circulation

Y# 17.1 SEN

Copper **Ruler:** Mutsuhito (Meiji) **Obv:** Square scales on dragon's body

Date	Mintage	F	VF	XF	Unc	BU
Yr.6(1873)	1,301,486	7.00	15.00	35.00	300	—
Yr.7(1874)	25,564,953	2.00	6.00	25.00	200	—
Yr.8(1875)	32,832,038	1.00	2.00	4.00	125	—
Yr.9(1876)	38,048,906	1.00	2.00	4.00	125	—
Yr.10(1877)	98,041,824	1.00	2.00	4.00	125	—

Y# 17.2 SEN

Copper **Ruler:** Mutsuhito (Meiji) **Obv:** V-scales on dragon's body

Date	Mintage	F	VF	XF	Unc	BU
Yr.13(1880)	33,947,810	1.00	2.00	5.00	85.00	—
Yr.14(1881)	16,123,612	2.00	4.00	10.00	125	—
Yr.14(1881) Large 4	Inc. above	25.00	50.00	100	225	—
Yr.15(1882)	19,150,666	2.00	3.00	6.00	90.00	—
Yr.16(1883)	47,613,017	1.00	2.00	5.00	85.00	—
Yr.17(1884)	53,702,768	1.00	2.00	5.00	85.00	—

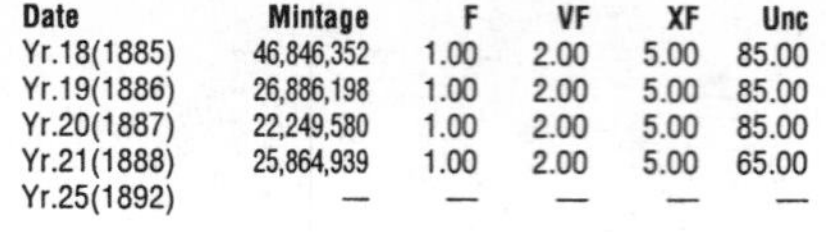

Date	Mintage	F	VF	XF	Unc	BU
Yr.18(1885)	46,846,352	1.00	2.00	5.00	85.00	—
Yr.19(1886)	26,886,198	1.00	2.00	5.00	85.00	—
Yr.20(1887)	22,249,580	1.00	2.00	5.00	85.00	—
Yr.21(1888)	25,864,939	1.00	2.00	5.00	65.00	—
Yr.25(1892)	—	—	—	—	—	—

Y# 20 SEN

7.1300 g., Bronze, 27.8 mm. **Ruler:** Mutsuhito (Meiji)

Date	Mintage	F	VF	XF	Unc	BU
Yr.31(1898)	3,649,498	3.00	7.50	25.00	150	—
Yr.32(1899)	9,764,028	2.00	5.00	17.00	125	—
Yr.33(1900)	3,086,524	5.00	9.00	25.00	200	—

Y# 18.1 2 SEN

Bronze **Ruler:** Mutsuhito (Meiji) **Obv:** Square scales on dragon's body

Date	Mintage	F	VF	XF	Unc	BU
Yr.6(1873)	3,949,758	35.00	75.00	150	1,000	—
Yr.7(1874)	Inc. above	3.50	15.00	50.00	600	—
Yr.8(1875)	22,835,255	2.00	3.50	6.00	265	—
Yr.9(1876)	25,817,570	2.00	3.50	6.00	265	—
Yr.10(1877)	33,097,868	2.00	5.00	15.00	350	—

Y# 18.2 2 SEN

Bronze **Ruler:** Mutsuhito (Meiji) **Obv:** V-scales on dragon's body

Date	Mintage	F	VF	XF	Unc	BU
Yr.10(1877)	43,290,398	2.00	5.00	10.00	150	—
Yr.13(1880)	33,142,307	2.00	3.50	6.00	115	—
Yr.14(1881)	38,475,569	2.00	3.50	6.00	115	—
Yr.15(1882)	43,527,187	2.00	3.50	6.00	115	—
Yr.16(1883)	19,476,164	2.00	3.50	6.00	115	—
Yr.17(1884)	12,090,586	3.00	6.00	12.00	350	—
Yr.25(1892)	—	—	—	—	—	—

Note: None struck for circulation

Y# 1 5 SEN

1.2500 g., 0.8000 Silver .0321 oz. **Ruler:** Mutsuhito (Meiji)

Date	Mintage	F	VF	XF	Unc	BU
Yr.3(1870) Shallow scales	1,501,473	150	250	350	550	—
Yr.3(1870) Deep scales	Inc. above	200	300	450	950	—
Yr.4(1871)	Inc. above	250	350	500	1,000	—

Y# 6.1 5 SEN

1.2500 g., 0.8000 Silver .0321 oz. **Ruler:** Mutsuhito (Meiji) **Rev:** 66 rays, 79 beads **Note:** Early variety.

Date	Mintage	F	VF	XF	Unc	BU
Yr.14(1871)	1,665,613	50.00	125	250	400	—

Y# 6.2 5 SEN

1.2500 g., 0.8000 Silver .0321 oz. **Ruler:** Mutsuhito (Meiji) **Rev:** 53 rays, 65 beads **Note:** Late variety.

Date	F	VF	XF	Unc	BU
Yr.4(1871)	40.00	90.00	150	325	—

明 Type I Characters not connected

明 Type II Characters connected

Y# A22 5 SEN

1.3400 g., 0.8000 Silver .0344 oz. **Ruler:** Mutsuhito (Meiji) **Note:** Varieties exist.

Date	Mintage	F	VF	XF	Unc	BU
Yr.6(1873) Type I	5,593,172	12.50	25.00	40.00	85.00	—
Yr.6(1873) Type II	Inc. above	50.00	75.00	125	250	—
Yr.7(1874)	7,806,493	100	200	325	800	—
Yr.8(1875)	6,396,784	12.50	25.00	40.00	75.00	—
Yr.9(1876) Type I	5,546,424	12.50	25.00	40.00	85.00	—
Yr.9(1876) Type II	Inc. above	15.00	30.00	45.00	150	—
Yr.10(1877) Type I	22,024,167	20.00	35.00	55.00	95.00	—
Yr.10(1877) Type II	Inc. above	22.00	45.00	75.00	150	—
Yr.13(1880)	79	—	—	—	—	—
Yr.25(1892)	—	—	—	—	—	—

Note: None struck for circulation

Y# 19 5 SEN

Copper-Nickel **Ruler:** Mutsuhito (Meiji) **Note:** Varieties exist.

Date	Mintage	F	VF	XF	Unc	BU
Yr.22(1889)	28,841,944	2.00	4.50	10.00	100	—
Yr.23(1890)	39,258,103	2.00	4.50	10.00	100	—
Yr.24(1891)	15,924,782	3.00	6.00	15.00	150	—
Yr.25(1892)	9,510,289	2.50	6.00	15.00	100	—
Yr.26(1893)	8,531,858	2.50	6.00	15.00	100	—
Yr.27(1894)	14,680,000	3.00	6.00	15.00	150	—
Yr.28(1895)	1,030,000	50.00	100	200	1,700	—
Yr.29(1896)	5,119,988	5.00	12.00	30.00	300	—
Yr.30(1897)	7,857,669	4.00	9.00	15.00	150	—

Y# 21 5 SEN

4.6700 g., Copper-Nickel **Ruler:** Mutsuhito (Meiji)

Date	Mintage	F	VF	XF	Unc	BU
Yr.30(1897)	4,167,020	7.50	15.00	35.00	400	—
Yr.31(1898)	18,197,271	6.00	12.00	25.00	125	—
Yr.32(1899)	10,658,052	6.00	12.00	25.00	125	—
Yr.33(1900)	2,426,632	10.00	20.00	35.00	235	—

Y# 2 10 SEN

2.5000 g., 0.8000 Silver .0643 oz. **Ruler:** Mutsuhito (Meiji)

Date	Mintage	F	VF	XF	Unc	BU
Yr.3(1870) Shallow scales	6,102,674	15.00	30.00	45.00	155	—
Yr.3(1870) Deep scales	Inc. above	20.00	45.00	60.00	250	—

Y# 23 10 SEN

2.6957 g., 0.8000 Silver .070 oz. **Ruler:** Mutsuhito (Meiji)

Date	Mintage	F	VF	XF	Unc	BU
Yr.6(1873) Type I	5,109,951	5.00	10.00	18.00	65.00	—
Yr.6(1873) Type II	Inc. above	60.00	120	165	600	—

Date	Mintage	F	VF	XF	Unc	BU

明 Type I Characters not connected — 明 Type II Characters connected

Date	Mintage	F	VF	XF	Unc	BU
Yr.7(1874)	10,221,571	160	275	425	950	—
Yr.8(1875) Type II	8,977,419	15.00	30.00	50.00	200	—
Yr.8(1875) Type I	Inc. above	8.00	14.00	22.00	55.00	—

銭 Type I Character Sen connected — 銭 Type II Character Sen not connected

Date	Mintage	F	VF	XF	Unc	BU
Yr.9(1876) Type I	11,890,000	8.00	14.00	25.00	55.00	—
Yr.9(1876) Type II	Inc. above	8.00	14.00	22.00	55.00	—
Yr.10(1877)	20,352,136	10.00	25.00	40.00	100	—
Yr.13(1880)	77	5,000	10,000	20,000	35,000	—
Yr.18(1885)	9,763,333	6.00	10.00	18.00	40.00	—
Yr.20(1887)	10,421,616	6.00	10.00	18.00	40.00	—
Yr.21(1888)	8,177,229	6.00	10.00	20.00	65.00	—
Yr.24(1891)	5,000,000	15.00	25.00	45.00	160	—
Yr.25(1892)	5,000,000	15.00	25.00	45.00	160	—
Yr.26(1893)	12,000,000	6.00	10.00	22.00	55.00	—
Yr.27(1894)	11,000,000	6.00	10.00	25.00	125	—
Yr.28(1895)	13,719,054	4.00	7.00	10.00	35.00	—
Yr.29(1896)	15,080,506	4.00	7.00	10.00	35.00	—
Yr.30(1897)	20,357,439	4.00	7.00	10.00	35.00	—
Yr.31(1898)	13,643,001	5.00	9.00	18.00	75.00	—
Yr.32(1899)	26,216,579	5.00	9.00	18.00	75.00	—
Yr.33(1900)	8,183,421	8.50	20.00	35.00	125	—

Y# 3 20 SEN
5.0000 g., 0.8000 Silver .1286 oz. **Ruler:** Mutsuhito (Meiji)

Date	Mintage	F	VF	XF	Unc	BU
Yr.3(1870) Shallow scales	4,313,015	15.00	25.00	45.00	135	—
Yr.3(1870) Deep scales	Inc. above	20.00	40.00	65.00	200	—
Yr.4(1871)	Inc. above	15.00	25.00	40.00	125	—
Yr.4(1871)	Inc. above	75.00	100	150	300	—

Note: Lower stroke in "Sen" incomplete

明 Type I Character closed — 明 Type II Character open

Y# 24 20 SEN
5.3900 g., 0.8000 Silver .1383 oz. **Ruler:** Mutsuhito (Meiji)

Date	Mintage	F	VF	XF	Unc	BU
Yr.6(1873) Type I	5,214,284	5.00	10.00	16.50	100	—
Yr.6(1873) Type II	Inc. above	65.00	125	250	1,000	—
Yr.7(1874)	3,024,242	20.00	40.00	65.00	200	—

明 Type I Characters not connected — 明 Type II Characters connected

Date	Mintage	F	VF	XF	Unc	BU
Yr.8(1875) Type I	612,736	100	150	275	975	—
Yr.8(1875) Type II	Inc. above	50.00	100	175	975	—
Yr.9(1876) Type II	9,200,892	20.00	35.00	65.00	325	—
Yr.9(1876) Type I	Inc. above	6.00	12.00	18.00	65.00	—
Yr.10(1877)	5,199,731	20.00	35.00	65.00	300	—
Yr.13(1880)	96	1,750	3,250	5,500	30,000	—
Yr.18(1885)	4,205,723	5.00	10.00	15.00	50.00	—
Yr.20(1887)	4,794,755	5.00	10.00	15.00	50.00	—
Yr.21(1888)	703,920	60.00	125	200	1,000	—
Yr.24(1891)	2,500,000	15.00	25.00	40.00	120	—
Yr.25(1892)	3,054,307	8.50	17.50	30.00	100	—
Yr.26(1893)	3,445,000	7.50	15.00	25.00	90.00	—
Yr.27(1894)	4,500,000	6.00	12.00	18.00	140	—
Yr.28(1895)	7,000,000	5.00	10.00	15.00	50.00	—
Yr.29(1896)	2,599,340	9.00	18.00	30.00	100	—
Yr.30(1897)	7,516,448	5.00	10.00	15.00	50.00	—
Yr.31(1898)	17,984,212	5.00	10.00	15.00	50.00	—

Date	Mintage	F	VF	XF	Unc	BU
Yr.32(1899)	15,000,000	5.00	10.00	15.00	50.00	—
Yr.33(1900)	800,000	25.00	50.00	75.00	325	—

Y# 4 50 SEN
12.5000 g., 0.8000 Silver .3215 oz. **Ruler:** Mutsuhito (Meiji)
Note: Varieties exist.

Date	Mintage	F	VF	XF	Unc	BU
Yr.3(1870)	1,806,293	32.50	65.00	100	325	—
Yr.4(1871)	Inc. above	30.00	60.00	85.00	300	—

Y# 4a.2 50 SEN
12.5000 g., 0.8000 Silver .3215 oz. **Ruler:** Mutsuhito (Meiji)
Note: Type II: 21 millimeter circle of dots around dragon.

Date	F	VF	XF	Unc	BU
Yr.4(1871)	500	900	1,500	3,500	—

Type II, Large dragon Flame tip overlaps third spine

Type I, Small dragon Flame tip extends between third and fourth spine

Y# 4a.1 50 SEN
12.5000 g., 0.8000 Silver .3215 oz., 30.5 mm. **Ruler:** Mutsuhito (Meiji) **Note:** Type I: 19mm circle of dots around dragon.

Date	Mintage	F	VF	XF	Unc	BU
Yr.4(1871)	2,648,309	50.00	100	150	300	—

Y# 25 50 SEN
13.4800 g., 0.8000 Silver .3472 oz. **Ruler:** Mutsuhito (Meiji)

Date	Mintage	F	VF	XF	Unc	BU
Yr.6(1873) Type I	3,447,733	150	200	300	1,200	—
Yr.6(1873) Type II	Inc. above	25.00	35.00	65.00	250	—
Yr.7(1874)	95,304	7,500	12,500	20,000	32,500	—
Yr.8(1875)	109	8,000	11,000	16,000	27,500	—
Yr.9(1876)	1,251	2,500	4,500	6,500	14,000	—
Yr.10(1877)	184,348	1,280	2,000	3,750	7,000	—
Yr.13(1880)	179	7,500	12,500	20,000	40,000	—
Yr.30(1897)	5,078,437	75.00	125	175	600	—
Yr.31(1898)	22,797,041	6.50	12.50	25.00	110	—
Yr.32(1899)	10,254,431	7.50	15.00	30.00	120	—
Yr.33(1900)	3,280,091	10.00	18.00	35.00	220	—

圓 Type I — 圓 Type II — 圓 Type III

Y# 5.1 YEN
26.9568 g., 0.9000 Silver .7800 oz. **Ruler:** Mutsuhito (Meiji)
Note: Dav. #273.

Date	Mintage	F	VF	XF	Unc	BU
Yr.3(1870) Type I	3,685,000	250	375	500	850	—

Y# 5.2 YEN
26.9568 g., 0.9000 Silver .7800 oz. **Ruler:** Mutsuhito (Meiji)

Date	F	VF	XF	Unc	BU
Yr.3(1870) Type II	325	500	700	1,000	—

Y# 5.3 YEN
26.9568 g., 0.9000 Silver .7800 oz. **Ruler:** Mutsuhito (Meiji)

Date	F	VF	XF	Unc	BU
Yr.3(1870) Type III	600	1,150	1,650	2,250	—

圓 Low dot

Y# 9 YEN
1.6700 g., 0.9000 Gold .0482 oz., 13.5 mm. **Ruler:** Mutsuhito (Meiji)

Date	Mintage	F	VF	XF	Unc	BU
Yr.4(1871) Low dot	1,841,288	600	900	1,500	2,500	—
Yr.4(1871) Proof	—	Value: 6,500				

圓 High dot

Date	Mintage	F	VF	XF	Unc	BU
Yr.4(1871) High dot	Inc. above	250	375	525	775	—

Y# 9a YEN
1.6700 g., 0.9000 Gold .0482 oz., 12 mm. **Ruler:** Mutsuhito (Meiji) **Note:** Reduced size.

Date	Mintage	F	VF	XF	Unc	BU
Yr.7(1874)	116,341	2,300	2,800	3,250	4,500	—
Yr.9(1876)	138	6,700	8,500	12,000	16,000	—
Yr.10(1877)	7,246	16,000	24,000	30,000	45,000	—
Yr.13(1880)	112	22,000	27,000	35,000	50,000	—
Yr.25(1892)	—	—	—	—	—	—

Note: None struck for circulation

Y# A25.2 YEN
Silver **Ruler:** Mutsuhito (Meiji) **Note:** Spiral on pearl curls clockwise direction from center.

Date	Mintage	F	VF	XF	Unc	BU
Yr.7(1874)	942,006	500	1,200	2,100	4,500	—
Yr.8(1875)	139,323	3,700	6,000	10,000	15,000	—
Yr.11(1878)	856,378	250	500	800	2,000	—
Yr.12(1879)	1,913,318	750	1,900	2,900	6,500	—
Yr.13(1880)	5,427,432	85.00	175	300	1,000	—
Yr.14(1881)	2,927,409	100	225	350	1,250	—
Yr.15(1882)	5,089,064	65.00	100	200	800	—
Yr.16(1883)	3,636,678	65.00	125	225	850	—
Yr.17(1884)	3,599,192	95.00	175	300	1,000	—
Yr.18(1885)	4,296,620	65.00	125	200	850	—
Yr.19(1886)	9,084,262	65.00	125	200	875	—
Yr.20(1887)	8,275,787	125	225	325	1,350	—

Y# A25.1 YEN
Silver, 38.6 mm. **Ruler:** Mutsuhito (Meiji) **Note:** Spiral on pearl held by dragon curls in counter clockwise direction from center. Dav. #274.

Date	Mintage	F	VF	XF	Unc	BU
Yr.7(1874)	942,006	600	1,300	2,300	5,000	—

Y# A25.3 YEN
26.9600 g., 0.9000 Silver .7800 oz., 38.1 mm. **Ruler:** Mutsuhito (Meiji) **Note:** Reduced size.

Date	Mintage	F	VF	XF	Unc	BU
Yr.19(1886)	Inc. above	500	900	1,750	4,000	—
Yr.20(1887)	Inc. above	45.00	75.00	150	850	—
Yr.21(1888)	9,477,414	25.00	50.00	75.00	400	—
Yr.22(1889)	9,295,348	25.00	45.00	65.00	225	—
Yr.23(1890)	7,292,877	25.00	45.00	65.00	220	—
Yr.24(1891)	7,518,021	23.00	30.00	50.00	185	—
Yr.25(1892)	11,187,613	100	200	400	1,350	—
Note: Flame extends between fourth and fifth spine						
Yr.25(1892)	Inc. above	20.00	35.00	55.00	210	—
Note: Flame overlaps third spine of dragon						
Yr.26(1893)	10,403,477	23.00	35.00	55.00	400	—
Yr.27(1894)	22,118,416	21.00	25.00	45.00	225	—
Yr.28(1895)	21,098,754	21.00	25.00	45.00	140	—
Yr.29(1896)	11,363,949	21.00	25.00	45.00	140	—
Yr.30(1897)	2,448,694	21.00	30.00	50.00	155	—

Y# 10 2 YEN
3.3333 g., 0.9000 Gold .0964 oz., 16.96 mm. **Ruler:** Mutsuhito (Meiji)

Date	Mintage	F	VF	XF	Unc	BU
Yr.3(1870)	883,000	800	900	1,150	1,650	—
Yr.3(1870) Proof	—	Value: 9,500				

Y# 10a 2 YEN
3.3333 g., 0.9000 Gold .0964 oz., 16.96 mm. **Ruler:** Mutsuhito (Meiji) **Note:** Reduced size, same weight.

Date	Mintage	F	VF	XF	Unc	BU
Yr.7(1874)	—	—	—	—	—	—
Note: Reported, not confirmed						
Yr.9(1876)	178	45,000	60,000	75,000	—	—
Yr.10(1877)	39	45,000	60,000	75,000	—	—
Yr.13(1880)	87	45,000	60,000	75,000	—	—
Yr.25(1892)	—	—	—	—	—	—
Note: None struck for circulation						

Y# 11 5 YEN
8.3333 g., 0.9000 Gold .2411 oz., 23.8 mm. **Ruler:** Mutsuhito (Meiji)

Date	Mintage	F	VF	XF	Unc	BU
Yr.3(1870)	273,000	1,750	2,150	2,600	3,500	—
Yr.4(1871)	Inc. above	1,250	1,850	2,400	3,400	—
Yr.4(1871) Proof	—	Value: 10,000				

Y# 11a 5 YEN
8.3333 g., 0.9000 Gold .2411 oz., 21.8 mm. **Ruler:** Mutsuhito (Meiji) **Note:** Reduced size, same weight.

Date	Mintage	F	VF	XF	Unc	BU
Yr.5(1872)	1,057,000	1,000	1,500	1,900	2,500	—
Yr.6(1873)	3,148,000	1,000	1,500	1,900	2,500	—
Yr.7(1874)	728,000	1,500	1,800	2,500	3,500	—
Yr.8(1875)	181,000	1,750	2,000	2,500	3,500	—
Yr.9(1876)	146,000	1,850	3,000	2,850	4,200	—
Yr.10(1877)	136,000	3,000	4,000	4,000	7,000	—
Yr.11(1878)	101,000	3,200	4,200	5,000	7,500	—
Yr.13(1880)	78,000	3,200	4,500	5,500	7,500	—
Yr.14(1881)	149,000	3,200	4,300	5,500	7,500	—
Yr.15(1882)	113,000	3,000	4,000	5,500	7,500	—
Yr.16(1883)	108,000	3,000	4,000	5,500	7,500	—
Yr.17(1884)	113,000	3,000	4,000	5,500	7,500	—
Yr.18(1885)	200,000	3,000	4,000	5,500	7,500	—
Yr.19(1886)	179,000	3,000	4,000	5,500	7,500	—
Yr.20(1887)	179,000	3,000	4,000	5,500	7,500	—
Yr.21(1888)	165,000	3,000	4,000	5,500	7,500	—
Yr.22(1889)	353,000	3,000	4,000	5,500	7,500	—
Yr.23(1890)	238,000	3,000	4,000	5,500	7,500	—
Yr.24(1891)	216,000	3,000	4,000	5,500	7,500	—
Yr.25(1892)	263,000	3,000	4,000	5,500	7,500	—
Yr.26(1893)	260,000	4,000	5,400	6,500	11,500	—
Yr.27(1894)	314,000	3,000	4,000	5,500	7,500	—
Yr.28(1895)	320,000	3,000	4,000	5,500	7,500	—
Yr.29(1896)	224,000	4,000	5,400	6,500	11,500	—
Yr.30(1897)	107,000	4,000	5,400	6,500	11,500	—

Y# 12 10 YEN
16.6666 g., 0.9000 Gold .4823 oz. **Ruler:** Mutsuhito (Meiji)

Date	Mintage	F	VF	XF	Unc	BU
Yr.4(1871)	1,867,000	3,000	3,750	4,500	6,000	—
Yr.4(1871) Proof	—	Value: 35,000				

Y# 12a 10 YEN
16.6666 g., 0.9000 Gold .4823 oz. **Ruler:** Mutsuhito (Meiji)
Note: Modified design.

Date	Mintage	F	VF	XF	Unc	BU
Yr.9(1876)	1,925	35,000	45,000	55,000	70,000	—
Yr.10(1877)	36	45,000	55,000	70,000	85,000	—
Yr.13(1880)	136	45,000	55,000	70,000	85,000	—
Yr.25(1892)	—	—	—	—	—	—
Note: None struck for circulation						

Y# 13 20 YEN
33.3332 g., 0.9000 Gold .9646 oz. **Ruler:** Mutsuhito (Meiji)

Date	Mintage	F	VF	XF	Unc	BU
Yr.3(1870)	46,000	20,000	26,000	30,000	37,500	—
Yr.3(1870) Proof	—	Value: 57,500				
Yr.9(1876)	954	35,000	50,000	65,000	100,000	—
Yr.10(1877)	29	45,000	70,000	85,000	110,000	—
Yr.13(1880)	103	40,000	60,000	75,000	100,000	—
Yr.25(1892)	—	—	—	—	—	—
Note: None struck for circulation						

REFORM COINAGE

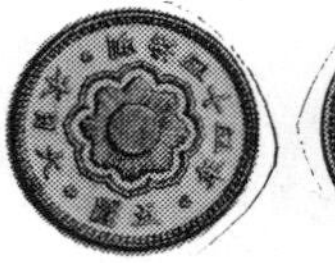

Y# 32 5 YEN
4.1666 g., 0.9000 Gold .1205 oz. **Ruler:** Mutsuhito (Meiji)

Date	Mintage	F	VF	XF	Unc	BU
Yr.30(1897)	111,776	1,200	1,600	2,000	2,500	—
Yr.31(1898)	55,888	1,200	1,600	2,000	2,500	—

Y# 33 10 YEN
8.3333 g., 0.9000 Gold .2411 oz. **Ruler:** Mutsuhito (Meiji)

Date	Mintage	F	VF	XF	Unc	BU
Yr.30(1897)	2,422,146	450	600	750	1,250	—
Yr.31(1898)	3,176,134	450	600	750	1,250	—
Yr.32(1899)	1,743,006	450	600	750	1,250	—
Yr.33(1900)	1,114,776	700	1,000	1,300	1,700	—

Y# 34 20 YEN
16.6666 g., 0.9000 Gold .4823 oz. **Ruler:** Mutsuhito (Meiji)

Date	Mintage	F	VF	XF	Unc	BU
Yr.30(1897)	1,861,000	1,200	1,500	1,750	2,400	—

TRADE COINAGE

Y# 14 TRADE DOLLAR
27.2200 g., 0.9000 Silver .7876 oz. **Ruler:** Mutsuhito (Meiji)
Note: Dav. #275.

Date	Mintage	F	VF	XF	Unc	BU
Yr.8(1875)	97,000	400	1,100	1,500	2,500	—
Yr.9(1876)	1,514,000	400	1,100	1,500	2,500	—
Yr.10(1877)	1,125,000	400	1,100	2,000	2,750	—

COUNTERMARKED COINAGE

1897

Y# 28 YEN

Silver **Ruler:** Mutsuhito (Meiji) **Countermark:** Gin **Note:** Countermark left on 1 Yen, Y#5.

CM Date	Host Date	Good	VG	F	VF	XF
ND	Yr.3(1870)	—	200	450	775	950

Y# 28.1 YEN

Silver **Ruler:** Mutsuhito (Meiji) **Countermark:** Gin **Note:** Countermark right on 1 Yen, Y#5.

CM Date	Host Date	Good	VG	F	VF	XF
ND	Yr.3(1870)	—	175	350	600	850

Y# 28a.1 YEN

Silver **Ruler:** Mutsuhito (Meiji) **Countermark:** Gin **Note:** Clockwise spiral on pearl.

CM Date	Host Date	Good	VG	F	VF	XF
ND	Yr.7(1874)	—	300	500	1,200	2,000
ND	Yr.8(1875)	—	1,700	3,700	6,100	8,500
ND	Yr.11(1878)	—	100	200	400	720
ND	Yr.12(1879)	—	350	750	1,900	3,000
ND	Yr.13(1880)	—	45.00	90.00	175	300
ND	Yr.14(1881)	—	50.00	100	225	325
ND	Yr.15(1882)	—	25.00	60.00	100	225
ND	Yr.16(1883)	—	35.00	65.00	125	225
ND	Yr.17(1884)	—	40.00	75.00	150	275
ND	Yr.18(1885)	—	25.00	60.00	125	225
ND	Yr.19(1886)	—	35.00	65.00	125	225
ND	Yr.20(1887)	—	60.00	125	225	325

Y# 28a.4 YEN

Silver **Ruler:** Mutsuhito (Meiji) **Countermark:** Gin **Note:** Clockwise spiral on pearl.

CM Date	Host Date	Good	VG	F	VF	XF
ND	Yr.7(1874)	—	300	500	1,300	2,200
ND	Yr.8(1875)	—	1,600	3,800	6,100	9,000
ND	Yr.11(1878)	—	100	200	600	750
ND	Yr.12(1879)	—	350	750	2,200	3,200
ND	Yr.13(1880)	—	50.00	95.00	175	325
ND	Yr.14(1881)	—	50.00	100	225	325
ND	Yr.15(1882)	—	35.00	65.00	125	250
ND	Yr.16(1883)	—	35.00	65.00	125	225
ND	Yr.17(1884)	—	35.00	75.00	225	325
ND	Yr.18(1885)	—	35.00	65.00	125	225
ND	Yr.19(1886)	—	35.00	65.00	125	225
ND	Yr.20(1887)	—	65.00	125	250	350

Y# 28a YEN

Silver, 38.6 mm. **Ruler:** Mutsuhito (Meiji) **Countermark:** Gin **Note:** Type I. Countermark left on 1 Yen, Y#A25. Counterclockwise spiral on pearl.

CM Date	Host Date	Good	VG	F	VF	XF
ND	Yr.7(1874)	—	400	650	1,400	2,300

Y# 28a.3 YEN

Silver, 38.6 mm. **Ruler:** Mutsuhito (Meiji) **Countermark:** Gin **Note:** Type I. Countermark right on 1 Yen, Y#A25. Counterclockwise spiral on pearl.

CM Date	Host Date	Good	VG	F	VF	XF
ND	Yr.7(1874)	—	400	650	150	2,500

Y# 28a.2 YEN

Silver, 38.1 mm. **Ruler:** Mutsuhito (Meiji) **Countermark:** Gin **Note:** Type II.

CM Date	Host Date	Good	VG	F	VF	XF
ND	Yr.19(1886)	—	300	500	800	1,200
ND	Yr.20(1887)	—	50.00	80.00	150	250
ND	Yr.21(1888)	—	25.00	35.00	65.00	125
ND	Yr.22(1889)	—	20.00	30.00	42.00	65.00
ND	Yr.23(1890)	—	20.00	30.00	42.00	60.00
ND	Yr.24(1891)	—	15.00	25.00	35.00	90.00
ND	Yr.25(1892) Early variety	—	75.00	150	300	500
ND	Yr.25(1892) Late variety	—	20.00	30.00	40.00	100
ND	Yr.26(1893)	—	25.00	45.00	85.00	125
ND	Yr.27(1894)	—	15.00	25.00	32.00	55.00
ND	Yr.28(1895)	—	15.00	25.00	32.00	55.00
ND	Yr.29(1896)	—	15.00	25.00	32.00	55.00
ND	Yr.30(1897)	—	20.00	35.00	70.00	100

Y# 28a.5 YEN

Silver, 38.1 mm. **Ruler:** Mutsuhito (Meiji) **Countermark:** Gin **Note:** Type II.

CM Date	Host Date	Good	VG	F	VF	XF
ND	Yr.19(1886)	—	350	550	850	1,250
ND	Yr.20(1887)	—	55.00	85.00	175	275
ND	Yr.21(1888)	—	15.00	30.00	75.00	125
ND	Yr.22(1889)	—	15.00	25.00	65.00	100
ND	Yr.23(1890)	—	15.00	25.00	55.00	100
ND	Yr.24(1891)	—	15.00	25.00	50.00	95.00
ND	Yr.25(1892) Note: Early variety	—	75.00	150	325	600
ND	Yr.25(1892) Note: Late variety	—	15.00	25.00	40.00	100
ND	Yr.26(1893)	—	25.00	50.00	100	150
ND	Yr.27(1894)	—	15.00	25.00	55.00	90.00
ND	Yr.28(1895)	—	15.00	25.00	50.00	90.00
ND	Yr.29(1896)	—	15.00	25.00	50.00	90.00
ND	Yr.30(1897)	—	25.00	45.00	90.00	150

Y# 28b.1 TRADE DOLLAR

Silver **Ruler:** Mutsuhito (Meiji) **Countermark:** Gin **Note:** Countermarked left on Trade Dollar, Y#14.

CM Date	Host Date	Good	VG	F	VF	XF
ND	Yr.8(1875)	—	250	500	1,100	1,600
ND	Yr.9(1876)	—	250	500	1,000	1,500
ND	Yr.10(1877)	—	250	500	1,100	1,700

Y# 28b.2 TRADE DOLLAR

Silver **Ruler:** Mutsuhito (Meiji) **Countermark:** Gin **Note:** Countermarked right on Trade Dollar, Y#14.

CM Date	Host Date	Good	VG	F	VF	XF
ND	Yr.8(1875)	—	275	550	1,100	1,600
ND	Yr.9(1876)	—	275	550	1,100	1,600
ND	Yr.10(1877)	—	275	550	1,100	1,700

PATTERNS

Including off metal strikes

KM#	Date	Mintage	Identification	Mkt Val
Pn1	ND(1861)	—	5 Momme. Cast Bronze.	—
Pn2	ND(1869)	—	Fun. Copper. Crossed flags and Mt. Fuji.	1,250

KM#	Date	Mintage	Identification	Mkt Val
Pn3	ND(1869)	—	5 Fun. Copper. Crossed flags and Mt. Fuji.	1,750
Pn4	ND(1869)	—	1 Momme. Copper. Crossed flags and Mt. Fuji.	3,000

Note: Above 3 coins struck by Heaton for a proposed (rejected) coinage

KM#	Date	Mintage	Identification	Mkt Val
Pn5	ND(1869)	—	Rin. Copper. Holed. Yr.2.	
Pn6	ND(1869)	—	Sen. Copper. Yr.2.	5,300
Pn7	ND(1870)	—	Rin. Copper. Yr.3.	6,000
Pn8	ND(1870)	—	1/2 Sen. Copper. Yr.3.	—

KM#	Date	Mintage	Identification	Mkt Val
Pn9	ND(1870)	—	Sen. Copper. Yr.3.	3,250
Pn10	ND(1870)	—	1/20 Yen. White Metal. Yr.2.	—
Pn11	ND(1870)	—	1/10 Yen. Copper. Yr.3.	—
Pn12	ND(1870)	—	1/10 Yen. White Metal. Yr.3.	—
Pn13	ND(1870)	—	1/4 Yen. Copper. Yr.3.	—

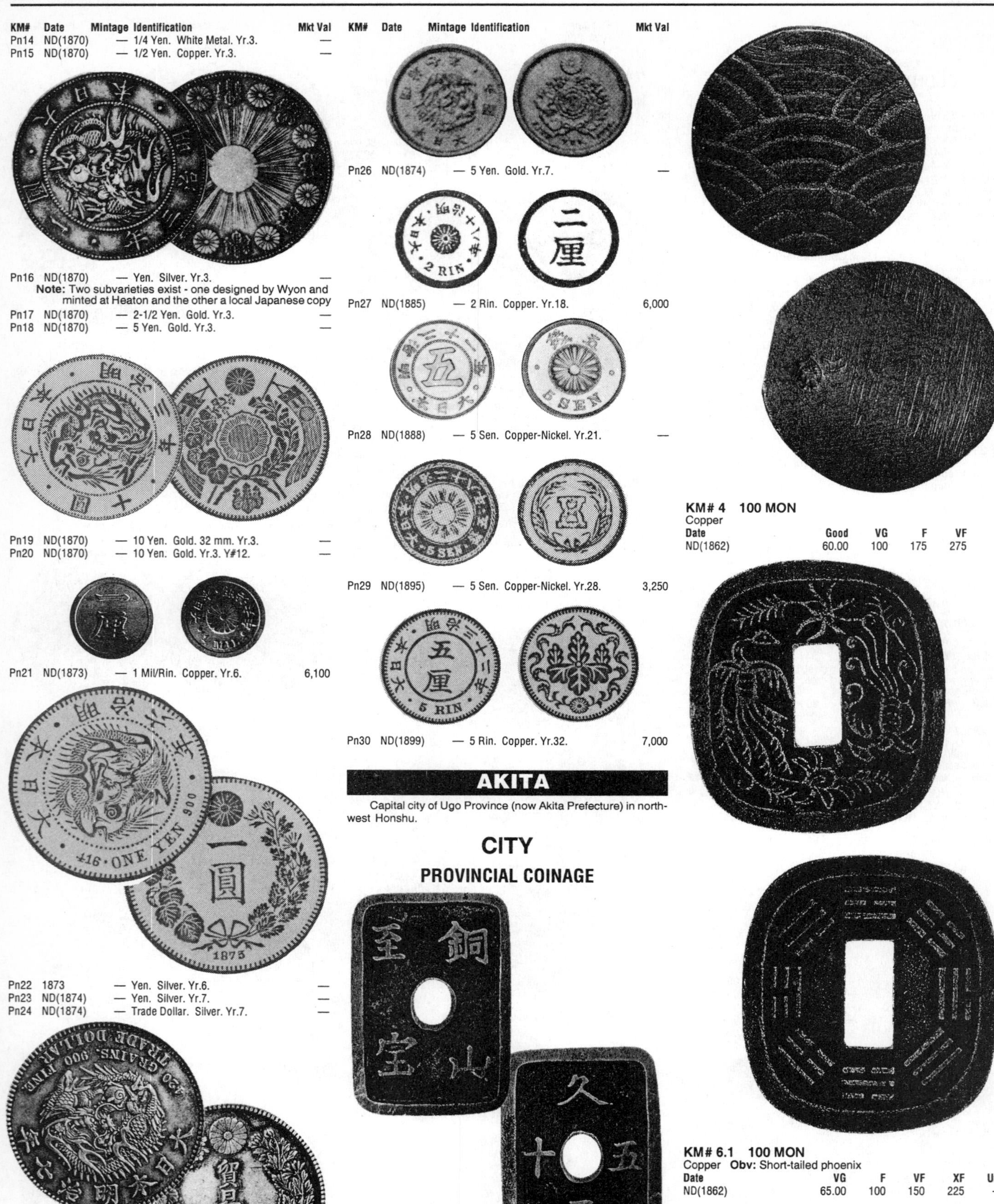

KM#	Date	Mintage	Identification	Mkt Val
Pn14	ND(1870)	—	1/4 Yen. White Metal. Yr.3.	—
Pn15	ND(1870)	—	1/2 Yen. Copper. Yr.3.	—
Pn16	ND(1870)	—	Yen. Silver. Yr.3.	—

Note: Two subvarieties exist - one designed by Wyon and minted at Heaton and the other a local Japanese copy

KM#	Date	Mintage	Identification	Mkt Val
Pn17	ND(1870)	—	2-1/2 Yen. Gold. Yr.3.	—
Pn18	ND(1870)	—	5 Yen. Gold. Yr.3.	—
Pn19	ND(1870)	—	10 Yen. Gold. 32 mm. Yr.3.	—
Pn20	ND(1870)	—	10 Yen. Gold. Yr.3. Y#12.	—
Pn21	ND(1873)	—	1 Mil/Rin. Copper. Yr.6.	6,100
Pn22	1873	—	Yen. Silver. Yr.6.	—
Pn23	ND(1874)	—	Yen. Silver. Yr.7.	—
Pn24	ND(1874)	—	Trade Dollar. Silver. Yr.7.	—
Pn25	ND(1874)	—	Trade Dollar. Silver. Yr.7.	—
Pn26	ND(1874)	—	5 Yen. Gold. Yr.7.	—
Pn27	ND(1885)	—	2 Rin. Copper. Yr.18.	6,000
Pn28	ND(1888)	—	5 Sen. Copper-Nickel. Yr.21.	—
Pn29	ND(1895)	—	5 Sen. Copper-Nickel. Yr.28.	3,250
Pn30	ND(1899)	—	5 Rin. Copper. Yr.32.	7,000

AKITA

Capital city of Ugo Province (now Akita Prefecture) in northwest Honshu.

CITY

PROVINCIAL COINAGE

KM# 2 50 MON

Lead or Copper-Plated Lead

Date	Good	VG	F	VF	XF
ND(1862)	80.00	110	175	250	—

KM# 4 100 MON

Copper

Date	Good	VG	F	VF	XF
ND(1862)	60.00	100	175	275	—

KM# 6.1 100 MON

Copper **Obv:** Short-tailed phoenix

Date	VG	F	VF	XF	Unc
ND(1862)	65.00	100	150	225	—

KM# 6.2 100 MON
Copper **Obv:** Long-tailed phoenix

Date	VG	F	VF	XF	Unc
ND(1862)	65.00	100	150	225	—

KM# 8 100 MON
Lead or Copper-Plated Lead

Date	Good	VG	F	VF	XF
ND(1862)	100	150	275	325	—

KM# 9 BU
Silver

Date	Good	VG	F	VF	XF
ND	900	1,200	1,500	2,000	—

KM# 7 1 MOMME 1 FUN
Silver

Date	Good	VG	F	VF	XF
ND(1863)	—	—	—	—	—

KM# 10 4 MOMME 6 FUN
17.2500 g., Silver

Date	VG	F	VF	XF	Unc
ND(1863)	150	250	350	450	—

KM# 12 9 MOMME 2 FUN
34.5100 g., Silver

Date	VG	F	VF	XF	Unc
ND(1863)	400	550	650	750	—

HAKODATE

City on the southern end of Hokkaido. One of the ports opened by Perry's Treaty of 1854.

CITY

PROVINCIAL COINAGE

KM# 20 MON
Iron **Obv:** Four characters around round hole **Rev:** One character above hole

Date	Good	VG	F	VF	XF
ND(1856)	3.00	6.00	12.00	25.00	—

KM# 20a MON
Copper

Date	Good	VG	F	VF	XF
ND(1856)	—	—	100	175	—

Note: KM#20a is the "bosen" or mother coin used in manufacturing KM#20

HOSOKURA

A lead mining district in Rikuchu Province (now Iwate Prefecture) in northern Honshu.

DISTRICT

PROVINCIAL COINAGE

KM# 30 100 MON
Lead

Date	Good	VG	F	VF	XF
ND(1863)	300	400	500	650	—

KOSHU

PROVINCE

PROVINCIAL COINAGE

KM# 90 KAKU SHU-NAKA KIN (Rectangular Half Shu Gold)
0.4000 g., Gold **Note:** 6x8 milimeters.

Date	VG	F	VF	XF	Unc
ND	700	900	1,200	1,600	—

KM# 91 SHU-NAKA KIN (Half Shu Gold)
Gold **Note:** Similar to Ichi-Bu KM#94. Weight varies: 0.40-0.50 grams. Size varies: 8.5-9.5mm.

Date	VG	F	VF	XF	Unc
ND	2,000	3,000	4,500	6,500	—

KM# 92 ISSHU KIN (One Shu Gold)
Gold **Note:** Similar to Ichi-Bu KM#94. Weight varies: 0.90-1.00 grams. Size varies: 11-12mm.

Date	VG	F	VF	XF	Unc
ND	425	650	850	1,100	—

KM# 93 NISSHU KIN (Two Shu Gold)
1.9000 g., Gold **Note:** Similar to Ichi-Bu KM#94. Size varies: 12-13mm.

Date	VG	F	VF	XF	Unc
ND	425	650	850	1,200	—

KM# 94 ICHI-BU KIN (One Bu Gold)
Gold **Note:** Similar to Ichi-Bu KM#94. Weight varies: 3.70-4.00 Size varies: 14-17mm.

Date	VG	F	VF	XF	Unc
ND	425	650	850	1,100	—

KM# 95 ICHI-BU ISSHU KIN (One Bu One Shu Gold)
4.8000 g., Gold, 18 mm. **Note:** Similar to Ichi-Bu KM#94.

Date	VG	F	VF	XF	Unc
ND Rare	—	—	—	—	—

KM# 96 ICHI-BU NISSHU KIN (One Bu Two Shu Gold)
5.0000 g., Gold, 16 mm. **Note:** Similar to Ichi-Bu KM#94.

Date	VG	F	VF	XF	Unc
ND Rare	—	—	—	—	—

KM# 97 NI-BU KIN (Two Bu Gold)
Gold **Note:** Similar to Ichi-Bu KM#94. Weight varies: 7.00-7.50 grams. Size varies: 18-19mm.

Date	VG	F	VF	XF	Unc
ND Rare	—	—	—	—	—

KM# 98 NI-BU ISSHU KIN (Two Bu One Shu Gold)
8.8000 g., Gold, 24 mm. **Note:** Similar to Ichi-Bu KM#94.

Date	VG	F	VF	XF	Unc
ND Rare	—	—	—	—	—

KM# 99 RYO KIN (One Ryo Gold)
Gold **Note:** Rounded "nugget" shape with stamps, similar to Ichi-Bu KM#94. Weight varies: 14.70-15.30 grams. Size varies: 16-19mm.

Date	VG	F	VF	XF	Unc
ND Rare	—	—	—	—	—

MORIOKA

Chief city of Rikuchu Province (now Iwate Prefecture) in northern Honshu.

CITY

PROVINCIAL COINAGE

KM# 50 100 MON
Copper

Date	Good	VG	F	VF	XF
ND	1,200	2,200	3,500	4,750	—

KM# 52 8 MOMME
30.0000 g., Silver

Date	VG	F	VF	XF	Unc
ND(1868)	1,000	1,500	2,000	2,500	—

RYUKYU ISLANDS

OKINAWA
(Also called Liu-kiu and Loo-choo)

PROVINCE

PROVINCIAL COINAGE

C# 100 100 MON
Copper

Date	VG	F	VF	XF	Unc
ND(1862)	40.00	70.00	100	125	—

C# 115 1/2 SHU
Copper

Date	VG	F	VF	XF	Unc
ND(1862)	70.00	80.00	100	150	—

TOSA

Province encompassing most of the southern coast of Shikoku, now Kochi Prefecture.

PROVINCE

PROVINCIAL COINAGE

KM# 70 100 MON
Copper

Date	VG	F	VF	XF	Unc
ND(1865) Rare	—	—	—	—	—

KM# 72 200 MON
Copper

Date	VG	F	VF	XF	Unc
ND(1865) Rare	—	—	—	—	—

Note: A total of eight types are reported for Tosa Province

PATTERNS

Including off metal strikes

KM#	Date	Mintage	Identification	Mkt Val
Pn1	ND	—	5 Momme. Bronze.	—

KM#	Date	Mintage	Identification	Mkt Val
Pn2	ND	—	10 Momme. Bronze.	—

YONEZAWA

City in Uzen Province (now in Yamagata Prefecture) in north-central Honshu.

CITY

PROVINCIAL COINAGE

KM# 80 200 MON
Lead

Date	Good	VG	F	VF	XF
ND(1866)	200	300	500	700	—

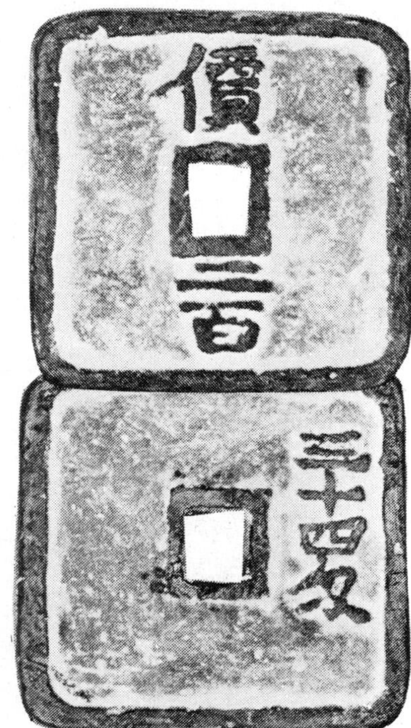

KM# 82 200 MON
Lead

Date	Good	VG	F	VF	XF
ND(1866)	250	350	550	750	—

JERSEY

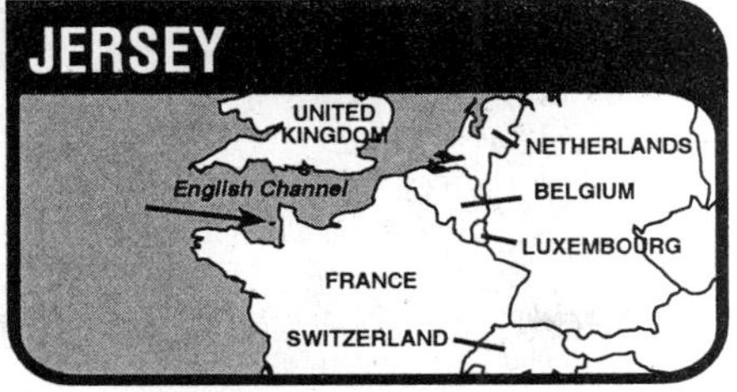

The Bailiwick of Jersey, a British Crown dependency located in the English Channel 12 miles (19 km.) west of Normandy, France, has an area of 45 sq. mi. (117 sq. km.) and a population of 74,000. Capital: St. Helier. The economy is based on agriculture and cattle breeding – the importation of cattle is prohibited to protect the purity of the island's world-famous strain of milch cows.

Jersey was occupied by Neanderthal man by 100,000 B.C., and by Iberians of 2000 B.C. who left their chamber tombs in the island's granite cliffs. Roman legions almost certainly visited the island although they left no evidence of settlement. The country folk of Jersey still speak an archaic form of Norman-French, lingering evidence of the Norman annexation of the island in 933 A.D. Jersey was annexed to England in 1206, 140 years after the Norman Conquest. The dependency is administered by its own laws and customs; laws enacted by the British Parliament do not apply to Jersey unless it is specifically mentioned.

Coins of pre-Roman Gaul and of Rome have been found in abundance on Jersey.

RULERS
British

MINT MARKS
H - Heaton, Birmingham

MONETARY SYSTEM

Until 1877
13 Pence (Jersey) = 1 Shilling
Commencing 1877
12 Pence = 1 Shilling
5 Shillings = 1 Crown
20 Shillings = 1 Pound
100 New Pence = 1 Pound

BRITISH DEPENDENCY

STANDARD COINAGE

KM# 1 1/52 SHILLING
Copper

Date	Mintage	F	VF	XF	Unc	BU
1841/0	116,000	10.00	30.00	80.00	160	—
1841 Proof	—	Value: 500				
1861 Proof	—	Value: 650				

KM# 1a 1/52 SHILLING
Bronze

Date	F	VF	XF	Unc	BU
1861 Proof, rare	—	—	—	—	—

KM# 6 1/48 SHILLING
Bronze

Date	F	VF	XF	Unc	BU
1877H	10.00	20.00	55.00	110	—

Note: Issue withdrawn except for 38,400 pieces

Date		
1877H Proof	—	Value: 200
1877 Proof	—	Value: 225

KM# 2 1/26 SHILLING
Copper

Date	Mintage	F	VF	XF	Unc	BU
1841	233,000	2.50	12.00	40.00	100	—
1841 Proof	—	Value: 650				
1844	233,000	3.00	12.00	40.00	100	—
1851	160,000	3.00	12.00	40.00	100	—
1858	173,000	3.00	12.00	40.00	100	—
1858 Proof	—	Value: 650				
1861	173,000	3.00	12.00	40.00	100	—
1861 Proof	—	Value: 650				

KM# 4 1/26 SHILLING
Bronze

Date	Mintage	F	VF	XF	Unc	BU
1866	173,000	1.00	6.00	30.00	50.00	—
1866 Proof	—	Value: 225				
1870	160,000	2.50	10.00	35.00	60.00	—
1870 Proof	—	Value: 350				
1871	160,000	2.00	8.00	32.00	55.00	—
1871 Proof	—	Value: 350				

KM# 7 1/24 SHILLING
Bronze

Date	Mintage	F	VF	XF	Unc	BU
1877H	336,000	1.25	4.00	12.00	30.00	—
1877H Proof	—	Value: 200				
1877 Proof	—	Value: 250				
1888	120,000	1.25	4.00	12.00	30.00	—
1894	120,000	1.25	4.00	12.00	30.00	—
1894 Proof	—	Value: 400				

KM# 3 1/13 SHILLING
Copper

Date	Mintage	F	VF	XF	Unc	BU
1841	116,000	1.00	13.50	50.00	175	—
1841 Proof	—	Value: 800				
1844	27,000	3.00	20.00	65.00	225	—
1844 Proof	—	Value: 800				
1851	160,000	1.50	13.50	50.00	160	—
1851 Proof	—	Value: 800				
1858	173,000	1.50	13.50	50.00	180	—
1858 Proof	—	Value: 600				
1861	173,000	1.50	13.50	50.00	160	—
1861	—	Value: 600				
1865	—	Value: 350				

KM# 5 1/13 SHILLING
Bronze

Date	Mintage	F	VF	XF	Unc	BU
1866	173,000	1.00	6.50	35.00	100	—
1866 Proof	—	Value: 225				
1866 Without LCW on bust, Proof	—	Value: 250				
1870	160,000	1.00	6.50	35.00	100	—
1870 Proof	—	Value: 225				
1871	160,000	1.00	6.50	35.00	100	—
1871 Proof	—	Value: 325				

KM# 8 1/12 SHILLING
Bronze

Date	Mintage	F	VF	XF	Unc	BU
1877H	240,000	0.50	2.00	15.00	50.00	—
1877H Proof	—	Value: 250				
1877 Proof	—	Value: 300				
1881	75,000	1.00	7.00	30.00	70.00	—
1888	180,000	0.50	2.00	15.00	50.00	—
1894	180,000	0.50	2.00	15.00	50.00	—
1894 Proof	—	Value: 400				

TOKEN COINAGE

KM# Tn2 1/2 PENNY
Copper **Obv:** Value within legend **Obv. Legend:** JERSEY, GUERNSEY & ALDERNEY **Rev:** Value, 3 plumes **Rev. Inscription:** TO FACILITATE TRADE

Date	VG	F	VF	XF	Unc
1813	35.00	60.00	125	350	—

KM# Tn1 PENNY
Copper **Obv:** Bust of George III **Obv. Legend:** JERSEY BANK TOKEN **Rev. Legend:** ELIAS NEEL JERSEY, A BANK OF ENGLAND...

Date	VG	F	VF	XF	Unc
1812 Rare	—	—	—	—	—

KM# Tn3 PENNY
Copper **Obv:** Bust of George III **Obv. Legend:** JERSEY BANK **Rev:** Seated female, value

Date	VG	F	VF	XF	Unc
1813	250	450	650	1,000	—

KM# Tn4 PENNY
Copper **Obv:** Bust of George III **Obv. Legend:** JERSEY BANK **Rev:** Seated female, value

Date	VG	F	VF	XF	Unc
1813	25.00	55.00	150	350	—

KM# Tn5 18 PENCE
0.8910 Silver **Obv:** Shield **Obv. Legend:** STATE OF JERSEY **Rev:** Value within wreath

Date		F	VF	XF	Unc	BU
1813		40.00	80.00	200	350	—
1813 Proof	—	Value: 500				

KM# Tn6 3 SHILLING
0.8910 Silver **Obv:** Shield **Rev:** Value within wreath

Date	Mintage	F	VF	XF	Unc	BU
1813	45,000	70.00	120	350	650	—
1813 Proof	—	Value: 950				

KM# Tn6a 3 SHILLING
Copper **Obv:** Arms **Rev:** Value within wreath

Date	F	VF	XF	Unc	BU
1813 Proof, rare	—	—	—	—	—

PATTERNS

Including off metal strikes

KM#	Date	Mintage	Identification	Mkt Val
Pn1	1866	—	1/26 Shilling. KM4.	2,500
Pn2	1877H	—	1/13 Shilling. Nickel. KM8.	—
Pn3	1877	—	1/13 Shilling. Nickel. KM8.	850
Pn4	1877	—	1/13 Shilling. Aluminum. KM8.	—

KOREA

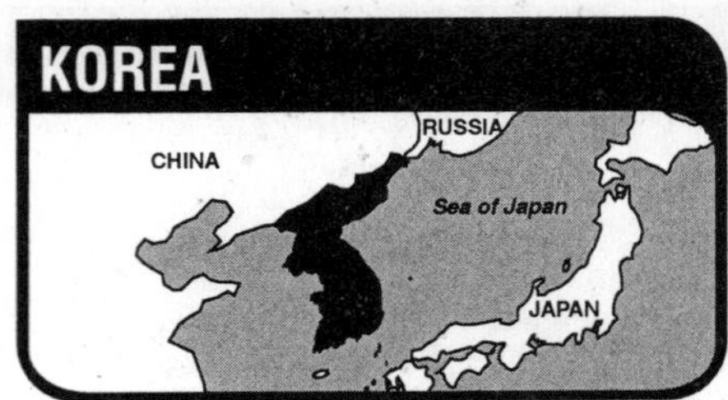

Korea, 'Land of the Morning Calm', occupies a mountainous peninsula in northeast Asia bounded by Manchuria, the Yellow Sea and the Sea of Japan.

According to legend, the first Korean dynasty, that of the House of Tangun, ruled from 2333 B.C. to 1122 B.C. It was followed by the dynasty of Kija, a Chinese scholar, which continued until 193 B.C. and brought a high civilization to Korea. The first recorded period in the history of Korea, the period of the Three Kingdoms, lasted from 57 B.C. to 935 A.D. and achieved the first political unification of the peninsula. The Kingdom of Koryo, from which Korea derived its name, was founded in 935 and continued until 1392, when it was superseded by the Yi Dynasty of King Yi. Sung Kye was to last until the Japanese annexation in 1910.

At the end of the 16th century Korea was invaded and occupied for 7 years by Japan, and from 1627 until the late 19th century it was a semi-independent tributary of China. Japan replaced China as the predominant foreign influence at the end of the Sino-Japanese War (1894-95), only to find her position threatened by Russian influence from 1896 to 1904. The Russian threat was eliminated by the Russo-Japanese War (1904-05) and in 1905 Japan established a direct protectorate over Korea. On Aug. 22,1910, the last Korean ruler signed the treaty that annexed Korea to Japan as a government generalcy in the Japanese Empire. Japanese suzerainty was maintained until the end of World War II.

From 1633 to 1891 the monetary system of Korea employed cast coins with a square center hole. Fifty-two agencies were authorized to procure these coins from a lesser number of coin foundries. They exist in thousands of varieties. Seed, or mother coins, were used to make the impressions in the molds in which the regular cash coins were cast. Czarist-Russian Korea experimented with Korean coins when Alexiev of Russia, Korea's Financial Advisor, founded the First Asian Branch of the Russo-Korean Bank on March 1, 1898, and authorized the issuing of a set of new Korean coins with a crowned Russian-style quasi-eagle. British-Japanese opposition and the Russo-Japanese War operated to end the Russian coinage experiment in 1904.

RULERS

Yi Sun (Chongjo Changhyo), 1777-1801
Yi Kwang (Sunjo Songhyo), 1801-1835
Yi Whan (Honjong Cholhyo), 1835-1850
Yi Chung (Choljong Yonghyo), 1850-1864
Yi Hyong (Kojong), 1864-1897
as Emperor Kwang Mu, 1897-1907

MONETARY UNITS

文 Mun	兩 Yang, Niang
分 Fun	圜 Hwan, Warn
錢 Chon	圓 Won Whan, Hwan

IDENTIFICATION CHART

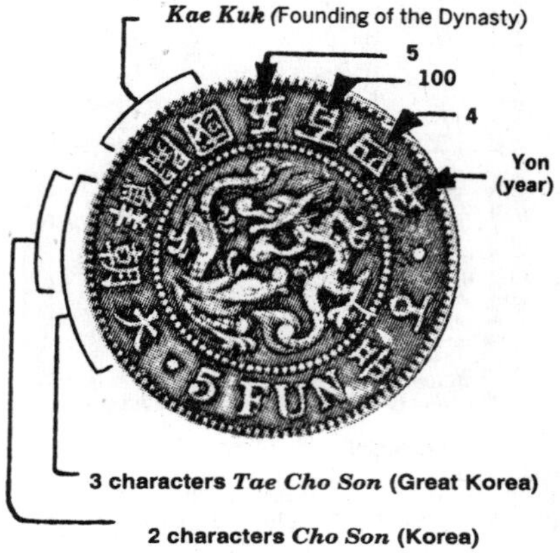

Obverse

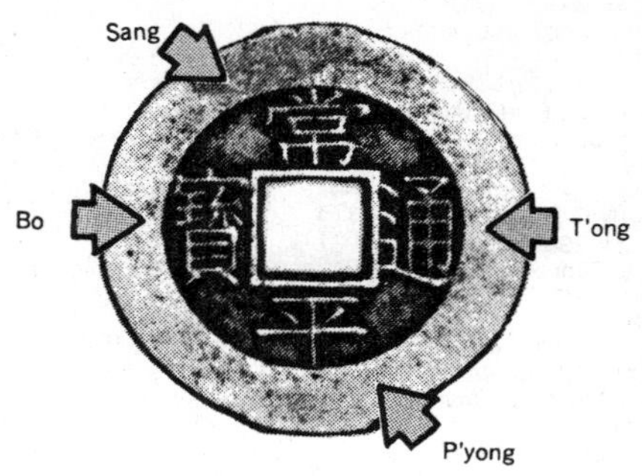

Sang P'yong T'ong Bo
"Always even currency"
Reverse

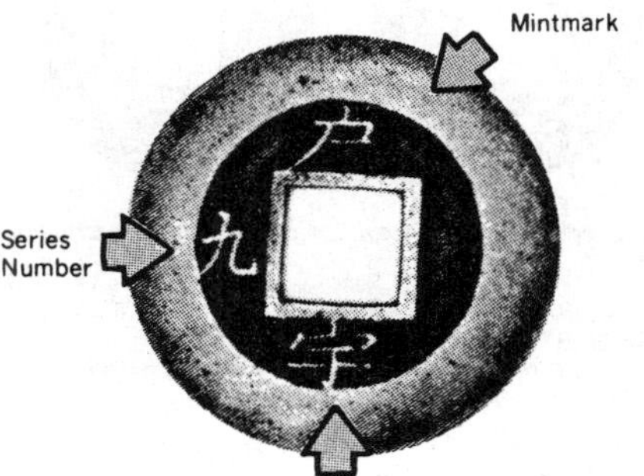

Furnace Designator

NOTE: The series number may be to the left, right or bottom of the center hole. The furnace designator may be either a numeral or a character from the *Thousand Character Classic.*

SEED COINS

Seed coins are specially prepared examples, perfectly round, with sharp characters, used in the preparation of clay or sand molds.

MINT MARKS

Ho	戸 or 户 or 戶 Treasury Department
Kyun	均 Government Tithe Office
Son	宣 Rice & Cloth Department
Chon	典 Central Government Mint
Mu	武 Palace Guard Office
Kum	禁 Court Guard Military Unit
Hun	訓 or 訓 Military Training Command
T'ong	統 or 綂 T'ongyong Naval Office Military Office in Seoul
Kyong	经 Government Office of Pukhan Mountain Fortress
Sim	沁 Kanghwa Township Military Office
Kae	開 Kaesong Township Military Office
Song	松 Kaesong Township Military Office
I	利 Iwon Township Military Office
Ch'un	春 or 春 Ch'unch'on Township Military Office
Ch'on	川 Tanch'on Township Military Office
Ch'ang	昌 Ch'angdok Palace Mint Ch'angwon Township Military Office
Ki	圻 Kwangju Township Military Office In Kyonggi Province
Kyong	京 Kyonggi Provincial Office
Kyong Su	京水 Kyonggi Naval Station
P'yong	平 P'yongan Provincial Office
Ham	咸 Hamgyong Provincial Office

KINGDOM

TREASURY DEPARTMENT

(Ho Jo)

KM# 21.1 MUN

Cast Copper or Bronze, 24 mm. **Rev:** Circle at right, series number at bottom

Date	Good	VG	F	VF	XF
ND(1757-1806) Series 1	3.00	5.00	7.00	10.00	—

KM# 21a.1 MUN

Cast Copper or Bronze **Obv:** 2 dot "Tong", and "P'yong" with hooks **Note:** Size varies 23-25 mm.

Date	Good	VG	F	VF	XF
ND(1757-1806) Series 1	3.00	5.00	7.00	10.00	—

KM# 21s.1 MUN

Cast Copper or Bronze

Date	Good	VG	F	VF	XF
ND(1757-1806) Series 1	—	—	—	—	60.00

KM# 21.2 MUN

Cast Copper or Bronze **Rev:** Circle at right, series number at bottom

Date	Good	VG	F	VF	XF
ND(1757-1806) Series 2	3.00	5.00	7.00	10.00	—

KM# 21a.2 MUN

Cast Copper or Bronze **Obv:** 2 dot "Tong", and "P'yong" with hooks **Note:** Size varies 23-25 mm.

Date	Good	VG	F	VF	XF
ND(1757-1806) Series 2	3.00	5.00	7.00	10.00	—

KM# 21s.2 MUN

Cast Copper or Bronze

Date	Good	VG	F	VF	XF
ND(1757-1806) Series 2	—	—	—	—	60.00

KM# 21.3 MUN

Cast Copper or Bronze **Rev:** Circle at right, series number at bottom

Date	Good	VG	F	VF	XF
ND(1757-1806) Series 3	3.00	5.00	7.00	10.00	—

KM# 21a.3 MUN

Cast Copper or Bronze **Obv:** 2 dot "Tong", and "P'yong" with hooks **Note:** Size varies 23-25 mm.

Date	Good	VG	F	VF	XF
ND(1757-1806) Series 3	3.00	5.00	7.00	10.00	—

KM# 21s.3 MUN

Cast Copper or Bronze

Date	Good	VG	F	VF	XF
ND(1757-1806) Series 3	—	—	—	—	60.00

KM# 21.4 MUN

Cast Copper or Bronze **Rev:** Circle at right, series number at bottom

Date	Good	VG	F	VF	XF
ND(1757-1806) Series 4	3.00	5.00	7.00	10.00	—

KM# 21a.4 MUN

Cast Copper or Bronze **Obv:** 2 dot "Tong", and "P'yong" with hooks **Note:** Size varies 23-25 mm.

Date	Good	VG	F	VF	XF
ND(1757-1806) Series 4	3.00	5.00	7.00	10.00	—

KM# 21s.4 MUN

Cast Copper or Bronze

Date	Good	VG	F	VF	XF
ND(1757-1806) Series 4	—	—	—	—	60.00

KM# 21.5 MUN

Cast Copper or Bronze **Rev:** Circle at right, series number at bottom

Date	Good	VG	F	VF	XF
ND(1757-1806) Series 5	3.00	5.00	7.00	10.00	—

KM# 21a.5 MUN

Cast Copper or Bronze **Obv:** 2 dot "Tong", and "P'yong" with hooks **Note:** Size varies 23-25 mm.

Date	Good	VG	F	VF	XF
ND(1757-1806) Series 5	3.00	5.00	7.00	10.00	—

KM# 21s.5 MUN

Cast Copper or Bronze

Date	Good	VG	F	VF	XF
ND(1757-1806) Series 5	—	—	—	—	60.00

KM# 21.6 MUN

Cast Copper or Bronze **Rev:** Circle at right, series number at bottom

Date	Good	VG	F	VF	XF
ND(1757-1806) Series 6	2.00	3.00	5.00	8.00	—

KM# 21a.6 MUN

Cast Copper or Bronze **Obv:** 2 dot "Tong", and "P'yong" with hooks **Note:** Size varies 23-25 mm.

Date	Good	VG	F	VF	XF
ND(1757-1806) Series 6	3.00	5.00	7.00	10.00	—

KM# 21s.6 MUN

Cast Copper or Bronze

Date	Good	VG	F	VF	XF
ND(1757-1806) Series 6	—	—	—	—	60.00

KM# 21.7 MUN

Cast Copper or Bronze **Rev:** Circle at right, series number at bottom

Date	Good	VG	F	VF	XF
ND(1757-1806) Series 7	3.00	5.00	7.00	10.00	—

KM# 21a.7 MUN

Cast Copper or Bronze **Obv:** 2 dot "Tong", and "P'yong" with hooks **Note:** Size varies 23-25 mm.

Date	Good	VG	F	VF	XF
ND(1757-1806) Series 7	3.00	5.00	7.00	10.00	—

KM# 21s.7 MUN

Cast Copper or Bronze

Date	Good	VG	F	VF	XF
ND(1757-1806) Series 7	—	—	—	—	60.00

KM# 21.8 MUN

Cast Copper or Bronze **Rev:** Circle at right, series number at bottom

Date	Good	VG	F	VF	XF
ND(1757-1806) Series 8	3.00	5.00	7.00	10.00	—

KM# 21a.8 MUN

Cast Copper or Bronze **Obv:** 2 dot "Tong", and "P'yong" with hooks **Note:** Size varies 23-25 mm.

Date	Good	VG	F	VF	XF
ND(1757-1803) Series 8	3.00	5.00	7.00	10.00	—

KM# 21s.8 MUN

Cast Copper or Bronze

Date	Good	VG	F	VF	XF
ND(1757-1806) Series 8	—	—	—	—	60.00

KM# 21.9 MUN

Cast Copper or Bronze **Rev:** Circle at right, series number at bottom

Date	Good	VG	F	VF	XF
ND(1757-1806) Series 9	3.00	5.00	7.00	10.00	—

KM# 21a.9 MUN

Cast Copper or Bronze **Obv:** 2 dot "Tong", and "P'yong" with hooks **Note:** Size varies 23-25 mm.

Date	Good	VG	F	VF	XF
ND(1757-1806) Series 9	3.00	5.00	7.00	10.00	—

KM# 21s.9 MUN
Cast Copper or Bronze

Date	Good	VG	F	VF	XF
ND(1757-1806) Series 9	—	—	—	—	60.00

KM# 21.10 MUN
Cast Copper or Bronze **Rev:** Circle at right, series number at bottom

Date	Good	VG	F	VF	XF
ND(1757-1806) Series 10	3.00	5.00	7.00	10.00	—

KM# 21s.10 MUN
Cast Copper or Bronze

Date	Good	VG	F	VF	XF
ND(1757-1806) Series 10	—	—	—	—	60.00

KM# 21a.10 MUN
Cast Copper or Bronze **Obv:** 2 dot "Tong", and "P'yong" with hooks **Note:** Size varies 23-25 mm.

Date	Good	VG	F	VF	XF
ND(1757-1806) Series 10	3.00	5.00	7.00	10.00	—

KM# 22.1 MUN
Cast Copper or Bronze, 23 mm. **Rev:** Circle at left, series number at bottom

Date	Good	VG	F	VF	XF
ND(1757-1806) Series 1	3.00	5.00	7.00	10.00	—

KM# 22a.1 MUN
Cast Copper or Bronze **Obv:** 2 dot "Tong" and "P'yong" with hooks

Date	Good	VG	F	VF	XF
ND(1757-1806) Series 1	3.00	5.00	7.00	10.00	—

KM# 22s.1 MUN
Cast Copper or Bronze

Date	Good	VG	F	VF	XF
ND(1757-1806) Series 1	—	—	—	—	50.00

KM# 22.2 MUN
Cast Copper or Bronze **Rev:** Circle at left, series number at bottom

Date	Good	VG	F	VF	XF
ND(1757-1806) Series 2	3.00	5.00	7.00	10.00	—

KM# 22a.2 MUN
Cast Copper or Bronze **Obv:** 2 dot "Tong" and "P'yong" with hooks

Date	Good	VG	F	VF	XF
ND(1757-1806) Series 2	3.00	5.00	7.00	10.00	—

KM# 22s.2 MUN
Cast Copper or Bronze

Date	Good	VG	F	VF	XF
ND(1757-1806) Series 2	—	—	—	—	60.00

KM# 22.3 MUN
Cast Copper or Bronze **Rev:** Circle at left, series number at bottom

Date	Good	VG	F	VF	XF
ND(1757-1806) Series 3	3.00	5.00	7.00	10.00	—

KM# 22a.3 MUN
Cast Copper or Bronze **Obv:** 2 dot "Tong" and "P'yong" with hooks

Date	Good	VG	F	VF	XF
ND(1757-1806) Series 3	3.00	5.00	7.00	10.00	—

KM# 22s.3 MUN
Cast Copper or Bronze

Date	Good	VG	F	VF	XF
ND(1757-1806) Series 3	—	—	—	—	60.00

KM# 22.4 MUN
Cast Copper or Bronze **Rev:** Circle at left, series number at bottom

Date	Good	VG	F	VF	XF
ND(1757-1806) Series 4	3.00	5.00	7.00	10.00	—

KM# 22a.4 MUN
Cast Copper or Bronze **Obv:** 2 dot "Tong" and "P'yong" with hooks

Date	Good	VG	F	VF	XF
ND(1757-1806) Series 4	3.00	5.00	7.00	10.00	—

KM# 22s.4 MUN
Cast Copper or Bronze

Date	Good	VG	F	VF	XF
ND(1757-1806) Series 4	—	—	—	—	60.00

KM# 22.5 MUN
Cast Copper or Bronze **Rev:** Circle at left, series number at bottom

Date	Good	VG	F	VF	XF
ND(1757-1806) Series 5	3.00	5.00	7.00	10.00	—

KM# 22a.5 MUN
Cast Copper or Bronze **Obv:** 2 dot "Tong" and "P'yong" with hooks

Date	Good	VG	F	VF	XF
ND(1757-1806) Series 5	3.00	5.00	7.00	10.00	—

KM# 22s.5 MUN
Cast Copper or Bronze

Date	Good	VG	F	VF	XF
ND(1757-1806) Series 5	—	—	—	—	60.00

KM# 22.6 MUN
Cast Copper or Bronze **Rev:** Circle at left, series number at bottom

Date	Good	VG	F	VF	XF
ND(1757-1806) Series 6	3.00	5.00	7.00	10.00	—

KM# 22a.6 MUN
Cast Copper or Bronze **Obv:** 2 dot "Tong" and "P'yong" with hooks

Date	Good	VG	F	VF	XF
ND(1757-1806) Series 6	3.00	5.00	7.00	10.00	—

KM# 22s.6 MUN
Cast Copper or Bronze

Date	Good	VG	F	VF	XF
ND(1757-1806) Series 6	—	—	—	—	60.00

KM# 22.7 MUN
Cast Copper or Bronze **Rev:** Circle at left, series number at bottom

Date	Good	VG	F	VF	XF
ND(1757-1806) Series 7	3.00	5.00	7.00	10.00	—

KM# 22a.7 MUN
Cast Copper or Bronze **Obv:** 2 dot "Tong" and "P'yong" with hooks

Date	Good	VG	F	VF	XF
ND(1757-1806) Series 7	3.00	5.00	7.00	10.00	—

KM# 22s.7 MUN
Cast Copper or Bronze

Date	Good	VG	F	VF	XF
ND(1757-1806) Series 7	—	—	—	—	60.00

KM# 22.8 MUN
Cast Copper or Bronze **Rev:** Circle at left, series number at bottom

Date	Good	VG	F	VF	XF
ND(1757-1806) Series 8	3.00	5.00	7.00	10.00	—

KM# 22a.8 MUN
Cast Copper or Bronze **Obv:** 2 dot "Tong" and "P'yong" with hooks

Date	Good	VG	F	VF	XF
ND(1757-1806) Series 8	3.00	5.00	7.00	10.00	—

KM# 22s.8 MUN
Cast Copper or Bronze

Date	Good	VG	F	VF	XF
ND(1757-1806) Series 8	—	—	—	—	60.00

KM# 22.9 MUN
Cast Copper or Bronze **Rev:** Circle at left, series number at bottom

Date	Good	VG	F	VF	XF
ND(1757-1806) Series 9	3.00	5.00	7.00	10.00	—

KM# 22a.9 MUN
Cast Copper or Bronze **Obv:** 2 dot "Tong" and "P'yong" with hooks

Date	Good	VG	F	VF	XF
ND(1757-1806) Series 9	3.00	5.00	7.00	10.00	—

KM# 22s.9 MUN
Cast Copper or Bronze

Date	Good	VG	F	VF	XF
ND(1757-1806) Series 9	—	—	—	—	60.00

KM# 22.10 MUN
Cast Copper or Bronze **Rev:** Circle at left, series number at bottom

Date	Good	VG	F	VF	XF
ND(1757-1806) Series 10	3.00	5.00	7.00	10.00	—

KM# 22s.10 MUN
Cast Copper or Bronze

Date	Good	VG	F	VF	XF
ND(1757-1806) Series 10	—	—	—	—	60.00

KM# 22a.10 MUN
Cast Copper or Bronze **Obv:** 2 dot "Tong" and "P'yong" with hooks

Date	Good	VG	F	VF	XF
ND(1757-1806) Series 10	3.00	5.00	7.00	10.00	—

KM# 29.1 MUN
Cast Copper or Bronze, 24 mm. **Rev:** Crescent at right, series number at bottom

Date	Good	VG	F	VF	XF
ND(1757-1806) Series 1	3.00	5.00	7.00	10.00	—

KM# 29a.1 MUN
Cast Copper or Bronze **Obv:** Without "P'yong" **Note:** Size varies 23-24 mm.

Date	Good	VG	F	VF	XF
ND(1757-1806) Series 1	3.00	5.00	7.00	10.00	—

KM# 29s.1 MUN
Cast Copper or Bronze

Date	Good	VG	F	VF	XF
ND(1757-1806) Series 1	—	—	—	—	60.00

KM# 29.2 MUN
Cast Copper or Bronze **Rev:** Crescent at right, series number at bottom

Date	Good	VG	F	VF	XF
ND(1757-1806) Series 2	3.00	5.00	7.00	10.00	—

KM# 29a.2 MUN
Cast Copper or Bronze **Obv:** Without "P'yong" **Note:** Size varies 23-24 mm.

Date	Good	VG	F	VF	XF
ND(1757-1806) Series 2	3.00	5.00	7.00	10.00	—

KM# 29s.2 MUN
Cast Copper or Bronze

Date	Good	VG	F	VF	XF
ND(1757-1806) Series 2	—	—	—	—	60.00

KM# 29.3 MUN
Cast Copper or Bronze **Rev:** Crescent at right, series number at bottom

Date	Good	VG	F	VF	XF
ND(1757-1806) Series 3	3.00	5.00	7.00	10.00	—

KM# 29a.3 MUN
Cast Copper or Bronze **Obv:** Without "P'yong" **Note:** Size varies 23-24 mm.

Date	Good	VG	F	VF	XF
ND(1757-1806) Series 3	3.00	5.00	7.00	10.00	—

KM# 29s.3 MUN
Cast Copper or Bronze

Date	Good	VG	F	VF	XF
ND(1757-1806) Series 3	—	—	—	—	60.00

KM# 29.4 MUN
Cast Copper or Bronze **Rev:** Crescent at right, series number at bottom

Date	Good	VG	F	VF	XF
ND(1757-1806) Series 4	3.00	5.00	7.00	10.00	—

KM# 29a.4 MUN
Cast Copper or Bronze **Obv:** Without "P'yong" **Note:** Size varies 23-24 mm.

Date	Good	VG	F	VF	XF
ND(1757-1806) Series 4	3.00	5.00	7.00	10.00	—

KM# 29s.4 MUN
Cast Copper or Bronze

Date	Good	VG	F	VF	XF
ND(1757-1806) Series 4	—	—	—	—	60.00

KM# 29.5 MUN
Cast Copper or Bronze **Rev:** Crescent at right, series number at bottom

Date	Good	VG	F	VF	XF
ND(1757-1806) Series 5	3.00	5.00	7.00	10.00	—

KM# 29a.5 MUN
Cast Copper or Bronze **Obv:** Without "P'yong" **Note:** Size varies 23-24 mm.

Date	Good	VG	F	VF	XF
ND(1757-1806) Series 5	3.00	5.00	7.00	10.00	—

KM# 29s.5 MUN
Cast Copper or Bronze

Date	Good	VG	F	VF	XF
ND(1757-1806) Series 5	—	—	—	—	60.00

KM# 29.6 MUN
Cast Copper or Bronze **Rev:** Crescent at right, series number at bottom

Date	Good	VG	F	VF	XF
ND(1757-1806) Series 6	3.00	5.00	7.00	10.00	—

KM# 29a.6 MUN
Cast Copper or Bronze **Obv:** Without "P'yong" **Note:** Size varies 23-24 mm.

Date	Good	VG	F	VF	XF
ND(1757-1806) Series 6	3.00	5.00	7.00	10.00	—

KM# 29s.6 MUN
Cast Copper or Bronze

Date	Good	VG	F	VF	XF
ND(1757-1806) Series 6	—	—	—	—	60.00

KM# 29.7 MUN
Cast Copper or Bronze **Rev:** Crescent at right, series number at bottom

Date	Good	VG	F	VF	XF
ND(1757-1806) Series 7	3.00	5.00	7.00	10.00	—

KM# 29.8 MUN
Cast Copper or Bronze **Rev:** Crescent at right, series number at bottom

Date	Good	VG	F	VF	XF
ND(1757-1806) Series 7	3.00	5.00	7.00	10.00	—

KM# 29a.7 MUN
Cast Copper or Bronze **Obv:** Without "P'yong" **Note:** Size varies 23-24 mm.

Date	Good	VG	F	VF	XF
ND(1757-1806) Series 7	3.00	5.00	7.00	10.00	—

KM# 29s.7 MUN
Cast Copper or Bronze

Date	Good	VG	F	VF	XF
ND(1757-1806) Series 7	—	—	—	—	60.00

KM# 29a.8 MUN
Cast Copper or Bronze **Obv:** Without "P'yong" **Note:** Size varies 23-24 mm.

Date	Good	VG	F	VF	XF
ND(1757-1806) Series 8	3.00	5.00	7.00	10.00	—

KM# 29s.8 MUN
Cast Copper or Bronze

Date	Good	VG	F	VF	XF
ND(1757-1806) Series 8	—	—	—	—	60.00

KM# 29.9 MUN
Cast Copper or Bronze **Rev:** Crescent at right, series number at bottom

Date	Good	VG	F	VF	XF
ND(1757-1806) Series 9	3.00	5.00	7.00	10.00	—

KM# 29a.9 MUN
Cast Copper or Bronze **Obv:** Without "P'yong" **Note:** Size varies 23-24 mm.

Date	Good	VG	F	VF	XF
ND(1757-1806) Series 9	3.00	5.00	7.00	10.00	—

KM# 29s.9 MUN
Cast Copper or Bronze

Date	Good	VG	F	VF	XF
ND(1757-1806) Series 9	—	—	—	—	60.00

KM# 29.10 MUN
Cast Copper or Bronze **Rev:** Crescent at right, series number at bottom

Date	Good	VG	F	VF	XF
ND(1757-1806) Series 10	3.00	5.00	7.00	10.00	—

KM# 29s.10 MUN
Cast Copper or Bronze

Date	Good	VG	F	VF	XF
ND(1757-1806) Series 10	—	—	—	—	60.00

KM# 29a.10 MUN
Cast Copper or Bronze **Obv:** Without "P'yong" **Note:** Size varies 23-24 mm.

Date	Good	VG	F	VF	XF
ND(1757-1806) Series 10	3.00	5.00	7.00	10.00	—

KM# 29b.6 MUN
Cast Copper or Bronze **Rev:** Star in crescent

Date	Good	VG	F	VF	XF
ND(1757-1806) Series 6	3.00	5.00	7.00	10.00	—

KM# 30.1 MUN
Cast Copper or Bronze **Rev:** Crescent at left, series number at bottom

Date	Good	VG	F	VF	XF
ND(1757-1806) Series 1	3.00	5.00	7.00	10.00	—

KM# 30c.1 MUN
Cast Copper or Bronze, 25 mm.

Date	Good	VG	F	VF	XF
ND(1757-1806) Series 1	3.00	5.00	7.00	10.00	—

KM# 30a.1 MUN
Cast Copper or Bronze **Obv:** Without "P'yong, tong" with 1 dot

Date	Good	VG	F	VF	XF
ND(1757-1806) Series 1	3.00	5.00	7.00	10.00	—

KM# 30s.1 MUN
Cast Copper or Bronze

Date	Good	VG	F	VF	XF
ND(1757-1806) Series 1	—	—	—	—	60.00

KM# 30c.2 MUN
Cast Copper or Bronze

Date	Good	VG	F	VF	XF
ND(1757-1806) Series 2	3.00	5.00	7.00	10.00	—

KM# 30.2 MUN
Cast Copper or Bronze **Rev:** Crescent at left, series number at bottom

Date	Good	VG	F	VF	XF
ND(1757-1806) Series 2	3.00	5.00	7.00	10.00	—

KM# 30a.2 MUN
Cast Copper or Bronze **Obv:** Without "P'yong, tong" with 1 dot

Date	Good	VG	F	VF	XF
ND(1757-1806) Series 2	3.00	5.00	7.00	10.00	—

KM# 30s.2 MUN
Cast Copper or Bronze

Date	Good	VG	F	VF	XF
ND(1757-1806) Series 2	—	—	—	—	60.00

KM# 30c.3 MUN
Cast Copper or Bronze

Date	Good	VG	F	VF	XF
ND(1757-1806) Series 3	3.00	5.00	7.00	10.00	—

KM# 30.3 MUN
Cast Copper or Bronze **Rev:** Crescent at left, series number at bottom

Date	Good	VG	F	VF	XF
ND(1757-1806) Series 3	3.00	5.00	7.00	10.00	—

KM# 30a.3 MUN
Cast Copper or Bronze **Obv:** Without "P'yong, tong" with 1 dot

Date	Good	VG	F	VF	XF
ND(1757-1806) Series 3	3.00	5.00	7.00	10.00	—

KM# 30s.3 MUN
Cast Copper or Bronze

Date	Good	VG	F	VF	XF
ND(1757-1806) Series 3	—	—	—	—	60.00

KM# 30c.4 MUN
Cast Copper or Bronze

Date	Good	VG	F	VF	XF
ND(1757-1806) Series 4	3.00	5.00	7.00	10.00	—

KM# 30.4 MUN
Cast Copper or Bronze **Rev:** Crescent at left, series number at bottom

Date	Good	VG	F	VF	XF
ND(1757-1806) Series 4	3.00	5.00	7.00	10.00	—

KM# 30a.4 MUN
Cast Copper or Bronze **Obv:** Without "P'yong, tong" with 1 dot

Date	Good	VG	F	VF	XF
ND(1757-1806) Series 4	3.00	5.00	7.00	10.00	—

KM# 30s.4 MUN
Cast Copper or Bronze

Date	Good	VG	F	VF	XF
ND(1757-1806) Series 4	—	—	—	—	60.00

KM# 30c.5 MUN
Cast Copper or Bronze

Date	Good	VG	F	VF	XF
ND(1757-1806) Series 5	3.00	5.00	7.00	10.00	—

KM# 30.5 MUN
Cast Copper or Bronze **Rev:** Crescent at left, series number at bottom

Date	Good	VG	F	VF	XF
ND(1757-1806) Series 5	3.00	5.00	7.00	10.00	—

KM# 30a.5 MUN
Cast Copper or Bronze **Obv:** Without "P'yong, tong" with 1 dot

Date	Good	VG	F	VF	XF
ND(1757-1806) Series 5	3.00	5.00	7.00	10.00	—

KM# 30s.5 MUN
Cast Copper or Bronze

Date	Good	VG	F	VF	XF
ND(1757-1806) Series 5	—	—	—	—	60.00

KM# 30c.6 MUN
Cast Copper or Bronze

Date	Good	VG	F	VF	XF
ND(1757-1806) Series 6	3.00	5.00	7.00	10.00	—

KM# 30.6 MUN
Cast Copper or Bronze **Rev:** Crescent at left, series number at bottom

Date	Good	VG	F	VF	XF
ND(1757-1806) Series 6	3.00	5.00	7.00	10.00	—

KM# 30a.6 MUN
Cast Copper or Bronze **Obv:** Without "P'yong, tong" with 1 dot

Date	Good	VG	F	VF	XF
ND(1757-1806) Series 6	3.00	5.00	7.00	10.00	—

KM# 30s.6 MUN
Cast Copper or Bronze

Date	Good	VG	F	VF	XF
ND(1757-1806) Series 6	—	—	—	—	60.00

KM# 30c.7 MUN
Cast Copper or Bronze

Date	Good	VG	F	VF	XF
ND(1757-1806) Series 7	3.00	5.00	7.00	10.00	—

KM# 30.7 MUN
Cast Copper or Bronze **Rev:** Crescent at left, series number at bottom

Date	Good	VG	F	VF	XF
ND(1757-1806) Series 7	3.00	5.00	7.00	10.00	—

KM# 30a.7 MUN
Cast Copper or Bronze **Obv:** Without "P'yong, tong" with 1 dot

Date	Good	VG	F	VF	XF
ND(1757-1806) Series 7	3.00	5.00	7.00	10.00	—

KM# 30s.7 MUN
Cast Copper or Bronze

Date	Good	VG	F	VF	XF
ND(1757-1806) Series 7	—	—	—	—	60.00

KM# 30c.8 MUN
Cast Copper or Bronze

Date	Good	VG	F	VF	XF
ND(1757-1806) Series 8	3.00	5.00	7.00	10.00	—

KM# 30.8 MUN
Cast Copper or Bronze **Rev:** Crescent at left, series number at bottom

Date	Good	VG	F	VF	XF
ND(1757-1806) Series 8	3.00	5.00	7.00	10.00	—

KM# 30a.8 MUN
Cast Copper or Bronze **Obv:** Without "P'yong, tong" with 1 dot

Date	Good	VG	F	VF	XF
ND(1757-1806) Series 8	3.00	5.00	7.00	10.00	—

KM# 30s.8 MUN
Cast Copper or Bronze

Date	Good	VG	F	VF	XF
ND(1757-1806) Series 8	—	—	—	—	60.00

KM# 30c.9 MUN
Cast Copper or Bronze

Date	Good	VG	F	VF	XF
ND(1757-1806) Series 9	3.00	5.00	7.00	10.00	—

KM# 30.9 MUN
Cast Copper or Bronze **Rev:** Crescent at left, series number at bottom

Date	Good	VG	F	VF	XF
ND(1757-1806) Series 9	3.00	5.00	7.00	10.00	—

KM# 30a.9 MUN
Cast Copper or Bronze **Obv:** Without "P'yong, tong" with 1 dot

Date	Good	VG	F	VF	XF
ND(1757-1806) Series 9	3.00	5.00	7.00	10.00	—

KM# 30s.9 MUN
Cast Copper or Bronze

Date	Good	VG	F	VF	XF
ND(1757-1806) Series 9	—	—	—	—	60.00

KM# 30c.10 MUN
Cast Copper or Bronze

Date	Good	VG	F	VF	XF
ND(1757-1806) Series 10	3.00	5.00	7.00	10.00	—

KM# 30.10 MUN
Cast Copper or Bronze **Rev:** Crescent at left, series number at bottom

Date	Good	VG	F	VF	XF
ND(1757-1806) Series 10	3.00	5.00	7.00	10.00	—

KM# 30s.10 MUN
Cast Copper or Bronze

Date	Good	VG	F	VF	XF
ND(1757-1806) Series 10	—	—	—	—	60.00

KM# 30a.10 MUN
Cast Copper or Bronze **Obv:** Without "P'yong, tong" with 1 dot

Date	Good	VG	F	VF	XF
ND(1757-1806) Series 10	3.00	5.00	7.00	10.00	—

KM# 30b.7 MUN
Cast Copper or Bronze **Obv:** Star at lower left

Date	Good	VG	F	VF	XF
ND(1757-1806) Series 7	3.00	5.00	7.00	10.00	—

KM# 19.4 MUN
Cast Copper or Bronze **Rev:** Dot at right, series number at bottom

Date	Good	VG	F	VF	XF
ND(1778-1806) Series 4	5.00	7.50	10.00	15.00	—

KM# 19s.4 MUN
Cast Copper or Bronze

Date	Good	VG	F	VF	XF
ND(1778-1806) Series 4	—	—	—	—	75.00

KM# 19.5 MUN
Cast Copper or Bronze **Rev:** Dot at right, series number at bottom

Date	Good	VG	F	VF	XF
ND(1778-1806) Series 5	3.00	5.00	7.50	10.00	—

KM# 19s.5 MUN
Cast Copper or Bronze

Date	Good	VG	F	VF	XF
ND(1778-1806) Series 5	—	—	—	—	60.00

KM# 19.6 MUN
Cast Copper or Bronze **Rev:** Dot at right, series number at bottom

Date	Good	VG	F	VF	XF
ND(1778-1806) Series 6	3.00	5.00	7.00	10.00	—

KM# 19s.6 MUN
Cast Copper or Bronze

Date	Good	VG	F	VF	XF
ND(1778-1806) Series 6	—	—	—	—	60.00

KM# 19.7 MUN
Cast Copper or Bronze **Rev:** Dot at right, series number at bottom

Date	Good	VG	F	VF	XF
ND(1778-1806) Series 7	3.00	5.00	7.00	10.00	—

KM# 19s.7 MUN
Cast Copper or Bronze

Date	Good	VG	F	VF	XF
ND(1778-1806) Series 7	—	—	—	—	60.00

KM# 19.8 MUN
Cast Copper or Bronze **Rev:** Dot at right, series number at bottom

Date	Good	VG	F	VF	XF
ND(1778-1806) Series 8	3.00	5.00	7.00	10.00	—

KM# 19s.8 MUN
Cast Copper or Bronze

Date	Good	VG	F	VF	XF
ND(1778-1806) Series 8	—	—	—	—	60.00

KM# 19.9 MUN
Cast Copper or Bronze **Rev:** Dot at right, series number at bottom

Date	Good	VG	F	VF	XF
ND(1778-1806) Series 9	3.00	5.00	7.00	10.00	—

KM# 19s.9 MUN
Cast Copper or Bronze

Date	Good	VG	F	VF	XF
ND(1778-1806) Series 9	—	—	—	—	60.00

KM# 20s.5 MUN
Cast Copper or Bronze

Date	Good	VG	F	VF	XF
ND(1778-1806) Series 5	—	—	—	—	50.00

KM# 20.6 MUN
Cast Copper or Bronze **Rev:** Dot at left, series number at bottom

Date	Good	VG	F	VF	XF
ND(1778-1806) Series 6	10.00	15.00	25.00	50.00	—

KM# 20s.6 MUN
Cast Copper or Bronze

Date	Good	VG	F	VF	XF
ND(1778-1806) Series 6	—	—	—	—	100

KM# 27.1 MUN
Cast Copper or Bronze **Rev:** Dot at right, circle at left, series number at bottom

Date	Good	VG	F	VF	XF
ND(1778-1806) Series 1	3.00	5.00	7.00	10.00	—

KM# 27s.1 MUN
Cast Copper or Bronze

Date	Good	VG	F	VF	XF
ND(1778-1806) Series 1	—	—	—	—	60.00

KM# 27.2 MUN
Cast Copper or Bronze **Rev:** Dot at right, circle at left, series number at bottom

Date	Good	VG	F	VF	XF
ND(1778-1806) Series 2	3.00	5.00	7.00	10.00	—

KM# 27s.2 MUN
Cast Copper or Bronze

Date	Good	VG	F	VF	XF
ND(1778-1806) Series 2	—	—	—	—	60.00

KM# 27.3 MUN
Cast Copper or Bronze **Rev:** Dot at right, circle at left, series number at bottom

Date	Good	VG	F	VF	XF
ND(1778-1806) Series 3	3.00	5.00	7.00	10.00	—

KM# 27s.3 MUN
Cast Copper or Bronze

Date	Good	VG	F	VF	XF
ND(1778-1806) Series 3	—	—	—	—	60.00

KM# 27.4 MUN
Cast Copper or Bronze **Rev:** Dot at right, circle at left, series number at bottom

Date	Good	VG	F	VF	XF
ND(1778-1806) Series 4	3.00	5.00	7.00	10.00	—

KM# 27s.4 MUN
Cast Copper or Bronze

Date	Good	VG	F	VF	XF
ND(1778-1806) Series 4	—	—	—	—	60.00

KM# 27.5 MUN
Cast Copper or Bronze **Rev:** Dot at right, circle at left, series number at bottom

Date	Good	VG	F	VF	XF
ND(1778-1806) Series 5	3.00	5.00	7.00	10.00	—

KM# 27s.5 MUN
Cast Copper or Bronze

Date	Good	VG	F	VF	XF
ND(1778-1806) Series 5	—	—	—	—	60.00

KM# 27.6 MUN
Cast Copper or Bronze **Rev:** Dot at right, circle at left, series number at bottom

Date	Good	VG	F	VF	XF
ND(1778-1806) Series 6	3.00	5.00	7.00	10.00	—

KM# 27s.6 MUN
Cast Copper or Bronze

Date	Good	VG	F	VF	XF
ND(1778-1806) Series 6	—	—	—	—	60.00

KM# 27.7 MUN
Cast Copper or Bronze **Rev:** Dot at right, circle at left, series number at bottom

Date	Good	VG	F	VF	XF
ND(1778-1806) Series 7	3.00	5.00	7.00	10.00	—

KM# 27s.7 MUN
Cast Copper or Bronze

Date	Good	VG	F	VF	XF
ND(1778-1806) Series 7	—	—	—	—	60.00

KM# 27.8 MUN
Cast Copper or Bronze **Rev:** Dot at right, circle at left, series number at bottom

Date	Good	VG	F	VF	XF
ND(1778-1806) Series 8	3.00	5.00	7.00	10.00	—

KM# 27s.8 MUN
Cast Copper or Bronze

Date	Good	VG	F	VF	XF
ND(1778-1806) Series 8	—	—	—	—	60.00

KM# 27.9 MUN
Cast Copper or Bronze **Rev:** Dot at right, circle at left, series number at bottom

Date	Good	VG	F	VF	XF
ND(1778-1806) Series 9	3.00	5.00	7.00	10.00	—

KM# 27s.9 MUN
Cast Copper or Bronze

Date	Good	VG	F	VF	XF
ND(1778-1806) Series 9	—	—	—	—	60.00

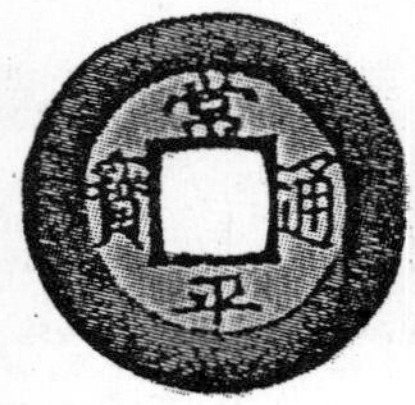

KM# 27.10 MUN
Cast Copper or Bronze **Rev:** Dot at right, circle at left, series number at bottom

Date	Good	VG	F	VF	XF
ND(1778-1806) Series 10	3.00	5.00	7.00	10.00	—

KM# 27s.10 MUN
Cast Copper or Bronze

Date	Good	VG	F	VF	XF
ND(1778-1806) Series 10	—	—	—	—	60.00

KM# 28.1 MUN
Cast Copper or Bronze **Rev:** Circle at right, dot at left, series number at bottom

Date	Good	VG	F	VF	XF
ND(1778-1806) Series 1	3.00	5.00	7.00	10.00	—

KM# 28s.1 MUN
Cast Copper or Bronze

Date	Good	VG	F	VF	XF
ND(1778-1806) Series 1	—	—	—	—	60.00

KM# 28.2 MUN
Cast Copper or Bronze **Rev:** Circle at right, dot at left, series number at bottom **Note:** Struck at Ho Jo.

Date	Good	VG	F	VF	XF
ND(1778-1806) Series 2	3.00	5.00	7.00	10.00	—

KM# 28s.2 MUN
Cast Copper or Bronze

Date	Good	VG	F	VF	XF
ND(1778-1806) Series 2	—	—	—	—	60.00

KM# 28.3 MUN
Cast Copper or Bronze **Rev:** Circle at right, dot at left, series number at bottom

Date	Good	VG	F	VF	XF
ND(1778-1806) Series 3	3.00	5.00	7.00	10.00	—

KM# 28s.3 MUN
Cast Copper or Bronze

Date	Good	VG	F	VF	XF
ND(1778-1806) Series 3	—	—	—	—	60.00

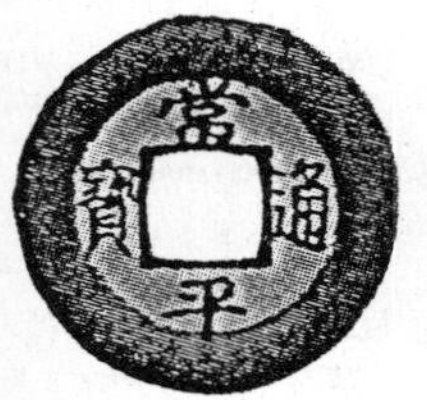

KM# 28.4 MUN
Cast Copper or Bronze **Rev:** Circle at right, dot at left, series number at bottom

Date	Good	VG	F	VF	XF
ND(1778-1806) Series 4	3.00	5.00	7.00	10.00	—

KM# 28s.4 MUN
Cast Copper or Bronze

Date	Good	VG	F	VF	XF
ND(1778-1806) Series 4	—	—	—	—	60.00

KM# 28.5 MUN
Cast Copper or Bronze **Rev:** Circle at right, dot at left, series number at bottom

Date	Good	VG	F	VF	XF
ND(1778-1806) Series 5	3.00	5.00	7.00	10.00	—

KM# 32s.1 MUN
Cast Copper or Bronze

Date	Good	VG	F	VF	XF
ND(1778-1806) Series 1	—	—	—	—	60.00

KM# 32s.2 MUN
Cast Copper or Bronze

Date	Good	VG	F	VF	XF
ND(1778-1806) Series 2	—	—	—	—	60.00

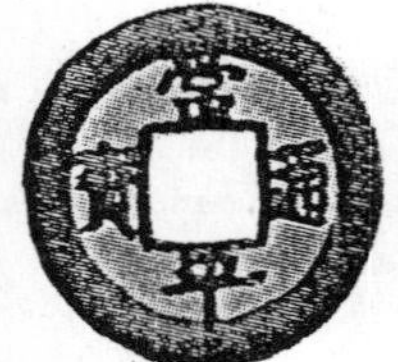

KM# 31.9 MUN
Cast Copper or Bronze **Rev:** Vertical line at right, crescent at left, number 9 at bottom

Date	Good	VG	F	VF	XF
ND(1778-1806) Series 9	2.00	3.00	5.00	8.00	—

KM# 31s.9 MUN
Cast Copper or Bronze

Date	Good	VG	F	VF	XF
ND(1778-1806) Series 9	—	—	—	—	50.00

KM# 32.1 MUN
Cast Copper or Bronze, 25 mm. **Rev:** Dot at right, crescent at left, series number at bottom

Date	Good	VG	F	VF	XF
ND(1778-1806) Series 1	3.00	5.00	8.00	12.00	—

KM# 32.2 MUN
Cast Copper or Bronze **Rev:** Dot at right, crescent at left, series number at bottom

Date	Good	VG	F	VF	XF
ND(1778-1806) Series 2	3.00	5.00	8.00	12.00	—

KM# 32.3 MUN
Cast Copper or Bronze **Rev:** Dot at right, crescent at left, series number at bottom

Date	Good	VG	F	VF	XF
ND(1778-1806) Series 3	3.00	5.00	8.00	12.00	—

KM# 32s.3 MUN
Cast Copper or Bronze

Date	Good	VG	F	VF	XF
ND(1778-1806) Series 3	—	—	—	—	60.00

KM# 32.4 MUN
Cast Copper or Bronze **Rev:** Dot at right, crescent at left, series number at bottom

Date	Good	VG	F	VF	XF
ND(1778-1806) Series 4	3.00	5.00	8.00	12.00	—

KM# 32s.4 MUN
Cast Copper or Bronze

Date	Good	VG	F	VF	XF
ND(1778-1806) Series 4	—	—	—	—	60.00

KM# 32.5 MUN
Cast Copper or Bronze **Rev:** Dot at right, crescent at left, series number at bottom

Date	Good	VG	F	VF	XF
ND(1778-1806) Series 5	3.00	5.00	8.00	12.00	—

KM# 32s.5 MUN
Cast Copper or Bronze

Date	Good	VG	F	VF	XF
ND(1778-1806) Series 5	—	—	—	—	60.00

KM# 32.6 MUN
Cast Copper or Bronze **Rev:** Dot at right, crescent at left, series number at bottom

Date	Good	VG	F	VF	XF
ND(1778-1806) Series 6	3.00	5.00	8.00	12.00	—

KM# 32s.6 MUN
Cast Copper or Bronze

Date	Good	VG	F	VF	XF
ND(1778-1806) Series 6	—	—	—	—	60.00

KM# 32.7 MUN
Cast Copper or Bronze **Rev:** Dot at right, crescent at left, series number at bottom

Date	Good	VG	F	VF	XF
ND(1778-1806) Series 7	3.00	5.00	8.00	12.00	—

KM# 32s.7 MUN
Cast Copper or Bronze

Date	Good	VG	F	VF	XF
ND(1778-1806) Series 7	—	—	—	—	60.00

KM# 32.8 MUN
Cast Copper or Bronze **Rev:** Dot at right, crescent at left, series number at bottom

Date	Good	VG	F	VF	XF
ND(1778-1806) Series 8	3.00	5.00	8.00	12.00	—

KM# 32s.8 MUN
Cast Copper or Bronze

Date	Good	VG	F	VF	XF
ND(1778-1806) Series 8	—	—	—	—	60.00

KM# 32.9 MUN
Cast Copper or Bronze **Rev:** Dot at right, crescent at left, series number at bottom

Date	Good	VG	F	VF	XF
ND(1778-1806) Series 9	3.00	5.00	8.00	12.00	—

KM# 32s.9 MUN
Cast Copper or Bronze

Date	Good	VG	F	VF	XF
ND(1778-1806) Series 9	—	—	—	—	60.00

KM# 32.10 MUN
Cast Copper or Bronze **Rev:** Dot at right, crescent at left, series number at bottom

Date	Good	VG	F	VF	XF
ND(1778-1806) Series 10	3.00	5.00	8.00	12.00	—

KM# 32s.10 MUN
Cast Copper or Bronze

Date	Good	VG	F	VF	XF
ND(1778-1806) Series 10	—	—	—	—	60.00

KM# 32.13 MUN
Cast Copper or Bronze **Rev:** Star in crescent

Date	Good	VG	F	VF	XF
ND(1778-1806) Series 3	1.75	2.50	3.50	5.00	—

KM# 33.1 MUN
Cast Copper or Bronze, 26 mm. **Rev:** Crescent at right, dot at left, series number at bottom

Date	Good	VG	F	VF	XF
ND(1778-1806) Series 1	3.00	5.00	8.00	12.00	—

KM# 33s.1 MUN
Cast Copper or Bronze **Note:** Seed type. Struck at Ho Jo.

Date	Good	VG	F	VF	XF
ND(1778-1806) Series 1	—	—	—	—	60.00

KM# 33.2 MUN
Cast Copper or Bronze **Rev:** Crescent at right, dot at left, series number at bottom

Date	Good	VG	F	VF	XF
ND(1778-1806) Series 2	3.00	5.00	8.00	12.00	—

KM# 33s.2 MUN
Cast Copper or Bronze

Date	Good	VG	F	VF	XF
ND(1778-1806) Series 2	—	—	—	—	60.00

KM# 33.3 MUN
Cast Copper or Bronze **Rev:** Crescent at right, dot at left, series number at bottom

Date	Good	VG	F	VF	XF
ND(1778-1806) Series 3	3.00	5.00	8.00	12.00	—

KM# 33s.3 MUN
Cast Copper or Bronze

Date	Good	VG	F	VF	XF
ND(1778-1806) Series 3	—	—	—	—	60.00

KM# 33.4 MUN
Cast Copper or Bronze **Rev:** Crescent at right, dot at left, series number at bottom

Date	Good	VG	F	VF	XF
ND(1778-1806) Series 4	3.00	5.00	8.00	12.00	—

KM# 33s.4 MUN
Cast Copper or Bronze

Date	Good	VG	F	VF	XF
ND(1778-1806) Series 4	—	—	—	—	60.00

KM# 33.5 MUN
Cast Copper or Bronze **Rev:** Crescent at right, dot at left, series number at bottom

Date	Good	VG	F	VF	XF
ND(1778-1806) Series 5	3.00	5.00	8.00	12.00	—

KM# 33s.5 MUN
Cast Copper or Bronze

Date	Good	VG	F	VF	XF
ND(1778-1806) Series 5	—	—	—	—	60.00

KM# 33.6 MUN
Cast Copper or Bronze **Rev:** Crescent at right, dot at left, series number at bottom

Date	Good	VG	F	VF	XF
ND(1778-1806) Series 6	3.00	5.00	8.00	12.00	—

KM# 33s.6 MUN
Cast Copper or Bronze

Date	Good	VG	F	VF	XF
ND(1778-1806) Series 6	—	—	—	—	60.00

KM# 33.7 MUN
Cast Copper or Bronze **Rev:** Crescent at right, dot at left, series number at bottom

Date	Good	VG	F	VF	XF
ND(1778-1806) Series 7	3.00	5.00	8.00	12.00	—

KM# 33s.7 MUN
Cast Copper or Bronze

Date	Good	VG	F	VF	XF
ND(1778-1806) Series 7	—	—	—	—	60.00

KM# 33.8 MUN
Cast Copper or Bronze **Rev:** Crescent at right, dot at left, series number at bottom

Date	Good	VG	F	VF	XF
ND(1778-1806) Series 8	3.00	5.00	8.00	12.00	—

KM# 33s.8 MUN
Cast Copper or Bronze

Date	Good	VG	F	VF	XF
ND(1778-1806) Series 8	—	—	—	—	60.00

KM# 33.9 MUN
Cast Copper or Bronze **Rev:** Crescent at right, dot at left, series number at bottom

Date	Good	VG	F	VF	XF
ND(1778-1806) Series 9	3.00	5.00	8.00	12.00	—

KM# 33s.9 MUN
Cast Copper or Bronze

Date	Good	VG	F	VF	XF
ND(1778-1806) Series 9	—	—	—	—	60.00

KM# 33.10 MUN
Cast Copper or Bronze **Rev:** Crescent at right, dot at left, series number at bottom

Date	Good	VG	F	VF	XF
ND(1778-1806) Series 10	3.00	5.00	8.00	12.00	—

KM# 33s.10 MUN
Cast Copper or Bronze

Date	Good	VG	F	VF	XF
ND(1778-1806) Series 10	—	—	—	—	60.00

KM# 10s.11 MUN
Cast Copper or Bronze **Ruler:** Yi Kwang (Sunjo Songhyo)

Date	Good	VG	F	VF	XF
ND(1806)	—	—	—	—	50.00
ND(1806) Series 11	—	—	—	—	50.00

KM# 9.1 MUN
Cast Copper or Bronze, 26 mm. **Ruler:** Yi Kweng (Sonjo Sog Yung) **Rev:** "Ho" at top in different style, series number at bottom

Date	Good	VG	F	VF	XF
ND(1806) Series 1	2.00	3.00	5.00	7.50	—

KM# 9s.1 MUN
Cast Copper or Bronze, 26 mm. **Ruler:** Yi Kwang (Sunjo Songhyo)

Date	Good	VG	F	VF	XF
ND(1806) Series 1	—	—	—	—	50.00

KM# 9.2 MUN
Cast Copper or Bronze, 26 mm. **Ruler:** Yi Kwang (Sunjo Songhyo) **Rev:** Ho at top in different style, series number at bottom

Date	Good	VG	F	VF	XF
ND(1806) Series 2	2.00	3.00	5.00	7.50	—

KM# 9s.2 MUN
Cast Copper or Bronze, 26 mm. **Ruler:** Yi Kwang (Sunjo Songhyo)

Date	Good	VG	F	VF	XF
ND(1806) Series 2	—	—	—	—	50.00

KM# 9.3 MUN
Cast Copper or Bronze, 26 mm. **Ruler:** Yi Kwang (Sunjo Songhyo)**Rev:** Ho at top in different style, series number at bottom

Date	Good	VG	F	VF	XF
ND(1806) Series 3	2.00	3.00	5.00	7.50	—

KM# 9s.3 MUN

Cast Copper or Bronze, 26 mm. **Ruler:** Yi Kwang (Sunjo Songhyo)

Date	Good	VG	F	VF	XF
ND(1806) Series 3	—	—	—	—	50.00

KM# 9.4 MUN

Cast Copper or Bronze, 26 mm. **Ruler:** Yi Kwang (Sunjo Songhyo) **Rev:** Ho at top in different style, series number at bottom

Date	Good	VG	F	VF	XF
ND(1806) Series 4	2.00	3.00	5.00	7.50	—

KM# 9s.4 MUN

Cast Copper or Bronze, 26 mm. **Ruler:** Yi Kwang (Sunjo Songhyo)

Date	Good	VG	F	VF	XF
ND(1806) Series 4	—	—	—	—	50.00

KM# 9.5 MUN

Cast Copper or Bronze, 26 mm. **Ruler:** Yi Kwang (Sunjo Songhyo) **Rev:** Ho at top in different style, series number at bottom

Date	Good	VG	F	VF	XF
ND(1806) Series 5	2.00	3.00	5.00	7.50	—

KM# 9s.5 MUN

Cast Copper or Bronze, 26 mm. **Ruler:** Yi Kwang (Sunjo Songhyo)

Date	Good	VG	F	VF	XF
ND(1806) Series 5	—	—	—	—	50.00

KM# 9.6 MUN

Cast Copper or Bronze, 26 mm. **Ruler:** Yi Kwang (Sunjo Songhyo) **Rev:** Ho at top in different style, series number at bottom

Date	Good	VG	F	VF	XF
ND(1806) Series 6	2.00	3.00	5.00	7.50	—

KM# 9s.6 MUN

Cast Copper or Bronze, 26 mm. **Ruler:** Yi Kwang (Sunjo Songhyo)

Date	Good	VG	F	VF	XF
ND(1806) Series 6	—	—	—	—	50.00

KM# 9.7 MUN

Cast Copper or Bronze, 26 mm. **Ruler:** Yi Kwang (Sunjo Songhyo) **Rev:** Ho at top in different style, series number at bottom

Date	Good	VG	F	VF	XF
ND(1806) Series 7	2.00	3.00	5.00	7.50	—

KM# 9s.7 MUN

Cast Copper or Bronze, 26 mm. **Ruler:** Yi Kwang (Sunjo Songhyo)

Date	Good	VG	F	VF	XF
ND(1806) Series 7	—	—	—	—	50.00

KM# 9.8 MUN

Cast Copper or Bronze, 26 mm. **Ruler:** Yi Kwang (Sunjo Songhyo) **Rev:** Ho at top in different style, series number at bottom

Date	Good	VG	F	VF	XF
ND(1806) Series 8	2.00	3.00	5.00	7.50	—

KM# 9s.8 MUN

Cast Copper or Bronze, 26 mm. **Ruler:** Yi Kwang (Sunjo Songhyo)

Date	Good	VG	F	VF	XF
ND(1806) Series 8	—	—	—	—	50.00

KM# 9.9 MUN

Cast Copper or Bronze, 26 mm. **Ruler:** Yi Kwang (Sunjo Songhyo) **Rev:** Ho at top in different style, series number at bottom

Date	Good	VG	F	VF	XF
ND(1806) Series 9	2.00	3.00	5.00	7.50	—

KM# 9s.9 MUN

Cast Copper or Bronze, 26 mm. **Ruler:** Yi Kwang (Sunjo Songhyo)

Date	Good	VG	F	VF	XF
ND(1806) Series 9	—	—	—	—	50.00

KM# 9.10 MUN

Cast Copper or Bronze, 26 mm. **Ruler:** Yi Kwang (Sunjo Songhyo) **Rev:** Ho at top in different style, series number at bottom

Date	Good	VG	F	VF	XF
ND(1806) Series 10	2.00	3.00	5.00	7.50	—

KM# 9s.10 MUN

Cast Copper or Bronze, 26 mm. **Ruler:** Yi Kwang (Sunjo Songhyo)

Date	Good	VG	F	VF	XF
ND(1806) Series 10	—	—	—	—	50.00

KM# 10.11 MUN

Cast Copper or Bronze, 25 mm. **Ruler:** Yi Kwang (Sunjo Songhyo) **Rev:** Sip (10) at bottom, additional series number at left

Date	Good	VG	F	VF	XF
ND(1806) Series 11	2.00	3.00	5.00	7.50	—

KM# 10s.11 MUN

Cast Copper or Bronze **Ruler:** Yi Kwang (Sunjo Songhyo)

Date	Good	VG	F	VF	XF
ND(1806)	—	—	—	—	50.00
ND(1806) Series 11	—	—	—	—	50.00

KM# 10.12 MUN

Cast Copper or Bronze, 25 mm. **Ruler:** Yi Kwang (Sunjo Songhyo) **Rev:** Sip (10) at bottom, additional series number at left

Date	Good	VG	F	VF	XF
ND(1806) Series 12	2.00	3.00	5.00	7.50	—

KM# 10s.12 MUN

Cast Copper or Bronze **Ruler:** Yi Kwang (Sunjo Songhyo)

Date	Good	VG	F	VF	XF
ND(1806) Series 12	—	—	—	—	50.00

KM# 10.13 MUN

Cast Copper or Bronze, 25 mm. **Ruler:** Yi Kwang (Sunjo Songhyo) **Rev:** Sip (10) at bottom, additional series number at left

Date	Good	VG	F	VF	XF
ND(1806) Series 13	2.00	3.00	5.00	7.50	—

KM# 10s.13 MUN

Cast Copper or Bronze **Ruler:** Yi Kwang (Sunjo Songhyo)

Date	Good	VG	F	VF	XF
ND(1806) Series 13	—	—	—	—	50.00

KM# 10.14 MUN

Cast Copper or Bronze, 25 mm. **Ruler:** Yi Kwang (Sunjo Songhyo) **Rev:** Sip (10) at bottom, additional series number at left

Date	Good	VG	F	VF	XF
ND(1806) Series 14	2.00	3.00	5.00	7.50	—

KM# 10s.14 MUN

Cast Copper or Bronze **Ruler:** Yi Kwang (Sunjo Songhyo)

Date	Good	VG	F	VF	XF
ND(1806) Series 14	—	—	—	—	50.00

KM# 10.15 MUN

Cast Copper or Bronze, 25 mm. **Ruler:** Yi Kwang (Sunjo Songhyo) **Rev:** Sip (10) at bottom, additional series number at left

Date	Good	VG	F	VF	XF
ND(1806) Series 15	2.00	3.00	5.00	7.50	—

KM# 10s.15 MUN

Cast Copper or Bronze **Ruler:** Yi Kwang (Sunjo Songhyo)

Date	Good	VG	F	VF	XF
ND(1806) Series 15	—	—	—	—	50.00

KM# 10.16 MUN

Cast Copper or Bronze, 25 mm. **Ruler:** Yi Kwang (Sunjo Songhyo) **Rev:** Sip (10) at bottom, additional series number at left

Date	Good	VG	F	VF	XF
ND(1806) Series 16	2.00	3.00	5.00	7.50	—

KM# 10s.16 MUN

Cast Copper or Bronze **Ruler:** Yi Kwang (Sunjo Songhyo)

Date	Good	VG	F	VF	XF
ND(1806) Series 16	—	—	—	—	50.00

KM# 71.1 MUN

Cast Copper or Bronze, 23 mm. **Rev:** "Ip" at bottom, series number at left

Date	Good	VG	F	VF	XF
ND(1806-14) Series 1	3.00	5.00	8.00	12.00	—

KM# 71a.1 MUN

Cast Copper or Bronze, 24 mm. **Obv:** 1 dot "Tong" and "P'yong" with hooks

Date	Good	VG	F	VF	XF
ND(1806-14) Series 1	3.00	5.00	8.00	12.00	—

KM# 71s.1 MUN

Cast Copper or Bronze

Date	Good	VG	F	VF	XF
ND(1806-14) Series 1	—	—	—	—	50.00

KM# 71.2 MUN

Cast Copper or Bronze **Rev:** "Ip" at bottom, series number at left

Date	Good	VG	F	VF	XF
ND(1806-14) Series 2	3.00	5.00	8.00	12.00	—

KM# 71a.2 MUN

Cast Copper or Bronze **Obv:** 1 dot "Tong" and "P'yong" with hooks

Date	Good	VG	F	VF	XF
ND(1806-14) Series 2	3.00	5.00	8.00	12.00	—

KM# 71s.2 MUN

Cast Copper or Bronze

Date	Good	VG	F	VF	XF
ND(1806-14) Series 2	—	—	—	—	50.00

KM# 71.3 MUN

Cast Copper or Bronze **Rev:** "Ip" at bottom, series number at left

Date	Good	VG	F	VF	XF
ND(1806-14) Series 3	3.00	5.00	8.00	12.00	—

KM# 71a.3 MUN

Cast Copper or Bronze **Obv:** 1 dot "Tong" and "P'yong" with hooks

Date	Good	VG	F	VF	XF
ND(1806-14) Series 3	3.00	5.00	8.00	12.00	—

KM# 71s.3 MUN

Cast Copper or Bronze

Date	Good	VG	F	VF	XF
ND(1806-14) Series 3	—	—	—	—	50.00

KM# 71.4 MUN

Cast Copper or Bronze **Rev:** "Ip" at bottom, series number at left

Date	Good	VG	F	VF	XF
ND(1806-14) Series 4	3.00	5.00	8.00	12.00	—

KM# 71a.4 MUN

Cast Copper or Bronze **Obv:** 1 dot "Tong" and "P'yong" with hooks

Date	Good	VG	F	VF	XF
ND(1806-14) Series 4	3.00	5.00	8.00	12.00	—

KM# 71s.4 MUN

Cast Copper or Bronze

Date	Good	VG	F	VF	XF
ND(1806-14) Series 4	—	—	—	—	50.00

KM# 71.5 MUN

Cast Copper or Bronze **Rev:** "Ip" at bottom, series number at left

Date	Good	VG	F	VF	XF
ND(1806-14) Series 5	3.00	5.00	8.00	12.00	—

KM# 71a.5 MUN

Cast Copper or Bronze **Obv:** 1 dot "Tong" and "P'yong" with hooks

Date	Good	VG	F	VF	XF
ND(1806-14) Series 5	3.00	5.00	8.00	12.00	—

KM# 71s.5 MUN

Cast Copper or Bronze

Date	Good	VG	F	VF	XF
ND(1806-14) Series 5	—	—	—	—	50.00

KM# 71.6 MUN

Cast Copper or Bronze **Rev:** "Ip" at bottom, series number at left

Date	Good	VG	F	VF	XF
ND(1806-14) Series 6	3.00	5.00	8.00	12.00	—

KM# 71a.6 MUN

Cast Copper or Bronze **Obv:** 1 dot "Tong" and "P'yong" with hooks

Date	Good	VG	F	VF	XF
ND(1806-14) Series 6	3.00	5.00	8.00	12.00	—

KM# 71s.6 MUN

Cast Copper or Bronze

Date	Good	VG	F	VF	XF
ND(1806-14) Series 6	—	—	—	—	50.00

KM# 71.7 MUN

Cast Copper or Bronze **Rev:** "Ip" at bottom, series number at left

Date	Good	VG	F	VF	XF
ND(1806-14) Series 7	3.00	5.00	8.00	12.00	—

KM# 71a.7 MUN

Cast Copper or Bronze **Obv:** 1 dot "Tong" and "P'yong" with hooks

Date	Good	VG	F	VF	XF
ND(1806-14) Series 7	3.00	5.00	8.00	12.00	—

KM# 71s.7 MUN

Cast Copper or Bronze

Date	Good	VG	F	VF	XF
ND(1806-14) Series 7	—	—	—	—	50.00

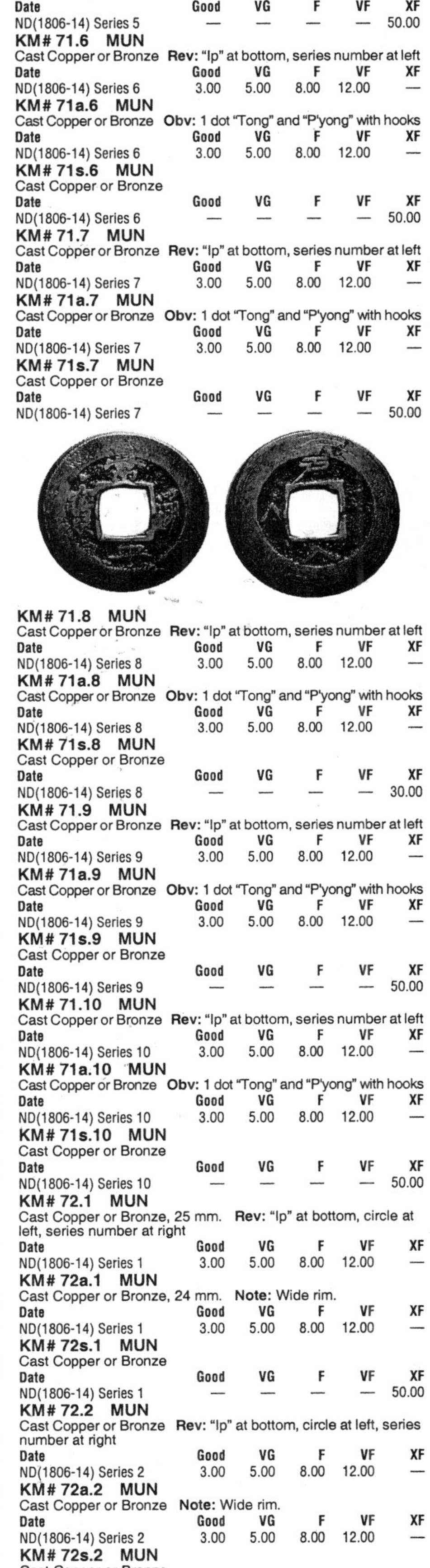

KM# 71.8 MUN

Cast Copper or Bronze **Rev:** "Ip" at bottom, series number at left

Date	Good	VG	F	VF	XF
ND(1806-14) Series 8	3.00	5.00	8.00	12.00	—

KM# 71a.8 MUN

Cast Copper or Bronze **Obv:** 1 dot "Tong" and "P'yong" with hooks

Date	Good	VG	F	VF	XF
ND(1806-14) Series 8	3.00	5.00	8.00	12.00	—

KM# 71s.8 MUN

Cast Copper or Bronze

Date	Good	VG	F	VF	XF
ND(1806-14) Series 8	—	—	—	—	30.00

KM# 71.9 MUN

Cast Copper or Bronze **Rev:** "Ip" at bottom, series number at left

Date	Good	VG	F	VF	XF
ND(1806-14) Series 9	3.00	5.00	8.00	12.00	—

KM# 71a.9 MUN

Cast Copper or Bronze **Obv:** 1 dot "Tong" and "P'yong" with hooks

Date	Good	VG	F	VF	XF
ND(1806-14) Series 9	3.00	5.00	8.00	12.00	—

KM# 71s.9 MUN

Cast Copper or Bronze

Date	Good	VG	F	VF	XF
ND(1806-14) Series 9	—	—	—	—	50.00

KM# 71.10 MUN

Cast Copper or Bronze **Rev:** "Ip" at bottom, series number at left

Date	Good	VG	F	VF	XF
ND(1806-14) Series 10	3.00	5.00	8.00	12.00	—

KM# 71a.10 MUN

Cast Copper or Bronze **Obv:** 1 dot "Tong" and "P'yong" with hooks

Date	Good	VG	F	VF	XF
ND(1806-14) Series 10	3.00	5.00	8.00	12.00	—

KM# 71s.10 MUN

Cast Copper or Bronze

Date	Good	VG	F	VF	XF
ND(1806-14) Series 10	—	—	—	—	50.00

KM# 72.1 MUN

Cast Copper or Bronze, 25 mm. **Rev:** "Ip" at bottom, circle at left, series number at right

Date	Good	VG	F	VF	XF
ND(1806-14) Series 1	3.00	5.00	8.00	12.00	—

KM# 72a.1 MUN

Cast Copper or Bronze, 24 mm. **Note:** Wide rim.

Date	Good	VG	F	VF	XF
ND(1806-14) Series 1	3.00	5.00	8.00	12.00	—

KM# 72s.1 MUN

Cast Copper or Bronze

Date	Good	VG	F	VF	XF
ND(1806-14) Series 1	—	—	—	—	50.00

KM# 72.2 MUN

Cast Copper or Bronze **Rev:** "Ip" at bottom, circle at left, series number at right

Date	Good	VG	F	VF	XF
ND(1806-14) Series 2	3.00	5.00	8.00	12.00	—

KM# 72a.2 MUN

Cast Copper or Bronze **Note:** Wide rim.

Date	Good	VG	F	VF	XF
ND(1806-14) Series 2	3.00	5.00	8.00	12.00	—

KM# 72s.2 MUN

Cast Copper or Bronze

Date	Good	VG	F	VF	XF
ND(1806-14) Series 2	—	—	—	—	50.00

KM# 72.3 MUN
Cast Copper or Bronze **Rev:** "Ip" at bottom, circle at left, series number at right

Date	Good	VG	F	VF	XF
ND(1806-14) Series 3	3.00	5.00	8.00	12.00	—

KM# 72a.3 MUN
Cast Copper or Bronze **Note:** Wide rim.

Date	Good	VG	F	VF	XF
ND(1806-14) Series 3	3.00	5.00	8.00	12.00	—

KM# 72s.3 MUN
Cast Copper or Bronze

Date	Good	VG	F	VF	XF
ND(1806-14) Series 3	—	—	—	—	50.00

KM# 72.4 MUN
Cast Copper or Bronze **Rev:** "Ip" at bottom, circle at left, series number at right

Date	Good	VG	F	VF	XF
ND(1806-14) Series 4	3.00	5.00	8.00	12.00	—

KM# 72a.4 MUN
Cast Copper or Bronze **Note:** Wide rim.

Date	Good	VG	F	VF	XF
ND(1806-14) Series 4	3.00	5.00	8.00	12.00	—

KM# 72s.4 MUN
Cast Copper or Bronze

Date	Good	VG	F	VF	XF
ND(1806-14) Series 4	—	—	—	—	50.00

KM# 72.5 MUN
Cast Copper or Bronze **Rev:** "Ip" at bottom, circle at left, series number at right

Date	Good	VG	F	VF	XF
ND(1806-14) Series 5	3.00	5.00	8.00	12.00	—

KM# 72a.5 MUN
Cast Copper or Bronze **Note:** Wide rim.

Date	Good	VG	F	VF	XF
ND(1806-14) Series 5	3.00	5.00	8.00	12.00	—

KM# 72s.5 MUN
Cast Copper or Bronze

Date	Good	VG	F	VF	XF
ND(1806-14) Series 5	—	—	—	—	50.00

KM# 72.6 MUN
Cast Copper or Bronze **Rev:** "Ip" at bottom, circle at left, series number at right

Date	Good	VG	F	VF	XF
ND(1806-14) Series 6	3.00	5.00	8.00	12.00	—

KM# 72a.6 MUN
Cast Copper or Bronze **Note:** Wide rim.

Date	Good	VG	F	VF	XF
ND(1806-14) Series 6	3.00	5.00	8.00	12.00	—

KM# 72s.6 MUN
Cast Copper or Bronze

Date	Good	VG	F	VF	XF
ND(1806-14) Series 6	—	—	—	—	50.00

KM# 72.7 MUN
Cast Copper or Bronze **Rev:** "Ip" at bottom, circle at left, series number at right

Date	Good	VG	F	VF	XF
ND(1806-14) Series 7	3.00	5.00	8.00	12.00	—

KM# 72a.7 MUN
Cast Copper or Bronze **Note:** Wide rim.

Date	Good	VG	F	VF	XF
ND(1806-14) Series 7	3.00	5.00	8.00	12.00	—

KM# 72s.7 MUN
Cast Copper or Bronze

Date	Good	VG	F	VF	XF
ND(1806-14) Series 7	—	—	—	—	50.00

KM# 72.8 MUN
Cast Copper or Bronze **Rev:** "Ip" at bottom, circle at left, series number at right

Date	Good	VG	F	VF	XF
ND(1806-14) Series 8	3.00	5.00	8.00	12.00	—

KM# 72a.8 MUN
Cast Copper or Bronze **Note:** Wide rim.

Date	Good	VG	F	VF	XF
ND(1806-14) Series 8	3.00	5.00	8.00	12.00	—

KM# 72s.8 MUN
Cast Copper or Bronze

Date	Good	VG	F	VF	XF
ND(1806-14) Series 8	—	—	—	—	50.00

KM# 72.9 MUN
Cast Copper or Bronze **Rev:** "Ip" at bottom, circle at left, series number at right

Date	Good	VG	F	VF	XF
ND(1806-14) Series 9	3.00	5.00	8.00	12.00	—

KM# 72a.9 MUN
Cast Copper or Bronze **Note:** Wide rim.

Date	Good	VG	F	VF	XF
ND(1806-14) Series 9	3.00	5.00	8.00	12.00	—

KM# 72s.9 MUN
Cast Copper or Bronze

Date	Good	VG	F	VF	XF
ND(1806-14) Series 9	—	—	—	—	50.00

KM# 72.10 MUN
Cast Copper or Bronze **Rev:** "Ip" at bottom, circle at left, series number at right

Date	Good	VG	F	VF	XF
ND(1806-14) Series 10	3.00	5.00	8.00	12.00	—

KM# 72s.10 MUN
Cast Copper or Bronze

Date	Good	VG	F	VF	XF
ND(1806-14) Series 10	—	—	—	—	50.00

KM# 72a.10 MUN
Cast Copper or Bronze **Note:** Wide rim.

Date	Good	VG	F	VF	XF
ND(1806-14) Series 10	3.00	5.00	8.00	12.00	—

KM# 73.1 MUN
Cast Copper or Bronze **Rev:** "Ip" at bottom, circle at right, series number at left

Date	Good	VG	F	VF	XF
ND(1806-14) Series 1	5.00	10.00	15.00	25.00	—

KM# 73s.1 MUN
Cast Copper or Bronze

Date	Good	VG	F	VF	XF
ND(1806-14) Series 1	—	—	—	—	75.00

KM# 73.2 MUN
Cast Copper or Bronze **Rev:** "Ip" at bottom, circle at right, series number at left

Date	Good	VG	F	VF	XF
ND(1806-14) Series 2	5.00	10.00	15.00	25.00	—

KM# 73s.2 MUN
Cast Copper or Bronze

Date	Good	VG	F	VF	XF
ND(1806-14) Series 2	—	—	—	—	75.00

KM# 73.3 MUN
Cast Copper or Bronze **Rev:** "Ip" at bottom, circle at right, series number at left

Date	Good	VG	F	VF	XF
ND(1806-14) Series 3	5.00	10.00	15.00	25.00	—

KM# 73s.3 MUN
Cast Copper or Bronze

Date	Good	VG	F	VF	XF
ND(1806-14) Series 3	—	—	—	—	75.00

KM# 73.4 MUN
Cast Copper or Bronze **Rev:** "Ip" at bottom, circle at right, series number at left

Date	Good	VG	F	VF	XF
ND(1806-14) Series 4	5.00	10.00	15.00	25.00	—

KM# 73s.4 MUN
Cast Copper or Bronze

Date	Good	VG	F	VF	XF
ND(1806-14) Series 4	—	—	—	—	75.00

KM# 73.5 MUN
Cast Copper or Bronze **Rev:** "Ip" at bottom, circle at right, series number at left

Date	Good	VG	F	VF	XF
ND(1806-14) Series 5	5.00	10.00	15.00	25.00	—

KM# 73s.5 MUN
Cast Copper or Bronze

Date	Good	VG	F	VF	XF
ND(1806-14) Series 5	—	—	—	—	75.00

KM# 23.1 MUN
Cast Copper or Bronze, 27 mm. **Rev:** Circle at right, "Il" (1) at left, series number at bottom

Date	Good	VG	F	VF	XF
ND(1814) Series 1	3.00	5.00	8.00	15.00	—

KM# 23s.1 MUN
Cast Copper or Bronze

Date	Good	VG	F	VF	XF
ND(1814) Series 1	—	—	—	—	50.00

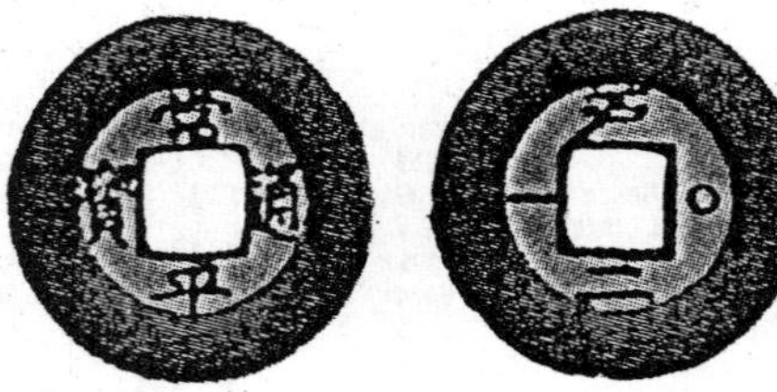

KM# 23.2 MUN
Cast Copper or Bronze **Rev:** Circle at right, "Il" (1) at left, series number at bottom

Date	Good	VG	F	VF	XF
ND(1814) Series 2	3.00	5.00	8.00	15.00	—

KM# 23s.2 MUN
Cast Copper or Bronze

Date	Good	VG	F	VF	XF
ND(1814) Series 2	—	—	—	—	50.00

KM# 23.3 MUN
Cast Copper or Bronze **Rev:** Circle at right, "Il" (1) at left, series number at bottom

Date	Good	VG	F	VF	XF
ND(1814) Series 3	3.00	5.00	8.00	15.00	—

KM# 23s.3 MUN
Cast Copper or Bronze

Date	Good	VG	F	VF	XF
ND(1814) Series 3	—	—	—	—	50.00

KM# 23.4 MUN
Cast Copper or Bronze **Rev:** Circle at right, "Il" (1) at left, series number at bottom

Date	Good	VG	F	VF	XF
ND(1814) Series 4	3.00	5.00	8.00	15.00	—

KM# 23s.4 MUN
Cast Copper or Bronze

Date	Good	VG	F	VF	XF
ND(1814) Series 4	—	—	—	—	50.00

KM# 24.1 MUN
Cast Copper or Bronze, 26 mm. **Rev:** Circle at left, "Il" (1) at right, series number at bottom

Date	Good	VG	F	VF	XF
ND(1814) Series 1	3.00	5.00	8.00	15.00	—

KM# 24s.1 MUN
Cast Copper or Bronze

Date	Good	VG	F	VF	XF
ND(1814) Series 1	—	—	—	—	50.00

KM# 24.2 MUN
Cast Copper or Bronze **Rev:** Circle at left, "Il" (1) at right, series number at bottom

Date	Good	VG	F	VF	XF
ND(1814) Series 2	3.00	5.00	8.00	15.00	—

KM# 24s.2 MUN
Cast Copper or Bronze

Date	Good	VG	F	VF	XF
ND(1814) Series 2	—	—	—	—	50.00

KM# 24.3 MUN
Cast Copper or Bronze **Rev:** Circle at left, "Il" (1) at right, series number at bottom

Date	Good	VG	F	VF	XF
ND(1814) Series 3	3.00	5.00	8.00	15.00	—

KM# 24s.3 MUN
Cast Copper or Bronze

Date	Good	VG	F	VF	XF
ND(1814) Series 3	—	—	—	—	50.00

KM# 24.4 MUN
Cast Copper or Bronze **Rev:** Circle at left, "Il" (1) at right, series number at bottom

Date	Good	VG	F	VF	XF
ND(1814) Series 4	3.00	5.00	8.00	15.00	—

KM# 24s.4 MUN
Cast Copper or Bronze

Date	Good	VG	F	VF	XF
ND(1814) Series 4	—	—	—	—	50.00

KM# 24.5 MUN
Cast Copper or Bronze **Rev:** Circle at left, "Il" (1) at right, series number at bottom

Date	Good	VG	F	VF	XF
ND(1814) Series 5	3.00	5.00	8.00	15.00	—

KM# 24s.5 MUN
Cast Copper or Bronze

Date	Good	VG	F	VF	XF
ND(1814) Series 5	—	—	—	—	50.00

KM# 24.6 MUN
Cast Copper or Bronze **Rev:** Circle at left, "Il" (1) at right, series number at bottom

Date	Good	VG	F	VF	XF
ND(1814) Series 6	3.00	5.00	8.00	15.00	—

KM# 24s.6 MUN
Cast Copper or Bronze

Date	Good	VG	F	VF	XF
ND(1814) Series 6	—	—	—	—	50.00

KM# 24.7 MUN
Cast Copper or Bronze **Rev:** Circle at left, "Il" (1) at right, series number at bottom

Date	Good	VG	F	VF	XF
ND(1814) Series 7	3.00	5.00	8.00	15.00	—

KM# 24s.7 MUN
Cast Copper or Bronze

Date	Good	VG	F	VF	XF
ND(1814) Series 7	—	—	—	—	50.00

KM# 24.8 MUN
Cast Copper or Bronze **Rev:** Circle at left, "Il" (1) at right, series number at bottom

Date	Good	VG	F	VF	XF
ND(1814) Series 8	3.00	5.00	8.00	15.00	—

KM# 24s.8 MUN
Cast Copper or Bronze

Date	Good	VG	F	VF	XF
ND(1814) Series 8	—	—	—	—	50.00

KM# 24.9 MUN
Cast Copper or Bronze **Rev:** Circle at left, "Il" (1) at right, series number at bottom

Date	Good	VG	F	VF	XF
ND(1814) Series 9	3.00	5.00	8.00	15.00	—

KM# 24s.9 MUN
Cast Copper or Bronze

Date	Good	VG	F	VF	XF
ND(1814) Series 9	—	—	—	—	50.00

KM# 24.10 MUN
Cast Copper or Bronze **Rev:** Circle at left, "Il" (1) at right, series number at bottom

Date	Good	VG	F	VF	XF
ND(1814) Series 10	3.00	5.00	8.00	15.00	—

KM# 24s.10 MUN
Cast Copper or Bronze

Date	Good	VG	F	VF	XF
ND(1814) Series 10	—	—	—	—	50.00

KM# 25.1 MUN
Cast Copper or Bronze **Rev:** Circle at right, “I” (2) at left, series number at bottom

Date	Good	VG	F	VF	XF
ND(1814) Series 1	3.00	5.00	8.00	15.00	—

KM# 25s.1 MUN
Cast Copper or Bronze

Date	Good	VG	F	VF	XF
ND(1814) Series 1	—	—	—	—	50.00

KM# 25.2 MUN
Cast Copper or Bronze **Rev:** Circle at right, “I” (2) at left, series number at bottom

Date	Good	VG	F	VF	XF
ND(1814) Series 2	3.00	5.00	8.00	15.00	—

KM# 25s.2 MUN
Cast Copper or Bronze

Date	Good	VG	F	VF	XF
ND(1814) Series 2	—	—	—	—	50.00

KM# 25.3 MUN
Cast Copper or Bronze **Rev:** Circle at right, “I” (2) at left, series number at bottom

Date	Good	VG	F	VF	XF
ND(1814) Series 3	3.00	5.00	8.00	15.00	—

KM# 25s.3 MUN
Cast Copper or Bronze

Date	Good	VG	F	VF	XF
ND(1814) Series 3	—	—	—	—	50.00

KM# 25.4 MUN
Cast Copper or Bronze **Rev:** Circle at right, “I” (2) at left, series number at bottom

Date	Good	VG	F	VF	XF
ND(1814) Series 4	3.00	5.00	8.00	15.00	—

KM# 25s.4 MUN
Cast Copper or Bronze

Date	Good	VG	F	VF	XF
ND(1814) Series 4	—	—	—	—	50.00

KM# 25.5 MUN
Cast Copper or Bronze **Rev:** Circle at right, “I” (2) at left, series number at bottom

Date	Good	VG	F	VF	XF
ND(1814) Series 5	3.00	5.00	8.00	15.00	—

KM# 25s.5 MUN
Cast Copper or Bronze

Date	Good	VG	F	VF	XF
ND(1814) Series 5	—	—	—	—	50.00

KM# 25.6 MUN
Cast Copper or Bronze **Rev:** Circle at right, “I” (2) at left, series number at bottom

Date	Good	VG	F	VF	XF
ND(1814) Series 6	3.00	5.00	8.00	15.00	—

KM# 25s.6 MUN
Cast Copper or Bronze

Date	Good	VG	F	VF	XF
ND(1814) Series 6	—	—	—	—	50.00

KM# 25.7 MUN
Cast Copper or Bronze **Rev:** Circle at right, “I” (2) at left, series number at bottom

Date	Good	VG	F	VF	XF
ND(1814) Series 7	3.00	5.00	8.00	15.00	—

KM# 25s.7 MUN
Cast Copper or Bronze

Date	Good	VG	F	VF	XF
ND(1814) Series 7	—	—	—	—	50.00

KM# 25.8 MUN
Cast Copper or Bronze **Rev:** Circle at right, “I” (2) at left, series number at bottom

Date	Good	VG	F	VF	XF
ND(1814) Series 8	3.00	5.00	8.00	15.00	—

KM# 25s.8 MUN
Cast Copper or Bronze

Date	Good	VG	F	VF	XF
ND(1814) Series 8	—	—	—	—	50.00

KM# 25.9 MUN
Cast Copper or Bronze **Rev:** Circle at right, “I” (2) at left, series number at bottom

Date	Good	VG	F	VF	XF
ND(1814) Series 9	3.00	5.00	8.00	15.00	—

KM# 25s.9 MUN
Cast Copper or Bronze

Date	Good	VG	F	VF	XF
ND(1814) Series 9	—	—	—	—	50.00

KM# 25.10 MUN
Cast Copper or Bronze **Rev:** Circle at right, “I” (2) at left, series number at bottom

Date	Good	VG	F	VF	XF
ND(1814) Series 10	3.00	5.00	8.00	15.00	—

KM# 25s.10 MUN
Cast Copper or Bronze

Date	Good	VG	F	VF	XF
ND(1814) Series 10	—	—	—	—	50.00

KM# 26.1 MUN
Cast Copper or Bronze, 25 mm. **Rev:** Circle at left, “I” (2) at right, series number at bottom

Date	Good	VG	F	VF	XF
ND(1814) Series 1	3.00	5.00	8.00	15.00	—

KM# 26s.1 MUN
Cast Copper or Bronze

Date	Good	VG	F	VF	XF
ND(1814) Series 1	—	—	—	—	50.00

KM# 26.2 MUN
Cast Copper or Bronze **Rev:** Circle at left, “I” (2) at right, series number at bottom

Date	Good	VG	F	VF	XF
ND(1814) Series 2	3.00	5.00	8.00	15.00	—

KM# 26s.2 MUN
Cast Copper or Bronze

Date	Good	VG	F	VF	XF
ND(1814) Series 2	—	—	—	—	50.00

KM# 26.3 MUN
Cast Copper or Bronze **Rev:** Circle at left, “I” (2) at right, series number at bottom

Date	Good	VG	F	VF	XF
ND(1814) Series 3	3.00	5.00	8.00	15.00	—

KM# 26s.3 MUN
Cast Copper or Bronze

Date	Good	VG	F	VF	XF
ND(1814) Series 3	—	—	—	—	50.00

KM# 26.4 MUN
Cast Copper or Bronze **Rev:** Circle at left, “I” (2) at right, series number at bottom

Date	Good	VG	F	VF	XF
ND(1814) Series 4	3.00	5.00	8.00	15.00	—

KM# 26s.4 MUN
Cast Copper or Bronze

Date	Good	VG	F	VF	XF
ND(1814) Series 4	—	—	—	—	50.00

KM# 26.5 MUN
Cast Copper or Bronze **Rev:** Circle at left, “I” (2) at right, series number at bottom

Date	Good	VG	F	VF	XF
ND(1814) Series 5	3.00	5.00	8.00	15.00	—

KM# 26s.5 MUN
Cast Copper or Bronze

Date	Good	VG	F	VF	XF
ND(1814) Series 5	—	—	—	—	50.00

KM# 26.6 MUN
Cast Copper or Bronze **Rev:** Circle at left, “I” (2) at right, series number at bottom

Date	Good	VG	F	VF	XF
ND(1814) Series 6	3.00	5.00	8.00	15.00	—

KM# 26s.6 MUN
Cast Copper or Bronze

Date	Good	VG	F	VF	XF
ND(1814) Series 6	—	—	—	—	50.00

KM# 26.7 MUN
Cast Copper or Bronze **Rev:** Circle at left, “I” (2) at right, series number at bottom

Date	Good	VG	F	VF	XF
ND(1814) Series 7	3.00	5.00	8.00	15.00	—

KM# 26s.7 MUN
Cast Copper or Bronze

Date	Good	VG	F	VF	XF
ND(1814) Series 7	—	—	—	—	50.00

KM# 26.8 MUN
Cast Copper or Bronze **Rev:** Circle at left, “I” (2) at right, series number at bottom

Date	Good	VG	F	VF	XF
ND(1814) Series 8	3.00	5.00	8.00	15.00	—

KM# 26s.8 MUN
Cast Copper or Bronze

Date	Good	VG	F	VF	XF
ND(1814) Series 8	—	—	—	—	50.00

KM# 26.9 MUN
Cast Copper or Bronze **Rev:** Circle at left, “I” (2) at right, series number at bottom

Date	Good	VG	F	VF	XF
ND(1814) Series 9	3.00	5.00	8.00	15.00	—

KM# 26s.9 MUN
Cast Copper or Bronze

Date	Good	VG	F	VF	XF
ND(1814) Series 9	—	—	—	—	50.00

KM# 26.10 MUN
Cast Copper or Bronze **Rev:** Circle at left, “I” (2) at right, series number at bottom

Date	Good	VG	F	VF	XF
ND(1814) Series 10	3.00	5.00	8.00	15.00	—

KM# 26s.10 MUN
Cast Copper or Bronze

Date	Good	VG	F	VF	XF
ND(1814) Series 10	—	—	—	—	50.00

KM# 34.1 MUN
Cast Copper or Bronze **Rev:** Crescent at right, “II” (1) at left, series number at bottom

Date	Good	VG	F	VF	XF
ND(1814) Series 1	4.00	6.00	9.00	15.00	—

KM# 34s.1 MUN
Cast Copper or Bronze

Date	Good	VG	F	VF	XF
ND(1814) Series 1	—	—	—	—	50.00

KM# 34.2 MUN
Cast Copper or Bronze **Rev:** Crescent at right, “II” (1) at left, series number at bottom

Date	Good	VG	F	VF	XF
ND(1814) Series 2	4.00	6.00	9.00	15.00	—

KM# 34s.2 MUN
Cast Copper or Bronze

Date	Good	VG	F	VF	XF
ND(1814) Series 2	—	—	—	—	50.00

KM# 34.3 MUN
Cast Copper or Bronze **Rev:** Crescent at right, “II” (1) at left, series number at bottom

Date	Good	VG	F	VF	XF
ND(1814) Series 3	4.00	6.00	9.00	15.00	—

KM# 34s.3 MUN
Cast Copper or Bronze

Date	Good	VG	F	VF	XF
ND(1814) Series 3	—	—	—	—	50.00

KM# 34.4 MUN
Cast Copper or Bronze **Rev:** Crescent at right, “II” (1) at left, series number at bottom

Date	Good	VG	F	VF	XF
ND(1814) Series 4	4.00	6.00	9.00	15.00	—

KM# 34s.4 MUN
Cast Copper or Bronze

Date	Good	VG	F	VF	XF
ND(1814) Series 4	—	—	—	—	50.00

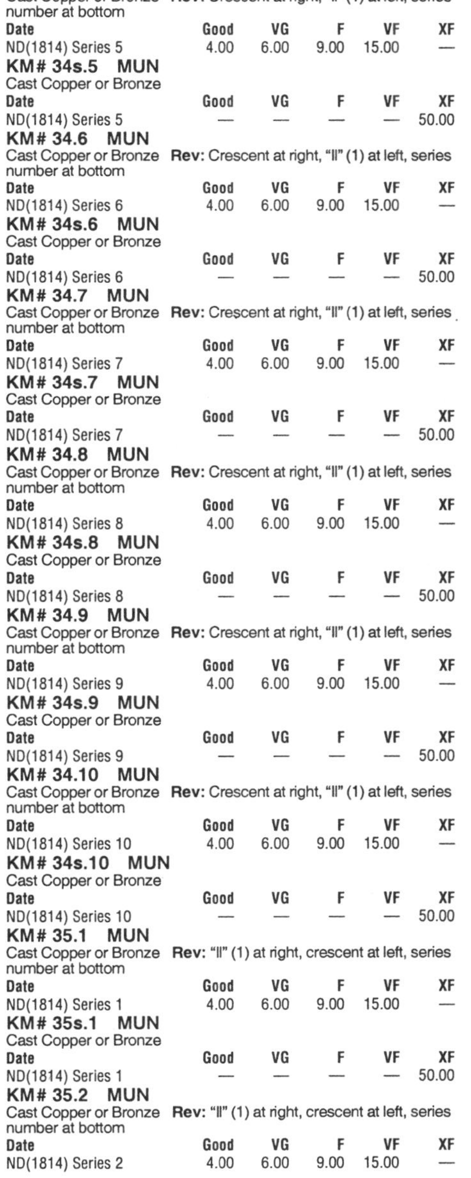

KM# 34.5 MUN
Cast Copper or Bronze **Rev:** Crescent at right, “II” (1) at left, series number at bottom

Date	Good	VG	F	VF	XF
ND(1814) Series 5	4.00	6.00	9.00	15.00	—

KM# 34s.5 MUN
Cast Copper or Bronze

Date	Good	VG	F	VF	XF
ND(1814) Series 5	—	—	—	—	50.00

KM# 34.6 MUN
Cast Copper or Bronze **Rev:** Crescent at right, “II” (1) at left, series number at bottom

Date	Good	VG	F	VF	XF
ND(1814) Series 6	4.00	6.00	9.00	15.00	—

KM# 34s.6 MUN
Cast Copper or Bronze

Date	Good	VG	F	VF	XF
ND(1814) Series 6	—	—	—	—	50.00

KM# 34.7 MUN
Cast Copper or Bronze **Rev:** Crescent at right, “II” (1) at left, series number at bottom

Date	Good	VG	F	VF	XF
ND(1814) Series 7	4.00	6.00	9.00	15.00	—

KM# 34s.7 MUN
Cast Copper or Bronze

Date	Good	VG	F	VF	XF
ND(1814) Series 7	—	—	—	—	50.00

KM# 34.8 MUN
Cast Copper or Bronze **Rev:** Crescent at right, “II” (1) at left, series number at bottom

Date	Good	VG	F	VF	XF
ND(1814) Series 8	4.00	6.00	9.00	15.00	—

KM# 34s.8 MUN
Cast Copper or Bronze

Date	Good	VG	F	VF	XF
ND(1814) Series 8	—	—	—	—	50.00

KM# 34.9 MUN
Cast Copper or Bronze **Rev:** Crescent at right, “II” (1) at left, series number at bottom

Date	Good	VG	F	VF	XF
ND(1814) Series 9	4.00	6.00	9.00	15.00	—

KM# 34s.9 MUN
Cast Copper or Bronze

Date	Good	VG	F	VF	XF
ND(1814) Series 9	—	—	—	—	50.00

KM# 34.10 MUN
Cast Copper or Bronze **Rev:** Crescent at right, “II” (1) at left, series number at bottom

Date	Good	VG	F	VF	XF
ND(1814) Series 10	4.00	6.00	9.00	15.00	—

KM# 34s.10 MUN
Cast Copper or Bronze

Date	Good	VG	F	VF	XF
ND(1814) Series 10	—	—	—	—	50.00

KM# 35.1 MUN
Cast Copper or Bronze **Rev:** “II” (1) at right, crescent at left, series number at bottom

Date	Good	VG	F	VF	XF
ND(1814) Series 1	4.00	6.00	9.00	15.00	—

KM# 35s.1 MUN
Cast Copper or Bronze

Date	Good	VG	F	VF	XF
ND(1814) Series 1	—	—	—	—	50.00

KM# 35.2 MUN
Cast Copper or Bronze **Rev:** “II” (1) at right, crescent at left, series number at bottom

Date	Good	VG	F	VF	XF
ND(1814) Series 2	4.00	6.00	9.00	15.00	—

KM# 35s.2 MUN
Cast Copper or Bronze

Date	Good	VG	F	VF	XF
ND(1814) Series 2	—	—	—	—	50.00

KM# 35.3 MUN
Cast Copper or Bronze **Rev:** "II" (1) at right, crescent at left, series number at bottom

Date	Good	VG	F	VF	XF
ND(1814) Series 3	4.00	6.00	9.00	15.00	—

KM# 35s.3 MUN
Cast Copper or Bronze

Date	Good	VG	F	VF	XF
ND(1814) Series 3	—	—	—	—	50.00

KM# 35.4 MUN
Cast Copper or Bronze **Rev:** "II" (1) at right, crescent at left, series number at bottom

Date	Good	VG	F	VF	XF
ND(1814) Series 4	4.00	6.00	9.00	15.00	—

KM# 35s.4 MUN
Cast Copper or Bronze

Date	Good	VG	F	VF	XF
ND(1814) Series 4	—	—	—	—	50.00

KM# 35.5 MUN
Cast Copper or Bronze **Rev:** "II" (1) at right, crescent at left, series number at bottom

Date	Good	VG	F	VF	XF
ND(1814) Series 5	4.00	6.00	9.00	15.00	—

KM# 35s.5 MUN
Cast Copper or Bronze

Date	Good	VG	F	VF	XF
ND(1814) Series 5	—	—	—	—	50.00

KM# 35.6 MUN
Cast Copper or Bronze **Rev:** "II" (1) at right, crescent at left, series number at bottom

Date	Good	VG	F	VF	XF
ND(1814) Series 6	4.00	6.00	9.00	15.00	—

KM# 35s.6 MUN
Cast Copper or Bronze

Date	Good	VG	F	VF	XF
ND(1814) Series 6	—	—	—	—	50.00

KM# 35.7 MUN
Cast Copper or Bronze **Rev:** "II" (1) at right, crescent at left, series number at bottom

Date	Good	VG	F	VF	XF
ND(1814) Series 7	4.00	6.00	9.00	15.00	—

KM# 35s.7 MUN
Cast Copper or Bronze

Date	Good	VG	F	VF	XF
ND(1814) Series 7	—	—	—	—	50.00

KM# 35.8 MUN
Cast Copper or Bronze **Rev:** "II" (1) at right, crescent at left, series number at bottom

Date	Good	VG	F	VF	XF
ND(1814) Series 8	4.00	6.00	9.00	15.00	—

KM# 35s.8 MUN
Cast Copper or Bronze

Date	Good	VG	F	VF	XF
ND(1814) Series 8	—	—	—	—	50.00

KM# 35.9 MUN
Cast Copper or Bronze **Rev:** "II" (1) at right, crescent at left, series number at bottom

Date	Good	VG	F	VF	XF
ND(1814) Series 9	4.00	6.00	9.00	15.00	—

KM# 35s.9 MUN
Cast Copper or Bronze

Date	Good	VG	F	VF	XF
ND(1814) Series 9	—	—	—	—	50.00

KM# 35.10 MUN
Cast Copper or Bronze **Rev:** "II" (1) at right, crescent at left, series number at bottom

Date	Good	VG	F	VF	XF
ND(1814) Series 10	4.00	6.00	9.00	15.00	—

KM# 35s.10 MUN
Cast Copper or Bronze

Date	Good	VG	F	VF	XF
ND(1814) Series 10	—	—	—	—	50.00

KM# 45 MUN
Cast Copper or Bronze, 25 mm. **Rev:** "U" at bottom

Date	Good	VG	F	VF	XF
ND(1814)	3.00	5.00	8.00	12.00	—

KM# 45s MUN
Cast Copper or Bronze

Date	Good	VG	F	VF	XF
ND(1814)	—	—	—	—	50.00

KM# 46.1 MUN
Cast Copper or Bronze **Rev:** 19mm inner circle, "U" at bottom, series number at right

Date	Good	VG	F	VF	XF
ND(1814) Series 1	3.00	5.00	8.00	12.00	—

KM# 46s.1 MUN
Cast Copper or Bronze

Date	Good	VG	F	VF	XF
ND(1814) Series 1	—	—	—	—	50.00

KM# 46.2 MUN
Cast Copper or Bronze **Rev:** 19mm inner circle, "U" at bottom, series number at right

Date	Good	VG	F	VF	XF
ND(1814) Series 2	3.00	5.00	8.00	12.00	—

KM# 46s.2 MUN
Cast Copper or Bronze

Date	Good	VG	F	VF	XF
ND(1814) Series 2	—	—	—	—	50.00

KM# 46.3 MUN
Cast Copper or Bronze **Rev:** 19mm inner circle, "U" at bottom, series number at right

Date	Good	VG	F	VF	XF
ND(1814) Series 3	3.00	5.00	8.00	12.00	—

KM# 46s.3 MUN
Cast Copper or Bronze

Date	Good	VG	F	VF	XF
ND(1814) Series 3	—	—	—	—	50.00

KM# 46.4 MUN
Cast Copper or Bronze **Rev:** 19mm inner circle, "U" at bottom, series number at right

Date	Good	VG	F	VF	XF
ND(1814) Series 4	3.00	5.00	8.00	12.00	—

KM# 46s.4 MUN
Cast Copper or Bronze

Date	Good	VG	F	VF	XF
ND(1814) Series 4	—	—	—	—	50.00

KM# 46.5 MUN
Cast Copper or Bronze **Rev:** 19mm inner circle, "U" at bottom, series number at right

Date	Good	VG	F	VF	XF
ND(1814) Series 5	3.00	5.00	8.00	12.00	—

KM# 46s.5 MUN
Cast Copper or Bronze

Date	Good	VG	F	VF	XF
ND(1814) Series 5	—	—	—	—	50.00

KM# 46.6 MUN
Cast Copper or Bronze **Rev:** 19mm inner circle, "U" at bottom, series number at right

Date	Good	VG	F	VF	XF
ND(1814) Series 6	3.00	5.00	8.00	12.00	—

KM# 46s.6 MUN
Cast Copper or Bronze

Date	Good	VG	F	VF	XF
ND(1814) Series 6	—	—	—	—	50.00

KM# 46.7 MUN
Cast Copper or Bronze **Rev:** 19mm inner circle, "U" at bottom, series number at right

Date	Good	VG	F	VF	XF
ND(1814) Series 7	3.00	5.00	8.00	12.00	—

KM# 46s.7 MUN
Cast Copper or Bronze

Date	Good	VG	F	VF	XF
ND(1814) Series 7	—	—	—	—	50.00

KM# 46.8 MUN
Cast Copper or Bronze **Rev:** 19mm inner circle, "U" at bottom, series number at right

Date	Good	VG	F	VF	XF
ND(1814) Series 8	3.00	5.00	8.00	12.00	—

KM# 46s.8 MUN
Cast Copper or Bronze

Date	Good	VG	F	VF	XF
ND(1814) Series 8	—	—	—	—	50.00

KM# 46.9 MUN
Cast Copper or Bronze **Rev:** 19mm inner circle, "U" at bottom, series number at right

Date	Good	VG	F	VF	XF
ND(1814) Series 9	3.00	5.00	8.00	12.00	—

KM# 46s.9 MUN
Cast Copper or Bronze

Date	Good	VG	F	VF	XF
ND(1814) Series 9	—	—	—	—	50.00

KM# 46.10 MUN
Cast Copper or Bronze **Rev:** 19mm inner circle, "U" at bottom, series number at right

Date	Good	VG	F	VF	XF
ND(1814) Series 10	3.00	5.00	8.00	12.00	—

KM# 46s.10 MUN
Cast Copper or Bronze

Date	Good	VG	F	VF	XF
ND(1814) Series 10	—	—	—	—	50.00

KM# 48.1 MUN
Cast Copper or Bronze **Rev:** "U" at bottom, series number at left **Note:** Size varies 23-26mm.

Date	Good	VG	F	VF	XF
ND(1814) Series 1	3.00	5.00	8.00	12.00	—

KM# 48s.1 MUN
Cast Copper or Bronze

Date	Good	VG	F	VF	XF
ND(1814) Series 1	—	—	—	—	50.00

KM# A48.1 MUN
Cast Copper or Bronze, 25 mm. **Obv:** Smaller "Po" at left

Date	Good	VG	F	VF	XF
ND(1814) Series 1	3.00	5.00	8.00	12.00	—

KM# 48.2 MUN
Cast Copper or Bronze **Rev:** "U" at bottom, series number at left **Note:** Size varies 23-26mm.

Date	Good	VG	F	VF	XF
ND(1814) Series 2	3.00	5.00	8.00	12.00	—

KM# 48s.2 MUN
Cast Copper or Bronze

Date	Good	VG	F	VF	XF
ND(1814) Series 2	—	—	—	—	50.00

KM# A48.2 MUN
Cast Copper or Bronze **Obv:** Smaller "Po" at left

Date	Good	VG	F	VF	XF
ND(1814) Series 2	3.00	5.00	8.00	12.00	—

KM# 48.3 MUN
Cast Copper or Bronze **Rev:** "U" at bottom, series number at left **Note:** Size varies 23-26mm.

Date	Good	VG	F	VF	XF
ND(1814) Series 3	3.00	5.00	8.00	12.00	—

KM# 48s.3 MUN
Cast Copper or Bronze

Date	Good	VG	F	VF	XF
ND(1814) Series 3	—	—	—	—	50.00

KM# A48.3 MUN
Cast Copper or Bronze **Obv:** Smaller "Po" at left

Date	Good	VG	F	VF	XF
ND(1814) Series 3	3.00	5.00	8.00	12.00	—

KM# 48.4 MUN
Cast Copper or Bronze **Rev:** "U" at bottom, series number at left **Note:** Size varies 23-26mm.

Date	Good	VG	F	VF	XF
ND(1814) Series 4	3.00	5.00	8.00	12.00	—

KM# 48s.4 MUN
Cast Copper or Bronze

Date	Good	VG	F	VF	XF
ND(1814) Series 4	—	—	—	—	50.00

KM# A48.4 MUN
Cast Copper or Bronze **Obv:** Smaller "Po" at left

Date	Good	VG	F	VF	XF
ND(1814) Series 4	3.00	5.00	8.00	12.00	—

KM# 48.5 MUN
Cast Copper or Bronze **Rev:** "U" at bottom, series number at left **Note:** Size varies 23-26mm.

Date	Good	VG	F	VF	XF
ND(1814) Series 5	3.00	5.00	8.00	12.00	—

KM# 48s.5 MUN
Cast Copper or Bronze

Date	Good	VG	F	VF	XF
ND(1814) Series 5	—	—	—	—	50.00

KM# A48.5 MUN
Cast Copper or Bronze **Obv:** Smaller "Po" at left

Date	Good	VG	F	VF	XF
ND(1814) Series 5	3.00	5.00	8.00	12.00	—

KM# 48.6 MUN
Cast Copper or Bronze **Rev:** "U" at bottom, series number at left **Note:** Size varies 23-26mm.

Date	Good	VG	F	VF	XF
ND(1814) Series 6	3.00	5.00	8.00	12.00	—

KM# 48s.6 MUN
Cast Copper or Bronze

Date	Good	VG	F	VF	XF
ND(1814) Series 6	—	—	—	—	50.00

KM# A48.6 MUN
Cast Copper or Bronze **Obv:** Smaller "Po" at left

Date	Good	VG	F	VF	XF
ND(1814) Series 6	3.00	5.00	8.00	12.00	—

KM# 48.7 MUN
Cast Copper or Bronze **Rev:** "U" at bottom, series number at left **Note:** Size varies 23-26mm.

Date	Good	VG	F	VF	XF
ND(1814) Series 7	3.00	5.00	8.00	12.00	—

KM# 48s.7 MUN
Cast Copper or Bronze

Date	Good	VG	F	VF	XF
ND(1814) Series 7	—	—	—	—	50.00

KM# A48.7 MUN
Cast Copper or Bronze **Obv:** Smaller "Po" at left

Date	Good	VG	F	VF	XF
ND(1814) Series 7	3.00	5.00	8.00	12.00	—

KM# 48.8 MUN
Cast Copper or Bronze **Rev:** "U" at bottom, series number at left **Note:** Size varies 23-26mm.

Date	Good	VG	F	VF	XF
ND(1814) Series 8	3.00	5.00	8.00	12.00	—

KM# 48s.8 MUN
Cast Copper or Bronze

Date	Good	VG	F	VF	XF
ND(1814) Series 8	—	—	—	—	50.00

KM# A48.8 MUN
Cast Copper or Bronze **Obv:** Smaller "Po" at left

Date	Good	VG	F	VF	XF
ND(1814) Series 8	3.00	5.00	8.00	12.00	—

KM# 48.9 MUN
Cast Copper or Bronze **Rev:** "U" at bottom, series number at left **Note:** Size varies 23-26mm.

Date	Good	VG	F	VF	XF
ND(1814) Series 9	3.00	5.00	8.00	12.00	—

KM# 48s.9 MUN
Cast Copper or Bronze

Date	Good	VG	F	VF	XF
ND(1814) Series 9	—	—	—	—	50.00

KM# A48.9 MUN
Cast Copper or Bronze **Obv:** Smaller "Po" at left

Date	Good	VG	F	VF	XF
ND(1814) Series 9	3.00	5.00	8.00	12.00	—

KM# 48.10 MUN
Cast Copper or Bronze **Rev:** "U" at bottom, series number at left **Note:** Size varies 23-26mm.

Date	Good	VG	F	VF	XF
ND(1814) Series 10	3.00	5.00	8.00	12.00	—

KM# 48s.10 MUN
Cast Copper or Bronze

Date	Good	VG	F	VF	XF
ND(1814) Series 10	—	—	—	—	50.00

KM# A48.10 MUN
Cast Copper or Bronze **Obv:** Smaller "Po" at left

Date	Good	VG	F	VF	XF
ND(1814) Series 10	3.00	5.00	8.00	12.00	—

KM# 70.1 MUN
Cast Copper or Bronze, 24 mm. **Rev:** "Ip" at bottom, series number at right

Date	Good	VG	F	VF	XF
ND(1814) Series 1	3.00	5.00	8.00	12.00	—

KM# 70a.1 MUN
Cast Copper or Bronze, 25 mm. **Rev:** "Ho" without stem

Date	Good	VG	F	VF	XF
ND(1814) Series 1	3.00	5.00	8.00	12.00	—

KM# 70s.1 MUN
Cast Copper or Bronze

Date	Good	VG	F	VF	XF
ND(1814) Series 1	—	—	—	—	50.00

KM# 70.2 MUN
Cast Copper or Bronze **Rev:** "Ip" at bottom, series number at right

Date	Good	VG	F	VF	XF
ND(1814) Series 2	3.00	5.00	8.00	12.00	—

KM# 70a.2 MUN
Cast Copper or Bronze **Rev:** "Ho" without stem

Date	Good	VG	F	VF	XF
ND(1814) Series 2	3.00	5.00	8.00	12.00	—

KM# 70s.2 MUN
Cast Copper or Bronze

Date	Good	VG	F	VF	XF
ND(1814) Series 2	—	—	—	—	50.00

KM# 70.3 MUN
Cast Copper or Bronze **Rev:** "Ip" at bottom, series number at right

Date	Good	VG	F	VF	XF
ND(1814) Series 3	3.00	5.00	8.00	12.00	—

KM# 70a.3 MUN
Cast Copper or Bronze **Rev:** "Ho" without stem

Date	Good	VG	F	VF	XF
ND(1814) Series 3	3.00	5.00	8.00	12.00	—

KM# 70s.3 MUN
Cast Copper or Bronze

Date	Good	VG	F	VF	XF
ND(1814) Series 3	—	—	—	—	50.00

KM# 70.4 MUN
Cast Copper or Bronze **Rev:** "Ip" at bottom, series number at right

Date	Good	VG	F	VF	XF
ND(1814) Series 4	3.00	5.00	8.00	12.00	—

KM# 70a.4 MUN
Cast Copper or Bronze **Rev:** "Ho" without stem

Date	Good	VG	F	VF	XF
ND(1814) Series 4	3.00	5.00	8.00	12.00	—

KM# 70s.4 MUN
Cast Copper or Bronze

Date	Good	VG	F	VF	XF
ND(1814) Series 4	—	—	—	—	50.00

KM# 70.5 MUN
Cast Copper or Bronze **Rev:** "Ip" at bottom, series number at right

Date	Good	VG	F	VF	XF
ND(1814) Series 5	3.00	5.00	8.00	12.00	—

KM# 70a.5 MUN
Cast Copper or Bronze **Rev:** "Ho" without stem

Date	Good	VG	F	VF	XF
ND(1814) Series 5	3.00	5.00	8.00	12.00	—

KM# 70s.5 MUN
Cast Copper or Bronze

Date	Good	VG	F	VF	XF
ND(1814) Series 5	—	—	—	—	50.00

KM# 70.6 MUN
Cast Copper or Bronze **Rev:** "Ip" at bottom, series number at right

Date	Good	VG	F	VF	XF
ND(1814) Series 6	3.00	5.00	8.00	12.00	—

KM# 70a.6 MUN
Cast Copper or Bronze **Rev:** "Ho" without stem

Date	Good	VG	F	VF	XF
ND(1814) Series 6	3.00	5.00	8.00	12.00	—

KM# 70s.6 MUN
Cast Copper or Bronze

Date	Good	VG	F	VF	XF
ND(1814) Series 6	—	—	—	—	50.00

KM# 70.7 MUN
Cast Copper or Bronze **Rev:** "Ip" at bottom, series number at right

Date	Good	VG	F	VF	XF
ND(1814) Series 7	3.00	5.00	8.00	12.00	—

KM# 70a.7 MUN
Cast Copper or Bronze **Rev:** "Ho" without stem

Date	Good	VG	F	VF	XF
ND(1814) Series 7	3.00	5.00	8.00	12.00	—

KM# 70s.7 MUN
Cast Copper or Bronze

Date	Good	VG	F	VF	XF
ND(1814) Series 7	—	—	—	—	50.00

KM# 70.8 MUN
Cast Copper or Bronze **Rev:** "Ip" at bottom, series number at right

Date	Good	VG	F	VF	XF
ND(1814) Series 8	3.00	5.00	8.00	12.00	—

KM# 70a.8 MUN
Cast Copper or Bronze **Rev:** "Ho" without stem

Date	Good	VG	F	VF	XF
ND(1814) Series 8	3.00	5.00	8.00	12.00	—

KM# 70s.8 MUN
Cast Copper or Bronze

Date	Good	VG	F	VF	XF
ND(1814) Series 8	—	—	—	—	50.00

KM# 70.9 MUN
Cast Copper or Bronze **Rev:** "Ip" at bottom, series number at right

Date	Good	VG	F	VF	XF
ND(1814) Series 9	3.00	5.00	8.00	12.00	—

KM# 70a.9 MUN
Cast Copper or Bronze **Rev:** "Ho" without stem

Date	Good	VG	F	VF	XF
ND(1814) Series 9	3.00	5.00	8.00	12.00	—

KM# 70s.9 MUN
Cast Copper or Bronze

Date	Good	VG	F	VF	XF
ND(1814) Series 9	—	—	—	—	50.00

KM# 70.10 MUN
Cast Copper or Bronze **Rev:** "Ip" at bottom, series number at right

Date	Good	VG	F	VF	XF
ND(1814) Series 10	3.00	5.00	8.00	12.00	—

KM# 70a.10 MUN
Cast Copper or Bronze **Rev:** "Ho" without stem

Date	Good	VG	F	VF	XF
ND(1814) Series 10	3.00	5.00	8.00	12.00	—

KM# 70s.10 MUN
Cast Copper or Bronze

Date	Good	VG	F	VF	XF
ND(1814) Series 10	—	—	—	—	50.00

KM# 15.1 MUN
Cast Copper or Bronze, 25 mm. **Rev:** "Sam" (3) at bottom, series number at right

Date	Good	VG	F	VF	XF
ND(1832) Series 1	8.00	14.00	20.00	40.00	—

KM# 15s.1 MUN
Cast Copper or Bronze

Date	Good	VG	F	VF	XF
ND(1832) Series 1	—	—	—	—	100

KM# 15.2 MUN
Cast Copper or Bronze, 25 mm. **Rev:** "Sam" (3) at bottom, series number at right

Date	Good	VG	F	VF	XF
ND(1832) Series 2	8.00	14.00	20.00	40.00	—

KM# 15s.2 MUN
Cast Copper or Bronze

Date	Good	VG	F	VF	XF
ND(1832) Series 2	—	—	—	—	100

KM# 15.3 MUN
Cast Copper or Bronze, 25 mm. **Rev:** "Sam" (3) at bottom, series number at right

Date	Good	VG	F	VF	XF
ND(1832) Series 3	8.00	14.00	20.00	40.00	—

KM# 15s.3 MUN
Cast Copper or Bronze

Date	Good	VG	F	VF	XF
ND(1832) Series 3	—	—	—	—	100

KM# 15.4 MUN
Cast Copper or Bronze, 25 mm. **Rev:** "Sam" (3) at bottom, series number at right

Date	Good	VG	F	VF	XF
ND(1832) Series 4	8.00	14.00	20.00	40.00	—

KM# 15s.4 MUN
Cast Copper or Bronze

Date	Good	VG	F	VF	XF
ND(1832) Series 4	—	—	—	—	100

KM# 15.5 MUN
Cast Copper or Bronze, 25 mm. **Rev:** "Sam" (3) at bottom, series number at right

Date	Good	VG	F	VF	XF
ND(1832) Series 5	8.00	14.00	20.00	40.00	—

KM# 15s.5 MUN
Cast Copper or Bronze

Date	Good	VG	F	VF	XF
ND(1832) Series 5	—	—	—	—	100

KM# 15.6 MUN
Cast Copper or Bronze, 25 mm. **Rev:** "Sam" (3) at bottom, series number at right

Date	Good	VG	F	VF	XF
ND(1832) Series 6	8.00	14.00	20.00	40.00	—

KM# 15s.6 MUN
Cast Copper or Bronze

Date	Good	VG	F	VF	XF
ND(1832) Series 6	—	—	—	—	100

KM# 15.7 MUN
Cast Copper or Bronze, 25 mm. **Rev:** "Sam" (3) at bottom, series number at right

Date	Good	VG	F	VF	XF
ND(1832) Series 7	8.00	14.00	20.00	40.00	—

KM# 15s.7 MUN
Cast Copper or Bronze

Date	Good	VG	F	VF	XF
ND(1832) Series 7	—	—	—	—	100

KM# 15.8 MUN
Cast Copper or Bronze, 25 mm. **Rev:** "Sam" (3) at bottom, series number at right

Date	Good	VG	F	VF	XF
ND(1832) Series 8	8.00	14.00	20.00	40.00	—

KM# 15s.8 MUN
Cast Copper or Bronze

Date	Good	VG	F	VF	XF
ND(1832) Series 8	—	—	—	—	100

KM# 15.9 MUN
Cast Copper or Bronze, 25 mm. **Rev:** "Sam" (3) at bottom, series number at right

Date	Good	VG	F	VF	XF
ND(1832) Series 9	8.00	14.00	20.00	40.00	—

KM# 15s.9 MUN
Cast Copper or Bronze

Date	Good	VG	F	VF	XF
ND(1832) Series 9	—	—	—	—	100

KM# 15.10 MUN
Cast Copper or Bronze, 25 mm. **Rev:** "Sam" (3) at bottom, series number at right

Date	Good	VG	F	VF	XF
ND(1832) Series 10	8.00	14.00	20.00	40.00	—

KM# 15s.10 MUN
Cast Copper or Bronze

Date	Good	VG	F	VF	XF
ND(1832) Series 10	—	—	—	—	100

KM# 15.11 MUN
Cast Copper or Bronze **Rev:** "Ho" without cross on top

Date	Good	VG	F	VF	XF
ND(1832) Series 1	8.00	14.00	20.00	40.00	—

KM# 15.14 MUN
Cast Copper or Bronze, 26 mm. **Rev:** Dot in lower right field

Date	Good	VG	F	VF	XF
ND(1832) Series 4	8.00	14.00	20.00	40.00	—

KM# 16.1 MUN
Cast Copper or Bronze, 24 mm. **Rev:** "Sam" (3) at bottom, series number at left

Date	Good	VG	F	VF	XF
ND(1832) Series 1	8.00	14.00	20.00	40.00	—

KM# 16s.1 MUN
Cast Copper or Bronze

Date	Good	VG	F	VF	XF
ND(1832) Series 1	—	—	—	—	100

KM# 16.2 MUN
Cast Copper or Bronze, 24 mm. **Rev:** "Sam" (3) at bottom, series number at left

Date	Good	VG	F	VF	XF
ND(1832) Series 2	8.00	14.00	20.00	40.00	—

KM# 16s.2 MUN
Cast Copper or Bronze

Date	Good	VG	F	VF	XF
ND(1832) Series 2	—	—	—	—	100

KM# 16.3 MUN
Cast Copper or Bronze, 24 mm. **Rev:** "Sam" (3) at bottom, series number at left

Date	Good	VG	F	VF	XF
ND(1832) Series 3	8.00	14.00	20.00	40.00	—

KM# 16s.3 MUN
Cast Copper or Bronze

Date	Good	VG	F	VF	XF
ND(1832) Series 3	—	—	—	—	100

KM# 16.4 MUN
Cast Copper or Bronze, 24 mm. **Rev:** "Sam" (3) at bottom, series number at left

Date	Good	VG	F	VF	XF
ND(1832) Series 4	8.00	14.00	20.00	40.00	—

KM# 16s.4 MUN
Cast Copper or Bronze

Date	Good	VG	F	VF	XF
ND(1832) Series 4	—	—	—	—	100

KM# 16.5 MUN
Cast Copper or Bronze, 24 mm. **Rev:** "Sam" (3) at bottom, series number at left

Date	Good	VG	F	VF	XF
ND(1832) Series 5	8.00	14.00	20.00	40.00	—

KM# 16s.5 MUN
Cast Copper or Bronze

Date	Good	VG	F	VF	XF
ND(1832) Series 5	—	—	—	—	100

KM# 16.6 MUN

Cast Copper or Bronze, 24 mm. **Rev:** "Sam" (3) at bottom, series number at left

Date	Good	VG	F	VF	XF
ND(1832) Series 6	8.00	14.00	20.00	40.00	—

KM# 16s.6 MUN

Cast Copper or Bronze

Date	Good	VG	F	VF	XF
ND(1832) Series 6	—	—	—	—	100

KM# 16.7 MUN

Cast Copper or Bronze, 24 mm. **Rev:** "Sam" (3) at bottom, series number at left

Date	Good	VG	F	VF	XF
ND(1832) Series 7	8.00	14.00	20.00	40.00	—

KM# 16s.7 MUN

Cast Copper or Bronze

Date	Good	VG	F	VF	XF
ND(1832) Series 7	—	—	—	—	100

KM# 16.8 MUN

Cast Copper or Bronze, 24 mm. **Rev:** "Sam" (3) at bottom, series number at left

Date	Good	VG	F	VF	XF
ND(1832) Series 8	8.00	14.00	20.00	40.00	—

KM# 16s.8 MUN

Cast Copper or Bronze

Date	Good	VG	F	VF	XF
ND(1832) Series 8	—	—	—	—	100

KM# 16.9 MUN

Cast Copper or Bronze, 24 mm. **Rev:** "Sam" (3) at bottom, series number at left

Date	Good	VG	F	VF	XF
ND(1832) Series 9	8.00	14.00	20.00	40.00	—

KM# 16s.9 MUN

Cast Copper or Bronze

Date	Good	VG	F	VF	XF
ND(1832) Series 9	—	—	—	—	100

KM# 16.10 MUN

Cast Copper or Bronze, 24 mm. **Rev:** "Sam" (3) at bottom, series number at left

Date	Good	VG	F	VF	XF
ND(1832) Series 10	8.00	14.00	20.00	40.00	—

KM# 16s.10 MUN

Cast Copper or Bronze

Date	Good	VG	F	VF	XF
ND(1832) Series 10	—	—	—	—	100

KM# 16.14 MUN

Cast Copper or Bronze **Rev:** "Ho" without cross on top

Date	Good	VG	F	VF	XF
ND(1832) Series 4	8.00	14.00	20.00	40.00	—

KM# 18.1 MUN

Cast Copper or Bronze **Rev:** "O" (5) at bottom, series number at left

Date	Good	VG	F	VF	XF
ND(1832) Series 1	1.50	2.50	3.50	5.00	—

KM# 18s MUN

Cast Copper or Bronze

Date	Good	VG	F	VF	XF
ND(1832) Series 1	—	—	—	—	30.00

KM# 37.1 MUN

Cast Copper or Bronze, 24 mm. **Rev:** "Ch'on" at bottom, series number at right **Note:** Small characters.

Date	Good	VG	F	VF	XF
ND(1832) Series 1	3.00	6.00	10.00	15.00	—

KM# 37s.1 MUN

Cast Copper or Bronze

Date	Good	VG	F	VF	XF
ND(1832) Series 1	—	—	—	—	50.00

KM# 37.2 MUN

Cast Copper or Bronze **Rev:** "Ch'on" at bottom, series number at right **Note:** Small characters.

Date	Good	VG	F	VF	XF
ND(1832) Series 2	3.00	6.00	10.00	15.00	—

KM# 37s.2 MUN

Cast Copper or Bronze

Date	Good	VG	F	VF	XF
ND(1832) Series 2	—	—	—	—	50.00

KM# 37.3 MUN

Cast Copper or Bronze **Rev:** "Ch'on" at bottom, series number at right **Note:** Small characters.

Date	Good	VG	F	VF	XF
ND(1832) Series 3	3.00	6.00	10.00	15.00	—

KM# 37s.3 MUN

Cast Copper or Bronze

Date	Good	VG	F	VF	XF
ND(1832) Series 3	—	—	—	—	50.00

KM# 37.4 MUN

Cast Copper or Bronze **Rev:** "Ch'on" at bottom, series number at right **Note:** Small characters.

Date	Good	VG	F	VF	XF
ND(1832) Series 4	3.00	6.00	10.00	15.00	—

KM# 37s.4 MUN

Cast Copper or Bronze

Date	Good	VG	F	VF	XF
ND(1832) Series 4	—	—	—	—	50.00

KM# 37.5 MUN

Cast Copper or Bronze **Rev:** "Ch'on" at bottom, series number at right **Note:** Small characters.

Date	Good	VG	F	VF	XF
ND(1832) Series 5	3.00	6.00	10.00	15.00	—

KM# 37s.5 MUN

Cast Copper or Bronze

Date	Good	VG	F	VF	XF
ND(1832) Series 5	—	—	—	—	50.00

KM# 37.6 MUN

Cast Copper or Bronze **Rev:** "Ch'on" at bottom, series number at right **Note:** Small characters.

Date	Good	VG	F	VF	XF
ND(1832) Series 6	3.00	6.00	10.00	15.00	—

KM# 37s.6 MUN

Cast Copper or Bronze

Date	Good	VG	F	VF	XF
ND(1832) Series 6	—	—	—	—	50.00

KM# 37.7 MUN

Cast Copper or Bronze **Rev:** "Ch'on" at bottom, series number at right **Note:** Small characters.

Date	Good	VG	F	VF	XF
ND(1832) Series 7	3.00	6.00	10.00	15.00	—

KM# 37s.7 MUN

Cast Copper or Bronze

Date	Good	VG	F	VF	XF
ND(1832) Series 7	—	—	—	—	50.00

KM# 37.8 MUN

Cast Copper or Bronze **Rev:** "Ch'on" at bottom, series number at right **Note:** Small characters.

Date	Good	VG	F	VF	XF
ND(1832) Series 8	3.00	6.00	10.00	15.00	—

KM# 37s.8 MUN

Cast Copper or Bronze

Date	Good	VG	F	VF	XF
ND(1832) Series 8	—	—	—	—	50.00

KM# 37.9 MUN

Cast Copper or Bronze **Rev:** "Ch'on" at bottom, series number at right **Note:** Small characters.

Date	Good	VG	F	VF	XF
ND(1832) Series 9	3.00	6.00	10.00	15.00	—

KM# 37s.9 MUN

Cast Copper or Bronze

Date	Good	VG	F	VF	XF
ND(1832) Series 9	—	—	—	—	50.00

KM# 37.10 MUN

Cast Copper or Bronze **Rev:** "Ch'on" at bottom, series number at right **Note:** Small characters.

Date	Good	VG	F	VF	XF
ND(1832) Series 10	3.00	6.00	10.00	15.00	—

KM# 37s.10 MUN

Cast Copper or Bronze

Date	Good	VG	F	VF	XF
ND(1832) Series 10	—	—	—	—	50.00

KM# 37.11 MUN

Cast Copper or Bronze **Rev:** "Ch'on" at bottom, series number at right **Note:** Small characters.

Date	Good	VG	F	VF	XF
ND(1832) Series 11	3.00	6.00	10.00	15.00	—

KM# 37s.11 MUN

Cast Copper or Bronze

Date	Good	VG	F	VF	XF
ND(1832) Series 11	—	—	—	—	50.00

KM# 39.1 MUN

Cast Copper or Bronze, 24 mm. **Rev:** "Ch'on" at bottom, series number at left **Note:** Small characters. Size varies 24mm.

Date	Good	VG	F	VF	XF
ND(1832) Series 1	3.00	6.00	10.00	15.00	—

KM# 39s.1 MUN

Cast Copper or Bronze

Date	Good	VG	F	VF	XF
ND(1832) Series 1	—	—	—	—	50.00

KM# 39.2 MUN

Cast Copper or Bronze **Rev:** "Ch'on" at bottom, series number at left **Note:** Small characters. Size varies 24mm.

Date	Good	VG	F	VF	XF
ND(1832) Series 2	3.00	6.00	10.00	15.00	—

KM# 39s.2 MUN

Cast Copper or Bronze

Date	Good	VG	F	VF	XF
ND(1832) Series 2	—	—	—	—	50.00

KM# 39.3 MUN

Cast Copper or Bronze **Rev:** "Ch'on" at bottom, series number at left **Note:** Small characters. Size varies 24mm.

Date	Good	VG	F	VF	XF
ND(1832) Series 3	3.00	6.00	10.00	15.00	—

KM# 39s.3 MUN

Cast Copper or Bronze

Date	Good	VG	F	VF	XF
ND(1832) Series 3	—	—	—	—	50.00

KM# 39.4 MUN

Cast Copper or Bronze **Rev:** "Ch'on" at bottom, series number at left **Note:** Small characters. Size varies 24mm.

Date	Good	VG	F	VF	XF
ND(1832) Series 4	3.00	6.00	10.00	15.00	—

KM# 39s.4 MUN

Cast Copper or Bronze

Date	Good	VG	F	VF	XF
ND(1832) Series 4	—	—	—	—	50.00

KM# 39.5 MUN

Cast Copper or Bronze **Rev:** "Ch'on" at bottom, series number at left **Note:** Small characters. Size varies 24mm.

Date	Good	VG	F	VF	XF
ND(1832) Series 5	3.00	6.00	10.00	15.00	—

KM# 39s.5 MUN

Cast Copper or Bronze

Date	Good	VG	F	VF	XF
ND(1832) Series 5	—	—	—	—	50.00

KM# 39.6 MUN

Cast Copper or Bronze **Rev:** "Ch'on" at bottom, series number at left **Note:** Small characters. Size varies 24mm.

Date	Good	VG	F	VF	XF
ND(1832) Series 6	3.00	6.00	10.00	15.00	—

KM# 39s.6 MUN

Cast Copper or Bronze

Date	Good	VG	F	VF	XF
ND(1832) Series 6	—	—	—	—	50.00

KM# 39.7 MUN

Cast Copper or Bronze **Rev:** "Ch'on" at bottom, series number at left **Note:** Small characters. Size varies 24mm.

Date	Good	VG	F	VF	XF
ND(1832) Series 7	3.00	6.00	10.00	15.00	—

KM# 39s.7 MUN

Cast Copper or Bronze

Date	Good	VG	F	VF	XF
ND(1832) Series 7	—	—	—	—	50.00

KM# 39.8 MUN

Cast Copper or Bronze **Rev:** "Ch'on" at bottom, series number at left **Note:** Small characters. Size varies 24mm.

Date	Good	VG	F	VF	XF
ND(1832) Series 8	3.00	6.00	10.00	15.00	—

KM# 39s.8 MUN

Cast Copper or Bronze

Date	Good	VG	F	VF	XF
ND(1832) Series 8	—	—	—	—	50.00

KM# 39.9 MUN

Cast Copper or Bronze **Rev:** "Ch'on" at bottom, series number at left **Note:** Small characters. Size varies 24mm.

Date	Good	VG	F	VF	XF
ND(1832) Series 9	3.00	6.00	10.00	15.00	—

KM# 39s.9 MUN

Cast Copper or Bronze

Date	Good	VG	F	VF	XF
ND(1832) Series 9	—	—	—	—	50.00

KM# 39.10 MUN

Cast Copper or Bronze **Rev:** "Ch'on" at bottom, series number at left **Note:** Small characters. Size varies 24mm.

Date	Good	VG	F	VF	XF
ND(1832) Series 10	3.00	6.00	10.00	15.00	—

KM# 39s.10 MUN

Cast Copper or Bronze

Date	Good	VG	F	VF	XF
ND(1832) Series 10	—	—	—	—	50.00

KM# 44.1 MUN

Cast Copper or Bronze **Rev:** "Hwang" (yellow) at bottom, series number at right

Date	Good	VG	F	VF	XF
ND(1832) Series 1	3.00	5.00	8.00	12.00	—

KM# 44s.1 MUN

Cast Copper or Bronze

Date	Good	VG	F	VF	XF
ND(1832) Series 1	—	—	—	—	50.00

KM# 44.2 MUN

Cast Copper or Bronze **Rev:** "Hwang" (yellow) at bottom, series number at right

Date	Good	VG	F	VF	XF
ND(1832) Series 2	3.00	5.00	8.00	12.00	—

KM# 44s.2 MUN

Cast Copper or Bronze

Date	Good	VG	F	VF	XF
ND(1832) Series 2	—	—	—	—	50.00

KM# 44.3 MUN

Cast Copper or Bronze **Rev:** "Hwang" (yellow) at bottom, series number at right

Date	Good	VG	F	VF	XF
ND(1832) Series 3	3.00	5.00	8.00	12.00	—

KM# 44s.3 MUN

Cast Copper or Bronze

Date	Good	VG	F	VF	XF
ND(1832) Series 3	—	—	—	—	50.00

KM# 44.4 MUN

Cast Copper or Bronze **Rev:** "Hwang" (yellow) at bottom, series number at right

Date	Good	VG	F	VF	XF
ND(1832) Series 4	3.00	5.00	8.00	12.00	—

KM# 44s.4 MUN

Cast Copper or Bronze

Date	Good	VG	F	VF	XF
ND(1832) Series 4	—	—	—	—	50.00

KM# 44.5 MUN

Cast Copper or Bronze **Rev:** "Hwang" (yellow) at bottom, series number at right

Date	Good	VG	F	VF	XF
ND(1832) Series 5	3.00	5.00	8.00	12.00	—

KM# 44s.5 MUN
Cast Copper or Bronze

Date	Good	VG	F	VF	XF
ND(1832) Series 5	—	—	—	—	50.00

KM# 44.6 MUN
Cast Copper or Bronze **Rev:** "Hwang" (yellow) at bottom, series number at right

Date	Good	VG	F	VF	XF
ND(1832) Series 6	3.00	5.00	8.00	12.00	—

KM# 44s.6 MUN
Cast Copper or Bronze

Date	Good	VG	F	VF	XF
ND(1832) Series 6	—	—	—	—	50.00

KM# 44.7 MUN
Cast Copper or Bronze **Rev:** "Hwang" (yellow) at bottom, series number at right

Date	Good	VG	F	VF	XF
ND(1832) Series 7	3.00	5.00	8.00	12.00	—

KM# 44s.7 MUN
Cast Copper or Bronze

Date	Good	VG	F	VF	XF
ND(1832) Series 7	—	—	—	—	50.00

KM# 44.8 MUN
Cast Copper or Bronze **Rev:** "Hwang" (yellow) at bottom, series number at right

Date	Good	VG	F	VF	XF
ND(1832) Series 8	3.00	5.00	8.00	12.00	—

KM# 44s.8 MUN
Cast Copper or Bronze

Date	Good	VG	F	VF	XF
ND(1832) Series 8	—	—	—	—	50.00

KM# 44.9 MUN
Cast Copper or Bronze **Rev:** "Hwang" (yellow) at bottom, series number at right

Date	Good	VG	F	VF	XF
ND(1832) Series 9	3.00	5.00	8.00	12.00	—

KM# 44s.9 MUN
Cast Copper or Bronze

Date	Good	VG	F	VF	XF
ND(1832) Series 9	—	—	—	—	50.00

KM# 44.10 MUN
Cast Copper or Bronze **Rev:** "Hwang" (yellow) at bottom, series number at right

Date	Good	VG	F	VF	XF
ND(1832) Series 10	3.00	5.00	8.00	12.00	—

KM# 44s.10 MUN
Cast Copper or Bronze

Date	Good	VG	F	VF	XF
ND(1832) Series 10	—	—	—	—	50.00

KM# 47.1 MUN
Cast Copper or Bronze, 23 mm. **Rev:** 16mm inner circle, "U" at bottom, series number at right

Date	Good	VG	F	VF	XF
ND(1832) Series 1	3.00	5.00	8.00	12.00	—

KM# 47s.1 MUN
Cast Copper or Bronze

Date	Good	VG	F	VF	XF
ND(1832) Series 1	—	—	—	—	50.00

KM# 47.2 MUN
Cast Copper or Bronze **Rev:** 16mm inner circle, "U" at bottom, series number at right

Date	Good	VG	F	VF	XF
ND(1832) Series 2	3.00	5.00	8.00	12.00	—

KM# 47s.2 MUN
Cast Copper or Bronze

Date	Good	VG	F	VF	XF
ND(1832) Series 2	—	—	—	—	50.00

KM# 47.3 MUN
Cast Copper or Bronze **Rev:** 16mm inner circle, "U" at bottom, series number at right

Date	Good	VG	F	VF	XF
ND(1832) Series 3	3.00	5.00	8.00	12.00	—

KM# 47s.3 MUN
Cast Copper or Bronze

Date	Good	VG	F	VF	XF
ND(1832) Series 3	—	—	—	—	50.00

KM# 47.4 MUN
Cast Copper or Bronze **Rev:** 16mm inner circle, "U" at bottom, series number at right

Date	Good	VG	F	VF	XF
ND(1832) Series 4	3.00	5.00	8.00	12.00	—

KM# 47s.4 MUN
Cast Copper or Bronze

Date	Good	VG	F	VF	XF
ND(1832) Series 4	—	—	—	—	50.00

KM# 47.5 MUN
Cast Copper or Bronze **Rev:** 16mm inner circle, "U" at bottom, series number at right

Date	Good	VG	F	VF	XF
ND(1832) Series 5	3.00	5.00	8.00	12.00	—

KM# 47s.5 MUN
Cast Copper or Bronze

Date	Good	VG	F	VF	XF
ND(1832) Series 5	—	—	—	—	50.00

KM# 47.6 MUN
Cast Copper or Bronze **Rev:** 16mm inner circle, "U" at bottom, series number at right

Date	Good	VG	F	VF	XF
ND(1832) Series 6	3.00	5.00	8.00	12.00	—

KM# 47s.6 MUN
Cast Copper or Bronze

Date	Good	VG	F	VF	XF
ND(1832) Series 6	—	—	—	—	50.00

KM# 47.7 MUN
Cast Copper or Bronze **Rev:** 16mm inner circle, "U" at bottom, series number at right

Date	Good	VG	F	VF	XF
ND(1832) Series 7	3.00	5.00	8.00	12.00	—

KM# 47s.7 MUN
Cast Copper or Bronze

Date	Good	VG	F	VF	XF
ND(1832) Series 7	—	—	—	—	50.00

KM# 47.8 MUN
Cast Copper or Bronze **Rev:** 16mm inner circle, "U" at bottom, series number at right

Date	Good	VG	F	VF	XF
ND(1832) Series 8	3.00	5.00	8.00	12.00	—

KM# 47s.8 MUN
Cast Copper or Bronze

Date	Good	VG	F	VF	XF
ND(1832) Series 8	—	—	—	—	50.00

KM# 47.9 MUN
Cast Copper or Bronze **Rev:** 16mm inner circle, "U" at bottom, series number at right

Date	Good	VG	F	VF	XF
ND(1832) Series 9	3.00	5.00	8.00	12.00	—

KM# 47s.9 MUN
Cast Copper or Bronze

Date	Good	VG	F	VF	XF
ND(1832) Series 9	—	—	—	—	50.00

KM# 47.10 MUN
Cast Copper or Bronze **Rev:** 16mm inner circle, "U" at bottom, series number at right

Date	Good	VG	F	VF	XF
ND(1832) Series 10	3.00	5.00	8.00	12.00	—

KM# 47s.10 MUN
Cast Copper or Bronze

Date	Good	VG	F	VF	XF
ND(1832) Series 10	—	—	—	—	50.00

KM# 50.1 MUN
Cast Copper or Bronze, 26 mm. **Rev:** "Chu" at bottom, "Chong" at left, series number at right

Date	Good	VG	F	VF	XF
ND(1832) Series 1	3.00	5.00	8.00	12.00	—

KM# 50s.1 MUN
Cast Copper or Bronze

Date	Good	VG	F	VF	XF
ND(1832) Series 1	—	—	—	—	50.00

KM# 50.2 MUN
Cast Copper or Bronze **Rev:** "Chu" at bottom, "Chong" at left, series number at right

Date	Good	VG	F	VF	XF
ND(1832) Series 2	1.50	2.25	3.50	5.00	—

KM# 50s.2 MUN
Cast Copper or Bronze

Date	Good	VG	F	VF	XF
ND(1832) Series 2	—	—	—	—	30.00

KM# 50.3 MUN
Cast Copper or Bronze **Rev:** "Chu" at bottom, "Chong" at left, series number at right

Date	Good	VG	F	VF	XF
ND(1832) Series 3	3.00	5.00	8.00	12.00	—

KM# 50s.3 MUN
Cast Copper or Bronze

Date	Good	VG	F	VF	XF
ND(1832) Series 3	—	—	—	—	50.00

KM# 50.4 MUN
Cast Copper or Bronze **Rev:** "Chu" at bottom, "Chong" at left, series number at right

Date	Good	VG	F	VF	XF
ND(1832) Series 4	3.00	5.00	8.00	12.00	—

KM# 50s.4 MUN
Cast Copper or Bronze

Date	Good	VG	F	VF	XF
ND(1832) Series 4	—	—	—	—	50.00

KM# 50.5 MUN
Cast Copper or Bronze **Rev:** "Chu" at bottom, "Chong" at left, series number at right

Date	Good	VG	F	VF	XF
ND(1832) Series 5	3.00	5.00	8.00	12.00	—

KM# 50s.5 MUN
Cast Copper or Bronze

Date	Good	VG	F	VF	XF
ND(1832) Series 5	—	—	—	—	50.00

KM# 50.6 MUN
Cast Copper or Bronze **Rev:** "Chu" at bottom, "Chong" at left, series number at right

Date	Good	VG	F	VF	XF
ND(1832) Series 6	3.00	5.00	8.00	12.00	—

KM# 50s.6 MUN
Cast Copper or Bronze

Date	Good	VG	F	VF	XF
ND(1832) Series 6	—	—	—	—	50.00

KM# 50.7 MUN
Cast Copper or Bronze **Rev:** "Chu" at bottom, "Chong" at left, series number at right

Date	Good	VG	F	VF	XF
ND(1832) Series 7	3.00	5.00	8.00	12.00	—

KM# 50s.7 MUN
Cast Copper or Bronze

Date	Good	VG	F	VF	XF
ND(1832) Series 7	—	—	—	—	50.00

KM# 50.8 MUN
Cast Copper or Bronze **Rev:** "Chu" at bottom, "Chong" at left, series number at right

Date	Good	VG	F	VF	XF
ND(1832) Series 8	3.00	5.00	8.00	12.00	—

KM# 50s.8 MUN
Cast Copper or Bronze

Date	Good	VG	F	VF	XF
ND(1832) Series 8	—	—	—	—	50.00

KM# 50.9 MUN
Cast Copper or Bronze **Rev:** "Chu" at bottom, "Chong" at left, series number at right

Date	Good	VG	F	VF	XF
ND(1832) Series 9	3.00	5.00	8.00	12.00	—

KM# 50s.9 MUN
Cast Copper or Bronze

Date	Good	VG	F	VF	XF
ND(1832) Series 9	—	—	—	—	50.00

KM# 50.10 MUN
Cast Copper or Bronze **Rev:** "Chu" at bottom, "Chong" at left, series number at right

Date	Good	VG	F	VF	XF
ND(1832) Series 10	3.00	5.00	8.00	12.00	—

KM# 50s.10 MUN
Cast Copper or Bronze

Date	Good	VG	F	VF	XF
ND(1832) Series 10	—	—	—	—	50.00

KM# 66.1 MUN
Cast Copper or Bronze, 24 mm. **Rev:** "Mun" at bottom, series number at left

Date	Good	VG	F	VF	XF
ND(1832) Series 1	3.00	5.00	8.00	12.00	—

KM# 66s.1 MUN
Cast Copper or Bronze

Date	Good	VG	F	VF	XF
ND(1832) Series 1	—	—	—	—	50.00

KM# 66.2 MUN
Cast Copper or Bronze **Rev:** "Mun" at bottom, series number at left

Date	Good	VG	F	VF	XF
ND(1832) Series 2	3.00	5.00	8.00	12.00	—

KM# 66s.2 MUN
Cast Copper or Bronze

Date	Good	VG	F	VF	XF
ND(1832) Series 2	—	—	—	—	50.00

KM# 66.3 MUN
Cast Copper or Bronze **Rev:** "Mun" at bottom, series number at left

Date	Good	VG	F	VF	XF
ND(1832) Series 3	3.00	5.00	8.00	12.00	—

KM# 66s.3 MUN
Cast Copper or Bronze

Date	Good	VG	F	VF	XF
ND(1832) Series 3	—	—	—	—	50.00

KM# 66.4 MUN
Cast Copper or Bronze **Rev:** "Mun" at bottom, series number at left

Date	Good	VG	F	VF	XF
ND(1832) Series 4	3.00	5.00	8.00	12.00	—

KM# 66s.4 MUN
Cast Copper or Bronze

Date	Good	VG	F	VF	XF
ND(1832) Series 4	—	—	—	—	50.00

KM# 66.5 MUN
Cast Copper or Bronze **Rev:** "Mun" at bottom, series number at left

Date	Good	VG	F	VF	XF
ND(1832) Series 5	3.00	5.00	8.00	12.00	—

KM# 66s.5 MUN
Cast Copper or Bronze

Date	Good	VG	F	VF	XF
ND(1832) Series 5	—	—	—	—	50.00

KM# 66.6 MUN
Cast Copper or Bronze **Rev:** "Mun" at bottom, series number at left

Date	Good	VG	F	VF	XF
ND(1832) Series 6	3.00	5.00	8.00	12.00	—

KM# 66s.6 MUN
Cast Copper or Bronze

Date	Good	VG	F	VF	XF
ND(1832) Series 6	—	—	—	—	50.00

KM# 66.7 MUN
Cast Copper or Bronze **Rev:** "Mun" at bottom, series number at left

Date	Good	VG	F	VF	XF
ND(1832) Series 7	3.00	5.00	8.00	12.00	—

KM# 66s.7 MUN
Cast Copper or Bronze

Date	Good	VG	F	VF	XF
ND(1832) Series 7	—	—	—	—	50.00

KM# 66.8 MUN
Cast Copper or Bronze **Rev:** "Mun" at bottom, series number at left

Date	Good	VG	F	VF	XF
ND(1832) Series 8	3.00	5.00	8.00	12.00	—

KM# 66s.8 MUN
Cast Copper or Bronze

Date	Good	VG	F	VF	XF
ND(1832) Series 8	—	—	—	—	50.00

KM# 66.9 MUN
Cast Copper or Bronze **Rev:** "Mun" at bottom, series number at left

Date	Good	VG	F	VF	XF
ND(1832) Series 9	3.00	5.00	8.00	12.00	—

KM# 66s.9 MUN
Cast Copper or Bronze

Date	Good	VG	F	VF	XF
ND(1832) Series 9	—	—	—	—	50.00

KM# 66.10 MUN
Cast Copper or Bronze **Rev:** "Mun" at bottom, series number at left

Date	Good	VG	F	VF	XF
ND(1832) Series 10	3.00	5.00	8.00	12.00	—

KM# 66s.10 MUN
Cast Copper or Bronze

Date	Good	VG	F	VF	XF
ND(1832) Series 10	—	—	—	—	50.00

KM# 67.1 MUN
Cast Copper or Bronze **Rev:** "Ho" in different style

Date	Good	VG	F	VF	XF
ND(1832) Series 1	3.00	5.00	8.00	12.00	—

KM# 67s.1 MUN
Cast Copper or Bronze

Date	Good	VG	F	VF	XF
ND(1832) Series 1	—	—	—	—	50.00

KM# 67.2 MUN
Cast Copper or Bronze **Rev:** "Ho" in different style

Date	Good	VG	F	VF	XF
ND(1832) Series 2	3.00	5.00	8.00	12.00	—

KM# 67s.2 MUN
Cast Copper or Bronze

Date	Good	VG	F	VF	XF
ND(1832) Series 2	—	—	—	—	50.00

KM# 67.3 MUN
Cast Copper or Bronze **Rev:** "Ho" in different style

Date	Good	VG	F	VF	XF
ND(1832) Series 3	3.00	5.00	8.00	12.00	—

KM# 67s.3 MUN
Cast Copper or Bronze

Date	Good	VG	F	VF	XF
ND(1832) Series 3	—	—	—	—	50.00

KM# 67.4 MUN
Cast Copper or Bronze **Rev:** "Ho" in different style

Date	Good	VG	F	VF	XF
ND(1832) Series 4	3.00	5.00	8.00	12.00	—

KM# 67s.4 MUN
Cast Copper or Bronze

Date	Good	VG	F	VF	XF
ND(1832) Series 4	—	—	—	—	50.00

KM# 67.5 MUN
Cast Copper or Bronze **Rev:** "Ho" in different style

Date	Good	VG	F	VF	XF
ND(1832) Series 5	3.00	5.00	8.00	12.00	—

KM# 67s.5 MUN
Cast Copper or Bronze

Date	Good	VG	F	VF	XF
ND(1832) Series 5	—	—	—	—	50.00

KM# 67.6 MUN
Cast Copper or Bronze **Rev:** "Ho" in different style

Date	Good	VG	F	VF	XF
ND(1832) Series 6	3.00	5.00	8.00	12.00	—

KM# 67s.6 MUN
Cast Copper or Bronze

Date	Good	VG	F	VF	XF
ND(1832) Series 6	—	—	—	—	50.00

KM# 67.7 MUN
Cast Copper or Bronze **Rev:** "Ho" in different style

Date	Good	VG	F	VF	XF
ND(1832) Series 7	3.00	5.00	8.00	12.00	—

KM# 67s.7 MUN
Cast Copper or Bronze

Date	Good	VG	F	VF	XF
ND(1832) Series 7	—	—	—	—	50.00

KM# 67.8 MUN
Cast Copper or Bronze **Rev:** "Ho" in different style

Date	Good	VG	F	VF	XF
ND(1832) Series 8	3.00	5.00	8.00	12.00	—

KM# 67s.8 MUN
Cast Copper or Bronze

Date	Good	VG	F	VF	XF
ND(1832) Series 8	—	—	—	—	50.00

KM# 67.9 MUN
Cast Copper or Bronze **Rev:** "Ho" in different style

Date	Good	VG	F	VF	XF
ND(1832) Series 9	3.00	5.00	8.00	12.00	—

KM# 67s.9 MUN
Cast Copper or Bronze

Date	Good	VG	F	VF	XF
ND(1832) Series 9	—	—	—	—	50.00

KM# 67.10 MUN
Cast Copper or Bronze **Rev:** "Ho" in different style

Date	Good	VG	F	VF	XF
ND(1832) Series 10	3.00	5.00	8.00	12.00	—

KM# 67s.10 MUN
Cast Copper or Bronze

Date	Good	VG	F	VF	XF
ND(1832) Series 10	—	—	—	—	50.00

KM# 67.18 MUN
Cast Copper or Bronze

Date	Good	VG	F	VF	XF
ND(1832) Series 8	3.00	5.00	8.00	12.00	—

KM# 68.1 MUN
Cast Copper or Bronze, 23 mm. **Rev:** "Mun" at bottom, circle at left, series number at right

Date	Good	VG	F	VF	XF
ND(1832) Series 1	4.00	8.00	13.00	20.00	—

KM# 68s.1 MUN
Cast Copper or Bronze

Date	Good	VG	F	VF	XF
ND(1832) Series 1	—	—	—	—	50.00

KM# 68.2 MUN
Cast Copper or Bronze **Rev:** "Mun" at bottom, circle at left, series number at right

Date	Good	VG	F	VF	XF
ND(1832) Series 2	4.00	8.00	13.00	20.00	—

KM# 68s.2 MUN
Cast Copper or Bronze

Date	Good	VG	F	VF	XF
ND(1832) Series 2	—	—	—	—	50.00

KM# 68.3 MUN
Cast Copper or Bronze **Rev:** "Mun" at bottom, circle at left, series number at right

Date	Good	VG	F	VF	XF
ND(1832) Series 3	4.00	8.00	13.00	20.00	—

KM# 68s.3 MUN
Cast Copper or Bronze

Date	Good	VG	F	VF	XF
ND(1832) Series 3	—	—	—	—	50.00

KM# 68.4 MUN
Cast Copper or Bronze **Rev:** "Mun" at bottom, circle at left, series number at right

Date	Good	VG	F	VF	XF
ND(1832) Series 4	4.00	8.00	13.00	20.00	—

KM# 68s.4 MUN
Cast Copper or Bronze

Date	Good	VG	F	VF	XF
ND(1832) Series 4	—	—	—	—	50.00

KM# 68.5 MUN
Cast Copper or Bronze **Rev:** "Mun" at bottom, circle at left, series number at right

Date	Good	VG	F	VF	XF
ND(1832) Series 5	4.00	8.00	13.00	20.00	—

KM# 68s.5 MUN
Cast Copper or Bronze

Date	Good	VG	F	VF	XF
ND(1832) Series 5	—	—	—	—	50.00

KM# 68.6 MUN
Cast Copper or Bronze **Rev:** "Mun" at bottom, circle at left, series number at right

Date	Good	VG	F	VF	XF
ND(1832) Series 6	4.00	8.00	13.00	20.00	—

KM# 68s.6 MUN
Cast Copper or Bronze

Date	Good	VG	F	VF	XF
ND(1832) Series 6	—	—	—	—	50.00

KM# 68.7 MUN
Cast Copper or Bronze **Rev:** "Mun" at bottom, circle at left, series number at right

Date	Good	VG	F	VF	XF
ND(1832) Series 7	4.00	8.00	13.00	20.00	—

KM# 68s.7 MUN
Cast Copper or Bronze

Date	Good	VG	F	VF	XF
ND(1832) Series 7	—	—	—	—	50.00

KM# 68.8 MUN
Cast Copper or Bronze **Rev:** "Mun" at bottom, circle at left, series number at right

Date	Good	VG	F	VF	XF
ND(1832) Series 8	4.00	8.00	13.00	20.00	—

KM# 68s.8 MUN
Cast Copper or Bronze

Date	Good	VG	F	VF	XF
ND(1832) Series 8	—	—	—	—	50.00

KM# 68.9 MUN
Cast Copper or Bronze **Rev:** "Mun" at bottom, circle at left, series number at right

Date	Good	VG	F	VF	XF
ND(1832) Series 9	4.00	8.00	13.00	20.00	—

KM# 68s.9 MUN
Cast Copper or Bronze

Date	Good	VG	F	VF	XF
ND(1832) Series 9	—	—	—	—	50.00

KM# 68.10 MUN
Cast Copper or Bronze **Rev:** "Mun" at bottom, circle at left, series number at right

Date	Good	VG	F	VF	XF
ND(1832) Series 10	4.00	8.00	13.00	20.00	—

KM# 68s.10 MUN
Cast Copper or Bronze

Date	Good	VG	F	VF	XF
ND(1832) Series 10	—	—	—	—	50.00

KM# 69.1 MUN
Cast Copper or Bronze, 25 mm. **Rev:** "Mun" at bottom, circle at right, series number at left

Date	Good	VG	F	VF	XF
ND(1832) Series 1	4.00	8.00	13.00	20.00	—

KM# 69s.1 MUN
Cast Copper or Bronze

Date	Good	VG	F	VF	XF
ND(1832) Series 1	—	—	—	—	50.00

KM# 69.2 MUN
Cast Copper or Bronze **Rev:** "Mun" at bottom, circle at right, series number at left

Date	Good	VG	F	VF	XF
ND(1832) Series 2	4.00	8.00	13.00	20.00	—

KM# 69s.2 MUN
Cast Copper or Bronze

Date	Good	VG	F	VF	XF
ND(1832) Series 2	—	—	—	—	50.00

KM# 69.3 MUN
Cast Copper or Bronze **Rev:** "Mun" at bottom, circle at right, series number at left

Date	Good	VG	F	VF	XF
ND(1832) Series 3	4.00	8.00	13.00	20.00	—

KM# 69s.3 MUN
Cast Copper or Bronze

Date	Good	VG	F	VF	XF
ND(1832) Series 3	—	—	—	—	50.00

KM# 69.4 MUN
Cast Copper or Bronze **Rev:** "Mun" at bottom, circle at right, series number at left

Date	Good	VG	F	VF	XF
ND(1832) Series 4	4.00	8.00	13.00	20.00	—

KM# 69s.4 MUN
Cast Copper or Bronze

Date	Good	VG	F	VF	XF
ND(1832) Series 4	—	—	—	—	50.00

KM# 69.5 MUN
Cast Copper or Bronze **Rev:** "Mun" at bottom, circle at right, series number at left

Date	Good	VG	F	VF	XF
ND(1832) Series 5	4.00	8.00	13.00	20.00	—

KM# 69s.5 MUN
Cast Copper or Bronze

Date	Good	VG	F	VF	XF
ND(1832) Series 5	—	—	—	—	50.00

KM# 63.6 MUN
Cast Copper or Bronze **Rev:** "Kwang" at bottom, dot at right, seeries number at left

Date	Good	VG	F	VF	XF
ND(1852) Series 6	4.00	8.00	13.00	20.00	—

KM# 64s MUN
Cast Copper or Bronze

Date	Good	VG	F	VF	XF
ND(1852) Series 2	—	—	—	—	50.00

KM# 38.1 MUN
Cast Copper or Bronze **Note:** Large characters, size varies 23-26mm.

Date	Good	VG	F	VF	XF
ND(1852) Series 1	4.00	8.00	13.00	20.00	—

KM# 38s.1 MUN
Cast Copper or Bronze

Date	Good	VG	F	VF	XF
ND(1852) Series 1	—	—	—	—	50.00

KM# 38.2 MUN
Cast Copper or Bronze **Note:** Large characters, size varies 23-26mm.

Date	Good	VG	F	VF	XF
ND(1852) Series 2	4.00	8.00	13.00	20.00	—

KM# 38s.2 MUN
Cast Copper or Bronze

Date	Good	VG	F	VF	XF
ND(1852) Series 2	—	—	—	—	50.00

KM# 38.3 MUN
Cast Copper or Bronze **Note:** Large characters, size varies 23-26mm.

Date	Good	VG	F	VF	XF
ND(1852) Series 3	4.00	8.00	13.00	20.00	—

KM# 38s.3 MUN
Cast Copper or Bronze

Date	Good	VG	F	VF	XF
ND(1852) Series 3	—	—	—	—	50.00

KM# 38.4 MUN
Cast Copper or Bronze **Note:** Large characters, size varies 23-26mm.

Date	Good	VG	F	VF	XF
ND(1852) Series 4	4.00	8.00	13.00	20.00	—

KM# 38s.4 MUN
Cast Copper or Bronze

Date	Good	VG	F	VF	XF
ND(1852) Series 4	—	—	—	—	50.00

KM# 38.5 MUN
Cast Copper or Bronze **Note:** Large characters, size varies 23-26mm.

Date	Good	VG	F	VF	XF
ND(1852) Series 5	4.00	8.00	13.00	20.00	—

KM# 38s.5 MUN
Cast Copper or Bronze

Date	Good	VG	F	VF	XF
ND(1852) Series 5	—	—	—	—	50.00

KM# 38.6 MUN
Cast Copper or Bronze **Note:** Large characters, size varies 23-26mm.

Date	Good	VG	F	VF	XF
ND(1852) Series 6	4.00	8.00	13.00	20.00	—

KM# 38s.6 MUN
Cast Copper or Bronze

Date	Good	VG	F	VF	XF
ND(1852) Series 6	—	—	—	—	50.00

KM# 38.7 MUN
Cast Copper or Bronze **Note:** Large characters, size varies 23-26mm.

Date	Good	VG	F	VF	XF
ND(1852) Series 7	4.00	8.00	13.00	20.00	—

KM# 38s.7 MUN
Cast Copper or Bronze

Date	Good	VG	F	VF	XF
ND(1852) Series 7	—	—	—	—	50.00

KM# 38.8 MUN
Cast Copper or Bronze **Note:** Large characters, size varies 23-26mm.

Date	Good	VG	F	VF	XF
ND(1852) Series 8	4.00	8.00	13.00	20.00	—

KM# 38s.8 MUN
Cast Copper or Bronze

Date	Good	VG	F	VF	XF
ND(1852) Series 8	—	—	—	—	50.00

KM# 38.9 MUN
Cast Copper or Bronze **Note:** Large characters, size varies 23-26mm.

Date	Good	VG	F	VF	XF
ND(1852) Series 9	4.00	8.00	13.00	20.00	—

KM# 38s.9 MUN
Cast Copper or Bronze

Date	Good	VG	F	VF	XF
ND(1852) Series 9	—	—	—	—	50.00

KM# 38.10 MUN
Cast Copper or Bronze **Note:** Large characters, size varies 23-26mm.

Date	Good	VG	F	VF	XF
ND(1852) Series 10	4.00	8.00	13.00	20.00	—

KM# 38s.10 MUN
Cast Copper or Bronze

Date	Good	VG	F	VF	XF
ND(1852) Series 10	—	—	—	—	50.00

KM# 38.11 MUN
Cast Copper or Bronze **Note:** Large characters, size varies 23-26mm.

Date	Good	VG	F	VF	XF
ND(1852) Series 11	1.50	2.25	3.50	5.00	—

KM# 38s.11 MUN
Cast Copper or Bronze

Date	Good	VG	F	VF	XF
ND(1852) Series 11	—	—	—	—	50.00

KM# 41.1 MUN
Cast Copper or Bronze, 24 mm. **Rev:** "Chi" at bottom, series number at left

Date	Good	VG	F	VF	XF
ND(1852) Series 1	3.00	5.00	8.00	12.00	—

KM# 41s.1 MUN
Cast Copper or Bronze

Date	Good	VG	F	VF	XF
ND(1852) Series 1	—	—	—	—	50.00

KM# 41.2 MUN
Cast Copper or Bronze **Rev:** "Chi" at bottom, series number at left

Date	Good	VG	F	VF	XF
ND(1852) Series 2	3.00	5.00	8.00	12.00	—

KM# 41s.2 MUN
Cast Copper or Bronze

Date	Good	VG	F	VF	XF
ND(1852) Series 2	—	—	—	—	50.00

KM# 41.3 MUN
Cast Copper or Bronze **Rev:** "Chi" at bottom, series number at left

Date	Good	VG	F	VF	XF
ND(1852) Series 3	3.00	5.00	8.00	12.00	—

KM# 41s.3 MUN
Cast Copper or Bronze

Date	Good	VG	F	VF	XF
ND(1852) Series 3	—	—	—	—	50.00

KM# 41.4 MUN
Cast Copper or Bronze **Rev:** "Chi" at bottom, series number at left

Date	Good	VG	F	VF	XF
ND(1852) Series 4	3.00	5.00	8.00	12.00	—

KM# 41s.4 MUN
Cast Copper or Bronze

Date	Good	VG	F	VF	XF
ND(1852) Series 4	—	—	—	—	50.00

KM# 41.5 MUN
Cast Copper or Bronze **Rev:** "Chi" at bottom, series number at left

Date	Good	VG	F	VF	XF
ND(1852) Series 5	2.00	3.00	5.00	8.00	—

KM# 41s.5 MUN
Cast Copper or Bronze

Date	Good	VG	F	VF	XF
ND(1852) Series 5	—	—	—	—	50.00

KM# 41.6 MUN
Cast Copper or Bronze **Rev:** "Chi" at bottom, series number at left

Date	Good	VG	F	VF	XF
ND(1852) Series 6	2.00	3.00	5.00	8.00	—

KM# 41s.6 MUN
Cast Copper or Bronze

Date	Good	VG	F	VF	XF
ND(1852) Series 6	—	—	—	—	50.00

KM# 41.7 MUN
Cast Copper or Bronze **Rev:** "Chi" at bottom, series number at left

Date	Good	VG	F	VF	XF
ND(1852) Series 7	2.00	3.00	5.00	8.00	—

KM# 41s.7 MUN
Cast Copper or Bronze

Date	Good	VG	F	VF	XF
ND(1852) Series 7	—	—	—	—	50.00

KM# 41.8 MUN
Cast Copper or Bronze **Rev:** "Chi" at bottom, series number at left

Date	Good	VG	F	VF	XF
ND(1852) Series 8	2.00	3.00	5.00	8.00	—

KM# 41s.8 MUN
Cast Copper or Bronze

Date	Good	VG	F	VF	XF
ND(1852) Series 8	—	—	—	—	50.00

KM# 41.9 MUN
Cast Copper or Bronze **Rev:** "Chi" at bottom, series number at left

Date	Good	VG	F	VF	XF
ND(1852) Series 9	2.00	3.00	5.00	8.00	—

KM# 41s.9 MUN
Cast Copper or Bronze

Date	Good	VG	F	VF	XF
ND(1852) Series 9	—	—	—	—	50.00

KM# 41.10 MUN
Cast Copper or Bronze **Rev:** "Chi" at bottom, series number at left

Date	Good	VG	F	VF	XF
ND(1852) Series 10	2.00	3.00	5.00	8.00	—

KM# 41s.10 MUN
Cast Copper or Bronze

Date	Good	VG	F	VF	XF
ND(1852) Series 10	—	—	—	—	50.00

KM# 42.1 MUN
Cast Copper or Bronze **Rev:** "Hyon" at bottom, series number at right

Date	Good	VG	F	VF	XF
ND(1852) Series 1	2.00	3.00	5.00	8.00	—

KM# 42s.1 MUN
Cast Copper or Bronze

Date	Good	VG	F	VF	XF
ND(1852) Series 1	—	—	—	—	50.00

KM# 42.2 MUN
Cast Copper or Bronze **Rev:** "Hyon" at bottom, series number at right

Date	Good	VG	F	VF	XF
ND(1852) Series 2	2.00	3.00	5.00	8.00	—

KM# 42s.2 MUN
Cast Copper or Bronze

Date	Good	VG	F	VF	XF
ND(1852) Series 2	—	—	—	—	50.00

KM# 42.3 MUN
Cast Copper or Bronze **Rev:** "Hyon" at bottom, series number at right

Date	Good	VG	F	VF	XF
ND(1852) Series 3	2.00	3.00	5.00	8.00	—

KM# 42s.3 MUN
Cast Copper or Bronze

Date	Good	VG	F	VF	XF
ND(1852) Series 3	—	—	—	—	30.00

KM# 42.4 MUN
Cast Copper or Bronze **Rev:** "Hyon" at bottom, series number at right

Date	Good	VG	F	VF	XF
ND(1852) Series 4	2.00	3.00	5.00	8.00	—

KM# 42s.4 MUN
Cast Copper or Bronze

Date	Good	VG	F	VF	XF
ND(1852) Series 4	—	—	—	—	50.00

KM# 42.5 MUN
Cast Copper or Bronze **Rev:** "Hyon" at bottom, series number at right

Date	Good	VG	F	VF	XF
ND(1852) Series 5	2.00	3.00	5.00	8.00	—

KM# 42s.5 MUN
Cast Copper or Bronze

Date	Good	VG	F	VF	XF
ND(1852) Series 5	—	—	—	—	50.00

KM# 42.6 MUN
Cast Copper or Bronze **Rev:** "Hyon" at bottom, series number at right

Date	Good	VG	F	VF	XF
ND(1852) Series 6	2.00	3.00	5.00	8.00	—

KM# 42s.6 MUN
Cast Copper or Bronze

Date	Good	VG	F	VF	XF
ND(1852) Series 6	—	—	—	—	50.00

KM# 42.7 MUN
Cast Copper or Bronze **Rev:** "Hyon" at bottom, series number at right

Date	Good	VG	F	VF	XF
ND(1852) Series 7	2.00	3.00	5.00	8.00	—

KM# 42s.7 MUN
Cast Copper or Bronze

Date	Good	VG	F	VF	XF
ND(1852) Series 7	—	—	—	—	50.00

KM# 42.8 MUN
Cast Copper or Bronze **Rev:** "Hyon" at bottom, series number at right

Date	Good	VG	F	VF	XF
ND(1852) Series 8	2.00	3.00	5.00	8.00	—

KM# 42s.8 MUN
Cast Copper or Bronze

Date	Good	VG	F	VF	XF
ND(1852) Series 8	—	—	—	—	50.00

KM# 42.9 MUN
Cast Copper or Bronze **Rev:** "Hyon" at bottom, series number at right

Date	Good	VG	F	VF	XF
ND(1852) Series 9	2.00	3.00	5.00	8.00	—

KM# 42s.9 MUN
Cast Copper or Bronze

Date	Good	VG	F	VF	XF
ND(1852) Series 9	—	—	—	—	50.00

KM# 42.10 MUN
Cast Copper or Bronze **Rev:** "Hyon" at bottom, series number at right

Date	Good	VG	F	VF	XF
ND(1852) Series 10	2.00	3.00	5.00	8.00	—

KM# 42s.10 MUN
Cast Copper or Bronze

Date	Good	VG	F	VF	XF
ND(1852) Series 10	—	—	—	—	50.00

KM# 42.16 MUN
Cast Copper or Bronze **Rev:** Star at upper right

Date	Good	VG	F	VF	XF
ND(1852) Series 6	1.50	2.25	3.50	5.00	—

KM# 43.1 MUN
Cast Copper or Bronze, 26 mm. **Obv:** Small characters **Rev:** Small characters, "Hyon" at bottom, series number at left

Date	Good	VG	F	VF	XF
ND(1852) Series 1	2.00	3.00	5.00	8.00	—

KM# A43.1 MUN
Cast Copper or Bronze **Obv:** Large characters **Rev:** Large characters, "Hyon" at bottom, series number at left

Date	Good	VG	F	VF	XF
ND(1852) Series 1	2.00	3.00	5.00	8.00	—

KM# 43s.1 MUN
Cast Copper or Bronze

Date	Good	VG	F	VF	XF
ND(1852) Series 1	—	—	—	—	50.00

KM# A43s.1 MUN
Cast Copper or Bronze

Date	Good	VG	F	VF	XF
ND(1852) Series 1	—	—	—	—	50.00

KM# 43.2 MUN
Cast Copper or Bronze **Obv:** Small characters **Rev:** Small characters, "Hyon" at bottom, series number at left

Date	Good	VG	F	VF	XF
ND(1852) Series 2	2.00	3.00	5.00	8.00	—

KM# A43.2 MUN
Cast Copper or Bronze **Obv:** Large characters **Rev:** Large characters, "Hyon" at bottom, series number at left

Date	Good	VG	F	VF	XF
ND(1852) Series 2	2.00	3.00	5.00	8.00	—

KM# 43s.2 MUN
Cast Copper or Bronze

Date	Good	VG	F	VF	XF
ND(1852) Series 2	—	—	—	—	50.00

KM# A43s.2 MUN
Cast Copper or Bronze

Date	Good	VG	F	VF	XF
ND(1852) Series 2	—	—	—	—	50.00

KM# 43.3 MUN
Cast Copper or Bronze **Obv:** Small characters **Rev:** Small characters, "Hyon" at bottom, series number at left

Date	Good	VG	F	VF	XF
ND(1852) Series 3	2.00	3.00	5.00	8.00	—

KM# A43.3 MUN
Cast Copper or Bronze **Obv:** Large characters **Rev:** Large characters, "Hyon" at bottom, series number at left

Date	Good	VG	F	VF	XF
ND(1852) Series 3	2.00	3.00	5.00	8.00	—

KM# 43s.3 MUN
Cast Copper or Bronze

Date	Good	VG	F	VF	XF
ND(1852) Series 3	—	—	—	—	50.00

KM# A43s.3 MUN
Cast Copper or Bronze

Date	Good	VG	F	VF	XF
ND(1852) Series 3	—	—	—	—	50.00

KM# 43.4 MUN
Cast Copper or Bronze **Obv:** Small characters **Rev:** Small characters, "Hyon" at bottom, series number at left

Date	Good	VG	F	VF	XF
ND(1852) Series 4	2.00	3.00	5.00	8.00	—

KM# A43.4 MUN
Cast Copper or Bronze **Obv:** Large characters **Rev:** Large characters, "Hyon" at bottom, series number at left

Date	Good	VG	F	VF	XF
ND(1852) Series 4	2.00	3.00	5.00	8.00	—

KM# 43s.4 MUN
Cast Copper or Bronze

Date	Good	VG	F	VF	XF
ND(1852) Series 4	—	—	—	—	50.00

KM# A43s.4 MUN
Cast Copper or Bronze

Date	Good	VG	F	VF	XF
ND(1852) Series 4	—	—	—	—	50.00

KM# 43.5 MUN
Cast Copper or Bronze **Obv:** Small characters **Rev:** Small characters, "Hyon" at bottom, series number at left

Date	Good	VG	F	VF	XF
ND(1852) Series 5	2.00	3.00	5.00	8.00	—

KM# A43.5 MUN
Cast Copper or Bronze **Obv:** Large characters **Rev:** Large characters, "Hyon" at bottom, series number at left

Date	Good	VG	F	VF	XF
ND(1852) Series 5	2.00	3.00	5.00	8.00	—

KM# 43s.5 MUN
Cast Copper or Bronze

Date	Good	VG	F	VF	XF
ND(1852) Series 5	—	—	—	—	50.00

KM# A43s.5 MUN
Cast Copper or Bronze

Date	Good	VG	F	VF	XF
ND(1852) Series 5	—	—	—	—	50.00

KM# 43.6 MUN
Cast Copper or Bronze **Obv:** Small characters **Rev:** Small characters, "Hyon" at bottom, series number at left

Date	Good	VG	F	VF	XF
ND(1852) Series 6	2.00	3.00	5.00	8.00	—

KM# A43.6 MUN
Cast Copper or Bronze **Obv:** Large characters **Rev:** Large characters, "Hyon" at bottom, series number at left

Date	Good	VG	F	VF	XF
ND(1852) Series 6	2.00	3.00	5.00	8.00	—

KM# A43s.6 MUN
Cast Copper or Bronze

Date	Good	VG	F	VF	XF
ND(1852) Series 6	—	—	—	—	50.00

KM# 43s.6 MUN
Cast Copper or Bronze

Date	Good	VG	F	VF	XF
ND(1852) Series 6	—	—	—	—	50.00

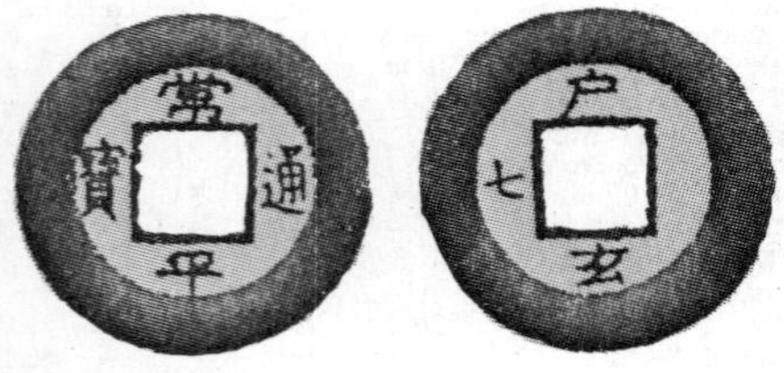

KM# 43.7 MUN
Cast Copper or Bronze **Obv:** Small characters **Rev:** Small characters, "Hyon" at bottom, series number at left

Date	Good	VG	F	VF	XF
ND(1852) Series 7	2.00	3.00	5.00	8.00	—

KM# A43.7 MUN
Cast Copper or Bronze **Obv:** Large characters **Rev:** Large characters, "Hyon" at bottom, series number at left

Date	Good	VG	F	VF	XF
ND(1852) Series 7	2.00	3.00	5.00	8.00	—

KM# A43s.7 MUN
Cast Copper or Bronze

Date	Good	VG	F	VF	XF
ND(1852) Series 7	—	—	—	—	50.00

KM# 43s.7 MUN
Cast Copper or Bronze

Date	Good	VG	F	VF	XF
ND(1852) Series 7	—	—	—	—	50.00

KM# 43.8 MUN
Cast Copper or Bronze **Obv:** Small characters **Rev:** Small characters, "Hyon" at bottom, series number at left

Date	Good	VG	F	VF	XF
ND(1852) Series 8	2.00	3.00	5.00	8.00	—

KM# A43.8 MUN
Cast Copper or Bronze **Obv:** Large characters **Rev:** Large characters, "Hyon" at bottom, series number at left

Date	Good	VG	F	VF	XF
ND(1852) Series 8	2.00	3.00	5.00	8.00	—

KM# A43s.8 MUN
Cast Copper or Bronze

Date	Good	VG	F	VF	XF
ND(1852) Series 8	—	—	—	—	50.00

KM# 43s.8 MUN
Cast Copper or Bronze

Date	Good	VG	F	VF	XF
ND(1852) Series 8	—	—	—	—	50.00

KM# 43.9 MUN
Cast Copper or Bronze **Obv:** Small characters **Rev:** Small characters, "Hyon" at bottom, series number at left

Date	Good	VG	F	VF	XF
ND(1852) Series 9	2.00	3.00	5.00	8.00	—

KM# A43.9 MUN
Cast Copper or Bronze **Obv:** Large characters **Rev:** Large characters, "Hyon" at bottom, series number at left

Date	Good	VG	F	VF	XF
ND(1852) Series 9	2.00	3.00	5.00	8.00	—

KM# A43s.9 MUN
Cast Copper or Bronze

Date	Good	VG	F	VF	XF
ND(1852) Series 9	—	—	—	—	50.00

KM# 43s.9 MUN
Cast Copper or Bronze

Date	Good	VG	F	VF	XF
ND(1852) Series 9	—	—	—	—	50.00

KM# 43.10 MUN
Cast Copper or Bronze **Obv:** Small characters **Rev:** Small characters, "Hyon" at bottom, series number at left

Date	Good	VG	F	VF	XF
ND(1852) Series 10	2.00	3.00	5.00	8.00	—

KM# 43s.10 MUN
Cast Copper or Bronze

Date	Good	VG	F	VF	XF
ND(1852) Series 10	—	—	—	—	50.00

KM# A43s.10 MUN
Cast Copper or Bronze

Date	Good	VG	F	VF	XF
ND(1852) Series 10	—	—	—	—	50.00

KM# A43.10 MUN
Cast Copper or Bronze **Obv:** Large characters **Rev:** Large characters, "Hyon" at bottom, series number at left

Date	Good	VG	F	VF	XF
ND(1852) Series 10	2.00	3.00	5.00	8.00	—

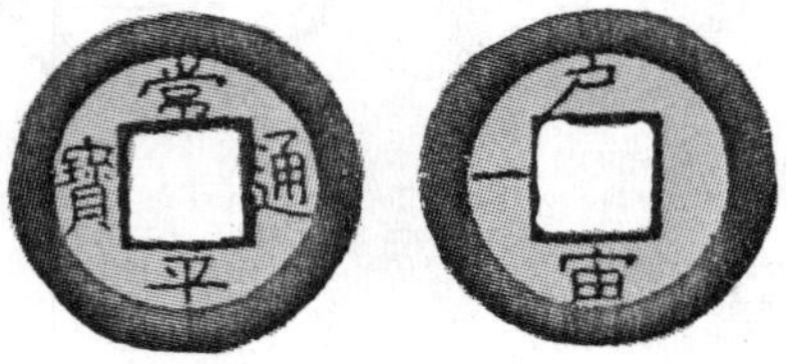

KM# 51.1 MUN
Cast Copper or Bronze **Rev:** "Chu" at bottom, series number at left **Note:** Size varies 23-25mm.

Date	Good	VG	F	VF	XF
ND(1852) Series 1	2.00	3.00	5.00	8.00	—

KM# 51s.1 MUN
Cast Copper or Bronze

Date	Good	VG	F	VF	XF
ND(1852) Series 1	—	—	—	—	50.00

KM# 51.2 MUN
Cast Copper or Bronze **Rev:** "Chu" at bottom, series number at left **Note:** Size varies 23-25mm.

Date	Good	VG	F	VF	XF
ND(1852) Series 2	2.00	3.00	5.00	8.00	—

KM# 51s.2 MUN
Cast Copper or Bronze

Date	Good	VG	F	VF	XF
ND(1852) Series 2	—	—	—	—	50.00

KM# 51.3 MUN
Cast Copper or Bronze **Rev:** "Chu" at bottom, series number at left **Note:** Size varies 23-25mm.

Date	Good	VG	F	VF	XF
ND(1852) Series 3	2.00	3.00	5.00	8.00	—

KM# 51s.3 MUN
Cast Copper or Bronze

Date	Good	VG	F	VF	XF
ND(1852) Series 3	—	—	—	—	50.00

KM# 51.4 MUN
Cast Copper or Bronze **Rev:** "Chu" at bottom, series number at left **Note:** Size varies 23-25mm.

Date	Good	VG	F	VF	XF
ND(1852) Series 4	2.00	3.00	5.00	8.00	—

KM# 51s.4 MUN
Cast Copper or Bronze

Date	Good	VG	F	VF	XF
ND(1852) Series 4	—	—	—	—	50.00

KM# 51.5 MUN
Cast Copper or Bronze **Rev:** "Chu" at bottom, series number at left **Note:** Size varies 23-25mm.

Date	Good	VG	F	VF	XF
ND(1852) Series 5	2.00	3.00	5.00	8.00	—

KM# 51s.5 MUN
Cast Copper or Bronze

Date	Good	VG	F	VF	XF
ND(1852) Series 5	—	—	—	—	50.00

KM# 51.6 MUN
Cast Copper or Bronze **Rev:** "Chu" at bottom, series number at left **Note:** Size varies 23-25mm.

Date	Good	VG	F	VF	XF
ND(1852) Series 6	2.00	3.00	5.00	8.00	—

KM# 51s.6 MUN
Cast Copper or Bronze

Date	Good	VG	F	VF	XF
ND(1852) Series 6	—	—	—	—	50.00

KM# 51.7 MUN
Cast Copper or Bronze **Rev:** "Chu" at bottom, series number at left **Note:** Size varies 23-25mm.

Date	Good	VG	F	VF	XF
ND(1852) Series 7	2.00	3.00	5.00	8.00	—

KM# 51s.7 MUN
Cast Copper or Bronze

Date	Good	VG	F	VF	XF
ND(1852) Series 7	—	—	—	—	50.00

KM# 51.8 MUN
Cast Copper or Bronze **Rev:** "Chu" at bottom, series number at left **Note:** Size varies 23-25mm.

Date	Good	VG	F	VF	XF
ND(1852) Series 8	2.00	3.00	5.00	8.00	—

KM# 51s.8 MUN
Cast Copper or Bronze

Date	Good	VG	F	VF	XF
ND(1852) Series 8	—	—	—	—	50.00

KM# 51.9 MUN
Cast Copper or Bronze **Rev:** "Chu" at bottom, series number at left **Note:** Size varies 23-25mm.

Date	Good	VG	F	VF	XF
ND(1852) Series 9	2.00	3.00	5.00	8.00	—

KM# 51s.9 MUN
Cast Copper or Bronze

Date	Good	VG	F	VF	XF
ND(1852) Series 9	—	—	—	—	50.00

KM# 51.10 MUN
Cast Copper or Bronze **Rev:** "Chu" at bottom, series number at left **Note:** Size varies 23-25mm.

Date	Good	VG	F	VF	XF
ND(1852) Series 10	2.00	3.00	5.00	8.00	—

KM# 51s.10 MUN
Cast Copper or Bronze

Date	Good	VG	F	VF	XF
ND(1852) Series 10	—	—	—	—	50.00

KM# 52.1 MUN
Cast Copper or Bronze, 26 mm. **Rev:** "Hong" at bottom, series number at left

Date	Good	VG	F	VF	XF
ND(1852) Series 1	3.00	5.00	8.00	12.00	—

KM# 52s.1 MUN
Cast Copper or Bronze

Date	Good	VG	F	VF	XF
ND(1852) Series 1	—	—	—	—	50.00

KM# 52.2 MUN
Cast Copper or Bronze **Rev:** "Hong" at bottom, series number at left

Date	Good	VG	F	VF	XF
ND(1852) Series 2	3.00	5.00	8.00	12.00	—

KM# 52s.2 MUN
Cast Copper or Bronze

Date	Good	VG	F	VF	XF
ND(1852) Series 2	—	—	—	—	50.00

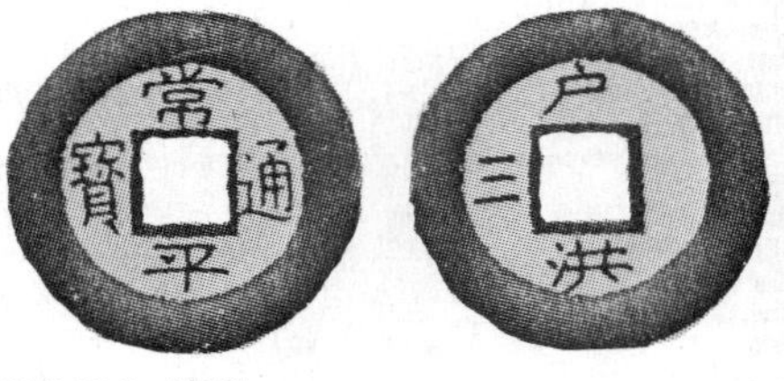

KM# 52.3 MUN
Cast Copper or Bronze **Rev:** "Hong" at bottom, series number at left

Date	Good	VG	F	VF	XF
ND(1852) Series 3	3.00	5.00	8.00	12.00	—

KM# 53.3 MUN
Cast Copper or Bronze **Note:** Size varies 22-24mm.

Date	Good	VG	F	VF	XF
ND(1852) Series 3	3.00	5.00	8.00	12.00	—

KM# 52s.3 MUN
Cast Copper or Bronze

Date	Good	VG	F	VF	XF
ND(1852) Series 3	—	—	—	—	50.00

KM# 52.4 MUN
Cast Copper or Bronze **Rev:** "Hong" at bottom, series number at left

Date	Good	VG	F	VF	XF
ND(1852) Series 4	3.00	5.00	8.00	12.00	—

KM# 52s.4 MUN
Cast Copper or Bronze

Date	Good	VG	F	VF	XF
ND(1852) Series 4	—	—	—	—	50.00

KM# 52.5 MUN
Cast Copper or Bronze **Rev:** "Hong" at bottom, series number at left

Date	Good	VG	F	VF	XF
ND(1852) Series 5	3.00	5.00	8.00	12.00	—

KM# 52s.5 MUN
Cast Copper or Bronze

Date	Good	VG	F	VF	XF
ND(1852) Series 5	—	—	—	—	50.00

KM# 52.6 MUN
Cast Copper or Bronze **Rev:** "Hong" at bottom, series number at left

Date	Good	VG	F	VF	XF
ND(1852) Series 6	3.00	5.00	8.00	12.00	—

KM# 52s.6 MUN
Cast Copper or Bronze

Date	Good	VG	F	VF	XF
ND(1852) Series 6	—	—	—	—	50.00

KM# 52.7 MUN
Cast Copper or Bronze **Rev:** "Hong" at bottom, series number at left

Date	Good	VG	F	VF	XF
ND(1852) Series 7	3.00	5.00	8.00	12.00	—

KM# 52s.7 MUN
Cast Copper or Bronze

Date	Good	VG	F	VF	XF
ND(1852) Series 7	—	—	—	—	50.00

KM# 52.8 MUN
Cast Copper or Bronze **Rev:** "Hong" at bottom, series number at left

Date	Good	VG	F	VF	XF
ND(1852) Series 8	3.00	5.00	8.00	12.00	—

KM# 52s.8 MUN
Cast Copper or Bronze

Date	Good	VG	F	VF	XF
ND(1852) Series 8	—	—	—	—	50.00

KM# 52.9 MUN
Cast Copper or Bronze **Rev:** "Hong" at bottom, series number at left

Date	Good	VG	F	VF	XF
ND(1852) Series 9	3.00	5.00	8.00	12.00	—

KM# 52s.9 MUN
Cast Copper or Bronze

Date	Good	VG	F	VF	XF
ND(1852) Series 9	—	—	—	—	50.00

KM# 52.10 MUN
Cast Copper or Bronze **Rev:** "Hong" at bottom, series number at left

Date	Good	VG	F	VF	XF
ND(1852) Series 10	3.00	5.00	8.00	12.00	—

KM# 52s.10 MUN
Cast Copper or Bronze

Date	Good	VG	F	VF	XF
ND(1852) Series 10	—	—	—	—	50.00

KM# 53.1 MUN
Cast Copper or Bronze **Note:** Size varies 22-24mm.

Date	Good	VG	F	VF	XF
ND(1852) Series 1	3.00	5.00	8.00	12.00	—

KM# 53a.1 MUN
Cast Copper or Bronze **Obv:** "Tong" with 1 dot

Date	Good	VG	F	VF	XF
ND(1852) Series 1	3.00	5.00	8.00	12.00	—

KM# 53s.1 MUN
Cast Copper or Bronze

Date	Good	VG	F	VF	XF
ND(1852) Series 1	—	—	—	—	50.00

KM# 53.2 MUN
Cast Copper or Bronze **Note:** Size varies 22-24mm.

Date	Good	VG	F	VF	XF
ND(1852) Series 2	3.00	5.00	8.00	12.00	—

KM# 53a.2 MUN
Cast Copper or Bronze **Obv:** "Tong" with 1 dot

Date	Good	VG	F	VF	XF
ND(1852) Series 2	3.00	5.00	8.00	12.00	—

KM# 53s.2 MUN
Cast Copper or Bronze

Date	Good	VG	F	VF	XF
ND(1852) Series 2	—	—	—	—	50.00

KM# 53a.3 MUN
Cast Copper or Bronze **Obv:** "Tong" with 1 dot

Date	Good	VG	F	VF	XF
ND(1852) Series 3	3.00	5.00	8.00	12.00	—

KM# 53s.3 MUN
Cast Copper or Bronze

Date	Good	VG	F	VF	XF
ND(1852) Series 3	—	—	—	—	50.00

KM# 53.4 MUN
Cast Copper or Bronze **Note:** Size varies 22-24mm.

Date	Good	VG	F	VF	XF
ND(1852) Series 4	3.00	5.00	8.00	12.00	—

KM# 53a.4 MUN
Cast Copper or Bronze **Obv:** "Tong" with 1 dot

Date	Good	VG	F	VF	XF
ND(1852) Series 4	3.00	5.00	8.00	12.00	—

KM# 53s.4 MUN
Cast Copper or Bronze

Date	Good	VG	F	VF	XF
ND(1852) Series 4	—	—	—	—	50.00

KM# 53.5 MUN
Cast Copper or Bronze **Note:** Size varies 22-24mm.

Date	Good	VG	F	VF	XF
ND(1852) Series 5	3.00	5.00	8.00	12.00	—

KM# 53a.5 MUN
Cast Copper or Bronze **Obv:** "Tong" with 1 dot

Date	Good	VG	F	VF	XF
ND(1852) Series 5	3.00	5.00	8.00	12.00	—

KM# 53s.5 MUN
Cast Copper or Bronze

Date	Good	VG	F	VF	XF
ND(1852) Series 5	—	—	—	—	50.00

KM# 53.6 MUN
Cast Copper or Bronze **Note:** Size varies 22-24mm.

Date	Good	VG	F	VF	XF
ND(1852) Series 6	3.00	5.00	8.00	12.00	—

KM# 53a.6 MUN
Cast Copper or Bronze **Obv:** "Tong" with 1 dot

Date	Good	VG	F	VF	XF
ND(1852) Series 6	3.00	5.00	8.00	12.00	—

KM# 53s.6 MUN
Cast Copper or Bronze

Date	Good	VG	F	VF	XF
ND(1852) Series 6	—	—	—	—	50.00

KM# 53.7 MUN
Cast Copper or Bronze **Note:** Size varies 22-24mm.

Date	Good	VG	F	VF	XF
ND(1852) Series 7	3.00	5.00	8.00	12.00	—

KM# 53a.7 MUN
Cast Copper or Bronze **Obv:** "Tong" with 1 dot

Date	Good	VG	F	VF	XF
ND(1852) Series 7	3.00	5.00	8.00	12.00	—

KM# 53s.7 MUN
Cast Copper or Bronze

Date	Good	VG	F	VF	XF
ND(1852) Series 7	—	—	—	—	50.00

KM# 53.8 MUN
Cast Copper or Bronze **Note:** Size varies 22-24mm.

Date	Good	VG	F	VF	XF
ND(1852) Series 8	3.00	5.00	8.00	12.00	—

KM# 53a.8 MUN
Cast Copper or Bronze **Obv:** "Tong" with 1 dot

Date	Good	VG	F	VF	XF
ND(1852) Series 8	3.00	5.00	8.00	12.00	—

KM# 53s.8 MUN
Cast Copper or Bronze

Date	Good	VG	F	VF	XF
ND(1852) Series 8	—	—	—	—	50.00

KM# 53.9 MUN
Cast Copper or Bronze **Note:** Size varies 22-24mm.

Date	Good	VG	F	VF	XF
ND(1852) Series 9	3.00	5.00	8.00	12.00	—

KM# 53a.9 MUN
Cast Copper or Bronze **Obv:** "Tong" with 1 dot

Date	Good	VG	F	VF	XF
ND(1852) Series 9	3.00	5.00	8.00	12.00	—

KM# 53s.9 MUN
Cast Copper or Bronze

Date	Good	VG	F	VF	XF
ND(1852) Series 9	—	—	—	—	50.00

KM# 53.10 MUN
Cast Copper or Bronze **Note:** Size varies 22-24mm.

Date	Good	VG	F	VF	XF
ND(1852) Series 10	3.00	5.00	8.00	12.00	—

KM# 53s.10 MUN
Cast Copper or Bronze

Date	Good	VG	F	VF	XF
ND(1852) Series 10	—	—	—	—	50.00

KM# 53a.10 MUN
Cast Copper or Bronze **Obv:** "Tong" with 1 dot

Date	Good	VG	F	VF	XF
ND(1852) Series 10	3.00	5.00	8.00	12.00	—

KM# 54.1 MUN
Cast Copper or Bronze **Rev:** "Il" (sun) at bottom, series number at left **Note:** Size varies 23-25mm.

Date	Good	VG	F	VF	XF
ND(1852) Series 1	2.00	3.00	5.00	8.00	—

KM# 54s.1 MUN
Cast Copper or Bronze

Date	Good	VG	F	VF	XF
ND(1852) Series 1	—	—	—	—	50.00

KM# 54.2 MUN
Cast Copper or Bronze **Rev:** "Il" (sun) at bottom, series numberat left **Note:** Size varies 23-25mm.

Date	Good	VG	F	VF	XF
ND(1852) Series 2	2.00	3.00	5.00	8.00	—

KM# 54s.2 MUN
Cast Copper or Bronze

Date	Good	VG	F	VF	XF
ND(1852) Series 2	—	—	—	—	50.00

KM# 54.3 MUN
Cast Copper or Bronze **Rev:** "Il" (sun) at bottom, series number at left **Note:** Size varies 23-25mm.

Date	Good	VG	F	VF	XF
ND(1852) Series 3	2.00	3.00	5.00	8.00	—

KM# 54s.3 MUN
Cast Copper or Bronze

Date	Good	VG	F	VF	XF
ND(1852) Series 3	—	—	—	—	50.00

KM# 54.4 MUN
Cast Copper or Bronze **Rev:** "Il" (sun) at bottom, series number at left **Note:** Size varies 23-25mm.

Date	Good	VG	F	VF	XF
ND(1852) Series 4	2.00	3.00	5.00	8.00	—

KM# 54s.4 MUN
Cast Copper or Bronze

Date	Good	VG	F	VF	XF
ND(1852) Series 4	—	—	—	—	50.00

KM# 54.5 MUN
Cast Copper or Bronze **Rev:** "Il" (sun) at bottom, series number at left **Note:** Size varies 23-25mm.

Date	Good	VG	F	VF	XF
ND(1852) Series 5	2.00	3.00	5.00	8.00	—

KM# 54s.5 MUN
Cast Copper or Bronze

Date	Good	VG	F	VF	XF
ND(1852) Series 5	—	—	—	—	50.00

KM# 54.6 MUN
Cast Copper or Bronze **Rev:** "Il" (sun) at bottom, series number at left **Note:** Size varies 23-25mm.

Date	Good	VG	F	VF	XF
ND(1852) Series 6	2.00	3.00	5.00	8.00	—

KM# 54s.6 MUN
Cast Copper or Bronze

Date	Good	VG	F	VF	XF
ND(1852) Series 6	—	—	—	—	50.00

KM# 54.7 MUN
Cast Copper or Bronze **Rev:** "Il" (sun) at bottom, series number at left **Note:** Size varies 23-25mm.

Date	Good	VG	F	VF	XF
ND(1852) Series 7	2.00	3.00	5.00	8.00	—

KM# 54s.7 MUN
Cast Copper or Bronze

Date	Good	VG	F	VF	XF
ND(1852) Series 7	—	—	—	—	50.00

KM# 54.8 MUN
Cast Copper or Bronze **Rev:** "Il" (sun) at bottom, series number at left **Note:** Size varies 23-25mm.

Date	Good	VG	F	VF	XF
ND(1852) Series 8	2.00	3.00	5.00	8.00	—

KM# 54s.8 MUN
Cast Copper or Bronze

Date	Good	VG	F	VF	XF
ND(1852) Series 8	—	—	—	—	50.00

KM# 54.9 MUN
Cast Copper or Bronze **Rev:** "Il" (sun) at bottom, series number at left **Note:** Size varies 23-25mm.

Date	Good	VG	F	VF	XF
ND(1852) Series 9	2.00	3.00	5.00	8.00	—

KM# 54s.9 MUN
Cast Copper or Bronze

Date	Good	VG	F	VF	XF
ND(1852) Series 9	—	—	—	—	50.00

KM# 54.10 MUN
Cast Copper or Bronze **Rev:** "Il" (sun) at bottom, series number at left **Note:** Size varies 23-25mm.

Date	Good	VG	F	VF	XF
ND(1852) Series 10	2.00	3.00	5.00	8.00	—

KM# 54s.10 MUN
Cast Copper or Bronze

Date	Good	VG	F	VF	XF
ND(1852) Series 10	—	—	—	—	50.00

KM# 55.1 MUN
Cast Copper or Bronze **Rev:** "Wol" (moon) at bottom, series number at left

Date	Good	VG	F	VF	XF
ND(1852) Series 1	2.00	3.00	5.00	8.00	—

KM# 55s.1 MUN
Cast Copper or Bronze, 26 mm. **Note:** Seed type.

Date	Good	VG	F	VF	XF
ND(1852) Series 1	—	—	—	—	50.00

KM# 55.2 MUN
Cast Copper or Bronze **Rev:** "Wol" (moon) at bottom, series number at left

Date	Good	VG	F	VF	XF
ND(1852) Series 2	2.00	3.00	5.00	8.00	—

KM# 55s.2 MUN
Cast Copper or Bronze

Date	Good	VG	F	VF	XF
ND(1852) Series 2	—	—	—	—	50.00

KM# 55.3 MUN
Cast Copper or Bronze **Rev:** "Wol" (moon) at bottom, series number at left

Date	Good	VG	F	VF	XF
ND(1852) Series 3	2.00	3.00	5.00	8.00	—

KM# 55s.3 MUN
Cast Copper or Bronze

Date	Good	VG	F	VF	XF
ND(1852) Series 3	—	—	—	—	50.00

KM# 55.4 MUN
Cast Copper or Bronze **Rev:** "Wol" (moon) at bottom, series number at left

Date	Good	VG	F	VF	XF
ND(1852) Series 4	2.00	3.00	5.00	8.00	—

KM# 55s.4 MUN
Cast Copper or Bronze

Date	Good	VG	F	VF	XF
ND(1852) Series 4	—	—	—	—	50.00

KM# 55.5 MUN
Cast Copper or Bronze **Rev:** "Wol" (moon) at bottom, series number at left

Date	Good	VG	F	VF	XF
ND(1852) Series 5	2.00	3.00	5.00	8.00	—

KM# 55s.5 MUN
Cast Copper or Bronze

Date	Good	VG	F	VF	XF
ND(1852) Series 5	—	—	—	—	50.00

KM# 55.6 MUN
Cast Copper or Bronze **Rev:** "Wol" (moon) at bottom, series number at left

Date	Good	VG	F	VF	XF
ND(1852) Series 6	2.00	3.00	5.00	8.00	—

KM# 55s.6 MUN
Cast Copper or Bronze

Date	Good	VG	F	VF	XF
ND(1852) Series 6	—	—	—	—	50.00

KM# 55.7 MUN
Cast Copper or Bronze **Rev:** "Wol" (moon) at bottom, series number at left

Date	Good	VG	F	VF	XF
ND(1852) Series 7	2.00	3.00	5.00	8.00	—

KM# 55s.7 MUN
Cast Copper or Bronze

Date	Good	VG	F	VF	XF
ND(1852) Series 7	—	—	—	—	50.00

KM# 55.8 MUN
Cast Copper or Bronze **Rev:** "Wol" (moon) at bottom, series number at left

Date	Good	VG	F	VF	XF
ND(1852) Series 8	2.00	3.00	5.00	8.00	—

KM# 55s.8 MUN
Cast Copper or Bronze

Date	Good	VG	F	VF	XF
ND(1852) Series 8	—	—	—	—	50.00

KM# 55.9 MUN
Cast Copper or Bronze **Rev:** "Wol" (moon) at bottom, series number at left

Date	Good	VG	F	VF	XF
ND(1852) Series 9	2.00	3.00	5.00	8.00	—

KM# 55s.9 MUN
Cast Copper or Bronze

Date	Good	VG	F	VF	XF
ND(1852) Series 9	—	—	—	—	50.00

KM# 55.10 MUN
Cast Copper or Bronze **Rev:** "Wol" (moon) at bottom, series number at left

Date	Good	VG	F	VF	XF
ND(1852) Series 10	2.00	3.00	5.00	8.00	—

KM# 55s.10 MUN
Cast Copper or Bronze

Date	Good	VG	F	VF	XF
ND(1852) Series 10	—	—	—	—	50.00

KM# 56.1 MUN
Cast Copper or Bronze **Rev:** "Chin" at bottom, series number at left

Date	Good	VG	F	VF	XF
ND(1852) Series 1	2.00	3.00	5.00	8.00	—

KM# 56s.1 MUN
Cast Copper or Bronze

Date	Good	VG	F	VF	XF
ND(1852) Series 1	—	—	—	—	50.00

KM# 56.2 MUN
Cast Copper or Bronze **Rev:** "Chin" at bottom, series number at left

Date	Good	VG	F	VF	XF
ND(1852) Series 2	2.00	3.00	5.00	8.00	—

KM# 56s.2 MUN
Cast Copper or Bronze

Date	Good	VG	F	VF	XF
ND(1852) Series 2	—	—	—	—	50.00

KM# 56.3 MUN
Cast Copper or Bronze **Rev:** "Chin" at bottom, series number at left

Date	Good	VG	F	VF	XF
ND(1852) Series 3	2.00	3.00	5.00	8.00	—

KM# 56s.3 MUN
Cast Copper or Bronze

Date	Good	VG	F	VF	XF
ND(1852) Series 3	—	—	—	—	50.00

KM# 56.4 MUN
Cast Copper or Bronze **Rev:** "Chin" at bottom, series number at left

Date	Good	VG	F	VF	XF
ND(1852) Series 4	2.00	3.00	5.00	8.00	—

KM# 56s.4 MUN
Cast Copper or Bronze

Date	Good	VG	F	VF	XF
ND(1852) Series 4	—	—	—	—	50.00

KM# 56.5 MUN
Cast Copper or Bronze **Rev:** "Chin" at bottom, series number at left

Date	Good	VG	F	VF	XF
ND(1852) Series 5	2.00	3.00	5.00	8.00	—

KM# 56s.5 MUN
Cast Copper or Bronze

Date	Good	VG	F	VF	XF
ND(1852) Series 5	—	—	—	—	50.00

KM# 56.6 MUN
Cast Copper or Bronze **Rev:** "Chin" at bottom, series number at left

Date	Good	VG	F	VF	XF
ND(1852) Series 6	2.00	3.00	5.00	8.00	—

KM# 56s.6 MUN
Cast Copper or Bronze

Date	Good	VG	F	VF	XF
ND(1852) Series 6	—	—	—	—	50.00

KM# 56.7 MUN
Cast Copper or Bronze **Rev:** "Chin" at bottom, series number at left

Date	Good	VG	F	VF	XF
ND(1852) Series 7	2.00	3.00	5.00	8.00	—

KM# 56s.7 MUN
Cast Copper or Bronze

Date	Good	VG	F	VF	XF
ND(1852) Series 7	—	—	—	—	50.00

KM# 56.8 MUN
Cast Copper or Bronze **Rev:** "Chin" at bottom, series number at left

Date	Good	VG	F	VF	XF
ND(1852) Series 8	2.00	3.00	5.00	8.00	—

KM# 56s.8 MUN
Cast Copper or Bronze

Date	Good	VG	F	VF	XF
ND(1852) Series 8	—	—	—	—	50.00

KM# 56.9 MUN
Cast Copper or Bronze **Rev:** "Chin" at bottom, series number at left

Date	Good	VG	F	VF	XF
ND(1852) Series 9	2.00	3.00	5.00	8.00	—

KM# 56s.9 MUN
Cast Copper or Bronze

Date	Good	VG	F	VF	XF
ND(1852) Series 9	—	—	—	—	50.00

KM# 56.10 MUN
Cast Copper or Bronze **Rev:** "Chin" at bottom, series number at left

Date	Good	VG	F	VF	XF
ND(1852) Series 10	2.00	3.00	5.00	8.00	—

KM# 56s.10 MUN
Cast Copper or Bronze

Date	Good	VG	F	VF	XF
ND(1852) Series 10	—	—	—	—	50.00

KM# 57.1 MUN
Cast Copper or Bronze, 24 mm. **Rev:** "Yol" at bottom, series number at left

Date	Good	VG	F	VF	XF
ND(1852) Series 1	2.00	3.00	5.00	8.00	—

KM# 57s.1 MUN
Cast Copper or Bronze

Date	Good	VG	F	VF	XF
ND(1852) Series 1	—	—	—	—	50.00

KM# 57.2 MUN
Cast Copper or Bronze **Rev:** "Yol" at bottom, series number at left

Date	Good	VG	F	VF	XF
ND(1852) Series 2	2.00	3.00	5.00	8.00	—

KM# 57s.2 MUN
Cast Copper or Bronze

Date	Good	VG	F	VF	XF
ND(1852) Series 2	—	—	—	—	50.00

KM# 57.3 MUN
Cast Copper or Bronze **Rev:** "Yol" at bottom, series number at left

Date	Good	VG	F	VF	XF
ND(1852) Series 3	2.00	3.00	5.00	8.00	—

KM# 57s.3 MUN
Cast Copper or Bronze

Date	Good	VG	F	VF	XF
ND(1852) Series 3	—	—	—	—	50.00

KM# 57.4 MUN
Cast Copper or Bronze **Rev:** "Yol" at bottom, series number at left

Date	Good	VG	F	VF	XF
ND(1852) Series 4	2.00	3.00	5.00	8.00	—

KM# 57s.4 MUN
Cast Copper or Bronze

Date	Good	VG	F	VF	XF
ND(1852) Series 4	—	—	—	—	50.00

KM# 57.5 MUN
Cast Copper or Bronze **Rev:** "Yol" at bottom, series number at left

Date	Good	VG	F	VF	XF
ND(1852) Series 5	2.00	3.00	5.00	8.00	—

KM# 57s.5 MUN
Cast Copper or Bronze

Date	Good	VG	F	VF	XF
ND(1852) Series 5	—	—	—	—	50.00

KM# 57.6 MUN
Cast Copper or Bronze **Rev:** "Yol" at bottom, series number at left

Date	Good	VG	F	VF	XF
ND(1852) Series 6	2.00	3.00	5.00	8.00	—

KM# 57s.6 MUN
Cast Copper or Bronze

Date	Good	VG	F	VF	XF
ND(1852) Series 6	—	—	—	—	50.00

KM# 57.7 MUN
Cast Copper or Bronze **Rev:** "Yol" at bottom, series number at left

Date	Good	VG	F	VF	XF
ND(1852) Series 7	2.00	3.00	5.00	8.00	—

KM# 57s.7 MUN
Cast Copper or Bronze

Date	Good	VG	F	VF	XF
ND(1852) Series 7	—	—	—	—	50.00

KM# 57.8 MUN
Cast Copper or Bronze **Rev:** "Yol" at bottom, series number at left

Date	Good	VG	F	VF	XF
ND(1852) Series 8	2.00	3.00	5.00	8.00	—

KM# 57s.8 MUN
Cast Copper or Bronze

Date	Good	VG	F	VF	XF
ND(1852) Series 8	—	—	—	—	50.00

KM# 57.9 MUN
Cast Copper or Bronze **Rev:** "Yol" at bottom, series number at left

Date	Good	VG	F	VF	XF
ND(1852) Series 9	2.00	3.00	5.00	8.00	—

KM# 57s.9 MUN
Cast Copper or Bronze

Date	Good	VG	F	VF	XF
ND(1852) Series 9	—	—	—	—	50.00

KM# 57.10 MUN
Cast Copper or Bronze **Rev:** "Yol" at bottom, series number at left

Date	Good	VG	F	VF	XF
ND(1852) Series 10	2.00	3.00	5.00	8.00	—

KM# 57s.10 MUN
Cast Copper or Bronze

Date	Good	VG	F	VF	XF
ND(1852) Series 10	—	—	—	—	50.00

KM# 58.1 MUN
Cast Copper or Bronze **Rev:** "Nae" at bottom, series number at left

Date	Good	VG	F	VF	XF
ND(1852) Series 1	2.00	3.00	5.00	8.00	—

KM# 58s.1 MUN
Cast Copper or Bronze

Date	Good	VG	F	VF	XF
ND(1852) Series 1	—	—	—	—	50.00

KM# 58.2 MUN
Cast Copper or Bronze **Rev:** "Nae" at bottom, series number at left

Date	Good	VG	F	VF	XF
ND(1852) Series 2	2.00	3.00	5.00	8.00	—

KM# 58s.2 MUN
Cast Copper or Bronze

Date	Good	VG	F	VF	XF
ND(1852) Series 2	—	—	—	—	50.00

KM# 58.3 MUN
Cast Copper or Bronze **Rev:** "Nae" at bottom, series number at left

Date	Good	VG	F	VF	XF
ND(1852) Series 3	2.00	3.00	5.00	8.00	—

KM# 58s.3 MUN
Cast Copper or Bronze

Date	Good	VG	F	VF	XF
ND(1852) Series 3	—	—	—	—	50.00

KM# 58.4 MUN
Cast Copper or Bronze **Rev:** "Nae" at bottom, series number at left

Date	Good	VG	F	VF	XF
ND(1852) Series 4	2.00	3.00	5.00	8.00	—

KM# 58s.4 MUN
Cast Copper or Bronze

Date	Good	VG	F	VF	XF
ND(1852) Series 4	—	—	—	—	50.00

KM# 58.5 MUN
Cast Copper or Bronze **Rev:** "Nae" at bottom, series number at left

Date	Good	VG	F	VF	XF
ND(1852) Series 5	2.00	3.00	5.00	8.00	—

KM# 58s.5 MUN
Cast Copper or Bronze

Date	Good	VG	F	VF	XF
ND(1852) Series 5	—	—	—	—	50.00

KM# 58.6 MUN
Cast Copper or Bronze **Rev:** "Nae" at bottom, series number at left

Date	Good	VG	F	VF	XF
ND(1852) Series 6	2.00	3.00	5.00	8.00	—

KM# 58s.6 MUN
Cast Copper or Bronze

Date	Good	VG	F	VF	XF
ND(1852) Series 6	—	—	—	—	50.00

KM# 58.7 MUN
Cast Copper or Bronze **Rev:** "Nae" at bottom, series number at left

Date	Good	VG	F	VF	XF
ND(1852) Series 7	2.00	3.00	5.00	8.00	—

KM# 58s.7 MUN
Cast Copper or Bronze

Date	Good	VG	F	VF	XF
ND(1852) Series 7	—	—	—	—	50.00

KM# 58.8 MUN
Cast Copper or Bronze **Rev:** "Nae" at bottom, series number at left

Date	Good	VG	F	VF	XF
ND(1852) Series 8	2.00	3.00	5.00	8.00	—

KM# 58s.8 MUN
Cast Copper or Bronze

Date	Good	VG	F	VF	XF
ND(1852) Series 8	—	—	—	—	50.00

KM# 58.9 MUN
Cast Copper or Bronze **Rev:** "Nae" at bottom, series number at left

Date	Good	VG	F	VF	XF
ND(1852) Series 9	2.00	3.00	5.00	8.00	—

KM# 58s.9 MUN
Cast Copper or Bronze

Date	Good	VG	F	VF	XF
ND(1852) Series 9	—	—	—	—	50.00

KM# 58.10 MUN
Cast Copper or Bronze **Rev:** "Nae" at bottom, series number at left

Date	Good	VG	F	VF	XF
ND(1852) Series 10	2.00	3.00	5.00	8.00	—

KM# 58s.10 MUN
Cast Copper or Bronze

Date	Good	VG	F	VF	XF
ND(1852) Series 10	—	—	—	—	50.00

KM# 59.1 MUN
Cast Copper or Bronze **Rev:** "Wang" at bottom, series number at left

Date	Good	VG	F	VF	XF
ND(1852) Series 1	2.00	3.00	5.00	8.00	—

KM# 59s.1 MUN

Cast Copper or Bronze

Date	Good	VG	F	VF	XF
ND(1852) Series 1	—	—	—	—	50.00

KM# 59.2 MUN

Cast Copper or Bronze **Rev:** "Wang" at bottom, series number at left

Date	Good	VG	F	VF	XF
ND(1852) Series 2	2.00	3.00	5.00	8.00	—

KM# 59s.2 MUN

Cast Copper or Bronze

Date	Good	VG	F	VF	XF
ND(1852) Series 2	—	—	—	—	50.00

KM# 59.3 MUN

Cast Copper or Bronze **Rev:** "Wang" at bottom, series number at left

Date	Good	VG	F	VF	XF
ND(1852) Series 3	2.00	3.00	5.00	8.00	—

KM# 59s.3 MUN

Cast Copper or Bronze

Date	Good	VG	F	VF	XF
ND(1852) Series 3	—	—	—	—	50.00

KM# 59.4 MUN

Cast Copper or Bronze **Rev:** "Wang" at bottom, series number at left

Date	Good	VG	F	VF	XF
ND(1852) Series 4	2.00	3.00	5.00	8.00	—

KM# 59s.4 MUN

Cast Copper or Bronze

Date	Good	VG	F	VF	XF
ND(1852) Series 4	—	—	—	—	50.00

KM# 59.5 MUN

Cast Copper or Bronze **Rev:** "Wang" at bottom, series number at left

Date	Good	VG	F	VF	XF
ND(1852) Series 5	2.00	3.00	5.00	8.00	—

KM# 59s.5 MUN

Cast Copper or Bronze

Date	Good	VG	F	VF	XF
ND(1852) Series 5	—	—	—	—	50.00

KM# 59.6 MUN

Cast Copper or Bronze **Rev:** "Wang" at bottom, series number at left

Date	Good	VG	F	VF	XF
ND(1852) Series 6	2.00	3.00	5.00	8.00	—

KM# 59s.6 MUN

Cast Copper or Bronze

Date	Good	VG	F	VF	XF
ND(1852) Series 6	—	—	—	—	50.00

KM# 59.7 MUN

Cast Copper or Bronze **Rev:** "Wang" at bottom, series number at left

Date	Good	VG	F	VF	XF
ND(1852) Series 7	2.00	3.00	5.00	8.00	—

KM# 59s.7 MUN

Cast Copper or Bronze

Date	Good	VG	F	VF	XF
ND(1852) Series 7	—	—	—	—	50.00

KM# 59.8 MUN

Cast Copper or Bronze **Rev:** "Wang" at bottom, series number at left

Date	Good	VG	F	VF	XF
ND(1852) Series 8	2.00	3.00	5.00	8.00	—

KM# 59s.8 MUN

Cast Copper or Bronze

Date	Good	VG	F	VF	XF
ND(1852) Series 8	—	—	—	—	50.00

KM# 59.9 MUN

Cast Copper or Bronze **Rev:** "Wang" at bottom, series number at left

Date	Good	VG	F	VF	XF
ND(1852) Series 9	2.00	3.00	5.00	8.00	—

KM# 59s.9 MUN

Cast Copper or Bronze

Date	Good	VG	F	VF	XF
ND(1852) Series 9	—	—	—	—	50.00

KM# 59.10 MUN

Cast Copper or Bronze **Rev:** "Wang" at bottom, series number at left

Date	Good	VG	F	VF	XF
ND(1852) Series 10	2.00	3.00	5.00	8.00	—

KM# 59s.10 MUN

Cast Copper or Bronze

Date	Good	VG	F	VF	XF
ND(1852) Series 10	—	—	—	—	50.00

KM# 60.1 MUN

Cast Copper or Bronze, 23 mm. **Rev:** "Saeng" at bottom, series number at left

Date	Good	VG	F	VF	XF
ND(1852) Series 1	2.00	3.00	5.00	8.00	—

KM# 60s.1 MUN

Cast Copper or Bronze

Date	Good	VG	F	VF	XF
ND(1852) Series 1	—	—	—	—	50.00

KM# 60.2 MUN

Cast Copper or Bronze **Rev:** "Saeng" at bottom, series number at left

Date	Good	VG	F	VF	XF
ND(1852) Series 2	2.00	3.00	5.00	8.00	—

KM# 60s.2 MUN

Cast Copper or Bronze

Date	Good	VG	F	VF	XF
ND(1852) Series 2	—	—	—	—	50.00

KM# 60.3 MUN

Cast Copper or Bronze **Rev:** "Saeng" at bottom, series number at left

Date	Good	VG	F	VF	XF
ND(1852) Series 3	2.00	3.00	5.00	8.00	—

KM# 60s.3 MUN

Cast Copper or Bronze

Date	Good	VG	F	VF	XF
ND(1852) Series 3	—	—	—	—	50.00

KM# 60.4 MUN

Cast Copper or Bronze **Rev:** "Saeng" at bottom, series number at left

Date	Good	VG	F	VF	XF
ND(1852) Series 4	2.00	3.00	5.00	8.00	—

KM# 60s.4 MUN

Cast Copper or Bronze

Date	Good	VG	F	VF	XF
ND(1852) Series 4	—	—	—	—	50.00

KM# 60.5 MUN

Cast Copper or Bronze **Rev:** "Saeng" at bottom, series number at left

Date	Good	VG	F	VF	XF
ND(1852) Series 5	2.00	3.00	5.00	8.00	—

KM# 60s.5 MUN

Cast Copper or Bronze

Date	Good	VG	F	VF	XF
ND(1852) Series 5	—	—	—	—	50.00

KM# 60.6 MUN

Cast Copper or Bronze **Rev:** "Saeng" at bottom, series number at left

Date	Good	VG	F	VF	XF
ND(1852) Series 6	2.00	3.00	5.00	8.00	—

KM# 60s.6 MUN

Cast Copper or Bronze

Date	Good	VG	F	VF	XF
ND(1852) Series 6	—	—	—	—	50.00

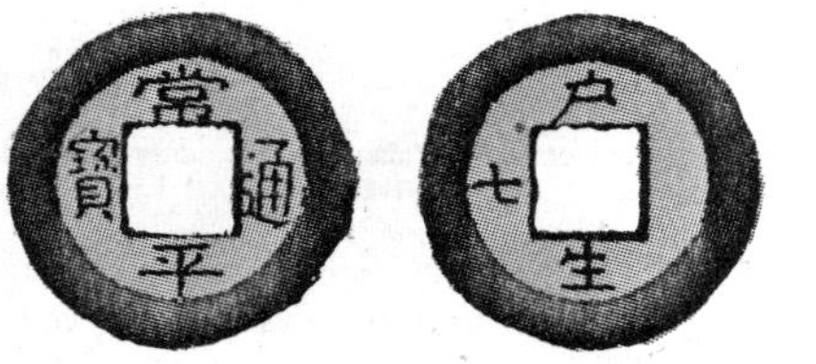

KM# 60.7 MUN

Cast Copper or Bronze **Rev:** "Saeng" at bottom, series number at left

Date	Good	VG	F	VF	XF
ND(1852) Series 7	2.00	3.00	5.00	8.00	—

KM# 60s.7 MUN

Cast Copper or Bronze

Date	Good	VG	F	VF	XF
ND(1852) Series 7	—	—	—	—	50.00

KM# 60.8 MUN

Cast Copper or Bronze **Rev:** "Saeng" at bottom, series number at left

Date	Good	VG	F	VF	XF
ND(1852) Series 8	2.00	3.00	5.00	8.00	—

KM# 60s.8 MUN

Cast Copper or Bronze

Date	Good	VG	F	VF	XF
ND(1852) Series 8	—	—	—	—	50.00

KM# 60.9 MUN

Cast Copper or Bronze **Rev:** "Saeng" at bottom, series number at left

Date	Good	VG	F	VF	XF
ND(1852) Series 9	2.00	3.00	5.00	8.00	—

KM# 60s.9 MUN

Cast Copper or Bronze

Date	Good	VG	F	VF	XF
ND(1852) Series 9	—	—	—	—	50.00

KM# 60.10 MUN

Cast Copper or Bronze **Rev:** "Saeng" at bottom, series number at left

Date	Good	VG	F	VF	XF
ND(1852) Series 10	2.00	3.00	5.00	8.00	—

KM# 60s.10 MUN

Cast Copper or Bronze

Date	Good	VG	F	VF	XF
ND(1852) Series 10	—	—	—	—	50.00

KM# 61.1 MUN

Cast Copper or Bronze, 24 mm. **Rev:** "Su" at bottom, series number at left

Date	Good	VG	F	VF	XF
ND(1852) Series 1	4.00	7.00	12.00	20.00	—

KM# 61s.1 MUN

Cast Copper or Bronze, 26 mm.

Date	Good	VG	F	VF	XF
ND(1852) Series 1	—	—	—	—	60.00

KM# 61.2 MUN

Cast Copper or Bronze **Rev:** "Su" at bottom, series number at left

Date	Good	VG	F	VF	XF
ND(1852) Series 2	4.00	7.00	12.00	20.00	—

KM# 61s.2 MUN

Cast Copper or Bronze

Date	Good	VG	F	VF	XF
ND(1852) Series 2	—	—	—	—	60.00

KM# 61.3 MUN

Cast Copper or Bronze **Rev:** "Su" at bottom, series number at left

Date	Good	VG	F	VF	XF
ND(1852) Series 3	4.00	7.00	12.00	20.00	—

KM# 61s.3 MUN

Cast Copper or Bronze

Date	Good	VG	F	VF	XF
ND(1852) Series 3	—	—	—	—	60.00

KM# 61.4 MUN

Cast Copper or Bronze **Rev:** "Su" at bottom, series number at left

Date	Good	VG	F	VF	XF
ND(1852) Series 4	4.00	7.00	12.00	20.00	—

KM# 61s.4 MUN

Cast Copper or Bronze

Date	Good	VG	F	VF	XF
ND(1852) Series 4	—	—	—	—	60.00

KM# 61.5 MUN

Cast Copper or Bronze **Rev:** "Su" at bottom, series number at left

Date	Good	VG	F	VF	XF
ND(1852) Series 5	4.00	7.00	12.00	20.00	—

KM# 61s.5 MUN

Cast Copper or Bronze

Date	Good	VG	F	VF	XF
ND(1852) Series 5	—	—	—	—	60.00

KM# 61.6 MUN

Cast Copper or Bronze **Rev:** "Su" at bottom, series number at left

Date	Good	VG	F	VF	XF
ND(1852) Series 6	4.00	7.00	12.00	20.00	—

KM# 61s.6 MUN

Cast Copper or Bronze

Date	Good	VG	F	VF	XF
ND(1852) Series 6	—	—	—	—	60.00

KM# 61.7 MUN

Cast Copper or Bronze **Rev:** "Su" at bottom, series number at left

Date	Good	VG	F	VF	XF
ND(1852) Series 7	4.00	7.00	12.00	20.00	—

KM# 61s.7 MUN

Cast Copper or Bronze **Note:** Seed type.

Date	Good	VG	F	VF	XF
ND(1852) Series 7	—	—	—	—	60.00

KM# 61.8 MUN

Cast Copper or Bronze **Rev:** "Su" at bottom, series number at left

Date	Good	VG	F	VF	XF
ND(1852) Series 8	4.00	7.00	12.00	20.00	—

KM# 61s.8 MUN

Cast Copper or Bronze

Date	Good	VG	F	VF	XF
ND(1852) Series 8	—	—	—	—	60.00

KM# 61.9 MUN

Cast Copper or Bronze **Rev:** "Su" at bottom, series number at left

Date	Good	VG	F	VF	XF
ND(1852) Series 9	4.00	7.00	12.00	20.00	—

KM# 61s.9 MUN

Cast Copper or Bronze

Date	Good	VG	F	VF	XF
ND(1852) Series 9	—	—	—	—	60.00

KM# 61.10 MUN

Cast Copper or Bronze **Rev:** "Su" at bottom, series number at left

Date	Good	VG	F	VF	XF
ND(1852) Series 10	4.00	7.00	12.00	20.00	—

KM# 61s.10 MUN

Cast Copper or Bronze

Date	Good	VG	F	VF	XF
ND(1852) Series 10	—	—	—	—	60.00

KM# 62.1 MUN

Cast Copper or Bronze **Rev:** "Kwang" at bottom, series number at left

Date	Good	VG	F	VF	XF
ND(1852) Series 1	2.00	3.00	5.00	8.00	—

KM# 62s.1 MUN

Cast Copper or Bronze

Date	Good	VG	F	VF	XF
ND(1852) Series 1	—	—	—	—	50.00

KM# 62.2 MUN

Cast Copper or Bronze **Rev:** "Kwang" at bottom, series number at left

Date	Good	VG	F	VF	XF
ND(1852) Series 2	2.00	3.00	5.00	8.00	—

KM# 62s.2 MUN

Cast Copper or Bronze

Date	Good	VG	F	VF	XF
ND(1852) Series 2	—	—	—	—	50.00

KM# 62.3 MUN

Cast Copper or Bronze **Rev:** "Kwang" at bottom, series number at left

Date	Good	VG	F	VF	XF
ND(1852) Series 3	2.00	3.00	5.00	8.00	—

KM# 62s.3 MUN

Cast Copper or Bronze

Date	Good	VG	F	VF	XF
ND(1852) Series 3	—	—	—	—	50.00

KM# 62.4 MUN

Cast Copper or Bronze **Rev:** "Kwang" at bottom, series number at left

Date	Good	VG	F	VF	XF
ND(1852) Series 4	2.00	3.00	5.00	8.00	—

KM# 62s.4 MUN

Cast Copper or Bronze

Date	Good	VG	F	VF	XF
ND(1852) Series 4	—	—	—	—	50.00

KM# 62.5 MUN

Cast Copper or Bronze **Rev:** "Kwang" at bottom, series number at left

Date	Good	VG	F	VF	XF
ND(1852) Series 5	2.00	3.00	5.00	8.00	—

KM# 62s.5 MUN

Cast Copper or Bronze

Date	Good	VG	F	VF	XF
ND(1852) Series 5	—	—	—	—	50.00

KM# 62.6 MUN

Cast Copper or Bronze **Rev:** "Kwang" at bottom, series number at left

Date	Good	VG	F	VF	XF
ND(1852) Series 6	2.00	3.00	5.00	8.00	—

KM# 62s.6 MUN

Cast Copper or Bronze

Date	Good	VG	F	VF	XF
ND(1852) Series 6	—	—	—	—	50.00

KM# 62.7 MUN

Cast Copper or Bronze **Rev:** "Kwang" at bottom, series number at left

Date	Good	VG	F	VF	XF
ND(1852) Series 7	2.00	3.00	5.00	8.00	—

KM# 62s.7 MUN

Cast Copper or Bronze

Date	Good	VG	F	VF	XF
ND(1852) Series 7	—	—	—	—	50.00

KM# 62.8 MUN

Cast Copper or Bronze **Rev:** "Kwang" at bottom, series number at left

Date	Good	VG	F	VF	XF
ND(1852) Series 8	2.00	3.00	5.00	8.00	—

KM# 62s.8 MUN

Cast Copper or Bronze

Date	Good	VG	F	VF	XF
ND(1852) Series 8	—	—	—	—	50.00

KM# 62.9 MUN

Cast Copper or Bronze **Rev:** "Kwang" at bottom, series number at left

Date	Good	VG	F	VF	XF
ND(1852) Series 9	2.00	3.00	5.00	8.00	—

KM# 62s.9 MUN

Cast Copper or Bronze

Date	Good	VG	F	VF	XF
ND(1852) Series 9	—	—	—	—	50.00

KM# 62.10 MUN

Cast Copper or Bronze **Rev:** "Kwang" at bottom, series number at left

Date	Good	VG	F	VF	XF
ND(1852) Series 10	2.00	3.00	5.00	8.00	—

KM# 62s.10 MUN

Cast Copper or Bronze

Date	Good	VG	F	VF	XF
ND(1852) Series 10	—	—	—	—	50.00

KM# 63s MUN

Cast Copper or Bronze

Date	Good	VG	F	VF	XF
ND(1852) Series 6	—	—	—	—	50.00

KM# 64.2 MUN

Cast Copper or Bronze, 25 mm. **Rev:** "Kwang" at bottom, series number at right

Date	Good	VG	F	VF	XF
ND(1852) Series 2	1.50	2.25	3.50	5.00	—

KM# 65.1 MUN

Cast Copper or Bronze, 23 mm. **Rev:** "Mun" at bottom, series number at right

Date	Good	VG	F	VF	XF
ND(1852) Series 1	2.00	3.00	5.00	8.00	—

KM# 65s.1 MUN

Cast Copper or Bronze

Date	Good	VG	F	VF	XF
ND(1852) Series 1	—	—	—	—	50.00

KM# 65.2 MUN

Cast Copper or Bronze **Rev:** "Mun" at bottom, series number at right

Date	Good	VG	F	VF	XF
ND(1852) Series 2	2.00	3.00	5.00	8.00	—

KM# 65s.2 MUN

Cast Copper or Bronze

Date	Good	VG	F	VF	XF
ND(1852) Series 2	—	—	—	—	50.00

KM# 65.3 MUN

Cast Copper or Bronze **Rev:** "Mun" at bottom, series number at right

Date	Good	VG	F	VF	XF
ND(1852) Series 3	2.00	3.00	5.00	8.00	—

KM# 65s.3 MUN

Cast Copper or Bronze

Date	Good	VG	F	VF	XF
ND(1852) Series 3	—	—	—	—	50.00

KM# 65.4 MUN

Cast Copper or Bronze **Rev:** "Mun" at bottom, series number at right

Date	Good	VG	F	VF	XF
ND(1852) Series 4	2.00	3.00	5.00	8.00	—

KM# 65s.4 MUN

Cast Copper or Bronze

Date	Good	VG	F	VF	XF
ND(1852) Series 4	—	—	—	—	50.00

KM# 65.5 MUN

Cast Copper or Bronze **Rev:** "Mun" at bottom, series number at right

Date	Good	VG	F	VF	XF
ND(1852) Series 5	2.00	3.00	5.00	8.00	—

KM# 65s.5 MUN

Cast Copper or Bronze

Date	Good	VG	F	VF	XF
ND(1852) Series 5	—	—	—	—	50.00

KM# 65.6 MUN

Cast Copper or Bronze **Rev:** "Mun" at bottom, series number at right

Date	Good	VG	F	VF	XF
ND(1852) Series 6	2.00	3.00	5.00	8.00	—

KM# 65s.6 MUN

Cast Copper or Bronze

Date	Good	VG	F	VF	XF
ND(1852) Series 6	—	—	—	—	50.00

KM# 65.7 MUN

Cast Copper or Bronze **Rev:** "Mun" at bottom, series number at right

Date	Good	VG	F	VF	XF
ND(1852) Series 7	2.00	3.00	5.00	8.00	—

KM# 65s.7 MUN

Cast Copper or Bronze

Date	Good	VG	F	VF	XF
ND(1852) Series 7	—	—	—	—	50.00

KM# 65.8 MUN

Cast Copper or Bronze **Rev:** "Mun" at bottom, series number at right

Date	Good	VG	F	VF	XF
ND(1852) Series 8	2.00	3.00	5.00	8.00	—

KM# 65s.8 MUN

Cast Copper or Bronze

Date	Good	VG	F	VF	XF
ND(1852) Series 8	—	—	—	—	50.00

KM# 65.9 MUN

Cast Copper or Bronze **Rev:** "Mun" at bottom, series number at right

Date	Good	VG	F	VF	XF
ND(1852) Series 9	2.00	3.00	5.00	8.00	—

KM# 65s.9 MUN

Cast Copper or Bronze

Date	Good	VG	F	VF	XF
ND(1852) Series 9	—	—	—	—	50.00

KM# 65.10 MUN

Cast Copper or Bronze **Rev:** "Mun" at bottom, series number at right

Date	Good	VG	F	VF	XF
ND(1852) Series 10	2.00	3.00	5.00	8.00	—

KM# 65s.10 MUN

Cast Copper or Bronze

Date	Good	VG	F	VF	XF
ND(1852) Series 10	—	—	—	—	50.00

KM# 13.1 MUN

Cast Copper or Bronze **Rev:** "I" (2) at bottom, series number at right

Date	Good	VG	F	VF	XF
ND(1857) Series 1	5.00	8.00	12.00	17.00	—

KM# 13s.1 MUN

Cast Copper or Bronze **Rev:** "I" (2) at bottom, series number at right

Date	Good	VG	F	VF	XF
ND(1857) Series 1	—	—	—	—	60.00

KM# 13.2 MUN

Cast Copper or Bronze **Rev:** "I" (2) at bottom, series number at right

Date	Good	VG	F	VF	XF
ND(1857) Series 2	8.00	15.00	25.00	40.00	—

KM# 13s.2 MUN

Cast Copper or Bronze **Rev:** "I" (2) at bottom, series number at right

Date	Good	VG	F	VF	XF
ND(1857) Series 2	—	—	—	—	100

KM# 13.3 MUN

Cast Copper or Bronze **Rev:** "I" (2) at bottom, series number at right

Date	Good	VG	F	VF	XF
ND(1857) Series 3	8.00	15.00	25.00	40.00	—

KM# 13s.3 MUN

Cast Copper or Bronze **Rev:** "I" (2) at bottom, series number at right

Date	Good	VG	F	VF	XF
ND(1857) Series 3	—	—	—	—	100

KM# 13.4 MUN

Cast Copper or Bronze **Rev:** "I" (2) at bottom, series number at right

Date	Good	VG	F	VF	XF
ND(1857) Series 4	8.00	15.00	25.00	40.00	—

KM# 13s.4 MUN

Cast Copper or Bronze **Rev:** "I" (2) at bottom, series number at right

Date	Good	VG	F	VF	XF
ND(1857) Series 4	—	—	—	—	100

KM# 13.5 MUN

Cast Copper or Bronze **Rev:** "I" (2) at bottom, series number at right

Date	Good	VG	F	VF	XF
ND(1857) Series 5	5.00	8.00	12.00	17.00	—

KM# 13s.5 MUN

Cast Copper or Bronze **Rev:** "I" (2) at bottom, series number at right

Date	Good	VG	F	VF	XF
ND(1857) Series 5	—	—	—	—	60.00

KM# 13.6 MUN

Cast Copper or Bronze **Rev:** "I" (2) at bottom, series number at right

Date	Good	VG	F	VF	XF
ND(1857) Series 6	8.00	15.00	25.00	40.00	—

KM# 13s.6 MUN

Cast Copper or Bronze **Rev:** "I" (2) at bottom, series number at right

Date	Good	VG	F	VF	XF
ND(1857) Series 6	—	—	—	—	100

KM# 13.7 MUN

Cast Copper or Bronze **Rev:** "I" (2) at bottom, series number at right

Date	Good	VG	F	VF	XF
ND(1857) Series 7	8.00	15.00	25.00	40.00	—

KM# 13s.7 MUN

Cast Copper or Bronze **Rev:** "I" (2) at bottom, series number at right

Date	Good	VG	F	VF	XF
ND(1857) Series 7	—	—	—	—	100

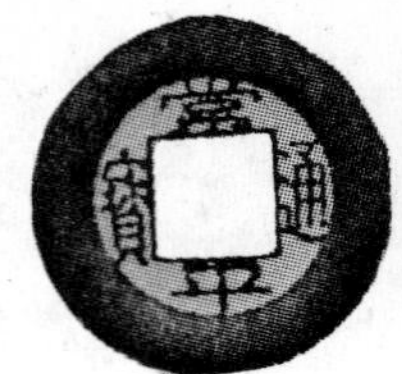

KM# 13.8 MUN

Cast Copper or Bronze **Rev:** "I" (2) at bottom, series number at right

Date	Good	VG	F	VF	XF
ND(1857) Series 8	8.00	15.00	25.00	40.00	—

KM# 13s.8 MUN

Cast Copper or Bronze **Rev:** "I" (2) at bottom, series number at right

Date	Good	VG	F	VF	XF
ND(1857) Series 8	—	—	—	—	100

KM# 13.9 MUN

Cast Copper or Bronze **Rev:** "I" (2) at bottom, series number at right

Date	Good	VG	F	VF	XF
ND(1857) Series 9	8.00	15.00	25.00	40.00	—

KM# 13s.9 MUN

Cast Copper or Bronze **Rev:** "I" (2) at bottom, series number at right

Date	Good	VG	F	VF	XF
ND(1857) Series 9	—	—	—	—	100

KM# 13.10 MUN

Cast Copper or Bronze **Rev:** "I" (2) at bottom, series number at right

Date	Good	VG	F	VF	XF
ND(1857) Series 10	8.00	15.00	25.00	40.00	—

KM# 13s.10 MUN

Cast Copper or Bronze **Rev:** "I" (2) at bottom, series number at right

Date	Good	VG	F	VF	XF
ND(1857) Series 10	—	—	—	—	100

KM# 14.1 MUN

Cast Copper or Bronze **Rev:** "I" (2) at bottom, series number at left

Date	Good	VG	F	VF	XF
ND(1857) Series 1	10.00	20.00	35.00	60.00	—

KM# 14s.1 MUN

Cast Copper or Bronze

Date	Good	VG	F	VF	XF
ND(1857) Series 1	—	—	—	—	100

KM# 14.2 MUN

Cast Copper or Bronze **Rev:** "I" (2) at bottom, series number at left

Date	Good	VG	F	VF	XF
ND(1857) Series 2	10.00	20.00	35.00	60.00	—

KM# 14s.2 MUN

Cast Copper or Bronze

Date	Good	VG	F	VF	XF
ND(1857) Series 2	—	—	—	—	100

KM# 14.3 MUN

Cast Copper or Bronze **Rev:** "I" (2) at bottom, series number at left

Date	Good	VG	F	VF	XF
ND(1857) Series 3	10.00	20.00	35.00	60.00	—

KM# 14s.3 MUN

Cast Copper or Bronze

Date	Good	VG	F	VF	XF
ND(1857) Series 3	—	—	—	—	100

KM# 14.4 MUN

Cast Copper or Bronze **Rev:** "I" (2) at bottom, series number at left

Date	Good	VG	F	VF	XF
ND(1857) Series 4	10.00	20.00	35.00	60.00	—

KM# 14s.4 MUN

Cast Copper or Bronze

Date	Good	VG	F	VF	XF
ND(1857) Series 4	—	—	—	—	100

KM# 14.5 MUN

Cast Copper or Bronze **Rev:** "I" (2) at bottom, series number at left

Date	Good	VG	F	VF	XF
ND(1857) Series 5	10.00	20.00	35.00	60.00	—

KM# 14s.5 MUN

Cast Copper or Bronze

Date	Good	VG	F	VF	XF
ND(1857) Series 5	—	—	—	—	100

KM# 14.6 MUN

Cast Copper or Bronze **Rev:** "I" (2) at bottom, series number at left

Date	Good	VG	F	VF	XF
ND(1857) Series 6	10.00	20.00	35.00	60.00	—

KM# 14s.6 MUN

Cast Copper or Bronze

Date	Good	VG	F	VF	XF
ND(1857) Series 6	—	—	—	—	100

KM# 14.7 MUN

Cast Copper or Bronze **Rev:** "I" (2) at bottom, series number at left

Date	Good	VG	F	VF	XF
ND(1857) Series 7	10.00	20.00	35.00	60.00	—

KM# 14s.7 MUN

Cast Copper or Bronze

Date	Good	VG	F	VF	XF
ND(1857) Series 7	—	—	—	—	100

KM# 14.8 MUN

Cast Copper or Bronze **Rev:** "I" (2) at bottom, series number at left

Date	Good	VG	F	VF	XF
ND(1857) Series 8	10.00	20.00	35.00	60.00	—

KM# 14s.8 MUN

Cast Copper or Bronze

Date	Good	VG	F	VF	XF
ND(1857) Series 8	—	—	—	—	100

KM# 14.9 MUN
Cast Copper or Bronze **Rev:** "I" (2) at bottom, series number at left

Date	Good	VG	F	VF	XF
ND(1857) Series 9	10.00	20.00	35.00	60.00	—

KM# 14s.9 MUN
Cast Copper or Bronze

Date	Good	VG	F	VF	XF
ND(1857) Series 9	—	—	—	—	100

KM# 14.10 MUN
Cast Copper or Bronze **Rev:** "I" (2) at bottom, series number at left

Date	Good	VG	F	VF	XF
ND(1857) Series 10	10.00	20.00	35.00	60.00	—

KM# 14s.10 MUN
Cast Copper or Bronze

Date	Good	VG	F	VF	XF
ND(1857) Series 10	—	—	—	—	100

KM# 17.1 MUN
Cast Copper or Bronze, 23 mm. **Rev:** "Ho" in different style, "Sam" (3) at bottom, series number at left

Date	Good	VG	F	VF	XF
ND(1857) Series 1	10.00	20.00	35.00	60.00	—

KM# 17s.1 MUN
Cast Copper or Bronze

Date	Good	VG	F	VF	XF
ND(1857) Series 1	—	—	—	—	100

KM# 17.2 MUN
Cast Copper or Bronze, 23 mm. **Rev:** "Ho" in different style, "Sam" (3) at bottom, series number at left

Date	Good	VG	F	VF	XF
ND(1857) Series 2	10.00	20.00	35.00	60.00	—

KM# 17s.2 MUN
Cast Copper or Bronze

Date	Good	VG	F	VF	XF
ND(1857) Series 2	—	—	—	—	100

KM# 17.3 MUN
Cast Copper or Bronze, 23 mm. **Rev:** "Ho" in different style, "Sam" (3) at bottom, series number at left

Date	Good	VG	F	VF	XF
ND(1857) Series 3	10.00	20.00	35.00	60.00	—

KM# 17s.3 MUN
Cast Copper or Bronze

Date	Good	VG	F	VF	XF
ND(1857) Series 3	—	—	—	—	100

KM# 17.4 MUN
Cast Copper or Bronze, 23 mm. **Rev:** "Ho" in different style, "Sam" (3) at bottom, series number at left

Date	Good	VG	F	VF	XF
ND(1857) Series 4	10.00	20.00	35.00	60.00	—

KM# 17s.4 MUN
Cast Copper or Bronze

Date	Good	VG	F	VF	XF
ND(1857) Series 4	—	—	—	—	100

KM# 17.5 MUN
Cast Copper or Bronze, 23 mm. **Rev:** "Ho" in different style, "Sam" (3) at bottom, series number at left

Date	Good	VG	F	VF	XF
ND(1857) Series 5	10.00	20.00	35.00	60.00	—

KM# 17s.5 MUN
Cast Copper or Bronze

Date	Good	VG	F	VF	XF
ND(1857) Series 5	—	—	—	—	100

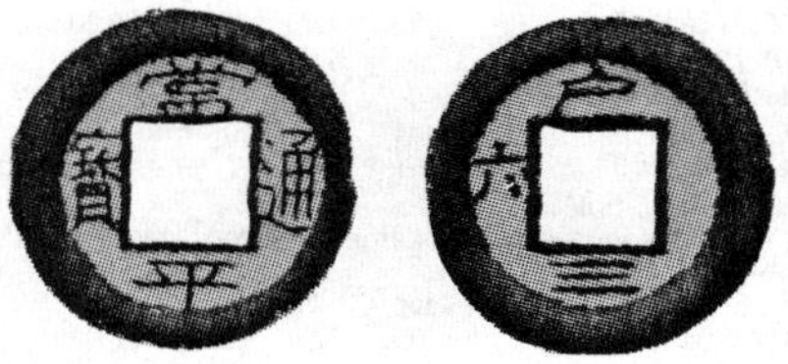

KM# 17.6 MUN
Cast Copper or Bronze, 23 mm. **Rev:** "Ho" in different style, "Sam" (3) at bottom, series number at left

Date	Good	VG	F	VF	XF
ND(1857) Series 6	10.00	20.00	35.00	60.00	—

KM# 17s.6 MUN
Cast Copper or Bronze

Date	Good	VG	F	VF	XF
ND(1857) Series 6	—	—	—	—	100

KM# 17.7 MUN
Cast Copper or Bronze, 23 mm. **Rev:** "Ho" in different style, "Sam" (3) at bottom, series number at left

Date	Good	VG	F	VF	XF
ND(1857) Series 7	10.00	20.00	35.00	60.00	—

KM# 17s.7 MUN
Cast Copper or Bronze

Date	Good	VG	F	VF	XF
ND(1857) Series 7	—	—	—	—	100

KM# 17.8 MUN
Cast Copper or Bronze, 23 mm. **Rev:** "Ho" in different style, "Sam" (3) at bottom, series number at left

Date	Good	VG	F	VF	XF
ND(1857) Series 8	10.00	20.00	35.00	60.00	—

KM# 17s.8 MUN
Cast Copper or Bronze

Date	Good	VG	F	VF	XF
ND(1857) Series 8	—	—	—	—	100

KM# 17.9 MUN
Cast Copper or Bronze, 23 mm. **Rev:** "Ho" in different style, "Sam" (3) at bottom, series number at left

Date	Good	VG	F	VF	XF
ND(1857) Series 9	10.00	20.00	35.00	60.00	—

KM# 17s.9 MUN
Cast Copper or Bronze

Date	Good	VG	F	VF	XF
ND(1857) Series 9	—	—	—	—	100

KM# 17.10 MUN
Cast Copper or Bronze, 23 mm. **Rev:** "Ho" in different style, "Sam" (3) at bottom, series number at left

Date	Good	VG	F	VF	XF
ND(1857) Series 10	10.00	20.00	35.00	60.00	—

KM# 17s.10 MUN
Cast Copper or Bronze

Date	Good	VG	F	VF	XF
ND(1857) Series 10	—	—	—	—	100

KM# 36.1 MUN
Cast Copper or Bronze, 26 mm. **Rev:** Crescent at right, "YuK" (6) at left, series number at bottom

Date	Good	VG	F	VF	XF
ND(1857) Series 1	10.00	20.00	35.00	60.00	—

KM# 36s.1 MUN
Cast Copper or Bronze

Date	Good	VG	F	VF	XF
ND(1857) Series 1	—	—	—	—	100

KM# 36.2 MUN
Cast Copper or Bronze **Rev:** Crescent at right, "YuK" (6) at left, series number at bottom

Date	Good	VG	F	VF	XF
ND(1857) Series 2	10.00	20.00	35.00	60.00	—

KM# 36s.2 MUN
Cast Copper or Bronze

Date	Good	VG	F	VF	XF
ND(1857) Series 2	—	—	—	—	100

KM# 36.3 MUN
Cast Copper or Bronze **Rev:** Crescent at right, "YuK" (6) at left, series number at bottom

Date	Good	VG	F	VF	XF
ND(1857) Series 3	10.00	20.00	35.00	60.00	—

KM# 36s.3 MUN
Cast Copper or Bronze **Note:** Seed type.

Date	Good	VG	F	VF	XF
ND(1857) Series 3	—	—	—	—	100

KM# 36.4 MUN
Cast Copper or Bronze **Rev:** Crescent at right, "YuK" (6) at left, series number at bottom

Date	Good	VG	F	VF	XF
ND(1857) Series 4	10.00	20.00	35.00	60.00	—

KM# 36s.4 MUN
Cast Copper or Bronze

Date	Good	VG	F	VF	XF
ND(1857) Series 4	—	—	—	—	100

KM# 36.5 MUN
Cast Copper or Bronze **Rev:** Crescent at right, "YuK" (6) at left, series number at bottom

Date	Good	VG	F	VF	XF
ND(1857) Series 5	10.00	20.00	35.00	60.00	—

KM# 36s.5 MUN
Cast Copper or Bronze

Date	Good	VG	F	VF	XF
ND(1857) Series 5	—	—	—	—	100

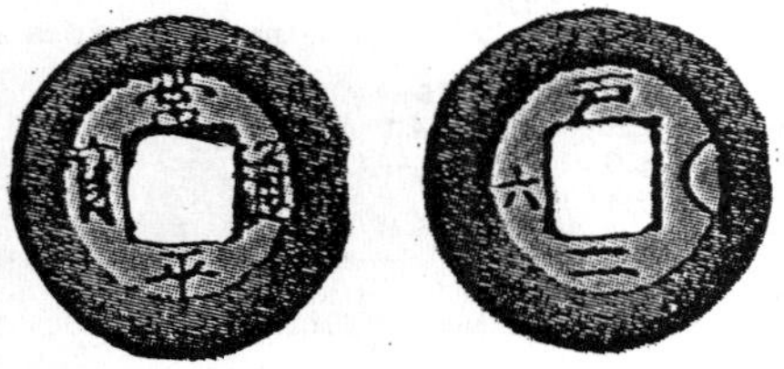

KM# 36.6 MUN
Cast Copper or Bronze **Rev:** Crescent at right, "YuK" (6) at left, series number at bottom

Date	Good	VG	F	VF	XF
ND(1857) Series 6	10.00	20.00	35.00	60.00	—

KM# 36s.6 MUN
Cast Copper or Bronze

Date	Good	VG	F	VF	XF
ND(1857) Series 6	—	—	—	—	100

KM# 36.7 MUN
Cast Copper or Bronze **Rev:** Crescent at right, "YuK" (6) at left, series number at bottom

Date	Good	VG	F	VF	XF
ND(1857) Series 7	10.00	20.00	35.00	60.00	—

KM# 36s.7 MUN
Cast Copper or Bronze

Date	Good	VG	F	VF	XF
ND(1857) Series 7	—	—	—	—	100

KM# 36.8 MUN
Cast Copper or Bronze **Rev:** Crescent at right, "YuK" (6) at left, series number at bottom

Date	Good	VG	F	VF	XF
ND(1857) Series 8	10.00	20.00	35.00	60.00	—

KM# 36s.8 MUN
Cast Copper or Bronze

Date	Good	VG	F	VF	XF
ND(1857) Series 8	—	—	—	—	100

KM# 36.9 MUN
Cast Copper or Bronze **Rev:** Crescent at right, "YuK" (6) at left, series number at bottom

Date	Good	VG	F	VF	XF
ND(1857) Series 9	10.00	20.00	35.00	60.00	—

KM# 36s.9 MUN
Cast Copper or Bronze

Date	Good	VG	F	VF	XF
ND(1857) Series 9	—	—	—	—	100

KM# 36.10 MUN
Cast Copper or Bronze **Rev:** Crescent at right, "YuK" (6) at left, series number at bottom

Date	Good	VG	F	VF	XF
ND(1857) Series 10	10.00	20.00	35.00	60.00	—

KM# 36s.10 MUN
Cast Copper or Bronze

Date	Good	VG	F	VF	XF
ND(1857) Series 10	—	—	—	—	100

KM# 40.1 MUN
Cast Copper or Bronze, 25 mm. **Note:** Large characters.

Date	Good	VG	F	VF	XF
ND(1857) Series 1	1.50	2.25	3.50	5.00	—

KM# 40s.1 MUN
Cast Copper or Bronze

Date	Good	VG	F	VF	XF
ND(1857) Series 1	—	—	—	—	30.00

KM# 40.2 MUN
Cast Copper or Bronze **Note:** Large characters.

Date	Good	VG	F	VF	XF
ND(1857) Series 2	1.50	2.25	3.50	5.00	—

KM# 40s.2 MUN
Cast Copper or Bronze

Date	Good	VG	F	VF	XF
ND(1857) Series 2	—	—	—	—	30.00

KM# 40.3 MUN
Cast Copper or Bronze **Note:** Large characters.

Date	Good	VG	F	VF	XF
ND(1857) Series 3	1.50	2.25	3.50	5.00	—

KM# 40s.3 MUN
Cast Copper or Bronze

Date	Good	VG	F	VF	XF
ND(1857) Series 3	—	—	—	—	30.00

KM# 40.4 MUN
Cast Copper or Bronze **Note:** Large characters.

Date	Good	VG	F	VF	XF
ND(1857) Series 4	1.50	2.25	3.50	5.00	—

KM# 40s.4 MUN
Cast Copper or Bronze

Date	Good	VG	F	VF	XF
ND(1857) Series 4	—	—	—	—	30.00

KM# 40.5 MUN
Cast Copper or Bronze **Note:** Large characters.

Date	Good	VG	F	VF	XF
ND(1857) Series 5	1.50	2.25	3.50	5.00	—

KM# 40s.5 MUN
Cast Copper or Bronze

Date	Good	VG	F	VF	XF
ND(1857) Series 5	—	—	—	—	30.00

KM# 40.6 MUN
Cast Copper or Bronze **Note:** Large characters.

Date	Good	VG	F	VF	XF
ND(1857) Series 6	1.50	2.25	3.50	5.00	—

KM# 40s.6 MUN
Cast Copper or Bronze

Date	Good	VG	F	VF	XF
ND(1857) Series 6	—	—	—	—	30.00

KM# 40.7 MUN
Cast Copper or Bronze **Note:** Large characters.

Date	Good	VG	F	VF	XF
ND(1857) Series 7	1.50	2.25	3.50	5.00	—

KM# 40s.7 MUN
Cast Copper or Bronze

Date	Good	VG	F	VF	XF
ND(1857) Series 7	—	—	—	—	30.00

KM# 40.8 MUN
Cast Copper or Bronze **Note:** Large characters.

Date	Good	VG	F	VF	XF
ND(1857) Series 8	1.50	2.25	3.50	5.00	—

KM# 40s.8 MUN
Cast Copper or Bronze

Date	Good	VG	F	VF	XF
ND(1857) Series 8	—	—	—	—	30.00

KM# 40.9 MUN
Cast Copper or Bronze **Note:** Large characters.

Date	Good	VG	F	VF	XF
ND(1857) Series 9	1.50	2.25	3.50	5.00	—

KM# 40s.9 MUN
Cast Copper or Bronze

Date	Good	VG	F	VF	XF
ND(1857) Series 9	—	—	—	—	30.00

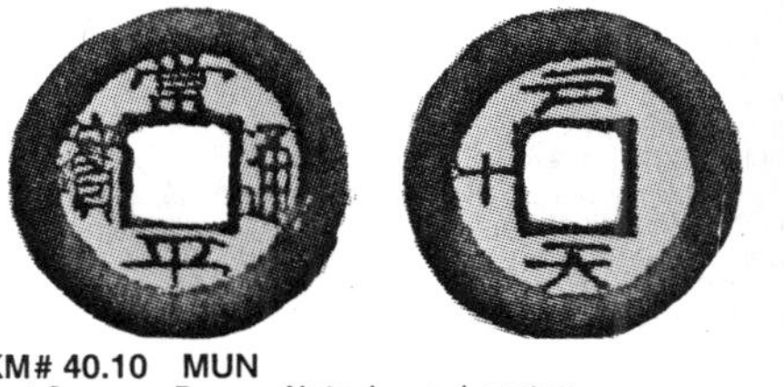

KM# 40.10 MUN
Cast Copper or Bronze **Note:** Large characters.

Date	Good	VG	F	VF	XF
ND(1857) Series 10	1.50	2.25	3.50	5.00	—

KM# 40s.10 MUN
Cast Copper or Bronze

Date	Good	VG	F	VF	XF
ND(1857) Series 10	—	—	—	—	30.00

KM# 40.11 MUN
Cast Copper or Bronze **Note:** Large characters.

Date	Good	VG	F	VF	XF
ND(1857) Series 11	1.50	2.25	3.50	5.00	—

KM# 40s.11 MUN
Cast Copper or Bronze

Date	Good	VG	F	VF	XF
ND(1857) Series 11	—	—	—	—	30.00

KM# 136.1 5 MUN
Cast Copper or Bronze, 30 mm. **Rev:** "Tang" at right, "0" (5) at left, series number at bottom **Note:** Small characters, inner circle 21-22mm.

Date	Good	VG	F	VF	XF
ND(1883) Series 1	4.00	7.00	12.00	20.00	—

KM# 136s.1 5 MUN
Cast Copper or Bronze

Date	Good	VG	F	VF	XF
ND(1883) Series 1	—	—	—	—	50.00

KM# 136.2 5 MUN
Cast Copper or Bronze **Rev:** "Tang" at right, "0" (5) at left, series number at bottom **Note:** Small characters, inner circle 21-22mm.

Date	Good	VG	F	VF	XF
ND(1883) Series 2	4.00	7.00	12.00	20.00	—

KM# 136s.2 5 MUN
Cast Copper or Bronze

Date	Good	VG	F	VF	XF
ND(1883) Series 2	—	—	—	—	50.00

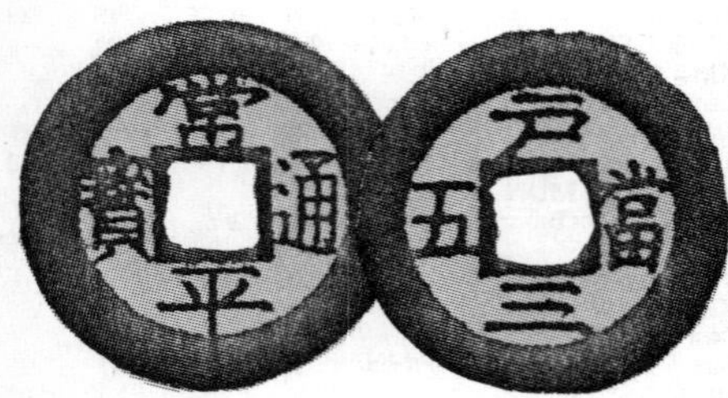

KM# 136.3 5 MUN
Cast Copper or Bronze **Rev:** "Tang" at right, "0" (5) at left, series number at bottom **Note:** Small characters, inner circle 21-22mm.

Date	Good	VG	F	VF	XF
ND(1883) Series 3	4.00	7.00	12.00	20.00	—

KM# 136s.3 5 MUN
Cast Copper or Bronze

Date	Good	VG	F	VF	XF
ND(1883) Series 3	—	—	—	—	50.00

KM# 136.4 5 MUN
Cast Copper or Bronze **Rev:** "Tang" at right, "0" (5) at left, series number at bottom **Note:** Small characters, inner circle 21-22mm.

Date	Good	VG	F	VF	XF
ND(1883) Series 4	4.00	7.00	12.00	20.00	—

KM# 136s.4 5 MUN
Cast Copper or Bronze

Date	Good	VG	F	VF	XF
ND(1883) Series 4	—	—	—	—	50.00

KM# 136.5 5 MUN
Cast Copper or Bronze **Rev:** "Tang" at right, "0" (5) at left, series number at bottom **Note:** Small characters, inner circle 21-22mm.

Date	Good	VG	F	VF	XF
ND(1883) Series 5	4.00	7.00	12.00	20.00	—

KM# 136s.5 5 MUN
Cast Copper or Bronze

Date	Good	VG	F	VF	XF
ND(1883) Series 5	—	—	—	—	50.00

KM# 136.6 5 MUN
Cast Copper or Bronze **Rev:** "Tang" at right, "0" (5) at left, series number at bottom **Note:** Small characters, inner circle 21-22mm.

Date	Good	VG	F	VF	XF
ND(1883) Series 6	4.00	7.00	12.00	20.00	—

KM# 136s.6 5 MUN
Cast Copper or Bronze

Date	Good	VG	F	VF	XF
ND(1883) Series 6	—	—	—	—	50.00

KM# 136.7 5 MUN
Cast Copper or Bronze **Rev:** "Tang" at right, "0" (5) at left, series number at bottom **Note:** Small characters, inner circle 21-22mm.

Date	Good	VG	F	VF	XF
ND(1883) Series 7	4.00	7.00	12.00	20.00	—

KM# 136s.7 5 MUN
Cast Copper or Bronze

Date	Good	VG	F	VF	XF
ND(1883) Series 7	—	—	—	—	50.00

KM# 136.8 5 MUN
Cast Copper or Bronze **Rev:** "Tang" at right, "0" (5) at left, series number at bottom **Note:** Small characters, inner circle 21-22mm.

Date	Good	VG	F	VF	XF
ND(1883) Series 8	4.00	7.00	12.00	20.00	—

KM# 136s.8 5 MUN
Cast Copper or Bronze

Date	Good	VG	F	VF	XF
ND(1883) Series 8	—	—	—	—	50.00

KM# 136.9 5 MUN
Cast Copper or Bronze **Rev:** "Tang" at right, "0" (5) at left, series number at bottom **Note:** Small characters, inner circle 21-22mm.

Date	Good	VG	F	VF	XF
ND(1883) Series 9	4.00	7.00	12.00	20.00	—

KM# 136s.9 5 MUN
Cast Copper or Bronze

Date	Good	VG	F	VF	XF
ND(1883) Series 9	—	—	—	—	50.00

KM# 136.10 5 MUN
Cast Copper or Bronze **Rev:** "Tang" at right, "0" (5) at left, series number at bottom **Note:** Small characters, inner circle 21-22mm.

Date	Good	VG	F	VF	XF
ND(1883) Series 10	4.00	7.00	12.00	20.00	—

KM# 136s.10 5 MUN
Cast Copper or Bronze

Date	Good	VG	F	VF	XF
ND(1883) Series 10	—	—	—	—	50.00

KM# 137.1 5 MUN
Cast Copper or Bronze, 31 mm. **Note:** Medium characters, inner circle 21-22mm.

Date	Good	VG	F	VF	XF
ND(1883) Series 1	4.00	7.00	12.00	20.00	—

KM# 137s.1 5 MUN
Cast Copper or Bronze

Date	Good	VG	F	VF	XF
ND(1883) Series 1	—	—	—	—	50.00

KM# 137.2 5 MUN
Cast Copper or Bronze **Note:** Medium characters, inner circle 21-22mm.

Date	Good	VG	F	VF	XF
ND(1883) Series 2	4.00	7.00	12.00	20.00	—

KM# 137s.2 5 MUN
Cast Copper or Bronze

Date	Good	VG	F	VF	XF
ND(1883) Series 2	—	—	—	—	50.00

KM# 137.3 5 MUN
Cast Copper or Bronze **Note:** Medium characters, inner circle 21-22mm.

Date	Good	VG	F	VF	XF
ND(1883) Series 3	4.00	7.00	12.00	20.00	—

KM# 137s.3 5 MUN
Cast Copper or Bronze

Date	Good	VG	F	VF	XF
ND(1883) Series 3	—	—	—	—	50.00

KM# 137.4 5 MUN
Cast Copper or Bronze **Note:** Medium characters, inner circle 21-22mm.

Date	Good	VG	F	VF	XF
ND(1883) Series 4	4.00	7.00	12.00	20.00	—

KM# 137s.4 5 MUN
Cast Copper or Bronze

Date	Good	VG	F	VF	XF
ND(1883) Series 4	—	—	—	—	50.00

KM# 137.5 5 MUN
Cast Copper or Bronze **Note:** Medium characters, inner circle 21-22mm.

Date	Good	VG	F	VF	XF
ND(1883) Series 5	4.00	7.00	12.00	20.00	—

KM# 137s.5 5 MUN
Cast Copper or Bronze

Date	Good	VG	F	VF	XF
ND(1883) Series 5	—	—	—	—	50.00

KM# 137.6 5 MUN
Cast Copper or Bronze **Note:** Medium characters, inner circle 21-22mm.

Date	Good	VG	F	VF	XF
ND(1883) Series 6	4.00	7.00	12.00	20.00	—

KM# 137s.6 5 MUN
Cast Copper or Bronze

Date	Good	VG	F	VF	XF
ND(1883) Series 6	—	—	—	—	50.00

KM# 137.7 5 MUN
Cast Copper or Bronze **Note:** Medium characters, inner circle 21-22mm.

Date	Good	VG	F	VF	XF
ND(1883) Series 7	4.00	7.00	12.00	20.00	—

KM# 137s.7 5 MUN
Cast Copper or Bronze

Date	Good	VG	F	VF	XF
ND(1883) Series 7	—	—	—	—	50.00

KM# 137.8 5 MUN
Cast Copper or Bronze **Note:** Medium characters, inner circle 21-22mm.

Date	Good	VG	F	VF	XF
ND(1883) Series 8	4.00	7.00	12.00	20.00	—

KM# 137s.8 5 MUN
Cast Copper or Bronze

Date	Good	VG	F	VF	XF
ND(1883) Series 8	—	—	—	—	50.00

KM# 137.9 5 MUN
Cast Copper or Bronze **Note:** Medium characters, inner circle 21-22mm.

Date	Good	VG	F	VF	XF
ND(1883) Series 9	4.00	7.00	12.00	20.00	—

KM# 137s.9 5 MUN
Cast Copper or Bronze

Date	Good	VG	F	VF	XF
ND(1883) Series 9	—	—	—	—	50.00

KM# 137.10 5 MUN
Cast Copper or Bronze **Note:** Medium characters, inner circle 21-22mm.

Date	Good	VG	F	VF	XF
ND(1883) Series 10	4.00	7.00	12.00	20.00	—

KM# 137s.10 5 MUN
Cast Copper or Bronze

Date	Good	VG	F	VF	XF
ND(1883) Series 10	—	—	—	—	50.00

KM# 137.11 5 MUN
Cast Copper or Bronze **Note:** Medium characters, inner circle 21-22mm.

Date	Good	VG	F	VF	XF
ND(1883) Series 11	4.00	7.00	12.00	20.00	—

KM# 137s.11 5 MUN
Cast Copper or Bronze

Date	Good	VG	F	VF	XF
ND(1883) Series 11	—	—	—	—	50.00

KM# 138.1 5 MUN
Cast Copper or Bronze, 30 mm. **Note:** Large characters, inner circle 21-22mm.

Date	Good	VG	F	VF	XF
ND(1883) Series 1	4.00	7.00	12.00	20.00	—

KM# 138s.1 5 MUN
Cast Copper or Bronze

Date	Good	VG	F	VF	XF
ND(1883) Series 1	—	—	—	—	50.00

KM# 138.2 5 MUN
Cast Copper or Bronze **Note:** Large characters, inner circle 21-22mm.

Date	Good	VG	F	VF	XF
ND(1883) Series 2	4.00	7.00	12.00	20.00	—

KM# 138s.2 5 MUN
Cast Copper or Bronze

Date	Good	VG	F	VF	XF
ND(1883) Series 2	—	—	—	—	50.00

KM# 138.3 5 MUN
Cast Copper or Bronze **Note:** Large characters, inner circle 21-22mm.

Date	Good	VG	F	VF	XF
ND(1883) Series 3	4.00	7.00	12.00	20.00	—

KM# 138s.3 5 MUN
Cast Copper or Bronze

Date	Good	VG	F	VF	XF
ND(1883) Series 3	—	—	—	—	50.00

KM# 138.4 5 MUN
Cast Copper or Bronze **Note:** Large characters, inner circle 21-22mm.

Date	Good	VG	F	VF	XF
ND(1883) Series 4	4.00	7.00	12.00	20.00	—

KM# 138s.4 5 MUN
Cast Copper or Bronze

Date	Good	VG	F	VF	XF
ND(1883) Series 4	—	—	—	—	50.00

KM# 138.5 5 MUN
Cast Copper or Bronze **Note:** Large characters, inner circle 21-22mm.

Date	Good	VG	F	VF	XF
ND(1883) Series 5	4.00	7.00	12.00	20.00	—

KM# 138s.5 5 MUN
Cast Copper or Bronze

Date	Good	VG	F	VF	XF
ND(1883) Series 5	—	—	—	—	50.00

KM# 138.6 5 MUN
Cast Copper or Bronze **Note:** Large characters, inner circle 21-22mm.

Date	Good	VG	F	VF	XF
ND(1883) Series 6	4.00	7.00	12.00	20.00	—

KM# 138s.6 5 MUN
Cast Copper or Bronze

Date	Good	VG	F	VF	XF
ND(1883) Series 6	—	—	—	—	50.00

KM# 138.7 5 MUN
Cast Copper or Bronze **Note:** Large characters, inner circle 21-22mm.

Date	Good	VG	F	VF	XF
ND(1883) Series 7	4.00	7.00	12.00	20.00	—

KM# 138s.7 5 MUN
Cast Copper or Bronze

Date	Good	VG	F	VF	XF
ND(1883) Series 7	—	—	—	—	50.00

KM# 138.8 5 MUN
Cast Copper or Bronze **Note:** Large characters, inner circle 21-22mm.

Date	Good	VG	F	VF	XF
ND(1883) Series 8	4.00	7.00	12.00	20.00	—

KM# 138s.8 5 MUN
Cast Copper or Bronze

Date	Good	VG	F	VF	XF
ND(1883) Series 8	—	—	—	—	50.00

KM# 138.9 5 MUN
Cast Copper or Bronze **Note:** Large characters, inner circle 21-22mm.

Date	Good	VG	F	VF	XF
ND(1883) Series 9	4.00	7.00	12.00	20.00	—

KM# 138s.9 5 MUN
Cast Copper or Bronze

Date	Good	VG	F	VF	XF
ND(1883) Series 9	—	—	—	—	50.00

KM# 138.10 5 MUN
Cast Copper or Bronze **Note:** Large characters, inner circle 21-22mm.

Date	Good	VG	F	VF	XF
ND(1883) Series 10	4.00	7.00	12.00	20.00	—

KM# 138s.10 5 MUN
Cast Copper or Bronze

Date	Good	VG	F	VF	XF
ND(1883) Series 10	—	—	—	—	50.00

KM# 138.11 5 MUN
Cast Copper or Bronze **Note:** Large characters, inner circle 21-22mm.

Date	Good	VG	F	VF	XF
ND(1883) Series 11	4.00	7.00	12.00	20.00	—

KM# 138s.11 5 MUN
Cast Copper or Bronze

Date	Good	VG	F	VF	XF
ND(1883) Series 11	—	—	—	—	50.00

KM# 139.1 5 MUN
Cast Copper or Bronze, 31 mm. **Note:** Inner circle 19mm.

Date	Good	VG	F	VF	XF
ND(1883) Series 1	4.00	7.00	12.00	20.00	—

KM# 139s.1 5 MUN
Cast Copper or Bronze

Date	Good	VG	F	VF	XF
ND(1883) Series 1	—	—	—	—	50.00

KM# 139.2 5 MUN
Cast Copper or Bronze **Note:** Inner circle 19mm.

Date	Good	VG	F	VF	XF
ND(1883) Series 2	4.00	7.00	12.00	20.00	—

KM# 139s.2 5 MUN
Cast Copper or Bronze

Date	Good	VG	F	VF	XF
ND(1883) Series 2	—	—	—	—	50.00

KM# 139.3 5 MUN
Cast Copper or Bronze **Note:** Inner circle 19mm.

Date	Good	VG	F	VF	XF
ND(1883) Series 3	4.00	7.00	12.00	20.00	—

KM# 139s.3 5 MUN
Cast Copper or Bronze

Date	Good	VG	F	VF	XF
ND(1883) Series 3	—	—	—	—	50.00

KM# 139.4 5 MUN
Cast Copper or Bronze **Note:** Inner circle 19mm.

Date	Good	VG	F	VF	XF
ND(1883) Series 4	4.00	7.00	12.00	20.00	—

KM# 139s.4 5 MUN
Cast Copper or Bronze

Date	Good	VG	F	VF	XF
ND(1883) Series 4	—	—	—	—	50.00

KM# 139.5 5 MUN
Cast Copper or Bronze **Note:** Inner circle 19mm.

Date	Good	VG	F	VF	XF
ND(1883) Series 5	4.00	7.00	12.00	20.00	—

KM# 139s.5 5 MUN
Cast Copper or Bronze

Date	Good	VG	F	VF	XF
ND(1883) Series 5	—	—	—	—	50.00

KM# 139.6 5 MUN
Cast Copper or Bronze **Note:** Inner circle 19mm.

Date	Good	VG	F	VF	XF
ND(1883) Series 6	4.00	7.00	12.00	20.00	—

KM# 139s.6 5 MUN
Cast Copper or Bronze

Date	Good	VG	F	VF	XF
ND(1883) Series 6	—	—	—	—	50.00

KM# 139.7 5 MUN
Cast Copper or Bronze **Note:** Inner circle 19mm.

Date	Good	VG	F	VF	XF
ND(1883) Series 7	4.00	7.00	12.00	20.00	—

KM# 139s.7 5 MUN
Cast Copper or Bronze

Date	Good	VG	F	VF	XF
ND(1883) Series 7	—	—	—	—	50.00

KM# 139.8 5 MUN
Cast Copper or Bronze **Note:** Inner circle 19mm.

Date	Good	VG	F	VF	XF
ND(1883) Series 8	4.00	7.00	12.00	20.00	—

KM# 139s.8 5 MUN
Cast Copper or Bronze

Date	Good	VG	F	VF	XF
ND(1883) Series 8	—	—	—	—	50.00

KM# 139.9 5 MUN
Cast Copper or Bronze **Note:** Inner circle 19mm.

Date	Good	VG	F	VF	XF
ND(1883) Series 9	4.00	7.00	12.00	20.00	—

KM# 139s.9 5 MUN
Cast Copper or Bronze

Date	Good	VG	F	VF	XF
ND(1883) Series 9	—	—	—	—	50.00

KM# 139.10 5 MUN
Cast Copper or Bronze **Note:** Inner circle 19mm.

Date	Good	VG	F	VF	XF
ND(1883) Series 10	4.00	7.00	12.00	20.00	—

KM# 139s.10 5 MUN
Cast Copper or Bronze

Date	Good	VG	F	VF	XF
ND(1883) Series 10	—	—	—	—	50.00

KM# 140.1 5 MUN
Cast Copper or Bronze **Rev:** Small "Ho" at top, crescent under series number at bottom

Date	Good	VG	F	VF	XF
ND(1883) Series 1	4.00	7.00	12.00	20.00	—

KM# 140s.1 5 MUN
Cast Copper or Bronze

Date	Good	VG	F	VF	XF
ND(1883) Series 1	—	—	—	—	50.00

KM# 140.2 5 MUN
Cast Copper or Bronze **Rev:** Small "Ho" at top, crescent under series number at bottom

Date	Good	VG	F	VF	XF
ND(1883) Series 2	4.00	7.00	12.00	20.00	—

KM# 140s.2 5 MUN
Cast Copper or Bronze

Date	Good	VG	F	VF	XF
ND(1883) Series 2	—	—	—	—	50.00

KM# 140.3 5 MUN
Cast Copper or Bronze **Rev:** Small "Ho" at top, crescent under series number at bottom

Date	Good	VG	F	VF	XF
ND(1883) Series 3	4.00	7.00	12.00	20.00	—

KM# 140s.3 5 MUN
Cast Copper or Bronze

Date	Good	VG	F	VF	XF
ND(1883) Series 3	—	—	—	—	50.00

KM# 140.4 5 MUN
Cast Copper or Bronze **Rev:** Small "Ho" at top, crescent under series number at bottom

Date	Good	VG	F	VF	XF
ND(1883) Series 4	4.00	7.00	12.00	20.00	—

KM# 140s.4 5 MUN
Cast Copper or Bronze

Date	Good	VG	F	VF	XF
ND(1883) Series 4	—	—	—	—	50.00

KM# 140.5 5 MUN
Cast Copper or Bronze **Rev:** Small "Ho" at top, crescent under series number at bottom

Date	Good	VG	F	VF	XF
ND(1883) Series 5	4.00	7.00	12.00	20.00	—

KM# 140s.5 5 MUN
Cast Copper or Bronze

Date	Good	VG	F	VF	XF
ND(1883) Series 5	—	—	—	—	50.00

KM# 140.6 5 MUN
Cast Copper or Bronze **Rev:** Small "Ho" at top, crescent under series number at bottom

Date	Good	VG	F	VF	XF
ND(1883) Series 6	4.00	7.00	12.00	20.00	—

KM# 140s.6 5 MUN
Cast Copper or Bronze

Date	Good	VG	F	VF	XF
ND(1883) Series 6	—	—	—	—	50.00

KM# 140.7 5 MUN
Cast Copper or Bronze **Rev:** Small "Ho" at top, crescent under series number at bottom

Date	Good	VG	F	VF	XF
ND(1883) Series 7	4.00	7.00	12.00	20.00	—

KM# 140s.7 5 MUN
Cast Copper or Bronze

Date	Good	VG	F	VF	XF
ND(1883) Series 7	—	—	—	—	50.00

KM# 140.8 5 MUN
Cast Copper or Bronze **Rev:** Small "Ho" at top, crescent under series number at bottom

Date	Good	VG	F	VF	XF
ND(1883) Series 8	4.00	7.00	12.00	20.00	—

KM# 140s.8 5 MUN
Cast Copper or Bronze

Date	Good	VG	F	VF	XF
ND(1883) Series 8	—	—	—	—	50.00

KM# 140.9 5 MUN
Cast Copper or Bronze **Rev:** Small "Ho" at top, crescent under series number at bottom

Date	Good	VG	F	VF	XF
ND(1883) Series 9	4.00	7.00	12.00	20.00	—

KM# 140s.9 5 MUN
Cast Copper or Bronze

Date	Good	VG	F	VF	XF
ND(1883) Series 9	—	—	—	—	50.00

KM# 140.10 5 MUN
Cast Copper or Bronze **Rev:** Small "Ho" at top, crescent under series number at bottom

Date	Good	VG	F	VF	XF
ND(1883) Series 10	4.00	7.00	12.00	20.00	—

KM# 140s.10 5 MUN
Cast Copper or Bronze

Date	Good	VG	F	VF	XF
ND(1883) Series 10	—	—	—	—	50.00

KM# 141.1 5 MUN
Cast Copper or Bronze, 30 mm. **Rev:** Wide "Ho" at top, crescent under series number at bottom

Date	Good	VG	F	VF	XF
ND(1883) Series 1	4.00	6.00	9.00	15.00	—

KM# 141s.1 5 MUN
Cast Copper or Bronze

Date	Good	VG	F	VF	XF
ND(1883) Series 1	—	—	—	—	50.00

KM# 141.2 5 MUN
Cast Copper or Bronze **Rev:** Wide "Ho" at top, crescent under series number at bottom

Date	Good	VG	F	VF	XF
ND(1883) Series 2	4.00	6.00	9.00	15.00	—

KM# 141s.2 5 MUN
Cast Copper or Bronze

Date	Good	VG	F	VF	XF
ND(1883) Series 2	—	—	—	—	50.00

KM# 141.3 5 MUN
Cast Copper or Bronze **Rev:** Wide "Ho" at top, crescent under series number at bottom

Date	Good	VG	F	VF	XF
ND(1883) Series 3	4.00	6.00	9.00	15.00	—

KM# 141s.3 5 MUN
Cast Copper or Bronze

Date	Good	VG	F	VF	XF
ND(1883) Series 3	—	—	—	—	50.00

KM# 141.4 5 MUN
Cast Copper or Bronze **Rev:** Wide "Ho" at top, crescent under series number at bottom

Date	Good	VG	F	VF	XF
ND(1883) Series 4	4.00	6.00	9.00	15.00	—

KM# 141s.4 5 MUN
Cast Copper or Bronze

Date	Good	VG	F	VF	XF
ND(1883) Series 4	—	—	—	—	50.00

KM# 141.5 5 MUN
Cast Copper or Bronze **Rev:** Wide "Ho" at top, crescent under series number at bottom

Date	Good	VG	F	VF	XF
ND(1883) Series 5	4.00	6.00	9.00	15.00	—

KM# 141s.5 5 MUN
Cast Copper or Bronze

Date	Good	VG	F	VF	XF
ND(1883) Series 5	—	—	—	—	50.00

KM# 141.6 5 MUN
Cast Copper or Bronze **Rev:** Wide "Ho" at top, crescent under series number at bottom

Date	Good	VG	F	VF	XF
ND(1883) Series 6	4.00	6.00	9.00	15.00	—

KM# 141s.6 5 MUN
Cast Copper or Bronze

Date	Good	VG	F	VF	XF
ND(1883) Series 6	—	—	—	—	50.00

KM# 141.7 5 MUN
Cast Copper or Bronze **Rev:** Wide "Ho" at top, crescent under series number at bottom

Date	Good	VG	F	VF	XF
ND(1883) Series 7	4.00	6.00	9.00	15.00	—

KM# 141s.7 5 MUN
Cast Copper or Bronze

Date	Good	VG	F	VF	XF
ND(1883) Series 7	—	—	—	—	50.00

KM# 141.8 5 MUN
Cast Copper or Bronze **Rev:** Wide "Ho" at top, crescent under series number at bottom

Date	Good	VG	F	VF	XF
ND(1883) Series 8	4.00	6.00	9.00	15.00	—

KM# 141s.8 5 MUN
Cast Copper or Bronze

Date	Good	VG	F	VF	XF
ND(1883) Series 8	—	—	—	—	50.00

KM# 141.9 5 MUN
Cast Copper or Bronze **Rev:** Wide "Ho" at top, crescent under series number at bottom

Date	Good	VG	F	VF	XF
ND(1883) Series 9	4.00	6.00	9.00	15.00	—

KM# 141s.9 5 MUN
Cast Copper or Bronze

Date	Good	VG	F	VF	XF
ND(1883) Series 9	—	—	—	—	50.00

KM# 141.10 5 MUN
Cast Copper or Bronze **Rev:** Wide "Ho" at top, crescent under series number at bottom

Date	Good	VG	F	VF	XF
ND(1883) Series 10	4.00	6.00	9.00	15.00	—

KM# 141s.10 5 MUN
Cast Copper or Bronze

Date	Good	VG	F	VF	XF
ND(1883) Series 10	—	—	—	—	50.00

KM# 142.1 5 MUN
Cast Copper or Bronze **Rev:** Crescent under series number at bottom **Note:** Small characters, inner circle 19mm.

Date	Good	VG	F	VF	XF
ND(1883) Series 1	5.00	8.00	12.00	20.00	—

KM# 142s.1 5 MUN
Cast Copper or Bronze

Date	Good	VG	F	VF	XF
ND(1883) Series 1	—	—	—	—	50.00

KM# 142.2 5 MUN
Cast Copper or Bronze **Rev:** Crescent under series number at bottom **Note:** Small characters, inner circle 19mm.

Date	Good	VG	F	VF	XF
ND(1883) Series 2	5.00	8.00	12.00	20.00	—

KM# 142s.2 5 MUN
Cast Copper or Bronze

Date	Good	VG	F	VF	XF
ND(1883) Series 2	—	—	—	—	50.00

KM# 142.3 5 MUN
Cast Copper or Bronze **Rev:** Crescent under series number at bottom **Note:** Small characters, inner circle 19mm.

Date	Good	VG	F	VF	XF
ND(1883) Series 3	5.00	8.00	12.00	20.00	—

KM# 142s.3 5 MUN
Cast Copper or Bronze

Date	Good	VG	F	VF	XF
ND(1883) Series 3	—	—	—	—	50.00

KM# 142.4 5 MUN
Cast Copper or Bronze **Rev:** Crescent under series number at bottom **Note:** Small characters, inner circle 19mm.

Date	Good	VG	F	VF	XF
ND(1883) Series 4	5.00	8.00	12.00	20.00	—

KM# 142s.4 5 MUN
Cast Copper or Bronze

Date	Good	VG	F	VF	XF
ND(1883) Series 4	—	—	—	—	50.00

KM# 142.5 5 MUN
Cast Copper or Bronze **Rev:** Crescent under series number at bottom **Note:** Small characters, inner circle 19mm.

Date	Good	VG	F	VF	XF
ND(1883) Series 5	5.00	8.00	12.00	20.00	—

KM# 142s.5 5 MUN
Cast Copper or Bronze

Date	Good	VG	F	VF	XF
ND(1883) Series 5	—	—	—	—	50.00

KM# 142.6 5 MUN
Cast Copper or Bronze **Rev:** Crescent under series number at bottom **Note:** Small characters, inner circle 19mm.

Date	Good	VG	F	VF	XF
ND(1883) Series 6	4.00	6.00	9.00	15.00	—

KM# 142s.6 5 MUN
Cast Copper or Bronze

Date	Good	VG	F	VF	XF
ND(1883) Series 6	—	—	—	—	50.00

KM# 142.7 5 MUN
Cast Copper or Bronze **Rev:** Crescent under series number at bottom **Note:** Small characters, inner circle 19mm.

Date	Good	VG	F	VF	XF
ND(1883) Series 7	4.00	6.00	9.00	15.00	—

KM# 142s.7 5 MUN
Cast Copper or Bronze

Date	Good	VG	F	VF	XF
ND(1883) Series 7	—	—	—	—	50.00

KM# 142.8 5 MUN
Cast Copper or Bronze **Rev:** Crescent under series number at bottom **Note:** Small characters, inner circle 19mm.

Date	Good	VG	F	VF	XF
ND(1883) Series 8	4.00	6.00	9.00	15.00	—

KM# 142s.8 5 MUN
Cast Copper or Bronze

Date	Good	VG	F	VF	XF
ND(1883) Series 8	—	—	—	—	50.00

KM# 142.9 5 MUN
Cast Copper or Bronze **Rev:** Crescent under series number at bottom **Note:** Small characters, inner circle 19mm.

Date	Good	VG	F	VF	XF
ND(1883) Series 9	4.00	6.00	9.00	15.00	—

KM# 142s.9 5 MUN
Cast Copper or Bronze

Date	Good	VG	F	VF	XF
ND(1883) Series 9	—	—	—	—	50.00

KM# 142.10 5 MUN
Cast Copper or Bronze **Rev:** Crescent under series number at bottom **Note:** Small characters, inner circle 19mm.

Date	Good	VG	F	VF	XF
ND(1883) Series 10	4.00	6.00	9.00	15.00	—

KM# 142s.10 5 MUN
Cast Copper or Bronze

Date	Good	VG	F	VF	XF
ND(1883) Series 10	—	—	—	—	50.00

KM# 143 100 MUN
24.0000 g., Cast Copper or Bronze **Note:** Size varies 39-40mm. More than 40 varieties exist.

Date	Good	VG	F	VF	XF
ND(1866)	10.00	20.00	35.00	60.00	—

KM# 143s 100 MUN
24.0000 g., Cast Copper or Bronze

Date	Good	VG	F	VF	XF
ND(1886)	—	—	—	—	125

GOVERNMENT TITHE OFFICE (KYUN YOK CH'ONG)

KM# 147.1 MUN
4.0000 g., Cast Copper or Bronze, 24 mm. **Rev:** "Kyun" at top, series number at bottom

Date	Good	VG	F	VF	XF
ND(1807) Series 1	2.00	3.00	5.00	7.00	—

KM# 147s.1 MUN
4.0000 g., Cast Copper or Bronze

Date	Good	VG	F	VF	XF
ND(1807) Series 1	—	—	—	—	50.00

KM# 147.2 MUN
4.0000 g., Cast Copper or Bronze **Rev:** "Kyun" at top, series number at bottom

Date	Good	VG	F	VF	XF
ND(1807) Series 2	2.00	3.00	5.00	7.00	—

KM# 147s.2 MUN
4.0000 g., Cast Copper or Bronze **Note:** Struck at Kyun Yok Ch'ong. Seed type.

Date	Good	VG	F	VF	XF
ND(1807) Series 2	—	—	—	—	50.00

KM# 147.3 MUN
4.0000 g., Cast Copper or Bronze **Rev:** "Kyun" at top, series number at bottom

Date	Good	VG	F	VF	XF
ND(1807) Series 3	2.00	3.00	5.00	7.00	—

KM# 147s.3 MUN
4.0000 g., Cast Copper or Bronze

Date	Good	VG	F	VF	XF
ND(1807) Series 3	—	—	—	—	50.00

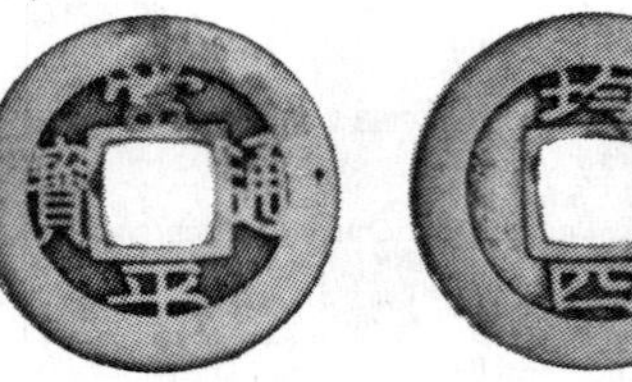

KM# 147.4 MUN
4.0000 g., Cast Copper or Bronze **Rev:** "Kyun" at top, series number at bottom

Date	Good	VG	F	VF	XF
ND(1807) Series 4	2.00	3.00	5.00	7.00	—

KM# 147s.4 MUN
4.0000 g., Cast Copper or Bronze

Date	Good	VG	F	VF	XF
ND(1807) Series 4	—	—	—	—	50.00

KM# 147.5 MUN
4.0000 g., Cast Copper or Bronze **Rev:** "Kyun" at top, series number at bottom

Date	Good	VG	F	VF	XF
ND(1807) Series 5	2.00	3.00	5.00	7.00	—

KM# 147s.5 MUN
4.0000 g., Cast Copper or Bronze

Date	Good	VG	F	VF	XF
ND(1807) Series 5	—	—	—	—	50.00

KM# 147.6 MUN
4.0000 g., Cast Copper or Bronze **Rev:** "Kyun" at top, series number at bottom

Date	Good	VG	F	VF	XF
ND(1807) Series 6	2.00	3.00	5.00	7.00	—

KM# 147s.6 MUN
4.0000 g., Cast Copper or Bronze

Date	Good	VG	F	VF	XF
ND(1807) Series 6	—	—	—	—	50.00

KM# 147.7 MUN
4.0000 g., Cast Copper or Bronze **Rev:** "Kyun" at top, series number at bottom

Date	Good	VG	F	VF	XF
ND(1807) Series 7	2.00	3.00	5.00	7.00	—

KM# 147s.7 MUN
4.0000 g., Cast Copper or Bronze

Date	Good	VG	F	VF	XF
ND(1807) Series 7	—	—	—	—	50.00

KM# 147.8 MUN
4.0000 g., Cast Copper or Bronze **Rev:** "Kyun" at top, series number at bottom

Date	Good	VG	F	VF	XF
ND(1807) Series 8	2.00	3.00	5.00	7.00	—

KM# 147s.8 MUN
4.0000 g., Cast Copper or Bronze

Date	Good	VG	F	VF	XF
ND(1807) Series 8	—	—	—	—	50.00

KM# 147.9 MUN
4.0000 g., Cast Copper or Bronze **Rev:** "Kyun" at top, series number at bottom

Date	Good	VG	F	VF	XF
ND(1807) Series 9	2.00	3.00	5.00	7.00	—

KM# 147s.9 MUN
4.0000 g., Cast Copper or Bronze

Date	Good	VG	F	VF	XF
ND(1807) Series 9	—	—	—	—	50.00

KM# 147.10 MUN
4.0000 g., Cast Copper or Bronze **Rev:** "Kyun" at top, series number at bottom

Date	Good	VG	F	VF	XF
ND(1807) Series 10	2.00	3.00	5.00	7.00	—

KM# 147s.10 MUN
4.0000 g., Cast Copper or Bronze

Date	Good	VG	F	VF	XF
ND(1807) Series 10	—	—	—	—	50.00

KM# 148.1 MUN
4.0000 g., Cast Copper or Bronze, 23 mm. **Rev:** "Il" (1) at bottom, series number at right

Date	Good	VG	F	VF	XF
ND(1857) Series 1	10.00	15.00	25.00	40.00	—

KM# 148s.1 MUN
4.0000 g., Cast Copper or Bronze

Date	Good	VG	F	VF	XF
ND(1857) Series 1	—	—	—	—	70.00

KM# 148.2 MUN
4.0000 g., Cast Copper or Bronze **Rev:** "Il" (1) at bottom, series number at right

Date	Good	VG	F	VF	XF
ND(1857) Series 2	10.00	15.00	25.00	40.00	—

KM# 148s.2 MUN
4.0000 g., Cast Copper or Bronze

Date	Good	VG	F	VF	XF
ND(1857) Series 2	—	—	—	—	70.00

KM# 148.3 MUN
4.0000 g., Cast Copper or Bronze **Rev:** "Il" (1) at bottom, series number at right

Date	Good	VG	F	VF	XF
ND(1857) Series 3	10.00	15.00	25.00	40.00	—

KM# 148s.3 MUN
4.0000 g., Cast Copper or Bronze

Date	Good	VG	F	VF	XF
ND(1857) Series 3	—	—	—	—	70.00

KM# 148.4 MUN
4.0000 g., Cast Copper or Bronze **Rev:** "Il" (1) at bottom, series number at right

Date	Good	VG	F	VF	XF
ND(1857) Series 4	10.00	15.00	25.00	40.00	—

KM# 148s.4 MUN
4.0000 g., Cast Copper or Bronze

Date	Good	VG	F	VF	XF
ND(1857) Series 4	—	—	—	—	70.00

KM# 148.5 MUN
4.0000 g., Cast Copper or Bronze **Rev:** "Il" (1) at bottom, series number at right

Date	Good	VG	F	VF	XF
ND(1857) Series 5	10.00	15.00	25.00	40.00	—

KM# 148s.5 MUN
4.0000 g., Cast Copper or Bronze

Date	Good	VG	F	VF	XF
ND(1857) Series 5	—	—	—	—	70.00

KM# 148.6 MUN
4.0000 g., Cast Copper or Bronze **Rev:** "Il" (1) at bottom, series number at right

Date	Good	VG	F	VF	XF
ND(1857) Series 6	10.00	15.00	25.00	40.00	—

KM# 148s.6 MUN
4.0000 g., Cast Copper or Bronze

Date	Good	VG	F	VF	XF
ND(1857) Series 6	—	—	—	—	70.00

KM# 148.7 MUN
4.0000 g., Cast Copper or Bronze **Rev:** "Il" (1) at bottom, series number at right

Date	Good	VG	F	VF	XF
ND(1857) Series 7	10.00	15.00	25.00	40.00	—

KM# 148s.7 MUN
4.0000 g., Cast Copper or Bronze

Date	Good	VG	F	VF	XF
ND(1857) Series 7	—	—	—	—	70.00

KM# 148.8 MUN
4.0000 g., Cast Copper or Bronze **Rev:** "Il" (1) at bottom, series number at right

Date	Good	VG	F	VF	XF
ND(1857) Series 8	10.00	15.00	25.00	40.00	—

KM# 148s.8 MUN

4.0000 g., Cast Copper or Bronze

Date	Good	VG	F	VF	XF
ND(1857) Series 8	—	—	—	—	70.00

KM# 148.9 MUN

4.0000 g., Cast Copper or Bronze **Rev:** "II" (1) at bottom, series number at right

Date	Good	VG	F	VF	XF
ND(1857) Series 9	10.00	15.00	25.00	40.00	—

KM# 148s.9 MUN

4.0000 g., Cast Copper or Bronze

Date	Good	VG	F	VF	XF
ND(1857) Series 9	—	—	—	—	70.00

KM# 149.1 MUN

4.0000 g., Cast Copper or Bronze **Rev:** "II" (1) at bottom, series number at left

Date	Good	VG	F	VF	XF
ND(1857) Series 1	10.00	15.00	25.00	40.00	—

KM# 149s.1 MUN

4.0000 g., Cast Copper or Bronze

Date	Good	VG	F	VF	XF
ND(1857) Series 1	—	—	—	—	70.00

KM# 149.2 MUN

4.0000 g., Cast Copper or Bronze **Rev:** "II" (1) at bottom, series number at left

Date	Good	VG	F	VF	XF
ND(1857) Series 2	10.00	15.00	25.00	40.00	—

KM# 149s.2 MUN

4.0000 g., Cast Copper or Bronze

Date	Good	VG	F	VF	XF
ND(1857) Series 2	—	—	—	—	70.00

KM# 149.3 MUN

4.0000 g., Cast Copper or Bronze **Rev:** "II" (1) at bottom, series number at left

Date	Good	VG	F	VF	XF
ND(1857) Series 3	10.00	15.00	25.00	40.00	—

KM# 149s.3 MUN

4.0000 g., Cast Copper or Bronze

Date	Good	VG	F	VF	XF
ND(1857) Series 3	—	—	—	—	70.00

KM# 149.5 MUN

4.0000 g., Cast Copper or Bronze **Rev:** "II" (1) at bottom, series number at left

Date	Good	VG	F	VF	XF
ND(1857) Series 5	10.00	15.00	25.00	40.00	—

KM# 149s.5 MUN

4.0000 g., Cast Copper or Bronze

Date	Good	VG	F	VF	XF
ND(1857) Series 5	—	—	—	—	70.00

KM# 149.6 MUN

4.0000 g., Cast Copper or Bronze **Rev:** "II" (1) at bottom, series number at left

Date	Good	VG	F	VF	XF
ND(1857) Series 6	10.00	15.00	25.00	40.00	—

KM# 149s.6 MUN

4.0000 g., Cast Copper or Bronze

Date	Good	VG	F	VF	XF
ND(1857) Series 6	—	—	—	—	70.00

KM# 149.7 MUN

4.0000 g., Cast Copper or Bronze **Rev:** "II" (1) at bottom, series number at left

Date	Good	VG	F	VF	XF
ND(1857) Series 7	10.00	15.00	25.00	40.00	—

KM# 149s.7 MUN

4.0000 g., Cast Copper or Bronze

Date	Good	VG	F	VF	XF
ND(1857) Series 7	—	—	—	—	70.00

KM# 149.8 MUN

4.0000 g., Cast Copper or Bronze **Rev:** "II" (1) at bottom, series number at left

Date	Good	VG	F	VF	XF
ND(1857) Series 8	10.00	15.00	25.00	40.00	—

KM# 149s.8 MUN

4.0000 g., Cast Copper or Bronze

Date	Good	VG	F	VF	XF
ND(1857) Series 8	—	—	—	—	70.00

KM# 149.9 MUN

4.0000 g., Cast Copper or Bronze **Rev:** "II" (1) at bottom, series number at left

Date	Good	VG	F	VF	XF
ND(1857) Series 9	10.00	15.00	25.00	40.00	—

KM# 149s.9 MUN

4.0000 g., Cast Copper or Bronze

Date	Good	VG	F	VF	XF
ND(1857) Series 9	—	—	—	—	70.00

KM# 149.10 MUN

4.0000 g., Cast Copper or Bronze **Rev:** "II" (1) at bottom, series number at left

Date	Good	VG	F	VF	XF
ND(1857) Series 10	10.00	15.00	25.00	40.00	—

KM# 149s.10 MUN

4.0000 g., Cast Copper or Bronze

Date	Good	VG	F	VF	XF
ND(1857) Series 10	—	—	—	—	70.00

KM# 150.1 5 MUN

Cast Bronze, 31 mm. **Rev:** "Tang" at right, "0" (5) at right, series number at bottom **Note:** Small characters.

Date	Good	VG	F	VF	XF
ND(1883) Series 1	5.00	7.50	10.00	15.00	—

KM# 150s.1 5 MUN

Cast Bronze

Date	Good	VG	F	VF	XF
ND(1883) Series 1	—	—	—	—	50.00

KM# 150.2 5 MUN

Cast Bronze **Rev:** "Tang" at right, "0" (5) at right, series number at bottom **Note:** Small characters.

Date	Good	VG	F	VF	XF
ND(1883) Series 2	5.00	7.00	5.00	10.00	15.00

KM# 150s.2 5 MUN

Cast Bronze

Date	Good	VG	F	VF	XF
ND(1883) Series 2	—	—	—	—	50.00

KM# 150.3 5 MUN

Cast Bronze **Rev:** "Tang" at right, "0" (5) at right, series number at bottom **Note:** Small characters.

Date	Good	VG	F	VF	XF
ND(1883) Series 3	5.00	7.50	10.00	15.00	—

KM# 150s.3 5 MUN

Cast Bronze

Date	Good	VG	F	VF	XF
ND(1883) Series 3	—	—	—	—	50.00

KM# 150.4 5 MUN

Cast Bronze **Rev:** "Tang" at right, "0" (5) at right, series number at bottom **Note:** Small characters.

Date	Good	VG	F	VF	XF
ND(1883) Series 4	5.00	7.50	10.00	15.00	—

KM# 150s.4 5 MUN

Cast Bronze

Date	Good	VG	F	VF	XF
ND(1883) Series 4	—	—	—	—	50.00

KM# 150.5 5 MUN

Cast Bronze **Rev:** "Tang" at right, "0" (5) at right, series number at bottom **Note:** Small characters.

Date	Good	VG	F	VF	XF
ND(1883) Series 5	5.00	7.50	10.00	15.00	—

KM# 150s.5 5 MUN

Cast Bronze

Date	Good	VG	F	VF	XF
ND(1883) Series 5	—	—	—	—	50.00

KM# 150.6 5 MUN

Cast Bronze **Rev:** "Tang" at right, "0" (5) at right, series number at bottom **Note:** Small characters.

Date	Good	VG	F	VF	XF
ND(1883) Series 6	5.00	7.50	10.00	15.00	—

KM# 150s.6 5 MUN

Cast Bronze

Date	Good	VG	F	VF	XF
ND(1883) Series 6	—	—	—	—	50.00

KM# 150.7 5 MUN

Cast Bronze **Rev:** "Tang" at right, "0" (5) at right, series number at bottom **Note:** Small characters.

Date	Good	VG	F	VF	XF
ND(1883) Series 7	5.00	7.50	10.00	15.00	—

KM# 150s.7 5 MUN

Cast Bronze

Date	Good	VG	F	VF	XF
ND(1883) Series 7	—	—	—	—	50.00

KM# 150.8 5 MUN

Cast Bronze **Rev:** "Tang" at right, "0" (5) at right, series number at bottom **Note:** Small characters.

Date	Good	VG	F	VF	XF
ND(1883) Series 8	5.00	7.50	10.00	15.00	—

KM# 150s.8 5 MUN

Cast Bronze

Date	Good	VG	F	VF	XF
ND(1883) Series 8	—	—	—	—	50.00

KM# 150.9 5 MUN

Cast Bronze **Rev:** "Tang" at right, "0" (5) at right, series number at bottom **Note:** Small characters.

Date	Good	VG	F	VF	XF
ND(1883) Series 9	5.00	7.50	10.00	15.00	—

KM# 150s.9 5 MUN

Cast Bronze

Date	Good	VG	F	VF	XF
ND(1883) Series 9	—	—	—	—	50.00

KM# 150.10 5 MUN

Cast Bronze **Rev:** "Tang" at right, "0" (5) at right, series number at bottom **Note:** Small characters.

Date	Good	VG	F	VF	XF
ND(1883) Series 10	5.00	7.50	10.00	15.00	—

KM# 150s.10 5 MUN

Cast Bronze

Date	Good	VG	F	VF	XF
ND(1883) Series 10	—	—	—	—	50.00

KM# 151.1 5 MUN

Cast Bronze, 32 mm. **Note:** Medium characters.

Date	Good	VG	F	VF	XF
ND(1883) Series 1	5.00	7.50	10.00	15.00	—

KM# 151s.1 5 MUN

Cast Bronze

Date	Good	VG	F	VF	XF
ND(1883) Series 1	—	—	—	—	50.00

KM# 151.2 5 MUN

Cast Bronze **Note:** Medium characters.

Date	Good	VG	F	VF	XF
ND(1883) Series 2	5.00	7.50	10.00	15.00	—

KM# 151s.2 5 MUN

Cast Bronze

Date	Good	VG	F	VF	XF
ND(1883) Series 2	—	—	—	—	50.00

KM# 151.3 5 MUN

Cast Bronze **Note:** Medium characters.

Date	Good	VG	F	VF	XF
ND(1883) Series 3	5.00	7.50	10.00	15.00	—

KM# 151s.3 5 MUN

Cast Bronze

Date	Good	VG	F	VF	XF
ND(1883) Series 3	—	—	—	—	50.00

KM# 151.4 5 MUN

Cast Bronze **Note:** Medium characters.

Date	Good	VG	F	VF	XF
ND(1883) Series 4	5.00	7.50	10.00	15.00	—

KM# 151s.4 5 MUN

Cast Bronze

Date	Good	VG	F	VF	XF
ND(1883) Series 4	—	—	—	—	50.00

KM# 151.5 5 MUN

Cast Bronze **Note:** Medium characters.

Date	Good	VG	F	VF	XF
ND(1883) Series 5	5.00	7.50	10.00	15.00	—

KM# 151s.5 5 MUN

Cast Bronze

Date	Good	VG	F	VF	XF
ND(1883) Series 5	—	—	—	—	50.00

KM# 151.6 5 MUN

Cast Bronze **Note:** Medium characters.

Date	Good	VG	F	VF	XF
ND(1883) Series 6	5.00	7.50	10.00	15.00	—

KM# 151s.6 5 MUN

Cast Bronze

Date	Good	VG	F	VF	XF
ND(1883) Series 6	—	—	—	—	50.00

KM# 151.7 5 MUN

Cast Bronze **Note:** Medium characters.

Date	Good	VG	F	VF	XF
ND(1883) Series 7	5.00	7.50	10.00	15.00	—

KM# 151s.7 5 MUN

Cast Bronze

Date	Good	VG	F	VF	XF
ND(1883) Series 7	—	—	—	—	50.00

KM# 151.8 5 MUN

Cast Bronze **Note:** Medium characters.

Date	Good	VG	F	VF	XF
ND(1883) Series 8	5.00	7.50	10.00	15.00	—

KM# 151s.8 5 MUN

Cast Bronze

Date	Good	VG	F	VF	XF
ND(1883) Series 8	—	—	—	—	50.00

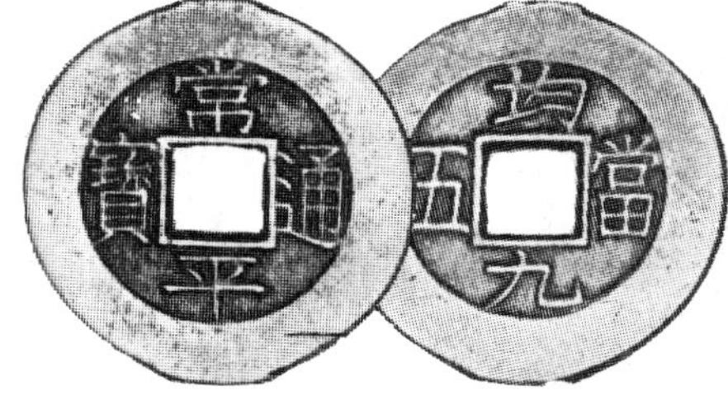

KM# 151.9 5 MUN

Cast Bronze **Note:** Medium characters.

Date	Good	VG	F	VF	XF
ND(1883) Series 9	5.00	7.50	10.00	15.00	—

KM# 151s.9 5 MUN

Cast Bronze

Date	Good	VG	F	VF	XF
ND(1883) Series 9	—	—	—	—	50.00

KM# 151.10 5 MUN

Cast Bronze **Note:** Medium characters.

Date	Good	VG	F	VF	XF
ND(1883) Series 10	5.00	7.50	10.00	15.00	—

KM# 151s.10 5 MUN

Cast Bronze

Date	Good	VG	F	VF	XF
ND(1883) Series 10	—	—	—	—	50.00

KM# 152.1 5 MUN

Cast Bronze, 31 mm. **Note:** Large characters.

Date	Good	VG	F	VF	XF
ND(1883) Series 1	5.00	7.50	10.00	15.00	—

KM# 152s.1 5 MUN

Cast Bronze

Date	Good	VG	F	VF	XF
ND(1883) Series 1	—	—	—	—	50.00

KM# 152.2 5 MUN

Cast Bronze **Note:** Large characters.

Date	Good	VG	F	VF	XF
ND(1883) Series 2	5.00	7.50	10.00	15.00	—

KM# 152s.2 5 MUN

Cast Bronze

Date	Good	VG	F	VF	XF
ND(1883) Series 2	—	—	—	—	50.00

KM# 152.3 5 MUN
Cast Bronze **Note:** Large characters.

Date	Good	VG	F	VF	XF
ND(1883) Series 3	5.00	7.50	10.00	15.00	—

KM# 152s.3 5 MUN
Cast Bronze

Date	Good	VG	F	VF	XF
ND(1883) Series 3	—	—	—	—	50.00

KM# 152.4 5 MUN
Cast Bronze **Note:** Large characters.

Date	Good	VG	F	VF	XF
ND(1883) Series 4	5.00	7.50	10.00	15.00	—

KM# 152s.4 5 MUN
Cast Bronze

Date	Good	VG	F	VF	XF
ND(1883) Series 4	—	—	—	—	50.00

KM# 152.5 5 MUN
Cast Bronze **Note:** Large characters.

Date	Good	VG	F	VF	XF
ND(1883) Series 5	5.00	7.50	10.00	15.00	—

KM# 152s.5 5 MUN
Cast Bronze

Date	Good	VG	F	VF	XF
ND(1883) Series 5	—	—	—	—	50.00

KM# 152.6 5 MUN
Cast Bronze **Note:** Large characters.

Date	Good	VG	F	VF	XF
ND(1883) Series 6	5.00	7.50	10.00	15.00	—

KM# 152s.6 5 MUN
Cast Bronze

Date	Good	VG	F	VF	XF
ND(1883) Series 6	—	—	—	—	50.00

KM# 152.7 5 MUN
Cast Bronze **Note:** Large characters.

Date	Good	VG	F	VF	XF
ND(1883) Series 7	5.00	7.50	10.00	15.00	—

KM# 152s.7 5 MUN
Cast Bronze

Date	Good	VG	F	VF	XF
ND(1883) Series 7	—	—	—	—	50.00

KM# 152.8 5 MUN
Cast Bronze **Note:** Large characters.

Date	Good	VG	F	VF	XF
ND(1883) Series 8	5.00	7.50	10.00	15.00	—

KM# 152s.8 5 MUN
Cast Bronze

Date	Good	VG	F	VF	XF
ND(1883) Series 8	—	—	—	—	50.00

KM# 152.9 5 MUN
Cast Bronze **Note:** Large characters.

Date	Good	VG	F	VF	XF
ND(1883) Series 9	5.00	7.50	10.00	15.00	—

KM# 152s.9 5 MUN
Cast Bronze

Date	Good	VG	F	VF	XF
ND(1883) Series 9	—	—	—	—	50.00

KM# 152.10 5 MUN
Cast Bronze **Note:** Large characters.

Date	Good	VG	F	VF	XF
ND(1883) Series 10	5.00	7.50	10.00	15.00	—

KM# 152s.10 5 MUN
Cast Bronze

Date	Good	VG	F	VF	XF
ND(1883) Series 10	—	—	—	—	50.00

KM# 153.1 5 MUN
Cast Bronze, 30 mm. **Note:** Different "Kyun".

Date	Good	VG	F	VF	XF
ND(1883) Series 1	5.00	7.50	10.00	15.00	—

KM# 153.2 5 MUN
Cast Bronze **Note:** Different "Kyun".

Date	Good	VG	F	VF	XF
ND(1883) Series 2	5.00	7.50	10.00	15.00	—

KM# 153.3 5 MUN
Cast Bronze **Note:** Different "Kyun".

Date	Good	VG	F	VF	XF
ND(1883) Series 3	5.00	7.50	10.00	15.00	—

KM# 153.4 5 MUN
Cast Bronze **Note:** Different "Kyun".

Date	Good	VG	F	VF	XF
ND(1883) Series 4	5.00	7.50	10.00	15.00	—

KM# 153.5 5 MUN
Cast Bronze **Note:** Different "Kyun".

Date	Good	VG	F	VF	XF
ND(1883) Series 5	5.00	7.50	10.00	15.00	—

KM# 153.6 5 MUN
Cast Bronze **Note:** Different "Kyun".

Date	Good	VG	F	VF	XF
ND(1883) Series 6	5.00	7.50	10.00	15.00	—

KM# 153.7 5 MUN
Cast Bronze **Note:** Different "Kyun".

Date	Good	VG	F	VF	XF
ND(1883) Series 7	5.00	7.50	10.00	15.00	—

KM# 153.8 5 MUN
Cast Bronze **Note:** Different "Kyun".

Date	Good	VG	F	VF	XF
ND(1883) Series 8	5.00	7.50	10.00	15.00	—

KM# 153.9 5 MUN
Cast Bronze **Note:** Different "Kyun".

Date	Good	VG	F	VF	XF
ND(1883) Series 9	5.00	7.50	10.00	15.00	—

KM# 153.10 5 MUN
Cast Bronze **Note:** Different "Kyun".

Date	Good	VG	F	VF	XF
ND(1883) Series 10	5.00	7.50	10.00	15.00	—

RICE AND CLOTH DEPARTMENT

(Son Hye Ch ong)

KM# 175.1 MUN
Cast Copper or Bronze **Rev:** "Hye" at top, series number at bottom **Note:** Large characters.

Date	Good	VG	F	VF	XF
ND(1806) Series 1	3.00	5.00	8.00	12.00	—

KM# 175s.1 MUN
Cast Copper or Bronze

Date	Good	VG	F	VF	XF
ND(1806) Series 1	—	—	—	—	50.00

KM# 175.2 MUN
Cast Copper or Bronze **Rev:** "Hye" at top, series number at bottom **Note:** Large characters.

Date	Good	VG	F	VF	XF
ND(1806) Series 2	3.00	5.00	8.00	12.00	—

KM# 175s.2 MUN
Cast Copper or Bronze

Date	Good	VG	F	VF	XF
ND(1806) Series 2	—	—	—	—	50.00

KM# 175.3 MUN
Cast Copper or Bronze **Rev:** "Hye" at top, series number at bottom **Note:** Large characters.

Date	Good	VG	F	VF	XF
ND(1806) Series 3	3.00	5.00	8.00	12.00	—

KM# 175s.3 MUN
Cast Copper or Bronze

Date	Good	VG	F	VF	XF
ND(1806) Series 3	—	—	—	—	50.00

KM# 175.4 MUN
Cast Copper or Bronze **Rev:** "Hye" at top, series number at bottom **Note:** Large characters.

Date	Good	VG	F	VF	XF
ND(1806) Series 4	3.00	5.00	8.00	12.00	—

KM# 175s.4 MUN
Cast Copper or Bronze

Date	Good	VG	F	VF	XF
ND(1806) Series 4	—	—	—	—	50.00

KM# 175.5 MUN
Cast Copper or Bronze **Rev:** "Hye" at top, series number at bottom

Date	Good	VG	F	VF	XF
ND(1806) Series 5	3.00	5.00	8.00	12.00	—

KM# 175s.5 MUN
Cast Copper or Bronze

Date	Good	VG	F	VF	XF
ND(1806) Series 5	—	—	—	—	50.00

KM# 175.6 MUN
Cast Copper or Bronze **Rev:** "Hye" at top, series number at bottom **Note:** Large characters.

Date	Good	VG	F	VF	XF
ND(1806) Series 6	3.00	5.00	8.00	12.00	—

KM# 175s.6 MUN
Cast Copper or Bronze

Date	Good	VG	F	VF	XF
ND(1806) Series 6	—	—	—	—	50.00

KM# 175.7 MUN
Cast Copper or Bronze **Rev:** "Hye" at top, series number at bottom **Note:** Large characters.

Date	Good	VG	F	VF	XF
ND(1806) Series 7	3.00	5.00	8.00	12.00	—

KM# 175s.7 MUN
Cast Copper or Bronze

Date	Good	VG	F	VF	XF
ND(1806) Series 7	—	—	—	—	50.00

KM# 175.8 MUN
Cast Copper or Bronze **Rev:** "Hye" at top, series number at bottom **Note:** Large characters.

Date	Good	VG	F	VF	XF
ND(1806) Series 8	3.00	5.00	8.00	12.00	—

KM# 175s.8 MUN
Cast Copper or Bronze

Date	Good	VG	F	VF	XF
ND(1806) Series 8	—	—	—	—	50.00

KM# 175.9 MUN
Cast Copper or Bronze **Rev:** "Hye" at top, series number at bottom **Note:** Large characters.

Date	Good	VG	F	VF	XF
ND(1806) Series 9	3.00	5.00	8.00	12.00	—

KM# 175s.9 MUN
Cast Copper or Bronze

Date	Good	VG	F	VF	XF
ND(1806) Series 9	—	—	—	—	50.00

KM# 175.10 MUN
Cast Copper or Bronze **Rev:** "Hye" at top, series number at bottom **Note:** Large characters.

Date	Good	VG	F	VF	XF
ND(1806) Series 10	3.00	5.00	8.00	12.00	—

KM# 175s.10 MUN
Cast Copper or Bronze

Date	Good	VG	F	VF	XF
ND(1806) Series 10	—	—	—	—	50.00

KM# 175.11 MUN
Cast Copper or Bronze **Rev:** "Hye" at top, series number at bottom **Note:** Large characters.

Date	Good	VG	F	VF	XF
ND(1806) Series 11	3.00	5.00	8.00	12.00	—

KM# 175s.11 MUN
Cast Copper or Bronze

Date	Good	VG	F	VF	XF
ND(1806) Series 11	—	—	—	—	50.00

KM# 175.12 MUN
Cast Copper or Bronze **Rev:** "Hye" at top, series number at bottom **Note:** Large characters.

Date	Good	VG	F	VF	XF
ND(1806) Series 12	3.00	5.00	8.00	12.00	—

KM# 176.1 MUN
Cast Copper or Bronze **Note:** Small characters.

Date	Good	VG	F	VF	XF
ND(1806) Series 1	3.00	5.00	8.00	12.00	—

KM# 176s.1 MUN
Cast Copper or Bronze

Date	Good	VG	F	VF	XF
ND(1806) Series 1	—	—	—	—	50.00

KM# 176.2 MUN
Cast Copper or Bronze **Note:** Small characters.

Date	Good	VG	F	VF	XF
ND(1806) Series 2	3.00	5.00	8.00	12.00	—

KM# 176s.2 MUN
Cast Copper or Bronze

Date	Good	VG	F	VF	XF
ND(1806) Series 2	—	—	—	—	50.00

KM# 176.3 MUN
Cast Copper or Bronze **Note:** Small characters.

Date	Good	VG	F	VF	XF
ND(1806) Series 3	3.00	5.00	8.00	12.00	—

KM# 176s.3 MUN
Cast Copper or Bronze

Date	Good	VG	F	VF	XF
ND(1806) Series 3	—	—	—	—	50.00

KM# 176.4 MUN
Cast Copper or Bronze **Note:** Small characters.

Date	Good	VG	F	VF	XF
ND(1806) Series 4	3.00	5.00	8.00	12.00	—

KM# 176s.4 MUN
Cast Copper or Bronze

Date	Good	VG	F	VF	XF
ND(1806) Series 4	—	—	—	—	50.00

KM# 176.5 MUN
Cast Copper or Bronze **Note:** Small characters.

Date	Good	VG	F	VF	XF
ND(1806) Series 5	3.00	5.00	8.00	12.00	—

KM# 176s.5 MUN
Cast Copper or Bronze

Date	Good	VG	F	VF	XF
ND(1806) Series 5	—	—	—	—	50.00

KM# 176.6 MUN
Cast Copper or Bronze **Note:** Small characters.

Date	Good	VG	F	VF	XF
ND(1806) Series 6	3.00	5.00	8.00	12.00	—

KM# 176s.6 MUN
Cast Copper or Bronze

Date	Good	VG	F	VF	XF
ND(1806) Series 6	—	—	—	—	50.00

KM# 176.7 MUN
Cast Copper or Bronze **Note:** Small characters.

Date	Good	VG	F	VF	XF
ND(1806) Series 7	3.00	5.00	8.00	12.00	—

KM# 176s.7 MUN
Cast Copper or Bronze

Date	Good	VG	F	VF	XF
ND(1806) Series 7	—	—	—	—	50.00

KM# 176.8 MUN
Cast Copper or Bronze

Date	Good	VG	F	VF	XF
ND(1806) Series 8	3.00	5.00	8.00	12.00	—

KM# 176s.8 MUN
Cast Copper or Bronze

Date	Good	VG	F	VF	XF
ND(1806) Series 8	—	—	—	—	50.00

KM# 176.9 MUN
Cast Copper or Bronze

Date	Good	VG	F	VF	XF
ND(1806) Series 9	3.00	5.00	8.00	12.00	—

KM# 176s.9 MUN
Cast Copper or Bronze

Date	Good	VG	F	VF	XF
ND(1806) Series 9	—	—	—	—	50.00

KM# 176.10 MUN
Cast Copper or Bronze **Note:** Small characters.

Date	Good	VG	F	VF	XF
ND(1806) Series 10	3.00	5.00	8.00	12.00	—

KM# 176s.10 MUN
Cast Copper or Bronze

Date	Good	VG	F	VF	XF
ND(1806) Series 10	—	—	—	—	50.00

KM# 176.11 MUN
Cast Copper or Bronze **Note:** Small characters.

Date	Good	VG	F	VF	XF
ND(1806) Series 11	3.00	5.00	8.00	12.00	—

KM# 176s.11 MUN

Cast Copper or Bronze

Date	Good	VG	F	VF	XF
ND(1806) Series 11	—	—	—	—	50.00

KM# 176.12 MUN

Cast Copper or Bronze **Note:** Small characters.

Date	Good	VG	F	VF	XF
ND(1806) Series 12	3.00	5.00	8.00	12.00	—

KM# 176s.12 MUN

Cast Copper or Bronze

Date	Good	VG	F	VF	XF
ND(1806) Series 12	—	—	—	—	50.00

KM# 174.1 MUN

4.0000 g., Cast Copper or Bronze, 25 mm. **Rev:** Series number at bottom

Date	Good	VG	F	VF	XF
ND(1814) Series 1	1.50	2.25	3.50	5.00	—

KM# 174s.1 MUN

Cast Copper or Bronze

Date	Good	VG	F	VF	XF
ND(1814) Series 1	—	—	—	—	30.00

KM# 174.2 MUN

4.0000 g., Cast Copper or Bronze **Rev:** Series number at bottom

Date	Good	VG	F	VF	XF
ND(1814) Series 2	1.50	2.25	3.50	5.00	—

KM# 174s.2 MUN

Cast Copper or Bronze

Date	Good	VG	F	VF	XF
ND(1814) Series 2	—	—	—	—	30.00

KM# 174.3 MUN

4.0000 g., Cast Copper or Bronze **Rev:** Series number at bottom

Date	Good	VG	F	VF	XF
ND(1814) Series 3	1.50	2.25	3.50	5.00	—

KM# 174s.3 MUN

Cast Copper or Bronze

Date	Good	VG	F	VF	XF
ND(1814) Series 3	—	—	—	—	30.00

KM# 174.4 MUN

4.0000 g., Cast Copper or Bronze **Rev:** Series number at bottom

Date	Good	VG	F	VF	XF
ND(1814) Series 4	1.50	2.25	3.50	5.00	—

KM# 174s.4 MUN

Cast Copper or Bronze

Date	Good	VG	F	VF	XF
ND(1814) Series 4	—	—	—	—	30.00

KM# 174.5 MUN

4.0000 g., Cast Copper or Bronze **Rev:** Series number at bottom

Date	Good	VG	F	VF	XF
ND(1814) Series 5	1.50	2.25	3.50	5.00	—

KM# 174s.5 MUN

Cast Copper or Bronze

Date	Good	VG	F	VF	XF
ND(1814) Series 5	—	—	—	—	30.00

KM# 174.6 MUN

4.0000 g., Cast Copper or Bronze **Rev:** Series number at bottom

Date	Good	VG	F	VF	XF
ND(1814) Series 6	1.50	2.25	3.50	5.00	—

KM# 174s.6 MUN

Cast Copper or Bronze

Date	Good	VG	F	VF	XF
ND(1814) Series 6	—	—	—	—	30.00

KM# 177.1 MUN

Cast Copper or Bronze **Rev:** "I" (2) at left, series number at bottom

Date	Good	VG	F	VF	XF
ND(1836) Series 1	3.00	5.00	8.00	12.00	—

KM# 177s.1 MUN

Cast Copper or Bronze

Date	Good	VG	F	VF	XF
ND(1836) Series 1	—	—	—	—	50.00

KM# 177.2 MUN

Cast Copper or Bronze **Rev:** "I" (2) at left, series number at bottom

Date	Good	VG	F	VF	XF
ND(1836) Series 2	3.00	5.00	8.00	12.00	—

KM# 177s.2 MUN

Cast Copper or Bronze

Date	Good	VG	F	VF	XF
ND(1836) Series 2	—	—	—	—	50.00

KM# 177.3 MUN

Cast Copper or Bronze **Rev:** "I" (2) at left, series number at bottom

Date	Good	VG	F	VF	XF
ND(1836) Series 3	3.00	5.00	8.00	12.00	—

KM# 177s.3 MUN

Cast Copper or Bronze

Date	Good	VG	F	VF	XF
ND(1836) Series 3	—	—	—	—	50.00

KM# 177.4 MUN

Cast Copper or Bronze **Rev:** "I" (2) at left, series number at bottom

Date	Good	VG	F	VF	XF
ND(1836) Series 4	3.00	5.00	8.00	12.00	—

KM# 177s.4 MUN

Cast Copper or Bronze

Date	Good	VG	F	VF	XF
ND(1836) Series 4	—	—	—	—	50.00

KM# 177.5 MUN

Cast Copper or Bronze **Rev:** "I" (2) at left, series number at bottom

Date	Good	VG	F	VF	XF
ND(1836) Series 5	3.00	5.00	8.00	12.00	—

KM# 177s.5 MUN

Cast Copper or Bronze

Date	Good	VG	F	VF	XF
ND(1836) Series 5	—	—	—	—	50.00

KM# 177.6 MUN

Cast Copper or Bronze **Rev:** "I" (2) at left, series number at bottom

Date	Good	VG	F	VF	XF
ND(1836) Series 6	3.00	5.00	8.00	12.00	—

KM# 177s.6 MUN

Cast Copper or Bronze

Date	Good	VG	F	VF	XF
ND(1836) Series 6	—	—	—	—	50.00

KM# 177.7 MUN

Cast Copper or Bronze **Rev:** "I" (2) at left, series number at bottom

Date	Good	VG	F	VF	XF
ND(1836) Series 7	3.00	5.00	8.00	12.00	—

KM# 177s.7 MUN

Cast Copper or Bronze

Date	Good	VG	F	VF	XF
ND(1836) Series 7	—	—	—	—	50.00

CENTRAL GOVERNMENT MINT

(Chon Hwan' Guk)

KM# 209.1 5 MUN

Cast Bronze, 31 mm. **Rev:** "Tang" at right, "O" (5) at left, series number at bottom **Note:** Large characters.

Date	Good	VG	F	VF	XF
ND(1883) Series 1	3.00	5.00	7.50	10.00	—

KM# 209s.1 5 MUN

Cast Bronze

Date	Good	VG	F	VF	XF
ND(1883) Series 1	—	—	—	—	40.00

KM# 209.2 5 MUN

Cast Bronze, 31 mm. **Rev:** "Tang" at right, "O" (5) at left, series number at bottom **Note:** Large characters.

Date	Good	VG	F	VF	XF
ND(1883) Series 2	3.00	5.00	7.50	10.00	—

KM# 209s.2 5 MUN

Cast Bronze

Date	Good	VG	F	VF	XF
ND(1883) Series 2	—	—	—	—	40.00

KM# 209.3 5 MUN

Cast Bronze, 31 mm. **Rev:** "Tang" at right, "O" (5) at left, series number at bottom **Note:** Large characters.

Date	Good	VG	F	VF	XF
ND(1883) Series 3	3.00	5.00	7.50	10.00	—

KM# 209s.3 5 MUN

Cast Bronze

Date	Good	VG	F	VF	XF
ND(1883) Series 3	—	—	—	—	40.00

KM# 209.4 5 MUN

Cast Bronze, 31 mm. **Rev:** "Tang" at right, "O" (5) at left, series number at bottom **Note:** Large characters.

Date	Good	VG	F	VF	XF
ND(1883) Series 4	3.00	5.00	7.50	10.00	—

KM# 209s.4 5 MUN

Cast Bronze

Date	Good	VG	F	VF	XF
ND(1883) Series 4	—	—	—	—	40.00

KM# 209.5 5 MUN

Cast Bronze, 31 mm. **Rev:** "Tang" at right, "O" (5) at left, series number at bottom **Note:** Large characters.

Date	Good	VG	F	VF	XF
ND(1883) Series 5	3.00	5.00	7.50	10.00	—

KM# 209s.5 5 MUN

Cast Bronze

Date	Good	VG	F	VF	XF
ND(1883) Series 5	—	—	—	—	40.00

KM# 209.6 5 MUN

Cast Bronze, 31 mm. **Rev:** "Tang" at right, "O" (5) at left, series number at bottom **Note:** Large characters.

Date	Good	VG	F	VF	XF
ND(1883) Series 6	3.00	5.00	7.50	10.00	—

KM# 209s.6 5 MUN

Cast Bronze

Date	Good	VG	F	VF	XF
ND(1883) Series 6	—	—	—	—	40.00

KM# 209.7 5 MUN

Cast Bronze, 31 mm. **Rev:** "Tang" at right, "O" (5) at left, series number at bottom **Note:** Large characters.

Date	Good	VG	F	VF	XF
ND(1883) Series 7	3.00	5.00	7.50	10.00	—

KM# 209s.7 5 MUN

Cast Bronze

Date	Good	VG	F	VF	XF
ND(1883) Series 7	—	—	—	—	40.00

KM# 209.8 5 MUN

Cast Bronze, 31 mm. **Rev:** "Tang" at right, "O" (5) at left, series number at bottom **Note:** Large characters.

Date	Good	VG	F	VF	XF
ND(1883) Series 8	3.00	5.00	7.50	10.00	—

KM# 209s.8 5 MUN

Cast Bronze

Date	Good	VG	F	VF	XF
ND(1883) Series 8	—	—	—	—	40.00

KM# 209.9 5 MUN

Cast Bronze, 31 mm. **Rev:** "Tang" at right, "O" (5) at left, series number at bottom **Note:** Large characters.

Date	Good	VG	F	VF	XF
ND(1883) Series 9	3.00	5.00	7.50	10.00	—

KM# 209s.9 5 MUN

Cast Bronze

Date	Good	VG	F	VF	XF
ND(1883) Series 9	—	—	—	—	40.00

KM# 209.10 5 MUN

Cast Bronze, 31 mm. **Rev:** "Tang" at right, "O" (5) at left, series number at bottom **Note:** Large characters.

Date	Good	VG	F	VF	XF
ND(1883) Series 10	3.00	5.00	7.50	10.00	—

KM# 209s.10 5 MUN

Cast Bronze

Date	Good	VG	F	VF	XF
ND(1883) Series 10	—	—	—	—	40.00

KM# 209.11 5 MUN

Cast Bronze, 31 mm. **Rev:** "Tang" at right, "O" (5) at left, series number at bottom **Note:** Large characters.

Date	Good	VG	F	VF	XF
ND(1883) Series 11	3.00	5.00	7.50	10.00	—

KM# 209s.11 5 MUN

Cast Bronze

Date	Good	VG	F	VF	XF
ND(1883) Series 11	—	—	—	—	40.00

KM# 209.12 5 MUN

Cast Bronze, 31 mm. **Rev:** "Tang" at right, "O" (5) at left, series number at bottom **Note:** Large characters.

Date	Good	VG	F	VF	XF
ND(1883) Series 12	3.00	5.00	7.50	10.00	—

KM# 209s.12 5 MUN

Cast Bronze

Date	Good	VG	F	VF	XF
ND(1883) Series 12	—	—	—	—	40.00

KM# 210.1 5 MUN

Cast Bronze, 32 mm. **Note:** Small characters.

Date	Good	VG	F	VF	XF
ND(1883) Series 1	3.00	5.00	7.50	10.00	—

KM# 210s.1 5 MUN

Cast Bronze

Date	Good	VG	F	VF	XF
ND(1883) Series 1	—	—	—	—	40.00

KM# 210.2 5 MUN

Cast Bronze, 32 mm. **Note:** Small characters.

Date	Good	VG	F	VF	XF
ND(1883) Series 2	3.00	5.00	7.50	10.00	—

KM# 210s.2 5 MUN

Cast Bronze

Date	Good	VG	F	VF	XF
ND(1883) Series 2	—	—	—	—	40.00

KM# 210.3 5 MUN

Cast Bronze, 32 mm. **Note:** Small characters.

Date	Good	VG	F	VF	XF
ND(1883) Series 3	3.00	5.00	7.50	10.00	—

KM# 210s.3 5 MUN

Cast Bronze

Date	Good	VG	F	VF	XF
ND(1883) Series 3	—	—	—	—	40.00

KM# 210.4 5 MUN

Cast Bronze, 32 mm. **Note:** Small characters.

Date	Good	VG	F	VF	XF
ND(1883) Series 4	3.00	5.00	7.50	10.00	—

KM# 210s.4 5 MUN

Cast Bronze

Date	Good	VG	F	VF	XF
ND(1883) Series 4	—	—	—	—	40.00

KM# 210.5 5 MUN

Cast Bronze, 32 mm. **Note:** Small characters.

Date	Good	VG	F	VF	XF
ND(1883) Series 5	3.00	5.00	7.50	10.00	—

KM# 210s.5 5 MUN

Cast Bronze

Date	Good	VG	F	VF	XF
ND(1883) Series 5	—	—	—	—	40.00

KM# 210.6 5 MUN
Cast Bronze, 32 mm. **Note:** Small characters.

Date	Good	VG	F	VF	XF
ND(1883) Series 6	3.00	5.00	7.50	10.00	—

KM# 210s.6 5 MUN
Cast Bronze

Date	Good	VG	F	VF	XF
ND(1883) Series 6	—	—	—	—	40.00

KM# 210.7 5 MUN
Cast Bronze, 32 mm. **Note:** Small characters.

Date	Good	VG	F	VF	XF
ND(1883) Series 7	3.00	5.00	7.50	10.00	—

KM# 210s.7 5 MUN
Cast Bronze

Date	Good	VG	F	VF	XF
ND(1883) Series 7	—	—	—	—	40.00

KM# 210.8 5 MUN
Cast Bronze, 32 mm. **Note:** Small characters.

Date	Good	VG	F	VF	XF
ND(1883) Series 8	3.00	5.00	7.50	10.00	—

KM# 210s.8 5 MUN
Cast Bronze

Date	Good	VG	F	VF	XF
ND(1883) Series 8	—	—	—	—	40.00

KM# 210s.9 5 MUN
Cast Bronze

Date	Good	VG	F	VF	XF
ND(1883) Series 9	—	—	—	—	40.00

KM# 210.10 5 MUN
Cast Bronze, 32 mm. **Note:** Small characters.

Date	Good	VG	F	VF	XF
ND(1883) Series 10	3.00	5.00	7.50	10.00	—

KM# 210s.10 5 MUN
Cast Bronze

Date	Good	VG	F	VF	XF
ND(1883) Series 10	—	—	—	—	40.00

KM# 210.11 5 MUN
Cast Bronze, 32 mm. **Note:** Small characters.

Date	Good	VG	F	VF	XF
ND(1883) Series 11	3.00	5.00	7.50	10.00	—

KM# 210s.11 5 MUN
Cast Bronze

Date	Good	VG	F	VF	XF
ND(1883) Series 11	—	—	—	—	40.00

KM# 210.12 5 MUN
Cast Bronze, 32 mm. **Note:** Small characters.

Date	Good	VG	F	VF	XF
ND(1883) Series 12	3.00	5.00	7.50	10.00	—

KM# 210s.12 5 MUN
Cast Bronze

Date	Good	VG	F	VF	XF
ND(1883) Series 12	—	—	—	—	40.00

KM# 210.13 5 MUN
Cast Bronze, 32 mm. **Note:** Small characters.

Date	Good	VG	F	VF	XF
ND(1883) Series 13	3.00	5.00	7.50	10.00	—

KM# 210s.13 5 MUN
Cast Bronze

Date	Good	VG	F	VF	XF
ND(1883) Series 13	—	—	—	—	40.00

KM# 210.14 5 MUN
Cast Bronze, 32 mm. **Note:** Small characters.

Date	Good	VG	F	VF	XF
ND(1883) Series 14	3.00	5.00	7.50	10.00	—

KM# 210s.14 5 MUN
Cast Bronze

Date	Good	VG	F	VF	XF
ND(1883) Series 14	—	—	—	—	40.00

KM# 210.15 5 MUN
Cast Bronze, 32 mm. **Note:** Small characters.

Date	Good	VG	F	VF	XF
ND(1883) Series 15	3.00	5.00	7.50	10.00	—

KM# 210s.15 5 MUN
Cast Bronze

Date	Good	VG	F	VF	XF
ND(1883) Series 15	—	—	—	—	40.00

KM# 211.1 5 MUN
Cast Bronze, 29 mm. **Note:** Reduced size.

Date	Good	VG	F	VF	XF
ND(1883) Series 1	5.00	7.50	10.00	15.00	—

KM# 211s.1 5 MUN
Cast Bronze

Date	Good	VG	F	VF	XF
ND(1883) Series 1	—	—	—	—	50.00

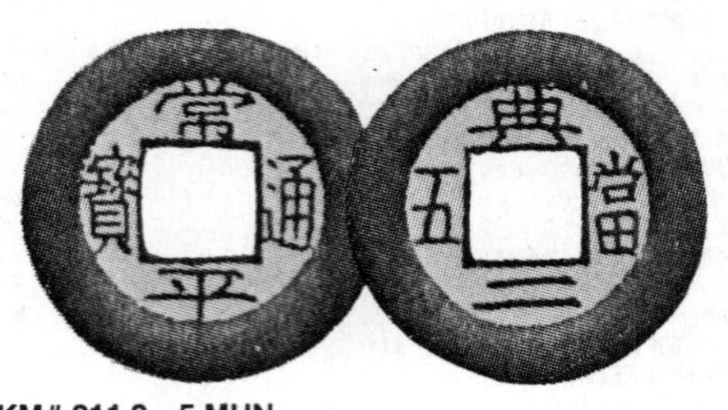

KM# 211.2 5 MUN
Cast Bronze, 29 mm. **Note:** Reduced size.

Date	Good	VG	F	VF	XF
ND(1883) Series 2	5.00	7.50	10.00	15.00	—

KM# 211s.2 5 MUN
Cast Bronze

Date	Good	VG	F	VF	XF
ND(1883) Series 2	—	—	—	—	40.00

KM# 211.3 5 MUN
Cast Bronze, 29 mm. **Note:** Reduced size.

Date	Good	VG	F	VF	XF
ND(1883) Series 3	5.00	7.50	10.00	15.00	—

KM# 211s.3 5 MUN
Cast Bronze

Date	Good	VG	F	VF	XF
ND(1883) Series 3	—	—	—	—	50.00

KM# 211.4 5 MUN
Cast Bronze, 29 mm. **Note:** Reduced size.

Date	Good	VG	F	VF	XF
ND(1883) Series 4	5.00	7.50	10.00	15.00	—

KM# 211s.4 5 MUN
Cast Bronze

Date	Good	VG	F	VF	XF
ND(1883) Series 4	—	—	—	—	50.00

KM# 211.5 5 MUN
Cast Bronze, 29 mm. **Note:** Reduced size.

Date	Good	VG	F	VF	XF
ND(1883) Series 5	5.00	7.50	10.00	15.00	—

KM# 211s.5 5 MUN
Cast Bronze

Date	Good	VG	F	VF	XF
ND(1883) Series 5	—	—	—	—	50.00

KM# 211.6 5 MUN
Cast Bronze, 29 mm. **Note:** Reduced size.

Date	Good	VG	F	VF	XF
ND(1883) Series 6	5.00	7.50	10.00	15.00	—

KM# 211s.6 5 MUN
Cast Bronze

Date	Good	VG	F	VF	XF
ND(1883) Series 6	—	—	—	—	50.00

KM# 211.7 5 MUN
Cast Bronze, 29 mm. **Note:** Reduced size.

Date	Good	VG	F	VF	XF
ND(1883) Series 7	5.00	7.50	10.00	15.00	—

KM# 211s.7 5 MUN
Cast Bronze

Date	Good	VG	F	VF	XF
ND(1883) Series 7	—	—	—	—	50.00

KM# 211.8 5 MUN
Cast Bronze, 29 mm. **Note:** Reduced size.

Date	Good	VG	F	VF	XF
ND(1883) Series 8	5.00	7.50	10.00	15.00	—

KM# 211s.8 5 MUN
Cast Bronze

Date	Good	VG	F	VF	XF
ND(1883) Series 8	—	—	—	—	50.00

KM# 211.9 5 MUN
Cast Bronze, 29 mm. **Note:** Reduced size.

Date	Good	VG	F	VF	XF
ND(1883) Series 9	5.00	7.50	10.00	15.00	—

KM# 211s.9 5 MUN
Cast Bronze

Date	Good	VG	F	VF	XF
ND(1883) Series 9	—	—	—	—	50.00

KM# 211.10 5 MUN
Cast Bronze, 29 mm. **Note:** Reduced size.

Date	Good	VG	F	VF	XF
ND(1883) Series 10	5.00	7.50	10.00	15.00	—

KM# 211s.10 5 MUN
Cast Bronze

Date	Good	VG	F	VF	XF
ND(1883) Series 10	—	—	—	—	50.00

KM# 211.11 5 MUN
Cast Bronze, 29 mm. **Note:** Reduced size.

Date	Good	VG	F	VF	XF
ND(1883) Series 11	5.00	7.50	10.00	15.00	—

KM# 211.12 5 MUN
Cast Bronze, 29 mm. **Note:** Reduced size.

Date	Good	VG	F	VF	XF
ND(1883) Series 12	5.00	7.50	10.00	15.00	—

KM# 212.1 5 MUN
Cast Bronze, 28 mm. **Rev:** Dot below series number at bottom

Date	Good	VG	F	VF	XF
ND(1883) Series 1	5.00	7.50	10.00	15.00	—

KM# 212s.1 5 MUN
Cast Bronze, 29 mm. **Note:** Reduced size.

Date	Good	VG	F	VF	XF
ND(1883) Series 1	—	—	—	—	50.00

KM# 212.2 5 MUN
Cast Bronze, 28 mm. **Rev:** Dot below series number at bottom

Date	Good	VG	F	VF	XF
ND(1883) Series 2	5.00	7.50	10.00	15.00	—

KM# 212s.2 5 MUN
Cast Bronze, 29 mm. **Note:** Reduced size.

Date	Good	VG	F	VF	XF
ND(1883) Series 2	—	—	—	—	50.00

KM# 212.3 5 MUN
Cast Bronze, 28 mm. **Rev:** Dot below series number at bottom

Date	Good	VG	F	VF	XF
ND(1883) Series 3	5.00	7.50	10.00	15.00	—

KM# 212s.3 5 MUN
Cast Bronze, 29 mm. **Note:** Reduced size.

Date	Good	VG	F	VF	XF
ND(1883) Series 3	—	—	—	—	50.00

PALACE GUARD OFFICE

(Mu Wi Yong)

KM# 337.1 MUN
4.0000 g., Cast Bronze **Rev:** "Ch'on" at bottom, series number at left **Note:** Size varies: 25-26 mm.

Date	Good	VG	F	VF	XF
ND(1881) Series 1	2.00	3.00	5.00	7.50	—

KM# 337s.1 MUN
4.0000 g., Cast Bronze

Date	Good	VG	F	VF	XF
ND(1881) Series 1	—	—	—	—	50.00

KM# 337.2 MUN
4.0000 g., Cast Bronze **Rev:** "Ch'on" at bottom, series number at left **Note:** Size varies: 25-26 mm.

Date	Good	VG	F	VF	XF
ND(1881) Series 2	2.00	3.00	5.00	7.50	—

KM# 337s.2 MUN
4.0000 g., Cast Bronze

Date	Good	VG	F	VF	XF
ND(1881) Series 2	—	—	—	—	50.00

KM# 337.3 MUN
4.0000 g., Cast Bronze **Rev:** "Ch'on" at bottom, series number at left **Note:** Size varies: 25-26 mm.

Date	Good	VG	F	VF	XF
ND(1881) Series 3	2.00	3.00	5.00	7.50	—

KM# 337s.3 MUN
4.0000 g., Cast Bronze

Date	Good	VG	F	VF	XF
ND(1881) Series 3	—	—	—	—	50.00

KM# 337.4 MUN
4.0000 g., Cast Bronze **Rev:** "Ch'on" at bottom, series number at left **Note:** Size varies: 25-26 mm.

Date	Good	VG	F	VF	XF
ND(1881) Series 4	2.00	3.00	5.00	7.50	—

KM# 337s.4 MUN
4.0000 g., Cast Bronze

Date	Good	VG	F	VF	XF
ND(1881) Series 4	—	—	—	—	50.00

KM# 337.5 MUN
4.0000 g., Cast Bronze **Rev:** "Ch'on" at bottom, series number at left **Note:** Size varies: 25-26 mm.

Date	Good	VG	F	VF	XF
ND(1881) Series 5	2.00	3.00	5.00	7.50	—

KM# 337s.5 MUN
4.0000 g., Cast Bronze

Date	Good	VG	F	VF	XF
ND(1881) Series 5	—	—	—	—	50.00

KM# 337.6 MUN
4.0000 g., Cast Bronze **Rev:** "Ch'on" at bottom, series number at left **Note:** Size varies: 25-26 mm.

Date	Good	VG	F	VF	XF
ND(1881) Series 6	2.00	3.00	5.00	7.50	—

KM# 337s.6 MUN
4.0000 g., Cast Bronze

Date	Good	VG	F	VF	XF
ND(1881) Series 6	—	—	—	—	50.00

KM# 337.7 MUN
4.0000 g., Cast Bronze **Rev:** "Ch'on" at bottom, series number at left **Note:** Size varies: 25-26 mm.

Date	Good	VG	F	VF	XF
ND(1881) Series 7	2.00	3.00	7.50	10.00	—

KM# 337s.7 MUN
4.0000 g., Cast Bronze

Date	Good	VG	F	VF	XF
ND(1881) Series 7	—	—	—	—	50.00

KM# 337.8 MUN
4.0000 g., Cast Bronze **Rev:** "Ch'on" at bottom, series number at left **Note:** Size varies: 25-26 mm.

Date	Good	VG	F	VF	XF
ND(1881) Series 8	2.00	3.00	5.00	7.50	—

KM# 337s.8 MUN
4.0000 g., Cast Bronze

Date	Good	VG	F	VF	XF
ND(1881) Series 8	—	—	—	—	50.00

KM# 337.9 MUN
4.0000 g., Cast Bronze **Rev:** "Ch'on" at bottom, series number at left **Note:** Size varies: 25-26 mm.

Date	Good	VG	F	VF	XF
ND(1881) Series 9	2.00	3.00	5.00	7.50	—

KM# 337s.9 MUN
4.0000 g., Cast Bronze

Date	Good	VG	F	VF	XF
ND(1881) Series 9	—	—	—	—	50.00

KM# 337.10 MUN
4.0000 g., Cast Bronze **Rev:** "Ch'on" at bottom, series number at left **Note:** Size varies: 25-26 mm.

Date	Good	VG	F	VF	XF
ND(1881) Series 10	2.00	3.00	5.00	7.50	—

KM# 337s.10 MUN
4.0000 g., Cast Bronze

Date	Good	VG	F	VF	XF
ND(1881) Series 10	—	—	—	—	50.00

KM# 337.11 MUN
4.0000 g., Cast Bronze **Rev:** "Ch'on" at bottom, series number at left **Note:** Size varies: 25-26 mm.

Date	Good	VG	F	VF	XF
ND(1881) Series 11	2.00	3.00	5.00	7.50	—

KM# 337s.11 MUN
4.0000 g., Cast Bronze

Date	Good	VG	F	VF	XF
ND(1881) Series 11	—	—	—	—	50.00

KM# 337.12 MUN
4.0000 g., Cast Bronze **Rev:** "Ch'on" at bottom, series number at left **Note:** Size varies: 25-26 mm.

Date	Good	VG	F	VF	XF
ND(1881) Series 12	2.00	3.00	5.00	7.50	—

KM# 337s.12 MUN
4.0000 g., Cast Bronze

Date	Good	VG	F	VF	XF
ND(1881) Series 12	—	—	—	—	50.00

KM# 337.13 MUN
4.0000 g., Cast Bronze **Rev:** "Ch'on" at bottom, series number at left **Note:** Size varies: 25-26 mm.

Date	Good	VG	F	VF	XF
ND(1881) Series 13	2.00	3.00	5.00	7.50	—

KM# 337s.13 MUN
4.0000 g., Cast Brass

Date	Good	VG	F	VF	XF
ND(1881) Series 13	—	—	—	—	50.00

KM# 337.14 MUN
4.0000 g., Cast Bronze **Rev:** "Ch'on" at bottom, series number at left **Note:** Size varies: 25-26 mm.

Date	Good	VG	F	VF	XF
ND(1881) Series 14	2.00	3.00	5.00	7.50	—

KM# 337s.14 MUN
4.0000 g., Cast Bronze

Date	Good	VG	F	VF	XF
ND(1881) Series 14	—	—	—	—	50.00

KM# 337.15 MUN
4.0000 g., Cast Bronze **Rev:** "Ch'on" at bottom, series number at left **Note:** Size varies: 25-26 mm.

Date	Good	VG	F	VF	XF
ND(1881) Series 15	2.00	3.00	5.00	7.50	—

KM# 337s.15 MUN
4.0000 g., Cast Bronze

Date	Good	VG	F	VF	XF
ND(1881) Series 15	—	—	—	—	50.00

KM# 337.16 MUN
4.0000 g., Cast Bronze **Rev:** "Ch'on" at bottom, series number at left **Note:** Size varies: 25-26 mm.

Date	Good	VG	F	VF	XF
ND(1881) Series 16	2.00	3.00	5.00	7.50	—

KM# 337s.16 MUN
4.0000 g., Cast Bronze

Date	Good	VG	F	VF	XF
ND(1881) Series 16	—	—	—	—	50.00

KM# 337.17 MUN
4.0000 g., Cast Bronze **Rev:** "Ch'on" at bottom, series number at left **Note:** Size varies: 25-26 mm.

Date	Good	VG	F	VF	XF
ND(1881) Series 17	2.00	3.00	5.00	7.50	—

KM# 337s.17 MUN
4.0000 g., Cast Bronze

Date	Good	VG	F	VF	XF
ND(1881) Series 17	—	—	—	—	50.00

KM# 337.18 MUN
4.0000 g., Cast Bronze **Rev:** "Ch'on" at bottom, series number at left **Note:** Size varies: 25-26 mm.

Date	Good	VG	F	VF	XF
ND(1881) Series 18	2.00	3.00	5.00	7.50	—

KM# 337s.18 MUN
4.0000 g., Cast Bronze

Date	Good	VG	F	VF	XF
ND(1881) Series 18	—	—	—	—	50.00

KM# 337.19 MUN
4.0000 g., Cast Bronze **Rev:** "Ch'on" at bottom, series number at left **Note:** Size varies: 25-26 mm.

Date	Good	VG	F	VF	XF
ND(1881) Series 19	2.00	3.00	5.00	7.50	—

KM# 337s.19 MUN
4.0000 g., Cast Bronze

Date	Good	VG	F	VF	XF
ND(1881) Series 19	—	—	—	—	50.00

KM# 337.20 MUN
4.0000 g., Cast Bronze **Rev:** "Ch'on" at bottom, series number at left **Note:** Size varies: 25-26 mm.

Date	Good	VG	F	VF	XF
ND(1881) Series 20	2.00	3.00	5.00	7.50	—

KM# 337s.20 MUN
4.0000 g., Cast Bronze

Date	Good	VG	F	VF	XF
ND(1881) Series 20	—	—	—	—	50.00

KM# 338.1 MUN
4.0000 g., Cast Bronze **Note:** Reduced size. Size varies: 23-24 mm.

Date	Good	VG	F	VF	XF
ND(1881) Series 1	2.00	3.00	5.00	7.50	—

KM# 338s.1 MUN
4.0000 g., Cast Bronze

Date	Good	VG	F	VF	XF
ND(1881) Series 1	—	—	—	—	40.00

KM# 338.2 MUN
4.0000 g., Cast Bronze **Note:** Reduced size. Size varies: 23-24 mm.

Date	Good	VG	F	VF	XF
ND(1881) Series 2	2.00	3.00	5.00	7.50	—

KM# 338s.2 MUN
4.0000 g., Cast Bronze

Date	Good	VG	F	VF	XF
ND(1881) Series 2	—	—	—	—	40.00

KM# 338.3 MUN
4.0000 g., Cast Bronze **Note:** Reduced size. Size varies: 23-24 mm.

Date	Good	VG	F	VF	XF
ND(1881) Series 3	2.00	3.00	5.00	7.50	—

KM# 338s.3 MUN
4.0000 g., Cast Bronze

Date	Good	VG	F	VF	XF
ND(1881) Series 3	—	—	—	—	40.00

KM# 338.4 MUN
4.0000 g., Cast Bronze **Note:** Reduced size. Size varies: 23-24 mm.

Date	Good	VG	F	VF	XF
ND(1881) Series 4	2.00	3.00	5.00	7.50	—

KM# 338s.4 MUN
4.0000 g., Cast Bronze

Date	Good	VG	F	VF	XF
ND(1881) Series 4	—	—	—	—	40.00

KM# 338.5 MUN
4.0000 g., Cast Bronze **Note:** Reduced size. Size varies: 23-24 mm.

Date	Good	VG	F	VF	XF
ND(1881) Series 5	2.00	3.00	5.00	7.50	—

KM# 338s.5 MUN
4.0000 g., Cast Bronze

Date	Good	VG	F	VF	XF
ND(1881) Series 5	—	—	—	—	40.00

KM# 338.6 MUN
4.0000 g., Cast Bronze **Note:** Reduced size. Size varies: 23-24 mm.

Date	Good	VG	F	VF	XF
ND(1881) Series 6	2.00	3.00	5.00	7.50	—

KM# 338s.6 MUN
4.0000 g., Cast Bronze

Date	Good	VG	F	VF	XF
ND(1881) Series 6	—	—	—	—	40.00

KM# 338.7 MUN
4.0000 g., Cast Bronze **Note:** Reduced size. Size varies: 23-24 mm.

Date	Good	VG	F	VF	XF
ND(1881) Series 7	2.00	3.00	5.00	7.50	—

KM# 338s.7 MUN
4.0000 g., Cast Bronze

Date	Good	VG	F	VF	XF
ND(1881) Series 7	—	—	—	—	40.00

KM# 338.8 MUN
4.0000 g., Cast Bronze **Note:** Reduced size. Size varies: 23-24 mm.

Date	Good	VG	F	VF	XF
ND(1881) Series 8	2.00	3.00	5.00	7.50	—

KM# 338s.8 MUN
4.0000 g., Cast Bronze

Date	Good	VG	F	VF	XF
ND(1881) Series 8	—	—	—	—	40.00

KM# 338.9 MUN
4.0000 g., Cast Bronze **Note:** Reduced size. Size varies: 23-24 mm.

Date	Good	VG	F	VF	XF
ND(1881) Series 9	2.00	3.00	5.00	7.50	—

KM# 338s.9 MUN
4.0000 g., Cast Bronze

Date	Good	VG	F	VF	XF
ND(1881) Series 9	—	—	—	—	40.00

KM# 338.10 MUN
4.0000 g., Cast Bronze **Note:** Reduced size. Size varies: 23-24 mm.

Date	Good	VG	F	VF	XF
ND(1881) Series 10	2.00	3.00	5.00	7.50	—

KM# 338.11 MUN
4.0000 g., Cast Bronze **Note:** Reduced size. Size varies: 23-24 mm.

Date	Good	VG	F	VF	XF
ND(1881) Series 11	2.00	3.00	5.00	7.50	—

KM# 338s.11 MUN
4.0000 g., Cast Bronze

Date	Good	VG	F	VF	XF
ND(1881) Series 11	—	—	—	—	40.00

KM# 338.12 MUN
4.0000 g., Cast Bronze **Note:** Reduced size. Size varies: 23-24 mm.

Date	Good	VG	F	VF	XF
ND(1881) Series 12	2.00	3.00	5.00	7.50	—

KM# 338s.12 MUN
4.0000 g., Cast Bronze

Date	Good	VG	F	VF	XF
ND(1881) Series 12	—	—	—	—	40.00

KM# 338.13 MUN
4.0000 g., Cast Bronze **Note:** Reduced size. Size varies: 23-24 mm.

Date	Good	VG	F	VF	XF
ND(1881) Series 13	2.00	3.00	5.00	7.50	—

KM# 338s.13 MUN
4.0000 g., Cast Bronze

Date	Good	VG	F	VF	XF
ND(1881) Series 13	—	—	—	—	40.00

KM# 338.14 MUN
4.0000 g., Cast Bronze **Note:** Reduced size. Size varies: 23-24 mm.

Date	Good	VG	F	VF	XF
ND(1881) Series 14	2.00	3.00	5.00	7.50	—

KM# 338s.14 MUN
4.0000 g., Cast Bronze

Date	Good	VG	F	VF	XF
ND(1881) Series 14	—	—	—	—	40.00

KM# 338.15 MUN
4.0000 g., Cast Bronze **Note:** Reduced size. Size varies: 23-24 mm.

Date	Good	VG	F	VF	XF
ND(1881) Series 15	2.00	3.00	5.00	7.50	—

KM# 338s.15 MUN
4.0000 g., Cast Bronze

Date	Good	VG	F	VF	XF
ND(1881) Series 15	—	—	—	—	40.00

KM# 338.16 MUN
4.0000 g., Cast Bronze **Note:** Reduced size. Size varies: 23-24 mm.

Date	Good	VG	F	VF	XF
ND(1881) Series 16	2.00	3.00	5.00	7.50	—

KM# 338s.16 MUN
4.0000 g., Cast Bronze

Date	Good	VG	F	VF	XF
ND(1881) Series 16	—	—	—	—	40.00

KM# 338.17 MUN
4.0000 g., Cast Bronze **Note:** Reduced size. Size varies: 23-24 mm.

Date	Good	VG	F	VF	XF
ND(1881) Series 17	2.00	3.00	5.00	7.50	—

KM# 338s.17 MUN
4.0000 g., Cast Bronze

Date	Good	VG	F	VF	XF
ND(1881) Series 17	—	—	—	—	40.00

KM# 338.18 MUN
4.0000 g., Cast Bronze **Note:** Reduced size. Size varies: 23-24 mm.

Date	Good	VG	F	VF	XF
ND(1881) Series 18	2.00	3.00	5.00	7.50	—

KM# 338s.18 MUN
4.0000 g., Cast Bronze

Date	Good	VG	F	VF	XF
ND(1881) Series 18	—	—	—	—	40.00

KM# 338.19 MUN
4.0000 g., Cast Bronze **Note:** Reduced size. Size varies: 23-24 mm.

Date	Good	VG	F	VF	XF
ND(1881) Series 19	2.00	3.00	5.00	7.50	—

KM# 338s.19 MUN
4.0000 g., Cast Bronze

Date	Good	VG	F	VF	XF
ND(1881) Series 19	—	—	—	—	40.00

KM# 338.20 MUN
4.0000 g., Cast Bronze **Note:** Reduced size. Size varies: 23-24 mm.

Date	Good	VG	F	VF	XF
ND(1881) Series 20	2.00	3.00	5.00	7.50	—

KM# 338s.20 MUN
4.0000 g., Cast Bronze

Date	Good	VG	F	VF	XF
ND(1881) Series 20	—	—	—	—	40.00

KM# 339.1 MUN
4.0000 g., Cast Bronze, 24 mm. **Rev:** "Wan" at bottom, series number at left

Date	Good	VG	F	VF	XF
ND(1881) Series 1	50.00	80.00	125	210	—

KM# 339s MUN
4.0000 g., Cast Bronze, 24 mm.

Date	Good	VG	F	VF	XF
ND(1881) Series 1	—	—	—	—	450

COURT GUARD

(Kum Wi Yong)

KM# 340.1 MUN
4.0000 g., Cast Bronze **Rev:** "Kum" at top, series number at bottom **Note:** Large characters. Size varies: 23-25 mm.

Date	Good	VG	F	VF	XF
ND(1823) Series 1	3.00	5.00	8.00	12.00	—

KM# 340.2 MUN
4.0000 g., Cast Bronze **Rev:** "Kum" at top, series number at bottom **Note:** Large characters. Size varies: 23-25 mm.

Date	Good	VG	F	VF	XF
ND(1823) Series 2	3.00	5.00	8.00	12.00	—

KM# 340s.2 MUN
4.0000 g., Cast Bronze

Date	Good	VG	F	VF	XF
ND(1823) Series 2	—	—	—	—	40.00

KM# 340.3 MUN

4.0000 g., Cast Bronze **Rev:** "Kum" at top, series number at bottom **Note:** Large characters. Size varies: 23-25 mm.

Date	Good	VG	F	VF	XF
ND(1823) Series 3	3.00	5.00	8.00	12.00	—

KM# 340s.3 MUN

4.0000 g., Cast Bronze

Date	Good	VG	F	VF	XF
ND(1823) Series 3	—	—	—	—	40.00

KM# 340.4 MUN

4.0000 g., Cast Bronze **Rev:** "Kum" at top, series number at bottom **Note:** Large characters. Size varies: 23-25 mm.

Date	Good	VG	F	VF	XF
ND(1823) Series 4	3.00	5.00	8.00	12.00	—

KM# 340s.4 MUN

4.0000 g., Cast Bronze

Date	Good	VG	F	VF	XF
ND(1823) Series 4	—	—	—	—	40.00

KM# 340.5 MUN

4.0000 g., Cast Bronze **Rev:** "Kum" at top, series number at bottom **Note:** Large characters. Size varies: 23-25 mm.

Date	Good	VG	F	VF	XF
ND(1823) Series 5	3.00	5.00	8.00	12.00	—

KM# 340s.5 MUN

4.0000 g., Cast Bronze

Date	Good	VG	F	VF	XF
ND(1823) Series 5	—	—	—	—	40.00

KM# 340.6 MUN

4.0000 g., Cast Bronze **Rev:** "Kum" at top, series number at bottom **Note:** Large characters. Size varies: 23-25 mm.

Date	Good	VG	F	VF	XF
ND(1823) Series 6	3.00	5.00	8.00	12.00	—

KM# 340s.6 MUN

4.0000 g., Cast Bronze

Date	Good	VG	F	VF	XF
ND(1823) Series 6	—	—	—	—	28.00

KM# 340.7 MUN

4.0000 g., Cast Bronze **Rev:** "Kum" at top, series number at bottom **Note:** Large characters. Size varies: 23-25 mm.

Date	Good	VG	F	VF	XF
ND(1823) Series 7	3.00	5.00	8.00	12.00	—

KM# 340s.7 MUN

4.0000 g., Cast Bronze

Date	Good	VG	F	VF	XF
ND(1823) Series 7	—	—	—	—	40.00

KM# 340.8 MUN

4.0000 g., Cast Bronze **Rev:** "Kum" at top, series number at bottom **Note:** Large characters. Size varies: 23-25 mm.

Date	Good	VG	F	VF	XF
ND(1823) Series 8	3.00	5.00	8.00	12.00	—

KM# 340s.8 MUN

4.0000 g., Cast Bronze

Date	Good	VG	F	VF	XF
ND(1823) Series 8	—	—	—	—	40.00

KM# 341.1 MUN

4.0000 g., Cast Bronze, 25 mm. **Note:** Small characters.

Date	Good	VG	F	VF	XF
ND(1823) Series 1	3.00	5.00	8.00	12.00	—

KM# 341a.1 MUN

4.0000 g., Cast Bronze, 25 mm. **Obv:** Hooks in "P'yong"

Date	Good	VG	F	VF	XF
ND(1823) Series 1	3.00	5.00	8.00	12.00	—

KM# 341b.1 MUN

4.0000 g., Cast Bronze, 23 mm. **Obv:** "P'yong" without hooks

Date	Good	VG	F	VF	XF
ND(1823) Series 1	3.00	5.00	8.00	12.00	—

KM# 341s.1 MUN

4.0000 g., Cast Bronze, 23 mm.

Date	Good	VG	F	VF	XF
ND(1823) Series 1	—	—	—	—	40.00

KM# 341.2 MUN

4.0000 g., Cast Bronze, 25 mm. **Note:** Small characters.

Date	Good	VG	F	VF	XF
ND(1823) Series 2	3.00	5.00	8.00	12.00	—

KM# 341a.2 MUN

4.0000 g., Cast Bronze, 25 mm. **Obv:** Hooks in "P'yong"

Date	Good	VG	F	VF	XF
ND(1823) Series 2	3.00	5.00	8.00	12.00	—

KM# 341b.2 MUN

4.0000 g., Cast Bronze, 23 mm. **Obv:** "P'yong" without hooks

Date	Good	VG	F	VF	XF
ND(1823) Series 2	3.00	5.00	8.00	12.00	—

KM# 341s.2 MUN

4.0000 g., Cast Bronze, 23 mm.

Date	Good	VG	F	VF	XF
ND(1823) Series 2	—	—	—	—	40.00

KM# 341.3 MUN

4.0000 g., Cast Bronze, 25 mm. **Note:** Small characters.

Date	Good	VG	F	VF	XF
ND(1823) Series 3	3.00	5.00	8.00	12.00	—

KM# 341a.3 MUN

4.0000 g., Cast Bronze, 25 mm. **Obv:** Hooks in "P'yong"

Date	Good	VG	F	VF	XF
ND(1823) Series 3	3.00	5.00	8.00	12.00	—

KM# 341b.3 MUN

4.0000 g., Cast Bronze, 23 mm. **Obv:** "P'yong" without hooks

Date	Good	VG	F	VF	XF
ND(1823) Series 3	3.00	5.00	8.00	12.00	—

KM# 341s.3 MUN

4.0000 g., Cast Bronze, 23 mm.

Date	Good	VG	F	VF	XF
ND(1823) Series 3	—	—	—	—	40.00

KM# 341.4 MUN

4.0000 g., Cast Bronze, 25 mm. **Note:** Small characters.

Date	Good	VG	F	VF	XF
ND(1823) Series 4	3.00	5.00	8.00	12.00	—

KM# 341a.4 MUN

4.0000 g., Cast Bronze, 25 mm. **Obv:** Hooks in "P'yong"

Date	Good	VG	F	VF	XF
ND(1823) Series 4	3.00	5.00	8.00	12.00	—

KM# 341b.4 MUN

4.0000 g., Cast Bronze, 23 mm. **Obv:** "P'yong" without hooks

Date	Good	VG	F	VF	XF
ND(1823) Series 4	3.00	5.00	8.00	12.00	—

KM# 341s.4 MUN

4.0000 g., Cast Bronze, 23 mm.

Date	Good	VG	F	VF	XF
ND(1823) Series 4	—	—	—	—	40.00

KM# 341.5 MUN

4.0000 g., Cast Bronze, 25 mm. **Note:** Small characters.

Date	Good	VG	F	VF	XF
ND(1823) Series 5	3.00	5.00	8.00	12.00	—

KM# 341a.5 MUN

4.0000 g., Cast Bronze, 25 mm. **Obv:** Hooks in "P'yong"

Date	Good	VG	F	VF	XF
ND(1823) Series 5	3.00	5.00	8.00	12.00	—

KM# 341b.5 MUN

4.0000 g., Cast Bronze, 23 mm. **Obv:** "P'yong" without hooks

Date	Good	VG	F	VF	XF
ND(1823) Series 5	3.00	5.00	8.00	12.00	—

KM# 341s.5 MUN

4.0000 g., Cast Bronze, 23 mm.

Date	Good	VG	F	VF	XF
ND(1823) Series 5	—	—	—	—	40.00

KM# 341.6 MUN

4.0000 g., Cast Bronze, 25 mm. **Note:** Small characters.

Date	Good	VG	F	VF	XF
ND(1823) Series 6	3.00	5.00	8.00	12.00	—

KM# 341a.6 MUN

4.0000 g., Cast Bronze, 25 mm. **Obv:** Hooks in "P'yong"

Date	Good	VG	F	VF	XF
ND(1823) Series 6	3.00	5.00	8.00	12.00	—

KM# 341b.6 MUN

4.0000 g., Cast Bronze, 23 mm. **Obv:** "P'yong" without hooks

Date	Good	VG	F	VF	XF
ND(1823) Series 6	3.00	5.00	8.00	12.00	—

KM# 341s.6 MUN

4.0000 g., Cast Bronze, 23 mm.

Date	Good	VG	F	VF	XF
ND(1823) Series 6	—	—	—	—	40.00

KM# 341.7 MUN

4.0000 g., Cast Bronze, 25 mm. **Note:** Small characters.

Date	Good	VG	F	VF	XF
ND(1823) Series 7	3.00	5.00	8.00	12.00	—

KM# 341a.7 MUN

4.0000 g., Cast Bronze, 25 mm. **Obv:** Hooks in "P'yong"

Date	Good	VG	F	VF	XF
ND(1823) Series 7	3.00	5.00	8.00	12.00	—

KM# 341b.7 MUN

4.0000 g., Cast Bronze, 23 mm. **Obv:** "P'yong" without hooks

Date	Good	VG	F	VF	XF
ND(1823) Series 7	3.00	5.00	8.00	12.00	—

KM# 341s.7 MUN

4.0000 g., Cast Bronze, 23 mm.

Date	Good	VG	F	VF	XF
ND(1823) Series 7	—	—	—	—	40.00

KM# 341.8 MUN

4.0000 g., Cast Bronze, 25 mm. **Note:** Small characters.

Date	Good	VG	F	VF	XF
ND(1823) Series 8	3.00	5.00	8.00	12.00	—

KM# 341a.8 MUN

4.0000 g., Cast Bronze, 25 mm. **Obv:** Hooks in "P'yong"

Date	Good	VG	F	VF	XF
ND(1823) Series 8	3.00	5.00	8.00	12.00	—

KM# 341b.8 MUN

4.0000 g., Cast Bronze, 23 mm. **Obv:** "P'yong without hooks

Date	Good	VG	F	VF	XF
ND(1823) Series 8	3.00	5.00	8.00	12.00	—

KM# 341s.8 MUN

4.0000 g., Cast Bronze, 23 mm.

Date	Good	VG	F	VF	XF
ND(1823) Series 8	—	—	—	—	40.00

MILITARY TRAINING COMMAND

(Hul Ly On Do Gam)

KM# 448.1 MUN

4.0000 g., Cast Bronze, 25 mm. **Rev:** "Hun" at top, series number at bottom

Date	Good	VG	F	VF	XF
ND(1828) Series 1	3.00	5.00	8.00	12.00	—

KM# 448s.1 MUN

4.0000 g., Cast Bronze, 25 mm.

Date	Good	VG	F	VF	XF
ND(1828) Series 1	—	—	—	—	40.00

KM# 448.2 MUN

4.0000 g., Cast Bronze, 25 mm. **Rev:** "Hun" at top, series number at bottom

Date	Good	VG	F	VF	XF
ND(1828) Series 2	3.00	5.00	8.00	12.00	—

KM# 448s.2 MUN

4.0000 g., Cast Bronze, 25 mm.

Date	Good	VG	F	VF	XF
ND(1828) Series 2	—	—	—	—	40.00

KM# 448.3 MUN

4.0000 g., Cast Bronze, 25 mm. **Rev:** "Hun" at top, series number at bottom

Date	Good	VG	F	VF	XF
ND(1828) Series 3	3.00	5.00	8.00	12.00	—

KM# 448s.3 MUN

4.0000 g., Cast Bronze, 25 mm.

Date	Good	VG	F	VF	XF
ND(1828) Series 3	—	—	—	—	40.00

KM# 448.4 MUN

4.0000 g., Cast Bronze, 25 mm. **Rev:** "Hun" at top, series number at bottom

Date	Good	VG	F	VF	XF
ND(1828) Series 4	3.00	5.00	8.00	12.00	—

KM# 448s.4 MUN

4.0000 g., Cast Bronze, 25 mm.

Date	Good	VG	F	VF	XF
ND(1828) Series 4	—	—	—	—	40.00

KM# 448.5 MUN

4.0000 g., Cast Bronze, 25 mm. **Rev:** "Hun" at top, series number at bottom

Date	Good	VG	F	VF	XF
ND(1828) Series 5	3.00	5.00	8.00	12.00	—

KM# 448s.5 MUN

4.0000 g., Cast Bronze, 25 mm.

Date	Good	VG	F	VF	XF
ND(1828) Series 5	—	—	—	—	40.00

KM# 448.6 MUN

4.0000 g., Cast Bronze, 25 mm. **Rev:** "Hun" at top, series number at bottom

Date	Good	VG	F	VF	XF
ND(1828) Series 6	3.00	5.00	8.00	12.00	—

KM# 448s.6 MUN

4.0000 g., Cast Bronze, 25 mm.

Date	Good	VG	F	VF	XF
ND(1828) Series 6	—	—	—	—	40.00

KM# 448.14 MUN

4.0000 g., Cast Bronze, 25 mm. **Rev:** Star at upper left

Date	Good	VG	F	VF	XF
ND(1828) Series 4	3.00	5.00	8.00	12.00	—

KM# 474.10 MUN

4.0000 g., Cast Bronze, 24 mm. **Rev:** "Kil" at bottom, series number at right

Date	Good	VG	F	VF	XF
ND(1857)	6.00	10.00	15.00	25.00	—

KM# 474s.10 MUN

4.0000 g., Cast Bronze, 24 mm.

Date	Good	VG	F	VF	XF
ND(1857) Series 10	—	—	—	—	100

KM# 449.1 MUN

4.0000 g., Cast Bronze, 25 mm. **Rev:** "Ch'on" at bottom, series number at left

Date	Good	VG	F	VF	XF
ND(1857) Series 1	2.00	4.00	7.00	10.00	—

KM# 449s.1 MUN

4.0000 g., Cast Bronze, 25 mm.

Date	Good	VG	F	VF	XF
ND(1857) Series 1	—	—	—	—	40.00

KM# 449.2 MUN

, 25 mm. **Rev:** "Ch'on" at bottom, series number at left

Date	Good	VG	F	VF	XF
ND(1857) Series 2	2.00	4.00	7.00	10.00	—

KM# 449s.2 MUN

4.0000 g., Cast Bronze, 25 mm.

Date	Good	VG	F	VF	XF
ND(1857) Series 2	—	—	—	—	40.00

KM# 449.3 MUN

4.0000 g., Cast Bronze, 25 mm. **Rev:** "Ch'on" at bottom, series number at left

Date	Good	VG	F	VF	XF
ND(1857) Series 3	2.00	4.00	7.00	10.00	—

KM# 449s.3 MUN

4.0000 g., Cast Bronze, 25 mm.

Date	Good	VG	F	VF	XF
ND(1857) Series 3	—	—	—	—	40.00

KM# 449.4 MUN

4.0000 g., Cast Bronze, 25 mm. **Rev:** "Ch'on" at bottom, series number at left

Date	Good	VG	F	VF	XF
ND(1857) Series 4	2.00	4.00	7.00	10.00	—

KM# 449s.4 MUN

4.0000 g., Cast Bronze, 25 mm.

Date	Good	VG	F	VF	XF
ND(1857) Series 4	—	—	—	—	40.00

KM# 449.5 MUN

4.0000 g., Cast Bronze, 25 mm. **Rev:** "Ch'on" at bottom, series number at left

Date	Good	VG	F	VF	XF
ND(1857) Series 5	2.00	4.00	7.00	10.00	—

KM# 449s.5 MUN

4.0000 g., Cast Bronze, 25 mm.

Date	Good	VG	F	VF	XF
ND(1857) Series 5	—	—	—	—	40.00

KM# 449.6 MUN

4.0000 g., Cast Bronze, 25 mm. **Rev:** "Ch'on" at bottom, series number at left

Date	Good	VG	F	VF	XF
ND(1857) Series 6	2.00	4.00	7.00	10.00	—

KM# 449s.6 MUN

4.0000 g., Cast Bronze, 25 mm.

Date	Good	VG	F	VF	XF
ND(1857) Series 6	—	—	—	—	40.00

KM# 449.7 MUN

4.0000 g., Cast Bronze, 25 mm. **Rev:** "Ch'on" at bottom, series number at left

Date	Good	VG	F	VF	XF
ND(1857) Series 7	2.00	4.00	7.00	10.00	—

KM# 449s.7 MUN

4.0000 g., Cast Bronze, 25 mm.

Date	Good	VG	F	VF	XF
ND(1857) Series 7	—	—	—	—	40.00

KM# 449.8 MUN

4.0000 g., Cast Bronze, 25 mm. **Rev:** "Ch'on" at bottom, series number at left

Date	Good	VG	F	VF	XF
ND(1857) Series 8	2.00	4.00	7.00	10.00	—

KM# 449s.8 MUN

4.0000 g., Cast Bronze, 25 mm.

Date	Good	VG	F	VF	XF
ND(1857) Series 8	—	—	—	—	40.00

KM# 449.9 MUN

4.0000 g., Cast Bronze, 25 mm. **Rev:** "Ch'on" at bottom, series number at left

Date	Good	VG	F	VF	XF
ND(1857) Series 9	2.00	4.00	7.00	10.00	—

KM# 449s.9 MUN

4.0000 g., Cast Bronze, 25 mm.

Date	Good	VG	F	VF	XF
ND(1857) Series 9	—	—	—	—	40.00

KM# 449.10 MUN

4.0000 g., Cast Bronze, 25 mm. **Rev:** "Ch'on" at bottom, series number at left

Date	Good	VG	F	VF	XF
ND(1857) Series 10	2.00	4.00	7.00	10.00	—

KM# 449s.10 MUN

4.0000 g., Cast Bronze, 25 mm.

Date	Good	VG	F	VF	XF
ND(1857) Series 10	—	—	—	—	40.00

KM# 450.1 MUN

4.0000 g., Cast Bronze, 25 mm. **Rev:** "Chong" at bottom, series number at left

Date	Good	VG	F	VF	XF
ND(1857) Series 1	2.00	4.00	7.00	10.00	—

KM# 450s.1 MUN

4.0000 g., Cast Bronze, 25 mm.

Date	Good	VG	F	VF	XF
ND(1857) Series 1	—	—	—	—	40.00

KM# 450.2 MUN

4.0000 g., Cast Bronze, 25 mm. **Rev:** "Chong" at bottom, series number at left

Date	Good	VG	F	VF	XF
ND(1857) Series 2	2.00	4.00	7.00	10.00	—

KM# 450s.2 MUN

4.0000 g., Cast Bronze, 25 mm.

Date	Good	VG	F	VF	XF
ND(1857) Series 2	—	—	—	—	40.00

KM# 450.3 MUN

4.0000 g., Cast Bronze, 25 mm. **Rev:** "Chong" at bottom, series number at left

Date	Good	VG	F	VF	XF
ND(1857) Series 3	2.00	4.00	7.00	10.00	—

KM# 450s.3 MUN

4.0000 g., Cast Bronze, 25 mm.

Date	Good	VG	F	VF	XF
ND(1857) Series 3	—	—	—	—	40.00

KM# 450.4 MUN

4.0000 g., Cast Bronze, 25 mm. **Rev:** "Chong" at bottom, series number at left

Date	Good	VG	F	VF	XF
ND(1857) Series 4	2.00	4.00	7.00	10.00	—

KM# 450s.4 MUN

4.0000 g., Cast Bronze, 25 mm.

Date	Good	VG	F	VF	XF
ND(1857) Series 4	—	—	—	—	40.00

KM# 450.5 MUN

4.0000 g., Cast Bronze, 25 mm. **Rev:** "Chong" at bottom, series number at left

Date	Good	VG	F	VF	XF
ND(1857) Series 5	2.00	4.00	7.00	10.00	—

KM# 450s.5 MUN

4.0000 g., Cast Bronze, 25 mm.

Date	Good	VG	F	VF	XF
ND(1857) Series 5	—	—	—	—	40.00

KM# 450.6 MUN

4.0000 g., Cast Bronze, 25 mm. **Rev:** "Chong" at bottom, series number at left

Date	Good	VG	F	VF	XF
ND(1857) Series 6	2.00	4.00	7.00	10.00	—

KM# 450s.6 MUN

4.0000 g., Cast Bronze, 25 mm.

Date	Good	VG	F	VF	XF
ND(1857) Series 6	—	—	—	—	40.00

KM# 450.7 MUN

4.0000 g., Cast Bronze, 25 mm. **Rev:** "Chong" at bottom, series number at left

Date	Good	VG	F	VF	XF
ND(1857) Series 7	2.00	4.00	7.00	10.00	—

KM# 450s.7 MUN

4.0000 g., Cast Bronze, 25 mm.

Date	Good	VG	F	VF	XF
ND(1857) Series 7	—	—	—	—	40.00

KM# 450.8 MUN

4.0000 g., Cast Bronze, 25 mm. **Rev:** "Chong" at bottom, series number at left

Date	Good	VG	F	VF	XF
ND(1857) Series 8	2.00	4.00	7.00	10.00	—

KM# 450s.8 MUN

4.0000 g., Cast Bronze, 25 mm.

Date	Good	VG	F	VF	XF
ND(1857) Series 8	—	—	—	—	40.00

KM# 450.9 MUN

4.0000 g., Cast Bronze, 25 mm. **Rev:** "Chong" at bottom, series number at left

Date	Good	VG	F	VF	XF
ND(1857) Series 9	2.00	4.00	7.00	10.00	—

KM# 450s.9 MUN

4.0000 g., Cast Bronze, 25 mm.

Date	Good	VG	F	VF	XF
ND(1857) Series 9	—	—	—	—	40.00

KM# 450.10 MUN

4.0000 g., Cast Bronze, 25 mm. **Rev:** "Chong" at bottom, series number at left

Date	Good	VG	F	VF	XF
ND(1857) Series 10	2.00	4.00	7.00	10.00	—

KM# 450s.10 MUN

4.0000 g., Cast Bronze, 25 mm.

Date	Good	VG	F	VF	XF
ND(1857) Series 10	—	—	—	—	40.00

KM# 451.1 MUN

4.0000 g., Cast Bronze, 25 mm. **Rev:** "Tae" at bottom, series number at left

Date	Good	VG	F	VF	XF
ND(1857) Series 1	2.00	4.00	7.00	10.00	—

KM# 451s.1 MUN

4.0000 g., Cast Bronze, 25 mm.

Date	Good	VG	F	VF	XF
ND(1857) Series 1	—	—	—	—	40.00

KM# 451.2 MUN

4.0000 g., Cast Bronze, 25 mm. **Rev:** "Tae" at bottom, series number at left

Date	Good	VG	F	VF	XF
ND(1857) Series 2	2.00	4.00	7.00	10.00	—

KM# 451s.2 MUN

4.0000 g., Cast Bronze, 25 mm.

Date	Good	VG	F	VF	XF
ND(1857) Series 2	—	—	—	—	40.00

KM# 451.3 MUN

4.0000 g., Cast Bronze, 25 mm. **Rev:** "Tae" at bottom, series number at left

Date	Good	VG	F	VF	XF
ND(1857) Series 3	2.00	4.00	7.00	10.00	—

KM# 451s.3 MUN

4.0000 g., Cast Bronze, 25 mm.

Date	Good	VG	F	VF	XF
ND(1857) Series 3	—	—	—	—	40.00

KM# 451.4 MUN

4.0000 g., Cast Bronze, 25 mm. **Rev:** "Tae" at bottom, series number at left

Date	Good	VG	F	VF	XF
ND(1857) Series 4	2.00	4.00	7.00	10.00	—

KM# 451s.4 MUN

4.0000 g., Cast Bronze, 25 mm.

Date	Good	VG	F	VF	XF
ND(1857) Series 4	—	—	—	—	40.00

KM# 451.5 MUN

4.0000 g., Cast Bronze, 25 mm. **Rev:** "Tae" at bottom, series number at left

Date	Good	VG	F	VF	XF
ND(1857) Series 5	2.00	4.00	7.00	10.00	—

KM# 451s.5 MUN

4.0000 g., Cast Bronze, 25 mm.

Date	Good	VG	F	VF	XF
ND(1857) Series 5	—	—	—	—	40.00

KM# 451.6 MUN

4.0000 g., Cast Bronze, 25 mm. **Rev:** "Tae" at bottom, series number at left

Date	Good	VG	F	VF	XF
ND(1857) Series 6	2.00	4.00	7.00	10.00	—

KM# 451s.6 MUN

4.0000 g., Cast Bronze, 25 mm.

Date	Good	VG	F	VF	XF
ND(1857) Series 6	—	—	—	—	40.00

KM# 451.7 MUN

4.0000 g., Cast Bronze, 25 mm. **Rev:** "Tae" at bottom, series number at left

Date	Good	VG	F	VF	XF
ND(1857) Series 7	2.00	4.00	7.00	10.00	—

KM# 451s.7 MUN

4.0000 g., Cast Bronze, 25 mm.

Date	Good	VG	F	VF	XF
ND(1857) Series 7	—	—	—	—	40.00

KM# 451.8 MUN

4.0000 g., Cast Bronze, 25 mm. **Rev:** "Tae" at bottom, series number at left

Date	Good	VG	F	VF	XF
ND(1857) Series 8	2.00	4.00	7.00	10.00	—

KM# 451s.8 MUN

4.0000 g., Cast Bronze, 25 mm.

Date	Good	VG	F	VF	XF
ND(1857) Series 8	—	—	—	—	40.00

KM# 451.9 MUN

4.0000 g., Cast Bronze, 25 mm. **Rev:** "Tae" at bottom, series number at left

Date	Good	VG	F	VF	XF
ND(1857) Series 9	2.00	4.00	7.00	10.00	—

KM# 451s.9 MUN

4.0000 g., Cast Bronze, 25 mm.

Date	Good	VG	F	VF	XF
ND(1857) Series 9	—	—	—	—	40.00

KM# 451.10 MUN

4.0000 g., Cast Bronze, 25 mm. **Rev:** "Tae" at bottom, series number at left

Date	Good	VG	F	VF	XF
ND(1857) Series 10	2.00	4.00	7.00	10.00	—

KM# 451s.10 MUN

4.0000 g., Cast Bronze, 25 mm.

Date	Good	VG	F	VF	XF
ND(1857) Series 10	—	—	—	—	40.00

KM# 452.1 MUN

4.0000 g., Cast Bronze, 25 mm. **Rev:** "Kong" at bottom, series number at left

Date	Good	VG	F	VF	XF
ND(1857) Series 1	2.00	4.00	7.00	10.00	—

KM# 452s.1 MUN

4.0000 g., Cast Bronze, 25 mm.

Date	Good	VG	F	VF	XF
ND(1857) Series 1	—	—	—	—	40.00

KM# 452.2 MUN

4.0000 g., Cast Bronze, 25 mm. **Rev:** "Kong" at bottom, series number at left

Date	Good	VG	F	VF	XF
ND(1857) Series 2	2.00	4.00	7.00	10.00	—

KM# 452s.2 MUN

4.0000 g., Cast Bronze, 25 mm.

Date	Good	VG	F	VF	XF
ND(1857) Series 2	—	—	—	—	40.00

KM# 452.3 MUN

4.0000 g., Cast Bronze, 25 mm. **Rev:** "Kong" at bottom, series number at left

Date	Good	VG	F	VF	XF
ND(1857) Series 3	2.00	4.00	7.00	10.00	—

KM# 452s.3 MUN

4.0000 g., Cast Bronze, 25 mm.

Date	Good	VG	F	VF	XF
ND(1857) Series 3	—	—	—	—	40.00

KM# 452.4 MUN

4.0000 g., Cast Bronze, 25 mm. **Rev:** "Kong" at bottom, series number at left

Date	Good	VG	F	VF	XF
ND(1857) Series 4	2.00	4.00	7.00	10.00	—

KM# 452s.4 MUN

4.0000 g., Cast Bronze, 25 mm.

Date	Good	VG	F	VF	XF
ND(1857) Series 4	—	—	—	—	40.00

KM# 452.5 MUN

4.0000 g., Cast Bronze, 25 mm. **Rev:** "Kong" at bottom, series number at left

Date	Good	VG	F	VF	XF
ND(1857) Series 5	2.00	4.00	7.00	10.00	—

KM# 452s.5 MUN

4.0000 g., Cast Bronze, 25 mm.

Date	Good	VG	F	VF	XF
ND(1857) Series 5	—	—	—	—	40.00

KM# 452.6 MUN

4.0000 g., Cast Bronze, 25 mm. **Rev:** "Kong" at bottom, series number at left

Date	Good	VG	F	VF	XF
ND(1857) Series 6	2.00	4.00	7.00	10.00	—

KM# 452s.6 MUN

4.0000 g., Cast Bronze, 25 mm.

Date	Good	VG	F	VF	XF
ND(1857) Series 6	—	—	—	—	40.00

KM# 452.7 MUN

4.0000 g., Cast Bronze, 25 mm. **Rev:** "Kong" at bottom, series number at left

Date	Good	VG	F	VF	XF
ND(1857) Series 7	2.00	4.00	7.00	10.00	—

KM# 452s.7 MUN

4.0000 g., Cast Bronze, 25 mm.

Date	Good	VG	F	VF	XF
ND(1857) Series 7	—	—	—	—	40.00

KM# 452.8 MUN

4.0000 g., Cast Bronze, 25 mm. **Rev:** "Kong" at bottom, series number at left

Date	Good	VG	F	VF	XF
ND(1857) Series 8	2.00	4.00	7.00	10.00	—

KM# 452s.8 MUN

4.0000 g., Cast Bronze, 25 mm.

Date	Good	VG	F	VF	XF
ND(1857) Series 8	—	—	—	—	40.00

KM# 452.9 MUN

4.0000 g., Cast Bronze, 25 mm. **Rev:** "Kong" at bottom, series number at left

Date	Good	VG	F	VF	XF
ND(1857) Series 9	2.00	4.00	7.00	10.00	—

KM# 452s.9 MUN

4.0000 g., Cast Bronze, 25 mm.

Date	Good	VG	F	VF	XF
ND(1857) Series 9	—	—	—	—	40.00

KM# 452.10 MUN

4.0000 g., Cast Bronze, 25 mm. **Rev:** "Kong" at bottom, series number at left

Date	Good	VG	F	VF	XF
ND(1857) Series 10	2.00	4.00	7.00	10.00	—

KM# 452s.10 MUN

4.0000 g., Cast Bronze, 25 mm.

Date	Good	VG	F	VF	XF
ND(1857) Series 10	—	—	—	—	40.00

KM# 453.1 MUN

4.0000 g., Cast Bronze, 25 mm. **Rev:** "Mun" at bottom, series number at right

Date	Good	VG	F	VF	XF
ND(1857) Series 1	2.00	4.00	7.00	10.00	—

KM# 453s MUN

4.0000 g., Cast Bronze, 25 mm.

Date	Good	VG	F	VF	XF
ND(1857) Series 1	—	—	—	—	40.00

KM# 454.1 MUN

4.0000 g., Cast Bronze, 25 mm. **Rev:** "Mun" at bottom, series number at left

Date	Good	VG	F	VF	XF
ND(1857) Series 1	2.00	4.00	7.00	10.00	—

KM# 454s.1 MUN

4.0000 g., Cast Bronze, 25 mm.

Date	Good	VG	F	VF	XF
ND(1857) Series 1	—	—	—	—	40.00

KM# 454.2 MUN

4.0000 g., Cast Bronze, 25 mm. **Rev:** "Mun" at bottom, series number at left

Date	Good	VG	F	VF	XF
ND(1857) Series 2	2.00	4.00	7.00	10.00	—

KM# 454s.2 MUN

4.0000 g., Cast Bronze, 25 mm.

Date	Good	VG	F	VF	XF
ND(1857) Series 2	—	—	—	—	40.00

KM# 454.3 MUN

4.0000 g., Cast Bronze, 25 mm. **Rev:** "Mun" at bottom, series number at left

Date	Good	VG	F	VF	XF
ND(1857) Series 3	2.00	4.00	7.00	10.00	—

KM# 454s.3 MUN

4.0000 g., Cast Bronze, 25 mm.

Date	Good	VG	F	VF	XF
ND(1857) Series 3	—	—	—	—	40.00

KM# 454.4 MUN

4.0000 g., Cast Bronze, 25 mm. **Rev:** "Mun" at bottom, series number at left

Date	Good	VG	F	VF	XF
ND(1857) Series 4	2.00	4.00	7.00	10.00	—

KM# 454s.4 MUN

4.0000 g., Cast Bronze, 25 mm.

Date	Good	VG	F	VF	XF
ND(1857) Series 4	—	—	—	—	40.00

KM# 454.5 MUN

4.0000 g., Cast Bronze, 25 mm. **Rev:** "Mun" at bottom, series number at left

Date	Good	VG	F	VF	XF
ND(1857) Series 5	2.00	4.00	7.00	10.00	—

KM# 454s.5 MUN

4.0000 g., Cast Bronze, 25 mm.

Date	Good	VG	F	VF	XF
ND(1857) Series 5	—	—	—	—	40.00

KM# 454.6 MUN

4.0000 g., Cast Bronze, 25 mm. **Rev:** "Mun" at bottom, series number at left

Date	Good	VG	F	VF	XF
ND(1857) Series 6	2.00	4.00	7.00	10.00	—

KM# 454s.6 MUN

4.0000 g., Cast Bronze, 25 mm.

Date	Good	VG	F	VF	XF
ND(1857) Series 6	—	—	—	—	40.00

KM# 454.7 MUN

4.0000 g., Cast Bronze, 25 mm. **Rev:** "Mun" at bottom, series number at left

Date	Good	VG	F	VF	XF
ND(1857) Series 7	2.00	4.00	7.00	10.00	—

KM# 454s.7 MUN

4.0000 g., Cast Bronze, 25 mm.

Date	Good	VG	F	VF	XF
ND(1857) Series 7	—	—	—	—	40.00

KM# 454.8 MUN

4.0000 g., Cast Bronze, 25 mm. **Rev:** "Mun" at bottom, series number at left

Date	Good	VG	F	VF	XF
ND(1857) Series 8	2.00	4.00	7.00	10.00	—

KM# 454s.8 MUN

4.0000 g., Cast Bronze, 25 mm.

Date	Good	VG	F	VF	XF
ND(1857) Series 8	—	—	—	—	40.00

KM# 454.9 MUN

4.0000 g., Cast Bronze, 25 mm. **Rev:** "Mun" at bottom, series number at left

Date	Good	VG	F	VF	XF
ND(1857) Series 9	2.00	4.00	7.00	10.00	—

KM# 454s.9 MUN

4.0000 g., Cast Bronze, 25 mm.

Date	Good	VG	F	VF	XF
ND(1857) Series 9	—	—	—	—	40.00

KM# 454.10 MUN

4.0000 g., Cast Bronze, 25 mm. **Rev:** "Mun" at bottom, series number at left

Date	Good	VG	F	VF	XF
ND(1857) Series 10	2.00	4.00	7.00	10.00	—

KM# 454s.10 MUN

4.0000 g., Cast Bronze, 25 mm.

Date	Good	VG	F	VF	XF
ND(1857) Series 10	—	—	—	—	40.00

KM# 455.1 MUN

4.0000 g., Cast Bronze, 25 mm. **Rev:** "Ch'on" (thousand) at bottom, series number at left

Date	Good	VG	F	VF	XF
ND(1857) Series 1	2.00	4.00	7.00	10.00	—

KM# 455s.1 MUN

4.0000 g., Cast Bronze, 25 mm.

Date	Good	VG	F	VF	XF
ND(1857) Series 1	—	—	—	—	40.00

KM# 455.2 MUN

4.0000 g., Cast Bronze, 25 mm. **Rev:** "Ch'on" (thousand) at bottom, series number at left

Date	Good	VG	F	VF	XF
ND(1857) Series 2	2.00	4.00	7.00	10.00	—

KM# 455s.2 MUN

4.0000 g., Cast Bronze, 25 mm.

Date	Good	VG	F	VF	XF
ND(1857) Series 2	—	—	—	—	40.00

KM# 455.3 MUN

4.0000 g., Cast Bronze, 25 mm. **Rev:** "Ch'on" (thousand) at bottom, series number at left

Date	Good	VG	F	VF	XF
ND(1857) Series 3	2.00	4.00	7.00	10.00	—

KM# 455s.3 MUN

4.0000 g., Cast Bronze, 25 mm.

Date	Good	VG	F	VF	XF
ND(1857) Series 3	—	—	—	—	40.00

KM# 455.4 MUN

4.0000 g., Cast Bronze, 25 mm. **Rev:** "Ch'on" (thousand) at bottom, series number at left

Date	Good	VG	F	VF	XF
ND(1857) Series 4	2.00	4.00	7.00	10.00	—

KM# 455s.4 MUN

4.0000 g., Cast Bronze, 25 mm.

Date	Good	VG	F	VF	XF
ND(1857) Series 4	—	—	—	—	40.00

KM# 455.5 MUN

4.0000 g., Cast Bronze, 25 mm. **Rev:** "Ch'on" (thousand) at bottom, series number at left

Date	Good	VG	F	VF	XF
ND(1857) Series 5	2.00	4.00	7.00	10.00	—

KM# 455s.5 MUN

4.0000 g., Cast Bronze, 25 mm.

Date	Good	VG	F	VF	XF
ND(1857) Series 5	—	—	—	—	40.00

KM# 455.6 MUN

4.0000 g., Cast Bronze, 25 mm. **Rev:** "Ch'on" (thousand) at bottom, series number at left

Date	Good	VG	F	VF	XF
ND(1857) Series 6	2.00	4.00	7.00	10.00	—

KM# 455s.6 MUN

4.0000 g., Cast Bronze, 25 mm.

Date	Good	VG	F	VF	XF
ND(1857) Series 6	—	—	—	—	40.00

KM# 455.7 MUN

4.0000 g., Cast Bronze, 25 mm. **Rev:** "Ch'on" (thousand) at bottom, series number at left

Date	Good	VG	F	VF	XF
ND(1857) Series 7	2.00	4.00	7.00	10.00	—

KM# 455s.7 MUN

4.0000 g., Cast Bronze, 25 mm.

Date	Good	VG	F	VF	XF
ND(1857) Series 7	—	—	—	—	40.00

KM# 455.8 MUN

4.0000 g., Cast Bronze, 25 mm. **Rev:** "Ch'on" (thousand) at bottom, series number at left

Date	Good	VG	F	VF	XF
ND(1857) Series 8	2.00	4.00	7.00	10.00	—

KM# 455s.8 MUN

4.0000 g., Cast Bronze, 25 mm.

Date	Good	VG	F	VF	XF
ND(1857) Series 8	—	—	—	—	40.00

KM# 455.9 MUN

4.0000 g., Cast Bronze, 25 mm. **Rev:** "Ch'on" (thousand) at bottom, series number at left

Date	Good	VG	F	VF	XF
ND(1857) Series 9	2.00	4.00	7.00	10.00	—

KM# 455s.9 MUN

, 25 mm.

Date	Good	VG	F	VF	XF
ND(1857) Series 9	—	—	—	40.00	—

KM# 455.10 MUN

4.0000 g., Cast Bronze, 25 mm. **Rev:** "Ch'on" (thousand) at bottom, series number at left

Date	Good	VG	F	VF	XF
ND(1857) Series 10	2.00	4.00	7.00	10.00	—

KM# 455s.10 MUN

4.0000 g., Cast Bronze, 25 mm.

Date	Good	VG	F	VF	XF
ND(1857) Series 10	—	—	—	—	40.00

KM# 456.1 MUN

4.0000 g., Cast Bronze, 25 mm. **Rev:** "Chung" at bottom, series number at right

Date	Good	VG	F	VF	XF
ND(1857) Series 1	2.00	4.00	7.00	10.00	—

KM# 456s MUN

4.0000 g., Cast Bronze, 25 mm.

Date	Good	VG	F	VF	XF
ND(1857) Series 1	—	—	—	—	40.00

KM# 457.1 MUN

4.0000 g., Cast Bronze, 24 mm. **Rev:** "Chung" at bottom, series number at left

Date	Good	VG	F	VF	XF
ND(1857) Series 1	2.00	4.00	7.00	10.00	—

KM# 457s.1 MUN

4.0000 g., Cast Bronze, 24 mm.

Date	Good	VG	F	VF	XF
ND(1857) Series 1	—	—	—	—	40.00

KM# 457.2 MUN

4.0000 g., Cast Bronze, 24 mm. **Rev:** "Chung" at bottom, series number at left

Date	Good	VG	F	VF	XF
ND(1857) Series 2	2.00	4.00	7.00	10.00	—

KM# 457s.2 MUN

4.0000 g., Cast Bronze, 24 mm.

Date	Good	VG	F	VF	XF
ND(1857) Series 2	—	—	—	—	40.00

KM# 457.3 MUN

4.0000 g., Cast Bronze, 24 mm. **Rev:** "Chung" at bottom, series number at left

Date	Good	VG	F	VF	XF
ND(1857) Series 3	2.00	4.00	7.00	10.00	—

KM# 457s.3 MUN

4.0000 g., Cast Bronze, 24 mm.

Date	Good	VG	F	VF	XF
ND(1857) Series 3	—	—	—	—	40.00

KM# 457.4 MUN

4.0000 g., Cast Bronze, 24 mm. **Rev:** "Chung" at bottom, series number at left

Date	Good	VG	F	VF	XF
ND(1857) Series 4	2.00	4.00	7.00	10.00	—

KM# 457s.4 MUN

4.0000 g., Cast Bronze, 24 mm.

Date	Good	VG	F	VF	XF
ND(1857) Series 4	—	—	—	—	40.00

KM# 457.5 MUN

4.0000 g., Cast Bronze, 24 mm. **Rev:** "Chung" at bottom, series number at left

Date	Good	VG	F	VF	XF
ND(1857) Series 5	2.00	4.00	7.00	10.00	—

KM# 457s.5 MUN

4.0000 g., Cast Bronze, 24 mm.

Date	Good	VG	F	VF	XF
ND(1857) Series 5	—	—	—	—	40.00

KM# 457.6 MUN

4.0000 g., Cast Bronze, 24 mm. **Rev:** "Chung" at bottom, series number at left

Date	Good	VG	F	VF	XF
ND(1857) Series 6	2.00	4.00	7.00	10.00	—

KM# 457s.6 MUN
4.0000 g., Cast Bronze, 24 mm.

Date	Good	VG	F	VF	XF
ND(1857) Series 6	—	—	—	—	40.00

KM# 457.7 MUN
4.0000 g., Cast Bronze, 24 mm. **Rev:** "Chung" at bottom, series number at left

Date	Good	VG	F	VF	XF
ND(1857) Series 7	2.00	4.00	7.00	10.00	—

KM# 457s.7 MUN
4.0000 g., Cast Bronze, 24 mm.

Date	Good	VG	F	VF	XF
ND(1857) Series 7	—	—	—	—	40.00

KM# 457.8 MUN
4.0000 g., Cast Bronze, 24 mm. **Rev:** "Chung" at bottom, series number at left

Date	Good	VG	F	VF	XF
ND(1857) Series 8	2.00	4.00	7.00	10.00	—

KM# 457s.8 MUN
4.0000 g., Cast Bronze, 24 mm.

Date	Good	VG	F	VF	XF
ND(1857) Series 8	—	—	—	—	40.00

KM# 457.9 MUN
4.0000 g., Cast Bronze, 24 mm. **Rev:** "Chung" at bottom, series number at left

Date	Good	VG	F	VF	XF
ND(1857) Series 9	2.00	4.00	7.00	10.00	—

KM# 457s.9 MUN
4.0000 g., Cast Bronze, 24 mm.

Date	Good	VG	F	VF	XF
ND(1857) Series 9	—	—	—	—	40.00

KM# 457.10 MUN
4.0000 g., Cast Bronze, 24 mm. **Rev:** "Chung" at bottom, series number at left

Date	Good	VG	F	VF	XF
ND(1857) Series 10	2.00	4.00	7.00	10.00	—

KM# 457s.10 MUN
4.0000 g., Cast Bronze, 24 mm.

Date	Good	VG	F	VF	XF
ND(1857) Series 10	—	—	—	—	40.00

KM# 457.14 MUN
4.0000 g., Cast Bronze, 24 mm. **Rev:** Star at lower right

Date	Good	VG	F	VF	XF
ND(1857) Series 4	2.00	4.00	7.00	10.00	—

KM# 457.16 MUN
4.0000 g., Cast Bronze, 24 mm. **Rev:** Star at right

Date	Good	VG	F	VF	XF
ND(1857) Series 6	2.00	4.00	7.00	10.00	—

KM# 457.17 MUN
4.0000 g., Cast Bronze, 24 mm. **Rev:** Star at right

Date	Good	VG	F	VF	XF
ND(1857) Series 7	2.00	4.00	7.00	10.00	—

KM# 458.1 MUN
4.0000 g., Cast Bronze, 25 mm. **Obv:** Small characters **Rev:** "T'o" at bottom, series number at right

Date	Good	VG	F	VF	XF
ND(1857) Series 1	2.00	4.00	7.00	10.00	—

KM# 458s.1 MUN
4.0000 g., Cast Bronze, 25 mm.

Date	Good	VG	F	VF	XF
ND(1857) Series 1	—	—	—	—	40.00

KM# 458.2 MUN
4.0000 g., Cast Bronze, 25 mm. **Obv:** Small characters **Rev:** "T'o" at bottom, series number at right

Date	Good	VG	F	VF	XF
ND(1857) Series 2	2.00	4.00	7.00	10.00	—

KM# 458s.2 MUN
4.0000 g., Cast Bronze, 25 mm.

Date	Good	VG	F	VF	XF
ND(1857) Series 2	—	—	—	—	40.00

KM# 458.3 MUN
4.0000 g., Cast Bronze, 25 mm. **Obv:** Small characters **Rev:** "T'o" at bottom, series number at right

Date	Good	VG	F	VF	XF
ND(1857) Series 3	2.00	4.00	7.00	10.00	—

KM# 458s.3 MUN
4.0000 g., Cast Bronze, 25 mm.

Date	Good	VG	F	VF	XF
ND(1857) Series 3	—	—	—	—	40.00

KM# 458.4 MUN
4.0000 g., Cast Bronze, 25 mm. **Obv:** Small characters **Rev:** "T'o" at bottom, series number at right

Date	Good	VG	F	VF	XF
ND(1857) Series 4	2.00	4.00	7.00	10.00	—

KM# 458s.4 MUN
4.0000 g., Cast Bronze, 25 mm.

Date	Good	VG	F	VF	XF
ND(1857) Series 4	—	—	—	—	40.00

KM# 458.5 MUN
4.0000 g., Cast Bronze, 25 mm. **Obv:** Small characters **Rev:** "T'o" at bottom, series number at right

Date	Good	VG	F	VF	XF
ND(1857) Series 5	2.00	4.00	7.00	10.00	—

KM# 458s.5 MUN
4.0000 g., Cast Bronze, 25 mm.

Date	Good	VG	F	VF	XF
ND(1857) Series 5	—	—	—	—	40.00

KM# 458.6 MUN
4.0000 g., Cast Bronze, 25 mm. **Obv:** Small characters **Rev:** "T'o" at bottom, series number at right

Date	Good	VG	F	VF	XF
ND(1857) Series 6	2.00	4.00	7.00	10.00	—

KM# 458s.6 MUN
4.0000 g., Cast Bronze, 25 mm.

Date	Good	VG	F	VF	XF
ND(1857) Series 6	—	—	—	—	40.00

KM# 458.7 MUN
4.0000 g., Cast Bronze, 25 mm. **Obv:** Small characters **Rev:** "T'o" at bottom, series number at right

Date	Good	VG	F	VF	XF
ND(1857) Series 7	2.00	4.00	7.00	10.00	—

KM# 458s.7 MUN
4.0000 g., Cast Bronze, 25 mm.

Date	Good	VG	F	VF	XF
ND(1857) Series 7	—	—	—	—	40.00

KM# 458.8 MUN
4.0000 g., Cast Bronze, 25 mm. **Obv:** Small characters **Rev:** "T'o" at bottom, series number at right

Date	Good	VG	F	VF	XF
ND(1857) Series 8	2.00	4.00	7.00	10.00	—

KM# 458s.8 MUN
4.0000 g., Cast Bronze, 25 mm.

Date	Good	VG	F	VF	XF
ND(1857) Series 8	—	—	—	—	40.00

KM# 458.9 MUN
4.0000 g., Cast Bronze, 25 mm. **Obv:** Small characters **Rev:** "T'o" at bottom, series number at right

Date	Good	VG	F	VF	XF
ND(1857) Series 9	2.00	4.00	7.00	10.00	—

KM# 458s.9 MUN
4.0000 g., Cast Bronze, 25 mm.

Date	Good	VG	F	VF	XF
ND(1857) Series 9	—	—	—	—	40.00

KM# 458.10 MUN
4.0000 g., Cast Bronze, 25 mm. **Obv:** Small characters **Rev:** "T'o" at bottom, series number at right

Date	Good	VG	F	VF	XF
ND(1857) Series 10	2.00	4.00	7.00	10.00	—

KM# 458s.10 MUN
4.0000 g., Cast Bronze, 25 mm.

Date	Good	VG	F	VF	XF
ND(1857) Series 10	—	—	—	—	40.00

KM# 459.1 MUN
4.0000 g., Cast Bronze, 25 mm. **Obv:** Large characters

Date	Good	VG	F	VF	XF
ND(1857) Series 1	2.00	4.00	7.00	10.00	—

KM# 459s.1 MUN
4.0000 g., Cast Bronze, 25 mm.

Date	Good	VG	F	VF	XF
ND(1857) Series 1	—	—	—	—	40.00

KM# 459.2 MUN
4.0000 g., Cast Bronze, 25 mm. **Obv:** Large characters

Date	Good	VG	F	VF	XF
ND(1857) Series 2	2.00	4.00	7.00	10.00	—

KM# 459s.2 MUN
4.0000 g., Cast Bronze, 25 mm.

Date	Good	VG	F	VF	XF
ND(1857) Series 2	—	—	—	—	40.00

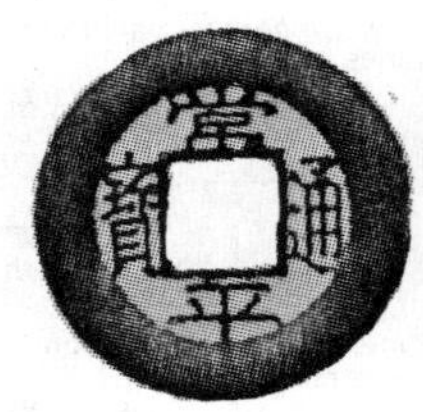

KM# 459.3 MUN
4.0000 g., Cast Bronze, 25 mm. **Obv:** Large characters

Date	Good	VG	F	VF	XF
ND(1857) Series 3	2.00	4.00	7.00	10.00	—

KM# 459s.3 MUN
4.0000 g., Cast Bronze, 25 mm.

Date	Good	VG	F	VF	XF
ND(1857) Series 3	—	—	—	—	40.00

KM# 459.4 MUN
4.0000 g., Cast Bronze, 25 mm. **Obv:** Large characters

Date	Good	VG	F	VF	XF
ND(1857) Series 4	2.00	4.00	7.00	10.00	—

KM# 459s.4 MUN
4.0000 g., Cast Bronze, 25 mm.

Date	Good	VG	F	VF	XF
ND(1857) Series 4	—	—	—	—	40.00

KM# 459.5 MUN
4.0000 g., Cast Bronze, 25 mm. **Obv:** Large characters

Date	Good	VG	F	VF	XF
ND(1857) Series 5	2.00	4.00	7.00	10.00	—

KM# 459s.5 MUN
4.0000 g., Cast Bronze, 25 mm.

Date	Good	VG	F	VF	XF
ND(1857) Series 5	—	—	—	—	40.00

KM# 459.6 MUN
4.0000 g., Cast Bronze, 25 mm. **Obv:** Large characters

Date	Good	VG	F	VF	XF
ND(1857) Series 6	2.00	4.00	7.00	10.00	—

KM# 459s.6 MUN
4.0000 g., Cast Bronze, 25 mm.

Date	Good	VG	F	VF	XF
ND(1857) Series 6	—	—	—	—	40.00

KM# 459.7 MUN
4.0000 g., Cast Bronze, 25 mm. **Obv:** Large characters

Date	Good	VG	F	VF	XF
ND(1857) Series 7	2.00	4.00	7.00	10.00	—

KM# 459s.7 MUN
4.0000 g., Cast Bronze, 25 mm.

Date	Good	VG	F	VF	XF
ND(1857) Series 7	—	—	—	—	40.00

KM# 459.8 MUN
4.0000 g., Cast Bronze, 25 mm. **Obv:** Large characters

Date	Good	VG	F	VF	XF
ND(1857) Series 8	2.00	4.00	7.00	10.00	—

KM# 459s.8 MUN
4.0000 g., Cast Bronze, 25 mm.

Date	Good	VG	F	VF	XF
ND(1857) Series 8	—	—	—	—	40.00

KM# 459.9 MUN
4.0000 g., Cast Bronze, 25 mm. **Obv:** Large characters

Date	Good	VG	F	VF	XF
ND(1857) Series 9	2.00	4.00	7.00	10.00	—

KM# 459s.9 MUN
4.0000 g., Cast Bronze, 25 mm.

Date	Good	VG	F	VF	XF
ND(1857) Series 9	—	—	—	—	40.00

KM# 459.10 MUN
4.0000 g., Cast Bronze, 25 mm. **Obv:** Large characters

Date	Good	VG	F	VF	XF
ND(1857) Series 10	2.00	4.00	7.00	10.00	—

KM# 459s.10 MUN
4.0000 g., Cast Bronze, 25 mm.

Date	Good	VG	F	VF	XF
ND(1857) Series 10	—	—	—	—	40.00

KM# 460.1 MUN
4.0000 g., Cast Bronze, 25 mm. **Obv:** Small characters **Rev:** "T'o" at bottom, series number at left

Date	Good	VG	F	VF	XF
ND(1857) Series 1	2.00	4.00	7.00	10.00	—

KM# 460s.1 MUN
4.0000 g., Cast Bronze, 25 mm.

Date	Good	VG	F	VF	XF
ND(1857) Series 1	—	—	—	—	40.00

KM# 460.2 MUN
4.0000 g., Cast Bronze, 25 mm. **Obv:** Small characters **Rev:** "T'o" at bottom, series number at left

Date	Good	VG	F	VF	XF
ND(1857) Series 2	2.00	4.00	7.00	10.00	—

KM# 460s.2 MUN
4.0000 g., Cast Bronze, 25 mm.

Date	Good	VG	F	VF	XF
ND(1857) Series 2	—	—	—	—	40.00

KM# 460.3 MUN
4.0000 g., Cast Bronze, 25 mm. **Obv:** Small characters **Rev:** "T'o" at bottom, series number at left

Date	Good	VG	F	VF	XF
ND(1857) Series 3	2.00	4.00	7.00	10.00	—

KM# 460s.3 MUN
4.0000 g., Cast Bronze, 25 mm.

Date	Good	VG	F	VF	XF
ND(1857) Series 3	—	—	—	—	40.00

KM# 460.4 MUN
4.0000 g., Cast Bronze, 25 mm. **Obv:** Small characters **Rev:** "T'o" at bottom, series number at left

Date	Good	VG	F	VF	XF
ND(1857) Series 4	2.00	4.00	7.00	10.00	—

KM# 460s.4 MUN
4.0000 g., Cast Bronze, 25 mm.

Date	Good	VG	F	VF	XF
ND(1857) Series 4	—	—	—	—	40.00

KM# 460.5 MUN
4.0000 g., Cast Bronze, 25 mm. **Obv:** Small characters **Rev:** "T'o" at bottom, series number at left

Date	Good	VG	F	VF	XF
ND(1857) Series 5	2.00	4.00	7.00	10.00	—

KM# 460s.5 MUN
4.0000 g., Cast Bronze, 25 mm.

Date	Good	VG	F	VF	XF
ND(1857) Series 5	—	—	—	—	40.00

KM# 460.6 MUN
4.0000 g., Cast Bronze, 25 mm. **Obv:** Small characters **Rev:** "T'o" at bottom, series number at left

Date	Good	VG	F	VF	XF
ND(1857) Series 6	2.00	4.00	7.00	10.00	—

KM# 460s.6 MUN
4.0000 g., Cast Bronze, 25 mm.

Date	Good	VG	F	VF	XF
ND(1857) Series 6	—	—	—	—	40.00

KM# 460.7 MUN
4.0000 g., Cast Bronze, 25 mm. **Obv:** Small characters **Rev:** "T'o" at bottom, series number at left

Date	Good	VG	F	VF	XF
ND(1857) Series 7	2.00	4.00	7.00	10.00	—

KM# 460s.7 MUN
4.0000 g., Cast Bronze, 25 mm.

Date	Good	VG	F	VF	XF
ND(1857) Series 7	—	—	—	—	40.00

KM# 460.8 MUN
4.0000 g., Cast Bronze, 25 mm. **Obv:** Small characters **Rev:** "T'o" at bottom, series number at left

Date	Good	VG	F	VF	XF
ND(1857) Series 8	2.00	4.00	7.00	10.00	—

KM# 460s.8 MUN
4.0000 g., Cast Bronze, 25 mm.

Date	Good	VG	F	VF	XF
ND(1857) Series 8	—	—	—	—	40.00

KM# 460.9 MUN

4.0000 g., Cast Bronze, 25 mm. **Obv:** Small characters **Rev:** "T'o" at bottom, series number at left

Date	Good	VG	F	VF	XF
ND(1857) Series 9	2.00	4.00	7.00	10.00	—

KM# 460s.9 MUN

4.0000 g., Cast Bronze, 25 mm.

Date	Good	VG	F	VF	XF
ND(1857) Series 9	—	—	—	—	40.00

KM# 460.10 MUN

4.0000 g., Cast Bronze, 25 mm. **Obv:** Small characters **Rev:** "T'o" at bottom, series number at left

Date	Good	VG	F	VF	XF
ND(1857) Series 10	2.00	4.00	7.00	10.00	—

KM# 460s.10 MUN

4.0000 g., Cast Bronze, 25 mm.

Date	Good	VG	F	VF	XF
ND(1857) Series 10	—	—	—	—	40.00

KM# 461.1 MUN

4.0000 g., Cast Bronze, 25 mm. **Obv:** Large characters

Date	Good	VG	F	VF	XF
ND(1857) Series 1	2.00	4.00	7.00	10.00	—

KM# 461s.1 MUN

4.0000 g., Cast Bronze, 25 mm.

Date	Good	VG	F	VF	XF
ND(1857) Series 1	—	—	—	—	40.00

KM# 461.2 MUN

4.0000 g., Cast Bronze, 25 mm. **Obv:** Large characters

Date	Good	VG	F	VF	XF
ND(1857) Series 2	2.00	4.00	7.00	10.00	—

KM# 461s.2 MUN

4.0000 g., Cast Bronze, 25 mm.

Date	Good	VG	F	VF	XF
ND(1857) Series 2	—	—	—	—	40.00

KM# 461.3 MUN

4.0000 g., Cast Bronze, 25 mm. **Obv:** Large characters

Date	Good	VG	F	VF	XF
ND(1857) Series 3	2.00	4.00	7.00	10.00	—

KM# 461s.3 MUN

4.0000 g., Cast Bronze, 25 mm.

Date	Good	VG	F	VF	XF
ND(1857) Series 3	—	—	—	—	40.00

KM# 461.4 MUN

4.0000 g., Cast Bronze, 25 mm. **Obv:** Large characters

Date	Good	VG	F	VF	XF
ND(1857) Series 4	2.00	4.00	7.00	10.00	—

KM# 461s.4 MUN

4.0000 g., Cast Bronze, 25 mm.

Date	Good	VG	F	VF	XF
ND(1857) Series 4	—	—	—	—	40.00

KM# 461.5 MUN

4.0000 g., Cast Bronze, 25 mm. **Obv:** Large characters

Date	Good	VG	F	VF	XF
ND(1857) Series 5	2.00	4.00	7.00	10.00	—

KM# 461s.5 MUN

4.0000 g., Cast Bronze, 25 mm.

Date	Good	VG	F	VF	XF
ND(1857) Series 5	—	—	—	—	40.00

KM# 461.6 MUN

4.0000 g., Cast Bronze, 25 mm. **Obv:** Large characters

Date	Good	VG	F	VF	XF
ND(1857) Series 6	2.00	4.00	7.00	10.00	—

KM# 461s.6 MUN

4.0000 g., Cast Bronze, 25 mm.

Date	Good	VG	F	VF	XF
ND(1857) Series 6	—	—	—	—	40.00

KM# 461.7 MUN

4.0000 g., Cast Bronze, 25 mm. **Obv:** Large characters

Date	Good	VG	F	VF	XF
ND(1857) Series 7	2.00	4.00	7.00	10.00	—

KM# 461s.7 MUN

4.0000 g., Cast Bronze, 25 mm.

Date	Good	VG	F	VF	XF
ND(1857) Series 7	—	—	—	—	40.00

KM# 461.8 MUN

4.0000 g., Cast Bronze, 25 mm. **Obv:** Large characters

Date	Good	VG	F	VF	XF
ND(1857) Series 8	2.00	4.00	7.00	10.00	—

KM# 461s.8 MUN

4.0000 g., Cast Bronze, 25 mm.

Date	Good	VG	F	VF	XF
ND(1857) Series 8	—	—	—	—	40.00

KM# 461.9 MUN

4.0000 g., Cast Bronze, 25 mm. **Obv:** Large characters

Date	Good	VG	F	VF	XF
ND(1857) Series 9	2.00	4.00	7.00	10.00	—

KM# 461s.9 MUN

4.0000 g., Cast Bronze, 25 mm.

Date	Good	VG	F	VF	XF
ND(1857) Series 9	—	—	—	—	40.00

KM# 461.10 MUN

4.0000 g., Cast Bronze, 25 mm. **Obv:** Large characters

Date	Good	VG	F	VF	XF
ND(1857) Series 10	2.00	4.00	7.00	10.00	—

KM# 461s.10 MUN

4.0000 g., Cast Bronze, 25 mm.

Date	Good	VG	F	VF	XF
ND(1857) Series 10	—	—	—	—	40.00

KM# 462.1 MUN

4.0000 g., Cast Bronze, 25 mm. **Rev:** "T'o" at bottom, series number at right, crescent at left

Date	Good	VG	F	VF	XF
ND(1857) Series 1	2.00	4.00	7.00	10.00	—

KM# 462s.1 MUN

4.0000 g., Cast Bronze, 25 mm.

Date	Good	VG	F	VF	XF
ND(1857) Series 1	—	—	—	—	40.00

KM# 462.2 MUN

4.0000 g., Cast Bronze, 25 mm. **Rev:** "T'o" at bottom, series number at right, crescent at left

Date	Good	VG	F	VF	XF
ND(1857) Series 2	2.00	4.00	7.00	10.00	—

KM# 462s.2 MUN

4.0000 g., Cast Bronze, 25 mm.

Date	Good	VG	F	VF	XF
ND(1857) Series 2	—	—	—	—	40.00

KM# 462.3 MUN

4.0000 g., Cast Bronze, 25 mm. **Rev:** "T'o" at bottom, series number at right, crescent at left

Date	Good	VG	F	VF	XF
ND(1857) Series 3	2.00	4.00	7.00	10.00	—

KM# 462s.3 MUN

4.0000 g., Cast Bronze, 25 mm.

Date	Good	VG	F	VF	XF
ND(1857) Series 3	—	—	—	—	40.00

KM# 462.4 MUN

4.0000 g., Cast Bronze, 25 mm. **Rev:** "T'o" at bottom, series number at right, crescent at left

Date	Good	VG	F	VF	XF
ND(1857) Series 4	2.00	4.00	7.00	10.00	—

KM# 462s.4 MUN

4.0000 g., Cast Bronze, 25 mm.

Date	Good	VG	F	VF	XF
ND(1857) Series 4	—	—	—	—	40.00

KM# 462.5 MUN

4.0000 g., Cast Bronze, 25 mm. **Rev:** "T'o" at bottom, series number at right, crescent at left

Date	Good	VG	F	VF	XF
ND(1857) Series 5	2.00	4.00	7.00	10.00	—

KM# 462s.5 MUN

4.0000 g., Cast Bronze, 25 mm.

Date	Good	VG	F	VF	XF
ND(1857) Series 5	—	—	—	—	40.00

KM# 463.1 MUN

4.0000 g., Cast Bronze, 25 mm. **Obv:** Small characters **Rev:** "T'o" at bottom, crescent at right, series number at left

Date	Good	VG	F	VF	XF
ND(1857) Series 1	2.00	4.00	7.00	10.00	—

KM# 463s.1 MUN

4.0000 g., Cast Bronze, 25 mm.

Date	Good	VG	F	VF	XF
ND(1857) Series 1	—	—	—	—	40.00

KM# 463.2 MUN

4.0000 g., Cast Bronze, 25 mm. **Obv:** Small characters **Rev:** "T'o" at bottom, crescent at right, series number at left

Date	Good	VG	F	VF	XF
ND(1857) Series 2	2.00	4.00	7.00	10.00	—

KM# 463s.2 MUN

4.0000 g., Cast Bronze, 25 mm.

Date	Good	VG	F	VF	XF
ND(1857) Series 2	—	—	—	—	40.00

KM# 463.3 MUN

4.0000 g., Cast Bronze, 25 mm. **Obv:** Small characters **Rev:** "T'o" at bottom, crescent at right, series number at left

Date	Good	VG	F	VF	XF
ND(1857) Series 3	2.00	4.00	7.00	10.00	—

KM# 463s.3 MUN

4.0000 g., Cast Bronze, 25 mm.

Date	Good	VG	F	VF	XF
ND(1857) Series 3	—	—	—	—	40.00

KM# 463.4 MUN

4.0000 g., Cast Bronze, 25 mm. **Obv:** Small characters **Rev:** "T'o" at bottom, crescent at right, series number at left

Date	Good	VG	F	VF	XF
ND(1857) Series 4	2.00	4.00	7.00	10.00	—

KM# 463s.4 MUN

4.0000 g., Cast Bronze, 25 mm.

Date	Good	VG	F	VF	XF
ND(1857) Series 4	—	—	—	—	40.00

KM# 463.5 MUN

4.0000 g., Cast Bronze, 25 mm. **Obv:** Small characters **Rev:** "T'o" at bottom, crescent at right, series number at left

Date	Good	VG	F	VF	XF
ND(1857) Series 5	2.00	4.00	7.00	10.00	—

KM# 463s.5 MUN

4.0000 g., Cast Bronze, 25 mm.

Date	Good	VG	F	VF	XF
ND(1857) Series 5	—	—	—	—	40.00

KM# 464.1 MUN

4.0000 g., Cast Bronze, 24 mm. **Obv:** Large characters

Date	Good	VG	F	VF	XF
ND(1857) Series 1	2.00	4.00	7.00	10.00	—

KM# 464s.1 MUN

4.0000 g., Cast Bronze, 24 mm.

Date	Good	VG	F	VF	XF
ND(1857) Series 1	—	—	—	—	40.00

KM# 464.2 MUN

4.0000 g., Cast Bronze, 24 mm. **Obv:** Large characters

Date	Good	VG	F	VF	XF
ND(1857) Series 2	2.00	4.00	7.00	10.00	—

KM# 464s.2 MUN

4.0000 g., Cast Bronze, 24 mm.

Date	Good	VG	F	VF	XF
ND(1857) Series 2	—	—	—	—	40.00

KM# 464.3 MUN

4.0000 g., Cast Bronze, 24 mm. **Obv:** Large characters

Date	Good	VG	F	VF	XF
ND(1857) Series 3	2.00	4.00	7.00	10.00	—

KM# 464s.3 MUN

4.0000 g., Cast Bronze, 24 mm.

Date	Good	VG	F	VF	XF
ND(1857) Series 3	—	—	—	—	40.00

KM# 464.4 MUN

4.0000 g., Cast Bronze, 24 mm. **Obv:** Large characters

Date	Good	VG	F	VF	XF
ND(1857) Series 4	2.00	4.00	7.00	10.00	—

KM# 464s.4 MUN

4.0000 g., Cast Bronze, 24 mm.

Date	Good	VG	F	VF	XF
ND(1857) Series 4	—	—	—	—	40.00

KM# 464.5 MUN

4.0000 g., Cast Bronze, 24 mm. **Obv:** Large characters

Date	Good	VG	F	VF	XF
ND(1857) Series 5	2.00	4.00	7.00	10.00	—

KM# 464s.5 MUN

4.0000 g., Cast Bronze, 24 mm.

Date	Good	VG	F	VF	XF
ND(1857) Series 5	—	—	—	—	40.00

KM# 465.1 MUN

4.0000 g., Cast Bronze, 24 mm. **Rev:** "Won" (first) at bottom, series number at right

Date	Good	VG	F	VF	XF
ND(1857) Series 1	2.00	4.00	7.00	10.00	—

KM# 465s.1 MUN

4.0000 g., Cast Bronze, 24 mm.

Date	Good	VG	F	VF	XF
ND(1857) Series 1	—	—	—	—	40.00

KM# 465.2 MUN

4.0000 g., Cast Bronze, 24 mm. **Rev:** "Won" (first) at bottom, series number at right

Date	Good	VG	F	VF	XF
ND(1857) Series 2	2.00	4.00	7.00	10.00	—

KM# 465s.2 MUN

4.0000 g., Cast Bronze, 24 mm.

Date	Good	VG	F	VF	XF
ND(1857) Series 2	—	—	—	—	40.00

KM# 465.3 MUN

4.0000 g., Cast Bronze, 24 mm. **Rev:** "Won" (first) at bottom, series number at right

Date	Good	VG	F	VF	XF
ND(1857) Series 3	2.00	4.00	7.00	10.00	—

KM# 465s.3 MUN

4.0000 g., Cast Bronze, 24 mm.

Date	Good	VG	F	VF	XF
ND(1857) Series 3	—	—	—	—	40.00

KM# 465.4 MUN

4.0000 g., Cast Bronze, 24 mm. **Rev:** "Won" (first) at bottom, series number at right

Date	Good	VG	F	VF	XF
ND(1857) Series 4	2.00	4.00	7.00	10.00	—

KM# 465s.4 MUN

4.0000 g., Cast Bronze, 24 mm.

Date	Good	VG	F	VF	XF
ND(1857) Series 4	—	—	—	—	40.00

KM# 465.5 MUN

4.0000 g., Cast Bronze, 24 mm. **Rev:** "Won" (first) at bottom, series number at right

Date	Good	VG	F	VF	XF
ND(1857) Series 5	2.00	4.00	7.00	10.00	—

KM# 465s.5 MUN

4.0000 g., Cast Bronze, 24 mm.

Date	Good	VG	F	VF	XF
ND(1857) Series 5	—	—	—	—	40.00

KM# 465.6 MUN

4.0000 g., Cast Bronze, 24 mm. **Rev:** "Won" (first) at bottom, series number at right

Date	Good	VG	F	VF	XF
ND(1857) Series 6	2.00	4.00	7.00	10.00	—

KM# 465s.6 MUN

4.0000 g., Cast Bronze, 24 mm.

Date	Good	VG	F	VF	XF
ND(1857) Series 6	—	—	—	—	40.00

KM# 465.7 MUN

4.0000 g., Cast Bronze, 24 mm. **Rev:** "Won" (first) at bottom, series number at right

Date	Good	VG	F	VF	XF
ND(1857) Series 7	2.00	4.00	7.00	10.00	—

KM# 465s.7 MUN

4.0000 g., Cast Bronze, 24 mm.

Date	Good	VG	F	VF	XF
ND(1857) Series 7	—	—	—	—	40.00

KM# 465.8 MUN

4.0000 g., Cast Bronze, 24 mm. **Rev:** "Won" (first) at bottom, series number at right

Date	Good	VG	F	VF	XF
ND(1857) Series 8	2.00	4.00	7.00	10.00	—

KM# 465s.8 MUN
4.0000 g., Cast Bronze, 24 mm.

Date	Good	VG	F	VF	XF
ND(1857) Series 8	—	—	—	—	40.00

KM# 465.9 MUN
4.0000 g., Cast Bronze, 24 mm. **Rev:** "Won" (first) at bottom, series number at right

Date	Good	VG	F	VF	XF
ND(1857) Series 9	2.00	4.00	7.00	10.00	—

KM# 465s.9 MUN
4.0000 g., Cast Bronze, 24 mm.

Date	Good	VG	F	VF	XF
ND(1857) Series 9	—	—	—	—	40.00

KM# 465.10 MUN
4.0000 g., Cast Bronze, 24 mm. **Rev:** "Won" (first) at bottom, series number at right

Date	Good	VG	F	VF	XF
ND(1857) Series 10	2.00	4.00	7.00	10.00	—

KM# 465s.10 MUN
4.0000 g., Cast Bronze, 24 mm.

Date	Good	VG	F	VF	XF
ND(1857) Series 10	—	—	—	—	40.00

KM# 466.1 MUN
4.0000 g., Cast Bronze, 25 mm. **Rev:** "Won" at bottom, series number at left

Date	Good	VG	F	VF	XF
ND(1857) Series 1	2.00	4.00	7.00	10.00	—

KM# 466s.1 MUN
4.0000 g., Cast Bronze, 25 mm.

Date	Good	VG	F	VF	XF
ND(1857) Series 1	—	—	—	—	40.00

KM# 466.2 MUN
4.0000 g., Cast Bronze, 25 mm. **Rev:** "Won" at bottom, series number at left

Date	Good	VG	F	VF	XF
ND(1857) Series 2	2.00	4.00	7.00	10.00	—

KM# 466s.2 MUN
4.0000 g., Cast Bronze, 25 mm.

Date	Good	VG	F	VF	XF
ND(1857) Series 2	—	—	—	—	40.00

KM# 466.3 MUN
4.0000 g., Cast Bronze, 25 mm. **Rev:** "Won" at bottom, series number at left

Date	Good	VG	F	VF	XF
ND(1857) Series 3	2.00	4.00	7.00	10.00	—

KM# 466s.3 MUN
4.0000 g., Cast Bronze, 25 mm. **Note:** Seed type. Struck at Hul Ly On Do Gam.

Date	Good	VG	F	VF	XF
ND(1857) Series 3	—	—	—	—	40.00

KM# 466.4 MUN
4.0000 g., Cast Bronze, 25 mm. **Rev:** "Won" at bottom, series number at left

Date	Good	VG	F	VF	XF
ND(1857) Series 4	2.00	4.00	7.00	10.00	—

KM# 466s.4 MUN
4.0000 g., Cast Bronze, 25 mm.

Date	Good	VG	F	VF	XF
ND(1857) Series 4	—	—	—	—	40.00

KM# 466.5 MUN
4.0000 g., Cast Bronze, 25 mm. **Rev:** "Won" at bottom, series number at left

Date	Good	VG	F	VF	XF
ND(1857) Series 5	2.00	4.00	7.00	10.00	—

KM# 466s.5 MUN
4.0000 g., Cast Bronze, 25 mm.

Date	Good	VG	F	VF	XF
ND(1857) Series 5	—	—	—	—	40.00

KM# 466.6 MUN
4.0000 g., Cast Bronze, 25 mm. **Rev:** "Won" at bottom, series number at left

Date	Good	VG	F	VF	XF
ND(1857) Series 6	2.00	4.00	7.00	10.00	—

KM# 466s.6 MUN
4.0000 g., Cast Bronze, 25 mm.

Date	Good	VG	F	VF	XF
ND(1857) Series 6	—	—	—	—	40.00

KM# 466.7 MUN
4.0000 g., Cast Bronze, 25 mm. **Rev:** "Won" at bottom, series number at left

Date	Good	VG	F	VF	XF
ND(1857) Series 7	2.00	4.00	7.00	10.00	—

KM# 466s.7 MUN
4.0000 g., Cast Bronze, 25 mm.

Date	Good	VG	F	VF	XF
ND(1857) Series 7	—	—	—	—	40.00

KM# 466.8 MUN
4.0000 g., Cast Bronze, 25 mm. **Rev:** "Won" at bottom, series number at left

Date	Good	VG	F	VF	XF
ND(1857) Series 8	2.00	4.00	7.00	10.00	—

KM# 466s.8 MUN
4.0000 g., Cast Bronze, 25 mm.

Date	Good	VG	F	VF	XF
ND(1857) Series 8	—	—	—	—	40.00

KM# 466.9 MUN
4.0000 g., Cast Bronze, 25 mm. **Rev:** "Won" at bottom, series number at left

Date	Good	VG	F	VF	XF
ND(1857) Series 9	2.00	4.00	7.00	10.00	—

KM# 466s.9 MUN
4.0000 g., Cast Bronze, 25 mm.

Date	Good	VG	F	VF	XF
ND(1857) Series 9	—	—	—	—	40.00

KM# 466.10 MUN
4.0000 g., Cast Bronze, 25 mm. **Rev:** "Won" at bottom, series number at left

Date	Good	VG	F	VF	XF
ND(1857) Series 10	2.00	4.00	7.00	10.00	—

KM# 466s.10 MUN
4.0000 g., Cast Bronze, 25 mm.

Date	Good	VG	F	VF	XF
ND(1857) Series 10	—	—	—	—	40.00

KM# 467.1 MUN
4.0000 g., Cast Bronze, 25 mm. **Rev:** "Won" at bottom, series number at right, crescent at left

Date	Good	VG	F	VF	XF
ND(1857) Series 1	2.00	4.00	7.00	10.00	—

KM# 467s.1 MUN
4.0000 g., Cast Bronze, 25 mm.

Date	Good	VG	F	VF	XF
ND(1857) Series 1	—	—	—	—	40.00

KM# 467.2 MUN
4.0000 g., Cast Bronze, 25 mm. **Rev:** "Won" at bottom, series number at right, crescent at left

Date	Good	VG	F	VF	XF
ND(1857) Series 2	2.00	4.00	7.00	10.00	—

KM# 467s.2 MUN
4.0000 g., Cast Bronze, 25 mm.

Date	Good	VG	F	VF	XF
ND(1857) Series 2	—	—	—	—	40.00

KM# 467.3 MUN
4.0000 g., Cast Bronze, 25 mm. **Rev:** "Won" at bottom, series number at right, crescent at left

Date	Good	VG	F	VF	XF
ND(1857) Series 3	2.00	4.00	7.00	10.00	—

KM# 467s.3 MUN
4.0000 g., Cast Bronze, 25 mm.

Date	Good	VG	F	VF	XF
ND(1857) Series 3	—	—	—	—	40.00

KM# 467.4 MUN
4.0000 g., Cast Bronze, 25 mm. **Rev:** "Won" at bottom, series number at right, crescent at left **Note:** Struck at Hul Ly On Do Gam.

Date	Good	VG	F	VF	XF
ND(1857) Series 4	2.00	4.00	7.00	10.00	—

KM# 467s.4 MUN
4.0000 g., Cast Bronze, 25 mm.

Date	Good	VG	F	VF	XF
ND(1857) Series 4	—	—	—	—	40.00

KM# 467.5 MUN
4.0000 g., Cast Bronze, 25 mm. **Rev:** "Won" at bottom, series number at right, crescent at left

Date	Good	VG	F	VF	XF
ND(1857) Series 5	2.00	4.00	7.00	10.00	—

KM# 467s.5 MUN
4.0000 g., Cast Bronze, 25 mm.

Date	Good	VG	F	VF	XF
ND(1857) Series 5	—	—	—	—	40.00

KM# 468.1 MUN
4.0000 g., Cast Bronze, 26 mm. **Rev:** "Saeng" at bottom, series number at right

Date	Good	VG	F	VF	XF
ND(1857) Series 1	2.00	4.00	7.00	10.00	—

KM# 468s.1 MUN
4.0000 g., Cast Bronze, 26 mm.

Date	Good	VG	F	VF	XF
ND(1857) Series 1	—	—	—	—	40.00

KM# 468.2 MUN
4.0000 g., Cast Bronze, 26 mm. **Rev:** "Saeng" at bottom, series number at right

Date	Good	VG	F	VF	XF
ND(1857) Series 2	2.00	4.00	7.00	10.00	—

KM# 468s.2 MUN
4.0000 g., Cast Bronze, 26 mm.

Date	Good	VG	F	VF	XF
ND(1857) Series 2	—	—	—	—	40.00

KM# 468.3 MUN
4.0000 g., Cast Bronze, 26 mm. **Rev:** "Saeng" at bottom, series number at right

Date	Good	VG	F	VF	XF
ND(1857) Series 3	2.00	4.00	7.00	10.00	—

KM# 468s.3 MUN
4.0000 g., Cast Bronze, 26 mm.

Date	Good	VG	F	VF	XF
ND(1857) Series 3	—	—	—	—	40.00

KM# 468.4 MUN
4.0000 g., Cast Bronze, 26 mm. **Rev:** "Saeng" at bottom, series number at right

Date	Good	VG	F	VF	XF
ND(1857) Series 4	2.00	4.00	7.00	10.00	—

KM# 468s.4 MUN
4.0000 g., Cast Bronze, 26 mm.

Date	Good	VG	F	VF	XF
ND(1857) Series 4	—	—	—	—	40.00

KM# 468.5 MUN
4.0000 g., Cast Bronze, 26 mm. **Rev:** "Saeng" at bottom, series number at right

Date	Good	VG	F	VF	XF
ND(1857) Series 5	2.00	4.00	7.00	10.00	—

KM# 468s.5 MUN
4.0000 g., Cast Bronze, 26 mm.

Date	Good	VG	F	VF	XF
ND(1857) Series 5	—	—	—	—	40.00

KM# 468.6 MUN
4.0000 g., Cast Bronze, 26 mm. **Rev:** "Saeng" at bottom, series number at right

Date	Good	VG	F	VF	XF
ND(1857) Series 6	2.00	4.00	7.00	10.00	—

KM# 468s.6 MUN
4.0000 g., Cast Bronze, 26 mm.

Date	Good	VG	F	VF	XF
ND(1857) Series 6	—	—	—	—	40.00

KM# 468.7 MUN
4.0000 g., Cast Bronze, 26 mm. **Rev:** "Saeng" at bottom, series number at right

Date	Good	VG	F	VF	XF
ND(1857) Series 7	2.00	4.00	7.00	10.00	—

KM# 468s.7 MUN
4.0000 g., Cast Bronze, 26 mm.

Date	Good	VG	F	VF	XF
ND(1857) Series 7	—	—	—	—	40.00

KM# 468.8 MUN
4.0000 g., Cast Bronze, 26 mm. **Rev:** "Saeng" at bottom, series number at right

Date	Good	VG	F	VF	XF
ND(1857) Series 8	2.00	4.00	7.00	10.00	—

KM# 468s.8 MUN
4.0000 g., Cast Bronze, 26 mm.

Date	Good	VG	F	VF	XF
ND(1857) Series 8	—	—	—	—	40.00

KM# 468.9 MUN
4.0000 g., Cast Bronze, 26 mm. **Rev:** "Saeng" at bottom, series number at right

Date	Good	VG	F	VF	XF
ND(1857) Series 9	2.00	4.00	7.00	10.00	—

KM# 468s.9 MUN
4.0000 g., Cast Bronze, 26 mm.

Date	Good	VG	F	VF	XF
ND(1857) Series 9	—	—	—	—	40.00

KM# 468.10 MUN
4.0000 g., Cast Bronze, 26 mm. **Rev:** "Saeng" at bottom, series number at right

Date	Good	VG	F	VF	XF
ND(1857) Series 10	2.00	4.00	7.00	10.00	—

KM# 468s.10 MUN
4.0000 g., Cast Bronze, 26 mm.

Date	Good	VG	F	VF	XF
ND(1857) Series 10	—	—	—	—	40.00

KM# 469.1 MUN
4.0000 g., Cast Bronze, 25 mm. **Rev:** "Saeng" at bottom, series number at left

Date	Good	VG	F	VF	XF
ND(1857) Series 1	2.00	4.00	7.00	10.00	—

KM# 469s.1 MUN
4.0000 g., Cast Bronze, 25 mm.

Date	Good	VG	F	VF	XF
ND(1857) Series 1	—	—	—	—	40.00

KM# 469.2 MUN
4.0000 g., Cast Bronze, 25 mm. **Rev:** "Saeng" at bottom, series number at left

Date	Good	VG	F	VF	XF
ND(1857) Series 2	2.00	4.00	7.00	10.00	—

KM# 469s.2 MUN
4.0000 g., Cast Bronze, 25 mm.

Date	Good	VG	F	VF	XF
ND(1857) Series 2	—	—	—	—	40.00

KM# 469.3 MUN
4.0000 g., Cast Bronze, 25 mm. **Rev:** "Saeng" at bottom, series number at left

Date	Good	VG	F	VF	XF
ND(1857) Series 3	2.00	4.00	7.00	10.00	—

KM# 469s.3 MUN
4.0000 g., Cast Bronze, 25 mm.

Date	Good	VG	F	VF	XF
ND(1857) Series 3	—	—	—	—	40.00

KM# 469.4 MUN
4.0000 g., Cast Bronze, 25 mm. **Rev:** "Saeng" at bottom, series number at left

Date	Good	VG	F	VF	XF
ND(1857) Series 4	2.00	4.00	7.00	10.00	—

KM# 469s.4 MUN
4.0000 g., Cast Bronze, 25 mm.

Date	Good	VG	F	VF	XF
ND(1857) Series 4	—	—	—	—	40.00

KM# 469.5 MUN
4.0000 g., Cast Bronze, 25 mm. **Rev:** "Saeng" at bottom, series number at left

Date	Good	VG	F	VF	XF
ND(1857) Series 5	2.00	4.00	7.00	10.00	—

KM# 469s.5 MUN

4.0000 g., Cast Bronze, 25 mm.

Date	Good	VG	F	VF	XF
ND(1857) Series 5	—	—	—	—	40.00

KM# 469.6 MUN

4.0000 g., Cast Bronze, 25 mm. **Rev:** "Saeng" at bottom, series number at left

Date	Good	VG	F	VF	XF
ND(1857) Series 6	2.00	4.00	7.00	10.00	—

KM# 469s.6 MUN

4.0000 g., Cast Bronze, 25 mm.

Date	Good	VG	F	VF	XF
ND(1857) Series 6	—	—	—	—	40.00

KM# 469.7 MUN

4.0000 g., Cast Bronze, 25 mm. **Rev:** "Saeng" at bottom, series number at left

Date	Good	VG	F	VF	XF
ND(1857) Series 7	2.00	4.00	7.00	10.00	—

KM# 469s.7 MUN

4.0000 g., Cast Bronze, 25 mm.

Date	Good	VG	F	VF	XF
ND(1857) Series 7	—	—	—	—	40.00

KM# 469.8 MUN

, 25 mm. **Rev:** "Saeng" at bottom, series number at left

Date	Good	VG	F	VF	XF
ND(1857) Series 8	2.00	4.00	7.00	10.00	—

KM# 469s.8 MUN

4.0000 g., Cast Bronze, 25 mm.

Date	Good	VG	F	VF	XF
ND(1857) Series 8	—	—	—	—	40.00

KM# 469.9 MUN

4.0000 g., Cast Bronze, 25 mm. **Rev:** "Saeng" at bottom, series number at left

Date	Good	VG	F	VF	XF
ND(1857) Series 9	2.00	4.00	7.00	10.00	—

KM# 469s.9 MUN

4.0000 g., Cast Bronze, 25 mm.

Date	Good	VG	F	VF	XF
ND(1857) Series 9	—	—	—	—	40.00

KM# 469.10 MUN

4.0000 g., Cast Bronze, 25 mm. **Rev:** "Saeng" at bottom, series number at left

Date	Good	VG	F	VF	XF
ND(1857) Series 10	2.00	4.00	7.00	10.00	—

KM# 469s.10 MUN

4.0000 g., Cast Bronze, 25 mm.

Date	Good	VG	F	VF	XF
ND(1857) Series 10	—	—	—	—	40.00

KM# 470.1 MUN

4.0000 g., Cast Bronze, 24 mm. **Rev:** "Saeng" at bottom, crescent at right, series number at left

Date	Good	VG	F	VF	XF
ND(1857) Series 1	2.00	4.00	7.00	10.00	—

KM# 470s.1 MUN

4.0000 g., Cast Bronze, 24 mm.

Date	Good	VG	F	VF	XF
ND(1857) Series 1	—	—	—	—	40.00

KM# 470.2 MUN

4.0000 g., Cast Bronze, 24 mm. **Rev:** "Saeng" at bottom, crescent at right, series number at left

Date	Good	VG	F	VF	XF
ND(1857) Series 2	2.00	4.00	7.00	10.00	—

KM# 470s.2 MUN

4.0000 g., Cast Bronze, 24 mm.

Date	Good	VG	F	VF	XF
ND(1857) Series 2	—	—	—	—	40.00

KM# 470.3 MUN

4.0000 g., Cast Bronze, 24 mm. **Rev:** "Saeng" at bottom, crescent at right, series number at left

Date	Good	VG	F	VF	XF
ND(1857) Series 3	2.00	4.00	7.00	10.00	—

KM# 470s.3 MUN

4.0000 g., Cast Bronze, 24 mm.

Date	Good	VG	F	VF	XF
ND(1857) Series 3	—	—	—	—	40.00

KM# 470.4 MUN

4.0000 g., Cast Bronze, 24 mm. **Rev:** "Saeng" at bottom, crescent at right, series number at left

Date	Good	VG	F	VF	XF
ND(1857) Series 4	2.00	4.00	7.00	10.00	—

KM# 470s.4 MUN

4.0000 g., Cast Bronze, 24 mm.

Date	Good	VG	F	VF	XF
ND(1857) Series 4	—	—	—	—	40.00

KM# 470.5 MUN

4.0000 g., Cast Bronze, 24 mm. **Rev:** "Saeng" at bottom, crescent at right, series number at left

Date	Good	VG	F	VF	XF
ND(1857) Series 5	2.00	4.00	7.00	10.00	—

KM# 470s.5 MUN

4.0000 g., Cast Bronze, 24 mm.

Date	Good	VG	F	VF	XF
ND(1857) Series 5	—	—	—	—	40.00

KM# 471.1 MUN

4.0000 g., Cast Bronze, 25 mm. **Rev:** "Chon" (perfect) at bottom, series number at right

Date	Good	VG	F	VF	XF
ND(1857) Series 1	2.00	4.00	7.00	10.00	—

KM# 471s.1 MUN

4.0000 g., Cast Bronze, 25 mm.

Date	Good	VG	F	VF	XF
ND(1857) Series 1	—	—	—	—	40.00

KM# 471.2 MUN

4.0000 g., Cast Bronze, 25 mm. **Rev:** "Chon" (perfect) at bottom, series number at right

Date	Good	VG	F	VF	XF
ND(1857) Series 2	2.00	4.00	7.00	10.00	—

KM# 471s.2 MUN

4.0000 g., Cast Bronze, 25 mm.

Date	Good	VG	F	VF	XF
ND(1857) Series 2	—	—	—	—	40.00

KM# 471.3 MUN

4.0000 g., Cast Bronze, 25 mm. **Rev:** "Chon" (perfect) at bottom, series number at right

Date	Good	VG	F	VF	XF
ND(1857) Series 3	2.00	4.00	7.00	10.00	—

KM# 471s.3 MUN

4.0000 g., Cast Bronze, 25 mm.

Date	Good	VG	F	VF	XF
ND(1857) Series 3	—	—	—	—	40.00

KM# 471.4 MUN

4.0000 g., Cast Bronze, 25 mm. **Rev:** "Chon" (perfect) at bottom, series number at right

Date	Good	VG	F	VF	XF
ND(1857) Series 4	2.00	4.00	7.00	10.00	—

KM# 471s.4 MUN

4.0000 g., Cast Bronze, 25 mm.

Date	Good	VG	F	VF	XF
ND(1857) Series 4	—	—	—	—	40.00

KM# 471.5 MUN

4.0000 g., Cast Bronze, 25 mm. **Rev:** "Chon" (perfect) at bottom, series number at right

Date	Good	VG	F	VF	XF
ND(1857) Series 5	2.00	4.00	7.00	10.00	—

KM# 471s.5 MUN

4.0000 g., Cast Bronze, 25 mm.

Date	Good	VG	F	VF	XF
ND(1857) Series 5	—	—	—	—	40.00

KM# 471.6 MUN

4.0000 g., Cast Bronze, 25 mm. **Rev:** "Chon" (perfect) at bottom, series number at right

Date	Good	VG	F	VF	XF
ND(1857) Series 6	2.00	4.00	7.00	10.00	—

KM# 471s.6 MUN

4.0000 g., Cast Bronze, 25 mm.

Date	Good	VG	F	VF	XF
ND(1857) Series 6	—	—	—	—	40.00

KM# 471.7 MUN

4.0000 g., Cast Bronze, 25 mm. **Rev:** "Chon" (perfect) at bottom, series number at right

Date	Good	VG	F	VF	XF
ND(1857) Series 7	2.00	4.00	7.00	10.00	—

KM# 471s.7 MUN

4.0000 g., Cast Bronze, 25 mm.

Date	Good	VG	F	VF	XF
ND(1857) Series 7	—	—	—	—	40.00

KM# 471.8 MUN

4.0000 g., Cast Bronze, 25 mm. **Rev:** "Chon" (perfect) at bottom, series number at right

Date	Good	VG	F	VF	XF
ND(1857) Series 8	2.00	4.00	7.00	10.00	—

KM# 471s.8 MUN

4.0000 g., Cast Bronze, 25 mm.

Date	Good	VG	F	VF	XF
ND(1857) Series 8	—	—	—	—	40.00

KM# 471.9 MUN

4.0000 g., Cast Bronze, 25 mm. **Rev:** "Chon" (perfect) at bottom, series number at right

Date	Good	VG	F	VF	XF
ND(1857) Series 9	2.00	4.00	7.00	10.00	—

KM# 471s.9 MUN

4.0000 g., Cast Bronze, 25 mm.

Date	Good	VG	F	VF	XF
ND(1857) Series 9	—	—	—	—	40.00

KM# 471.10 MUN

4.0000 g., Cast Bronze, 25 mm. **Rev:** "Chon" (perfect) at bottom, series number at right

Date	Good	VG	F	VF	XF
ND(1857) Series 10	2.00	4.00	7.00	10.00	—

KM# 471s.10 MUN

4.0000 g., Cast Bronze, 25 mm.

Date	Good	VG	F	VF	XF
ND(1857) Series 10	—	—	—	—	40.00

KM# 472.1 MUN

4.0000 g., Cast Brass, 24 mm. **Rev:** "Chon" at bottom, series number at left

Date	Good	VG	F	VF	XF
ND(1857) Series 1	2.00	4.00	7.00	10.00	—

KM# 472s.1 MUN

4.0000 g., Cast Bronze, 24 mm.

Date	Good	VG	F	VF	XF
ND(1857) Series 1	—	—	—	—	40.00

KM# 472.2 MUN

4.0000 g., Cast Bronze, 24 mm. **Rev:** "Chon" at bottom, series number at left

Date	Good	VG	F	VF	XF
ND(1857) Series 2	2.00	4.00	7.00	10.00	—

KM# 472s.2 MUN

4.0000 g., Cast Bronze, 24 mm.

Date	Good	VG	F	VF	XF
ND(1857) Series 2	—	—	—	—	40.00

KM# 472.3 MUN

4.0000 g., Cast Bronze, 24 mm. **Rev:** "Chon" at bottom, series number at left

Date	Good	VG	F	VF	XF
ND(1857) Series 3	2.00	4.00	7.00	10.00	—

KM# 472s.3 MUN

4.0000 g., Cast Bronze, 24 mm.

Date	Good	VG	F	VF	XF
ND(1857) Series 3	—	—	—	—	40.00

KM# 472.4 MUN

4.0000 g., Cast Bronze, 24 mm. **Rev:** "Chon" at bottom, series number at left

Date	Good	VG	F	VF	XF
ND(1857) Series 4	2.00	4.00	7.00	10.00	—

KM# 472s.4 MUN

4.0000 g., Cast Bronze, 24 mm.

Date	Good	VG	F	VF	XF
ND(1857) Series 4	—	—	—	—	40.00

KM# 472.5 MUN

4.0000 g., Cast Bronze, 24 mm. **Rev:** "Chon" at bottom, series number at left

Date	Good	VG	F	VF	XF
ND(1857) Series 5	2.00	4.00	7.00	10.00	—

KM# 472s.5 MUN

4.0000 g., Cast Bronze, 24 mm.

Date	Good	VG	F	VF	XF
ND(1857) Series 5	—	—	—	—	40.00

KM# 472.6 MUN

4.0000 g., Cast Bronze, 24 mm. **Rev:** "Chon" at bottom, series number at left

Date	Good	VG	F	VF	XF
ND(1857) Series 6	2.00	4.00	7.00	10.00	—

KM# 472s.6 MUN

4.0000 g., Cast Bronze, 24 mm.

Date	Good	VG	F	VF	XF
ND(1857) Series 6	—	—	—	—	40.00

KM# 472.7 MUN

4.0000 g., Cast Bronze, 24 mm. **Rev:** "Chon" at bottom, series numbrer at left

Date	Good	VG	F	VF	XF
ND(1857) Series 7	2.00	4.00	7.00	10.00	—

KM# 472s.7 MUN

4.0000 g., Cast Bronze, 24 mm.

Date	Good	VG	F	VF	XF
ND(1857) Series 7	—	—	—	—	40.00

KM# 472.8 MUN

4.0000 g., Cast Bronze, 24 mm. **Rev:** "Chon" at bottom, series number at left

Date	Good	VG	F	VF	XF
ND(1857) Series 8	2.00	4.00	7.00	10.00	—

KM# 472s.8 MUN

4.0000 g., Cast Bronze, 24 mm.

Date	Good	VG	F	VF	XF
ND(1857) Series 8	—	—	—	—	40.00

KM# 472.9 MUN

4.0000 g., Cast Bronze, 24 mm. **Rev:** "Chon" at bottom, series number at left

Date	Good	VG	F	VF	XF
ND(1857) Series 9	2.00	4.00	7.00	10.00	—

KM# 472s.9 MUN

4.0000 g., Cast Bronze, 24 mm.

Date	Good	VG	F	VF	XF
ND(1857) Series 9	—	—	—	—	40.00

KM# 472.10 MUN

4.0000 g., Cast Bronze, 24 mm. **Rev:** "Chon" at bottom, series number at left

Date	Good	VG	F	VF	XF
ND(1857) Series 10	2.00	4.00	7.00	10.00	—

KM# 472s.10 MUN

4.0000 g., Cast Bronze, 24 mm.

Date	Good	VG	F	VF	XF
ND(1857) Series 10	—	—	—	—	40.00

KM# 473.1 MUN

4.0000 g., Cast Bronze **Rev:** "Chon" at bottom, crescent at right, series number at left **Note:** Size varies: 23-25 mm.

Date	Good	VG	F	VF	XF
ND(1857) Series 1	2.00	4.00	7.00	10.00	—

KM# 473s.1 MUN

4.0000 g., Cast Bronze **Note:** Size varies: 23-25 mm.

Date	Good	VG	F	VF	XF
ND(1857) Series 1	—	—	—	—	40.00

KM# 473.2 MUN

4.0000 g., Cast Bronze **Rev:** "Chon" at bottom, crescent at right, series number at left **Note:** Size varies: 23-25 mm.

Date	Good	VG	F	VF	XF
ND(1857) Series 2	2.00	4.00	7.00	10.00	—

KM# 473s.2 MUN

4.0000 g., Cast Bronze **Note:** Size varies: 23-25 mm.

Date	Good	VG	F	VF	XF
ND(1857) Series 2	—	—	—	—	40.00

KM# 473.3 MUN

4.0000 g., Cast Bronze **Rev:** "Chon" at bottom, crescent at right, series number at left **Note:** Size varies: 23-25 mm.

Date	Good	VG	F	VF	XF
ND(1857) Series 3	2.00	4.00	7.00	10.00	—

KM# 473s.3 MUN
4.0000 g., Cast Bronze **Note:** Size varies: 23-25 mm.

Date	Good	VG	F	VF	XF
ND(1857) Series 3	—	—	—	—	40.00

KM# 473.4 MUN
4.0000 g., Cast Bronze **Rev:** "Chon" at bottom, crescent at right, series number at left **Note:** Size varies: 23-25 mm.

Date	Good	VG	F	VF	XF
ND(1857) Series 4	2.00	4.00	7.00	10.00	—

KM# 473s.4 MUN
4.0000 g., Cast Bronze **Note:** Size varies: 23-25 mm.

Date	Good	VG	F	VF	XF
ND(1857) Series 4	—	—	—	—	40.00

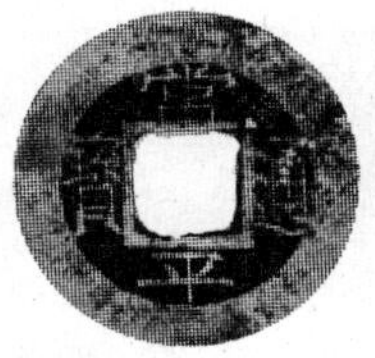

KM# 473.5 MUN
4.0000 g., Cast Bronze **Rev:** "Chon" at bottom, crescent at right, series number at left **Note:** Size varies: 23-25 mm.

Date	Good	VG	F	VF	XF
ND(1857) Series 5	2.00	4.00	7.00	10.00	—

KM# 473s.5 MUN
4.0000 g., Cast Bronze **Note:** Size varies: 23-25 mm.

Date	Good	VG	F	VF	XF
ND(1857) Series 5	—	—	—	—	40.00

KM# 474.1 MUN
4.0000 g., Cast Bronze, 24 mm. **Rev:** "Kil" at bottom, series number at right

Date	Good	VG	F	VF	XF
ND(1857) Series 1	10.00	20.00	40.00	75.00	—

KM# 474s.1 MUN
4.0000 g., Cast Bronze, 24 mm.

Date	Good	VG	F	VF	XF
ND(1857) Series 1	—	—	—	—	100

KM# 474.2 MUN
4.0000 g., Cast Bronze, 24 mm. **Rev:** "Kil" at bottom, series number at right

Date	Good	VG	F	VF	XF
ND(1857) Series 2	10.00	20.00	40.00	75.00	—

KM# 474s.2 MUN
4.0000 g., Cast Bronze, 24 mm.

Date	Good	VG	F	VF	XF
ND(1857) Series 2	—	—	—	—	100

KM# 474.3 MUN
4.0000 g., Cast Bronze **Rev:** "Kil" at bottom, series number at right

Date	Good	VG	F	VF	XF
ND(1857) Series 3	10.00	20.00	40.00	75.00	—

KM# 474s.3 MUN
4.0000 g., Cast Bronze, 24 mm.

Date	Good	VG	F	VF	XF
ND(1857) Series 3	—	—	—	—	100

KM# 474.4 MUN
4.0000 g., Cast Bronze, 24 mm. **Rev:** "Kil" at bottom, series number at right

Date	Good	VG	F	VF	XF
ND(1857) Series 4	10.00	20.00	40.00	75.00	—

KM# 474s.4 MUN
4.0000 g., Cast Bronze, 24 mm.

Date	Good	VG	F	VF	XF
ND(1857) Series 4	—	—	—	—	100

KM# 474.5 MUN
4.0000 g., Cast Bronze, 24 mm. **Rev:** "Kil" at bottom, series number at right

Date	Good	VG	F	VF	XF
ND(1857) Series 5	10.00	20.00	40.00	75.00	—

KM# 474s.5 MUN
4.0000 g., Cast Bronze, 24 mm.

Date	Good	VG	F	VF	XF
ND(1857) Series 5	—	—	—	—	100

KM# 474.6 MUN
4.0000 g., Cast Bronze, 24 mm. **Rev:** "Kil" at bottom, series number at right

Date	Good	VG	F	VF	XF
ND(1857) Series 6	10.00	20.00	40.00	75.00	—

KM# 474s.6 MUN
4.0000 g., Cast Bronze, 24 mm.

Date	Good	VG	F	VF	XF
ND(1857) Series 6	—	—	—	—	100

KM# 474.7 MUN
4.0000 g., Cast Bronze, 24 mm. **Rev:** "Kil" at bottom, series number at right

Date	Good	VG	F	VF	XF
ND(1857) Series 7	10.00	20.00	40.00	75.00	—

KM# 474s.7 MUN
4.0000 g., Cast Bronze, 24 mm.

Date	Good	VG	F	VF	XF
ND(1857) Series 7	—	—	—	—	100

KM# 474.8 MUN
4.0000 g., Cast Bronze, 24 mm. **Rev:** "Kil" at bottom, series number at right

Date	Good	VG	F	VF	XF
ND(1857) Series 8	10.00	20.00	40.00	75.00	—

KM# 474s.8 MUN
4.0000 g., Cast Bronze, 24 mm.

Date	Good	VG	F	VF	XF
ND(1857) Series 8	—	—	—	—	100

KM# 474.9 MUN
4.0000 g., Cast Bronze, 24 mm. **Rev:** "Kil" at bottom, series number at right

Date	Good	VG	F	VF	XF
ND(1857) Series 9	10.00	20.00	40.00	75.00	—

KM# 474s.9 MUN
4.0000 g., Cast Bronze, 24 mm.

Date	Good	VG	F	VF	XF
ND(1857) Series 9	—	—	—	—	100

KM# 475.1 MUN
4.0000 g., Cast Bronze, 24 mm. **Rev:** "Kil" at bottom, series number at left

Date	Good	VG	F	VF	XF
ND(1857) Series 1	10.00	20.00	40.00	75.00	—

KM# 475s.1 MUN
4.0000 g., Cast Bronze, 24 mm.

Date	Good	VG	F	VF	XF
ND(1857) Series 1	—	—	—	—	100

KM# 475.2 MUN
4.0000 g., Cast Bronze, 24 mm. **Rev:** "Kil" at bottom, series number at left

Date	Good	VG	F	VF	XF
ND(1857) Series 2	10.00	20.00	40.00	75.00	—

KM# 475s.2 MUN
4.0000 g., Cast Bronze, 24 mm.

Date	Good	VG	F	VF	XF
ND(1857) Series 2	—	—	—	—	100

KM# 475.3 MUN
4.0000 g., Cast Bronze, 24 mm. **Rev:** "Kil" at bottom, series number at left

Date	Good	VG	F	VF	XF
ND(1857) Series 3	10.00	20.00	40.00	75.00	—

KM# 475s.3 MUN
4.0000 g., Cast Bronze, 24 mm.

Date	Good	VG	F	VF	XF
ND(1857) Series 3	—	—	—	—	100

KM# 475.4 MUN
4.0000 g., Cast Bronze, 24 mm. **Rev:** "Kil" at bottom, series number at left

Date	Good	VG	F	VF	XF
ND(1857) Series 4	10.00	20.00	40.00	75.00	—

KM# 475s.4 MUN
4.0000 g., Cast Bronze, 24 mm.

Date	Good	VG	F	VF	XF
ND(1857) Series 4	—	—	—	—	100

KM# 475.5 MUN
4.0000 g., Cast Bronze, 24 mm. **Rev:** "Kil" at bottom, series number at left

Date	Good	VG	F	VF	XF
ND(1857) Series 5	10.00	20.00	40.00	75.00	—

KM# 475s.5 MUN
4.0000 g., Cast Bronze, 24 mm.

Date	Good	VG	F	VF	XF
ND(1857) Series 5	—	—	—	—	100

KM# 475.6 MUN
4.0000 g., Cast Bronze, 24 mm. **Rev:** "Kil" at bottom, series number at left

Date	Good	VG	F	VF	XF
ND(1857) Series 6	10.00	20.00	40.00	75.00	—

KM# 475s.6 MUN
4.0000 g., Cast Bronze, 24 mm.

Date	Good	VG	F	VF	XF
ND(1857) Series 6	—	—	—	—	100

KM# 475.7 MUN
4.0000 g., Cast Bronze, 24 mm. **Rev:** "Kil" at bottom, series number at left

Date	Good	VG	F	VF	XF
ND(1857) Series 7	10.00	20.00	40.00	75.00	—

KM# 475s.7 MUN
4.0000 g., Cast Bronze, 24 mm.

Date	Good	VG	F	VF	XF
ND(1857) Series 7	—	—	—	—	100

KM# 475.8 MUN
4.0000 g., Cast Bronze, 24 mm. **Rev:** "Kil" at bottom, series number at left

Date	Good	VG	F	VF	XF
ND(1857) Series 8	10.00	20.00	40.00	75.00	—

KM# 475s.8 MUN
4.0000 g., Cast Bronze, 24 mm.

Date	Good	VG	F	VF	XF
ND(1857) Series 8	—	—	—	—	100

KM# 475.9 MUN
4.0000 g., Cast Bronze, 24 mm. **Rev:** "Kil" at bottom, series number at left

Date	Good	VG	F	VF	XF
ND(1857) Series 9	10.00	20.00	40.00	75.00	—

KM# 475s.9 MUN
4.0000 g., Cast Bronze, 24 mm.

Date	Good	VG	F	VF	XF
ND(1857) Series 9	—	—	—	—	100

KM# 475.10 MUN
4.0000 g., Cast Bronze, 24 mm. **Rev:** "Kil" at bottom, series number at left

Date	Good	VG	F	VF	XF
ND(1857) Series 10	10.00	20.00	40.00	75.00	—

KM# 475s.10 MUN
4.0000 g., Cast Bronze, 24 mm.

Date	Good	VG	F	VF	XF
ND(1857) Series 10	—	—	—	—	100

KM# 476.1 MUN
4.0000 g., Cast Bronze, 24 mm. **Rev:** "Kil" at bottom, crescent at right, series number at left

Date	Good	VG	F	VF	XF
ND(1857) Series 1	10.00	20.00	40.00	75.00	—

KM# 476s.1 MUN
4.0000 g., Cast Bronze, 24 mm.

Date	Good	VG	F	VF	XF
ND(1857) Series 1	—	—	—	—	100

KM# 476.2 MUN
4.0000 g., Cast Bronze, 24 mm. **Rev:** "Kil" at bottom, crescent at right, series number at left

Date	Good	VG	F	VF	XF
ND(1857) Series 2	10.00	20.00	40.00	75.00	—

KM# 476s.2 MUN
4.0000 g., Cast Bronze, 24 mm.

Date	Good	VG	F	VF	XF
ND(1857) Series 2	—	—	—	—	100

KM# 476.3 MUN
4.0000 g., Cast Bronze, 24 mm. **Rev:** "Kil" at bottom, crescent at right, series number at left

Date	Good	VG	F	VF	XF
ND(1857) Series 3	10.00	20.00	40.00	75.00	—

KM# 476s.3 MUN
4.0000 g., Cast Bronze, 24 mm.

Date	Good	VG	F	VF	XF
ND(1857) Series 3	—	—	—	—	100

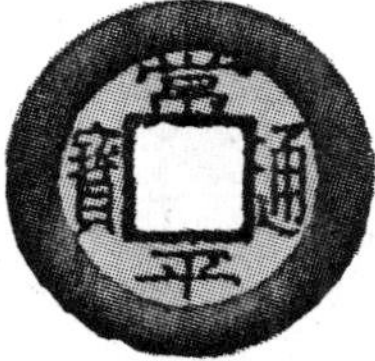

KM# 476.4 MUN
4.0000 g., Cast Bronze, 24 mm. **Rev:** "Kil" at bottom, crescent at right, series number at left

Date	Good	VG	F	VF	XF
ND(1857) Series 4	10.00	20.00	40.00	75.00	—

KM# 476s.4 MUN
4.0000 g., Cast Bronze, 24 mm.

Date	Good	VG	F	VF	XF
ND(1857) Series 4	—	—	—	—	100

KM# 476.5 MUN
4.0000 g., Cast Bronze, 24 mm. **Rev:** "Kil" at bottom, crescent at right, series number at left

Date	Good	VG	F	VF	XF
ND(1857) Series 5	10.00	20.00	40.00	75.00	—

KM# 476s.5 MUN
4.0000 g., Cast Bronze, 24 mm.

Date	Good	VG	F	VF	XF
ND(1857) Series 5	—	—	—	—	100

SEOUL MILITARY OFFICE

(T'ong Wi Yong)

KM# 763.1 5 MUN
Cast Bronze, 32 mm. **Rev:** "Tang" at right, "O" (5) at left, series number at bottom **Note:** Inside diameter 20-22 mm.

Date	Good	VG	F	VF	XF
ND(1883) Series 1	5.00	9.00	15.00	25.00	—

KM# 763s.1 5 MUN
Cast Bronze, 32 mm.

Date	Good	VG	F	VF	XF
ND(1883) Series 1	—	—	—	—	75.00

KM# 763.2 5 MUN
Cast Bronze, 32 mm. **Rev:** "Tang" at right, "O" (5) at left, series number at bottom **Note:** Inside diameter 20-22 mm.

Date	Good	VG	F	VF	XF
ND(1883) Series 2	5.00	9.00	15.00	25.00	—

KM# 763s.2 5 MUN
Cast Bronze, 32 mm.

Date	Good	VG	F	VF	XF
ND(1883) Series 2	—	—	—	—	75.00

KM# 763.3 5 MUN
Cast Bronze, 32 mm. **Rev:** "Tang" at right, "O" (5) at left, series number at bottom **Note:** Inside diameter 20-22 mm.

Date	Good	VG	F	VF	XF
ND(1883) Series 3	5.00	9.00	15.00	25.00	—

KM# 763s.3 5 MUN
Cast Bronze, 32 mm.

Date	Good	VG	F	VF	XF
ND(1883) Series 3	—	—	—	—	75.00

KM# 763.4 5 MUN
Cast Bronze, 32 mm. **Rev:** "Tang" at right, "O" (5) at left, series number at bottom **Note:** Inside diameter 20-22 mm.

Date	Good	VG	F	VF	XF
ND(1883) Series 4	5.00	9.00	15.00	25.00	—

KM# 763s.4 5 MUN
Cast Bronze, 32 mm.

Date	Good	VG	F	VF	XF
ND(1883) Series 4	—	—	—	—	75.00

KM# 763.5 5 MUN
Cast Bronze, 32 mm. **Rev:** "Tang" at right, "O" (5) at left, series number at bottom **Note:** Inside diameter 20-22 mm.

Date	Good	VG	F	VF	XF
ND(1883) Series 5	5.00	9.00	15.00	25.00	—

KM# 763s.5 5 MUN
Cast Bronze, 32 mm.

Date	Good	VG	F	VF	XF
ND(1883) Series 5	—	—	—	—	75.00

KM# 763.6 5 MUN
Cast Bronze, 32 mm. **Rev:** "Tang" at right, "O" (5) at left, series number at bottom **Note:** Inside diameter 20-22 mm.

Date	Good	VG	F	VF	XF
ND(1883) Series 6	5.00	9.00	15.00	25.00	—

KM# 763s.6 5 MUN
Cast Bronze, 32 mm.

Date	Good	VG	F	VF	XF
ND(1883) Series 6	—	—	—	—	75.00

KM# 763.7 5 MUN
Cast Bronze, 32 mm. **Rev:** "Tang" at right, "O" (5) at left, series number at bottom **Note:** Inside diameter 20-22 mm.

Date	Good	VG	F	VF	XF
ND(1883) Series 7	5.00	9.00	15.00	25.00	—

KM# 763s.7 5 MUN
Cast Bronze, 32 mm.

Date	Good	VG	F	VF	XF
ND(1883) Series 7	—	—	—	—	75.00

KM# 763.8 5 MUN
Cast Bronze, 32 mm. **Rev:** "Tang" at right, "O" (5) at left, series number at bottom **Note:** Inside diameter 20-22 mm.

Date	Good	VG	F	VF	XF
ND(1883) Series 8	5.00	9.00	15.00	25.00	—

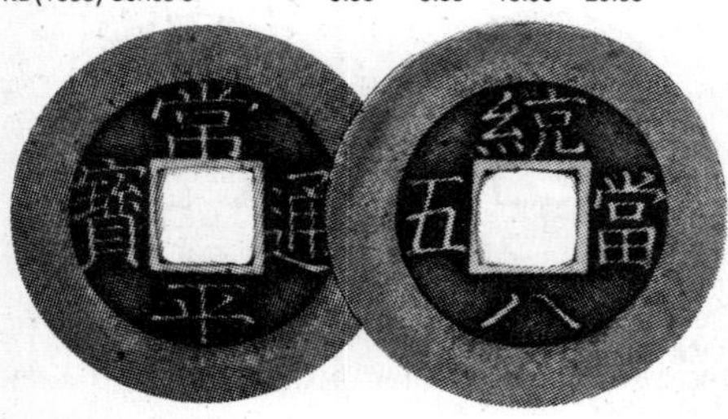

KM# 763s.8 5 MUN
Cast Bronze, 32 mm.

Date	Good	VG	F	VF	XF
ND(1883) Series 8	—	—	—	—	75.00

KM# 763.9 5 MUN
Cast Bronze, 32 mm. **Rev:** "Tang" at right, "O" (5) at left, series number at bottom **Note:** Inside diameter 20-22 mm.

Date	Good	VG	F	VF	XF
ND(1883) Series 9	5.00	9.00	15.00	25.00	—

KM# 763s.9 5 MUN
Cast Bronze, 32 mm.

Date	Good	VG	F	VF	XF
ND(1883) Series 9	—	—	—	—	75.00

KM# 763.10 5 MUN
Cast Bronze, 32 mm. **Rev:** "Tang" at right, "O" (5) at left, series number at bottom **Note:** Inside diameter 20-22 mm.

Date	Good	VG	F	VF	XF
ND(1883) Series 10	5.00	9.00	15.00	25.00	—

KM# 763s.10 5 MUN
Cast Bronze, 32 mm.

Date	Good	VG	F	VF	XF
ND(1883) Series 10	—	—	—	—	75.00

KM# 763.11 5 MUN
Cast Bronze, 32 mm. **Rev:** "Tang" at right, "O" (5) at left, series number at bottom **Note:** Inside diameter 20-22 mm.

Date	Good	VG	F	VF	XF
ND(1883) Series 11	5.00	9.00	15.00	25.00	—

KM# 763s.11 5 MUN
Cast Bronze, 32 mm.

Date	Good	VG	F	VF	XF
ND(1883) Series 11	—	—	—	—	75.00

KM# 763.12 5 MUN
Cast Bronze, 32 mm. **Rev:** "Tang" at right, "O" (5) at left, series number at bottom **Note:** Inside diameter 20-22 mm.

Date	Good	VG	F	VF	XF
ND(1883) Series 12	5.00	9.00	15.00	25.00	—

KM# 763s.12 5 MUN
Cast Bronze, 32 mm.

Date	Good	VG	F	VF	XF
ND(1883) Series 12	—	—	—	—	75.00

KM# 763.13 5 MUN
Cast Bronze, 32 mm. **Rev:** "Tang" at right, "O" (5) at left, series number at bottom **Note:** Inside diameter 20-22 mm.

Date	Good	VG	F	VF	XF
ND(1883) Series 13	5.00	9.00	15.00	25.00	—

KM# 763s.13 5 MUN
Cast Bronze, 32 mm.

Date	Good	VG	F	VF	XF
ND(1883) Series 13	—	—	—	—	75.00

KM# 763.14 5 MUN
Cast Bronze, 32 mm. **Rev:** "Tang" at right, "O" (5) at left, series number at bottom **Note:** Inside diameter 20-22 mm.

Date	Good	VG	F	VF	XF
ND(1883) Series 14	5.00	9.00	15.00	25.00	—

KM# 763s.14 5 MUN
Cast Bronze, 32 mm.

Date	Good	VG	F	VF	XF
ND(1883) Series 14	—	—	—	—	75.00

KM# 763.15 5 MUN
Cast Bronze, 32 mm. **Rev:** "Tang" at right, "O" (5) at left, series number at bottom **Note:** Inside diameter 20-22 mm.

Date	Good	VG	F	VF	XF
ND(1883) Series 15	5.00	9.00	15.00	25.00	—

KM# 763s.15 5 MUN
Cast Bronze, 32 mm.

Date	Good	VG	F	VF	XF
ND(1883) Series 15	—	—	—	—	75.00

KM# 763.16 5 MUN
Cast Bronze, 32 mm. **Rev:** "Tang" at right, "O" (5) at left, series number at bottom **Note:** Inside diameter 20-22 mm.

Date	Good	VG	F	VF	XF
ND(1883) Series 16	5.00	9.00	15.00	25.00	—

KM# 763s.16 5 MUN
Cast Bronze, 32 mm.

Date	Good	VG	F	VF	XF
ND(1883) Series 16	—	—	—	—	75.00

KM# 763.17 5 MUN
Cast Bronze, 32 mm. **Rev:** "Tang" at right, "O" (5) at left, series number at bottom **Note:** Inside diameter 20-22 mm.

Date	Good	VG	F	VF	XF
ND(1883) Series 17	5.00	9.00	15.00	25.00	—

KM# 763s.17 5 MUN
Cast Bronze, 32 mm.

Date	Good	VG	F	VF	XF
ND(1883) Series 17	—	—	—	—	75.00

KM# 763.18 5 MUN
Cast Bronze, 32 mm. **Rev:** "Tang" at right, "O" (5) at left, series number at bottom **Note:** Inside diameter 20-22 mm.

Date	Good	VG	F	VF	XF
ND(1883) Series 18	5.00	9.00	15.00	25.00	—

KM# 763s.18 5 MUN
Cast Bronze, 32 mm.

Date	Good	VG	F	VF	XF
ND(1883) Series 18	—	—	—	—	75.00

KM# 763.19 5 MUN
Cast Bronze, 32 mm. **Rev:** "Tang" at right, "O" (5) at left, series number at bottom **Note:** Inside diameter 20-22 mm.

Date	Good	VG	F	VF	XF
ND(1883) Series 19	5.00	9.00	15.00	25.00	—

KM# 763s.19 5 MUN
Cast Bronze, 32 mm.

Date	Good	VG	F	VF	XF
ND(1883) Series 19	—	—	—	—	75.00

KM# 763.20 5 MUN
Cast Bronze, 32 mm. **Rev:** "Tang" at right, "O" (5) at left, series number at bottom **Note:** Inside diameter 20-22 mm.

Date	Good	VG	F	VF	XF
ND(1883) Series 20	5.00	9.00	15.00	25.00	—

KM# 763s.20 5 MUN
Cast Bronze, 32 mm.

Date	Good	VG	F	VF	XF
ND(1883) Series 20	—	—	—	—	75.00

KM# 764.1 5 MUN
Cast Bronze, 29 mm. **Note:** Reduced size. Inside diameter 18-19 mm.

Date	Good	VG	F	VF	XF
ND(1883) Series 1	5.00	9.00	15.00	25.00	—

KM# 764s.1 5 MUN
Cast Bronze, 29 mm.

Date	Good	VG	F	VF	XF
ND(1883) Series 1	—	—	—	—	75.00

KM# 764.2 5 MUN
Cast Bronze, 29 mm. **Note:** Reduced size. Inside diameter 18-19 mm.

Date	Good	VG	F	VF	XF
ND(1883) Series 2	5.00	9.00	15.00	25.00	—

KM# 764s.2 5 MUN
Cast Bronze, 29 mm.

Date	Good	VG	F	VF	XF
ND(1883) Series 2	—	—	—	—	75.00

KM# 764.3 5 MUN
Cast Bronze, 29 mm. **Note:** Reduced size. Inside diameter 18-19 mm.

Date	Good	VG	F	VF	XF
ND(1883) Series 3	5.00	9.00	15.00	25.00	—

KM# 764s.3 5 MUN
Cast Bronze, 29 mm.

Date	Good	VG	F	VF	XF
ND(1883) Series 3	—	—	—	—	75.00

KM# 764.4 5 MUN
Cast Bronze, 29 mm. **Note:** Reduced size. Inside diameter 18-19 mm.

Date	Good	VG	F	VF	XF
ND(1883) Series 4	5.00	9.00	15.00	25.00	—

KM# 764s.4 5 MUN
Cast Bronze, 29 mm.

Date	Good	VG	F	VF	XF
ND(1883) Series 4	—	—	—	—	75.00

KM# 764.5 5 MUN
Cast Bronze, 29 mm. **Note:** Reduced size. Inside diameter 18-19 mm.

Date	Good	VG	F	VF	XF
ND(1883) Series 5	5.00	9.00	15.00	25.00	—

KM# 764s.5 5 MUN
Cast Bronze, 29 mm.

Date	Good	VG	F	VF	XF
ND(1883) Series 5	—	—	—	—	75.00

KM# 764.6 5 MUN
Cast Bronze, 29 mm. **Note:** Reduced size. Inside diameter 18-19 mm.

Date	Good	VG	F	VF	XF
ND(1883) Series 6	5.00	9.00	15.00	25.00	—

KM# 764s.6 5 MUN
Cast Bronze, 29 mm.

Date	Good	VG	F	VF	XF
ND(1883) Series 6	—	—	—	—	75.00

KM# 764.7 5 MUN
Cast Bronze, 29 mm. **Note:** Reduced size. Inside diameter 18-19 mm.

Date	Good	VG	F	VF	XF
ND(1883) Series 7	5.00	9.00	15.00	25.00	—

KM# 764s.7 5 MUN
Cast Bronze, 29 mm.

Date	Good	VG	F	VF	XF
ND(1883) Series 7	—	—	—	—	75.00

KM# 764.8 5 MUN
Cast Bronze, 29 mm. **Note:** Reduced size. Inside diameter 18-19 mm.

Date	Good	VG	F	VF	XF
ND(1883) Series 8	5.00	9.00	15.00	25.00	—

KM# 764s.8 5 MUN
Cast Bronze, 29 mm.

Date	Good	VG	F	VF	XF
ND(1883) Series 8	—	—	—	—	75.00

KM# 764.9 5 MUN
Cast Bronze, 29 mm. **Note:** Reduced size. Inside diameter 18-19 mm.

Date	Good	VG	F	VF	XF
ND(1883) Series 9	5.00	9.00	15.00	25.00	—

KM# 764s.9 5 MUN
Cast Bronze, 29 mm.

Date	Good	VG	F	VF	XF
ND(1883) Series 9	—	—	—	—	75.00

KM# 764.10 5 MUN
Cast Bronze, 29 mm. **Note:** Reduced size. Inside diameter 18-19 mm.

Date	Good	VG	F	VF	XF
ND(1883) Series 10	5.00	9.00	15.00	25.00	—

KM# 764s.10 5 MUN
Cast Bronze, 29 mm.

Date	Good	VG	F	VF	XF
ND(1883) Series 10	—	—	—	—	75.00

KM# 764.11 5 MUN
Cast Bronze, 29 mm. **Note:** Reduced size. Inside diameter 18-19 mm.

Date	Good	VG	F	VF	XF
ND(1883) Series 11	5.00	9.00	15.00	25.00	—

KM# 764s.11 5 MUN
Cast Bronze, 29 mm.

Date	Good	VG	F	VF	XF
ND(1883) Series 11	—	—	—	—	75.00

KM# 764.12 5 MUN
Cast Bronze, 29 mm. **Note:** Reduced size. Inside diameter 18-19 mm.

Date	Good	VG	F	VF	XF
ND(1883) Series 12	5.00	9.00	15.00	25.00	—

KM# 764s.12 5 MUN
Cast Bronze, 29 mm.

Date	Good	VG	F	VF	XF
ND(1883) Series 12	—	—	—	—	75.00

KM# 764.13 5 MUN
Cast Bronze, 29 mm. **Note:** Reduced size. Inside diameter 18-19 mm.

Date	Good	VG	F	VF	XF
ND(1883) Series 13	5.00	9.00	15.00	25.00	—

KM# 764s.13 5 MUN
Cast Bronze, 29 mm.

Date	Good	VG	F	VF	XF
ND(1883) Series 13	—	—	—	—	75.00

KM# 764.14 5 MUN
Cast Bronze, 29 mm. **Note:** Reduced size. Inside diameter 18-19 mm.

Date	Good	VG	F	VF	XF
ND(1883) Series 14	5.00	9.00	15.00	25.00	—

KM# 764s.14 5 MUN
Cast Bronze, 29 mm.

Date	Good	VG	F	VF	XF
ND(1883) Series 14	—	—	—	—	75.00

KM# 764.15 5 MUN
Cast Bronze, 29 mm. **Note:** Reduced size. Inside diameter 18-19 mm.

Date	Good	VG	F	VF	XF
ND(1883) Series 15	5.00	9.00	15.00	25.00	—

KM# 764s.15 5 MUN
Cast Bronze, 29 mm.

Date	Good	VG	F	VF	XF
ND(1883) Series 15	—	—	—	—	75.00

KM# 764.16 5 MUN
Cast Bronze, 29 mm. **Note:** Reduced size. Inside diameter 18-19 mm.

Date	Good	VG	F	VF	XF
ND(1883) Series 16	5.00	9.00	15.00	25.00	—

KM# 764s.16 5 MUN
Cast Bronze, 29 mm.

Date	Good	VG	F	VF	XF
ND(1883) Series 16	—	—	—	—	75.00

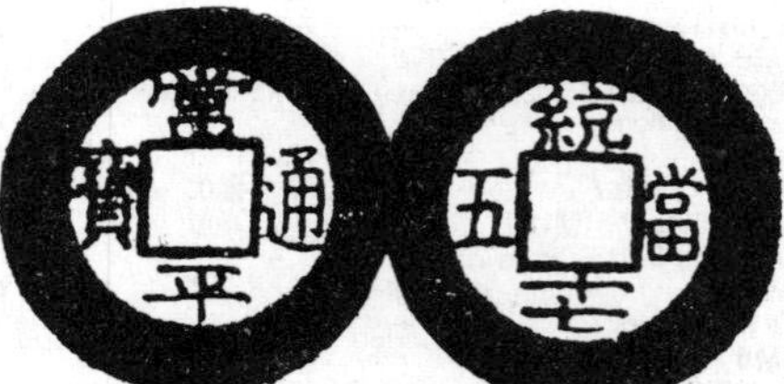

KM# 764.17 5 MUN
Cast Bronze, 29 mm. **Note:** Reduced size. Inside diameter 18-19 mm.

Date	Good	VG	F	VF	XF
ND(1883) Series 17	5.00	9.00	15.00	25.00	—

KM# 764s.17 5 MUN
Cast Bronze, 29 mm.

Date	Good	VG	F	VF	XF
ND(1883) Series 17	—	—	—	—	75.00

KM# 764.18 5 MUN
Cast Bronze, 29 mm. **Note:** Reduced size. Inside diameter 18-19 mm.

Date	Good	VG	F	VF	XF
ND(1883) Series 18	5.00	9.00	15.00	25.00	—

KM# 764s.18 5 MUN
Cast Bronze, 29 mm.

Date	Good	VG	F	VF	XF
ND(1883) Series 18	—	—	—	—	75.00

KM# 764.19 5 MUN
Cast Bronze, 29 mm. **Note:** Reduced size. Inside diameter 18-19 mm.

Date	Good	VG	F	VF	XF
ND(1883) Series 19	5.00	9.00	15.00	25.00	—

KM# 764s.19 5 MUN
Cast Bronze, 29 mm.

Date	Good	VG	F	VF	XF
ND(1883) Series 19	—	—	—	—	75.00

KM# 764.20 5 MUN
Cast Bronze, 29 mm. **Note:** Reduced size. Inside diameter 18-19 mm.

Date	Good	VG	F	VF	XF
ND(1883) Series 20	5.00	9.00	15.00	25.00	—

KM# 764s.20 5 MUN
Cast Bronze, 29 mm.

Date	Good	VG	F	VF	XF
ND(1883) Series 20	—	—	—	—	75.00

GOVERNMENT OFFICE PUKHAN MOUNTAIN FORTRESS

(Kyong Ni Ch'ong)

KM# 765.1 MUN
4.0000 g., Cast Bronze, 26 mm. **Rev:** "Kyong" at top, series number at bottom

Date	Good	VG	F	VF	XF
ND(1830) Series 1	3.00	5.00	8.00	12.00	—

KM# 765s.1 MUN
4.0000 g., Cast Bronze, 26 mm.

Date	Good	VG	F	VF	XF
ND(1830) Series 1	—	—	—	—	35.00

KM# 765.2 MUN
4.0000 g., Cast Bronze, 26 mm. **Rev:** "Kyong" at top, series number at bottom

Date	Good	VG	F	VF	XF
ND(1830) Series 2	3.00	5.00	8.00	12.00	—

KM# 765s.2 MUN
4.0000 g., Cast Bronze, 26 mm.

Date	Good	VG	F	VF	XF
ND(1830) Series 2	—	—	—	—	35.00

KM# 765.3 MUN
4.0000 g., Cast Bronze, 26 mm. **Rev:** "Kyong" at top, series number at bottom

Date	Good	VG	F	VF	XF
ND(1830) Series 3	3.00	5.00	8.00	12.00	—

KM# 765s.3 MUN
4.0000 g., Cast Bronze, 26 mm.

Date	Good	VG	F	VF	XF
ND(1830) Series 3	—	—	—	—	35.00

KM# 765.4 MUN
4.0000 g., Cast Bronze, 26 mm. **Rev:** "Kyong" at top, series number at bottom

Date	Good	VG	F	VF	XF
ND(1830) Series 4	3.00	5.00	8.00	12.00	—

KM# 765s.4 MUN
4.0000 g., Cast Bronze, 26 mm.

Date	Good	VG	F	VF	XF
ND(1830) Series 4	—	—	—	—	35.00

KM# 765.5 MUN
4.0000 g., Cast Bronze, 26 mm. **Rev:** "Kyong" at top, series number at bottom

Date	Good	VG	F	VF	XF
ND(1830) Series 5	3.00	5.00	8.00	12.00	—

KM# 765s.5 MUN
4.0000 g., Cast Bronze, 26 mm.

Date	Good	VG	F	VF	XF
ND(1830) Series 5	—	—	—	—	35.00

KM# 765.6 MUN
4.0000 g., Cast Bronze, 26 mm. **Rev:** "Kyong" at top, series number at bottom

Date	Good	VG	F	VF	XF
ND(1830) Series 6	3.00	5.00	8.00	12.00	—

KM# 765s.6 MUN
4.0000 g., Cast Bronze, 26 mm.

Date	Good	VG	F	VF	XF
ND(1830) Series 6	—	—	—	—	35.00

KM# 765.7 MUN
4.0000 g., Cast Bronze, 26 mm. **Rev:** "Kyong" at top, series number at bottom

Date	Good	VG	F	VF	XF
ND(1830) Series 7	3.00	5.00	8.00	12.00	—

KM# 765s.7 MUN
4.0000 g., Cast Bronze, 26 mm.

Date	Good	VG	F	VF	XF
ND(1830) Series 7	—	—	—	—	35.00

KM# 765.8 MUN
4.0000 g., Cast Bronze, 26 mm. **Rev:** "Kyong" at top, series number at bottom

Date	Good	VG	F	VF	XF
ND(1830) Series 8	3.00	5.00	8.00	12.00	—

KM# 765s.8 MUN
4.0000 g., Cast Bronze, 26 mm.

Date	Good	VG	F	VF	XF
ND(1830) Series 8	—	—	—	—	35.00

KM# 765.9 MUN
4.0000 g., Cast Bronze, 26 mm. **Rev:** "Kyong" at top, series number at bottom

Date	Good	VG	F	VF	XF
ND(1830) Series 9	3.00	5.00	8.00	12.00	—

KM# 765s.9 MUN
4.0000 g., Cast Bronze, 26 mm.

Date	Good	VG	F	VF	XF
ND(1830) Series 9	—	—	—	—	35.00

KM# 765.10 MUN
4.0000 g., Cast Bronze, 26 mm. **Rev:** "Kyong" at top, series number at bottom

Date	Good	VG	F	VF	XF
ND(1830) Series 10	3.00	5.00	8.00	12.00	—

KM# 765s.10 MUN
4.0000 g., Cast Bronze, 26 mm.

Date	Good	VG	F	VF	XF
ND(1830) Series 10	—	—	—	—	35.00

KM# 766.1 MUN
4.0000 g., Cast Bronze, 26 mm. **Rev:** "Sip" (10) at bottom and additional series number at left

Date	Good	VG	F	VF	XF
ND(1830) Series 1	3.00	5.00	8.00	12.00	—

KM# 766s.1 MUN
4.0000 g., Cast Bronze, 26 mm.

Date	Good	VG	F	VF	XF
ND(1830) Series 1	—	—	—	—	35.00

KM# 766.2 MUN
4.0000 g., Cast Bronze, 26 mm. **Rev:** "Sip" (10) at bottom and additional series number at left

Date	Good	VG	F	VF	XF
ND(1830) Series 2	3.00	5.00	8.00	12.00	—

KM# 766s.2 MUN
4.0000 g., Cast Bronze, 26 mm.

Date	Good	VG	F	VF	XF
ND(1830) Series 2	—	—	—	—	35.00

KM# 766.3 MUN
4.0000 g., Cast Bronze, 26 mm. **Rev:** "Sip" (10) at bottom and additional series number at left

Date	Good	VG	F	VF	XF
ND(1830) Series 3	3.00	5.00	8.00	12.00	—

KM# 766s.3 MUN
4.0000 g., Cast Bronze, 26 mm.

Date	Good	VG	F	VF	XF
ND(1830) Series 3	—	—	—	—	35.00

KM# 766.4 MUN
4.0000 g., Cast Bronze, 26 mm. **Rev:** "Sip" (10) at bottom and additional series number at left

Date	Good	VG	F	VF	XF
ND(1830) Series 4	3.00	5.00	8.00	12.00	—

KM# 766s.4 MUN
4.0000 g., Cast Bronze, 26 mm.

Date	Good	VG	F	VF	XF
ND(1830) Series 4	—	—	—	—	35.00

KM# 766.5 MUN
4.0000 g., Cast Bronze, 26 mm. **Rev:** "Sip" (10) at bottom and additional series number at left

Date	Good	VG	F	VF	XF
ND(1830) Series 5	3.00	5.00	8.00	12.00	—

KM# 766s.5 MUN
4.0000 g., Cast Bronze, 26 mm.

Date	Good	VG	F	VF	XF
ND(1830) Series 5	—	—	—	—	35.00

KM# 766.6 MUN
4.0000 g., Cast Bronze, 26 mm. **Rev:** "Sip" (10) at bottom and additional series number at left

Date	Good	VG	F	VF	XF
ND(1830) Series 6	3.00	5.00	8.00	12.00	—

KM# 766s.6 MUN
4.0000 g., Cast Bronze, 26 mm.

Date	Good	VG	F	VF	XF
ND(1830) Series 6	—	—	—	—	35.00

KM# 766.11 MUN
4.0000 g., Cast Bronze, 26 mm. **Rev:** Star at left

Date	Good	VG	F	VF	XF
ND(1830) Series 1	1.75	2.25	3.50	5.00	—

KANGWHA TOWNSHIP MILITARY OFFICE

(Kang Hwa Kwal Li Yong)

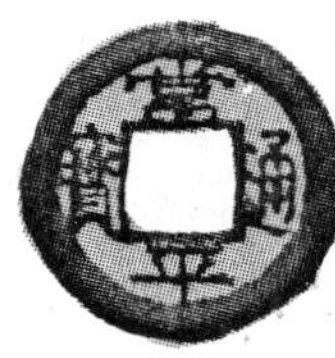

KM# 771 MUN
4.0000 g., Cast Bronze, 22 mm. **Rev:** "Sim" at top, "Won" (first) at bottom, dot at left **Note:** Struck at Kang Hwa Kwal Li Yong.

Date	Good	VG	F	VF	XF
ND(1883)	2.75	3.00	4.00	6.00	—

KM# 772.1 MUN
4.0000 g., Cast Bronze, 25 mm. **Rev:** "Won" (first) at bottom, series number at left

Date	Good	VG	F	VF	XF
ND(1883) Series 1	6.00	10.00	16.50	25.00	—

KM# 772.2 MUN
4.0000 g., Cast Bronze, 25 mm. **Rev:** "Won" (first) at bottom, series number at left

Date	Good	VG	F	VF	XF
ND(1883) Series 2	6.00	10.00	16.50	25.00	—

KM# 772.3 MUN
4.0000 g., Cast Bronze, 25 mm. **Rev:** "Won" (first) at bottom, series number at left

Date	Good	VG	F	VF	XF
ND(1883) Series 3	6.00	10.00	16.50	25.00	—

KM# 772.4 MUN
4.0000 g., Cast Bronze, 25 mm. **Rev:** "Won" (first) at bottom, series number at left

Date	Good	VG	F	VF	XF
ND(1883) Series 4	6.00	10.00	16.50	25.00	—

KM# 772.5 MUN
4.0000 g., Cast Bronze, 25 mm. **Rev:** "Won" (first) at bottom, series number at left

Date	Good	VG	F	VF	XF
ND(1883) Series 5	6.00	10.00	16.50	25.00	—

KM# 772.6 MUN
4.0000 g., Cast Bronze, 25 mm. **Rev:** "Won" (first) at bottom, series number at left

Date	Good	VG	F	VF	XF
ND(1883) Series 6	6.00	10.00	16.50	25.00	—

KM# 772.7 MUN
4.0000 g., Cast Bronze, 25 mm. **Rev:** "Won" (first) at bottom, series number at left

Date	Good	VG	F	VF	XF
ND(1883) Series 7	6.00	10.00	16.50	25.00	—

KM# 772.8 MUN
4.0000 g., Cast Bronze, 25 mm. **Rev:** "Won" (first) at bottom, series number at left

Date	Good	VG	F	VF	XF
ND(1883) Series 8	6.00	10.00	16.50	25.00	—

KM# 772.9 MUN
4.0000 g., Cast Bronze, 25 mm. **Rev:** "Won" (first) at bottom, series number at left

Date	Good	VG	F	VF	XF
ND(1883) Series 9	6.00	10.00	16.50	25.00	—

KM# 772.10 MUN
4.0000 g., Cast Bronze, 25 mm. **Rev:** "Won" (first) at bottom, series number at left

Date	Good	VG	F	VF	XF
ND(1883) Series 10	6.00	10.00	16.50	25.00	—

KM# 773 MUN
4.0000 g., Cast Bronze, 22 mm. **Rev:** "Won" (first) at bottom, series number at right, circle at left

Date	Good	VG	F	VF	XF
ND(1883)	40.00	80.00	125	200	—

KM# 774.1 MUN
4.0000 g., Cast Bronze, 23 mm. **Rev:** "Won" (first) at bottom, series number at right, crescent at left **Note:** Wide rim.

Date	Good	VG	F	VF	XF
ND(1883) Series 1	6.00	10.00	16.50	25.00	—

KM# 774.2 MUN
4.0000 g., Cast Bronze, 23 mm. **Rev:** "Won" (first) at bottom, series number at right, crescent at left **Note:** Wide rim.

Date	Good	VG	F	VF	XF
ND(1883) Series 2	6.00	10.00	16.50	25.00	—

KM# 774.3 MUN
4.0000 g., Cast Bronze, 23 mm. **Rev:** "Won" (first) at bottom, series number at right, crescent at left **Note:** Wide rim.

Date	Good	VG	F	VF	XF
ND(1883) Series 3	6.00	10.00	16.50	25.00	—

KM# 774.4 MUN
4.0000 g., Cast Bronze, 23 mm. **Rev:** "Won" (first) at bottom, series number at right, crescent at left **Note:** Wide rim.

Date	Good	VG	F	VF	XF
ND(1883) Series 4	6.00	10.00	16.50	25.00	—

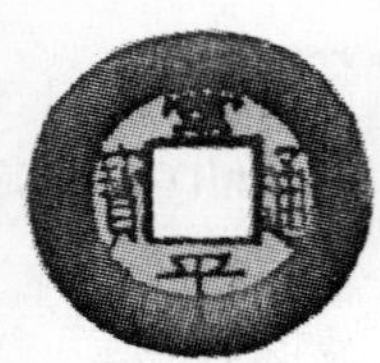

KM# 774.5 MUN
4.0000 g., Cast Bronze, 23 mm. **Rev:** "Won" (first) at bottom, series number at right, crescent at left **Note:** Wide rim.

Date	Good	VG	F	VF	XF
ND(1883) Series 5	6.00	10.00	16.50	25.00	—

KM# 774.6 MUN
4.0000 g., Cast Bronze, 23 mm. **Rev:** "Won" (first) at bottom, series number at right, crescent at left **Note:** Wide rim.

Date	Good	VG	F	VF	XF
ND(1883) Series 6	6.00	10.00	16.50	25.00	—

KM# 774.7 MUN
4.0000 g., Cast Bronze, 23 mm. **Rev:** "Won" (first) at bottom, series number at right, crescent at left **Note:** Wide rim.

Date	Good	VG	F	VF	XF
ND(1883) Series 7	6.00	10.00	16.50	25.00	—

KM# 774.8 MUN
4.0000 g., Cast Bronze, 23 mm. **Rev:** "Won" (first) at bottom, series number at right, crescent at left **Note:** Wide rim.

Date	Good	VG	F	VF	XF
ND(1883) Series 8	6.00	10.00	16.50	25.00	—

KM# 774.9 MUN
4.0000 g., Cast Bronze, 23 mm. **Rev:** "Won" (first) at bottom, series number at right, crescent at left **Note:** Wide rim.

Date	Good	VG	F	VF	XF
ND(1883) Series 9	6.00	10.00	16.50	25.00	—

KM# 774.10 MUN
4.0000 g., Cast Bronze, 23 mm. **Rev:** "Won" (first) at bottom, series number at right, crescent at left **Note:** Wide rim.

Date	Good	VG	F	VF	XF
ND(1883) Series 10	6.00	10.00	16.50	25.00	—

KM# A774.1 MUN
4.0000 g., Cast Bronze, 21 mm. **Rev:** "Won" (first) at bottom, series number at right, crescent at left **Note:** Narrow rim.

Date	Good	VG	F	VF	XF
ND(1883) Series 1	6.00	10.00	16.50	25.00	—

KM# A774.2 MUN
4.0000 g., Cast Bronze, 21 mm. **Rev:** "Won" (first) at bottom, series number at right, crescent at left **Note:** Narrow rim.

Date	Good	VG	F	VF	XF
ND(1883) Series 2	6.00	10.00	16.50	25.00	—

KM# A774.3 MUN
4.0000 g., Cast Bronze, 21 mm. **Rev:** "Won" (first) at bottom, series number at right, crescent at left **Note:** Narrow rim.

Date	Good	VG	F	VF	XF
ND(1883) Series 3	6.00	10.00	16.50	25.00	—

KM# A774.4 MUN
4.0000 g., Cast Bronze, 21 mm. **Rev:** "Won" (first) at bottom, series number at right, crescent at left **Note:** Narrow rim.

Date	Good	VG	F	VF	XF
ND(1883) Series 4	6.00	10.00	16.50	25.00	—

KM# A774.5 MUN
4.0000 g., Cast Bronze, 21 mm. **Rev:** "Won" (first) at bottom, series number at right, crescent at left **Note:** Narrow rim.

Date	Good	VG	F	VF	XF
ND(1883) Series 5	6.00	10.00	16.50	25.00	—

KM# A774.6 MUN
4.0000 g., Cast Bronze, 21 mm. **Rev:** "Won" (first) at bottom, series number at right, crescent at left **Note:** Narrow rim.

Date	Good	VG	F	VF	XF
ND(1883) Series 6	6.00	10.00	16.50	25.00	—

KM# A774.7 MUN
4.0000 g., Cast Bronze, 21 mm. **Rev:** "Won" (first) at bottom, series number at right, crescent at left **Note:** Narrow rim.

Date	Good	VG	F	VF	XF
ND(1883) Series 7	6.00	10.00	16.50	25.00	—

KM# A774.8 MUN
4.0000 g., Cast Bronze, 21 mm. **Rev:** "Won" (first) at bottom, series number at right, crescent at left **Note:** Narrow rim.

Date	Good	VG	F	VF	XF
ND(1883) Series 8	6.00	10.00	16.50	25.00	—

KM# A774.9 MUN
4.0000 g., Cast Bronze, 21 mm. **Rev:** "Won" (first) at bottom, series number at right, crescent at left **Note:** Narrow rim.

Date	Good	VG	F	VF	XF
ND(1883) Series 9	6.00	10.00	16.50	25.00	—

KM# A774.10 MUN
4.0000 g., Cast Bronze, 21 mm. **Rev:** "Won" (first) at bottom, series number at right, crescent at left **Note:** Narrow rim.

Date	Good	VG	F	VF	XF
ND(1883) Series 10	6.00	10.00	16.50	25.00	—

KM# 775 5 MUN
Cast Bronze, 31 mm. **Rev:** "Sim" at top, "Won" at bottom, "Tang" at right, "O" (5) at left

Date	Good	VG	F	VF	XF
ND(1883)	5.00	9.00	18.00	25.00	—

KM# 776.1 5 MUN
Cast Bronze, 30 mm. **Rev:** Series number at bottom **Note:** Large characters.

Date	Good	VG	F	VF	XF
ND(1883) Series 1	2.00	2.75	3.50	5.00	—

KM# 776.2 5 MUN
Cast Bronze, 30 mm. **Rev:** Series number at bottom **Note:** Large characters.

Date	Good	VG	F	VF	XF
ND(1883) Series 2	2.00	2.75	3.50	5.00	—

KM# 776.3 5 MUN
Cast Bronze, 30 mm. **Rev:** Series number at bottom **Note:** Large characters.

Date	Good	VG	F	VF	XF
ND(1883) Series 3	2.00	2.75	3.50	5.00	—

KM# 776.4 5 MUN
Cast Bronze, 30 mm. **Rev:** Series number at bottom **Note:** Large characters.

Date	Good	VG	F	VF	XF
ND(1883) Series 4	2.00	2.75	3.50	5.00	—

KM# 776.5 5 MUN
Cast Bronze, 30 mm. **Rev:** Series number at bottom **Note:** Large characters.

Date	Good	VG	F	VF	XF
ND(1883) Series 5	2.00	2.75	3.50	5.00	—

KM# 776.6 5 MUN
Cast Bronze, 30 mm. **Rev:** Series number at bottom **Note:** Large characters.

Date	Good	VG	F	VF	XF
ND(1883) Series 6	2.00	2.75	3.50	5.00	—

KM# 776.7 5 MUN
Cast Bronze, 30 mm. **Rev:** Series number at bottom **Note:** Large characters.

Date	Good	VG	F	VF	XF
ND(1883) Series 7	2.00	2.75	3.50	5.00	—

KM# 776.8 5 MUN
Cast Bronze, 30 mm. **Rev:** Series number at bottom **Note:** Large characters.

Date	Good	VG	F	VF	XF
ND(1883) Series 8	2.00	2.75	3.50	5.00	—

KM# 776.9 5 MUN
Cast Bronze, 30 mm. **Rev:** Series number at bottom **Note:** Large characters.

Date	Good	VG	F	VF	XF
ND(1883) Series 9	2.00	2.75	3.50	5.00	—

KM# 776.10 5 MUN
Cast Bronze, 30 mm. **Rev:** Series number at bottom **Note:** Large characters.

Date	Good	VG	F	VF	XF
ND(1883) Series 10	2.00	2.75	3.50	5.00	—

KM# 776.11 5 MUN
Cast Bronze, 30 mm. **Rev:** Series number at bottom **Note:** Large characters.

Date	Good	VG	F	VF	XF
ND(1883) Series 11	2.00	2.75	3.50	5.00	—

KM# 777.1 5 MUN
Cast Bronze, 32 mm. **Note:** Small characters.

Date	Good	VG	F	VF	XF
ND(1883) Series 1	2.00	2.75	3.50	5.00	—

KM# 777.2 5 MUN
Cast Bronze, 32 mm. **Note:** Small characters.

Date	Good	VG	F	VF	XF
ND(1883) Series 2	2.00	2.75	3.50	5.00	—

KM# 777.3 5 MUN
Cast Bronze, 32 mm. **Note:** Small characters.

Date	Good	VG	F	VF	XF
ND(1883) Series 3	2.00	2.75	3.50	5.00	—

KM# 777.4 5 MUN
Cast Bronze, 32 mm. **Note:** Small characters.

Date	Good	VG	F	VF	XF
ND(1883) Series 4	2.00	2.75	3.50	5.00	—

KM# 777.5 5 MUN
Cast Bronze, 32 mm. **Note:** Small characters.

Date	Mintage	Good	VG	F	VF	XF
ND(1883) Series 5	1	2.00	2.75	3.50	5.00	—

KM# 777.6 5 MUN
Cast Bronze, 32 mm. **Note:** Small characters.

Date	Good	VG	F	VF	XF
ND(1883) Series 6	2.00	2.75	3.50	5.00	—

KM# 777.7 5 MUN
Cast Bronze, 32 mm. **Note:** Small characters.

Date	Good	VG	F	VF	XF
ND(1883) Series 7	2.00	2.75	3.50	5.00	—

KM# 777.8 5 MUN
Cast Bronze, 32 mm. **Note:** Small characters.

Date	Good	VG	F	VF	XF
ND(1883) Series 8	2.00	2.75	3.50	5.00	—

KM# 777.9 5 MUN
Cast Bronze, 32 mm. **Note:** Small characters.

Date	Good	VG	F	VF	XF
ND(1883) Series 9	2.00	2.75	3.50	5.00	—

KM# 777.10 5 MUN
Cast Bronze, 32 mm. **Note:** Small characters.

Date	Good	VG	F	VF	XF
ND(1883) Series 10	2.00	2.75	3.50	5.00	—

KM# 778.1 5 MUN
Cast Bronze, 32 mm. **Rev:** Crescednt below series number

Date	Good	VG	F	VF	XF
ND(1883) Series 1	8.00	12.00	20.00	30.00	—

KM# 778.2 5 MUN
Cast Bronze, 32 mm. **Rev:** Crescent below series number

Date	Good	VG	F	VF	XF
ND(1883) Series 2	8.00	12.00	20.00	30.00	—

KM# 778.3 5 MUN
Cast Bronze, 32 mm. **Rev:** Crescent below series number

Date	Good	VG	F	VF	XF
ND(1883) Series 3	8.00	12.00	20.00	30.00	—

KM# 778.4 5 MUN
Cast Bronze, 32 mm. **Rev:** Crescent below series number

Date	Good	VG	F	VF	XF
ND(1883) Series 4	8.00	12.00	20.00	30.00	—

KM# 778.5 5 MUN
Cast Bronze, 32 mm. **Rev:** Crescent below series number

Date	Good	VG	F	VF	XF
ND(1883) Series 5	8.00	12.00	20.00	30.00	—

KM# 778.6 5 MUN
Cast Bronze, 32 mm. **Rev:** Crescent below series number

Date	Good	VG	F	VF	XF
ND(1883) Series 6	8.00	12.00	20.00	30.00	—

KM# 778.7 5 MUN
Cast Bronze, 32 mm. **Rev:** Crescent below series number

Date	Good	VG	F	VF	XF
ND(1883) Series 7	8.00	12.00	20.00	30.00	—

KM# 779.1 5 MUN
Cast Bronze, 32 mm. **Rev:** Crescent at lower left

Date	Good	VG	F	VF	XF
ND(1883) Series 1	8.00	12.00	20.00	30.00	—

KM# 779.2 5 MUN
Cast Bronze, 32 mm. **Rev:** Crescent at lower left

Date	Good	VG	F	VF	XF
ND(1883) Series 2	8.00	12.00	20.00	30.00	—

KM# 779.3 5 MUN
Cast Bronze, 32 mm. **Rev:** Crescent at lower left

Date	Good	VG	F	VF	XF
ND(1883) Series 3	8.00	12.00	20.00	30.00	—

KM# 779.4 5 MUN
Cast Bronze, 32 mm. **Rev:** Crescent at lower left

Date	Good	VG	F	VF	XF
ND(1883) Series 4	8.00	12.00	20.00	30.00	—

KM# 779.5 5 MUN
Cast Bronze, 32 mm. **Rev:** Crescent at lower left

Date	Good	VG	F	VF	XF
ND(1883) Series 5	8.00	12.00	20.00	30.00	—

KM# 779.6 5 MUN
Cast Bronze, 32 mm. **Rev:** Crescent at lower left

Date	Good	VG	F	VF	XF
ND(1883) Series 6	8.00	12.00	20.00	30.00	—

KM# 779.7 5 MUN
Cast Bronze, 32 mm. **Rev:** Crescent at lower left

Date	Good	VG	F	VF	XF
ND(1883) Series 7	8.00	12.00	20.00	30.00	—

KM# 779.9 5 MUN
Cast Bronze, 32 mm. **Rev:** Crescent at lower left

Date	Good	VG	F	VF	XF
ND(1883) Series 9	8.00	12.00	20.00	3.00	—

KM# 779.10 5 MUN
Cast Bronze, 32 mm. **Rev:** Crescent at lower left

Date	Good	VG	F	VF	XF
ND(1883) Series 10	8.00	12.00	20.00	30.00	—

KM# 779.11 5 MUN
Cast Bronze, 32 mm. **Rev:** Crescent at lower left

Date	Good	VG	F	VF	XF
ND(1883) Series 11	8.00	12.00	20.00	30.00	—

KM# 779.12 5 MUN
Cast Bronze, 32 mm. **Rev:** Crescent at lower left

Date	Good	VG	F	VF	XF
ND(1883) Series 12	8.00	12.00	20.00	30.00	—

KM# 779.13 5 MUN
Cast Bronze, 32 mm. **Rev:** Crescent at lower left

Date	Good	VG	F	VF	XF
ND(1883) Series 13	8.00	12.00	20.00	30.00	—

KAESONG TOWNSHIP MILITARY OFFICE

(Kae Song Kwal Li Yong)

KM# 793.1 MUN
4.0000 g., Cast Bronze, 24.5 mm. **Rev:** Circle at right, series number at bottom

Date	Good	VG	F	VF	XF
ND(1816) Series 1	3.00	5.00	8.00	12.00	—

KM# 793.2 MUN
4.0000 g., Cast Bronze, 32 mm. **Rev:** Circle at right, series number at bottom

Date	Good	VG	F	VF	XF
ND(1816) Series 2	3.00	5.00	8.00	12.00	—

KM# 793.3 MUN
4.0000 g., Cast Bronze, 32 mm. **Rev:** Circle at right, series number at bottom

Date	Good	VG	F	VF	XF
ND(1816) Series 3	3.00	5.00	8.00	12.00	—

KM# 793.4 MUN
4.0000 g., Cast Bronze, 32 mm. **Rev:** Circle at right, series number at bottom

Date	Good	VG	F	VF	XF
ND(1816) Series 4	3.00	5.00	8.00	12.00	—

KM# 793.6 MUN
4.0000 g., Cast Bronze, 32 mm. **Rev:** Circle at right, series number at bottom

Date	Good	VG	F	VF	XF
ND(1816) Series 6	3.00	5.00	8.00	12.00	—

KM# 793.7 MUN
4.0000 g., Cast Bronze, 32 mm. **Rev:** Circle at right, series number at bottom

Date	Good	VG	F	VF	XF
ND(1816) Series 7	3.00	5.00	8.00	12.00	—

KM# 793.8 MUN
4.0000 g., Cast Bronze, 32 mm. **Rev:** Circle at right, series number at bottom

Date	Good	VG	F	VF	XF
ND(1816) Series 8	3.00	5.00	8.00	12.00	—

KM# 793.9 MUN
4.0000 g., Cast Bronze, 32 mm. **Rev:** Circle at right, series number at bottom

Date	Good	VG	F	VF	XF
ND(1816) Series 9	3.00	5.00	8.00	12.00	—

KM# 793.10 MUN
4.0000 g., Cast Bronze, 32 mm. **Rev:** Circle at right, series number at bottom

Date	Good	VG	F	VF	XF
ND(1816) Series 10	3.00	5.00	8.00	12.00	—

KM# 793.11 MUN
4.0000 g., Cast Bronze, 32 mm. **Rev:** Star at lower left

Date	Good	VG	F	VF	XF
ND(1816) Series 1	3.00	5.00	8.00	12.00	—

KM# 793.17 MUN
4.0000 g., Cast Bronze, 32 mm. **Rev:** Star at upper left

Date	Good	VG	F	VF	XF
ND(1816) Series 7	3.00	5.00	8.00	12.00	—

KM# 794.1 MUN
4.0000 g., Cast Bronze, 24 mm. **Rev:** Circle at left, series number at bottom

Date	Good	VG	F	VF	XF
ND(1816) Series 1	3.00	5.00	8.00	12.00	—

KM# 794.2 MUN
4.0000 g., Cast Bronze, 24 mm. **Rev:** Circle at left, series number at bottom

Date	Good	VG	F	VF	XF
ND(1816) Series 2	3.00	5.00	8.00	12.00	—

KM# 794.3 MUN
4.0000 g., Cast Bronze, 24 mm. **Rev:** Circle at left, series number at bottom

Date	Good	VG	F	VF	XF
ND(1816) Series 3	3.00	5.00	8.00	12.00	—

KM# 794.4 MUN
4.0000 g., Cast Bronze, 24 mm. **Rev:** Circle at left, series number at bottom

Date	Good	VG	F	VF	XF
ND(1816) Series 4	3.00	5.00	8.00	12.00	—

KM# 794.5 MUN
4.0000 g., Cast Bronze, 24 mm. **Rev:** Circle at left, series number at bottom

Date	Good	VG	F	VF	XF
ND(1816) Series 5	3.00	5.00	8.00	12.00	—

KM# 794.6 MUN
4.0000 g., Cast Bronze, 24 mm. **Rev:** Circle at left, series number at bottom

Date	Good	VG	F	VF	XF
ND(1816) Series 6	3.00	5.00	8.00	12.00	—

KM# 794.7 MUN
4.0000 g., Cast Bronze, 24 mm. **Rev:** Circle at left, series number at bottom

Date	Good	VG	F	VF	XF
ND(1816) Series 7	3.00	5.00	8.00	12.00	—

KM# 794.8 MUN
4.0000 g., Cast Bronze, 24 mm. **Rev:** Circle at left, series number at bottom

Date	Good	VG	F	VF	XF
ND(1816) Series 8	3.00	5.00	8.00	12.00	—

KM# 794.9 MUN
4.0000 g., Cast Bronze, 24 mm. **Rev:** Circle at left, series number at bottom

Date	Good	VG	F	VF	XF
ND(1816) Series 9	3.00	5.00	8.00	12.00	—

KM# 794.10 MUN
4.0000 g., Cast Bronze, 24 mm. **Rev:** Circle at left, series number at bottom

Date	Good	VG	F	VF	XF
ND(1816) Series 10	3.00	5.00	8.00	12.00	—

KM# 795.1 MUN
4.0000 g., Cast Bronze, 25 mm. **Rev:** Crescent at right, series number at bottom

Date	Good	VG	F	VF	XF
ND(1816) Series 1	3.00	5.00	8.00	12.00	—

KM# 795.2 MUN
4.0000 g., Cast Bronze, 25 mm. **Rev:** Crescent at right, series number at bottom

Date	Good	VG	F	VF	XF
ND(1816) Series 2	3.00	5.00	8.00	12.00	—

KM# 795.3 MUN
4.0000 g., Cast Bronze, 25 mm. **Rev:** Crescent at right, series number at bottom

Date	Good	VG	F	VF	XF
ND(1816) Series 3	3.00	5.00	8.00	12.00	—

KM# 795.4 MUN
4.0000 g., Cast Bronze, 25 mm. **Rev:** Crescent at right, series number at bottom **Note:** Struck at Kae Song Kwal Li Yong.

Date	Good	VG	F	VF	XF
ND(1816) Series 4	3.00	5.00	8.00	12.00	—

KM# 795.5 MUN
4.0000 g., Cast Bronze, 25 mm. **Rev:** Crescent at right, series number at bottom

Date	Good	VG	F	VF	XF
ND(1816) Series 5	3.00	5.00	8.00	12.00	—

KM# 795.6 MUN
4.0000 g., Cast Bronze, 25 mm. **Rev:** Crescent at right, series number at bottom

Date	Good	VG	F	VF	XF
ND(1816) Series 6	3.00	5.00	8.00	12.00	—

KM# 795.7 MUN
4.0000 g., Cast Bronze, 25 mm. **Rev:** Crescent at right, series number at bottom

Date	Good	VG	F	VF	XF
ND(1816) Series 7	3.00	5.00	8.00	12.00	—

KM# 795.8 MUN
4.0000 g., Cast Bronze, 25 mm. **Rev:** Crescent at right, series number at bottom

Date	Good	VG	F	VF	XF
ND(1816) Series 8	3.00	5.00	8.00	12.00	—

KM# 795.9 MUN
4.0000 g., Cast Bronze, 25 mm. **Rev:** Crescent at right, series number at bottom

Date	Good	VG	F	VF	XF
ND(1816) Series 9	3.00	5.00	8.00	12.00	—

KM# 795.10 MUN
4.0000 g., Cast Bronze, 25 mm. **Rev:** Crescent at right, series number at bottom

Date	Good	VG	F	VF	XF
ND(1816) Series 10	3.00	5.00	8.00	12.00	—

KM# 797.4 MUN
4.0000 g., Cast Bronze, 25 mm. **Rev:** "Ch'on" at bottom, "Sip" (10) at right, additional series number at left

Date	Good	VG	F	VF	XF
ND(1836) Series 4	3.00	5.00	8.00	12.00	—

KM# 797.5 MUN
4.0000 g., Cast Bronze, 25 mm. **Rev:** Struck at Kae Song Kwal Li Yong.

Date	Good	VG	F	VF	XF
ND(1836) Series 5	3.00	5.00	8.00	12.00	—

KM# A795.1 MUN
4.0000 g., Cast Bronze, 25.5 mm. **Rev:** Crescent at right, series number at bottom **Note:** Small characters.

Date	Good	VG	F	VF	XF
ND(1836) Series 1	3.00	6.00	10.00	15.00	—

KM# A795.2 MUN
4.0000 g., Cast Bronze, 25.5 mm. **Rev:** Crescent at right, series number at bottom **Note:** Small characters.

Date	Good	VG	F	VF	XF
ND(1836) Series 2	3.00	6.00	10.00	15.00	—

KM# A795.3 MUN
4.0000 g., Cast Bronze, 25.5 mm. **Rev:** Crescent at right, series number at bottom **Note:** Small characters.

Date	Good	VG	F	VF	XF
ND(1836) Series 3	3.00	6.00	10.00	15.00	—

KM# A795.4 MUN
4.0000 g., Cast Bronze, 25.5 mm. **Rev:** Crescent at right, series number at bottom **Note:** Small characters.

Date	Good	VG	F	VF	XF
ND(1836) Series 4	3.00	6.00	10.00	15.00	—

KM# A795.5 MUN
4.0000 g., Cast Bronze, 25.5 mm. **Rev:** Crescent at right, series number at bottom **Note:** Small characters.

Date	Good	VG	F	VF	XF
ND(1836) Series 5	3.00	6.00	10.00	15.00	—

KM# A795.6 MUN
4.0000 g., Cast Bronze, 25.5 mm. **Rev:** Crescent at right, series number at bottom **Note:** Small characters.

Date	Good	VG	F	VF	XF
ND(1836) Series 6	3.00	6.00	10.00	15.00	—

KM# A795.7 MUN
4.0000 g., Cast Bronze, 25.5 mm. **Rev:** Crescent at right, series number at bottom **Note:** Small characters.

Date	Good	VG	F	VF	XF
ND(1836) Series 7	3.00	6.00	10.00	15.00	—

KM# A795.8 MUN
4.0000 g., Cast Bronze, 25.5 mm. **Rev:** Crescent at right, series number at bottom **Note:** Small characters.

Date	Good	VG	F	VF	XF
ND(1836) Series 8	3.00	6.00	10.00	15.00	—

KM# A795.9 MUN
4.0000 g., Cast Bronze, 25.5 mm. **Rev:** Crescent at right, series number at bottom **Note:** Small characters.

Date	Good	VG	F	VF	XF
ND(1836) Series 9	3.00	6.00	10.00	15.00	—

KM# A795.10 MUN
4.0000 g., Cast Bronze, 25.5 mm. **Rev:** Crescent at right, series number at bottom **Note:** Small characters.

Date	Good	VG	F	VF	XF
ND(1836) Series 10	3.00	6.00	10.00	15.00	—

KM# A795.13 MUN
4.0000 g., Cast Bronze, 25.5 mm. **Rev:** Star at lower left **Note:** Small characters.

Date	Good	VG	F	VF	XF
ND(1836) Series 3	3.00	6.00	10.00	15.00	—

KM# B795.1 MUN
4.0000 g., Cast Bronze, 25 mm. **Rev:** Crescent at left, series number at bottom **Note:** Small characters.

Date	Good	VG	F	VF	XF
ND(1836) Series 1	3.00	5.00	8.00	12.00	—

KM# B795.2 MUN
4.0000 g., Cast Bronze, 25 mm. **Rev:** Crescent at left, series number at bottom **Note:** Small characters.

Date	Good	VG	F	VF	XF
ND(1836) Series 2	3.00	5.00	8.00	12.00	—

KM# B795.3 MUN
4.0000 g., Cast Bronze, 25 mm. **Rev:** Crescent at left, series number at bottom **Note:** Small characters.

Date	Good	VG	F	VF	XF
ND(1836) Series 3	3.00	5.00	8.00	12.00	—

KM# B795.4 MUN
4.0000 g., Cast Bronze, 25 mm. **Rev:** Crescent at left, series number at bottom **Note:** Small characters.

Date	Good	VG	F	VF	XF
ND(1836) Series 4	3.00	5.00	8.00	12.00	—

KM# B795.5 MUN
4.0000 g., Cast Bronze, 25 mm. **Rev:** Crescent at left, series number at bottom **Note:** Small characters.

Date	Good	VG	F	VF	XF
ND(1836) Series 5	3.00	5.00	8.00	12.00	—

KM# B795.6 MUN
4.0000 g., Cast Bronze, 25 mm. **Rev:** Crescent at left, series number at bottom **Note:** Small characters.

Date	Good	VG	F	VF	XF
ND(1836) Series 6	3.00	5.00	8.00	12.00	—

KM# B795.7 MUN
4.0000 g., Cast Bronze, 25 mm. **Rev:** Crescent at left, series number at bottom **Note:** Small characters.

Date	Good	VG	F	VF	XF
ND(1836) Series 7	3.00	5.00	8.00	12.00	—

KM# B795.8 MUN
4.0000 g., Cast Bronze, 25 mm. **Rev:** Crescent at left, series number at bottom **Note:** Small characters.

Date	Good	VG	F	VF	XF
ND(1836) Series 8	3.00	5.00	8.00	12.00	—

KM# B795.9 MUN
4.0000 g., Cast Bronze, 25 mm. **Rev:** Crescent at left, series number at bottom **Note:** Small characters.

Date	Good	VG	F	VF	XF
ND(1836) Series 9	3.00	5.00	8.00	12.00	—

KM# B795.10 MUN
4.0000 g., Cast Bronze, 25 mm. **Rev:** Crescent at left, series number at bottom **Note:** Small characters.

Date	Good	VG	F	VF	XF
ND(1836) Series 10	3.00	5.00	8.00	12.00	—

KM# C795.1 MUN
4.0000 g., Cast Bronze, 25 mm. **Rev:** Small crescent **Note:** Small characters, wider rims.

Date	Good	VG	F	VF	XF
ND(1836) Series 1	3.00	6.00	10.00	15.00	—

KM# C795.2 MUN
4.0000 g., Cast Bronze, 25 mm. **Rev:** Small crescent **Note:** Small characters, wider rims.

Date	Good	VG	F	VF	XF
ND(1836) Series 2	3.00	6.00	10.00	15.00	—

KM# C795.3 MUN
4.0000 g., Cast Bronze, 25 mm. **Rev:** Small crescent **Note:** Small characters, wider rims.

Date	Good	VG	F	VF	XF
ND(1836) Series 3	3.00	6.00	10.00	15.00	—

KM# C795.4 MUN
4.0000 g., Cast Bronze, 25 mm. **Rev:** Small crescent **Note:** Small characters, wider rims.

Date	Good	VG	F	VF	XF
ND(1836) Series 4	3.00	6.00	10.00	15.00	—

KM# C795.5 MUN
4.0000 g., Cast Bronze, 25 mm. **Rev:** Small crescent **Note:** Small characters, wider rims.

Date	Good	VG	F	VF	XF
ND(1836) Series 5	3.00	6.00	10.00	15.00	—

KM# C795.6 MUN
4.0000 g., Cast Bronze, 25 mm. **Rev:** Small crescent **Note:** Small characters, wider rims.

Date	Good	VG	F	VF	XF
ND(1836) Series 6	3.00	6.00	10.00	15.00	—

KM# C795.7 MUN
4.0000 g., Cast Bronze, 25 mm. **Rev:** Small crescent **Note:** Small characters, wider rims.

Date	Good	VG	F	VF	XF
ND(1836) Series 7	3.00	6.00	10.00	15.00	—

KM# C795.8 MUN
4.0000 g., Cast Bronze, 25 mm. **Rev:** Small crescent **Note:** Small characters, wider rims.

Date	Good	VG	F	VF	XF
ND(1836) Series 8	3.00	6.00	10.00	15.00	—

KM# C795.9 MUN
4.0000 g., Cast Bronze, 25 mm. **Rev:** Small crescent **Note:** Small characters, wider rims.

Date	Good	VG	F	VF	XF
ND(1836) Series 9	3.00	6.00	10.00	15.00	—

KM# C795.10 MUN
4.0000 g., Cast Bronze, 25 mm. **Rev:** Small crescent **Note:** Small characters, wider rims.

Date	Good	VG	F	VF	XF
ND(1836) Series 10	3.00	6.00	10.00	15.00	—

KM# 796.1 MUN
4.0000 g., Cast Bronze, 25 mm. **Rev:** "Ch'on" at bottom, series number at right

Date	Good	VG	F	VF	XF
ND(1836) Series 1	3.00	5.00	8.00	12.00	—

KM# 796.2 MUN
4.0000 g., Cast Bronze, 25 mm. **Rev:** "Ch'on" at bottom, series number at right

Date	Good	VG	F	VF	XF
ND(1836) Series 2	3.00	5.00	8.00	12.00	—

KM# 796.3 MUN
4.0000 g., Cast Bronze, 25 mm. **Rev:** "Ch'on" at bottom, series number at right

Date	Good	VG	F	VF	XF
ND(1836) Series 3	3.00	5.00	8.00	12.00	—

KM# 796.4 MUN
4.0000 g., Cast Bronze, 25 mm. **Rev:** "Ch'on" at bottom, series number at right

Date	Good	VG	F	VF	XF
ND(1836) Series 4	3.00	5.00	8.00	12.00	—

KM# 796.5 MUN
4.0000 g., Cast Bronze, 25 mm. **Rev:** "Ch'on" at bottom, series number at right

Date	Good	VG	F	VF	XF
ND(1836) Series 5	3.00	5.00	8.00	12.00	—

KM# 796.6 MUN
4.0000 g., Cast Bronze, 25 mm. **Rev:** "Ch'on" at bottom, series number at right

Date	Good	VG	F	VF	XF
ND(1836) Series 6	3.00	5.00	8.00	12.00	—

KM# 796.7 MUN
4.0000 g., Cast Bronze, 25 mm. **Rev:** "Ch'on" at bottom, series number at right

Date	Good	VG	F	VF	XF
ND(1836) Series 7	3.00	5.00	8.00	12.00	—

KM# 796.8 MUN
4.0000 g., Cast Bronze, 25 mm. **Rev:** "Ch'on" at bottom, series number at right

Date	Good	VG	F	VF	XF
ND(1836) Series 8	3.00	5.00	8.00	12.00	—

KM# 796.9 MUN
4.0000 g., Cast Bronze, 25 mm. **Rev:** "Ch'on" at bottom, series number at right

Date	Good	VG	F	VF	XF
ND(1836) Series 9	3.00	5.00	8.00	12.00	—

KM# 796.10 MUN
4.0000 g., Cast Bronze, 25 mm. **Rev:** "Ch'on" at bottom, series number at right

Date	Good	VG	F	VF	XF
ND(1836) Series 10	3.00	5.00	8.00	12.00	—

KM# 797.1 MUN
4.0000 g., Cast Bronze, 25 mm. **Rev:** "Ch'on" at bottom, "Sip" (10) at right, additional series number at left

Date	Good	VG	F	VF	XF
ND(1836) Series 1	3.00	5.00	8.00	12.00	—

KM# 797.2 MUN
4.0000 g., Cast Bronze, 25 mm. **Rev:** "Ch'on" at bottom, "Sip" (10) at right, additional series number at left

Date	Good	VG	F	VF	XF
ND(1836) Series 2	3.00	5.00	8.00	12.00	—

KM# 797.3 MUN
4.0000 g., Cast Bronze, 25 mm. **Rev:** "Ch'on" at bottom, "Sip" (10) at right, additional series number at left

Date	Good	VG	F	VF	XF
ND(1836) Series 3	3.00	5.00	8.00	12.00	—

KM# 798.1 MUN
4.0000 g., Cast Bronze, 25 mm. **Rev:** "Ch'on" at bottom, series number at right, crescent at left

Date	Good	VG	F	VF	XF
ND(1836) Series 1	3.00	5.00	8.00	12.00	—

KM# 798.2 MUN
4.0000 g., Cast Bronze, 25 mm. **Rev:** "Ch'on" at bottom, series number at right, crescent at left

Date	Good	VG	F	VF	XF
ND(1836) Series 2	3.00	5.00	8.00	12.00	—

KM# 798.3 MUN
4.0000 g., Cast Bronze, 25 mm. **Rev:** "Ch'on" at bottom, series number at right, crescent at left

Date	Good	VG	F	VF	XF
ND(1836) Series 3	3.00	5.00	8.00	12.00	—

KM# 799.1 MUN
4.0000 g., Cast Bronze, 25.5 mm. **Rev:** "Chi" at bottom, series number at right

Date	Good	VG	F	VF	XF
ND(1836) Series 1	3.00	5.00	8.00	12.00	—

KM# 799.2 MUN
4.0000 g., Cast Bronze, 25.5 mm. **Rev:** "Chi" at bottom, series number at right

Date	Good	VG	F	VF	XF
ND(1836) Series 2	3.00	5.00	8.00	12.00	—

KM# 799.3 MUN
4.0000 g., Cast Bronze, 25.5 mm. **Rev:** "Chi" at bottom, series number at right

Date	Good	VG	F	VF	XF
ND(1836) Series 3	3.00	5.00	8.00	12.00	—

KM# 799.4 MUN
4.0000 g., Cast Bronze, 25.5 mm. **Rev:** "Chi" at bottom, series number at right

Date	Good	VG	F	VF	XF
ND(1836) Series 4	3.00	5.00	8.00	12.00	—

KM# 799.5 MUN
4.0000 g., Cast Bronze, 25.5 mm. **Rev:** "Chi" at bottom, series number at right

Date	Good	VG	F	VF	XF
ND(1836) Series 5	3.00	5.00	8.00	12.00	—

KM# 799.6 MUN
4.0000 g., Cast Bronze, 25.5 mm. **Rev:** "Chi" at bottom, series number at right

Date	Good	VG	F	VF	XF
ND(1836) Series 6	3.00	5.00	8.00	12.00	—

KM# 799.7 MUN
4.0000 g., Cast Bronze, 25.5 mm. **Rev:** "Chi" at bottom, series number at right

Date	Good	VG	F	VF	XF
ND(1836) Series 7	3.00	5.00	8.00	12.00	—

KM# 799.8 MUN
4.0000 g., Cast Bronze, 25.5 mm. **Rev:** "Chi" at bottom, series number at right

Date	Good	VG	F	VF	XF
ND(1836) Series 8	3.00	5.00	8.00	12.00	—

KM# 799.9 MUN
4.0000 g., Cast Bronze, 25.5 mm. **Rev:** "Chi" at bottom, series number at right

Date	Good	VG	F	VF	XF
ND(1836) Series 9	3.00	5.00	8.00	12.00	—

KM# 799.10 MUN
4.0000 g., Cast Bronze, 25.5 mm. **Rev:** "Chi" at bottom, series number at right

Date	Good	VG	F	VF	XF
ND(1836) Series 10	3.00	5.00	8.00	12.00	—

KM# 800.1 MUN
4.0000 g., Cast Bronze, 24.5 mm. **Rev:** "Chi" at bottom, "Sip" (10) at right, additional series number at left

Date	Good	VG	F	VF	XF
ND(1836) Series 1	3.00	5.00	8.00	12.00	—

KM# 800.2 MUN
4.0000 g., Cast Bronze, 24.5 mm. **Rev:** "Chi" at bottom, "Sip" (10) at right, additional series number at left

Date	Good	VG	F	VF	XF
ND(1836) Series 2	3.00	5.00	8.00	12.00	—

KM# 800.3 MUN
4.0000 g., Cast Bronze, 24.5 mm. **Rev:** "Chi" at bottom, "Sip" (10) at right, additional series number at left

Date	Good	VG	F	VF	XF
ND(1836) Series 3	3.00	5.00	8.00	12.00	—

KM# 800.4 MUN
4.0000 g., Cast Bronze, 24.5 mm. **Rev:** "Chi" at bottom, "Sip" (10) at right, additional series number at left

Date	Good	VG	F	VF	XF
ND(1836) Series 4	3.00	5.00	8.00	12.00	—

KM# 800.5 MUN
4.0000 g., Cast Bronze, 24.5 mm. **Rev:** "Chi" at bottom, "Sip" (10) at right, additional series number at left

Date	Good	VG	F	VF	XF
ND(1836) Series 5	3.00	5.00	8.00	12.00	—

KM# 800.6 MUN
4.0000 g., Cast Bronze, 24.5 mm. **Rev:** "Chi" at bottom, "Sip" (10) at right, additional series number at left

Date	Good	VG	F	VF	XF
ND(1836) Series 6	3.00	5.00	8.00	12.00	—

KM# 800.7 MUN
4.0000 g., Cast Bronze, 24.5 mm. **Rev:** "Chi" at bottom, "Sip" (10) at right, additional series number at left

Date	Good	VG	F	VF	XF
ND(1836) Series 7	3.00	5.00	8.00	12.00	—

KM# 800.8 MUN
4.0000 g., Cast Bronze, 24.5 mm. **Rev:** "Chi" at bottom, "Sip" (10) at right, additional series number at left

Date	Good	VG	F	VF	XF
ND(1836) Series 8	3.00	5.00	8.00	12.00	—

KM# 800.9 MUN
4.0000 g., Cast Bronze, 24.5 mm. **Rev:** "Chi" at bottom, "Sip" (10) at right, additional series number at left

Date	Good	VG	F	VF	XF
ND(1836) Series 9	3.00	5.00	8.00	12.00	—

KM# 801.2 MUN
4.0000 g., Cast Bronze, 25 mm. **Rev:** "Chi" at bottom, "I" (2) at right, "Sip" (10) at left

Date	Good	VG	F	VF	XF
ND(1836) Series 2	3.00	5.00	8.00	12.00	—

KM# 802.1 MUN
4.0000 g., Cast Bronze, 25 mm. **Rev:** "Il" (sun) at bottom, series number at right

Date	Good	VG	F	VF	XF
ND(1836) Series 1	3.00	5.00	8.00	12.00	—

KM# 802.2 MUN
4.0000 g., Cast Bronze, 25 mm. **Rev:** "Il" (sun) at bottom, series number at right

Date	Good	VG	F	VF	XF
ND(1836) Series 2	3.00	5.00	8.00	12.00	—

KM# 802.3 MUN
4.0000 g., Cast Bronze, 25 mm. **Rev:** "Il" (sun) at bottom, series number at right

Date	Good	VG	F	VF	XF
ND(1836) Series 3	3.00	5.00	8.00	12.00	—

KM# 802.4 MUN
4.0000 g., Cast Bronze, 25 mm. **Rev:** "Il" (sun) at bottom, series number at right

Date	Good	VG	F	VF	XF
ND(1836) Series 4	3.00	5.00	8.00	12.00	—

KM# 802.5 MUN
4.0000 g., Cast Bronze, 25 mm. **Rev:** "Il" (sun) at bottom, series number at right

Date	Good	VG	F	VF	XF
ND(1836) Series 5	3.00	5.00	8.00	12.00	—

KM# 802.6 MUN
4.0000 g., Cast Bronze, 25 mm. **Rev:** "Il" (sun) at bottom, series number at right

Date	Good	VG	F	VF	XF
ND(1836) Series 6	3.00	5.00	8.00	12.00	—

KM# 802.7 MUN
4.0000 g., Cast Bronze, 25 mm. **Rev:** "Il" (sun) at bottom, series number at right

Date	Good	VG	F	VF	XF
ND(1836) Series 7	3.00	5.00	8.00	12.00	—

KM# 802.8 MUN
4.0000 g., Cast Bronze, 25 mm. **Rev:** "Il" (sun) at bottom, series number at right

Date	Good	VG	F	VG	XF
ND(1836)	1.75	2.75	3.50	5.00	—

KM# 802.9 MUN
4.0000 g., Cast Brass or Copper, 25 mm. **Rev:** "Il" (sun) at bottom, series number at right

Date	Good	VG	F	VF	XF
ND(1836) Series 9	3.00	5.00	8.00	12.00	—

KM# 802.10 MUN
4.0000 g., Cast Bronze, 25 mm. **Rev:** "Il" (sun) at bottom, series number at right

Date	Good	VG	F	VF	XF
ND(1836) Series 10	3.00	5.00	8.00	12.00	—

KM# 802.13 MUN
4.0000 g., Cast Bronze, 22 mm.

Date	Good	VG	F	VF	XF
ND(1836) Series 3	3.00	5.00	8.00	12.00	—

KM# 803.1 MUN
4.0000 g., Cast Bronze, 24.5 mm. **Rev:** "Il" (sun) at bottom, series number at left

Date	Good	VG	F	VF	XF
ND(1836) Series 1	4.00	7.00	11.00	16.00	—

KM# 803.2 MUN
4.0000 g., Cast Bronze, 24.5 mm. **Rev:** "Il" (sun) at bottom, series number at left

Date	Good	VG	F	VF	XF
ND(1836) Series 2	4.00	7.00	11.00	16.00	—

KM# 803.3 MUN
4.0000 g., Cast Bronze, 24.5 mm. **Rev:** "Il" (sun) at bottom, series number at left

Date	Good	VG	F	VF	XF
ND(1836) Series 3	4.00	7.00	11.00	16.00	—

KM# 803.4 MUN
4.0000 g., Cast Bronze, 24.5 mm. **Rev:** "Il" (sun) at bottom, series number at left

Date	Good	VG	F	VF	XF
ND(1836) Series 4	4.00	7.00	11.00	16.00	—

KM# 803.5 MUN
4.0000 g., Cast Bronze, 24.5 mm. **Rev:** "Il" (sun) at bottom, series number at left

Date	Good	VG	F	VF	XF
ND(1836) Series 5	4.00	7.00	11.00	16.00	—

KM# 803.6 MUN
4.0000 g., Cast Bronze, 24.5 mm. **Rev:** "Il" (sun) at bottom, series number at left

Date	Good	VG	F	VF	XF
ND(1836) Series 6	4.00	7.00	11.00	16.00	—

KM# 803.7 MUN
4.0000 g., Cast Bronze, 24.5 mm. **Rev:** "Il" (sun) at bottom, series number at left

Date	Good	VG	F	VF	XF
ND(1836) Series 7	4.00	7.00	11.00	16.00	—

KM# 803.8 MUN
4.0000 g., Cast Bronze, 24.5 mm. **Rev:** "Il" (sun) at bottom, series number at left

Date	Good	VG	F	VF	XF
ND(1836) Series 8	4.00	7.00	11.00	16.00	—

KM# 803.9 MUN
4.0000 g., Cast Bronze, 24.5 mm. **Rev:** "Il" (sun) at bottom, series number at left

Date	Good	VG	F	VF	XF
ND(1836) Series 9	4.00	7.00	11.00	16.00	—

KM# 803.10 MUN
4.0000 g., Cast Bronze, 24.5 mm. **Rev:** "Il" (sun) a bottom, series number at left

Date	Good	VG	F	VF	XF
ND(1836) Series 10	4.00	7.00	11.00	16.00	—

KM# 804.10 MUN
4.0000 g., Cast Bronze, 24 mm. **Rev:** "T'o" at bottom, series number at left

Date	Good	VG	F	VF	XF
ND(1836) Series 10 Rare	—	—	—	—	—

SONG (SONG DO KWAL LI YONG)

(Song Do is another name for Kae Song)

KM# 805.1 MUN
4.0000 g., Cast Bronze, 25 mm. **Rev:** "Song" at top, series number at bottom **Note:** Struck at Song Do Kwai Li Yong. (Song Do = "Kae Song").

Date	Good	VG	F	VF	XF
ND(1882) Series 1	3.00	5.00	8.00	12.00	—

KM# 805s.1 MUN
4.0000 g., Cast Bronze, 25 mm. **Note:** Struck at Song Do Kwai Li Yong. (Song Do = "Kae Song").

Date	Good	VG	F	VF	XF
ND(1882) Series 1	—	—	—	—	45.00

KM# 805.2 MUN
4.0000 g., Cast Bronze, 25 mm. **Rev:** "Song" at top, series number at bottom **Note:** Struck at Song Do Kwai Li Yong. (Song Do = "Kae Song").

Date	Good	VG	F	VF	XF
ND(1882) Series 2	3.00	5.00	8.00	12.00	—

KM# 805s.2 MUN
4.0000 g., Cast Bronze, 25 mm. **Note:** Struck at Song Do Kwai Li Yong. (Song Do = "Kae Song").

Date	Good	VG	F	VF	XF
ND(1882) Series 2	—	—	—	—	45.00

KM# 805.3 MUN
4.0000 g., Cast Bronze, 25 mm. **Rev:** "Song" at top, series number at bottom **Note:** Struck at Song Do Kwai Li Yong. (Song Do = "Kae Song").

Date	Good	VG	F	VF	XF
ND(1882) Series 3	3.00	5.00	8.00	12.00	—

KM# 805s.3 MUN
4.0000 g., Cast Bronze, 25 mm. **Note:** Struck at Song Do Kwai Li Yong. (Song Do = "Kae Song").

Date	Good	VG	F	VF	XF
ND(1882) Series 3	—	—	—	—	45.00

KM# 805.4 MUN
4.0000 g., Cast Bronze, 25 mm. **Rev:** "Song" at top, series number at bottom **Note:** Struck at Song Do Kwai Li Yong. (Song Do = "Kae Song").

Date	Good	VG	F	VF	XF
ND(1882) Series 4	3.00	5.00	8.00	12.00	—

KM# 805s.4 MUN
4.0000 g., Cast Bronze, 25 mm. **Note:** Struck at Song Do Kwai Li Yong. (Song Do = "Kae Song").

Date	Good	VG	F	VF	XF
ND(1882) Series 4	—	—	—	—	45.00

KM# 805.5 MUN
4.0000 g., Cast Bronze, 25 mm. **Rev:** "Song" at top, series number at bottom **Note:** Struck at Song Do Kwai Li Yong. (Song Do = "Kae Song").

Date	Good	VG	F	VF	XF
ND(1882) Series 5	3.00	5.00	8.00	12.00	—

KM# 805s.5 MUN
4.0000 g., Cast Bronze, 25 mm. **Note:** Struck at Song Do Kwai Li Yong. (Song Do = "Kae Song").

Date	Good	VG	F	VF	XF
ND(1882) Series 5	—	—	—	—	45.00

KM# 805.6 MUN
4.0000 g., Cast Bronze, 25 mm. **Rev:** "Song" at top, series number at bottom **Note:** Struck at Song Do Kwai Li Yong. (Song Do = "Kae Song").

Date	Good	VG	F	VF	XF
ND(1882) Series 6	3.00	5.00	8.00	12.00	—

KM# 805s.6 MUN
4.0000 g., Cast Bronze, 25 mm. **Note:** Struck at Song Do Kwai Li Yong. (Song Do = "Kae Song").

Date	Good	VG	F	VF	XF
ND(1882) Series 6	—	—	—	—	45.00

KM# 805.7 MUN
4.0000 g., Cast Bronze, 25 mm. **Rev:** "Song" at top, series number at bottom **Note:** Struck at Song Do Kwai Li Yong. (Song Do = "Kae Song").

Date	Good	VG	F	VF	XF
ND(1882) Series 7	3.00	5.00	8.00	12.00	—

KM# 805s.7 MUN
4.0000 g., Cast Bronze, 25 mm. **Note:** Struck at Song Do Kwai Li Yong. (Song Do = "Kae Song").

Date	Good	VG	F	VF	XF
ND(1882) Series 7	—	—	—	—	45.00

KM# 805.8 MUN
4.0000 g., Cast Bronze, 25 mm. **Rev:** "Song" at top, series number at bottom **Note:** Struck at Song Do Kwai Li Yong. (Song Do = "Kae Song").

Date	Good	VG	F	VF	XF
ND(1882) Series 8	3.00	5.00	8.00	12.00	—

KM# 805s.8 MUN
4.0000 g., Cast Bronze, 25 mm. **Note:** Struck at Song Do Kwai Li Yong. (Song Do = "Kae Song").

Date	Good	VG	F	VF	XF
ND(1882) Series 8	—	—	—	—	45.00

KM# 805.9 MUN
4.0000 g., Cast Bronze, 25 mm. **Rev:** "Song" at top, series number at bottom **Note:** Struck at Song Do Kwai Li Yong. (Song Do = "Kae Song").

Date	Good	VG	F	VF	XF
ND(1882) Series 9	3.00	5.00	8.00	12.00	—

KM# 805s.9 MUN
4.0000 g., Cast Bronze, 25 mm. **Note:** Struck at Song Do Kwai Li Yong. (Song Do = "Kae Song").

Date	Good	VG	F	VF	XF
ND(1882) Series 9	—	—	—	—	45.00

KM# 805s.10 MUN
4.0000 g., Cast Bronze, 25 mm. **Note:** Struck at Song Do Kwai Li Yong. (Song Do = "Kae Song").

Date	Good	VG	F	VF	XF
ND(1882) Series 10	—	—	—	—	45.00

KM# 805.10 MUN
4.0000 g., Cast Bronze, 25 mm. **Rev:** "Song" at top, series number at bottom **Note:** Struck at Song Do Kwai Li Yong. (Song Do = "Kae Song").

Date	Good	VG	F	VF	XF
ND(1882) Series 10	3.00	5.00	8.00	12.00	—

IWON TOWNSHIP MILITARY OFFICE

(I Won Kwal Li Yong)

KM# 834.1 MUN
4.0000 g., Cast Bronze, 24 mm. **Rev:** "Chon" at bottom, series number at left

Date	Good	VG	F	VF	XF
ND(1882) Series 1	5.00	7.50	10.00	15.00	—

KM# 834s.1 MUN
4.0000 g., Cast Bronze, 24 mm.

Date	Good	VG	F	VF	XF
ND(1882) Series 1	—	—	—	—	60.00

KM# 834s.3 MUN
4.0000 g., Cast Bronze, 24 mm.

Date	Good	VG	F	VF	XF
ND(1882) Series 3	—	—	—	—	35.00

KM# 835.4 MUN
4.0000 g., Cast Bronze, 23 mm. **Rev:** "Chi" at bottom, series number at right

Date	Good	VG	F	VF	XF
ND(1882) Series 4	10.00	15.00	25.00	40.00	—

KM# 835s.4 MUN
4.0000 g., Cast Bronze, 23 mm. **Note:** Seed type. Struck at I Won Kwal Li Yong.

Date	Good	VG	F	VF	XF
ND(1882) Series 4	—	—	—	—	75.00

KM# 836.1 MUN
4.0000 g., Cast Bronze, 24 mm. **Rev:** "Chi" at bottom, series number at left **Note:** Large characters.

Date	Good	VG	F	VF	XF
ND(1882) Series 1	15.00	20.00	30.00	50.00	—

KM# 836s.1 MUN
4.0000 g., Cast Bronze, 24 mm.

Date	Good	VG	F	VF	XF
ND(1882) Series 1	—	—	—	—	100

KM# 836.2 MUN
4.0000 g., Cast Bronze, 24 mm. **Rev:** "Chi" at bottom, series number at left **Note:** Large characters.

Date	Good	VG	F	VF	XF
ND(1882) Series 2	10.00	20.00	30.00	50.00	—

KM# 836s.2 MUN
4.0000 g., Cast Bronze, 24 mm.

Date	Good	VG	F	VF	XF
ND(1882) Series 2	—	—	—	—	100

KM# 836.3 MUN
4.0000 g., Cast Bronze, 24 mm. **Rev:** "Chi" at bottom, series number at left **Note:** Large characters.

Date	Good	VG	F	VF	XF
ND(1882) Series 3	10.00	20.00	30.00	50.00	—

KM# 836s.3 MUN
4.0000 g., Cast Bronze, 24 mm.

Date	Good	VG	F	VF	XF
ND(1882) Series 3	—	—	—	—	100

KM# 836.4 MUN
4.0000 g., Cast Bronze, 24 mm. **Rev:** "Chi" at bottom, series number at left **Note:** Large characters.

Date	Good	VG	F	VF	XF
ND(1882) Series 4	10.00	20.00	30.00	50.00	—

KM# 836s.4 MUN
4.0000 g., Cast Bronze, 24 mm.

Date	Good	VG	F	VF	XF
ND(1882) Series 4	—	—	—	—	100

KM# 836.5 MUN
4.0000 g., Cast Bronze, 24 mm. **Rev:** "Chi" at bottom, series number at left **Note:** Large characters.

Date	Good	VG	F	VF	XF
ND(1882) Series 5	10.00	20.00	30.00	50.00	—

KM# 836s.5 MUN
4.0000 g., Cast Bronze, 24 mm.

Date	Good	VG	F	VF	XF
ND(1882) Series 5	—	—	—	—	100

KM# 837.1 MUN
4.0000 g., Cast Bronze, 22 mm. **Note:** Small characters.

Date	Good	VG	F	VF	XF
ND(1882) Series 1	10.00	20.00	30.00	50.00	—

KM# 837.2 MUN
, 22 mm. **Note:** Small characters.

Date	Good	VG	F	VF	XF
ND(1882) Series 2	10.00	20.00	30.00	50.00	—

KM# 837.3 MUN
4.0000 g., Cast Bronze, 22 mm. **Note:** Small characters.

Date	Good	VG	F	VF	XF
ND(1882) Series 3	10.00	20.00	30.00	50.00	—

KM# 837.4 MUN
4.0000 g., Cast Bronze, 22 mm. **Note:** Small characters.

Date	Good	VG	F	VF	XF
ND(1882) Series 4	10.00	20.00	30.00	50.00	—

KM# 837.5 MUN
4.0000 g., Cast Bronze, 22 mm. **Note:** Small characters.

Date	Good	VG	F	VF	XF
ND(1882) Series 5	10.00	20.00	30.00	50.00	—

CH'UNCH'ON TOWNSHIP MILITARY OFFICE

(Ch'un Ch'on Kwal Li Yong)

KM# 886.1 5 MUN
Cast Bronze, 31 mm. **Rev:** Crescent at bottom under series number **Note:** Large characters.

Date	Good	VG	F	VF	XF
ND(1888) Series 1	5.00	7.50	10.00	15.00	—

KM# 874.1 5 MUN
Cast Bronze, 31 mm. **Rev:** "Ch'un" at top, "Tang" at right, "O" (5) at left, series number at bottom **Note:** Large characters.

Date	Good	VG	F	VF	XF
ND(1888) Series 1	3.00	5.00	7.50	10.00	—

KM# 874s.1 5 MUN
Cast Bronze, 31 mm.

Date	Good	VG	F	VF	XF
ND(1888) Series 1	—	—	—	—	50.00

KM# 874.2 5 MUN
Cast Bronze, 31 mm. **Rev:** "Ch'un" at top, "Tang" at right, "O" (5) at left, series number at bottom **Note:** Large characters.

Date	Good	VG	F	VF	XF
ND(1888) Series 2	3.00	5.00	7.50	10.00	—

KM# 874s.2 5 MUN
Cast Bronze, 31 mm.

Date	Good	VG	F	VF	XF
ND(1888) Series 2	—	—	—	—	50.00

KM# 874.3 5 MUN
Cast Bronze, 31 mm. **Rev:** "Ch'un" at top, "Tang" at right, "O" (5) at left, series number at bottom **Note:** Large characters.

Date	Good	VG	F	VF	XF
ND(1888) Series 3	3.00	5.00	7.50	10.00	—

KM# 874s.3 5 MUN
Cast Bronze, 31 mm.

Date	Good	VG	F	VF	XF
ND(1888) Series 3	—	—	—	—	50.00

KM# 874.4 5 MUN
Cast Bronze, 31 mm. **Rev:** "Ch'un" at top, "Tang" at right, "O" (5) at left, series number at bottom **Note:** Large characters.

Date	Good	VG	F	VF	XF
ND(1888) Series 4	3.00	5.00	7.50	10.00	—

KM# 874s.4 5 MUN
Cast Bronze, 31 mm.

Date	Good	VG	F	VF	XF
ND(1888) Series 4	—	—	—	—	50.00

KM# 874.5 5 MUN
Cast Bronze, 31 mm. **Rev:** "Ch'un" at top, "Tang" at right, "O" (5) at left, series number at bottom **Note:** Large characters.

Date	Good	VG	F	VF	XF
ND(1888) Series 5	3.00	5.00	7.50	10.00	—

KM# 874s.5 5 MUN
Cast Bronze, 31 mm.

Date	Good	VG	F	VF	XF
ND(1888) Series 5	—	—	—	—	50.00

KM# 874.6 5 MUN
Cast Bronze, 31 mm. **Rev:** "Ch'un" at top, "Tang" at right, "O" (5) at left, series number at bottom **Note:** Large characters.

Date	Good	VG	F	VF	XF
ND(1888) Series 6	3.00	5.00	7.50	10.00	—

KM# 874s.6 5 MUN
Cast Bronze, 31 mm.

Date	Good	VG	F	VF	XF
ND(1888) Series 6	—	—	—	—	50.00

KM# 875s.6 5 MUN
Cast Bronze, 30 mm.

Date	Good	VG	F	VF	XF
ND(1888) Series 6	—	—	—	—	35.00

KM# 874.7 5 MUN
Cast Bronze, 31 mm. **Rev:** "Ch'un" at top, "Tang" at right, "O" (5) at left, series number at bottom **Note:** Large characters.

Date	Good	VG	F	VF	XF
ND(1888) Series 7	3.00	5.00	7.50	10.00	—

KM# 874s.7 5 MUN
Cast Bronze, 31 mm.

Date	Good	VG	F	VF	XF
ND(1888) Series 7	—	—	—	—	50.00

KM# 874.8 5 MUN
Cast Bronze, 31 mm. **Rev:** "Ch'un" at top, "Tang" at right, "O" (5) at left, series number at bottom **Note:** Large characters.

Date	Good	VG	F	VF	XF
ND(1888) Series 8	5.00	7.50	10.00	15.00	—

KM# 874s.8 5 MUN
Cast Bronze, 31 mm.

Date	Good	VG	F	VF	XF
ND(1888) Series 8	—	—	—	—	60.00

KM# 874.9 5 MUN
Cast Bronze, 31 mm. **Rev:** "Ch'un" at top, "Tang" at right, "O" (5) at left, series number at bottom **Note:** Large characters.

Date	Good	VG	F	VF	XF
ND(1888) Series 9	5.00	7.50	10.00	15.00	—

KM# 874s.9 5 MUN
Cast Bronze, 31 mm.

Date	Good	VG	F	VF	XF
ND(1888) Series 9	—	—	—	—	60.00

KM# 874.10 5 MUN
Cast Bronze, 31 mm. **Rev:** "Ch'un" at top, "Tang" at right, "O" (5) at left, series number at bottom **Note:** Large characters.

Date	Good	VG	F	VF	XF
ND(1888) Series 10	5.00	7.50	10.00	15.00	—

KM# 874s.10 5 MUN
Cast Bronze, 31 mm.

Date	Good	VG	F	VF	XF
ND(1888) Series 10	—	—	—	—	60.00

KM# 875.1 5 MUN
Cast Bronze, 30 mm. **Note:** Medium characters.

Date	Good	VG	F	VF	XF
ND(1888) Series 1	3.00	5.00	7.50	10.00	—

KM# 875s.1 5 MUN
Cast Bronze, 30 mm.

Date	Good	VG	F	VF	XF
ND(1888) Series 1	—	—	—	—	50.00

KM# 875.2 5 MUN
Cast Bronze, 30 mm. **Note:** Medium characters.

Date	Good	VG	F	VF	XF
ND(1888) Series 2	3.00	5.00	7.50	10.00	—

KM# 875s.2 5 MUN
Cast Bronze, 30 mm.

Date	Good	VG	F	VF	XF
ND(1888) Series 2	—	—	—	—	50.00

KM# 875.3 5 MUN
Cast Bronze, 30 mm. **Note:** Medium characters.

Date	Good	VG	F	VF	XF
ND(1888) Series 3	3.00	5.00	7.50	10.00	—

KM# 875s.3 5 MUN
Cast Bronze, 30 mm.

Date	Good	VG	F	VF	XF
ND(1888) Series 3	—	—	—	—	50.00

KM# 875.4 5 MUN
Cast Bronze, 30 mm. **Note:** Medium characters.

Date	Good	VG	F	VF	XF
ND(1888) Series 4	3.00	5.00	7.50	10.00	—

KM# 875s.4 5 MUN
Cast Bronze, 30 mm.

Date	Good	VG	F	VF	XF
ND(1888) Series 4	—	—	—	—	50.00

KM# 875.5 5 MUN
Cast Bronze, 30 mm. **Note:** Medium characters.

Date	Good	VG	F	VF	XF
ND(1888) Series 5	3.00	5.00	7.50	10.00	—

KM# 875s.5 5 MUN
Cast Bronze, 30 mm.

Date	Good	VG	F	VF	XF
ND(1888) Series 5	—	—	—	—	50.00

KM# 875.6 5 MUN
Cast Bronze, 30 mm. **Note:** Medium characters.

Date	Good	VG	F	VF	XF
ND(1888) Series 6	3.00	5.00	7.50	10.00	—

KM# 875.7 5 MUN
Cast Bronze, 30 mm. **Note:** Medium characters.

Date	Good	VG	F	VF	XF
ND(1888) Series 7	5.00	7.50	10.00	15.00	—

KM# 875s.7 5 MUN
Cast Bronze, 30 mm.

Date	Good	VG	F	VF	XF
ND(1888) Series 7	—	—	—	—	60.00

KM# 875.8 5 MUN
Cast Bronze, 30 mm. **Note:** Medium characters.

Date	Good	VG	F	VF	XF
ND(1888) Series 8	5.00	7.00	10.00	15.00	—

KM# 875s.8 5 MUN
Cast Bronze, 30 mm.

Date	Good	VG	F	VF	XF
ND(1888) Series 8	—	—	—	—	60.00

KM# 875.9 5 MUN
Cast Bronze, 30 mm. **Note:** Medium characters.

Date	Good	VG	F	VF	XF
ND(1888) Series 9	5.00	7.50	10.00	15.00	—

KM# 875s.9 5 MUN
Cast Bronze, 30 mm.

Date	Good	VG	F	VF	XF
ND(1888) Series 9	—	—	—	—	60.00

KM# 875.10 5 MUN
Cast Bronze, 30 mm. **Note:** Medium characters.

Date	Good	VG	F	VF	XF
ND(1888) Series 10	5.00	7.50	10.00	15.00	—

KM# 875s.10 5 MUN
Cast Bronze, 30 mm.

Date	Good	VG	F	VF	XF
ND(1888) Series 10	—	—	—	—	60.00

KM# 876.1 5 MUN
Cast Bronze, 27 mm. **Note:** Reduced size.

Date	Good	VG	F	VF	XF
ND(1888) Series 1	7.50	10.00	15.00	20.00	—

KM# 876s.1 5 MUN
Cast Bronze, 27 mm.

Date	Good	VG	F	VF	XF
ND(1888) Series 1	—	—	—	—	60.00

KM# 876.2 5 MUN
Cast Bronze, 27 mm. **Note:** Reduced size.

Date	Good	VG	F	VF	XF
ND(1888) Series 2	7.50	10.00	15.00	20.00	—

KM# 876s.2 5 MUN
Cast Bronze, 27 mm.

Date	Good	VG	F	VF	XF
ND(1888) Series 2	—	—	—	—	60.00

KM# 876.3 5 MUN
Cast Bronze, 27 mm. **Note:** Reduced size.

Date	Good	VG	F	VF	XF
ND(1888) Series 3	7.50	10.00	15.00	20.00	—

KM# 876s.3 5 MUN
Cast Bronze, 27 mm.

Date	Good	VG	F	VF	XF
ND(1888) Series 3	—	—	—	—	60.00

KM# 876.4 5 MUN
Cast Bronze, 27 mm. **Note:** Reduced size.

Date	Good	VG	F	VF	XF
ND(1888) Series 4	7.50	10.00	15.00	20.00	—

KM# 876s.4 5 MUN
Cast Bronze, 27 mm.

Date	Good	VG	F	VF	XF
ND(1888) Series 4	—	—	—	—	60.00

KM# 876.5 5 MUN
Cast Bronze, 27 mm. **Note:** Reduced size.

Date	Good	VG	F	VF	XF
ND(1888) Series 5	7.50	10.00	15.00	20.00	—

KM# 876s.5 5 MUN
Cast Bronze, 27 mm.

Date	Good	VG	F	VF	XF
ND(1888) Series 5	—	—	—	—	60.00

KM# 876.6 5 MUN
Cast Bronze, 27 mm. **Note:** Reduced size.

Date	Good	VG	F	VF	XF
ND(1888) Series 6	7.50	10.00	15.00	20.00	—

KM# 876s.6 5 MUN
Cast Bronze, 27 mm.

Date	Good	VG	F	VF	XF
ND(1888) Series 6	—	—	—	—	60.00

KM# 876.7 5 MUN
Cast Bronze, 27 mm. **Note:** Reduced size.

Date	Good	VG	F	VF	XF
ND(1888) Series 7	7.50	10.00	15.00	20.00	—

KM# 876s.7 5 MUN
Cast Bronze, 27 mm.

Date	Good	VG	F	VF	XF
ND(1888) Series 7	—	—	—	—	60.00

KM# 876.8 5 MUN
Cast Bronze, 27 mm. **Note:** Reduced size.

Date	Good	VG	F	VF	XF
ND(1888) Series 8	7.50	10.00	15.00	20.00	—

KM# 876s.8 5 MUN
Cast Bronze, 27 mm.

Date	Good	VG	F	VF	XF
ND(1888) Series 8	—	—	—	—	60.00

KM# 876.9 5 MUN
Cast Bronze, 27 mm. **Note:** Reduced size.

Date	Good	VG	F	VF	XF
ND(1888) Series 9	7.50	10.00	15.00	20.00	—

KM# 876s.9 5 MUN
Cast Bronze, 27 mm.

Date	Good	VG	F	VF	XF
ND(1888) Series 9	—	—	—	—	60.00

KM# 876.10 5 MUN
Cast Bronze, 27 mm. **Note:** Reduced size.

Date	Good	VG	F	VF	XF
ND(1888) Series 10	7.50	10.00	15.00	20.00	—

KM# 876s.10 5 MUN
Cast Bronze, 27 mm.

Date	Good	VG	F	VF	XF
ND(1888) Series 10	—	—	—	—	60.00

KM# 877.1 5 MUN
Cast Bronze, 28 mm. **Rev:** "Ch'un" at top in different style

Date	Good	VG	F	VF	XF
ND(1888) Series 1	7.50	10.00	15.00	20.00	—

KM# 877a.1 5 MUN
Cast Bronze, 30 mm.

Date	Good	VG	F	VF	XF
ND(1888) Series 1	7.50	10.00	15.00	20.00	—

KM# 877s.1 5 MUN
Cast Bronze, 30 mm.

Date	Good	VG	F	VF	XF
ND(1888) Series 1	—	—	—	—	60.00

KM# 877.2 5 MUN
Cast Bronze, 28 mm. **Rev:** "Ch'un" at top in different style

Date	Good	VG	F	VF	XF
ND(1888) Series 2	7.50	10.00	15.00	20.00	—

KM# 877a.2 5 MUN
Cast Bronze, 30 mm.

Date	Good	VG	F	VF	XF
ND(1888) Series 2	7.50	10.00	15.00	20.00	—

KM# 877s.2 5 MUN
Cast Bronze, 30 mm.

Date	Good	VG	F	VF	XF
ND(1888) Series 2	—	—	—	—	60.00

KM# 877.3 5 MUN
Cast Bronze, 28 mm. **Rev:** "Ch'un" at top in different style

Date	Good	VG	F	VF	XF
ND(1888) Series 3	7.50	10.00	15.00	20.00	—

KM# 877a.3 5 MUN
Cast Bronze, 30 mm.

Date	Good	VG	F	VF	XF
ND(1888) Series 3	7.50	10.00	15.00	20.00	—

KM# 877s.3 5 MUN
Cast Bronze, 30 mm.

Date	Good	VG	F	VF	XF
ND(1888) Series 3	—	—	—	—	60.00

KM# 877.4 5 MUN
Cast Bronze, 28 mm. **Rev:** "Ch'un" at top in different style

Date	Good	VG	F	VF	XF
ND(1888) Series 4	7.50	10.00	15.00	20.00	—

KM# 877a.4 5 MUN
Cast Bronze, 30 mm.

Date	Good	VG	F	VF	XF
ND(1888) Series 4	7.50	10.00	15.00	20.00	—

KM# 877s.4 5 MUN
Cast Bronze, 30 mm.

Date	Good	VG	F	VF	XF
ND(1888) Series 4	—	—	—	—	60.00

KM# 877.5 5 MUN
Cast Bronze, 28 mm. **Rev:** "Ch'un" at top in different style

Date	Good	VG	F	VF	XF
ND(1888) Series 5	7.50	10.00	15.00	20.00	—

KM# 877a.5 5 MUN
Cast Bronze, 30 mm.

Date	Good	VG	F	VF	XF
ND(1888) Series 5	7.50	10.00	15.00	20.00	—

KM# 877s.5 5 MUN
Cast Bronze, 30 mm.

Date	Good	VG	F	VF	XF
ND(1888) Series 5	—	—	—	—	60.00

KM# 877.6 5 MUN
Cast Bronze, 28 mm. **Rev:** "Ch'un" at top in different style

Date	Good	VG	F	VF	XF
ND(1888) Series 6	7.50	10.00	15.00	20.00	—

KM# 877a.6 5 MUN
Cast Bronze, 30 mm.

Date	Good	VG	F	VF	XF
ND(1888) Series 6	2.00	3.00	5.00	7.00	—

KM# 877s.6 5 MUN
Cast Bronze, 30 mm.

Date	Good	VG	F	VF	XF
ND(1888) Series 6	—	—	—	—	60.00

KM# 877.7 5 MUN
Cast Bronze, 28 mm. **Rev:** "Ch'un" at top in different style

Date	Good	VG	F	VF	XF
ND(1888) Series 7	7.50	10.00	15.00	20.00	—

KM# 877a.7 5 MUN
Cast Bronze, 30 mm.

Date	Good	VG	F	VF	XF
ND(1888) Series 7	2.00	3.00	5.00	7.00	—

KM# 877s.7 5 MUN
Cast Bronze, 30 mm.

Date	Good	VG	F	VF	XF
ND(1888) Series 7	—	—	—	—	60.00

KM# 877.8 5 MUN
Cast Bronze, 28 mm. **Rev:** "Ch'un" at top in different style

Date	Good	VG	F	VF	XF
ND(1888) Series 8	7.50	10.00	15.00	20.00	—

KM# 877s.8 5 MUN
Cast Bronze, 30 mm.

Date	Good	VG	F	VF	XF
ND(1888) Series 8	—	—	—	—	60.00

KM# 877.9 5 MUN
Cast Bronze, 28 mm. **Rev:** "Ch'un" at top in different style

Date	Good	VG	F	VF	XF
ND(1888) Series 9	7.50	10.00	15.00	20.00	—

KM# 877a.9 5 MUN
Cast Bronze, 30 mm.

Date	Good	VG	F	VF	XF
ND(1888) Series 9	2.00	3.00	5.00	7.00	—

KM# 877s.9 5 MUN
Cast Bronze, 30 mm.

Date	Good	VG	F	VF	XF
ND(1888) Series 9	—	—	—	—	60.00

KM# 877.10 5 MUN
Cast Bronze, 28 mm. **Rev:** "Ch'un" at top in different style

Date	Good	VG	F	VF	XF
ND(1888) Series 10	7.50	10.00	15.00	20.00	—

KM# 877a.10 5 MUN
Cast Bronze, 30 mm.

Date	Good	VG	F	VF	XF
ND(1888) Series 10	7.50	10.00	15.00	20.00	—

KM# 877s.10 5 MUN
Cast Bronze, 30 mm.

Date	Good	VG	F	VF	XF
ND(1888) Series 10	—	—	—	—	60.00

KM# 877.11 5 MUN
Cast Bronze, 28 mm. **Rev:** "Ch'un" at top in different style

Date	Good	VG	F	VF	XF
ND(1888) Series 11	7.50	10.00	15.00	20.00	—

KM# 877s.11 5 MUN
Cast Bronze, 30 mm.

Date	Good	VG	F	VF	XF
ND(1888) Series 11	—	—	—	—	60.00

KM# 877.12 5 MUN
Cast Bronze, 28 mm. **Rev:** "Ch'un" at top in different style

Date	Good	VG	F	VF	XF
ND(1888) Series 12	7.50	10.00	15.00	20.00	—

KM# 877s.12 5 MUN
Cast Bronze, 30 mm.

Date	Good	VG	F	VF	XF
ND(1888) Series 12	—	—	—	—	60.00

KM# 877.13 5 MUN
Cast Bronze, 28 mm. **Rev:** "Ch'un" at top in different style

Date	Good	VG	F	VF	XF
ND(1888) Series 13	7.50	10.00	15.00	20.00	—

KM# 877s.13 5 MUN
Cast Bronze, 30 mm.

Date	Good	VG	F	VF	XF
ND(1888) Series 13	—	—	—	—	60.00

KM# 877.14 5 MUN
Cast Bronze, 28 mm. **Rev:** "Ch'un" at top in different style

Date	Good	VG	F	VF	XF
ND(1888) Series 14	7.50	10.00	15.00	20.00	—

KM# 877s.14 5 MUN
Cast Bronze, 30 mm.

Date	Good	VG	F	VF	XF
ND(1888) Series 14	—	—	—	—	60.00

KM# 877.15 5 MUN
Cast Bronze, 28 mm. **Rev:** "Ch'un" at top in different style

Date	Good	VG	F	VF	XF
ND(1888) Series 15	2.00	3.00	5.00	7.00	—

KM# 877s.15 5 MUN
Cast Brass, 30 mm.

Date	Good	VG	F	VF	XF
ND(1888) Series 15	—	—	—	—	60.00

KM# 877.16 5 MUN
Cast Bronze, 28 mm. **Rev:** "Ch'un" at top in different style

Date	Good	VG	F	VF	XF
ND(1888) Series 16	7.50	10.00	15.00	20.00	—

KM# 877.17 5 MUN
Cast Bronze, 28 mm. **Rev:** "Ch'un" at top in different style

Date	Good	VG	F	VF	XF
ND(1888) Series 17	7.50	10.00	15.00	20.00	—

KM# 877s.17 5 MUN
Cast Bronze, 30 mm.

Date	Good	VG	F	VF	XF
ND(1888) Series 17	—	—	—	—	60.00

KM# 877.18 5 MUN
Cast Bronze, 28 mm. **Rev:** "Ch'un" at top in different style

Date	Good	VG	F	VF	XF
ND(1888) Series 18	7.50	10.00	15.00	20.00	—

KM# 877s.18 5 MUN
Cast Bronze, 30 mm.

Date	Good	VG	F	VF	XF
ND(1888) Series 18	—	—	—	—	60.00

KM# 877.19 5 MUN
Cast Bronze, 28 mm. **Rev:** "Ch'un" at top in different style

Date	Good	VG	F	VF	XF
ND(1888) Series 19	7.50	10.00	15.00	20.00	—

KM# 877s.19 5 MUN
Cast Bronze, 30 mm.

Date	Good	VG	F	VF	XF
ND(1888) Series 19	—	—	—	—	60.00

KM# 877.20 5 MUN
Cast Bronze, 28 mm. **Rev:** "Ch'un" at top in different style

Date	Good	VG	F	VF	XF
ND(1888) Series 20	7.50	10.00	15.00	20.00	—

KM# 877s.20 5 MUN
Cast Bronze, 30 mm.

Date	Good	VG	F	VF	XF
ND(1888) Series 20	—	—	—	—	60.00

KM# 878.1 5 MUN
Cast Bronze, 29 mm. **Rev:** Crescent at bottom under series number

Date	Good	VG	F	VF	XF
ND(1888) Series 1	5.00	7.50	9.00	15.00	—

KM# 878s.1 5 MUN
Cast Bronze, 29 mm.

Date	Good	VG	F	VF	XF
ND(1888) Series 1	—	—	—	—	60.00

KM# 878.2 5 MUN
Cast Bronze, 29 mm. **Rev:** Crescent at bottom under series number

Date	Good	VG	F	VF	XF
ND(1888) Series 2	2.75	3.50	5.00	7.00	—

KM# 878s.2 5 MUN
Cast Bronze, 29 mm.

Date	Good	VG	F	VF	XF
ND(1888) Series 2	—	—	—	—	60.00

KM# 878.3 5 MUN
Cast Bronze, 29 mm. **Rev:** Crescent at bottom under series number

Date	Good	VG	F	VF	XF
ND(1888) Series 3	5.00	7.00	9.00	15.00	—

KM# 878s.3 5 MUN
Cast Bronze, 29 mm.

Date	Good	VG	F	VF	XF
ND(1888) Series 3	—	—	—	—	60.00

KM# 878.4 5 MUN
Cast Bronze, 29 mm. **Rev:** Crescent at bottom under series number

Date	Good	VG	F	VF	XF
ND(1888) Series 4	5.00	7.00	9.00	15.00	—

KM# 878s.4 5 MUN
Cast Bronze, 29 mm.

Date	Good	VG	F	VF	XF
ND(1888) Series 4	—	—	—	—	60.00

KM# 878.5 5 MUN
Cast Bronze, 29 mm. **Rev:** Crescent at bottom under series number

Date	Good	VG	F	VF	XF
ND(1888) Series 5	5.00	7.00	9.00	15.00	—

KM# 878s.5 5 MUN
Cast Bronze, 29 mm.

Date	Good	VG	F	VF	XF
ND(1888) Series 5	—	—	—	—	60.00

KM# 878.6 5 MUN
Cast Bronze, 29 mm. **Rev:** Crescent at bottom under series number

Date	Good	VG	F	VF	XF
ND(1888) Series 6	5.00	7.00	9.00	15.00	—

KM# 878s.6 5 MUN
Cast Bronze, 29 mm.

Date	Good	VG	F	VF	XF
ND(1888) Series 6	—	—	—	—	60.00

KM# 878.7 5 MUN
Cast Bronze, 29 mm. **Rev:** Crescent at bottom under series number

Date	Good	VG	F	VF	XF
ND(1888) Series 7	5.00	7.00	9.00	15.00	—

KM# 878s.7 5 MUN
Cast Bronze, 29 mm.

Date	Good	VG	F	VF	XF
ND(1888) Series 7	—	—	—	—	60.00

KM# 878.8 5 MUN
Cast Bronze, 29 mm. **Rev:** Crescent at bottom under series number

Date	Good	VG	F	VF	XF
ND(1888) Series 8	5.00	7.00	9.00	15.00	—

KM# 878s.8 5 MUN
Cast Bronze, 29 mm.

Date	Good	VG	F	VF	XF
ND(1888) Series 8	—	—	—	—	60.00

KM# 878.9 5 MUN
Cast Bronze, 29 mm. **Rev:** Crescent at bottom under series number

Date	Good	VG	F	VF	XF
ND(1888) Series 9	5.00	7.00	9.00	15.00	—

KM# 878s.9 5 MUN
Cast Bronze, 29 mm.

Date	Good	VG	F	VF	XF
ND(1888) Series 9	—	—	—	—	60.00

KM# 878.10 5 MUN
Cast Bronze, 29 mm. **Rev:** Crescent at bottom under series number

Date	Good	VG	F	VF	XF
ND(1888) Series 10	5.00	7.00	9.00	15.00	—

KM# 878s.10 5 MUN
Cast Bronze, 29 mm.

Date	Good	VG	F	VF	XF
ND(1888) Series 10	—	—	—	—	60.00

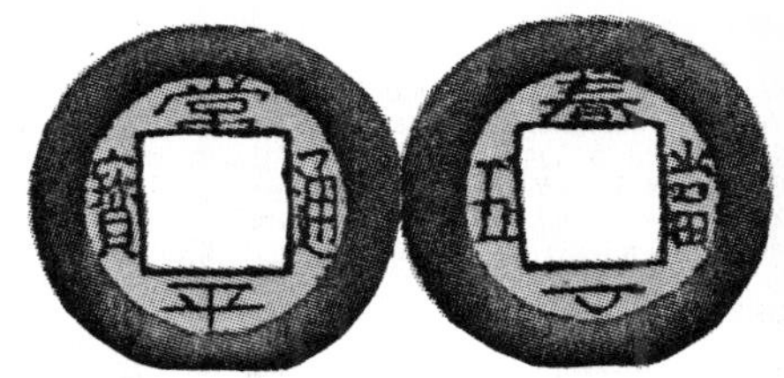

KM# 879.1 5 MUN
Cast Bronze, 28 mm. **Rev:** Inverted crescent at bottom under series number

Date	Good	VG	F	VF	XF
ND(1888) Series 1	5.00	7.00	9.00	15.00	—

KM# 879s 5 MUN
Cast Bronze, 28 mm.

Date	Good	VG	F	VF	XF
ND(1888) Series 1	—	—	—	—	60.00

KM# 879.2 5 MUN
Cast Bronze, 28 mm. **Rev:** Inverted crescent at bottom under series number

Date	Good	VG	F	VF	XF
ND(1888) Series 2	5.00	7.00	9.00	15.00	—

KM# 879.3 5 MUN
Cast Bronze, 28 mm. **Rev:** Inverted crescent at bottom under series number

Date	Good	VG	F	VF	XF
ND(1888) Series 3	5.00	7.00	9.00	15.00	—

KM# 879.4 5 MUN
Cast Bronze, 28 mm. **Rev:** Inverted crescent at bottom under series number

Date	Good	VG	F	VF	XF
ND(1888) Series 4	5.00	7.00	9.00	15.00	—

KM# 879.5 5 MUN
Cast Bronze, 28 mm. **Rev:** Inverted crescent at bottom under series number

Date	Good	VG	F	VF	XF
ND(1888) Series 5	5.00	7.00	9.00	15.00	—

KM# 879.6 5 MUN
Cast Bronze, 28 mm. **Rev:** Inverted crescent at bottom under series number

Date	Good	VG	F	VF	XF
ND(1888) Series 6	5.00	7.00	9.00	15.00	—

KM# 879.7 5 MUN
Cast Bronze, 28 mm. **Rev:** Inverted crescent at bottom under series number

Date	Good	VG	F	VF	XF
ND(1888) Series 7	5.00	7.00	9.00	15.00	—

KM# 879.8 5 MUN
Cast Bronze, 28 mm. **Rev:** Inverted crescent at bottom under series number

Date	Good	VG	F	VF	XF
ND(1888) Series 8	5.00	7.00	9.00	15.00	—

KM# 879.9 5 MUN
Cast Bronze, 28 mm. **Rev:** Inverted crescent at bottom under series number

Date	Good	VG	F	VF	XF
ND(1888) Series 9	5.00	7.00	9.00	15.00	—

KM# 879.10 5 MUN
Cast Bronze, 28 mm. **Rev:** Inverted crescent at bottom under series number

Date	Good	VG	F	VF	XF
ND(1888) Series 10	5.00	7.00	9.00	15.00	—

KM# 880.1 5 MUN
Cast Bronze **Rev:** "Ch'un" at top in different style, crescent at bottom under series number **Note:** Size varies: 29-30 millimeters.

Date	Good	VG	F	VF	XF
ND(1888) Series 1	6.00	9.00	15.00	20.00	—

KM# 880s.1 5 MUN
Cast Bronze **Note:** Seed type. Size varies: 29-30 millimeters.

Date	Good	VG	F	VF	XF
ND(1888) Series 1	—	—	—	—	70.00

KM# 880.2 5 MUN
Cast Bronze **Rev:** "Ch'un" at top in different style, crescent at bottom under series number **Note:** Size varies: 29-30 millimeters.

Date	Good	VG	F	VF	XF
ND(1888) Series 2	6.00	9.00	15.00	20.00	—

KM# 880s.2 5 MUN
Cast Bronze **Note:** Size varies: 29-30 millimeters.

Date	Good	VG	F	VF	XF
ND(1888) Series 2	—	—	—	—	70.00

KM# 880.3 5 MUN
Cast Bronze **Rev:** "Ch'un" at top in different style, crescent at bottom under series number **Note:** Size varies: 29-30 millimeters.

Date	Good	VG	F	VF	XF
ND(1888) Series 3	6.00	9.00	15.00	20.00	—

KM# 880s.3 5 MUN
Cast Bronze **Note:** Size varies: 29-30 millimeters.

Date	Good	VG	F	VF	XF
ND(1888) Series 3	—	—	—	—	70.00

KM# 880.4 5 MUN
Cast Bronze **Rev:** "Ch'un" at top in different style, crescent at bottom under series number **Note:** Size varies: 29-30 millimeters.

Date	Good	VG	F	VF	XF
ND(1888) Series 4	6.00	9.00	15.00	20.00	—

KM# 880s.4 5 MUN
Cast Bronze **Note:** Size varies: 29-30 mm.

Date	Good	VG	F	VF	XF
ND(1888) Series 4	—	—	—	—	27.50

KM# 880.5 5 MUN
Cast Bronze **Rev:** "Ch'un" at top in different style, crescent at bottom under series number **Note:** Size varies: 29-30 millimeters.

Date	Good	VG	F	VF	XF
ND(1888) Series 5	6.00	9.00	15.00	20.00	—

KM# 880s.5 5 MUN
Cast Bronze **Note:** Size varies: 29-30 mm.

Date	Good	VG	F	VF	XF
ND(1888) Series 5	—	—	—	—	70.00

KM# 880.6 5 MUN
Cast Bronze **Rev:** "Ch'un" at top in different style, crescent at bottom under series number **Note:** Size varies: 29-30 millimeters.

Date	Good	VG	F	VF	XF
ND(1888) Series 6	6.00	9.00	15.00	20.00	—

KM# 880s.6 5 MUN
Cast Bronze **Note:** Size varies: 29-30 mm.

Date	Good	VG	F	VF	XF
ND(1888) Series 6	—	—	—	—	70.00

KM# 880.7 5 MUN
Cast Bronze **Rev:** "Ch'un" at top in different style, crescent at bottom under series number **Note:** Size varies: 29-30 millimeters.

Date	Good	VG	F	VF	XF
ND(1888) Series 7	6.00	9.00	15.00	20.00	—

KM# 880s.7 5 MUN
Cast Bronze **Note:** Size varies: 29-30 mm.

Date	Good	VG	F	VF	XF
ND(1888) Series 7	—	—	—	—	70.00

KM# 880.8 5 MUN
Cast Bronze **Rev:** "Ch'un" at top in different style, crescent at bottom under series number **Note:** Size varies: 29-30 millimeters.

Date	Good	VG	F	VF	XF
ND(1888) Series 8	6.00	9.00	15.00	20.00	—

KM# 880s.8 5 MUN
Cast Bronze **Note:** Size varies: 29-30 mm.

Date	Good	VG	F	VF	XF
ND(1888) Series 8	—	—	—	—	70.00

KM# 880.9 5 MUN
Cast Bronze **Rev:** "Ch'un" at top in different style, crescent at bottom under series number **Note:** Size varies: 29-30 millimeters.

Date	Good	VG	F	VF	XF
ND(1888) Series 9	6.00	9.00	15.00	20.00	—

KM# 880s.9 5 MUN
Cast Bronze **Note:** Size varies: 29-30 mm.

Date	Good	VG	F	VF	XF
ND(1888) Series 9	—	—	—	—	70.00

KM# 880.10 5 MUN
Cast Bronze **Rev:** "Ch'un" at top in different style, crescent at bottom under series number **Note:** Size varies: 29-30 millimeters.

Date	Good	VG	F	VF	XF
ND(1888) Series 10	2.75	3.50	4.50	7.00	—

KM# 880s.10 5 MUN
Cast Bronze **Note:** Size varies: 29-30 millimeters.

Date	Good	VG	F	VF	XF
ND(1888) Series 10	—	—	—	—	70.00

TANCH'ON TOWNSHIP MILITARY OFFICE

(Tan Ch'on Kwal Li Yong)

KM# 881.1 5 MUN
Cast Bronze, 32 mm. **Rev:** "Ch'on" at top, "Tang" at right, "O" (5) at left, series number at bottom **Note:** Inner diameter hole 22 x 22 mm.

Date	Good	VG	F	VF	XF
ND(1883) Series 1	5.00	10.00	15.00	25.00	—

KM# 881s.1 5 MUN
Cast Bronze, 32 mm. **Note:** Inner diameter hole 22 x 22 mm.

Date	Good	VG	F	VF	XF
ND(1883) Series 1	—	—	—	—	75.00

KM# 881.2 5 MUN
Cast Bronze, 32 mm. **Rev:** "Ch'on" at top, "Tang" at right, "O" (5) at left, series number at bottom **Note:** Inner diameter hole 22 x 22 mm.

Date	Good	VG	F	VF	XF
ND(1883) Series 2	5.00	10.00	15.00	25.00	—

KM# 881s.2 5 MUN
Cast Bronze, 32 mm. **Note:** Inner diameter hole 22 x 22 mm.

Date	Good	VG	F	VF	XF
ND(1883) Series 2	—	—	—	—	75.00

KM# 881.3 5 MUN
Cast Bronze, 32 mm. **Rev:** "Ch'on" at top, "Tang" at right, "O" (5) at left, series number at bottom **Note:** Inner diameter hole 22 x 22 mm.

Date	Good	VG	F	VF	XF
ND(1883) Series 3	3.00	4.50	6.50	9.00	—

KM# 881s.3 5 MUN
Cast Bronze, 32 mm. **Note:** Inner diameter hole 22 x 22 mm.

Date	Good	VG	F	VF	XF
ND(1883) Series 3	—	—	—	—	75.00

KM# 881.4 5 MUN
Cast Bronze, 32 mm. **Rev:** "Ch'on" at top, "Tang" at right, "O" (5) at left, series number at bottom **Note:** Inner diameter hole 22 x 22 mm.

Date	Good	VG	F	VF	XF
ND(1883) Series 4	3.00	4.50	6.50	9.00	—

KM# 881.8 5 MUN
Cast Bronze, 32 mm. **Note:** Inner diameter hole 22 x 22 mm.

Date	Good	VG	F	VF	XF
ND(1883) Series 8	7.50	15.00	25.00	40.00	—

KM# 881s.8 5 MUN
Cast Bronze, 32 mm. **Note:** Inner diameter hole 22 x 22 mm.

Date	Good	VG	F	VF	XF
ND(1883) Series 8	—	—	—	—	100

KM# 882.1 5 MUN
Cast Bronze, 28 mm. **Note:** Reduced size, Inner diameter hole 20 x 20 mm.

Date	Good	VG	F	VF	XF
ND(1883) Series 1	5.00	7.50	15.00	25.00	—

KM# 882s.1 5 MUN
Cast Bronze, 28 mm. **Note:** Reduced size, inner diameter hole 20 x 20 mm.

Date	Good	VG	F	VF	XF
ND(1883) Series 1	—	—	—	—	50.00

KM# 882.2 5 MUN
Cast Bronze, 28 mm. **Note:** Reduced size, inner diameter hole 20 x 20 mm.

Date	Good	VG	F	VF	XF
ND(1883) Series 2	5.00	7.50	15.00	25.00	—

KM# 882s.2 5 MUN
Cast Bronze, 28 mm. **Note:** Reduced size, inner diameter hole 20 x 20 mm.

Date	Good	VG	F	VF	XF
ND(1883) Series 2	—	—	—	—	50.00

KM# 882.3 5 MUN
Cast Bronze, 28 mm. **Note:** Reduced size, inner diameter hole 20 x 20 mm.

Date	Good	VG	F	VF	XF
ND(1883) Series 3	5.00	7.50	15.00	25.00	—

KM# 882s.3 5 MUN
Cast Bronze, 28 mm. **Note:** Reduced size, inner diameter hole 20 x 20 mm.

Date	Good	VG	F	VF	XF
ND(1883) Series 3	—	—	—	—	50.00

KM# 882.7 5 MUN
Cast Bronze, 28 mm. **Note:** Reduced size, inner diameter hole 20 x 20 mm.

Date	Good	VG	F	VF	XF
ND(1883) Series 7	10.00	15.00	25.00	40.00	—

KM# 882s.7 5 MUN
Cast Bronze, 28 mm. **Note:** Reduced size, inner diameter hole 20 x 20 mm.

Date	Good	VG	F	VF	XF
ND(1883) Series 7	—	—	—	—	100

CH'ANG DOK PALACE MINT

(Ch'ang Dok Kung)

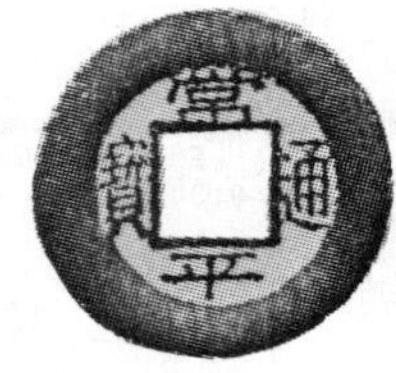

KM# 883.1 MUN
4.0000 g., Cast Bronze, 23.5 mm. **Rev:** "Ch'ang" at top, series number at bottom **Note:** Similar pieces without a series number are considered to be spurious.

Date	Good	VG	F	VF	XF
ND(1864-95) Series 1	10.00	15.00	25.00	40.00	—

KM# 883s MUN
4.0000 g., Cast Bronze, 23.5 mm.

Date	Good	VG	F	VF	XF
ND(1864-95) Series 1	—	—	—	—	100

CH'ANG WON TOWNSHIP MILITARY OFFICE

(Ch'ang Won Kwal Li Yong)

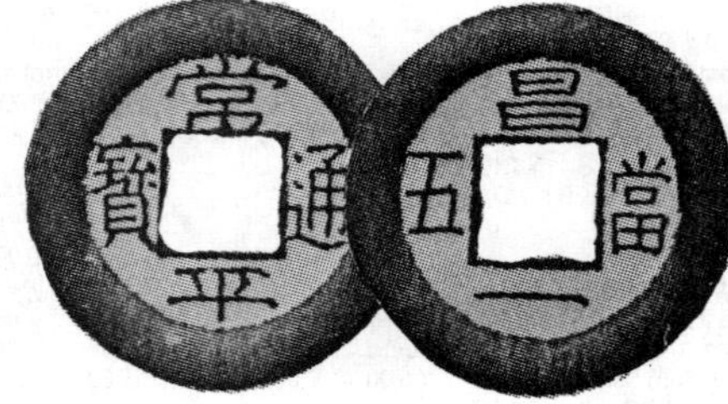

KM# 884.1 5 MUN
Cast Bronze, 31 mm. **Rev:** "Ch'ang" at top, "Tang" at right, "O" (5) at left, series number at bottom **Note:** Large characters.

Date	Good	VG	F	VF	XF
ND(1887) Series 1	4.00	7.00	12.50	20.00	—

KM# 884s.1 5 MUN
Cast Bronze, 31 mm. **Note:** Large characters.

Date	Good	VG	F	VF	XF
ND(1887) Series 1	—	—	—	—	50.00

KM# 884.2 5 MUN
Cast Bronze, 31 mm. **Rev:** "Ch'ang" at top, "Tang" at right, "O" (5) at left, series number at bottom **Note:** Large characters.

Date	Good	VG	F	VF	XF
ND(1887) Series 2	4.00	7.00	12.50	20.00	—

KM# 884s.2 5 MUN
Cast Bronze, 31 mm. **Note:** Large characters.

Date	Good	VG	F	VF	XF
ND(1887) Series 2	—	—	—	—	50.00

KM# 884.3 5 MUN
Cast Bronze, 31 mm. **Rev:** "Ch'ang" at top, "Tang" at right, "O" (5) at left, series number at bottom **Note:** Large characters.

Date	Good	VG	F	VF	XF
ND(1887) Series 3	4.00	7.00	12.50	20.00	—

KM# 884s.3 5 MUN
Cast Bronze, 31 mm. **Note:** Large characters.

Date	Good	VG	F	VF	XF
ND(1887) Series 3	—	—	—	—	50.00

KM# 884.4 5 MUN
Cast Bronze, 31 mm. **Rev:** "Ch'ang" at top, "Tang" at right, "O" (5) at left, series number at bottom **Note:** Large characters.

Date	Good	VG	F	VF	XF
ND(1887) Series 4	10.00	15.00	20.00	40.00	—

KM# 884s.4 5 MUN
Cast Bronze, 31 mm. **Note:** Large characters.

Date	Good	VG	F	VF	XF
ND(1887) Series 4	—	—	—	—	75.00

KM# 884.5 5 MUN
Cast Bronze, 31 mm. **Rev:** "Ch'ang" at top, "Tang" at right, "O" (5) at left, series number at bottom **Note:** Large characters.

Date	Good	VG	F	VF	XF
ND(1887) Series 5	10.00	15.00	20.00	40.00	—

KM# 884s.5 5 MUN
Cast Bronze, 31 mm. **Note:** Large characters.

Date	Good	VG	F	VF	XF
ND(1887) Series 5	—	—	—	—	75.00

KM# 884.6 5 MUN
Cast Bronze, 31 mm. **Rev:** "Ch'ang" at top, "Tang" at right, "O" (5) at left, series number at bottom **Note:** Large characters.

Date	Good	VG	F	VF	XF
ND(1887) Series 6	10.00	15.00	20.00	40.00	—

KM# 884s.6 5 MUN
Cast Bronze, 31 mm. **Note:** Large characters.

Date	Good	VG	F	VF	XF
ND(1887) Series 6	—	—	—	—	75.00

KM# 884.7 5 MUN
Cast Bronze, 31 mm. **Rev:** "Ch'ang" at top, "Tang" at right, "O" (5) at left, series number at bottom

Date	Good	VG	F	VF	XF
ND(1887) Series 7	10.00	15.00	20.00	40.00	—

KM# 884s.7 5 MUN
Cast Bronze, 31 mm. **Note:** Large characters.

Date	Good	VG	F	VF	XF
ND(1887) Series 7	—	—	—	—	75.00

KM# 884s.8 5 MUN
Cast Bronze, 31 mm. **Note:** Large characters.

Date	Good	VG	F	VF	XF
ND(1887) Series 8	—	—	—	—	75.00

KM# 884.9 5 MUN
Cast Bronze, 31 mm. **Rev:** "Ch'ang" at top, "Tang" at right, "O" (5) at left, series number at bottom **Note:** Large characters.

Date	Good	VG	F	VF	XF
ND(1887) Series 9	2.75	4.00	6.00	9.00	—

KM# 884s.9 5 MUN
Cast Bronze, 31 mm. **Note:** Large characters.

Date	Good	VG	F	VF	XF
ND(1887) Series 9	—	—	—	—	30.00

KM# 884s.10 5 MUN
Cast Bronze, 31 mm. **Note:** Large characters.

Date	Good	VG	F	VF	XF
ND(1887) Series 10	—	—	—	—	30.00

KM# 884.10 5 MUN
Cast Bronze, 31 mm. **Rev:** "Ch'ang" at top, "Tang" at right, "O" (5) at left, series number at bottom **Note:** Large characters.

Date	Good	VG	F	VF	XF
ND(1887) Series 10	2.75	4.00	6.00	9.00	—

KM# 884.11 5 MUN
Cast Bronze, 31 mm. **Rev:** "Ch'ang" at top, "Tang" at right, "O" (5) at left, series number at bottom **Note:** Large characters.

Date	Good	VG	F	VF	XF
ND(1887) Series 11	2.75	4.00	6.00	9.00	—

KM# 884s.11 5 MUN
Cast Bronze, 31 mm. **Note:** Large characters.

Date	Good	VG	F	VF	XF
ND(1887) Series 11	—	—	—	—	30.00

KM# 884.12 5 MUN
Cast Bronze, 31 mm. **Rev:** "Ch'ang" at top, "Tang" at right, "O" (5) at left, series number at bottom **Note:** Large characters.

Date	Good	VG	F	VF	XF
ND(1887) Series 12	2.75	4.00	6.00	9.00	—

KM# 884s.12 5 MUN
Cast Bronze, 31 mm. **Note:** Large characters.

Date	Good	VG	F	VF	XF
ND(1887) Series 12	—	—	—	—	30.00

KM# 885.1 5 MUN
Cast Bronze, 29 mm. **Note:** Reduced size; Small characters.

Date	Good	VG	F	VF	XF
ND(1887) Series 1	10.00	15.00	20.00	40.00	—

KM# 885s.1 5 MUN
Cast Bronze, 29 mm. **Note:** Reduced size; Small characters.

Date	Good	VG	F	VF	XF
ND(1887) Series 1	—	—	—	—	75.00

KM# A885.1 5 MUN
Cast Bronze, 30 mm. **Rev:** Sun or circle at upper right

Date	Good	VG	F	VF	XF
ND(1887) Series 1	3.00	4.50	6.50	10.00	—

KM# 885.2 5 MUN
Cast Bronze, 29 mm. **Note:** Reduced size; Small characters.

Date	Good	VG	F	VF	XF
ND(1887) Series 2	10.00	15.00	20.00	40.00	—

KM# 885s.2 5 MUN
Cast Bronze, 29 mm. **Note:** Reduced size; Small characters.

Date	Good	VG	F	VF	XF
ND(1887) Series 2	—	—	—	—	75.00

KM# A885.2 5 MUN
Cast Bronze, 30 mm. **Rev:** Sun or circle at upper right

Date	Good	VG	F	VF	XF
ND(1887) Series 2	10.00	15.00	20.00	40.00	—

KM# 885.3 5 MUN
Cast Bronze, 29 mm. **Note:** Reduced size; Small characters.

Date	Good	VG	F	VF	XF
ND(1887) Series 3	10.00	15.00	20.00	40.00	—

KM# 885s.3 5 MUN
Cast Bronze, 29 mm. **Note:** Reduced size; Small characters.

Date	Good	VG	F	VF	XF
ND(1887) Series 3	—	—	—	—	75.00

KM# A885.3 5 MUN
Cast Bronze, 30 mm. **Rev:** Sun or circle at upper right

Date	Good	VG	F	VF	XF
ND(1887) Series 3	10.00	15.00	20.00	40.00	—

KM# 885.4 5 MUN
Cast Bronze, 29 mm. **Note:** Reduced size; Small characters.

Date	Good	VG	F	VF	XF
ND(1887) Series 4	10.00	15.00	20.00	40.00	—

KM# 885s.4 5 MUN
Cast Bronze, 29 mm. **Note:** Reduced size; Small characters.

Date	Good	VG	F	VF	XF
ND(1887) Series 4	—	—	—	—	75.00

KM# A885.4 5 MUN
Cast Bronze, 30 mm. **Rev:** Sun or circle at upper right

Date	Good	VG	F	VF	XF
ND(1887) Series 4	10.00	15.00	20.00	40.00	—

KM# 885.5 5 MUN
Cast Bronze, 29 mm. **Note:** Reduced size; Small characters.

Date	Good	VG	F	VF	XF
ND(1887) Series 5	10.00	15.00	20.00	40.00	—

KM# 885s.5 5 MUN
Cast Bronze, 29 mm. **Note:** Reduced size; Small characters.

Date	Good	VG	F	VF	XF
ND(1887) Series 5	—	—	—	—	75.00

KM# A885.5 5 MUN
Cast Bronze, 30 mm. **Rev:** Sun or circle at upper right

Date	Good	VG	F	VF	XF
ND(1887) Series 5	10.00	15.00	20.00	40.00	—

KM# 885.6 5 MUN
Cast Bronze, 29 mm. **Note:** Reduced size; Small characters.

Date	Good	VG	F	VF	XF
ND(1887) Series 6	2.75	4.00	6.00	9.00	—

KM# A885.9 5 MUN
Cast Bronze, 30 mm. **Rev:** Sun or circle at upper right

Date	Good	VG	F	VF	XF
ND(1887) Series 9	3.00	4.50	6.50	10.00	—

KM# A885.10 5 MUN
Cast Bronze, 30 mm. **Rev:** Sun or circle at upper right

Date	Good	VG	F	VF	XF
ND(1887) Series 10	3.00	4.50	6.50	10.00	—

KM# 886s.1 5 MUN
Cast Bronze, 31 mm. **Note:** Large characters.

Date	Good	VG	F	VF	XF
ND(1887) Series 1	—	—	—	—	50.00

KM# 886.2 5 MUN
Cast Bronze, 31 mm. **Rev:** Crescent at bottom under series number **Note:** Large characters.

Date	Good	VG	F	VF	XF
ND(1887) Series 2	5.00	7.50	15.00	25.00	—

KM# 886s.2 5 MUN
Cast Bronze, 31 mm. **Note:** Large characters.

Date	Good	VG	F	VF	XF
ND(1887) Series 2	—	—	—	—	75.00

KM# 886.4 5 MUN
Cast Bronze, 31 mm. **Rev:** Crescent at bottom under series number **Note:** Large characters.

Date	Good	VG	F	VF	XF
ND(1887) Series 4	5.00	7.50	15.00	25.00	—

KM# 886s.4 5 MUN
Cast Bronze, 31 mm. **Note:** Large characters.

Date	Good	VG	F	VF	XF
ND(1887) Series 4	—	—	—	—	50.00

KM# 886.5 5 MUN
Cast Bronze, 31 mm. **Rev:** Crescent at bottom under series number **Note:** Large characters.

Date	Good	VG	F	VF	XF
ND(1887) Series 5	5.00	7.50	15.00	25.00	—

KM# 886s.5 5 MUN
Cast Bronze, 31 mm. **Note:** Large characters.

Date	Good	VG	F	VF	XF
ND(1887) Series 5	—	—	—	—	50.00

KM# 886.6 5 MUN
Cast Bronze, 31 mm. **Rev:** Crescent at bottom under series number **Note:** Large characters.

Date	Good	VG	F	VF	XF
ND(1887) Series 6	5.00	7.50	15.00	25.00	—

KM# 886s.6 5 MUN
Cast Bronze, 31 mm. **Note:** Large characters.

Date	Good	VG	F	VF	XF
ND(1887) Series 6	—	—	—	—	50.00

KM# 886.7 5 MUN
Cast Bronze, 31 mm. **Rev:** Crescent at bottom under series number **Note:** Large characters.

Date	Good	VG	F	VF	XF
ND(1887) Series 7	5.00	7.50	15.00	25.00	—

KM# 886s.7 5 MUN
Cast Bronze, 31 mm. **Note:** Large characters.

Date	Good	VG	F	VF	XF
ND(1887) Series 7	—	—	—	—	50.00

KM# 886.8 5 MUN
Cast Bronze, 31 mm. **Rev:** Crescent at bottom under series number **Note:** Large characters.

Date	Good	VG	F	VF	XF
ND(1887) Series 8	5.00	7.50	15.00	25.00	—

KM# 886s.8 5 MUN
Cast Bronze, 31 mm. **Note:** Large characters.

Date	Good	VG	F	VF	XF
ND(1887) Series 8	—	—	—	—	50.00

KM# 886.9 5 MUN
Cast Bronze, 31 mm. **Rev:** Crescent at bottom under series number **Note:** Large characters.

Date	Good	VG	F	VF	XF
ND(1887) Series 9	2.75	4.00	6.00	9.00	—

KM# 886s.9 5 MUN
Cast Bronze, 31 mm. **Note:** Large characters.

Date	Good	VG	F	VF	XF
ND(1887) Series 9	—	—	—	—	50.00

KM# A887.1 5 MUN
Cast Bronze, 30 mm. **Rev:** Crescent at upper right

Date	Good	VG	F	VF	XF
ND(1887) Series 1	3.00	4.50	6.50	10.00	—

KM# 887.2 5 MUN
Cast Bronze, 29 mm. **Rev:** Crescent at bottom under series number **Note:** Reduced size; Small characters.

Date	Good	VG	F	VF	XF
ND(1887) Series 2	5.00	7.50	15.00	25.00	—

KM# 887.4 5 MUN
Cast Bronze, 29 mm. **Rev:** Crescent at bottom under series number **Note:** Reduced size; Small characters.

Date	Good	VG	F	VF	XF
ND(1887) Series 4	5.00	7.50	15.00	25.00	—

KM# 887s.4 5 MUN
Cast Bronze, 29 mm. **Note:** Reduced size; Small characters.

Date	Good	VG	F	VF	XF
ND(1887) Series 4	—	—	—	—	50.00

KM# 887.5 5 MUN
Cast Bronze, 29 mm. **Rev:** Crescent at bottom under series number **Note:** Reduced size; Small characters.

Date	Good	VG	F	VF	XF
ND(1887) Series 5	5.00	7.50	15.00	25.00	—

KM# 887s.5 5 MUN
Cast Bronze, 29 mm. **Note:** Reduced size; Small characters.

Date	Good	VG	F	VF	XF
ND(1887) Series 5	—	—	—	—	50.00

KM# 887.6 5 MUN
Cast Bronze, 29 mm. **Rev:** Crescent at bottom under series number **Note:** Reduced size; Small characters.

Date	Good	VG	F	VF	XF
ND(1887) Series 6	5.00	7.50	15.00	25.00	—

KM# 887s.6 5 MUN
Cast Bronze, 29 mm. **Note:** Reduced size; Small characters.

Date	Good	VG	F	VF	XF
ND(1887) Series 6	—	—	—	—	50.00

KM# 887.7 5 MUN
Cast Bronze, 29 mm. **Rev:** Crescent at bottom under series number **Note:** Reduced size; Small characters.

Date	Good	VG	F	VF	XF
ND(1887) Series 7	2.75	4.00	6.00	9.00	—

KM# 887.8 5 MUN
Cast Bronze, 29 mm. **Rev:** Crescent at bottom under series number **Note:** Reduced size; Small characters.

Date	Good	VG	F	VF	XF
ND(1887) Series 8	5.00	7.50	15.00	25.00	—

KM# 887s.8 5 MUN
Cast Bronze, 29 mm. **Note:** Reduced size; Small characters.

Date	Good	VG	F	VF	XF
ND(1887) Series 8	—	—	—	—	50.00

KM# 887.9 5 MUN
Cast Bronze, 29 mm. **Rev:** Crescent at bottom under series number **Note:** Reduced size; Small characters.

Date	Good	VG	F	VF	XF
ND(1887) Series 9	2.75	4.00	6.00	9.00	—

KM# 887s.9 5 MUN
Cast Bronze, 29 mm. **Note:** Reduced size; Small characters.

Date	Good	VG	F	VF	XF
ND(1887) Series 9	—	—	—	—	50.00

KM# 887.10 5 MUN
Cast Bronze, 29 mm. **Rev:** Crescent at bottom under series number **Note:** Reduced size; Small characters.

Date	Good	VG	F	VF	XF
ND(1887) Series 10	5.00	7.50	15.00	25.00	—

KM# 887s.10 5 MUN
Cast Bronze, 29 mm. **Note:** Reduced size; Small characters.

Date	Good	VG	F	VF	XF
ND(1887) Series 10	—	—	—	—	50.00

KM# A887.10 5 MUN
, 30 mm. **Rev:** Crescent at upper right

Date	Good	VG	F	VF	XF
ND(1887) Series 10	5.00	7.50	15.00	25.00	—

KWANG JU TOWNSHIP MILITARY OFFICE

(Kwang Ju Kwal Li Yong)

KM# 889.1 MUN
4.0000 g., Cast Bronze, 25 mm. **Rev:** "Ch'on" at bottom, series number at right

Date	Good	VG	F	VF	XF
ND(1836) Series 1	3.00	5.00	8.00	12.00	—

KM# 889s.1 MUN
4.0000 g., Cast Bronze, 25 mm.

Date	Good	VG	F	VF	XF
ND(1836) Series 1	—	—	—	—	45.00

KM# 889.2 MUN
4.0000 g., Cast Bronze, 25 mm. **Rev:** "Ch'on" at bottom, series number at right

Date	Good	VG	F	VF	XF
ND(1836) Series 2	3.00	5.00	8.00	12.00	—

KM# 889s.2 MUN
4.0000 g., Cast Bronze, 25 mm.

Date	Good	VG	F	VF	XF
ND(1836) Series 2	—	—	—	—	45.00

KM# 889.3 MUN
4.0000 g., Cast Bronze, 25 mm. **Rev:** "Ch'un" at bottom, series number at right

Date	Good	VG	F	VF	XF
ND(1836) Series 3	3.00	5.00	8.00	12.00	—

KM# 889s.3 MUN
4.0000 g., Cast Bronze, 25 mm.

Date	Good	VG	F	VF	XF
ND(1836) Series 3	—	—	—	—	45.00

KM# 889.4 MUN
4.0000 g., Cast Bronze, 25 mm. **Rev:** "Ch'on" at bottom, series number at right

Date	Good	VG	F	VF	XF
ND(1836) Series 4	1.75	2.25	3.00	5.00	—

KM# 889s.4 MUN
4.0000 g., Cast Bronze, 25 mm.

Date	Good	VG	F	VF	XF
ND(1836) Series 4	—	—	—	—	25.00

KM# 889.5 MUN
4.0000 g., Cast Bronze, 25 mm. **Rev:** "Ch'on" at bottom, series number at right

Date	Good	VG	F	VF	XF
ND(1836) Series 5	1.75	2.25	3.00	5.00	—

KM# 889s.5 MUN
4.0000 g., Cast Bronze, 25 mm.

Date	Good	VG	F	VF	XF
ND(1836) Series 5	—	—	—	—	25.00

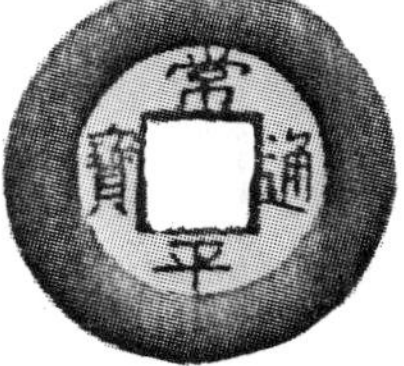

KM# 890.1 MUN
4.0000 g., Cast Bronze, 26 mm. **Rev:** "Ch'on" at bottom, series number at left **Note:** Large characters.

Date	Good	VG	F	VF	XF
ND(1836) Series 1	1.75	2.25	3.00	5.00	—

KM# 890s.1 MUN
4.0000 g., Cast Bronze, 26 mm. **Note:** Large characters.

Date	Good	VG	F	VF	XF
ND(1836) Series 1	—	—	—	—	25.00

KM# A890.1 MUN
4.0000 g., Cast Bronze, 24 mm. **Note:** Small characters.

Date	Good	VG	F	VF	XF
ND(1836) Series 1	1.75	2.25	3.00	5.00	—

KM# A890s.1 MUN
4.0000 g., Cast Bronze, 24 mm. **Note:** Small characters.

Date	Good	VG	F	VF	XF
ND(1836) Series 1	—	—	—	—	25.00

KM# 890.2 MUN
4.0000 g., Cast Bronze, 26 mm. **Rev:** "Ch'on" at bottom, series number at left **Note:** Large characters.

Date	Good	VG	F	VF	XF
ND(1836) Series 2	1.75	2.25	3.00	5.00	—

KM# 890s.2 MUN
4.0000 g., Cast Bronze, 26 mm. **Note:** Large characters.

Date	Good	VG	F	VF	XF
ND(1836) Series 2	—	—	—	—	25.00

KM# A890.2 MUN
4.0000 g., Cast Bronze, 24 mm. **Note:** Small characters.

Date	Good	VG	F	VF	XF
ND(1836) Series 2	1.75	2.25	3.00	5.00	—

KM# A890s.2 MUN
4.0000 g., Cast Bronze, 24 mm. **Note:** Small characters.

Date	Good	VG	F	VF	XF
ND(1836) Series 2	—	—	—	—	25.00

KM# 890.3 MUN
4.0000 g., Cast Bronze, 26 mm. **Rev:** "Ch'on" at bottom, series number at left **Note:** Large characters.

Date	Good	VG	F	VF	XF
ND(1836) Series 3	1.75	2.25	3.00	5.00	—

KM# 890s.3 MUN
4.0000 g., Cast Bronze, 26 mm. **Note:** Large characters.

Date	Good	VG	F	VF	XF
ND(1836) Series 3	—	—	—	—	25.00

KM# A890.3 MUN
4.0000 g., Cast Bronze, 24 mm. **Note:** Small characters.

Date	Good	VG	F	VF	XF
ND(1836) Series 3	1.75	2.25	3.00	5.00	—

KM# A890s.3 MUN
4.0000 g., Cast Bronze, 24 mm. **Note:** Small characters.

Date	Good	VG	F	VF	XF
ND(1836) Series 3	—	—	—	—	25.00

KM# 890.4 MUN
4.0000 g., Cast Bronze, 26 mm. **Rev:** "Ch'on" at bottom, series number at left **Note:** Large characters.

Date	Good	VG	F	VF	XF
ND(1836) Series 4	1.75	2.25	3.00	5.00	—

KM# 890s.4 MUN
4.0000 g., Cast Bronze, 26 mm. **Note:** Large characters.

Date	Good	VG	F	VF	XF
ND(1836) Series 4	—	—	—	—	25.00

KM# A890.4 MUN
4.0000 g., Cast Bronze, 24 mm. **Note:** Small characters.

Date	Good	VG	F	VF	XF
ND(1836) Series 4	1.75	2.25	3.00	5.00	—

KM# A890s.4 MUN
4.0000 g., Cast Bronze, 24 mm. **Note:** Small characters.

Date	Good	VG	F	VF	XF
ND(1836) Series 4	—	—	—	—	25.00

KM# 890.5 MUN
4.0000 g., Cast Bronze, 26 mm. **Rev:** "Ch'on" at bottom, series number at left **Note:** Large characters.

Date	Good	VG	F	VF	XF
ND(1836) Series 5	1.75	2.25	3.00	5.00	—

KM# 890s.5 MUN
4.0000 g., Cast Bronze, 26 mm. **Note:** Large characters.

Date	Good	VG	F	VF	XF
ND(1836) Series 5	—	—	—	—	25.00

KM# A890.5 MUN
4.0000 g., Cast Bronze, 24 mm. **Note:** Small characters.

Date	Good	VG	F	VF	XF
ND(1836) Series 5	1.75	2.25	3.00	5.00	—

KM# A890s.5 MUN
4.0000 g., Cast Bronze, 24 mm. **Note:** Small characters.

Date	Good	VG	F	VF	XF
ND(1836) Series 5	—	—	—	—	25.00

KM# 890.6 MUN
4.0000 g., Cast Bronze, 26 mm. **Rev:** "Ch'on" at bottom, series number at left **Note:** Large characters.

Date	Good	VG	F	VF	XF
ND(1836) Series 6	1.75	2.25	3.00	5.00	—

KM# 890s.6 MUN
4.0000 g., Cast Bronze, 26 mm. **Note:** Large characters.

Date	Good	VG	F	VF	XF
ND(1836) Series 6	—	—	—	—	25.00

KM# A890.6 MUN
4.0000 g., Cast Bronze, 24 mm. **Note:** Small characters.

Date	Good	VG	F	VF	XF
ND(1836) Series 6	1.75	2.25	3.00	5.00	—

KM# A890s.6 MUN
4.0000 g., Cast Bronze, 24 mm. **Note:** Small characters.

Date	Good	VG	F	VF	XF
ND(1836) Series 6	—	—	—	—	25.00

KM# 890.7 MUN
4.0000 g., Cast Bronze, 26 mm. **Rev:** "Ch'on" at bottom, series number at left **Note:** Large characters.

Date	Good	VG	F	VF	XF
ND(1836) Series 7	1.75	2.25	3.00	5.00	—

KM# 890s.7 MUN
4.0000 g., Cast Bronze, 26 mm. **Note:** Large characters.

Date	Good	VG	F	VF	XF
ND(1836) Series 7	—	—	—	—	25.00

KM# A890.7 MUN
4.0000 g., Cast Bronze, 24 mm. **Note:** Small characters.

Date	Good	VG	F	VF	XF
ND(1836) Series 7	1.75	2.25	3.00	5.00	—

KM# A890s.7 MUN
4.0000 g., Cast Bronze, 24 mm. **Note:** Seed type.

Date	Good	VG	F	VF	XF
ND(1836) Series 7	—	—	—	—	25.00

KM# 890.8 MUN
4.0000 g., Cast Bronze, 26 mm. **Rev:** "Ch'on" at bottom, series number at left **Note:** Large characters.

Date	Good	VG	F	VF	XF
ND(1836) Series 8	1.75	2.25	3.00	5.00	—

KM# 890s.8 MUN
4.0000 g., Cast Bronze, 26 mm. **Note:** Large characters.

Date	Good	VG	F	VF	XF
ND(1836) Series 8	—	—	—	—	25.00

KM# A890.8 MUN
4.0000 g., Cast Bronze, 24 mm. **Note:** Small characters.

Date	Good	VG	F	VF	XF
ND(1836) Series 8	1.75	2.25	3.00	5.00	—

KM# A890s.8 MUN
4.0000 g., Cast Bronze, 24 mm. **Note:** Small characters.

Date	Good	VG	F	VF	XF
ND(1836) Series 8	—	—	—	—	25.00

KM# 890.9 MUN
4.0000 g., Cast Bronze, 26 mm. **Rev:** "Ch'on" at bottom, series number at left **Note:** Large characters.

Date	Good	VG	F	VF	XF
ND(1836) Series 9	1.75	2.25	3.00	5.00	—

KM# 890s.9 MUN
4.0000 g., Cast Bronze, 26 mm. **Note:** Large characters.

Date	Good	VG	F	VF	XF
ND(1836) Series 9	—	—	—	—	25.00

KM# A890.9 MUN
4.0000 g., Cast Bronze, 24 mm. **Note:** Small characters.

Date	Good	VG	F	VF	XF
ND(1836) Series 9	1.75	2.25	3.00	5.00	—

KM# A890s.9 MUN
4.0000 g., Cast Bronze, 24 mm. **Note:** Small characters.

Date	Good	VG	F	VF	XF
ND(1836) Series 9	—	—	—	—	25.00

KM# 890.10 MUN
4.0000 g., Cast Bronze, 26 mm. **Rev:** "Ch'on" at bottom, series number at left **Note:** Large characters.

Date	Good	VG	F	VF	XF
ND(1836) Series 10	1.75	2.25	3.00	5.00	—

KM# 890s.10 MUN
4.0000 g., Cast Bronze, 26 mm. **Note:** Large characters.

Date	Good	VG	F	VF	XF
ND(1836) Series 10	—	—	—	—	25.00

KM# A890.10 MUN
4.0000 g., Cast Bronze, 24 mm. **Note:** Small characters.

Date	Good	VG	F	VF	XF
ND(1836) Series 10	1.75	2.25	3.00	5.00	—

KM# A890s.10 MUN
4.0000 g., Cast Bronze, 24 mm. **Note:** Small characters.

Date	Good	VG	F	VF	XF
ND(1836) Series 10	—	—	—	—	25.00

KM# 892.1 MUN
4.0000 g., Cast Bronze, 25 mm. **Rev:** Crescent at left, series number at right

Date	Good	VG	F	VF	XF
ND(1836) Series 1	4.00	6.00	10.00	18.00	—

KM# 892s.1 MUN
4.0000 g., Cast Bronze, 25 mm.

Date	Good	VG	F	VF	XF
ND(1836) Series 1	—	—	—	—	60.00

KM# 892.2 MUN
4.0000 g., Cast Bronze, 25 mm. **Rev:** Crescent at left, series number at right

Date	Good	VG	F	VF	XF
ND(1836) Series 2	4.00	6.00	10.00	18.00	—

KM# 892s.2 MUN
4.0000 g., Cast Bronze, 25 mm.

Date	Good	VG	F	VF	XF
ND(1836) Series 2	—	—	—	—	35.00

KM# 892.3 MUN
4.0000 g., Cast Bronze, 25 mm. **Rev:** Crescent at left, series number at right

Date	Good	VG	F	VF	XF
ND(1836) Series 3	4.00	6.00	10.00	18.00	—

KM# 892s.3 MUN
4.0000 g., Cast Bronze, 25 mm.

Date	Good	VG	F	VF	XF
ND(1836) Series 3	—	—	—	—	60.00

KM# 892.4 MUN
4.0000 g., Cast Bronze, 25 mm. **Rev:** Crescent at left, series number at right

Date	Good	VG	F	VF	XF
ND(1836) Series 4	4.00	6.00	10.00	18.00	—

KM# 892s.4 MUN
4.0000 g., Cast Bronze, 25 mm.

Date	Good	VG	F	VF	XF
ND(1836) Series 4	—	—	—	—	60.00

KM# 892.5 MUN
4.0000 g., Cast Bronze, 25 mm. **Rev:** Crescent at left, series number at right

Date	Good	VG	F	VF	XF
ND(1836) Series 5	4.00	6.00	10.00	18.00	—

KM# 892s.5 MUN
4.0000 g., Cast Bronze, 25 mm.

Date	Good	VG	F	VF	XF
ND(1836) Series 5	—	—	—	—	60.00

KM# 892.6 MUN
4.0000 g., Cast Bronze, 25 mm. **Rev:** Crescent at left, series number at right

Date	Good	VG	F	VF	XF
ND(1836) Series 6	4.00	6.00	10.00	18.00	—

KM# 892s.6 MUN
4.0000 g., Cast Bronze, 25 mm.

Date	Good	VG	F	VF	XF
ND(1836) Series 6	—	—	—	—	60.00

KM# 892.7 MUN
4.0000 g., Cast Bronze, 25 mm. **Rev:** Crescent at left, series number at right

Date	Good	VG	F	VF	XF
ND(1836) Series 7	4.00	6.00	10.00	18.00	—

KM# 892s.7 MUN
4.0000 g., Cast Bronze, 25 mm.

Date	Good	VG	F	VF	XF
ND(1836) Series 7	—	—	—	—	60.00

KM# 892.8 MUN
4.0000 g., Cast Bronze, 25 mm. **Rev:** Crescent at left, series number at right

Date	Good	VG	F	VF	XF
ND(1836) Series 8	4.00	6.00	10.00	18.00	—

KM# 892s.8 MUN
4.0000 g., Cast Bronze, 25 mm.

Date	Good	VG	F	VF	XF
ND(1836) Series 8	—	—	—	—	60.00

KM# 892.9 MUN
4.0000 g., Cast Bronze, 25 mm. **Rev:** Crescent at left, series number at right

Date	Good	VG	F	VF	XF
ND(1836) Series 9	4.00	6.00	10.00	18.00	—

KM# 892s.9 MUN
4.0000 g., Cast Bronze, 25 mm.

Date	Good	VG	F	VF	XF
ND(1836) Series 9	—	—	—	—	60.00

KM# 892.10 MUN
4.0000 g., Cast Bronze, 25 mm. **Rev:** Crescent at left, series number at right

Date	Good	VG	F	VF	XF
ND(1836) Series 10	4.00	6.00	10.00	18.00	—

KM# 892s.10 MUN
4.0000 g., Cast Bronze, 25 mm.

Date	Good	VG	F	VF	XF
ND(1836) Series 10	—	—	—	—	60.00

KM# 891.1 MUN
4.0000 g., Cast Bronze, 27 mm. **Rev:** "Ch'on" at bottom, series number at right, circle at left

Date	Good	VG	F	VF	XF
ND(1839) Series 1	4.00	6.00	10.00	18.00	—

KM# 891s.1 MUN
4.0000 g., Cast Bronze, 27 mm.

Date	Good	VG	F	VF	XF
ND(1839) Series 1	—	—	—	—	60.00

KM# 891.2 MUN
4.0000 g., Cast Bronze, 27 mm. **Rev:** "Ch'on" at bottom, series number at right, circle at left

Date	Good	VG	F	VF	XF
ND(1839) Series 2	4.00	6.00	10.00	18.00	—

KM# 891s.2 MUN
4.0000 g., Cast Bronze, 27 mm.

Date	Good	VG	F	VF	XF
ND(1839) Series 2	—	—	—	—	60.00

KM# 891.3 MUN
4.0000 g., Cast Bronze, 27 mm. **Rev:** "Ch'on" at bottom, series number at right, circle at left

Date	Good	VG	F	VF	XF
ND(1839) Series 3	4.00	6.00	10.00	18.00	—

KM# 891s.3 MUN
4.0000 g., Cast Bronze, 27 mm.

Date	Good	VG	F	VF	XF
ND(1839) Series 3	—	—	—	—	60.00

KM# 891.4 MUN
4.0000 g., Cast Bronze, 27 mm. **Rev:** "Ch'on" at bottom, series number at right, circle at left

Date	Good	VG	F	VF	XF
ND(1839) Series 4	4.00	6.00	10.00	18.00	—

KM# 891s.4 MUN
4.0000 g., Cast Bronze, 27 mm.

Date	Good	VG	F	VF	XF
ND(1839) Series 4	—	—	—	—	60.00

KM# 891.5 MUN
4.0000 g., Cast Bronze, 27 mm.

Date	Good	VG	F	VF	XF
ND(1839) Series 5	4.00	6.00	10.00	18.00	—

KM# 891s.5 MUN
4.0000 g., Cast Bronze, 27 mm.

Date	Good	VG	F	VF	XF
ND(1839) Series 5	—	—	—	—	60.00

KM# 893.1 MUN
4.0000 g., Cast Bronze, 26.5 mm. **Rev:** Crescent at right, series number at left

Date	Good	VG	F	VF	XF
ND(1839) Series 1	4.00	6.00	9.00	16.00	—

KM# 893s.1 MUN
4.0000 g., Cast Bronze, 26.5 mm.

Date	Good	VG	F	VF	XF
ND(1839) Series 1	—	—	—	—	60.00

KM# 893.2 MUN
4.0000 g., Cast Bronze, 26.5 mm. **Rev:** Crescent at right, series number at left

Date	Good	VG	F	VF	XF
ND(1839) Series 2	4.00	6.00	9.00	16.00	—

KM# 893s.2 MUN
4.0000 g., Cast Bronze, 26.5 mm.

Date	Good	VG	F	VF	XF
ND(1839) Series 2	—	—	—	—	60.00

KM# 893.3 MUN
4.0000 g., Cast Bronze, 26.5 mm. **Rev:** Crescent at right, series number at left

Date	Good	VG	F	VF	XF
ND(1839) Series 3	4.00	6.00	9.00	16.00	—

KM# 893s.3 MUN
4.0000 g., Cast Bronze, 26.5 mm.

Date	Good	VG	F	VF	XF
ND(1839) Series 3	—	—	—	—	60.00

KM# 893.4 MUN
4.0000 g., Cast Bronze, 26.5 mm. **Rev:** Crescent at right, series number at left

Date	Good	VG	F	VF	XF
ND(1839) Series 4	4.00	6.00	9.00	16.00	—

KM# 893s.4 MUN
4.0000 g., Cast Bronze, 26.5 mm.

Date	Good	VG	F	VF	XF
ND(1839) Series 4	—	—	—	—	60.00

KM# 893.5 MUN
4.0000 g., Cast Bronze, 26.5 mm. **Rev:** Crescent at right, series number at left

Date	Good	VG	F	VF	XF
ND(1839) Series 5	4.00	6.00	9.00	16.00	—

KM# 893s.5 MUN
4.0000 g., Cast Bronze, 26.5 mm.

Date	Good	VG	F	VF	XF
ND(1839) Series 5	—	—	—	—	60.00

KM# 893.6 MUN
4.0000 g., Cast Bronze, 26.5 mm. **Rev:** Crescent at right, series number at left

Date	Good	VG	F	VF	XF
ND(1839) Series 6	4.00	6.00	9.00	16.00	—

KM# 893s.6 MUN
4.0000 g., Cast Bronze, 26.5 mm.

Date	Good	VG	F	VF	XF
ND(1839) Series 6	—	—	—	—	60.00

KM# 893.7 MUN
4.0000 g., Cast Bronze, 26.5 mm. **Rev:** Crescent at right, series number at left

Date	Good	VG	F	VF	XF
ND(1839) Series 7	4.00	6.00	9.00	16.00	—

KM# 893s.7 MUN
4.0000 g., Cast Bronze, 26.5 mm.

Date	Good	VG	F	VF	XF
ND(1839) Series 7	—	—	—	—	60.00

KM# 893.8 MUN
4.0000 g., Cast Bronze, 26.5 mm. **Rev:** Crescent at right, series number at left

Date	Good	VG	F	VF	XF
ND(1839) Series 8	4.00	6.00	9.00	16.00	—

KM# 893s.8 MUN
4.0000 g., Cast Bronze, 26.5 mm.

Date	Good	VG	F	VF	XF
ND(1839) Series 8	—	—	—	—	60.00

KM# 893.9 MUN
4.0000 g., Cast Bronze, 26.5 mm. **Rev:** Crescent at right, series number at left

Date	Good	VG	F	VF	XF
ND(1839) Series 9	4.00	6.00	9.00	16.00	—

KM# 893s.9 MUN
4.0000 g., Cast Bronze, 26.5 mm.

Date	Good	VG	F	VF	XF
ND(1839) Series 9	—	—	—	—	60.00

KM# 893.10 MUN
4.0000 g., Cast Bronze, 26.5 mm. **Rev:** Crescent at right, series number at left

Date	Good	VG	F	VF	XF
ND(1839) Series 10	4.00	6.00	9.00	16.00	—

KM# 893s.10 MUN
4.0000 g., Cast Bronze, 26.5 mm.

Date	Good	VG	F	VF	XF
ND(1839) Series 10	—	—	—	—	60.00

KM# 894.1 MUN
4.0000 g., Cast Bronze, 26 mm. **Rev:** "I" (2) at bottom, series number at right

Date	Good	VG	F	VF	XF
ND(1839) Series 1	5.00	8.50	13.50	20.00	—

KM# 894s.1 MUN
4.0000 g., Cast Bronze, 26 mm. **Rev:** "I" (2) at bottom, series number at right

Date	Good	VG	F	VF	XF
ND(1839) Series 1	—	—	—	—	60.00

KM# 894.2 MUN
4.0000 g., Cast Bronze, 26 mm. **Rev:** "I" (2) at bottom, series number at right

Date	Good	VG	F	VF	XF
ND(1839) Series 2	5.00	8.50	13.50	20.00	—

KM# 894s.2 MUN
4.0000 g., Cast Bronze, 26 mm.

Date	Good	VG	F	VF	XF
ND(1839) Series 2	—	—	—	—	60.00

KM# 894.3 MUN
4.0000 g., Cast Bronze, 26 mm. **Rev:** "I" (2) at bottom, series number at right

Date	Good	VG	F	VF	XF
ND(1839) Series 3	5.00	8.50	13.50	20.00	—

KM# 894s.3 MUN
4.0000 g., Cast Bronze, 26 mm.

Date	Good	VG	F	VF	XF
ND(1839) Series 3	—	—	—	—	60.00

KM# 894.4 MUN
4.0000 g., Cast Bronze, 26 mm. **Rev:** "I" (2) at bottom, series number at right

Date	Good	VG	F	VF	XF
ND(1839) Series 4	5.00	8.50	13.50	20.00	—

KM# 894s.4 MUN
4.0000 g., Cast Bronze, 26 mm.

Date	Good	VG	F	VF	XF
ND(1839) Series 4	—	—	—	—	60.00

KM# 894.5 MUN
4.0000 g., Cast Bronze, 26 mm. **Rev:** "I" (2) at bottom, series number at right

Date	Good	VG	F	VF	XF
ND(1839) Series 5	5.00	8.50	13.50	20.00	—

KM# 894s.5 MUN
4.0000 g., Cast Bronze, 26 mm.

Date	Good	VG	F	VF	XF
ND(1839) Series 5	—	—	—	—	60.00

KM# 894.6 MUN
4.0000 g., Cast Bronze, 26 mm. **Rev:** "I" (2) at bottom, series number at right

Date	Good	VG	F	VF	XF
ND(1839) Series 6	5.00	8.50	13.50	20.00	—

KM# 894s.6 MUN
4.0000 g., Cast Bronze, 26 mm.

Date	Good	VG	F	VF	XF
ND(1839) Series 6	—	—	—	—	60.00

KM# 894.7 MUN
4.0000 g., Cast Bronze, 26 mm. **Rev:** "I" (2) at bottom, series number at right

Date	Good	VG	F	VF	XF
ND(1839) Series 7	5.00	8.50	13.50	20.00	—

KM# 894s.7 MUN
4.0000 g., Cast Bronze, 26 mm.

Date	Good	VG	F	VF	XF
ND(1839) Series 7	—	—	—	—	60.00

KM# 894.8 MUN
4.0000 g., Cast Bronze, 26 mm. **Rev:** "I" (2) at bottom, series number at right

Date	Good	VG	F	VF	XF
ND(1839) Series 8	5.00	8.50	13.50	20.00	—

KM# 894s.8 MUN
4.0000 g., Cast Bronze, 26 mm.

Date	Good	VG	F	VF	XF
ND(1839) Series 8	—	—	—	—	60.00

KM# 894.9 MUN
4.0000 g., Cast Bronze, 26 mm. **Rev:** "I" (2) at bottom, series number at right

Date	Good	VG	F	VF	XF
ND(1839) Series 9	5.00	8.50	13.50	20.00	—

KM# 894s.9 MUN
4.0000 g., Cast Bronze, 26 mm.

Date	Good	VG	F	VF	XF
ND(1839) Series 9	—	—	—	—	60.00

KM# 894.10 MUN
4.0000 g., Cast Bronze, 26 mm. **Rev:** "I" (2) at bottom, series number at right

Date	Good	VG	F	VF	XF
ND(1839) Series 10	5.00	8.50	13.50	20.00	—

KM# 894s.10 MUN
4.0000 g., Cast Bronze, 26 mm.

Date	Good	VG	F	VF	XF
ND(1839) Series 10	—	—	—	—	60.00

KM# 895.1 MUN
4.0000 g., Cast Bronze, 26 mm. **Rev:** "I" (2) at bottom, series number at left

Date	Good	VG	F	VF	XF
ND(1839) Series 1	5.00	8.00	13.50	20.00	—

KM# 895s.1 MUN
4.0000 g., Cast Bronze, 26 mm.

Date	Good	VG	F	VF	XF
ND(1839) Series 1	—	—	—	—	60.00

KM# 895.2 MUN
4.0000 g., Cast Bronze, 26 mm. **Rev:** "I" (2) at bottom, series number at left

Date	Good	VG	F	VF	XF
ND(1839) Series 2	5.00	8.00	12.50	20.00	—

KM# 895s.2 MUN
4.0000 g., Cast Bronze, 26 mm.

Date	Good	VG	F	VF	XF
ND(1839) Series 2	—	—	—	—	60.00

KM# 895.3 MUN
4.0000 g., Cast Bronze, 26 mm. **Rev:** "I" (2) at bottom, series number at left

Date	Good	VG	F	VF	XF
ND(1839) Series 3	5.00	8.00	13.50	20.00	—

KM# 895s.3 MUN
4.0000 g., Cast Bronze, 26 mm.

Date	Good	VG	F	VF	XF
ND(1839) Series 3	—	—	—	—	60.00

KM# 895.4 MUN
4.0000 g., Cast Bronze, 26 mm. **Rev:** "I" (2) at bottom, series number at left

Date	Good	VG	F	VF	XF
ND(1839) Series 4	5.00	8.00	13.50	20.00	—

KM# 895s.4 MUN
4.0000 g., Cast Bronze, 26 mm.

Date	Good	VG	F	VF	XF
ND(1839) Series 4	—	—	—	—	60.00

KM# 895.5 MUN
4.0000 g., Cast Bronze, 26 mm. **Rev:** "I" (2) at bottom, series number at left

Date	Good	VG	F	VF	XF
ND(1839) Series 5	5.00	8.00	13.50	20.00	—

KM# 895s.5 MUN
4.0000 g., Cast Bronze, 26 mm.

Date	Good	VG	F	VF	XF
ND(1839) Series 5	—	—	—	—	60.00

KM# 895.6 MUN
4.0000 g., Cast Bronze, 26 mm. **Rev:** "I" (2) at bottom, series number at left

Date	Good	VG	F	VF	XF
ND(1839) Series 6	5.00	8.00	13.50	20.00	—

KM# 895s.6 MUN
4.0000 g., Cast Bronze, 26 mm.

Date	Good	VG	F	VF	XF
ND(1839) Series 6	—	—	—	—	60.00

KM# 895.7 MUN
4.0000 g., Cast Bronze, 26 mm. **Rev:** "I" (2) at bottom, series number at left

Date	Good	VG	F	VF	XF
ND(1839) Series 7	5.00	8.00	13.50	20.00	—

KM# 895s.7 MUN
4.0000 g., Cast Bronze, 26 mm.

Date	Good	VG	F	VF	XF
ND(1839) Series 7	—	—	—	—	60.00

KM# 895.8 MUN
4.0000 g., Cast Bronze, 26 mm. **Rev:** "I" (2) at bottom, series number at left

Date	Good	VG	F	VF	XF
ND(1839) Series 8	5.00	8.00	13.50	20.00	—

KM# 895s.8 MUN
4.0000 g., Cast Bronze, 26 mm.

Date	Good	VG	F	VF	XF
ND(1839) Series 8	—	—	—	—	60.00

KM# 895.9 MUN
4.0000 g., Cast Bronze, 26 mm. **Rev:** "I" (2) at bottom, series number at left

Date	Good	VG	F	VF	XF
ND(1839) Series 9	5.00	8.00	13.50	20.00	—

KM# 895s.9 MUN
4.0000 g., Cast Bronze, 26 mm.

Date	Good	VG	F	VF	XF
ND(1839) Series 9	—	—	—	—	60.00

KM# 895.10 MUN
4.0000 g., Cast Bronze, 26 mm. **Rev:** "I" (2) at bottom, series number at left

Date	Good	VG	F	VF	XF
ND(1839) Series 10	5.00	8.00	13.50	20.00	—

KM# 895s.10 MUN
4.0000 g., Cast Bronze, 26 mm.

Date	Good	VG	F	VF	XF
ND(1839) Series 10	—	—	—	—	60.00

KM# 896.1 MUN
4.0000 g., Cast Bronze, 26 mm. **Rev:** "I" (2) at bottom, crescent at right, series number at left

Date	Good	VG	F	VF	XF
ND(1839) Series 1	5.00	8.00	12.50	20.00	—

KM# 896s.1 MUN
4.0000 g., Cast Bronze, 26 mm.

Date	Good	VG	F	VF	XF
ND(1839) Series 1	—	—	—	—	60.00

KM# 896.2 MUN
4.0000 g., Cast Bronze, 6 mm. **Rev:** "I" (2) at bottom, crescent at right, series number at left

Date	Good	VG	F	VF	XF
ND(1839) Series 2	5.00	8.00	12.50	20.00	—

KM# 896s.2 MUN
4.0000 g., Cast Bronze, 26 mm.

Date	Good	VG	F	VF	XF
ND(1839) Series 2	—	—	—	—	60.00

KM# 896.3 MUN
4.0000 g., Cast Bronze, 26 mm. **Rev:** "I" (2) at bottom, crescent at right, series number at left

Date	Good	VG	F	VF	XF
ND(1839) Series 3	5.00	8.00	12.50	20.00	—

KM# 896s.3 MUN
4.0000 g., Cast Bronze, 26 mm.

Date	Good	VG	F	VF	XF
ND(1839) Series 3	—	—	—	—	60.00

KM# 896.4 MUN
4.0000 g., Cast Bronze, 26 mm. **Rev:** "I" (2) at bottom, crescent at right, series number at left

Date	Good	VG	F	VF	XF
ND(1839) Series 4	5.00	8.00	12.50	20.00	—

KM# 896s.4 MUN
4.0000 g., Cast Bronze, 26 mm.

Date	Good	VG	F	VF	XF
ND(1839) Series 4	—	—	—	—	60.00

KM# 896.5 MUN
4.0000 g., Cast Bronze, 26 mm. **Rev:** "I" (2) at bottom, crescent at right, series number at left

Date	Good	VG	F	VF	XF
ND(1839) Series 5	5.00	8.00	12.50	20.00	—

KM# 896s.5 MUN
4.0000 g., Cast Bronze, 26 mm.

Date	Good	VG	F	VF	XF
ND(1839) Series 5	—	—	—	—	60.00

KM# 896.6 MUN
4.0000 g., Cast Bronze, 26 mm. **Rev:** "I" (2) at bottom, crescent at right, series number at left

Date	Good	VG	F	VF	XF
ND(1839) Series 6	5.00	8.00	12.50	20.00	—

KM# 896s.6 MUN
4.0000 g., Cast Bronze, 26 mm.

Date	Good	VG	F	VF	XF
ND(1839) Series 6	—	—	—	—	60.00

KM# 896.7 MUN
4.0000 g., Cast Bronze, 26 mm. **Rev:** "I" (2) at bottom, crescent at right, series number at left

Date	Good	VG	F	VF	XF
ND(1839) Series 7	5.00	8.00	12.50	20.00	—

KM# 896s.7 MUN
4.0000 g., Cast Bronze, 26 mm.

Date	Good	VG	F	VF	XF
ND(1839) Series 7	—	—	—	—	60.00

KM# 896.8 MUN
4.0000 g., Cast Bronze, 26 mm. **Rev:** "I" (2) at bottom, crescent at right, series number at left

Date	Good	VG	F	VF	XF
ND(1839) Series 8	5.00	8.00	12.50	20.00	—

KM# 896s.8 MUN
4.0000 g., Cast Bronze, 26 mm.

Date	Good	VG	F	VF	XF
ND(1839) Series 8	—	—	—	—	60.00

KM# 896.9 MUN
4.0000 g., Cast Bronze, 26 mm. **Rev:** "I" (2) at bottom, crescent at right, series number at left

Date	Good	VG	F	VF	XF
ND(1839) Series 9	5.00	8.00	12.50	20.00	—

KM# 896s.9 MUN
4.0000 g., Cast Bronze, 26 mm.

Date	Good	VG	F	VF	XF
ND(1839) Series 9	—	—	—	—	60.00

KM# 896.10 MUN
4.0000 g., Cast Bronze, 26 mm. **Rev:** "I" (2) at bottom, crescent at right, series number at left

Date	Good	VG	F	VF	XF
ND(1839) Series 10	5.00	8.00	12.50	20.00	—

KM# 896s.10 MUN
4.0000 g., Cast Bronze, 26 mm.

Date	Good	VG	F	VF	XF
ND(1839) Series 10	—	—	—	—	60.00

KYONGGI PROVINCIAL OFFICE

(Kyong Gi Kam Yong)

KM# 907.1 5 MUN

Cast Bronze **Rev:** "Kyong" at top, "Tang" at right, "O" (5) at left, series number at bottom **Note:** Size varies: 29-30 mm.

Date	Good	VG	F	VF	XF
ND(1888) Series 1	2.00	3.00	5.00	10.00	—

KM# 907s.1 5 MUN

Cast Bronze **Note:** Size varies: 29-30 mm.

Date	Good	VG	F	VF	XF
ND(1888) Series 1	—	—	—	—	50.00

KM# 907.2 5 MUN

Cast Bronze **Rev:** "Kyong" at top, "Tang" at right, "O" (5) at left, series number at bottom **Note:** Size varies: 29-30 mm.

Date	Good	VG	F	VF	XF
ND(1888) Series 2	2.00	3.00	5.00	10.00	—

KM# 907s.2 5 MUN

Cast Bronze **Note:** Size varies: 29-30 mm.

Date	Good	VG	F	VF	XF
ND(1888) Series 2	—	—	—	—	50.00

KM# 907.3 5 MUN

Cast Bronze **Rev:** "Kyong" at top, "Tang" at right, "O" (5) at left, series number at bottom **Note:** Size varies: 29-30 mm.

Date	Good	VG	F	VF	XF
ND(1888) Series 3	2.00	3.00	5.00	10.00	—

KM# 907s.3 5 MUN

Cast Bronze **Note:** Size varies: 29-30 mm.

Date	Good	VG	F	VF	XF
ND(1888) Series 3	—	—	—	—	50.00

KM# 907.4 5 MUN

Cast Bronze **Rev:** "Kyong" at top, "Tang" at right, "O" (5) at left, series number at bottom **Note:** Size varies: 29-30 mm.

Date	Good	VG	F	VF	XF
ND(1888) Series 4	2.00	3.00	5.00	10.00	—

KM# 907s.4 5 MUN

Cast Bronze **Note:** Size varies: 29-30 mm.

Date	Good	VG	F	VF	XF
ND(1888) Series 4	—	—	—	—	50.00

KM# 907.5 5 MUN

Cast Bronze **Rev:** "Kyong" at top, "Tang" at right, "O" (5) at left, series number at bottom **Note:** Size varies: 29-30 mm.

Date	Good	VG	F	VF	XF
ND(1888) Series 5	2.00	3.00	5.00	10.00	—

KM# 907s.5 5 MUN

Cast Bronze **Note:** Size varies: 29-30 mm.

Date	Good	VG	F	VF	XF
ND(1888) Series 5	—	—	—	—	50.00

KM# 907.6 5 MUN

Cast Bronze **Rev:** "Kyong" at top, "Tang" at right, "O" (5) at left, series number at bottom **Note:** Size varies: 29-30 mm.

Date	Good	VG	F	VF	XF
ND(1888) Series 6	2.00	3.00	5.00	10.00	—

KM# 907s.6 5 MUN

Cast Bronze **Note:** Size varies: 29-30 mm.

Date	Good	VG	F	VF	XF
ND(1888) Series 6	—	—	—	—	50.00

KM# 907.7 5 MUN

Cast Bronze **Rev:** "Kyong" at top, "Tang" at right, "O" (5) at left, series number at bottom **Note:** Size varies: 29-30 mm.

Date	Good	VG	F	VF	XF
ND(1888) Series 7	2.00	3.00	5.00	10.00	—

KM# 907s.7 5 MUN

Cast Bronze **Note:** Size varies: 29-30 mm.

Date	Good	VG	F	VF	XF
ND(1888) Series 7	—	—	—	—	50.00

KM# 907.8 5 MUN

Cast Bronze **Rev:** "Kyong" at top, "Tang" at right, "O" (5) at left, series number at bottom **Note:** Size varies: 29-30 mm.

Date	Good	VG	F	VF	XF
ND(1888) Series 8	2.00	3.00	5.00	10.00	—

KM# 907s.8 5 MUN

Cast Bronze **Note:** Size varies: 29-30 mm.

Date	Good	VG	F	VF	XF
ND(1888) Series 8	—	—	—	—	50.00

KM# 907.9 5 MUN

Cast Bronze **Rev:** "Kyong" at top, "Tang" at right, "O" (5) at left, series number at bottom **Note:** Size varies: 29-30 mm.

Date	Good	VG	F	VF	XF
ND(1888) Series 9	2.00	3.00	5.00	10.00	—

KM# 907s.9 5 MUN

Cast Bronze **Note:** Size varies: 29-30 mm.

Date	Good	VG	F	VF	XF
ND(1888) Series 9	—	—	—	—	50.00

KM# 907.10 5 MUN

Cast Bronze **Rev:** "Kyong" at top, "Tang" at right, "O" (5) at left, series number at bottom **Note:** Size varies: 29-30 mm.

Date	Good	VG	F	VF	XF
ND(1888) Series 10	1.75	2.25	3.00	5.00	—

KM# 907s.10 5 MUN

Cast Bronze **Note:** Size varies: 29-30 mm.

Date	Good	VG	F	VF	XF
ND(1888) Series 10	—	—	—	—	50.00

KM# 907.11 5 MUN

Cast Bronze **Rev:** "Kyong" at top, "Tang" at right, "O" (5) at left, series number at bottom **Note:** Size varies: 29-30 mm.

Date	Good	VG	F	VF	XF
ND(1888) Series 11	2.00	3.00	5.00	10.00	—

KM# 907s.11 5 MUN

Cast Bronze **Note:** Size varies: 29-30 mm.

Date	Good	VG	F	VF	XF
ND(1888) Series 11	—	—	—	—	50.00

KM# 907.12 5 MUN

Cast Bronze **Rev:** "Kyong" at top, "Tang" at right, "O" (5) at left, series number at bottom **Note:** Size varies: 29-30 mm.

Date	Good	VG	F	VF	XF
ND(1888) Series 12	2.00	3.00	5.00	10.00	—

KM# 907s.12 5 MUN

Cast Bronze **Note:** Size varies: 29-30 mm.

Date	Good	VG	F	VF	XF
ND(1888) Series 12	—	—	—	—	50.00

KM# 907.13 5 MUN

Cast Bronze **Rev:** "Kyong" at top, "Tang" at right, "O" (5) at left, series number at bottom **Note:** Size varies: 29-30 mm.

Date	Good	VG	F	VF	XF
ND(1888) Series 13	2.00	3.00	5.00	10.00	—

KM# 907s.13 5 MUN

Cast Bronze **Note:** Size varies: 29-30 mm.

Date	Good	VG	F	VF	XF
ND(1888) Series 13	—	—	—	—	50.00

KM# 907.14 5 MUN

Cast Bronze **Rev:** "Kyong" at top, "Tang" at right, "O" (5) at left, series number at bottom **Note:** Size varies: 29-30 mm.

Date	Good	VG	F	VF	XF
ND(1888) Series 14	2.00	3.00	5.00	10.00	—

KM# 907s.14 5 MUN

Cast Bronze **Note:** Size varies: 29-30 mm.

Date	Good	VG	F	VF	XF
ND(1888) Series 14	—	—	—	—	50.00

KM# 907.15 5 MUN

Cast Bronze **Rev:** "Kyong" at top, "Tang" at right, "O" (5) at left, series number at bottom **Note:** Size varies: 29-30 mm.

Date	Good	VG	F	VF	XF
ND(1888) Series 15	2.00	3.00	5.00	10.00	—

KM# 907s.15 5 MUN

Cast Bronze **Note:** Size varies: 29-30 mm.

Date	Good	VG	F	VF	XF
ND(1888) Series 15	—	—	—	—	50.00

KM# 907.16 5 MUN

Cast Bronze **Rev:** "Kyong" at top, "Tang" at right, "O" (5) at left, series number at bottom **Note:** Size varies: 29-30 mm.

Date	Good	VG	F	VF	XF
ND(1888) Series 16	2.00	3.00	5.00	10.00	—

KM# 907s.16 5 MUN

Cast Bronze **Note:** Size varies: 29-30 mm.

Date	Good	VG	F	VF	XF
ND(1888) Series 16	—	—	—	—	30.00

KM# 907.17 5 MUN

Cast Bronze **Rev:** "Kyong" at top, "Tang" at right, "O" (5) at left, series number at bottom **Note:** Size varies: 29-30 mm.

Date	Good	VG	F	VF	XF
ND(1888) Series 17	2.00	3.00	5.00	10.00	—

KM# 907s.17 5 MUN

Cast Bronze **Note:** Size varies: 29-30 mm.

Date	Good	VG	F	VF	XF
ND(1888) Series 17	—	—	—	—	50.00

KM# 907.18 5 MUN

Cast Bronze **Rev:** "Kyong" at top, "Tang" at right, "O" (5) at left, series number at bottom **Note:** Size varies: 29-30 mm.

Date	Good	VG	F	VF	XF
ND(1888) Series 18	2.00	3.00	5.00	10.00	—

KM# 907s.18 5 MUN

Cast Bronze **Note:** Size varies: 29-30 mm.

Date	Good	VG	F	VF	XF
ND(1888) Series 18	—	—	—	—	50.00

KM# 907.19 5 MUN

Cast Bronze **Rev:** "Kyong" at top, "Tang" at right, "O" (5) at left, series number at bottom **Note:** Size varies: 29-30 mm.

Date	Good	VG	F	VF	XF
ND(1888) Series 19	2.00	3.00	5.00	10.00	—

KM# 907s.19 5 MUN

Cast Bronze **Note:** Size varies: 29-30 mm.

Date	Good	VG	F	VF	XF
ND(1888) Series 19	—	—	—	—	50.00

KM# 907.20 5 MUN

Cast Bronze **Rev:** "Kyong" at top, "Tang" at right, "O" (5) at left, series number at bottom **Note:** Size varies: 29-30 mm.

Date	Good	VG	F	VF	XF
ND(1888) Series 20	2.00	3.00	5.00	10.00	—

KM# 907s.20 5 MUN

Cast Bronze **Note:** Size varies: 29-30 mm.

Date	Good	VG	F	VF	XF
ND(1888) Series 20	—	—	—	—	50.00

KM# 907.21 5 MUN

Cast Bronze **Rev:** "Kyong" at top, "Tang" at right, "O" (5) at left, series number at bottom **Note:** Size varies: 29-30 mm.

Date	Good	VG	F	VF	XF
ND(1888) Series 21	2.00	3.00	5.00	10.00	—

KM# 907s.21 5 MUN

Cast Bronze **Note:** Size varies: 29-30 mm.

Date	Good	VG	F	VF	XF
ND(1888) Series 21	—	—	—	—	50.00

KM# 907.22 5 MUN

Cast Bronze **Rev:** "Kyong" at top, "Tang" at right, "O" (5) at left, series number at bottom **Note:** Size varies: 29-30 mm.

Date	Good	VG	F	VF	XF
ND(1888) Series 22	2.00	3.00	5.00	10.00	—

KM# 907s.22 5 MUN

Cast Bronze **Note:** Size varies: 29-30 mm.

Date	Good	VG	F	VF	XF
ND(1888) Series 22	—	—	—	—	50.00

KM# 907.23 5 MUN

Cast Bronze **Rev:** "Kyong" at top, "Tang" at right, "O" (5) at left, series number at bottom **Note:** Size varies: 29-30 mm.

Date	Good	VG	F	VF	XF
ND(1888) Series 23	4.00	7.50	12.00	20.00	—

KM# 907s.23 5 MUN

Cast Bronze **Note:** Size varies: 29-30 mm.

Date	Good	VG	F	VF	XF
ND(1888) Series 23	—	—	—	—	60.00

KM# 907.24 5 MUN

Cast Bronze **Rev:** "Kyong" at top, "Tang" at right, "O" (5) at left, series number at bottom **Note:** Size varies: 29-30 mm.

Date	Good	VG	F	VF	XF
ND(1888) Series 24	4.00	7.50	12.00	20.00	—

KM# 907s.24 5 MUN

Cast Bronze **Note:** Size varies: 29-30 mm.

Date	Good	VG	F	VF	XF
ND(1888) Series 24	—	—	—	—	50.00

KM# 907.25 5 MUN

Cast Bronze **Rev:** "Kyong" at top, "Tang" at right, "O" (5) at left, series number at bottom **Note:** Size varies: 29-30 mm.

Date	Good	VG	F	VF	XF
ND(1888) Series 25	5.00	9.00	14.00	25.00	—

KM# 907s.25 5 MUN

Cast Bronze **Note:** Size varies: 29-30 mm.

Date	Good	VG	F	VF	XF
ND(1888) Series 25	—	—	—	—	60.00

KM# 907.26 5 MUN

Cast Bronze **Rev:** "Kyong" at top, "Tang" at right, "O" (5) at left, series number at bottom **Note:** Size varies: 29-30 mm.

Date	Good	VG	F	VF	XF
ND(1888) Series 26	4.00	7.00	12.00	20.00	—

KM# 907s.26 5 MUN

Cast Bronze **Note:** Size varies: 29-30 mm.

Date	Good	VG	F	VF	XF
ND(1888) Series 26	—	—	—	—	60.00

KM# 907.27 5 MUN

Cast Bronze **Rev:** "Kyong" at top, "Tang" at right, "O" (5) at left, series number at bottom **Note:** Size varies: 29-30 mm.

Date	Good	VG	F	VF	XF
ND(1888) Series 27	6.00	10.00	15.00	25.00	—

KM# 907s.27 5 MUN

Cast Bronze **Note:** Size varies: 29-30 mm.

Date	Good	VG	F	VF	XF
ND(1888) Series 27	—	—	—	—	75.00

P'YONGAN PROVINCIAL OFFICE

(P'yong An Kam Yong)

KM# 915.1 MUN

4.0000 g., Cast Bronze, 22 mm.

Date	Good	VG	F	VF	XF
ND(1883) Series 1	2.00	3.00	5.00	8.00	—

KM# 915s.1 MUN

4.0000 g., Cast Bronze, 22 mm.

Date	Good	VG	F	VF	XF
ND(1883) Series 1	—	—	—	—	50.00

KM# 915.2 MUN

4.0000 g., Cast Bronze, 22 mm.

Date	Good	VG	F	VF	XF
ND(1883) Series 2	2.00	3.00	5.00	8.00	—

KM# 915s.2 MUN

4.0000 g., Cast Bronze, 22 mm.

Date	Good	VG	F	VF	XF
ND(1883) Series 2	—	—	—	—	50.00

KM# 915.3 MUN

4.0000 g., Cast Bronze, 22 mm.

Date	Good	VG	F	VF	XF
ND(1883) Series 3	2.00	3.00	5.00	8.00	—

KM# 915s.3 MUN

4.0000 g., Cast Bronze, 22 mm.

Date	Good	VG	F	VF	XF
ND(1883) Series 3	—	—	—	—	50.00

KM# 915.4 MUN

4.0000 g., Cast Bronze, 22 mm.

Date	Good	VG	F	VF	XF
ND(1883) Series 4	2.00	3.00	5.00	8.00	—

KM# 915s.4 MUN

4.0000 g., Cast Bronze, 22 mm.

Date	Good	VG	F	VF	XF
ND(1883) Series 4	—	—	—	—	50.00

KM# 915.5 MUN

4.0000 g., Cast Bronze, 22 mm.

Date	Good	VG	F	VF	XF
ND(1883) Series 5	2.00	3.00	5.00	8.00	—

KM# 915s.5 MUN

4.0000 g., Cast Bronze, 22 mm.

Date	Good	VG	F	VF	XF
ND(1883) Series 5	—	—	—	—	50.00

KM# 915.6 MUN

4.0000 g., Cast Bronze, 22 mm.

Date	Good	VG	F	VF	XF
ND(1883) Series 6	2.00	3.00	5.00	8.00	—

KM# 915s.6 MUN
4.0000 g., Cast Bronze, 22 mm.

Date	Good	VG	F	VF	XF
ND(1883) Series 6	—	—	—	—	50.00

KM# 915.7 MUN
4.0000 g., Cast Bronze, 22 mm.

Date	Good	VG	F	VF	XF
ND(1883) Series 7	2.00	3.00	5.00	8.00	—

KM# 915s.7 MUN
4.0000 g., Cast Bronze, 22 mm.

Date	Good	VG	F	VF	XF
ND(1883) Series 7	—	—	—	—	50.00

KM# 915.8 MUN
4.0000 g., Cast Bronze, 22 mm.

Date	Good	VG	F	VF	XF
ND(1883) Series 8	2.00	3.00	5.00	8.00	—

KM# 915s.8 MUN
4.0000 g., Cast Bronze, 22 mm.

Date	Good	VG	F	VF	XF
ND(1883) Series 8	—	—	—	—	50.00

KM# 915.9 MUN
4.0000 g., Cast Bronze, 22 mm.

Date	Good	VG	F	VF	XF
ND(1883) Series 9	4.00	6.00	9.00	16.00	—

KM# 915s.9 MUN
4.0000 g., Cast Bronze, 22 mm.

Date	Good	VG	F	VF	XF
ND(1883) Series 9	—	—	—	—	50.00

KM# 915.10 MUN
4.0000 g., Cast Bronze, 22 mm.

Date	Good	VG	F	VF	XF
ND(1883) Series 10	4.00	6.00	9.00	16.00	—

KM# 915s.10 MUN
4.0000 g., Cast Bronze, 22 mm.

Date	Good	VG	F	VF	XF
ND(1883) Series 10	—	—	—	—	50.00

KM# 915.11 MUN
4.0000 g., Cast Bronze, 22 mm.

Date	Good	VG	F	VF	XF
ND(1883) Series 11	4.00	6.00	9.00	16.00	—

KM# 915s.11 MUN
4.0000 g., Cast Bronze, 22 mm.

Date	Good	VG	F	VF	XF
ND(1883) Series 11	—	—	—	—	50.00

KM# 917.1 MUN
4.0000 g., Cast Bronze, 22 mm. **Rev:** Circle at left, series number at bottom

Date	Good	VG	F	VF	XF
ND(1883) Series 1	2.00	3.00	5.00	8.00	—

KM# 917s.1 MUN
4.0000 g., Cast Bronze, 22 mm.

Date	Good	VG	F	VF	XF
ND(1883) Series 1	—	—	—	—	50.00

KM# 917.2 MUN
4.0000 g., Cast Bronze, 22 mm. **Rev:** Circle at left, series number at bottom

Date	Good	VG	F	VF	XF
ND(1883) Series 2	2.00	3.00	5.00	8.00	—

KM# 917s.2 MUN
4.0000 g., Cast Bronze, 22 mm.

Date	Good	VG	F	VF	XF
ND(1883) Series 2	—	—	—	—	50.00

KM# 917.3 MUN
4.0000 g., Cast Bronze, 22 mm. **Rev:** Circle at left, series number at bottom

Date	Good	VG	F	VF	XF
ND(1883) Series 3	2.00	3.00	5.00	8.00	—

KM# 917s.3 MUN
4.0000 g., Cast Bronze, 22 mm.

Date	Good	VG	F	VF	XF
ND(1883) Series 3	—	—	—	—	50.00

KM# 917.4 MUN
4.0000 g., Cast Bronze, 22 mm. **Rev:** Circle at left, series number at bottom

Date	Good	VG	F	VF	XF
ND(1883) Series 4	2.00	3.00	5.00	8.00	—

KM# 917s.4 MUN
4.0000 g., Cast Bronze, 22 mm.

Date	Good	VG	F	VF	XF
ND(1883) Series 4	—	—	—	—	50.00

KM# 917.5 MUN
4.0000 g., Cast Bronze, 22 mm. **Rev:** Circle at left, series number at bottom

Date	Good	VG	F	VF	XF
ND(1883) Series 5	2.00	3.00	5.00	8.00	—

KM# 917s.5 MUN
4.0000 g., Cast Bronze, 22 mm.

Date	Good	VG	F	VF	XF
ND(1883) Series 5	—	—	—	—	50.00

KM# 918.1 MUN
4.0000 g., Cast Bronze, 23 mm. **Rev:** "Ch'on" at bottom, series number at left

Date	Good	VG	F	VF	XF
ND(1891) Series 1	2.00	3.00	5.00	8.00	—

KM# 918s.1 MUN
Cast Bronze

Date	Good	VG	F	VF	XF
ND(1891) Series 1	—	—	—	—	50.00

KM# 918.2 MUN
4.0000 g., Cast Bronze, 23 mm. **Rev:** "Ch'on" at bottom, series number at left

Date	Good	VG	F	VF	XF
ND(1891) Series 2	2.00	3.00	5.00	8.00	—

KM# 918s.2 MUN
Cast Bronze

Date	Good	VG	F	VF	XF
ND(1891) Series 2	—	—	—	—	50.00

KM# 918.3 MUN
4.0000 g., Cast Bronze, 23 mm. **Rev:** "Ch'on" at bottom, series number at left

Date	Good	VG	F	VF	XF
ND(1891) Series 3	2.00	3.00	5.00	8.00	—

KM# 918s.3 MUN
Cast Bronze

Date	Good	VG	F	VF	XF
ND(1891) Series 3	—	—	—	—	50.00

KM# 918.4 MUN
4.0000 g., Cast Bronze, 23 mm. **Rev:** "Ch'on" at bottom, series number at left

Date	Good	VG	F	VF	XF
ND(1891) Series 4	2.00	3.00	5.00	8.00	—

KM# 918s.4 MUN
Cast Bronze

Date	Good	VG	F	VF	XF
ND(1891) Series 4	—	—	—	—	50.00

KM# 918.5 MUN
4.0000 g., Cast Bronze, 23 mm. **Rev:** "Ch'on" at bottom, series number at left

Date	Good	VG	F	VF	XF
ND(1891) Series 5	2.00	3.00	5.00	8.00	—

KM# 918s.5 MUN
Cast Bronze

Date	Good	VG	F	VF	XF
ND(1891) Series 5	—	—	—	—	50.00

KM# 918.6 MUN
4.0000 g., Cast Bronze, 23 mm. **Rev:** "Ch'on" at bottom, series number at left

Date	Good	VG	F	VF	XF
ND(1891) Series 6	2.00	3.00	5.00	8.00	—

KM# 918s.6 MUN
Cast Bronze

Date	Good	VG	F	VF	XF
ND(1891) Series 6	—	—	—	—	50.00

KM# 918.7 MUN
4.0000 g., Cast Bronze, 23 mm. **Rev:** "Ch'on" at bottom, series number at left

Date	Good	VG	F	VF	XF
ND(1891) Series 7	2.00	3.00	5.00	8.00	—

KM# 918s.7 MUN
Cast Bronze

Date	Good	VG	F	VF	XF
ND(1891) Series 7	—	—	—	—	50.00

KM# 918.8 MUN
4.0000 g., Cast Bronze, 23 mm. **Rev:** "Ch'on" at bottom, series number at left

Date	Good	VG	F	VF	XF
ND(1891) Series 8	2.00	3.00	5.00	8.00	—

KM# 918s.8 MUN
Cast Bronze

Date	Good	VG	F	VF	XF
ND(1891) Series 8	—	—	—	—	50.00

KM# 918.9 MUN
4.0000 g., Cast Bronze, 23 mm. **Rev:** "Ch'on" at bottom, series number at left

Date	Good	VG	F	VF	XF
ND(1891) Series 9	2.00	3.00	5.00	8.00	—

KM# 918s.9 MUN
Cast Bronze

Date	Good	VG	F	VF	XF
ND(1891) Series 9	—	—	—	—	50.00

KM# 918.10 MUN
4.0000 g., Cast Bronze, 23 mm. **Rev:** "Ch'on" at bottom, series number at left

Date	Good	VG	F	VF	XF
ND(1891) Series 10	2.00	3.00	5.00	8.00	—

KM# 918s.10 MUN
Cast Bronze

Date	Good	VG	F	VF	XF
ND(1891) Series 10	—	—	—	—	50.00

KM# 919.1 MUN
Cast Bronze, 22 mm. **Rev:** "Chi" at bottom, series number at left

Date	Good	VG	F	VF	XF
ND(1891) Series 1	4.00	7.00	12.00	20.00	—

KM# 919s.1 MUN
Cast Bronze, 22 mm.

Date	Good	VG	F	VF	XF
ND(1891) Series 1	—	—	—	—	50.00

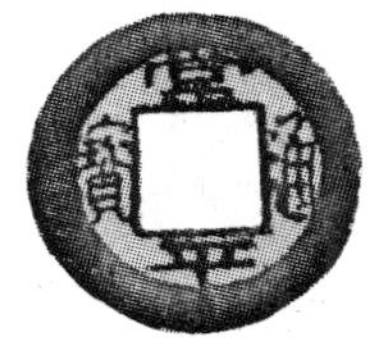

KM# 919.4 MUN
Cast Bronze, 22 mm. **Rev:** "Chi" at bottom, series number at left

Date	Good	VG	F	VF	XF
ND(1891) Series 4	3.00	5.00	8.00	12.00	—

KM# 919s.4 MUN
Cast Bronze, 22 mm.

Date	Good	VG	F	VF	XF
ND(1891) Series 4	—	—	—	—	50.00

KM# 920 MUN
Cast Bronze, 21 mm. **Rev:** "Il" (sun) at bottom

Date	Good	VG	F	VF	XF
ND(1891)	2.00	3.00	5.00	8.00	—

KM# 920s MUN
Cast Bronze, 21 mm.

Date	Good	VG	F	VF	XF
ND(1891)	—	—	—	—	40.00

KM# 921.1 MUN
Cast Bronze, 22 mm. **Rev:** "Il" (sun) at bottom, series number at right

Date	Good	VG	F	VF	XF
ND(1891) Series 1	2.00	3.00	5.00	8.00	—

KM# 921s.1 MUN
Cast Bronze, 22 mm.

Date	Good	VG	F	VF	XF
ND(1891) Series 1	—	—	—	—	40.00

KM# 921.2 MUN
Cast Bronze, 22 mm. **Rev:** "Il" (sun) at bottom, series number at right

Date	Good	VG	F	VF	XF
ND(1891) Series 2	2.00	3.00	5.00	8.00	—

KM# 921s.2 MUN
Cast Bronze, 22 mm.

Date	Good	VG	F	VF	XF
ND(1891) Series 2	—	—	—	—	40.00

KM# 921.3 MUN
Cast Bronze, 22 mm. **Rev:** "Il" (sun) at bottom, series number at right

Date	Good	VG	F	VF	XF
ND(1891) Series 3	2.00	3.00	5.00	8.00	—

KM# 921s.3 MUN
Cast Bronze, 22 mm.

Date	Good	VG	F	VF	XF
ND(1891) Series 3	—	—	—	—	40.00

KM# 921.4 MUN
Cast Bronze, 22 mm. **Rev:** "Il" (sun) at bottom, series number at right

Date	Good	VG	F	VF	XF
ND(1891) Series 4	2.00	3.00	5.00	8.00	—

KM# 921s.4 MUN
Cast Bronze, 22 mm.

Date	Good	VG	F	VF	XF
ND(1891) Series 4	—	—	—	—	40.00

KM# 921.5 MUN
Cast Bronze, 22 mm.

Date	Good	VG	F	VF	XF
ND(1891) Series 5	2.00	3.00	5.00	8.00	—

KM# 921s.5 MUN
Cast Bronze, 22 mm.

Date	Good	VG	F	VF	XF
ND(1891) Series 5	—	—	—	—	40.00

KM# 921.6 MUN
Cast Bronze, 22 mm. **Rev:** "Il" (sun) at bottom, series number at right

Date	Good	VG	F	VF	XF
ND(1891) Series 6	2.00	3.00	5.00	8.00	—

KM# 921s.6 MUN
Cast Bronze, 22 mm.

Date	Good	VG	F	VF	XF
ND(1891) Series 6	—	—	—	—	40.00

KM# 921.7 MUN
Cast Bronze, 22 mm. **Rev:** "Il" (sun) at bottom, series number at right

Date	Good	VG	F	VF	XF
ND(1891) Series 7	2.00	3.00	5.00	8.00	—

KM# 921s.7 MUN
Cast Bronze, 22 mm.

Date	Good	VG	F	VF	XF
ND(1891) Series 7	—	—	—	—	40.00

KM# 921.8 MUN
Cast Bronze, 22 mm. **Rev:** "Il" (sun) at bottom, series number at right

Date	Good	VG	F	VF	XF
ND(1891) Series 8	2.00	3.00	5.00	8.00	—

KM# 921s.8 MUN
Cast Bronze, 22 mm.

Date	Good	VG	F	VF	XF
ND(1891) Series 8	—	—	—	—	40.00

KM# 921.9 MUN
Cast Bronze, 22 mm. **Rev:** "Il" (sun) at bottom, series number at right

Date	Good	VG	F	VF	XF
ND(1891) Series 9	2.00	3.00	5.00	8.00	—

KM# 921s.9 MUN
Cast Bronze, 22 mm.

Date	Good	VG	F	VF	XF
ND(1891) Series 9	—	—	—	—	40.00

KM# 921.10 MUN
Cast Bronze, 22 mm. **Rev:** "Il" (sun) at bottom, series number at right

Date	Good	VG	F	VF	XF
ND(1891) Series 10	2.00	3.00	5.00	8.00	—

KM# 921s.10 MUN
Cast Bronze, 22 mm.

Date	Good	VG	F	VF	XF
ND(1891) Series 10	—	—	—	—	30.00

KM# 922.1 MUN
Cast Bronze, 22 mm. **Rev:** "Il" (sun) at bottom, series number at left

Date	Good	VG	F	VF	XF
ND(1891) Series 1	2.00	3.00	5.00	8.00	—

KM# 922s.1 MUN
Cast Bronze, 22 mm.

Date	Good	VG	F	VF	XF
ND(1891) Series 1	—	—	—	—	40.00

KM# 922.2 MUN
Cast Bronze, 22 mm. **Rev:** "Il" (sun) at bottom, series number at left

Date	Good	VG	F	VF	XF
ND(1891) Series 2	2.00	3.00	5.00	8.00	—

KM# 922s.2 MUN
Cast Bronze, 22 mm.

Date	Good	VG	F	VF	XF
ND(1891) Series 2	—	—	—	—	40.00

KM# 922.3 MUN
Cast Bronze, 22 mm. **Rev:** "Il" (sun) at bottom, series number at left

Date	Good	VG	F	VF	XF
ND(1891) Series 3	2.00	3.00	5.00	8.00	—

KM# 922s.3 MUN
Cast Bronze, 22 mm.

Date	Good	VG	F	VF	XF
ND(1891) Series 3	—	—	—	—	40.00

KM# 922.4 MUN
Cast Bronze, 22 mm. **Rev:** "Il" (sun) at bottom, series number at left

Date	Good	VG	F	VF	XF
ND(1891) Series 4	2.00	3.00	5.00	8.00	—

KM# 922s.4 MUN
Cast Bronze, 22 mm.

Date	Good	VG	F	VF	XF
ND(1891) Series 4	—	—	—	—	40.00

KM# 922.5 MUN
Cast Bronze, 22 mm. **Rev:** "Il" (sun) at bottom, series number at left

Date	Good	VG	F	VF	XF
ND(1891) Series 5	2.00	3.00	5.00	8.00	—

KM# 922s.5 MUN
Cast Bronze, 22 mm.

Date	Good	VG	F	VF	XF
ND(1891) Series 5	—	—	—	—	40.00

KM# 922.6 MUN
Cast Bronze, 22 mm. **Rev:** "Il" (sun) at bottom, series number at left

Date	Good	VG	F	VF	XF
ND(1891) Series 6	2.00	3.00	5.00	8.00	—

KM# 922s.6 MUN
Cast Bronze, 22 mm.

Date	Good	VG	F	VF	XF
ND(1891) Series 6	—	—	—	—	40.00

KM# 922.7 MUN
Cast Bronze, 22 mm. **Rev:** "Il" (sun) at bottom, series number at left

Date	Good	VG	F	VF	XF
ND(1891) Series 7	2.00	3.00	5.00	8.00	—

KM# 922s.7 MUN
Cast Bronze, 22 mm.

Date	Good	VG	F	VF	XF
ND(1891) Series 7	—	—	—	—	40.00

KM# 922.8 MUN
Cast Bronze, 22 mm. **Rev:** "Il" (sun) at bottom, series number at left

Date	Good	VG	F	VF	XF
ND(1891) Series 8	2.00	3.00	5.00	8.00	—

KM# 922s.8 MUN
Cast Bronze, 22 mm.

Date	Good	VG	F	VF	XF
ND(1891) Series 8	—	—	—	—	40.00

KM# 922.9 MUN
Cast Bronze, 22 mm. **Rev:** "Il" (sun) at bottom, series number at left

Date	Good	VG	F	VF	XF
ND(1891) Series 9	2.00	3.00	5.00	8.00	—

KM# 922s.9 MUN
Cast Bronze, 22 mm.

Date	Good	VG	F	VF	XF
ND(1891) Series 9	—	—	—	—	40.00

KM# 922.10 MUN
Cast Bronze, 22 mm. **Rev:** "Il" (sun) at bottom, series number at left

Date	Good	VG	F	VF	XF
ND(1891) Series 10	2.00	3.00	5.00	8.00	—

KM# 922s.10 MUN
Cast Bronze, 22 mm.

Date	Good	VG	F	VF	XF
ND(1891) Series 10	—	—	—	—	40.00

KM# 922.11 MUN
Cast Bronze, 22 mm. **Rev:** "Il" (sun) at bottom, series number at left

Date	Good	VG	F	VF	XF
ND(1891) Series 11	2.00	3.00	5.00	8.00	—

KM# 922s.11 MUN
Cast Bronze, 22 mm.

Date	Good	VG	F	VF	XF
ND(1891) Series 11	—	—	—	—	40.00

KM# 922.12 MUN
Cast Bronze, 22 mm. **Rev:** "Il" (sun) at bottom, series number at left

Date	Good	VG	F	VF	XF
ND(1891) Series 12	2.00	3.00	5.00	8.00	—

KM# 922s.12 MUN
Cast Bronze, 22 mm.

Date	Good	VG	F	VF	XF
ND(1891) Series 12	—	—	—	—	40.00

KM# 922s.13 MUN
Cast Bronze, 22 mm.

Date	Good	VG	F	VF	XF
ND(1891) Series 13	—	—	—	—	40.00

KM# 922.13 MUN
Cast Bronze, 22 mm. **Rev:** "Il" (sun) at bottom, series number at left

Date	Good	VG	F	VF	XF
ND(1891) Series 13	2.00	3.00	5.00	8.00	—

KM# 922.14 MUN
Cast Bronze, 22 mm. **Rev:** "Il" (sun) at bottom, series number at left

Date	Good	VG	F	VF	XF
ND(1891) Series 14	2.00	3.00	5.00	8.00	—

KM# 922s.14 MUN
Cast Bronze, 22 mm.

Date	Good	VG	F	VF	XF
ND(1891) Series 14	—	—	—	—	40.00

KM# 923.1 MUN
Cast Bronze, 22.5 mm. **Rev:** "Saeng" at bottom, series number at left

Date	Good	VG	F	VF	XF
ND(1891) Series 1	3.00	5.00	8.00	12.00	—

KM# 923s.1 MUN
Cast Bronze, 22.5 mm.

Date	Good	VG	F	VF	XF
ND(1891) Series 1	—	—	—	—	45.00

KM# 923.2 MUN
Cast Bronze, 22.5 mm. **Rev:** "Saeng" at bottom, series number at left

Date	Good	VG	F	VF	XF
ND(1891) Series 2	3.00	5.00	8.00	12.00	—

KM# 923s.2 MUN
Cast Bronze, 22.5 mm.

Date	Good	VG	F	VF	XF
ND(1891) Series 2	—	—	—	—	45.00

KM# 923.3 MUN
Cast Bronze, 22.5 mm. **Rev:** "Saeng" at bottom, series number at left

Date	Good	VG	F	VF	XF
ND(1891) Series 3	3.00	5.00	8.00	12.00	—

KM# 923s.3 MUN
Cast Bronze, 22.5 mm.

Date	Good	VG	F	VF	XF
ND(1891) Series 3	—	—	—	—	45.00

KM# 923.4 MUN
Cast Bronze, 22.5 mm. **Rev:** "Saeng" at bottom, series number at left

Date	Good	VG	F	VF	XF
ND(1891) Series 4	3.00	5.00	8.00	12.00	—

KM# 923s.4 MUN
Cast Bronze, 22.5 mm.

Date	Good	VG	F	VF	XF
ND(1891) Series 4	—	—	—	—	45.00

KM# 923.5 MUN
Cast Bronze, 22.5 mm. **Rev:** "Saeng" at bottom, series number at left

Date	Good	VG	F	VF	XF
ND(1891) Series 5	3.00	5.00	8.00	12.00	—

KM# 923s.5 MUN
Cast Bronze, 22.5 mm.

Date	Good	VG	F	VF	XF
ND(1891) Series 5	—	—	—	—	45.00

KM# 923.6 MUN
Cast Bronze, 22.5 mm. **Rev:** "Saeng" at bottom, series number at left **Note:** Struck at P'yong An Kam Yong.

Date	Good	VG	F	VF	XF
ND(1891) Series 6	3.00	5.00	8.00	12.00	—

KM# 923s.6 MUN
Cast Bronze, 22.5 mm.

Date	Good	VG	F	VF	XF
ND(1891) Series 6	—	—	—	—	45.00

KM# 923.7 MUN
Cast Bronze, 22.5 mm. **Rev:** "Saeng" at bottom, series number at left

Date	Good	VG	F	VF	XF
ND(1891) Series 7	3.00	5.00	8.00	12.00	—

KM# 923s.7 MUN
Cast Bronze, 22.5 mm.

Date	Good	VG	F	VF	XF
ND(1891) Series 7	—	—	—	—	45.00

KM# 923.8 MUN
Cast Bronze, 22.5 mm. **Rev:** "Saeng" at bottom, series number at left

Date	Good	VG	F	VF	XF
ND(1891) Series 8	3.00	5.00	8.00	12.00	—

KM# 923s.8 MUN
Cast Bronze, 22.5 mm.

Date	Good	VG	F	VF	XF
ND(1891) Series 8	—	—	—	—	45.00

KM# 923.9 MUN
Cast Bronze, 22.5 mm. **Rev:** "Saeng" at bottom, series number at left

Date	Good	VG	F	VF	XF
ND(1891) Series 9	3.00	5.00	8.00	12.00	—

KM# 923s.9 MUN
Cast Cannon Metal, 22.5 mm.

Date	Good	VG	F	VF	XF
ND(1891) Series 9	—	—	—	—	45.00

KM# 923.10 MUN
Cast Bronze, 22.5 mm. **Rev:** "Saeng" at bottom, series number at left

Date	Good	VG	F	VF	XF
ND(1891) Series 10	3.00	5.00	8.00	12.00	—

KM# 923s.10 MUN
Cast Bronze, 22.5 mm.

Date	Good	VG	F	VF	XF
ND(1891) Series 10	—	—	—	—	45.00

KM# 923.11 MUN
Cast Bronze, 22.5 mm. **Rev:** "Saeng" at bottom, series number at left

Date	Good	VG	F	VF	XF
ND(1891) Series 11	3.00	5.00	8.00	12.00	—

KM# 923s.11 MUN
Cast Bronze, 22.5 mm.

Date	Good	VG	F	VF	XF
ND(1891) Series 11	—	—	—	—	45.00

KM# 923.12 MUN
Cast Bronze, 22.5 mm. **Rev:** "Saeng" at bottom, series number at left

Date	Good	VG	F	VF	XF
ND(1891) Series 12	3.00	5.00	8.00	12.00	—

KM# 923s.12 MUN
Cast Bronze, 22.5 mm.

Date	Good	VG	F	VF	XF
ND(1891) Series 12	—	—	—	—	45.00

KM# 923.13 MUN
Cast Bronze, 22.5 mm. **Rev:** "Saeng" at bottom, series number at left

Date	Good	VG	F	VF	XF
ND(1891) Series 13	3.00	5.00	8.00	12.00	—

KM# 923s.13 MUN
Cast Bronze, 22.5 mm.

Date	Good	VG	F	VF	XF
ND(1891) Series 13	—	—	—	—	45.00

KM# 924.1 MUN
Cast Bronze, 22 mm. **Rev:** "Saeng" at bottom, series number at right, circle at left

Date	Good	VG	F	VF	XF
ND(1891) Series 1	4.00	7.00	12.00	20.00	—

KM# 924s.1 MUN
Cast Bronze, 22 mm.

Date	Good	VG	F	VF	XF
ND(1891) Series 1	—	—	—	—	50.00

KM# 924.2 MUN
Cast Bronze, 22 mm. **Rev:** "Saeng" at bottom, series number at right, circle at left

Date	Good	VG	F	VF	XF
ND(1891) Series 2	4.00	7.00	12.00	20.00	—

KM# 924s.2 MUN
Cast Bronze, 22 mm.

Date	Good	VG	F	VF	XF
ND(1891) Series 2	—	—	—	—	50.00

KM# 924.3 MUN
Cast Bronze, 22 mm. **Rev:** "Saeng" at bottom, series number at right, circle at left

Date	Good	VG	F	VF	XF
ND(1891) Series 3	1.50	2.25	3.50	5.00	—

KM# 924s.3 MUN
Cast Bronze, 22 mm.

Date	Good	VG	F	VF	XF
ND(1891) Series 3	—	—	—	—	50.00

KM# 924.4 MUN
Cast Bronze, 22 mm. **Rev:** "Saeng" at bottom, series number at right, circle at left

Date	Good	VG	F	VF	XF
ND(1891) Series 4	4.00	7.00	12.00	20.00	—

KM# 924s.4 MUN
Cast Bronze, 22 mm.

Date	Good	VG	F	VF	XF
ND(1891) Series 4	—	—	—	—	50.00

KM# 924.5 MUN
Cast Bronze, 22 mm. **Rev:** "Saeng" at bottom, series number at right, circle at left

Date	Good	VG	F	VF	XF
ND(1891) Series 5	4.00	7.00	12.00	20.00	—

KM# 924s.5 MUN
Cast Bronze, 22 mm.

Date	Good	VG	F	VF	XF
ND(1891) Series 5	—	—	—	—	50.00

KM# 924.6 MUN
Cast Bronze, 22 mm. **Rev:** "Saeng" at bottom, series number at right, circle at left

Date	Good	VG	F	VF	XF
ND(1891) Series 6	4.00	7.00	12.00	20.00	—

KM# 924s.6 MUN
Cast Bronze, 22 mm.

Date	Good	VG	F	VF	XF
ND(1891) Series 6	—	—	—	—	50.00

KM# 924.7 MUN
Cast Bronze, 22 mm. **Rev:** "Saeng" at bottom, series number at right, circle at left

Date	Good	VG	F	VF	XF
ND(1891) Series 7	4.00	7.00	12.00	20.00	—

KM# 924s.7 MUN
Cast Bronze, 22 mm.

Date	Good	VG	F	VF	XF
ND(1891) Series 7	—	—	—	—	50.00

KM# 924.8 MUN
Cast Bronze, 22 mm. **Rev:** "Saeng" at bottom, series number at right, circle at left

Date	Good	VG	F	VF	XF
ND(1891) Series 8	4.00	7.00	12.00	20.00	—

KM# 924s.8 MUN
Cast Bronze, 22 mm.

Date	Good	VG	F	VF	XF
ND(1891) Series 8	—	—	—	—	50.00

KM# 924.9 MUN
Cast Bronze, 22 mm. **Rev:** "Saeng" at bottom, series number at right, circle at left

Date	Good	VG	F	VF	XF
ND(1891) Series 9	4.00	7.00	12.00	20.00	—

KM# 924s.9 MUN
Cast Bronze, 22 mm.

Date	Good	VG	F	VF	XF
ND(1891) Series 9	—	—	—	—	50.00

KM# 924.10 MUN
Cast Bronze, 22 mm. **Rev:** "Saeng" at bottom, series number at right, circle at left

Date	Good	VG	F	VF	XF
ND(1891) Series 10	4.00	7.00	12.00	20.00	—

KM# 924s.10 MUN
Cast Bronze, 22 mm.

Date	Good	VG	F	VF	XF
ND(1891) Series 10	—	—	—	—	50.00

HAMGYONG PROVINCIAL OFFICE

(Ham Gyong Kam Yong)

KM# 974.1 MUN
4.0000 g., Cast Bronze, 24 mm. **Rev:** "Ham" at top, series number at bottom

Date	Good	VG	F	VF	XF
ND(1891) Series 1	3.00	5.00	8.00	12.00	—

KM# 974s.1 MUN
4.0000 g., Cast Bronze, 24 mm.

Date	Good	VG	F	VF	XF
ND(1891) Series 1	—	—	—	—	50.00

KM# 974.2 MUN
4.0000 g., Cast Bronze, 24 mm. **Rev:** "Ham" at top, series number at bottom

Date	Good	VG	F	VF	XF
ND(1891) Series 2	3.00	5.00	8.00	12.00	—

KM# 974s.2 MUN
4.0000 g., Cast Bronze, 24 mm.

Date	Good	VG	F	VF	XF
ND(1891) Series 2	—	—	—	—	50.00

KM# 974s.3 MUN
4.0000 g., Cast Bronze, 24 mm.

Date	Good	VG	F	VF	XF
ND(1891) Series 3	—	—	—	—	50.00

KM# 974.3 MUN
4.0000 g., Cast Bronze, 22 mm. **Rev:** "Ham" at top, series number at bottom

Date	Good	VG	F	VF	XF
ND(1891) Series 4	3.00	5.00	8.00	12.00	—

KM# 974s.4 MUN
4.0000 g., Cast Bronze, 24 mm.

Date	Good	VG	F	VF	XF
ND(1891) Series 4	—	—	—	—	50.00

TAE DONG TREASURY DEPARTMENT

Cast Coinage with Cloisonné

Due to the added expense of adding the "cloissonne" enamel during production the silver one, two and three Chon KM#1081-83 were discontinued in June, 1883. Examples with cloissonne missing are valued at about one half normal valuations. There are many types of trial sets of 1, 2 and 3 Chon in existence.

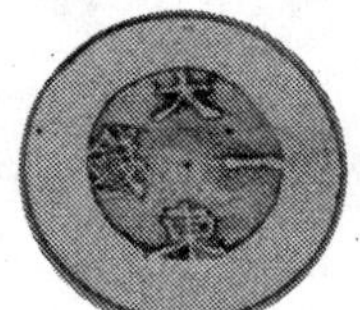

KM# 1081 CHON
Silver, 22 mm. **Rev:** "Ho" in green, black or blue cloisonne enameled center circle

Date	VG	F	VF	XF	Unc
ND(1882-83)	100	150	200	300	—

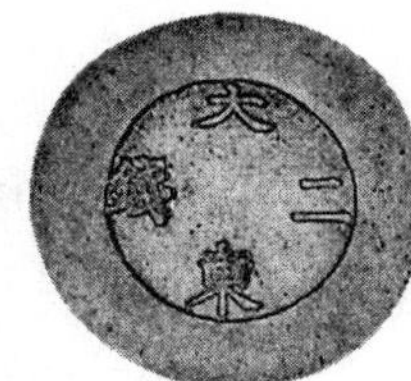
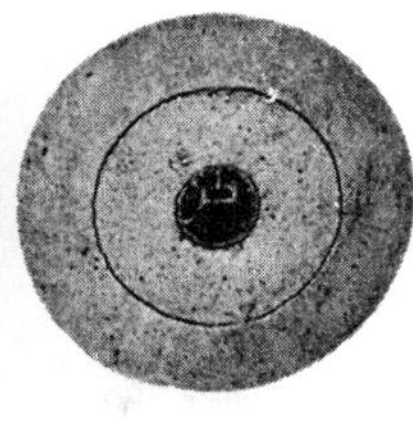

KM# 1082 CHON
Silver, 27 mm. **Rev:** "Ho" in green, black or blue cloissonne enameled center circle

Date	Good	VG	F	VF	XF
ND(1882-83)	—	275	400	550	800

KM# 1083 3 CHON
Silver, 32.5 mm. **Rev:** "Ho" in green, black or blue cloisonne enameled center circle

Date	VG	F	VF	XF	Unc
ND(1882-83)	275	400	550	800	—

MILLED COINAGE

During the 1880's and 1890's, Korea experimented with several different types of machine-struck coins including a struck "Cash" coin with round center hole, KM#1100. Some pattern coins of this period exist, some of which may have actually entered circulation.

KM# 1100 5 MUN
Brass

Date	F	VF	XF	Unc	BU
ND(1884)	250	450	700	950	—

KM# 1101 5 MUN
3.2500 g., Copper

Date	F	VF	XF	Unc	BU
497 (1888)	60.00	120	250	450	—

KM# 1102 10 MUN
6.5000 g., Copper

Date	F	VF	XF	Unc	BU
497 (1888)	125	265	450	750	—

KM# 1103 WARN
26.9500 g., 0.9000 Silver 0.7798 oz.

Date	F	VF	XF	Unc	BU
497 (1888)	5,500	13,500	15,000	20,000	—

Note: Heritage Piedmont Sale 6-2000 AU realized $18,975.

MILLED COINAGE

Coinage Reform of 1892

KM# 1104 FUN
3.5000 g., Brass **Obv:** 3 characters, "Tae Cho-son" (Great Korea), to left of denomination

Date	F	VF	XF	Unc	BU
501 (1892)	10.00	35.00	75.00	250	—
501 (1892) Proof	Value: 1,000				
504 (1895)	20.00	75.00	150	450	—
505 (1896)	20.00	75.00	150	450	—

KM# 1105 FUN
3.5000 g., Brass **Obv:** 2 characters, "Cho-son" (Korea), to left of denomination

Date	F	VF	XF	Unc	BU
502 (1893)	15.00	50.00	100	250	—
504 (1895)	8.00	25.00	50.00	150	—

KM# 1106 5 FUN
17.2000 g., Copper **Obv:** 3 small characters, "Tae Cho-son", legend above dragon divided into two parts by a dot

Date	F	VF	XF	Unc	BU
501 (1892)	2.50	6.00	15.00	80.00	—
501 (1892) Proof	Value: 1,200				
505 (1896)	2.50	6.00	14.00	75.00	—

KM# 1107 5 FUN
17.2000 g., Copper **Obv:** 2 characters, "Cho-son" (Korea), to left of denomination

Date	F	VF	XF	Unc	BU
502 (1893) Small characters obverse	2.50	6.00	15.00	85.00	—
502 (1893) Large characters obverse	20.00	45.00	80.00	300	—
503 (1894) Large characters obverse	4.00	8.50	18.00	90.00	—
504 (1895) Large characters obvrerse	2.50	6.00	14.00	80.00	—
505 (1896) Small characters obverse	2.50	5.00	12.00	75.00	—

KM# 1108 5 FUN
17.2000 g., Copper **Obv:** 3 large characters, "Tae Cho-son"

(Great Korea) to left of denomination, without dot in legend above dragon

Date	F	VF	XF	Unc	BU
504 (1895)	2.50	5.00	12.00	75.00	—
505 (1896)	3.00	8.00	18.00	90.00	—

KM# 1109 1/4 YANG
Copper-Nickel **Obv:** 3 characters, "Tae Cho-son" (Great Korea), to left of denomination

Date	F	VF	XF	Unc	BU
501 (1892)	10.00	25.00	55.00	175	—
501 (1892) Proof	Value: 2,000				
504 (1895)	10.00	25.00	55.00	—	—

KM# 1110 1/4 YANG
Copper Around Silver **Obv:** 2 characters, "Cho-son" (Korea), to left of denomination

Date	F	VF	XF	Unc	BU
502 (1893)	6.00	20.00	40.00	125	—
503 (1894)	50.00	120	225	350	—
504 (1895)	165	375	600	1,200	—
505 (1896)	6.00	20.00	40.00	125	—

KM# 1112 YANG
5.2000 g., 0.8000 Silver 0.1337 oz. **Obv:** 3 characters, "Tae Cho-son"

Date	F	VF	XF	Unc	BU
501 (1892)	65.00	100	150	400	—
501 (1892) Proof	Value: 4,000				

KM# 1113 YANG
5.2000 g., 0.8000 Silver 0.1337 oz. **Obv:** 2 characters, "Cho-son"

Date	F	VF	XF	Unc	BU
502 (1893)	50.00	85.00	135	385	—

KM# 1114 5 YANG
26.9500 g., 0.9000 Silver 0.7798 oz.

Date	Mintage	F	VF	XF	Unc	BU
501 (1892)	20,000	700	1,250	2,000	3,500	—
501 (1892) Proof	—	Value: 9,500				

KM# 1115 WHAN
26.9500 g., 0.9000 Silver 0.7798 oz.

Date	F	VF	XF	Unc	BU
502 (1893)	2,750	5,925	10,000	16,500	—

Note: Heritage Piedmont sale 6-2000 prooflike uncirculated realized, $17,825.

KM# 1116 5 FUN
17.2000 g., Copper **Ruler:** Kuang Mu

Date	F	VF	XF	Unc	BU
2 (1898) Small characters obverse	2.00	4.00	10.00	80.00	—
2 (1898) Medium characters obverse	15.00	40.00	70.00	250	—
2 (1898) Large characters obverse	55.00	115	200	425	—

KM# 1117 1/4 YANG
Copper-Nickel **Ruler:** Kuang Mu **Obv:** Dragon crowded by small tight circle

Date	F	VF	XF	Unc	BU
1 (1897)	225	350	600	1,250	—
2 (1898)	1.00	2.00	3.50	10.00	—

Note: Many varieties of character size and style exist for year 2 coins

Date	F	VF	XF	Unc	BU
3 (1899) Large characters obverse	200	300	550	1,200	—
3 (1899) Small characters obverse	200	300	550	1,200	—
4 (1900)	275	450	1,250	2,000	—

KM# 1118 1/4 YANG
Copper-Nickel **Obv:** Larger circle around dragon **Note:** KM#1118 were counterfeits made on machinery supplied by the Japanese. These couterfeits were authorized for circulation by the Korean Government.

Date	F	VF	XF	Unc	BU
2 (1898)	5.00	8.50	17.50	100	—

KM# 1119 YANG
5.2000 g., 0.8000 Silver 0.1337 oz. **Obv:** Wide spaced "Yang"

Date	F	VF	XF	Unc	BU
2 (1898)	85.00	160	275	485	—

KM# 1120 YANG
5.2000 g., 0.8000 Silver 0.1337 oz. **Obv:** Closely spaced "Yang"

Date	F	VF	XF	Unc	BU
2 (1898)	75.00	140	245	450	—

TEST COINAGE
Treasury Department

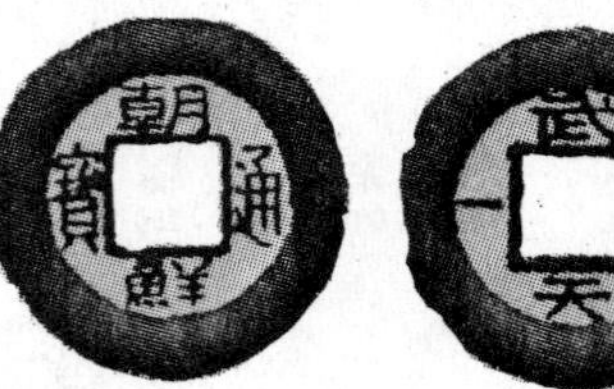

KM# Tc1 MUN
Cast Bronze **Obv. Legend:** Cho Son T'ong Bo **Rev:** "Mu" at top, "Chon" at bottom

Date	VG	F	VF	XF	Unc
ND(1881) Rare	—	—	—	—	—

KM# Tc2 10 MUN
Cast Bronze **Obv. Legend:** Cho Son T'ong Bo **Rev:** Blank

Date	VG	F	VF	XF	Unc
ND Rare	—	—	—	—	—

KM# Tc4 CHON
Cast Bronze **Obv. Legend:** Cho Son T'ong Bo **Rev:** "Ho" at top, "Il" (1) Chon at right

Date	VG	F	VF	XF	Unc
ND(1881) Rare	—	—	—	—	—

KM# Tc3 10 CHON
Cast Bronze **Rev:** "Sip" (10) at top

Date	VG	F	VF	XF	Unc
ND Rare	—	—	—	—	—

TEST COINAGE
Central Government Mint

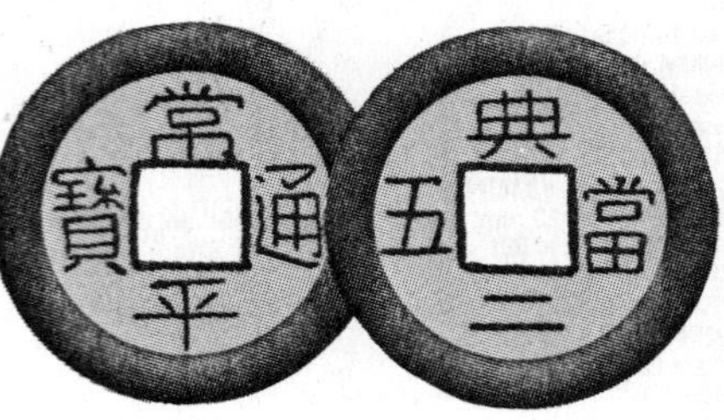

KM# Tc6 5 MUN
Bronze **Obv. Legend:** Sang P'yong T'ong Bo **Rev:** "I" at bottom, "Tang" at right, "O" (5) at left

Date	VG	F	VF	XF	Unc
ND(1884) Rare	—	—	—	—	—

TEST COINAGE
Ch'ung Ch'ong Provincial Office

KM# Tc7 10 MUN
Struck Brass **Obv. Legend:** Sang P'yong T'ong Bo **Rev:** "Ch'ung" at top, "Tang" at right, "Sip" (10) at left

Date	VG	F	VF	XF	Unc
ND(1884)	—	—	700	1,000	—

TEST COINAGE
Without Mint Mark

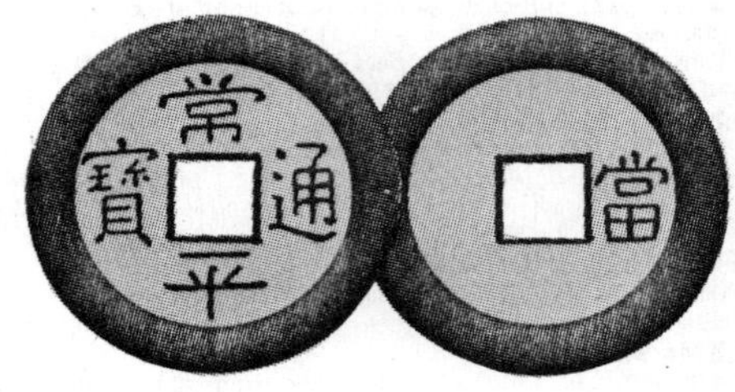

KM# Tc8 10 MUN
Struck Brass **Obv. Legend:** Sang P'yong T'ong Bo **Rev:** "Tang" at right

Date	VG	F	VF	XF	Unc
ND(1884) Rare	—	—	—	—	—

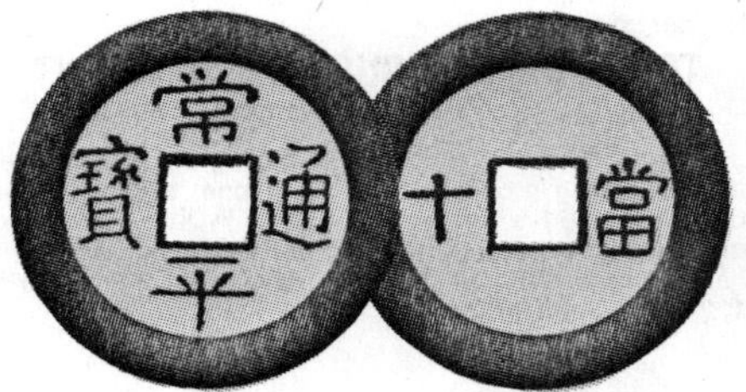

KM# Tc9 10 MUN
Struck Brass **Obv. Legend:** Sang P'yong T'ong Bo **Rev:** "Tang" at right, "Sip" (10) at left

Date	VG	F	VF	XF	Unc
ND(1884) Rare	—	—	—	—	—

PATTERNS
Including off metal strikes

KM#	Date	Mintage	Identification	Mkt Val
Pn6	CD1885	—	5 Mun. White Metal (Tin Alloy).	12,650

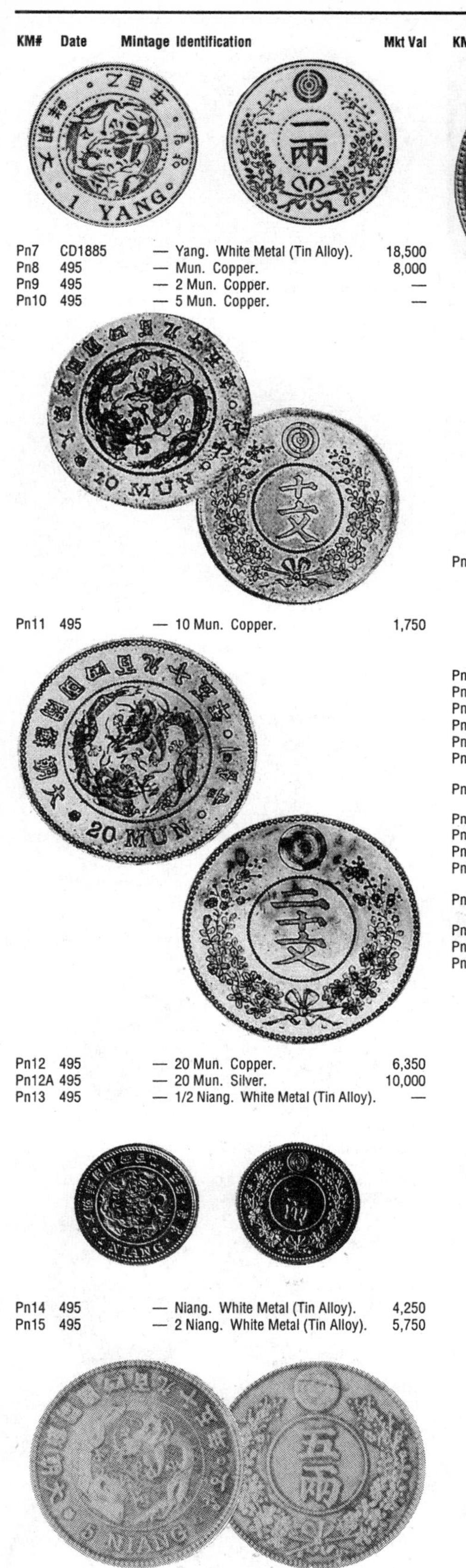

KM#	Date	Mintage	Identification	Mkt Val
Pn7	CD1885	—	Yang. White Metal (Tin Alloy).	18,500
Pn8	495	—	Mun. Copper.	8,000
Pn9	495	—	2 Mun. Copper.	—
Pn10	495	—	5 Mun. Copper.	—
Pn11	495	—	10 Mun. Copper.	1,750
Pn12	495	—	20 Mun. Copper.	6,350
Pn12A	495	—	20 Mun. Silver.	10,000
Pn13	495	—	1/2 Niang. White Metal (Tin Alloy).	—
Pn14	495	—	Niang. White Metal (Tin Alloy).	4,250
Pn15	495	—	2 Niang. White Metal (Tin Alloy).	5,750
Pn16	495	—	5 Niang. White Metal (Tin Alloy).	8,650

KM#	Date	Mintage	Identification	Mkt Val
Pn17	495	—	Warn. White Metal (Tin Alloy).	11,500

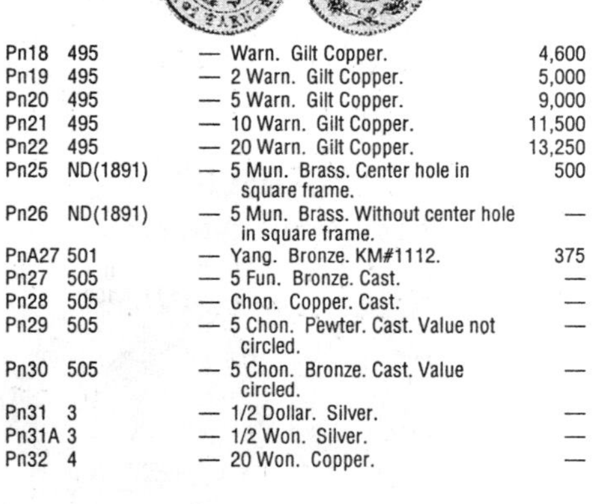

KM#	Date	Mintage	Identification	Mkt Val
Pn18	495	—	Warn. Gilt Copper.	4,600
Pn19	495	—	2 Warn. Gilt Copper.	5,000
Pn20	495	—	5 Warn. Gilt Copper.	9,000
Pn21	495	—	10 Warn. Gilt Copper.	11,500
Pn22	495	—	20 Warn. Gilt Copper.	13,250
Pn25	ND(1891)	—	5 Mun. Brass. Center hole in square frame.	500
Pn26	ND(1891)	—	5 Mun. Brass. Without center hole in square frame.	—
PnA27	501	—	Yang. Bronze. KM#1112.	375
Pn27	505	—	5 Fun. Bronze. Cast.	—
Pn28	505	—	Chon. Copper. Cast.	—
Pn29	505	—	5 Chon. Pewter. Cast. Value not circled.	—
Pn30	505	—	5 Chon. Bronze. Cast. Value circled.	—
Pn31	3	—	1/2 Dollar. Silver.	—
Pn31A	3	—	1/2 Won. Silver.	—
Pn32	4	—	20 Won. Copper.	—

KUWAIT

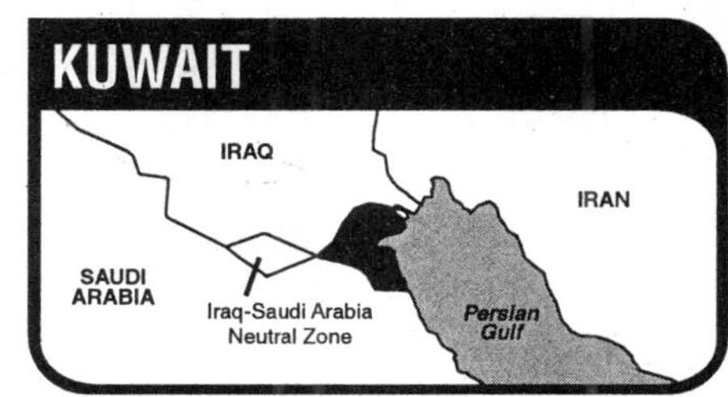

Kuwait is located on the Arabian Peninsula at the northwestern corner of the Persian Gulf. The modern history of Kuwait began with the founding of the city of Kuwait, 1740, by tribesmen who wandered northward from the region of the Qatar Peninsula of eastern Arabia. Fearing that the Turks would take over the sheikhdom, Sheikh Mubarak entered into an agreement with Great Britain, 1899, placing Kuwait under the protection of Britain and empowering Britain to conduct its foreign affairs. Britain terminated the protectorate on June19, 1961, giving Kuwait its independence (by a simple exchange of notes) but agreeing to furnish military aid on request.

TITLES

الكويت

al-Kuwait

RULERS

British Protectorate, until 1961

LOCAL

Al Sabah Dynasty

Abdallah Ibn Sabah, 1762-1812
Jabir Ibn Abdallah, 1812-1859
Sabah Ibn Jabir, 1859-1866
Abdullah Ibn Sabah, 1866-1892
Muhammad Ibn Sabah, 1892-1896
Mubarak Ibn Sabah, 1896-1915

BRITISH PROTECTORATE

Local - Al Sabah Dynasty

EARLY COINAGE

KM# A2 BAIZA

5.1300 g., Copper **Obv:** Abdallah Ibn Sabah, date

Date	Good	VG	F	VF	XF
AH1304 Rare	—	—	—	—	—

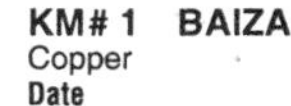

KM# 1 BAIZA

Copper

Date	Good	VG	F	VF	XF
AH1304 Rare	—	—	—	—	—

LAHEJ

A rather small partially independent sultanate situated north of the port city of Aden. Lahej had entered into a protective treaty relationship with Britain following Britain's capture of the port of Aden in 1839.

TITLES

Lahej

LOCAL RULERS
Ali ibn Muhassin,
AH1265-1279/1849-1863AD
Fadl ibn Ali,
AH1291-1315/1874-1898AD

SULTANATE

STANDARD COINAGE

KM# 1 1/2 BAIZA
Copper

Date	F	VF	XF	Unc	BU
ND(1860)	20.00	35.00	60.00	175	—

KM# 2 1/2 BAIZA
Copper

Date	Mintage	F	VF	XF	Unc	BU
ND(1896)	678,000	22.50	40.00	70.00	200	—
ND(1896) Proof	—	Value: 350				

LIBERIA

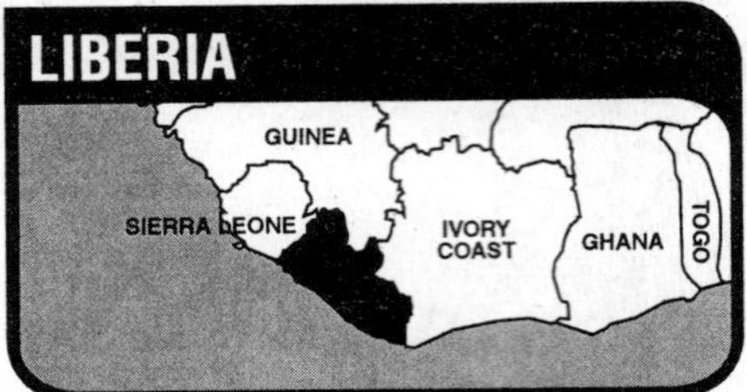

Liberia is located on the southern side of the West African bulge between Sierra Leone and Ivory Coast. The Liberian coast was explored and charted by Portuguese navigator Pedro de Cintra in 1461. For the following three centuries Portuguese traders visited the area regularly to trade for gold, slaves and pepper. The modern country of Liberia, Africa's first republic, was settled in 1822 by the American Colonization Society as a homeland for American freed slaves, with the U.S. government furnishing funds and assisting in negotiations for procurement of land from the native chiefs. The various settlements united in 1839 to form the Commonwealth of Liberia, and in 1847 established the country as a republic with a constitution modeled after that of the United States.

U.S. money was declared legal tender in Liberia in 1943, replacing British West African currency.

Most of the Liberian pattern series, particularly of the 1888-90 period are acknowledged to have been 'unofficial' privately sponsored issues, but they are nonetheless avidly collected by many collectors of Liberian coins. The 'K' number designations on these pieces refer to a listing of Liberian patterns compiled and published by Ernst Kraus.

MINT MARKS
B - Bern, Switzerland
H - Heaton, Birmingham
(l) - London
(s) - San Francisco, U.S.

MONETARY SYSTEM
100 Cents = 1 Dollar

REPUBLIC

STANDARD COINAGE

100 Cents = 1 Dollar

KM# 1 CENT
Copper **Obv:** Palm tree, two stars in legend

Date	F	VF	XF	Unc	BU
1847	6.00	15.00	30.00	110	—
1847 Proof	Value: 195				

KM# 3 CENT
Copper **Rev:** Palm tree, four stars at edge

Date	F	VF	XF	Unc	BU
1862	7.00	20.00	35.00	125	—
1862/42	10.00	25.00	50.00	185	—
1862 Proof	Value: 250				

KM# 5 CENT
Bronze

Date	Mintage	F	VF	XF	Unc	BU
1896H	358,000	3.50	7.50	18.00	45.00	—
1896H Proof	—	Value: 120				

KM# 2 2 CENTS
Rev: Palm tree, two stars at edge

Date	F	VF	XF	Unc	BU
1847	12.00	30.00	75.00	250	—
1847 Proof	Value: 350				

KM# 4 2 CENTS
Copper **Rev:** Palm tree, four stars at edge

Date	F	VF	XF	Unc	BU
1862	15.00	35.00	85.00	275	—
1862 Proof	Value: 375				

KM# 6 2 CENTS
Bronze

Date	Mintage	F	VF	XF	Unc	BU
1896H	323,000	5.00	10.00	25.00	60.00	—
1896H Proof	—	Value: 150				

KM# 7 10 CENTS
2.3200 g., 0.9250 Silver .0690 oz.

Date	Mintage	F	VF	XF	Unc	BU
1896H	20,000	5.00	15.00	40.00	150	—
1896H Proof	—	Value: 250				

KM# 8 25 CENTS
5.8000 g., 0.9250 Silver .1725 oz.

Date	Mintage	F	VF	XF	Unc	BU
1896H	15,000	10.00	20.00	60.00	250	—
1896H Proof	—	Value: 375				

KM# 9 50 CENTS
11.6000 g., 0.9250 Silver .3450 oz.

Date	Mintage	F	VF	XF	Unc	BU
1896H	5,000	15.00	35.00	90.00	450	—
1896H Proof	—	Value: 600				

TOKEN COINAGE

CH-1. Obverse: 1 in date left of tree trunk, small ship, 15 rays, 13 palm tree leaves, bush top at water line. Reverse: wide-spaced AD, single period between.

CH-2. Obverse: 1 in date under tree trunk, large ship, 14 rays, 12 palm tree leaves, bush top above water. Reverse: narrow-spaced AD, double periods between.

CH-3. Obverse: 1 in date under tree trunk, large ship, 14 rays with second touching ship, 10 palm tree leaves with leaf between LI, bush top at water line. Reverse: narrow-spaced AD, double periods between.

CH-4. Obverse: 1 in date left of tree trunk, large ship, 11 rays, 12 palm tree leaves with leaf between BE, bush top above water. Reverse: wide spaced AD, single period between, and first N in COLONIZATION tilted upward.

CH-5: Obverse: as CH-1. Reverse: very narrow AD.

CH-6: Obverse: as CH-2. Reverse: as CH-4.

KM# Tn1 CENT

Copper **Obv:** Large ship (CH-2, 3, 4, 5).

Date	VG	F	VF	XF	Unc
1833	5.00	10.00	27.50	70.00	350

KM# Tn2 CENT

Copper **Obv:** Small ship (CH-1, 5)

Date	VG	F	VF	XF	Unc
1833	4.00	8.00	25.00	65.00	325

PATTERNS

Including off metal strikes

KM#	Date	Mintage	Identification	Mkt Val
Pn1	1847	—	Cent. Copper.	200
Pn2	1847	—	2 Cents. Copper.	300
Pn3	1847	—	10 Cents. Silver.	1,500
Pn4	1847	—	10 Cents. Bronze.	850
Pn4a	1847	—	10 Cents. Bronze. Struck on a 1834 U.S. Cent	—
Pn5	1862	—	Cent. Copper. Struck on thick planchet	250
Pn6	1862	—	2 Cents. Copper. 2-1/2mm thick planchet	300
Pn7	1864	—	10 Cents. Silver.	1,750
Pn8	1864	—	10 Cents. Bronze.	900
Pn9	1865	—	25 Cents. Silver.	1,250
Pn10	1865	—	25 Cents. Bronze.	800
Pn11	1866	—	Cent. Copper.	210
Pn12	1866	—	Cent. Copper.	275
Pn13	1866	—	2 Cents. Copper.	250
Pn14	1866	—	2 Cents. Copper.	350
Pn15	1868	—	Cent. Copper.	175
Pn16	1868	—	2 Cents. Copper.	185
Pn17	1888	—	Cent. Copper.	150
Pn18	1889	—	Cent. Copper. Small shield.	135
Pn19	1889	—	25 Cents. Silver. Reported, not confirmed.	200
Pn20	1889	—	25 Cents. Bronze.	275
Pn21	1889	—	25 Cents. Aluminum.	175
Pn22	1889	—	25 Cents. Copper Nickel.	185
Pn23	1889	—	25 Cents. Silver. Reported, not confirmed.	250
Pn24	1889	—	25 Cents. Bronze.	300
Pn25	1889	—	25 Cents. Aluminum.	200
Pn26	1889	—	25 Cents. Copper Nickel.	225
Pn27	1889	—	25 Cents. Silver. Reported, not confirmed.	—
Pn28	1889	—	25 Cents. Bronze.	250
Pn29	1889	—	25 Cents. Aluminum.	175
Pn30	1889	—	25 Cents. Copper Nickel.	185
Pn31	1889	—	50 Cents. Silver. 1-1/4mm thick planchet. Reported, not confirmed.	—
Pn32	1889	—	50 Cents. Silver. 2-1/2mm thick planchet. Reported, not confirmed.	—
Pn33	1889	—	50 Cents. Copper Silvered.	550
Pn34	1889	—	50 Cents. Bronze.	350
Pn35	1889	—	50 Cents. Aluminum.	250
Pn36	1889	—	50 Cents. Copper Nickel.	275

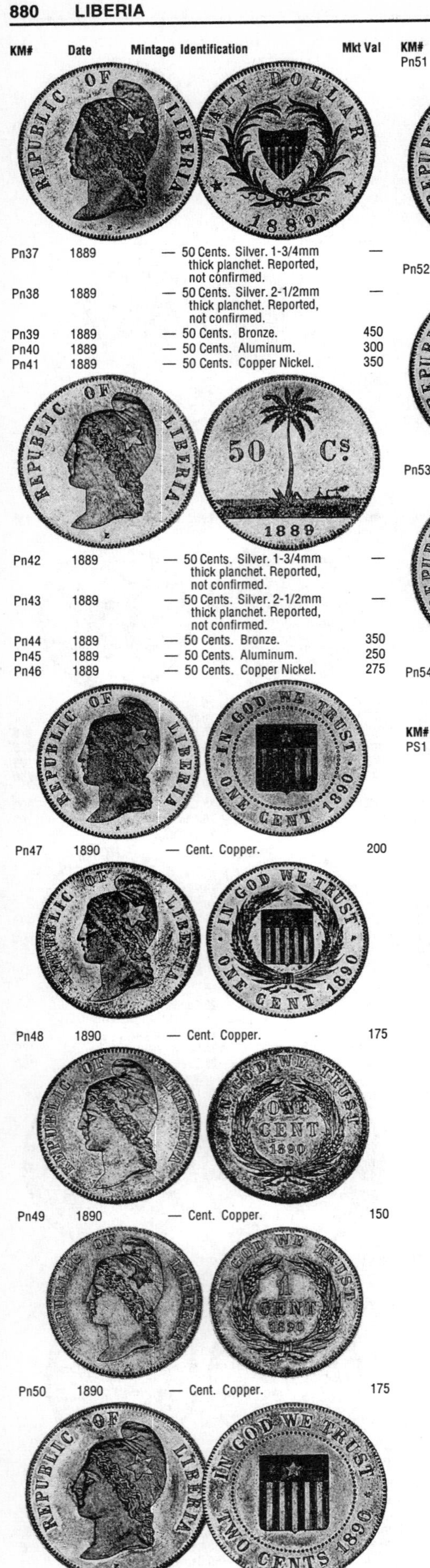

KM#	Date	Mintage	Identification	Mkt Val
Pn37	1889	—	50 Cents. Silver. 1-3/4mm thick planchet. Reported, not confirmed.	—
Pn38	1889	—	50 Cents. Silver. 2-1/2mm thick planchet. Reported, not confirmed.	—
Pn39	1889	—	50 Cents. Bronze.	450
Pn40	1889	—	50 Cents. Aluminum.	300
Pn41	1889	—	50 Cents. Copper Nickel.	350
Pn42	1889	—	50 Cents. Silver. 1-3/4mm thick planchet. Reported, not confirmed.	—
Pn43	1889	—	50 Cents. Silver. 2-1/2mm thick planchet. Reported, not confirmed.	—
Pn44	1889	—	50 Cents. Bronze.	350
Pn45	1889	—	50 Cents. Aluminum.	250
Pn46	1889	—	50 Cents. Copper Nickel.	275
Pn47	1890	—	Cent. Copper.	200
Pn48	1890	—	Cent. Copper.	175
Pn49	1890	—	Cent. Copper.	150
Pn50	1890	—	Cent. Copper.	175

KM#	Date	Mintage	Identification	Mkt Val
Pn51	1890	—	2 Cents. Copper.	250

KM#	Date	Mintage	Identification	Mkt Val
Pn52	1890	—	2 Cents. Copper.	225

KM#	Date	Mintage	Identification	Mkt Val
Pn53	1890	—	2 Cents. Copper.	185

KM#	Date	Mintage	Identification	Mkt Val
Pn54	1890	—	2 Cents. Copper.	225

PROOF SETS

KM#	Date	Mintage	Identification	Issue Price	Mkt Val
PS1	1896H (5)	—	KM#5-9	—	1,625

LIBYA

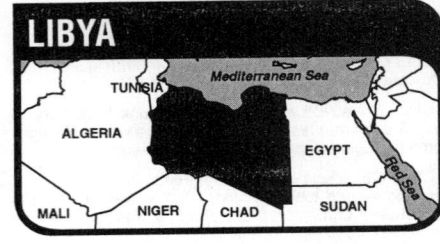

Libya is located on the north-central coast of Africa between Tunisia and Egypt. Libya has been subjected to foreign rule throughout most of its history, various parts of it having been ruled by the Phoenicians, Carthaginians, Vandals, Byzantines, Greeks, Romans, Egyptians, and in the following centuries the Arabs' language, culture and religion were adopted by the indigenous population. Libya was conquered by the Ottoman Turks in 1553, and remained under Turkish domination, becoming a Turkish vilayet in 1835, until it was conquered by Italy and made into a colony in 1911. The name 'Libya', the ancient Greek name for North Africa exclusive of Egypt, was given to the colony by Italy in 1934.

TITLES

المملكة الليبية

al-Mamlaka(t) al-Libiya(t)

الجمهورية الليبية

al-Jomhuriya(t) al-Arabiya(t) al-Libiya(t)

TRIPOLI

Tripoli (formerly Ottoman Empire Area of antique Tripolitania, 700-146 B.C.), the capital city and chief port of the Libyan Arab Jamahiriya, is situated on the North African coast on a promontory stretching out into the Mediterranean Sea. It was probably founded by Phoenicians from Sicily, but was under Roman control from 146 B.C. until 450 A.D. Invasion by Vandals and conquest by the Byzantines preceded the Arab invasions of the 11th century which, by destroying the commercial centers of Sabratha and Leptis, greatly enhanced the importance of Tripoli, an importance maintained through periods of Norman and Spanish control. Tripoli fell to the Turks, who made it the capital of the vilayet of Tripoli in 1551 and remained in their hands until 1911, when it was occupied by the Italians who made it the capital of the Italian province of Tripolitania. British forces entered the city on Jan. 23, 1943, and administered it until establishment of the independent Kingdom of Libya on Dec. 24, 1951.

RULERS

Ottoman, 1836-1911
refer to Turkey

LOCAL PASHAS

Yusuf Pasha Qaramanli,
AH1210-1248/1796-1833AD (resigned)
Ali Pasha Qaramanli II,
AH1248-1250/1833-1835AD

MINT NAME

طرابس

Tarabalus

طرابلس غرب

Tarabalus Gharb = (Tripoli West)

The appellation *west* serving to distinguish it from Tripoli in Lebanon, which had been an Ottoman Mint in the 16th century. On some of the copper coins, *Gharb* is omitted; several types come both with and without *Gharb*. The mint closed between the 28th and 29th year of the reign of Mahmud II.

MONETARY SYSTEM

The monetary system of Tripoli was confused and is poorly understood. Theoretically, 40 Para were equal to one Piastre, but due to the debasement of the silver coinage, later issues are virtually pure copper, though the percentage of alloy varies radically even within a given year. The 10 Para and 20 Para pieces were a little heavier than the copper Paras, with which they could easily be confounded, except that the copper Paras were generally thicker, and bear simpler inscriptions. It is not known how many of the coppers were tariffed to the debased Piastre and its fractions. Some authorities consider the copper pieces to be Beshliks (5 Para coins).

The gold coinage came in two denominations, the Zeri Mahbub (2.4-2.5 g), and the Sultani Altin (3.3-3.4 g). The ratio of the billon Piastres to the gold coins fluctuated from day to day.

COPPER COINAGE Under MAHMUD II

Under this rubric are included all pieces intended as paras. Many of the billon coins are so debased as to be nearly pure copper, but they can be distinguished from those coins intended as paras as they are much thinner, and bear different devices and inscriptions. Some pieces are also struck in brass.

In addition to pieces bearing no regnal year, the issuance of coppers seems to be restricted to two series, the first bearing years 12 & 13, the other years 20-27. The first group is related to an anomalous billon issue in the same years (Type D below), the second issue seems to be connected to the reduced weight series of years 21-25. The undated pieces were most probably struck during one of these two periods.

All of the following pieces appear to be of one denomination, probably a para, but vary in size from about 17-23mm.

BILLON COINAGE of Mahmud II

The billon coinage of Mahmud II is extremely varied, with a plethora of types deriving largely from contemporary Turkish, Egyptian, and Tunisian prototypes. There is considerable controversy over the denominations of these coins, although they seem to be based on a Piastre (40 Paras, Kuruns) of about 16 grams from yrs. 1-13, of about 12 grams from yrs. 13-21, and of 10 grams from yrs. 21-25. A new style coinage was introduced in yr. 28, but it was apparently never issued in sizable quantities and confined to the one year.

There is considerable weight variation within each denomination, in some cases up to 20 percent higher or lower than the theoretical norm. There is not yet discernible correlation between type, denomination, year, and standard. Recent evidence indicates that the net silver content was frequently and repeatedly reduced, probably in rather small increments. Thus the existence of several types for a single denomination and regnal year may indicate a multiplicity of issues with a single year, but as the full series is still not known, the complete sequence for each denomination cannot yet be reconstructed Debasements were frequent: In the 4-year period covering years 21-24, ten changes in the values of coinage are recorded, but not all changes need have referred to the denominations and designs.

Except for a few isolated miscellaneous types, all of the billon coinage can be classed into five basic types:

TYPE A: Obv: Toughra, sometimes with adjacent symbol, (i.e. flower, tamgha with arrow heads, large tamgha, crescent, letter "nun", and figures "22" and "23"). Rev: Year/mintname/*1223.*

TYPE B: Obv: Toughra/mintname/*1223.* Rev: 4-line leg. giving Sultan's titles: *Sultan al-Bahrayn Wa Khaqan al-Bahrayn al Sultan Ibn al Sultan* (sometimes with stars).

TYPE C: Obv: Sultan's name/benediction/mintname/*1223.* (4-line leg.) Rev: Same as rev. of Type B.

TYPE D: Obv: Sultan's name (sometimes with *1223*). Rev: Year/mintname/*1223* (1223 omitted when on obv.)

TYPE E: Obv: 4-line leg: *Sultan al Barrayn wa Khaqan al Bahrayn al Sultan Mahmud Khan Azza Nasruhu* /year. Rev: Mintname/*1223,* this type copied from Tunis piastre & fractions).

In addition to the variations in type, there is considerable variation in the borders. No attempt has been made in these listings to distinguish the various types of borders, though it is quite possible that such distinctions may have been monetarily important.

STANDARD COINAGE

The following listings are arranged by standard, and then by denomination within each standard. The sizes of the coins can vary considerably within each issue. The weight can vary by up to 20 percent higher or lower than the amounts shown.

All of the coins were struck in low-grade billon, tending toward pure copper on some of the later issues. Most of the coins originally were lightly silver-washed, and specimens with the silver wash intact are now quite scarce.

OTTOMAN EMPIRE

OTTOMAN COINAGE

KM# 63 5 PARA

Silver, 20 mm. **Ruler:** Selim III **Note:** Weight varies 0.85-1.20 grams.

Date	VG	F	VF	XF	Unc
AH1203//14 (1802)	40.00	60.00	200	400	—

KM# 61 10 PARA

Silver, 26 mm. **Ruler:** Selim III **Note:** Weight varies 1.94-3.30 grams. There exists 3 different marks in place of the normal numeral for the regnal year.

Date	VG	F	VF	XF	Unc
AH1203//14 (1802)	50.00	100	200	500	—

KM# 64 20 PARA

Silver **Ruler:** Selim III **Note:** Similar to Piastre, KM#60.

Date	VG	F	VF	XF	Unc
AH1203//14 (1788)	100	150	250	400	—

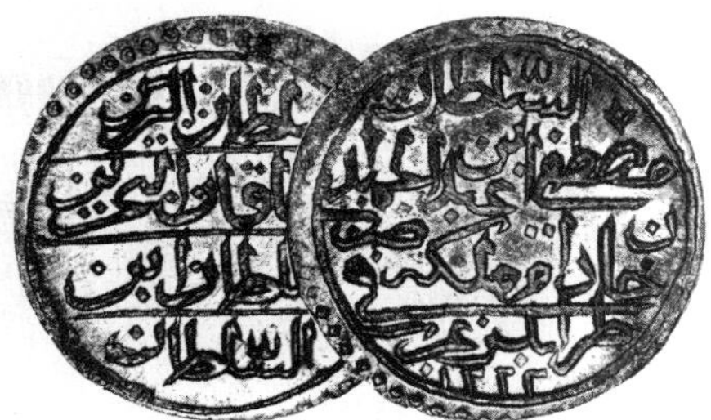

KM# 70 30 PARA

12.5000 g., Silver, 35 mm. **Ruler:** Mustafa IV

Date	VG	F	VF	XF	Unc
AH1222 (1807) Rare	—	—	—	—	—

KM# 66 50 PARA

Silver **Ruler:** Selim III **Note:** Weight varies 23.80-24.35 grams. Size varies 42-44mm.

Date	VG	F	VF	XF	Unc
AH1203//16 (1805)	150	250	400	600	—
AH1203//17 (1806)	—	—	—	—	—

KM# 67 100 PARA

Silver, 45 mm. **Ruler:** Selim III **Note:** Weight varies 30.60-31.32 grams.

Date	VG	F	VF	XF	Unc
AH1203//16	200	300	450	650	—

KM# 65 ZERI MAHBUB

2.0000 g., Gold, 27 mm. **Ruler:** Selim III

Date	VG	F	VF	XF	Unc
AH1203//14 (1803)	200	400	700	1,500	—

KM# 72 ZERI MAHBUB

2.4500 g., Gold, 21 mm. **Ruler:** Mustafa IV **Note:** Similar to Zeri Mahbub, KM#56.

Date	VG	F	VF	XF	Unc
AH1222 Rare	—	—	—	—	—

KM# 62 SULTANI

3.5000 g., Gold **Ruler:** Selim III **Note:** Size varies 23-27mm.

Date	VG	F	VF	XF	Unc
AH1203//14	200	400	700	1,500	—
AH1203//15	200	400	700	1,500	—
AH1203//17	200	400	700	1,500	—
AH1203//19	200	400	700	1,500	—

KM# 73 SULTANI

3.3300 g., Gold, 25 mm. **Ruler:** Mustafa IV

Date	VG	F	VF	XF	Unc
AH1222 Rare	—	—	—	—	—

COPPER COINAGE

KM# 81.1 PARA

Copper **Ruler:** Mahmud II **Obv:** Toughra **Rev:** Similar to KM#75 with Gharb

Date	Good	VG	F	VF	XF
AH1221 (1806) Error	8.00	12.50	20.00	45.00	—
AH1222 (1807) Error	8.00	12.50	20.00	45.00	—
AH1223 (1808)	6.00	10.00	18.00	30.00	—

KM# 75 PARA

Copper **Ruler:** Mahmud II

Date	Good	VG	F	VF	XF
AH1223 (1808)	5.00	8.00	12.50	20.00	—
ND (1808)	4.00	8.00	12.00	18.00	—
AH1223 (1820) 12 obverse and 13 reverse	—	—	—	—	—
AH1223//12 (1820)	10.00	15.00	18.50	35.00	—
AH1223//13 (1821)	10.00	15.00	18.50	35.00	—
AH1223//20 (1828)	10.00	15.00	17.50	30.00	—

KM# 77 PARA

Copper **Ruler:** Mahmud II **Obv. Legend:** SULTAN/MAHMUD KHAN/AZZA NASRUHU

Date	Good	VG	F	VF	XF
AH1223 (1808)	10.00	15.00	16.50	22.50	—
AH1223//20 (1828)	10.00	15.00	17.00	25.00	—

KM# 83 PARA

2.5000 g., Copper **Ruler:** Mahmud II **Rev:** Without Gharb

Date	Good	VG	F	VF	XF
AH1223 (1808)	2.50	5.00	10.00	20.00	—

KM# 91.1 PARA

Copper **Ruler:** Mahmud II **Obv:** Without dot above "B" in "DARB"

Date	Good	VG	F	VF	XF
ND (1808)	8.00	10.00	15.00	20.00	—

KM# 91.2 PARA

Copper **Ruler:** Mahmud II **Obv. Legend:** DURIBA **Rev. Legend:** FI TRABLUS

Date	Good	VG	F	VF	XF
ND (1808)	10.00	12.00	15.00	20.00	—

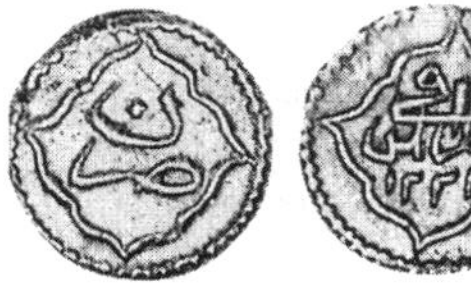

KM# 93 PARA
Copper **Ruler:** Mahmud II **Obv:** Legend within lozenge **Rev:** Legend within lozenge

Date	Good	VG	F	VF	XF
AH1223 (1808)	10.00	15.00	20.00	30.00	—

KM# 115 PARA
Copper **Ruler:** Mahmud II **Obv. Legend:** DURIBA/FI/TARABALUS/1223 **Rev:** Hexagram with central dot

Date	Good	VG	F	VF	XF
AH1223 (1808)	9.00	12.00	15.00	30.00	—
AH1223//25 (1832)	9.00	12.00	15.00	30.00	—
AH1223//27 (1834)	9.00	12.00	15.00	30.00	—

KM# 117 PARA
Copper **Ruler:** Mahmud II **Rev:** Hexagram with 4-7 dots

Date	Good	VG	F	VF	XF
AH1223 (1808)	10.00	12.00	15.00	25.00	—

KM# 85 PARA
2.5000 g., Copper **Ruler:** Mahmud II **Obv:** Toughra and reverse legend within square and 8 loops

Date	Good	VG	F	VF	XF
AH1223 (1810)	10.00	12.00	15.00	30.00	—

KM# 99 PARA
Copper **Ruler:** Mahmud II **Obv. Legend:** DURIBA/FI/1223 **Rev. Legend:** TARABALUS/R.Y

Date	Good	VG	F	VF	XF
AH1223//12 (1819)	9.00	12.00	16.50	30.00	—
AH1223//13 (1820)	9.00	12.00	16.50	30.00	—
AH1223//20 (1827)	9.00	12.00	16.50	30.00	—
AH1223//21 (1828)	9.00	12.00	16.50	30.00	—

KM# 101 PARA
Copper **Ruler:** Mahmud II **Obv. Legend:** DURIBA/FI/1223 **Rev. Legend:** TARABALUS/R.Y

Date	Good	VG	F	VF	XF
AH1223//13 (1820)	10.00	12.50	16.50	35.00	—
AH1223//21 (1828)	10.00	12.50	16.50	35.00	—

KM# 87 PARA
2.5000 g., Copper **Ruler:** Mahmud II **Obv:** Toughra **Rev:** 6-line legend

Date	Good	VG	F	VF	XF
AH1223 (1826)	12.00	15.00	20.00	35.00	—

KM# 103 PARA
Copper **Ruler:** Mahmud II **Rev:** 5 dots within wreath

Date	Good	VG	F	VF	XF
AH1223//20 (1827)	10.00	12.50	15.00	25.00	—

KM# 105 PARA
Copper **Ruler:** Mahmud II **Rev:** Arabesque within garland

Date	Good	VG	F	VF	XF
AH1223//21 (1828)	10.00	12.50	16.00	30.00	—

KM# 112 PARA
Copper **Ruler:** Mahmud II **Obv:** Ornament **Rev:** Gharb

Date	Good	VG	F	VF	XF
AH1223//21 (1828)	8.00	10.00	15.00	25.00	—

KM# 111 PARA
Copper **Ruler:** Mahmud II **Obv. Legend:** DURIBA/FI/TARABALUS/1223 **Rev:** Gharb

Date	Good	VG	F	VF	XF
AH1223//21 (1828)	8.00	10.00	15.00	25.00	—

KM# 107 PARA
Copper **Ruler:** Mahmud II **Obv:** Without "Gharb" **Rev:** Rose within garland

Date	Good	VG	F	VF	XF
AH1223//22 (1829)	10.00	12.50	15.00	25.00	—

KM# 102 PARA
3.7900 g., Copper, 22 mm. **Ruler:** Mahmud II **Rev:** "Tarabalus 22" in looped star of David

Date	Good	VG	F	VF	XF
AH1223//22 (1829)	10.00	15.00	20.00	35.00	—

KM# 119 PARA
Copper **Ruler:** Mahmud II **Obv:** Similar to KM#111 **Rev:** Hexagram with 1723

Date	Good	VG	F	VF	XF
AH1223//22 (1829)	12.00	15.00	18.00	30.00	—
AH1223//23 (1830)	12.00	15.00	18.00	30.00	—

KM# 95 PARA
Copper Or Brass **Ruler:** Mahmud II **Obv:** Legend arranged differently **Rev:** Legend arranged differently

Date	Good	VG	F	VF	XF
AH1223//23 (1830)	12.00	18.00	22.00	45.00	—

KM# 97 PARA
Copper **Ruler:** Mahmud II **Obv:** Legend within 10-pointed stars **Rev:** Legend within 10-pointed stars

Date	Good	VG	F	VF	XF
AH1223//23 (1830)	10.00	12.00	15.00	25.00	—

KM# 79 PARA
Copper **Ruler:** Mahmud II **Obv. Legend:** SULTAN/1223 **Rev. Legend:** MAHMUD/24

Date	Good	VG	F	VF	XF
AH1223//24 (1832)	10.00	15.00	18.00	30.00	—

KM# 81.2 PARA
2.5000 g., Copper **Ruler:** Mahmud II **Note:** Reduced size: 17 millimeters.

Date	Good	VG	F	VF	XF
AH1223 (1832)	12.00	20.00	35.00	75.00	—

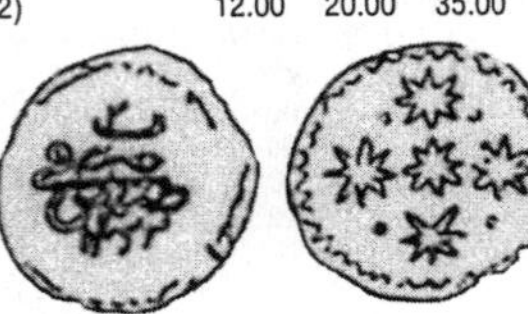

KM# 109 PARA
Copper **Ruler:** Mahmud II **Rev:** 5 stars

Date	Good	VG	F	VF	XF
AH1223//25 (1832)	10.00	12.50	16.50	25.00	—

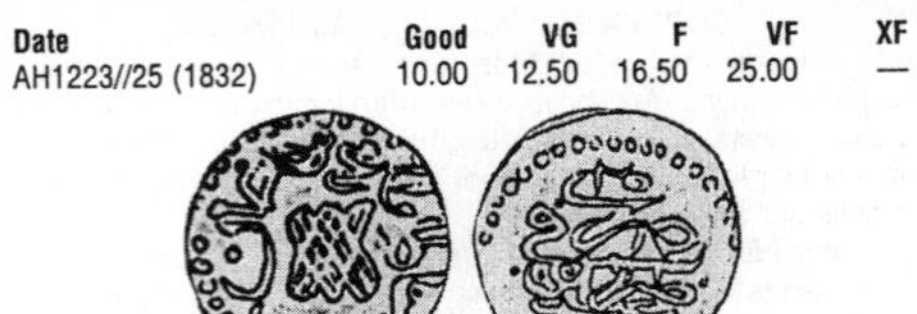

KM# 90.1 PARA
Copper **Ruler:** Mahmud II **Note:** Similar to KM#89 but year below arabesque.

Date	Good	VG	F	VF	XF
AH1223//25 (1833)	8.00	10.00	15.00	25.00	—

KM# 89 PARA
2.5000 g., Copper **Ruler:** Mahmud II **Obv:** Year above arabesque **Obv. Legend:** SULTAN MAHMUD KHAN 1223

Date	Good	VG	F	VF	XF
AH1223//25 (1833)	8.00	10.00	15.00	25.00	—
AH1223//26 (1834)	8.00	10.00	15.00	25.00	—
AH1223//62 (1834) Error for year 26--	8.00	10.00	15.00	35.00	—

Note: Several variations are found in the arrangement of the obverse legend. Year 29 is reported, but is likely a misreading of year 26

KM# 90.2 PARA
Copper **Ruler:** Mahmud II

Date	Good	VG	F	VF	XF
AH1223//25 (1833) Year inverted	10.00	12.00	18.00	30.00	—

STANDARD COINAGE

First Standard - Based on a Piastre (40 Para) of about 16.00 g.

KM# 126 5 PARA
Billon **Ruler:** Mahmud II **Note:** Size varies 22-23 millimeters. Type B.

Date	Good	VG	F	VF	XF
AH1223//1 (1808)	20.00	35.00	60.00	100	—
AH1223//2 (1809)	20.00	35.00	60.00	100	—
AH1223//7 (1814)	20.00	35.00	60.00	100	—
AH1223//8 (1815)	25.00	40.00	75.00	125	—
AH1223//9 (1816)	20.00	35.00	60.00	100	—
AH1223//10 (1817)	20.00	35.00	60.00	100	—
AH1223//11 (1818)	20.00	35.00	60.00	100	—
AH1223//17 (1824)	20.00	35.00	60.00	100	—

KM# 127 10 PARA
1.3500 g., Silver, 18 mm. **Ruler:** Mahmud II **Rev:** Ornament in circle for regnal year

Date	Good	VG	F	VF	XF
AH1223 (1808)	30.00	50.00	75.00	125	—

KM# 128 10 PARA
2.4600 g., Billon **Ruler:** Mahmud II **Note:** Size varies 22-24 millimeters. Type A.

Date	Good	VG	F	VF	XF
AH1223 (1808)	30.00	40.00	75.00	125	—
AH1223//2 (1810)	30.00	40.00	75.00	125	—

KM# 129 10 PARA
Copper Or Billon, 25 mm. **Ruler:** Mahmud II **Obv:** "Sultan Mahmud" 2 lines in beaded circle **Rev:** "DURIBE FI AH1223 TRABLUS GHARB" within breaded circle **Note:** Type D.

Date	Good	VG	F	VF	XF
AH1223 (1809)	35.00	50.00	75.00	125	—

KM# 135 10 PARA
1.8000 g., Copper Or Billon, 25 mm. **Ruler:** Mahmud II **Note:** Type D.

Date	Good	VG	F	VF	XF
AH1223//3 (1811)	35.00	50.00	60.00	100	—

KM# 130 10 PARA
3.3500 g., Copper Or Billon **Ruler:** Mahmud II

Date	Good	VG	F	VF	XF
AH1223//7 (1814)	30.00	50.00	75.00	125	—

KM# 131 10 PARA
Copper Or Billon **Ruler:** Mahmud II

Date	Good	VG	F	VF	XF
AH1223//9 (1816)	50.00	60.00	75.00	125	—

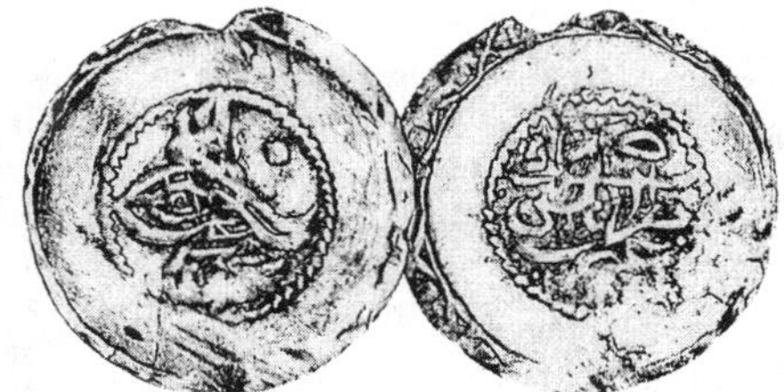

KM# 134 10 PARA
3.8900 g., Copper Or Billon **Ruler:** Mahmud II **Note:** Size varies 29-31 millimeters.

Date	Good	VG	F	VF	XF
AH1223//9 (1816)	35.00	50.00	60.00	100	—
AH1223//10 (1817)	35.00	50.00	60.00	100	—

KM# 132 15 PARA
Billon **Ruler:** Mahmud II

Date	Good	VG	F	VF	XF
AH1223//7 (1814)	35.00	50.00	60.00	80.00	—

KM# 136 20 PARA
Billon, 31 mm. **Ruler:** Mahmud II **Note:** Weight varies 5.38-6.65 grams. Type A.

Date	Good	VG	F	VF	XF
AH1223//2 (1809)	30.00	40.00	75.00	125	—
AH1223//7 (1814)	30.00	40.00	75.00	125	—

KM# 137 20 PARA
Billon **Ruler:** Mahmud II

Date	Good	VG	F	VF	XF
AH1223//8 (1815)	30.00	40.00	75.00	125	—

KM# 138 20 PARA
Billon **Ruler:** Mahmud II

Date	Good	VG	F	VF	XF
AH1223//9 (1816)	30.00	50.00	75.00	125	—

KM# 139 20 PARA
Billon **Ruler:** Mahmud II

Date	Good	VG	F	VF	XF
AH1223//10 (1817)	30.00	50.00	75.00	125	—
AH1223//11 (1818)	30.00	50.00	75.00	125	—

KM# 140 40 PARA
15.6800 g., Billon, 37 mm. **Ruler:** Mahmud II **Note:** Type A.

Date	Good	VG	F	VF	XF
AH1223 (1808)	85.00	100	125	200	—

KM# 141 40 PARA
12.0250 g., Billon **Ruler:** Mahmud II **Note:** Type B.

Date	Good	VG	F	VF	XF
AH1223//1 (1808)	80.00	150	175	300	—
AH1223 (1808) Ornament	80.00	100	130	300	—
AH1223//2 (1809)	80.00	100	150	400	—
AH1223//3 (1810)	80.00	100	125	300	—

KM# 142 100 PARA
24.6800 g., Billon **Ruler:** Mahmud II **Note:** Size varies 43-44 millimeters. Ornament with dot on either side.

Date	Good	VG	F	VF	XF
AH1223 (1808)	200	250	375	400	—

KM# 143 100 PARA
Billon **Ruler:** Mahmud II **Obv:** Ornament right of toughra

Date	Good	VG	F	VF	XF
AH1223//3 (1810) Rare	—	—	—	—	—
AH1223//4 (1812) Rare	—	—	—	—	—
AH1223//5 (1813) Rare	—	—	—	—	—

KM# 144 100 PARA
24.6800 g., Billon **Ruler:** Mahmud II **Obv:** Flower right of toughra **Note:** Size varies 43-44 millimeters.

Date	Good	VG	F	VF	XF
AH1223//4 (1812) Rare	—	—	—	—	—
AH1227//4 (1812) Error; Rare	—	—	—	—	—
AH1223//5 (1813) Special form; Rare	—	—	—	—	—
AH1223//5 (1813) Rare	—	—	—	—	—

STANDARD COINAGE

Second Standard - Years 12-13;
Based on a Piastre of about 14.00 g.

KM# 145 10 PARA
2.9000 g., Billon, 19 mm. **Ruler:** Mahmud II **Note:** Type D.

Date	Good	VG	F	VF	XF
AH1223//12 (1819)	30.00	40.00	75.00	125	—
AH1223//13 (1820)	30.00	40.00	75.00	125	—

KM# 147 20 PARA
4.4100 g., Billon, 23 mm. **Ruler:** Mahmud II **Note:** Type D.

Date	Good	VG	F	VF	XF
AH1223//12 (1819)	30.00	50.00	60.00	100	—
AH1223//13 (1820)	30.00	50.00	60.00	100	—

KM# 149 20 PARA
6.3500 g., Billon, 28 mm. **Ruler:** Mahmud II **Note:** Type B.

Date	Good	VG	F	VF	XF
AH1223//13 (1820)	35.00	60.00	100	150	—

KM# 150.2 40 PARA
Billon **Ruler:** Mahmud II **Obv:** Flower beside toughra ornament

Date	Good	VG	F	VF	XF
AH1223//13 (1820)	100	125	150	200	—

KM# 150.1 40 PARA
Billon, 35 mm. **Ruler:** Mahmud II **Note:** Weight varies 11.30-12.22 grams. Type B.

Date	Good	VG	F	VF	XF
AH1223//13 (1820)	100	125	150	200	—

STANDARD COINAGE

Third Standard - Years 14-21;
Based on a Piastre of about 12.00 g.

KM# 156 10 PARA
Billon **Ruler:** Mahmud II **Note:** Weight varies 1.69-1.90 grams. Size varies 22-25 millimeters. Type B.

Date	Good	VG	F	VF	XF
AH1223//16 (1823)	30.00	50.00	70.00	100	—
AH1223//17 (1824)	30.00	50.00	70.00	100	—
AH1223//18 (1825)	30.00	50.00	70.00	125	—

KM# 154 10 PARA
3.0900 g., Billon **Ruler:** Mahmud II **Note:** Size varies 22-28 millimeters. Type A.

Date	Good	VG	F	VF	XF
AH1223//19 (1826)	30.00	50.00	70.00	100	—

KM# 155 10 PARA
Billon **Ruler:** Mahmud II **Rev:** Legend within square

Date	Good	VG	F	VF	XF
AH1223//20 (1827)	30.00	50.00	70.00	100	—

KM# 162 15 PARA
3.7000 g., Billon, 29 mm. **Ruler:** Mahmud II **Note:** Type E.

Date	Good	VG	F	VF	XF
AH1223//17 (1824)	35.00	50.00	75.00	125	—

KM# 168.2 20 PARA
5.5900 g., Billon **Ruler:** Mahmud II **Obv:** Sprig beside toughra

Date	Good	VG	F	VF	XF
AH1223//15 (1822)	50.00	75.00	100	150	—

KM# 168.3 20 PARA
5.5900 g., Billon **Ruler:** Mahmud II **Obv:** Without stars

Date	Good	VG	F	VF	XF
AH1223//15 (1822)	50.00	75.00	100	150	—

KM# 166 20 PARA
5.5900 g., Billon, 31 mm. **Ruler:** Mahmud II **Note:** Type A.

Date	Good	VG	F	VF	XF
AH1223//15 (1822)	50.00	75.00	100	125	—
AH1223//20 (1827)	50.00	75.00	100	125	—
AH1223//21 (1828)	50.00	75.00	100	125	—

KM# 168.1 20 PARA
5.5900 g., Billon **Ruler:** Mahmud II **Note:** Type B.

Date	Good	VG	F	VF	XF
AH1223//15 (1822)	50.00	75.00	100	150	—

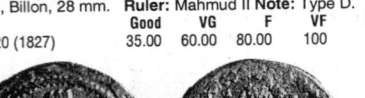

KM# 170 20 PARA
6.4300 g., Billon, 29 mm. **Ruler:** Mahmud II **Note:** Type C.

Date	Good	VG	F	VF	XF
AH1223//17 (1824)	40.00	75.00	100	120	—
AH1223//18 (1825)	40.00	75.00	100	120	—
AH1223//20 (1827)	40.00	75.00	100	120	—

KM# 172 20 PARA
5.1000 g., Billon, 28 mm. **Ruler:** Mahmud II **Note:** Type D.

Date	Good	VG	F	VF	XF
AH1223//20 (1827)	35.00	60.00	80.00	100	—

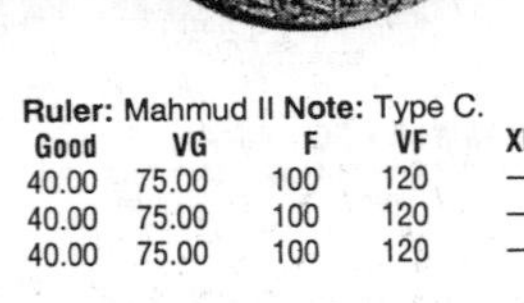

KM# 164 20 PARA
5.6000 g., Billon, 23 mm. **Ruler:** Mahmud II **Note:** Type A.

Date	Good	VG	F	VF	XF
AH1223//20 (1827)	30.00	40.00	50.00	100	—

KM# 176 30 PARA
Billon **Ruler:** Mahmud II **Note:** Size varies 27-29 millimeters. Type A.

Date	Good	VG	F	VF	XF
AH1223//2 (1809)	30.00	50.00	70.00	100	—

KM# 174 30 PARA
Billon, 34 mm. **Ruler:** Mahmud II **Note:** Type A.

Date	Good	VG	F	VF	XF
AH1223//3 (1811)	100	150	250	400	—

KM# A178 30 PARA
22.1300 g., Billon, 37 mm. **Ruler:** Mahmud II **Note:** Type B.

Date	Good	VG	F	VF	XF
AH1223//14 (1821)	80.00	90.00	125	185	—

KM# 178 30 PARA
7.7300 g., Billon **Ruler:** Mahmud II **Note:** Size varies 33-34 millimeters.

Date	Good	VG	F	VF	XF
AH1223//17 (1824)	75.00	85.00	100	125	—
AH1223//18 (1825)	75.00	85.00	100	125	—

KM# 179 30 PARA
6.4300 g., Billon **Ruler:** Mahmud II **Note:** Type E.

Date	Good	VG	F	VF	XF
AH1223//20 (1827)	75.00	85.00	100	125	—

KM# 186.1 40 PARA
Billon **Ruler:** Mahmud II **Note:** Weight viares 12.15-12.68 grams. Size varies 35-37 millimeters. Type B.

Date	Good	VG	F	VF	XF
AH1223//13 (1820)	80.00	100	125	150	—
AH1223//14 (1821)	80.00	100	125	150	—
AH1223//18 (1825)	80.00	100	125	150	—
AH1223//20 (1827)	80.00	100	125	150	—

KM# 187.2 40 PARA
Billon **Ruler:** Mahmud II **Obv:** Sprig beside toughra

Date	Good	VG	F	VF	XF
AH1223//14 (1821)	200	300	400	500	—

KM# 187.1 40 PARA
Billon **Ruler:** Mahmud II **Rev:** Stars on lines 1, 2 and 3 **Note:** Similar to KM#186 but letter "nun" beside toughra

Date	Good	VG	F	VF	XF
AH1223//14 (1821)	100	150	185	250	—

KM# 184 40 PARA
11.9800 g., Billon **Ruler:** Mahmud II **Note:** Size varies 36-39 millimeters. Type A, circular ornate borders.

Date	Good	VG	F	VF	XF
AH1223//15 (1822)	80.00	100	125	150	—
AH1223//18 (1825)	80.00	100	125	150	—
AH1223//19 (1826)	80.00	100	125	150	—
AH1223//21 (1828)	150	200	225	350	—

KM# 190.1 40 PARA
Billon, 34 mm. **Ruler:** Mahmud II **Note:** Type D.

Date	Good	VG	F	VF	XF
AH1223//18 (1825)	75.00	100	150	200	—

KM# 188 40 PARA
11.9800 g., Billon, 35 mm. **Ruler:** Mahmud II **Note:** Type A, lozenge borders.

Date	Good	VG	F	VF	XF
AH1223//19 (1826)	75.00	100	150	200	—
AH1223//20 (1827)	75.00	100	150	200	—

KM# 182 40 PARA
11.9800 g., Billon, 32 mm. **Ruler:** Mahmud II **Note:** Type A, plain borders.

Date	Good	VG	F	VF	XF
AH1223//20 (1827)	80.00	100	125	150	—

KM# 186.2 40 PARA
Billon **Ruler:** Mahmud II **Obv:** Without toughra

Date	Good	VG	F	VF	XF
AH1223//20 (1827)	90.00	120	150	200	—

KM# 190.2 40 PARA
15.3500 g., Billon, 37 mm. **Ruler:** Mahmud II **Note:** Type E.

Date	Good	VG	F	VF	XF
AH1223//20 (1827) Rare	—	—	—	—	—

KM# 192 40 PARA
11.7500 g., Billon, 33 mm. **Ruler:** Mahmud II **Note:** Type E.

Date	Good	VG	F	VF	XF
AH1243 (1828) Rare	—	—	—	—	—

Note: KM#192 is dated to the actual year AH1243, as on similar coins of Tunis

KM# 180 40 PARA
11.9800 g., Billon, 35 mm. **Ruler:** Mahmud II **Note:** Type A, lozenge borders.

Date	Good	VG	F	VF	XF
AH1223//21 (1828)	80.00	100	125	160	—

KM# 194 50 PARA
15.4400 g., Billon, 37 mm. **Ruler:** Mahmud II **Note:** Type A.

Date	Good	VG	F	VF	XF
AH1243 (1828) Rare	—	—	—	—	—

Note: Refer to KM#182. The denomination of the above coin is very uncertain

KM# 196 60 PARA
18.2700 g., Billon **Ruler:** Mahmud II **Note:** Type A. Varieties exist.

Date	Good	VG	F	VF	XF
AH1223//20 (1827)	50.00	75.00	85.00	100	—

KM# 197 100 PARA
12.0500 g., Billon, 42 mm. **Ruler:** Mahmud II **Note:** Varieties exist.

Date	Good	VG	F	VF	XF
AH1223//15 (1822) Rare	—	—	—	—	—

STANDARD COINAGE

Fourth Standard - Years 21-25;
Based on a Piastre of approximately 10.00 g.

KM# 201 10 PARA
Billon, 24 mm. **Ruler:** Mahmud II **Note:** Type B.

Date	Good	VG	F	VF	XF
AH1223//22 (1829)	30.00	40.00	50.00	75.00	—
AH1223//24 (1830)	30.00	40.00	50.00	75.00	—
AH1223//25 (1831)	30.00	40.00	50.00	75.00	—

KM# 203 20 PARA
Billon **Ruler:** Mahmud II **Obv:** Type D **Rev:** Type E **Note:** Size varies 29-30 millimeters.

Date	Good	VG	F	VF	XF
AH1223//22 (1829)	35.00	50.00	75.00	100	—
AH1223//23 (1830)	35.00	50.00	75.00	100	—

KM# 205 20 PARA
Billon **Ruler:** Mahmud II **Note:** Type B.

Date	Good	VG	F	VF	XF
AH1223//22 (1829)	35.00	50.00	75.00	100	—
AH1223//24 (1831)	35.00	50.00	75.00	100	—
AH1223//25 (1832)	35.00	50.00	75.00	100	—

KM# 207 30 PARA
Billon, 32 mm. **Ruler:** Mahmud II **Note:** Type D.

Date	Good	VG	F	VF	XF
AH1223//22 (1829)	60.00	90.00	150	200	—

KM# 209 30 PARA
Billon, 34 mm. **Ruler:** Mahmud II

Date	Good	VG	F	VF	XF
AH1223//23 (1830) Rare	—	—	—	—	—

KM# 211 30 PARA
Billon, 35 mm. **Ruler:** Mahmud II **Note:** Similar to Type A, but with large crescents at both sides similar to Turkey 10 Para, C#197 but without wreaths.

Date	Good	VG	F	VF	XF
AH1223//24 (1831)	65.00	85.00	100	125	—

KM# 206 30 PARA
Billon, 35 mm. **Ruler:** Mahmud II **Note:** Type A.

Date	Good	VG	F	VF	XF
AH1223//24 (1831)	60.00	90.00	150	200	—

KM# 213 40 PARA
Billon **Ruler:** Mahmud II **Note:** Type A.

Date	Good	VG	F	VF	XF
AH1223//21 (1828)	40.00	70.00	100	150	—
AH1223//22 (1829)	60.00	90.00	150	200	—
AH1223//24 (1831)	40.00	70.00	100	125	—

KM# 215 40 PARA
Billon **Ruler:** Mahmud II **Note:** Type B.

Date	Good	VG	F	VF	XF
AH1223//21 (1828)	85.00	100	150	225	—
AH1223//22 (1829)	85.00	100	150	200	—
AH1223//24 (1831)	85.00	100	150	200	—
AH1223//25 (1832)	85.00	100	150	200	—

STANDARD COINAGE

Fifth Standard - Year 28 only; Uncertain metrology

KM# 217 MANGIR
0.9140 g., Copper, 16 mm. **Ruler:** Mahmud II **Obv:** Toughra with "Nuhas" (= copper) to right, year 28 to left **Rev. Legend:** DURIBA / FI / TARABALUS GHARB / 1223 **Note:** Varieties exist.

Date	Good	VG	F	VF	XF
AH1223//28 (1835)	25.00	35.00	50.00	75.00	—

KM# 216 5 PARA
Silver, 19 mm. **Ruler:** Mahmud II **Note:** Weight varies 1.855-1.91 grams. Type A, but obverse and reverse legend within wreaths. With Fidda (Silver) to right of toughra, regnal year at left.

Date	Good	VG	F	VF	XF
AH1223//28 (1835) Rare	—	—	—	—	—

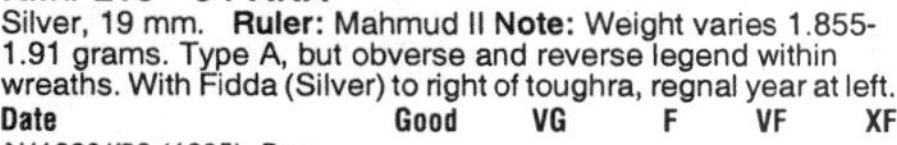

KM# 220 10 PARA
Silver **Ruler:** Mahmud II **Note:** Weight varies 3.680-3.820 grams. Type A, but obverse and rever legend within wreaths. W Fidda (Silver) to right of toughra, regnal year at left.

Date	Good	VG	F	VF	XF
AH1223//28 (1835) Rare	—	—	—	—	—

KM# 218 20 PARA
Billon **Ruler:** Mahmud II **Note:** Weight varies 7.05-7.73 grams. Size varies 25-30 millimeters. Type A, but obverse and reverse legend within wreaths. With Fidda (Silver) to right of toughra, regnal year at left.

Date	Good	VG	F	VF	XF
AH1223//28 (1835) Rare	—	—	—	—	—

KM# 219 40 PARA
Silver **Ruler:** Mahmud II **Note:** Weight varies 14.50-15.27 grams. Size varies 36-38 millimeters. Type A, but obverse and reverlegend within wreaths. With Fidda (Silver) to right of toughra, regnal year at left.

Date	Good	VG	F	VF	XF
AH1223//28 (1835) Rare	—	—	—	—	—

KM# 222 ZERI MAHBUB
Gold **Ruler:** Mahmud II **Note:** Weight varies 2.30-2.50 grams. Size varies 21-24 millimeters. Type B.

Date	VG	F	VF	XF	Unc
AH1223//12	150	200	400	800	—
AH1223//13	150	200	400	800	—
AH1223//14	150	200	400	800	—

KM# 224 ZERI MAHBUB
Gold **Ruler:** Mahmud II **Rev:** Mintname above date **Note:** Type E.

Date	VG	F	VF	XF	Unc
AH1223//18	150	200	400	800	—

KM# 226 ZERI MAHBUB
Gold **Ruler:** Mahmud II

Date	VG	F	VF	XF	Unc
AH1223//20	200	250	400	800	—

KM# 232 SULTANI
Gold **Ruler:** Mahmud II **Rev:** Without lines dividing legend

Date	VG	F	VF	XF	Unc
AH1223	200	250	400	800	—

KM# 228 SULTANI
Gold **Ruler:** Mahmud II **Note:** Weight varies 3.20-3.40 grams. Size varies 24-26 millimeters. Type C (variant).

Date	VG	F	VF	XF	Unc
AH1223 Ornament	150	200	400	800	—
AH1223//6	150	200	400	800	—
AH1223//19	150	200	400	800	—

KM# 227 SULTANI
5.5800 g., Gold, 33 mm. **Ruler:** Mahmud II **Obv:** Toughra

Date	VG	F	VF	XF	Unc
AH1223//5	300	350	500	1,000	—

KM# 230 SULTANI
Gold **Ruler:** Mahmud II **Note:** Similar, but broader and thinner.

Date	VG	F	VF	XF	Unc
AH1223//14 Rare	—	—	—	—	—

LIECHTENSTEIN

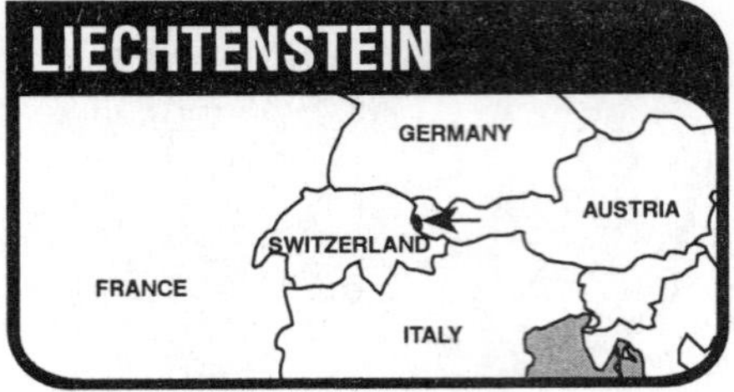

The Principality of Liechtenstein, is located in central Europe on the east bank of the Rhine between Austria and Switzerland. The lordships of Schellenburg and Vaduz were merged into the principality of Liechtenstein. It was a member of the Rhine Confederation from 1806 to 1815, and of the German Confederation from 1815 to 1866 when it became independent. Liechtenstein's long and close association with Austria was terminated by World War I. In 1921 it adopted the coinage of Switzerland, and two years later entered into a customs union with the Swiss, who also operated its postal and telegraph systems and represented it in international affairs. The tiny principality abolished its army in 1868 and has avoided involvement in all European wars since that time.

RULERS
Prince John II, 1858-1929

MINT MARKS
A - Vienna
B - Bern
M - Munich (restrikes)

MONETARY SYSTEM
(1857-1868)
1-1/2 Florins = 1 Vereinsthaler

PRINCIPALITY

STANDARD COINAGE

1-1/2 Florins = 1 Vereinsthaler

Y# 1 THALER (Ein)
18.5200 g., 0.9000 Silver 0.5359 oz. **Ruler:** Prince John II **Note:** Vereins Thaler.

Date	Mintage	F	VF	XF	Unc	BU
1862A	1,920	950	1,500	2,500	3,500	—
1862A M Proof, restrike	—	Value: 37.50				

Y# 1a THALER (Ein)
29.5000 g., 0.9000 Gold 0.8536 oz. **Ruler:** Prince John II

Date	Mintage	F	VF	XF	Unc	BU
1862A M Proof, restrike	50,000	Value: 400				

Y# 1b THALER (Ein)
33.3400 g., Platinum **Ruler:** Prince John II

Date	F	VF	XF	Unc	BU
1862A M Proof, restrike	— Value: 935				

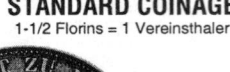

REFORM COINAGE

100 Heller = 1 Krone

Y# 2 KRONE
5.0000 g., 0.8350 Silver .1342 oz. **Ruler:** Prince John II

Date	Mintage	F	VF	XF	Unc	BU
1900	50,000	10.00	15.00	20.00	40.00	—

Y# 4 5 KRONEN
24.0000 g., 0.9000 Silver .6944 oz. **Ruler:** Prince John II

Date	Mintage	F	VF	XF	Unc	BU
1900	5,000	150	250	425	775	—

Y# 5 10 KRONEN
3.3875 g., 0.9000 Gold 0.098 oz. **Ruler:** Prince John II

Date	Mintage	F	VF	XF	Unc	BU
1900	1,500	—	—	2,500	4,500	—

Y# 6 20 KRONEN
6.7750 g., 0.9000 Gold 0.196 oz. **Ruler:** Prince John II

Date	F	VF	XF	Unc	BU
1898	—	—	2,250	4,250	—

ESSAIS

KM#	Date	Mintage	Identification	Mkt Val
E1	1898	125	Krone. Silver. Y2	1,250
E2	1898	100	5 Kronen. Silver. Y4	4,000
E3	1898	35	10 Kronen. Gold. Y5	9,000
E4	1898	35	20 Kronen. Gold. Y6	8,000

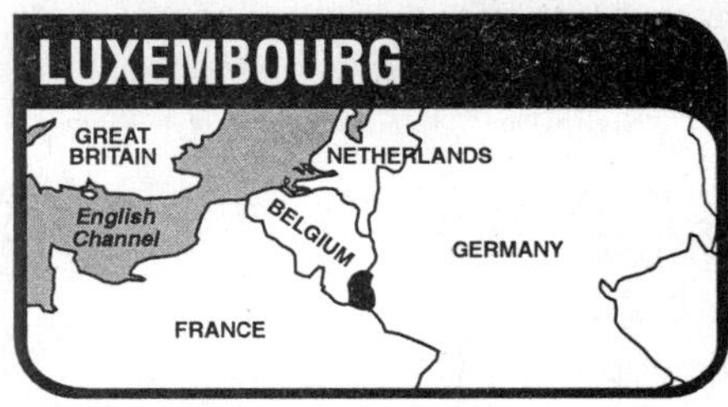

The Grand Duchy of Luxembourg is located in western Europe between Belgium, Germany and France. Founded about 963, Luxembourg was a prominent country of the Holy Roman Empire; one of its sovereigns became Holy Roman Emperor as Henry VII, 1308. After being made a duchy by Emperor Charles IV, 1354, Luxembourg passed under the domination of Burgundy, Spain, Austria and France, 1443-1815, regaining autonomy under the Treaty of Vienna, 1815, as a grand duchy in union with the Netherlands, though ostensibly a member of the German Confederation. When Belgium seceded from the Kingdom of the Netherlands, 1830, Luxembourg was forced to cede its greater western section to Belgium. The tiny duchy left the German Confederation in 1867 when the Treaty of London recognized it as an independent state and guaranteed its perpetual neutrality. Luxembourg was occupied by Germany and liberated by American troops in both World Wars.

RULERS
William III (Netherlands), 1849-1890
Adolphe, 1890-1905

MINT MARKS
A - Paris
(b) - Brussels, privy marks only
H - Gunzburg
(u) - Utrecht, privy marks only

PRIVY MARKS
Angel's head, two headed eagle - Brussels
Anchor, hand - Paris, (1846-60)
Anchor, bee - Paris, (1860-79)
Sword, Caduceus - Utrecht (1846-74 although struck at Brussels until 1909)

MONETARY SYSTEM
100 Centimes = 1 Franc

GRAND DUCHY

STANDARD COINAGE RESUMED

100 Centimes = 1 Franc

KM# 21 2-1/2 CENTIMES
Bronze

Date	Mintage	F	VF	XF	Unc	BU
1854(u)	640,000	3.00	9.00	45.00	120	—
1854(u)	—	10.00	30.00	70.00	180	—
Note: Without serif on "E" of DUCHE						
1870(u)	210,000	10.00	30.00	100	240	—
Note: Dot above BARTH on reverse						
1870(u)	Inc. above	20.00	60.00	120	300	—
Note: Without dot above BARTH on reverse						

KM# 22.1 5 CENTIMES
Bronze

Date	Mintage	F	VF	XF	Unc	BU
1854(u)	680,000	5.00	15.00	60.00	120	—
1870(u)	304,000	15.00	40.00	120	240	—

KM# 22.2 5 CENTIMES
Bronze

Date	Mintage	F	VF	XF	Unc	BU
1855 A	600,000	7.00	22.00	85.00	175	—
1860 A	200,000	20.00	60.00	180	350	—

KM# 23.1 10 CENTIMES
Bronze

Date	Mintage	F	VF	XF	Unc	BU
1854(u)	500,000	10.00	30.00	90.00	200	—
1855(u) Rare	—	—	—	—	—	—
1870(u)	1,313,000	3.00	6.00	40.00	120	—
Note: Dot above BATRH on reverse						
1870(u)	Inc. above	30.00	70.00	180	285	—
Note: Without dot above BARTH on reverse.						

KM# 23.2 10 CENTIMES
Bronze

Date	Mintage	F	VF	XF	Unc	BU
1855A	1,200,000	3.00	6.00	40.00	120	—
1860A	900,000	3.50	7.00	60.00	145	—
1865A	1,000,000	3.00	6.00	50.00	135	—

ESSAIS

KM#	Date	Mintage	Identification	Mkt Val
E1	1853	—	10 Centimes. Copper.	500
E2	1853	—	10 Centimes. Tin.	400
E5	1854	—	10 Centimes. Copper.	500
E6	1854	—	5 Centimes. Silver.	600
E7	1854	—	10 Centimes. Copper.	500
E8	1854	—	10 Centimes. Silver.	600
E9	1855	—	5 Centimes. Copper.	650
E10	1870	—	5 Centimes. Copper.	600
E11	1870	—	5 Centimes. Silver.	600
E12	1870	—	10 Centimes. Silver.	700

KM#	Date	Mintage	Identification	Mkt Val
E13	1889	100	5 Centimes. Copper.	90.00
E14	1889	—	5 Centimes. Silver.	350

KM#	Date	Mintage	Identification	Mkt Val
E15	1889	—	10 Centimes. Copper. Large arms.	90.00
E16	1889	—	5 Centimes. Silver.	350

KM#	Date	Mintage	Identification	Mkt Val
E17	1889	50	10 Centimes. Copper. Small arms.	150

KM#	Date	Mintage	Identification	Mkt Val
E18	1889	—	5 Francs. Copper.	450
E19	1889	50	5 Francs. Tin.	450
E20	1889	50	5 Francs. Silver.	1,250
Note: Beware of counterfeits				
E21	1889	—	5 Francs. Gold.	5,000

PATTERNS

Including off metal strikes

KM#	Date	Mintage	Identification	Mkt Val
PnA1	1852	—	Franc. Nickel.	400
Pn1	1854(u)	—	5 Centimes. Silver.	600
Pn2	1854(u)	—	10 Centimes. Silver.	650
PnA3	1870(u)	—	2-1/2 Centimes. Nickel.	350
Pn3	1870(u)	—	2-1/2 Centimes. Silver.	600
Pn4	1870(u)	—	5 Centimes. Silver.	650
Pn5	1870(u)	—	10 Centimes. Silver.	750

PIEFORTS AND PIEFORTS WITH ESSAI

KM#	Date	Mintage	Identification	Mkt Val
PE1	1854	—	5 Centimes. Copper.	600
PE2	1889	—	5 Francs. Tin.	600
PE3	1889	—	10 Centimes. Silver.	500

MADEIRA ISLANDS

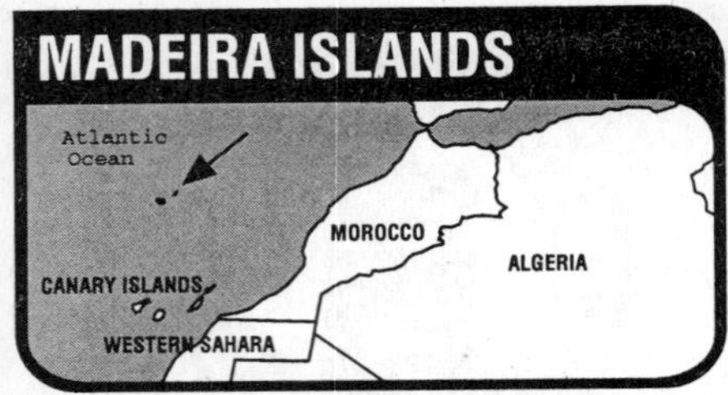

The Madeira Islands, which belong to Portugal, are located 360 miles (492 km.) off the northwest coast of Africa. They have an area of 307 sq. mi. (795 sq. km.). The group consists of two inhabited islands named Madeira and Porto Santo and two groups of uninhabited rocks named Desertas and Selvagens. Capital: Funchal. The two staple products are wine and sugar. Bananas and pineapples are also produced for export.

Although the evidence is insufficient, it is thought that the Phoenicians visited Madeira at an early period. It is also probable that the entire archipelago was explored by Genoese adventurers; an Italian map dated 1351 shows the Madeira Islands quite clearly. The Portuguese navigator Goncalvez Zarco first sighted Porto Santo in 1418, having been driven there by a storm while he was exploring the coast of West Africa. Madeira itself was discovered in 1420. The islands were uninhabited when visited by Zarco, but soon after 1418 Madeira was quickly colonized by Prince Henry the Navigator, aided by the knights of the Order of Christ. British troops occupied the islands in 1801, and again in 1807-14.

RULERS
Portuguese

PORTUGUESE COLONY

EARLY COINAGE

KM# 1 5 REIS (V Reis)
Copper **Obv:** Crowned ornate arms **Obv. Legend:** MARIA.II.D.G.PORTUG.ET.ALG.REGINA **Rev:** Value in sprays **Rev. Legend:** PECUNIA.MADEIRENSIS

Date	VG	F	VF	XF	Unc
1850	100	200	375	600	—

KM# 2 10 REIS (X Reis)
Copper **Obv:** Crowned ornate arms **Obv. Legend:** MARIA.II.D.G.PORTUG.ET.ALG.REGINA **Rev:** Value in sprays **Rev. Legend:** PECUNIA.MADEIRENSIS

Date	VG	F	VF	XF	Unc
1842	10.00	20.00	85.00	175	—
1850 Unique	—	—	—	—	—
1852	10.00	20.00	70.00	150	—

KM# 3 20 REIS (XX Reis)
Copper **Obv:** Crowned ornate arms **Obv. Legend:** MARIA.II.D.G.PORTUG.ET.ALG.REGINA **Rev:** Value in sprays **Rev. Legend:** PECUNIA.MADEIRENSIS

Date	VG	F	VF	XF	Unc
1842	20.00	40.00	100	220	—
1852 Rare	—	—	—	—	—

PATTERNS

KM#	Date	Mintage	Identification	Mkt Val
Pn1	1842	—	10 Reis. Silver. KM2.	—
Pn2	1842	—	10 Reis. Gold. KM2.	—

MALAYSIA

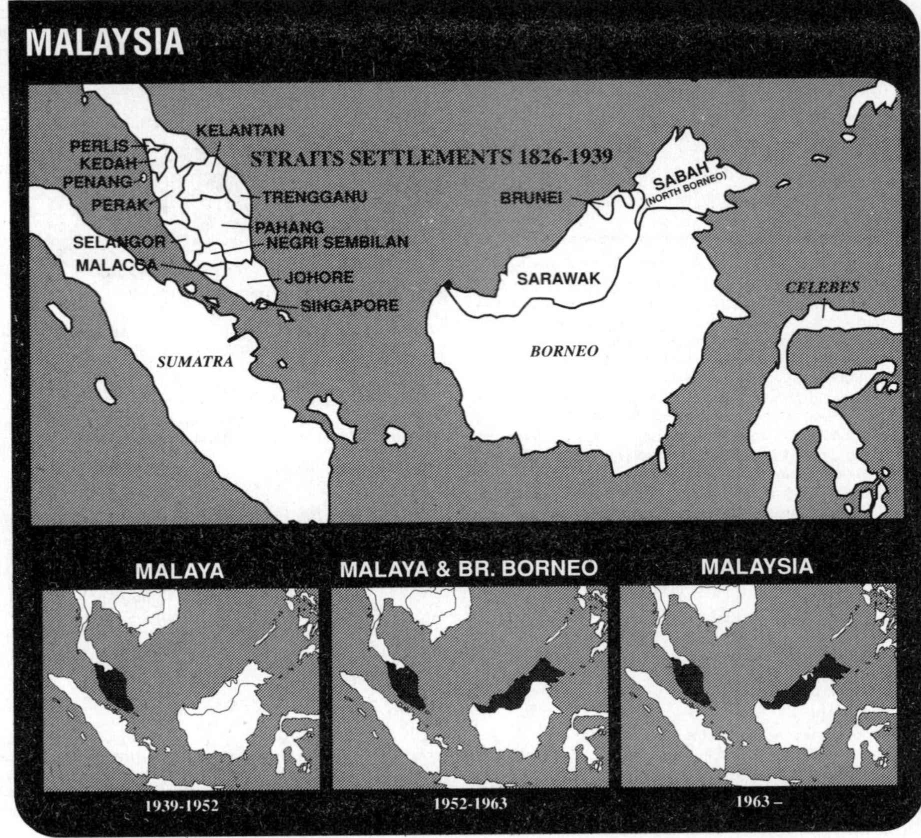

MONETARY SYSTEM
10 Pitis = 1 Keping
900-4,000 Pitis = 1 Ringgit (Dollar)
1280 Trah = 1 Ringgit
100 Pice (cents) = 1 Ringgit

DENOMINATIONS
The following Arabic legends appear for the denomination with an Arabic number above.

كفڠ	سكفڠ	سات كڤڠ
(1) Keping	Sakeping	Satkeping

دو كڤڠ

(2) Dua Keping

NOTE: Many local merchant tokens, inscribed mainly in Chinese, exist for most of the Malay states. These have not been listed.

KEDAH

A state in northwestern Malaysia. Islam introduced in 15th century. Subject to Thailand from 1821-1909. Coins issued under Governor Tengku Anum.

TITLES

كداه

Kedah

SULTANS
Ahmad Taju'd-din Halim Shah, 1798-1843
Zainal Rashid al-Muazzam Shah, 1843-54
Ahmad Taju'd-din Mukarram Shah, 1854-79
Abdul-Hamim, 1882-1909

From 1821-1843, Kedah was actually under the control of the Siamese, and was ruled by Governor Tengku Anum.

ISLAMIC STATE

HAMMERED COINAGE

KM# 13 TRA
Tin, 23 mm. **Obv:** Arabic legend **Obv. Legend:** Tahun Alif 1224 **Rev:** Arabic legend **Rev. Legend:** Balad Kedah Daru'l/Aman **Note:** Irregular center hole.

Date	Good	VG	F	VF	XF
AH1224	28.00	48.00	72.00	110	—

KM# 14 TRA
Tin, 24 mm. **Obv:** Five petaled lotus blossom **Rev:** Arabic legend **Rev. Legend:** Belanja Balad al-Perlis Kedah-Senat 1262 **Note:** Irregular center hole.

Date	Good	VG	F	VF	XF
AH1262	28.00	48.00	72.00	110	—

KM# 15 TRA
Tin, 18 mm. **Obv:** Crude 12-pointed star **Rev:** Arabic legend **Rev. Legend:** "Belanja Balad Kedah Daru'l-Aman" **Note:** Irregular center hole.

Date	Good	VG	F	VF	XF
ND	25.00	40.00	60.00	90.00	—

KELANTAN

A state in northern Malaysia, colonized by the Javanese in 1300's. It was subject to Thailand from 1780 to 1909.

TITLES

Kelantan

خليفة المؤمنين

Khalifa(t) Al-Mu'minin

كماسن

Kemasin

SULTANS
Muhammed I, 1800-1835
Muhammed II, 1835-1886
Ahmad, 1886-1889
Muhammed III, 1889-1891
Mansur, 1891-1899
Interregnum, 1899-1902

STATE

STANDARD COINAGE

KM# 1 PITIS
Tin, 24-29 mm. **Obv:** Arabic legend **Obv. Legend:** Khalifat al-Mu'minin **Rev:** Arabic legend **Note:** Many minor variations.

Date	VG	F	VF	XF	Unc
ND	6.00	12.00	25.00	45.00	—

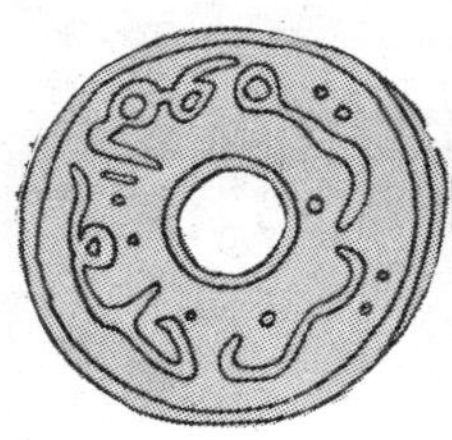
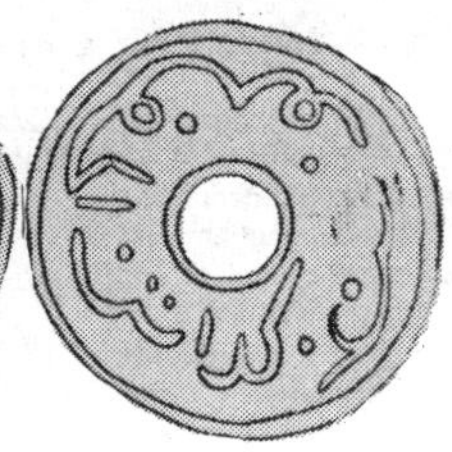

KM# 2 PITIS
Tin **Obv:** Similar to KM#1 **Rev:** Arabic legend **Rev. Legend:** Al-Julus Kelantan

Date	VG	F	VF	XF	Unc
ND	12.00	25.00	42.00	72.00	—

KM# 4 PITIS
Tin, 28 mm. **Obv:** Arabic legend **Obv. Legend:** Legend similar to KM#1 **Rev:** Sanat 1256 **Note:** This type has also been attributed to Legeh.

Date	VG	F	VF	XF	Unc
AH1256	9.00	20.00	35.00	46.00	—

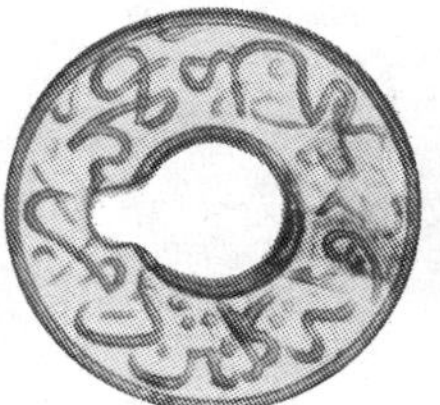

KM# 5 PITIS
Tin **Obv:** Arabic legend **Obv. Legend:** Dama Sama Mulka Daulat Kelantan **Rev:** Arabic legend **Rev. Legend:** Duriba Fi Jamadal Akhir 1300

Date	VG	F	VF	XF	Unc
AH1300	9.00	20.00	35.00	46.00	—

KM# 10 PITIS
Tin **Obv:** Arabic legend **Obv. Legend:** Adim Mulkahu Belanjaan Kera Jaan Kelantan **Rev:** Arabic legend **Rev. Legend:** Sunia Fi Jumadal Ula Sanat 1314

Date	VG	F	VF	XF	Unc
AH1314	6.00	12.00	25.00	42.00	—

Note: Legends are incuse

KEMASIN LOCAL COINAGE

KM# 30 JOKOH
Tin, 29-30 mm. **Obv:** Jawi legend **Obv. Legend:** Ini Pakai Di Kemasin Sanat 1300 **Rev:** Chinese inscription and 5 countermark; two variations

Date	VG	F	VF	XF	Unc
AH1300	25.00	50.00	85.00	160	—

MALACCA

A state of Malaysia on the west coast. It was settled from Sumatra in the 1300's, occupied by the Portuguese in 1511. Captured by the Dutch in 1641. Held by the British from 1795 to 1802 and 1811 to 1818 and finally ceded to Britain in 1824.

The attribution of the following coins to Malacca is uncertain. All were struck in England, on behalf of merchants in Singapore. All have an Arabic legend *Tanah Melayu* Land of the Malays, above a rooster.

BRITISH ADMINISTRATION

TOKEN COINAGE

KM# 8.1 KEPING
Copper **Rev:** Denomination at top written like a fraction

Date	F	VF	XF	Unc	BU
AH1247	4.00	8.00	18.00	48.00	—

KM# 8.1a KEPING
Brass

Date	F	VF	XF	Unc	BU
AH1247	—	—	—	—	—

KM# 8.2 KEPING
Copper **Rev:** Denomination written simply 1

Date	F	VF	XF	Unc	BU
AH1247	3.00	6.00	14.00	50.00	—
AH1251	—	—	—	—	—
Note: Reported, not confirmed					
AH1147 Error	40.00	70.00	100	150	—
AH1219 Error	6.00	10.00	25.00	70.00	—
AH1241 Error	40.00	70.00	100	150	—
AH1411 Error	6.00	10.00	25.00	70.00	—

KM# 14 2 KEPING
Copper

Date	F	VF	XF	Unc	BU
AH1247	25.00	50.00	60.00	95.00	—

PAHANG

A state on the east coast of Malaysia. Subject to the Suvyaya kingdom in Sumatra in the 1200's. Shuttled from native kingdom to native kingdom after 1450. Became one of the Federated Malay States in 1895.

The following coins were minted by prominent Chinese Pahang by permission of Sultan Ahmed. They were intended for general circulation within Pahang. Many other pieces issued by merchants and gambling houses exist, but will not be listed here.

TITLES

Pahang

GOVERNORS
Bendahara Sewa Raja Tun Ali, 1806-1857
Bendahara Sewa Raja Tun Mutahir, 1857-1863
Bendahara Sewa Raja Ahmad 1863-1884

SULTANS
Ahmed Al Muazzam, 1884-1914
(Who ruled as Governor Bendahara Sewa Raja Ahmad from 1863 to 1884.)

STATE

STANDARD COINAGE

KM# 6 1/2 CENT
Tin **Obv:** 4 Chinese characters Ch'ien Sheng T'ung Pao **Rev:** Value and Arabic legend **Rev. Legend:** Pahang Company and 1/2 C **Note:** Minted between 1884 and 1896.

Date	Good	VG	F	VF	XF
ND	30.00	48.00	72.00	110	—

KM# 9 CENT
Tin **Rev:** 1 C **Note:** Minted between 1884 and 1896.

Date	Good	VG	F	VF	XF
ND	30.00	48.00	72.00	110	—

KM# 11 CENT
Tin **Obv:** Value and Chinese Ch'ien Sheng T'ung Pao **Rev:** Date and Arabic legend

Date	Good	VG	F	VF	XF
AH1301	25.00	42.00	65.00	95.00	—

PENANG

Pulu Penang-Prince of Wales Island

An island off the west coast of Malaysia. Ceded to the British in 1791 by the sultan of Kedah and was the first British settlement in Malaya. Also known as Pulu Penang and Prince of Wales Island - which title it retained until1867.

The currency system depended on the Spanish dollar divided into 100 pice (or cents) until 1826 when 48 pice were deemed the equivalent of one Bengal rupee until1830. The coins are considered in three groups:

(a) The Company bale mark series, consisting of copper1/10, 1/2 and 1 pice of 1786/1787, and silver tenth, quarter and half dollars, dated 1788;

(b) Company coat of arms issues in copper between1810 and 1828 in denominations of 1/2, 1 and double pice pieces; and

(c) Tin issues of local mintage pice pieces of 1800-1809,which are extremely rare.

TITLES

Pulu Penang
Acquired by the British East India Company in 1786.

MONETARY SYSTEM
100 Cents (Pice) = 1 Dollar

BRITISH ADMINISTRATION

STANDARD COINAGE

KM# 12 1/2 CENT (1/2 Pice)
Copper

Date	Mintage	F	VF	XF	Unc	BU
1810	1	20.00	40.00	72.00	150	—
1810 Proof	—	Value: 460				

KM# 13 1/2 CENT (1/2 Pice)
Copper

Date	Mintage	F	VF	XF	Unc	BU
1825	145,000	65.00	110	170	320	—
1828	414,000	65.00	110	170	320	—

Note: Wreath varies from 21 to 26 lily cups

KM# 8 CENT (Pice)
40.3500 g., Tin **Note:** Uniface; initial 'GL' (Governor Leith) in ring; countermark of Chinese character for Yuan.

Date	Good	VG	F	VF	XF
ND(ca.1800-1803)	—	1,450	3,350	5,000	6,750

KM# 9 CENT (Pice)
Tin, 30.50 mm. **Note:** Initials GF (Governor Farguhar) in ring, countmark Chinese character Ch'i.

Date	VG	F	VF	XF	Unc
ND(c.1805)	700	1,350	2,600	3,800	—

KM# 10 CENT (Pice)
Tin, 30.00-32.00 mm. **Note:** Native initials A & C (Anderson and Clubley), countmark Chinese character Mei.

Date	VG	F	VF	XF	Unc
1809	1,000	1,750	3,200	5,000	—

KM# 11 CENT (Pice)
Tin **Note:** English initials A & C (Anderson and Clubley), countmark Chinese character Mei.

Date	VG	F	VF	XF	Unc
1809	1,000	1,750	3,200	5,000	—

KM# 14 CENT (Pice)
Copper **Rev:** Leaves on wreath go clockwise

Date	Mintage	F	VF	XF	Unc	BU
1810	1,827,000	16.00	32.00	75.00	115	—
Note: small date, small shield						
1810 Proof	—	Value: 400				

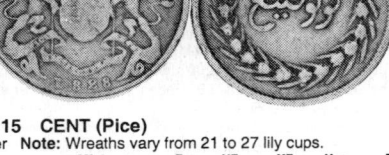

KM# 15 CENT (Pice)
Copper **Note:** Wreaths vary from 21 to 27 lily cups.

Date	Mintage	F	VF	XF	Unc	BU
1825	137,000	40.00	80.00	150	280	—
1828	236,000	40.00	80.00	150	280	—

KM# 16 2 CENTS (2 Pice)
Copper **Note:** Wreaths vary from 24 to 28 lily cups.

Date	Mintage	F	VF	XF	Unc	BU
1825	130,000	40.00	90.00	160	280	—
1825 Proof	—	Value: 430				
1828	720,000	20.00	50.00	145	225	—

PATTERNS

KM#	Date	Mintage	Identification	Mkt Val
Pn1	1810	—	Cent. Copper. Leaves on wreath counterclockwise.	800
Pn2	1810	—	Cent. Copper. Leaves on wreath clockwise.	925

PERAK

A state on the west coast of Malaysia. Important tin deposits are in this state. Part of Malay kingdoms from early times. Perak was an independent state from 1824-1874. The only coin is one made in Birmingham, England and distributed by a Singapore importer.

TITLES

Negri Peraq

SULTANS
Ahmadin, 1706-1806
Abdul-Malik Mansur, 1806-1825
Abdullah Muazzam, 1825-1830
Shahabud-Din Riayat, 1831-1851
Abdullah Muhammad, 1851-1857
Jafar Muazzam, 1857-1865
Ali Al-Mukammal Inayat, 1865-1871
Ismail Muabidin, 1871-1874
Abdullah Muhammad, 1874-1877
Yusuf Sharifud-Din Mufzal, 1877-1887
Sir Idris Murshid Al-Azzam, 1887-1916

STATE

TOKEN COINAGE

KM# 4 KEPING
Copper **Ruler:** Shahabud-Din Riayat **Obv:** Arabic lgend **Obv. Legend:** Negri Perak (State of Perak) **Rev:** Arabic legend **Rev. Legend:** Satu Kepang 1251 (one Keping AH 1251)

Date	F	VF	XF	Unc	BU
AH1251	12.00	25.00	40.00	70.00	—
AH1251 Proof	—	Value: 120			

Note: See Indonesia for similar tokens with differing legends

PATTERNS

Including off metal strikes

KM#	Date	Mintage	Identification	Mkt Val
Pn1	AH1251	—	Keping. Tin. KM#4.	—
Pn2	AH1251	—	Keping. Silver Or Silvered. KM#4.	—

SELANGOR

A state on the west coast of Malaysia. Played a part in the trading programs of both the Dutch and the British. Signed a treaty with Britain in 1818 and Britain took control of the state in 1874.

TITLES

نكري سلاغور

Negri Selangor

SULTANS

Ibrahim, 1777-1826
Muhammad, 1826-1857
Abdul-Samad, 1857-1898
Sulaiman, 1898-1938

STATE

TOKEN COINAGE

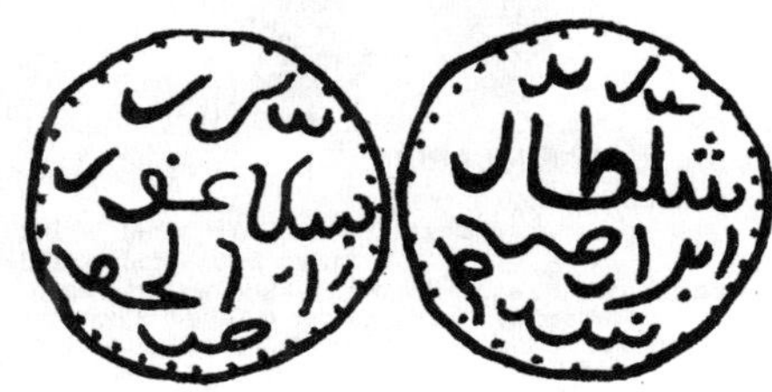

KM# 1 PITIS
Tin **Obv. Legend:** Arabic Negri Selangor Darul Ihsan **Rev. Legend:** Arabic Baginda Sultan Ibrahim Shah

Date	F	VF	XF	Unc	BU
ND	—	—	—	—	—

KM# 3 KEPING
Copper **Ruler:** Muhammad **Obv:** Arabic legend **Obv. Legend:** Negri Selangor **Rev:** Arabic legend **Rev. Legend:** Satu Keping 1251

Date	F	VF	XF	Unc	BU
AH1251	12.00	22.00	38.00	70.00	—

Note: See Indonesia for similar tokens with differing legends

TRENGGANU

A state in eastern Malaysia on the shore of the south China Sea. Area of dispute between Malacca and Thailand with the latter emerging with possession. Trengganu became a British dependency in 1909.

TITLES

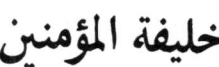

خليفة المؤمنين

Khalifa(t) al-Mu'minin

ترغكانو

Trengganu

SULTANS

Zainal Abidin II, 1793-1808
Ahmad I, 1808-1827
Abdul Rahman, 1827-1831
Daud, 1831
Mansur II, 1831-1836
Muhammed, 1836-1839
Baginda Omar, 1839-1876
Ahmad II, 1876-1881
Zainal Abidin III, 1881-1918

STATE

STANDARD COINAGE

KM# 9 PITIS
Ruler: Zainal Abidin II

Date	VG	F	VF	XF	Unc
AH1222	25.00	38.00	60.00	95.00	—

KM# 10 PITIS
Ruler: Zainal Abidin II **Note:** Legend points outward instead of inward.

Date	VG	F	VF	XF	Unc
AH1222	25.00	45.00	70.00	110	—

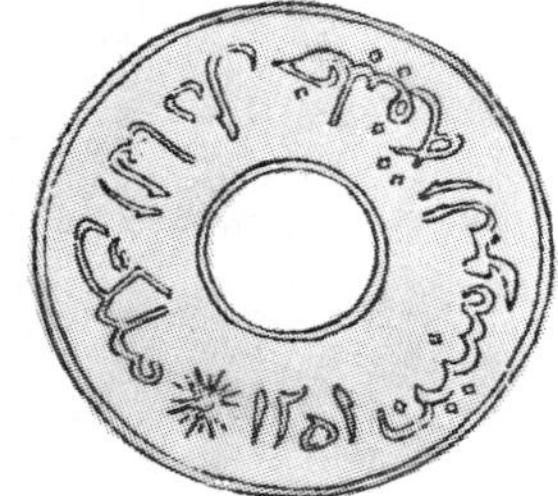

KM# 11 PITIS
Ruler: Mansur II **Note:** Khalifat al-Muminin 1251 Malik al-Adil.

Date	VG	F	VF	XF	Unc
AH1251	40.00	75.00	110	180	—

KM# 13 PITIS
Ruler: Baginda Omar

Date	VG	F	VF	XF	Unc
AH1265	32.00	55.00	90.00	150	—

KM# 14 PITIS
Ruler: Zainal Abidin III **Note:** Belanja Trengganu Sanat 1299.

Date	VG	F	VF	XF	Unc
AH1299	30.00	60.00	90.00	150	—

KM# 12 KEPING
Copper **Ruler:** Mansur II **Obv:** Arabic legend **Obv. Legend:** Negri Trengganu (State of Trengganu) **Rev:** Arabic legend **Rev. Legend:** Satu Keping 1251

Date	VG	F	VF	XF	Unc
AH1251	8.00	15.00	35.00	70.00	—
AH1251 Proof	—	Value: 220			

KM# 15 10 KEPINGS
Tin **Ruler:** Zainal Abidin III

Date	VG	F	VF	XF	Unc
AH1310	15.00	35.00	45.00	85.00	—

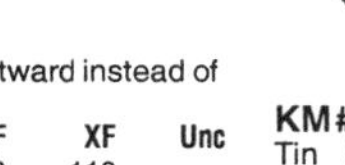

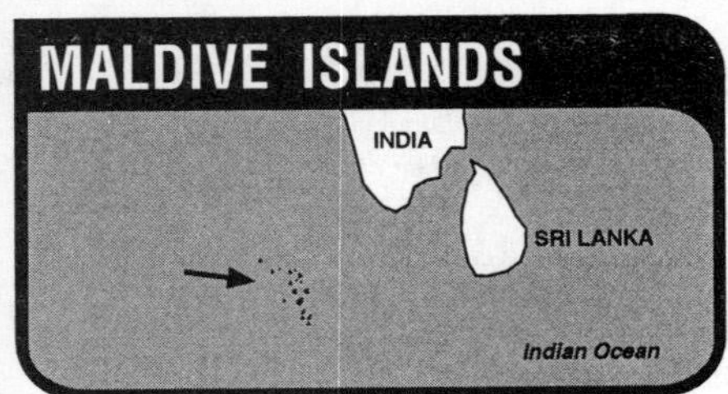

The Maldives are an archipelago of 2,000 coral islets in the northern Indian Ocean 417 miles (671 km.) west of Ceylon.

The Maldive Islands were visited by Arab traders and converted to Islam in 1153. After being harassed in the16th and 17th centuries by Mopla pirates of the Malabar coast and Portuguese raiders, the Maldivians voluntarily placed themselves under the suzeraínty of Ceylon. In 1887 the islands became an internally self-governing British protectorate and a nominal dependency of Ceylon. Traditionally a sultanate, the Maldives became a republic in 1953 but restored the sultanate in 1954. The Sultanate of the Maldive Islands attained complete internal and external autonomy on July 26, 1965, and on Nov. 11,1968, again became a republic.

RULERS

Muhammad Mu'in al-Din, AH1213-1250/1798-1835AD
Muhammad Imad al-Din IV, AH1250-1300/1835-1882AD
Ibrahim Nur al-Din, AH1300-1318/1882-1900AD
Muhammad Imad al-Din V, AH1318-1322/1900-1904AD

MINT NAME

Mahle (Male)

MONETARY SYSTEM

100 Lari = 1 Rupee (Rufiyaa)

NOTE: The metrology of the early coinage is problematical. There seem to have been three denominations: a double Larin of 8-10 g, a Larin of approximately 4.8 g, and a half Larin that varied from 1.1 to 2.4 g, known as the Bodu Larin, Larin and Kuda Larin, respectively. In some years probably when copper was cheap (AH1276 & 1294),the Kuda (1/2) Larin is found with weights as high as 3.5 g. During the rule of Muhammad Imad Al-Din II Al-Muzaffar Bin Muhammad (1704-1721AD) additional denominations in the form of the 1/4, 1/8 and 1/16 Larin (1.17 g, 0.55 g and 0.29 g) were introduced on an experimental basis. This experiment was not followed by later rulers with the exception of Muhammad Imad Al-Din IV (1835-1882AD) who struck some light weight coins of about 1.1 g which can be considered 1/4 Larins.

SULTANATE

Muhammad Mu'in al-Din Iskandar

AH 1213-50 / 1798-1835 AD

STANDARD COINAGE

100 Lari = 1 Rupee (Rufiyaa)

KM# 32 1/2 LARIN (Kuda)

Copper, Bronze Or Brass, 1.40-2.40 mm. **Note:** Weight and size varies: 1.40-2.40 grams; 9-11 mm.

Date	Mintage	Good	VG	F	VF	XF
AH1216	—	3.00	5.00	7.50	10.00	—
AH1219	—	3.00	5.00	7.50	10.00	—
AH1220	—	5.00	7.50	12.00	18.00	—
AH1221	—	3.00	5.00	7.50	10.00	—
AH1230	—	5.00	7.50	12.00	18.00	—
AH1238	—	3.50	6.00	9.00	12.50	—
AH1239	—	4.00	6.50	10.00	15.00	—
AH1248	—	3.00	5.00	7.50	9.00	—

Note: Varieties exist. Some specimens are also struck on lightweight (1.4-1.9g) planchets, som also being square in shape (1219, 1221 and 1248). The year on the reverse occurs in 2nd, 3rd and 4th line

Muhammad Imad al-Din IV

AH 1250-1300 / 1835-1882 AD

STANDARD COINAGE

100 Lari = 1 Rupee (Rufiyaa)

KM# 34.1 1/4 LARIN

Bronze Or Brass, 8-9 mm. **Note:** 0.70-1.20 grams.

Date	Mintage	Good	VG	F	VF	XF
AH1251	—	—	—	—	—	—
AH1286	—	5.00	7.50	12.00	17.50	—
AH1292	—	5.00	7.50	12.00	17.50	—
AH1294	—	5.00	7.50	12.00	17.50	—
AH1298	—	4.00	6.50	10.00	15.00	—

Note: These lightweight coins are believed tohave been intended as 1/4 Larins since the dies with which they were struck are smaller than those for the kuda (1/2) larin. The issues dated AH1251 and 1298 are square or round. Varieties exist. Some authorities consider all 1/4 Larins as 1/2 Larins

KM# 35.1 1/2 LARIN (Kuda)

Bronze, 9-13 mm. **Note:** 1.20-2.80 grams.

Date	Mintage	Good	VG	F	VF	XF
AH1257	—	2.50	3.50	6.00	9.00	—
AH1258	—	2.50	3.50	6.00	9.00	—
AH1276	—	2.50	3.50	6.00	9.00	—
AH1280	—	2.50	3.50	6.00	9.00	—
AH1286	—	2.50	3.00	5.00	8.00	—
AH1292	—	2.50	3.50	6.00	9.00	—
AH1294	—	3.00	5.00	7.50	10.00	—
AH1298	—	0.50	1.25	2.50	4.50	—

Note: Varieties exist. Date year second and third lines on reverse

KM# 35.4 1/2 LARIN (Kuda)

Bronze **Obv:** Within circular, saw-toothed borders **Rev:** Within circular, saw-toothed borders **Note:** Square planchet. The 1/2 Larin, KM#35.1, 35.2 and 35.3 are struck on planchets cut from bronze sheets.

Date	Mintage	Good	VG	F	VF	XF
AH1276 Rare	—	—	—	—	—	—

KM# 35.2 1/2 LARIN (Kuda)

Bronze **Rev:** Year in top line

Date	Mintage	Good	VG	F	VF	XF
AH1286	—	4.00	6.50	10.00	15.00	—

KM# 35.3 1/2 LARIN (Kuda)

Bronze **Obv:** Legend within border of small circles **Rev:** Legend within quadrifoil

Date	Mintage	Good	VG	F	VF	XF
AH1286 Rare	—	—	—	—	—	—

KM# A36 LARIN

Bronze, 14.4 mm. **Note:** 3.55 grams.

Date	Mintage	Good	VG	F	VF	XF
AH1294 Rare	—	—	—	—	—	—
AH1296 Rare	—	—	—	—	—	—

Note: Although this Larin is lightweight, it is of Larin size and its planchet was produced with a mold like the planchets of almost all other Larins and 1/2 Larins of earlier rulers

KM# 36.1 2 LARI (Bodu)

Bronze **Rev:** Year in third line **Note:** Varieties exist. 8.60 grams.

Date	Mintage	Good	VG	F	VF	XF
AH1294	—	5.00	8.50	12.50	18.50	—
AH1298	—	5.00	8.50	12.50	18.50	—

KM# 36.2 2 LARI (Bodu)

Bronze 8.60 oz. **Rev:** Year in second line **Note:** Varieties exist.

Date	Mintage	Good	VG	F	VF	XF
AH1298	—	7.50	12.50	20.00	30.00	—

Ibrahim Nur al-Din

AH 1300-18 / 1882-1900 AD

STANDARD COINAGE

100 Lari = 1 Rupee (Rufiyaa)

KM# 37 1/4 LARIN/LARIN

Bronze **Note:** 0.70-1.40 grams.

Date	Mintage	F	VF	XF	Unc
AH1300	—	2.00	3.00	4.50	6.00

Note: Toward the end of this reign the standard was reportedly revised by a factory of four, making this denomination officially one larin. The year occurs on second and third lines on the reverse

Muhammad Imad al-Din V

AH 1318-22 / 1900-04 AD

STANDARD COINAGE

100 Lari = 1 Rupee (Rufiyaa)

KM# 38 LARIN

Copper Or Brass **Note:** 0.80-1.10 grams.

Date	Mintage	F	VF	XF	Unc
AH1318	—	1.00	1.50	2.00	4.00

Note: Die varieties exist

KM# 39 2 LARIAT

Copper-Brass, 13 mm. **Note:** 1.4-2.2 grams. Previously listed date AH1311 is merely poor die cutting of AH1319. Many die varieties exist.

Date	Mintage	F	VF	XF	Unc
AH1318 (1900)	—	1.50	3.50	5.00	7.50
AH1319 (1901)	—	1.50	3.50	5.00	7.50

MARTINIQUE

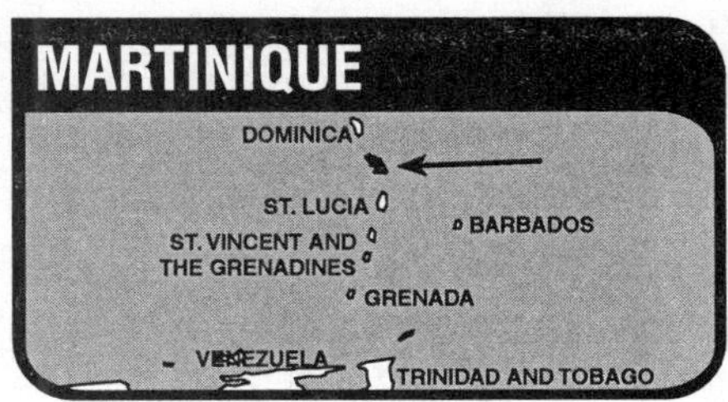

The French Overseas Department of Martinique, located in the Lesser Antilles off the West Indies between Dominica and Saint Lucia, has an area of 425 sq. mi.(1,100 sq. km.).

Christopher Columbus discovered Martinique, probably on June 15, 1502. France took possession on June 25, 1635, and has maintained possession since that time except for three short periods of British occupation during the Napoleonic Wars. A French department since 1946, Martinique voted a reaffirmation of that status in 1958, remaining within the new French Community. Martinique was the birthplace of Napoleon's Empress Josephine, and the site of the eruption of Mt. Pelee in 1902 that claimed 40,000 lives.

RULERS

British, 1793-1801

FRENCH COLONY

COUNTERMARKED COINAGE

1802-1809

6400 Reis = 22 Livres

KM# 31 20 LIVRES

Gold **Countermark:** 20 above eagle **Note:** Countermark on false Brazil 6400 Reis, type of KM#199.

CM Date	Host Date	Good	VG	F	VF	XF
ND(c. 1802)	ND(1777-86)	—	750	1,150	1,650	3,000

KM# 32 20 LIVRES

Gold **Countermark:** 20 above eagle **Note:** Countermark on false or lightweight Brazil 6400 Reis, KM#172.2.

CM Date	Host Date	Good	VG	F	VF	XF
ND(c. 1802)	ND(1751-77)	—	1,000	1,500	2,000	3,500
ND(c. 1802)	ND(1778-79)	—	700	1,000	1,500	2,800

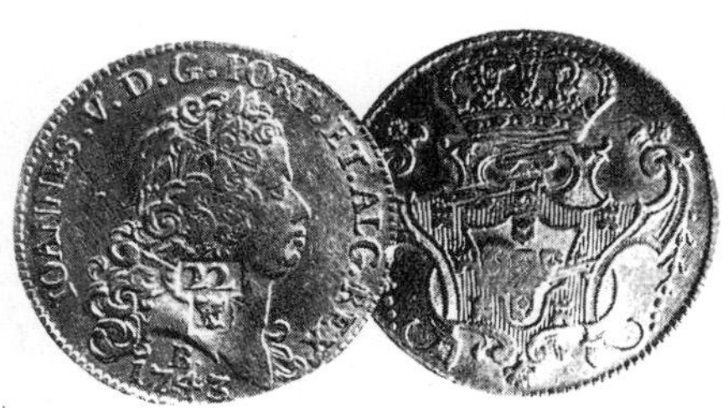

KM# 39 22 LIVRES

Gold **Countermark:** 22 above eagle **Note:** Countermark on Brazil 6400 Reis, KM#151.

CM Date	Host Date	Good	VG	F	VF	XF
ND(c. 1802)	ND(1735-50)	—	2,000	3,500	4,500	7,500

KM# 33 22 LIVRES

Gold **Countermark:** 22 above eagle **Note:** Countermark on Brazil 6400 Reis, KM#199.1.

CM Date	Host Date	Good	VG	F	VF	XF
ND(c. 1802)	ND(1777-86)	—	1,000	1,500	1,800	3,000

KM# 34 22 LIVRES

Gold **Countermark:** 22 above eagle **Note:** Countermark on Brazil 6400 Reis, KM#218.2.

CM Date	Host Date	Good	VG	F	VF	XF
ND(c. 1802)	ND(1786-90)	—	1,000	1,500	1,800	3,000

KM# 35 22 LIVRES

Gold **Countermark:** 22 above eagle **Note:** Countermark on Brazil 6400 Reis, KM#226.1.

CM Date	Host Date	Good	VG	F	VF	XF
ND(c. 1802)	ND(1789-1805)	—	950	1,400	1,700	2,850

KM# 37 22 LIVRES

Gold **Countermark:** 22 above eagle **Note:** Countermark on false Brazil 6400 Reis, type of KM#172.1.

CM Date	Host Date	Good	VG	F	VF	XF
ND(c. 1802)	ND(1751-77)	—	1,500	2,500	3,000	5,000

KM# 36 22 LIVRES

Gold **Countermark:** 22 above eagle **Note:** Countermark on Portugal 4 Escudos, KM#240.

CM Date	Host Date	Good	VG	F	VF	XF
ND(c. 1802)	ND(1750-76)	—	1,250	2,000	2,450	4,000

KM# 38 22 LIVRES

Gold **Countermark:** 22 above eagle **Note:** Countermark on Portuguese 4000 Reis, KM#184.

CM Date	Host Date	Good	VG	F	VF	XF
ND(c. 1802)	ND(1707-22)	—	2,500	4,000	5,500	8,500

DECIMAL COINAGE

KM# 40 50 CENTIMES

Copper-Nickel

Date	Mintage	VG	F	VF	XF	Unc
1897	600,000	15.00	25.00	50.00	135	320

KM# 41 FRANC

Copper-Nickel

Date	Mintage	VG	F	VF	XF	Unc
1897	300,000	18.00	30.00	60.00	160	350

ESSAIS

Standard thickness

KM#	Date	Mintage	Identification	Issue Price	Mkt Val
E1	1897	—	50 Centimes. KM#40.	—	200
E2	1897	—	Franc. KM#41	—	275
E3	1(897)	—	50 Centimes. KM#40	—	250
E4	1(897)	—	Franc. KM#41	—	325

PIEFORTS WITH ESSAIS

Double thickness, standard metals unless otherwise noted

KM#	Date	Mintage	Identification	Issue Price	Mkt Val
PE1	1897	—	50 Centimes.	—	450
PE2	1897	—	Franc.	—	550

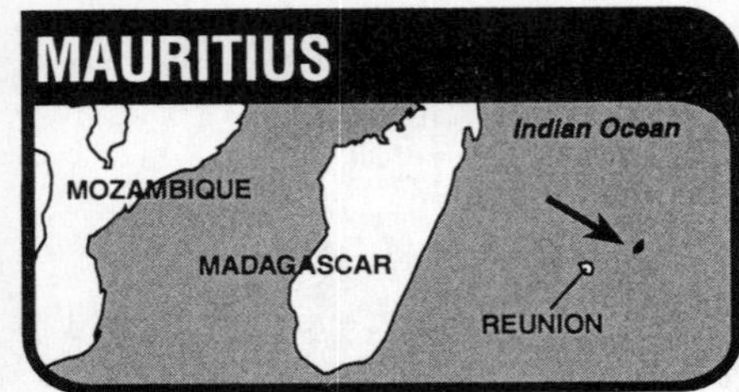

The Republic of Mauritius, is located in the Indian Ocean 500 miles (805 km.) east of Madagascar, has an area of 790 sq. mi. (1,860 sq. km.) and a population of 1 million. Capital: Port Louis. Sugar provides 90 percent of the export revenue.

Cartographic evidence indicates that Arabs and Malays arrived at Mauritius during the Middle Ages. Domingo Fernandez, a Portuguese navigator, visited the island in the early 16th century, but Portugal made no attempt at settlement. The Dutch took possession, and named the island, in 1598. Their colony failed to prosper and was abandoned in 1710. France claimed Mauritius in 1715 and developed a strong and prosperous colony that endured until the island was captured by the British, 1810, during the Napoleonic Wars. British possession was confirmed by the 1814 Treaty of Paris. Mauritius became independent on March 12, 1968. It is a member of the Commonwealth of Nations.

The first coins struck under British auspices for Mauritius were undated (1822) and bore French legends.

RULERS
British, until 1968

MINT MARKS
H - Heaton, Birmingham
SA - Pretoria Mint

MONETARY SYSTEM
100 Cents = 1 Rupee

REPUBLIC

FRENCH COINAGE

20 Sols (Sous) = 1 Livre; 100 Cents = 1 Rupee

KM# 1 25 SOUS
0.5000 Silver

Date	Mintage	VG	F	VF	XF	Unc
ND(1822)	311,000	15.00	30.00	50.00	150	—
ND(1822) Proof	—	Value: 550				

KM# 2 50 SOUS
0.5000 Silver

Date	Mintage	VG	F	VF	XF	Unc
ND(1822)	286,000	20.00	40.00	75.00	200	—
ND(1822) Proof	—	Value: 700				

STANDARD COINAGE

100 Cents = 1 Rupee

KM# 7 CENT
Bronze

Date	Mintage	F	VF	XF	Unc	BU
1877 Proof	—	Value: 175				
1877H	700,000	2.00	4.00	22.50	65.00	—
1877H Proof	—	Value: 125				
1878	250,000	3.00	13.00	50.00	135	—
1878 Proof	—	Value: 350				
1882H	300,000	1.50	5.00	30.00	80.00	—
1882H Proof	—	Value: 150				
1883	500,000	1.25	2.50	18.50	50.00	—
1883 Proof	—	Value: 175				
1884	500,000	1.25	2.50	18.50	45.00	—
1884 Proof	—	Value: 175				
1888	500,000	1.25	2.50	18.50	50.00	—
1890H	500,000	1.25	2.50	18.50	50.00	—
1896	500,000	1.25	2.50	18.50	50.00	—
1896	500,000	1.25	2.50	18.50	50.00	—
1897	1,000,000	1.00	2.00	12.50	40.00	—
1897 Proof	—	Value: 175				

KM# 8 2 CENTS
Bronze

Date	Mintage	F	VF	XF	Unc	BU
1877 Proof	—	Value: 150				
1877H	350,000	1.00	6.50	27.50	100	250
1877H Proof	—	Value: 300				
1878	130,000	2.50	12.00	65.00	150	300
1878 Proof	—	Value: 150				
1882H	150,000	2.00	8.00	30.00	125	250
1882H Proof	—	Value: 275				
1883	250,000	1.00	6.50	27.50	75.00	—
1884	250,000	1.00	6.50	27.50	75.00	225
1884 Proof	—	Value: 550				
1888	250,000	0.75	4.00	20.00	60.00	180
1888 Proof	—	Value: 400				
1890H	250,000	1.00	5.00	25.00	75.00	—
1896	188,000	1.00	5.00	25.00	85.00	—
1896	188,000	1.00	5.00	25.00	85.00	—
1897	1,000,000	0.75	4.00	20.00	50.00	—
1897 Proof	—	Value: 375				

KM# 9 5 CENTS
Bronze

Date	Mintage	F	VF	XF	Unc	BU
1877 Proof	—	Value: 375				
1877H	3,000,000	3.00	10.00	55.00	165	400
1877H Proof	—	Value: 900				
1878	50,000	6.00	20.00	90.00	275	500
1878 Proof	—	Value: 200				
1882H	60,000	5.00	15.00	65.00	245	400
1882 Proof	—	Value: 375				
1883	100,000	3.00	12.00	55.00	135	—
1884	100,000	3.00	12.00	55.00	135	200
1884 Proof	—	Value: 250				
1888	100,000	1.50	7.50	40.00	90.00	—
1890H	100,000	2.50	12.00	60.00	185	—
1897	600,000	1.50	7.50	45.00	110	—
1897 Proof	—	Value: 185				

KM# 10.1 10 CENTS
1.1660 g., 0.8000 Silver .0300 oz.

Date	Mintage	F	VF	XF	Unc	BU
1877 Proof	—	Value: 400				
1877H	250,000	1.50	6.50	27.50	100	200
1877H Proof	—	Value: 300				
1878	50,000	5.00	18.00	50.00	220	400
1878 Proof	—	Value: 275				
1882H	30,000	15.00	35.00	150	250	—
1883	100,000	3.00	10.00	40.00	200	375
1883 Proof	—	Value: 275				
1886	750,000	1.25	5.00	22.00	80.00	200
1886 Proof	—	Value: 275				
1889H	500,000	2.00	7.50	25.00	90.00	200
1889 Proof	—	Value: 275				
1897	500,000	2.00	7.50	25.00	80.00	250
1897 Proof	—	Value: 400				

KM# 10.2 10 CENTS
1.1660 g., 0.8000 Silver .0300 oz. **Edge:** Plain

Date		F	VF	XF	Unc	BU
1877H Proof	—	Value: 225				

KM# 11.1 20 CENTS
2.3320 g., 0.8000 Silver .0600 oz.

Date	Mintage	F	VF	XF	Unc	BU
1877 Proof	—	Value: 750				
1877H	375,000	5.00	20.00	75.00	300	500
1877H Proof	—	Value: 400				
1878	50,000	10.00	30.00	150	400	600
1878 Proof	—	Value: 300				
1882H	15,000	15.00	50.00	225	475	—
1883	100,000	6.00	22.50	100	275	400
1883 Proof	—	Value: 300				
1886	750,000	4.00	16.00	40.00	150	300
1886 Proof	—	Value: 300				
1889H	250,000	5.00	20.00	60.00	200	—
1899	500,000	4.00	16.00	55.00	185	325
1899 Proof	—	Value: 300				

KM# 11.2 20 CENTS
2.3320 g., 0.8000 Silver .0600 oz. **Edge:** Plain

Date		F	VF	XF	Unc	BU
1877H Proof	—	Value: 750				

PIEFORTS

KM#	Date	Mintage	Identification	Issue Price	Mkt Val
P1	ND(1822)	—	25 Sous. Copper. KM1.	—	375

MEXICO

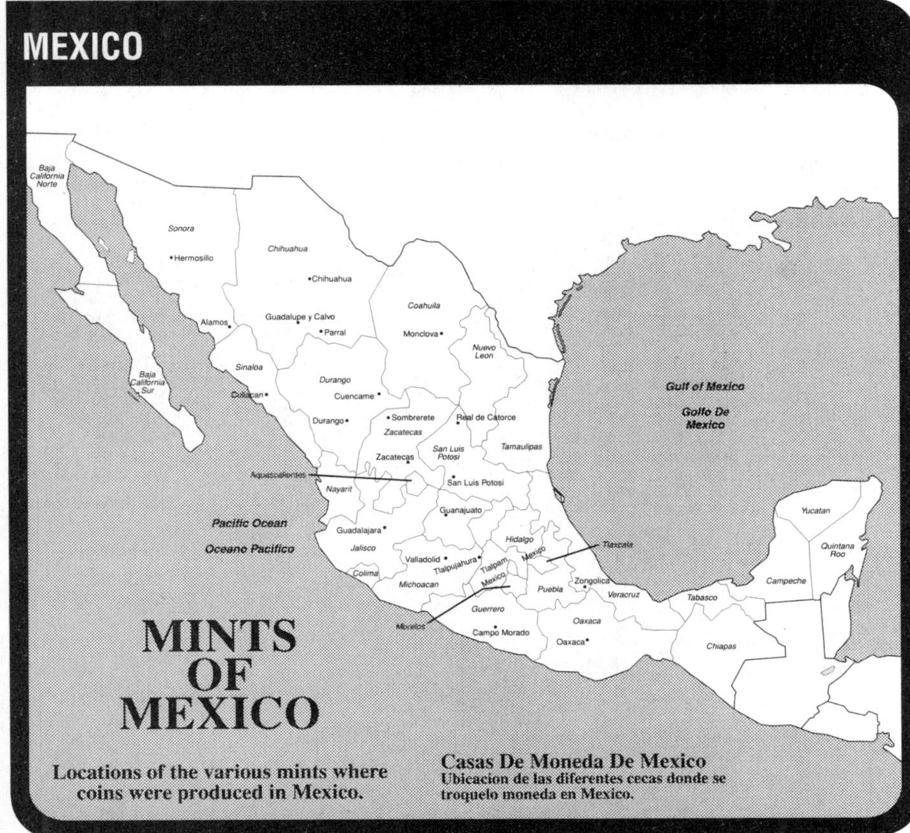

The United States of Mexico, located immediately south of the United States has an area of 759,529 sq. mi. (1,967,183 sq. km.) and an estimated population of 88 million. Capital: Mexico City. The economy is based on agriculture, manufacturing and mining. Oil, cotton, silver, coffee, and shrimp are exported.

Mexico was the site of highly advanced Indian civilizations 1,500 years before conquistador Hernando Cortes conquered the wealthy Aztec empire of Montezuma,1519-21, and founded a Spanish colony which lasted for nearly 300 years. During the Spanish period, Mexico, then called New Spain, stretched from Guatemala to the present states of Wyoming and California, its present northern boundary having been established by the secession of Texas during 1836 and the war of 1846-48 with the United States.

Independence from Spain was declared by Father Miguel Hidalgo on Sept. 16, 1810, (Mexican Independence Day) and was achieved by General Agustin de Iturbide in1821. Iturbide became emperor in 1822 but was deposed when a republic was established a year later. For more than fifty years following the birth of the republic, the political scene of Mexico was characterized by turmoil which saw two emperors (including the unfortunate Maximilian), several dictators and an average of one new government every nine months passing swiftly from obscurity to oblivion. The land, social, economic and labor reforms promulgated by the Reform Constitution of Feb. 5, 1917 established the basis for sustained economic development and participative democracy that have made Mexico one of the most politically stable countries of modern Latin America.

RULERS

Charles and Johanna, 1516-1556
Philip II, 1556-1598
Philip III, 1598-1621
Philip IV, 1621-1665
Charles II, 1665-1700
Philip V, 1700-1724, 1724-1746
Luis I, 1724
Ferdinand VI, 1746-1759
Charles III, 1760-1788
Charles IV, 1788-1808
Ferdinand VII, 1808-1821

MINT MARKS

A, AS – Alamos
CE – Real de Catorce
C, CH, CL – Chihuahua
C, Cn, Gn (error) – Culiacan
D, Do – Durango
EoMo – Estado de Mexico
Ga – Guadalajara
GC – Guadalupe y Calvo
Go, G – Guanajuato
Ho, H – Hermosillo
M, Mo, oMo, MXo – Mexico City
OA, O – Oaxaca
SLP, PI, P, I/P – San Luis Potosi
Z, Zs – Zacatecas

ASSAYER'S' INITIALS

A	?	?
F	1538-40	Estaban Franco
G	1538-40	Juan Gutierrez
L		Luis Rodriguez
O	?	?
P	1541-42	Pedro de Espina
R	1536-38	Francisco del Rincon
S	?	Gomez de Santillan
A	1600-09	?
F	1603-16	?
Ne	1611	?
D	1614-32	?
P	1635-65	?
G	1667-76	Geronimo Becerra
L	1678-1703	Martin Lopez
J	1708-23	Jose E. de Leon
D	1724-27	?
R	1729-30	Nicolas de Roxas
G	1730	?
F	1730-33	Felipe Rivas de Angulo
F	1733-84	Francisco de la Pena
M	1733-63	Manuel de la Pena
F	1733-84	Francisco de la Pena
M	1754-1770	Manuel Assorin
F	1762-70	Francisco de Rivera
M	1770-77	Manuel de Rivera
F	1777-1803	Francisco Arance Cobos
M	1784-1801	Mariano Rodriguez
T	1801-10	Tomas Butron Miranda
H	1803-1814	Henrique Buenaventura Azorin
J	1809-33	Joaquin Davila Madrid
J	1812-33	Jose Garcia Ansaldo

COLONIAL

The United States of Mexico, located immediately south of the United States has an area of 759,529 sq. mi. (1,967,183 sq. km.).

Mexico was the site of highly advanced Indian civilizations 1,500 years before conquistador Hernando Cortes conquered the wealthy Aztec empire of Montezuma,1519-21, and founded a Spanish colony which lasted for nearly 300 years. During the Spanish period, Mexico, then called New Spain, stretched from Guatemala to the present states of Wyoming and California, its present northern boundary having been established by the secession of Texas during 1836 and the war of 1846-48 with the United States.

Independence from Spain was declared by Father Miguel Hidalgo on Sept. 16, 1810, (Mexican Independence Day) and was achieved by General Agustin de Iturbide in1821. Iturbide became emperor in 1822 but was deposed when a republic was established a year later. For more than fifty years following the birth of the republic, the political scene of Mexico was characterized by turmoil which saw two emperors (including the unfortunate Maximilian), several dictators and an average of one new government every nine months passing swiftly from obscurity to oblivion. The land, social, economic and labor reforms promulgated by the Reform Constitution of Feb. 5, 1917 established the basis for sustained economic development and participative democracy that have made Mexico one of the most politically stable countries of modern Latin America.

RULERS

Charles IV, 1788-1808
Ferdinand VII, 1808-1821

MINT MARKS

M, Mo, oMo, MXo – Mexico City

ASSAYER'S' INITIALS

Initial	Date	Name
FM	1783-1802	Francisco Arance y Cobos and Mariano Rodriguez
FT	1801-1803	Francisco Arance y Cobos and Tomas Butron Miranda
TH	1803-1810	Tomas Butron Miranda and Henrique B Azorin
HJ	1809-1814	Henrique B Azorin and Joaquin Davila Madrid
JJ	1812-1821	Joaquin Davila Madrid and Jose García Ansaldo

MONETARY SYSTEM

16 Pilones = 1 Real
8 Tlaco = 1 Real
16 Reales = 1 Escudo

MILLED COINAGE

16 Pilones = 1 Real; 8 Tlaco = 1 Real;
16 Reales = 1 Escudo

Mint: Mexico City

KM# 59 1/16 REAL

Copper **Obv:** Crowned F VII monogram **Rev:** Castles and lions in wreath **Note:** Mint mark M, Mo.

Date	VG	F	VF	XF	Unc
1814	10.00	20.00	45.00	120	—
1815	10.00	20.00	45.00	120	—

Mint: Mexico City

KM# 63 1/8 REAL

Copper **Obv:** Legend around crowned F. VII **Obv. Legend:** FERDIN. VII... **Note:** Mint mark M, Mo.

Date	VG	F	VF	XF	Unc
1814	12.00	25.00	50.00	150	—
1815	12.00	25.00	50.00	150	—
1816	12.00	25.00	50.00	150	—

Mint: Mexico City

KM# 62 1/4 REAL

0.8458 g., 0.8960 Silver .0244 oz. ASW **Obv:** Castle **Rev:** Lion **Note:** Mint mark M, Mo.

Date	VG	F	VF	XF	Unc
1801/0	10.00	20.00	40.00	70.00	—
1801	10.00	20.00	40.00	70.00	—
1802	10.00	20.00	40.00	70.00	—
1803	10.00	20.00	40.00	70.00	—
1804	10.00	20.00	40.00	75.00	—
1805/4	12.50	25.00	55.00	85.00	—
1805	10.00	22.00	50.00	75.00	—
1806	10.00	22.00	50.00	80.00	—
1807/797	15.00	30.00	55.00	85.00	—
1807	12.50	25.00	50.00	80.00	—
1808	12.50	25.00	50.00	80.00	—
1809/8	12.50	25.00	50.00	80.00	—
1809	12.50	25.00	50.00	80.00	—
1810	12.50	25.00	50.00	75.00	—
1811	12.50	25.00	50.00	75.00	—
1812	12.50	25.00	50.00	75.00	—
1813	10.00	20.00	40.00	70.00	—
1815	12.50	22.00	50.00	75.00	—
1816	10.00	20.00	40.00	70.00	—

Mint: Mexico City
KM# 64 1/4 REAL

Copper **Obv:** Legend around crowned F. VII **Obv. Legend:** FERDIN. VII... **Note:** Mint mark M, Mo.

Date	VG	F	VF	XF	Unc
1814	12.00	25.00	50.00	150	—
1815/4	15.00	30.00	60.00	165	—
1815	12.00	25.00	50.00	150	—
1816	12.00	25.00	50.00	150	—
1821	20.00	40.00	75.00	200	—

Mint: Mexico City
KM# 72 1/2 REAL

1.6900 g., 0.9030 Silver .0490 oz. ASW **Obv:** Armored bust of Charles IIII **Rev:** Pillars and arms **Note:** Mint mark M, Mo.

Date	VG	F	VF	XF	Unc
1801 FM	7.50	15.00	30.00	80.00	—
1801 FT	4.00	10.00	22.00	45.00	—
1802 FT	4.00	10.00	22.00	45.00	—
1803 FT	5.00	11.50	25.00	50.00	—
1804 TH	4.00	10.00	22.00	45.00	—
1805 TH	4.00	10.00	22.00	45.00	—
1806 TH	4.00	10.00	22.00	45.00	—
1807/6 TH	5.00	11.50	25.00	50.00	—
1807 TH	4.00	10.00	22.00	45.00	—
1808/7 TH	5.00	11.50	25.00	50.00	—
1808 TH	4.00	10.00	22.00	45.00	—

Mint: Mexico City
KM# 73 1/2 REAL

1.6900 g., 0.9030 Silver .0490 oz. ASW **Obv:** Armored bust of Ferdinand VII **Rev:** Pillars and arms **Note:** Mint mark M, Mo.

Date	VG	F	VF	XF	Unc
1808 TH	3.50	8.00	20.00	35.00	—
1809 TH	3.50	8.00	20.00	35.00	—
1810 TH	5.00	10.00	22.00	45.00	—
1810 HJ	3.50	8.00	20.00	35.00	—
1811 HJ	3.50	8.00	20.00	35.00	—
1812/1 HJ	7.50	15.00	35.00	80.00	—
1812 HJ	3.50	8.00	20.00	35.00	—
1812 JJ	12.00	25.00	45.00	100	—
1813/2 JJ	12.00	25.00	45.00	100	—
1813 JJ	6.00	12.00	25.00	75.00	—
1813 TH	3.50	8.00	20.00	35.00	—
1813 HJ	7.50	15.00	35.00	90.00	—
1814/3 JJ	7.50	15.00	35.00	90.00	—
1814 JJ	5.00	10.00	22.00	45.00	—

Mint: Mexico City
KM# 74 1/2 REAL

1.6900 g., 0.9030 Silver .0490 oz. ASW **Obv:** Draped bust of Ferdinand VII **Rev:** Pillars and arms **Note:** Mint mark M, Mo.

Date	VG	F	VF	XF	Unc
1815 JJ	3.50	8.00	20.00	40.00	—
1816 JJ	3.50	8.00	20.00	40.00	—
1817/6 JJ	12.00	25.00	50.00	120	—
1817 JJ	3.50	8.00	28.00	45.00	—
1818/7 JJ	3.50	8.00	25.00	50.00	—
1818 JJ	3.50	8.00	25.00	50.00	—
1819/8 JJ	6.00	12.00	35.00	90.00	—
1819 JJ	3.50	8.00	20.00	40.00	—
1820 JJ	3.50	8.00	25.00	50.00	—
1821 JJ	3.50	8.00	20.00	40.00	—

Mint: Mexico City
KM# 81 REAL

3.3834 g., 0.8960 Silver .0975 oz. ASW **Obv:** Armored bust of Charles IIII **Note:** Mint mark M, Mo.

Date	VG	F	VF	XF	Unc
1801 FT/M	5.00	10.00	25.00	60.00	—
1801 FM	8.00	15.00	28.00	80.00	—
1801 FT	5.00	10.00	25.00	60.00	—
1802 FM	5.00	10.00	25.00	60.00	—
1802 FT	5.00	10.00	25.00	60.00	—
1802/1 FT	5.00	10.00	25.00	60.00	—
1802 FT/M	5.00	10.00	25.00	60.00	—
1803 FT	5.00	10.00	25.00	60.00	—
1804 TH	5.00	10.00	25.00	60.00	—
1805 TH	5.00	10.00	25.00	60.00	—
1806 TH	5.00	10.00	25.00	60.00	—
1807/6 TH	5.00	10.00	25.00	65.00	—
1807 TH	5.00	10.00	25.00	60.00	—
1808/7 TH	5.00	10.00	25.00	65.00	—
1808 FM	5.00	10.00	25.00	60.00	—

Mint: Mexico City
KM# 82 REAL

3.3800 g., 0.9030 Silver .0981 oz. ASW **Obv:** Armored bust of Ferdinand VII **Note:** Mint mark M, Mo.

Date	VG	F	VF	XF	Unc
1809 TH	8.00	15.00	28.00	90.00	—
1810/09 TH	8.00	15.00	28.00	90.00	—
1810 TH	8.00	15.00	28.00	90.00	—
1811 TH	25.00	35.00	60.00	250	—
1811 HJ	8.00	15.00	28.00	90.00	—
1812 HJ	4.00	9.00	28.00	80.00	—
1812 JJ	10.00	20.00	40.00	120	—
1813 HJ	10.00	20.00	40.00	120	—
1813 JJ	50.00	100	150	250	—
1814 HJ	15.00	30.00	150	150	—
1814 JJ	50.00	100	175	300	—

Mint: Mexico City
KM# 83 REAL

3.3800 g., 0.9030 Silver .0981 oz. ASW **Obv:** Draped bust of Ferdinand VII **Note:** Mint mark M, Mo.

Date	VG	F	VF	XF	Unc
1814 JJ	25.00	50.00	100	350	—
1815 HJ	15.00	30.00	60.00	150	—
1815 JJ	10.00	20.00	40.00	120	—
1816 JJ	5.00	10.00	25.00	70.00	—
1817 JJ	5.00	10.00	25.00	70.00	—
1818 JJ	30.00	60.00	125	500	—
1819 JJ	5.00	10.00	25.00	70.00	—
1820 JJ	5.00	10.00	25.00	70.00	—
1821/0 JJ	8.00	15.00	30.00	110	—
1821 JJ	5.00	10.00	25.00	50.00	—

Mint: Mexico City
KM# 91 2 REALES

6.7668 g., 0.8960 Silver .1949 oz. ASW **Obv:** Armored bust of Carolus IIII **Note:** Mint mark M, Mo.

Date	VG	F	VF	XF	Unc
1801 FT/M	7.00	15.00	30.00	85.00	—
1801 FT	7.00	15.00	30.00	85.00	—
1801 FM	20.00	40.00	75.00	250	—
1802 FT	7.00	15.00	30.00	85.00	—
1803 FT	7.00	15.00	30.00	85.00	—
1804/3 TH	7.00	15.00	30.00	85.00	—
1804 TH	7.00	15.00	30.00	85.00	—
1805 TH	7.00	15.00	30.00	85.00	—
1806/5 TH	7.00	15.00	32.00	90.00	—
1806 TH	7.00	15.00	30.00	85.00	—
1807/5 TH	7.00	15.00	32.00	90.00	—
1807/6 TH	15.00	30.00	60.00	200	—
1807 TH	7.00	15.00	30.00	85.00	—
1808/7 TH	7.00	15.00	32.00	90.00	—
1808 TH	7.00	15.00	30.00	85.00	—

Mint: Mexico City
KM# 92 2 REALES

6.7700 g., 0.9030 Silver .1965 oz. ASW **Obv:** Armored bust of Ferdinand VII **Note:** Mint mark M, Mo.

Date	VG	F	VF	XF	Unc
1809 TH	15.00	30.00	75.00	200	—
181/00 TH	15.00	30.00	75.00	200	—
181/00 HJ/TH	15.00	30.00	75.00	200	—
1810 TH	15.00	30.00	75.00	200	—
181/00 HJ	15.00	30.00	75.00	200	—
1810 HJ	15.00	30.00	75.00	200	—
1811 TH	150	250	350	750	—
1811 HJ/TH	40.00	80.00	150	300	—
1811 HJ	15.00	30.00	75.00	200	—

Mint: Mexico City
KM# 93 2 REALES

6.7700 g., 0.9030 Silver .1965 oz. ASW **Obv:** Draped bust of Ferdinand VII **Note:** Mint mark M, Mo.

Date	VG	F	VF	XF	Unc
1812 TH	60.00	125	250	550	—
1812 HJ	40.00	100	200	500	—
1812 JJ	10.00	20.00	60.00	200	—
1813 TH	15.00	30.00	100	400	—
1813 JJ	20.00	60.00	125	350	—
1813 HJ	40.00	100	200	500	—
1814/2 JJ	15.00	30.00	100	400	—
1814 JJ	15.00	30.00	100	400	—
1815 JJ	6.00	12.00	28.00	85.00	—
1816 JJ	6.00	12.00	28.00	85.00	—
1817 JJ	6.00	12.00	28.00	85.00	—
1818 JJ	6.00	12.00	28.00	85.00	—
1819/8 JJ	5.50	12.00	30.00	85.00	—
1819 JJ	6.00	12.00	28.00	85.00	—
1820 JJ	175	—	—	—	—
1821/0 JJ	7.00	15.00	30.00	90.00	—
1821 JJ	6.00	12.00	28.00	85.00	—

Mint: Mexico City
KM# 100 4 REALES

13.5337 g., 0.8960 Silver .3899 oz. ASW **Obv:** Armored bust of Charles IIII **Rev:** Pillars, arms **Note:** Mint mark M, Mo.

Date	VG	F	VF	XF	Unc
1801 FM	35.00	65.00	150	400	—
1801 FT	60.00	120	200	500	—
1802 FT	200	300	500	1,000	—
1803 FT	75.00	135	225	550	—
1803 FM	200	300	500	1,000	—
1804 TH	40.00	75.00	175	450	—
1805 TH	35.00	65.00	150	400	—
1806 TH	35.00	65.00	150	400	—
1807 TH	35.00	65.00	150	400	—
1808/7 TH	40.00	75.00	175	450	—
1808 TH	40.00	75.00	175	450	—

Mint: Mexico City

KM# 101 4 REALES

13.5400 g., 0.9030 Silver .3931 oz. ASW **Obv:** Armored bust of Ferdinand VII **Note:** Mint mark M, Mo.

Date	VG	F	VF	XF	Unc
1809 HJ	75.00	135	250	750	—
1810 HJ	75.00	135	250	750	—
1811 HJ	75.00	135	250	750	—
1812 HJ	400	650	900	1,850	—

Mint: Mexico City

KM# 102 4 REALES

13.5400 g., 0.9030 Silver .3931 oz. ASW **Obv:** Draped bust of Ferdinand VII **Note:** Mint mark M, Mo.

Date	VG	F	VF	XF	Unc
1816 JJ	150	200	325	700	—
1817 JJ	250	400	500	1,000	—
1818/7 JJ	250	400	500	1,000	—
1819 JJ	175	250	325	700	—
1820 JJ	175	250	325	700	—
1821 JJ	75.00	135	250	650	—

Mint: Mexico City

KM# 109 8 REALES

27.0674 g., 0.8960 Silver .7797 oz. ASW **Obv:** Armored bust of Charles IIII **Note:** Mint mark M, Mo.

Date	VG	F	VF	XF	Unc
1800 FM	20.00	35.00	50.00	100	—
1801/0 FT/FM	20.00	35.00	50.00	100	—
1801/791 FM	35.00	60.00	100	250	—
1801/0 FM	35.00	60.00	100	250	—
1801 FM	20.00	40.00	100	250	—
1801 FT/M	35.00	60.00	100	250	—
1801 FT	20.00	35.00	50.00	100	—
1802/1 FT	35.00	60.00	100	250	—
1802 FT	20.00	35.00	50.00	100	—
1802 FT/M	20.00	35.00	50.00	100	—
1803 FT	20.00	35.00	50.00	110	—
1803 FT/M	20.00	35.00	50.00	100	—
1803 TH	75.00	150	250	500	—
1804/3 TH	35.00	60.00	100	250	—
1804 TH CARLUS (error)	20.00	35.00	50.00	100	—
1805/4 TH	40.00	80.00	125	275	—
1805 TH Narrow date	20.00	35.00	50.00	100	—
1805 Wide date	20.00	35.00	50.00	100	—
1806 TH	20.00	35.00	50.00	100	—
1807/6 TH	150	250	350	700	—
1807 TH	20.00	35.00	50.00	100	—
1808/7 TH	20.00	35.00	50.00	100	—
1808 TH	20.00	35.00	50.00	100	—

Mint: Mexico City

KM# 110 8 REALES

27.0674 g., 0.8960 Silver .7797 oz. ASW **Obv:** Armored bust of Ferdinand VII **Note:** Mint mark M, Mo.

Date	VG	F	VF	XF	Unc
1808 TH	25.00	40.00	75.00	145	—
1809/8 TH	25.00	40.00	75.00	145	—
1809 TH	20.00	35.00	55.00	120	—
1809 HJ	25.00	40.00	75.00	145	—
1809 HJ/TH	20.00	35.00	55.00	120	—
1810/09 HJ	25.00	40.00	75.00	145	—
1810 TH	75.00	150	300	600	—
1810 HJ/TH	25.00	40.00	75.00	145	—
1810 HJ	25.00	40.00	75.00	145	—
1811/0 HJ	20.00	35.00	55.00	120	—
1811 HJ	20.00	35.00	55.00	120	—
1811 HJ/TH	20.00	35.00	50.00	100	—

Mint: Mexico City

KM# 111 8 REALES

27.0700 g., 0.9030 Silver .7859 oz. ASW **Obv:** Draped bust of Ferdinand VII **Note:** Mint mark M, Mo.

Date	VG	F	VF	XF	Unc
1811 HJ	20.00	40.00	60.00	125	—
1812 HJ	50.00	75.00	125	250	—
1812 JJ/HJ	20.00	35.00	50.00	100	—
1812 JJ	20.00	35.00	50.00	100	—
1813 HJ	50.00	75.00	125	250	—
1813 JJ	20.00	35.00	50.00	100	—
1814/3 HJ	1,200	2,500	5,000	—	—
1814/3 JJ	20.00	35.00	50.00	100	—
1814 JJ	20.00	35.00	50.00	100	—
1815/4 JJ	20.00	35.00	50.00	100	—
1815 JJ	20.00	35.00	50.00	100	—
1816/5 JJ	20.00	35.00	50.00	90.00	—
1816 JJ	20.00	35.00	50.00	90.00	—
1817 JJ	20.00	35.00	50.00	90.00	—
1818 JJ	20.00	35.00	50.00	90.00	—
1819 JJ	20.00	35.00	50.00	90.00	—
1820 JJ	20.00	35.00	50.00	90.00	—
1821 JJ	20.00	35.00	50.00	90.00	—

Mint: Mexico City

KM# 112 1/2 ESCUDO

1.6917 g., 0.8750 Gold .0476 oz. AGW **Obv. Legend:** FERD. VII. D. G. HISP. ET IND **Note:** Mint mark M, Mo.

Date	VG	F	VF	XF	Unc
1814 JJ	100	150	225	375	—
1815/4 JJ	150	200	250	400	—
1815 JJ	150	200	250	400	—
1816 JJ	100	150	225	375	—
1817 JJ	150	200	250	400	—
1818 JJ	150	200	250	400	—
1819 JJ	150	200	250	400	—
1820 JJ	200	300	400	550	—

Mint: Mexico City

KM# 120 ESCUDO

3.3834 g., 0.8750 Gold .0952 oz. AGW **Obv:** Armored bust of Charles IV **Obv. Legend:** CAROLUS. IV. D. G... **Rev:** Initial letters and mint mark upright **Rev. Legend:** FELIX. A. D **Note:** Mint mark M, Mo.

Date	VG	F	VF	XF	Unc
1801 FM	125	165	235	345	—
1801 FT	125	165	235	345	—
1802 FT	125	165	235	345	—
1803 FT	125	165	235	345	—
1804/3 TH	125	165	235	345	—
1804 TH	125	165	235	345	—
1805 TH	125	165	235	345	—
1806/5 TH	125	165	235	345	—
1806 TH	125	165	235	345	—
1807 TH	125	165	235	345	—
1808 TH	125	165	235	345	—

Mint: Mexico City

KM# 121 ESCUDO

3.3834 g., 0.8750 Gold .0952 oz. AGW **Obv:** Armored bust of Ferdinand VII **Obv. Legend:** CAROLUS. IV. D. G... **Rev:** Initial letters and mint mark upright **Rev. Legend:** FELIX. A. D **Note:** Mint mark M, Mo.

Date	VG	F	VF	XF	Unc
1809 HJ/TH	125	165	235	400	—
1809 HJ	125	165	235	400	—
1811/0 HJ	125	165	235	400	—
1812 HJ	150	250	300	500	—

Mint: Mexico City

KM# 122 ESCUDO

3.3834 g., 0.8750 Gold .0952 oz. AGW **Obv:** Undraped bust of Ferdinand VII **Obv. Legend:** CAROLUS. IV. D. G... **Rev:** Initial letters and mint mark upright **Rev. Legend:** FELIX. A. D **Note:** Mint mark M, Mo.

Date	VG	F	VF	XF	Unc
1814 HJ	150	250	300	500	—
1815 HJ	150	250	300	500	—
1815 JJ	150	250	300	500	—
1816 JJ	175	275	325	550	—

Date	VG	F	VF	XF	Unc
1817 JJ	150	250	300	500	—
1818 JJ	150	250	300	500	—
1819 JJ	150	250	300	500	—
1820 JJ	150	250	300	500	—

Mint: Mexico City

KM# 132 2 ESCUDOS

6.7668 g., 0.8750 Gold .1904 oz. AGW **Obv:** Armored bust of Charles IV **Obv. Legend:** CAROL. IV. D. G... **Rev:** Initials and mint mark upright **Rev. Legend:** IN. UTROQ. FELIX. AUSPICE. DEO **Note:** Mint mark M, Mo.

Date	VG	F	VF	XF	Unc
1801 FT	125	225	350	575	—
1802 FT	125	225	350	575	—
1803 FT	125	225	350	575	—
1804 TH	125	225	350	575	—
1805 TH	125	225	350	575	—
1806/5 TH	125	225	350	575	—
1807 TH	125	225	350	575	—
1808 TH	125	225	350	575	—

Mint: Mexico City

KM# 134 2 ESCUDOS

6.7668 g., 0.8750 Gold .1904 oz. AGW **Obv:** Undraped bust of Ferdinand VII **Obv. Legend:** CAROL. IV. D. G... **Rev:** Initials and mint mark upright **Rev. Legend:** IN. UTROQ. FELIX. AUSPICE. DEO **Note:** Mint mark M, Mo.

Date	VG	F	VF	XF	Unc
1814 JJ	250	425	700	1,200	—
1815 JJ	250	425	700	1,200	—
1816 JJ	250	425	700	1,200	—
1817 JJ	250	425	700	1,200	—
1818 JJ	250	425	700	1,200	—
1819 JJ	250	425	700	1,200	—
1820 JJ	250	425	700	1,200	—
1821 JJ	250	425	700	1,200	—

Mint: Mexico City

KM# 144 4 ESCUDOS

13.5337 g., 0.8750 Gold .3807 oz. AGW **Obv:** Armored bust of Charles IIII **Obv. Legend:** CAROL. IIII D. G... **Rev:** Initials and mint mark upright **Rev. Legend:** IN. UTROQ. FELIX. AUSPICE. DEO **Note:** Mint mark M, Mo.

Date	VG	F	VF	XF	Unc
1801 FM	300	500	750	1,500	—
1801 FT	300	500	750	1,500	—
1802 FT	300	500	750	1,500	—
1803 FT	300	500	750	1,500	—
1804/3 TH	300	500	750	1,500	—
1804 TH	300	500	750	1,500	—
1805 TH	300	500	750	1,500	—
1806/5 TH	300	500	750	1,500	—
1807 TH	300	500	750	1,500	—
1808/0 TH	300	500	750	1,500	—
1808 TH	300	500	750	1,500	—

Mint: Mexico City

KM# 145 4 ESCUDOS

13.5337 g., 0.8750 Gold .3807 oz. AGW **Obv:** Armored bust of Ferdinand VII **Obv. Legend:** CAROL. IIII D. G... **Rev:** Initials and mint mark upright **Rev. Legend:** IN. UTROQ. FELIX. AUSPICE. DEO **Note:** Mint mark M, Mo.

Date	VG	F	VF	XF	Unc
1810 HJ	350	500	850	1,700	—
1811 HJ	350	500	850	1,700	—
1812 HJ	350	500	850	1,700	—

Mint: Mexico City

KM# 146 4 ESCUDOS

13.5337 g., 0.8750 Gold .3807 oz. AGW **Obv:** Undraped bust of Ferdinand VII **Obv. Legend:** CAROL. IIII D. G... **Rev:** Initials and mint mark upright **Rev. Legend:** IN. UTROQ. FELIX. AUSPICE. DEO **Note:** Mint mark M, Mo.

Date	VG	F	VF	XF	Unc
1814 HJ	400	700	1,200	2,700	—
1815 HJ	400	700	1,200	2,700	—
1815 JJ	400	700	1,200	2,700	—
1816 JJ	400	700	1,200	2,700	—
1817 JJ	400	700	1,200	2,700	—
1818 JJ	400	700	1,200	2,700	—
1819 JJ	400	700	1,200	2,700	—
1820 JJ	400	700	1,200	2,700	—

Mint: Mexico City

KM# 159 8 ESCUDOS

27.0674 g., 0.8750 Gold .7615 oz. AGW **Obv:** Armored bust of Charles IIII **Obv. Legend:** CAROL. IIII. D. G... **Rev:** Arms, Order chain **Rev. Legend:** IN UTROQ. FELIX **Note:** Mint mark M, Mo.

Date	VG	F	VF	XF	Unc
1801/0 FT	400	500	700	1,150	—
1801 FM	350	450	625	1,000	—
1801 FT	350	450	625	1,000	—
1802 FT	350	450	625	1,000	—
1803 FT	350	450	625	1,000	—
1804/3 TH	400	500	700	1,150	—
1804 TH	350	450	625	1,000	—
1805 TH	350	450	625	1,000	—
1806 TH	350	450	625	1,000	—
1807/6 TH	400	500	700	1,150	—
1807 TH Mo over inverted Mo	400	500	700	1,150	—
1808/7 TH	450	600	800	1,250	—
1807 TH	350	450	625	1,000	—
1808 TH	450	600	800	1,250	—

Mint: Mexico City

KM# 160 8 ESCUDOS

27.0674 g., 0.8750 Gold .7615 oz. AGW **Obv:** Armored bust of Ferdinand VII **Obv. Legend:** CAROL. IIII. D. G... **Rev:** Arms, Order chain **Rev. Legend:** IN UTROQ. FELIX **Note:** Mint mark M, Mo.

Date	VG	F	VF	XF	Unc
1808 TH	400	500	750	1,250	—
1809 HJ	400	500	750	1,350	—
1810 HJ	375	475	700	1,200	—
1811/0 HJ	425	525	800	1,350	—
1811 HJ H/T	425	525	800	1,350	—
1811 HJ	425	525	800	1,350	—
1811 JJ	375	475	700	1,200	—
1812 JJ	375	475	700	1,200	—

Mint: Mexico City

KM# 161 8 ESCUDOS

27.0674 g., 0.8750 Gold .7615 oz. AGW **Obv:** Undraped bust of Ferdinand VII **Obv. Legend:** CAROL. IIII. D. G... **Rev:** Arms, Order chain **Rev. Legend:** IN UTROQ. FELIX **Note:** Mint mark M, Mo.

Date	VG	F	VF	XF	Unc
1814 JJ	360	465	650	1,000	—
1815/4 JJ	400	500	700	1,150	—
1815/4 HJ	400	500	700	1,150	—
1815 JJ	360	465	650	1,000	—
1815 HJ	360	465	650	1,000	—
1816 JJ	360	465	650	1,000	—
1817 JJ	400	500	700	1,150	—
1818/7 JJ	360	465	675	1,100	—
1818 JJ	360	465	675	1,100	—
1819 JJ	360	465	675	1,100	—
1820 JJ	360	465	675	1,100	—
1821 JJ	400	500	750	1,300	—

PROCLAMATION MEDALLIC COINAGE

The Q used in the following listings refer to Standard Catalog of Mexican Coins, Paper Money, Stocks, Bonds, and Medals by Krause Publications, Inc., ©1981.

KM# Q8 REAL

Silver **Issuer:** Chiapa **Obv:** Crowned arms between pillars, IR below **Obv. Legend:** FERNANDO VII REY DE ESPANA Y DE SUS INDIAS **Rev:** Legend in 5 lines within wreath **Rev. Legend:** PROCLA/MADO/ENCIUD/R. DECHIAPPA/1808

Date	F	VF	XF	Unc
1808	20.00	32.50	47.50	75.00

KM# Q10 2 REALES

Silver **Issuer:** Chiapa **Obv. Legend:** FERNANDO VII REY DE ESPANA Y DE SUS INDIAS

Date	F	VF	XF	Unc
1808	37.50	57.50	78.50	115

KM# Q64 2 REALES

Silver **Issuer:** Queretaro **Obv. Legend:** FERNANDO VII REY DE ESPANA

Date	F	VF	XF	Unc
1808	20.00	37.50	67.50	100

KM# Q-A66 4 REALES
Silver **Issuer:** Queretaro **Obv. Legend:** FERNANDO VII REY DE ESPANA

Date	F	VF	XF	Unc
1808	85.00	135	200	325

KM# Q68 8 REALES
Silver **Issuer:** Queretaro **Obv. Legend:** FERNANDO VII REY DE ESPANA

Date	F	VF	XF	Unc
1808	185	350	475	625

LOCAL COINAGE

AHUALULCO

KM# L1 1/8 REAL
Copper **Issuer:** Ahualulco **Obv:** AHUALULCO and 1813 arfound 1/8 in circle **Note:** Uniface.

Date	Good	VG	F	VF	XF
1813	15.00	25.00	35.00	55.00	—

KM# L2 1/8 REAL
Copper **Issuer:** Ahualulco **Obv:** Script AHO, 1/8 below **Note:** Uniface.

Date	Good	VG	F	VF	XF
ND	10.00	17.50	25.00	40.00	—

AMECA

KM# L7 1/8 REAL
Copper **Issuer:** Ameca **Obv:** QTG monogram in toothed circle **Obv. Legend:** TLACO DE AMECA

Date	Good	VG	F	VF	XF
ND(1812)	10.00	17.50	25.00	40.00	—

KM# L9 1/8 REAL
Copper **Issuer:** Ameca **Obv:** AME/CA 1811 in circle **Note:** Octagonal planchet.

Date	Good	VG	F	VF	XF
1811	16.50	27.50	38.50	65.00	—

KM# L10 1/8 REAL
Copper **Issuer:** Ameca **Obv:** F 1/8 Z within wavy circle **Note:** Octagonal planchet.

Date	Good	VG	F	VF	XF
ND	16.50	25.00	33.50	57.50	—

KM# L11 1/8 REAL
Copper **Issuer:** Ameca **Obv:** T.Z. AMECA 1833 around value **Note:** Octagonal planchet.

Date	Good	VG	F	VF	XF
1833	10.00	15.00	22.50	35.00	—

KM# L12 1/8 REAL
Copper **Issuer:** Ameca **Obv:** V.F AMECA 1858 below value **Note:** Octagonal planchet.

Date	Good	VG	F	VF	XF
1858	12.50	17.50	25.00	40.00	—

KM# L6 1/8 REAL
Copper **Issuer:** Ameca **Obv:** Church flanked by trees **Note:** Uniface.

Date	Good	VG	F	VF	XF
1824	10.00	17.50	25.00	40.00	—

KM# L8 1/8 REAL
Copper **Issuer:** Ameca **Obv:** AME/CA 1811 in circle **Note:** Uniface.

Date	Good	VG	F	VF	XF
1811	15.00	25.00	35.00	55.00	—

AMESCUA

KM# L15 1/8 REAL
Copper **Issuer:** Amescua **Obv:** Mexican eagle

Date	Good	VG	F	VF	XF
1828	10.00	15.00	22.50	35.00	—

KM# L16 1/8 REAL
Copper **Issuer:** Amescua **Obv:** Darte below eagle

Date	Good	VG	F	VF	XF
1838	13.50	20.00	28.50	45.00	—

ATENCINCO

KM# L19 1/8 REAL
Copper **Issuer:** Atencinco **Obv:** ATENCINCO in outer border, 8-leaved rosette above branch in center

Date	Good	VG	F	VF	XF
ND	13.50	20.00	28.00	45.00	—

ATOTONILCO

KM# L22 1/8 REAL
Copper **Issuer:** Atotonilco **Obv:** ATOTONILCO ANO DE 1808 in outer border, L. S. S. / JUSU/ESES in circle

Date	Good	VG	F	VF	XF
1808	25.00	37.50	55.00	80.00	—

KM# L23 1/8 REAL
Copper **Issuer:** Atotonilco **Obv:** Legend in outer border, 1821 in center **Obv. Legend:** ANTOTONILCO ANO DE **Rev:** Legend around outer border **Rev. Legend:** E T P D Z

Date	Good	VG	F	VF	XF
1821	15.00	25.00	35.00	55.00	—

KM# L24 1/8 REAL
Copper **Issuer:** Atotonilco **Obv:** Legend in outer border, 1826 in center **Obv. Legend:** VILL ANTOTONILCO **Rev:** Legend in center, stars in outer border **Rev. Legend:** 1/8

Date	Good	VG	F	VF	XF
1826	15.00	25.00	35.00	55.00	—

CAMPECHE

KM# L27 CENTAVO
Brass **Issuer:** Campeche

Date	Good	VG	F	VF	XF
1861	7.00	10.00	17.50	27.50	—

CATORCE

KM# L30 1/4 REAL
Copper **Issuer:** Catorce **Obv:** Legend around border, 1/4 below flower and raised rectangle **Obv. Legend:** FONDOS PUVBLICO **Rev:** Legend around border, eagle on cactus **Rev. Legend:** DE CATORCE 1822

Date	Good	VG	F	VF	XF
1822	12.00	18.50	30.00	45.00	—

CELAYA

KM# L33 1/8 REAL
Copper **Issuer:** Celaya **Obv. Legend:** EN/CELAYA/DE/1803 **Rev:** Branches below legend, flower above **Rev. Legend:** LUIS/VASQUE S

Date	Good	VG	F	VF	XF
1803	25.00	37.50	55.00	80.00	—

KM# L34 1/8 REAL
Copper **Issuer:** Celaya **Obv. Legend:** VINDERI/QUE/CELALLA/1808 **Rev:** Branches below legend, flower above **Rev. Legend:** LUIS/VASQUE S **Note:** Uniface.

Date	Good	VG	F	VF	XF
1808	25.00	37.50	55.00	80.00	—

KM# L35 1/8 REAL
Copper **Issuer:** Celaya **Obv. Legend:** VISCARA/CELAYA/1814 with ornament above **Rev:** Branches below legend, flower above **Rev. Legend:** LUIS/VASQUE S **Note:** Uniface.

Date	Good	VG	F	VF	XF
1814	17.50	25.00	35.00	55.00	—

CHILCHOTA

KM# L38 1/8 REAL
Copper **Issuer:** Chilchota **Obv:** Head to right, date below legend **Obv. Legend:** CHILCHOTA UN OCTAVO **Rev:** Wreath in center **Rev. Legend:** RESPONSAVIDAD DE MURGVIA

Date	Good	VG	F	VF	XF
1858	15.00	25.00	35.00	55.00	—

COLIMA

KM# L41 1/8 REAL
Copper **Issuer:** Colima **Obv:** Legend around border as continuos legend **Obv. Legend:** VILLA DE COLIMA **Rev:** Blank

Date	Good	VG	F	VF	XF
1813	12.50	17.50	25.00	42.50	—

KM# L42 1/8 REAL
Copper **Issuer:** Colima **Obv:** Legend and date in three lines **Obv. Legend:** VILLA DE COLIMA **Rev:** Blank

Date	Good	VG	F	VF	XF
1814	12.50	17.50	25.00	42.50	—

KM# L44 1/8 REAL
Copper **Issuer:** Colima **Obv:** Legend and date in three lines **Obv. Legend:** OCT. DE COLI **Rev:** Date

Date	Good	VG	F	VF	XF
1819	15.00	22.50	30.00	50.00	—

KM# L46 1/8 REAL
Copper **Issuer:** Colima **Obv:** Legend around border, date in center circle **Obv. Legend:** OCTO DE COLIMA **Rev:** Legend within wreath, pellet in center **Rev. Legend:** OCTAVO

Date	Good	VG	F	VF	XF
1824	13.50	17.50	25.00	42.00	—

KM# L47 1/8 REAL
Copper **Issuer:** Colima **Obv:** Legend in three lines **Obv. Legend:** OCTO DE COLA **Rev:** Legend within wreath, pellet in center **Rev. Legend:** OCTAVO

Date	Good	VG	F	VF	XF
1824	13.50	17.50	25.00	42.50	—
1828	13.50	17.50	25.00	42.50	—

KM# L48 1/8 REAL
Copper **Issuer:** Colima **Obv:** Legend in three lines **Obv. Legend:** OCTO DE COLIMA **Rev:** Legend in three lines **Rev. Legend:** ANO DE 1830

Date	Good	VG	F	VF	XF
1830	13.50	17.50	25.00	42.50	—

KM# L43 1/4 REAL
Copper **Issuer:** Colima **Obv:** Legend in three lines in wreath **Obv. Legend:** QUART COLIMA 1816 **Rev:** Colima monogram in wreath

Date	Good	VG	F	VF	XF
1816	10.00	16.50	22.50	40.00	—

KM# L45 1/4 REAL
Copper **Issuer:** Colima **Obv:** Legend around border, date in center circle **Obv. Legend:** QUARTo DE COLIMA **Rev:** Colima monogram in wreath

Date	Good	VG	F	VF	XF
1824	12.50	16.50	22.50	40.00	—

COTIJA

KM# L51 1/4 REAL
Copper **Issuer:** Cotija **Obv:** Seated Liberty with staff and liberty cap **Obv. Legend:** DE. D. JOSE NUNES **Rev:** Value and date in wreath **Rev. Legend:** COMMERCIO. D. COTIJA

Date	Good	VG	F	VF	XF
ND	12.50	18.50	25.00	42.50	—

CUIDO

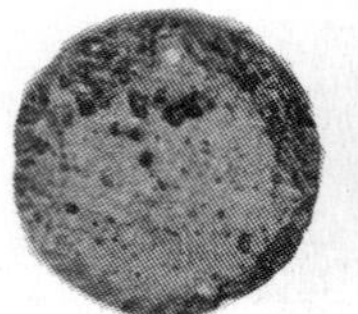

KM# L52 1/8 REAL
Copper **Issuer:** Cuido **Note:** Uniface. "CUIDO" above "1/8" in spray.

Date	Good	VG	F	VF	XF
ND	12.50	20.00	28.50	45.00	—

GUADALAJARA

KM# L57 1/8 REAL
Copper **Issuer:** Guadalajara **Obv:** Eagle with wings spread **Obv. Legend:** GUADALAXARA **Note:** Uniface.

Date	Good	VG	F	VF	XF
ND	27.50	37.50	55.00	80.00	—

LAGOS

KM# L59 1/4 REAL
Bronze **Issuer:** Lagos **Obv:** 2 globes with crown above, wreath and 1/4 below **Rev:** Coat of arms of Lagos

Date	Good	VG	F	VF	XF
ND	60.00	75.00	120	185	—

KM# L59a 1/4 REAL
Silver **Issuer:** Lagos **Obv:** 2 globes with crown above, wreath and 1/4 below **Rev:** Coat of arms of Lagos

Date	Good	VG	F	VF	XF
ND	150	200	300	500	—

MERIDA

KM# L60 1/2 GRANO
Lead **Issuer:** Merida **Obv:** First part of legend in center, second part of legend around border, 1859 below **Obv. Legend:** PART/DE LA SO/CIED • MERIDADE YUCATAN **Rev. Legend:** 1/2/GRAND/DE PESO/FUERTE

Date	Good	VG	F	VF	XF
1859	10.00	16.00	32.50	55.00	—

PAZCUARO

KM# L63 1/8 REAL
Copper **Issuer:** Pazcuaro **Obv:** Town at base of mountains, lake in foreground, value 1/8 above **Rev:** Woman walking right, carrying bag, fish net and fish

Date	Good	VG	F	VF	XF
ND	11.00	16.50	22.50	35.00	—

Note: Also in brass and cast in bronze; minor die varieties have been observed.

KM# L64 1/8 REAL
Copper **Issuer:** Pazcuaro **Obv:** 1/8 PAZCUARO **Rev:** Woman walking right, carrying bag, fish net and fish

Date	Good	VG	F	VF	XF
ND	12.50	17.50	25.00	40.00	—

PROGRESO

KM# L66 1/8 REAL
Copper **Issuer:** Progreso **Obv:** Radiant star above open book **Rev:** Value 1/8 in double wreath

Date	Good	VG	F	VF	XF
1858	15.00	22.50	35.00	55.00	—

KM# L67 CENTAVO
Lead **Issuer:** Progreso **Obv:** Legend and 1873 in center **Obv. Legend:** MUNICIPALIDAD DE PROGRESSO UN CENT **Rev:** Flank in oval band

Date	Good	VG	F	VF	XF
1873	12.50	20.00	30.00	50.00	—

QUITUPAN

KM# L69 1/8 REAL
Copper **Issuer:** Quitupan **Obv:** Bow and two arrows in center **Obv. Legend:** QUITUPAN ... 1854 **Rev:** 1/8 in center, mongram countermark **Rev. Legend:** IGNACIO BUENROSTO

Date	Good	VG	F	VF	XF
1854	15.00	22.50	32.50	55.00	—

TACAMBARO

KM# L72 1/8 REAL
Copper **Issuer:** Tacambaro **Obv:** Winged caduceus in sprays **Rev:** Value 1/8 in sprays

Date	Good	VG	F	VF	XF
ND	12.50	18.50	25.00	40.00	—

TARETAN

KM# L75 1/8 REAL
Copper **Issuer:** Taretan **Obv:** Head of man right **Rev:** Tree

Date	Good	VG	F	VF	XF
1858	15.00	25.00	37.50	60.00	—

TLAZASALCA

KM# L78 1/8 REAL
Copper **Issuer:** Tlazasalca **Obv:** Two mountains, date below **Rev:** Value 1/8 in wreath

Date	Good	VG	F	VF	XF
1853	16.50	25.00	35.00	55.00	—

XALOSTOTITLAN

KM# L54 1/8 REAL
Copper **Issuer:** Xalostotitlan **Obv:** Crown in center **Obv. Legend:** AYVNTANIENTO ILVSTRE **Rev:** 4 in center **Rev. Legend:** DE XALOSTOTITLAN. 1820

Date	Good	VG	F	VF	XF
1820	22.50	35.00	55.00	80.00	—

ZAMORA

KM# L80 1/8 REAL
Copper **Issuer:** Zamora

Date	Good	VG	F	VF	XF
1842	6.00	12.50	22.50	37.50	—
1848	6.00	12.50	22.50	37.50	—
1854	6.00	12.50	22.50	37.50	—
1858	6.00	12.50	22.50	37.50	—

KM# L81 1/8 REAL
Copper Or Bronze **Issuer:** Zamora **Obv:** Eagle on cactus above sprays **Rev:** Liberty cap, bow and arrows above sprays. With or without various countermarks

Date	Good	VG	F	VF	XF
1852	6.00	12.50	22.50	37.50	—
1853	6.00	12.50	22.50	37.50	—
1854	6.00	12.50	22.50	37.50	—
1856	6.00	12.50	22.50	37.50	—
1857	6.00	12.50	22.50	37.50	—
1858	6.00	12.50	22.50	37.50	—

Note: These pieces are also found with various countermarks. "Za" in a dentilated circle is the most common. "1/8" in a circular countermark is also encountered.

ZAPOTLAN

KM# L84 1/8 REAL
Copper **Issuer:** Zapotlan **Obv. Legend:** ZAPO/TLAN/1813

Date	Good	VG	F	VF	XF
1813	17.50	27.50	40.00	60.00	—

CHIHUAHUA

The Chihuahua Mint was established by a decree of October 8, 1810 as a temporary mint. Their first coins were cast 8 Reales using Mexico City coins as patterns and obliterating/changing the mint mark and moneyer initials. Two c/m were placed on the obverse - on the left, a T designating receipt by the Royal Treasurer, crowned pillars of Hercules on the right with pomegranate beneath, the comptrollers symbol.

In 1814, standard dies were made available, thus machine struck 8 Reales were produced until 1822. Only the one denomination was made at Chihuahua.

Mint mark: CA.

WAR OF INDEPENDENCE

ROYALIST COINAGE

KM# 123 8 REALES
Cast Silver **Ruler:** Ferdinand VII **Mint:** Chihuahua **Countermark:** T at left, pillars at right, pomegranate below **Obverse:** Imaginary bust of Ferdinand VII **Obv. Legend:** FERDIN. VII. DEI. GRATIA

Date	Good	VG	F	VF	XF
1810CA RP Rare	—	—	—	—	—
1811CA RP	45.00	60.00	100	150	—
1812CA RP	30.00	40.00	60.00	90.00	—
1813CA RP	30.00	40.00	60.00	90.00	—

KM# 111.1 8 REALES
27.0700 g., 0.9030 Silver .7860 oz. ASW **Ruler:** Ferdinand VII **Obverse:** Draped bust of Ferdinand VII **Obv. Legend:** FERDIN. VII. DEI. GRATIA **Reverse:** Similar to KM#123

Date	VG	F	VF	XF	Unc
1815CA RP	200	275	350	500	—
1816CA RP	80.00	125	150	275	—
1817CA RP	100	150	185	275	—
1818CA RP	100	150	185	275	—
1819/8 RP	125	175	250	350	—
1819CA RP	125	175	250	350	—
1820CA RP	200	275	350	500	—
1821CA RP	200	275	350	500	—
1822CA RP	400	600	800	1,100	—

Note: KM#111.1 is normally found struck over earlier cast 8 Reales, KM#123 and Monclova (MVA) 1812 cast countermark 8 Reales, KM#202 and Zacatecas 8 Reales, KM#190

DURANGO

The Durango mint was authorized as a temporary mint on the same day as the Chihuahua Mint, October 8, 1810. The mint opened in 1811 and made coins of 6 denominations between 1811 and 1822.

Mint mark: D.

WAR OF INDEPENDENCE

ROYALIST COINAGE

KM# 60 1/8 REAL
Copper **Ruler:** Ferdinand VII **Mint:** Durango **Obverse:** Crown above double F7 monogram **Reverse:** EN DURANGO, value, date

Date	VG	F	VF	XF	Unc
1812D	32.50	75.00	125	250	—
1813D Rare	—	—	—	—	—
1814D Rare	—	—	—	—	—

KM# 61 1/8 REAL
Copper **Ruler:** Ferdinand VII **Mint:** Durango **Obverse:** Crown above double F7 monogram **Reverse:** Spray added above date

Date	VG	F	VF	XF	Unc
1814D	15.00	30.00	50.00	90.00	—
1815D	18.00	35.00	60.00	100	—
1816D	18.00	35.00	60.00	100	—
1817D	15.00	30.00	50.00	90.00	—
1818D	15.00	30.00	50.00	90.00	—
1818D OCTAVO DD REAL (error)	45.00	80.00	125	225	—

KM# 74.1 1/2 REAL
1.6900 g., 0.9030 Silver .0491 oz. ASW **Ruler:** Ferdinand VII **Mint:** Durango **Obverse:** Draped bust of Ferdinand VII

Date	VG	F	VF	XF	Unc
1813D RM	250	450	750	1,800	—
1814D MZ	250	450	750	1,850	—
1816D MZ	250	450	750	1,850	—

KM# 83.1 REAL
3.3800 g., 0.9030 Silver .0981 oz. ASW **Ruler:** Ferdinand VII **Mint:** Durango **Obverse:** Draped bust of Ferdinand VII

Date	VG	F	VF	XF	Unc
1813D RM	250	450	650	1,650	—
1814D MZ	250	450	650	1,650	—
1815D MZ	250	450	650	1,650	—

KM# 92.2 2 REALES
6.7700 g., 0.9030 Silver .1966 oz. ASW **Ruler:** Ferdinand VII **Mint:** Durango **Obverse:** Armored bust of Ferdinand VII **Rev. Legend:** MON PROV DE DURANGO...

Date	VG	F	VF	XF	Unc
1811D RM	375	450	850	1,750	—

KM# 92.3 2 REALES
6.7700 g., 0.9030 Silver .1966 oz. ASW **Ruler:** Ferdinand VII **Obverse:** Armored bust of Ferdinand VII **Rev. Legend:** HISPAN ET IND REX...

Date	VG	F	VF	XF	Unc
1812 RM	250	400	750	1,650	—

KM# 93.1 2 REALES
6.7700 g., 0.9030 Silver .1966 oz. ASW **Ruler:** Ferdinand VII **Mint:** Durango **Obverse:** Draped bust of Ferdinand VII

Date	VG	F	VF	XF	Unc
1812D RM	250	400	750	1,650	—
1813D RM	300	600	1,000	2,750	—
1813D MZ	300	600	1,000	2,750	—
1814D MZ	300	600	1,000	2,750	—
1815D MZ	300	600	1,000	2,750	—
1816D MZ	300	600	1,000	2,750	—
1817D MZ	300	600	1,000	2,750	—

KM# 102.1 4 REALES

13.5400 g., 0.9030 Silver .3931 oz. ASW **Ruler:** Ferdinand VII
Mint: Durango **Obverse:** Draped bust of Ferdinand VII

Date	VG	F	VF	XF	Unc
1814D MZ	550	1,000	1,650	4,500	—
1816D MZ	450	900	1,400	4,000	—
1817D MZ	450	900	1,400	4,000	—

KM# 110.1 8 REALES

27.0700 g., 0.9030 Silver .7860 oz. ASW **Ruler:** Ferdinand VII
Mint: Durango **Obverse:** Armored bust of Ferdinand VII

Date	VG	F	VF	XF	Unc
1811D RM	600	1,000	1,750	5,000	—
1812D RM	350	650	1,000	3,500	—
1814D MZ	350	650	1,000	3,500	—

KM# 111.2 8 REALES

27.0700 g., 0.9030 Silver .7860 oz. ASW **Ruler:** Ferdinand VII
Mint: Durango **Obverse:** Draped bust of Ferdinand VII

Date	VG	F	VF	XF	Unc
1812D RM	125	175	275	800	—
1813D RM	150	200	325	850	—
1813D MZ	125	175	275	750	—
1814/2D MZ	150	200	300	750	—
1814D MZ	150	200	300	750	—
1815D MZ	75.00	125	225	600	—
1816D MZ	50.00	75.00	125	325	—
1817D MZ	30.00	50.00	90.00	250	—
1818D MZ	50.00	75.00	125	350	—
1818D RM	50.00	75.00	125	325	—
1818D CG/RM	100	125	150	350	—
1818D CG	50.00	75.00	125	325	—
1819D CG/RM	50.00	100	150	300	—
1819D CG	30.00	60.00	100	250	—
1820D CG	30.00	60.00	100	250	—
1821D CG	30.00	40.00	80.00	200	—
1822D CG	30.00	50.00	90.00	240	—

Note: Occasionally these are found struck over cast Chihuahua 8 reales and are very rare in general, specimens dated prior to 1816 are rather crudely struck

GUADALAJARA

The Guadalajara Mint made its first coins in 1812 and the mint operated until April 30, 1815. It was to reopen in 1818 and continue operations until 1822. It was the only Royalist mint to strike gold coins, both 4 and 8 Escudos. In addition to these it struck the standard 5 denominations in silver.

Mint mark: GA.

WAR OF INDEPENDENCE

ROYALIST COINAGE

KM# 74.2 1/2 REAL

1.6900 g., 0.9030 Silver .0491 oz. ASW **Ruler:** Ferdinand VII
Mint: Guadalajara **Obverse:** Draped bust of Ferdinand VII

Date	VG	F	VF	XF	Unc
1812GA MR Rare	—	—	—	—	—
1814GA MR	40.00	100	200	300	—
1815GA MR	200	350	500	1,000	—

KM# 83.2 REAL

3.3800 g., 0.9030 Silver .0981 oz. ASW **Ruler:** Ferdinand VII
Mint: Guadalajara **Obverse:** Draped bust of Ferdinand VII

Date	VG	F	VF	XF	Unc
1813GA MR	300	500	800	—	—
1814GA MR	150	200	350	650	—
1815GA MR	300	500	800	—	—

KM# 93.2 2 REALES

6.7700 g., 0.9030 Silver .1966 oz. ASW **Ruler:** Ferdinand VII
Mint: Guadalajara **Obverse:** Draped bust of Ferdinand VII

Date	VG	F	VF	XF	Unc
1812GA MR	300	500	800	2,500	—
1814/2GA MR	75.00	125	250	600	—
1814GA MR	75.00	125	250	600	—
1815/4GA MR	425	725	1,100	3,600	—
1815GA MR	400	700	1,000	3,500	—
1821GA FS	200	250	350	900	—

KM# 102.2 4 REALES

13.5400 g., 0.9030 Silver .3931 oz. ASW **Ruler:** Ferdinand VII
Mint: Guadalajara **Obverse:** Draped small bust of Ferdinand VII

Date	VG	F	VF	XF	Unc
1814GA MR	40.00	65.00	150	250	—
1815GA MR	80.00	150	300	500	—

KM# 102.3 4 REALES

13.5400 g., 0.9030 Silver .3931 oz. ASW **Ruler:** Ferdinand VII
Mint: Guadalajara **Obverse:** Large bust

Date	VG	F	VF	XF	Unc
1814GA MR	50.00	100	200	400	—

KM# 102.4 4 REALES

13.5400 g., 0.9030 Silver .3931 oz. ASW **Ruler:** Ferdinand VII
Mint: Guadalajara **Obverse:** Large bust with berries in laurel

Date	VG	F	VF	XF	Unc
1814GA MR	60.00	120	250	450	—

KM# 111.3 8 REALES

27.0700 g., 0.9030 Silver .7860 oz. ASW **Ruler:** Ferdinand VII
Mint: Guadalajara **Obverse:** Draped bust of Ferdinand VII

Date	VG	F	VF	XF	Unc
1812GA MR	2,000	3,500	5,000	7,000	—
1813/2GA MR	60.00	100	150	400	—
1813GA MR	60.00	100	150	400	—
1814GA MR	20.00	35.00	60.00	180	—
Note: Several bust varieties exist for the 1814 issue					
1815GA MR	150	200	350	750	—
1818GA FS	30.00	50.00	75.00	200	—
1821/18GA FS	30.00	50.00	75.00	200	—
1821GA FS	25.00	35.00	60.00	165	—
1821/2GA FS	30.00	50.00	75.00	200	—
1822/1GA FS	30.00	50.00	75.00	200	—
1822GA FS	30.00	50.00	75.00	200	—

Note: Die varieties exist. Early dates are also encountered struck over other types

KM# 147 4 ESCUDOS

13.5400 g., 0.8750 Gold .3809 oz. AGW **Ruler:** Ferdinand VII
Mint: Guadalajara **Obverse:** Uniformed bust of Ferdinand VII

Date	VG	F	VF	XF	Unc
1812GA MR Rare	—	—	—	—	—

KM# 162 8 ESCUDOS

27.0700 g., 0.8750 Gold .7616 oz. AGW **Ruler:** Ferdinand VII **Mint:** Guadalajara **Obverse:** Large uniformed bust of Ferdinand VII

Date	VG	F	VF	XF	Unc
1812GA MR Rare	—	—	—	—	—
1813GA MR	5,250	8,250	12,500	21,000	—

KM# 163 8 ESCUDOS
27.0700 g., 0.8750 Gold .7616 oz. AGW **Ruler:** Ferdinand VII **Mint:** Guadalajara **Obverse:** Small uniformed bust of Ferdinand VII

Date	VG	F	VF	XF	Unc
1813GA MR	10,000	16,000	30,000	45,000	—

Note: Spink America Gerber sale 6-96 VF or better realized $46,200

KM# 161.1 8 ESCUDOS
27.0700 g., 0.8750 Gold .7616 oz. AGW **Ruler:** Ferdinand VII **Mint:** Guadalajara **Obverse:** Undraped bust of Ferdinand VII

Date	VG	F	VF	XF	Unc
1821GA FS	1,200	2,000	4,000	6,500	—

KM# 164 8 ESCUDOS
27.0700 g., 0.8750 Gold .7616 oz. AGW **Ruler:** Ferdinand VII **Mint:** Guadalajara **Obverse:** Draped bust of Ferdinand VII

Date	VG	F	VF	XF	Unc
1821GA FS	5,000	7,500	14,000	23,000	—

GUANAJUATO

The Guanajuato Mint was authorized December 24, 1812 and started production shortly thereafter; closing for unknown reasons on May 15, 1813. The mint was reopened in April, 1821 by the insurgents, who struck coins of the old royal Spanish design to pay their army, even after independence, well into 1822.

Only the 2 and 8 Reales coins were made.

Mint mark: Go.

WAR OF INDEPENDENCE

ROYALIST COINAGE

KM# 93.3 2 REALES
6.7700 g., 0.9030 Silver .1966 oz. ASW **Ruler:** Ferdinand VII **Mint:** Guanajuato **Obverse:** Draped bust of Ferdinand VII

Date	VG	F	VF	XF	Unc
1821Go JM	35.00	65.00	100	185	—
1822Go JM	30.00	50.00	75.00	145	—

KM# 111.4 8 REALES
27.0700 g., 0.9030 Silver .7860 oz. ASW **Ruler:** Ferdinand VII **Mint:** Guanajuato **Obverse:** Draped bust of Ferdinand VII

Date	VG	F	VF	XF	Unc
1812Go JJ	1,250	2,500	—	—	—
1813Go JJ	125	175	275	600	—
1821Go JM	25.00	50.00	75.00	200	—
1822Go JM	20.00	35.00	60.00	185	—

NUEVA GALICIA

(Later became Jalisco State)

In early colonial times, Nueva Galicia was an extensive province which substantially combined later provinces of Zacatecas and Jalisco. These are states of Mexico today although the name was revived during the War of Independence. The only issue was 2 Reales of rather enigmatic origin. No decrees or other authorization to strike this coin has yet been located or reported.

WAR OF INDEPENDENCE

INSURGENT COINAGE

KM# 218 2 REALES
0.9030 Silver **Obverse:** N. G. in center, date **Obv. Legend:** PROVYCIONAL... **Reverse:** 2R in center **Rev. Legend:** ... A. JUNIANA...

Date	Good	VG	F	VF	XF
1813	1,000	2,500	4,500	—	—

Note: Excellent struck counterfeits exist

NUEVA VISCAYA

(Later became Durango State)

This 8 Reales, intended for the province of Nueva Viscaya, was minted in the newly-opened Durango Mint during February and March of 1811, before the regular coinage of Durango was started.

WAR OF INDEPENDENCE

ROYALIST COINAGE

KM# 181 8 REALES
27.0700 g., 0.9030 Silver .7860 oz. ASW **Ruler:** Ferdinand VII **Obverse:** Arms of Durango **Obv. Legend:** MON. PROV. DE NUEV. VIZCAYA **Reverse:** Royal arms

Date	Good	VG	F	VF	XF
1811 RM	1,000	2,250	2,850	5,500	—

Note: Several varieties exist.

OAXACA

The city of Oaxaca was in the midst of a coin shortage when it became apparent the city would be taken by the Insurgents. Royalist forces under Lt. Gen. Saravia had coins made. They were cast in a blacksmith shop. 1/2, 1, and 8 Reales were made only briefly in 1812 before the Royalists surrendered the city.

WAR OF INDEPENDENCE

ROYALIST COINAGE

KM# 166 1/2 REAL
0.9030 Silver **Ruler:** Ferdinand VII **Obverse:** Cross separating castle, lion, Fo, 7o **Reverse:** Legend around shield **Rev. Legend:** PROV. D. OAXACA

Date	Good	VG	F	VF	XF
1812	1,000	1,500	2,500	3,500	—

KM# 167 REAL
0.9030 Silver **Ruler:** Ferdinand VII **Obverse:** Cross separating castle, lion, Fo, 7o **Reverse:** Legend around shield **Rev. Legend:** PROV. D. OAXACA

Date	Good	VG	F	VF	XF
1812	350	650	1,200	2,500	—

KM# 168.5 8 REALES
0.9030 Silver **Ruler:** Ferdinand VII **Obverse:** Countermark O between crowned pillars **Reverse:** Countermark K

Date	Good	VG	F	VF	XF
1812	1,300	1,900	3,300	4,750	—

KM# 168 8 REALES
0.9030 Silver **Obverse:** Cross seperating castle, lion, Fo, 7o **Reverse:** Shield, authorization mark above **Note:** These issues usually display a second mark 'O' between the crowned pillars on the obverse. Varieties of large and small lion in shield also exist.

Date	Good	VG	F	VF	XF
1812 "A"	1,300	1,900	3,300	5,000	—
1812 "B"	1,300	1,900	3,300	5,000	—
1812 "C"	1,300	1,900	3,300	5,000	—
1812 "D"	1,300	1,900	3,300	5,000	—
1812 "K"	1,300	1,900	3,300	5,000	—
1812 "L"	1,300	1,900	3,300	5,000	—
1812 "Mo"	1,300	1,900	3,300	5,000	—
1812 "N"	1,300	1,900	3,300	5,000	—
1812 "O"	1,300	1,900	3,300	5,000	—
1812 "R"	1,300	1,900	3,300	5,000	—
1812 "V"	1,300	1,900	3,300	5,000	—
1812 "Z"	1,300	1,900	3,300	5,000	—

INSURGENT COINAGE

Oaxaca was the hub of Insurgent activity in the south where coinage started in July 1811 and continued until October 1814. The Oaxaca issues represent episodic strikings, usually under dire circumstances by various individuals. Coins were commonly made of copper due to urgency and were intended to be redeemed at face value in gold or silver once silver was available to the Insurgents. Some were later made in silver, but most appear to be of more recent origin, to satisfy collectors.

KM# 219 1/2 REAL
Struck Copper **Issuer:** SUD, Under General Morelos **Obverse:** Bow, arrow, SUD **Reverse:** Morelos monogram Mo, date

Date	Good	VG	F	VF	XF
1811	6.75	11.50	20.00	35.00	—
1812	6.75	11.50	20.00	35.00	—
1813	5.50	9.00	17.50	30.00	—
1814	9.00	16.50	25.00	40.00	—

Note: Uniface strikes exist of #219

KM# 220.1 1/2 REAL
Struck Silver **Issuer:** SUD, Under General Morelos **Obverse:** Bow, arrow, SUD **Reverse:** Morelos monogram Mo, date

Date	Good	VG	F	VF	XF
1811	—	—	—	—	—
1812	—	—	—	—	—
1813	—	—	—	—	—

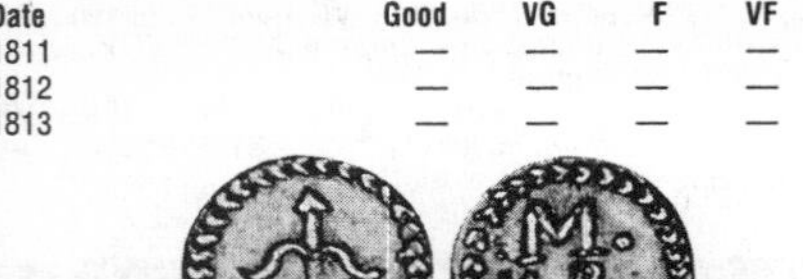

KM# 220.2 1/2 REAL
Struck Silver **Issuer:** SUD, Under General Morelos **Obverse:** Bow, arrow, SUD **Reverse:** Morelos monogram Mo, date

Date	Good	VG	F	VF	XF
1811	—	—	—	—	—
1812	—	—	—	—	—
1813	25.00	50.00	100	150	—

Note: Use caution as silver specimens appear questionable and may be considered spurious

KM# 221 1/2 REAL
Struck Silver **Issuer:** SUD, Under General Morelos **Obverse:** Bow, arrow **Obv. Legend:** PROVICIONAL DE OAXACA **Reverse:** Lion **Rev. Legend:** AMERICA MORELOS

Date	Good	VG	F	VF	XF
1812	35.00	60.00	100	150	—
1813	35.00	60.00	100	150	—

KM# 221a 1/2 REAL
Struck Copper **Issuer:** SUD, Under General Morelos **Obverse:** Bow, arrow **Obv. Legend:** PROVICIONAL DE OAXACA **Reverse:** Lion **Rev. Legend:** AMERICA MORELOS

Date	Good	VG	F	VF	XF
1812	27.50	42.50	70.00	100	—
1813	20.00	35.00	60.00	85.00	—

KM# A222 1/2 REAL
Struck Copper **Issuer:** SUD, Under General Morelos **Obverse:** Similar to KM#220 **Reverse:** Similar to KM#221 but with 1/2 at left of lion **Rev. Legend:** AMERICA MORELOS

Date	Good	VG	F	VF	XF
1813	27.50	42.50	70.00	100	—

KM# 243 1/2 REAL
Struck Copper **Issuer:** Tierra Caliente (Hot Country), Under General Morelos **Obverse:** Bow, T.C., SUD **Reverse:** Morelos monogram, value, date

Date	Good	VG	F	VF	XF
1813	37.50	70.00	125	200	—

KM# 222 REAL
Struck Copper **Issuer:** SUD, Under General Morelos **Obverse:** Bow, arrow, SUD **Reverse:** Morelos monogram, 1 R., date

Date	Good	VG	F	VF	XF
1811	4.75	9.00	18.00	38.00	—
1812	3.75	7.00	14.00	30.00	—
1813	3.75	7.00	14.00	30.00	—

KM# 222a REAL
Struck Silver **Issuer:** SUD, Under General Morelos **Obverse:** Bow, arrow, SUD **Reverse:** Morelos monogram, 1 R., date

Date	Good	VG	F	VF	XF
1812	—	—	—	—	—
1813	—	—	—	—	—

KM# 223 REAL
Cast Silver **Issuer:** SUD, Under General Morelos **Obverse:** Bow, arrow, SUD with floral ornaments **Reverse:** Morelos monogram, 1 R., date

Date	Good	VG	F	VF	XF
1812	—	—	—	—	—
1813	27.50	60.00	115	160	—

Note: Use caution as many silver specimens appear questionable and may be considered spurious

KM# 224 REAL
Struck Copper **Issuer:** SUD, Under General Morelos **Obverse:** Bow, arrow/SUD **Reverse:** Lion **Rev. Legend:** AMERICA MORELOS

Date	Good	VG	F	VF	XF
1813	27.50	42.50	75.00	110	—

KM# 225 REAL
Silver **Issuer:** SUD, Under General Morelos **Obverse:** Bow, arrow/SUD **Reverse:** Lion **Rev. Legend:** AMERICA MORELOS

Date	Good	VG	F	VF	XF
1813 Rare	—	—	—	—	—

KM# 244 REAL
Struck Copper **Issuer:** Tierra Caliente (Hot Country), Under General Morelos **Obverse:** Bow, T.C., SUD **Reverse:** Morelos monogram, value, date

Date	Good	VG	F	VF	XF
1813	13.50	25.00	50.00	80.00	—

KM# 226.1 2 REALES
Struck Copper **Issuer:** SUD, Under General Morelos **Obverse:** Bow, arrow/SUD **Reverse:** Morelos monogram, .2.R., date

Date	Good	VG	F	VF	XF
1811	12.50	25.00	55.00	100	—
1811 inverted 2	15.00	30.00	60.00	120	—
1812	2.50	4.00	6.50	12.00	—
1813	3.00	5.00	8.00	15.00	—
1814	13.50	28.00	65.00	120	—

KM# 226.1a 2 REALES
Struck Silver **Issuer:** SUD, Under General Morelos **Obverse:** Bow, arrow/SUD **Reverse:** Morelos monogram, .2.R., date

Date	Good	VG	F	VF	XF
1812	175	300	500	750	—

KM# 229 2 REALES
Cast Silver **Issuer:** SUD, Under General Morelos **Obverse:** Bow, arrow, SUD **Reverse:** Morelos monogram, value, date in center with ornamentation around

Date	Good	VG	F	VF	XF
1812	60.00	100	150	225	—
1812 Filled in D in SUD	60.00	100	150	225	—

Note: Use caution as many silver specimens appear questionable and may be considered spurious

KM# 245 2 REALES
Struck Copper **Issuer:** Tierra Caliente (Hot Country), Under General Morelos **Obverse:** Bow, T.C., SUD **Reverse:** Morelos monogram, value, date

Date	Good	VG	F	VF	XF
1813	9.00	22.50	35.00	50.00	—

KM# 227 2 REALES
Struck Silver **Issuer:** SUD, Under General Morelos **Obverse:** Bow, arrow **Obv. Legend:** SUD-OXA **Reverse:** Morelos monogram, value, date

Date	Good	VG	F	VF	XF
1813	60.00	100	200	300	—
1814	60.00	100	200	300	—

KM# 226.2 2 REALES
Struck Silver **Issuer:** SUD, Under General Morelos **Obverse:** Three large stars added **Reverse:** Morelos monogram, .2.R., date

Date	Good	VG	F	VF	XF
1814	10.00	20.00	40.00	60.00	—

KM# 246 2 REALES
Struck Copper **Issuer:** Tierra Caliente (Hot Country), Under General Morelos **Obverse:** Bow, T.C., SUD **Reverse:** Morelos monogram, value, date

Date	Good	VG	F	VF	XF
1814	22.50	50.00	100	175	—

KM# 228 2 REALES
Struck Silver **Issuer:** SUD, Under General Morelos **Obverse:** Bow, arrow **Obv. Legend:** SUD. OAXACA **Reverse:** Morelos monogram, value, date

Date	Good	VG	F	VF	XF
1814	60.00	100	200	325	—

KM# 234 8 REALES
Copper **Issuer:** SUD, Under General Morelos **Obverse:** Bow, arrow, SUD in floral ornamentation **Obv. Legend:** SUD-OXA **Reverse:** Morelos monogram, .8.R., date surrounded by ornate flowery fields

Date	Good	VG	F	VF	XF
1811	75.00	125	150	225	—
1812	4.00	6.00	10.00	20.00	—
1813	4.00	6.00	10.00	20.00	—
1814	10.00	15.00	25.00	50.00	—

KM# 234a 8 REALES
Struck Silver **Issuer:** SUD, under General Morelos **Obverse:** Bow, arrow, SUD in floral ornamentation **Reverse:** Morelos monogram, .8.R., date surrounded by ornate flowery fields

Date	Good	VG	F	VF	XF
1811	—	—	2,500	4,000	—
1812	—	—	1,200	2,000	—

KM# 235 8 REALES
Cast Silver **Issuer:** SUD, Under General Morelos **Obverse:** Bow, arrow, SUD in floral ornamentation **Reverse:** Morelos monogram, value, date surrounded by ornate flowery fields

Date	Good	VG	F	VF	XF
1811	—	—	—	—	—
1812	75.00	125	200	350	—
1813	60.00	100	175	300	—
1814	—	—	—	—	—

Note: Most silver specimens available in today's market are considered spurious

KM# 236 8 REALES
0.9030 Struck Silver **Issuer:** SUD, Under General Morelos **Obverse:** M monogram **Obv. Legend:** PROV. D. OAXACA **Reverse:** Lion shield with or without bow above

Date	Good	VG	F	VF	XF
1812 Rare	—	—	—	—	—

KM# 233.1 8 REALES
Copper **Issuer:** SUD, Under General Morelos **Obverse:** Bow, arrow, SUD **Reverse:** Morelos monogram, 8.R., date, plain fields

Date	Good	VG	F	VF	XF
1812	15.00	30.00	60.00	90.00	—

KM# 233.5a 8 REALES
Silver **Issuer:** SUD, Under General Morelos **Obverse:** 8 dots below bow, SUD, plain fields **Reverse:** Morelos monogram, 8.R., date

Date	Good	VG	F	VF	XF
1812	—	—	1,200	2,000	—

KM# 233.1a 8 REALES
Struck Silver **Issuer:** SUD, Under General Morelos **Obverse:** Bow, arrow, SUD **Reverse:** Morelos monogram, 8.R., date, plain fields

Date	Good	VG	F	VF	XF
1812	100	150	250	450	—

KM# 233.2 8 REALES
Copper **Issuer:** SUD, Under General Morelos **Obverse:** Bow, arrow, SUD **Reverse:** Morelos monogram, 8 R, date, plain fields

Date	Good	VG	F	VF	XF
1812	6.00	8.00	12.00	15.00	—
1813	6.00	8.00	12.00	15.00	—
1814	10.00	12.00	15.00	20.00	—

Note: Similar to KM#233.4 but lines below bow slant left

KM# 233.2a 8 REALES
Silver **Issuer:** SUD, Under General Morelos **Obverse:** bow, arrow, SUD **Reverse:** Morelos monogram, 8R, date, plain fields

Date	Good	VG	F	VF	XF
1813	—	—	1,200	2,000	—

KM# 242 8 REALES
Copper **Issuer:** Huautla, Under General Morelos **Obverse:** Legend around bow, arrow/SUD **Obv. Legend:** MONEDA PROVI. CIONAL PS. ES. **Rev. Legend:** FABRICADO EN HUAUTLA

Date	Good	VG	F	VF	XF
1812	1,000	1,500	2,000	—	—

KM# 248 8 REALES
Struck Copper **Issuer:** Tierra Caliente (Hot Country), Under General Morelos **Obverse:** Bow, T.C., SUD **Reverse:** Morelos monogram, value, date

Date	Good	VG	F	VF	XF
1813	9.00	20.00	40.00	75.00	—

KM# 249 8 REALES
Cast Silver **Issuer:** Tierra Caliente (Hot Country), Under General Morelos **Obverse:** Bow, T.C., SUD **Reverse:** Morelos monogram, value, date

Date	Good	VG	F	VF	XF
1813	—	—	—	—	—

Note: Use caution as many silver specimens appear questionable and may be considered spurious

KM# 233.3 8 REALES
Struck Copper **Issuer:** SUD, Under General Morelos **Obverse:** Bow, arrow, SUD, with left slant lines below bow **Reverse:** Morelos monogram, 8.R., date, plain fields

Date	Good	VG	F	VF	XF
1813	10.00	17.50	30.00	50.00	—

KM# 233.4 8 REALES
Struck Copper **Issuer:** SUD, Under General Morelos **Obverse:** Bow, arrow, SUD, with right slant lines below bow **Reverse:** Morelos monogram, 8.R., date, plain fields

Date	Good	VG	F	VF	XF
1813	10.00	17.50	30.00	50.00	—

KM# 237 8 REALES
0.9030 Sterling Silver **Issuer:** SUD, Under General Morelos **Obverse:** M monogram, without legend **Reverse:** Lion shield with or without bow above

Date	Good	VG	F	VF	XF
1813 Rare	—	—	—	—	—

KM# 238 8 REALES
0.9030 Struck Silver **Issuer:** SUD, Under General Morelos **Obverse:** Bow/M/SUD **Reverse:** PROV. DE. ... arms

Date	Good	VG	F	VF	XF
1813 Rare	—	—	—	—	—

KM# 239 8 REALES
Cast Silver **Issuer:** SUD, Under General Morelos **Obverse:** Bow, arrow **Obv. Legend:** SUD-OXA **Reverse:** Morelos monogram

Date	Good	VG	F	VF	XF
1814 Rare	—	—	—	—	—

KM# 240 8 REALES
Copper **Issuer:** SUD, Under General Morelos **Obverse:** Bow, arrow **Obv. Legend:** SUD-OXA **Reverse:** Morelos monogram, 8.R., date

Date	Good	VG	F	VF	XF
1814	35.00	70.00	150	250	—

KM# 241 8 REALES
Copper **Issuer:** SUD, Under General Morelos **Obverse:** Bow, arrow **Obv. Legend:** SUD-OAXACA **Reverse:** Morelos monogram, 8.R., date

Date	Good	VG	F	VF	XF
1814	100	200	350	550	—

PUEBLA

The coins of Puebla emanated from Zacatlan, the headquarters of the hit-and-run Insurgent leader Osorno. The mint opened in April 1812 and operated through 1813.

WAR OF INDEPENDENCE

INSURGENT COINAGE

KM# 250 1/2 REAL
Copper **Issuer:** Zacatlan, struck by General Osorno **Obverse:** Osorno monogram, ZACATLAN, date **Reverse:** Crossed arrows, wreath, value

Date	Good	VG	F	VF	XF
1813 Rare	—	—	—	—	—

KM# 251 REAL
Copper **Issuer:** Zacatlan, struck by General Osorno **Obverse:** Osorno monogram, ZACATLAN, date **Reverse:** Crossed arrows, wreath, value

Date	Good	VG	F	VF	XF
1813	100	150	225	450	—

KM# 252 2 REALES
Copper **Issuer:** Zacatlan, struck by General Osorno **Obverse:** Osorno monogram, ZACATLAN, date **Reverse:** Crossed arrows, wreath, value

Date	Good	VG	F	VF	XF
1813	125	175	275	500	—

REAL DEL CATORCE

(City in San Luis Potosi)

Real del Catorce is an important mining center in the Province of San Luis Potosi. In 1811 an 8 Reales coin was issued under very primitive conditions while the city was still in Royalist hands. Few survive.

WAR OF INDEPENDENCE

ROYALIST COINAGE

KM# 169 8 REALES
0.9030 Silver **Ruler:** Ferdinand VII **Obv. Legend:** EL R. D. CATORC. POR FERNA. VII **Rev. Legend:** MONEDA. PROVISIONAL. VALE. 8R

Date	VG	F	VF	XF	Unc
1811	7,000	15,000	35,000	65,000	—

Note: Spink America Gerber Sale 6-96 VF or XF realized $63,800

SAN FERNANDO DE BEXAR

San Fernando de Bexar, known today as San Antonio, was a military center and capital of the Province of Texas in New Spain. In the early part of the 19th century it experienced a shortage of small denomination coinage, which caused problems with the flow of local trade.

In 1817, Manual Barrera, a local merchant was granted the right by the Governor of the Province to issue small denomination pieces to relieve this problem. No examples of the Barrera tokens resulting from March 20, 1817 decree are known to exist.

Later that year a new Governor was appointed and in 1818 Jose Antonio de la Garza, the city's Postmaster applied for and was granted, by Governor Martinez decree of November 30, 1818, permission to strike and circulate small copper pieces of 1/2 Real denomination. De la Garza was required to redeem any Barrera pieces still in circulation within 12 days, exchanging them for his new copper jolas, to be bonded and to redeem his own pieces on command. The Governor's proclamation of December 6, 1818 made these details known to the public.

It is presumed that all Barrera pieces were destroyed upon redemption. Similarly the tokens of Jose Antonio de la Garza were mostly destroyed after redemption, with most of the few remaining examples being discovered along the banks of the San Antonio River, where de la Garza owned property.

WAR OF INDEPENDENCE

ROYALIST COINAGE

KM# Tn1 1/2 REAL (Jola)

Copper **Ruler:** Ferdinand VII **Note:** Prev. KM#170.

Date	Mintage	Good	VG	F	VF	XF
1818	8,000	350	650	1,250	2,500	—

KM# Tn2 1/2 REAL (Jola)

Copper **Ruler:** Ferdinand VII **Note:** Prev. KM#171.

Date	Good	VG	F	VF	XF
1818	500	750	1,500	3,000	—

SAN LUIS POTOSI

Sierra de Pinos

WAR OF INDEPENDENCE

ROYALIST COINAGE

KM# A172 1/4 REAL

Copper **Ruler:** Ferdinand VII **Issuer:** Sierra de Pinos, Villa

Date	Good	VG	F	VF	XF
1814	75.00	125	200	350	—

KM# A172a 1/4 REAL

Silver **Ruler:** Ferdinand VII

Date	Good	VG	F	VF	XF
1814 Rare	—	—	—	—	—

SOMBRERETE

(Under Royalist Vargas)

The Sombrerete Mint opened on October 8, 1810 in an area that boasted some of the richest mines in Mexico. The mint operated only until July 16, 1811, only to reopen in 1812 and finally close for good at the end of the year. Mines Administrator Fernando Vargas, was also in charge of the coining, all coins bear his name.

WAR OF INDEPENDENCE

ROYALIST COINAGE

KM# 172 1/2 REAL

0.9030 Silver **Ruler:** Ferdinand VII **Obverse:** Legend around crowned globes **Obv. Legend:** FERDIN. VII. SOMBRERETE... **Reverse:** Legend above lys in oval, sprays, date below **Rev. Legend:** VARGAS

Date	Good	VG	F	VF	XF
1811	45.00	70.00	150	250	—
1812	50.00	90.00	175	275	—

KM# 173 REAL

0.9030 Silver **Ruler:** Ferdinand VII **Obverse:** Legend around crowned globes **Obv. Legend:** FERDIN. VII. SOMBRERETE... **Reverse:** Legend above lys in oval with denomination flanking, sprays, date below **Rev. Legend:** VARGAS

Date	Good	VG	F	VF	XF
1811	45.00	70.00	150	250	—
	Note: For 1811, denomination reads as '1R' or 'R1'				
1812	50.00	90.00	175	275	—

KM# 174 2 REALES

0.9030 Silver **Ruler:** Ferdinand VII **Countermark:** VARGAS **Obverse:** Royal arms **Obv. Legend:** R.CAXA. DE. SOMBRERETE **Reverse:** 1811, S between crowned pillars

Date	Good	VG	F	VF	XF
1811 SE	100	250	450	700	—

KM# 175 4 REALES

0.9030 Silver **Ruler:** Ferdinand VII **Obverse:** Crowned Royal arms **Obv. Legend:** R. CAXA. DE. SOMBRERETE **Reverse:** Large legend **Rev. Legend:** VARGAS/1811 **Note:** Prev. KM#172.

Date	Good	VG	F	VF	XF
1812	50.00	100	200	450	—

KM# 176 8 REALES

0.9030 Silver **Ruler:** Ferdinand VII **Countermark:** VARGAS, date, S **Obverse:** Royal arms **Obv. Legend:** R. CAXA. DE SOMBRERETE **Reverse:** Several countermarks between crowned pillars

Date	Good	VG	F	VF	XF
1810	1,000	1,750	2,750	4,000	—
1811	225	325	450	600	—

KM# 177 8 REALES

0.9030 Silver **Ruler:** Ferdinand VII **Obverse:** Crowned Royal arms **Obv. Legend:** R. CAXA. DE SOMBRETE **Rev. Legend:** VARGAS/date/3, S between crowned pillars

Date	Good	VG	F	VF	XF
1811	125	185	245	500	—
1812	125	175	225	475	—

VALLADOLID MICHOACAN

(Now Morelia)

Valladolid, capitol of Michoacan province, was a strategically important center for military thrusts into the adjoining provinces. The Royalists made every effort to retain the position. In 1813, with the advance of the insurgent forces, it became apparent that to maintain the position would be very difficult. During 1813 it was necessary to make coins in the city due to lack of traffic with other areas. These were made only briefly before the city fell and were also used by the insurgents with appropriate countermarks.

WAR OF INDEPENDENCE

ROYALIST COINAGE

KM# 178 8 REALES

0.9030 Silver **Ruler:** Ferdinand VII **Obverse:** Royal arms in wreath, value at sides **Reverse:** PROVISIONAL/DE VALLADOLID/1813

Date	Good	VG	F	VF	XF
1813 Rare	—	—	—	—	—

KM# 179 8 REALES

0.9030 Silver **Ruler:** Ferdinand VII **Obverse:** Bust **Obv. Legend:** FERDIN. VII. **Reverse:** Arms, pillars, P. D. V. in legend

Date	Good	VG	F	VF	XF
1813 Rare	—	—	—	—	—

Note: Spink America Gerber sale 6-96 good realized $23,100

VERACRUZ

In Zongolica, in the province of Veracruz, 2 priests and a lawyer decided to raise an army to fight for independence. Due to isolation from other Insurgent forces, they decided to make their own coins. Records show that they intended to mint coins of 1/2, 1, 2, 4, and 8 Reales, but specimens are extant of only the three higher denominations.

WAR OF INDEPENDENCE

INSURGENT COINAGE

KM# 253 2 REALES

0.9030 Silver **Issuer:** Zongolica **Obverse:** Bow and arrow **Obv. Legend:** VIVA FERNANDO VII Y AMERICA **Reverse:** Value, crossed palm branch, sword, date **Rev. Legend:** ZONGOLICA

Date	Good	VG	F	VF	XF
1812	85.00	175	300	500	—

KM# 255 8 REALES

0.9030 Silver **Issuer:** Zongolica **Obverse:** Bow and arrow **Obv. Legend:** VIVA FERNANDO VII Y AMERICA **Reverse:** Value, crossed palm branch, sword, date **Rev. Legend:** ZONGOLICA **Note:** Similar to 2 Reales, KM#253.

Date	Good	VG	F	VF	XF
1812 Rare	—	—	—	—	—

Note: Spink America Gerber sale 6-96 VF to XF realized $57,200

INSURGENT COUNTERMARKED COINAGE

GENERAL VICENTE GUERRERO

The countermark of an eagle facing left within a pearled oval has been attributed by some authors as that of General Vicente Guerrero, a leader of the insurgents in the south, 1816-1821.

KM# 276 1/2 REAL
Silver **Issuer:** General Vicente Guerrero **Countermark:** Eagle **Note:** Countermark on Mexico City KM#72.

CM Date	Host Date	Good	VG	F	VF	XF
ND	ND	40.00	60.00	80.00	175	—

KM# 277 REAL
Silver **Issuer:** General Vicente Guerrero **Countermark:** Eagle **Note:** Countermark on Mexico City KM#78.

CM Date	Host Date	Good	VG	F	VF	XF
ND	1772 FM	35.00	50.00	75.00	165	—

KM# 278.1 2 REALES
Silver **Issuer:** General Vicente Guerrero **Countermark:** Eagle **Note:** Countermark on Mexico City KM#88.

CM Date	Host Date	Good	VG	F	VF	XF
ND	1784 FM	40.00	60.00	100	225	—
ND	1798	40.00	60.00	100	225	—

KM# 278.2 2 REALES
Silver **Issuer:** General Vicente Guerrero **Countermark:** Eagle **Note:** Countermark on Mexico City KM#91.

CM Date	Host Date	Good	VG	F	VF	XF
ND	1807 PJ	30.00	50.00	80.00	200	—

KM# 279 8 REALES
Silver **Issuer:** General Vicente Guerrero **Countermark:** Eagle **Note:** Countermark on Zacatecas KM#191.

CM Date	Host Date	Good	VG	F	VF	XF
ND	1811	100	150	200	350	—

ZMY

KM# 286 8 REALES
Silver **Issuer:** Unknown, presumed insurgent **Countermark:** ZMY **Note:** Countermark on Zacatecas KM#191.

CM Date	Host Date	Good	VG	F	VF	XF
ND	1812	100	150	200	350	—

CONGRESS OF CHILPANZINGO

Type A: Hand holding bow and arrow between quiver with arrows, sword and bow.

Type B: Crowned eagle on bridge.

KM# 256.1 1/2 REAL
Silver **Issuer:** Congress of Chilpanzingo **Countermark:** Type A hand holding bow and arrow between quiver with arrows, sword and bow **Note:** Countermark on cast Mexico City KM#72.

CM Date	Host Date	Good	VG	F	VF	XF
ND	1812	42.50	70.00	90.00	120	—

KM# 256.2 1/2 REAL
Silver **Issuer:** Congress of Chilpanzingo **Countermark:** Type A hand holding bow and arrow between quiver with arrows, sword and bow **Note:** Countermark on Zacatecas KM#181.

CM Date	Host Date	Good	VG	F	VF	XF
ND	1811	50.00	75.00	100	125	—

KM# A257 REAL
Cast Silver **Issuer:** Congress of Chilpanzingo **Countermark:** Type A hand holding bow and arrow between quiver with arrows, sword and bow **Note:** Countermark on cast Mexico City KM#81.

CM Date	Host Date	Good	VG	F	VF	XF
ND	1803	18.50	30.00	50.00	80.00	—

KM# 257.1 2 REALES
Silver **Issuer:** Congress of Chilpanzingo **Countermark:** Type B crowned eagle on bridge **Note:** Countermark on 1/4 cut of 8 Reales.

CM Date	Host Date	Good	VG	F	VF	XF
	ND Unique	—	—	—	—	—

KM# 257.2 2 REALES
Silver **Issuer:** Congress of Chilpanzingo **Countermark:** Type B crowned eagle on bridge **Note:** Countermark on Zacatecas KM#186.

CM Date	Host Date	Good	VG	F	VF	XF
ND	1811 Unique	—	—	—	—	—

KM# 258.1 8 REALES
Silver **Issuer:** Congress of Chilpanzingo **Countermark:** Type A hand holding bow and arrow between quiver with arrows, sword and bow **Note:** Countermark on cast Mexico City KM#109.

CM Date	Host Date	Good	VG	F	VF	XF
ND	1805	45.00	65.00	85.00	125	—

Note: A countermark appears on coins dated 1805 TH

KM# 258.2 8 REALES
Silver **Issuer:** Congress of Chilpanzingo **Countermark:** Type A hand holding bow and arrow between quiver with arrows, sword and bow **Note:** Countermark on cast Mexico City KM#110.

CM Date	Host Date	Good	VG	F	VF	XF
ND	1810 HJ	50.00	75.00	100	150	—

KM# 258.3 8 REALES
Silver **Issuer:** Congress of Chilpanzingo **Countermark:** Type A hand holding bow and arrow between quiver with arrows, sword and bow **Note:** Countermark on cast Mexico City KM#111.

CM Date	Host Date	Good	VG	F	VF	XF
ND	1811 HJ	45.00	65.00	85.00	125	—
ND	1812 HJ	100	125	175	275	—

KM# 259.1 8 REALES
Silver **Issuer:** Congress of Chilpanzingo **Countermark:** Type B crowned eagle on bridge **Note:** Countermark on Chihuahua KM#111.1.

CM Date	Host Date	Good	VG	F	VF	XF
ND	1816 RP	200	250	300	350	—

KM# 259.2 8 REALES
Silver **Issuer:** Congress of Chilpanzingo **Countermark:** Type B crowned eagle on bridge **Note:** Countermark on cast Mexico City KM#111.

CM Date	Host Date	Good	VG	F	VF	XF
ND	1811 HJ	130	140	150	175	—

KM# 259.3 8 REALES
Silver **Issuer:** Congress of Chilpanzingo **Countermark:** Type B crowned eagle on bridge **Note:** Countermark on Valladolid KM#178.

CM Date	Host Date	Good	VG	F	VF	XF
ND	1813	1,000	2,000	3,000	5,000	—

KM# 259.4 8 REALES
Silver **Issuer:** Congress of Chilpanzingo **Countermark:** Type B crowned eagle on bridge **Note:** Countermark on Zacatecas KM#190.

CM Date	Host Date	Good	VG	F	VF	XF
ND	1810	400	500	600	750	—

DON JOSE MARIA DE LINARES

KM# 263.1 8 REALES
Silver **Issuer:** Don Jose Maria De Linares **Countermark:** LINA/RES* **Note:** Countermark on Mexico City KM#110.

CM Date	Host Date	Good	VG	F	VF	XF
ND	1808 TH	250	300	375	500	—

KM# 263.2 8 REALES
Silver **Issuer:** Don Jose Maria De Linares **Countermark:** LINA/RES * **Note:** Countermark on Zacatecas KM#190.

CM Date	Host Date	Good	VG	F	VF	XF
ND	1811	300	375	450	575	—

KM# 263.3 8 REALES
Silver **Issuer:** Don Jose Maria De Linares **Countermark:** LINA/RES* **Note:** Countermark on Zacatecas KM#191.

CM Date	Host Date	Good	VG	F	VF	XF
ND	1812	250	300	375	500	—

ENSAIE

KM# 260.3 8 REALES
Silver **Issuer:** Ensaie **Countermark:** Eagle over ENSAIE, crude sling below **Note:** Countermark on Zacatecas KM#190.

CM Date	Host Date	Good	VG	F	VF	XF
ND	1810	—	—	—	—	—
ND	1811	100	150	200	300	—

KM# 260.4 8 REALES
Silver **Issuer:** Ensaie **Countermark:** Eagle over ENSAIE, crude sling below **Note:** Countermark on Zacatecas KM#191.

CM Date	Host Date	Good	VG	F	VF	XF
ND	1810	500	700	900	1,200	—
ND	1811	250	300	375	500	—
ND	1812	200	250	285	400	—

KM# 260.1 8 REALES
Silver **Issuer:** Ensaie **Countermark:** Eagle over ENSAIE, crude sling below **Note:** Countermark on Mexico City KM#110.

CM Date	Host Date	Good	VG	F	VF	XF
ND	1811 HJ	150	200	275	350	—

KM# 260.2 8 REALES
Silver **Issuer:** Ensaie **Countermark:** Eagle over ENSAIE, crude sling below **Note:** Countermark on Zacatecas KM#189.

CM Date	Host Date	Good	VG	F	VF	XF
ND	1811	200	400	600	800	—

JOSE MARIA LICEAGA

J.M.L. with banner on cross, crossed olive branches.

(J.M.L./V., D.s, S.M., S.Y.S.L., Ve, A.P., s.r.a., Sea, P.G., S., S.M., El)

KM# A260 1/2 REAL
Silver **Issuer:** Jose Maria Liceaga **Countermark:** JML/SM with banner on cross, crossed olive branches **Note:** Countermark on cast Mexico City 1/2 Real.

CM Date	Host Date	Good	VG	F	VF	XF
ND	ND	100	150	200	275	—

KM# 261.6 2 REALES
Silver **Issuer:** Jose Maria Liceaga **Countermark:** J.M.L./V. with banner on cross, crossed olive branches **Note:** Countermark on Zacatecas KM#187.

CM Date	Host Date	Good	VG	F	VF	XF
ND	1811	200	225	250	300	—

KM# 261.7 2 REALES
Silver **Issuer:** Jose Maria Liceaga **Countermark:** J.M.L./DS with banner on cross, crossed olive branches **Note:** Countermark on Zacatecas KM#187.

CM Date	Host Date	Good	VG	F	VF	XF
ND	1811	200	235	275	325	—

KM# 261.8 2 REALES
Silver **Issuer:** Jose Maria Liceaga **Countermark:** J.M.L./S.M. with banner on cross, crossed olive branches **Note:** Countermark on Zacatecas KM#187.

CM Date	Host Date	Good	VG	F	VF	XF
ND	1811	200	235	275	325	—

KM# 261.9 2 REALES
Silver **Issuer:** Jose Maria Liceaga **Countermark:** J.M.L./S.Y. with banner on cross, crossed olive branches **Note:** Countermark on Zacatecas KM#187.

CM Date	Host Date	Good	VG	F	VF	XF
ND	1811	200	235	275	325	—

KM# 261.1 2 REALES
Silver **Issuer:** Jose Maria Liceaga **Countermark:** J.M.L./Ve with banner on cross, crossed olive branches **Note:** Countermark on 1/4 cut of 8 Reales.

CM Date	Host Date	Good	VG	F	VF	XF
ND	ND	175	225	300	—	—

KM# 261.2 2 REALES
Silver **Issuer:** Jose Maria Liceaga **Countermark:** J.M.L./V with banner on cross, crossed olive branchs **Note:** Countermark on Zacatecas KM#186.

CM Date	Host Date	Good	VG	F	VF	XF
ND	1811	200	225	250	300	—

KM# 261.3 2 REALES
Silver **Issuer:** Jose Maria Liceaga **Countermark:** J.M.L./DS with banner on cross, crossed olive branches **Note:** Countermark on Zacatecas KM#186.

CM Date	Host Date	Good	VG	F	VF	XF
ND	1811	200	235	275	325	—

KM# 261.4 2 REALES
Silver **Issuer:** Jose Maria Liceaga **Countermark:** J.M.L./S.M. with banner on cross, crossed olive branches **Note:** Countermark on Zacatecas KM#186.

CM Date	Host Date	Good	VG	F	VF	XF
ND	1811	200	235	275	325	—

KM# 261.5 2 REALES
Silver **Issuer:** Jose Maria Liceaga **Countermark:** J.M.L./S.Y. with banner on cross, crossed olive branches **Note:** Countermark on Zacatecas KM#186.

CM Date	Host Date	Good	VG	F	VF	XF
ND	1811	200	235	275	325	—

KM# 262.1 8 REALES
Silver **Issuer:** Jose Maria Liceaga **Countermark:** J.M.L./D.S. with banner on cross, crossed olive branches **Note:** Countermark on Zacatecas KM#190.

CM Date	Host Date	Good	VG	F	VF	XF
ND	1811	250	325	425	550	—

KM# 262.4 8 REALES
Silver **Issuer:** Jose Maria Liceaga **Countermark:** J.M.L./S.F. with banner on cross, crossed olive branches **Note:** Countermark on Zacatecas KM#190.

CM Date	Host Date	Good	VG	F	VF	XF
ND	1811	200	275	375	525	—

KM# 262.2 8 REALES
Silver **Issuer:** Jose Maria Liceaga **Countermark:** J.M.L./E with banner on cross, crossed olive branches **Note:** Countermark on Zacatecas KM#190.

CM Date	Host Date	Good	VG	F	VF	XF
ND	1811	225	300	400	550	—

KM# 262.3 8 REALES
Silver **Issuer:** Jose Maria Liceaga **Countermark:** J.M.L./P.G. with banner on cross, crossed olive branches **Note:** Countermark on Durango KM#111.2.

CM Date	Host Date	Good	VG	F	VF	XF
ND	1813 RM	200	275	375	525	—

KM# 262.5 8 REALES
Silver **Issuer:** Jose Maria Liceaga **Countermark:** J.M.L./S.M. with banner on cross, crossed olive branches **Note:** Countermark on Zacatecas KM#190.

CM Date	Host Date	Good	VG	F	VF	XF
ND	1811	200	275	375	525	—

KM# 262.6 8 REALES
Silver **Issuer:** Jose Maria Liceaga **Countermark:** J.M.L./V.E. with banner on cross, cross olive branches **Note:** Countermark on Zacatecas KM#190.

CM Date	Host Date	Good	VG	F	VF	XF
ND	1811	200	275	375	525	—

L.V.S. - LABOR VINCIT SEMPER

Some authorities believe L.V.S. is for La Villa de Sombrerete.

KM# 264.1 8 REALES
Cast Silver **Issuer:** Labor Vincit Semper, Some authorities believe L.V.S. is for "La Villa de Sombrerete" **Countermark:** L.V.S. **Note:** Countermark on Chihuahua KM#123.

CM Date	Host Date	Good	VG	F	VF	XF
ND	1811 RP	275	350	450	550	—
ND	1812 RP	200	250	300	375	—

KM# 264.2 8 REALES

Silver **Issuer:** Labor Vincit Semper, Some authorities believe L.V.S. is for "La Villa de Sombrerete" **Countermark:** L.V.S. **Note:** Countermark on Chihuahua KM#111.1 overstruck on KM#123.

CM Date	Host Date	Good	VG	F	VF	XF
ND	1816 RP	250	300	325	375	—
ND	1817 RP	250	300	325	375	—
ND	1818 RP	250	300	325	375	—
ND	1819 RP	400	450	500	600	—
ND	1820 RP	450	500	550	650	—

KM# 264.3 8 REALES

Silver **Issuer:** Labor Vincit Semper, Some authorities believe L.V.S. is for "La Villa de Sombrerete" **Countermark:** L.V.S. **Note:** Countermark on Guadalajara KM#111.3.

CM Date	Host Date	Good	VG	F	VF	XF
ND	1817	185	220	250	310	—

KM# 264.4 8 REALES

Silver **Issuer:** Labor Vincit Semper, Some authorities believe L.V.S. is for "La Villa de Sombrerete" **Countermark:** L.V.S. **Note:** Countermark on Nueva Vizcaya KM#165.

CM Date	Host Date	Good	VG	F	VF	XF
ND	1811 RM	1,150	3,150	5,250	8,250	—

KM# 264.5 8 REALES

Silver **Issuer:** Labor Vincit Semper, Some authorities believe L.V.S. is for "La Villa de Sombrerete" **Countermark:** L.V.S. **Note:** Countermark on Sombrerete KM#177.

CM Date	Host Date	Good	VG	F	VF	XF
ND	1811	300	350	450	550	—
ND	1812	300	350	450	550	—

KM# 264.6 8 REALES

Silver **Issuer:** Labor Vincit Semper, Some authorities believe L.V.S. is for "La Villa de Sombrerete" **Countermark:** L.V.S. **Note:** Countermark on Zacatecas KM#190.

CM Date	Host Date	Good	VG	F	VF	XF
ND	1811	350	400	450	550	—

KM# 264.7 8 REALES

Silver **Issuer:** Labor Vincit Semper, Some authorities believe L.V.S. is for "La Villa de Sombrerete" **Countermark:** L.V.S. **Note:** Countermark on Zacatecas KM#192.

CM Date	Host Date	Good	VG	F	VF	XF
ND	1813	350	400	450	550	—

MORELOS

Morelos monogram

Type A: Stars above and below monogram in circle.

Type B: Dots above and below monogram in oval.

Type C: Monogram in rectangle.

Note: Many specimens of Type C available in todays market are considered spurious.

KM# A265 2 REALES

Copper **Issuer:** Morelos **Countermark:** Type A stars above and below monogram in circle **Note:** Countermark on Oaxaca Sud, KM#226.1.

CM Date	Host Date	Good	VG	F	VF	XF
ND	1812	—	—	—	—	—

KM# A267 8 REALES

Silver **Note:** Countermark Type C on Zacatecas KM#189-190.

CM Date	Host Date	Good	VG	F	VF	XF
ND	ND	300	350	425	650	—

KM# 265.1 8 REALES

Silver **Issuer:** Morelos **Countermark:** Type A star above and below monogram in circle **Note:** Countermark on Mexico City KM#109.

CM Date	Host Date	Good	VG	F	VF	XF
ND	1797 FM	45.00	50.00	60.00	85.00	—
ND	1798 FM	45.00	50.00	60.00	85.00	—
ND	1800 FM	45.00	50.00	60.00	85.00	—
ND	1807 TH	45.00	50.00	60.00	85.00	—

KM# 265.2 8 REALES

Silver **Issuer:** Morelos **Countermark:** Type A stars above and below monogram in circle **Note:** Countermark on Mexico City KM#110.

CM Date	Host Date	Good	VG	F	VF	XF
ND	1809 TH	55.00	65.00	85.00	120	—
ND	1811 HJ	55.00	65.00	85.00	120	—

KM# 265.3 8 REALES

Silver **Issuer:** Morelos **Countermark:** Type A stars above and below monogram in circle **Note:** Countermark on Mexico City KM#111.

CM Date	Host Date	Good	VG	F	VF	XF
ND	1812 JJ	50.00	60.00	75.00	110	—

KM# 265.5 8 REALES

Cast Silver **Issuer:** Morelos **Countermark:** Type A stars above and below monogram in circle **Note:** Countermark on Supreme National Congress KM#206.

CM Date	Host Date	Good	VG	F	VF	XF
ND	1811	200	250	375	600	—

KM# 266.1 8 REALES

Silver **Issuer:** Morelos **Countermark:** Type B dots above and below monogram in oval **Note:** Countermark on Guatamala 8 Reales, C#67.

CM Date	Host Date	Good	VG	F	VF	XF
ND	1810 M Rare	—	—	—	—	—

KM# 266.2 8 REALES

Silver **Issuer:** Morelos **Countermark:** Type B dots above and below monogram in oval **Note:** Countermark on Mexico City KM#110.

CM Date	Host Date	Good	VG	F	VF	XF
ND	1809 TH	45.00	55.00	65.00	90.00	—

KM# 267.1 8 REALES

Silver **Issuer:** Morelos **Countermark:** Type C monogram in rectangle **Note:** Countermark on Zacatecas KM#189. Many specimens of Type C available in today's market are considered spurious.

CM Date	Host Date	Good	VG	F	VF	XF
ND	1811	300	350	425	650	—

KM# 265.4 8 REALES

Copper **Issuer:** Morelos **Countermark:** Type A stars above and below monogram in circle **Note:** Countermark on Oaxaca Sud KM#233.2.

CM Date	Host Date	Good	VG	F	VF	XF
ND	1812	12.50	17.50	25.00	40.00	—
ND	1813	12.50	17.50	25.00	40.00	—
ND	1814	12.50	17.50	25.00	40.00	—

KM# 265.6 8 REALES

Silver **Issuer:** Morelos **Countermark:** Type A stars above and below monogram in circle **Note:** Countermark on Zacatecas KM#190.

CM Date	Host Date	Good	VG	F	VF	XF
ND	1811	200	250	375	600	—

KM# 265.7 8 REALES

Silver **Issuer:** Morelos **Countermark:** Type A stars above and below monogram in circle **Note:** Countermark on Zacatecas KM#191.

CM Date	Host Date	Good	VG	F	VF	XF
ND	1811	200	250	375	600	—

KM# 267.2 8 REALES

Silver **Issuer:** Morelos **Countermark:** Type C: monogram in rectangle **Note:** Countermark Type C on Zacatecas KM#190. Many specimens of Type C available in today's market are considered spurious.

CM Date	Host Date	Good	VG	F	VF	XF
ND	1811	300	350	425	650	—

NORTE

Issued by the Supreme National Congress and the Army of the North.

Countermark: Eagle on cactus; star to left; NORTE below.

KM# 268 1/2 REAL

Silver **Issuer:** Supreme National Congress and the Army of the North **Countermark:** Eagle on cactus; star to left; NORTE below **Note:** Countermark on Zacatecas KM#180.

CM Date	Host Date	Good	VG	F	VF	XF
ND	1811	250	300	375	450	—

KM# 269 2 REALES
Silver **Issuer:** Supreme National Congress and the Army of the North **Countermark:** Eagle on cactus; star to left; NORTE below **Note:** Countermark on Zacatecas KM#187.

CM Date	Host Date	Good	VG	F	VF	XF
ND	1811	225	275	325	400	—

KM# A269 2 REALES
Silver **Issuer:** Supreme National Congress and the Army of the North **Countermark:** Eagle on cactus; star to left; NORTE below **Note:** Countermark on Zacatecas KM#188.

CM Date	Host Date	Good	VG	F	VF	XF
ND	1812	—	—	—	—	—

KM# B269 4 REALES
Silver **Issuer:** Supreme National Congress and the Army of the North **Countermark:** Eagle on cactus; star to left; NORTE below **Note:** Countermark on Sombrerete KM#175.

CM Date	Host Date	Good	VG	F	VF	XF
ND	1812	100	150	200	275	—

KM# 270.4 8 REALES
Silver **Issuer:** Supreme National Congress and the Army of the North **Countermark:** Eagle on cactus; star to left; NORTE below **Note:** Countermark on Zacatecas KM#191.

CM Date	Host Date	Good	VG	F	VF	XF
ND	1811	200	300	400	550	—
ND	1811	200	300	400	550	—
ND	1812	200	300	400	550	—

KM# 270.1 8 REALES
Silver **Issuer:** Supreme National Congress and the Army of the North **Countermark:** Eagle on cactus; star to left; NORTE below **Note:** Countermark on Chihuahua KM#111.1.

CM Date	Host Date	Good	VG	F	VF	XF
ND	1813 RP	250	350	450	550	—

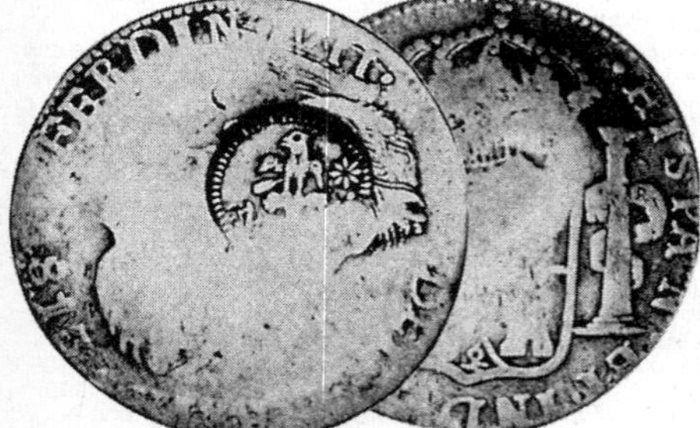

KM# 270.2 8 REALES
Silver **Issuer:** Supreme National Congress and the Army of the North **Countermark:** Eagle on cactus; star to left; NORTE below **Note:** Countermark on Guanajuato KM#111.4.

CM Date	Host Date	Good	VG	F	VF	XF
ND	1813 JM	400	550	700	800	—

KM# 270.3 8 REALES
Silver **Issuer:** Supreme National Congress and the Army of the North **Countermark:** Eagle on cactus; star to left; NORTE below **Note:** Countermark on Zacatecas KM#190.

CM Date	Host Date	Good	VG	F	VF	XF
ND	1811	300	400	500	650	—

OSORNO

Countermark: Osorno monogram. (Jose Francisco Osorno)

KM# 271.1 1/2 REAL
Silver **Issuer:** Jose Francisco Osorno **Countermark:** Osorno monogram **Note:** Countermark on Mexico City KM#72.

CM Date	Host Date	Good	VG	F	VF	XF
ND	1798 FM	65.00	100	150	200	—
ND	1802 FT	65.00	100	150	200	—
ND	1806	65.00	100	150	200	—

KM# 271.2 1/2 REAL
Silver **Issuer:** Jose Francisco Osorno **Countermark:** Osorno monogram **Note:** Countermark on Mexico City KM#73.

CM Date	Host Date	Good	VG	F	VF	XF
ND	1809 TH	65.00	100	150	200	—

KM# 272.1 REAL
Silver **Issuer:** Jose Francisco Osorno **Countermark:** Osorno monogram **Note:** Countermark on Mexico City KM#81.

CM Date	Host Date	Good	VG	F	VF	XF
ND	1803 FT	65.00	100	150	200	—

KM# 272.2 REAL
Silver **Issuer:** Jose Francisco Osorno **Countermark:** Osorno monogram **Note:** Countermark on Potosi KM#70.

CM Date	Host Date	Good	VG	F	VF	XF
ND	ND	75.00	115	175	250	—

KM# 272.3 REAL
Silver **Issuer:** Jose Francisco Osorno **Countermark:** Osorno monogram **Note:** Countermark on Guatemala KM#54.

CM Date	Host Date	Good	VG	F	VF	XF
ND	1804	75.00	115	175	250	—

KM# A272.1 2 REALES
Silver **Issuer:** Jose Francisco Osorno **Countermark:** Osorno monogram **Note:** Countermark on Mexico City KM#88.2.

CM Date	Host Date	Good	VG	F	VF	XF
ND	1788 FM	75.00	125	175	250	—

KM# A272.2 2 REALES
Silver **Issuer:** Jose Francisco Osorno **Countermark:** Osorno monogram **Note:** Countermark on Mexico City KM#91.

CM Date	Host Date	Good	VG	F	VF	XF
ND	1808 TH	75.00	125	175	250	—

KM# A272.3 2 REALES
Silver **Issuer:** Jose Francisco Osorno **Countermark:** Osorno monogram **Note:** Countermark on Mexico City KM#92.

CM Date	Host Date	Good	VG	F	VF	XF
ND	1809 TH	75.00	125	175	250	—

KM# A272.4 2 REALES
Silver **Issuer:** Jose Francisco Osorno **Countermark:** Osorno monogram **Note:** Countermark on Zacatlian KM#252.

CM Date	Host Date	Good	VG	F	VF	XF
ND	1813	150	200	300	400	—

KM# 273.1 4 REALES
Silver **Issuer:** Jose Francisco Osorno **Countermark:** Osorno monogram **Note:** Countermark on Mexico City KM#97.2.

CM Date	Host Date	Good	VG	F	VF	XF
ND	1782 FF	85.00	150	200	275	—

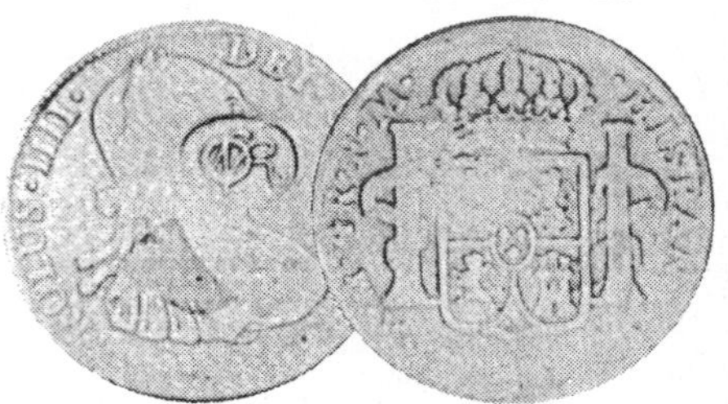

KM# 273.2 4 REALES
Silver **Issuer:** Jose Francisco Osorno **Countermark:** Osorno monogram **Note:** Countermark on Mexico City KM#100.

CM Date	Host Date	Good	VG	F	VF	XF
ND	1799 FM	85.00	150	200	275	—

KM# 274.1 8 REALES
Silver **Issuer:** Jose Francisco Osorno **Countermark:** Osorno monogram **Note:** Countermark on Lima 8 Reales, C#101.

CM Date	Host Date	Good	VG	F	VF	XF
ND	1811 JP	200	225	250	300	—

KM# 274.2 8 REALES
Silver **Issuer:** Jose Francisco Osorno **Countermark:** Osorno monogram **Note:** Countermark on Mexico City KM#110.

CM Date	Host Date	Good	VG	F	VF	XF
ND	1809 TH	125	150	225	300	—
ND	1810 HJ	125	150	225	300	—
ND	1811 HJ	125	150	225	300	—

VILLA / GRAN

(Julian Villagran)

KM# 298 2 REALES
Cast Silver , Julian Villagran **Countermark:** VILLA/GRAN **Note:** Countermark on cast Mexico City KM#91.

CM Date	Host Date	Good	VG	F	VF	XF
ND	1799 FM	150	200	250	350	—
ND	1802 FT	150	200	250	350	—

KM# 275 8 REALES
Cast Silver **Issuer:** Julian Villagran **Countermark:** VILLA/GRAN **Note:** Countermark on cast Mexico City KM#109.

CM Date	Host Date	Good	VG	F	VF	XF
ND	1796 FM	200	250	300	400	—
ND	1806 TH	200	250	300	400	—

COUNTERMARKED COINAGE

MULTIPLE COUNTERMARKS

Many combinations of Royalist and Insurgent countermarks are usually found on the cast copies produced by Chihuahua and Mexico City and on the other crude provisional issues of this period. Struck Mexico City coins were used to make molds for casting necessity issues and countermarked afterwards to show issuing authority. Some were marked again by either both or separate opposing friendly forces to authorize circulation in their areas of occupation. Some countermarks are only obtainable with companion markings.

KM# 289 2 REALES
Silver **Issuer:** C.M.S. and S.C.M. **Countermark:** C.M.S. (Comandancia Militar Suriana) and eagle with S.C.M. (Soberano Congreso Mexicano) **Note:** Countermark on Mexico City KM#91.

CM Date	Host Date	Good	VG	F	VF	XF
ND	ND	—	—	—	—	—

KM# 295 2 REALES
Silver **Issuer:** Militar del Sur and Soberano Congreso Mexicano **Countermark:** M.d.S. and eagle with S.C.M **Note:** Countermark on Mexico City KM#91.

CM Date	Host Date	Good	VG	F	VF	XF
ND	ND	150	250	450	—	—

KM# 296 2 REALES
Silver **Issuer:** Jose Francisco Osorno and Julian Villagran **Countermark:** Osorno monogram and VILLA/GRAN **Note:** Countermark on cast Mexico City KM#110.

CM Date	Host Date	Good	VG	F	VF	XF
ND	1809 TH	—	—	—	—	—

KM# A286 2 REALES
Silver **Issuer:** Jose Maria Liceaga and VTIL **Countermark:** J.M.L./D.S. AND VTIL **Note:** Countermark on Zacatecas KM#186.

CM Date	Host Date	Good	VG	F	VF	XF
ND	1811	75.00	125	175	250	—

KM# B286 2 REALES
Silver **Issuer:** Jose Maria Liceaga and VTIL **Countermark:** J.M.L./V.E. and VTIL **Note:** Countermark on Zacatecas KM#186.

CM Date	Host Date	Good	VG	F	VF	XF
ND	1810	75.00	125	175	250	—
ND	1811	75.00	125	175	250	—

KM# 285.2 8 REALES
Silver **Issuer:** Chilpanzingo and Morelos **Countermark:** Chilpanzingo Type A and Morelos monogram Type A **Note:** Countermark on cast Mexico City KM#110.

CM Date	Host Date	Good	VG	F	VF	XF
ND	1810 HJ	35.00	45.00	60.00	140	—
ND	1811 HJ	35.00	45.00	60.00	140	—

KM# C286 8 REALES
Silver **Issuer:** Chilpanzingo and Morelos and LVS **Countermark:** Chilpanzingo Type A, Morelos Type A and LVS monogram on cast Mexico City KM#110

CM Date	Host Date	Good	VG	F	VF	XF
ND	1809 HJ	50.00	75.00	125	275	—

KM# A298 8 REALES
Silver **Issuer:** S.J.N.G. and VTIL **Countermark:** S.J.N.G and VTIL on Zacatecas KM#191

CM Date	Host Date	Good	VG	F	VF	XF
ND	ND	35.00	50.00	75.00	200	—

KM# A297 8 REALES
Silver **Issuer:** Chilpanzingo and ENSAIE **Countermark:** Chilpanzingo Type B and ENSAIE **Note:** Countermark on Zacatecas KM#189.

CM Date	Host Date	Good	VG	F	VF	XF
ND	ND	175	250	350	—	—

KM# 297 8 REALES
Silver **Issuer:** Chilpanzingo and LVA **Countermark:** Chilpanzingo Type A and LVA **Note:** Countermark on Mexico City KM#109.

CM Date	Host Date	Good	VG	F	VF	XF
ND	1805 TH	45.00	75.00	145	250	—

KM# 281 8 REALES

Silver **Issuer:** Chilpanzingo and LVS **Countermark:** Chilpanzingo Type A and script LVS **Note:** Countermark on cast Mexico City KM#110.

CM Date	Host Date	Good	VG	F	VF	XF
ND	1809 HJ	45.00	65.00	135	250	—

KM# 288.2 8 REALES
Silver **Issuer:** Chilpanzingo and Suprema Junta Nacional Gubernativa **Countermark:** Chilpanzingo Type B **Note:** Countermark on Zacatecas KM#190. Prev. KM#288.

CM Date	Host Date	Good	VG	F	VF	XF
ND	1811	—	—	—	—	—

KM# 290.2 8 REALES
Silver **Issuer:** ENSAIE and VTIL **Countermark:** ENSAIE and VTIL **Note:** Countermark on Zacatecas KM#190. Prev. KM#290.

CM Date	Host Date	Good	VG	F	VF	XF
ND	1811	100	175	275	350	—

KM# 291 8 REALES
Silver **Issuer:** Jose Maria Liceaga and VTIL **Countermark:** J.M.L./D.S. and VTIL **Note:** Countermark on Mexico City KM#110.

CM Date	Host Date	Good	VG	F	VF	XF
ND	1810 HJ	85.00	150	250	400	—

KM# 282 8 REALES
Silver **Issuer:** La Comandancia Militar and Morelos **Countermark:** L.C.M and Morelos monogram Type A **Note:** Countermark on cast Mexico City KM#109.

CM Date	Host Date	Good	VG	F	VF	XF
ND	1792 FM	—	—	—	—	—

KM# 283 8 REALES
Silver **Issuer:** Morelos and Morelos **Countermark:** Morelos Type A and C **Note:** Countermark on cast Mexico City KM#109.

CM Date	Host Date	Good	VG	F	VF	XF
ND	1806 TH	—	—	—	—	—

KM# 284 8 REALES
Silver **Issuer:** Chilpanzingo and Morelos **Countermark:** Chilpanzingo Type A and Morelos monogram Type A **Note:** Countermark on cast Mexico City KM#109.

CM Date	Host Date	Good	VG	F	VF	XF
ND	1806 TH	35.00	50.00	100	200	—
ND	1807 TH	35.00	50.00	100	200	—

KM# 285.1 8 REALES
Silver **Issuer:** Chilpanzingo and Morelos **Countermark:** Chilpanzingo Type A and Morelos monogram Type A **Note:** Countermark on struck Mexico City KM#110.

CM Date	Host Date	Good	VG	F	VF	XF
ND	1809 TH	45.00	65.00	135	250	—

KM# 285.3 8 REALES
Silver **Issuer:** Chilpanzingo and Morelos **Countermark:** Chilpanzingo Type A and Morelos monogram Type A **Note:** Countermark on cast Mexico City KM#111.

CM Date	Host Date	Good	VG	F	VF	XF
ND	1811 HJ	75.00	120	175	275	—

KM# A290 8 REALES
Silver **Issuer:** ENSAIE and Jose Maria Liceaga **Countermark:** ENSAIE and J.M.L. **Note:** Countermark on Zacatecas KM#190.

CM Date	Host Date	Good	VG	F	VF	XF
ND	1811	100	175	275	350	—

KM# 294 8 REALES
Silver **Issuer:** L.V.A. and Morelos **Countermark:** Script LVA and Morelos monogram Type A **Note:** Countermark on cast Mexico City KM#110.

CM Date	Host Date	Good	VG	F	VF	XF
ND	ND HJ	45.00	75.00	135	250	—

KM# 288.1 8 REALES
Silver **Issuer:** Chilpanzingo and Suprema Junta Nacional Gubernativa **Countermark:** Chilpanzingo Type B and S.J.N.G **Note:** Countermark on Zacatecas KM#189.

CM Date	Host Date	Good	VG	F	VF	XF
ND	1811	—	—	—	—	—

KM# 280.1 8 REALES
Silver **Issuer:** Chilpanzingo and Crown and flag **Countermark:** Chilpanzingo Type B and Crown and flag **Note:** Countermark on Zacatecas KM#189.

CM Date	Host Date	Good	VG	F	VF	XF
ND	1811	—	—	—	—	—

KM# 290.1 8 REALES
Silver **Issuer:** ENSAIE and VTIL **Countermark:** ENSAIE and VTIL **Note:** Countermark on Zacatecas KM#189.

CM Date	Host Date	Good	VG	F	VF	XF
ND	1811	100	175	275	350	—

KM# 280.2 8 REALES
Silver **Issuer:** Chilpanzingo and crown and flag **Countermark:** Chilpanzingo Type B and crown and flag **Note:** Countermark on Zacatecas KM#190.

CM Date	Host Date	Good	VG	F	VF	XF
ND	1811	—	—	—	—	—

KM# 287 8 REALES
Silver **Issuer:** Chilpanzingo - Provisional De Valladolid **Countermark:** Chilpanzingo Type B and P.D.V **Note:** Countermark on Valladolid KM#178.

CM Date	Host Date	Good	VG	F	VF	XF
ND	1813	—	—	—	—	—

ZACATECAS

The city of Zacatecas, in a rich mining region has provided silver for the world since mid-1500. On November 14, 1810 a mint began production for the Royalist cause. Zacatecas was the most prolific during the War of Independence. Four of the 5 standard silver denominations were made here, 4 Reales were not. The first, a local type showing mountains of silver on the coins were made only in 1810 and 1811. Some 1811 coins were made by the Insurgents who took the city on April 15, 1811, later retaken by the Royalists on May 21, 1811. Zacatecas struck the standard Ferdinand VII bust type until 1922.

Mint marks: Z, ZS, Zs.

WAR OF INDEPENDENCE

ROYALIST COINAGE

KM# 180 1/2 REAL
0.9030 Silver **Ruler:** Ferdinand VII **Mint:** Zacatecas **Obverse:** Local arms with flowers and castles **Reverse:** Mountain **Note:** Mint marks: Z, ZS, Zs.

Date	Mintage	Good	VG	F	VF	XF
1810	—	75.00	125	200	400	—
1811	—	30.00	50.00	90.00	175	—

Note: Date aligned with legend

KM# 181 1/2 REAL
0.9030 Silver **Ruler:** Ferdinand VII **Mint:** Zacatecas **Obverse:** Royal arms **Reverse:** Mountain **Rev. Legend:** MONEDA PROVISIONAL DE ZACATECAS **Note:** Mint marks: Z, ZS, Zs.

Date	Mintage	Good	VG	F	VF	XF
1811	—	30.00	50.00	90.00	175	—

KM# 182 1/2 REAL
0.9030 Silver **Ruler:** Ferdinand VII **Mint:** Zacatecas **Obverse:** Provincial bust **Obv. Legend:** FERDIN. VII **Reverse:** Mountain **Rev. Legend:** MONEDA PROVISIONAL DE ZACATECAS **Note:** Mint marks: Z, ZS, Zs.

Date	Mintage	Good	VG	F	VF	XF
1811	—	30.00	40.00	65.00	135	—
1812	—	25.00	35.00	60.00	120	—

KM# 73.1 1/2 REAL
1.6900 g., 0.9030 Silver .0491 oz. ASW **Ruler:** Ferdinand VII **Mint:** Zacatecas **Obverse:** Armored bust of Ferdinand VII **Reverse:** Crowned arms, pillars **Note:** Mint marks: Z, ZS, Zs.

Date	Mintage	Good	VG	F	VF	XF
1813 AG	—	20.00	40.00	60.00	100	—
1813 FP	—	25.00	45.00	85.00	175	—
1814 AG	—	15.00	30.00	60.00	100	—
1815 AG	—	12.50	25.00	40.00	60.00	—
1816 AG	—	10.00	15.00	25.00	50.00	—
1817 AG	—	10.00	15.00	25.00	50.00	—
1818 AG	—	10.00	15.00	25.00	50.00	—
1819 AG	—	10.00	15.00	25.00	50.00	—

KM# 74.3 1/2 REAL
1.6900 g., 0.9030 Silver .0491 oz. ASW **Ruler:** Ferdinand VII **Mint:** Zacatecas **Obverse:** Draped bust Ferdinand VII **Reverse:** Crowned arms, pillars **Note:** Mint marks: Z, ZS, Zs.

Date	Mintage	VG	F	VF	XF	Unc
1819 AG	—	8.00	12.00	25.00	50.00	—
1820 AG	—	8.00	12.00	25.00	50.00	—
1820 RG	—	5.00	10.00	20.00	45.00	—
1821 AG	—	150	250	450	850	—
1821 RG	—	5.00	10.00	20.00	45.00	—

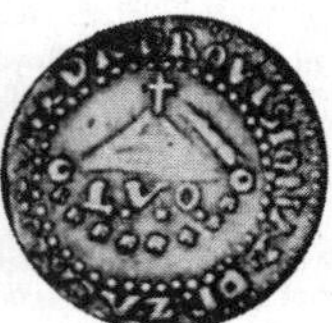

KM# 183 REAL
0.9030 Silver **Ruler:** Ferdinand VII **Mint:** Zacatecas **Obverse:** Local arms with flowers and castles **Reverse:** Mountain **Note:** Mint marks: Z, ZS, Zs.

Date	Mintage	Good	VG	F	VF	XF
1810	—	100	150	300	500	—
1811	—	20.00	40.00	75.00	150	—

Note: Date aligned with legend

KM# 184 REAL
0.9030 Silver **Ruler:** Ferdinand VII **Mint:** Zacatecas **Obverse:** Royal arms **Reverse:** Mountain **Rev. Legend:** MONEDA PROVISIONAL DE ZACATECAS **Note:** Mint marks: Z, ZS, Zs.

Date	Mintage	Good	VG	F	VF	XF
1811	—	15.00	30.00	60.00	135	—

KM# 185 REAL
0.9030 Silver **Ruler:** Ferdinand VII **Mint:** Zacatecas **Obverse:** Provincial bust **Obv. Legend:** FERDIN. VII. **Reverse:** Crowned arms, pillars **Rev. Legend:** MONEDA PROVISIONAL DE ZACATECAS **Note:** Mint marks: Z, ZS, Zs.

Date	Mintage	Good	VG	F	VF	XF
1811	—	50.00	85.00	120	200	—
1812	—	40.00	70.00	100	175	—

KM# 82.1 REAL
3.3800 g., 0.9030 Silver .0981 oz. ASW **Ruler:** Ferdinand VII **Mint:** Zacatecas **Obverse:** Armored bust of Ferdinand VII **Obv. Legend:** FERDIN. VII. **Reverse:** Crowned arms, pillars **Note:** Mint marks: Z, ZS, Zs.

Date	Mintage	Good	VG	F	VF	XF
1813 FP	—	50.00	100	150	250	—
1814 FP	—	20.00	35.00	50.00	85.00	—
1814 AG	—	20.00	35.00	50.00	85.00	—
1815 AG	—	20.00	35.00	50.00	85.00	—
1816 AG	—	10.00	20.00	30.00	65.00	—
1817 AG	—	6.50	12.50	20.00	45.00	—
1818 AG	—	6.50	12.50	20.00	45.00	—
1819 AG	—	5.00	9.00	15.00	35.00	—

KM# 83.3 REAL
3.3800 g., 0.9030 Silver .0981 oz. ASW **Ruler:** Ferdinand VII **Mint:** Zacatecas **Obverse:** Draped bust of Ferdinand VII **Obv. Legend:** FERDIN. VII. **Reverse:** Crowned arms, pillars **Note:** Mint marks: Z, ZS, Zs.

Date	Mintage	VG	F	VF	XF	Unc
1820 AG	—	5.00	10.00	20.00	60.00	—
1820 RG	—	5.00	10.00	20.00	60.00	—
1821 AG	—	15.00	30.00	45.00	90.00	—
1821 AZ	—	10.00	20.00	40.00	85.00	—
1821 RG	—	6.00	12.00	25.00	65.00	—
1822 AZ	—	6.00	12.00	25.00	65.00	—
1822 RG	—	15.00	30.00	45.00	90.00	—

KM# 186 2 REALES
0.9030 Silver **Ruler:** Ferdinand VII **Mint:** Zacatecas **Obverse:** Local arms with flowers and castles **Reverse:** Mountain **Note:** Mint marks: Z, ZS, Zs.

Date	Mintage	Good	VG	F	VF	XF
1810 Rare	—	—	—	—	—	—
1811	—	25.00	40.00	70.00	120	—

Note: Date aligned with legend

KM# 187 2 REALES
0.9030 Silver **Ruler:** Ferdinand VII **Mint:** Zacatecas **Obverse:** Royal arms **Reverse:** Mountain above L. V. O **Rev. Legend:** MONEDA PROVISIONAL DE ZACATECAS **Note:** Mint marks: Z, ZS, Zs.

Date	Mintage	Good	VG	F	VF	XF
1811	—	15.00	30.00	60.00	100	—

KM# 188 2 REALES
0.9030 Silver **Ruler:** Ferdinand VII **Mint:** Zacatecas **Obverse:** Armored bust **Obv. Legend:** FERDIN. VII **Reverse:** Crowned arms, pillars **Rev. Legend:** MONEDA PROVISIONAL DE ZACATECAS **Note:** Mint marks: Z, ZS, Zs.

Date	Mintage	Good	VG	F	VF	XF
1811	—	35.00	65.00	135	225	—
1812	—	30.00	60.00	125	200	—

KM# 92.1 2 REALES
6.7700 g., 0.9030 Silver .1966 oz. ASW **Ruler:** Ferdinand VII **Mint:** Zacatecas **Obverse:** Large armored bust of Ferdinand VII **Obv. Legend:** FERDIN. VII **Reverse:** Crowned arms, pillars **Note:** Mint marks: Z, ZS, Zs.

Date	Mintage	Good	VG	F	VF	XF
1813 FP	—	35.00	50.00	75.00	125	—
1814 FP	—	35.00	50.00	75.00	125	—
1814 AG	—	35.00	50.00	75.00	125	—
1815 AG	—	6.50	12.50	25.00	55.00	—
1816 AG	—	6.50	12.50	25.00	55.00	—
1817 AG	—	6.50	12.50	25.00	55.00	—
1818 AG	—	6.50	12.50	25.00	55.00	—

KM# 93.4 2 REALES
6.7700 g., 0.9030 Silver .1966 oz. ASW **Ruler:** Ferdinand VII **Mint:** Zacatecas **Obverse:** Draped bust of Ferdinand VII **Obv. Legend:** FERDIN. VII **Reverse:** Crowned arms, pillars **Note:** Mint marks: Z, ZS, Zs.

Date	Mintage	VG	F	VF	XF	Unc
1818 AG	—	6.50	12.50	25.00	50.00	—
1819 AG	—	10.00	20.00	40.00	85.00	—
1819 AG Reversed 'S' in HISPAN	—	10.00	20.00	40.00	85.00	—
1820 AG	—	10.00	20.00	40.00	85.00	—
1820 RG	—	10.00	20.00	40.00	85.00	—
1821 AG	—	10.00	20.00	40.00	85.00	—
1821 AZ/RG	—	10.00	20.00	40.00	85.00	—
1821 AZ	—	10.00	20.00	40.00	85.00	—
1821 RG	—	10.00	20.00	40.00	85.00	—
1822 AG	—	10.00	20.00	40.00	85.00	—
1822 RG	—	10.00	20.00	40.00	85.00	—

KM# A92 2 REALES
6.7700 g., 0.9030 Silver .1966 oz. ASW **Ruler:** Ferdinand VII **Mint:** Zacatecas **Obverse:** Small armored bust of Ferdinand VII **Obv. Legend:** FERDIN. VII **Reverse:** Crowned arms, pillars **Note:** Mint marks: Z, ZS, Zs.

Date	Mintage	Good	VG	F	VF	XF
1819 AG	—	45.00	100	200	400	—

KM# 189 8 REALES
0.9030 Silver **Ruler:** Ferdinand VII **Mint:** Zacatecas **Obverse:** Local arm with flowers and castles **Reverse:** Mountain above L.V.O. **Note:** Mint Zacatecas.

Date	Mintage	Good	VG	F	VF	XF
1810	—	300	500	750	1,250	—
1811	—	100	150	225	350	—

Note: Date aligned with legend. Also exists with incomplete date

KM# 190 8 REALES
0.9030 Silver **Ruler:** Ferdinand VII **Mint:** Zacatecas **Obverse:** Royal arms **Obv. Legend:** FERDIN. VII. DEI... **Reverse:** Mountain above L. V. O **Rev. Legend:** MONEDA PROVISIONAL DE ZACATECAS

Date	Mintage	Good	VG	F	VF	XF
1811	—	65.00	100	135	220	—

Note: Date aligned with legend

KM# 191 8 REALES
0.9030 Silver **Ruler:** Ferdinand VII **Mint:** Zacatecas **Obverse:** Armored bust of Ferdinand VII **Obv. Legend:** FERDIN. VII. 8.R. DEI... **Reverse:** Crowned arms, pillars **Rev. Legend:** MONEDA PROVISIONAL DE ZACATECAS

Date	Mintage	Good	VG	F	VF	XF
1811	—	45.00	75.00	145	275	—
1812	—	50.00	85.00	160	300	—

KM# 192 8 REALES
0.9030 Silver **Ruler:** Ferdinand VII **Mint:** Zacatecas **Obverse:** Draped bust of Ferdinand VII **Obv. Legend:** FERDIN. VII. DEI... **Reverse:** Crowned arms, pillars **Rev. Legend:** MONEDA PROVISIONAL DE ZACATECAS

Date	Mintage	Good	VG	F	VF	XF
1812	—	75.00	150	275	450	—

KM# 111.5 8 REALES
27.0700 g., 0.9030 Silver .7860 oz. ASW **Ruler:** Ferdinand VII **Mint:** Zacatecas **Obverse:** Draped bust of Ferdinand VII **Obv. Legend:** FERDIN. VII. DEI. GRATIA **Reverse:** Crowned arms, pillars **Rev. Legend:** HISPAN. ET IND. REX **Note:** Mint mark: Zs. Several bust types exist for the 1821 issues.

Date	Mintage	VG	F	VF	XF	Unc
1813 FP	—	75.00	125	175	275	—
1814 FP	—	150	250	350	450	—
1814 AG	—	100	150	200	300	—
1814 AG D over horizontal D in IND	—	125	175	225	325	—
1814 AG/FP	—	100	150	200	300	—
1815 AG	—	50.00	100	150	250	—
1816 AG	—	35.00	50.00	65.00	125	—
1817 AG	—	35.00	50.00	65.00	125	—
1818 AG	—	30.00	40.00	50.00	100	—
1819 AG	—	30.00	40.00	50.00	100	—
1819 AG 'GRATIA' error	—	100	200	300	400	—
1820 AG 18/11 error	—	100	200	300	400	—
1820 AG	—	30.00	40.00	50.00	100	—
1820 RG	—	30.00	40.00	50.00	100	—
1821/81 RG	—	75.00	150	225	300	—
1821 RG	—	15.00	25.00	35.00	65.00	—
1821 AZ/RG	—	50.00	100	150	200	—
1821 AZ	—	50.00	100	150	200	—
1822 RG	—	40.00	60.00	100	175	—

KM# 111.6 8 REALES
27.0700 g., 0.9030 Silver .7860 oz. ASW **Ruler:** Ferdinand VII **Mint:** Zacatecas **Obverse:** Draped bust of Ferdinand VII **Obv. Legend:** FERDIN. VII. DEI. GRATIA **Reverse:** Crown with lower rear arc **Rev. Legend:** HISAV. ET IND. REX

Date	Mintage	VG	F	VF	XF	Unc
1821 Zs	—	160	320	550	750	—

ROYALIST COUNTERMARKED COINAGE

LCM - LA COMANDANCIA MILITAR

Crown and Flag

This countermark exists in 15 various sizes.

KM# 193.1 2 REALES
0.9030 Silver **Issuer:** La Comandancia Militar **Countermark:** LCM **Note:** Countermark on Mexico KM#92.

CM Date	Host Date	Good	VG	F	VF	XF
ND	1809 TH	85.00	165	250	400	—

KM# 193.2 2 REALES
0.9030 Silver **Issuer:** La Comandancia Militar, (The LCM countermark exists in 15 various sizes) **Countermark:** LCM **Note:** Countermark on Mexico KM#186.

CM Date	Host Date	Good	VG	F	VF	XF
ND	1811	85.00	165	250	400	—

KM# 194.1 8 REALES
Cast Silver **Issuer:** La Comandancia Militar, (The LCM countermark exists in 15 various sizes) **Countermark:** LCM **Note:** Countermark on Chihuahua KM#123.

CM Date	Host Date	Good	VG	F	VF	XF
ND	1811 RP	100	200	300	450	—
ND	1812 RP	100	200	300	450	—

KM# 194.2 8 REALES
0.9030 Silver **Issuer:** La Comandancia Militar, The LCM countermark exists in 15 different sizes **Countermark:** LCM **Note:** Countermark on Chihuahua KM#111.1 struck over KM#123.

CM Date	Host Date	Good	VG	F	VF	XF
ND	1815 RP	200	275	400	550	—
ND	1817 RP	125	175	225	300	—
ND	1820 RP	125	175	225	300	—
ND	1821 RP	125	175	225	300	—

KM# 194.3 8 REALES
0.9030 Silver **Issuer:** La Comandancia Militar, The LCM countermark exists in 15 different sizes **Countermark:** LCM **Note:** Countermark on Durango KM#111.2.

CM Date	Host Date	Good	VG	F	VF	XF
ND	1812 RM	70.00	125	190	250	—
ND	1821 CG	70.00	125	190	250	—

KM# 194.4 8 REALES
0.9030 Silver **Issuer:** La Comandancia Militar, The LCM countermark exists in 15 different sizes **Countermark:** LCM **Note:** Countermark on Guadalajara KM#111.3.

CM Date	Host Date	Good	VG	F	VF	XF
ND	1813 MR	150	225	300	475	—

KM# 194.5 8 REALES
0.9030 Silver **Issuer:** La Comandancia Militar, The LCM countermark exists in 15 different sizes **Countermark:** LCM **Note:** Countermark on Guanajuato KM#111.4.

CM Date	Host Date	Good	VG	F	VF	XF
ND	1813 JJ	225	350	475	650	—

KM# 194.6 8 REALES
0.9030 Silver **Issuer:** La Comandancia Militar, The LCM countermark exists in 15 different sizes **Countermark:** LCM **Note:** Countermark on Nueva Viscaya KM#165.

CM Date	Host Date	Good	VG	F	VF	XF
ND	1811 RM Rare	—	—	—	—	—

KM# 194.7 8 REALES
0.9030 Silver **Issuer:** La Comandancia Militar, The LCM countermark exists in 15 different sizes **Countermark:** LCM **Note:** Countermark on Mexico KM#111.

CM Date	Host Date	Good	VG	F	VF	XF
ND	1811 HJ	125	225	350	600	—
ND	1812 JJ	110	135	190	325	—
ND	1817 JJ	50.00	65.00	85.00	125	—
ND	1818 JJ	50.00	65.00	85.00	125	—
ND	1820 JJ	—	—	—	—	—

KM# 194.8 8 REALES
0.9030 Silver **Issuer:** La Comandancia Militar, The LCM countermark exists in 15 different sizes **Countermark:** LCM **Note:** Countermark on Sombrerete KM#176.

CM Date	Host Date	Good	VG	F	VF	XF
ND	1811 Rare	—	—	—	—	—
ND	1812 Rare	—	—	—	—	—

KM# 194.9 8 REALES
0.9030 Silver **Issuer:** La Comandancia Militar, The LCM countermark exists in 15 different sizes **Countermark:** LCM **Note:** Countermark on Zacatecas KM#190.

CM Date	Host Date	Good	VG	F	VF	XF
ND	1811	225	350	450	—	—

KM# 194.10 8 REALES
0.9030 Silver **Issuer:** La Comandancia Militar, The LCM countermark exists in 15 different sizes **Countermark:** LCM **Note:** Countermark on Zacatecas KM#111.5.

CM Date	Host Date	Good	VG	F	VF	XF
ND	1813 FP	—	—	—	—	—
ND	1814 AG	—	—	—	—	—
ND	1822 RG	—	—	—	—	—

LCV - LAS CAJAS DE VERACRUZ

The Royal Treasury of the City of Veracruz

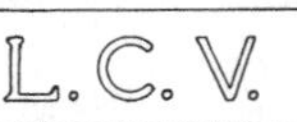

KM# 195 7 REALES
Silver **Issuer:** Las Cajas de Veracruz, The Royal Treasury of the City of Veracruz **Countermark:** LCV **Note:** Countermark and 7 on underweight 8 Reales.

CM Date	Host Date	Good	VG	F	VF	XF
ND	ND Rare	—	—	—	—	—

Note: Most examples are counterfeit

KM# 196 7-1/4 REALES
Silver **Issuer:** Las Cajas de Veracruz, The Royal Treasury of the City of Veracruz **Countermark:** LCV **Note:** Countermark and 7-1/4 on underweight 8 Reales.

CM Date	Host Date	Good	VG	F	VF	XF
ND	ND Rare	—	—	—	—	—

Note: Most examples are counterfeit

KM# 197 7-1/2 REALES
Silver **Issuer:** Las Cajas de Veracruz, The Royal Treasury of the City of Veracruz **Countermark:** LCV **Note:** Countermark and 7-1/2 on underweight 8 Reales.

CM Date	Host Date	Good	VG	F	VF	XF
ND	ND Rare	—	—	—	—	—

Note: Most examples are counterfeit

KM# 198 7-3/4 REALES
Silver **Issuer:** Las Cajas de Veracruz, The Royal Treasury of the City of Veracruz **Countermark:** LCV **Note:** Countermark and 7-3/4 on underweight 8 Reales.

CM Date	Host Date	Good	VG	F	VF	XF
ND	ND	300	375	450	600	—

Note: Many examples are counterfeit

KM# A198 8 REALES
Cast Silver **Issuer:** Las Cajas de Veracruz, The Royal Treasury of the City of Veracruz **Countermark:** LCV **Note:** Countermark on Chihuahua KM#123.

CM Date	Host Date	Good	VG	F	VF	XF
ND	1811 RP	150	250	400	500	—

KM# 199 8 REALES
Silver **Issuer:** Las Cajas de Veracruz, The Royal Treasury of the City of Veracruz **Countermark:** LCV **Note:** Countermark on Zacatecas KM#191.

CM Date	Host Date	Good	VG	F	VF	XF
ND	1811	175	225	275	350	—
ND	1812	175	225	275	350	—

MS (MONOGRAM) - MANUEL SALCEDO

KM# 200 8 REALES
Silver **Issuer:** Manuel Salcedo **Countermark:** MS monogram **Note:** Countermark on Mexico KM#110.

CM Date	Host Date	Good	VG	F	VF	XF
ND	1809 TH	150	250	400	500	—
ND	1810 HJ	150	250	400	500	—
ND	1811 HJ	150	250	400	500	—

MVA - MONCLOVA

KM# 202.3 8 REALES
Silver **Issuer:** Monclova, MVA **Countermark:** MVA/1812 **Note:** Countermark on cast Mexico KM#110.

CM Date	Host Date	Good	VG	F	VF	XF
1812	1809 HJ	100	150	250	350	—
1812	1809 TH	100	150	250	350	—
1812	1810 HJ	100	150	250	350	—

KM# 201 8 REALES
Silver **Issuer:** Monclova, MVA **Countermark:** MVA/1811 **Note:** Countermark on Chihuahua KM#111.1; struck over cast Mexico KM#110.

CM Date	Host Date	Good	VG	F	VF	XF
ND	1809	250	450	700	1,000	—
ND	1816 RP	250	450	700	1,000	—
ND	1821 RP	250	450	700	1,000	—

KM# 202.1 8 REALES
Silver **Issuer:** Monclova, MVA **Countermark:** MVA/1812 **Note:** Countermark on Chihuahua KM#111.1; struck over cast Mexico KM#109.

CM Date	Host Date	Good	VG	F	VF	XF
1812	1810	125	175	250	350	—

KM# 202.5 8 REALES
Silver **Issuer:** Monclova, MVA **Countermark:** MVA/1812 **Note:** Countermark on Zacatecas KM#189.

CM Date	Host Date	Good	VG	F	VF	XF
1812	1813	300	350	450	550	—

KM# 202.2 8 REALES
Silver **Issuer:** Monclova, MVA **Countermark:** MVA/1812 **Note:** Countermark on cast Mexico KM#109.

CM Date	Host Date	Good	VG	F	VF	XF
1812	1798 FM	100	150	250	350	—
1812	1802 FT	100	150	250	350	—

INSURGENT COINAGE

AMERICAN CONGRESS

KM# 216 REAL
0.9030 Silver **Issuer:** American Congress **Mint:** Mexico City **Obverse:** Eagle on cactus **Obv. Legend:** CONGRESO AMERICANO **Reverse:** F. 7 on spread mantle **Rev. Legend:** DEPOSIT D.L. AUCTORI J

Date	Mintage	Good	VG	F	VF	XF
ND(1813)	—	35.00	75.00	120	200	—

KM# 217 REAL
0.9030 Silver **Issuer:** American Congress **Mint:** Mexico City **Obverse:** Eagle on cactus **Obv. Legend:** CONGR. AMER. **Reverse:** F. 7 on spread mantle **Rev. Legend:** DEPOS. D. L. AUT. D.

Date	Mintage	Good	VG	F	VF	XF
ND(1813)	—	35.00	75.00	120	200	—

NATIONAL CONGRESS

KM# 209 1/2 REAL
Struck Copper **Issuer:** National Congress **Obverse:** Eagle on bridge **Obv. Legend:** VICE FERD. VII DEI GRATIA ET **Reverse:** Value, bow quiver, etc **Rev. Legend:** S. P. CONG. NAT. IND.

Date	Mintage	Good	VG	F	VF	XF
1811	—	45.00	85.00	150	200	—
1812	—	27.50	60.00	100	150	—
1813	—	27.50	60.00	100	150	—
1814	—	45.00	85.00	150	200	—

KM# 210 1/2 REAL
0.9030 Silver **Issuer:** National Congress **Obverse:** Eagle on bridge **Obv. Legend:** VICE FERD. VII DEI GRATIA ET **Reverse:** Value, bow quiver, etc **Rev. Legend:** S. P. CONG. NAT. IND.

Date	Mintage	Good	VG	F	VF	XF
1812	—	27.50	60.00	100	150	—
1813	—	45.00	90.00	175	275	—

Note: 1812 exists with the date reading inwards and outwards

KM# 211 REAL
0.9030 Silver **Issuer:** National Congress **Obverse:** Eagle on bridge **Obv. Legend:** VICE FERD. VII DEI GRATIA ET **Reverse:** Value, bow quiver, etc **Rev. Legend:** S. P. CONG. NAT. IND.

Date	Mintage	Good	VG	F	VF	XF
1812	—	22.50	45.00	80.00	125	—
1813	—	22.50	45.00	80.00	125	—

Note: 1812 exists with the date reading either inward or outward

KM# 212 2 REALES
Struck Copper **Issuer:** National Congress **Obverse:** Eagle on bridge **Obv. Legend:** VICE FERD. VII DEI GRATIA ET **Reverse:** Value, bow quiver, etc **Rev. Legend:** S. P. CONG. NAT. IND.

Date	Mintage	Good	VG	F	VF	XF
1812	—	100	150	200	275	—
1813	—	23.50	50.00	75.00	120	—
1814	—	32.50	75.00	110	165	—

KM# A213 2 REALES
Struck Silver **Issuer:** National Congress **Obverse:** Eagle on bridge **Obv. Legend:** VICE FERD. VII DEI GRATIA ET **Reverse:** Value, bow, quiver, etc **Rev. Legend:** S. P. CONG. NAT. IND.

Date	Mintage	Good	VG	F	VF	XF
1813	—	950	1,750	3,000	4,850	—

KM# 213 2 REALES
0.9030 Silver **Issuer:** National Congress **Obverse:** Eagle on bridge in shield, denomination at sides **Obv. Legend:** VICE FERD. VII DEI GRATIA ET **Reverse:** Canon, quiver, arm, etc

Date	Mintage	Good	VG	F	VF	XF
1813	—	75.00	155	265	375	—

Note: These dies were believed to be intended for the striking of 2 Escudos

KM# 214 4 REALES
0.9030 Silver **Issuer:** National Congress **Mint:** Mexico City **Obverse:** Eagle on bridge **Obv. Legend:** VICE FERD. VII DEI GRATIA ET **Reverse:** Value, bow, quiver, etc **Rev. Legend:** S. P. CONG. NAT. IND.

Date	Mintage	Good	VG	F	VF	XF
1813	—	600	1,200	2,450	4,400	—

KM# 215.1 8 REALES
0.9030 Silver **Issuer:** National Congress **Mint:** Mexico City
Obverse: Small crowned eagle **Obv. Legend:** VICE FERD. VII DEI GRATIA ET **Reverse:** Value, bow, quiver, etc **Rev. Legend:** S. P. CONG. NAT. IND.

Date	Mintage	Good	VG	F	VF	XF
1812Mo	—	600	1,150	2,350	4,250	—

KM# 215.2 8 REALES
0.9030 Silver **Issuer:** National Congress **Mint:** Mexico City
Obverse: Large crowned eagle **Obv. Legend:** VICE FERD. VII DEI GRATIA ET **Reverse:** Value, bow, quiver, etc **Rev. Legend:** S. P. CONG. NAT. IND.

Date	Mintage	Good	VG	F	VF	XF
1813Mo	—	600	1,150	2,350	4,250	—

SUPREME NATIONAL CONGRESS OF AMERICA

PDV - Provisional de Valladolid

VTIL - Util = useful

(Refer to Multiple countermarks)

KM# 203 1/2 REAL
Struck Copper **Issuer:** Supreme National Congress of America
Obverse: Eagle on bridge **Obv. Legend:** FERDIN. VII DEI GRATIA **Reverse:** Value, bow, quiver, etc **Rev. Legend:** S. P. CONG. NAT. IND. GUV.T.

Date	Mintage	Good	VG	F	VF	XF
1811	—	27.50	45.00	60.00	100	—
1812	—	27.50	45.00	60.00	100	—
1813	—	27.50	45.00	60.00	100	—
1814	—	27.50	45.00	60.00	100	—

KM# 204 REAL
Struck Copper **Issuer:** Supreme National Congress of America
Obverse: Eagle on bridge **Obv. Legend:** FERDIN. VII DEI GRATIA **Reverse:** Value, bow, quiver, etc **Rev. Legend:** S. P. CONG. NAT. IND. GUV.T.

Date	Mintage	Good	VG	F	VF	XF
1811	—	45.00	75.00	125	200	—

KM# 205 2 REALES
Struck Copper **Issuer:** Supreme National Congress of America
Obverse: Eagle on bridge **Obv. Legend:** FERDIN. VII DEI GRATIA **Reverse:** Value, bow, quiver, etc

Date	Mintage	Good	VG	F	VF	XF
1812	—	225	325	475	750	—

KM# 206 8 REALES
Cast Silver **Issuer:** Supreme National Congress of America
Obverse: Eagle on bridge **Obv. Legend:** FERDIN. VII DEI GRATIA **Reverse:** Value, bow, quiver, etc

Date	Mintage	Good	VG	F	VF	XF
1811	—	150	250	350	500	—
1812	—	150	250	350	500	—

KM# 207 8 REALES
Struck Silver **Issuer:** Supreme National Congress of America
Obverse: Eagle on bridge **Obv. Legend:** FERDIN. VII DEI GRATIA **Reverse:** Value, bow, quiver, etc

Date	Mintage	Good	VG	F	VF	XF
1811	—	—	—	—	—	—
1812	—	300	600	1,000	1,500	—

KM# 208 8 REALES
Struck Copper **Issuer:** Supreme National Congress of America
Obverse: Eagle on bridge **Obv. Legend:** FERDIN. VII...
Reverse: Bow, sword and quiver **Rev. Legend:** PROVICIONAL POR LA SUPREMA JUNTA DE AMERICA

Date	Mintage	Good	VG	F	VF	XF
1811	—	100	150	225	450	—
1812	—	100	150	225	450	—

EMPIRE OF ITURBIDE

RULERS
Augustin I Iturbide, 1822-1823

MINT MARKS
Mo - Mexico City

ASSAYERS INITIALS
JA - Jose Garcia Ansaldo, 1812-1833
JM - Joaquin Davila Madrid, 1809-1833

Augustin I Iturbide

MILLED COINAGE

16 Pilones = 1 Real; 8 Tlaco = 1 Real; 16 Reales = 1 Escudo

Mint: Durango
KM# 299 1/8 REAL
Copper **Rev. Inscription:** DE LA PROVINCIA DE NUEVA VISCAYA

Date	Good	VG	F	VF	XF
1821D	22.50	50.00	85.00	150	—
1822D	7.50	13.50	28.50	60.00	—
1823D	7.50	12.50	25.00	50.00	—

Mint: Durango
KM# 300 1/4 REAL
Copper **Rev. Inscription:** DE LA PROVINCIA DE NUEVA VISCAYA

Date	Good	VG	F	VF	XF
1822D	160	275	400	550	—

Mint: Mexico City
KM# 301 1/2 REAL
0.9030 Silver

Date	F	VF	XF	Unc
1822Mo JM	20.00	40.00	80.00	300
1823Mo JM	15.00	30.00	60.00	250

Mint: Mexico City
KM# 302 REAL
0.9030 Silver

Date	VG	F	VF	XF	Unc
1822Mo JM	100	175	350	550	900

Mint: Mexico City
KM# 303 2 REALES
6.7667 g., 0.9030 Silver

Date	F	VF	XF	Unc
1822Mo JM	50.00	100	350	1,000
1823Mo JM	40.00	80.00	250	850

Mint: Mexico City
KM# 304 8 REALES
27.0674 g., 0.9030 Silver

Date	F	VF	XF	Unc
1822Mo JM	75.00	150	300	950
1822Mo JM Proof, 3 known	—	—	—	—

Note: Ponterio & Associates Sale #86, 04-97, choice AU Proof realized $12,650.

Mint: Mexico City
KM# 305 8 REALES
0.9030 Silver **Obv:** Bust similar to 8 Escudos, KM#131 **Rev:** Similar to KM#304

Date	F	VF	XF	Unc
1822Mo JM Rare	—	—	—	—

Mint: Mexico City
KM# 306.1 8 REALES
0.9030 Silver **Obv:** Legend divided **Rev:** 8 R.J.M. at upper left of eagle **Note:** Type I.

Date	F	VF	XF	Unc
1822Mo JM	90.00	170	450	1,300

Mint: Mexico City
KM# 306.2 8 REALES
0.9030 Silver **Obv:** Legend divided **Rev:** Cross on crown **Note:** Type I.

Date	F	VF	XF	Unc
1822Mo JM	650	1,000	—	—

Mint: Mexico City
KM# 307 8 REALES
0.9030 Silver **Obv:** Similar to KM#306 **Rev:** Similar to KM#310 **Note:** Type II.

Date	F	VF	XF	Unc
1822Mo JM	150	350	650	2,250

Mint: Mexico City
KM# 308 8 REALES
0.9030 Silver **Obv:** Continous legend with long smooth truncation **Rev:** Similar to KM#306 **Note:** Type III.

Date	F	VF	XF	Unc
1822Mo JM	175	500	950	2,250

Note: Variety with long, straight truncation is valued at $5,000 in uncirculated condition

Mint: Mexico City
KM# 309 8 REALES
0.9030 Silver **Obv:** Similar to KM#308 **Rev:** Similar to KM#310 **Note:** Type IV.

Date	F	VF	XF	Unc
1822Mo JM	50.00	120	250	850

Mint: Mexico City
KM# 310 8 REALES
0.9030 Silver **Obv:** Continuous legend with short irregular truncation **Rev:** 8 R.J.M. below eagle **Note:** Type V.

Date	F	VF	XF	Unc
1822Mo JM	50.00	120	225	900
1823Mo JM	50.00	120	225	900

Mint: Mexico City
KM# 311 8 REALES
0.9030 Silver **Obv:** Bust with long truncation **Rev:** Similar to KM#310 **Note:** Type VI.

Date	F	VF	XF	Unc
1822Mo JM Rare	—	—	—	—

Mint: Mexico City
KM# 312 4 SCUDOS
13.5334 g., 0.8750 Gold **Obv:** Bust **Rev:** Eagle in shield

Date	F	VF	XF	Unc
1823Mo JM	1,000	1,750	2,850	5,500

Mint: Mexico City
KM# 313.1 8 SCUDOS
27.0674 g., 0.8750 Gold **Obv. Legend:** AUGUSTINUS

Date	F	VF	XF	Unc
1822Mo JM	1,200	2,000	3,750	—

Note: Superior Casterline sale 5-89 choice AU realized $11,000

Mint: Mexico City
KM# 313.2 8 SCUDOS
0.8750 Gold **Obv:** Error in legend **Obv. Legend:** AUGSTINUS

Date	F	VF	XF	Unc
1822Mo JM	1,250	2,250	4,200	—

Mint: Mexico City
KM# 314 8 SCUDOS
0.8750 Gold **Obv:** Large bust **Rev:** Eagle in shield

Date	F	VF	XF	Unc
1823Mo JM	1,000	1,800	3,250	6,000

REPUBLIC

First

MINT MARKS

A, AS - Alamos
CE - Real de Catorce
CA,CH - Chihuahua
C, Cn, Gn(error) - Culiacan
D, Do - Durango
EoMo - Estado de Mexico
Ga - Guadalajara
GC - Guadalupe y Calvo
G, Go - Guanajuato
H, Ho - Hermosillo
M, Mo - Mexico City
O, OA - Oaxaca
SLP, PI, P, I/P - San Luis Potosi
Z, Zs – Zacatecas

ASSAYERS' INITIALS

ALAMOS MINT

PG	1862-68	Pascual Gaxiola
DL, L	1866-79	Domingo Larraguibel
AM	1872-74	Antonio Moreno
ML, L	1878-95	Manuel Larraguibel

REAL DE CATORCE MINT

ML	1863	Mariano Cristobal Ramirez

CHIHUAHUA MINT

MR	1831-34	Mariano Cristobal Ramirez
AM	1833-39	Jose Antonio Mucharraz
MJ	1832	Jose Mariano Jimenez
RG	1839-56	Rodrigo Garcia
JC	1856-65	Joaquin Campa
BA	1858	Bruno Arriada
FP	1866	Francisco Potts
JC	1866-1868	Jose Maria Gomez del Campo
MM, M	1868-95	Manuel Merino
AV	1873-80	Antonio Valero
EA	1877	Eduardo Avila
JM	1877	Jacobo Mucharraz
GR	1877	Guadalupe Rocha
MG	1880-82	Manuel Gameros

CULIACAN MINT

CE	1846-70	Clemente Espinosa de los Monteros
C	1870	???
PV	1860-61	Pablo Viruega
MP, P	1871-76	Manuel Onofre Parodi
GP	1876	Celso Gaxiola & Manuel Onofre Parodi
CG, G	1876-78	Celso Gaxiola
JD, D	1878-82	Juan Dominguez
AM, M	1882-1899	Antonio Moreno
F	1870	Fernando Ferrari
JQ, Q	1899-1903	Jesus S. Quiroz

DURANGO MINT

RL	1825-1832	???
RM	1830-48	Ramon Mascarenas
OMC	1840	Octavio Martinez de Castro
CM	1848-76	Clemente Moron
JMR	1849-52	Jose Maria Ramirez
CP, P	1853-64, 1867-73	Carlos Leon de la Pena
LT	1864-65	???
JMP, P	1877	Carlos Miguel de la Palma
PE, E	1878	Pedro Espejo
TB, B	1878-80	Trinidad Barrera
JP	1880-94	J. Miguel Palma
MC, C,	1882-90	Manuel M. Canseco or Melchor Calderon
JB	1885	Jocobo Blanco
ND, D	1892-95	Norberto Dominguez

ESTADO DE MEXICO MINT

L	1828-30	Luis Valazquez de la Cadena
F	1828-30	Francisco Parodi

GUADALAJARA MINT

FS	1818-35	Francisco Suarez
JM	1830-32	???
JG	1836-39, 1842-67	Juan de Dios Guzman
MC	1839-46	Manuel Cueras
JM	1867-69	Jesus P. Manzano
IC, C	1869-77	Ignacio Canizo y Soto
MC	1874-75	Manuel Contreras
JA, A	1877-81	Julio Arancivia
FS, S	1880-82	Fernando Sayago
TB, B	1883-84	Trinidad Barrera
AH, H	1884-85	Antonio Hernandez y Prado
JS, S	1885-95	Jose S. Schiafino

GUADALUPE Y CALVO MINT

MP	1844-52	Manuel Onofre Parodi

GUANAJUATO MINT

JJ	1825-26	Jose Mariano Jimenez
MJ, MR, JM, PG, PJ, PF		???
PM	1841-48, 1853-61	Patrick Murphy
YF	1862-68	Yldefonso Flores
YE	1862-63	Ynocencio Espinoza
FR	1870-78	Faustino Ramirez
SB, RR		???
RS	1891-1900	Rosendo Sandoval

HERMOSILLO MINT

PP	1835-36	Pedro Peimbert
FM	1871-76	Florencio Monteverde
MP	1866	Manuel Onofre Parodi
PR	1866-75	Pablo Rubio
R	1874-75	Pablo Rubio
GR	1877	Guadalupe Rocha
AF, F	1876-77	Alejandro Fourcade
JA, A	1877-83	Jesus Acosta
FM, M	1883-86	Fernando Mendez
FG, G	1886-95	Fausto Gaxiola

MEXICO CITY MINT

Because of the great number of assayers for this mint (Mexico City is a much larger mint than any of the others)there is much confusion as to which initial stands for which assayer at any one time. Therefore we feel that it would be of no value to list the assayers.

OAXACA MINT

AE	1859-91	Agustin Endner
E	1889-90	Agustin Endner
FR	1861-64	Francisco de la Rosa
EN	1890	Eduardo Navarro Luna
N	1890	Eduardo Navarro Luna

POTOSI MINT

JS	1827-42	Juan Sanabria
AM	1838, 1843-49	Jose Antonio Mucharraz
PS	1842-43, 1848-49, 1857-61, 1867-70	Pompaso Sanabria
S	1869-70	Pomposo Sanabria
MC	1849-59	Mariano Catano
RO	1859-65	Romualdo Obregon
MH, H	1870-85	Manuel Herrera Razo
O	1870-73	Juan R. Ochoa
CA, G	1867-70	Carlos Aguirre Gomez
BE, E	1879-81	Blas Escontria
LC, C	1885-86	Luis Cuevas
MR, R	1886-93	Mariano Reyes

ZACATECAS MINT

A	1825-29	Adalco
Z	1825-26	Mariano Zaldivar
V	1824-31	Jose Mariano Vela
O	1829-67	Manuel Ochoa
M	1831-67	Manuel Miner
VL	1860-66	Vicente Larranaga
JS	1867-68, 1876-86	J.S. de Santa Ana
YH	1868-74	Ygnacio Hierro
JA	1874-76	Juan H. Acuna
FZ	18861905	Francisco de P. Zarate

Die Varieties

Similar basic designs were utilized by all the Mexican mints, but many variations are noticeable, particularly in the eagle, cactus and sprays.

1835 Durango, 8 Escudos
Illustration enlarged.

A large winged eagle was portrayed on the earlier coinage of the new republic.

1849 Mexico City, 8 Escudos
Illustration enlarged.
The later eagle featured undersized wings.

1844 Durango, 8 Escudos
Illustration enlarged.

The early renditions of the hand held Liberty cap over open book were massive in the gold escudo series.

1864 Durango, 8 Escudos
Illustration enlarged.

A finer, more petite style was adopted later on in the gold escudo series.

PROFILE EAGLE COINAGE

The first coins of the Republic were of the distinctive Profile Eagle style, sometimes called the "Hooked Neck Eagle". They were struck first in Mexico City in 1823 in denominations of eight reales and eight escudos. In 1824, they were produced at the Durango and Guanajuato mints in addition to Mexico City. Denominations included the one half, one, two and eight reales. No gold escudos of this design were struck in 1824. In 1825, only the eight reales were struck briefly at the Guanajuato mint.

NOTE: For a more extensive examination of Profile Eagle Coinage, please refer to Hookneck - El Aguilade Perfil by Clyde Hubbard and David O Harrow.

Mint: Mexico City
KM# 369 1/2 REAL
1.6900 g., 0.9030 Silver .0490 oz. ASW **Obv:** Full breast Profile eagle **Rev:** Cap and rays **Note:** Die varieties exist.

Date	F	VF	XF	Unc
1824Mo JM	45.00	75.00	150	600

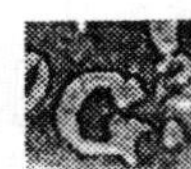

Mint: Durango
KM# 371.1 REAL
3.3800 g., 0.9030 Silver .081 oz. ASW **Obv:** Thin Profile eagle **Rev:** Superscript S reversed

Date	F	VF	XF	Unc
1824Do RL	3,750	7,500	10,000	15,000

Mint: Durango
KM# 371.2 REAL
3.3800 g., 0.9030 Silver .081 oz. ASW **Obv:** Thin Profile eagle **Rev:** Superscript S normal

Date	F	VF	XF	Unc
1824Do RL 3 known	—	—	—	—

Mint: Durango
KM# 373.2 2 REALES
6.7600 g., 0.9030 Silver .1962 oz. ASW **Obv:** Thin Profile eagle **Rev:** Type I, dot before 2R in legend

Date	F	VF	XF	Unc
1824D RL	100	200	1,000	3,000

Mint: Durango
KM# 373.3 2 REALES
6.7600 g., 0.9030 Silver .1962 oz. ASW **Obv:** Thin Profile eagle **Rev:** Type II, no dot before 2R in legend

Date	F	VF	XF	Unc
1824D RL	100	200	1,000	3,000

Mint: Durango
KM# 373.1 2 REALES
6.7600 g., 0.9030 Silver .1962 oz. ASW **Obv:** Profile eagle **Rev:** Cap and rays **Note:** Die varieties exist.

Date	F	VF	XF	Unc
1824Do RL	50.00	125	850	2,200

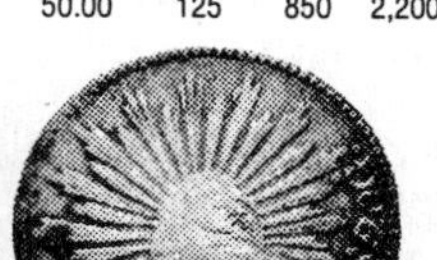
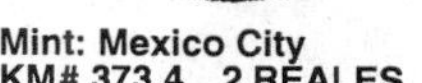

Mint: Mexico City
KM# 373.4 2 REALES
Obv: Profile eagle **Note:** Varieties exist.

Date	F	VF	XF	Unc
1824Mo JM	30.00	70.00	450	2,000

Note: No coins are known with visible feather details on the eagle's breast

Typical Defiant Snake Obverse

Typical Submissive Snake Obverse

Typical Folded Snake Obverse

NOTE: Legible Libertads on the Cap are common on Durango eight reales.

Med. Libertad Cap Reverse

Small Libertad Cap Reverse

Large Libertad Cap Reverse

NOTE: The three styles of obverses and the three styles of reverses were combined to make six distinct varieties of coins.

Mint: Durango
KM# 376.1 8 REALES
27.0700 g., 0.9030 Silver .7859 oz. ASW **Obv:** Thin profile eagle, defiant snake **Rev:** Medium Libertad

Date	F	VF	XF	Unc
1824Do RL	500	1,200	4,500	7,000

Note: Five die varieties are known, all are rare

Mint: Durango
KM# 376.2 8 REALES
27.0700 g., 0.9030 Silver .7859 oz. ASW **Obv:** Thin profile eagle, defiant snake **Rev:** Small Libertad

Date	F	VF	XF	Unc
1824Do RL	300	400	1,600	3,500

Note: Eleven die varieties are known, some are rare

Mint: Durango
KM# 376.3 8 REALES
27.0700 g., 0.9030 Silver .7859 oz. ASW **Obv:** Thin profile eagle, submissive snake **Rev:** Small Libertad

Date	F	VF	XF	Unc
1824Do RL	200	350	1,250	2,750

Note: Seven die varieties are known, some are rare

Mint: Durango
KM# 376.4 8 REALES
27.0700 g., 0.9030 Silver .7859 oz. ASW **Obv:** Thin profile eagle, submissive snake **Rev:** Large Libertad

Date	F	VF	XF	Unc
1824Do RL	200	350	1,250	2,750

Note: Twelve die varieties known, some are rare

Mint: Durango
KM# 376.5 8 REALES
27.0700 g., 0.9030 Silver .7859 oz. ASW **Obv:** Thin profile eagle, folded snake **Rev:** Small Libertad

Date	F	VF	XF	Unc
1824Do RL	200	350	1,200	2,500

Note: Only one die variety is known

Mint: Durango
KM# 376.6 8 REALES
27.0700 g., 0.9030 Silver .7859 oz. ASW **Obv:** Thin profile eagle, folded snake **Rev:** Large Libertad

Date	F	VF	XF	Unc
1824Do RL	200	400	1,500	3,000

Note: Eleven die varieties known, some are rare

Mint: Guanajuato
KM# A376.1 8 REALES
27.0700 g., 0.9030 Silver .7859 oz. ASW **Obv:** Full breast profile eagle

Date	F	VF	XF	Unc
1824Go JM	250	400	1,100	3,500
1825/4Go JJ	600	1,200	2,750	7,000
1825Go JJ	500	750	1,400	5,500

1825/4 JJ overdate

NOTE: Most examples of this overdate exhibit the results of a warped obverse die.

NOTE: Other easily identified die varieties are the 1824 w/the missing superscript "s" for granos and the 1825 w/a dash under the "I" of MEXICANA resulting from a die chip, but these die varieties are not rare.

NOTE: Guanajuato eight reales are characterized by flat strikes on large, thin planchets. Visible feather details on the eagle's breast and legible Libertads on the cap are the exception.

Tight snake loop at eagle's beak.

Open snake loop at eagle's beak.

The Standard or Republic Edge

The Colonial or Circle & Rectangle

The standard Flat-Topped Three

Mint: Mexico City
KM# A376.2 8 REALES
27.0700 g., 0.9030 Silver .7859 oz. ASW **Obv:** Full breast profile eagle **Edge:** Standard or Republic

Date	F	VF	XF	Unc
1823Mo JM	150	300	800	4,500
1824Mo JM	125	250	700	4,000

Mint: Mexico City
KM# A376.3 8 REALES
27.0700 g., 0.9030 Silver .7859 oz. ASW **Obv:** Full breast profile eagle **Edge:** Colonial or circle and rectangle

Date	F	VF	XF	Unc
1823Mo JM Rare	—	—	—	—

The Round-Topped Three

Mint: Mexico City
KM# A376.4 8 REALES
27.0700 g., 0.9030 Silver .7859 oz. ASW **Obv:** Full breast profile eagle **Rev:** Round topped three **Edge:** Standard or Republic

Date	F	VF	XF	Unc
1823Mo JM	2,000	4,000	6,000	8,000

Note: Many die varieties exist. Illustrations of one of the die differences is the size of the snake loop at the eagle's beak. This difference is not apparent except on the 1824 Mo 8 Reales

Mint: Mexico City
KM# A376.5 8 REALES
27.0700 g., 0.9030 Silver .7859 oz. ASW **Obv:** REPULICA (error)

Date	F	VF	XF	Unc
1824Mo JM	6,000	9,000	11,000	—

Note: Legible Libertads on the cap are not as prevalent on the Mexico City 8 Reales as on the Durango 8 Reales. They are much more numerous than on the Guanajuato 8 Reales

Type I Obverse/Reverse

NOTE: The cap on the reverse of the curved tail Type I points to the "A" of LIBERTAD.

Mint: Mexico City
KM# 382.1 8 ESCUDOS
27.0700 g., 0.6750 Gold .7616 oz. AGW **Obv:** Profile eagle, snakes tail curved **Rev:** Cap points to "A" of LIBERTAD

Date	F	VF	XF	Unc
1823Mo JM	6,000	9,000	12,500	20,000

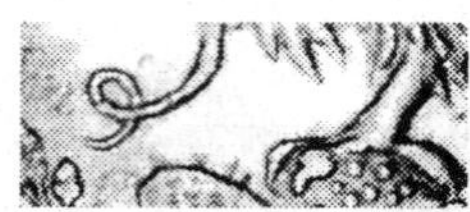

Type II Obverse/Reverse

NOTE: The cap on the reverse of the looped tail Type II points to the "T" of LIBERTAD.

Mint: Mexico City
KM# 382.2 8 ESCUDOS
27.0700 g., 0.6750 Gold .7616 oz. AGW **Obv:** Profile eagle, snake's tail looped **Rev:** Cap points to "T" of LIBERTAD

Date	F	VF	XF	Unc
1823Mo JM	5,000	8,000	12,000	18,000

Note: The quality of the strikes of Type I coins is almost always superior to that of the Type II. Details of the eagle feathers, cactus and lettering on the open book are better on most Type I coins but the Type II coins are scarcer. Type I coins outnumber Type II coins by about two to one

STATE COINAGE

Mint: Guadalajara
KM# 316 1/16 REAL
4.7500 g., Copper, 21 mm. **Obv. Legend:** DEPARTMENTO DE JALISCO **Edge:** Oblique reeding

Date	Good	VG	F	VF	XF
1860	3.00	8.00	17.50	55.00	—

Mint: Guadalajara
KM# 317 1/16 REAL
4.7500 g., Copper, 21 mm. **Obv. Legend:** ESTADO LIBRE DE JALISCO **Edge:** Oblique reeding

Date	Good	VG	F	VF	XF
1861	2.50	6.00	13.50	32.50	—

Mint: Alamos
KM# 335 1/8 REAL
Copper **Obv. Legend:** ESTADO DE OCCIDENTE **Edge:** Oblique reeding **Note:** Size varies: 17-18mm, weight varies: 2-3 g. The C before date on reverse may be a mint mark standing for Concepcion de Alamos.

Date	Good	VG	F	VF	XF
1828 Reverse S	15.00	32.50	57.50	140	—
1829	13.50	30.00	50.00	120	—

Mint: Chihuahua
KM# 318 1/8 REAL
3.5400 g., Copper, 20 mm. **Obv. Legend:** ESTADO SOBERANO DE CHIHUAHUA **Edge:** Plain

Date	Good	VG	F	VF	XF
1833	350	750	—	—	—
1834	350	750	—	—	—
1835/3	350	750	—	—	—

Mint: Chihuahua
KM# 319 1/8 REAL
3.5400 g., Copper, 20 mm. **Obv. Legend:** ESTADO DE CHIHUAHUA **Edge:** Plain

Date	Good	VG	F	VF	XF
1855	5.00	8.50	25.00	75.00	—

Mint: Durango
KM# 322 1/8 REAL
3.5000 g., Copper, 20 mm. **Obv. Legend:** ESTADO DE DURANGO

Date	Good	VG	F	VF	XF
1833 Rare	—	—	—	—	—

Mint: Durango
KM# 320 1/8 REAL
Copper **Rev. Legend:** LIBERTAD **Edge:** Oblique reeding **Note:** Size varies 17-18mm. Weight varies 2.5-4 g. These pieces were frequently struck over 1/8 Real, dated 1821-23 of Nueva Vizcaya. All known examples struck over these coins are believed to be contemporary counterfeits.

Date	Good	VG	F	VF	XF
1824D	5.00	12.50	35.00	85.00	—
1828D	150	250	400	1,000	—

Mint: Durango
KM# 321 1/8 REAL
3.3000 g., Copper **Rev:** Date **Rev. Legend:** OCTo. DE. R. DE DO **Edge:** Oblique reeding **Note:** Size varies 18-19mm.

Date	Good	VG	F	VF	XF
1828D	7.50	18.50	40.00	115	—

Mint: Durango
KM# 323 1/8 REAL
3.5000 g., Copper **Obv. Legend:** REPUBLICA MEXICANA **Note:** Size varies: 19-23mm.

Date	Good	VG	F	VF	XF
1842/33	12.50	22.50	42.50	115	—
1842	8.50	15.00	32.50	100	—

Mint: Durango
KM# 324 1/8 REAL
Copper, 19 mm. **Obv. Legend:** REPUBLICA MEXICANA **Rev. Legend:** DEPARTAMENTO DE DURANGO **Edge:** Ornamented with arc and dot pattern **Note:** Weight varies: 3.5-3.8 g.

Date	Good	VG	F	VF	XF
1845	22.50	55.00	115	250	—
1846 Rare	—	—	—	—	—
1847	3.50	7.50	17.50	37.50	—

Mint: Durango
KM# 325 1/8 REAL
Copper, 19 mm. **Obv. Legend:** REPUBLICA MEXICANA **Rev. Legend:** ESTADO DE DURANGO **Edge:** Ornamented with arc and dot pattern **Note:** Weight varies: 3.5-3.8 g.

Date	Good	VG	F	VF	XF
1851	3.50	8.00	12.50	33.50	—
1852/1	3.50	6.50	11.00	33.50	—
1852	3.00	5.00	8.00	30.00	—
1854	7.00	13.50	28.50	62.50	—

Mint: Guadalajara
KM# 329 1/8 REAL
4.8000 g., Copper, 21 mm. **Obv. Legend:** ESTADO LIBRE DE JALISCO **Edge:** Oblique reeding

Date	Good	VG	F	VF	XF
1828	3.00	5.00	8.00	22.50	—
1831	62.50	100	185	275	—
1832/28	4.50	6.50	11.00	27.50	—
1832	4.50	6.00	10.00	25.00	—
1833	3.50	5.50	9.00	23.50	—
1834	37.50	80.00	150	235	—

Mint: Guadalajara
KM# 330 1/8 REAL
9.5000 g., Copper, 28 mm. **Obv. Legend:** ESTADO LIBRE DE JALISCO **Edge:** Oblique reeding

Date	Good	VG	F	VF	XF
1856	3.00	6.00	9.00	18.50	—
1857	3.00	6.00	9.00	18.50	—
1858	3.00	6.00	9.00	18.50	—
1861	75.00	135	200	300	—
1862/1	4.00	7.00	10.00	22.50	—
1862	4.00	7.00	10.00	22.50	—

Mint: Guadalajara
KM# 331 1/8 REAL
9.5000 g., Copper, 28 mm. **Obv. Legend:** DEPARTMENTO DE JALISCO **Edge:** Oblique reeding

Date	Good	VG	F	VF	XF
1858	4.00	7.00	13.50	28.50	—
1859	3.00	5.75	8.00	20.00	—
1860/59	3.25	6.00	9.00	22.50	—
1860	3.25	6.00	9.00	22.50	—
1862	4.00	8.00	17.50	37.50	—

Mint: Guanajuato
KM# 326 1/8 REAL
3.5000 g., Copper, 21 mm. **Obv. Legend:** ESTADO LIBRE DE GUANAJUATO **Edge:** Ornamented with incuse dots

Date	Good	VG	F	VF	XF
1829	3.00	5.00	10.00	26.50	—
1829 error w/GUANJUATO	4.00	6.50	12.50	28.50	—
1830	8.00	13.50	28.50	62.50	—

Mint: Guanajuato
KM# 327 1/8 REAL
7.2000 g., Brass, 29 mm. **Obv. Legend:** ESTADO LIBRE DE GUANAJUATO **Edge:** Plain

Date	Good	VG	F	VF	XF
1856	7.50	12.00	20.00	75.00	—

Mint: Guanajuato
KM# 328 1/8 REAL
Brass, 25 mm. **Obv. Legend:** ESTADO LIBRE DE GUANAJUATO **Edge:** Plain **Note:** Weight varies: 7.1-7.2 g.

Date	Good	VG	F	VF	XF
1856	4.00	7.50	12.50	35.00	—
1857	3.50	6.00	10.00	30.00	—

Mint: Guanajuato
KM# 328a 1/8 REAL
Copper, 25 mm. **Obv. Legend:** ESTADO LIBRE DE GUANAJUATO **Edge:** Plain **Note:** Weight varies: 7.1-7.2 g.

Date	Good	VG	F	VF	XF
1857	7.00	16.50	32.50	55.00	—

Mint: Hermosillo
KM# 337 1/8 REAL
6.7000 g., Copper, 28 mm. **Obv. Legend:** ESTO LIBE Y SOBO DE SONORA **Edge:** Reeded

Date	Good	VG	F	VF	XF
1859 Rare	—	—	—	—	—

Mint: San Luis Potosi
KM# 336 1/8 REAL
Copper, 21 mm. **Obv. Legend:** ESTADO LIBRE DE SAN LUIS POTOSI **Edge:** Oblique reeding **Note:** Weight varies (1829-31) 4.5-5.5 g; (1859) 4-4.5 g.

Date	Good	VG	F	VF	XF
1829	6.00	11.00	26.50	62.50	—
1830	8.50	15.00	30.00	70.00	—
1831	6.00	9.50	18.50	47.50	—
1859	5.00	8.00	16.50	45.00	—
1865/1 Reported, not confirmed	—	—	—	—	—

Mint: Zacatecas
KM# 338 1/8 REAL
4.0000 g., Brass, 21 mm. **Obv. Legend:** ESTo LIBe FEDo DE ZACATECAS **Edge:** Oblique reeding

Date	Good	VG	F	VF	XF
1825	3.00	5.50	12.00	25.00	—
1827	3.00	5.50	12.00	25.00	—
1827 Inverted A for V in OCTAVO	12.00	20.00	40.00	100	—
1827 OCTAVA (error)	15.00	25.00	50.00	120	—
1827 Inverted 1	12.00	20.00	40.00	100	—
1829 Rare	—	—	—	—	—
1830	2.75	5.00	8.00	20.00	—
1831	4.50	6.75	13.50	27.50	—
1832	2.75	5.00	8.00	20.00	—
1833	2.75	5.00	8.00	20.00	—
1835	3.50	6.00	10.00	25.00	—
1846	3.50	6.00	10.00	25.00	—
1851	38.00	70.00	115	220	—
1852	3.50	6.00	10.00	25.00	—
1858	2.75	5.00	8.00	20.00	—
1859	2.75	5.00	8.00	20.00	—
1862	2.75	5.00	8.00	20.00	—
1863 Reversed 6 in date	2.75	5.00	8.00	20.00	—

Mint: Zacatecas
KM# 339 1/8 REAL
4.0000 g., Copper, 21 mm. **Obv. Legend:** DEPARTMENTO DE ZACATECAS **Edge:** Oblique reeding

Date	Good	VG	F	VF	XF
1836	5.00	8.50	17.50	40.00	—
1845	7.50	12.50	22.50	50.00	—
1846	8.50	10.00	20.00	45.00	—

Mint: Chihuahua
KM# 340 1/4 REAL
Copper, 27 mm. **Obv. Legend:** ESTADO SOBERANO DE CHIHUAHUA **Edge:** Herringbone pattern

Date	Good	VG	F	VF	XF
1833	7.50	16.50	37.50	85.00	—
1834	6.50	13.50	28.00	55.00	—
1835	5.00	10.00	22.00	50.00	—
1835 Plain edge	5.00	8.00	12.00	50.00	—

Mint: Chihuahua
KM# 341 1/4 REAL
7.0800 g., Copper, 27 mm. **Obv. Legend:** ESTADO LIBRE DE CHIHUAHUA **Edge:** Plain

Date	Good	VG	F	VF	XF
1846 With fraction bar	3.50	6.00	12.00	37.50	—
1846 Without fraction bar	5.00	8.50	15.00	45.00	—

Mint: Chihuahua
KM# 342 1/4 REAL
7.0800 g., Copper, 27 mm. **Obv. Legend:** ESTADO DE CHIHUAHUA **Edge:** Plain

Date	Good	VG	F	VF	XF
1855	2.50	5.75	13.50	40.00	—
1856	2.50	5.75	13.50	40.00	—

Mint: Chihuahua
KM# 343 1/4 REAL
7.0800 g., Copper, 27 mm. **Obv. Legend:** DEPARTMENTO DE CHIHUAHUA **Edge:** Plain

Date	Good	VG	F	VF	XF
1855	3.00	5.75	13.00	36.50	—
1855 DE (reversed D)	4.50	8.50	17.50	40.00	—

Mint: Chihuahua
KM# 344 1/4 REAL
Copper, 28 mm. **Obv. Legend:** E. CHIHA LIBERTAD **Edge:** Plain **Note:** Weight varies 11-11.5 g.

Date	Good	VG	F	VF	XF
1860	2.00	4.00	11.00	25.00	—
1861	2.00	4.00	11.00	25.00	—
1865/1	2.50	5.50	13.50	30.00	—
1865	6.00	14.00	28.50	65.00	—
1866/5	5.00	9.50	25.00	60.00	—

Date	Good	VG	F	VF	XF
1866 Coin rotation	2.00	4.00	11.00	25.00	—
1866 Medal rotation	2.00	4.00	11.00	25.00	—

Mint: Culiacan
KM# 363 1/4 REAL
27.0000 g., Copper, 27 mm. **Obv. Legend:** ESTADO LIBRE Y SOBERANO DE SINALOA **Edge:** Reeded

Date	Mintage	Good	VG	F	VF	XF
1847	—	3.50	5.50	12.00	23.50	—
1848	—	3.50	5.50	11.00	22.00	—
1859	—	3.00	4.50	7.50	16.50	—
1861	—	1.75	3.00	4.00	10.00	—
1862	—	1.75	3.00	4.00	11.00	—
1863	—	2.50	4.00	5.00	11.00	—
1864/3	—	2.50	4.00	5.00	11.00	—
1864	—	1.75	3.00	4.75	10.00	—
1865	—	3.00	5.50	8.50	18.50	—
1866/5	7,401,000	2.50	3.50	5.00	11.00	—
1866	Inc. above	1.75	3.00	4.00	10.00	—

Mint: Culiacan
KM# 363a 1/4 REAL
7.0000 g., Brass, 27 mm. **Obv. Legend:** ESTADO LIBRE Y SOBERANO DE SINALOA **Edge:** Reeded

Date	Good	VG	F	VF	XF
1847	5.00	10.00	18.50	40.00	—

Mint: Durango
KM# 345 1/4 REAL
7.0000 g., Copper, 27 mm. **Obv. Legend:** REPUBLICA MEXICANA **Rev:** DURANGO above in wreath

Date	Good	VG	F	VF	XF
1845 Rare	—	—	—	—	—

Mint: Durango
KM# 346 1/4 REAL
7.5000 g., Copper, 27 mm. **Obv. Legend:** REPUBLICA MEXICANA **Rev:** Date, value **Rev. Legend:** DURANGO **Edge:** Ornamented with arc and dot pattern

Date	Good	VG	F	VF	XF
1858 Rare	—	—	—	—	—

Mint: Durango
KM# 347 1/4 REAL
7.5000 g., Copper, 27 mm. **Obv. Legend:** ESTADO DE DURANGO **Rev. Legend:** CONSTITUCION **Edge:** Ornamented wiht arc and dot pattern **Note:** Brass examples have been reported, but not confirmed.

Date	Good	VG	F	VF	XF
1858	4.00	8.50	22.00	50.00	—

Mint: Durango
KM# 350 1/4 REAL
7.5000 g., Copper, 27 mm. **Obv. Legend:** ESTADO DE DURANGO **Rev. Legend:** SUFRAGIO LIBRE **Edge:** Ornamented with arc and dot pattern **Note:** Brass examples have been reported, but not confirmed.

Date	Good	VG	F	VF	XF
1872	2.00	3.75	8.50	18.50	—

Mint: Durango
KM# 349 1/4 REAL
7.0000 g., Copper **Obv. Legend:** ESTADO DE DURANGO **Rev. Legend:** INDEPENDENCIA Y LIBERTAD **Edge:** Ornamented wiht arc and dot pattern **Note:** Size varies: 26-27mm.

Date	Good	VG	F	VF	XF
1866	3.75	8.50	22.00	50.00	—

Mint: Durango
KM# 348 1/4 REAL
Copper, 27 mm. **Obv. Legend:** DEPARTMENTO DE DURANGO **Rev. Legend:** LIBERTAD EN EL ORDEN **Edge:** Ornamented wiht arc and dot pattern **Note:** Weight varies: 7-7.5 g.

Date	Good	VG	F	VF	XF
1860	2.25	6.00	15.00	38.50	—
1866	3.00	7.50	16.50	42.50	—

Mint: Guadalajara
KM# 353 1/4 REAL
9.3500 g., Copper, 28 mm. **Obv:** Oblique reeding **Obv. Legend:** ESTADO LIBRE DE JALISCO

Date	Good	VG	F	VF	XF
1828	3.75	7.00	15.00	37.50	—
1829/8	3.00	6.00	13.00	33.00	—
1829	3.00	6.00	13.00	33.00	—
1830/20	3.00	5.00	10.00	28.50	—
1830/29	3.00	5.00	10.00	28.50	—
1830	3.00	5.00	10.00	28.50	—
1831 Rare	—	—	—	—	—
1832/20	3.00	5.00	10.00	28.50	—
1832/28	3.00	5.00	10.00	28.50	—
1832	2.50	5.00	9.00	27.50	—
1833/2	3.00	5.00	9.00	27.50	—
1834	2.50	5.00	9.00	27.50	—
1835/3	3.00	5.00	9.00	27.50	—
1835	2.50	5.00	9.00	27.50	—
1836 Rare	—	—	—	—	—

Mint: Guadalajara
KM# 354 1/4 REAL
9.3500 g., Copper, 28 mm. **Obv. Legend:** DEPARTMENTO DE JALISCO **Edge:** Oblique reeding

Date	Good	VG	F	VF	XF
1836 Rare	—	—	—	—	—

Mint: Guadalajara
KM# 355 1/4 REAL
19.0000 g., Copper, 32 mm. **Obv. Legend:** ESTADO LIBRE DE JALISCO **Edge:** Oblique reeding

Date	Good	VG	F	VF	XF
1858	3.00	5.50	10.00	22.50	—
1861	3.50	7.50	15.00	30.00	—
1862	3.00	5.50	10.00	22.50	—

Mint: Guadalajara
KM# 356 1/4 REAL
19.0000 g., Copper, 32 mm. **Obv. Legend:** DEPARTMENTO DE JALISCO **Edge:** Oblique reeding

Date	Good	VG	F	VF	XF
1858	2.75	5.00	8.50	18.50	—
1859/8	2.75	5.00	8.50	18.50	—
1859	2.75	5.00	8.50	18.50	—
1860	2.75	5.00	8.50	18.50	—

Mint: Guanajuato
KM# 351 1/4 REAL
7.0000 g., Copper, 27 mm. **Obv. Legend:** ESTADO LIBRE DE GUANAJUATO **Edge:** Ornamented with incuse dots

Date	Good	VG	F	VF	XF
1828	3.75	8.00	18.50	40.00	—
1828 Error with GUANJUATO	4.00	9.00	20.00	42.50	—
1829	5.50	12.00	22.50	47.50	—

Mint: Guanajuato
KM# 352 1/4 REAL

14.0000 g., Copper, 32 mm. **Obv. Legend:** EST. LIB. DE GUANAXUATO **Rev. Legend:** OMNIA VINCIT LABOR **Edge:** Plain

Date	Good	VG	F	VF	XF
1856	7.50	18.50	37.50	65.00	—
1857	6.50	13.50	27.50	48.00	—

Mint: Guanajuato
KM# 352a 1/4 REAL
14.0000 g., Brass, 32 mm. **Obv. Legend:** EST. LIB. DE GUANAXUATO **Rev. Legend:** OMNIA VINCIT LABOR **Edge:** Plain

Date	Good	VG	F	VF	XF
1856	3.25	6.75	13.50	30.00	—
1857	3.25	6.75	13.50	30.00	—

Mint: Hermosillo
KM# 365 1/4 REAL
14.3000 g., Copper, 32 mm. **Obv. Legend:** ESTO. LIBE. Y SOBO. DE SONORA **Edge:** Reeded

Date	Good	VG	F	VF	XF
1859	2.00	5.00	8.00	20.00	—
1861/59	2.75	6.50	11.00	25.00	—
1861	2.00	5.00	8.00	20.00	—
1862	2.00	5.00	8.00	20.00	—
1863/2	5.00	12.50	25.00	55.00	—

Mint: Hermosillo
KM# 364 1/4 REAL
Copper **Obv. Legend:** EST. D. SONORA UNA CUART **Edge:** Oblique reeding **Note:** Size varies: 21-22mm. Weight varies: 2.3-5.5 g.

Date	Good	VG	F	VF	XF
1831 L.S. Rare	—	—	—	—	—
1832 L.S.	2.75	5.50	15.00	50.00	—
1833/2 L.S.	2.00	4.00	12.50	37.50	—
1833 L.S.	2.00	4.00	12.50	37.50	—
1834 L.S.	2.00	4.00	12.50	37.50	—
1835/3 L.S.	2.50	5.50	15.00	40.00	—
1835 L.S.	2.00	4.00	12.50	37.50	—
1836 L.S.	2.00	4.00	12.50	37.50	—

Mint: San Luis Potosi
KM# 362 1/4 REAL
Copper **Obv. Legend:** ESTADO LIBRE Y SOBERANO DE S.L. POTOSI **Rev. Legend:** LIBERTAD Y REFORMA **Edge:** Plain

Date	Good	VG	F	VF	XF
1867	2.50	3.75	6.50	15.00	—
1867 AFG	2.50	3.75	6.50	15.00	—

Note: AFG are the coin designer/engraver initials

Mint: San Luis Potosi
KM# 359 1/4 REAL
Copper **Obv. Legend:** ESTADO LIBRE DE SAN LUIS POTOSI **Rev. Legend:** MEXICO LIBRE **Edge:** Oblique reeding **Note:** Size varies: 25-31mm, weight varies: (1828-32) 9-10 g.; (1859-60) 8-9 g.

Date	Good	VG	F	VF	XF
1828	2.00	3.50	8.00	17.50	—
1829	3.00	4.50	8.50	18.50	—
1830	2.00	3.50	7.00	15.00	—
1832	3.25	5.00	9.00	20.00	—
1859 Large LIBRE	2.50	4.00	7.50	16.50	—
1859 Small LIBRE	2.50	4.00	7.50	16.50	—
1860	2.50	4.00	7.00	16.50	—

Mint: San Luis Potosi
KM# 360 1/4 REAL
Copper **Obv. Legend:** ESTADO LIBRE DE SAN LUIS POTOSI **Rev. Legend:** REPUBLICA MEXICANA **Edge:** Oblique reeding **Note:** Size varies: 25-31mm.

Date	Mintage	Good	VG	F	VF	XF
1862	1,367	2.50	4.00	7.00	15.00	—
1862 LIBR	Inc. above	3.25	5.00	8.00	16.50	—

Mint: San Luis Potosi
KM# 361 1/4 REAL
Copper **Obv. Legend:** ESTADO LIBRE Y SOBERANO DE S.L. POTOSI **Rev. Legend:** LIBERTAD Y REFORMA **Edge:** Reeded or plain **Note:** Size varies: 27-28mm. Weight varies: 9-10 g.

Date	Mintage	Good	VG	F	VF	XF
1867	3,177,000	2.50	3.75	6.50	15.00	—
1867 AFG	Inc. above	2.50	3.75	6.50	15.00	—

Note: AFG are the coin designer/engraver initials

Mint: Zacatecas
KM# 366 1/4 REAL
8.0000 g., Brass **Obv. Legend:** ESTO LIBE FEDO DE ZACATECAS **Edge:** Oblique reeding **Note:** Size varies: 28-29mm.

Date	Good	VG	F	VF	XF
1824 Rare	—	—	—	—	—
1825	2.50	5.00	10.00	20.00	—
1826	75.00	130	220	325	—
1827/17	2.50	5.00	9.00	20.00	—
1829	2.50	5.00	9.00	20.00	—
1830	2.50	5.00	8.50	20.00	—
1831	40.00	85.00	140	220	—
1832	2.50	5.00	9.00	20.00	—
1833	2.50	5.00	9.00	20.00	—
1834 Rare	—	—	—	—	—
1835	2.50	5.00	9.00	20.00	—
1846	2.50	5.00	8.50	20.00	—
1847	2.50	5.00	8.50	20.00	—
1852	2.50	5.00	8.50	20.00	—
1853	2.50	5.00	8.50	20.00	—
1855	4.50	10.00	25.00	65.00	—
1858	2.50	5.00	8.50	20.00	—
1859	2.50	5.00	8.50	20.00	—
1860	75.00	125	200	310	—
1862/57	2.50	5.00	8.50	20.00	—
1862/59/7	8.00	18.00	37.50	75.00	—
1862	2.50	5.00	8.00	20.00	—
1863/2	2.50	5.00	8.00	20.00	—
1863	2.50	5.00	8.00	20.00	—
1864	4.00	11.00	25.00	60.00	—

Mint: Zacatecas
KM# 367 1/4 REAL
8.0000 g., Brass **Obv. Legend:** DEPARTMENTO DE ZACATECAS **Edge:** Oblique reeding **Note:** Size varies: 28-29mm.

Date	Good	VG	F	VF	XF
1836	4.00	8.50	13.50	25.00	—
1845 Rare	—	—	—	—	—
1846	3.50	6.75	9.00	20.00	—

FEDERAL COINAGE

Mint: Mexico City
KM# 315 1/16 REAL
1.7500 g., Copper, 17 mm. **Obv. Legend:** REPUBLICA MEXICANA **Edge:** Ornamented with small incuse rectangles

Date	VG	F	VF	XF	Unc
1831	10.00	20.00	50.00	100	—
1832/1	12.00	22.00	55.00	125	—
1832	10.00	20.00	50.00	100	—
1833	10.00	20.00	50.00	100	—

Mint: Mexico City
KM# 315a 1/16 REAL
1.7500 g., Brass, 17 mm. **Obv. Legend:** REPUBLICA MEXICANA **Edge:** Ornamented with small incuse rectangles

Date	VG	F	VF	XF	Unc
1832	13.50	22.50	60.00	165	—
1833	10.00	17.50	50.00	135	—
1835	400	800	1,250	2,500	—

Mint: Mexico City
KM# 333 1/8 REAL
3.5000 g., Copper, 21 mm. **Obv. Legend:** REPUBLICA MEXICANA **Edge:** Ornamented wiht small incuse rectangles

Date	Good	VG	F	VF	XF
1829	7.50	12.00	25.00	55.00	—
1830	1.00	2.00	6.00	20.00	—
1831	1.50	3.50	7.00	25.00	—
1832	1.50	3.50	7.00	25.00	—
1833/2	1.50	3.50	7.00	25.00	—
1833	1.50	2.75	6.00	20.00	—
1834	1.50	2.75	6.00	20.00	—
1835/4	1.75	3.50	7.00	25.00	—
1835	1.50	2.75	6.00	20.00	—

Mint: Mexico City
KM# 334 1/8 REAL
14.0000 g., Copper **Obv. Legend:** LIBERTAD **Edge:** Lettered (1841-41); Plain (1850-61) **Edge Lettering:** REPUBLICA MEXICANA **Note:** Size varies: 29-30mm.

Date	Good	VG	F	VF	XF
1841	6.00	15.00	30.00	75.00	—
1842	2.50	5.00	10.00	30.00	—
1850	12.50	20.00	30.00	80.00	—
1861	5.00	12.00	25.00	70.00	—

Mint: Mexico City
KM# 332 1/8 REAL
7.0000 g., Copper, 27 mm. **Obv. Legend:** REPUBLICA MEXICANA **Edge:** Ornamented with small incuse rectangles

Date	VG	F	VF	XF	Unc
1829	450	900	1,500	2,500	—

Mint: Chihuahua
KM# 368 1/4 REAL
0.8450 g., 0.9030 Silver .0245 oz. ASW **Note:** Mint mark CA.

Date	VG	F	VF	XF	Unc
1843CA RG	75.00	125	300	500	—

Mint: Culiacan
KM# 368.1 1/4 REAL
0.8450 g., 0.9030 Silver .0245 oz. ASW **Note:** Mint mark C.

Date	VG	F	VF	XF	Unc
1855C LR	50.00	100	200	400	—

Mint: Durango
KM# 368.2 1/4 REAL
0.8450 g., 0.9030 Silver .0245 oz. ASW **Note:** Struck at Durango Mint, mint mark Do.

Date	VG	F	VF	XF	Unc
1842Do LR	12.00	20.00	40.00	125	—
1843Do	20.00	25.00	60.00	150	—

Mint: Guadalajara

KM# 368.3 1/4 REAL

0.8450 g., 0.9030 Silver .0245 oz. ASW **Note:** Mint mark Ga.

Date	VG	F	VF	XF	Unc
1842Ga JG	2.50	5.50	8.00	20.00	—
1843/2Ga JG	—	—	—	—	—
1843Ga JG	6.00	9.00	12.50	30.00	—
1843Ga MC	4.00	6.50	9.00	25.00	—
1844Ga MC	4.00	6.50	9.00	25.00	—
1844Ga LR	2.50	5.00	7.50	15.00	—
1845Ga LR	2.50	4.50	7.50	15.00	—
1846Ga LR	5.00	8.00	10.00	25.00	—
1847Ga LR	4.00	6.50	9.00	25.00	—
1848Ga LR Rare	—	—	—	—	—
1850Ga LR Rare	—	—	—	—	—
1851Ga LR	6.00	10.00	20.00	50.00	—
1852Ga LR	50.00	100	135	200	—
1854/3Ga LR	50.00	100	135	200	—
1854Ga LR	5.00	10.00	12.50	30.00	—
1855Ga LR	5.00	8.00	10.00	30.00	—
1857Ga LR	6.50	10.00	15.00	27.50	—
1862Ga LR	5.50	10.00	15.00	30.00	—

Mint: Guadalupe y Calvo

KM# 368.4 1/4 REAL

0.8450 g., 0.9030 Silver .0245 oz. ASW **Note:** Mint mark GC.

Date	VG	F	VF	XF	Unc
1844GC LR	50.00	75.00	125	300	—

Mint: Guanajuato

KM# 368.5 1/4 REAL

0.8450 g., 0.9030 Silver .0245 oz. ASW **Note:** Mint mark Go.

Date	VG	F	VF	XF	Unc
1842Go PM	4.00	6.00	10.00	20.00	—
1842Go LR	2.00	4.00	8.00	15.00	—
1843/2Go LR	4.00	6.00	10.00	20.00	—
1843Go LR	2.00	4.00	8.00	15.00	—
1844/3Go LR	—	—	—	—	—
1844Go LR	2.00	4.00	8.00	15.00	—
1845Go LR	8.00	15.00	30.00	60.00	—
1846/5Go LR	—	—	—	—	—
1846Go LR	4.00	6.00	10.00	20.00	—
1847Go LR	2.00	4.00	8.00	15.00	—
1848/7Go LR	2.00	4.00	8.00	15.00	—
1848Go LR	2.00	4.00	8.00	15.00	—
1849/7Go LR	8.00	15.00	30.00	60.00	—
1849Go LR	2.00	4.00	8.00	15.00	—
1850Go LR	2.00	4.00	8.00	15.00	—
1851Go LR	2.00	4.00	8.00	15.00	—
1852Go LR	2.00	4.00	8.00	15.00	—
1853Go LR	2.00	4.00	8.00	15.00	—
1855Go LR	4.00	8.00	15.00	30.00	—
1856/4Go LR	—	—	—	—	—
1856Go LR	5.00	10.00	20.00	35.00	—
1862/1Go LR	3.00	5.00	10.00	20.00	—
1862Go LR	2.00	4.00	8.00	15.00	—
1863Go	2.00	4.00	8.00	15.00	—

Mint: Mexico City

KM# 357 1/4 REAL

14.0000 g., Copper, 33 mm. **Obv. Legend:** REPUBLICA MEXICANA **Edge:** Ornamented with small incuse rectangles

Date	VG	F	VF	XF	Unc
1829	8.00	30.00	75.00	250	—

Mint: Mexico City

KM# 368.6 1/4 REAL

0.8450 g., 0.9030 Silver .0245 oz. ASW **Note:** Mint mark Mo.

Date	VG	F	VF	XF	Unc
1842Mo LR	2.00	4.00	8.00	15.00	—
1843Mo LR	2.00	4.00	8.00	15.00	—
1844/3Mo LR	8.00	12.00	20.00	40.00	—
1844Mo LR	4.00	6.00	10.00	20.00	—
1845Mo LR	4.00	6.00	10.00	20.00	—
1846Mo LR	2.00	4.00	8.00	15.00	—
1850Mo LR	5.00	10.00	20.00	35.00	—
1858Mo LR	4.00	8.00	15.00	30.00	—
1859Mo LR	4.00	6.00	10.00	20.00	—
1860Mo LR	4.00	6.00	10.00	20.00	—
1861Mo LR	4.00	6.00	10.00	20.00	—
1862Mo LR	4.00	6.00	10.00	20.00	—
1863/53Mo LR	—	—	—	—	—
1863Mo LR	4.00	6.00	10.00	20.00	—

Mint: Mexico City

KM# 358 1/4 REAL

7.0000 g., Copper, 27 mm. **Obv. Legend:** REPUBLICA MEXICANA **Edge:** Ornamented with small incuse rectangles **Note:** Reduced size.

Date	VG	F	VF	XF	Unc
1829	12.00	25.00	50.00	150	—
1830	1.50	2.75	5.00	10.00	—
1831	1.50	2.75	5.00	10.00	—
1832	5.50	10.00	20.00	35.00	—
1833	1.50	2.75	5.00	10.00	—
1834/3	1.75	3.00	6.00	12.00	—
1834	1.50	2.75	5.00	10.00	—
1835	1.50	2.75	5.00	10.00	—
1836	1.50	2.75	5.00	10.00	—
1837	6.50	13.50	22.50	45.00	—

Mint: Mexico City

KM# 358a.1 1/4 REAL

7.0000 g., Brass, 27 mm. **Countermark:** JM **Obv. Legend:** REPUBLICA MEXICANA **Edge:** Ornamented with small incuse rectangles **Note:** Reduced size.

Date	VG	F	VF	XF	Unc
1831	8.00	13.50	27.50	50.00	—

Mint: Mexico City

KM# 358a.2 1/4 REAL

7.0000 g., Brass, 27 mm. **Obv. Legend:** REPUBLICA MEXICANA **Edge:** Ornamented with small incuse rectangles **Note:** Without countermark.

Date	VG	F	VF	XF	Unc
1831	—	—	—	—	—

Mint: San Luis Potosi

KM# 368.7 1/4 REAL

0.8450 g., 0.9030 Silver .0245 oz. ASW **Note:** Mint mark SLP, PI, P, I/P.

Date	VG	F	VF	XF	Unc
1842S.L.Pi	2.00	4.00	8.00	15.00	—
1843/2S.L.Pi	4.00	6.00	10.00	20.00	—
1843S.L.Pi	2.00	4.00	8.00	15.00	—
1844S.L.Pi	2.00	4.00	8.00	15.00	—
1845/3S.L.Pi	4.00	6.00	10.00	25.00	—
1845/4S.L.Pi	4.00	6.00	10.00	25.00	—
1845S.L.Pi	2.00	4.00	8.00	15.00	—
1847/5S.L.Pi	4.00	6.00	10.00	20.00	—
1847S.L.Pi	2.00	4.00	8.00	15.00	—
1851/47S.L.Pi	4.00	8.00	15.00	30.00	—
1854S.L.Pi	125	200	275	400	—
1856S.L.Pi	4.00	8.00	15.00	30.00	—
1857S.L.Pi	5.00	10.00	20.00	35.00	—
1862/57S.L.Pi	10.00	20.00	40.00	85.00	—

Mint: Zacatecas

KM# 368.8 1/4 REAL

0.8450 g., 0.9030 Silver .0245 oz. ASW **Note:** Mint mark Zs.

Date	VG	F	VF	XF	Unc
1842/1Zs LR	4.00	8.00	15.00	30.00	—
1842Zs LR	4.00	6.00	10.00	20.00	—

Mint: Alamos

KM# 370 1/2 REAL

1.6900 g., 0.9030 Silver .0490 oz. ASW **Obv:** Hook-necked eagle

Date	F	VF	XF	Unc
1862A PG Rare	—	—	—	—

Mint: Chihuahua

KM# 370.1 1/2 REAL

1.6900 g., 0.9030 Silver .0490 oz. ASW **Obv:** Facing eagle

Date	F	VF	XF	Unc
1844 Ca RG	75.00	125	175	275
1845 Ca RG	75.00	125	150	250

Mint: Culiacan

KM# 370.2 1/2 REAL

1.6900 g., 0.9030 Silver .0490 oz. ASW **Obv:** Facing eagle **Note:** Mint mark C, Co.

Date	F	VF	XF	Unc
1846 CE	30.00	50.00	75.00	150
1848/7 CE	15.00	25.00	45.00	90.00
1849/8 CE	15.00	25.00	45.00	90.00
1849 CE	—	—	—	—
1852 CE	12.50	20.00	40.00	80.00
1853/1 CE	12.50	20.00	40.00	80.00
1854 CE	20.00	35.00	50.00	100
1856 CE	12.50	20.00	40.00	80.00
1857/6 CE	20.00	35.00	50.00	100
1857 CE	15.00	25.00	45.00	90.00
1858 CE Error 1 for 1/2	12.50	20.00	40.00	80.00

Date	F	VF	XF	Unc
1860/59 PV	20.00	35.00	50.00	100
1860 PV	12.50	20.00	40.00	80.00
1861 PV	12.50	20.00	40.00	80.00
1863 CE Error 1 for 1/2	15.00	25.00	45.00	90.00
1867 CE	12.50	20.00	40.00	80.00
1869 6/5 CE Error 1 for 1/2	12.50	20.00	40.00	80.00

Mint: Durango

KM# 370.3 1/2 REAL

1.6900 g., 0.9030 Silver .0490 oz. ASW **Obv:** Facing eagle **Note:** Mint mark D, Do.

Date	F	VF	XF	Unc
1832 RM	125	225	350	600
1832 RM/L	—	—	—	—
1833/2 RM/L	75.00	100	150	225
1833/1 RM/L	12.50	20.00	40.00	80.00
1833 RM	25.00	40.00	75.00	150
1834/1 RM	25.00	40.00	75.00	150
1834 RM	12.50	20.00	40.00	80.00
1837/1 RM	12.50	30.00	60.00	200
1837/4 RM	12.50	30.00	60.00	200
1837/6 RM	12.50	30.00	60.00	200
1841/33 RM	15.00	30.00	60.00	250
1842/32 RM	12.50	20.00	40.00	80.00
1842 RM	12.50	20.00	40.00	80.00
1842 8R RM Error	12.50	20.00	40.00	80.00
1842 1/2/8R RM	12.50	20.00	40.00	80.00
1843/33 RM	15.00	25.00	50.00	100
1843 RM	15.00	25.00	50.00	100
1845/31 RM	12.50	20.00	40.00	80.00
1845/34 RM	12.50	20.00	40.00	80.00
1845/35 RM	12.50	20.00	40.00	80.00
1845 RM	15.00	25.00	50.00	100
1846 RM	30.00	50.00	80.00	200
1848/5 RM	35.00	55.00	110	250
1848/36 RM	25.00	40.00	75.00	200
1849 JMR	25.00	40.00	75.00	200
1850 RM Rare	—	—	—	—
1850 JMR	25.00	40.00	75.00	200
1851 JMR	20.00	35.00	50.00	100
1852/1 JMR	65.00	125	250	600
1852 JMR	30.00	50.00	80.00	200
1853 CP	12.50	20.00	40.00	80.00
1854 CP	25.00	40.00	75.00	200
1855 CP	25.00	40.00	60.00	150
1856/5 CP	20.00	35.00	50.00	100
1857 CP	20.00	35.00	50.00	100
1858/7 CP	20.00	35.00	50.00	100
1859 CP	20.00	35.00	50.00	100
1860/59 CP	40.00	65.00	135	300
1861 CP	125	250	400	700
1862 CP	25.00	40.00	60.00	125
1864 LT	100	300	500	1,000
1869 CP	40.00	65.00	125	275

Mint: Estado de Mexico

KM# 370.4 1/2 REAL

1.6900 g., 0.9030 Silver .0490 oz. ASW **Obv:** Facing eagle

Date	F	VF	XF	Unc
1829EoMo LF	175	300	500	1,400

Mint: Guadalajara

KM# 370.5 1/2 REAL

1.6900 g., 0.9030 Silver .0490 oz. ASW **Obv:** Facing eagle

Date	F	VF	XF	Unc
1825Ga FS	25.00	40.00	75.00	200
1826Ga FS	10.00	15.00	35.00	80.00
1828/7Ga FS	12.50	20.00	40.00	90.00
1829Ga FS	7.50	15.00	30.00	70.00
1830/29Ga FS	40.00	60.00	100	200
1831Ga LP Rare	—	—	—	—
1832Ga FS	10.00	20.00	35.00	80.00
1834/3Ga FS	65.00	100	175	250
1834Ga FS	10.00	20.00	35.00	80.00
1835/4/3Ga FS/LP	15.00	25.00	40.00	90.00
1837/6Ga JG	100	250	500	1,000
1838/7Ga JG	15.00	25.00	40.00	90.00
1839/8Ga JG/FS	35.00	75.00	150	250
1839Ga MC	10.00	20.00	35.00	80.00
1840/39Ga MC/JG	—	—	—	—
1840Ga MC	15.00	25.00	40.00	90.00
1841Ga MC	20.00	35.00	50.00	100
1842/1Ga JG	15.00	25.00	40.00	90.00
1842Ga JG	10.00	20.00	35.00	80.00
1843/2Ga JG	15.00	30.00	50.00	100
1843Ga JG	10.00	20.00	35.00	80.00
1843Ga MC/JG	10.00	20.00	35.00	80.00
1843Ga MC	10.00	20.00	35.00	80.00
1844Ga MC	10.00	20.00	35.00	80.00
1845Ga MC	10.00	20.00	35.00	80.00
1845Ga JG	10.00	20.00	35.00	80.00
1846Ga MC	10.00	20.00	35.00	80.00
1846Ga JG	10.00	20.00	35.00	80.00
1847Ga JG	10.00	20.00	35.00	80.00
1848/7Ga JG	10.00	20.00	35.00	80.00
1849Ga JG	10.00	20.00	35.00	80.00
1850/49Ga JG	—	—	—	—
1850Ga JG	10.00	20.00	35.00	80.00
1851/0Ga JG	10.00	20.00	35.00	80.00
1852Ga JG	10.00	20.00	35.00	80.00
1853Ga JG	10.00	20.00	35.00	80.00
1854Ga JG	10.00	20.00	35.00	80.00
1855/4Ga JG	10.00	20.00	35.00	80.00
1855Ga JG	10.00	20.00	35.00	80.00

Date	F	VF	XF	Unc
1856Ga JG	10.00	20.00	35.00	80.00
1857Ga JG	10.00	20.00	35.00	80.00
1858/7Ga JG	10.00	20.00	35.00	80.00
1858Ga JG	10.00	20.00	35.00	80.00
1859/7Ga JG	10.00	20.00	35.00	80.00
1860/59Ga JG	10.00	20.00	35.00	80.00
1861Ga JG	5.00	12.50	25.00	60.00
1862/1Ga JG	15.00	25.00	40.00	90.00

Mint: Guadalupe y Calvo
KM# 370.6 1/2 REAL

1.6900 g., 0.9030 Silver .0490 oz. ASW **Obv:** Facing eagle

Date	F	VF	XF	Unc
1844GC MP	50.00	100	150	350
1845GC MP	25.00	50.00	100	200
1846GC MP	25.00	50.00	100	200
1847GC MP	25.00	50.00	100	300
1848GC MP	20.00	40.00	75.00	150
1849GC MP	25.00	50.00	100	200
1850GC MP	30.00	60.00	125	250
1851GC MP	25.00	50.00	100	200

Mint: Guanajuato
KM# 370.7 1/2 REAL

1.6900 g., 0.9030 Silver .0490 oz. ASW **Obv:** Facing eagle
Note: Varieties exist.

Date	F	VF	XF	Unc
1826Go MJ	125	250	400	1,000
1827/6Go MJ	7.50	15.00	30.00	75.00
1828/7Go MJ	7.50	15.00	30.00	75.00
1828Go MJ Denomination 2/1	—	—	—	—
1828Go JG	—	—	—	—
1828Go MR	50.00	100	150	250
1829/8Go MJ	5.00	10.00	25.00	50.00
1829Go MJ	5.00	10.00	25.00	50.00
1829Go MJ Reversed N in MEXICANA	5.00	10.00	25.00	50.00
1830Go MJ	5.00	10.00	25.00	50.00
1831/29Go MJ	15.00	30.00	60.00	150
1831Go MJ	10.00	20.00	40.00	80.00
1832/1Go MJ	7.50	15.00	30.00	75.00
1832Go MJ	7.50	15.00	30.00	75.00
1833Go MJ Round top 3	10.00	20.00	40.00	80.00
1833Go MJ Flat top 3	10.00	20.00	40.00	80.00
1834Go PJ	5.00	10.00	25.00	50.00
1835Go PJ	5.00	10.00	25.00	50.00
1836/5Go PJ	7.50	15.00	30.00	75.00
1836Go PJ	5.00	10.00	25.00	50.00
1837Go PJ	5.00	10.00	25.00	50.00
1838/7Go PJ	5.00	10.00	25.00	50.00
1839Go PJ	5.00	10.00	25.00	50.00
1839Go PJ Error: REPUBLIGA	5.00	10.00	25.00	50.00
1840/39Go PJ	7.50	10.00	25.00	75.00
1840Go PJ Straight J	5.00	10.00	25.00	50.00
1840Go PJ Curved J	5.00	10.00	25.00	50.00
1841/31Go PJ	5.00	10.00	25.00	50.00
1841Go PJ	5.00	10.00	25.00	50.00
1842/1Go PJ	5.00	10.00	25.00	50.00
1842/1Go PM	5.00	10.00	25.00	50.00
1842Go PM/J	5.00	10.00	25.00	50.00
1842Go PJ	5.00	10.00	25.00	50.00
1842Go PM	5.00	10.00	25.00	50.00
1843/33Go PM 1/2 over 8	5.00	10.00	25.00	50.00
1843Go PM Convex wings	5.00	10.00	25.00	50.00
1843Go PM Concave wings	5.00	10.00	25.00	50.00
1844/3Go PM	5.00	10.00	25.00	50.00
1844Go PM	10.00	20.00	40.00	90.00
1845/4Go PM	5.00	10.00	25.00	50.00
1845Go PM	5.00	10.00	25.00	50.00
1846/4Go PM	5.00	10.00	25.00	50.00
1846/5Go PM	5.00	10.00	25.00	50.00
1846Go PM	5.00	10.00	25.00	50.00
1847/6Go PM	7.50	15.00	30.00	60.00
1847Go PM	7.50	15.00	30.00	60.00
1848/35Go PM	5.00	10.00	25.00	50.00
1848Go PM	5.00	10.00	25.00	50.00
1848Go PF/M	5.00	10.00	25.00	50.00
1849/39Go PF	5.00	10.00	25.00	50.00
1849Go PF	5.00	10.00	25.00	50.00
1849Go PF Error: MEXCANA	5.00	10.00	25.00	50.00
1850Go PF	5.00	10.00	25.00	50.00
1851Go PF	5.00	10.00	25.00	50.00
1852/1Go PF	5.00	10.00	25.00	50.00
1852Go PF	2.50	7.50	17.50	40.00
1853Go PF/R	5.00	10.00	25.00	50.00
1853Go PF	5.00	10.00	25.00	50.00
1854Go PF	5.00	10.00	25.00	50.00
1855Go PF	5.00	10.00	25.00	50.00
1856/4Go PF	5.00	10.00	25.00	50.00
1856/5Go PF	5.00	10.00	25.00	50.00
1856Go PF	5.00	10.00	25.00	50.00
1857/6Go PF	5.00	10.00	25.00	50.00
1857Go PF	5.00	10.00	25.00	50.00
1858/7Go PF	7.50	15.00	30.00	60.00
1858Go PF	5.00	10.00	25.00	50.00
1859Go PF	5.00	10.00	25.00	50.00
1860Go PF Small 1/2	5.00	10.00	25.00	50.00
1860Go PF Large 1/2	5.00	10.00	25.00	50.00
1860/59Go PF	5.00	10.00	25.00	50.00
1861Go PF Small 1/2	5.00	10.00	25.00	50.00
1861Go PF Large 1/2	5.00	10.00	25.00	50.00
1862/1Go YE	5.00	10.00	25.00	50.00
1862Go YE	2.50	7.50	17.50	40.00
1862Go YF	5.00	10.00	25.00	50.00
1867Go YF	2.50	7.50	17.50	40.00
1868Go YF	2.50	7.50	17.50	40.00

Mint: Hermosillo
KM# 370.8 1/2 REAL

1.6900 g., 0.9030 Silver .0490 oz. ASW **Obv:** Facing eagle

Date	F	VF	XF	Unc
1839Ho PP Unique	—	—	—	—
1862Ho FM	500	650	1,000	—
1867Ho PR/FM Inverted 6, and 7/1	100	175	250	500

Mint: Mexico City
KM# 370.9 1/2 REAL

1.6900 g., 0.9030 Silver .0490 oz. ASW **Obv:** Facing eagle

Date	F	VF	XF	Unc
1825Mo JM Short top 5	10.00	20.00	40.00	80.00
1825Mo JM Long top 5	10.00	20.00	40.00	80.00
1826/5Mo JM	10.00	20.00	40.00	80.00
1826Mo JM	5.00	10.00	20.00	60.00
1827/6Mo JM	5.00	10.00	20.00	60.00
1827Mo JM	5.00	10.00	20.00	60.00
1828/7Mo JM	7.50	15.00	25.00	85.00
1828Mo JM	10.00	20.00	40.00	90.00
1829Mo JM	7.50	15.00	25.00	75.00
1830Mo JM	5.00	10.00	20.00	60.00
1831Mo JM	5.00	10.00	20.00	60.00
1832Mo JM	7.50	12.50	27.50	60.00
1833Mo MJ	7.50	12.50	27.50	60.00
1834Mo ML	5.00	10.00	20.00	60.00
1835Mo ML	5.00	10.00	20.00	60.00
1836/5Mo ML/MF	7.50	15.00	25.00	65.00
1836Mo ML	7.50	15.00	25.00	65.00
1838Mo ML	5.00	10.00	20.00	60.00
1839/8Mo ML	5.00	10.00	25.00	65.00
1839Mo ML	5.00	10.00	20.00	50.00
1840Mo ML	5.00	10.00	20.00	50.00
1841Mo ML	5.00	10.00	20.00	50.00
1842Mo ML	5.00	10.00	20.00	50.00
1842Mo MM	5.00	10.00	20.00	50.00
1843Mo MM	10.00	20.00	40.00	80.00
1844Mo MF	5.00	10.00	20.00	50.00
1845/4Mo MF	5.00	10.00	25.00	60.00
1845Mo MF	5.00	10.00	20.00	50.00
1846Mo MF	5.00	10.00	20.00	50.00
1847Mo RC	10.00	20.00	40.00	80.00
1847Mo RC R/M	10.00	20.00	40.00	80.00
1848/7Mo GC/RC	5.00	10.00	20.00	50.00
1849Mo GC	5.00	10.00	20.00	50.00
1850Mo GC	5.00	10.00	20.00	50.00
1851Mo GC	5.00	10.00	20.00	50.00
1852Mo GC	5.00	10.00	20.00	50.00
1853Mo GC	5.00	10.00	20.00	50.00
1854Mo GC	5.00	10.00	20.00	50.00
1855Mo GC	5.00	10.00	20.00	50.00
1855Mo GF/GC	7.50	12.50	25.00	65.00
1856/5Mo GF	7.50	12.50	25.00	65.00
1857Mo GF	5.00	10.00	20.00	50.00
1858Mo FH	3.00	5.00	12.50	40.00
1858Mo FH F/G	5.00	10.00	20.00	50.00
1858/9Mo FH	5.00	10.00	20.00	50.00
1859Mo FH	3.00	6.00	15.00	50.00
1860Mo FH/GC	5.00	10.00	20.00	50.00
1860Mo FH	3.00	6.00	15.00	50.00
1860Mo TH	25.00	50.00	100	200
1860/59Mo FH	7.50	12.50	25.00	65.00
1861Mo CH	3.00	6.00	15.00	45.00
1862/52Mo CH	5.00	10.00	20.00	50.00
1862Mo CH	3.00	6.00	15.00	45.00
1863/55Mo TH/GC	5.00	10.00	20.00	50.00
1863Mo CH/GC	5.00	10.00	20.00	50.00
1863Mo CH	3.00	6.00	15.00	45.00

Mint: San Luis Potosi
KM# 370.10 1/2 REAL

1.6900 g., 0.9030 Silver .0490 oz. ASW **Obv:** Facing eagle

Date	F	VF	XF	Unc
1831 Pi JS	7.50	12.50	25.00	65.00
1841/36 Pi JS	20.00	40.00	75.00	125
1842/1 Pi PS	20.00	40.00	75.00	125
1842/1 Pi PS P/J	60.00	80.00	150	300
1842 Pi PS/PJ	50.00	75.00	125	250
1842 PS	60.00	80.00	150	300
1842 Pi JS	20.00	40.00	75.00	125
1843/2 Pi PS	17.50	25.00	40.00	80.00
1843 Pi PS	15.00	25.00	35.00	70.00
1843 Pi AM	10.00	15.00	25.00	60.00
1844 Pi AM	10.00	15.00	30.00	65.00
1845 Pi AM	250	375	500	1,500
1846/5 Pi AM	40.00	75.00	125	200
1847/6 Pi AM	15.00	25.00	40.00	80.00
1848 Pi AM	15.00	25.00	40.00	80.00
1849 Pi MC/AM	15.00	25.00	40.00	80.00
1849 Pi MC	12.50	20.00	35.00	70.00
1850/49 Pi MC	—	—	—	—
1850 Pi MC	10.00	15.00	25.00	60.00
1850P MC	—	—	—	—
1851 Pi MC	10.00	15.00	25.00	60.00
1852 Pi MC	10.00	20.00	30.00	65.00
1853 Pi MC	7.50	12.50	20.00	60.00
1854 Pi MC	7.50	12.50	20.00	60.00
1855 Pi MC	15.00	20.00	35.00	70.00
1856 Pi MC	15.00	25.00	50.00	100
1856PI (no I)	—	—	—	—
1857 Pi MC	7.50	12.50	20.00	60.00
1857 Pi PS	10.00	15.00	30.00	65.00
1858 Pi MC	12.50	20.00	35.00	70.00
1858 Pi PS	12.50	20.00	35.00	70.00
1859 Pi MC Rare	—	—	—	—
1860/59 Pi PS	125	200	600	—
1861 Pi RO	10.00	15.00	30.00	60.00
1862/1 Pi RO	15.00	25.00	50.00	125
1862 Pi RO	15.00	25.00	50.00	125
1863/2 Pi RO	15.00	25.00	45.00	100

Mint: Zacatecas
KM# 370.11 1/2 REAL

1.6900 g., 0.9030 Silver .0490 oz. ASW **Obv:** Facing eagle
Note: Mint mark Z, Zs.

Date	F	VF	XF	Unc
1826 AZ	5.00	10.00	20.00	60.00
1826 AO	5.00	10.00	20.00	60.00
1827 AO	5.00	10.00	20.00	60.00
1828/7 AO	5.00	10.00	20.00	60.00
1829 AO	5.00	10.00	20.00	60.00
1830 OV	5.00	10.00	20.00	60.00
1831 OV	25.00	50.00	75.00	150
1831 OM	5.00	10.00	20.00	60.00
1832 OM	5.00	10.00	20.00	60.00
1833 OM	5.00	10.00	20.00	60.00
1834 OM	5.00	10.00	20.00	60.00
1835/4 OM	5.00	10.00	20.00	60.00
1835 OM	5.00	10.00	20.00	60.00
1836 OM	5.00	10.00	20.00	60.00
1837 OM	10.00	20.00	40.00	80.00
1838 OM	5.00	10.00	20.00	60.00
1839 OM	7.50	15.00	30.00	65.00
1840 OM	10.00	25.00	45.00	90.00
1841 OM	10.00	25.00	45.00	90.00
1842/1 OM	5.00	10.00	20.00	60.00
1842 OM	5.00	10.00	20.00	60.00
1843 OM	40.00	75.00	115	250
1844 OM	5.00	10.00	20.00	60.00
1845 OM	5.00	10.00	20.00	60.00
1846 OM	7.50	15.00	30.00	65.00
1847 OM	5.00	10.00	20.00	50.00
1848 OM	5.00	10.00	20.00	50.00
1849 OM	5.00	10.00	20.00	50.00
1850 OM	5.00	10.00	20.00	50.00
1851 OM	5.00	10.00	20.00	50.00
1852 OM	5.00	10.00	20.00	50.00
1853 OM	5.00	10.00	20.00	50.00
1854/3 OM	5.00	10.00	20.00	50.00
1854 OM	5.00	10.00	20.00	50.00
1855/3 OM	7.50	15.00	30.00	65.00
1855 OM	5.00	10.00	20.00	50.00
1856 OM	5.00	10.00	20.00	50.00
1857 MO	5.00	10.00	20.00	50.00
1858 MO	5.00	10.00	20.00	50.00
1859 MO	6.00	8.50	17.50	35.00
1859 VL	6.00	8.50	17.50	40.00
1860/50 VL Inverted A for V	5.00	10.00	20.00	50.00
1860/59 VL Inverted A for V	5.00	10.00	20.00	50.00
1860 MO	5.00	10.00	20.00	50.00
1860 VL	5.00	10.00	20.00	50.00
1861/0 VL Inverted A for V	7.50	15.00	30.00	65.00
1861 VL Inverted A for V	5.00	10.00	20.00	50.00
1862 VL Inverted A for V	5.00	10.00	20.00	50.00
1863/1 VL Inverted A for V	7.50	15.00	30.00	65.00
1863 VL Inverted A for V	5.00	10.00	20.00	50.00
1869 YH	5.00	10.00	20.00	50.00

Mint: Chihuahua
KM# 372 REAL

3.3800 g., 0.9030 Silver .0981 oz. ASW

Date	F	VF	XF	Unc
1844 Ca RG	500	1,000	1,500	2,750
1845 Ca RG	500	1,000	1,500	2,750
1855 Ca RG	100	150	225	450

Mint: Culiacan
KM# 372.1 REAL

3.3800 g., 0.9030 Silver .0981 oz. ASW

Date	F	VF	XF	Unc
1846C CE	12.50	25.00	40.00	110
1848C CE	12.50	25.00	40.00	110
1850C CE	12.50	25.00	40.00	110
1851/0C CE	12.50	25.00	40.00	110
1852/1C CE	7.50	15.00	30.00	100
1853/2C CE	7.50	15.00	30.00	100
1854C CE	7.50	15.00	30.00	100
1856C CE	40.00	65.00	100	225
1857/4C CE	10.00	20.00	35.00	100
1857/6C CE	10.00	20.00	35.00	100
1858C CE	5.00	7.50	15.00	100
1859C CE	—	—	—	—
1860C PV	5.00	7.50	15.00	100
1861C PV	5.00	7.50	15.00	100
1863C CE 3 known	—	—	1,650	2,250
1869C CE	—	7.50	15.00	100

Mint: Durango
KM# 372.2 REAL

3.3800 g., 0.9030 Silver .0981 oz. ASW

Date	F	VF	XF	Unc
1832/1Do RM	5.00	10.00	20.00	90.00
1832Do RM/RL	10.00	15.00	30.00	100
1832Do RM	5.00	10.00	20.00	100
1834/24Do RM/RL	15.00	25.00	50.00	150
1834/3Do RM/RL	15.00	25.00	50.00	150

Date	F	VF	XF	Unc
1834Do RM	10.00	20.00	40.00	110
1836/4Do RM	5.00	7.50	15.00	100
1836Do RM	5.00	7.50	15.00	100
1837Do RM 3/2	12.50	20.00	40.00	110
1837Do RM	12.50	20.00	40.00	110
1841Do RM	7.50	15.00	30.00	100
1842/32Do RM	10.00	20.00	40.00	110
1842Do RM	7.50	15.00	30.00	100
1843Do RM	5.00	7.50	15.00	100
1844/34Do RM	15.00	25.00	45.00	125
1845Do RM	5.00	7.50	15.00	100
1846Do RM	7.50	15.00	30.00	100
1847Do RM	10.00	15.00	35.00	100
1848/31Do RM	10.00	15.00	35.00	100
1848/33Do RM	10.00	15.00	35.00	100
1848/5Do RM	10.00	15.00	35.00	100
1848Do RM	7.50	12.50	20.00	100
1849/8Do CM	10.00	15.00	30.00	100
1850Do JMR	20.00	40.00	75.00	175
1851Do JMR	20.00	40.00	75.00	175
1852Do JMR	20.00	40.00	75.00	175
1853Do CP	12.50	20.00	35.00	100
1854/1Do CP	10.00	15.00	25.00	100
1854Do CP	7.50	12.50	20.00	100
1855Do CP	10.00	15.00	25.00	100
1856Do CP	12.50	20.00	35.00	100
1857Do CP	12.50	20.00	35.00	100
1858Do CP	12.50	20.00	35.00	100
1859Do CP	7.50	12.50	20.00	100
1860/59Do CP	10.00	15.00	25.00	100
1861Do CP	15.00	25.00	40.00	110
1862/1Do CP	225	300	450	1,250
1864Do LT	15.00	25.00	40.00	110

Mint: Estado de Mexico
KM# 372.3 REAL
3.3800 g., 0.9030 Silver .0981 oz. ASW

Date	F	VF	XF	Unc
1828EoMo LF	200	300	450	1,500

Mint: Guadalajara
KM# 372.4 REAL
3.3800 g., 0.9030 Silver .0981 oz. ASW

Date	F	VF	XF	Unc
1826Ga FS	15.00	30.00	50.00	125
1828/7Ga FS	15.00	30.00	50.00	125
1829/8/7Ga FS	—	—	—	—
1829Ga FS	15.00	30.00	50.00	125
1830Ga FS	250	425	600	—
1831Ga LP	15.00	30.00	50.00	125
1831Ga LP/FS	300	450	600	—
1832Ga FS	250	350	500	—
1833/2Ga G FS	100	150	275	550
1833Ga FS	75.00	125	225	500
1834/3Ga FS	75.00	125	225	500
1835Ga FS	—	—	—	—
1837/6Ga JG/FS	12.50	20.00	35.00	100
1838/7Ga JG/FS	100	200	400	—
1839Ga JG	250	350	500	—
1840Ga JG	12.50	20.00	35.00	100
1840Ga MC	7.50	12.50	25.00	70.00
1841Ga MC	50.00	75.00	125	250
1842/0Ga JG/MC	10.00	15.00	30.00	100
1842Ga JG	7.50	12.50	20.00	100
1843Ga JG	150	200	300	750
1843Ga MC	5.00	7.50	15.00	100
1844Ga MC	7.50	12.50	20.00	100
1845Ga MC	10.00	15.00	25.00	100
1845Ga JG	5.00	7.50	20.00	100
1846Ga JG	12.50	20.00	35.00	100
1847/6Ga JG	10.00	15.00	25.00	100
1847Ga JG	10.00	15.00	25.00	100
1848Ga JG	400	550	700	—
1849Ga JG	7.50	12.50	20.00	100
1850Ga JG	175	275	400	—
1851Ga JG	10.00	15.00	25.00	100
1852Ga JG	10.00	15.00	25.00	100
1853/2Ga JG	10.00	15.00	25.00	100
1854Ga JG	10.00	15.00	25.00	100
1855Ga JG	15.00	25.00	40.00	100
1856Ga JG	7.50	12.50	20.00	100
1857/6Ga JG	12.50	20.00	35.00	100
1858/7Ga JG	15.00	25.00	40.00	110
1859/8Ga JG	25.00	50.00	75.00	150
1860/59Ga JG	30.00	60.00	90.00	225
1861/0Ga JG	20.00	30.00	50.00	125
1861Ga JG	25.00	50.00	100	250
1862Ga JG	7.50	12.50	20.00	100

Mint: Guadalupe y Calvo
KM# 372.5 REAL
3.3800 g., 0.9030 Silver .0981 oz. ASW

Date	F	VF	XF	Unc
1844GC MP	40.00	60.00	100	250
1845GC MP	40.00	60.00	100	250
1846GC MP	40.00	60.00	100	250
1847GC MP	40.00	60.00	100	250
1848GC MP	40.00	60.00	100	250
1849/7GC MP	40.00	60.00	100	250
1849/8GC MP	40.00	60.00	100	250
1849GC MP	40.00	60.00	100	250
1850GC MP	40.00	60.00	100	250
1851GC MP	40.00	60.00	100	250

Mint: Guanajuato
KM# 372.6 REAL
3.3800 g., 0.9030 Silver .0981 oz. ASW

Date	F	VF	XF	Unc
1826/5Go JJ	5.00	7.50	15.00	85.00
1826Go MJ	4.00	6.00	15.00	85.00
1827Go MJ	4.00	6.00	15.00	65.00
1827Go JM	10.00	15.00	25.00	75.00
1828/7Go MR	4.00	6.00	15.00	85.00
1828Go MJ	4.00	6.00	15.00	85.00
Note: Straight J, small 8				
1828Go MJ	4.00	6.00	15.00	85.00
Note: Full J, large 8				
1828G MR/JJ	4.00	6.00	15.00	85.00
1828Go MR	4.00	6.00	15.00	85.00
1829/8Go MG Small eagle	4.00	6.00	15.00	85.00
1829Go MJ Small eagle	4.00	6.00	15.00	85.00
1829Go MJ Large eagle	4.00	6.00	15.00	85.00
1830Go MJ Small initials	4.00	6.00	15.00	85.00
1830Go MJ Medium initials	4.00	6.00	15.00	85.00
1830Go MJ Large initials	4.00	6.00	15.00	85.00
1830Go MJ	4.00	6.00	15.00	85.00
Note: Reversed N in MEXICANA				
1830GC MJ 3/2	4.00	6.00	15.00	85.00
1831/0Go MJ	4.00	6.00	15.00	85.00
Note: Reversed N in MEXICANA				
1831Go MJ	4.00	6.00	15.00	85.00
1832/1Go MJ	15.00	30.00	50.00	125
1832Go MJ	15.00	30.00	50.00	125
1833Go MJ Top of 3 round	4.00	6.00	15.00	85.00
1833Go MJ Top of 3 flat	4.00	6.00	15.00	85.00
1834Go PJ	4.00	6.00	15.00	85.00
1835Go PJ	7.50	12.50	20.00	85.00
1836Go PJ	4.00	6.00	15.00	85.00
1837Go PJ	15.00	30.00	50.00	125
1838/7Go PJ	10.00	20.00	35.00	85.00
1839Go PJ	4.00	6.00	15.00	85.00
1840/39Go PJ	4.00	6.00	15.00	85.00
1840Go PJ	4.00	6.00	15.00	85.00
1841/31Go PJ	10.00	20.00	35.00	85.00
1841Go PJ	4.00	6.00	15.00	85.00
1842Go PJ	4.00	6.00	15.00	85.00
1842Go PM	4.00	6.00	15.00	85.00
1843Go PM Convex wings	4.00	6.00	15.00	85.00
1843Go PM Concave wings	4.00	6.00	15.00	85.00
1844Go PM	4.00	6.00	15.00	85.00
1845/4Go PM	4.00	6.00	15.00	85.00
1845Go PM	4.00	6.00	15.00	85.00
1846/5Go PM	7.50	12.50	20.00	85.00
1846Go PM	4.00	6.00	15.00	85.00
1847/6Go PM	4.00	6.00	15.00	85.00
1847Go PM	4.00	6.00	15.00	85.00
1848Go PM	4.00	6.00	15.00	85.00
1849Go PF	10.00	20.00	35.00	85.00
1850Go PF	4.00	6.00	15.00	85.00
1851Go PF	10.00	20.00	35.00	100
1853/2Go PF	7.50	12.50	20.00	75.00
1853Go PF	4.00	6.00	15.00	75.00
1853Go PF/M 5/4	7.50	12.50	20.00	75.00
1854/3Go PF	4.00	6.00	15.00	75.00
1854Go PF Large eagle	4.00	6.00	15.00	75.00
1854Go PF Small eagle	4.00	6.00	15.00	75.00
1855/3Go PF	4.00	6.00	15.00	75.00
1855/4Go PF	4.00	6.00	15.00	75.00
1855Go PF	4.00	6.00	15.00	75.00
1856/5Go PF	4.00	6.00	15.00	75.00
1856Go PF	4.00	6.00	15.00	75.00
1857/6Go PF	4.00	6.00	15.00	75.00
1857Go PF	4.00	6.00	15.00	75.00
1858Go PF	4.00	6.00	15.00	75.00
1859Go PF	4.00	6.00	15.00	75.00
1860/50Go PF	4.00	6.00	15.00	75.00
1860Go PF	4.00	6.00	15.00	75.00
1861Go PF	4.00	6.00	15.00	75.00
1862Go YE	4.00	6.00	15.00	75.00
1862/1Go YF	7.50	12.50	20.00	75.00
1862Go YF	4.00	6.00	15.00	75.00
1867Go YF	4.00	6.00	15.00	75.00
1868/7Go YF	4.00	6.00	15.00	75.00

Mint: Hermosillo
KM# 372.7 REAL
3.3800 g., 0.9030 Silver .0981 oz. ASW

Date	F	VF	XF	Unc
1867Ho PR	38.50	75.00	120	250
Note: Small 7/1				
1867Ho PR	38.50	75.00	120	250
Note: Large 7/ small 7				
1868Ho PR	38.50	75.00	120	250

Mint: Mexico City
KM# 372.8 REAL
3.3800 g., 0.9030 Silver .0981 oz. ASW

Date	F	VF	XF	Unc
1825Mo JM	10.00	20.00	40.00	110
1826Mo JM	7.50	15.00	30.00	100
1827/6Mo JM	7.50	15.00	30.00	75.00
1827Mo JM	5.00	10.00	20.00	70.00
1828Mo JM	7.50	15.00	30.00	100
1830/29Mo JM	5.00	10.00	20.00	100
1830Mo JM	5.00	12.50	25.00	100
1831Mo JM	100	200	300	750
1832Mo JM	5.00	10.00	20.00	100
1833/2Mo MJ	5.00	10.00	20.00	100
1850Mo GC	5.00	10.00	20.00	100
1852Mo GC	275	425	575	—
1854Mo GC	10.00	20.00	40.00	100
1855Mo GF	5.00	10.00	20.00	80.00
1856Mo GF	5.00	10.00	20.00	80.00
1857Mo GF	5.00	10.00	20.00	80.00
1858Mo FH	5.00	10.00	20.00	80.00
1859Mo FH	5.00	10.00	20.00	80.00
1861Mo CH	5.00	10.00	20.00	80.00
1862Mo CH	5.00	10.00	20.00	80.00
1863/2Mo CH	7.50	12.50	25.00	80.00

Mint: San Luis Potosi
KM# 372.9 REAL
3.3800 g., 0.9030 Silver .0981 oz. ASW

Date	F	VF	XF	Unc
1831 Pi JS	5.00	10.00	20.00	125
1837 Pi JS	600	750	1,000	—
1838/7 Pi JS	250	300	375	—
1838 Pi JS	20.00	35.00	60.00	125
1840/39 Pi JS	7.50	15.00	30.00	125
1840 Pi JS	7.50	15.00	30.00	125
1841 Pi JS	7.50	15.00	30.00	125
1842 Pi JS	15.00	30.00	55.00	150
1842 Pi PS	5.00	10.00	20.00	125
1843 Pi PS	12.50	20.00	35.00	125
1843 Pi AM	40.00	60.00	80.00	150
1844 Pi AM	40.00	60.00	80.00	150
1845 Pi AM	7.50	15.00	30.00	125
1846/5 Pi AM	7.50	15.00	30.00	125
1847/6 Pi AM	7.50	15.00	30.00	125
1847 Pi AM	7.50	15.00	30.00	125
1848/7 Pi AM	7.50	15.00	30.00	125
1849 Pi PS	7.50	15.00	30.00	125
1849/8 Pi SP	60.00	100	150	—
1849 Pi SP	15.00	25.00	40.00	125
1850 Pi MC	5.00	10.00	20.00	125
1851/0 Pi MC	7.50	15.00	30.00	125
1851 Pi MC	7.50	15.00	30.00	125
1852/1/0 Pi MC	10.00	20.00	35.00	125
1852 Pi MC	7.50	15.00	30.00	125
1853/1 Pi MC	12.50	20.00	35.00	125
1853 Pi MC	10.00	20.00	35.00	125
1854/2 Pi MO	30.00	60.00	100	—
1854/3 Pi MC	20.00	40.00	60.00	150
1855/4 Pi MC	20.00	40.00	60.00	150
1855 Pi MC	15.00	25.00	45.00	125
1856 Pi MC	15.00	25.00	45.00	125
1857 Pi PS	20.00	35.00	55.00	135
1857 Pi MC	20.00	40.00	60.00	150
1858 Pi MC	12.50	20.00	35.00	125
1859 Pi PS	10.00	15.00	30.00	125
1860/59 Pi PS	10.00	15.00	30.00	125
1861 Pi PS	7.50	12.50	20.00	125
1861 Pi RO	12.50	20.00	35.00	125
1862/1 Pi RO	12.50	20.00	35.00	90.00
1862 Pi RO	7.50	12.50	20.00	125

Mint: Zacatecas
KM# 372.10 REAL
3.3800 g., 0.9030 Silver .0981 oz. ASW

Date	F	VF	XF	Unc
1826Zs AZ	5.00	12.50	35.00	120
1826Zs AO	5.00	12.50	35.00	120
1827Zs AO	5.00	12.50	35.00	120
1828/7Zs AO	5.00	12.50	35.00	120
1828Zs AO	5.00	12.50	35.00	120
1828Zs AO Inverted V for A	5.00	12.50	35.00	120
1829Zs AO	5.00	12.50	35.00	120
1830Zs ZsOV	5.00	12.50	35.00	120
1830Zs ZOV	5.00	12.50	35.00	120
1831Zs OV	5.00	12.50	35.00	120
1831Zs OM	5.00	12.50	30.00	120
1832Zs OM	5.00	12.50	30.00	120
1833/2Zs OM	5.00	12.50	30.00	120
1833/2Zs OM/V	5.00	12.50	30.00	120
1833Zs OM	5.00	12.50	30.00	120
1834/3Zs OM	5.00	12.50	30.00	120
1834Zs OM	5.00	12.50	30.00	120
1835/4Zs OM	20.00	35.00	60.00	150
1835Zs OM	4.00	8.00	20.00	65.00
1836/5Zs OM	4.00	8.00	20.00	85.00
1836Zs OM	4.00	8.00	20.00	85.00
1837Zs OM	4.00	8.00	20.00	85.00
1838Zs OM	4.00	8.00	20.00	85.00
1839Zs OM	4.00	8.00	20.00	85.00
1840Zs OM	4.00	8.00	20.00	85.00
1841Zs OM	20.00	40.00	60.00	150
1842/1Zs OM	4.00	8.00	20.00	85.00
1842Zs OM	4.00	8.00	20.00	85.00
1843Zs OM	4.00	8.00	20.00	85.00
1844Zs OM	4.00	8.00	20.00	85.00
1845/4Zs OM	5.00	12.50	30.00	100
1845Zs OM	4.00	8.00	20.00	85.00

Date	F	VF	XF	Unc
1846Zs OM	4.00	8.00	20.00	85.00
Note: Old font and obverse				
1846Zs OM	4.00	8.00	20.00	85.00
Note: New font and obverse				
1847Zs OM	4.00	8.00	20.00	85.00
1848Zs OM	4.00	8.00	20.00	85.00
1849Zs OM	10.00	25.00	50.00	125
1850Zs OM	4.00	6.00	15.00	85.00
1851Zs OM	4.00	6.00	15.00	85.00
1852Zs OM	4.00	6.00	15.00	85.00
1853Zs OM	4.00	6.00	15.00	85.00
1854/2Zs OM	4.00	6.00	15.00	85.00
1854/3Zs OM	4.00	6.00	15.00	85.00
1854Zs OM	4.00	6.00	15.00	85.00
1855/4Zs OM	4.00	6.00	15.00	85.00
1855Zs OM	4.00	6.00	15.00	85.00
1855Zs MO	4.00	6.00	15.00	85.00
1856Zs MO	4.00	6.00	15.00	85.00
1856Zs MO/OM	4.00	6.00	15.00	85.00
1857Zs MO	4.00	6.00	15.00	85.00
1858Zs MO	4.00	6.00	15.00	85.00
1859Zs MO	4.00	6.00	15.00	75.00
1860 MO	250	—	—	—
1860Zs VL	4.00	6.00	15.00	75.00
1860Zs VL Inverted A for V	4.00	6.00	15.00	75.00
1861Zs VL	4.00	6.00	15.00	75.00
1861Zs VL Inverted A for V	4.00	6.00	15.00	75.00
1862Zs VL	5.00	12.50	30.00	100
1868Zs JS	25.00	45.00	90.00	175
1869Zs YH	4.00	8.00	20.00	75.00

Mint: Alamos
KM# 374 2 REALES
6.7600 g., 0.9030 Silver .1962 oz. ASW **Obv:** Facing eagle
Edge: Reeded

Date	Mintage	F	VF	XF	Unc
1872A AM	15,000	50.00	115	225	550

Mint: Chihuahua
KM# 374.2 2 REALES
6.7600 g., 0.9030 Silver .1962 oz. ASW **Obv:** Facing eagle
Edge: Reeded

Date	F	VF	XF	Unc
1832 Ca MR	30.00	60.00	100	200
1833 Ca MR	30.00	60.00	125	500
1834 Ca MR	35.00	75.00	125	500
1834 Ca AM	35.00	75.00	125	500
1835 Ca AM	35.00	75.00	125	500
1836 Ca AM	20.00	40.00	80.00	200
1844 Ca AM Rare	—	—	—	—
1844 Ca RG Unique	—	—	—	—
1845 Ca RG	20.00	40.00	80.00	200
1855 Ca RG	20.00	40.00	80.00	200

Mint: Culiacan
KM# 374.3 2 REALES
6.7600 g., 0.9030 Silver .1962 oz. ASW **Obv:** Facing eagle
Edge: Reeded

Date	F	VF	XF	Unc
1846/1146C CE	25.00	50.00	100	225
1847C CE	12.50	20.00	40.00	200
1848C CE	12.50	20.00	40.00	200
1850C CE	25.00	50.00	75.00	200
1851C CE	12.50	20.00	40.00	200
1852/1C CE	12.50	20.00	40.00	200
1853/2C CE	12.50	20.00	40.00	200
1854C CE	15.00	30.00	50.00	200
1856C CE	20.00	35.00	70.00	200
1857C CE	12.50	20.00	40.00	200
1860C PV	12.50	20.00	40.00	200
1861C PV	12.50	20.00	40.00	200
1869C CE	12.50	20.00	40.00	200

Mint: Durango
KM# 374.4 2 REALES
6.7600 g., 0.9030 Silver .1962 oz. ASW **Obv:** Facing eagle
Edge: Reeded

Date	F	VF	XF	Unc
1826Do RL	20.00	40.00	60.00	200
1832Do RM	20.00	40.00	60.00	200
Note: Style of pre-1832				
1832Do RM	20.00	40.00	60.00	200
Note: Style of post-1832				
1834/2Do RM	20.00	40.00	60.00	200
1834/3Do RM	20.00	40.00	60.00	200
1835/4Do RM/RL	200	300	500	—
1841/31Do RM	50.00	75.00	125	250
1841Do RM	50.00	75.00	125	250
1842/32Do RM	12.50	20.00	40.00	200
1843Do RM/RL	12.50	20.00	40.00	200
1844Do RM	35.00	50.00	80.00	200
1845/34Do RM/RL	12.50	20.00	40.00	200
1846/36Do RM	100	150	200	350
1848/36Do RM	12.50	20.00	40.00	200
1848/37Do RM	12.50	20.00	40.00	200
1848/7Do RM	12.50	20.00	40.00	200
1848Do RM	12.50	20.00	40.00	200
1849Do CM/RM	12.50	20.00	40.00	200
1849Do CM	12.50	20.00	40.00	200
1851Do JMR/RL	12.50	20.00	40.00	200
1852Do JMR	12.50	20.00	40.00	200
1854Do CP/CR	30.00	50.00	80.00	200
1855Do CP	250	350	500	—
1856Do CP	100	150	250	500
1858Do CP	12.50	20.00	40.00	200

Date	F	VF	XF	Unc
1859/8Do CP	12.50	20.00	40.00	200
1861Do CP	12.50	20.00	40.00	200

Mint: Estado de Mexico
KM# 374.5 2 REALES
6.7600 g., 0.9030 Silver .1962 oz. ASW **Obv:** Facing eagle
Edge: Reeded

Date	F	VF	XF	Unc
1828EoMo LF	325	525	900	2,500

Mint: Guadalajara
KM# 374.6 2 REALES
6.7600 g., 0.9030 Silver .1962 oz. ASW **Obv:** Facing eagle
Edge: Reeded

Date	F	VF	XF	Unc
1825Ga FS	20.00	40.00	80.00	200
1826Ga FS	20.00	40.00	80.00	200
1828/7Ga FS	100	150	225	400
1829Ga FS Rare	—	—	—	—
1832/0Ga FS/LP	100	150	225	350
1832Ga FS	12.50	20.00	40.00	200
1833/2Ga FS/LP	12.50	20.00	40.00	200
1834/27Ga FS Rare	—	—	—	—
1834Ga FS	12.50	20.00	40.00	200
1835Ga FS	2,100	—	—	—
1837Ga JG	12.50	20.00	40.00	200
1838Ga JG	12.50	20.00	40.00	200
1840/30Ga MC	12.50	20.00	40.00	200
1841Ga MC	30.00	50.00	200	500
1842/32Ga JG/MC	35.00	50.00	100	200
1842Ga JG	20.00	40.00	80.00	200
1843Ga JG	12.50	20.00	40.00	200
1843Ga MC/JG	12.50	20.00	40.00	200
1844Ga MC	12.50	20.00	40.00	200
1845/3Ga MC/JG	12.50	20.00	40.00	200
1845/4Ga MC/JG	12.50	20.00	40.00	200
1845Ga JG	12.50	20.00	40.00	200
1846Ga JG	12.50	20.00	40.00	200
1847/6Ga JG	25.00	40.00	80.00	200
1848/7Ga JG	12.50	20.00	40.00	200
1849Ga JG	12.50	20.00	40.00	200
1850/40Ga JG	12.50	20.00	40.00	200
1851Ga JG	250	350	500	—
1852Ga JG	12.50	20.00	40.00	200
1853/1Ga JG	12.50	20.00	40.00	200
1854/3Ga JG	250	350	500	—
1855Ga JG	35.00	50.00	80.00	200
1856Ga JG	12.50	20.00	40.00	200
1857Ga JG	250	350	500	—
1859/8Ga JG	12.50	20.00	40.00	200
1859Ga JG	12.50	20.00	40.00	200
1862/1Ga JG	12.50	20.00	40.00	200

Mint: Guadalupe y Calvo
KM# 374.7 2 REALES
6.7600 g., 0.9030 Silver .1962 oz. ASW **Obv:** Facing eagle
Edge: Reeded

Date	F	VF	XF	Unc
1844GC MP	40.00	60.00	125	275
1845GC MP	40.00	60.00	125	275
1846GC MP	50.00	100	150	300
1847GC MP	35.00	50.00	100	250
1848GC MP	50.00	100	150	300
1849GC MP	50.00	100	150	300
1850GC MP	125	250	—	—
1851/0GC MP	50.00	100	150	300
1851GC MP	50.00	100	150	300

Mint: Guanajuato
KM# 374.8 2 REALES
6.7600 g., 0.9030 Silver .1962 oz. ASW **Obv:** Facing eagle
Edge: Reeded **Note:** Varieties exist.

Date	F	VF	XF	Unc
1825Go JJ	7.50	15.00	30.00	150
1826/5Go JJ	7.50	15.00	30.00	150
1826Go JJ	7.50	10.00	25.00	150
1826Go MJ	7.50	10.00	25.00	150
1827/6Go MJ	7.50	10.00	25.00	150
1827Go MJ	7.50	10.00	25.00	150
1828/7Go MR	7.50	15.00	30.00	150
1828Go MJ	7.50	10.00	20.00	150
1828Go JM	7.50	10.00	20.00	150
1829Go MJ	7.50	10.00	20.00	150
1831Go MJ	7.50	10.00	20.00	150
1832Go MJ	7.50	10.00	20.00	150
1833Go MJ	7.50	10.00	20.00	150
1834Go PJ	7.50	10.00	20.00	150
1835/4Go PJ	7.50	15.00	30.00	150
1835Go PJ	7.50	10.00	20.00	150
1836Go PJ	7.50	10.00	20.00	150
1837/6Go PJ	7.50	10.00	20.00	150
1837Go PJ	7.50	10.00	20.00	150
1838/7Go PJ	7.50	10.00	20.00	150
1838Go PJ	7.50	10.00	20.00	150
1839/8Go PJ	7.50	15.00	30.00	150
1839Go PJ	7.50	10.00	20.00	150
1840Go PJ	7.50	10.00	20.00	150
1841Go PJ	7.50	10.00	20.00	150
1842Go PJ	7.50	10.00	20.00	150
1842Go PM/PJ	7.50	10.00	20.00	150
1842Go PM	7.50	10.00	20.00	150
1843/2Go PM	7.50	10.00	20.00	150
Note: Concave wings, thin rays, small letters				
1843Go PM	7.50	10.00	20.00	150
Note: Convex wings, thick rays, large letters				
1844Go PM	7.50	10.00	20.00	150
1845/4Go PM	7.50	10.00	20.00	150
1845Go PM	7.50	10.00	20.00	150
1846/5Go PM	10.00	15.00	35.00	150
1846Go PM	7.50	10.00	20.00	150
1847Go PM	7.50	10.00	20.00	150
1848/7Go PM	7.50	15.00	30.00	150
1848Go PM	7.50	15.00	30.00	150
1848Go PF	100	150	250	500
1849/8Go PF/PM	7.50	10.00	20.00	150
1849Go PF	7.50	10.00	20.00	150
1850/40Go PF	7.50	10.00	20.00	150
1850Go PF	7.50	10.00	20.00	150
1851Go PF	7.50	10.00	20.00	150
1852/1Go PF	7.50	10.00	20.00	150
1852Go PF	7.50	10.00	20.00	150
1853Go PF	7.50	10.00	20.00	150
1854/3Go PF	7.50	10.00	20.00	150
1854Go PF	7.50	10.00	20.00	150
Note: Old font and obverse				
1854Go PF	7.50	10.00	20.00	150
Note: New font and obverse				
1855Go PF	7.50	10.00	20.00	150
1855Go PF	7.50	10.00	20.00	150
Note: Star in G of mint mark				
1856/5Go PF	10.00	15.00	35.00	150
1856Go PF	10.00	15.00	25.00	150
1857/6Go PF	7.50	10.00	20.00	150
1857Go PF	7.50	10.00	20.00	150
1858/7Go PF	7.50	10.00	20.00	150
1858Go PF	7.50	10.00	20.00	150
1859/7Go PF	7.50	10.00	20.00	150
1859Go PF	7.50	10.00	20.00	150
1860/7Go PF	7.50	10.00	20.00	150
1860/50Go PF	7.50	10.00	20.00	150
1860/59Go PF	7.50	10.00	20.00	150
1860Go PF	7.50	10.00	20.00	150
1861/51Go PF	7.50	10.00	20.00	150
1861/57Go PF	7.50	10.00	20.00	150
1861/0Go PF	7.50	10.00	20.00	150
1861Go PF	7.50	10.00	20.00	150
1862/1Go YE	7.50	10.00	20.00	125
1862Go YE	7.50	10.00	20.00	125
1862/57Go YE	7.50	10.00	20.00	125
1862Go YE/PF	7.50	10.00	20.00	125
1862Go YF	7.50	10.00	20.00	125
1863/52Go YF	7.50	10.00	20.00	125
1863Go YF	7.50	10.00	20.00	125
1867/57Go YF	7.50	10.00	20.00	125
1868/57Go YF	10.00	15.00	25.00	125

Mint: Hermosillo
KM# 374.9 2 REALES
6.7600 g., 0.9030 Silver .1962 oz. ASW **Obv:** Facing eagle
Edge: Reeded

Date	F	VF	XF	Unc
1861Ho FM	200	300	400	650
1862/52Ho FM/C. CE	250	350	500	—
1867/1Ho PR/FM	75.00	150	250	500

Mint: Mexico City
KM# 374.10 2 REALES
6.7600 g., 0.9030 Silver .1962 oz. ASW **Obv:** Facing eagle
Edge: Reeded **Note:** Varieties exist.

Date	F	VF	XF	Unc
1825Mo JM	10.00	15.00	30.00	175
1826Mo JM	10.00	15.00	30.00	175
1827Mo JM	10.00	15.00	30.00	175
1828Mo JM	10.00	15.00	30.00	175
1829/8Mo JM	10.00	15.00	30.00	175
1829Mo JM	10.00	15.00	30.00	175
1830Mo JM	40.00	60.00	125	250
1831Mo JM	10.00	15.00	30.00	175
1832Mo JM	100	200	400	—
1833/2Mo MJ/JM	10.00	15.00	30.00	175
1834Mo ML	50.00	100	200	400
1836Mo MF	10.00	15.00	30.00	175
1837Mo ML	10.00	15.00	30.00	175
1840/7Mo ML	150	225	350	—
1840Mo ML	150	225	350	—
1841Mo ML	15.00	40.00	100	250
1842 ML Rare	—	—	—	—
1847Mo RC Narrow date	10.00	15.00	30.00	175
1847Mo RC Wide date	10.00	15.00	30.00	175
1848Mo GC	10.00	15.00	30.00	175
1849Mo GC	10.00	15.00	30.00	175
1850Mo GC	10.00	15.00	30.00	175
1851Mo GC	40.00	60.00	125	250
1852Mo GC	10.00	15.00	30.00	175
1853Mo GC	10.00	15.00	30.00	175
1854/44Mo GC	10.00	15.00	30.00	175
1855Mo GC	10.00	15.00	30.00	175
1855Mo GF/GC	10.00	15.00	30.00	175

Date	F	VF	XF	Unc
1855Mo GF	10.00	15.00	30.00	175
1856/5Mo GF/GC	10.00	15.00	30.00	175
1857Mo GF	10.00	15.00	30.00	175
1858Mo FH	7.50	12.50	25.00	150
1858Mo FH/GF	7.50	12.50	25.00	150
1859Mo FH	7.50	12.50	25.00	150
1860Mo FH	7.50	12.50	25.00	150
1860Mo TH	7.50	12.50	25.00	150
1861Mo CH	7.50	12.50	25.00	150
1862Mo CH	7.50	12.50	25.00	150
1863Mo CH	7.50	12.50	25.00	150
1863Mo TH	7.50	12.50	25.00	150
1867Mo CH	7.50	12.50	25.00	150
1868Mo CH	10.00	15.00	30.00	150
1868Mo PH	7.50	12.50	25.00	150

Mint: Real de Catorce
KM# 374.1 2 REALES
6.7600 g., 0.9030 Silver .1962 oz. ASW **Obv:** Facing eagle
Edge: Reeded

Date	F	VF	XF	Unc
1863 Ce ML	125	200	325	675

Mint: San Luis Potosi
KM# 374.11 2 REALES
6.7600 g., 0.9030 Silver .1962 oz. ASW **Obv:** Facing eagle
Edge: Reeded

Date	F	VF	XF	Unc
1829 Pi JS	10.00	15.00	30.00	200
1830/20 Pi JS	20.00	30.00	60.00	200
1837 Pi JS	10.00	15.00	30.00	200
1841 Pi JS	10.00	15.00	30.00	200
1842/1 Pi JS	10.00	15.00	30.00	200
1842 Pi JS	10.00	15.00	30.00	200
1842 Pi PS	20.00	35.00	60.00	200
1843 Pi PS	12.50	20.00	40.00	200
1843 Pi AM	10.00	15.00	30.00	200
1844 Pi AM	10.00	15.00	30.00	200
1845 Pi AM	10.00	15.00	30.00	200
1846 Pi AM	10.00	15.00	30.00	200
1849 Pi MC	10.00	15.00	30.00	200
1850 Pi MC	10.00	15.00	30.00	200
1856 Pi MC	40.00	60.00	125	250
1857 Pi MC	—	—	—	—
1858 Pi MC	12.50	20.00	40.00	200
1859 Pi MC	50.00	70.00	100	200
1861 Pi PS	10.00	15.00	30.00	200
1862 Pi RO	12.50	20.00	40.00	200
1863 Pi RO	100	250	350	500
1868 Pi PS	10.00	15.00	30.00	200
1869/8 Pi PS	10.00	15.00	30.00	200
1869 Pi PS	10.00	15.00	30.00	200

Mint: Zacatecas
KM# 374.12 2 REALES
6.7600 g., 0.9030 Silver .1962 oz. ASW **Obv:** Facing eagle
Edge: Reeded **Note:** Varieties exist.

Date	F	VF	XF	Unc
1825Zs AZ	10.00	15.00	30.00	150
1826Zs AV	7.50	10.00	25.00	150
Note: A is inverted V				
1826Zs AZ	7.50	10.00	25.00	150
Note: A is inverted V				
1826Zs AO	10.00	15.00	30.00	150
1827Zs AO	6.00	8.00	12.00	150
Note: A is inverted V				
1827Zs AO	6.00	8.00	12.00	150
1828/7Zs AO	15.00	30.00	60.00	175
1828Zs AO	7.50	10.00	25.00	100
1828Zs AO	7.50	10.00	25.00	150
Note: A is inverted V				
1829Zs AO	7.50	10.00	25.00	150
1829Zs OV	7.50	10.00	25.00	150
1830Zs OV	7.50	10.00	25.00	150
1831Zs OV	7.50	10.00	25.00	150
1831Zs OM/OV	7.50	10.00	25.00	150
1831Zs OM	7.50	10.00	25.00	150
1832/1Zs OM	15.00	30.00	60.00	150
1832Zs OM	7.50	10.00	25.00	150
1833/27Zs OM	7.50	10.00	25.00	150
1833/2Zs OM	7.50	10.00	25.00	150
1833Zs OM	7.50	10.00	25.00	150
1834Zs OM	40.00	60.00	125	200
1835Zs OM	7.50	10.00	25.00	150
1836Zs OM	7.50	10.00	25.00	150
1837Zs OM	7.50	10.00	25.00	150
1838Zs OM	15.00	30.00	60.00	150
1839Zs OM	7.50	10.00	20.00	150
1840Zs OM	7.50	10.00	20.00	150
1841/0Zs OM	7.50	10.00	20.00	150
1841Zs OM	7.50	10.00	20.00	150
1842Zs OM Narrow date	7.50	10.00	20.00	150
1842Zs OM Wide date	7.50	10.00	20.00	150
1843Zs OM	7.50	10.00	20.00	150
1844Zs OM	7.50	10.00	20.00	150
1845Zs OM	7.50	10.00	20.00	150
Note: Small letters with leaves				
1845Zs OM	7.50	10.00	20.00	150
Note: Large letters with leaves				
1846Zs OM	7.50	10.00	20.00	150
1847Zs OM	7.50	10.00	20.00	150
1848Zs OM	7.50	10.00	20.00	150
1849Zs OM	7.50	10.00	20.00	150
1850Zs OM	7.50	10.00	20.00	150
1851Zs OM	7.50	10.00	20.00	150
1852Zs OM	7.50	10.00	20.00	150
1853Zs OM	7.50	10.00	20.00	150
1854/3Zs OM	7.50	10.00	20.00	150
1854Zs OM	7.50	10.00	20.00	150
1855/4Zs OM	7.50	10.00	20.00	150
1855Zs OM	7.50	10.00	20.00	150
1855Zs MO	7.50	10.00	20.00	150
1856/5Zs MO	7.50	10.00	20.00	150
1856Zs MO	7.50	10.00	20.00	150
1857Zs MO	7.50	10.00	20.00	150
1858Zs MO	7.50	10.00	20.00	150
1859Zs MO	7.50	10.00	20.00	150
1860/59Zs MO	7.50	10.00	20.00	150
1860Zs MO	7.50	10.00	20.00	100
1860Zs VL	7.50	10.00	20.00	150
1861Zs VL	7.50	10.00	20.00	150
1862Zs VL	7.50	10.00	20.00	100
1863Zs MO	12.50	20.00	40.00	150
1863Zs VL	7.50	10.00	20.00	150
1864Zs MO	7.50	10.00	20.00	150
1864Zs VL	7.50	10.00	20.00	150
1865Zs MO	7.50	10.00	20.00	150
1867Zs JS	7.50	10.00	20.00	150
1868Zs JS	10.00	15.00	35.00	150
1868Zs YH	7.50	10.00	20.00	150
1869Zs YH	7.50	10.00	20.00	150
1870Zs YH	7.50	10.00	20.00	150

Mint: Culiacan
KM# 375.1 4 REALES
13.5400 g., 0.9030 Silver .3925 oz. ASW **Obv:** Facing eagle

Date	F	VF	XF	Unc
1846C CE	400	550	900	—
1850C CE	75.00	125	250	700
1852C CE	200	300	500	1,250
1857C CE Rare	—	—	—	—
1858C CE	100	200	350	1,000
1860C PV	25.00	50.00	125	650

Mint: Guadalajara
KM# 375.2 4 REALES
13.5400 g., 0.9030 Silver .3925 oz. ASW **Obv:** Facing eagle

Date	F	VF	XF	Unc
1843Ga MC	20.00	40.00	80.00	600
1844/3Ga MC	30.00	60.00	125	600
1844Ga MC	20.00	40.00	80.00	600
1845Ga MC	20.00	40.00	80.00	600
1845Ga JG	20.00	40.00	80.00	600
1846Ga JG	20.00	40.00	80.00	600
1847Ga JG	40.00	80.00	150	600
1848/7Ga JG	40.00	80.00	150	600
1849Ga JG	40.00	80.00	150	600
1850Ga JG	65.00	125	250	650
1852Ga JG Rare	—	—	—	—
1854Ga JG Rare	—	—	—	—
1855Ga JG	100	200	400	1,250
1856Ga JG Rare	—	—	—	—
1857/6Ga JG	65.00	125	250	700
1858Ga JG	125	250	450	1,250
1859/8Ga JG	125	250	450	1,250
1860Ga JG	850	1,450	—	—
1863/2Ga JG	150	300	1,250	7,500
1863Ga JG	150	300	1,250	7,500

Mint: Guadalupe y Calvo
KM# 375.3 4 REALES
13.5400 g., 0.9030 Silver .3925 oz. ASW **Obv:** Facing eagle

Date	F	VF	XF	Unc
1844GC MP	3,000	5,000	6,000	—
1845GC MP	3,000	4,000	5,000	9,000
1846GC MP	1,700	2,800	—	—
1847GC MP	1,500	2,500	—	—
1849GC MP	2,000	3,000	—	—
1850GC MP	500	1,000	—	—

Mint: Guanajuato
KM# 375.4 4 REALES
13.5400 g., 0.9030 Silver .3925 oz. ASW **Obv:** Facing eagle
Note: Varieties exist. Some 1862 dates appear to be 1869 because of weak dies.

Date	F	VF	XF	Unc
1835Go PJ	12.50	25.00	60.00	600
1836/5Go PJ	15.00	30.00	75.00	600
1836Go PJ	15.00	30.00	75.00	600
1837Go PJ	12.50	25.00	60.00	600
1838/7Go PJ	15.00	30.00	75.00	600
1838Go PJ	12.50	30.00	75.00	600
1839Go PJ	12.50	25.00	60.00	600
1840/30Go PJ	20.00	50.00	100	600
1840 PJ	20.00	50.00	100	600
1841/30 PJ	200	325	600	1,500
1841/31Go PJ	150	250	450	1,250
1842Go PJ Rare	—	—	—	—
1842Go PM	15.00	30.00	75.00	400
1843/2Go PM	12.50	25.00	60.00	400
Note: Eagle with convex wings, thick rays				
1843Go PM	12.50	25.00	60.00	400
Note: Eagle with concave wings, thin rays				
1844/3Go PM	15.00	30.00	75.00	600
1844Go PM	20.00	50.00	100	600
1845/4Go PM	20.00	50.00	100	600
1845Go PM	20.00	50.00	100	600
1846/5Go PM	15.00	30.00	75.00	600
1846Go PM	15.00	30.00	75.00	600
1847/6Go PM	15.00	30.00	75.00	600
1847Go PM	15.00	30.00	75.00	600
1848/7Go PM	20.00	50.00	100	600
1848Go PM	20.00	50.00	100	600
1849Go PF	20.00	50.00	100	600
1850Go PF	12.50	25.00	60.00	600
1851Go PF	12.50	25.00	60.00	600
1852Go PF	15.00	30.00	75.00	600
1852Go PF 5/4	20.00	50.00	100	600
1853Go PF	15.00	30.00	75.00	600
1854Go PF Large eagle	15.00	30.00	75.00	600
1854Go PF Small eagle	15.00	30.00	75.00	600
1855/4Go PF	15.00	30.00	75.00	600
1855Go PF	12.50	25.00	60.00	600
1856Go PF	12.50	25.00	60.00	600
1857Go PF	20.00	50.00	100	600
1858Go PF	20.00	50.00	100	600
1859Go PF	20.00	50.00	100	600
1860/59Go PF	15.00	30.00	75.00	600
1860Go PF	15.00	30.00	75.00	600
1861/51Go PF	15.00	30.00	75.00	600
1861Go PF	20.00	50.00	100	600
1862/1Go YE	15.00	30.00	75.00	600
1862/1Go YF	15.00	30.00	75.00	600
1862Go YE/PF	15.00	30.00	75.00	600
1862Go YE	15.00	30.00	75.00	600
1862Go YF	15.00	30.00	75.00	600
1863/53Go YF	15.00	30.00	75.00	600
1863Go YF/PF	15.00	30.00	75.00	600
1863Go YF	15.00	30.00	75.00	600
1867/57Go YF/PF	15.00	30.00	75.00	600
1868/58Go YF/PF	15.00	30.00	75.00	600
1870Go FR	15.00	30.00	75.00	600

Mint: Hermosillo
KM# 375.5 4 REALES
13.5400 g., 0.9030 Silver .3925 oz. ASW **Obv:** Facing eagle

Date	F	VF	XF	Unc
1861Ho FM	200	350	500	2,500
1867/1Ho PR/FM	150	275	400	2,500

Mint: Mexico City
KM# 375.6 4 REALES
13.5400 g., 0.9030 Silver .3925 oz. ASW **Obv:** Facing eagle

Date	F	VF	XF	Unc
1827/6Mo JM	200	400	800	—
1850Mo GC Rare	—	—	—	—
1852Mo GC Rare	—	—	—	—
1854Mo GC Rare	—	—	—	—
1855Mo GF/GC	50.00	100	200	1,250
1855Mo GF	100	200	350	1,500
1856Mo GF/GC	50.00	125	400	1,200
1856Mo GF Rare	—	—	—	—
1859Mo FH	20.00	50.00	150	1,000
1861Mo CH	15.00	35.00	125	1,000
1862Mo CH	20.00	50.00	150	1,000
1863/2Mo CH	20.00	50.00	150	1,000
1863Mo CH	75.00	150	300	1,500
1867Mo CH	20.00	50.00	150	1,000
1868Mo CH/PH	30.00	75.00	150	1,000
1868Mo CH	20.00	50.00	150	1,000
1868Mo PH	30.00	75.00	200	1,250

Mint: Oaxaca
KM# 375.7 4 REALES
13.5400 g., 0.9030 Silver .3925 oz. ASW **Obv:** Facing eagle

Date	F	VF	XF	Unc
1861O FR	225	450	750	2,750
Note: Ornamental edge				
1861O FR	300	550	850	2,850
Note: Herringbone edge				
1861O FR	200	400	700	—
Note: Obliquely reeded edge				

Mint: Real de Catorce
KM# 375 4 REALES

13.5400 g., 0.9030 Silver .3925 oz. ASW **Obv:** Facing eagle

Date	F	VF	XF	Unc
1863 Ce ML Large C	200	500	850	4,000
1863 Ce ML Small C	225	650	1,500	6,000

Mint: San Luis Potosi
KM# 375.8 4 REALES

13.5400 g., 0.9030 Silver .3925 oz. ASW **Obv:** Facing eagle

Date	F	VF	XF	Unc
1837 Pi JS	200	350	—	—
1838 Pi JS	150	250	400	650
1842 Pi PS	50.00	100	200	650
1843/2 Pi PS	50.00	100	200	650
1843/2 Pi PS	50.00	100	200	650
Note: 3 cut from 8 punch				
1843 Pi AM	30.00	75.00	150	650
1843 Pi PS	50.00	100	200	650
1844 Pi AM	30.00	75.00	150	650
1845/4 Pi AM	20.00	50.00	100	650
1845 Pi AM	20.00	50.00	100	650
1846 Pi AM	20.00	50.00	100	650
1847 Pi AM	75.00	150	250	700
1848 Pi AM Rare	—	—	—	—
1849 Pi MC/AM	20.00	50.00	100	650
1849 Pi MC	20.00	50.00	100	650
1849 Pi PS	20.00	50.00	100	650
1850 Pi MC	20.00	50.00	100	650
1851 Pi MC	20.00	50.00	100	650
1852 Pi MC	20.00	50.00	100	650
1853 Pi MC	20.00	50.00	100	650
1854 Pi MC	100	200	400	1,100
1855 Pi MC	175	300	750	2,000
1856 Pi MC	250	400	700	—
1857 Pi MC Rare	—	—	—	—
1857 Pi PS Rare	—	—	—	—
1858 Pi MC	100	200	400	1,000
1859 Pi MC	2,000	3,000	—	—
1860 Pi PS	300	450	700	—
1861 Pi PS	30.00	75.00	150	650
1861 Pi RO/PS	30.00	75.00	150	650
1861 Pi RO	50.00	100	200	650
1862 Pi RO	30.00	75.00	150	650
1863 Pi RO	30.00	75.00	150	650
1864 Pi RO	1,600	2,600	—	—
1868 Pi PS	30.00	75.00	150	650
1869/8 Pi PS	30.00	75.00	150	650
1869 Pi PS	30.00	75.00	150	650

Mint: Zacatecas
KM# 375.9 4 REALES

13.5400 g., 0.9030 Silver .3925 oz. ASW **Obv:** Facing eagle

Date	F	VF	XF	Unc
1830Zs OM	20.00	50.00	100	600
1831Zs OM	15.00	30.00	75.00	600
1832/1Zs OM	20.00	50.00	100	600
1832Zs OM	20.00	50.00	100	600
1833/2Zs OM	20.00	50.00	100	600
1833/27Zs OM	15.00	30.00	75.00	600
1833Zs OM	15.00	30.00	75.00	600
1834/3Zs OM	20.00	50.00	100	600
1834Zs OM	15.00	30.00	75.00	600
1835Zs OM	15.00	30.00	75.00	600
1836Zs OM	15.00	30.00	75.00	600
1837/5Zs OM	20.00	50.00	100	600
1837/6Zs OM	20.00	50.00	100	600
1837Zs OM	20.00	50.00	100	600
1838/7Zs OM	15.00	30.00	75.00	600
1839Zs OM	250	375	500	—
1840Zs OM	500	1,300	—	—
1841Zs OM	15.00	30.00	75.00	600
1842Zs OM Small letters	15.00	40.00	85.00	600
1842Zs OM Large letters	15.00	30.00	75.00	600
1843Zs OM	15.00	30.00	75.00	600
1844Zs OM	20.00	50.00	100	600
1845Zs OM	20.00	50.00	100	600
1846/5Zs OM	25.00	60.00	125	600
1846Zs OM	20.00	50.00	100	600
1847Zs OM	15.00	30.00	75.00	600
1848/6Zs OM	50.00	75.00	125	600
1848Zs OM	20.00	50.00	100	600
1849Zs OM	20.00	50.00	100	600
1850Zs OM	20.00	50.00	100	600
1851Zs OM	15.00	30.00	75.00	600
1852Zs OM	15.00	30.00	75.00	600
1853Zs OM	20.00	50.00	100	600
1854/3Zs OM	30.00	75.00	150	600
1855/4Zs OM	20.00	50.00	100	600
1855Zs OM	15.00	30.00	75.00	600
1856Zs OM	15.00	30.00	75.00	600
1856Zs MO	20.00	50.00	100	600
1857/5Zs MO	20.00	50.00	100	600
1857Zs O/M	20.00	50.00	100	600
1857Zs MO	15.00	30.00	75.00	600
1858Zs MO	20.00	50.00	100	600
1859Zs MO	15.00	30.00	75.00	600
1860/59Zs MO	20.00	50.00	100	600
1860Zs MO	15.00	30.00	75.00	600
1860Zs VL	20.00	50.00	100	600
1861/0Zs VL	20.00	50.00	100	600
1861Zs VL	15.00	30.00	75.00	600
1861Zs VL 6/5	20.00	50.00	100	600
1862/1Zs VL	20.00	50.00	100	600
1862Zs VL	20.00	50.00	100	600
1863Zs VL	20.00	50.00	100	600
1863Zs MO	20.00	50.00	100	600
1864Zs VL	15.00	30.00	75.00	600
1868Zs JS	20.00	50.00	100	600
1868Zs YH	15.00	30.00	75.00	600
1869Zs YH	15.00	30.00	75.00	600
1870Zs YH	15.00	30.00	75.00	600

Mint: Alamos
KM# 377 8 REALES

27.0700 g., 0.9030 Silver .7859 oz. ASW **Obv:** Facing eagle
Note: Mint mark A, As. Varieties exist.

Date	Mintage	F	VF	XF	Unc
1864 PG	—	750	1,250	2,000	—
1865/4 PG Rare	—	—	—	—	—
1865 PG	—	500	750	1,000	—
1866/5 PG Rare	—	—	—	—	—
1866 PG	—	1,250	2,250	—	—
1866 DL Rare	—	—	—	—	—
1867 DL	—	1,150	2,150	—	—
1868 DL	—	50.00	90.00	150	300
1869/8 DL	—	50.00	90.00	150	—
1869 DL	—	50.00	80.00	120	300
1870 DL	—	30.00	60.00	120	300
1871 DL	—	20.00	35.00	75.00	200
1872 AM/DL	—	25.00	50.00	100	300
1872 AM	—	25.00	50.00	100	250
1873 AM	509,000	15.00	25.00	50.00	150
1874/3 As DL	—	25.00	50.00	100	250
1874 DL	—	15.00	25.00	50.00	150
1875A DL 7/7	—	40.00	80.00	120	300
1875A DL	—	15.00	25.00	50.00	150
1875 As DL	—	30.00	60.00	110	250
1876 DL	—	15.00	25.00	50.00	150
1877 DL	515,000	15.00	25.00	50.00	150
1878 DL	513,000	15.00	25.00	50.00	150
1879 DL	—	20.00	35.00	75.00	175
1879 ML	—	30.00	60.00	125	350
1880 ML	—	12.00	15.00	30.00	140
1881 ML	966,000	12.00	15.00	30.00	140
1882 ML	480,000	12.00	15.00	30.00	140
1883 ML	464,000	12.00	15.00	30.00	140
1884 ML	—	12.00	15.00	30.00	140
1885 ML	280,000	12.00	15.00	30.00	140
1886 ML	857,000	12.00	15.00	25.00	110
1886/0As/Cn ML/JD	Inc. above	15.00	20.00	35.00	160
1887 ML	650,000	12.00	15.00	25.00	110
1888/7 ML	508,000	30.00	60.00	100	400
1888 ML	Inc. above	12.00	15.00	25.00	110
1889 ML	427,000	12.00	15.00	25.00	110
1890 ML	450,000	12.00	15.00	25.00	110
1891 ML	533,000	12.00	15.00	25.00	110
1892/0 ML	—	20.00	30.00	60.00	160
1892 ML	465,000	12.00	15.00	25.00	110
1893 ML	734,000	10.00	12.00	22.00	85.00
1894 ML	725,000	10.00	12.00	22.00	85.00
1895 ML	477,000	10.00	12.00	22.00	85.00

Mint: Chihuahua
KM# 377.2 8 REALES

27.0700 g., 0.9030 Silver .7859 oz. ASW **Obv:** Facing eagle
Note: Varieties exist.

Date	Mintage	F	VF	XF	Unc
1831 Ca MR	—	1,000	1,750	2,250	3,250
1832 Ca MR	—	125	200	300	600
1833 Ca MR	—	250	550	1,000	—
1834 Ca MR	—	300	600	1,150	—
1834 Ca AM	—	350	500	700	—
1835 Ca AM	—	150	250	475	900
1836 Ca AM	—	100	200	300	600
1837 Ca AM	—	550	1,150	—	—
1838 Ca AM	—	100	200	300	600
1839 Ca RG	—	750	1,250	2,500	—
1840 Ca RG	—	300	500	800	1,500
Note: 1 dot after date					
1840 Ca RG	—	300	500	800	1,500
Note: 3 dots after date					
1841 Ca RG	—	50.00	100	150	300
1842 Ca RG	—	25.00	40.00	75.00	150
1843 Ca RG	—	40.00	80.00	125	250
1844/1 Ca RG	—	35.00	70.00	100	200
1844 Ca RG	—	25.00	40.00	75.00	160
1845 Ca RG	—	25.00	40.00	75.00	160
1846 Ca RG	—	30.00	60.00	100	250
1847 Ca RG	—	40.00	80.00	125	250
1848 Ca RG	—	35.00	70.00	125	250
1849 Ca RG	—	30.00	60.00	100	200
1850/40 Ca RG	—	40.00	80.00	125	250
1850 Ca RG	—	30.00	60.00	100	200
1851/41 Ca RG	—	100	200	300	500
1851 Ca RG	—	150	250	400	750
1852/42 Ca RG	—	150	250	400	750
1852 Ca RG	—	150	250	400	750
1853/43 Ca RG	—	150	250	400	750
1853 Ca RG	—	150	250	350	700
1854/44 Ca RG	—	100	200	300	500
1854 Ca RG	—	50.00	100	150	300
1855/45 Ca RG	—	100	200	350	650
1855 Ca RG	—	50.00	100	150	300
1856/45 Ca RG	—	275	450	750	1,250
1856/5 Ca RG	—	400	700	1,500	3,500
1857 Ca JC/RG	—	40.00	80.00	125	250
1857 Ca JC	—	50.00	100	150	250
1858 Ca JC	—	35.00	70.00	125	250
1858 Ca BA	—	2,000	3,500	—	—
1859 Ca JC	—	40.00	80.00	125	250
1860 Ca JC	—	20.00	40.00	90.00	175
1861 Ca JC	—	15.00	25.00	55.00	125
1862 Ca JC	—	15.00	25.00	55.00	125
1863 Ca JC	—	20.00	35.00	75.00	150
1864 Ca JC	—	20.00	35.00	75.00	150
1865 Ca JC	—	100	200	350	600
1865 Ca FP	—	1,350	2,150	3,250	—
1866 Ca JC	—	750	1,150	2,250	—
1866 Ca FP	—	1,000	2,000	3,250	5,000
1866 Ca JG	—	850	1,650	2,750	4,250
1867 Ca JG	—	100	200	350	600
1868 Ca JG	—	75.00	150	250	400
1868 Ca MM	—	65.00	125	200	350
1869 Ca MM	—	20.00	35.00	65.00	135
1870 Ca MM	—	20.00	35.00	65.00	135
1871/0 Ca MM	—	15.00	25.00	55.00	125
1871 Ca MM	—	15.00	25.00	55.00	125
1871 Ca MM	—	20.00	35.00	65.00	135
Note: First M over inverted M					
1873 Ca MM	—	20.00	35.00	65.00	135
1873 Ca MM/T	—	15.00	25.00	55.00	125
1874 Ca MM	—	12.00	15.00	30.00	100
1875 Ca MM	—	12.00	15.00	30.00	100
1876 Ca MM	—	12.00	15.00	30.00	100
1877 Ca EA	472,000	20.00	40.00	85.00	200
1877 Ca GR	Inc. above	25.00	45.00	65.00	150
1877 Ca JM	Inc. above	12.00	15.00	30.00	100
1877 Ca AV	Inc. above	100	200	350	750
1878 Ca AV	439,000	12.00	15.00	25.00	80.00
1879 Ca AV	—	12.00	15.00	25.00	80.00
1880 Ca AV	—	200	350	600	1,250
1880 Ca PM	—	500	800	1,250	2,500
1880 Ca MG	—	12.00	15.00	25.00	100
Note: Normal initials					
1880 Ca MG	—	12.00	15.00	25.00	100
Note: Tall initials					
1880 Ca MM	—	12.00	15.00	25.00	100
1881 Ca MG	1,085,000	10.00	12.00	20.00	65.00
1882 Ca MG	779,000	10.00	12.00	20.00	65.00
1882 Ca MM	Inc. above	10.00	12.00	20.00	65.00
1882 Ca MM	Inc. above	20.00	45.00	100	175
Note: M sideways					
1883 Ca MM	818,000	—	—	—	—
Note: Sideways M					
1883/2 Ca MM/G	—	12.00	15.00	30.00	80.00
1883 Ca MM	Inc. above	10.00	12.00	20.00	65.00
1884/3 Ca MM	—	12.00	15.00	30.00	90.00
1884 Ca MM	—	10.00	12.00	20.00	65.00
1885/4 Ca MM	1,345,000	15.00	25.00	55.00	125
1885/6 Ca MM	Inc. above	15.00	25.00	55.00	125
1885 Ca MM	Inc. above	10.00	12.00	20.00	65.00
1886 Ca MM	2,483,000	10.00	12.00	20.00	65.00
1887 Ca MM	2,625,000	10.00	12.00	20.00	65.00
1888/7 Ca MM	2,434,000	15.00	25.00	65.00	135
1888 Ca MM	Inc. above	10.00	12.00	20.00	65.00
1889 Ca MM	2,681,000	10.00	12.00	20.00	65.00
1890/89 Ca MM	—	15.00	25.00	55.00	125
1890 Ca MM	2,137,000	10.00	12.00	20.00	65.00
1891/0 Ca MM	2,268,000	15.00	25.00	55.00	135
1891 Ca MM	Inc. above	10.00	12.00	20.00	80.00
1892 Ca MM	2,527,000	10.00	12.00	20.00	65.00
1893 Ca MM	2,632,000	10.00	12.00	20.00	65.00
1894 Ca MM	2,642,000	10.00	12.00	20.00	65.00
1895 Ca MM	1,112,000	10.00	12.00	20.00	65.00

Mint: Culiacan
KM# 377.3 8 REALES

27.0700 g., 0.9030 Silver .7859 oz. ASW **Obv:** Facing eagle
Note: Mint mark C, Cn. Varieties exist.

Date	Mintage	F	VF	XF	Unc
1846 CE	—	150	300	800	1,500
1846 CE	—	175	385	900	1,650
Note: Dot after G					
1846 CE	—	125	265	750	1,450
Note: No dot after G					
1847 CE	—	400	700	1,500	—
1848 CE	—	125	250	450	1,000
1849 CE	—	75.00	125	200	400
1850 CE	—	75.00	125	200	400
1851 CE	—	125	250	450	1,000
1852/1 CE	—	100	150	250	500
1852 CE	—	100	200	300	600
1853/0 CE	—	200	350	700	1,300
1853/2/0	—	200	400	750	1,400
1853 CE	—	100	175	300	600
Note: Thick rays					
1853 CE	—	200	350	650	—
Note: Error: MEXIGANA					
1854 CE	—	750	1,250	—	—
1854 CE	—	175	350	750	1,200
Note: Large eagle and hat					
1855/6 CE	—	40.00	60.00	100	200
1855 CE	—	25.00	40.00	75.00	150
1856 CE	—	50.00	100	175	350
1857 CE	—	20.00	35.00	75.00	150
1858 CE	—	30.00	40.00	75.00	150
1859 CE	—	20.00	35.00	75.00	150
1860/9 PV/CV	—	50.00	70.00	100	200
1860/9 PV/E	—	50.00	70.00	100	200
1860 CE	—	25.00	40.00	75.00	150
1860 PV	—	40.00	60.00	90.00	175
1861/0 CE	—	50.00	80.00	120	250
1861 PV/CE	—	75.00	125	200	350
1861 CE	—	20.00	35.00	60.00	150
1862 CE	—	20.00	35.00	60.00	150
1863/2 CE	—	30.00	50.00	75.00	200
1863 CE	—	20.00	30.00	60.00	150
1864 CE	—	30.00	60.00	100	300
1865 CE	—	125	200	325	650
1866 CE	—	400	750	1,250	2,250
1867 CE	—	125	200	350	700
1868/7 CE	—	30.00	40.00	75.00	150
1868/8	—	50.00	100	150	300
1868 CE	—	30.00	40.00	75.00	150
1869 CE	—	30.00	40.00	75.00	175
1870 CE	—	50.00	100	150	350
1873 MP	—	50.00	100	150	300
1874/3 MP	—	30.00	40.00	75.00	150
1874C MP	—	20.00	30.00	45.00	100
1874 CN MP	—	125	200	300	600
1875 MP	—	12.00	15.00	22.00	80.00
1876 GP	—	12.00	15.00	30.00	90.00
1876 CG	—	12.00	15.00	22.00	80.00
1877 CG	339,000	12.00	15.00	22.00	80.00
1877Gn CG Error	—	65.00	125	200	400
1877 JA	Inc. above	35.00	75.00	125	250
1878/7 CG	483,000	35.00	75.00	125	250
1878 CG	Inc. above	15.00	25.00	35.00	125
1878 JD/CG	—	25.00	35.00	50.00	150
1878 JD	Inc. above	15.00	20.00	30.00	125
1878 JD	Inc. above	20.00	30.00	40.00	150
Note: D over retrograde D					
1879 JD	—	12.00	15.00	30.00	135
1880/70 JD	—	15.00	20.00	30.00	90.00
1880 JD	—	12.00	15.00	22.00	120
1881/0 JD	1,032,000	15.00	20.00	30.00	90.00
1881C JD	Inc. above	12.00	15.00	22.00	80.00
1881Cn JD	Inc. above	40.00	60.00	90.00	150
1882 JD	397,000	12.00	15.00	22.00	80.00
1882 AM	Inc. above	12.00	15.00	22.00	80.00
1883 AM	333,000	12.00	15.00	22.00	125
1884 AM	—	12.00	15.00	22.00	80.00
1885/6 AM	227,000	20.00	30.00	45.00	110
1885C AM	Inc. above	35.00	70.00	150	350
1885Cn AM	Inc. above	12.00	15.00	22.00	80.00
1885Gn AM Error	Inc. above	25.00	50.00	100	275
1886 AM	571,000	12.00	15.00	22.00	80.00
1887 AM	732,000	12.00	15.00	22.00	80.00
1888 AM	768,000	12.00	15.00	22.00	80.00
1889 AM	1,075,000	12.00	15.00	22.00	80.00
1890 AM	874,000	10.00	12.00	20.00	65.00
1891 AM	777,000	10.00	12.00	20.00	65.00
1892 AM	681,000	10.00	12.00	20.00	65.00
1893 AM	1,144,000	10.00	12.00	20.00	65.00
1894 AM	2,118,000	10.00	12.00	20.00	65.00
1895 AM	1,834,000	10.00	12.00	20.00	65.00
1896 AM	2,134,000	10.00	12.00	20.00	65.00
1897 AM	1,580,000	10.00	12.00	20.00	65.00

Mint: Durango
KM# 377.4 8 REALES

27.0700 g., 0.9030 Silver .7859 oz. ASW **Obv:** Facing eagle
Note: Varieties exist.

Date	Mintage	F	VF	XF	Unc
1825Do RL	—	30.00	65.00	150	375
1826Do RL	—	40.00	85.00	200	475
1827/6Do RL	—	35.00	60.00	85.00	200
1827/8Do RL	—	150	275	500	—
1827Do RL	—	30.00	50.00	90.00	200
1828/7Do RL	—	35.00	60.00	90.00	200
1828Do RL	—	25.00	50.00	80.00	175
1829Do RL	—	25.00	50.00	80.00	175
1830Do RM	—	25.00	50.00	90.00	200
Note: B on eagle's claw					
1831Do RM	—	20.00	30.00	60.00	150
Note: B on eagle's claw					
1832Do RM	—	35.00	60.00	120	300
Note: Mexican dies, B on eagle's claw					
1832/1Do RM/RL	—	25.00	35.00	75.00	165
Note: French dies					
1833/2Do RM/RL	—	20.00	35.00	75.00	165
1833Do RM	—	15.00	30.00	60.00	150
1834/3/2Do RM/RL	—	20.00	35.00	75.00	165
1834Do RM	—	15.00	25.00	50.00	150
1835/4Do RM/RL	—	20.00	35.00	65.00	150
1835Do RM	—	20.00	35.00	65.00	150
1836/1Do RM	—	20.00	35.00	65.00	150
1836/4Do RM	—	20.00	35.00	65.00	150
1836/5/4Do RM/RL	—	75.00	150	250	500
1836Do RM	—	20.00	30.00	55.00	150
1836Do RM	—	20.00	30.00	55.00	150
Note: M on snake					
1837/1Do RM	—	20.00	30.00	55.00	150
1837Do RM	—	20.00	30.00	55.00	150
1838/1Do RM	—	20.00	30.00	60.00	165
1838/7Do RM	—	20.00	30.00	60.00	165
1838Do RM	—	20.00	30.00	55.00	150
1839/1Do RM/RL	—	20.00	30.00	55.00	150
1839/1Do RM	—	20.00	30.00	55.00	150
1839Do RM	—	20.00	30.00	55.00	150
1840/38/31Do RM	—	20.00	30.00	55.00	150
1840/39Do RM	—	20.00	30.00	55.00	150
1840Do RM	—	20.00	30.00	55.00	150
1841/31Do RM	—	65.00	125	275	450
1841/39Do RM/L	—	25.00	50.00	85.00	200
1841/39Do RM	—	25.00	50.00	85.00	200
1842/31Do RM	—	125	250	400	750
Note: B below cactus					
1842/31Do RM	—	40.00	80.00	125	250
1842/32Do RM	—	40.00	80.00	125	250
1842Do RM	—	20.00	30.00	55.00	150
Note: Eagle of 1832-41					
1842Do RM	—	20.00	30.00	55.00	150
Note: Pre-1832 eagle resumed					
1842Do RM	—	40.00	80.00	125	250
1843/33Do RM	—	50.00	90.00	150	250
1843Do RM	—	50.00	90.00	150	250
1844/34Do RM	—	100	200	300	500
1844/35Do RM	—	100	200	300	500
1844/43Do RM	—	60.00	120	220	425
1845/31Do RM	—	100	200	300	500
1845/34Do RM	—	35.00	75.00	125	250
1845/35Do RM	—	35.00	75.00	125	250
1845Do RM	—	20.00	30.00	55.00	150
1846/31Do RM	—	20.00	30.00	55.00	150
1846/36Do RM	—	20.00	30.00	55.00	150
1846Do RM	—	20.00	30.00	55.00	150
1847Do RM	—	25.00	50.00	80.00	185
1848/7Do RM	—	125	250	400	750
1848/7Do CM/RM	—	100	200	350	700
1848Do CM/RM	—	100	200	350	700
1848Do RM	—	100	200	300	600
1848Do CM	—	50.00	100	200	400
1849/39Do CM	—	100	200	350	700
1849Do CM	—	65.00	125	250	550
1849Do JMR/CM Oval 0	—	200	400	450	800
1849Do JMR Oval 0	—	200	325	450	800
1849Do JMR Round 0	—	200	400	600	1,000
1850Do JMR	—	100	150	250	500
1851/0Do JMR	—	65.00	125	225	475
1851Do JMR	—	100	150	250	500
1852Do CP/JMR	—	450	800	1,500	—
1852Do CP	—	750	1,200	2,250	—
1852Do JMR	—	175	250	375	650
1853Do CP/JMR	—	125	235	350	600
1853Do CP	—	200	350	600	1,200
1854Do CP	—	25.00	35.00	65.00	300
1855Do CP	—	50.00	100	175	350
Note: Eagle type of 1854					
1855Do CP	—	50.00	100	175	350
Note: Eagle type of 1856					
1856Do CP	—	50.00	100	175	350
1857Do CP	—	35.00	65.00	125	250
1858/7Do CP	—	25.00	35.00	70.00	165
1858Do CP	—	20.00	30.00	60.00	165
1859Do CP	—	20.00	30.00	60.00	165
1860/59Do CP	—	30.00	50.00	100	200
1860Do CP	—	20.00	30.00	60.00	165
1861/0Do CP	—	20.00	30.00	60.00	165
1861Do CP	—	20.00	30.00	50.00	125
1862/1Do CP	—	25.00	35.00	60.00	125
1862Do CP	—	20.00	30.00	60.00	175
1863/1Do CP	—	30.00	60.00	90.00	200
1863/2Do CP	—	25.00	50.00	75.00	175
1863/53Do CP	—	30.00	60.00	90.00	200
1863Do CP	—	25.00	50.00	75.00	175
1864Do CP	—	100	150	250	500
1864Do LT	—	25.00	40.00	80.00	175
1864Do LT/T	—	25.00	40.00	80.00	175
1864Do LT/CP	—	50.00	100	175	350
1865Do LT Rare	—	—	—	—	—
1866/4Do CM	—	2,750	5,500	—	—
1866Do CM	—	1,750	3,250	5,500	8,000
1867Do CM	—	3,500	—	—	—
1867/6Do CP	—	200	400	600	1,200
1867Do CP	—	175	300	500	1,000
1867Do CP/CM	—	125	250	400	900
1867Do CP/LT	—	200	400	650	1,250
1868Do CP	—	25.00	40.00	80.00	175
1869Do CP	—	20.00	30.00	50.00	135
1870/69Do CP	—	20.00	30.00	50.00	125
1870/9Do CP	—	20.00	30.00	50.00	125
1870Do CP	—	20.00	30.00	50.00	125
1873Do CP	—	125	225	325	600
1873Do CM	—	30.00	50.00	100	200
1874/3Do CM	—	12.00	15.00	22.00	100
1874Do CM	—	10.00	15.00	22.00	80.00
1874Do JH	—	1,150	1,750	2,750	—
1875Do CM	—	10.00	15.00	22.00	80.00
1875Do JH	—	80.00	150	250	450
1876Do CM	—	10.00	15.00	22.00	80.00
1877Do CM	431,000	1,450	2,500	—	—
1877Do CP	Inc. above	10.00	15.00	22.00	80.00
1877Do JMP	Inc. above	750	1,250	2,000	—
1878Do PE	409,000	15.00	25.00	40.00	100
1878Do TB	Inc. above	10.00	15.00	25.00	90.00
1879Do TB	—	10.00	15.00	22.00	80.00
1880/70Do TB	—	60.00	100	175	350
1880/70Do TB/JP	—	150	250	375	650
1880/70Do JP	—	15.00	25.00	40.00	100
1880Do TB	—	150	250	375	650
1880Do JP	—	10.00	15.00	22.00	80.00
1881Do JP	928,000	10.00	15.00	25.00	90.00
1882Do JP	414,000	10.00	15.00	22.00	80.00
1882Do MC/JP	Inc. above	30.00	60.00	100	200
1882Do MC	Inc. above	25.00	50.00	75.00	150
1883/73Do MC	452,000	15.00	25.00	40.00	90.00
1883Do MC	Inc. above	10.00	15.00	22.00	80.00
1884/3Do MC	—	15.00	25.00	40.00	90.00
1884Do MC	—	10.00	15.00	22.00	80.00
1885Do MC	547,000	10.00	12.00	20.00	70.00
1885Do JB	Inc. above	25.00	35.00	50.00	125
1886/5Do MC	—	15.00	25.00	40.00	100
1886/3Do MC	955,000	15.00	25.00	40.00	100
1886Do MC	Inc. above	10.00	12.00	20.00	70.00
1887Do MC	1,004,000	10.00	12.00	20.00	70.00
1888/7Do MC	—	65.00	125	250	450
1888Do MC	996,000	10.00	12.00	20.00	70.00
1889Do MC	874,000	10.00	12.00	20.00	70.00
1890Do MC	1,119,000	10.00	12.00	20.00	70.00
1890Do JP	Inc. above	10.00	12.00	20.00	70.00
1891Do JP	1,487,000	10.00	12.00	20.00	70.00
1892Do JP	1,597,000	10.00	12.00	20.00	70.00
1892Do ND	Inc. above	25.00	50.00	100	200
1893Do ND	1,617,000	10.00	12.00	20.00	70.00
1894Do ND	1,537,000	10.00	12.00	20.00	70.00
1895/3Do ND	761,000	15.00	25.00	40.00	100
1895Do ND	Inc. above	10.00	12.00	20.00	70.00
1895Do ND/P	—	15.00	25.00	40.00	100

Mint: Estado de Mexico
KM# 377.5 8 REALES

27.0700 g., 0.9030 Silver .7859 oz. ASW **Obv:** Facing eagle

Date	F	VF	XF	Unc
1828EoMo LF/LP	350	850	2,150	—
1828EoMo LF	350	850	2,150	5,500
1829EoMo LF	300	750	1,850	4,500
1830/20EoMo LF	1,250	2,750	4,250	—
1830EoMo LF	1,000	2,000	3,250	6,000

Mint: Guadalajara

KM# 377.6 8 REALES

27.0700 g., 0.9030 Silver .7859 oz. ASW **Obv:** Facing eagle
Note: Varieties exist.

Date	Mintage	F	VF	XF	Unc
1825Ga FS	—	150	275	475	1,000
1826/5Ga FS	—	125	250	450	1,000
1826Ga FS	—	125	250	450	1,000
1827/87Ga FS	—	125	250	450	1,000
1827Ga FS	—	125	250	450	1,000
1287Ga FS Error	—	8,500	9,500	—	—
1828Ga FS	—	200	375	550	1,200
1829/8Ga FS	—	200	375	550	1,200
1829Ga FS	—	175	325	475	950
1830/29Ga FS	—	100	175	300	600
1830Ga FS	—	100	175	300	600
1830Ga LP/FS	—	800	1,450	—	—
Note: The 1830 LP/FS is currently only known with a Philippine countermark.					
1831Ga LP	—	200	400	600	1,200
1831Ga FS/LP	—	300	500	750	1,500
1831Ga FS	—	125	275	400	—
1832/1Ga FS	—	50.00	100	175	300
1832/1Ga FS/LP	—	50.00	100	175	300
1832Ga FS/LP	—	75.00	150	285	550
1832Ga FS	—	25.00	50.00	100	225
1833/2/1Ga FS/LP	—	45.00	75.00	125	250
1833/2Ga FS	—	25.00	50.00	100	225
1834/2Ga FS	—	60.00	125	200	350
1834/3Ga FS	—	60.00	125	200	350
1834/0Ga FS	—	50.00	100	150	300
1834Ga FS	—	50.00	100	150	300
1835Ga FS	—	25.00	50.00	100	225
1836/5Ga FS	—	175	350	—	—
1836/1Ga JG/FS	—	40.00	80.00	125	250
1836Ga FS	—	275	450	750	—
1836Ga JG/FS	—	25.00	50.00	100	225
1836Ga JG	—	25.00	50.00	100	225
1837/6Ga JG/FS	—	50.00	100	175	300
1837/6Ga JG	—	45.00	90.00	160	285
1837Ga JG	—	40.00	80.00	125	250
1838/7Ga JG	—	100	175	300	550
1838Ga JG	—	100	150	275	500
1839Ga MC	—	100	200	350	600
1839Ga MC/JG	—	100	200	300	550
1839Ga JG	—	60.00	125	200	350
1840/30Ga MC	—	50.00	75.00	150	275
1840Ga MC	—	30.00	60.00	125	250
1841Ga MC	—	30.00	60.00	125	250
1842/1Ga JG/MG	—	100	150	250	450
1842/1Ga JG/MC	—	100	150	250	450
1842Ga JG	—	25.00	50.00	100	225
1842Ga JG/MG	—	25.00	50.00	100	225
1843/2Ga MC/JG	—	25.00	50.00	100	225
1843Ga MC/JG	—	25.00	50.00	100	225
1843Ga JG	—	400	600	900	1,650
1843Ga MC	—	50.00	100	150	300
1844Ga MC	—	50.00	100	150	300
1845Ga MC	—	75.00	150	300	700
1845Ga JG	—	500	850	1,250	1,850
1846Ga JG	—	40.00	80.00	150	300
1847Ga JG	—	100	150	225	400
1848/7Ga JG	—	55.00	85.00	125	250
1848Ga JG	—	50.00	75.00	100	225
1849Ga JG	—	90.00	125	175	325
1849/39Ga JG	—	250	500	—	—
1850Ga JG	—	50.00	100	150	300
1851Ga JG	—	125	200	350	650
1852Ga JG	—	100	150	250	450
1853/2Ga JG	—	125	175	250	475
1853Ga JG	—	90.00	125	175	300
1854/3Ga JG	—	65.00	90.00	125	250
1854Ga JG	—	50.00	75.00	110	225
1855/4Ga JG	—	50.00	100	150	275
1855Ga JG	—	25.00	50.00	100	225
1856/4Ga JG	—	60.00	125	175	300
1856/5Ga 56	—	60.00	125	175	300
1856Ga JG	—	50.00	100	150	275
1857Ga JG	—	50.00	100	225	450
1858Ga JG	—	100	150	300	500
1859/7Ga JG	—	25.00	50.00	110	225
1859/8Ga JG	—	25.00	50.00	100	200
1859Ga JG	—	20.00	40.00	80.00	175
1860Ga JG Without dot	—	350	750	1,200	2,250
1860Ga JG	—	2,000	3,250	4,500	—
Note: Dot in loop of snake's tail, base alloy					
1861Ga JG	—	2,200	5,750	—	—
1862Ga JG	—	850	1,350	2,750	4,500
1863/52Ga JG	—	—	—	—	—
1863/59Ga JG	—	45.00	50.00	85.00	145
1863/2Ga JG	—	30.00	50.00	90.00	175
1863/4Ga JG	—	40.00	75.00	150	250
1863Ga JG	—	25.00	45.00	75.00	150
1863Ga FV Rare	—	—	—	—	—
1867Ga JM Rare	—	—	—	—	—
1868/7Ga JM	—	50.00	75.00	125	200
1868Ga JM	—	50.00	75.00	125	200
1869Ga JM	—	50.00	75.00	125	200
1869Ga IC	—	75.00	125	200	375
1870/60Ga IC	—	60.00	90.00	150	275
1870Ga IC	—	60.00	90.00	150	275
1873Ga IC	—	15.00	25.00	50.00	125
1874Ga IC	—	10.00	15.00	22.00	90.00
1874Ga MC	—	25.00	50.00	100	200
1875Ga IC	—	15.00	30.00	60.00	125
1875Ga MC	—	10.00	15.00	22.00	90.00
1876Ga IC	559,000	15.00	30.00	50.00	100
1876Ga MC	Inc. above	125	175	250	375
1877Ga IC	928,000	10.00	15.00	22.00	90.00
1877/6Ga JA	—	10.00	15.00	22.00	90.00
1877Ga JA	Inc. above	10.00	15.00	22.00	90.00
1878Ga JA	764,000	10.00	15.00	22.00	90.00
1879Ga JA	—	10.00	15.00	22.00	90.00
1880/70Ga FS	—	15.00	25.00	50.00	125
1880Ga JA	—	10.00	15.00	22.00	90.00
1880Ga FS	—	10.00	15.00	22.00	90.00
1881Ga FS	1,300,000	10.00	15.00	22.00	90.00
1882/1Ga FS	537,000	15.00	25.00	50.00	125
1882Ga FS	Inc. above	10.00	15.00	22.00	90.00
1882Ga TB/FS	Inc. above	50.00	100	175	300
1882Ga TB	Inc. above	50.00	100	175	300
1883Ga TB	561,000	15.00	25.00	40.00	125
1884Ga TB	—	10.00	12.00	20.00	85.00
1884Ga AH	—	10.00	12.00	20.00	85.00
1885Ga AH	443,000	10.00	12.00	20.00	90.00
1885Ga JS	Inc. above	30.00	60.00	100	200
1886Ga JS/H	—	10.00	12.00	20.00	85.00
1886Ga JS	1,038,999	10.00	12.00	20.00	85.00
1887Ga JS	878,000	10.00	12.00	20.00	85.00
1888Ga JS	1,159,000	10.00	12.00	20.00	85.00
1889Ga JS	1,583,000	10.00	12.00	20.00	85.00
1890Ga JS	1,658,000	10.00	12.00	20.00	85.00
1891Ga JS	1,507,000	10.00	12.00	20.00	85.00
1892/1Ga JS	1,627,000	15.00	25.00	50.00	125
1892Ga JS	Inc. above	10.00	12.00	20.00	80.00
1893Ga JS	1,952,000	10.00	12.00	20.00	80.00
1894Ga JS	2,045,999	10.00	12.00	20.00	80.00
1895/3Ga JS	—	12.00	20.00	35.00	100
1895Ga JS	1,146,000	10.00	12.00	20.00	65.00

Mint: Guadalupe y Calvo

KM# 377.7 8 REALES

27.0700 g., 0.9030 Silver .7859 oz. ASW **Obv:** Facing eagle

Date	F	VF	XF	Unc
1844GC MP	350	500	1,000	2,000
1844GC MP Error, reversed S in Ds, Gs	400	600	1,200	2,250
1845GC MP Eagle's tail square	125	200	325	700
1845GC MP Eagle's tail round	175	350	650	1,200
1846GC MP Eagle's tail square	175	350	750	1,650
1846GC MP Eagle's tail round	125	200	350	750
1847GC MP	150	250	400	800
1848GC MP	175	300	500	900
1849GC MP	175	300	525	1,000
1850GC MP	175	300	575	1,100
1851GC MP	300	500	900	1,600
1852GC MP	350	600	1,250	2,500

Mint: Guanajuato

KM# 377.8 8 REALES

27.0700 g., 0.9030 Silver .7859 oz. ASW **Obv:** Facing eagle
Note: Varieties exist.

Date	Mintage	F	VF	XF	Unc
1825Go JJ	—	40.00	70.00	150	300
1825G JJ	—	1,250	1,650	—	—
Note: Error mint mark G					
1826Go JJ	—	40.00	80.00	175	350
Note: Straight J's					
1826Go JJ	—	30.00	60.00	125	250
Note: Full J's					
1826Go MJ	—	250	450	850	—
1827Go MJ	—	40.00	75.00	125	250
1827Go MJ/JJ	—	—	—	—	—
1827Go MR	—	100	200	350	600
1828Go MJ	—	—	—	—	—
Note: Error mint mark Goo					
1828Go MJ	—	30.00	60.00	125	250
1828/7Go MR	—	150	300	600	1,200
1828Go MR	—	150	300	600	1,200
1829Go MJ	—	20.00	35.00	55.00	165
1830Go MJ	—	20.00	30.00	55.00	165
Note: Oblong beading and narrow J					
1830Go MJ	—	20.00	30.00	55.00	165
Note: Regular beading and wide J					
1831Go MJ	—	12.00	20.00	40.00	150
Note: Colon after date					
1831Go MJ	—	12.00	20.00	40.00	150
Note: 2 stars after date					
1832Go MJ	—	12.00	20.00	40.00	150
1832Go MJ	—	20.00	35.00	65.00	175
Note: 1 of date over inverted 1					
1833Go MJ/1	—	20.00	35.00	65.00	175
1833Go MJ	—	12.00	20.00	40.00	150
1833Go JM	—	400	750	1,250	2,500
1834Go PJ	—	12.00	20.00	40.00	150
1835Go PJ	—	12.00	20.00	40.00	150
Note: Star on cap					
1835Go PJ	—	12.00	20.00	40.00	150
Note: Dot on cap					
1836Go PJ	—	12.00	20.00	40.00	150
1837Go PJ	—	12.00	20.00	40.00	150
1838Go PJ	—	12.00	20.00	40.00	150
1839Go PJ/JJ	—	12.00	20.00	40.00	150
1839Go PJ	—	12.00	20.00	40.00	150
1840/30Go PJ	—	20.00	30.00	50.00	150
1840Go PJ	—	12.00	20.00	35.00	125
1841/31Go PJ	—	12.00	20.00	35.00	125
1841Go PJ	—	12.00	20.00	35.00	125
1842/1Go PM	—	20.00	30.00	50.00	125
1842/31Go PM/PJ	—	25.00	35.00	60.00	150
1842Go PJ	—	20.00	30.00	50.00	125
1842Go PM/PJ	—	12.00	20.00	35.00	125
1842Go PM	—	12.00	20.00	35.00	125
1843Go PM	—	12.00	20.00	35.00	125
Note: Dot after date					
1843Go PM	—	12.00	20.00	35.00	125
Note: Triangle of dots after date					
1844Go PM	—	12.00	20.00	35.00	125
1845Go PM	—	12.00	20.00	35.00	125
1846/5Go PM	—	20.00	30.00	50.00	150
Note: Eagle type of 1845					
1846Go PM	—	15.00	25.00	40.00	135
Note: Early type of 1847					
1847Go PM Narrow date	—	12.00	20.00	35.00	125
1847Go PM Wide date	—	12.00	20.00	35.00	125
1848/7Go PM	—	20.00	35.00	65.00	150
1848Go PM	—	20.00	35.00	65.00	150
1848Go PF	—	12.00	20.00	35.00	125
1849Go PF	—	12.00	20.00	35.00	125
1850Go PF	—	12.00	20.00	35.00	125
1851/0Go PF	—	20.00	30.00	50.00	150
1851Go PF	—	12.00	20.00	35.00	125

Date	Mintage	F	VF	XF	Unc
1852/1Go PF	—	20.00	30.00	50.00	150
1852Go PF	—	12.00	20.00	35.00	125
1853/2Go PF	—	20.00	30.00	50.00	150
1853Go PF	—	12.00	20.00	35.00	125
1854Go PF	—	12.00	20.00	35.00	125
1855Go PF Large letters	—	12.00	20.00	35.00	125
1855Go PF Small letters	—	12.00	20.00	35.00	125
1856/5Go PF	—	20.00	30.00	50.00	150
1856Go PF	—	12.00	20.00	35.00	125
1857/5Go PF	—	20.00	30.00	50.00	150
1857/6Go PF	—	20.00	35.00	70.00	200
1857Go PF	—	12.00	15.00	20.00	75.00
1858/7Go PI	—	12.00	20.00	35.00	125
1858Go PF	—	12.00	20.00	35.00	125
1859/7Go PF	—	12.00	20.00	35.00	125
1859/8Go PF	—	20.00	30.00	50.00	150
1859Go PF	—	12.00	20.00	35.00	125
1860/50Go PF	—	20.00	30.00	50.00	150
1860/59Go PF	—	12.00	18.00	25.00	85.00
1860Go PF	—	12.00	15.00	20.00	75.00
1861/51Go PF	—	15.00	20.00	30.00	100
1861/0Go PF	—	12.00	15.00	20.00	75.00
1861Go PF	—	12.00	15.00	20.00	75.00
186/52Go YE	—	—	—	—	—
1862Go YE/PF	—	12.00	15.00	20.00	75.00
1862Go YE	—	12.00	15.00	20.00	75.00
1862Go YF	—	12.00	15.00	20.00	75.00
1862Go YF/PF	—	12.00	15.00	20.00	75.00
1863/53Go YF	—	12.00	18.00	25.00	75.00
1863/54Go YF	—	15.00	20.00	30.00	100
1863Go YE Rare	—	—	—	—	—
1863Go YF	—	12.00	15.00	20.00	75.00
1867/57Go YF	—	15.00	20.00	30.00	100
1867Go YF	—	12.00	15.00	20.00	75.00
1868/58Go YF	—	15.00	20.00	30.00	100
1868/7Go YF	—	15.00	20.00	30.00	100
1868Go YF	—	12.00	15.00	20.00	75.00
1870/60Go FR	—	20.00	30.00	50.00	150
1870Go YF	—	1,800	3,000	5,000	7,500
1870Go FR/YF	—	20.00	35.00	70.00	200
1870Go FR	—	12.00	15.00	20.00	75.00
1873Go FR	—	12.00	15.00	20.00	75.00
1874/3Go FR	—	15.00	20.00	30.00	85.00
1874Go FR	—	15.00	25.00	35.00	100
1875/3Go FR	—	15.00	20.00	30.00	85.00
1875/6Go FR	—	15.00	20.00	30.00	85.00
1875Go FR	—	12.00	15.00	20.00	75.00
Note: Small circle with dot on eagle					
1876/5Go FR	—	15.00	20.00	30.00	85.00
1876Go FR	—	12.00	15.00	20.00	60.00
1877Go FR	2,477,000	12.00	15.00	20.00	60.00
1878/7Go FR	2,273,000	15.00	20.00	30.00	75.00
1878/7Go SM	—	15.00	20.00	30.00	75.00
1878Go FR	Inc. above	12.00	15.00	20.00	65.00
1878Go SM, S/F	—	15.00	20.00	25.00	70.00
1878Go SM	—	12.00	15.00	20.00	65.00
1879/7Go SM	—	15.00	20.00	30.00	75.00
1879/8Go SM	—	15.00	20.00	30.00	75.00
1879/8Go SM/FR	—	15.00	20.00	30.00	75.00
1879Go SM	—	12.00	15.00	20.00	65.00
1879Go SM/FR	—	15.00	20.00	30.00	75.00
1880/70Go SB	—	15.00	20.00	30.00	75.00
1880Go SB/SM	—	12.00	15.00	20.00	65.00
1880Go SB	—	12.00	15.00	20.00	65.00
1881/71Go SB	3,974,000	15.00	20.00	30.00	75.00
1881/0Go SB	Inc. above	15.00	20.00	30.00	75.00
1881Go SB	Inc. above	12.00	15.00	20.00	65.00
1882Go SB	2,015,000	12.00	15.00	20.00	75.00
1883Go SB	2,100,000	35.00	75.00	125	250
1883Go BR	Inc. above	12.00	15.00	20.00	65.00
1883Go BR/SR	—	12.00	15.00	20.00	65.00
1883Go BR/SB	Inc. above	12.00	15.00	20.00	65.00
1884/73Go BR	—	20.00	30.00	40.00	100
1884/74Go BR	—	20.00	30.00	40.00	100
1884/3Go BR	—	20.00	30.00	60.00	150
1884Go BR	—	12.00	15.00	20.00	65.00
1884/74Go RR	—	50.00	100	175	350
1884Go RR	—	25.00	50.00	100	250
1885/75Go RR	2,363,000	15.00	20.00	30.00	75.00
1885Go RR	Inc. above	12.00	15.00	20.00	65.00
1886/75Go RR	4,127,000	15.00	20.00	25.00	70.00
1886/76Go RR	Inc. above	12.00	15.00	20.00	65.00
1886/5Go RR/BR	Inc. above	12.00	15.00	20.00	65.00
1886Go RR	Inc. above	12.00	15.00	20.00	65.00
1887Go RR	4,205,000	10.00	15.00	20.00	65.00
1888Go RR	3,985,000	10.00	15.00	20.00	65.00
1889Go RR	3,646,000	10.00	15.00	20.00	65.00
1890Go RR	3,615,000	10.00	15.00	20.00	65.00
1891Go RS/R	—	10.00	15.00	20.00	65.00
1891Go RS	3,197,000	10.00	15.00	20.00	65.00
1892/0Go RS	—	10.00	15.00	20.00	65.00
1892Go RS	3,672,000	10.00	15.00	20.00	65.00
1893Go RS	3,854,000	10.00	15.00	20.00	65.00
1894Go RS	4,127,000	10.00	15.00	20.00	65.00
1895/1Go RS	3,768,000	15.00	20.00	25.00	75.00
1895/3Go RS	Inc. above	15.00	20.00	25.00	75.00
1895Go RS	Inc. above	10.00	15.00	20.00	65.00
1896/1Go/As RS/ML	5,229,000	15.00	20.00	25.00	75.00
1896/1Go RS	Inc. above	12.00	15.00	20.00	65.00
1896Go/Ga RS	Inc. above	—	—	—	—
1896Go RS	Inc. above	10.00	12.00	18.00	60.00
1897Go RS	4,344,000	10.00	12.00	18.00	60.00

Mint: Hermosillo

KM# 377.9 8 REALES

27.0700 g., 0.9030 Silver .7859 oz. ASW **Obv:** Facing eagle

Note: Varieties exist.

Date	Mintage	F	VF	XF	Unc
1835Ho PP Rare	—	—	—	—	—
1836Ho PP Rare	—	—	—	—	—
1839Ho PR Unique	—	—	—	—	—
1861Ho FM Reeded edge	—	4,500	7,500	—	—
1862Ho FM Rare	—	—	—	—	—
Note: Plain edge, snakes tail left, long ray over *8R					
1862Ho FM	—	1,550	2,700	—	—
Note: Plain edge, snake's tail left					
1862Ho FM	—	1,650	2,750	—	—
Note: Reeded edge, snakes tail right					
1863Ho FM	—	150	300	800	—
1864Ho FM	—	850	1,650	2,750	—
1864Ho PR/FM	—	1,200	2,200	—	—
1864Ho PR	—	650	1,250	2,150	3,350
1865Ho FM	—	250	500	950	1,850
1866Ho FM	—	1,150	2,150	3,500	5,500
1866Ho MP	—	950	1,750	3,000	4,650
1867Ho PR	—	100	175	275	500
1868Ho PR	—	20.00	35.00	65.00	175
1869Ho PR	—	40.00	60.00	125	250
1870Ho PR	—	100	175	275	550
1871/0Ho PR	—	50.00	75.00	125	250
1871Ho PR	—	30.00	50.00	90.00	200
1872/1Ho PR	—	35.00	60.00	90.00	200
1872Ho PR	—	30.00	50.00	75.00	175
1873Ho PR	351,000	30.00	50.00	85.00	150
1874Ho PR	—	15.00	20.00	40.00	125
1875Ho PR	—	15.00	20.00	40.00	125
1876Ho AF	—	15.00	20.00	40.00	125
1877Ho AF	410,000	20.00	30.00	50.00	150
1877Ho GR	Inc. above	100	150	225	400
1877Ho JA	Inc. above	25.00	50.00	85.00	175
1878Ho JA	451,000	15.00	20.00	40.00	120
1879Ho JA	—	15.00	20.00	40.00	120
1880Ho JA	—	15.00	20.00	40.00	120
1881Ho JA	586,000	15.00	20.00	40.00	120
1882Ho JA	240,000	25.00	40.00	65.00	125
Note: O above H					
1882Ho JA	Inc. above	25.00	40.00	65.00	125
Note: O after H					
1883/2Ho JA	204,000	200	350	500	1,000
1883/2Ho FM/JA	Inc. above	25.00	40.00	75.00	150
1883Ho FM/JA	—	27.00	45.00	85.00	165
1883Ho FM	Inc. above	20.00	30.00	60.00	125
1883Ho JA	Inc. above	275	450	800	1,500
1884/3Ho FM	—	20.00	25.00	50.00	125
1884Ho FM	—	15.00	20.00	40.00	120
1885Ho FM	132,000	15.00	20.00	40.00	120
1886Ho FM	225,000	20.00	30.00	45.00	125
1886Ho FG	Inc. above	20.00	30.00	45.00	125
1887/6Ho FG	—	20.00	35.00	65.00	150
1887Ho FG	150,000	20.00	35.00	65.00	150
1888Ho FG	364,000	12.00	18.00	25.00	100
1889Ho FG	490,000	12.00	18.00	25.00	100
1890Ho FG	565,000	12.00	18.00	25.00	100
1891Ho FG	738,000	12.00	18.00	25.00	100
1892Ho FG	643,000	12.00	18.00	25.00	100
1893Ho FG	518,000	12.00	18.00	25.00	100
1894Ho FG	504,000	12.00	18.00	25.00	100
1895Ho FG	320,000	12.00	18.00	25.00	100

Mint: Mexico City

KM# 377.10 8 REALES

27.0700 g., 0.9030 Silver .7859 oz. ASW **Obv:** Facing eagle

Note: Varieties exist. 1874 CP is a die struck counterfeit.

Date	Mintage	F	VF	XF	Unc
1824Mo JM Round tail	—	75.00	125	250	500
1824Mo JM Square tail	—	75.00	125	250	500
1825Mo JM	—	25.00	40.00	75.00	200
1826/5Mo JM	—	25.00	40.00	75.00	200
1826Mo JM	—	20.00	30.00	55.00	165
1827Mo JM	—	25.00	35.00	60.00	175
Note: Medal alignment					
1827Mo JM	—	25.00	35.00	60.00	175
Note: Coin alignment					
1828Mo JM	—	30.00	60.00	100	250
1829Mo JM	—	20.00	30.00	90.00	220
1830/20Mo JM	—	35.00	5.00	150	300
1830Mo JM	—	30.00	50.00	90.00	220
1831Mo JM	—	30.00	50.00	100	240
1832/1Mo JM	—	25.00	40.00	65.00	180
1832Mo JM	—	20.00	30.00	55.00	165
1833Mo MJ	—	25.00	40.00	80.00	200
1833Mo ML	—	450	650	950	2,000
1834/3Mo ML	—	25.00	35.00	60.00	175
1834Mo ML	—	20.00	30.00	55.00	165
1835Mo ML Narrow date	—	20.00	30.00	55.00	165
1835Mo ML Wide date	—	20.00	30.00	55.00	165
1836Mo ML	—	50.00	100	150	325
1836Mo ML/MF	—	50.00	100	150	325
1836Mo MF	—	30.00	50.00	90.00	220
1836Mo MF/ML	—	35.00	60.00	100	240
1837/6Mo ML	—	30.00	50.00	80.00	200
1837/6Mo MM	—	30.00	50.00	80.00	200
1837/6Mo MM/ML	—	30.00	50.00	80.00	200
1837/6Mo MM/MF	—	30.00	50.00	80.00	200
1837Mo ML	—	30.00	50.00	80.00	200
1837Mo MM	—	75.00	125	175	325
1838Mo MM	—	30.00	50.00	80.00	200
1838Mo ML	—	20.00	35.00	60.00	180
1838Mo ML/MM	—	20.00	35.00	60.00	180
1839Mo ML Narow date	—	15.00	25.00	50.00	165
1839Mo ML Wide date	—	15.00	25.00	50.00	165
1840Mo ML	—	15.00	25.00	50.00	165
1841Mo ML	—	15.00	25.00	45.00	150
1842Mo ML	—	15.00	25.00	45.00	150
1842Mo MM	—	15.00	25.00	45.00	150
1843Mo MM	—	15.00	25.00	45.00	150
1844Mo MF/MM	—	—	—	—	—
1844Mo MF	—	15.00	25.00	45.00	150
1845/4Mo MF	—	15.00	25.00	45.00	150
1845Mo MF	—	15.00	25.00	45.00	150
1846/5Mo MF	—	15.00	25.00	50.00	165
1846Mo MF	—	15.00	25.00	50.00	165
1847/6Mo MF	—	2,000	3,550	—	—
1847Mo MF	—	1,650	3,000	5,000	7,500
1847Mo RC	—	20.00	30.00	55.00	165
1847Mo RC/MF	—	15.00	25.00	45.00	150
1848Mo GC	—	15.00	25.00	45.00	150
1849/8Mo GC	—	20.00	35.00	60.00	180
1849Mo GC	—	15.00	25.00	45.00	150
1850/40Mo GC	—	25.00	50.00	100	240
1850/49Mo GC	—	25.00	50.00	100	240
1850Mo GC	—	20.00	40.00	75.00	200
1851Mo GC	—	20.00	40.00	60.00	175
1852Mo GC	—	20.00	40.00	75.00	200
1853Mo GC	—	15.00	25.00	50.00	160
1854Mo GC	—	12.00	15.00	30.00	125
1855Mo GC	—	20.00	35.00	65.00	180
1855Mo GF	—	12.00	15.00	30.00	125
1855Mo GF/GC	—	12.00	15.00	30.00	125
1856/4Mo GF	—	15.00	25.00	45.00	145
1856/5Mo GF	—	15.00	25.00	45.00	145
1856Mo GF	—	12.00	15.00	30.00	125
1857Mo GF	—	10.00	15.00	30.00	125
1858/7Mo FH/GF	—	10.00	15.00	30.00	125
1858Mo FH Narrow date	—	10.00	15.00	30.00	125
1858Mo FH Wide date	—	10.00	15.00	30.00	125
1859Mo FH	—	10.00	15.00	30.00	125
1859/8Mo FH	—	25.00	50.00	100	240
1860/59Mo FH	—	15.00	20.00	30.00	125
1860Mo FH	—	10.00	15.00	30.00	125
1860Mo TH	—	12.00	18.00	40.00	145
1861Mo TH	—	12.00	18.00	40.00	145
1861Mo CH	—	10.00	15.00	20.00	75.00
1862Mo CH	—	10.00	15.00	20.00	75.00
1863Mo CH	—	10.00	15.00	20.00	75.00
1863Mo CH/TH	—	10.00	15.00	20.00	75.00
1863Mo TH	—	10.00	15.00	20.00	75.00
1867Mo CH	—	10.00	15.00	20.00	65.00
1867Mo CH/TH	—	20.00	45.00	70.00	185
1868Mo CH	—	10.00	15.00	20.00	65.00
1868Mo PH	—	10.00	15.00	20.00	65.00
1868Mo CH/PH	—	10.00	15.00	20.00	65.00
1868Mo PH Narrow date	—	10.00	15.00	20.00	65.00
1868Mo PH Wide date	—	10.00	15.00	20.00	65.00
1869Mo CH	—	10.00	15.00	20.00	65.00
1873Mo MH	—	10.00	15.00	20.00	65.00
1873Mo MH/HH	—	12.00	18.00	25.00	75.00
1874/69Mo MH	—	20.00	45.00	70.00	185
1874Mo MH	—	12.00	18.00	25.00	75.00
1874Mo BH/MH	—	12.00	18.00	25.00	75.00
1874Mo BH	—	12.00	18.00	25.00	85.00
1875Mo BH	—	10.00	15.00	20.00	65.00
1876/4Mo BH	—	12.00	18.00	25.00	75.00
1876/5Mo BH	—	12.00	18.00	25.00	75.00
1876Mo BH	—	10.00	15.00	20.00	65.00
1877Mo MH	898,000	10.00	15.00	20.00	65.00

Date	Mintage	F	VF	XF	Unc
1877Mo MH/BH	Inc. above	12.00	18.00	25.00	75.00
1878Mo MH	2,154,000	10.00	15.00	20.00	65.00
1879/8Mo MH	—	10.00	15.00	20.00	75.00
1879Mo MH	—	10.00	15.00	20.00	65.00
1880/79Mo MH	—	15.00	20.00	30.00	75.00
1880Mo MH	—	10.00	15.00	20.00	75.00
1881Mo MH	5,712,000	10.00	15.00	20.00	65.00
1882/1Mo MH	2,746,000	12.00	15.00	20.00	75.00
1882Mo MH	Inc. above	10.00	15.00	20.00	65.00
1883/2Mo MH	2,726,000	12.00	18.00	25.00	85.00
1883Mo MH Narrow date	Inc. above	10.00	15.00	20.00	65.00
1883Mo MH Wide date	—	10.00	15.00	20.00	65.00
1884/3Mo MH	—	15.00	20.00	30.00	75.00
1884Mo MH	—	10.00	15.00	20.00	65.00
1885Mo MH	3,649,000	10.00	15.00	20.00	65.00
1886Mo MH	7,558,000	10.00	12.00	18.00	60.00
1887Mo MH	7,681,000	10.00	12.00	18.00	60.00
1888Mo MH Narrow date	7,179,000	10.00	12.00	18.00	60.00
1888Mo MH Wide date	—	10.00	12.00	18.00	60.00
1889Mo MH	7,332,000	10.00	15.00	20.00	65.00
1890Mo MH Narrow date	7,412,000	10.00	12.00	18.00	60.00
1890Mo AM Wide date	—	10.00	12.00	18.00	60.00
1890Mo AM	Inc. above	10.00	12.00	18.00	60.00
1891Mo AM	8,076,000	10.00	12.00	18.00	60.00
1892Mo AM	9,392,000	10.00	12.00	18.00	60.00
1893Mo AM	10,773,000	10.00	12.00	18.00	55.00
1894Mo AM	12,394,000	10.00	12.00	18.00	45.00
1895Mo AM	10,474,000	10.00	12.00	18.00	45.00
1895Mo AB	Inc. above	10.00	12.00	18.00	60.00
1896Mo AB	9,327,000	10.00	12.00	18.00	60.00
1896Mo AM	Inc. above	10.00	12.00	18.00	60.00
1897Mo AM	8,621,000	10.00	12.00	18.00	60.00

Mint: Real de Catorce

KM# 377.1 8 REALES

27.0700 g., 0.9030 Silver .7859 oz. ASW **Obv:** Facing eagle

Date	F	VF	XF	Unc
1863 Ce ME	425	700	1,350	3,000
1863 Ce /PI ML/MC	425	750	1,500	3,250

Mint: Oaxaca

KM# 377.11 8 REALES

27.0700 g., 0.9030 Silver .7859 oz. ASW **Obv:** Facing eagle
Note: Mint mark O, Oa. Varieties exist.

Date	Mintage	F	VF	XF	Unc
18580 AE	—	2,500	4,000	—	—
1858 Oa AE Unique	—	—	—	—	—
1859 AE	—	500	900	1,750	—
Note: A in O of mint mark					
1860 AE	—	200	450	800	—
Note: A in O of mint mark					
18610 FR	—	125	250	550	1,350
1861 Oa FR	—	150	350	700	—
18620 FR	—	40.00	80.00	200	375
1862 Oa FR	—	65.00	125	250	450
18630 FR	—	30.00	60.00	100	250
18630 AE	—	30.00	60.00	100	250
1863 Oa AE	—	100	150	250	450
Note: A in O of mint mark					
1863 Oa AE	—	1,000	1,750	2,750	—
Note: A above O in mint mark					
1864 FR	—	25.00	50.00	75.00	200
1865 AE	—	1,850	3,000	—	—
1867 AE	—	40.00	80.00	150	400
1868 AE	—	40.00	80.00	150	400
1869 AE	—	30.00	60.00	100	250
1873 AE	—	200	300	550	1,350
1874 AE	142,000	15.00	30.00	50.00	200
1875/4 AE	131,000	25.00	50.00	75.00	200
1875 AE	Inc. above	15.00	30.00	40.00	135
1876 AE	140,000	20.00	35.00	55.00	200
1877 AE	139,000	20.00	30.00	50.00	200
1878 AE	125,000	20.00	30.00	50.00	200
1879 AE	153,000	20.00	30.00	50.00	200
1880 AE	143,000	15.00	30.00	45.00	150
1881 AE	134,000	20.00	35.00	60.00	150
1882 AE	100,000	20.00	35.00	60.00	150
1883 AE	122,000	15.00	30.00	45.00	150
1884 AE	142,000	15.00	30.00	50.00	150
1885 AE	158,000	15.00	25.00	40.00	135
1886 AE	120,000	15.00	30.00	45.00	150
1887/6 AE	115,000	25.00	50.00	80.00	200
1887 AE	Inc. above	15.00	25.00	40.00	135
1888 AE	145,000	15.00	25.00	40.00	135
1889 AE	150,000	20.00	30.00	60.00	175
1890 AE	181,000	20.00	30.00	60.00	175
1891 EN	160,000	15.00	25.00	40.00	135
1892 EN	120,000	15.00	25.00	40.00	135
1893 EN	66,000	45.00	75.00	115	300

Mint: San Luis Potosi

KM# 377.12 8 REALES

27.0700 g., 0.9030 Silver .7859 oz. ASW **Obv:** Facing eagle
Note: Varieties exist.

Date	Mintage	F	VF	XF	Unc
1827 Pi JS	—	3,800	—	—	—
1827 Pi SA	—	6,000	9,000	—	—
1828/7 Pi JS	—	275	425	650	1,250
1828 Pi JS	—	225	375	550	1,100
1829 Pi JS	—	35.00	65.00	125	250
1830 Pi JS	—	30.00	50.00	100	200
1831/0 Pi JS	—	35.00	75.00	200	350
1831 Pi JS	—	25.00	35.00	75.00	200
1832/22 Pi JS	—	25.00	35.00	65.00	165
18/032 Pi JS	—	40.00	80.00	175	300
1832 Pi JS	—	25.00	35.00	65.00	165
1833/2 Pi JS	—	30.00	45.00	80.00	250
1833 Pi JS Narrow date	—	20.00	30.00	50.00	150
1833 Pi JS Wide date	—	20.00	30.00	50.00	150
1834/3 Pi JS	—	35.00	65.00	125	300
1834 Pi JS	—	15.00	25.00	50.00	150
1835/4 Pi JS	—	60.00	125	250	500
1835 Pi JS	—	20.00	30.00	65.00	175
Note: Denomination as 8R					
1835 Pi JS	—	15.00	25.00	50.00	150
Note: Denomination as 8Rs					
1836 Pi JS	—	20.00	30.00	55.00	150
1837 Pi JS	—	30.00	50.00	85.00	200
1838 Pi JS	—	20.00	30.00	55.00	150
1839 Pi JS	—	20.00	40.00	70.00	150
1840 Pi JS	—	20.00	30.00	60.00	150
1841 Pi JS	—	25.00	40.00	85.00	200
1841iP JS Error	—	200	350	550	—
1842/1 Pi JS	—	40.00	65.00	125	300
1842/1 Pi JS/PS	—	35.00	55.00	90.00	200
1842 Pi JS	—	30.00	50.00	80.00	175
Note: Eagle type of 1843					
1842 Pi PS	—	30.00	50.00	80.00	175
1842 Pi PS/JS	—	30.00	50.00	80.00	175
Note: Eagle type of 1841					
1843/2 Pi PS Round top 3	—	50.00	75.00	150	300
1843 Pi PS Flat top 3	—	60.00	100	200	475
1843 Pi AM Round top 3	—	20.00	30.00	55.00	150
1843 Pi AM Flat top 3	—	20.00	30.00	55.00	150
1844 Pi AM	—	20.00	30.00	55.00	150
1845/4 Pi AM	—	35.00	55.00	120	250
1845 Pi AM	—	25.00	50.00	100	225
1846/5 Pi AM	—	40.00	65.00	125	300
1846 Pi AM	—	15.00	25.00	50.00	150
1847 Pi AM	—	30.00	50.00	85.00	175
1848/7 Pi AM	—	30.00	60.00	100	200
1848 Pi AM	—	30.00	50.00	85.00	175
1849/8 Pi PS/AM	—	950	1,750	—	—
1849 Pi PS	—	950	1,750	—	—
1849 Pi MC/PS	—	60.00	125	250	500
1849 Pi AM	—	1,850	3,250	5,000	—
1849 Pi MC	—	60.00	125	250	500
1850 Pi MC	—	40.00	80.00	150	300
1851 Pi MC	—	75.00	150	275	550
1852 Pi MC	—	75.00	125	200	400
1853 Pi MC	—	150	275	400	850
1854 Pi MC	—	100	150	250	500
1855 Pi MC	—	100	150	250	500
1856 Pi MC	—	65.00	100	200	400
1857 Pi MC	—	400	700	1,250	—
1857 Pi PS/MC	—	150	250	450	1,000
1857 Pi PS	—	125	200	350	650
1858 Pi MC/PS	—	250	400	650	1,200
1858 Pi MC	—	250	400	650	1,200
1858 Pi PS	—	650	1,150	1,750	—
1859/8 Pi MC/PS	—	3,650	5,750	—	—
1859 Pi MC/PS	—	900	1,750	—	—
1859 Pi MC	—	2,000	3,500	5,000	—
1859 Pi PS/MC	—	800	1,500	2,500	—
1860 Pi FC Rare	—	—	—	—	—
1860 Pi FE Rare	—	—	—	—	—
1860 Pi MC	—	1,750	2,750	6,000	—
1860 Pi PS/FE	—	500	1,000	—	—
1860 Pi RO Rare	—	—	—	—	—
Note: Spink America Gerber sale 6-96 cleaned VF or better realized $33,000					
1860 Pi PS	—	400	600	900	1,750
1861 Pi PS	—	30.00	60.00	90.00	175
1861 Pi RO	—	25.00	35.00	55.00	125
1862/1 Pi RO	—	20.00	25.00	50.00	125
1862 Pi RO	—	15.00	20.00	40.00	100
1862 Pi RO	—	15.00	20.00	40.00	100
Note: Oval O in RO					
1862 Pi RO	—	20.00	30.00	50.00	125
Note: Round O in RO, 6 is an inverted 9					
1863/2 Pi RO	—	25.00	35.00	65.00	150
1863 Pi RO	—	15.00	20.00	40.00	125
1863	—	25.00	35.00	55.00	125
Note: 6 over inverted 6					
1863 Pi FC	—	2,750	4,750	—	—
1864 Pi RO Rare	—	—	—	—	—
1867 Pi CA	—	300	500	—	—
1867 Pi LR	—	250	400	650	—
1867 Pi PS/CA	—	850	—	—	—
1867 Pi PS	—	30.00	60.00	125	275
1868/7 Pi PS	—	30.00	60.00	125	250
1868 Pi PS	—	20.00	30.00	50.00	125
1869/8 Pi PS	—	20.00	25.00	45.00	125
1869 Pi PS	—	15.00	20.00	40.00	125
1870/69 Pi PS	—	750	1,450	3,500	—
1870 Pi PS	—	650	1,250	2,500	—
1873 Pi MH	—	18.00	25.00	45.00	150
1874/3 Pi MH	—	25.00	50.00	120	250
1874 Pi MH	—	10.00	12.00	22.00	120
1875 Pi MH	—	10.00	12.00	22.00	100
1876/5 Pi MH	—	18.00	25.00	45.00	150
1876 Pi MH	—	10.00	12.00	22.00	100
1877/6 Pi MH	—	165	325	550	—
1877 Pi MH	1,018,000	10.00	12.00	22.00	120
1878 Pi MH	1,046,000	15.00	30.00	100	225
1879/8 Pi MH	—	15.00	20.00	30.00	125
1879 Pi MH	—	10.00	12.00	22.00	100
1879 Pi BE	—	25.00	50.00	75.00	150
1879 Pi MR	—	30.00	50.00	100	200
1880 Pi MR	—	250	375	750	—
1880 Pi MH/R	—	10.00	12.00	22.00	100
1880 Pi MH	—	10.00	12.00	22.00	100
1881 Pi MH/R	—	10.00	12.00	22.00	100
1881 Pi MH	2,100,000	10.00	12.00	22.00	100
1882/1 Pi MH	1,602,000	15.00	20.00	30.00	125
1882 Pi MH	Inc. above	10.00	12.00	22.00	100
1883/2 Pi MH	—	15.00	20.00	30.00	125
1883 Pi MH	1,545,000	10.00	12.00	22.00	100
1884/3 Pi MH	—	15.00	20.00	30.00	125
1884 Pi MH/MM	—	12.00	15.00	22.00	90.00
1884 Pi MH	—	10.00	12.00	20.00	80.00
1885/4 Pi MH	1,736,000	15.00	20.00	30.00	125
1885/8 Pi MH	Inc. above	15.00	20.00	30.00	125
1885 Pi MH	Inc. above	10.00	12.00	20.00	80.00
1885 Pi LC	Inc. above	12.00	18.00	25.00	100
1886 Pi LC	3,347,000	10.00	12.00	20.00	80.00
1886 Pi MR	Inc. above	10.00	12.00	20.00	80.00
1887 Pi MR	2,922,000	10.00	12.00	20.00	80.00
1888/7 Pi MR	—	15.00	20.00	30.00	125
1888 Pi MR	2,438,000	10.00	12.00	20.00	70.00
1889 Pi MR	2,103,000	10.00	12.00	20.00	80.00
1890 Pi MR	1,562,000	10.00	12.00	20.00	70.00
1891 Pi MR	1,184,000	10.00	12.00	20.00	70.00
1892 Pi MR	1,336,000	10.00	12.00	20.00	70.00
1893 Pi MR	530,000	10.00	12.00	20.00	80.00

Mint: Zacatecas

KM# 377.13 8 REALES

27.0700 g., 0.9030 Silver .7859 oz. ASW **Obv:** Facing eagle
Note: Varieties exist.

Date	Mintage	F	VF	XF	Unc
1825Zs AZ	—	25.00	35.00	65.00	175
1826/5Zs AZ	—	25.00	45.00	85.00	200
1826Zs AZ	—	100	200	400	800
1826Zs AV	—	175	350	600	1,500
1826/5Zs AO/AZ	—	300	600	1,000	2,000
1826Zs AO	—	200	350	750	2,000
1827Zs AO/AZ	—	35.00	50.00	125	250
1827Zs AO	—	25.00	45.00	85.00	200
1828Zs AO	—	15.00	20.00	45.00	165
1829Zs AO	—	15.00	20.00	45.00	165
1829Zs OV	—	50.00	90.00	150	300
1830Zs OV	—	15.00	20.00	45.00	165

Date	Mintage	F	VF	XF	Unc
1831Zs OV	—	25.00	50.00	90.00	200
1831Zs OM	—	15.00	25.00	55.00	165
1832/1Zs OM	—	20.00	25.00	45.00	165
1832Zs OM	—	15.00	20.00	40.00	150
1833/2Zs OM	—	20.00	30.00	45.00	165
1833Zs OM/MM	—	15.00	25.00	40.00	150
1833Zs OM	—	15.00	20.00	35.00	150
1834Zs OM	—	15.00	20.00	35.00	150
1835Zs OM	—	15.00	20.00	40.00	150
1836/4Zs OM	—	20.00	30.00	50.00	165
1836/5Zs OM	—	20.00	30.00	50.00	165
1836Zs OM	—	15.00	20.00	35.00	150
1837Zs OM	—	15.00	20.00	35.00	150
1838/7Zs OM	—	20.00	30.00	45.00	165
1838Zs OM	—	15.00	20.00	35.00	150
1839Zs OM	—	15.00	20.00	35.00	150
1840Zs OM	—	15.00	20.00	35.00	150
1841Zs OM	—	15.00	20.00	35.00	150
1842Zs OM	—	15.00	20.00	35.00	150
Note: Eagle type of 1841					
1842Zs OM	—	15.00	20.00	35.00	150
Note: Eagle type of 1843					
1843Zs OM	—	15.00	20.00	35.00	150
1844Zs OM	—	15.00	20.00	35.00	150
1845Zs OM	—	15.00	20.00	35.00	150
1846Zs OM	—	15.00	20.00	35.00	150
1847Zs OM	—	15.00	20.00	35.00	150
1848/7Zs OM	—	20.00	30.00	45.00	165
1848Zs OM	—	15.00	20.00	35.00	150
1849Zs OM	—	15.00	20.00	35.00	150
1850Zs OM	—	15.00	20.00	35.00	150
1851Zs OM	—	15.00	20.00	35.00	150
1852Zs OM	—	15.00	20.00	35.00	150
1853Zs OM	—	30.00	45.00	75.00	200
1854/3Zs OM	—	20.00	30.00	60.00	175
1854Zs OM	—	15.00	25.00	45.00	165
1855Zs OM	—	20.00	30.00	60.00	175
1855Zs MO	—	30.00	60.00	90.00	200
1856/5Zs MO	—	20.00	30.00	45.00	165
1856Zs MO	—	15.00	20.00	35.00	150
1857/5Zs MO	—	20.00	30.00	45.00	165
1857Zs MO	—	15.00	20.00	35.00	150
1858/7Zs MO	—	15.00	20.00	35.00	150
1858Zs MO	—	15.00	20.00	35.00	150
1859/8Zs MO	—	15.00	20.00	35.00	150
1859Zs MO	—	15.00	20.00	35.00	150
1859Zs VL/MO	—	25.00	50.00	75.00	175
1859Zs VL	—	20.00	40.00	60.00	165
1860/50Zs MO	—	10.00	12.00	20.00	80.00
1860/59Zs MO	—	10.00	12.00	20.00	80.00
1860Zs MO	—	10.00	12.00	20.00	80.00
1860Zs VL/MO	—	10.00	12.00	20.00	80.00
1860Zs VL	—	10.00	12.00	20.00	80.00
1861/0Zs VL/MO	—	10.00	12.00	20.00	80.00
1861Zs VL	—	10.00	12.00	20.00	80.00
1861/0Zs VL	—	10.00	12.00	20.00	80.00
1862/1Zs VL	—	15.00	20.00	35.00	100
1862Zs VL	—	10.00	12.00	20.00	80.00
1863Zs VL	—	10.00	12.00	20.00	80.00
1863Zs MO	—	10.00	12.00	20.00	80.00
1864/3Zs VL	—	15.00	20.00	35.00	100
1864Zs VL	—	10.00	12.00	20.00	80.00
1864Zs MO	—	15.00	20.00	35.00	100
1865/4Zs MO	—	200	450	800	1,550
1865Zs MO	—	150	300	600	1,250
1866Zs VL	—	—	—	—	—
Note: Contemporary counterfeit					
1867Zs JS Rare	—	—	—	—	—
1868Zs JS	—	10.00	12.00	20.00	80.00
1868Zs YH	—	10.00	12.00	20.00	80.00
1869Zs YH	—	10.00	12.00	20.00	80.00
1870Zs YH Rare	—	—	—	—	—
1873Zs YH	—	10.00	12.00	20.00	80.00
1874Zs YH	—	10.00	12.00	20.00	80.00
1874Zs JA/YA	—	10.00	12.00	20.00	80.00
1874Zs JA	—	10.00	12.00	20.00	80.00
1875Zs JA	—	10.00	12.00	20.00	80.00
1876Zs JA	—	10.00	12.00	20.00	80.00
1876Zs JS	—	10.00	12.00	20.00	80.00
1877Zs JS	2,700,000	10.00	12.00	20.00	80.00
1878Zs JS	2,310,000	10.00	12.00	20.00	80.00
1879/8Zs JS	—	15.00	20.00	35.00	100
1879Zs JS	—	10.00	12.00	20.00	80.00
1880Zs JS	—	10.00	12.00	20.00	80.00
1881Zs JS	5,592,000	10.00	12.00	20.00	80.00
1882/1Zs JS	2,485,000	15.00	20.00	35.00	100
1882Zs JS Straight J	Inc. above	10.00	12.00	20.00	65.00
1882Zs JS Full J	Inc. above	10.00	12.00	20.00	65.00
1883/2Zs JS	2,563,000	15.00	20.00	35.00	100
1883Zs JS	Inc. above	10.00	12.00	20.00	80.00
1884Zs JS	—	10.00	12.00	20.00	80.00
1885Zs JS	2,252,000	10.00	12.00	20.00	65.00
1886/5Zs JS	5,303,000	15.00	20.00	35.00	100
1886/8Zs JS	Inc. above	15.00	20.00	35.00	100
1886Zs JS	Inc. above	10.00	12.00	20.00	65.00
1886Zs FZ	Inc. above	10.00	12.00	20.00	65.00
1887Zs FZ	4,733,000	10.00	12.00	20.00	65.00
1887Z FZ	Inc. above	20.00	30.00	50.00	100
1888/7Zs FZ	5,132,000	12.00	15.00	25.00	80.00
1888Zs FZ	Inc. above	10.00	12.00	20.00	65.00
1889Zs FZ	4,344,000	10.00	12.00	20.00	65.00
1890Zs FZ	3,887,000	10.00	12.00	20.00	65.00
1891Zs FZ	4,114,000	10.00	12.00	20.00	65.00
1892/1Zs FZ	4,238,000	12.00	15.00	25.00	80.00
1892Zs FZ Narrow date	Inc. above	10.00	12.00	20.00	65.00
1892Zs FZ Wide date	—	10.00	12.00	20.00	65.00
1893Zs FZ	3,872,000	10.00	12.00	20.00	65.00
1894Zs FZ	3,081,000	10.00	12.00	20.00	65.00
1895Zs FZ	4,718,000	10.00	12.00	20.00	65.00
1896Zs FZ	4,226,000	10.00	12.00	20.00	55.00
1897Zs FZ	4,877,000	10.00	12.00	20.00	55.00

Mint: Culiacan
KM# 378 1/2 ESCUDO
1.6900 g., 0.8750 Gold .0475 oz. AGW **Obv:** Facing eagle

Date	VG	F	VF	XF	Unc
1848C CE	35.00	50.00	75.00	150	—
1853C CE	35.00	50.00	75.00	150	—
1854C CE	35.00	50.00	75.00	150	—
1856C CE	50.00	100	150	250	—
1857C CE	35.00	50.00	75.00	150	—
1859C CE	35.00	50.00	75.00	150	—
1860C CE	35.00	50.00	75.00	150	—
1862C CE	35.00	50.00	75.00	125	—
1863C CE	35.00	50.00	75.00	125	—
1866C CE	35.00	50.00	75.00	125	—
1867C CE	35.00	50.00	75.00	125	—
1870C CE	75.00	150	275	450	—

Mint: Durango
KM# 378.1 1/2 ESCUDO
1.6900 g., 0.8750 Gold .0475 oz. AGW **Obv:** Facing eagle

Date	VG	F	VF	XF	Unc
1833Do RM/RL	35.00	50.00	75.00	150	—
1834/1Do RM	35.00	50.00	75.00	150	—
1834/3Do RM	35.00	50.00	75.00	150	—
1835/2Do RM	35.00	50.00	75.00	150	—
1835/3Do RM	35.00	50.00	75.00	150	—
1835/4Do RM	35.00	50.00	75.00	150	—
1836/4Do RM	35.00	50.00	75.00	150	—
1837Do RM	35.00	50.00	75.00	150	—
1838Do RM	40.00	60.00	100	175	—
1843Do RM	40.00	60.00	100	175	—
1844/33Do RM	40.00	60.00	100	175	—
1844/33Do R./RL	65.00	125	275	450	—
1845Do CM	40.00	60.00	100	175	—
1846Do RM	40.00	60.00	100	175	—
1848Do RM	40.00	60.00	100	175	—
1850/33Do JMR	40.00	60.00	100	175	—
1851Do JMR	40.00	60.00	100	200	—
1852Do JMR	40.00	60.00	100	175	—
1853/33Do CP	75.00	150	300	500	—
1853Do CP	35.00	50.00	75.00	150	—
1854Do CP	35.00	50.00	75.00	150	—
1855Do CP	35.00	50.00	75.00	150	—
1859Do CP	35.00	50.00	75.00	150	—
1861Do CP	35.00	50.00	75.00	150	—
1862Do CP	35.00	50.00	75.00	150	—
1864Do LT	75.00	125	250	400	—

Mint: Guadalajara
KM# 378.2 1/2 ESCUDO
1.6900 g., 0.8750 Gold .0475 oz. AGW **Obv:** Facing eagle

Date	VG	F	VF	XF	Unc
1825Ga FS	40.00	60.00	100	175	—
1829Ga FS	40.00	60.00	100	175	—
1831Ga FS	40.00	60.00	100	175	—
1834Ga FS	40.00	60.00	100	175	—
1835Ga FS	40.00	60.00	100	175	—
1837Ga JG	40.00	60.00	100	175	—
1838Ga JG	40.00	60.00	100	175	—
1839Ga JG	—	—	—	—	—
1842Ga JG	—	—	—	—	—
1847Ga JG	40.00	60.00	100	175	—
1850Ga JG	35.00	50.00	75.00	150	—
1852Ga JG	35.00	50.00	75.00	150	—
1859Ga JG	40.00	60.00	100	175	—
1861Ga JG	35.00	50.00	75.00	150	—

Mint: Guadalupe y Calvo
KM# 378.3 1/2 ESCUDO
1.6900 g., 0.8750 Gold .0475 oz. AGW **Obv:** Facing eagle

Date	VG	F	VF	XF	Unc
1846GC MP	50.00	75.00	100	175	—
1847GC MP	50.00	75.00	100	175	—
1848/7GC MP	50.00	75.00	100	200	—
1850GC MP	50.00	75.00	100	175	—
1851GC	50.00	75.00	100	175	—

Mint: Guanajuato
KM# 378.4 1/2 ESCUDO
1.6900 g., 0.8750 Gold .0475 oz. AGW **Obv:** Facing eagle

Date	VG	F	VF	XF	Unc
1845Go PM	30.00	40.00	65.00	125	—
1849Go PF	30.00	40.00	65.00	125	—
1851/41Go PF	30.00	40.00	65.00	125	—
1851Go PF	30.00	40.00	65.00	125	—
1852Go PF	30.00	40.00	65.00	125	—
1853Go PF	30.00	40.00	65.00	125	—
1855Go PF	30.00	50.00	80.00	150	—
1857Go PF	30.00	40.00	65.00	125	—
1858/7Go PF	30.00	40.00	65.00	125	—
1859Go PF	30.00	40.00	65.00	125	—
1860Go PF	30.00	40.00	65.00	125	—
1861Go PF	30.00	40.00	65.00	125	—
1862/1Go YE	30.00	40.00	65.00	125	—
1863Go PF	30.00	50.00	80.00	150	—
1863Go YF	30.00	40.00	65.00	125	—

Mint: Mexico City
KM# 378.5 1/2 ESCUDO
1.6900 g., 0.8750 Gold .0475 oz. AGW **Obv:** Facing eagle

Date	VG	F	VF	XF	Unc
1825/1Mo JM	50.00	75.00	125	200	—
1825/4Mo JM	50.00	75.00	125	200	—
1825Mo JM	30.00	40.00	80.00	150	—
1827/6Mo JM	30.00	40.00	80.00	150	—
1827Mo JM	30.00	40.00	80.00	150	—
1829Mo JM	30.00	40.00	80.00	150	—
1831/0Mo JM	30.00	40.00	80.00	150	—
1831Mo JM	30.00	40.00	60.00	125	—
1832Mo	30.00	40.00	60.00	125	—
1833Mo MJ Olive and oak branches reversed	30.00	50.00	90.00	175	—
1834Mo ML	30.00	40.00	60.00	125	—
1835Mo ML	30.00	40.00	80.00	150	—
1838Mo ML	30.00	50.00	90.00	175	—
1839Mo ML	30.00	50.00	90.00	175	—
1840Mo ML	30.00	40.00	60.00	125	—
1841Mo ML	30.00	40.00	60.00	125	—
1842Mo ML	30.00	40.00	80.00	150	—
1842Mo MM	30.00	40.00	80.00	150	—
1843Mo MM	30.00	40.00	60.00	125	—
1844Mo MF	30.00	40.00	60.00	125	—
1845Mo MF	30.00	40.00	60.00	125	—
1846/5Mo MF	30.00	40.00	60.00	125	—
1846Mo MF	30.00	40.00	60.00	125	—
1848Mo GC	30.00	40.00	60.00	125	—
1850Mo GC	30.00	40.00	60.00	125	—
1851Mo GC	30.00	40.00	60.00	125	—
1852Mo GC	30.00	40.00	60.00	125	—
1853Mo GC	30.00	40.00	60.00	125	—
1854Mo GC	30.00	40.00	60.00	125	—
1855Mo GF	30.00	40.00	60.00	125	—
1856/4Mo GF	30.00	40.00	60.00	125	—
1857Mo GF	30.00	40.00	60.00	125	—
1858/7Mo FH/GF	35.00	50.00	75.00	150	—
1858Mo FH	30.00	40.00	60.00	125	—
1859Mo FH	30.00	40.00	60.00	125	—
1860/59Mo FH	30.00	40.00	60.00	125	—
1861Mo CH/FH	30.00	40.00	80.00	150	—
1862Mo CH	30.00	40.00	60.00	125	—
1863/57Mo CH/GF	30.00	40.00	60.00	125	—
1868/58Mo PH	30.00	40.00	80.00	150	—
1869/59Mo CH	30.00	40.00	80.00	150	—

Mint: Zacatecas
KM# 378.6 1/2 ESCUDO
1.6900 g., 0.8750 Gold .0475 oz. AGW **Obv:** Facing eagle

Date	VG	F	VF	XF	Unc
1860Zs VL	35.00	50.00	75.00	150	—
1862/1Zs VL	35.00	50.00	75.00	150	—
1862Zs VL	30.00	40.00	65.00	125	—

Mint: Culiacan
KM# 379 ESCUDO
3.3800 g., 0.8750 Gold .0950 oz. AGW **Obv:** Facing eagle

Date	VG	F	VF	XF	Unc
1846C CE	75.00	100	200	350	—
1847C CE	50.00	75.00	125	175	—
1848C CE	50.00	75.00	125	175	—
1849/8C CE	60.00	100	150	225	—
1850C CE	50.00	75.00	125	175	—
1851C CE	60.00	100	150	225	—
1853/1C CE	60.00	100	150	225	—
1854C CE	50.00	75.00	125	175	—
1856/5/4C CE	60.00	100	150	225	—
1856C CE	50.00	75.00	125	175	—
1857/1C CE	60.00	100	150	225	—
1857C CE	50.00	75.00	125	175	—
1861C PV	50.00	75.00	125	175	—
1862C CE	50.00	75.00	125	175	—
1863C CE	50.00	75.00	125	175	—
1866C CE	50.00	75.00	125	175	—
1870C CE	50.00	75.00	125	175	—

Mint: Durango
KM# 379.1 ESCUDO
3.3800 g., 0.8750 Gold .0950 oz. AGW **Obv:** Facing eagle

Date	VG	F	VF	XF	Unc
1833/2Do RM/RL	75.00	125	200	300	—
1834Do RM	60.00	100	150	200	—
1835Do RM	—	—	—	—	—
1836Do RM/RL	60.00	100	150	200	—
1838Do RM	60.00	100	150	200	—
1846/38Do RM	75.00	125	200	300	—
1850Do JMR	75.00	125	175	225	—
1851/31Do JMR	75.00	125	200	300	—
1851Do JMR	75.00	125	175	225	—
1853Do CP	75.00	125	175	225	—
1854/34Do CP	75.00	125	175	225	—
1854/44Do CP/RP	75.00	125	175	225	—
1855Do CP	75.00	125	175	225	—
1859Do CP	75.00	125	175	225	—
1861Do CP	75.00	125	175	225	—
1864Do LT/CP	75.00	125	175	225	—

Mint: Guadalajara
KM# 379.2 ESCUDO
3.3800 g., 0.8750 Gold .0950 oz. AGW **Obv:** Facing eagle

Date	VG	F	VF	XF	Unc
1825Ga FS	60.00	90.00	125	200	—
1826Ga FS	60.00	90.00	125	200	—
1829Ga FS	—	—	—	—	—
1831Ga FS	60.00	90.00	125	200	—
1834Ga FS	60.00	90.00	125	200	—
1835Ga JG	60.00	90.00	125	200	—
1842Ga JG/MC	60.00	90.00	125	200	—
1843Ga MC	60.00	90.00	125	200	—
1847Ga JG	60.00	90.00	125	200	—
1848/7Ga JG	60.00	90.00	125	200	—
1849Ga JG	60.00	90.00	125	200	—
1850/40Ga JG	65.00	125	225	325	—
1850Ga JG	60.00	90.00	125	200	—
1852/1Ga JG	60.00	90.00	125	200	—
1856Ga JG	60.00	90.00	125	200	—
1857Ga JG	60.00	90.00	125	200	—
1859/7Ga JG	60.00	90.00	125	200	—
1860/59Ga JG	65.00	100	175	275	—
1860Ga	60.00	90.00	125	200	—

Mint: Guadalupe y Calvo
KM# 379.3 ESCUDO
3.3800 g., 0.8750 Gold .0950 oz. AGW **Obv:** Facing eagle

Date	VG	F	VF	XF	Unc
1844GC MP	75.00	100	175	250	—
1845GC MP	75.00	100	175	250	—
1846GC MP	75.00	100	175	250	—
1847GC MP	75.00	100	175	250	—
1848GC MP	75.00	100	175	250	—
1849GC MP	75.00	100	175	250	—
1850GC MP	75.00	100	175	250	—
1851GC MP	75.00	100	175	250	—

Mint: Guanajuato
KM# 379.4 ESCUDO
3.3800 g., 0.8750 Gold .0950 oz. AGW **Obv:** Facing eagle

Date	VG	F	VF	XF	Unc
1845Go PM	60.00	75.00	125	200	—
1849Go PF	60.00	75.00	125	200	—
1851Go PF	60.00	75.00	125	200	—
1853Go PF	60.00	75.00	125	200	—
1860Go PF	75.00	125	200	300	—
1862Go PE	60.00	75.00	125	200	—

Mint: Mexico City
KM# 379.5 ESCUDO
3.3800 g., 0.8750 Gold .0950 oz. AGW **Obv:** Facing eagle

Date	VG	F	VF	XF	Unc
1825Mo JM	50.00	70.00	100	150	—
1827/6Mo JM	50.00	70.00	100	150	—
1827Mo JM	50.00	70.00	100	150	—
1830/29Mo JM	50.00	70.00	100	150	—
1831Mo JM	50.00	70.00	100	150	—
1832Mo JM	50.00	70.00	125	175	—
1833Mo MJ	50.00	70.00	100	150	—
1834Mo ML	50.00	70.00	125	175	—
1841Mo ML	50.00	70.00	125	175	—
1843Mo MM	50.00	70.00	100	150	—
1845Mo MF	50.00	70.00	100	150	—
1846/5Mo MF	50.00	70.00	100	150	—
1848Mo GC	50.00	70.00	125	175	—
1850Mo GC	50.00	70.00	125	175	—
1856/4Mo GF	50.00	70.00	100	150	—
1856/5Mo GF	50.00	70.00	100	150	—
1856Mo GF	50.00	70.00	100	150	—
1858Mo FH	50.00	70.00	125	175	—
1859Mo FH	50.00	70.00	100	150	—
1860Mo TH	50.00	70.00	125	175	—
1861Mo CH	50.00	70.00	100	150	—
1862Mo CH	50.00	70.00	125	175	—
1863Mo TH	50.00	70.00	100	150	—
1869Mo CH	50.00	70.00	100	150	—

Mint: Zacatecas
KM# 379.6 ESCUDO
3.3800 g., 0.8750 Gold .0950 oz. AGW **Obv:** Facing eagle
Note: Struck at Zacatecas Mint, mint mark Zs.

Date	VG	F	VF	XF	Unc
1853Zs OM	100	125	200	300	—
1860/59Zs VL V is inverted A	75.00	100	200	350	—
1860Zs VL	75.00	100	150	200	—
1862Zs VL	75.00	100	150	200	—

Mint: Culiacan
KM# 380 2 ESCUDOS
6.7700 g., 0.8750 Gold .1904 oz. AGW **Obv:** Facing eagle

Date	VG	F	VF	XF	Unc
1846C CE	100	150	225	325	—
1847C CE	100	150	225	325	—
1848C CE	100	150	225	325	—
1852C CE	100	150	225	325	—
1854C CE	100	175	250	375	—
1856/4C CE	100	175	250	375	—
1857C CE	100	150	225	325	—

Mint: Durango
KM# 380.1 2 ESCUDOS
6.7700 g., 0.8750 Gold .1904 oz. AGW **Obv:** Facing eagle

Date	VG	F	VF	XF	Unc
1833Do RM	300	450	700	1,200	—
1837/4Do RM	—	—	—	—	—
1837Do RM	—	—	—	—	—
1844Do RM	275	400	600	1,000	—

Mint: Estado de Mexico
KM# 380.2 2 ESCUDOS
6.7700 g., 0.8750 Gold .1904 oz. AGW **Obv:** Facing eagle

Date	VG	F	VF	XF	Unc
1828EoMo LF	700	1,000	1,750	2,500	—

Mint: Guadalajara
KM# 380.3 2 ESCUDOS
6.7700 g., 0.8750 Gold .1904 oz. AGW **Obv:** Facing eagle

Date	VG	F	VF	XF	Unc
1835Ga FS	100	150	225	325	—
1836/5Ga JG	125	200	400	500	—
1839/5Ga JG	—	—	—	—	—
1839Ga JG	100	150	200	285	—
1840Ga MC	100	150	200	285	—
1841Ga MC	100	150	250	400	—
1847/6Ga JG	100	150	225	300	—
1848/7Ga JG	100	150	225	300	—
1850/40Ga JG	100	150	200	285	—
1851Ga JG	100	150	200	285	—
1852Ga JG	100	150	225	325	—
1853Ga JG	100	150	200	285	—
1854/2Ga JG	—	—	—	—	—
1858Ga JG	100	150	200	285	—
1859/8Ga JG	100	150	225	300	—
1859Ga JG	100	150	200	285	—
1860/50Ga JG	100	150	225	300	—
1860Ga JG	100	150	225	300	—
1861/59Ga JG	100	150	200	285	—
1861/0Ga JG	100	150	200	285	—
1863/1Ga JG	100	150	200	285	—
1870Ga IC	100	150	200	285	—

Mint: Guadalupe y Calvo
KM# 380.4 2 ESCUDOS
6.7700 g., 0.8750 Gold .1904 oz. AGW **Obv:** Facing eagle

Date	VG	F	VF	XF	Unc
1844GC MP	150	200	275	400	—
1845GC MP	750	1,250	2,000	3,000	—
1846GC MP	750	1,250	2,000	3,000	—
1847GC MP	125	175	350	500	—
1848GC MP	150	200	350	450	—
1849GC MP	150	200	300	400	—
1850GC MP	150	200	300	400	—

Mint: Guanajuato
KM# 380.5 2 ESCUDOS
6.7700 g., 0.8750 Gold .1904 oz. AGW **Obv:** Facing eagle

Date	VG	F	VF	XF	Unc
1845Go PM	100	150	250	400	—
1849Go PF	100	150	250	400	—
1853Go PF	100	150	250	400	—
1856Go PF	100	150	250	400	—
1859Go PF	100	150	250	400	—
1860/59Go PF	100	150	250	400	—
1860Go PF	100	150	250	400	—
1862Go YE	100	150	250	400	—

Mint: Hermosillo
KM# 380.6 2 ESCUDOS
6.7700 g., 0.8750 Gold .1904 oz. AGW **Obv:** Facing eagle

Date	VG	F	VF	XF	Unc
1861Ho FM	500	1,000	1,500	2,000	—

Mint: Mexico City
KM# 380.7 2 ESCUDOS
6.7700 g., 0.8750 Gold .1904 oz. AGW **Obv:** Facing eagle

Date	VG	F	VF	XF	Unc
1825Mo JM	100	150	200	285	—
1827/6Mo JM	100	150	200	285	—
1827Mo JM	100	150	200	285	—
1830/29Mo JM	100	150	200	285	—
1831Mo JM	100	150	200	285	—
1833Mo ML	100	150	200	285	—
1841Mo ML	100	150	200	285	—
1844Mo MF	100	150	200	285	—
1845Mo MF	100	150	200	285	—
1846Mo MF	125	200	400	600	—
1848Mo GC	100	150	200	285	—
1850Mo GC	100	150	200	285	—
1856/5Mo GF	100	150	200	285	—
1856Mo GF	100	150	200	285	—
1858Mo FH	100	150	200	285	—
1859Mo FH	100	150	200	285	—
1861Mo TH	100	150	200	285	—
1861Mo CH	100	150	200	300	—
1862Mo CH	100	150	200	300	—
1863Mo TH	100	150	200	300	—
1868Mo PH	100	150	200	300	—
1869Mo CH	100	150	200	300	—

Mint: Zacatecas
KM# 380.8 2 ESCUDOS
6.7700 g., 0.8750 Gold .1904 oz. AGW **Obv:** Facing eagle

Date	VG	F	VF	XF	Unc
1860Zs VL	150	300	600	1,200	—
1862Zs VL	250	500	800	1,200	—
1864Zs MO	150	300	600	1,200	—

Mint: Culiacan
KM# 381 4 ESCUDOS
13.5400 g., 0.8750 Gold .3809 oz. AGW **Obv:** Facing eagle

Date	VG	F	VF	XF	Unc
1846C CE	1,200	1,700	—	—	—
1847C CE	400	650	850	1,350	—
1848C CE	600	900	1,250	1,850	—

Mint: Durango
KM# 381.1 4 ESCUDOS
13.5400 g., 0.8750 Gold .3809 oz. AGW **Obv:** Facing eagle

Date	VG	F	VF	XF	Unc
1832Do RM/LR Rare	—	—	—	—	—
1832Do RM	600	900	1,250	1,850	—
1833Do RM/RL Rare	—	—	—	—	—
1852Do JMR Rare	—	—	—	—	—

Mint: Guadalajara
KM# 381.2 4 ESCUDOS
13.5400 g., 0.8750 Gold .3809 oz. AGW **Obv:** Facing eagle

Date	VG	F	VF	XF	Unc
1844Ga MC	500	750	1,000	1,600	—
1844Ga JG	400	650	850	1,350	—

Mint: Guadalupe y Calvo
KM# 381.3 4 ESCUDOS
13.5400 g., 0.8750 Gold .3809 oz. AGW **Obv:** Facing eagle

Date	VG	F	VF	XF	Unc
1844GC MP	400	650	850	1,350	—
1845GC MP	350	500	700	1,000	—
1846GC MP	400	650	850	1,350	—
1848GC MP	400	650	850	1,350	—
1850GC MP	500	750	1,000	1,600	—

Mint: Guanajuato
KM# 381.4 4 ESCUDOS
13.5400 g., 0.8750 Gold .3809 oz. AGW **Obv:** Facing eagle

Date	VG	F	VF	XF	Unc
1829/8Go MJ	200	300	450	850	—
1829Go JM	200	300	450	850	—
1829Go MJ	200	300	450	850	—
1831Go MJ	200	300	450	850	—
1832Go MJ	200	300	450	850	—
1833Go MJ	200	300	500	900	—
1834Go PJ	250	450	650	1,000	—
1835Go PJ	250	450	650	1,000	—
1836Go PJ	200	300	500	900	—
1837Go PJ	200	300	500	900	—
1838Go PJ	200	300	500	900	—
1839Go PJ	250	450	650	1,000	—
1840Go PJ	200	300	500	900	—
1841Go PJ	250	450	650	1,000	—
1845Go PM	200	300	500	900	—
1847/5Go YE	250	450	650	1,000	—
1847Go PM	250	450	650	1,000	—
1849Go PF	250	450	650	1,000	—
1851Go PF	250	450	650	1,000	—
1852Go PF	200	300	500	900	—
1855Go PF	200	300	500	900	—
1857/5Go PF	200	300	500	900	—
1858/7Go PF	200	300	500	900	—
1858Go PF	200	300	500	900	—
1859/7Go PF	250	450	650	1,000	—
1860Go PF	275	475	750	1,200	—
1862Go YE	200	300	500	900	—
1863Go YF	200	300	500	900	—

Mint: Hermosillo
KM# 381.5 4 ESCUDOS
13.5400 g., 0.8750 Gold .3809 oz. AGW **Obv:** Facing eagle

Date	VG	F	VF	XF	Unc
1861Ho FM	1,000	1,500	2,500	3,750	—

Mint: Mexico City
KM# 381.6 4 ESCUDOS
13.5400 g., 0.8750 Gold .3809 oz. AGW **Obv:** Facing eagle

Date	VG	F	VF	XF	Unc
1825Mo JM	200	300	525	950	—
1827/6Mo JM	200	300	500	900	—
1829Mo JM	200	350	650	1,000	—
1831Mo JM	200	350	650	1,000	—
1832Mo JM	275	475	750	1,200	—
1844Mo MF	200	350	650	1,000	—
1850Mo GC	200	350	650	1,000	—
1856Mo GF	200	300	500	900	—
1857/6Mo GF	200	300	500	900	—
1857Mo GF	200	300	500	900	—
1858Mo FH	200	350	650	1,000	—
1859/8Mo FH	200	350	650	1,000	—
1861Mo CH	400	800	1,200	1,750	—
1863Mo CH	200	350	650	1,000	—
1868Mo PH	200	300	500	900	—
1869Mo CH	200	300	500	900	—

Mint: Oaxaca
KM# 381.7 4 ESCUDOS
13.5400 g., 0.8750 Gold .3809 oz. AGW **Obv:** Facing eagle
Note: Mint mark O, Oa.

Date	VG	F	VF	XF	Unc
1861 FR	1,500	2,500	4,000	6,500	—

Mint: Zacatecas
KM# 381.8 4 ESCUDOS
13.5400 g., 0.8750 Gold .3809 oz. AGW **Obv:** Facing eagle

Date	VG	F	VF	XF	Unc
1860Zs VL Rare	—	—	—	—	—
1862Zs VL	750	1,250	2,250	3,750	—

Mint: Alamos
KM# 383 8 ESCUDOS
27.0700 g., 0.8750 Gold .7616 oz. AGW **Obv:** Facing eagle

Date	F	VF	XF	Unc
1864A PG	650	1,250	2,250	—
1866A DL	—	—	7,500	—
1868/7A DL	1,500	2,250	3,250	—
1869A DL	650	1,250	2,250	—
1870A DL	1,500	2,250	3,250	—
1872A AM Rare	—	—	—	—

Mint: Chihuahua
KM# 383.1 8 ESCUDOS
27.0700 g., 0.8750 Gold .7616 oz. AGW **Obv:** Facing eagle

Date	F	VF	XF	Unc
1841 Ca RG	400	750	1,250	1,750
1842 Ca RG	350	500	1,000	1,500
1843 Ca RG	350	500	1,000	1,500
1844 Ca RG	350	500	1,000	1,500
1845 Ca RG	350	500	1,000	1,500
1846 Ca RG	500	1,250	1,500	2,000
1847 Ca RG	1,000	2,500	—	—
1848 Ca RG	350	500	1,000	1,500
1849 Ca RG	350	500	1,000	1,500
1850/40 Ca RG	350	500	1,000	1,500
1851/41 Ca RG	50.00	500	1,000	1,500
1852/42 Ca RG	350	500	1,000	1,500
1853/43 Ca RG	350	500	1,000	1,500
1854/44 Ca RG	350	500	1,000	1,500
1855/43 Ca RG	350	500	1,000	1,500
1856/46 Ca RG	400	650	1,250	1,750
1857 Ca JC/RG	325	475	750	1,250
1858 Ca JC	325	475	750	1,250
1858 Ca BA/RG	325	475	750	1,250
1859 Ca JC/RG	325	475	750	1,250
1860 Ca JC/RG	350	500	1,000	1,500
1861 Ca JC	350	475	750	1,250
1862 Ca JC	350	475	750	1,250
1863 Ca JC	500	1,000	1,750	2,250
1864 Ca JC	400	750	1,250	1,750
1865 Ca JC	750	1,500	2,500	3,500
1866 Ca JC	350	500	1,000	1,500
1866 Ca FP	600	1,250	2,000	2,500
1866 Ca JG	350	500	1,000	1,500
1867 Ca JG	350	475	750	1,250
1868 Ca JG Concave wings	350	475	750	1,250
1869 Ca MM Regular eagle	350	475	750	1,250
1870/60 Ca MM	350	475	750	1,250
1871/61 Ca MM	350	475	750	1,250

Mint: Culiacan
KM# 383.2 8 ESCUDOS
27.0700 g., 0.8750 Gold .7616 oz. AGW **Obv:** Facing eagle

Date	F	VF	XF	Unc
1846C CE	350	500	1,000	1,750
1847C CE	350	500	800	1,250
1848C CE	350	500	1,000	1,750
1849C CE	325	450	700	1,250
1850C CE	325	450	700	1,250
1851C CE	350	500	800	1,250
1852C CE	350	500	800	1,250
1853/1C CE	325	450	700	1,250
1854C CE	325	450	700	1,250
1855/4C CE	350	500	1,000	1,750
1855C CE	350	500	800	1,250
1856C CE	325	450	700	1,250
1857C CE	325	450	700	1,250
1857C CE	—	—	—	—
Note: Without periods after C's				
1858C CE	325	450	700	1,250
1859C CE	325	450	700	1,250
1860/58C CE	350	500	800	1,250
1860C CE	350	500	800	1,250
1860C PV	325	450	700	1,250
1861C PV	350	500	800	1,250
1861C CE	350	500	800	1,250
1862C CE	350	500	800	1,250
1863C CE	350	500	800	1,250
1864C CE	325	450	700	1,250
1865C CE	350	500	800	1,250
1866/5C CE	325	450	700	1,250
1866C CE	325	450	700	1,250
1867C CB Error	325	450	700	1,250
1867C CE/CB	325	450	700	1,250
1868C CB Error	350	500	800	1,250
1869C CE	350	500	800	1,250
1870C CE	350	500	800	1,250

Mint: Durango
KM# 383.3 8 ESCUDOS
27.0700 g., 0.8750 Gold .7616 oz. AGW **Obv:** Facing eagle

Date	F	VF	XF	Unc
1832Do RM	850	1,750	2,000	3,000
1833Do RM/RL	350	500	800	1,250
1834Do RM	350	500	800	1,250
1835Do RM	350	500	800	1,250
1836Do RM/RL	350	500	800	1,250
1836Do RM	350	500	800	1,250
Note: M on snake				
1837Do RM	350	500	800	1,250
1838/6Do RM	350	500	800	1,250
1838Do RM	350	500	800	1,250
1839Do RM	325	450	700	1,250
1840/30Do RM/RL	400	600	1,000	1,750
1841/30Do RM	550	750	1,250	2,000
1841/31Do RM	350	500	800	1,250
1841/34Do RM	350	500	800	1,250
1841Do RM/RL	350	500	800	1,250
1842/32Do RM	350	500	800	1,250
1843/33Do RM	550	750	1,250	2,000
1843/1Do RM	350	500	800	1,250
1843Do RM	350	500	800	1,250
1844/34Do RM/RL	500	1,000	1,500	2,500
1844Do RM	450	800	1,250	2,000
1845/36Do RM	400	600	1,000	1,750
1845Do RM	400	600	1,000	1,750
1846Do RM	350	500	800	1,250
1847/37Do RM	350	500	800	1,250
1848/37Do RM	—	—	—	—
1848/38Do CM	350	500	800	1,250
1849/39Do CM	350	500	800	1,250
1849Do JMR	400	750	1,250	2,000
1850Do JMR	400	750	1,250	2,000
1851Do JMR	400	750	1,250	2,000
1852/1Do JMR	450	800	1,250	2,000
1852Do CP	450	800	1,250	2,000
1853Do CP	450	800	1,250	2,000
1854Do CP	400	600	1,000	1,750
1855/4Do CP	350	500	800	1,250
1855Do CP	350	500	800	1,250
1856Do CP	400	600	1,000	1,750
1857Do CP	350	500	800	1,250
Note: French style eagle, 1832-57				
1857Do CP	350	500	800	1,250
Note: Mexican style eagle				
1858Do CP	350	500	800	1,250
1859Do CP	350	500	800	1,250
1860/59Do CP	450	700	1,250	2,200
1861/0Do CP	400	600	1,000	1,750
1862/52Do CP	350	500	800	1,250
1862/1Do CP	350	500	800	1,250
1862Do CP	350	500	800	1,250
1863/53Do CP	350	500	800	1,250
1864Do LT	350	500	800	1,250
1865/4Do LT	500	1,000	1,650	2,750
1866/4Do CM	1,250	2,000	2,500	—
1866Do CM	400	600	1,000	1,750
1867/56Do CP	400	600	1,000	1,750
1867/4Do CP	350	500	800	1,250
1868/4Do CP/LT	—	—	—	—
1869Do CP	500	1,250	1,750	2,750
1870Do CP	400	600	1,000	1,750

Mint: Estado de Mexico
KM# 383.4 8 ESCUDOS
27.0700 g., 0.8750 Gold .7616 oz. AGW **Obv:** Facing eagle

Date	F	VF	XF	Unc
1828EoMo LF	3,500	5,500	8,500	—
1829EoMo LF	3,500	5,500	8,500	—

Mint: Guadalajara

KM# 383.5 8 ESCUDOS

27.0700 g., 0.8750 Gold .7616 oz. AGW **Obv:** Facing eagle

Date	F	VF	XF	Unc
1825Ga FS	500	1,000	1,250	1,750
1826Ga FS	500	1,000	1,250	1,750
1830Ga FS	500	1,000	1,250	1,750
1836Ga FS	750	1,500	2,000	3,000
1836Ga JG	1,000	2,500	3,500	—
1837Ga JG	1,000	2,500	3,500	—
1840Ga MC	750	1,500	2,000	3,000
1841/31Ga MC	1,000	2,500	—	—
1841Ga MC	850	1,650	2,250	—
1842Ga JG	—	—	—	—
1843Ga MC	—	—	—	—
1845Ga MC	400	850	1,100	1,650
1847Ga JG	2,250	—	—	—
1849Ga JG	500	1,000	1,250	1,750
1850Ga JG	400	850	1,100	1,650
1851Ga JG	400	850	1,100	1,650
1852/1Ga JG	500	1,000	1,250	1,750
1855Ga JG	1,000	2,500	3,500	—
1856Ga JG	400	850	1,100	1,650
1857Ga JG	400	850	1,100	1,650
1861/0Ga JG	500	1,000	1,250	1,750
1861Ga JG	400	700	1,200	1,750
1863/1Ga JG	500	1,000	1,250	1,750
1866Ga JG	400	850	1,100	1,650

Mint: Guadalupe y Calvo

KM# 383.6 8 ESCUDOS

27.0700 g., 0.8750 Gold .7616 oz. AGW **Obv:** Facing eagle

Date	F	VF	XF	Unc
1844GC MP	550	750	1,250	2,000
1845GC MP	550	750	1,250	2,000
Note: Eagle's tail square				
1845GC MP	550	750	1,250	2,000
Note: Eagle's tail round				
1846GC MP	450	650	1,000	1,750
Note: Eagle's tail square				
1846GC MP	450	650	1,000	1,750
Note: Eagle's tail round				
1847GC MP	450	650	1,000	1,750
1848GC MP	550	750	1,250	2,000
1849GC MP	550	750	1,250	2,000
1850GC MP	450	650	1,000	1,750
1851GC MP	450	650	1,000	1,750
1852GC MP	550	750	1,250	2,000

Mint: Guanajuato

KM# 383.7 8 ESCUDOS

27.0700 g., 0.8750 Gold .7616 oz. AGW **Obv:** Facing eagle

Date	F	VF	XF	Unc
1828Go MJ	700	1,750	2,250	3,000
1829Go MJ	600	1,500	2,000	2,750
1830Go MJ	350	500	750	1,000
1831Go MJ	600	1,500	2,000	2,750
1832Go MJ	500	1,250	1,750	2,500
1833Go MJ	350	500	700	1,000
1834Go PJ	350	500	700	1,000
1835Go PJ	350	500	700	1,000
1836Go PJ	400	650	900	1,250
1837Go PJ	400	650	900	1,250
1838/7Go PJ	350	500	700	1,000
1838Go PJ	350	500	800	1,200
1839/8Go PJ	350	500	700	1,000
1839Go PJ	350	500	800	1,200
Note: Regular eagle				
1840Go PJ	350	500	700	1,000
Note: Concave wings				
1841Go PJ	350	500	700	1,000
1842Go PJ	325	400	500	900
1842Go PM	350	500	700	1,000
1843Go PM	350	500	700	1,000
Note: Small eagle				
1844/3Go PM	400	650	900	1,250
1844Go PM	350	500	700	1,000
1845Go PM	350	500	700	1,000
1846/5Go PM	350	500	800	1,200
1846Go PM	350	500	700	1,000
1847Go PM	400	650	900	1,250
1848/7Go PM	350	500	700	1,000
1848Go PM	350	500	700	1,000
1848Go PF	350	500	700	1,000
1849Go PF	325	400	500	900
1850Go PF	325	400	500	900
1851Go PF	375	500	700	1,000
1852Go PF	375	500	700	1,000
1853Go PF	325	400	500	900
1854Go PF	350	500	700	1,000
Note: Eagle of 1853				
1854Go PF	350	500	700	1,000
Note: Eagle of 1855				
1855/4Go PF	400	650	900	1,250
1855Go PF	350	500	700	1,000
1856Go PF	350	500	700	1,000
1857Go PF	350	500	700	1,000
1858Go PF	350	500	700	1,000
1859Go PF	325	400	500	800
1860/50Go PF	325	400	500	900
1860/59Go PF	400	650	900	1,250
1860Go PF	375	500	700	1,100
1861/0Go PF	325	400	500	800
1861Go PF	325	400	500	800
1862/1Go YE	350	500	700	1,000
1862Go YE	350	500	700	1,000
1862Go YF	—	—	—	—
1863/53Go YF	350	500	700	1,000
1863Go PF	350	500	700	1,000
1867/57Go YF/PF	350	500	700	1,000
1867Go YF	350	500	700	1,000
1868/58Go YF	350	500	700	1,000
1870Go FR	325	400	500	900

Mint: Hermosillo

KM# 383.8 8 ESCUDOS

27.0700 g., 0.8750 Gold .7616 oz. AGW **Obv:** Facing eagle

Date	F	VF	XF	Unc
1863Ho FM	400	650	1,000	2,000
1864Ho FM	600	1,250	1,750	2,750
1864Ho PR/FM	400	650	1,000	2,000
1865Ho FM/PR	500	800	1,250	2,500
1867/57Ho PR	400	650	1,000	2,000
1868Ho PR	500	800	1,250	2,500
1868Ho PR/FM	500	800	1,250	2,500
1869Ho PR/FM	400	650	1,000	2,000
1869Ho PR	400	650	1,000	2,000
1870Ho PR	400	650	1,000	2,000
1871/0Ho PR	500	800	1,250	2,500
1871Ho PR	500	800	1,250	2,500
1872/1Ho PR	600	1,250	1,750	2,750
1873Ho PR	400	650	1,000	2,000

Mint: Mexico City

KM# 383.9 8 ESCUDOS

27.0700 g., 0.8750 Gold .7616 oz. AGW **Obv:** Facing eagle **Note:** Formerly reported 1825/3 JM is merely a reworked 5.

Date	F	VF	XF	Unc
1824Mo JM	500	1,000	1,250	2,000
Note: Large book reverse				
1825Mo JM	325	400	500	1,000
Note: Small book reverse				
1826/5Mo JM	700	1,750	2,250	3,000
1827Mo JM	350	500	700	1,000
1828Mo JM	350	500	700	1,000
1829Mo JM	350	500	700	1,000
1830Mo JM	350	500	700	1,000
1831Mo JM	350	500	700	1,000
1832/1Mo JM	350	500	700	1,000
1832Mo JM	350	500	700	1,000
1833Mo MJ	400	750	1,000	1,500
1833Mo ML	325	400	500	900
1834Mo ML	400	750	1,000	1,500
1835/4Mo ML	500	1,000	1,250	2,000
1836Mo ML	325	400	500	900
1836Mo MF	500	700	1,200	2,000
1837/6Mo ML	325	400	500	900
1838Mo ML	325	400	500	900
1839Mo ML	325	400	500	900
1840Mo ML	325	400	500	900
1841Mo ML	325	400	500	900
1842/1Mo ML	—	—	—	—
1842Mo ML	325	400	500	900
1842Mo MM	—	—	—	—
1843Mo MM	325	400	500	900
1844Mo MF	325	400	500	900
1845Mo MF	325	400	500	900
1846Mo MF	500	1,000	1,250	2,000
1847Mo MF	950	2,250	—	—
1847Mo RC	325	500	800	1,250
1848Mo GC	325	400	500	900
1849Mo GC	325	400	500	900
1850Mo GC	325	400	500	900
1851Mo GC	325	400	500	900
1852Mo GC	325	400	500	900
1853Mo GC	325	400	500	900
1854/44Mo GC	325	400	500	900
1854/3Mo GC	325	400	500	900
1855Mo GF	325	400	500	900
1856/5Mo GF	325	400	500	900
1856Mo GF	325	400	500	900
1857Mo GF	325	400	500	900
1858Mo FH	325	400	500	900
1859Mo FH	400	750	1,000	1,500
1860Mo FH	325	400	500	900
1860Mo TH	325	400	500	900
1861/51Mo CH	325	400	500	900
1862Mo CH	325	400	500	900
1863/53Mo CH	325	400	500	900
1863/53Mo TH	325	400	500	900
1867Mo CH	325	400	500	900
1868Mo CH	325	400	500	900
1868Mo PH	325	400	500	900
1869Mo CH	325	400	500	900

Mint: Oaxaca
KM# 383.10 8 ESCUDOS
27.0700 g., 0.8750 Gold .7616 oz. AGW **Obv:** Facing eagle

Date	F	VF	XF	Unc
18580 AE	2,000	3,000	4,000	6,000
18590 AE	1,000	2,500	3,750	5,500
18600 AE	1,000	2,500	3,750	5,500
18610 FR	450	850	1,250	2,750
18620 FR	450	850	1,250	2,750
18630 FR	450	850	1,250	2,750
18640 FR	450	850	1,250	2,750
18670 AE	450	850	1,250	2,750
18680 AE	450	850	1,250	2,750
18690 AE	450	850	1,250	2,750

Mint: Zacatecas
KM# 383.11 8 ESCUDOS
27.0700 g., 0.8750 Gold .7616 oz. AGW **Obv:** Facing eagle

Date	F	VF	XF	Unc
1858Zs MO	400	750	1,000	2,000
1859Zs MO	325	400	500	900
1860/59Zs VL/MO	2,000	3,000	4,000	—
1860/9Zs MO	400	750	1,000	2,000
1860Zs MO	375	500	700	1,000
1861/0Zs VL	375	500	700	1,000
1861Zs VL	375	500	700	1,000
1862Zs VL	375	500	700	1,100
1863Zs VL	375	525	750	1,150
1863Zs MO	375	500	700	1,000
1864Zs MO	750	1,000	1,500	3,000
1865Zs MO	375	500	700	1,000
1865Zs MP	—	—	—	—
Note: Contemporary counterfeit				
1868Zs JS	400	600	800	1,250
1868Zs YH	400	600	800	1,250
1869Zs YH	400	600	800	1,250
1870Zs YH	400	600	800	1,250
1871Zs YH	400	600	800	1,250

EMPIRE OF MAXIMILIAN

Maximilian

MILLED COINAGE

16 Pilones = 1 Real; 8 Tlaco = 1 Real; 16 Reales = 1 Escudo

Mint: Mexico City
KM# 384 CENTAVO
Copper

Date	F	VF	XF	Unc
1864M	40.00	75.00	225	1,100

Mint: Guanajuato
KM# 385 5 CENTAVOS
1.3537 g., 0.9030 Silver .0393 oz. ASW

Date	Mintage	F	VF	XF	Unc
1864G	90,000	17.50	35.00	75.00	320
1865G	—	20.00	30.00	55.00	285
1866G	—	75.00	150	300	1,800

Mint: Mexico City
KM# 385.1 5 CENTAVOS
1.3537 g., 0.9030 Silver .0393 oz. ASW

Date	F	VF	XF	Unc
1864M	12.50	20.00	55.00	285
1866/4M	25.00	40.00	75.00	385
1866M	20.00	35.00	65.00	375

Mint: San Luis Potosi
KM# 385.2 5 CENTAVOS
1.3537 g., 0.9030 Silver .0393 oz. ASW

Date	F	VF	XF	Unc
1864P	150	400	1,500	2,500

Mint: Zacatecas
KM# 385.3 5 CENTAVOS
1.3537 g., 0.9030 Silver .0393 oz. ASW

Date	F	VF	XF	Unc
1865Z	25.00	45.00	150	425

Mint: Guanajuato
KM# 386 10 CENTAVOS
2.7073 g., 0.9030 Silver .0786 oz. ASW

Date	Mintage	F	VF	XF	Unc
1864G	45,000	20.00	45.00	90.00	325
1865G	—	30.00	60.00	110	375

Mint: Mexico City
KM# 386.1 10 CENTAVOS
2.7073 g., 0.9030 Silver .0786 oz. ASW **Note:** Struck at Mexico City Mint, mint mark M.

Date	F	VF	XF	Unc
1864M	15.00	25.00	55.00	285
1866/4M	25.00	35.00	70.00	320
1866/5M	25.00	40.00	85.00	375
1866M	25.00	35.00	75.00	375

Mint: San Luis Potosi
KM# 386.2 10 CENTAVOS
2.7073 g., 0.9030 Silver .0786 oz. ASW

Date	F	VF	XF	Unc
1864P	70.00	150	300	600

Mint: Zacatecas
KM# 386.3 10 CENTAVOS
2.7073 g., 0.9030 Silver .0786 oz. ASW

Date	F	VF	XF	Unc
1865Z	25.00	55.00	165	475

Mint: Mexico City
KM# 387 50 CENTAVOS
13.5365 g., 0.9030 Silver .3929 oz. ASW

Date	Mintage	F	VF	XF	Unc
1866Mo	31,000	40.00	95.00	200	600

Mint: Guanajuato
KM# 388 PESO
27.0700 g., 0.9030 Silver .7857 oz. ASW

Date	F	VF	XF	Unc
1866Go	300	400	900	3,500

Mint: Mexico City
KM# 388.1 PESO
27.0700 g., 0.9030 Silver .7857 oz. ASW

Date	Mintage	F	VF	XF	Unc
1866Mo	2,148,000	30.00	45.00	125	375
1867Mo	1,238,000	40.00	65.00	175	425

Mint: San Luis Potosi
KM# 388.2 PESO
27.0700 g., 0.9030 Silver .7857 oz. ASW

Date	F	VF	XF	Unc
1866 Pi	45.00	90.00	275	725

Mint: Mexico City
KM# 389 20 PESOS
33.8400 g., 0.8750 Gold .9520 oz. AGW

Date	Mintage	F	VF	XF	Unc
1866Mo	8,274	500	900	1,350	2,500

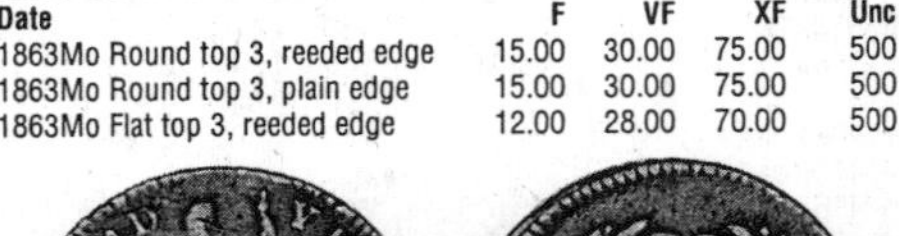

REPUBLIC

Second

DECIMAL COINAGE

100 CENTAVOS = 1 PESO

KM# 390 CENTAVO
Copper, 25 mm. **Mint:** Mexico City **Obverse:** Seated Liberty **Reverse:** Thick wreath.

Date	F	VF	XF	Unc
1863Mo Round top 3, reeded edge	15.00	30.00	75.00	500
1863Mo Round top 3, plain edge	15.00	30.00	75.00	500
1863Mo Flat top 3, reeded edge	12.00	28.00	70.00	500

KM# 390.1 CENTAVO
Copper, 26.5 mm. **Mint:** San Luis Potosi **Obverse:** Seated Liberty **Reverse:** Thin wreath

Date	Mintage	F	VF	XF	Unc
1863SLP	1,024,999	15.00	30.00	60.00	400

KM# 391 CENTAVO
Copper **Mint:** Alamos **Obverse:** Standing eagle **Edge:** Reeded.

Date	Mintage	F	VF	XF	Unc
1875 As Rare	—	—	—	—	—
1876 As	50,000	100	200	300	650
1880 As	—	25.00	50.00	125	400
1881 As	—	30.00	60.00	125	350

KM# 391.1 CENTAVO
Copper **Mint:** Culiacan **Obverse:** Standing eagle **Edge:** Plain

Date	Mintage	F	VF	XF	Unc
1874Cn	266,000	12.50	17.50	35.00	250
1875/4Cn	153,000	15.00	20.00	45.00	250
1875Cn	Inc. above	10.00	15.00	25.00	250
1876Cn	154,000	5.00	8.00	15.00	200
1877/6Cn	993,000	7.50	11.50	17.50	200
1877Cn	Inc. above	6.00	9.00	15.00	200
1880Cn	142,000	7.50	10.00	12.50	200
1881Cn	167,000	7.50	10.00	25.00	200
1897Cn Large N in mint mark	300,000	2.50	5.00	12.00	50.00
1897Cn Small N in mint mark	Inc. above	2.50	5.00	9.00	45.00

KM# 391.2 CENTAVO
Copper **Mint:** Durango **Obverse:** Standing eagle

Date	Mintage	F	VF	XF	Unc
1879Do	110,000	10.00	17.50	35.00	150
1880Do	69,000	40.00	90.00	175	500
1891Do	—	8.00	11.00	30.00	150
1891Do/Mo	—	8.00	11.00	30.00	150

KM# 391.3 CENTAVO

Copper **Mint:** Guadalajara **Obverse:** Standing eagle

Date	Mintage	F	VF	XF	Unc
1872Ga	263,000	15.00	30.00	60.00	200
1873Ga	333,000	6.00	9.00	25.00	150
1874Ga	76,000	15.00	25.00	50.00	175
1875Ga	—	10.00	15.00	30.00	150
1876Ga	303,000	3.00	6.00	17.50	150
1877Ga	108,000	4.00	6.00	20.00	150
1878Ga	543,000	4.00	6.00	15.00	150
1881/71Ga	975,000	7.00	9.00	20.00	175
1881Ga	Inc. above	7.00	9.00	20.00	175
1889Ga/Mo	—	3.50	5.00	25.00	125
1890Ga	—	4.00	7.50	20.00	100

KM# 391.4 CENTAVO

Copper **Mint:** Guanajuato **Obverse:** Standing eagle

Date	Mintage	F	VF	XF	Unc
1874Go	—	20.00	40.00	80.00	250
1875Go	190,000	11.50	20.00	60.00	200
1876Go	—	125	200	350	750
1877Go Rare	—	—	—	—	—
1878Go	576,000	8.00	11.00	30.00	175
1880Go	890,000	6.00	10.00	25.00	175

KM# 391.5 CENTAVO

Copper **Mint:** Hermosillo **Obverse:** Standing eagle

Date	Mintage	F	VF	XF	Unc
1875Ho	3,500	450	—	—	—
1876Ho	8,508	50.00	100	225	500
1880Ho Short H, round O	102,000	7.50	15.00	35.00	150
1880Ho Tall H, oval O	Inc. above	7.50	15.00	35.00	150
1881Ho	459,000	5.00	10.00	25.00	150

KM# 391.7 CENTAVO

Copper **Mint:** Oaxaca **Obverse:** Standing eagle

Date	Mintage	F	VF	XF	Unc
1872 Oa	16,000	300	500	1,200	—
1873 Oa	11,000	350	600	—	—
1874 Oa	4,835	450	—	—	—
1875 Oa	2,860	500	—	—	—

KM# 391.8 CENTAVO

Copper **Mint:** San Luis Potosi **Obverse:** Standing eagle

Date	Mintage	F	VF	XF	Unc
1871 Pi Rare	—	—	—	—	—
1877 Pi	249,000	15.00	50.00	200	—
1878 Pi	751,000	12.50	25.00	50.00	200
1878 Pp error mintmark - rare	—	—	—	—	—
1891Pi/Mo	—	10.00	50.00	150	300
1891 Pi	—	8.00	25.00	125	250

KM# 391.9 CENTAVO

Copper **Mint:** Zacatecas **Obverse:** Standing eagle **Note:** Struck at Zacatecas Mint, mint mark Zs.

Date	Mintage	F	VF	XF	Unc
1872Zs	55,000	22.50	30.00	100	300
1873Zs	1,460,000	4.00	8.00	25.00	150
1874/3Zs	685,000	5.50	11.00	30.00	250
1874Zs	Inc. above	4.00	8.00	25.00	200
1875/4Zs	200,000	8.50	17.00	45.00	250
1875Zs	Inc. above	7.00	14.00	35.00	200
1876Zs	—	5.00	10.00	25.00	200
1877Zs	—	50.00	125	300	750
1878Zs	—	4.50	9.00	25.00	200
1880Zs	100,000	5.00	10.00	30.00	200
1881Zs	1,200,000	4.25	8.00	25.00	150

KM# 391.6 CENTAVO

Copper **Mint:** Mexico City **Obverse:** Standing eagle **Note:** Varieties exist.

Date	Mintage	F	VF	XF	Unc
1869Mo	1,874,000	7.50	25.00	60.00	200
1870/69Mo	1,200,000	10.00	25.00	60.00	225
1870Mo	Inc. above	8.00	20.00	50.00	200
1871Mo	918,000	8.00	15.00	40.00	200
1872/1Mo	1,625,000	6.50	10.00	30.00	200
1872Mo	Inc. above	6.00	9.00	25.00	200
1873Mo	1,605,000	4.00	7.50	20.00	200
1874/3Mo	1,700,000	5.00	7.00	15.00	100
1874Mo	Inc. above	3.00	5.50	15.00	100
1874Mo	Inc. above	5.00	10.00	25.00	200
1875Mo	1,495,000	6.00	8.00	30.00	100
1876Mo	1,600,000	3.00	5.50	12.50	100
1877Mo	1,270,000	3.00	5.50	13.50	100
1878/5Mo	1,900,000	7.50	11.00	22.50	125
1878/6Mo	Inc. above	7.50	11.00	22.50	125
1878/7Mo	Inc. above	7.50	11.00	20.00	125
1878Mo	Inc. above	6.00	9.00	13.50	100
1879/8Mo	1,505,000	4.50	6.50	13.50	100
1879Mo	Inc. above	3.00	5.50	12.50	75.00
1880/70Mo	1,130,000	5.50	7.50	15.00	100
1880/72Mo	Inc. above	20.00	50.00	100	250
1880/79Mo	Inc. above	15.00	35.00	75.00	175
1880Mo	Inc. above	4.25	6.00	12.50	75.00
1881Mo	1,060,000	4.50	7.00	15.00	75.00
1886Mo	12,687,000	1.50	2.00	10.00	40.00
1887Mo	7,292,000	1.50	2.00	10.00	35.00
1888/78Mo	9,984,000	2.50	3.00	10.00	30.00
1888/7Mo	Inc. above	2.50	3.00	10.00	30.00
1888Mo	Inc. above	1.50	2.00	10.00	30.00
1889Mo	19,970,000	2.00	3.00	10.00	30.00
1890/89Mo	18,726,000	2.50	3.00	12.00	40.00
1890/990Mo	Inc. above	2.50	3.00	12.00	40.00
1890Mo	Inc. above	1.50	2.00	10.00	30.00
1891Mo	14,544,000	1.50	2.00	10.00	30.00
1892Mo	12,908,000	1.50	2.00	10.00	30.00
1893/2Mo	5,078,000	2.50	3.00	12.00	35.00
1893Mo	Inc. above	1.50	2.00	10.00	30.00
1894/3Mo	1,896,000	3.00	6.00	15.00	50.00
1894Mo	Inc. above	2.00	3.00	12.00	35.00
1895/3Mo	3,453,000	3.00	4.50	12.50	35.00
1895/85Mo	Inc. above	3.00	6.00	15.00	50.00
1895Mo	Inc. above	2.00	3.00	10.00	30.00
1896Mo	3,075,000	2.00	3.00	10.00	30.00
1897Mo	4,150,000	1.50	2.00	10.00	30.00

KM# 392 CENTAVO

Copper-Nickel **Mint:** Mexico City

Date	Mintage	F	VF	XF	Unc
1882Mo	99,955,000	7.50	12.50	17.50	35.00
1883Mo	Inc. above	0.50	0.75	1.00	1.50

KM# 393 CENTAVO

Copper **Mint:** Mexico City **Obverse:** Restyled eagle **Note:** Varieties exist.

Date	Mintage	F	VF	XF	Unc
1898Mo	1,529,000	4.00	6.00	15.00	50.00

KM# 394.1 CENTAVO

Copper **Mint:** Mexico City **Note:** Mint mark M, Mo. Reduced size. Varieties exist.

Date	Mintage	F	VF	XF	Unc
1899M	51,000	150	175	300	800
1900M Wide date	4,010,000	2.50	4.00	8.00	28.00
1900M Narrow date	Inc. above	2.50	4.00	8.00	28.00

KM# 395 2 CENTAVOS

Copper-Nickel **Mint:** Mexico City

Date	Mintage	F	VF	XF	Unc
1882	50,023,000	2.00	3.00	7.50	15.00
1883/2	Inc. above	2.00	3.00	7.50	15.00
1883	Inc. above	0.50	0.75	1.00	2.50

KM# 396.1 5 CENTAVOS

1.3530 g., 0.9030 Silver .0392 oz. ASW **Mint:** San Luis Potosi **Obverse:** Facing eagle **Reverse:** Deonomination in wreath

Date	F	VF	XF	Unc
1863SLP	37.50	135	350	1,200

KM# 397 5 CENTAVOS

1.3530 g., 0.9030 Silver .0392 oz. ASW **Mint:** Mexico City **Obverse:** Facing eagle **Reverse:** Cap and rays **Note:** Varieties exist.

Date	F	VF	XF	Unc
1867/3Mo	22.50	50.00	125	425
1867Mo	18.50	42.50	100	400
1868/7Mo	22.50	50.00	150	500
1868Mo	18.50	42.50	100	400

KM# 396 5 CENTAVOS

1.3530 g., 0.9030 Silver .0392 oz. ASW **Mint:** Chihuahua **Obverse:** Facing eagle **Reverse:** Denomination in wreath

Date	Mintage	F	VF	XF	Unc
1868 Ca	—	40.00	65.00	125	450
1869 Ca	30,000	25.00	40.00	100	400
1870/69 Ca	—	35.00	55.00	120	425
1870 Ca	35,000	30.00	50.00	100	400

KM# 397.1 5 CENTAVOS

1.3530 g., 0.9030 Silver .0392 oz. ASW **Mint:** San Luis Potosi **Obverse:** Facing eagle **Reverse:** Cap and rays

Date	Mintage	F	VF	XF	Unc
1868/7P	34,000	25.00	50.00	125	450
1868P	Inc. above	20.00	45.00	100	400
1869P	14,000	200	300	600	—

KM# 398 5 CENTAVOS

1.3530 g., 0.9030 Silver .0392 oz. ASW **Mint:** Alamos **Obverse:** Standing eagle **Reverse:** Cap and rays

Date	Mintage	F	VF	XF	Unc
1874 As DL	—	10.00	20.00	40.00	150
1875 As DL	—	10.00	20.00	40.00	150
1876 As L	—	22.00	45.00	70.00	160
1878 As L Mule, gold peso reverse	—	250	350	650	—
1879 As L Mule, gold peso obverse	—	40.00	65.00	120	275
1880 As L Mule, gold peso obverse	12,000	55.00	85.00	165	325
1886 As L	43,000	12.00	25.00	50.00	165
1886 As L Mule, gold peso obverse	Inc. above	55.00	85.00	165	300
1887 As L	20,000	25.00	50.00	75.00	165
1888 As L	32,000	12.00	25.00	50.00	125
1889 As L	16,000	25.00	50.00	100	200
1890 As L	30,000	25.00	50.00	85.00	175
1891 As L	8,000	65.00	125	200	400
1892 As L	13,000	20.00	40.00	60.00	125
1893 As L	24,000	10.00	20.00	45.00	90.00
1895 As L	20,000	10.00	20.00	45.00	90.00

KM# 398.2 5 CENTAVOS

1.3530 g., 0.9030 Silver .0392 oz. ASW **Mint:** Culiacan **Obverse:** Standing eagle **Reverse:** Cap and rays

Date	Mintage	F	VF	XF	Unc
1871Cn P	—	125	200	350	—
1873Cn P	4,992	50.00	100	200	400
1874Cn P	—	25.00	50.00	100	200
1875Cn P Rare	—	—	—	—	—
1876Cn P	—	25.00	50.00	100	200
1886Cn M	10,000	25.00	50.00	100	200
1887Cn M	10,000	25.00	50.00	100	200
1888Cn M	119,000	1.50	3.00	6.00	30.00
1889Cn M	66,000	4.00	7.50	15.00	50.00
1890Cn M	180,000	1.50	3.00	6.00	25.00
1890/9Cn M	—	2.00	4.00	8.00	40.00
1890Cn D Error	Inc. above	125	175	250	—
1891Cn M	87,000	2.00	4.00	7.50	25.00
1894Cn M	24,000	4.00	7.50	15.00	40.00
1896Cn M	16,000	7.50	12.50	25.00	75.00
1897Cn M	223,000	1.50	2.50	5.00	20.00

KM# 398.3 5 CENTAVOS

1.3530 g., 0.9030 Silver .0392 oz. ASW **Mint:** Durango **Obverse:** Standing eagle **Reverse:** Cap and rays

Date	Mintage	F	VF	XF	Unc
1874Do M	—	100	150	225	500
1877Do P	4,795	75.00	125	225	450
1878/7Do E/P	4,300	200	300	450	—
1879Do B	—	125	200	350	—
1880Do B Rare	—	—	—	—	—
1881Do P	3,020	300	500	800	—
1887Do C	42,000	5.00	8.00	17.50	60.00
1888/9Do C	91,000	6.00	10.00	20.00	70.00
1888Do C	Inc. above	4.00	7.50	15.00	55.00
1889Do C	49,000	3.50	6.00	12.50	50.00
1890Do C	136,000	4.00	7.50	15.00	55.00
1890Do P	Inc. above	5.00	8.00	17.50	60.00
1891/0Do P	48,000	3.50	6.00	12.50	50.00
1891Do P	Inc. above	3.00	5.00	10.00	45.00
1894Do D	38,000	3.50	6.00	12.50	50.00

KM# 398.4 5 CENTAVOS

1.3530 g., 0.9030 Silver .0392 oz. ASW **Mint:** Guadalajara **Obverse:** Standing eagle **Reverse:** Cap and rays

Date	Mintage	F	VF	XF	Unc
1877Ga A	—	15.00	30.00	60.00	150
1881Ga S	156,000	4.00	7.50	15.00	60.00
1886Ga S	87,000	2.00	4.00	7.50	25.00
1888Ga S Large G	262,000	2.00	4.00	10.00	30.00
1888Ga S Small G	Inc. above	2.00	4.00	10.00	30.00
1889Ga S	178,000	1.50	3.00	7.50	25.00
1890Ga S	68,000	4.00	7.50	12.50	35.00

Date	Mintage	F	VF	XF	Unc
1891Ga S	50,000	4.00	6.50	10.00	35.00
1892Ga S	78,000	2.00	4.00	7.50	25.00
1893Ga S	44,000	4.00	7.50	15.00	45.00

KM# 398.5 5 CENTAVOS
1.3530 g., 0.9030 Silver .0392 oz. ASW **Mint:** Guanajuato
Obverse: Standing eagle **Reverse:** Cap and rays

Date	Mintage	F	VF	XF	Unc
1869Go S	80,000	15.00	30.00	75.00	175
1871Go S	100,000	5.00	10.00	25.00	75.00
1872Go S	30,000	30.00	60.00	125	250
1873Go S	40,000	30.00	60.00	125	250
1874Go S	—	7.00	12.00	25.00	75.00
1875Go S	—	8.00	15.00	30.00	75.00
1876Go S	—	8.00	15.00	30.00	75.00
1877Go S	—	7.00	12.00	20.00	75.00
1878/7Go S	20,000	8.00	15.00	25.00	75.00
1879Go S	—	8.00	15.00	25.00	75.00
1880Go S	55,000	15.00	30.00	60.00	200
1881/0Go S	160,000	5.00	8.00	17.50	60.00
1881Go S	Inc. above	4.00	6.00	12.00	45.00
1886Go R	230,000	1.50	3.00	6.00	30.00
1887Go R/S	—	1.50	3.00	6.00	30.00
1887Go R	230,000	1.50	2.50	5.00	30.00
1888Go R	320,000	1.50	2.50	5.00	20.00
1889Go R	60,000	4.00	6.00	12.00	45.00
1890/5Go R/S	—	1.50	3.00	6.00	30.00
1890Go R	250,000	1.50	2.50	5.00	20.00
1891/0Go R	168,000	1.80	3.00	6.00	30.00
1891Go R	Inc. above	1.50	2.50	5.00	20.00
1892Go R	138,000	1.50	3.00	6.00	25.00
1893Go R	200,000	1.25	2.50	5.00	20.00
1894Go R	200,000	1.25	2.50	5.00	20.00
1896Go R	525,000	1.25	2.00	4.00	15.00
1896Go R/S	—	1.50	3.00	6.00	25.00
1897Go R	596,000	1.50	2.00	4.00	15.00
1898Go R	—	—	—	—	—

KM# 398.6 5 CENTAVOS
1.3530 g., 0.9030 Silver .0392 oz. ASW **Mint:** Hermosillo
Obverse: Standing eagle **Reverse:** Cap and rays

Date	Mintage	F	VF	XF	Unc
1874/69Ho R	—	125	225	350	—
1874Ho R	—	100	200	325	—
1878/7Ho A Rare	22,000	—	—	—	—
1878Ho A	Inc. above	20.00	40.00	80.00	175
1878Ho A Mule, gold peso obverse	Inc. above	40.00	80.00	150	300
1880Ho A	43,000	7.50	15.00	30.00	75.00
1886Ho G	44,000	5.00	10.00	20.00	75.00
1887Ho G	20,000	5.00	10.00	20.00	75.00
1888Ho G	12,000	7.50	15.00	30.00	85.00
1889Ho G	67,000	3.00	6.00	12.50	40.00
1890Ho G	50,000	3.00	6.00	12.50	40.00
1891Ho G	46,000	3.00	6.00	12.50	40.00
1893Ho G	84,000	2.50	5.00	10.00	30.00
1894Ho G	68,000	2.00	4.00	10.00	30.00

KM# 398.1 5 CENTAVOS
1.3530 g., 0.9030 Silver .0392 oz. ASW **Mint:** Chihuahua
Obverse: Standing eagle **Reverse:** Cap and rays **Note:** Mint mark Ca, Ch.

Date	Mintage	F	VF	XF	Unc
1871 M	14,000	20.00	40.00	100	250
1873 M Crude date	—	100	150	250	500
1874 M Crude date	—	25.00	50.00	75.00	150
1886 M	25,000	7.50	15.00	30.00	100
1887 M	37,000	7.50	15.00	30.00	100
1887 Ca/MoM	Inc. above	10.00	20.00	40.00	125
1888 M	145,000	1.50	3.00	6.00	25.00
1889 M	44,000	5.00	10.00	20.00	50.00
1890 M	102,000	1.50	3.00	6.00	25.00
1891 M	164,000	1.50	3.00	6.00	25.00
1892 M	85,000	1.50	3.00	6.00	25.00
1892 M 9/inverted 9	Inc. above	2.00	4.00	7.50	30.00
1893 M	133,000	1.50	3.00	6.00	25.00
1894 M	108,000	1.50	3.00	6.00	25.00
1895 M	74,000	2.00	4.00	7.50	30.00

KM# 398.7 5 CENTAVOS
1.3530 g., 0.9030 Silver .0392 oz. ASW **Mint:** Mexico City
Obverse: Standing eagle **Reverse:** Cap and rays **Note:** Struck at Mexico City Mint, mint mark Mo. Varieties exist.

Date	Mintage	F	VF	XF	Unc
1869/8Mo C	40,000	8.00	15.00	40.00	120
1870Mo C	140,000	4.00	7.00	20.00	60.00
1871Mo C	103,000	9.00	20.00	40.00	100
1871Mo M	Inc. above	7.50	12.50	25.00	60.00
1872Mo M	266,000	5.00	8.00	20.00	55.00
1873Mo M	20,000	40.00	60.00	100	225
1874/69Mo M	—	7.50	15.00	30.00	75.00
1874Mo M	—	4.00	7.00	17.50	50.00
1874/3Mo B	—	5.00	8.00	22.50	55.00
1874Mo B	—	5.00	8.00	22.50	55.00
1875Mo B	—	4.00	7.00	15.00	50.00
1875Mo B/M	—	6.00	9.00	17.50	60.00
1876/5Mo B	—	4.00	7.00	15.00	50.00
1876Mo B	—	4.00	7.00	12.50	50.00
1877/6Mo M	80,000	4.00	7.00	15.00	60.00
1877Mo M	Inc. above	4.00	7.00	12.50	60.00
1878/7Mo M	100,000	4.00	7.00	15.00	55.00
1878Mo M	Inc. above	2.50	5.00	12.50	45.00
1879/8Mo M	—	8.00	12.50	22.50	55.00
1879Mo M	—	4.50	7.00	15.00	50.00
1879Mo M 9/inverted 9	—	10.00	15.00	25.00	75.00
1880/76Mo M/B	—	5.00	7.50	15.00	50.00
1880/76Mo M	—	5.00	7.50	15.00	50.00
1880Mo M	—	4.00	6.00	12.00	40.00
1881/0Mo M	180,000	4.00	6.00	10.00	35.00
1881Mo M	Inc. above	3.00	4.50	9.00	35.00
1886/0Mo M	398,000	2.00	2.75	7.50	25.00
1886/1Mo M	Inc. above	2.00	2.75	7.50	25.00
1886Mo M	Inc. above	1.75	2.25	6.00	20.00
1887Mo m	720,000	1.75	2.00	5.00	20.00
1887Mo M/m	Inc. above	1.75	2.00	6.00	20.00
1888/7Mo M	1,360,000	2.25	2.50	6.00	20.00
1888Mo M	Inc. above	1.75	2.00	5.00	20.00
1889/8Mo M	1,242,000	2.25	2.50	6.00	20.00
1889Mo M	Inc. above	1.75	2.00	5.00	20.00
1890/00Mo M	1,694,000	1.75	2.75	6.00	20.00
1890Mo M	Inc. above	1.50	2.00	5.00	20.00
1891Mo M	1,030,000	1.75	2.00	5.00	20.00
1892Mo M	1,400,000	1.75	2.00	5.00	20.00
1892Mo M 9/inverted 9	Inc. above	2.00	2.75	7.50	20.00
1893Mo M	220,000	1.75	2.00	5.00	15.00
1894Mo M	320,000	1.75	2.00	5.00	15.00
1895Mo M	78,000	3.00	5.00	8.00	25.00
1896Mo B	80,000	1.75	2.00	5.00	20.00
1897Mo B	160,000	1.75	2.00	5.00	15.00

KM# 398.9 5 CENTAVOS
1.3530 g., 0.9030 Silver .0392 oz. ASW **Mint:** San Luis Potosi
Obverse: Standing eagle **Reverse:** Cap and rays **Note:** Varieties exist.

Date	Mintage	F	VF	XF	Unc
1869 Pi S	—	300	400	500	—
1870 Pi G/MoC Rare	20,000	150	250	400	—
1870 Pi O	Inc. above	200	300	450	—
1871 Pi O Rare	5,400	—	—	—	—
1872 Pi O	—	75.00	100	175	400
1873 Pi Rare	5,000	—	—	—	—
1874 Pi H	—	30.00	50.00	100	225
1875 Pi H	—	7.50	12.50	30.00	75.00
1876 Pi H	—	10.00	20.00	45.00	100
1877 Pi H	—	7.50	12.50	20.00	60.00
1878/7 Pi H Rare	—	—	—	—	—
1878 Pi H	—	60.00	90.00	150	300
1879 H	—	200	400	—	—
1880 Pi H Rare	6,200	—	—	—	—
1881 Pi H Rare	4,500	—	—	—	—
1886 Pi R	33,000	12.50	25.00	50.00	125
1887/0 Pi R	169,000	4.00	7.50	15.00	45.00
1887 Pi R	Inc. above	3.00	5.00	10.00	32.00
1888 Pi R	210,000	2.00	4.00	9.00	30.00
1889/7 Pi R	197,000	2.50	5.00	10.00	32.00
1889 Pi R	Inc. above	2.00	4.00	9.00	30.00
1890 Pi R	221,000	2.00	3.00	6.00	25.00
1891/89 Pi R/B	176,000	2.00	4.00	8.00	25.00
1891 Pi R	Inc. above	2.00	3.00	6.00	20.00
1892/89 Pi R	182,000	2.00	4.00	8.00	25.00
1892/0 Pi R	Inc. above	2.00	4.00	8.00	25.00
1892 Pi R	Inc. above	2.00	3.00	6.00	20.00
1893 Pi R	41,000	5.00	10.00	20.00	60.00

KM# 398.8 5 CENTAVOS
1.3530 g., 0.9030 Silver .0392 oz. ASW **Mint:** Oaxaca **Obverse:** Standing eagle **Reverse:** Cap and rays

Date	Mintage	F	VF	XF	Unc
1890 Oa E Rare	48,000	—	—	—	—
1890 Oa N	Inc. above	65.00	125	200	350

KM# 398.10 5 CENTAVOS
1.3530 g., 0.9030 Silver .0392 oz. ASW **Mint:** Zacatecas
Obverse: Standing eagle **Reverse:** Cap and rays

Date	Mintage	F	VF	XF	Unc
1871Zs H	40,000	12.50	25.00	50.00	125
1872Zs H	40,000	12.50	25.00	50.00	125
1873/2Zs H	20,000	35.00	65.00	125	275
1873Zs H	Inc. above	25.00	50.00	100	250
1874Zs H	—	7.50	12.50	25.00	75.00
1874Zs A	—	40.00	75.00	150	300
1875Zs A	—	7.50	12.50	25.00	75.00
1876Zs A	—	50.00	75.00	150	500
1876/5Zs S	—	15.00	30.00	60.00	150
1876Zs S	—	12.50	25.00	50.00	125
1877Zs S	—	3.00	6.00	12.00	40.00
1878Zs S	60,000	3.00	6.00	12.00	40.00
1879/8Zs S	—	3.00	6.00	15.00	50.00
1879Zs S	—	3.00	6.00	12.00	40.00
1880/79Zs S	130,000	6.00	10.00	20.00	60.00
1880Zs S	Inc. above	5.00	8.00	16.00	45.00
1881Zs S	210,000	2.50	5.00	10.00	35.00
1886/4Zs S	360,000	6.00	10.00	20.00	60.00
1886Zs S	Inc. above	2.00	3.00	6.00	20.00
1886Zs Z	Inc. above	5.00	10.00	25.00	65.00
1887Zs Z	400,000	2.00	3.00	6.00	25.00
1888/7Zs Z	500,000	2.00	3.00	6.00	25.00
1888Zs Z	Inc. above	2.00	3.00	6.00	25.00
1889Zs Z	520,000	2.00	3.00	6.00	25.00
1889Zs Z 9/inverted 9	Inc. above	2.00	3.00	6.00	25.00
1889Zs Z/MoM	Inc. above	2.00	3.00	6.00	25.00
1890Zs Z	580,000	1.75	2.50	5.00	20.00
1890Zs Z/MoM	Inc. above	2.00	3.00	6.00	25.00
1890Zs ZsZ 9/8	—	2.00	3.00	6.00	25.00
1890Zs ZsZ 0/9 Z/M	—	2.00	3.00	6.00	25.00
1891Zs Z	420,000	1.75	2.50	5.00	20.00
1892Zs Z	346,000	1.75	2.50	5.00	20.00
1893Zs Z	258,000	1.75	2.50	5.00	20.00
1894Zs Z	228,000	1.75	2.50	5.00	20.00
1894Zs ZoZ Error	Inc. above	2.00	4.00	8.00	30.00
1895Zs Z	260,000	1.75	2.50	5.00	20.00
1895Zs Z	260,000	1.75	2.50	5.00	20.00
1895/4Zs ZsZ	—	2.00	3.00	6.00	25.00
1896Zs Z	200,000	1.75	2.50	5.00	20.00
1896Zs 6/inverted 6	Inc. above	2.00	3.00	6.00	25.00
1897/6Zs Z	200,000	2.00	3.00	6.00	25.00
1897Zs Z	Inc. above	1.75	2.50	5.00	20.00
1870Zs H	40,000	12.50	25.00	50.00	125

KM# 399 5 CENTAVOS
Copper-Nickel **Mint:** Mexico City

Date	F	VF	XF	Unc
1882	0.50	1.00	2.50	7.50
1883	25.00	50.00	80.00	250

KM# 400.2 5 CENTAVOS
0.9030 Silver **Mint:** Mexico City **Obverse:** Restyled eagle

Date	Mintage	F	VF	XF	Unc
1898Mo M	80,000	2.00	4.00	7.00	25.00
1899Mo M	168,000	1.75	2.50	4.50	15.00
1900/800Mo M	300,000	4.50	6.50	10.00	30.00
1900Mo M	Inc. above	1.75	2.50	4.50	15.00

KM# 400.3 5 CENTAVOS
0.9030 Silver **Mint:** Zacatecas **Obverse:** Restyled eagle

Date	Mintage	F	VF	XF	Unc
1898Zs Z	100,000	1.75	2.25	4.50	12.50
1899Zs Z	50,000	2.00	3.00	7.00	20.00
1900Zs Z	55,000	1.75	2.50	5.00	16.50

KM# 400 5 CENTAVOS
0.9030 Silver **Mint:** Culiacan **Obverse:** Restyled eagle **Note:** Varieties exist.

Date	Mintage	F	VF	XF	Unc
1898Cn M	44,000	1.75	4.00	8.00	20.00
1899Cn M	111,000	5.50	8.50	20.00	50.00
1899Cn Q	Inc. above	1.75	2.50	4.50	15.00
1900/800Cn Q	239,000	3.50	5.00	12.50	30.00
1900Cn Q Round Q, single tail	Inc. above	1.75	3.00	6.00	16.50
1900Cn Q Narrow C, oval Q	Inc. above	1.75	3.00	6.00	16.50
1900Cn Q Wide C, oval Q	Inc. above	1.75	3.00	6.00	16.50

KM# 400.1 5 CENTAVOS
0.9030 Silver **Mint:** Guanajuato **Obverse:** Restyled eagle **Note:** Varieties exist.

Date	Mintage	F	VF	XF	Unc
1898Go R Mule, gold peso obverse	180,000	7.50	15.00	30.00	75.00
1899Go R	260,000	1.75	2.50	4.50	15.00
1900Go R	200,000	1.75	2.50	4.50	15.00

KM# 401 10 CENTAVOS
2.7070 g., 0.9030 Silver .0785 oz. ASW **Mint:** Chihuahua
Obverse: Eagle **Reverse:** Value within wreath

Date	Mintage	F	VF	XF	Unc
1868/7 Ca	—	30.00	60.00	150	550
1868 Ca	—	30.00	60.00	150	550
1869 Ca	15,000	25.00	50.00	125	600
1870 Ca	17,000	22.50	45.00	100	550

KM# 401.2 10 CENTAVOS

2.7070 g., 0.9030 Silver .0785 oz. ASW **Mint:** San Luis Potosi
Obverse: Eagle **Reverse:** Value within wreath

Date	F	VF	XF	Unc
1863SLP	75.00	150	275	900

KM# 402 10 CENTAVOS

2.7070 g., 0.9030 Silver .0785 oz. ASW **Mint:** Mexico City
Obverse: Eagle **Reverse:** Value within wreath

Date	F	VF	XF	Unc
1867/3Mo	50.00	100	200	550
1867Mo	20.00	50.00	150	450
1868/7Mo	20.00	50.00	175	500
1868Mo	20.00	55.00	175	500

KM# 402.1 10 CENTAVOS

2.7070 g., 0.9030 Silver .0785 oz. ASW **Mint:** San Luis Potosi
Obverse: Eagle **Reverse:** Value within wreath

Date	Mintage	F	VF	XF	Unc
1868/7P	38,000	45.00	90.00	175	650
1868P	Inc. above	20.00	40.00	100	550
1869/7P	4,900	55.00	125	250	800

KM# 403 10 CENTAVOS

2.7070 g., 0.9030 Silver .0785 oz. ASW **Mint:** Alamos **Obverse:** Eagle **Reverse:** Value within wreath **Note:** Varieties exist.

Date	Mintage	F	VF	XF	Unc
1874 As DL	—	20.00	40.00	80.00	175
1875 As L	—	5.00	10.00	25.00	90.00
1876 As L	—	10.00	18.00	40.00	110
1878/7 As L	—	10.00	18.00	45.00	120
1878 As L	—	5.00	10.00	30.00	100
1879 As L	—	10.00	18.00	40.00	110
1880 As L	13,000	10.00	18.00	40.00	110
1882 As L	22,000	10.00	18.00	40.00	110
1883 As L	8,520	25.00	50.00	100	225
1884 As L	—	7.50	12.50	35.00	100
1885 As L	15,000	7.50	12.50	35.00	100
1886 As L	45,000	7.50	12.50	35.00	100
1887 As L	15,000	7.50	12.50	35.00	100
1888 As L	38,000	7.50	12.50	35.00	100
1889 As L	20,000	7.50	12.50	35.00	100
1890 As L	40,000	7.50	12.50	35.00	100
1891 As L	38,000	7.50	12.50	35.00	100
1892 As L	57,000	5.00	10.00	25.00	90.00
1893 As L	70,000	10.00	18.00	40.00	110

Note: An 1891 As L over 1889 HoG exists which was evidently produced at the Alamos Mint using dies sent from the Hermosillo Mint

KM# 403.1 10 CENTAVOS

2.7070 g., 0.9030 Silver .0785 oz. ASW **Mint:** Chihuahua
Obverse: Eagle **Reverse:** Value within wreath **Note:** Mint mark CH, Ca. Varieties exist.

Date	Mintage	F	VF	XF	Unc
1871 M	8,150	15.00	30.00	60.00	150
1873 M Crude date	—	35.00	75.00	125	175
1874 M	—	10.00	17.50	35.00	100
1880/70 G	7,620	20.00	40.00	80.00	175
1880 G/g	Inc. above	15.00	25.00	50.00	125
1881 Rare	340	—	—	—	—
1883 M	9,000	10.00	20.00	40.00	125
1884/73	—	5.00	30.00	60.00	150
1884 M	—	10.00	20.00	40.00	125
1886 M	45,000	7.50	12.50	30.00	100
1887/3 M/G	96,000	5.00	10.00	20.00	75.00
1887 M/G	—	2.00	4.00	8.00	75.00
1887 M	Inc. above	2.00	4.00	8.00	75.00
1888 M/G	—	2.00	4.00	8.00	75.00
1888 M	299,000	1.50	2.50	5.00	75.00
1888 Ca/Mo	Inc. above	1.50	2.50	5.00	75.00
1889/8 M	115,000	2.00	4.00	8.00	75.00
1889 M Small 89 (5 Centavo font)	Inc. above	2.00	4.00	8.00	75.00
1890/80 M	140,000	2.00	4.00	8.00	75.00
1890/89 M	Inc. above	2.00	4.00	8.00	75.00
1890 M	Inc. above	1.50	3.00	7.00	75.00
1891 M	163,000	1.50	3.00	7.00	75.00
1892 M	169,000	1.50	3.00	7.00	75.00
1892 M 9/inverted 9	Inc. above	2.00	4.00	8.00	75.00
1893 M	246,000	1.50	3.00	7.00	75.00
1894 M	163,000	1.50	3.00	7.00	75.00
1895 M	127,000	1.50	3.00	7.00	75.00

KM# 403.2 10 CENTAVOS

2.7070 g., 0.9030 Silver .0785 oz. ASW **Mint:** Culiacan
Obverse: Eagle **Reverse:** Value within wreath

Date	Mintage	F	VF	XF	Unc
1871Cn P Rare	—	—	—	—	—
1873Cn P	8,732	20.00	50.00	100	225
1881Cn D	9,440	75.00	175	325	500
1882Cn D	12,000	75.00	125	200	400
1885Cn M Mule, gold 2-1/2 peso obverse	18,000	25.00	50.00	100	200
1886Cn M Mule, gold 2-1/2 peso obverse	13,000	50.00	100	150	300
1887Cn M	11,000	20.00	40.00	75.00	175
1888Cn M	56,000	5.00	10.00	25.00	125
1889Cn M	42,000	5.00	10.00	20.00	75.00
1890Cn M	132,000	2.00	4.00	7.50	75.00
1891Cn M	84,000	5.00	10.00	20.00	75.00
1892/1Cn M	37,000	4.00	8.00	15.00	75.00
1892Cn M	Inc. above	2.50	5.00	10.00	75.00
1894Cn M	43,000	2.50	5.00	10.00	75.00
1895Cn M	23,000	2.50	5.00	10.00	60.00
1896Cn M	121,000	1.50	2.50	5.00	50.00

KM# 403.3 10 CENTAVOS

2.7070 g., 0.9030 Silver .0785 oz. ASW **Mint:** Durango
Obverse: Eagle **Reverse:** Value within wreath

Date	Mintage	F	VF	XF	Unc
1878Do E	2,500	100	175	300	600
1879Do B Rare	—	—	—	—	—
1880/70Do B Rare	—	—	—	—	—
1880/79Do B Rare	—	—	—	—	—
1884Do C	—	30.00	60.00	100	225
1886Do C	13,000	75.00	150	300	500
1887Do C	81,000	4.00	8.00	15.00	100
1888Do C	31,000	6.00	12.00	30.00	100
1889Do C	55,000	4.00	8.00	15.00	100
1890Do C	50,000	4.00	8.00	15.00	100
1891Do P	139,000	2.00	4.00	8.00	80.00
1892Do P	212,000	2.00	4.00	8.00	80.00
1892Do D	Inc. above	2.00	4.00	8.00	80.00
1893Do D	258,000	2.00	4.00	8.00	80.00
1893Do D/C	Inc. above	2.50	5.00	10.00	80.00
1894Do D	184,000	1.50	3.00	6.00	80.00
1894Do D/C	Inc. above	2.00	4.00	8.00	80.00
1895Do D	142,000	1.50	3.00	6.00	80.00

KM# 403.4 10 CENTAVOS

2.7070 g., 0.9030 Silver .0785 oz. ASW **Mint:** Guadalajara
Obverse: Eagle **Reverse:** Value within wreath **Note:** Varieties exist.

Date	Mintage	F	VF	XF	Unc
1871Ga C	4,734	75.00	125	200	500
1873/1Ga C	25,000	10.00	15.00	35.00	150
1873Ga C	Inc. above	10.00	15.00	35.00	150
1874Ga C	—	10.00	15.00	35.00	150
1877Ga A	—	10.00	15.00	30.00	150
1881Ga S	115,000	5.00	10.00	25.00	150
1883Ga B	90,000	4.00	8.00	15.00	90.00
1884Ga B	—	5.00	10.00	20.00	90.00
1884Ga B/S	—	6.00	12.50	25.00	90.00
1884Ga H	—	3.00	5.00	10.00	90.00
1885Ga H	93,000	3.00	5.00	10.00	90.00
1886Ga S	151,000	2.50	4.00	9.00	90.00
1887Ga S	162,000	1.50	3.00	6.00	90.00
1888Ga S	225,000	1.50	3.00	6.00	90.00
1888Ga GaS/HoG	Inc. above	1.50	3.00	6.00	90.00
1889Ga S	310,000	1.50	3.00	6.00	40.00
1890Ga S	303,000	1.50	3.00	6.00	40.00
1891Ga S	199,000	5.00	10.00	20.00	45.00
1892Ga S	329,000	1.50	3.00	6.00	40.00
1893Ga S	225,000	1.50	3.00	6.00	40.00
1894Ga S	243,000	3.00	6.00	12.00	40.00
1895Ga S	80,000	1.50	3.00	6.00	40.00

KM# 403.5 10 CENTAVOS

2.7070 g., 0.9030 Silver .0785 oz. ASW **Mint:** Guanajuato
Obverse: Eagle **Reverse:** Value within wreath **Note:** Varieties exist.

Date	Mintage	F	VF	XF	Unc
1869Go S	7,000	20.00	40.00	80.00	200
1871/0Go S	60,000	15.00	25.00	50.00	125
1872Go S	60,000	15.00	25.00	50.00	125
1873Go S	50,000	15.00	25.00	50.00	125
1874Go S	—	15.00	25.00	50.00	125
1875Go S	—	250	350	500	800
1876Go S	—	10.00	20.00	40.00	100
1877Go S	—	80.00	120	200	400
1878/7Go S	10,000	10.00	20.00	45.00	110
1878Go S	Inc. above	7.50	12.00	20.00	75.00
1879Go S	—	7.50	12.00	20.00	75.00
1880Go S	—	100	200	300	450
1881/71Go S	100,000	3.00	5.00	10.00	75.00
1881/0Go S	Inc. above	3.50	5.00	10.00	75.00
1881Go S	Inc. above	3.00	5.00	10.00	75.00
1882/1Go S	40,000	3.00	6.00	12.00	75.00
1883Go B	—	3.00	5.00	10.00	75.00
1884Go B	—	1.50	3.00	6.00	75.00
1884Go S	—	6.00	12.50	25.00	90.00
1885Go R	100,000	1.50	3.00	6.00	75.00
1886Go R	95,000	3.00	5.00	10.00	75.00
1887Go R	330,000	2.50	5.00	10.00	75.00
1888Go R	270,000	1.50	3.00	6.00	75.00
1889Go R	205,000	2.00	4.00	8.00	75.00
1889Go GoR/HoG	Inc. above	3.00	5.00	10.00	75.00
1890Go R	270,000	1.50	3.00	6.00	35.00
1890Go GoR/Cn M	Inc. above	1.50	3.00	6.00	35.00
1891Go R	523,000	1.50	3.00	6.00	35.00
1891Go R/G	—	1.50	3.00	6.00	35.00
1891Go GoR/HoG	Inc. above	1.50	3.00	6.00	35.00
1892Go R	440,000	1.50	3.00	6.00	35.00
1893/1Go R	389,000	3.00	5.00	10.00	35.00
1893Go R	Inc. above	1.50	3.00	6.00	35.00
1894Go R	400,000	1.50	2.50	5.00	35.00
1895Go R	355,000	1.50	2.50	5.00	35.00
1896Go R	190,000	1.50	2.50	5.00	35.00
1897Go R	205,000	1.50	2.50	5.00	35.00

KM# 403.6 10 CENTAVOS

2.7070 g., 0.9030 Silver .0785 oz. ASW **Mint:** Hermosillo
Obverse: Eagle **Reverse:** Value within wreath

Date	Mintage	F	VF	XF	Unc
1874Ho R	—	30.00	60.00	100	200
1876Ho F	3,140	200	300	450	750
1878Ho A	—	5.00	10.00	15.00	85.00
1879Ho A	—	25.00	50.00	90.00	175
1880Ho A	—	3.00	6.00	12.50	85.00
1881Ho A	28,000	4.00	7.00	15.00	85.00
1882/1Ho A	25,000	5.00	10.00	20.00	85.00
1882/1Ho a	Inc. above	6.00	12.50	25.00	85.00
1882Ho A	Inc. above	4.00	7.00	15.00	85.00
1883Ho	7,000	65.00	100	200	400
1884Ho A	—	35.00	75.00	150	300
1884/3Ho M	—	10.00	20.00	40.00	90.00
1884Ho M	—	7.50	15.00	30.00	85.00
1885Ho M	21,000	12.50	25.00	50.00	100
1886Ho M Rare	10,000	—	—	—	—
1886Ho G	Inc. above	7.50	12.50	25.00	85.00
1887Ho G	—	25.00	50.00	75.00	150
1888Ho G	25,000	6.00	12.50	25.00	85.00
1889Ho G	42,000	3.00	6.00	10.00	85.00
1890Ho G	48,000	3.00	6.00	10.00	85.00
1891/80Ho G	136,000	3.00	6.00	10.00	85.00
1891/0Ho G	Inc. above	3.00	6.00	10.00	85.00
1891Ho G	Inc. above	3.00	6.00	10.00	85.00
1892Ho G	67,000	3.00	6.00	10.00	85.00
1893Ho G	67,000	3.00	6.00	10.00	85.00

KM# 403.7 10 CENTAVOS

2.7070 g., 0.9020 Silver .0785 oz. ASW **Mint:** Mexico City
Obverse: Eagle **Reverse:** Value within wreath **Note:** Varieties exist.

Date	Mintage	F	VF	XF	Unc
1869/8Mo C	30,000	10.00	20.00	40.00	100
1869Mo C	Inc. above	8.00	17.50	35.00	90.00
1870Mo C	110,000	3.00	7.50	15.00	50.00
1871Mo C	84,000	50.00	75.00	125	250
1871Mo M	Inc. above	12.00	17.50	45.00	125
1872/69Mo M	198,000	10.00	20.00	35.00	100
1872Mo M	Inc. above	3.00	7.50	15.00	65.00
1873Mo M	40,000	10.00	15.00	30.00	75.00
1874Mo M	—	5.00	10.00	20.00	65.00
1874Mo M/C	—	5.00	10.00	20.00	65.00
1874/64Mo B	—	5.00	10.00	20.00	65.00
1874Mo B/M	—	20.00	40.00	60.00	125
1874Mo B	—	5.00	10.00	15.00	65.00
1875Mo B	—	20.00	40.00	60.00	125
1876/5Mo B	—	3.00	5.00	9.00	65.00
1876/5Mo B/M	—	3.00	5.00	9.00	65.00
1877/6Mo M	—	3.00	5.00	9.00	65.00
1877/6Mo M/B	—	3.00	5.00	9.00	65.00
1877Mo M	—	3.00	5.00	9.00	65.00
1878/7Mo M	100,000	3.00	5.00	9.00	65.00
1878Mo M	Inc. above	3.00	5.00	9.00	65.00
1879/69Mo M	—	3.00	5.00	9.00	65.00
1879Mo M/C	—	3.00	5.00	9.00	65.00
1880/79Mo M	—	3.00	5.00	9.00	65.00
1881/0Mo M	510,000	3.00	5.00	9.00	35.00
1881Mo M	Inc. above	3.00	5.00	9.00	35.00
1882/1Mo M	550,000	3.00	5.00	9.00	35.00
1882Mo M	Inc. above	3.00	5.00	9.00	35.00
1883/2Mo M	250,000	3.00	5.00	9.00	35.00
1884Mo M	—	3.00	5.00	9.00	35.00
1885Mo M	470,000	3.00	5.00	9.00	35.00
1886Mo M	603,000	3.00	5.00	9.00	35.00
1887Mo M	580,000	3.00	5.00	9.00	35.00
1888/7Mo MoM	710,000	3.00	5.00	9.00	35.00
1888Mo MoM	Inc. above	3.00	5.00	9.00	35.00
1888Mo MOM	Inc. above	3.00	5.00	9.00	35.00
1889/8Mo M	622,000	3.00	5.00	9.00	35.00
1889Mo M	Inc. above	3.00	5.00	9.00	35.00
1890/89Mo M	815,000	3.00	5.00	9.00	35.00
1890Mo M	Inc. above	3.00	5.00	9.00	35.00
1891Mo M	859,000	1.50	2.50	7.00	25.00
1892Mo M	1,030,000	1.50	2.50	7.00	25.00
1893Mo M	310,000	1.50	2.50	7.00	25.00
1893Mo M/C	Inc. above	1.50	2.50	7.00	25.00
1893Mo Mo/Ho M/G	—	1.50	2.50	7.00	25.00
1894/3Mo M	—	5.00	10.00	20.00	60.00
1894Mo M	350,000	5.00	10.00	20.00	60.00
1895Mo M	320,000	1.50	2.50	7.00	25.00
1896Mo B/G	340,000	1.50	2.50	7.00	25.00
1896Mo M	Inc. above	35.00	70.00	100	150
1897Mo M	170,000	1.50	2.50	5.00	20.00

KM# 403.8 10 CENTAVOS

2.7070 g., 0.9030 Silver .0785 oz. ASW **Mint:** Oaxaca **Obverse:** Eagle **Reverse:** Value within wreath

Date	Mintage	F	VF	XF	Unc
1889 Oa E	21,000	200	400	600	—
1890 Oa N Rare	Inc. above	—	—	—	—
1890 Oa E	31,000	100	150	250	500

KM# 403.9 10 CENTAVOS

2.7070 g., 0.9030 Silver .0785 oz. ASW **Mint:** San Luis Potosi
Obverse: Eagle **Reverse:** Value within wreath **Note:** Varieties exist.

Date	Mintage	F	VF	XF	Unc
1869/8 Pi S Rare	4,000	—	—	—	—
1870/69 Pi O Rare	18,000	—	—	—	—
1870 Pi G	Inc. above	125	200	325	600
1871 Pi O	21,000	50.00	100	150	300
1872 Pi O	16,000	150	225	350	650

Date	Mintage	F	VF	XF	Unc
1873 Pi O Rare	4,750	—	—	—	—
1874 Pi H	—	25.00	50.00	100	200
1875 Pi H	—	75.00	125	200	400
1876 Pi H	—	75.00	125	200	400
1877 Pi H	—	75.00	125	200	400
1878 Pi H	—	250	500	750	—
1879 Pi H	—	—	—	—	—
1880 Pi H	—	150	250	350	—
1881 Pi H	7,600	250	350	500	—
1882 Pi H Rare	4,000	—	—	—	—
1883 Pi H	—	125	200	300	500
1884 Pi H	—	25.00	50.00	100	200
1885 Pi H	51,000	25.00	50.00	100	200
1885 Pi C Rare	Inc. above	—	—	—	—
1886 Pi C	52,000	15.00	30.00	60.00	150
1886 Pi R	Inc. above	5.00	10.00	20.00	65.00
1887 Pi R	118,000	2.50	5.00	10.00	50.00
1888 Pi R	136,000	2.50	5.00	10.00	50.00
1889/8 Pi R/G	—	7.50	12.50	20.00	60.00
1889/7 Pi R	131,000	7.50	12.50	20.00	60.00
1890 Pi R	204,000	1.50	3.00	7.50	40.00
1891/89 Pi R	163,000	2.50	5.00	10.00	40.00
1891 Pi R	Inc. above	1.50	3.50	6.00	30.00
1892/0 Pi R	200,000	2.00	4.00	8.00	40.00
1892 Pi R	Inc. above	1.50	2.50	5.00	40.00
1892 Pi R/G	—	2.00	4.00	8.00	40.00
1893 Pi R	48,000	7.50	10.00	17.50	60.00
1893 Pi R/G	—	1.50	10.00	17.50	60.00

KM# 403.10 10 CENTAVOS

2.7070 g., 0.9030 Silver .0785 oz. ASW **Mint:** Zacatecas
Obverse: Eagle **Reverse:** Value within wreath **Note:** Varieties exist.

Date	Mintage	F	VF	XF	Unc
1870Zs H	20,000	100	150	200	400
1871/0Zs H	10,000	—	—	—	—
1871Zs H	Inc. above	—	—	—	—
1872Zs H	10,000	150	200	275	500
1873Zs H	10,000	250	350	600	—
1874/3Zs H	—	50.00	75.00	150	300
1874Zs A	—	200	300	500	—
1875Zs A	—	5.00	10.00	25.00	100
1876Zs A	—	5.00	10.00	25.00	100
1876Zs S	—	100	200	300	500
1877Zs S Small S	—	7.50	12.50	25.00	100
1877Zs S Regular S	—	7.50	12.50	25.00	100
1878/7Zs S	30,000	5.00	10.00	20.00	80.00
1878Zs S	Inc. above	5.00	10.00	20.00	80.00
1879Zs S	—	5.00	10.00	20.00	80.00
1880Zs S	—	5.00	10.00	20.00	80.00
1881/0Zs S	120,000	3.00	6.00	12.50	50.00
1881Zs S	Inc. above	3.00	6.00	12.50	50.00
1882/1Zs S	64,000	12.50	25.00	50.00	125
1882Zs S	Inc. above	12.50	25.00	50.00	125
1883/73Zs S	102,000	2.00	4.00	8.00	50.00
1883Zs S	Inc. above	2.00	4.00	8.00	50.00
1884/3Zs S	—	2.00	4.00	8.00	50.00
1884Zs S	—	2.00	4.00	8.00	50.00
1885Zs S	297,000	1.50	2.50	5.00	50.00
1885Zs S Small S in mint mark	Inc. above	2.50	4.00	8.00	50.00
1885Zs Z Without assayers initials (error)	Inc. above	3.50	7.50	15.00	65.00
1886Zs S	274,000	1.50	2.50	5.00	30.00
1886Zs Z	Inc. above	12.50	25.00	50.00	125
1887Zs ZsZ	233,000	1.50	2.50	5.00	30.00
1887Zs Z Z (Error)	Inc. above	3.50	10.00	25.00	100
1888Zs ZsZ	270,000	1.50	2.50	5.00	30.00
1888Zs Z Z (Error)	Inc. above	3.50	10.00	25.00	100
1889/7Zs Z/S	240,000	4.00	8.00	12.50	40.00
1889Zs ZS	Inc. above	1.50	4.00	8.00	30.00
1889Zs Z/G	—	1.50	4.00	8.00	30.00
1889Zs Z	Inc. above	1.50	2.50	5.00	30.00
1890Zs ZsZ	410,000	1.50	2.50	5.00	30.00
1890Zs Z Z (Error)	Inc. above	3.75	10.00	25.00	100
1891Zs Z	1,105,000	1.50	2.50	5.00	30.00
1891Zs ZsZ Double s	Inc. above	2.00	4.00	7.00	30.00
1892Zs Z	1,102,000	1.50	2.50	5.00	30.00
1892Zs Z/G	—	2.00	4.00	7.00	30.00
1893/2Zs Z	—	2.00	4.00	8.00	40.00
1893Zs Z	1,010,999	1.50	2.50	5.00	25.00
1894Zs Z	892,000	1.50	2.50	5.00	30.00
1895Zs Z	920,000	1.50	2.50	5.00	30.00
1895Zs Z 9/5	—	2.00	4.00	7.00	30.00
1896/5Zs Z/G	—	1.50	2.50	5.00	30.00
1896Zs Z/G	—	1.50	2.50	5.00	30.00
1896/5Zs ZsZ	700,000	1.50	2.50	5.00	30.00
1896Zs ZsZ	Inc. above	1.50	2.50	5.00	30.00
1896Zs Z Z (Error)	Inc. above	3.75	10.00	25.00	100
1897/6Zs ZsZ	900,000	2.00	5.00	10.00	30.00
1897/6Zs Z Z (Error)	Inc. above	3.75	10.00	25.00	100
1897Zs Z	Inc. above	1.50	2.50	5.00	30.00

KM# 404 10 CENTAVOS

2.7070 g., 0.9030 Silver .0785 oz. ASW **Mint:** Culiacan
Obverse: Restyled eagle **Note:** Varieties exist.

Date	Mintage	F	VF	XF	Unc
1898Cn M	9,870	50.00	100	200	500
1899Cn Q Round Q, single tail	80,000	5.00	7.50	25.00	100
1899Cn Q Oval Q, double tail	Inc. above	5.00	7.50	25.00	100
1900Cn Q	160,000	1.50	2.50	5.00	20.00

KM# 404.1 10 CENTAVOS

2.7070 g., 0.9030 Silver .0785 oz. ASW **Mint:** Guanajuato
Obverse: Restyled eagle

Date	Mintage	F	VF	XF	Unc
1898Go R	435,000	1.50	2.50	5.00	20.00
1899Go R	270,000	1.50	2.50	5.00	25.00
1900Go R	130,000	7.50	12.50	25.00	60.00

KM# 404.2 10 CENTAVOS

2.7070 g., 0.9030 Silver .0785 oz. ASW **Mint:** Mexico City
Obverse: Restyled eagle

Date	Mintage	F	VF	XF	Unc
1898Mo M	130,000	1.50	2.50	5.00	20.00
1899Mo M	190,000	1.50	2.50	5.00	20.00
1900Mo M	311,000	1.50	2.50	5.00	20.00

KM# 404.3 10 CENTAVOS

2.7070 g., 0.9020 Silver .0785 oz. ASW **Mint:** Zacatecas
Obverse: Restyled eagle

Date	Mintage	F	VF	XF	Unc
1898Zs Z	240,000	1.50	2.50	7.50	20.00
1899Zs Z	105,000	1.50	3.00	10.00	22.00
1900Zs Z	219,000	7.50	10.00	20.00	45.00

KM# 405 20 CENTAVOS

5.4150 g., 0.9030 Silver .1572 oz. ASW **Mint:** Culiacan
Obverse: Restyled eagle

Date	Mintage	F	VF	XF	Unc
1898Cn M	114,000	5.00	12.50	35.00	140
1899Cn M	44,000	12.00	20.00	45.00	225
1899Cn Q	Inc. above	20.00	35.00	100	250
1900Cn Q	68,000	6.50	12.50	35.00	140

KM# 405.1 20 CENTAVOS

5.4150 g., 0.9027 Silver .1572 oz. ASW **Mint:** Guanajuato
Obverse: Restyled eagle

Date	Mintage	F	VF	XF	Unc
1898Go R	135,000	4.00	8.00	20.00	100
1899Go R	215,000	4.00	8.00	20.00	100
1900/800Go R	38,000	10.00	20.00	60.00	250

KM# 405.2 20 CENTAVOS

5.4150 g., 0.9030 Silver .1572 oz. ASW **Mint:** Mexico City
Obverse: Restyled eagle **Note:** Varieties exist.

Date	Mintage	F	VF	XF	Unc
1898Mo M	150,000	4.00	8.00	20.00	90.00
1899Mo M	425,000	4.00	8.00	20.00	90.00
1900/800Mo M	295,000	4.00	8.00	20.00	90.00

KM# 405.3 20 CENTAVOS

5.4150 g., 0.9027 Silver .1572 oz. ASW **Mint:** Zacatecas
Obverse: Restyled eagle

Date	Mintage	F	VF	XF	Unc
1898Zs Z	195,000	5.00	10.00	20.00	100
1899Zs Z	210,000	5.00	10.00	20.00	100
1900/800Zs Z	97,000	5.00	10.00	20.00	100

KM# 406 25 CENTAVOS

6.7680 g., 0.9030 Silver .1965 oz. ASW **Mint:** Alamos **Note:** Mint mark A, As.

Date	Mintage	F	VF	XF	Unc
1874 L	—	20.00	40.00	90.00	200
1875 L	—	15.00	30.00	70.00	200
1876 L	—	30.00	50.00	100	200
1877 L	11,000	200	300	500	—
1877.	Inc. above	10.00	25.00	60.00	200
1878 L	25,000	10.00	25.00	60.00	200
1879 L	—	10.00	25.00	60.00	200
1880 L	—	10.00	25.00	60.00	200
1880. L	—	10.00	25.00	60.00	200
1881 L	8,800	500	700	—	—
1882 L	7,777	15.00	35.00	80.00	200
1883 L	28,000	10.00	25.00	60.00	200
1884 L	—	10.00	25.00	60.00	200
1885 L	—	20.00	40.00	90.00	200
1886 L	46,000	15.00	30.00	70.00	200
1887 L	12,000	12.50	27.50	65.00	200
1888 L	20,000	12.50	27.50	65.00	200
1889 L	14,000	12.50	27.50	65.00	200
1890 L	23,000	10.00	25.00	60.00	200

KM# 406.1 25 CENTAVOS

6.7680 g., 0.9030 Silver .1965 oz. ASW **Mint:** Chihuahua **Note:** Mint mark CA, CH, Ca.

Date	Mintage	F	VF	XF	Unc
1871 M	18,000	25.00	50.00	100	200
1872 M Very crude date	24,000	50.00	100	150	300
1883 M	12,000	10.00	25.00	50.00	175
1885/3 M	35,000	10.00	25.00	50.00	175
1885 M	Inc. above	10.00	25.00	50.00	175
1886 M	22,000	10.00	25.00	50.00	175
1887/6 M	26,000	10.00	15.00	30.00	175
1887 M	Inc. above	10.00	15.00	30.00	175
1888 M	14,000	10.00	25.00	50.00	175
1889 M	50,000	10.00	15.00	30.00	175

KM# 406.2 25 CENTAVOS

6.7680 g., 0.9030 Silver .1965 oz. ASW **Mint:** Culiacan

Date	Mintage	F	VF	XF	Unc
1871Cn P	—	250	500	750	—
1872Cn P	2,780	300	550	800	—
1873Cn P	20,000	100	150	250	500
1874Cn P	—	20.00	50.00	125	250
1875Cn P	—	250	500	750	—
1876Cn P Rare	—	—	—	—	—
1878/7Cn D/S	—	100	150	250	500
1878Cn Cn/Go D/S	—	100	150	250	500
1878Cn D	—	100	150	250	500
1879Cn D	—	15.00	35.00	70.00	175
1880Cn D	—	250	500	750	—
1881/0Cn D	18,000	15.00	30.00	60.00	175
1882Cn D	—	200	350	600	—
1882Cn M Rare	—	—	—	—	—
1883Cn M	15,000	50.00	100	150	300
1884Cn M	—	20.00	40.00	80.00	175
1885/4Cn M	19,000	20.00	40.00	80.00	175
1886Cn M	22,000	12.50	20.00	50.00	175
1887Cn M	32,000	12.50	20.00	50.00	175
1888Cn M	86,000	7.50	15.00	30.00	175
1888Cn M Cn/Mo	—	—	—	—	—
1889Cn M	50,000	10.00	25.00	50.00	175
1890Cn M 9/8	—	7.50	17.50	40.00	175
1890Cn M	91,000	7.50	17.50	40.00	175
1892/0Cn M	16,000	20.00	40.00	80.00	200
1892Cn M	Inc. above	20.00	40.00	80.00	200

KM# 406.3 25 CENTAVOS

6.7680 g., 0.9030 Silver .1965 oz. ASW **Mint:** Durango

Date	Mintage	F	VF	XF	Unc
1873Do P Rare	892	—	—	—	—
1877Do P	—	25.00	50.00	100	200
1878/7Do E	—	250	500	750	—
1878Do B Rare	—	—	—	—	—
1879Do B	—	50.00	75.00	125	250
1880Do B Rare	—	—	—	—	—
1882Do C	17,000	25.00	50.00	100	225
1884/3Do C	—	25.00	50.00	100	200
1885Do C	15,000	20.00	40.00	80.00	200
1885Do C/S	—	20.00	40.00	80.00	200
1886Do C	33,000	15.00	30.00	60.00	200
1887Do C	27,000	10.00	20.00	50.00	200
1888Do C	25,000	10.00	20.00	50.00	200
1889Do C	29,000	10.00	20.00	50.00	200
1890Do C	68,000	7.50	15.00	40.00	200

KM# 406.4 25 CENTAVOS

6.7680 g., 0.9030 Silver .1965 oz. ASW **Mint:** Guadalajara

Date	Mintage	F	VF	XF	Unc
1880Ga A	38,000	25.00	50.00	100	200
1881/0Ga S	39,000	25.00	50.00	100	200
1881Ga S	Inc. above	25.00	50.00	100	200
1882Ga S	18,000	25.00	50.00	100	200
1883/2Ga B/S	—	50.00	100	150	300
1884Ga B	—	20.00	40.00	80.00	150
1889Ga S	30,000	20.00	40.00	80.00	150

KM# 406.5 25 CENTAVOS

6.7680 g., 0.9030 Silver .1965 oz. ASW **Mint:** Guanajuato **Note:** Varieties exist.

Date	Mintage	F	VF	XF	Unc
1870Go S	128,000	10.00	20.00	50.00	125
1871Go S	172,000	10.00	20.00	50.00	125
1872/1Go S	178,000	10.00	20.00	50.00	125
1872Go S	Inc. above	10.00	20.00	50.00	125
1873Go S	120,000	10.00	20.00	50.00	125
1874Go S	—	15.00	30.00	60.00	150
1875/4Go S	—	15.00	30.00	60.00	150
1875Go S	—	10.00	20.00	50.00	125
1876Go S	—	20.00	40.00	80.00	175
1877Go S	124,000	10.00	20.00	50.00	125
1878Go S	146,000	10.00	20.00	50.00	125
1879Go S	—	10.00	20.00	50.00	125
1880Go S	—	20.00	40.00	80.00	175
1881Go S	408,000	7.50	17.50	45.00	125
1882Go S	204,000	7.50	17.50	45.00	125
1883Go B	168,000	7.50	17.50	45.00	125
1884/69Go B	—	7.50	17.50	45.00	125
1884/3Go B	—	7.50	17.50	45.00	125
1884/3Go B/R	—	7.50	17.50	45.00	125
1884Go B	—	7.50	17.50	45.00	125
1885/65Go R	300,000	7.50	17.50	45.00	125

Date	Mintage	F	VF	XF	Unc
1885/69Go R	Inc. above	7.50	17.50	45.00	125
1885Go R	Inc. above	7.50	17.50	45.00	125
1886/66Go R	322,000	7.50	17.50	45.00	125
1886/69Go R/S	Inc. above	7.50	17.50	45.00	125
1886/5/69Go R	Inc. above	7.50	15.00	45.00	125
1886Go R	Inc. above	7.50	15.00	45.00	125
1887Go R	254,000	7.50	15.00	45.00	125
1887Go/Cn R/D	Inc. above	7.50	15.00	45.00	125
1888Go R	312,000	7.50	15.00	45.00	125
1889/8Go R	304,000	7.50	15.00	45.00	125
1889/8Go/Cn R/D	Inc. above	7.50	15.00	45.00	125
1889Go R	Inc. above	7.50	15.00	45.00	125
1890Go R	236,000	7.50	15.00	45.00	125

KM# 406.6 25 CENTAVOS

6.7680 g., 0.9030 Silver .1965 oz. ASW **Mint:** Hermosillo **Note:** Varieties exist.

Date	Mintage	F	VF	XF	Unc
1874/64Ho R	Inc. above	10.00	20.00	40.00	125
1874/69Ho R	—	10.00	20.00	40.00	125
1874Ho R	23,000	10.00	20.00	40.00	125
1875Ho R Rare	—	—	—	—	—
1876/4Ho F/R	34,000	10.00	20.00	50.00	150
1876Ho F/R	Inc. above	10.00	25.00	60.00	150
1876Ho F	Inc. above	10.00	25.00	55.00	135
1877Ho F	—	10.00	20.00	50.00	125
1878Ho A	23,000	10.00	20.00	50.00	125
1879Ho A	—	10.00	20.00	50.00	125
1880Ho A	—	15.00	30.00	60.00	125
1881Ho A	19,000	15.00	30.00	60.00	125
1882Ho A	8,120	20.00	40.00	80.00	150
1883Ho M	2,000	100	200	300	600
1884Ho M	—	12.50	25.00	50.00	150
1885Ho M	—	10.00	20.00	50.00	125
1886Ho G	6,400	30.00	60.00	125	250
1887Ho G	12,000	10.00	20.00	40.00	125
1888Ho G	20,000	10.00	20.00	40.00	125
1889Ho G	28,000	10.00	20.00	40.00	125
1890/80Ho G	18,000	25.00	50.00	100	125
1890Ho G	Inc. above	25.00	50.00	100	125

KM# 406.7 25 CENTAVOS

6.7680 g., 0.9027 Silver .1965 oz. ASW **Mint:** Mexico City **Note:** Varieties exist.

Date	Mintage	F	VF	XF	Unc
1869Mo C	76,000	10.00	25.00	50.00	125
1870/69Mo C	—	6.00	12.00	30.00	125
1870/9Mo C	136,000	6.00	12.00	30.00	125
1870Mo C	Inc. above	6.00	12.00	30.00	125
1871Mo M	138,000	6.00	12.00	30.00	125
1872Mo M	220,000	6.00	12.00	30.00	125
1873/1Mo M	48,000	10.00	25.00	50.00	125
1873Mo M	Inc. above	10.00	25.00	50.00	125
1874/69Mo B/M	—	10.00	25.00	50.00	125
1874/3Mo M	—	10.00	25.00	50.00	125
1874/3Mo B	—	10.00	25.00	50.00	125
1874/3Mo B/M	—	10.00	25.00	50.00	125
1874Mo M	—	6.00	12.00	30.00	125
1874Mo B/M	—	10.00	25.00	50.00	125
1875Mo B	—	6.00	12.00	30.00	125
1876/5Mo B	—	7.50	15.00	40.00	125
1876Mo B	—	6.00	12.00	30.00	125
1877Mo M	56,000	10.00	25.00	50.00	125
1878/1Mo M	120,000	10.00	25.00	50.00	125
1878/7Mo M	Inc. above	10.00	25.00	50.00	125
1878Mo M	Inc. above	6.00	12.00	30.00	125
1879Mo M	—	10.00	20.00	40.00	125
1880Mo M	—	7.50	15.00	35.00	125
1881/0Mo M	300,000	10.00	25.00	50.00	125
1881Mo M	Inc. above	10.00	25.00	50.00	125
1882Mo M	212,000	7.50	15.00	35.00	125
1883Mo M	108,000	7.50	15.00	35.00	125
1884/3Mo M	—	10.00	25.00	50.00	125
1884Mo M	—	10.00	20.00	40.00	125
1885Mo M	216,000	10.00	20.00	40.00	125
1886/5Mo M	436,000	7.50	15.00	35.00	125
1886Mo M	Inc. above	7.50	15.00	35.00	125
1887Mo M	376,000	7.50	15.00	35.00	125
1888Mo M	192,000	7.50	15.00	35.00	125
1889Mo M	132,000	7.50	15.00	35.00	125
1890Mo M	60,000	10.00	20.00	40.00	125

KM# 406.8 25 CENTAVOS

6.7680 g., 0.9030 Silver .1965 oz. ASW **Mint:** San Luis Potosi **Note:** Varieties exist.

Date	Mintage	F	VF	XF	Unc
1869 Pi S	—	25.00	75.00	150	300
1870 Pi G	50,000	10.00	30.00	75.00	150
1870 Pi O	Inc. above	15.00	35.00	85.00	175
1871 Pi O	30,000	10.00	30.00	75.00	150
1872 Pi O	46,000	10.00	30.00	75.00	150
1873 Pi O	13,000	15.00	40.00	90.00	175
1874 Pi H	—	15.00	40.00	90.00	200
1875 Pi H	—	10.00	20.00	60.00	150
1876/5 Pi H	—	15.00	30.00	80.00	175
1876 Pi H	—	10.00	25.00	65.00	150
1877 Pi H	19,000	10.00	25.00	65.00	150
1878 Pi H	—	15.00	30.00	60.00	150
1879/8 Pi H	—	10.00	25.00	60.00	150
1879 Pi H	—	10.00	25.00	60.00	150
1879 Pi E	—	100	200	300	600
1880 Pi H	—	20.00	40.00	100	200
1880 Pi H/M	—	20.00	40.00	100	200
1881 Pi H	50,000	20.00	40.00	80.00	175
1881 Pi E Rare	Inc. above	—	—	—	—
1882 Pi H	20,000	10.00	20.00	60.00	150
1883 Pi H	17,000	10.00	25.00	65.00	150
1884 Pi H	—	10.00	25.00	65.00	150
1885/4 Pi H	—	10.00	20.00	60.00	150
1885 Pi H	43,000	10.00	20.00	60.00	150
1886 Pi C	78,000	10.00	25.00	65.00	150
1886 Pi R	Inc. above	7.50	20.00	50.00	150
1886 Pi R 6/inverted 6	Inc. above	7.50	20.00	50.00	150
1887Pi/ZsR	92,000	7.50	20.00	50.00	150
1887Pi/ZsB	Inc. above	100	150	300	500
1887 Pi R	—	7.50	20.00	50.00	150
1888 Pi R	106,000	7.50	20.00	50.00	150
1888Pi/ZsR	Inc. above	10.00	20.00	50.00	150
1888 Pi R/B	Inc. above	10.00	20.00	50.00	150
1889 Pi R	115,000	7.50	15.00	40.00	150
1889Pi/ZsR	Inc. above	10.00	20.00	50.00	150
1889 Pi R/B	Inc. above	10.00	20.00	50.00	150
1890 Pi R	64,000	10.00	20.00	50.00	150
1890Pi/ZsR/B	Inc. above	7.50	15.00	40.00	150
1890 Pi R/B	Inc. above	10.00	20.00	50.00	150

KM# 406.9 25 CENTAVOS

6.7680 g., 0.9030 Silver .1965 oz. ASW **Mint:** Zacatecas **Note:** Varieties exist.

Date	Mintage	F	VF	XF	Unc
1870Zs H	152,000	6.00	15.00	50.00	125
1871Zs H	250,000	6.00	15.00	50.00	125
1872Zs H	260,000	6.00	15.00	50.00	125
1872Zs H	—	—	—	—	—
1873Zs H	132,000	6.00	15.00	50.00	125
1874Zs H	—	10.00	20.00	60.00	125
1874Zs A	—	10.00	20.00	60.00	125
1875Zs A	—	7.00	20.00	60.00	125
1876Zs A	—	6.00	15.00	50.00	125
1876Zs S	—	6.00	15.00	50.00	125
1877Zs S	350,000	6.00	15.00	50.00	125
1878Zs S	252,000	6.00	15.00	50.00	125
1878/1Zs S	—	7.00	20.00	60.00	125
1878/7Zs S	—	7.00	20.00	60.00	125
1879Zs S	—	6.00	15.00	50.00	125
1880Zs S	—	6.00	15.00	50.00	125
1881/0Zs S	570,000	6.00	15.00	50.00	125
1881Zs S	Inc. above	6.00	15.00	50.00	125
1882/1Zs S	300,000	10.00	17.50	55.00	125
1882Zs S	Inc. above	6.00	15.00	50.00	125
1883/2Zs S	193,000	10.00	17.50	55.00	125
1883Zs S	Inc. above	6.00	15.00	50.00	125
1884/3Zs S	—	10.00	17.50	55.00	125
1884Zs S	—	6.00	15.00	50.00	125
1885Zs S	309,000	6.00	15.00	50.00	125
1886/2Zs S	—	10.00	17.50	55.00	125
1886/5Zs S	613,000	6.00	15.00	50.00	125
1886Zs S	Inc. above	6.00	15.00	50.00	125
1886Zs Z	Inc. above	6.00	15.00	55.00	125
1887Zs Z	389,000	6.00	15.00	50.00	125
1888Zs Z	408,000	6.00	15.00	50.00	125
1889Zs Z	400,000	6.00	15.00	50.00	125
1890Zs Z	269,000	6.00	15.00	50.00	125

KM# 407 50 CENTAVOS

13.5360 g., 0.9030 Silver .3930 oz. ASW **Mint:** Alamos
Reverse: Balance scale **Note:** Mint mark A, As.

Date	Mintage	F	VF	XF	Unc
1875 L	—	12.00	25.00	70.00	400
1876/5 L	—	25.00	50.00	120	450
1876 L	—	12.00	25.00	70.00	400
1876 L	—	—	—	—	—
1877 L	26,000	15.00	30.00	85.00	450
1878 L	—	12.00	25.00	70.00	400
1879 L	—	25.00	50.00	120	450
1880 L	57,000	12.00	25.00	70.00	400
1881 L	18,000	15.00	30.00	80.00	450
1884 L	6,286	65.00	120	250	650
1885As/HoL	21,000	15.00	35.00	90.00	450
1888 L	—	4,000	5,000	7,000	—

KM# 407.1 50 CENTAVOS

13.5360 g., 0.9030 Silver .3930 oz. ASW **Mint:** Chihuahua
Reverse: Balance scale **Note:** Mint mark Ca, CHa.

Date	Mintage	F	VF	XF	Unc
1883 M	12,000	30.00	60.00	125	500
1884 M	—	25.00	50.00	125	500
1885 M	13,000	15.00	35.00	90.00	400
1886 M	18,000	20.00	40.00	100	450
1887 M	26,000	25.00	65.00	150	500

KM# 407.2 50 CENTAVOS

13.5360 g., 0.9030 Silver .3930 oz. ASW **Mint:** Culiacan
Reverse: Balance scale

Date	Mintage	F	VF	XF	Unc
1871Cn P	—	400	550	750	1,500
1873Cn P	—	400	550	750	1,500
1874Cn P	—	200	300	500	1,000
1875/4Cn P	—	20.00	40.00	75.00	450
1875Cn P	—	12.00	25.00	50.00	450
1876Cn P	—	15.00	30.00	60.00	450
1877/6Cn G	—	15.00	30.00	60.00	450
1877Cn G	—	12.00	25.00	50.00	450
1878Cn G	18,000	20.00	40.00	75.00	450
1878Cn/Mo D	Inc. above	30.00	60.00	100	450
1878Cn D	Inc. above	15.00	35.00	75.00	450
1879Cn D	—	12.00	25.00	50.00	450
1879Cn D/G	—	12.00	25.00	50.00	450
1880/8Cn D	—	15.00	30.00	60.00	450
1880Cn D	—	15.00	30.00	60.00	450
1881/0Cn D	188,000	15.00	30.00	60.00	450
1881Cn D	Inc. above	15.00	30.00	60.00	450
1881Cn G	Inc. above	125	175	275	550
1882Cn D	—	175	300	500	2,000
1882Gn G	—	100	250	300	1,000
1883 D	19,000	25.00	50.00	100	500
1885/3Cn M/H	9,254	30.00	60.00	100	500
1886Cn M/G	7,030	50.00	100	300	1,500
1886Cn M	Inc. above	40.00	80.00	150	800
1887Cn M	76,000	20.00	40.00	100	450
1888Cn M	—	4,000	6,000	—	—
1892Cn M	8,200	40.00	80.00	150	650

KM# 407.3 50 CENTAVOS

13.5360 g., 0.9030 Silver .3930 oz. ASW **Mint:** Durango
Reverse: Balance scale

Date	Mintage	F	VF	XF	Unc
1871Do P Rare	591	—	—	—	—
1873Do P	4,010	150	250	500	1,250
1873Do M/P	Inc. above	150	250	500	1,250
1874Do M	—	20.00	40.00	175	750
1875Do M	—	20.00	40.00	80.00	350
1875Do H	—	150	250	450	1,000
1876/5Do M	—	35.00	70.00	150	500
1876Do M	—	35.00	70.00	150	500
1877Do P	2,000	30.00	45.00	150	1,250
1878Do B Rare	—	—	—	—	—
1879Do B Rare	—	—	—	—	—
1880Do P	—	30.00	60.00	125	500
1881Do P	10,000	40.00	80.00	150	550
1882Do C	8,957	30.00	75.00	200	800
1884/2Do C	—	20.00	50.00	125	600
1884Do C	—	—	—	—	—
1885Do B	—	15.00	40.00	100	500
1885Do B/P	—	15.00	40.00	100	500
1886Do C	16,000	15.00	40.00	100	500
1887Do/Mo C	28,000	15.00	40.00	100	500
1887Do C	—	15.00	40.00	100	500

KM# 407.4 50 CENTAVOS

13.5360 g., 0.9030 Silver .3930 oz. ASW **Mint:** Guanajuato
Reverse: Balance scale **Note:** Struck at Guanajuato Mint, mitn mark Go. Varieties exist.

Date	Mintage	F	VF	XF	Unc
1869Go S	—	15.00	35.00	75.00	550
1870Go S	166,000	12.00	25.00	50.00	450
1871Go S	148,000	12.00	25.00	50.00	450
1872/1Go S	144,000	15.00	30.00	60.00	500
1872Go S	Inc. above	12.00	25.00	50.00	450
1873Go S	50,000	12.00	25.00	50.00	450
1874Go S	—	12.00	25.00	50.00	450
1875Go S	—	15.00	35.00	75.00	450
1876/5Go S	—	12.00	25.00	50.00	450
1877Go S	76,000	12.00	25.00	60.00	450
1878Go S	37,000	15.00	30.00	75.00	550
1879/8Go S	—	15.00	30.00	60.00	500
1879Go S	—	12.00	25.00	50.00	450
1880Go S	—	12.00	25.00	50.00	450
1881/79Go S	32,000	15.00	30.00	60.00	500
1881Go S	Inc. above	12.00	25.00	50.00	450
1882Go S	18,000	12.00	25.00	50.00	450
1883/2Go B/S	—	15.00	30.00	60.00	500
1883Go B	—	12.00	25.00	50.00	450
1883Go S Rare	—	—	—	—	—
1884Go B/S	—	15.00	30.00	60.00	500
1885/4Go R/B	—	15.00	30.00	60.00	500
1885Go R	53,000	12.00	25.00	50.00	450
1886/5Go R/B	59,000	15.00	30.00	60.00	500
1886/5Go R/S	Inc. above	20.00	40.00	75.00	500
1886Go R	Inc. above	20.00	40.00	75.00	450
1887Go R	18,000	20.00	40.00	75.00	550
1888Go R 1 known; Rare	—	—	—	—	—

KM# 407.5 50 CENTAVOS

13.5360 g., 0.9030 Silver .3930 oz. ASW **Mint:** Hermosillo
Reverse: Balance scale **Note:** Varieties exist.

Date	Mintage	F	VF	XF	Unc
1874Ho R	—	20.00	40.00	100	600
1875/4Ho R	—	20.00	50.00	125	600
1875Ho R	—	20.00	50.00	125	600
1876/5Ho F/R	—	15.00	35.00	100	550
1876Ho F	—	15.00	35.00	100	550

Date	Mintage	F	VF	XF	Unc
1877Ho F	—	50.00	75.00	150	650
1880/70Ho A	—	15.00	35.00	100	550
1880Ho A	—	15.00	35.00	100	550
1881Ho A	13,000	15.00	35.00	100	550
1882Ho A	—	75.00	150	250	750
1888Ho G	—	2,000	3,000	6,000	—
1894Ho G	59,000	15.00	30.00	100	450
1895Ho G	8,000	250	350	700	1,500

KM# 407.6 50 CENTAVOS
13.5360 g., 0.9027 Silver .3930 oz. ASW **Mint:** Mexico City
Reverse: Balance scale

Date	Mintage	F	VF	XF	Unc
1869Mo C	46,000	15.00	35.00	95.00	600
1870Mo C	52,000	15.00	30.00	90.00	550
1871Mo C	14,000	40.00	75.00	150	650
1871Mo M/C	Inc. above	35.00	75.00	150	600
1872/1Mo M	60,000	35.00	75.00	150	550
1872Mo M	Inc. above	35.00	75.00	150	550
1873Mo M	6,000	35.00	75.00	150	600
1874/3Mo M	—	200	400	600	1,250
1874/2Mo B	—	15.00	30.00	75.00	500
1874/2Mo B/M	—	15.00	30.00	75.00	500
1874/3Mo B/M	—	15.00	30.00	75.00	500
1874Mo B	—	15.00	30.00	75.00	500
1875Mo B	—	15.00	30.00	75.00	550
1876/5Mo B	—	15.00	30.00	75.00	500
1876Mo B	—	12.00	25.00	75.00	500
1877/2Mo M	—	20.00	40.00	100	550
1877Mo M	—	15.00	30.00	90.00	500
1878/7Mo M	8,000	25.00	50.00	125	600
1878Mo M	Inc. above	15.00	35.00	100	550
1879Mo M	—	25.00	50.00	125	550
1880Mo M	—	100	150	250	750
1881Mo M	16,000	25.00	50.00	125	600
1881/0Mo M	—	30.00	50.00	125	600
1882/1Mo M	2,000	30.00	60.00	150	750
1883/2Mo M	4,000	150	225	350	1,000
1884Mo M	—	150	225	350	1,000
1885Mo M	12,000	30.00	60.00	150	600
1886/5Mo M	66,000	15.00	35.00	90.00	475
1886Mo M	Inc. above	12.00	25.00	75.00	450
1887/6Mo M	88,000	15.00	35.00	90.00	475
1887Mo M	Inc. above	15.00	35.00	75.00	475
1888Mo M	—	3,000	4,000	6,000	—

KM# 407.7 50 CENTAVOS
13.5360 g., 0.9030 Silver .3930 oz. ASW **Mint:** San Luis Potosi
Reverse: Balance scale

Date	Mintage	F	VF	XF	Unc
1870 Pi G	Inc. above	20.00	40.00	100	450
1870/780 Pi G	50,000	25.00	45.00	110	500
1870 Pi O	Inc. above	20.00	40.00	100	450
1871 Pi O	—	15.00	30.00	80.00	400
1871 Pi O/G	64,000	15.00	30.00	80.00	400
1872 Pi O	52,000	15.00	30.00	80.00	400
1872 Pi O/G	Inc. above	15.00	30.00	80.00	400
1873 Pi O	32,000	20.00	40.00	100	450
1873 Pi H	Inc. above	25.00	50.00	125	550
1874 Pi H/O	—	15.00	30.00	80.00	400
1875/3 Pi H	—	15.00	30.00	80.00	400
1875 Pi H	—	15.00	30.00	80.00	400
1876 Pi H	—	30.00	60.00	150	700
1877 Pi H	34,000	20.00	40.00	100	450
1878 Pi H	9,700	20.00	40.00	100	450
1879/7 Pi H	—	15.00	35.00	90.00	450
1879 Pi H	—	15.00	35.00	90.00	400
1880 Pi H	—	20.00	40.00	100	450
1881 Pi H	28,000	20.00	40.00	100	450
1882 Pi H	22,000	15.00	30.00	80.00	400
1883 Pi H 8/8	29,000	50.00	100	200	750
1883 Pi H	Inc. above	15.00	30.00	80.00	400
1884 Pi H	—	50.00	100	175	600
1885/3 Pi H	—	20.00	40.00	100	450
1885/0 Pi H	45,000	20.00	40.00	100	450
1885/4 Pi H	Inc. above	20.00	40.00	100	450
1885 Pi H	Inc. above	25.00	50.00	125	450
1885 Pi C	Inc. above	15.00	30.00	80.00	400
1886/1 Pi R	92,000	50.00	100	175	600
1886/1 Pi C	—	25.00	40.00	100	450
1886 Pi C	Inc. above	15.00	30.00	80.00	400
1886 Pi R	Inc. above	15.00	30.00	80.00	400
1887 Pi R	32,000	15.00	30.00	90.00	450

KM# 407.8 50 CENTAVOS
13.5360 g., 0.9030 Silver .3930 oz. ASW **Mint:** Zacatecas
Reverse: Balance scale **Note:** Varieties exist.

Date	Mintage	F	VF	XF	Unc
1870Zs H	86,000	12.00	25.00	60.00	450
1871Zs H	146,000	12.00	25.00	50.00	400
1872Zs H	132,000	12.00	25.00	50.00	400
1873Zs H	56,000	12.00	25.00	50.00	400
1874Zs H	—	12.00	25.00	50.00	400
1874Zs A Rare	—	—	—	—	—
1875Zs A	—	12.00	25.00	50.00	400
1876/5Zs A	—	15.00	30.00	60.00	450
1876Zs A	—	12.00	25.00	50.00	400
1876Zs S	—	100	200	350	750
1877Zs S	100,000	12.00	25.00	50.00	400
1878/7Zs S	254,000	15.00	30.00	60.00	450
1878Zs S	Inc. above	15.00	30.00	60.00	400
1879Zs S	—	12.00	25.00	50.00	400
1880Zs S	—	12.00	25.00	50.00	400
1881Zs S	201,000	12.00	25.00	50.00	400
1882/1Zs S	2,000	50.00	100	250	650
1882Zs S	Inc. above	50.00	100	250	650
1883Zs/Za S	31,000	30.00	60.00	100	450
1883Zs S	Inc. above	25.00	50.00	100	450
1884/3Zs S	—	15.00	30.00	60.00	450
1884Zs S	—	12.00	25.00	50.00	400
1885/4Zs S	2,000	25.00	50.00	125	450
1885Zs S	Inc. above	25.00	50.00	125	450
1886Zs Z	2,000	150	275	400	1,000
1887Zs Z	63,000	30.00	60.00	125	450

KM# 408 PESO
27.0730 g., 0.9030 Silver .7860 oz. ASW **Mint:** Chihuahua
Reverse: Balance scale

Date	Mintage	F	VF	XF	Unc
1872CH M	Inc. above	17.50	25.00	50.00	250
1872CH P/M	747,000	750	1,500	3,500	—
1872CH P	Inc. above	350	700	1,500	—
1872/1CH M	Inc. above	25.00	40.00	75.00	400
1873CH M	320,000	20.00	30.00	60.00	265
1873CH M/P	Inc. above	25.00	40.00	75.00	350

KM# 408.1 PESO
27.0730 g., 0.9030 Silver .7860 oz. ASW **Mint:** Culiacan
Reverse: Balance scale

Date	Mintage	F	VF	XF	Unc
1870Cn E	—	40.00	80.00	150	500
1871/11Cn P	478,000	25.00	45.00	100	450
1871Cn P	Inc. above	20.00	40.00	75.00	300
1872/1Cn P	—	20.00	40.00	75.00	300
1872Cn P	209,000	20.00	40.00	75.00	300
1873Cn P narrow date	527,000	20.00	40.00	75.00	300
1873Cn P wide date	Inc. above	20.00	40.00	75.00	300

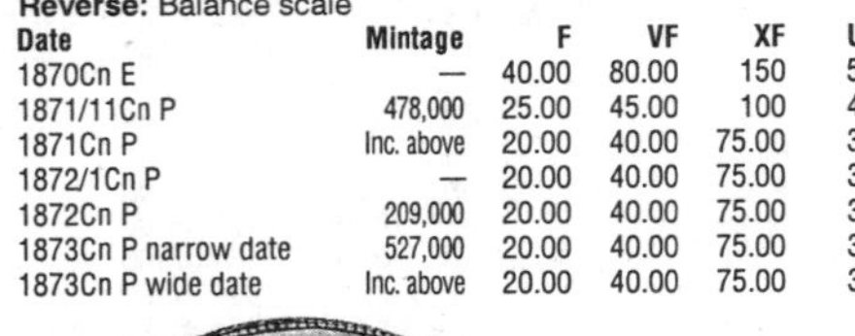

KM# 408.2 PESO
27.0730 g., 0.9027 Silver .7860 oz. ASW **Mint:** Durango
Reverse: Balance scale

Date	Mintage	F	VF	XF	Unc
1870Do P	—	50.00	100	175	450
1871Do P	427,000	25.00	50.00	75.00	300
1872Do P	296,000	20.00	40.00	75.00	350
1872Do PT	Inc. above	100	175	250	850
1873Do P	203,000	25.00	45.00	85.00	350

KM# 408.3 PESO
27.0730 g., 0.9030 Silver .7860 oz. ASW **Mint:** Guadalajara
Reverse: Balance scale

Date	Mintage	F	VF	XF	Unc
1870Ga C	—	650	850	—	—
1871Ga C	829,000	25.00	65.00	135	600
1872Ga C	485,000	40.00	90.00	175	650
1873/2Ga C	277,000	40.00	90.00	175	700
1873Ga C	Inc. above	25.00	65.00	135	600

KM# 408.4 PESO
27.0730 g., 0.9027 Silver .7860 oz. ASW **Mint:** Guanajuato
Reverse: Balance scale

Date	Mintage	F	VF	XF	Unc
1871/0Go S	3,946,000	30.00	50.00	90.00	350
1871/3Go S	Inc. above	20.00	35.00	70.00	275
1871Go S	Inc. above	12.00	20.00	40.00	220
1872Go S	4,067,000	12.00	20.00	40.00	250
1873/2Go S	1,560,000	15.00	25.00	50.00	250
1873Go S	Inc. above	12.00	20.00	45.00	250
1873Go/Mo/S/M	Inc. above	12.00	20.00	45.00	250

KM# 408.5 PESO
27.0730 g., 0.9030 Silver .7860 oz. ASW **Mint:** Mexico City
Reverse: Balance scale

Date	Mintage	F	VF	XF	Unc
1869Mo C	—	35.00	65.00	135	600
1870/69Mo C	5,115,000	15.00	25.00	55.00	275
1870Mo C	Inc. above	12.00	20.00	40.00	250
1870Mo M/C	Inc. above	18.00	30.00	60.00	275
1870Mo M	Inc. above	18.00	30.00	60.00	275
1871/0Mo M	6,974,000	15.00	25.00	55.00	275
1871Mo M	Inc. above	12.00	20.00	40.00	250
1872/1Mo M	—	15.00	25.00	50.00	275
1872/1Mo M/C	4,801,000	15.00	25.00	50.00	275
1872Mo M	Inc. above	12.00	20.00	40.00	250
1873Mo M	1,765,000	12.00	20.00	40.00	250

Note: The 1869 C with large LEY on the scroll is a pattern

KM# 408.6 PESO
27.0730 g., 0.9030 Silver .7860 oz. ASW **Mint:** Oaxaca
Reverse: Balance scale

Date	Mintage	F	VF	XF	Unc
1869 Oa E	—	275	400	600	2,000
1870 Oa E Small A	Inc. above	15.00	30.00	75.00	400
1870OA E Large A	Inc. above	100	150	300	900
1871/69 Oa E	140,000	30.00	50.00	125	550
1871 Oa E Small A	Inc. above	15.00	30.00	60.00	300
1871 Oa E Large A	Inc. above	15.00	30.00	75.00	400
1872 Oa E Small A	180,000	15.00	30.00	75.00	400
1872 Oa E Large A	Inc. above	50.00	100	200	450
1873 Oa E	105,000	15.00	30.00	75.00	350

KM# 408.7 PESO
27.0730 g., 0.9030 Silver .7860 oz. ASW **Mint:** San Luis Potosi
Reverse: Balance scale **Note:** Varieties exist.

Date	Mintage	F	VF	XF	Unc
1870 Pi S	1,967,000	200	350	500	1,000
1870 Pi S/A	Inc. above	200	350	550	1,200
1870 Pi G	Inc. above	25.00	40.00	75.00	550
1870 Pi H Contemporary counterfeits	Inc. above	—	—	—	—
1870 Pi O/G	Inc. above	25.00	40.00	75.00	550
1870 Pi O	Inc. above	20.00	30.00	100	400
1871/69 Pi O	2,103,000	75.00	100	200	500
1871 Pi O/G	Inc. above	15.00	30.00	60.00	500
1871 Pi O	—	15.00	30.00	60.00	500
1872 Pi O	1,873,000	15.00	30.00	60.00	500
1873 Pi O	893,000	15.00	30.00	60.00	500
1873 Pi H	Inc. above	15.00	30.00	60.00	500

KM# 408.8 PESO
27.0730 g., 0.9030 Silver .7860 oz. ASW **Mint:** Zacatecas
Reverse: Balance scale **Note:** Varieties exist.

Date	Mintage	F	VF	XF	Unc
1870Zs H	4,519,000	12.00	30.00	40.00	220
1871Zs H	4,459,000	12.00	20.00	40.00	220
1872Zs H	4,039,000	12.00	20.00	40.00	220
1873/1Zs H	Inc. above	12.00	20.00	40.00	220
1873Zs H	1,782,000	12.00	20.00	40.00	220

KM# 409 PESO
27.0730 g., 0.9030 Silver .7860 oz. ASW **Mint:** Culiacan
Reverse: Liberty cap

Date	Mintage	F	VF	XF	Unc
1898Cn AM	1,720,000	10.00	15.00	25.00	65.00
1898Cn/MoAM	Inc. above	15.00	30.00	90.00	150
1899Cn AM	1,722,000	25.00	50.00	90.00	175
1899Cn JQ	Inc. above	10.00	15.00	50.00	125
1900Cn JQ	1,804,000	10.00	15.00	25.00	75.00

KM# 409.1 PESO
27.0730 g., 0.9030 Silver .7860 oz. ASW **Mint:** Guanajuato
Reverse: Liberty cap **Note:** Varieties exist.

Date	Mintage	F	VF	XF	Unc
1898Go RS	4,256,000	10.00	15.00	35.00	75.00
1898Go/MoRS	Inc. above	20.00	30.00	60.00	125
1899Go RS	3,207,000	10.00	15.00	30.00	75.00
1900Go RS	1,489,000	25.00	50.00	100	250

KM# 409.2 PESO
27.0730 g., 0.9027 Silver .7860 oz. ASW **Mint:** Mexico City
Reverse: Liberty cap **Note:** Varieties exist.

Date	Mintage	F	VF	XF	Unc
1898Mo AM Original strike - reverse with 139 beads	10,156,000	9.00	11.50	18.50	60.00
1898Mo AM Restrike (1949) - reverse with 134 beads	10,250,000	9.00	11.50	16.50	40.00
1899Mo AM	7,930,000	10.00	12.50	20.00	70.00
1900Mo AM	8,226,000	10.00	12.50	20.00	70.00

KM# 409.3 PESO
27.0730 g., 0.9030 Silver .7860 oz. ASW **Mint:** Zacatecas
Reverse: Liberty cap **Note:** Struck at Zacatecas Mint, mint mark Zs. Varieties exist.

Date	Mintage	F	VF	XF	Unc
1898Zs FZ	5,714,000	10.00	12.50	20.00	60.00
1899Zs FZ	5,618,000	10.00	12.50	20.00	65.00
1900Zs FZ	5,357,000	10.00	12.50	20.00	65.00

KM# 410 PESO
1.6920 g., 0.8750 Gold .0476 oz. AGW **Mint:** Alamos

Date	F	VF	XF	Unc
1888AsL/MoM Rare	—	—	—	—
1888 As L Rare	—	—	—	—

KM# 410.1 PESO
1.6920 g., 0.8750 Gold .0476 oz. AGW **Mint:** Chihuahua

Date	Mintage	F	VF	XF	Unc
1888Ca/MoM Rare	104	—	—	—	—

KM# 410.2 PESO
1.6920 g., 0.8750 Gold .0476 oz. AGW **Mint:** Culiacan

Date	Mintage	F	VF	XF	Unc
1873Cn P	1,221	75.00	100	150	250
1875Cn P	—	85.00	125	150	250
1878Cn G	248	100	175	225	475
1879Cn D	—	100	150	175	285
1881/0Cn D	338	100	150	175	285
1882Cn D	340	100	150	175	285
1883Cn D	—	100	150	175	285
1884Cn M	—	100	150	175	285
1886/4Cn M	277	100	150	225	450
1888/7Cn M	2,586	100	175	225	450
1888Cn M	Inc. above	65.00	100	150	265
1889Cn M Rare	—	—	—	—	—
1891/89Cn M	969	75.00	100	150	265
1892Cn M	780	75.00	100	150	265
1893Cn M	498	85.00	125	150	265
1894Cn M	493	80.00	125	150	265
1895Cn M	1,143	65.00	100	150	250
1896/5Cn M	1,028	65.00	100	150	250
1897Cn M	785	65.00	100	150	250
1898Cn M	3,521	65.00	100	150	225
1898Cn/MoM	Inc. above	65.00	100	150	250
1899Cn Q	2,000	65.00	100	150	225

KM# 410.3 PESO
1.6920 g., 0.8750 Gold .0476 oz. AGW **Mint:** Guanajuato

Date	Mintage	F	VF	XF	Unc
1870Go S	—	100	125	150	265
1871Go S	500	100	175	225	475
1888Go R	210	125	200	250	550
1890Go R	1,916	75.00	100	150	265
1892Go R	533	100	150	175	350
1894Go R	180	150	200	250	550
1895Go R	676	100	150	175	325
1896/5Go R	4,671	65.00	100	150	250
1897/6Go R	4,280	65.00	100	150	250
1897Go R	Inc. above	65.00	100	150	250
1898Go R Regular obverse	5,193	65.00	100	150	250
1898Go R Mule, 5 Centavos obverse, normal reverse	Inc. above	75.00	100	150	250
1899Go R	2,748	65.00	100	150	250
1900/800Go R	864	75.00	125	150	285

KM# 410.4 PESO
1.6920 g., 0.8750 Gold .0476 oz. AGW **Mint:** Hermosillo

Date	Mintage	F	VF	XF	Unc
1875Ho R Rare	310	—	—	—	—
1876Ho F Rare	—	—	—	—	—
1888Ho G/MoM Rare	—	—	—	—	—

KM# 410.5 PESO
1.6920 g., 0.8750 Gold .0476 oz. AGW **Mint:** Mexico City

Date	Mintage	F	VF	XF	Unc
1870Mo C	2,540	40.00	60.00	90.00	185
1871Mo M/C	1,000	50.00	100	150	250
1872Mo M/C	3,000	40.00	60.00	90.00	185
1873/1Mo M	2,900	40.00	60.00	90.00	185
1873Mo M	Inc. above	40.00	60.00	90.00	185
1874Mo M	—	40.00	60.00	90.00	185
1875Mo B/M	—	40.00	60.00	90.00	185
1876/5Mo B/M	—	40.00	60.00	90.00	185
1877Mo M	—	40.00	60.00	90.00	185
1878Mo M	2,000	40.00	60.00	90.00	185
1879Mo M	—	40.00	60.00	90.00	185
1880/70Mo M	—	40.00	60.00	90.00	185
1881/71Mo M	1,000	40.00	60.00	90.00	185
1882/72Mo M	—	40.00	60.00	90.00	185
1883/72Mo M	1,000	40.00	60.00	90.00	185
1884Mo M	—	40.00	60.00	90.00	185
1885/71Mo M	—	40.00	60.00	90.00	185
1885Mo M	—	40.00	60.00	90.00	185
1886Mo M	1,700	40.00	60.00	90.00	185
1887Mo M	2,200	40.00	60.00	90.00	185
1888Mo M	1,000	40.00	60.00	90.00	185
1889Mo M	500	100	150	200	285
1890Mo M	570	100	150	200	285
1891Mo M	746	100	150	200	285
1892/0Mo M	2,895	40.00	60.00	90.00	185
1893Mo M	5,917	40.00	60.00	90.00	185
1894/3MMo	—	40.00	60.00	90.00	185
1894Mo M	6,244	40.00	60.00	90.00	185
1895Mo M	8,994	40.00	60.00	90.00	185
1895Mo B	Inc. above	40.00	60.00	90.00	185
1896Mo B	7,166	40.00	60.00	90.00	185
1896Mo M	Inc. above	40.00	60.00	90.00	185
1897Mo M	5,131	40.00	60.00	90.00	185
1898/7Mo M	5,368	40.00	60.00	90.00	185
1899Mo M	9,515	40.00	60.00	90.00	185
1900/800Mo M	9,301	40.00	60.00	90.00	185
1900/880Mo M	Inc. above	40.00	60.00	90.00	185
1900/890Mo M	Inc. above	40.00	60.00	90.00	185
1900Mo M	Inc. above	40.00	60.00	90.00	185

KM# 410.6 PESO
1.6920 g., 0.8750 Gold .0476 oz. AGW **Mint:** Zacatecas

Date	Mintage	F	VF	XF	Unc
1872Zs H	2,024	125	150	175	275
1875/3Zs A	—	125	150	200	325
1878Zs S	—	125	150	175	275
1888Zs Z	280	175	225	325	700
1889Zs Z	492	150	175	225	450
1890Zs Z	738	150	175	225	450

KM# 411 2-1/2 PESOS
4.2300 g., 0.8750 Gold .1190 oz. AGW **Mint:** Alamos

Date	F	VF	XF	Unc
1888As/MoL Rare	—	—	—	—

KM# 411.1 2-1/2 PESOS
4.2300 g., 0.8750 Gold .1190 oz. AGW **Mint:** Culiacan

Date	Mintage	F	VF	XF	Unc
1893Cn M	141	1,500	2,000	2,500	3,500

KM# 411.2 2-1/2 PESOS
4.2300 g., 0.8750 Gold .1190 oz. AGW **Mint:** Durango

Date	F	VF	XF	Unc
1888Do C Rare	—	—	—	—

KM# 411.3 2-1/2 PESOS
4.2300 g., 0.8750 Gold .1190 oz. AGW **Mint:** Guanajuato

Date	Mintage	F	VF	XF	Unc
1871Go S	600	1,250	2,000	2,500	3,250
1888Go/MoR	110	1,750	2,250	2,750	3,500

KM# 411.4 2-1/2 PESOS
4.2300 g., 0.8750 Gold .1190 oz. AGW **Mint:** Hermosillo

Date	F	VF	XF	Unc
1874Ho R Rare	—	—	—	—
1888Ho G Rare	—	—	—	—

KM# 411.5 2-1/2 PESOS
4.2300 g., 0.8750 Gold .1190 oz. AGW **Mint:** Mexico City

Date	Mintage	F	VF	XF	Unc
1870Mo C	820	150	250	350	750
1872Mo M/C	800	150	250	350	750
1873/2Mo M	—	200	350	750	1,350
1874Mo M	—	200	350	750	1,350
1874Mo B/M	—	200	350	750	1,350
1875Mo B	—	200	350	750	1,350
1876Mo B	—	250	500	1,000	1,600
1877Mo M	—	200	350	750	1,350
1878Mo M	400	200	350	750	1,350
1879Mo M	—	200	350	750	1,350
1880/79Mo M	—	200	350	750	1,350
1881Mo M	400	200	350	750	1,350
1882Mo M	—	200	350	750	1,350
1883/73Mo M	400	200	350	750	1,350
1884Mo M	—	250	500	1,000	1,600
1885Mo M	—	200	350	750	1,350
1886Mo M	400	200	350	750	1,350
1887Mo M	400	200	350	750	1,350
1888Mo M	540	200	350	750	1,350
1889Mo M	240	150	300	525	950
1890Mo M	420	200	350	750	1,350
1891Mo M	188	200	350	750	1,350
1892Mo M	240	200	350	750	1,350

KM# 411.6 2-1/2 PESOS
4.2300 g., 0.8750 Gold .1190 oz. AGW **Mint:** Zacatecas

Date	Mintage	F	VF	XF	Unc
1872Zs H	1,300	200	350	500	1,200
1873Zs H	—	175	325	450	850
1875/3Zs A	—	200	350	750	1,350
1877Zs S	—	200	350	750	1,350
1878Zs S	300	200	350	750	1,350
1888Zs/MoS	80	300	500	1,000	1,800
1889Zs/Mo Z	184	250	450	950	1,600
1890Zs Z	326	200	350	750	1,350

KM# 412 5 PESOS
8.4600 g., 0.8750 Gold .2380 oz. AGW **Mint:** Alamos

Date	Mintage	F	VF	XF	Unc
1875 As L	—	—	—	—	—
1878 As L	383	900	1,700	3,000	4,500

KM# 412.1 5 PESOS
8.4600 g., 0.8750 Gold .2380 oz. AGW **Mint:** Chihuahua

Date	Mintage	F	VF	XF	Unc
1888 Ca M Rare	120	—	—	—	—

KM# 412.2 5 PESOS
8.4600 g., 0.8750 Gold .2380 oz. AGW **Mint:** Culiacan

Date	Mintage	F	VF	XF	Unc
1873Cn P	—	300	600	1,000	1,500
1874Cn P	—	—	—	—	—
1875Cn P	—	300	500	700	1,250
1876Cn P	—	300	500	700	1,250
1877Cn G	—	300	500	700	1,250
1882Cn Rare	174	—	—	—	—
1888Cn M	—	500	1,000	1,350	2,000
1890Cn M	435	250	500	750	1,250
1891Cn M	1,390	250	400	500	1,000
1894Cn M	484	250	500	750	1,600
1895Cn M	142	500	750	1,500	2,500
1900Cn Q	1,536	150	300	400	900

KM# 412.3 5 PESOS
8.4600 g., 0.8750 Gold .2380 oz. AGW **Mint:** Durango

Date	F	VF	XF	Unc
1873/2Do P	700	1,250	1,800	3,000
1877Do P	700	1,250	1,800	3,000
1878Do E	700	1,250	1,800	3,000
1879/7Do B	700	1,250	1,800	3,000
1879Do B	700	1,250	1,800	3,000

KM# 412.4 5 PESOS
8.4600 g., 0.8750 Gold .2380 oz. AGW **Mint:** Guanajuato

Date	Mintage	F	VF	XF	Unc
1871Go S	1,600	400	800	1,250	2,500
1887Go R	140	600	1,200	1,500	2,750
1888Go R Rare	65	—	—	—	—
1893Go R Rare	16	—	—	—	—

KM# 412.5 5 PESOS
8.4600 g., 0.8750 Gold .2380 oz. AGW **Mint:** Hermosillo

Date	Mintage	F	VF	XF	Unc
1877Ho R	990	750	1,250	2,000	3,000
1877Ho A	Inc. above	650	1,100	1,750	2,750
1888Ho G Rare	—	—	—	—	—
1874Ho R	—	1,750	2,500	3,000	4,500

KM# 412.6 5 PESOS
8.4600 g., 0.8750 Gold .2380 oz. AGW **Mint:** Mexico City

Date	Mintage	F	VF	XF	Unc
1870Mo C	550	200	400	550	900
1871/69Mo M	1,600	150	300	400	650
1871Mo M	Inc. above	150	300	400	650
1872Mo M	1,600	150	300	400	650
1873/2Mo M	—	200	400	550	850
1874Mo M	—	200	400	550	850
1875/3Mo B/M	—	200	400	550	950

Date	Mintage	F	VF	XF	Unc
1875Mo B	—	200	400	550	950
1876/5Mo B/M	—	200	400	550	1,000
1877Mo M	—	250	450	750	1,250
1878/7Mo M	400	200	400	550	1,250
1878Mo M	Inc. above	200	400	550	1,250
1879/8Mo M	—	200	400	550	1,250
1880Mo M	—	200	400	550	1,250
1881Mo M	—	200	400	550	1,250
1882Mo M	200	250	450	750	1,250
1883Mo M	200	250	450	750	1,250
1884Mo M	—	250	450	750	1,250
1886Mo M	200	250	450	750	1,250
1887Mo M	200	250	450	750	1,250
1888Mo M	250	200	400	550	1,250
1889Mo M	190	250	450	750	1,250
1890Mo M	149	250	450	750	1,250
1891Mo M	156	250	450	750	1,250
1892Mo M	214	250	450	750	1,250
1893Mo M	1,058	200	400	500	800
1897Mo M	370	200	400	550	1,000
1898Mo M	376	200	400	550	1,000
1900Mo M	1,014	150	300	400	650

KM# 412.7 5 PESOS
8.4600 g., 0.8750 Gold .2380 oz. AGW **Mint:** Zacatecas

Date	Mintage	F	VF	XF	Unc
1874Zs A	—	250	500	750	1,500
1875Zs A	—	200	400	500	1,000
1877Zs S/A	—	200	400	550	1,000
1878/7Zs S/A	—	200	400	550	1,000
1883Zs S	—	150	300	450	700
1888Zs Z	70	1,000	1,500	2,000	3,000
1889Zs Z	373	200	300	500	850
1892Zs Z	1,229	150	300	450	700

KM# 413 10 PESOS
16.9200 g., 0.8750 Gold .4760 oz. AGW **Mint:** Alamos **Reverse:** Balance scale

Date	Mintage	F	VF	XF	Unc
1874 As DL Rare	—	—	—	—	—
1875 As L	642	600	1,250	2,500	3,500
1878 As L	977	500	1,000	2,000	3,000
1879 As L	1,078	500	1,000	2,000	3,000
1880 As L	2,629	500	1,000	2,000	3,000
1881 As L	2,574	500	1,000	2,000	3,000
1882 As L	3,403	500	1,000	2,000	3,000
1883 As L	3,597	500	1,000	2,000	3,000
1884 As L Rare	—	—	—	—	—
1885 As L	4,562	500	1,000	2,000	3,000
1886 As L	4,643	500	1,000	2,000	3,000
1887 As L	3,667	500	1,000	2,000	3,000
1888 As L	4,521	500	1,000	2,000	3,000
1889 As L	5,615	500	1,000	2,000	3,000
1890 As L	4,920	500	1,000	2,000	3,000
1891 As L	568	500	1,000	2,000	3,000
1892 As L	—	—	—	—	—
1893 As L	817	500	1,000	2,000	3,000
1894/3 As L	1,658	—	—	—	—
1894 As L	Inc. above	500	1,000	2,000	3,000
1895 As L	1,237	500	1,000	2,000	3,000

KM# 413.1 10 PESOS
16.9200 g., 0.8750 Gold .4760 oz. AGW **Mint:** Chihuahua
Reverse: Balance scale

Date	Mintage	F	VF	XF	Unc
1888 Ca M	175	—	—	7,500	—

KM# 413.2 10 PESOS
16.9200 g., 0.8750 Gold .4760 oz. AGW **Mint:** Culiacan
Reverse: Balance scale

Date	Mintage	F	VF	XF	Unc
1881Cn D	—	400	600	1,000	1,750
1882Cn D	874	400	600	1,000	1,750
1882Cn E	Inc. above	400	600	1,000	1,750
1883Cn D	221	—	—	—	—
1883Cn M	Inc. above	400	600	1,000	1,750
1884Cn D	—	400	600	1,000	1,750
1884Cn M	—	400	600	1,000	1,750
1885Cn M	1,235	400	600	1,000	1,750
1886Cn M	981	400	600	1,000	1,750
1887Cn M	2,289	400	600	1,000	1,750
1888Cn M	767	400	600	1,000	1,750
1889Cn M	859	400	600	1,000	1,750
1890Cn M	1,427	400	600	1,000	1,750
1891Cn M	670	400	600	1,000	1,750
1892Cn M	379	400	600	1,000	1,750
1893Cn M	1,806	400	600	1,000	1,750
1895Cn M	179	500	1,000	1,500	2,500

KM# 413.3 10 PESOS
16.9200 g., 0.8750 Gold .4760 oz. AGW **Mint:** Durango
Reverse: Balance scale

Date	Mintage	F	VF	XF	Unc
1872Do P	1,755	350	500	800	1,250
1873/2Do P	1,091	350	550	900	1,450
1873/2Do M/P	Inc. above	350	550	900	1,450
1874Do M	—	350	550	900	1,450
1875Do M	—	350	550	900	1,450
1876Do M	—	450	750	1,250	2,000
1877Do P	—	350	550	900	1,450
1878Do E	582	350	550	900	1,450
1879/8Do B	—	350	550	900	1,450
1879Do B	—	350	550	900	1,450
1880Do P	2,030	350	550	900	1,450
1881/79Do P	2,617	350	550	900	1,450
1882Do P Rare	1,528	—	—	—	—
1882Do C	Inc. above	350	550	900	1,450
1883Do C	793	450	750	1,250	2,000
1884Do C	108	450	750	1,250	2,000

KM# 413.4 10 PESOS
16.9200 g., 0.8750 Gold .4760 oz. AGW **Mint:** Guadalajara
Reverse: Balance scale

Date	Mintage	F	VF	XF	Unc
1870Ga C	490	500	800	1,000	1,550
1871Ga C	1,910	400	800	1,500	2,250
1872Ga C	780	500	1,000	2,000	2,500
1873Ga C	422	500	1,000	2,000	3,000
1874/3Ga C	477	500	1,000	2,000	3,000
1875Ga C	710	500	1,000	2,000	3,000
1878Ga A	183	600	1,200	2,500	3,500
1879Ga A	200	600	1,200	2,500	3,500
1880Ga S	404	500	1,000	2,000	3,000
1881Ga S	239	600	1,200	2,500	3,500
1891Ga S	196	600	1,200	2,500	3,500

KM# 413.5 10 PESOS
16.9200 g., 0.8750 Gold .4760 oz. AGW **Mint:** Guanajuato
Reverse: Balance scale

Date	Mintage	F	VF	XF	Unc
1872Go S	1,400	2,000	4,000	6,500	10,000
1887Go R Rare	80	—	—	—	—
Note: Stack's Rio Grande Sale 6-93, P/L AU realized, $12,650					
1888Go R Rare	68	—	—	—	—

KM# 413.6 10 PESOS
16.9200 g., 0.8750 Gold .4760 oz. AGW **Mint:** Hermosillo
Reverse: Balance scale

Date	Mintage	F	VF	XF	Unc
1874Ho R Rare	—	—	—	—	—
1876Ho F Rare	357	—	—	—	—
1878Ho A	814	1,750	3,000	3,500	5,500
1879Ho A	—	1,000	2,000	2,500	4,000
1880Ho A	—	1,000	2,000	2,500	4,000
1881Ho A Rare	—	—	—	—	—

KM# 413.7 10 PESOS
16.9200 g., 0.8750 Gold .4760 oz. AGW **Mint:** Mexico City
Reverse: Balance scale

Date	Mintage	F	VF	XF	Unc
1870Mo C	480	500	900	1,200	2,000
1872/1Mo M/C	2,100	350	550	900	1,350
1873Mo M	—	400	600	950	1,450
1874/3Mo M	—	400	600	950	1,450
1875Mo B/M	—	400	600	950	1,450
1876Mo B Rare	—	—	—	—	—
1878Mo M	300	400	600	950	1,450
1879Mo M	—	—	—	—	—
1881Mo M	100	500	1,000	1,600	2,500
1882Mo M	—	400	600	950	1,450
1883Mo M	100	600	1,000	1,600	2,500
1884Mo M	—	600	1,000	1,600	2,500
1885Mo M	—	400	600	950	1,450
1886Mo M	100	600	1,000	1,600	2,500
1887Mo M	100	600	1,000	1,625	2,750
1888Mo M	144	450	750	1,200	2,000
1889Mo M	88	600	1,000	1,600	2,500
1890Mo M	137	600	1,000	1,600	2,500
1891Mo M	133	600	1,000	1,600	2,500
1892Mo M	45	600	1,000	1,600	2,500
1893Mo M	1,361	350	550	900	1,350
1897Mo M	239	400	600	950	1,450
1898/7Mo M	244	425	625	1,000	1,750
1900Mo M	733	400	600	950	1,450

KM# 413.8 10 PESOS
16.9200 g., 0.8750 Gold .4760 oz. AGW **Mint:** Oaxaca **Reverse:** Balance scale

Date	Mintage	F	VF	XF	Unc
1870 Oa E	4,614	400	600	900	1,350
1871 Oa E	2,705	400	600	900	1,350
1872 Oa E	5,897	400	600	900	1,350
1873 Oa E	3,537	400	600	950	1,500
1874 Oa E	2,205	400	600	1,200	1,800
1875 Oa E	312	450	750	1,400	2,250
1876 Oa E	766	450	750	1,400	2,250
1877 Oa E	463	450	750	1,400	2,250
1878 Oa E	229	450	750	1,400	2,250
1879 Oa E	210	450	750	1,400	2,250
1880 Oa E	238	450	750	1,400	2,250
1881 Oa E	961	400	600	1,200	2,000
1882 Oa E	170	600	1,000	1,500	2,500
1883 Oa E	111	600	1,000	1,500	2,500
1884 Oa E	325	450	750	1,400	2,250
1885 Oa E	370	450	750	1,400	2,250
1886 Oa E	400	450	750	1,400	2,250
1887 Oa E	—	700	1,250	2,250	4,000
1888 Oa E	—	—	—	—	—

KM# 413.9 10 PESOS
16.9200 g., 0.8750 Gold .4760 oz. AGW **Mint:** Zacatecas
Reverse: Balance scale

Date	Mintage	F	VF	XF	Unc
1871Zs H	2,000	350	500	800	1,250
1872Zs H	3,092	300	500	750	1,150
1873Zs H	936	400	600	950	1,450
1874Zs H	—	400	600	950	1,450
1875/3Zs A	—	400	600	1,000	1,750
1876/5Zs S	—	400	600	1,000	1,750
1877Zs S/H	506	400	600	1,000	1,750
1878Zs S	711	400	600	1,000	1,750
1879/8Zs S	—	450	750	1,400	2,250
1879Zs S	—	450	750	1,400	2,250
1880Zs S	2,089	350	550	950	1,450
1881Zs S	736	400	600	1,000	1,750
1882Zs S	1,599	350	550	950	1,450
1883/2Zs S	256	400	600	1,000	1,750
1884/3Zs S	—	350	550	950	1,600
1884Zs S	—	350	550	950	1,600
1885Zs S	1,588	350	550	950	1,450
1886Zs S	5,364	350	550	950	1,450
1887Zs Z	2,330	350	550	950	1,450
1888Zs Z	4,810	350	550	950	1,450
1889Zs Z	6,154	300	500	750	1,250
1890Zs Z	1,321	350	550	950	1,450
1891Zs Z	1,930	350	550	950	1,450
1892Zs Z	1,882	350	550	950	1,450
1893Zs Z	2,899	350	550	950	1,450
1894Zs Z	2,501	350	550	950	1,450
1895Zs Z	1,217	350	550	950	1,450

KM# 414 20 PESOS
33.8400 g., 0.8750 Gold .9520 oz. AGW **Mint:** Alamos **Reverse:** Balance scale

Date	Mintage	F	VF	XF	Unc
1876 As L Rare	276	—	—	—	—
1877 As L Rare	166	—	—	—	—
1878 As L	—	—	—	—	—
1888 As L Rare	—	—	—	—	—

KM# 414.1 20 PESOS
33.8400 g., 0.8750 Gold .9520 oz. AGW **Mint:** Chihuahua
Reverse: Balance scale **Note:** Mint mark CH, Ca.

Date	Mintage	F	VF	XF	Unc
1872 M	995	500	700	1,000	2,500
1873 M	950	500	700	1,000	2,500
1874 M	1,116	450	675	950	2,500
1875 M	750	500	700	1,000	2,500
1876 M	600	500	800	1,250	2,750
1877 Rare	55	—	—	—	—
1882 M	1,758	450	675	950	2,500
1883 M	161	600	1,000	1,500	3,000
1884 M	496	500	700	1,000	2,500
1885 M	122	600	1,000	1,500	3,000
1887 M	550	500	700	1,000	2,500
1888 M	351	500	700	1,000	2,500
1889 M	464	500	700	1,000	2,500
1890 M	1,209	450	675	950	2,500
1891 M	2,004	425	650	900	2,250
1893 M	418	500	700	950	2,500
1895 M	133	600	1,000	1,500	3,000

KM# 414.2 20 PESOS
33.8400 g., 0.8750 Gold .9520 oz. AGW **Mint:** Culiacan
Reverse: Balance scale

Date	Mintage	F	VF	XF	Unc
1870Cn E	3,749	450	675	950	2,000
1871Cn P	3,046	450	675	950	2,000
1872Cn P	972	450	675	950	2,000
1873Cn P	1,317	450	675	950	2,000
1874Cn P	—	450	675	950	2,000
1875Cn P	—	600	1,200	1,800	2,500
1876Cn P	—	450	675	950	2,000
1876Cn G	—	450	675	950	2,000
1877Cn G	167	600	1,000	1,500	3,000
1878Cn Rare	842	—	—	—	—
1881/0Cn D	2,039	—	—	—	—
1881Cn D	Inc. above	450	675	950	2,000
1882/1Cn D	736	450	675	950	2,000
1883Cn M	1,836	450	675	950	2,000
1884Cn M	—	450	675	950	2,000
1885Cn M	544	450	675	950	2,000
1886Cn M	882	450	675	950	2,000
1887Cn M	837	450	675	950	2,000
1888Cn M	473	450	675	950	2,000
1889Cn M	1,376	450	675	950	2,000

Date	Mintage	F	VF	XF	Unc
1890Cn M	—	450	675	950	2,000
1891Cn M	237	500	900	1,200	2,250
1892Cn M	526	450	675	950	2,000
1893Cn M	2,062	450	675	950	2,000
1894Cn M	4,516	450	675	950	2,000
1895Cn M	3,193	450	675	950	2,000
1896Cn M	4,072	450	675	950	2,000
1897/6Cn M	959	450	675	950	2,000
1897Cn M	Inc. above	450	675	950	2,000
1898Cn M	1,660	450	675	950	2,000
1899Cn M	1,243	450	675	950	2,000
1899Cn Q	Inc. above	500	900	1,200	2,250
1900Cn Q	1,558	450	675	950	2,000

KM# 414.3 20 PESOS

33.8400 g., 0.8750 Gold .9520 oz. AGW **Mint:** Durango
Reverse: Balance scale

Date	Mintage	F	VF	XF	Unc
1870Do P	416	1,000	1,500	2,000	2,500
1871/0Do P	1,073	1,000	1,750	2,250	2,750
1871Do P	Inc. above	1,000	1,500	2,000	2,500
1872/1Do PT	—	1,500	3,000	4,500	7,000
1876Do M	—	1,000	1,500	2,000	2,500
1877Do P	94	1,500	2,250	2,750	3,250
1878Do Rare	258	—	—	—	—

KM# 414.4 20 PESOS

33.8400 g., 0.8750 Gold .9520 oz. AGW **Mint:** Guanajuato
Reverse: Balance scale

Date	Mintage	F	VF	XF	Unc
1870Go S	3,250	425	650	900	1,500
1871Go S	20,000	425	650	900	1,500
1872Go S	18,000	425	650	900	1,500
1873Go S	7,000	425	650	900	1,500
1874Go S	—	425	650	900	1,500
1875Go S	—	425	650	900	1,500
1876Go S	—	425	650	900	1,500
1876Go M/S	—	—	—	—	—
1877Go M/S Rare	15,000	—	—	—	—
1877Go R	Inc. above	425	650	900	1,500
1877Go S Rare	Inc. above	—	—	—	—
1878/7Go M/S	13,000	650	1,250	2,000	2,800
1878Go M	Inc. above	650	1,250	2,000	2,800
1878Go S	Inc. above	425	650	900	1,500
1879Go S	8,202	500	800	1,200	2,300
1880Go S	7,375	425	650	900	1,500
1881Go S	4,909	425	650	900	1,500
1882Go S	4,020	425	650	900	1,500
1883/2Go B	3,705	500	750	1,150	2,250
1883Go B	Inc. above	425	650	900	1,500
1884Go B	1,798	425	650	900	1,500
1885Go R	2,660	425	650	900	1,500
1886Go R	1,090	550	800	1,250	2,500
1887Go R	1,009	550	800	1,250	2,500
1888Go R	1,011	550	800	1,250	2,500
1889Go R	956	550	800	1,250	2,500
1890Go R	879	550	800	1,250	2,500
1891Go R	818	550	800	1,250	2,500
1892Go R	730	550	800	1,250	2,500
1893Go R	3,343	425	650	1,000	2,000
1894/3Go R	6,734	425	650	900	1,500
1894Go R	Inc. above	425	650	900	1,500
1895/3Go R	7,118	425	650	900	1,500
1895Go R	Inc. above	425	650	900	1,500
1896Go R	9,219	425	650	900	1,500
1897/6Go R	6,781	425	650	900	1,500
1897Go R	Inc. above	425	650	900	1,500
1898Go R	7,710	425	650	900	1,500
1899Go R	8,527	425	650	900	1,500
1900Go R	4,512	550	800	1,250	2,350

KM# 414.5 20 PESOS

33.8400 g., 0.8750 Gold .9520 oz. AGW **Mint:** Hermosillo
Reverse: Balance scale

Date	F	VF	XF	Unc
1874Ho R Rare	—	—	—	—
1875Ho R Rare	—	—	—	—
1876Ho F Rare	—	—	—	—
1888Ho g Rare	—	—	—	—

KM# 414.6 20 PESOS

33.8400 g., 0.8750 Gold .9520 oz. AGW **Mint:** Mexico City
Reverse: Balance scale

Date	Mintage	F	VF	XF	Unc
1870Mo C	14,000	420	600	850	1,450
1871Mo M	21,000	420	600	850	1,450
1872/1Mo M	11,000	420	600	850	1,600
1872Mo M	Inc. above	420	600	850	1,450
1873Mo M	5,600	420	600	850	1,450
1874/2Mo M	—	420	600	850	1,450
1874/2Mo B	—	450	700	1,000	1,600
1875Mo B	—	435	650	900	1,500
1876Mo B	—	435	650	900	1,500
1876Mo M Reported, not confirmed	—	—	—	—	—
1877Mo M	2,000	450	700	1,100	2,000
1878Mo M	7,000	435	650	900	1,500
1879Mo M	—	435	650	900	1,750
1880Mo M	—	435	650	900	1,750
1881/0Mo M	11,000	425	600	850	1,450
1881Mo M	Inc. above	425	600	850	1,450
1882/1Mo M	5,800	425	600	850	1,450
1882Mo M	Inc. above	425	600	850	1,450
1883/1Mo M	4,000	425	600	850	1,450
1883Mo M	Inc. above	425	600	850	1,450
1884/3Mo M	—	435	650	900	1,500
1884Mo M	—	435	650	900	1,500
1885Mo M	6,000	435	650	900	1,750
1886Mo M	10,000	420	600	850	1,450
1887Mo M	12,000	600	800	1,500	2,500
1888Mo M	7,300	420	600	850	1,450
1889Mo M	6,477	420	600	900	1,650
1890Mo M	7,852	420	600	850	1,500
1891/0Mo M	8,725	420	600	850	1,500
1891Mo M	Inc. above	420	600	850	1,500
1892Mo M	11,000	420	600	850	1,450
1893Mo M	15,000	420	600	850	1,450
1894Mo M	14,000	420	600	850	1,450
1895Mo M	13,000	420	600	850	1,450
1896Mo B	14,000	420	600	850	1,450
1897/6Mo M	12,000	420	600	850	1,450
1897Mo M	Inc. above	420	600	850	1,450
1898Mo M	20,000	420	600	850	1,450
1899Mo M	23,000	420	600	850	1,450
1900Mo M	21,000	420	600	850	1,450

KM# 414.7 20 PESOS

33.8400 g., 0.8750 Gold .9520 oz. AGW **Mint:** Oaxaca **Reverse:** Balance scale

Date	Mintage	F	VF	XF	Unc
1870 Oa E	1,131	750	1,500	2,500	5,000
1871 Oa E	1,591	750	1,500	2,500	5,000
1872 Oa E	255	1,000	1,750	3,000	7,000
1888 Oa E	170	2,000	3,000	5,000	—

KM# 414.8 20 PESOS

33.8400 g., 0.8750 Gold .9520 oz. AGW **Mint:** Zacatecas
Reverse: Balance scale

Date	Mintage	F	VF	XF	Unc
1871Zs H	1,000	3,500	6,500	7,000	9,000
1875Zs A	—	4,000	6,000	7,500	9,500
1878Zs S	441	4,000	6,000	7,500	9,500
1888Zs Z Rare	50	—	—	—	—
1889Zs Z	640	3,500	5,500	7,000	9,000

PRIVATE COINAGE - 1838 LIBERTY HEAD ISSUE

KM# NC1 1/4 REAL (Una Quartilla)

Brass **Issuer:** Chihuahua **Mint:** Chihuahua

Date	F	VF	XF	Unc
1838CA	—	250	500	850

KM# NC1a 1/4 REAL (Una Quartilla)

Silver **Issuer:** Chihuahua **Mint:** Chihuahua

Date	F	VF	XF	Unc
1838CA	—	500	1,000	1,500

KM# NC2 1/4 REAL (Una Quartilla)

Copper **Issuer:** Chihuahua **Mint:** Chihuahua

Date	F	VF	XF	Unc
1838	—	250	500	850

KM# NC2a 1/4 REAL (Una Quartilla)

Brass **Issuer:** Chihuahua **Mint:** Chihuahua

Date	F	VF	XF	Unc
1838	—	250	500	850

KM# NC3 1/4 REAL (Una Quartilla)

Brass **Issuer:** Durango **Mint:** Durango

Date	F	VF	XF	Unc
1838Do	—	250	500	850

KM# NC4 1/4 REAL (Una Quartilla)

Brass **Issuer:** Guadalajara **Mint:** Guadalajara

Date	F	VF	XF	Unc
1838Ga	—	250	500	850

KM# NC5 1/4 REAL (Una Quartilla)

Brass **Issuer:** Guanajuato **Mint:** Guanajuato

Date	F	VF	XF	Unc
1838Go	—	250	500	850

KM# NC6 1/4 REAL (Una Quartilla)

Brass **Issuer:** Mexico City **Mint:** Mexico City

Date	F	VF	XF	Unc
1838Mo	—	175	375	750

KM# NC7 1/4 REAL (Una Quartilla)
Brass **Issuer:** Mexico City **Mint:** Mexico City

Date	F	VF	XF	Unc
1838Mo	—	175	375	750

KM# NC8 1/4 REAL (Una Quartilla)
Brass **Issuer:** Mexico City **Mint:** Mexico City **Reverse:** Column with flying eagle above in wreath

Date	F	VF	XF	Unc
1838	—	250	500	850

KM# NC9 1/4 REAL (Una Quartilla)
Brass **Issuer:** San Luis Potosi **Mint:** San Luis Potosi

Date	F	VF	XF	Unc
1838SLP	—	250	500	850

KM# NC10 1/4 REAL (Una Quartilla)
Copper **Issuer:** Tuxtla

Date	F	VF	XF	Unc
1838	—	30.00	60.00	100

KM# NC11 1/4 REAL (Una Quartilla)
Brass **Issuer:** Zacatecas **Mint:** Zacatecas

Date	F	VF	XF	Unc
1838Zs	—	250	500	850

KM# NC11a 1/4 REAL (Una Quartilla)
Silver **Issuer:** Zacatecas **Mint:** Zacatecas

Date	F	VF	XF	Unc
1838Zs	—	500	1,000	1,500

PRIVATE COINAGE - 1890 LIBERTY HEAD ISSUE

KM# NC12 2 CENTAVOS
Bronze **Issuer:** Campeche **Note:** Struck by the firm of L. Chr. Lauer, Nurnberg, Germany.

Date	F	VF	XF	Unc
1890	—	20.00	40.00	70.00

KM# NC12a 2 CENTAVOS
Copper Nickel **Issuer:** Campeche **Note:** Struck by the firm of L. Chr. Lauer, Nurnberg, Germany.

Date	F	VF	XF	Unc
1890	—	50.00	100	150

KM# NC13 2 CENTAVOS
Bronze **Issuer:** Coahuila **Note:** Similar to NC15. Struck by the firm of L. Chr. Lauer, Nurnberg, Germany.

Date	F	VF	XF	Unc
1890	—	20.00	40.00	70.00

KM# NC13a 2 CENTAVOS
Copper-Nickel **Issuer:** Coahuila **Note:** Similar to NC15. Struck by the firm of L. Chr. Lauer, Nurnberg, Germany.

Date	F	VF	XF	Unc
1890	—	50.00	100	150

KM# NC14 2 CENTAVOS
Bronze **Issuer:** Mexico **Note:** Similar to NC15. Struck by the firm of L. Chr. Lauer, Nurnberg, Germany.

Date	F	VF	XF	Unc
1890	—	20.00	40.00	70.00

KM# NC14a 2 CENTAVOS
Copper-Nickel **Issuer:** Mexico **Note:** Similar to NC15. Struck by the firm of L. Chr. Lauer, Nurnberg, Germany.

Date	F	VF	XF	Unc
1890	—	50.00	100	150

KM# NC15 2 CENTAVOS
Bronze **Issuer:** Nuevo Leon **Note:** Struck by the firm of L. Chr. Lauer, Nurnberg, Germany.

Date	F	VF	XF	Unc
1890	—	20.00	40.00	70.00

KM# NC15a 2 CENTAVOS
Copper-Nickel **Issuer:** Nuevo Leon **Note:** Struck by the firm of L. Chr. Lauer, Nurnberg, Germany.

Date	F	VF	XF	Unc
1890	—	50.00	100	150

KM# NC16 2 CENTAVOS
Bronze **Issuer:** Puebla **Note:** Struck by the firm of L. Chr. Lauer, Nurnberg, Germany.

Date	F	VF	XF	Unc
1890	—	20.00	40.00	70.00

KM# NC16a 2 CENTAVOS
Copper-Nickel **Issuer:** Puebla **Note:** Struck by the firm of L. Chr. Lauer, Nurnberg, Germany.

Date	F	VF	XF	Unc
1890	—	50.00	100	150

KM# NC17 2 CENTAVOS
Bronze **Issuer:** Queretaro **Note:** Struck by the firm of L. Chr. Lauer, Nurnberg, Germany.

Date	F	VF	XF	Unc
1890	—	20.00	40.00	70.00

KM# NC17a 2 CENTAVOS
Copper-Nickel **Issuer:** Queretaro **Note:** Struck by the firm of L. Chr. Lauer, Nurnberg, Germany.

Date	F	VF	XF	Unc
1890	—	50.00	100	150

KM# NC18 2 CENTAVOS
Bronze **Issuer:** San Luis Potosi **Note:** Struck by the firm of L. Chr. Lauer, Nurnberg, Germany.

Date	F	VF	XF	Unc
1890	—	20.00	40.00	70.00

KM# NC18a 2 CENTAVOS
Copper-Nickel **Issuer:** San Luis Potosi **Note:** Struck by the firm of L. Chr. Lauer, Nurnberg, Germany.

Date	F	VF	XF	Unc
1890	—	50.00	100	150

KM# NC19 2 CENTAVOS
Bronze **Issuer:** Tlaxcala **Note:** Struck by the firm of L. Chr. Lauer, Nurnberg, Germany.

Date	F	VF	XF	Unc
1890	—	20.00	40.00	70.00

KM# NC19a 2 CENTAVOS
Copper-Nickel **Issuer:** Tlaxcala **Note:** Struck by the firm of L. Chr. Lauer, Nurnberg, Germany.

Date	F	VF	XF	Unc
1890	—	50.00	100	150

KM# NC20 2 CENTAVOS
Bronze **Issuer:** Zacatecas **Note:** Struck by the firm of L. Chr. Lauer, Nurnberg, Germany.

Date	F	VF	XF	Unc
1890	—	20.00	40.00	70.00

KM# NC20a 2 CENTAVOS
Copper-Nickel **Issuer:** Zacatecas **Note:** Struck by the firm of L. Chr. Lauer, Nurnberg, Germany.

Date	F	VF	XF	Unc
1890	—	50.00	100	150

KM# NC21 2 CENTAVOS
Bronze **Subject:** 80th Anniversary of Independence **Note:** Medallic Issue.

Date	F	VF	XF	Unc
1890	—	40.00	80.00	120

KM# NC21a 2 CENTAVOS
Silvered Bronze **Subject:** 80th Anniversary of Independence **Note:** Medallic Issue.

Date	F	VF	XF	Unc
1890	—	65.00	125	180

KM# NC21b 2 CENTAVOS
Copper-Nickel **Subject:** 80th Anniversary of Independence **Note:** Medallic Issue.

Date	F	VF	XF	Unc
1890	—	100	200	250

PRIVATE COINAGE - REPUBLIC OF NORTH MEXICO

KM# NC22 2 CENTS

Bronze **Note:** Medallic Issue.

Date	F	VF	XF	Unc
1890	—	75.00	150	225

PRIVATE COINAGE - REPUBLIC OF THE RIO GRANDE

KM# NC23 2 CENTS

Bronze **Note:** Medallic Issue.

Date	F	VF	XF	Unc
1890	—	100	200	300

PATTERNS

Including off metal strikes

KM#	Date	Mintage	Identification	Mkt Val
Pn1	1822Mo	—	8 Reales. Lead. Iturbide.	—

KM#	Date	Mintage	Identification	Mkt Val
Pn2	1823Mo	—	8 Reales. Silver.	—

Note: Christie's Norweb Sale 11-85, EF realized $11,550.

KM#	Date	Mintage	Identification	Mkt Val
Pn3	1823Mo	—	8 Reales. Silver.	—
Pn4	1823Mo	—	8 Reales. Copper.	—
Pn5	1823Mo	—	8 Reales. Silver.	—
Pn6	1823Mo	—	8 Escudos. Silver.	—
Pn7	1823Mo	—	8 Escudos. Brass.	—
Pn8	1824Do	—	1/8 Real. Silver.	—
Pn9	1825Zs	—	1/8 Real. Silver.	—
Pn10	1826Go	—	8 Reales. Sterling Silver.	9,000
Pn11	1826Go	—	8 Escudos. Gold.	—

KM#	Date	Mintage	Identification	Mkt Val
Pn12	1827Go	—	8 Reales. Sterling Silver.	9,000

KM#	Date	Mintage	Identification	Mkt Val
Pn13	1828 Pi	—	8 Reales. Silver.	—
Pn14	1828	—	1/8 Real. Gold.	—
Pn15	1828	—	1/4 Real. Silver.	—
Pn16	1828	—	1/4 Real. Silver.	—

KM#	Date	Mintage	Identification	Mkt Val
Pn17	1828	—	1/4 Real. Copper.	400
Pn18	1828Go	—	1/4 Real. Silver.	2,650
Pn19	1829Go	—	1/8 Real. Silver.	—

KM#	Date	Mintage	Identification	Mkt Val
Pn20	1829 Pi	—	8 Reales. Silver.	3,000
Pn21	1829	—	8 Reales. Bronze.	1,150
Pn22	183xG	—	8 Reales. Silver.	2,000
Pn23	183xG	—	8 Reales. Silver.	—
Pn24	183x	—	8 Reales. Copper.	1,250

KM#	Date	Mintage	Identification	Mkt Val
Pn25	1831Do	—	8 Reales. Silver Plated Bronze.	900
Pn26	1831Do	—	Escudo. Gilt Bronze.	650
Pn27	1831G	—	8 Escudos. Silver.	3,000
Pn28	1831	—	8 Escudos. Copper.	1,550
Pn29	1832	—	1/8 Real. Silver.	—
Pn30	1832Zs	—	1/4 Real. Silver.	—
Pn31	1832Do	—	2 Reales. Silver Plated Bronze. Eagle. Liberty cap	550
Pn32	1832Do	—	2 Escudos. Gilt Bronze. Eagle. Liberty cap	550

KM#	Date	Mintage	Identification	Mkt Val
Pn33	1832	—	2 Escudos. Brass. Eagle. Liberty cap	650

KM#	Date	Mintage	Identification	Mkt Val
Pn34	1832Do	—	4 Escudos. Gilt Bronze.	1,550
Pn35	1832Do	—	4 Escudos. Brass.	1,550

KM#	Date	Mintage	Identification	Mkt Val
Pn36	1832Do	—	8 Escudos. Gilt Bronze.	750
Pn37	1832Do	—	8 Escudos. Brass.	750
Pn38	1832Do	—	8 Escudos. Bronze.	750
Pn39	1832Do	—	8 Escudos. Copper.	750
Pn40	1833Zs	—	1/8 Real. Silver.	—
Pn41	1833Zs	—	1/4 Real. Silver.	—

KM#	Date	Mintage	Identification	Mkt Val
Pn42	1833Do	—	1/2 Real. Silver Plated Bronze.	350
Pn43	1833	—	1/2 Real. Silver.	500

KM#	Date	Mintage	Identification	Mkt Val
Pn44	1833Do	—	Real. Silver Plated Bronze.	500
Pn45	1833Do	—	Real. White Metal.	500
Pn46	1833/2Do	—	1/2 Escudo. Gilt Bronze. Eagle. Hand holding Liberty cap	700

KM#	Date	Mintage	Identification	Mkt Val
Pn47	1833Do	—	1/2 Escudo. Brass.	675
Pn48	1834Mo	—	1/4 Real. Silver.	—

KM#	Date	Mintage	Identification	Mkt Val
Pn49	1834Zs	—	Real. Silver.	1,500

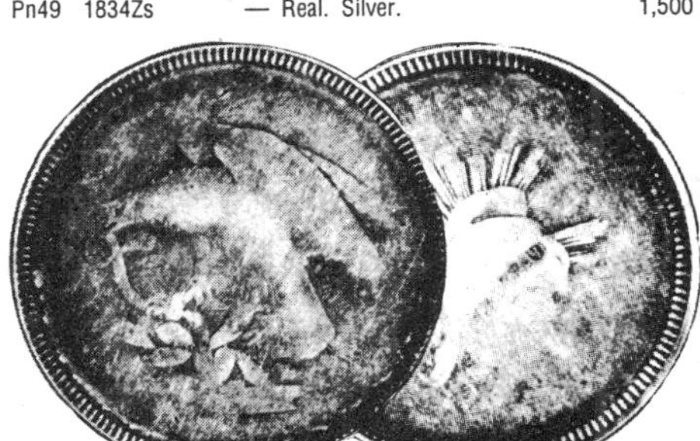

KM#	Date	Mintage	Identification	Mkt Val
Pn50	1834Zs	—	8 Reales. Copper.	3,500
Pn51	1834Zs	—	8 Reales. Silver. Reeded edge	12,500
Pn52	1835/4Mo	—	4 Escudos. Copper.	—

KM#	Date	Mintage	Identification	Mkt Val
Pn53	1836	—	1/4 Real. Copper.	350
Pn54	1836Do	—	1/2 Real. Silver.	250
Pn55	1836Do	—	1/2 Real. Silver.	250
Pn56	1836G	—	8 Reales. Copper.	—
Pn57	1836Do	—	8 Reales. Silver.	1,500
Pn59	1840Do	—	8 Reales. Silver Plated Bronze.	—
PnA58	184x	—	8 Reales. Copper.	1,000
Pn58	1840Do	—	8 Reales. White Metal.	1,250
Pn60	1841	—	Centavo. Copper.	1,000
Pn61	1842Mo	—	Peso. Silver. Eagle. Liberty cap on pole	—

KM#	Date	Mintage	Identification	Mkt Val
Pn62	1843Go	—	8 Reales. Copper.	3,550
Pn63	1843	—	8 Reales. Silver.	1,350
Pn64	1843Mo	—	8 Reales. Copper. Plain edge	1,250
Pn65	1843Mo	—	8 Reales. Copper. Reeded edge	1,350
Pn66	1843Zs	—	8 Reales. Silver.	3,000
Pn67	1844Go	—	8 Reales. Copper.	1,250
Pn68	1844Mo	—	8 Reales. Copper. Eagle on cactus. Radiant Liberty cap	—
Pn69	1844Zs	—	8 Reales. Copper.	—
Pn71	1846Zs	—	1/8 Real. Silver.	—
Pn72	1846Zs	—	1/4 Real. Silver.	—
Pn73	1848Mo	—	2 Escudos. Copper.	—
Pn74	1854C	—	8 Reales. Copper.	1,250
Pn75	1854C	—	8 Escudos. Copper.	—
Pn76	1856Go	—	1/8 Real. White Metal.	—
Pn77	1856	—	1/8 Real. Silver.	—
Pn78	1856Mo	—	1/2 Escudo. Silver.	450
Pn79	1857	—	1/8 Real. Silver.	650
Pn80	1857Zs	—	Escudo. Silver.	—
Pn81	1860Mo	—	1/2 Escudo. Copper.	—
Pn82	1861C	—	1/4 Real. Copper.	900
Pn83	NULL	—	8 Escudos. Silver.	500
Pn84	1862Zs	—	1/8 Real. Silver.	—
Pn85	1862 Pi	—	1/4 Real. Silver.	800
Pn86	1862Mo	—	Centavo. Copper.	1,000
Pn87	1862Mo	—	Centavo. Silver.	1,500
Pn88	1862Mo	—	Centavo. Silver Plated Copper.	1,000

KM#	Date	Mintage	Identification	Mkt Val
Pn89	1863Mo	—	1/8 Real. Silver.	—
Pn90	1863Mo	—	Centavo. Lead.	350
Pn91	1863Mo	—	Centavo. White Metal.	—
Pn92	1863Mo	—	Centavo. Silver.	—
Pn93	1863Mo	—	Centavo. Copper. Plain edge	—
Pn94	1863Mo	—	5 Centavos. Silver. Eagle on cactus. Liberty cap	2,000
Pn95	1863Mo	—	10 Centavos. Silver.	2,000
Pn96	1864Mo	—	Centavo. Silver Plated Copper.	—
Pn97	1865Ho	—	8 Escudos. Silver.	—
Pn98	1866Mo	—	50 Centavos. White Metal.	—
Pn99	1866Mo	—	50 Centavos. Silver.	2,500
Pn100	1866Mo	—	Peso. Silver. Small letters	2,000
Pn101	1866Mo	—	Peso. Silver Plated Copper.	900
Pn102	1866Mo	—	Peso. Copper-Nickel.	1,500
Pn103	1866Mo	—	Peso. Copper.	1,250
Pn104	1866Mo	—	Peso. Copper.	1,250
Pn105	1866Mo	—	Peso. Lead.	—
Pn106	1866Mo	—	20 Pesos. Gilt Copper.	—
Pn107	1868Mo	—	Centavo. Copper.	1,500
Pn108	1868Mo	—	5 Centavos. Silver. Value in branches	—
Pn109	1868Mo	—	10 Centavos. Silver. Value in branches	—

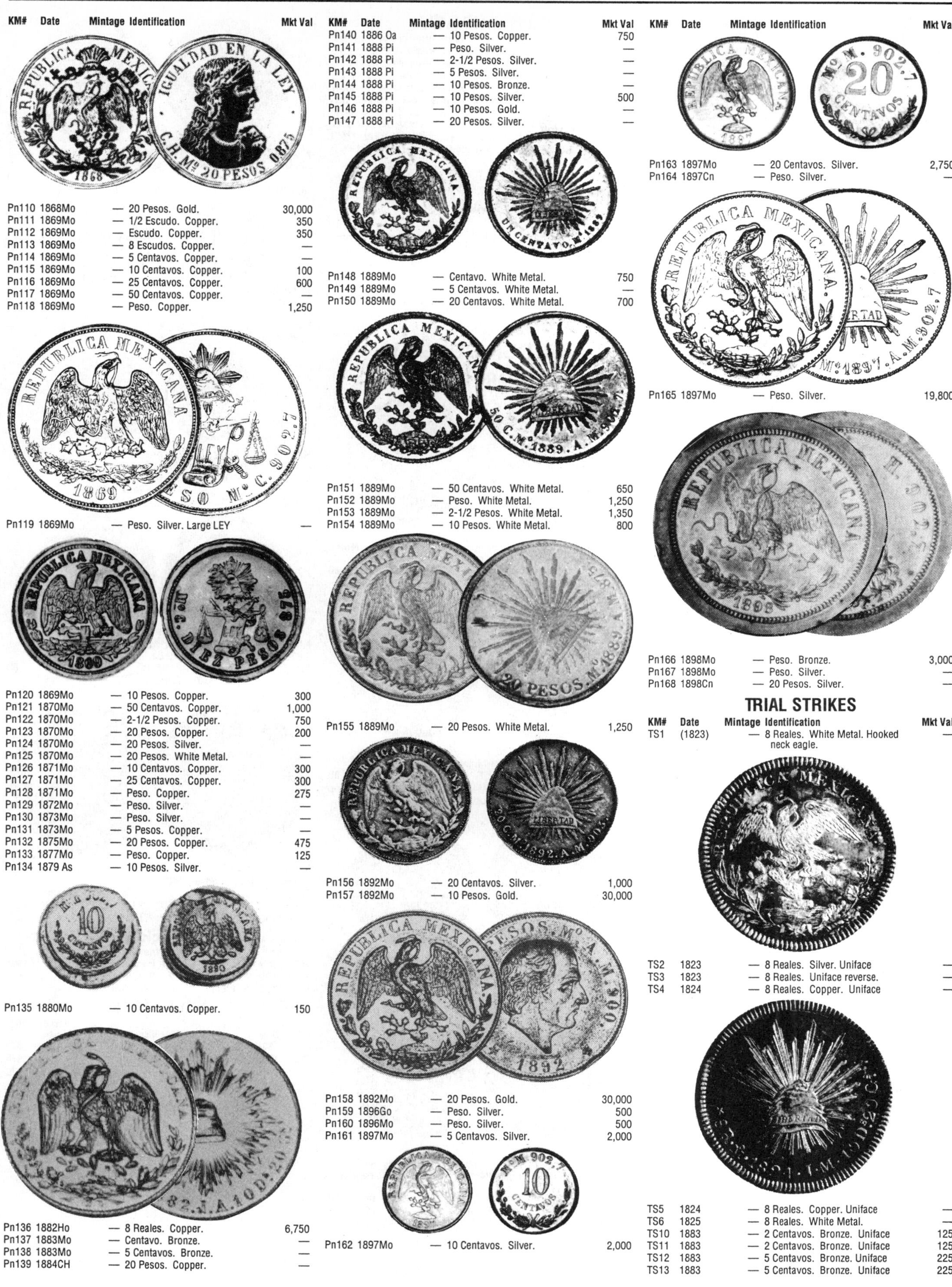

KM#	Date	Mintage	Identification	Mkt Val
Pn110	1868Mo	—	20 Pesos. Gold.	30,000
Pn111	1869Mo	—	1/2 Escudo. Copper.	350
Pn112	1869Mo	—	Escudo. Copper.	350
Pn113	1869Mo	—	8 Escudos. Copper.	—
Pn114	1869Mo	—	5 Centavos. Copper.	—
Pn115	1869Mo	—	10 Centavos. Copper.	100
Pn116	1869Mo	—	25 Centavos. Copper.	600
Pn117	1869Mo	—	50 Centavos. Copper.	—
Pn118	1869Mo	—	Peso. Copper.	1,250
Pn119	1869Mo	—	Peso. Silver. Large LEY	—
Pn120	1869Mo	—	10 Pesos. Copper.	300
Pn121	1870Mo	—	50 Centavos. Copper.	1,000
Pn122	1870Mo	—	2-1/2 Pesos. Copper.	750
Pn123	1870Mo	—	20 Pesos. Copper.	200
Pn124	1870Mo	—	20 Pesos. Silver.	—
Pn125	1870Mo	—	20 Pesos. White Metal.	—
Pn126	1871Mo	—	10 Centavos. Copper.	300
Pn127	1871Mo	—	25 Centavos. Copper.	300
Pn128	1871Mo	—	Peso. Copper.	275
Pn129	1872Mo	—	Peso. Silver.	—
Pn130	1873Mo	—	Peso. Silver.	—
Pn131	1873Mo	—	5 Pesos. Copper.	—
Pn132	1875Mo	—	20 Pesos. Copper.	475
Pn133	1877Mo	—	Peso. Copper.	125
Pn134	1879 As	—	10 Pesos. Silver.	—
Pn135	1880Mo	—	10 Centavos. Copper.	150
Pn136	1882Ho	—	8 Reales. Copper.	6,750
Pn137	1883Mo	—	Centavo. Bronze.	—
Pn138	1883Mo	—	5 Centavos. Bronze.	—
Pn139	1884CH	—	20 Pesos. Copper.	—

KM#	Date	Mintage	Identification	Mkt Val
Pn140	1886 Oa	—	10 Pesos. Copper.	750
Pn141	1888 Pi	—	Peso. Silver.	—
Pn142	1888 Pi	—	2-1/2 Pesos. Silver.	—
Pn143	1888 Pi	—	5 Pesos. Silver.	—
Pn144	1888 Pi	—	10 Pesos. Bronze.	—
Pn145	1888 Pi	—	10 Pesos. Silver.	500
Pn146	1888 Pi	—	10 Pesos. Gold.	—
Pn147	1888 Pi	—	20 Pesos. Silver.	—
Pn148	1889Mo	—	Centavo. White Metal.	750
Pn149	1889Mo	—	5 Centavos. White Metal.	—
Pn150	1889Mo	—	20 Centavos. White Metal.	700
Pn151	1889Mo	—	50 Centavos. White Metal.	650
Pn152	1889Mo	—	Peso. White Metal.	1,250
Pn153	1889Mo	—	2-1/2 Pesos. White Metal.	1,350
Pn154	1889Mo	—	10 Pesos. White Metal.	800
Pn155	1889Mo	—	20 Pesos. White Metal.	1,250
Pn156	1892Mo	—	20 Centavos. Silver.	1,000
Pn157	1892Mo	—	10 Pesos. Gold.	30,000
Pn158	1892Mo	—	20 Pesos. Gold.	30,000
Pn159	1896Go	—	Peso. Silver.	500
Pn160	1896Mo	—	Peso. Silver.	500
Pn161	1897Mo	—	5 Centavos. Silver.	2,000
Pn162	1897Mo	—	10 Centavos. Silver.	2,000
Pn163	1897Mo	—	20 Centavos. Silver.	2,750
Pn164	1897Cn	—	Peso. Silver.	—
Pn165	1897Mo	—	Peso. Silver.	19,800
Pn166	1898Mo	—	Peso. Bronze.	3,000
Pn167	1898Mo	—	Peso. Silver.	—
Pn168	1898Cn	—	20 Pesos. Silver.	—

TRIAL STRIKES

KM#	Date	Mintage	Identification	Mkt Val
TS1	(1823)	—	8 Reales. White Metal. Hooked neck eagle.	—
TS2	1823	—	8 Reales. Silver. Uniface	—
TS3	1823	—	8 Reales. Uniface reverse.	—
TS4	1824	—	8 Reales. Copper. Uniface	—
TS5	1824	—	8 Reales. Copper. Uniface	—
TS6	1825	—	8 Reales. White Metal.	—
TS10	1883	—	2 Centavos. Bronze. Uniface	125
TS11	1883	—	2 Centavos. Bronze. Uniface	125
TS12	1883	—	5 Centavos. Bronze. Uniface	225
TS13	1883	—	5 Centavos. Bronze. Uniface	225

MOLDAVIA & WALLACHIA

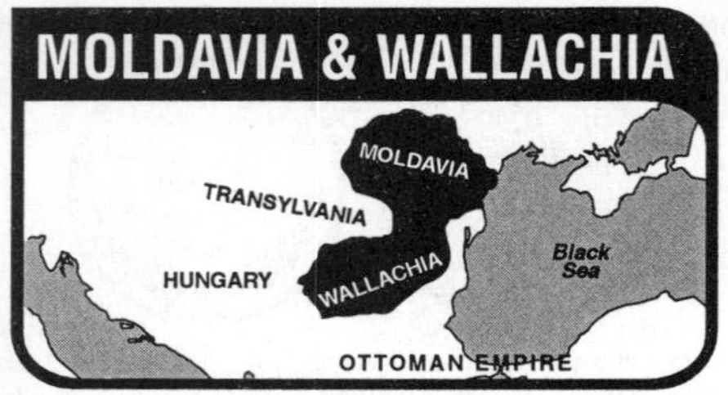

These two principalities have constituted the base of modern Romania. Wallachia and Moldova were established early in the 14th century. Following some wars against Hungarian kings, both principalities became independent.

Union of the principalities was voted for unanimously in 1848 and the two assemblies elected a prince in the person of Alexander Cuza on Jan. 17, 1859, accomplishing the de facto union of Romania. The prince, through lack of agrarian reform, was compelled to abdicate in Feb. 1866, and was succeeded by Prince Carol I who later became King in 1881.

PATTERNS

Including off metal strikes

KM#	Date	Mintage	Identification	Mkt Val
Pn11	1860	—	5 Parale. Bronze. Mantled arms.	—
Pn12	1864	—	5 Satimi. Bronze. head of Ion Cuza.	—
Pn13	1864	—	10 Satimi. Bronze.	—

MOMBASA

Mombasa was a thriving Arabic commercial center when first visited by Portuguese navigator Vasco da Gama in 1498. During the following two centuries Portugal made repeated efforts to capture the island stronghold but was unable to hold it against the assaults of the Muscat Arabs. In 1823 the ruling Mazuri family placed the city under British protection. Britain repudiated the protectorate and it was then seized by Seyyid Said of Oman, 1837, and annexed to Zanzibar. In 1887 the sultan of Zanzibar relinquished the port of Mombasa to British administration. It was occupied by the Imperial British East Africa Company and for the following two decades was the capital of British East Africa.

TITLES

ممباسه

Mombasa

MINT MARKS

H – Birmingham

C/M – Calcutta

MONETARY SYSTEM

4 Pice = 1 Anna

16 Annas = 1 Rupee

BRITISH COLONY

STANDARD COINAGE

KM# 1.1 PICE

Bronze, 24.9 mm. **Obv:** Small letters **Rev:** Small letters **Note:** Varieties in planchet thickness exist.

Date	Mintage	F	VF	XF	Unc	BU
1888//AH1306C/M	630,000	1.00	2.50	8.00	25.00	—
1888//AH1306C/M Proof	—	Value: 150				

KM# 1.2 PICE

Bronze, 25.4 mm. **Obv:** Small letters **Rev:** Medium letters

Date	Mintage	F	VF	XF	Unc	BU
1888//AH1306C/M	Inc. above	0.75	2.00	7.00	22.00	—
1888//AH1306C/M Proof	—	Value: 200				

KM# 1.3 PICE

Bronze **Obv:** Medium letters **Rev:** Medium letters

Date	Mintage	F	VF	XF	Unc	BU
1888//AH1306H	2,352,000	0.50	1.25	5.00	16.50	—
1888//AH1306H Proof	—	Value: 125				

KM# 1.4 PICE

Bronze, 24.9 mm. **Obv:** Large letters without serifs, dots between words **Rev:** Large letters without serifs, dots between words

Date	Mintage	F	VF	XF	Unc	BU
1888//AH1306H	Inc. above	0.35	1.00	4.00	13.50	—
1888//AH1306H Proof	—	Value: 100				

KM# 1.5 PICE

Bronze **Obv:** Medium letters **Rev:** Medium letters

Date	Mintage	F	VF	XF	Unc	BU
1888//AH1306C/M	Inc. above	0.75	2.00	7.00	22.00	—

KM# 2 2 ANNAS

1.4600 g., 0.9170 Silver .0430 oz.

Date	Mintage	F	VF	XF	Unc	BU
1890H	16,000	12.00	20.00	40.00	85.00	—
1890H Proof	—	Value: 125				

KM# 3 1/4 RUPEE (4 Annas)

2.9200 g., 0.9170 Silver .0860 oz.

Date	Mintage	F	VF	XF	Unc	BU
1890H	12,000	15.00	28.00	55.00	115	—
1890H Proof	—	Value: 150				

KM# 4 1/2 RUPEE (8 Annas)

5.8300 g., 0.9170 Silver .1719 oz.

Date	Mintage	F	VF	XF	Unc	BU
1890H	10,000	20.00	45.00	85.00	165	—
1890H Proof	—	Value: 200				

KM# 5 RUPEE

11.6600 g., 0.9170 Silver .3438 oz.

Date	Mintage	F	VF	XF	Unc	BU
1888H	94,000	12.00	28.00	60.00	145	—
1888H Proof	—	Value: 275				

PATTERNS

Including off metal strikes

KM#	Date	Mintage	Identification	Mkt Val
Pn1	1888//AH1306H	—	Pice. Silver. KM#1.4.	350
Pn2	1888//AH1306H	—	Pice. Gold. KM#1.4.	—

PROOF SETS

KM#	Date	Mintage	Identification	Issue Price	Mkt Val
PS1	1888H (2)	—	KM1.4, 5	—	375
PS2	1890H (3)	—	KM#2-4	—	475

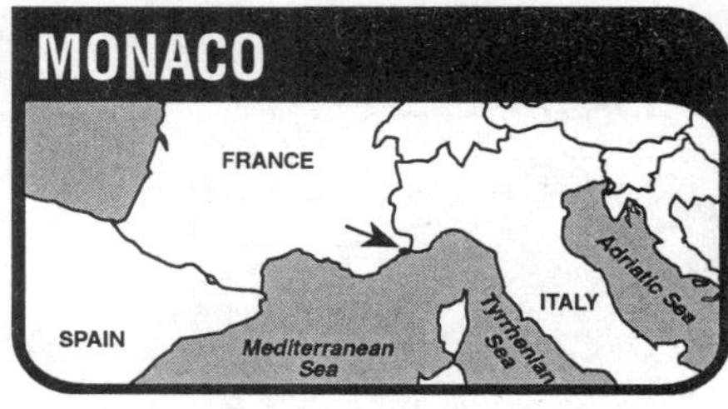

The Principality of Monaco, located on the Mediterranean coast nine miles from Nice, has an area of 0.58 sq. mi. (1.9 sq. km.). Capital: Monaco-Ville.

Monaco derives its name from Monoikos', the Greek surname for Hercules, the mythological strong man who, according to legend, formed the Monacan headland during one of his twelve labors. Monaco has been ruled by the Grimaldi dynasty since 1297 - Prince Rainier III, the present and 31st monarch of Monaco, is still of that line - except for a period during the French Revolution until Napoleon's downfall when the Principality was annexed to France. Since 1865, Monaco has maintained a customs union with France which guarantees its privileged position as long as the royal line remains intact.

RULERS
Honore IV, 1795-1819
Honore V, 1819-1841
Florestan I, 1841-1856
Charles III, 1856-1889
Albert I, 1889-1922

MINT MARKS
M - Monaco
A – Paris

MINT PRIVY MARKS
(a) - Paris (privy marks only)
C and clasped hands - Francois Cabinas, mint director, 1837-1838
(p) - Thunderbolt - Poissy

MONETARY SYSTEM
10 Centimes = 1 Decime
10 Decimes = 1 Franc

PRINCIPALITY

DECIMAL COINAGE

10 Centimes = 1 Decime; 10 Decimes = 1 Franc

KM# 95.1 5 CENTIMES (Cinq)

Cast Brass **Obv:** Large head BORREL F. below

Date	Mintage	VG	F	VF	XF	Unc
1837M C	—	5.00	12.00	25.00	60.00	125

KM# 95.1a 5 CENTIMES (Cinq)

Copper Struck

Date	Mintage	VG	F	VF	XF	Unc
1837M C	—	3.50	7.00	15.00	50.00	100

KM# 95.2 5 CENTIMES (Cinq)

Cast Brass **Obv:** Small hed BORREL F. below

Date	Mintage	VG	F	VF	XF	Unc
1837M C	—	4.00	10.00	35.00	75.00	200
1838M C Reported, not confirmed	—	—	—	—	—	—

KM# 95.2a 5 CENTIMES (Cinq)

Copper Struck

Date	Mintage	VG	F	VF	XF	Unc
1837M C	—	3.50	7.00	15.00	45.00	90.00
1838M C	—	12.00	25.00	50.00	125	250

KM# 97.1 DECIME

Copper Struck **Obv:** BORREL F. below head **Rev:** Knot of wreath tied

Date	Mintage	VG	F	VF	XF	Unc
1838M C	—	10.00	15.00	50.00	110	240

KM# 97.1a DECIME

Brass Cast

Date	Mintage	VG	F	VF	XF	Unc
1838M C	—	7.50	12.00	60.00	115	250

KM# 97.2 DECIME

Copper Struck **Obv:** Smaller head, BORREL F. below **Rev:** Knot of wreath untied

Date	Mintage	VG	F	VF	XF	Unc
1838M C	—	35.00	75.00	175	350	—

KM# 97.2a DECIME

Brass Struck

Date	Mintage	VG	F	VF	XF	Unc
1838M C	—	50.00	150	250	400	—

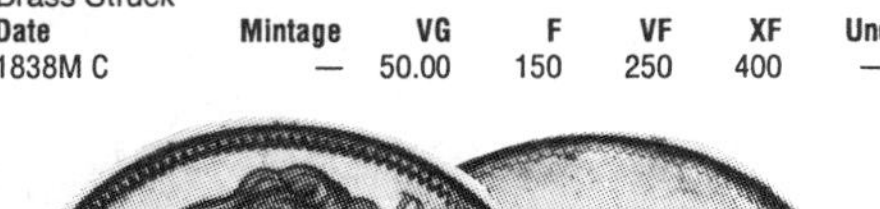

KM# 96 5 FRANCS

25.0000 g., 0.9000 Silver .7234 oz.

Date	Mintage	F	VF	XF	Unc	BU
1837M	—	350	750	1,250	3,500	—

KM# 98 20 FRANCS (Vingt)

6.4516 g., 0.9000 Gold .1867 oz.

Date	Mintage	F	VF	XF	Unc	BU
1878A	25,000	120	200	300	600	—
1879A	50,000	80.00	150	200	500	—

KM# 99 100 FRANCS (Cent)

32.2580 g., 0.9000 Gold .9335 oz.

Date	Mintage	F	VF	XF	Unc	BU
1882A	5,000	400	600	800	1,200	—
1884A	15,000	BV	450	550	775	—
1886A	15,000	BV	450	550	775	—

KM# 105 100 FRANCS (Cent)

32.2580 g., 0.9000 Gold .9335 oz. **Obv:** Head of Prince Albert I left

Date	Mintage	F	VF	XF	Unc	BU
1891A	20,000	BV	420	500	775	900
1895A	20,000	BV	420	500	775	900
1896A	20,000	BV	420	500	775	900
1901A	15,000	BV	420	500	775	900
1904A	10,000	BV	420	500	775	900

PATTERNS

Including off metal strikes

KM#	Date	Mintage	Identification	Mkt Val
Pn1	1837	—	5 Francs. 0.9000 Silver.	3,500
Pn2	1837	—	10 Centimes. Tin. E. Roger	—

KM#	Date	Mintage	Identification	Mkt Val
Pn3	1838	—	5 Centimes. Copper. E Roger below bust	275
Pn4	1838	—	5 Centimes. Copper And Tin Alloy.	275

KM#	Date	Mintage	Identification	Mkt Val
Pn5	1838	—	Decime. Copper.	250
Pn6	1838	—	Decime. Copper And Tin Alloy.	250
Pn7	1838	—	1/4 Franc. 0.9000 Silver.	275
Pn8	1838	—	1/2 Franc. 0.9000 Silver.	350
Pn9	1838	—	Franc. 0.9000 Silver.	450

KM#	Date	Mintage	Identification	Mkt Val
Pn10	1838	—	2 Francs. 0.9000 Silver.	550
Pn11	1838	—	10 Francs. Tin.	500

KM#	Date	Mintage	Identification	Mkt Val
Pn12	1838	—	20 Francs. Gold.	—
Pn13	1838	—	40 Francs. Gold.	—
Pn14	1892A	—	20 Francs. 0.9000 Gold.	3,000

TRIAL STRIKES

KM#	Date	Mintage	Identification	Mkt Val
TS1	1837	—	5 Francs. 0.9000 Silver. Pn2 obverse.	—
TS2	1837	—	5 Francs. 0.9000 Silver. Pn1 reverse.	—
TS3	1838	—	5 Centimes. Copper. Pn2 obverse.	—
TS4	1838	—	5 Centimes. Copper. Pn2 reverse.	—
TS5	1838	—	5 Centimes. Copper And Tin Alloy. Pn3 obverse.	—
TS6	1838	—	5 Centimes. Copper And Tin Alloy. Pn3 reverse.	—
TS7	1838	—	Decime. Copper. Pn4 obverse.	—
TS8	1838	—	Decime. Copper. Pn4 reverse.	—
TS9	1838	—	Decime. Copper And Tin Alloy. Pn5 obverse.	—
TS10	1838	—	Decime. Copper And Tin Alloy. Pn5 reverse.	—
TS11	1838	—	1/4 Franc. 0.9000 Silver. Pn6 obverse.	—
TS12	1838	—	1/4 Franc. 0.9000 Silver. Pn6 reverse.	—
TS13	1838	—	1/2 Franc. 0.9000 Silver. Pn7 obverse.	—
TS14	1838	—	1/2 Franc. 0.9000 Silver. Pn7 reverse.	—
TS15	1838	—	Franc. 0.9000 Silver. Pn8 obverse.	—
TS16	1838	—	Franc. 0.9000 Silver. Pn8 reverse.	—
TS17	1838	—	2 Francs. 0.9000 Silver. Pn9 obverse.	—
TS18	1838	—	2 Francs. 0.9000 Silver. Pn9 reverse.	—
TS19	1838	—	20 Francs. Gold. Pn10 obverse.	—
TS20	1838	—	20 Francs. Gold. Pn10 reverse.	—
TS21	1838	—	40 Francs. Gold. Pn11 obverse.	5,000
TS22	1838	—	40 Francs. Gold. Pn11 reverse.	5,000

MONTENEGRO

The former independent kingdom of Montenegro, now one of the nominally autonomous federated units of Yugoslavia, was located in southeastern Europe north of Albania. As a kingdom, it had an area of 5,333 sq. mi. (13,812 sq. km.).

Montenegro became an independent state in 1355 following the break-up of the Serb empire. During the Turkish invasion of Albania and Herzegovina in the 15th century, the Montenegrins moved their capital to the remote mountain village of Cetinje where they maintained their independence through two centuries of intermittent attack, emerging as the only one of the Balkan states not subjugated by the Turks.

The coinage, issued under the autocratic rule of Prince Nicholas, is obsolete.

RULERS

Nicholas I as Prince 1860-1910
...as King 1910-1918

MINT MARKS

- Paris, privy marks only

MONETARY SYSTEM

100 Para = 1 Perper

CATTARO

A seaport of Montenegro, Yugoslavia, occupies a ledge between the Montenegrin mountains and an inlet of the Adriatic Sea which forms one of the finest natural harbors in the world. It has at various times been occupied by Turks, Venetians, Spaniards, French, English and Austrians. It became a part of Yugoslavia in 1918. Cattarowas united to the French Empire during the period of 1807-13. In 1813, while the city was besieged by Montenegrins and a British fleet, the French defenders issued an emergency cast silver coinage.

FRENCH OCCUPATION

FRENCH SEIGE COINAGE

KM# 1 FRANC

Cast Silver **Note:** Weight varies: 5.50-6.30 grams.

Date	Mintage	Good	VG	F	VF	XF
1813	—	200	250	350	500	—

KM# 2 5 FRANCS

Cast Silver **Note:** Weight varies: 28.00-30.00 grams.

Date	Mintage	Good	VG	F	VF	XF
1813	—	800	1,200	1,800	2,300	—

KM# 3 10 FRANCS

Cast Silver **Note:** Weight varies: 59.00-59.60 grams.

Date	Mintage	Good	VG	F	VF	XF
1813	—	1,000	1,700	2,600	3,600	—

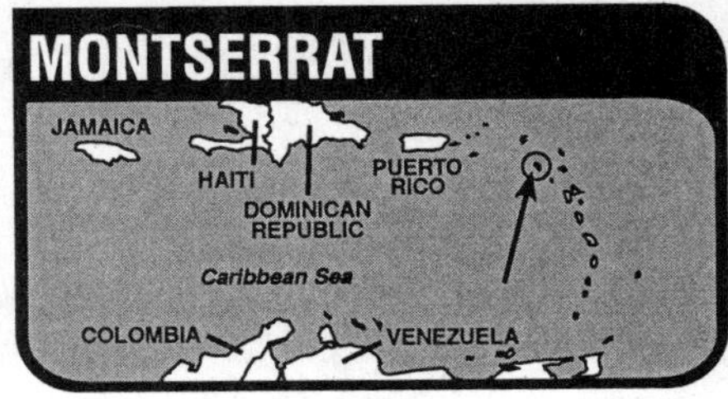

Montserrat, a British crown colony located in the Lesser Antilles of the West Indies 27 miles (43 km.) southwest of Antigua, has an area of 38 sq. mi. (100 sq. km.) and a population of 18,500. Capital: Plymouth. The island - actually a range of volcanic peaks rising from the Caribbean - exports cotton, limes and vegetables.

Columbus discovered Montserrat in 1493 and named it after Monserrado, a mountain in Spain. It was colonized by the English in 1632 and, except for brief periods of French occupancy in 1667 and 1782-83, has remained a British possession from that time. Currency of the British Caribbean Territories (Eastern Group) was used until later when the East Caribbean States coinage was introduced. Until becoming a separate colony in 1956, Montserrat was a presidency of the Leeward Islands.

The early 19th century countermarks of a crowned 3, 4,7, 9 or 18 over M as documented by Major Pridmore have been more correctly listed under St. Bartholomew.

RULERS

British

MONETARY SYSTEM

100 Cents = 1 Dollar

CROWN COLONY

COUNTERMARKED COINAGE

KM# 3 3 DOGS (4-1/2 Pence - 1/2 Bit)

Silver **Countermark:** M **Note:** Countermark on 1/4 cut of Spanish Colonial 2 Reales.

CM Date	Host Date	Good	VG	F	VF	XF
ND	1772-99	150	250	400	600	—

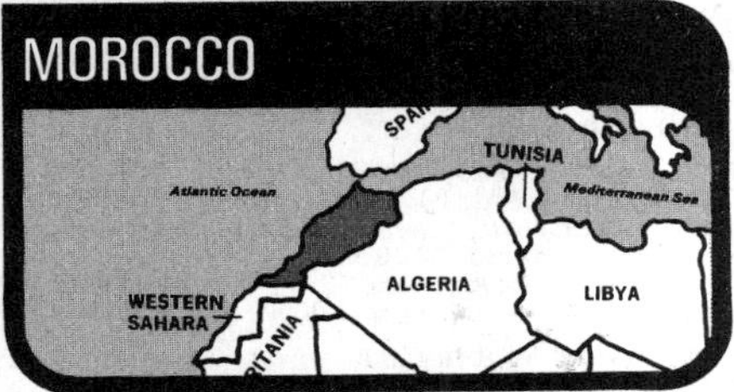

The Kingdom of Morocco, situated on the northwest corner of Africa, has an area of 432,620 sq. mi. (710,850 sq. km.). Capital: Rabat.

Morocco's strategic position at the gateway to western Europe has been the principal determinant of its violent, frequently unfortunate history. Time and again the fertile plain between the rugged Atlas Mountains and the sea has echoed the battle's trumpet as Phoenicians, Romans, Vandals, Visigoths, Byzantine Greeks and Islamic Arabs successively conquered and occupied the land. Modern Morocco is a remnant of an early empire formed by the Arabs at the close of the 7th century which encompassed all of northwest Africa and most of the Iberian Peninsula. During the 17th and 18th centuries, while under the control of native dynasties, it was the headquarters of the famous Sale pirates. Morocco's strategic position involved it in the competition of 19th century European powers for political influence in Africa, and resulted in the division of Morocco into French and Spanish spheres of interest which were established as protectorates in 1912. Morocco became independent on March 2, 1956, after France agreed to end its protectorate. Spain signed similar agreements on April 7 of the same year.

TITLES

المعربية

Al-Maghribiya(t)

المملكة المغربية

Al-Mamlaka(t) al-Maghribiya(t)

المحمدية الشريفة

Al-Mohammediya(t) esh-Sherifiya(t)

RULERS

Moulay Suleiman, AH1207-1238/1793-1822AD
Moulay 'Abd al-Rahman II, AH1238-1276/1822-1859AD
Sidi Mohammed IV, AH1276-1290/1859-1873AD
Moulay al-Hasan I, AH1290-1311/1873-1894AD
'Abd al-Aziz, AH1311-1326/1894-1908AD

EARLY COINAGE

Prior to the introduction of modern machine-struck coinage in Morocco in AH1299/1882AD the coinage of the Filali Sharifs contained of a variety of primitive hammered copper and cast bronze coins as well as of crudely hammered silver and gold issues which were in circulation together with considerable quantities of foreign coins.

The cast bronze (starting with Al-Yazid in AH1204/1790AD) were produced in several denominations, multiples and fractions of the basic unit of the Falus (Felous). The expression Zelagh (Zalagh) was used for all fractions of the Falus. After the Monetary Reform of 1902AD the Mazuna (or Muzuna, Mouzuna, Mawzuna) was the standard bronze unit. The size and weights of the pre-1902AD coins vary, which sometimes makes its distinction difficult, in particular for earlier rulers. Early types are varied, with different ornamentation and designs, some undated and/or without mint name, which makes a complete presentation of all varieties impossible. Beginning in AH1208, the obverse bears the Seal of Solomon (hexagram) and the reverse includes the date and/or mint name. All cast bronzes with only ornaments or the Seal of Solomon on both sides are issues of Sulayman. The mint (if present) is in Arabic script and starting with issues of Mohammed III the date (when present) is in Western numerals. The bronze pieces were cast in "trees" and occasionally entire or partial "trees" are found in the market.

Some bronze issues of Mohammed IV with illegible dates and mints and often light in weight are considered contemporary counterfeits. The war with Spain led to a chaotic and bad economic period in Morocco, during which Dirhams have been counterfeited by silver-plating hammered copper and brass pieces with dates AH1283-89/1866-72AD of Mohammed IV.

The silver and gold coins usually have the mint name on one side and the date on the other side. The original silver unit was the "legal dirham" of 2.931 grams standard weight, changing to several lower standards depending on the economic situation. A ¼ Dirham was called Mazuna until AH1213. The gold units Dinar and beginning with Sulayman, the Benduqi (Bonduqi) had 3.52 grams standard weight.

All weights indicated in the following listings for bronze, silver and gold coins are standards weights; actual weights of coins found can differ considerably. Anonymous strikes can be assigned to individual rulers by date, design and weight standard. Prices are for specimens with clearly legible dates (if any) and mint names (if any). Illegible and defectively produced pieces are worth much less.

To have more information on Moroccan issues from AH1075-1400/1664-1980AD, refer to Corpus des Monnaies Alawites by Daniel Eustache, Rabat 1984. For professional comments and estimate of rarity for all weights standards, see A Checklist of Islamic Coins by Stephen Album, Santa Rosa 1998. Information on Mazuna-strikes of Fes of AH1320-1323/1902-1205AD can be found in Monedas de Marruecos by Sanchez-Giron Blasco, Ceuta 1980. For details of Moroccan issues from AH1297-1380/1879-1960AD, refer to Monnaies et Jetons des Colonies Francaises by Jean Lecompte, Monaco 2000. Excellent drawings of bronze coins of Morocco, from AH1184-1321/1770-1903AD, can be found in Modern Copper Coins of the Muhammadan States by W. H. Valentine, London 1911 (reprint 1969).

MINTS

(a) = Paris privy marks only

اسفي

As = Asfi (Safi)

برلين

Be = Berlin

بانكلند

Bi – bi-Ankland, England (Birmingham)

By = (al-Madinat) al-Bayda (Fes al-Jadid)

الصويرة . الصوير

EM = Essaouira (al-Suwairah) (Mogador)

Fd = Fedala (Fadala al-Mohammedia)

فاس حضره

FH = Fes Hazrat

فاس

Fs = Fes (Fas, Fez)

H = Hazrat (Royal residence)

Hw = Hawz

حضره الكتوه

KH = al-Kitaoua Hazrat

بانكلند

Ln = bi-Ankland (London)

Lr = al-Ara'is (Larache)

مدريد

Ma = Madrid

مولاي ابراهيم

MB = Moulay-Ibrahim (Mawley)

مراكش

MH = Marakesh Hazrat

مكناس

Mk = Meknes (Miknas)

مكناسة

Miknasah

MK = Meknes Hazrat

مراكش

Mr = Marrakesh (Marakesh, Marrakush)

(NM) = No mintname on coin.

بباريز

Pa = bi-Bariz (Paris)

مولاي ابراهيم

Py - Poissy Inscribed "Paris" but with thunderbolt privy mark.

رباط

Rb = Rabat (Ribat)

Rd = Rudana (Taroudant)

رباط الفتح

RF = Rabat (Ribat) al-Fath

سا

Sa = Sala (Sale)

الصويرة

Sh = al-Suwairah

سجلماسه

Si = Sijilmasah (Sizilmassa)

سوس

Sus

الصوير

Sr = al-Suwair

تطوان

Te = Tetuan (Tetouan, Titwan)

طنجة

Tg = Tanjah (Tangier)

زا

Za (Taorirt)

NOTE: Some of the above forms of the mintnames are shown as they appear on the coins, not in regular Arabic script.

KINGDOM

Filali Sharifs - Alawi Dynasty

Sulayman II

AH1207-38/1793-1822AD

HAMMERED COINAGE

Mint: Without Mint Name
KM# 90.1 1/2 FALUS
1.7000 g., Cast Bronze **Obv:** Square design **Rev:** Flower design **Note:** Size varies 12-16 mm.

Date	Mintage	Good	VG	F	VF	XF
ND(1792-1822)	—	8.00	15.00	30.00	60.00	—

Mint: Without Mint Name
KM# 90.2 1/2 FALUS
1.7000 g., Cast Bronze **Obv:** Seal of solomon **Rev:** Ornamental design **Note:** Size varies 12-16 mm.

Date	Mintage	Good	VG	F	VF	XF
ND(1792-1822)	—	8.00	15.00	30.00	60.00	—

Mint: Without Mint Name
KM# 91 1/2 FALUS
1.7000 g., Cast Bronze **Obv:** Seal of Solomon **Rev:** Seal of Solomon **Note:** Size varies 12-16 mm.

Date	Mintage	Good	VG	F	VF	XF
ND(1792-1822)	—	10.00	20.00	40.00	80.00	—

Mint: Marrakesh
KM# 92.2 1/2 FALUS
1.7000 g., Cast Bronze **Obv:** Seal of Solomon **Rev:** Mint **Note:** Size varies 12-16 mm.

Date	Mintage	Good	VG	F	VF	XF
ND(1792-1822)	—	12.00	25.00	50.00	100	—

Mint: Rabat
KM# 92.3c 1/2 FALUS
1.7000 g., Cast Bronze **Obv:** Seal of Solomon **Rev:** Year and mint **Note:** Size varies 12-16 mm.

Date	Mintage	Good	VG	F	VF	XF
AH1230	—	12.00	25.00	50.00	100	—

Mint: Tetuan
KM# 92.4 1/2 FALUS
1.7000 g., Cast Bronze **Obv:** Interlacing lines in circle **Rev:** Year and mint **Note:** Size varies 12-16 mm.

Date	Mintage	Good	VG	F	VF	XF
AH1219 Rare	—	—	—	—	—	—

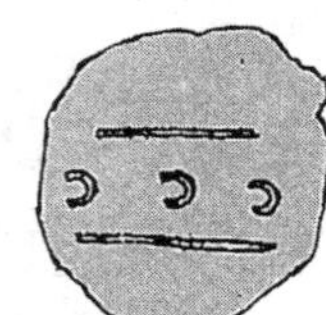

Mint: Without Mint Name
KM# A95.2 FALUS
3.5000 g., Cast Bronze **Obv:** Seal of Solomon **Rev:** Symbols composed of retrograde CCCs between lines **Note:** Size varies 17-22 mm.

Date	Mintage	Good	VG	F	VF	XF
ND(1792-1822)	—	12.00	25.00	50.00	100	—

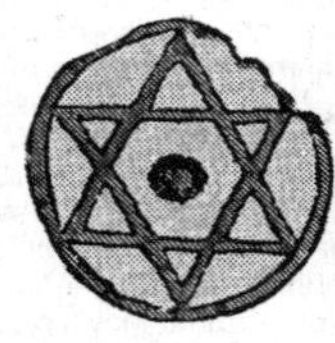

Mint: Without Mint Name
KM# 95.1 FALUS
3.5000 g., Cast Bronze, 17-22 mm. **Obv:** Seal of Solomon **Rev:** Year **Note:** Previous C#95.1.

Date	Mintage	Good	VG	F	VF	XF
AH1216 Rare	—	—	—	—	—	—
AH1218	—	8.00	15.00	30.00	60.00	—
AH1220	—	4.00	8.00	15.00	30.00	—
AH1225	—	4.00	8.00	15.00	30.00	—
AH1229	—	4.00	8.00	15.00	30.00	—
AH1231 Rare	—	—	—	—	—	—
AH1234 Rare	—	—	—	—	—	—
AH1235	—	8.00	15.00	30.00	60.00	—
AH1236	—	8.00	15.00	30.00	60.00	—
AH1237	—	8.00	15.00	30.00	60.00	—
AH1238	—	8.00	15.00	30.00	60.00	—

Mint: Without Mint Name
KM# 93 FALUS
3.5000 g., Cast Bronze **Obv:** Seal of Solomon **Rev:** Ornamental design **Note:** Size varies 17-22 mm.

Date	Mintage	Good	VG	F	VF	XF
ND(1792-1822)	—	8.00	15.00	30.00	60.00	—

Mint: Without Mint Name
KM# 94 FALUS
3.5000 g., Cast Bronze **Obv:** Seal of Solomon **Rev:** Seal of Solomon **Note:** Size varies 17-22 mm.

Date	Mintage	Good	VG	F	VF	XF
ND(1792-1822)	—	8.00	15.00	30.00	60.00	—

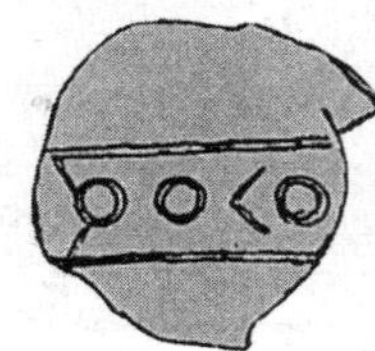

Mint: Without Mint Name
KM# A95.1 FALUS
3.5000 g., Cast Bronze **Obv:** Seal of Solomon **Rev:** Combination of symbols composed of circles and right or left angles between lines **Note:** Size varies 17-22 mm.

Date	Mintage	Good	VG	F	VF	XF
ND(1792-1822)	—	10.00	20.00	40.00	80.00	—

Mint: al-Araisah
KM# 95.2 FALUS
3.5000 g., Cast Bronze **Obv:** Seal of Solomon **Rev:** Year and mint **Note:** Size varies 17-22 mm.

Date	Mintage	Good	VG	F	VF	XF
AH1228 Rare	—	—	—	—	—	—

Mint: Asfi
KM# 95.3 FALUS
3.5000 g., Cast Bronze, 17-22 mm. **Obv:** Seal of Solomon **Rev:** Year and mint **Note:** Previous C#95.2.

Date	Mintage	Good	VG	F	VF	XF
AH1231	—	20.00	40.00	80.00	160	—

Mint: Essaouira
KM# 95.4 FALUS
3.5000 g., Cast Bronze, 17-22 mm. **Note:** Previous C#95.3.

Date	Mintage	Good	VG	F	VF	XF
AH1228 Rare	—	—	—	—	—	—
AH1229	—	15.00	30.00	60.00	120	—
AH1230	—	5.00	10.00	20.00	40.00	—
AH1231	—	10.00	20.00	40.00	80.00	—
AH1233 Rare	—	—	—	—	—	—
AH1234	—	15.00	30.00	60.00	120	—
AH1235 Rare	—	—	—	—	—	—

Mint: Fes
KM# 95.5 FALUS
3.5000 g., Cast Bronze, 17-22 mm. **Note:** Previous C#95.4.

Date	Mintage	Good	VG	F	VF	XF
AH1235 Rare	—	—	—	—	—	—

Mint: Marrakesh
KM# 95.6 FALUS
3.5000 g., Cast Bronze, 17-22 mm. **Note:** Previous C#95.5.

Date	Mintage	Good	VG	F	VF	XF
AH1217 Rare	—	—	—	—	—	—
AH1231 Rare	—	—	—	—	—	—

Mint: Rabat
KM# 95.7 FALUS
3.5000 g., Cast Bronze **Note:** Previous C#95.6; Size varies 17-22 mm.

Date	Mintage	Good	VG	F	VF	XF
AH1230 Rare	—	—	—	—	—	—

Mint: Rabat al-Fath
KM# 95.8 FALUS
3.5000 g., Cast Bronze, 17-22 mm. **Note:** Previous C#95.7.

Date	Mintage	Good	VG	F	VF	XF
AH1221 Rare	—	—	—	—	—	—

Mint: Tetuan
KM# 95.9 FALUS
3.5000 g., Cast Bronze **Note:** Previous C#95.8.

Date	Mintage	Good	VG	F	VF	XF
AH1228	—	10.00	20.00	40.00	80.00	—
AH1229	—	12.00	25.00	50.00	100	—
AH1230 Rare	—	—	—	—	—	—

Mint: Without Mint Name
KM# 96.1 2 FALUS
7.1000 g., Cast Bronze **Obv:** Ornamental design **Rev:** Ornamental design **Note:** Size varies 20-23 mm.

Date	Mintage	Good	VG	F	VF	XF
ND(1792-1822)	—	15.00	30.00	60.00	120	—

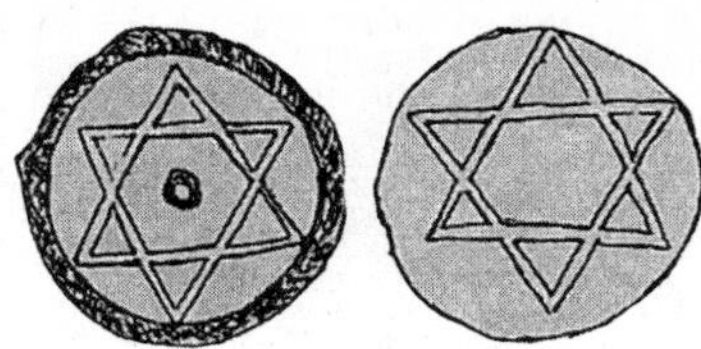

Mint: Without Mint Name
KM# 96.2 2 FALUS
7.1000 g., Cast Bronze **Obv:** Seal of Solomon **Rev:** Seal of Solomon **Note:** Size varies 20-23 mm.

Date	Mintage	Good	VG	F	VF	XF
ND(1792-1822)	—	10.00	20.00	30.00	60.00	—

Mint: Without Mint Name
KM# 97.1 2 FALUS
7.1000 g., Cast Bronze **Obv:** Seal of Solomon **Rev:** Year **Note:** Size varies 20-23 mm.

Date	Mintage	Good	VG	F	VF	XF
AH1221	—	8.00	15.00	32.50	60.00	—
AH1222	—	8.00	15.00	32.50	60.00	—
AH1226	—	8.00	15.00	32.50	60.00	—
AH1230	—	8.00	15.00	32.50	60.00	—
AH1231	—	8.00	15.00	32.50	60.00	—

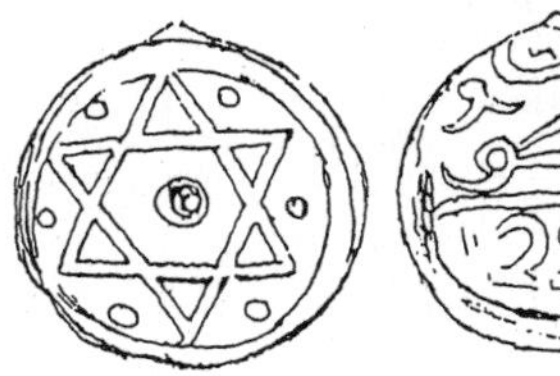

Mint: Essaouira
KM# 97.2 2 FALUS
7.1000 g., Cast Bronze **Obv:** Seal of Solomon **Rev:** Year and mint **Note:** Size varies 20-23 mm.

Date	Mintage	Good	VG	F	VF	XF
AH1229	—	8.00	15.00	32.50	60.00	—
AH1230	—	15.00	30.00	60.00	120	—
AH1231	—	10.00	20.00	40.00	80.00	—

Mint: Fes
KM# 97.3 2 FALUS
7.1000 g., Cast Bronze **Note:** Size varies 20-23 mm.

Date	Mintage	Good	VG	F	VF	XF
AH1237 Rare	—	—	—	—	—	—

Mint: Marrakesh
KM# 97.4 2 FALUS
7.1000 g., Cast Bronze **Note:** Size varies 20-23 mm.

Date	Mintage	Good	VG	F	VF	XF
ND	—	15.00	30.00	60.00	120	—
AH1228 Rare	—	—	—	—	—	—
AH1230	—	15.00	30.00	60.00	120	—
AH1231	—	5.00	10.00	20.00	40.00	—
AH1232 Rare	—	—	—	—	—	—

Mint: Tetuan
KM# 97.5 2 FALUS
7.1000 g., Cast Bronze **Obv:** Mint in circle **Rev:** Year in circular design **Note:** Size varies 20-23 mm.

Date	Mintage	Good	VG	F	VF	XF
AH1231 Rare	—	—	—	—	—	—

Mint: Without Mint Name
KM# 99.1 3 FALUS
10.6000 g., Cast Bronze **Obv:** Seal of Solomon **Rev:** Ornamental design **Note:** Size varies 24-27 mm.

Date	Mintage	Good	VG	F	VF	XF
ND(1792-1822)	—	15.00	25.00	50.00	100	—

Mint: Without Mint Name
KM# 99.2 3 FALUS
10.6000 g., Cast Bronze **Obv:** Seal of Solomon **Rev:** Seal of Solomon **Note:** Size varies 24-27 mm.

Date	Mintage	Good	VG	F	VF	XF
ND(1792-1822)	—	10.00	15.00	25.00	50.00	—

Mint: Without Mint Name
KM# 100.1 3 FALUS
10.6000 g., Cast Bronze **Obv:** Seal of Solomon **Rev:** Year **Note:** Size varies 24-27 mm.

Date	Mintage	Good	VG	F	VF	XF
AH1217	—	15.00	25.00	40.00	80.00	—

Mint: Essaouira
KM# 100.2 3 FALUS
10.6000 g., Cast Bronze **Obv:** Seal of Solomon with year **Rev:** Octogram with mint **Note:** Size varies 24-27 mm.

Date	Mintage	Good	VG	F	VF	XF
AH1219 Rare	—	—	—	—	—	—

Mint: Fes
KM# 100.3 3 FALUS
10.6000 g., Cast Bronze, 24-27 mm.

Date	Mintage	Good	VG	F	VF	XF
AH1215	—	10.00	20.00	40.00	80.00	—

Mint: Meknes
KM# 100.4 3 FALUS
Cast Bronze **Obv:** Seal of Solomon **Rev:** Mintname with 4 besant squared in the field

Date	Mintage	Good	VG	F	VF	XF
ND-	—	20.00	40.00	80.00	160	—

Mint: Tetuan
KM# 100.5 3 FALUS
10.6000 g., Cast Bronze **Note:** Size varies 24-27 mm.

Date	Mintage	Good	VG	F	VF	XF
AH1217	—	15.00	25.00	40.00	75.00	—

Mint: Without Mint Name
KM# 101 4 FALUS
14.1000 g., Cast Bronze **Obv:** Ornamental design **Rev:** Ornamental design **Note:** Size varies 28-34 mm.

Date	Mintage	Good	VG	F	VF	XF
ND(1792-1822)	—	15.00	30.00	70.00	150	—

Mint: Without Mint Name
KM# 102 4 FALUS
Cast Bronze 14.1 **Obv:** Seal of Solomon **Rev:** Flower in octogram **Note:** Size varies 28-34 mm.

Date	Mintage	Good	VG	F	VF	XF
ND(1792-1822)	—	20.00	40.00	90.00	200	—

Mint: Without Mint Name
KM# 103 4 FALUS
14.1000 g., Cast Bronze **Obv:** Seal of Solomon **Rev:** Seal of Solomon **Note:** Size varies 28-34 mm.

Date	Mintage	Good	VG	F	VF	XF
ND(1792-1822)	—	12.00	25.00	60.00	120	—

Mint: Essaouira
KM# 108d.1 DIRHAM
2.1500 g., Silver

Date	Mintage	Good	VG	F	VF	XF
AH1216	—	12.00	25.00	50.00	100	—

Mint: Fes Hazrat
KM# 108d.2 DIRHAM
2.1500 g., Silver

Date	Mintage	Good	VG	F	VF	XF
AH1216	—	12.00	25.00	50.00	100	—
AH1217	—	12.00	25.00	50.00	100	—

Mint: Essaouira
KM# 108e.1 DIRHAM
2.9300 g., Silver **Note:** Retuns to legal weight.

Date	Mintage	Good	VG	F	VF	XF
AH1219 Rare	—	—	—	—	—	—

Mint: Fes Hazrat
KM# 108e.2 DIRHAM
2.9300 g., Silver

Date	Mintage	Good	VG	F	VF	XF
AH1218	—	10.00	15.00	20.00	40.00	—

Mint: Rabat al-Fath
KM# 108e.3 DIRHAM
2.9300 g., Silver

Date	Mintage	Good	VG	F	VF	XF
AH1218	—	10.00	20.00	30.00	50.00	—

Mint: Fes Hazrat
KM# 108f DIRHAM
1.9500 g., Silver

Date	Mintage	Good	VG	F	VF	XF
AH1221	—	10.00	15.00	20.00	30.00	—
AH1236	—	15.00	30.00	50.00	100	—
AH1237	—	15.00	30.00	50.00	100	—
AH1238	—	20.00	40.00	80.00	150	—

Note: KM#108f of AH1238 shows the obverse with an anchored line between the 2n & 3rd line of the legend on the obverse. 'Abd al-Rahman also struck a Dirham dated AH1238 at Fes Hazrat. Refer to C#140.1

Mint: Fes
C# 114 1/2 BENDUQI
1.7000 g., Gold

Date	Mintage	Good	VG	F	VF	XF
AH1232	—	100	200	350	600	—
AH1236	—	100	200	350	600	—
AH1237	—	100	200	350	600	—

Mint: Fes Hazrat
C# 115 BENDUQI
3.5200 g., Gold

Date	Mintage	VG	F	VF	XF	Unc
AH1216	—	90.00	125	250	375	—
AH1217	—	90.00	125	250	375	—
AH1218	—	90.00	125	250	375	—
AH1219	—	100	150	300	500	—
AH1220	—	100	150	300	500	—
AH1224	—	100	150	300	500	—
AH1234	—	100	150	300	500	—
AH1235	—	100	150	300	500	—
AH1238	—	100	150	300	500	—

Moulay 'Abd al-Rahman
AH1238-76/1822-59AD
HAMMERED COINAGE

Mint: Without Mint Name
C# 119 1/4 FALUS
1.1700 g., Cast Bronze, 15 mm. **Obv:** Seal of Solomon **Rev:** Date

Date	Mintage	Good	VG	F	VF	XF
AH126x Rare	—	—	—	—	—	—

Mint: Without Mint Name
C# 121 1/2 FALUS
2.3500 g., Cast Bronze **Obv:** Seal of Solomon **Rev:** Date **Note:** Size varies 13-14 mm.

Date	Mintage	Good	VG	F	VF	XF
AH1258	—	15.00	35.00	65.00	100	—
AH1261	—	15.00	35.00	65.00	100	—
AH1263	—	8.00	20.00	37.50	60.00	—
AH1265 Rare	—	—	—	—	—	—
AH1268	—	8.00	20.00	37.50	60.00	—

Mint: Without Mint Name
C# 121a 1/2 FALUS
1.7000 g., Cast Bronze

Date	Mintage	Good	VG	F	VF	XF
AH1271	—	15.00	35.00	65.00	100	—
AH1274	—	15.00	35.00	65.00	100	—

Mint: Without Mint Name
C# 122.1 FALUS
3.5000 g., Cast Bronze **Obv:** Seal of Solomon **Rev:** Mintname (if it appears), date **Note:** Size varies 18-20 mm.

Date	Mintage	Good	VG	F	VF	XF
AH1239	—	15.00	35.00	65.00	100	—
AH1240	—	7.50	12.50	20.00	30.00	—
AH1241	—	7.50	12.50	20.00	30.00	—
AH1242 Rare	—	—	—	—	—	—
AH1244 Rare	—	—	—	—	—	—
AH1245	—	8.00	12.50	20.00	30.00	—
AH1246	—	10.00	20.00	30.00	60.00	—
AH1247	—	10.00	20.00	30.00	60.00	—
AH1248	—	10.00	20.00	30.00	60.00	—
AH1248/7	—	15.00	35.00	65.00	100	—

Mint: Marrakesh
C# 122.2 FALUS
3.5000 g., Cast Bronze **Note:** 18-20mm.

Date	Mintage	Good	VG	F	VF	XF
AH1241 Rare	—	—	—	—	—	—
AH1242	—	7.50	12.50	20.00	30.00	—
AH1243	—	7.50	12.50	20.00	30.00	—
AH1245	—	15.00	35.00	65.00	100	—
AH1249 Rare	—	—	—	—	—	—

Mint: Without Mint Name
C# 122a.1 FALUS
4.7000 g., Cast Bronze **Note:** Size varies: 20-22 mm.

Date	Mintage	Good	VG	F	VF	XF
AH1250	—	10.00	20.00	30.00	60.00	—
AH1251	—	2.00	4.00	8.00	15.00	—
AH1252	—	2.00	4.00	8.00	15.00	—
AH1253	—	2.00	4.00	8.00	15.00	—
AH1254	—	2.00	4.00	8.00	15.00	—
AH1255	—	2.00	4.00	8.00	15.00	—
AH1256	—	2.00	4.00	8.00	15.00	—
AH1257/6	—	10.00	20.00	40.00	80.00	—
AH1257	—	2.00	4.00	8.00	15.00	—
AH1258	—	2.00	4.00	8.00	15.00	—
AH1259	—	2.00	4.00	8.00	15.00	—
AH1260	—	2.00	4.00	8.00	15.00	—
AH1621 Error for 1261	—	10.00	20.00	30.00	60.00	—
AH1261	—	2.00	4.00	8.00	15.00	—
AH1262	—	2.00	4.00	8.00	15.00	—
AH1263	—	2.00	4.00	8.00	15.00	—
AH1264	—	2.00	4.00	8.00	15.00	—
AH1265	—	2.00	4.00	8.00	15.00	—
AH1266	—	2.00	4.00	8.00	15.00	—
AH1267	—	2.00	4.00	8.00	15.00	—
AH1268	—	2.00	4.00	8.00	15.00	—
AH1269	—	10.00	20.00	30.00	60.00	—

Mint: Asfi
C# A122a.2 FALUS
Cast Bronze **Note:** Size varies 20-22 mm.

Date	Mintage	Good	VG	F	VF	XF
AH1252 Rare	—	—	—	—	—	—

Mint: Fes
C# 122a.2 FALUS
4.7000 g., Cast Bronze **Note:** Size varies: 20-22 mm.

Date	Mintage	Good	VG	F	VF	XF
AH1256 Rare	—	—	—	—	—	—
AH1257	—	15.00	35.00	65.00	100	—
AH1260	—	15.00	35.00	65.00	100	—
AH1261 Rare	—	—	—	—	—	—
AH1263 Rare	—	—	—	—	—	—
AH1265	—	2.00	4.50	8.50	15.00	—
AH1266	—	2.00	4.50	8.50	15.00	—
AH1267	—	2.00	4.50	8.50	15.00	—
AH1269	—	10.00	20.00	30.00	60.00	—

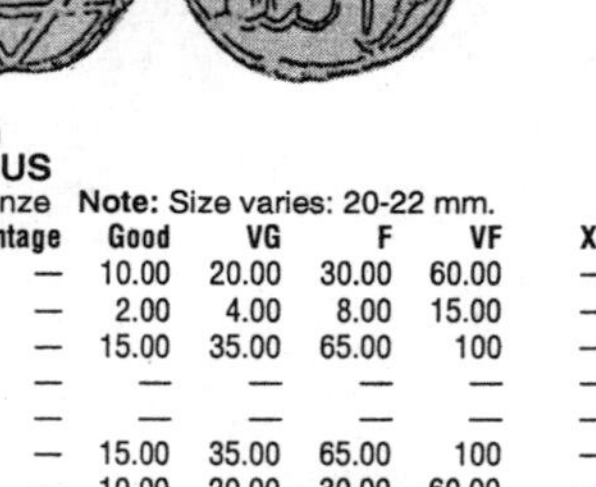

Mint: Marrakesh
C# 122a.3 FALUS
4.7000 g., Cast Bronze **Note:** Size varies: 20-22 mm.

Date	Mintage	Good	VG	F	VF	XF
AH1250	—	10.00	20.00	30.00	60.00	—
AH1251	—	2.00	4.00	8.00	15.00	—
AH1254	—	15.00	35.00	65.00	100	—
AH1256 Rare	—	—	—	—	—	—
AH1257 Rare	—	—	—	—	—	—
AH1259	—	15.00	35.00	65.00	100	—
AH1260	—	10.00	20.00	30.00	60.00	—
AH1262 Rare	—	—	—	—	—	—
AH1265 Rare	—	—	—	—	—	—
AH1266	—	2.00	4.00	8.00	15.00	—
AH1267	—	2.00	4.00	8.00	15.00	—
AH1268	—	2.00	4.00	8.00	15.00	—
AH1269	—	2.00	4.00	8.00	15.00	—

Mint: Rabat
C# 122a.4 FALUS
4.7000 g., Cast Bronze **Note:** Size varies: 20-22 mm.

Date	Mintage	Good	VG	F	VF	XF
AH1253	—	15.00	35.00	65.00	100	—
AH1255 Rare	—	—	—	—	—	—
AH1256 Rare	—	—	—	—	—	—
AH1257	—	15.00	35.00	65.00	100	—
AH1258	—	8.00	14.00	20.00	30.00	—
AH1259	—	8.00	14.00	20.00	30.00	—
AH1260 Rare	—	—	—	—	—	—
AH1264	—	8.00	14.00	20.00	30.00	—
AH1265 Rare	—	—	—	—	—	—

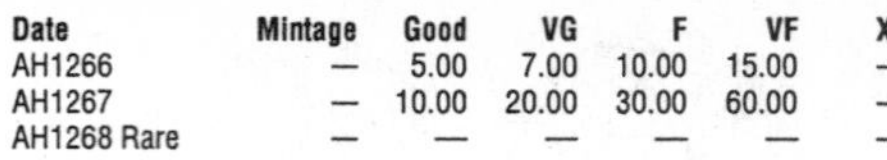

Date	Mintage	Good	VG	F	VF	XF
AH1266	—	5.00	7.00	10.00	15.00	—
AH1267	—	10.00	20.00	30.00	60.00	—
AH1268 Rare	—	—	—	—	—	—

Mint: Rabat al-Fath
C# 122a.5 FALUS
4.7000 g., Cast Bronze **Note:** Size varies: 20-22 mm.

Date	Mintage	Good	VG	F	VF	XF
AH1250	—	5.00	7.00	10.00	15.00	—
AH1251	—	15.00	35.00	65.00	100	—
AH1252 Rare	—	—	—	—	—	—
AH1260	—	5.00	7.00	10.00	15.00	—
AH1261	—	8.00	14.00	20.00	30.00	—
AH1262	—	15.00	35.00	65.00	100	—
AH1263	—	5.00	7.00	10.00	15.00	—
AH1264	—	8.00	14.00	20.00	30.00	—

Mint: Sale
C# 122a.6 FALUS
4.7000 g., Cast Bronze **Note:** Previous C#122a.5; size varies: 20-22 mm.

Date	Mintage	Good	VG	F	VF	XF
AH1257	—	20.00	40.00	80.00	150	—
AH1158 Error for 1258	—	30.00	50.00	100	180	—
AH1258	—	20.00	40.00	80.00	150	—
AH1259/8	—	30.00	50.00	100	180	—
AH1259	—	15.00	30.00	60.00	120	—
AH1261 Rare	—	—	—	—	—	—

Mint: Za
C# 122a.7 FALUS
4.7000 g., Cast Bronze **Note:** Size varies: 20-22 mm; previous C#122a.6.

Date	Mintage	Good	VG	F	VF	XF
AH1253	—	8.50	20.00	35.00	65.00	—
AH1254	—	10.00	15.00	25.00	50.00	—
AH1255	—	8.50	20.00	35.00	60.00	—
AH1256	—	15.00	35.00	65.00	120	—
AH1852 Error for 1258	—	30.00	50.00	100	180	—
AH1258	—	15.00	35.00	65.00	120	—

Mint: Without Mint Name
C# 122b.1 FALUS
3.5000 g., Cast Bronze **Note:** Size varies 17-18 mm.

Date	Mintage	Good	VG	F	VF	XF
AH1270	—	2.00	4.00	6.50	10.00	—
AH1721 Error for 1271	—	10.00	20.00	40.00	80.00	—
AH1271	—	2.00	4.00	6.50	10.00	—
AH1272	—	2.00	4.00	6.50	10.00	—
AH1372 Error for 1273	—	12.00	25.00	50.00	100	—
AH1273	—	2.00	4.00	6.50	10.00	—
AH1274	—	2.00	4.00	6.50	10.00	—
AH1275	—	10.00	20.00	30.00	60.00	—
AH1276	—	15.00	35.00	65.00	100	—

Mint: Fes
C# 122b.2 FALUS
3.5000 g., Cast Bronze **Note:** Size varies 17-18 mm.

Date	Mintage	Good	VG	F	VF	XF
AH1270	—	2.00	4.00	6.50	10.00	—
AH1271	—	2.00	4.00	6.50	10.00	—
AH1272	—	2.00	4.00	6.50	10.00	—
AH1273	—	10.00	20.00	30.00	60.00	—
AH1274	—	10.00	20.00	30.00	60.00	—
AH1275	—	10.00	20.00	30.00	60.00	—
AH1276 Rare	—	—	—	—	—	—

Mint: Marrakesh
C# 122b.3 FALUS
3.5000 g., Cast Bronze **Note:** Size varies 17-18 mm.

Date	Mintage	Good	VG	F	VF	XF
AH1270	—	15.00	35.00	65.00	100	—
AH1272 Rare	—	—	—	—	—	—
AH1273	—	15.00	35.00	65.00	100	—
AH1275	—	15.00	35.00	65.00	100	—

Mint: Rabat
C# 122b.4 FALUS
3.5000 g., Cast Bronze **Note:** Size varies 17-18 mm.

Date	Mintage	Good	VG	F	VF	XF
AH1270 Normal date	—	4.00	8.00	12.00	20.00	—
AH1270 Reversed date	—	12.00	25.00	50.00	100	—
AH1721 Error for 1271	—	10.00	20.00	40.00	80.00	—
AH1271	—	4.00	8.00	12.00	20.00	—
AH1272	—	10.00	20.00	30.00	60.00	—
AH1273/2 With reversed 3	—	12.00	25.00	50.00	100	—
AH1273	—	15.00	35.00	65.00	100	—
AH1275	—	15.00	35.00	65.00	100	—

Mint: Tetuan
C# 122b.5 FALUS
3.5000 g., Cast Bronze **Note:** Size varies 17-18 mm.

Date	Mintage	Good	VG	F	VF	XF
AH1271	—	10.00	15.00	20.00	30.00	—
AH1272	—	10.00	15.00	20.00	30.00	—

Mint: Without Mint Name
C# 126 2 FALUS
7.0000 g., Cast Bronze **Obv:** Seal of Solomon **Rev:** Date **Note:** Without mintname; size varies 20-22 mm.

Date	Mintage	Good	VG	F	VF	XF
AH1240	—	5.00	8.50	12.50	20.00	—
AH1245	—	8.00	17.50	20.00	30.00	—
AH1248 Rare	—	—	—	—	—	—

Mint: Without Mint Name
C# 126a 2 FALUS
9.4000 g., Cast Bronze **Note:** 26-28mm.

Date	Mintage	Good	VG	F	VF	XF
AH1260	—	8.50	12.50	20.00	30.00	—
AH1261	—	10.00	20.00	30.00	60.00	—
AH1263	—	10.00	20.00	30.00	60.00	—
AH1264	—	8.50	12.50	20.00	30.00	—
AH1265	—	10.00	20.00	30.00	60.00	—
AH1266	—	15.00	35.00	65.00	100	—
AH1267	—	3.00	6.00	10.00	15.00	—
AH1268	—	3.00	6.00	10.00	15.00	—
AH1269	—	8.50	12.50	20.00	30.00	—

Mint: Without Mint Name
C# 126b.1 2 FALUS
7.0000 g., Cast Bronze **Note:** Without mintname. 22-26mm.

Date	Mintage	Good	VG	F	VF	XF
AH1270 Rare	—	—	—	—	—	—
AH1274 Rare	—	—	—	—	—	—
AH1275	—	15.00	35.00	65.00	100	—
AH1276	—	8.00	14.00	20.00	30.00	—

Mint: Fes
C# 126b.2 2 FALUS
7.0000 g., Cast Bronze **Note:** 22-26mm.

Date	Mintage	Good	VG	F	VF	XF
AH1270	—	15.00	35.00	65.00	100	—
AH1271	—	8.00	14.00	20.00	30.00	—
AH1272	—	15.00	35.00	65.00	100	—
AH1274	—	2.50	4.50	9.00	15.00	—
AH1275	—	8.00	14.00	20.00	30.00	—
AH1276	—	8.00	14.00	20.00	30.00	—

Mint: Marrakesh
C# 126b.3 2 FALUS
7.0000 g., Cast Bronze **Note:** 22-26mm.

Date	Mintage	Good	VG	F	VF	XF
AH1270 Rare	—	—	—	—	—	—
AH1274	—	15.00	35.00	65.00	100	—
AH1275	—	5.00	10.00	20.00	40.00	—
AH1276	—	5.00	10.00	20.00	40.00	—

Mint: Rabat
C# 126b.4 2 FALUS
7.0000 g., Cast Bronze **Note:** 22-26mm.

Date	Mintage	Good	VG	F	VF	XF
AH1275 Rare	—	—	—	—	—	—

Mint: Rabat al-Fath
C# 126b.5 2 FALUS
7.0000 g., Cast Bronze

Date	Mintage	Good	VG	F	VF	XF
AH1270 Rare	—	—	—	—	—	—
AH1271	—	15.00	35.00	65.00	100	—

Mint: Tetuan
C# 126b.6 2 FALUS
7.0000 g., Cast Bronze **Note:** 22-26mm.

Date	Mintage	Good	VG	F	VF	XF
AH1271	—	5.00	7.00	10.00	15.00	—
AH1272	—	8.00	14.00	20.00	30.00	—
AH1273	—	15.00	35.00	65.00	100	—
AH1274 Rare	—	—	—	—	—	—
AH1275 Rare	—	—	—	—	—	—

Mint: Marrakesh
C# 127 1/4 DIRHAM
0.4900 g., Silver

Date	Mintage	Good	VG	F	VF	XF
AH1241	—	25.00	50.00	100	200	—

Mint: Rabat al-Fath
C# 128 1/4 DIRHAM
0.4100 g., Silver

Date	Mintage	Good	VG	F	VF	XF
AH1254	—	25.00	50.00	100	200	—

Mint: Fes Hazrat
C# 140.1 DIRHAM
2.7400 g., Silver **Obv:** No line between 2nd and 3rd line of legend **Note:** Size varies 17-20 mm.

Date	Mintage	Good	VG	F	VF	XF
AH1238	—	20.00	40.00	80.00	150	—
AH1239	—	20.00	40.00	80.00	150	—

Mint: Marrakesh
C# 140.3 DIRHAM
2.7400 g., Silver

Date	Mintage	Good	VG	F	VF	XF
AH1241	—	15.00	35.00	65.00	100	—

Mint: Meknes Hazrat
C# 140.2 DIRHAM
2.7400 g., Silver

Date	Mintage	Good	VG	F	VF	XF
AH1240	—	10.00	20.00	40.00	75.00	—
AH1241	—	10.00	20.00	40.00	75.00	—

Mint: Fes Hazrat
C# 140a.1 DIRHAM
1.9500 g., Silver

Date	Mintage	Good	VG	F	VF	XF
AH1240	—	10.00	20.00	30.00	60.00	—
AH1241	—	10.00	20.00	30.00	60.00	—
AH1242	—	15.00	35.00	65.00	100	—
AH1243 Rare	—	—	—	—	—	—
AH1244	—	15.00	35.00	65.00	100	—
AH1245	—	20.00	40.00	80.00	150	—
AH1246	—	20.00	40.00	80.00	150	—

Mint: Marrakesh
C# 140a.2 DIRHAM
1.9500 g., Silver

Date	Mintage	Good	VG	F	VF	XF
AH1241	—	13.50	32.50	60.00	90.00	—
AH1242 Rare	—	—	—	—	—	—

Mint: Meknes
C# 140a.3 DIRHAM
1.9500 g., Silver

Date	Mintage	Good	VG	F	VF	XF
AH1240	—	20.00	40.00	80.00	150	—
AH1241	—	20.00	40.00	80.00	150	—

Mint: Rabat al-Fath
C# 140a.4 DIRHAM
1.9500 g., Silver

Date	Mintage	Good	VG	F	VF	XF
AH1242 Rare	—	—	—	—	—	—

Mint: Fes Hazrat
C# 140b.1 DIRHAM
1.6600 g., Silver

Date	Mintage	Good	VG	F	VF	XF
AH1247 Rare	—	—	—	—	—	—
AH1248 Rare	—	—	—	—	—	—
AH1249	—	20.00	40.00	80.00	150	—
AH1250	—	20.00	40.00	80.00	150	—
AH1251 Rare	—	—	—	—	—	—
AH1252	—	20.00	40.00	80.00	150	—
AH1253	—	8.50	13.50	20.00	30.00	—
AH1254	—	8.50	13.50	20.00	30.00	—
AH1255	—	15.00	35.00	65.00	100	—
AH1256	—	15.00	35.00	65.00	100	—
AH1257	—	10.00	20.00	30.00	60.00	—
AH1258	—	20.00	40.00	80.00	150	—
AH1259	—	10.00	20.00	30.00	60.00	—
AH1260	—	20.00	40.00	80.00	150	—

Mint: Marakesh Hazrat
C# 140b.3 DIRHAM
1.6600 g., Silver

Date	Mintage	Good	VG	F	VF	XF
AH1253	—	20.00	40.00	80.00	150	—

Mint: Marrakesh
C# 140b.2 DIRHAM
1.6600 g., Silver

Date	Mintage	Good	VG	F	VF	XF
AH1254	—	8.50	13.50	20.00	30.00	—
AH1255	—	10.00	20.00	30.00	60.00	—
AH1256	—	10.00	20.00	30.00	60.00	—
AH1257	—	15.00	35.00	65.00	100	—
AH1258	—	15.00	35.00	65.00	100	—
AH1259	—	15.00	35.00	65.00	100	—
AH1260	—	10.00	20.00	30.00	60.00	—
AH1261	—	15.00	35.00	65.00	100	—

Mint: Meknes
C# 140b.4 DIRHAM
1.6600 g., Silver

Date	Mintage	Good	VG	F	VF	XF
AH1247	—	20.00	40.00	80.00	150	—
AH1252 Rare	—	—	—	—	—	—
AH1253 Rare	—	—	—	—	—	—

Mint: Rabat al-Fath
C# 140b.5 DIRHAM
1.6600 g., Silver

Date	Mintage	Good	VG	F	VF	XF
AH1251 Rare	—	—	—	—	—	—
AH1253	—	8.50	18.50	32.50	60.00	—
AH1254	—	8.50	18.50	32.50	60.00	—
AH1255	—	8.50	18.50	32.50	60.00	—
AH1256	—	15.00	35.00	65.00	100	—
AH1257	—	20.00	40.00	80.00	150	—
AH1258	—	20.00	40.00	80.00	150	—

Mint: Tetuan
C# 140b.6 DIRHAM
1.6600 g., Silver

Date	Mintage	Good	VG	F	VF	XF
AH1249	—	13.50	32.50	60.00	90.00	—
AH1256	—	10.00	20.00	30.00	60.00	—
AH1257	—	10.00	20.00	30.00	60.00	—
AH1258 Rare	—	—	—	—	—	—

Mint: Fes Hazrat
C# 140c.1 DIRHAM
1.4700 g., Silver

Date	Mintage	Good	VG	F	VF	XF
AH1261 Rare	—	—	—	—	—	—
AH1262	—	20.00	40.00	80.00	150	—
AH1263	—	20.00	40.00	80.00	150	—
AH1264	—	15.00	35.00	65.00	100	—
AH1265 Rare	—	—	—	—	—	—
AH1266	—	15.00	35.00	65.00	100	—
AH1267	—	20.00	40.00	80.00	150	—
AH1268	—	20.00	40.00	80.00	150	—

Mint: Marrakesh
C# 140c.2 DIRHAM
1.4700 g., Silver

Date	Mintage	Good	VG	F	VF	XF
AH1262	—	15.00	35.00	65.00	100	—
AH1263	—	15.00	35.00	65.00	100	—
AH1264	—	15.00	35.00	65.00	100	—
AH1265	—	15.00	35.00	65.00	100	—
AH1266	—	20.00	40.00	80.00	150	—
AH1267	—	15.00	35.00	65.00	100	—

Mint: Rabat al-Fath
C# 140c.3 DIRHAM
1.4700 g., Silver

Date	Mintage	Good	VG	F	VF	XF
AH1262	—	13.50	30.00	50.00	80.00	—
AH1264 Rare	—	—	—	—	—	—
AH1266	—	20.00	40.00	80.00	150	—

Mint: Fes
C# 140d.1 DIRHAM
2.1500 g., Silver

Date	Mintage	Good	VG	F	VF	XF
AH1270	—	15.00	35.00	65.00	100	—
AH1271	—	20.00	40.00	80.00	150	—
AH1272 Rare	—	—	—	—	—	—
AH1273	—	15.00	35.00	65.00	100	—
AH1274	—	15.00	35.00	65.00	100	—
AH1275	—	15.00	35.00	65.00	100	—
AH1276	—	15.00	35.00	65.00	100	—

Mint: Fes Hazrat
C# 140d.2 DIRHAM
2.1500 g., Silver

Date	Mintage	Good	VG	F	VF	XF
AH1268	—	10.00	20.00	30.00	60.00	—
AH1269	—	10.00	20.00	30.00	60.00	—

Mint: Marrakesh
C# 140d.3 DIRHAM
2.1500 g., Silver

Date	Mintage	Good	VG	F	VF	XF
AH1268	—	15.00	35.00	65.00	100	—
AH1269	—	20.00	40.00	80.00	150	—
AH1270 Rare	—	—	—	—	—	—
AH1271 Rare	—	—	—	—	—	—
AH1272	—	15.00	35.00	65.00	100	—
AH1273 Rare	—	—	—	—	—	—
AH1274 Rare	—	—	—	—	—	—
AH1276 Rare	—	—	—	—	—	—

Mint: Rabat al-Fath
C# 140d.4 DIRHAM
2.1500 g., Silver

Date	Mintage	Good	VG	F	VF	XF
AH1270	—	10.00	20.00	30.00	60.00	—
AH1271	—	20.00	40.00	80.00	150	—
AH1272	—	15.00	35.00	65.00	100	—
AH1273	—	15.00	35.00	65.00	100	—
AH1274	—	15.00	35.00	65.00	100	—
AH1275	—	15.00	35.00	65.00	100	—
AH1276	—	15.00	35.00	65.00	100	—

Mint: Fes Hazrat
C# 145 1/2 BENDUQI
1.7600 g., Gold

Date	Mintage	VG	F	VF	XF	Unc
AH1240	—	100	200	350	600	—
AH1247	—	100	200	350	600	—
AH1248	—	90.00	150	250	375	—
AH1250	—	100	200	350	600	—
AH1252	—	100	200	350	600	—

Mint: Fes
C# 150.1 BENDUQI
3.5200 g., Gold

Date	Mintage	VG	F	VF	XF	Unc
AH1270	—	75.00	100	150	200	—
AH1271	—	80.00	110	175	300	—
AH1272	—	75.00	100	150	200	—
AH1273	—	80.00	110	175	300	—
AH1274 Rare	—	—	—	—	—	—
AH1275 Rare	—	—	—	—	—	—

Mint: Fes Hazrat
C# 150.2 BENDUQI
3.5200 g., Gold

Date	Mintage	VG	F	VF	XF	Unc
AH1241	—	80.00	110	175	300	—
AH1242	—	80.00	110	175	300	—
AH1243	—	75.00	100	150	200	—
AH1244	—	75.00	100	150	200	—
AH1245	—	75.00	100	150	200	—
AH1246	—	80.00	110	175	300	—
AH1247	—	75.00	100	150	200	—
AH1248	—	75.00	100	150	200	—
AH1249	—	75.00	100	150	200	—
AH1250	—	75.00	100	150	200	—
AH1251	—	80.00	110	175	300	—
AH1252	—	100	150	300	500	—
AH1253	—	80.00	110	175	300	—
AH1254	—	80.00	110	175	300	—
AH1255	—	80.00	110	175	300	—
AH1256	—	80.00	110	175	300	—
AH1257	—	75.00	100	150	200	—
AH1258	—	100	150	300	500	—
AH1259	—	75.00	100	150	200	—
AH1261	—	100	150	300	500	—
AH1266 Rare	—	—	—	—	—	—
AH1267	—	80.00	110	175	300	—
AH1268 Rare	—	—	—	—	—	—
AH1269	—	80.00	110	175	300	—

Mint: Meknes
C# 150.3 BENDUQI
3.5200 g., Gold

Date	Mintage	VG	F	VF	XF	Unc
AH1247 Rare	—	—	—	—	—	—

Sidi Mohammed IV
AH1276-90/1859-73

HAMMERED COINAGE

Mint: Without Mint Name
C# 160.1 FALUS
3.5300 g., Cast Bronze **Obv:** Seal of Solomon **Rev:** Date **Note:** Size varies 17-18 mm.

Date	Mintage	Good	VG	F	VF	XF
AH1277	—	4.50	8.50	18.50	30.00	—
AH1278 Rare	—	—	—	—	—	—
AH1279	—	4.50	8.50	18.50	30.00	—

Mint: Rabat
C# 160.2 FALUS
3.5300 g., Cast Bronze **Note:** Size varies 17-18 mm.

Date	Mintage	Good	VG	F	VF	XF
AH1277	—	4.50	8.50	18.50	30.00	—
AH1278 Rare	—	—	—	—	—	—

Mint: Tetuan
C# 160.3 FALUS
3.5300 g., Cast Bronze **Note:** Size varies 17-18 mm.

Date	Mintage	Good	VG	F	VF	XF
AH1277	—	6.50	13.50	22.50	40.00	—

Mint: Without Mint Name
C# 160a.1 FALUS
2.8800 g., Cast Bronze **Obv:** Seal of Solomon **Rev:** Date between lines **Note:** Size varies 17-18 mm.

Date	Mintage	Good	VG	F	VF	XF
AH1280	—	6.50	12.50	25.00	50.00	—
AH1281 Rare	—	—	—	—	—	—
AH1283 Rare	—	—	—	—	—	—
AH1288 Rare	—	—	—	—	—	—

Mint: Fes
C# 160a.2 FALUS
2.8800 g., Cast Bronze **Note:** Size varies 17-18 mm.

Date	Mintage	Good	VG	F	VF	XF
AH1280	—	4.50	10.00	18.50	30.00	—
AH1283	—	4.50	10.00	18.50	30.00	—
AH1284	—	3.00	6.00	10.00	15.00	—
AH1285	—	3.00	6.00	10.00	15.00	—
AH1286/5	—	8.00	15.00	25.00	50.00	—
AH1286	—	3.00	6.00	10.00	15.00	—
AH1287	—	4.50	6.00	10.00	30.00	—
AH1288	—	3.00	6.00	10.00	15.00	—
AH1289	—	4.50	10.00	18.50	30.00	—
AH1290	—	4.50	10.00	18.50	30.00	—

Mint: Marrakesh
C# 160a.3 FALUS
2.8800 g., Cast Bronze **Note:** Size varies 17-18 mm.

Date	Mintage	Good	VG	F	VF	XF
AH1283	—	4.50	10.50	18.50	30.00	—
AH1288 Rare	—	—	—	—	—	—

Mint: Rabat al-Fath
C# 160a.4 FALUS
2.8800 g., Cast Bronze **Note:** Size varies 17-18 mm.

Date	Mintage	Good	VG	F	VF	XF
AH1281 Rare	—	—	—	—	—	—

Mint: Without Mint Name
C# 163.1 2 FALUS
7.0600 g., Cast Bronze **Obv:** Seal of Solomon **Rev:** Date **Note:** Size varies 21-23 mm.

Date	Mintage	Good	VG	F	VF	XF
AH1277	—	3.00	6.00	10.00	15.00	—
AH1278	—	3.00	6.00	10.00	15.00	—

Mint: Fes
C# 163.2 2 FALUS
7.0600 g., Cast Bronze **Note:** Size varies 21-23 mm.

Date	Mintage	Good	VG	F	VF	XF
AH1277	—	4.50	10.00	18.50	30.00	—
AH1278	—	4.50	10.00	18.50	30.00	—
AH1279	—	4.50	10.00	18.50	30.00	—

Mint: Hawz
C# 163.5 2 FALUS
7.0600 g., Cast Bronze

Date	Mintage	Good	VG	F	VF	XF
AH1277 Rare	—	—	—	—	—	—
AH1278/7	—	10.00	20.00	30.00	50.00	—
AH1278	—	5.00	10.00	18.00	30.00	—
AH1279 Rare	—	—	—	—	—	—

Mint: Marrakesh
C# 163.3 2 FALUS
7.0600 g., Cast Bronze **Note:** Size varies 21-23 mm.

Date	Mintage	Good	VG	F	VF	XF
AH1277	—	4.50	10.00	18.50	30.00	—
AH1278	—	6.50	12.50	22.50	40.00	—

Mint: Tetuan
C# 163.4 2 FALUS
7.0600 g., Cast Bronze **Note:** Size varies 21-23 mm.

Date	Mintage	Good	VG	F	VF	XF
AH1277	—	4.50	10.00	18.50	30.00	—
AH1278	—	4.00	8.00	12.00	20.00	—
AH1279	—	4.50	10.00	18.50	30.00	—

Mint: Without Mint Name
C# 163a.1 2 FALUS
5.7700 g., Cast Bronze **Note:** Without mintname; Size varies 22-23 mm.

Date	Mintage	Good	VG	F	VF	XF
AH1281	—	4.50	10.00	18.50	30.00	—

Mint: Fes
C# 163a.2 2 FALUS
5.7700 g., Cast Bronze **Note:** Size varies 22-23mm.

Date	Mintage	Good	VG	F	VF	XF
AH1280	—	4.50	10.00	18.50	30.00	—
AH1281/0	—	8.00	15.00	25.00	50.00	—
AH1281	—	3.00	6.00	10.00	15.00	—
AH0821 Error for 1280	—	15.00	25.00	50.00	100	—
AH1282 Rare	—	—	—	—	—	—
AH1283	—	3.00	6.00	10.00	15.00	—
AH1284	—	3.00	6.00	10.00	15.00	—
AH1285	—	3.00	6.00	10.00	15.00	—
AH1286	—	3.00	6.00	10.00	15.00	—
AH1287	—	3.00	6.00	10.00	15.00	—
AH1288/7	—	6.50	12.50	22.50	40.00	—
AH1288	—	3.00	6.00	10.00	15.00	—
AH1289/8	—	6.50	12.50	22.50	40.00	—
AH1289	—	4.50	10.00	18.50	30.00	—
AH1290	—	3.00	6.00	10.00	15.00	—

Mint: Hawz
C# 163a.4 2 FALUS
5.7700 g., Cast Bronze **Note:** Size varies 22-23 mm.

Date	Mintage	Good	VG	F	VF	XF
AH1280	—	4.50	10.00	18.50	30.00	—
AH1281	—	4.50	10.00	18.50	30.00	—

Mint: Marrakesh
C# 163a.3 2 FALUS
5.7700 g., Cast Bronze **Note:** Size varies 22-23 mm.

Date	Mintage	Good	VG	F	VF	XF
AH1280	—	4.50	10.00	18.50	30.00	—
AH1283	—	3.00	6.00	10.00	15.00	—
AH1284	—	3.00	6.00	10.00	15.00	—
AH1285	—	3.00	6.00	10.00	15.00	—
AH1288	—	3.00	6.00	10.00	15.00	—

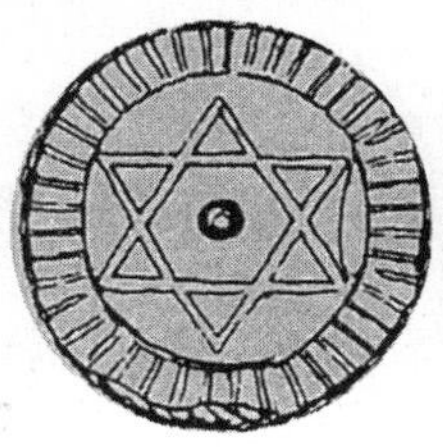

Mint: Fes
C# 166.1 4 FALUS
11.5400 g., Cast Bronze **Obv:** Seal of Solomon **Rev:** Mintname, date within 2 circles **Note:** Size varies 27-29 mm.

Date	Mintage	Good	VG	F	VF	XF
AH1280	—	4.50	10.00	18.50	30.00	—
AH1281	—	4.50	10.00	18.50	30.00	—
AH1283	—	2.00	3.50	6.00	10.00	—
AH1284	—	2.00	3.50	6.00	10.00	—
AH1285	—	2.00	3.50	6.00	10.00	—
AH1286/5	—	8.00	15.00	25.00	50.00	—
AH1286	—	2.00	3.50	6.00	10.00	—
AH1287/6	—	6.50	12.50	22.50	40.00	—
AH1287	—	2.00	3.50	6.00	10.00	—
AH1288/7	—	6.50	12.50	22.50	40.00	—
AH1288	—	2.00	3.50	6.00	10.00	—
AH1289/8	—	6.50	12.50	22.50	40.00	—
AH1289	—	2.00	3.50	6.00	10.00	—
AH1290/89	—	8.00	15.00	25.00	50.00	—
AH1290	—	2.00	3.50	6.00	10.00	—

Mint: Marrakesh
C# 166.2 4 FALUS
11.5400 g., Cast Bronze **Note:** Underweight 6.00 grams or less, with mintnames of Fes or Marrakesh, or with illegible inscriptions and dates are contemporary forgeries, often with smaller diameters; size varies 27-29 mm.

Date	Mintage	Good	VG	F	VF	XF
AH1280	—	4.50	10.00	18.50	30.00	—
AH1281	—	4.50	10.00	18.50	30.00	—
AH1282	—	4.50	10.00	18.50	30.00	—
AH1283	—	2.00	3.50	6.00	10.00	—
AH1284	—	2.00	3.50	6.00	10.00	—
AH1285	—	2.00	3.50	6.00	10.00	—
AH1286	—	2.00	3.50	6.00	10.00	—
AH1287	—	4.50	10.00	18.50	30.00	—
AH1288	—	2.00	3.50	6.00	10.00	—
AH1289	—	4.50	10.00	18.50	30.00	—
AH1290	—	4.50	10.00	18.50	30.00	—

Mint: Fes
C# 170.1 1/4 DIRHAM
0.7300 g., Silver

Date	Mintage	Good	VG	F	VF	XF
AH1284	—	15.00	35.00	65.00	100	—
AH1286 Rare	—	—	—	—	—	—
AH1288	—	10.00	20.00	30.00	60.00	—

Mint: Marrakesh
C# 170.2 1/4 DIRHAM
0.7300 g., Silver

Date	Mintage	Good	VG	F	VF	XF
AH1284	—	15.00	35.00	65.00	100	—

Mint: Fes
C# 175.1 1/2 DIRHAM
1.4600 g., Silver

Date	Mintage	Good	VG	F	VF	XF
AH1283	—	8.00	14.00	20.00	30.00	—
AH1284	—	8.00	14.00	20.00	30.00	—
AH1285	—	15.00	35.00	65.00	100	—
AH1286 Rare	—	—	—	—	—	—
AH1287	—	20.00	40.00	80.00	150	—
AH1288	—	15.00	35.00	65.00	100	—

Mint: Marrakesh
C# 175.2 1/2 DIRHAM
1.4600 g., Silver

Date	Mintage	Good	VG	F	VF	XF
AH1283	—	15.00	35.00	65.00	100	—
AH1284	—	15.00	35.00	65.00	100	—
AH1286 Rare	—	—	—	—	—	—

Mint: Rabat al-Fath
C# 175.3 1/2 DIRHAM
1.4600 g., Silver

Date	Mintage	Good	VG	F	VF	XF
AH1284	—	20.00	40.00	80.00	150	—

Mint: Fes
C# 176.1 DIRHAM
1.9500 g., Silver

Date	Mintage	Good	VG	F	VF	XF
AH1277	—	15.00	35.00	65.00	100	—
AH1278	—	15.00	35.00	65.00	100	—
AH1279	—	20.00	40.00	80.00	150	—

Mint: Rabat al-Fath
C# 176.2 DIRHAM
1.9500 g., Silver

Date	Mintage	Good	VG	F	VF	XF
AH1277 Rare	—	—	—	—	—	—

Mint: Without Mint Name
C# 176.3 DIRHAM
2.9300 g., Silver

Date	Mintage	Good	VG	F	VF	XF
AH1284 Rare	—	—	—	—	—	—

Mint: Fes
C# 176a.1 DIRHAM
2.9300 g., Silver

Date	Mintage	Good	VG	F	VF	XF
AH1283	—	8.00	14.00	20.00	30.00	—
AH1284	—	8.00	14.00	20.00	30.00	—
AH1285	—	8.00	14.00	20.00	30.00	—
AH1286	—	8.00	14.00	20.00	30.00	—
AH1287 Rare	—	—	—	—	—	—
AH1289 Rare	—	—	—	—	—	—

Mint: Marrakesh
C# 176a.2 DIRHAM
2.9300 g., Silver

Date	Mintage	Good	VG	F	VF	XF
AH1283	—	10.00	20.00	30.00	60.00	—
AH1284	—	4.50	10.00	18.50	30.00	—
AH1285	—	10.00	20.00	30.00	60.00	—
AH1286	—	15.00	35.00	65.00	100	—
AH1287 Rare	—	—	—	—	—	—

Mint: Rabat al-Fath
C# 176a.3 DIRHAM
2.9300 g., Silver

Date	Mintage	Good	VG	F	VF	XF
AH1284	—	4.50	10.00	18.50	30.00	—
AH1285	—	20.00	40.00	80.00	150	—
AH1286	—	20.00	40.00	80.00	150	—

Mint: Fes
C# 178 BENDUQI
3.5200 g., Gold

Date	Mintage	VG	F	VF	XF	Unc
AH1277 Rare	—	—	—	—	—	—
AH1284 Rare	—	—	—	—	—	—
AH1286 Rare	—	—	—	—	—	—

Moulay al-Hasan I

AH1290-1311/1873-94AD

HAMMERED COINAGE

Mint: Without Mint Name
C# 181 FALUS
3.5280 g., Cast Bronze, 19 mm.

Date	Mintage	Good	VG	F	VF	XF
AH1291	—	8.50	13.50	22.50	40.00	—
AH1297	—	8.50	13.50	22.50	40.00	—

Mint: Fes
C# 181.1 FALUS
2.8830 g., Cast Bronze **Note:** Size varies: 16 - 17 mm.

Date	Mintage	Good	VG	F	VF	XF
AH1299 Rare	—	—	—	—	—	—

Mint: Without Mint Name
C# 182.3 2 FALUS
7.0560 g., Cast Bronze, 23 mm.

Date	Mintage	Good	VG	F	VF	XF
AH1297	—	8.50	13.50	22.50	40.00	—

Mint: Fes
C# 182.2 2 FALUS
5.7700 g., Cast Bronze, 21 mm.

Date	Mintage	Good	VG	F	VF	XF
AH1291	—	8.50	13.50	22.50	40.00	—
AH1299	—	20.00	40.00	80.00	150	—

Mint: Fes
C# 183.1 4 FALUS
11.5400 g., Cast Bronze **Note:** Size varies 27 - 28 mm.

Date	Mintage	Good	VG	F	VF	XF
AH1291	—	8.50	13.50	22.50	40.00	—
AH1299	—	12.00	25.00	50.00	100	—

Mint: Marrakesh
C# 183.2 4 FALUS
11.5400 g., Cast Bronze **Note:** Size varies 27 - 29 mm.

Date	Mintage	Good	VG	F	VF	XF
AH1291	—	8.50	13.50	22.50	40.00	—
AH1292	—	10.00	16.00	30.00	60.00	—
AH1295	—	8.50	13.50	22.50	40.00	—

Mint: Fes
C# 187 DIRHAM
2.9300 g., Silver

Date	Mintage	Good	VG	F	VF	XF
AH1291	—	20.00	40.00	80.00	160	—

MILLED COINAGE

Mint: Fes
Y# C1 1/4 FALUS
0.7200 g., Bronze **Note:** Previously listed as "1/2 Muzuna".

Date	Mintage	F	VF	XF	Unc
AH1306Fs	—	400	700	1,200	2,000
AH1310Fs	—	200	350	600	1,000

Mint: Fes
Y# B1 1/2 FALUS
1.4400 g., Bronze **Note:** Previously listed as "Muzuna".

Date	Mintage	F	VF	XF	Unc
AH1306Fs	—	350	650	1,100	1,800
AH1310Fs	—	150	300	550	900

Mint: Fes
Y# 1 FALUS
2.8800 g., Bronze **Note:** Previously listed as "2 1/2 Muzunas".

Date	Mintage	F	VF	XF	Unc
AH1306Fs	—	300	500	1,000	1,600
AH1310Fs	—	125	250	500	800

Mint: Fes
Y# 2 2 FALUS
5.7700 g., Bronze **Note:** Previously listed as "5 Muzunas".

Date	Mintage	F	VF	XF	Unc
AH1306Fs	—	300	500	1,000	1,600
AH1310Fs	—	60.00	100	200	500

Note: Varieties exist

Mint: Fes
Y# 3 4 FALUS
11.5400 g., Bronze **Note:** Previously listed as "10 Muzunas".

Date	Mintage	F	VF	XF	Unc
AH1306Fs	—	300	500	1,000	1,600
AH1310Fs	—	65.00	125	250	600

Mint: Paris
Y# 4 1/2 DIRHAM
1.4558 g., 0.8350 Silver .0391 oz. ASW **Note:** AH1312-1314Pa were struck posthumously under 'Abd al-Aziz'

Date	Mintage	F	VF	XF	Unc
AH1299Pa	2,200,000	2.00	3.50	6.00	12.00
AH1299Pa Proof; 2 known	—	—	—	—	—
AH1309Pa	1,143,000	3.50	8.50	16.50	35.00
AH1310Pa	1,142,000	3.50	8.50	16.50	35.00
AH1311Pa	1,716,000	3.00	6.50	13.50	25.00
AH1312Pa	1,700,000	2.00	4.00	9.00	20.00
AH1313Pa	1,700,000	2.00	4.00	9.00	20.00
AH1314Pa Mintage included with Y#9.2	—	10.00	22.50	40.00	80.00

Mint: Paris
Y# 5 DIRHAM
2.9116 g., 0.8350 Silver .0782 oz. ASW **Note:** AH1312-1314Pa were struck posthumously under 'Abd al-Aziz'

Date	Mintage	F	VF	XF	Unc
AH1299Pa	6,800,000	2.00	4.00	8.00	20.00
AH1299Pa Proof; 2 known	—	—	—	—	—
AH1309Pa	571,000	6.00	12.50	25.00	60.00
AH1310Pa	1,144,000	3.50	8.50	16.50	35.00
AH1311Pa	1,890,000	3.00	6.50	13.50	25.00
AH1312Pa	800,000	2.75	7.50	17.00	35.00
AH1313Pa	800,000	3.00	8.00	22.50	35.00
AH1314Pa Mintage included with Y#10.2	—	20.00	42.50	80.00	160

Mint: Paris
Y# 6 2-1/2 DIRHAMS
7.2790 g., 0.8350 Silver .1954 oz. ASW **Note:** AH1312-1314Pa were struck posthumously under 'Abd al-Aziz'

Date	Mintage	F	VF	XF	Unc
AH1299Pa	2,100,000	3.00	10.00	20.00	30.00
AH1299Pa Proof; 2 known	—	—	—	—	—
AH1309Pa	229,000	10.00	25.00	50.00	100
AH1310Pa	400,000	4.00	12.00	30.00	60.00
AH1311Pa	800,000	4.00	12.00	30.00	60.00
AH1312Pa	300,000	4.00	12.00	32.00	65.00
AH1313Pa	300,000	4.00	12.00	32.00	65.00
AH1314Pa Mintage included with Y#11.2	—	50.00	100	200	400

Mint: Paris
Y# 7 5 DIRHAMS
14.5580 g., 0.8350 Silver .3908 oz. ASW **Note:** AH1312-1314Pa were struck posthumously under 'Abd al-Aziz'

Date	Mintage	F	VF	XF	Unc
AH1299Pa	1,400,000	10.00	22.50	40.00	80.00
AH1299Pa Proof; 2 known	—	—	—	—	—
AH1309Pa	114,000	20.00	45.00	80.00	160
AH1310Pa	170,000	12.50	25.00	50.00	100
AH1311Pa	170,000	12.50	25.00	50.00	100
AH1312Pa	170,000	12.50	25.00	50.00	100
AH1313Pa	170,000	12.50	25.00	50.00	100
AH1314Pa Mintage included with Y#12.2	—	150	300	600	950

Mint: Paris
Y# 8 10 DIRHAMS
29.1160 g., 0.9000 Silver .8425 oz. ASW

Date	Mintage	F	VF	XF	Unc
AH1299Pa	870,000	15.00	30.00	50.00	120
AH1299Pa Proof; 2 known	—	—	—	—	—

Abd al-Aziz

AH1311-1326 / 1894-1908AD

MILLED COINAGE

Mint: Berlin
Y# 9.1 1/2 DIRHAM
1.4558 g., 0.8350 Silver .0391 oz. ASW **Rev:** Arrow heads point outward

Date	Mintage	F	VF	XF	Unc
AH1313Be	560,000	8.50	17.50	32.50	60.00

Mint: Paris
Y# 9.2 1/2 DIRHAM
1.4558 g., 0.8350 Silver .0391 oz. ASW **Rev:** Arrow heads point inward

Date	Mintage	F	VF	XF	Unc
AH1314Pa	1,714,000	3.00	6.50	13.50	25.00
AH1315Pa	2,230,000	3.00	6.50	13.50	25.00
AH1316Pa	1,193,000	4.50	8.50	16.50	35.00
AH1317Pa	2,285,000	3.00	6.50	13.50	25.00
AH1318Pa	1,715,000	4.00	8.00	12.00	25.00
AH1319Pa	572,000	8.00	16.00	30.00	60.00

Mint: Berlin
Y# 10.1 DIRHAM
2.9116 g., 0.8350 Silver .0782 oz. ASW **Rev:** Arrow heads point outward

Date	Mintage	F	VF	XF	Unc
AH1313Be	430,000	9.00	18.50	35.00	70.00

Mint: Paris
Y# 10.2 DIRHAM
2.9116 g., 0.8350 Silver .0782 oz. ASW **Rev:** Arrow heads point inward

Date	Mintage	F	VF	XF	Unc
AH1314Pa	1,400,000	3.00	7.00	15.00	30.00
AH1315Pa	1,141,000	3.00	7.00	15.00	30.00
AH1316Pa	860,000	3.00	7.00	15.00	30.00
AH1317Pa	860,000	3.00	7.00	15.00	30.00
AH1318Pa	1,144,000	3.00	7.00	15.00	30.00

Mint: Berlin
Y# 11.1 2-1/2 DIRHAMS
7.2790 g., 0.8350 Silver .1954 oz. ASW **Rev:** Arrow heads point outward

Date	Mintage	F	VF	XF	Unc
AH1313Be	220,000	7.50	15.00	25.00	80.00
AH1315Be	640,000	5.00	10.00	15.00	55.00
AH1318Be	146,000	25.00	50.00	100	200

Mint: Paris
Y# 11.2 2-1/2 DIRHAMS
7.2790 g., 0.8350 Silver .1954 oz. ASW **Rev:** Arrow heads point inward

Date	Mintage	F	VF	XF	Unc
AH1314Pa	1,036,000	6.00	15.00	32.50	80.00
AH1315Pa	1,036,000	4.00	10.00	20.00	40.00
AH1316Pa	344,000	6.00	15.00	32.50	80.00
AH1317Pa	451,000	6.00	15.00	32.50	80.00
AH1318Pa	452,000	6.00	15.00	32.50	80.00

Mint: Berlin
Y# 12.1 5 DIRHAMS
14.5580 g., 0.8350 Silver .3908 oz. ASW

Date	Mintage	F	VF	XF	Unc
AH1313Be	110,000	20.00	42.50	80.00	160
AH1315Be	288,000	10.00	22.50	40.00	80.00
AH1318Be	73,000	50.00	100	200	400

Mint: Paris
Y# 12.2 5 DIRHAMS
14.5580 g., 0.8350 Silver .3908 oz. ASW

Date	Mintage	F	VF	XF	Unc
AH1314Pa	517,000	15.00	32.50	65.00	125
AH1315Pa	517,000	8.00	16.50	30.00	60.00
AH1316Pa	160,000	15.00	32.50	65.00	125
AH1317Pa	225,000	12.50	25.00	50.00	100
AH1318Pa	231,000	12.50	25.00	50.00	100

Mint: Berlin
Y# 13 10 DIRHAMS
29.1160 g., 0.9000 Silver .8425 oz. ASW

Date	Mintage	F	VF	XF	Unc
AH1313Be	55,000	80.00	160	325	650
AH1313Be Proof	10	Value: 1,400			

PATTERNS

Including off metal strikes

KM#	Date	Mintage	Identification	Mkt Val
Pn1	AH1295Mr	—	4 Falus. Cast Bronze. 14.1100 g. 29 mm.	—
Pn2	AH1295Mr	—	8 Falus. Cast Bronze. 28.2200 g. 35 mm.	—

KM#	Date	Mintage	Identification	Mkt Val
Pn3	AH1297	—	Dirham. Bronze.	1,200

KM#	Date	Mintage	Identification	Mkt Val
Pn4	AH1297	—	5 Miscals.	5,000
Pn5	AH1297	—	10 Mitqals. Silver.	2,000

KM#	Date	Mintage	Identification	Mkt Val
Pn6	AH1297	—	4 Ryals. Gold.	5,500

KM#	Date	Mintage	Identification	Mkt Val
PnA7	AH(1880-90)	—	Dirham. Silver. In the name of Marrakush Mint.	700

KM#	Date	Mintage	Identification	Mkt Val
Pn7	AH1298	—	1/2 Mitqal. Silver.	10,000

KM#	Date	Mintage	Identification	Mkt Val
Pn8	AH1298	—	10 Dirhems. Silver.	13,000
Pn9	AH1301	—	Falus. Cast Bronze. Octangular central designs.	—
Pn10	AH1301	—	Falus. Cast Bronze. Stars in border.	—
Pn11	AH1301	—	Falus. Cast Bronze. Floral and leaf borders.	—

KM#	Date	Mintage	Identification	Mkt Val
Pn12	AH1301	—	2 Falus. Cast Bronze.	850
Pn13	AH1301	—	2 Falus. Cast Bronze.	—
Pn14	AH1301	—	4 Falus. Cast Bronze.	—
Pn15	AH1301	—	4 Falus. Cast Bronze.	—
Pn21	AH1311	—	2 Falus. Cast Bronze.	—

KM#	Date	Mintage	Identification	Mkt Val
Pn22	AH1311	—	4 Falus. Cast Bronze.	—
Pn23	AH1311	—	6 Falus. Cast Bronze.	—

KM#	Date	Mintage	Identification	Mkt Val
Pn24	AH1311	—	8 Falus. Cast Bronze.	—
Pn25	AH1311Fs	—	1/2 Dirham. Silver. 1.4000 g. 15 mm.	—

KM#	Date	Mintage	Identification	Mkt Val
Pn26	AH1311Fs	—	Dirham. Silver. 2.9000 g. 17 mm.	—
Pn27	AH1313Fs	—	1/2 Falus. Bronze. 1.4430 g. 13 mm.	—

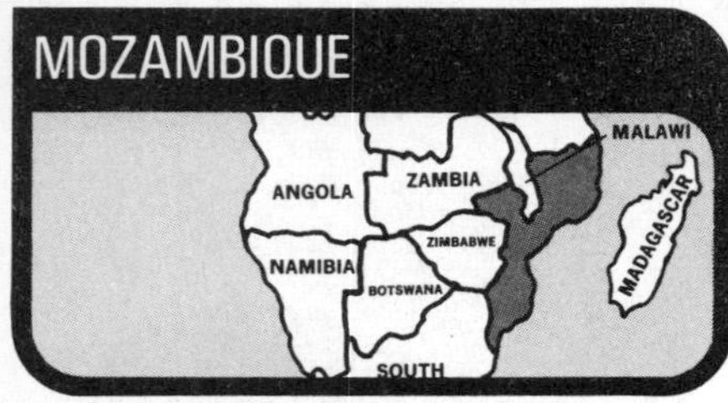

The Republic of Mozambique, a former overseas province of Portugal, stretches for 1,430 miles (2,301km.) along the southeast coast of Africa, has an area of 302,330 sq. mi. (801,590 sq. km.).

Vasco de Gama explored all the coast of Mozambique in 1498 and found Arab trading posts already established along the coast. Portuguese settlement dates from the establishment of the trading post of Mozambique in 1505. Within five years Portugal absorbed all the former Arab sultanates along the east African coast.

RULERS
Portuguese, until 1975

MONETARY SYSTEM
100 Centavos = 1 Escudo

PORTUGUESE COLONY

COLONIAL COINAGE

KM# 24 REAL
Copper

Date	Mintage	F	VF	XF	Unc	BU
1853	100,000	12.00	25.00	70.00	120	—

KM# 25 2 REIS (II)
Copper

Date	Mintage	F	VF	XF	Unc	BU
1853	100,000	12.00	25.00	70.00	120	—

Note: The V Reis, X Reis and XX Reis pieces dated 1853 were issued primarily for circulation in Mozambique. These are also attributed to Portugal and will be found under their appropriate listings

KM# 18 20 REIS
Copper

Date	Mintage	F	VF	XF	Unc	BU
1820	—	16.00	30.00	75.00	155	—

Note: For coins with countermark 10' refer to Brazil listings. Some 20 Reis coins previously listed here are now listed in St. Thomas and Prince Island

KM# 21 20 REIS
Copper **Note:** Similar to 40 Reis, KM#22.

Date	Mintage	F	VF	XF	Unc	BU
1840	40,000	25.00	50.00	100	200	—

KM# 19 40 REIS
Copper

Date	Mintage	F	VF	XF	Unc	BU
1820	—	16.00	35.00	80.00	170	—

Note: For coins with countermark 20' refer to Brazil listings. Some 40 Reis coins previously listed here are now listed in St. Thomas and Prince Islands

KM# 22 40 REIS
Copper

Date	Mintage	F	VF	XF	Unc	BU
1840	20,000	22.50	45.00	95.00	185	—

KM# 20 80 REIS
Copper

Date	Mintage	F	VF	XF	Unc	BU
1820	—	22.50	45.00	90.00	180	—

Note: Other 80 Reis coins previously listed here are now listed in St. Thomas and Prince Islands

KM# 23 80 REIS
Copper **Note:** Similar to 40 Reis, KM#22.

Date	Mintage	F	VF	XF	Unc	BU
1840	10,000	25.00	50.00	120	210	—

KM# 26.1 ONCA
Silver **Obv:** Small date, lettering

Date	Mintage	VG	F	VF	XF	Unc
1843	—	75.00	200	325	—	—

KM# 26.2 ONCA
Silver **Obv:** Large date, lettering

Date	Mintage	VG	F	VF	XF	Unc
1845	—	80.00	225	365	—	—
1847	—	65.00	200	300	—	—

Note: NOTE: Varieties of reverse exist.</p>

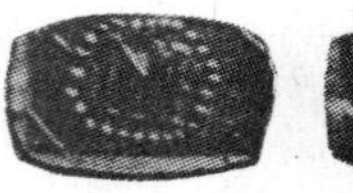

KM# 31 1-1/4 MATICAES
7.2000 g., Gold, 11 x 17 mm. **Note:** Rectangular.

Date	Mintage	VG	F	VF	XF	Unc
ND	—	750	1,600	3,500	—	—

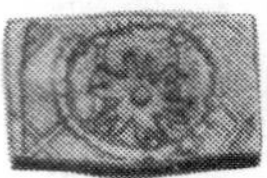
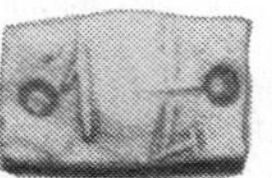

KM# 32 1-1/4 MATICAES
7.2000 g., Gold **Countermark:** Rosette **Note:** Countermark on KM#31

Date	Mintage	VG	F	VF	XF	Unc
ND	—	500	1,000	2,500	—	—

KM# 33 2-1/2 MATICAES
14.5000 g., Gold

Date	Mintage	VG	F	VF	XF	Unc
ND	—	750	1,400	3,000	—	—

KM# 34 2-1/2 MATICAES
14.5000 g., Gold **Countermark:** Rosette **Note:** Countermark on KM#33

Date	Mintage	VG	F	VF	XF	Unc
ND	—	250	450	750	—	—

COUNTERMARKED COINAGE

Decree of January 5, 1889

This decree ordained that all foreign silver coinage circulating in Mozambique was to be countermarked with a crowned PM within a circle. These coins were eventually to be replaced or exchanged by current Portuguese coinage upon their entry into the public treasury. The following list is a basic guide. Caution should be exercised as counterfeits exist. Grades noted are for the basic coin as the countermark is normally found in better condition than the coin bearing it.

KM# 35 6 PENCE
0.9250 Silver **Countermark:** Crowned PM **Note:** Countermark on Great Britain 6 Pence, KM#751.

CM Date	Host Date	Good	VG	F	VF	XF
ND	(1867-80)	25.00	40.00	65.00	110	—

KM# 36 SHILLING
0.9250 Silver **Countermark:** Crowned PM **Note:** Countermark on Great Britain Shilling, KM#734

CM Date	Host Date	Good	VG	F	VF	XF
ND	(1838-87)	25.00	40.00	65.00	110	—

KM# 37.1 1/2 RUPEE
0.9170 Silver **Countermark:** Crowned PM **Note:** Previous KM#A37; countermark on India 1/2 Rupee, KM#455.

CM Date	Host Date	Good	VG	F	VF	XF
ND	ND(1840)	12.50	20.00	35.00	75.00	—

KM# 37.2 1/2 RUPEE
0.9170 Silver **Countermark:** Crowned PM **Note:** Countermark on India 1/2 Rupee, KM#456.

CM Date	Host Date	Good	VG	F	VF	XF
ND	ND(1840)	12.50	20.00	35.00	75.00	—

KM# 38.1 1/2 RUPEE
0.9170 Silver **Countermark:** Crowned PM **Note:** Previous KM#A38; countermark on India 1/2 Rupee, KM#472.

CM Date	Host Date	Good	VG	F	VF	XF
ND	(1862-76)	12.50	20.00	35.00	75.00	—

KM# 38.2 1/2 RUPEE
0.9170 Silver **Countermark:** Crowned PM **Note:** Previous KM#38; countermark on India 1/2 Rupee, KM#471.

CM Date	Host Date	Good	VG	F	VF	XF
ND	ND	12.50	20.00	35.00	75.00	—

KM# 39 RUPEE
0.9170 Silver **Countermark:** Crowned PM **Note:** Countermark on India Rupee, KM#450.

CM Date	Host Date	Good	VG	F	VF	XF
ND	(1835)	35.00	60.00	100	165	—

KM# 40.1 RUPEE
0.9170 Silver **Countermark:** Crowned PM **Note:** Previous KM#A40; countermark on India Rupee, KM#457.

CM Date	Host Date	Good	VG	F	VF	XF
ND	(1877-88)	27.50	42.50	70.00	115	—

KM# 40.2 RUPEE
0.9170 Silver **Countermark:** Crowned PM **Note:** Previous KM#40; countermark on India Rupee, KM#458.

CM Date	Host Date	Good	VG	F	VF	XF
ND	(1840)	27.50	42.50	70.00	115	—

KM# 41.1 RUPEE
0.9170 Silver **Countermark:** Crowned PM **Note:** Previous KM#A41; countermark on India Rupee, KM#473.

CM Date	Host Date	Good	VG	F	VF	XF
ND	(1862-76)	27.50	42.50	70.00	115	—

KM# 41.2 RUPEE
0.9170 Silver **Countermark:** Crowned PM **Note:** Previous KM#41; countermark on India Rupee, KM#472.

CM Date	Host Date	Good	VG	F	VF	XF
ND	ND	27.50	42.50	70.00	115	—

KM# 42 RUPEE
0.9170 Silver **Countermark:** Crowned PM **Note:** Countermark on India-Portuguese Rupee, KM#12.

CM Date	Host Date	Good	VG	F	VF	XF
ND	(1881-82)	27.50	42.50	70.00	115	—

KM# 43 RUPEE
0.9170 Silver **Countermark:** Crowned PM **Note:** Countermark on Mombasa Rupee, KM#5.

CM Date	Host Date	Good	VG	F	VF	XF
ND	ND	27.50	42.50	70.00	115	—

KM# 44.1 8 REALES
27.0700 g., 0.9030 Silver .7859 oz. **Countermark:** Crowned PM **Note:** Countermark on Guanajuato 8 Reales, KM#377.8.

CM Date	Host Date	Good	VG	F	VF	XF
ND	(1825-88)	45.00	85.00	145	235	—

KM# 44.2 8 REALES
27.0700 g., 0.9030 Silver 0.7859 oz. **Note:** Countermark: Crowned PM on Hermosilla 8 Reales, KM#377.9.

CM Date	Host Date	Good	VG	F	VF	XF
ND	(1835-88)	45.00	85.00	145	235	—

KM# 44.3 8 REALES
27.0700 g., 0.9030 Silver 0.7859 oz. **Note:** Countermark: Crowned PM on Mexico City 8 Reales, KM#377.10.

CM Date	Host Date	Good	VG	F	VF	XF
ND	(1824-88)	45.00	85.00	145	235	—

KM# 44.4 8 REALES
27.0700 g., 0.9030 Silver 0.7859 oz. **Note:** Countermark: Crowned PM on Potosi 8 Reales, KM#377.12.

CM Date	Host Date	Good	VG	F	VF	XF
ND	(1827-88)	45.00	85.00	145	235	—

KM# 44.5 8 REALES
27.0700 g., 0.9030 Silver 0.7859 oz. **Note:** Countermark: Crowned PM on Zacatecas 8 Reales, KM#377.13.

CM Date	Host Date	Good	VG	F	VF	XF
ND	(1825-88)	45.00	85.00	145	235	—

KM# 45 THALER
28.0668 g., 0.8330 Silver .7517 oz. **Countermark:** Crowned PM **Note:** Countermark on Austria Maria Theresa (restrike) Thaler, KM#T1.

CM Date	Host Date	Good	VG	F	VF	XF
ND	(1780)	25.00	40.00	65.00	125	—

KM# 46.1 THALER
28.0668 g., 0.8330 Silver .7517 oz. **Countermark:** Crowned PM **Note:** Previous KM#AA46; countermark on Austria Thaler, KM#2160.

CM Date	Host Date	Good	VG	F	VF	XF
ND	ND	—	50.00	100	160	250

KM# 46.2 THALER
Silver **Countermark:** Crowned PM **Note:** Previous KM#A46; countermark on Austria Thaler, KM#2161.

CM Date	Host Date	Good	VG	F	VF	XF
ND	(1811-15)	—	50.00	100	160	250

KM# 46.3 THALER
Silver **Countermark:** Crowned PM **Note:** Previous KM#46; Countermark on Austria Thaler, KM#2162.

CM Date	Host Date	Good	VG	F	VF	XF
ND	(1817-24)	—	50.00	100	160	250

KM# 47 THALER
Silver **Countermark:** Crowned PM **Note:** Countermark on Austria Thaler, KM#2163.

CM Date	Host Date	Good	VG	F	VF	XF
ND	(1824-30)	—	50.00	100	160	250

Decree of January 19, 1889
1889-1895

During the reign of D. Carlos I, a substitution of an indented PM (Provincia de Mocambique) which replaced the crowned PM of D. Luis I, was countermarked on all foreign silver coinage circulating in Mozambique. These coins were to be replaced or exchanged by Portuguese coinage on their entry into the public treasury.

KM# 48.1 1/4 RUPEE
0.9170 Silver **Countermark:** PM on India 1/4 Rupee, KM#470

CM Date	Host Date	Good	VG	F	VF	XF
ND	(1862-76)	15.00	22.50	37.50	75.00	—

KM# 48.2 1/4 RUPEE
0.9170 Silver **Countermark:** PM on India 1/4 Rupee, KM#490

CM Date	Host Date	Good	VG	F	VF	XF
ND	(1877-88)	15.00	22.50	37.50	75.00	—

KM# 49.1 1/2 RUPEE
0.9170 Silver **Countermark:** PM on India 1/2 Rupee, KM#455

CM Date	Host Date	Good	VG	F	VF	XF
ND	(1840)	15.00	22.50	37.50	75.00	—

KM# 49.2 1/2 RUPEE
0.9170 Silver **Countermark:** PM on India 1/2 Rupee, KM#456

CM Date	Host Date	Good	VG	F	VF	XF
ND	(1840)	15.00	22.50	37.50	75.00	—

KM# 50 1/2 RUPEE
0.9170 Silver **Countermark:** PM on India 1/2 Rupee, KM#472

CM Date	Host Date	Good	VG	F	VF	XF
ND	(1862-76)	15.00	22.50	37.50	75.00	—

KM# 51 1/2 RUPEE
0.9170 Silver **Countermark:** PM on German East Africa 1/2 Rupie, KM#4

CM Date	Host Date	Good	VG	F	VF	XF
ND	(1891)	40.00	75.00	125	200	—

KM# 52 RUPEE
0.9170 Silver **Countermark:** PM on India Rupee, KM#450

CM Date	Host Date	Good	VG	F	VF	XF
ND	(1835)	35.00	60.00	100	150	—

KM# 53.1 RUPEE
0.9170 Silver **Countermark:** PM on India Rupee KM#457

CM Date	Host Date	Good	VG	F	VF	XF
ND	(1840)	20.00	30.00	50.00	85.00	—

KM# 53.2 RUPEE
0.9170 Silver **Countermark:** PM on India Rupee KM#458

CM Date	Host Date	Good	VG	F	VF	XF
ND	(1840)	20.00	30.00	50.00	85.00	—

KM# 54.1 RUPEE
0.9170 Silver **Countermark:** PM on India Rupee KM#473

CM Date	Host Date	Good	VG	F	VF	XF
ND	(1862-76)	20.00	30.00	50.00	85.00	—

KM# 54.2 RUPEE
0.9170 Silver **Countermark:** PM on India Rupee KM#492

CM Date	Host Date	Good	VG	F	VF	XF
ND	(1877-88)	20.00	30.00	50.00	85.00	—

KM# 55 RUPEE
0.9170 Silver **Countermark:** PM on India-Portuguese Rupia, KM#12

CM Date	Host Date	Good	VG	F	VF	XF
ND	(1881)	20.00	30.00	50.00	85.00	—

KM# 56 RUPEE
0.9170 Silver **Countermark:** PM on Mombasa Rupee, KM#5

CM Date	Host Date	Good	VG	F	VF	XF
ND	(1888)	25.00	37.50	62.50	100	—

KM# 57 RUPEE
0.9170 Silver **Countermark:** PM on German East Africa Rupie, KM#2

CM Date	Host Date	Good	VG	F	VF	XF
ND	(1890-94)	40.00	75.00	125	200	—

KM# 58 THALER
Silver **Countermark:** PM on Austria Marie Theresa Thaler, KM#T1

CM Date	Host Date	Good	VG	F	VF	XF
ND	(1780)	40.00	85.00	125	240	—

KM# 59 THALER
Silver **Countermark:** PM on Austria Thaler, KM#2162

CM Date	Host Date	Good	VG	F	VF	XF
ND	(1817-24)	50.00	100	160	250	—

KM# 60 THALER
Silver **Countermark:** PM on Austria Thaler, KM#2163

CM Date	Host Date	Good	VG	F	VF	XF
ND	(1824-30)	50.00	100	160	250	—

PRIVATE TOKEN COINAGE

KM# Tn1 10 REIS
Copper **Issuer:** Companhia Do Nyassa

Date	Mintage	F	VF	XF	Unc	BU
1894	508,000	—	—	250	450	—

KM# Tn2 20 REIS
Copper

Date	Mintage	F	VF	XF	Unc	BU
1894	423,000	—	—	200	400	—

KM# Tn3 500 REIS
Silver

Date	Mintage	F	VF	XF	Unc	BU
1894	—	—	—	2,000	3,500	—

KM# Tn4 1000 REIS
Silver

Date	Mintage	F	VF	XF	Unc	BU
1894	—	—	—	6,000	—	—

KM# Tn4a 1000 REIS
Bronze

Date	Mintage	F	VF	XF	Unc	BU
1894	—	—	—	—	—	—

Note: The above issues were produced at the Birmingham Mint to match the standards of the coins circulating in Portugal

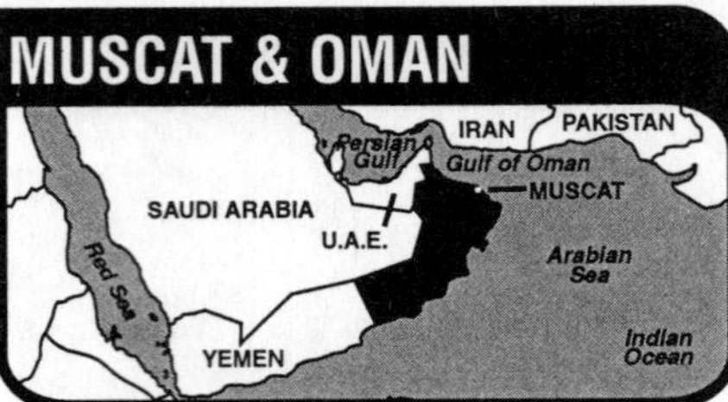

The Sultanate of Oman (formerly Muscat and Oman), an independent monarchy located in the southeastern part of the Arabian Peninsula, has an area of 82,030 sq. mi. (212,460 sq. km.) and a population of *1.3 million. Capital: Muscat. The economy is based on agriculture, herding and petroleum. Petroleum products, dates, fish and hides are exported.

The Portuguese who captured Muscat, the capital and chief port, in 1508, made the first European contact with Muscat and Oman. They occupied the city, utilizing it as a naval base and factory and holding it against land and sea attacks by Arabs and Persians until finally ejected by local Arabs in 1650. It was next occupied by the Persians who maintained control until 1741,when it was taken by Ahmed ibn Sa'id of the present ruling family. Muscat and Oman was the most powerful state in Arabia during the first half of the 19th century, until weakened by the persistent attack of interior nomadic tribes. British influence, initiated by the signing of a treaty of friendship with the Sultanate in 1798,remains a dominant fact of the civil and military phases of the government, although Britain recognizes the Sultanate as a sovereign state.

Sultan Sa'id bin Taimur was overthrown by his son, Qabus bin Sa'id, on July 23, 1970. The new sultan changed the nation's name to Sultanate of Oman.

TITLES

Muscat مسقط

Oman عمان

RULERS

al-Bu Sa'id Dynasty

Sultan bin Ahmad, AH1207-1219/1792-1804AD
Sultan bin Sultan, AH1219-1273/1804-1856AD
Thuwaini bin Sa'id, AH1273-1283/1856-1866AD
Salim bin Thuwaini, AH1283-1285/1866-1868AD
Azzan bin Quais, AH1285-1288/1868-1871AD
Turkee bin Sa'id, AH1288-1306/1871-1888AD
Faisal bin Turkee, AH1306-1332/1888-1913AD

MONETARY SYSTEM

Until 1970

4 Baiza = 1 Anna
64 Baiza = 1 Rupee
200 Baiza = 1 Saidi (Dasin Dog)/Dhofari Rial

SULTANATE

REGULAR COINAGE

KM# 1 1/12 ANNA
Copper **Ruler:** Faisal bin Turkee

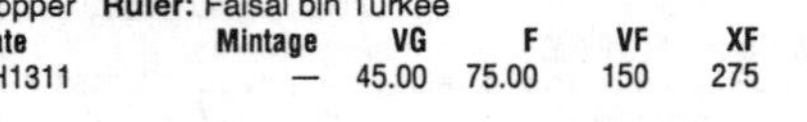

Date	Mintage	VG	F	VF	XF	Unc
AH1311	—	45.00	75.00	150	275	—

KM# 2 1/4 ANNA
Copper **Ruler:** Faisal bin Turkee

Date	Mintage	VG	F	VF	XF	Unc
AH1311	—	10.00	20.00	40.00	85.00	—

KM# 3.1 1/4 ANNA
Copper Or Brass **Ruler:** Faisal bin Turkee **Note:** Level 5.

Date	Mintage	VG	F	VF	XF	Unc
AH1315	19,110,000	0.50	1.00	2.00	4.00	—

KM# 3.2 1/4 ANNA
Copper Or Brass **Ruler:** Faisal bin Turkee **Note:** Small, angled 5.

Date	Mintage	VG	F	VF	XF	Unc
AH1315	Inc. above	0.75	1.50	3.00	6.00	—

Note: This type is considered a crude issue with many die varieties known. It was perhaps struch in Bombay, India.

LOCAL COINAGE

There are numerous varieties of each year of the native issues, varying in both obverse and reverse legends presentation, with the presence or absence of borders, etc.

KM# 4.1 1/4 ANNA
Copper **Ruler:** Faisal bin Turkee **Obv. Legend:** ...IMAM.MUSCAT

Date	Mintage	VG	F	VF	XF	Unc
AH1312	—	12.00	25.00	50.00	90.00	—

KM# 4.2 1/4 ANNA
Copper **Ruler:** Faisal bin Turkee **Obv:** Without inner circle

Date	Mintage	VG	F	VF	XF	Unc
AH1312	—	12.00	25.00	50.00	90.00	—

KM# 5 1/4 ANNA
Copper **Ruler:** Faisal bin Turkee **Obv. Legend:** ...IMAM.MUSCAT.OMAN. **Rev:** Similar to KM#2

Date	Mintage	VG	F	VF	XF	Unc
AH1312//1311	—	20.00	35.00	75.00	140	—

KM# 6 1/4 ANNA
Copper **Ruler:** Faisal bin Turkee

Date	Mintage	VG	F	VF	XF	Unc
AH1312	—	5.00	10.00	20.00	40.00	—
AH1313	—	6.00	12.00	25.00	45.00	—

KM# 7 1/4 ANNA
Copper **Ruler:** Faisal bin Turkee **Obv:** Similar to KM#6. **Rev:** Similar to KM#2 **Note:** Mule.

Date	Mintage	VG	F	VF	XF	Unc
AH1313//1311	—	35.00	60.00	100	185	—

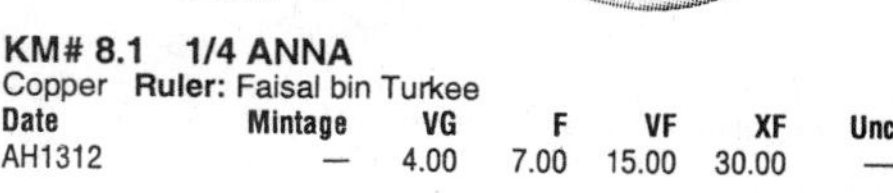

KM# 8.1 1/4 ANNA
Copper **Ruler:** Faisal bin Turkee

Date	Mintage	VG	F	VF	XF	Unc
AH1312	—	4.00	7.00	15.00	30.00	—

KM# 8.2 1/4 ANNA
Copper **Ruler:** Faisal bin Turkee **Rev:** Long dentilated borders

Date	Mintage	VG	F	VF	XF	Unc
AH1312	—	5.00	10.00	20.00	35.00	—

KM# 9.1 1/4 ANNA
Copper **Ruler:** Faisal bin Turkee

Date	Mintage	VG	F	VF	XF	Unc
AH1313	—	5.00	10.00	20.00	35.00	—

KM# 9.2 1/4 ANNA
Copper **Ruler:** Faisal bin Turkee **Obv:** Legend begins at top with star or dot **Rev:** 5-line inscription with denticled border

Date	Mintage	VG	F	VF	XF	Unc
AH1313	—	6.00	12.00	25.00	40.00	—

KM# 10.1 1/4 ANNA
Copper **Ruler:** Faisal bin Turkee

Date	Mintage	VG	F	VF	XF	Unc
AH1314	—	5.00	10.00	20.00	35.00	—

KM# 10.2 1/4 ANNA
Copper **Ruler:** Faisal bin Turkee **Obv:** Large date, value on one line

Date	Mintage	VG	F	VF	XF	Unc
AH1314	—	5.00	10.00	20.00	35.00	—

KM# 11 1/4 ANNA
Copper **Ruler:** Faisal bin Turkee

Date	Mintage	VG	F	VF	XF	Unc
AH1314	—	5.00	10.00	20.00	35.00	—

KM# 12.1 1/4 ANNA
Copper **Ruler:** Faisal bin Turkee **Note:** Varieties exist.

Date	Mintage	VG	F	VF	XF	Unc
AH1315	—	3.00	5.00	10.00	18.00	—

KM# 12.2 1/4 ANNA
Copper **Ruler:** Faisal bin Turkee **Rev:** Legend style varies

Date	Mintage	VG	F	VF	XF	Unc
AH1315	—	3.00	5.00	10.00	18.00	—

KM# 12.3 1/4 ANNA
Copper **Ruler:** Faisal bin Turkee **Obv:** Legend style varies

Date	Mintage	VG	F	VF	XF	Unc
AH1315	—	3.00	5.00	10.00	18.00	—

KM# 12.4 1/4 ANNA
Copper **Ruler:** Faisal bin Turkee

Date	Mintage	VG	F	VF	XF	Unc
AH1315	—	3.00	5.00	10.00	18.00	—

KM# 13 1/4 ANNA
Copper **Ruler:** Faisal bin Turkee **Note:** Error: Date retrograde.

Date	Mintage	VG	F	VF	XF	Unc
AH5131	—	6.00	12.00	25.00	40.00	—

KM# 14 1/4 ANNA
Copper **Ruler:** Faisal bin Turkee **Rev:** Without star

Date	Mintage	VG	F	VF	XF	Unc
AH1316	—	5.00	10.00	20.00	35.00	—

KM# 15 1/4 ANNA
Copper **Ruler:** Faisal bin Turkee **Rev:** Star between wreath points

Date	Mintage	VG	F	VF	XF	Unc
AH1316	—	15.00	25.00	45.00	90.00	—

KM# 16 1/4 ANNA
Copper **Ruler:** Faisal bin Turkee **Note:** Reading of date is questionable.

Date	Mintage	VG	F	VF	XF	Unc
AH1318/5	—	15.00	25.00	45.00	90.00	—

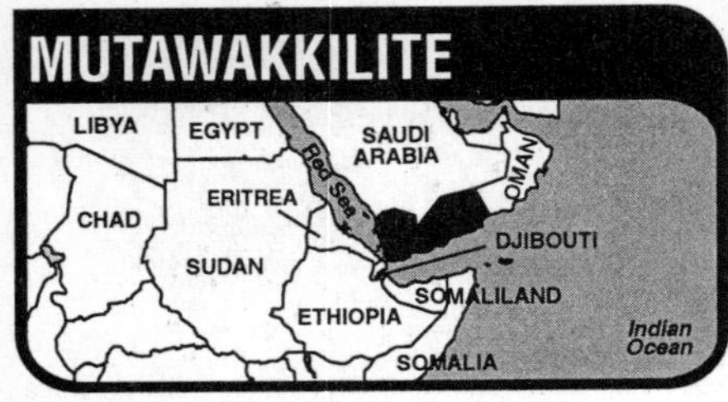

One of the oldest centers of civilization in the Middle East, Yemen was once part of the Minaean Kingdom and of the ancient Kingdom of Sheba, after which it was captured successively by Egyptians, Ethiopians and Romans. It was converted to Islam in 628 A.D. and administered as a caliphate until 1538, when it came under Ottoman occupation in 1849. The second Ottoman occupation which began in 1872 was maintained until 1918 when autonomy was achieved through revolution.

TITLES

المملكة المتوكلية اليمنية

al-Mamlaka(t) al-Mutawakkiliya(t) al-Yamaniya(t)

RULERS

QASIMID 19th century IMAMS

Repeatedly more than one imam ruled in Yemen at the same time. Sometimes they ruled separately in and for various cities and areas, some of them declared as counter imams. Frequently imams also regained power again, some of them used different names in their later periods of reign. Therefore overlapping periods of reigns appear in the following list of rulers.

Not all Yemeni imams struck coins. On coins we sometimes fine 'Abd Allah' (Abdullah), meaning 'servant of allah' and as such it was not the name of the imam.

Since coins also in the name of some of the Governors of Sana'a (Shaikhs of Sana'a) exist, they are mentioned below as well.

al-Mansur Ali I,
AH1189-1224/1775-1809AD
al-Mutawakkil Ahmad,
AH1224-1231/1809-1816AD
al-Mahdi Abdullah,
AH1231-1251/1816-1835AD
al-Mansir Ali II,
First reign, AH1251-1252/1835-1837AD and
as al-Mahdi Ali, second reign
AH1259-1261/1844-1845AD and
as al-Mahdi Ali and as al-Hadi Ali,
third reign, AH1265-1266/1848-1849 and
as al-Mutawakkil Ali, fourth reign,
AH1267-1277/1851-1860AD and
As al-Mahdi Ali, fifth reign,
AH1274/1857AD
al-Nasir Abdullah,
AH1252-1256/1837-1840AD
al-Hadi Muhammad,
AH1256-1259/1840-1844AD
al-Mutawakkil Muhammad,
AH1261-1265/1845-1849AD
al-Mansur Ahmad,
AH1265-1269/1849-1853AD
al-Mansur Muhammad bin Yahya,
(Imam Mansur) AH1307-1322/1890-1904AD

OTTOMAN

First Ottoman occupation, AH1265/1849AD
Second Ottoman occupation, AH1289-1337/1872-1918AD

GOVERNORS of SANA'A

Al-Hajj Ahmad bin Ahmad al-Haymi al-Suwaydi,
AH1270-1275/1854-1858AD
Abdullah bin Yusuf Huwaydir,
First rule, AH1275/1858AD
Second rule, AH1279-80/1862-1863AD
Muhsin bin Ali Mu'id,
First rule, AH1276-79/1859-1862AD
Second rule, AH1280-89/1863-1872AD

MINTS

ابو عريش

Abu Arish

الزهرة

Al Zuhra

مختارة

Mukhtara

صعدة

Sa'da

صنعاء

Sana'a
(Sanaa, San'a)

دار الخلافة

'dar al-Khalifa(t)
(Seat of the ruler)

TITLES

امير المومنين

Amir al-Mu'minin
(Prince of the believers)

MONETARY SYSTEM

(until AH1322/1904AD)
1 Buqsha = 1/80 Riyal
1 Riyal = 80 Buqsha = Maria Theresa Thaler
(After Accession of Iman Yahya, AH1322/1904AD)
1 Zalat = 1/160 Riyal
2 Zalat = 1 Halala = 1/80 Riyal
2 Halala = 1 Buqsha = 1/40 Riyal
40 Buqsha = 1 Riyal

NOTE: The Riyal was called an IMADI (RIYAL) during the reign of Imam Yahya "Imadi" honorific name instead of Yahyawi and an AHMADI (RIYAL) during the reign of Imam Ahmad. The 1 Zalat, Y#2.1, D1, A3, A4 and all Imam Yahya gold strikes except Y#F10, bear no indication of value. Many of the Mutawakkilite coins after AH1322/1904AD bear the denomination expressed as fraction of the Riyal as follows.

BRONZE and ALUMINUM

Thumn ushr = 1/80 Riyal = 1/2 Buqsha = 1 Halala
Rub ushr = 1/40 Riyal = 1 Buqsha
Nisf ushr = 1/20 Riyal = 2 Buqsha = 1/2 Bawlah
Nisf thumn = 1/16 Riyal = 2-1/2 Buqsha
Ushr = 1/10 Riyal = 4 Buqsha = 1 Bawlah
Thumn = 1/8 Riyal = 5 Buqsha
Rub = 1/4 Riyal = 10 Buqsha
Nisf = 1/2 Riyal = 20 Buqsha
1 Riyal (Imadi, Ahmadi) = 40 Buqsha

DATING

All coins of Imam Yahya have accession date AH1322 on obverse and actual date of issue on reverse. All coins of Imam Ahmad bear accession date AH1367 on obverse and actual date on reverse.

NOTE: If not otherwise noted, all coins of Imam Yahya and Imam Ahmad as well as the early issues of the Republic (Y#20 through Y#A25 and Y#32), were struck at the mint in Sana'a. The Sana'a Mint was essentially a medieval mint, using hand-cut dies and crudely machined blanks. There is a large amount of variation from one die to the next in arrangement of legends and ornaments, form of crescents, number of stars, size of the circle, etc., and literally hundreds of subtypes could be identified. Types are divided only when there are changes in the inscriptions, or major variations in the basic type, such as the presence or absence of *Rabb al-Alamin* in the legend or the position of the word *Sana* (= year) in relation to the year.

KINGDOM

al-Mansur Ali I
1775-1809AD

HAMMERED COINAGE

KM# 300 HARF
Billon **Note:** Weight varies: 0.25-0.40 grams.

Date	Mintage	Good	VG	F	VF	XF
ND	—	15.00	25.00	35.00	50.00	—

KM# 302 KABIR
Billon **Note:** Weight varies: 0.70-1.10 grams.

Date	Mintage	Good	VG	F	VF	XF
ND	—	15.00	25.00	35.00	50.00	—

LOCAL HAMMERED COINAGE

Issues of The Sulayman Sharifs. Rulers in the Mikhlaf Sulayman, a region in what is now The Asir district of Saudi Arabia and the northern part of Yemen. Anonymous issues in the time of Hammud bin Muhammad of the Banu Qatada clan, (known as Ibn Mismar) AH1217-32/1802-17AD.

KM# 304 BUQSHA
0.8000 g., Billon **Obv:** Al hamd/Allah **Rev:** Duriba/Zabid/1223

Date	Mintage	Good	VG	F	VF	XF
AH1223 Rare	—	—	—	—	—	—

KM# 303 PARA
Billon **Obv:** Allah hasbi/date **Rev:** Duriba Abu Arish **Note:** Allah hasbi = "God suffieceth". Weight varies: 0.55-0.70 grams.

Date	Mintage	Good	VG	F	VF	XF
AH1222 Rare	—	—	—	—	—	—
AH1227	—	—	—	—	—	—

KM# 307 PARA
0.6800 g., Billon **Obv:** xxx/Al Zuhra/1224 **Rev:** xxx

Date	Mintage	Good	VG	F	VF	XF
AH1224 Rare	—	—	—	—	—	—

KM# 308 PARA
0.5500 g., Billon **Obv:** xxx/122x **Rev:** xxx/122x **Note:** Mukhtara was a fortress near Hodeidah.

Date	Mintage	Good	VG	F	VF	XF
AH122x Rare	—	—	—	—	—	—

al-Mutawakkil Ahmad
AH1224-1231 / 1809-1816AD

HAMMERED COINAGE

KM# 305 HARF
Billon **Note:** Weight varies: 0.25-0.45 grams.

Date	Mintage	Good	VG	F	VF	XF
ND	—	15.00	25.00	35.00	50.00	—

KM# 306 KABIR
Billon **Note:** Weight varies: 00.70-1.10 grams.

Date	Mintage	Good	VG	F	VF	XF
ND	—	15.00	25.00	35.00	50.00	—

al-Mahdi Abdullah
AH1224-1231 / 1816-1835AD

HAMMERED COINAGE

KM# 315 BUQSHA
Billon **Note:** Weight varies: 0.75-1.10 grams.

Date	Mintage	Good	VG	F	VF	XF
ND	—	7.00	10.00	15.00	25.00	—

KM# 310 KABIR
Copper-Billon **Note:** Weight varies: 0.25-0.40 grams.

Date	Mintage	Good	VG	F	VF	XF
ND	—	10.00	15.00	20.00	30.00	—

al-Mansir Ali II
First Reign AH1251-1252 / 1835-1837AD

HAMMERED COINAGE

KM# 325 HARF
Billon **Note:** Weight varies: 0.25-0.40 grams.

Date	Mintage	Good	VG	F	VF	XF
AH1251-52 Rare	—	—	—	—	—	—

al-Nasir Abdullah
AH1252-1256 / 1837-1840AD

HAMMERED COINAGE

KM# 340 HARF
Billon **Note:** Weight varies: 0.25-0.40 grams.

Date	Mintage	Good	VG	F	VF	XF
AH1252-56 Rare	—	—	—	—	—	—

al-Mutawakkil al-Hadi Muhammad
AH1256-1259 / 1840-1844AD

HAMMERED COINAGE

KM# 345 HARF
Billon **Note:** Weight varies: 0.25-0.40 grams.

Date	Mintage	Good	VG	F	VF	XF
ND Rare	—	—	—	—	—	—

al-Mutawakkil Muhammad
AH1261-1265 / 1845-1849AD

HAMMERED COINAGE

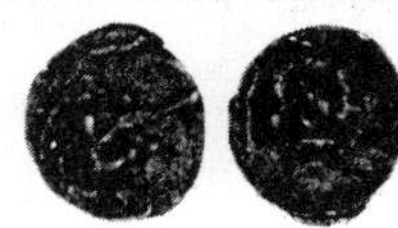

KM# 350 HARF
Billon To Copper **Note:** Weight varies: 0.25-0.40 grams.

Date	Mintage	Good	VG	F	VF	XF
ND	—	12.50	20.00	20.00	40.00	—

al-Mansur Ali II as al-Mahdi Ali and al-Hadi Ali
AH1265-1266 / 1848-1849AD

HAMMERED COINAGE

KM# 330 HARF
Billon **Note:** Weight varies: 0.25-0.40 grams.

Date	Mintage	Good	VG	F	VF	XF
AH1265-66 Rare	—	—	—	—	—	—

al-Hadi Ghalib
First Reign AH1267-1269 / 1851-1853AD

HAMMERED COINAGE

KM# 360 KABIR
0.8700 g., Silver **Obv. Legend:** 'azza nasruhu/duriba fi/sa'da/1267 **Rev. Legend:** 'abd/allah/al-hadi/li-din **Note:** Size varies: 15.5-16.0 millimeters.

Date	Mintage	VG	F	VF	XF	Unc
AH1267 Rare	—	—	—	—	—	—

al-Mansur Ahmad
AH1264-1267 / 1848-1851AD

HAMMERED COINAGE

KM# 355 HARF
Billon **Note:** Weight varies: 0.25-0.40 grams.

Date	Mintage	Good	VG	F	VF	XF
ND Rare	—	—	—	—	—	—

al-Mansur Muhammad bin Yahya (Imam Mansur)
AH1307-1322 / 1890-1904AD

Coins for this ruler were struck at Qaflat Idhar. Harf and Kabir strikes have similar inscriptions with varieties in position of date, legend arrangements and ornamentation. No indication of denomination on coins.

HAMMERED COINAGE

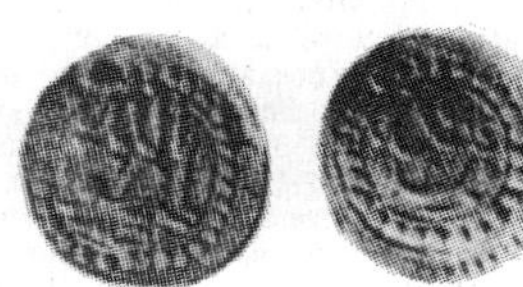

KM# 402.1 HARF
Bronze **Obv. Legend:** Billah/al-Mansur/date/Sana **Rev. Legend:** Allah/Abd **Note:** Size varies: 16.0-18.0 millimeters. Weight varies: 1.20-2.10 grams.

Date	Mintage	Good	VG	F	VF	XF
AH1312	—	—	—	—	—	—

KM# 402.2 HARF
1.3000 g., Bronze **Obv. Legend:** Without "Sana"

Date	Mintage	Good	VG	F	VF	XF
AH1313	—	—	—	—	—	—

KM# 405 BUQSHA
3.0000 g., Bronze, 23 mm. **Obv. Legend:** Billah/al-Mansur/Rabg/al-Alamin **Rev. Legend:** Amir/sana/al-mu'minin/1312

Date	Mintage	Good	VG	F	VF	XF
AH1312	—	—	—	—	—	—

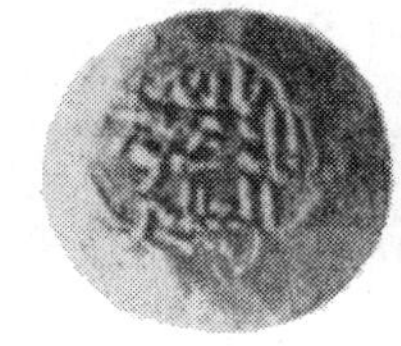
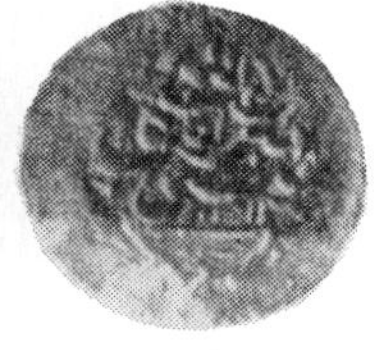

KM# 406 BUQSHA
3.1000 g., Bronze, 24 mm. **Obv:** Similar to KM#405 **Rev. Legend:** Allah/Abd/Amir al-mu'/minin/date/sana

Date	Mintage	Good	VG	F	VF	XF
AH1313	—	—	—	—	—	—

KM# 407.1 KABIR
0.5000 g., Silver **Obv:** Billah/al-Mansur, flower below **Rev:** Allah/Abd/1311/xxx

Date	Mintage	Good	VG	F	VF	XF
AH1311	—	—	—	—	—	—

KM# 408.1 KABIR
Silver **Obv:** Ornament below legend **Obv. Legend:** "Bilah/al-Mansu/r" **Rev:** Legend as circle **Rev. Legend:** "Allah/", date, "Abd" **Note:** Weight varies: 0.40-0.80 grams. Size varies: 15-17 millimeters. Varieties of shape of ornaments exist.

Date	Mintage	Good	VG	F	VF	XF
AH1312	—	—	—	—	—	—
AH1316	—	—	—	—	—	—
AH1318	—	—	—	—	—	—

KM# 408.2 KABIR
Silver **Obv:** Billah/al-Mansur/date **Rev:** Allah/Abd, ornament below **Note:** Weight varies: 0.70-0.80 grams. Varieties of shape of ornament exist.

Date	Mintage	Good	VG	F	VF	XF
AH1312	—	—	—	—	—	—
AH1314	—	—	—	—	—	—

KM# 409 KABIR
Silver **Obv:** Billah/al-Mansu/r **Rev:** Allah/Abd/1315, ornament below, without four circular segments **Note:** Weight varies: 0.70-1.00 grams.

Date	Mintage	Good	VG	F	VF	XF
AH1315	—	—	—	—	—	—

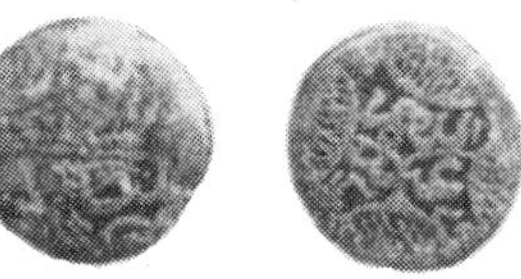

KM# 410 KABIR
Silver **Obv:** Similar to KM#409 **Rev:** "Allah/Abd/" date, divided by ornament, wtih four circular segments **Note:** Weight varies: 0.60-1.00 gram. Size varies: 15-16 millimeters. Varieties with three and four stars on reverse exist. Varieties of planchet thickness exist.

Date	Mintage	Good	VG	F	VF	XF
AH1316	—	15.00	30.00	50.00	150	—
AH1319	—	15.00	30.00	50.00	150	—
AH1320	—	15.00	30.00	50.00	150	—
AH1321	—	15.00	30.00	50.00	150	—

KM# 407.2 KABIR
Silver **Rev:** Date at bottom **Note:** Weight varies: 0.60-0.70 grams.

Date	Mintage	Good	VG	F	VF	XF
AH1318	—	—	—	—	—	—

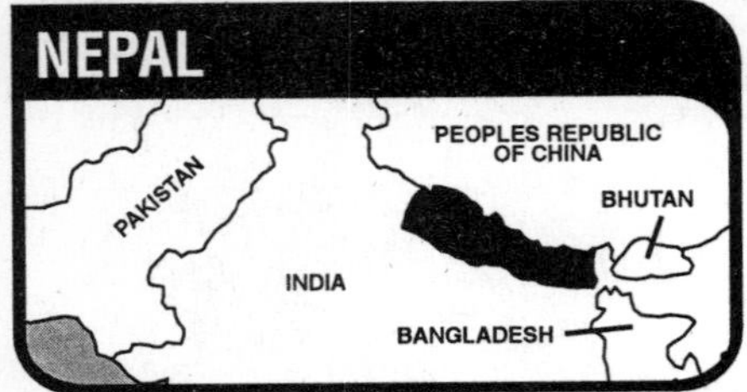

The Kingdom of Nepal, the world's only surviving Hindu kingdom, is a landlocked country occupying the southern slopes of the Himalayas. It has an area of 56,136 sq. mi. (140,800 sq. km.).

Apart from a brief Muslim invasion in the 14th century, Nepal was able to avoid the mainstream of Northern Indian politics, due to its impregnable position in the mountains. It is therefore a unique survivor of the medieval Hindu and Buddhist culture of Northern India which was largely destroyed by the successive waves of Muslim invasions.

Prior to the late 18th century, Nepal was divided among a number of small states. Unless otherwise stated, the term *Nepal* applies to the small fertile valley, about 4,500 ft. above sea level, in which the three main cities of Kathmandu, Patan and Bhatgaon are situated.

During the reign of King Yaksha Malla (1428-1482AD), the Nepalese kingdom, with capital at Bhatgaon, was extended northwards into Tibet, and also controlled a considerable area to the south of the hills. After Yaksha Malla's death, the Kingdom was divided among his sons, so four kingdoms were established with capitals at Bhatgaon, Patan, Kathmandu and Banepa, all situated within the small valley, less than 20 miles square. Banepa was quickly absorbed within the territory of Bhatgaon, but the other three kingdoms remained until 1769. The internecine strife between the three kings effectively stopped Nepal from becoming a major military force during this period, although with its fertile land and strategic position, it was by far the wealthiest and most powerful of the Himalayan states.

Apart from agriculture, Nepal owed its prosperity to its position on one of the easiest trade routes between the great monasteries of central Tibet, and India. Nepal made full use of this, and a trading community was set up in Lhasa during the 16th century, and Nepalese coins became the accepted currency medium in Tibet.

The seeds of discord between Nepal and Tibet were sown during the first half of the 18th century, when the Nepalese debased the coinage, and the fate of the Malla kings of Nepal was sealed when Prithvi Narayan Shah, King of the small state of Gorkha, to the west of Kathmandu, was able to gain control of the trans-himalayan trade routes during the years after 1750.

Prithvi Narayan spent several years consolidating his position in hill areas before he finally succeeded in conquering the Kathmandu Valley in 1768, where he established the Shah dynasty, and moved his capital to Kathmandu.

After Prithvi Narayan's death a period of political instability ensued which lasted until the 1840's when the Rana family reduced the monarch to a figurehead and established the post of hereditary Prime Minister.

DATING

Nepal Samvat Era (NS)

All coins of the Malla kings of Nepal are dated in the Nepal Samvat era (NS). Year 1 NS began in 881, so to arrive at the AD date add 880 to the NS date. This era was exclusive to Nepal, except for one gold coin of Prana Narayan of Cooch Behar.

Saka Era (SE)

Up until 1888AD all coins of the Gorkha Dynasty were dated in the Saka era (SE). To convert from Saka to AD take Saka date and add 78 to arrive at the AD date. Coins dated with this era have SE before the date in the following listing.

Vikrama Samvat Era (VS)

From 1888AD most copper coins were dated in the Vikram Samvat (VS) era. To convert take VS date - 57 =AD date. Coins with this era have VS before the year in the listing. With the exception of a few gold coins struck in 1890 & 1892, silver and gold coins only changed to the VS era in 1911AD, but now this era is used for all coins struck in Nepal.

RULERS

SHAH DYNASTY

गीर्वाण युद्ध विक्रम सा

Girvan Yuddha Vikrama
SE1720-1738/1799-1816AD

Queens of Girvan Yuddha Vikrama:

सिद्धि लक्ष्मी

Siddhi Lakshmi

गोरक्ष राज्य लक्ष्मी

Goraksha Rajya Lakshmi

राजेन्द्र विक्रम

Rajendra Vikrama
SE1738-1769/1816-1847AD

Queens of Rajendra Vikrama:

साम्राज्य लक्ष्मी

Samrajya Lakshmi

राज्य लक्ष्मी

Rajya Lakshmi

सुरेन्द्र विक्रम सा

Surendra Vikrama
SE1769-1803/1847-1881AD

Queens of Surendra Vikrama:

त्रैलोक्य राज लक्ष्मी

Trailokya Raja Lakshmi

सुर राज लक्ष्मी

Sura Raja Lakshmi

देवराज लक्ष्मी

Deva Raja Lakshmi

पुण्यकुमारी राज लक्ष्मी

Punyakumari Raja Lakshmi

पृथ्वी वीर विक्रम

Prithvi Vira Vikrama
SE1803-1833/1881-1911AD, VS1938-1968

Queen of Prithvi Vira Vikrama:

लक्ष्मी दिव्येश्वरी

Lakshmi Divyeswari

MONETARY SYSTEM

COPPER

Initially the copper paisa was not fixed in value relative to the silver coins, and generally fluctuated in value from1/32 mohar in 1865AD to around 1/50 mohar afterc1880AD, and was fixed at that value in 1903AD.
4 Dam = 1 Paisa
2 Paisa = 1 Dyak, Adhani

GOLD COINAGE

Nepalese gold coinage until recently did not carry any denominations and was traded for silver, etc. at the local bullion exchange rate. The three basic weight standards used in the following listing are distinguished for convenience, although all were known as Asarphi (gold coin) locally as follows:

GOLD MOHAR

5.60 g multiples and fractions

TOLA

12.48 g multiples and fractions

GOLD RUPEE or ASARPHI

11.66 g multiples and fractions
(Reduced to 10.00 g in 1966)

NOTE: In some instances the gold and silver issues were struck from the same dies.

NUMERALS

Nepal has used more variations of numerals on theircoins than any other nation. The most common areillustrated in the numeral chart in the introduction. Thechart below illustrates some variations encompassing thelast four centuries.

1	2	3	4	5	6	7	8	9	0
१	२	३	४	५	६	७	८	९	०

NUMERICS

Half	आधा
One	एक
Two	दुइ
Four	चार
Five	पाच
Ten	दसा
Twenty	विसा
Twenty-five	पचीसा
Fifty	पचासा
Hundred	सय

DENOMINATIONS

Paisa	पैसा
Dam	दाम
Mohar	मोहरु
Rupee	रुपैयाँ
Ashrapi	असार्फी
Asarfi	अश्रफी

DIE VARIETIES

Although the same dies were usually used both for silver and gold minor denominations, the gold Mohar is easily recognized being less ornate. The following illustrations are of a silver Mohar, KM#602 and a gold Mohar KM#615 issued by Surendra Vikrama Saha Deva in the period SE1769-1803/1847-1881AD. Note the similar reverse legend. The obverse usually will start with the character for the word Shri in single or multiples, the latter as Shri Shri Shri or Shri 3.

OBVERSE

SILVER SE1791 GOLD SE1793

LEGEND

श्री श्री श्री सुरेन्द्र विक्रम साहदेव

Shri Shri Shri Surendra Vikrama Saha Deva (date)

REVERSE

SILVER GOLD

LEGEND
(in center)

श्री ३ भवानी

Shri 3 Bhavani
(around outer circle)

श्री श्री श्री गोरषनाथ

Shri Shri Shri Gorakhanatha

SHAH DYNASTY

KINGDOM

Rana Bahadur
SE1699-1720 / 1777-1799AD

SILVER COINAGE

KM# 496 1/4 MOHAR
1.4000 g., Silver **Note:** In the name of Queen Raja Rajesvari.

Date	Mintage	VG	F	VF	XF	Unc
SE1723 (1801)	—	7.00	10.00	15.00	22.50	—
SE1724 (1802)	—	7.00	10.00	15.00	22.50	—

KM# 498 1/4 MOHAR
1.4000 g., Silver **Note:** In the name of Queen Suvarna Prabha.

Date	Mintage	VG	F	VF	XF	Unc
SE1723 (1801)	—	5.50	9.00	13.50	20.00	—

KM# 497 1/4 MOHAR
1.4000 g., Silver **Note:** In the name of Queen Amara Rajesvari.

Date	Mintage	VG	F	VF	XF	Unc
SE1725 (1802)	—	50.00	75.00	85.00	100	—

KM# 499 1/4 MOHAR
1.4000 g., Silver **Note:** In the name of Queen Mahamahesvari.

Date	Mintage	VG	F	VF	XF	Unc
SE1725 (1803)	—	65.00	75.00	85.00	100	—

KM# 500 1/4 MOHAR
1.4000 g., Silver **Note:** In the name of Queen Lalita Tripura Sundari.

Date	Mintage	VG	F	VF	XF	Unc
SE1728 (1806)	—	10.00	13.50	18.50	28.00	—
SE1729 (1807)	—	10.00	13.50	18.50	28.00	—
SE1738 (1816)	—	7.00	10.00	15.00	25.00	—
SE1741 (1819)	—	5.00	8.50	12.50	20.00	—
SE1744 (1822)	—	10.00	13.50	18.50	28.00	—

KM# A501 3/8 MOHAR

श्री श्रीश्री सुरेन्द्र विक्रम साहदेव

GOLD COINAGE

KM# 509 1/4 MOHAR
1.4000 g., Gold **Note:** In the name of Queen Raja Rajesvari.

Date	Mintage	Good	VG	F	VF	XF
SE1723 (1801)	—	40.00	50.00	70.00	90.00	—
SE1724 (1802)	—	40.00	50.00	70.00	90.00	—

KM# 511.1 1/4 MOHAR
1.4000 g., Gold **Note:** In the name of Queen Suvarna Prabha.

Date	Mintage	Good	VG	F	VF	XF
SE1723 (1801)	—	40.00	50.00	70.00	90.00	—

KM# 510 1/4 MOHAR
1.4000 g., Gold **Note:** In the name of Queen Amara Rajesvari.

Date	Mintage	Good	VG	F	VF	XF
SE1724 (1802)	—	85.00	100	125	150	—

KM# 511.2 3/8 MOHAR
1.4000 g., Gold **Note:** In the name of Queen Mahamahesvari.

Date	Mintage	Good	VG	F	VF	XF
SE1725 (1803)	—	150	250	350	500	—

KM# 512 3/8 MOHAR
1.4000 g., Gold **Note:** In the name of Queen Lalita Tripura Sundari.

Date	Mintage	VG	F	VF	XF	Unc
SE1728 (1806)	—	40.00	50.00	65.00	85.00	—
SE1729 (1807)	—	40.00	50.00	65.00	85.00	—
SE1741 (1819)	—	40.00	50.00	65.00	85.00	—

Girvan Yuddha Vikrama
SE1720-1738 / 1799-1816AD

COPPER COINAGE

KM# 517 DAM
1.0000 g., Copper

Date	Mintage	VG	F	VF	XF	Unc
VS1861 (1804)	—	0.75	1.25	2.25	3.50	—

KM# A517 2 DAM
2.0000 g., Copper

Date	Mintage	VG	F	VF	XF	Unc
VS1861 (1804)	—	1.50	2.00	4.00	8.00	—

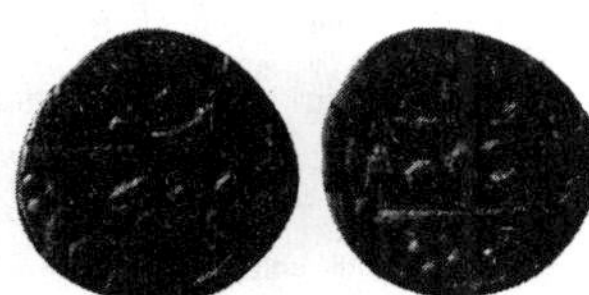

KM# C517 PAISA
7.6000 g., Copper

Date	Mintage	VG	F	VF	XF	Unc
VS1859 (1802)	—	—	7.00	15.00	20.00	—

SILVER COINAGE

Actual size 2x actual size

KM# 518 DAM
0.0400 g., Silver **Note:** Uniface; Size varies 7 - 8 mm.

Date	Mintage	VG	F	VF	XF	Unc
ND(1799-1816)	—	4.00	8.00	11.50	16.00	—

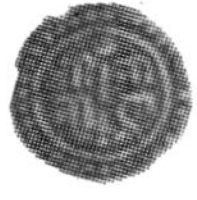

KM# 519 1/32 MOHAR
0.1800 g., Silver **Note:** Uniface.

Date	Mintage	VG	F	VF	XF	Unc
ND(1799-1816)	—	8.00	13.50	18.50	25.00	—

KM# 520 1/16 MOHAR
0.3500 g., Silver **Note:** Varieties exist.

Date	Mintage	VG	F	VF	XF	Unc
ND(1799-1816)	—	7.50	11.50	16.50	22.50	—

KM# 521 1/8 MOHAR
0.7000 g., Silver **Obv:** Shri above sword

Date	Mintage	VG	F	VF	XF	Unc
ND(1799-1816)	—	6.00	10.00	13.50	18.50	—

KM# 522 1/8 MOHAR
0.7000 g., Silver **Obv:** Umbrella above sword

Date	Mintage	VG	F	VF	XF	Unc
ND(1799-1816)	—	6.00	10.00	13.50	18.50	—

KM# 523 1/8 MOHAR
0.7000 g., Silver **Obv:** Wreath above sword

Date	Mintage	VG	F	VF	XF	Unc
ND(1799-1816)	—	6.00	10.00	13.50	18.50	—

KM# 524 1/4 MOHAR
1.4000 g., Silver **Note:** In the name of Queen Siddi Lakshmi.

Date	Mintage	VG	F	VF	XF	Unc
SE1730 (1808)	—	10.00	13.50	18.50	25.00	—
SE1733 (1811)	—	10.00	13.50	18.50	25.00	—
SE1735 (1813)	—	10.00	13.50	18.50	25.00	—

KM# 525 1/4 MOHAR
1.4000 g., Silver **Note:** In the name of Queen Goraksha Rajya Lakshmi.

Date	Mintage	VG	F	VF	XF	Unc
SE1738 (1816)	—	65.00	75.00	85.00	100	—

KM# 526 1/2 MOHAR
2.7700 g., Silver

Date	Mintage	VG	F	VF	XF	Unc
SE1728 (1806)	—	7.50	12.50	20.00	30.00	—
SE1729 (1807)	—	7.50	12.50	20.00	30.00	—
SE1730 (1808)	—	5.00	8.50	15.00	22.50	—
SE1733 (1811)	—	7.50	12.50	20.00	30.00	—

KM# 527 3/4 MOHAR
4.2000 g., Silver

Date	Mintage	VG	F	VF	XF	Unc
SE1727 (1805)	—	100	200	250	300	—

KM# 529 MOHAR
5.6000 g., Silver **Obv:** 3 "Shri's" above square

Date	Mintage	VG	F	VF	XF	Unc
SE1723 (1801)	—	4.50	6.50	9.00	11.50	—
SE1724 (1802)	—	4.50	6.50	9.00	11.50	—
SE1725 (1803)	—	4.50	6.50	9.00	11.50	—
SE1728 (1806)	—	4.50	6.50	9.00	11.50	—
SE1729 (1807)	—	4.50	6.50	9.00	11.50	—
SE1730 (1808)	—	4.50	6.50	9.00	11.50	—
SE1731 (1809)	—	4.50	6.50	9.00	11.50	—
SE1732 (1810)	—	4.50	6.50	9.00	11.50	—
SE1733 (1811)	—	4.50	6.50	9.00	11.50	—
SE1734 (1812)	—	4.50	6.50	9.00	11.50	—
SE1735 (1813)	—	4.50	6.50	9.00	11.50	—
SE1736 (1814)	—	4.50	6.50	9.00	11.50	—
SE1737 (1815)	—	4.50	6.50	9.00	11.50	—
SE1738 (1816)	—	4.50	6.50	9.00	11.50	—

KM# 530 MOHAR
5.6000 g., Silver **Obv:** KM#547 **Rev:** KM#529 **Note:** Mule.

Date	Mintage	VG	F	VF	XF	Unc
SE1728 (1806)	—	50.00	80.00	100	125	—
SE1729 (1807)	—	50.00	80.00	100	125	—

KM# 531 1-1/2 MOHARS
8.4000 g., Silver

Date	Mintage	VG	F	VF	XF	Unc
SE1725 (1803)	—	25.00	35.00	50.00	75.00	—
SE1726 (1804)	—	25.00	35.00	50.00	75.00	—

KM# 532 1-1/2 MOHARS
8.4000 g., Silver

Date	Mintage	VG	F	VF	XF	Unc
SE1727 (1805)	—	75.00	125	175	250	—

KM# A533 3 MOHARS
16.8000 g., Silver **Obv:** Flourishes outside central legend

Date	Mintage	VG	F	VF	XF	Unc
SE1725 (1803)	—	—	150	200	250	—

KM# 533 3 MOHARS
16.8000 g., Silver **Obv:** Without flourishes outside central legend

Date	Mintage	VG	F	VF	XF	Unc
SE1725 (1803)	—	—	150	200	250	—

KM# 534 3 MOHARS
16.8000 g., Silver **Note:** Similar to 1-1/2 Mohars, KM#532.

Date	Mintage	VG	F	VF	XF	Unc
SE1726 (1804)	—	—	200	300	400	—

GOLD COINAGE

KM# 535 DAM
0.0440 g., Gold **Note:** Uniface.

Date	Mintage	VG	F	VF	XF	Unc
ND(1799-1816)	—	10.00	14.00	20.00	30.00	—

KM# 536 1/32 MOHAR
0.1750 g., Gold **Note:** Uniface.

Date	Mintage	VG	F	VF	XF	Unc
ND(1799-1816)	—	14.00	20.00	25.00	40.00	—

KM# 537 1/16 MOHAR
0.3500 g., Gold **Note:** Three varieties exist.

Date	Mintage	VG	F	VF	XF	Unc
ND(1799-1816)	—	14.00	20.00	25.00	40.00	—

KM# 538 1/8 MOHAR
0.7000 g., Gold **Obv:** "Shr" above sword

Date	Mintage	VG	F	VF	XF	Unc
ND(1799-1816)	—	22.50	27.50	40.00	60.00	—

KM# 539 1/8 MOHAR
0.7000 g., Gold **Obv:** Umbrella above sword

Date	Mintage	VG	F	VF	XF	Unc
ND(1799-1816)	—	22.50	27.50	40.00	60.00	—

KM# 540.1 1/4 MOHAR
1.4000 g., Gold **Note:** In the name of Queen Siddhi Lakshmi.

Date	Mintage	VG	F	VF	XF	Unc
SE1730 (1808)	—	40.00	50.00	65.00	85.00	—

KM# 540.3 1/4 MOHAR
1.4000 g., Gold **Note:** In the name of Queen Siddhi Lakshmi.

Date	Mintage	VG	F	VF	XF	Unc
SE1732 (1810)	—	40.00	50.00	65.00	85.00	—
SE1733 (1811)	—	40.00	50.00	65.00	85.00	—

KM# 540.4 1/4 MOHAR
1.4000 g., Gold **Note:** In the name of Queen Siddhi Lakshmi.

Date	Mintage	VG	F	VF	XF	Unc
SE1736 (1814)	—	40.00	50.00	65.00	85.00	—

KM# 540.2 1/4 MOHAR
1.4000 g., Gold **Note:** In the name of Queen Goraksha Rajyalakshmi.

Date	Mintage	VG	F	VF	XF	Unc
SE1738 (1816)	—	120	150	170	200	—

KM# 541 1/2 MOHAR
2.8000 g., Gold

Date	Mintage	VG	F	VF	XF	Unc
SE1728 (1806)	—	70.00	80.00	100	130	—
SE1728 (1806)	—	70.00	80.00	100	130	—
SE1729 (1807)	—	70.00	80.00	100	130	—
SE1730 (1808)	—	70.00	80.00	100	130	—

KM# 542 1/2 MOHAR
2.8000 g., Gold

Date	Mintage	VG	F	VF	XF	Unc
SE1732 (1810)	—	150	200	250	325	—
SE1733 (1811)	—	150	200	250	325	—

KM# 543 1/2 MOHAR
2.8000 g., Gold

Date	Mintage	VG	F	VF	XF	Unc
SE1736 (1814)	—	150	200	250	325	—

KM# 544 MOHAR
5.6000 g., Gold **Note:** Similar to 1 Mohar, KM#529.

Date	Mintage	VG	F	VF	XF	Unc
SE1723 (1801)	—	125	150	175	225	—
SE1723 (1801)	—	125	150	175	225	—
SE1724 (1802)	—	125	150	175	225	—
SE1728 (1806)	—	125	150	175	225	—

KM# 546 MOHAR
5.6000 g., Gold **Obv:** Square in center

Date	Mintage	VG	F	VF	XF	Unc
SE1733 (1811)	—	150	175	225	265	—

KM# 547 1-1/2 MOHARS
8.4000 g., Gold

Date	Mintage	VG	F	VF	XF	Unc
SE1726 (1804)	—	185	225	275	350	—
SE1728 (1806)	—	185	225	275	350	—
SE1729 (1807)	—	185	225	275	350	—

KM# 548 1-1/2 MOHARS
8.4000 g., Gold **Rev:** Hexagon

Date	Mintage	VG	F	VF	XF	Unc
SE1736 (1814)	—	185	225	275	350	—

KM# 550 2 MOHARS
11.2000 g., Gold **Obv:** Square in center

Date	Mintage	VG	F	VF	XF	Unc
SE1733 (1811)	—	250	275	325	385	—

ANONYMOUS COINAGE

KM# E517 PAISA
Copper **Note:** Local issues. No inscription, plain both sides. Weight varies: 8-12 gr.

Date	Mintage	VG	F	VF	XF	Unc
ND(1799-1816)	—	3.00	5.00	10.00	15.00	—

KM# E517a PAISA
Copper Alloys **Note:** Local issues. No inscription, plain both sides. Weight varies: 8-12 gr. Magnetic - Iron alloy.

Date	Mintage	VG	F	VF	XF	Unc
ND(1799-1816)	—	3.00	5.00	10.00	15.00	—

KM# B517 2 PAISA (Dhyak)
Copper **Note:** No incscription, plain both sides. Weight varies: 18-22 gr.

Date	Mintage	VG	F	VF	XF	Unc
ND(1799-1816)	—	3.00	5.00	10.00	15.00	—

KM# B517a 2 PAISA (Dhyak)
Copper **Note:** No inscription, plain both sides. Magnetic, copper-iron alloy. Weight varies: 18-22 gr.

Date	Mintage	VG	F	VF	XF	Unc
(1799-1816)	—	3.00	5.00	10.00	15.00	—

KM# D517a 4 PAISA (Ganda)
Copper **Note:** Local issue. No inscription, plain both sides. Weight varies: 40-44 gr. Copper-iron alloy, magnetic.

Date	Mintage	VG	F	VF	XF	Unc
ND(1799-1816)	—	3.00	5.00	10.00	15.00	—

KM# F517 4 PAISA (Ganda)
Copper **Note:** Local issues. No inscription, plain both sides. Weight varies 39-42gr. Slight traces of former Arabic inscription.

Date	Mintage	VG	F	VF	XF	Unc
ND(1799-1816)	—	3.00	5.00	10.00	15.00	—

KM# D517 4 PAISA (Ganda)
40.0000 g., Copper **Note:** Local Issues. No inscription, plain both sides. Weight varies: 40-44 gr.

Date	Mintage	VG	F	VF	XF	Unc
ND(1799-1816)	—	4.00	6.00	10.00	15.00	—

PRESENTATION COINAGE

KM# 551 2 MOHARS
11.6600 g., Gold **Obv:** Square in center **Note:** In the name of Queen Goraksha Rajya Lakshmi.

Date	Mintage	VG	F	VF	XF	Unc
SE1735 (1813)	—	400	500	550	625	—

Rajendra Vikrama
SE1738-1769/ 1816-1847AD

SILVER COINAGE

Actual size

2x actual size

KM# 553 DAM
0.0400 g., Silver **Note:** Uniface.

Date	Mintage	VG	F	VF	XF	Unc
ND(1816-47)	—	4.00	6.00	8.00	12.50	—

KM# 554 1/32 MOHAR
0.1800 g., Silver **Note:** Uniface.

Date	Mintage	VG	F	VF	XF	Unc
ND(1816-47)	—	5.50	9.00	12.50	17.50	—

KM# 555 1/16 MOHAR
0.3500 g., Silver

Date	Mintage	VG	F	VF	XF	Unc
ND(1816-47)	—	5.00	8.50	12.00	17.00	—

KM# 556 1/8 MOHAR
0.7000 g., Silver **Obv:** "Shri" above sword

Date	Mintage	VG	F	VF	XF	Unc
ND(1816-47)	—	3.00	5.00	8.50	15.00	—

KM# 557 1/8 MOHAR
0.7000 g., Silver **Obv:** Umbrella above sword

Date	Mintage	VG	F	VF	XF	Unc
ND(1816-47)	—	3.00	5.00	8.50	15.00	—

KM# 558 1/4 MOHAR
1.4000 g., Silver **Note:** In the name of Queen Samrajya Lakshmi.

Date	Mintage	VG	F	VF	XF	Unc
SE1745 (1823)	—	8.50	12.50	18.50	25.00	—
SE1746 (1824)	—	5.00	8.50	12.50	18.50	—
SE1753 (1831)	—	5.00	8.50	12.50	18.50	—
SE1755 (1833)	—	5.00	8.50	12.50	18.50	—

KM# 559 1/4 MOHAR
1.4000 g., Silver **Note:** In the name of Queen Samrajya Lakshmi.

Date	Mintage	VG	F	VF	XF	Unc
SE1746 (1824)	—	5.00	8.50	12.50	18.50	—
SE1759 (1837)	—	5.00	8.50	12.50	18.50	—

KM# 560 1/4 MOHAR
1.4000 g., Silver **Obv:** Wreath above vase **Note:** In the name of Queen Samrajya Lakshmi.

Date	Mintage	VG	F	VF	XF	Unc
SE1746 (1824)	—	5.00	8.50	12.50	18.50	—
SE1753 (1831)	—	5.00	8.50	12.50	18.50	—
SE1759 (1837)	—	5.00	8.50	12.50	18.50	—

KM# 561.1 1/4 MOHAR
1.4000 g., Silver **Note:** In the name of Queen Rajya Lakshmi.

Date	Mintage	VG	F	VF	XF	Unc
SE1764 (1842)	—	8.50	12.50	18.50	25.00	—
SE1766 (1844)	—	8.50	12.50	18.50	25.00	—
SE1767 (1845)	—	8.50	12.50	18.50	25.00	—

KM# 561.2 1/4 MOHAR
1.4000 g., Silver **Rev:** Circle **Note:** In the name of Queen Rajya Lakshmi. Struck with gold dies.

Date	Mintage	VG	F	VF	XF	Unc
SE1764 (1842)	—	30.00	40.00	55.00	75.00	—

KM# 562 1/2 MOHAR
2.8000 g., Silver **Obv:** KM#563 **Rev:** KM#526 **Note:** Mule.

Date	Mintage	VG	F	VF	XF	Unc
SE1730 (1808)	—	15.00	25.00	40.00	60.00	—

KM# 563 1/2 MOHAR
2.8000 g., Silver

Date	Mintage	VG	F	VF	XF	Unc
SE1738 (1816)	—	3.50	6.50	10.00	15.00	—
SE1744 (1822)	—	7.50	12.50	20.00	30.00	—
SE1746 (1824)	—	4.50	7.50	12.50	17.50	—

KM# 564 1/2 MOHAR
2.8000 g., Silver

Date	Mintage	VG	F	VF	XF	Unc
SE1746 (1824)	—	3.50	6.50	10.00	15.00	—
SE1753 (1831)	—	3.50	6.50	10.00	15.00	—
SE1755 (1833)	—	3.50	6.50	10.00	15.00	—
SE1757 (1835)	—	3.50	6.50	10.00	15.00	—
SE1759 (1837)	—	3.50	6.50	10.00	15.00	—
SE1762 (1840)	—	3.50	7.50	12.50	16.50	—
SE1764 (1842)	—	3.50	7.50	12.00	16.50	—
SE1765 (1843)	—	3.50	7.50	12.00	16.50	—
SE1766 (1844)	—	3.50	7.50	12.00	16.50	—

KM# 565.1 MOHAR
5.6000 g., Silver **Rev:** Moon and sun

Date	Mintage	VG	F	VF	XF	Unc
SE1738 (1816)	—	50.00	90.00	120	150	—

KM# 565.2 MOHAR
5.6000 g., Silver

Date	Mintage	VG	F	VF	XF	Unc
SE1738 (1816)	—	4.50	6.50	9.00	11.50	—
SE1739 (1817)	—	4.50	6.50	9.00	11.50	—
SE1740 (1818)	—	4.50	6.50	9.00	11.50	—
SE1741 (1819)	—	4.50	6.50	9.00	11.50	—
SE1742 (1820)	—	4.50	6.50	9.00	11.50	—
SE1743 (1821)	—	4.50	6.50	9.00	11.50	—
SE1744 (1822)	—	4.50	6.50	9.00	11.50	—
SE1745 (1823)	—	4.50	6.50	9.00	11.50	—
SE1746 (1824)	—	4.50	6.50	9.00	11.50	—
SE1747 (1825)	—	4.50	6.50	9.00	11.50	—
SE1748 (1826)	—	4.50	6.50	9.00	11.50	—
SE1749 (1827)	—	4.50	6.50	9.00	11.50	—
SE1750 (1828)	—	4.50	6.50	9.00	11.50	—
SE1751 (1829)	—	4.50	6.50	9.00	11.50	—
SE1752 (1830)	—	4.50	6.50	9.00	11.50	—
SE1753 (1831)	—	4.50	6.50	9.00	11.50	—
SE1754 (1832)	—	4.50	6.50	9.00	11.50	—
SE1755 (1833)	—	4.50	6.50	9.00	11.50	—
SE1756 (1834)	—	4.50	6.50	9.00	11.50	—
SE1757 (1835)	—	4.50	6.50	9.00	11.50	—
SE1758 (1836)	—	4.50	6.50	9.00	11.50	—
SE1759 (1837)	—	4.50	6.50	9.00	11.50	—
SE1760 (1838)	—	4.50	6.50	9.00	11.50	—
SE1761 (1839)	—	7.00	10.00	13.50	17.50	—
SE1762 (1840)	—	7.00	10.00	13.50	17.50	—
SE1764 (1842)	—	4.50	6.50	9.00	11.50	—
SE1765 (1843)	—	7.00	10.00	13.50	17.50	—
SE1766 (1844)	—	4.50	6.50	9.00	11.50	—
SE1767 (1845)	—	4.50	6.50	9.00	11.50	—
SE1768 (1846)	—	4.50	7.50	12.50	16.50	—
SE1769 (1847)	—	7.00	10.00	13.50	17.50	—

KM# 566 MOHAR
5.6000 g., Silver **Obv:** "Sri 3" at top

Date	Mintage	VG	F	VF	XF	Unc
SE1740 (1818)	—	7.00	10.00	13.50	17.50	—

KM# 567 MOHAR
5.6000 g., Silver **Obv:** Ornamentation reversed

Date	Mintage	VG	F	VF	XF	Unc
SE1762 (1840)	—	7.00	10.00	13.50	17.50	—

KM# 568 2 MOHARS
11.2000 g., Silver

Date	Mintage	VG	F	VF	XF	Unc
SE1738 (1816)	—	25.00	35.00	50.00	75.00	—
SE1740 (1818)	—	25.00	35.00	50.00	75.00	—
SE1742 (1820)	—	25.00	35.00	50.00	75.00	—
SE1743 (1821)	—	25.00	35.00	50.00	75.00	—
SE1744 (1822)	—	25.00	35.00	50.00	75.00	—
SE1753 (1831)	—	25.00	35.00	50.00	75.00	—
SE1757 (1835)	—	25.00	35.00	50.00	75.00	—
SE1764 (1842)	—	25.00	35.00	50.00	75.00	—

GOLD COINAGE

KM# 569 DAM
0.0400 g., Gold **Note:** Uniface.

Date	Mintage	VG	F	VF	XF	Unc
ND(1816-47)	—	10.00	14.00	20.00	30.00	—

KM# 570 1/32 MOHAR
0.1800 g., Gold **Note:** Uniface.

Date	Mintage	VG	F	VF	XF	Unc
ND(1816-47)	—	14.00	20.00	25.00	40.00	—

KM# 571 1/16 MOHAR
0.3500 g., Gold

Date	Mintage	VG	F	VF	XF	Unc
ND(1816-47)	—	14.00	20.00	25.00	40.00	—

KM# 572 1/8 MOHAR
0.7000 g., Gold

Date	Mintage	VG	F	VF	XF	Unc
ND(1816-47)	—	22.50	27.50	35.00	50.00	—

KM# 573.1 1/4 MOHAR
0.7000 g., Gold **Note:** In the name of Queen Samrajya Lakshmi. Varieties exist.

Date	Mintage	VG	F	VF	XF	Unc
SE1746 (1824)	—	40.00	50.00	65.00	85.00	—
SE1757 (1835)	—	40.00	50.00	65.00	85.00	—
SE1758 (1836)	—	40.00	50.00	65.00	85.00	—
SE1759 (1837)	—	40.00	50.00	65.00	85.00	—

KM# 573.2 1/4 MOHAR
0.7000 g., Gold **Note:** In the name of Queen Samrajya Lakshmi.

Date	Mintage	VG	F	VF	XF	Unc
SE1757 (1835)	—	40.00	50.00	65.00	85.00	—

KM# 574 1/4 MOHAR
0.7000 g., Gold **Note:** In the name of Queen Rajya Lakshmi.

Date	Mintage	VG	F	VF	XF	Unc
SE1764 (1842)	—	40.00	50.00	65.00	85.00	—

KM# 575 1/2 MOHAR
2.8000 g., Gold

Date	Mintage	VG	F	VF	XF	Unc
SE1741 (1819)	—	150	200	250	325	—

KM# 576 1/2 MOHAR
2.8000 g., Gold

Date	Mintage	VG	F	VF	XF	Unc
SE1744 (1822)	—	65.00	75.00	85.00	100	—
SE1746 (1824)	—	65.00	75.00	85.00	100	—
SE1753 (1831)	—	65.00	75.00	85.00	100	—

KM# 577 1/2 MOHAR
2.8000 g., Gold

Date	Mintage	VG	F	VF	XF	Unc
SE1757 (1835)	—	65.00	75.00	85.00	100	—

KM# 578 1/2 MOHAR
2.8000 g., Gold

Date	Mintage	VG	F	VF	XF	Unc
SE1757 (1835)	—	65.00	75.00	85.00	100	—
SE1758 (1836)	—	65.00	75.00	85.00	100	—
SE1762 (1840)	—	65.00	75.00	85.00	100	—
SE1764 (1842)	—	65.00	75.00	85.00	100	—
SE1766 (1844)	—	65.00	75.00	85.00	100	—

KM# 579 MOHAR
5.6000 g., Gold, 24 mm. **Obv:** Square in center

Date	Mintage	VG	F	VF	XF	Unc
SE1738 (1816)	—	125	150	175	225	—

KM# 580 MOHAR
5.6000 g., Gold, 27 mm. **Obv:** Circle in center

Date	Mintage	VG	F	VF	XF	Unc
SE1741 (1819)	—	125	150	175	225	—
SE1758 (1836)	—	125	150	175	225	—
SE1760 (1838)	—	125	150	175	225	—
SE1764 (1842)	—	125	150	175	225	—
SE1766 (1844)	—	125	150	175	225	—
SE1768 (1846)	—	125	150	175	225	—

KM# 581 MOHAR
5.6000 g., Gold **Obv:** Square in center

Date	Mintage	VG	F	VF	XF	Unc
SE1746 (1824)	—	135	160	200	265	—
SE1757 (1835)	—	135	160	200	265	—

KM# 582 2 MOHARS
11.2000 g., Gold

Date	Mintage	VG	F	VF	XF	Unc
SE1738 (1816)	—	250	275	325	385	—
SE1741 (1819)	—	250	275	325	385	—
SE1766 (1844)	—	250	275	325	385	—
SE1768 (1846)	—	250	275	325	385	—

KM# 583 2 MOHARS
11.2000 g., Gold **Obv:** Square in center

Date	Mintage	VG	F	VF	XF	Unc
SE1746 (1824)	—	250	275	325	385	—
SE1757 (1835)	—	—	—	—	—	—

PRESENTATION COINAGE

KM# 584 RUPEE
11.6600 g., Gold **Note:** In the name of Queen Rajendra Vikrama.

Date	Mintage	VG	F	VF	XF	Unc
SE1759 (1837)	—	400	500	550	625	—

KM# 585 2 RUPEES
23.3200 g., Gold **Note:** In the name of Queen Rajendra Vikrama.

Date	Mintage	VG	F	VF	XF	Unc
SE1762 (1840)	—	750	1,000	1,250	1,500	—

Surendra Vikrama
SE1769-1803 / 1847-1881AD

COPPER COINAGE

KM# 586.1 DAM
Copper **Rev. Inscription:** "Sarkar" **Note:** Prev. KM#586. Handstruck.

Date	Mintage	Good	VG	F	VF	XF
SE(17)88 (1866)	—	2.00	3.50	5.00	7.50	—
SE(17)90 (1868)	—	0.75	1.25	2.25	3.50	—
SE(17)91 (1869)	—	0.75	1.25	2.25	3.50	—
SE(17)92 (1870)	—	0.75	1.25	2.25	3.50	—
SE(17)93 (1871)	—	0.75	1.25	2.25	3.50	—
SE(17)94 (1872)	—	0.75	1.25	2.25	3.50	—
SE(17)96 (1874)	—	0.75	1.25	2.25	3.50	—
SE(17)97 (1875)	—	0.75	1.25	2.25	3.50	—
SE(17)98 (1876)	—	0.75	1.25	2.25	3.50	—
SE(17)99 (1877)	—	0.75	1.25	2.25	3.50	—
SE(18)02 (1880)	—	—	—	—	—	—

KM# 586.2 DAM
Copper **Note:** Machine struck. Prev. KM#586.1.

Date	Mintage	Good	VG	F	VF	XF
SE(17)90 (1868)	—	30.00	45.00	85.00	175	—

KM# 586.3 DAM
Copper **Rev. Inscription:** "Sarkarla" **Note:** Handstruck

Date	Mintage	Good	VG	F	VF	XF
SE(17)90 (1868)	—	20.00	40.00	60.00	90.00	—

KM# 587 1/2 PAISA
Copper

Date	Mintage	Good	VG	F	VF	XF
SE1802 (1880)	—	45.00	75.00	125	200	—

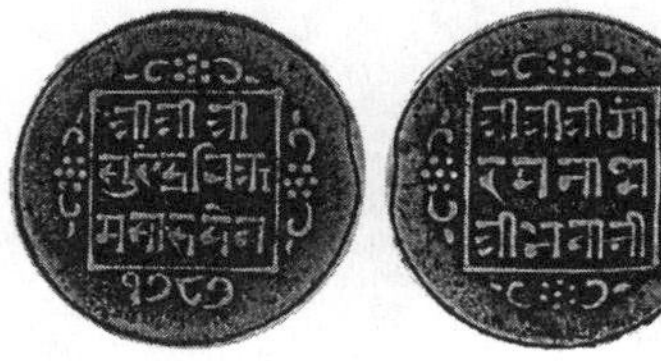

KM# 588 PAISA
Copper **Rev:** Twelve characters in legend

Date	Mintage	Good	VG	F	VF	XF
SE1787 (1865)	—	1.75	3.00	5.00	9.00	—

KM# 589 PAISA
Copper **Obv:** Border of dots **Rev:** Border of dots

Date	Mintage	Good	VG	F	VF	XF
SE1787 (1865)	—	3.00	5.00	7.50	10.00	—

KM# 590 PAISA
Copper **Rev:** Nine characters **Note:** Varieties exist.

Date	Mintage	Good	VG	F	VF	XF
SE1787 (1865)	—	1.50	2.00	3.50	5.00	—
SE1788 (1866)	—	1.50	2.00	3.50	5.00	—
SE1789 (1867)	—	1.50	2.00	3.50	5.00	—
SE1790 (1868)	—	1.50	2.00	3.50	5.00	—
SE1791 (1869)	—	1.50	2.00	3.50	5.00	—
SE1792 (1870)	—	1.50	2.00	3.50	5.00	—
SE1793 (1871)	—	1.50	2.00	3.50	5.00	—
SE1794 (1872)	—	1.50	2.00	3.50	5.00	—
SE1796 (1874)	—	1.50	2.00	3.50	5.00	—
SE1797 (1875)	—	1.50	2.00	3.50	5.00	—
SE1798 (1876)	—	1.50	2.00	3.50	5.00	—
SE1799 (1877)	—	1.50	2.00	3.50	5.00	—
SE1802 (1880)	—	15.00	20.00	25.00	35.00	—

KM# 591 2 PAISA (Dak)
10.6000 g., Copper **Rev:** Twelve characters in legend

Date	Mintage	Good	VG	F	VF	XF
SE1787 (1865)	—	30.00	40.00	50.00	75.00	—

KM# 592.1 2 PAISA (Dak)
Copper **Obv:** Sun on top shows dots **Rev:** Nine characters **Note:** Varieties exist.

Date	Mintage	Good	VG	F	VF	XF
SE1788 (1866)	—	2.00	3.50	5.00	10.00	—
SE1790 (1868)	—	1.50	2.50	3.50	6.00	—

KM# 592.2 2 PAISA (Dak)
Copper **Obv:** Sun on top shows flames pointing up or down **Note:** Varieties exist in planchet size and thickness.

Date	Mintage	Good	VG	F	VF	XF
SE1790	—	1.50	2.50	3.50	6.00	—
SE1791	—	1.50	2.50	3.50	6.00	—
SE1796	—	1.75	3.00	4.00	8.00	—
SE1798	—	1.75	3.00	4.00	8.00	—
SE1802	—	30.00	40.00	50.00	75.00	—

SILVER COINAGE

KM# 593 DAM
0.0400 g., Silver **Note:** Uniface.

Date	Mintage	VG	F	VF	XF	Unc
ND(1847-81)	—	5.00	7.50	10.00	15.00	—

KM# 594 1/32 MOHAR
0.1800 g., Silver **Note:** Uniface.

Date	Mintage	VG	F	VF	XF	Unc
ND(1847-81)	—	6.00	10.00	13.50	18.50	—

KM# 595 1/16 MOHAR
0.3500 g., Silver

Date	Mintage	VG	F	VF	XF	Unc
ND(1847-81)	—	6.00	10.00	13.50	18.50	—

KM# 596 1/8 MOHAR
0.7000 g., Silver

Date	Mintage	VG	F	VF	XF	Unc
ND(1847-81)	—	5.00	8.50	12.50	17.50	—

KM# 599 1/4 MOHAR
1.4000 g., Silver **Note:** In the name of Queen Deva Raja Lakshmi.

Date	Mintage	VG	F	VF	XF	Unc
SE1769 (1847)	—	9.00	13.50	20.00	30.00	—
SE1770 (1848)	—	9.00	13.50	20.00	30.00	—
SE1772 (1850)	—	9.00	13.50	20.00	30.00	—
SE1773 (1851)	—	9.00	13.50	20.00	30.00	—
SE1775 (1853)	—	9.00	13.50	20.00	30.00	—
SE1776 (1854)	—	9.00	13.50	20.00	30.00	—

KM# 598.1 1/4 MOHAR
1.4000 g., Silver **Note:** In the name of Queen Sura Raja Lakshmi.

Date	Mintage	VG	F	VF	XF	Unc
SE1769 (1847)	—	15.00	25.00	35.00	45.00	—
SE1770 (1848)	—	15.00	25.00	35.00	45.00	—
SE1772 (1850)	—	15.00	25.00	35.00	45.00	—
SE1775 (1853)	—	15.00	25.00	35.00	45.00	—
SE1776 (1854)	—	15.00	25.00	35.00	45.00	—
SE1782 (1860)	—	15.00	25.00	35.00	45.00	—
SE1787 (1865)	—	15.00	25.00	35.00	45.00	—
SE1788 (1866)	—	15.00	25.00	35.00	45.00	—

KM# 597 1/4 MOHAR
1.4000 g., Silver **Note:** In the name of Queen Trailokya Raja Lakshmi.

Date	Mintage	VG	F	VF	XF	Unc
SE1769 (1847)	—	15.00	20.00	30.00	40.00	—
SE1770 (1848)	—	15.00	20.00	30.00	40.00	—
SE1772 (1850)	—	15.00	20.00	30.00	40.00	—

KM# 598.2 1/4 MOHAR
1.4000 g., Silver **Note:** In the name of Queen Sura Raja Lakshmi. Struck with gold dies.

Date	Mintage	VG	F	VF	XF	Unc
SE1777 (1855)	—	40.00	50.00	75.00	100	—

KM# 600 1/4 MOHAR
1.4000 g., Silver **Note:** In the name of Queen Punyakumari Raja Lakshmi.

Date	Mintage	VG	F	VF	XF	Unc
SE1802 (1880)	—	40.00	50.00	75.00	100	—

KM# 601 1/2 MOHAR
2.8000 g., Silver

Date	Mintage	VG	F	VF	XF	Unc
SE1769 (1847)	—	5.00	8.50	13.50	20.00	—
SE1770 (1848)	—	5.00	8.50	13.50	20.00	—
SE1771 (1849)	—	5.00	8.50	13.50	20.00	—
SE1772 (1850)	—	5.00	8.50	13.50	20.00	—
SE1773 (1851)	—	15.00	20.00	25.00	30.00	—
SE1775 (1853)	—	15.00	20.00	25.00	30.00	—
SE1776 (1854)	—	15.00	20.00	25.00	30.00	—
SE1787 (1865)	—	15.00	20.00	25.00	30.00	—
SE1802 (1880)	—	15.00	20.00	25.00	30.00	—

KM# 602 MOHAR
5.6000 g., Silver

Date	Mintage	VG	F	VF	XF	Unc
SE1769 (1847)	—	4.50	6.50	9.00	11.50	—
SE1770 (1848)	—	4.50	6.50	9.00	11.50	—
SE1771 (1849)	—	4.50	6.50	9.00	11.50	—
SE1772 (1850)	—	4.50	6.50	9.00	11.50	—
SE1773 (1851)	—	4.50	6.50	9.00	11.50	—
SE1774 (1852)	—	7.00	10.00	13.50	17.50	—
SE1775 (1853)	—	4.50	6.50	9.00	11.50	—
SE1776 (1854)	—	4.50	6.50	9.00	11.50	—
SE1777 (1855)	—	4.50	6.50	9.00	11.50	—
SE1778 (1856)	—	4.50	6.50	9.00	11.50	—
SE1779 (1857)	—	4.50	6.50	9.00	11.50	—
SE1780 (1858)	—	4.50	6.50	9.00	11.50	—
SE1781 (1859)	—	4.50	6.50	9.00	11.50	—
SE1782 (1860)	—	4.50	7.50	12.50	16.50	—
SE1785 (1863)	—	7.00	10.00	13.50	17.50	—
SE1786 (1864)	—	4.50	6.50	9.00	11.50	—
SE1787 (1865)	—	4.50	6.50	9.00	11.50	—
SE1788 (1866)	—	4.50	6.50	9.00	11.50	—
SE1789 (1867)	—	4.50	6.50	9.00	11.50	—
SE1790 (1868)	—	4.50	6.50	9.00	11.50	—
SE1791 (1869)	—	4.50	6.50	9.00	11.50	—
SE1792 (1870)	—	4.50	6.50	9.00	11.50	—
SE1793 (1871)	—	4.50	6.50	9.00	11.50	—
SE1794 (1872)	—	4.50	6.50	9.00	11.50	—
SE1796 (1874)	—	4.50	6.50	9.00	11.50	—
SE1797 (1875)	—	4.50	6.50	9.00	11.50	—
SE1800 (1878)	—	4.50	6.50	9.00	11.50	—
SE1801 (1879)	—	4.50	6.50	9.00	11.50	—
SE1802 (1880)	—	4.50	6.50	9.00	11.50	—
SE1803 (1881)	—	4.50	6.50	9.00	11.50	—

KM# 602.1 MOHAR
5.6000 g., Silver **Edge:** Plain **Note:** Machine struck.

Date	Mintage	VG	F	VF	XF	Unc
SE1786 (1864)	—	12.50	15.00	20.00	27.50	—
SE1787 (1865)	—	7.50	10.00	15.00	22.50	—
SE1788 (1866)	—	12.50	15.00	20.00	27.50	—
SE1789 (1867)	—	12.50	15.00	20.00	27.50	—

KM# 602.2 MOHAR
5.6000 g., Silver **Note:** Struck using gold dies.

Date	Mintage	VG	F	VF	XF	Unc
SE1801 (1879)	—	12.50	15.00	20.00	27.50	—

KM# 603 2 MOHARS
11.2000 g., Silver **Edge:** Plain

Date	Mintage	VG	F	VF	XF	Unc
SE1769 (1847)	—	22.50	30.00	40.00	55.00	—
SE1770 (1848)	—	22.50	30.00	40.00	55.00	—
SE1771 (1849)	—	22.50	30.00	40.00	55.00	—
SE1772 (1850)	—	22.50	30.00	40.00	55.00	—
SE1777 (1855)	—	22.50	30.00	40.00	55.00	—
SE1782 (1860)	—	22.50	30.00	40.00	55.00	—
SE1796 (1874)	—	22.50	30.00	40.00	55.00	—
SE1797 (1875)	—	22.50	30.00	40.00	55.00	—
SE1801 (1879)	—	17.50	20.00	25.00	40.00	—
SE1802 (1880)	—	22.50	30.00	40.00	55.00	—

KM# 603.1 2 MOHARS
11.2000 g., Silver **Edge:** Milled **Note:** Machine struck.

Date	Mintage	VG	F	VF	XF	Unc
SE1786 (1864) Rare	—	—	—	—	—	—

KM# 603.2 2 MOHARS
11.2000 g., Silver **Note:** Struck with regular gold dies. Size varies: 26-28 millimeters.

Date	Mintage	VG	F	VF	XF	Unc
SE1801 (1879)	—	11.50	20.00	28.50	50.00	—
SE1802 (1880)	—	22.50	30.00	40.00	55.00	—

GOLD COINAGE

Actual size 2x actual size

KM# 604 DAM
0.0400 g., Gold **Note:** Uniface. Legend in two lines.

Date	Mintage	VG	F	VF	XF	Unc
ND(1847-81)	—	7.50	10.00	12.50	16.00	—

Actual size 2x actual size

KM# A604 DAM
0.0400 g., Gold **Note:** Legend in three lines.

Date	Mintage	VG	F	VF	XF	Unc
ND(1847-81)	—	15.00	20.00	25.00	32.00	—

KM# 605 1/32 MOHAR
0.1800 g., Gold **Note:** Uniface.

Date	Mintage	VG	F	VF	XF	Unc
ND(1847-81)	—	14.00	20.00	25.00	35.00	—

KM# 606 1/16 MOHAR
0.3500 g., Gold

Date	Mintage	VG	F	VF	XF	Unc
ND(1847-81)	—	14.00	20.00	25.00	35.00	—

KM# 607 1/8 MOHAR
0.7000 g., Gold

Date	Mintage	VG	F	VF	XF	Unc
ND(1847-81)	—	22.50	27.50	35.00	50.00	—

KM# 608 1/4 MOHAR
1.4000 g., Gold **Note:** In the name of Queen Sura Raja Lakshmi.

Date	Mintage	VG	F	VF	XF	Unc
SE1769 (1847)	—	40.00	50.00	65.00	85.00	—
SE1787 (1865)	—	40.00	50.00	65.00	85.00	—
SE1790 (1868)	—	40.00	50.00	65.00	85.00	—

KM# A608 1/4 MOHAR
1.4000 g., Gold **Note:** In the name of Queen Trailokya Raja Lakshmi.

Date	Mintage	VG	F	VF	XF	Unc
SE1769 (1847)	—	40.00	50.00	65.00	85.00	—
SE1770 (1848)	—	40.00	50.00	65.00	85.00	—

KM# 609 1/4 MOHAR
1.4000 g., Gold **Note:** In the name of Queen Deva Raja Lakshmi.

Date	Mintage	VG	F	VF	XF	Unc
SE1770 (1848)	—	40.00	50.00	65.00	85.00	—

KM# 610 1/4 MOHAR
1.4000 g., Gold **Note:** In the name of Queen Punyakumari Raja Lakshmi.

Date	Mintage	VG	F	VF	XF	Unc
SE1802 (1880)	—	55.00	75.00	100	135	—

KM# 611 1/2 MOHAR
2.8000 g., Gold

Date	Mintage	VG	F	VF	XF	Unc
SE1769 (1847)	—	65.00	75.00	85.00	100	—
SE1770 (1848)	—	65.00	75.00	85.00	100	—
SE1802 (1880)	—	65.00	75.00	85.00	100	—

KM# 612 1/2 MOHAR
2.8000 g., Gold **Rev:** Without horizontal lines

Date	Mintage	VG	F	VF	XF	Unc
SE1790 (1868)	—	65.00	75.00	85.00	100	—

KM# 613 MOHAR
2.8000 g., Gold **Note:** In the name of Queen Deva Raja Lakshmi.

Date	Mintage	VG	F	VF	XF	Unc
SE1769 (1847)	—	115	125	145	175	—
SE1791 (1869)	—	115	125	145	175	—
SE1794 (1872)	—	115	125	145	175	—
SE1802 (1880)	—	115	125	145	175	—

KM# 616 2 RUPEES
Gold **Note:** Similar to 1 Tola, KM#615.

Date	Mintage	VG	F	VF	XF	Unc
SE1794 (1872)	—	450	525	650	800	—

KM# 614.1 1/2 TOLA
6.2400 g., Gold, 21.5 mm.

Date	Mintage	VG	F	VF	XF	Unc
SE1773 (1851)	—	125	135	160	200	—

KM# 614.2 1/2 TOLA
6.2400 g., Gold, 26.5 mm. **Note:** Larger size.

Date	Mintage	VG	F	VF	XF	Unc
SE1786 (1864)	—	125	135	160	200	—
SE1787 (1865)	—	125	135	160	200	—

KM# 615 TOLA
12.4800 g., Gold

Date	Mintage	VG	F	VF	XF	Unc
SE1769 (1847)	—	265	285	310	350	—
SE1773 (1851)	—	265	285	310	350	—
SE1774 (1852)	—	265	285	310	350	—
SE1778 (1856)	—	265	285	310	350	—
SE1780 (1858)	—	265	285	310	350	—
SE1786 (1864)	—	265	285	310	350	—
SE1787 (1865)	—	265	285	310	350	—
SE1791 (1869)	—	265	285	310	350	—
SE1793 (1871)	—	265	285	310	350	—
SE1794 (1872)	—	265	285	310	350	—
SE1802 (1880)	—	265	285	310	350	—

PRESENTATION COINAGE

KM# 617.1 RUPEE
11.6600 g., Gold **Note:** In the name of Queen Trailokyaraja Lakshmi.

Date	Mintage	VG	F	VF	XF	Unc
SE1769 (1847)	—	400	500	550	625	—

KM# 617.2 RUPEE
11.6600 g., Gold **Note:** In the name of Queen Trailokyaraja Lakshmi.

Date	Mintage	VG	F	VF	XF	Unc
SE1771 (1849)	—	285	350	425	525	—

KM# A618 2 RUPEES
Silver **Note:** In the name of King Surendra.

Date	Mintage	VG	F	VF	XF	Unc
SE1769 (1847)	—	—	750	1,000	1,250	—

KM# B618 2 RUPEES
23.3200 g., Gold **Note:** In the name of King Surendra.

Date	Mintage	VG	F	VF	XF	Unc
SE1769 (1847)	—	750	1,000	1,250	1,500	—
SE1771 (1849)	—	750	1,000	1,250	1,500	—

KM# A619 2 RUPEES
Silver **Note:** In the name of (Crown Prince) Trailokya Vira Vikrama.

Date	Mintage	VG	F	VF	XF	Unc
SE1771 (1849)	—	—	1,000	1,250	1,500	—

KM# 619 2 RUPEES
Gold **Note:** In the name of (Crown Prince) Trailokya Vira Vikrama.

Date	Mintage	VG	F	VF	XF	Unc
SE1771 (1849)	—	—	1,500	1,800	2,200	—

Prithvi Bir Bikram
VS1938-1968 / 1881-1911AD
COPPER COINAGE

KM# 620.1 DAM
Copper

Date	Mintage	F	VF	XF	Unc
SE(18)18 (1896)	—	7.50	12.00	15.00	20.00
Note: Reverse inscription SARKAR					
SE(18)19 (1897)	—	7.50	12.00	15.00	20.00
Note: Reverse inscription SURKAR (error)					

KM# 623 PAISA
Copper **Obv:** Trident **Rev:** Legend in four lines

Date	Mintage	Good	VG	F	VF	XF
SE1810 (1888)	—	30.00	50.00	75.00	100	—

KM# 625 PAISA
Copper **Obv:** Two footprints above khukris

Date	Mintage	Good	VG	F	VF	XF
VS1945 (1888)	—	3.00	5.00	8.50	13.50	—
VS1948 (1891)	—	9.00	15.00	22.50	35.00	—

KM# 624 PAISA
Copper **Obv:** Crossed khukris, circular legend, border of flowers **Note:** Two reverse die varieties

Date	Mintage	Good	VG	F	VF	XF
VS1945 (1888)	—	30.00	50.00	75.00	100	—
VS1945 (1888)	—	30.00	50.00	75.00	100	—
Note: Without obverse footprints						

KM# 626 PAISA
Copper **Obv:** Border of XXX's **Rev:** Border of XXX's

Date	Mintage	Good	VG	F	VF	XF
VS1948 (1891)	—	1.00	1.50	3.00	5.00	—
VS1948 (1891) Inverted date	—	2.00	3.00	5.00	8.00	—
VS1949 (1892)	—	2.00	3.00	5.00	8.00	—

KM# 627 PAISA
Copper **Obv:** Border of crescents **Rev:** Border of crescents

Date	Mintage	Good	VG	F	VF	XF
VS1949 (1892)	—	1.00	1.50	3.00	5.00	—
VS1950 (1893)	—	1.00	1.50	3.00	5.00	—
VS1951 (1894)	—	1.25	1.75	3.50	6.00	—

KM# 628 PAISA
Copper **Obv:** Legend within sprays **Rev:** Legend within sprays **Note:** Varieties in sprays exist. Coin and medal alignment varieties exist.

Date	Mintage	Good	VG	F	VF	XF
VS1949 (1892)	—	1.00	1.50	3.00	5.00	—
VS1950 (1893)	—	1.00	1.50	3.00	5.00	—
VS1951 (1894)	—	1.00	1.50	3.00	5.00	—
VS1952 (1895)	—	1.00	1.50	3.00	5.00	—
VS1953 (1896)	—	1.00	1.50	3.00	5.00	—
VS1954 (1897)	—	1.00	1.50	3.00	5.00	—
VS1955 (1898)	—	1.00	1.50	3.00	5.00	—
VS1956 (1899)	—	1.00	1.50	3.00	5.00	—

KM# 632 2 PAISA (Dak)
Copper **Obv:** Circular legends **Rev:** Circular legends **Note:** Varieties exist with dot or with cross below khukris.

Date	Mintage	Good	VG	F	VF	XF
VS1948 (1891)	—	2.00	3.00	5.00	8.00	—
VS1949 (1892)	—	2.50	3.50	5.00	8.00	—
VS1950 (1893)	—	2.50	3.50	5.00	8.00	—

SILVER COINAGE

KM# 635 DAM
0.0400 g., Silver **Note:** Uniface. Five characters around sword.

Date	Mintage	VG	F	VF	XF	Unc
ND(1881-1911)	—	—	8.00	10.00	15.00	25.00

KM# 636 DAM
0.0400 g., Silver **Note:** Four characters around sword.

Date	Mintage	VG	F	VF	XF	Unc
ND(1881-1911)	—	—	15.00	25.00	30.00	40.00

KM# 637 1/32 MOHAR
0.1800 g., Silver **Obv:** Sun and moon

Date	Mintage	VG	F	VF	XF	Unc
ND(1881-1911)	—	5.00	8.50	12.50	16.50	—

KM# 638 1/32 MOHAR
0.1800 g., Silver **Obv:** Without sun and moon

Date	Mintage	VG	F	VF	XF	Unc
ND(1881-1911)	—	5.00	8.50	12.50	16.50	—

KM# 639 1/16 MOHAR
0.3500 g., Silver **Note:** Varieties exist.

Date	Mintage	VG	F	VF	XF	Unc
ND(1881-1911)	—	—	6.00	10.00	13.50	20.00

KM# 640 1/8 MOHAR
0.7000 g., Silver **Note:** Varieties exist.

Date	Mintage	VG	F	VF	XF	Unc
ND(1881-1911)	—	—	7.50	12.50	18.50	27.50

KM# 641 1/4 MOHAR
1.4000 g., Silver **Rev:** Two moons **Note:** Handstruck

Date	Mintage	VG	F	VF	XF	Unc
SE1804 (1882)	—	15.00	17.50	25.00	35.00	—
SE1806 (1884)	—	20.00	25.00	35.00	45.00	—
SE1808 (1886)	—	15.00	17.50	25.00	35.00	—
SE1811 (1889)	—	20.00	25.00	35.00	45.00	—

KM# 642 1/4 MOHAR
1.4000 g., Silver **Rev:** Moon and spiral sun **Note:** Machine struck

Date	Mintage	VG	F	VF	XF	Unc
SE1816 (1894)	—	1.75	3.00	5.00	7.00	—
SE1817 (1895)	—	1.75	3.00	5.00	7.00	—

KM# 645 1/2 MOHAR
2.7700 g., Silver **Note:** Hand struck

Date	Mintage	VG	F	VF	XF	Unc
SE1803 (1881)	—	15.00	20.00	25.00	30.00	—
SE1804 (1882)	—	15.00	20.00	25.00	30.00	—

KM# 646 1/2 MOHAR
2.7700 g., Silver **Obv:** Legend modified **Note:** Hand struck

Date	Mintage	VG	F	VF	XF	Unc
SE1805 (1883)	—	15.00	20.00	25.00	30.00	—

KM# 647 1/2 MOHAR
2.7700 g., Silver **Edge:** Plain **Note:** Machine struck. Varieties exist.

Date	Mintage	F	VF	XF	Unc
SE1816 (1894)	—	3.00	5.00	7.00	10.00
SE1817 (1895)	—	3.00	5.00	7.00	10.00
SE1824 (1902)	—	20.00	25.00	30.00	35.00

KM# 650 MOHAR
5.6000 g., Silver **Edge:** Milled **Note:** Hand struck.

Date	Mintage	VG	F	VF	XF	Unc
SE1803 (1881)	—	4.50	6.50	9.00	11.50	—
SE1804 (1882)	—	4.50	6.50	9.00	11.50	—

KM# 651.1 MOHAR
5.6000 g., Silver **Edge:** Plain **Note:** Machine struck.

Date	Mintage	F	VF	XF	Unc
SE1803 (1881)	—	15.00	25.00	35.00	50.00
SE1804 (1882)	—	4.50	6.50	8.00	10.00
SE1805 (1883)	—	4.50	6.50	8.00	10.00
SE1806 (1884)	—	4.50	6.50	8.00	10.00
SE1807 (1885)	—	4.50	6.50	8.00	10.00
SE1808 (1886)	—	4.50	6.50	8.00	10.00
SE1809 (1887)	—	4.50	6.50	8.00	10.00
SE1810 (1888)	—	4.50	6.50	8.00	10.00
SE1811 (1889)	—	15.00	25.00	35.00	50.00
SE1816 (1894)	—	4.50	6.50	8.00	10.00
SE1817 (1895)	—	4.50	6.50	8.00	10.00
SE1818 (1896)	—	4.50	6.50	8.00	10.00
SE1819 (1897)	—	4.50	6.50	8.00	10.00
SE1820 (1898)	—	4.50	6.50	8.00	10.00
SE1821 (1899)	—	4.50	6.50	8.00	10.00

Date	Mintage	F	VF	XF	Unc
SE1822 (1900)	—	4.50	6.50	8.00	10.00
SE1823 (1901)	—	4.50	6.50	8.00	10.00
SE1824 (1902)	—	4.50	6.50	8.00	10.00
SE1825 (1903)	—	4.50	6.50	8.00	10.00
SE1826 (1904)	—	4.50	6.50	8.00	10.00
SE1827 (1905)	—	4.50	6.50	8.00	10.00

KM# A653 2 MOHARS
11.2000 g., Silver, 27 mm. **Note:** Hand struck using gold dies.

Date	Mintage	F	VF	XF	Unc
SE1803 (1881)	—	40.00	60.00	80.00	100

KM# 653 2 MOHARS
11.2000 g., Silver, 27 mm. **Note:** Machine struck.

Date		Mintage	F	VF	XF	Unc
SE1804 (1882)	Milled edge	—	40.00	60.00	80.00	100
SE1811 (1889)	Plain edge	—	40.00	60.00	80.00	100
SE1817 (1895)	Plain edge	—	8.00	12.50	17.50	25.00

KM# 654 2 MOHARS
11.2000 g., Silver, 29 mm. **Edge:** Plain **Note:** Machine struck using gold dies.

Date	Mintage	F	VF	XF	Unc
SE1821 (1899)	—	10.00	15.00	25.00	45.00

KM# 657 4 MOHARS
22.4000 g., Silver **Edge:** Plain

Date	Mintage	F	VF	XF	Unc
SE1817 (1895)	—	60.00	100	140	200

GOLD COINAGE

KM# 659 DAM
0.0400 g., Gold **Note:** Uniface. Five characters around sword. Similar to 1/64 Mohar, KM#664.

Date	Mintage	VG	F	VF	XF	Unc
ND(1881-1911)	—	—	10.00	14.00	20.00	27.50

KM# 660 DAM
0.0400 g., Gold **Note:** Uniface. Four characters around sword. Similar to 1/64 Mohar, KM#663.

Date	Mintage	VG	F	VF	XF	Unc
ND(1881-1911)	—	—	10.00	14.00	20.00	27.50

Actual Size 2 x Actual Size

KM# 661 DAM
0.0400 g., Gold **Note:** Uniface. Circle around characters.

Date	Mintage	VG	F	VF	XF	Unc
ND(1881-1911)	—	—	10.00	14.00	20.00	27.50

Actual Size 2 x Actual Size

KM# 662 DAM
0.0400 g., Gold **Note:** Uniface. Two characters below sword. Varieties exist.

Date	Mintage	VG	F	VF	XF	Unc
ND(1881-1911)	—	—	10.00	14.00	20.00	27.50

Actual Size 2 x Actual Size

KM# 663 1/64 MOHAR
0.0900 g., Gold **Note:** Uniface. Four characters around sword.

Date	Mintage	VG	F	VF	XF	Unc
ND(1881-1911)	—	—	12.50	17.50	22.50	30.00

Actual Size 2 x Actual Size

KM# 664 1/64 MOHAR
0.0900 g., Gold **Note:** Uniface. Five characters around sword.

Date	Mintage	VG	F	VF	XF	Unc
ND(1881-1911)	—	—	12.50	17.50	22.50	30.00

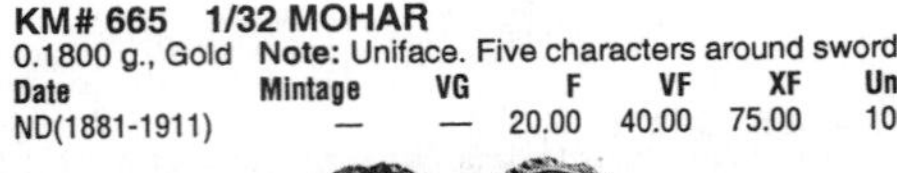

KM# 665 1/32 MOHAR
0.1800 g., Gold **Note:** Uniface. Five characters around sword.

Date	Mintage	VG	F	VF	XF	Unc
ND(1881-1911)	—	—	20.00	40.00	75.00	100

KM# 666 1/32 MOHAR
0.1800 g., Gold **Note:** Uniface. Four characters around sword.

Date	Mintage	VG	F	VF	XF	Unc
ND(1881-1911)	—	—	15.00	30.00	75.00	100

KM# 667 1/16 MOHAR
0.3500 g., Gold

Date	Mintage	VG	F	VF	XF	Unc
ND(1881-1911)	—	—	15.00	40.00	75.00	100

KM# 669.1 1/8 MOHAR
0.7000 g., Gold **Obv:** Six characters

Date	Mintage	F	VF	XF	Unc
ND (1881)	—	22.50	40.00	75.00	100

KM# 669.2 1/8 MOHAR
0.7000 g., Gold **Obv:** Five characters **Note:** Varieties exist.

Date	Mintage	F	VF	XF	Unc
ND (1881)	—	22.50	40.00	75.00	100

KM# 671.1 1/4 MOHAR
1.4000 g., Gold

Date	Mintage	F	VF	XF	Unc
SE1808 (1886)	—	45.00	60.00	80.00	100
SE1811 (1889)	—	45.00	60.00	80.00	100
SE1817 (1895)	—	40.00	50.00	60.00	80.00

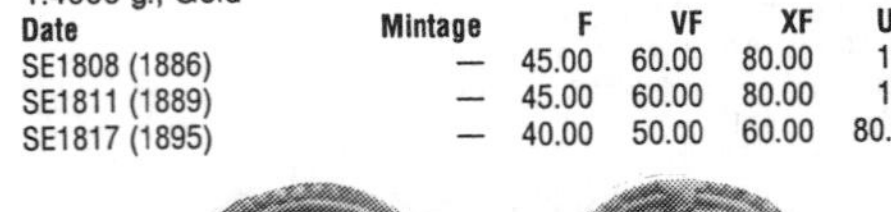

KM# 672.1 1/2 MOHAR
2.8000 g., Gold

Date	Mintage	F	VF	XF	Unc
SE1805 (1883)	—	65.00	75.00	85.00	100

KM# 672.2 1/2 MOHAR
2.8000 g., Gold

Date	Mintage	F	VF	XF	Unc
SE1817 (1895)	—	65.00	75.00	85.00	100

KM# 673.1 MOHAR
5.6000 g., Gold

Date	Mintage	F	VF	XF	Unc
SE1804 (1882)	—	115	125	150	200
SE1805 (1883)	—	115	125	150	200
SE1809 (1887)	—	115	125	150	200
SE1817 (1895)	—	115	125	150	200
SE1820 (1898)	—	115	125	150	200

KM# 673.3 MOHAR
5.6000 g., Gold

Date	Mintage	F	VF	XF	Unc
VS1949 (1892)	—	115	125	145	175

KM# 674.1 TOLA
12.4800 g., Gold **Note:** Oblique edge milling.

Date	Mintage	F	VF	XF	Unc
SE1803 (1881)	—	235	255	285	325
SE1805 (1883)	—	235	255	285	325
SE1810 (1888)	—	235	255	285	325
SE1811 (1889)	—	235	255	285	325

KM# 674.2 TOLA
12.4800 g., Gold **Note:** Vertical edge milling.

Date	Mintage	F	VF	XF	Unc
SE1803 (1881)	—	235	255	285	325
SE1804 (1882)	—	235	255	285	325

KM# 674.3 TOLA
12.4800 g., Gold **Edge:** Plain

Date	Mintage	F	VF	XF	Unc
SE1807 (1885)	—	235	255	275	300
SE1817 (1895)	—	235	255	275	300
SE1820 (1898)	—	235	255	275	300

KM# 675.2 TOLA
12.4800 g., Gold **Edge:** Plain

Date	Mintage	F	VF	XF	Unc
VS1947 (1890)	—	235	255	275	300

KM# 675.3 TOLA
12.4800 g., Gold **Note:** Oblique edge milling.

Date	Mintage	F	VF	XF	Unc
VS1949 (1892)	—	235	255	275	300

KM# 676 DUITOLA ASARPHI
23.3200 g., Gold

Date	Mintage	F	VF	XF	Unc
SE1811 (1889)	—	600	700	800	1,000

KM# 677 DUITOLA ASARPHI
23.3200 g., Gold **Rev:** Die of 4 Mohars, KM#657

Date	Mintage	F	VF	XF	Unc
SE1817 (1895)	—	600	700	800	1,000

PATTERNS

Including off metal strikes

KM#	Date	Mintage Identification	Mkt Val

Pn1	SE1810	— Paisa.	—

Pn2	SE(ca.1888)	— Paisa.	—

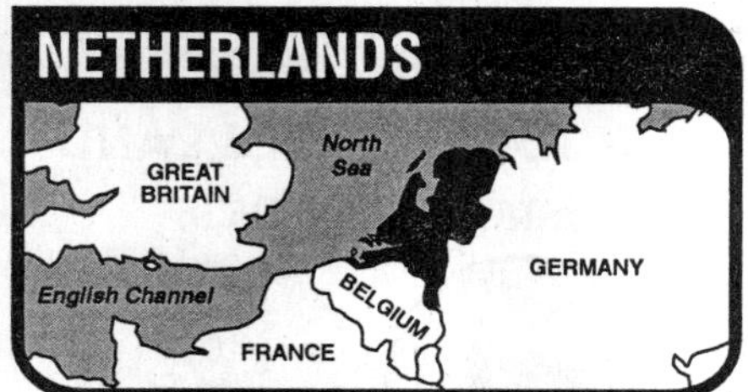

The Kingdom of the Netherlands, a country of western Europe fronting on the North Sea and bordered by Belgium and Germany, has an area of 15,770 sq. mi. (41,500 sq. km.).

After being a part of Charlemagne's empire in the 8th and 9th centuries, the Netherlands came under control of Burgundy and the Austrian Hapsburgs, and finally was subjected to Spanish dominion in the 16th century. Led by William of Orange, the Dutch revolted against Spain in 1568. The seven northern provinces formed the Union of Utrecht and declared their independence in 1581, becoming the Republic of the United Netherlands. In the following century, the *Golden Age* of Dutch history, the Netherlands became a great sea and colonial power, a patron of the arts and a refuge for the persecuted. The United Dutch Republic ended in 1795 when the French formed the Batavian Republic. Napoleon made his brother Louis, the King of Holland in 1806, however he abdicated in 1810 when Napoleon annexed Holland. The French were expelled in 1813, and all the provinces of Holland and Belgium were merged into the Kingdom of the United Netherlands under William I, in 1814. The Belgians withdrew in 1830 to form their own kingdom, the last substantial change in the configuration of European Netherlands.

RULERS

United Netherlands, 1543-1795

BATAVIAN REPUBLIC

French domination, 1795-1806

KINGDOM OF HOLLAND

French Protectorate

Louis Napoleon, 1806-1810

FRENCH ANNEXATION

Napoleon I, 1810-1814

KINGDOM OF THE NETHERLANDS

William I, 1815-1840
William II, 1840-1849
William III, 1849-1890
Wilhelmina I, 1890-1948

MINT MARKS

B - Brussels (Belgium), 1821-1830
D - Denver, 1943-1945
P - Philadelphia, 1941-1945
S - San Francisco, 1944-1945

MINT PRIVY MARKS

Harderwijk (Gelderland)

Date	Privy Mark
1782-1806	Ear of corn

Dordrecht (Holland)

Date	Privy Mark
1600-1806	Rosette
1795-1806	None

Enkhuizen (West Friesland)

Date	Privy Mark
1796-1803	Star

Hoorn (West Friesland)

Date	Privy Mark
1803-1809	Star

Utrecht (Utrecht)

Date	Privy Mark
1738-1805	Shield

Utrecht

Date	Privy Mark
1806-present	Caduceus

MINT OFFICIALS' PRIVY MARKS

Brussels Mint

Date	Privy Mark
1821-1830	Palm branch

Utrecht Mint

Date	Privy Mark
1806-1810	Bee
1810-1813	Mast
1815-1816	Cloverleaf
1817	Child in swaddling clothes
1818-1840	Torch
1839-1846	Fleur de lis
1846-1874	Sword
1874	Sword in scabbard
1875-87	Broadaxe
1887	Broadaxe and star
1888-1909	Halberd

NOTE: A star adjoining the privy mark indicates that the piece was struck at the beginning of the term of office of a successor. (The star was used only if the successor had not chosen his own mark yet.)

MONETARY SYSTEM

1 Penning = 1/2 Duit
2 Duits = 1 Oord
8 Duits = 1 Stuiver (Stiver)
6 Stuiver = 1 Schelling
20 Stuiver = 1 Gulden (Guilder or Florin)
50 Stuiver = 1 Rijksdaalder (Silver Ducat)
60 Stuiver = 1 Ducaton (Silver Rider)
14 Gulden = 1 Golden Rider

Commencing 1815

100 Cents = 1 Gulden
2-1/2 Gulden = 1 Rijksdaalder

BATAVIAN REPUBLIC

From 1796 to 1806, the Netherlands was a confederation of seven provinces, each producing coins similar in design but differing in the coat of arms or inscription. Generally the coins of each province contained an abbreviation of the name of the province somewhere in the inscription. Under the Batavian Republic, the following abbreviations were used.

PROVINCE ABBREVIATIONS

G, GEL - Gelderland
HOL, HOLL - Holland
TRANSI - Overijsel
TRA, TRAI, TRAIECTUM - Utrecht
WESTF, WESTRI - Westfriesland
ZEL, ZEELANDIA - Zeeland

STANDARD COINAGE

KM# 10.1 RIJKSDAALDER (2-1/2 Gulden)
0.8680 Silver **Obv. Legend:** ...D: GEL: &: C: Z: **Rev:** Crowned weapon between date

Date	Mintage	F	VF	XF	Unc	BU
1800	253,925	180	400	600	1,100	—
1801	Inc. above	300	450	600	1,100	—
1801	—	300	450	600	1,100	—
1802	Inc. above	300	450	600	1,100	—

KM# 10.2 RIJKSDAALDER (2-1/2 Gulden)
0.8680 Silver **Obv. Legend:** ...HOLL: or Hol:

Date	Mintage	F	VF	XF	Unc	BU
1801/0	Inc. above	300	450	600	850	1,200
1801	Inc. above	75.00	150	250	300	400
1802	Inc. above	75.00	150	250	300	400
1806	Inc. above	350	600	1,000	1,400	1,600

KM# 10.4 RIJKSDAALDER (2-1/2 Gulden)
0.8680 Silver **Obv:** Legend ends:...TRA or TRAI.

Date	Mintage	F	VF	XF	Unc	BU
1801	Inc. above	65.00	100	150	200	—
1801	—	65.00	100	150	300	—

Date	Mintage	F	VF	XF	Unc	BU
1801	—	—	—	—	—	—
1801 small 8-0	Inc. above	65.00	100	150	300	—
1802	Inc. above	65.00	100	150	300	—
1803 long sword	Inc. above	65.00	100	150	200	300
1803	—	—	—	—	—	—
1803	—	—	—	—	—	—
1803 short sword	Inc. above	65.00	100	150	300	—
1804	Inc. above	65.00	100	150	200	300
1805/797	Inc. above	65.00	100	150	250	350
1805	Inc. above	65.00	100	150	200	300

KM# 9.2 3 GULDEN
0.9150 Silver **Obv. Legend:** ...HOL: or HOLL **Rev:** Standing maiden, date below

Date	Mintage	F	VF	XF	Unc	BU
1795/3	1,084,000	70.00	125	180	250	—
1795	Inc. above	60.00	100	160	225	—
1796	Inc. above	60.00	100	160	225	—
1797	Inc. above	60.00	100	160	225	—
1798	Inc. above	110	250	350	500	—
1800	Inc. above	60.00	125	200	275	—
1801	Inc. above	90.00	160	240	350	—
1801	—	90.00	160	240	350	—

TRADE COINAGE

KM# 11.2 DUCAT
3.5000 g., 0.9860 Gold .1109 oz. **Obv. Legend:** ends:...Hol **Note:** Coins with the star were struck at the Enkhuizen Mint with a total mintage of 630,455. Coins without the star were struck at the Dordrecht Mint with a total mintage of 2,861,825.

Date	Mintage	F	VF	XF	Unc	BU
1801/1800 without star	—	300	600	800	1,000	1,250
1801 without star	—	90.00	150	225	300	375
1801 star	—	200	400	600	800	1,000
1802 without star	—	150	250	400	600	800
1802 star	—	150	300	400	550	650
1803 without star	—	80.00	120	165	250	350
1804 without star	—	80.00	120	165	250	350
1805 without star	—	150	300	400	600	850

KM# 11.1 DUCAT
3.5000 g., 0.9860 Gold .1109 oz. **Obv. Legend:** ends:...G or GEL.

Date	Mintage	F	VF	XF	Unc	BU
1801	Inc. above	80.00	150	300	400	—
1802	Inc. above	150	250	450	600	—
1803	—	650	1,300	2,000	3,250	—

KM# 11.3 DUCAT
3.5000 g., 0.9860 Gold .1109 oz. **Obv. Legend:** ends:...CRES: TRA • **Note:** 1788, 1795, 1800 and 1802 has also been struck at the Stuttgarter Munzstatte in Germany, quanity unknown. Struck in 1812 as payment for soliders value unknown (recently discovered).

Date	Mintage	F	VF	XF	Unc	BU
1801	960,000	70.00	130	200	275	400
1802	1,705,000	70.00	130	200	275	400
1803	2,089,000	70.00	130	200	275	400
1804/3	870,000	100	200	300	400	600
1804	Inc. above	70.00	130	200	275	400
1805	1,300,000	70.00	130	200	275	400

KM# 12.2 2 DUCAT
7.0000 g., 0.9860 Gold .2219 oz. **Obv. Legend:** ends:...CRES: TRA. **Note:** Similar to 1 Ducat KM#11.3

Date	Mintage	F	VF	XF	Unc	BU
1801	215,000	325	650	1,000	1,350	1,750
1801	215,000	325	650	1,000	1,350	1,750
1802	115,000	450	1,000	1,500	2,000	2,750
1803	365,000	325	650	1,000	1,350	1,750
1804	250,000	325	650	1,000	1,350	1,750
1805	301,000	325	650	1,000	1,350	1,750

KM# 12.1 2 DUCAT
7.0000 g., 0.9860 Gold .2219 oz. **Obv. Inscription:** ends:...HOL or HOLL **Note:** Similar to 1 Ducat KM#11.2.

Date	Mintage	F	VF	XF	Unc	BU
1802	—	750	1,350	2,250	3,500	5,000
1802	—	750	1,350	2,250	3,500	5,000

KINGDOM OF HOLLAND

STANDARD COINAGE

KM# 30 10 STUIVERS
Silver **Obv:** Head right **Rev:** Crowned shield flanked by value

Date	Mintage	F	VF	XF	Unc	BU
1807 Rare	—	—	—	—	—	—
1808 Rare	—	—	—	—	—	—
1809	—	300	700	1,200	1,500	—

KM# 28 50 STUIVERS
0.9120 Silver **Obv:** Head right **Rev:** Crowned shield flanked by value

Date	Mintage	F	VF	XF	Unc	BU
1807	300	300	800	1,250	2,000	2,500
1808	2,466,000	100	175	250	325	500

KM# 25 RIJKSDAALDER
28.0780 g., 0.8680 Silver .7836 oz. **Rev:** Crowned weapon flanked by date **Rev. Legend:** ...TRAI

Date	Mintage	F	VF	XF	Unc	BU
1806	580,000	125	220	300	350	600
1807	151,000	150	250	325	450	700
1808	343,000	125	220	300	350	600

KM# 36 RIJKSDAALDER
26.3480 g., 0.9120 Silver .7726 oz. **Obv:** Head right **Rev:** Crowned shield between R-DR

Date	Mintage	F	VF	XF	Unc	BU
1809	—	600	1,500	2,500	4,000	5,500

KM# 37 RIJKSDAALDER
26.3480 g., 0.9120 Silver .7726 oz. **Obv:** Head right **Rev:** Standing knight with sword

Date	Mintage	F	VF	XF	Unc	BU
1809	—	1,500	2,500	4,000	6,000	10,000

KM# 29 FLORIN
10.5300 g., 0.9120 Silver **Obv:** Head right **Rev:** Crowned shield with I-F flanking

Date	Mintage	F	VF	XF	Unc	BU
1807	—	550	1,200	1,750	2,500	3,250

KM# 31 GULDEN
10.5300 g., 0.9120 Silver **Obv:** Head right **Rev:** Crowned shield flanked by I-G **Edge Lettering:** DE NAAM DES HEEREN ZY GELOOFD

Date	Mintage	F	VF	XF	Unc	BU
1808	—	300	700	1,200	1,500	2,250
1809	—	300	700	1,200	1,500	2,250
1810	—	350	800	1,500	2,500	3,250

KM# 32 2-1/2 GULDEN
26.3480 g., 0.9120 Silver **Obv:** Head right **Rev:** Crowned shield, 2 1/2-G flanking **Edge Lettering:** DE NAAM DES HEEREN ZY GELOOFD

Date	Mintage	F	VF	XF	Unc	BU
1808	—	800	1,600	2,500	3,000	—

KM# 33 10 GULDEN
6.8250 g., 0.9170 Gold .2012 oz. **Obv:** Head left **Rev:** Crowned shield, 10-G flanking

Date	Mintage	F	VF	XF	Unc	BU
1808	—	1,200	2,500	4,000	6,000	8,000
1810	—	1,200	2,500	4,000	6,000	8,000

KM# 34 20 GULDEN
13.6500 g., 0.9170 Gold .4024 oz. **Obv:** Head left **Rev:** Crowned shield, 20-G flanking **Edge Lettering:** DE NAAM DES HEEREN ZY GELOOFD

Date	Mintage	F	VF	XF	Unc	BU
1808	—	1,700	3,500	7,000	10,000	13,000
1810	—	1,700	3,500	7,000	10,000	13,000

TRADE COINAGE

KM# 26.1 DUCAT
3.5000 g., 0.9860 Gold .1109 oz. **Obv. Legend:** ...HOL •

Date	Mintage	F	VF	XF	Unc	BU
1806	526	600	900	1,300	1,800	2,300

KM# 26.2 DUCAT
3.5000 g., 0.9860 Gold .1109 oz. **Obv. Legend:** ...TRAIECTUM, TRA or TRAI

Date	Mintage	F	VF	XF	Unc	BU
1806 small date	794,000	110	190	260	450	525
1807 small date, straight 7	622,000	110	190	260	350	425
1808/7	37,000	175	300	350	550	800
1808	Inc. above	140	250	325	500	750

KM# 26.3 DUCAT
3.5000 g., 0.9860 Gold .1109 oz. **Obv. Legend:** ...TRAIECTUM, TRA or TRAI

Date	Mintage	F	VF	XF	Unc	BU
1806 large date	1,300,000	110	190	260	350	425
1807 larage date, curved 7	1,940,000	110	190	260	350	425

KM# 35 DUCAT
3.5000 g., 0.9860 Gold .1109 oz. **Obv:** Head left **Rev:** Standing knight, date flanking

Date	Mintage	F	VF	XF	Unc	BU
1808	282,870	200	375	525	1,100	—
1809	Inc. above	200	375	525	1,100	—

KM# 38 DUCAT
3.5000 g., 0.9860 Gold .1109 oz. **Obv:** Head left **Rev:** Crowned shield

Date	Mintage	F	VF	XF	Unc	BU
1809	2,370,620	200	375	525	900	—
1810	Inc. above	200	375	525	900	—

KM# 27 2 DUCAT
7.0000 g., 0.9860 Gold .2218 oz. **Obv. Legend:** ...TRA

Date	Mintage	F	VF	XF	Unc	BU
1806	199,000	500	800	1,200	1,500	2,000
1807	156,000	500	800	1,200	1,500	2,000
1808	—	500	800	1,200	1,500	2,000

KINGDOM OF THE NETHERLANDS

STANDARD COINAGE

KM# 46 RIJKSDAALDER
28.0780 g., 0.8680 Silver .7836 oz., 38.5 mm. **Obv:** Knight with sword **Rev:** Crowned weapon, date flanking

Date	Mintage	F	VF	XF	Unc	BU
1815 Proof	12	Value: 12,500				
1816	174,092	450	750	1,000	1,800	—
1816 Proof	—	Value: 2,500				

KM# 51 1/2 CENT
1.9200 g., Copper **Obv:** Crowned W, date flanking **Rev:** Crowned weapon, 1/2-C flanking

Date	Mintage	F	VF	XF	Unc	BU
1818	—	750	2,000	4,000	6,000	8,000
1818 Proof	—	—	—	—	—	—
1819	144,000	300	750	1,750	3,000	4,000
1821	1,648,000	30.00	65.00	125	200	300
1821B	261,146	75.00	150	300	700	1,000
1821B Proof	—	Value: 1,300				
1822	11,240,000	15.00	35.00	100	150	150
1822B	4,066,133	30.00	65.00	125	250	400
1823	9,850,000	15.00	35.00	100	150	250
1823B	14,093,168	15.00	35.00	100	150	200
1824	2,552,287	40.00	100	200	350	500
1824B	3,429,761	50.00	125	250	600	850
1826	—	700	8,000	4,500	7,000	8,500
1826 Proof	—	—	—	—	—	—
1826B	1,560,879	50.00	125	250	500	700
1827	5,374,000	15.00	28.00	75.00	200	300
1827B	2,396,514	20.00	50.00	100	250	350
1828	1,700,000	60.00	150	300	600	850
1828B	4,234,131	20.00	50.00	100	250	350
1829	2,946,596	35.00	90.00	185	325	450
1831	3,849,608	16.50	32.50	85.00	200	300
1832	10,327,943	15.00	28.00	75.00	150	200
1833	150,379	200	400	1,000	2,000	3,000
1837	2,601,910	12.00	35.00	80.00	125	200

KM# 68 1/2 CENT
Copper

Date	Mintage	F	VF	XF	Unc	BU
1841	2,600,000	17.50	35.00	90.00	200	2,500
1843	3,120,000	17.50	30.00	90.00	175	225
1846	600,000	20.00	30.00	90.00	175	225
1847	2,000,000	20.00	35.00	90.00	200	250

KM# 90 1/2 CENT
Copper

Date	Mintage	F	VF	XF	Unc	BU
1850	2,000,400	10.00	25.00	50.00	100	160
1851	2,051,400	10.00	25.00	50.00	100	160
1852	2,027,560	40.00	80.00	175	350	500
1853	2,000,000	10.00	25.00	50.00	100	150
1854	3,000,000	8.00	18.00	45.00	90.00	120
1855	998,800	80.00	200	350	800	1,000
1857	4,154,800	5.00	15.00	30.00	65.00	100
1859	4,052,000	5.00	15.00	30.00	65.00	100
1861	1,446,000	15.00	35.00	65.00	90.00	120
1862	2,026,000	5.00	18.00	45.00	90.00	120
1863	2,428,000	5.00	18.00	45.00	90.00	120
1864	2,016,000	5.00	18.00	45.00	90.00	160
1865	2,006,000	5.00	18.00	45.00	90.00	120
1867	2,008,000	5.00	18.00	45.00	90.00	120
1869	2,014,000	5.00	18.00	45.00	90.00	120
1870	2,004,000	5.00	15.00	30.00	80.00	100
1872	2,026,000	5.00	15.00	30.00	80.00	100
1873	2,026,000	5.00	15.00	30.00	80.00	100
1875	2,026,000	5.00	15.00	30.00	80.00	100
1876	2,020,000	5.00	15.00	30.00	80.00	100
1877	1,400,000	10.00	25.00	50.00	80.00	100

KM# 47 CENT
3.8450 g., Copper **Obv:** Crowned W, date flanking **Rev:** Crowned weapon, I-C flanking

Date	Mintage	F	VF	XF	Unc	BU
1817	—	700	2,250	5,000	10,000	12,000
1817 Proof, rare	—	—	—	—	—	—
1818	—	700	2,250	5,000	10,000	12,000
1818 Proof, rare	—	—	—	—	—	—
1819	165,000	220	700	1,500	2,750	4,500
1821	6,435,000	10.00	40.00	75.00	150	250
1821B	113,132	220	600	1,150	2,000	3,000
1822	20,462,000	9.00	18.00	50.00	100	150
1822B	5,739,000	10.00	28.00	80.00	200	—
1823	22,300,142	9.00	18.00	50.00	100	150
1823B	11,530,819	10.00	25.00	80.00	150	200
1824	3,454,000	30.00	80.00	145	250	350
1824B	144,000	—	—	—	—	—
Note: Reported, not confirmed						
1826	8,400,000	10.00	28.00	80.00	150	200
1826B	5,331,600	10.00	28.00	80.00	150	200
1827	25,650,000	9.00	18.00	50.00	100	150
1827B	30,026,006	9.00	18.00	50.00	100	150
1828	7,343,393	9.00	18.00	50.00	100	150
1828B	8,907,671	10.00	28.00	80.00	175	225
1830	800,000	30.00	60.00	150	300	450
1831	4,860,912	10.00	28.00	80.00	175	225
1837	5,202,040	8.00	16.00	45.00	100	120

KM# 52 5 CENTS
0.8200 g., 0.5690 Silver .0150 oz., 12.5 mm.

Date	Mintage	F	VF	XF	Unc	BU
1818	2,500	450	800	1,600	2,500	3,000
1818 Proof	—	Value: 3,500				
1819	3,000	300	600	1,200	1,800	2,250
1819 Proof	—	Value: 2,650				
1822	47,489	220	440	650	1,000	1,250
1825B	900,012	32.50	60.00	120	200	250
1826B	1,021,362	32.50	60.00	120	200	250
1827	534,000	25.00	50.00	75.00	125	150
1827B	283,553	40.00	80.00	130	250	325
1828B	396,690	35.00	70.00	120	250	325

KM# 74 5 CENTS
0.6850 g., 0.6400 Silver .0141 oz. **Obv:** Head left **Rev:** Value and date within wreath

Date	Mintage	F	VF	XF	Unc	BU
1848	100	500	800	1,200	2,500	3,000
1848 Proof	—	Value: 3,500				

KM# 91 5 CENTS

0.6850 g., 0.6400 Silver .0141 oz., 12.5 mm. **Obv:** Head right **Rev:** Value and date within wreath

Date	Mintage	F	VF	XF	Unc	BU
1850	Inc. above	—	—	—	—	—
Note: Without dot after date						
1850.	3,037,000	2.00	5.00	12.00	25.00	35.00
Note: Dot after date						
1853	11,170	150	400	600	1,200	1,500
1853 Proof	2	Value: 2,500				
1855	515,000	5.00	12.00	20.00	40.00	50.00
1859	400,000	5.00	12.00	20.00	40.00	50.00
1862.	400,000	5.00	12.00	20.00	40.00	50.00
Note: Dot after date						
1862	Inc. above	5.00	12.00	20.00	40.00	50.00
Note: Without dot after date						
1863	640,000	5.00	12.00	20.00	40.00	50.00
1868	200,000	35.00	65.00	130	200	275
1869	500,000	5.00	12.00	20.00	40.00	50.00
1876	200,000	7.00	20.00	35.00	50.00	60.00
1879	200,000	7.00	20.00	35.00	50.00	60.00
1879 Proof	—	Value: 160				
1887	100,000	20.00	35.00	45.00	60.00	80.00

KM# 53 10 CENTS

1.6900 g., 0.5690 Silver .0309 oz., 18 mm. **Obv:** Crowned W flanked by date **Rev:** Crowned weapon flanked by 10-C

Date	Mintage	F	VF	XF	Unc	BU
1818 Proof	48	Value: 10,000				
1819	25,030	275	600	1,200	2,000	2,500
1822	113,142	200	400	800	1,400	1,800
1823B	178,449	110	220	500	1,000	1,300
1825	972,400	22.00	45.00	90.00	170	250
1825B	17,500,000	22.00	45.00	90.00	170	250
1826	2,138,000	18.00	40.00	85.00	150	200
1826B	1,032,000	22.00	50.00	100	200	275
1827	5,895,000	10.00	25.00	50.00	100	150
1827B	1,335,000	22.00	50.00	100	200	275
1828	2,035,860	18.00	40.00	85.00	130	180
1828B	1,168,174	22.00	50.00	100	200	275

KM# 75 10 CENTS

1.4000 g., 0.6400 Silver .0288 oz., 15 mm. **Obv:** Head left **Rev:** Value and date within wreath

Date	Mintage	F	VF	XF	Unc	BU
1848	6,859,006	20.00	50.00	100	200	240
1848 Proof	—	Value: 500				
1849.	4,050,589	10.00	30.00	70.00	110	150
Note: Dot after date						
1849	Inc. above	50.00	125	400	600	800
Note: Without dot after date						

KM# 80 10 CENTS

1.4000 g., 0.6400 Silver .0288 oz., 15 mm. **Obv:** Head right **Rev:** Value and date within legend

Date	Mintage	F	VF	XF	Unc	BU
1849	6,204,000	20.00	45.00	100	225	275
1850	7,270,000	25.00	55.00	120	250	300
1853	1,104,000	50.00	100	150	275	325
1855	745,000	60.00	120	160	300	375
1855 Low 5	Inc. above	60.00	120	160	300	375
1856	1,000,000	10.00	35.00	80.00	175	225
1859	1,000,000	10.00	35.00	80.00	175	225
1862	800,000	35.00	80.00	140	275	325
1863	1,240,000	10.00	35.00	70.00	150	200
1868	200,000	80.00	250	450	900	1,200
1869	1,000,000	10.00	35.00	70.00	140	180
1871	1,000,000	10.00	35.00	70.00	140	180
1873	1,000,000	10.00	35.00	70.00	140	180
1874	800,000	80.00	225	500	1,500	2,000
Note: Sword privy mark						
1874	Inc. above	30.00	80.00	125	200	250
Note: Sword in scabbard privy mark						
1876	1,000,000	8.00	25.00	60.00	100	130
1877	1,000,000	8.00	25.00	60.00	100	130
1878	1,000,000	8.00	25.00	60.00	100	130
1879	1,000,000	8.00	25.00	60.00	100	130
1880	1,000,000	8.00	25.00	60.00	100	130
1881.	2,000,000	8.00	25.00	60.00	100	130
Note: Dot after date						
1881	Inc. above	8.00	25.00	60.00	100	130
Note: Without dot after date						
1882	2,000,000	8.00	25.00	60.00	100	130
1884	1,000,000	8.00	25.00	60.00	100	130
1885	2,000,000	8.00	25.00	60.00	100	130
1887	1,600,000	8.00	25.00	60.00	100	130
1889	2,800,000	5.00	20.00	50.00	90.00	130
1890	2,600,000	5.00	20.00	50.00	90.00	130

KM# 48 25 CENTS

4.2300 g., 0.5690 Silver .0773 oz., 21 mm. **Obv:** Crowned W, date flanking **Rev:** Crowned weapon, 25-C flanking

Date	Mintage	F	VF	XF	Unc	BU
1817 Proof	—	Value: 11,000				
1818 Proof	—	Value: 11,000				
1819	13,000	350	800	1,500	2,750	3,500
1819 Proof	—	Value: 3,500				
1822	116,000	220	450	850	1,500	2,000
1823/22B	1,334,000	75.00	200	400	700	900
1823B	Inc. above	25.00	75.00	200	300	400
1824B	6,033,000	15.00	40.00	85.00	150	200
1825	10,311,000	15.00	30.00	65.00	130	175
1825B	2,608,000	25.00	45.00	100	175	250
1826	12,282,000	15.00	28.00	70.00	120	150
1826B	7,299,000	15.00	28.00	70.00	120	150
1827B	2,021,999	30.00	75.00	150	200	275
1828B	334,000	150	350	750	1,200	1,500
1829	106,000	175	450	900	1,500	1,800
1829B	1,256,000	28.00	55.00	145	250	350
1830	1,534,000	28.00	55.00	145	250	350
1830B	902,000	25.00	75.00	200	300	400

KM# 76 25 CENTS

3.5750 g., 0.6400 Silver .0736 oz., 19 mm. **Obv:** Head left **Rev:** Value and date within wreath

Date	Mintage	F	VF	XF	Unc	BU
1848.	10,730,203	10.00	25.00	75.00	120	175
Note: Dot after date						
1848. Proof	—	Value: 300				
1848	Inc. above	12.00	40.00	100	200	300
Note: Without dot after date						
1849/8	8,059,000	150	330	500	625	—
1849	Inc. above	7.00	20.00	60.00	100	150

KM# 81 25 CENTS

3.5750 g., 0.6400 Silver .0736 oz., 19 mm. **Obv:** Head right **Rev:** Value and date within wreath

Date	Mintage	F	VF	XF	Unc	BU
1849	1,909,567	115	275	450	900	1,150
1850/49	2,207,000	200	350	600	1,100	1,400
1850	Inc. above	125	350	500	1,000	1,300
1853	7,974	350	1,000	2,000	3,000	4,000
1853 Proof	—	Value: 3,500				
1887	100,000	125	200	500	850	1,150
1889	200,000	100	250	325	500	700
1890.	600,000	60.00	150	250	400	500
Note: Dot after date						
1890	Inc. above	110	215	400	650	850
Note: Without dot after date						

KM# 54 1/2 GULDEN

5.3800 g., 0.8930 Silver .1544 oz. **Obv:** Head right **Rev:** Crowned weapon, 1/2-G flanking **Edge Lettering:** GOD ZY MET ONS

Date	Mintage	F	VF	XF	Unc	BU
1818	51,558	150	280	650	1,000	1,250
1819	43,342	150	280	650	1,000	1,250
1819 Proof	—	Value: 1,500				
1822	118,739	150	280	500	800	—
Note: Engraver's name below bust						
1822	Inc. above	200	400	700	1,000	1,250
Note: Without engraver's name						
1829B	180,336	150	300	600	800	1,000
1830B/1820	—	150	300	650	900	1,100
1830B	100,186	150	300	650	900	1,100

KM# 73.1 1/2 GULDEN

5.0000 g., 0.9450 Silver .1519 oz. **Obv:** Head left **Rev:** Crowned weapon, 1/2-G flanking **Edge:** Reeded

Date	Mintage	F	VF	XF	Unc	BU
1846 Proof	—	Value: 4,000				
1847	1,110,882	22.00	50.00	200	350	500
1847 Proof	—	Value: 700				
1848/47	—	25.00	50.00	150	200	300
1848	4,049,904	10.00	50.00	125	250	350

KM# 73.2 1/2 GULDEN

5.0000 g., 0.9450 Silver .1519 oz. **Obv:** Head left **Rev:** Crowned weapon, 1/2-G flanking **Edge:** Lettered

Date	Mintage	F	VF	XF	Unc	BU
1846 Proof	—	Value: 5,000				

KM# 92 1/2 GULDEN

5.0000 g., 0.9450 Silver .1519 oz.

Date	Mintage	F	VF	XF	Unc	BU
1850	—	800	1,800	2,500	3,500	4,500
1850 Proof	—	Value: 5,000				
1853/43.	1,711	700	1,500	2,250	3,200	4,000
1853	Inc. above	700	1,500	2,250	3,200	4,000
1857	3,606,444	10.00	28.00	60.00	165	200
1858	7,604,462	8.00	25.00	50.00	125	175
1859	3,000,510	10.00	28.00	60.00	165	200
1860	6,602,687	8.00	25.00	50.00	135	185
1861	6,001,252	8.00	25.00	50.00	135	185
1862	4,001,577	8.00	25.00	50.00	135	185
1863	5,152,084	8.00	25.00	50.00	135	185
1864	4,001,385	8.00	25.00	50.00	135	185
1866	1,402,446	15.00	50.00	150	250	325
1868 open 8	4,004,161	8.00	25.00	50.00	125	175
1868 closed 8	Inc. above	8.00	25.00	50.00	120	170

KM# 55 GULDEN

10.7660 g., 0.8930 Silver .3089 oz. **Obv:** Head right **Rev:** Weapon, 1-G flanking **Edge Lettering:** GOD ZY MET ONS

Date	Mintage	F	VF	XF	Unc	BU
1818	43,000	400	750	1,500	2,500	3,000
1818 Proof	—	Value: 2,750				
1819	252,000	200	450	750	1,000	1,250
1820	543,000	70.00	125	300	550	800
1821	1,145,000	70.00	125	325	500	700
1822	80,000	350	800	1,600	2,500	3,500
1823	743,000	70.00	150	300	550	800
1823 Proof	—	Value: 900				
1823B	25,000	650	1,500	2,000	2,750	3,500
1824	1,096,000	70.00	150	325	550	800
1824	Inc. above	60.00	125	250	525	725
Note: Dash between crown and shield						
1828	62,000	300	600	1,250	1,800	2,300
1829B	383,000	200	400	750	1,100	1,400
1831/21	120,000	200	400	750	1,100	1,400
1831	Inc. above	200	400	750	1,100	1,400
1832/21	1,362,000	75.00	135	325	700	1,100
1832/23	Inc. above	75.00	135	325	700	1,100
1832/24	Inc. above	75.00	135	325	700	1,100
1832/24	Inc. above	75.00	135	325	700	1,100
Note: Dash between crown and shield						
1832/28	Inc. above	75.00	135	325	700	1,100
1832	Inc. above	75.00	135	325	700	1,100
1837	383,000	75.00	135	325	650	1,000

KM# 65 GULDEN

10.0000 g., 0.9450 Silver .3038 oz., 28 mm. **Obv:** Head right **Rev:** Weapon, I-G flanking **Edge Lettering:** GOD ZY MET ONS

Date	Mintage	F	VF	XF	Unc	BU
1840	99,000	50.00	110	300	550	750
1840 Proof	—	Value: 2,000				

KM# 66 GULDEN

10.0000 g., 0.9450 Silver .3038 oz., 28 mm. **Obv:** Head left **Rev:** Weapon, 1-G flanking **Edge Lettering:** GOD ZY MET ONS

Date	Mintage	F	VF	XF	Unc	BU
1840 Proof	2	—	—	—	—	—
1842	660,815	75.00	175	450	850	1,250
1842 Proof	—	Value: 1,000				
1842 shorter bust	Inc. above	150	300	700	1,250	1,750
1842 Proof	—	Value: 1,650				
1843	1,739,623	35.00	80.00	200	400	600
1844	1,574,618	35.00	80.00	200	400	600
1845	3,802,556	12.00	35.00	95.00	170	250
1845	221,105	35.00	80.00	200	450	700
Note: Dash between crown and shield						
1846	900,558	20.00	50.00	125	250	350
Note: Fleur de lis privy mark						
1846	3,772,335	10.00	30.00	90.00	170	250
Note: Sword privy mark						
1847	8,279,321	8.00	25.00	60.00	150	200
1848	13,615,913	8.00	25.00	60.00	150	200
1849	650,000	35.00	80.00	200	450	700

KM# 93 GULDEN

10.0000 g., 0.9450 Silver .3038 oz., 28 mm. **Obv:** Head right **Rev:** Weapon, 1-G flanking **Edge:** GOD ZY MET ONS

Date	Mintage	F	VF	XF	Unc	BU
1850 Proof	—	Value: 4,750				
1850 Rare, reeded edge	—	—	—	—	—	—
1851	2,125,148	15.00	40.00	100	175	250
1853/0	652,035	200	300	550	950	1,250
1853/1	Inc. above	200	300	550	950	12,500
1853	Inc. above	100	200	350	750	1,100
1854	4,511,054	12.00	25.00	45.00	120	175
1855	5,133,283	12.00	25.00	45.00	120	175
1856	4,954,661	12.00	25.00	45.00	120	175
1857	2,125,500	15.00	30.00	60.00	150	200
1858	4,199,241	12.00	25.00	55.00	130	180
1859	2,717,216	12.00	25.00	55.00	150	200
1860	4,035,791	10.00	20.00	40.00	130	180
1861	5,078,886	10.00	20.00	40.00	120	170
1863	7,986,113	10.00	20.00	40.00	120	170
1864	3,600,143	10.00	20.00	40.00	120	170
1865	6,401,755	10.00	20.00	40.00	120	170
1866	1,002,450	20.00	45.00	100	200	300
1867 Proof	4	Value: 20,000				

KM# 67 2-1/2 GULDEN

25.0000 g., 0.9450 Silver .7596 oz., 38 mm. **Obv:** Head right **Rev:** Weapon, 2 1/2-G flanking **Edge:** GOD ZY MET ONS

Date	Mintage	F	VF	XF	Unc	BU
1840	44,376	125	250	500	1,000	1,250
1840 Proof	—	Value: 1,600				

KM# 69 2-1/2 GULDEN

25.0000 g., 0.9450 Silver .7596 oz., 38 mm. **Obv:** Head left **Rev:** Weapon, 2 1/2-G flanking **Edge Lettering:** GOD ZY MET ONS

Date	Mintage	F	VF	XF	Unc	BU
1841	53,535	175	450	1,000	2,000	2,500
1841 Proof	—	Value: 2,200				
1842	909,883	40.00	80.00	250	600	900
1843	742,659	50.00	110	300	700	1,000
1843 Proof	—	Value: 1,000				
1844	278,534	80.00	175	400	850	1,250
1845	3,589,217	20.00	60.00	200	400	60.00
1845 dash between crown and shield	505,330	30.00	70.00	225	450	650
1845 dot on band of privy mark	163,868	50.00	150	425	650	950
1846 Fleur de lis privy mark	3,023,712	25.00	60.00	200	400	500
1846 Proof	—	Value: 950				
1846 Sword privy mark	—	25.00	60.00	150	350	500
1847	8,958,675	10.00	25.00	90.00	250	400
1848	88,339,330	10.00	25.00	90.00	250	400
1849	1,582,927	25.00	60.00	200	400	500

KM# 82 2-1/2 GULDEN

25.0000 g., 0.9450 Silver .7596 oz., 38 mm. **Obv:** Head right **Rev:** Crowned weapon, 2 1/2-G flanking **Edge Lettering:** GOD ZY MET ONS

Date	Mintage	F	VF	XF	Unc	BU
1849	439,307	50.00	150	250	500	800
1849 Proof	—	Value: 1,000				
1850	5,008,210	12.00	25.00	70.00	200	250
1851	3,647,493	12.00	25.00	70.00	200	250
1852	4,546,764	12.00	25.00	70.00	200	250
1853/2	234,128	100	300	500	950	150
1853	Inc. above	60.00	200	400	625	1,250
1854/2	4,334,526	50.00	175	350	600	1,200
1854	Inc. above	12.00	25.00	70.00	200	250
1855	2,082,046	12.00	25.00	70.00	200	250
1856	909,545	40.00	90.00	250	400	600
1857	3,353,072	12.00	25.00	70.00	200	250
1858	8,357,486	12.00	25.00	70.00	150	200
1859	4,306,594	12.00	25.00	80.00	175	225
1860	847,104	40.00	80.00	175	375	550
1861	876,003	30.00	80.00	175	375	550
1862	3,304,118	12.00	25.00	80.00	175	225
1863	50,652	350	1,000	1,750	2,000	4,000
1864	2,033,644	12.00	20.00	50.00	150	200
1865	2,287,612	12.00	20.00	50.00	150	200
1866	3,562,608	12.00	20.00	50.00	150	200
1867	4,948,886	10.00	18.00	50.00	125	175
1868	4,040,021	10.00	18.00	50.00	125	175
1869	5,046,192	10.00	18.00	50.00	125	175
1870	6,639,947	8.00	15.00	40.00	100	150
1871	6,875,035	8.00	15.00	40.00	100	150
1872	13,416,378	8.00	15.00	40.00	100	150
1873	5,515,073	8.00	15.00	40.00	100	150
1874	3,040,000	8.00	15.00	50.00	125	175
Note: Sword privy mark						
1874	9,755,726	8.00	15.00	40.00	100	150
Note: Sword in scabbard privy mark						

KM# 49 3 GULDEN

39.2900 g., 0.8930 Silver .9270 oz., 40 mm. **Obv:** Head left **Rev:** Crowned weapon, 3-G flanking **Edge:** GOD ZY MET ONS

Date	Mintage	F	VF	XF	Unc	BU
1817 Proof	12	Value: 15,000				
1818	116,346	250	450	900	1,500	2,250
1819/8	150,612	600	1,000	1,500	2,250	3,000
1819	Inc. above	250	450	900	1,500	2,250
1820	712,961	250	450	900	1,500	2,250
1821	276,659	250	450	900	1,500	2,250
1821	Inc. above	400	750	1,000	1,600	2,500
Note: Without engraver's name						
1821 medal rotation	—	600	1,000	1,500	2,250	3,000
1822	296,200	400	750	1,000	1,700	2,500
1822	Inc. above	500	900	1,600	2,000	2,750
Note: Without engraver's name						
1823	235,100	400	750	950	1,500	2,250
1823B	13,817	1,200	3,000	7,000	10,000	12,500
1824	644,126	250	450	900	1,500	2,250
1824	Inc. above	250	450	900	1,500	2,250
Note: Dash between crown and shield						
1830/20	246,233	250	450	900	1,500	2,250
1830/24	Inc. above	250	450	900	1,500	2,250
1830/24	Inc. above	375	750	1,000	1,750	2,500
Note: Dash between crown and shield						
1830	Inc. above	250	450	900	1,500	2,250
1831/24	117,400	250	450	900	1,500	2,250
1831/24	Inc. above	250	450	900	1,500	50.00
Note: Dash between crown and shield						
1831	Inc. above	250	450	900	1,500	2,250
1832/21	371,363	250	450	900	1,500	2,250
1832/22	Inc. above	250	450	900	1,500	2,250
1832/23	Inc. above	250	450	900	1,500	2,250
1832/24	Inc. above	250	450	900	1,500	2,250
1832/24	Inc. above	250	450	900	1,500	2,250
Note: Dash between crown and shield						
1832	Inc. above	200	400	800	1,250	2,000

KM# 60 5 GULDEN

3.3645 g., 0.9000 Gold .0973 oz., 18.5 mm. **Obv:** Head left **Rev:** Crowned weapon, 5-G flanking

Date	Mintage	F	VF	XF	Unc	BU
1826B	842,694	120	300	400	600	800
1827	517,826	175	275	375	850	1,000
1827B	1,628,218	70.00	175	250	450	600

KM# 72 5 GULDEN

3.3645 g., 0.9000 Gold .0973 oz., 18.5 mm. **Obv:** Head right **Rev:** Crowned weapon, 5-G flanking

Date	Mintage	F	VF	XF	Unc	BU
1843	1,595	300	900	1,900	2,500	3,000

KM# 77 5 GULDEN
3.3645 g., 0.9000 Gold .0973 oz., 18.5 mm. **Obv:** Bust right **Rev:** Crowned arms within branches

Date	Mintage	F	VF	XF	Unc	BU
1848 Proof	50	Value: 6,000				

KM# 94 5 GULDEN
3.3645 g., 0.9000 Gold .0973 oz., 18.5 mm. **Obv:** Bust left **Rev:** Crowned arms within branches

Date	Mintage	F	VF	XF	Unc	BU
1850 Proof	—	Value: 4,000				
1851	10,000	300	1,000	1,500	2,000	2,500

KM# 56 10 GULDEN
6.7290 g., 0.9000 Gold .1947 oz., 22.5 mm. **Obv:** Bust left **Rev:** Crowned weapon, 10-G flanking **Edge Lettering:** GOD ZY MET ONS

Date	Mintage	F	VF	XF	Unc	BU
1818	—	1,500	4,000	5,500	7,000	8,500
1819	107,000	650	1,750	3,000	4,500	5,000
1820	33,000	650	1,750	3,000	4,000	5,000
1822	48,000	650	1,750	3,000	4,000	5,000
1823	266,000	150	300	500	900	1,250
1824	336,000	150	275	450	850	1,200
1824B	3,735,000	150	275	350	800	1,150
1825	228,000	150	300	500	900	1,250
1825B	3,821,000	150	275	350	800	1,150
1826	—	1,000	4,000	5,000	7,000	9,000
1826B	79,000	650	1,400	2,000	3,000	4,000
1827B	134,000	400	850	1,600	2,500	3,250
1828	15,000	1,000	4,000	5,000	7,000	9,000
1828B/27B	—	175	300	500	1,000	1,350
1828B	562,000	150	275	350	800	1,150
1829	9,484	850	2,000	3,250	5,000	7,000
1829B	84,000	650	1,400	2,000	3,000	4,000
1830/20	—	250	500	1,000	2,000	2,750
1830/28	568,000	1,000	1,200	1,500	3,000	4,000
1830	Inc. above	150	375	650	1,000	1,350
1831/0	99,000	500	850	1,600	2,500	3,250
1831	Inc. above	150	375	650	1,000	1,350
1832/1	1,372,000	600	850	1,200	2,000	3,250
1832	Inc. above	150	375	650	1,000	1,350
1833	721,000	150	375	650	1,000	1,350
1837	458,000	150	375	650	1,000	1,350
1839	326,000	150	375	650	1,000	1,350
1840/37	—	650	1,400	2,000	3,000	4,000
1840	2,760,000	150	275	350	600	800

KM# 71 10 GULDEN
6.7290 g., 0.9000 Gold .1947 oz., 22.5 mm. **Obv:** Bust right **Rev:** Crowned weapon, 10-G flanking **Edge Lettering:** GOD ZY MET ONS

Date	Mintage	F	VF	XF	Unc	BU
1842	860	1,100	2,000	3,500	5,000	6,500

KM# 78 10 GULDEN
6.7290 g., 0.9000 Gold .1947 oz., 22.5 mm. **Obv:** Bust right **Rev:** Crowned weapon in wreath **Edge Lettering:** GOD ZY MET ONS

Date	Mintage	F	VF	XF	Unc	BU
1848 Proof	50	Value: 8,000				

KM# 95 10 GULDEN
6.7290 g., 0.9000 Gold .1947 oz., 22.5 mm. **Obv:** Bust left **Rev:** Crowned weapon in wreath **Edge Lettering:** GOD ZY MET ONS

Date	Mintage	F	VF	XF	Unc	BU
1850 Proof	—	Value: 5,500				
1851	10,000	500	1,000	1,750	2,500	3,000

KM# 79 20 GULDEN
13.4580 g., 0.9000 Gold .3894 oz., 27 mm. **Obv:** Head right **Rev:** Crowned arms within branches **Edge Lettering:** GOD ZY MET ONS

Date	Mintage	F	VF	XF	Unc	BU
1848 Proof	50	Value: 12,000				

KM# 96 20 GULDEN
13.4580 g., 0.9000 Gold .3894 oz. **Obv:** Head left **Rev:** Crowned arms within branches **Edge Lettering:** GOD ZY MET ONS

Date	Mintage	F	VF	XF	Unc	BU
1850 Proof	—	Value: 8,000				
1851	2,500	600	2,000	3,000	4,000	5,000
1853	136	2,000	4,000	5,000	6,500	7,500

DECIMAL COINAGE

KM# 109 1/2 CENT
1.2500 g., Bronze, 14 mm. **Obv:** 17 small shields in field **Obv. Legend:** KONINGRIJK DER NEDERLANDEN **Rev:** Value within wreath **Edge:** Reeded

Date	Mintage	F	VF	XF	Unc	BU
1878	4,000,000	4.00	8.00	15.00	35.00	50.00
1883	800,000	40.00	80.00	120	180	260
1884	17,200,000	1.50	4.00	10.00	25.00	30.00
1885	7,800,000	2.00	6.00	12.00	30.00	35.00
1886	2,200,000	20.00	50.00	90.00	130	160
1891	5,000,000	4.00	8.00	15.00	35.00	50.00
1894	5,000,000	4.00	8.00	15.00	35.00	50.00
1898	2,000,000	10.00	30.00	60.00	120	150
1900	3,000,000	8.00	15.00	40.00	70.00	90.00

KM# 100 CENT
Copper

Date	Mintage	F	VF	XF	Unc	BU
1860	2,032,000	6.00	15.00	35.00	75.00	100
1861	2,050,000	6.00	12.00	32.00	65.00	90.00
1862	2,026,000	6.00	15.00	35.00	75.00	100
1863	10,246,000	2.50	5.50	12.50	28.00	35.00
1864	2,026,000	6.00	15.00	35.00	75.00	100
1870	4,010,000	4.00	9.00	24.00	45.00	60.00
1873	3,026,000	5.00	10.00	28.00	55.00	80.00
1875	3,015,000	5.00	10.00	28.00	55.00	60.00
1876	13,047,000	2.50	5.50	12.50	25.00	30.00
1877	11,026,000	2.50	5.50	12.50	25.00	30.00

KM# 107 CENT
2.5000 g., Bronze, 19 mm. **Obv:** 17 small shields in field **Obv. Legend:** KONINGRIJK DER NEDERLANDEN **Rev:** Value within wreath

Date	Mintage	F	VF	XF	Unc	BU
1877	6,100,000	3.50	8.00	20.00	50.00	70.00
1878	53,900,000	0.50	2.00	6.00	15.00	20.00
1880	20,000,000	1.50	4.00	10.00	30.00	35.00
1881	10,000,000	1.50	4.00	10.00	30.00	35.00
1882/1	—	4.00	15.00	35.00	80.00	120
1882	5,000,000	3.00	6.00	15.00	45.00	65.00
1883	15,000,000	1.50	4.00	10.00	30.00	35.00
1884	10,000,000	1.50	4.00	10.00	30.00	35.00
1892	5,000,000	3.50	10.00	30.00	70.00	100
1896	3,000,000	5.00	15.00	35.00	85.00	120
1897	2,500,000	6.00	17.00	40.00	90.00	130
1898	5,000,000	2.50	5.00	12.00	50.00	70.00
1899	5,100,000	2.50	5.00	12.00	50.00	70.00
1900 large date	12,400,000	2.00	4.00	10.00	45.00	60.00
1900 small date	Inc. above	2.00	4.00	10.00	45.00	60.00
1900 Proof	—	Value: 200				

KM# 108 2-1/2 CENT
4.0000 g., Bronze, 23.5 mm. **Obv:** 17 small shields in field **Obv. Legend:** KONINGRIJK DER NEDERLANDEN

Date	Mintage	F	VF	XF	Unc	BU
1877	4,000,000	2.50	5.00	15.00	45.00	55.00
1880	4,000,000	2.50	5.00	15.00	45.00	55.00
1881	4,000,000	2.50	5.00	15.00	45.00	55.00
1883	400,000	15.00	25.00	50.00	125	150
1884	3,600,000	3.50	7.00	18.00	50.00	60.00
1886	2,000,000	4.00	10.00	20.00	55.00	65.00
1890	2,000,000	4.00	10.00	20.00	55.00	65.00
1894	1,000,000	15.00	25.00	50.00	185	225
1898	1,600,000	10.00	20.00	40.00	100	140

KM# 116 10 CENTS
1.4000 g., 0.6400 Silver .0288 oz., 15 mm. **Obv:** Queen head left with long hair **Obv. Legend:** Value and date in wreath

Date	Mintage	F	VF	XF	Unc	BU
1892 Thin head	2,000,000	10.00	20.00	50.00	100	150
1893	2,000,000	10.00	20.00	50.00	100	150
1894	1,500,000	10.00	20.00	50.00	100	150
1895	1,000,000	20.00	60.00	100	150	200
1896	2,000,000	10.00	20.00	50.00	100	150
1897	7,850,000	5.00	15.00	30.00	65.00	90.00

KM# 119 10 CENTS
1.4000 g., 0.6400 Silver .0288 oz., 15 mm. **Obv:** Small head, divided legend **Rev:** Value within wreath **Edge:** Reeded

Date	Mintage	F	VF	XF	Unc	BU
1898	2,000,000	15.00	35.00	80.00	150	225

KM# 115 25 CENTS
3.5750 g., 0.6400 Silver .0736 oz.

Date	Mintage	F	VF	XF	Unc	BU
1891	2	—	—	—	—	—
1892	800,000	15.00	60.00	125	225	300
1893	800,000	15.00	60.00	125	225	300
1894	1,000,000	15.00	60.00	125	225	300
1895	1,200,000	15.00	60.00	125	225	300
1895 slanted mintmasters mark	Inc. above	120	275	450	900	1,300

Date	Mintage	F	VF	XF	Unc	BU
1896	600,000	30.00	85.00	225	450	600
1897	3,100,000	6.00	25.00	60.00	120	160

KM# 120.1 25 CENTS
3.5750 g., 0.6400 Silver .0736 oz., 19 mm. **Obv:** Bust with wide truncation **Rev:** Value within wreath **Edge:** Reeded

Date	Mintage	F	VF	XF	Unc	BU
1898	400,000	90.00	200	400	750	1,000

KM# 121.1 1/2 GULDEN
5.0000 g., 0.9450 Silver .1519 oz., 22 mm. **Obv:** Queen's head left **Rev:** Weapon, 1/2-G flanking, 50 C below

Date	Mintage	F	VF	XF	Unc	BU
1898	2,000,000	25.00	60.00	110	180	250
1898 Proof	—	Value: 700				

KM# 117 GULDEN
10.0000 g., 0.9450 Silver .3038 oz., 28 mm. **Obv:** Queen's head left with long hair **Rev:** Weapon, 1-G flanking **Edge Lettering:** GOD ZY MET ONS

Date	Mintage	F	VF	XF	Unc	BU
1892	3,500,000	6.00	20.00	60.00	150	200
1896	100,000	150	400	800	1,500	2,000
1896 Proof	—	Value: 2,500				
1897	2,500,000	10.00	22.00	80.00	175	225

KM# 122.1 GULDEN
10.0000 g., 0.9450 Silver .3038 oz., 28 mm. **Obv:** Young head left **Rev:** Crowned shield with 100 C below **Edge Lettering:** GOD * ZIJ * MET * ONS *

Date	Mintage	F	VF	XF	Unc	BU
1898	2,000,000	25.00	55.00	125	325	375

KM# 123 2-1/2 GULDEN
25.0000 g., 0.9450 Silver .7596 oz., 38 mm. **Obv:** Yound head left **Rev:** Crowned shield, 2 1/2-G flanking

Date	Mintage	F	VF	XF	Unc	BU
1898 P. Pander	100,000	150	275	500	1,000	1,250
1898 P. Pander. Proof	—	Value: 3,000				
1898 P Pander	—	175	350	800	1,250	1,750

KM# 123a 2-1/2 GULDEN
88.5000 g., Gold, 38 mm.

Date	Mintage	F	VF	XF	Unc	BU
1898 Rare	2	—	—	—	—	—

KM# 105 10 GULDEN
6.7290 g., 0.9000 Gold .1947 oz., 22.5 mm. **Obv:** Bust right **Rev:** Crowned weapon, 10-G flanking, date above crown

Date	Mintage	F	VF	XF	Unc	BU
1875	4,110,000	—	BV	65.00	90.00	100

KM# 106 10 GULDEN
6.7290 g., 0.9000 Gold .1947 oz., 22.5 mm. **Obv:** Crowned weapon, 10-G flanking, date under weapon

Date	Mintage	F	VF	XF	Unc	BU
1876	1,581,106	—	BV	70.00	100	110
1877	1,108,149	—	BV	90.00	110	120
1879/7	581,036	125	175	250	350	450
1879	Inc. above	—	BV	100	120	130
1880	50,100	BV	110	145	175	200
1885	67,095	BV	100	135	165	175
1886	51,141	BV	110	145	175	200
1887	40,754	BV	110	145	175	200
1888	35,585	125	200	300	400	500
1889	204,691	—	BV	90.00	110	120

KM# 118 10 GULDEN
6.7290 g., 0.9000 Gold .1947 oz., 22.5 mm. **Obv:** Bust left with long hair **Rev:** Crowned weapon, 10-G flanking

Date	Mintage	F	VF	XF	Unc	BU
1892	61	2,500	4,500	8,000	10,000	12,000
1892 Proof	—	Value: 13,500				
1895/1	149	1,400	2,500	4,500	6,000	7,000
1895/1 Proof	—	Value: 7,500				
1895	Inc. above	900	2,000	3,500	5,500	6,500
1897	453,696	—	BV	90.00	135	160

KM# 124 10 GULDEN
6.7290 g., 0.9000 Gold .1947 oz., 22.5 mm. **Obv:** Crowned head right **Rev:** Crowned weapon, 10-G flanking

Date	Mintage	F	VF	XF	Unc	BU
1898	99,239	100	150	200	350	400

TRADE COINAGE

KM# 45 DUCAT
3.5000 g., 0.9830 Gold .1106 oz.

Date	Mintage	F	VF	XF	Unc	BU
1814	2,930,000	100	175	275	400	—
1815	673,000	100	175	300	450	—
1815 cloverleaf	614,000	100	250	400	600	—
1816	221,000	110	250	400	600	—

KM# 50.1 DUCAT
3.5000 g., 0.9830 Gold .1106 oz. **Obv:** Standing knight with sword and arrows **Rev:** Text within decorated square **Note:** Size varies: 20.5-21.5 mm.

Date	Mintage	F	VF	XF	Unc	BU
1817	498,013	200	350	600	750	1,000
1818	1,561,407	75.00	125	200	300	400
1819	111,301	100	200	350	500	650
1820	10,419	175	300	500	700	950
1821	15,073	175	300	500	700	950
1822	11,971	175	350	600	800	1,200
1824B	—	400	1,500	2,750	4,000	5,000
Note: Mintage included with 1825B						
1825	119,276	100	200	375	550	600
1825B	48,003	200	425	700	1,000	1,300
1827	138,110	110	225	325	450	600
1827B	27,032	200	425	700	1,000	1,300
1828/7	631,800	200	425	700	1,000	1,300
1828	Inc. above	100	175	275	400	500
1828B	454,114	100	200	375	550	650
1829/28	Inc. below	200	425	700	1,000	1,300
1829	1,153,100	75.00	125	175	250	300
1829B	247,000	175	400	650	900	1,250
1830B	11,186	800	1,500	2,000	2,500	2,500
1831	410,915	75.00	125	175	250	300
1833	247,303	100	175	275	400	500
1836/5	235,801	250	725	1,000	1,500	2,000
1836	Inc. above	100	255	400	600	700
1839	118,604	100	200	300	450	550
1840	—	100	200	300	450	550
1840 Fleur de lis privy mark	103,321	125	250	350	550	650

KM# 50.2 DUCAT
3.5000 g., 0.9830 Gold .1106 oz. **Obv:** Standing knight with sword and arrows **Rev:** Text within decorated square

Date	Mintage	F	VF	XF	Unc	BU
1818	1,350,000	80.00	130	175	250	—
1827	350,000	130	250	325	450	—
1828	1,300,000	120	225	275	375	—
1829	150,000	80.00	130	175	200	—
1830	2,000,000	80.00	130	175	200	—
1831	1,000,000	80.00	130	175	200	—
1832	1,000,000	100	200	275	350	—
1833	350,000	100	200	275	350	—
1834	150,000	200	350	500	700	—
1835	650,000	110	225	325	425	—
1836	300,000	110	225	325	450	—
1837	1,400,000	80.00	170	250	350	—
1838	1,200,000	80.00	170	250	350	—
1839	1,350,000	80.00	170	250	350	—
1840 torch privy mark	—	80.00	175	250	350	—

KM# 70.1 DUCAT
3.5000 g., 0.9830 Gold .1106 oz. **Obv:** Standing knight with sword and arrows **Rev:** Text within decorated sqaure

Date	Mintage	F	VF	XF	Unc	BU
1841 torch privy mark	3,904,240	80.00	300	400	600	700

KM# 70.2 DUCAT
3.5000 g., 0.9830 Gold .1106 oz. **Obv:** Standing knight with sword and arrows **Rev:** Text within decorated square

Date	Mintage	F	VF	XF	Unc	BU
1841 Fleur de lis privy mark	95,760	100	200	350	450	500

KM# 83.1 DUCAT
3.4940 g., 0.9830 Gold .1106 oz., 21 mm. **Obv:** Standing knight with sword **Rev:** Text within decorated square

Date	Mintage	F	VF	XF	Unc	BU
1849	14,344	80.00	175	250	350	450
1872	30,095	300	1,250	2,500	3,750	4,500
1873	40,041	300	1,250	2,500	3,750	4,500
1874	44,005	300	1,250	2,500	3,750	4,500
1876	44,409	300	1,250	2,500	3,750	4,500
1877	14,875	300	1,250	2,750	4,000	4,750
1878	87,310	300	800	1,300	1,900	2,500
1879	20,103	300	1,250	2,500	3,750	4,500
1880	25,372	300	1,250	2,500	3,750	4,500
1885	81,205	300	850	1,500	2,250	2,750
1894	30,407	175	350	750	1,000	1,500
1895/55	58,444	175	500	850	1,200	1,700
1895/59	Inc. above	175	500	850	1,200	1,700
1895	Inc. above	150	300	600	850	1,100
1899	60,686	150	350	700	950	1,200

KM# 83.2 DUCAT
3.5000 g., 0.9830 Gold .1106 oz., 21 mm. **Obv:** Standing knight with sword and arrows **Rev:** Text within decorated square

Date	Mintage	F	VF	XF	Unc	BU
1849	4,750,000	70.00	140	200	300	—

KM# 83.1a DUCAT
Bronze

Date	Mintage	F	VF	XF	Unc	BU
1868 Rare	—	—	—	—	—	—

KM# 190.1 DUCAT
3.4940 g., 0.9830 Gold .1106 oz., 21 mm. **Obv:** Knight with right leg bent, larger letters in legend **Rev:** Decorated square with text

Date	Mintage	F	VF	XF	Unc	BU
1972 Prooflike	29,205	—	—	—	—	70.00
1974 Prooflike	86,558	—	—	—	—	70.00
1974 medal struck	Est. 2,000	65.00	125	250	350	475
1975 Prooflike	204,788	—	—	—	—	60.00
1976 Prooflike	37,844	—	—	50.00	100	150
Note: Of 37,844 pieces struck, 32,000 were melted						
1978 Prooflike	29,305	—	—	—	60.00	90.00
1985 Prooflike	103,863	—	—	—	—	55.00

KM# 97 2 DUCAT
6.9880 g., 0.9830 Gold .2209 oz., 27 mm. **Obv:** Standing knight with sword and arrows **Rev:** Text within decorated square

Date	Mintage	F	VF	XF	Unc	BU
1854 Proof	—	Value: 9,000				
1867 Proof; 6 known	—	—	—	—	20,000	—

PATTERNS

Including off metal strikes

KM#	Date	Mintage	Identification	Mkt Val
Pn7	1801	—	Ducat. Copper. Over 1797 Zeeland Duit, KM11.2.	—
Pn8	1801	—	2 Ducat. Copper. c/s: DD, KM12.2.	—
Pn9	1804	—	Silver Ducat. Bronze. KM10.4.	—
Pn10	1806	—	Silver Ducat. Copper. Km10.2.	—
Pn11	1808	—	10 Stuivers. Bronze. KM30.	—
Pn12	1808	—	Gulden. Bronze. KM31.	—
Pn14	1808	—	Rijksdaalder. Bronze. KM36.	—
Pn13	1808	—	20 Gulden. Bronze. Without value.	1,500
Pn17	1809	—	2-1/2 Gulden. Lead.	2,750
Pn15	1809	—	10 Stuivers. Bronze. KM30.	—
Pn16	1809	—	Gulden. Bronze. KM31.	—
Pn18	1809	—	Rijksdaalder. Bronze. KM37.	—
Pn19	1809	—	Rijksdaalder. Copper. KM37.	—
Pn20	1810	—	10 Gulden. Silver. KM33.	—
Pn21	1810	—	10 Gulden. Tin. KM33.	350
Pn22	1817	—	25 Cents. Bronze. KM48.	—
Pn23	1817	—	3 Gulden. Tin. KM49.	—
Pn24	1818	—	1/2 Cent. Silver. KM51.	—
Pn26	1818	—	5 Cents. Bronze. KM52.	—
Pn27	1818	—	1/2 Gulden. Bronze. KM54.	—
Pn28	1818	—	Gulden. Bronze. KM55.	—

KM#	Date	Mintage	Identification	Mkt Val
Pn25	1818	—	5 Cents. Gold. KM52.	3,500
Pn29	1818	—	3 Gulden. Bronze. KM49.	1,000
Pn30	1818	—	10 Gulden. Bronze. KM56.	500
Pn31	1819	—	1/2 Cent. Gold. KM51.	7,500
Pn34	1819/8	—	3 Gulden. Bronze. KM49.	600
Pn35	1819	—	10 Gulden. Bronze. KM56.	500
Pn32	1819	—	1/2 Gulden. Bronze. KM54.	—
Pn33	1819	—	Gulden. Bronze. KM55.	—
Pn36	1820	—	Gulden. Gold. KM55.	—
Pn37	1820	—	Gulden. Silver. KM55.	—
Pn38	1820	—	3 Gulden. Bronze. KM49.	—
Pn40	1821	—	Gulden. Silver. KM55.	—
Pn39	1821	—	Gulden. Gold. KM55.	—
Pn41	1822	—	1/2 Cent. Gold. KM51.	—
Pn44	1822	—	3 Gulden. Bronze. KM49.	—
Pn42	1822	—	5 Cents. Gold. 1.8600 g. KM52.	6,000
Pn43	1822	—	10 Cents. Gold. 2.5000 g. KM53.	5,500
Pn46	1823	—	Cent. Gold. 5.3900 g. KM47.	5,000
Pn45	1823	—	Cent. Silver. KM47.	—
Pn47	1823	—	3 Gulden. Gold. KM49.	—
Pn48	1824	—	1/2 Cent. Gold. KM51.	—
Pn50	1826	—	5 Gulden. Bronze. KM60.	—
Pn49	1826	—	Cent. Gold. 3.6600 g. KN47.	5,000
Pn51	1827	—	Cent. Gold. 3.3000 g. KM47.	7,000
Pn52	1840	2	2-1/2 Gulden. Gold. KM46.	—

KM#	Date	Mintage	Identification	Mkt Val
Pn53	1843	—	10 Cents. Gold.	1,500
Pn54	1843	—	10 Cents. Silver.	—
Pn55	1843	—	10 Cents. Bronze.	—
Pn56	1848	—	5 Cents. Gold. KM74.	—
Pn57	1848	—	10 Cents. Gold. KM74.	—
Pn58	1849	—	25 Cents. Gold. KM81.	—
Pn59	1849	—	Ducat. Copper. KM83.1	—

KM#	Date	Mintage	Identification	Mkt Val
Pn60	1850	—	5 Gulden. 0.9000 Gold. KM94.	2,250
Pn61	1850	—	10 Gulden. 0.9000 Gold. KM95.	3,750

KM#	Date	Mintage	Identification	Mkt Val
Pn62	1850	—	20 Gulden. 0.9000 Gold. KM96.	5,000

KM#	Date	Mintage	Identification	Mkt Val
Pn63	1851	—	5 Cents. Bronze.	—
Pn64	1851	—	5 Cents. Bronze.	—
Pn65	1853	—	5 Cents. 0.7180 Silver. C/m: 718, KM91.	—
Pn66	1853	—	10 Cents. 0.7180 Silver. C/m: 718, KM80.	—
Pn67	1853	—	25 Cents. 0.7180 Silver. C/m: 718, KM81.	—

KM#	Date	Mintage	Identification	Mkt Val
PnA68	1860	—	Cent. Bronze.	—
Pn68	1866	—	1/2 Gulden. Bronze. KM92.	—
Pn69	1867	—	Gulden. Gold. KM93.	—
PnA71	1868	—	2 Ducat. Bronze. KM97.	500
Pn70	1868/58	—	1/2 Gulden. Gold. 9.3500 g. KM92.	10,000
Pn72	1872	—	1/2 Cent. Gold. 3.6300 g. KM90.	3,500
Pn71	1872	—	1/2 Cent. Silver. KM90.	—
Pn73	1873	—	1/2 Cent. Gold. KM90.	—
Pn74	1874	—	2-1/2 Gulden. Gold. Sword in scabbard privy mark, KM82.	—
Pn75	1875	—	Cent. Gold. KM100.	—
Pn76	1875	—	Cent. Silver. KM100.	—
Pn77	1876	—	Cent. Gold. KM100.	—
Pn78	1876	—	Cent. Silver. KM100.	—
Pn79	1877	—	Cent. Gold. 7.6700 g. KM100.	8,000
Pn80	1879	—	5 Cents. Gold. KM91.	—
Pn81	1884	—	1/2 Cent. Gold. KM109.	—
Pn82	1884	—	Cent. Gold. KM107.	—
Pn83	1884	—	2-1/2 Cent. Gold. KM108.	—
Pn84	1884	—	10 Cents. Gold. KM80.	—
Pn85	1885	—	10 Cents. Gold. KM80.	—
Pn86	1887	—	5 Cents. Gold. KM91.	—
Pn87	1888	—	10 Gulden. Bronze. KM106.	—
Pn88	1891	—	10 Gulden. Gold. KM118.	—
Pn89	1891	—	10 Gulden. Silver. KM118.	—
Pn90	1892	—	10 Cents. Bronze. KM116.	—
Pn91	1892	—	Gulden. Bronze. KM117.	—
Pn92	1898	—	1/2 Gulden. Gold. 9.3400 g. KM121.1	10,000
Pn93	1898	2	Gulden. Gold. KM122.1	—
Pn94	1898	—	2-1/2 Gulden. Gold. KM123.	—

PIEFORTS

KM#	Date	Mintage	Identification	Mkt Val
P2	1808	—	50 Stuivers. Gold.	—
P3	1820	—	1/2 Gulden. 0.8930 Silver.	—
P4	1822	—	Cent. Copper.	—
P6	1822	—	3 Gulden. Silver.	—
P5	1822	—	3 Gulden. Gold.	5,000
P7	1823	—	1/2 Cent. Copper. KM51.	—
P8	1823	—	1/2 Cent. Copper. KM51.	—
P9	1823	—	Cent. Gold. KM47.	—
P10	1827	—	1/2 Cent. Copper. KM51.	—
P11	1827	—	Cent. Copper. KM47.	—
P12	1828	—	Cent. Copper. KM47.	—
P13	1837	—	Cent. Copper. KM47.	—
P14	1840	—	2-1/2 Gulden. Silver. KM46.	—
P15	1848	—	10 Cents. Silver. KM74.	—
P16	1868/58	—	1/2 Gulden. 0.9450 Silver.	—
P17	1876	—	Cent. Silver.	—
P18	1898	—	2-1/2 Gulden. 0.9450 Silver.	—

SELECT SETS (FLEUR DE COIN)

KM#	Date	Mintage	Identification	Issue Price	Mkt Val
SS1	1819 (9)	—	KM47-49, 51-56 1 set	—	50,000

The Netherlands East Indies of the 19th century, ruled by the Dutch with brief sojourns under the British would now be provinces of Sumatra, a part of the Republic of Indonesia. The islands of Indonesia are made up partly of the Malay Archipelago, which encompasses 3,000 islands, which is the largest in the world.

Had Columbus succeeded in reaching the fabled Spice Islands, he would have found advanced civilizations a millennium old, and temples still ranked among the finest examples of ancient art. During the opening centuries of the Christian era, the islands were influenced by Hindu priests and traders who spread their culture and religion. Moslem invasions began in the 13th century, fragmenting the island kingdoms into small states which were unable to resist Western colonial infiltration. Portuguese traders established posts in the 16th century, but they were soon outnumbered by the Dutch who arrived in 1596 and gradually asserted control over the islands comprising present-day Indonesia. Dutch dominance, interrupted by British incursions during the Napoleonic Wars, established the Netherlands East Indies as one of the richest colonial possessions in the world.

The VOC (United East India Company) struck coins and emergency issues for the Indonesian Archipelago and for the islands at various mints in the Netherlands and the islands. In 1798 the VOC was subsumed by the Dutch government, which issued VOC type transitional and regal types during the Batavian Republic and the Kingdom of the Netherlands until independence. The British issued a coinage during the various occupations by the British East Indian Company, 1811-24. Modern coinage issued by the Republic of Indonesia includes separate series for West Irian and for the Riau Archipelago, an area of small islands between Singapore and Sumatra.

RULERS

Batavian Republic, 1799-1806
Louis Napoleon, King of Holland, 1806-1811
Dutch, 1816-1942

MINT MARKS

H - Amsterdam (H)
Hk - Harderwijk (star, rosette, cock, cross, Z)
Hn - Hoorn (star)
E - Enkhuizen (star)
Dt - Dordrecht (rosette)
K - Kampen (eagle)
S - Utrecht
Sa - Soerabaja (Za)

MONETARY SYSTEM

120 Duits = 120 Cents
1 Gulden = 1 Java Rupee
16 Silver Rupees = 1 Gold Mohur

BONKS: Because of the slow delivery of coins from the Netherlands, the government in the East Indies often resorted to the manufacture of "Bonks". These were simply lumps cut from the copper (or tin) rods used for coining. This eliminated the problems inherent in casting round coins and allowed the production of large quantities of legal tender very quickly. The thicker rods were used for the 2 and 8 Stuiver Bonks and the thinner rod for the smaller denominations.

DUITS: On many of the Duit and 1/2 Duit coins of the East Indies dated 1802-1826, the value appears as 5-1/32-G (1/2 Duit) and 5-1/16-G (Duit). This is interpreted as; 5 of the pieces equal 1/16 Guilder or 5 equal 1/32 Guilder. However, in 1802 the rate of exchange was set so that 6 Duiten should equal 1/16 Guilder which would mean the Duit actually equaled 1/96 Guilder and the1/2 Duit equaled 1/192 Guilder, but because of the perennial shortage of small coins, the error was ignored and the coins released to circulation.

CENTS: Although some coins in 1833-1841 appear with value as 1 CT (1 Cent) and 2 CT (2 Cent) they are considered Duiten and Double Duiten and were exchanged at the rate of 1 Duit = 1/96 Guilder, not on a decimal system.

KINGDOM OF NETHERLANDS

Dutch Administration 1817-1949

DECIMAL COINAGE

KM# 306 1/2 CENT

2.3000 g., Copper, 17 mm. **Obv:** Crowned Dutch weapon shield, legend begins and ends beside date **Rev:** Javanes and Malayan text

Date	Mintage	F	VF	XF	Unc	BU
1855(u) Proof	—	Value: 250				
1856(u)	10,800,000	10.00	20.00	40.00	60.00	80.00
1857(u)	36,800,000	7.50	12.50	25.00	50.00	65.00
1858(u)	53,588,017	4.00	7.50	15.00	30.00	45.00
1858(u) Proof	—	Value: 250				
1859(u)	219,600,000	2.50	5.00	10.00	20.00	30.00
1860(u)	107,123,913	2.50	5.00	10.00	20.00	30.00

KM# 307.1 CENT
Copper **Obv:** Legend begins and ends above date

Date	Mintage	F	VF	XF	Unc	BU
1855(u)	100,000	25.00	50.00	100	200	—
1855(u) Proof	—	Value: 80.00				
1856(u)	67,900,000	3.50	7.00	15.00	25.00	—
1856(u) Proof	—	Value: 65.00				

KM# 307.2 CENT
4.8000 g., Copper, 23 mm. **Obv:** Crowned Dutch weapon shield, legend begins and ends beside date **Rev:** Javanes and Malayan text

Date	Mintage	F	VF	XF	Unc	BU
1856(u)	Inc. above	3.50	7.00	15.00	25.00	30.00
1856(u) Proof	—	Value: 60.00				
1857(u)	162,000,000	2.00	4.00	8.00	15.00	25.00
1858(u)	119,431,741	2.00	4.00	8.00	15.00	25.00
1859(u)	40,800,000	3.00	5.00	10.00	17.50	30.00
1860(u)	14,455,000	3.50	7.00	15.00	25.00	45.00
1896(u)	60,400,000	3.00	5.00	10.00	17.50	30.00
1896(u) Proof	—	Value: 80.00				
1897(u)	69,600,000	7.50	12.50	25.00	50.00	65.00
1897(u) Proof	—	Value: 100				
1898(u)	36,600,000	3.00	5.00	10.00	20.00	32.00
1899(u)	18,400,000	5.00	12.50	25.00	50.00	65.00
1899(u) Proof	—	Value: 90.00				
1902(u)	10,000,000	4.00	8.00	15.0C	30.00	50.00

KM# 308 2-1/2 CENTS
12.5000 g., Copper, 31 mm. **Obv:** Crowned Dutch weapon shield **Rev:** Javanes and Malayan text

Date	Mintage	F	VF	XF	Unc	BU
1856	2,480,000	20.00	40.00	80.00	150	175
1856 Proof	—	Value: 200				
1857	36,560,000	7.50	12.50	25.00	50.00	65.00
1857 Proof	—	Value: 135				
1858	40,989,806	7.50	12.50	25.00	50.00	65.00
1896	1,120,000	20.00	40.00	80.00	150	175
1897	18,105,000	5.00	10.00	20.00	40.00	55.00
1898	7,600,000	7.50	12.50	25.00	50.00	65.00
1899	10,400,000	5.00	10.00	20.00	40.00	55.00

KM# 304 1/10 GULDEN
1.2500 g., 0.7200 Silver .0289 oz., 15 mm. **Obv:** Crowned Dutch weapon shield **Rev:** Javanes and Malayan text **Edge:** Reeded

Date	Mintage	F	VF	XF	Unc	BU
1854(u)	3,550,000	2.00	4.00	8.00	15.00	25.00
1854(u) Proof	—	Value: 50.00				
1855(u)	6,452,000	2.00	4.00	8.00	15.00	25.00
1855(u) Proof	—	Value: 75.00				
1856(u)	3,000,000	2.50	5.00	10.00	20.00	30.00
1857(u)	11,000,000	2.00	4.00	8.00	15.00	20.00
1857(u) Proof	—	Value: 50.00				
1858(u)	14,000,000	2.00	4.00	8.00	15.00	20.00
1882(u)	7,500,000	2.00	4.00	8.00	15.00	25.00
1884(u)	3,550,000	2.00	4.00	8.00	15.00	25.00
1884(u) Proof	—	Value: 100				
1885(u)	825,000	10.00	20.00	40.00	80.00	125
1891(u)	5,000,000	2.00	4.00	8.00	15.00	25.00
1891(u) Proof	—	Value: 85.00				
1893(u)	5,000,000	2.00	4.00	8.00	15.00	25.00
1893(u) Proof	—	Value: 85.00				

Date	Mintage	F	VF	XF	Unc	BU
1896(u)	3,075,000	2.00	4.00	8.00	15.00	25.00
1896(u) Proof	—	Value: 100				
1898(u)	2,500,000	4.00	8.00	15.00	30.00	45.00
1898(u) Proof	—	Value: 120				
1900(u)	6,850,000	2.00	4.00	8.00	15.00	25.00

KM# 305 1/4 GULDEN
3.1800 g., 0.7200 Silver .0736 oz., 15 mm. **Obv:** Crowned Dutch weapon shield **Rev:** Javanese and Malayan text **Edge:** Reeded

Date	Mintage	F	VF	XF	Unc	BU
1854(u)	11,460,000	7.50	15.00	30.00	45.00	60.00
1854(u) Proof	—	Value: 75.00				
1855(u)	4,541,000	7.50	15.00	25.00	40.00	60.00
1855(u) Proof	—	Value: 95.00				
1857(u)	2,400,000	9.00	15.00	30.00	45.00	70.00
1858(u)	4,800,000	8.00	15.00	25.00	40.00	60.00
1858(u) Proof	—	Value: 90.00				
1882(u)	2,200,000	10.00	20.00	35.00	50.00	75.00
1883(u)	800,000	25.00	80.00	100	150	175
1883(u) Proof	—	Value: 225				
1885(u)	1,750,000	12.50	22.50	45.00	80.00	110
1890(u)	1,140,000	12.50	22.50	45.00	80.00	110
1891(u)	860,000	30.00	60.00	120	200	300
1893(u)	2,000,000	10.00	20.00	35.00	50.00	75.00
1893(u) Proof	—	Value: 175				
1896(u)	1,230,000	10.00	20.00	40.00	75.00	95.00
1898(u)	3,000,000	7.50	12.50	32.50	50.00	70.00
1898(u) Proof	—	Value: 120				
1900(u)	2,800,000	7.50	12.50	32.50	50.00	70.00

BANJARMASIN

Sultanate of So. Indonesia on the Martapura River where it meets the Barito. It has a population of 481,371. It is about 24 mi. from the sea. It was settled by the Dutch 1711; held by English 1811-17; bombed by Japanese and taken in Feb. 13, 1942; retaken by Allies August 1945.

TITLES

بنجرمسن

Banjarmasin

RULERS

S. Tamjid Illah III, 1785-1808

NOTE: From around 1790 until at least 1817 various native minted copper coins have been circulating in the Sultanate of Banjarmasin. There is a very large variety in design of these Banjarmasin-Kepings, the majority are crude imitations of Duits of the Dutch East India Co. showing a range of crowned shields on the obverse. Some of them have inscriptions in Malay within the shield, some show the name Banjarmasin in Malay in 2 lines; also mirror script types are known. Most coins have the company's VOC mark on the reverse, usually with badly executed date numerals below. There are other scarcer talismanic numeral type reverses as well as scarce pieces bearing an imitation of the English United East Indian Company's bale mark 'C-E-V-I' or the scales design found on the company's Bombay Presidency series. Sizes vary from 20-25mm with rare specimens of 15-16mm. The weight of this copper series ranges from 1.35-2.50g. Combinations of obv. and rev. of all types exist.

SULTANATE

STANDARD COINAGE

KM# 2 KEPING
Copper **Obv:** Crowned shield **Rev:** VOC, date below **Note:** Many varieties and designs exist.

Date	Mintage	VG	F	VF	XF	Unc
ND(1790-1817)	—	35.00	55.00	75.00	120	—

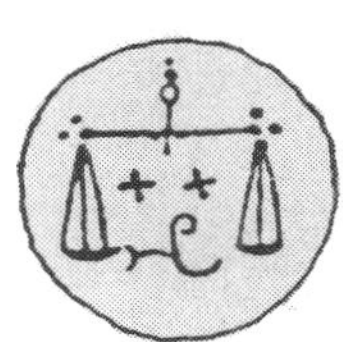

KM# 3 KEPING
Copper **Obv:** Crowned shield **Rev:** Scales **Note:** Many varieties and designs exist.

Date	Mintage	VG	F	VF	XF	Unc
ND(1790-1817)	—	35.00	55.00	75.00	120	—

KM# 4 KEPING
Copper **Obv:** Shield **Rev:** Numerals inscription **Note:** Many varieties and designs exist.

Date	Mintage	VG	F	VF	XF	Unc
ND(1790-1817)	—	35.00	55.00	75.00	120	—

KM# 5 KEPING
Copper **Rev:** Crude CEVI in sections of heart-shaped shield **Note:** Many varieties and designs exist.

Date	Mintage	VG	F	VF	XF	Unc
ND(1790-1817)	—	35.00	55.00	75.00	120	—

KM# 1 KEPING
Copper **Obv:** Legend in shield **Obv. Legend:** Arabic "Banjarmasin" **Rev:** Date and value **Note:** Many varieties exist, some have VOC monogram with date below.

Date	Mintage	VG	F	VF	XF	Unc
ND(1790-1817)	—	25.00	45.00	65.00	110	—

COUNTERMARKED COINAGE

KM# 6 1/4 RUPEE
Silver **Countermark:** "Banjar" **Note:** Countermark on Malay on Dutch West Indies (Utrecht) 1/4 Gulden, 1794, KM#2.

CM Date	Host Date	Good	VG	F	VF	XF
ND	ND	—	—	—	—	—

KM# 7 RUPEE
Silver **Countermark:** "Banjar" **Note:** Countermark on Malay on Dutch West Indies (Utrecht) 1/4 Gulden, 1794, KM#3.

CM Date	Host Date	Good	VG	F	VF	XF
ND	ND	—	—	—	—	—

GELDERLAND

MINTMASTER PRIVY MARKS

Privy Mark	Date	Name
Ear of corn	1782-1809	Martin Hendrik Lohse

MONETARY SYSTEM

4 Duits = 1 Stuiver
20 Stuivers = 1 Gulden

DUCHY

COLONIAL COINAGE

KM# 50.2 DUIT
3.6190 g., Copper **Obv. Legend:** IN DEO • EST • SPES • NOSTRA **Note:** Varieties exist.

Date	Mintage	VG	F	VF	XF	Unc
1802	—	2.75	4.50	7.50	12.50	—
1803	—	2.75	4.50	7.50	12.50	—
1804	—	4.50	7.50	12.50	20.00	—
1805	—	4.50	7.50	12.50	20.00	—
1085 Error	—	—	—	—	—	—
1806	—	2.00	3.50	6.00	10.00	—

KM# 50.2a DUIT
8.2000 g., Silver **Edge:** Milled

Date	Mintage	VG	F	VF	XF	Unc
1806	—	—	—	—	—	—

HOLLAND

MINT MARKS
H – Heus, Amsterdam
Rosette – Dordrecht, 1601-1806
Star – Enkhuizen, 1796-1803
Star – Hoorn, 1803-1809

UNITED EAST INDIA COMPANY

COLONIAL COINAGE

KM# 70 DUIT
3.6190 g., Copper **Obv:** Crowned arms of Holland **Rev:** VOC monogram above date **Note:** Special presentation strikes produced by the mintmaster on demand. Varieties exist.

Date	Mintage	VG	F	VF	XF	Unc
1802 Star	—	7.50	12.00	20.00	32.50	—
1802 Rosette	—	7.50	12.00	20.00	32.50	—
1803	—	7.50	12.00	20.00	32.50	—
1804	—	3.50	6.00	10.00	20.00	—

JAVA

LOCAL COINAGE

A mountainous island, 661 miles long by 124 miles at widest part, in greater Sunda island group. Early cultural influence from India. Islam introduced in late 1400's. Java was mainly a Dutch possession from 1619 to 1947 with the exception of a few periods of British occupation, principally 1811-1816.

MONETARY SYSTEM
4 Duit = 1 Stiver
30 Stivers = 1 Rupee (Silver)
66 Stivers = 1 Dollar

DATING SYSTEM

The coins listed are found with AD (Christian) dates, AD and AH (Hejira) dates, and with AD, AH and AS (Aji Saka = Javanese) dates which are explained in the introduction in this catalog.

BATAVIAN REPUBLIC

1799-1806

HAMMERED DUMP COINAGE

KM# 207 STUIVER
46.3200 g., Copper Bonk **Obv:** Value **Rev:** Date **Note:** Varieties exist.

Date	Mintage	Good	VG	F	VF	XF
1800	—	25.00	40.00	60.00	100	—
1801	—	15.00	27.50	45.00	75.00	—
1802	—	10.00	18.00	30.00	50.00	—
1803	—	10.00	18.00	30.00	50.00	—

Note: Roman I in date of post 1800 issues

KM# 206 STUIVER
23.1600 g., Copper Bonk **Obv:** Value **Rev:** Date **Note:** Varieties exist.

Date	Mintage	Good	VG	F	VF	XF
1801	—	8.50	15.00	25.00	40.00	—
1802	—	6.00	10.00	20.00	35.00	—
Note: Roman I in date of 1802 issues						
1803	—	8.50	15.00	25.00	40.00	—

KM# 208 RUPEE
13.1500 g., 0.7920 Silver .3349 oz. **Note:** Thick planchet. Varieties exist.

Date	Mintage	VG	F	VF	XF	Unc
1801 Z	—	20.00	35.00	60.00	100	—
1802 Z	—	20.00	35.00	60.00	100	—
1803 Z	—	20.00	35.00	60.00	100	—

KM# 209 1/2 GOLD RUPEE
8.0060 g., 0.7500 Gold .1929 oz.

Date	Mintage	VG	F	VF	XF	Unc
1801	—	300	500	800	1,350	—
1802	—	300	500	800	1,350	—
1803 Unique	—	—	—	—	—	—
1807	—	600	1,100	1,650	2,500	—

MADURA ISLAND

Sumenep is a sultanate on the island of Madura.

RULERS
Sultan Paku Nata Ningrat, 1811-1854

TITLES

Sumenep

SULTANATE OF SUMENEP

COUNTERMARKED COINAGE

Madura Star Series

KM# 201.3 DUCATON (Thaler, Daalder)
Silver **Countermark:** "Madura Star" in shield **Note:** Countermark on Mexico City Mint 8 Reales, KM#109.

CM Date	Host Date	Good	VG	F	VF	XF
ND(1798-99)	ND(1790-1808)	40.00	60.00	90.00	150	—

KM# 201.4 DUCATON (Thaler, Daalder)
Silver **Countermark:** "Madura Star" in shield **Note:** Countermark on Potosi Mint 8 Reales, KM#73.1.

CM Date	Host Date	Good	VG	F	VF	XF
ND(1798-99)	ND(1791-1808)	50.00	70.00	100	160	—

PONTIANAK

Sultanate in West Borneo.

RULER
S. Syarif Kasim Alkadrie, 1808-1819

SULTANATE

HAMMERED COINAGE

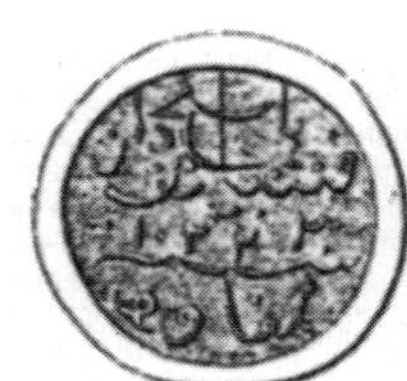

KM# 1 KEPING
Obv: Inscription **Rev:** Scales with x at center

Date	Mintage	Good	VG	F	VF	XF
AH1223	—	—	10.00	20.00	40.00	85.00

KM# 2 KEPING
Copper **Obv:** Inscription **Rev:** Scales with dot at center

Date	Mintage	Good	VG	F	VF	XF
AH1226	—	—	10.00	20.00	40.00	85.00

KM# 3 KEPING
Copper **Obv:** Retrograde inscription **Rev:** Scales with 3 dots at center

Date	Mintage	Good	VG	F	VF	XF
AH1226	—	—	10.00	20.00	40.00	85.00

NEVIS

Nevis, a component of one of the West Indies Associated States, is located in the Leeward Islands and has an area of 50 sq. mi. (105 sq. km.).

Nevis was discovered by Columbus in 1493. It was first colonized by the English in 1628. Admiral De Grasse captured the island for France in 1782, but it was restored to Britain the following year. Alexander Hamilton, first Secretary of the Treasury, was born on Nevis in 1757.

RULERS
British

MONETARY SYSTEM
72 Black Dogs = 1 Dollar

BRITISH ADMINISTRATION

COUNTERMARKED COINAGE

72 Black Dogs = 1 Dollar

KM# 1 BLACK DOG
Billon **Countermark:** NEVIS **Note:** Countermark on French Guiana 2 Sous.

CM Date	Host Date	Good	VG	F	VF	XF
ND	1801	75.00	125	200	250	—

KM# 2 4 BLACK DOGS
Silver **Countermark:** NEVIS **Note:** Countermark above incuse 4.

CM Date	Host Date	Good	VG	F	VF	XF
ND	ND	500	1,000	1,650	2,750	—

KM# 3 6 BLACK DOGS
Silver **Countermark:** NEVIS **Note:** Countermark above incuse 6.

CM Date	Host Date	Good	VG	F	VF	XF
ND	ND	650	1,200	1,850	3,000	—

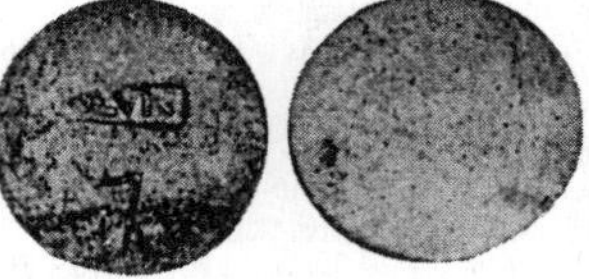

KM# 4 7 BLACK DOGS
Silver **Countermark:** NEVIS **Note:** Countermark above incuse 7.

CM Date	Host Date	Good	VG	F	VF	XF
ND	ND	350	700	1,250	2,275	—

KM# 5.2 9 BLACK DOGS
Silver **Countermark:** NEVIS **Note:** Countermark above incuse 9 on Potosi 1 Real.

CM Date	Host Date	Good	VG	F	VF	XF
ND	ND1684	350	750	1,150	1,850	—

KM# 5.1 9 BLACK DOGS
Silver **Countermark:** NEVIS **Note:** Countermark above incuse 9 Spanish Colonial 1 Real.

CM Date	Host Date	Good	VG	F	VF	XF
ND	ND	300	600	1,000	1,750	—

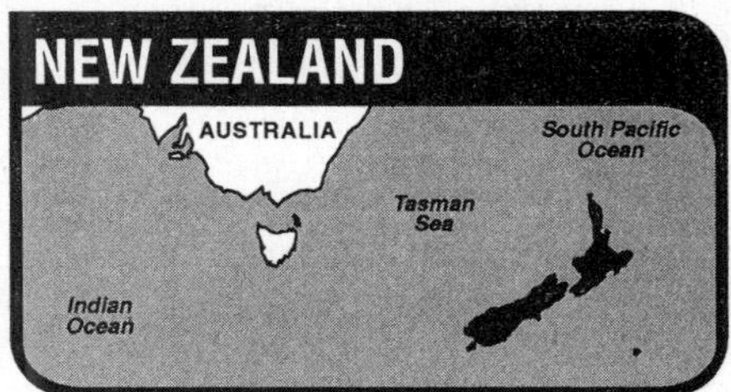

New Zealand, a parliamentary state located in the Southwest Pacific 1,250 miles (2,011 km.) east of Australia, has an area of 103,883 sq. mi. (268,680 sq. km.).

The first European to sight New Zealand was the Dutch navigator Abel Tasman in 1642. The islands were explored by British navigator Capt. James Cook who surveyed it in 1769 and annexed the land to Great Britain. The British government disavowed the annexation and for the next 70 years the only white settlers to arrive were adventurers attracted by the prospects of lumbering, sealing and whaling. Great Britain annexed the land in 1840 by treaty with the native chiefs and made it a dependency of New South Wales. Full internal and external autonomy, which New Zealand had in effect possessed for many years, was formally extended in 1947.

RULERS

British

MONETARY SYSTEM

12 Pence = 1 Shilling
2 Shillings = 1 Florin
2 Shillings & 6 Pence = Half Crown
5 Shillings = 1 Crown
20 Shillings = 1 Pound
2 Dollars = 1 Pound

TOKEN COINAGE

Because of a shortage of British money, New Zealand merchant tokens were issued beginning in 1857. There were some 147 varieties issued in 10 cities, although the majority were issued in Auckland, Christchurch, Wellington and Dunedin. Issuance was discontinued in 1881, but they continued to circulate until 1897 when British copper and silver and Australian gold became plentiful. Almost all tokens bear the name of the city and the issuing merchant, but few have a stated value so the user had to rely on size and weight – a very irregular standard to determine value. Most tokens are of copper, a few are bronze.

BRITISH PARLIAMENTARY STATE

TOKEN COINAGE

ALLIANCE TEA CO.

Christchurch

KM# Tn1.1 PENNY

Copper, 34 mm. **Issuer:** Alliance Tea Co., Christchurch **Obv:** "Y" of "COMPANY" level with "D" of " ZEALAND"

Date	Mintage	VG	F	VF	XF	Unc
1866	—	50.00	100	175	325	600

KM# Tn1.2 PENNY

Copper, 34 mm. **Obv:** "Y" of "COMPANY" below "D" of " ZEALAND"

Date	Mintage	VG	F	VF	XF	Unc
1866	—	150	300	600	1,000	—

D. ANDERSONS

Wellington

KM# Tn2 1/2 PENNY

Copper, 27.5 mm. **Issuer:** D. Andersons, Wellington

Date	Mintage	VG	F	VF	XF	Unc
ND	—	75.00	175	325	500	—

KM# Tn3 PENNY

Copper, 34 mm.

Date	Mintage	VG	F	VF	XF	Unc
ND	—	75.00	175	350	500	—

H. ASHTON

Auckland

KM# Tn4 1/2 PENNY

Copper, 27.5 mm. **Issuer:** H. Ashton, Auckland **Obv:** Legend above seated Justice **Obv. Legend:** "NEW ZEALAND" **Rev. Legend:** "H. ASHTON"...

Date	Mintage	VG	F	VF	XF	Unc
1858	—	35.00	75.00	125	225	325
1859	—	50.00	100	175	325	500

KM# Tn5 PENNY

Copper, 34 mm. **Obv:** Legend above standing Justice **Obv. Legend:** "NEW ZEALAND" **Rev:** Similar to 1/2 Penny, KM#Tn4

Date	Mintage	VG	F	VF	XF	Unc
1862	—	35.00	75.00	145	275	500
1863	—	35.00	75.00	150	250	500

Note: 3 varieties of 1863 exist

AUCKLAND LICENSED VICTUALLERS ASSOCIATION

Auckland

KM# Tn6 PENNY

Bronze, 31 mm. **Issuer:** Auckland Licensed Victuallers/Association, Auckland

Date	Mintage	VG	F	VF	XF	Unc
ND	—	15.00	30.00	75.00	150	250

Note: 4 varieties exist

CHARLES C. BARLEY

Auckland

KM# Tn7 PENNY

Bronze, 34 mm. **Issuer:** Charles C. Barley , Auckland **Obv. Legend:** "CHARLES C. BARLEY..." **Rev:** Legend above seated Justice **Rev. Legend:** "GOD SAVE THE QUEEN"

Date	Mintage	VG	F	VF	XF	Unc
1858	—	35.00	75.00	145	275	450

G. L. BEATH & CO.

Christchurch

KM# Tn8 PENNY

Bronze, 31 mm. **Obv. Legend:** "G. L. BEATH & CO..." **Rev:** Legend above facing rampant lions **Rev. Legend:** "ARGYE HOUSE" **Note:** 5 Varieties exist.

Date	Mintage	VG	F	VF	XF	Unc
ND(1858)	—	35.00	75.00	150	275	500

Note: A uniface obverse die trial sold at Spinks Australia for U.S. $600 in 1979.

S. BEAVEN

Invercargill

KM# Tn9 PENNY

Bronze, 31 mm. **Issuer:** S. Beaven, Invercargill

Date	Mintage	VG	F	VF	XF	Unc
1863	—	150	300	600	1,000	—

BROWN & DUTHIE

New Plymouth

KM# Tn10 PENNY

Copper, 31 mm. **Issuer:** Brown & Duthie, New Plymouth

Date	Mintage	VG	F	VF	XF	Unc
1866	—	30.00	60.00	125	225	350

J. CARO & CO.
Christchurch

KM# Tn11 PENNY
Copper, 34 mm. **Issuer:** J. Caro & Co., Christchurch **Note:** Restrikes exist.

Date	Mintage	VG	F	VF	XF	Unc
ND	—	35.00	75.00	150	275	500

ARCHIBALD CLARK
Auckland

KM# Tn12 PENNY
Copper, 34 mm. **Issuer:** Archibald Clark, Auckland **Note:** Believed to be the first token struck for New Zealand.

Date	Mintage	VG	F	VF	XF	Unc
1857	—	50.00	100	175	300	500

S. CLARKSON
Christchurch

KM# Tn13 PENNY
Copper, 34 mm. **Issuer:** S. Clarkson, Christchurch **Obv. Legend:** "S. CLARKSON. . ." **Rev:** Similar to KM#Tn12 **Note:** 4 varieties exist.

Date	Mintage	VG	F	VF	XF	Unc
1875	—	35.00	75.00	145	275	500

CLARKSON & TURNBULL
Timaru

KM# Tn14 PENNY
Copper, 34 mm. **Issuer:** Clarkson & Turnbull, Timaru **Note:** 3 varieties exist

Date	Mintage	VG	F	VF	XF	Unc
1865	—	50.00	100	180	325	600

SAMUEL COOMBES
Auckland

KM# Tn15 PENNY
Copper, 34 mm. **Issuer:** Samuel Coombes, Auckland **Note:** 3 varieties exist

Date	Mintage	VG	F	VF	XF	Unc
ND	—	30.00	60.00	125	225	350

DAY & MIEVILLE
Dunedin

KM# Tn16 PENNY
Copper, 34 mm. **Issuer:** Day & Mieville, Dunedin **Obv. Legend:** "DAY & MIEVILLE..." **Rev:** Similar to KM#Tn12

Date	Mintage	VG	F	VF	XF	Unc
1857	—	25.00	50.00	100	200	350

E. DE CARLE & CO.
Dunedin

KM# Tn17 PENNY
Bronze, 31 mm. **Issuer:** E. De Carle & Co., Dunedin **Note:** 3 varieties exist

Date	Mintage	VG	F	VF	XF	Unc
1862	—	35.00	75.00	150	275	450

T. S. FORSAITH
Auckland

KM# Tn18 1/2 PENNY
Copper, 28 mm. **Issuer:** T. S. Forsaith, Auckland

Date	Mintage	VG	F	VF	XF	Unc
1858	—	50.00	100	175	325	600

KM# Tn19 PENNY
Copper, 34 mm. **Note:** Similar to 1/2 Penny, KM#Tn18.

Date	Mintage	VG	F	VF	XF	Unc
1858	—	75.00	150	325	500	750

GAISFORD & EDMONDS
Christchurch

KM# Tn20 PENNY
Copper **Issuer:** Gaisford & Edmonds, Christchurch **Obv. Legend:** "GAISFORD & EDMONDS. . ."

Date	Mintage	VG	F	VF	XF	Unc
1875	—	50.00	100	175	300	500

JOHN GILMOUR
New Plymouth

KM# Tn21 PENNY
Copper, 31 mm. **Issuer:** John Gilmour, New Plymouth **Obv. Legend:** "JOHN GILMOUR. . ." **Rev:** Kiwi bird below Mt. Egmont **Note:** 2 varieties exist

Date	Mintage	VG	F	VF	XF	Unc
ND	—	30.00	60.00	125	225	300

B. GITTOS
Auckland

KM# Tn22 PENNY
Copper, 34 mm. **Issuer:** B. Gittos, Auckland **Obv. Legend:** "B. GITTOS. . ." **Rev. Legend:** "WHOLESALE & RETAIL. . ."

Date	Mintage	VG	F	VF	XF	Unc
1864	—	30.00	60.00	100	200	300

T. W. GOURLAY & CO.
Christchurch

KM# Tn23 PENNY
Copper **Issuer:** T. W. Gourlay & Co., Christchurch **Note:** 2 varieties exist

Date	Mintage	VG	F	VF	XF	Unc
ND	—	50.00	100	175	350	600

R. GRATTEN
Auckland

KM# Tn24 PENNY
Copper, 32 mm. **Issuer:** R. Gratten, Auckland **Obv. Legend:** "THAMES HOTEL/R. GRATTEN. . ." **Rev:** Indian paddling boat within sprays

Date	Mintage	VG	F	VF	XF	Unc
1872	—	35.00	75.00	150	275	500

HENRY J. HALL
Christchurch

KM# Tn25 1/2 PENNY
Copper, 28 mm. **Issuer:** Henry J. Hall, Christchurch **Obv. Legend:** "HENRY J. HALL. . ." **Rev. Legend:** "FAMILY GROCER. . ."

Date	Mintage	VG	F	VF	XF	Unc
ND	—	50.00	100	175	300	500

KM# Tn27 1/2 PENNY
, 28 mm. **Note:** Mule, Obverse of KM#Tn25 and reverse of Lipman Levy 1/2 Penny, KM#Tn38.

Date	Mintage	VG	F	VF	XF	Unc
ND	—	—	—	150	1,200	1,800

KM# Tn26 1/2 PENNY
, 28 mm. **Note:** Mule, Reverse of KM#Tn25 and obverse of E.F. Dease (Australian) 1/2 Penny, KM#Tn50.

Date	Mintage	VG	F	VF	XF	Unc
ND	—	—	—	150	1,200	1,800

KM# Tn29 PENNY
Copper, 33 mm. **Obv:** KM#Tn30 **Rev:** Similar to obverse KM#Tn28A

Date	Mintage	VG	F	VF	XF	Unc
ND	—	50.00	100	175	325	500

KM# Tn28 PENNY
Copper, 34 mm. **Note:** H.J. HALL in large letters. 4 varieties exist, restrikes exist.

Date	Mintage	VG	F	VF	XF	Unc
ND	—	50.00	100	185	350	600

KM# Tn28a PENNY
Copper **Note:** H.J. HALL in small letters. 6 varieties exist.

Date	Mintage	VG	F	VF	XF	Unc
ND	—	35.00	75.00	125	275	500

KM# Tn30 PENNY
Copper, 33 mm. **Note:** Mule. Obverse of KM#Tn29 & reverse of Emu and kangaroo (Australian) Penny.

Date	Mintage	VG	F	VF	XF	Unc
ND	—	—	—	2,000	3,000	—

HOBDAY & JOBBERNS
Christchurch

KM# Tn31 PENNY
Copper, 33.5 mm. **Issuer:** Hobday & Jobberns, Christchurch **Obv. Legend:** "HOBDAY & JOBBERNS. . ." **Rev:** Legend below shield **Rev. Legend:** "ADVANCE CANTERBURY" **Note:** 2 major varieties exist.

Date	Mintage	VG	F	VF	XF	Unc
ND	—	35.00	75.00	150	275	500

HOLLAND & BUTLER
Auckland

KM# Tn32 PENNY
Copper, 32 mm. **Issuer:** Holland & Butler, Auckland **Obv. Legend:** "HOLLAND & BUTLER" **Rev. Legend:** "IMPORTERS OF. . ."

Date	Mintage	VG	F	VF	XF	Unc
ND	—	8.00	15.00	40.00	100	—

J. HURLEY & CO.
Wanganui

KM# Tn33 1/2 PENNY
Copper, 33 mm. **Issuer:** J. Hurley & Co., Wanganui

Date	Mintage	VG	F	VF	XF	Unc
ND	—	35.00	75.00	150	250	400

KM# Tn34 PENNY
Copper, 31 mm. **Note:** Similar to 1/2 Penny, KM#Tn33.

Date	Mintage	VG	F	VF	XF	Unc
ND	—	30.00	60.00	100	175	300

JONES & WILLIAMSON
Dunedin

KM# Tn35 PENNY
Copper, 34 mm. **Issuer:** Jones & Williamson, Dunedin

Date	Mintage	VG	F	VF	XF	Unc
1858	—	50.00	100	175	325	500

KIRKCALDIE & STAINS
Wellington

KM# Tn36 1/2 PENNY
Bronze, 25 mm. **Issuer:** Kirkcaldie & Stains, Welington **Obv. Legend:** "KIRKCALDIE & STAINS. . ." **Rev:** Legend above helmeted shield **Rev. Legend:** "KIRKCALDIE & STAINS"

Date	Mintage	VG	F	VF	XF	Unc
ND	—	30.00	60.00	100	200	300

KM# Tn37 PENNY
Bronze, 31 mm. **Note:** Similar to 1/2 Penny, KM#Tn36.

Date	Mintage	VG	F	VF	XF	Unc
ND	—	30.00	60.00	100	200	300

LIPMAN LEVY
Wellington

KM# Tn38 1/2 PENNY
Copper, 28 mm. **Issuer:** Lipman Levy, Wellington

Date	Mintage	VG	F	VF	XF	Unc
ND	—	120	250	500	750	—

KM# Tn39.2 PENNY
Copper, 34 mm. **Note:** Die rotated 180 degrees. Specimen strike for collectors.

Date	Mintage	VG	F	VF	XF	Unc
ND	—	—	—	—	400	500

KM# Tn39.1 PENNY
Copper, 34 mm. **Note:** Similar to 1/2 Penny, KM#T38, normal die alignment.

Date	Mintage	VG	F	VF	XF	Unc
ND	—	75.00	175	325	750	1,000

KM# Tn41 PENNY
Copper, 34 mm. **Note:** Mule. Obverse of KM#Tn39 and reverse of AUSTRALIA above seated woman penny token. Specimen strike for collectors.

Date	Mintage	F	VF	XF	Unc	BU
ND	—	—	—	1,000	1,250	—

KM# Tn40 PENNY
Copper, 34 mm. **Rev:** Legend around laureate head of Wellington. **Rev. Legend:** "WELLINGTON & ERIN GOBRACH" **Note:** Mule. Obverse of KM#Tn39. Specimen strike for collectors.

Date	Mintage	F	VF	XF	Unc	BU
ND	—	—	—	750	1,000	—

MORRIS MARKS
Auckland

KM# Tn42 PENNY
Brass **Issuer:** Morris Marks, Auckland

Date	Mintage	VG	F	VF	XF	Unc
ND	—	120	250	500	750	—

MASON STRUTHERS & CO.
Christchurch

KM# Tn43 PENNY
Bronze, 30.5 mm. **Issuer:** Mason Struthers & Co., Christchurch **Obv. Legend:** "MASON STRUTHERS & CO. . ." **Rev:** Legend around Maori head right **Rev. Legend:** "ONE PENNY TOKEN" **Note:** 2 varieties exist.

Date	Mintage	VG	F	VF	XF	Unc
ND	—	35.00	75.00	150	275	500

GEORGE MCCAUL
Grahamstown

KM# Tn44 PENNY
Copper, 34 mm. **Issuer:** George McCaul, Grahamstown **Obv. Legend:** "GEORGE MCCAUL. . ." **Rev:** Poppet head of gold mine

Date	Mintage	VG	F	VF	XF	Unc
1874	—	20.00	40.00	75.00	125	250

J. W. MEARS
Wellington

KM# Tn45 1/2 PENNY
Copper, 29 mm. **Issuer:** J. W. Mears, Wellington

Date	Mintage	VG	F	VF	XF	Unc
ND	—	150	300	500	750	—

J. M. MERRINGTON & CO.
Nelson

KM# Tn46 PENNY
Copper, 34 mm. **Issuer:** J. M. Merrington & Co., Nelson **Obv. Legend:** "J. M. MERRINGTON & CO. . ." **Rev:** Legend above standing Justice **Rev. Legend:** "ADVANCE NEW ZEALAND"

Date	Mintage	VG	F	VF	XF	Unc
ND	—	35.00	75.00	150	285	500

MILNER & THOMPSON
Christchurch

KM# Tn49 PENNY
Copper, 34 mm.

Date	Mintage	VG	F	VF	XF	Unc
ND	—	—	75.00	125	250	400

KM# Tn53 PENNY
Bronze, 32 mm. **Obv:** Similar to reverse of KM#Tn49 **Rev:** Similar to reverse of KM#Tn54

Date	Mintage	VG	F	VF	XF	Unc
ND	—	—	60.00	100	175	300

KM# Tn54 PENNY
Bronze, 32 mm. **Obv:** Scene **Rev:** Inscription

Date	Mintage	VG	F	VF	XF	Unc
ND	—	—	75.00	125	250	400

KM# Tn55 PENNY
Bronze, 32 mm. **Obv:** Similar to reverse of KM#Tn49 **Rev:** Similar to obverse of KM#Tn54

Date	Mintage	F	VF	XF	Unc	BU
ND 2 known	—	—	—	—	6,000	—

KM# Tn50 PENNY
Bronze, 32 mm. **Note:** Reduced size. Similar to KM#Tn47.

Date	Mintage	VG	F	VF	XF	Unc
1881	—	—	60.00	100	175	300

KM# Tn51 PENNY
Bronze, 32 mm. **Note:** Similar to KM#Tn48.

Date	Mintage	VG	F	VF	XF	Unc
1881	—	—	—	22.50	75.00	—

KM# Tn52 PENNY
Bronze, 32 mm. **Obv:** Similar to obverse of KM#Tn48 **Rev:** Similar to reverse of KM#Tn54

Date	Mintage	VG	F	VF	XF	Unc
1881	—	—	60.00	100	175	300

KM# Tn47 PENNY
Copper, 34 mm. **Issuer:** Milner & Thompson, Christchurch **Obv:** Legend around winged head of angel above musical instruments **Obv. Legend:** "MILNER & THOMPSON. . ." **Rev:** Scene

Date	Mintage	VG	F	VF	XF	Unc
1881	—	—	75.00	125	250	400

KM# Tn48 PENNY
Copper, 34 mm. **Obv:** Similar to KM#Tn47 **Rev:** Similar to KM#Tn49

Date	Mintage	VG	F	VF	XF	Unc
1881	—	—	75.00	125	250	400

MORRIN & CO.
Auckland

KM# Tn56.1 PENNY
Copper, 34 mm. **Issuer:** Morrin & Co., Auckland **Obv:** Left hand palm branch lower **Rev:** Head of Justice below "A" of AUCKLAND"

Date	Mintage	VG	F	VF	XF	Unc
ND	—	35.00	75.00	150	275	450

KM# Tn56.3 PENNY
Copper, 34 mm. **Obv:** "T" of "STREET" points to "S" of "MERCHANTS" **Rev:** Head of Justice below "AU" of "AUCKLAND"

Date	Mintage	VG	F	VF	XF	Unc
ND	—	200	400	1,200	1,800	—

KM# Tn56.2 PENNY
Copper, 34 mm. **Obv:** Palm branches even

Date	Mintage	VG	F	VF	XF	Unc
ND	—	35.00	75.00	150	275	350

KM# Tn56.4 PENNY
Copper, 34 mm. **Obv:** Right hand palm branch lower, last "T" of "STREET" points to "TS" of "MERCHANTS"

Date	Mintage	VG	F	VF	XF	Unc
ND	—	400	650	1,800	2,750	—

PERKINS & CO.
Dunedin

KM# Tn57 1/2 PENNY
Bronze, 25 mm. **Issuer:** Perkins & Co., Dunedin

Date	Mintage	VG	F	VF	XF	Unc
ND	—	120	245	500	750	—

KM# Tn58 PENNY
Bronze, 30 mm.

Date	Mintage	VG	F	VF	XF	Unc
ND	—	50.00	100	175	350	600

W. PETERSON
Christchurch

KM# Tn59 PENNY
Copper, 34 mm. **Issuer:** W. Peterson, Christchurch

Date	Mintage	VG	F	VF	XF	Unc
ND	—	125	250	500	750	—

WILLIAM PRATT
Christchurch

KM# Tn60 PENNY
Copper, 34 mm. **Issuer:** William Pratt, Christchurch **Obv. Legend:** "WILLIAM PRATT. . ." **Rev. Legend:** "DUNSTABLE HOUSE. . ." **Note:** 4 varieties exist.

Date	Mintage	VG	F	VF	XF	Unc
ND	—	75.00	175	325	500	—

EDWARD REECE
Christchurch

KM# Tn61.2 1/2 PENNY
Copper, 28 mm. **Rev:** Legends, small letters

Date	Mintage	VG	F	VF	XF	Unc
ND	—	450	650	1,750	2,750	—

KM# Tn61.1 1/2 PENNY
Copper, 28 mm. **Issuer:** Edward Reece, Christchurch **Rev:** Legends, large letters **Note:** 2 varieties exist.

Date	Mintage	VG	F	VF	XF	Unc
ND	—	75.00	35.00	175	325	—

KM# Tn62 PENNY
Copper, 34 mm.

Date	Mintage	VG	F	VF	XF	Unc
ND	—	75.00	175	325	500	750

S. HAGUE SMITH
Auckland

KM# Tn63 PENNY
Copper, 34 mm. **Issuer:** S. Hague Smith, Auckland **Note:** 8 varieties exist.

Date	Mintage	VG	F	VF	XF	Unc
ND	—	35.00	75.00	150	275	500

M. SOMERVILLE
Auckland

KM# Tn64 PENNY
Copper, 34 mm. **Issuer:** M. Sommerville, Auckland **Note:** 4 varieties exist.

Date	Mintage	VG	F	VF	XF	Unc
1857	—	30.00	60.00	125	225	350

UNION BAKERY CO.
Christchurch

KM# Tn65 PENNY
Bronze, 30 mm. **Issuer:** Union Bakery Co., Christchurch

Date	Mintage	VG	F	VF	XF	Unc
ND	—	50.00	100	180	325	600

UNITED SERVICE HOTEL
Auckland

KM# Tn66 PENNY
Copper, 34 mm. **Issuer:** United Service Hotel, Auckland **Obv:** Similar to KM#Tn67 **Rev:** Similar to KM#Tn67 but "UNITED HOTEL" in straight line

Date	Mintage	VG	F	VF	XF	Unc
1874	—	30.00	60.00	125	250	350

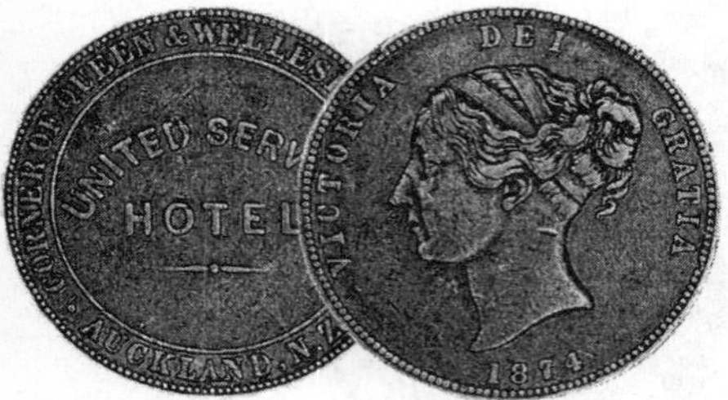

KM# Tn67 PENNY
Copper, 34 mm.

Date	Mintage	VG	F	VF	XF	Unc
1874	—	30.00	60.00	125	250	350

JAMES WALLACE
Wellington

KM# Tn68 1/2 PENNY
Copper, 28 mm. **Issuer:** James Wallace, Wellington

Date	Mintage	VG	F	VF	XF	Unc
1859	—	125	250	500	750	—

KM# Tn69 PENNY
Copper, 34 mm. **Note:** Obverse and reverse: Similar to 1/2 Penny, KM#Tn68.

Date	Mintage	VG	F	VF	XF	Unc
1859	—	75.00	175	350	500	—

EDWARD WATERS
Auckland

KM# Tn70.1 PENNY
Copper, 33 mm. **Issuer:** Edward Waters, Auckland **Obv. Legend:** "WHOLESALE & RETAIL. . .QUEEN ST" **Rev:** Legend around Maori head right **Rev. Legend:** "ONE PENNY TOKEN" **Note:** 23mm.

Date	Mintage	VG	F	VF	XF	Unc
ND	—	75.00	175	350	500	—

KM# Tn70.2 PENNY
Copper, 33 mm. **Obv. Legend:** "....QUEEN ST." **Note:** 19mm.

Date	Mintage	VG	F	VF	XF	Unc
ND	—	30.00	60.00	120	250	350

A. S. WILSON
Dunedin

KM# Tn71 PENNY
Copper **Issuer:** A. S. Wilson, Dunedin

Date	Mintage	VG	F	VF	XF	Unc
1857	—	50.00	100	200	500	—

KM# Tn72 PENNY
30 mm. **Note:** Considered by some to be a pattern.

Date	Mintage	VG	F	VF	XF	Unc
ND 2 known	—	—	—	—	15,000	—

PATTERNS
INCLUDING OFF METAL STRIKES

KM#	Date	Mintage	Identification	Mkt Val
Pn1	1879	—	Penny. Bronze.	2,250

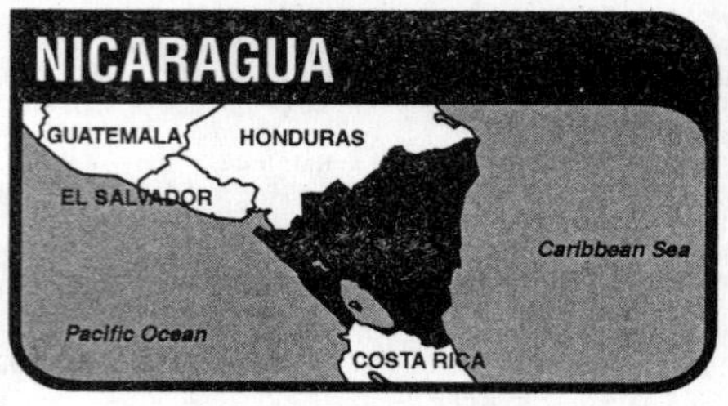

The Republic of Nicaragua, situated in Central America between Honduras and Costa Rica, has an area of 50,193 sq. mi. (129,494 sq. km.).

Columbus sighted the coast of Nicaragua on Sept. 12,1502 during the course of his last voyage of discovery. It was first visited in 1522 by conquistadors from Panama, under the command of Gil Gonzalez. Francisco Hernandez de Cordoba established the first settlements in 1524 at Granada and Leon. Nicaragua was incorporated, for administrative purpose, in the Captaincy General of Guatemala, which included every Central American state but Panama. On September 15, 1821 the Captaincy General of Guatemala declared itself and all the Central American provinces independent of Spain. The next year Nicaragua united with the Mexican Empire of Augustin de Iturbide, only to join in 1823 the federation of the Central American Republic. Within Nicaragua rival cities or juntas such as Leon, Granada and El Viejo vied for power, wealth and influence, often attacking each other at will. To further prove their legitimacy as well as provide an acceptable circulating coinage in those turbulent times (1821-1825), provisional mints functioned intermittently at Granada, Leon and ElViejo. The early coinage reflected traditional but crude Spanish colonial cob-style designs. Nicaragua's first governor was Pedro Arias Davila, appointed on June 1, 1827. When the federation was dissolved, Nicaragua declared itself an independent republic on April 30, 1838.

Dissension between the Liberals and Conservatives of the contending cities kept Nicaragua in turmoil, which made it possible for William Walker to make himself President in 1855. The two major political parties finally united to drive him out and in 1857 he was expelled. A relative peace followed, but by 1912, Nicaragua had requested the U.S. Marines to restore order, which began a U.S. involvement that lasted until the Good Neighbor Policy was adopted in 1933.

MINT MARKS
H - Heaton, Birmingham
HF - Huguenin Freres, Le Locle, Switzerland
Mo - Mexico City

MONETARY SYSTEM
100 Centavos = 1 Peso

NOTE: Former listing for 1823 IL 1/2 Real of Leon has been identified by recognized authorities as a Honduras issue 1823 TL 1/2 Real cataloged there as KM#9.

VICE-ROYALTY OF NEW SPAIN

MEDALLIC COINAGE

KM# M1 REAL
Silver **Note:** This was a proclamation issue, struck at the Guatemala City mint for Ferdinand VII as the new King of Spain while he was under Napoleonic French Guard.

Date	Mintage	F	VF	XF	Unc	BU
1808	1,600	85.00	135	225	550	—

KM# M2 REAL
Silver **Note:** This was a proclamation issue, most likely struck at the Guatemala City mint for Augustin I Iturbide, Emperor during the brief period that Central America was part of the short-lived Mexican Empire.

Date	Mintage	F	VF	XF	Unc	BU
1822	—	125	250	450	750	—

REPUBLIC

GENERAL COINAGE

KM# 1 CENTAVO
Copper Nickel

Date	Mintage	F	VF	XF	Unc	BU
1878	500,000	3.00	6.00	20.00	85.00	—
1878 Proof	—	Value: 650				

KM# 2 5 CENTAVOS
1.2500 g., 0.8000 Silver .0322 oz. **Note:** Examples known in coin and medal alignment.

Date	Mintage	F	VF	XF	Unc	BU
1880H	256,000	2.50	5.00	15.00	125	—
1880H Proof	—	Value: 450				

KM# 5 5 CENTAVOS
1.2500 g., 0.8000 Silver .0322 oz.

Date	Mintage	F	VF	XF	Unc	BU
1887H	1,000,000	2.00	4.00	10.00	50.00	—
1887H Proof	—	Value: 500				

KM# 8 5 CENTAVOS
Copper Nickel

Date	Mintage	F	VF	XF	Unc	BU
1898	2,000,000	0.75	2.00	8.00	35.00	—

KM# 9 5 CENTAVOS
Copper Nickel

Date	Mintage	F	VF	XF	Unc	BU
1899	2,000,000	0.50	1.50	7.00	25.00	—

KM# 3 10 CENTAVOS
2.5000 g., 0.8000 Silver .0643 oz.

Date	Mintage	F	VF	XF	Unc	BU
1880H	552,000	4.00	8.00	25.00	80.00	—
1880H Proof	—	Value: 500				

KM# 6 10 CENTAVOS
2.5000 g., 0.8000 Silver .0643 oz.

Date	Mintage	F	VF	XF	Unc	BU
1887H	1,500,000	1.00	2.50	10.00	60.00	—
1887H Proof	—	Value: 550				

KM# 4 20 CENTAVOS
5.0000 g., 0.8000 Silver .1286 oz. **Note:** Examples known in coin and medal alignment.

Date	Mintage	F	VF	XF	Unc	BU
1880H	288,000	3.00	7.50	35.00	140	—
1880H Proof	—	Value: 600				

KM# 7 20 CENTAVOS
5.0000 g., 0.8000 Silver .1286 oz.

Date	Mintage	F	VF	XF	Unc	BU
1887H	1,000,000	2.00	5.00	20.00	70.00	—
1887H Proof	—	Value: 700				

PATTERNS

INCLUDING OFF METAL STRIKES.

KM#	Date	Mintage	Identification	Mkt Val
Pn1	1860	—	Centavo.	2,250

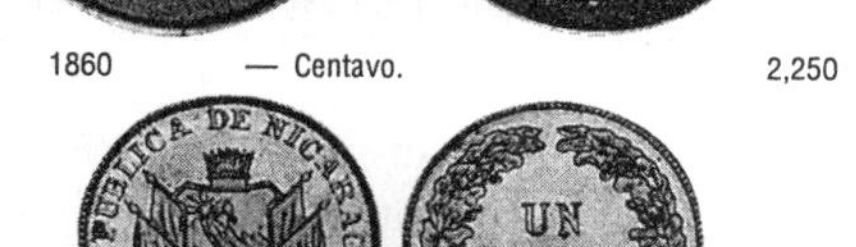

KM#	Date	Mintage	Identification	Mkt Val
Pn2	1878	—	Centavo. Copper.	400

KM#	Date	Mintage	Identification	Mkt Val
Pn3	1887E	—	2 Centavos. Copper.	450
PnA3	1880H	—	5 Centavos. Plain edge. KM2.	500
PnB3	1880 H	—	10 Centavos. Plain edge. KM3.	550
PnC3	1880H	—	20 Centavos. Plain edge. KM4.	650

KM#	Date	Mintage	Identification	Mkt Val
Pn4	1892	—	Centavo. Copper-Nickel.	325
Pn5	1892	—	Centavo. Copper.	325
Pn6	1892	—	Centavo. Aluminum.	375

KM#	Date	Mintage	Identification	Mkt Val
Pn7	1892	—	Centavo. Copper-Nickel.	325
Pn8	1892	—	Centavo. Copper.	325
Pn9	1892	—	Centavo. Aluminum.	375

PIEFORTS

KM#	Date	Mintage	Identification	Mkt Val
P1	1892	—	Centavo. Copper-Nickel.	325
P2	1892	—	Centavo. Copper.	325
P3	1892	—	Centavo. Aluminum.	375
P4	1892	—	Centavo. Copper-Nickel.	325
P5	1892	—	Centavo. Copper.	325
P6	1892	—	Centavo. Aluminum.	375

EL VIEJO

SPANISH COLONY

COLONIAL COINAGE

KM# 5 2 REALS
Silver **Obv:** V/IE/JO P/24 V **Note:** Type I.

Date	Mintage	Good	VG	F	VF	XF
(18)24	—	1,600	2,250	4,000	6,500	—

KM# 6 2 REALS
Silver **Obv:** V/IE/JO P/24/V **Rev:** P. L. 1824 **Note:** Type II - Sun over mountains.

Date	Mintage	Good	VG	F	VF	XF
1824	—	1,750	2,450	4,250	6,750	—

KM# 7 4 REALS
Silver **Obv:** V/IE/JO P/24/V **Note:** Type I.

Date	Mintage	Good	VG	F	VF	XF
(18)24 Rare	—	—	—	—	—	—

GRANADA

SPANISH COLONY

COLONIAL COINAGE

KM# 5 1/2 REAL
Silver **Rev:** J G/1823

Date	Mintage	Good	VG	F	VF	XF
1823	—	1,500	2,000	3,500	6,000	—

KM# 6 REAL
Silver **Rev:** D/24/G

Date	Mintage	Good	VG	F	VF	XF
(18)24	—	1,000	1,800	3,250	5,500	—

KM# 7 2 REALS
Silver **Rev:** D/24/G

Date	Mintage	Good	VG	F	VF	XF
(18)24	—	1,250	2,000	3,500	6,000	—

KM# 8 4 REALS
Silver **Obv:** J cross G **Rev:** D/24/G

Date	Mintage	Good	VG	F	VF	XF
(18)24 rare	—	—	—	—	—	—

MERCADO DE LEON

By executive decree, the government of Nicaragua on September 12, 1859, authorized the municipality of Leon to mint between 100 and 200 Pesos in copper cents and half cents. The first known documentation of this right being exercised came in

1877 when the Heaton Mint was contracted to strike the following pieces. The 1/12 Dime and 1/24 Dime were valued at a fraction of the United States dime as both the U.S. half dime and dime were authorized as legal tender and circulated heavily in Nicaragua during this period.

STATE

STANDARD COINAGE

KM# S1 1/24 DIME
Copper, 21.5 mm. **Edge:** Plain

Date	Mintage	F	VF	XF	Unc	BU
ND(1877)	13,000	75.00	150	300	550	—

KM# S2 1/12 DIME
Copper, 26.5 mm. **Edge:** Plain

Date	Mintage	F	VF	XF	Unc	BU
ND(1877)	6,600	100	200	400	650	—

NIGERIA

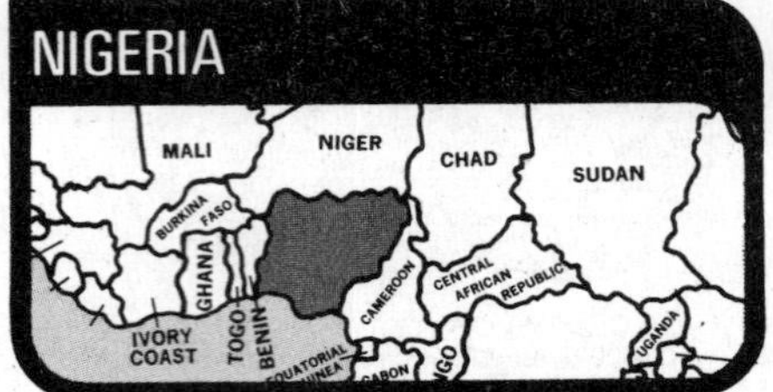

Nigeria, situated on the Atlantic coast of West Africa has an area of 356,669 sq. mi. (923,770 sq. km.).

Following the Napoleonic Wars, the British expanded their trade with the interior of Nigeria. The Berlin Conference of 1885 recognized British claims to a sphere of influence in that area, and in the following year the Royal Niger Company was chartered. Direct British control of the territory was initiated in 1900, and in 1914 the amalgamation of Northern and Southern Nigeria into the Colony and Protectorate of Nigeria was effected.

For earlier coinage refer to British West Africa.

REPUBLIC

TOKEN COINAGE

KM# Tn2 LAIRD (1/8 Penny)
Copper **Issuer:** Mac Gregor

Date	Mintage	F	VF	XF	Unc	BU
AH1274	1,858	50.00	100	180	300	—

Note: Three die varieties exist. Variously attributed to Guinea, Gold Coast, Sierra Leone and West Africa, this token, struck in 1858, was intended to circulate at the MacGregor Laird trading posts located along the Niger and Benue rivers. In 1885 this region became the British Protectorate of Nigeria

NORWAY

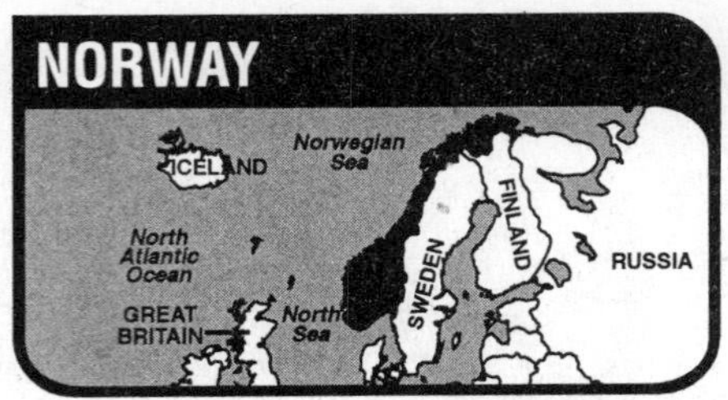

The Kingdom of Norway (*Norge, Noreg*), a constitutional monarchy located in northwestern Europe, has an area of 150,000sq. mi. (324,220 sq. km.), including the island territories of Spitzbergen (Svalbard) and Jan Mayen. Capital: Oslo (Christiana).

A united Norwegian kingdom was established in the 9th century, the era of the indomitable Norse Vikings who ranged far and wide, visiting the coasts of northwestern Europe, the Mediterranean, Greenland and North America. In the 13th century the Norse kingdom was united briefly with Sweden, then passed through inheritance in 1380 to the rule of Denmark which was maintained until 1814. In 1814 Norway fell again under the rule of Sweden.

RULERS
Danish, until 1814
Swedish, 1814-1905

MINT MARKS
(h) - Crossed hammers – Kongsberg

MINT OFFICIALS' INITIALS

Initial	Date	Name
B	1861	Brynjulf Bergslien
CHL, star(s)	1836-88	Caspar Herman Langberg in Kongsberg
I, IT	1880-1918	Ivar Trondsen, engraver
IAR		Angrid Austlid Rise, engraver
IGM	1797-1806	Johan Georg Madelung in Altona
IGP	1807-24	Johan Georg Prahm in Kongsberg
JMK	1825-36	Johan Michael Kruse in Kongsberg
M	1815-30	Gregorius Middelthun

MONETARY SYSTEM

1794-1873

120 Skilling = 1 Speciedaler

KINGDOM

STANDARD COINAGE

KM# 305.1 1/2 SKILLING
Copper

Date	Mintage	VG	F	VF	XF	Unc
1839	613,000	2.50	5.00	15.00	40.00	—
1840	2,558,000	2.00	4.00	12.00	35.00	—
1841	1,683,000	2.00	4.00	10.00	25.00	—

KM# 305.2 1/2 SKILLING
Copper **Rev:** Star below hammers

Date	Mintage	VG	F	VF	XF	Unc
1841	Inc. above	1.00	4.00	8.00	20.00	—

KM# 324 1/2 SKILLING
Copper

Date	Mintage	VG	F	VF	XF	Unc
1863	480,000	2.00	5.00	17.50	45.00	125

KM# 329 1/2 SKILLING
Copper

Date	Mintage	VG	F	VF	XF	Unc
1867	3,600,000	0.50	1.00	2.00	7.00	25.00

KM# 274.1 SKILLING
Copper, 25 mm. **Obv:** Crowned FR monogram **Rev:** Five-petalled rosettes, by 1 and below date

Date	Mintage	VG	F	VF	XF	Unc
1809	346,000	7.50	12.50	20.00	50.00	—

KM# 274.2 SKILLING

Copper **Rev:** Eight-petalled rosettes, by 1 and below date

Date	Mintage	VG	F	VF	XF	Unc
1809	Inc. above	7.50	12.50	20.00	50.00	—

KM# 274.3 SKILLING

Copper **Rev:** Ovals by 1 and below date

Date	Mintage	VG	F	VF	XF	Unc
1809	Inc. above	7.50	12.50	20.00	50.00	—

KM# 281 SKILLING

Copper

Date	Mintage	VG	F	VF	XF	Unc
1812	5,453,000	1.00	2.50	5.00	10.00	—
1812 Without crossed hammers below date	Inc. above	15.00	35.00	65.00	120	—

Note: Beware of removed mint mark or altered coin

KM# 284 SKILLING

Copper

Date	Mintage	VG	F	VF	XF	Unc
1816	1,659,000	4.00	10.00	30.00	100	—

KM# 286 SKILLING

Copper

Date	Mintage	VG	F	VF	XF	Unc
1819	3,817,000	4.00	12.00	35.00	75.00	—
1820	Inc. above	3.00	7.00	20.00	50.00	—
1824	6,000	30.00	60.00	125	325	—
1825	—	250	500	850	1,500	—
1827	34,000	25.00	45.00	100	250	—
1828	38,000	600	1,500	2,500	—	—
1831/28	1,440,000	35.00	60.00	135	265	—
1831	Inc. above	35.00	65.00	150	300	—
1832	Inc. above	20.00	40.00	85.00	200	—
1833	126,000	20.00	40.00	85.00	200	—
1834	—	1,250	1,750	—	—	—

KM# 335 SKILLING

Copper

Date	Mintage	VG	F	VF	XF	Unc
1870	1,200,000	1.00	2.00	10.00	20.00	75.00

KM# 270 2 SKILLING

1.5000 g., 0.2500 Silver .0120 oz.

Date	Mintage	VG	F	VF	XF	Unc
1801 IGM	1,109,000	2.00	5.00	10.00	20.00	—
1802 IGM	2,854,000	2.00	5.00	10.00	20.00	—
1803 IGM	2,410,000	2.00	5.00	10.00	20.00	—
1804 IGM	3,634,000	4.00	10.00	18.00	35.00	—
1805 IGM	2,412,000	3.00	8.00	15.00	30.00	—
1807 IGP	3,507,000	2.00	5.00	10.00	18.00	—

KM# 280.1 2 SKILLING

Copper **Rev:** Eight-petalled rosettes by 2 and below date

Date	Mintage	VG	F	VF	XF	Unc
1810	3,449,000	2.00	4.00	8.00	20.00	—

KM# 280.2 2 SKILLING

Copper **Rev:** Cross

Date	Mintage	VG	F	VF	XF	Unc
1810	Inc. above	2.00	4.00	8.00	20.00	—
1811	1,190,000	2.50	6.00	12.00	25.00	—

KM# 280.3 2 SKILLING

Copper **Rev:** Five-petalled rosettes by 2 and below date

Date	Mintage	VG	F	VF	XF	Unc
1811	—	2.50	6.00	12.00	25.00	—

KM# 295 2 SKILLING

Copper

Date	Mintage	VG	F	VF	XF	Unc
1822	963,000	7.00	15.00	45.00	110	—
1824	549,000	7.00	15.00	45.00	110	—
1825	510,000	10.00	30.00	85.00	200	—
1827	288,000	12.50	30.00	70.00	150	—
1828	453,000	12.50	30.00	70.00	150	—
1831/28	723,000	7.00	17.50	40.00	100	—
1831	Inc. above	7.00	20.00	45.00	115	—
1832	Inc. above	7.00	20.00	45.00	115	—
1833	60,000	8.00	22.50	50.00	120	—
1834	880,000	40.00	90.00	175	375	—

KM# 297 2 SKILLING

1.5000 g., 0.2500 Silver .0120 oz.

Date	Mintage	VG	F	VF	XF	Unc
1825	240,000	5.00	12.00	25.00	75.00	—

KM# 310 2 SKILLING

1.5000 g., 0.2500 Silver .0120 oz.

Date	Mintage	VG	F	VF	XF	Unc
1842	1,500,000	2.00	4.00	10.00	25.00	—
1843	Inc. above	3.00	10.00	20.00	40.00	—

KM# 336.1 2 SKILLING

1.5000 g., 0.2500 Silver .0120 oz. **Rev:** Rosettes

Date	Mintage	VG	F	VF	XF	Unc
1870	900,000	1.00	3.00	5.00	10.00	30.00
1871	900,000	1.00	3.00	5.00	10.00	30.00

KM# 336.2 2 SKILLING

1.5000 g., 0.2500 Silver .0120 oz. **Rev:** Stars

Date	Mintage	VG	F	VF	XF	Unc
1871	1,140,000	1.00	3.00	5.00	10.00	30.00

KM# 330.1 3 SKILLING

2.2500 g., 0.2500 Silver .0181 oz. **Rev:** Rosettes

Date	Mintage	VG	F	VF	XF	Unc
1868	499,000	2.00	5.00	10.00	20.00	55.00
1869	103,000	5.00	15.00	25.00	45.00	110

KM# 330.2 3 SKILLING

2.2500 g., 0.2500 Silver .0181 oz. **Rev:** Stars

Date	Mintage	VG	F	VF	XF	Unc
1869	600,000	2.00	5.00	10.00	20.00	55.00

KM# 338.1 3 SKILLING

2.2500 g., 0.2500 Silver .0181 oz. **Rev:** Rosettes

Date	Mintage	VG	F	VF	XF	Unc
1872	504,000	2.00	5.00	10.00	20.00	45.00

KM# 338.2 3 SKILLING

2.2500 g., 0.2500 Silver .0181 oz. **Rev:** Stars

Date	Mintage	VG	F	VF	XF	Unc
1872	576,000	2.00	5.00	8.00	16.00	45.00
1873	600,000	2.00	5.00	8.00	16.00	45.00

KM# 275.1 4 SKILLING

Copper **Rev:** Rosettes by 4 and below date

Date	Mintage	VG	F	VF	XF	Unc
1809	251,000	12.50	30.00	70.00	150	—

KM# 275.2 4 SKILLING

Copper **Rev:** Stars by 4 and below date

Date	Mintage	VG	F	VF	XF	Unc
1809	Inc. above	17.50	40.00	85.00	190	—
1810 Rare	—	—	—	—	—	—

KM# 276.1 4 SKILLING

Date	Mintage	VG	F	VF	XF	Unc
1809 IGP	2,228,000	6.00	1.00	35.50	—	—

KM# 276.2 4 SKILLING

2.0500 g., 0.2500 Silver .0165 oz. **Rev. Legend:** SKILLE =

Date	Mintage	VG	F	VF	XF	Unc
1809 IGP	Inc. above	3.00	6.00	14.00	32.50	—

KM# 298 4 SKILLING

3.0000 g., 0.2500 Silver .0241 oz.

Date	Mintage	VG	F	VF	XF	Unc
1825 JMK	333,000	5.00	10.00	25.00	60.00	—

KM# 311 4 SKILLING

3.0000 g., 0.2500 Silver .0241 oz.

Date	Mintage	VG	F	VF	XF	Unc
1842	750,000	3.00	7.00	25.00	75.00	—

KM# 337 4 SKILLING
3.0000 g., 0.2500 Silver .0241 oz.

Date	Mintage	VG	F	VF	XF	Unc
1871	559,000	3.00	10.00	15.00	25.00	65.00

KM# 282 6 SKILLING
Copper **Obv:** Crowned shield **Rev:** Dot after value

Date	Mintage	VG	F	VF	XF	Unc
1813	109,000	3.00	6.00	15.00	32.50	—

KM# 277 8 SKILLING (1/2 Mark)
2.7300 g., 0.3750 Silver .0329 oz.

Date	Mintage	VG	F	VF	XF	Unc
1809 IGP	1,350,000	5.00	10.00	20.00	50.00	—

KM# 285 8 SKILLING (1/2 Mark)
3.3700 g., 0.5000 Silver .0542 oz.

Date	Mintage	VG	F	VF	XF	Unc
1817 IGP	241,000	10.00	20.00	60.00	165	—

KM# 287 8 SKILLING (1/2 Mark)
3.3700 g., 0.5000 Silver .0542 oz.

Date	Mintage	VG	F	VF	XF	Unc
1819 IGP	101,000	15.00	35.00	100	200	—

KM# 299 8 SKILLING (1/2 Mark)
1.9300 g., 0.8750 Silver .0543 oz.

Date	Mintage	VG	F	VF	XF	Unc
1825	16,000	10.00	25.00	50.00	125	—
1827/5	14,000	15.00	30.00	65.00	140	—

KM# 283 12 SKILLING
Copper **Obv:** Crowned shield **Rev:** Damaged 3 in value

Date	Mintage	VG	F	VF	XF	Unc
1813	739,000	3.00	6.00	12.50	30.00	—

KM# 314.1 12 SKILLING
2.8900 g., 0.8750 Silver .813 oz. **Note:** Plain border.

Date	Mintage	VG	F	VF	XF	Unc
1845	631,000	5.00	10.00	22.50	50.00	—
1846	250,000	5.00	10.00	25.00	55.00	—
1847	256,000	5.00	10.00	25.00	55.00	—
1848	316,000	5.00	10.00	25.00	55.00	—

KM# 314.2 12 SKILLING
2.8900 g., 0.8750 Silver .813 oz. **Note:** Beaded border.

Date	Mintage	VG	F	VF	XF	Unc
1850	287,000	5.00	10.00	25.00	55.00	—
1850	Inc. above	5.00	10.00	25.00	55.00	—
1852	313,000	5.00	10.00	22.50	50.00	—
1853	360,000	5.00	10.00	22.50	50.00	—
1854	301,000	5.00	10.00	22.50	50.00	—
1855	450,000	5.00	10.00	22.50	50.00	—
1856/5	812,000	4.50	9.00	20.00	45.00	—
1856	Inc. above	4.00	7.00	19.00	40.00	—

KM# 320 12 SKILLING
2.8900 g., 0.8750 Silver .813 oz. **Obv:** Small head

Date	Mintage	VG	F	VF	XF	Unc
1861	2,500	250	500	950	1,700	3,000
1862	2,500,000	250	500	950	1,700	3,000

KM# 326 12 SKILLING
2.8900 g., 0.8750 Silver .813 oz. **Obv:** Large head

Date	Mintage	VG	F	VF	XF	Unc
1865	152,000	20.00	40.00	90.00	200	425

KM# 339 12 SKILLING
2.8900 g., 0.8750 Silver .813 oz.

Date	Mintage	VG	F	VF	XF	Unc
1873	490,000	15.00	25.00	50.00	100	200

KM# 288 24 SKILLING
7.3100 g., 0.6870 Silver .1615 oz.

Date	Mintage	VG	F	VF	XF	Unc
1819 IGP	50,000	25.00	50.00	90.00	175	—

KM# 296 24 SKILLING
5.7300 g., 0.8750 Silver .1612 oz.

Date	Mintage	VG	F	VF	XF	Unc
1823	125,000	40.00	80.00	160	350	—
1824	7,800	45.00	95.00	200	400	—

KM# 300 24 SKILLING
5.7300 g., 0.8750 Silver .1612 oz.

Date	Mintage	VG	F	VF	XF	Unc
1825	4,600	50.00	110	225	400	—
1827/5	27,000	40.00	75.00	150	300	—
1827	Inc. above	40.00	75.00	150	300	—
1830	5,800	80.00	165	275	550	—
1831 Rare	2,400	—	—	—	—	—
1833	—	125	250	400	700	—
1834	—	125	250	400	700	—
1835	2,500	85.00	175	325	600	—
1836	2,500	110	220	375	650	—

KM# 315.1 24 SKILLING
5.7800 g., 0.8750 Silver .1626 oz. **Note:** Plain border.

Date	Mintage	VG	F	VF	XF	Unc
1845	357,000	8.00	20.00	40.00	75.00	—
1846	383,000	8.00	20.00	40.00	75.00	—
1847	217,000	10.00	25.00	50.00	100	—
1848	150,000	15.00	30.00	60.00	125	—

KM# 315.2 24 SKILLING
5.7800 g., 0.8750 Silver .1626 oz. **Note:** Beaded border.

Date	Mintage	VG	F	VF	XF	Unc
1850	102,000	10.00	25.00	50.00	125	—
1852	254,000	10.00	25.00	50.00	100	—
1853	327,000	10.00	25.00	50.00	100	—
1854	212,000	15.00	30.00	60.00	125	—
1855	204,000	10.00	25.00	50.00	100	—

KM# 321 24 SKILLING
5.7800 g., 0.8750 Silver .1626 oz. **Obv:** Small head

Date	Mintage	VG	F	VF	XF	Unc
1861 Rare	13	—	—	—	—	—
Note: Heritage Long Beach sale 10-88 P/L BU realized $11,275						
1862	1,200	300	600	1,100	2,100	3,600

KM# 327 24 SKILLING
5.7800 g., 0.8750 Silver .1626 oz. **Obv:** Large head

Date	Mintage	VG	F	VF	XF	Unc
1865	79,000	40.00	75.00	150	325	600

KM# 271 1/15 SPECIE DALER
3.3700 g., 0.5000 Silver .0542 oz. **Obv:** Crowned oval arms **Rev:** Value, date

Date	Mintage	VG	F	VF	XF	Unc
1801 IGM	382,000	5.00	10.00	18.00	55.00	—
1802 IGM	149,000	5.00	10.00	18.00	55.00	—

KM# 272 1/5 SPECIE DALER
7.3100 g., 0.6870 Silver .1615 oz.

Date	Mintage	VG	F	VF	XF	Unc
1801 IGM	163,000	15.00	30.00	65.00	120	—
1803 IGM	92,000	15.00	30.00	65.00	120	—

KM# 266 1/3 SPECIE DALER
9.6300 g., 0.8750 Silver .2709 oz. **Note:** Similar to KM#273.

Date	Mintage	VG	F	VF	XF	Unc
1801 IGM	108,000	25.00	55.00	110	250	—
1802 IGM	65,000	30.00	60.00	120	275	—
1803 IGM	24,000	35.00	65.00	125	285	—

KM# 273 1/3 SPECIE DALER
9.6300 g., 0.8750 Silver .2709 oz. **Obv:** Bust right without bow, P.G. below portrait

Date	Mintage	VG	F	VF	XF	Unc
1803 IGM	Inc. above	125	250	500	1,250	—

KM# 289 1/2 SPECIE DALER
14.4500 g., 0.8750 Silver .4065 oz.

Date	Mintage	VG	F	VF	XF	Unc
1819	302,000	55.00	100	235	500	—
1821	69,000	35.00	55.00	125	225	—
1823/1	6,100	100	200	400	750	—
1824/1	33,000	40.00	80.00	150	275	—
1824	Inc. above	40.00	80.00	150	275	—

KM# 302 1/2 SPECIE DALER
14.4500 g., 0.8750 Silver .4065 oz.

Date	Mintage	VG	F	VF	XF	Unc
1827 SKI:	70,000	35.00	70.00	125	265	—
1827. SKI.	Inc. above	35.00	70.00	125	265	—
1829	5,100	250	450	800	1,250	—
1830	8,000	90.00	175	350	625	—
1831	9,000	90.00	175	350	625	—
1832	4,700	90.00	175	350	625	—
1833	1,500	250	450	800	1,250	—
1834/29	18,000	40.00	80.00	150	350	—
1834	Inc. above	40.00	80.00	150	350	—
1835	9,000	40.00	80.00	150	350	—
1835 Rare, star below mint mark	Inc. above	—	—	—	—	—
1836	4,000	60.00	125	250	425	—

KM# 312 1/2 SPECIE DALER
14.4500 g., 0.8750 Silver .4065 oz.

Date	Mintage	VG	F	VF	XF	Unc
1844	231,000	25.00	50.00	100	225	—

KM# 316 1/2 SPECIE DALER
14.4500 g., 0.8750 Silver .4065 oz.

Date	Mintage	VG	F	VF	XF	Unc
1846	146,000	35.00	60.00	125	250	—
1847	47,000	35.00	60.00	125	250	—
1848	15,000	40.00	75.00	150	350	—
1849	142,000	30.00	50.00	100	225	—
1850	Inc. above	30.00	50.00	100	225	—
1855	10,000	125	250	500	900	—

KM# 322 1/2 SPECIE DALER
14.4500 g., 0.8750 Silver .4065 oz.

Date	Mintage	VG	F	VF	XF	Unc
1861 Rare	500	—	—	—	—	—

Note: Oslo Mynthandel sale 10/98, XF realized approximately $12,000. Heritage Long Beach sale 10-88 P/L BU realized $14,575

Date	Mintage	VG	F	VF	XF	Unc
1861 B below bust, Rare	13	—	—	—	—	—

Note: Oslo Mynthandel sale 4/02, uncirculated realized approximately $43,200.

Date	Mintage	VG	F	VF	XF	Unc
1862	64,000	150	250	400	700	—

KM# 328 1/2 SPECIE DALER
14.4500 g., 0.8750 Silver .4065 oz. **Obv:** Larger head

Date	Mintage	VG	F	VF	XF	Unc
1865 Rare	700	—	—	—	—	—

Note: Oslo Mynthandel sale 10/97, F/VF realized approximately $9,300. Oslo Mynthandel sale 10-89 VF realized $12,750

KM# 340 1/2 SPECIE DALER
14.4500 g., 0.8750 Silver .4065 oz.

Date	Mintage	VG	F	VF	XF	Unc
1873	4,200	3,000	4,500	6,000	8,800	13,000

KM# 290 SPECIE DALER
28.8900 g., 0.8750 Silver .8127 oz.

Date	Mintage	VG	F	VF	XF	Unc
1819 IGP	24,000	125	250	600	1,000	—
1821 IGP	101,000	85.00	135	300	625	—
1823 IGP	16,000	250	500	1,000	1,850	—
1824/1 JMK	121,000	75.00	125	275	625	—
1824 JMK	Inc. above	75.00	125	275	625	—

KM# 301 SPECIE DALER
28.8900 g., 0.8750 Silver .8127 oz.

Date	Mintage	VG	F	VF	XF	Unc
1826	25,000	80.00	150	325	650	—
1826 Initial M	Inc. above	750	1,500	3,000	5,500	—
1827/6	132,000	60.00	115	225	425	—
1827	Inc. above	60.00	115	225	425	—
1829/7	16,000	100	200	425	750	—
1829	Inc. above	100	200	425	750	—
1830	26,000	85.00	135	300	600	—
1831	31,000	100	225	475	800	—
1832	24,000	100	225	475	800	—
1833	2,732	425	850	1,600	2,600	—
1834	103,000	60.00	100	225	425	—
1835	40,000	60.00	100	225	425	—
1835 Star below mint mark	Inc. above	200	500	950	1,600	—
1836	52,000	65.00	150	275	500	—

KM# 313 SPECIE DALER
28.8900 g., 0.8750 Silver .8127 oz.

Date	Mintage	VG	F	VF	XF	Unc
1844	302,000	50.00	100	200	475	—

KM# 317 SPECIE DALER
28.8900 g., 0.8750 Silver .8127 oz.

Date	Mintage	VG	F	VF	XF	Unc
1846	67,000	60.00	100	200	350	—
1847	140,000	60.00	100	200	350	—
1848	81,000	60.00	100	200	350	—
1849	114,000	60.00	100	200	350	—
1850	124,000	60.00	100	200	350	—
1855	148,000	60.00	100	200	350	—
1856	114,000	60.00	100	200	350	—
1857	160,000	60.00	100	200	350	—

KM# 323 SPECIE DALER
28.8900 g., 0.8750 Silver .8127 oz. **Rev:** Similar to KM#313

Date	Mintage	VG	F	VF	XF	Unc
1861	44,000	150	250	500	950	1,900
1861 Rare, B below bust	13	—	—	—	—	—
1862	62,000	125	225	450	800	1,750

KM# 325 SPECIE DALER
28.8900 g., 0.8750 Silver .8127 oz. **Rev:** Similar to KM#313

Date	Mintage	VG	F	VF	XF	Unc
1864	130,000	90.00	175	350	600	1,200
1865	86,000	90.00	175	350	600	1,200
1867	30,000	200	400	750	1,300	2,750
1868	114,000	120	200	400	750	1,750
1869	57,000	110	175	375	650	1,450

DECIMAL COINAGE

KM# 352 ORE
2.0000 g., Bronze **Note:** Varieties exist.

Date	Mintage	VG	F	VF	XF	BU
1876	8,000,000	—	5.00	10.00	20.00	80.00
1877	2,166,000	—	15.00	25.00	50.00	150
1878	1,834,000	—	25.00	40.00	60.00	200
1884	3,378,000	—	6.00	10.00	20.00	80.00
1885	622,000	—	70.00	115	150	250
1889	3,000,000	—	7.00	10.00	20.00	55.00
1891	3,000,000	—	7.00	10.00	20.00	55.00
1893	3,000,000	—	7.00	10.00	20.00	55.00
1897	3,000,000	—	7.00	10.00	20.00	55.00
1899	4,500,000	—	2.00	4.00	12.00	45.00
1902	4,500,000	—	2.00	4.00	12.00	45.00

KM# 353 2 ORE
4.0000 g., Bronze

Date	Mintage	VG	F	VF	XF	BU
1876	1,774,000	—	4.00	7.00	25.00	100
1877	1,976,000	—	3.00	6.00	15.00	80.00
1884	1,000,000	—	5.00	9.00	20.00	100
1889	1,000,000	—	3.00	6.00	13.50	65.00
1891	1,000,000	—	2.00	5.00	12.00	60.00
1893	1,000,000	—	2.00	5.00	12.00	60.00
1897	1,000,000	—	2.00	5.00	12.00	60.00
1899	1,000,000	—	2.00	5.00	12.00	60.00
1902	1,005,000	—	1.50	4.00	12.00	125

KM# 349 5 ORE
8.0000 g., Bronze

Date	Mintage	VG	F	VF	XF	BU
1875	354,000	—	22.00	45.00	130	650
1876	1,647,000	—	3.50	10.00	50.00	200
1878	500,000	—	6.00	25.00	85.00	400
1896	1,000,000	—	2.50	6.00	40.00	185
1899	700,000	—	2.50	6.00	40.00	185
1902	705,000	—	2.50	6.00	45.00	300

KM# 345 10 ORE
1.5000 g., 0.4000 Silver 0.0193 oz.

Date	Mintage	VG	F	VF	XF	BU
1874	2,000,000	—	10.00	25.00	60.00	200
1875	996,000	—	25.00	45.00	100	275

KM# 350 10 ORE
1.5000 g., 0.4000 Silver .0192 oz.

Date	Mintage	VG	F	VF	XF	BU
1875	1,008,000	—	45.00	75.00	150	500
1876	1,992,000	—	10.00	20.00	40.00	150
1877	588,000	—	60.00	100	225	625
1878	612,000	—	30.00	60.00	125	500
1880	600,000	—	25.00	45.00	75.00	200
1882	760,000	—	17.50	30.00	50.00	95.00
1883	1,250,000	—	12.50	20.00	40.00	70.00
1888	500,000	—	20.00	35.00	65.00	125
1889	750,000	—	12.50	20.00	32.50	75.00
1890	1,000,000	—	8.00	15.00	27.50	60.00
1892	2,000,000	—	8.00	15.00	27.50	60.00
1894	1,500,000	—	8.00	15.00	27.50	60.00
1897	1,500,000	—	5.00	10.00	25.00	55.00
1898	2,000,000	—	5.00	10.00	25.00	55.00
1899	2,500,000	—	5.00	10.00	25.00	55.00
1901	2,021,100	—	5.00	10.00	22.50	50.00
1903	1,500,700	—	5.00	10.00	22.50	50.00

KM# 354 25 ORE
2.4000 g., 0.6000 Silver .0463 oz.

Date	Mintage	VG	F	VF	XF	BU
1876	3,200,000	—	10.00	20.00	50.00	165

KM# 360 25 ORE
2.4200 g., 0.6000 Silver .0463 oz.

Date	Mintage	VG	F	VF	XF	BU
1896	400,000	10.00	25.00	40.00	100	300
1898	400,000	10.00	25.00	40.00	100	300
1899	600,000	5.00	10.00	20.00	50.00	125
1900	400,000	7.00	20.00	40.00	85.00	250
1901	606,900	5.00	10.00	25.00	55.00	120
1902	611,700	5.00	10.00	25.00	55.00	120
1904	600,000	5.00	10.00	25.00	55.00	120

KM# 346 50 ORE (15 Skilling)
5.0000 g., 0.6000 Silver .0964 oz.

Date	Mintage	VG	F	VF	XF	BU
1874	160,000	—	70.00	100	225	650
1875	640,000	—	75.00	110	250	700

KM# 356 50 ORE (15 Skilling)
5.0000 g., 0.6000 Silver .0964 oz. **Rev:** Without 15 SK

Date	Mintage	VG	F	VF	XF	BU
1877	800,000	7.50	20.00	65.00	175	550
1880	120,000	40.00	80.00	175	350	800
1885	100,000	40.00	80.00	175	375	850
1887	200,000	15.00	30.00	65.00	125	350
1888	100,000	25.00	60.00	100	250	700
1889	200,000	9.00	17.50	35.00	75.00	225
1891	400,000	5.00	10.00	26.00	65.00	185
1893	600,000	4.00	7.50	24.00	65.00	185
1895	200,000	6.50	12.50	26.00	65.00	185
1896	500,000	6.50	12.50	26.00	70.00	225
1897	200,000	12.00	22.50	40.00	85.00	275
1898	300,000	6.50	12.50	26.00	70.00	190
1899	200,000	7.50	15.00	30.00	85.00	300
1900	300,000	4.00	8.00	24.00	65.00	185
1901	404,000	4.00	8.00	24.00	65.00	185
1902	301,200	4.00	8.00	24.00	65.00	185
1904	100,500	35.00	70.00	120	260	550

KM# 351 KRONE (30 Skilling)
7.5000 g., 0.8000 Silver .1929 oz.

Date	Mintage	VG	F	VF	XF	BU
1875	600,000	—	100	175	325	1,400

KM# 357 KRONE (30 Skilling)
7.5000 g., 0.8000 Silver .1929 oz. **Note:** Without 30 SK

Date	Mintage	VG	F	VF	XF	BU
1877	1,000,000	—	20.00	60.00	185	625
1878	60,000	—	500	950	2,100	6,500
1879	140,000	—	50.00	165	425	1,150
1881	80,000	—	80.00	200	500	1,200
1882	120,000	—	50.00	125	375	1,000
1885	100,000	—	45.00	90.00	275	725
1887	100,000	—	40.00	85.00	250	650
1888	75,000	—	100	275	550	1,800
1889	200,000	—	25.00	50.00	115	400
1890	200,000	—	25.00	50.00	115	400
1892	150,000	—	30.00	50.00	125	425
1893	100,000	—	30.00	50.00	125	425
1894	100,000	—	35.00	65.00	150	500
1895/4	100,000	—	32.50	55.00	125	425
1895	Inc. above	—	35.00	65.00	165	450
1897	250,000	—	25.00	45.00	90.00	275
1898	150,000	—	25.00	50.00	125	475
1900	250,000	—	20.00	45.00	90.00	250
1901	151,800	10.00	20.00	50.00	120	500
1904	100,100	30.00	60.00	125	215	525

KM# 359 2 KRONER
15.0000 g., 0.8000 Silver .3858 oz. **Note:** Restrikes are made by the Royal Mint, Norway, in gold, silver and bronze.

Date	Mintage	VG	F	VF	XF	BU
1878	300,000	15.00	30.00	95.00	300	900
1885	25,000	150	275	475	1,100	2,800
1887	25,000	150	275	475	1,100	2,800
1888	25,000	150	300	525	1,350	3,500
1890	100,000	20.00	45.00	75.00	200	625
1892	50,000	30.00	60.00	150	325	1,200
1893	75,000	25.00	50.00	100	250	800
1894	75,000	25.00	50.00	100	250	800
1897	50,000	30.00	70.00	175	400	1,500
1898	50,000	30.00	70.00	135	300	1,250
1900	125,000	20.00	35.00	55.00	140	450
1902	153,100	20.00	35.00	55.00	140	450
1904	75,600	22.00	45.00	85.00	200	500

KM# 347 10 KRONER (2-1/2 Speciedaler)
4.4803 g., 0.9000 Gold .1296 oz.

Date	Mintage	VG	F	VF	XF	Unc
1874	24,000	—	200	450	700	1,000

KM# 358 10 KRONER (2-1/2 Speciedaler)
4.4803 g., 0.9000 Gold .1296 oz.

Date	Mintage	VG	F	VF	XF	Unc
1877	20,000	—	250	450	650	950
1902	24,100	—	100	200	375	600

KM# 348 20 KRONER (5 Speciedaler)
8.9606 g., 0.9000 Gold .2593 oz.

Date	Mintage	VG	F	VF	XF	Unc
1874	198,000	—	100	150	300	500
1875	105,000	—	100	150	300	450

KM# 355 20 KRONER (5 Speciedaler)
8.9600 g., 0.9000 Gold .2593 oz.

Date	Mintage	VG	F	VF	XF	Unc
1876	109,000	—	110	150	250	400
1877	38,000	—	150	250	450	700
1878	139,000	—	110	150	225	375
1879	46,000	—	110	150	225	375
1883	36,000	—	3,000	6,000	9,000	12,500
1886	101,000	—	110	150	225	400

PATTERNS

Including off metal strikes

KM#	Date	Mintage	Identification	Mkt Val

KM#	Date	Mintage	Identification	Mkt Val
Pn39	1837	—	1/2 Skilling.	—

KM#	Date	Mintage	Identification	Mkt Val
PnA39	1813	—	Skilling. Copper.	—
PnB39	1809	—	Skilling. Copper.	—
PnC39	1813	—	Skilling. Copper.	—
PnD39	1816	—	Skilling. Copper.	—
PnE39	1836	—	2 Skilling. Copper.	—
PnF39	1837	—	1/2 Skilling. Copper.	—
PnA40	1837	—	Skilling. Copper.	—
PnB40	1849	—	12 Skilling. Silver. 2.8900 g.	—
PnC40	1849	—	24 Skilling. Silver. 5.7800 g.	—
PnD40	1866	—	1/2 Skilling. Copper.	—
PnE40	1870	—	Skilling. Copper. with PROVE.	—

PARAGUAY

The Republic of Paraguay, a landlocked country in the heart of South America surrounded by Argentina, Bolivia and Brazil, has an area of 157,048 sq. mi. (406,750 sq. km.).

Paraguay was first visited by Alejo Garcia, a shipwrecked Spaniard, in 1524. The interior was explored by Sebastian Cabot in 1527 and 1528, when he sailed up the Parana and Paraguay rivers. Asuncion, which would become the center of a Spanish colonial province embracing much of southern South America, was established by the Spanish explorer Juan de Salazar on Aug. 15,1537. For 150 years the history of Paraguay was largely the history of the agricultural colonies established by the Jesuits in the south and east to Christianize the Indians. In 1811, following the outbreak of the South American wars of independence, Paraguayan patriots overthrew the local Spanish authorities and proclaimed their country's independence.

During the Triple Alliance War (1864-1870) in which Paraguay faced Argentina, Brazil and Uruguay, Asuncion's ladies gathered in an Assembly on Feb. 24, 1867 and decided to give up their jewelry in order to help the national defense. The President of the Republic, Francisco Solano Lopez accepted the offering and ordered one twentieth of it be used to mint the first Paraguayan gold coins according to the Decree of the 11th of Sept.,1867.

Two dies were made, one by Bouvet, and another by an American, Leonard Charles, while only the die made by Bouvet was eventually used.

MINT MARKS
HF – Hugillen Ferres, LeLocle, Switzerland

CONTRACTORS
(Chas. J.) SHAW - for Ralph Heaton, Birmingham Mint

MONETARY SYSTEM
100 Centesimos = 1 Peso

REPUBLIC

REAL COINAGE

KM# 1.1 1/12 REAL
Copper **Obv:** Denomination and date **Rev:** Lion in wreath, liberty cap on pole above **Note:** Struck at Birmingham. Varieties exist in the lions tail, the wreath and bow.

Date	Mintage	F	VF	XF	Unc	BU
1845	2,880,000	7.00	20.00	60.00	175	—

KM# 1.2 1/12 REAL
Copper **Note:** Crude issue struck at Asuncion Mint.

Date	Mintage	F	VF	XF	Unc	BU
1845	288,000	15.00	45.00	125	285	—

Note: Struck with medal die alignment. Coin strike varieties exist. After 1847 they were revalued at 1/24th Real.

KM# A2 4 PESOS FUERTES
6.5700 g., 0.9000 Gold .1901 oz. **Note:** First Paraguayan gold coin.

Date	Mintage	F	VF	XF	Unc	BU
1867	—	5,500	8,500	11,500	—	—

CUT AND COUNTERMARKED COINAGE

WAR OF THE TRIPLE ALLIANCE

In 1864 Brazil sent troops into Uruguay to help quell a civil war. Paraguay, which had harbored border disputes with both Brazil and Argentina, took this occasion to declare war on Brazil. In 1865, the Paraguayan military attempted to cross Argentina with hopes of attacking southern Brazil. This armed aggression pushed Argentina, Brazil and Uruguay to form a triple alliance against Paraguay with the intent to overthrow their government and settle all boundary disputes on the terms of the allies.

The resulting War of the Triple Alliance lasted until March of 1870, decimating the Paraguayan population and leaving them at the mercy of their neighbors. New borders were established with Brazil in 1872 and Argentina in 1876, at which time all occupation troops were withdrawn.

During the war both Brazil and Paraguay used some cut and countermarked coins as emergency currency. Spanish and Spanish colonial coins were already in circulation and cut fractions were often being used in local trade. These pieces became the hosts for Brazilian countermarks in denominations of 100 Reis, 200 Reis and 400 Reis, as well as Paraguayan countermarks in denominations of 1 Real, 2 Reales and 4 Pesos Fuertes. Many examples have crenulated, curved or wavy edge cuts.

All cut coins, including these emergency countermarked issues, were outlawed in Paraguay by decree of February 24, 1872.

KM# B2 REAL
3.2000 g., Silver **Countermark:** 1 on rounded hexagonal field of horizontal lines **Note:** Countermark applied to 1/4 cut of Bolivian 4 Soles.

Date	Host Date	Good	VG	F	VF	XF
ND(1865-1872)	1830	75.00	140	200	300	—

KM# C2 REAL
Silver **Countermark:** Incuse 1 **Note:** Countermark applied to 1/4 cut of Bolivian 4 Soles.

Date	Host Date	Good	VG	F	VF	XF
ND(1865-1872)	18xx	60.00	100	185	250	—

KM# D2 2 REALES
6.0000 g., Silver **Countermark:** 2 on rounded hexagonal field of horizontal lines **Note:** Countermark applied to 1/2 cut of Bolivian 4 Soles.

Date	Host Date	Good	VG	F	VF	XF
ND(1865-1872)	1830 Rare	—	—	—	—	—

KM# E2 4 PESOS FUERTES
6.2470 g., Gold **Countermark:** Incuse 4 **Edge:** Oblique edge reeding **Note:** Countermark applied to 1/4 cut of Spanish or Spanish Colonial 8 Escudos. Of the two know examples of this type, one has a weight of 6.247g, while the other weighs 6.70g.

Date	Host Date	Good	VG	F	VF	XF
ND(1865-1872)	17xx 2 Known	—	—	—	—	—

DECIMAL COINAGE

100 CENTAVOS (CENTESIMOS) = PESO

KM# 2 CENTESIMO

Copper **Rev:** SHAW to right of date

Date	Mintage	F	VF	XF	Unc	BU
1870	—	2.00	5.00	20.00	45.00	—

KM# 3 2 CENTESIMOS

Copper **Rev:** SHAW to right of date

Date	Mintage	F	VF	XF	Unc	BU
1870	—	3.00	8.00	30.00	65.00	—

KM# 4.1 4 CENTESIMOS

Copper **Rev:** SHAW to right of date

Date	Mintage	F	VF	XF	Unc	BU
1870	—	4.00	12.00	40.00	85.00	—

KM# 4.2 4 CENTESIMOS

Copper **Obv:** Without ribbon bow on sprays **Rev:** Without SHAW to right of date **Note:** Crude issue struck at Asuncion.

Date	Mintage	VG	F	VF	XF	Unc
1870	—	50.00	100	200	500	—

KM# 4.3 4 CENTESIMOS

Copper **Obv:** Without ribbon bow on sprays **Rev:** SAEZ to right of date **Note:** Crude issue struck at Asuncion. Varieties exist.

Date	Mintage	VG	F	VF	XF	Unc
1870	—	50.00	75.00	150	300	—

KM# 6 5 CENTAVOS

Copper-Nickel

Date	Mintage	F	VF	XF	Unc	BU
1900	400,000	2.00	9.00	27.50	85.00	—

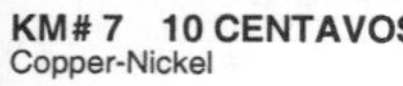

KM# 7 10 CENTAVOS

Copper-Nickel

Date	Mintage	F	VF	XF	Unc	BU
1900	800,000	1.50	5.00	18.00	45.00	—

KM# 8 20 CENTAVOS

Copper-Nickel

Date	Mintage	F	VF	XF	Unc	BU
1900	500,000	1.50	5.00	22.50	75.00	—

KM# 5 PESO

25.0000 g., 0.9000 Silver .7233 oz.

Date	Mintage	F	VF	XF	Unc	BU
1889	600,000	65.00	125	250	425	—

Note: Unknown quantity melted

PATTERNS

INCLUDING OFF METAL STRIKES

KM#	Date	Mintage	Identification	Mkt Val
Pn1	1854	—	10 Reales. Lead center. Silver Shell outer limit. Medal rotation.	3,500
Pn2	1854	—	10 Reales. Lead center. Silver Shell outer limit. Coin die rotation.	3,500
PnA2	1854	—	10 Reales. Tin center. Silver Shell outer limit.	3,500
PnA3	1854	—	10 Reales. Silver. Reeded edge.	6,500
Pn3	1855	—	4 Pesos. Gold.	—
Pn4	1855	—	4 Pesos. Silver.	—
Pn5	1855	—	4 Pesos. Gilt Silver.	—
Pn6	1855	—	4 Pesos. Copper.	—
Pn7	1855	—	10 Reales. Silver. Reeded edge. Medal die rotation.	6,500
Pn8	1855	—	10 Reales. Silver. Reeded edge. Coin die rotation.	6,500
Pn9	1855	—	10 Reales. Silver. Plain edge. Coin die rotation.	6,500
Pn10	1855	—	10 Reales. Pewter.	6,000
Pn11	1864	—	10 Reales. Silver. Coarse reeded edge.	5,750
Pn12	1864	—	10 Reales. Silver. Fine reeded edge.	5,750
Pn13	1864	—	10 Reales. Pewter. Plain edge.	5,750
Pn14	1866	—	10 Reales. Silver. Reeded edge.	5,750
Pn15	1867	—	10 Reales. Silver. Reeded edge. Small 7.	5,250
Pn16	1867	—	10 Reales. Silver. Reeded edge. Large 7.	5,250
Pn17	1867	—	10 Reales. Copper. Reeded edge. Small 7.	5,000
Pn18	1867	—	4 Pesos. Gold.	16,500
PnA19	1867	—	4 Pesos. Silver.	—
Pn19	1867	—	4 Pesos. Copper.	—

KM#	Date	Mintage Identification	Mkt Val
Pn20	1867	— 1/4 Real. Gold.	—
Pn21	1868	— 2 Centimos. Brass.	165
Pn22	1868	— 2 Centimes. German Silver.	300
Pn24	1868	— 2 Reales. Copper. Thin planchet.	—
Pn26	1868	— 2 Reales. Silver. 24 mm. Reeded edge. large date.	1,250
Pn27	1868	— 2 Reales. Silver. 22 mm.	850
Pn23	1868	— 2 Reales. Copper. Thick planchet.	—
Pn29	1869	— 2 Reales. Silver. Thin planchet, broad flan.	1,850
Pn30	1869	— 2 Reales. Silver. 24 mm. Thick planchet, small flan.	1,750
Pn31	1869	— 2 Reales. Copper. Thick planchet.	—
Pn32	1869	— 2 Reales. Copper. Thin planchet.	—
Pn34	1870	— 2 Centesimos. Silvered Copper. KM4.1.	—
Pn33	1870	— 2 Centesimos. Silvered Copper. KM3.	—
Pn35	1873	— 5 Pesos. Gold.	7,500
Pn36	1873	— 5 Pesos. Silver.	—

KM#	Date	Mintage Identification	Mkt Val
Pn37	1888	— Peso. Silver.	1,650
Pn38	1888	— Peso. Aluminum.	1,650
Pn39	1888	— Peso. Copper.	1,650

PIEFORTS

KM#	Date	Mintage Identification	Mkt Val
P1	1888	— Peso. Silver.	3,500

TRIAL STRIKES

KM#	Date	Mintage Identification	Mkt Val
TS1	1854	— 10 Reales. Lead center. Silver Shell outer limit. Reverse.	—
TS2	1854	— 10 Reales. Silvered Copper. Reverse.	—
TS3	1855	— 10 Reales. Lead center. Silver Shell outer limit. Reverse.	—

The Republic of Peru, located on the Pacific coast of South America has an area of 496,225 sq. mi. (1,285,220sq. km.).

Once part of the great Inca Empire that reached from northern Ecuador to central Chile, the conquest of Peru by Francisco Pizarro began in 1531. Desirable as the richest of the Spanish viceroyalties, it was torn by warfare between avaricious Spaniards until the arrival in 1569 of Francisco de Toledo, who initiated 2-1/2 centuries of efficient colonial rule, which made Lima the most aristocratic colonial capital and the stronghold of Spain's American possessions. Jose de San Martin of Argentina proclaimed Peru's independence on July 28, 1821; Simon Bolivar of Venezuela secured it in December, 1824 when he defeated the last Spanish army in South America. After several futile attempts to re-establish its South American empire, Spain recognized Peru's independence in 1879.

Andres de Santa Cruz, whose mother was a high-ranking Inca, was the best of Bolivia's early presidents, and temporarily united Peru and Bolivia 1836-39, thus realizing his dream of a Peruvian/Bolivian confederation. This prompted the separate coinages of North and South Peru. Peruvian resistance and Chilean intervention finally broke up the confederation, sending Santa Cruz into exile. A succession of military strongman presidents ruled Peru until Marshall Castilla revitalized Peruvian politics in themid-19th century and repulsed Spain's attempt to reclaim its one-time colony. Subsequent loss of southern territory to Chile in the War of the Pacific, 1879-81, and gradually increasing rejection of foreign economic domination, combined with recent serious inflation, affected the country numismatically.

As a result of the discovery of silver at Potosi in 1545, a mint was eventually authorized in 1565with the first coinage taking place in 1568. The mint had an uneven life span during the Spanish Colonial period from 1568-72. It was closed from 1573-76, reopened from 1577-88. It remained closed until 1659-1660 when an unauthorized coinage in both silver and gold were struck. After being closed in 1660, it remained closed until 1684 when it struck cob style coins until 1752.

RULERS

Spanish until 1822

MINT MARKS

AREQUIPA, AREQ = Arequipa
AYACUCHO = Ayacucho
(B) = Brussels
CUZCO (monogram), Cuzco, Co. Cuzco
L, LIMAE (monogram), Lima
(monogram), LIMA = Lima
(L) = London
PASCO (monogram), Pasco, Paz, Po= Pasco

NOTE: The LIMAE monogram appears in three forms. The early LM monogram form looks like a dotted L with M. The later LIMAE monogram has all the letters of LIMAE more readily distinguishable. The third form appears as an M monogram during early Republican issues.

MINT ASSAYERS INITIALS

The letter(s) following the dates of Peruvian coins are the assayer's initials appearing on the coins. They generally appear at the 11 o'clock position on the Colonial coinage and at the 5 o'clock position along the rim on the obverse or reverse on the Republican coinage.

MONETARY SYSTEM

16 Reales = 2 Pesos = 1 Escudo

SPANISH COLONY

MILLED COINAGE

KM# 102.2 1/4 REAL

0.8458 g., 0.8960 Silver .0244 oz. ASW **Mint:** Lima **Obverse:** Castle, L at left, 1/4 at right

Date	VG	F	VF	XF	Unc
1801L	10.00	60.00	80.00	100	—
1802L	40.00	60.00	80.00	100	—
1803L	40.00	60.00	80.00	100	—
1804L	40.00	60.00	80.00	100	—
1805L	40.00	60.00	80.00	100	—
1806L	40.00	60.00	80.00	100	—

Date	VG	F	VF	XF	Unc
1807L	40.00	60.00	80.00	100	—
1808L	40.00	60.00	80.00	100	—

KM# 108 1/4 REAL
0.8458 g., 0.8960 Silver .0244 oz. ASW **Mint:** Lima **Obverse:** Castle, L at left, 1/4 at right

Date	VG	F	VF	XF	Unc
1809L	40.00	60.00	80.00	100	—

Note: Most "1809" dates found are actually dated 1802, where the base of the 2 is weakly struck

Date	VG	F	VF	XF	Unc
1810L	40.00	60.00	80.00	100	—
1811L	40.00	60.00	80.00	100	—
1812L	40.00	60.00	80.00	100	—
1813L	40.00	60.00	80.00	100	—
1814L	40.00	60.00	80.00	100	—
1815L	40.00	60.00	80.00	100	—
1816L	40.00	60.00	80.00	100	—
1817L	40.00	60.00	80.00	100	—
1818L	40.00	60.00	80.00	100	—
1819L	40.00	60.00	80.00	100	—
1820L	40.00	60.00	80.00	100	—
1821L	40.00	60.00	80.00	100	—
1823L	40.00	60.00	80.00	100	—

KM# 93 1/2 REAL
1.6917 g., 0.8960 Silver .0487 oz. ASW **Mint:** Lima **Obverse:** Bust of Charles IV **Obv. Legend:** CAROLUS IIII... **Reverse:** Crowned arms, pillars **Note:** Mint mark in monogram.

Date	VG	F	VF	XF	Unc
1802LIMAE IJ	10.00	20.00	30.00	50.00	—
1803LIMAE IJ	10.00	20.00	30.00	50.00	—
1803LIMAE JP	10.00	20.00	30.00	50.00	—
1804LIMAE IJ	15.00	25.00	35.00	60.00	—
1804LIMAE JP	10.00	20.00	30.00	50.00	—
1805LIMAE JP	10.00	20.00	30.00	50.00	—
1805LIMAE IJ	20.00	40.00	60.00	80.00	—
1806LIMAE JP	10.00	20.00	30.00	50.00	—
1807LIMAE JP	10.00	20.00	30.00	50.00	—
1808LIMAE JP	10.00	20.00	30.00	50.00	—

KM# 103.1 1/2 REAL
1.6917 g., 0.8960 Silver .0487 oz. ASW **Mint:** Lima **Obverse:** Lima (imaginary) bust of Ferdinand VII **Obv. Legend:** FERDND • VII... **Reverse:** Crowned arms, pillars **Note:** Mint mark in monogram.

Date	VG	F	VF	XF	Unc
1808LIMAE JP	40.00	70.00	125	175	—

KM# 103.2 1/2 REAL
1.6917 g., 0.8960 Silver .0487 oz. ASW **Mint:** Lima **Obverse:** Lima bust of Ferdinand **Obv. Legend:** FERDIN VII... **Reverse:** Crowned arms, pillars **Note:** Mint mark in monogram.

Date	VG	F	VF	XF	Unc
1809LIMAE JP	20.00	40.00	60.00	80.00	—
1810LIMAE JP	20.00	40.00	60.00	80.00	—
1811LIMAE JP	10.00	20.00	30.00	60.00	—

KM# 113.1 (KM113) 1/2 REAL
1.6917 g., 0.8960 Silver .0487 oz. ASW **Mint:** Lima **Obverse:** Standard bust of Ferdinand **Note:** Mint mark in monogram.

Date	VG	F	VF	XF	Unc
1811LIMAE JP	20.00	40.00	60.00	80.00	—
1811LIMAE JP	20.00	40.00	60.00	80.00	—
1812LIMAE JP	10.00	20.00	30.00	50.00	—
1812LIMAE JP	10.00	20.00	30.00	50.00	—
1813LIMAE JP	10.00	20.00	30.00	50.00	—
1813LIMAE JP	10.00	20.00	30.00	50.00	—

KM# 113.2 1/2 REAL
1.6917 g., 0.8960 Silver .0487 oz. ASW **Mint:** Lima **Obverse:** Larger standard bust **Note:** Mint mark in monogram.

Date	VG	F	VF	XF	Unc
1814LIMAE JP	10.00	20.00	30.00	50.00	—
1815LIMAE JP	10.00	20.00	30.00	50.00	—
1816LIMAE JP	10.00	20.00	30.00	50.00	—
1817LIMAE JP	10.00	20.00	30.00	50.00	—
1818LIMAE JP	10.00	20.00	30.00	50.00	—
1819LIMAE JP	10.00	20.00	30.00	50.00	—
1820LIMAE JP	10.00	20.00	30.00	50.00	—
1821LIMAE JP	10.00	20.00	30.00	50.00	—

KM# 94 REAL
3.3834 g., 0.8960 Silver .0975 oz. ASW **Mint:** Lima **Obverse:** Bust of Charles IV **Obv. Legend:** CAROLUS IIII... **Reverse:** Crowned arms, pillars **Note:** Mint mark in monogram.

Date	VG	F	VF	XF	Unc
1802LIMAE IJ	12.50	30.00	45.00	60.00	—
1803LIMAE IJ	12.50	30.00	45.00	60.00	—
1803LIMAE JP	12.50	30.00	45.00	60.00	—
1804LIMAE IJ	12.00	30.00	45.00	60.00	—
1804LIMAE JP	12.00	30.00	45.00	60.00	—
1805LIMAE JP	12.00	30.00	45.00	60.00	—
1806LIMAE JP	12.00	30.00	45.00	60.00	—
1807LIMAE JP	12.50	30.00	45.00	60.00	—
1808LIMAE JP	12.50	30.00	45.00	60.00	—

KM# 109 REAL
3.3834 g., 0.8960 Silver .0975 oz. ASW **Mint:** Lima **Obverse:** Lima (imaginary) bust of Ferdinand VII **Obv. Legend:** FERDIN VII... **Reverse:** Crowned arms, pillars **Note:** Mint mark in monogram.

Date	VG	F	VF	XF	Unc
1808LIMAE JP	40.00	80.00	150	300	—
1809LIMAE JP	25.00	50.00	90.00	150	—
1810LIMAE JP	25.00	50.00	90.00	150	—
1811LIMAE JP	20.00	40.00	70.00	100	—

KM# 114.1 REAL
3.3834 g., 0.8960 Silver .0975 oz. ASW **Mint:** Lima **Obverse:** Standard bust of Ferdinand VII **Obv. Legend:** FERDIN VII... **Reverse:** Crowned arms, pillars **Note:** Mint mark in monogram.

Date	VG	F	VF	XF	Unc
1811LIMAE JP	30.00	50.00	95.00	150	—
1812LIMAE JP	12.50	30.00	45.00	60.00	—
1813LIMAE JP	12.50	30.00	45.00	60.00	—
1814LIMAE JP	12.50	30.00	45.00	60.00	—
1815LIMAE JP	12.50	30.00	45.00	60.00	—
1816LIMAE JP	12.50	30.00	45.00	60.00	—
1817LIMAE JP	12.50	30.00	45.00	60.00	—
1818LIMAE JP	12.50	30.00	45.00	60.00	—
1819LIMAE JP	12.50	30.00	45.00	60.00	—
1820LIMAE JP	12.50	30.00	45.00	60.00	—
1821LIMAE JP	12.50	30.00	45.00	60.00	—
1823LIMAE JP	20.00	40.00	70.00	100	—

KM# 114.2 REAL
3.3834 g., 0.8960 Silver 0.0975 oz. ASW **Mint:** Cuzco **Obverse:** Standard bust of Ferdinand VII **Obv. Legend:** FERDIN VII... **Reverse:** Crowned arms, pillars **Note:** Mint mark in monogram.

Date	VG	F	VF	XF	Unc
1824/3CUZCO T	45.00	80.00	175	300	—
1824CUZCO T	60.00	120	200	400	—

KM# 95 2 REALES
6.7668 g., 0.8960 Silver .1949 oz. ASW **Mint:** Lima **Obverse:** Bust of Charles IV **Obv. Legend:** CAROLUS IIII... **Reverse:** Crowned arms, pillars **Note:** Mint mark in monogram.

Date	VG	F	VF	XF	Unc
1802LIMAE IJ	17.50	35.00	50.00	65.00	—
1803/2LIMAE IJ	17.50	35.00	50.00	65.00	—
1803LIMAE IJ	17.50	35.00	50.00	65.00	—
1803LIMAE JP	17.50	35.00	50.00	65.00	—
1804LIMAE JP	17.50	35.00	50.00	65.00	—
1805LIMAE JP	17.50	35.00	50.00	65.00	—
1806LIMAE JP	17.50	35.00	50.00	65.00	—
1807/0LIMAE JP	17.50	35.00	50.00	65.00	—
1807LIMAE JP	17.50	35.00	50.00	65.00	—
1808LIMAE JP	17.50	35.00	50.00	65.00	—

KM# 104.1 2 REALES
6.7668 g., 0.8960 Silver .1949 oz. ASW **Mint:** Lima **Obverse:** Lima (imaginary) bust **Obv. Legend:** FERDND • VII... **Reverse:** Crowned arms, pillars **Note:** Mint mark in monogram.

Date	VG	F	VF	XF	Unc
1808LIMAE JP	40.00	70.00	175	285	—
1809LIMAE JP Rare	—	—	—	—	—

KM# 104.2 2 REALES
6.7668 g., 0.8960 Silver .1949 oz. ASW **Mint:** Lima **Obverse:** Lima (imaginary) bust of Ferdinand VII **Obv. Legend:** FERDND • VII... **Reverse:** Crowned arms, pillars **Note:** Mint mark in monogram.

Date	VG	F	VF	XF	Unc
1808LIMAE JP	100	170	280	450	—
1809LIMAE JP Rare	—	—	—	—	—
1810LIMAE JP	25.00	50.00	75.00	90.00	—
1811LIMAE JP	25.00	50.00	75.00	90.00	—

KM# 115.1 2 REALES
6.7668 g., 0.8960 Silver .1949 oz. ASW **Mint:** Lima **Obverse:** Standard bust of Ferdinand VII **Obv. Legend:** FERDND • VII... **Reverse:** Crowned arms, pillars **Note:** Mint mark in monogram.

Date	VG	F	VF	XF	Unc
1811LIMAE JP Rare	—	—	—	—	—
1812LIMAE JP	17.50	35.00	50.00	65.00	—
1813LIMAE JP	17.50	35.00	50.00	65.00	—
1814LIMAE JP	17.50	35.00	50.00	65.00	—
1815LIMAE JP	17.50	35.00	50.00	65.00	—
1816LIMAE JP	17.50	35.00	50.00	65.00	—
1817LIMAE JP	17.50	35.00	50.00	65.00	—
1818LIMAE JP	17.50	35.00	50.00	65.00	—
1819LIMAE JP	17.50	35.00	50.00	65.00	—
1820LIMAE JP	17.50	35.00	50.00	65.00	—
1821LIMAE JP	17.50	35.00	50.00	65.00	—
1823LIMAE JP	17.50	35.00	50.00	65.00	—

KM# 115.2 2 REALES
6.7668 g., 0.8960 Silver .1949 oz. ASW **Mint:** Cuzco **Obverse:** Standard bust of Ferdinand VI **Obv. Legend:** FERDND • VII... **Reverse:** Crowned arms, pillars **Note:** Mint mark in monogram.

Date	VG	F	VF	XF	Unc
1824CUZCO T	125	250	500	—	—

KM# 115.3 2 REALES
6.7668 g., 0.8960 Silver .1949 oz. ASW **Mint:** Lima **Obverse:** Standard bust of Ferdinand VI **Obv. Legend:** FERDND • VII... **Reverse:** Crowned arms, pillars **Note:** Mint mark in monogram.

Date	VG	F	VF	XF	Unc
1826LIMAE IR	85.00	145	285	425	—

Note: KM#115.3 was struck in Callao by Royalists prior to final capitulation on January 22, 1826

KM# 96 4 REALES
13.5337 g., 0.8960 Silver .3899 oz. ASW **Mint:** Lima **Obverse:** Bust of Charles IIII **Obv. Legend:** CAROLUS IIII.. **Reverse:** Crowned arms, pillars

Date	VG	F	VF	XF	Unc
1802LIMAE IJ	35.00	60.00	125	300	—
1803LIMAE IJ	35.00	60.00	125	300	—
1803LIMAE JP	35.00	60.00	125	300	—
1804LIMAE JP	35.00	60.00	125	300	—
1805LIMAE JP	35.00	60.00	125	300	—
1806LIMAE JP	35.00	60.00	125	300	—
1807LIMAE JP	35.00	60.00	125	300	—
1808LIMAE JP	35.00	60.00	125	300	—

KM# 105.1 4 REALES
13.5337 g., 0.8960 Silver .3899 oz. ASW **Mint:** Lima **Obverse:** Lima (imaginary) bust of Ferdinand VII **Obv. Legend:** FERDND VII... **Reverse:** Crowned arms, pillars **Note:** Mint mark in monogram.

Date	VG	F	VF	XF	Unc
1808LIMAE JP	35.00	60.00	125	300	—
1809LIMAE JP Rare	—	—	—	—	—

KM# 105.2 4 REALES
13.5337 g., 0.8960 Silver .3899 oz. ASW **Mint:** Lima **Obverse:** Lima (imaginary) bust of Ferdinand VII **Obv. Legend:** FERDIN • VII... **Reverse:** Crowned arms, pillars **Note:** Mint mark in monogram.

Date	VG	F	VF	XF	Unc
1810LIMAE JP	35.00	60.00	125	300	—
1811LIMAE JP	35.00	60.00	125	300	—

KM# 116 4 REALES
13.0000 g., 0.9030 Silver .3774 oz. ASW **Mint:** Lima **Obverse:** Standard bust of Ferdinand VII **Obv. Legend:** FERDIN • VII... **Reverse:** Crowned arms, pillars **Note:** Mint mark in monogram.

Date	VG	F	VF	XF	Unc
1811LIMAE JP Rare	—	—	—	—	—
1812LIMAE JP	30.00	55.00	110	275	—
1813LIMAE JP	30.00	55.00	110	275	—
1814LIMAE JP	30.00	55.00	110	275	—
1815LIMAE JP	30.00	55.00	110	275	—

Date	VG	F	VF	XF	Unc
1816LIMAE JP	30.00	55.00	110	275	—
1817LIMAE JP	30.00	55.00	110	275	—
1818LIMAE JP	30.00	55.00	110	275	—
1819LIMAE JP	30.00	55.00	110	275	—
1820LIMAE JP	30.00	55.00	110	275	—
1821LIMAE JP	30.00	55.00	110	275	—

KM# 97 8 REALES
27.0674 g., 0.8960 Silver .7797 oz. ASW **Mint:** Lima **Obverse:** Bust of Charles IV **Obv. Legend:** CAROLUS IIII... **Reverse:** Crowned arms, pillars **Note:** Mint mark in monogram.

Date	Mintage	VG	F	VF	XF	Unc
1802LIMAE IJ	3,875,000	25.00	50.00	75.00	125	—
1803LIMAE IJ	—	35.00	60.00	100	125	—
1803/2LIMAE JP	—	35.00	60.00	100	125	—
1803LIMAE JP	—	25.00	50.00	75.00	90.00	—
1804LIMAE JP	3,979,000	25.00	50.00	75.00	90.00	—
1805LIMAE JP	4,030,000	25.00	50.00	75.00	90.00	—
1806LIMAE JP	4,199,000	25.00	50.00	75.00	90.00	—
1807LIMAE JP	3,562,000	25.00	50.00	75.00	90.00	—
1808LIMAE JP	4,017,000	25.00	50.00	75.00	90.00	—

KM# 106.1 8 REALES
27.0674 g., 0.8960 Silver .7797 oz. ASW **Mint:** Lima **Obverse:** Large imaginary bust of Ferdinand VII **Obv. Legend:** FERDND VII... **Reverse:** Crowned arms, pillars **Note:** Mint mark in monogram.

Date	Mintage	VG	F	VF	XF	Unc
1808LIMAE JP	Inc. above	450	750	1,250	2,500	—
1809LIMAE JP	4,197,000	75.00	150	275	465	—

KM# 106.2 8 REALES
27.0674 g., 0.8960 Silver .7797 oz. ASW **Mint:** Lima **Obverse:** Smaller imaginary bust of Ferdinand VII **Obv. Legend:** FERDIN VII... **Reverse:** Crowned arms, pillars **Note:** Mint mark in monogram.

Date	Mintage	VG	F	VF	XF	Unc
1809LIMAE JP	Inc. above	30.00	60.00	90.00	200	—
1810LIMAE JP	4,380,000	30.00	50.00	75.00	165	—
1811LIMAE JP	4,412,000	30.00	50.00	75.00	165	—

KM# 117.1 8 REALES
27.0674 g., 0.8960 Silver .7797 oz. ASW **Mint:** Lima **Obverse:** Standard bust of Ferdinand VII **Obv. Legend:** FERDIN VII... **Reverse:** Crowned arms, pillars **Note:** Mint mark in monogram.

Date	Mintage	VG	F	VF	XF	Unc
1811LIMAE JP	Inc. above	50.00	90.00	140	225	—
1812LIMAE JP	3,800,000	25.00	50.00	75.00	90.00	—
1813LIMAE JP	4,033,000	25.00	50.00	75.00	90.00	—
1814LIMAE JP	3,599,000	25.00	50.00	75.00	90.00	—
1815/4LIMAE JP	3,642,000	25.00	50.00	75.00	90.00	—
1815LIMAE JP	Inc. above	25.00	50.00	75.00	90.00	—
1816LIMAE JP	—	25.00	50.00	75.00	90.00	—
1817LIMAE JP Wide date	—	25.00	50.00	75.00	90.00	—
1817LIMAE JP Narrow date	—	25.00	50.00	75.00	90.00	—
1818LIMAE JP	—	25.00	50.00	75.00	90.00	—
1819LIMAE JP	3,139,000	25.00	50.00	75.00	90.00	—
1820LIMAE JP	—	25.00	50.00	75.00	90.00	—
1821LIMAE JP	—	25.00	50.00	75.00	90.00	—
1823LIMAE JP	—	100	175	250	400	—
1824LIMAE JM	—	120	250	450	950	—

KM# 117.3 8 REALES
25.0000 g., 0.9030 Silver .7259 oz. ASW **Mint:** Lima **Note:** Struck over Republican Provisional 8 Reales, KM#136.

Date	VG	F	VF	XF	Unc
1823LIMAE JP Rare	—	—	—	—	—

Note: A small number of "Peru Libre" 8 Reales were directly overstruck with colonial dies of Ferdinand VII when Royalist forces, under General Cantarac, recaptured Lima

KM# 117.2 8 REALES
27.6674 g., 0.8960 Silver .7797 oz. ASW **Mint:** Cuzco **Obverse:** Standard bust of Ferdinand VII **Obv. Legend:** FERDIN VII... **Reverse:** Crowned arms, pillars **Note:** Mint mark in monogram.

Date	VG	F	VF	XF	Unc
1824/3CUZCO T	125	200	350	700	—
1824CUZCO T	100	175	300	650	—
1824CUZCO G/T	100	165	275	600	—
1824CUZCO G	90.00	150	250	550	—

KM# 125 1/2 ESCUDO
1.6875 g., 0.8730 Gold .0475 oz. AGW **Mint:** Lima **Obverse:** Bust of Ferdinand VII **Obv. Legend:** FERDND • VII... **Reverse:** Crowned arms in order chain

Date	VG	F	VF	XF	Unc
1814L JP	225	450	800	1,400	—
1815L JP	225	450	800	1,400	—
1816L JP	225	450	800	1,400	—
1817L JP	225	450	800	1,400	—
1818L JP	225	450	800	1,400	—
1819L JP	225	450	800	1,400	—
1820L JP	225	450	800	1,400	—
1821L JP	225	450	800	1,400	—

KM# 89 ESCUDO
3.3834 g., 0.8750 Gold .0952 oz. AGW **Mint:** Lima **Obverse:** Bust of Charles IV **Obv. Legend:** CAROL • IIII... **Reverse:** Crowned arms in order chain **Note:** Mint mark in monogram.

Date	VG	F	VF	XF	Unc
1802LIMAE IJ	100	175	265	450	—
1803LIMAE IJ	100	175	265	450	—
1803LIMAE JP	100	175	265	450	—
1804LIMAE JP	100	175	265	450	—
1805LIMAE JP	100	175	265	450	—
1806LIMAE JP	100	175	265	450	—
1807LIMAE JP	100	175	265	450	—
1808LIMAE JP	125	200	300	500	—

KM# 110 ESCUDO
3.3834 g., 0.8750 Gold .0952 oz. AGW **Mint:** Lima **Obverse:** Uniformed Lima (imaginary) bust of Ferdinand VII **Obv. Legend:** FERDIN • VII... **Reverse:** Crowned arms in order chain **Note:** Mint mark in monogram.

Date	VG	F	VF	XF	Unc
1809LIMAE JP Rare	—	—	—	—	—
1810LIMAE JP	200	400	650	1,000	—
1811LIMAE JP	300	600	1,000	1,650	—

KM# 119 ESCUDO
3.3834 g., 0.8750 Gold .0952 oz. AGW **Mint:** Lima **Obverse:** Standard small bust of Ferdinand VII **Obv. Legend:** FERDIN • VII... **Reverse:** Crowned arms in order chain **Note:** Mint mark in monogram.

Date	VG	F	VF	XF	Unc
1812LIMAE JP	175	300	500	850	—
1813LIMAE JP	150	250	400	750	—
1814LIMAE JP	150	300	500	850	—

KM# 126 ESCUDO
3.3834 g., 0.8750 Gold .0952 oz. AGW **Mint:** Lima **Obverse:** Laureate undraped bust of Ferdinand VII **Obv. Legend:** FERDIN • VII... **Reverse:** Crowned arms in order chain **Note:** Mint mark in monogram.

Date	VG	F	VF	XF	Unc
1814LIMAE JP	125	200	300	400	—
1815LIMAE JP	125	200	300	400	—
1816LIMAE JP	125	200	300	400	—
1817LIMAE JP	125	200	300	400	—
1818LIMAE JP	150	225	350	500	—
1819LIMAE JP	150	225	350	500	—
1820LIMAE JP	125	200	300	400	—
1821LIMAE JP	125	200	300	400	—

KM# 100 2 ESCUDOS

6.7668 g., 0.8750 Gold .1904 oz. AGW **Mint:** Lima **Obverse:** Bust of Charles IV **Obv. Legend:** CAROL IIII... **Reverse:** Crowned arms in order chain **Note:** Mint mark in monogram.

Date	VG	F	VF	XF	Unc
1802LIMAE IJ	175	375	675	900	—
1804LIMAE JP	150	300	575	750	—
1805LIMAE JP	150	300	575	750	—
1806LIMAE JP	175	375	675	900	—
1807LIMAE JP	175	375	675	900	—
1808LIMAE JP	150	300	575	750	—

KM# 111 2 ESCUDOS

6.7668 g., 0.8750 Gold .1904 oz. AGW **Mint:** Lima **Obverse:** Uniformed Lima (imaginary)bust of Ferdinand VII **Obv. Legend:** FERDIN • VII... **Reverse:** Crowned arms in order chain **Note:** Mint mark in monogram.

Date	VG	F	VF	XF	Unc
1809LIMAE JP	300	550	1,000	1,650	—
1810LIMAE JP	300	550	1,000	1,650	—
1811LIMAE JP	300	550	1,000	1,650	—
Smaller bust					

KM# 120 2 ESCUDOS

6.7668 g., 0.8750 Gold .1904 oz. AGW **Mint:** Lima **Obverse:** Standard bust of Ferdinand VII **Obv. Legend:** FERDIN • VII... **Reverse:** Crowned arms in order chain **Note:** Mint mark in monogram.

Date	VG	F	VF	XF	Unc
1812LIMAE JP	225	450	750	1,250	—
1813LIMAE JP	225	450	750	1,250	—

KM# 127 2 ESCUDOS

6.7668 g., 0.8750 Gold .1904 oz. AGW **Mint:** Lima **Obverse:** Laureate undraped bust of Ferdinand VII **Obv. Legend:** FERDIN • VII... **Reverse:** Crowned arms in order chain **Note:** Mint mark in monogram.

Date	VG	F	VF	XF	Unc
1814LIMAE JP	175	375	675	900	—
1815LIMAE JP	175	325	600	800	—
1816LIMAE JP	175	400	700	1,000	—
1817LIMAE JP	200	400	700	950	—
1818LIMAE JP	150	300	575	750	—
1819LIMAE JP	150	300	575	750	—
1820LIMAE JP	200	400	700	1,000	—
1821LIMAE JP	175	325	600	800	—

KM# 98 4 ESCUDOS

13.5337 g., 0.8750 Gold .3807 oz. AGW **Mint:** Lima **Obverse:** Bust of Charles IV **Obv. Legend:** CAROL • IIII... **Reverse:** Crowned arms in order chain **Note:** Mint mark in monogram.

Date	VG	F	VF	XF	Unc
1804LIMAE JP	475	650	900	1,250	—
1805LIMAE JP	475	650	900	1,250	—
1806LIMAE JP	475	650	900	1,250	—
1807LIMAE JP	475	650	900	1,250	—
1808LIMAE JP Rare	—	—	—	—	—

KM# 112 4 ESCUDOS

13.5337 g., 0.8750 Gold .3807 oz. AGW **Mint:** Lima **Obverse:** Uniformed Lima (imaginary) bust of Ferdinand VII **Obv. Legend:** FERDIN • VII... **Reverse:** Crowned arms in order chain **Note:** Mint mark in monogram.

Date	VG	F	VF	XF	Unc
1809LIMAE JP	1,250	1,750	2,500	4,000	—
1810LIMAE JP	1,000	1,600	2,250	3,500	—

KM# 121 4 ESCUDOS

13.5337 g., 0.8750 Gold .3807 oz. AGW **Mint:** Lima **Obverse:** Large laureate draped bust of Ferdinand VII **Obv. Legend:** FERDIN • VII... **Reverse:** Crowned arms in order chains **Note:** Mint mark in monogram.

Date	VG	F	VF	XF	Unc
1812LIMAE JP	1,250	1,750	2,350	3,650	—

KM# 122 4 ESCUDOS

13.5337 g., 0.8750 Gold .3807 oz. AGW **Mint:** Lima **Obverse:** Small laureate draped bust of Ferdinand VII **Obv. Legend:** FERDIN • VII... **Reverse:** Crowned arms in order chain **Note:** Mint mark in monogram.

Date	VG	F	VF	XF	Unc
1812LIMAE JP	800	1,250	1,850	2,750	—
1813LIMAE JP	800	1,250	1,850	2,750	—

KM# 128 4 ESCUDOS

13.5337 g., 0.8750 Gold .3807 oz. AGW **Mint:** Lima **Obverse:** Laureate, undraped bust of Ferdinand VII **Obv. Legend:** FERDIN • VII... **Reverse:** Crowned arms in order chain **Note:** Mint mark in monogram.

Date	VG	F	VF	XF	Unc
1814LIMAE JP	575	750	1,000	1,500	—
1815LIMAE JP	300	450	750	1,000	—
1816LIMAE JP	275	375	675	900	—
1817LIMAE JP	600	900	1,500	2,000	—
1818LIMAE JP	300	450	750	1,000	—
1819LIMAE JP	475	650	900	1,100	—
1820LIMAE JP	275	375	675	900	—
1821LIMAE JP	575	750	1,000	1,500	—

KM# 101 8 ESCUDOS

27.0674 g., 0.8750 Gold .7615 oz. AGW **Mint:** Lima **Obverse:** Bust of Charles IV **Obv. Legend:** CAROL • IIII... **Reverse:** Crowned arms in order chain **Rev. Legend:** VTROQ • FELIX • AUSPICE • DEO **Note:** Mint mark in monogram.

Date	VG	F	VF	XF	Unc
1801LIMAE IJ	375	475	650	1,000	—
1802LIMAE IJ	375	475	650	1,000	—
1803LIMAE IJ	375	475	650	1,000	—
1803LIMAE JP	375	475	750	1,200	—
1804LIMAE IJ	600	900	1,800	3,000	—
1804LIMAE JP	375	475	750	1,200	—
1805LIMAE JP	375	475	650	1,000	—
1806/5LIMAE JP	375	475	650	1,000	—
1806LIMAE JP	375	475	650	1,000	—
1807LIMAE JP	375	475	650	1,000	—
1808LIMAE JP	375	475	650	1,000	—

KM# 107 8 ESCUDOS

27.0000 g., 0.8750 Gold .7596 oz. AGW **Mint:** Lima **Obverse:** Uniformed Lima (imaginary) bust of Ferdinand VII **Obv. Legend:** FERDIN • VII... **Reverse:** Crowned arms in order chain **Rev. Legend:** VTROQ • FELIX • AUSPICE • DEO **Note:** Mint mark in monogram.

Date	VG	F	VF	XF	Unc
1808LIMAE JP	750	1,350	2,500	4,000	—
1809LIMAE JP	500	800	1,500	2,250	—
1810LIMAE JP	500	800	1,500	2,250	—
1811LIMAE JP	500	800	1,500	2,250	—

KM# 118 8 ESCUDOS

27.0674 g., 0.8750 Gold .7615 oz. AGW **Mint:** Lima **Obverse:** Large laureate draped bust of Ferdinand VII **Obv. Legend:** FERDIN • VII... **Reverse:** Crowned arms in order chain **Rev. Legend:** VTROQ • FELIX • AUSPICE • DEO **Note:** Mint mark in monogram.

Date	VG	F	VF	XF	Unc
1811LIMAE JP Rare	—	—	—	—	—
1812LIMAE JP	500	700	1,000	1,600	—

KM# 124 8 ESCUDOS

27.0674 g., 0.8750 Gold .7615 oz. AGW **Mint:** Lima **Obverse:** Small laureate draped bust of Ferdinand VII **Obv. Legend:** FERDIN • VII... **Reverse:** Crowned arms in order chain **Rev. Legend:** VTROQ • FELIX • AUSPICE • DEO **Note:** Mint mark in monogram.

Date	VG	F	VF	XF	Unc
1812LIMAE JP	400	675	900	1,500	—
1813LIMAE JP	400	675	900	1,500	—

KM# 129.1 8 ESCUDOS

27.0674 g., 0.8750 Gold .7615 oz. AGW **Mint:** Lima **Obverse:** Small laureate bust, undraped, of Ferdinand VII **Obv. Legend:** FERDIN • VII... **Reverse:** Crowned arms in order chain **Rev. Legend:** VTROQ • FELIX • AUSPICE • DEO **Note:** Mint mark in monogram.

Date	VG	F	VF	XF	Unc
1814LIMAE JP	375	475	650	1,000	—
1815LIMAE JP	375	475	650	1,000	—
1816LIMAE JP	375	475	750	1,200	—
1817LIMAE JP	375	475	650	1,000	—
1818LIMAE JP	375	475	650	1,000	—
1819LIMAE JP	375	475	650	1,000	—
1820LIMAE JP	375	475	650	1,000	—
1821LIMAE JP	375	475	750	1,200	—

KM# 129.2 8 ESCUDOS
27.0674 g., 0.8750 Gold .7615 oz. AGW **Mint:** Lima **Obverse:** Similar to KM#129.1 **Obv. Legend:** FERDIN • VII... **Reverse:** Crowned arms in order chain **Rev. Legend:** VTROQ • FELIX • AUSPICE • DEO

Date	VG	F	VF	XF	Unc
1824Co G	750	1,250	2,000	2,750	—

PROVISIONAL COINAGE

REPUBLICAN

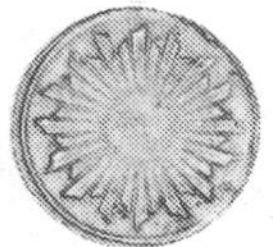

KM# 135 1/4 REAL
Copper **Mint:** Lima **Reverse:** Sunface

Date	VG	F	VF	XF	Unc
1822	7.00	15.00	30.00	75.00	—

KM# 136 8 REALES
25.0000 g., 0.9030 Silver .7259 oz. ASW **Mint:** Lima **Note:** "Peru Libre" Type. Mint mark in monogram.

Date	VG	F	VF	XF	Unc
1822 LIMA JP	60.00	90.00	175	450	—
1823 LIMA JP	50.00	80.00	150	400	—

KM# 137 1/8 PESO (Octavo De)
Copper **Mint:** Lima **Note:** Mint mark in monogram. Official restrikes of KM#137 and 138 were issued in 1921, using the original dies, to commemorate the Centennial of Independence.

Date	VG	F	VF	XF	Unc
1823 LIMA	4.00	9.00	18.00	48.00	—
1823 LIMA V	16.50	37.50	65.00	140	—

KM# 138 1/4 PESO (Quarto De; 2 Reales)
Copper **Mint:** Lima **Note:** Mint mark in monogram.

Date	VG	F	VF	XF	Unc
1823 LIMA	3.00	7.00	15.00	45.00	—
1823 LIMA V	10.00	20.00	40.00	90.00	—

COUNTERMARKED COINAGE

ROYALIST

KM# 130 8 REALES
Silver **Mint:** Lima **Countermark:** Crown above 1824 **Note:** Countermark on KM#136.

CM Date	Host Date	Good	VG	F	VF	XF
1824	1823 JP	—	50.00	90.00	175	425

Note: The crown/1824 countermark appears to have been applied without any discretion to obverse or reverse. Although being very collectable, neither variety carries a premium over the other

CM Date	Host Date	Good	VG	F	VF	XF
1824	1822 JP	—	75.00	135	250	575

REPUBLIC

REAL - ESCUDO COINAGE

KM# 143.1 1/4 REAL
0.8400 g., 0.9030 Silver .0243 oz. ASW **Mint:** Lima **Note:** LIMAE mint mark in monogram.

Date	VG	F	VF	XF	Unc
1826	3.50	6.50	14.00	27.50	—
1827	2.50	4.75	10.00	17.50	—
1828	3.50	6.50	14.00	27.50	—
1829/8 Inverted 1/4	4.75	8.50	17.50	37.50	—
1830/28	3.00	6.00	14.00	27.50	—
1831/0	2.50	4.75	10.00	17.50	—
1831	3.50	6.00	13.00	25.00	—
1832	5.25	11.00	22.50	45.00	—
1833	3.00	5.75	12.00	25.00	—
1834/3	5.00	7.50	15.00	30.00	—
1834	3.50	6.00	13.00	27.50	—
1835	6.50	13.50	26.00	55.00	—
1836/5	10.00	15.00	30.00	50.00	—
1836	5.00	10.00	22.50	45.00	—
1837	5.00	10.00	22.50	45.00	—
1839/8	5.00	10.00	22.50	45.00	—
1839	4.25	8.50	17.00	35.00	—
1840	4.25	8.50	17.00	35.00	—
1841/0	3.50	6.00	13.00	25.00	—
1841	4.00	8.00	16.00	35.00	—
1842/32	4.00	8.00	16.00	35.00	—
1842	2.50	4.75	10.00	17.50	—
1843/33	4.00	8.00	16.00	35.00	—
1843	2.50	4.75	10.00	17.50	—
1845/36	4.00	8.00	16.00	35.00	—
1845	3.00	5.75	12.00	22.50	—
1846	2.50	4.75	10.00	17.50	—
1846/3	3.00	6.00	15.00	25.00	—
1847/6	5.00	12.50	25.00	50.00	—
1847	3.50	7.00	16.00	30.00	—
1848/38	4.25	8.50	20.00	40.00	—
1848	4.25	8.50	20.00	40.00	—
1849/38	4.25	8.50	20.00	40.00	—
1849/8	4.25	8.50	20.00	40.00	—
1849	3.50	7.00	16.00	30.00	—
1850	2.50	5.00	12.00	20.00	—
1851/21	3.00	6.00	15.00	25.00	—
1851/31	3.00	6.00	15.00	25.00	—
1853/31	2.00	4.00	10.00	18.00	—
1853/1	2.50	5.00	12.00	20.00	—
1855/35	2.50	5.00	12.00	20.00	—
1855/3	2.50	5.00	12.00	20.00	—
1855	1.50	3.00	5.00	15.00	—
1856/26	2.50	5.00	12.00	20.00	—
1856/36	2.50	5.00	12.00	20.00	—
1856/45	2.50	5.00	12.00	20.00	—
1856 5/3	2.50	5.00	12.00	20.00	—
1856	1.50	3.00	5.00	15.00	—

KM# 143.2 1/4 REAL
0.8400 g., 0.9030 Silver .0243 oz. ASW **Mint:** Arequipa **Note:** Struck at the Arequipa mint.

Date	VG	F	VF	XF	Unc
1839AREQ	250	500	750	1,000	—

KM# 144.1 1/2 REAL
1.6900 g., 0.9030 Silver .0490 oz. ASW **Mint:** Lima **Obv. Legend:** REPUB. PERUANA **Note:** LIMAE mint mark in monogram.

Date	VG	F	VF	XF	Unc
1826 JM	5.00	10.00	17.50	30.00	—
1827/6 JM/J	20.00	40.00	60.00	90.00	—
1827 JM	5.50	12.50	25.00	40.00	—
1828 JM	3.50	7.50	15.00	25.00	—
1829/8 JM	7.00	15.00	35.00	60.00	—
1830 JM	7.00	15.00	35.00	60.00	—
1831 MM	4.00	7.50	17.50	30.00	—
1832 MM	4.00	7.50	17.50	30.00	—
1833/2	4.00	7.50	17.50	30.00	—
1833 MM	2.50	6.00	12.50	20.00	—
1834 MM	3.00	7.50	15.00	30.00	—
1835/3 MM	4.50	9.00	18.50	32.00	—
1835 MM	4.50	9.00	18.50	32.00	—
1835 MT/M	7.00	15.00	35.00	60.00	—
1836/5 MT	5.00	10.00	20.00	40.00	—
1836 MT	3.50	7.50	17.50	30.00	—
1839 MB	3.00	6.50	15.00	25.00	—
1840 MB	3.00	6.50	15.00	25.00	—

KM# 144.2 1/2 REAL
1.6900 g., 0.9030 Silver .0490 oz. ASW **Mint:** Cuzco **Obv. Legend:** REPUB. PERUANA **Note:** CUZCO mint mark in monogram.

Date	VG	F	VF	XF	Unc
1827 GM	12.50	25.00	50.00	95.00	—
1828 G	12.50	25.00	50.00	95.00	—
1829/8 G	10.00	20.00	40.00	80.00	—
1829 G	12.50	25.00	50.00	95.00	—
1830/28 G	10.00	20.00	40.00	80.00	—
1830 G	7.50	15.00	25.00	50.00	—
1831 G	7.50	15.00	25.00	50.00	—
1835 B	7.50	15.00	25.00	50.00	—

KM# 144.3 1/2 REAL
1.6900 g., 0.9030 Silver .0490 oz. ASW **Mint:** Cuzco **Obv. Legend:** REPUB. PERUANA **Note:** CUZCO mint mark in monogram.

Date	VG	F	VF	XF	Unc
1833 B	5.00	10.00	20.00	40.00	—
1834 B	5.00	10.00	20.00	45.00	—

KM# 144.4 1/2 REAL
1.6500 g., 0.9030 Silver .0354 oz. ASW **Mint:** Arequipa **Obv. Legend:** REPUB. PERUANA **Note:** Struck at Arequipa with AREQ mint mark.

Date	VG	F	VF	XF	Unc
1836 M	10.00	20.00	40.00	85.00	—

KM# 144.5 1/2 REAL
1.6500 g., 0.9030 Silver .0479 oz. ASW **Mint:** Lima **Note:** LIMA mint mark in monogram.

Date	VG	F	VF	XF	Unc
1840 MMB	10.00	20.00	35.00	65.00	—
1841/0 MMB	15.00	30.00	50.00	85.00	—

KM# 144.7 1/2 REAL
1.6500 g., 0.9030 Silver .0479 oz. ASW **Mint:** Lima **Obv. Legend:** REP. PERUANA 10D 20G **Note:** LIMA mint mark in monogram; varieties exist.

Date	VG	F	VF	XF	Unc
1840 MB	5.50	12.00	25.00	55.00	—
1841 MB	5.50	12.00	25.00	45.00	—
1842 MB	5.50	12.00	25.00	45.00	—
1843 MB	4.00	8.00	16.00	32.00	—
1845 MB	4.00	8.00	15.00	25.00	—
1846 MB	4.00	8.00	17.50	30.00	—
1847 MB	9.00	15.00	28.00	65.00	—
1849 MB	6.00	12.00	25.00	55.00	—
1850 MB	5.00	10.00	20.00	45.00	—
1851 MB	5.00	10.00	20.00	45.00	—
1852 MB	5.00	10.00	20.00	45.00	—
1853/1 MB	15.00	20.00	30.00	75.00	—
1853 MB	15.00	20.00	30.00	75.00	—
1854 MB	4.00	7.50	15.00	30.00	—
1855 MB	3.50	6.50	12.50	25.00	—
1856 MB	3.50	6.50	12.50	25.00	—

KM# 145.1 REAL
3.3800 g., 0.9030 Silver .0981 oz. ASW **Obv. Legend:** REPUB. PERUANA **Note:** LIMAE mint mark in monogram.

Date	VG	F	VF	XF	Unc
1826 JM	17.50	35.00	55.00	100	—
1827 JM	5.00	10.00	17.50	35.00	—
1828 JM	5.00	10.00	17.50	35.00	—
1829 JM Reported, not confirmed	—	—	—	—	—
1830 JM	8.50	17.50	35.00	60.00	—
1831 JM	10.00	20.00	42.50	80.00	—
1831 MM	—	—	—	—	—
1832 MM	7.50	15.00	27.50	50.00	—

Date	VG	F	VF	XF	Unc
1833/2 MM	10.00	20.00	40.00	75.00	—
1834 MM	5.00	10.00	17.50	35.00	—
1835/3 Reported, not confirmed	—	—	—	—	—
1836 MT	10.00	20.00	40.00	75.00	—
1838 MB	7.50	15.00	27.50	50.00	—
1839 MB	7.50	15.00	27.50	50.00	—
1840 MB	5.00	10.00	17.50	35.00	—

KM# 145.2 REAL
3.3800 g., 0.9030 Silver .0981 oz. ASW **Mint:** Cuzco **Obv. Legend:** REPUB. PERUANA **Note:** CUZco mint mark in monogram.

Date	VG	F	VF	XF	Unc
1827 GM	17.50	35.00	60.00	100	—
1828 G	17.50	35.00	60.00	100	—
1829/8 G	20.00	40.00	75.00	125	—
1829 G	20.00	40.00	75.00	125	—
1830 G	20.00	40.00	75.00	125	—
1831/21 G	20.00	40.00	75.00	125	—
1831/0 G	20.00	40.00	75.00	125	—
1831 G	20.00	40.00	75.00	125	—

KM# 145.3 REAL
3.3800 g., 0.9030 Silver .0981 oz. ASW **Mint:** Cuzco **Obv. Legend:** REPUB. PERUANA **Note:** CUZCO mint mark in monogram.

Date	VG	F	VF	XF	Unc
1834 B	45.00	80.00	150	225	—

KM# 145.4 REAL
3.3800 g., 0.9030 Silver .0981 oz. ASW **Mint:** Lima **Obv. Legend:** REP. PERUANA 10D 20G **Note:** LIMAE mint mark in monogram.

Date	VG	F	VF	XF	Unc
1841 MB	—	—	—	—	—
1842/1 MB	12.00	25.00	47.50	90.00	—
1842 MB	10.00	20.00	40.00	75.00	—
1843 MB	10.00	20.00	40.00	75.00	—
1846 MB	10.00	20.00	40.00	75.00	—
1847/6 MB	12.00	25.00	47.50	90.00	—
1849 MB	5.50	10.00	18.00	35.00	—
1850 MB PBRUANA	3.50	7.00	12.50	20.00	—
1851 MB	4.00	8.00	14.00	25.00	—
1855 MB	4.50	9.00	16.00	30.00	—
1856/5 MB	3.50	7.00	12.50	20.00	—
1856	4.50	9.00	16.00	30.00	—

KM# 141.1 2 REALES
6.7700 g., 0.9030 Silver .1965 oz. ASW **Mint:** Lima **Obv. Legend:** REPUB. PERUANA **Note:** Mint mark in monogram.

Date	VG	F	VF	XF	Unc
1825 LIMA JM	30.00	65.00	100	—	—
1826 LIMA JM	5.00	10.00	18.00	40.00	—
1827 LIMA JM	5.00	10.00	18.00	40.00	—
1828/27 LIMA JM	5.00	10.00	18.00	40.00	—
1828 LIMA JM	4.00	10.00	18.00	40.00	—
1828 LIMA JM Inverted reverse	6.00	12.00	25.00	50.00	—
1829 LIMA JM	16.00	35.00	65.00	125	—
1830/29 LIMA JM	9.00	17.50	35.00	75.00	—
1830 LIMA JM	9.00	17.50	35.00	75.00	—
1831 LIMA MM	15.00	35.00	60.00	—	—
1832/1 LIMA MM	9.00	17.50	35.00	75.00	—
1832 LIMA MM	5.00	10.00	18.00	40.00	—
1833 LIMA MM	8.00	15.00	25.00	50.00	—
1834/3 LIMA MM	10.00	20.00	40.00	80.00	—
1834 LIMA MM	8.00	15.00	25.00	50.00	—
1835 LIMA MM	150	300	—	—	—
1836 LIMA MT	150	350	—	—	—
1839 LIMA MB	8.00	15.00	25.00	50.00	—
1840 LIMA MB	5.00	10.00	18.00	40.00	—

KM# 141.2 2 REALES
6.7700 g., 0.9030 Silver .1965 oz. ASW **Mint:** Cuzco **Obv. Legend:** REPUB. PERUANA **Note:** Mint mark in monogram.

Date	VG	F	VF	XF	Unc
1827 CUZco GM	35.00	65.00	100	165	—
1828 CUZco G	25.00	55.00	80.00	145	—
1829 CUZco G	25.00	55.00	80.00	145	—
1830 CUZco G	30.00	60.00	85.00	150	—
1831 CUZco G	35.00	65.00	100	165	—

KM# 141.2a 2 REALES
6.7700 g., 0.9030 Silver .1452 oz. ASW **Mint:** Cuzco **Obv. Legend:** REPUB. PERUANA **Note:** Mint mark in monogram.

Date	VG	F	VF	XF	Unc
1835 CUZco B	10.00	20.00	35.00	70.00	—

KM# 141.3 2 REALES
6.7700 g., 0.9030 Silver .1452 oz. ASW **Mint:** Lima **Obv. Legend:** REPUB. PERUANA 10D 20G **Note:** Mint mark in monogram; Varieties exist.

Date	VG	F	VF	XF	Unc
1840LIMAE MB	12.00	25.00	40.00	80.00	—
1841/0LIMAE MB	10.00	22.00	35.00	65.00	—
1841LIMAE MB	4.50	10.00	20.00	45.00	—
1842LIMAE MB Iinverted V's in PERUANA	4.50	10.00	20.00	45.00	—
1843LIMAE MB Inverted V's in PERUANA	10.00	20.00	45.00	90.00	—
1845LIMAE MB	10.00	20.00	40.00	80.00	—
1846LIMAE MB	15.00	30.00	50.00	100	—
1848/6LIMAE MB	5.00	12.00	22.00	50.00	—
1848LIMAE MB	5.00	12.00	22.00	50.00	—
1849LIMAE MB	4.00	8.00	15.00	30.00	—
1850LIMAE MB	4.00	8.00	15.00	30.00	—
1851LIMAE MB	4.50	10.00	20.00	45.00	—
1854LIMAE MB	8.00	15.00	25.00	60.00	—
1855LIMAE MB	10.00	20.00	40.00	80.00	—
1856LIMAE MB	8.00	15.00	25.00	60.00	—

KM# 141.4 2 REALES
6.7700 g., 0.9030 Silver .1452 oz. ASW **Mint:** Pasco **Obv. Legend:** REPUB. PERUANA

Date	VG	F	VF	XF	Unc
1843 M	400	750	—	—	—

KM# 151.1 4 REALES
13.0000 g., 0.6670 Silver .2788 oz. ASW **Mint:** Cuzco **Note:** Mint mark in monogram; many die varieties.

Date	VG	F	VF	XF	Unc
1835 CUZco B	5.00	10.00	20.00	60.00	—
1836 CUZco B	4.00	9.00	17.50	45.00	—

KM# 151.2 4 REALES
13.0000 g., 0.6670 Silver .2788 oz. ASW **Mint:** Arequipa **Obv. Legend:** REPUB PERUANA

Date	VG	F	VF	XF	Unc
1836/26AREQ M	40.00	75.00	150	300	—
1836AREQ M	30.00	60.00	125	250	—
1839AREQ MV	30.00	60.00	125	250	—
1840AREQ MV	30.00	60.00	125	250	—

KM# 151.3 4 REALES
13.5400 g., 0.9030 Silver .3931 oz. ASW **Mint:** Lima **Obv. Legend:** REPUB. PERUANA **Note:** Mint mark in monogram.

Date	VG	F	VF	XF	Unc
1842 LIMA MB	20.00	35.00	70.00	150	—
1843/2 LIMA MB	10.00	17.50	35.00	85.00	—
1843 LIMA MB	10.00	17.50	35.00	85.00	—
1845 LIMA MB	15.00	25.00	50.00	125	—
1846 LIMA MB	20.00	35.00	70.00	150	—
1848 LIMA MB	7.00	15.00	30.00	50.00	—
1849 LIMA MB	15.00	25.00	50.00	125	—
1850 LIMA MB	9.00	20.00	35.00	75.00	—
1851 LIMA MB	8.00	17.50	32.50	70.00	—
1854 LIMA MB	6.00	12.00	25.00	45.00	—
1855/4 LIMA MB	6.00	12.00	25.00	45.00	—
1855 LIMA MB	10.00	15.00	30.00	65.00	—
1856 LIMA MB	40.00	75.00	125	250	—

KM# 151.4 4 REALES
13.5400 g., 0.9030 Silver .3931 oz. ASW **Mint:** Pasco **Obv. Legend:** REPUB. PERUANA 10Ds 20Gs **Note:** Mint mark in monogram.

Date	VG	F	VF	XF	Unc
1843PAZCO M	25.00	50.00	120	250	—

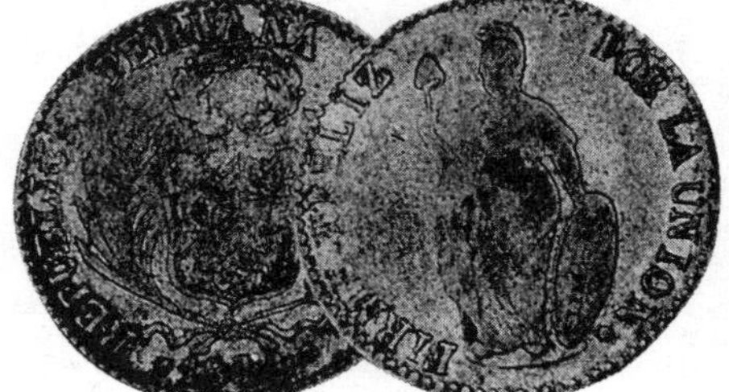

KM# 151.6 4 REALES
13.5400 g., 0.9030 Silver .3931 oz. ASW **Mint:** Pasco **Obverse:** Without fineness **Obv. Legend:** REPUB. PERUANA **Note:** Mint mark in monogram.

Date	VG	F	VF	XF	Unc
1844PASCO M	25.00	50.00	120	250	—
1845PASCO M 4 known	140	180	—	—	—

KM# 151.5 4 REALES
13.5400 g., 0.9030 Silver .3931 oz. ASW **Mint:** Pasco **Obv. Legend:** REPUB. PERUANA 10Ds 20Gs

Date	VG	F	VF	XF	Unc
1844PASCO M	10.00	20.00	50.00	150	—

KM# 151.7 4 REALES
13.5400 g., 0.9030 Silver .3931 oz. ASW **Mint:** Pasco **Obv. Legend:** REPUB. PERUANA 10Ds 20Gs **Note:** Mint mark in monogram.

Date	VG	F	VF	XF	Unc
1844PASCO M Reported, not confirmed	—	—	—	—	—
1855PASCO N. S. Rare	—	—	—	—	—

KM# 151.8 4 REALES
13.5400 g., 0.9030 Silver .3931 oz. ASW **Mint:** Pasco **Obv. Legend:** REPUB. PERUANA 10Ds 20Gs

Date	VG	F	VF	XF	Unc
1855PASCO	25.00	55.00	120	275	—

KM# 151.9 4 REALES
13.5400 g., 0.9030 Silver .3931 oz. ASW **Mint:** Pasco **Obv. Legend:** REP. PERUANA 10Ds 20Gs

Date	VG	F	VF	XF	Unc
1855PASCO M	12.00	25.00	55.00	145	—

Note: Most coins of this variety have small engraver's initial B in wreath above arms; at least one example is known with JB in relief

KM# 151.10 4 REALES
13.5400 g., 0.9030 Silver .3931 oz. ASW **Mint:** Pasco **Obv. Legend:** REP. PERUANA

Date	VG	F	VF	XF	Unc
1856PASCO Z in O	75.00	175	300	—	—
1857PASCO Z in O	25.00	50.00	100	200	—
1857PASCO AF	85.00	190	325	—	—
1857PASCO	150	350	750	—	—

KM# 142.1 8 REALES
27.0700 g., 0.9030 Silver .7859 oz. ASW **Mint:** Lima **Obv. Legend:** REPUB. PERUANA **Reverse:** Small figure of Liberty
Note: Mint mark in monogram; Varieties exist.

Date	VG	F	VF	XF	Unc
1825 LIMA JM	30.00	60.00	125	275	—
1826 LIMA JM	15.00	25.00	45.00	135	—
1827 LIMA JM	15.00	25.00	45.00	135	—
1828 LIMA JM	75.00	150	250	550	—

KM# 142.2 8 REALES
27.0700 g., 0.9030 Silver .7859 oz. ASW **Mint:** Cuzco **Obv. Legend:** REPUB. PERUANA **Reverse:** Small figure of Liberty
Note: Mint mark in monogram.

Date	VG	F	VF	XF	Unc
1826 CUZco GM	35.00	55.00	100	250	—
1826 CUZco G	15.00	30.00	60.00	145	—
1827 CUZco GM	15.00	30.00	60.00	145	—
1827 CUZco G	35.00	55.00	100	250	—
1828/7 CUZco G	15.00	30.00	60.00	145	—
1828 CUZco G	15.00	30.00	60.00	145	—
1829 CUZco G	35.00	55.00	100	250	—
1829 CUZco G REPMB (error), Rare	—	—	—	—	—

KM# 142.3 8 REALES
27.0700 g., 0.9030 Silver .7859 oz. ASW **Mint:** Lima **Obv. Legend:** REPUB. PERUANA **Reverse:** Small figure of Liberty
Note: Mint mark in monogram.

Date	VG	F	VF	XF	Unc
1828LIMAE JM	10.00	15.00	25.00	65.00	—
1829LIMAE JM	11.00	17.00	30.00	75.00	—
1830LIMAE JM	11.00	17.00	30.00	75.00	—
1831LIMAE JM	50.00	100	200	420	—
1831LIMAE MM	11.00	17.00	30.00	75.00	—
1832LIMAE MM	10.00	15.00	25.00	60.00	—
1833LIMAE MM	10.00	15.00	25.00	60.00	—
1833LIMAE MM POR AL UNION (error), Rare	—	—	—	—	—
1834LIMAE MM	10.00	15.00	25.00	60.00	—
1835LIMAE MM	11.00	17.00	30.00	75.00	—
1835LIMAE MM POR AL UNION (error), Rare	—	—	—	—	—
1835LIMAE MT	11.00	17.00	30.00	75.00	—
1836LIMAE MT	10.00	15.00	25.00	60.00	—
1836LIMAE TM	30.00	50.00	100	250	—
1838LIMAE MB	20.00	30.00	55.00	125	—
1839LIMAE MB	12.00	20.00	40.00	90.00	—
1840LIMAE MB	10.00	15.00	25.00	60.00	—

KM# 142.4 8 REALES
27.0700 g., 0.9030 Silver .7859 oz. ASW **Mint:** Cuzco **Obv. Legend:** REPUB. PERUANA **Reverse:** Small figure of Liberty

Date	VG	F	VF	XF	Unc
1830CUZCO G	12.00	20.00	35.00	80.00	—
1831CUZCO G	12.00	20.00	35.00	80.00	—
1832CUZCO B	12.50	22.50	40.00	90.00	—
1833CUZCO B	15.00	25.00	45.00	100	—
1833CUZCO BoAr	15.00	25.00	45.00	100	—
1834CUZCO BoAr	15.00	25.00	45.00	100	—

KM# 142.5 8 REALES
27.0700 g., 0.9030 Silver .7859 oz. ASW **Mint:** Cuzco **Obv. Legend:** REPUB. PERUANA **Reverse:** Small figure of Liberty
Note: Mint mark in monogram.

Date	VG	F	VF	XF	Unc
1835/4 CUZco B	30.00	60.00	125	250	—
1835 CUZco B	30.00	60.00	125	250	—

KM# 142.6 8 REALES
27.0700 g., 0.9030 Silver .7859 oz. ASW **Mint:** Pasco **Obv. Legend:** REPUB. PERUANA

Date	VG	F	VF	XF	Unc
1836 MO Rare	—	—	—	—	—

Note: Swiss Bank Corp. sale 20 9-88 holed fine realized $10,500

KM# 142.7 8 REALES
27.0700 g., 0.9030 Silver .7859 oz. ASW **Mint:** Arequipa **Obv. Legend:** REPUB. PERUANA **Reverse:** Small figure of Liberty

Date	VG	F	VF	XF	Unc
1839AREQ MV	800	1,500	3,500	7,000	—
1840AREQ MV	600	1,200	3,000	6,000	—

KM# 142.8 8 REALES
27.0700 g., 0.9030 Silver .7859 oz. ASW **Mint:** Lima **Obv. Legend:** REPUB. PERUANA 10DS 20GS **Reverse:** Similar to KM#142.3 **Note:** Mint mark in monogram.

Date	VG	F	VF	XF	Unc
1840LIMAE MB	30.00	55.00	100	200	—
1841/0LIMAE MB	25.00	50.00	85.00	100	—
1841LIMAE MB	12.00	22.00	32.00	75.00	—

KM# 142.9 8 REALES
27.0700 g., 0.9030 Silver .7859 oz. ASW **Mint:** Cuzco **Obv. Legend:** 10Ds20Gs **Note:** Mint mark in monogram.

Date	VG	F	VF	XF	Unc
1840 CUZco A	15.00	30.00	60.00	145	—

KM# 142.10 8 REALES
27.0700 g., 0.9030 Silver .7859 oz. ASW **Mint:** Lima **Obv. Legend:** REPUB. PERUANA 10Ds20Gs **Note:** Mint mark in monogram.

Date	VG	F	VF	XF	Unc
1841LIMAE MB	3,000	5,000	8,000	—	—
1842LIMAE MB	15.00	30.00	75.00	200	—
1843LIMAE MB	10.00	17.50	50.00	140	—
1843LIMAE MB POR AL UNION (error)	120	150	175	350	—
1843LIMAE MB Inverted V in LA	125	150	175	350	—
1844LIMAE MB	20.00	35.00	85.00	250	—
1845LIMAE MB	10.00	17.50	50.00	140	—
1846LIMAE MB	10.00	25.00	75.00	200	—
1847/6LIMAE MB	25.00	50.00	100	325	—
1847LIMAE MB	25.00	50.00	100	325	—
1848/7LIMAE MB	10.00	25.00	75.00	200	—
1848LIMAE MB	10.00	25.00	75.00	200	—
1849/8/7LIMAE MB	50.00	125	300	600	—
1849LIMAE MB	50.00	125	300	600	—
1850/49LIMAE MB	50.00	100	200	300	—
1850LIMAE MB Ornamented edge	10.00	25.00	75.00	200	—
1850LIMAE MB Roped edge	30.00	60.00	150	450	—
1851LIMAE MB	15.00	35.00	95.00	250	—
1852LIMAE MB	20.00	45.00	120	300	—

KM# 142.11 8 REALES
27.0700 g., 0.9030 Silver .7859 oz. ASW **Mint:** Arequipa **Obv. Legend:** REPUB. PERUANA 10Ds20Gs

Date	VG	F	VF	XF	Unc
1841AREQ M	2,500	4,500	7,500	12,000	—

KM# 142.12 8 REALES
27.0700 g., 0.9030 Silver .7859 oz. ASW **Mint:** Lima **Obverse:** Small date **Obv. Legend:** Small REPUBLICA PERUANA **Reverse:** Small letters in legend **Note:** Mint mark in monogram.

Date	VG	F	VF	XF	Unc
1853LIMAE MB	40.00	90.00	200	500	—

KM# 142.10a 8 REALES
23.9734 g., 0.9030 Silver .6960 oz. ASW **Mint:** Lima **Obv. Legend:** REPUB. PERUANA 10Ds20Gs **Edge:** Reeded edge **Note:** Mint mark in monogram.

Date	VG	F	VF	XF	Unc
1855LIMAE MB	10.00	20.00	50.00	120	—

KM# 142.13 8 REALES
27.0700 g., 0.9030 Silver .7859 oz. ASW **Mint:** Pasco **Obverse:** Small date **Obv. Legend:** REPUB PERUANA 10Ds20Gs

Date	VG	F	VF	XF	Unc
1857 Z in O PRO LA UNION (error); Rare	—	—	—	—	—

Note: Superior December sale 12-90 VF realized $20,900

Date	VG	F	VF	XF	Unc
1857 Z in O	—	—	10,000	20,000	—

KM# 146.2 1/2 ESCUDO
1.6873 g., 0.8750 Gold .0475 oz. AGW **Mint:** Cuzco

Date	VG	F	VF	XF	Unc
1826CUZCO GM	35.00	75.00	120	210	—

KM# 146.1 1/2 ESCUDO
1.6873 g., 0.8750 Gold .0475 oz. AGW **Mint:** Lima **Note:** Mint mark in monogram.

Date	VG	F	VF	XF	Unc
1826LIMAE JM	45.00	90.00	150	275	—
1827LIMAE JM	60.00	125	225	425	—
1828LIMAE JM	35.00	70.00	115	200	—
1829LIMAE JM	30.00	50.00	80.00	150	—
1833LIMAE MM	35.00	70.00	115	200	—
1836LIMAE TM	35.00	70.00	115	200	—
1836LIMAE MM	—	—	—	—	—
1839LIMAE MB	60.00	125	225	425	—
1840LIMAE MB	30.00	50.00	80.00	150	—
1841LIMAE MB	35.00	70.00	115	200	—
1842LIMAE MB	60.00	125	225	425	—
1850LIMAE MB	35.00	70.00	115	200	—
1851LIMAE MB	75.00	150	300	600	—
1856LIMAE MB	45.00	90.00	150	275	—

Note: For coins of this type dated 1838 M, see North Peru

KM# 147.2 ESCUDO
3.3750 g., 0.8750 Gold .0949 oz. AGW **Mint:** Cuzco **Obv. Legend:** REPUBLICA PERUANA

Date	VG	F	VF	XF	Unc
1826CUZCO GM	100	160	285	550	—
1830CUZCO G	100	160	285	550	—

KM# 147.1 ESCUDO
3.3750 g., 0.8750 Gold .0949 oz. AGW **Mint:** Lima **Obv. Legend:** REPUBLICA PERUANA **Note:** Mint mark in monogram.

Date	VG	F	VF	XF	Unc
1826LIMAE JM	70.00	120	240	425	—
1827LIMAE JM	95.00	165	300	500	—
1828/7LIMAE JM	70.00	120	240	425	—
1828LIMAE JM	70.00	120	240	425	—
1829LIMAE JM	55.00	85.00	165	275	—

KM# 147.3 ESCUDO
3.3750 g., 0.8750 Gold .0949 oz. AGW **Mint:** Cuzco **Obv. Legend:** REPUBLICA PERUANA **Note:** Mint mark in monogram.

Date	VG	F	VF	XF	Unc
1840 CUZco A	55.00	85.00	165	275	—
1845 CUZco A	55.00	70.00	115	200	—
1846 CUZco A	55.00	85.00	165	275	—

KM# 147.4 ESCUDO
3.3750 g., 0.8750 Gold .0949 oz. AGW **Mint:** Lima **Obv. Legend:** REPUB PERUANA **Note:** Mint mark in monogram.

Date	VG	F	VF	XF	Unc
1850LIMAE MB	—	—	—	—	—
1855LIMAE MB	70.00	120	240	425	—

KM# 149.1 2 ESCUDOS
6.8500 g., 0.8750 Gold .1899 oz. AGW **Mint:** Lima **Obv. Legend:** REPUBLICA PERUANA **Note:** Mint mark in monogram.

Date	VG	F	VF	XF	Unc
1828/7LIMAE JM	150	200	325	700	—
1828LIMAE JM	150	200	325	700	—
1829LIMAE JM	100	130	200	350	—

KM# 149.2 2 ESCUDOS
6.8500 g., 0.8750 Gold .1899 oz. AGW **Mint:** Lima **Obv. Legend:** REPUB. PERUANA **Note:** Mint mark in monogram.

Date	VG	F	VF	XF	Unc
1850LIMAE MB	125	175	300	550	—
1851LIMAE MB	110	150	240	425	—
1853LIMAE MB	95.00	115	145	275	—
1854LIMAE MB	125	175	300	550	—
1855LIMAE MB	125	175	300	550	—

KM# 150.1 4 ESCUDOS
13.5000 g., 0.8750 Gold .3798 oz. AGW **Mint:** Lima **Obv. Legend:** REPUB. PERUANA

Date	VG	F	VF	XF	Unc
1828 LIMA JM Rare	—	—	—	—	—

KM# 150.2 4 ESCUDOS
13.5000 g., 0.8750 Gold .3798 oz. AGW **Mint:** Lima **Obv. Legend:** REPUB. PERUANA **Note:** Mint mark in monogram.

Date	VG	F	VF	XF	Unc
1850LIMAE MB	225	350	600	1,000	—
1853LIMAE MB	300	475	750	1,500	—

KM# 150.3 4 ESCUDOS
13.5000 g., 0.8750 Gold .3798 oz. AGW **Mint:** Lima **Obverse:** Small lettering in legend **Reverse:** Flat base below Liberty **Note:** Mint mark in monogram.

Date	VG	F	VF	XF	Unc
1854LIMAE MB	200	300	550	900	—

KM# 150.4 4 ESCUDOS
13.5000 g., 0.8750 Gold .3798 oz. AGW **Mint:** Lima **Obv. Legend:** REPUB. PERVANA **Note:** Mint mark in monogram.

Date	VG	F	VF	XF	Unc
1855LIMAE MB	185	210	350	650	—

KM# 148.2 8 ESCUDOS
27.0000 g., 0.8750 Gold .7596 oz. AGW **Mint:** Cuzco **Obv. Legend:** REPUBLICA PERVANA

Date	VG	F	VF	XF	Unc
1826CUZCO GM	325	550	750	1,400	—
1827CUZCO G	325	550	750	1,400	—
1828/7CUZCO G	325	450	600	1,100	—
1828CUZCO G	325	450	600	1,100	—
1829CUZCO G	325	550	750	1,400	—
1830CUZCO G	325	450	600	1,100	—
1831CUZCO G	325	375	550	900	—
1832CUZCO VOARSH	325	400	600	1,000	—
1833CUZCO BoAr	325	375	550	900	—
1834CUZCO BoAr	325	400	600	1,000	—

KM# 148.1 8 ESCUDOS
27.0000 g., 0.8750 Gold .7596 oz. AGW **Mint:** Lima **Obv. Legend:** REPUBLICA PERVANA **Note:** Mint mark in monogram.

Date	VG	F	VF	XF	Unc
1826LIMAE JM	325	375	500	800	—
1827LIMAE JM	325	400	550	1,000	—
1828LIMAE JM	325	500	800	1,500	—
1829/8LIMAE JM	325	400	550	1,000	—
1829LIMAE JM	325	400	550	1,000	—
1830LIMAE JM	325	400	550	1,000	—
1833LIMAE MM	325	375	500	800	—
1840LIMAE MB	325	500	800	1,500	—

KM# 148.3 8 ESCUDOS
27.0000 g., 0.8750 Gold .7596 oz. AGW **Mint:** Cuzco **Obv. Legend:** REPUBLICA PERVANA **Note:** Mint mark in monogram.

Date	VG	F	VF	XF	Unc
1835 CUZco B	325	450	650	1,200	—
1836 CUZco B	325	500	800	1,500	—
1839 CUZco A	325	500	800	1,500	—
1840 CUZco A	325	400	600	1,000	—
1843 CUZco A	325	450	650	1,200	—
1844 CUZco A	325	500	800	1,500	—
1845 CUZco A	325	375	550	900	—

KM# 148.6 8 ESCUDOS
27.0000 g., 0.8750 Gold .7596 oz. AGW **Mint:** Lima **Obverse:** Large letters in legends **Obv. Legend:** REPUBLICA PERVANA **Reverse:** Large letters in legends **Note:** Mint mark in monogram.

Date	VG	F	VF	XF	Unc
1850 LIMA MB	325	375	500	900	—

KM# 148.4 8 ESCUDOS
27.0000 g., 0.8750 Gold .7596 oz. AGW **Mint:** Lima **Obverse:** Small letters in legends **Obv. Legend:** REPUBLICA PERVANA **Reverse:** Small letters in legends **Note:** Mint mark in monogram.

Date	VG	F	VF	XF	Unc
1853 LIMA MB	375	600	900	1,500	—
1854 LIMA MB	325	375	450	750	—
1855 LIMA MB	325	375	500	850	—

KM# 148.5 8 ESCUDOS
27.0000 g., 0.8750 Gold .7596 oz. AGW **Mint:** Lima **Obv. Legend:** REPUB. PERVANA **Note:** Mint mark in monogram.

Date	VG	F	VF	XF	Unc
1855 LIMA MB	325	375	450	750	—

DECIMAL COINAGE

100 Centavos (10 Dineros) = 1 Sol; 10 Soles = 1 Libra

KM# 206.2 1/2 DINERO
1.2500 g., 0.9000 Silver .0362 oz. ASW **Mint:** Lima **Obverse:** Without JR on stems **Reverse:** Denomination in straight line **Note:** Most coins 1900-06 show faint to strong traces of 9/8 or 90/89 in date. Non-overdates without such traces are scarce. Most coins of 1907-17 have engraver's initial R at left of shield tip on reverse. Many other varieties exist. Struck at Lima.

Date	Mintage	F	VF	XF	Unc
1893 TF	—	25.00	50.00	95.00	200
1895 TF	422,000	1.00	2.00	5.00	14.00
1896 TF	456,000	2.00	4.00	9.00	22.50
1896, F. Error; PBRUANA	Inc. above	—	—	—	—
1896 F.	Inc. above	1.00	2.00	4.50	12.00
1896. F.	Inc. above	1.00	2.00	4.50	12.00
1897 JF	320,000	0.75	1.25	2.50	6.00
1897 VN	Inc. above	3.50	7.00	16.00	37.50
1898/7 VN	600,000	1.00	2.00	5.00	14.00
1898 VN	Inc. above	0.75	1.50	3.50	10.00
1898 JF	Inc. above	0.60	1.25	2.50	6.00
1899/8 JF	500,000	1.00	1.75	4.00	11.00

Date	Mintage	F	VF	XF	Unc
1899 JF	Inc. above	0.60	1.25	2.50	6.00
1900/890 JF	400,000	6.00	1.25	2.50	6.00

KM# 204.2 DINERO
2.5000 g., 0.9000 Silver .0723 oz. ASW **Mint:** Lima **Obverse:** Large wreath **Reverse:** Denomination in curved line **Note:** Varieties exist. Struck at Lima.

Date	Mintage	F	VF	XF	Unc
1893 TF	23,000	4.00	8.00	17.50	60.00
1894/3 TF	—	15.00	30.00	60.00	175
1895/3 TF	90,000	5.00	15.00	25.00	45.00
1895 TF	Inc. above	4.00	8.00	17.50	70.00
1896/5 TF	534,000	2.50	6.00	12.50	25.00
1896 TF	Inc. above	5.00	10.00	20.00	50.00
1896/5 F	Inc. above	3.00	6.00	12.00	30.00
1896 F	Inc. above	3.00	6.00	12.00	28.00
1896 F	Inc. above	1.00	1.75	3.50	10.00
Note: Inverted E in Firme					
1897 JF	511,000	1.00	1.75	3.50	10.00
1897 VN	Inc. above	1.00	1.75	3.50	10.00
1898/7 JF	200,000	3.00	6.00	12.00	28.00
1898 JF	Inc. above	1.25	2.25	4.00	12.50
1900/90 JF	550,000	1.00	2.00	3.25	10.00
1900/98 JF	Inc. above	1.25	2.25	4.00	12.50
1900/890 JF	Inc. above	1.00	2.00	3.50	10.00
1900/898 JF	Inc. above	1.00	2.00	3.50	10.00
1900/897 JF	Inc. above	1.25	2.25	4.00	12.50
1900/89 JF	Inc. above	1.00	2.00	3.50	10.00
1900 JF	Inc. above	1.00	2.00	3.50	10.00

KM# 205.2 1/5 SOL
5.0000 g., 0.9000 Silver .1447 oz. ASW **Mint:** Lima **Reverse:** Libertad incuse **Edge:** Plain **Note:** Die varieties exist. Some coins 1893-1900 have engraver's initials JR left of shield on reverse and some 1911-17 have R in same location. Struck at Lima.

Date	Mintage	F	VF	XF	Unc
1893 TF-JR	49,000	5.00	10.00	20.00	75.00
1895 TF-JR	Inc. above	7.00	15.00	30.00	90.00
1896 TF-JR	586,000	1.50	3.00	5.50	14.00
1896 F-JR	Inc. above	1.75	3.50	7.00	20.00
1897 JF	745,000	1.50	3.00	5.50	14.00
1897 JF-JR	Inc. above	1.50	3.00	5.50	14.00
1897 VN	Inc. above	1.75	3.50	6.00	15.00
1898 JF Closed 9	350,000	1.50	3.00	5.50	14.00
1898 JF Open 9	Inc. above	2.00	4.00	8.00	25.00
1899/88 JF-JR	700,000	1.50	3.00	5.50	12.50
1899/8	Inc. above	1.50	3.00	5.50	12.50
1899 JF	Inc. above	1.50	3.00	5.50	12.00
1899 JF-JR	Inc. above	1.50	3.00	5.50	12.00
1900/800 JF	750,000	2.00	4.00	8.00	17.50
1900/800 JF-JR	Inc. above	1.75	3.50	6.00	15.00
1900/890 JF	Inc. above	1.50	3.00	5.50	12.00
1900 JF	Inc. above	2.00	4.00	8.00	17.50

KM# 196.26 SOL
25.0000 g., 0.9000 Silver .7234 oz. ASW **Reverse:** Libertad incuse **Note:** Type XII. Legends have smaller lettering. Varieties exist.

Date	Mintage	F	VF	XF	Unc
1393/893 TF Error date	—	30.00	45.00	90.00	200
1893 TF	—	6.00	7.00	10.00	27.50
1894 TF	4,358,000	6.00	7.00	10.00	27.50
1895 TF	4,111,000	6.00	7.00	10.00	27.50
1896 TF	2,511,000	6.00	8.00	12.00	40.00
1896 F	Inc. above	6.00	7.00	10.00	27.50
1897 JF	234,000	7.00	12.00	20.00	90.00

TRADE COINAGE

KM# 207 LIBRA (Pound)
7.9881 g., 0.9170 Gold .2354 oz. AGW

Date	Mintage	F	VF	XF	Unc
1898 ROZF	—	—	BV	110	165
1899 ROZF	—	—	BV	110	165
1900 ROZF	64,000	—	BV	110	165

TRIAL STRIKES

KM#	Date	Mintage	Identification	Mkt Val
TS1	1836	—	8 Reales. Silver. KM142	—

NORTH PERU

STATE

Estado Nor-Peruano

STATE COINAGE

KM# 154 1/2 REAL
1.6900 g., 0.9030 Silver .0490 oz. ASW **Mint:** Lima **Note:** Struck at Lima.

Date	VG	F	VF	XF	Unc
1836 TM	13.50	32.50	80.00	185	—
1837 TM	9.00	18.50	42.50	75.00	—
1837 M	10.00	22.50	50.00	85.00	—
1838 M	10.00	22.50	50.00	85.00	—
1838 MB	10.00	22.50	50.00	85.00	—

KM# 158 REAL
3.3800 g., 0.9030 Silver .0981 oz. ASW **Mint:** Lima **Note:** Struck at Lima.

Date	VG	F	VF	XF	Unc
1838/7	115	200	325	475	—
1838 MB	100	185	300	450	—

KM# 157 2 REALES
6.7700 g., 0.9030 Silver .1965 oz. ASW **Mint:** Lima **Note:** Struck at Lima

Date	VG	F	VF	XF	Unc
1837 JM Rare	—	—	—	—	—
1838 MB Rare	—	—	—	—	—

KM# 155 8 REALES
27.0700 g., 0.9030 Silver .7859 oz. ASW **Mint:** Lima **Note:** Struck at Lima.

Date	VG	F	VF	XF	Unc
1836 TM	12.00	20.00	35.00	125	—
1837 TM	11.00	18.50	32.00	100	—
1837 M	12.00	20.00	35.00	100	—
1838 M	12.00	20.00	35.00	100	—
1838 MB	11.00	18.50	32.00	100	—
1839 MB	12.00	20.00	35.00	100	—

KM# 159 1/2 ESCUDO
1.6875 g., 0.8750 Gold .0475 oz. AGW **Mint:** Lima **Note:** Struck at Lima.

Date	VG	F	VF	XF	Unc
1838 M	100	200	350	550	—

Note: This coin is identical to the Republic type, KM#146.1 and can only be identified by the date

KM# 160 ESCUDO
3.3750 g., 0.8750 Gold .0949 oz. AGW **Mint:** Lima **Note:** Struck at Lima.

Date	VG	F	VF	XF	Unc
1838 M	500	1,000	1,500	2,500	—

KM# 161 2 ESCUDOS
6.7500 g., 0.8750 Gold .1899 oz. AGW **Mint:** Lima **Note:** Struck at Lima.

Date	VG	F	VF	XF	Unc
1838 M	1,500	2,000	2,500	3,500	—

KM# 162 4 ESCUDOS
13.5000 g., 0.8750 Gold .3798 oz. AGW **Mint:** Lima **Note:** Struck at Lima.

Date	VG	F	VF	XF	Unc
1838 M	2,000	3,500	6,000	11,500	—

KM# 156 8 ESCUDOS
27.0000 g., 0.8750 Gold .7596 oz. AGW **Mint:** Lima **Note:** Struck at Lima.

Date	VG	F	VF	XF	Unc
1836 TM Rare	—	—	—	—	—
1838 TM	1,500	2,500	4,000	7,000	—

REPUBLIC

Republic Nor-Peruano

STATE COINAGE

KM# 163 1/2 REAL
1.6900 g., 0.9030 Silver .0490 oz. ASW **Mint:** Lima **Note:** Struck at Lima.

Date	VG	F	VF	XF	Unc
1839 MB	42.50	100	175	300	—

KM# 164 8 REALES
27.0700 g., 0.9030 Silver .7859 oz. ASW **Mint:** Lima **Note:** Struck at Lima.

Date	VG	F	VF	XF	Unc
1839 MB	350	650	1,150	2,000	—

SOUTH PERU

STATE

Estado Sud Peruano

STATE COINAGE

KM# 166 1/2 REAL
1.6900 g., 0.6670 Silver .0362 oz. ASW **Mint:** Cuzco **Note:** Struck at Cuzco.

Date	VG	F	VF	XF	Unc
1837 B	10.00	25.00	50.00	175	—

KM# 167 8 ESCUDOS
27.0000 g., 0.8750 Gold .7596 oz. AGW **Mint:** Cuzco

Date	VG	F	VF	XF	Unc
1837 BA	400	600	850	1,450	—

REPUBLIC

Republic Sud Peruano

REPUBLIC COINAGE

KM# 168 1/2 REAL
1.6500 g., 0.6670 Silver .0354 oz. ASW **Mint:** Arequipa

Date	VG	F	VF	XF	Unc
1837AREQ	10.00	20.00	45.00	135	—
1838/7AREQ	—	—	—	—	—

KM# 169.1 2 REALES
6.5000 g., 0.6670 Silver .1391 oz. ASW **Mint:** Cuzco

Date	VG	F	VF	XF	Unc
1837 BA	4.00	12.00	30.00	75.00	—

KM# 169.2 2 REALES
6.5000 g., 0.6670 Silver .1391 oz. ASW **Mint:** Arequipa

Date	VG	F	VF	XF	Unc
1838AREQ	5.00	15.00	37.50	90.00	—

KM# 172 4 REALES
13.5400 g., 0.6670 Silver .2899 oz. ASW **Mint:** Arequipa

Date	VG	F	VF	XF	Unc
1838AREQ MV	10.00	25.00	60.00	165	—

KM# 170.1 8 REALES
27.0700 g., 0.9030 Silver .7859 oz. ASW **Mint:** Cuzco **Rev. Legend:** REDERACION

Date	VG	F	VF	XF	Unc
1837CUZCO BA BA incuse edge lettering	20.00	45.00	80.00	175	—
1837CUZCO BA Raised edge lettering, 5 known	200	350	500	—	—

KM# 170.2 8 REALES
27.0700 g., 0.9030 Silver .7859 oz. ASW **Mint:** Cuzco **Reverse:** Small letters on legend **Rev. Legend:** CONFEDERATION • B • A •

Date	VG	F	VF	XF	Unc
1837CUZCO BA	25.00	55.00	120	300	—

KM# 170.4 8 REALES
27.0700 g., 0.9030 Silver .7859 oz. ASW **Mint:** Cuzco **Reverse:** Large letters in legend **Rev. Legend:** CONFEDERATION • B • A •

Date	VG	F	VF	XF	Unc
1837CUZCO MS	45.00	70.00	140	350	—
1838 CUZCO BA	20.00	45.00	75.00	125	—
1838CUZCO MS	20.00	45.00	75.00	125	—
1839CUZCO MS	50.00	100	225	375	—

KM# 170.3 8 REALES
27.0700 g., 0.9030 Silver .7859 oz. ASW **Mint:** Arequipa

Date	VG	F	VF	XF	Unc
1838AREQ MV	600	1,200	2,500	5,500	—
1839AREQ MV	1,650	3,250	5,250	—	—

KM# 173 1/2 ESCUDO
1.6875 g., 0.8750 Gold .0475 oz. AGW **Mint:** Cuzco **Note:** Mint mark in monogram.

Date	VG	F	VF	XF	Unc
1838CUZCO MS	75.00	140	220	450	—

KM# 174 ESCUDO
3.3750 g., 0.8750 Gold .0949 oz. AGW **Mint:** Cuzco

Date	VG	F	VF	XF	Unc
1838 MS	90.00	160	280	525	—

KM# 171 8 ESCUDOS
27.0000 g., 0.8750 Gold .7596 oz. AGW **Mint:** Cuzco

Date	VG	F	VF	XF	Unc
1837 BA	400	600	900	1,800	—
1838 MS	400	550	800	1,650	—

Republic of Peru

TRANSITIONAL COINAGE

ISSUED DURING THE CHANGEOVER TO THE DECIMAL SYSTEM

KM# 177 1/2 REAL (Medio)
1.2500 g., 0.9000 Silver .0361 oz. ASW **Mint:** Lima

Date	F	VF	XF	Unc
1858/68 MB	5.00	12.50	35.00	100
1858 MB	4.75	11.00	27.50	60.00

KM# 180 1/2 REAL (Medio)
1.2500 g., 0.9000 Silver .0361 oz. ASW **Mint:** Lima **Note:** Die and date varieties exist.

Date	F	VF	XF	Unc
1859 YB	4.00	9.50	22.50	50.00
1859 Y.B.	4.50	10.00	30.00	75.00
1860/59 YB	4.00	9.50	22.50	50.00
1860 YB/YO	4.00	9.50	22.50	50.00
1860 YB	3.00	8.00	17.50	40.00
1861 YB	4.00	9.50	22.50	50.00

KM# 181 REAL
2.5000 g., 0.9000 Silver .0723 oz. ASW **Mint:** Lima **Note:** Die varieties exist.

Date	F	VF	XF	Unc
1859 Y.B.	4.50	11.00	25.00	75.00
1860 Y.B.	2.75	6.00	12.50	55.00
1861 Y.B	5.00	13.50	30.00	85.00

KM# 184 4 ESCUDOS
13.5000 g., 0.8750 Gold .3798 oz. AGW **Mint:** Lima

Date	F	VF	XF	Unc
1863 YB Rare	—	—	—	—

KM# 183 8 ESCUDOS
27.0000 g., 0.8750 Gold .7596 oz. AGW **Mint:** Lima

Date	F	VF	XF	Unc
1862(no Mint Mark) YB	400	500	700	1,250
1863/2 YB	350	450	600	950
1863	350	450	600	950

KM# 182 25 CENTAVOS
6.2500 g., 0.9000 Silver .1808 oz. ASW **Mint:** Lima **Obverse:** RB below shield **Note:** Die varieties exist.

Date	F	VF	XF	Unc
1859/8 YB	22.50	47.50	110	250
1859 YB	35.00	65.00	150	300

KM# 179.1 50 CENTAVOS
12.0000 g., 0.9000 Silver .3501 oz. ASW **Mint:** Lima **Reverse:** Liberty with short hair

Date	F	VF	XF	Unc
1858 MB	15.00	30.00	75.00	275
1858 YB	12.00	25.00	65.00	235
1859 YB/Y	13.50	27.50	70.00	250

KM# 179.2 50 CENTAVOS
12.0000 g., 0.9000 Silver .3501 oz. ASW **Mint:** Lima **Reverse:** Liberty with long hair **Note:** Die varieties exist.

Date	F	VF	XF	Unc
1858 YB	10.00	22.50	48.00	145
1859/8 YB/Y	10.00	22.50	48.00	145
1859 YB/Y	9.00	20.00	40.00	125

KM# 178 50 CENTIMOS
12.0000 g., 0.9000 Silver .3501 oz. ASW **Mint:** Lima

Date	F	VF	XF	Unc
1858 MB	15.00	28.00	65.00	250
1858 MB Proof	—	—	—	—

DECIMAL COINAGE

100 CENTAVOS (10 DINEROS) = 1 SOL; 10 SOLES = 1 LIBRA

KM# 187.1 CENTAVO
Copper Nickel **Obverse:** Date at top **Reverse:** Straight centavo **Note:** Wreath varieties exist.

Date	Mintage	F	VF	XF	Unc
1863	1,000,000	1.00	2.50	6.00	22.50
1863 Proof	—	—	—	—	—
1864	Inc. above	1.25	3.50	7.50	25.00

KM# 187.1a CENTAVO
Bronze **Obverse:** Date at top **Reverse:** Straight centavo **Note:** Date varieties exist.

Date	F	VF	XF	Unc
1875	1.50	3.50	8.00	22.00
1876	1.50	3.50	9.00	22.00
1877	2.00	5.00	10.00	30.00
1878	10.00	15.00	25.00	65.00

KM# 188.1 2 CENTAVOS
Copper Nickel **Obverse:** Date at top

Date	Mintage	F	VF	XF	Unc
1863	1,000,000	1.50	4.00	12.50	27.50
1863 Proof	—	—	—	—	—
1864	Inc. above	1.50	4.00	12.50	27.50

KM# 188.1a 2 CENTAVOS
Copper Or Bronze **Obverse:** Date at top

Date	F	VF	XF	Unc
1864	3.00	9.00	20.00	50.00
1876	1.00	3.00	6.00	17.50
1877	1.00	4.00	8.50	25.00
1878	1.00	3.00	7.00	20.00
1879	1.00	3.00	7.00	20.00

Note: Coin and medal rotations exist

KM# 188.2 2 CENTAVOS
Copper Or Bronze **Note:** Modified dies.

Date	F	VF	XF	Unc
1895 (W)	0.75	1.75	4.00	25.00

KM# 189 1/2 DINERO
1.2500 g., 0.9000 Silver .0362 oz. ASW **Mint:** Lima **Obverse:** Small wreath **Reverse:** Denomination in curved line

Date	F	VF	XF	Unc
1863 YB	1.00	2.00	5.00	25.00
Note: Engraver's initials RB appear left of shield on reverse. Roman numeral I in 1/2 on 1863 dated coins				
1864 YB	1.50	3.00	7.50	35.00

KM# 189a 1/2 DINERO
1.2500 g., 0.9000 Silver .0362 oz. ASW **Mint:** Cuzco **Obverse:** Small wreath **Reverse:** Denomination in curved line

Date	VG	F	VF	XF	Unc
1885 JM	100	225	550	800	—

Note: S in wreath on obverse and engravers initials left of shield, Roman numeral I in 1/2 on reverse

KM# 206.1 1/2 DINERO
1.2500 g., 0.9000 Silver .0362 oz. ASW **Mint:** Lima **Obverse:** Large wreath, JR incuse on stems **Reverse:** Denomination in straight line

Date	Mintage	F	VF	XF	Unc
1890 TF	870,000	1.50	3.00	6.00	15.00
1891 TF	160,000	2.00	3.50	8.00	20.00
1892 TF	228,000	1.00	2.00	4.50	12.00

KM# 190 DINERO
2.5000 g., 0.9000 Silver .0723 oz. ASW **Mint:** Lima **Obverse:** Small wreath **Reverse:** Denomination in curved line

Date	F	VF	XF	Unc
1863 YB	1.25	2.25	4.50	20.00
1864/3 YB	1.25	2.25	4.00	15.00
1864 YB	1.50	2.50	5.00	22.00
1865/3 YB	3.50	7.50	15.00	45.00
1865 YB	2.00	5.00	10.00	45.00
1866/5 YB	1.25	2.25	4.00	15.00
1866 YB	1.00	1.75	3.50	12.50
1867 YB Reported, not confirmed	—	—	—	—
1870/60 YJ	3.00	6.00	15.00	45.00
1870/60 YJ/YB	—	—	—	—
1870/69 YJ/YB	1.25	2.25	4.00	15.00
1870 YJ	1.25	2.25	4.50	17.50
1870 YJ/B	1.25	2.25	4.00	15.00
1872/62 YJ/B	65.00	125	250	600
1872 YJ/B	50.00	100	200	450
1872 YJ	35.00	75.00	125	200

Date	F	VF	XF	Unc
1874 YJ	1.25	2.25	4.50	17.50
1875 YJ	1.00	1.75	3.50	12.50
1877 YJ	2.00	5.00	10.00	35.00
1877 Y.J.	3.00	5.00	15.00	50.00
1877 YJ Feilz (error)	4.00	8.00	20.00	60.00

KM# 190a DINERO
2.5000 g., 0.9000 Silver .0723 oz. ASW **Mint:** Cuzco **Obverse:** Small wreath **Reverse:** Denomination in curved line

Date	VG	F	VF	XF	Unc
1886 JM	16.50	35.00	65.00	150	—

Note: Engravers initials FB left of shield on reverse

KM# 204.1 DINERO
2.5000 g., 0.9000 Silver .0723 oz. ASW **Mint:** Lima **Obverse:** Large wreath **Reverse:** Denomination in straight line

Date	Mintage	F	VF	XF	Unc
1888(no Mint Mark) TF	10,000	50.00	90.00	150	250
1890(no Mint Mark) TF	400,000	1.25	2.25	5.00	20.00
1891(no Mint Mark) TF	60,000	3.00	8.00	20.00	42.00
1892(no Mint Mark) TF	69,000	3.00	8.00	20.00	42.00

KM# 191 1/5 SOL
5.0000 g., 0.9000 Silver .1447 oz. ASW **Mint:** Lima **Obverse:** Small wreath **Reverse:** Denomination in curved line **Edge:** Plain **Note:** Varieties exist.

Date	F	VF	XF	Unc
1863 YB	1.75	4.00	8.00	60.00
1864/3 YB	2.00	5.00	10.00	65.00
1864/3 YB-DD	—	25.00	55.00	250
1864 YB	1.50	3.50	7.00	60.00
1864 YB-DD	20.00	40.00	65.00	250
1865/4 YB	2.00	5.00	10.00	65.00
1865 YB	1.50	3.50	7.00	60.00
1866/5 YB	2.00	4.50	8.50	65.00
1866 YB	1.50	3.00	6.00	40.00
1867 YB	1.50	3.50	7.00	55.00
1869 YB	8.00	15.00	25.00	200
1874 YJ	1.75	4.00	7.50	60.00
1874 YJ/YB	—	—	—	—
1875 YB	—	—	—	—
1875/65 YJ	2.50	5.00	10.00	65.00
1875 YJ	1.75	4.00	7.50	60.00

Note: Engraver's initials RB appear left of shield on reverse.

KM# 191a 1/5 SOL
5.0000 g., 0.9000 Silver .1447 oz. ASW **Mint:** Arequipa **Edge:** Plain

Date	VG	F	VF	XF	Unc
1885 A. C.	350	575	900	1,500	2,500

KM# 205.1 1/5 SOL
5.0000 g., 0.9000 Silver .1447 oz. ASW **Mint:** Lima **Obverse:** Large wreath **Reverse:** Denomination in straight line, Libertad in relief **Edge:** Plain

Date	Mintage	F	VF	XF	Unc
1888 TF	550,000	1.75	3.50	6.00	17.50
1889 TF Rare	—	—	—	—	—
1890/88 TF	85,000	4.50	9.00	18.00	45.00
1890 TF	Inc. above	3.50	7.00	15.00	40.00
1891 TF	64,000	5.00	10.00	20.00	60.00
1892 TF	128,000	1.75	3.50	7.00	20.00

KM# 195 1/2 SOL
12.5000 g., 0.9000 Silver .3617 oz. ASW **Mint:** Lima **Obverse:** Small wreath **Reverse:** Denomination in curved line **Note:** Date varieties exist.

Date	F	VF	XF	Unc
1864 YB	5.00	10.00	20.00	60.00
1864(no Mint Mark) YB-D	100	150	250	400
Note: Engraver's initials RB appear left of shield on reverse				
1865 YB	4.00	8.50	15.00	100

Note: See 1 Sol, KM#196.2

KM# 196.2 SOL
250000.0000 g., 0.9000 Silver .7234 oz. ASW **Mint:** Lima **Obverse:** DERTEANO on bottom row of coins falling from cornucopia

Date	F	VF	XF	Unc
1864/54 Y. B. Arabic date	60.00	150	400	1,500
1864/54 Y. B. Roman I in date	100	175	500	1,700
1864 Y. B. Arabic date, Rare	—	—	—	—

Note: There are numerous minor die varieties such as D's in the denticles around the border on the obv

KM# 196.1 SOL
25.0000 g., 0.9000 Silver .7234 oz. ASW **Mint:** Lima **Obverse:** Small wreath above shield has ribbon ties **Reverse:** Shield below liberty's hand is tilted. Santiago issues have LIMA onthe coin **Note:** Type I.

Date	F	VF	XF	Unc
1864/54 YB	6.00	8.50	15.00	55.00
1864/54 Y. B.	6.00	8.50	15.00	55.00
1864/54 Y. B. Roman I in date	6.00	8.50	15.00	55.00
1864/54 Y. B. with Y. B. inverted	6.00	8.50	15.00	55.00
1864/54 Y. B. R-B on stems/ribbon by date	9.00	16.00	30.00	90.00
1865/55 YB	6.00	9.00	17.50	65.00
1865/55 Y. B.	6.00	9.00	14.00	65.00
1865/55 Y. B./B. B	6.00	9.00	17.50	65.00
1866/56 YB	6.00	8.00	12.00	40.00
1866/56 Y. B.	6.00	9.00	17.50	65.00
1866/56 Y. B.	6.00	8.00	12.00	40.00
1867/57 Y. B.	6.00	8.00	12.00	40.00
1868/58 Y. B.	6.00	8.00	12.00	40.00
1868/58 Y. B. BP on rev., left side	6.00	9.00	17.50	65.00

Note: Many minor die varieities, left side

KM# 196.3 SOL
250000.0000 g., 0.9000 Silver .7234 oz. ASW **Mint:** Lima **Note:** Type II; Many minor die varieties exist.

Date	F	VF	XF	Unc
1868 YB Roman I	6.00	9.00	17.50	65.00
1868 YB Arabic 1/Roman I	10.00	20.00	35.00	100
1868 YB Arabic 1	10.00	20.00	35.00	100
1868 YB Arabic BP on rev, left side	6.00	8.00	12.00	40.00
1868(no Mint Mark) YB Arabic 1 llama has 5 legs	6.00	9.00	17.50	70.00
1869 YB Arabic 1	6.00	7.50	11.00	30.00
1869 YB Arabic 1 BP on rev, left side	6.00	7.50	12.00	40.00
1869 YB Roman I	6.00	8.00	12.00	40.00
1870 YB Reported, but not confirmed	—	—	—	—
1870 YJ	6.00	7.50	12.00	40.00
1870 YJ dot below 7 in date	6.00	7.50	12.00	40.00
1871 YJ	6.00	7.50	11.00	30.00
1871 YJ dot above 1 in date	6.00	7.50	11.00	30.00
1871 YJ dot below i in date	6.00	7.50	11.00	30.00
1871 YJ dot below 7 in date	6.00	7.50	11.00	30.00
1872 YJ	6.00	7.50	11.00	30.00
1872 YJ dot below 7 in date	7.00	10.00	15.00	35.00
1873 YJ	10.00	20.00	40.00	135
1874 YJ	6.00	7.50	11.00	30.00
1875 YJ	6.00	7.50	11.00	35.00
1876 YJ Reported, not confirmed	—	—	—	—

KM# 196.4 SOL
250000.0000 g., 0.9000 Silver .7234 oz. ASW **Mint:** Santiago **Note:** Many minor die varieties exist.

Date	Mintage	F	VF	XF	Unc
1873 LD Arabic 1	445,000	7.50	15.00	25.00	75.00
1873 LD/backwards D. Arabic 1	—	12.00	20.00	35.00	100
1873 LD Arabic 1/Roman I	—	12.00	20.00	35.00	100
1873(no Mint Mark) LD Roman I	—	9.00	17.50	30.00	90.00

KM# 196.5 SOL
250000.0000 g., 0.9000 Silver .7234 oz. ASW **Mint:** Santiago **Note:** Type III. Letters R B on stems flanking date.

Date	F	VF	XF	Unc
1879 YJ	6.00	8.50	15.00	55.00
1880/70 YJ	17.50	37.50	75.00	250
1880/8 YJ	12.00	25.00	50.00	200
1880 YJ	12.00	25.00	50.00	150

KM# 196.7 SOL
250000.0000 g., 0.9000 Silver .7234 oz. ASW **Mint:** Santiago **Note:** 3 berries in bunch.

Date	F	VF	XF	Unc
1880 YJ	15.00	35.00	75.00	200

KM# 196.6 SOL
250000.0000 g., 0.9000 Silver .7234 oz. ASW **Mint:** Santiago **Note:** Letters R B on ribbon of wreath. 3 berries in bunch.

Date	F	VF	XF	Unc
1880 YJ	20.00	45.00	85.00	350

KM# 196.29 SOL
250000.0000 g., 0.9000 Silver .7234 oz. ASW **Mint:** Santiago **Note:** Without extra letters on stem, 3 berries.

Date	F	VF	XF	Unc
1880 YJ	12.00	25.00	50.00	150

KM# 196.8 SOL
250000.0000 g., 0.9000 Silver .7234 oz. ASW **Mint:** Santiago **Note:** Without extra letters. 2 berries in bunch; Many minor die varieties exist.

Date	F	VF	XF	Unc
1880 YJ	12.00	25.00	50.00	200

KM# 196.9 SOL
250000.0000 g., 0.9000 Silver .7234 oz. ASW **Mint:** Santiago **Note:** Type IV.

Date	F	VF	XF	Unc
1881 BF	6.00	12.00	20.00	60.00

KM# 196.11 SOL
250000.0000 g., 0.9000 Silver .7234 oz. ASW **Mint:** Santiago **Note:** Type V. B. F. on rev, left side.

Date	F	VF	XF	Unc
1881 BF	6.00	9.00	17.50	65.00

KM# 196.12 SOL
250000.0000 g., 0.9000 Silver .7234 oz. ASW **Mint:** Santiago **Note:** R.B. on rev, left side.

Date	F	VF	XF	Unc
1881 BF	6.00	9.00	17.50	65.00
1882 BF	6.00	8.50	15.00	55.00

KM# 196.10 SOL
250000.0000 g., 0.9000 Silver .7234 oz. ASW **Mint:** Santiago **Reverse:** Letters R. L. on base of column **Note:** Many minor die varieties exist.

Date	F	VF	XF	Unc
1881 BF	6.00	12.00	20.00	60.00

KM# 196.17 SOL
250000.0000 g., 0.9000 Silver .7234 oz. ASW **Mint:** Santiago **Reverse:** FD RB at base of column **Note:** Many minor die varieties exist.

Date	F	VF	XF	Unc
1882 FN	6.00	9.00	17.50	65.00

KM# 196.13 SOL
250000.0000 g., 0.9000 Silver .7234 oz. ASW **Mint:** Santiago **Note:** F. D. on rev, left side.

Date	F	VF	XF	Unc
1882 BF	6.00	8.50	15.00	55.00

KM# 196.14 SOL
250000.0000 g., 0.9000 Silver .7234 oz. ASW **Mint:** Santiago **Note:** FD on rev at base of column; Many minor die varieties exist.

Date	F	VF	XF	Unc
1882 BF	6.00	10.00	20.00	75.00
1882 FN	6.00	12.00	25.00	80.00

KM# 196.16 SOL
250000.0000 g., 0.9000 Silver .7234 oz. ASW **Mint:** Santiago **Reverse:** FD at base of column

Date	F	VF	XF	Unc
1882 FN	6.00	9.00	17.50	65.00

KM# 196.15 SOL
250000.0000 g., 0.9000 Silver .7234 oz. ASW **Mint:** Santiago **Reverse:** F. D. n left side **Note:** Type VI.

Date	F	VF	XF	Unc
1882 FN	6.00	9.00	17.50	65.00
1882 FN/BN	—	—	—	—

KM# 196.18 SOL
250000.0000 g., 0.9000 Silver .7234 oz. ASW **Mint:** Santiago **Reverse:** B. F. on left side **Note:** Type VII

Date	F	VF	XF	Unc
1883 FN	6.00	8.50	15.00	55.00

KM# 196.19 SOL
250000.0000 g., 0.9000 Silver .7234 oz. ASW **Mint:** Santiago **Reverse:** F. D. on left side. Libertad in relief **Note:** Many minor die varieties exist.

Date	F	VF	XF	Unc
1883 FN	6.00	8.50	15.00	55.00
1884 BD	6.00	7.50	11.00	35.00
1884 RD	6.00	7.50	11.00	35.00

KM# 196.20 SOL
250000.0000 g., 0.9000 Silver .7234 oz. ASW **Mint:** Santiago **Reverse:** F. D. on left side **Note:** Type VIII

Date	F	VF	XF	Unc
1884 BD	6.00	7.50	11.00	35.00
1884 BD/BF	6.00	8.00	12.00	40.00
1884 RD	6.00	7.50	11.00	35.00

KM# 196.21 SOL
250000.0000 g., 0.9000 Silver .7234 oz. ASW **Mint:** Santiago **Note:** Type IX. Without extra initials.

Date	F	VF	XF	Unc
1884 RD	7.00	9.00	15.00	50.00

KM# 196.22 SOL
250000.0000 g., 0.9000 Silver .7234 oz. ASW **Mint:** Santiago **Reverse:** Libertad incuse **Note:** Type X; Many minor die varieties exist.

Date	F	VF	XF	Unc
1885 RD	6.00	7.50	15.00	30.00
1885 RD/BD	6.00	7.50	15.00	30.00
1885 RD/BF	6.00	7.50	15.00	30.00
1885 TD	6.00	7.50	15.00	30.00
1885 TD/BD	6.00	7.50	15.00	30.00
1885 TD/BF	6.00	7.50	15.00	30.00
1885 TD/TF	6.00	7.50	15.00	30.00
1886/5 TF	17.50	37.50	75.00	300
1886/5 TF/BR	17.50	37.50	100	200
1886 TF	6.00	8.50	15.00	55.00
1887/6 TF	6.00	7.50	11.00	30.00
1887/6 TF/BF	6.00	7.50	11.00	30.00
1887 TF	6.00	7.00	10.00	27.50
1887 TF/BF	6.00	7.00	10.00	27.50

KM# 196.23 SOL
250000.0000 g., 0.9000 Silver .7234 oz. ASW **Mint:** Santiago **Reverse:** R on base of column

Date	F	VF	XF	Unc
1885 RD	6.00	8.50	15.00	50.00

KM# 196.24 SOL
250000.0000 g., 0.9000 Silver .7234 oz. ASW **Mint:** Santiago **Reverse:** Shield below Liberty's hand is tilted. UN SOL is in a stright line, Libertad in relief **Note:** Type XI; Date varieties exist.

Date	Mintage	F	VF	XF	Unc
1888 TF	3,147,000	6.00	7.00	11.00	30.00
1888 TF/BF	Inc. above	6.00	7.00	11.00	30.00
1889 TF	2,842,000	6.00	7.00	10.00	27.50
1889 TF/BF	Inc. above	6.00	7.00	10.00	27.50
1890/80 TF/BF	2,304,000	6.00	9.00	15.00	55.00
1890 TF/BF	Inc. above	6.00	7.00	10.00	27.50
1890 TF	Inc. above	6.00	7.00	10.00	27.50
1891/81 TF	2,981,000	6.00	8.00	12.00	32.50
1891/81 TF/BF	Inc. above	6.00	8.00	12.00	32.50
1891 TF/BF	Inc. above	6.00	7.00	10.00	27.50
1891 TF	Inc. above	6.00	7.00	10.00	27.50
1892/82 TF/BF	—	6.00	8.00	12.00	32.50
1892 TF/BF	Inc. above	6.00	7.00	10.00	27.50
1892 TF	2,270,000	6.00	7.00	10.00	27.50

KM# 196.25 SOL
250000.0000 g., 0.9000 Silver .7234 oz. ASW **Mint:** Santiago **Reverse:** Legend: Inverted V for A in LA **Note:** Many minor die varieties exist, especially for the 1888 issues.

Date	F	VF	XF	Unc
1889 TF/BF	15.00	30.00	60.00	100

KM# 192 5 SOLES
8.0645 g., 0.9000 Gold .2334 oz. AGW **Mint:** Lima **Note:** Mint mark: LIMA

Date	F	VF	XF	Unc
1863LIMA YB	125	150	225	375

KM# 193 10 SOLES
16.1290 g., 0.9000 Gold .4667 oz. AGW **Mint:** Lima **Note:** Mint mark: LIMA

Date	F	VF	XF	Unc
1863LIMA YB	225	250	300	500

KM# 194 20 SOLES
32.2581 g., 0.9000 Gold .9334 oz. AGW **Mint:** Lima **Subject:** 150th Anniversary - Birth of Admiral Grau **Note:** Mint mark: LIMA

Date	F	VF	XF	Unc
1863LIMA YB	450	475	500	650

PROVISIONAL COINAGE

KM# 197 5 CENTAVOS
Copper Nickel **Mint:** Lima

Date	Mintage	F	VF	XF	Unc
1879	12,000,000	1.00	1.75	3.50	6.00
1880	2,000,000	1.50	3.00	6.00	10.00

KM# 198 10 CENTAVOS
Copper Nickel **Mint:** Lima

Date	Mintage	F	VF	XF	Unc
1879	3,005,000	1.00	2.00	6.00	10.00
1880	4,000,000	1.00	1.50	2.50	5.00

KM# 199 20 CENTAVOS
Copper Nickel **Mint:** Lima

Date	Mintage	F	VF	XF	Unc
1879	498,000	4.50	8.50	20.00	55.00

PESETA COINAGE

KM# 202 1/2 REAL
1.2500 g., 0.9000 Silver .0362 oz. ASW **Mint:** Ayacucho

Date	VG	F	VF	XF	Unc
1882 LM	150	275	500	850	1,800

Note: Most specimens have been holed or soldered (and sometimes repaired) and are worth less than half of market valuations shown

KM# 200.1 PESETA
5.0000 g., 0.9000 Silver .1447 oz. ASW **Mint:** Lima **Obverse:** B below wreath

Date	F	VF	XF	Unc
1880 BF	3.00	5.00	12.50	40.00

KM# 200.2 PESETA
5.0000 g., 0.9000 Silver .1447 oz. ASW **Mint:** Lima **Obverse:** With dot after B below wreath **Note:** Die varieties exist.

Date	F	VF	XF	Unc
1880 BF	3.00	5.00	12.50	40.00

KM# 201.1 5 PESETAS
25.0000 g., 0.9000 Silver .7234 oz. ASW **Mint:** Lima **Obverse:** B below wreath

Date	F	VF	XF	Unc
1880 BF	15.00	25.00	60.00	225

KM# 201.2 5 PESETAS
25.0000 g., 0.9000 Silver .7234 oz. ASW **Mint:** Lima **Obverse:** With dot after B below wreath

Date	F	VF	XF	Unc
1880 BF	12.00	20.00	45.00	185

KM# 201.3 5 PESETAS
25.0000 g., 0.9000 Silver .7234 oz. ASW **Mint:** Ayacucho **Reverse:** Similar to KM#201.1

Date	F	VF	XF	Unc
1881 B	90.00	220	500	1,000
1882 LM	45.00	100	200	500

TRIAL STRIKES

KM#	Date	Mintage	Identification	Mkt Val
TS2	1864	—	Centavo. Bronze. KM187.1a	—
TS3	1864	—	2 Centavos. Copper Or Bronze. KM188.1a.	—

PATTERNS

Including off metal strikes

KM#	Date	Mintage	Identification	Mkt Val
Pn4	1837	—	8 Reales. Bronze.	500
Pn5	1837	—	8 Reales. Silver.	—
Pn6	1855	—	1/2 Centimo. Copper. 5.5000 g.	220
Pn7	1855	—	Centimo. Copper. 10.7000 g.	300
Pn9	1855	—	5 Centimos. Silver.	1,000
Pn10	1855	—	10 Centimos. Silver.	1,000
Pn11	1855	—	20 Centimos. Silver.	800
PnA11	1855	—	50 Centimos. Silver. 12.5000 g.	2,000
Pn12	1855	—	Peso. Silver.	9,000
Pn13	1855	—	2 Pesos. 0.9000 Gold.	12,650
Pn14	1855	—	5 Pesos. 0.9000 Gold.	29,900
Pn15	1855	—	10 Pesos. 0.9000 Gold.	—
Pn16	1855	—	20 Pesos. 0.9000 Gold.	—

Note: KM#Pn6-16 were the first foreign coins struck at the United States Philadelphia Mint

KM#	Date	Mintage	Identification	Mkt Val
Pn17	1860	—	Real. Bust without legend	—
Pn18	1860	—	2 Reales. (No Composition).	—
Pn19	1860	—	Peseta. (No Composition).	—
Pn20	1863	—	1/2 Sol. 0.9000 Silver.	—
Pn21	1863	—	Sol. 0.9000 Silver.	—
Pn23	1875	—	1/2 Centimo. (No Composition).	1,700
PnA24	1876	—	Sol. 0.9000 Silver.	400
PnA25	1886	—	Centavo. Bronze. KM187.1a	—
Pn25	1886	—	2 Centavos. Copper Or Bronze. KM188.1a	—
PnA26	1886	6	1/2 Dinero. 0.9000 Silver. KM206.1	750
PnB26	1886	6	Dinero. 0.9000 Silver. KM204.1	950
PnC26	1886	6	1/5 Sol. 0.9000 Silver. KM205	1,250
PnD26	1886	—	1/2 Sol. 0.9000 Silver. KM203	1,750
PnE26	1886	—	Sol. 0.9000 Silver. KM196.22.	2,500

PROOF SETS

KM#	Date	Mintage	Identification	Issue Price	Mkt Val
PS1	1886 (7)	6	KMPnA25, 25, A26-E26	—	4,500

PHILIPPINES

The Philippines, an archipelago in the western Pacific 500 miles (805 km.) from the southeast coast of Asia, has an area of 115,830 sq. mi. (300,000 sq. km.).

Migration to the Philippines began about 30,000 years ago when land bridges connected the islands with Borneo and Sumatra. Ferdinand Magellan claimed the islands for Spain in 1521. The first permanent settlement was established by Miguel de Legazpi at Cebu April 1565. Manila was established in 1572. A British expedition captured Manila and occupied the Spanish colony in October 1762, but returned it to Spain by the treaty of Paris, 1763. Spain held the Philippines despite growing Filipino nationalism until 1898 when they were ceded to the United States at the end of the Spanish-American War.

MINT MARKS

(b) Brussels, privy marks only
BSP - Bangko Sentral Pilipinas
(Lt) - Llantrisant
M, MA - Manila
(Sh) - Sherritt
(VDM) - Vereinigte Deutsche Metall ...Werks; Altona, Germany
Star - Manila (Spanish) = Manila

MONETARY SYSTEM

4 Quartos = 1 Real
8 Reales = 1 Peso

SPANISH COLONIAL

COLONIAL COINAGE

For copper issues until 1833, minor variations in die work, planchet size and weight are relatively commonplace, compared to later issues from the up-graded Manila Mint (ca.1860).

KM# 5 OCTAVO
Copper

Date	Mintage	Good	VG	F	VF	XF
1798M F	—	50.00	75.00	125	175	—
1805M F	—	25.00	40.00	75.00	125	—
1806M F	—	25.00	40.00	75.00	125	—

KM# 8 OCTAVO
Copper

Date	Mintage	F	VF	XF	Unc	BU
1820 F	—	10.00	25.00	50.00	125	—
1829 F	—	50.00	75.00	250	750	—
1830 F	—	15.00	40.00	75.00	350	—

KM# 6 QUARTO
Copper **Note:** Similar to KM#7.

Date	Mintage	Good	VG	F	VF	XF
1805M F	—	7.50	15.00	40.00	65.00	—
1806M F	—	7.50	15.00	40.00	65.00	—
1807M F	—	7.50	15.00	40.00	65.00	—

KM# 7 QUARTO
Copper **Note:** Varieties exist.

Date	Mintage	VG	F	VF	XF	Unc
1817 F	—	60.00	90.00	125	200	—
1817 F Retrograde 7	—	75.00	100	—	—	—
1819 F Error, 9181 with retrograde 9	—	75.00	125	250	500	—
1820 F	—	10.00	20.00	40.00	60.00	—
1821 F	—	20.00	40.00	75.00	100	—
1822 F Rare	—	—	—	—	—	—
1822 F Error, 2281 with retrograde 2s	—	60.00	75.00	100	175	—
1823 F	—	15.00	30.00	50.00	85.00	—
1824 F	—	200	350	—	—	—
1826 F	—	12.50	30.00	50.00	75.00	—
1827 F Rare	—	—	—	—	—	—
1828 F	—	10.00	20.00	75.00	100	—
1829 F	—	10.00	20.00	60.00	85.00	—
1829 F Retrograde	—	—	100	175	—	—
1830 F	—	10.00	25.00	60.00	85.00	—
1831 F	—	50.00	80.00	100	175	—
1833 F	—	50.00	80.00	100	175	—

KM# 9 QUARTO
Copper **Obv:** Ferdinand VII bust r. **Rev:** Crowned Spanish shield

Date	Mintage	Good	VG	F	VF	XF
1822 F	—	35.00	50.00	75.00	150	—
1823 F	—	30.00	40.00	50.00	100	—
1824 F	—	35.00	55.00	80.00	200	—

KM# 10 QUARTO
Copper **Obv:** Crowned Spanish shield **Obv. Legend:** FERD • VII...

Date	Mintage	Good	VG	F	VF	XF
1834MA F	—	10.00	20.00	50.00	75.00	—

KM# 13 QUARTO
Copper **Obv:** Crowned Spanish shield **Obv. Legend:** YSAB • II...

Date	Mintage	Good	VG	F	VF	XF
1835MA F	—	50.00	75.00	125	300	—

KM# 11 2 QUARTOS
Copper **Obv:** Crowned Spanish shield **Obv. Legend:** FERD • VII...

Date	Mintage	Good	VG	F	VF	XF
1834MA F	—	100	200	300	500	—

KM# 14 2 QUARTOS
Copper **Obv:** Crowned Spanish shield **Obv. Inscription:** YSAB • II...

Date	Mintage	Good	VG	F	VF	XF
1835	—	50.00	100	200	300	—

KM# 12 4 QUARTOS
Copper **Obv:** Crowned Spanish shield **Obv. Legend:** FERD • VII...

Date	Mintage	Good	VG	F	VF	XF
1834	—	150	225	400	700	—

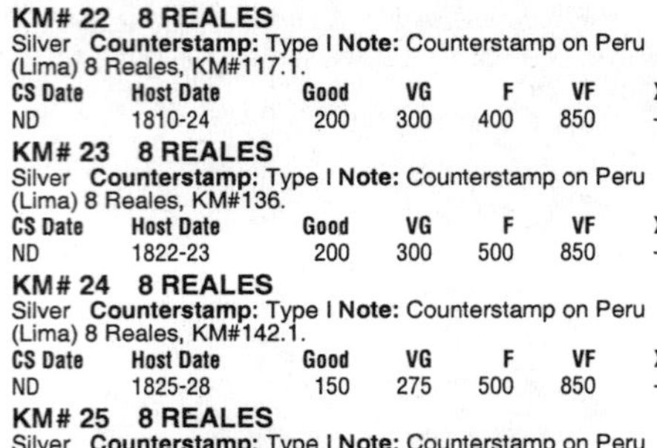

KM# 15 4 QUARTOS
Copper **Obv:** Crowned Spanish shield **Obv. Legend:** YSAB • II...

Date	Mintage	Good	VG	F	VF	XF
1835 F	—	225	400	650	1,000	—

COUNTERSTAMPED COINAGE

MANILA/1828 TYPE I

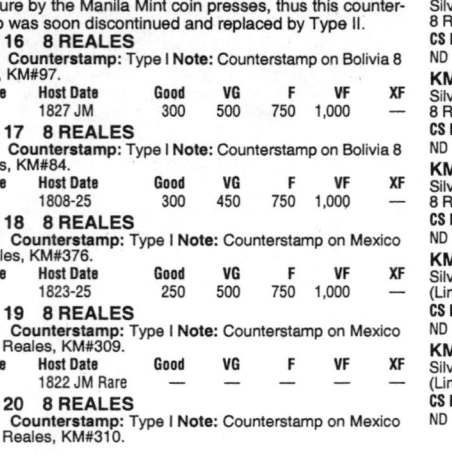

Obverse counterstamp: MANILA/1828 within serrated circle. Reverse legend: HABILITADO POR EL REY N. S. D. FERN. VII. around crowned Spanish royal arms.

This counterstamp was inaugurated on October 13, 1828 by the Captain-General of the Philippines. The outer border and reverse legend of the Type I counterstamp were intended to obliterate the legends on the foreign dollars being overstruck. This failed to work satisfactorily due to inadequate pressure by the Manila Mint coin presses, thus this counterstamp was soon discontinued and replaced by Type II.

KM# 16 8 REALES
Silver **Counterstamp:** Type I **Note:** Counterstamp on Bolivia 8 Soles, KM#97.

CS Date	Host Date	Good	VG	F	VF	XF
ND	1827 JM	300	500	750	1,000	—

KM# 17 8 REALES
Silver **Counterstamp:** Type I **Note:** Counterstamp on Bolivia 8 Reales, KM#84.

CS Date	Host Date	Good	VG	F	VF	XF
ND	1808-25	300	450	750	1,000	—

KM# 18 8 REALES
Silver **Counterstamp:** Type I **Note:** Counterstamp on Mexico 8 Reales, KM#376.

CS Date	Host Date	Good	VG	F	VF	XF
ND	1823-25	250	500	750	1,000	—

KM# 19 8 REALES
Silver **Counterstamp:** Type I **Note:** Counterstamp on Mexico City 8 Reales, KM#309.

CS Date	Host Date	Good	VG	F	VF	XF
ND	1822 JM Rare	—	—	—	—	—

KM# 20 8 REALES
Silver **Counterstamp:** Type I **Note:** Counterstamp on Mexico City 8 Reales, KM#310.

CS Date	Host Date	Good	VG	F	VF	XF
ND	1822-23 JM	300	500	800	1,100	—

KM# 21 8 REALES
Silver **Counterstamp:** Type I **Note:** Counterstamp on Mexico 8 Reales, KM#377.

CS Date	Host Date	Good	VG	F	VF	XF
ND	1824-28	200	400	700	950	—

KM# 22 8 REALES
Silver **Counterstamp:** Type I **Note:** Counterstamp on Peru (Lima) 8 Reales, KM#117.1.

CS Date	Host Date	Good	VG	F	VF	XF
ND	1810-24	200	300	400	850	—

KM# 23 8 REALES
Silver **Counterstamp:** Type I **Note:** Counterstamp on Peru (Lima) 8 Reales, KM#136.

CS Date	Host Date	Good	VG	F	VF	XF
ND	1822-23	200	300	500	850	—

KM# 24 8 REALES
Silver **Counterstamp:** Type I **Note:** Counterstamp on Peru (Lima) 8 Reales, KM#142.1.

CS Date	Host Date	Good	VG	F	VF	XF
ND	1825-28	150	275	500	850	—

KM# 25 8 REALES
Silver **Counterstamp:** Type I **Note:** Counterstamp on Peru (Lima) 8 Reales, KM#142.3.

CS Date	Host Date	Good	VG	F	VF	XF
ND	1828	250	500	750	900	—

KM# 26.1 8 REALES
Silver **Counterstamp:** Type I **Note:** Prev. KM#26. Counterstamp on Peru (Cuzco) 8 Reales, KM#142.2.

CS Date	Host Date	Good	VG	F	VF	XF
ND	1826-28	500	750	1,000	1,250	—

Note: Other coin types may exist with this particular counterstamp

KM# 38 8 REALES
Silver **Counterstamp:** Type I **Note:** Counterstamp on Mexico 8 Reales, KM#376.

CS Date	Host Date	Good	VG	F	VF	XF
ND	1823-24	250	500	750	1,000	—

KM# 26.2 8 REALES
Silver **Countermark:** Type I **Note:** Counterstamp on Peru (Cuzco), 8 Reales, KM#142.2.

CS Date	Host Date	Good	VG	F	VF	XF
ND	1828	—	750	1,000	1,500	—

MANILA/1828 TYPE II

Obverse counterstamp: MANILA/1828. Reverse: Crowned Spanish royal arms without legends and serrated circles.

KM# 27 8 REALES
Silver **Counterstamp:** Type II **Note:** Counterstamp on Bolivia 8 Reales, KM#84.

CS Date	Host Date	Good	VG	F	VF	XF
ND	1808-25	250	550	800	950	—

KM# 28 8 REALES
Silver **Counterstamp:** Type II **Note:** Counterstamp on Mexico 8 Reales, KM#376.

CS Date	Host Date	Good	VG	F	VF	XF
ND	1823-25	300	600	900	1,100	—

KM# 29 8 REALES
Silver **Counterstamp:** Type II **Note:** Counterstamp on Mexico 8 Reales, KM#377.

CS Date	Host Date	Good	VG	F	VF	XF
ND	1824-28	200	500	800	950	—

KM# 30 8 REALES
Silver **Counterstamp:** Type II **Note:** Counterstamp on Peru (Lima) 8 Reales, KM#117.1.

CS Date	Host Date	Good	VG	F	VF	XF
ND	1810-24	200	500	750	900	—

KM# 31 8 REALES
Silver **Counterstamp:** Type II **Note:** Counterstamp on Peru (Lima) 8 Reales, KM#136.

CS Date	Host Date	Good	VG	F	VF	XF
ND	1822-23	200	500	750	900	—

KM# 32 8 REALES
Silver **Counterstamp:** Type II **Note:** Counterstamp on Peru (Lima) 8 Reales, KM#142.1.

CS Date	Host Date	Good	VG	F	VF	XF
ND	1825-28	200	500	750	900	—

KM# 33 8 REALES
Silver **Counterstamp:** Type II **Note:** Counterstamp on Peru (Lima) 8 Reales, KM#142.3.

CS Date	Host Date	Good	VG	F	VF	XF
ND	1828	250	550	800	900	—

Note: Other coin types may exist with this particular counterstamp

MANILA/1828 TYPE III

Reverse: Crowned Spanish royal arms.

KM# 34 8 ESCUDOS
Gold **Counterstamp:** Type III **Note:** Counterstamp on Mexico City 8 Escudos, KM#383.

CS Date	Host Date	Good	VG	F	VF	XF
ND	1825 JM Rare	—	—	—	—	—

Note: The above is in the collection of Fabrica Nacional de Moneda y Timbre de Madrid (Spain)

MANILA/1830 TYPE IV

Counterstamp: MANILA/1830 within serrated circle. Reverse legend: HABILITADO POR EL REY N. S. D. FERN. VII. around crowned Spanish royal arms.

KM# 35 8 REALES
Silver **Counterstamp:** Type IV **Note:** Counterstamp on Bolivia 8 Soles, KM#97.

CS Date	Host Date	Good	VG	F	VF	XF
ND	1827-30 Rare	—	—	—	—	—

Note: Rare double stamped obverse coin illustrated, Bank Leu Bostonian sale 10-90 VF realized $16,380. In the Stack's sale of 1-04 an XF realized $16,000.

KM# 36 8 REALES
Silver **Counterstamp:** Type IV **Note:** Counterstamp on Mexico 8 Reales, KM#376.

CS Date	Host Date	Good	VG	F	VF	XF
ND	1823-25 Rare	—	—	—	—	—

KM# 37 8 REALES
Silver **Counterstamp:** Type IV **Note:** Counterstamp on Mexico 8 Reales, KM#377.

CS Date	Host Date	Good	VG	F	VF	XF
ND	1824-30	—	—	—	—	—

Note: Other coin types may exist with this particular counterstamp

FERDINAND VII

Silver

Oval Type V and Round Type V

Round Type V

Actual size 9-10mm

These countermarks were introduced by decree of October 27, 1832 due to the problems encountered with the larger countermarks of 1828-1830. Pierced or holed coins were declared not valid but later were countermarked directly over the hole with Type V or Type VI countermarks and circulated freely. The latter types exist countermarked on both sides directly over the hole and are very scarce. These countermarks were retired in 1834 after the death of Ferdinand VII and replaced with a similar design showing ""Y II"" for Isabel II, Type VI. Coins dated 1835 and later with either Type V countermark should be considered counterfeit.

KM# 40 REAL
Silver **Countermark:** F. 7. o **Note:** Countermark on Mexico 1 Real.

CM Date	Host Date	Good	VG	F	VF	XF
ND	ND Rare	—	—	—	—	—

KM# A42 2 REALS
Silver **Countermark:** F. 7. o. **Note:** Countermark on Spain 2 Reales, KM 430.2.

CM Date	Host Date	Good	VG	F	VF	XF
ND	1806 Rare	—	—	—	—	—

KM# 41 2 REALS
Silver **Countermark:** F. 7. o **Note:** Countermark on Mexico 2 Reales, KM#372.

CM Date	Host Date	Good	VG	F	VF	XF
ND	1825-34	75.00	100	200	300	—

KM# 42 2 REALS
Silver **Countermark:** F. 7. o **Note:** Countermark on Peru 2 Reales, KM#141.

CM Date	Host Date	Good	VG	F	VF	XF
ND	1825-34	300	400	500	750	—

KM# 43 4 REALS
Silver **Countermark:** F. 7. o **Note:** Countermark on Mexico 4 Reales.

CM Date	Host Date	Good	VG	F	VF	XF
ND	ND Rare	—	—	—	—	—

KM# 44.1 8 REALES
Silver **Countermark:** F. 7. o **Note:** Countermark on Argentina 8 Reales, KM#5.

CM Date	Host Date	Good	VG	F	VF	XF
ND	1813	350	550	850	1,250	—

KM# 44.2 8 REALES
Silver **Countermark:** F. 7. o **Note:** Countermark on Argentina 8 Reales, KM#14.

CM Date	Host Date	Good	VG	F	VF	XF
ND	1815	350	500	750	1,000	—

KM# 45 8 REALES
Silver **Countermark:** F. 7. o **Note:** Countermark on Argentina 8 Soles, KM#15.

CM Date	Host Date	Good	VG	F	VF	XF
ND	1815	350	550	650	900	—

KM# 46 8 REALES
Silver **Countermark:** F. 7. o **Note:** Countermark on Argentina 8 Reales, KM#20.

CM Date	Host Date	Good	VG	F	VF	XF
ND	1826-34	350	550	650	900	—

KM# 47 8 REALES
Silver **Countermark:** F. 7. o **Note:** Countermark on Bolivia 8 Reales, KM#55.

CM Date	Host Date	Good	VG	F	VF	XF
ND	1773-89	150	300	425	650	—

KM# 48 8 REALES
Silver **Countermark:** F. 7. o **Note:** Countermark on Bolivia 8 Reales, KM#64.

CM Date	Host Date	Good	VG	F	VF	XF
ND	1789-91	100	150	200	300	—

KM# 49 8 REALES
Silver **Countermark:** F. 7. o **Note:** Countermark on Bolivia 8 Reales, KM#73.

CM Date	Host Date	Good	VG	F	VF	XF
ND	1791-1808	—	200	300	500	—

KM# 50 8 REALES
Silver **Countermark:** F. 7. o **Note:** Countermark on Bolivia 8 Reales, KM#84.

CM Date	Host Date	Good	VG	F	VF	XF
ND	1808-25	75.00	125	175	275	—

KM# 51 8 REALES
Silver **Countermark:** F. 7. o **Note:** Countermark on Bolivia 8 Soles, KM#97.

CM Date	Host Date	Good	VG	F	VF	XF
ND	1827-34	50.00	75.00	125	250	—

KM# 52 8 REALES
Silver **Countermark:** F. 7. o **Note:** Countermark on Brazil 960 Reis, KM#307.

CM Date	Host Date	Good	VG	F	VF	XF
ND	1809-18 Rare	—	—	—	—	—

KM# 53 8 REALES
Silver **Countermark:** F. 7. o **Note:** Countermark on Brazil 960 Reis, KM#326.

CM Date	Host Date	Good	VG	F	VF	XF
ND	1818-22 Rare	—	—	—	—	—

KM# 54 8 REALES
Silver **Countermark:** F. 7. o **Note:** Countermark on Brazil 960 Reis, KM#368.

CM Date	Host Date	Good	VG	F	VF	XF
ND	1823-27 Rare	—	—	—	—	—

KM# 55 8 REALES
Silver **Countermark:** F. 7. o **Note:** Countermark on Central American Republic (Guatemala) 8 Reales, KM#4.

CM Date	Host Date	Good	VG	F	VF	XF
ND	1824-34	200	300	450	600	—

KM# 56 8 REALES
Silver **Countermark:** F. 7. o **Note:** Countermark on Chile 1 Peso, KM#82.

CM Date	Host Date	Good	VG	F	VF	XF
ND	1817-34	150	200	300	400	—

KM# 57 8 REALES
Silver **Countermark:** F. 7. o **Note:** Countermark on Columbia, Cundinamarca Province 8 Reales, KM#6.

CM Date	Host Date	Good	VG	F	VF	XF
ND	1820-21	125	200	300	450	—

KM# A58 8 REALES
Silver **Countermark:** F. 7. o **Note:** Countermark on France 5 Francs, C#189.

CM Date	Host Date	Good	VG	F	VF	XF
ND	1826D Rare	—	—	—	—	—

KM# 58 8 REALES
Silver **Countermark:** F. 7. o **Note:** Countermark in oval on Kingdom of Italy 5 Lire, C#10.1.

CM Date	Host Date	Good	VG	F	VF	XF
ND	1809 Rare	—	—	—	—	—

KM# 59 8 REALES
Silver **Countermark:** F. 7. o **Note:** Countermark on Mexico City 8 Reales, KM#105.

CM Date	Host Date	Good	VG	F	VF	XF
ND	1760-71 Rare	—	—	—	—	—

KM# 60 8 REALES
Silver **Countermark:** F. 7. o **Note:** Countermark on Mexico City 8 Reales, KM#106.

CM Date	Host Date	Good	VG	F	VF	XF
ND	1772-89	125	200	300	400	—

KM# 61 8 REALES
Silver **Countermark:** F. 7. o **Note:** Countermark on Mexico City 8 Reales, KM#107.

CM Date	Host Date	Good	VG	F	VF	XF
ND	1789-90FM	60.00	125	200	300	—

KM# 62 8 REALES
Silver **Countermark:** F. 7. o **Note:** Countermark on Mexico City 8 Reales, KM#108.

CM Date	Host Date	Good	VG	F	VF	XF
ND	1790FM	60.00	125	200	300	—

KM# 63 8 REALES
Silver **Countermark:** F. 7. o **Note:** Countermark on Mexico City 8 Reales, KM#109.

CM Date	Host Date	Good	VG	F	VF	XF
ND	1791-1808	150	200	300	500	—

KM# 64 8 REALES
Silver **Countermark:** F. 7. o **Note:** Countermark on Mexico City 8 Reales, KM#110.

CM Date	Host Date	Good	VG	F	VF	XF
ND	1808-11	60.00	100	175	275	—

KM# 65 8 REALES
Silver **Countermark:** F. 7. o **Note:** Countermark on Mexico City 8 Reales, KM#111.

CM Date	Host Date	Good	VG	F	VF	XF
ND	1811-21	60.00	110	150	250	—

KM# 66 8 REALES
Silver **Countermark:** F. 7. o **Note:** Countermark on Mexico City 8 Reales, KM#304.

CM Date	Host Date	Good	VG	F	VF	XF
ND	1822 JM	50.00	100	200	300	—

KM# 67 8 REALES
Silver **Countermark:** F. 7. o **Note:** Countermark on Mexico City 8 Reales, KM#305.

CM Date	Host Date	Good	VG	F	VF	XF
ND	1822 JM	50.00	100	200	300	—

KM# 68 8 REALES
Silver **Countermark:** F. 7. o **Note:** Countermark on Mexico City 8 Reales, KM#306.

CM Date	Host Date	Good	VG	F	VF	XF
ND	1822 JM	50.00	100	200	300	—

KM# 69 8 REALES
Silver **Countermark:** F. 7. o **Note:** Countermark on Mexico City 8 Reales, KM#307.

CM Date	Host Date	Good	VG	F	VF	XF
ND	1822 JM	75.00	150	250	450	—

KM# 70 8 REALES
Silver **Countermark:** F. 7. o **Note:** Countermark on Mexico City 8 Reales, KM#308.

CM Date	Host Date	Good	VG	F	VF	XF
ND	1822 JM	70.00	140	200	350	—

KM# 71 8 REALES
Silver **Countermark:** F. 7. o **Note:** Countermark on Mexico City 8 Reales, KM#309.

CM Date	Host Date	Good	VG	F	VF	XF
ND	1822 Rare	—	—	—	—	—

KM# 72 8 REALES
Silver **Countermark:** F. 7. o **Note:** Countermark on Mexico City 8 Reales, KM#310.

CM Date	Host Date	Good	VG	F	VF	XF
ND	1822-23 JM	75.00	125	200	300	—

KM# 73 8 REALES
Silver **Countermark:** F. 7. o **Note:** Countermark on Mexico (Guanajuato) 8 Reales, KM#376.1.

CM Date	Host Date	Good	VG	F	VF	XF
ND	1823-25	175	300	500	600	—

KM# A74 8 REALES
Silver **Countermark:** F.7.o. **Note:** Countermark on Mexico 8 Reales, KM #376.2.

CM Date	Host Date	Good	VG	F	VF	XF
ND	1824	—	300	450	600	—

KM# 74 8 REALES
Silver **Countermark:** F. 7. o **Note:** Countermark on Mexico 8 Reales, KM#377.

CM Date	Host Date	Good	VG	F	VF	XF
ND	1824-34	75.00	100	150	250	—

KM# 75 8 REALES
Silver **Countermark:** F. 7. o **Note:** Countermark on Peru (Lima) 8 Reales, KM#78.

CM Date	Host Date	Good	VG	F	VF	XF
ND	1772-89	60.00	100	150	250	—

KM# 76 8 REALES
Silver **Countermark:** F. 7. o **Note:** Countermark on Peru (Lima) 8 Reales, KM#87.

CM Date	Host Date	Good	VG	F	VF	XF
ND	1789-91	60.00	100	175	250	—

KM# 77 8 REALES
Silver **Countermark:** F. 7. o **Note:** Countermark on Peru (Lima) 8 Reales, KM#97.

CM Date	Host Date	Good	VG	F	VF	XF
ND	1791-1808	60.00	100	175	250	—

KM# 78 8 REALES
Silver **Countermark:** F. 7. o **Note:** Countermark on Peru (Lima) 8 Reales, KM#106.

CM Date	Host Date	Good	VG	F	VF	XF
ND	1808-11	60.00	85.00	130	200	—

KM# 79 8 REALES
Silver **Countermark:** F. 7. o **Note:** Countermark on Peru (Lima) 8 Reales, KM#117.1.

CM Date	Host Date	Good	VG	F	VF	XF
ND	1810-24	60.00	80.00	125	175	—

KM# 80 8 REALES
Silver **Countermark:** F. 7. o **Note:** Countermark on Peru (Lima) 8 Reales, KM#136.

CM Date	Host Date	Good	VG	F	VF	XF
ND	1822-23	50.00	100	200	275	—

KM# 81 8 REALES
Silver **Countermark:** F. 7. o **Note:** Countermark on Peru (Lima) 8 Reales, KM#130.

CM Date	Host Date	Good	VG	F	VF	XF
ND	1824	60.00	90.00	150	200	—

KM# 82 8 REALES
Silver **Countermark:** F. 7. o **Note:** Countermark in oval on Peru (Lima) 8 Reales, KM#142.1.

CM Date	Host Date	Good	VG	F	VF	XF
ND	1825-28 Rare	—	—	—	—	—

KM# 83 8 REALES
Silver **Countermark:** F. 7. o **Note:** Countermark on Peru (Lima) 8 Reales, KM#142.3.

CM Date	Host Date	Good	VG	F	VF	XF
ND	1828-34	30.00	40.00	50.00	65.00	125

KM# A84 8 REALES
Silver **Countermark:** F.7.o. **Note:** Countermark on Peru (Cuzco) 8 Reales, KM#142.2

CM Date	Host Date	Good	VG	F	VF	XF
ND	1829	—	200	300	400	—

KM# 84 8 REALES
Silver **Countermark:** F. 7. o **Note:** Countermark on Peru (Cuzco) 8 Reales, KM#142.4.

CM Date	Host Date	Good	VG	F	VF	XF
ND	1830-34	75.00	100	175	300	—

KM# 85 8 ESCUDOS
Gold **Countermark:** F. 7. o **Note:** Countermark on Chile 8 Escudos, KM#84.

CM Date	Host Date	Good	VG	F	VF	XF
ND	1822 FD	3,000	3,500	5,000	7,500	—
ND	1825 I Unique	—	—	—	—	—
ND	1826 I Unique	—	—	—	—	—

KM# A86 8 ESCUDOS
Gold **Countermark:** F. 7. o **Note:** Countermark on Colombia 8 Escudos, KM#82.2.

CM Date	Host Date	Good	VG	F	VF	XF
ND	1825 Rare	—	—	—	—	—

Note: Superior Ebsen sale 6-87 VF realized $13,750.

KM# 86 8 ESCUDOS
Gold **Countermark:** F. 7. o **Note:** Countermark on Mexico - Estado 8 Escudos, KM#383.4.

CM Date	Host Date	Good	VG	F	VF	XF
ND	1829 LF Unique	—	—	—	—	—

Note: Other coin types may exist with this particular countermark

ISABEL II

Silver

Type VI

This countermark was introduced after the death of Ferdinand VII on December 20, 1834. It exists with several varieties of crowns. Countermarking of foreign coins was halted in Manila by the edict of March 31, 1837 after Spain had recognized the independence of Mexico, Peru, Colombia, Bolivia, Chile and other former colonies in Central and South America. Coins bearing the Type VI countermark dated 1838 or later should be considered counterfeit.

KM# A87 REAL
Silver **Countermark:** Y • II • **Note:** Countermark on Mexico City Real, KM#76.

CM Date	Host Date	Good	VG	F	VF	XF
ND	1747-60	—	350	500	750	—

KM# 87 REAL
Silver **Countermark:** Y • II • **Note:** Countermark on Mexico - Zacatecas Real, KM#372.10.

CM Date	Host Date	Good	VG	F	VF	XF
ND	1826-37	—	250	375	500	—

KM# 88 2 REALS
Silver **Countermark:** Y • II • **Note:** Countermark on Mexico - Zacatecas 2 Reales, KM#372.12.

CM Date	Host Date	Good	VG	F	VF	XF
ND	1825-37	—	325	475	625	—

KM# A90 2 REALS
Silver **Countermark:** Y • II • **Note:** Countermark on Peru (Lima) 2 Reales, KM#104.2.

CM Date	Host Date	Good	VG	F	VF	XF
ND	1808-11	—	375	475	650	—

KM# 90 2 REALS
Silver **Countermark:** Y • II • **Note:** Countermark on Peru (Lima) 2 Reales, KM#141.

CM Date	Host Date	Good	VG	F	VF	XF
ND	1825-37	—	350	450	600	—

KM# 91 4 REALS
Silver **Countermark:** Y • II • **Note:** Countermark on Bolivia 4 Reales, KM#54.

CM Date	Host Date	Good	VG	F	VF	XF
ND	1788	—	500	700	1,000	—

KM# A92 4 REALS
Silver **Countermark:** Y • II • **Note:** Countermark over both sides of hole on holes "ARAS" Mexico City 4 Reales, KM#102.

CM Date	Host Date	Good	VG	F	VF	XF
ND	1816-21 Rare	—	—	—	—	—

KM# 92 4 REALS
Silver **Countermark:** Y • II • **Note:** Countermark on Mexico - Zacatecas 4 Reales, KM#375.9.

CM Date	Host Date	Good	VG	F	VF	XF
ND	1832	—	400	525	775	—

KM# 89 GULDEN
Silver **Countermark:** Y • II • **Note:** Countermark on Netherlands-Holland 1 Gulden, C#13.1

CM Date	Host Date	Good	VG	F	VF	XF
ND	1793 Rare	—	—	—	—	—

KM# 93.1 8 REALES
Silver **Countermark:** Y • II • **Note:** Countermark on Argentina 8 Reales, KM#5.

CM Date	Host Date	Good	VG	F	VF	XF
ND	1813	—	225	350	500	—

KM# 93.2 8 REALES
Silver **Countermark:** Y • II • **Note:** Countermark on Argentina 8 Reales, KM#14.

CM Date	Host Date	Good	VG	F	VF	XF
ND	1815	—	400	600	900	—

KM# 94 8 REALES
Silver **Countermark:** Y • II • **Note:** Countermark on Argentina 8 Soles, KM#15.

CM Date	Host Date	Good	VG	F	VF	XF
ND	1815	—	225	350	500	—

KM# 95 8 REALES
Silver **Countermark:** Y • II • **Note:** Countermark on Argentina 8 Reales, KM#20.

CM Date	Host Date	Good	VG	F	VF	XF
ND	1826-37	—	225	350	500	—

KM# 96 8 REALES
Silver **Countermark:** Y • II • **Note:** Countermark on Bolivia 8 Reales, KM#55.

CM Date	Host Date	Good	VG	F	VF	XF
ND	1773-89	—	125	175	300	—

KM# 97 8 REALES
Silver **Countermark:** Y • II • **Note:** Countermark on Bolivia 8 Reales, KM#64.

CM Date	Host Date	Good	VG	F	VF	XF
ND	1789-91	—	125	175	300	—

KM# 98 8 REALES
Silver **Countermark:** Y • II • **Note:** Countermark on Bolivia 8 Reales, KM#73

CM Date	Host Date	Good	VG	F	VF	XF
ND	1791-1808	—	125	175	300	—

KM# 99 8 REALES
Silver **Countermark:** Y • II • **Note:** Countermark on Bolivia 8 Reales, KM#84.

CM Date	Host Date	Good	VG	F	VF	XF
ND	1808-25	—	100	140	200	—

KM# 100 8 REALES
Silver **Countermark:** Y • II • **Note:** Countermark on Bolivia 8 Sueldos, KM#97.

CM Date	Host Date	Good	VG	F	VF	XF
ND	1827-37	—	100	150	225	—

KM# 101 8 REALES
Silver **Countermark:** Y • II • **Note:** Countermark on Brazil 960 Reis, KM#307.

CM Date	Host Date	Good	VG	F	VF	XF
ND	1809-18 Rare	—	—	—	—	—

KM# 102 8 REALES
Silver **Countermark:** Y • II • **Note:** Countermark on Brazil 960 Reis, KM#326.

CM Date	Host Date	Good	VG	F	VF	XF
ND	1818-22 Rare	—	—	—	—	—

KM# 103 8 REALES
Silver **Countermark:** Y • II • **Note:** Countermark on Brazil 960 Reis, KM#368.

CM Date	Host Date	Good	VG	F	VF	XF
ND	1823-30 Rare	—	—	—	—	—

KM# 104 8 REALES
Silver **Countermark:** Y • II • **Note:** Countermark on Brazil 960 Reis, KM#385.

CM Date	Host Date	Good	VG	F	VF	XF
ND	1832-34 Rare	—	—	—	—	—

KM# 105 8 REALES
Silver **Countermark:** Y • II • **Note:** Countermark on Brazil 1200 Reis, KM#454.

CM Date	Host Date	Good	VG	F	VF	XF
ND	1834-37 Rare	—	—	—	—	—

KM# 106.1 8 REALES
Silver **Countermark:** Y • II • **Note:** Countermark on Central American Republic - Guatemala 8 Reales, KM#4.

CM Date	Host Date	Good	VG	F	VF	XF
ND	1824-37	—	200	300	500	—

KM# 106.2 8 REALES
Silver **Countermark:** Y • II • **Note:** Countermark on obverse and reverse of Central American Republic - Guatemala 8 Reales, KM#4.

CM Date	Host Date	Good	VG	F	VF	XF
ND	1824 NG	—	275	400	625	—

KM# 107 8 REALES
Silver **Countermark:** Y • II • **Note:** Countermark on Central American Republic - Costa Rica 8 Reales, KM#22.

CM Date	Host Date	Good	VG	F	VF	XF
ND	1831 Rare	—	—	—	—	—

KM# 108 8 REALES
Silver **Countermark:** Y • II • **Note:** Countermark on Chile 1 Peso, KM#82.

CM Date	Host Date	Good	VG	F	VF	XF
ND	1817-34	—	150	250	325	—

KM# 109 8 REALES
Silver **Countermark:** Y • II • **Note:** Countermark on Columbia 8 Reales, KM#89.

CM Date	Host Date	Good	VG	F	VF	XF
ND	1834-36	—	225	300	400	—

KM# 110 8 REALES
Silver **Countermark:** Y • II • **Note:** Countermark on Mexico City 8 Reales, KM#104.

CM Date	Host Date	Good	VG	F	VF	XF
ND	1747-60 Rare	—	—	—	—	—

KM# 111 8 REALES
Silver **Countermark:** Y • II • **Note:** Countermark on Mexico City 8 Reales, KM#105.

CM Date	Host Date	Good	VG	F	VF	XF
ND	1760-71 Rare	—	—	—	—	—

KM# 112 8 REALES
Silver **Countermark:** Y • II • **Note:** Countermark on Mexico City 8 Reales, KM#106.

CM Date	Host Date	Good	VG	F	VF	XF
ND	1772-89	—	150	200	300	—

KM# 113 8 REALES
Silver **Countermark:** Y • II • **Note:** Countermark on Mexico City 8 Reales, KM#107.

CM Date	Host Date	Good	VG	F	VF	XF
ND	1789-90FM	—	175	300	400	—

KM# 114 8 REALES
Silver **Countermark:** Y • II • **Note:** Countermark on Mexico City 8 Reales, KM#108.

CM Date	Host Date	Good	VG	F	VF	XF
ND	1790FM	—	175	300	400	—

KM# 115 8 REALES
Silver **Countermark:** Y • II • **Note:** Countermark on Mexico City 8 Reales, KM#109.

CM Date	Host Date	Good	VG	F	VF	XF
ND	1791-1808	—	150	300	425	—

KM# 116 8 REALES
Silver **Countermark:** Y • II • **Note:** Countermark on Mexico City 8 Reales, KM#110.

CM Date	Host Date	Good	VG	F	VF	XF
ND	1808-11	—	100	150	200	—

KM# 117.1 8 REALES
Silver **Countermark:** Y • II • **Note:** Countermark on Mexico - Chihuahua 8 Reales, KM#111.1.

CM Date	Host Date	Good	VG	F	VF	XF
ND	1815-22	—	300	450	600	—

KM# 117.2 8 REALES
Silver **Countermark:** Y • II • **Note:** Countermark on Mexico - Durango 8 Reales, KM#111.2.

CM Date	Host Date	Good	VG	F	VF	XF
ND	1812-21	—	225	300	400	—

KM# A118 8 REALES
Silver **Countermark:** Y • II • **Note:** Countermark on Mexico Sombrete 8 Reales, KM#177.

CM Date	Host Date	Good	VG	F	VF	XF
ND	1811-12 Rare	—	—	—	—	—

KM# 118 8 REALES
Silver **Countermark:** Y • II • **Note:** Countermark on Mexico - Zacatecas 8 Reales, KM#111.5.

CM Date	Host Date	Good	VG	F	VF	XF
ND	1813-22	—	225	300	400	—

KM# 119 8 REALES
Silver **Countermark:** Y • II • **Note:** Countermark on Mexico City 8 Reales, KM#111.

CM Date	Host Date	Good	VG	F	VF	XF
ND	1811-21	—	125	200	300	—

KM# 120 8 REALES
Silver **Countermark:** Y • II • **Note:** Countermark on Mexico - Zacatecas 8 Reales, KM#189.

CM Date	Host Date	Good	VG	F	VF	XF
ND	1811 Rare	—	—	—	—	—

KM# 121 8 REALES
Silver **Countermark:** Y • II • **Note:** Countermark on Mexico City 8 Reales, KM#304.

CM Date	Host Date	Good	VG	F	VF	XF
ND	1822 JM	—	200	300	400	—

KM# 122 8 REALES
Silver **Countermark:** Y • II • **Note:** Countermark on Mexico City 8 Reales, KM#305.

CM Date	Host Date	Good	VG	F	VF	XF
ND	1822 JM Rare	—	—	—	—	—

KM# 123 8 REALES
Silver **Countermark:** Y • II • **Note:** Countermark on Mexico City 8 Reales, KM#306.

CM Date	Host Date	Good	VG	F	VF	XF
ND	1822 JM	—	300	400	500	—

KM# 124 8 REALES
Silver **Countermark:** Y • II • **Note:** Countermark on Mexico City 8 Reales, KM#307.

CM Date	Host Date	Good	VG	F	VF	XF
ND	1822 JM Rare	—	—	—	—	—

KM# 125 8 REALES
Silver **Countermark:** Y • II • **Note:** Countermark on Mexico City 8 Reales, KM#308.

CM Date	Host Date	Good	VG	F	VF	XF
ND	1822 JM Rare	—	—	—	—	—

KM# 126 8 REALES
Silver **Countermark:** Y • II • **Note:** Countermark on Mexico City 8 Reales, KM#309.

CM Date	Host Date	Good	VG	F	VF	XF
ND	1822 JM	—	300	400	500	—

KM# 127 8 REALES
Silver **Countermark:** Y • II • **Note:** Countermark on Mexico City 8 Reales, KM#310..

CM Date	Host Date	Good	VG	F	VF	XF
ND	1822-23 JM	—	125	200	300	—

KM# 128 8 REALES
Silver **Countermark:** Y • II • **Note:** Countermark on Mexico 8 Reales, KM#376.

CM Date	Host Date	Good	VG	F	VF	XF
ND	1823-24	—	300	500	600	—

KM# 129 8 REALES
Silver **Countermark:** Y • II • **Note:** Countermark on Mexico 8 Reales, KM#377.

CM Date	Host Date	Good	VG	F	VF	XF
ND	1824-37	—	750	125	200	—

KM# 130 8 REALES
Silver **Countermark:** Y • II • **Note:** Countermark on Peru (Lima) 8 Reales, KM#64.

CM Date	Host Date	Good	VG	F	VF	XF
ND	1760-72 Rare	—	—	—	—	—

KM# 131 8 REALES
Silver **Countermark:** Y • II • **Note:** Countermark on Peru (Lima) 8 Reales, KM#78.

CM Date	Host Date	Good	VG	F	VF	XF
ND	1772-89	—	100	150	200	—

KM# 132 8 REALES
Silver **Countermark:** Y • II • **Note:** Countermark on Peru (Lima) 8 Reales, KM#87.

CM Date	Host Date	Good	VG	F	VF	XF
ND	1789-91	—	125	225	300	—

KM# 133 8 REALES
Silver **Countermark:** Y • II • **Note:** Countermark on Peru (Lima) 8 Reales, KM#97.

CM Date	Host Date	Good	VG	F	VF	XF
ND	1791-1808	—	125	225	300	—

KM# 134 8 REALES
Silver **Countermark:** Y • II • **Note:** Countermark on Peru (Lima) 8 Reales, KM#106.

CM Date	Host Date	Good	VG	F	VF	XF
ND	1808-11	—	100	150	200	—

KM# 135 8 REALES
Silver **Countermark:** Y • II • **Note:** Countermark on Peru (Lima) 8 Reales, KM#117.1.

CM Date	Host Date	Good	VG	F	VF	XF
ND	1810-24	—	150	225	325	—

KM# 136 8 REALES
Silver **Countermark:** Y • II • **Note:** Countermark on Peru (Lima) 8 Reales, KM#136.

CM Date	Host Date	Good	VG	F	VF	XF
ND	1822-23	—	200	275	375	—

KM# 137 8 REALES
Silver **Countermark:** Y • II • **Note:** Countermark on Peru (Lima) 8 Reales, KM#130.

CM Date	Host Date	Good	VG	F	VF	XF
ND	1824	—	150	225	325	—

KM# 138.1 8 REALES
Silver **Countermark:** Y • II • **Note:** Countermark on Peru (Lima) 8 Reales, KM#142.1.

CM Date	Host Date	Good	VG	F	VF	XF
ND	1825-28	—	45.00	65.00	85.00	—

KM# 138.2 8 REALES
Silver **Countermark:** Y • II • **Note:** Countermark on Peru (Lima) 8 Reales, KM#142.3.

CM Date	Host Date	Good	VG	F	VF	XF
ND	1828-37	—	30.00	50.00	65.00	—

KM# 138.4 8 REALES
Silver **Countermark:** Y • II • **Note:** Countermark on Peru (Cuzco) 8 Reales, KM#142.4.

CM Date	Host Date	Good	VG	F	VF	XF
ND	1830-34	—	100	150	250	—

KM# A139 8 REALES
Silver **Countermark:** Y • II • **Note:** Countermark over both sides of hole on holed Philippines 8 Reales, KM#83.

CM Date	Host Date	Good	VG	F	VF	XF
ND	1828-34	—	500	700	1,000	—

KM# B139 8 REALES
Silver **Countermark:** Y • II • **Note:** Countermark over both sides of hole on Philippines 8 Reales, KM#135 (original host Peru, KM112.1)

CM Date	Host Date	Good	VG	F	VF	XF
ND	ND	—	—	—	—	—

KM# 139 8 REALES
Silver **Countermark:** Y • II • **Note:** Countermark on Philippines KM#80.

CM Date	Host Date	Good	VG	F	VF	XF
ND	1822-23	—	500	700	1,000	—

DECIMAL COINAGE

100 CENTAVOS = 1 PESO

KM# 145 10 CENTIMOS
2.5960 g., 0.9000 Silver .0751 oz.

Date	Mintage	F	VF	XF	Unc	BU
1864	4,586	200	300	650	2,500	—
1865	82,000	50.00	75.00	150	1,000	—
1866	39,000	75.00	100	175	1,200	—
1867/6	124,000	75.00	200	400	1,200	—
1867	Inc. above	40.00	60.00	150	950	—
1868	Est. 139,000	7.00	12.00	50.00	200	225

Note: An additional 450,000 pieces were struck between 1870-74, all dated 1868.

KM# 148 10 CENTIMOS
2.5960 g., 0.8350 Silver .0697 oz.

Date	Mintage	F	VF	XF	Unc	BU
1880	15,000	300	425	750	3,500	—
1881/0	624,000	25.00	45.00	125	2,000	—
1881	Inc. above	20.00	45.00	100	2,000	—
1882/1	525,000	25.00	50.00	160	2,500	—
1882	Inc. above	25.00	50.00	150	2,500	—
1883/1	983,000	25.00	40.00	100	2,000	—
1883/2	Inc. above	25.00	40.00	100	2,000	—
1883	Inc. above	20.00	40.00	100	2,000	—
1884	10,000	400	525	800	5,000	—
1885/3	—	7.50	12.00	25.00	75.00	—
1885	Inc. above	2.50	5.00	12.50	60.00	85.00

Note: An additional 5,432,614 pieces were struck between 1886-98, all dated 1885.

KM# 142 PESO
1.6915 g., 0.8750 Gold .0476 oz.

Date	Mintage	F	VF	XF	Unc	BU
1861/0	237,000	45.00	80.00	140	350	—
1861	Inc. above	45.00	80.00	125	350	—
1862/1	143,000	45.00	80.00	135	350	—
1862	Inc. above	45.00	80.00	135	375	—
1863/2	236,000	45.00	80.00	140	375	—
1863	Inc. above	45.00	75.00	125	350	—
1864/0	274,000	45.00	80.00	135	350	—
1864	Inc. above	45.00	75.00	120	350	—
1865/0	189,000	50.00	85.00	145	400	—
1865/3	Inc. above	75.00	80.00	200	450	—
1865	Inc. above	45.00	85.00	135	400	—
1866/5	77,000	150	250	400	1,200	—
1866	Inc. above	150	250	400	1,200	—
1867	12,000	350	700	1,250	3,500	—
1868/6	28,000	45.00	75.00	125	250	—
Note: An additional 372,724 pieces were struck between 1869-74, all dated 1868.						
1868/7	Inc. above	45.00	75.00	125	250	—
1868	Inc. above	40.00	60.00	85.00	200	—

KM# 154 PESO
25.0000 g., 0.9000 Silver .7234 oz.

Date	Mintage	F	VF	XF	Unc	BU
1897 SGV	6,000,000	25.00	40.00	65.00	300	350

KM# 143 2 PESOS
3.3830 g., 0.8750 Gold .0952 oz.

Date	Mintage	F	VF	XF	Unc	BU
1861/0	265,000	75.00	135	200	500	—
1861	Inc. above	75.00	125	175	500	—
1862/1	237,000	75.00	135	200	500	—
1862	Inc. above	75.00	125	175	500	—
1863/2	176,000	75.00	135	200	500	—
1863	Inc. above	75.00	125	175	500	—
1864/0	181,000	75.00	135	200	500	—
1864/3	Inc. above	75.00	135	200	500	—
1864	Inc. above	75.00	135	175	500	—
1865	34,000	135	190	325	800	—
1866/5	16,000	400	600	1,250	3,000	—
1866	Inc. above	400	600	1,250	3,000	—
1868/6	48,000	75.00	130	180	375	—
Note: An additional 304,691 pieces were struck between 1869-73, all dated 1868.						
1868	Inc. above	65.00	100	160	350	—

KM# 144 4 PESOS
6.7661 g., 0.8750 Gold .1903 oz.

Date	Mintage	F	VF	XF	Unc	BU
1861	183,000	120	175	245	475	—
1862/0	—	—	165	225	—	—
1862/1	507,000	120	165	225	450	—
1862	Inc. above	110	145	200	450	—
1863	475,000	110	145	200	450	—
1864	461,000	110	145	200	500	—
1865	241,000	120	225	325	700	—
1866/65	44,000	400	600	1,500	3,000	—
1866	Inc. above	400	600	1,500	3,000	—
1867	1,530	1,200	1,800	3,000	8,000	—
1868	36,000	100	125	165	375	—

Note: 51,521,505 were struck between 1869-73, all dated 1868.

KM# 151 4 PESOS
6.7661 g., 0.8750 Gold .1903 oz.

Date	Mintage	F	VF	XF	Unc	BU
1880 Rare	—	—	—	—	—	—
1881	—	—	—	6,000	10,000	—
1882	—	800	1,200	1,500	2,250	—
1885	—	—	—	4,000	8,000	—

REVOLUTIONARY COINAGE

ISLAND OF PANAY

KM# 156 CENTAVO
Copper **Issuer:** Island of Panay **Obv:** Helmeted head right, legend **Rev:** Sun in triangle, legend

Date	Mintage	VG	F	VF	XF	Unc
1899	—	—	—	5,000	7,500	—

KM# 157 CENTAVO
Copper **Issuer:** Island of Panay **Obv:** Countermark M behind head **Rev:** NACIONAL LIBERTAD at sides of triangle

Date	Mintage	VG	F	VF	XF	Unc
1899	—	—	—	5,500	8,000	—

TOWN OF MALOLOS

KM# 158.1 2 CENTAVOS
Copper **Issuer:** Town of Malolos **Obv:** Large date

Date	Mintage	VG	F	VF	XF	Unc
1899	—	—	—	4,500	7,000	—

KM# 158.2 2 CENTAVOS
Copper **Issuer:** Town of Malolos **Obv:** Small date

Date	Mintage	VG	F	VF	XF	Unc
1899	—	—	—	4,750	7,250	—

KM# 159 2 CENTAVOS
Copper **Issuer:** Town of Malolos

Date	Mintage	VG	F	VF	XF	Unc
1899	—	—	—	6,000	9,000	—

REPUBLIC

PRETENDER COINAGE

CHARLES VII OF SPAIN

KM# PT1 5 PESETAS
Copper **Obv:** Laureated head of Charles right, date below **Rev:** Value in branches

Date	Mintage	F	VF	XF	Unc	BU
1874(b) Unique	—	—	—	—	—	—

PATTERNS

INCLUDING OFF METAL STRIKES

KM#	Date	Mintage	Identification	Mkt Val
Pn9	1855	—	5 Pesetas. Silver.	15,000
Pn10	1857	—	Silver.	4,000
Pn11	1857	—	Copper.	3,200

KM#	Date	Mintage	Identification	Mkt Val
Pn12	1859	—	2 Centavos. Copper.	400
Pn13	1859	—	2 Centavos. Copper.	450

KM#	Date	Mintage	Identification	Mkt Val
Pn14	1859	—	Copper.	500

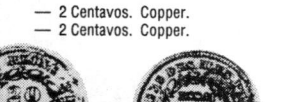

KM#	Date	Mintage	Identification	Mkt Val
Pn15	1859	—	Copper.	600

KM#	Date	Mintage	Identification	Mkt Val
Pn16	1859	—	Copper.	700

KM#	Date	Mintage	Identification	Mkt Val
Pn17	1880	—	50 Centimos. Bronze.	3,000
Pn18	1894	—	Centavo. Copper.	5,000

KM#	Date	Mintage	Identification	Mkt Val
Pn19	1894	—	2 Centavos. Copper.	7,000

TRIAL STRIKES

KM#	Date	Mintage	Identification	Mkt Val
TS1	1859	—	4 Pesos. Gold-Plated Bronze.	1,000
TS2	1859	—	4 Pesos. Gold-Plated Bronze.	1,000
TS3	1861	—	Peso. Gold-Plated Bronze.	—
TS4	1861	—	Peso. Gold-Plated Bronze.	—
TS5	1861	—	Gold-Plated Bronze.	—
TS6	1861	—	Gold-Plated Bronze.	—
TS7	ND(b)	—	5 Pesetas. Bronze.	—

POLAND

Poland is located in central Europe and has an area of 120,725 sq. mi. (312,680 sq. km.).

Poland, which began as a Slavic duchy in the 10th century and reached its peak of power between the 14th and16th centuries, has had a turbulent history of invasion, occupation or partition by Mongols, Turkey, Transylvania, Sweden, Austria, Prussia and Russia.

The first partition took place in 1772. Prussia took Polish Pomerania, Russia took part of the eastern provinces, and Austria occupied Galicia, in which lay the capital city of Lwów. The second partition occurred in 1793 when Russia took another slice of the eastern provinces and Prussia took what remained of western Poland. The third partition, 1795, literally removed Poland from the map. Russia took what was left of the eastern provinces. Prussia seized most of central Poland, including Warsaw. Austria took what was left of the south. Napoleon restored to Poland much of the territory lost to Prussia and Austria, but after his defeat another partition returned the Duchy of Warsaw to Prussia, made Kracow into a tiny republic, and declared what remained to be the Kingdom of Poland under the czar and in permanent union with Russia.

RULERS

Friedrich August I, King of Saxony,
... as Duke, 1807-1814
Alexander I, Czar of Russia,
... as King, 1815-1825
Nicholas I, Czar of Russia,
... as King, 1825-1855

MINT MARKS

Other letters appearing with date denote the Mintmaster at the time the coin was struck.

MINT OFFICIALS' INITIALS

Mintmasters initials usually appear flanking the shield or by the date.

WARSAW MINT

Initial	Date	Name
FA	1815-27	Friedrich Hunger
IB	1811-27	Jakub Benik
IP	1834-35	Jerzy (George) Pusch
JS	1810-11	Jan Sztokman
KG	1829-34	Karol Gronau

SAINT PETERSBURG

Initial	Date	Name
HR	1832-41	Nikolay Grachov
MA	1834-38	Pavel Danilov
MY	1835-36	Pavel Utkin
P.M.		YTKMHb
A4	1839-41	Aleksander Chadov

MONETARY SYSTEM

Until 1815

1 Solidus = 1 Schilling
3 Solidi = 2 Poltura = 1 Grosz
3 Poltura = 1-1/2 Grosze = 1 Polturak
6 Groszy = 1 Szostak
18 Groszy = 1 Tympf
30 Groszy = 4 Silbergroschen = 1 Zloty
1 Talar = 1 Zloty
6 Zlotych = 1 Reichsthaler
8 Zlotych = 1 Speciesthaler
5 Speciesthaler = 1 August D'or
3 Ducats = 1 Stanislaus D'or

GRAND DUCHY OF WARSZAWA

STANDARD COINAGE

C# 81 GROSZ
Copper

Date	Mintage	VG	F	VF	XF	Unc
1810 IS	742,000	2.00	5.00	8.00	20.00	—
1811 IS	4,358,000	2.00	4.00	6.00	14.00	—
1811 IB	Inc. above	2.00	4.00	6.00	14.00	—
1812 IB	6,377,000	2.00	4.00	6.00	14.00	—
1814 IB	3,072,000	2.00	4.00	6.00	14.00	—

C# 82 3 GROSZE
Copper

Date	Mintage	VG	F	VF	XF	Unc
1810 IS	1,008,000	2.00	5.00	12.00	20.00	—
1811 IS	5,479,000	2.00	5.00	10.00	16.00	—
1811 IB	Inc. above	2.00	5.00	10.00	16.00	—
1812 IB	6,816,000	2.00	5.00	10.00	16.00	—
1813 IB	1,139,000	2.00	5.00	12.00	20.00	—
1814 IB	3,427,000	2.00	5.00	10.00	16.00	—

C# 83 5 GROSZY
2.2000 g., 0.2100 Silver .0148 oz.

Date	Mintage	VG	F	VF	XF	Unc
1811 IS	11,595,000	5.00	10.00	18.00	30.00	—
1811 IB	Inc. above	5.00	10.00	18.00	30.00	—
1812 IB	3,405,000	5.00	10.00	18.00	30.00	—

C# 84 10 GROSZY
2.9900 g., 0.2450 Silver .0235 oz.

Date	Mintage	VG	F	VF	XF	Unc
1810 IS	—	30.00	55.00	—	—	—
1812 IB	951,000	5.00	10.00	20.00	45.00	—
1813 IB	3,549,000	5.00	10.00	16.00	32.00	—

C# 85 1/6 TALARA
4.9800 g., 0.5350 Silver .0856 oz.

Date	Mintage	VG	F	VF	XF	Unc
1811 IS	113,000	10.00	15.00	45.00	100	—
1812 IB	223,000	10.00	15.00	45.00	100	—
1813 IB	106,000	15.00	25.00	70.00	160	—
1814 IB	1,492,000	10.00	15.00	40.00	80.00	—

C# 86 1/3 TALARA
8.6600 g., 0.6250 Silver .1740 oz.

Date	Mintage	VG	F	VF	XF	Unc
1810 IS	123,000	12.00	25.00	65.00	120	—
1811 IS	993,000	12.00	20.00	30.00	75.00	—
1812 IB	2,804,000	12.00	20.00	30.00	75.00	—
1813 IB	1,916,000	12.00	20.00	30.00	75.00	—
1814 IB	4,611,000	10.00	20.00	30.00	75.00	—

C# 87 TALAR
22.9200 g., 0.7200 Silver .5305 oz.

Date	Mintage	VG	F	VF	XF	Unc
1811 IB	4,488	95.00	200	375	800	—
1812 IB	36,000	75.00	150	250	400	—
1814 IB	14,000	75.00	150	275	550	—

TRADE COINAGE

C# 88 DUKAT
3.5000 g., 0.9860 Gold .1109 oz.

Date	Mintage	VG	F	VF	XF	Unc
1812 IB	8,546	250	450	750	1,500	—
1813 IB	3,000	450	800	2,000	3,000	—

CONGRESS - KINGDOM OF POLAND

STANDARD COINAGE

C# 93 GROSZ
Copper **Note:** Varieties of eagles exist. Varieties of crown exist for 1816 and 1817.

Date	Mintage	VG	F	VF	XF	Unc
1816 IB	1,873,000	1.00	2.00	5.00	10.00	—
1817 IB	3,092,000	1.00	2.00	5.00	10.00	—
1818 IB	4,035,000	1.00	2.00	5.00	10.00	—
1818	Inc. above	7.50	15.00	25.00	60.00	—
1819 IB	—	1.00	3.00	5.00	10.00	—
1820 IB	372,000	1.00	3.00	5.00	10.00	—
1821 IB	571,000	1.00	3.00	5.00	10.00	—
1822 IB	—	6.00	10.00	17.50	35.00	—

C# 94 GROSZ
Copper **Rev. Legend:** Z MIEDZI KRAIOWEY

Date	Mintage	VG	F	VF	XF	Unc
1822 IB	2,721,000	1.75	2.50	5.00	15.00	—
1823 IB	5,046,000	1.75	2.50	5.00	15.00	—
1824 IB	5,413,000	1.75	2.50	5.00	15.00	—
1825 IB	2,108,000	1.75	2.50	5.00	15.00	—
1826 IB	1,096,000	—	—	—	15.00	—

C# 105 GROSZ
Copper

Date	Mintage	VG	F	VF	XF	Unc
1828 FH	1,190,000	1.00	2.00	5.00	12.00	—
1829 FH	931,000	1.00	2.00	5.00	12.00	—
1830 FH	1,569,000	1.00	2.00	5.00	12.00	—
1830 KG	Inc. above	1.00	2.00	5.00	12.00	—
1831 KG	1,777,000	1.00	2.00	5.00	12.00	—
1832 KG	1,559,000	1.00	2.00	5.00	12.00	—
1833 KG	375,000	1.00	2.00	5.00	12.00	—
1834 KG	427,000	1.00	2.00	5.00	12.00	—
1834 IP	Inc. above	1.00	2.00	5.00	12.00	—
1835 IP	542,000	1.00	2.00	5.00	12.00	—

C# 106 GROSZ
Copper **Note:** Varieties exist.

Date	Mintage	VG	F	VF	XF	Unc
1835MW	Inc. above	2.00	4.00	8.00	15.00	—
1836MW	839,000	2.00	4.00	8.00	15.00	—
1837MW	1,016,000	1.00	2.00	5.00	12.00	—
1837WM Rare	Inc. above	—	—	—	—	—
1838MW	488,000	1.00	2.00	5.00	12.00	—
1839MW	670,000	1.00	2.00	5.00	12.00	—
1840MW	243,000	1.00	2.00	5.00	12.00	—

C# 106a GROSZ
Copper **Rev:** Without wreath, pearl rim

Date	Mintage	VG	F	VF	XF	Unc
1840MW	Inc. above	10.00	15.00	25.00	50.00	—

C# 107 GROSZ
Copper **Rev:** JEDEN or IEDEN above value

Date	Mintage	VG	F	VF	XF	Unc
1840MW Rare	—	—	—	—	—	—
Note: Mintage included in C#106						
1841MW Rare	372,000	—	—	—	—	—

C# 95.1 3 GROSZE
Copper **Edge:** Plain **Note:** Struck without collar. Varieties of eagles exist.

Date	Mintage	VG	F	VF	XF	Unc
1817 IB	843,000	2.00	5.00	10.00	25.00	—
1818 IB	157,000	5.00	10.00	20.00	40.00	—

C# 95.2 3 GROSZE
Copper **Edge:** Reeded **Note:** Struck in collar. Varieties in edge for 1818.

Date	Mintage	VG	F	VF	XF	Unc
1818 IB Rare	—	—	—	—	—	—
1819 IB	187,000	2.00	5.00	10.00	20.00	—
1820 IB	89,000	2.00	5.00	12.00	30.00	—

C# 108 3 GROSZE
Copper **Rev. Legend:** Z MIEDZI KRAIOWEY

Date	Mintage	VG	F	VF	XF	Unc
1826 IB	570,000	7.00	10.00	15.00	35.00	—
1827 IB	Inc. above	7.00	10.00	15.00	35.00	—

C# 109 3 GROSZE
Copper **Rev. Legend:** 3/GROSZE/POLSKI

Date	Mintage	VG	F	VF	XF	Unc
1827 FH	495,000	3.00	5.00	10.00	30.00	—
1828 FH	1,159,000	3.00	5.00	8.00	25.00	—
1829 FH	1,057,000	3.00	5.00	8.00	25.00	—
1829	—	7.00	10.00	15.00	35.00	—
1830 FH	891,000	3.00	5.00	8.00	25.00	—
1830 KG	Inc. above	12.50	20.00	40.00	95.00	—
1831 FH Rare	1,773,000	—	—	—	—	—
1831 KG	1,343,000	3.00	5.00	8.00	25.00	—
1832 FH Rare	30,000	—	—	—	—	—
1832 KG	7,117	3.00	5.00	8.00	25.00	—
1833 KG	515,000	3.00	5.00	8.00	25.00	—
1834 KG	346,000	3.00	5.00	10.00	30.00	—
1834 IP	Inc. above	3.00	5.00	10.00	30.00	—
1835 IP	185,000	4.00	8.00	16.00	35.00	—

C# 110.1 3 GROSZE
Copper **Rev:** Wreath surrounds value **Note:** Varieties exist.

Date	Mintage	VG	F	VF	XF	Unc
1835MW	Inc. above	3.00	5.00	8.00	25.00	—
1836MW	244,000	3.00	5.00	8.00	25.00	—
1837MW	398,000	3.00	5.00	8.00	25.00	—
1838MW	288,000	3.00	5.00	8.00	25.00	—
1839MW	333,000	3.00	5.00	8.00	25.00	—

C# 110.2 3 GROSZE
Copper **Obv:** Eagle's head larger, shield smaller

Date	Mintage	VG	F	VF	XF	Unc
1839MW	Inc. above	3.00	6.00	8.00	22.00	—
1840MW	118,000	3.00	7.50	12.00	22.00	—
1840MW	Inc. above	7.00	12.00	25.00	35.00	—
1841MW	242,000	4.00	7.50	15.00	35.00	—

C# 96.1 5 GROSZY
1.4500 g., 0.1920 Silver .0090 oz. **Obv:** Eagle's wings smaller **Rev:** Value: 5 GROSZY **Edge:** Smooth

Date	Mintage	VG	F	VF	XF	Unc
1816 IB	2,700,000	6.00	8.50	12.00	25.00	—

C# 96.2 5 GROSZY
1.4500 g., 0.1920 Silver .0090 oz. **Edge:** Reeded

Date	Mintage	VG	F	VF	XF	Unc
1817 IB Rare	Inc. above	—	—	—	—	—

C# 96.3 5 GROSZY
1.4500 g., 0.1920 Silver .0090 oz. **Obv:** Redesigned shield

Date	Mintage	VG	F	VF	XF	Unc
1818 IB	3,056,000	2.50	5.00	12.00	25.00	—
1819 IB	5,532,000	2.50	5.00	12.00	25.00	—
1820 IB	3,481,000	2.50	5.00	12.00	25.00	—
1821 IB	1,651,000	2.50	5.00	12.00	25.00	—
1822 IB	1,282,000	2.50	5.00	12.00	25.00	—
1823 IB	2,098,000	2.50	5.00	12.00	25.00	—
1824 IB	235,000	5.00	7.50	25.00	50.00	—
1825 IB	350,000	2.50	6.00	20.00	40.00	—

C# 111 5 GROSZY
1.4500 g., 0.1920 Silver .0090 oz.

Date	Mintage	VG	F	VF	XF	Unc
1826 IB	2,079,000	2.50	5.00	12.00	25.00	—
1827 IB	1,904,000	2.50	5.00	12.00	25.00	—
1827 FH	Inc. above	2.50	5.00	15.00	25.00	—
1828 FH	403,000	2.50	5.00	15.00	25.00	—
1829 FH	714,000	2.50	5.00	15.00	25.00	—
1829 KG Rare	Inc. above	—	—	—	—	—
1830 FH	571,000	2.50	5.00	15.00	25.00	—
1831 KG	Inc. above	3.00	8.00	20.00	40.00	—
1832 KG	154,000	12.00	20.00	40.00	75.00	—

C# 111a 5 GROSZY
1.4500 g., 0.1920 Silver .0090 oz.

Date	Mintage	VG	F	VF	XF	Unc
1836MW	159,000	2.50	5.00	15.00	25.00	—
1838MW	173,000	2.50	5.00	15.00	25.00	—
1839MW	380,000	2.50	5.00	15.00	25.00	—
1840MW	127,000	2.50	5.00	17.50	20.00	—

C# 112 5 GROSZY
1.4500 g., 0.1920 Silver .0090 oz. **Obv:** Similar to 25 Zlotych, C#118

Date	Mintage	VG	F	VF	XF	Unc
1841 Proof, rare	—	—	—	—	—	—

C# 97 10 GROSZY
2.9000 g., 0.1920 Silver .0180 oz. **Obv:** Eagle

Date	Mintage	VG	F	VF	XF	Unc
1816 IB	750,000	5.00	12.00	17.50	35.00	—
1820 IB	793,000	8.00	12.00	17.50	35.00	—
1821 IB	707,000	5.00	10.00	15.00	27.50	—
1822 IB	1,238,000	5.00	10.00	15.00	27.50	—
1823 IB	262,000	10.00	15.00	20.00	40.00	—
1825 IB	750,000	7.50	10.00	15.00	35.00	—

C# 113 10 GROSZY
2.9000 g., 0.1920 Silver .0180 oz.

Date	Mintage	VG	F	VF	XF	Unc
1826 IB	750,000	4.00	7.50	12.50	25.00	—
1827 IB	737,000	4.00	7.50	12.50	25.00	—
1827 FH	Inc. above	8.00	12.50	20.00	40.00	—
1828 FH	529,000	4.00	7.50	12.50	25.00	—
1830 FH	145,000	6.00	10.00	15.00	30.00	—
1830 KG	Inc. above	4.00	7.50	12.50	25.00	—
1831 KG	16,604,000	6.00	10.00	15.00	30.00	—
1832 KG Rare	—	—	—	—	—	—
1833 KG Rare	—	—	—	—	—	—

C# 113a 10 GROSZY
2.9000 g., 0.1920 Silver .0180 oz.

Date	Mintage	VG	F	VF	XF	Unc
1835MW	869,000	4.00	7.50	12.50	25.00	—
1836MW	1,736,000	4.00	7.50	12.50	25.00	—
1837MW	767,000	4.00	7.50	12.50	25.00	—
1838MW	1,735,000	4.00	7.50	12.50	25.00	—
1839MW	60,000	4.00	8.00	15.00	30.00	—
1840MW	63,349,000	2.50	6.00	10.00	15.00	—
1840MW	Inc. above	6.00	12.00	17.50	40.00	—

C# 130 40 GROSZY-20 KOPEKS
4.1000 g., 0.8680 Silver .1144 oz.

Date	Mintage	VG	F	VF	XF	Unc
1842MW	51,000	10.00	17.50	25.00	50.00	—
1843MW	37,000	10.00	17.50	25.00	50.00	—
1844MW	—	10.00	17.50	25.00	50.00	—
1845MW	62,000	10.00	17.50	25.00	50.00	—
1846MW Rare	—	—	—	—	—	—
1848MW	27,000	10.00	17.50	25.00	50.00	—
1850MW	38,000	10.00	17.50	25.00	50.00	—

C# 131 50 GROSZY-25 KOPEKS
5.1800 g., 0.8680 Silver .1445 oz.

Date	Mintage	VG	F	VF	XF	Unc
1842MW	57,000	10.00	17.50	30.00	65.00	—
1843MW	28,000	10.00	17.50	30.00	50.00	—
1844MW	—	10.00	24.00	45.00	100	—
1845MW	52,000	10.00	17.50	30.00	50.00	—
1846MW	561,000	10.00	17.50	30.00	50.00	—
1847MW	485,000	10.00	17.50	30.00	50.00	—
1848MW	168,000	10.00	17.50	30.00	50.00	—
1850MW	1,489,000	10.00	17.50	30.00	50.00	—

C# 98a ZLOTY
4.5500 g., 0.5930 Silver .0872 oz. **Obv:** Smaller head

Date	Mintage	VG	F	VF	XF	Unc
1818 IB Rare	Inc. above	—	—	—	—	—
1822 IB	287,000	6.00	10.00	20.00	40.00	—
1823 IB	52,000	6.00	10.00	20.00	40.00	—
1824 IB	119,000	6.00	10.00	20.00	40.00	—
1825 IB	84,000	6.00	10.00	20.00	40.00	—

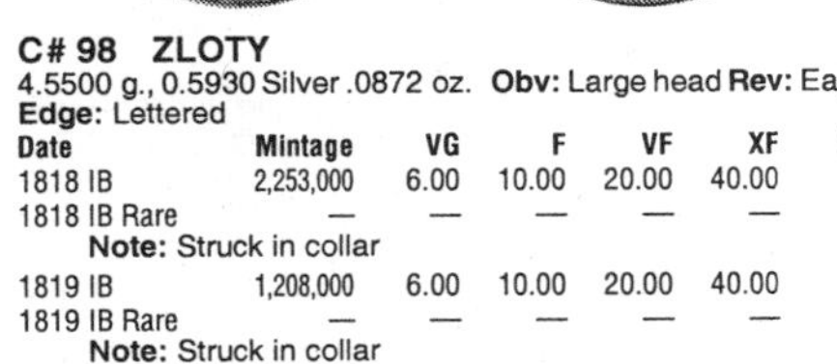

C# 98 ZLOTY
4.5500 g., 0.5930 Silver .0872 oz. **Obv:** Large head **Rev:** Eagle **Edge:** Lettered

Date	Mintage	VG	F	VF	XF	Unc
1818 IB	2,253,000	6.00	10.00	20.00	40.00	—
1818 IB Rare	—	—	—	—	—	—

Note: Struck in collar

Date	Mintage	VG	F	VF	XF	Unc
1819 IB	1,208,000	6.00	10.00	20.00	40.00	—
1819 IB Rare	—	—	—	—	—	—

Note: Struck in collar

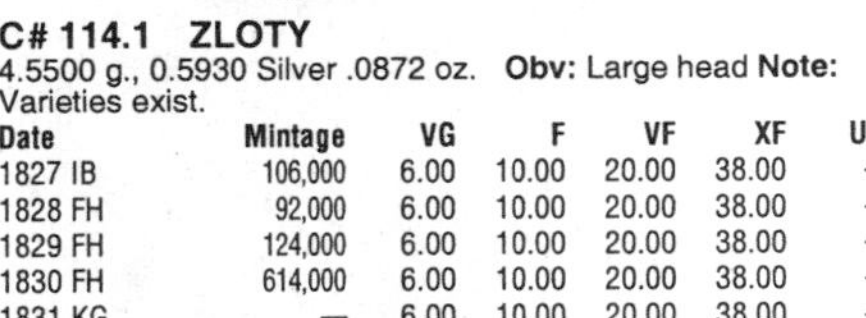

C# 114.1 ZLOTY
4.5500 g., 0.5930 Silver .0872 oz. **Obv:** Large head **Note:** Varieties exist.

Date	Mintage	VG	F	VF	XF	Unc
1827 IB	106,000	6.00	10.00	20.00	38.00	—
1828 FH	92,000	6.00	10.00	20.00	38.00	—
1829 FH	124,000	6.00	10.00	20.00	38.00	—
1830 FH	614,000	6.00	10.00	20.00	38.00	—
1831 KG	—	6.00	10.00	20.00	38.00	—
1832 KG	1,112,000	6.00	10.00	20.00	38.00	—

C# 114.2 ZLOTY
4.5500 g., 0.5930 Silver .0872 oz. **Obv:** Small head

Date	Mintage	VG	F	VF	XF	Unc
1832 KG	Inc. above	6.00	10.00	20.00	38.00	—
1833 KG	41,000	6.50	11.00	25.00	45.00	—
1834 IP	201,000	6.00	10.00	20.00	38.00	—

C# 129 ZLOTY - 15 KOPEKS
3.0700 g., 0.8680 Silver .0857 oz. **Note:** Varieties exist.

Date	Mintage	VG	F	VF	XF	Unc
1832 НГ	49,000	7.50	12.50	20.00	40.00	—
1833 НГ	655,000	6.50	10.00	15.00	30.00	—
1834 НГ	30,000	7.50	12.50	20.00	40.00	—
1834MW	42,000	15.00	30.00	60.00	100	—
1835 НГ	150,000	6.50	10.00	15.00	30.00	—
1835MW	2,192,000	5.00	7.50	10.00	25.00	—
1836 НГ	1,450,000	6.50	10.00	15.00	30.00	—
1836MW	3,331,000	5.00	7.50	10.00	25.00	—
1837 НГ	80,000	6.50	10.00	15.00	30.00	—
1837MW	3,028,000	5.00	7.50	10.00	25.00	—
1838 НГ	1,410,000	10.00	20.00	40.00	80.00	—
1838MW	3,617,000	5.00	7.50	10.00	25.00	—
1839 НГ	1,510,000	6.50	10.00	15.00	30.00	—
1839 НГ Proof, rare	Inc. above	—	—	—	—	—
1839MW	3,586,000	5.00	7.50	10.00	25.00	—
1840 НГ	1,060,000	6.50	10.00	15.00	30.00	—
1840MW	487,000	6.50	10.00	15.00	30.00	—
1841 НГ Proof, rare	1,060,000	—	—	—	—	—
1841MW	1,320,000	10.00	17.50	30.00	60.00	—

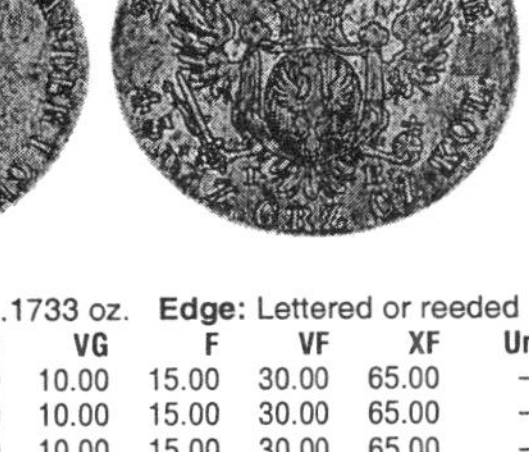

C# 99 2 ZLOTE
9.0900 g., 0.5930 Silver .1733 oz. **Edge:** Lettered or reeded

Date	Mintage	VG	F	VF	XF	Unc
1816 IB	1,393,000	10.00	15.00	30.00	65.00	—
1817 IB	1,084,000	10.00	15.00	30.00	65.00	—
1818 IB	1,321,000	10.00	15.00	30.00	65.00	—
1819 IB	1,241,000	10.00	15.00	30.00	65.00	—
1820 IB	1,970,000	10.00	20.00	40.00	80.00	—

C# 99b 2 ZLOTE
9.0900 g., 0.5930 Silver .1733 oz. **Obv:** Large head

Date	Mintage	VG	F	VF	XF	Unc
1819 IB	—	10.00	15.00	25.00	60.00	—
1820 IB	Inc. above	10.00	15.00	25.00	60.00	—
1821 IB	997,000	10.00	15.00	25.00	50.00	—
1822 IB	93,000	10.00	15.00	25.00	60.00	—
1823 IB	446,000	10.00	15.00	25.00	50.00	—
1824 IB	348,000	10.00	15.00	25.00	50.00	—
1825 IB	229,000	10.00	15.00	25.00	50.00	—

C# 99a 2 ZLOTE
9.0900 g., 0.5930 Silver .1733 oz. **Obv:** Medium head **Edge:** Reeded **Note:** Struck in collar.

Date	Mintage	VG	F	VF	XF	Unc
1819 IB Rare	—	—	—	—	—	—

C# 115 2 ZLOTE
9.0900 g., 0.5930 Silver .1733 oz. **Obv:** Laureated head

Date	Mintage	VG	F	VF	XF	Unc
1826 IB	65,000	10.00	17.50	35.00	75.00	—
1828 FH	119,000	10.00	15.00	25.00	55.00	—
1830 FH	306,000	10.00	15.00	25.00	55.00	—

C# 132 2 ZLOTE - 30 KOPEKS
6.2100 g., 0.8680 Silver .1733 oz.

Date	Mintage	VG	F	VF	XF	Unc
1834MW	24,000	12.00	20.00	40.00	75.00	—
1835MW	2,229,000	7.50	10.00	20.00	40.00	—
1836MW	2,589,000	7.50	10.00	20.00	40.00	—
1837MW	1,544	10.00	15.00	35.00	60.00	—

Date	Mintage	VG	F	VF	XF	Unc
1838MW	1,978	10.00	15.00	35.00	60.00	—
1839MW	2,037	10.00	15.00	35.00	60.00	—
1840MW	306,000	10.00	15.00	35.00	50.00	—
1841MW	1,261	10.00	15.00	35.00	60.00	—

C# 100 5 ZLOTYCH
15.5900 g., 0.8680 Silver .4351 oz. **Note:** Large and small crown varieties exist.

Date	Mintage	VG	F	VF	XF	Unc
1816 IB	971,000	30.00	60.00	125	265	—
1817 IB	2,585,000	25.00	45.00	90.00	220	—
1818 IB	201,000	35.00	75.00	135	285	—

C# 116 5 ZLOTYCH
15.5900 g., 0.8680 Silver .4351 oz. **Note:** Large and small bust varieties exist.

Date	Mintage	VG	F	VF	XF	Unc
1829 FH	1,234,000	15.00	25.00	45.00	100	—
1830 FH	287,000	22.50	32.50	60.00	125	—
1830 KG	Inc. above	22.50	32.50	60.00	125	—
1831 KG	23,000	15.00	25.00	45.00	100	—
1832 KG	639,000	15.00	25.00	45.00	100	—
1833 KG	445,000	15.00	25.00	45.00	100	—
1834 KG	414,000	22.50	32.50	60.00	125	—
1834 IP	—	22.50	32.50	55.00	135	—

C# 116a 5 ZLOTYCH
15.5900 g., 0.8680 Silver .4351 oz. **Obv:** Legend with retrograde "S"

Date	Mintage	VG	F	VF	XF	Unc
1833 KG	Inc. above	22.50	32.50	60.00	120	—

C# 133 5 ZLOTYCH - 3/4 RUBLE
15.5400 g., 0.8680 Silver .4337 oz.

Date	Mintage	VG	F	VF	XF	Unc
1833 НГ	258,000	12.00	20.00	30.00	50.00	—
1834 НГ	206,000	12.00	20.00	30.00	50.00	—
1834MW	86,000	12.00	20.00	30.00	60.00	—
1835 НГ	107,000	12.00	20.00	30.00	50.00	—
1835MW	540,000	12.00	20.00	30.00	55.00	—
1836 НГ	78,000	12.00	20.00	30.00	50.00	—
1836MW	1,196,000	12.00	20.00	30.00	45.00	—
1837 НГ	262,000	12.00	20.00	30.00	50.00	—
1837MW	1,000,000	12.00	20.00	30.00	45.00	—
1838 НГ	12,000	50.00	85.00	135	225	—
1838MW	1,996,000	12.00	20.00	30.00	45.00	—
1839 НГ Rare	—	—	—	—	—	—
1839 НГ Proof, rare	—	—	—	—	—	—
1839MW	2,689,000	10.00	15.00	20.00	40.00	—
1840 НГ	2,001	—	—	—	—	—
1840MW	2,482,000	10.00	15.00	20.00	40.00	—
1841 НГ	—	—	—	—	—	—
1841MW	1,274,000	12.00	20.00	30.00	45.00	—

C# 101.1 10 ZLOTYCH
31.1000 g., 0.8680 Silver .8679 oz.

Date	Mintage	VG	F	VF	XF	Unc
1820 IB Rare	534	—	—	—	—	—
1821 IB	1,195	150	250	400	600	—
1822 IB Rare	233	—	—	—	—	—

C# 101.2 10 ZLOTYCH
31.1000 g., 0.8680 Silver .8679 oz.

Date	Mintage	VG	F	VF	XF	Unc
1823	1,124	150	250	400	600	—
1824	513	400	1,000	2,000	3,500	—
1825 Rare	—	—	—	—	—	—

C# 117 10 ZLOTYCH
31.1000 g., 0.8680 Silver .8679 oz. **Obv:** Laureate head

Date	Mintage	VG	F	VF	XF	Unc
1827 IB Rare	123	—	—	—	—	—
1827 FH Rare	Inc. above	—	—	—	—	—

C# 134 10 ZLOTYCH - 1-1/2 RUBLES
31.1000 g., 0.8680 Silver .8679 oz.

Date	Mintage	VG	F	VF	XF	Unc
1833 НГ	127,000	20.00	30.00	60.00	100	—
1834 НГ	64,000	25.00	40.00	80.00	150	—
1835 НГ	262,000	20.00	35.00	60.00	100	—
1835MW	3,081	40.00	80.00	140	225	—
1836 НГ	134,000	20.00	35.00	60.00	100	—
1836MW	220,000	20.00	35.00	60.00	100	—
1837 НГ	36,000	40.00	80.00	120	200	—
1837MW	194,000	20.00	35.00	60.00	100	—
1838 НГ Rare	13	—	—	—	—	—
1838MW	10,000	100	200	350	500	—
1839 НГ	7,006	125	275	450	750	—
1839 НГ Proof, rare	Inc. above	—	—	—	—	—
1839MW	2,295	40.00	80.00	150	350	—
1840 НГ Rare	2,001	—	—	—	—	—
1840MW	2,747	40.00	80.00	150	350	—
1841 НГ	—	—	—	—	—	—
1841MW	37,000	40.00	80.00	120	200	—

C# 136.1 20 ZLOTYCH - 3 RUBLES
3.8900 g., 0.9170 Gold .1147 oz.

Date	Mintage	F	VF	XF	Unc	BU
1834MW	243	500	1,400	2,500	4,500	—
1835MW	350	500	1,400	2,500	4,500	—
1836MW	307	500	1,400	2,500	4,500	—
1837MW	423	500	1,400	2,500	4,500	—
1838MW	66	1,000	2,000	4,000	7,000	—
1839MW	57	1,000	2,000	4,000	7,000	—
1840MW	—	1,600	3,000	4,000	8,500	—

C# 136.2 20 ZLOTYCH - 3 RUBLES
3.8900 g., 0.9170 Gold .1147 oz. **Note:** Mint mark: St. Petersburg "USB".

Date	Mintage	F	VF	XF	Unc	BU
1834MW ПД	77,000	195	275	500	850	—
1835MW ПД	52,000	195	275	500	850	—
1836MW ПД	10,000	195	275	500	850	—
1837MW ПД	30,000	195	275	500	850	—
1838MW ПД	17,000	195	275	500	850	—
1839MW ПД	11,000	195	275	500	850	—
1840MW ПД	—	195	275	500	850	—

C# 136.3 20 ZLOTYCH - 3 RUBLES
3.8900 g., 0.9170 Gold .1147 oz.

Date	Mintage	F	VF	XF	Unc	BU
1840 ПД	5,473,000	225	375	450	1,000	—
1841 ПД Proof, unique	—	—	—	—	—	—

Note: Superior Pipito sale 12-87 Proof realized $12,100

C# 102 25 ZLOTYCH

4.8900 g., 0.9170 Gold .1442 oz.

Date	Mintage	F	VF	XF	Unc	BU
1817 IB	96,000	175	550	650	1,800	—
1818 IB	55,000	175	550	650	2,000	—
1819 IB	1,124	175	550	650	2,000	—

C# 102a 25 ZLOTYCH

4.8900 g., 0.9170 Gold .1442 oz. **Note:** Struck in collar.

Date	Mintage	F	VF	XF	Unc	BU
1818 IB Rare	86,000	—	—	—	—	—
1822 IB	479	550	850	2,000	3,600	—
1823 IB	612	700	1,250	2,500	4,000	—
1824 IB	636	550	850	2,000	3,600	—
1825 IB	134	550	850	2,000	3,600	—
1828 IB	385	550	850	2,000	3,600	—

C# 118 25 ZLOTYCH

4.8900 g., 0.9170 Gold .1442 oz. **Note:** Struck in collar.

Date	Mintage	F	VF	XF	Unc	BU
1828 FH	241	700	1,250	3,000	4,500	—
1829 FH	66	850	1,400	3,500	4,800	—
1830	618	700	1,250	3,000	4,500	—
1832 KG	152	700	1,250	3,000	4,500	—
1833 KG	424	700	1,250	3,000	4,500	—

C# 103 50 ZLOTYCH

9.7800 g., 0.9170 Gold .2884 oz.

Date	Mintage	F	VF	XF	Unc	BU
1817 IB	17,000	350	550	950	2,500	—
1818 IB	50,000	350	700	1,100	2,750	—
1819 IB	20,000	350	700	1,200	3,000	—

C# 103.1 50 ZLOTYCH

9.7367 g., 0.9170 Gold .2871 oz.

Date	Mintage	F	VF	XF	Unc	BU
1817 IB Proof, rare	—	—	—	—	—	—

C# 103a 50 ZLOTYCH

9.7800 g., 0.9170 Gold .2884 oz. **Obv:** Small head

Date	Mintage	F	VF	XF	Unc	BU
1819 IB	Inc. above	375	600	1,000	2,500	—
1820 IB	7,098	375	600	1,200	2,500	—
1821 IB	2,638	375	750	1,400	3,000	—
1822 IB	1,610	375	750	1,400	3,200	—
1823 IB	251	700	1,500	2,250	4,500	—
1827 IB	62	975	1,725	2,400	4,800	—

C# 119 50 ZLOTYCH

9.7800 g., 0.9170 Gold .2884 oz.

Date	Mintage	F	VF	XF	Unc	BU
1827 FH	62	1,000	1,700	2,400	5,000	—
1829 FH	238	700	1,650	2,250	4,500	—

C# 119.1 50 ZLOTYCH

9.7367 g., 0.9170 Gold .2871 oz.

Date	Mintage	F	VF	XF	Unc	BU
1829 FH Proof	237	—	—	—	—	—

REVOLUTIONARY COINAGE

1830-1831

C# 120 3 GROSZE

Copper **Note:** Varieties in eagle exist.

Date	Mintage	VG	F	VF	XF	Unc
1831 KG	1,112,000	5.00	10.00	25.00	60.00	—

C# 121 10 GROSZY

2.8000 g., 0.1920 Silver .0173 oz. **Note:** Varieties in eagle exist.

Date	Mintage	VG	F	VF	XF	Unc
1831 KG	6,038,000	5.00	10.00	20.00	55.00	—

C# 123 2 ZLOTE

8.9800 g., 0.5930 Silver .1712 oz. **Note:** Varieties exist.

Date	Mintage	VG	F	VF	XF	Unc
1831 KG	171,000	17.50	30.00	50.00	100	—

C# 124 5 ZLOTYCH

15.4900 g., 0.8680 Silver .4323 oz. **Note:** Varieties in fraction numerator fineness exist.

Date	Mintage	VG	F	VF	XF	Unc
1831 KG	23,000	30.00	55.00	100	185	—

TRADE COINAGE

C# 125 DUKAT

3.5000 g., 0.9860 Gold .1109 oz. **Obv:** Eagle in legend at one o'clock

Date	Mintage	F	VF	XF	Unc	BU
1831	163,000	110	250	375	750	—

PATTERNS

INCLUDING OFF METAL STRIKES

KM#	Date	Mintage	Identification	Mkt Val
Pn122	1811 IS	—	Grosz. Silver. C#81.	—
Pn123	1813 IB	—	Dukat. Copper.	—
Pn124	1815 IB	—	Grosz. Copper. Wing feathers close together.	—
Pn125	1815 IB	—	Grosz. Copper. Wing feathers spread.	—
Pn126	1815 IB	—	3 Grosze. Copper. Plain edge.	—
Pn127	1815 IB	—	3 Grosze. Copper.	—
Pn128	1815 IB	—	3 Grosze. Copper.	—
Pn129	1816 IB	—	Grosz. Copper. Plain edge.	—
Pn130	1816 IB	—	3 Grosze. Copper.	—
Pn131	1817 IB	—	Grosz. Copper.	—
Pn133	1817 IB	—	3 Grosze. Copper.	—
Pn132	1817 IB	—	Grosz. Copper.	175
Pn134	1818 IB	—	Grosz. Copper.	—
Pn136	1818 IB	—	3 Grosze. Copper.	—
Pn137	1818 IB	—	3 Grosze. Copper. Plain rim.	—
Pn138	1818 IB	—	5 Groszy. Silver.	—
Pn139	1818 IB	—	Zloty. Silver.	—
Pn140	1818 IB	—	2 Zlote. Silver.	—
Pn141	1818 IB	—	25 Zlotych. Gold.	—
Pn142	1819 IB	—	Grosz. Copper.	—
Pn143	1819 IB	—	3 Grosze. Copper.	—
Pn144	1819 IB	—	Zloty. Silver.	—
Pn145	1819 IB	—	Zloty. Copper.	—
Pn146	1820 IB	—	Grosz. Copper.	—
Pn147	1820 IB	—	3 Grosze. Copper.	—
Pn148	1821 IB	—	Grosz. Copper.	—
Pn149	1822 IB	—	Grosz. Copper.	—
Pn150	1823 IB	—	Grosz. Copper.	—
Pn151	1824 IB	—	Grosz. Copper.	—
Pn152	1824 IB	—	Grosz. Copper.	—
Pn153	1824 IB	—	3 Grosze. (No Composition).	—
Pn154	1825 IB	—	Grosz. Copper.	—
Pn155	1826 IB	—	Grosz. Copper.	—
Pn156	1826 IB	—	3 Grosze. Copper.	—
Pn157	1827 IB	—	3 Grosze. Copper.	—
Pn158	1827 FH	—	3 Grosze. Copper.	—
Pn159	1827 FH	—	3 Grosze. Copper.	—
Pn160	1827 IB	—	10 Zlotych. Silver.	—
Pn161	1828 FH	—	Grosz. Copper.	—
Pn162	1828 FH	—	3 Grosze. Copper.	—
Pn163	1829 FH	—	Grosz. Copper.	—
Pn164	1829 FH	—	3 Grosze. Copper.	—
Pn165	1829 KG	—	5 Groszy. Silver.	—
Pn166	1830 FH	—	Grosz. Copper.	—
Pn167	1830 KG	—	Grosz. Copper.	—
Pn168	1830 FH	—	3 Grosze. Copper.	—
Pn169	1831 KG	—	Grosz. Copper.	—
Pn171	1831 KG	—	5 Groszy.	—
Pn172	1831 KG	—	10 Groszy. Silver.	—
Pn173	1831 IC	—	10 Groszy. Copper.	—
Pn174	1831 KG	—	Zloty. (No Composition).	—
Pn170	1831 KG	—	3 Grosze. Copper.	200
Pn175	1831 KG	—	2 Zloty. Silver.	200
Pn176	1832 KG	—	Grosz. Copper.	—
Pn177	1832 KG	—	3 Grosze. Copper.	—
Pn178	1832	—	5 Groszy. Silver.	—
Pn179	1832 KG	—	10 Groszy. Silver. C#113.	—
Pn180	1833	—	Grosz. Copper.	—
Pn181	1833 KG	—	3 Grosze. Copper.	—
Pn182	1833 KG	—	10 Groszy. Silver. C#113.	—
Pn184	1834 IP	—	Grosz. Copper.	—
Pn185	1834 KG	—	3 Grosze. Copper.	—
Pn186	1834 IP	—	3 Grosze. Copper.	—
Pn183	1834 KG	—	Grosz. Copper.	175
Pn187	1835 IP	—	Grosz. Copper.	—
Pn188	1835 IP	—	3 Grosze. Copper.	—
Pn189	1835	—	10 Zlotych - 1-1/2 Rubles. Silver.	—
Pn190	1836MW	—	Grosz. Copper.	—
Pn191	1836MW	—	3 Grosze. Copper.	—
Pn192	1836 РП@07	—	10 Zlotych - 1-1/2 Rubles. Silver.	—
Pn193	1836 РП@07	—	10 Zlotych - 1-1/2 Rubles. Silver.	—
Pn194	1837MW	—	Grosz. Copper.	—
Pn195	1837MW	—	3 Grosze. Copper.	—
Pn196	1838MW	—	Grosz. Copper.	—
Pn197	1838MW	—	3 Grosze. Copper.	—
Pn198	1838 НГ@07	—	10 Zlotych - 1-1/2 Rubles. Silver.	—
Pn199	1839MW	—	Grosz. Copper.	—
Pn200	1839MW	—	3 Grosze. Copper.	—
Pn201	1839 НГ@07	—	5 Zlotych - 3/4 Ruble. Silver.	—
Pn202	1840MW	—	Grosz. Copper. Large date, value in wreath.	—
Pn203	1840MW	—	Grosz. Copper. Small date, value in wreath.	—
Pn204	1840MW	—	Grosz. Copper. Large date and value.	—
Pn205	1840MW	—	Grosz. Copper. Small eagle. Large date and value.	—
Pn206	1840MW	—	Grosz. Silver.	—
Pn207	1840MW	—	Jeden Grosz. Copper. Small eagle.	—
Pn208	1840MW	—	Jeden Grosz. Copper. Large eagle.	—
Pn209	1840MW	—	3 Grosze. Copper.	—
Pn210	1840MW	—	10 Groszy. Copper. Large eagle.	—
Pn211	1840MW	—	10 Groszy. Silver.	—
Pn212	1840MW	—	10 Groszy. Tin.	—
Pn213	1840MW	—	10 Groszy. Silver.	—
Pn214	1840MW	—	10 Groszy. Silver. Without wreath.	—
Pn215	1840MW	—	20 Zlotych - 3 Rubles. Gold.	—
Pn227	1840 АЧ@07	—	20 Zlotych - 3 Rubles. Gold.	—
Pn223	1841MW	—	10 Groszy. Silver.	—
Pn224	1841 НГ@07	—	Zloty - 15 Kopeks. Silver.	—
Pn225	1841 НГ@07	—	5 Zlotych - 3/4 Ruble. Silver.	—

KM#	Date	Mintage	Identification	Mkt Val
Pn226	1841 НГ@07	—	10 Zlotych - 1-1/2 Rubles. Silver.	—
Pn216	1841MW	—	Grosz. Copper.	—
Pn217	1841MW	—	Jeden Groschen. Copper.	—
Pn218	1841MW	—	Jeden Grosz. Copper. Large eagle.	—
Pn219	1841MW	—	Jeden Grosz. Copper. Small eagle.	—
Pn220	1841MW	—	3 Grosze. Copper.	—
Pn221	1841MW	—	5 Groszy. Silver. Eagle.	—
Pn222	1841MW	—	5 Groszy. Silver. Head.	—
Pn228	1842 Mw	—	10 Groszy. Silver.	—
Pn229	1842MW	—	10 Kopecks/20 Groszy. Silver.	—
Pn230	1846MW	—	20 Kopecks/40 Groszy. Silver.	—
Pn231	1848	—	2 Zlote. Silver.	—

SPECIMEN SETS (SS)

KM#	Date	Mintage	Identification	Issue Price	Mkt Val
SS1	1831 (5)	—	C#120, 121, 123-125 including 1 Zloty banknote	—	1,950

EAST PRUSSIA

East Prussia is an area on the southeastern coast of the Baltic Sea. Part of the area is in present day Poland and part in Russia. A possession of Prussia from 1525 until 1945, coinage for the area made by the Prussian kings except for brief occupation by Russia from 1756-1762 when Russia produced special coin types for the area.

RULERS
Friedrich Wilhelm III (of Prussia), ...1797-1840

MINT MARKS
A - Berlin
E - Konigsberg
G - Glatz, Silesia

NOTE: For gold listings refer to Konigsberg Mint under Brandenburg and Prussia (German States).

PRUSSIAN POSSESSION

STANDARD COINAGE

C# 53 SCHILLING
Copper

Date	Mintage	VG	F	VF	XF	Unc
1804A	—	4.00	7.00	15.00	40.00	—
1805A	—	4.00	7.00	15.00	40.00	—
1806A	—	4.00	7.00	15.00	40.00	—

C# 54 SCHILLING
Copper

Date	Mintage	VG	F	VF	XF	Unc
1810A	—	4.00	7.00	15.00	40.00	—

C# 56 1/2 GROSCHEN
Copper

Date	Mintage	VG	F	VF	XF	Unc
1811A	—	10.00	20.00	50.00	120	—

C# 58 GROSCHEN
Copper

Date	Mintage	VG	F	VF	XF	Unc
1810A	—	5.00	10.00	20.00	75.00	—
1811A	—	5.00	10.00	20.00	75.00	—

C# 60 3 GROSCHEN
Billon **Ruler:** Friedrich III (of Prussia)

Date	Mintage	VG	F	VF	XF	Unc
1801 A	—	7.00	18.00	30.00	90.00	—
1802 A	—	7.00	18.00	30.00	90.00	—
1803 A	—	7.00	18.00	30.00	90.00	—
1805 A	—	7.00	18.00	30.00	90.00	—
1806 A	—	7.00	18.00	30.00	90.00	—
1807 A	—	7.00	18.00	30.00	90.00	—

C# 60a 3 GROSCHEN
Billon

Date	Mintage	VG	F	VF	XF	Unc
1807G	—	6.00	12.00	28.00	90.00	—
1808G	—	6.00	12.00	28.00	90.00	—

KRAKOW

Krakow is located in southern Poland and is the third largest city in the country. From 1815 thru 1846 it was an independent republic, after which it reverted to Austria. Coins made for the republic in 1835.

RULERS
Cajetan Soltyk, 1759-1782

MONETARY SYSTEM
30 Groszy = 1 Zloty

CITY

STANDARD COINAGE

C# 11 5 GROSZY
Billon **Ruler:** Cajetan Soltyk

Date	Mintage	VG	F	VF	XF	Unc
1835	180,000	10.00	20.00	35.00	60.00	—

C# 12 10 GROSZY
3.1000 g., Silver **Ruler:** Cajetan Soltyk

Date	Mintage	VG	F	VF	XF	Unc
1835	150,000	10.00	20.00	35.00	60.00	—

C# 13 ZLOTY
Silver **Ruler:** Cajetan Soltyk

Date	Mintage	VG	F	VF	XF	Unc
1835	20,000	15.00	30.00	50.00	90.00	—

PATTERNS

INCLUDING OFF METAL STRIKES

KM#	Date	Mintage	Identification	Mkt Val
Pn1	1835	—	3 Groszy. Copper. Value and date in wreath.	450
Pn2	1835	—	3 Groszy. Copper. Value and date.	—
Pn3	1835	—	2 Zlote. Silver.	—
Pn4	1835	—	2 Zlote. Lead.	—

POSEN

Posen was part of Poland until 1793, then a province of Prussia from 1793-1918. It became part of the Grand Duchy of Warsaw (Warszawa). Returned to Prussia after the Congress of Vienna (1815). A special coin issue was made as a provincial issue for the Grand Duchy (Frederich August, Grand Duke) of Posen by Prussia immediately after repossession.

RULERS
Friedrich Wilhelm III (of Prussia), 1797-1840

MINT MARKS
A - Berlin
B - Breslau

KINGDOM

STANDARD COINAGE

KM# 30 GROSCHEN
Silver

Date	Mintage	VG	F	VF	XF	Unc
1816A	—	6.00	12.00	25.00	80.00	—
1816B	—	6.00	12.00	25.00	80.00	—
1817A	—	7.00	15.00	30.00	100	—

KM# 31 3 GROSCHEN
Copper

Date	Mintage	VG	F	VF	XF	Unc
1816A Rare	—	—	—	—	—	—
1816B	—	7.00	15.00	30.00	100	—
1817A	—	10.00	20.00	40.00	110	—

ZAMOSC

Zamosc is a fortress commune in southeastern Poland twice besieged by Russians.

MONETARY SYSTEM
30 Groszy = 1 Zloty

FORTRESS COMMUNE

SIEGE COINAGE

KM# 1 6 GROSZY
Copper

Date	Mintage	VG	F	VF	XF	Unc
1813	1,330	200	275	525	850	—

KM# 2 6 GROSZY
Copper **Rev:** Without outer legend

Date	Mintage	VG	F	VF	XF	Unc
1813	Inc. above	250	350	600	1,000	—

KM# 3 6 GROSZY
Copper **Rev:** Without palm fronds

Date	Mintage	VG	F	VF	XF	Unc
1813 Rare	Inc. above	—	—	—	—	—

KM# 5 2 ZLOTY
Silver

Date	Mintage	VG	F	VF	XF	Unc
1813(b)	7,830	200	250	300	400	—

KM# 6 2 ZLOTY
Silver **Obv:** Without mint mark

Date	Mintage	VG	F	VF	XF	Unc
1813	Inc. above	225	275	350	500	—

KM# 7 2 ZLOTY
Silver **Obv:** Legend in four lines **Note:** Varieties exist.

Date	Mintage	VG	F	VF	XF	Unc
1813	Inc. above	225	275	350	500	—

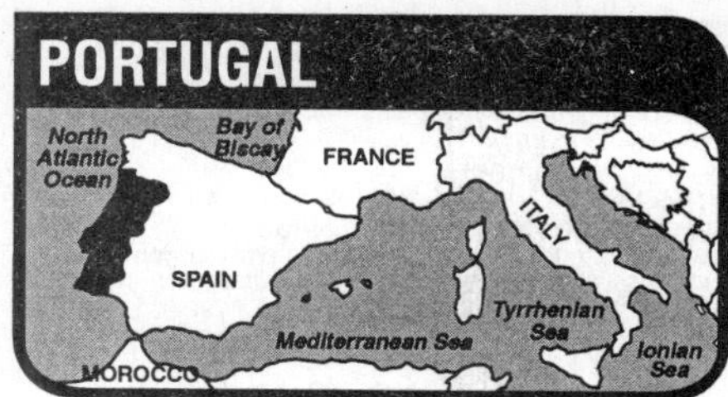

Portugal is located in the western part of the Iberian Peninsula in southwestern Europe and has an area of 35,553 sq. mi. (92,080 sq. km.). Portugal has become Europe's number one producer of copper and the world's largest producer of cork.

After centuries of domination by Romans, Visigoths and Moors, Portugal emerged in the 12th century as an independent kingdom financially and philosophically prepared for the great period of exploration that would soon follow. Attuned to the inspiration of Prince Henry the Navigator (1394-1460), Portugal's daring explorers of the 15th and 16th centuries roamed the world's oceans from Brazil to Japan in an unprecedented burst of energy and endeavor that culminated in 1494 with Portugal laying claim to half the transoceanic world. Unfortunately for the fortunes of the tiny kingdom, the Portuguese population was too small to colonize this vast territory. Less than a century after Portugal laid claim to half the world, English, French and Dutch trading companies had seized the lion's share of the world's colonies and commerce, and Portugal's place as an imperial power was lost forever.

RULERS

Joao, As Prince Regent, 1799-1816
Joao, As King (Joao VI), 1816-1826
Pedro IV, 1826-1828
Miguel, 1828-1834
Maria II, 1834-1853
Pedro V, 1853-1861
Luiz I, 1861-1889
Carlos I, 1889-1908

MINT MARKS

A - Paris (1891-1892, Copper only)
E - Evora
L - Lisbon
P - Porto
No Mint mark – Lisbon

MONETARY SYSTEM

Until 1825

20 Reis = 1 Vintem
100 Reis = 1 Tostao
480 Reis = 24 Vintens = 1 Cruzado
1600 Reis = 1 Escudo
6400 Reis = 4 Escudos = 1 Peca

1826-1836

7500 Reis = 1 Peca

Beginning in 1836 all coins were expressed in terms of Reis and arranged in a decimal sequence (until 1910).

NOTE: The primary denomination was the Peca, weighing 14.34 g, tariffed at 6400 Reis until 1825, and at 7500 Reis after 1826. The weight was not changed.

KINGDOM

MILLED COINAGE

KM# 334 3 REIS (III)
Copper **Obv:** Cround shield **Obv. Legend:** JOANNES... **Rev:** Legend around wreath, date and denomination within

Date	Mintage	VG	F	VF	XF	Unc
1804	123,000	6.00	12.00	32.00	80.00	—

KM# 354 3 REIS (III)
Copper **Obv:** Crowned arms **Obv. Legend:** JOANNES VI... **Rev:** Value and date in branches

Date	Mintage	VG	F	VF	XF	Unc
1818	—	45.00	90.00	280	540	—

KM# 325 5 REIS (V)
Copper **Obv:** Crowned arms **Obv. Legend:** JOANNES... **Rev:** Legend ends: ...PRINCEPS

Date	Mintage	VG	F	VF	XF	Unc
1800	—	60.00	120	250	500	—
1801 Rare	—	—	—	—	—	—

KM# 335 5 REIS (V)
Copper **Obv:** Crowned arms **Rev:** Legend ends: ...REGENS

Date	Mintage	VG	F	VF	XF	Unc
1804	—	—	—	—	—	—

Note: Reported, not confirmed.

KM# 346 5 REIS (V)
Copper **Obv:** Crowned arms **Obv. Legend:** JOANNES • DEI • GRATIA **Rev:** Value in wreath

Date	Mintage	VG	F	VF	XF	Unc
1812	399,000	2.00	5.00	22.00	45.00	—
1813	539,000	2.00	5.00	22.00	45.00	—
1814	448,000	2.50	6.00	26.00	55.00	—

KM# 347 5 REIS (V)
Copper **Obv:** KM#305 **Rev:** KM#346 **Note:** Mule.

Date	Mintage	VG	F	VF	XF	Unc
1812	—	14.00	28.00	55.00	100	—

KM# 355 5 REIS (V)
Copper **Obv:** Arms **Obv. Legend:** JOANNES VI... **Rev:** Value in wreath **Rev. Legend:** PORTUGALIAE...REX

Date	Mintage	VG	F	VF	XF	Unc
1818	—	200	500	1,000	1,800	—
1819	11,000	20.00	50.00	110	220	—
1820	—	9.00	28.00	70.00	135	—
1823	32,000	20.00	45.00	90.00	180	—
1824	98,000	9.00	28.00	70.00	135	—

KM# 389 5 REIS (V)
Copper **Obv:** Crowned arms **Obv. Legend:** MICHAEL I DEI GRATIA **Rev:** Legend around wreath, value within, date below

Date	Mintage	VG	F	VF	XF	Unc
1829	401,000	7.00	18.00	35.00	70.00	—

Note: For similar coins dated 1830 but with titles of Maria II, see Azores/Terceira Islands

KM# 398 5 REIS (V)
Copper **Obv:** Square shield **Obv. Legend:** MARIA II... **Rev:** Legend around wreath, value within, date below

Date	Mintage	VG	F	VF	XF	Unc
1833	—	100	250	400	700	—

KM# 408 5 REIS (V)
Copper **Obv:** Square shield **Obv. Legend:** MARIA II DEI GRATIA **Rev:** Legend around wreath, value within, date below

Date	Mintage	VG	F	VF	XF	Unc
1836	5,593	15.00	32.00	90.00	160	—

KM# 327 10 REIS (X; 1/2 Vinten)
Copper **Obv:** Arms **Obv. Legend:** JOANNES... **Rev:** Legend ends: ...PRINCEPS

Date	Mintage	VG	F	VF	XF	Unc
1800	—	70.00	150	300	600	—
1801 Rare	—	—	—	—	—	—

KM# 333 10 REIS (X; 1/2 Vinten)
Copper **Obv:** Arms **Obv. Legend:** JOANNES... **Rev:** Legend ends: ...REGENS

Date	Mintage	VG	F	VF	XF	Unc
1803	—	—	—	—	—	—

Note: Reported, not confirmed.

KM# 348 10 REIS (X; 1/2 Vinten)
Copper **Obv:** Arms **Obv. Legend:** JOANNES... **Rev:** Legend ends REGENS

Date	Mintage	VG	F	VF	XF	Unc
1812	332,000	3.00	6.00	25.00	50.00	—
1813	276,000	3.00	7.00	32.00	60.00	—

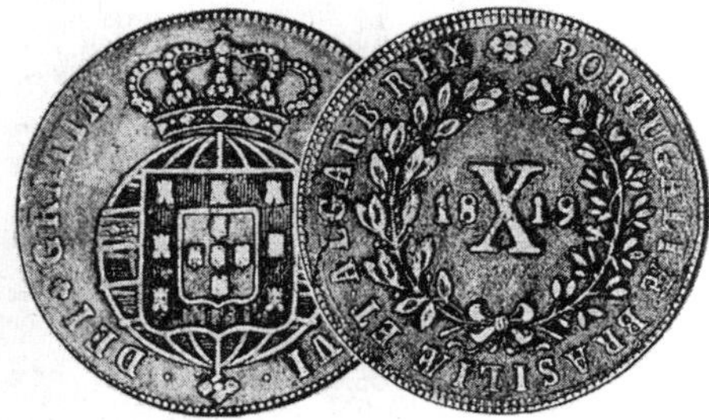

KM# 356 10 REIS (X; 1/2 Vinten)
Copper **Obv:** Crowned arms on globe **Obv. Legend:** JOANNES VI... **Rev:** Value in wreath **Rev. Legend:** PORTUGALIAE...REX

Date	Mintage	VG	F	VF	XF	Unc
1818	—	30.00	70.00	200	350	—
1819	806,000	4.00	6.00	20.00	40.00	—
1820	6,773	25.00	70.00	180	300	—
1822	21,000	20.00	45.00	140	250	—
1823	44,000	7.00	20.00	55.00	100	—
1824	64,000	7.00	20.00	55.00	100	—

KM# 390 10 REIS (X; 1/2 Vinten)
Copper **Obv:** Arms **Obv. Legend:** MICHAEL I DEI GRATIA **Rev:** Value in wreath **Rev. Legend:** PORTUGALIAE...REX **Note:** Previous #C89. For similar coins dated 1830 but with titles of Maria II see Azores/Terceira Islands.

Date	Mintage	VG	F	VF	XF	Unc
1829	56,000	4.00	10.00	25.00	55.00	—
1831	345,000	4.00	10.00	25.00	55.00	—
1833	70,000	12.00	30.00	60.00	130	—

KM# 399 10 REIS (X; 1/2 Vinten)
Copper **Obv:** Arms **Obv. Legend:** MARIA II... **Rev:** Value in wreath **Rev. Legend:** PORTUGALIAE.. **Note:** Similar to 5 Reis, KM#408

Date	Mintage	VG	F	VF	XF	Unc
1833 Struck at Porto	—	100	270	450	775	—

KM# 406 10 REIS (X; 1/2 Vinten)
Copper **Obv:** Large crowned shield **Obv. Legend:** MARIA II DEI GRATIA **Rev:** Value in wreath **Rev. Legend:** PORTUGALIAE...REGINA

Date	Mintage	VG	F	VF	XF	Unc
1835	287,000	7.00	20.00	55.00	120	—
1836	227,000	7.00	20.00	45.00	100	—
1837	360,000	10.00	35.00	75.00	160	—

KM# 409 10 REIS (X; 1/2 Vinten)
Copper **Obv:** Small crowned shield **Obv. Legend:** MARIA II DEI GRATIA **Rev:** Value in wreath **Rev. Legend:** PORTUGALIAE...REGINA

Date	Mintage	VG	F	VF	XF	Unc
1837	Inc. above	7.00	20.00	40.00	100	—
1838	645,000	5.00	18.00	35.00	80.00	—
1839	469,000	5.00	18.00	35.00	80.00	—

KM# 328 20 REIS (Vinten)
Copper, 34 mm. **Obv:** Arms **Obv. Legend:** JOANNES... **Rev:** Date, value within wreath **Rev. Legend:** PORTUGALIAE

Date	Mintage	VG	F	VF	XF	Unc
1800	—	70.00	150	350	750	—

KM# 329 20 REIS (Vinten)
Copper **Obv:** Arms **Obv. Legend:** JOANNES... **Rev:** Date, value within wreath **Rev. Legend:** PORTUGALIAE **Note:** Large planchet

Date	Mintage	VG	F	VF	XF	Unc
1800	—	60.00	125	300	700	—

KM# 330 20 REIS (Vinten)
Silver **Obv:** Globe **Rev:** Cross with rosettes in angles

Date	Mintage	VG	F	VF	XF	Unc
ND(1799-1816)	—	6.00	15.00	50.00	100	—

KM# 400 20 REIS (Vinten)
Bronze **Obv:** Globe **Rev:** Cross with rosettes in angles **Note:** Titles of Maria II, struck at Porto.

Date	Mintage	VG	F	VF	XF	Unc
1833	—	40.00	90.00	160	320	—

KM# 345.1 40 REIS (Pataco)
Bronze **Obv:** Bust right **Obv. Legend:** JOANNES • D • G •... **Rev:** Crowned oval shield, value below. **Edge:** Plain **Note:** Varieties exist.

Date	Mintage	VG	F	VF	XF	Unc
1811	163,000	9.00	20.00	40.00	85.00	—

Note: There are 5 additional edge varieties of 1811 date which are found listed in the pattern section

Date	Mintage	VG	F	VF	XF	Unc
1812	1,384,000	7.00	15.00	50.00	110	—
1813	1,762,000	7.00	15.00	50.00	110	—
1814	542,000	7.00	15.00	50.00	110	—
1815	118,000	22.00	52.00	300	650	—

KM# 345.2 40 REIS (Pataco)
Bronze **Obv:** Bust right **Obv. Legend:** JOANNES • D • G •... **Rev:** Crowned oval shield, value below **Edge:** Milled

Date	Mintage	VG	F	VF	XF	Unc
1814	Inc. above	10.00	20.00	45.00	90.00	—

KM# 365 40 REIS (Pataco)
Bronze **Obv:** Bust right **Obv. Legend:** JOANNES • D • G •...

Date	Mintage	VG	F	VF	XF	Unc
1819	422,000	7.00	15.00	70.00	140	—

KM# 370 40 REIS (Pataco)
Bronze **Obv:** Bust right **Obv. Legend:** JOANNES VI D G... **Rev:** Shield on crowned globe, value below.

Date	Mintage	VG	F	VF	XF	Unc
1820	1,579,000	7.00	15.00	75.00	150	—
1821	1,575,000	7.00	15.00	75.00	150	—
1822	2,370,000	7.00	15.00	75.00	150	—
1823	2,621,000	7.00	15.00	75.00	150	—
1824	3,051,000	7.00	15.00	75.00	150	—
1825	1,124,000	7.00	15.00	95.00	190	—

KM# 371 40 REIS (Pataco)
Bronze **Obv:** Bust right **Obv. Legend:** JOANNES VI D G... **Rev:** Shield on crowned globe, value below **Note:** Similar to KM#345.1

Date	Mintage	VG	F	VF	XF	Unc
1821	—	50.00	90.00	200	450	—
1823	—	50.00	90.00	200	450	—

KM# 373 40 REIS (Pataco)
Bronze **Obv:** Bust right **Obv. Legend:** PETRUS IV... **Rev:** Similar to KM#345.1

Date	Mintage	VG	F	VF	XF	Unc
1826	1,253,000	11.00	28.00	95.00	300	—
1827	1,447,000	9.00	21.00	70.00	260	—
1828	1,378,000	9.00	21.00	95.00	300	—

KM# 380 40 REIS (Pataco)
Bronze **Obv:** Crowned shield, large high crown **Rev:** Similar to KM#345.1

Date	Mintage	VG	F	VF	XF	Unc
1828	1,378,000	9.00	21.00	70.00	250	—
1829	1,678,000	7.00	15.00	45.00	170	—

KM# 391 40 REIS (Pataco)
Bronze **Obv:** Crowned shield, small lower crown **Rev:** Similar to KM#345.1

Date	Mintage	VG	F	VF	XF	Unc
1829 Inc. KM380	—	7.00	15.00	45.00	140	—
1830	1,783,000	7.00	15.00	45.00	140	—
1831	1,391,000	7.00	15.00	45.00	140	—
1832	1,780,000	7.00	15.00	45.00	140	—
1833	1,631,000	7.00	15.00	45.00	170	—

KM# 401 40 REIS (Pataco)
Bronze **Obv:** Crowned shield flared outward at upper corners **Obv. Legend:** MARIA II.. **Rev:** Value within wreath **Note:** Similar to 20 Reis, KM#400. Struck at Porto.

Date	Mintage	VG	F	VF	XF	Unc
1833 Struck at Porto	—	22.00	50.00	225	450	—

KM# 402 40 REIS (Pataco)
Bronze **Obv:** Crowned shield with right-angle upper corners **Obv. Legend:** MARIA II... **Rev:** Value within wreath **Note:** Struck at Lisbon, 1833-34; Struck at Porto, 1847.

Date	Mintage	VG	F	VF	XF	Unc
1833	—	7.00	15.00	45.00	250	—

Note: 1833 variety with vertical axis instead of horizontal. Value $50 in XF

Date	Mintage	VG	F	VF	XF	Unc
1834	—	7.00	15.00	55.00	250	—

Note: 1834 variety with vertical axis instead of horizontal. Value $60 in XF

Date	Mintage	VG	F	VF	XF	Unc
1847	—	8.50	22.50	67.50	210	—

KM# 311 50 REIS (1/2 Tostao)
Silver **Obv:** Value: XXXX, crown above **Obv. Legend:** JOANNES...ET ALG...P REGENS **Rev:** Cross **Rev. Legend:** IN HOC..

Date	Mintage	VG	F	VF	XF	Unc
ND(1799-1816)	—	10.00	25.00	55.00	150	—

KM# 350 50 REIS (1/2 Tostao)
Silver **Obv:** Value XXXX, crown above **Obv. Legend:** JOANNES VI...ET ALG REX **Rev:** Cross **Rev. Legend:** IN HOC...

Date	Mintage	VG	F	VF	XF	Unc
ND(1816-26)	10,000	8.00	20.00	55.00	125	—

KM# 381 50 REIS (1/2 Tostao)
Silver **Obv:** Crowned value **Obv. Legend:** MICHAEL I...REX **Rev:** Cross **Rev. Legend:** IN HOC...

Date	Mintage	VG	F	VF	XF	Unc
ND(1828-34)	—	12.00	25.00	50.00	135	—

KM# 312 60 REIS (3 Vintens)
1.8300 g., Silver **Obv:** Arms **Obv. Legend:** JOANNES...ET ALG **Rev:** Cross **Rev. Legend:** IN HOC...

Date	Mintage	VG	F	VF	XF	Unc
ND(1799-1816)	—	5.00	10.00	25.00	60.00	—

KM# 313 60 REIS (3 Vintens)
1.8300 g., Silver **Obv. Legend:** JOANNES...P REGENS **Rev:** Cross **Rev. Legend:** IN HOC...

Date	Mintage	VG	F	VF	XF	Unc
ND(1799-1816)	—	5.00	10.00	27.00	55.00	—

KM# 351 60 REIS (3 Vintens)
1.8300 g., Silver **Obv:** Crowned arms above globe **Obv. Legend:** JOANNES VI...ET ALG REX **Rev:** Cross **Rev. Legend:** IN HOC...

Date	Mintage	VG	F	VF	XF	Unc
ND(1816-26)	—	5.50	13.50	32.00	65.00	—

KM# 374 60 REIS (3 Vintens)
1.8300 g., Silver **Obv:** Arms **Obv. Legend:** PETRUS IV...REX **Rev:** Cross **Rev. Legend:** IN HOC...

Date	Mintage	VG	F	VF	XF	Unc
ND(1826-28)	36,000	110	230	450	950	—

KM# 382 60 REIS (3 Vintens)
1.8300 g., Silver **Obv:** Crowned arms **Obv. Legend:** MICHAEL I... **Rev:** Cross **Rev. Legend:** IN HOC...

Date	Mintage	VG	F	VF	XF	Unc
ND(1828-34)	—	9.50	22.00	45.00	90.00	—

KM# 314 80 REIS (LXXX; Tostao)
Silver **Obv:** Crown **Obv. Legend:** JOANNES...ET.ALG **Rev:** Cross **Rev. Legend:** IN HOC...

Date	Mintage	VG	F	VF	XF	Unc
ND(1799-1816)	—	6.00	14.50	30.00	65.00	—

KM# 315 80 REIS (LXXX; Tostao)
Silver **Obv:** Value LXXX, crown above **Obv. Legend:** JOANNES...P REGENS **Rev:** Cross **Rev. Legend:** IN HOC...

Date	Mintage	VG	F	VF	XF	Unc
ND(1799-1816)	—	5.00	12.50	27.50	60.00	—

KM# 352 80 REIS (LXXX; Tostao)
Silver **Obv:** Value LXXX, crown above **Obv. Legend:** JOANNES VI...ET ALG REX **Rev:** Cross **Rev. Legend:** IN HOC...

Date	Mintage	VG	F	VF	XF	Unc
ND(1799-1816)	—	5.00	12.50	27.50	60.00	—

KM# 375 80 REIS (LXXX; Tostao)
Silver **Obv:** Crowned value **Obv. Legend:** PETRUS IV... REX **Rev:** Cross **Rev. Legend:** IN HOC...

Date	Mintage	VG	F	VF	XF	Unc
ND(1816-26)	9,986	300	680	2,000	3,250	—

KM# 383 80 REIS (LXXX; Tostao)
Silver **Obv:** Crowned value, large high crown **Obv. Legend:** MICHAEL I... **Rev:** Cross **Rev. Legend:** IN HOC...

Date	Mintage	VG	F	VF	XF	Unc
ND(1828-34)	—	17.50	37.50	65.00	135	—

KM# 384 80 REIS (LXXX; Tostao)
Silver **Obv:** Crowned value, small lower crown **Obv. Legend:** MICHAEL I... **Rev:** Cross **Rev. Legend:** IN HOC...

Date	Mintage	VG	F	VF	XF	Unc
ND(1828-34)	—	300	600	1,000	1,650	—

KM# 316 120 REIS (6 Vintens)
Silver **Obv:** Crowned arms **Obv. Legend:** JOANNES...ET ALG **Rev:** Cross **Rev. Legend:** IN HOC...

Date	Mintage	VG	F	VF	XF	Unc
ND(1799-1816)	—	6.50	15.00	35.00	95.00	—

KM# 317 120 REIS (6 Vintens)
Silver **Obv:** Crowned arms **Obv. Legend:** JOANNES...P REGENS **Rev:** Cross **Rev. Legend:** IN HOC...

Date	Mintage	VG	F	VF	XF	Unc
ND(1799-1816)	—	5.50	12.50	30.00	70.00	—

KM# 353 120 REIS (6 Vintens)
Silver **Obv:** Crowned arms **Obv. Legend:** JOANNES...ET ALG REX **Rev:** Cross **Rev. Legend:** IN HOC...

Date	Mintage	VG	F	VF	XF	Unc
ND(1816-26)	—	6.50	15.00	35.00	95.00	—

KM# 376 120 REIS (6 Vintens)
Silver **Obv:** Crowned arms **Obv. Legend:** PETRUS IV...REX

Date	Mintage	VG	F	VF	XF	Unc
ND(1826-28)	18,000	200	450	900	2,000	—

KM# 385 120 REIS (6 Vintens)
Silver **Obv:** Crowned arms **Obv. Legend:** MICHAEL I...

Date	Mintage	VG	F	VF	XF	Unc
ND(1828-34)	—	8.50	20.00	40.00	85.00	—

KM# 340 200 REIS (12 Vintens, 200 = 240 Reis)
Silver **Obv:** Crowned arms **Obv. Legend:** JOANNES...P • REGENS **Rev:** Cross of Jerusalem, rosettes in angles

Date	Mintage	VG	F	VF	XF	Unc
1806	—	75.00	180	400	850	—
1807 Rare	—	—	—	—	—	—
1808	—	20.00	45.00	170	380	—
1809	22,000	35.00	60.00	185	400	—
1816	—	65.00	140	370	750	—

KM# 357 200 REIS (12 Vintens, 200 = 240 Reis)
Silver **Obv:** Crowned arms **Obv. Legend:** JOANNES VI...ET ALGARB REX **Rev:** Cross of Jerusalem, rosettes in angles

Date	Mintage	VG	F	VF	XF	Unc
1818	21,000	30.00	60.00	140	310	—
1819	24,000	32.50	70.00	160	350	—
1820	2,818	32.50	70.00	160	350	—
1821	2,293	190	410	1,850	3,700	—
1822	6,483	65.00	160	370	800	—

KM# 392 200 REIS (12 Vintens, 200 = 240 Reis)
Silver **Obv:** Crowned arms **Obv. Legend:** MICHAEL I...

Date	Mintage	VG	F	VF	XF	Unc
1829	3,584,000	25.00	55.00	110	250	—
1830	6,594,000	35.00	80.00	145	300	—

KM# 318 400 REIS (Pinto, 480 Reis)
Silver **Obv:** Legend ends: ...ET. ALG **Obv. Legend:** MARIA I **Rev:** Similar to KM#331 **Rev. Legend:** IN HOC... **Note:** Dav. #1633

Date	Mintage	VG	F	VF	XF	Unc
1801	—	50.00	90.00	150	350	—
1802 Rare	—	—	—	—	—	—

KM# 331 400 REIS (Pinto, 480 Reis)
Silver **Obv. Legend:** JOANNES...P REGENS **Rev:** Cross of Jerusalem, rosettes in angles

Date	Mintage	VG	F	VF	XF	Unc
1802	—	30.00	70.00	145	310	—
1805	—	22.50	47.50	95.00	200	—
1807	—	9.00	20.00	45.00	100	—
1808	—	9.00	20.00	45.00	100	—
1809	—	9.00	20.00	45.00	100	—
1810	—	9.00	20.00	47.50	125	—
1811	—	9.00	20.00	47.50	125	—
1812	—	7.00	15.00	40.00	80.00	—
1813	—	7.00	15.00	40.00	80.00	—
1814	—	7.00	15.00	35.00	65.00	—
1815	—	7.00	15.00	35.00	65.00	—
1816	—	7.00	15.00	35.00	65.00	—
1816 VINECS (Error for VINCES.)	—	125	300	625	1,500	—

KM# 341 400 REIS (Pinto, 480 Reis)
1.0720 g., 0.9170 Gold .0316 oz. **Obv:** Legend in crowned wreath **Obv. Legend:** JOANNES P R...

Date	Mintage	VG	F	VF	XF	Unc
1807	8,857	240	525	700	950	—

KM# 358 400 REIS (Pinto, 480 Reis)
Silver **Obv:** Crowned arms on globe **Obv. Legend:** JOANNES VI...ET ALGARB REX

Date	Mintage	VG	F	VF	XF	Unc
1818	2,337,000	17.50	40.00	75.00	160	—
1819	1,432,000	9.00	20.00	42.50	95.00	—
1820	1,845,000	9.00	20.00	42.50	95.00	—
1821	1,937,000	9.00	20.00	42.50	95.00	—
1822	568,000	11.00	25.00	70.00	150	—

Date	Mintage	VG	F	VF	XF	Unc
1823	667,000	15.00	30.00	70.00	150	—
1825	28,000	60.00	120	275	550	—

KM# 359 400 REIS (Pinto, 480 Reis)
1.0720 g., 0.9170 Gold .0316 oz. **Obv:** Legend in crowned wreath **Obv. Legend:** JOAN VI...

Date	Mintage	VG	F	VF	XF	Unc
1818	4,401	350	700	1,050	1,600	—
1819	1,387	900	1,800	2,750	3,700	—
1820 Rare	200	—	—	—	—	—
1821	266	1,300	2,750	3,700	4,600	—

KM# 377 400 REIS (Pinto, 480 Reis)
Silver **Obv:** Arms **Obv. Legend:** PETRUS IV...REX

Date	Mintage	VG	F	VF	XF	Unc
1826	259,000	40.00	95.00	140	230	—
1827	—	—	—	—	—	—

Note: None are known to have survived

KM# 386 400 REIS (Pinto, 480 Reis)
0.9060 Silver **Obv:** Arms **Obv. Legend:** MICHAEL I...REX **Rev:** Cross of Jerusalem, rosettes in angles.

Date	Mintage	VG	F	VF	XF	Unc
1828	135,000	50.00	95.00	190	400	—
1829 Rare	22,000	—	—	—	—	—
1830	29,000	40.00	80.00	140	280	—
1831	65,000	35.00	72.50	120	240	—
1832	108,000	35.00	72.50	120	240	—
1833	708,000	50.00	95.00	190	400	—
1834 Rare	705,000	—	—	—	—	—

KM# 403.2 400 REIS (Pinto, 480 Reis)
0.9060 Silver **Obv:** Arms, no stars in legend **Note:** Struck at Lisbon

Date	Mintage	VG	F	VF	XF	Unc
1833	798,000	15.00	35.00	75.00	140	—
1834	1,864,000	10.00	25.00	50.00	95.00	—
1835	3,433,000	10.00	25.00	45.00	80.00	—
1836	829,000	12.50	30.00	70.00	115	—
1837	194,000	200	450	1,150	2,000	—

KM# 403.1 400 REIS (Pinto, 480 Reis)
0.9060 Silver **Obv:** Arms **Obv. Legend:** *MARIA II...REGINA* **Rev:** Cross of Jerusalem, rosettes in angles **Note:** Struck at Porto.

Date	Mintage	VG	F	VF	XF	Unc
1833 Rare	—	—	—	—	—	—

KM# 337 1/2 ESCUDO (800 Reis)
1.7920 g., 0.9170 Gold .0528 oz. **Obv:** Bust right **Obv. Legend:** JOANNES D. G. PORT. ET ALG. P. REGENS **Rev:** Crowned oval arms

Date	Mintage	VG	F	VF	XF	Unc
1805	3,278	200	450	680	1,000	—
1806	—	650	1,450	2,000	2,750	—
1807	5,253	150	360	550	850	—

KM# 361 1/2 ESCUDO (800 Reis)
1.7920 g., 0.9170 Gold .0528 oz. **Obv:** Bust right **Obv. Legend:** JOANNES VI D. G. PORT... **Rev:** Crowned arms

Date	Mintage	VG	F	VF	XF	Unc
1818	270	300	750	1,400	3,400	—
1819	5,536	250	700	1,400	2,250	—
1820 Rare	82	—	—	—	—	—
1821	286	300	750	1,400	3,400	—

KM# 360 1000 REIS (Quartinho, 1200 Reis)
2.6800 g., 0.9170 Gold .0790 oz. **Obv:** Crowned arms on globe **Obv. Legend:** JOANNES VI D G PORT... **Rev:** Cross with rosettes in angles, date at top **Rev. Legend:** IN HOC...

Date	Mintage	VG	F	VF	XF	Unc
1818	3,144	400	850	1,450	2,350	—
1819	1,247	850	1,200	1,800	2,750	—
1820	270	800	1,700	2,750	4,500	—
1821	275	800	1,700	2,750	4,500	—

KM# 338 ESCUDO (1600 Reis)
3.5800 g., 0.9170 Gold .1057 oz. **Obv:** Bust right **Obv. Legend:** JOANNES D. G. PORT ET ALG P. REGENS **Rev:** Crowned arms in cartouche

Date	Mintage	VG	F	VF	XF	Unc
1805 Rare	143	—	—	—	—	—
1807	800	280	700	1,050	1,450	—

KM# 339 1/2 PECA (3200 Reis)
7.1500 g., 0.9170 Gold .2107 oz. **Obv:** Bust right, large letters **Obv. Legend:** JOANNES D. G. PORT ET ALG. P. REGENS **Rev:** Crowned oval arms in cartouche **Note:** Revalued to 3750 Reis in 1826.

Date	Mintage	VG	F	VF	XF	Unc
1805 Rare	74	—	—	—	—	—

KM# 342 1/2 PECA (3200 Reis)
7.1500 g., 0.9170 Gold .2107 oz. **Obv:** Bust right, small letters **Obv. Legend:** JOANNES D. G. PORT ET ALG. P. REGENS **Rev:** Crowned oval arms in cartouche **Note:** Revalued to 3750 Reis in 1826.

Date	Mintage	VG	F	VF	XF	Unc
1807	483	250	520	850	1,400	—

KM# 363 1/2 PECA (3200 Reis)
7.1500 g., 0.9170 Gold .2107 oz. **Obv:** Bust right **Obv. Legend:** JOANNES VI D G... **Rev:** Shield on crowned globe within wreath **Note:** Revalued to 3750 Reis in 1826.

Date	Mintage	VG	F	VF	XF	Unc
1818	100	—	300	600	1,050	1,850
1819 Rare	1,700	—	—	—	—	—
1820	242	—	900	2,000	3,500	6,500
1821	196	—	900	2,000	3,500	8,500
1822	14,000	—	100	150	275	450
1823 Rare	—	—	—	—	—	—

KM# 379 1/2 PECA (3200 Reis)
7.1500 g., 0.9170 Gold .2107 oz. **Obv:** Bust right **Obv. Legend:** PETRUS IV D G... **Rev:** Crowned oval arms in wreath **Note:** Revalued to 3750 Reis in 1826.

Date	Mintage	VG	F	VF	XF	Unc
1827	1,713	—	300	500	800	1,450

KM# 387 1/2 PECA (3200 Reis)
7.1500 g., 0.9170 Gold .2107 oz. **Obv:** Draped laureate bust right **Obv. Legend:** MICHAEL I... **Rev:** Crowned shield in palm wreath **Note:** Revalued to 3750 Reis in 1826.

Date	Mintage	VG	F	VF	XF	Unc
1828	242	—	700	1,400	2,100	3,000

KM# 396 1/2 PECA (3200 Reis)
7.1500 g., 0.9170 Gold .2107 oz. **Obv:** Armored bust right **Obv. Legend:** MICHAEL I... **Rev:** Crowned shield, crossed palms behind **Note:** Revalued to 3750 Reis in 1826.

Date	Mintage	VG	F	VF	XF	Unc
1830	525	—	500	800	1,350	2,500
1831	225	—	600	900	1,650	3,000

KM# 332 PECA (6400 Reis)
14.3420 g., 0.9170 Gold .4228 oz. **Obv:** Laureate and draped bust right **Obv. Legend:** IOANNES D. G. PORT ET ALG. P. REGENS **Rev:** Crowned oval arms in frame **Note:** Revalued to 7500 Reis in 1826.

Date	Mintage	VG	F	VF	XF	Unc
1802	30,000	800	1,600	3,250	5,000	—

KM# 336 PECA (6400 Reis)
14.3420 g., 0.9170 Gold .4228 oz. **Obv:** Laureate and draped bust right **Obv. Legend:** JOANNES D. G. PORT ET ALG. P. REGENS **Rev:** Crowned oval shield in floral frame **Note:** Revalued to 7500 Reis in 1826. Similar pieces with "R" after date were struck in Rio de Janeiro and are found listed under Brazil.

Date	Mintage	VG	F	VF	XF	Unc
1804 Rare	476	—	—	—	—	—
1805	27,000	250	550	1,000	1,200	—
1806	41,000	225	500	850	1,100	—
1807	36,000	400	850	1,400	1,600	—
1808	27,000	250	550	1,000	1,200	—
1809	13,000	250	500	850	1,100	—
1812	25,000	250	500	850	1,100	—
1813	5,590	600	1,200	2,100	3,500	—
1814 Rare	21	—	—	—	—	—
1815	305	650	1,300	2,400	4,250	—
1816 Rare	—	—	—	—	—	—

KM# 364 PECA (6400 Reis)
14.3420 g., 0.9170 Gold .4228 oz. **Obv:** Laureate and draped bust right **Rev:** Shield on crowned globe within wreath **Note:** Revalued to 7500 Reis in 1826. Similar pieces with "R" after date were struck in Rio de Janeiro and are listed under Brazil.

Date	Mintage	VG	F	VF	XF	Unc
1818 Rare	291	—	—	—	—	—
1819	1,727	—	2,900	5,200	8,500	14,000
1820	1,687	—	2,900	5,200	8,500	14,000
1821	391	—	9,500	12,500	16,000	18,500
1822	30,000	—	250	375	550	750
1823	27,000	—	350	520	650	950
1824	1,553	—	320	480	600	900

KM# 378 PECA (6400 Reis)
14.3420 g., 0.9170 Gold .4228 oz. **Obv:** Laureate head right **Rev:** Crowned oval shield in wreath **Note:** Revalued to 7500 Reis in 1826. Similar pieces dated 1825 with square shield on reverse are patterns.

Date	Mintage	VG	F	VF	XF	Unc
1826	10,883	—	450	850	1,500	2,500
1828	1,255	—	600	1,200	2,500	4,500

KM# 388 PECA (6400 Reis)
14.3420 g., 0.9170 Gold .4228 oz. **Obv:** Laureate and draped bust right **Obv. Legend:** MICHAEL I... **Rev:** Crowned shield in palm wreath with floral garland

Date	Mintage	VG	F	VF	XF	Unc
1828	—	—	650	1,300	2,100	3,200

KM# 397 PECA (6400 Reis)
14.3420 g., 0.9170 Gold .4228 oz. **Note:** Modified design.

Date	Mintage	F	VF	XF	Unc	BU
1830	2,274	325	650	1,100	2,000	—
1831	1,618	450	950	1,600	2,450	—

KM# 405 PECA (6400 Reis)
14.3420 g., 0.9170 Gold .4228 oz. **Obv:** Draped bust left, hair breaks legend at top **Rev:** Crowned shield in wreath

Date	Mintage	VG	F	VF	XF	Unc
1833	—	—	850	1,650	3,000	4,750
1834	32,000	—	250	450	900	1,500

KM# 404 PECA (6400 Reis)
14.3420 g., 0.9170 Gold .4228 oz. **Obv:** Head left **Rev:** Crowned shield in wreath **Note:** Modified design.

Date	Mintage	VG	F	VF	XF	Unc
1833	1,265	—	1,000	2,000	4,000	6,000

KM# 407 PECA (6400 Reis)
14.3420 g., 0.9170 Gold .4228 oz. **Obv:** Draped bust left, continious legend **Rev:** Crowned shield in wreath

Date	Mintage	VG	F	VF	XF	Unc
1835	2,989	—	350	700	1,450	1,900

COUNTERMARKED COINAGE

(870 REIS)

Countermark: Crowned arms of Portugal.

In 1834, the Portuguese government ordered that the countermarking of all Spanish Colonial 8 Reales in circulation with the crowned arms of Portugal, to indicate a revaluation to 870 Reis.

KM# 440.21 40 REIS (870 Reis)
Silver **Countermark:** Crowned arms of Portugal **Note:** Countermark on Peru (Lima) 8 Reales, KM#97.

CM Date	Host Date	Good	VG	F	VF	XF
ND(1834)	1812-1822	50.00	80.00	120	200	—

KM# 440.1 870 REIS
Silver **Countermark:** Crowned arms of Portugal **Note:** Countermark on Bolivia (Potosi) 8 Reales, KM#55.

CM Date	Host Date	Good	VG	F	VF	XF
ND(1834)	1773-1789	60.00	120	180	250	—

KM# 440.2 870 REIS
Silver **Countermark:** Crowned arms of Portugal **Note:** Countermark on Bolivia (Potosi) 8 Reales, KM#74.

CM Date	Host Date	Good	VG	F	VF	XF
ND(1834)	1789-1791	70.00	140	210	300	—

KM# 440.3 870 REIS
Silver **Countermark:** Crowned arms of Portugal **Note:** Countermark on Bolivia (Potosi) 8 Reales, KM#73.

CM Date	Host Date	Good	VG	F	VF	XF
ND(1834)	1791-1808	50.00	100	150	210	—

KM# 440.4 870 REIS
Silver **Countermark:** Crowned arms of Portugal **Note:** Countermark on Bolivia (Potosi) 8 Reales, KM#84.

CM Date	Host Date	Good	VG	F	VF	XF
ND(1834)	1808-1825	50.00	85.00	150	200	—

KM# 440.5 870 REIS
Silver **Countermark:** Crowned arms of Portugal **Note:** Countermark on Brazil 960 Reis, KM#326.

CM Date	Host Date	Good	VG	F	VF	XF
ND(1834)	1818-1822	65.00	125	200	250	—

KM# 440.6 870 REIS
Silver **Countermark:** Crowned arms of Portugal **Note:** Countermark on Chile (Santiago) 8 Reales, KM#51.

CM Date	Host Date	Good	VG	F	VF	XF
ND(1834)	1791-1808	225	450	700	925	—

KM# 440.7 870 REIS
Silver **Countermark:** Crowned arms of Portugal **Note:** Countermark on Guatemala 8 Reales, KM#69.

CM Date	Host Date	Good	VG	F	VF	XF
ND(1834)	1808-1822	200	320	410	600	—

KM# 440.8 870 REIS
Silver **Countermark:** Crowned arms of Portugal **Note:** Countermark on Mexico 8 Reales, KM#103.

CM Date	Host Date	Good	VG	F	VF	XF
ND(1834)	1732-1747	125	220	290	400	—

KM# 440.9 870 REIS
Silver **Countermark:** Crowned arms of Portugal **Note:** Countermark on Mexico 8 Reales, KM#104.

CM Date	Host Date	Good	VG	F	VF	XF
ND(1834)	1747-1760	95.00	160	240	330	—

KM# 440.10 870 REIS
Silver **Countermark:** Crowned arms of Portugal **Note:** Countermark on Mexico 8 Reales, KM#105.

CM Date	Host Date	Good	VG	F	VF	XF
ND(1834)	1760-1772	95.00	160	240	330	—

KM# 440.11 870 REIS
Silver **Countermark:** Crowned arms of Portugal **Note:** Countermark on Mexico 8 Reales, KM#106.

CM Date	Host Date	Good	VG	F	VF	XF
ND(1834)	1772-1789	55.00	110	170	240	—

KM# 440.12 870 REIS
Silver **Countermark:** Crowned arms of Portugal **Note:** Countermark on Mexico 8 Reales, KM#107.

CM Date	Host Date	Good	VG	F	VF	XF
ND(1834)	1789-1790	50.00	90.00	150	200	—

KM# 440.13 870 REIS
Silver **Countermark:** Crowned arms of Portugal **Note:** Countermark on Mexico 8 Reales, KM#109.

CM Date	Host Date	Good	VG	F	VF	XF
ND(1834)	1791-1808	50.00	90.00	150	200	—

KM# 440.14 870 REIS
Silver **Countermark:** Crowned arms of Portugal **Note:** Countermark on Mexico 8 Reales, KM#110.

CM Date	Host Date	Good	VG	F	VF	XF
ND(1834)	1808-1811	50.00	90.00	150	200	—

KM# 440.15 870 REIS
Silver **Countermark:** Crowned arms of Portugal **Note:** Countermark on Mexico 8 Reales, KM#111.

CM Date	Host Date	Good	VG	F	VF	XF
ND(1834)	1811-1821	50.00	90.00	150	200	—

KM# 440.16 870 REIS
Silver **Countermark:** Crowned arms of Portugal **Note:** Countermark on Mexico (Durango) 8 Reales, KM#111.2

CM Date	Host Date	Good	VG	F	VF	XF
ND(1834)	1812-1822	130	260	400	580	—

KM# 440.17 870 REIS
Silver **Countermark:** Crowned arms of Portugal **Note:** Countermark on Mexico (Guadalajara) 8 Reales, KM#111.3.

CM Date	Host Date	Good	VG	F	VF	XF
ND(1834)	1812-1822	70.00	140	170	260	—

KM# 440.18 870 REIS
Silver **Countermark:** Crowned arms of Portugal **Note:** Countermark on Mexico (Guanajuato) 8 Reales, KM#111.4.

CM Date	Host Date	Good	VG	F	VF	XF
ND(1834)	1812-1822	85.00	170	210	320	—

KM# 440.19 870 REIS
Silver **Countermark:** Crowned arms of Portugal **Note:** Countermark on Mexico (Zacatecas) 8 Reales, KM#111.5.

CM Date	Host Date	Good	VG	F	VF	XF
ND(1834)	1813-1822	60.00	120	160	240	—

KM# A440.20 870 REIS
Silver **Countermark:** Crowned arms of Portugal **Note:** Countermark on Peru (Lima) 8 Reales, KM#87.

CM Date	Host Date	Good	VG	F	VF	XF
ND(1834)	ND(1774)	—	—	—	—	—

KM# 440.20 870 REIS
Silver **Countermark:** Crowned arms of Portugal **Note:** Countermark on Peru (Lima) 8 Reales, KM#87.

CM Date	Host Date	Good	VG	F	VF	XF
ND(1834)	1789-1791	50.00	90.00	150	200	—

KM# 440.22 870 REIS
Silver **Countermark:** Crowned arms of Portugal **Note:** Countermark on Peru (Lima) 8 Reales, KM#106.

CM Date	Host Date	Good	VG	F	VF	XF
ND(1834)	1808-1811	50.00	80.00	150	200	—

KM# 440.33 870 REIS
Silver **Countermark:** Crowned arms of Portugal **Note:** Countermark on Peru (Lima) 8 Reales, KM#117.

CM Date	Host Date	Good	VG	F	VF	XF
ND(1834)	1810-1824	50.00	80.00	150	200	—

KM# 440.34 870 REIS
Silver **Countermark:** Crowned arms of Portugal **Note:** Countermark on Spain (Cadiz) 8 Reales, C#136.

CM Date	Host Date	Good	VG	F	VF	XF
ND(1834)	1810-1815	160	325	500	680	—

KM# 440.35 870 REIS
Silver **Countermark:** Crowned arms of Portugal **Note:** Countermark on Spain (Madrid) 8 Reales, C#71.

CM Date	Host Date	Good	VG	F	VF	XF
ND(1834)	1789-1808	115	230	320	450	—

KM# 440.36 870 REIS
Silver **Countermark:** Crowned arms of Portugal **Note:** Countermark on Spain (Madrid) 20 Reales, C#92.

CM Date	Host Date	Good	VG	F	VF	XF
ND(1834)	1808-1813	160	320	460	680	—

KM# 440.37 870 REIS
Silver **Countermark:** Crowned arms of Portugal **Note:** Countermark on Spain (Madrid)8 Reales, C#136.

CM Date	Host Date	Good	VG	F	VF	XF
ND(1834)	1812-1833	65.00	130	190	280	—

KM# 440.38 870 REIS
Silver **Countermark:** Crowned arms of Portugal **Note:** Countermark on Spain (Seville) 8 Reales, C#40.

CM Date	Host Date	Good	VG	F	VF	XF
ND(1834)	1772-1788	140	280	400	580	—

KM# 440.39 870 REIS
Silver **Countermark:** Crowned arms of Portugal **Note:** Countermark on Spain (Seville) 8 Reales, C#71.

CM Date	Host Date	Good	VG	F	VF	XF
ND(1834)	1788-1808	105	210	320	550	—

KM# 440.40 870 REIS
Silver **Countermark:** Crowned arms of Portugal **Note:** Countermark on Spain (Seville) 8 Reales, C#136.

CM Date	Host Date	Good	VG	F	VF	XF
ND(1834)	1809-1830	65.00	130	190	280	—

KM# 440.41 870 REIS
Silver **Countermark:** Crowned arms of Portugal **Note:** Countermark on Spain (Valencia) 8 Reales, C#136a.

CM Date	Host Date	Good	VG	F	VF	XF
ND(1834)	1809-1811	160	320	460	640	—

KM# 440.42 870 REIS
Silver **Countermark:** Crowned arms of Portugal **Note:** Countermark on Mozambique 8 Reales, KM#28.

CM Date	Host Date	Good	VG	F	VF	XF
ND(1834)	1834	200	300	500	750	—

KM# 467 4 CRUZADOS (30,000 Reis)
12.2400 g., 0.9170 Gold .3609 oz. **Note:** Crowned arms on Brazil 20,000 Reis, KM#117.

CM Date	Host Date	Good	VG	F	VF	XF
ND(1847)	1724 Rare	—	—	—	—	—
ND(1847)	1725	1,000	2,000	3,100	4,600	—
ND(1847)	1726	1,500	2,500	4,000	5,500	—
ND(1847)	1727	1,500	2,500	4,000	5,500	—

GOVERNO CIVIL DO PORTO 1847

KM# 415.1 40 REIS
Copper **Countermark:** GCP **Note:** Countermark in a circle on 40 Reis, KM#402.

CM Date	Host Date	Good	VG	F	VF	XF
ND(1847)	(1833)	10.00	22.50	45.00	95.00	—
ND(1847)	1847	30.00	80.00	160	350	—

KM# 415.2 40 REIS
Copper **Countermark:** GCP **Note:** Dot added below GCP on 40 Reis, KM#402.

CM Date	Host Date	Good	VG	F	VF	XF
ND(1847)	1847	10.00	22.50	45.00	95.00	—

DECIMAL COINAGE

New denominations, all expressed in terms of Reis were introduced by Maria II in 1836, to bring Portugal's currency into decimal form. Some of the coins retained old names, as follows:

1000 Reis Silver - Coroa

100 Reis Silver - Tostao

The diameter of the new copper coins, first minted by Maria II in 1837, was smaller than the earlier coinage, but the weight was unaltered. However, in 1882, Luis I reduced the size and weight of the copper currency.

The Real and 2 Reis pieces dated 1853 were issued for circulation in Mozambique and will be found in those listings.

KM# 517 3 REIS
Copper

Date	Mintage	F	VF	XF	Unc	BU
1868	100,000	3.00	8.00	11.00	30.00	—
1874	280,000	3.00	8.50	13.00	36.00	—
1875	1,200,000	3.00	8.00	11.00	30.00	—

KM# 480 5 REIS
Copper **Obv. Legend:** MARIA II...

Date	Mintage	VG	F	VF	XF	Unc
1840	174,000	3.00	6.00	30.00	110	—
1843	3,621	6.00	12.00	50.00	140	—
1848	147,000	2.50	5.00	18.00	75.00	—
1850	180,000	2.50	5.00	18.00	75.00	—
1852	292,000	2.00	4.00	18.00	75.00	—
1853	Est. 97,000	2.50	5.00	25.00	85.00	—

Note: Struck for circulation primarily in Mozambique.

KM# 513 5 REIS
Copper **Obv:** Bust of Luiz I left

Date	Mintage	F	VF	XF	Unc	BU
1867	737,000	4.00	5.00	15.00	30.00	—
1868	740,000	4.00	5.00	15.00	30.00	—
1871	240,000	14.00	40.00	85.00	170	—
1872	700,000	5.00	7.00	35.00	70.00	—
1873	600,000	14.00	40.00	70.00	140	—
1874	1,080,000	4.00	5.00	20.00	250	—
1874 Proof	—	Value: 250				
1875	2,200,000	2.00	4.50	15.00	30.00	—
1876	320,000	13.00	40.00	85.00	170	—
1877	620,000	13.00	40.00	85.00	170	—
1878	Inc. above	4.50	7.00	20.00	40.00	—
1879	332,000	4.50	7.00	20.00	40.00	—

KM# 525 5 REIS
Bronze

Date	Mintage	F	VF	XF	Unc	BU
1882	5,200,000	1.00	1.50	7.00	20.00	—
1883	4,700,000	1.00	2.00	10.00	28.00	—
1884	1,730,000	1.50	3.00	25.00	50.00	—
1885	3,200,000	1.00	2.00	13.00	45.00	—
1886	4,170,000	1.50	4.00	30.00	60.00	—

KM# 530 5 REIS
Bronze **Obv:** Bust of Carlos I right

Date	Mintage	F	VF	XF	Unc	BU
1890	430,000	1.00	2.00	10.00	20.00	—
1891	Inc. above	1.00	2.00	10.00	20.00	—
1892/1	1,510,000	1.00	5.00	11.50	25.00	—
1892	Inc. above	0.75	1.50	6.00	20.00	—
1893	3,280,000	1.00	1.75	7.50	15.00	—

Date	Mintage	F	VF	XF	Unc	BU
1897	1,120,000	4.00	15.00	40.00	80.00	—
1898	700,000	1.00	1.75	20.00	40.00	—
1899	1,220,000	1.00	1.50	6.00	20.00	—
1900	1,110,000	4.00	14.00	40.00	80.00	—

KM# 470 10 REIS
Copper **Obv:** Plain shield, struck in collared dies

Date	Mintage	VG	F	VF	XF	Unc
1837	—	2.00	7.00	20.00	80.00	—
1838	—	2.00	7.00	15.00	60.00	—
1839	—	2.00	7.00	15.00	60.00	—

KM# 481 10 REIS
Copper **Obv:** Ornate shield **Obv. Legend:** MARIA II...

Date	Mintage	VG	F	VF	XF	Unc
1840	392,000	2.50	5.00	15.00	50.00	—
1841	476,000	2.25	4.50	15.00	50.00	—
1842	1,131,000	2.25	4.50	15.00	50.00	—
1843	837,000	2.00	4.00	10.00	45.00	—
1844	620,000	2.00	4.00	10.00	45.00	—
1845	545,000	2.00	4.00	10.00	45.00	—
1846	1,166,000	2.50	5.00	10.00	125	—
1847	57,000	10.00	15.00	50.00	45.00	—
1850	443,000	2.00	4.00	10.00	40.00	—
1851	1,236,000	2.00	4.00	10.00	40.00	—
1852	558,000	1.75	3.75	10.00	40.00	—
1853	Est. 46,000	2.50	5.00	10.00	40.00	—

Note: Struck for circulation primarily in Mozambique.

KM# 514 10 REIS
Copper **Obv. Legend:** LUDOVICUS I... **Obv. Designer:** Ornate shield

Date	Mintage	VG	F	VF	XF	Unc
1867	300,000	2.00	5.00	7.00	25.00	—
1868	450,000	6.50	12.00	20.00	75.00	—
1870	Inc. above	25.00	90.00	100	250	—
1871	360,000	4.00	8.00	15.00	50.00	—
1873	2,000,000	3.00	6.00	10.00	20.00	—
1874	220,000	6.00	15.00	25.00	75.00	—

KM# 526 10 REIS
Bronze **Obv:** Bust of Luiz I left

Date	Mintage	F	VF	XF	Unc	BU
1882	14,795,000	1.25	2.50	12.00	35.00	—
1883	Inc. above	1.25	2.50	12.00	35.00	—
1883 Proof	—	Value: 250				
1884	10,190,000	1.25	2.50	11.00	35.00	—
1885	8,100,000	1.50	7.00	11.00	45.00	—
1886	3,915,000	2.25	8.00	30.00	75.00	—

KM# 532 10 REIS
Bronze **Obv:** Bust of Carlos I right

Date	Mintage	F	VF	XF	Unc	BU
1891	3,445,000	1.25	2.50	8.00	20.00	—
1891A	895,000	2.50	6.00	17.50	35.00	—
1892	9,298,000	1.25	2.50	7.00	20.00	—
1892A	5,769,000	2.25	5.00	8.00	20.00	—

KM# 482 20 REIS
Copper **Obv. Legend:** MARIA II...

Date	Mintage	VG	F	VF	XF	Unc
1847	2,484,000	6.00	12.00	20.00	50.00	—
1848	801,000	6.00	9.00	20.00	50.00	—
1849	2,269,000	5.00	9.00	20.00	50.00	—
1850	1,803,000	5.00	12.00	20.00	50.00	—
1851	842,000	7.00	15.00	20.00	50.00	—
1852	1,215,000	5.00	12.00	20.00	50.00	—
1853	Est. 946,000	5.00	9.00	14.00	50.00	—

Note: Struck for circulation primarily in Mozambique.

KM# 515 20 REIS
Copper **Obv. Legend:** LUDOVICUS I...

Date	Mintage	VG	F	VF	XF	Unc
1867	745,000	5.00	14.00	45.00	80.00	—
1870	—	50.00	100	300	600	—
1871	360,000	7.00	30.00	100	200	—
1873	2,500,000	4.00	8.00	14.00	50.00	—
1874	1,575,000	4.00	8.00	14.00	50.00	—

KM# 527 20 REIS
Bronze **Obv:** Bust of Luis I left

Date	Mintage	F	VF	XF	Unc	BU
1882	17,235,000	1.00	2.00	10.00	30.00	—
1883	Inc. above	1.00	2.00	8.00	25.00	—
1884	17,200,000	1.00	2.00	8.00	25.00	—
1885	18,493,000	1.50	4.50	13.00	35.00	—
1886	4,573,000	2.00	7.00	20.00	60.00	—

KM# 533 20 REIS
Bronze **Obv:** Bust of Carlos I right

Date	Mintage	F	VF	XF	Unc	BU
1891	3,282,000	1.00	2.00	8.00	24.00	—
1891A	6,016,000	1.50	2.75	12.00	28.00	—
1892/1	15,411,000	1.25	2.50	13.00	30.00	—
1892	Inc. above	1.00	2.00	9.00	24.00	—
1892A	658,000	4.00	15.00	50.00	100	—

KM# 493 50 REIS
1.2500 g., 0.9170 Silver .0368 oz. **Obv. Legend:** PETRUS V..

Date	Mintage	VG	F	VF	XF	Unc
1855	48,000	8.50	17.50	40.00	80.00	—
1861	800,000	3.00	6.00	12.00	24.00	—

KM# 506.1 50 REIS
1.2500 g., 0.9170 Silver .0368 oz., 15 mm. **Obv. Legend:** LUDOVICUS I...

Date	Mintage	VG	F	VF	XF	Unc
1862	17,000	6.00	10.00	20.00	50.00	—
1863	215,000	2.50	5.00	15.00	30.00	—
1864	50,000	4.00	9.00	20.00	40.00	—

KM# 506.2 50 REIS
1.2500 g., 0.9170 Silver .0368 oz., 15.5 mm. **Obv:** LUDOVICUS I...

Date	Mintage	VG	F	VF	XF	Unc
1874	60,000	—	3.50	7.00	20.00	40.00
1875	Inc. above	—	10.00	25.00	50.00	100
1876	100,000	—	2.00	4.00	9.50	20.00
1877	100,000	—	2.00	4.00	9.50	15.00
1879	80,000	—	1.75	3.50	7.00	12.00
1880	320,000	—	1.75	3.50	7.00	12.00
1886	60,000	—	2.00	3.75	7.00	12.00
1887	40,000	—	10.00	20.00	40.00	75.00
1888 Rare	Inc. below	—	—	—	—	—
1889	1,000,000	—	1.00	2.00	5.00	10.00

KM# 536 50 REIS
1.2500 g., 0.9170 Silver .0368 oz. **Obv. Legend:** CARLOS I...

Date	Mintage	VG	F	VF	XF	Unc
1893	620,000	2.25	4.50	6.50	12.50	—

KM# 545 50 REIS
Copper Nickel

Date	Mintage	F	VF	XF	Unc	BU
1900	8,000,000	0.75	1.50	10.00	20.00	—

KM# 473 100 REIS
2.9600 g., 0.9170 Silver .0873 oz. **Obv:** Young head of Maria II **Edge:** Reeded

Date	Mintage	VG	F	VF	XF	Unc
1836 Rare	—	—	—	—	—	—
1838	2,505	35.00	50.00	100	200	—
1843	—	12.50	25.00	50.00	100	—

KM# 485 100 REIS
2.9600 g., 0.9170 Silver .0873 oz. **Obv:** Mature head of Maria II

Date	Mintage	VG	F	VF	XF	Unc
1851	9,205	7.50	15.00	30.00	60.00	—

KM# 488 100 REIS
2.9600 g., 0.9170 Silver .0873 oz. **Obv:** Older head of Maria II

Date	Mintage	VG	F	VF	XF	Unc
1853	66,000	4.50	10.00	20.00	50.00	—

KM# 490 100 REIS
2.5000 g., 0.9070 Silver .0737 oz. **Obv:** Child's head right **Obv. Legend:** PETRVS V...

Date	Mintage	VG	F	VF	XF	Unc
1854	535,000	5.00	10.00	38.00	75.00	—

KM# 497 100 REIS
2.5000 g., 0.9070 Silver .0737 oz. **Obv:** Young head **Obv. Legend:** PETRVS V...

Date	Mintage	VG	F	VF	XF	Unc
1857	43,000	30.00	60.00	140	280	—
1858	—	30.00	60.00	140	280	—
1859	455,000	5.00	10.00	38.00	70.00	—
1861	762,000	5.00	10.00	30.00	50.00	—

KM# 510 100 REIS
2.5000 g., 0.9070 Silver .0737 oz. **Obv:** Young head **Obv. Legend:** LUDOVICUS I...

Date	Mintage	VG	F	VF	XF	Unc
1864	198,000	7.50	15.00	80.00	200	—
1865	100,000	7.50	15.00	80.00	250	—
1866	10,000	70.00	140	300	650	—
1869	10,000	47.50	95.00	200	500	—
1871	60,000	5.00	10.00	50.00	100	—
1872	60,000	5.00	10.00	50.00	100	—
1874	170,000	3.00	6.00	25.00	75.00	—
1875	130,000	3.00	6.00	25.00	75.00	—
1876	220,000	3.00	6.00	30.00	80.00	—
1877	120,000	5.00	10.00	30.00	80.00	—
1878	30,000	5.00	10.00	32.50	90.00	—
1879	560,000	2.50	5.00	15.00	30.00	—
1880	440,000	2.50	5.00	16.50	30.00	—
1881	Inc. above	25.00	50.00	150	300	—
1886	750,000	2.00	4.00	12.50	35.00	—
1888	500,000	3.00	6.00	25.00	55.00	—
1889	1,500,000	2.00	3.50	6.00	18.00	—

KM# 531 100 REIS
2.5000 g., 0.9170 Silver .0737 oz. **Obv. Legend:** CARLOS I...

Date	Mintage	VG	F	VF	XF	Unc
1890	700,000	5.00	10.00	20.00	55.00	—
1891	270,000	7.50	15.00	40.00	70.00	—
1893	1,050,000	4.00	5.00	14.00	42.00	—
1894	Inc. above	37.50	75.00	150	300	—
1898	655,000	3.00	5.00	18.50	40.00	—

KM# 546 100 REIS
Copper Nickel

Date	Mintage	F	VF	XF	Unc	BU
1900	16,000,000	0.30	1.50	10.00	20.00	—

KM# 474 200 REIS
5.9200 g., 0.9170 Silver .1746 oz. **Obv:** Young head of Maria II **Edge:** Reeded

Date	Mintage	VG	F	VF	XF	Unc
1836 Rare	—	—	—	—	—	—
1838	2,177	37.50	75.00	150	300	—
1841	868	47.50	85.00	185	350	—
1843	1,181	15.00	30.00	60.00	150	—

KM# 491 200 REIS
5.0000 g., 0.9170 Silver .1474 oz. **Obv:** Child's head right **Obv. Legend:** PETRUS V...

Date	Mintage	VG	F	VF	XF	Unc
1854	292,000	3.50	7.00	37.50	75.00	—
1855	793,000	3.50	7.00	30.00	100	—

KM# 499 200 REIS
5.0000 g., 0.9170 Silver .1474 oz. **Obv:** Young head **Obv. Legend:** PETRUS V...

Date	Mintage	VG	F	VF	XF	Unc
1858	—	3.50	7.00	37.50	110	—
1860	—	6.00	10.00	40.00	140	—
1861	202,000	30.00	60.00	120	350	—

KM# 507 200 REIS
5.0000 g., 0.9170 Silver .1474 oz. **Obv:** First bust right **Obv. Legend:** LUDOVICUS I...

Date	Mintage	VG	F	VF	XF	Unc
1862	696,000	3.50	7.00	37.50	90.00	—
1863	421,000	6.00	12.00	40.00	100	—

KM# 512 200 REIS
5.0000 g., 0.9170 Silver .1474 oz. **Obv. Legend:** LUDOVICUS I... **Note:** Second bust.

Date	Mintage	VG	F	VF	XF	Unc
1865	50,000	12.50	25.00	70.00	200	—
1866	10,000	90.00	175	550	1,400	—
1867	10,000	75.00	140	500	1,100	—
1868	5,000	70.00	145	500	1,100	—
1871	75,000	10.00	20.00	50.00	120	—
1872	70,000	12.00	25.00	60.00	120	—
1875	70,000	10.00	20.00	50.00	120	—
1876	80,000	80.00	150	500	1,100	—
1877	30,000	15.00	30.00	90.00	230	—
1878	20,000	70.00	120	400	900	—
1879	5,050	100	200	500	1,200	—
1880	150,000	5.00	10.00	35.00	60.00	—
1886	340,000	3.50	7.00	20.00	50.00	—
1887	3,600,000	2.00	4.00	10.00	20.00	—
1888	700,000	3.00	6.00	20.00	50.00	—

KM# 534 200 REIS
5.0000 g., 0.9170 Silver .1474 oz. **Obv:** Bust right **Obv. Legend:** CARLOS I...

Date	Mintage	VG	F	VF	XF	Unc
1891	2,365,000	5.00	10.00	14.00	20.00	—
1892	788,000	4.00	8.50	20.00	30.00	—
1893	Inc. above	8.00	15.00	30.00	50.00	—
1893/2	1,205,000	8.50	17.50	35.00	65.00	—

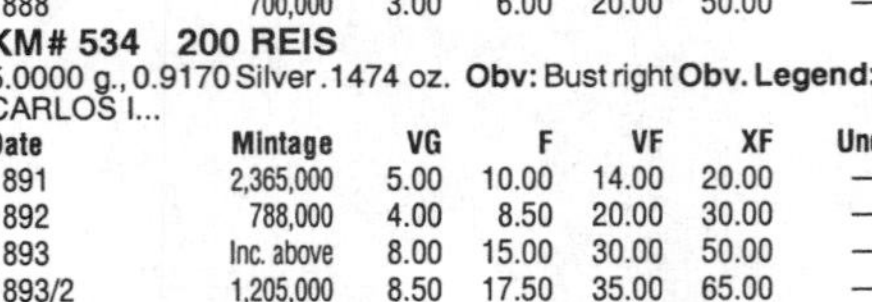

KM# 537 200 REIS
5.0000 g., 0.9170 Silver .1474 oz. **Subject:** 400th Anniversary Discovery of India **Obv:** Conjoined busts left

Date	Mintage	VG	F	VF	XF	Unc
1898	250,000	2.50	5.50	8.00	12.50	—
1898 Prooflike	—	—	—	—	—	22.50

KM# 471 500 REIS
14.8000 g., 0.9170 Silver .4364 oz. **Obv:** Bust left **Obv. Legend:** MARIA II...

Date	Mintage	VG	F	VF	XF	Unc
1837	1,266	175	365	675	1,000	—
1838	2,645	140	280	550	800	—
1839	2,084	175	365	550	800	—
1841	22,000	10.00	15.00	40.00	60.00	—
1842	135,000	10.00	15.00	40.00	60.00	—
1843	105,000	15.00	30.00	80.00	100	—
1844	4,265	22.50	45.00	85.00	135	—
1845	—	22.50	45.00	85.00	135	—
1846	74,000	10.00	15.00	25.00	60.00	—
1847	775,000	10.00	15.00	30.00	60.00	—
1848	24,000	20.00	40.00	80.00	125	—
1849	59,000	10.00	15.00	30.00	60.00	—
1850	41,000	20.00	40.00	60.00	100	—
1851	155,000	10.00	15.00	30.00	60.00	—
1853	22,000	50.00	100	200	350	—

KM# 492 500 REIS
12.5000 g., 0.9170 Silver .3684 oz. **Obv:** Young head **Obv. Legend:** PETRUS V...

Date	Mintage	VG	F	VF	XF	Unc
1854	592,000	7.50	15.00	40.00	120	—

KM# 494 500 REIS
12.5000 g., 0.9170 Silver .3684 oz. **Obv:** Young head **Obv. Legend:** PETRUS V...

Date	Mintage	VG	F	VF	XF	Unc
1855	1,210,000	10.00	20.00	40.00	90.00	—
1856	1,478,000	7.00	15.00	25.00	65.00	—

KM# 498 500 REIS
12.5000 g., 0.9170 Silver .3684 oz. **Obv:** Mature head **Obv. Legend:** PETRUS V...

Date	Mintage	VG	F	VF	XF	Unc
1857	1,949,000	7.50	15.00	50.00	150	—
1858	3,091,000	5.00	8.00	25.00	65.00	—
1859	2,660,000	5.00	8.00	25.00	65.00	—

KM# 509 500 REIS
12.5000 g., 0.9170 Silver .3684 oz. **Obv:** Head left **Obv. Legend:** LUDOVICUS I...

Date	Mintage	VG	F	VF	XF	Unc
1863	148,000	7.50	15.00	120	—	—
1864	341,000	6.00	12.00	95.00	—	—
1865	406,000	6.00	12.00	80.00	—	—
1866	378,000	5.00	9.00	30.00	120	—
1867	458,000	5.00	9.00	30.00	120	—
1868	388,000	5.00	9.50	35.00	120	—
1870	314,000	5.00	9.50	35.00	110	—
1871	228,000	5.00	9.00	30.00	110	—
1872	576,000	80.00	150	450	800	—
1875	140,000	17.50	35.00	70.00	165	—
1876	280,000	40.00	80.00	200	400	—
1877	50,000	22.50	45.00	80.00	150	—
1879	788,000	5.00	9.00	15.00	40.00	—
1886	300,000	5.00	9.00	15.00	30.00	—
1887	432,000	5.00	9.00	12.00	25.00	—
1888	2,740,000	5.00	9.00	12.00	25.00	—
1889	960,000	5.00	9.00	12.00	25.00	—

KM# 535 500 REIS
12.5000 g., 0.9170 Silver .3684 oz. **Obv:** Head right **Obv. Legend:** CARLOS I...

Date	Mintage	VG	F	VF	XF	Unc
1891	12,476,000	3.50	5.50	12.00	18.00	—
1892/1	4,716,000	6.00	12.00	22.00	50.00	—
1892	Inc. above	3.50	5.50	12.00	18.00	—
1893	2,494,000	4.00	7.00	15.00	30.00	—
1894	254,000	175	350	700	—	—
1895	216,000	25.00	50.00	85.00	140	—
1896	5,120,000	3.50	7.00	14.00	20.00	—
1898	1,320,000	4.50	9.00	16.00	32.00	—
1899	3,100,000	3.50	5.00	12.00	18.00	—
1900	200,000	100	200	350	650	—
1903	680,000	4.00	9.00	15.00	30.00	—
1906/3	240,000	15.00	35.00	70.00	100	—
1906	Inc. above	12.00	30.00	60.00	90.00	—
1907	384,000	4.00	6.00	10.00	18.00	—
1908	1,840,000	4.00	6.00	10.00	16.00	25.00

KM# 538 500 REIS
12.5000 g., 0.9170 Silver .3684 oz. **Subject:** 400th Anniversary Discover of India **Obv:** Conjoined busts left

Date	Mintage	VG	F	VF	XF	Unc
1898	300,000	5.00	8.50	10.00	20.00	—
1898 Prooflike	—	—	—	—	—	35.00

KM# 472 1000 REIS
29.6000 g., 0.9170 Silver .8727 oz. **Obv. Legend:** MARIA II...

Date	Mintage	VG	F	VF	XF	Unc
1837	2,295	80.00	120	275	500	—
1838	3,959	50.00	100	225	400	—
1842 Rare	1,515	—	—	—	—	—
1844	—	35.00	75.00	150	225	—
1845	10,724	35.00	75.00	150	225	—

KM# 486 1000 REIS
1.7900 g., 0.9170 Gold .0528 oz. **Obv. Legend:** MARIA II...

Date	Mintage	VG	F	VF	XF	Unc
1851	12,000	60.00	80.00	100	150	—

KM# 495 1000 REIS
1.7735 g., 0.9170 Gold .0523 oz. **Obv. Legend:** PETRVS V...

Date	Mintage	VG	F	VF	XF	Unc
1855	68,000	60.00	80.00	100	145	—

KM# 539 1000 REIS
25.0000 g., 0.9170 Silver .7368 oz. **Subject:** 400th Anniversary Discovery of India **Obv:** Conjoined busts left

Date	Mintage	VG	F	VF	XF	Unc
1898	300,000	10.00	17.50	27.50	40.00	—
1898 Prooflike	—	—	—	—	—	200

KM# 540 1000 REIS
25.0000 g., 0.9170 Silver .7368 oz. **Obv. Legend:** CARLOS I...

Date	Mintage	VG	F	VF	XF	Unc
1899	1,500,000	10.00	17.50	25.00	35.00	—
1900 3 known; Rare	—	—	—	—	—	—

KM# 496 2000 REIS
3.5470 g., 0.9170 Gold .1045 oz. **Obv:** Boy head **Obv. Legend:** PETRVS V...

Date	Mintage	F	VF	XF	Unc	BU
1856	38,000	110	170	225	325	—
1857	44,000	110	170	225	265	—

KM# 500 2000 REIS
3.5470 g., 0.9170 Gold .1045 oz. **Obv:** Young head **Obv. Legend:** PETRVS V...

Date	Mintage	F	VF	XF	Unc	BU
1858	13,000	110	170	225	375	—
1859	16,000	110	170	225	375	—
1860	53,000	110	170	225	375	—

KM# 511 2000 REIS
3.5470 g., 0.9170 Gold .1045 oz. **Obv. Legend:** LUDOVICUS I... **Rev:** Arms in spray

Date	Mintage	F	VF	XF	Unc	BU
1864	101,000	80.00	130	200	350	—
1865	95,000	80.00	130	200	350	—
1866	86,000	80.00	130	200	350	—

KM# 518 2000 REIS
3.5470 g., 0.9170 Gold .1045 oz. **Obv. Legend:** LUDOVICUS I... **Rev:** Mantled arms

Date	Mintage	F	VF	XF	Unc	BU
1868	24,000	80.00	130	200	350	—
1869	11,000	90.00	150	240	425	—
1870	500	800	1,600	—	—	—
1871	500	380	750	1,100	1,500	—
1872	1,000	150	280	550	875	—
1874	5,000	90.00	150	225	425	—
1875	2,000	130	260	375	650	—
1876	5,000	130	260	375	650	—
1877	2,250	100	175	275	450	—
1878	22,000	100	175	275	450	—
1881	1,000	230	460	700	1,100	—
1888	500	900	1,850	2,800	4,400	—

KM# 475 2500 REIS
4.7800 g., 0.9170 Gold .1410 oz. **Obv:** Young head **Obv. Legend:** MARIA II...

Date	Mintage	F	VF	XF	Unc	BU
1838	1,114	400	700	1,200	2,000	—

KM# 487 2500 REIS
4.4800 g., 0.9170 Gold .1321 oz. **Obv:** Mature head **Obv. Legend:** MARIA II...

Date	Mintage	F	VF	XF	Unc	BU
1851	58,000	120	210	300	450	—

KM# 489 2500 REIS
4.4800 g., 0.9170 Gold .1321 oz. **Obv:** Mature head **Obv. Legend:** MARIA II...

Date	Mintage	F	VF	XF	Unc	BU
1853	1,010	400	700	1,200	2,000	—

KM# 476.1 5000 REIS
9.5600 g., 0.9170 Gold .2819 oz. **Obv:** Young head **Obv. Legend:** MARIA II...

Date	Mintage	F	VF	XF	Unc	BU
1838	2,410	550	700	1,200	2,000	—
1845 Rare	401	—	—	—	—	—

KM# 476.2 5000 REIS
8.9600 g., 0.9170 Gold .2642 oz.

Date	Mintage	F	VF	XF	Unc	BU
1851	57,000	175	225	350	600	—

KM# 505 5000 REIS
8.8675 g., 0.9170 Gold .2613 oz. **Obv:** Young head **Obv. Legend:** PETRUS V...

Date	Mintage	F	VF	XF	Unc	BU
1860	52,000	175	210	300	550	—
1861	81,000	175	210	300	550	—

KM# 508 5000 REIS
8.8675 g., 0.9170 Gold .2613 oz. **Obv. Legend:** LUDOVICUS I... **Rev:** Arms in wreath

Date	Mintage	F	VF	XF	Unc	BU
1862	166,000	160	200	275	475	—
1863	38,000	160	200	275	475	—

KM# 516 5000 REIS
8.8675 g., 0.9170 Gold .2613 oz. **Obv. Legend:** LUDOVICUS I... **Rev:** Mantled arms

Date	Mintage	F	VF	XF	Unc	BU
1867	45,000	160	200	275	475	—
1868	64,000	160	200	275	475	—
1869	77,000	160	200	275	475	—
1870	61,000	160	200	275	475	—
1871	47,000	160	200	275	475	—
1872	28,000	160	200	275	475	—
1874	6,800	160	200	275	475	—
1875	10,000	160	200	275	475	—
1876	15,000	160	200	275	475	—
1877	9,400	300	350	575	1,000	—
1878	8,400	160	200	275	475	—
1880	7,000	375	575	925	1,400	—
1883	23,000	160	200	275	475	—
1886	27,000	160	200	275	475	—
1887	44,000	160	200	275	475	—
1888	4,800	160	200	275	475	—
1889	9,000	160	200	275	475	—

KM# 520 10000 REIS
17.7350 g., 0.9170 Gold .5227 oz. **Obv. Legend:** LUDOVICUS I... **Rev:** Crowned and mantled shield

Date	Mintage	F	VF	XF	Unc	BU
1878	23,000	320	400	550	950	—
1879	36,000	320	400	550	950	—
1880	30,000	320	400	550	950	—
1881	19,000	320	400	550	950	—
1882	15,000	320	400	550	950	—
1883	8,500	360	450	550	950	—
1884	13,000	340	425	550	950	—
1885	21,000	340	425	550	950	—
1886	1,800	400	525	650	1,100	—
1888	7,000	425	575	850	1,500	—
1889	4,400	425	575	800	1,400	—

PATTERNS

INCLUDING OFF METAL STRIKES

KM#	Date	Mintage	Identification	Mkt Val
Pn29	1803	—	Peca. Copper. Circular wreath.	1,000
Pn30	1803	—	Peca. Copper Gilt. Circular wreath.	1,200
Pn31	1803	—	Peca. Copper Gilt.	1,200
Pn32	1803	—	Peca. Copper Gilt. Wreath connected to shield.	1,200
Pn33	ND	—	Peca. Lead. Royal bust.	350
Pn34	ND	—	Peca. Lead. Bust and legend.	350
Pn35	ND	—	Peca. Lead Gilt. Bust and legend.	650
Pn36	1804	—	Peca. Lead. Date incuse.	400
Pn37	1804	—	Peca. Lead. Date in relief.	450
Pn38	1811	—	20 Reis. Bronze. Simple shield.	1,000
Pn39	1811	—	20 Reis. Bronze. Reduced size.	—
Pn40	1811	—	30 Reis. Bronze. Simple shield.	1,250
Pn41	1811	—	30 Reis. Bronze. Thin planchet.	1,150
Pn42	1811	—	30 Reis. Bronze. Ornate shield.	—
Pn43	1811	—	40 Reis. Lead.	600
Pn44	1811	—	40 Reis. Bronze. Experimental edge.	1,850
Pn45	1811	—	40 Reis. Bronze. Experimental edge.	1,850
Pn46	1811	—	40 Reis. Bronze. Experimental edge.	1,850
Pn47	1811	—	40 Reis. Bronze. Experimental edge.	1,850
Pn48	1811	—	40 Reis. Bronze. Experimental edge.	1,850
Pn49	1813	—	40 Reis. Bronze. Reeded edge.	750
Pn50	1814	—	40 Reis. Bronze. Reeded edge.	750
Pn51	1820	—	10 Reis. Copper. Roman numeral.	500
Pn52	1822	—	40 Reis. Bronze.	—
Pn53	1822	—	40 Reis. Bronze. Coarse reeding.	900
Pn54	1822	—	40 Reis. Bronze. Fine reeding.	900
Pn55	1822	—	40 Reis. Bronze. Laurel leaved edge.	1,650
Pn56	1822	—	Peca. Silver. Shield over wreath.	1,750
Pn57	1826	—	Peca. Copper Gilt. Square arms.	—
Pn58	1826	—	Peca. Copper. Square arms.	—
Pn59	1826	—	Peca. Copper. Oval arms, KM378	—
Pn60	1828	—	40 Reis. Bronze. Oval shield.	—
Pn61	1828	—	1/2 Peca. Copper Gilt. KM387.	1,000
Pn62	1828	—	Peca. Lead. KM388.	800
Pn63	1828	—	Peca. Nickel-Silver. KM388.	1,000
Pn64	1828	—	Peca. Copper Gilt. For royal approval, KM388.	1,250
Pn65	1829	—	40 Reis. Cast Lead. Crowned value in arms/wreath.	1,500
Pn66	1829	—	40 Reis. Gun Metal. Crowned arms/value in wreath.	1,750
Pn67	1829	—	80 Reis. Copper. Crowned arms/value in wreath.	4,500
Pn68	1829	—	600 Reis. Copper. Crowned arms/value in wreath.	4,000
Pn69	1829	—	Peca. Copper. Engraved by Dubois.	600
Pn70	1830	—	Peca. Copper. KM397.	950
Pn71	1830	—	Peca. Copper. Inward palms.	950
Pn72	1831	—	Peca. Copper. Inward palms.	—
Pn73	1833	—	5 Reis. Lead. Without collar, Roman numerals.	500
Pn74	1833	—	10 Reis. Copper. Roman numerals.	550
Pn75	1833	—	20 Reis. Bronze.	—
Pn76	1833	—	20 Reis. Bronze. Wreath variety.	450
Pn77	1833	—	40 Reis. Bronze.	—
Pn78	1833	—	40 Reis. Bronze. Wreath variety.	675
Pn79	1833	—	40 Reis. Silver.	—
Pn80	1833	—	1/2 Peca. Tin. Maria II.	1,750
Pn81	1833	—	Peca. Tin. Maria II.	2,000
Pn82	1833	—	Peca. Silver. High neck.	—
Pn83	1834	—	400 Reis. Silver. W. Wyon	2,750
Pn84	1835	—	400 Reis. Silver. W. Wyon	—
Pn85	1836	—	100 Reis. 0.9170 Silver.	350
Pn86	1836	—	200 Reis. Copper. Reeded edge.	300
Pn87	1836	—	200 Reis. Copper. Plain edge.	300
Pn88	1836	—	200 Reis. 0.9170 Silver. Plain edge.	500
Pn89	1836	—	500 Reis. Copper. Plain edge.	500
Pn90	1836	—	500 Reis. Copper. Reeded edge.	500
Pn91	1836	—	500 Reis. 0.9170 Silver.	1,000
Pn92	1836	—	1000 Reis. Copper. Fine reeding edge.	500
Pn93	1836	—	1000 Reis. Copper. Reeded edge.	500
Pn94	1836	—	1000 Reis. Copper. Plain edge.	500
Pn95	1836	—	1000 Reis. 0.9170 Silver.	1,000
Pn96	1836	—	2500 Reis. 0.9170 Gold. W. Wyon	4,500
Pn97	1836	—	5000 Reis. Copper. W. Wyon	450
Pn98	1836	—	5000 Reis. 0.9170 Gold. W. Wyon	5,000
Pn99	1838	—	200 Reis. Silver. Plain edge.	350
Pn100	1842	—	500 Reis. Copper. Plain edge.	500
Pn101	1842	—	500 Reis. Copper. Reeded edge.	500
Pn102	1842	—	500 Reis. Gold. Plain edge.	—
Pn103	1842	—	500 Reis. Gold. Reeded edge.	—
Pn104	1842	—	1000 Reis. Copper.	600
Pn105	1842	—	1000 Reis. Gold. Reeded edge.	—
Pn106	1852	—	500 Reis. Copper. Reeded edge.	550
Pn107	1854	—	500 Reis. Copper.	150
Pn108	1854	—	500 Reis. Silver.	400

KM#	Date	Mintage	Identification	Mkt Val
Pn109	1855	—	200 Reis. Brass.	350
Pn110	1855	—	500 Reis. Silver.	450
Pn111	1856	—	5000 Reis. Gold. Maria II.	6,500
Pn112	1857	—	Silver.	450
Pn113	1858	—	Copper.	350
Pn114	ND	—	10000 Reis. Porcelain.	200
PnA114	1858	—	2500 Reis. (No Composition).	—
Pn115	1858	—	10000 Reis. Copper Gilt.	1,200
PN116	1859	—	Silver.	500
Pn117	1859	—	10000 Reis. Copper Gilt. Mantled arms.	1,200
Pn118	1860	—	200 Reis. Silver.	450
Pn119	1861	—	50 Reis. Silver. Crowned date.	200
Pn120	1861	—	200 Reis. Silver. Smooth hair, vlaue between palms.	200
Pn121	1861	—	1000 Reis. Copper.	150
Pn122	1861	—	10000 Reis. Gold. Mantled arms.	—
Pn123	1861	—	10000 Reis. Copper. Mantled arms.	1,250
Pn124	1862	—	5 Reis. Copper.	400
Pn125	1862	—	5 Reis. Nickel.	450
Pn126	1862	—	10 Reis. Copper.	500
Pn127	1862	—	10 Reis. Copper. Roman numeral.	500
Pn128	1862	—	20 Reis. Copper.	600
Pn129	1862	—	20 Reis. Copper. Roman numeral.	600
Pn130	1863	—	5 Reis. Copper. Roman numeral.	400
Pn131	1863	—	5 Reis. Copper. Roman numeral, large type.	800
Pn132	1863	—	5 Reis. Nickel.	750
Pn133	1863	—	10 Reis. Copper. Roman numeral.	200
Pn134	1863	—	10 Reis. Nickel.	450
Pn135	1863	—	20 Reis. Copper. Roman numeral.	300
Pn136	1863	—	20 Reis. Nickel. Roman numeral.	500
Pn137	1863	—	100 Reis. Copper. Wavy hair.	200
Pn138	1863	—	200 Reis. Copper. Wavy hair.	200
Pn139	ND	—	500 Reis. Copper. Royal bust.	400
Pn140	1863	—	500 Reis. Silver. Wavy hair, shield between palms.	1,200
Pn141	1863	—	500 Reis. Silver. Smooth hair, shield between palms.	1,250
Pn142	ND	—	5000 Reis. Copper. Queen Victoria.	1,500
Pn143	1863	—	5000 Reis. Copper. Charles Wiener engraver.	1,500
Pn144	1864	—	500 Reis. Copper. Smooth hair, value between palms.	—
Pn145	1865	—	200 Reis. Copper. Wavy hair.	200

KM#	Date	Mintage	Identification	Mkt Val
Pn146	1865	—	5000 Reis. Copper. Charles Wiener engraver.	500
Pn147	1865	—	5000 Reis. Silver.	800
Pn148	1866	—	5000 Reis. Gold. Charles Wiener engraver.	1,250
Pn149	1866	—	5000 Reis. Silver. Charles Wiener engraver.	300
Pn150	1866	—	5000 Reis. Copper. Charles Wiener engraver.	200
Pn151	1866	—	5000 Reis. Copper Gilt. Charles Wiener engraver.	300
Pn152	1866	—	5000 Reis. Tin. Charles Wiener engraver.	200
Pn153	1866	—	5000 Reis. Lead.	200
Pn154	1867	—	5 Reis. Brass. Roman numeral.	150
Pn155	1874	—	3 Reis. Brass.	250
Pn156	1877	—	5 Reis. Copper.	175
Pn157	1877	—	100 Reis. Brass.	200
Pn158	1877	—	200 Reis. Copper.	250
Pn159	1878	—	10000 Reis. Copper. Shield over royal mantle.	300
Pn160	1879	—	50 Reis. Copper. Crowned date,	175
Pn161	1879	—	500 Reis. Copper. Plain edge. Rotated 90 degrees.	200
Pn162	1879	—	500 Reis. Gold. Plain edge. Rotated 90 degrees.	—
Pn163	1879	—	500 Reis. Copper. 'ENS' incuse.	200
Pn164	1879	—	1000 Reis. Gold. Value between palms.	—
Pn165	1879	—	1000 Reis. Gold. Crowned date.	—
Pn166	1879	—	1000 Reis. Copper. Royal bust with date.	175
Pn167	1879	—	1000 Reis. Copper. Crowned date, 50 Reis type.	175
Pn168	1879	—	1000 Reis. Gold. Shield over royal mantle.	—
Pn169	1879	—	5000 Reis. Copper. Shield over royal mantle.	450
Pn170	1879	—	5000 Reis. Gold.	1,450
Pn171	1880	—	200 Reis. Copper.	175
Pn172	1880	—	2200 Reis. Copper.	175
Pn173	1880	—	5000 Reis. Copper.	185
Pn174	1880	—	5000 Reis. Copper. 'ENS' incuse.	150
Pn175	1882	—	5 Reis. Brass. Roman numeral.	150
Pn176	1883	—	1000 Reis. Gold. Value inside wreath.	—
Pn177	1886	—	200 Reis. Copper. Wavy hair.	—
Pn178	1888	—	100 Reis. Silver.	350
Pn179	1888	—	100 Reis. Nickel.	200
Pn180	1888	—	5000 Reis. Nickel. Small type, old monarch.	175
Pn181	1888	—	5000 Reis. Copper. Small type, old monarch.	175
Pn182	1890	—	10 Reis. Copper. Legend of 1891.	200
Pn183	1890	—	20 Reis. Copper. Legend of 1891.	220
Pn184	ND	—	5 Reis. Nickel. Two reverses.	245
Pn185	1891	—	5 Reis. Copper Nickel. Royal bust, value between palms.	200
Pn186	1891	—	20 Reis. Bronze.	200
Pn187	1892	—	10 Reis. Copper Nickel.	200

KM#	Date	Mintage	Identification	Mkt Val
Pn188	1892	—	20 Reis. Aluminum.	125
Pn189	1892	—	20 Reis. Copper Nickel.	165
Pn190	1892	—	200 Reis. Copper Nickel. Plain edge. Reduced type.	350
Pn191	1895	—	5000 Reis. Silver Gilt.	15,000
Pn192	1895	—	5000 Reis. Gold.	—
Pn193	1898	—	100 Reis. Copper Nickel. Reduced type.	350
Pn194	1898	—	1000 Reis. Copper.	450
Pn195	1899	—	20 Reis. Copper Nickel.	250
PnA196	1899	—	500 Reis. Copper. Mantled arms without wreath.	350
Pn196	1900	—	50 Reis. Nickel. Plain edge.	150
Pn197	1900	—	100 Reis. Copper Nickel. Plain edge.	175
Pn198	1900	—	100 Reis. Aluminum. Plain edge.	175
Pn199	1900	—	10000 Reis. Gold.	—

PROVAS

STAMPED

KM#	Date	Mintage	Identification	Mkt Val
PrA1	1863	—	500 Reis. Silver. PROVA above crown, KM506.	300
PrB1	1863	—	500 Reis. Copper. PROVA above crown, KM506.	250
PrC1	1864	—	500 Reis. Copper. PROVA above crown, KM506.	250
Pr1	1868	—	5 Reis. Copper. Roman numeral, KM513.	100
Pr2	1868	—	5 Reis. Copper. 1 above Roman numeral V, KM513.	75.00
Pr3	1868	—	5 Reis. Copper. 1 above Roman numeral V, KM513.	75.00
Pr4	1868	—	5 Reis. Copper. 3 above Roman numeral V, KM513.	75.00
Pr5	1871	—	10 Reis. Copper. Roman numeral, KM514.	125
Pr6	ND	—	500 Reis. Copper. Two busts, KM535	—

TRIAL STRIKES

KM#	Date	Mintage	Identification	Mkt Val
TS1	1802	—	6400 Reis. Lead. Obverse.	850
TS2	1803	—	6400 Reis. Lead. Obverse type of 1805.	350
TS3	ND	—	6400 Reis. Lead. Reverse.	350
TS5	ND	—	800 Reis. Lead. Reverse.	275
TS6	1805	—	1600 Reis. Lead. Obverse.	300
TS7	ND	—	1600 Reis. Lead. Reverse.	300
TS8	1805	—	3200 Reis. Lead. Obverse.	350
TS9	ND	—	3200 Reis. Lead. Obverse.	350
TS10	ND	—	3200 Reis. Lead. Reverse.	350
TS4	1805	—	200 Reis. Lead. Obverse.	250
TS11	1817	—	400 Reis. Lead. Obverse.	350
TS12	ND	—	7500 Reis. Lead.	—
TS13	ND	—	7500 Reis. Copper. Obverse.	—

KM#	Date	Mintage	Identification	Mkt Val
TS16	1829	—	7500 Reis. Lead. Obverse, radiant field.	—
TS17	1829	—	7500 Reis. Lead. Obverse, ray variety.	250
TS14	1829	—	7500 Reis. Lead. Obverse, Dubois.	250
TS15	1829	—	7500 Reis. Lead. Reverse, Dubois.	250
TS18	1866	—	5000 Reis. Silver. Obverse, Charlies Wiener.	100
TS19	1866	—	5000 Reis. Silver. Reverse, Charlies Wiener.	100
TS21	1866	—	5000 Reis. Copper. Reverse, Charlies Wiener.	60.00
TS22	1866	—	5000 Reis. Lead. Obverse, Charlies Wiener.	60.00
TS23	1866	—	5000 Reis. Lead. Reverse, Charlies Wiener.	60.00
TS24	1868	—	3 Reis. Copper. Obverse Roman numeral.	80.00
TS25	ND	—	3 Reis. Copper. Reverse Roman numeral.	80.00
TS26	1871	—	5 Reis. Copper. Obverse Roman numeral.	60.00
TS31	1871	—	20 Reis. Copper. Reverse Roman numeral.	70.00
TS27	ND	—	10 Reis. Copper. Reverse Roman numeral.	70.00
TS28	ND	—	10 Reis. Copper. Obverse Roman numeral.	70.00
TS29	1871	—	10 Reis. Copper. Reverse Roman numeral.	70.00
TS30	ND	—	20 Reis. Copper. Obverse Roman numeral.	—
TS32	ND	—	10000 Reis. Tin. Reverse.	—

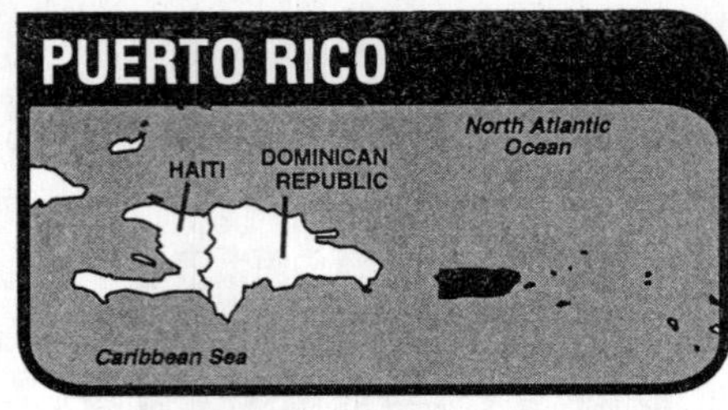

The Commonwealth of Puerto Rico, the eastern-most island of the Greater Antilles in the West Indies, has an area of 3,435 sq. mi. (9,104 sq. km.).

Columbus discovered Puerto Rico (*Rich Port*) and took possession for Spain on Oct. 19, 1493 - the only time Columbus set foot on the soil of what is now a possession of the United States. The first settlement, Caparra, was established by Ponce de Leon in 1508. The early years of the colony were not promising. Considerable gold was found, but the supply was soon exhausted. Efforts to enslave the Indians caused violent reprisals. Hurricanes destroyed crops and homes. French, Dutch, and English freebooters burned the towns. Puerto Rico remained a Spanish possession until 1898, when it was ceded to the United States following the Spanish-American War.

RULERS

Spanish, until 1898

ASSAYERS INITIALS

G - Antonio Garcia Gonzalez

P - Felix Miguel Peiro Rodrigo

MONETARY SYSTEM

100 Centavos = 1 Peso

SPANISH COLONY

COUNTERMARKED COINAGE

In 1884, a large number of holed coins were countermarked at Puerto Ricos seven customs houses to legitimatize them with a device very similar to a fleur-de-lys. These coins were redeemed in 1894.

KM# 1 5 CENTIMOS

Bronze **Countermark:** Lys **Note:** Countermark on Spanish 5 Centimos, KM#674.

CM Date	Host Date	Good	VG	F	VF	XF
ND(1884)	1877-79	75.00	125	175	275	—

KM# 2 10 CENTIMOS

Bronze **Countermark:** Lys **Note:** Countermark on Spanish 5 Centimos, KM#675.

CM Date	Host Date	Good	VG	F	VF	XF
ND(1884)	1877-79	75.00	125	175	275	—

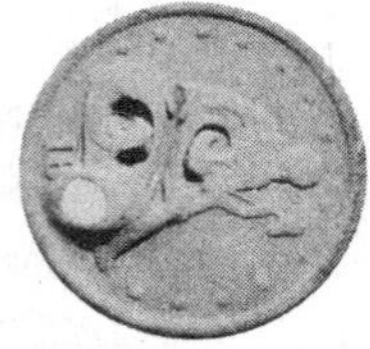

KM# 3 1/5 DOLLAR

Silver **Countermark:** Lys **Note:** Countermark on U.S. 20 cent, KM#109.

CM Date	Host Date	Good	VG	F	VF	XF
ND(1884)	1875-78	250	350	500	800	—

KM# 5 1/4 DOLLAR

Silver **Countermark:** Lys **Note:** Countermark on U.S. Seated Liberty quarter.

CM Date	Host Date	Good	VG	F	VF	XF
ND(1884)	1853	100	150	250	350	—

KM# 4 1/4 DOLLAR

Silver **Countermark:** Lys **Note:** Countermark on U.S. Bust quarter, KM#44.

CM Date	Host Date	Good	VG	F	VF	XF
ND(1884)	1815-28	125	175	275	425	—

KM# 6.1 1/4 DOLLAR

Silver **Countermark:** Lys **Note:** Countermark on U.S. Seated Liberty quarter, KM#78. Prev. KM#5.

CM Date	Host Date	Good	VG	F	VF	XF
ND(1884)	1853	100	150	250	350	—

KM# 6.2 1/4 DOLLAR

Silver **Countermark:** Lys **Note:** Countermark on U.S. Seated Liberty quarter, KM#81. Prev. KM#6.

CM Date	Host Date	Good	VG	F	VF	XF
ND(1884)	1854-55	100	150	275	375	—

KM# 6.3 1/4 DOLLAR

Silver **Countermark:** Lys **Note:** Countermark on U.S. Seated quarter, KM#64.2. Prev. KM#6.2.

CM Date	Host Date	Good	VG	F	VF	XF
ND(1884)	1856-65	100	150	265	375	—

KM# 6.4 1/4 DOLLAR

Silver **Countermark:** Lys **Note:** Countermark on U.S. Seated Liberty quarter, KM#98.

CM Date	Host Date	Good	VG	F	VF	XF
ND(1884)	1875-83	100	150	250	350	—

KM# 8.1 1/4 DOLLAR

Silver **Countermark:** Lys **Note:** Countermark on Lima 2 Reales, KM#62.

CM Date	Host Date	Good	VG	F	VF	XF
ND(1884)	1760-72	75.00	125	200	300	—

KM# 8.2 1/4 DOLLAR

Silver **Countermark:** Lys **Note:** Countermark on Spanish 2 reales, KM#388

CM Date	Host Date	Good	VG	F	VF	XF
ND(1884)	(1759-71)	75.00	125	200	300	—

KM# 16 1/4 DOLLAR

Silver **Countermark:** Lys **Note:** Countermark on Spanish 2 Reales, KM#388.

CM Date	Host Date	Good	VG	F	VF	XF
ND(1884)	1759-71	75.00	125	200	300	—

KM# 12 1/2 DOLLAR
Silver **Countermark:** Lys **Note:** Countermark on Potosi 4 Reales, KM#72.

CM Date	Host Date	Good	VG	F	VF	XF
ND(1884)	1791-1809	200	300	400	550	—

KM# 9 1/2 DOLLAR
Silver **Countermark:** Lys **Note:** Countermark on U.S. 1/2 dollar, KM#37.

CM Date	Host Date	Good	VG	F	VF	XF
ND(1884)	1807-36	250	350	450	750	—

KM# 10 1/2 DOLLAR
Silver **Countermark:** Lys **Note:** Countermark on U.S. Seated Liberty 1/2 dollar, KM#68.

CM Date	Host Date	Good	VG	F	VF	XF
ND(1884)	1839-66	125	175	275	450	—

KM# 11 1/2 DOLLAR
Silver **Countermark:** Lys **Note:** Countermark on U.S. Seated Liberty 1/2 dollar, KM#99.

CM Date	Host Date	Good	VG	F	VF	XF
ND(1884)	ND1866-83	125	175	275	450	—

KM# 15 DOLLAR
Silver **Countermark:** Lys **Note:** Countermark on Lima 8 Reales, KM#78.

CM Date	Host Date	Good	VG	F	VF	XF
ND(1884)	1772-89	250	375	525	850	—

KM# 13 DOLLAR
Silver **Countermark:** Lys **Note:** Countermark on U.S. Bust type dollar, KM#32.

CM Date	Host Date	Good	VG	F	VF	XF
ND(1884)	1798-1803	500	650	850	1,250	—

KM# 14 DOLLAR
Silver **Countermark:** Lys **Note:** Countermark on U.S. Trade dollar, KM#108.

CM Date	Host Date	Good	VG	F	VF	XF
ND(1884)	1873-78	250	375	550	900	—

DECIMAL COINAGE

KM# 20 5 CENTAVOS
1.2500 g., 0.9000 Silver .0361 oz. **Ruler:** Alfonso XIII **Obv:** Denomination **Rev:** Crowned arms between columns

Date	Mintage	F	VF	XF	Unc	BU
1896 PGV	600,000	30.00	45.00	85.00	200	—

KM# 21 10 CENTAVOS
2.5000 g., 0.9000 Silver .0723 oz. **Ruler:** Alfonso XIII **Obv:** Bust of young Alfonso XIII left **Rev:** Crowned arms between columns

Date	Mintage	F	VF	XF	Unc	BU
1896 PGV	700,000	35.00	60.00	110	275	—

KM# 22 20 CENTAVOS
5.0000 g., 0.9000 Silver .1446 oz. **Ruler:** Alfonso XIII **Obv:** Bust of young Alfonso XIII left **Rev:** Crowned arms between columns

Date	Mintage	F	VF	XF	Unc	BU
1895 PGV	3,350,000	45.00	70.00	135	325	—

KM# 23 40 CENTAVOS
10.0000 g., 0.9000 Silver .2893 oz. **Ruler:** Alfonso XIII **Obv:** Bust of young Alfonso XIII left **Rev:** Crowned arms between columns

Date	Mintage	F	VF	XF	Unc	BU
1896 PGV	725,000	250	325	750	2,850	—

KM# 24 PESO
25.0000 g., 0.9000 Silver .7234 oz. **Ruler:** Alfonso XIII **Obv:** Bust of young Alfonso XIII left **Rev:** Crowned arms between columns

Date	Mintage	F	VF	XF	Unc	BU
1895 PGV	8,500,000	275	350	800	1,650	—

TRIAL STRIKES

KM#	Date	Mintage	Identification	Mkt Val
TS1	1895	—	Peso. Copper. KM#24	—
TS2	ND(1895)	—	Peso. Copper. KM#24.	—

PATTERNS

INCLUDING OFF METAL STRIKES

KM#	Date	Mintage	Identification	Mkt Val

KM#	Date	Mintage	Identification	Mkt Val
Pn1	1890	—	10 Centimos. Copper.	1,650

VIEQUES ISLAND

(Crab Island)

Vieques (Crab) Island, located to the east of Puerto Rico is the largest of the Commonwealth's offshore islands. Two-thirds of the island is leased to the U.S. Navy. The neighboring island to the north, Culebra, was leased to the Navy until 1974, when the naval station was closed and bombardment exercises ceased. Puerto Rico's offshore island to the west, Mona, situated between the main island and the Dominican Republic, has been unpopulated since the late 16th century, and has no numismatic legacy.

COUNTERMARKED COINAGE

KM# 2 2 SKILLING
0.2500 Silver **Countermark:** 12-rayed sunburst **Note:** Countermark on Danish West Indies 2 Skilling, KM#13.

CM Date	Host Date	Good	VG	F	VF	XF
ND(ca.1858)	1837	40.00	60.00	90.00	175	—
ND(ca.1858)	1816	40.00	55.00	85.00	150	—

KM# 3 2 SKILLING
0.2500 Silver **Countermark:** 12-rayed sunburst **Note:** Countermark on Danish West Indies 2 Skilling, KM#19.

CM Date	Host Date	Good	VG	F	VF	XF
ND(ca.1858)	1848	40.00	75.00	125	225	—

KM# 9 2 SKILLING
0.2500 Silver **Countermark:** 12-rayed sunburst **Note:** Countermark on Danish West Indies 2 Skilling, KM#18.

CM Date	Host Date	Good	VG	F	VF	XF
ND(ca.1858)	1847	—	—	—	—	—

KM# 6 8 SKILLING
Silver **Countermark:** 12-rayed sunburst **Note:** Countermark on Denmark 8 Skilling, KM#470.

CM Date	Host Date	Good	VG	F	VF	XF
ND(ca.1858)	ND(1701-05)	85.00	135	175	275	—

KM# 5 20 SKILLING
0.6250 Silver **Countermark:** 12-rayed sunburst **Note:** Countermark on Danish West Indies 20 Skilling, KM#17.

CM Date	Host Date	Good	VG	F	VF	XF
ND(ca.1858)	1840	50.00	80.00	145	250	—

KM# 11 20 SKILLING
0.6250 Silver **Countermark:** 12-rayed sunburst **Note:** Countermark on Danish West Indies 20 Skilling, KM#15.

CM Date	Host Date	Good	VG	F	VF	XF
ND(ca.1858)	1816	—	—	—	—	—

KM# 12 20 SKILLING
0.6250 Silver **Countermark:** 12-rayed sunburst **Note:** Countermark on Danish West Indies 20 Skilling, KM#21.1.

CM Date	Host Date	Good	VG	F	VF	XF
ND(ca.1858)	1848	—	—	—	—	—

KM# 7 2 REALES
0.9030 Silver **Countermark:** 12-rayed sunburst **Note:** Countermark on Spanish 2 Reales, KM#460.

CM Date	Host Date	Good	VG	F	VF	XF
ND(ca.1858)	1825	85.00	135	175	275	—

CUT & COUNTERMARKED COINAGE

KM# 8 REAL
Silver **Countermark:** V in 12 rayed sunburst **Note:** Countermark on 1/2 cut of Spanish Colonial 2 Reales

Date	Mintage	Good	VG	F	VF	XF
ND(ca.1858)	—	100	145	185	285	—

QAITI STATE

Between 1200 B.C. and the 6th century A.D., what is now the Peoples Democratic Republic of Yemen was part of the Minaean kingdom. In subsequent years it was controlled by Persians, Egyptians and Turks. Aden, one of the cities mentioned in the Bible, had been a port for trade between the East and West for 2,000 years. British rule began in 1839 when the British East India Co. seized control to put an end to the piracy threatening trade with India. To protect their foothold in Aden, the British found it necessary to extend their control into the area known historically as the Hadhramaut, and to sign protection treaties with the sheiks of the hinterland.

STATE

TITLES

Qa'iti 

RULERS

Munassar bin Abdullah bin Umar,
AH1246-1283/1830-1866AD

Awadh bin Umar,
AH1283-1327/1866-1909AD

Countermarked Coinage

The countermarks on the following coins will have one of two possible legend varieties. They are:

a. 1307 Magar/ad-Dawlah/bin 'Abd Allah/Al Qaiti (1307, seat of government, Abd Allah Al Qa'iti).

b. Magar/ad-Dawlah/1307/sana (seat of government, 1307).

COUNTERMARKED COINAGE

KM# 1 1/12 ANNA

Copper **Obv:** Arabic countermark in 10mm circle **Note:** Countermark on India 1/12 Anna.

CM Date	Host Date	Good	VG	F	VF	XF
AH1307	1835 (b)	8.50	16.50	30.00	50.00	—
AH1307	1835 (m)	8.50	16.50	30.00	50.00	—
AH1307	1848 (c)	8.50	16.50	30.00	50.00	—

KM# 5 1/4 ANNA

Copper **Obv:** Arabic countermark in 15mm circle **Note:** Countermark on India-Bombay Presidency E.I.Co. 1/4 Anna, KM#232.

CM Date	Host Date	Good	VG	F	VF	XF
AH1307	1833	8.50	16.50	30.00	50.00	—

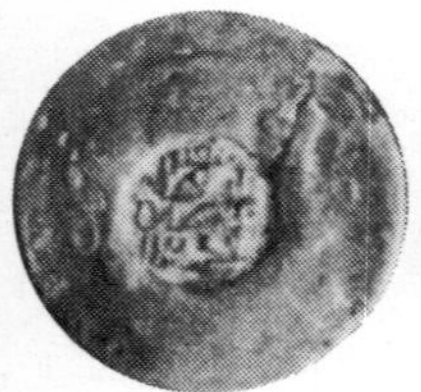

KM# 6 1/4 ANNA

Copper **Obv:** Arabic countermark in 10mm circle **Note:** Countermark on India-Bombay Presidency E.I.Co. 1/4 Anna, KM#231.

CM Date	Host Date	Good	VG	F	VF	XF
AH1307	1830	6.50	13.50	25.00	40.00	—
AH1307	1832	6.50	13.50	25.00	40.00	—

KM# 7.1 1/4 ANNA

Copper **Obv:** Arabic countermark in 10mm circle **Note:** Prev. KM#7. Countermark on India 1/4 Anna, KM#446.1.

CM Date	Host Date	Good	VG	F	VF	XF
AH1307	1833 (b)	6.50	13.50	25.00	40.00	—
AH1307	1835 (m)	6.50	13.50	25.00	40.00	—

KM# 7.2 1/4 ANNA

Copper **Obv:** Arabic countermark in 10mm circle **Note:** Countermark on India 1/4 Anna, KM#446.2.

CM Date	Host Date	Good	VG	F	VF	XF
AH1307	1835 (b)	6.50	13.50	25.00	40.00	—
AH1307	1835 (c)	6.50	13.50	25.00	40.00	—
AH1307	1835 (m)	6.50	13.50	25.00	40.00	—

KM# 8 1/4 ANNA

Copper **Obv:** Arabic countermark in 15mm circle **Note:** Countermark on India 1/4 Anna, KM#447.

CM Date	Host Date	Good	VG	F	VF	XF
AH1307	1862-76	6.50	13.50	25.00	40.00	—

KM# 9 1/4 ANNA

Copper **Obv:** Arabic countermark in 10mm circle **Note:** Countermark on Mombasa 1/4 Anna, KM#1.

CM Date	Host Date	Good	VG	F	VF	XF
AH1307	1888	7.50	15.00	27.50	45.00	—

KM# 10 1/4 ANNA

Copper **Obv:** Arabic countermark in 10mm circle **Note:** Countermark on Zanzibar Pysa, KM#1.

CM Date	Host Date	Good	VG	F	VF	XF
AH1307	1881	7.50	15.00	27.50	45.00	—

KM# 15 1/2 ANNA

Copper **Obv:** Arabic countermark in 15mm circle **Note:** Countermark on India-Bombay Presidency 1/2 Anna, KM#251.

CM Date	Host Date	Good	VG	F	VF	XF
AH1307	1834	8.50	16.50	30.00	50.00	—

KM# 16 1/2 ANNA

Copper **Obv:** Arabic countermark in 15mm circle **Note:** Countermark on India 1/2 Anna, KM#447.

CM Date	Host Date	Good	VG	F	VF	XF
AH1307	1835-45	8.50	16.50	30.00	50.00	—

KM# 17 1/2 ANNA

Copper **Obv:** Arabic countermark in 15mm circle **Note:** Countermark on India 1/2 Anna, KM#468.

CM Date	Host Date	Good	VG	F	VF	XF
AH1307	1862-76	8.50	16.50	30.00	50.00	—

KM# 20 1/4 RUPEE

Silver **Obv:** Arabic countermark in 10mm circle **Note:** Countermark on India-Bengal Presidency 1/4 Rupee, KM#96.

CM Date	Host Date	Good	VG	F	VF	XF
AH1307	AH1204	12.50	25.00	45.00	75.00	—

KM# 25 1/2 RUPEE

Silver **Obv:** Arabic countermark in 10mm circle **Note:** Countermark on India 1/2 Rupee, KM#491.

CM Date	Host Date	Good	VG	F	VF	XF
AH1307	1877-99	7.50	15.00	27.50	45.00	—

KM# 26 1/2 RUPEE

Silver **Obv:** Arabic countermark in 10mm circle **Note:** Countermark on English 1 Shilling, KM#734.

CM Date	Host Date	Good	VG	F	VF	XF
AH1307	1838-87	7.50	15.00	27.50	45.00	—

KM# 27 1/2 RUPEE

Silver **Obv:** Arabic countermark in 15mm circle **Note:** Countermark on India 1/2 Rupee, KM#491.

CM Date	Host Date	Good	VG	F	VF	XF
AH1307	1877-99	10.00	20.00	35.00	55.00	—

KM# 28 1/2 RUPEE

Silver **Obv:** Arabic countermark in 15mm circle **Note:** Countermark on Mexico 2 Reales, KM#88.

CM Date	Host Date	Good	VG	F	VF	XF
AH1307	1772-89	10.00	20.00	35.00	55.00	—

KM# A30 RUPEE

Silver **Obv:** Arabic countermark in 10mm circle **Note:** Countermark on India Bengal Presidency Rupee, KM#99.

CM Date	Host Date	Good	VG	F	VF	XF
AH1307	1793-1813	—	60.00	100	175	—

KM# 30 RUPEE

Silver **Obv:** Arabic countermark in 10mm circle **Note:** Countermark on India Rupee, KM#457.

CM Date	Host Date	Good	VG	F	VF	XF
AH1307	1840	15.00	22.50	32.50	65.00	—

Note: Prices for single countermark on coin; add 15% for each additional countermark

KM# 31 RUPEE

Silver **Obv:** Arabic countermark in 10mm circle **Note:** Countermark on India Rupee, KM#458.

CM Date	Host Date	Good	VG	F	VF	XF
AH1307	1840	—	17.50	25.00	35.00	70.00

KM# 32 RUPEE

Silver **Obv:** Arabic countermark in 10mm circle **Note:** Countermark on India Rupee, KM#458.

CM Date	Host Date	Good	VG	F	VF	XF
AH1307	1840	15.00	22.50	32.50	65.00	—

KM# 33 RUPEE
Silver , Arabic countermark in 15mm circle **Note:** Countermark on India Rupee, KM#473.1.

CM Date	Host Date	Good	VG	F	VF	XF
AH1307	1862-74	17.50	25.00	35.00	70.00	—

KM# 34 RUPEE
Silver **Obv:** Arabic countermark in 10mm circle **Note:** Countermark on India Rupee, KM#492.

CM Date	Host Date	Good	VG	F	VF	XF
AH1307	1877-1901	17.50	25.00	35.00	70.00	—

KM# 35 RYAL
Silver **Obv:** Arabic countermark in 10mm circle **Note:** Countermark on Austria MTT, KM#T1.

CM Date	Host Date	Good	VG	F	VF	XF
AH1307	1780	30.00	45.00	60.00	90.00	—

KM# 36 RYAL
Silver **Obv:** Arabic countermark in 15mm circle **Note:** Countermark on Austria MTT, KM#T1.

CM Date	Host Date	Good	VG	F	VF	XF
AH1307	1780	35.00	50.00	70.00	100	—

KM# 40 SOVEREIGN
Gold **Countermark:** Arabic **Note:** Countermark on English Sovereign, KM#767.

CM Date	Host Date	Good	VG	F	VF	XF
AH1307	1887-92 Rare	—	—	—	—	—

STANDARD COINAGE

KM# 45 5 KHUMSI
Copper Or Bronze

Date	Mintage	Good	VG	F	VF	XF
AH1315 (1897)	—	7.00	10.00	20.00	35.00	—

KM# 48 5 KHUMSI
Copper Or Bronze **Obv:** Toughra **Note:** Overstrikes on East India Co. 1/4 Annas exist.

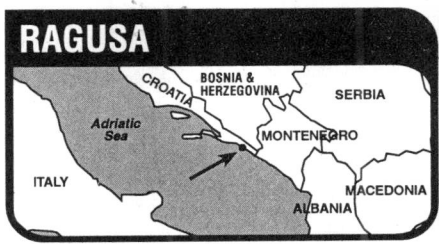

Date	Mintage	Good	VG	F	VF	XF
AH1318 (1900)	—	6.00	8.00	18.00	30.00	—

KM# 46 1/3 RIYAL
Silver

Date	Mintage	Good	VG	F	VF	XF
AH1315	—	150	250	350	500	—

KM# 47 1/2 RIYAL
Silver

Date	Mintage	Good	VG	F	VF	XF
AH1316	—	175	300	450	600	—

RAGUSA

A port city in Croatia on the Dalmatian coast of the Adriatic Sea. Ragusa was once a great mercantile power, the merchant fleets of which sailed as far abroad as India and America.

Refugees from the destroyed Latin communities of Salona and Epidaurus, and a colony of Slavs colonized the island rock of Ragusa during the 7th century. For four centuries Ragusa successfully defended itself against attacks by foreign powers, but from 1205 to 1358 recognized Venetian suzeranity. From 1358 to 1526, Ragusa was a vassal state of Hungary. The fall of Hungary in 1526 freed Ragusa, permitting it to become one of the foremost commercial powers of the Mediterranean and a leader in the development of literature and art. After this period its importance declined, due in part to the discovery of America, which reduced the importance of Mediterranean ports. A measure of its former economic importance was regained during the Napoleonic Wars when the republic, by adopting a policy of neutrality (1800-1805), became the leading carrier of the Mediterranean. This favored position was terminated by French seizure in 1805. In 1814 Ragusa was annexed by Austria, remaining a part of the Austrian Empire until its incorporation in the newly formed state of Yugoslavia in 1918.

MONETARY SYSTEM
6 Soldi = 1 Grosetto
12 Grosetti = 1 Perpero
3 Perpero = 1 Scudo
36 Grosetti = 1 Scudo
40 Grosetti = 1 Ducato
60 Grosetti = 1 Tallero
5 Perpero = 1 Tallero

REPUBLIC

STANDARD COINAGE

KM# 25.1 6 GROSETTI
Billon **Obv:** St. Blaze **Obv. Legend:** PROT. REIP. RHAGUSIN... **Rev:** Value

Date	Mintage	VG	F	VF	XF	Unc
1801	—	17.00	35.00	70.00	125	—

KM# 25.2 6 GROSETTI
Billon **Obv. Legend:** PROT. REIPV. RHACVSI...

Date	Mintage	VG	F	VF	XF	Unc
1801	—	17.00	35.00	70.00	125	—

KM# 7 PERPERO
Billon **Obv:** St. Blaze **Obv. Legend:** PROT. RAEIP. RHAGVSINAE **Rev:** Christ

Date	Mintage	VG	F	VF	XF	Unc
1801	—	16.50	27.50	55.00	90.00	—
1802	—	16.50	27.50	55.00	90.00	—
1803	—	16.50	27.50	55.00	90.00	—

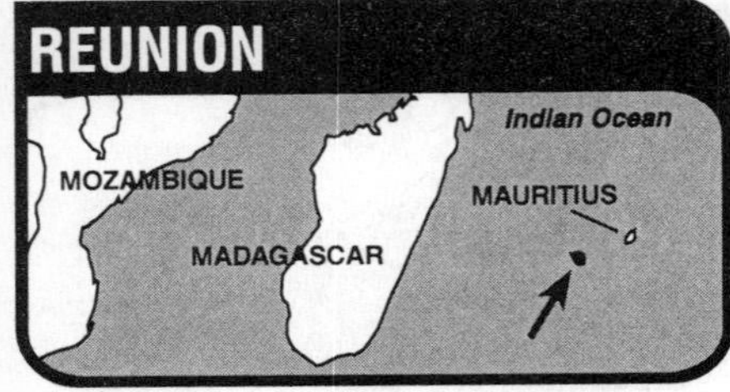

The Department of Reunion, an overseas department of France located in the Indian Ocean 400 miles (640 km.) east of Madagascar, has an area of 969 sq. mi. (2,510 sq. km.).

Although first visited by Portuguese navigators in the 16th century, Reunion was uninhabited when claimed for France by Capt. Goubert in 1638. The French first colonized the Isle de Bourbon in 1662 as a layover station for ships rounding the Cape of Good Hope to India. It was renamed Reunion in 1793. The island remained in French possession except for the period of 1810-15, when the British occupied it. Reunion became an overseas department of France in 1946, and in 1958 voted to continue that status within the new French Union.

During the first half of the 19th century, Reunion was officially known as Isle de Bonaparte (1801-14) and Isle de Bourbon (1814-48). Reunion coinage of those periods is so designated.

Mint Marks
(a) – Paris, privy marks only

MONETARY SYSTEM
100 Centimes = 1 Franc

FRENCH DEPARTMENT

STANDARD COINAGE

KM# 4 50 CENTIMES
Copper-Nickel

Date	Mintage	F	VF	XF	Unc	BU
1896	1,000,000	20.00	45.00	125	375	700

KM# 5 FRANC
Copper Nickel

Date	Mintage	F	VF	XF	Unc	BU
1896	500,000	35.00	60.00	175	425	800

ESSAIS

Standard metals unless otherwise noted

KM#	Date	Mintage	Identification	Mkt Val
E1	1896	—	50 Centimes. Copper Nickel. KM#4	275
E2	1896	—	Franc. Copper Nickel. KM#5	350

PIEFORTS WITH ESSAI

Double thickness; standard metals unless otherwise noted

KM#	Date	Mintage	Identification	Mkt Val
PE1	1896	—	50 Centimes. Copper Nickel.	450
PE1a	1896	—	50 Centimes. Bronze. KM#4.	600
PE2	1896	—	50 Centimes. Copper Nickel. KM#5.	600

Romania (formerly the Socialist Republic of Romania), a country in southeast Europe, has an area of 91,699 sq. mi. (237,500 sq. km.).

The area of Romania, generally referred to as Dacia, existed as early as 200 BC, it was inhabited by Dacians or Getae, a people of Thracian stock.

Because of the decline of Turkish power during the eighteenth century, the Austrian and later Russian influence became preeminent in the area.

Between 1718-1734, the Hapsburgs annexed the region of Oltenia, in western Wallachia. In 1775 Moldavia lost its northern region Bukovina to Austria and in 1812 Russia annexed its eastern portion, Bessarabia.

The erosion of Turkish influence became more evident after the national movement of Tudor Vladimirescu in 1821 in Wallachia. The Phanariot system was ended, Romanian rulers were reestablished. The principalities, although remaining under Sultan control, were more autonomous. As such, in 1829, the Turkish monopoly of commerce was abolished. Important institutional reforms were adopted.

The European insurrectionist movements in 1848 reached The European insurrectionist movements reached the region in 1848, in Moldova and Wallachia the provisional the area. In Moldova and Wallachia the provisional revolutionary governments were put down by a Russo-Turkish military intervention. In 1859 Wallachia and Moldavia unified, and in 1862 officially proclaimed as Romania. In Transylvania the Romanians, as native and majority of the population, continued to the revolution had another aspect. The Romanians, as native and majority of the population, continued to fight for social and national emancipation, which went unrecognized by the Hungarian revolutionary government. In 1867, Transylvania was incorporated under Hungarian administration during establishment of the dual Austro-Hungarian Empire. After the Russian defeat in the Crimean War, the great European powers ended the Russian protectorate and returned south of Bessarabia to Moldavia. The question of union of Wallachia and Moldavia was resolved in 1859. The union was voted in unanimously on January 5 at Iasi, the Moldavian capital; and on January 24 at Bucharest. The two assemblies elected a single prince in the person of Alexandru Ioanperson of Alexandru Ioan Cuza, establishing the fruition of Romania. Prince A. I. Cuza was deposed by a conspiracy in 1866. A provisional government then elected Prince Karl of Hohenzollern-Sigmaringen, who took office as Carol I and was vested as hereditary prince. A constitution was adopted on his arrival. A rapid modernization of the country was perceived. Romania, successfully involved in war against Turkey (1877-78), proclaimed itself to be completely independent. The historical region of Dobruja, including the Delta of Danube, was returned, but Romania was forced to cede its southern area of Bessarabia to Russia.

In 1881, Carol I became king. In 1888, Romania became a constitutional monarchy with a bicameral legislature. Neutral during the First Balkan War (1912), Romania joined Serbia and Greece in the Second Balkan War (1913) against Bulgaria The intervention and deployment of Romanian troops into Bulgaria resulted in the acquisition of southern Dobruja.

RULERS
Carol I (as Prince), 1866-81 (as King), 1881-1914

MINT MARKS
(a) - Paris, privy marks only
(b) - Brussels, privy marks only
...angel head (1872-1876),
no marks (1894-1924)
B - Bucharest (1870-1900)
B - Hamburg, Germany
C - Candescu, chief engineer of the Bucharest Mint
...(1870-)
H - Heaton, Birmingham, England
HF - Huguenin Freres & Co., Le Locle, Switzerland
J - Hamburg
KN - Kings Norton, Birmingham, England
(p) - Thunderbolt - Poissy, France
...zig zag (1924)
V - Vienna, Austria
W - Watt (James Watt & Co.)
Huguenin - Le Locle, Switzerland

MINT OFFICIALS' INITIALS

Initial	Date	Name
C	1870	Candescu
KULLRICH, C	1879-1901	Wilhelm Kullrich
A. SCHARFF	1894-1901	Anton Scharff
STERN	1872	
LEOP. WIENER	1879	Wiener Leopold Wyon

MONETARY SYSTEM
100 Bani = 1 Leu

KINGDOM

STANDARD COINAGE

KM# 1.1 BANU
Copper, 15 mm. **Ruler:** Carol I

Date	Mintage	F	VF	XF	Unc	BU
1867H	2,500,000	6.00	12.00	32.00	65.00	—
1867H Proof	Inc. above	Value: 95.00				

KM# 1.2 BANU
Copper, 15 mm. **Ruler:** Carol I

Date	Mintage	F	VF	XF	Unc	BU
1867 WATT & CO.	2,500,000	8.00	16.00	40.00	85.00	—
1867 WATT & CO. Proof	—	Value: 120				

KM# A18 BAN
Bronze, 15 mm. **Ruler:** Carol I **Note:** Similar to 2 Bani, KM#18.

Date	Mintage	F	VF	XF	Unc	BU
1883	100	—	—	850	1,400	—

KM# A18a BAN
Gilt Bronze, 15 mm. **Ruler:** Carol I **Note:** Presentation issues for Queen Elizabeth of Romania.

Date	Mintage	F	VF	XF	Unc	BU
1888	500	—	—	750	1,200	—

KM# 26 BAN
Copper **Ruler:** Carol I **Note:** Varieties exist.

Date	Mintage	F	VF	XF	Unc	BU
1900B	20,007,000	2.00	3.00	8.00	26.00	—
1900B Proof	—	Value: 55.00				

KM# 2.1 2 BANI
Copper, 20 mm. **Ruler:** Carol I

Date	Mintage	F	VF	XF	Unc	BU
1867 HEATON	5,000,000	3.00	6.00	15.00	40.00	—
1867 HEATON Proof	—	Value: 70.00				

KM# 2.2 2 BANI
Copper, 20 mm. **Ruler:** Carol I

Date	Mintage	F	VF	XF	Unc	BU
1867 WATT & CO.	5,000,000	5.00	12.00	26.00	55.00	—
1867 WATT & CO. Proof	—	Value: 85.00				

KM# 11.1 2 BANI
Copper, 19.5 mm. **Ruler:** Carol I **Obv. Legend:** CAROL I DOMNUL (Prince)

Date	Mintage	F	VF	XF	Unc	BU
1879B	500,000	6.00	12.00	32.00	65.00	—

KM# 11.2 2 BANI
Copper, 20 mm. **Ruler:** Carol I **Note:** Varieties exist.

Date	Mintage	F	VF	XF	Unc	BU
1879B	Inc. above	4.00	8.00	18.00	40.00	—
1880/79B	10,500,000	7.00	15.00	35.00	100	—
1880B	Inc. above	3.00	6.00	12.00	32.00	—
1881B	1,250,000	15.00	25.00	60.00	145	—

KM# 18 2 BANI
Copper **Ruler:** Carol I **Obv. Legend:** CAROL I REGE (King) **Note:** Varieties exist.

Date	Mintage	F	VF	XF	Unc	BU
1882B	5,000,000	5.00	12.00	27.50	60.00	—

KM# 27 2 BANI
Copper **Ruler:** Carol I **Rev:** ROMANIA added above shield **Note:** Varieties exist.

Date	Mintage	F	VF	XF	Unc	BU
1900B	20,000,000	1.50	3.00	7.00	25.00	—

KM# 3.1 5 BANI
Copper, 25 mm. **Ruler:** Carol I

Date	Mintage	F	VF	XF	Unc	BU
1867 HEATON	12,500,000	3.00	7.00	12.00	32.00	—
1867 HEATON Proof	—	Value: 85.00				

KM# 3.2 5 BANI
Copper, 25 mm. **Ruler:** Carol I

Date	Mintage	F	VF	XF	Unc	BU
1867 WATT & CO.	12,500,000	3.00	8.00	17.00	50.00	—
1867 WATT & CO. Proof	—	Value: 100				

KM# 19 5 BANI
Copper **Ruler:** Carol I **Obv. Legend:** CAROL I REGE (King)

Date	Mintage	F	VF	XF	Unc	BU
1882B	5,000,000	1.00	2.50	12.00	40.00	—
1883B	3,000,000	1.00	3.00	13.00	42.00	—
1884B	8,400,000	1.00	2.00	10.00	35.00	—
1885B	3,600,000	2.00	6.00	20.00	52.00	—

KM# 28 5 BANI
Copper-Nickel **Ruler:** Carol I **Note:** Varieties exist.

Date	Mintage	F	VF	XF	Unc	BU
1900	20,000,000	1.00	3.00	9.00	22.00	—

KM# 4.2 10 BANI
Copper, 30 mm. **Ruler:** Carol I

Date	Mintage	F	VF	XF	Unc	BU
1867 WATT & CO.	12,500,000	3.00	8.00	18.00	45.00	—
1867 WATT & CO. Proof	—	Value: 95.00				

KM# 4.1 10 BANI
Copper, 30 mm. **Ruler:** Carol I **Note:** Medal and coin alignment.

Date	Mintage	F	VF	XF	Unc	BU
1867 HEATON	12,500,000	2.50	7.50	16.00	35.00	—
1867 HEATON Proof	—	Value: 75.00				

KM# 29 10 BANI
Copper-Nickel, 22 mm. **Ruler:** Carol I

Date	Mintage	F	VF	XF	Unc	BU
1900	15,000,000	1.00	2.50	8.00	22.00	—
1900 Proof	—	Value: 65.00				

KM# 30 20 BANI
Copper-Nickel, 25 mm. **Ruler:** Carol I

Date	Mintage	F	VF	XF	Unc	BU
1900	2,500,000	4.00	12.00	32.00	85.00	—

KM# 9 50 BANI
2.5000 g., 0.8350 Silver .0671 oz., 18 mm. **Ruler:** Carol I

Date	Mintage	F	VF	XF	Unc	BU
1873(b)	4,810,000	2.50	8.00	25.00	100	—
1873(b)	Inc. above	4.00	10.00	27.00	110	—
Note: Medal rotation						
1876(b)	2,169,800	3.00	12.00	32.00	160	—

KM# 13 50 BANI
2.5000 g., 0.8350 Silver .0671 oz. **Ruler:** Carol I

Date	Mintage	F	VF	XF	Unc	BU
1881V	1,000,000	6.50	20.00	60.00	300	—

KM# 21 50 BANI
2.5000 g., 0.8350 Silver .0671 oz. **Ruler:** Carol I **Rev:** Large 50 and letters

Date	Mintage	F	VF	XF	Unc	BU
1884	Inc. above	—	—	—	—	—
1884B	1,000,000	3.00	12.00	30.00	95.00	—
1885B	200,000	6.00	20.00	60.00	250	—

KM# 23 50 BANI
2.5000 g., 0.8350 Silver .0671 oz. **Ruler:** Carol I **Rev:** Small 50 and letters

Date	Mintage	F	VF	XF	Unc	BU
1894	600,000	4.00	13.00	24.00	90.00	—
1900	3,838,000	2.50	12.00	22.00	85.00	—

KM# 6 LEU
5.0000 g., 0.8350 Silver .1342 oz., 23 mm. **Ruler:** Carol I

Date	Mintage	F	VF	XF	Unc	BU
1870C	400,000	35.00	65.00	210	650	—
1870C	Inc. above	120	180	475	1,000	—
Note: Medal rotation						
1870B	Inc. above	250	350	750	1,800	—

KM# 10 LEU
5.0000 g., 0.8350 Silver .1342 oz. **Ruler:** Carol I **Note:** Varieties exist.

Date	Mintage	F	VF	XF	Unc	BU
1873(b)	4,443,393	4.00	9.00	18.00	160	—
1874(b)	4,511,607	5.00	12.00	25.00	200	—
1876(b)	225,000	400	600	1,100	2,250	—

KM# 14 LEU
5.0000 g., 0.8350 Silver .1342 oz. **Ruler:** Carol I **Obv. Legend:** CAROL I DOMNUL (Prince)

Date	Mintage	F	VF	XF	Unc	BU
1881V	1,800,000	12.00	22.00	65.00	225	—
1881V Proof	—	—	—	—	—	—

KM# 22 LEU
5.0000 g., 0.8350 Silver .1342 oz. **Ruler:** Carol I **Obv. Legend:** CAROL I REGE (King)

Date	Mintage	F	VF	XF	Unc	BU
1884B	1,000,000	8.00	16.00	40.00	125	—
1885B	400,000	16.00	45.00	160	650	—
1885B Proof	—	—	—	—	—	—

KM# 24 LEU
5.0000 g., 0.8350 Silver .1342 oz. **Ruler:** Carol I

Date	Mintage	F	VF	XF	Unc	BU
1894	1,500,000	4.00	12.00	40.00	190	—
1894 Proof	—	—	—	—	—	—
1900	798,800	4.00	9.00	26.00	95.00	—

KM# 8 2 LEI
10.0000 g., 0.8350 Silver .2684 oz. **Ruler:** Carol I

Date	Mintage	F	VF	XF	Unc	BU
1872(b)	262,000	7.00	18.00	75.00	300	—
1872 Proof	—	Value: 700				
1873(b)	1,745,000	4.00	10.00	30.00	160	—
1875(b)	3,092,500	4.00	10.00	32.00	185	—
1876(b)	653,255	8.00	19.50	75.00	280	—

KM# 15 2 LEI
10.0000 g., 0.8350 Silver .2684 oz. **Ruler:** Carol I

Date	Mintage	F	VF	XF	Unc	BU
1881V	1,150,000	22.00	46.00	125	350	—

KM# 25 2 LEI
10.0000 g., 0.8350 Silver .2684 oz. **Edge:** Reeded

Date	Mintage	F	VF	XF	Unc	BU
1894	600,000	10.00	22.00	110	350	—
1894 Proof	—	Value: 650				
1900	87,279	12.00	30.00	90.00	360	—

KM# 12 5 LEI
25.0000 g., 0.9000 Silver .7234 oz. **Ruler:** Carol I **Obv. Legend:** CAROL I DOMNUL ROMANIEI **Note:** Carol I as Prince

Date	Mintage	F	VF	XF	Unc	BU
1880B Name near rim	1,800,000	17.50	35.00	85.00	500	—
1880B Name near truncation	Inc. above	20.00	40.00	90.00	550	—
1881B	2,200,000	16.00	30.00	55.00	400	—

KM# 16 5 LEI
25.0000 g., 0.9000 Silver .7234 oz. **Ruler:** Carol I **Obv. Legend:** CAROL I REGE AL ROMANIEI **Note:** Carol I as King

Date	Mintage	F	VF	XF	Unc	BU
1881B	570,000	30.00	65.00	160	580	—

KM# 17.1 5 LEI
25.0000 g., 0.9000 Silver .7234 oz. **Ruler:** Carol I **Edge:** Lettered **Note:** Five or six stars on lettered edge varieties exist.

Date	Mintage	F	VF	XF	Unc	BU
1881B	1,230,000	15.00	35.00	85.00	575	—
1882B	1,100,000	16.00	40.00	90.00	575	—
1883B	Est. 2,300,000	15.00	30.00	50.00	400	—
Note: Varieties in crown on mantle exist						
1884B	300,000	25.00	65.00	160	650	—
1885B	40,000	120	220	650	1,500	—

KM# 5 20 LEI
6.4516 g., 0.9000 Gold .1867 oz. **Ruler:** Carol I **Obv:** Light beard **Obv. Legend:** CAROL I DOMNULU (Prince) **Edge:** Reeded

Date	Mintage	F	VF	XF	Unc	BU
1868(b)	200	—	4,000	8,000	11,500	—

KM# 7 20 LEI
6.4516 g., 0.9000 Gold .1867 oz. **Ruler:** Carol I **Obv:** Heavy beard **Obv. Legend:** CAROL I DOMNUL (Prince)

Date	Mintage	F	VF	XF	Unc	BU
1870C	5,000	600	1,000	1,800	3,000	—

KM# 20 20 LEI
6.4516 g., 0.9000 Gold .1867 oz. **Ruler:** Carol I **Obv. Legend:** CAROL I REGE (King) **Note:** Varieties exist.

Date	Mintage	F	VF	XF	Unc	BU
1883B	150,000	95.00	125	150	220	—
1884 Rare	35,290	—	—	—	—	—
1890B	196,000	100	145	165	235	—

PATTERNS

Including off metal strikes

KM#	Date	Mintage	Identification	Mkt Val
PnA1	1860	—	5 Parale.	—
PnC1	1864	—	10 Sutimi.	—
PnB1	1864	—	5 Sutimi.	5,000
Pn11	1867	—	20 Lei. Gold. Berlin Mint. KM#5.	10,000
Pn1	1867 HEATON	—	Ban.	—
Pn2	1867 WATT	—	Ban.	—
Pn3	1867 HEATON	—	2 Bani.	—
Pn4	1867 WATT	—	2 Bani.	—
Pn5	1867	—	5 Bani. Bronze. 1-1/2 times normal thickness.	—
Pn6	1867	—	5 Bani. Copper-Nickel. 1-1/2 times normal thickness.	400

KM#	Date	Mintage	Identification	Mkt Val
Pn7	1867 WATT	—	5 Bani. Nickel.	—
Pn8	1867	—	10 Bani. Copper-Nickel. 1-1/2 times normal thickness.	130
Pn9	1867	—	10 Bani. Copper-Nickel. Regular thickness.	—
Pn10	1867 WATT	—	10 Bani. Nickel. Plain edge.	—
Pn12	1868	—	20 Lei. Gold. Plain edge.	8,000

KM#	Date	Mintage	Identification	Mkt Val
Pn13	1869	—	50 Bani. Copper. Reeded edge.	—
Pn14	1869	—	50 Bani. Zinc.	350
Pn15	1869	—	50 Bani. Brass.	100
Pn16	1869	—	50 Bani. Bronze.	100
Pn17	1869	—	50 Bani. White Metal.	125

KM#	Date	Mintage	Identification	Mkt Val
Pn18	1869	—	50 Bani. Silver.	225
Pn19	1869	—	Leu. Copper. Reeded edge.	—
Pn20	1869	—	Leu. Pewter.	350
Pn21	1869	—	Leu. Bronze.	125
Pn22	1869	—	Leu. White Metal.	200
Pn23	1869	—	Leu. Silver.	275

KM#	Date	Mintage	Identification	Mkt Val
Pn24	1869	—	2 Lei. Copper Or Bronze.	—
Pn25	1869	—	2 Lei. Zinc.	400
Pn26	1869	—	2 Lei. White Metal.	225
Pn27	1869	—	2 Lei. Silver. Plain edge.	350
Pn28	1870B	—	Leu. 0.8350 Silver. Medal rotation.	800
Pn29	1870	—	20 Lei. Gold.	2,500
Pn30	1873	—	Leu.	—
Pn31	1875	—	2 Lei. Copper-Nickel.	275
Pn32	1876	—	20 Bani. German Silver.	125
Pn33	1876	—	50 Bani. Copper-Nickel. Reeded edge.	—
Pn34	1876	—	Leu. Copper-Nickel. Reeded edge.	—
Pn35	1876	—	2 Lei. Copper-Nickel. Reeded edge.	—
Pn36	1879	—	5 Lei. Zinc.	—

KM#	Date	Mintage	Identification	Mkt Val
Pn37	1879	—	5 Lei. Copper.	200
Pn38	1879	—	5 Lei. Bronze.	—
Pn39	1879	—	5 Lei. Silver.	—
Pn40	1881(b)	—	Leu. Silver.	900
Pn41	1881(b)	—	2 Lei. Silver.	1,600
Pn42	1883	—	5 Lei. Silver.	—

KM#	Date	Mintage	Identification	Mkt Val

KM#	Date	Mintage	Identification	Mkt Val
Pn44	1888	100	Ban. Copper.	150
Pn46	1890	—	20 Lei. Gold.	1,500
Pn47	1894	—	Leu. Bronze.	300
Pn48	1894	—	Leu. Copper-Nickel.	—

PIEFORTS

KM#	Date	Mintage	Identification	Mkt Val
P1	1869	—	Leu. Copper-Nickel.	200
P2	1876	—	20 Bani. Copper-Nickel. ESSAI.	300

RUSSIA (U.S.S.R.)

Russia, formerly the central power of the Union of Soviet Socialist Republics and now of the Commonwealth of Independent States occupies the northern part of Asia and the eastern part of Europe, has an area of 17,075,400 sq. km. Capital: Moscow.

The first Russian dynasty was founded in Novgorod by the Viking Rurik in 862 A.D. under Yaroslav the Wise (1019-54). The subsequent Kievan state became one of the great commercial and cultural centers of Europe before falling to the Mongols of the Batu Khan, 13th century, who were suzerains of Russia until late in the 15th century when Ivan III threw off the Mongol yoke. The Russian Empire was enlarged, solidified and Westernized during the reigns of Ivan the Terrible, Peter the Great and Catherine the Great, and by 1881 extended to the Pacific and into Central Asia. Contemporary Russian history began in March of 1917 when Tsar Nicholas II abdicated under pressure and was replaced by a provisional government composed of both radical and conservative elements. This government rapidly lost ground to the Bolshevik wing of the Socialist Democratic Labor Party which attained power following the Bolshevik Revolution which began on Nov. 7, 1917. After the Russian Civil War, the regional governments, national states and armies became federal republics of the Russian Socialist Federal Soviet Republic. These autonomous republics united to form the Union of Soviet Socialist Republics that was established as a federation under the premiership of Lenin on Dec. 30, 1922.

EMPIRE

RULERS

Alexander I, 1801-1825
Nicholas I, 1825-1855
Alexander II, 1855-1881
Alexander III, 1881-1894
Nicholas II, 1894-1917

MINT MARKS

ЕМ - Ekaterinburg, 1763-1876
КМ - Kolpino (Izhora), 1810-1821
КМ - Kolyvan, 1767-1830 (later Suzun)
КМ - Kolpina, 1810
СМ - St. Petersburg (gold), 1796-1801
СПБ - St. Petersburg, 1724-1914
ИМ - Izhora, 1811-1821
СПМ St. Petersburg (Izhora), 1840-1843
СМ - Suzun (Kolyvan), 1831-1847
ВМ - Warsaw, 1850-1864
MW - Warsaw, 1842-1854
Star (on rim) - Paris, 1896-1899
2 Stars (on rim) - Brussels, 1897-1899

MINTMASTERS INITIALS

EKATERINBURG MINT

Initials	Years	Mintmaster
НМ	1810-21	Nicholai Mundt
ИФ	1811	Ivan Felkner
ФГ	1811-23	Franz German
ПГ	1823-25	Peter Gramatchikov
ИШ	1825	Ivan Shevkunov
ИК	1825-30	Ivan Kolobov
ФХ	1830-37	Fedor Khvochinski
КТ	1837	Konstantin Tomson
НА	1837-39	Nicholai Alexeev

IZHORA (KOLPINO) MINT

Initials	Years	Mintmaster
МК	1810-11	Mikhail Kleiner
ПС	1811-14	Paul Stupitzyn
ЯБ	1820-21	Yakov Wilson

KOLYVAN and SOUZAN MINTS

Initials	Years	Mintmaster
ПБ	1810-11	Peter Berezowski
АМ	1812-17	Alexei Maleev
ДБ	1817-18	Dmitri Bikhtov
АД	1818-21	Alexander Deichmann
АМ	1821-30	Andrei Mevius

ST. PETERSBURG MINT

Initials	Years	Mintmaster
ФЦ	1797-1801	Fedor Tsetreus
ОМ	1798-1801	Ossip Medzher
АИ	1801-03	Alexie Ivanov
ФГ	1803-17	Fedor Gelman
ХЛ	1804-05	Christopher Leo
МК	1808-09	Mikhail Kleiner
МФ	1812-22	Mikhail Fedorov
ПС	1811-25	Paul Stupitzyn
ПД	1820-38	Paul Danilov
НГ	1825-42	Nikolai Grachev
АЧ	1839-43	Alexei Chadov
КБ	1844-46	Constantine Butenev
АГ	1846-57	Alexander Gertov
ПА	1847-52	Paul Alexiev
НІ	1848-77	Nicholai Iossa
ФБ	1856-61	Fedor Blum
ПФ	1858-62	Paul Follendorf
МИ	1861-63	Mikhail Ivanov
АБ	1863	Alexander Belozerov
АС	1864-65	Aggei Svechin
НФ	1864-82	Nikolai Follendorf
СШ	1865-66	Sergei Shostak
ДС	1882-83	Dmitri Sabaneev
Initials	**Years**	**Mintmaster**
АГ	1883-99	Appolon Grasgov
ЭБ	1899-1913	Elikum Babayantz
ФЗ	1899-1901	Felix Zaleman

MONETARY SYSTEM

1/4 Kopek = Polushka ПОЛУШКА
1/2 Kopek = Denga, Denezhka
ДЕНГА, ДЕНЕЖКА

Kopek КОПѢИКА
(2, 3 & 4) Kopeks КОПѢИКИ
(5 and up) Kopeks КОПѢЕКЪ
3 Kopeks = Altyn, Altynnik
АЛТЫНЪ, АЛТЫННИКЪ
10 Kopeks = Grivna, Grivennik
ГРИВНА, ГРИВЕННИКЪ
25 Kopeks = Polupoltina, Polupoltinnik
ПОЛУПОЛТИНА
ПОЛУПОЛТИННИКЪ
50 Kopeks = Poltina, Poltinnik
ПОЛТИНА, ПОЛТИННИКЪ
100 Kopeks = Rouble, Ruble РУБЛЪ
10 Roubles = Imperial ИМПЕРIАЛЪ
10 Roubles = Chervonetz ЧЕРВОНЕЦ

NOTE: Mintage figures for years after 1885 are for fiscal years and may or may not reflect actual rarity, the commemorative silver figures being exceptions.

NOTE: For silver coins with Zlotych and Kopek or Ruble denominations see Poland.

NOTE: For gold coins with Zlotych and Ruble denominations see Poland.

POLUSHKA

(1/4 Kopek)

NOTE: Polushka dated 1801 #C92.2 previously listed here is now recognized as Novodel #N340.

STANDARD COINAGE

C# 111.1 POLUSHKA (1/4 Kopek)

3.0000 g., Copper **Ruler:** Alexander I

Date	Mintage	VG	F	VF	XF	Unc
1803EM	12,000	15.00	30.00	60.00	120	—

C# 111.2 POLUSHKA (1/4 Kopek)

3.0000 g., Copper **Ruler:** Alexander I

Date	Mintage	VG	F	VF	XF	Unc
1804KM	—	20.00	40.00	80.00	160	—
1805KM	—	20.00	40.00	80.00	160	—
1807KM	—	20.00	40.00	80.00	160	—

C# 142.3 POLUSHKA (1/4 Kopek)

3.0000 g., Copper **Ruler:** Nicholas I

Date	Mintage	VG	F	VF	XF	Unc
1839CM	450,000	12.50	25.00	50.00	100	—
1840CM	2,573,000	4.00	7.50	15.00	30.00	—
1841CM	3,571,000	4.00	7.50	15.00	30.00	—
1842CM	3,960,000	4.00	7.50	15.00	30.00	—
1843CM	2,005,999	4.00	7.50	15.00	30.00	—
1844CM	3,400,000	4.00	7.50	15.00	30.00	—
1845CM	3,000,000	4.00	7.50	15.00	30.00	—
1846CM	3,000,000	4.00	7.50	15.00	30.00	—

C# 142.1 POLUSHKA (1/4 Kopek)

3.0000 g., Copper **Ruler:** Nicholas I

Date	Mintage	VG	F	VF	XF	Unc
1840EM	10,793,000	2.00	4.00	8.00	20.00	—
1841EM	3,230,000	2.00	4.00	8.00	20.00	—
1842EM	1,600,000	2.00	4.00	8.00	20.00	—
1843EM	1,664,000	2.00	4.00	8.00	20.00	—

C# 142.2 POLUSHKA (1/4 Kopek)

3.0000 g., Copper **Ruler:** Nicholas I

Date	Mintage	VG	F	VF	XF	Unc
1840СПМ	6,400,000	4.00	7.50	15.00	30.00	—
1841СПМ	6,400,000	3.00	6.00	12.00	24.00	—
1842СПМ	12,800,000	3.00	6.00	12.00	24.00	—

C# 147.1 POLUSHKA (1/4 Kopek)

3.0000 g., Copper **Ruler:** Nicholas I

Date	Mintage	VG	F	VF	XF	Unc
1850EM	5,184,000	1.50	3.00	5.00	10.00	—
1851/0EM	7,776,000	2.00	4.00	7.00	15.00	—
1851EM	Inc. above	1.50	3.00	5.00	10.00	—
1852EM	1,178,000	1.50	3.00	5.00	10.00	—
1853EM	5,382,000	1.50	3.00	5.00	10.00	—
1854/3EM	4,538,000	2.00	4.00	7.00	15.00	—
1854EM	Inc. above	1.50	3.00	5.00	10.00	—
1855EM	6,442,000	3.00	6.00	13.00	25.00	—

C# 147.3 POLUSHKA (1/4 Kopek)

3.0000 g., Copper **Ruler:** Nicholas I

Date	Mintage	VG	F	VF	XF	Unc
1850BM	—	7.00	12.00	25.00	50.00	—
1851BM	80,000	7.00	12.00	25.00	50.00	—
1852BM	80,000	7.00	12.00	25.00	50.00	—
1853BM	40,000	7.00	12.00	25.00	50.00	—

Y# 1.2 POLUSHKA (1/4 Kopek)

3.0000 g., Copper **Ruler:** Alexander II

Date	Mintage	F	VF	XF	Unc	BU
1855BM	40,000	7.00	15.00	30.00	60.00	—
1860BM	—	60.00	120	200	300	—

Y# 1.1 POLUSHKA (1/4 Kopek)

3.0000 g., Copper **Ruler:** Alexander II **Note:** Plain border.

Date	Mintage	F	VF	XF	Unc	BU
1855EM	6,422,000	2.00	4.00	8.00	20.00	—
1856EM	6,000,000	2.00	4.00	8.00	20.00	—
1857EM	6,000,000	2.00	4.00	8.00	20.00	—
1858EM	6,970,000	2.00	4.00	8.00	20.00	—
1859EM	3,834,000	2.00	4.00	8.00	20.00	—

Y# 1.3 POLUSHKA (1/4 Kopek)

3.0000 g., Copper **Ruler:** Alexander II **Note:** Toothed border.

Date	Mintage	F	VF	XF	Unc	BU
1858EM Rare	—	—	—	—	—	—
1859EM	—	2.00	4.00	8.00	20.00	—
1860EM	—	60.00	120	200	300	—
1861EM	192,000	3.00	6.00	12.00	25.00	—
1862EM	992,000	2.00	4.00	8.00	20.00	—
1863EM	300,000	4.00	8.00	15.00	30.00	—
1864EM	403,000	4.00	8.00	15.00	30.00	—
1865EM	122,000	2.00	4.00	8.00	20.00	—
1866EM	326,000	2.00	4.00	8.00	20.00	—
1867EM	832,000	10.00	20.00	40.00	80.00	—

Y# 1.4 POLUSHKA (1/4 Kopek)

3.0000 g., Copper **Ruler:** Alexander II

Date	Mintage	F	VF	XF	Unc	BU
1861BM	3,160,000	3.00	6.00	15.00	35.00	—

Y# 7.1 POLUSHKA (1/4 Kopek)

3.0000 g., Copper **Ruler:** Alexander II

Date	Mintage	F	VF	XF	Unc	BU
1867EM	—	10.00	17.00	35.00	70.00	—
Note: Mintage included in Y#1.3						
1868EM	700,000	2.00	5.00	10.00	20.00	—
1869EM	615,000	2.00	5.00	10.00	20.00	—
1870EM	435,000	2.00	5.00	10.00	20.00	—
1871EM	155,000	2.00	5.00	10.00	20.00	—
18721EM	540,000	2.00	5.00	10.00	20.00	—
1873EM	823,000	2.00	5.00	10.00	20.00	—
1874EM	340,000	2.00	5.00	10.00	20.00	—
1875EM	300,000	1.25	2.50	5.00	10.00	—

Y# 7.2 POLUSHKA (1/4 Kopek)

3.0000 g., Copper **Ruler:** Alexander II

Date	Mintage	F	VF	XF	Unc	BU
1867СПБ	—	3.00	6.00	12.00	25.00	—
1868СПБ	60,000	3.00	6.00	12.00	25.00	—
1869СПБ	92,000	3.00	6.00	12.00	25.00	—
1870СПБ	20,000	3.50	7.50	15.00	30.00	—
1871СПБ Rare	—	—	—	—	—	—
1876СПБ	800,000	1.25	2.50	5.00	15.00	—
1877СПБ	720,000	1.25	2.50	5.00	15.00	—
1878СПБ	1,100,000	1.25	2.50	5.00	15.00	—
1879СПБ	280,000	1.50	3.00	6.00	15.00	—
1880СПБ	180,000	7.00	12.00	25.00	50.00	—
1881СПБ	60,000	3.00	5.00	9.00	20.00	—

Y# 29 POLUSHKA (1/4 Kopek)

3.0000 g., Copper **Ruler:** Alexander II

Date	Mintage	F	VF	XF	Unc	BU
1881СПБ	200,000	2.50	5.00	10.00	20.00	—
1882СПБ	60,000	2.50	5.00	10.00	20.00	—
1883СПБ	240,000	1.50	3.00	6.00	12.00	—
1884СПБ	140,000	2.50	4.00	8.00	20.00	—
1885СПБ	480,000	1.50	3.00	6.00	12.00	—
1886СПБ	1,060,000	1.25	2.50	5.00	10.00	—
1887СПБ	1,000,000	1.25	2.50	5.00	10.00	—
1888СПБ	200,000	1.50	3.00	6.00	12.00	—
1889СПБ	181,000	3.00	5.00	10.00	30.00	—
1890СПБ	Inc. above	1.50	3.00	6.00	12.00	—
1891СПБ	400,000	1.50	3.00	6.00	12.00	—
1892СПБ	918,000	1.25	2.50	5.00	12.00	—
1893СПБ	740,000	1.25	2.50	5.00	12.00	—

Y# 47.1 POLUSHKA (1/4 Kopek)

3.0000 g., Copper

Date	Mintage	F	VF	XF	Unc	BU
1894СПБ	—	50.00	100	300	500	—
1895СПБ	60,000	2.50	5.00	10.00	20.00	—
1896СПБ	5,960,000	0.50	1.00	2.00	7.00	—
1897СПБ	3,040,000	0.50	1.00	2.00	7.00	—
1898СПБ	8,000,000	0.50	1.00	2.00	7.00	—
1899СПБ	8,000,000	0.50	1.00	2.00	7.00	—
1900СПБ	4,000,000	0.50	1.00	2.00	7.00	—
Common date Proof	—	Value: 125				

C# 116.4 1/2 KOPEK

6.5000 g., Copper **Ruler:** Alexander I

Date	Mintage	VG	F	VF	XF	Unc
1810ИМ ФГ	26,000	25.00	50.00	100	200	—
1810ИМ МК	Inc. above	3.50	7.00	15.00	30.00	—
1811ИМ МК	160,000	2.50	5.00	10.00	20.00	—
1812ИМ ПС	510,000	2.50	5.00	10.00	20.00	—
1813ИМ ПС	1,220,000	2.50	5.00	10.00	20.00	—
1814ИМ ПС	2,250,000	2.50	5.00	10.00	20.00	—
1814ИМ СП	Inc. above	2.50	5.00	10.00	20.00	—

C# 116.6 1/2 KOPEK

6.5000 g., Copper **Ruler:** Alexander I

Date	Mintage	VG	F	VF	XF	Unc
1810СПБ ФГ	—	6.00	12.00	25.00	50.00	—
1811СПБ МК	75,000	3.00	6.00	12.00	25.00	—
1812СПБ ПС	—	25.00	50.00	100	200	—

C# 116.5 1/2 KOPEK

6.5000 g., Copper **Ruler:** Alexander I

Date	Mintage	VG	F	VF	XF	Unc
1812KM AM	—	4.00	8.00	15.00	30.00	—
1813KM AM	—	4.00	8.00	15.00	30.00	—
1814KM AM	—	4.00	8.00	15.00	30.00	—
1815KM AM	—	4.00	8.00	15.00	30.00	—
1816KM AM	—	4.00	8.00	15.00	30.00	—
1817KM AM	—	4.00	8.00	15.00	30.00	—

Y# 48.1 1/2 KOPEK

4.0000 g., Copper

Date	Mintage	F	VF	XF	Unc	BU
1894СПБ	—	—	—	—	—	—
1895СПБ	2,992,000	—	—	—	—	—
1896СПБ	1,340,000	—	—	—	—	—
1897СПБ	60,000,000	—	—	—	—	—
1898СПБ	76,000,000	—	—	—	—	—
1899СПБ	76,000,000	—	—	—	—	—
1900СПБ	36,000,000	—	—	—	—	—
Common date Proof	—	Value: 125				

C# 93.2 DENGA (1/2 Kopek)
6.5000 g., Copper **Ruler:** Paul I **Obv:** Monogram **Rev:** Value, date

Date	Mintage	VG	F	VF	XF	Unc
1801EM	26,000	7.50	15.00	30.00	60.00	—

C# 112.1 DENGA (1/2 Kopek)
6.5000 g., Copper **Ruler:** Alexander I

Date	Mintage	VG	F	VF	XF	Unc
1804EM Rare	20	—	—	—	—	—
1805EM	40,000	50.00	100	175	225	—
1808EM Rare	—	—	—	—	—	—
1810EM Rare	—	—	—	—	—	—

C# 112.2 DENGA (1/2 Kopek)
6.5000 g., Copper **Ruler:** Alexander I

Date	Mintage	VG	F	VF	XF	Unc
1804KM	—	40.00	80.00	150	300	—
1805KM	—	40.00	80.00	150	300	—
1807KM	—	40.00	80.00	150	300	—

C# 116.3 DENGA (1/2 Kopek)
6.5000 g., Copper **Ruler:** Alexander I **Obv:** Type 3 eagle

Date	Mintage	VG	F	VF	XF	Unc
1810EM HM Rare	—	—	—	—	—	—
1811EM HM	135,000	3.75	7.50	15.00	30.00	—
1811EM HM Reeded edge	Inc. above	3.75	7.50	15.00	30.00	—
1813EM HM	24,000	4.00	8.00	15.00	30.00	—
1815EM HM	59,000	4.00	8.00	15.00	30.00	—
1818EM HM	23,410,000	2.00	4.00	8.00	15.00	—
1819EM HM	1,360,000	2.00	4.00	8.00	15.00	—
1822EM ФГ	—	25.00	50.00	100	200	—
1825EM ИК	555,000	3.00	6.00	12.00	25.00	—
1827EM ИК	2,165,000	3.00	6.00	12.00	25.00	—
1828EM ИК	—	3.00	6.00	12.00	25.00	—

C# 116.2 DENGA (1/2 Kopek)
6.5000 g., Copper **Ruler:** Alexander I **Obv:** Type 2 eagle

Date	Mintage	VG	F	VF	XF	Unc
1811ПБ	—	5.00	10.00	20.00	40.00	—

C# 135 DENGA (1/2 Kopek)
6.5000 g., Copper **Ruler:** Nicholas I **Note:** Prev. KM#135.2.

Date	Mintage	VG	F	VF	XF	Unc
1828СПБ	—	25.00	50.00	100	200	—

C# 143.4 DENGA (1/2 Kopek)
4.0000 g., Copper **Ruler:** Nicholas I

Date	Mintage	VG	F	VF	XF	Unc
1839CM	454,000	4.00	8.00	15.00	30.00	—
1840CM	2,560,000	2.00	4.00	8.00	15.00	—
1841CM	3,542,000	2.00	4.00	8.00	15.00	—
1842CM	3,960,000	2.00	4.00	8.00	15.00	—
1843CM	2,006,000	2.00	4.00	8.00	15.00	—
1844CM	3,400,000	2.00	4.00	8.00	15.00	—
1845CM	3,000,000	2.00	4.00	8.00	15.00	—
1846CM	3,000,000	2.00	4.00	8.00	15.00	—
1847CM	2,532,000	2.00	4.00	8.00	15.00	—

C# 143.1 DENGA (1/2 Kopek)
4.0000 g., Copper **Ruler:** Nicholas I

Date	Mintage	VG	F	VF	XF	Unc
1840EM	10,999,000	2.00	4.00	8.00	15.00	—
1841EM	3,384,000	2.00	4.00	8.00	15.00	—
1842EM	3,600,000	2.00	4.00	8.00	15.00	—
1843EM	2,580,000	2.00	4.00	8.00	15.00	—

C# 143.2 DENGA (1/2 Kopek)
4.0000 g., Copper **Ruler:** Nicholas I

Date	Mintage	VG	F	VF	XF	Unc
1840СПБ	—	6.00	12.00	25.00	50.00	—

C# 143.3 DENGA (1/2 Kopek)
4.0000 g., Copper **Ruler:** Nicholas I

Date	Mintage	VG	F	VF	XF	Unc
1840СПМ	6,400,000	2.00	4.00	8.00	15.00	—
1841СПМ	6,400,000	2.00	4.00	8.00	15.00	—
1842СПМ	12,800,000	2.00	4.00	8.00	15.00	—

C# 143.5 DENGA (1/2 Kopek)
4.0000 g., Copper **Ruler:** Nicholas I

Date	Mintage	VG	F	VF	XF	Unc
1848MW	87,000	30.00	60.00	120	225	—

C# 148.1 DENGA (1/2 Kopek)
4.0000 g., Copper **Ruler:** Nicholas I

Date	Mintage	VG	F	VF	XF	Unc
1850EM	3,562,000	1.00	2.00	4.00	8.00	—
1851EM	6,426,000	1.00	2.00	4.00	8.00	—
1852EM	14,672,000	1.00	2.00	4.00	8.00	—
1853EM	12,243,000	1.00	2.00	4.00	8.00	—
1854/3EM	13,754,000	1.25	2.50	5.00	10.00	—
1854EM	Inc. above	1.00	2.00	4.00	8.00	—
1855EM	20,510,000	1.50	3.00	6.00	12.00	—

C# 148.3 DENGA (1/2 Kopek)
4.0000 g., Copper **Ruler:** Nicholas I

Date	Mintage	VG	F	VF	XF	Unc
1850BM	1,840,000	2.00	4.00	8.00	15.00	—
1851BM	1,200,000	2.00	4.00	8.00	15.00	—
1852BM	1,231,000	2.00	4.00	8.00	15.00	—
1853BM	804,000	2.00	4.00	8.00	15.00	—
1854BM	352,000	2.00	4.00	8.00	15.00	—
1855BM	6,380,000	4.00	8.00	15.00	30.00	—

Y# 2.2 DENGA (1/2 Kopek)
4.0000 g., Copper **Ruler:** Alexander II

Date	Mintage	F	VF	XF	Unc	BU
1855BM	6,380,000	5.00	10.00	20.00	40.00	—
1856BM	4,278,000	5.00	10.00	20.00	40.00	—
1857BM	1,909,000	5.00	10.00	20.00	40.00	—
1858BM	311,000	5.00	10.00	20.00	40.00	—
1859BM	3,719,000	5.00	10.00	20.00	40.00	—
1860BM	1,861,000	4.00	8.00	16.00	35.00	—

Y# 2.1 DENGA (1/2 Kopek)
4.0000 g., Copper **Ruler:** Alexander II **Note:** Plain border.

Date	Mintage	F	VF	XF	Unc	BU
1855EM	—	2.00	4.00	8.00	20.00	—
Note: Mintage included in C#148.1						
1856EM	6,000,000	2.00	4.00	8.00	20.00	—
1857EM	6,000,000	2.00	4.00	8.00	20.00	—
1858EM	11,147,000	2.00	4.00	8.00	20.00	—
1859EM	5,871,000	2.00	4.00	8.00	20.00	—

Y# 2.3 DENGA (1/2 Kopek)
4.0000 g., Copper **Ruler:** Alexander II **Note:** Toothed border.

Date	Mintage	F	VF	XF	Unc	BU
1859EM	—	2.00	4.00	8.00	20.00	—
1860EM	2,838,000	2.00	5.00	10.00	20.00	—
1861EM	2,277,000	2.00	5.00	10.00	20.00	—
1862EM	3,072,000	2.00	5.00	10.00	20.00	—
1863EM	1,011,000	2.00	5.00	10.00	20.00	—
1864EM	1,116,000	3.00	6.00	12.00	30.00	—
1865EM	560,000	50.00	100	200	300	—
1866EM	333,000	4.00	8.00	15.00	40.00	—
1867EM	390,000	8.00	15.00	30.00	70.00	—

Y# 2.4 DENGA (1/2 Kopek)
4.0000 g., Copper **Ruler:** Alexander II

Date	Mintage	F	VF	XF	Unc	BU
1861BM	2,819,000	4.00	8.00	15.00	30.00	—
1862BM	1,036,000	4.00	8.00	15.00	30.00	—
1863BM	2,400,000	6.00	12.50	25.00	50.00	—

Y# 8.1 DENGA (1/2 Kopek)
4.0000 g., Copper **Ruler:** Alexander II

Date	Mintage	F	VF	XF	Unc	BU
1867EM	—	7.00	15.00	30.00	60.00	—
Note: Mintage included in Y#2.3						
1868EM	1,190,000	1.50	3.00	6.00	12.00	—
1869EM	593,000	1.50	3.00	6.00	12.00	—
1870EM	510,000	2.00	4.00	8.00	15.00	—
1871EM	223,000	1.50	3.00	6.00	12.00	—
1872EM	365,000	1.50	3.00	6.00	12.00	—
1873EM	963,000	1.50	3.00	6.00	12.00	—
1874EM	300,000	1.50	3.00	6.00	12.00	—
1875EM	321,000	3.00	6.00	12.00	25.00	—

Y# 8.2 DENGA (1/2 Kopek)
4.0000 g., Copper **Ruler:** Alexander II

Date	Mintage	F	VF	XF	Unc	BU
1867СПБ	—	5.00	10.00	20.00	40.00	—
1868СПБ	60,000	3.00	6.00	12.00	25.00	—
1869СПБ	145,000	2.00	4.50	9.00	17.50	—
1870СПБ	25,000	5.00	10.00	20.00	40.00	—
1871СПБ Rare	—	—	—	—	—	—
1876СПБ	770,000	1.00	2.25	4.50	9.00	—
1877СПБ	1,290,000	1.00	2.25	4.50	9.00	—
1878СПБ	1,120,000	1.00	2.25	4.50	9.00	—
1879СПБ	740,000	1.00	2.25	4.50	9.00	—
1880СПБ	1,260,000	1.00	2.25	4.50	9.00	—
1881СПБ	420,000	1.00	2.25	4.50	9.00	—

Y# 30 DENGA (1/2 Kopek)
4.0000 g., Copper **Ruler:** Alexander III

Date	Mintage	F	VF	XF	Unc	BU
1881СПБ	440,000	5.00	10.00	20.00	40.00	—
1882СПБ	350,000	1.00	2.25	4.50	9.00	—
1883СПБ	540,000	1.00	2.25	4.50	9.00	—
1884СПБ	550,000	1.00	2.25	4.50	9.00	—
1885СПБ	680,000	1.00	2.25	4.50	9.00	—
1886СПБ	560,000	1.00	2.25	4.50	9.00	—
1887СПБ	600,000	1.00	2.25	4.50	9.00	—
1888СПБ	610,000	1.00	2.25	4.50	9.00	—
1889СПБ	4,650,000	1.00	2.00	4.00	7.50	—
1890СПБ	2,040,000	1.00	2.00	4.00	7.50	—
1892СПБ	2,271,000	1.00	2.00	4.00	7.50	—
1893СПБ	3,900,000	1.00	2.00	4.00	7.50	—
1894СПБ	—	1.00	2.00	4.00	7.50	—

C# 94.2 KOPEK
4.0000 g., Copper **Ruler:** Paul I **Obv:** Monogram **Rev:** Value, date

Date	Mintage	VG	F	VF	XF	Unc
1801EM	1,708,000	3.00	6.00	12.00	25.00	—

C# 113.1 KOPEK
4.0000 g., Copper **Ruler:** Alexander I

Date	Mintage	VG	F	VF	XF	Unc
1804EM Rare	20	—	—	—	—	—
1805EM	114,000	20.00	40.00	80.00	150	—

C# 113.2 KOPEK
4.0000 g., Copper **Ruler:** Alexander I

Date	Mintage	VG	F	VF	XF	Unc
1804KM	—	20.00	40.00	80.00	160	—
1805KM	—	25.00	50.00	100	200	—
1807KM	—	25.00	50.00	100	200	—

C# 117.2 KOPEK
4.0000 g., Copper **Ruler:** Alexander I **Obv:** Type 2 eagle

Date	Mintage	VG	F	VF	XF	Unc
1810 Rare	—	—	—	—	—	—
1811 ПБ Rare	—	—	—	—	—	—

C# 117.6 KOPEK
4.0000 g., Copper **Ruler:** Alexander I

Date	Mintage	VG	F	VF	XF	Unc
1810СПБ ФГ	93,000	25.00	50.00	100	200	—
1810СПБ МК	Inc. above	25.00	50.00	100	200	—
1811/0СПБ МК	260,000	2.50	3.00	10.00	20.00	—
1811СПБ МК	Inc. above	1.50	3.00	6.00	10.00	—
1828СПБ	—	25.00	50.00	100	225	—

C# 117.3 KOPEK
4.0000 g., Copper **Ruler:** Alexander I **Obv:** Type 3 eagle **Note:** Varieties exist.

Date	Mintage	VG	F	VF	XF	Unc
1810ЕМ НМ Rare	—	—	—	—	—	—
1711ЕМ НМ Rare	—	—	—	—	—	—
1811ЕМ НМ	1,926,000	3.00	6.00	12.00	25.00	—
1813ЕМ НМ	30,000	25.00	50.00	100	200	—
1815ЕМ НМ	31,000	25.00	50.00	100	200	—
1818ЕМ НМ	55,750,000	3.00	6.00	12.00	25.00	—
1819ЕМ НМ	35,030,000	3.00	6.00	12.00	25.00	—
1821ЕМ НМ	10,160,000	3.00	6.00	12.00	25.00	—
1822ЕМ НМ	10,265,000	3.00	6.00	12.00	25.00	—
1823ЕМ НМ	10,350,000	3.00	6.00	12.00	25.00	—
1824ЕМ НМ	—	3.00	6.00	12.00	25.00	—
1825ЕМ НМ	—	3.00	6.00	12.00	25.00	—
1827ЕМ ИК	2,646,000	3.00	6.00	12.00	25.00	—
1828ЕМ ИК	43,015,000	3.00	6.00	12.00	25.00	—
1829ЕМ ИК	48,215,000	3.00	6.00	12.00	25.00	—
1830ЕМ ИК	2,100,000	3.00	6.00	12.00	25.00	—

C# 117.4 KOPEK
4.0000 g., Copper **Ruler:** Alexander I

Date	Mintage	VG	F	VF	XF	Unc
1811ИМ МК	490,000	1.50	3.00	7.00	15.00	—
1812ИМ ПС	1,040,000	1.50	3.00	7.00	15.00	—
1813ИМ ПС	1,980,000	1.50	3.00	7.00	15.00	—
1814ИМ ПС	3,740,000	1.50	3.00	7.00	15.00	—
1820ИМ ЯВ	—	1.50	3.00	7.00	15.00	—
1821ИМ ЯВ	—	1.50	3.00	7.00	15.00	—

C# 117.5 KOPEK
4.0000 g., Copper **Ruler:** Alexander I

Date	Mintage	VG	F	VF	XF	Unc
1812КМ АМ	—	2.50	5.00	10.00	20.00	—
1813КМ АМ	—	2.50	5.00	10.00	20.00	—
1814КМ АМ	—	2.50	5.00	10.00	20.00	—
1815КМ АМ	—	2.50	5.00	10.00	20.00	—
1816КМ АМ	—	2.50	5.00	10.00	20.00	—
1817КМ АМ	—	2.50	5.00	10.00	20.00	—
1818КМ АМ	—	2.50	5.00	10.00	20.00	—

Date	Mintage	VG	F	VF	XF	Unc
1818КМ АМ	—	2.50	5.00	10.00	20.00	—
1819КМ АМ	—	2.50	5.00	10.00	20.00	—
1820КМ АМ	—	2.50	5.00	10.00	20.00	—
1821КМ АМ	—	2.50	5.00	10.00	20.00	—
1822КМ АМ	—	2.50	5.00	10.00	20.00	—
1823КМ АМ	—	2.50	5.00	10.00	20.00	—
1824КМ АМ	—	2.50	5.00	10.00	20.00	—
1825КМ АМ	—	2.50	5.00	10.00	20.00	—
1826КМ АМ	6,250,000	2.50	5.00	10.00	20.00	—
1827КМ АМ	6,250,000	2.50	5.00	10.00	20.00	—
1828КМ АМ	5,000,000	2.50	5.00	10.00	20.00	—
1829КМ АМ	5,000,000	2.50	5.00	10.00	20.00	—
1830КМ АМ	5,000,000	2.50	5.00	10.00	20.00	—

C# 138.1 KOPEK
4.0000 g., Copper **Ruler:** Nicholas I

Date	Mintage	VG	F	VF	XF	Unc
1831ЕМ ФХ	13,050,000	1.50	3.00	6.00	12.00	—
1832ЕМ ФХ	3,400,000	1.50	3.00	6.00	12.00	—
1833ЕМ ФХ	2,883,000	1.50	3.00	6.00	12.00	—
1834/3ЕМ ФХ	5,020,000	2.00	4.00	8.00	15.00	—
1834ЕМ ФХ	Inc. above	1.50	3.00	6.00	12.00	—
1835ЕМ ФХ	6,570,000	1.50	3.00	6.00	12.00	—
1836ЕМ ФХ	2,100,000	1.50	3.00	6.00	12.00	—
1837ЕМ ФХ	4,890,000	1.50	3.00	6.00	12.00	—
1837ЕМ ФХ	Inc. above	1.50	3.00	6.00	12.00	—
1838/7ЕМ ФХ	1,042,999	25.00	50.00	100	200	—

C# 138.3 KOPEK
4.0000 g., Copper **Ruler:** Nicholas I

Date	Mintage	VG	F	VF	XF	Unc
1831СМ	2,000,000	2.50	5.00	10.00	20.00	—
1832СМ	2,000,000	2.50	5.00	10.00	20.00	—
1833СМ	45,000	20.00	40.00	80.00	120	—
1834СМ	2,000,000	2.50	5.00	10.00	20.00	—
1835СМ	2,000,000	7.00	12.00	25.00	50.00	—
1836СМ	100,000	2.50	5.00	10.00	20.00	—
1837СМ	1,000,000	2.50	5.00	10.00	20.00	—
1838СМ	1,800,000	2.50	5.00	10.00	20.00	—
1839СМ	20,000	20.00	40.00	80.00	120	—

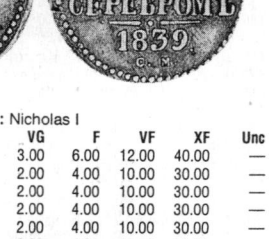

C# 144.4 KOPEK
4.0000 g., Copper **Ruler:** Nicholas I

Date	Mintage	VG	F	VF	XF	Unc
1839СМ	795,000	3.00	6.00	12.00	40.00	—
1840СМ	4,500,000	2.00	4.00	10.00	30.00	—
1841СМ	6,120,000	2.00	4.00	10.00	30.00	—
1842СМ	7,002,000	2.00	4.00	10.00	30.00	—
1843СМ	3,498,000	2.00	4.00	10.00	30.00	—
1844СМ	5,250,000	2.00	4.00	10.00	30.00	—
1845СМ	5,250,000	2.00	4.00	10.00	30.00	—
1846СМ	5,250,000	2.00	4.00	10.00	30.00	—
1847СМ	2,368,000	4.00	8.00	18.00	65.00	—

C# 144.3 KOPEK
4.0000 g., Copper **Ruler:** Nicholas I

Date	Mintage	VG	F	VF	XF	Unc
1840СПМ	Inc. above	1.50	3.00	7.50	22.50	—
1841СПМ	11,200,000	1.50	3.00	7.50	22.50	—
1842СПМ	11,200,000	1.50	3.00	7.50	22.50	—
1843СПМ	11,200,000	1.50	3.00	7.50	22.50	—

C# 144.1 KOPEK
4.0000 g., Copper **Ruler:** Nicholas I

Date	Mintage	VG	F	VF	XF	Unc
1840ЕМ	20,778,000	1.50	3.00	7.50	22.50	—
1841ЕМ	19,341,000	1.50	3.00	7.50	22.50	—
1842ЕМ	13,851,000	1.50	3.00	7.50	22.50	—
1843ЕМ	12,520,000	1.50	3.00	7.50	22.50	—
1844ЕМ	—	1.50	3.00	7.50	22.50	—

C# 144.2 KOPEK
4.0000 g., Copper **Ruler:** Nicholas I

Date	Mintage	VG	F	VF	XF	Unc
1840СПБ	11,200,000	7.00	15.00	30.00	60.00	—

C# 149.1 KOPEK
4.0000 g., Copper **Ruler:** Nicholas I

Date	Mintage	VG	F	VF	XF	Unc
1850ЕМ	1,843,000	0.50	1.00	3.00	7.00	—
1851ЕМ	4,790,000	0.50	1.00	3.00	7.00	—
1852ЕМ	14,006,000	0.50	1.00	3.00	7.00	—
1853ЕМ	21,328,000	0.50	1.00	3.00	7.00	—
1854ЕМ	22,397,000	0.50	1.00	3.00	7.00	—
1855ЕМ	24,594,000	1.00	2.00	4.00	10.00	—

C# 149.3 KOPEK
4.0000 g., Copper **Ruler:** Nicholas I

Date	Mintage	VG	F	VF	XF	Unc
1850ВМ	—	2.00	4.00	8.00	15.00	—
1851ВМ	797,000	2.00	4.00	8.00	15.00	—
1852ВМ	311,000	2.00	4.00	8.00	15.00	—
1853ВМ	391,000	2.00	4.00	8.00	15.00	—
1855ВМ	—	2.00	4.00	8.00	15.00	—
Note: Mintage included in C#149.1						
1856ВМ Error, rare	—	—	—	—	—	—

Y# 3.1 KOPEK
4.0000 g., Copper **Ruler:** Alexander II **Obv:** Crowned small A **Edge:** Plain

Date	Mintage	F	VF	XF	Unc	BU
1854ЕМ Error, rare	—	—	—	—	—	—
1855ЕМ	—	1.00	2.00	6.00	15.00	—
Note: Mintage included in C#149.1						
1856ЕМ	10,641,000	1.00	2.00	6.00	15.00	—
1857ЕМ	5,659,000	1.00	2.00	6.00	15.00	—
1858ЕМ	13,731,000	1.00	2.00	6.00	15.00	—
1859ЕМ	11,059,000	1.00	2.00	6.00	15.00	—

Y# 3.2 KOPEK
4.0000 g., Copper **Ruler:** Alexander II **Obv:** Crowned tall A **Rev:** Large date

Date	Mintage	F	VF	XF	Unc	BU
1855ВМ	—	2.00	4.00	12.00	25.00	—
Note: Mintage included in C#149.3						
1856ВМ	3,337,000	2.00	4.00	12.00	25.00	—
1858ВМ	1,528,000	2.00	4.00	12.00	25.00	—
1859ВМ	3,109,000	2.00	4.00	12.00	25.00	—
1860ВМ	3,766,000	2.00	4.00	12.00	25.00	—

Y# 3.3 KOPEK
4.0000 g., Copper **Ruler:** Alexander II **Obv:** Crowned small A **Note:** Toothed border.

Date	Mintage	F	VF	XF	Unc	BU
1859ЕМ	—	1.00	2.00	4.00	10.00	—
1860ЕМ	8,306,000	1.00	2.00	4.00	10.00	—
1861ЕМ	10,130,000	1.00	2.00	4.00	10.00	—
1862ЕМ	10,165,000	1.00	2.00	4.00	10.00	—
1863ЕМ	6,544,000	1.00	2.00	4.00	10.00	—
1864/2ЕМ	4,400,000	1.50	3.00	6.00	15.00	—
1864ЕМ	Inc. above	1.00	2.00	4.00	10.00	—
1865ЕМ	14,230,000	1.00	2.00	4.00	10.00	—
1866ЕМ	12,304,000	1.00	2.00	4.00	10.00	—
1867ЕМ	5,851,000	5.00	10.00	20.00	40.00	—

Y# 3.4 KOPEK

4.0000 g., Copper **Ruler:** Alexander II **Obv:** Crowned tall A

Date	Mintage	F	VF	XF	Unc	BU
1861BM	1,800,000	2.50	5.00	10.00	20.00	—
1862BM	2,100,000	2.50	5.00	10.00	20.00	—
1863BM	2,854,000	2.50	5.00	10.00	20.00	—
1864BM	1,046,000	2.50	5.00	10.00	20.00	—

Y# 9.2 KOPEK

4.0000 g., Copper

Date	Mintage	F	VF	XF	Unc	BU
1867СПБ	Inc. below	2.00	4.00	8.00	20.00	—
1868СПБ	750,000	1.00	2.00	4.00	10.00	—
1869СПБ	739,000	1.00	2.00	4.00	10.00	—
1870СПБ	1,143,000	1.00	2.00	4.00	10.00	—
1871СПБ Rare	—	—	—	—	—	—
1876СПБ	2,930,000	0.50	1.00	2.00	9.00	—
1877СПБ	7,065,000	0.50	1.00	2.00	9.00	—
1878СПБ	8,241,000	0.50	1.00	2.00	9.00	—
1879СПБ	9,045,000	0.50	1.00	2.00	9.00	—
1880СПБ	7,730,000	0.50	1.00	2.00	9.00	—
1881СПБ	8,415,000	0.50	1.00	2.00	9.00	—
1882СПБ	5,685,000	0.50	1.00	2.00	9.00	—
1883СПБ	7,830,000	0.50	1.00	2.00	9.00	—
1884СПБ	2,500,000	0.50	1.00	2.00	9.00	—
1885СПБ	3,400,000	0.50	1.00	2.00	9.00	—
1886СПБ	3,210,000	0.50	1.00	2.00	9.00	—
1887СПБ	6,000,000	0.25	0.50	1.50	8.00	—
1888СПБ	6,000,000	0.25	0.50	1.50	8.00	—
1889СПБ	9,000,000	0.25	0.50	1.50	8.00	—
1890СПБ	6,905,000	0.25	0.50	1.50	8.00	—
1891СПБ	10,875,000	0.25	0.50	1.50	8.00	—
1892СПБ	5,640,000	0.25	0.50	1.50	8.00	—
1893СПБ	13,395,000	0.25	0.50	1.50	8.00	—
1894СПБ	15,490,000	0.25	0.50	1.50	8.00	—
1895СПБ	18,200,000	0.25	0.50	1.50	8.00	—
1896СПБ	22,960,000	0.25	0.50	1.50	8.00	—
1898СПБ	50,000,000	0.25	0.50	1.50	8.00	—
1899СПБ	50,000,000	0.25	0.50	1.50	8.00	—
1900СПБ	30,000,000	0.25	0.50	1.50	8.00	—

Y# 9.1 KOPEK

4.0000 g., Copper **Ruler:** Alexander II

Date	Mintage	F	VF	XF	Unc	BU
1867EM	—	3.00	6.00	12.00	25.00	—
1868EM	6,305,000	0.50	1.00	3.00	10.00	—
1869EM	10,230,000	0.50	1.00	3.00	10.00	—
1870EM	9,875,000	0.50	1.00	3.00	10.00	—
1871EM	2,880,000	0.50	1.00	3.00	10.00	—
1872EM	5,713,000	0.50	1.00	3.00	10.00	—
1873EM	5,213,000	0.50	1.00	3.00	10.00	—
1874EM	5,013,000	0.50	1.00	3.00	10.00	—
1875EM	6,438,000	0.50	1.00	3.00	10.00	—
1876EM	1,755,000	2.00	4.00	7.50	15.00	—

C# 95.3 2 KOPEKS

Copper **Ruler:** Paul I

Date	Mintage	VG	F	VF	XF	Unc
1801EM	27,380,000	4.00	8.00	15.00	30.00	—

C# 95.4 2 KOPEKS

Copper **Ruler:** Paul I

Date	Mintage	VG	F	VF	XF	Unc
1801KM	—	7.50	15.00	30.00	60.00	—

C# 114.1 2 KOPEKS

Copper **Ruler:** Alexander I

Date	Mintage	VG	F	VF	XF	Unc
1802EM	45,798,000	10.00	20.00	40.00	100	—
1803EM	298,000	25.00	50.00	100	200	—
1804EM Rare	—	—	—	—	—	—

C# 114.2 2 KOPEKS

Copper **Ruler:** Alexander I

Date	Mintage	VG	F	VF	XF	Unc
1804KM	—	100	200	400	800	—
1805KM	—	50.00	100	200	400	—
1807KM	—	50.00	100	200	400	—

C# 118.2 2 KOPEKS

Copper **Ruler:** Alexander I **Obv:** Type 2 eagle

Date	Mintage	VG	F	VF	XF	Unc
1810KM	—	4.00	8.00	15.00	30.00	—
1810KM ПБ	—	4.00	8.00	15.00	30.00	—
1811KM ПБ	—	4.00	8.00	15.00	30.00	—
1812KM	—	4.00	8.00	15.00	30.00	—

C# 118.7 2 KOPEKS

Copper **Ruler:** Alexander I

Date	Mintage	VG	F	VF	XF	Unc
1810 MK	—	20.00	40.00	80.00	150	—

Note: The Kolpino mint mark was changed to |J|O in 1810

C# 118.4 2 KOPEKS

Copper **Ruler:** Alexander I

Date	Mintage	VG	F	VF	XF	Unc
1810ИМ МК	—	1.50	3.00	7.00	15.00	—
1811ИМ ПС	Inc. above	1.50	3.00	7.00	15.00	—
1811ИМ МК	—	1.50	3.00	7.00	15.00	—
1812ИМ ПС	—	1.50	3.00	7.00	15.00	—
1813ИМ ПС	—	1.50	3.00	7.00	15.00	—
1814ИМ ПС	—	1.50	3.00	7.00	15.00	—
1814ИМ	—	7.00	12.00	25.00	50.00	—

C# 118.6 2 KOPEKS

Copper **Ruler:** Alexander I

Date	Mintage	VG	F	VF	XF	Unc
1810СПБ ФГ	—	1.50	2.50	5.00	10.00	—
1810СПБ МК	—	1.50	2.50	5.00	10.00	—
1810СПБ ПС	—	3.00	6.00	12.00	25.00	—
1811СПБ МК	—	1.50	2.50	5.00	10.00	—
1811СПБ ПС	—	1.50	2.50	5.00	10.00	—
1812СПБ ПС	—	1.50	2.50	5.00	10.00	—
1813СПБ ПС	—	1.50	2.50	5.00	10.00	—
1814СПБ ПС	—	3.00	6.00	12.00	25.00	—
1818СПБ	—	20.00	40.00	80.00	150	—
1828СПБ	—	25.00	50.00	100	200	—

C# 118.1 2 KOPEKS

Copper **Ruler:** Alexander I **Obv:** Type 1 eagle **Note:** Exists with large and small date.

Date	Mintage	VG	F	VF	XF	Unc
1810EM HM	79,364,000	1.50	2.50	5.00	10.00	—

C# 118.3 2 KOPEKS

Copper **Ruler:** Alexander I **Obv:** Type 3 eagle **Note:** Varieties exist.

Date	Mintage	VG	F	VF	XF	Unc
1810EM HM	129,000,000	2.50	5.00	10.00	20.00	—
1811EM HM Plain edge	Inc. above	2.50	5.00	10.00	20.00	—
1811EM HM Reeded edge	Inc. above	2.50	5.00	10.00	20.00	—
1812EM HM	132,085,000	2.50	5.00	10.00	20.00	—
1812EM HM Inverted 2	Inc. above	2.50	5.00	10.00	20.00	—
1813EM HM	64,980,000	2.50	5.00	10.00	20.00	—
1814EM HM	110,000,000	2.50	5.00	10.00	20.00	—
1815EM HM	44,970,000	2.50	5.00	10.00	20.00	—
1816EM HM	64,150,000	2.50	5.00	10.00	20.00	—
1817EM HM	75,000,000	2.50	5.00	10.00	20.00	—
1818EM HM	60,625,000	2.50	5.00	10.00	20.00	—
1818EM ФГ	Inc. above	2.50	5.00	10.00	20.00	—
1819EM HM	100,468,000	2.50	5.00	10.00	20.00	—
1820EM HM	75,180,000	2.50	5.00	10.00	20.00	—
1821EM HM	55,170,000	2.50	5.00	10.00	20.00	—
1821EM ФГ	Inc. above	2.50	5.00	10.00	20.00	—
1822EM ФГ	44,867,000	2.50	5.00	10.00	20.00	—
1823EM ФГ	44,935,000	2.50	5.00	10.00	20.00	—
1823EM ПГ Rare	Inc. above	—	—	—	—	—
1824EM S\D	36,600,000	2.50	5.00	10.00	20.00	—
1825EM ПГ	73,856,000	2.50	5.00	10.00	20.00	—
1825EM ИШ	Inc. above	2.50	5.00	10.00	20.00	—
1825EM ИК	Inc. above	2.50	5.00	10.00	20.00	—
1826EM ИК	50,450,000	3.00	6.00	12.00	25.00	—
1827EM ИК	34,065,000	3.00	6.00	12.00	25.00	—
1828EM JK	14,475,000	3.00	6.00	12.00	25.00	—
1829EM JK	13,790,000	3.00	6.00	12.00	25.00	—
1830EM JK	15,450,000	3.00	6.00	12.00	25.00	—

C# 118.5 2 KOPEKS

Copper

Date	Mintage	VG	F	VF	XF	Unc
1812KM AM	—	1.50	2.50	5.00	10.00	—
1813KM AM	—	1.50	2.50	5.00	10.00	—
1814KM AM	—	1.50	2.50	5.00	10.00	—
1815KM AM	—	1.50	2.50	5.00	10.00	—
1816KM AM	—	1.50	2.50	5.00	10.00	—
1817KM AM	—	1.50	2.50	5.00	10.00	—
1817KM АБ	—	1.50	2.50	5.00	10.00	—
1818KM ДБ	—	1.50	2.50	5.00	10.00	—
1818KM АД Rare	—	—	—	—	—	—
1819KM АД	—	1.50	2.50	5.00	10.00	—

Date	Mintage	VG	F	VF	XF	Unc
1820КМ АД	—	1.50	2.50	5.00	10.00	—
1821КМ АД	—	1.50	2.50	5.00	10.00	—
1821КМ АМ	—	1.50	2.50	5.00	10.00	—
1822КМ АМ	—	1.50	2.50	5.00	10.00	—
1823КМ АМ	—	1.50	2.50	5.00	10.00	—
1824КМ АМ	—	1.50	2.50	5.00	10.00	—
1825КМ АМ	—	1.50	2.50	5.00	10.00	—
1826КМ АМ	9,375,000	2.50	5.00	10.00	20.00	—
1827КМ АМ	Inc. above	2.50	5.00	10.00	20.00	—
1828КМ АМ	15,000,000	2.50	5.00	10.00	20.00	—
1829КМ АМ	15,000,000	2.50	5.00	10.00	20.00	—
1830КМ АМ	15,000,000	2.50	5.00	10.00	20.00	—

C# 139.1 2 KOPEKS
Copper **Ruler:** Nicholas I

Date	Mintage	VG	F	VF	XF	Unc
1831ЕМ ФХ	—	20.00	40.00	80.00	150	—
1833ЕМ ФХ	261,000	3.00	6.00	12.00	25.00	—
1837ЕМ НА	16,845,000	3.00	6.00	12.00	25.00	—
1838/7ЕМ НА	6,623,000	3.50	7.00	14.00	30.00	—
1838ЕМ НА	Inc. above	3.00	6.00	12.00	25.00	—
1839ЕМ НА	8,250,000	3.00	6.00	12.00	25.00	—

C# 139.3 2 KOPEKS
Copper **Ruler:** Nicholas I

Date	Mintage	VG	F	VF	XF	Unc
1831СМ	1,500,000	2.50	4.50	8.00	15.00	—
1832СМ	1,500,000	2.50	4.50	8.00	15.00	—
1833СМ	539,000	2.50	4.50	8.00	15.00	—
1834СМ	1,500,000	2.50	4.50	8.00	15.00	—
1835СМ	1,500,000	2.50	4.50	8.00	15.00	—
1836СМ	1,350,000	2.50	4.50	8.00	15.00	—
1837СМ	1,000,000	2.50	4.50	8.00	15.00	—
1838СМ	10,500,000	2.50	4.50	8.00	15.00	—
1839СМ	7,073,000	2.50	4.50	8.00	15.00	—

C# 145.4 2 KOPEKS
Copper **Ruler:** Nicholas I

Date	Mintage	VG	F	VF	XF	Unc
1839СМ	341,000	2.00	4.00	8.00	20.00	—
1840СМ	1,929,000	2.00	4.00	8.00	20.00	—
1841СМ	2,636,000	2.00	4.00	8.00	20.00	—
1842СМ	3,000,000	2.00	4.00	8.00	20.00	—
1843СМ	1,500,000	2.00	4.00	8.00	20.00	—
1844СМ	2,250,000	2.00	4.00	8.00	20.00	—
1845СМ	2,250,000	2.00	4.00	8.00	20.00	—
1846СМ	2,250,000	2.00	4.00	8.00	20.00	—
1847СМ	2,209,000	2.00	4.00	8.00	20.00	—

C# 145.1 2 KOPEKS
Copper **Ruler:** Nicholas I

Date	Mintage	VG	F	VF	XF	Unc
1840ЕМ	20,778,000	2.00	4.00	8.00	25.00	—
1841ЕМ	14,999,000	2.00	4.00	8.00	25.00	—
1842ЕМ	12,446,000	2.00	4.00	8.00	25.00	—
1843ЕМ	11,020,000	2.00	4.00	8.00	25.00	—
1844ЕМ	5,500,000	2.00	4.00	8.00	25.00	—

C# 145.2 2 KOPEKS
Copper **Ruler:** Nicholas I

Date	Mintage	VG	F	VF	XF	Unc
1840СПБ	—	6.00	12.00	25.00	75.00	—
1841СПБ	—	25.00	50.00	100	200	—

C# 145.3 2 KOPEKS
Copper **Ruler:** Nicholas I

Date	Mintage	VG	F	VF	XF	Unc
1840СПМ	4,800,000	2.00	4.00	8.00	20.00	—
1841СПМ	Inc. above	2.00	4.00	8.00	20.00	—
1842СПМ	4,800,000	2.00	4.00	8.00	20.00	—
1843СПМ	4,800,000	2.00	4.00	8.00	20.00	—

C# 145.5 2 KOPEKS
Copper **Ruler:** Nicholas I

Date	Mintage	VG	F	VF	XF	Unc
1848MW	31,000	20.00	40.00	80.00	150	—

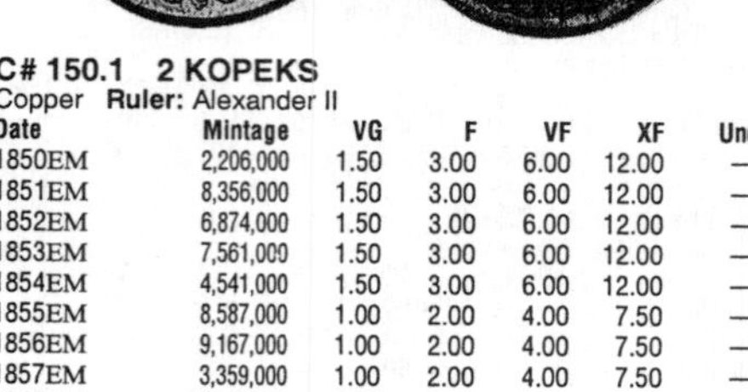

C# 150.1 2 KOPEKS
Copper **Ruler:** Alexander II

Date	Mintage	VG	F	VF	XF	Unc
1850ЕМ	2,206,000	1.50	3.00	6.00	12.00	—
1851ЕМ	8,356,000	1.50	3.00	6.00	12.00	—
1852ЕМ	6,874,000	1.50	3.00	6.00	12.00	—
1853ЕМ	7,561,000	1.50	3.00	6.00	12.00	—
1854ЕМ	4,541,000	1.50	3.00	6.00	12.00	—
1855ЕМ	8,587,000	1.00	2.00	4.00	7.50	—
1856ЕМ	9,167,000	1.00	2.00	4.00	7.50	—
1857ЕМ	3,359,000	1.00	2.00	4.00	7.50	—
1858ЕМ	10,028,000	1.00	2.00	4.00	7.50	—
1859ЕМ	14,772,000	1.00	2.00	4.00	7.50	—

C# 150.3 2 KOPEKS
Copper **Ruler:** Alexander II

Date	Mintage	VG	F	VF	XF	Unc
1850ВМ	—	10.00	20.00	40.00	80.00	—
1851ВМ	298,000	5.00	10.00	20.00	40.00	—
1852ВМ	202,000	5.00	10.00	20.00	40.00	—
1853ВМ Rare	2,642	—	—	—	—	—
1854ВМ	148,000	5.00	10.00	20.00	40.00	—
1855ВМ	1,347,000	2.00	4.00	8.00	15.00	—
1856ВМ	1,190,000	2.00	4.00	8.00	15.00	—
1858ВМ	750,000	2.00	4.00	8.00	15.00	—
1859ВМ	1,595,000	2.00	4.00	8.00	15.00	—
1860ВМ	1,605,000	2.00	4.00	8.00	15.00	—

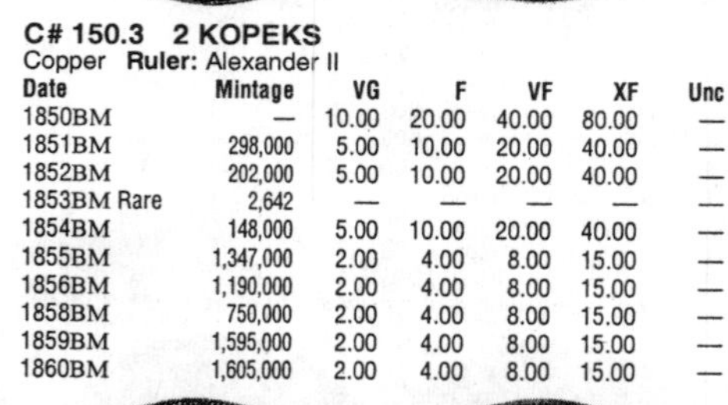

Y# 4a.1 2 KOPEKS
Copper **Ruler:** Alexander II **Obv:** Ribbons added to crown

Date	Mintage	F	VF	XF	Unc	BU
1859ЕМ	14,772,000	1.25	3.00	6.50	8.00	—
1860ЕМ	19,239,000	1.25	3.00	6.50	8.00	—
1861ЕМ	18,547,000	1.25	3.00	6.50	8.00	—
1862ЕМ	16,889,000	1.25	3.00	6.50	8.00	—
1863ЕМ	21,703,000	1.25	3.00	6.50	8.00	—
1864ЕМ	14,175,000	1.25	3.00	6.50	8.00	—
1865ЕМ	26,921,000	1.25	3.00	6.50	8.00	—
1866ЕМ	21,890,000	1.25	3.00	6.50	8.00	—
1867ЕМ	8,970,000	1.25	3.00	6.50	8.00	—

Y# 4a.2 2 KOPEKS
Copper **Ruler:** Alexander II

Date	Mintage	F	VF	XF	Unc	BU
1860ВМ	1,605,000	3.00	6.00	12.00	25.00	—
1861ВМ	586,000	3.00	6.00	12.00	25.00	—
1862ВМ	966,000	3.00	6.00	12.00	25.00	—
1863ВМ	1,739,000	3.00	6.00	12.00	25.00	—

Y# 10.1 2 KOPEKS
Copper **Ruler:** Alexander II

Date	Mintage	F	VF	XF	Unc	BU
1867ЕМ	150,000	5.00	10.00	20.00	40.00	—
1868ЕМ	18,200,000	0.50	1.00	3.00	12.00	—
1869ЕМ	22,174,000	0.50	1.00	3.00	12.00	—
1870ЕМ	21,884,000	0.50	1.00	3.00	12.00	—
1871ЕМ	7,058,000	0.50	1.00	3.00	12.00	—
1872ЕМ	12,734,000	0.50	1.00	3.00	12.00	—
1873ЕМ	7,364,000	0.50	1.00	3.00	12.00	—
1874ЕМ	8,551,000	0.50	1.00	3.00	12.00	—
1875ЕМ	10,451,000	0.50	1.00	3.00	12.00	—
1876ЕМ	2,905,000	0.50	1.00	3.00	12.00	—

Y# 10.2 2 KOPEKS
Copper

Date	Mintage	F	VF	XF	Unc	BU
1867СПБ	Inc. below	3.00	6.00	12.00	25.00	—
1868СПБ	659,000	1.50	3.00	6.00	15.00	—
1869СПБ	643,000	1.50	3.00	6.00	15.00	—
1870СПБ	231,000	2.00	4.00	8.00	20.00	—
1871СПБ Rare	—	—	—	—	—	—
1876СПБ	3,240,000	0.50	1.00	2.50	10.00	—
1877СПБ	5,010,000	0.50	1.00	2.50	10.00	—
1878СПБ	8,093,000	0.50	1.00	2.50	10.00	—
1879СПБ	7,380,000	0.50	1.00	2.50	10.00	—
1880СПБ	6,525,000	0.50	1.00	2.50	10.00	—
1881СПБ	7,299,000	0.50	1.00	2.50	10.00	—
1882СПБ	4,478,000	0.50	1.00	2.50	10.00	—
1883СПБ	6,230,000	0.50	1.00	2.50	10.00	—
1884СПБ	2,625,000	0.50	1.00	2.50	10.00	—
1885СПБ	3,070,000	0.50	1.00	2.50	10.00	—
1886СПБ	3,123,000	0.50	1.00	2.50	10.00	—
1887СПБ	1,725,000	0.50	1.00	2.50	10.00	—
1888СПБ	1,823,000	0.50	1.00	2.50	10.00	—
1889СПБ	2,815,000	0.50	1.00	2.50	10.00	—
1890СПБ	2,538,000	0.50	1.00	2.50	10.00	—
1891СПБ	2,788,000	0.50	1.00	2.50	10.00	—
1892СПБ	918,000	2.00	4.00	8.00	20.00	—
1893СПБ	10,295,000	0.50	1.00	2.00	8.00	—
1894СПБ	8,600,000	0.50	1.00	2.00	8.00	—
1895СПБ	9,122,000	0.50	1.00	2.00	8.00	—
1896СПБ	14,675,000	0.50	1.00	2.00	8.00	—
1897СПБ	9,500,000	0.50	1.00	2.00	8.00	—
1898СПБ	17,500,000	0.50	1.00	2.00	8.00	—
1899СПБ	17,500,000	0.50	1.00	2.00	8.00	—
1900СПБ	20,500,000	0.50	1.00	2.00	8.00	—
Common date Proof	—	Value: 165				

C# 146.4 3 KOPEKS
Copper **Ruler:** Nicholas I

Date	Mintage	VG	F	VF	XF	Unc
1839СМ	142,000	7.00	15.00	30.00	75.00	—
1840СМ	827,000	5.00	10.00	22.00	55.00	—
1841СМ	1,171,000	5.00	10.00	22.00	55.00	—
1842СМ	1,360,000	7.50	15.00	50.00	70.00	—
1843СМ	669,000	5.00	10.00	22.00	55.00	—
1844СМ	1,000,000	5.00	10.00	22.00	55.00	—
1845СМ	1,000,000	5.00	10.00	22.00	55.00	—
1846СМ	1,000,000	5.00	10.00	22.00	55.00	—
1847СМ	1,000,000	6.00	12.00	25.00	65.00	—

C# 146.3 3 KOPEKS
Copper **Ruler:** Nicholas I

Date	Mintage	VG	F	VF	XF	Unc
1840СПМ	2,133,000	6.00	12.00	25.00	65.00	—
1841СПМ	2,133,000	6.00	12.00	25.00	65.00	—
1842СПМ	2,133,000	6.00	12.00	25.00	65.00	—
1843СПМ	2,133,000	6.00	12.00	25.00	65.00	—

C# 146.1 3 KOPEKS
Copper **Ruler:** Nicholas I

Date	Mintage	VG	F	VF	XF	Unc
1840EM	5,230,000	4.00	8.00	18.00	45.00	—
1841EM	13,417,000	4.00	8.00	18.00	45.00	—
1842EM	13,700,000	4.00	8.00	18.00	45.00	—
1843EM	14,578,000	4.00	8.00	18.00	45.00	—
1844EM	4,840,000	4.00	8.00	18.00	45.00	—

C# 146.2 3 KOPEKS
Copper **Ruler:** Nicholas I

Date	Mintage	VG	F	VF	XF	Unc
1840СПБ	—	20.00	40.00	90.00	175	—

C# 146.5 3 KOPEKS
Copper **Ruler:** Nicholas I

Date	Mintage	VG	F	VF	XF	Unc
1848MW	17,000	65.00	150	400	1,000	—

C# 151.1 3 KOPEKS
Copper **Obv:** First variety - 6 coats of arms, no ribbons at crown

Date	Mintage	VG	F	VF	XF	Unc
1850EM	184,000	2.00	4.00	7.50	15.00	—
1851EM	3,448,000	2.00	4.00	7.50	15.00	—
1852EM	5,444,000	2.00	4.00	7.50	15.00	—
1853EM	3,719,000	2.00	4.00	7.50	15.00	—
1854EM	1,351,000	2.00	4.00	7.50	15.00	—
1855EM	2,835,000	1.00	2.00	5.00	10.00	—
1856EM	6,700,000	1.00	2.00	5.00	10.00	—
1857EM	4,726,000	1.00	2.00	5.00	10.00	—
1858EM	10,662,000	1.00	2.00	5.00	10.00	—
1859EM	15,821,000	1.00	2.00	5.00	10.00	—
Common date Proof	—	Value: 300				

C# 151.3 3 KOPEKS
Copper

Date	Mintage	VG	F	VF	XF	Unc
1850BM	50,000	4.00	7.50	15.00	30.00	—
1851BM	100,000	4.00	7.50	15.00	30.00	—
1852BM	100,000	4.00	7.50	15.00	30.00	—
1853BM	89,000	4.00	7.50	15.00	30.00	—
1854BM	161,000	4.00	7.50	15.00	30.00	—
1856BM	417,000	2.50	5.00	10.00	20.00	—
1857BM	21,000	7.50	12.50	25.00	50.00	—
1858BM	712,000	2.50	5.00	10.00	20.00	—
1859BM	400,000	5.00	7.50	15.00	30.00	—

Y# 5a.1 3 KOPEKS
Copper **Ruler:** Alexander II **Obv:** Second variety - 8 coats of arms, ribbons from crown

Date	Mintage	F	VF	XF	Unc	BU
1859EM	—	2.00	4.00	8.00	25.00	—
1860EM	14,010,000	2.00	4.00	8.00	25.00	—
1861EM	7,738,000	2.00	4.00	8.00	25.00	—
1862EM	10,377,000	2.00	4.00	8.00	25.00	—
1863EM	3,939,000	2.00	4.00	8.00	25.00	—
1864EM	6,121,000	4.00	8.00	15.00	30.00	—
1865EM	5,740,000	40.00	80.00	150	250	—
1866EM	6,611,000	2.00	4.00	8.00	25.00	—
1867EM	1,786,000	4.00	8.00	15.00	30.00	—

Y# 5a.2 3 KOPEKS
Copper **Ruler:** Alexander II

Date	Mintage	F	VF	XF	Unc	BU
1860BM	283,000	7.50	15.00	30.00	75.00	—
1861BM	284,000	6.00	12.50	25.00	60.00	—
1862BM	200,000	6.00	12.50	25.00	60.00	—
1863BM	401,000	9.00	17.50	35.00	80.00	—

Y# 11.1 3 KOPEKS
Copper **Ruler:** Alexander II **Note:** Similar to 2 Kopeks, Y#10.2

Date	Mintage	F	VF	XF	Unc	BU
1867EM	160,000	2.00	4.00	8.00	20.00	—
1868EM	6,059,000	1.00	2.00	4.00	15.00	—
1869EM	5,526,000	1.00	2.00	4.00	15.00	—
1870EM	5,018,000	1.00	2.00	4.00	15.00	—
1871EM	1,585,000	1.00	2.00	4.00	15.00	—
1872EM	3,018,000	1.00	2.00	4.00	15.00	—
1873EM	4,704,000	1.00	2.00	4.00	15.00	—
1874EM	4,419,000	1.00	2.00	4.00	15.00	—
1875EM	3,595,000	1.00	2.00	4.00	15.00	—
1876EM	890,000	1.00	2.00	4.00	15.00	—

Y# 11.2 3 KOPEKS
Copper **Obv:** Double-headed eagle

Date	Mintage	F	VF	XF	Unc	BU
1867СПБ	Inc. below	4.00	7.50	15.00	30.00	—
1868СПБ	910,000	2.00	4.00	8.00	20.00	—
1869СПБ	723,000	2.00	4.00	8.00	20.00	—
1870СПБ	80,000	6.00	12.00	25.00	50.00	—
1871СПБ Rare	—	—	—	—	—	—
1876СПБ	4,863,000	1.00	2.00	4.00	18.00	—
1877СПБ	5,902,000	1.00	2.00	4.00	18.00	—
1878СПБ	6,355,000	1.00	2.00	4.00	18.00	—
1879СПБ	7,355,000	1.00	2.00	4.00	18.00	—
1880СПБ	6,773,000	1.00	2.00	4.00	18.00	—
1881СПБ	6,141,000	1.00	2.00	4.00	18.00	—
1882СПБ	4,280,000	1.00	2.00	4.00	18.00	—
1883СПБ	1,061,000	1.00	2.00	4.00	18.00	—
1884СПБ	2,975,000	1.00	2.00	4.00	18.00	—
1899СПБ	11,667,000	2.00	3.00	6.00	20.00	—
1891СПБ	1,983,000	2.00	3.00	6.00	20.00	—
1892СПБ	648,000	0.75	1.50	3.00	15.00	—
1893СПБ	6,365,000	0.75	1.50	3.00	15.00	—
1894СПБ	4,803,000	0.75	1.50	3.00	15.00	—
1895СПБ	5,417,000	0.75	1.50	3.00	15.00	—
1896СПБ	7,923,000	0.75	1.50	3.00	15.00	—
1897СПБ	6,667,000	0.75	1.50	3.00	15.00	—
1898СПБ	11,667,000	0.75	1.50	3.00	15.00	—
1900СПБ	16,667,000	0.75	1.50	3.00	15.00	—
Common date Proof	—	Value: 175				

C# 96.1a 5 KOPEKS
1.0400 g., 0.8680 Silver .0290 oz. **Ruler:** Paul I

Date	Mintage	VG	F	VF	XF	Unc
1801CM АИ	10,000	17.50	35.00	70.00	120	—
1801CM ФЧ Rare	Inc. above	—	—	—	—	—

C# 115.1 5 KOPEKS
Copper **Ruler:** Alexander I **Note:** Varieties exist.

Date	Mintage	VG	F	VF	XF	Unc
1802EM	12,592,000	10.00	20.00	40.00	80.00	—
1803/2EM	31,820,000	12.00	24.00	50.00	100	—
1803EM	Inc. above	9.00	17.50	32.50	65.00	—
1804EM	26,268,000	9.00	17.50	32.50	65.00	—
1805EM	16,518,999	10.00	20.00	40.00	80.00	—
1806EM	38,416,000	7.50	15.00	30.00	65.00	—
1807EM	10,667,000	10.00	20.00	40.00	80.00	—
1808EM	10,001,000	10.00	20.00	40.00	80.00	—
1809EM	10,140,000	10.00	20.00	40.00	80.00	—
1810EM	15,802,000	10.00	20.00	40.00	80.00	—

C# 115.2 5 KOPEKS
Copper **Ruler:** Alexander I **Note:** Varieties exist.

Date	Mintage	VG	F	VF	XF	Unc
1802KM	4,000,000	12.50	25.00	50.00	100	—
1803KM	3,600,000	12.50	25.00	50.00	100	—
1804/3KM	4,000,000	15.00	30.00	60.00	120	—
1804KM	Inc. above	12.50	25.00	50.00	100	—
1805KM	5,000,000	12.50	25.00	50.00	100	—
1806KM	5,000,000	15.00	30.00	60.00	120	—
1807KM	5,000,000	15.00	30.00	60.00	120	—
1808KM	5,000,000	15.00	30.00	60.00	120	—
1809KM	5,000,000	15.00	30.00	60.00	120	—
1810KM	—	15.00	30.00	60.00	120	—

C# 126 5 KOPEKS
1.0366 g., 0.8680 Silver .0289 oz. **Ruler:** Alexander I

Date	Mintage	VG	F	VF	XF	Unc
1810СПБ ФГ	—	50.00	100	200	300	—
1811СПБ ФГ	80,000	10.00	20.00	40.00	80.00	—
1811СПБ Rare	Inc. above	—	—	—	—	—
1812СПБ МФ Rare	—	—	—	—	—	—
1813СПБ ПС	620,000	3.00	6.00	12.00	25.00	—
1814СПБ ПС	1,300,000	3.00	6.00	12.00	25.00	—
1814СПБ МФ	Inc. above	3.00	6.00	12.00	25.00	—
1815СПБ МФ	3,000,000	3.00	6.00	12.00	25.00	—
1815СПБ Rare	Inc. above	—	—	—	—	—
1816/5СПБ МФ	1,040,000	3.50	7.00	14.00	30.00	—
1816СПБ МФ	Inc. above	3.00	6.00	12.00	25.00	—
1816СПБ ПС	Inc. above	3.00	6.00	12.00	25.00	—
1817СПБ ПС	120,000	3.00	6.00	12.00	25.00	—
1818СПБ ПС	340,000	3.00	6.00	12.00	25.00	—
1819СПБ ПС	920,000	3.00	6.00	12.00	25.00	—
1820/19СПБ ПС	460,000	3.50	7.00	14.00	30.00	—
1820СПБ ПС	Inc. above	3.00	6.00	12.00	25.00	—
1820СПБ ПД	Inc. above	3.00	6.00	12.00	25.00	—
1821СПБ ПД	2,000,000	3.00	6.00	12.00	25.00	—
1822/1СПБ ПД	1,060,000	3.50	7.00	14.00	30.00	—
1822СПБ ПД	Inc. above	3.00	6.00	12.00	25.00	—

Date	Mintage	VG	F	VF	XF	Unc
1823СПБ ПД	2,300,000	3.00	6.00	12.00	25.00	—
1824СПБ ПД	1,740,000	3.00	6.00	12.00	25.00	—
1825СПБ ПД	1,160,000	3.00	6.00	12.00	25.00	—
1825СПБ НГ Rare	Inc. above	—	—	—	—	—
1826СПБ НГ	1,340,000	4.00	8.00	16.00	35.00	—

C# 156 5 KOPEKS

1.0366 g., 0.8680 Silver .0289 oz. **Ruler:** Nicholas I

Date	Mintage	VG	F	VF	XF	Unc
1826СПБ НГ	—	3.00	6.00	12.00	25.00	—
Note: Mintage included in C#152.3						
1827СПБ НГ	1,769,000	3.00	6.00	12.00	25.00	—
1828СПБ НГ	60,000	5.00	10.00	20.00	40.00	—
1829СПБ НГ	80,000	5.00	10.00	20.00	40.00	—
1830СПБ НГ	1,500,000	3.00	6.00	12.00	25.00	—
1831СПБ НГ	520,000	3.00	6.00	12.00	25.00	—
Common date Proof	—	Value: 300				

C# 140.1 5 KOPEKS

Copper **Ruler:** Nicholas I

Date	Mintage	VG	F	VF	XF	Unc
1831ЕМ ФХ	41,120,000	3.50	6.50	12.50	25.00	—
1831ЕМ	—	4.00	8.00	15.00	30.00	—
1832ЕМ ФХ	30,080,000	3.50	6.50	12.50	25.00	—
1833ЕМ ФХ	14,332,000	3.50	6.50	12.50	25.00	—
1834ЕМ ФХ	41,785,000	3.50	6.50	12.50	25.00	—
1835ЕМ ФХ	41,763,000	3.50	6.50	12.50	25.00	—
1836ЕМ ФХ	31,332,000	3.50	6.50	12.50	25.00	—
1837/6ЕМ ФХ	19,745,000	4.00	8.00	15.00	30.00	—
1837ЕМ ФХ	Inc. above	4.00	8.00	15.00	30.00	—
1837ЕМ КТ	Inc. above	3.50	6.50	12.50	25.00	—
1837ЕМ НА	Inc. above	3.50	6.50	12.50	25.00	—
1838ЕМ НА	24,430,000	3.50	6.50	12.50	25.00	—
1839ЕМ НА	1,400,000	4.00	8.00	15.00	30.00	—

C# 140.3 5 KOPEKS

Copper **Ruler:** Nicholas I

Date	Mintage	VG	F	VF	XF	Unc
1831СМ	5,900,000	4.00	7.50	15.00	30.00	—
1832СМ	5,900,000	4.00	7.50	15.00	30.00	—
1833СМ	6,295,000	4.00	7.50	15.00	30.00	—
1834СМ	5,900,000	4.00	7.50	15.00	30.00	—
1835СМ	5,000,000	4.00	7.50	15.00	30.00	—
1836СМ	5,240,000	4.00	7.50	15.00	30.00	—
1837СМ	5,200,000	4.00	7.50	15.00	30.00	—
1838СМ	1,420,000	4.00	7.50	15.00	30.00	—
1839СМ	1,400,000	4.00	7.50	15.00	30.00	—

C# 163 5 KOPEKS

1.0366 g., 0.8680 Silver .0289 oz. **Ruler:** Nicholas I

Date	Mintage	VG	F	VF	XF	Unc
1832СПБ НГ	224,000	1.50	2.75	4.00	12.00	—
1833СПБ НГ	1,026,000	1.50	2.75	4.00	12.00	—
1834СПБ НГ	780,000	1.50	2.75	4.00	12.00	—
1835СПБ НГ	1,010,000	1.50	2.75	4.00	12.00	—
1836СПБ НГ	900,000	1.50	2.75	4.00	12.00	—
1837СПБ НГ	1,140,000	1.50	2.75	4.00	12.00	—
1838СПБ НГ	2,400,000	1.50	2.75	4.00	12.00	—
1839СПБ НГ	1,002	20.00	40.00	80.00	150	—
1840СПБ НГ	420,000	2.00	4.00	6.00	15.00	—
Common date Proof	—	Value: 175				
1841СПБ НГ	100,000	2.00	4.00	6.00	15.00	—
1842СПБ АЧ	Inc. above	2.00	4.00	6.00	15.00	—
1843СПБ АЧ	400,000	2.00	4.00	6.00	15.00	—
1844СПБ КБ	401,000	2.00	4.00	6.00	15.00	—
1845СПБ КБ	1,740,000	1.50	2.75	4.00	10.00	—
1846СПБ ПА	280,000	1.50	2.75	4.00	10.00	—
1847СПБ ПА	1,010,000	1.50	2.75	4.00	10.00	—
1848СПБ НI	1,000,000	1.50	2.75	4.00	10.00	—
1849СПБ ПА	1,020,000	1.50	2.75	4.00	10.00	—
1850СПБ ПА	1,300,000	1.50	2.75	4.00	10.00	—
1851СПБ ПА	1,000,000	1.50	2.75	4.00	10.00	—
1852СПБ ПА	900,000	1.50	2.75	4.00	10.00	—

Date	Mintage	VG	F	VF	XF	Unc
1852СПБ НI Rare	Inc. above	—	—	—	—	—
1853СПБ НI	900,000	1.50	2.75	7.50	20.00	—
1854СПБ НI	500,000	1.50	2.75	7.50	20.00	—
1855СПБ НI	640,000	1.50	2.75	4.00	10.00	—
1856СПБ ФБ	680,000	1.50	2.75	4.00	10.00	—
1857СПБ ФБ	80,000	2.00	4.00	8.00	15.00	—
1858СПБ ФБ	40,000	2.50	5.00	10.00	20.00	—
Common date Proof	—	Value: 150				

C# 152.1 5 KOPEKS

Copper **Obv:** 6 coats of arms, no ribbons at crown

Date	Mintage	F	VF	XF	Unc	BU
1850ЕМ	373,000	4.00	7.50	15.00	40.00	—
1851ЕМ	2,241,000	4.00	7.50	15.00	40.00	—
1852ЕМ	3,961,000	4.00	7.50	15.00	40.00	—
1853ЕМ	1,474,000	30.00	60.00	120	200	—
1854ЕМ	356,000	4.00	7.50	15.00	40.00	—
1855ЕМ	740,000	3.00	6.00	12.00	25.00	—
1856ЕМ	5,146,000	2.00	4.00	8.00	20.00	—
1857ЕМ	8,675,000	2.00	4.00	8.00	20.00	—
1858ЕМ	19,561,000	2.00	4.00	8.00	20.00	—
1859ЕМ	19,441,000	2.00	4.00	8.00	20.00	—

C# 152.4 5 KOPEKS

Copper

Date	Mintage	F	VF	XF	Unc	BU
1850ВМ	—	15.00	25.00	50.00	120	—
1851ВМ	24,000	15.00	25.00	50.00	120	—
1852ВМ	16,000	15.00	25.00	50.00	120	—
1853ВМ	40,000	15.00	25.00	50.00	120	—
1856ВМ	40,000	15.00	25.00	50.00	120	—

Y# 6a 5 KOPEKS

Copper **Ruler:** Alexander II **Obv:** 8 coats of arms, ribbons at crown

Date	Mintage	F	VF	XF	Unc	BU
1858ЕМ Rare	—	—	—	—	—	—
1859ЕМ	Inc. above	2.00	4.00	8.00	20.00	—
1860ЕМ	25,260,000	2.00	4.00	8.00	20.00	—
1861ЕМ	28,022,000	2.00	4.00	8.00	20.00	—
1862ЕМ	22,055,000	2.00	4.00	8.00	20.00	—
1863ЕМ	22,511,000	2.00	4.00	8.00	20.00	—
1864ЕМ	26,042,000	2.00	4.00	8.00	20.00	—
1865ЕМ	38,943,000	2.00	4.00	8.00	20.00	—
1866ЕМ	24,767,000	2.00	4.00	8.00	20.00	—
1867ЕМ	11,697,000	4.00	8.00	16.00	40.00	—

Y# 19.1 5 KOPEKS

1.0366 g., 0.7500 Silver .0250 oz. **Ruler:** Alexander II **Obv:** Ribbons added to crown

Date	Mintage	F	VF	XF	Unc	BU
1859СПБ Rare	120,000	—	—	—	—	—
1859СПБ ФБ	Inc. above	4.00	8.00	16.00	90.00	—
1860СПБ ФБ	20,000	10.00	20.00	40.00	100	—

Y# 19.2 5 KOPEKS

1.0366 g., 0.7500 Silver .0250 oz. **Ruler:** Alexander II **Obv:** Redesigned eagle, engrailed edge

Date	Mintage	F	VF	XF	Unc	BU
1860СПБ ФБ	180,000	2.00	4.00	10.00	40.00	—
1861СПБ ФБ	360,000	2.00	4.00	10.00	40.00	—
1861СПБ МИ	Inc. above	7.50	15.00	30.00	75.00	—
1861СПБ Rare	—	—	—	—	—	—
1862СПБ МИ	400,000	2.00	4.00	10.00	40.00	—
1863СПБ АБ	200,000	2.00	4.00	10.00	40.00	—
1864СПБ НФ	240,000	2.00	4.00	10.00	40.00	—
1865СПБ НФ	240,000	2.00	4.00	10.00	40.00	—
1866СПБ НФ	190,000	2.00	4.00	10.00	40.00	—
1866СПБ НI	Inc. above	25.00	50.00	100	140	—
Common date Proof	—	Value: 150				

Y# 12.1 5 KOPEKS

Copper **Ruler:** Alexander II

Date	Mintage	F	VF	XF	Unc	BU
1867ЕМ	1,459,000	3.00	6.00	12.00	25.00	—
1868ЕМ	23,019,000	1.00	3.00	6.00	20.00	—
1869ЕМ	20,277,000	1.00	3.00	6.00	20.00	—
1870ЕМ	21,158,000	1.00	3.00	6.00	20.00	—
1871ЕМ	6,304,000	1.00	3.00	6.00	20.00	—
1872ЕМ	11,890,000	1.00	3.00	6.00	20.00	—
1873ЕМ	13,052,000	1.00	3.00	6.00	20.00	—
1874ЕМ	12,879,000	1.00	3.00	6.00	20.00	—
1875ЕМ	19,624,000	1.00	3.00	6.00	20.00	—
1876ЕМ	5,329,000	1.00	3.00	6.00	20.00	—

Y# 19a.1 5 KOPEKS

0.8998 g., 0.5000 Silver .0144 oz. **Obv:** Eagle **Edge:** Reeded

Date	Mintage	F	VF	XF	Unc	BU
1867СПБ НI	180,000	1.75	3.50	7.50	40.00	—
1868СПБ НI	240,000	1.75	3.50	7.50	40.00	—
1869СПБ НI	170,000	1.75	3.50	7.50	40.00	—
1870СПБ НI	220,000	1.75	3.50	7.50	40.00	—
1871СПБ НI	200,000	1.75	3.50	7.50	40.00	—
1872СПБ НI	180,000	1.75	3.50	7.50	40.00	—
1873СПБ НI	160,000	1.75	3.50	7.50	40.00	—
1874СПБ НI	200,000	1.75	3.50	7.50	40.00	—
1875СПБ НI	200,000	1.75	3.50	7.50	40.00	—
1876СПБ НI	240,000	1.75	3.50	7.50	40.00	—
1877СПБ НI	200,000	1.75	3.50	7.50	40.00	—
1877СПБ НФ	Inc. above	5.00	10.00	20.00	75.00	—
1878СПБ НФ	220,000	1.75	3.50	7.50	40.00	—
1878СПБ НI	Inc. above	7.50	15.00	30.00	100	—
1879СПБ НФ	140,000	1.75	3.50	7.50	40.00	—
1880СПБ НФ	240,000	1.75	3.50	7.50	40.00	—
1881СПБ НФ	200,000	1.75	3.50	7.50	40.00	—
1882СПБ НФ	1,760,000	1.00	2.00	4.00	15.00	—
1883СПБ ДС	1,000,000	1.00	2.00	4.00	15.00	—
1883СПБ АГ	Inc. above	1.00	2.00	4.00	15.00	—
1884СПБ АГ	3,460,000	1.00	2.00	4.00	15.00	—
1885СПБ АГ	1,700,000	1.00	2.00	4.00	15.00	—
1886СПБ АГ	2,000,000	1.00	2.00	4.00	15.00	—
1887СПБ АГ	3,000,000	1.00	2.00	4.00	15.00	—
1888СПБ АГ	4,000,000	1.00	2.00	4.00	15.00	—
1889СПБ АГ	3,500,000	1.00	2.00	4.00	15.00	—
1890СПБ АГ	8,000,000	1.00	2.00	4.00	15.00	—
1891СПБ АГ	2,000,000	1.00	2.00	4.00	15.00	—
1892СПБ АГ	8,000,000	1.00	2.00	4.00	15.00	—
1893СПБ АГ	2,000,000	1.00	2.00	4.00	15.00	—
1897СПБ АГ	2,029,000	1.00	2.00	4.00	15.00	—
1898СПБ АГ	3,980,000	1.00	2.00	4.00	15.00	—
1899СПБ АГ	4,605,000	1.00	2.00	4.00	15.00	—
1899СПБ ЭБ	Inc. above	1.00	2.00	4.00	15.00	—
1900СПБ ФЗ	5,205,000	1.00	2.00	4.00	15.00	—
Common date Proof	—	Value: 150				

Y# 12.2 5 KOPEKS

Copper

Date	Mintage	F	VF	XF	Unc	BU
1867СПБ	Inc. below	4.00	7.50	15.00	40.00	—
1868СПБ	821,000	2.00	4.00	8.00	30.00	—
1869СПБ	942,000	2.00	4.00	8.00	30.00	—
1870СПБ	28,000	5.00	10.00	20.00	40.00	—
1871СПБ Rare	—	—	—	—	—	—
1876СПБ	4,655,000	1.00	3.00	6.00	20.00	—
1877СПБ	7,184,000	1.00	3.00	6.00	20.00	—
1878СПБ	12,542,000	1.00	3.00	6.00	20.00	—
1879СПБ	14,652,000	1.00	3.00	6.00	20.00	—
1880СПБ	6,773,000	1.00	3.00	6.00	20.00	—
1881СПБ	13,824,000	1.00	3.00	6.00	20.00	—
Common date Proof	—	Value: 265				

C# 97.1a 10 KOPEKS (Grivennik)

2.0700 g., 0.8680 Silver .0578 oz. **Ruler:** Paul I

Date	Mintage	VG	F	VF	XF	Unc
1801 АИ	10,000	25.00	50.00	100	200	—
1801 ФЦ Rare	Inc. above	—	—	—	—	—

C# 119 10 KOPEKS (Grivennik)

2.0732 g., 0.8680 Silver .0578 oz. **Ruler:** Alexander I

Date	Mintage	VG	F	VF	XF	Unc
1802СПБ АИ	190,000	25.00	50.00	100	200	—
1803СПБ АИ	40,000	50.00	100	200	450	—
1804/2СПБ ФГ	380,000	30.00	60.00	120	250	—
1804СПБ ФГ	Inc. above	25.00	50.00	100	200	—
1805/4СПБ ФГ	112,000	30.00	60.00	120	250	—
1805СПБ ФГ	Inc. above	25.00	50.00	100	200	—

C# 119a 10 KOPEKS (Grivennik)

2.0732 g., 0.8680 Silver .0578 oz. **Ruler:** Alexander I

Date	Mintage	VG	F	VF	XF	Unc
1808СПБ ФГ Rare	—	—	—	—	—	—
1809СПБ МК	35,000	35.00	70.00	130	250	—
1810СПБ ФГ	77,000	25.00	50.00	100	200	—

C# 127 10 KOPEKS (Grivennik)

2.0732 g., 0.8680 Silver .0578 oz. **Ruler:** Alexander I

Date	Mintage	VG	F	VF	XF	Unc
1810СПБ ФГ	—	5.00	10.00	20.00	40.00	—
1811СПБ ФГ	930,000	3.50	5.00	10.00	20.00	—
1812СПБ МФ	—	—	—	—	—	—
1813СПБ ПС	1,010,000	3.50	5.00	10.00	20.00	—
1814СПБ ПС	2,120,000	3.50	5.00	10.00	20.00	—
1814СПБ СП	Inc. above	—	—	—	—	—
1814СПБ МФ	Inc. above	3.50	5.00	10.00	20.00	—
1815СПБ МФ	2,000,000	3.50	5.00	10.00	20.00	—
1816/5СПБ ПС	250,000	4.00	6.00	12.00	25.00	—
1816СПБ МФ	Inc. above	3.50	5.00	10.00	20.00	—
1816СПБ ПС	Inc. above	3.50	5.00	10.00	20.00	—
1817СПБ ПС	160,000	3.50	5.00	10.00	20.00	—
1818СПБ ПС	630,000	3.50	5.00	10.00	20.00	—
1819СПБ ПС	1,520,000	3.50	5.00	10.00	20.00	—
1820СПБ ПС	520,000	3.50	5.00	10.00	20.00	—
1820СПБ ПД	Inc. above	3.50	5.00	10.00	20.00	—
1821/0СПБ ПД	2,250,000	4.00	6.00	12.00	25.00	—
1821СПБ ПД	Inc. above	3.50	5.00	10.00	20.00	—
1822СПБ ПД	2,069,999	3.50	5.00	10.00	20.00	—
1823СПБ ПД	3,850,000	3.50	5.00	10.00	20.00	—
1824/3СПБ ПД	1,330,000	4.00	6.00	12.00	25.00	—
1824СПБ ПД	Inc. above	3.50	5.00	10.00	20.00	—
1825СПБ ПД	1,350,000	3.50	5.00	10.00	20.00	—
1825СПБ НГ	Inc. above	7.50	15.00	30.00	75.00	—
1826/5СПБ НГ	2,049,999	4.00	6.00	12.00	25.00	—
1826СПБ НГ	Inc. above	3.50	5.00	10.00	20.00	—

C# 157 10 KOPEKS (Grivennik)

2.0732 g., 0.8680 Silver .0578 oz. **Ruler:** Nicholas I

Date	Mintage	VG	F	VF	XF	Unc
1826СПБ НГ	—	3.50	5.00	10.00	20.00	—

Note: Mintage included in C#152.7

Date	Mintage	VG	F	VF	XF	Unc
1827СПБ НГ	1,290,000	3.50	5.00	10.00	20.00	—
1828СПБ НГ	370,000	4.00	6.00	12.00	25.00	—
1829СПБ НГ	40,000	5.00	10.00	20.00	40.00	—
1830СПБ НГ	500,000	4.00	6.00	12.00	25.00	—
1831СПБ НГ	450,000	4.00	6.00	12.00	25.00	—
Common date Proof	—	Value: 375				

C# 141.1 10 KOPEKS (Grivennik)

Copper **Ruler:** Nicholas I

Date	Mintage	VG	F	VF	XF	Unc
1831ЕМ ФХ	2,640,000	7.50	15.00	30.00	60.00	—
1832ЕМ ФХ	7,620,000	7.50	15.00	30.00	60.00	—
1833ЕМ ФХ	6,968,000	7.50	15.00	30.00	60.00	—
1834ЕМ ФХ	9,134,000	7.50	15.00	30.00	60.00	—
1835ЕМ ФХ	5,175,000	7.50	15.00	30.00	60.00	—
1836ЕМ ФХ	7,240,000	7.50	15.00	30.00	60.00	—
1837/6ЕМ КТ	9,728,000	9.00	18.00	35.00	70.00	—
1837ЕМ ФХ	Inc. above	10.00	20.00	40.00	75.00	—
1837ЕМ КТ	Inc. above	7.50	15.00	30.00	60.00	—
1837ЕМ НА	Inc. above	7.50	15.00	30.00	60.00	—
1838ЕМ НА	5,468,000	7.50	15.00	30.00	60.00	—
1839ЕМ НА	350,000	8.50	17.50	35.00	70.00	—

C# 141.3 10 KOPEKS (Grivennik)

Copper **Ruler:** Nicholas I

Date	Mintage	VG	F	VF	XF	Unc
1831СМ	510,000	15.00	25.00	50.00	125	—
1832СМ	510,000	15.00	25.00	50.00	125	—
1833СМ	700,000	15.00	25.00	50.00	125	—
1834СМ	510,000	15.00	25.00	50.00	125	—
1835СМ	500,000	15.00	25.00	50.00	125	—
1836СМ	600,000	15.00	25.00	50.00	125	—
1837СМ	500,000	15.00	25.00	50.00	125	—
1838СМ	350,000	15.00	25.00	50.00	125	—
1839СМ	350,000	20.00	35.00	60.00	140	—

C# 164.1 10 KOPEKS (Grivennik)

2.0700 g., 0.8680 Silver .0577 oz.

Date	Mintage	VG	F	VF	XF	Unc
1832СПБ НГ	104,000	10.00	25.00	50.00	100	—
1833СПБ НГ	880,000	2.00	4.00	8.00	15.00	—
1834/3СПБ НГ	400,000	2.50	5.00	10.00	20.00	—
1834СПБ НГ	Inc. above	2.00	4.00	8.00	15.00	—
1835СПБ НГ	940,000	2.00	4.00	8.00	15.00	—
1836СПБ НГ	490,000	2.00	4.00	8.00	15.00	—
1837СПБ НГ	2,360,000	2.00	4.00	8.00	15.00	—
1838СПБ НГ	500,000	2.00	4.00	8.00	15.00	—
1839СПБ НГ	2,411,000	2.00	4.00	8.00	15.00	—
1840СПБ НГ	190,000	2.00	4.00	8.00	15.00	—
Common date Proof	—	Value: 200				
1841/0СПБ НГ	500,000	2.50	5.00	10.00	20.00	—
1841СПБ НГ	Inc. above	2.00	4.00	8.00	15.00	—
1842СПБ АЧ	300,000	2.00	4.00	8.00	15.00	—
1843СПБ АЧ	180,000	2.00	4.00	8.00	15.00	—
1844СПБ КБ	461,000	2.00	4.00	8.00	15.00	—
1845СПБ КБ	2,435,000	2.00	4.00	8.00	15.00	—
1846/5СПБ ПА	810,000	2.50	5.00	10.00	20.00	—
1846СПБ ПА	Inc. above	2.00	4.00	8.00	15.00	—
1847СПБ ПА	3,180,000	2.00	4.00	8.00	15.00	—
1848СПБ НІ	1,860,000	2.00	4.00	8.00	15.00	—
1849СПБ ПА	3,110,000	2.00	4.00	8.00	15.00	—
1850СПБ ПА	2,450,000	2.00	4.00	8.00	15.00	—
1851СПБ ПА	1,500,000	2.00	4.00	8.00	15.00	—
1852СПБ ПА	1,350,000	2.00	4.00	8.00	15.00	—
1852СПБ НІ	Inc. above	3.00	6.00	12.00	25.00	—
1853СПБ НІ	1,350,000	2.00	4.00	8.00	15.00	—
1854СПБ НІ	1,000,000	2.00	4.00	8.00	15.00	—
1855СПБ НІ	3,201,000	2.00	4.00	8.00	15.00	—
1856СПБ ФБ	1,940,000	2.00	4.00	8.00	15.00	—
1857СПБ ФБ	3,110,000	2.00	4.00	8.00	15.00	—
1858СПБ ФБ	2,600,000	2.00	4.00	8.00	15.00	—
Common date Proof	—	Value: 150				

C# 164.2 10 KOPEKS (Grivennik)

2.0700 g., 0.8680 Silver .0577 oz. **Ruler:** Nicholas I

Date	Mintage	VG	F	VF	XF	Unc
1854MW Rare	—	—	—	—	—	—
1855MW	103,000	25.00	50.00	100	200	—

Y# 20.1 10 KOPEKS (Grivennik)

2.0732 g., 0.7500 Silver .0499 oz. **Ruler:** Alexander II **Note:** Type 1, reticulated edge.

Date	Mintage	F	VF	XF	Unc	BU
1859СПБ ФБ	3,920,000	1.00	2.00	4.00	30.00	—
1860СПБ ФБ	580,000	4.00	8.00	15.00	50.00	—

Y# 20.2 10 KOPEKS (Grivennik)

2.0732 g., 0.7500 Silver .0499 oz. **Ruler:** Alexander II **Note:** Type 2, eagle redesigned.

Date	Mintage	F	VF	XF	Unc	BU
1860СПБ ФБ	2,810,000	1.00	2.00	4.00	30.00	—
1861СПБ ФБ	5,660,000	1.00	2.00	4.00	30.00	—
1861СПБ МИ	Inc. above	2.00	4.00	8.00	30.00	—
1861СПБ	19,300,000	1.00	2.00	4.00	30.00	—
1862СПБ МИ	5,800,000	1.00	2.00	4.00	30.00	—
1863СПБ АБ	5,750,000	1.00	2.00	4.00	30.00	—
1864СПБ НФ	3,740,000	1.00	2.00	4.00	30.00	—
1865СПБ НФ	3,886,000	1.00	2.00	4.00	30.00	—
1866СПБ НФ	2,533,000	1.00	2.00	4.00	30.00	—
1866СПБ НІ	Inc. above	1.00	2.00	4.00	30.00	—
Common date Proof	—	Value: 265				

Y# 20a.2 10 KOPEKS

1.7996 g., 0.5000 Silver .0289 oz. **Edge:** Reeded

Date	Mintage	F	VF	XF	Unc	BU
1874СПБ НІ	2,520,000	0.50	1.00	3.00	25.00	—
1875СПБ НІ	3,590,000	0.50	1.00	3.00	25.00	—
1876СПБ НІ	4,900,000	0.50	1.00	3.00	25.00	—
1877СПБ НІ	2,090,000	0.50	1.00	3.00	25.00	—
1877СПБ НФ	Inc. above	3.00	6.00	12.00	60.00	—
1878СПБ НФ	6,920,000	0.50	1.00	3.00	25.00	—
1878СПБ НІ	Inc. above	5.00	10.00	20.00	80.00	—
1879СПБ НФ	6,890,000	0.50	1.00	3.00	25.00	—
1880/7СПБ НФ	6,740,000	0.75	1.25	5.00	30.00	—
1880СПБ НФ	Inc. above	0.50	1.00	3.00	25.00	—
1881СПБ НФ	2,950,000	0.50	1.00	3.00	25.00	—
1882СПБ НФ	920,000	0.50	1.00	3.00	25.00	—
1883СПБ ДС	1,520,000	0.50	1.00	3.00	25.00	—
1883СПБ АГ	Inc. above	1.00	2.00	5.00	25.00	—
1884СПБ АГ	1,710,000	0.50	1.00	3.00	25.00	—
1885СПБ АГ	1,300,000	0.50	1.00	3.00	25.00	—
1886СПБ АГ	2,000,000	0.50	1.00	3.00	25.00	—
1887СПБ АГ	4,000,000	0.50	1.00	3.00	25.00	—
1888СПБ АГ	2,000,000	0.50	1.00	3.00	25.00	—
1889СПБ АГ	5,000,000	0.50	1.00	3.00	25.00	—
1890СПБ АГ	3,750,000	0.50	1.00	3.00	25.00	—
1891СПБ АГ	3,240,000	0.50	1.00	3.00	25.00	—
1893СПБ АГ	4,250,000	0.50	1.00	3.00	25.00	—
1894СПБ АГ	4,000,000	0.50	1.00	3.00	25.00	—
1895СПБ АГ	1,000,000	0.50	1.00	3.00	25.00	—
1896СПБ АГ	2,010,000	0.50	1.00	3.00	25.00	—
1897СПБ АГ	3,150,000	0.50	1.00	3.00	25.00	—
1898СПБ АГ	6,610,000	0.50	1.00	2.00	15.00	—
1899СПБ АГ	14,000,000	0.50	1.00	2.00	15.00	—
1899СПБ ЭБ	Inc. above	0.50	1.00	2.00	15.00	—
1900СПБ ФЗ	2,603,000	0.50	1.00	2.00	15.00	—
Common date Proof	—	Value: 250				

Y# 21 15 KOPEKS

3.1097 g., 0.7500 Silver .0750 oz. **Ruler:** Alexander II **Edge:** Reticulated

Date	Mintage	F	VF	XF	Unc	BU
1860СПБ ФБ	4,480,000	1.25	1.50	3.00	30.00	—
1861СПБ ФБ	10,120,000	1.25	1.50	3.00	30.00	—
1861СПБ МИ	Inc. above	2.00	4.00	8.00	30.00	—

Date	Mintage	F	VF	XF	Unc	BU
1861СПБ	13,300,000	1.25	1.50	3.00	30.00	—
1862СПБ МИ	10,000,000	1.25	1.50	3.00	30.00	—
1863СПБ АБ	9,960,000	1.25	1.50	3.00	30.00	—
1864СПБ НФ	10,715,000	1.25	1.50	3.00	30.00	—
1865СПБ НФ	10,703,000	1.25	1.50	3.00	30.00	—
1866СПБ НФ	6,329,000	1.25	1.50	3.00	30.00	—
1866СПБ НІ	Inc. above	1.25	1.50	3.00	30.00	—
Common date Proof	—	Value: 265				

Y# 21a.2 15 KOPEKS

2.6994 g., 0.5000 Silver .0434 oz. **Edge:** Reeded

Date	Mintage	F	VF	XF	Unc	BU
1867СПБ НІ	8,720,000	0.75	1.00	3.00	25.00	—
1868СПБ НІ	7,460,000	0.75	1.00	3.00	25.00	—
1869СПБ НІ	8,120,000	0.75	1.00	3.00	25.00	—
1870СПБ НІ	9,380,000	0.75	1.00	3.00	25.00	—
1871СПБ НІ	9,460,000	0.75	1.00	3.00	25.00	—
1872СПБ НІ	5,880,000	0.75	1.00	3.00	25.00	—
1873СПБ НІ	7,960,000	0.75	1.00	3.00	25.00	—
1874СПБ НІ	6,960,000	0.75	1.00	3.00	25.00	—
1875СПБ НІ	7,480,000	0.75	1.00	3.00	25.00	—
1876СПБ НІ	9,760,000	0.75	1.00	3.00	25.00	—
1877СПБ НІ	4,360,000	0.75	1.00	3.00	25.00	—
1877СПБ НФ	Inc. above	2.00	5.00	12.50	40.00	—
1878СПБ НФ	1,116,000	0.75	1.00	3.00	25.00	—
1879СПБ НФ	12,504,000	0.75	1.00	3.00	25.00	—
1880/7СПБ НФ	11,655,000	1.00	1.25	5.00	30.00	—
1880СПБ НФ	Inc. above	0.75	1.00	3.00	25.00	—
1881СПБ НФ	4,900,000	0.75	1.00	3.00	25.00	—
1882СПБ НФ	1,470,000	0.75	1.00	3.00	25.00	—
1882СПБ ДС	Inc. above	10.00	20.00	30.00	80.00	—
1883СПБ ДС	4,020,000	3.00	6.00	12.00	40.00	—
1883СПБ АГ	Inc. above	0.75	1.00	3.00	25.00	—
1884СПБ АГ	2,720,000	0.75	1.00	3.00	25.00	—
1885СПБ АГ	1,420,000	0.75	1.00	3.00	25.00	—
1886СПБ АГ	1,840,000	0.75	1.00	3.00	25.00	—
1887СПБ АГ	3,000,000	0.75	1.00	3.00	25.00	—
1888СПБ АГ	—	3.00	6.00	12.00	40.00	—
1889СПБ АГ	2,835,000	0.75	1.00	2.00	15.00	—
1890СПБ АГ	3,500,000	0.75	1.00	2.00	15.00	—
1891СПБ АГ	4,710,000	0.75	1.00	2.00	15.00	—
1893СПБ АГ	6,500,000	0.75	1.00	2.00	15.00	—
1896СПБ АГ	3,160,000	0.75	1.00	2.00	15.00	—
1897СПБ АГ	Inc. above	0.75	1.00	2.00	15.00	—
1898СПБ АГ	3,000,000	0.75	1.00	2.00	15.00	—
1899СПБ АГ	12,665,000	0.75	1.00	2.00	15.00	—
1899СПБ ЗБ	Inc. above	5.00	10.00	20.00	70.00	—
1900СПБ ФЗ	12,665,000	0.75	1.00	202	10.00	—
Common date Proof	—	Value: 250				

C# 128 20 KOPEKS

4.1463 g., 0.8680 Silver .1157 oz. **Ruler:** Alexander I

Date	Mintage	VG	F	VF	XF	Unc
1810СПБ ФГ	250,000	5.00	10.00	20.00	30.00	—
1811СПБ ФГ	1,969,000	3.00	5.00	10.00	20.00	—
1813СПБ ПС	1,900,000	3.00	5.00	10.00	20.00	—
1814/3СПБ МФ	1,850,000	4.00	6.00	12.00	25.00	—
1814СПБ ПС	Inc. above	3.00	5.00	10.00	20.00	—
1814СПБ МФ	Inc. above	3.00	5.00	10.00	20.00	—
1815/4СПБ МФ	1,024,999	4.00	6.00	12.00	25.00	—
1815СПБ МФ	Inc. above	3.00	5.00	10.00	20.00	—
1816/5СПБ МФ	115,000	4.00	6.00	12.00	25.00	—
1816СПБ МФ	Inc. above	6.00	12.50	25.00	50.00	—
1816СПБ ПС	Inc. above	3.00	5.00	10.00	20.00	—
1817СПБ ПС	1,545,000	3.00	5.00	10.00	20.00	—
1818СПБ ПС	2,000,000	3.00	5.00	10.00	20.00	—
1819СПБ ПС	1,705,000	3.00	5.00	10.00	20.00	—
1820/19СПБ ПС	1,895,000	4.00	6.00	12.00	25.00	—
1820/19СПБ ПД	Inc. above	4.00	6.00	12.00	25.00	—
1820СПБ ПС	Inc. above	4.00	6.00	12.00	25.00	—
1820СПБ ПД	Inc. above	3.00	5.00	10.00	20.00	—
1821/0СПБ ПД	3,025,000	4.00	6.00	12.00	25.00	—
1821/1СПБ ПД	Inc. above	4.00	6.00	12.00	25.00	—
1821СПБ ПД	Inc. above	3.00	5.00	10.00	20.00	—
1822/1СПБ ПД	2,100,000	4.00	6.00	12.00	25.00	—
1822СПБ ПД	Inc. above	3.00	5.00	10.00	20.00	—
1823/18СПБ ПД	7,075,000	4.00	6.00	12.00	25.00	—
1823/1СПБ ПД	Inc. above	4.00	6.00	12.00	25.00	—
1823СПБ ПД	Inc. above	3.00	5.00	10.00	20.00	—
1824СПБ ПД	1,750,000	3.00	5.00	10.00	20.00	—
1825/23/19СПБ ПД	1,375,000	4.00	6.00	12.00	25.00	—
1825СПБ ПД	Inc. above	3.00	5.00	10.00	20.00	—
1825СПБ НГ	Inc. above	6.00	12.50	25.00	50.00	—
1826/5СПБ НГ	2,815,000	4.00	6.00	12.00	25.00	—
1826СПБ НГ	Inc. above	3.00	5.00	10.00	20.00	—

C# 158 20 KOPEKS

4.1463 g., 0.8680 Silver .1157 oz. **Ruler:** Nicholas I

Date	Mintage	VG	F	VF	XF	Unc
1826 НГ	—	4.50	9.00	17.50	35.00	—
Note: Mintage included in C#153						
1827 НГ	465,000	4.50	9.00	17.50	35.00	—
1828 НГ	50,000	7.50	15.00	30.00	60.00	—
1829 НГ	250,000	4.50	9.00	17.50	35.00	—
1830 НГ	1,175,000	6.00	12.00	25.00	50.00	—
1831 НГ	385,000	4.50	9.00	17.50	35.00	—
Common date Proof	—	Value: 375				

C# 165 20 KOPEKS

4.1463 g., 0.8680 Silver .1157 oz. **Ruler:** Nicholas I **Obv:** Variety I eagle

Date	Mintage	VG	F	VF	XF	Unc
1832 НГ	97,000	3.00	6.00	10.00	25.00	—
1833 НГ	435,000	2.50	5.00	10.00	20.00	—
1834 НГ	320,000	2.50	5.00	10.00	20.00	—
1835 НГ	500,000	2.50	5.00	10.00	20.00	—
1836 НГ	1,280,000	2.50	5.00	10.00	20.00	—
1837 НГ	1,300,000	2.50	5.00	10.00	20.00	—
1838 НГ	1,635,000	2.50	5.00	10.00	20.00	—
1839 НГ	4,030,000	2.50	5.00	10.00	20.00	—
1840 НГ	2,075,000	2.50	5.00	10.00	20.00	—
Common date Proof	—	Value: 190				
1841 НГ	25,000	6.00	12.00	20.00	40.00	—
1842 АЧ	—	20.00	40.00	80.00	150	—
1843 АЧ	—	20.00	40.00	80.00	150	—
1844 КБ	—	20.00	40.00	80.00	150	—
1845 КБ	105,000	2.50	5.00	10.00	20.00	—
1846 ПА	630,000	2.50	5.00	10.00	20.00	—
1847 ПА	3,923,000	2.50	5.00	10.00	20.00	—
1848 НІ	2,636,000	2.50	5.00	10.00	20.00	—
1849 ПА	3,250,000	2.50	5.00	10.00	20.00	—
1850 ПА	3,075,000	2.50	5.00	10.00	20.00	—
1851 ПА	2,000,000	2.50	5.00	10.00	20.00	—
1852 ПА	Inc. above	2.50	5.00	10.00	20.00	—
1852 НІ Rare	1,800,000	—	—	—	—	—
1853 НІ	1,800,000	2.50	5.00	10.00	20.00	—
1854 НІ	990,000	2.50	5.00	10.00	20.00	—
1855 НІ	3,090,000	2.50	5.00	10.00	20.00	—
1856 ФБ	3,240,000	2.50	5.00	10.00	20.00	—
1857 ФБ	4,275,000	2.50	5.00	10.00	20.00	—
1857 MW	27,000	6.00	12.50	25.00	50.00	—
1858 ФБ	4,150,000	2.50	5.00	10.00	20.00	—
Common date Proof	—	Value: 150				

Y# 22.1 20 KOPEKS

4.1463 g., 0.7500 Silver .0999 oz. **Ruler:** Alexander II **Edge:** Reticulated

Date	Mintage	F	VF	XF	Unc	BU
1859 ФБ	3,960,000	1.50	3.00	5.00	30.00	—
1860 ФБ	1,070,000	3.00	5.00	30.00	—	—

Y# 22.2 20 KOPEKS

4.1463 g., 0.7500 Silver .0999 oz. **Ruler:** Alexander II **Obv:** Eagle redesigned **Note:** Varieties of eagle exist for 1860 dated coins.

Date	Mintage	F	VF	XF	Unc	BU
1860 ФБ	14,440,000	1.50	3.00	5.00	30.00	—
1861 ФБ	19,500,000	1.50	3.00	5.00	30.00	—
1861 МИ	Inc. above	2.00	4.00	8.00	35.00	—
1861	19,000,000	1.50	3.00	5.00	30.00	—
1862 МИ	19,500,000	1.50	3.00	5.00	30.00	—
1863 АБ	19,230,000	1.50	3.00	5.00	30.00	—
1864 НФ	20,060,000	1.50	3.00	5.00	30.00	—
1865 НФ	20,048,000	1.50	3.00	5.00	30.00	—
1866 НФ	10,067,000	1.50	3.00	5.00	30.00	—
1866 НІ	Inc. above	1.50	3.00	5.00	30.00	—
Common date Proof	—	Value: 265				

Y# 22a.1 20 KOPEKS

3.5992 g., 0.5000 Silver .0579 oz.

Date	Mintage	F	VF	XF	Unc	BU
1867СПБ НФ Error, rare	—	—	—	—	—	—
1867СПБ НІ	15,355,000	1.00	2.00	3.00	25.00	—
1868СПБ НІ	11,975,000	1.00	2.00	3.00	25.00	—
1869СПБ НІ	17,017,000	1.00	2.00	3.00	25.00	—
1870СПБ НІ	16,255,000	1.00	2.00	3.00	25.00	—
1871СПБ НІ	18,860,000	1.00	2.00	3.00	25.00	—
1872СПБ НІ	11,980,000	1.00	2.00	3.00	25.00	—
1873СПБ НІ	15,185,000	1.00	2.00	3.00	25.00	—
1874СПБ НІ	14,850,000	1.00	2.00	3.00	25.00	—
1875СПБ НІ	15,545,000	1.00	2.00	3.00	25.00	—
1876СПБ НІ	16,255,000	1.00	2.00	3.00	25.00	—
1877СПБ НІ	6,950,000	1.00	2.00	3.00	25.00	—
1877СПБ НФ	Inc. above	2.00	4.00	8.00	25.00	—
1878СПБ НФ	25,335,000	1.00	2.00	3.00	25.00	—
1878СПБ НІ	Inc. above	5.00	10.00	20.00	50.00	—
1879СПБ НФ	23,070,000	1.00	2.00	3.00	25.00	—
1880/7СПБ НФ	22,605,000	1.25	2.50	4.00	25.00	—
1880СПБ НФ	Inc. above	1.00	2.00	3.00	25.00	—
1881СПБ НФ	9,350,000	1.00	2.00	3.00	25.00	—
1882СПБ НФ	3,535,000	1.00	2.00	3.00	25.00	—
1883СПБ ДС	4,270,000	1.00	2.00	3.00	25.00	—
1883СПБ АГ	Inc. above	2.00	4.00	8.00	25.00	—
1884СПБ АГ	2,595,000	1.00	2.00	3.00	25.00	—
1885СПБ АГ	1,610,000	1.00	2.00	3.00	25.00	—
1886СПБ АГ	2,625,000	1.00	2.00	3.00	25.00	—
1887СПБ АГ	2,500,000	1.00	2.00	3.00	25.00	—
1888СПБ АГ	3,035,000	1.00	2.00	3.00	25.00	—
1889СПБ АГ	1,964,000	1.00	2.00	3.00	25.00	—
1890СПБ АГ	3,500,000	1.00	2.00	3.00	25.00	—
1891СПБ АГ	6,105,000	1.00	2.00	3.00	25.00	—
1893СПБ АГ	7,500,000	1.00	2.00	3.00	25.00	—
Common date Proof	—	Value: 250				

C# 159 25 KOPEKS

5.1830 g., 0.8680 Silver .1446 oz. **Ruler:** Nicholas I **Note:** For similar coins not listed here refer to Poland.

Date	Mintage	VG	F	VF	XF	Unc
1827СПБ НГ	1,860,000	5.00	10.00	25.00	50.00	—
1828СПБ НГ	320,000	6.00	12.50	35.00	65.00	—
Note: The 1828 with reeded edge is a rare pattern						
1829СПБ НГ	1,200,000	5.00	10.00	20.00	50.00	—
1830СПБ НГ	1,160,000	5.00	10.00	20.00	50.00	—
1831СПБ НГ	484,000	5.00	10.00	20.00	50.00	—
Common date Proof	—	Value: 375				

C# 166.1 25 KOPEKS

5.1830 g., 0.8680 Silver .1446 oz. **Ruler:** Nicholas I **Obv:** Variety I eagle **Note:** Varieties of eagle and crown exist.

Date	Mintage	VG	F	VF	XF	Unc
1832 НГ	308,000	3.50	8.00	15.00	30.00	—
1833 НГ	260,000	3.50	8.00	15.00	30.00	—
1834 НГ	260,000	3.50	8.00	15.00	30.00	—
1835 НГ	356,000	3.50	8.00	15.00	30.00	—
1836/5 НГ	1,072,000	4.00	9.00	17.00	35.00	—
1836 НГ	Inc. above	3.50	8.00	15.00	30.00	—

Date	Mintage	VG	F	VF	XF	Unc
1837 НГ	1,144,000	3.50	8.00	15.00	30.00	—
1838 НГ	2,672,000	3.50	8.00	15.00	30.00	—
1839 НГ	2,738,000	3.50	8.00	15.00	30.00	—
1840 НГ	604,000	3.50	8.00	15.00	30.00	—
Common date Proof	—	Value: 450				
1841/0 НГ	20,000	4.00	9.00	17.00	35.00	—
1841 НГ	Inc. above	20.00	40.00	80.00	150	—
1842 АЧ	—	20.00	40.00	80.00	150	—
1843 АЧ	—	20.00	40.00	80.00	150	—
1844 КБ	21,000	3.50	8.00	15.00	30.00	—
1845 КБ	569,000	3.50	8.00	15.00	30.00	—
1846 ПА	576,000	3.50	8.00	15.00	30.00	—
1847 ПА	4,824,000	2.50	6.00	12.50	25.00	—
1848 НІ	2,636,000	2.50	6.00	12.50	25.00	—
1849 ПА	3,440,000	2.50	6.00	12.50	25.00	—
1850 ПА	3,740,000	2.50	6.00	12.50	25.00	—
1851 ПА	2,400,000	2.50	6.00	12.50	25.00	—
1852 ПА	2,160,000	2.50	6.00	12.50	25.00	—
1852 НІ	Inc. above	10.00	20.00	40.00	80.00	—
1853 НІ	2,160,000	2.50	6.00	12.50	25.00	—
1853	—	10.00	20.00	40.00	80.00	—
1854 НІ	1,148,000	2.50	6.00	12.50	25.00	—
1855 НІ	10,396,000	2.50	5.00	7.50	12.50	—
1856 ФБ	4,444,000	2.50	5.00	10.00	20.00	—
1857 ФБ	5,420,000	2.50	5.00	10.00	20.00	—
1858 ФБ	5,528,000	2.50	5.00	10.00	20.00	—
1858	Inc. above	5.00	10.00	20.00	40.00	—
Common date Proof	—	Value: 350				

C# 166.2 25 KOPEKS

5.1830 g., 0.8680 Silver .1446 oz.

Date	Mintage	VG	F	VF	XF	Unc
1854MW	9,000	12.00	25.00	50.00	100	—
1857MW	33,000	10.00	20.00	45.00	90.00	—

Y# 23 25 KOPEKS

5.1830 g., 0.8680 Silver .1446 oz. **Ruler:** Alexander II **Obv:** Eagle redesigned

Date	Mintage	F	VF	XF	Unc	BU
1859СПБ ФБ	4,400,000	5.00	10.00	20.00	60.00	—
1860СПБ ФБ	1,052,000	7.50	15.00	30.00	80.00	—
1861СПБ ФБ	116,000	12.50	25.00	50.00	125	—
1861СПБ МИ	Inc. above	30.00	60.00	125	250	—
1862СПБ МИ	36,000	20.00	40.00	85.00	175	—
1863СПБ АБ	36,000	20.00	40.00	85.00	175	—
1864СПБ НФ	68,000	15.00	37.50	75.00	150	—
1865СПБ НФ	16,000	15.00	37.50	75.00	150	—
1866СПБ НФ	36,000	15.00	37.50	75.00	150	—
1866СПБ НІ	Inc. above	15.00	37.50	75.00	150	—
1867СПБ НІ	48,000	15.00	37.50	75.00	150	—
1868СПБ НІ	40,000	15.00	37.50	75.00	150	—
1869СПБ НІ	20,000	30.00	60.00	125	250	—
1870СПБ НІ	44,000	15.00	37.50	75.00	150	—
1871СПБ НІ	24,000	15.00	37.50	75.00	150	—
1872СПБ НІ	44,000	15.00	37.50	75.00	150	—
1873СПБ НІ	36,000	15.00	37.50	75.00	150	—
1874СПБ НІ	32,000	15.00	37.50	75.00	150	—
1875СПБ НІ	24,000	15.00	37.50	75.00	150	—
1876СПБ НІ	40,000	15.00	37.50	75.00	150	—
1877СПБ НІ	1,776,000	7.50	15.00	30.00	80.00	—
1877СПБ Rare	Inc. above	—	—	—	—	—
1877СПБ НФ	Inc. above	7.50	15.00	30.00	80.00	—
1878СПБ НФ	1,768,000	5.00	10.00	20.00	40.00	—
1879СПБ НФ	32,000	15.00	37.50	75.00	150	—
1880СПБ НФ	78,000	12.50	25.00	50.00	125	—
1881СПБ НФ	2,001	25.00	50.00	75.00	150	—
1882СПБ НФ	2,007	25.00	50.00	75.00	150	—
1883СПБ ДС	2,008	25.00	50.00	75.00	175	—
1883СПБ АГ	Inc. above	30.00	60.00	125	250	—
1884СПБ АГ	2,004	25.00	50.00	75.00	175	—
1885СПБ АГ	1,011	25.00	50.00	75.00	200	—
Common date Proof	—	Value: 425				

Y# 44 25 KOPEKS

4.9990 g., 0.9000 Silver .1446 oz. **Ruler:** Alexander III **Note:** Without mint mark.

Date	Mintage	F	VF	XF	Unc	BU
1886 АГ	4,058	25.00	50.00	90.00	175	—
1887 АГ	28,000	20.00	40.00	80.00	150	—
1888 АГ	4,007	25.00	50.00	90.00	175	—
1889 АГ	1,002	75.00	125	200	400	—
1890 АГ	2,006	25.00	50.00	90.00	175	—
1891 АГ	24,000	25.00	50.00	90.00	175	—
1892 АГ	4,006	25.00	50.00	90.00	175	—
1893 АГ	8,008	25.00	50.00	90.00	175	—
1894/3 АГ	—	17.00	34.00	66.00	110	—
1894 АГ	—	15.00	30.00	60.00	100	—
Common date Proof	—	Value: 500				

Y# 57 25 KOPEKS

4.9990 g., 0.9000 Silver .1446 oz. **Note:** Struck at St. Petersburg without mint mark.

Date	Mintage	F	VF	XF	Unc	BU
1895	2,660,000	8.00	15.00	40.00	150	—
1896	27,212,000	5.00	10.00	20.00	70.00	—
1898 Proof	1	Value: 20,000				
1900	560,000	15.00	30.00	60.00	250	—

C# 98.1a POLUPOLTINNIK (1/4 Rouble)

5.1800 g., 0.8680 Silver .1446 oz. **Ruler:** Paul I

Date	Mintage	VG	F	VF	XF	Unc
1801СМ АИ	68,000	35.00	70.00	150	300	—
1801СМ ОЦ Rare	Inc. above	—	—	—	—	—

C# 121 POLUPOLTINNIK (1/4 Rouble)

4.1400 g., 0.8680 Silver .1155 oz. **Ruler:** Alexander I

Date	Mintage	VG	F	VF	XF	Unc
1802СПБ АИ	324,000	50.00	100	175	250	—
1803СПБ АИ	152,000	60.00	110	200	275	—
1804СПБ ФГ	168,000	50.00	100	175	250	—
1805СПБ ФГ	137,000	60.00	110	200	275	—

C# 121a POLUPOLTINNIK (1/4 Rouble)

4.1400 g., 0.8680 Silver .1155 oz. **Ruler:** Alexander I

Date	Mintage	VG	F	VF	XF	Unc
1808СПБ ФГ Rare	—	—	—	—	—	—
1809СПБ МК	40,000	75.00	150	250	350	—
1809СПБ ФГ Rare	Inc. above	—	—	—	—	—
1810СПБ ФГ	66,000	60.00	120	200	275	—

Y# 45 50 KOPEKS

9.9980 g., 0.9000 Silver .2893 oz. **Ruler:** Alexander III **Note:** Without mint mark.

Date	Mintage	F	VF	XF	Unc	BU
1886 АГ	2,058	15.00	30.00	80.00	250	—
1887 АГ	26,000	20.00	40.00	80.00	250	—
1888 АГ	2,007	15.00	30.00	80.00	250	—
1889 АГ	1,002	75.00	125	200	500	—
1890 АГ	2,006	15.00	30.00	80.00	250	—
1891 АГ	24,000	20.00	40.00	80.00	250	—
1892 АГ	2,006	15.00	30.00	80.00	250	—
1893 АГ	4,008	15.00	30.00	80.00	250	—
1894 АГ	—	15.00	25.00	75.00	200	—
Common date Proof	—	Value: 850				

Y# 58.2 50 KOPEKS

9.9980 g., 0.9000 Silver .2893 oz. **Note:** Struck at St. Petersburg without mint mark.

Date	Mintage	F	VF	XF	Unc	BU
1895 АГ	5,400,000	5.00	10.00	25.00	100	—
1896 АГ	17,402,000	5.00	8.00	15.00	75.00	—
1898 АГ Proof	—	Value: 1,250				
1899 ЭБ	15,442,000	5.00	10.00	25.00	100	—
1899 ФЗ	Inc. above	5.00	10.00	25.00	100	—
1899 АГ	Inc. above	5.00	10.00	25.00	100	—
1900 ФЗ	3,360,000	5.00	10.00	25.00	100	—
Common date Proof	—	Value: 500				

Y# 58.1 50 KOPEKS

9.9980 g., 0.9000 Silver .2893 oz. **Ruler:** Nicholas II **Note:** Mint mark: Star on rim.

Date	Mintage	F	VF	XF	Unc	BU
1896	245,000	10.00	20.00	40.00	80.00	—
1897	46,755,000	7.50	12.50	25.00	60.00	—
1899	10,000,000	7.50	12.50	25.00	60.00	—
Common date Proof	—	Value: 600				

C# 99.1a POLTINA (1/2 Rouble)

10.3700 g., 0.8680 Silver .2894 oz. **Ruler:** Paul I **Note:** Reduced size.

Date	Mintage	VG	F	VF	XF	Unc
1801СМ ОМ	172,000	40.00	75.00	150	275	—
1801СМ ФЦ	Inc. above	50.00	100	200	350	—
1801СМ АИ	Inc. above	40.00	75.00	150	275	—

C# 123 POLTINA (1/2 Rouble)

10.3600 g., 0.8680 Silver .2892 oz. **Ruler:** Alexander I

Date	Mintage	VG	F	VF	XF	Unc
1802СПБ АИ	104,000	25.00	50.00	100	250	—
1803СПБ АИ	242,000	25.00	50.00	100	250	—
1804СПБ ФГ	230,000	25.00	50.00	100	250	—
1805СПБ ФГ	315,000	35.00	70.00	140	300	—

C# 123a POLTINA (1/2 Rouble)

10.3600 g., 0.8680 Silver .2892 oz. **Ruler:** Alexander I

Date	Mintage	VG	F	VF	XF	Unc
1809 МК Rare	11,000	—	—	—	—	—
1810 ФГ	79,000	75.00	150	300	750	—

C# 129 POLTINA (1/2 Rouble)

10.3600 g., 0.8680 Silver .2892 oz. **Ruler:** Alexander I

Date	Mintage	VG	F	VF	XF	Unc
1810 ФГ	—	12.50	25.00	50.00	125	—
Note: Mintage included in C#123a						
1811/0 ФГ	90,000	7.00	14.00	35.00	80.00	—
1811 ФГ	Inc. above	6.00	12.00	30.00	70.00	—
1812/1 МФ	45,000	7.00	14.00	35.00	80.00	—
1812 МФ	Inc. above	6.00	12.00	30.00	70.00	—
1813 ПС	580,000	6.00	12.00	30.00	70.00	—
1814/3 ПС	662,000	7.00	14.00	35.00	80.00	—
1814 ПС	Inc. above	6.00	12.00	30.00	70.00	—
1814 МФ	Inc. above	6.00	12.00	30.00	70.00	—
1815 МФ	1,700,000	6.00	12.00	30.00	70.00	—
1816 МФ	270,000	6.00	12.00	30.00	70.00	—
1816 ПС	Inc. above	6.00	12.00	30.00	70.00	—
1817 ПС	2,820,000	6.00	12.00	30.00	70.00	—
1818 ПС	4,250,000	6.00	12.00	30.00	70.00	—
1819 Rare	Inc. above	—	—	—	—	—
1819 ПС	2,430,000	6.00	12.00	30.00	70.00	—
1820 ПС Rare	1,356,000	—	—	—	—	—
1820 ПД	Inc. above	6.00	12.00	30.00	70.00	—
1821/0 ПД	480,000	7.00	14.00	35.00	80.00	—
1821 ПД	Inc. above	6.00	12.00	30.00	70.00	—
1822/1 ПД	90,000	7.00	14.00	35.00	80.00	—
1822/0 ПД	90,000	7.00	14.00	35.00	80.00	—
1822 ПД	Inc. above	6.00	12.00	30.00	70.00	—
1823 ПД	200,000	6.00	12.00	30.00	70.00	—
1824/3 ПД	320,000	7.00	14.00	35.00	80.00	—
1824 ПД	Inc. above	6.00	12.00	30.00	70.00	—
1825/4 ПД	152,000	7.00	14.00	35.00	80.00	—
1825 ПД	Inc. above	6.00	12.00	30.00	70.00	—
1826 НГ	201,000	6.00	12.00	30.00	70.00	—

C# 160 POLTINA (1/2 Rouble)

10.3600 g., 0.8680 Silver .2892 oz. **Ruler:** Nicholas I

Date	Mintage	VG	F	VF	XF	Unc
1826 НГ	—	15.00	30.00	70.00	165	—
Note: Mintage included in C#129						
1827 НГ	164,000	15.00	30.00	70.00	165	—
1828 НГ	274,000	15.00	30.00	70.00	165	—
1829 НГ	880,000	12.50	25.00	50.00	125	—
1830 НГ	290,000	15.00	30.00	70.00	165	—
1831 НГ	140,000	15.00	30.00	70.00	165	—
Common date Proof	—	Value: 700				

C# 167.1 POLTINA (1/2 Rouble)

10.3600 g., 0.8680 Silver .2892 oz. **Ruler:** Nicholas I **Note:** Variety I eagle. Varieties of eagle and wreath exist.

Date	Mintage	VG	F	VF	XF	Unc
1832 НГ	50,000	10.00	20.00	40.00	100	—
1833 НГ	82,000	10.00	20.00	40.00	100	—
1834 НГ	46,000	10.00	20.00	40.00	100	—
1835 НГ	20,000	12.50	25.00	50.00	125	—
1836 НГ	140,000	7.50	15.00	30.00	60.00	—
1837/6 НГ	104,000	8.00	16.00	32.00	65.00	—
1837 НГ	Inc. above	7.50	15.00	30.00	60.00	—
1838 НГ Rare	4,000	—	—	—	—	—
1839/7 НГ	1,830,000	6.00	12.00	30.00	60.00	—
1839 НГ	Inc. above	5.00	10.00	25.00	45.00	—
1840/3 НГ	960,000	20.00	40.00	80.00	150	—
1840 НГ	Inc. above	5.00	10.00	25.00	45.00	—
Common date Proof	—	Value: 600				
1841/0 НГ	10,000	20.00	40.00	80.00	150	—
1841 НГ	Inc. above	15.00	30.00	60.00	125	—
1842 НГ Rare	—	—	—	—	—	—
1842/39 АЧ	214,000	6.00	12.00	30.00	50.00	—
1842 АЧ	Inc. above	5.00	10.00	25.00	40.00	—
1843 АЧ	—	10.00	20.00	40.00	100	—
1844 КБ	348,000	5.00	10.00	25.00	45.00	—
1845 КБ	2,009,000	5.00	10.00	25.00	45.00	—
1846 ПА	460,000	5.00	10.00	25.00	45.00	—
1847 ПА	615,000	5.00	10.00	25.00	45.00	—
1848 НI	1,560,000	5.00	10.00	25.00	45.00	—
1849 ПА	450,000	5.00	10.00	25.00	45.00	—
1850 ПА	530,000	5.00	10.00	25.00	45.00	—
1851 ПА	800,000	5.00	10.00	25.00	45.00	—
1852 ПА	720,000	5.00	10.00	25.00	45.00	—
1852 НI	Inc. above	7.50	15.00	35.00	60.00	—
1853 НI	720,000	5.00	10.00	25.00	45.00	—
1854/0 НI	440,000	6.00	12.00	30.00	50.00	—
1854 НI	Inc. above	5.00	10.00	25.00	45.00	—
1855 НI	714,000	5.00	15.00	25.00	45.00	—
1856 ФБ	450,000	5.00	15.00	25.00	45.00	—
1857/6 ФБ	1,650,000	6.00	17.00	30.00	50.00	—
1857 ФБ	Inc. above	5.00	15.00	25.00	45.00	—
1858 ФБ	1,112,000	5.00	15.00	25.00	50.00	—
Common date Proof	—	Value: 450				

C# 167.2 POLTINA (1/2 Rouble)

10.3600 g., 0.8680 Silver .2892 oz. **Ruler:** Nicholas I **Note:** Varieties of eagle exist.

Date	Mintage	VG	F	VF	XF	Unc
1842MW	76,000	7.50	15.00	30.00	60.00	—
1843MW	23,000	10.00	20.00	40.00	80.00	—
1844MW	116,000	7.50	15.00	30.00	60.00	—
1845MW	138,000	7.50	15.00	30.00	60.00	—
1846MW	308,000	7.50	15.00	30.00	60.00	—
1847MW	783,000	7.50	15.00	30.00	60.00	—
1854MW	269,000	7.50	15.00	30.00	60.00	—
Common date Proof	—	Value: 450				

Y# 24 POLTINA (1/2 Rouble)

10.3600 g., 0.8680 Silver .2892 oz. **Ruler:** Alexander II **Note:** Variety II eagle. Edge varieties exist.

Date	Mintage	F	VF	XF	Unc	BU
1859СПБ ФБ	1,392,000	10.00	20.00	40.00	100	—
1859СПБ ФБ Proof	—	Value: 700				
1860СПБ ФБ	192,000	20.00	40.00	85.00	175	—
1861СПБ ФБ	64,000	25.00	50.00	100	200	—
1861СПБ МИ	Inc. above	50.00	100	200	400	—
1862СПБ МИ	24,000	30.00	60.00	125	250	—
1863СПБ АБ	22,000	30.00	60.00	125	250	—
1864СПБ НФ	34,000	30.00	60.00	125	250	—
1865СПБ НФ	24,000	30.00	60.00	125	250	—
1866СПБ НФ	22,000	30.00	60.00	125	250	—
1866СПБ НI	Inc. above	30.00	60.00	125	250	—
1867СПБ НI	26,000	30.00	60.00	125	250	—
1868СПБ НI	30,000	50.00	100	200	400	—
1869СПБ НI	20,000	30.00	60.00	125	250	—
1870СПБ НI	6,000	40.00	80.00	150	300	—
1871СПБ НI	20,000	30.00	60.00	125	250	—
1872СПБ НI	22,000	30.00	60.00	125	250	—
1873СПБ НI	36,000	30.00	60.00	125	250	—
1874СПБ НI	16,000	30.00	60.00	125	250	—
1875СПБ НI	14,000	30.00	60.00	125	250	—
1876СПБ НI	24,000	30.00	60.00	125	250	—
1876СПБ	Inc. above	40.00	80.00	150	300	—
1877СПБ НI	1,034,000	10.00	20.00	40.00	100	—
1877СПБ НФ	Inc. above	15.00	30.00	60.00	125	—
1878СПБ НФ	778,000	10.00	20.00	40.00	100	—
1879СПБ НФ	14,000	30.00	60.00	125	250	—
1880СПБ НФ	42,000	25.00	50.00	100	200	—
1881СПБ НФ	1,011	40.00	80.00	150	300	—
1882СПБ НФ	1,007	40.00	80.00	150	300	—
1883СПБ ДС	1,008	40.00	80.00	150	300	—
1883СПБ АГ	Inc. above	50.00	100	200	400	—
1884СПБ АГ	1,004	40.00	80.00	150	300	—
1885СПБ АГ	511	50.00	100	200	400	—

C# 101a ROUBLE

20.7300 g., 0.8680 Silver .5785 oz. **Ruler:** Paul I **Note:** Reduced size, 38 millimeter. Dav. #1688.

Date	Mintage	VG	F	VF	XF	Unc
1801СМ АИ	3,143,000	20.00	40.00	90.00	200	—
1801СМ АИ	3,143,000	20.00	40.00	90.00	200	—
1801СМ ФЦ	Inc. above	20.00	40.00	90.00	200	—
1801СМ ОМ	Inc. above	30.00	60.00	120	300	—

C# 125 ROUBLE

20.7300 g., 0.8680 Silver .5785 oz. **Ruler:** Alexander I

Date	Mintage	VG	F	VF	XF	Unc
1802СПБ АИ	5,360,000	30.00	60.00	150	300	—
1803СПБ АИ	2,429,000	30.00	60.00	150	300	—
1803СПБ ФГ	Inc. above	35.00	75.00	200	400	—
1804СПБ ФГ	4,355,000	30.00	60.00	150	300	—
1805СПБ ФГ	2,020,000	30.00	60.00	150	300	—

C# 125a ROUBLE

20.7300 g., 0.8680 Silver .5785 oz. **Ruler:** Alexander I

Date	Mintage	VG	F	VF	XF	Unc
1807 ФГ	533,000	40.00	85.00	250	500	—
1808/7 ФГ	1,701,000	35.00	75.00	185	425	—
1808 ФГ	Inc. above	35.00	75.00	185	425	—
1808/7 МК	Inc. above	35.00	75.00	185	425	—
1808 МК	Inc. above	35.00	75.00	185	425	—
1809 МК	2,177,000	35.00	75.00	185	425	—
1809 ФГ	Inc. above	35.00	75.00	185	425	—
1810 ФГ	1,682,000	40.00	85.00	250	500	—

C# 130 ROUBLE

20.7300 g., 0.8680 Silver .5785 oz. **Ruler:** Alexander I

Date	Mintage	VG	F	VF	XF	Unc
1810 ФГ	—	175	375	700	1,500	—
Note: Mintage included in C#125a						
1811 ФГ	2,675,000	15.00	30.00	75.00	150	—
1812/1 МФ	4,076,000	16.00	35.00	80.00	165	—
1812 МФ	Inc. above	15.00	30.00	75.00	150	—
1813/2 ПС	5,210,000	16.00	35.00	80.00	165	—
1813 ПС	Inc. above	15.00	30.00	75.00	150	—
1814 МФ	3,600,000	15.00	30.00	75.00	150	—
1814 ПС	Inc. above	15.00	30.00	75.00	150	—
1814	Inc. above	30.00	60.00	150	300	—
1815 МФ	4,750,000	10.00	30.00	75.00	150	—
1816/5 МФ	1,782,000	16.00	35.00	80.00	165	—
1816 ПС	Inc. above	15.00	30.00	75.00	150	—
1816 МФ	Inc. above	15.00	30.00	75.00	150	—
1816 ПС	Inc. above	15.00	30.00	75.00	150	—
1817 ПС	11,775,000	15.00	30.00	75.00	150	—
1818 ПС	16,275,000	15.00	30.00	75.00	150	—
1818 СП	Inc. above	20.00	50.00	100	200	—
1818	Inc. above	30.00	60.00	150	300	—
1819 ПС	6,355,000	15.00	30.00	75.00	150	—
1820/1 ПД	1,962,000	15.00	35.00	80.00	165	—
1820/19 ПД	Inc. above	15.00	35.00	80.00	165	—
1820 ПС	Inc. above	100	220	450	800	—
1820 ПД	Inc. above	15.00	30.00	75.00	150	—
1821/0 ПД	840,000	16.00	35.00	80.00	165	—
1821 ПД	Inc. above	15.00	30.00	75.00	150	—
1822/1 ПД	3,120,000	16.00	35.00	80.00	165	—
1822 ПД	Inc. above	15.00	30.00	75.00	150	—
1823 ПД	2,955,000	15.00	30.00	75.00	150	—
1824/3 ПД	2,035,000	16.00	35.00	80.00	165	—
1824 ПД	Inc. above	15.00	30.00	75.00	150	—
1825/4 ПД	1,461,000	16.00	35.00	80.00	165	—
1825 ПД	Inc. above	15.00	30.00	75.00	150	—
1825 НГ	Inc. above	20.00	50.00	100	200	—
1826 НГ	730,000	20.00	55.00	150	250	—

C# 161 ROUBLE

20.7300 g., 0.8680 Silver .5785 oz. **Ruler:** Nicholas I **Note:** Edge varieties exist.

Date	Mintage	F	VF	XF	Unc	BU
1826 НГ	—	70.00	145	375	1,100	—
Note: Mintage included in C#155						
1827/6 НГ	584,000	65.00	135	360	1,000	—
1827 НГ	Inc. above	60.00	125	350	975	—
1828 НГ	2,530,000	60.00	125	350	975	—
1829 НГ	5,510,000	60.00	125	350	975	—
1830/2 НГ	6,010,000	65.00	135	360	1,000	—
1830 НГ	Inc. above	60.00	125	350	975	—
1831/0 НГ	3,670,000	65.00	135	360	1,000	—
1831 НГ	Inc. above	60.00	125	350	975	—

C# 168.1 ROUBLE

20.7300 g., 0.8680 Silver .5785 oz. **Note:** Superior Goodman sale 2-91 P/L Unc realized $10,450.

Date	Mintage	F	VF	XF	Unc	BU
1832 НГ	1,941,000	18.00	38.00	120	300	—
1833 НГ	1,711,000	18.00	38.00	120	300	—
1834 НГ	2,270,000	18.00	38.00	120	300	—
1835/4 НГ	244,000	27.00	68.00	165	400	—
1835 НГ	Inc. above	25.00	60.00	150	350	—
1836/4 НГ	1,102,000	20.00	45.00	140	350	—
1836 НГ	Inc. above	18.00	38.00	120	300	—
1837 НГ	1,478,000	18.00	38.00	120	300	—
1838 НГ	232,000	25.00	60.00	150	350	—
1839 НГ Rare	36,000	—	—	—	—	—
1840/3 НГ	2,627,000	20.00	45.00	140	350	—
1840 НГ	Inc. above	18.00	38.00	120	300	—
1841/0 НГ	6,155,000	20.00	45.00	140	350	—
1841/3 НГ	Inc. above	20.00	45.00	140	350	—
1841 НГ	Inc. above	18.00	38.00	120	300	—
1842/1 АЧ	4,965,000	20.00	45.00	140	350	—
1842 АЧ	Inc. above	18.00	38.00	120	300	—
1843/2 АЧ	5,320,000	20.00	45.00	140	350	—
1843 A\b	Inc. above	18.00	38.00	120	300	—
1844/3 КБ	2,933,000	20.00	45.00	140	350	—
1844 КБ	Inc. above	18.00	38.00	120	300	—
1845 КБ	683,000	18.00	38.00	120	300	—
1846/5 ПА	3,523,000	20.00	45.00	140	350	—
1846 ПА	Inc. above	18.00	38.00	120	300	—
1847 ПА	563,000	20.00	45.00	140	325	—
1848 HI	1,542,000	18.00	38.00	120	300	—
1849 ПА	1,708,000	18.00	38.00	120	300	—
1850 ПА	1,600,000	18.00	38.00	120	300	—
1851/0 ПА	2,400,000	20.00	45.00	140	350	—
1851 ПА	Inc. above	18.00	38.00	120	300	—
1852 ПА	2,560,000	18.00	38.00	120	300	—
1852 HI	Inc. above	25.00	60.00	150	350	—
1853 HI	2,160,000	18.00	38.00	120	300	—
1854 HI	3,070,000	18.00	38.00	120	300	—
1855 HI	—	18.00	38.00	120	300	—
1856/5 ФБ	1,388,000	20.00	45.00	140	350	—
1856 ФБ	Inc. above	18.00	38.00	120	300	—
1857 ФБ	250,000	25.00	60.00	150	400	—
1858 ФБ	570,000	25.00	60.00	150	400	—
Common date Proof	—	Value: 1,600				

C# 169 ROUBLE

20.7300 g., 0.8680 Silver .5785 oz. **Ruler:** Nicholas I **Note:** Alexander I monument.

Date	Mintage	F	VF	XF	Unc	BU
1834СПБ Rare; Proof	—	—	—	—	—	—
1834СПБ	15,000	75.00	150	325	700	—

C# 170 ROUBLE

20.7300 g., 0.8680 Silver .5785 oz. **Ruler:** Nicholas I **Subject:** Battle of Borodino Memorial **Note:** Large portion of mintage melted. The 1841 Marriage "Rouble" is a medal.

Date	Mintage	F	VF	XF	Unc	BU
1839 НГ	160,000	100	250	400	750	—

C# 168.2 ROUBLE

20.7300 g., 0.8680 Silver .5785 oz. **Ruler:** Nicholas I

Date	Mintage	F	VF	XF	Unc	BU
1842MW	257,000	25.00	45.00	100	275	—
1843MW	267,000	25.00	45.00	100	275	—
1844MW	2,364,000	25.00	45.00	100	275	—
1845MW	345,000	30.00	55.00	120	300	—
1846MW	511,000	25.00	45.00	100	275	—
1847MW	987,000	25.00	45.00	100	275	—

Y# 25 ROUBLE

20.7300 g., 0.8680 Silver .5785 oz. **Ruler:** Alexander II

Date	Mintage	F	VF	XF	Unc	BU
1859СПБ ФБ	14,000	100	225	450	1,000	—
1860СПБ ФБ	18,000	100	250	600	1,500	—
1861СПБ ФБ	76,000	60.00	120	225	700	—
1861СПБ МИ	Inc. above	150	300	750	2,000	—
1862СПБ МИ	22,000	60.00	120	225	700	—
1863СПБ АБ	5,000	150	300	750	2,000	—
1864СПБ НФ	114,000	35.00	70.00	150	450	—
1865СПБ НФ	115,000	35.00	70.00	150	450	—
1866СПБ HI	110,000	35.00	70.00	150	450	—
1866СПБ НФ	Inc. above	35.00	70.00	150	450	—
1867СПБ HI	425,000	20.00	35.00	75.00	275	—
1868СПБ HI	775,000	20.00	35.00	75.00	275	—
1869СПБ HI	285,000	20.00	35.00	75.00	275	—
1870СПБ HI	386,000	20.00	35.00	75.00	275	—
1871СПБ HI	884,000	20.00	35.00	75.00	275	—
1872СПБ HI	978,000	20.00	35.00	75.00	275	—
1873СПБ HI	673,000	20.00	35.00	75.00	275	—
1874СПБ HI	648,000	20.00	35.00	75.00	275	—
1875СПБ HI	687,000	20.00	35.00	75.00	275	—
1876СПБ HI	778,000	20.00	35.00	75.00	275	—
1877СПБ HI	6,923,000	17.50	30.00	55.00	275	—
1877СПБ НФ	Inc. above	17.50	30.00	55.00	275	—
1878СПБ НФ	8,087,000	17.50	30.00	55.00	275	—
1879СПБ НФ	611,000	20.00	35.00	75.00	275	—
1880СПБ НФ	521,000	20.00	35.00	75.00	275	—
1881СПБ НФ	699,000	20.00	35.00	75.00	275	—
1882СПБ НФ	434,000	20.00	35.00	75.00	275	—
1883СПБ ДС	425,000	20.00	35.00	75.00	275	—
1883СПБ АГ	Inc. above	150	300	750	2,000	—
1884СПБ АГ	355,000	20.00	35.00	75.00	275	—
1885СПБ АГ	500,000	20.00	35.00	75.00	275	—
Common date Proof	—	Value: 1,250				

Y# 28 ROUBLE

20.7300 g., 0.8680 Silver .5785 oz. **Ruler:** Alexander II **Subject:** Nicholas I Memorial **Note:** Without mint mark.

Date	Mintage	F	VF	XF	Unc	BU
1859	50,000	100	150	275	450	—

Y# 43 ROUBLE

20.7300 g., 0.8680 Silver .5785 oz. **Ruler:** Alexander III **Subject:** Alexander III Coronation **Note:** Without mint mark.

Date	Mintage	F	VF	XF	Unc	BU
1883	279,000	35.00	75.00	150	300	—
1883 Proof	—	Value: 1,000				

Y# 46 ROUBLE

19.9960 g., 0.9000 Silver .5786 oz. **Ruler:** Alexander III **Note:** Mintmasters initials and stars found on edge

Date	Mintage	F	VF	XF	Unc	BU
1886 АГ	488,000	30.00	60.00	150	450	—
1887 АГ	491,000	30.00	60.00	150	450	—
1888 АГ	498,000	30.00	60.00	150	450	—
1889 АГ	1,002	300	900	1,800	4,000	—
1890 АГ	90,000	40.00	75.00	175	485	—
1891 АГ	117,000	30.00	60.00	160	465	—
1892 АГ	2,131,000	30.00	60.00	150	435	—
1893 АГ	1,485,000	30.00	60.00	150	435	—
1894 АГ	3,007	75.00	150	375	700	—
Common date Proof	—	Value: 2,000				

Y# 59.3 ROUBLE

19.9960 g., 0.9000 Silver .5786 oz. **Note:** Struck at St. Petersburg without mint mark.

Date	Mintage	F	VF	XF	Unc	BU
1895 АГ	1,240,000	15.00	30.00	75.00	300	—
1896 АГ	12,540,000	12.00	25.00	65.00	225	—
1897 АГ	18,515,000	12.00	25.00	65.00	225	—
1898 АГ	18,725,000	12.00	25.00	65.00	225	—
1899 ЭБ	6,503,000	12.00	25.00	65.00	225	—
1899 ФЗ	Inc. above	12.00	25.00	65.00	225	—
1900 ФЗ	3,484,000	15.00	30.00	75.00	325	—
Common date Proof	—	Value: 1,500				

Y# 60 ROUBLE
19.9960 g., 0.9000 Silver .5786 oz. **Ruler:** Nicholas II **Subject:** Nicholas II Coronation

Date	Mintage	F	VF	XF	Unc	BU
1896 АГ	191,000	25.00	45.00	100	250	—
1896 АГ Proof	—	Value: 900				

Y# 59.2 ROUBLE
19.9960 g., 0.9000 Silver .5786 oz. **Ruler:** Nicholas II **Note:** Mint mark: Star on rim.

Date	Mintage	F	VF	XF	Unc	BU
1896	12,000,000	12.00	25.00	60.00	225	—
1898	5,000,000	12.00	25.00	60.00	225	—
Common date Proof	—	Value: 1,500				

Y# 59.1 ROUBLE
19.9960 g., 0.9000 Silver .5786 oz. **Ruler:** Nicholas II **Note:** Without mint mark.

Date	Mintage	F	VF	XF	Unc	BU
1897	26,000,000	12.00	25.00	60.00	225	—
1898	14,000,000	12.00	25.00	60.00	225	—
1899	10,000,000	12.00	25.00	60.00	225	—
Common date Proof	—	Value: 1,500				

Y# 61 ROUBLE
19.9960 g., 0.9000 Silver .5786 oz. **Ruler:** Nicholas II **Subject:** Alexander II Memorial

Date	Mintage	F	VF	XF	Unc	BU
1898 АГ	Est. 5,000	175	350	500	1,000	—
1898 АГ Proof	—	Value: 2,200				

C# A172 1-1/2 ROUBLES - 10 ZLOTYCH
31.1000 g., 0.8680 Silver .8679 oz. **Ruler:** Nicholas I **Note:** Without mint mark.

Date	Mintage	F	VF	XF	Unc	BU
1835	36	—	—	20,000	35,000	—

C# 172.4 1-1/2 ROUBLES - 10 ZLOTYCH
31.1000 g., 0.8680 Silver .8679 oz. **Ruler:** Nicholas I **Obv:** Without designer's name or initials **Note:** This coin was struck as a presentation piece.

Date	Mintage	F	VF	XF	Unc	BU
1836	Inc. above	—	—	30,000	40,000	—

C# 172.1 1-1/2 ROUBLES - 10 ZLOTYCH
31.1000 g., 0.8680 Silver .8679 oz. **Ruler:** Nicholas I **Obv:** Designer's initials ПУ on truncation

Date	Mintage	F	VF	XF	Unc	BU
1836	50	—	—	11,000	15,000	—

C# 172.2 1-1/2 ROUBLES - 10 ZLOTYCH
31.1000 g., 0.8680 Silver .8679 oz. **Ruler:** Nicholas I **Rev:** Die break at rim lower right

Date	Mintage	F	VF	XF	Unc	BU
1836 Restrike	—	—	—	9,000	12,000	—

C# 172.3 1-1/2 ROUBLES - 10 ZLOTYCH
31.1000 g., 0.8680 Silver .8679 oz. **Ruler:** Nicholas I **Obv:** Designer's name below bust

Date	Mintage	F	VF	XF	Unc	BU
1836	Inc. above	—	—	18,000	25,000	—

C# 173.1 1-1/2 ROUBLES - 10 ZLOTYCH
31.1000 g., 0.8680 Silver .8679 oz. **Ruler:** Nicholas I **Subject:** Battle of Borodino Memorial **Obv:** Long rays

Date	Mintage	F	VF	XF	Unc	BU
1839	6,000	600	1,000	2,500	5,500	—

C# 173.2 1-1/2 ROUBLES - 10 ZLOTYCH
31.1000 g., 0.8680 Silver .8679 oz. **Ruler:** Nicholas I **Obv:** Short rays

Date	Mintage	F	VF	XF	Unc	BU
1839	Inc. above	600	1,000	2,500	5,500	—

Note: Large portion of the mintage melted

C# 177 3 ROUBLES
10.3500 g., Platinum .3327 oz. **Ruler:** Nicholas I **Note:** The low mintage figures incorporated in the following listings of Russian platinum issues are not necessarily reflective of relative scarcity as many of the issues were restruck at later dates, using original dies in unrecorded quantities.

Date	Mintage	F	VF	XF	Unc	BU
1828СПБ	20,000	250	425	850	1,250	—
1829СПБ	43,000	225	350	675	1,500	—
1830СПБ	106,000	225	350	675	1,500	—
1831СПБ	87,000	225	350	675	1,500	—
1832СПБ	66,000	225	350	675	1,500	—
1833СПБ	85,000	250	400	800	1,500	—
1834СПБ	91,000	225	300	650	1,500	—
1835СПБ	139,000	250	400	800	1,500	—
1836СПБ	44,000	275	350	700	1,500	—
1837СПБ	46,000	275	350	700	1,500	—
1838СПБ	49,000	275	350	700	1,500	—
1839СПБ Proof; Rare	6	—	—	—	—	—
1840СПБ Proof; Rare	3	—	—	—	—	—
1841СПБ	17,000	250	400	800	1,850	—
1842СПБ	146,000	225	350	650	1,500	—
1843СПБ	172,000	225	350	675	1,500	—
1844СПБ	215,000	225	375	800	1,850	—
1845СПБ	50,000	250	425	900	2,000	—
Common date Proof	—	Value: 2,500				

Y# 26 3 ROUBLES
3.9260 g., 0.9170 Gold .1157 oz.

Date	Mintage	F	VF	XF	Unc	BU
1869 НІ	143,000	175	225	400	600	—
1870 НІ	200,000	175	225	400	600	—
1871 НІ	200,000	175	225	400	600	—
1872 НІ	100,000	175	225	400	600	—
1873 НІ	77,000	175	225	400	600	—
1874 НІ	270,000	175	225	400	600	—
1875 НІ	100,000	175	225	400	600	—
1876 НІ	63,000	175	225	400	600	—
1877 НІ	50,000	175	225	400	—	—
1877 НФ	Inc. above	175	225	400	—	—
1878 НФ	194,000	175	225	400	600	—
1879 НФ	—	—	—	—	3,000	—
1880 НФ	100,000	175	225	400	600	—
1881 НФ	48,000	175	225	400	600	—
1882 НФ	—	—	2,200	3,500	5,000	—
1883 ДС	9,007	175	225	350	750	—
1883 АГ Rare	Inc. above	—	—	—	—	—
1884 АГ	47,000	175	225	350	750	—
1885 АГ	29,000	175	250	375	700	—
Common date Proof	—	Value: 2,000				

C# 104.1 5 ROUBLES
6.0800 g., 0.9860 Gold .1928 oz. **Ruler:** Paul I **Obv:** Monograms of Paul I in cruciform **Rev:** Legend in ornate square

Date	Mintage	F	VF	XF	Unc	BU
1801СМ АИ	180,000	250	400	1,700	2,500	—
1801СМ АИ	180,000	250	400	1,700	2,500	—

C# 131 5 ROUBLES
6.0800 g., 0.9860 Gold .1928 oz. **Ruler:** Alexander I

Date	Mintage	F	VF	XF	Unc	BU
1802СПБ Rare	15	—	—	—	—	—
1803СПБ ХЛ Rare	6	—	—	—	—	—
1804СПБ ХЛ	37,000	250	400	3,500	5,500	—
1805СПБ ХЛ	8,109	250	400	3,500	5,500	—

C# 132 5 ROUBLES
6.5440 g., 0.9170 Gold .1929 oz. **Ruler:** Alexander I

Date	Mintage	F	VF	XF	Unc	BU
1817 ФГ	710,000	130	180	600	1,600	—
1818 МФ	1,520,000	130	200	600	1,600	—
1819 МФ	963,000	130	180	600	1,600	—
1822 МФ	—	130	180	600	1,600	—
1823 ПС	440,000	130	180	600	1,600	—
1824 ПС	276,000	130	180	600	1,600	—
1825 ПС	101,000	400	700	2,000	3,000	—
1825 ПС Proof	—	Value: 5,000				
1825 ПД	Inc. above	300	500	1,250	2,000	—
Common date Proof	—	Value: 3,500				

C# 174 5 ROUBLES
6.5440 g., 0.9170 Gold .1929 oz. **Ruler:** Nicholas I

Date	Mintage	F	VF	XF	Unc	BU
1826 ПД	212,000	130	180	600	1,600	—
1827 ПД	—	300	500	2,000	3,500	—
1828 ПД	604,000	130	180	600	1,600	—
1829 ПД	733,000	130	180	600	1,600	—
1830 ПД	490,000	130	180	600	1,600	—
1831 ПД	846,000	130	180	600	1,600	—

C# 176 5 ROUBLES
6.5440 g., 0.9170 Gold .1929 oz. **Ruler:** Nicholas I **Subject:** Discovery of Gold at Kolyvan Mines

Date	Mintage	F	VF	XF	Unc	BU
1832 ПД	1,000	600	1,200	2,200	6,000	—
1832 Proof	—	Value: 8,500				

C# 175.1 5 ROUBLES
6.5440 g., 0.9170 Gold .1929 oz. **Ruler:** Nicholas I

Date	Mintage	F	VF	XF	Unc	BU
1832 ПД	481,000	100	120	150	400	—
1833 ПД	829,000	100	120	150	400	—
1834 ПД	1,346,000	100	120	150	400	—
1835 ПД	1,440,000	100	120	150	400	—
1835 Rare	Inc. above	—	—	—	—	—
1835 ПД Without mintmark, rare	Inc. above	—	—	—	—	—
1836 ПД	953,000	100	120	150	400	—
1837 ПД	48,000	150	200	250	900	—
1838 ПД	302,000	100	120	150	300	—
1839 АЧ	1,609,000	100	120	150	300	—
1840 АЧ	1,277,000	100	120	150	300	—
1841 АЧ	1,668,000	100	120	140	300	—
1842 АЧ	2,180,000	100	120	140	300	—
1843 АЧ	1,852,000	100	120	140	300	—
1844 КБ	2,365,000	100	120	140	300	—
1845 КБ	2,842,000	100	120	140	300	—
1846 КБ	3,442,000	100	120	140	300	—
Common date Proof	—	Value: 3,750				

C# 175.2 5 ROUBLES
6.5440 g., 0.9170 Gold .1929 oz. **Ruler:** Nicholas I

Date	Mintage	F	VF	XF	Unc	BU
1842MW	695	700	1,000	2,500	5,000	—
1846MW	62	1,000	1,500	3,000	7,000	—
1848MW	485	700	1,000	2,500	5,000	—
1849MW	133	700	1,000	2,500	5,000	—
Common date Proof	—	Value: 6,000				

C# 175.3 5 ROUBLES
6.5440 g., 0.9170 Gold .1929 oz. **Ruler:** Nicholas I **Note:** Different eagle.

Date	Mintage	F	VF	XF	Unc	BU
1846	—	—	—	—	—	—
1846СПБ АГ	—	100	120	140	300	—
Note: Mintage included in C#175.1						
1847СПБ АГ	3,900,000	100	150	200	350	—
1848СПБ АГ	2,900,000	100	120	140	300	—
1849СПБ АГ	3,100,000	100	120	140	300	—
1850СПБ АГ	3,900,000	100	120	140	300	—
1851СПБ АГ	3,400,000	100	120	140	300	—
1852СПБ АГ	3,900,000	100	120	140	300	—
1853СПБ АГ	3,900,000	100	120	140	300	—
1854СПБ АГ	3,900,000	100	120	140	300	—
Common date Proof	—	Value: 3,000				

Y# A26 5 ROUBLES
6.5440 g., 0.9170 Gold .1929 oz. **Ruler:** Alexander II

Date	Mintage	F	VF	XF	Unc	BU
1855 АГ	3,400,000	100	120	140	275	—
1856 АГ	3,800,000	100	120	140	275	—
1857 АГ	4,500,000	100	120	140	275	—
1858 АГ	3,500,000	100	120	140	275	—
1858 ПУ	—	100	120	140	275	—
Common date Proof	—	Value: 3,000				

Y# B26 5 ROUBLES
6.5440 g., 0.9170 Gold .1929 oz.

Date	Mintage	F	VF	XF	Unc	BU
1859 ПФ	3,900,000	100	120	140	275	—
1860 ПФ	3,600,000	100	120	140	275	—
1861 ПФ	3,500,000	100	120	140	275	—
1862 ПФ	6,354,000	100	120	140	275	—
1863 МИ	7,200,000	100	120	140	275	—
1864 АС	3,900,000	100	120	140	275	—
1865 АС	3,902,000	100	120	140	275	—
1865 СШ	Inc. above	100	120	140	275	—
1866 СШ	3,900,000	100	120	140	275	—
1866 НІ	Inc. above	100	120	140	275	—
1867 НІ	3,494,000	100	120	140	275	—
1868 НІ	3,400,000	100	120	140	275	—
1869 НІ	3,900,000	100	120	140	275	—
1870 НІ	5,000,000	100	120	140	275	—
1871 НІ	800,000	100	120	140	275	—
1872 НІ	2,400,000	100	120	140	275	—
1873 НІ	3,000,000	100	120	140	275	—
1874 НІ	4,800,000	100	120	140	275	—
1875 НІ	4,000,000	100	120	140	275	—
1876 НІ	6,000,000	100	120	140	275	—
1877 НІ	6,600,000	100	120	140	275	—
1877 НФ	Inc. above	125	150	175	350	—
1878 НФ	6,800,000	100	120	140	275	—
1879 НФ	7,225,000	100	120	140	275	—
1880 НФ	6,200,000	100	120	140	275	—
1881 НФ	5,500,000	100	120	140	275	—
1882 НФ	4,547,000	100	120	140	275	—
1883 ДС	5,632,000	100	120	140	275	—
1883 АГ	Inc. above	100	120	140	275	—
1884 АГ	4,801,000	100	120	140	275	—
1885 АГ	5,433,000	100	120	140	275	—
Common date Proof	—	Value: 3,000				

Y# 42 5 ROUBLES
6.4516 g., 0.9000 Gold .1867 oz. **Ruler:** Alexander III **Note:** Without mint mark. Edge varieties exist.

Date	Mintage	F	VF	XF	Unc	BU
1886 АГ	351,000	100	115	130	225	—
1887 АГ	3,261,000	100	115	130	225	—
1888 АГ	5,257,000	100	115	130	225	—
1889 АГ	4,200,000	100	115	130	225	—
1890 АГ	5,600,000	100	115	130	225	—
1891 АГ	541,000	100	115	130	225	—
1892 АГ	128,000	125	150	175	275	—
1893 АГ	598,000	100	115	130	225	—
1894 АГ	598,000	100	115	130	225	—
Common date Proof	—	Value: 3,250				

Y# A61 5 ROUBLES
6.4516 g., 0.9000 Gold .1867 oz. **Ruler:** Nicholas II **Note:** Without mint mark.

Date	Mintage	F	VF	XF	Unc	BU
1895 АГ	36	—	6,000	10,000	15,000	—
1896 АГ	33	—	6,000	10,000	15,000	—

Y# 62 5 ROUBLES
6.4516 g., 0.9000 Gold .1244 oz. **Note:** Struck at St. Petersburg without mint mark.

Date	Mintage	F	VF	XF	Unc	BU
1897 АГ	5,372,000	—	BV	60.00	90.00	—
1898 АГ	52,378,000	—	BV	60.00	90.00	—
1899 ЗБ	20,400,000	—	BV	60.00	90.00	—
1899 ФЗ	Inc. above	—	BV	60.00	90.00	—
1900 ФЗ	31,000	—	BV	70.00	95.00	—
Common date Proof	—	Value: 1,500				

C# 178 6 ROUBLES
20.7100 g., Platinum .6655 oz. **Ruler:** Nicholas I

Date	Mintage	F	VF	XF	Unc	BU
1829СПБ	828	1,250	2,500	3,500	5,500	—
1830СПБ	8,610	1,250	2,200	3,250	5,000	—
1831СПБ	2,784	1,250	2,200	3,250	5,000	—
1832СПБ	1,502	1,250	2,500	3,500	5,500	—
1833СПБ	302	1,250	2,500	3,500	5,500	—
1834СПБ	11	1,500	2,500	4,000	8,000	—
1835СПБ	107	1,250	2,500	3,250	8,000	—
1836СПБ Proof	11	Value: 12,000				
1837СПБ	253	1,250	2,500	3,500	6,500	—
1838СПБ Rare	12	—	—	—	—	—
1839СПБ Rare	2	—	—	—	—	—
1840СПБ Rare	—	—	—	—	—	—
1841СПБ	170	1,200	2,500	3,500	6,500	—
1842СПБ	121	1,200	2,500	3,500	6,500	—
1843СПБ	127	1,200	2,500	3,500	6,500	—
1844СПБ Rare	4	—	—	—	—	—
1845СПБ Rare	2	—	—	—	—	—
Common date Proof	—	Value: 5,000				

Y# 63 7 ROUBLES 50 KOPEKS

6.4516 g., 0.9000 Gold .1867 oz. **Ruler:** Nicholas II **Note:** Without mint mark.

Date	Mintage	F	VF	XF	Unc	BU
1897 АГ	16,829,000	100	120	190	300	—

C# 133 10 ROUBLES

12.1700 g., 0.9860 Gold .3858 oz. **Ruler:** Alexander I

Date	Mintage	F	VF	XF	Unc	BU
1802СПБ	74,000	2,500	3,000	3,500	7,500	—
1802СПБ АИ	Inc. above	2,500	3,000	3,500	7,500	—
1804СПБ ХЛ	72,000	2,500	3,000	3,500	7,500	—
1805СПБ ХЛ	55,000	1,500	2,000	2,150	7,000	—

Y# A42 10 ROUBLES

12.9039 g., 0.9000 Gold .3734 oz. **Ruler:** Alexander III **Note:** Without mint mark.

Date	Mintage	F	VF	XF	Unc	BU
1886 АГ	57,000	250	350	600	1,400	—
1887 АГ	475,000	250	300	425	1,400	—
1888 АГ	23,000	250	350	600	1,400	—
1889 АГ	343,000	250	300	425	1,400	—
1890 АГ	15,000	250	350	600	1,700	—
1891 АГ	3,010	300	475	725	1,700	—
1892 АГ	8,006	300	475	725	2,200	—
1893 АГ	1,008	300	475	725	2,200	—
1894 АГ	1,007	250	300	425	1,100	—
Common date Proof	—	Value: 4,500				

Y# A63 10 ROUBLES

12.9039 g., 0.9000 Gold .3734 oz. **Ruler:** Nicholas II **Rev. Legend:** ИМПЕРIАЛЪ (IMPERIAL)

Date	Mintage	F	VF	XF	Unc	BU
1895 АГ	125	—	6,000	8,000	18,000	—
1895 АГ	125	—	6,000	8,000	18,000	—
1896 АГ	125	—	6,000	8,000	18,000	—
1897 АГ	125	—	6,000	8,000	18,000	—

Y# 64 10 ROUBLES

8.6026 g., 0.9000 Gold .2489 oz. **Note:** Struck at St. Petersburg without mint mark.

Date	Mintage	F	VF	XF	Unc	BU
1898 АГ	200,000	—	BV	120	180	—
1899 АГ	27,600,000	—	BV	110	160	—
1899 ФЗ	Inc. above	—	BV	110	160	—
1899 ЗБ	Inc. above	—	BV	120	180	—
1900 ФЗ	6,021,000	—	BV	120	170	—
Common date Proof	—	Value: 2,500				

C# 179 12 ROUBLES

41.4100 g., Platinum 1.3311 oz. **Ruler:** Nicholas I **Note:** Varieties exist.

Date	Mintage	F	VF	XF	Unc	BU
1830СПБ	119	2,750	4,400	6,250	15,000	—
1831СПБ	1,463	2,250	3,800	6,000	8,500	—
1832СПБ	1,102	2,250	3,800	6,000	11,000	—
1833СПБ	255	2,750	4,400	6,250	15,000	—
1834СПБ Proof	11	Value: 15,000				
1835СПБ	127	2,750	4,400	6,250	14,000	—
1836СПБ Proof	11	Value: 15,000				
1837СПБ	53	2,750	4,700	7,250	15,000	—
1838СПБ Rare	12	—	—	—	—	—
1839СПБ Rare	2	—	—	—	—	—
1840СПБ Rare	—	—	—	—	—	—
1841СПБ	75	2,750	4,700	7,250	18,000	—
1842СПБ	115	2,750	4,400	7,250	18,000	—
1843СПБ	122	2,750	4,700	7,250	18,000	—
1844СПБ Proof; Rare	4	—	—	—	—	—
1845СПБ Rare	2	—	—	—	—	—
Common date Proof	—	Value: 10,000				

Y# 65.1 15 ROUBLES

12.9039 g., 0.9000 Gold .3734 oz. **Ruler:** Nicholas II **Note:** Without mint mark. Wide rim, legend ends at back of neck.

Date	Mintage	F	VF	XF	Unc	BU
1897 АГ	11,900,000	BV	170	190	300	—

Y# 65.2 15 ROUBLES

12.9039 g., 0.9000 Gold .3734 oz. **Ruler:** Nicholas II **Note:** Narrow rim, 4 letters of legend under neck.

Date	Mintage	F	VF	XF	Unc	BU
1897	Inc. above	BV	170	190	300	—

Y# 27 25 ROUBLES

32.7200 g., 0.9170 Gold .9640 oz. **Ruler:** Alexander II **Note:** Realized in Stack's International sale 3-88.

Date	Mintage	F	VF	XF	Unc	BU
1876СПБ Proof	100	Value: 30,000				

Y# A65 25 ROUBLES

32.2500 g., 0.9000 Gold .9332 oz. **Rev. Legend:** 2-1/2 ИМПЕРIАЛЪ@A|05 (IMPERIALS) **Note:** Struck at St. Petersburg without mint mark.

Date	Mintage	F	VF	XF	Unc	BU
1896	300	—	7,500	12,000	18,000	—

NOVODELS

KM#	Date	Mintage	Identification	Mkt Val
N341	1801КМ	—	Denga. Copper. Oblique milling edge.	—
N342	1801	—	Denga. Copper. Oblique milling edge.	—
N343	1801КМ	—	Kopek. Copper. Reversed oblique milling edge.	—
N345	1801	—	2 Kopeks. Copper. Oblique milling edge.	—
N346	1801СМ	—	10 Kopeks. Silver. Oblique milling edge.	—
N347	1801СМ	—	Rouble. Silver. Oblique milling edge.	—
N340	1801КМ	—	Polushka. Copper. Oblique milling edge.	250
N344	1801КМ	—	2 Kopeks. Copper. Oblique milling edge.	225

KM#	Date	Mintage	Identification	Mkt Val
N348	1802ЕМ	—	Polushka. Copper. Oblique milling edge. mm below eagle.	450
N349	1802ЕМ	—	Polushka. Copper. Plain edge. mm below eagle.	325
N350	1802ЕМ	—	Polushka. Copper. Oblique milling edge. High relief.	300
N351	1802ЕМ	—	Polushka. Copper. Plain edge. mm below date.	300

KM#	Date	Mintage	Identification	Mkt Val
N352	1802ЕМ	—	Polushka. Copper. Oblique milling edge. Low relief.	275
N353	1802ЕМ	—	Polushka. Copper. Struck with Denga die. Oblique milling edge.	350
N354	1802КМ	—	Polushka. Copper. Oblique milling edge. With outer ring.	300

KM#	Date	Mintage	Identification	Mkt Val
N355	1802КМ	—	Polushka. Copper. Oblique milling edge. Without outer ring.	300

KM#	Date	Mintage	Identification	Mkt Val
N356	1802ЕМ	—	Denga. Copper. Oblique milling edge. High relief.	300
N357	1802ЕМ	—	Denga. Copper. Oblique milling edge. Low relief.	275
N358	1802ЕМ	—	Denga. Copper. Plain edge. Low relief.	275

KM#	Date	Mintage	Identification	Mkt Val
N359	1802КМ	—	Denga. Copper. Oblique milling edge. With outer ring.	300
N360	1802КМ	—	Denga. Copper. Oblique milling edge. Without outer ring.	300
N361	1802	—	Denga. Copper. Oblique milling edge.	300

KM#	Date	Mintage	Identification	Mkt Val
N362	1802	—	Denga. Copper. Plain edge.	300

KM#	Date	Mintage	Identification	Mkt Val
N363	1802ЕМ	—	Kopek. Copper. Oblique milling edge. High relief.	350
N364	1802ЕМ	—	Kopek. Copper. Oblique milling edge. Low relief.	300
N365	1802КМ	—	Kopek. Copper. Oblique milling edge. With outer ring.	300
N366	1802КМ	—	Kopek. Copper. Oblique milling edge. Without outer ring.	300
N367	1802	—	Kopek. Copper. Oblique milling edge.	350
N368	1802	—	Kopek. Copper. Plain edge.	300
N369	1802ЕМ	—	2 Kopeks. Copper. Oblique milling edge. mm below eagle.	450
N370	1802ЕМ	—	2 Kopeks. Copper. Plain edge. mm below eagle.	400
N371	1802ЕМ	—	2 Kopeks. Copper. Oblique milling edge. High relief.	350
N372	1802ЕМ	—	2 Kopeks. Copper. Oblique milling edge. Low relief.	300
N373	1802ЕМ	—	2 Kopeks. Copper. Diagonal reeded edge. Low relief.	300
N374	1802КМ	—	2 Kopeks. Copper. Oblique milling edge. With outer ring.	300
N375	1802КМ	—	2 Kopeks. Copper. Oblique milling edge. Without outer ring.	350
N376	1802ЕМ	—	5 Kopeks. Copper. Oblique milling edge. mm below eagle.	750
N377	1802ЕМ	—	5 Kopeks. Copper. Oblique milling edge. High relief.	550
N378	1802ЕМ	—	5 Kopeks. Copper. Oblique milling edge. Low relief.	500
N379	1802КМ	—	5 Kopeks. Copper. Oblique milling edge. With outer ring.	450
N380	1802КМ	—	5 Kopeks. Copper. Oblique milling edge. Without outer ring.	450
N386	1802СП Б ХЛ	—	10 Roubles. Gold. Oblique milling edge.	4,000
N387	1802СП Б АИ	—	10 Roubles. Gold. Oblique milling edge. Double weight.	20,000
N381	1802СП Б ФГ	—	10 Kopeks. Silver. Oblique milling edge.	—
N382	1802СП Б	—	1/4 Rouble. Silver. Plain edge.	—
N383	1802СП Б	—	1/4 Rouble. Copper. Plain edge.	—
N384	1802СП Б	—	Rouble. Silver. Plain edge.	—
N385	1802СП Б	—	Rouble. Silver. Oblique milling edge.	—
N393	1803СП Б ФГ	—	10 Kopeks. Silver. Plain edge.	—
N394	1803СП Б АИ	—	1/4 Rouble. Silver. Plain edge.	—
N395	1803СП Б ФГ	—	1/4 Rouble. Silver. Plain edge.	—
N396	1803СП Б АИ	—	Rouble. Silver. Plain edge.	—
N397	1803СП Б ФГ	—	Rouble. Silver. Incuse lettered edge.	—
N388	1803КМ	—	Polushka. Copper. Oblique milling edge.	300
N389	1803КМ	—	Denga. Copper. Oblique milling edge.	300
N390	1803КМ	—	Kopek. Copper. Oblique milling edge.	300
N391	1803КМ	—	2 Kopeks. Copper. Oblique milling edge.	350
N392	1803КМ	—	5 Kopeks. Copper. Oblique milling edge.	500
N398	1803СП Б ХЛ	—	5 Roubles. Gold. Oblique milling edge.	15,000
N399	1803СП Б ХЛ	—	10 Roubles. Gold. Oblique milling edge.	15,000
N400	1804КМ	—	Polushka. Copper. Oblique milling edge.	300
N401	1804КМ	—	Denga. Copper. Oblique milling edge.	300
N402	1804КМ	—	Kopek. Copper. Oblique milling edge.	300
N403	1804КМ	—	2 Kopeks. Copper. Oblique milling edge.	300
N404	1804КМ	—	5 Kopeks. Copper. Oblique milling edge.	450
N405	1805КМ	—	Polushka. Copper. Oblique milling edge.	300
N406	1805КМ	—	Denga. Copper. Oblique milling edge.	300
N407	1805КМ	—	Kopek. Copper. Oblique milling edge.	300
N408	1805КМ	—	2 Kopeks. Copper. Oblique milling edge.	300
N409	1805КМ	—	5 Kopeks. Copper. Oblique milling edge.	450
N410	1806КМ	—	Polushka. Copper. Oblique milling edge. Without outer ring.	300
N411	1806КМ	—	Denga. Copper. Oblique milling edge.	300
N412	1806КМ	—	Kopek. Copper. Oblique milling edge.	300
N413	1806КМ	—	2 Kopeks. Copper. Oblique milling edge.	300
N414	1806КМ	—	5 Kopeks. Copper. Oblique milling edge.	450
N415	1807КМ	—	Polushka. Copper. Oblique milling edge. Without outer ring.	300
N416	1807КМ	—	Denga. Copper. Oblique milling edge.	300
N417	1807КМ	—	Kopek. Copper. Oblique milling edge.	300
N418	1807КМ	—	2 Kopeks. Copper. Oblique milling edge.	300
N419	1807КМ	—	5 Kopeks. Copper. Oblique milling edge.	450
N420	1808КМ	—	Polushka. Copper. Oblique milling edge. Without outer ring.	300
N421	1808КМ	—	Denga. Copper. Oblique milling edge.	300
N422	1808КМ	—	Kopek. Copper. Oblique milling edge.	300
N423	1808КМ	—	2 Kopeks. Copper. Oblique milling edge.	300
N424	1808КМ	—	5 Kopeks. Copper. Oblique milling edge.	450
N425	1808СП Б ФГ	—	1/4 Rouble. Silver. Plain edge.	—
N431	1809СП Б ФГ	—	10 Kopeks. Silver. Plain edge.	—
N432	1809СП Б	—	10 Kopeks. Silver. Plain edge.	—
N433	1809СП Б	—	1/2 Rouble. Silver. Plain edge.	—
N426	1809КМ	—	Polushka. Copper. Oblique milling edge. Without outer ring.	300
N427	1809КМ	—	Denga. Copper. Oblique milling edge.	300
N428	1809КМ	—	Kopek. Copper. Oblique milling edge.	300
N429	1809КМ	—	2 Kopeks. Copper. Oblique milling edge.	300
N430	1809КМ	—	5 Kopeks. Copper. Oblique milling edge.	450
N434	1809СП Б ХЛ	—	10 Roubles. Gold. Oblique milling edge.	15,000
N435	1810КМ	—	Polushka. Copper. Oblique milling edge.	300
N436	1810КМ	—	Denga. Copper. Oblique milling edge.	300
N437	1810КМ	—	Kopek. Copper. Oblique milling edge.	300
N438	1810КМ	—	2 Kopeks. Copper. Oblique milling edge.	300
N439	1810КМ	—	5 Kopeks. Copper. Oblique milling edge.	450
N440	1810ЕМ НМ	—	Denga. Copper. Plain edge. Curved date.	200
N441	1810ЕМ	—	Denga. Copper. Plain edge. Without initials.	200
N442	1810КМ ПБ	—	Denga. Copper. Plain edge.	225
N443	1810ЕМ НМ	—	Kopek. Copper. Plain edge. Curved date.	200
N444	1810КМ ПБ	—	Kopek. Copper. Plain edge. Without initials.	200
N445	1810ЕМ НМ	—	2 Kopeks. Copper. Plain edge. Curved date.	200
N446	1810ЕМ НМ	—	2 Kopeks. Copper. Plain edge. Small initials.	200
N447	1810КМ	—	2 Kopeks. Copper. Plain edge.	200
N448	1810КМ ПБ	—	2 Kopeks. Copper. Plain edge. Small eagle.	200
N449	1810СП Б ФГ	—	2 Kopeks. Copper. Plain edge.	200
N-A435	1810КМ	—	1/4 Kopek. Copper. Oblique milling edge.	—
N450	1810СП Б МК	—	10 Kopeks. Silver. Plain edge. Old type.	—
N451	1810СП Б ФГ	—	1/4 Rouble. Silver. Plain edge. Old type.	—
N452	1810СП Б ФГ	—	Rouble. Silver. Plain edge. Old type.	—
N453	1810СП Б ФГ	—	10 Kopeks. Silver. Plain edge. New type.	—
N454	1810СП Б	—	1/2 Rouble. Silver. Plain edge.	—
N461	1811СП Б ФГ	—	5 Kopeks. Silver. Plain edge.	—
N462	1811СП Б ФГ	—	10 Kopeks. Silver. Plain edge. Broad crown.	—
N463	1811СП Б ФГ	—	1/2 Rouble. Silver. Plain edge. Tapered crown.	—
N455	1811КМ ПБ	—	Denga. Copper. Plain edge. Wings far from rim.	175
N456	1811СП Б МК	—	Denga. Copper. Plain edge.	225
N457	1811КМ ПБ	—	Kopek. Copper. Plain edge.	200
N458	1811СП Б ПС	—	Kopek. Copper. Plain edge.	200
N459	1811ЕМ ИФ	—	2 Kopeks. Copper. Oblique milling edge.	450
N460	1811СП Б ФГ	—	2 Kopeks. Copper. Plain edge. Small eagle.	200
N464	1813СП Б ПС	—	10 Kopeks. Silver. Plain edge. Broad crown.	—
N465	1813СП Б	—	1/2 Rouble. Silver. Plain edge.	—
N468	1814СП Б	—	5 Kopeks. Silver. Plain edge. Tapered crown.	—
N469	1814СП Б	—	20 Kopeks. Silver. Plain edge.	—
N470	1814СП Б	—	1/2 Rouble. Silver. Plain edge.	—
N466	1814СП Б ПС	—	Denga. Copper. Plain edge.	275
N467	1814СП Б ПС	—	Kopek. Copper. Plain edge.	225
N471	1815СП Б	—	20 Kopeks. Silver. Plain edge. Open 2 in value.	—
N472	1815СП Б	—	1/2 Rouble. Silver. Plain edge. Tapered crown.	—
N473	1815СП Б	—	Rouble. Silver. Plain edge.	—
N474	1816СП Б	—	5 Kopeks. Silver. Plain edge. Large crown.	—
N475	1816СП Б	—	20 Kopeks. Silver. Plain edge. Large crown.	—
N476	1816СП Б	—	1/2 Rouble. Silver. Plain edge. Tapered crown.	—
N477	1817СП Б	—	1/2 Rouble. Silver. Plain edge. Tapered crown.	—
N479	1818КМ АД	—	2 Kopeks. Copper. Plain edge.	—
N480	1818СП Б	—	1/2 Rouble. Silver. Plain edge. Tapered crown.	—
N478	1818КМ АМ	—	Kopek. Copper. Plain edge.	325
N481	1819КМ АД	—	Kopek. Copper. Plain edge.	175
N482	1819КМ ДБ	—	2 Kopeks. Copper. Plain edge.	300
N483	1819СП Б	—	10 Kopeks. Silver. Plain edge. Tapered crown.	—
N484	1819СП Б	—	1/2 Rouble. Silver. Plain edge. Tapered crown.	—
N485	1819СП Б	—	Rouble. Silver. Plain edge.	—
N487	1820СП Б	—	5 Kopeks. Silver. Plain edge. Broad crown.	—
N486	1820КМ АД	—	Kopek. Copper. Plain edge.	175
N488	1821КМ АД	—	Kopek. Copper. Plain edge.	200
N489	1821СП Б	—	5 Kopeks. Silver. Plain edge.	—
N490	1821СП Б	—	Rouble. Silver. Plain edge.	—

KM#	Date	Mintage	Identification	Mkt Val
N491	1823КМ АМ	—	Denga. Copper. Plain edge.	—
N492	1825СП Б	—	20 Kopeks. Silver. Plain edge. Tapered crown.	—
N493	1826СП Б	—	20 Kopeks. Silver. Plain edge. Open 2 in value.	—
N494	1826СП Б	—	20 Kopeks. Silver. Plain edge. New type, large crown.	—
N495	1826СП Б ПД	—	1/2 Rouble. Silver. Lettered edge. New type.	—
N496	1830ЕМ	—	Kopek. Copper. Plain edge.	250
N497	1830ЕМ	—	2 Kopeks. Copper. Plain edge.	300
N498	1830ЕМ	—	5 Kopeks. Copper. Plain edge.	450
N499	1830ЕМ	—	10 Kopeks. Copper. Plain edge. Without initials.	550
N500	1831СМ	—	Kopek. Copper. Plain edge.	175
N501	1831СМ	—	2 Kopeks. Copper. Plain edge.	200
N502	1831СМ	—	5 Kopeks. Copper. Plain edge.	250
N503	1831СМ	—	10 Kopeks. Copper. Plain edge.	425
N504	1832СМ	—	Kopek. Copper. Plain edge.	175
N505	1832СМ	—	2 Kopeks. Copper. Plain edge.	200
N506	1832СМ	—	5 Kopeks. Copper. Plain edge.	250
N507	1832СМ	—	10 Kopeks. Copper. Plain edge.	425
N508	1833СМ	—	Kopek. Copper. Plain edge.	175
N509	1833СМ	—	2 Kopeks. Copper. Plain edge.	200
N510	1833СМ	—	5 Kopeks. Copper. Plain edge.	250
N511	1833СМ	—	10 Kopeks. Copper. Plain edge.	425
N512	1833СП Б НГ	—	3/4 Rouble. Silver. Plain edge. St. George with mantle.	—
N513	1834СМ	—	Kopek. Copper. Plain edge.	175
N514	1834СМ	—	2 Kopeks. Copper. Plain edge.	200
N515	1834СМ	—	5 Kopeks. Copper. Plain edge.	250
N516	1834СМ	—	10 Kopeks. Copper. Plain edge.	425
N517	1835СМ	—	Kopek. Copper. Plain edge.	175
N518	1835СМ	—	2 Kopeks. Copper. Plain edge.	200
N519	1835СМ	—	5 Kopeks. Copper. Plain edge.	250
N520	1835СМ	—	10 Kopeks. Copper. Plain edge.	425
N521	1836СМ	—	Kopek. Copper. Plain edge.	175
N522	1836СМ	—	2 Kopeks. Copper. Plain edge.	200
N523	1836СМ	—	5 Kopeks. Copper. Plain edge.	250
N524	1836СМ	—	10 Kopeks. Copper. Plain edge.	425
N525	1837СМ	—	Kopek. Copper. Plain edge.	175
N526	1837СМ	—	2 Kopeks. Copper. Plain edge.	200
N527	1837СМ	—	5 Kopeks. Copper. Plain edge.	250
N528	1837СМ	—	10 Kopeks. Copper. Plain edge.	425
N529	1838СМ	—	Kopek. Copper. Plain edge.	175
N530	1838СМ	—	2 Kopeks. Copper. Plain edge.	200
N531	1838СМ	—	5 Kopeks. Copper. Plain edge.	250
N532	1838СМ	—	10 Kopeks. Copper. Plain edge.	425
N533	1839СМ	—	Kopek. Copper. Plain edge.	175
N534	1839СМ	—	2 Kopeks. Copper. Plain edge.	200
N535	1839СМ	—	5 Kopeks. Copper. Plain edge.	250
N536	1839СМ	—	10 Kopeks. Copper. Plain edge.	425
N537	1839СМ	—	Polushka. Copper. Plain edge.	175
N538	1839СМ	—	Denga. Copper. Plain edge.	175
N539	1839СМ	—	Kopek. Copper. Plain edge.	200
N540	1839СМ	—	2 Kopeks. Copper. Plain edge.	225
N541	1839СМ	—	3 Kopeks. Copper. Plain edge.	275
N542	1840СМ	—	Polushka. Copper. Plain edge.	175
N543	1840СМ	—	Denga. Copper. Plain edge.	175
N545	1840СМ	—	Kopek. Copper. Plain edge.	200
N546	1840	—	Kopek. Copper. Plain edge.	450
N547	1840СМ	—	2 Kopeks. Copper. Plain edge.	250
N549	1840СМ	—	3 Kopeks. Copper. Plain edge.	250
N544	1840	—	Denga. Copper. Plain edge.	—
N548	1840	—	2 Kopeks. Copper. Plain edge.	—
N550	1840	—	3 Kopeks. Copper. Plain edge.	—
N551	1840	—	25 Kopeks. Silver. Plain edge. Lis missing on scepter.	—
N552	1840	—	Rouble. Silver. Plain edge. St. George with mantle.	—
N553	1841СМ	—	Polushka. Copper. Plain edge.	175
N554	1841СМ	—	Denga. Copper. Plain edge.	175
N555	1841СМ	—	Kopek. Copper. Plain edge.	200
N556	1841СМ	—	2 Kopeks. Copper. Plain edge.	225
N557	1841СМ	—	3 Kopeks. Copper. Plain edge.	250
N558	1842СМ	—	Polushka. Copper. Plain edge.	175
N559	1842СМ	—	Denga. Copper. Plain edge.	175
N560	1842СМ	—	Kopek. Copper. Plain edge.	200
N561	1842СМ	—	2 Kopeks. Copper. Plain edge.	225
N562	1842СМ	—	3 Kopeks. Copper. Plain edge.	250
N563	1842НГ	—	10 Kopeks. Silver. Plain edge.	—
N564	1842АЧ	—	1/2 Rouble. Silver. Plain edge. Large center tail feather.	—
N565	1842НГ	—	1/2 Rouble. Silver. Plain edge.	—
N566	1842НГ	—	Rouble. Silver. Plain edge. St. George with mantle.	—
N567	1843СМ	—	Polushka. Copper. Plain edge.	175
N568	1843СМ	—	Denga. Copper. Plain edge.	175
N569	1843СМ	—	Kopek. Copper. Plain edge.	200
N570	1843СМ	—	2 Kopeks. Copper. Plain edge.	225
N571	1843СМ	—	3 Kopeks. Copper. Plain edge.	250
N572	1844СМ	—	Polushka. Copper. Plain edge.	175
N573	1844СМ	—	Denga. Copper. Plain edge.	175
N574	1844СМ	—	Kopek. Copper. Plain edge.	200
N575	1844СМ	—	2 Kopeks. Copper. Plain edge.	225
N576	1844СМ	—	3 Kopeks. Copper. Plain edge.	250
N577	1845СМ	—	Polushka. Copper. Plain edge.	175
N578	1845СМ	—	Denga. Copper. Plain edge.	175
N579	1845СМ	—	Kopek. Copper. Plain edge.	200
N580	1845СМ	—	2 Kopeks. Copper. Plain edge.	225
N581	1845СМ	—	3 Kopeks. Copper. Plain edge.	250
N582	1846СМ	—	Polushka. Copper. Plain edge.	175
N583	1846СМ	—	Denga. Copper. Plain edge.	175
N584	1846СМ	—	Kopek. Copper. Plain edge.	200
N585	1846СМ	—	2 Kopeks. Copper. Plain edge.	225
N586	1846СМ	—	3 Kopeks. Copper. Plain edge.	250
N587	1846СП Б	—	1/2 Rouble. Silver. Plain edge. Wave-shaped tail feathers.	—
N588	1847СМ	—	Denga. Copper. Plain edge.	175
N589	1847СМ	—	Kopek. Copper. Plain edge.	200
N590	1847СМ	—	2 Kopeks. Copper. Plain edge.	225
N591	1847СМ	—	3 Kopeks. Copper. Plain edge.	250
N592	1849ЕМ	—	3 Kopeks. Copper. Plain edge. Small 3.	450
N593	1852ПА	—	Rouble. Silver. Plain edge. St. George with mantle.	—
N594	1855ЕМ	—	2 Kopeks. Copper. Plain edge. Small 2.	325
N595	1857ЕМ	—	Denga. Copper. Plain edge.	—
N596	1859ЕМ	—	2 Kopeks. Copper. Plain edge. Small 2.	250
N597	1859ЕМ	—	3 Kopeks. Copper. Plain edge. Small 3.	250
N598	1859ЕМ	—	5 Kopeks. Copper. Plain edge. Small 5.	300
N599	1860	—	20 Kopeks. Silver. Plain edge. Old type large shield.	—
N600	1860	—	1/2 Rouble. Silver. Lettered edge. New type short shield.	—
N601	1860	—	1/2 Rouble. Silver. Plain edge. New type tall shield.	—
N602	1861	—	5 Kopeks. Silver. Plain edge. No mm.	—

PATTERNS

Including off metal strikes

KM#	Date	Mintage	Identification	Mkt Val
Pn52	1801AI	—	Rouble. Silver. Eagle in circle. Value in wreath.	—
Pn53	1801АИ	—	Rouble. Silver.	

KM#	Date	Mintage	Identification	Mkt Val
Pn54	1801AI	—	Rouble. Silver.	—
Pn55	1801AИ	—	Rouble. Silver.	—
Pn56	1802	—	2 Kopeks. Copper.	—
Pn57	1802	—	2 Kopeks. Copper.	—
Pn58	1802	—	2 Kopeks. Copper.	—
Pn59	1802	—	Rouble. Silver.	—
Pn60	180-(1803)	—	5 Kopeks. Copper. C#115.1.	—
Pn62	ND(1804)	—	1/2 Rouble. Copper.	—
Pn63	ND(1804)	—	1/2 Rouble. Silver.	—
Pn64	ND(1804)	—	1/2 Rouble. Gold.	—
Pn66	1804	—	Rouble. Silver.	—
Pn61	ND(1804)	—	1/2 Rouble. Gilt.	650
Pn65	1804	—	Rouble. Copper.	600
PnA67	1805СПБ	—	Rouble. Silver.	—
Pn68	180x	—	Rouble. Silver.	—
Pn67	1806	—	Rouble. Silver. C#125a.	6,000
Pn69	1806	—	Rouble. Silver. Uniformed bust of Alexander. Eagle in circle.	6,000

KM#	Date	Mintage	Identification	Mkt Val
Pn70	180x	—	Rouble. Silver.	8,000
Pn71	1807	—	Rouble. Silver.	6,000
Pn72	1807	—	Rouble. Silver.	—
Pn73	1810EM	—	Denga. Copper. C#116.1.	—
Pn74	1810	—	Kopek. Copper.	—
Pn75	1810	—	Kopek. Copper. Different eagle.	—
Pn76	1810СПБ	—	Kopek. Copper.	—
Pn77	1810СПБ	—	Kopek. Copper.	—
Pn78	1810EM HM	—	Kopek. Copper. C#117.1.	—
Pn79	1810	—	2 Kopeks. Copper.	—
Pn80	ND(1810)	—	Rouble. Silver.	—
Pn81	1811	—	Denga. Copper.	—
Pn82	1811	—	Denga. Copper.	—
Pn83	1811	—	Kopek. Copper.	—
Pn84	1811	—	Kopek. Copper.	—
Pn85	1811	—	2 Kopeks. Copper.	—
Pn86	1811	—	2 Kopeks. Copper.	—
Pn87	1816	—	2 Kopeks. Copper.	450
Pn88	1825	—	Rouble. Silver.	—

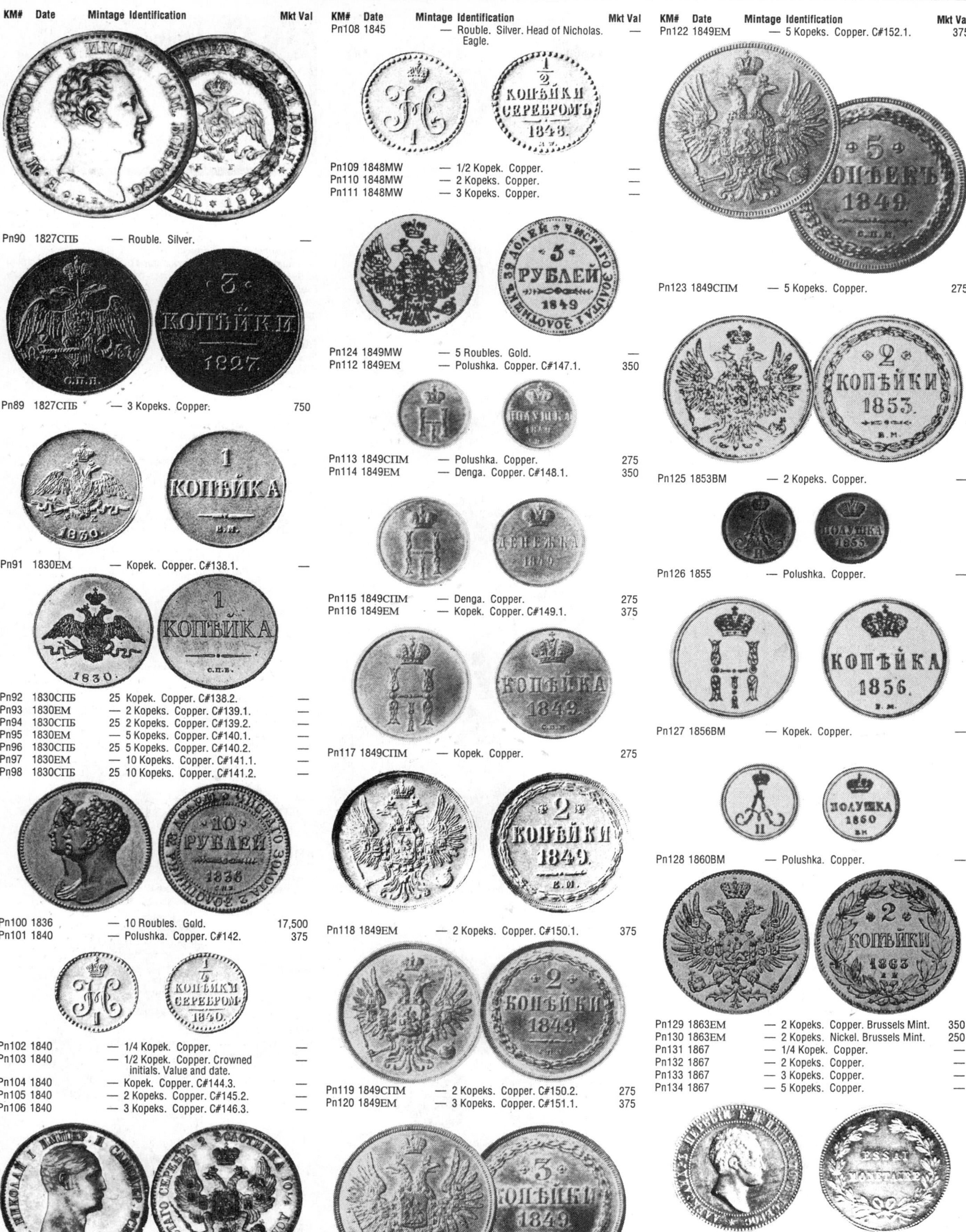

KM#	Date	Mintage	Identification	Mkt Val
Pn90	1827СПБ	—	Rouble. Silver.	—
Pn89	1827СПБ	—	3 Kopeks. Copper.	750
Pn91	1830ЕМ	—	Kopek. Copper. C#138.1.	—
Pn92	1830СПБ	25	Kopek. Copper. C#138.2.	—
Pn93	1830ЕМ	—	2 Kopeks. Copper. C#139.1.	—
Pn94	1830СПБ	25	2 Kopeks. Copper. C#139.2.	—
Pn95	1830ЕМ	—	5 Kopeks. Copper. C#140.1.	—
Pn96	1830СПБ	25	5 Kopeks. Copper. C#140.2.	—
Pn97	1830ЕМ	—	10 Kopeks. Copper. C#141.1.	—
Pn98	1830СПБ	25	10 Kopeks. Copper. C#141.2.	—
Pn100	1836	—	10 Roubles. Gold.	17,500
Pn101	1840	—	Polushka. Copper. C#142.	375
Pn102	1840	—	1/4 Kopek. Copper.	—
Pn103	1840	—	1/2 Kopek. Copper. Crowned initials. Value and date.	—
Pn104	1840	—	Kopek. Copper. C#144.3.	—
Pn105	1840	—	2 Kopeks. Copper. C#145.2.	—
Pn106	1840	—	3 Kopeks. Copper. C#146.3.	—
Pn107	1845	—	1/2 Rouble. Silver.	—
Pn108	1845	—	Rouble. Silver. Head of Nicholas. Eagle.	—
Pn109	1848MW	—	1/2 Kopek. Copper.	—
Pn110	1848MW	—	2 Kopeks. Copper.	—
Pn111	1848MW	—	3 Kopeks. Copper.	—
Pn124	1849MW	—	5 Roubles. Gold.	—
Pn112	1849ЕМ	—	Polushka. Copper. C#147.1.	350
Pn113	1849СПМ	—	Polushka. Copper.	275
Pn114	1849ЕМ	—	Denga. Copper. C#148.1.	350
Pn115	1849СПМ	—	Denga. Copper.	275
Pn116	1849ЕМ	—	Kopek. Copper. C#149.1.	375
Pn117	1849СПМ	—	Kopek. Copper.	275
Pn118	1849ЕМ	—	2 Kopeks. Copper. C#150.1.	375
Pn119	1849СПМ	—	2 Kopeks. Copper. C#150.2.	275
Pn120	1849ЕМ	—	3 Kopeks. Copper. C#151.1.	375
Pn121	1849СПМ	—	3 Kopeks. Copper.	275
Pn122	1849ЕМ	—	5 Kopeks. Copper. C#152.1.	375
Pn123	1849СПМ	—	5 Kopeks. Copper.	275
Pn125	1853ВМ	—	2 Kopeks. Copper.	—
Pn126	1855	—	Polushka. Copper.	—
Pn127	1856ВМ	—	Kopek. Copper.	—
Pn128	1860ВМ	—	Polushka. Copper.	—
Pn129	1863ЕМ	—	2 Kopeks. Copper. Brussels Mint.	350
Pn130	1863ЕМ	—	2 Kopeks. Nickel. Brussels Mint.	250
Pn131	1867	—	1/4 Kopek. Copper.	—
Pn132	1867	—	2 Kopeks. Copper.	—
Pn133	1867	—	3 Kopeks. Copper.	—
Pn134	1867	—	5 Kopeks. Copper.	—
Pn139	1871	—	10 Kopeks. Nickel.	—

KM#	Date	Mintage	Identification	Mkt Val
Pn135	1871	—	10 Kopeks. Copper-Nickel.	900
Pn136	1871	—	10 Kopeks. Nickel.	700
Pn137	1871	—	10 Kopeks. Copper-Nickel.	950
Pn138	1871	—	10 Kopeks. Nickel.	750
Pn140	1882	—	3 Kopeks. Nickel.	—
Pn141	1886	—	5 Roubles. Gold. Plain edge.	—
Pn142	1895	36	5 Roubles. Gold. C#A61.	20,000
Pn143	1895	125	10 Roubles. Gold. C#A63.	15,000
Pn144	1895	5	1/3 Imperial. Gold. 1/3 Imperial (5 Russ).	18,000
Pn145	1895	5	2/3 Imperial. Gold. Head of Nicholas. Eagle in circle. 2/3 Imperial (10 Russ).	20,000

KM#	Date	Mintage	Identification	Mkt Val
Pn146	1895	5	Imperial. Gold. Head of Nicholas. Eagle in circle. Imperial (15 Russ).	20,000
Pn147	1896	5	5 Roubles. Gold. C#A61.	20,000
Pn148	1896	125	10 Roubles. Gold. C#A63.	15,000
Pn149	1897	—	1/2 Kopek. Copper. Inverted W. Retrograde lgend. Berlin Mint.	—
Pn150	1897	—	1/2 Kopek. Nickel.	—
Pn152	1898	—	1/2 Kopek. Nickel Alloy.	600
Pn158	1898	—	Rouble. Silver. Y#61, no value.	2,500
Pn159	1898	—	Rouble. Copper. Y#61, no value.	850
Pn156	1898	—	2 Kopeks. Copper. Berlin Mint.	—
Pn157	1898	—	3 Kopeks. Copper. Berlin Mint.	—
Pn151	1898	—	1/4 Kopek. Copper. Inverted W. Retrograde legend. Berlin Mint.	—
Pn153	1898	—	Kopek. Copper.	—
Pn154	1898	—	Kopek. Aluminum. Berlin Mint.	—
Pn155	1898	—	Kopek. Nickel. Berlin Mint.	—

ST. BARTHOLOMEW

Saint Bartholomew (Saint Barthelemy, Saint Barts), a French island possession located in the Leeward Islands of the West Indies about 15 miles northwest of Guadeloupe, of which it is a dependency, has an area of 10 sq. mi. (26 sq. km.).

Saint Bartholomew was occupied by France in 1648 and sold to Sweden in 1784. In 1877 it was reacquired, by purchase, by France.

The coins issued under Sweden for Saint Bartholomew, crown-countermarked U.S. coins, Cayenne sous, Swedish and Polish billon -- have been extensively counterfeited.

RULERS

French, until 1784, 1877--
Swedish, 1784-1877

MONETARY SYSTEM

1797-1821

6 Stivers = 1 Bit
12 Bits = 8 Spanish Reales

1821-1846 (actually used to 1864)

6 Stivers = 1 Bit (Courant)
18-3/4 Bits (Courant) = 8 Reales

1864-1878

100 Cents = 1 Dollar

SWEDISH OCCUPATION

COUNTERMARKED COINAGE

Proclamation of December 30, 1808

KM# 4 3 STIVERS
Silver **Countermark:** Crowned 3/M **Note:** Countermark on Spanish Colonial 1/2 Real.

CM Date	Host Date	Good	VG	F	VF	XF
ND	ND	150	250	500	950	—

KM# 5 4 STIVERS
Silver **Countermark:** Crowned 4/M **Note:** Countermark on Spanish Colonial 1/2 Real.

CM Date	Host Date	Good	VG	F	VF	XF
ND	ND	150	250	500	950	—

KM# 7 7 STIVERS
Silver **Countermark:** Crowned 7/M **Note:** Countermark on Spanish Colonial 1 Real.

CM Date	Host Date	Good	VG	F	VF	XF
ND	ND	150	250	500	950	—

KM# 8 9 STIVERS
Silver **Countermark:** Crowned 9/M **Note:** Countermark on Spanish Colonial 1 Real.

CM Date	Host Date	Good	VG	F	VF	XF
ND	ND	175	275	600	1,150	—

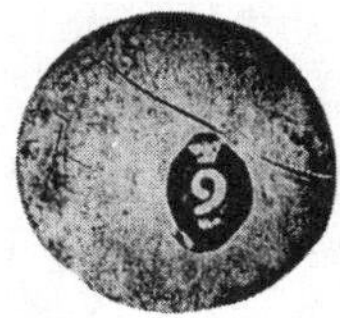

KM# 9 9 STIVERS
Silver **Countermark:** Crowned 9/M **Note:** Countermark on Spanish Colonial 1 Real.

CM Date	Host Date	Good	VG	F	VF	XF
ND	ND	175	275	550	1,000	—

KM# 11 14 STIVERS
Silver **Countermark:** Crowned 14/M **Note:** Countermark on Spanish Colonial 2 Reales.

CM Date	Host Date	Good	VG	F	VF	XF
ND	ND	200	300	600	1,200	—

Note: For St. Bartholomew countermarked 14 Stivers with additional countermark P in circle of dots see Saint Eustatius in Netherlands Antilles

KM# 13 18 STIVERS
Silver **Countermark:** Crowned 18/M **Note:** Countermark on Spanish Colonial 2 Reales.

CM Date	Host Date	Good	VG	F	VF	XF
ND	ND	350	550	1,350	2,850	—

Note: Many contemporary counterfeits of the 1808 countermarks exist

COUNTERMARKED COINAGE

Proclamation of July 9, 1834

KM# 3 STIVER
Silver **Countermark:** Type I crown **Note:** Countermark on Curacao Stiver, KM#24.

CM Date	Host Date	Good	VG	F	VF	XF
ND	ND(1834)	75.00	150	300	500	—

KM# 2.1 2 SOU
Billon **Countermark:** Type II crown **Note:** Countermark on Cayenne 2 Sou, KM#1.

CM Date	Host Date	Good	VG	F	VF	XF
ND	ND(1834-64)	65.00	115	160	225	—

KM# 2.2 2 SOU
Billon **Countermark:** Type III crown **Note:** Countermark on Cayenne 2 Sou, KM#1.

CM Date	Host Date	Good	VG	F	VF	XF
ND	ND(1834-64)	65.00	115	160	225	—

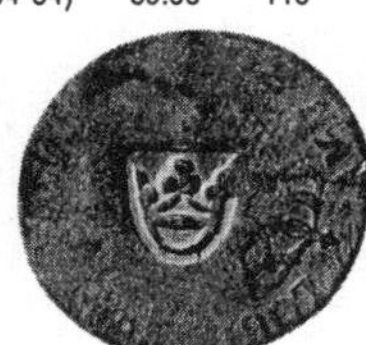

KM# 2.3 2 SOU
Billon **Countermark:** Type IV crown **Note:** Countermark on Cayenne 2 Sou, KM#1.

CM Date	Host Date	Good	VG	F	VF	XF
ND	ND(1834-64)	75.00	125	175	250	—

KM# 2.4 2 SOU
Billon **Countermark:** Type V crown **Note:** Countermark on Cayenne 2 Sou, KM#1.

CM Date	Host Date	Good	VG	F	VF	XF
ND	ND(1834-64)	75.00	125	175	250	—

KM# 2.5 2 SOU
Billon **Countermark:** Type VI crown **Note:** Countermark on Cayenne 2 Sou, KM#1.

CM Date	Host Date	Good	VG	F	VF	XF
ND	ND(1834-64)	85.00	135	190	275	—

KM# 2.6 2 SOU
Billon **Countermark:** Type VII crown **Note:** Countermark on Cayenne 2 Sou, KM#1.

CM Date	Host Date	Good	VG	F	VF	XF
ND	ND(1834-64)	85.00	135	190	275	—

Note: The crown countermark of 1834 was extensively counterfeited and imitated for over a century and a half from the period of issue; Spanish and Spanish Colonial hosts are almost assuredly counterfeit

SAINT EUSTATIUS

St. Eustatius (*Sint Eustatius, Statia*), a Netherlands West Indian island located in the Leeward Islands of the Lesser Antilles nine miles northwest of St. Kitts, has an area of 12 sq. mi. (21 sq. km.). It is part of the Netherlands Antilles.

Between 1630 and 1640 the Dutch seized Curacao, Saba, St. Martin and St. Eustatius, all valuable as piloting and smuggling depots. The territorial acquisitions were confirmed to the Dutch by the Treaty of Munster in 1648. Under the guidance of merchants from Flushing, St. Eustatius became a prosperous entry port of neutral trade. On Feb. 3, 1781, British Admiral George Rodney, acting under orders, captured the island and confiscated much valuable booty. Before passing permanently into Dutch hands, St. Eustatius was attacked or captured several times by the French and English, and was in English hands during the Napoleonic Wars from 1810 to 1814.

RULERS
Dutch

MONETARY SYSTEM
6 Stuivers = 1 Reaal

BRITISH OCCUPATION

COUNTERMARKED COINAGE

SE incuse countermark on French Guiana 2 Sous coins was official.

These were followed by raised SE countermarks (on a variety of worn billon & silver coins) generally thought to be forgeries.

From 1809 all coins had to be revalidated with a P countermark, which stood for Pierre dit Flamand, the artisan who designed the mark. Both raised and incuse SE varieties as well as unmarked coins were revalidated.

KM# 1.2 STUIVER
Copper **Countermark:** SE **Note:** Raised countermark.

CM Date	Host Date	Good	VG	F	VF	XF
ND	ND(1797-1809)	40.00	70.00	120	200	—

KM# 1.2a STUIVER
Billon **Countermark:** SE **Note:** Raised countermark.

CM Date	Host Date	Good	VG	F	VF	XF
ND	ND(1797-1809)	40.00	65.00	100	175	—

KM# 1.2b STUIVER
Silver **Countermark:** SE **Note:** Raised countermark.

CM Date	Host Date	Good	VG	F	VF	XF
ND	ND(1797-1809)	100	150	200	250	—

KM# 4 STUIVER
Various Metals **Countermark:** P **Note:** Countermark on older SE.

CM Date	Host Date	Good	VG	F	VF	XF
ND	ND(1809-12)	35.00	60.00	100	175	—

KM# 5 STUIVER
Silver **Countermark:** P **Note:** Countermark in circle of dots on St. Bartholomew 4 Stivers, KM#5.

CM Date	Host Date	Good	VG	F	VF	XF
ND	ND(1810-12) Rare	—	—	—	—	—

KM# 6.1 REAL
Silver **Countermark:** P **Note:** Countermark in circle of dots on St. Bartholomew 7 Stivers, KM#7.

CM Date	Host Date	Good	VG	F	VF	XF
ND	ND(1810-12) Rare	—	—	—	—	—

KM# 6.2 REAL
Silver **Countermark:** P **Note:** Countermark in circle of dots on St. Bartholomew 9 Stivers, KM#8.

CM Date	Host Date	Good	VG	F	VF	XF
ND	ND(1810-12) Rare	—	—	—	—	—

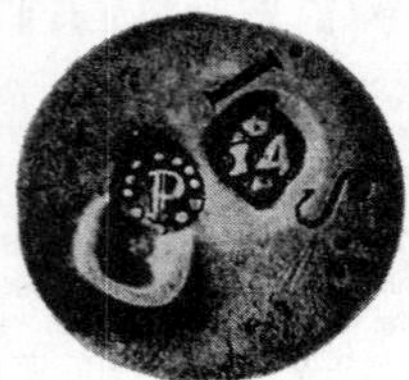

KM# 7.2 2 REALES
Silver **Countermark:** P **Note:** Countermark in circle of dots on St. Bartholomew.

CM Date	Host Date	Good	VG	F	VF	XF
ND	ND(1810-12) Rare	—	—	—	—	—

KM# 7.1 2 REALES
Silver **Countermark:** P **Note:** Countermark in circle of dots.

CM Date	Host Date	Good	VG	F	VF	XF
ND	ND(1810-12)	30.00	50.00	80.00	120	—

SAINT HELENA & ASCENSION

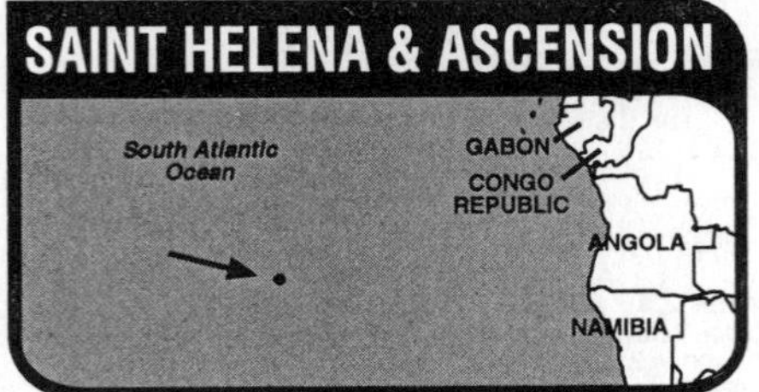

Saint Helena, a British colony located about 1,150 miles (1,850 km.) from the west coast of Africa, has an area of 47 sq. mi. (410 sq. km.). Ascension and Tristan da Cunha are dependencies of Saint Helena.

The island was discovered and named by the Portuguese navigator Joao de Nova Castella in 1502. The Portuguese imported livestock, fruit trees, and vegetables but established no permanent settlement. The Dutch occupied the island temporarily, 1645-51. The original European settlement was founded by representatives of the British East India Company sent to annex the island after the departure of the Dutch. The Dutch returned and captured Saint Helena from the British on New Year's Day, 1673, but were in turn ejected by a British force under Sir Richard Munden. Thereafter Saint Helena was the undisputed possession of Great Britain. The island served as the place of exile for Napoleon, several Zulu chiefs, and an ex-sultan of Zanzibar.

RULERS
British

MONETARY SYSTEM
12 Pence = 1 Shilling

BRITISH EAST INDIA COMPANY

STANDARD COINAGE

100 Pence = 1 Pound

KM# A4 1/2 PENNY
Copper

Date	Mintage	F	VF	XF	Unc	BU
1821	—	10.00	20.00	70.00	175	—
1821 Proof	—	Value: 225				

KM# 4a 1/2 PENNY
Bronze

Date	Mintage	F	VF	XF	Unc	BU
1821 Proof	—	Value: 250				

KM# 4b 1/2 PENNY
Gilt Bronze

Date	Mintage	F	VF	XF	Unc	BU
1821 Proof, rare	—	—	—	—	—	—

SAINT HELENA

Under British Administration

TOKEN COINAGE

KM# Tn1 HALFPENNY
Issuer: Slomon, Dickson and Taylor

Date	Mintage	VG	F	VF	XF	Unc
ND(1821)	71,000	8.00	15.00	40.00	100	225

PATTERNS

Including off metal strikes

KM#	Date	Mintage	Identification	Mkt Val
Pn1	1833	—	Sixpence. Copper. Plain edge.	2,250
Pn2	1833	—	Shilling. Copper. Plain edge.	3,500

KM#	Date	Mintage	Identification	Mkt Val
Pn3	1833	—	1/2 Crown. Copper. Plain edge.	4,500

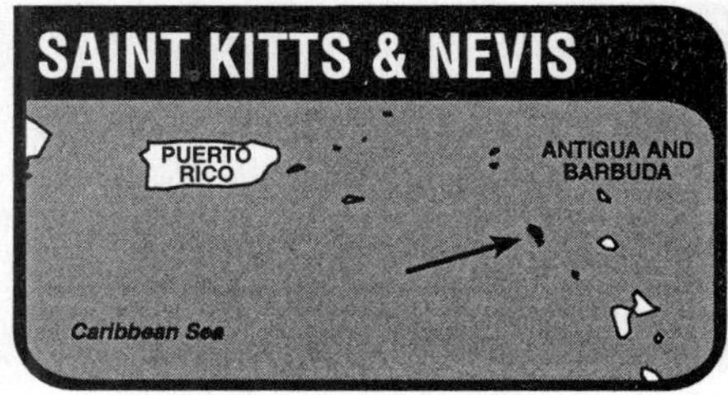

Saint Kitts (Saint Christopher), a West Indian island located in the Leeward Islands southeast of Puerto Rico, is the principal component of a British associated state composed of the islands of Saint Kitts, Nevis, and Anguilla. The associated state has an area of 104 sq. mi. (360 sq. km.).

Saint Kitts was discovered by Columbus in 1493 and was settled by Thomas Warner, an Englishman, in 1623. The island was ceded to the British by the Treaty of Utrecht, 1713. France protested British occupancy, and on three occasions between 1616 and 1782 seized the island and held it for short periods. Saint Kitts used the coins and currency of the British Caribbean Territories (Eastern Group).

From approximately 1750-1830, billon 2 sous of the French colony of Cayenne were countermarked SK' and used on Saint Kitts. They were valued at 1-1/3 Pence.

RULERS
British

MONETARY SYSTEM
100 Cents = 1 Dollar

NOTE: The grades shown describe the condition of the raised countermarks, not the host coin itself, which is typically well worn.

BRITISH ADMINISTRATION

COUNTERMARKED COINAGE

108 Pence = 9 Shillings = 12 Bits = 1 Dollar; 100 Cents = 1 Dollar

KM# 1 1-1/2 PENCE (Black Dog)
Billon **Countermark:** S **Note:** Countermark on French Colonies 24 Deniers, C#6.

CM Date	Host Date	Good	VG	F	VF	XF
ND	1801	50.00	75.00	100	135	—

KM# 2 2-1/4 PENCE
Billon **Countermark:** S K **Note:** Countermark on French Guyana 2 Sous, C#1.

CM Date	Host Date	Good	VG	F	VF	XF
ND	1809-1812	50.00	75.00	100	135	—

KM# 3 1/8 DOLLAR
Silver **Countermark:** S **Note:** Countermark on cut 1/8 section of Spanish 8 Reales.

CM Date	Host Date	Good	VG	F	VF	XF
ND	1801	550	1,250	2,000	2,500	—

KM# 4 1/4 DOLLAR
Silver **Countermark:** S **Note:** Countermark on cut 1/4 section of Spanish 8 Reales.

CM Date	Host Date	Good	VG	F	VF	XF
ND	1801	150	300	550	750	—

KM# 5 1/2 DOLLAR
Silver **Countermark:** S **Note:** Countermark on cut 1/2 section of Spanish 8 Reales.

CM Date	Host Date	Good	VG	F	VF	XF
ND	1801	200	400	700	950	—

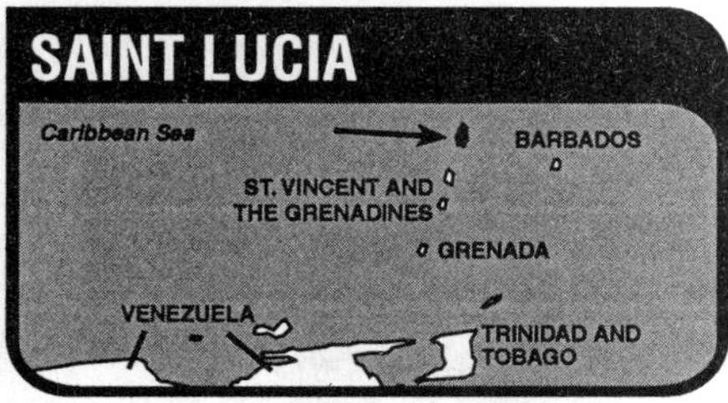

Saint Lucia, an island located in the Windward Islands of the West Indies between Saint Vincent and Martinique, has an area of 238 sq. mi. (620 sq. km.).

Columbus discovered Saint Lucia in 1502. The first attempts at settlement undertaken by the British in 1605 and 1638 were frustrated by sickness and the determined hostility of the fierce Carib inhabitants. The French settled it in 1650 and made a treaty with the natives. Until 1814, when the island became a definite British possession, it was the scene of a continuous conflict between the British and French, which saw the island change, hands on at least 14 occasions.

RULERS
British

FRENCH COLONIAL

COUNTERMARKED COINAGE

Series of 1811

KM# 5 3 STAMPEES
Silver **Countermark:** Circle with crenalated edges **Note:** Countermark on 1/4 cut of Spanish or Spanish Colonial 2 Reales.

CM Date	Host Date	Good	VG	F	VF	XF
ND	ND(1811)	—	—	—	—	—

KM# 6 ESCALIN
2.0000 g., Silver **Countermark:** Circle **Note:** Countermark on 1/3 cut of Spanish or Spanish Colonial 2 Reales.

CM Date	Host Date	Good	VG	F	VF	XF
ND	ND(1811)	200	300	550	850	—

KM# 7 1-1/2 ESCALINS
2.0000 g., Silver **Countermark:** Two circles **Note:** Countermark on 1/4 cut of Spanish or Spanish Colonial 4 Reales.

CM Date	Host Date	Good	VG	F	VF	XF
ND	ND(1811)	300	600	900	1,250	—

KM# 8 2 ESCALINS
4.0000 g., Silver **Countermark:** Three circles **Note:** Countermark on 1/3 cut of Spanish or Spanish Colonial 4 Reales.

CM Date	Host Date	Good	VG	F	VF	XF
ND	ND(1811)	350	650	950	1,350	—

COUNTERMARKED COINAGE

Series of 1813

KM# 9 2 LIVRES 5 SOUS
5.3000 g., Silver **Countermark:** S:Lucie **Note:** Countermark on 1/3 outer cut of Spanish or Spanish Colonial 8 Reales.

CM Date	Host Date	Good	VG	F	VF	XF
ND	ND(1813)	50.00	100	200	400	—

KM# 10 6 LIVRES 15 SOUS
15.0000 g., Silver **Countermark:** S:Lucie **Note:** Countermark on 1/3 center cut of Spanish or Spanish Colonial 8 Reales.

CM Date	Host Date	Good	VG	F	VF	XF
ND	ND(1813)	100	200	400	750	—

Note: There are no known genuine examples existing today of any other similar varieties cut from Spanish or Spanish Colonial 2 and 4 Reales with this countermark

SAINT MARTIN

St. Martin (*Sint Maarten*), the only island in the Antilles owned by two European powers (France and the Netherlands), is located in the Leeward Islands of the Lesser Antilles five miles south of the British island of Anguilla. The French northern section of the island (St.Martin) is a dependency of the French Department of Guadeloupe. It has an area of 20 sq. mi. (51 sq. km.). The Dutch southern section of the island (Sint Maarten) has an area of 17 sq. mi. (34 sq. km.).

Although nominally a Spanish possession at the time, St. Martin was occupied by French freebooters in 1638, but when Spain relinquished claim to the island in 1648 it was peaceably divided between France and Holland in recognition of the merchant communities already established on the island by nationals of both powers. St. Martin has remained under dual French-Dutch ownership to the present time, except for a period during the Napoleonic Wars when the British seized and occupied it.

The northern section of the island uses the coins and currency of France.

MONETARY SYSTEM
6 Stuivers = 1 Reaal
20 Stuivers = 1 Gulden
12 (later 15) Reaals = 1 Peso

COLONIAL

COUNTERMARKED COINAGE

KM# 4 2 STUIVERS
Billon **Countermark:** StM **Note:** Incuse Fleur-de-Lys countermark on French Guiana 2 Sous.

CM Date	Host Date	Good	VG	F	VF	XF
ND	ND(1805)	100	150	200	250	—

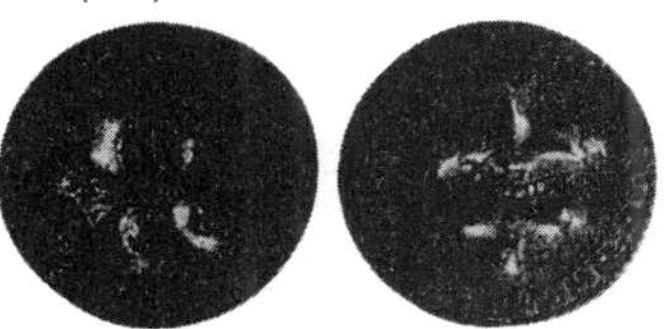

KM# 6 2 STUIVERS
Silver **Note:** Incuse Fleur-de-Lys plus S t M countermark in beaded circle.

CM Date	Host Date	Good	VG	F	VF	XF
ND	ND(1805)	35.00	60.00	100	170	—

KM# 5 2 STUIVERS
Silver **Note:** Raised Fleur-de-lis countermark.

CM Date	Host Date	Good	VG	F	VF	XF
ND	ND(1805)	30.00	50.00	75.00	100	—

KM# 3 2 STUIVERS
Billon **Countermark:** StM **Note:** Countermrk in beaded circle plus incuse M on French Guiana 2 Sous.

CM Date	Host Date	Good	VG	F	VF	XF
ND	ND(1820)	70.00	110	140	175	—

KM# 12 18 STUIVERS
Silver **Note:** Countermark ST. MARTIN and arrows on 1/5 cut of Spanish or Spanish Colonial 8 Reales.

CM Date	Host Date	Good	VG	F	VF	XF
ND	ND(1817-20)	45.00	75.00	185	250	—

SAINT THOMAS & PRINCE

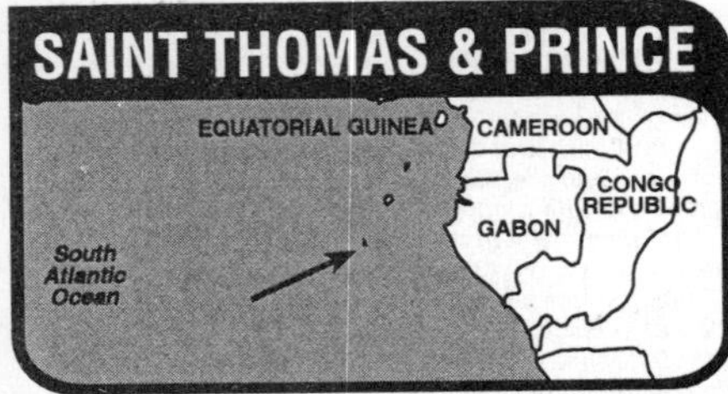

The Democratic Republic of Sao Tome and Principe (formerly the Portuguese overseas province of Saint Thomas and Prince Islands) is located in the Gulf of Guinea 150 miles (241 km.) off the western coast of Africa. It has an area of 372 sq. mi. (960 sq. km.).

Saint Thomas and Saint Prince were uninhabited when discovered by Portuguese navigators Joao de Santarem and Pedro de Escobar in 1470. After the failure of their initial settlement of 1485, the Portuguese successfully colonized St. Thomas with a colony of prisoners and exiled Jews in 1493. An initial prosperity based on the sugar trade gave way to a time of misfortune, 1567-1709, that saw the colony attacked and occupied or plundered by the French and Dutch, ravaged by the slave revolt of 1595; and finally rendered destitute by the transfer of the world sugar trade to Brazil. In the late 1800s, the colony turned from the production of sugar to cocoa, the basis of its present economy

RULERS
Portuguese, until 1975

MINT MARKS
R – Rio

MONETARY SYSTEM
100 Centavos = 1 Escudo

PORTUGUESE COLONY

STANDARD COINAGE

100 Centimos = 1 Dobra

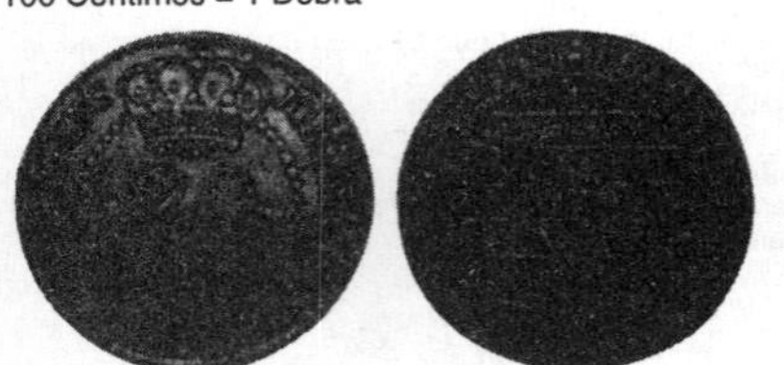

KM# A1 20 REIS
Copper

Date	Mintage	VG	F	VF	XF	Unc
1813R	10,000	10.00	20.00	45.00	100	180
1815R	—	10.00	20.00	45.00	100	180

KM# D1 20 REIS
Copper **Note:** Examples with a countermark of a small crown exist.

Date	Mintage	VG	F	VF	XF	Unc
1819 Bahaia	—	4.00	9.00	25.00	60.00	—
1825 Lisbon	28,000	5.00	10.00	28.00	65.00	—

KM# B1 40 REIS
Copper

Date	Mintage	VG	F	VF	XF	Unc
1813R	15,000	12.00	20.00	35.00	110	—
1815R	—	20.00	30.00	60.00	120	—

KM# E1 40 REIS
Copper **Note:** The difference between the Bahia and Lisbon coins is slight. The crown on the Bahia issue being rounder, approximately 2mm between the crown and rim. Strikes over earlier issues known. Examples exist with a small crown countermark.

Date	Mintage	VG	F	VF	XF	Unc
1819 Bahia	—	6.00	15.00	35.00	75.00	—
1821 Bahia	—	5.00	10.00	28.00	65.00	—
1822 Bahia; Rare	—	—	—	—	—	—
1825 Lisbon	24,000	6.00	15.00	30.00	70.00	—

KM# C1 80 REIS
Copper

Date	Mintage	VG	F	VF	XF	Unc
1813R	15,000	10.00	20.00	40.00	80.00	—

KM# F1 80 REIS
Copper **Note:** Examples exist with a small crown countermark.

Date	Mintage	VG	F	VF	XF	Unc
1819 Bahia	—	7.50	15.00	35.00	75.00	—
1825 Lisbon	14,000	6.00	12.00	30.00	70.00	—

SAINT VINCENT

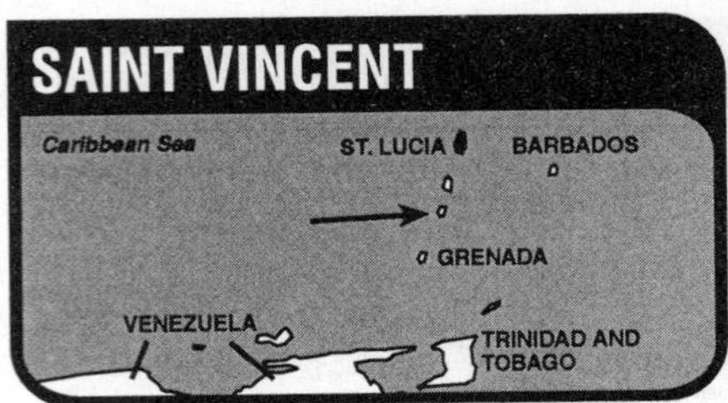

Saint Vincent and the Grenadines, consisting of the island of Saint Vincent and the northern Grenadines (a string of islets stretching southward from Saint Vincent), is located in the Windward Islands of the West Indies, West of Barbados and south of Saint Lucia. The tiny nation has an area of 150sq. mi. (340 sq. km.).

Saint Vincent was discovered by Columbus on Jan. 22, 1498, but was left undisturbed for more than a century. The British began colonization early in the 18th century against bitter and prolonged Carib resistance. The island was taken by the French in 1779, but was restored to the British in 1783, at the end of the American Revolution. Saint Vincent and the northern Grenadines became a British associated state in Oct. 1969. Independence under the name of Saint Vincent and the Grenadines was attained at midnight of Oct. 26, 1979. The new nation chose to become a member of the Commonwealth of Nations with Elizabeth II as Head of State and Queen of Saint Vincent.

A local coinage was introduced in 1797, with the gold withdrawn in 1818 and the silver in 1823. This was replaced by sterling.

RULERS
British

MONETARY SYSTEM
6 Black Dogs = 4 Stampees = 1 Bit = 9 Pence
1797-1811
8 Shillings, 3 Pence = 11 Bits = 1 Dollar
Commencing 1811
9 Shillings = 12 Bits = 1 Dollar

BRITISH ADMINISTRATION

COUNTERMARKED COINAGE

(1797-1818)

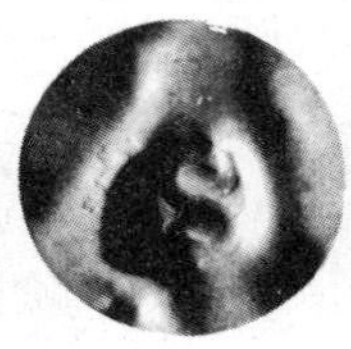

KM# 7 BLACK DOG
Billon **Countermark:** Retrograde S within octagonal indent

CM Date	Host Date	Good	VG	F	VF	XF
ND	ND(1814)	25.00	50.00	75.00	100	—

KM# 8 STAMPEE
Billon **Countermark:** Retrograde S within octagonal indent
Note: Countermark on French Colonial coin bearing a crowned C.

CM Date	Host Date	Good	VG	F	VF	XF
ND	ND(1814)	25.00	50.00	75.00	100	—

KM# 9.1 IV-1/2 BITS
Silver **Countermark:** S/IV 1/2/B **Note:** Countermark on Mexico 2 Reales, KM#86.

CM Date	Host Date	Good	VG	F	VF	XF
ND	ND(1754 M)	300	500	750	1,200	—

KM# 9.2 IV-1/2 BITS
Silver **Countermark:** S/IV 1/2/B **Note:** Countermark on Mexico 2 Reales, KM#88.2.

CM Date	Host Date	Good	VG	F	VF	XF
	ND(1786 FM)	300	500	750	1,200	—

KM# 10 VI BITS

Silver **Countermark:** S/VI **Note:** Countermark on 23 milimeter center disk cut from Spanish or Spanish Colonial 8 Reales.

CM Date	Host Date	Good	VG	F	VF	XF
ND	ND(1811-14)	275	450	700	1,150	—

KM# 11 IX BITS

Silver **Countermark:** S/IX **Note:** Countermark on Spanish or Spanish American 4 Reales.

CM Date	Host Date	Good	VG	F	VF	XF
	ND(1811-14)	2,500	3,500	4,750	6,500	—

KM# 12.1 XII BITS

Silver **Countermark:** S/XII **Note:** Countermark on holed Bolivia 8 Reales, KM#64.

CM Date	Host Date	Good	VG	F	VF	XF
ND	ND(1789-90 PR)	2,750	3,750	5,000	6,750	—

KM# 12.2 XII BITS

Silver **Countermark:** S/XII **Note:** Countermark on holed Mexico 8 Reales, KM#109.

CM Date	Host Date	Good	VG	F	VF	XF
ND	ND(1802 FT)	2,750	3,750	5,000	6,750	—

KM# 12.3 XII BITS

Silver **Countermark:** S/XII **Note:** Countermark on holed Mexico 8 Reales, KM#110.

CM Date	Host Date	Good	VG	F	VF	XF
ND	ND(1809 TH)	2,750	3,750	5,000	6,750	—

COUNTERMARKED COINAGE

Gold (1798-1818)

The countermarking of various gold coins in circulation on Saint Vincent was authorized by an Act of August 1, 1798. Standard weight for a gold Joe was set at 11.66 grams with a denomination of 66 Shillings. Full weight gold was marked 3 times with the letter S. Underweight gold could be brought up to proper weight by plugging and marking the plug with a letter S, under the guidance of at least 1 council member and 2 assemblymen.

Ongoing concerns and practical implementation made this act subject to review and in all likelihood alterations were made resulting in the various plugged and full weight examples listed below. All countermarked Joes were recalled in 1818.

KM# 17 66 SHILLINGS

Gold **Countermark:** S (three times) **Note:** Weight varies: 11.50-11.66 grams. Countermark on Brazil 6400 Reis, KM#149.

CM Date	Host Date	Good	VG	F	VF	XF
ND	ND17x8	1,500	2,250	3,500	5,000	—

KM# 18 66 SHILLINGS

Gold **Countermark:** S (three times) **Note:** Weight varies: 11.50-11.66 grams. Countermark on Brazil 6400 Reis, KM#199.2.

CM Date	Host Date	Good	VG	F	VF	XF
ND	ND1786	1,500	2,250	3,500	5,000	—

KM# 19 66 SHILLINGS

Gold **Countermark:** S (three times) **Note:** Weight varies: 11.50-11.66 grams. Countermark on plugged Brazil 6400 Reis, KM#199.2.

CM Date	Host Date	Good	VG	F	VF	XF
ND	ND1779	1,500	2,500	4,000	6,000	—

KM# 5.1 66 SHILLINGS

Gold **Countermark:** Obverse: S (three times); Reverse: IS **Note:** Weight varies: 11.50-11.66 grams. Countermark on the plug of a false Brazil 6400 Reis, KM#172.2

CM Date	Host Date	Good	VG	F	VF	XF
ND	ND1773 Rare	—	—	—	—	—

KM# 6 66 SHILLINGS

Gold **Countermark:** S (three times) and GH **Note:** Weight varies: 11.50-11.66 grams. Countermark on the plug of a false Brazil 6400 Reis, KM#172.2

CM Date	Host Date	Good	VG	F	VF	XF
ND	ND1767 Rare	—	—	—	—	—

KM# 5.2 66 SHILLINGS

Gold **Countermark:** Obverse: S (three times); Reverse: IS **Note:** Weight varies: 11.50-11.66 grams. Countermark on the plug of a false Brazil 6400 Reis, KM#199.2

CM Date	Host Date	Good	VG	F	VF	XF
ND	ND178x Rare	—	—	—	—	—

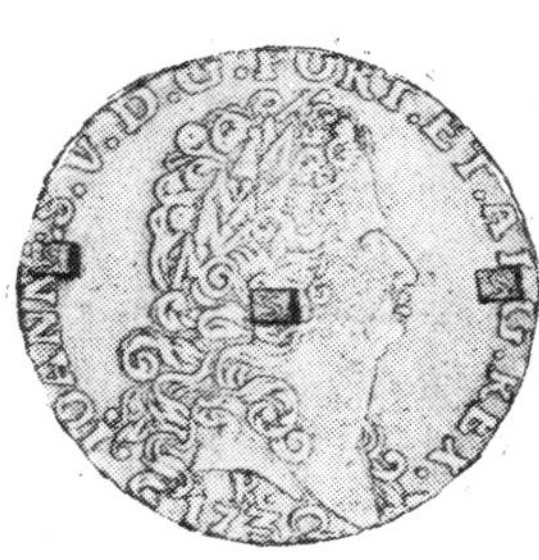

KM# 16 6 POUNDS 12 SHILLING

23.4000 g., Gold **Countermark:** S (three times) **Note:** Countermark on Brazil 12,800 Reis, KM#150.

CM Date	Host Date	Good	VG	F	VF	XF
ND	ND(1732) Rare	—	—	—	—	—

Note: Glendining's Ford sale 9-89 VF realized $12,800

SAN MARINO

The Republic of San Marino, the oldest and smallest republic in the world is located in north central Italy entirely surrounded by the Province of Emilia-Romagna. It has an area of 24 sq. mi. (60 sq. km.) and a population of *23,000. Capital: San Marino. The principal economic activities are farming, livestock raising, cheese making, tourism and light manufacturing. Building stone, lime, wheat, hides and baked goods are exported. The government derives most of its revenue from the sale of postage stamps for philatelic purposes.

According to tradition, San Marino was founded about 350AD by a Christian stonecutter as a refuge against religious persecution. While gradually acquiring the institutions of an independent state, it avoided the factional fights of the Middle Ages and, except for a brief period in fief to Cesare Borgia, retained its freedom despite attacks on its sovereignty by the Papacy, the Lords of Rimini, Napoleon and Mussolini. In 1862 San Marino established a customs union with, and put itself under the protection of, Italy. A Communist-Socialist coalition controlled the Government for 12 years after World War II. The Christian Democratic Party has been the core of government since 1957. In 1978 a Communist-Socialist coalition again came into power and remained in control until 1991.

San Marino has its own coinage, but Italian and Vatican City coins and currency are also in circulation.

MINT MARKS
M - Milan
R – Rome

MONETARY SYSTEM
100 Centesimi = 1 Lira

REPUBLIC

STANDARD COINAGE

100 Centesimi = 1 Lira

KM# 1 5 CENTESIMI
Copper

Date	Mintage	F	VF	XF	Unc	BU
1864M	280,000	4.00	9.00	40.00	175	—
1869M	600,000	3.00	7.50	22.50	55.00	—
1894R	600,000	3.00	6.50	20.00	50.00	—

KM# 2 10 CENTESIMI
Copper

Date	Mintage	F	VF	XF	Unc	BU
1875	150,000	4.50	9.00	30.00	100	—
1893R	150,000	4.00	8.00	28.00	65.00	—
1894R	150,000	4.00	7.50	25.00	60.00	—

KM# 3 50 CENTESIMI
2.5000 g., 0.8350 Silver 0.0671 oz.

Date	Mintage	F	VF	XF	Unc	BU
1898R	40,000	10.00	20.00	30.00	60.00	—

KM# 4 LIRA
5.0000 g., 0.8350 Silver .1342 oz.

Date	Mintage	F	VF	XF	Unc	BU
1898R	20,000	20.00	30.00	50.00	95.00	—

KM# 5 2 LIRE
10.0000 g., 0.8350 Silver .2684 oz.

Date	Mintage	F	VF	XF	Unc	BU
1898R	10,000	30.00	50.00	110	200	—

KM# 6 5 LIRE
25.0000 g., 0.9000 Silver 0.7234 oz.

Date	Mintage	F	VF	XF	Unc	BU
1898R	18,000	75.00	135	225	425	—

SARAWAK

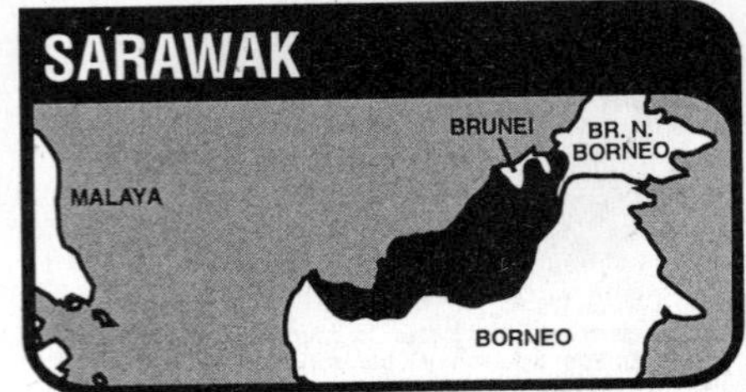

Sarawak is a former British colony located on the north-west coast of Borneo. The Japanese occupation during World War II so thoroughly devastated the economy that Rajah Sir Charles Vyner Brooke ceded it to Great Britain on July 1, 1946. In September, 1963 the colony joined the Federation of Malaysia.

RULERS
Charles J. Brooke, Rajah, 1868-1917
Charles V. Brooke, Rajah, 1917-1946

MINT MARKS
H - Heaton, Birmingham

MONETARY SYSTEM
100 Cents = 1 Dollar

BRITISH COLONY

STANDARD COINAGE

100 Cents = 1 Dollar

KM# 1 1/4 CENT
Copper **Ruler:** James Brooke Rajah

Date	Mintage	F	VF	XF	Unc	BU
1863	—	50.00	150	240	410	—
1863 Proof	—	Value: 600				

KM# 1a 1/4 CENT
Bronzed Copper **Ruler:** James Brooke Rajah

Date	Mintage	F	VF	XF	Unc	BU
1863 Proof	—	Value: 825				

KM# 4 1/4 CENT
Copper **Ruler:** Charles J. Brooke Rajah

Date	Mintage	F	VF	XF	Unc	BU
1870	100,000	15.00	35.00	120	200	—
1870 Proof	—	Value: 450				
1896H	283,000	10.00	27.00	78.00	200	—
1896H Proof	—	Value: 375				

KM# 2 1/2 CENT
Copper **Ruler:** James Brooke Rajah

Date	Mintage	F	VF	XF	Unc	BU
1863	—	27.00	60.00	180	350	—
1863 Proof	—	Value: 575				

KM# 2a 1/2 CENT
Bronzed Copper **Ruler:** James Brooke Rajah

Date	Mintage	F	VF	XF	Unc	BU
1863 Proof	—	Value: 720				

KM# 5 1/2 CENT
Copper **Ruler:** Charles J. Brooke Rajah

Date	Mintage	F	VF	XF	Unc	BU
1870	250,000	12.00	30.00	60.00	145	—
1879	640,000	12.00	30.00	60.00	145	—
1879 Proof	—	Value: 365				
1896	327,000	10.00	20.00	50.00	115	—
1896H Proof	—	Value: 365				

KM# 3 CENT
Copper **Ruler:** James Brooke Rajah

Date	Mintage	F	VF	XF	Unc	BU
1863	—	20.00	35.00	90.00	200	—
1863 Proof	—	Value: 540				

KM# 3a CENT
Bronzed Copper **Ruler:** James Brooke Rajah

Date	Mintage	F	VF	XF	Unc	BU
1863 Proof	—	Value: 785				

KM# 6 CENT
Copper **Ruler:** Charles J. Brooke Rajah **Note:** Varieties exist.

Date	Mintage	F	VF	XF	Unc	BU
1870	—	4.00	8.00	25.00	90.00	—
1870 Proof	—	Value: 290				
1870 Gilt Proof	—	Value: 290				
1879	750,000	6.00	12.00	35.00	115	—
1879 Proof	—	Value: 290				
1880	1,070,000	5.00	9.00	32.00	115	—
1882	1,070,000	4.00	8.00	27.00	85.00	—
1882 Proof	—	Value: 270				
1884	1,070,000	4.00	8.00	27.00	85.00	—
1884 Proof	—	Value: 270				
1885	2,140,000	4.00	8.00	27.00	85.00	—
1885 Proof	—	Value: 270				
1886	3,210,000	4.00	8.00	27.00	85.00	—
1887	1,605,000	4.00	8.00	27.00	85.00	—
1887 Proof	—	Value: 270				
1888	2,140,000	4.00	8.00	27.00	85.00	—
1888 Proof	—	Value: 270				
1889	535,000	4.00	8.00	27.00	85.00	—
1889/8H	2,675,000	4.00	8.00	27.00	85.00	—
1889H	Inc. above	4.00	8.00	27.00	85.00	—
1889H Proof	—	Value: 270				
1890H	3,210,000	4.00	8.00	27.00	85.00	—
1891	535,000	7.00	15.00	60.00	120	—
1891H	1,070,000	4.00	8.00	27.00	85.00	—

KM# 7 CENT
Copper **Ruler:** Charles J. Brooke Rajah

Date	Mintage	F	VF	XF	Unc	BU
1892H	2,178,000	4.00	8.00	27.00	85.00	—
1892H Proof	—	Value: 260				
1893H	1,634,000	4.00	8.00	27.00	85.00	—
1894H	1,633,000	4.00	8.00	27.00	85.00	—
1896H	2,178,000	4.00	8.00	27.00	85.00	—
1896H Proof	—	Value: 260				
1897H	1,089,000	4.00	8.00	27.00	85.00	—

KM# 8 5 CENTS
1.3500 g., 0.8000 Silver .0347 oz. **Ruler:** Charles J. Brooke Rajah

Date	Mintage	F	VF	XF	Unc	BU
1900H	200,000	30.00	60.00	100	170	—
1900H Proof	—	Value: 390				

KM# 9 10 CENTS
2.7100 g., 0.8000 Silver .0697 oz. **Ruler:** Charles J. Brooke Rajah

Date	Mintage	F	VF	XF	Unc	BU
1900H	150,000	20.00	35.00	60.00	130	—
1900H Proof	—	Value: 400				

KM# 10 20 CENTS
5.4300 g., 0.8000 Silver .1396 oz. **Ruler:** Charles J. Brooke Rajah

Date	Mintage	F	VF	XF	Unc	BU
1900H	75,000	38.00	85.00	200	360	—
1900H Proof	—	Value: 630				

KM# 11 50 CENTS
13.5700 g., 0.8000 Silver .349 oz. **Ruler:** Charles V. Brooke Rajah

Date	Mintage	F	VF	XF	Unc	BU
1900H	40,000	125	245	350	485	—
1900H Proof	—	Value: 1,850				

TOKEN COINAGE

KM# Tn1 KEPING
Copper **Ruler:** James Brooke Rajah **Note:** Accession Date: Sept. 24, 1841.

Date	Mintage	VG	F	VF	XF	Unc
AH1247	—	950	1,350	2,600	4,250	8,500

KM# Tn1a KEPING
Brass **Ruler:** James Brooke Rajah **Note:** Accession Date: Sept. 24, 1841.

Date	Mintage	VG	F	VF	XF	Unc
AH1247	—	1,250	1,750	2,880	4,850	9,400

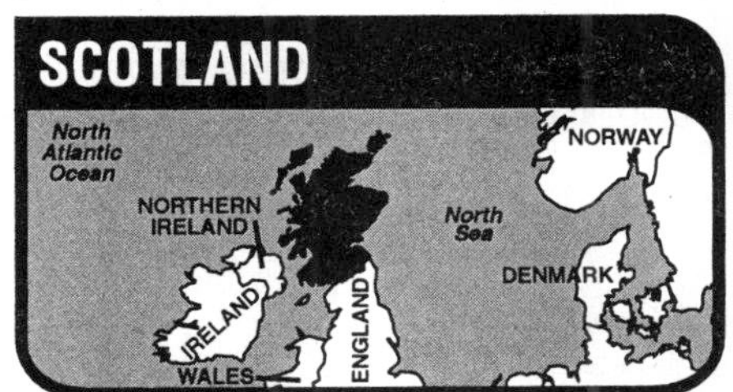

Scotland is located on the northern part of the island of Great Britain. It has an area of 30,414 square miles (78,772 sq. km.).

Scotland was the traditional home of the Picts in ancient times. The Romans invaded the area after 80 A.D. and Hadrian's Wall was built from 122-126 A.D. to keep the Picts from the Roman settlements to the south. In the 5th century Scotland had 4 kingdoms: Northumbria (Anglo-Saxon), Picts, Scots (of Irish extraction) and Strathclyde. St. Columba converted the Picts to Christianity in the late 6th century. Norse invasions started in the late 8th century. The Picts conquered the Scots in the 9th century and under Malcolm II (1005-1034) the Scottish kingdoms were united. The Scottish King became a vassal of the English king in 1174 (a circumstance that was to lead to many disputes). The Scots gained independence in 1314 at Bannockburn under Robert Bruce. From 1371-1714 it was ruled by the Stuarts, and in 1603 when James VI of Scotland succeeded Elizabeth I as James I, King of England, a personal union of the two kingdoms was formed. Parliamentary Act in 1707 made final union of the two kingdoms. In 1999 the Scottish Parliament was re-formed to make local decisions.

RULERS
George III, 1760-1820
George IV, 1820-1830
William IV, 1830-1837
Victoria, 1837-1901

KINGDOM

COUNTERMARKED COINAGE

Commercial

Private issue silver tokens appeared from 1811-12. For various reasons, the Spanish "dollars" themselves were preferred in Scotland where they circulated bearing a countermark of the merchant or company responsible for its issue. Sometimes other foreign crown-sized pieces were similarly countermarked. Many pieces are found with a grill-like cancellation over the countermark and have a considerably lower market value.

KM# CC94 1 SHILLING/8 PENCE
Silver **Mint:** Rothsay, Buteshire **Note:** Countermark similar to CC92 but value 1/8 in circle and on a cut third-dollar (or cut third 8 reales).

CM Date	Host Date	Good	VG	F	VF	XF
ND(1811)	ND	100	200	300	—	—

KM# CC95 2 SHILLINGS/4 PENCE
Silver **Mint:** Rothsay, Buteshire **Note:** Countermark similar to CC93 but value 2/4 in rectangle on half of wool sack countermark and on a cut half-dollar (same as above).

CM Date	Host Date	Good	VG	F	VF	XF
ND(1811)	ND	—	—	—	—	—

KM# CC8 2 SHILLINGS/6 PENCE
Silver **Mint:** Ballindallock, Balfron, Stirlingshire **Countermark:** BALLINDALLOCH COTTON WORK **Note:** Countermark in a circle around a cotton bale on French half-ecus.

CM Date	Host Date	Good	VG	F	VF	XF
ND(1811)	ND	—	400	600	—	—

KM# CC23 2 SHILLINGS/6 PENCE
Silver **Mint:** Dalzell, Lanarkshire **Countermark:** ADELPHI COTTON WORK **Note:** Countermark in circle around cotton bale.

CM Date	Host Date	Good	VG	F	VF	XF
ND(1811)	ND	250	450	600	—	—

KM# CC69 2 SHILLINGS/6 PENCE
Silver **Issuer:** Lanark, New, Lanarkshire **Mint:** Lanark, New, Lanarkshire **Note:** Similar to #CC66 but value 2/6.

CM Date	Host Date	Good	VG	F	VF	XF
ND(1811)	ND	600	800	1,000	—	—

Note: All of the 4/6 denomination and about half of the 2/6 denomination have an additional countermark of quatrefoil * within a small shield; Struck on French half-ecus

KM# CC96 2 SHILLINGS/6 PENCE
Silver **Mint:** Rothsay, Buteshire **Note:** Countermark similar to CC92 but value 2/6 in oval and on a cut half-dollar (or a cut half 8 reales).

CM Date	Host Date	Good	VG	F	VF	XF
ND(1811)	ND	800	1,000	1,200	—	—

KM# CC97 2 SHILLINGS/6 PENCE
Silver **Mint:** Rothsay, Buteshire **Note:** Countermark similar to CC93 but value 2/6 in rectangle and on a cut half-dollar (same as above), additional with 6-pointed star countermark.

CM Date	Host Date	Good	VG	F	VF	XF
ND(1811)	ND	600	800	1,000	—	—

KM# CC52 4 SHILLINGS/6 PENCE
Silver **Mint:** Greenock, Renfrewshire **Countermark:** R. & G. BLAIR. GREENOCK. **Note:** Countermark in oval around 4/6.

CM Date	Host Date	Good	VG	F	VF	XF
ND(1811)	ND Rare	—	—	—	—	—

KM# CC53 4 SHILLINGS/6 PENCE

Silver **Mint:** Greenock, Renfrewshire **Countermark:** GREENOCK DRAPER'S SOCIETY. **Note:** Countermark around 4/6 within a triangle.

CM Date	Host Date	Good	VG	F	VF	XF
ND(1811)	ND Rare	—	—	—	—	—

KM# CC56 4 SHILLINGS/6 PENCE

Silver **Mint:** Greenock, Renfrewshire **Note:** Similar to #CC55, but value 4/6.

CM Date	Host Date	Good	VG	F	VF	XF
ND(1811)	ND	525	675	900	—	—

KM# CC57 4 SHILLINGS/6 PENCE

Silver **Mint:** Greenock, Renfrewshire **Countermark:** J. McK. & SON GREENOCK **Note:** Countermark around 4/6.

CM Date	Host Date	Good	VG	F	VF	XF
ND(1811)	ND	300	400	550	—	—

KM# CC58 4 SHILLINGS/6 PENCE

Silver **Mint:** Greenock, Renfrewshire **Countermark:** McFIE LINDSAY & COY *GREENOCK* **Note:** Countermark around 4/6.

CM Date	Host Date	Good	VG	F	VF	XF
ND(1811)	ND	350	500	700	—	—

KM# CC59 4 SHILLINGS/6 PENCE

Silver **Mint:** Greenock, Renfrewshire **Countermark:** * J & A, MUIR * GREENOCK. **Note:** Countermark around 4/6.

CM Date	Host Date	Good	VG	F	VF	XF
ND(1811)	ND	300	400	550	—	—

KM# CC60 4 SHILLINGS/6 PENCE

Silver **Mint:** Greenock, Renfrewshire **Countermark:** JOHN RODGER JUNR. * GREENOCK * **Note:** Countermark around 4/6.

CM Date	Host Date	Good	VG	F	VF	XF
ND(1811)	ND	700	900	1,200	—	—

KM# CC65 4 SHILLINGS/6 PENCE

Silver **Issuer:** Johnstone, Renfrewshire **Mint:** Johnstone, Renfrewshire **Countermark:** CAMPBELL HALL & WATT around JOHNSTONE 4/6

CM Date	Host Date	Good	VG	F	VF	XF
ND(1811)	ND Rare	—	—	—	—	—

KM# CC68 4 SHILLINGS/6 PENCE

Silver **Issuer:** Lanark, New, Lanarkshire **Mint:** Lanark, New, Lanarkshire **Note:** Similar to #CC66 but value 4/6.

CM Date	Host Date	Good	VG	F	VF	XF
ND(1811)	ND	—	1,400	1,800	—	—

KM# CC89 4 SHILLINGS/6 PENCE

Silver **Mint:** Port Glasgow, Renfrewshire **Countermark:** ROBt. CRIGHTON Pt. GLASGOW. **Note:** Countermark in circle around 4/6.

CM Date	Host Date	Good	VG	F	VF	XF
ND(1811)	ND Rare	—	—	—	—	—

KM# CC91 4 SHILLINGS/6 PENCE

Silver **Mint:** Port Glasgow, Renfrewshire **Countermark:** A, STEVEN & SONS Pt GLASGOW **Note:** Countermark in circle around 4/6.

CM Date	Host Date	Good	VG	F	VF	XF
ND(1811)	ND	1,200	1,600	—	—	—

KM# CC100 4 SHILLINGS/6 PENCE

Silver **Mint:** Rothsay, Buteshire **Countermark:** ROTHSAY COTTON WORKS. **Note:** Countermark between beaded and cable circles around 4/6 above 1820.

CM Date	Host Date	Good	VG	F	VF	XF
ND(1811)	ND	200	300	450	—	—

KM# CC17 4 SHILLINGS/9 PENCE

Silver **Mint:** Catrine, Ayrshire **Note:** Countermark similar to CC14 but 4/9.

CM Date	Host Date	Good	VG	F	VF	XF
ND(1811)	ND	500	800	1,400	—	—

Note: All the Catrine countermarks have an individual number stamped in, the highest known being "5067"

KM# CC45 4 SHILLINGS/9 PENCE

Silver **Mint:** Glasgow, Lanarkshire **Note:** Similar to #CC44 but without ++ or inner circle, and with value 4/9.

CM Date	Host Date	Good	VG	F	VF	XF
ND(1811)	ND Rare	—	—	—	—	—

KM# CC49 4 SHILLINGS/9 PENCE

Silver **Mint:** Glasgow, Lanarkshire **Countermark:** THISTLE BANK. **Reverse:** Countermark: Thistle **Note:** Countermark in a circle around 4/9.

CM Date	Host Date	Good	VG	F	VF	XF
ND(1811)	ND	200	350	500	—	—

Note: This countermark is also known on counterfeit or false dollars struck in England

KM# CC50 4 SHILLINGS/9 PENCE

Silver **Mint:** Glasgow, Lanarkshire **Note:** Similar to #CC49 but without reverse thistle countermark.

CM Date	Host Date	Good	VG	F	VF	XF
ND(1811)	ND	300	500	800	—	—

KM# CC54 4 SHILLINGS/9 PENCE

Silver **Mint:** Glasgow, Lanarkshire **Countermark:** W G & CO, 4/9 **Note:** Countermark in a toothed T-shape indent.

CM Date	Host Date	Good	VG	F	VF	XF
ND(1811)	ND Rare	—	—	—	—	—

KM# CC61 4 SHILLINGS/9 PENCE

Silver **Mint:** Greenock, Renfrewshire **Countermark:** PAYABLE BY I & W SCOTT. GREENOCK **Note:** Countermark around 4/9 wtihin a rectangle.

CM Date	Host Date	Good	VG	F	VF	XF
ND(1811)	ND Rare	—	—	—	—	—

KM# CC67 4 SHILLINGS/9 PENCE

Silver **Issuer:** Lanark, New, Lanarkshire **Mint:** Lanark, New, Lanarkshire **Note:** Similar to #CC66 but value 4/9.

CM Date	Host Date	Good	VG	F	VF	XF
ND(1811)	ND	350	450	600	—	—

KM# CCA91 5 SHILLINGS

Silver **Mint:** Port Glasgow, Renfrewshire **Countermark:** A. STEVEN. PORT. GLASGOW **Note:** Countermark in circle around 5/.

CM Date	Host Date	Good	VG	F	VF	XF
ND(1811)	ND Rare	—	—	—	—	—

KM# CC1 5 SHILLINGS

Silver **Mint:** Ballindallock, Balfron, Stirlingshire **Countermark:** PAYABLE AT ALLOA COLLIERY **Note:** Countermark in a circle around an incuse 5.

CM Date	Host Date	Good	VG	F	VF	XF
ND(1811)	ND	200	300	500	—	—

Note: This countermark is only known on counterfeit or false dollars struck in England. Specimens retaining the silver plating command a premium

KM# CC7 5 SHILLINGS

Silver **Mint:** Ballindallock, Balfron, Stirlingshire **Countermark:** *BALLINDALLOCH*COTTON*WORKS **Note:** Countermark in two circlular lines around 5/.

CM Date	Host Date	Good	VG	F	VF	XF
ND(1811)	ND	275	850	1,300	—	—

KM# CC11 5 SHILLINGS

Silver **Mint:** Blantyre, Lanarkshire **Countermark:** BLANTYRE WORKS **Note:** Countermark in circle around 5/.

CM Date	Host Date	Good	VG	F	VF	XF
ND(1811)	ND	—	1,400	1,800	—	—

KM# CC12 5 SHILLINGS
Silver **Mint:** Calton, Lanarkshire **Countermark:** * HENRY REID * CALTON **Note:** Countermark in a circle around 5/.

CM Date	Host Date	Good	VG	F	VF	XF
ND(1811)	ND	—	1,400	1,800	—	—

Note: All known pieces are partly obliterated by cuts

KM# CC13 5 SHILLINGS
Silver **Mint:** Campsie, Lanarkshire **Countermark:** J. LECKIE CAMPSIE **Note:** Countermark around 5/ in beaded circle.

CM Date	Host Date	Good	VG	F	VF	XF
ND(1811)	ND Rare	—	—	—	—	—

KM# CC15 5 SHILLINGS
Silver **Mint:** Catrine, Ayrshire **Countermark:** CATRINE WORKS. No and number in oval, 5/

CM Date	Host Date	Good	VG	F	VF	XF
ND(1811)	ND Rare	—	—	—	—	—

KM# CC16 5 SHILLINGS
Silver **Mint:** Catrine, Ayrshire **Note:** Countermark similar to CC15 but value in circle.

CM Date	Host Date	Good	VG	F	VF	XF
ND(1811)	ND Rare	—	—	—	—	—

KM# CC19 5 SHILLINGS
Silver **Mint:** Culcreuch, Stirlingshire **Countermark:** PAYABLE AT CULCREUCH MILL * **Note:** Countermark around 5/.

CM Date	Host Date	Good	VG	F	VF	XF
ND(1811)	ND Rare	—	—	—	—	—

KM# CC21 5 SHILLINGS
Silver **Mint:** Dalry, Ayrshire **Countermark:** JAMIESON & HARVEY DALRY **Note:** Countermark around 5.

CM Date	Host Date	Good	VG	F	VF	XF
ND(1811)	ND Rare	—	—	—	—	—

KM# CC22 5 SHILLINGS
Silver **Mint:** Dalzell, Lanarkshire **Countermark:** PAYABLE AT DALZELL FARM * **Note:** Countermark without value.

CM Date	Host Date	Good	VG	F	VF	XF
ND(1811)	ND	275	375	500	—	—

Note: The Dalzell countermarks are only known on French 5 Franc pieces

KM# CC24 5 SHILLINGS
Silver **Mint:** Dalzell, Lanarkshire **Note:** Countermark similar to #CC23. Struck on French half-ecus.

CM Date	Host Date	Good	VG	F	VF	XF
ND(1811)	ND Rare	—	—	—	—	—

KM# CC28 5 SHILLINGS
Silver **Mint:** Deanston, Kilmarnock, Perthshire **Countermark:** DEANSTON COTTON MILL **Note:** Countermark in circle around 5/ within a toothed octagon.

CM Date	Host Date	Good	VG	F	VF	XF
ND(1811)	ND	—	—	2,000	—	—

KM# CC30 5 SHILLINGS
Silver **Mint:** Denny, Stirlingshire **Countermark:** T. SHIELS & CO. DENNY (value cancelled) **Reverse:** Countermark: PAYABLE AT HERBERTSHIRE **Note:** Reverse countermark: PAYABLE AT HERBERTSHIRE

CM Date	Host Date	Good	VG	F	VF	XF
ND(1811)	ND Rare	—	—	—	—	—

KM# CC33 5 SHILLINGS
Silver **Mint:** Fintry, Stirlingshire **Countermark:** *P. BY ROBERT McNEE FINTRY **Note:** Countermark around 5/.

CM Date	Host Date	Good	VG	F	VF	XF
ND(1811)	ND Rare	—	—	—	—	—

KM# CC35 5 SHILLINGS
Silver **Mint:** Fintry, Stirlingshire **Countermark:** J. STEWART FINTRY. **Note:** Countermark around 5/.

CM Date	Host Date	Good	VG	F	VF	XF
ND(1811)	ND Rare	—	—	—	—	—

KM# CC36 5 SHILLINGS
Silver **Mint:** Galston, Kilmarnock, Ayrshire **Countermark:** GALSTON above SOC. Y around 5s No. 12 **Note:** Countermark all in small circular indent.

CM Date	Host Date	Good	VG	F	VF	XF
ND(1811)	ND	800	1,100	1,500	—	—

Note: This countermark is also known on a French Ecu and on a Charles II crown

KM# CC37 5 SHILLINGS
Silver **Mint:** Glasgow, Lanarkshire **Countermark:** ADAMSON & LOGAN GLASGOW around FIVE SHIL

CM Date	Host Date	Good	VG	F	VF	XF
ND(1811)	ND Rare	—	—	—	—	—

KM# CC38 5 SHILLINGS
Silver **Mint:** Glasgow, Lanarkshire **Countermark:** T. & R. ARTHUR GLASGOW . around 5/ **Note:** This countermark is usually found cancelled with a grill pattern. Uncancelled examples are considered rare.

CM Date	Host Date	Good	VG	F	VF	XF
ND(1811)	ND Rare	—	—	—	—	—

KM# CC39 5 SHILLINGS
Silver **Mint:** Glasgow, Lanarkshire **Countermark:** W. BILTON 630 ARGYLE STREET TOBACCONISt **Reverse:** Countermark: a tree (the arms of Glasgow) **Note:** Countermark in two lines around 5/.

CM Date	Host Date	Good	VG	F	VF	XF
ND(1811)	ND Rare	—	—	—	—	—

KM# CCA39.1 5 SHILLINGS
Silver **Mint:** Glasgow, Lanarkshire **Countermark:** CBCo **Note:** Countermark in rectangle on Lima 8 Reales, KM#87.

CM Date	Host Date	Good	VG	F	VF	XF
ND(1811)	ND	—	—	650	—	—

KM# CCA39.2 5 SHILLINGS
Silver **Mint:** Glasgow, Lanarkshire **Countermark:** CBCo **Note:** Countermark in rectangle on Mexico City 8 Reales, KM#109.

CM Date	Host Date	Good	VG	F	VF	XF
ND(1811)	ND	—	—	650	—	—

KM# CC40 5 SHILLINGS
Silver **Mint:** Glasgow, Lanarkshire **Countermark:** D C **Note:** Countermark above large 12-pointed rosette without value.

CM Date	Host Date	Good	VG	F	VF	XF
ND(1811)	ND	400	600	800	—	—

Note: Possibly issued by D. Campbell & Co., Shuttle St., Glasgow

KM# CC44 5 SHILLINGS
Silver **Mint:** Glasgow, Lanarkshire **Countermark:** ++GLASGOW BANK **Note:** Countermark in a circle around 5/. within an inner circle.

CM Date	Host Date	Good	VG	F	VF	XF
ND(1811)	ND	400	600	800	—	—

KM# CC46 5 SHILLINGS
Silver **Mint:** Glasgow, Lanarkshire **Countermark:** PAYABLE BY J. INGLIS 32 TRONGATE GLASGOW **Reverse:** Countermark: A tree (arms of Glasgow)

CM Date	Host Date	Good	VG	F	VF	XF
ND(1811)	ND Rare	—	—	—	—	—

Note: The only specimen now known has the countermark obliterated and the value has not been determined

KM# CC48 5 SHILLINGS
Silver **Mint:** Glasgow, Lanarkshire **Countermark:** THISTLE BANK. **Reverse:** Countermark: Thistle **Note:** Countermark in a circle around 5/.

CM Date	Host Date	Good	VG	F	VF	XF
ND(1811)	ND	300	500	800	—	—

KM# CC51 5 SHILLINGS
Silver **Mint:** Glasgow, Lanarkshire **Countermark:** WM. THOMSON ++ FLESHER ++, BELL STREET GLASGOW **Note:** Countermark in inner circle around 5/.

CM Date	Host Date	Good	VG	F	VF	XF
ND(1811)	ND Rare	—	—	—	—	—

KM# CC55 5 SHILLINGS
Silver **Mint:** Greenock, Renfrewshire **Countermark:** A. KING *GREENOCK* **Note:** Countermark around 5/.

CM Date	Host Date	Good	VG	F	VF	XF
ND(1811)	ND	—	—	—	—	—

Note: Reported, not confirmed

KM# CC62 5 SHILLINGS
Silver **Mint:** Greenock, Renfrewshire **Countermark:** J. WATT & CO. . GREENOCK. **Note:** Countermark around 5/.

CM Date	Host Date	Good	VG	F	VF	XF
ND(1811)	ND Rare	—	—	—	—	—

KM# CC63 5 SHILLINGS
Silver **Mint:** Hurlet, Renfrewshire **Countermark:** J. & J. W. HURLET. **Note:** Countermark around 5/.

CM Date	Host Date	Good	VG	F	VF	XF
ND(1811)	ND	350	450	675	—	—

Note: There are two types of countermark, differing slightly in punctuation; Type I has an additional three dots punched in a triangle; A specimen of this countermark is known on a U.S. Dollar which has the three dots

KM# CC64 5 SHILLINGS

Silver **Issuer:** Hutchesontown, Renfrewshire, Purvey **Mint:** Hutchesontown, Renfrewshire, Purvey **Countermark:** FORSTER & CORBET HUTCHESONTOWN, 5/

CM Date	Host Date	Good	VG	F	VF	XF
ND(1811)	ND	600	800	1,000	—	—

KM# CC66 5 SHILLINGS
Silver **Issuer:** Lanark, New, Lanarkshire **Mint:** Lanark, New, Lanarkshire **Countermark:** PAYABLE AT LANARK MILLS-, around 5/

CM Date	Host Date	Good	VG	F	VF	XF
ND(1811)	ND	150	200	275	—	—

KM# CC74 5 SHILLINGS
Silver **Issuer:** Levern, Renfrewshire, Barrhead **Mint:** Levern, Renfrewshire, Barrhead **Countermark:** LEVERN. MILL. S. D & CO **Note:** Similar to #CC73 but value 5 and without additional countermark.

CM Date	Host Date	Good	VG	F	VF	XF
ND(1811)	ND Rare	—	—	—	—	—

KM# CC76 5 SHILLINGS
Silver **Issuer:** Lochwinnock, Renfrewshire **Mint:** Lochwinnock, Renfrewshire **Countermark:** N (?) ARTHUR & CO (LOCH)WINNOCH **Note:** Countermark in an oval around a large 5.

CM Date	Host Date	Good	VG	F	VF	XF
ND(1811)	ND Rare	—	—	—	—	—

KM# CC77 5 SHILLINGS
Silver **Issuer:** Lochwinnock, Renfrewshire **Mint:** Lochwinnock, Renfrewshire **Countermark:** A. GIBSON. & CO. LOCHWINNOCK. **Note:** Countermark within a circle around 5.

CM Date	Host Date	Good	VG	F	VF	XF
ND(1811)	ND Rare	—	—	—	—	—

KM# CC80 5 SHILLINGS
Silver **Issuer:** Paisley, Renfrewshire **Mint:** Paisley, Renfrewshire **Countermark:** CORCER PAISLEY **Reverse:** Countermark: View of blast furnace with smoke stack, etc., dated 1809 **Note:** Countermark around 5.

CM Date	Host Date	Good	VG	F	VF	XF
ND(1811)	ND					

Note: The only known specimen was reported in the 19th century but has since disappeared; a very indistinct electrotype copy exists

KM# CC81 5 SHILLINGS
Silver **Issuer:** Paisley, Renfrewshire **Mint:** Paisley, Renfrewshire **Countermark:** McG & C. PAISLEY **Note:** Countermark in a circle around 5. Presumably issued by McGavin & Clarkson.

CM Date	Host Date	Good	VG	F	VF	XF
ND(1811)	ND Rare	—	—	—	—	—

KM# CC84 5 SHILLINGS
Silver **Mint:** Paisley, Renfrewshire **Countermark:** JNo. & ROBt. McKERRELL. PAISLEY **Note:** Countermark in triangle around 5/.

CM Date	Host Date	Good	VG	F	VF	XF
ND(1811)	ND Rare	—	—	—	—	—

KM# CCA86 5 SHILLINGS
Silver **Mint:** Paisley, Renfrewshire **Countermark:** MCLEAN & DOBIE PAISLEY **Note:** Countermark in circle around 5/.

CM Date	Host Date	Good	VG	F	VF	XF
ND(1811)	ND Rare	—	—	—	—	—

KM# CC87 5 SHILLINGS
Silver **Mint:** Paisley, Renfrewshire **Countermark:** J. MUIR Manufr .PAISLEY. **Reverse:** Countermark: Prince of Wales plumes **Note:** Countermark in circle around 5/.

CM Date	Host Date	Good	VG	F	VF	XF
ND(1811)	ND	700	1,000	1,400	—	—

Note: The majority of specimens are cancelled with a grill pattern; these bring somewhat lower prices

KM# CC88 5 SHILLINGS
Silver **Mint:** Paisley, Renfrewshire **Countermark:** R. PEACOCK & SONS . PAISLEY. **Note:** Countermark in circle around 5/.

CM Date	Host Date	Good	VG	F	VF	XF
ND(1811)	ND	—	1,000	1,400	—	—

Note: The majority of specimens are cancelled with a grill pattern; these bring somewhat lower prices

KM# CC93 5 SHILLINGS
Silver **Mint:** Rothsay, Buteshire **Countermark:** PAYABLE AT ROTHSAY COTTON MILLS **Note:** Countermark around a wool sack on which is stamped 5 above Sh in a rectangle with additional 6-pointed star countermark.

CM Date	Host Date	Good	VG	F	VF	XF
ND(1811)	ND	—	—	—	—	—

KM# CC102 5 SHILLINGS
Silver **Mint:** Tobermoray, Argyllshire **Countermark:** DUGD. McLACHLAN MERCHT. ++ TOBERMORY ++ **Note:** Countermark in circle around 5/ in center on lined background.

CM Date	Host Date	Good	VG	F	VF	XF
ND(1811)	ND Rare	—	—	—	—	—

Note: A specimen of this countermark is known on a French 5 franc piece

KM# CC103 5 SHILLINGS
Silver **Mint:** Stevenston, Ayrshire **Countermark:** J. LOCKHART STEVENSON **Note:** Countermark around 5 Sh within oval.

CM Date	Host Date	Good	VG	F	VF	XF
ND(1811)	ND Rare	—	—	—	—	—

KM# CC10 5 SHILLINGS/3 PENCE
Silver **Mint:** Beith, Ayrshire **Countermark:** J. FAULDS & CO. BEITH **Note:** Countermark around 5/3.

CM Date	Host Date	Good	VG	F	VF	XF
ND(1811)	ND Rare	—	—	—	—	—

KM# CC82 5 SHILLINGS/3 PENCE
Silver **Issuer:** Paisley, Renfrewshire **Mint:** Paisley, Renfrewshire **Countermark:** JOHN LANG MERCHT. PAISLEY **Note:** Countermark in a oval around 5/3.

CM Date	Host Date	Good	VG	F	VF	XF
ND(1811)	ND Rare	—	—	—	—	—

KM# CC83 5 SHILLINGS/3 PENCE
Silver **Mint:** Paisley, Renfrewshire **Countermark:** PAYABLE BY W. LANGMUIR. **Reverse:** Countermark: PAISELY DOLLAR SOCIETY. around 5/3 within wreath **Note:** Countermark around arms of Paisley. About half of the known examples are cancelled with a grill pattern over the denomination; these bring somewhat lower prices than listed.

CM Date	Host Date	Good	VG	F	VF	XF
ND(1811)	ND	400	600	900	—	—

Note: Countermark around arms of Paisley. About half of the known examples are cancelled with a grill pattern over the denomination; these bring somewhat lower prices.

KM# CC85 5 SHILLINGS/3 PENCE
Silver **Mint:** Paisley, Renfrewshire **Countermark:** J. Mc.LEAN "Cott. St. Paisley" **Note:** Countermark in oval around 5/3.

CM Date	Host Date	Good	VG	F	VF	XF
ND(1811)	ND	—	—	—	—	—

Note: This countermark also is known on a U.S. Dollar dated 1799, which is unique

KM# CC86 5 SHILLINGS/3 PENCE
Silver **Mint:** Paisley, Renfrewshire **Countermark:** JOHN MORRIS . PAISLEY . **Note:** Countermark in circle around 5/3.

CM Date	Host Date	Good	VG	F	VF	XF
ND(1811)	ND Rare	—	—	—	—	—

KM# CC101 5 SHILLINGS/6 PENCE
Silver **Mint:** Salcoats, Ayrshire **Countermark:** SALTCOATS "Merchants" **Note:** Countermark within wreathed border around 5/6.

CM Date	Host Date	Good	VG	F	VF	XF
ND(1811)	ND Rare	—	—	—	—	—

KM# CC14 5 SHILLINGS/6 PENCE
Silver **Mint:** Catrine, Ayrshire **Countermark:** CATRINE.COTTON.WORKS/ No. followed by incuse number in oval, 5/6 in center **Note:** Over 4/9.

CM Date	Host Date	Good	VG	F	VF	XF
ND(1811)	ND	—	1,200	1,600	—	—

KM# CC73 5 SHILLINGS/6 PENCE
Silver **Issuer:** Levern, Renfrewshire, Barrhead **Mint:** Levern, Renfrewshire, Barrhead **Countermark:** LEVERN. MILL. S. D & CO **Note:** Countermark around 5/6 and additional countermark: S. D in a small beaded circle.

CM Date	Host Date	Good	VG	F	VF	XF
ND(1811)	ND Rare	—	—	—	—	—

KM# CC78 5 SHILLINGS/6 PENCE
Silver **Issuer:** Muirkirk, Ayshire **Mint:** Muirkirk, Ayshire **Countermark:** MUIRKIRK IRON WORKS++ **Reverse:** Countermark: View of blast furnace with smoke stack, etc., dated 1809 **Note:** Countermark around 5/6.

CM Date	Host Date	Good	VG	F	VF	XF
ND(1811)	ND	—	—	—	—	—

KM# CC47 6 SHILLING
Silver **Mint:** Glasgow, Lanarkshire **Countermark:** THISTLE BANK. **Reverse:** Countermark: Thistle **Note:** Countermark in a circle around 6/.

CM Date	Host Date	Good	VG	F	VF	XF
ND(1811)	ND Rare	—	—	—	—	—

KM# CCA14 6 SHILLINGS/6 PENCE
Silver **Mint:** Catrine, Ayrshire **Countermark:** CATRINE WORKS/ No. followed by incuse number, in oval, 6/6 in center

CM Date	Host Date	Good	VG	F	VF	XF
ND(1811)	ND Rare	—	—	—	—	—

Serbia, a former inland Balkan kingdom has an area of 34,116 sq. mi. (88,361 sq. km.). Capital: Belgrade.

Serbia emerged as a separate kingdom in the 12th century and attained its greatest expansion and political influence in the mid-14th century. After the Battle of Kosovo, 1389, Serbia became a vassal principality of Turkey and remained under Turkish suzerainty until it was re-established as an independent kingdom by the 1887 Treaty of Berlin. Following World War I, which had its immediate cause in the assassination of Austrian Archduke Francis Ferdinand by a Serbian nationalist, Serbia joined with the Croats and Slovenes to form the new Kingdom of the South Slavs with Peter I of Serbia asking. The name of the kingdom was later changed to Yugoslavia. Invaded by Germany during World War II, Serbia emerged as a constituent republic of the Socialist Federal Republic of Yugoslavia.

RULERS
Michael, Obrenovich III
...as Prince, 1839-1842, 1860-1868
Milan, Obrenovich IV,
...as Prince, 1868-1882
...as King, 1882-1889
Alexander I, 1889-1902

MINT MARKS
A - Paris
(a) - Paris, privy mark only
H - Birmingham
V - Vienna
БП - (BP) Budapest

MONETARY SYSTEM
100 Para = 1 Dinara

DENOMINATIONS
ПАРА = Para
ПАРЕ = Pare
ДИНАР = Dinar
ДИНАРА = Dinara

KINGDOM

STANDARD COINAGE

KM# 1.1 PARA
Bronze **Note:** SERBIA spelled: **СРБСКИ.**

Date	Mintage	F	VF	XF	Unc	BU
1868	7,500,000	5.00	12.50	30.00	76.00	—

KM# 1.2 PARA
Bronze **Note:** SERBIA spelled: **СРЂСКИ.**

Date	Mintage	F	VF	XF	Unc	BU
1868	Inc. above	6.00	15.00	35.00	95.00	—

KM# 2 5 PARA
Bronze **Note:** Coin and medal rotation exist.

Date	Mintage	F	VF	XF	Unc	BU
1868	7,420,000	4.00	12.00	35.00	95.00	—
1868 Proof	—	Value: 275				

KM# 7 5 PARA
Bronze

Date	Mintage	F	VF	XF	Unc	BU
1879	6,000,000	3.50	8.50	28.50	80.00	—
1879 Proof	—	Value: 200				

KM# 18 5 PARA
Copper-Nickel **Ruler:** Peter I **Note:** Medallic die alignment.

Date	Mintage	F	VF	XF	Unc	BU
1883	4,000,000	2.00	4.00	9.00	24.00	—
1884H	3,000,000	1.00	5.00	10.00	28.00	—
1884H Proof	—	Value: 200				

KM# 3 10 PARA
Bronze **Note:** Coin and medal rotation exist.

Date	Mintage	F	VF	XF	Unc	BU
1868	6,590,000	6.00	14.50	36.00	95.00	—
1868 Proof	—	Value: 325				

KM# 8 10 PARA
Bronze

Date	Mintage	F	VF	XF	Unc	BU
1879	9,000,000	5.00	10.00	30.00	75.00	—
1879 Proof	—	Value: 200				

KM# 19 10 PARA
Copper-Nickel **Ruler:** Peter I **Note:** Medallic die alignment.

Date	Mintage	F	VF	XF	Unc	BU
1883	5,000,000	1.00	2.00	6.00	18.00	—
1884H	6,500,000	1.00	2.00	5.00	14.00	—
1884H Proof	—	Value: 250				

KM# 20 20 PARA
Copper-Nickel **Ruler:** Peter I **Note:** Medallic die alignment.

Date	Mintage	F	VF	XF	Unc	BU
1883	2,500,000	2.00	4.00	14.00	28.00	—
1884H	6,000,000	1.50	3.50	10.00	20.00	—
1884H Proof	—	Value: 300				

KM# 4 50 PARA
2.5000 g., 0.8350 Silver .0671 oz.

Date	Mintage	F	VF	XF	Unc	BU
1875	2,000,000	7.50	20.00	70.00	260	—
1875 Proof	—	Value: 500				

KM# 9 50 PARA
2.5000 g., 0.8350 Silver .0671 oz.

Date	Mintage	F	VF	XF	Unc	BU
1879	600,000	4.50	15.00	35.00	165	—
1879 Proof	—	Value: 400				

KM# 5 DINAR
5.0000 g., 0.8350 Silver .1342 oz.

Date	Mintage	F	VF	XF	Unc	BU
1875	3,000,000	14.00	35.00	120	360	—
1875 Proof	—	Value: 750				

KM# 10 DINAR
5.0000 g., 0.8350 Silver .1342 oz.

Date	Mintage	F	VF	XF	Unc	BU
1879	800,000	6.00	18.00	60.00	330	—
1879 Proof	—	Value: 600				

KM# 21 DINAR
5.0000 g., 0.8350 Silver .1342 oz.

Date	Mintage	F	VF	XF	Unc	BU
1897	4,001,000	2.50	6.50	18.50	100	—

KM# 6 2 DINARA
10.0000 g., 0.8350 Silver .2684 oz.

Date	Mintage	F	VF	XF	Unc	BU
1875	1,000,000	32.00	85.00	180	575	—
1875 Proof	—	Value: 1,200				

KM# 11 2 DINARA
10.0000 g., 0.8350 Silver .2684 oz.

Date	Mintage	F	VF	XF	Unc	BU
1879	750,000	8.00	24.00	65.00	420	—
1879 Proof	—	Value: 1,000				

KM# 22 2 DINARA
10.0000 g., 0.8350 Silver .2684 oz.

Date	Mintage	F	VF	XF	Unc	BU
1897	1,000,000	6.00	14.00	36.00	180	—
1897 Proof	—	Value: 400				

KM# 12 5 DINARA
25.0000 g., 0.9000 Silver .7234 oz. **Edge:** Type 1 **Edge Lettering:** БОГ*ЧУВА*СРБИЈУ***

Date	Mintage	F	VF	XF	Unc	BU
1879	200,000	32.00	65.00	175	650	—
1879 Proof	—	Value: 1,400				

KM# 13 5 DINARA
25.0000 g., 0.9000 Silver .7234 oz. **Edge:** Type 2 **Edge Lettering:** БОГ*СРБИЈУ*ЧУВА***

Date	Mintage	F	VF	XF	Unc	BU
1879	Inc. above	45.00	85.00	185	760	—

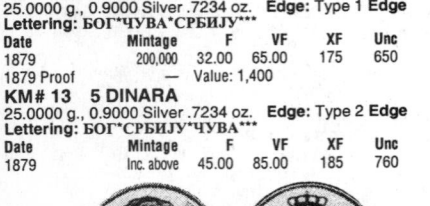

KM# 16 10 DINARA
3.2258 g., 0.9000 Gold .0933 oz. **Obv. Legend:** Short title like KM#17

Date	Mintage	F	VF	XF	Unc	BU
1882	300,000	80.00	140	180	320	—

KM# 14 20 DINARA
6.4516 g., 0.9000 Gold .1867 oz. **Obv. Legend:** Full title

Date	Mintage	F	VF	XF	Unc	BU
1879A	50,000	130	175	320	550	—
1879A Proof	—	Value: 5,000				

KM# 17 20 DINARA
6.4516 g., 0.9000 Gold .1867 oz. **Obv. Legend:** Short title

Date	Mintage	F	VF	XF	Unc	BU
1882V	300,000	100	150	200	340	—

PATTERNS

Including off metal strikes

KM#	Date	Mintage	Identification	Mkt Val
Pn1	1882V	—	20 Dinara. Copper.	1,250
Pn2	1890	—	Dinar. Silver.	5,000
Pn3	1890	—	2 Dinara. Silver.	6,000
Pn4	1890	—	2 Dinara. Aluminum-Bronze.	—
Pn5	1890	—	2 Dinara. Gilt Bronze.	—
PnA6	1892	—	Dinar. Silver.	7,000
PnB6	1892	—	2 Dinara. Silver.	8,000

SHIHR AND MUKALLA

The Qa'iti State of Shihr and Mukalla was comprised in Eastern Aden Protectorate located in southern Arabia.

Kasadi of Mukalla

A port, city sultanate and capital of the Qa'iti state of Shihr and Mukalla in Eastern Aden Protectorate in southern Arabia, was a principal port servicing trade between the Middle East and India and Java.

TITLES

المكلا

al-Mukala

RULERS

Salah bin Muhammad,
AH12xx-1290/18xx-1873AD
Umar bin Salah,
AH1290-1298/1873-1881AD

KASADI OF MUKALLA SULTANATE

STANDARD COINAGE

KM# A1 1/2 KHUMSI
Bronze

Date	Mintage	Good	VG	F	VF	XF
AH1276 (1859)	—	25.00	45.00	75.00	125	—

KM# 2 KHUMSI
Bronze

Date	Mintage	Good	VG	F	VF	XF
AH1276	—	20.00	40.00	65.00	110	—

Sierra Leone is located in western Africa between Guinea and Liberia, has an area of 27,699 sq. mi. (71,740 sq. km).

The coast of Sierra Leone was first visited by Portuguese and British slavers in the 15th and 16th centuries. The first settlement, at Freetown, 1787, was established as a refuge for freed slaves within the British Empire, runaway slaves from the United States and Negroes discharged from the British armed forces. The first settlers were virtually wiped out by tribal attacks and disease. The colony was re-established under the auspices of the Sierra Leone Company and transferred to the British Crown in 1807. The interior region was secured and established as a protectorate in 1896.

For similar coinage refer to British West Africa.

RULERS
British, until 1971

MONETARY SYSTEM

Until 1906

100 Cents = 1 Dollar

SIERRA LEONE COMPANY

British Colony

STANDARD COINAGE

KM# 3 10 CENTS
0.9020 Silver **Obv:** Lion **Rev:** Clasped hands

Date	Mintage	F	VF	XF	Unc	BU
1805	6,100	45.00	115	185	325	—

COUNTERMARKED COINAGE

KM# 10 1/4 DOLLAR
0.9030 Silver **Countermark:** Crowned WR **Note:** Countermark on 1/4-cut of Spanish or Colonial 8 Reales.

CM Date	Host Date	Good	VG	F	VF	XF
ND(1832)	ND	—	275	500	850	1,350

KM# 13 1/2 DOLLAR
0.9030 Silver **Countermark:** Crowned WR **Note:** Countermark on Spanish or Spanish Colonial 4 Reales.

CM Date	Host Date	Good	VG	F	VF	XF
ND(1832)	ND	—	250	450	750	1,250

TOKEN COINAGE

KM# Tn1.2 PENNY
16.8400 g., Copper **Obv:** Without engraver's initials

Date	Mintage	F	VF	XF	Unc	BU
ND(1814)	—	7.50	15.00	45.00	125	—

KM# Tn1.1 PENNY
16.8400 g., Copper **Obv. Legend:** SLAVE TRADE ABOLISHED/BY GREAT BRITAIN/1807 **Rev:** Similar in Arabic

Date	Mintage	F	VF	XF	Unc	BU
(1814) GFP	50,000	7.50	15.00	45.00	125	—
(1814) GFP Proof, restrike	—	Value: 200				

Note: Heavier specimens weighing 24.94-26.75 g exist, probably struck later as medals

KM# Tn1.1a PENNY
Gilt Copper

Date	Mintage	F	VF	XF	Unc	BU
ND(1830-32) Proof, restrike	—	Value: 350				

KM# Tn1.1b PENNY
Silver

Date	Mintage	F	VF	XF	Unc	BU
ND(1830-32) Proof, restrike	—	Value: 450				

SOUTH AFRICA

The Republic of South Africa, located at the southern tip of Africa, has an area, including the enclave of Walvis Bay, of 472,359 sq. mi. (1,221,040 sq. km.). Capitals: Administrative, Pretoria; Legislative, Cape Town; Judicial, Bloemfontein.

Portuguese navigator Bartholomew Diaz became the first European to sight the region of South Africa when he rounded the Cape of Good Hope in 1488, but throughout the 16th century the only white men to come ashore were the survivors of ships wrecked while attempting the stormy Cape passage. Jan van Riebeeck of the Dutch East India Company established the first permanent settlement in 1652. In subsequent decades additional Dutch, German and Huguenot refugees from France settled in the Cape area to form the Afrikaner segment of today's population.

Great Britain captured the Cape colony in 1795, and again in 1806, receiving permanent title in 1814. To escape British political rule and cultural dominance, many Afrikaner farmers (Boers) migrated northward (the Great Trek) beginning in 1836, and established the independent Boer Republics of the Transvaal (the South African Republic, Zuid Afrikaansche Republic) in 1852, and the Orange Free State in 1854. British political intrigues against the two republics, coupled with the discovery of diamonds and gold in the Boer-settled regions, led to the bitter Boer Wars (1880-81, 1899-1902) and the incorporation of the Boer republics into the British Empire.

On May 31, 1910, the two former Boer Republics (Transvaal and Orange Free State) were joined with the British colonies of Cape of Good Hope and Natal to form the Union of South Africa, a dominion of the British Empire. In 1934 the Union achieved status as a sovereign state within the British Empire.

South African coins and currency bear inscriptions in tribal languages, Afrikaans and English.

RULERS
British, until 1934

MONETARY SYSTEM

Until 1961

12 Pence = 1 Shilling
2 Shillings = 1 Florin
20 Shillings = 1 Pound (Pond)

ZUID-AFRIKAANSCHE REPUBLIEK

Beware of counterfeit double shafts. Aside from there being two shafts on the wagon in the coat of arms (reverse), the two wheels of the wagon must be the same size. On single shaft wagons, the rear wheel is noticeably larger than the front wheel.

STANDARD COINAGE

12 Pence = 1 Shilling; 20 Shillings = 1 Pond

KM# 2 PENNY
Bronze **Note:** In 1900, just prior to the Boer evacuation of Pretoria, blank penny planchets were released into circulation. Reasonably preserved examples have sold for about $50.00 each.

Date	Mintage	F	VF	XF	Unc	BU
1892	83,000	3.50	7.00	20.00	60.00	—
1892 Proof	6	Value: 4,500				
1893	11,000	30.00	60.00	120	250	—
1894	182,000	5.00	15.00	50.00	150	—
1898	263,000	1.00	3.00	7.00	30.00	—

KM# 3 3 PENCE
1.4138 g., 0.9250 Silver 0.042 oz.

Date	Mintage	F	VF	XF	Unc	BU
1892	24,000	3.00	6.00	40.00	100	—
1892 35-40 pieces	—	Value: 800				
1893	135,000	3.00	10.00	65.00	150	—
1894	104,000	4.00	12.50	85.00	200	—
1895	113,000	3.00	20.00	100	250	—
1896	166,000	2.00	4.00	8.00	50.00	—
1897	201,000	2.00	4.00	8.00	40.00	—

KM# 4 6 PENCE
2.8276 g., 0.9250 Silver 0.0841 oz.

Date	Mintage	F	VF	XF	Unc	BU
1892	28,000	4.00	7.50	45.00	125	—
1892 Proof, 40-50 pieces	—	Value: 500				
1893	96,000	3.00	6.00	100	225	—
1894	168,000	3.00	6.00	120	250	—
1895	179,000	3.00	6.00	120	275	—
1896	205,000	2.00	4.00	10.00	50.00	—
1896 Proof, 1 known	—	—	—	—	—	—
1897	220,000	1.50	3.00	8.00	35.00	—
1897 Proof, 1 known	—	—	—	—	—	—

KM# 5 SHILLING
5.6555 g., 0.9250 Silver 0.1682 oz.

Date	Mintage	F	VF	XF	Unc	BU
1892	130,000	7.50	15.00	55.00	135	—
1892 Proof, 40-50 pieces	—	Value: 550				
1893	137,000	10.00	65.00	500	1,200	—
1894	366,000	4.00	6.00	150	400	—
1895	327,000	4.00	10.00	250	500	—
1896	437,000	4.00	10.00	135	275	—
1897	397,000	2.00	4.00	15.00	40.00	—

KM# 6 2 SHILLINGS
11.3100 g., 0.9250 Silver 0.3364 oz.

Date	Mintage	F	VF	XF	Unc	BU
1892	55,000	10.00	25.00	65.00	175	—
1892 Proof, 50-60 pieces	—	Value: 850				
1893	107,000	15.00	75.00	550	1,100	—
1894	173,000	6.00	25.00	275	750	—
1895	150,000	7.50	32.00	500	900	—
1896	353,000	4.00	8.00	25.00	65.00	—
1897	148,000	3.00	6.00	20.00	60.00	—

KM# 7 2-1/2 SHILLINGS
14.1380 g., 0.9250 Silver 0.4205 oz.

Date	Mintage	F	VF	XF	Unc	BU
1892	16,000	15.00	30.00	90.00	250	—
1892 Proof, 50-60 pieces	—	Value: 1,000				
1893	135,000	20.00	60.00	400	1,100	—
1894	135,000	10.00	30.00	225	750	—
1895	182,000	10.00	40.00	350	900	—
1896	285,000	5.00	10.00	30.00	75.00	—
1897	149,000	5.00	10.00	30.00	75.00	—

KM# 8.1 5 SHILLINGS
28.2759 g., 0.9250 Silver 0.8409 oz. **Rev:** Single shaft on wagon tongue

Date	Mintage	F	VF	XF	Unc	BU
1892	14,000	60.00	150	350	850	—

KM# 8.2 5 SHILLINGS
28.2759 g., 0.9250 Silver 0.8409 oz. **Rev:** Double shaft on wagon tongue

Date	Mintage	F	VF	XF	Unc	BU
1892	4,327	90.00	200	450	1,100	—
1892 Proof, 25-30 pieces	—	Value: 3,250				

KM# 9.1 1/2 POND
3.9940 g., 0.9160 Gold 0.1176 oz. **Rev:** Double shaft wagon tongue

Date	Mintage	F	VF	XF	Unc	BU
1892	10,000	100	150	200	550	—
1892 Proof, 20-25 pieces	—	Value: 5,500				

KM# 9.2 1/2 POND
3.9940 g., 0.9160 Gold 0.1176 oz. **Rev:** Single shaft wagon tongue

Date	Mintage	F	VF	XF	Unc	BU
1892 Unique	—	—	—	—	—	—
1893	—	350	900	1,950	3,000	—
1894	39,000	60.00	80.00	250	450	—
1895	135,000	65.00	90.00	275	600	—
1896	104,000	50.00	70.00	170	400	—
1897	75,000	50.00	70.00	170	400	—

KM# 1.1 POND (Een)
7.9880 g., 0.9160 Gold 0.2352 oz. **Obv:** Coarse beard

Date	Mintage	F	VF	XF	Unc	BU
1874	174	200	3,000	5,500	10,000	—

KM# 1.2 POND (Een)
7.9880 g., 0.9160 Gold 0.2352 oz. **Obv:** Fine beard

Date	Mintage	F	VF	XF	Unc	BU
1874	695	1,500	2,500	5,000	8,500	—

KM# 10.1 POND (Een)
7.9880 g., 0.9160 Gold 0.2352 oz. **Rev:** Double shaft wagon tongue

Date	Mintage	F	VF	XF	Unc	BU
1892	16,000	120	150	250	600	—
1892 Proof, Rare, 12-15 pieces	—	—	—	—	—	—

Note: David Akers John Jay Pittman sale 8-99, choice proof realized $12,650, hairlined proof realized $4,600.

KM# 10.2 POND (Een)
7.9880 g., 0.9160 Gold 0.2352 oz. **Rev:** Single shaft wagon tongue

Date	Mintage	F	VF	XF	Unc	BU
1892	—	450	800	200	4,500	—
1893	62,000	100	135	275	750	—
1894	318,000	100	125	225	700	—
1895	336,000	100	135	350	850	—
1896	235,000	100	125	225	600	—
1897	311,000	100	125	175	450	—
1898	137,000	90.00	110	150	350	—
1898/99	130	2,500	3,000	5,000	7,500	—
1898/9 Unique	—	—	—	—	—	—
1900	788,000	100	125	155	265	—

STANDARD COINAGE

12 Pence = 1 Shilling; 20 Shillings = 1 Pond

KM#	Date	Mintage	Identification	Mkt Val
PnA5	1874	—	2 Pence. Bronze.	325

KM#	Date	Mintage	Identification	Mkt Val
PnA6	1874	—	2-1/2 Shillings. Gilt Bronze. Milled edge.	2,750
PnA11	1874	—	5 Shillings. Gilt Bronze. Milled edge.	2,750
PnA13	1874	—	5 Shillings. Aluminum. Milled edge.	2,750
PnA19	1874	—	Pond. Bronze. Short beard.	1,850
PnA12	1874	—	5 Shillings. Gilt Bronze. Plain edge.	3,000
PnA7	1874	—	2-1/2 Shillings. Silver. Milled edge.	3,500
PnA20	1874	—	Pond. Bronze. Long beard.	—

KM#	Date	Mintage	Identification	Mkt Val
PnA1	1874	—	Penny. Bronze. 1 PENNY.	325
PnA2	1874	—	Penny. Bronze. Double thickness	450
PnA3	1874	—	Penny. Bronze. Triple thickness.	650
PnA8	1874	—	2-1/2 Shillings. Silver. Plain edge.	2,750

KM#	Date	Mintage	Identification	Mkt Val
PnA21	1874	—	Pond. Aluminum. Long beard.	2,000

KM#	Date	Mintage	Identification	Mkt Val
PnA14	1874.	—	5 Shillings. Gilt Copper. Milled edge.	2,500

KM#	Date	Mintage	Identification	Mkt Val
PnA4	1874	—	Penny. Bronze. EEN PENNY.	325
PnA15	1874.	—	5 Shillings. Gilt Copper. Plain edge.	2,750
PnA9	1874	—	2-1/2 Shillings. Aluminum. Milled edge.	2,250

KM#	Date	Mintage	Identification	Mkt Val
PnA10	1874	—	2-1/2 Shillings. Aluminum. Plain edge.	1,750
PnA16	1874.	—	5 Shillings. Silver.	6,000
PnA17	1874.	—	5 Shillings. Silver. Plain edge. Piefort.	5,000
PnA18	1874.	—	5 Shillings. Aluminum. Milled edge.	2,250

KM#	Date	Mintage	Identification	Mkt Val
PnA22	1890	—	Penny. Bronze.	325
PnA23	1898	215	3 Pence. Gold. KM#3.	4,000

Note: Struck for mining magnate Sammie Marks.

CAPE

Griquatown

Griquatown is located in the Griqualand West region of northern Cape Province, 90 miles west of Kimberley. Griqualand West occupies an area of 15,400 sq. mi. (50,500 sq. km.) north of the Orange River and west of Orange Free State. It is dry desert country, noted for its diamond fields. Chief town: Kimberley. Following the discovery of diamonds in 1867, a bitter dispute over possession erupted between the British and Orange Free State. Britain annexed the territory in 1871. It was joined to Cape Colony in 1880. Tokens for the area were commissioned by Rev. John Campbell and produced by Thomas Halliday in 1815-16, but are undated. They were eventually retired from circulation and melted. In 1890, two pattern types were struck by Otto Nolte & Co. of Berlin for advertising purposes.

RULERS

British, until 1961

NOTE: Similar pieces struck in silver w/100 are modern fantasies.

GRIQUATOWN

MISSIONARY TOKEN COINAGE

KM# Tn1 1/4 PENNY
Copper

Date	Mintage	F	VF	XF	Unc	BU
ND (1815-16)	—	—	450	650	1,200	—

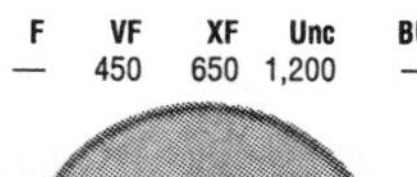

KM# Tn2 1/2 PENNY
Copper

Date	Mintage	F	VF	XF	Unc	BU
ND (1815-16)	—	—	500	750	1,500	—
ND (1815-16) Proof	—	Value: 1,700				

KM# Tn4 5 PENCE
Silver

Date	Mintage	F	VF	XF	Unc	BU
ND (1815-16)	—	—	500	900	1,750	—
ND (1815-16) Proof	—	Value: 1,950				

KM# Tn5 10 PENCE TOKEN
Silver

Date	Mintage	F	VF	XF	Unc	BU
ND (1815-16)	—	—	650	1,100	2,200	—
ND (1815-16) Proof	—	Value: 2,500				

PATTERNS

Including off metal strikes

KM#	Date	Mintage	Identification	Mkt Val
Pn1	ND (1815-16)	—	1/4 Penny. Lead. KM#1.	500
Pn2	ND (1815-16)	—	1/2 Penny. Lead. KM#2.	550
Pn3	ND (1815-16)	—	5 Pence. Copper.	650
Pn4	ND (1815-16)	—	10 Pence Token. Copper.	750

KM#	Date	Mintage	Identification	Mkt Val
Pn5	1890	—	Penny. Copper.	550

KM#	Date	Mintage	Identification	Mkt Val
Pn6	ND (1890)	—	Penny. Copper.	450
Pn7	ND (1890)	—	Penny. Nickel.	—

CAPE OF GOOD HOPE

Cape of Good Hope, the largest of the four provinces of the Republic of South Africa, has an area of 278,380 sq. mi. (721,001 sq. km.). The colony of Cape of Good Hope was founded by the Dutch in 1652 and was occupied by the British in 1795-1803 and 1806-14. The Dutch ceded it to the British in 1814. It was united for administrative purpose with Natal, 1843-56; annexed British Kaffraria in 1865 and British Becchuanaland in 1895; and administered Basutoland (now Lesotho), 1871-84. Cape Colony attained internal self-government in 1872, and joined the Union of South Africa in 1910. An extensive token series exists. One penny patterns are known for 1889.

RULERS

British, 1814-1961

MONETARY SYSTEM

12 Pence = 1 Shilling
20 Shillings = 1 Pound

PATTERNS

Including off metal strikes

KM#	Date	Mintage	Identification	Mkt Val
Pn1	1889	—	Penny. Bronze. I of BRITANNIAR above hair ribbon.	450
Pn2	1889	—	Penny. Copper Nickel. I of BRITANNIAR above hair ribbon.	485
Pn3	1889	—	Penny. Bronze.	450
Pn4	1889	—	Penny. Copper Nickel.	485
Pn5	1889	—	Penny. Aluminum.	600
Pn6	1889	—	Penny. Tin.	600
Pn7	1889	—	Penny. Silver.	1,500

ORANGE FREE STATE

Orange Free State, a province of the Republic of South Africa bounded by Natal and Lesotho on the east, Cape Province on the south and west, and the Transvaal on the north, has an area of 49,866 sq. mi. (129,152 sq. km.) and a population of 1.8 million. Capital: Bloemfontein. The first settlements in the Orange region were established 1810-20, but general occupancy began with the great trek of the Boers in 1836. The British annexed it in 1848, then withdrew their sovereignty and recognized the independence of the Boer state, 1854. It joined Transvaal in the Boer War of 1899-1902, after which it was annexed by Britain and established as the Orange River Colony, May 28, 1900. It attained internal self-government in 1907 and joined the Union of South Africa in 1910. A series of patterns was struck by Otto Nolte & Co. of Berlin, but no regular-issue coins were produced. Tokens are known.

RULERS

British, 1848-1854, 1900-1961

MONETARY SYSTEM

12 Pence = 1 Shilling
20 Shillings = 1 Kroon

NOTE: In 1900, just prior to the Boer evacuation of Pretoria, blank penny planchets were released into circulation. Reasonably preserved examples have sold for about $50.00 each.

PATTERNS

Including off metal strikes

KM#	Date	Mintage	Identification	Mkt Val
Pn5	1874	—	2 Pence. Bronze. Mule, Pn3 and Zuid Afrikaansche Republic Pn5.	—

KM#	Date	Mintage	Identification	Mkt Val
Pn1	1874	—	Penny. Bronze.	450
Pn2	1874	—	Penny. Bronze. Double thickness.	550
Pn3	1874	—	Penny. Bronze. Triple thickness.	650
Pn4	1874	—	Penny. Bronze. Like Pn7.	—

KM#	Date	Mintage	Identification	Mkt Val
Pn6	1887	—	Kroon. Silver. ESSAY.	6,500
Pn7	1887	—	Kroon. Lead. ESSAY.	3,000

KM#	Date	Mintage	Identification	Mkt Val
Pn9	1888	—	Penny. Bronze. Ornamental shield.	425
Pn10	1888	—	Penny. Copper Nickel.	500
Pn11	1888	—	Penny. Bronze. with LLC below PENNY.	425

KM#	Date	Mintage	Identification	Mkt Val
Pn12	1888	—	Penny. Copper Nickel.	485
Pn13	1888	—	Penny. Bronze. Plain shield.	475
Pn14	1888	—	Penny. Bronze. Double thickness.	550
Pn15	1888	—	Penny. Bronze. Triple thickness.	650
Pn16	1888	—	Penny. Aluminum.	500
Pn17	1888	—	Penny. Silver.	1,500

SPAIN

The Spanish State, forming the greater part of the Iberian Peninsula of southwest Europe, has an area of 195,988 sq. mi. (504,714 sq. km.).

It isn't known when man first came to the Iberian Peninsula - the Altamira caves off the Cantabrian coast approximately 50 miles west of Santander were fashioned in Paleolithic times. Spain was a battleground for centuries before it became a united nation, fought for by Phoenicians, Carthaginians, Greeks, Celts, Romans, Vandals, Visigoths and Moors. Ferdinand and Isabella destroyed the last Moorish stronghold in 1492, freeing the national energy and resources for the era of discovery and colonization that would make Spain the most powerful country in Europe during the 16th century. After the destruction of the Spanish Armada, 1588, Spain never again played a major role in European politics. Forcing Ferdinand to give up his throne and placing him under military guard at Valencay in 1808, Napoleonic France ruled Spain until 1814. When the monarchy was restored in 1814 it continued, only interrupted by the short-lived republic of 1873-74, until the exile of Alfonso XIII in 1931 when the Second Republic was established.

Discontent against the mother country increased after1808 as colonists faced new imperialist policies from Napoleon or Spanish liberals. The revolutionary movement was established which resulted in the eventual independence of the Vice-royalties of New Spain, New Granada and Rio de la Plata within 2 decades.

RULERS

Carlos IV, 1788-1808
Jose Napoleon, 1808-1813
Ferdinand VII, 1808-1833 (in exile until 1814)
Isabel II, 1833-1868
Carlos IV, 1833-1840 (pretender)
Provisional Government, 1868-1871
Amadeo I, 1871-1873
1st Republic, 1873-1874
Carlos VII, 1872-1875 (pretender)
Alfonso XII, 1874-1885
Regency, 1885-1886
Alfonso XIII, 1886-1931

NOTE: From 1868 to 1982, two dates may be found on most Spanish coinage. The larger date is the year of authorization and the smaller date incused on the two 6--pointed-stars found on most types is the year of issue. The latter appears in parentheses in these listings.

HOMELAND MINT MARKS

Until 1851

CA – Cuenca
G – Flower over G – Granada
J, JA – Jubia
M, MD – Madrid
P, p., P., P.L., PA – Pamplona
S, S/L – Seville
Sr – Santander
T, To, Tole – Toledo
V, VA, VAL – Valencia
Crowned C – Cadiz
Crowned M – Madrid
Aqueduct – Segovia, until 1864

NOTE: The Catalonia Mint was located at Reus between February 1-25, 1809 and March 31, 1809 to May 20, 1810 and again from April 14 to August 15, 1810. It was then temporarily located at Tarragonia until May 9, 1811 and finally located at Palma de Mallorca from June 2, 1811 to June 20, 1814.

Until 1980

OM - Oeschger Mesdach & Co.
3-pointed star - Segovia after 1868
4-pointed star - Jubia
6-pointed star - Madrid
7-pointed star - Seville
8-pointed star – Barcelona

NOTE: Letters after date are initials of mint officials.

COLONIAL MINT MARKS

Many Spanish Colonial mints struck coins similar to regular Spanish issues until the 1820's. These issues are easily distinguished from regular Spanish issues by the following mint marks.

C, CH, Ch - Chihuahua, Mexico
D, DO, Do - Durango, Mexico
Ga - Guadalajara, Mexico
G, GG - Guatemala
G, Go - Guanajuato, Mexico
L, L*M, LI*M, LIMAE, LIMA - Lima, Peru
M, MA - Manila, Philippines
M, Mo - Mexico City, Mexico
MZ - Durango, Mexico
NG - Nueva Grenada, Guatemala
NR - Nueva Reino, Colombia
PDV - Valladolid Michoacan, Mexico
P, P* - Peru, Lima
P, PN, Pn - Popayan, Colombia
P, POTOSI - Potosi, Bolivia
So - Santiago, Chile
Z, Zs - Zacatecas, Mexico
5-pointed Star - Manila, Philippines

MINT OFFICIALS' INITIALS

BARCELONA MINT

Initial	Date	Name
CC	1842-43	?
PS	1836-41, 1843-48	Francisco Paradaltas and Simeon Sola y Roca
SM	1850	Simeon Sola y Roca and Francisco Miro
SP	1822-23	Pablo Sala and Francisco Paradaltas

MADRID MINT

Initial	Date	Name
AF	1808	Antonio de Goycoechea
AI	1807-08	Antonio de Goycoechea and Ildefonso de Urquiza
AI	1808-12	Antonio Rafael Narvaez and Isidoro Ramos del Manzano
FA	1799-1808	Francisco Herrera and Antonio Goicoechea
FM	1801	Francisco Herrera and Manuel de Lamas
IA	1808	Ildefonso de Urquiza and Antonio Goycoechea
IA	1810	Isidoro Ramos del Manzano and Antonio Rafael Narvaez
IG	1808-10	Ildefonso de Urquiza and Gregorio Lazaro Labrqandero
MF	1788-1802	Manuel de Lamas and Francisco Herrera
RN	1812-13	Antonio Rafael Narvaez
RS	1810-12	Antonio Rafael Narvaez and Jose Sanchez Delgado

SEVILLE MINT

Initial	Date	Name
C	1790-91, 1801-08	Carlos Tiburcio de Roxas
CJ	1815-21	Carlos Tiburcio de Roxas and Joaquin Delgado Diaz
CN	1791-1810, 1812	Carlos Tiburcio de Roxas and Nicolas Lamas
DR	1835-38	Joaquin Delgado Diaz and Benito de Roxas
J	1823	Jose Sanchez Delgado o Joaquin Delgado
JB	1824-33	Joaquin Delgado Diaz and Benito de Roxas
LA	1810, 1812	Leonardo Carrero and Antonio de Larra
RD	1821-23	Carlos Tiburcio de Roxas and Joaquin Delgado Diaz
RD	1835	Benito de Roxas and Joaquin Delgado

VALENCIA MINT

Initial	Date	Name
GS	1811	Gregorio Lazaro Labrandero and Sixto Giber Polo
R	1821	?
SG	1809-14	Sixto Giber Polo

MONETARY SYSTEM

34 Maravedi = 1 Real (of Silver)
16 Reales = 1 Escudo

NOTE: The early coinage of Spain is listed by denomination based on a system of 16 Reales de Plata (silver) = 1 Escudo (gold). However, in the Constitutional period from 1808-1850, a concurrent system was introduced in which 20 Reales de Vellon (billon) = 8 Reales de Plata. This system does not necessarily refer to the composition of the coin itself. To avoid confusion we have listed the coins using the value as it appears on each coin, ignoring the monetary base.

KINGDOM, PRE-1931

EARLY REAL COINAGE

KM# 445 MARAVEDI

Copper **Obv:** Bust of Charles IV right **Rev:** Castles and lions in angles of cross **Note:** Similar to 4 Maravedis, KM#427. Mint mark: Aqueduct.

Date	Mintage	VG	F	VF	XF	Unc
1802	—	15.00	25.00	40.00	60.00	—

KM# 503 MARAVEDI

Copper **Obv:** Head of Ferdinand VII right **Rev:** Castles and lions in angles of cross **Note:** Mint mark: J, JA.

Date	Mintage	VG	F	VF	XF	Unc
1824	—	15.00	20.00	35.00	55.00	—

KM# 525.1 MARAVEDI

Copper **Obv:** Head of Isabel II right **Rev:** Castles and lions in angles of cross **Note:** Mint mark: J, JA.

Date	Mintage	VG	F	VF	XF	Unc
1842	—	10.00	20.00	65.00	90.00	—
1843	—	75.00	150	300	425	—

KM# 525.3 MARAVEDI

Copper **Obv:** Head of Isabel II right **Rev:** Castles and lions in angles of cross **Note:** Mint mark: Aqueduct.

Date	Mintage	VG	F	VF	XF	Unc
1842	—	10.00	20.00	35.00	50.00	75.00

KM# 525.2 MARAVEDI

Copper **Obv:** Head of Isabel II right **Rev:** Castles and lions in angles of cross **Note:** Mint mark: Crowned M.

Date	Mintage	VG	F	VF	XF	Unc
1842 DG	—	75.00	125	200	300	500

KM# 426 2 MARAVEDIS

Copper **Obv:** Head of Charles IV right **Rev:** Cross with castles and lions in angles, all within sprays **Note:** Mint mark: Aqueduct.

Date	Mintage	VG	F	VF	XF	Unc
1801	—	3.00	6.00	12.00	30.00	—
1802	—	3.00	7.00	12.00	35.00	—
1803	—	10.00	25.00	40.00	65.00	—
1804	—	6.00	12.50	20.00	35.00	—
1805	—	3.00	6.00	15.00	30.00	—
1806	—	6.00	12.50	20.00	35.00	—
1807	—	3.00	6.00	12.00	25.00	—
1808	—	3.00	6.00	10.00	25.00	—

KM# 471 2 MARAVEDIS

Copper **Obv:** Bare head of Ferdinand VII right **Rev:** Cross with castles and lions in angles, all within sprays **Note:** Mint mark: J, JA.

Date	Mintage	VG	F	VF	XF	Unc
1812 Rare	—	—	—	—	—	—
1813	—	7.00	15.00	35.00	75.00	—
1814	—	5.00	11.00	25.00	50.00	—
1815	—	3.00	5.00	20.00	35.00	—
1816	—	5.00	10.00	22.00	40.00	—
1817	—	5.00	11.00	25.00	50.00	—

KM# 487.1 2 MARAVEDIS

Copper **Obv:** Laureate head of Ferdinand VII right **Rev:** Cross with castles and lions in angles, all within sprays **Note:** Mint mark: Aqueduct.

Date	Mintage	VG	F	VF	XF	Unc
1816	—	4.00	8.00	30.00	50.00	—
1817	—	3.00	6.00	15.00	28.00	—
1818	—	3.00	6.00	12.00	25.00	—
1819	—	3.00	6.00	12.00	25.00	—
1820	—	3.00	6.00	10.00	15.00	—
1824	—	1.00	2.00	4.00	8.00	—
1825	—	2.00	4.00	8.00	17.00	—
1826	—	6.00	10.00	20.00	40.00	—
1827	—	1.00	2.00	4.00	8.00	—
1828	—	1.00	2.00	4.00	8.00	—
1829	—	1.00	2.00	4.00	8.00	—
1830	—	0.75	1.50	3.50	6.00	—
1831	—	0.75	1.50	3.50	6.00	—
1832	—	0.75	1.50	3.00	5.00	—
1833	—	0.75	1.50	3.00	5.00	—

KM# 488 2 MARAVEDIS

Copper **Obv:** Thin laureate bust of Ferdinand VII right **Note:** Mint mark: J, JA.

Date	Mintage	VG	F	VF	XF	Unc
1817	—	2.00	7.00	12.00	30.00	—
1818	—	2.00	6.00	8.00	20.00	—
1819	—	2.00	6.00	7.00	15.00	—
1820	—	2.00	6.00	7.00	15.00	—
1821	—	35.00	60.00	100	150	—

KM# 504 2 MARAVEDIS

Copper **Obv:** Large bare head of Ferdinand VII right **Note:** Mint mark: J. JA.

Date	Mintage	VG	F	VF	XF	Unc
1824	—	5.00	8.00	15.00	28.00	—
1826	—	4.00	7.00	13.50	25.00	—
1827	—	6.00	10.00	25.00	45.00	—

KM# 487.2 2 MARAVEDIS

Copper **Obv. Legend:** FERDIN. IIV (error) **Note:** Mint mark: Aqueduct.

Date	Mintage	VG	F	VF	XF	Unc
1832	—	10.00	15.00	30.00	50.00	—

KM# 532.4 2 MARAVEDIS

Copper **Obv:** Bust of Isabel II right **Rev:** Cross with castles and lion in angles **Note:** Mint mark: Aqueduct.

Date	Mintage	VG	F	VF	XF	Unc
1836	—	25.00	60.00	150	250	—
1837	—	25.00	60.00	150	250	—
1838	—	5.00	7.00	12.50	20.00	—
1839	—	5.00	7.00	12.50	20.00	—
1840	—	5.00	7.00	12.50	20.00	—
1841	—	5.00	7.00	12.50	20.00	—
1842	—	5.00	7.00	12.50	20.00	—
1843	—	5.00	7.00	12.50	20.00	—
1844	—	5.00	7.00	12.50	20.00	—
1845	—	5.00	7.50	15.00	25.00	—
1846	—	5.00	7.50	15.00	25.00	—
1847	—	5.00	7.50	15.00	25.00	—
1848	—	5.00	7.50	15.00	25.00	—
1849	—	5.00	7.00	12.50	20.00	—
1850	—	5.00	7.00	12.50	20.00	—

KM# 532.3 2 MARAVEDIS

Copper **Obv:** Bust of Isabel II right **Rev:** Cross with castles and lions in angles **Note:** Mint mark: Crowned M.

Date	Mintage	VG	F	VF	XF	Unc
1837 DG	—	75.00	150	275	500	—

KM# 532.2 2 MARAVEDIS

Copper **Obv:** Bust of Isabel II right **Rev:** Cross with castles and lions in angles **Note:** Mint mark: J, JA.

Date	Mintage	VG	F	VF	XF	Unc
1838	—	10.00	20.00	45.00	75.00	—
1840	—	50.00	100	250	350	—
1841	—	35.00	60.00	150	200	—
1842	—	50.00	100	200	275	—
1844	—	40.00	75.00	125	225	—
1848	—	4.00	8.00	25.00	50.00	—
1849	—	4.00	7.00	20.00	40.00	—

KM# 532.1 2 MARAVEDIS

Copper **Obv:** Bust of Isabel II right **Rev:** Cross with castles and lions in angles **Note:** Mint mark: B, BA.

Date	Mintage	VG	F	VF	XF	Unc
1855	—	15.00	25.00	50.00	100	—
1858	—	10.00	20.00	30.00	50.00	—

KM# 427 4 MARAVEDIS

Copper **Obv:** Head of Charles IV right **Rev:** Cross with castles and lions in angles, all within wreath **Note:** Mint mark: Aqueduct.

Date	Mintage	VG	F	VF	XF	Unc
1801	—	3.00	6.00	8.00	15.00	—
1802	—	3.00	6.00	8.00	15.00	—
1803	—	3.00	6.00	8.00	15.00	—
1804	—	5.00	10.00	13.00	20.00	—
1805	—	5.00	10.00	13.00	20.00	—
1806	—	5.00	10.00	13.00	20.00	—
1807	—	5.00	9.00	12.50	18.50	—
1808	—	3.00	6.00	8.00	15.00	—

KM# 472 4 MARAVEDIS

Copper **Obv:** Bare head of Ferdinand VII right **Rev:** Cross with castles and lions in angles **Note:** Mint mark: J, JA.

Date	Mintage	VG	F	VF	XF	Unc
1812	—	8.00	20.00	40.00	70.00	—
1813	—	4.50	11.00	20.00	35.00	—
1814	—	4.00	10.00	20.00	35.00	—
1815	—	4.50	11.00	20.00	35.00	—
1816	—	4.00	10.00	20.00	35.00	—
1817	—	10.00	22.00	45.00	75.00	—

KM# 489.2 4 MARAVEDIS

Copper **Obv:** Laureate head of Ferdinand VII right **Rev:** Cross with castles and lions in angles **Note:** Mint mark: Aqueduct.

Date	Mintage	VG	F	VF	XF	Unc
1816	—	4.00	7.00	10.00	20.00	—
1818	—	5.00	10.00	16.00	30.00	—
1819	—	4.00	7.00	14.00	25.00	—
1820	—	4.00	7.00	10.00	20.00	—
1823	—	3.00	6.00	10.00	20.00	—
1824	—	3.00	6.00	10.00	20.00	—
1825	—	3.00	6.00	10.00	20.00	—
1826	—	3.00	6.00	10.00	20.00	—
1827	—	3.00	6.00	9.00	15.00	—
1828	—	3.00	6.00	9.00	15.00	—
1829	—	3.00	6.00	8.00	12.00	—
1830	—	3.00	6.00	8.00	12.00	—
1831	—	3.00	6.00	8.00	12.00	—
1832	—	3.00	6.00	9.00	15.00	—
1833	—	3.00	6.00	8.00	12.00	—

KM# 490.1 4 MARAVEDIS

Copper **Obv:** Small, thin laureate head of Ferdinand VII right. **Rev:** Cross with castles and lions in angles **Note:** Mint mark: J, JA.

Date	Mintage	VG	F	VF	XF	Unc
1817	—	5.00	9.00	14.00	25.00	—
1818	—	5.00	9.00	17.50	27.50	—
1819	—	5.00	10.00	18.00	28.00	—
1820	—	5.00	9.00	14.00	30.00	—

KM# 489.1 4 MARAVEDIS

Copper **Obv:** Laureate head of Ferdinand VII right **Rev:** Cross with castles and lions in angles **Note:** Mint mark: J, JA.

Date	Mintage	VG	F	VF	XF	Unc
1817	—	4.50	11.00	20.00	35.00	—
1818	—	8.00	16.00	25.00	40.00	—

KM# 490.2 4 MARAVEDIS

Copper **Obv:** Small, thin laureate head of Ferdinand VII right **Rev:** Cross with castles and lions in angles **Note:** Mint mark: Aqueduct.

Date	Mintage	VG	F	VF	XF	Unc
1817	—	5.00	9.00	14.00	30.00	—

KM# 505 4 MARAVEDIS

Copper **Obv:** Large head of Ferdinand VII right. **Rev:** Cross with castles and lions in angles **Note:** Mint mark: J, JA.

Date	Mintage	VG	F	VF	XF	Unc
1824	—	4.00	8.00	12.00	25.00	—
1825	—	6.00	12.00	30.00	55.00	—
1826	—	4.00	7.00	12.00	18.00	—
1827	—	4.00	7.00	10.00	15.00	—

KM# 511.1 4 MARAVEDIS

Copper **Obv:** Bust of Isabel II right **Rev:** Cross with castles and lions in angles **Note:** Mint mark: J, JA.

Date	Mintage	VG	F	VF	XF	Unc
1835	—	10.00	17.50	30.00	65.00	—
1836	—	35.00	65.00	150	300	—

KM# 511.3 4 MARAVEDIS

Copper **Obv:** Bust of Isabel II right **Rev:** Cross with castles and lions in angles **Note:** Mint mark: Aqueduct.

Date	Mintage	VG	F	VF	XF	Unc
1835	—	12.50	25.00	50.00	125	—
1836	—	7.50	15.00	30.00	50.00	—

KM# 511.2 4 MARAVEDIS

Copper **Obv:** Bust of Isabel II right **Rev:** Cross with castles and lions in angles **Note:** Mint mark: Crowned M.

Date	Mintage	VG	F	VF	XF	Unc
1836 DG	—	225	400	750	1,400	—

KM# 530.3 4 MARAVEDIS

Copper **Obv:** Bust of Isabel II right **Rev:** Cross with castles and lions in angles, legend around **Note:** Mint mark: Aqueduct.

Date	Mintage	VG	F	VF	XF	Unc
1837	—	5.00	12.50	25.00	40.00	—
1838	—	4.00	8.00	12.00	22.00	—
1839	—	4.00	10.00	15.00	30.00	—
1840	—	4.00	10.00	15.00	30.00	—
1841	—	4.00	10.00	17.00	32.00	—
1842	—	3.00	7.00	12.00	22.00	—
1843	—	3.00	7.00	18.00	30.00	—
1844	—	3.00	7.00	18.00	30.00	—
1845	—	3.00	7.00	18.00	30.00	—
1846	—	3.00	6.00	15.00	25.00	—
1847	—	3.00	6.00	15.00	25.00	—
1848	—	3.00	6.00	15.00	25.00	—
1849	—	3.00	6.00	15.00	25.00	—
1850	—	20.00	50.00	85.00	135	—

KM# 530.2 4 MARAVEDIS

Copper **Obv:** Bust of Isabel II right **Rev:** Cross with castles and lions in angles, legend around **Note:** Mint mark: J, JA.

Date	Mintage	VG	F	VF	XF	Unc
1837	—	7.00	14.00	30.00	50.00	—
1840	—	30.00	80.00	150	225	—
1841	—	5.00	14.00	40.00	60.00	—
1842	—	20.00	50.00	100	375	—
1843	—	7.00	14.00	60.00	180	—
1844	—	7.00	14.00	75.00	225	—
1845	—	2.00	5.00	15.00	35.00	—
1846	—	2.00	5.00	8.00	30.00	—
1847	—	2.00	5.00	8.00	25.00	—
1848	—	4.00	8.00	15.00	50.00	—
1849	—	4.00	8.00	15.00	50.00	—
1850	—	2.00	5.00	8.00	30.00	—

KM# 530.1 4 MARAVEDIS

Copper **Obv:** Bust of Isabel II right **Rev:** Cross with castles and lions in angles, legend around **Note:** Mint mark: B, BA.

Date	Mintage	VG	F	VF	XF	Unc
1853	—	50.00	100	225	600	—
1855	—	15.00	35.00	75.00	125	—

KM# 428 8 MARAVEDIS

Copper **Obv:** Head of Charles IV right **Rev:** Cross with castles and lions in angles, all within sprays **Note:** Mint mark: Aqueduct.

Date	Mintage	VG	F	VF	XF	Unc
1801	—	4.00	8.00	12.00	18.00	—
1802	—	4.00	8.00	12.00	18.00	—
1803	—	4.00	8.00	12.00	18.00	—
1804	—	5.00	9.00	13.00	20.00	—
1805	—	4.00	8.00	12.00	18.00	—
1806	—	5.00	9.00	13.00	20.00	—
1807	—	4.00	8.00	12.00	18.00	—
1808	—	3.00	7.00	9.00	16.00	—

KM# 450 8 MARAVEDIS

Copper **Obv:** Head of Joseph Napoleon left **Rev:** Cross with castles and lions in angles, all within sprays **Note:** Mint mark: Aqueduct.

Date	Mintage	VG	F	VF	XF	Unc
1809	—	25.00	50.00	75.00	110	—
1810	—	20.00	40.00	65.00	90.00	—
1811	—	14.00	28.00	45.00	60.00	—
1812	—	10.00	20.00	35.00	50.00	—
1813	—	16.00	32.50	50.00	70.00	—

KM# 461 8 MARAVEDIS

Copper **Obv:** Head of Ferdinand VII right **Rev:** Cross wtih castles and lions, all within sprays **Note:** Mint mark: J, JA.

Date	Mintage	VG	F	VF	XF	Unc
1811	—	20.00	40.00	85.00	140	—
1812	—	15.00	35.00	65.00	100	—
1813	—	7.00	14.00	30.00	50.00	—
1814	—	7.00	14.00	30.00	50.00	—
1815	—	7.00	14.00	30.00	50.00	—
1816	—	5.00	10.00	20.00	35.00	—
1817	—	4.00	9.00	18.00	30.00	—

KM# 486.1 8 MARAVEDIS

Copper **Obv:** Head laureate of Ferdinand VII right **Rev:** Cross with castles and lions in angles, all within sprays **Note:** Mint mark: Aqueduct.

Date	Mintage	VG	F	VF	XF	Unc
1815	—	9.00	18.00	30.00	50.00	—
1816	—	5.00	10.00	25.00	40.00	—
1817	—	5.00	10.00	20.00	35.00	—
1818	—	5.00	10.00	20.00	35.00	—
1819	—	6.00	12.00	12.50	25.00	—
1820	—	5.00	10.00	20.00	30.00	—
1821	—	10.00	25.00	40.00	60.00	—
1822	—	9.00	18.00	40.00	60.00	—
1823	—	5.00	10.00	20.00	30.00	—
1824	—	5.00	8.00	12.00	18.00	—
1825	—	5.00	9.00	15.00	22.00	—
1826	—	5.00	9.00	15.00	22.00	—
1827	—	5.00	10.00	17.00	25.00	—
1828	—	8.00	15.00	25.00	40.00	—
1829	—	4.00	6.00	8.00	12.00	—
1830	—	5.00	7.00	10.00	15.00	—
1831	—	4.00	6.00	8.00	12.00	—
1832	—	4.00	6.00	8.00	12.00	—
1833	—	4.00	6.00	8.00	12.00	—

KM# 491 8 MARAVEDIS

Copper **Obv:** Head laureate of Ferdinand VII right **Obv. Legend:** FERDIN. VII. D. G. HISP. REX **Rev:** Cross with castles and lions in angles, all within sprays **Note:** Mint mark: J, JA.

Date	Mintage	VG	F	VF	XF	Unc
1817	—	4.00	8.00	10.00	25.00	—
1818	—	4.00	7.00	10.00	18.00	—
1819	—	4.00	7.00	10.00	20.00	—
1820	—	4.00	7.00	10.00	20.00	—
1821	—	3.00	6.00	9.00	15.00	—

KM# 500 8 MARAVEDIS

Copper **Obv:** Head laureate of Ferdinand VII right **Obv. Legend:** FERN 7o POR LA.. **Rev:** Cross with castles and lions in angles, all within sprays **Note:** Mint mark: J, JA.

Date	Mintage	VG	F	VF	XF	Unc
1822	—	6.00	12.00	20.00	35.00	—
1823	—	5.00	10.00	17.50	32.00	—

KM# 502.1 8 MARAVEDIS

Copper **Obv:** Head laureate of Ferdinand VII right **Obv. Legend:** FERDIN. VII D. G. HISP. REX **Rev:** Cross with castles and lions in angles, all within sprays **Note:** Mint mark: J, JA.

Date	Mintage	VG	F	VF	XF	Unc
1823	—	6.00	11.00	18.00	32.00	—
1824	—	6.00	11.00	18.00	28.00	—
1825	—	6.00	11.00	18.00	28.00	—
1826	—	5.00	8.00	12.00	20.00	—
1827	—	5.00	9.00	16.00	27.00	—

KM# 486.2 8 MARAVEDIS

Copper **Obv:** Head laureate of Ferdinand VII right **Obv. Legend:** FERDIN. VII. D. G. HISP. REX **Rev:** Cross with castles and lions in angles, all within sprays **Note:** Mint mark: P, P.P., P.L., PA.

Date	Mintage	VG	F	VF	XF	Unc
1823	—	12.00	25.00	45.00	65.00	—

KM# 501 8 MARAVEDIS

Copper **Obv:** Head laureate of Ferdinand VII right, without value flanking **Obv. Legend:** FERN 7o POR LA.. **Rev:** Cross with castles and lions in angles, all within sprays **Note:** Mint mark: J, JA.

Date	Mintage	VG	F	VF	XF	Unc
1823	—	6.00	12.00	20.00	35.00	—

KM# 502.2 8 MARAVEDIS

Copper **Obv:** Head laureate of Ferdinand VII right **Obv. Legend:** FERDIN. VII D. G. HISP. REX **Rev:** Cross with castles and lions in angles, all within sprays **Note:** Mint mark: Aqueduct.

Date	Mintage	VG	F	VF	XF	Unc
1823	—	5.00	9.00	15.00	25.00	—

KM# 512.1 8 MARAVEDIS

Copper **Obv:** Head of Isabel II right **Obv. Legend:** FERDIN. VII D. G. HISP. REX **Rev:** Cross with castles and lions in angles, legend around **Note:** Mint mark: J, JA.

Date	Mintage	VG	F	VF	XF	Unc
1835	—	10.00	20.00	45.00	75.00	—
1836	—	10.00	17.50	35.00	60.00	—

KM# 512.3 8 MARAVEDIS

Copper **Obv:** Head of Isabel II right **Rev:** Cross with castles and lions in angles, legend around **Note:** Mint mark: Aqueduct.

Date	Mintage	VG	F	VF	XF	Unc
1835	—	4.00	10.00	25.00	45.00	—
1836	—	4.00	10.00	25.00	45.00	—

KM# 512.2 8 MARAVEDIS

Copper **Obv:** Head of Isabel II right **Rev:** Cross with castles and lions in angles, legend around **Note:** Mint mark: Crowned M.

Date	Mintage	VG	F	VF	XF	Unc
1835 DG	—	150	300	600	1,000	—

KM# 531.2 8 MARAVEDIS

Copper **Obv:** Head of Isabel II right **Rev:** Cross with castles and lions in angles, legend around **Note:** Mint mark: J, JA.

Date	Mintage	VG	F	VF	XF	Unc
1836	—	25.00	75.00	150	275	—
1837	—	5.00	10.00	20.00	50.00	—
1838	—	4.00	8.00	15.00	35.00	—
1839	—	6.00	10.00	18.00	75.00	—
1840	—	4.00	7.00	15.00	30.00	—
1841	—	4.00	8.00	15.00	35.00	—
1842	—	4.00	8.00	15.00	35.00	—
1843	—	4.00	8.00	15.00	35.00	—
1844	—	4.00	8.00	15.00	35.00	—
1845	—	4.00	8.00	15.00	35.00	—
1846	—	4.00	8.00	15.00	35.00	—
1847	—	4.00	8.00	15.00	35.00	—
1848	—	4.00	8.00	15.00	35.00	—
1849	—	4.00	8.00	15.00	35.00	—
1850	—	3.00	7.00	12.00	28.00	—

KM# 531.3 8 MARAVEDIS

Copper **Obv:** Head of Isabel II right **Rev:** Cross with castles and lions in angles, legend around **Note:** Mint mark: Aqueduct.

Date	Mintage	VG	F	VF	XF	Unc
1837	—	4.00	10.00	20.00	45.00	—
1838	—	4.00	7.00	17.00	35.00	—
1839	—	4.00	7.00	15.00	32.00	—
1840	—	4.00	7.00	15.00	32.00	—
1841	—	4.00	10.00	18.00	50.00	—
1842	—	4.00	7.00	15.00	32.00	—
1842 Ryena	—	20.00	60.00	125	200	—
1843	—	4.00	7.00	15.00	32.00	—
1844	—	3.00	7.00	14.00	30.00	—
1845	—	3.00	7.00	14.00	30.00	—
1846	—	3.00	7.00	14.00	28.00	—
1847	—	3.00	7.00	14.00	28.00	—
1848	—	3.00	7.00	14.00	30.00	—
1849	—	3.00	7.00	14.00	30.00	—
1850	—	4.00	12.00	20.00	40.00	—

KM# 516 8 MARAVEDIS

Copper **Obv:** Head of Charles V right **Rev:** Cross with castles and lions in angles, all within wreath **Note:** Charles V - Pretender issue. Mint mark: Aqueduct.

Date	Mintage	VG	F	VF	XF	Unc
1837	—	400	700	1,000	1,600	—

KM# 517.1 8 MARAVEDIS

Cast Bell Metal **Obv:** Head of Isabel II right **Rev:** Cross with castles and lions in angles, legend around **Note:** Mint mark: P, P.P., P.L., PA.

Date	Mintage	Good	VG	F	VF	XF
1837	—	50.00	75.00	100	175	—

KM# 517.2 8 MARAVEDIS
Cast Bell Metal **Obv:** Head of Isabel II right **Rev:** Cross with castles and lions in angles, legend around **Note:** Mint mark within oval.

Date	Mintage	Good	VG	F	VF	XF
1837	—	50.00	75.00	100	175	—

KM# 531.1 8 MARAVEDIS
Copper **Obv:** Head of Isabel II right **Rev:** Cross with castles and lions in angles, legend around **Note:** Mint mark: B, BA.

Date	Mintage	VG	F	VF	XF	Unc
1852	—	50.00	125	300	600	—
1853	—	35.00	60.00	100	235	—
1854	—	—	—	—	—	—
Note: Only counterfeits seen						
1855	—	10.00	25.00	40.00	80.00	—
1858	—	10.00	20.00	35.00	70.00	—

KM# 438.1 1/2 REAL
1.6900 g., 0.8120 Silver .0441 oz. **Obv:** Bust of Charles IV right **Rev:** Crowned arms **Note:** Mint mark: Crowned M.

Date	Mintage	VG	F	VF	XF	Unc
1802 FA	—	8.00	15.00	27.50	35.00	—
1803 FA	—	5.00	10.00	18.50	30.00	—
1804 FA	—	7.00	13.00	22.50	30.00	—
1808 AI	—	7.00	14.00	25.00	35.00	—
1808 FA	—	8.00	16.00	27.50	40.00	—

KM# 438.2 1/2 REAL
1.6900 g., 0.8120 Silver .0441 oz. **Obv:** Bust of Charles IV right **Rev:** Crowned arms **Note:** Mint mark: S, SL.

Date	Mintage	VG	F	VF	XF	Unc
1802 CN	—	8.00	16.00	32.50	40.00	—
1805 CN	—	8.00	16.00	32.50	40.00	—
1807 CN	—	7.00	13.00	25.00	30.00	—

KM# 473.1 1/2 REAL
1.6900 g., 0.8120 Silver .0441 oz. **Obv:** Laureate bust of Ferdinand VII right **Rev:** Crowned arms

Date	Mintage	VG	F	VF	XF	Unc
1812C SF	—	15.00	30.00	50.00	70.00	—
1813C SF	—	15.00	30.00	50.00	70.00	—
1814C SF	—	20.00	35.00	55.00	75.00	—

KM# 473.2 1/2 REAL
1.6900 g., 0.8120 Silver .0441 oz. **Obv:** Laureate bust of Ferdinand VII right **Rev:** Crowned arms **Note:** Mint mark: Crowned M.

Date	Mintage	VG	F	VF	XF	Unc
1813 IJ	—	9.00	18.00	30.00	45.00	—
1813 GJ	—	10.00	20.00	35.00	55.00	—
1814 GJ	—	10.00	20.00	35.00	50.00	—

KM# 482.1 1/2 REAL
1.6900 g., 0.8120 Silver .0441 oz. **Obv:** Laureate bust of Ferdinand VII right **Rev:** Crowned arms **Note:** Mint mark: Crowned C.

Date	Mintage	VG	F	VF	XF	Unc
1814 CI	—	5.00	10.00	22.50	35.00	—
1814 CJ	—	5.00	10.00	25.00	40.00	—

KM# 482.2 1/2 REAL
1.6900 g., 0.8120 Silver .0441 oz. **Obv:** Laureate bust of Ferdinand VII right **Rev:** Crowned arms **Note:** Mint mark: Crowned M.

Date	Mintage	VG	F	VF	XF	Unc
1815 GJ	—	6.00	12.50	27.50	40.00	—
1816 GJ	—	6.00	12.00	18.00	30.00	—
1817 GJ	—	6.00	12.00	18.00	35.00	—
1818 GJ	—	6.00	12.00	16.00	30.00	—
1819 GJ	—	6.00	12.00	18.00	35.00	—
1820 GJ	—	6.00	12.50	18.00	30.00	—
1824 AJ	—	8.00	15.00	25.00	35.00	—
1826 AJ	—	6.00	12.50	25.00	30.00	—
1828 AJ	—	8.00	15.00	25.00	30.00	—
1830 AJ	—	6.00	12.00	17.50	35.00	—
1831 AJ	—	9.00	17.50	25.00	35.00	—
1832 AJ	—	6.00	12.00	20.00	30.00	—
1833 AJ	—	6.00	12.00	25.00	35.00	—
1833 JI	—	11.00	22.00	40.00	65.00	—

KM# 482.3 1/2 REAL
1.6900 g., 0.8120 Silver .0441 oz. **Obv:** Laureate bust of Ferdinand VII right **Rev:** Crowned arms **Note:** Mint mark: Crowned S, SL.

Date	Mintage	VG	F	VF	XF	Unc
1825 JB	—	4.00	7.00	15.00	25.00	—
1831 JB	—	4.00	7.00	15.00	25.00	—
1832 JB	—	6.00	12.00	20.00	35.00	—
1833 JB	—	7.00	13.00	20.00	35.00	—

KM# 429.1 REAL
3.3800 g., 0.8120 Silver .0882 oz. **Obv:** Bust of Charles IV right **Rev:** Crowned arms at Castile and Leon **Note:** Mint mark: Crowned M.

Date	Mintage	VG	F	VF	XF	Unc
1801 FA	—	5.00	10.00	16.00	25.00	—
1802 FA	—	5.00	10.00	20.00	35.00	—
1803 FA	—	6.00	12.00	18.00	25.00	—
1805 FA	—	6.00	12.00	19.00	30.00	—
1807 FA	—	6.00	12.00	18.00	25.00	—
1807 AI	—	7.00	14.00	20.00	40.00	—
1808 AI	—	7.00	14.00	19.00	30.00	—

KM# 429.2 REAL
3.3800 g., 0.8120 Silver .0882 oz. **Obv:** Bust of Charles IV right **Rev:** Crowned arms at Castile and Leon **Note:** Mint mark: S, S/L.

Date	Mintage	VG	F	VF	XF	Unc
1802 CN	—	10.00	20.00	45.00	65.00	—
1807 CN	—	9.00	18.00	35.00	50.00	—

KM# 463.1 REAL
3.3800 g., 0.8120 Silver .0882 oz. **Obv:** Small draped bust of Ferdinand VII **Rev:** Crowned arms at Castile and Leon

Date	Mintage	VG	F	VF	XF	Unc
1811C SF	—	13.50	25.00	45.00	65.00	—
1814C SF	—	22.50	40.00	80.00	130	—

KM# 462.1 REAL
3.3800 g., 0.8120 Silver .0882 oz. **Obv:** Large laureate bust of Ferdinand VII **Rev:** Crowned arms at Castile and Leon

Date	Mintage	VG	F	VF	XF	Unc
1811 C SF	—	12.50	22.50	40.00	55.00	—

KM# 463.2 REAL
3.3800 g., 0.8120 Silver .0882 oz. **Obv:** Small draped bust of Ferdinand VII **Rev:** Crowned arms at Castile and Leon **Note:** Mint mark: Crowned M.

Date	Mintage	VG	F	VF	XF	Unc
1813 IJ	—	22.50	40.00	60.00	85.00	—
1814 IJ	—	15.00	30.00	45.00	75.00	—
1814 GJ	—	9.00	18.50	30.00	50.00	—

KM# 462.2 REAL
3.3800 g., 0.8120 Silver .0882 oz. **Obv:** Large laureate bust of Ferdinand VII **Rev:** Crowned arms at Castile and Leon **Note:** Mint mark: Crowned C.

Date	Mintage	VG	F	VF	XF	Unc
1813 CJ	—	10.00	20.00	30.00	45.00	—

KM# 462.3 REAL
3.3800 g., 0.8120 Silver .0882 oz. **Obv:** Large laureate bust of Ferdinand VII **Rev:** Crowned arms of Castile and Leon **Note:** Mint mark: Crowned M.

Date	Mintage	VG	F	VF	XF	Unc
1815 GJ	—	8.00	16.50	32.50	50.00	—
1816 GJ	—	8.00	16.50	30.00	50.00	—
1817 GJ	—	8.00	16.50	25.00	45.00	—
1819 GJ	—	10.00	20.00	27.50	45.00	—
1820 GJ	—	9.00	18.50	25.00	55.00	—
1824 AJ	—	15.00	30.00	55.00	80.00	—
1826 AJ	—	10.00	20.00	40.00	60.00	—
1828 AJ	—	10.00	20.00	40.00	60.00	—
1830 AJ	—	7.00	15.00	22.00	35.00	—
1831 AJ	—	8.00	17.00	30.00	45.00	—
1832 AJ	—	7.00	15.00	20.00	40.00	—
1833 AJ	—	10.00	20.00	30.00	50.00	—
1833 JI	—	11.00	22.50	38.50	60.00	—
1833 JJ	—	9.00	18.00	30.00	40.00	—

KM# 462.4 REAL
3.3800 g., 0.8120 Silver .0882 oz. **Obv:** Laureate bust of Ferdinand VII right **Rev:** Crowned arms of Castile and Leon **Note:** Mint mark: S, SL.

Date	Mintage	VG	F	VF	XF	Unc
1830 JB	—	10.00	19.00	32.00	50.00	—
1831 JB	—	6.00	12.00	25.00	35.00	—
1832 JB	—	7.00	14.00	25.00	35.00	—
1833 JB	—	7.00	14.00	20.00	30.00	—

KM# 518.1 REAL
3.3800 g., 0.8120 Silver .0882 oz. **Obv:** Head of Isabel II right **Rev:** Crowned arms of Castile and Leon within Order of The Golden Fleece collar **Note:** Mint mark: Crowned M.

Date	Mintage	VG	F	VF	XF	Unc
1837 CL	—	65.00	125	225	325	—
1838 CL	—	9.00	18.00	22.00	30.00	—
1838 DG	—	125	200	375	600	—
1839 CL	—	8.00	16.50	35.00	65.00	—
1840 CL	—	15.00	30.00	60.00	115	—
1841 CL	—	30.00	60.00	115	225	—
1842 CL	—	35.00	70.00	140	180	—
1843 CL	—	16.00	32.50	60.00	115	—
1844 CL	—	7.00	15.00	30.00	60.00	—
1845 CL	—	5.00	10.00	20.00	35.00	—
1847 CL	—	4.00	8.00	15.00	25.00	—
1848 CL	—	4.00	8.00	15.00	25.00	—
1849 CL	—	4.00	8.00	15.00	25.00	—

KM# 518.2 REAL
3.3800 g., 0.8120 Silver .0882 oz. **Obv:** Small draped bust of Isabel II right **Rev:** Crowned arms of Castile and Leon within Order of The Golden Fleece collar **Note:** Mint mark: S, SL.

Date	Mintage	VG	F	VF	XF	Unc
1840 RD	—	10.00	30.00	50.00	150	—

KM# 518.4 REAL
3.3800 g., 0.8120 Silver .0882 oz. **Obv:** Head of Isabel II right **Rev:** Crowned arms of Castile and Leon within Order of The Golden Fleece collar **Note:** Different bust from 518.2 and 518.3.

Date	Mintage	VG	F	VF	XF	Unc
1850 RD	—	6.00	14.00	25.00	40.00	—
1851 RD	—	6.00	14.00	25.00	40.00	—
1852 RD	—	6.00	14.00	25.00	40.00	—

KM# 430.1 2 REALES
6.7700 g., 0.8120 Silver .1767 oz. **Obv:** Bust of Charles IV right **Obv. Legend:** CAROLUS IIII • DEI • G • **Rev:** Crowned arms of Castile and Leon **Note:** Mint mark: Crowned M.

Date	Mintage	VG	F	VF	XF	Unc
1801 FA	—	7.00	15.00	22.00	35.00	—
1802 FA	—	7.00	15.00	22.00	35.00	—
1803 FA	—	7.00	15.00	22.00	35.00	—
1804 FA	—	7.00	15.00	22.00	35.00	—
1805 FA	—	7.00	15.00	22.00	35.00	—
1806 FA	—	7.00	15.00	22.00	35.00	—
1807 FA	—	7.00	15.00	22.00	35.00	—
1807 AI	—	8.00	17.00	30.00	50.00	—
1808 FA	—	7.00	15.00	22.00	35.00	—
1808 IG	—	8.00	17.00	30.00	50.00	—
1808 AI	—	7.00	15.00	25.00	40.00	—

KM# 430.2 2 REALES
6.7700 g., 0.8120 Silver .1767 oz. **Obv:** Bust of Charles IV right **Obv. Legend:** CAROLUS IIII • DEI • G • **Rev:** Crowned arms of Castile and Leon **Note:** Mint mark: S.

Date	Mintage	VG	F	VF	XF	Unc
1801 CN	—	8.00	16.00	25.00	40.00	—
1802 CN	—	8.00	16.00	25.00	40.00	—
1803 CN	—	8.00	16.00	25.00	40.00	—
1804 CN	—	8.00	16.00	25.00	40.00	—
1805 CN	—	8.00	16.00	25.00	40.00	—
1806 CN	—	8.00	16.00	25.00	40.00	—
1807 CN	—	8.00	16.00	25.00	40.00	—
1808 CN	—	8.00	16.00	25.00	40.00	—

KM# 474.2 2 REALES
6.7700 g., 0.8120 Silver .1767 oz. **Obv:** Bust of Ferdinand VII right **Obv. Legend:** FERDIN • VII • DEI • G • **Rev:** Crowned arms of Castile and Leon **Note:** Struck at Cataluna. Mint mark: C.

Date	Mintage	VG	F	VF	XF	Unc
1810 FS	—	14.00	27.50	45.00	60.00	—
1810 SF	—	30.00	55.00	80.00	140	—
1811 SF	—	11.00	22.50	35.00	50.00	—
1811 FS	—	15.00	30.00	45.00	60.00	—

KM# 460.1 2 REALES
6.7700 g., 0.8120 Silver .1767 oz. **Obv:** Bust of Ferdinand VII right **Obv. Legend:** FERDIN • VII • DEI • GRATIA **Rev:** Crowned arms of Castile and Leon **Note:** Mint mark: Crowned C.

Date	Mintage	VG	F	VF	XF	Unc
1810 CI	—	9.00	18.00	25.00	40.00	—
1810 CI With small crowned C	—	11.00	21.00	35.00	60.00	—
1811 CI	—	9.00	18.00	25.00	40.00	—
1812 CI	—	9.00	18.00	25.00	40.00	—

KM# 464 2 REALES
6.7700 g., 0.8120 Silver .1767 oz. **Obv:** Laureate bust of Ferdinand VII right **Rev:** Crowned arms of Castile and Leon **Note:** Struck at Cataluna.

Date	Mintage	VG	F	VF	XF	Unc
1811 SF	—	8.00	17.00	30.00	50.00	—
1812 SF	—	40.00	60.00	100	150	—
1813 SF	—	8.00	17.00	30.00	50.00	—
1814 SF	—	14.00	27.50	35.00	55.00	—

KM# 474.4 2 REALES
6.7700 g., 0.8120 Silver .1767 oz. **Obv:** Bust of Ferdinand VII right **Obv. Legend:** FERDIN • VII • DEI • G • **Rev:** Crowned arms of Castile and Leon **Note:** Mint mark: V, VAL.

Date	Mintage	VG	F	VF	XF	Unc
1811 GS	—	70.00	125	175	225	—
1812 GS	—	65.00	100	135	175	—

KM# 474.3 2 REALES
6.7700 g., 0.8120 Silver .1767 oz. **Obv:** Bust of Ferdinand VII right **Obv. Legend:** FERDIN • VII • DEI • GRATIA **Rev:** Crowned arms of Castile and Leon **Note:** Mint mark: Crowned M.

Date	Mintage	VG	F	VF	XF	Unc
1812 IJ	—	9.00	17.50	25.00	40.00	—
1813 IJ	—	7.00	15.00	20.00	30.00	—
1813 IG	—	12.00	25.00	40.00	60.00	—
1813 GJ	—	7.00	15.00	20.00	30.00	—
1814 GJ	—	12.00	25.00	40.00	60.00	—

KM# 474.1 2 REALES
6.7700 g., 0.8120 Silver .1767 oz. **Obv:** Bust of Ferdinand VII right **Obv. Legend:** FERDIN • VII • DEI • DRATIA • **Rev:** Crowned arms of Castile and Leon **Note:** Mint mark: •B•.

Date	Mintage	VG	F	VF	XF	Unc
1812 SP	—	80.00	150	275	400	—

KM# 460.2 2 REALES
6.7700 g., 0.8120 Silver .1767 oz. **Obv:** Laureate bust of Ferdinand VII right **Obv. Legend:** FERDIN • VII • DEI • GRATIA **Rev:** Crowned Spanish shield **Note:** Mint mark: Crowned M.

Date	Mintage	VG	F	VF	XF	Unc
1814 GJ	—	8.00	16.00	23.00	35.00	—
1815 GJ	—	8.00	16.00	23.00	35.00	—
1816 GJ	—	8.00	16.00	25.00	40.00	—
1817 GJ	—	8.00	16.00	23.00	35.00	—
1818 GJ	—	9.00	19.00	25.00	40.00	—
1819 GJ	—	9.00	19.00	25.00	45.00	—
1820 GJ	—	8.00	16.00	23.00	35.00	—
1821 AJ	—	7.00	15.00	30.00	50.00	—
1822 AJ	—	16.00	32.50	40.00	65.00	—
1823 AJ	—	8.00	16.00	25.00	40.00	—
1824 AJ	—	8.00	16.00	25.00	40.00	—
1825 AJ	—	8.00	16.00	25.00	40.00	—
1826 AJ	—	8.00	16.00	23.00	35.00	—
1827 AJ	—	8.00	16.00	25.00	40.00	—
1828 AJ	—	8.00	16.00	23.00	35.00	—
1829 AJ	—	8.00	16.00	23.00	35.00	—
1830 AJ	—	8.00	16.00	23.00	30.00	—
1831 AJ	—	8.00	16.00	25.00	40.00	—
1832 AJ	—	8.00	16.00	23.00	35.00	—
1833 AJ	—	9.00	18.00	25.00	40.00	—

KM# 460.3 2 REALES
6.7700 g., 0.8120 Silver .1767 oz. **Obv:** Laureate bust of Ferdinand VII right **Obv. Legend:** FERDIN • VII • DEI • GRATIA • **Rev:** Crowned Spanish shield **Note:** Mint mark: S, S/L.

Date	Mintage	VG	F	VF	XF	Unc
1815 CJ	—	10.00	20.00	30.00	50.00	—
1820 CJ	—	8.00	16.00	25.00	40.00	—
1821 CJ	—	7.00	14.00	20.00	30.00	—
1823 CJ	—	8.00	16.00	25.00	40.00	—
1824 J	—	15.00	30.00	40.00	65.00	—
1824 JB	—	8.00	16.00	25.00	40.00	—
1825 JB	—	8.00	16.00	25.00	40.00	—
1826 JB	—	8.00	16.00	25.00	40.00	—
1827 JB	—	8.00	16.00	25.00	40.00	—
1828 JB	—	8.00	16.00	25.00	40.00	—
1829 JB	—	8.00	16.00	25.00	40.00	—
1830 JB	—	8.00	16.00	25.00	40.00	—
1831 JB	—	8.00	16.00	25.00	40.00	—
1832 JB	—	8.00	16.00	25.00	45.00	—
1833 JB	—	9.00	18.00	27.00	50.00	—

KM# A513.1 2 REALES
6.7700 g., 0.8120 Silver .1767 oz. **Obv:** Young head of Isabella II right **Obv. Legend:** ...GRACIA DE DIOS **Rev:** Crowned arms of Castile and Leon within collar of the Order of the Golden Fleece **Note:** Mint mark: Crowned M.

Date	Mintage	VG	F	VF	XF	Unc
1836 DG	—	200	400	800	1,100	—
1836 CR	—	20.00	40.00	80.00	110	—

KM# A513.2 2 REALES
6.7700 g., 0.8120 Silver .1767 oz. **Obv:** Young head of Isabella II right **Obv. Legend:** ... GRACIA DE DIOS **Rev:** Crowned arms of Castile and Leon within collar of the Order of the Golden Fleece **Note:** Mint mark: S.

Date	Mintage	VG	F	VF	XF	Unc
1836 DR	—	20.00	40.00	95.00	150	—

KM# 513.1 2 REALES
6.7700 g., 0.8120 Silver .1767 oz. **Obv:** Young head of Isabella II right **Obv. Legend:** ...DIOS Y LA CONST **Rev:** Crowned arms of Castile and Leon within Order of the Golden Fleece collar **Note:** Mint mark: Crowned M.

Date	Mintage	VG	F	VF	XF	Unc
1837 CR	—	60.00	125	250	350	—
1838 CL	—	60.00	115	230	300	—
1839 CL	—	45.00	90.00	200	300	—
1841 CL	—	75.00	150	800	1,250	—
1842 CL	—	45.00	90.00	200	325	—
1843 CL	—	17.50	35.00	75.00	110	—

KM# 513.2 2 REALES
6.7700 g., 0.8120 Silver .1767 oz. **Obv:** Young head of Isabella right **Obv. Legend:** ... DIOS Y LA CONST **Rev:** Crowned arms of Castile and Leon within Order of the Golden Fleece collar **Note:** Mint mark: S.

Date	Mintage	VG	F	VF	XF	Unc
1839 RD	—	17.00	35.00	60.00	100	—
1840 RD	—	22.00	45.00	90.00	140	—

KM# 526.1 2 REALES
6.7700 g., 0.8120 Silver .1767 oz. **Subject:** Charles V - Pretender Issue **Obv:** Head of Isabel II right **Rev:** Crowned arms of Castile and Leon in collar of the Order of the Golden Fleece **Note:** Mint mark: Crowned M.

Date	Mintage	VG	F	VF	XF	Unc
1844 CL	—	11.00	22.50	35.00	60.00	—
1845 CL	—	11.00	22.50	35.00	50.00	—
1847 CL	—	10.00	20.00	30.00	45.00	—
1848 CL	—	11.00	22.50	35.00	55.00	—
1849 CL	—	10.00	20.00	30.00	40.00	—

KM# 526.2 2 REALES
6.7700 g., 0.8120 Silver .1767 oz. **Obv:** Head of Isabel II right **Rev:** Crowned arms of Castile and Leon in collar of the Order of the Golden Fleece **Note:** Mint mark: S.

Date	Mintage	VG	F	VF	XF	Unc
1845 RD	—	22.00	45.00	100	165	—
1848 RD	—	17.00	35.00	65.00	80.00	—
1850/45 RD	—	30.00	60.00	100	150	—
1850 RD	—	20.00	40.00	70.00	100	—
1851 RD	—	10.00	20.00	30.00	40.00	—

KM# 431.2 4 REALES
13.5400 g., 0.8960 Silver .3900 oz. **Obv:** Bust of Charles III right **Rev:** Crowned arms **Note:** Mint mark: S, S/L.

Date	Mintage	VG	F	VF	XF	Unc
1803 CN	—	20.00	40.00	55.00	85.00	—
1807 CN	—	20.00	40.00	60.00	90.00	—

KM# 431.1 4 REALES
13.5400 g., 0.8960 Silver .3900 oz. **Obv:** Bust of Charles IV right **Rev:** Crowned shield of Castile and Leon **Note:** Similar to 2 Reales, KM#430.2. Mint mark: Crowned M.

Date	Mintage	VG	F	VF	XF	Unc
1804 FA	—	20.00	30.00	55.00	85.00	—
1805 FA	—	20.00	30.00	55.00	80.00	—
1806 FA	—	25.00	40.00	80.00	140	—
1808 AI	—	30.00	50.00	70.00	120	—
1808 FA	—	30.00	50.00	70.00	120	—

KM# 453.2 4 REALES
13.5400 g., 0.8960 Silver .3900 oz. **Obv:** Bust draped of Ferdinand VII right **Rev:** Crowned shield of Castile and Leon **Note:** Mint mark: V, VAL.

Date	Mintage	VG	F	VF	XF	Unc
1809 SG	—	90.00	150	200	300	—
1810 SG	—	35.00	65.00	100	150	—
1811 SG	—	40.00	70.00	125	175	—

KM# 453.1 4 REALES
13.5400 g., 0.8960 Silver .3900 oz. **Obv:** Bust draped of Ferdinand VII right **Rev:** Crowned shield of Castile and Leon

Date	Mintage	VG	F	VF	XF	Unc
1809C MP	—	65.00	125	225	600	—
1809C SF	—	75.00	150	250	650	—
1810C SF	—	100	200	325	775	—
1814C SF	—	175	325	525	900	—

KM# 465 4 REALES
13.5400 g., 0.8960 Silver .3900 oz. **Obv:** Bust laureate and armored of Ferdinand VII right **Rev:** Crowned shield of Castile and Leon

Date	Mintage	VG	F	VF	XF	Unc
1811C SF	—	60.00	150	300	450	—

KM# 475 4 REALES
13.5400 g., 0.8960 Silver .3900 oz. **Obv:** Bust laureate and draped of Ferdinand VII right **Rev:** Crowned shield of Castile and Leon

Date	Mintage	VG	F	VF	XF	Unc
1812C SF	—	100	225	350	500	—
1813C SF	—	275	550	800	1,000	—

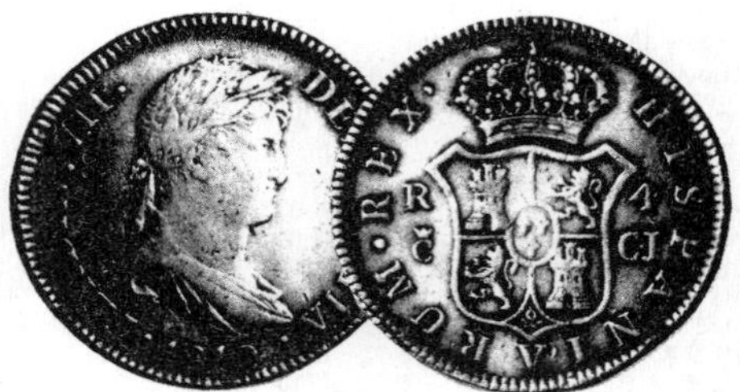

KM# 476.1 4 REALES
13.5400 g., 0.8960 Silver .3900 oz. **Obv:** Bust laureate and draped of Ferdinand VII right **Rev:** Crowned shield of Castile and Leon **Note:** Mint mark: Crowned C.

Date	Mintage	VG	F	VF	XF	Unc
1812 CJ	—	25.00	40.00	60.00	90.00	—
1812 CI	—	35.00	65.00	90.00	135	—

KM# 479 4 REALES
13.5400 g., 0.8960 Silver .3900 oz. **Obv:** Bust draped of Ferdinand VII right **Obv. Legend:** FERDINANDUS VII.. **Rev:** Crowned shield of Castile and Leon **Note:** Mint mark: Crowned M.

Date	Mintage	VG	F	VF	XF	Unc
1813 IJ	—	75.00	150	250	400	—
1813 GJ	—	90.00	165	275	450	—
1814 GJ	—	90.00	165	275	450	—

KM# 476.2 4 REALES
13.5400 g., 0.8960 Silver .3900 oz. **Obv:** Bust laureate and draped of Ferdinand VII right **Rev:** Crowned shield of Castile and Leon **Note:** Mint mark: Crowned M.

Date	Mintage	VG	F	VF	XF	Unc
1814 GJ	—	90.00	175	300	400	—
1815 GJ	—	12.00	25.00	40.00	65.00	—
1816 GJ	—	20.00	40.00	65.00	110	—
1817 GJ	—	18.00	35.00	60.00	90.00	—
1818 GJ	—	18.00	35.00	60.00	100	—
1819 GJ	—	60.00	100	165	250	—
1822 SR	—	30.00	55.00	90.00	160	—
1824 AJ	—	16.00	32.50	40.00	70.00	—
1830 AJ	—	15.00	30.00	40.00	70.00	—

KM# 476.3 4 REALES
13.5400 g., 0.8960 Silver .3900 oz. **Obv:** Bust laureate and draped of Ferdinand VII right **Rev:** Crowned shield of Castile and Leon **Note:** Mint mark: S, S/L.

Date	Mintage	VG	F	VF	XF	Unc
1818 CJ	—	20.00	40.00	65.00	110	—
1818 J	—	25.00	45.00	85.00	145	—
1819 CJ	—	20.00	40.00	55.00	85.00	—
1820 CJ	—	20.00	40.00	60.00	90.00	—
1824 J	—	20.00	40.00	90.00	155	—
1824 JB	—	20.00	40.00	45.00	70.00	—
1825 JB	—	15.00	30.00	50.00	80.00	—
1826 JB	—	20.00	35.00	55.00	90.00	—
1828 JB	—	20.00	40.00	75.00	125	—
1830 JB	—	15.00	30.00	50.00	80.00	—
1832 JB	—	15.00	30.00	45.00	70.00	—
1833 JB	—	20.00	35.00	55.00	90.00	—

KM# 510.1 4 REALES
13.5400 g., 0.8960 Silver .3900 oz. **Obv:** Head of Isabel II right **Obv. Legend:** ...GRACIA DE DIOS.. **Rev:** Crowned shield of Castile and Leon **Note:** Mint mark: Crowned M.

Date	Mintage	VG	F	VF	XF	Unc
1834 CR	—	60.00	125	185	300	—
1834 DG	—	175	500	800	1,500	—
1835 CR	—	20.00	35.00	70.00	110	—
1836 CR	—	20.00	40.00	80.00	135	—

KM# 510.2 4 REALES
13.5400 g., 0.8960 Silver .3900 oz. **Obv:** Head of Isabel II right **Obv. Legend:** ...GRACIA DE DIOS.. **Rev:** Crowned shield of Castile and Leon **Note:** Mint mark: S, S/L.

Date	Mintage	VG	F	VF	XF	Unc
1835 DR	—	20.00	35.00	70.00	110	—
1836 DR	—	20.00	35.00	70.00	110	—

KM# 514 4 REALES
13.5400 g., 0.8960 Silver .3900 oz. **Obv:** Head of Isabel II right **Obv. Legend:** ...GRACIA DE DIOS Y CONSTITUCION **Rev:** Crowned shield of Castile and Leon **Note:** Mint mark: B, BA.

Date	Mintage	VG	F	VF	XF	Unc
1836 PS	—	35.00	65.00	155	225	—
1837 PS	—	35.00	70.00	130	175	—
1837 RS	—	20.00	40.00	85.00	125	—

KM# 519.1 4 REALES
13.5400 g., 0.8960 Silver .3900 oz. **Obv:** Head of Isabel II right **Obv. Legend:** ...GRACIA DE DIOS Y CONST **Rev:** Crowned shield of Castile and Leon in collar of The Golden Fleece **Note:** Mint mark: B, BA.

Date	Mintage	VG	F	VF	XF	Unc
1837 PJ	—	15.00	25.00	50.00	70.00	—
1838 PS	—	25.00	50.00	80.00	110	—
1839 PS	—	80.00	175	375	525	—
1840 PS	—	25.00	50.00	85.00	120	—
1841 PS	—	15.00	25.00	45.00	65.00	—
1842 CC	—	20.00	40.00	60.00	85.00	—
1843 CC	—	75.00	150	350	425	—
1843 PS	—	75.00	150	350	450	—
1844 PS	—	20.00	40.00	70.00	100	—
1845 PS	—	35.00	70.00	135	200	—
1846 PS	—	75.00	150	250	350	—
1847 PS	—	35.00	70.00	120	175	—

KM# 519.3 4 REALES
13.5400 g., 0.8960 Silver .3900 oz. **Obv:** Head of Isabel II right **Obv. Legend:** ...GRACIA DE DIOS Y CONST **Rev:** Crowned shield of Castile and Leon in collar of The Golden Fleece **Note:** Mint mark: S, S/L.

Date	Mintage	VG	F	VF	XF	Unc
1837 DR	—	20.00	40.00	70.00	100	—
1838 DR	—	25.00	50.00	100	200	—
1838 RD	—	25.00	45.00	85.00	160	—
1839 DR	—	35.00	70.00	180	300	—
1839 RD	—	35.00	70.00	140	250	—
1840 RD	—	50.00	100	210	400	—
1841 RD	—	20.00	40.00	75.00	150	—
1842 RD	—	20.00	40.00	70.00	150	—
1843 RD	—	15.00	30.00	50.00	80.00	—
1844 RD	—	40.00	80.00	185	375	—
1845 RD	—	40.00	80.00	160	350	—

KM# 519.2 4 REALES
13.5400 g., 0.8960 Silver .3900 oz. **Obv:** Head of Isabel II right **Obv. Legend:** ...GRACIA DE DIOS Y CONST **Rev:** Crowned shield of Castile and Leon in collar of The Golden Fleece **Note:** Mint mark: Crowned M.

Date	Mintage	VG	F	VF	XF	Unc
1837 CR	—	25.00	45.00	65.00	90.00	—
1838 CL	—	45.00	90.00	150	225	—
1839 CL	—	30.00	60.00	100	150	—
1840 CL	—	30.00	50.00	100	150	—
1841 CL	—	30.00	50.00	100	150	—
1842 CL	—	40.00	80.00	140	250	—
1843 CL	—	40.00	80.00	140	200	—
1844 CL	—	45.00	90.00	175	275	—
1845 CL	—	40.00	80.00	160	250	—
1846 CL	—	35.00	65.00	110	175	—
1847 CL	—	30.00	65.00	110	175	—
1848 CL	—	15.00	25.00	35.00	50.00	—
1848 DG	—	275	425	1,000	1,600	—
1849 CL	—	15.00	25.00	35.00	50.00	—

KM# 432.2 8 REALES
27.0700 g., 0.9030 Silver .7859 oz. **Obv:** Bust of Charles IV right **Rev:** Crowned shield of Castile and Leon **Note:** Mint mark: S, S/L. Similar to 2 Reales, KM#430.2.

Date	Mintage	VG	F	VF	XF	Unc
1802 CN	—	120	240	365	500	—
1803 CN	—	150	300	500	650	—

KM# 432.1 8 REALES
27.0700 g., 0.9030 Silver .7859 oz. **Obv:** Bust of Charles IV right **Rev:** Crowned shield of Castile and Leon **Note:** Similar to 2 Reales, KM#430.2. Dav. #1701. Mint mark: Crowned M.

Date	Mintage	VG	F	VF	XF	Unc
1802 MF	—	200	375	500	700	—
1802 FA	—	100	185	265	400	—
1803 FA	—	150	300	450	550	—
1805 FA	—	100	185	250	350	—
1808 FA	—	150	300	500	600	—
1808 AI	—	140	280	425	650	—
1808 IG	—	200	375	475	750	—

KM# 451 8 REALES
27.0700 g., 0.9030 Silver .7859 oz. **Obv:** Bust of Ferd VII right **Rev:** Crowned shield of Castile and Leon **Note:** Mint mark: S, S/L

Date	Mintage	VG	F	VF	XF	Unc
1808 CN	—	50.00	100	185	275	—
1809 CN	—	50.00	100	185	275	—

KM# 466.4 8 REALES
27.0700 g., 0.9030 Silver .7859 oz. **Obv:** Bust of Fedinand VII right **Rev:** Crowned shield of Castile and Leon **Note:** Mint mark: S, S/L.

Date	Mintage	VG	F	VF	XF	Unc
1809 CN	—	75.00	125	200	350	—
1810 CN	—	450	900	1,350	2,000	—
1812 CN	—	825	1,650	2,400	3,600	—
1814 CJ	—	250	500	1,150	1,600	—
1815 CJ	—	65.00	125	175	275	—
1816 CJ	—	50.00	100	150	220	—
1817 CJ	—	50.00	100	150	220	—
1818 CJ	—	50.00	100	150	220	—
1819 CJ	—	65.00	125	200	325	—
1820 CJ	—	50.00	100	150	220	—

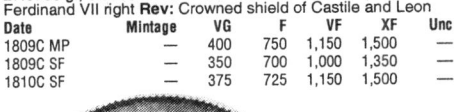

KM# 455.1 8 REALES
27.0700 g., 0.9030 Silver .7859 oz. **Obv:** Bust draped of Ferdinand VII right **Rev:** Crowned shield of Castile and Leon

Date	Mintage	VG	F	VF	XF	Unc
1809C MP	—	400	750	1,150	1,500	—
1809C SF	—	350	700	1,000	1,350	—
1810C SF	—	375	725	1,150	1,500	—

KM# 454 8 REALES
27.0700 g., 0.9030 Silver .7859 oz. **Obv:** Head of Joseph Napoleon left **Rev:** Crowned shield of Castile and Leon **Note:** Mint mark: Crowned M.

Date	Mintage	VG	F	VF	XF	Unc
1809 IG	—	40.00	80.00	200	350	—
1810 JG	—	550	1,100	2,500	3,250	—

KM# 466.2 8 REALES
27.0700 g., 0.9030 Silver .7859 oz. **Obv:** Bust of Ferdinand VII right **Rev:** Crowned shield of Castile and Leon **Note:** Mint mark: Crowned C.

Date	Mintage	VG	F	VF	XF	Unc
1810 CI	—	300	600	1,000	1,450	—
1811 CI	—	150	300	550	900	—
1811 CJ	—	190	425	700	1,000	—
1812 CJ	—	175	400	650	950	—
1813 CJ	—	85.00	140	220	350	—
1814 CJ	—	85.00	140	220	350	—
1815 CJ	—	500	1,000	2,000	2,800	—

KM# 466.1 8 REALES
27.0700 g., 0.9030 Silver .7859 oz. **Obv:** Bust of Ferdinand VII right **Rev:** Crowned shield of Castile and Leon

Date	Mintage	VG	F	VF	XF	Unc
1811C SF	—	625	1,250	—	—	—
1812C SF	—	450	850	1,550	—	—
1813C SF	—	475	950	1,650	2,200	—
1814C SF	—	625	1,250	—	—	—

KM# 455.2 8 REALES
27.0700 g., 0.9030 Silver .7859 oz. **Obv:** Bust of Ferdinand VII right **Rev:** Crowned shield of Castile and Leon **Note:** Mint mark: V, VAL.

Date	Mintage	VG	F	VF	XF	Unc
1811 GS	—	300	700	1,100	1,500	—
1811 SG	—	250	600	1,000	1,200	—

KM# 477 8 REALES
27.0700 g., 0.9030 Silver .7859 oz. **Obv:** Bust of Ferdinand VII right **Rev:** Crowned shield of Castile and Leon **Note:** Mint mark: Crowned M.

Date	Mintage	VG	F	VF	XF	Unc
1812 IJ	—	200	425	600	800	—
1813 IJ	—	175	375	550	750	—
1813 IG	—	200	425	600	800	—
1813 GJ	—	225	475	700	900	—

KM# 466.3 8 REALES
27.0700 g., 0.9030 Silver .7859 oz. **Obv:** Bust of Ferdinand VII right **Rev:** Crowned shield of Castile and Leon **Note:** Mint mark: Crowned M.

Date	Mintage	VG	F	VF	XF	Unc
1814 GJ	—	50.00	100	150	250	—
1815 GJ	—	50.00	100	150	250	—
1816 GJ	—	50.00	100	150	250	—
1817 GJ	—	65.00	125	200	325	—
1818 GJ	—	50.00	100	150	250	—
1823 AJ	—	425	850	1,400	1,700	—
1824 AJ	—	275	550	900	1,250	—
1825 AJ	—	300	600	1,100	1,600	—
1830 AJ	—	400	800	1,600	2,000	—

KM# 492 1/2 ESCUDO
1.6900 g., 0.8750 Gold .0475 oz. **Obv:** Laureate head of Ferdinand VII right **Rev:** Crowned shield in collar of The Golden Fleece **Note:** Mint mark: Crowned M.

Date	Mintage	VG	F	VF	XF	Unc
1817 GJ	—	50.00	90.00	150	175	—

KM# 434 ESCUDO
3.3800 g., 0.8785 Gold .0951 oz. **Obv:** Bust of Charles IV right **Rev:** Crowned shield in Order chain **Note:** Mint mark: Crowned M.

Date	Mintage	VG	F	VF	XF	Unc
1801 FA	—	65.00	80.00	100	150	—
1807 FA	—	65.00	80.00	100	150	—

KM# 493 ESCUDO
3.3800 g., 0.8785 Gold .0951 oz. **Obv:** head of Ferdinand VII right **Rev:** Crowned shield in Order chain **Note:** Similar to 1/2 Escudo, KM#492. Mint mark: Crowned M.

Date	Mintage	VG	F	VF	XF	Unc
1817 GJ	—	150	300	500	800	—

KM# 435.1 2 ESCUDOS
6.7700 g., 0.8750 Gold .1905 oz. **Obv:** Bust of Charles IV right **Rev:** Crowned arms **Note:** Mint mark: Crowned M.

Date	Mintage	VG	F	VF	XF	Unc
1801 MF	—	125	150	175	235	—
1801 FM	—	150	200	350	500	—
1801 FA/MF	—	125	150	175	235	—
1801 FA	—	125	150	175	235	—
1802 FA	—	125	150	175	235	—
1803 FA	—	125	150	175	235	—
1804 FA	—	125	150	175	235	—
1805 FA	—	125	150	175	235	—
1806 FA	—	125	150	175	235	—
1807 FA	—	125	150	175	235	—
1807 AI	—	125	150	175	235	—
1808 AI	—	125	150	175	235	—
1808 FA	—	300	600	1,000	1,500	—

KM# 435.2 2 ESCUDOS
6.7700 g., 0.8750 Gold .1905 oz. **Obv:** Bust of Charles IV right **Rev:** Crowned arms **Note:** Mint mark: S, S/L.

Date	Mintage	VG	F	VF	XF	Unc
1801 CN	—	125	150	175	250	—
1802 CN	—	125	150	175	250	—
1803 CN	—	125	150	175	250	—
1804 CN	—	125	150	175	250	—
1805 CN	—	150	200	350	500	—
1806 CN	—	125	150	175	250	—
1807 CN	—	125	150	175	250	—
1808 CN	—	125	150	175	250	—

KM# 457 2 ESCUDOS
6.7700 g., 0.8750 Gold .1905 oz. **Obv:** Wide armored bust of Ferdinand VII right **Rev:** Crowned arms

Date	Mintage	F	VF	XF	Unc	BU
1808S CN	—	150	200	325	—	—
1809S CN	—	175	250	375	—	—

KM# 455 2 ESCUDOS
6.7700 g., 0.8750 Gold .1905 oz. **Ruler:** Ferdinand VII In exile until 1814 **Obv:** Wide armored, bare head of Ferdinand facing right

Date	Mintage	VG	F	VF	XF	Unc
1808S CN	—	125	150	200	325	—
1809S CN	—	135	175	250	375	—

KM# 456.1 2 ESCUDOS
6.7700 g., 0.8750 Gold .1905 oz. **Obv:** Draped bust of Ferdinand VII right **Rev:** Crowned arms

Date	Mintage	VG	F	VF	XF	Unc
1809S CN	—	150	250	400	650	—

KM# 468 2 ESCUDOS
6.7700 g., 0.8750 Gold .1905 oz. **Obv:** Laureate bust of Ferdinand VII right **Rev:** Crowned arms in collar of The Golden Fleece **Note:** Mint mark: Crowned C, large and small varieties exist.

Date	Mintage	VG	F	VF	XF	Unc
1811 CI	—	125	150	225	350	—
1812 CI	—	125	150	225	350	—
1813 CI	—	150	175	275	450	—
1813 CJ	—	125	150	225	350	—
1814 CJ	—	125	150	225	350	—

KM# 469 2 ESCUDOS
6.7700 g., 0.8750 Gold .1905 oz. **Obv:** Laureate head of Ferdinand VII right **Rev:** Crowned arms in collar of The Golden Fleece **Note:** Varieties in the bust design exist.

Date	Mintage	VG	F	VF	XF	Unc
1811C SF	—	500	1,000	1,750	2,500	—
1812C SF	—	450	900	1,400	2,000	—
1813C SF	—	350	750	1,200	1,750	—

KM# 456.2 2 ESCUDOS
6.7700 g., 0.8750 Gold .1905 oz. **Obv:** Draped bust of Ferdinand VII right **Rev:** Crowned arms **Note:** Mint mark: Crowned C.

Date	Mintage	VG	F	VF	XF	Unc
1811 CI	—	250	450	750	1,250	—

KM# 467 2 ESCUDOS
6.7700 g., 0.8750 Gold .1905 oz. **Obv:** Laureate armored bust of Ferdinand VII right **Rev:** Crowned arms in collar of The Golden Fleece **Note:** Mint mark: Crowned C.

Date	Mintage	VG	F	VF	XF	Unc
1811 CI	—	125	200	300	500	—

KM# 478 2 ESCUDOS
6.7700 g., 0.8750 Gold .1905 oz. **Obv:** Large laureate military bust of Ferdinand VII right **Rev:** Crowned arms in collar of The Golden Fleece **Note:** Mint mark: Crowned M.

Date	Mintage	VG	F	VF	XF	Unc
1812 IJ	—	175	350	600	950	—

KM# 480 2 ESCUDOS
6.7700 g., 0.8750 Gold .1905 oz. **Obv:** Small laureate military bust of Ferdinand VII right **Rev:** Crowned arms in collar of The Golden Fleece **Note:** Mint mark: Crowned M.

Date	Mintage	VG	F	VF	XF	Unc
1813 IG	—	250	500	900	1,400	—
1813 IJ	—	150	275	400	600	—
1813 GJ	—	125	150	225	350	—
1814 GJ	—	125	225	350	500	—

KM# 483.1 2 ESCUDOS
6.7700 g., 0.8750 Gold .1905 oz. **Obv:** Laureate head of Ferdinand VII right **Rev:** Crowned arms in collar of The Golden Fleece **Note:** Mint mark: Crowned M.

Date	Mintage	VG	F	VF	XF	Unc
1814 GJ	—	125	175	225	300	—
1815 GJ	—	135	225	350	500	—
1816 GJ	—	150	275	475	600	—
1817 GJ	—	150	275	475	600	—
1818 GJ	—	125	150	200	300	—
1819 GJ	—	125	150	200	300	—
1820 GJ	—	125	125	175	250	—
1822 AJ	—	150	275	475	600	—
1823 AJ	—	150	300	500	750	—
1824 AJ	—	125	125	175	250	—
1825 AJ	—	125	125	175	250	—
1826 AJ	—	135	175	250	350	—
1827 AJ	—	135	200	300	450	—
1828 AJ	—	135	225	350	500	—
1829 AJ	—	125	125	175	250	—
1830 AJ	—	125	125	175	250	—
1831 AJ	—	125	125	175	250	—
1832 AJ	—	125	125	175	250	—
1833 AJ	—	125	125	175	250	—

KM# 483.2 2 ESCUDOS
6.7700 g., 0.8750 Gold .1905 oz. **Obv:** Laureate head of Ferdinand VII right **Rev:** Crowned arms in collar of The Golden Fleece **Note:** Mint mark: S, S/L.

Date	Mintage	VG	F	VF	XF	Unc
1815 CJ	—	125	125	175	225	—
1816 CJ	—	125	125	175	225	—
1817 CJ	—	135	175	250	350	—
1818 CJ	—	125	125	175	225	—
1819 CJ	—	125	125	175	225	—
1820 CJ	—	125	125	175	225	—
1821 CJ	—	125	150	200	300	—
1824 J	—	400	700	1,250	1,850	—
1824 JB	—	135	175	275	400	—
1825 JB	—	125	125	175	225	—
1826 JB	—	125	125	175	225	—
1827 JB	—	125	125	175	225	—
1828 JB	—	135	175	275	400	—
1829 JB	—	135	175	275	400	—
1830 JB	—	135	225	350	500	—
1831 JB	—	125	125	175	225	—
1832 JB	—	125	125	175	225	—
1833 JB	—	125	125	175	225	—

KM# 436.1 4 ESCUDOS
13.5400 g., 0.8750 Gold .3809 oz. **Obv:** Bust of Charles IV right **Rev:** Crowned arms in collar of The Golden Fleece **Note:** Mint mark: Crowned M.

Date	Mintage	VG	F	VF	XF	Unc
1801 FA	—	200	250	350	500	—
1801 MF	—	300	600	850	1,250	—
1803 FA	—	225	300	425	600	—

KM# 436.2 4 ESCUDOS
13.5400 g., 0.8750 Gold .3809 oz. **Obv:** Bust of Charles IV right **Rev:** Crowned arms in collar of The Golden Fleece **Note:** Mint mark: S, S/L.

Date	Mintage	VG	F	VF	XF	Unc
1801 C	—	1,000	2,200	3,000	4,500	—
1808 C	—	1,000	2,200	3,000	4,500	—

KM# 484 4 ESCUDOS
13.5400 g., 0.8750 Gold .3809 oz. **Obv:** Bust of Ferdinand VII right **Rev:** Crowned arms in collar of The Golden Fleece **Note:** Mint mark: Crowned M.

Date	Mintage	VG	F	VF	XF	Unc
1814 GJ	—	225	400	550	800	—
1815 GJ	—	225	350	500	700	—
1816 GJ	—	300	600	800	1,200	—
1818 GJ	—	225	400	550	800	—
1819 GJ	—	225	350	500	700	—
1820 GJ	—	200	250	350	500	—
1824 AI	—	750	1,500	2,100	3,000	—

KM# 437.1 8 ESCUDOS
27.0700 g., 0.8750 Gold .7616 oz. **Obv:** Older bust of Charles IV right **Rev:** Crowned arms in Order of the Golden Fleece collar **Note:** Mint mark: Crowned M.

Date	Mintage	VG	F	VF	XF	Unc
1802 FA	—	400	650	950	1,450	—
1803 FA	—	900	1,700	2,500	4,000	—
1805 FA	—	550	1,100	1,600	2,600	—

KM# 470 8 ESCUDOS
27.0700 g., 0.8750 Gold .7616 oz. **Obv:** Laureate armored bust of Ferdinand VII right **Rev:** Crowned arms in Order of the Golden Fleece collar **Note:** Mint mark: Crowned C.

Date	Mintage	VG	F	VF	XF	Unc
1811 CI	—	550	850	2,500	4,250	—

KM# 481 8 ESCUDOS
27.0700 g., 0.8750 Gold .7616 oz. **Obv:** Laureate head of Ferdinand VII right **Rev:** Crowned arms in Order of the Golden Fleece collar

Date	Mintage	VG	F	VF	XF	Unc
1813C SF	—	3,000	7,000	10,000	15,000	—
1814C SF	—	3,500	7,500	11,000	—	—

Note: Stack's CICF sale 4-89, XF realized $16,500

KM# 485 8 ESCUDOS
27.0700 g., 0.8750 Gold .7616 oz. **Obv:** Laureate head of Ferdinand VII right **Rev:** Crowned shield in order chain **Note:** Mint mark: Crowned M.

Date	Mintage	VG	F	VF	XF	Unc
1814 GJ	—	1,000	2,000	2,800	4,000	—
1816 GJ	—	1,500	3,000	4,200	6,000	—
1817 GJ	—	1,100	2,250	3,100	4,500	—
1819 GJ	—	1,800	3,500	5,000	7,500	—
1820 GJ	—	450	750	1,150	1,650	—

DE VELLON COINAGE

1808-1850

KM# 553 REAL
1.3540 g., 0.9030 Silver .0393 oz. **Obv:** Head of Joseph Napoleon left **Rev:** Crowned shield **Note:** Mint Mark: Crowned M.

Date	Mintage	VG	F	VF	XF	Unc
1812 AI	—	17.50	45.00	135	250	—
1813 RN	—	25.00	60.00	160	350	—

KM# 550 2 REALES
2.7080 g., 0.9030 Silver .0786 oz. **Obv:** Head of Joseph Napoleon left **Rev:** Crowned shield **Note:** Mint Mark: Crowned M.

Date	Mintage	VG	F	VF	XF	Unc
1811 AI	—	40.00	100	200	300	—
1812 AI	—	35.00	80.00	160	240	—
1812 RN	—	25.00	60.00	120	180	—
1813 RN	—	60.00	150	300	450	—

KM# 540.1 4 REALES

5.4160 g., 0.9030 Silver .1572 oz. **Obv:** Head of Joseph Napoleon left **Note:** Mint Mark: Crowned M.

Date	Mintage	VG	F	VF	XF	Unc
1808 AI	—	25.00	65.00	130	200	—
1809 AI	—	10.00	17.50	30.00	45.00	—
1810 AI	—	7.50	12.50	22.50	35.00	—
1811 AI	—	6.50	10.00	20.00	30.00	—
1811 RS	—	20.00	50.00	100	150	—
1812 AI	—	7.50	12.50	22.50	35.00	—
1812 RS	—	25.00	40.00	80.00	120	—
1812 RN	—	10.00	17.50	30.00	45.00	—
1813 RN	—	12.50	25.00	47.50	70.00	—

KM# 540.2 4 REALES

5.4160 g., 0.9030 Silver .1572 oz. **Obv:** Head of Joseph Napoleon left **Rev:** Crowned shield **Note:** Mint mark: S, S/L.

Date	Mintage	VG	F	VF	XF	Unc
1810 LA	—	30.00	70.00	140	210	—
1812 LA	—	12.50	30.00	60.00	90.00	—

KM# 562.2 4 REALES

5.4160 g., 0.9030 Silver .1572 oz. **Obv:** Head of Ferdinand VII right **Rev:** Crowned shield **Note:** Mint Mark: Crowned M.

Date	Mintage	VG	F	VF	XF	Unc
1822 SR	—	12.50	27.50	55.00	85.00	—
1823 SR	—	15.00	35.00	65.00	100	—

KM# 562.1 4 REALES

5.4160 g., 0.9030 Silver .1572 oz. **Obv:** Head of Ferdinand VII right **Rev:** Crowned shield **Note:** Mint mark: •B•.

Date	Mintage	VG	F	VF	XF	Unc
1822 SP	—	10.00	20.00	32.50	50.00	—
1823 SP	—	12.50	30.00	60.00	90.00	—

KM# 562.3 4 REALES

5.4160 g., 0.9030 Silver .1572 oz. **Obv:** Head of Ferdinand VII right **Rev:** Crowned shield **Note:** Mint mark: S.

Date	Mintage	VG	F	VF	XF	Unc
1823 RD	—	12.50	27.50	55.00	85.00	—

KM# 567 4 REALES

5.4160 g., 0.9030 Silver .1572 oz. **Obv:** Small bare head draped bust of Ferdinand VII right **Rev:** Crowned shield **Note:** Mint mark: V, VAL.

Date	Mintage	VG	F	VF	XF	Unc
1823 R Spanish arms	—	10.00	20.00	35.00	55.00	—

KM# 541 10 REALES

13.5400 g., 0.9030 Silver .3931 oz. **Obv:** Head of Joseph Napoleon left **Rev:** Crowned shield **Note:** Mint Mark: Crowned M.

Date	Mintage	VG	F	VF	XF	Unc
1809 AI	—	200	500	1,000	1,500	—
1810 AI	—	120	300	600	900	—
1811 AI	58,000	60.00	150	300	475	—
1812 AI	490,000	40.00	100	225	350	—
1812 RN	Inc. above	40.00	100	225	350	—
1813 RN	135,000	70.00	175	400	600	—

KM# 560.1 10 REALES

13.5400 g., 0.9030 Silver .3931 oz. **Obv:** Bust of Ferdinand VII right **Rev:** RESELLADO 10 RS in sprays **Note:** Mint mark: Bo.

Date	Mintage	VG	F	VF	XF	Unc
1821 UG	—	15.00	35.00	70.00	200	—

KM# 560.2 10 REALES

13.5400 g., 0.9030 Silver .3931 oz. **Obv:** Bust of Ferdinand VII right **Rev:** RESELLADO 10 Rs in sprays **Note:** Mint Mark: Crowned M.

Date	Mintage	VG	F	VF	XF	Unc
1821 SR	—	10.00	17.50	30.00	175	—

KM# 560.3 10 REALES

13.5400 g., 0.9030 Silver .3931 oz. **Obv:** Bust of Ferdinand VII right **Rev:** RESEKKADI 19 Rs ub sprays **Note:** Mint mark: Sr.

Date	Mintage	VG	F	VF	XF	Unc
1821 LT	—	15.00	35.00	70.00	175	—

KM# 560.4 10 REALES

13.5400 g., 0.9030 Silver .3931 oz. **Obv:** Bust of Ferdinand VII right **Rev:** RESELLADO 10 Rs in sprays **Note:** Mint mark: S, S/L.

Date	Mintage	VG	F	VF	XF	Unc
1821 RD	—	17.50	40.00	80.00	250	—

KM# 585.1 10 REALES

13.5400 g., 0.9030 Silver .3931 oz. **Obv:** Head of Isabel II right **Rev:** Crownes shield in order chain **Note:** Mint Mark: Crowned M.

Date	Mintage	VG	F	VF	XF	Unc
1840 CL	—	70.00	175	350	525	—
1840 DG	—	325	900	1,800	2,750	—
1841 CL	—	65.00	165	325	500	—
1842 CL	—	70.00	175	350	525	—
1843 CL	—	55.00	140	275	425	—
1844 CL	—	70.00	175	350	525	—
1845 CL	—	100	250	500	750	—

KM# 585.2 10 REALES

13.5400 g., 0.9030 Silver .3931 oz. **Obv:** Head of Isabel II right **Rev:** Crowned shield in order chain **Note:** Mint mark: S, S/L.

Date	Mintage	VG	F	VF	XF	Unc
1841 RD	—	75.00	150	300	600	—
1842 RD	—	75.00	150	300	600	—
1843 RD	—	75.00	150	300	600	—

KM# 551.2 20 REALES

27.0800 g., 0.9030 Silver .7863 oz. **Obv:** Head of Joseph Napoleon left **Rev:** Crowned shield **Note:** Mint Mark: Crowned M.

Date	Mintage	VG	F	VF	XF	Unc
1809 AI	700,000	35.00	80.00	160	250	—
1811 AI	460,000	30.00	75.00	150	225	—
1812 AI	250,000	65.00	140	275	425	—
1813 RN	68,000	100	240	480	725	—

KM# 551.1 20 REALES

27.0800 g., 0.9030 Silver .7863 oz. **Obv:** Head of Joseph Napoleon left **Rev:** Crowned shield **Note:** Mint mark: B, BA.

Date	Mintage	VG	F	VF	XF	Unc
1811	—	75.00	180	360	550	—
1812	—	110	275	550	850	—

KM# 551.3 20 REALES

27.0800 g., 0.9030 Silver .7863 oz. **Obv:** Head of Joseph Napoleon left **Rev:** Crowned shield **Note:** Mint mark: S, S/L.

Date	Mintage	VG	F	VF	XF	Unc
1812 LA	13,000	120	300	600	900	—

KM# 561 20 REALES

27.0800 g., 0.9030 Silver .7863 oz. **Obv:** Head of Ferdinand VII right **Rev:** Crowned shield between pillars of Heronles **Note:** Smaller legends; Mint Mark: Crowned M.

Date	Mintage	VG	F	VF	XF	Unc
1821 SR	—	400	1,000	2,000	3,000	—
1822 SR	—	25.00	50.00	100	175	—
1823 SR	—	60.00	125	200	300	—

KM# 563.1 20 REALES

27.0800 g., 0.9030 Silver .7863 oz. **Obv:** Head of Ferdinand VII right **Rev:** Crowned shield between pillars of Heronles **Note:** Large legends. Mint mark: B, BA.

Date	Mintage	VG	F	VF	XF	Unc
1822 SP	—	120	250	400	850	—
1823 SP	—	40.00	80.00	150	300	—

KM# 563.2 20 REALES

27.0800 g., 0.9030 Silver .7863 oz. **Obv:** Head of Ferdinand VII right **Rev:** Crowned shield between pillars of Heronles **Note:** Large legends. Mint mark: S, S/L.

Date	Mintage	VG	F	VF	XF	Unc
1822 RD	—	40.00	100	150	300	—
1823 RD	—	50.00	125	225	400	—

KM# 575 20 REALES

27.0800 g., 0.9030 Silver .7863 oz. **Obv:** Laureate head of Ferdinand VII right **Rev:** Crowned shield in order chain **Note:** Mint mark: S, S/L.

Date	Mintage	VG	F	VF	XF	Unc
1833 DG	—	400	1,000	2,000	3,000	—

KM# 576 20 REALES

27.0800 g., 0.9030 Silver .7863 oz. **Obv:** Legend ends: DIOS, head of Isabel II right **Rev:** Crowned arms in order chain

Date	Mintage	VG	F	VF	XF	Unc
1834 DG	—	700	1,700	3,400	5,400	—
1834 NC	4,769	200	500	1,000	1,500	—
1835 CR	13,000	160	400	800	1,200	—
1836 CR	48,000	125	300	600	1,000	—

KM# 579.1 20 REALES
27.0800 g., 0.9030 Silver .7863 oz. **Obv:** Head of Isabel II right **Rev:** Crowned arms in order chain

Date	Mintage	VG	F	VF	XF	Unc
1837 CR	115,000	70.00	175	400	750	—
1838 CL	231,000	65.00	165	400	750	—
1839 CL	74,000	400	1,000	2,000	3,000	—
1840 CL	6,012	975	2,450	4,800	7,500	—
1847 DG	—	800	1,900	3,800	5,800	—
1848 CL	67,000	50.00	125	350	675	—
1849 CL	120,000	70.00	175	400	750	—
1850 DG	—	950	2,400	4,750	7,150	—

KM# 579.2 20 REALES
27.0800 g., 0.9030 Silver .7863 oz. **Obv:** Legend ends: DIOS, head of Isabel II right **Rev:** Crowned arms in order chain **Note:** Mint mark: S, S/L.

Date	Mintage	VG	F	VF	XF	Unc
1842 RD	12,000	225	500	1,000	1,500	—

KM# 542 80 REALES
6.7700 g., 0.8750 Gold .1905 oz. **Obv:** Head of Joseph Napoleon left **Rev:** Crowned arms in order chain **Note:** Mint Mark: Crowned M.

Date	Mintage	VG	F	VF	XF	Unc
1809 AI	—	100	150	250	375	—
1810 AI	—	200	500	1,000	1,500	—

KM# 552 80 REALES
6.7700 g., 0.8750 Gold .1905 oz. **Obv:** Laureate head of Joseph Napoleon left **Rev:** Crowned arms in order chain **Note:** Mint Mark: Crowned M.

Date	Mintage	VG	F	VF	XF	Unc
1811 AI	440,000	100	150	275	450	—
1812/1 AI	—	100	200	400	650	—
1812 AI	238,000	100	200	400	650	—
1813 RN	161,000	125	250	450	750	—

KM# 564.2 80 REALES
6.7700 g., 0.8750 Gold .1905 oz. **Obv:** Head of Ferdinand VII right **Rev:** Crowned arms in order chain **Note:** Mint Mark: Crowned M.

Date	Mintage	VG	F	VF	XF	Unc
1822 SR	—	100	125	175	250	—
1823 SR	—	100	135	225	375	—

KM# 564.1 80 REALES
6.7700 g., 0.8750 Gold .1905 oz. **Obv:** Head of Ferdinand VII right **Rev:** Crowned arms in order chain **Note:** Mint mark: B, BA.

Date	Mintage	VG	F	VF	XF	Unc
1822 SP	—	125	250	500	800	—
1823 SP	—	100	125	200	300	—

KM# 564.3 80 REALES
6.7700 g., 0.8750 Gold .1905 oz. **Obv:** Head of Ferdinand VII right **Rev:** Crowned arms in order chain **Note:** Mint mark: S, S/L.

Date	Mintage	VG	F	VF	XF	Unc
1823 RD	—	140	300	600	900	—

KM# 578.2 80 REALES
6.7700 g., 0.8750 Gold .1905 oz. **Obv:** Head of Isabel II right **Obv. Legend:** ...CONST **Rev:** Crowned shield in order chain **Note:** Mint Mark: Crowned M.

Date	Mintage	VG	F	VF	XF	Unc
1834 CR	—	100	120	145	200	—
1835 CR	—	100	120	135	190	—
1836 CL	—	100	125	250	400	—
1836 CR	—	120	265	525	800	—
1837 CR	—	135	320	625	950	—
1838 CL	—	130	300	600	900	—
1839 CL	—	135	325	650	1,000	—
1840 CL	—	110	200	400	600	—
1841 CL	—	100	165	325	500	—
1842 CL	—	175	300	550	850	—
1843 CL	—	100	120	145	200	—
1844 CL	—	100	125	200	300	—
1845 CL	—	100	120	135	190	—
1846 CL	—	100	150	300	450	—
1847 CL	—	110	200	400	600	—
1848 CL	—	100	150	300	450	—
1849 CL	—	200	500	1,000	1,500	—

KM# 577.2 80 REALES
6.7700 g., 0.8750 Gold .1905 oz. **Obv:** Head of Isabel II right **Obv. Legend:** ...DIOS **Rev:** Crowned shield in order chain **Note:** Mint Mark: Crowned M.

Date	Mintage	VG	F	VF	XF	Unc
1834 CR	—	100	120	145	200	—
1835 CR	—	100	120	145	200	—
1836 CL	—	100	125	200	325	—
1836 CR	—	110	150	300	500	—

KM# 577.3 80 REALES
6.7700 g., 0.8750 Gold .1905 oz. **Obv:** Head of Isabel II right **Obv. Legend:** ...DIOS **Rev:** Crowned shield in order chain **Note:** Mint mark: S, S/L.

Date	Mintage	VG	F	VF	XF	Unc
1835 DR	—	125	215	425	650	—
1835 RD	—	110	175	350	525	—
1836 DR	—	110	175	350	525	—
1837 DR	—	110	175	350	525	—

KM# 578.3 80 REALES
6.7700 g., 0.8750 Gold .1905 oz. **Obv:** Head of Isabel II right **Obv. Legend:** ...CONST **Rev:** Crowned shield in order chain **Note:** Mint mark: S, S/L.

Date	Mintage	VG	F	VF	XF	Unc
1835 DR	—	110	220	425	650	—
1835 RD	—	100	125	250	375	—
1836 DR	—	100	175	350	525	—
1837 DR	—	100	170	375	550	—
1838 DR	—	130	300	600	900	—
1838 RD	—	165	400	800	1,200	—
1839 RD	—	100	150	300	475	—
1840 RD	—	100	140	275	425	—
1841 RD	—	100	150	300	450	—
1842 RD	—	100	140	275	425	—
1843 RD	—	100	150	300	450	—
1844 RD	—	100	150	300	450	—
1845 RD	—	100	125	225	350	—
1846 RD	—	100	175	350	525	—
1847 RD	—	100	165	325	500	—
1848 RD	—	200	500	1,000	1,600	—

KM# 578.1 80 REALES
6.7700 g., 0.8750 Gold .1905 oz. **Obv:** Head of Isabel II right **Obv. Legend:** ...CONST **Rev:** Crowned shield in order chain **Note:** Mint mark: B, BA.

Date	Mintage	VG	F	VF	XF	Unc
1836 PS	—	400	700	1,500	2,200	—
1838 PS	—	110	200	400	600	—
1839 PS	—	100	125	225	350	—
1840 PS	—	100	120	135	190	—
1841 PS	—	100	120	135	190	—
1842 CC	—	100	125	200	300	—
1842 PS	—	600	1,500	3,000	4,500	—
1843 CC	—	450	750	1,650	2,500	—
1843 PS	—	325	800	1,600	2,400	—
1844 PS	—	100	125	200	300	—
1845 PS	—	100	125	200	300	—
1846 PS	—	100	120	145	200	—
1847 PS	—	100	125	210	325	—
1848 PS	—	150	325	625	950	—

KM# 577.1 80 REALES
6.7700 g., 0.8750 Gold .1905 oz. **Obv:** Legend ends: DIOS, head of Isabel II right **Rev:** Crowned shield in order chain **Note:** Mint mark: B, B/A.

Date	Mintage	VG	F	VF	XF	Unc
1836 PS	—	400	1,000	2,000	3,000	—

KM# 580 80 REALES
6.7700 g., 0.8750 Gold .1905 oz. **Obv:** Head of Isabel II right **Obv. Legend:** ...CONSTITUCION **Rev:** Crowned shield in order chain **Note:** Mint mark: B, BA.

Date	Mintage	VG	F	VF	XF	Unc
1837 PS	—	110	250	500	750	—
1838 PS	—	100	125	225	350	—

KM# 565 160 REALES
13.5400 g., 0.8750 Gold .3809 oz. **Obv:** Head of Ferdinand VII right **Rev:** Crowned arms in order chain **Note:** Mint Mark: Crowned M.

Date	Mintage	VG	F	VF	XF	Unc
1822 SR	—	250	400	700	1,150	—

KM# 545 320 REALES
27.0700 g., 0.8750 Gold .7616 oz. **Obv:** Laureate head of Joseph Napoleon left **Rev:** Crowned arms in order chain **Note:** Mint Mark: Crowned M.

Date	Mintage	VG	F	VF	XF	Unc
1810 AI	64,000	1,500	3,250	6,500	10,000	—
1810 RS	Inc. above	1,750	4,000	7,000	11,500	—
1812 RS	60,000	1,500	3,000	6,000	9,500	—

KM# 566 320 REALES
27.0700 g., 0.8750 Gold .7616 oz. **Obv:** Head of Ferdinand VII right **Rev:** Crowned arms in order chain **Note:** Mint Mark: Crowned M.

Date	Mintage	VG	F	VF	XF	Unc
1822 SR	—	600	1,300	2,750	4,750	—
1823 SR	—	1,100	2,400	5,000	7,500	—

DECIMAL COINAGE

Real System

100 Centimos = 10 Decimos = 1 Real

KM# 597 1/20 REAL
Copper **Note:** Mint Mark: Aqueduct.

Date	Mintage	VG	F	VF	XF	Unc
1852	—	5.00	12.50	35.00	70.00	—
1853	—	2.00	3.50	7.50	12.50	—

KM# 602 5 CENTIMOS
Copper **Note:** Mint Mark: Aqueduct.

Date	Mintage	VG	F	VF	XF	Unc
1854	—	90.00	225	400	650	—
1855	—	5.00	12.50	22.50	35.00	—
1856	—	2.00	4.50	7.50	12.50	—
1857	—	2.25	5.50	9.00	15.00	—
1858	—	10.00	25.00	40.00	70.00	—
1859	—	2.00	4.50	7.50	12.50	—
1860	—	2.50	6.50	12.00	20.00	—
1861	—	3.50	9.00	15.00	25.00	—
1862	—	3.50	9.00	15.00	25.00	—
1863	—	2.50	6.50	12.00	20.00	—
1864	—	5.00	12.50	22.50	35.00	—

KM# 590 1/10 REAL
Copper **Note:** Mint Mark: Aqueduct.

Date	Mintage	VG	F	VF	XF	Unc
1850	—	3.00	7.50	12.50	28.00	—
1851	—	10.00	22.50	40.00	65.00	—
1852	—	3.00	7.50	30.00	50.00	—
1853	—	2.50	4.00	7.00	22.00	—

KM# 603 10 CENTIMOS
Copper **Note:** Mint Mark: Aqueduct.

Date	Mintage	VG	F	VF	XF	Unc
1854	—	100	250	450	750	—
1855	—	5.00	12.50	21.00	35.00	—
1856	—	2.75	7.00	12.00	20.00	—
1857	—	2.00	4.50	7.50	12.50	—
1858	—	5.00	12.50	21.00	35.00	—
1859	—	2.00	4.50	7.50	12.50	—
1860	—	2.00	4.50	7.50	12.50	—
1861	—	2.50	6.50	11.00	18.00	—
1862	—	2.75	7.00	12.00	20.00	—
1863	—	3.50	9.00	15.00	25.00	—
1864	—	8.50	21.00	35.00	60.00	—

KM# 601 1/5 REAL
Copper **Note:** Mint Mark: Aqueduct.

Date	Mintage	VG	F	VF	XF	Unc
1853	—	12.50	28.00	50.00	150	350

KM# 615.2 25 CENTIMOS
Copper **Ruler:** Isabel II **Note:** Mint Mark: Aqueduct.

Date	Mintage	VG	F	VF	XF	Unc
1854	—	2.75	7.00	14.00	25.00	—
1855	—	2.00	4.50	8.00	15.00	—
1856	—	2.00	4.50	8.00	15.00	—
1857	—	2.25	5.50	10.00	18.00	—
1858	—	2.00	4.50	8.00	15.00	—
1859	—	2.00	4.50	8.00	15.00	—
1860	—	2.00	4.50	8.00	15.00	—
1861	—	2.00	4.50	8.00	15.00	—
1862	—	2.00	4.50	8.00	15.00	—
1863	—	2.00	4.50	8.00	15.00	—
1864	—	2.50	6.50	12.00	20.00	—

KM# 615.1 25 CENTIMOS
Copper **Ruler:** Isabel II **Note:** Mint mark: 8-pointed star.

Date	Mintage	VG	F	VF	XF	Unc
1863BA	—	50.00	125	200	350	—
1864BA	—	17.50	40.00	70.00	120	—

KM# 591.3 1/2 REAL
Copper **Note:** Mint Mark: Aqueduct.

Date	Mintage	VG	F	VF	XF	Unc
1848	—	75.00	150	400	700	—
1849	—	75.00	150	400	700	—
1850	—	5.00	10.00	25.00	75.00	—
1851	—	5.00	10.00	25.00	75.00	—
1852	—	5.00	10.00	25.00	75.00	—
1853	—	5.00	10.00	25.00	75.00	—

KM# 591.2 1/2 REAL
Copper **Note:** Mint mark: 6-pointed star.

Date	Mintage	VG	F	VF	XF	Unc
1848 DG	—	150	375	950	1,700	—
1848	—	5.00	10.00	27.50	60.00	—

KM# 591.1 1/2 REAL
Copper **Note:** Similar to 1/5 Real, KM#601. Mint mark: 4-pointed star.

Date	Mintage	VG	F	VF	XF	Unc
1850	—	17.50	40.00	90.00	200	—

KM# 598.2 REAL
1.3146 g., 0.9000 Silver .0380 oz. **Note:** Mint mark: 6-pointed star.

Date	Mintage	VG	F	VF	XF	Unc
1852	—	3.00	7.00	15.00	25.00	—
1853	—	3.00	7.00	15.00	25.00	—

KM# 598.3 REAL
1.3146 g., 0.9000 Silver .0380 oz. **Note:** Mint mark: 7-pointed star.

Date	Mintage	VG	F	VF	XF	Unc
1852	—	3.00	7.00	15.00	25.00	—
1853	—	3.00	7.00	15.00	25.00	—
1854	—	3.00	7.00	15.00	25.00	—
1855	—	3.00	10.00	18.00	28.00	—

KM# 598.1 REAL
1.3146 g., 0.9000 Silver .0380 oz. **Note:** Mint mark: 8-pointed star.

Date	Mintage	VG	F	VF	XF	Unc
1852	—	4.00	10.00	18.00	28.00	—
1853	—	3.00	7.00	15.00	25.00	—
1854	—	3.00	7.00	15.00	25.00	—
1855	—	4.00	10.00	18.00	28.00	—

KM# 606.1 REAL
1.3146 g., 0.9000 Silver .0380 oz. **Note:** Mint mark: 8-pointed star.

Date	Mintage	VG	F	VF	XF	Unc
1857	—	3.00	7.00	15.00	25.00	—
1858	—	3.00	10.00	18.00	30.00	—
1859	—	3.00	12.00	25.00	40.00	—
1860/59	—	3.00	7.00	15.00	25.00	—
1860	—	3.00	7.00	15.00	25.00	—
1861	—	3.00	7.00	15.00	25.00	—
1862	—	3.00	10.00	18.00	30.00	—
1863	—	3.00	12.00	25.00	40.00	—

KM# 606.3 REAL
1.3146 g., 0.9000 Silver .0380 oz. **Note:** Mint mark: 7-pointed star.

Date	Mintage	VG	F	VF	XF	Unc
1857	—	20.00	65.00	100	140	—
1858	—	15.00	35.00	55.00	100	—
1859	—	15.00	35.00	55.00	100	—
1860	—	7.00	25.00	30.00	55.00	—
1862	—	5.00	20.00	25.00	40.00	—
1863	—	4.00	18.00	20.00	35.00	—
1864	—	4.00	18.00	20.00	35.00	—

KM# 606.2 REAL
1.3146 g., 0.9000 Silver .0380 oz. **Note:** Mint mark: 6-pointed star.

Date	Mintage	VG	F	VF	XF	Unc
1857	—	5.00	10.00	20.00	28.00	—
1859	—	3.00	7.00	15.00	25.00	—
1860	—	3.00	7.00	15.00	25.00	—
1861	—	3.00	7.00	15.00	30.00	—
1862	—	3.00	7.00	15.00	30.00	—
1863	—	3.00	7.00	15.00	25.00	—
1864	—	3.00	7.00	15.00	25.00	—

KM# 599.2 2 REALES
2.6291 g., 0.9000 Silver .0761 oz. **Note:** Mint mark: 6-pointed star.

Date	Mintage	VG	F	VF	XF	Unc
1852	—	10.00	25.00	40.00	70.00	—
1853	—	8.00	18.00	30.00	55.00	—
1854	—	6.00	15.00	25.00	50.00	—
1855	—	5.00	12.50	22.00	45.00	—

KM# 599.3 2 REALES
2.6291 g., 0.9000 Silver .0761 oz. **Note:** Mint mark: 7-pointed star.

Date	Mintage	VG	F	VF	XF	Unc
1852	—	5.00	12.50	30.00	50.00	—
1853	—	3.00	7.50	25.00	45.00	—
1854	—	5.00	12.50	30.00	50.00	—
1855	—	5.00	12.50	30.00	50.00	—

KM# 599.1 2 REALES
2.6291 g., 0.9000 Silver .0761 oz. **Note:** Mint mark: 8-pointed star.

Date	Mintage	VG	F	VF	XF	Unc
1852	—	12.50	21.00	35.00	50.00	—
1853	—	5.00	12.50	17.50	32.00	—
1854	—	18.00	45.00	75.00	110	—
1855	—	12.50	21.00	35.00	50.00	—

KM# 607.1 2 REALES
2.6291 g., 0.9000 Silver .0761 oz. **Note:** Mint mark: 8-pointed star.

Date	Mintage	VG	F	VF	XF	Unc
1857	—	4.25	10.00	17.50	28.00	—
1858	—	10.00	25.00	60.00	120	—
1860	—	7.50	19.00	30.00	50.00	—
1861	—	7.50	19.00	30.00	50.00	—

KM# 607.3 2 REALES
2.6291 g., 0.9000 Silver .0761 oz. **Note:** Mint mark: 7-pointed star.

Date	Mintage	VG	F	VF	XF	Unc
1857	—	15.00	30.00	60.00	125	—
1858	—	25.00	45.00	90.00	150	—
1859	—	30.00	60.00	125	225	—
1860	—	30.00	60.00	125	225	—
1861	—	15.00	30.00	60.00	125	—
1863	—	15.00	25.00	45.00	100	—
1864	—	15.00	30.00	60.00	125	—

KM# 607.2 2 REALES
2.6291 g., 0.9000 Silver .0761 oz. **Note:** Mint mark: 6-pointed star.

Date	Mintage	VG	F	VF	XF	Unc
1857	—	15.00	35.00	90.00	175	—
1859	—	7.00	18.00	40.00	75.00	—
1860	—	9.00	20.00	45.00	100	—
1861	—	7.00	18.00	40.00	75.00	—
1862	—	6.00	15.00	40.00	100	—
1864	—	15.00	35.00	75.00	175	—

KM# 600.2 4 REALES
5.2582 g., 0.9000 Silver .1521 oz. **Note:** Mint mark: 6-pointed star.

Date	Mintage	VG	F	VF	XF	Unc
1852	—	5.00	10.00	20.00	32.00	—
1853	—	16.00	40.00	65.00	95.00	—
1854	—	7.50	19.00	30.00	50.00	—
1855	—	15.00	37.50	60.00	90.00	—

KM# 600.3 4 REALES
5.2582 g., 0.9000 Silver .1521 oz. **Note:** Mint mark: 7-pointed star.

Date	Mintage	VG	F	VF	XF	Unc
1852	—	5.00	12.50	22.00	35.00	—
1853	—	5.00	12.50	22.00	35.00	—
1854	—	4.25	10.00	17.50	28.00	—
1855	—	12.50	21.00	35.00	50.00	—

KM# 600.1 4 REALES
5.2582 g., 0.9000 Silver .1521 oz. **Note:** Mint mark: 8-pointed star.

Date	Mintage	VG	F	VF	XF	Unc
1852	—	7.50	15.00	35.00	55.00	—
1853	—	10.00	25.00	40.00	60.00	—
1854	—	9.25	22.50	37.50	57.50	—
1855	—	60.00	150	250	350	—

KM# 608.2 4 REALES
5.2582 g., 0.9000 Silver .1521 oz. **Note:** Mint mark: 6-pointed star.

Date	Mintage	VG	F	VF	XF	Unc
1856	—	12.50	25.00	50.00	80.00	—
1857	—	7.50	15.00	30.00	50.00	—
1858	—	6.00	12.50	25.00	38.00	—
1859	—	5.00	10.00	22.00	35.00	—
1860	—	32.50	85.00	140	200	—
1861	—	7.50	15.00	30.00	50.00	—
1862	—	5.00	10.00	20.00	32.00	—
1863	—	5.00	10.00	20.00	32.00	—
1864	—	20.00	50.00	85.00	120	—

KM# 608.3 4 REALES
5.2582 g., 0.9000 Silver .1521 oz. **Note:** Mint Mark: 7-pointed star.

Date	Mintage	VG	F	VF	XF	Unc
1857	—	30.00	70.00	120	175	—
1858	—	40.00	100	175	250	—
1859	—	30.00	70.00	120	175	—
1860	—	10.00	25.00	40.00	60.00	—
1861	—	12.50	30.00	50.00	80.00	—
1862	—	15.00	37.50	60.00	90.00	—
1863	—	12.50	21.00	35.00	50.00	—
1864	—	10.00	25.00	40.00	60.00	—

KM# 608.1 4 REALES
5.2582 g., 0.9000 Silver .1521 oz. **Note:** Mint mark: 8-pointed star.

Date	Mintage	VG	F	VF	XF	Unc
1857	—	65.00	160	275	400	—
1858	—	35.00	80.00	125	250	—
1859	—	10.00	25.00	40.00	60.00	—
1860	—	10.00	25.00	40.00	60.00	—
1861	—	7.50	15.00	30.00	50.00	—
1862	—	60.00	150	250	350	—
1864	—	65.00	155	260	375	—

KM# 595.2 10 REALES
13.1455 g., 0.9000 Silver .3804 oz. **Note:** Mint mark: 6-pointed star.

Date	Mintage	VG	F	VF	XF	Unc
1851	—	25.00	60.00	100	160	—
1852	—	10.00	20.00	40.00	65.00	—
1853	—	10.00	20.00	40.00	65.00	—
1854	—	14.00	35.00	60.00	85.00	—
1855	—	50.00	125	200	300	—

KM# 595.3 10 REALES
13.1455 g., 0.9000 Silver .3804 oz. **Note:** Mint mark: 7-pointed star.

Date	Mintage	VG	F	VF	XF	Unc
1851	—	75.00	180	300	450	—
1852	—	7.50	20.00	35.00	55.00	—
1853	—	10.00	25.00	40.00	65.00	—
1854	—	10.00	25.00	40.00	65.00	—
1855	—	16.00	40.00	70.00	110	—
1856	—	275	750	1,300	1,800	—

KM# 595.1 10 REALES
13.1455 g., 0.9000 Silver .3804 oz. **Note:** Similar to 4 Reales, KM#600.1. Mint mark: 8-pointed star.

Date	Mintage	VG	F	VF	XF	Unc
1851	—	150	375	625	900	—
1852	—	25.00	60.00	100	160	—
1853	—	10.00	25.00	40.00	65.00	—
1854	—	15.00	37.50	60.00	100	—
1855	—	30.00	70.00	120	180	—

KM# 611.3 10 REALES
13.1455 g., 0.9000 Silver .3804 oz. **Note:** Mint mark: 7-pointed star.

Date	Mintage	VG	F	VF	XF	Unc
1857	—	65.00	165	275	400	—
1858	—	55.00	135	225	325	—
1859	—	60.00	150	250	350	—
1860	—	100	250	425	600	—
1861	—	25.00	60.00	100	160	—
1863	—	40.00	100	175	250	—
1864	—	125	325	550	800	—

KM# 611.2 10 REALES
13.1455 g., 0.9000 Silver .3804 oz. **Note:** Mint mark: 6-pointed star.

Date	Mintage	VG	F	VF	XF	Unc
1857	—	32.50	85.00	140	200	—
1858	—	20.00	50.00	85.00	125	—
1859	—	20.00	50.00	85.00	125	—
1860	—	15.00	30.00	45.00	90.00	—
1861	—	20.00	50.00	85.00	125	—
1862	—	12.50	21.00	35.00	55.00	—
1863	—	7.50	15.00	25.00	45.00	—
1864	—	20.00	40.00	65.00	90.00	—
1865	—	125	300	500	750	—

KM# 611.1 10 REALES
13.1455 g., 0.9000 Silver .3804 oz. **Note:** Mint mark: 8-pointed star.

Date	Mintage	VG	F	VF	XF	Unc
1859	—	60.00	150	250	350	—
1860	—	60.00	150	250	350	—
1861	—	37.50	90.00	150	225	—
1862	—	125	350	550	800	—
1863	—	100	275	450	650	—
1864	—	55.00	135	225	325	—

KM# 593.2 20 REALES
26.2910 g., 0.9000 Silver .7607 oz. **Note:** Mint mark: 6-pointed star.

Date	Mintage	VG	F	VF	XF	Unc
1850	500,000	20.00	60.00	100	200	—
1851	—	20.00	60.00	100	200	—
1852	—	30.00	75.00	125	250	—
1854	1,355,000	20.00	60.00	100	200	—
1855	1,229,000	20.00	60.00	100	200	—

KM# 593.3 20 REALES
26.2910 g., 0.9000 Silver .7607 oz. **Note:** Mint mark: 7-pointed star.

Date	Mintage	VG	F	VF	XF	Unc
1850	—	500	1,000	1,700	2,800	—
1851	—	30.00	75.00	125	225	—
1852	—	30.00	75.00	125	225	—
1854	—	20.00	60.00	100	200	—
1855	—	20.00	60.00	100	200	—

KM# 593.1 20 REALES
26.2910 g., 0.9000 Silver .7607 oz. **Note:** Mint mark: 8-pointed star.

Date	Mintage	VG	F	VF	XF	Unc
1850	—	500	1,200	2,200	4,000	—
1851	1,055,000	200	350	650	1,150	—
1852	1,053,000	350	650	1,000	1,800	—

KM# 592.1 20 REALES
26.2910 g., 0.9000 Silver .7607 oz. **Note:** Mint Mark: Crowned M.

Date	Mintage	VG	F	VF	XF	Unc
1850 CL	126,000	35.00	75.00	135	225	375
1850 DG	—	1,100	2,000	3,500	5,500	7,500

KM# 592.2 20 REALES
26.2910 g., 0.9000 Silver .7607 oz.

Date	Mintage	VG	F	VF	XF	Unc
1850S RD	—	350	900	1,400	1,800	—

KM# 609.2 20 REALES
26.2910 g., 0.9000 Silver .7607 oz. **Note:** Mint mark: 6-pointed star.

Date	Mintage	VG	F	VF	XF	Unc
1856	1,021,000	30.00	75.00	125	225	—
1857	—	30.00	75.00	125	225	—
1858	1,626,000	30.00	75.00	125	225	—
1859	—	30.00	75.00	125	225	—
1860	941,000	40.00	100	150	275	—
1861	1,352,000	30.00	75.00	125	225	—
1862	—	30.00	75.00	125	225	—
1863	—	70.00	140	250	400	—
1864	2,776,000	30.00	75.00	125	225	—

KM# 609.3 20 REALES
26.2910 g., 0.9000 Silver .7607 oz. **Note:** Mint mark: 7-pointed star.

Date	Mintage	VG	F	VF	XF	Unc
1856	—	70.00	175	300	700	—
1857	—	30.00	70.00	225	400	—
1858	—	30.00	70.00	225	375	—
1859	—	70.00	175	300	700	—
1860	—	45.00	115	225	400	—
1861	—	50.00	125	300	700	—
1862	—	75.00	185	250	500	—
1863	—	75.00	185	250	475	—

KM# 609.1 20 REALES
26.2910 g., 0.9000 Silver .7607 oz. **Note:** Mint mark: 8-pointed star.

Date	Mintage	VG	F	VF	XF	Unc
1857	713,000	200	475	850	1,250	—
1859	880,000	240	600	1,000	1,450	—
1862	1,594,000	400	900	1,650	2,500	—
1863	520,000	400	900	1,650	2,500	—

KM# 610 20 REALES
1.6674 g., 0.9000 Gold .0482 oz. **Note:** Mint mark: 6-pointed star.

Date	Mintage	F	VF	XF	Unc	BU
1857	—	250	500	825	1,250	—
1861	—	50.00	90.00	150	220	—
1862	—	220	400	700	1,100	—
1863	—	500	1,000	1,850	2,650	—

KM# 616.2 40 REALES
3.3349 g., 0.9000 Gold .0965 oz. **Note:** Mint mark: 6-pointed star.

Date	Mintage	F	VF	XF	Unc	BU
1861	—	100	225	400	600	—
1862	—	60.00	75.00	100	165	—
1863	—	60.00	75.00	90.00	130	—

KM# 616.1 40 REALES
3.3349 g., 0.9000 Gold .0965 oz. **Note:** Mint mark: 8-pointed star.

Date	Mintage	F	VF	XF	Unc	BU
1863	—	60.00	75.00	100	165	—
1864	—	450	900	1,600	2,250	—

KM# 618.1 40 REALES
3.3349 g., 0.9000 Gold .0965 oz. **Obv:** Draped bust of Isabel II left **Rev:** Crowned draped arms **Note:** Mint Mark: 6-pointed star.

Date	Mintage	F	VF	XF	Unc	BU
1864	—	60.00	75.00	85.00	125	—

KM# 618.2 40 REALES
3.3349 g., 0.9000 Gold .0965 oz. **Obv:** Draped bust of Isabel II left **Rev:** Crowned draped arms **Note:** Mint Mark: 7-pointed star.

Date	Mintage	F	VF	XF	Unc	BU
1864	—	185	375	650	950	—

KM# 594.2 100 REALES
8.3371 g., 0.9000 Gold .2412 oz. **Note:** Mint mark: 6-pointed star.

Date	Mintage	F	VF	XF	Unc	BU
1850 CL	—	125	160	220	350	—
1850 DG	—	1,750	3,500	6,500	9,500	—
1851 CL	—	200	500	825	1,250	—

KM# 594.1 100 REALES
8.3371 g., 0.9000 Gold .2412 oz. **Note:** Mint mark: 8-pointed star.

Date	Mintage	F	VF	XF	Unc	BU
1850 SM	—	400	850	1,450	2,200	—

KM# 594.3 100 REALES
8.3371 g., 0.9000 Gold .2412 oz. **Note:** Mint mark: 7-pointed star.

Date	Mintage	F	VF	XF	Unc	BU
1850 RD	—	450	900	1,500	2,200	—

KM# 596.3 100 REALES
8.3371 g., 0.9000 Gold .2412 oz. **Note:** Mint mark: 7-pointed star.

Date	Mintage	F	VF	XF	Unc	BU
1851	—	1,500	3,000	5,000	7,500	—
1852	—	650	1,400	2,500	3,500	—
1854	—	125	160	200	300	—
1855	—	125	160	190	250	—

KM# 596.2 100 REALES
8.3371 g., 0.9000 Gold .2412 oz. **Note:** Mint mark: 6-pointed star.

Date	Mintage	F	VF	XF	Unc	BU
1851	—	700	1,500	2,500	3,750	—
1852	—	600	1,200	2,000	3,000	—
1854	—	125	160	265	385	—
1855	—	125	160	220	280	—

KM# 596.1 100 REALES
8.3371 g., 0.9000 Gold .2412 oz. **Note:** Mint mark: 8-pointed star.

Date	Mintage	F	VF	XF	Unc	BU
1851	—	700	1,500	2,750	4,000	—
1854	—	125	175	250	350	—
1855	—	120	160	220	325	—

KM# 605.1 100 REALES
8.3371 g., 0.9000 Gold .2412 oz. **Note:** Mint mark: 8-pointed star.

Date	Mintage	F	VF	XF	Unc	BU
1856	—	375	750	1,150	1,850	—
1857	—	125	160	190	275	—
1858	—	135	180	215	400	—
1859	—	125	160	190	220	—
1860	—	125	160	190	220	—
1861	—	375	625	950	1,500	—
1862	—	175	350	475	650	—

KM# 605.2 100 REALES
8.3371 g., 0.9000 Gold .2412 oz. **Note:** Mint mark: 6-pointed star.

Date	Mintage	F	VF	XF	Unc	BU
1856	—	125	160	190	225	—
1857	—	200	400	650	1,000	—
1858	—	130	175	300	500	—
1859	—	125	160	190	250	—
1860	—	125	160	190	225	—
1861	—	125	160	180	215	—
1862	—	125	160	180	215	—

KM# 605.3 100 REALES
8.3371 g., 0.9000 Gold .2412 oz. **Note:** Mint mark: 7-pointed star.

Date	Mintage	F	VF	XF	Unc	BU
1856	—	275	600	1,100	1,650	—
1857	—	125	160	190	225	—
1858	—	125	160	250	385	—
1859	—	125	160	190	220	—
1860	—	125	160	190	220	—
1861	—	125	160	190	215	—
1862	—	125	160	190	215	—

KM# 617.2 100 REALES
8.3371 g., 0.9000 Gold .2412 oz. **Rev:** Crowned and mantled rectangular arms **Note:** Mint mark: 7-pointed star.

Date	Mintage	F	VF	XF	Unc	BU
1863	—	250	400	650	950	—
1864	—	300	450	750	1,250	—

Note: For similar coins, with denominations expressed Cs. de Peso, see Philippines

KM# 617.1 100 REALES
8.3371 g., 0.9000 Gold .2412 oz. **Rev:** Crowned and mantled rectangular arms **Note:** Mint mark: 6-pointed star.

Date	Mintage	F	VF	XF	Unc	BU
1863	—	125	160	190	220	—
1864	—	125	160	190	220	—

SECOND DECIMAL COINAGE
Escudo System

100 Centimos = 1 Escudo

KM# 632.3 1/2 CENTIMO
Copper **Note:** Mint mark: 6-pointed star.

Date	Mintage	VG	F	VF	XF	Unc
1866	—	—	175	375	750	—

KM# 632.4 1/2 CENTIMO
Copper **Note:** Mint mark: 3-pointed star.

Date	Mintage	VG	F	VF	XF	Unc
1866 OM	—	2.25	5.50	9.00	15.00	—
1867 OM	—	2.00	4.00	7.00	12.50	—
1868 OM	—	4.00	9.00	12.50	20.00	—

KM# 632.2 1/2 CENTIMO
Copper **Note:** Mint mark: 4-pointed star.

Date	Mintage	VG	F	VF	XF	Unc
1866 OM	—	3.50	9.00	15.00	25.00	—
1867 OM	—	2.25	5.50	9.00	15.00	—
1868 OM	—	1.50	3.50	6.00	10.00	—

KM# 632.1 1/2 CENTIMO
Copper **Note:** Mint mark: 8-pointed star.

Date	Mintage	VG	F	VF	XF	Unc
1866 Rare	—	—	—	—	—	—
1866 OM	—	5.00	12.50	21.00	35.00	—
1867 OM	—	2.25	5.50	9.00	15.00	—
1868 OM	—	2.25	5.50	9.00	15.00	—

KM# 632.5 1/2 CENTIMO
Copper **Note:** Mint mark: 7-pointed star.

Date	Mintage	VG	F	VF	XF	Unc
1867 OM	—	6.00	14.00	25.00	40.00	—
1868 OM	—	3.50	9.00	15.00	25.00	—

KM# 633.3 CENTIMO
Copper **Note:** Mint mark: 6-pointed star.

Date	Mintage	VG	F	VF	XF	Unc
1865	—	—	150	325	650	—

KM# 633.4 CENTIMO
Copper **Note:** Mint mark: 3-pointed star.

Date	Mintage	VG	F	VF	XF	Unc
1866	—	6.00	14.00	25.00	40.00	—
1866 OM	—	4.00	8.00	16.00	30.00	—
1867	—	20.00	50.00	90.00	150	—
1867 OM	—	2.25	5.50	9.00	15.00	—
1868 OM	—	2.25	5.50	9.00	15.00	—

KM# 633.2 CENTIMO
Copper **Note:** Mint mark: 4-pointed star.

Date	Mintage	VG	F	VF	XF	Unc
1866	—	8.50	21.00	35.00	60.00	—
1866 OM	—	6.00	14.00	25.00	40.00	—
1867 OM	—	4.50	11.00	18.00	30.00	—
1868 OM	—	1.50	3.50	6.00	10.00	—

KM# 633.1 CENTIMO
Copper **Note:** Mint mark: 8-pointed star.

Date	Mintage	VG	F	VF	XF	Unc
1866	—	6.00	14.00	25.00	40.00	—
1866 OM	—	3.50	7.00	10.00	15.00	—
1867	—	10.00	25.00	40.00	70.00	—
1867 OM	—	3.50	7.00	10.00	15.00	—
1868 OM	—	2.00	4.00	7.00	12.50	—

KM# 633.5 CENTIMO
Copper **Note:** Mint mark: 7-pointed star.

Date	Mintage	VG	F	VF	XF	Unc
1867 OM	—	2.00	5.00	9.00	15.00	—
1868 OM	—	2.00	5.00	9.00	15.00	—

KM# 634.3 2-1/2 CENTIMOS
Copper **Note:** Mint mark: 6-pointed star.

Date	Mintage	VG	F	VF	XF	Unc
1865	—	65.00	175	275	475	—
1867 OM	—	17.50	40.00	70.00	120	—

KM# 634.4 2-1/2 CENTIMOS
Copper **Note:** Mint mark: 3-pointed star.

Date	Mintage	VG	F	VF	XF	Unc
1866 OM	—	25.00	60.00	100	175	—
1867 OM	—	2.50	6.50	11.00	18.00	—
1868 OM	—	2.00	4.50	7.50	12.50	—

KM# 634.2 2-1/2 CENTIMOS
Copper **Note:** Mint mark: 4-pointed star.

Date	Mintage	VG	F	VF	XF	Unc
1866	—	30.00	75.00	125	250	—
1866 OM	—	10.00	25.00	45.00	75.00	—
1867 OM	—	2.00	3.00	10.00	18.00	—
1868 OM	—	2.00	3.00	10.00	18.00	—

KM# 634.1 2-1/2 CENTIMOS
Copper **Note:** Mint mark: 8-pointed star.

Date	Mintage	VG	F	VF	XF	Unc
1866	—	2.75	7.00	12.00	20.00	—
1866 OM	—	2.75	7.00	12.00	20.00	—
1867 OM	—	2.00	5.00	8.00	12.50	—
1868 OM	—	2.00	5.00	8.00	12.50	—

KM# 634.5 2-1/2 CENTIMOS
Copper **Note:** Mint mark: 7-pointed star.

Date	Mintage	VG	F	VF	XF	Unc
1867 OM	—	2.00	4.50	7.50	12.50	—
1868 OM	—	2.75	7.00	12.00	20.00	—

KM# 635.3 5 CENTIMOS
Copper **Note:** Mint mark: 6-pointed star.

Date	Mintage	VG	F	VF	XF	Unc
1865	—	80.00	200	325	550	—

KM# 635.4 5 CENTIMOS
Copper **Note:** Mint mark: 3-pointed star.

Date	Mintage	VG	F	VF	XF	Unc
1866 OM	—	3.50	9.00	15.00	25.00	—
1867 OM	—	3.50	9.00	15.00	25.00	—
1868 OM	—	2.50	6.50	11.00	18.00	—

KM# 635.2 5 CENTIMOS
Copper **Note:** Mint mark: 4-pointed star.

Date	Mintage	VG	F	VF	XF	Unc
1866	—	8.50	21.00	35.00	60.00	—
1867 OM	—	2.00	4.50	7.50	12.50	—
1868 OM	—	3.50	9.00	15.00	25.00	—

KM# 635.1 5 CENTIMOS
Copper **Note:** Mint mark: 8-pointed star.

Date	Mintage	VG	F	VF	XF	Unc
1866	—	10.00	25.00	40.00	70.00	—
1866 OM	—	7.00	18.00	30.00	50.00	—
1867	—	75.00	175	300	525	—
1867 OM	—	2.00	4.50	7.50	12.50	—
1868 OM	—	2.00	4.50	7.50	12.50	—

KM# 635.5 5 CENTIMOS
Copper **Note:** Mint mark: 7-pointed star.

Date	Mintage	VG	F	VF	XF	Unc
1867 OM	—	4.50	11.00	18.00	30.00	—
1868 OM	—	2.00	4.50	7.50	12.50	—

KM# 627.2 10 CENTIMOS
1.2980 g., 0.8100 Silver .0338 oz. **Note:** Mint mark: 7-pointed star.

Date	Mintage	VG	F	VF	XF	Unc
1864	—	16.00	40.00	65.00	95.00	—
1865	—	5.00	12.50	20.00	30.00	—
1866	—	12.50	21.00	35.00	50.00	—
1868	—	60.00	150	275	400	—

KM# 627.1 10 CENTIMOS
1.2980 g., 0.8100 Silver .0338 oz. **Note:** Mint mark: 6-pointed star. Similar to 20 Centimos, KM#628.1.

Date	Mintage	VG	F	VF	XF	Unc
1865	—	5.00	12.50	21.00	30.00	—
1866	—	12.00	30.00	50.00	70.00	—
1867	—	100	250	425	600	—
1868 (68)	—	5.00	12.50	21.00	30.00	—

KM# 625.1 20 CENTIMOS
2.5960 g., 0.8100 Silver .0676 oz. **Note:** Mint mark: 6-pointed star.

Date	Mintage	VG	F	VF	XF	Unc
1864	—	25.00	60.00	100	150	—
1865	—	7.00	16.00	27.50	40.00	—
1866	—	50.00	125	200	300	—
1867	—	125	250	450	650	—
1868 (68)	—	3.50	8.50	14.00	20.00	—

KM# 625.2 20 CENTIMOS
2.5960 g., 0.8100 Silver .0676 oz. **Note:** Mint mark: 7-pointed star.

Date	Mintage	VG	F	VF	XF	Unc
1864	—	9.00	22.50	37.50	55.00	—
1865	—	10.00	25.00	40.00	60.00	—
1866	—	12.00	30.00	50.00	70.00	—

KM# 628.2 40 CENTIMOS
5.1920 g., 0.8100 Silver .1352 oz. **Note:** Mint mark: 6-pointed star.

Date	Mintage	VG	F	VF	XF	Unc
1864	—	12.50	21.00	35.00	50.00	—
1865	—	5.00	10.00	12.50	25.00	—
1866	—	3.50	7.50	12.50	25.00	—
1867	—	3.50	7.50	12.50	20.00	—
1868 (68)	—	3.50	7.50	12.50	20.00	—

KM# 628.3 40 CENTIMOS
5.1920 g., 0.8100 Silver .1352 oz. **Note:** Mint mark: 7-pointed star.

Date	Mintage	VG	F	VF	XF	Unc
1864	—	60.00	150	250	350	—
1865	—	7.50	19.00	30.00	45.00	—
1866	—	6.00	12.50	22.50	35.00	—

KM# 628.1 40 CENTIMOS
5.1920 g., 0.8100 Silver .1352 oz. **Note:** Mint mark: 8-pointed star.

Date	Mintage	VG	F	VF	XF	Unc
1865	—	80.00	200	350	500	—

KM# 626.2 ESCUDO
12.9800 g., 0.9000 Silver .3756 oz. **Note:** Mint mark: 7-pointed star.

Date	Mintage	VG	F	VF	XF	Unc
1864	—	175	450	750	1,000	—
1866	—	75.00	175	300	450	—

KM# 626.1 ESCUDO
12.9800 g., 0.9000 Silver .3756 oz. **Note:** Mint mark: 6-pointed star.

Date	Mintage	VG	F	VF	XF	Unc
1865	—	20.00	50.00	85.00	150	—
1866	—	12.00	20.00	35.00	80.00	—
1867	—	7.00	15.00	30.00	70.00	—
1868 (68)	—	7.00	15.00	25.00	60.00	—

KM# 629 2 ESCUDOS
25.9600 g., 0.9000 Silver .7512 oz. **Note:** Mint mark: 6-pointed star.

Date	Mintage	VG	F	VF	XF	Unc
1865	—	800	2,000	3,750	5,500	—
1866	—	1,000	2,250	4,000	6,000	—
1867	4,234,000	12.50	25.00	40.00	70.00	—
1868 (68)	2,225,000	25.00	60.00	100	150	—

KM# 630 2 ESCUDOS
1.6774 g., 0.9000 Gold .0485 oz. **Note:** Mint mark: 6-pointed star.

Date	Mintage	F	VF	XF	Unc	BU
1865	—	35.00	60.00	100	175	—
1867	—	300	550	900	1,500	—
1868 (68)	—	225	450	750	1,200	—

KM# 631.1 4 ESCUDOS
3.3548 g., 0.9000 Gold .0971 oz. **Note:** Mint mark: 6-pointed star.

Date	Mintage	F	VF	XF	Unc	BU
1865	—	55.00	70.00	90.00	140	—
1866	—	55.00	70.00	90.00	140	—
1867	—	55.00	65.00	80.00	120	—
1868 (68)	—	75.00	100	125	185	—

KM# 631.2 4 ESCUDOS
3.3548 g., 0.9000 Gold .0971 oz. **Note:** Mint mark: 7-pointed star.

Date	Mintage	F	VF	XF	Unc	BU
1865	—	275	550	950	1,300	—
1866	—	200	400	700	1,000	—

KM# 636.2 10 ESCUDOS
8.3870 g., 0.9000 Gold .2427 oz. **Note:** Mint mark: 7-pointed star.

Date	Mintage	F	VF	XF	Unc	BU
1865	—	1,200	2,500	4,500	6,500	—

KM# 636.1 10 ESCUDOS
8.3870 g., 0.9000 Gold .2427 oz. **Note:** Mint mark: 6-pointed star.

Date	Mintage	F	VF	XF	Unc	BU
1866	—	200	300	450	650	—
1867	—	125	150	250	350	—
1868 (68)	—	125	150	185	215	—

KM# 636.3 10 ESCUDOS
8.3870 g., 0.9000 Gold .2427 oz. **Note:** Mint mark: 6-pointed star.

Date	Mintage	F	VF	XF	Unc	BU
1868 (73)	—	125	150	190	225	—

PROVISIONAL COINAGE

1868

KM# 645 25 MILESIMAS DE ESCUDO
Bronze **Subject:** Battle of Alcolea Bridge **Note:** Mint mark: 3-pointed star.

Date	Mintage	F	VF	XF	Unc	BU
1868	10,000	—	200	285	375	—

DECIMAL COINAGE

Peseta System

100 Centimos = 1 Peseta

KM# 660 CENTIMO
Copper **Note:** Mint mark: 8-pointed star.

Date	Mintage	F	VF	XF	Unc	BU
1870 OM	169,891,000	0.50	1.50	8.00	20.00	—

KM# 661 2 CENTIMOS
Copper **Note:** Mint mark: 8-pointed star.

Date	Mintage	F	VF	XF	Unc	BU
1870 OM	115,869,000	0.50	2.00	9.00	30.00	—

KM# 662 5 CENTIMOS
Copper **Note:** Mint mark: 8-pointed star.

Date	Mintage	F	VF	XF	Unc	BU
1870 OM	287,381,000	2.00	10.00	40.00	100	—

KM# 669 5 CENTIMOS
Copper **Obv:** Charles VII head r. **Note:** Pretender issue. Mint mark: 8-pointed star.

Date	Mintage	F	VF	XF	Unc	BU
1875 (b)	50,000	25.00	50.00	75.00	125	—

KM# 674 5 CENTIMOS
Bronze **Note:** Mint mark: 8-pointed star.

Date	Mintage	F	VF	XF	Unc	BU
1877 OM	34,376,000	0.75	10.00	45.00	125	—
1878 OM	67,954,000	0.75	12.00	50.00	125	—
1879 OM	54,994,000	0.75	10.00	40.00	100	—

KM# 663 10 CENTIMOS
Copper **Obv:** Lion standing with shield

Date	Mintage	F	VF	XF	Unc	BU
1870 OM	170,088,000	2.00	10.00	75.00	200	—

KM# 670 10 CENTIMOS
Copper **Obv:** Charles VII head r. **Note:** Pretender issue

Date	Mintage	F	VF	XF	Unc	BU
1875 (b)	100,000	15.00	50.00	100	150	—

KM# 675 10 CENTIMOS
Bronze

Date	Mintage	F	VF	XF	Unc	BU
1877 OM	29,567,000	0.75	12.00	75.00	150	—
1878 OM	68,740,000	0.75	10.00	70.00	125	—
1879 OM	56,313,000	0.75	15.00	75.00	150	—

KM# 650 20 CENTIMOS
1.0000 g., 0.8350 Silver .0268 oz. **Note:** Mint mark: 6-pointed star.

Date	Mintage	F	VF	XF	Unc	BU
1869 (69) SN-M	91	1,200	1,850	3,000	6,000	—
1870 (70) SN-M	5,000	350	500	1,000	1,500	—

KM# 651 50 CENTIMOS
2.5000 g., 0.8350 Silver .0671 oz. **Note:** Mint mark: 6-pointed star.

Date	Mintage	F	VF	XF	Unc	BU
1869 (69) SN-M	453,000	12.50	50.00	250	600	—
1870 (70) SN-M	540,000	35.00	100	450	1,000	—

KM# 685 50 CENTIMOS
2.5000 g., 0.8350 Silver .0671 oz. **Note:** Mint mark: 6-pointed stars.

Date	Mintage	F	VF	XF	Unc	BU
1880 (80) MS-M	2,787,000	1.50	5.00	40.00	150	—
1881 (81) MS-M	5,647,000	1.50	5.00	40.00	125	—
1885/1 (86) MS-M	1,468,000	6.00	12.00	45.00	175	—
1885 (86) MS-M	Inc. above	1.50	10.00	40.00	125	—

Note: 1885 (85) coins have been modified from another date

KM# 690 50 CENTIMOS
2.5000 g., 0.8350 Silver .0671 oz. **Note:** Mint mark: 6-pointed star. Varieties exist.

Date	Mintage	F	VF	XF	Unc	BU
1889 (89) MP-M	537,000	7.00	20.00	50.00	110	—
1892/89 (92) PG-M	3,954,000	6.00	15.00	40.00	120	—
1892 (92) PG-M	Inc. above	1.50	3.00	10.00	25.00	—
1892 (22) PG-M	—	20.00	40.00	75.00	120	—
1892/82 (82) PG-M	—	15.00	30.00	40.00	100	—
1892 (82) PG-M	—	15.00	40.00	90.00	165	—
1892 (62) PG-M	—	17.50	50.00	100	175	—
1892 (62) PG-M/MP-M	—	—	—	—	—	—

KM# 703 50 CENTIMOS
2.5000 g., 0.8350 Silver .0671 oz. **Note:** Mint mark: 6-pointed star.

Date	Mintage	F	VF	XF	Unc	BU
1894 (94) PG-V	1,109,000	3.50	10.00	25.00	60.00	—

KM# 705 50 CENTIMOS
2.5000 g., 0.8350 Silver .0671 oz. **Note:** Mint mark: 6-pointed star.

Date	Mintage	F	VF	XF	Unc	BU
1896 (96) PG-V	297,000	25.00	50.00	100	150	—
1900 (00) SM-V	2,128,000	4.00	10.00	20.00	45.00	—

KM# 653 PESETA
5.0000 g., 0.8350 Silver .1342 oz. **Obv. Legend:** ESPANA **Note:** Mint mark: 6-pointed star.

Date	Mintage	F	VF	XF	Unc	BU
1869 (69) SN-M	367,000	50.00	250	2,000	4,000	—
1870 (70) SN-M	3,865,000	10.00	75.00	250	600	—
1870 (73) DE-M	5,165,000	10.00	70.00	200	450	—

KM# 652 PESETA
5.0000 g., 0.8350 Silver .1342 oz. **Obv. Legend:** GOBIERNO PROVISIONAL **Note:** Mint mark: 6-pointed star.

Date	Mintage	F	VF	XF	Unc	BU
1869 (69) SN-M	7,000,000	10.00	50.00	250	500	—

KM# 672 PESETA
5.0000 g., 0.8350 Silver .1342 oz. **Note:** Mint mark: 6-pointed star.

Date	Mintage	F	VF	XF	Unc	BU
1876 (76) DE-M	4,427,000	10.00	100	250	500	—

KM# 686 PESETA
5.0000 g., 0.8350 Silver .1342 oz. **Note:** Mint mark: 6-pointed star.

Date	Mintage	F	VF	XF	Unc	BU
1881 (81) MS-M	799,000	25.00	250	1,500	3,500	—
1882/81 (82) MS-M	3,506,000	15.00	100	300	1,000	—
1882 (82) MS-M	Inc. above	10.00	40.00	200	450	—
1883 (83) MS-M	8,440,000	8.00	30.00	150	350	—
1884/3 (84) MS-M	5,839	400	600	2,500	5,000	—
1885 (85) MS-M	3,336,000	10.00	75.00	200	500	—
1885 (86) MS-M	3,954,000	10.00	100	250	600	—

KM# 691 PESETA
5.0000 g., 0.8350 Silver .1342 oz. **Note:** Mint mark: 6-pointed star.

Date	Mintage	F	VF	XF	Unc	BU
1889 (89) MP-M	760,000	50.00	350	1,500	2,500	—
1891 (91) PG-M	4,948,000	3.00	50.00	100	200	—

KM# 702 PESETA
5.0000 g., 0.8350 Silver .1342 oz. **Note:** Mint mark: 6-pointed star.

Date	Mintage	F	VF	XF	Unc	BU
1893 (93) PG-L	1,958,000	10.00	75.00	225	500	—
1894 (94) PG-V	1,044,000	35.00	150	600	1,400	—

KM# 706 PESETA
5.0000 g., 0.8350 Silver .1342 oz. **Note:** Mint mark: 6-pointed star. Prices are for coins with full right star dates. Partial right star dates sell for less. Examples with no visable right star date have limited collector appeal.

Date	Mintage	F	VF	XF	Unc	BU
1896 (96) PG-V	6,412,000	4.00	15.00	35.00	75.00	100
1899 (99) SG-V	7,472,000	3.50	12.50	30.00	70.00	85.00
1900 (00) SM-V	18,650,000	3.50	12.50	30.00	70.00	85.00

KM# 654 2 PESETAS
10.0000 g., 0.8350 Silver .2685 oz. **Note:** Mint mark: 6-pointed star.

Date	Mintage	F	VF	XF	Unc	BU
1869 (68) SN-M	—	25.00	75.00	180	500	—
1869 (69) SN-M	3,270,000	5.00	10.00	150	400	—
1870 (70) SN-M	1,504,000	6.50	12.50	175	400	—
1870 (73) DE-M	11,880,000	5.00	9.00	40.00	200	—
1870 (74) DE-M	14,893,000	5.00	9.00	40.00	200	—
1870 (75) DE-M	4,997,000	6.00	11.50	150	400	—

KM# 678.1 2 PESETAS
10.0000 g., 0.8350 Silver 0.2685 oz. **Note:** Mint mark: 6-pointed star.

Date	Mintage	F	VF	XF	Unc	BU
1879(79) EM-M	5,578,000	5.50	10.00	150	400	—

KM# 678.2 2 PESETAS
10.0000 g., 0.8350 Silver .2685 oz. **Obv:** Revised whiskers
Note: Mint mark: 6-pointed star.

Date	Mintage	F	VF	XF	Unc	BU
1881 (81) MS-M	3,639,000	5.50	10.00	150	400	—
1882/1 (82) MS-M	20,343,000	4.50	10.00	150	400	—
1882 (82) MS-M	Inc. above	4.50	7.50	50.00	150	—
1883 (83) MS-M	3,318,000	5.00	40.00	250	600	—
1884 (84) MS-M	2,839,000	5.50	15.00	150	400	—

KM# 692 2 PESETAS
10.0000 g., 0.8350 Silver .2685 oz. **Note:** Mint mark: 6-pointed star.

Date	Mintage	F	VF	XF	Unc	BU
1889 (89) MP-M	559,000	25.00	100	400	800	—
1891 (91) PG-M	93,000	100	200	500	900	—
1892 (92) PG-M	1,379,000	10.00	50.00	100	200	—

KM# 704 2 PESETAS
10.0000 g., 0.8350 Silver .2685 oz. **Note:** Mint mark: 6-pointed star.

Date	Mintage	F	VF	XF	Unc	BU
1894 (94) PG-V	279,000	50.00	250	450	650	—

KM# 655 5 PESETAS
25.0000 g., 0.9000 Silver .7234 oz. **Note:** Mint mark: 6-pointed star.

Date	Mintage	F	VF	XF	Unc	BU
1869 (69) SN-M	100	5,000	7,500	15,000	25,000	—
1870 (70) SN-M	5,923,000	10.00	20.00	200	500	—

KM# 666 5 PESETAS
25.0000 g., 0.9000 Silver .7234 oz. **Note:** Mint mark: 6-pointed star.

Date	Mintage	F	VF	XF	Unc	BU
1871 (71) SD-M	13,641,000	10.00	15.00	75.00	250	—
1871 (73) DE-M	2,870,000	100	500	1,500	2,500	—
1871 (74) DE-M	5,075,000	8.00	15.00	75.00	250	—
1871 (75) DE-M	3,000,000	8.00	20.00	150	450	—

KM# 671 5 PESETAS
25.0000 g., 0.9000 Silver .7234 oz. **Note:** Mint mark: 6-pointed star.

Date	Mintage	F	VF	XF	Unc	BU
1875 (75) DE-M	8,641,000	10.00	20.00	200	400	—
1876 (76) DE-M	8,548,000	10.00	20.00	200	350	—

KM# 676 5 PESETAS
25.0000 g., 0.9000 Silver .7234 oz. **Note:** Mint mark: 6-pointed star.

Date	Mintage	F	VF	XF	Unc	BU
1877 (77) DE-M	6,987,000	10.00	15.00	100	350	—
1878 (78) DE-M	5,000,000	10.00	20.00	125	375	—
1878 (78) EM-M	4,147,000	10.00	25.00	150	400	—
1879 (79) EM-M	1,634,000	15.00	50.00	300	750	—
1881 (81) MS-M	699,000	25.00	75.00	500	1,500	—

KM# 688 5 PESETAS
25.0000 g., 0.9000 Silver .7234 oz. **Note:** Mint mark: 6-pointed star.

Date	Mintage	F	VF	XF	Unc	BU
1882 (81) MS-M	—	35.00	90.00	285	700	—
1882/1(82) MS-M	—	30.00	75.00	225	575	—
1882 (82) MS-M	1,662,000	10.00	25.00	150	450	—
1883 (83) MS-M	5,507,000	8.00	15.00	125	450	—
1884 (84) MS-M	5,848,000	8.00	15.00	125	450	—
1885 (85) MS-M	3,144,000	8.00	20.00	165	500	—
1885 (86) MS-M	1,951,000	10.00	25.00	170	500	—
1885 (87) MS-M	9,000,000	8.00	12.00	85.00	250	—
1885 (87) MP-M	2,803,000	15.00	25.00	170	500	—

KM# 689 5 PESETAS
25.0000 g., 0.9000 Silver .7234 oz. **Note:** Mint mark: 6-pointed star.

Date	Mintage	F	VF	XF	Unc	BU
1888 (88) MS-M	—	200	1,500	3,000	4,500	—
1888 (88) MP-M	10,644,000	8.00	12.00	50.00	150	—
1889 (89) MP-M	4,681,000	10.00	15.00	100	200	—
1890 (90) MP-M	4,275,000	10.00	20.00	100	225	—
1890 (90) PG-M	3,000,000	10.00	25.00	150	300	—
1891 (91) PG-M	11,660,000	8.00	12.00	50.00	150	—
1892 (92) PG-M	1,294,000	12.50	30.00	175	450	—

KM# 700 5 PESETAS
25.0000 g., 0.9000 Silver .7234 oz. **Note:** Mint mark: 6-pointed star.

Date	Mintage	F	VF	XF	Unc	BU
1892 (92) PG-M	7,000,000	10.00	20.00	75.00	200	—
1893 (93) PG-L	2,500,000	12.00	25.00	75.00	200	—
1893 (93) PG-V	518,000	40.00	100	350	750	—
1894 (94) PG-V	3,871,000	12.00	30.00	150	300	—

KM# 707 5 PESETAS
25.0000 g., 0.9000 Silver .7234 oz. **Note:** Mint mark: 6-pointed star. All other date and mintmasters or assayers initial combinations on crowns of this era are contemporary counterfeits.

Date	Mintage	F	VF	XF	Unc	BU
1896 (96) PG-V	4,272,000	10.00	18.00	75.00	200	—
1897 (97) SG-V	6,733,000	8.00	12.00	50.00	150	—
1898 (98) SG-V	39,977,000	8.00	10.00	25.00	75.00	—
1899 (99) SG-V	13,930,000	10.00	20.00	50.00	100	—

KM# 677 10 PESETAS
3.2258 g., 0.9000 Silver .0933 oz. **Note:** Mint mark: 6-pointed star.

Date	Mintage	F	VF	XF	Unc	BU
1878 (78) EM-M	91,000	—	200	300	400	—
1879 (79) EM-M	33,000	—	1,000	1,500	2,500	—
1878 (61) DE-M	496	—	—	—	1,000	—
1878 (62) DE-M	18,000	—	—	—	100	—

Note: The above 2 coins dated (61) and (62) were restruck by the Spanish Mint from original dies in 1961 and 1962 and are considered official restrike issues

KM# 693 20 PESETAS
6.4516 g., 0.9000 Gold .1867 oz. **Note:** Mint mark: 6-pointed star.

Date	Mintage	F	VF	XF	Unc	BU
1889 (89) MP-M	875,000	—	200	250	400	—
1890 (90) MP-M	2,344,000	—	145	155	200	—
1887 (61) PG-V	800	—	—	550	800	—
1887 (62) PG-V	11,000	—	—	80.00	100	—

Note: For above 2 coins dated (61) and (62), see note after 10 Pesetas, KM#677

KM# 701 20 PESETAS
6.4516 g., 0.9000 Gold .1867 oz. **Note:** Mint mark: 6-pointed star.

Date	Mintage	F	VF	XF	Unc	BU
1892 (92) PG-M	2,430,000	—	1,400	2,000	2,750	—

KM# 709 20 PESETAS
6.4516 g., 0.9000 Gold .1867 oz. **Note:** Mint mark: 6-pointed star.

Date	Mintage	F	VF	XF	Unc	BU
1899 (99) SM-V	2,086,000	—	225	300	400	—
1896 (61) PG-V	900	—	—	400	500	—
1896 (62) PG-V	12,000	—	—	125	150	—

Note: The above 2 coins dated (61) and (62) were restruck by the Spanish Mint from original dies in 1961 and 1962 and are considered official restrike issues

KM# 667 25 PESETAS
8.0645 g., 0.9000 Gold .2333 oz. **Note:** Mint mark: 6-pointed star.

Date	Mintage	F	VF	XF	Unc	BU
1871 (75) SD-M Rare	25	—	—	—	—	—

KM# 673 25 PESETAS
8.0645 g., 0.9000 Gold .2333 oz. **Note:** Mint mark: 6-pointed star.

Date	Mintage	F	VF	XF	Unc	BU
1876 (76) DE-M	1,281,000	—	135	150	200	—
1877 (77) DE-M	10,048,000	—	135	150	175	—
1878 (78) DE-M	5,192,000	—	135	150	175	—
1878 (78) EM-M	3,000,000	—	135	150	175	—
1879 (79) EM-M	3,478,000	—	135	150	175	—
1880 (80) MS-M	6,863,000	—	135	150	175	—
1876 (61) DE-M	300	—	—	1,500	1,750	—
1876 (62) DE-M	6,000	—	—	250	300	—

Note: For above 2 coins dated (61) and (62) see note after 10 Pesetas, KM#677

KM# 687 25 PESETAS
8.0645 g., 0.9000 Gold .2333 oz. **Note:** Mint mark: 6-pointed star.

Date	Mintage	F	VF	XF	Unc	BU
1881 (81) MS-M	4,366,000	—	135	150	200	—
1882 (82) MS-M	414,000	—	400	600	700	—
1883 (83) MS-M	669,000	—	400	500	600	—
1884 (84) MS-M	1,033,000	—	225	300	400	—
1885 (85) MS-M	503,000	—	1,000	1,500	1,800	—
1885 (86) MS-M	491,000	—	2,250	3,000	5,000	—

KM# 664 100 PESETAS
32.2581 g., 0.9000 Gold .9334 oz. **Subject:** Provisional Government **Note:** Mint mark: 6-pointed star.

Date	Mintage	F	VF	XF	Unc	BU
1870 (70) SD-M Rare	12	—	—	—	—	—

KM# 668a 100 PESETAS
0.9000 Yellow Gold **Subject:** Provisional Government **Note:** Mint mark: 6-pointed star.

Date	Mintage	F	VF	XF	Unc	BU
1871 (71) SD-M Rare	25	—	—	—	—	—

KM# 668b 100 PESETAS
0.9000 Red Gold **Subject:** Provisional Government **Note:** Mint mark: 6-pointed star.

Date	Mintage	F	VF	XF	Unc	BU
1871 (71) SD-M Rare	50	—	—	—	—	—

KM# 708 100 PESETAS
0.9000 Red Gold **Subject:** Provisional Government **Note:** Mint mark: 6-pointed star.

Date	Mintage	F	VF	XF	Unc	BU
1897 (97) SG-V	150,000	600	1,000	1,500	2,000	—
1897 (61) SG-V	810	—	—	1,000	1,500	—
1897 (62) SG-V	6,000	—	—	550	750	—

Note: The above 2 coins were restruck by the Spanish Mint from original dies in 1961 and 1962 and are considered official restrike issues

REVOLUTIONARY COINAGE

1873

Former Y#62, 2 Pesetas, 1873 Cartagena Mint, Cantonal issue similar to KM#715, 10 Reales and KM#716, 5 Pesetas, are all considered fantasies struck later for collectors. Refer to Unusual World Coins, 3rd edition, Krause Publications, Inc.

KM# 715 10 REALES (2-1/2 Pesetas)
13.5000 g., 0.9000 Silver .3907 oz. **Note:** Mint: Cartagena.

Date	Mintage	F	VF	XF	Unc	BU
1873	—	150	350	650	1,200	—

KM# 716 5 PESETAS (20 Reales)
25.0000 g., 0.9000 Silver .7234 oz. **Note:** Several varieties exist.

Date	Mintage	F	VF	XF	Unc	BU
1873	—	75.00	150	225	450	—

PRETENDER COINAGE

CHARLES V 1835-1840

Charles V, brother of Ferdinand VII, claimed the throne upon the death of his brother, but Isabella II became the ruler. Charles V fled to Portugal and set up, what he called, the true monarchy of Spain.

NOTE: For 4 Reales issues of 1838, see regular coinage.

KM# PT6 8 MARAVEDIS
Copper **Ruler:** Charles V **Countermark:** CAB/BER/A **Note:** Countermark on 8 Maravedi of Ferdinand VII; Mint Mark: Aqueduct.

Date	Mintage	F	VF	XF	Unc	BU
1835	—	175	300	400	—	—

KM# PT7 2 REALES
2.6291 g., 0.9030 Silver .0761 oz. **Ruler:** Charles V **Obv:** Mint mark above, asterisk below inscription **Note:** Mint Mark: Aqueduct.

Date	Mintage	Good	VG	F	VF	XF
1837	—	225	375	450	600	—

KM# PT8 2 REALES
2.6291 g., 0.9030 Silver .0761 oz. **Ruler:** Charles V **Obv:** Without mint mark and asterisk

Date	Mintage	Good	VG	F	VF	XF
1837	—	225	375	450	600	—

CHARLES VII 1872-1875

A grandson of Charles V who claimed the throne and maintained a court and government in exile. All Charles VII pieces were made at the Brussels Mint.

NOTE: Some pretender issues which circulated are listed in the regular coinage.

KM# PT13 50 CENTIMOS
2.0875 g., 0.8350 Silver .0671 oz. **Ruler:** Charles VII

Date	Mintage	F	VF	XF	Unc	BU
1876(b)	—	—	350	450	650	—

KM# PT9.1a 5 PESETAS
Bronze **Ruler:** Charles VII

Date	Mintage	F	VF	XF	Unc	BU
1874	—	—	—	—	1,200	—
1875	—	—	—	—	1,200	—

KM# PT9.1 5 PESETAS
25.0000 g., 0.9000 Silver .7234 oz. **Ruler:** Charles VII **Rev:** Crowned arms divide value, 5-P **Edge:** Reeded **Note:** Struck at Paris.

Date	Mintage	F	VF	XF	Unc	BU
1874	—	—	—	—	2,200	—
1875	—	—	—	—	2,200	—

KM# PT9.2 5 PESETAS
25.0000 g., 0.9000 Silver .7234 oz. **Ruler:** Charles VII **Note:** Piedfort (double thickness).

Date	Mintage	F	VF	XF	Unc	BU
1874	—	—	—	—	3,500	—

KM# PT9.3 5 PESETAS
25.0000 g., 0.9000 Silver .7234 oz. **Ruler:** Charles VII **Edge:** Plain

Date	Mintage	F	VF	XF	Unc	BU
1874	—	—	—	—	3,500	—

KM# PT9.4 5 PESETAS
25.0000 g., 0.9000 Silver .7234 oz. **Ruler:** Charles VII **Note:** Triple piedfort.

Date	Mintage	F	VF	XF	Unc	BU
1874	—	—	—	—	4,500	—

KM# PT10.1 5 PESETAS
Silver 25.50 oz. **Ruler:** Charles VII **Rev:** Crowned arms divide value, P-5, diamond and C below **Edge:** Plain

Date	Mintage	F	VF	XF	Unc	BU
1874	—	—	—	—	2,500	—

KM# PT10.1a 5 PESETAS
Bronze **Ruler:** Charles VII **Obv:** Bust of Carolus VII facing right **Note:** Uniface.

Date	Mintage	F	VF	XF	Unc	BU
1874	—	—	—	—	1,000	—

KM# PT10.1b 5 PESETAS
Bronze **Ruler:** Charles VII **Rev:** Crowned arms **Note:** Uniface.

Date	Mintage	F	VF	XF	Unc	BU
1874	—	—	—	—	1,000	—

KM# PT10.2 5 PESETAS
Silver 25.50 oz. **Ruler:** Charles VII **Note:** Piedfort (double thickness).

Date	Mintage	F	VF	XF	Unc	BU
1874	—	—	—	—	4,000	—

KM# PT10.3 5 PESETAS
Silver 25.50 oz. **Ruler:** Charles VII **Edge:** Reeded

Date	Mintage	F	VF	XF	Unc	BU
1874	—	—	—	—	3,500	—

KM# PT11.1 5 PESETAS
Silver 25.50 oz. **Ruler:** Charles VII **Rev:** Crowned arms divide value, 5-P, date below

Date	Mintage	F	VF	XF	Unc	BU
1874	—	—	—	—	2,500	—

KM# PT11.1a 5 PESETAS
Bronze **Ruler:** Charles VII

Date	Mintage	F	VF	XF	Unc	BU
1874	—	—	—	—	1,200	—

KM# PT11.1b 5 PESETAS
Tin **Ruler:** Charles VII

Date	Mintage	F	VF	XF	Unc	BU
1874	—	—	—	—	1,200	—

KM# PT11.2 5 PESETAS
Silver **Ruler:** Charles VII **Note:** Piedfort (double thickness).

Date	Mintage	F	VF	XF	Unc	BU
1874	—	—	—	—	4,000	—

KM# PT12 5 PESETAS
1.6129 g., 0.9000 Gold .0467 oz. **Ruler:** Charles VII **Obv:** Laureate head right **Rev:** Crowned arms divide value

Date	Mintage	F	VF	XF	Unc	BU
1874 Rare	—	—	—	—	—	—

KM# PT14 5 PESETAS
Silver 25.50 oz. **Ruler:** Charles VII **Note:** Struck at Brussels

Date	Mintage	F	VF	XF	Unc	BU
1885	—	Value: 850				

Note: The private patterns of Charles VII, were of a purely political speculative nature

PATTERNS

Including off metal strikes

KM#	Date	Mintage	Identification	Mkt Val
Pn10	1868	—	5 Pesetas. Copper.	—

KM#	Date	Mintage	Identification	Mkt Val
Pn11	1869	—	10 Centimos. Copper. Lion with shield right	—

KM#	Date	Mintage	Identification	Mkt Val
Pn12	1870	—	10 Centimos. Copper. Lion with shield left	—
Pn13	1878	—	Centimo. Copper. Alphonso VII	—
Pn14	1878	—	2 Centimos. Copper. Alphonso XII	6,000

BARCELONA

Barcelona was a maritime province located in northeast Spain. The city was the provincial capital of Barcelona. Barcelona is a major port and commercial center.

RULERS
Joseph (Jose) Napoleon, 1808-1814
Ferdinand (Fernando) VII, restored 1814-1833

MINT MARKS
Ba - Barcelona

MONETARY SYSTEM
4 Quartos = 1 Sueldo
6 Sueldos = 1 Peseta

PROVINCE

STANDARD COINAGE

KM# 75 1/2 QUARTO
Copper **Note:** Similar to 4 Quartos, KM#67.

Date	Mintage	Good	VG	F	VF	XF
ND(1811)	—	20.00	40.00	65.00	100	—

KM# 65 QUARTO
Copper **Note:** Similar to 4 Quartos, KM#67.

Date	Mintage	Good	VG	F	VF	XF
1808	—	17.50	35.00	70.00	110	—
1809	—	10.00	20.00	35.00	55.00	—
1810	—	10.00	20.00	35.00	55.00	—
1811	—	20.00	40.00	80.00	125	—
1812	—	10.00	20.00	35.00	55.00	—
1813	—	20.00	40.00	75.00	165	—

KM# 66 2 QUARTOS
Copper **Note:** Similar to 4 Quartos, KM#67.

Date	Mintage	Good	VG	F	VF	XF
1808	—	10.00	25.00	50.00	85.00	—
1809	—	10.00	20.00	30.00	45.00	—
1810	—	20.00	40.00	80.00	125	—
1813	—	10.00	25.00	50.00	75.00	—
1814	—	20.00	60.00	125	200	—

KM# 80 3 QUARTOS
Copper

Date	Mintage	Good	VG	F	VF	XF
1823	—	2.00	5.00	15.00	25.00	—

KM# 67 4 QUARTOS
Copper

Date	Mintage	Good	VG	F	VF	XF
1808	—	10.00	30.00	60.00	90.00	—
1809	—	5.00	10.00	20.00	35.00	—
1810	—	3.00	10.00	15.00	22.00	—
1811	—	4.00	10.00	15.00	22.00	—
1812	—	3.00	10.00	15.00	22.00	—

KM# 67a 4 QUARTOS
Cast Copper

Date	Mintage	Good	VG	F	VF	XF
1808	—	5.00	11.50	15.00	22.00	—
1809	—	3.00	9.50	15.00	22.00	—
1810	—	2.00	9.50	15.00	22.00	—
1811	—	4.00	10.00	17.50	28.00	—
1812	—	3.00	9.50	15.00	22.00	—

KM# 77 4 QUARTOS
Copper **Obv:** Obverse legend widely spaced

Date	Mintage	Good	VG	F	VF	XF
1813	—	5.00	12.50	25.00	35.00	—
1814	—	7.50	15.00	30.00	45.00	—

KM# 77a 4 QUARTOS
Cast Copper

Date	Mintage	Good	VG	F	VF	XF
1813	—	5.00	11.50	15.00	22.00	—
1814	—	5.00	11.50	15.00	22.00	—

KM# 81 6 QUARTOS
Copper

Date	Mintage	Good	VG	F	VF	XF
1823	—	10.00	20.00	30.00	50.00	—

KM# 70 PESETA
Silver

Date	Mintage	Good	VG	F	VF	XF
1809	—	20.00	40.00	55.00	90.00	—
1810	—	15.00	25.00	30.00	50.00	—
1811	—	15.00	25.00	30.00	50.00	—
1812	—	18.00	35.00	45.00	75.00	—
1813	—	20.00	40.00	50.00	80.00	—
1814	—	35.00	65.00	120	200	—

KM# 68 2-1/2 PESETAS
Silver

Date	Mintage	Good	VG	F	VF	XF
1808	—	125	250	300	400	—
1809	—	100	165	225	300	—
1810	—	200	400	500	650	—
1814	—	300	575	725	975	—

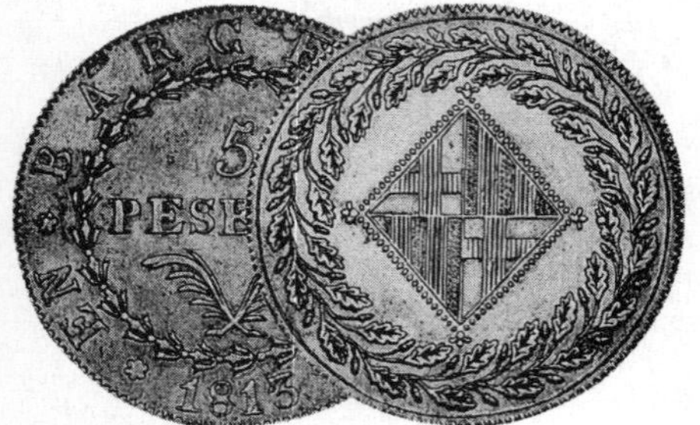

KM# 69 5 PESETAS
Silver

Date	Mintage	Good	VG	F	VF	XF
1808	—	100	225	375	600	—
1809	—	100	225	375	600	—
1810	—	100	225	375	600	—
1811	—	100	225	325	450	—
1812	—	125	250	400	700	—
1813	—	300	600	900	1,250	—
1814	—	1,000	2,100	2,800	3,500	—

KM# 76 20 PESETAS
Gold

Date	Mintage	Good	VG	F	VF	XF
1812Ba	—	250	600	850	1,250	—
1813Ba	—	350	750	1,100	1,650	—
1814Ba	—	1,000	2,500	3,500	5,000	—

CATALONIA

Catalonia, a triangular territory forming the northeast corner of the Iberian Peninsula, was formerly a province of Spain and also formerly a principality of Aragon. In1833 the region was divided into four provinces, Barcelona, Gerona, Lerida and Tarragona.

RULERS
Ferdinand (Fernando) VII, 1808-1833
Isabel II, 1833-1868

MINT MARKS
C – Catalonia

MONETARY SYSTEM
12 Ardites (Dineros) = 8 Ochavos =
4 Quartos = 1 Sueldo
6 Sueldos = 1 Peseta
5 Pesetas = 1 Duro

PROVINCE

STANDARD COINAGE

KM# 118 OCHAVO
Copper

Date	Mintage	Good	VG	F	VF	XF
1813	—	10.00	20.00	30.00	45.00	—

KM# 119 QUARTO
Copper **Obv:** Crowned spade Catalonian arms **Rev:** Crowned Spanish arms

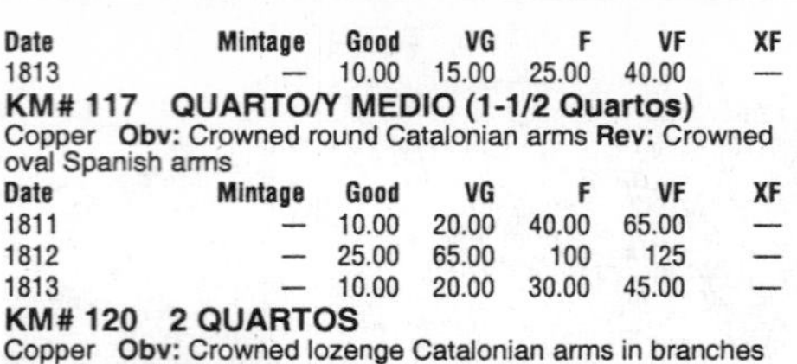

Date	Mintage	Good	VG	F	VF	XF
1813	—	10.00	15.00	25.00	40.00	—

KM# 117 QUARTO/Y MEDIO (1-1/2 Quartos)
Copper **Obv:** Crowned round Catalonian arms **Rev:** Crowned oval Spanish arms

Date	Mintage	Good	VG	F	VF	XF
1811	—	10.00	20.00	40.00	65.00	—
1812	—	25.00	65.00	100	125	—
1813	—	10.00	20.00	30.00	45.00	—

KM# 120 2 QUARTOS
Copper **Obv:** Crowned lozenge Catalonian arms in branches **Rev:** Crowned Spanish arms

Date	Mintage	Good	VG	F	VF	XF
1813	—	7.50	15.00	25.00	40.00	—
1814	—	10.00	22.50	32.50	50.00	—

KM# 115 3 QUARTOS
Copper

Date	Mintage	Good	VG	F	VF	XF
1810	—	9.00	17.50	22.50	37.50	—
1811	—	7.00	12.50	17.50	30.00	—
1812	—	5.00	7.50	10.00	20.00	—
1813	—	5.00	7.50	10.00	20.00	—
1814	—	5.00	7.50	10.00	20.00	—

KM# 125 3 QUARTOS
Copper

Date	Mintage	VG	F	VF	XF	Unc
1836 CATHAL	—	50.00	125	225	300	—
1836 CATALUNA	—	40.00	80.00	120	150	—

KM# 126 3 QUARTOS
Copper

Date	Mintage	VG	F	VF	XF	Unc
1836	—	12.50	25.00	32.50	40.00	—
1837	—	5.00	7.50	12.50	25.00	—
1838	—	6.00	10.00	15.00	30.00	—
1839	—	6.00	10.00	15.00	30.00	—
1840	—	12.00	25.00	40.00	65.00	—
1841	—	5.00	7.50	12.50	25.00	—
1842	—	20.00	40.00	80.00	110	—
1843	—	22.00	45.00	65.00	80.00	—
1844	—	10.00	15.00	20.00	30.00	—
1845	—	20.00	40.00	75.00	100	—
1846	—	10.00	20.00	25.00	35.00	—

KM# 116 6 QUARTOS
Copper

Date	Mintage	Good	VG	F	VF	XF
1810	—	10.00	20.00	30.00	50.00	—
1811/0	—	12.00	25.00	40.00	60.00	—
1811	—	10.00	20.00	30.00	50.00	—
1812	—	7.50	12.50	20.00	35.00	—
1813	—	7.50	12.50	20.00	35.00	—
1814	—	12.00	25.00	40.00	60.00	—

KM# 127 6 QUARTOS
Copper

Date	Mintage	VG	F	VF	XF	Unc
1836	—	110	250	400	500	—

KM# 128 6 QUARTOS
Copper

Date	Mintage	VG	F	VF	XF	Unc
1836	—	12.00	25.00	40.00	55.00	—
1837	—	7.50	12.50	22.50	45.00	—
1838	—	7.50	12.50	20.00	40.00	—
1839	—	7.50	12.50	20.00	40.00	—
1840	—	7.50	12.50	20.00	40.00	—
1841	—	12.50	20.00	30.00	45.00	—
1842	—	100	225	375	625	—
1843	—	30.00	70.00	125	300	—
1844	—	7.50	12.50	20.00	40.00	—
1845	—	7.50	12.50	20.00	40.00	—
1846	—	7.50	12.50	20.00	40.00	—
1847	—	90.00	250	400	500	—
1848	—	90.00	250	400	500	—

KM# 129 PESETA
Silver

Date	Mintage	VG	F	VF	XF	Unc
1836B PS	—	20.00	50.00	80.00	150	—
1837B PS	—	25.00	65.00	110	175	—

PRETENDER COINAGE

Charles V

KM# 135 6 QUARTOS
Copper **Rev:** Crowned Catalonian arms within legend

Date	Mintage	Good	VG	F	VF	XF
1840BGA	—	450	750	1,000	1,200	—

KM# 136 REAL
Silver **Rev:** Crowned Spanish arms within legend

Date	Mintage	Good	VG	F	VF	XF
1840	—	300	500	650	800	—

GERONA

Gerona, a maritime frontier province in the extreme northeast corner of Spain and the provincial capital city of Gerona. The city of Gerona is the ancient city of Gerunda where St. Paul and St. James known as Santiago, patron saint of Spain and one of the twelve apostles, first rested when they came to Spain.

RULERS
Ferdinand (Fernando) VII, 1808-1833

MONETARY SYSTEM
12 Ardites (Dineros) = 8 Ochavos =
4 Quartos = 1 Sueldo
6 Sueldos = 1 Peseta
5 Pesetas = 1 Duro

PROVINCE

PROVISIONAL COINAGE

KM# 10 DURO (5 Pesetas)
Silver

Date	Mintage	VG	F	VF	XF	Unc
1808	—	50.00	90.00	140	250	—

KM# 11 DURO (5 Pesetas)
Copper

Date	Mintage	VG	F	VF	XF	Unc
1809	—	60.00	100	160	275	—

Note: Rim reeding on the Duro is hand cut making each example unique

KM# 12 5 PESETAS
Copper **Obv:** Bust of Ferndinand VII **Obv. Legend:** FERNANDO • VII • REY • DE • ESPANA **Rev. Legend:** GERONA...

Date	Mintage	VG	F	VF	XF	Unc
1809	—	4,000	7,000	12,000	15,000	—

LERIDA

Lerida is a frontier province of northern Spain with the provincial capital city of Lerida. The province is bounded on the north by France and on the east by Barcelona and Gerona.

RULERS
Ferdinand VII, 1808-1833

MONETARY SYSTEM
12 Ardites (Dineros) = 8 Ochavos =
4 Quartos = 1 Sueldo
6 Sueldos = 1 Peseta
5 Pesetas = 1 Duro

PROVINCE

STANDARD COINAGE

KM# 10 5 PESETAS
Silver

Date	Mintage	VG	F	VF	XF	Unc
1809	—	2,000	3,000	4,500	6,000	—

KM# 11 5 PESETAS
Silver **Obv:** Bust of Fernando VII right **Rev:** Crowned arms **Rev. Legend:** LERIDA * ANO * DE * 1809

Date	Mintage	VG	F	VF	XF	Unc
1809	—	1,800	2,500	4,000	5,500	—

MAJORCA

Majorca (Mallorca)

The Balearic Islands, an archipelago located in the Mediterranean Sea off the east coast of Spain including Majorca, Minorca, Cabrera, Ibiza, Formentera and a number of islets. Majorca, largest of the Balearic Islands is famous for its 1,000-year-old olive trees.

RULERS
Philip III of Spain, 1598-1621
Philip IV of Spain, 1621-1665
Charles II, 1665-1700
Philip V, 1700-1746

MONETARY SYSTEM
12 Dineros = 6 Doblers = 1 Sueldo (Sou)
30 Sueldos = 1 Duro

PROVINCE

STANDARD COINAGE

C# L51 12 DINEROS
Copper **Ruler:** Ferdinand VII **Obv. Legend:** FERDIN • VII • DEI • GRATIA **Rev. Legend:** HISP • ET • BALEARIUM • REX •

Date	Mintage	VG	F	VF	XF	Unc
1811	—	40.00	75.00	125	275	—
1812 DEI GRATIA, small date	—	5.00	8.00	15.00	35.00	—
1812 DEI GRATIA, large date	—	5.00	8.00	15.00	35.00	—
1812 DEI GRAT	—	12.50	20.00	35.00	85.00	—

C# L7.1 30 SUELDOS (Sous)
Silver **Ruler:** Ferdinand VII **Obv:** Ornate trim **Rev:** Crowned arms, ornate trim around edge

Date	Mintage	VG	F	VF	XF	Unc
1808	—	50.00	85.00	120	240	—

C# L7.2 30 SUELDOS (Sous)
Silver **Ruler:** Ferdinand VII **Obv:** FER. VII, value and date in depression **Rev:** Crowned arms

Date	Mintage	VG	F	VF	XF	Unc
1808	—	40.00	60.00	110	200	—

C# L52.1 30 SUELDOS (Sous)
Silver **Ruler:** Ferdinand VII **Rev:** Similar to C#L52.2

Date	Mintage	VG	F	VF	XF	Unc
1808	—	90.00	165	225	340	—

C# L52.2 30 SUELDOS (Sous)
Silver **Ruler:** Ferdinand VII **Obv:** Without FER VII **Rev:** Arms

Date	Mintage	VG	F	VF	XF	Unc
1808	—	150	300	700	1,250	—

C# L53.1 30 SUELDOS (Sous)
Silver **Ruler:** Ferdinand VII **Rev:** Arms

Date	Mintage	VG	F	VF	XF	Unc
1821 FRo. VII	—	40.00	60.00	110	200	—

C# L53.2 30 SUELDOS (Sous)
Silver **Ruler:** Ferdinand VII **Obv:** Error: FRo. VII inverted **Rev:** Arms

Date	Mintage	VG	F	VF	XF	Unc
1821	—	300	600	1,000	1,500	—

C# L9.1 5 PESETAS
Silver **Ruler:** Ferdinand VII **Obv:** Legend ends...CONST **Rev. Inscription:** YSLAS BALEARES in sprays

Date	Mintage	VG	F	VF	XF	Unc
1823	—	40.00	65.00	115	200	—

C# L9.2 5 PESETAS
Silver **Ruler:** Ferdinand VII **Obv:** Legend ends...EYND. **Rev. Inscription:** YSLAS BALEARES in sprays

Date	Mintage	VG	F	VF	XF	Unc
1823	—	60.00	90.00	150	275	—

NAVARRE

Navarre, a frontier province of northern Spain and a former kingdom lies on the western end of the border between France and Spain. From the 10th through the12th centuries Navarre was a solid power in the region. After 1234 the kingdom fell under French dominance. In 1516 Ferdinand annexed Navarre to Spain and it was under this vice royalty that coinage was struck at the mint in Pamplona.

The Kingdom of Navarre was ultimately divided and absorbed by France and Spain.

RULERS
Carlos VII (IV in Spain), 1788-1808
Ferdinand (Fernando) III
(VII in Spain), 1808-1833

MINT MARKS
B - Banyoles
P - Pamplona

PROVINCE

STANDARD COINAGE

KM# 120 1/2 MARAVEDI
Copper **Note:** Struck at Pamplona. Similar to 6 Maravedi, KM#125.

Date	Mintage	VG	F	VF	XF	Unc
1818PP	—	15.00	27.50	35.00	40.00	—
1819PP	—	20.00	40.00	50.00	60.00	—

KM# 135 1/2 MARAVEDI
Copper

Date	Mintage	VG	F	VF	XF	Unc
1831PP	—	12.00	25.00	35.00	45.00	—
1381PP Error	—	90.00	165	200	250	—
1832PP	—	90.00	165	200	250	—

KM# 121 MARAVEDI
Copper

Date	Mintage	VG	F	VF	XF	Unc
1818PP	—	10.00	20.00	30.00	40.00	—
1824Ja	—	10.00	20.00	27.50	35.00	—
1825PP	—	8.00	12.50	22.50	30.00	—
1826PP	—	8.00	12.50	22.50	30.00	—

KM# 122 MARAVEDI
Copper **Obv:** Laureate bust **Rev:** Arms

Date	Mintage	VG	F	VF	XF	Unc
1818PP	—	9.00	17.50	22.50	30.00	—
1819PP	—	9.00	17.50	22.50	30.00	—
1820PP	—	10.00	20.00	27.50	35.00	—

KM# 130 MARAVEDI
Copper **Note:** Similar to 1/2 Maravedi, KM#135.

Date	Mintage	VG	F	VF	XF	Unc
1829PP	—	7.50	15.00	20.00	25.00	—
1830/20PP	—	7.50	15.00	20.00	25.00	—
1830PP	—	7.50	15.00	20.00	25.00	—
1831PP	—	9.00	17.50	22.50	30.00	—
1832PP	—	9.00	17.50	22.50	30.00	—
1833PP	—	15.00	30.00	45.00	50.00	—

KM# 124 3 MARAVEDIS
Copper **Note:** Similar to 6 Maravedi, KM#126, but legend: FERDIN.III...

Date	Mintage	VG	F	VF	XF	Unc
1818	—	15.00	30.00	45.00	65.00	—
1819	—	15.00	30.00	45.00	65.00	—

KM# 123 3 MARAVEDIS
Copper **Note:** Similar to 6 Maravedi, KM#126.

Date	Mintage	VG	F	VF	XF	Unc
1818PP	—	25.00	45.00	65.00	85.00	—
1819PP	—	20.00	35.00	55.00	70.00	—
1820PP	—	20.00	35.00	55.00	70.00	—
1825PP	—	20.00	35.00	55.00	70.00	—
1826PP	—	20.00	35.00	55.00	70.00	—

KM# 131 3 MARAVEDIS
Copper

Date	Mintage	VG	F	VF	XF	Unc
1829	—	12.50	25.00	40.00	60.00	—
1830	—	10.00	15.00	20.00	40.00	—
1831	—	15.00	30.00	45.00	65.00	—
1832	—	12.50	25.00	40.00	60.00	—
1833	—	12.50	25.00	40.00	60.00	—

KM# 125 6 MARAVEDIS
Copper **Obv:** Young bust, bare head **Rev:** Arms

Date	Mintage	VG	F	VF	XF	Unc
1818	—	25.00	50.00	80.00	100	—

KM# 126 6 MARAVEDIS
Copper **Obv:** Laureate bust

Date	Mintage	VG	F	VF	XF	Unc
1818PP	—	35.00	70.00	120	150	—
1819PP	—	25.00	50.00	80.00	100	—
1820PP	—	30.00	55.00	90.00	125	—

TARRAGONA

Tarragona is a maritime province in northeast Spain, south of Barcelona and Lerida, with the provincial capital city of Tarragona. The province produces excellent wines; the city is a flourishing seaport.

RULERS
Ferdinand (Fernando) III,
(VII in Spain) 1808-1833

PROVINCE

STANDARD COINAGE

KM# 5 5 PESETAS
Silver **Obv. Legend:** FER • VII • (raised periods) **Rev:** Crowned shield, curved base crown

Date	Mintage	VG	F	VF	XF	Unc
1809. Small 0	—	50.00	85.00	125	200	—

KM# 6 5 PESETAS
Silver **Obv. Legend:** FER • VII • (raised periods) **Rev:** Curved base crown/shield

Date	Mintage	VG	F	VF	XF	Unc
1809. Large 0	—	50.00	85.00	125	200	—

KM# 7 5 PESETAS
Silver **Obv. Legend:** FER VII **Rev:** Crowned shield, straight base crown

Date	Mintage	VG	F	VF	XF	Unc
1809. Small 0	—	50.00	85.00	125	200	—

KM# 8 5 PESETAS
Silver **Obv. Legend:** FER VII **Rev:** Crowned shield, curved base crown

Date	Mintage	VG	F	VF	XF	Unc
1809. Small 0	—	50.00	85.00	125	200	—

KM# 9 5 PESETAS
Silver **Obv. Legend:** FER VII **Rev:** Crowned shield, straight base crown

Date	Mintage	VG	F	VF	XF	Unc
1809. Small 0, lazy 9	—	50.00	85.00	125	200	—

KM# 10 5 PESETAS
Silver **Obv. Legend:** FER // F.o.

Date	Mintage	VG	F	VF	XF	Unc
1809. Rare	—	—	—	—	—	—

TORTOSA

Tortosa is a fortified city of Spain located in Tarragona province.

RULERS
Fernando VII, 1808-1833

CITY

STANDARD COINAGE

KM# 5 DURO (5 Pesetas)
Silver **Countermark:** Tower, 1, DURO & TOR. raised R • SA
Note: 4 countermarks.

Date	Mintage	VG	F	VF	XF	Unc
1808-09	—	450	850	1,350	2,250	—

VALENCIA

Valencia is a maritime province of eastern Spain with a capital city of Valencia. Once a former kingdom, Valencia included the present provinces of Castellon de la Plana and Alicante.

RULERS
Ferdinand (Fernando) VII, 1808-1833

PROVINCE

STANDARD COINAGE

KM# 80 REAL (2 Reales de Vellon)
Silver

Date	Mintage	VG	F	VF	XF	Unc
1809LL	—	17.50	32.50	55.00	90.00	—

KM# 85 2 REALES (4 Reales de Vellon)
Silver

Date	Mintage	VG	F	VF	XF	Unc
1823LL	—	12.50	22.50	37.50	65.00	—

Note: The 4 Reales de Vellon circulated as a regular issue 2 Reales while the 2 Reales de Vellon circulated as a regular 1 Real

STRAITS SETTLEMENTS

THAILAND
PERLIS
KEDAH
PENANG
PERAK
SELANGOR
MALACCA
KELANTAN
South China Sea
TRENGGANU
PAHANG
NEGRI SEMBILAN
JOHORE
SINGAPORE
Indian Ocean
SUMATRA

Straits Settlements, a former British crown colony situated on the Malay Peninsula of Asia, was formed in 1826 by combining the territories of Singapore, Penang and Malacca. The colony was administered by the East India Company until its abolition in 1853. Straits Settlements was a part of British India from 1858 to 1867 at which time it became a Crown Colony. This name was changed to Malaya in 1939.

RULERS
British

MINT MARKS
H - Heaton, Birmingham
W - Soho Mint
B - Bombay

MONETARY SYSTEM
100 Cents = 1 Dollar

EAST INDIA COMPANY
1826-1858

STANDARD COINAGE

KM# 1 1/4 CENT
Copper **Rev. Legend:** EAST INDIA COMPANY

Date	Mintage	F	VF	XF	Unc	BU
1845	34,327,000	10.00	20.00	40.00	140	—
1845 Proof	—	Value: 550				

Note: WW on truncation

KM# 2 1/2 CENT
Copper

Date	Mintage	F	VF	XF	Unc	BU
1845	18,737,000	12.00	18.00	85.00	135	—
1845 Proof	—	Value: 530				
1845	Inc. above	12.00	16.00	75.00	135	—

Note: WW on truncation

Date	Mintage	F	VF	XF	Unc	BU
1845 Proof	—	Value: 550				

Note: WW on truncation

KM# 3 CENT
Copper

Date	Mintage	F	VF	XF	Unc	BU
1845	18,526,000	6.00	16.00	38.00	85.00	—
1845 Proof	—	Value: 530				

Note: WW on truncation

BRITISH INDIA GOVERNMENT
1858-1867

STANDARD COINAGE

KM# 4 1/4 CENT
Copper **Rev. Legend:** INDIA STRAITS

Date	Mintage	F	VF	XF	Unc	BU
1862	3,368,000	85.00	180	380	715	—
1862 Proof	—	Value: 1,150				

KM# 5 1/2 CENT
Copper

Date	Mintage	F	VF	XF	Unc	BU
1862	4,590,000	50.00	100	260	500	—
1862 Proof	—	Value: 900				

KM# 6 CENT
Copper

Date	Mintage	F	VF	XF	Unc	BU
1862	9,321,000	9.00	22.00	85.00	245	—
1862 Proof	—	Value: 635				

BRITISH COLONY
1867-1939

STANDARD COINAGE

KM# 7 1/4 CENT
Copper **Rev. Legend:** STRAITS SETTLEMENTS **Edge:** Plain

Date	Mintage	F	VF	XF	Unc	BU
1872 Proof	—	Value: 580				
1872H	9,240,000	12.00	26.00	90.00	200	—
1872H Proof	—	Value: 515				
1873	—	150	250	600	1,500	—
1873 Proof	—	Value: 2,600				
1875 Proof	—	Value: 1,000				
1875W Proof	—	Value: 1,000				
1883	200,000	520	1,200	2,280	3,500	—

KM# 7a 1/4 CENT
Bronze

Date	Mintage	F	VF	XF	Unc	BU
1884	8,000,000	10.00	16.00	80.00	170	—
1884 Proof	—	Value: 460				

KM# 14 1/4 CENT
Bronze **Obv:** Head of Queen Victoria left **Edge:** Reeded

Date	Mintage	F	VF	XF	Unc	BU
1889	2,000,000	10.00	16.00	80.00	170	—
1889 Proof	—	Value: 460				
1890 Proof	—	Value: 880				

Date	Mintage	F	VF	XF	Unc	BU
1891 Proof	—	Value: 660				
1898	1,600,000	9.00	15.00	48.00	150	—
1898 Proof	—	Value: 360				
1899	2,400,000	9.00	15.00	48.00	150	—

KM# 8 1/2 CENT

Copper **Edge:** Plain

Date	Mintage	F	VF	XF	Unc	BU
1872 Proof	—	Value: 1,150				
1872H	5,610,000	30.00	75.00	145	330	—
1872H Proof	—	Value: 630				
1873	—	55.00	120	280	600	—
1874 Proof	—	Value: 630				
1875 Proof	—	Value: 780				
1875W Proof	—	Value: 630				
1883	2,740,000	75.00	145	450	850	—

KM# 8a 1/2 CENT

Bronze

Date	Mintage	F	VF	XF	Unc	BU
1884	4,000,000	16.00	30.00	125	250	—
1884 Proof	—	Value: 635				

KM# 15 1/2 CENT

Bronze **Edge:** Reeded

Date	Mintage	F	VF	XF	Unc	BU
1889	2,000,000	25.00	45.00	135	260	—
1890 Proof	—	Value: 630				
1891 Proof	—	Value: 2,500				

KM# 9 CENT

Copper **Edge:** Plain

Date	Mintage	F	VF	XF	Unc	BU
1872 Proof	—	Value: 550				
1872H	5,770,000	4.50	12.50	60.00	145	—
1872H Proof	—	Value: 550				
1873	—	9.00	18.00	75.00	180	—
1874	10,000,000	4.50	12.50	60.00	145	—
1874H	10,000,000	4.50	12.50	60.00	145	—
1874H Proof	—	Value: 450				
1875	6,000,000	7.50	15.00	65.00	150	—
1875 Proof	—	Value: 450				
1875W	—	7.50	15.00	65.00	150	—
1875 Proof	—	Value: 450				

Note: W on truncation

Date	Mintage	F	VF	XF	Unc	BU
1876	—	7.50	15.00	65.00	150	—
1877	—	7.50	15.00	65.00	150	—
1878	—	150	380	780	1,800	—
1883	8,640,000	7.50	15.00	70.00	200	—

KM# 9a CENT

Bronze

Date	Mintage	F	VF	XF	Unc	BU
1884	6,000,000	2.50	8.00	28.00	145	—
1884 Proof	—	Value: 450				
1885	7,412,000	12.00	60.00	145	320	—
1886	1,512,000	22.00	65.00	170	380	—

KM# 16 CENT

Bronze **Obv:** Bust of Queen Victoria left **Edge:** Reeded

Date	Mintage	F	VF	XF	Unc	BU
1887	8,988,000	2.50	9.00	45.00	160	—
1888	10,000,000	2.50	9.00	45.00	160	—
1889	6,010,000	2.50	9.00	45.00	160	—
1890	11,006,000	2.50	9.00	45.00	160	—
1890 Proof	—	Value: 450				
1891	6,004,000	2.00	7.00	30.00	135	—
1894	9,034,000	2.00	7.00	30.00	135	—
1895	4,466,000	2.00	7.00	30.00	135	—
1897	18,040,000	2.00	7.00	30.00	135	—

Date	Mintage	F	VF	XF	Unc	BU
1898	2,085,999	8.00	16.00	60.00	170	—
1898 Proof	—	Value: 450				
1900	2,914,000	1.50	6.00	27.00	125	—

KM# 10 5 CENTS

1.3600 g., 0.8000 Silver .0349 oz. **Obv:** Bust of Queen Victoria left

Date	Mintage	F	VF	XF	Unc	BU
1871	62,000	440	880	1,750	2,880	—
1871 Proof	—	Value: 5,150				
1873	60,000	560	1,580	2,450	3,330	—
1874H	60,000	65.00	170	320	600	—
1876H	40,000	560	1,580	2,450	3,330	—
1877	60,000	480	975	1,665	2,720	—
1878	260,000	17.00	37.00	145	290	—
1878 Proof	—	Value: 700				
1879H	100,000	145	255	550	780	—
1880H	90,000	175	350	850	1,150	—
1881	180,000	22.00	48.00	190	320	—
1881 Proof	—	Value: 700				
1882H	380,000	17.00	35.00	110	260	—
1882H Proof	—	Value: 700				
1883	80,000	180	300	580	1,100	—
1884	440,000	7.00	15.00	80.00	180	—
1884 Proof	—	Value: 700				
1885	220,000	18.00	50.00	150	400	—
1885 Proof	—	Value: 700				
1886	340,000	10.00	15.00	50.00	170	—
1887	400,000	7.00	12.00	50.00	150	—
1888	590,000	7.00	12.00	50.00	150	—
1889	1,000,000	5.00	7.00	23.00	128	—
1889 Proof	—	Value: 700				
1890H	400,000	10.00	25.00	80.00	160	—
1890H Proof	—	Value: 700				
1891	800,000	5.00	7.00	23.00	128	—
1893	440,000	4.50	8.00	30.00	130	—
1894	340,000	4.50	8.00	23.00	128	—
1895	1,480,000	4.50	8.00	23.00	128	—
1896	960,000	4.50	6.00	22.00	120	—
1897	320,000	8.00	12.00	40.00	145	—
1897H	440,000	8.00	12.00	40.00	145	—
1898	1,200,000	3.50	5.00	22.00	120	—
1899	78,000	6.00	9.00	33.00	145	—
1900	2,720,000	4.00	6.00	23.00	128	—
1900H	400,000	8.00	12.00	30.00	145	—

KM# 11 10 CENTS

2.7100 g., 0.8000 Silver .0697 oz.

Date	Mintage	F	VF	XF	Unc	BU
1871	248,000	17.00	30.00	120	290	—
1871 Proof	—	Value: 2,900				
1872H	230,000	17.00	30.00	120	290	—
1872H Proof	—	Value: 1,800				
1873	210,000	30.00	60.00	180	320	—
1874H	180,000	15.00	22.00	90.00	175	—
1876H	120,000	42.00	75.00	180	380	—
1877	160,000	20.00	48.00	85.00	220	—
1878	470,000	8.00	13.00	33.00	120	—
1878 Proof	—	Value: 380				
1879H	250,000	15.00	23.00	85.00	160	—
1879H Proof	—	Value: 380				
1880H	235,000	18.00	36.00	110	245	—
1881	460,000	6.00	12.00	45.00	115	—
1881 Proof	—	Value: 380				
1882H	430,000	6.00	12.00	45.00	115	—
1882H Proof	—	Value: 380				
1883	160,000	45.00	90.00	160	410	—
1883H	610,000	190	400	780	1,600	—
1883H Proof	—	Value: 2,600				
1884 Crosslet 4	1,240,000	3.50	6.00	18.00	120	—
1884 Plain 4	Inc. above	3.50	6.00	18.00	120	—
1884 Proof	—	Value: 380				
1885	400,000	18.00	28.00	48.00	180	—
1885 Proof	—	Value: 410				
1886	790,000	4.00	6.00	18.00	120	—
1886 Proof	—	Value: 380				
1887	640,000	4.00	6.00	18.00	120	—
1887 Proof	—	Value: 380				
1888	1,075,000	3.00	6.00	18.00	120	—
1888 Proof	—	Value: 380				
1889	1,500,000	3.00	5.00	16.00	110	—
1889 Proof	—	Value: 380				
1890H	730,000	4.00	6.00	20.00	120	—
1890H Proof	—	Value: 380				
1891	1,380,000	4.00	6.00	12.00	90.00	—
1891 Proof	—	Value: 380				

Date	Mintage	F	VF	XF	Unc	BU
1893	980,000	4.00	6.00	12.00	90.00	—
1893 Proof	—	Value: 380				
1894	1,640,000	4.00	6.00	12.00	90.00	—
1895	2,324,000	4.00	6.00	12.00	90.00	—
1896	2,256,000	4.00	6.00	12.00	90.00	—
1897	700,000	5.00	7.00	30.00	135	—
1897H	390,000	6.00	10.00	35.00	135	—
1898	1,960,000	4.00	6.00	20.00	95.00	—
1899	286,000	4.00	6.00	20.00	95.00	—
1900	2,960,000	4.00	6.00	20.00	95.00	—
1900H	1,000,000	5.00	7.00	30.00	100	—
1900H Proof	—	Value: 750				

KM# 12 20 CENTS

5.4300 g., 0.8000 Silver .1396 oz.

Date	Mintage	F	VF	XF	Unc	BU
1871	16,000	400	840	1,580	2,575	—
1871 Proof	—	Value: 3,480				
1872H	40,000	120	275	550	1,050	—
1873	30,000	400	730	1,360	2,360	—
1874H	45,000	65.00	120	220	560	—
1876H	30,000	130	290	560	1,050	—
1877	55,000	60.00	100	215	550	—
1877 Proof	—	Value: 750				
1878	150,000	15.00	20.00	95.00	22.00	—
1878 Proof	—	Value: 515				
1879H	50,000	75.00	145	265	560	—
1879H Proof	—	Value: 630				
1880H	85,000	35.00	65.00	125	350	—
1880H Proof	—	Value: 500				
1881/71	100,000	60.00	120	180	600	—
1881	Inc. above	18.00	40.00	125	300	—
1882H	245,000	12.00	22.00	60.00	260	—
1882H Proof	—	Value: 600				
1883	200,000	15.00	25.00	75.00	200	—
1884	220,000	7.50	12.00	35.00	135	—
1884 Proof	—	Value: 460				
1885	100,000	16.00	36.00	127	320	—
1886	245,000	6.00	9.00	45.00	115	—
1886 Proof	—	Value: 500				
1887	220,000	6.00	9.00	45.00	115	—
1888	295,000	6.00	9.00	45.00	115	—
1889	420,000	5.00	8.00	28.00	100	—
1890H	270,000	9.00	18.00	75.00	145	—
1890H Proof	—	Value: 410				
1891	510,000	4.50	7.50	22.00	90.00	—
1893	310,000	4.50	7.50	22.00	90.00	—
1894	495,000	4.50	7.50	22.00	90.00	—
1895	580,000	4.50	7.50	22.00	90.00	—
1896	600,000	4.50	7.50	22.00	90.00	—
1897	150,000	10.00	18.00	45.00	160	—
1897H	185,000	10.00	18.00	45.00	160	—
1898	580,000	4.50	7.50	22.00	100	—
1899	204,000	4.50	7.50	22.00	100	—
1900	620,000	4.50	7.50	22.00	100	—
1900H	300,000	9.00	12.00	30.00	120	—
1900H Proof	—	Value: 1,250				
1901	600,000	4.50	8.00	18.00	90.00	—

KM# 13 50 CENTS

13.5769 g., 0.8000 Silver .3492 oz.

Date	Mintage	F	VF	XF	Unc	BU
1886	60,000	110	245	480	1,100	—
1886 Proof	—	Value: 4,800				
1887	94,000	60.00	145	330	820	—
1887 Proof	—	Value: 4,800				
1888	96,000	60.00	145	330	820	—
1889	32,000	1,210	1,950	2,660	5,000	—
1890H	42,000	175	330	665	1,335	—
1891	121,000	45.00	85.00	200	440	—
1891 Proof	—	Value: 4,800				
1893	24,000	665	1,120	1,880	3,650	—
1893 Proof	—	Value: 5,900				
1894	52,000	75.00	200	350	720	—
1895	56,000	75.00	200	350	720	—
1896	120,000	42.00	75.00	200	485	—
1897	36,000	120	235	515	1,000	—

Date	Mintage	F	VF	XF	Unc	BU
1897H	44,000	120	230	420	900	—
1898	160,000	35.00	75.00	220	460	—
1899	136,000	35.00	75.00	220	460	—
1900	88,000	60.00	100	275	515	—
1900H	40,000	145	275	550	970	—
1900H Proof	—	Value: 6,000				
1901	120,000	28.00	55.00	180	360	—

PATTERNS

Including off metal strikes

KM#	Date	Mintage	Identification	Mkt Val
Pn1	1872H	—	10 Cents. Copper. KM#11.	1,120
Pn2	1873	—	10 Cents. Copper. KM#11.	1,120
Pn4	1890	—	Cent. Silver. KM#16.	11,000
Pn5	1891	—	1/4 Cent. Silver. KM#14.	12,420
Pn6	1891	—	1/4 Cent. Gold. KM#14.	17,270
Pn7	1891	—	1/2 Cent. Silver. KM#15.	12,420
Pn8	1891	—	1/2 Cent. Gold. KM#15.	17,270
Pn9	1891	—	Cent. Silver. KM#16.	11,000
Pn10	1891	—	Cent. Gold. KM#16.	15,000
Pn11	1898	—	1/4 Cent. Silver. KM#14.	7,300
Pn12	1898	—	Cent. Silver. KM#16.	10,600

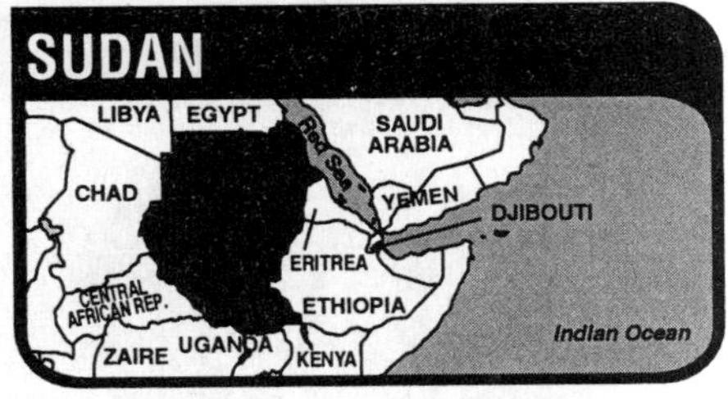

The Democratic Republic of the Sudan, located in northeast Africa on the Red Sea between Egypt and Ethiopia, has an area of 967,500 sq. mi. (2,505,810 sq. km.) and a population of *24.5 million. Capital: Khartoum. Agriculture and livestock raising are the chief occupations. Cotton, gum arabic and peanuts are exported.

The Sudan, site of the powerful Nubian kingdom of Roman times, was a collection of small independent states from the 14th century until 1820-22 when it was conquered and united by Mohammed Ali, Pasha of Egypt. Egyptian forces were driven from the area during the Mahdist revolt, 1881-98, but the Sudan was retaken by Anglo-Egyptian expeditions, 1896-98, and established as an Anglo-Egyptian condominium in 1899. Britain supplied the administrative apparatus and personnel, but the appearance of joint Anglo-Egyptian administration was continued until Jan. 9, 1954, when the first Sudanese self-government parliament was inaugurated. The Sudan achieved independence on Jan. 1, 1956 with the consent of the British and Egyptian government.

TITLES

جمهورية السودان

Jumhuriya(t) as-Sudan

الجمهورية السودان

الديمقراطية

al-Jumhuriya(t) as-Sudan ad-Dimiqratiya(t)

MINTNAME

ام درمان

Omdurman

RULERS

Mohammed Ahmed (the Mahdi),
AH1298-1302/1881-1885AD

Abdullah Ibn Mohammed (the Khalifa),
AH1302-1316/1885-1898AD

MONETARY SYSTEM

40 Para = 1 Ghirsh = Piastre

KINGDOM

Mohammed Ahmed

AH1298-1302/1881-85AD

(the Mahdi)

MINT

Khartoum

Translation of Arabic legends on Mahdi silver coinage:

بامر المهدى = By order of the Mahdi (in Toughra)

٥ = 5 (regnal year)

ضرب = Struck (Duriba)

فى = In (Fi)

الهجرة = Hejira(t)

١٣٠٢ = 1302(AH)

سنة = Sana(t) (year)

STANDARD COINAGE

Mint: Khartoum
KM# 1 10 PIASTRES
Silver

Date	Mintage	VG	F	VF	XF	Unc
AH1302 Rare	—	—	—	—	—	—

Mint: Khartoum
KM# 2 20 PIASTRES
Silver

Date	Mintage	VG	F	VF	XF	Unc
AH1302	—	225	400	750	1,500	—

Mint: Khartoum
KM# 3 100 PIASTRES
Gold **Note:** Struck by the Mahdi, which is a copy of the Egyptian coin 100 Qirsh, KM#235.1 under the Ottoman sultan. This issue is more crude than the Egyptian type and has crude edge milling. Reverse Arabic legend "Struck in Misr AH1255 Year 2" (Egypt); however they were struck in the Sudan about AH1302.

Date	Mintage	VG	F	VF	XF	Unc
AH1255-2	—	—	2,000	3,500	—	—

Abdullah Ibn Mohammed

AH1302-16/1885-98AD

STANDARD COINAGE

Mint: Without Mint Name
KM# A8 5 PARA
Copper **Note:** Probably a pattern.

Date	Mintage	VG	F	VF	XF	Unc
AH1308 Unique	—	—	—	—	—	—

Mint: Omdurman
KM# 8 10 PARA
Copper, 25 mm. **Note:** Probably a pattern.

Date	Mintage	VG	F	VF	XF	Unc
AH1308 Unique	—	—	—	—	—	—

Mint: Omdurman
KM# 4 PIASTRE
Debased Silver/Billon, 18 mm. **Note:** Plain borders.

Date	Mintage	VG	F	VF	XF	Unc
AH1304-1 (1886)	—	200	500	1,000	—	—
AH1311-9 (1893)	—	150	400	850	—	—
AH1311-11 (1894)	—	150	400	750	—	—

Mint: Omdurman
KM# 22.3 2 PIASTRES

Debased Silver/Billon **Note:** Borders of crescents and roses.

Date	Mintage	VG	F	VF	XF	Unc
AH1312	—	60.00	125	250	500	—

Mint: Omdurman
KM# 22.2 2 PIASTRES
Debased Silver/Billon **Note:** Borders of crescents, stars and roses.

Date	Mintage	VG	F	VF	XF	Unc
AH1312	—	60.00	15.00	250	500	—

Mint: Omdurman
KM# 22.1 2 PIASTRES
Debased Silver/Billon **Note:** Borders of small crescrnts and few stars.

Date	Mintage	VG	F	VF	XF	Unc
AH1311	—	150	400	750	—	—

Mint: Omdurman
KM# 9 2 PIASTRES
Debased Silver/Billon, 18 mm. **Note:** Plain borders.

Date	Mintage	VG	F	VF	XF	Unc
AH1310-8	—	200	500	1,000	—	—
AH1311-9	—	150	400	850	—	—
AH1311-11	—	150	400	850	—	—

Mint: Omdurman
KM# 18 2 PIASTRES
Debased Silver/Billon **Note:** Wreath borders.

Date	Mintage	VG	F	VF	XF	Unc
AH1311-8	—	60.00	125	250	500	—
AH1311-11	—	40.00	100	200	450	—

Mint: Omdurman
KM# 23.2 2-1/2 PIASTRES
Debased Silver/Billon **Obv:** "Maqbul" below toughra

Date	Mintage	VG	F	VF	XF	Unc
AH1312	—	120	300	500	—	—

Mint: Omdurman
KM# 24 2-1/2 PIASTRES
Debased Silver/Billon **Note:** Borders of crescents only.

Date	Mintage	VG	F	VF	XF	Unc
AH1312	—	100	200	400	—	—

Mint: Omdurman
KM# 23.1 2-1/2 PIASTRES
Debased Silver/Billon **Obv:** "Umla Jadida" below toughra **Note:** Borders of crescents, stars, and roses.

Date	Mintage	VG	F	VF	XF	Unc
AH1312	—	60.00	120	200	300	—

Note: KM#23.1 differs from KM#22.2 by the presence of the "Shadda" which looks like the letter W, after the numeral "2" on the reverse

Mint: Omdurman
KM# 10.1 4 PIASTRES
Debased Silver/Billon, 25 mm. **Note:** Plain borders.

Date	Mintage	VG	F	VF	XF	Unc
AH1310	—	350	800	1,500	—	—

Mint: Omdurman
KM# 10.2 4 PIASTRES
Debased Silver/Billon **Note:** Wreath borders.

Date	Mintage	VG	F	VF	XF	Unc
AH1310	—	350	800	1,500	—	—

Mint: Omdurman
KM# 5.2 5 PIASTRES
Debased Silver/Billon **Obv:** Denomination below toughra

Date	Mintage	VG	F	VF	XF	Unc
AH1311-11	—	60.00	120	200	400	—

Mint: Omdurman
KM# 19 5 PIASTRES
Debased Silver/Billon **Note:** Borders of crescents and stars.

Date	Mintage	VG	F	VF	XF	Unc
AH1311	—	60.00	120	200	400	—

Mint: Omdurman
KM# 20 5 PIASTRES
Debased Silver/Billon **Note:** Borders of crescents only.

Date	Mintage	VG	F	VF	XF	Unc
AH1311	—	70.00	150	300	—	—

Mint: Omdurman
KM# 5.1 5 PIASTRES
Debased Silver/Billon **Note:** Borders of double crescents.

Date	Mintage	VG	F	VF	XF	Unc
AH1304-4	—	65.00	125	250	500	—
AH1304-5	—	70.00	150	300	550	—
AH1311-11	—	40.00	80.00	150	280	—

Note: Coins of AH1304/yr. "4" comes in two varieties, one with numeral 1 at top on reverse and one with 4.

Mint: Omdurman
KM# 11 5 PIASTRES
Debased Silver/Billon, 21-22 mm. **Note:** Plain borders.

Date	Mintage	VG	F	VF	XF	Unc
AH1310	—	65.00	150	250	—	—

Mint: Omdurman
KM# 6 10 PIASTRES
Debased Silver/Billon **Note:** Borders of double crescents. Edge varieties exist.

Date	Mintage	VG	F	VF	XF	Unc
AH1304	—	150	400	750	—	—
AH1304-4	—	150	400	750	—	—
AH1311-11	—	100	200	400	—	—

Mint: Omdurman
KM# 12 10 PIASTRES
Debased Silver/Billon **Note:** Plain borders.

Date	Mintage	VG	F	VF	XF	Unc
AH1310-8	—	250	500	1,000	—	—

Mint: Omdurman
KM# 13 10 PIASTRES
Debased Silver/Billon **Note:** Wreath borders.

Date	Mintage	VG	F	VF	XF	Unc
AH1310-8	—	300	600	1,250	—	—

Mint: Omdurman
KM# 7.2 20 PIASTRES
Debased Silver/Billon

Date	Mintage	VG	F	VF	XF	Unc
AH1309-5	—	40.00	80.00	150	280	—
Note: Date on obverse with 1 on reverse, normal date						
AH1309-5	—	40.00	80.00	150	280	—
Note: Date on obverse with 1 on reverse, 9 of date retrograde						
AH1309-5	—	40.00	80.00	150	280	—
Note: Date on obverse without 1 on reverse, normal date						

Mint: Omdurman
KM# 25 20 PIASTRES
Debased Silver/Billon **Rev:** With "Azza Nasruhu"

Date	Mintage	VG	F	VF	XF	Unc
AH1311-11	—	30.00	60.00	125	225	—
AH1312-11	—	30.00	60.00	125	225	—

Mint: Omdurman
KM# 16 20 PIASTRES
Debased Silver/Billon **Obv:** Wreath with spears below **Rev:** Wreath with spears below

Date	Mintage	VG	F	VF	XF	Unc
AH1310 (8)	—	20.00	50.00	100	160	—
AH1311-12	—	20.00	50.00	100	160	—

Mint: Omdurman
KM# 21 20 PIASTRES
Debased Silver/Billon **Rev:** Without "Azza Nasruhu" **Note:** Borders of crescents only. Varieties exist.

Date	Mintage	VG	F	VF	XF	Unc
AH1302-9	—	35.00	80.00	150	225	—
Note: The date 1302 on the year 9 is in error for 1312, and is not to be confused with the Mahdi coinage						
AH1311-11	—	20.00	45.00	100	175	—
AH1312-11	—	20.00	45.00	100	175	—

Mint: Omdurman
KM# 14 20 PIASTRES
Debased Silver/Billon **Rev:** "Azza Nasruhu" **Note:** Borders of crescents, stars, and roses.

Date	Mintage	VG	F	VF	XF	Unc
AH1311	—	14.00	28.00	45.00	85.00	—
AH1311-9	—	12.00	25.00	40.00	75.00	—
AH1310-10	—	12.00	25.00	40.00	75.00	—
AH1312-11	—	12.00	25.00	40.00	75.00	—
AH1311-11	—	12.00	25.00	40.00	75.00	—
AH1312-12	—	10.00	15.00	25.00	45.00	—
AH1312	—	10.00	15.00	25.00	45.00	—

Mint: Omdurman
KM# 7.1 20 PIASTRES
Debased Silver/Billon **Note:** Borders of double crescents. Early years of 7.1 have larger diameter and larger circles on obverse and reverse.

Date	Mintage	VG	F	VF	XF	Unc
AH1304-4	—	40.00	80.00	150	280	—
AH1304-5	—	40.00	80.00	150	280	—

Note: Date on obverse with 1 on reverse

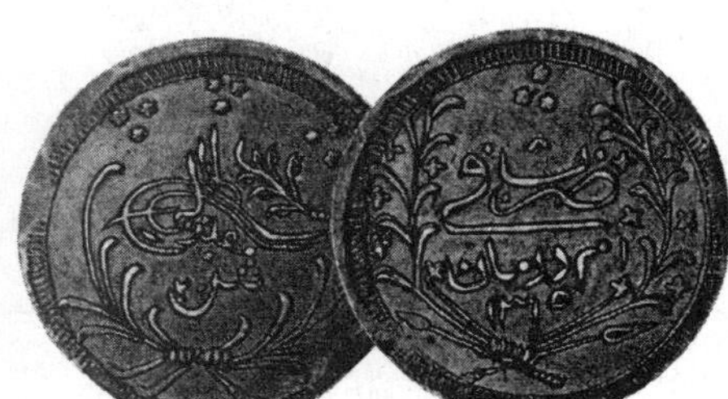

AH1315, R.Y. 8

AH1315, R.Y. 12

Mint: Omdurman
KM# 15 20 PIASTRES
Debased Silver/Billon **Rev:** Wreath borders with spears below **Note:** Many die varieties of this type exist.

Date	Mintage	VG	F	VF	XF	Unc
AH1310-8	—	15.00	30.00	50.00	90.00	—
AH1311-11	—	12.00	25.00	40.00	75.00	—
AH1312-12	—	7.00	12.50	20.00	40.00	—
AH1315-8	—	6.00	11.50	18.50	35.00	—

Mint: Omdurman
KM# 26 20 PIASTRES
Debased Silver/Billon **Obv:** Spears below **Note:** Wreath borders. Many die varieties of this type exist.

Date	Mintage	VG	F	VF	XF	Unc
AH1312-12	—	6.00	12.00	17.50	25.00	—
AH1312-16	—	20.00	40.00	70.00	125	—
AH1313-13	—	12.00	25.00	40.00	75.00	—
AH1315-8	—	7.00	13.50	20.00	35.00	—
AH1315-12	—	7.00	13.50	20.00	35.00	—

Mint: Omdurman
KM# 17 20 PIASTRES
Debased Silver/Billon **Note:** Wreath borders. Without spears on either side.

Date	Mintage	VG	F	VF	XF	Unc
AH1310-8	—	15.00	30.00	50.00	90.00	—
AH1315-12	—	12.00	25.00	40.00	75.00	—

The Kingdom of Sweden, a limited constitutional monarchy located in northern Europe between Norway and Finland, has an area of 173,732 sq. mi. (449,960 sq. km.).

Sweden was founded as a Christian stronghold by Olaf Skottkonung late in the 10th century. After conquering Finland late in the 13th century, Sweden, together with Norway, came under the rule of Denmark, 1397-1523, in an association known as the Union of Kalmar. Modern Sweden had its beginning in 1523 when Gustaf Vasa drove the Danes out of Sweden and was himself chosen king. Under Gustaf Adolphus II and Charles XII, Sweden was one of the great powers of 17th century Europe – until Charles invaded Russia in 1708, and was defeated at the Battle of Pultowa in June, 1709. Early in the 18th century, a coalition of Russia, Poland and Denmark took away Sweden's Baltic empire and in 1809 Sweden was forced to cede Finland to Russia. Norway was ceded to Sweden by the Treaty of Kiel in January, 1814. The Norwegians resisted for a time but later signed the Act of Union at the Convention of Moss in August, 1814,The Union was dissolved in 1905 and Norway became independent.

RULERS

Gustaf IV Adolf, 1792-1809
Carl XIII, 1809-1818
Carl XIV Johan, 1818-1844
Oscar I, 1844-1859
Carl XV Adolf, 1859-1872
Oscar II, 1872-1907

MINT OFFICIALS' INITIALS

Initials	Date	Name
AG, G	1838-55	Alexander Grandinson
AL	1898-1916	Adolf Lindberg, engraver
CB	1821-37	Christopher Borg
EB	1876-1908	Emil Brusewitz
G	1799-1830	Lars Grandel, engraver
G	1830-53	Ludvig Persson Lundgren
LA	1854-97	Lea Ahlborn, engraver
LB	1819-21	Lars Bergencreutz
OL	1773-1819	Olof Lidijn
ST, T	1855-76	Sebastian Tham

MONETARY SYSTEM

1798-1830

48 Skilling = 1 Riksdaler Species
2 Riksdaler (Speciesdaler) = 1 Ducat

1830-1855

32 Skilling Banco = 1 Riksdaler Riksgalds
12 Riksdaler Riksgalds = 3 Riksdaler Species

1855-1873

100 Ore = 4 Riksdaler Riksmynt
4 Riksdaler Riksmynt = 1 Riksdaler Species

Commencing 1873

100 Ore = 1 Riksdaler Riksmynt = 1 Krona

KINGDOM

REFORM COINAGE

1798-1830

KM# 563 1/12 SKILLING
Copper

Date	Mintage	VG	F	VF	XF	Unc
1802	3,393,000	0.75	1.50	4.00	16.00	—
1803	1,008,000	1.00	2.50	6.00	18.50	—
1805	2,526,000	0.75	1.50	4.00	16.00	—
1808	3,476,000	1.00	1.00	4.00	16.00	—

KM# 584 1/12 SKILLING
Copper

Date	Mintage	VG	F	VF	XF	Unc
1812	2,880,000	0.75	2.00	6.00	18.00	—

KM# 616 1/12 SKILLING
Copper

Date	Mintage	VG	F	VF	XF	Unc
1825	576,000	1.50	3.00	8.00	27.50	—
Note: Reeded edge						
1825	—	10.00	20.00	40.00	90.00	—
Note: Plain edge						

KM# 564 1/4 SKILLING
Copper **Ruler:** Gustaf IV Adolf

Date	Mintage	VG	F	VF	XF	Unc
1802	3,383,000	1.00	2.00	7.00	25.00	—
1803	3,217,000	1.00	2.00	8.00	27.50	—
1805	5,189,000	1.00	2.00	7.00	25.00	—
1806	8,141,000	1.00	2.00	7.00	25.00	—
1807	641,000	1.50	2.50	8.00	30.00	—
1808 Narrow crown	7,480,000	1.00	2.50	8.00	30.00	—
1808 Wider crown	Inc. above	3.00	7.00	17.50	50.00	—

KM# 592 1/4 SKILLING
Copper

Date	Mintage	VG	F	VF	XF	Unc
1817	1,152,000	10.00	30.00	75.00	160	—

KM# 595 1/4 SKILLING
Copper

Date	Mintage	VG	F	VF	XF	Unc
1819	2,450,000	1.00	3.00	10.00	35.00	—
1820	2,610,000	1.00	3.00	12.50	37.50	—
1821	2,208,000	1.00	3.00	10.00	35.00	—
1824	768,000	5.00	20.00	75.00	160	—
Note: Space between crown and monogram						
1824	Inc. above	5.00	20.00	75.00	160	—
Note: Crown touches monogram						
1825	2,496,000	1.00	3.00	10.00	35.00	—
Note: Open 4 in denomination						
1825	Inc. above	1.00	3.00	10.00	35.00	—
Note: Closed 4 in denomination						
1827	3,200,000	1.00	3.00	10.00	35.00	—
Note: Open 4 in denomination						
1827	Inc. above	1.00	3.00	10.00	35.00	—
Note: Closed 4 in denomination						
1828	4,320,000	1.00	2.50	8.00	30.00	—
1829	4,896,000	1.00	2.50	8.00	30.00	—
1830	256,000	10.00	20.00	75.00	175	—

KM# 549 1/2 SKILLING
Copper **Ruler:** Gustaf IV Adolf **Obv:** 3 crowns on orb **Rev:** Value, date

Date	Mintage	VG	F	VF	XF	Unc
1801	3,203,000	1.00	2.50	5.00	20.00	—
1802	1,188,000	1.00	2.50	5.00	20.00	—

KM# 565 1/2 SKILLING
Copper

Date	Mintage	VG	F	VF	XF	Unc
1802	Est. 2,340,000	2.00	5.00	10.00	40.00	—
Note: Struck over 18th century 1 ore - worth 50 to 100 percent more if earlier date visible.						
1803	Est. 5,048,000	2.00	5.00	10.00	37.50	—
Note: Struck over 18th century 1 ore - worth 50 to 100 percent more if earlier date visible.						
1804	595,000	125	200	400	1,500	—
1805	Est. 173,000	2.00	5.00	10.00	40.00	—
Note: Struck over 18th century 1 ore - worth 50 to 100 percent more if earlier date visible.						
1807	1,950,000	2.00	5.00	10.00	40.00	—
1809	4,845,000	2.00	5.00	10.00	40.00	—
Note: Struck over 18th century 1 ore - worth 50 to 100 percent more if earlier date visible.						

KM# 590 1/2 SKILLING
Copper

Date	Mintage	VG	F	VF	XF	Unc
1815	1,421,000	2.00	6.00	15.00	50.00	—
1816	566,000	2.50	9.00	18.00	70.00	—
1817	Inc. above	3.00	12.50	25.00	70.00	—

KM# 596 1/2 SKILLING
Copper

Date	Mintage	VG	F	VF	XF	Unc
1819	1,264,000	1.50	3.50	10.00	45.00	—
1820	1,296,000	1.50	3.50	10.00	45.00	—
1821	1,840,000	1.50	3.50	10.00	45.00	—
1822	944,000	1.50	3.50	10.00	75.00	—
1822	Inc. above	17.50	35.00	85.00	325	—
Note: L and S reversed						
1824	640,000	2.00	10.00	30.00	100	—
1825	816,000	4.50	15.00	40.00	140	—
1827	800,000	1.75	3.00	10.00	42.50	—
Note: SKIL- - LING						
1827	Inc. above	5.00	10.00	25.00	100	—
Note: SKIL LING						
1828	1,872,000	1.75	3.50	10.00	45.00	—
1829	2,560,000	1.75	3.50	10.00	45.00	—
1830	588,000	2.50	5.00	15.00	65.00	—

KM# 566 SKILLING
Copper

Date	Mintage	VG	F	VF	XF	Unc
1802	—	3.00	7.00	17.50	180	—
1803	—	20.00	40.00	100	375	—
1805	—	3.50	8.00	20.00	220	—
Note: Struck over 18th century 2 Ore - worth 50 to 100 percent more if earlier date visible.						

KM# 585 SKILLING
Copper

Date	Mintage	VG	F	VF	XF	Unc
1812	480,000	5.00	11.00	27.50	100	—
1814	730,000	6.00	12.50	27.50	100	—
1815	Inc. above	5.00	11.00	25.00	90.00	—
1816	230,000	7.50	16.00	32.50	100	—
1817	202,000	9.00	17.50	40.00	140	—

KM# 597 SKILLING
Copper

Date	Mintage	VG	F	VF	XF	Unc
1819	1,176,000	2.00	6.00	20.00	80.00	—
1820	1,376,000	8.00	13.50	37.50	135	—
Note: Oblique milling						
1820	Inc. above	2.00	6.00	20.00	85.00	—
Note: Square milling						
1821	704,000	2.00	6.00	20.00	85.00	—
1822	520,000	3.00	7.50	22.50	90.00	—
1825	472,000	2.00	6.00	20.00	85.00	—
1827	504,000	5.50	15.00	40.00	140	—
1828	664,000	4.00	8.00	25.00	95.00	—
1829	344,000	2.00	6.50	20.00	85.00	—
1830	312,000	3.50	7.50	22.50	90.00	—

KM# 580 1/24 RIKSDALER
0.3820 Silver

Date	Mintage	VG	F	VF	XF	Unc
1810 OL	742,000	5.00	10.00	22.50	50.00	—
1811 OL	378,000	5.00	10.00	25.00	50.00	—
1812 OL	537,000	6.00	12.50	25.00	55.00	—
1813 OL	444,000	5.00	10.00	25.00	50.00	—
1814 OL	101,000	8.00	17.50	37.50	80.00	—
1816 OL	160,000	7.50	15.00	32.50	70.00	—

KM# 583 1/12 RIKSDALER
0.5070 Silver

Date	Mintage	VG	F	VF	XF	Unc
1811 OL	735,000	15.00	30.00	80.00	175	—

KM# 560 1/6 RIKSDALER
6.2500 g., 0.6910 Silver .1388 oz.

Date	Mintage	VG	F	VF	XF	Unc
1800 OL	106,000	15.00	35.00	75.00	160	—
1801 OL	420,000	10.00	25.00	45.00	100	—
1802 OL	1,254,000	7.00	17.50	32.50	90.00	—
1803 OL	2,341,000	7.00	17.50	35.00	80.00	—
1804 OL	2,156,000	7.00	17.50	35.00	85.00	—
1805 OL	978,000	7.00	17.50	35.00	85.00	—
1806 OL	341,000	8.00	20.00	40.00	85.00	—
1807 OL	909,000	7.00	17.50	35.00	80.00	—
1808 OL	943,000	7.00	17.50	35.00	80.00	—
1809 OL	707,000	8.00	20.00	40.00	90.00	—

KM# 568 1/6 RIKSDALER
6.2500 g., 0.6910 Silver .1388 oz.

Date	Mintage	VG	F	VF	XF	Unc
1809 OL	—	50.00	150	325	675	—
1810 OL	297,000	20.00	50.00	100	225	—
1814/0 OL	199,000	22.50	60.00	125	275	—
1814 OL	Inc. above	20.00	55.00	100	225	—

KM# 589 1/6 RIKSDALER
6.2500 g., 0.6910 Silver .1388 oz. **Obv:** NORR in legends

Date	Mintage	VG	F	VF	XF	Unc
1815 OL	59,000	70.00	150	300	675	—
1817 OL	91,000	65.00	150	300	625	—

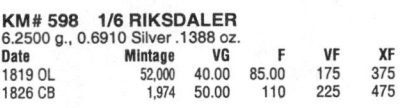

KM# 598 1/6 RIKSDALER
6.2500 g., 0.6910 Silver .1388 oz.

Date	Mintage	VG	F	VF	XF	Unc
1819 OL	52,000	40.00	85.00	175	375	—
1826 CB	1,974	50.00	110	225	475	—

KM# 615 1/6 RIKSDALER
6.1900 g., 0.6910 Silver .1378 oz.

Date	Mintage	VG	F	VF	XF	Unc
1828 CB Rare	1,974	—	—	—	—	—
Note: Edge inscription						
1828 CB Rare	1,024	—	—	—	—	—
Note: Without edge inscription						
1829 CB	2,039	25.00	50.00	100	235	—

KM# 587 1/3 RIKSDALER
0.8780 Silver

Date	Mintage	VG	F	VF	XF	Unc
1813 OL	63,000	65.00	130	235	525	—
1814 OL	33,000	80.00	160	300	700	—

KM# 612 1/3 RIKSDALER
9.7500 g., 0.8780 Silver .2752 oz.

Date	Mintage	VG	F	VF	XF	Unc
1827 CB Rare	—	—	—	—	—	—
1828 CB	61,000	32.00	65.00	140	375	—
1829 CB	109,000	35.00	70.00	145	300	—

Note: Previously listed 1828 and 1829 plain edge varieties are normal but weakly struck examples.

KM# 561 RIKSDALER
29.3600 g., 0.8780 Silver .8287 oz.

Date	Mintage	VG	F	VF	XF	Unc
1801 OL	91,000	100	100	200	425	—
1805 OL	150,000	32.50	100	200	350	—
1806 OL	205,000	30.00	75.00	165	385	—
1807 OL	37,000	35.00	80.00	190	450	—

KM# 586 RIKSDALER
29.3600 g., 0.8780 Silver .8287 oz.

Date	Mintage	VG	F	VF	XF	Unc
1812 OL	43,000	100	185	300	700	—
1814/2 OL	Inc. above	125	250	375	800	—
1814 OL	6,600	125	250	375	800	—

KM# 588 RIKSDALER
29.3600 g., 0.8780 Silver .8287 oz. **Obv:** NORR added to legend

Date	Mintage	VG	F	VF	XF	Unc
1814 OL	Inc. above	250	535	985	1,700	—
1815 OL	66,000	80.00	175	300	700	—
1816/5 OL	12,000	80.00	175	300	700	—
1816 OL	Inc. above	80.00	175	300	700	—
1817 OL	9,895	85.00	200	375	850	—
1818 OL	15,000	100	225	460	950	—

KM# 593 RIKSDALER
29.2500 g., 0.8780 Silver .8256 oz.

Date	Mintage	VG	F	VF	XF	Unc
1818 OL	—	65.00	125	320	650	—
Note: Mintage included with KM403.						
1819 OL	14,000	75.00	150	350	675	—
1819 LB	Inc. above	80.00	160	375	750	—
1820 LB Large bust	11,000	125	225	425	850	—

Date	Mintage	VG	F	VF	XF	Unc
1820 LB Small bust	Inc. above	125	225	425	850	—
1820 LB Rare	Inc. above	—	—	—	—	—
Note: Bust of Carl XIII						
1821 LB	29,000	50.00	100	300	480	—
1822 CB	34,000	40.00	120	200	480	—
1823 CB Large bust	26,000	40.00	120	200	525	—
1823 CB Small bust	Inc. above	40.00	120	200	525	—
1824 CB	53,000	40.00	80.00	200	525	—
1825 CB	20,000	40.00	80.00	200	525	—
1826 CB	7,538	100	225	500	975	—
1827 CB	17,000	50.00	110	225	550	—

KM# 610 RIKSDALER
29.2500 g., 0.8780 Silver .8256 oz. **Subject:** 300 Hundred Years of Political and Religious Freedom

Date	Mintage	VG	F	VF	XF	Unc
1821 CB	7,339	60.00	125	250	475	—

KM# 613 RIKSDALER
29.2500 g., 0.8780 Silver .8256 oz. **Obv:** Similar to KM#614 **Rev:** Seven angel heads around arms

Date	Mintage	VG	F	VF	XF	Unc
1827 CB	610	250	500	1,000	1,750	—

KM# 614 RIKSDALER
29.2500 g., 0.8780 Silver .8256 oz. **Rev:** Nine angel heads around arms

Date	Mintage	VG	F	VF	XF	Unc
1827 CB	Inc. above	350	750	1,500	3,000	—
1829 CB	409	350	750	1,500	3,000	—

REFORM COINAGE

1830-1855

KM# 625 1/6 SKILLING
Copper

Date	Mintage	VG	F	VF	XF	Unc
1830	2,544,000	0.90	1.50	4.00	17.50	—
Note: Reeded edge						
1830	Inc. above	5.00	12.00	25.00	80.00	—
Note: Plain edge						
1831	Inc. above	4.00	9.00	20.00	50.00	—

KM# 633 1/6 SKILLING
Copper **Note:** Draped bust with pearl border.

Date	Mintage	VG	F	VF	XF	Unc
1832	912,000	6.50	12.50	25.00	80.00	—

KM# 634 1/6 SKILLING
Copper **Note:** Plain border.

Date	Mintage	VG	F	VF	XF	Unc
1832	Inc. above	1.25	3.00	6.00	16.00	—

KM# 635 1/6 SKILLING
Copper **Obv:** Naked bust with pearl border

Date	Mintage	VG	F	VF	XF	Unc
1832	Inc. above	5.00	10.00	22.00	60.00	—

KM# 639 1/6 SKILLING
Copper

Date	Mintage	VG	F	VF	XF	Unc
1835	538,000	1.25	2.50	5.00	13.00	—
1836/5	1,498,000	1.25	2.50	5.00	13.00	—
1836	Inc. above	1.25	2.50	5.00	13.00	—
1838	427,000	2.50	6.50	12.00	29.00	—
1839	827,000	1.25	2.50	5.00	13.00	—
1840/35	860,000	0.90	2.00	4.50	10.00	—
1840	Inc. above	0.90	2.00	4.50	15.00	—
1840/35	865,000	2.00	4.00	15.00	45.00	—
1843	Inc. above	2.50	5.00	10.00	40.00	—
1844	71,000	30.00	60.00	120	350	—

KM# 656 1/6 SKILLING
Copper

Date	Mintage	VG	F	VF	XF	Unc
1844/35	291,000	5.00	15.00	40.00	175	—
1844	Inc. above	0.75	2.00	6.00	16.00	—
1845	92,000	3.00	6.00	17.50	50.00	—
1846	67,000	3.00	6.00	15.00	40.00	—
1847	823,000	0.90	1.75	4.50	13.00	—
1849	537,000	0.90	1.75	4.50	13.50	—
1850	407,000	1.00	2.00	5.00	22.00	—
1851	486,000	0.90	1.75	4.50	15.00	—
1852	462,000	0.90	1.75	4.50	15.00	—
1853	126,000	2.00	5.00	7.50	35.00	—
1854	422,000	0.90	1.75	4.50	13.00	—
1855	311,000	0.90	1.75	4.50	13.00	—

KM# 636 1/4 SKILLING
Copper

Date	Mintage	VG	F	VF	XF	Unc
1832	160,000	9.00	15.00	45.00	130	—
1833/2	96,000	3.50	10.00	30.00	75.00	—

KM# 640 1/3 SKILLING
Copper

Date	Mintage	VG	F	VF	XF	Unc
1835	483,000	3.00	6.00	16.00	45.00	—
1836	985,000	1.00	2.50	8.00	22.00	—
1837	1,096,000	1.00	2.50	8.00	22.00	—
1839/37	921,000	3.00	7.45	20.00	50.00	—
1839	Inc. above	1.00	2.50	8.00	22.00	—
1840/37	692,000	3.50	8.00	20.00	55.00	—
1840	Inc. above	2.00	4.50	10.00	35.00	—
1841	13,000	30.00	70.00	160	375	—
1842	612,000	1.00	3.00	8.00	22.00	—
1843	593,000	3.00	12.50	30.00	90.00	—

KM# 657 1/3 SKILLING
Copper

Date	Mintage	VG	F	VF	XF	Unc
1844	226,000	1.75	3.50	10.00	27.50	—
1845	192,000	2.00	4.50	15.00	30.00	—
1845/3	Inc. above	2.00	6.00	15.00	45.00	—
1846	79,000	2.50	5.00	10.00	30.00	—
1847	783,000	1.00	3.00	8.00	24.00	—
1848/7	933,000	1.50	3.00	10.00	30.00	—
1848	Inc. above	1.00	3.00	6.00	18.00	—
1850	537,000	1.00	3.00	8.00	24.00	—
Note: BANCO						
1850	Inc. above	4.00	8.00	30.00	85.00	—
Note: BANCO with two dots above A (error)						
1851	538,000	1.00	3.00	8.00	24.00	—
1852	489,000	1.00	3.00	8.00	24.00	—
1853	70,000	2.50	6.00	20.00	60.00	—
1854	495,000	1.00	3.00	8.00	24.00	—
1855	377,000	1.00	2.00	7.00	22.00	—

KM# 637 1/2 SKILLING
Copper

Date	Mintage	VG	F	VF	XF	Unc
1832	288,000	6.00	12.50	25.00	80.00	—
1833 Rare	3	—	—	—	—	—

KM# 641 2/3 SKILLING
Copper

Date	Mintage	VG	F	VF	XF	Unc
1835	198,000	5.00	10.00	35.00	120	—
1836	928,000	1.50	3.50	12.50	50.00	—
1837	1,026,000	1.50	4.00	12.50	50.00	—
1839	654,000	2.00	3.50	12.50	50.00	—
1840	646,000	2.50	6.50	15.00	60.00	—
1842	526,000	1.50	4.00	12.50	50.00	—
1843	626,000	2.50	6.50	15.00	60.00	—

KM# 658 2/3 SKILLING

Copper

Date	Mintage	VG	F	VF	XF	Unc
1844	266,000	2.50	5.00	15.00	45.00	—
1845/4	495,000	3.00	6.00	17.50	55.00	—
1845	Inc. above	3.00	6.00	17.50	45.00	—

KM# 663 2/3 SKILLING

Copper **Note:** Redesigned, smaller head.

Date	Mintage	VG	F	VF	XF	Unc
1845/4	—	3.00	6.50	18.50	60.00	—
Note: Mintage included in KM453						
1845	—	2.50	5.00	16.00	50.00	—
Note: Mintage included in KM453						
1846/4	123,000	1.90	5.00	16.00	55.00	—
1846	Inc. above	1.50	5.00	15.00	45.00	—
1847	89,000	1.50	5.00	12.50	40.00	—
1849/4	219,000	2.00	4.00	12.50	42.50	—
1849	Inc. above	1.50	3.00	12.50	40.00	—
1850	329,000	1.50	5.00	16.00	55.00	—
1851	467,000	1.50	3.00	12.50	37.50	—
1852	297,000	1.50	3.00	12.50	40.00	—
1853	52,000	4.00	8.00	30.00	90.00	—
1854	408,000	1.50	3.00	12.50	42.50	—
1855	506,000	1.50	3.00	10.00	35.00	—

KM# 638 SKILLING

Copper

Date	Mintage	VG	F	VF	XF	Unc
1832	8,000	100	200	375	650	—

KM# 642 SKILLING

Copper

Date	Mintage	VG	F	VF	XF	Unc
1835	186,000	40.00	100	275	750	—
1835	Inc. above	5.00	10.00	30.00	120	—
1836/5	651,000	4.00	6.50	25.00	85.00	—
1836	Inc. above	3.00	6.50	25.00	85.00	—
1837	628,000	5.00	7.50	27.50	90.00	—
1838	140,000	5.00	10.00	30.00	110	—
1839	360,000	5.00	7.50	27.50	95.00	—
1840	278,000	5.00	6.00	2.50	80.00	—
1842	499,000	5.00	6.00	22.50	75.00	—
1843	361,000	5.00	7.50	26.50	90.00	—

KM# 659 SKILLING

Copper **Note:** Large head of Oscar I.

Date	Mintage	VG	F	VF	XF	Unc
1844	93,000	9.00	15.00	40.00	135	—
1845/4	97,000	6.00	15.00	40.00	130	—

KM# 671 SKILLING

Copper **Note:** Redesigned, smaller head.

Date	Mintage	VG	F	VF	XF	Unc
1847	150,000	3.00	6.00	17.50	60.00	—
1849	306,000	3.50	7.50	20.00	65.00	—
1850	137,000	6.50	17.50	35.00	120	—
1851	151,000	3.50	7.50	20.00	70.00	—
1852	154,000	3.50	7.50	18.50	65.00	—
1853	31,000	10.00	20.00	60.00	200	—
1854	64,000	7.50	15.00	30.00	110	—
1855	40,000	10.00	17.50	50.00	200	—

KM# 643 2 SKILLING

Copper

Date	Mintage	VG	F	VF	XF	Unc
1835	79,000	10.00	20.00	67.50	225	—
1836	583,000	175	350	800	1,750	—
Note: Wide wreath						
1836	Inc. above	4.00	10.00	32.50	130	—
Note: Narrow wreath						
1837	388,000	4.00	10.00	32.50	130	—
1839	270,000	6.00	15.00	40.00	140	—
1840	69,000	6.00	15.00	40.00	140	—
1841	93,000	7.50	17.50	50.00	175	—
1842	123,000	10.00	20.00	60.00	200	—
1843	162,000	6.00	15.00	40.00	140	—

KM# 660 2 SKILLING

Copper

Date	Mintage	VG	F	VF	XF	Unc
1844	89,000	7.50	15.00	60.00	200	—
1845	120,000	7.50	15.00	75.00	250	—

KM# 664 2 SKILLING

Copper **Obv:** Smaller head **Rev:** Simalar to KM#442

Date	Mintage	VG	F	VF	XF	Unc
1845	Inc. above	8.50	17.50	60.00	160	—
1846	56,000	12.50	15.00	50.00	140	—
1847	115,000	10.00	10.00	32.50	100	—
1849	138,000	7.50	20.00	60.00	175	—
1850	81,000	12.50	25.00	72.50	240	—
1851	83,000	10.00	15.00	40.00	110	—
1852	61,000	12.50	15.00	45.00	130	—
1853	23,000	7.50	20.00	60.00	175	—
1854	38,000	7.50	25.00	70.00	185	—
1855	11,000	10.00	45.00	100	275	—

KM# 672 4 SKILLING

Copper

Date	Mintage	VG	F	VF	XF	Unc
1849	444,000	4.00	10.00	30.00	125	—
1850	170,000	7.50	15.00	50.00	180	—
1851	38,000	10.00	25.00	70.00	200	—
1852	38,000	10.00	25.00	70.00	200	—
1855	74,000	10.00	25.00	70.00	200	—
1855	Inc. above	25.00	80.00	160	425	—
Note: Denomination and BANCO larger						

KM# 681 1/32 RIKSDALER

1.0600 g., 0.7500 Silver .0255 oz.

Date	Mintage	VG	F	VF	XF	Unc
1851 AG Rare	—	—	—	—	—	—
1852/1 AG	480,000	2.50	5.00	10.00	30.00	—
1852 AG	Inc. above	2.00	4.00	8.50	20.00	—
1853 AG	775,000	2.00	4.00	8.50	20.00	—
1853 AG Small AG	Inc. above	2.50	4.50	9.00	25.00	—

KM# 644 1/16 RIKSDALER

2.1300 g., 0.7500 Silver .0513 oz.

Date	Mintage	VG	F	VF	XF	Unc
1835 CB	433,000	5.00	10.00	22.50	55.00	—
1836/5 CB	88,000	8.00	16.00	32.50	75.00	—

KM# 665 1/16 RIKSDALER

2.1300 g., 0.7500 Silver .0513 oz.

Date	Mintage	VG	F	VF	XF	Unc
1845 AG	4,185	25.00	30.00	100	225	—
1846/5 AG	34,000	15.00	30.00	60.00	140	—
1846 AG	Inc. above	15.00	25.00	50.00	130	—
1848/5 AG	4,173,000	3.50	8.00	20.00	45.00	—
1848 AG	Inc. above	2.00	5.00	12.50	37.50	—
1849 AG Rare	—	—	—	—	—	—
1850 AG	1,006,000	2.50	6.00	15.00	40.00	—
1851 AG	847,000	2.50	6.00	15.00	40.00	—

Date	Mintage	VG	F	VF	XF	Unc
1852 AG	934,000	2.50	6.00	15.00	40.00	—
1855 AG	830,000	2.50	6.00	15.00	40.00	—

KM# 630 1/12 RIKSDALER

2.8300 g., 0.7500 Silver .0682 oz.

Date	Mintage	VG	F	VF	XF	Unc
1831 CB	212,000	7.50	17.50	35.00	75.00	—
1832/1 CB	1,463,000	10.00	22.50	45.00	95.00	—
1832 CB	Inc. above	6.00	15.00	35.00	80.00	—
1833/1 CB	157,000	8.50	17.50	35.00	75.00	—
1833	Inc. above	7.00	15.00	30.00	65.00	—

KM# 626 1/8 RIKSDALER

4.2500 g., 0.7500 Silver .1024 oz.

Date	Mintage	VG	F	VF	XF	Unc
1830 CB	1,796,000	12.50	35.00	80.00	225	—
Note: Reeded edge						
1830 CB	Inc. above	—	—	—	—	—
Note: Stars and flowers on edge						
1831 CB	1,470,000	5.00	10.00	19.00	50.00	—
1832 CB	2,829,000	5.00	9.00	19.00	45.00	—
1833 CB	1,032,000	5.00	11.00	23.00	55.00	—
1834 CB	103,000	9.00	20.00	45.00	125	—
1835 CB	103,000	11.00	23.00	50.00	145	—
1836 CB	9,024,000	35.00	70.00	150	500	—
1837 CB	4,818	45.00	100	175	550	—

KM# 682 1/8 RIKSDALER

4.2500 g., 0.7500 Silver .1024 oz.

Date	Mintage	VG	F	VF	XF	Unc
1852 AG	46,000	40.00	80.00	175	425	—

KM# 627 1/4 RIKSDALER

0.5000 g., 0.7500 Silver .2049 oz.

Date	Mintage	VG	F	VF	XF	Unc
1830 CB	704,000	17.50	30.00	70.00	150	—
Note: Previously listed 1830 plain edge variety is normal but a weakly struck example.						
1831 CB	2,470,000	12.50	25.00	55.00	120	—
1832 CB	522,000	17.50	30.00	70.00	150	—
1833 CB	63,000	50.00	125	250	550	—
1834/3 CB	953,000	17.50	35.00	75.00	160	—
1834 CB	Inc. above	12.50	25.00	50.00	110	—
1836 CB	2,766	50.00	120	250	525	—

KM# 669 1/4 RIKSDALER

0.5000 g., 0.7500 Silver .2049 oz.

Date	Mintage	VG	F	VF	XF	Unc
1846/4 AG	221,000	22.50	45.00	90.00	300	—
1848/4 AG	130,000	22.50	45.00	100	300	—
1852/44 AG Rare	—	—	—	—	—	—
1852 AG Rare	—	—	—	—	—	—

KM# 631 1/2 RIKSDALER

17.0000 g., 0.7500 Silver .4099 oz.

Date	Mintage	VG	F	VF	XF	Unc
1831 CB	270,000	25.00	50.00	100	225	—
Note: Previously listed 1831 plain edge variety is normal but a weakly struck example.						
1832 CB	142,000	50.00	100	200	400	—
1833/1 CB	191,000	40.00	80.00	130	275	—
1833 CB	Inc. above	40.00	80.00	130	275	—
1836/1 CB	2,482	80.00	150	250	600	—
1836 CB	Inc. above	125	225	400	800	—
1838 CB Rare	4	—	—	—	—	—

KM# 666 1/2 RIKSDALER

17.0000 g., 0.7500 Silver .4099 oz.

Date	Mintage	VG	F	VF	XF	Unc
1845 AG	22,000	60.00	125	275	525	—
1846/5 AG	82,000	55.00	100	225	425	—
1846 AG	Inc. above	50.00	100	200	400	—
1848/7 AG	74,000	40.00	80.00	175	400	—
1848/5 AG	Inc. above	35.00	75.00	160	450	—
1848 AG	Inc. above	30.00	60.00	150	325	—
1852/45 AG	1,104	1,000	1,500	2,650	4,600	—
1852 AG	Inc. above	1,000	1,500	2,650	4,500	—

KM# 632 RIKSDALER

34.0000 g., 0.7500 Silver .8198 oz.

Date	Mintage	VG	F	VF	XF	Unc
1831 CB	47,000	50.00	100	200	500	—
1832/1 CB	2,100	175	350	750	1,600	—
1832 CB	Inc. above	150	300	650	1,400	—
1833/1 CB	39,000	50.00	80.00	250	525	—
1833 CB	Inc. above	50.00	70.00	150	375	—
1834/1 CB	68,000	30.00	60.00	150	375	—
1834 CB	Inc. above	30.00	60.00	150	375	—
Note: Previously listed 1834 plain edge variety is normal but a weakly struck example.						
1835 CB	331,000	30.00	60.00	150	375	—
1836 CB	93,000	40.00	80.00	200	450	—
1837 CB	177,000	50.00	100	300	700	—
1837 CB-G	Inc. above	100	200	400	850	—
1838 AG	834,000	40.00	80.00	150	375	—
1838 AG-G	Inc. above	125	250	525	1,150	—
1839 AG	212,000	50.00	100	200	425	—
1840 AG	68,000	75.00	150	250	545	—
1841 AG	549,000	35.00	65.00	125	325	—
1842 AG	288,000	100	250	475	975	—

KM# 655 RIKSDALER

34.0000 g., 0.7500 Silver .8198 oz. **Rev:** Arms with three crowns

Date	Mintage	VG	F	VF	XF	Unc
1842 AG	Inc. above	50.00	90.00	160	375	—
1843/2 AG Rare	3	—	—	—	—	—

KM# 661 RIKSDALER

34.0000 g., 0.7500 Silver .8198 oz.

Date	Mintage	F	VF	XF	Unc	BU
1844 AG	88,000	60.00	125	300	500	—
1845 AG	43,000	90.00	175	375	700	—
Note: Large head						

KM# 667 RIKSDALER

34.0000 g., 0.7500 Silver .8198 oz.

Date	Mintage	F	VF	XF	Unc	BU
1845 AG	—	90.00	175	375	750	—
Note: Small head. Mintage included in KM456						
1846 AG	111,000	60.00	125	300	550	—
Note: Obverse: GOTH.						
1846 AG	Inc. above	60.00	125	375	600	—
Note: Obverse: GOTH without period						
1847 AG	60,000	80.00	160	375	600	—
1848 AG	185,000	60.00	100	250	525	—
1850 AG	70,000	75.00	150	300	600	—
1851 AG	122,000	60.00	100	225	475	—
1852 AG	54,000	65.00	125	300	750	—
1853 AG	109,000	70.00	150	325	600	—
Note: Small date, GOTH.						
1853 AG	Inc. above	70.00	150	325	600	—
Note: Small date, GOTH without period						
1853	Inc. above	70.00	150	350	600	—
Note: Large date						
1854 AG	34,000	70.00	150	350	650	—
1855 AG	161,000	60.00	110	240	500	—
Note: Small date						
1855 AG	Inc. above	60.00	125	325	600	—
Note: Large date						

REFORM COINAGE

1855-1873

100 Ore = 1 Riksdaler Riksmynt;
4 Riksdaler Riksmynt = 1 Riksmynt = 1 Riksdaler Specie

KM# 686 1/2 ORE
Bronze

Date	Mintage	VG	F	VF	XF	Unc
1856	26,000	25.00	52.00	100	280	—
1857	1,312,000	0.90	2.00	4.50	10.00	—
1858/7	1,849,000	2.50	6.00	12.50	35.00	—
1858	Inc. above	1.50	1.50	3.50	8.00	—

KM# 715 1/2 ORE
Bronze

Date	Mintage	VG	F	VF	XF	Unc
1867	64,000	15.00	30.00	60.00	130	—
Note: Large date						
1867	Inc. above	7.50	15.00	32.00	60.00	—
Note: Small date						

KM# 687 ORE
Bronze

Date	Mintage	F	VF	XF	Unc	BU
1856	24,000	60.00	100	350	700	—
1857	1,596,000	2.00	4.50	14.00	35.00	—
1858/57	6,290,000	6.00	12.00	35.00	70.00	—
1858/7	Inc. above	4.50	8.00	17.50	35.00	—
1858 L.A.	Inc. above	2.00	4.50	18.50	50.00	—
1858 L.A	Inc. above	2.00	4.50	13.00	35.00	—
1858 LA	Inc. above	2.00	4.50	13.00	35.00	—

KM# 705 ORE
Bronze

Date	Mintage	F	VF	XF	Unc	BU
1860/57	46,000	15.00	30.00	250	700	—
1860	Inc. above	15.00	30.00	250	700	—
1861	300,000	3.00	8.00	40.00	100	—
1862	79,000	5.00	12.00	50.00	100	—
1863	450,000	5.00	12.00	50.00	100	—
1864 L. A.	1,848,000	1.75	3.00	20.00	40.00	—
1864 LA	Inc. above	1.75	3.00	20.00	40.00	—
1865/2	561,000	7.00	15.00	200	400	—
1865/4	Inc. above	7.00	15.00	95.00	200	—
1865	Inc. above	2.50	6.00	45.00	100	—
1866	327,000	3.00	7.00	50.00	100	—
1867	956,000	1.75	3.00	19.00	50.00	—
1870	1,079,000	1.75	3.00	19.00	40.00	—
1871/61	1,063,000	2.50	6.00	35.00	80.00	—
1871 L. A.	Inc. above	1.75	3.00	20.00	50.00	—
1871 LA	Inc. above	1.75	3.00	20.00	50.00	—
1872 L. A.	1,897,000	1.00	3.00	15.00	30.00	—
1872 LA.	Inc. above	1.00	3.00	15.00	30.00	—
1872 LA	Inc. above	1.00	2.50	15.00	30.00	—

KM# 728 ORE
Bronze

Date	Mintage	F	VF	XF	Unc	BU
1873 LA	1,867,000	3.00	9.00	55.00	125	—
1873 L. A.	Inc. above	3.00	9.00	45.00	110	—
1873 LA.	Inc. above	3.00	9.00	45.00	110	—
1873 SVFRIGES Error	Inc. above	20.00	60.00	125	275	—

KM# 688 2 ORE
Bronze

Date	Mintage	F	VF	XF	Unc	BU
1856	22,000	65.00	130	300	600	—
1857	1,143,000	3.00	7.50	25.00	50.00	—
Note: Long beard						
1857	Inc. above	3.00	7.50	25.00	50.00	—
Note: Short beard						
1858/7	2,831,000	5.00	10.00	65.00	130	—
1858	Inc. above	3.00	7.50	20.00	40.00	—

KM# 706 2 ORE
Bronze

Date	Mintage	F	VF	XF	Unc	BU
1860/57	197,000	10.00	30.00	65.00	175	—
1860	Inc. above	10.00	25.00	65.00	175	—
1861	1,626,000	2.50	6.00	15.00	37.50	—
1862	213,000	6.00	15.00	40.00	90.00	—
1863/2	1,621,000	3.00	7.50	25.00	60.00	—
1863	Inc. above	2.50	6.00	16.00	37.50	—
1864	600,000	2.50	6.00	16.00	37.50	—
1865	603,000	4.00	10.00	20.00	70.00	—
1866/5	400,000	6.00	15.00	27.50	80.00	—
1866	Inc. above	3.00	7.50	20.00	50.00	—
1867 L. A.	428,000	2.50	6.00	17.50	45.00	—
1867 LA	Inc. above	2.50	6.00	18.50	45.00	—
1871/61	718,000	3.00	7.00	16.50	50.00	—
1871	Inc. above	2.50	6.00	16.50	40.00	—
1872/1	1,646,000	5.00	12.00	30.00	80.00	—
1872	Inc. above	2.00	5.00	10.00	27.50	—

KM# 729 2 ORE
Bronze

Date	Mintage	F	VF	XF	Unc	BU
1873	1,294,000	6.00	17.50	40.00	100	—

Note: Previously dated 1873 without dots above "O" in GOTH is a weakly struck example.

KM# 690 5 ORE
Bronze

Date	Mintage	F	VF	XF	Unc	BU
1857	731,000	4.00	10.00	45.00	100	—
Note: Small L. A						
1857	Inc. above	4.00	10.00	45.00	100	—
Note: Large L. A						
1857	Inc. above	20.00	60.00	165	375	—
Note: Curved-top 5						
1858/7	1,193,000	4.00	10.00	45.00	100	—
1858	Inc. above	10.00	20.00	50.00	125	—

KM# 707 5 ORE
Bronze

Date	Mintage	F	VF	XF	Unc	BU
1860/57	68,000	25.00	60.00	120	240	—
1860	Inc. above	20.00	50.00	100	175	—
1861/57	343,000	8.00	25.00	50.00	120	—
1861	Inc. above	6.00	15.00	30.00	90.00	—
1862 Star	136,000	7.00	17.50	35.00	100	—
1862 Rose	Inc. above	30.00	75.00	150	375	—
1863/2	633,000	9.00	16.50	32.50	85.00	—
1863	Inc. above	9.00	15.00	35.00	100	—
1864/2	264,000	9.00	16.50	32.50	95.00	—
1864	Inc. above	9.00	15.00	30.00	90.00	—
1865	104,000	10.00	20.00	45.00	115	—
1866/5	120,000	12.50	22.50	60.00	125	—
1866	Inc. above	30.00	70.00	150	325	—
1867/6	741,000	4.50	11.00	27.50	55.00	—
1867	Inc. above	4.50	10.00	25.00	75.00	—
1872/66	620,000	8.00	18.00	42.00	110	—
1872	Inc. above	3.00	10.00	25.00	60.00	—

KM# 730 5 ORE
Bronze

Date	Mintage	F	VF	XF	Unc	BU
1873/2	783,000	25.00	40.00	75.00	150	—

Note: Previously dated 1873 without dots above "O" in GOTH is a weakly struck example.

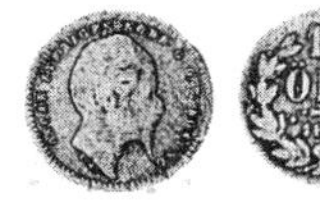

KM# 683 10 ORE
0.8500 g., 0.7500 Silver .0204 oz.

Date	Mintage	F	VF	XF	Unc	BU
1855 AG Small AG	1,359,000	40.00	80.00	175	350	—
1855 AG Larger AG	Inc. above	50.00	100	215	450	—
1855 G Long beard	Inc. above	4.00	10.00	25.00	60.00	—
1855 G Shorter beard	Inc. above	4.00	10.00	25.00	60.00	—
1855 T	Inc. above	4.00	10.00	35.00	75.00	—
1857 ST	1,007,000	4.00	10.00	30.00	75.00	—
1858/7 ST	354,000	5.00	12.00	35.00	75.00	—
1858 ST	Inc. above	4.00	10.00	35.00	75.00	—
1859/7 ST	1,684,000	4.00	10.00	32.00	70.00	—
1859/8 ST	Inc. above	4.00	10.00	32.00	70.00	—
1859 ST	Inc. above	3.00	7.50	35.00	70.00	—

KM# 710 10 ORE
0.8500 g., 0.7500 Silver .0204 oz.

Date	Mintage	F	VF	XF	Unc	BU
1861 ST	579,000	4.00	10.00	30.00	70.00	—
1862 ST	Inc. above	250	500	700	1,400	—
1863 ST	449,000	9.00	15.00	50.00	100	—
1864 ST	Inc. above	4.00	10.00	30.00	60.00	—
1865 ST	560,000	4.00	10.00	30.00	60.00	—
1867 ST	609,000	4.00	10.00	30.00	60.00	—
1869 ST	210,000	5.00	12.50	35.00	70.00	—
1870 ST	384,000	4.00	10.00	30.00	60.00	—
1871 ST	1,162,000	3.00	6.00	20.00	45.00	—

KM# 727 10 ORE
0.8500 g., 0.7500 Silver .0204 oz.

Date	Mintage	F	VF	XF	Unc	BU
1872 ST	120,000	60.00	90.00	150	265	—
1873 ST	635,000	50.00	75.00	100	215	—
1873 ST	Inc. above	65.00	130	200	425	—
Note: Inverted A in Sverige (error)						
1873 ST	Inc. above	60.00	125	250	500	—
Note: SVF.RIGES (error)						

KM# 684 25 ORE
2.1300 g., 0.7500 Silver .0513 oz.

Date	Mintage	F	VF	XF	Unc	BU
1855 ST	437,000	6.00	15.00	55.00	120	—
1856 ST	1,763,000	5.00	12.00	45.00	100	—
1857/6 ST	434,000	16.00	30.00	135	275	—
1857 ST	Inc. above	16.00	25.00	90.00	200	—
1858/7 ST	1,183,000	19.00	35.00	135	275	—
1858 ST	Inc. above	19.00	35.00	130	250	—
1859/7 ST	—	6.50	16.50	55.00	100	—
1859/8 ST	—	9.00	16.50	60.00	125	—
1859 ST	—	6.00	15.00	40.00	80.00	—

KM# 712 25 ORE
2.1300 g., 0.7500 Silver .0513 oz.

Date	Mintage	F	VF	XF	Unc	BU
1862 ST	1,740	450	800	1,200	1,800	—
1864/2 ST	266,000	16.50	32.50	70.00	145	—
1864 ST	Inc. above	15.00	30.00	100	200	—
1865 ST	400,000	15.00	30.00	60.00	110	—
1866 ST	39,000	17.50	35.00	75.00	160	—
1867/6 ST	198,000	18.00	37.50	90.00	185	—
1867 ST	Inc. above	15.00	35.00	75.00	150	—
1871/61 ST	660,000	12.00	22.50	50.00	100	—
1871 ST	Inc. above	11.00	20.00	40.00	90.00	—

KM# 691 50 ORE
4.2500 g., 0.7500 Silver .1024 oz.

Date	Mintage	F	VF	XF	Unc	BU
1857 ST	492,000	50.00	100	215	450	—

KM# 713 50 ORE
4.2500 g., 0.7500 Silver .1024 oz.

Date	Mintage	F	VF	XF	Unc	BU
1862 ST	2,319	500	800	1,250	1,750	—

KM# 692 RIKSDALER RIKSMYNT
8.5000 g., 0.7500 Silver .2049 oz. **Obv:** Short goatee

Date	Mintage	F	VF	XF	Unc	BU
1857 ST	645,000	50.00	90.00	235	600	—

KM# 693 RIKSDALER RIKSMYNT
8.5000 g., 0.7500 Silver .2049 oz. **Obv:** Long goatee

Date	Mintage	F	VF	XF	Unc	BU
1857 ST	Inc. above	35.00	75.00	215	550	—

KM# 708 RIKSDALER RIKSMYNT
8.5000 g., 0.7500 Silver .2049 oz.

Date	Mintage	F	VF	XF	Unc	BU
1860 ST	125,000	50.00	90.00	180	375	—
1861/0 ST	158,000	70.00	125	225	535	—
1861 ST	Inc. above	50.00	90.00	180	350	—
1862 ST	—	850	1,250	2,000	4,500	—
1864 ST	85,000	60.00	100	225	450	—
Note: Previously listed 1864 without edge lettering variety is a weakly struck example.						
1865 ST	59,000	100	200	400	800	—
1867/6 ST	106,000	60.00	100	225	375	—
1867 ST	Inc. above	50.00	90.00	180	350	—
1871/61 ST	208,000	60.00	100	225	275	—
1871 ST	Inc. above	40.00	80.00	160	350	—

KM# 731 RIKSDALER RIKSMYNT
8.5000 g., 0.7500 Silver .2049 oz. **Obv:** Deepened hairlines

Date	Mintage	F	VF	XF	Unc	BU
1873 ST	166,000	350	600	1,000	1,300	—

KM# 694 2 RIKSDALER RIKSMYNT
17.0000 g., 0.7500 Silver .4099 oz.

Date	Mintage	F	VF	XF	Unc	BU
1857 ST	288,000	85.00	175	375	800	—

KM# 714 2 RIKSDALER RIKSMYNT
17.0000 g., 0.7500 Silver .4099 oz.

Date	Mintage	F	VF	XF	Unc	BU
1862 ST	640	400	800	1,200	2,150	—
1864/2 ST	38,000	150	320	500	1,000	—
1864 ST	Inc. above	150	325	600	1,000	—
1871 ST	19,000	125	300	500	1,000	—
Note: Small date and large head						

KM# 725 2 RIKSDALER RIKSMYNT
17.0000 g., 0.7500 Silver .4099 oz. **Obv:** Small head **Rev:** Large date

Date	Mintage	F	VF	XF	Unc	BU
1871 ST	Inc. above	125	300	500	925	—

KM# 711 RIKSDALER SPECIE
(4 Riksdaler Riksmynt)
34.0061 g., 0.7500 Silver .8201 oz.

Date	Mintage	F	VF	XF	Unc	BU
	—	—	—	—	—	—
1861 ST	207,000	65.00	125	325	650	—
862/1 ST	943,000	35.00	75.00	215	450	—
1862 ST L. A.	Inc. above	35.00	75.00	215	450	—
Note: Large and small edge lettering						
1862 ST L A	Inc. above	35.00	75.00	215	450	—
1862 ST	Inc. above	75.00	135	335	675	—
Note: Without engraver's initials						
1862 ST	Inc. above	115	225	335	675	—
Note: Without edge lettering; Previously listed 1862 without edge lettering varieties are normal but weakly struck examples.						
1863 ST	268,000	55.00	110	325	650	—
1864 ST	535,000	45.00	100	235	475	—
1865 ST	107,000	65.00	125	350	700	—
1866/5 ST	41,000	70.00	125	375	750	—
1866 ST	Inc. above	70.00	125	375	750	—
Note: Previously listed 1866 without edge lettering varieties are normal but weakly struck examples.						
1867 ST	64,000	70.00	150	375	750	—
1868 ST	120,000	80.00	125	425	850	—
1869 ST	314,000	45.00	70.00	235	475	—
1870 ST	161,000	55.00	100	275	550	—

KM# 685 RIKSDALER SPECIE
(4 Riksdaler Riksmynt)
34.0061 g., 0.7500 Silver .8201 oz. **Obv:** Bust right with short goatee **Rev:** Crowned, supported arms, small mintmaster's initials

Date	Mintage	F	VF	XF	Unc	BU
1855 ST Rare	2,117	—	—	—	—	—
1856/5 ST	776,000	250	500	2,000	3,000	—
1856 ST	Inc. above	200	400	1,000	2,500	—

KM# 689 RIKSDALER SPECIE (4 Riksdaler Riksmynt)
34.0061 g., 0.7500 Silver .8201 oz. **Obv:** Long goatee **Rev:** Large mintmaster's initials

Date	Mintage	F	VF	XF	Unc	BU
1856 ST	Inc. above	50.00	100	240	500	—
1857 ST	483,000	60.00	125	300	600	—
1859 ST	101,000	100	200	425	850	—

KM# 726 RIKSDALER SPECIE (4 Riksdaler Riksmynt)
34.0061 g., 0.7500 Silver .8201 oz. **Obv:** Larger head

Date	Mintage	F	VF	XF	Unc	BU
1871 ST	260,000	55.00	100	215	475	—

REFORM COINAGE

1873 - present

100 Ore = 1 Krona

KM# 734 ORE
Bronze **Obv:** Small lettering

Date	Mintage	F	VF	XF	Unc	BU
1874	2,370,000	6.00	14.00	30.00	85.00	—
1875/4	2,829,000	40.00	70.00	120	275	—
1875	Inc. above	7.50	15.00	35.00	95.00	—
1876	1,889,000	25.00	40.00	80.00	200	—
1877	1,590,000	12.50	25.00	55.00	120	—

KM# 745 ORE
Bronze **Obv:** Large lettering

Date	Mintage	F	VF	XF	Unc	BU
1877	Inc. above	17.00	27.50	55.00	120	—
1878	1,570,000	12.50	23.50	55.00	125	—
1879	1,630,000	7.50	12.50	30.00	75.00	—
1880	1,713,000	300	450	700	1,400	—

KM# 750 ORE
Bronze **Obv:** Legend lengthened

Date	Mintage	F	VF	XF	Unc	BU
1879	Inc. above	250	350	575	1,200	—
1880	Inc. above	22.50	35.00	57.50	135	—
1881	1,984,000	5.00	15.00	30.00	80.00	—
1882	2,587,000	3.00	7.50	15.00	45.00	—
1883	2,587,000	2.50	9.00	18.50	50.00	—
1884	2,626,000	3.00	8.50	17.50	50.00	—
1885	2,464,000	3.00	8.50	17.50	50.00	—
1886	1,234,000	4.00	16.50	30.00	80.00	—
1888	1,738,000	4.00	12.50	22.50	65.00	—
1889	1,189,000	4.00	12.50	22.50	70.00	—
1890	1,949,000	2.00	7.50	17.50	50.00	—
1891	2,723,000	2.00	6.00	15.00	40.00	—
1892	Inc. above	45.00	70.00	130	300	—
1893	2,145,000	2.00	5.00	12.50	32.50	—
1894	590,000	20.00	35.00	60.00	125	—
1895/3	2,012,000	8.00	17.50	40.00	110	—
1895	Inc. above	1.00	4.50	10.00	25.00	—
1896	1,463,000	1.00	4.00	10.00	25.00	—
1897	2,544,000	1.00	3.00	8.00	22.50	—
1898	2,959,000	1.00	3.00	8.00	22.50	—
1899	2,821,000	1.00	3.00	8.00	22.50	—
1900	2,929,000	1.00	3.00	8.00	22.50	—

KM# 735 2 ORE
Bronze **Obv:** Small lettering

Date	Mintage	F	VF	XF	Unc	BU
1874	1,914,000	2.50	12.50	30.00	100	—
1875/74	2,441,000	30.00	55.00	60.00	165	—
1875	Inc. above	3.00	12.50	35.00	110	—
1876/5	1,402,000	30.00	60.00	140	350	—
1876	Inc. above	5.00	20.00	65.00	175	—
1877	1,015,000	5.00	20.00	50.00	140	—
1878	865,000	70.00	135	300	750	—

KM# 746 2 ORE
Bronze **Obv:** Large lettering

Date	Mintage	F	VF	XF	Unc	BU
1877	Inc. above	3.00	15.00	60.00	150	—
1878	Inc. above	4.00	15.00	65.00	175	—
1879	935,000	2.00	10.00	35.00	100	—
1879/76	—	2.50	12.50	40.00	110	—
1879 Inverted 9	—	2.50	12.50	40.00	110	—
1880	825,000	3.00	15.00	60.00	150	—
1881	1,244,000	1.00	5.00	20.00	75.00	—
1882	1,777,000	1.00	5.00	22.50	80.00	—
1883	1,483,000	1.00	5.00	20.00	75.00	—
1884 Open 4	1,316,000	1.00	5.00	20.00	75.00	—
1884 Closed 4	Inc. above	17.50	32.50	90.00	250	—
1885	615,000	2.00	13.50	40.00	125	—
1886	1,241,000	1.00	5.00	20.00	75.00	—
1888	865,000	1.00	8.00	25.00	90.00	—
1889	589,000	1.00	7.00	20.00	70.00	—
1890/89	912,000	40.00	90.00	200	435	—
1890	Inc. above	1.00	5.00	15.00	60.00	—
1891	942,000	1.00	5.00	15.00	60.00	—
1892	688,000	1.00	5.00	17.00	75.00	—
1893	558,000	1.00	5.00	20.00	85.00	—
1894 Open 4	586,000	2.50	8.00	25.00	85.00	—
1894	Inc. above	18.00	40.00	90.00	260	—
1895	781,000	1.25	5.00	15.00	60.00	—
1896	908,000	1.00	4.00	12.50	55.00	—
1897	1,300,000	1.00	4.00	11.00	55.00	—
1898	1,527,000	1.00	3.50	11.00	50.00	—
1899	2,172,000	1.00	3.50	11.00	50.00	—
1900 Oval 00	688,000	1.75	6.00	19.00	75.00	—
1900 Round 00	Inc. above	15.00	65.00	175	325	—

KM# 736 5 ORE
Bronze **Obv:** Small lettering

Date	Mintage	F	VF	XF	Unc	BU
1874	866,000	5.00	25.00	80.00	230	—
1875/4	1,234,000	40.00	80.00	200	425	—
1875	Inc. above	4.00	25.00	85.00	240	—
1876	609,000	4.00	30.00	100	250	—
1877	514,000	20.00	80.00	200	500	—
1878	364,000	4.00	20.00	65.00	200	—
1879	350,000	22.50	85.00	200	500	—
1880/70	403,000	20.00	85.00	200	500	—
1880	Inc. above	15.00	60.00	150	365	—
1881	625,000	4.00	20.00	60.00	160	—
1882/1	825,000	15.00	60.00	150	365	—
1882	Inc. above	4.00	20.00	60.00	165	—
1883	578,000	4.00	20.00	60.00	165	—
1884	784,000	4.00	20.00	60.00	165	—
1885	282,000	4.00	20.00	65.00	190	—
1886	269,000	7.50	25.00	80.00	225	—
1887	251,000	5.00	25.00	75.00	225	—
1888	214,000	10.00	30.00	90.00	250	—
1889	220,000	12.50	35.00	95.00	275	—

KM# 757 5 ORE
Bronze **Obv:** Large lettering

Date	Mintage	F	VF	XF	Unc	BU
1888	Inc. above	375	600	1,000	3,000	—
1889	Inc. above	3.00	15.00	45.00	150	—
1890	339,000	3.00	15.00	60.00	160	—
1891/81	374,000	2.00	10.00	35.00	120	—
1891	Inc. above	2.00	10.00	35.00	110	—
1892	586,000	1.00	7.00	30.00	110	—
1895	529,000	1.00	7.00	30.00	125	—
1896	309,000	2.00	10.00	35.00	100	—
1897	570,000	1.00	6.00	20.00	95.00	—
1898	721,000	1.00	6.00	20.00	125	—
Note: Varieties exist						
1899	1,225,000	1.00	6.00	20.00	90.00	—
1900	365,000	1.00	7.00	30.00	120	—

KM# 737 10 ORE
1.4500 g., 0.4000 Silver .0186 oz. **Obv:** Small lettering

Date	Mintage	F	VF	XF	Unc	BU
1874 ST	2,875,000	12.00	20.00	55.00	140	—
1875/4 ST	1,503,000	60.00	90.00	200	375	—
1875 ST	Inc. above	50.00	80.00	160	360	—
1876/5 ST	1,814,000	15.00	30.00	80.00	250	—
1876 ST	Inc. above	12.50	25.00	70.00	200	—

KM# 755 10 ORE
1.4500 g., 0.4000 Silver .0186 oz. **Obv:** Large lettering **Note:** Varieties exist.

Date	Mintage	F	VF	XF	Unc	BU
1880 EB	851,000	30.00	45.00	90.00	210	—
1881 EB	763,000	30.00	45.00	90.00	215	—
1882/1 EB	735,000	65.00	100	100	215	—
1882/2	Inc. above	4.00	10.00	75.00	225	—
1882 EB	Inc. above	30.00	45.00	50.00	165	—
1883 EB	694,000	20.00	35.00	50.00	140	—
1884 EB	1,560,000	12.00	25.00	60.00	140	—
1887 EB	1,513,000	12.00	25.00	60.00	140	—
1890 EB	922,000	12.00	25.00	60.00	145	—
1890 EB Close pearls at border	Inc. above	50.00	100	200	500	—
1891 EB	827,000	12.00	25.00	65.00	175	—
1892 EB	1,215,000	4.00	10.00	30.00	100	—
1892/2 EB	—	4.00	10.00	25.00	100	—
1894 EB	1,733,000	2.50	7.50	22.00	60.00	—
1896 EB	2,084,000	2.00	6.00	20.00	65.00	—
1897 EB	819,000	2.50	7.50	25.00	70.00	—
1898 EB	2,087,000	1.00	4.50	16.50	45.00	—
1899 EB	2,041,000	1.00	4.50	15.00	42.50	—
1900 EB	1,173,000	1.50	6.00	17.50	55.00	—

KM# 739 25 ORE
2.4200 g., 0.6000 Silver 0.0467 oz. **Obv:** Large lettering

Date	Mintage	F	VF	XF	Unc	BU
1874 ST	Inc. above	6.00	17.50	65.00	220	—
1880 EB	1,180,000	6.00	17.50	70.00	225	—
1881 EB	1,392,000	5.00	15.00	50.00	185	—
1883 EB	1,100,000	3.00	10.00	35.00	125	—
1885 EB	1,168,000	4.50	12.00	40.00	150	—
1889 EB	422,000	4.50	12.00	75.00	250	—
1890 EB	469,000	3.00	10.00	50.00	175	—
1896 EB	794,000	2.50	8.50	27.50	90.00	—
1897 EB	1,097,000	1.75	8.00	25.00	82.00	—
1898 EB	1,458,000	2.00	8.00	25.00	82.00	—
1899 EB	1,458,000	2.00	8.00	25.00	82.00	—

KM# 738 25 ORE
2.4200 g., 0.6000 Silver .0467 oz. **Obv:** Small lettering

Date	Mintage	F	VF	XF	Unc	BU
1874 ST	2,100,000	12.00	50.00	100	275	—
1875/4 ST	1,131,000	45.00	100	225	500	—
1875 ST	Inc. above	40.00	80.00	175	440	—
1876 ST	2,225,000	12.00	30.00	65.00	240	—
1877 EB	894,000	15.00	32.50	80.00	275	—
1878/7 EB	859,000	70.00	200	500	1,175	—
1878 EB	Inc. above	60.00	150	325	975	—

KM# 740 50 ORE
5.0000 g., 0.6000 Silver .0965 oz.

Date	Mintage	F	VF	XF	Unc	BU
1875 ST	1,908,000	10.00	50.00	150	500	—
Note: Large obverse letters						
1875 ST	Inc. above	50.00	100	325	1,000	—
Note: Small obverse letters						
1877 EB	149,000	60.00	150	400	1,100	—
1878 EB	319,000	15.00	65.00	200	650	—
1880 EB	188,000	20.00	75.00	250	850	—
1881 EB	268,000	19.00	70.00	200	750	—
1883 EB	770,000	8.00	40.00	110	325	—
1898 EB	505,000	6.00	30.00	95.00	300	—
1899 EB	720,000	6.00	30.00	95.00	300	—

KM# 741 KRONA
7.5000 g., 0.8000 Silver .1929 oz.

Date	Mintage	F	VF	XF	Unc	BU
1875 ST	3,531,000	15.00	60.00	175	525	—
1876/5 ST	2,510,000	20.00	75.00	200	675	—
1876 ST	Inc. above	15.00	65.00	175	540	—

KM# 747 KRONA
7.5000 g., 0.8000 Silver .1929 oz. **Obv:** OCH replaces "O" in royal title

Date	Mintage	F	VF	XF	Unc	BU
1877 EB	554,000	19.00	85.00	250	850	—
1879 EB	77,000	55.00	135	375	1,200	—
1880 EB	177,000	17.50	75.00	250	850	—
1381 EB	619,000	20.00	85.00	275	825	—
1883 EB	205,000	25.00	100	300	—	—
1884 EB	382,000	17.50	75.00	250	800	—
1887 EB	58,000	50.00	130	350	1,200	—
1888 EB	62,000	50.00	130	375	1,300	—
1889 EB	425,000	17.00	70.00	200	650	—
1889 EB	Inc. above	100	325	750	2,200	—
Note: Lock of hair below NO in NORGES						

KM# 760 KRONA
7.5000 g., 0.8000 Silver .1929 oz. **Obv:** Without initials below bust

Date	Mintage	F	VF	XF	Unc	BU
1890 EB	594,000	9.00	60.00	150	600	—
1897 EB	735,000	6.00	40.00	100	375	—
1898 EB	1,860,000	3.50	30.00	85.00	300	—

KM# 742 2 KRONOR
15.0000 g., 0.8000 Silver .3858 oz.

Date	Mintage	F	VF	XF	Unc	BU
1876 EB	370,000	500	1,100	2,250	—	—
Note: Wide date, 6mm wide, large E. B.						
1876 EB	Inc. above	225	525	1,400	2,800	—
Note: Wide date, Small E. B.						
1876 EB	Inc. above	20.00	100	450	1,000	—
Note: Smaller date, 5mm wide						
1877 EB	168,000	25.00	125	475	1,100	—
1878 EB	193,000	20.00	100	450	1,050	—
1880 EB	128,000	40.00	150	700	1,700	—

KM# 749 2 KRONOR
15.0000 g., 0.8000 Silver .3858 oz. **Obv:** OCH replaces "O" in royal title

Date	Mintage	F	VF	XF	Unc	BU
1878 EB	Inc. above	550	950	1,750	3,250	—
1880 EB	Inc. above	40.00	190	725	1,800	—

KM# 761 2 KRONOR
15.0000 g., 0.8000 Silver .3858 oz. **Obv:** Without initials below bust

Date	Mintage	F	VF	XF	Unc	BU
1890 EB	72,000	30.00	120	400	1,100	—
1892 EB	87,000	25.00	120	420	1,100	—
1893 EB	49,000	35.00	135	435	1,100	—
1897 EB	207,000	12.00	45.00	200	500	—
1898 EB	141,000	12.00	45.00	225	500	—
1900 EB	131,000	12.00	45.00	225	500	—

KM# 762 2 KRONOR
Silver **Ruler:** Oscar II **Subject:** Silver Jubilee

Date	Mintage	VG	F	VF	XF	Unc
ND(1897) EB	—	—	6.50	9.00	15.00	40.00

KM# 756 5 KRONOR
2.2402 g., 0.9000 Gold .0648 oz.

Date	Mintage	F	VF	XF	Unc	BU
1881 EB	65,000	45.00	60.00	120	200	—
1882 EB	30,000	55.00	70.00	200	300	—
1883 EB	28,000	60.00	90.00	200	300	—
1886/3 EB	42,000	40.00	55.00	150	275	—
1886 EB	Inc. above	40.00	55.00	150	275	—
1894 EB	51,000	40.00	55.00	100	200	—
1899 EB	104,000	35.00	50.00	80.00	175	—

KM# 732 10 KRONOR
4.4803 g., 0.9000 Gold .1296 oz.

Date	Mintage	F	VF	XF	Unc	BU
1873 ST	200,000	65.00	85.00	140	250	—
1874/3 ST	461,000	60.00	80.00	100	200	—
1874 ST	Inc. above	60.00	80.00	100	200	—
1874 ST Proof	—	Value: 1,500				
1876 ST	133,000	60.00	80.00	175	300	—

KM# 743 10 KRONOR
4.4803 g., 0.9000 Gold .1296 oz. **Obv:** OCH substituted for "O" in royal title

Date	Mintage	F	VF	XF	Unc	BU
1876 EB	37,000	65.00	100	215	350	—
1877 EB	55,000	75.00	150	375	500	—
1880 EB	27,000	75.00	150	400	475	—
1880 EB L. A.	Inc. above	75.00	150	450	600	—
1883 EB L. A.	149,000	60.00	75.00	85.00	150	—
1883 LA	Inc. above	60.00	75.00	95.00	160	—
1883 L. A.	Inc. above	60.00	75.00	95.00	160	—
Note: Larger L. A.						
1894 EB	36,000	65.00	80.00	130	200	—
1895 EB	65,000	65.00	85.00	160	215	—

KM# 733 20 KRONOR
8.9606 g., 0.9000 Gold .2593 oz.

Date	Mintage	F	VF	XF	Unc	BU
1873 ST	115,000	110	150	275	525	—
1874 ST	240,000	100	125	250	500	—
1875 ST	359,000	100	125	225	450	—
1876/5 ST	240,000	150	300	850	1,250	—
1876 ST	Inc. above	150	300	850	1,250	—

KM# 744 20 KRONOR
8.9606 g., 0.9000 Gold .2593 oz. **Rev:** Arms wider

Date	Mintage	F	VF	XF	Unc	BU
1876 EB	Inc. above	100	125	250	400	—
1877 EB	103,000	100	125	220	425	—

KM# 748 20 KRONOR
8.9606 g., 0.9000 Gold .2593 oz. **Obv:** OCH substituted for O in royal title

Date	Mintage	F	VF	XF	Unc	BU
1877 EB	Inc. above	125	150	275	450	—
1878/7 EB	245,000	125	150	250	400	—
1878 EB	Inc. above	125	150	250	400	—
1879 EB	75,000	125	150	275	450	—
1879 EB Unique	—	Value: 10,000				
1880 EB	127,000	125	150	240	450	—
1881 EB	47,000	150	250	375	750	—
1884 EB	191,000	125	150	220	350	—
1885 EB	6,250	400	700	1,600	2,250	—

Date	Mintage	F	VF	XF	Unc	BU
1886 EB	173,000	125	150	220	400	—
1887 EB	59,000	125	225	375	500	—
1889 EB	202,000	125	150	200	375	—
1890 EB	155,000	125	150	210	350	—
1895 EB	135,000	125	150	210	350	—
1898 EB	313,000	125	150	200	325	—
1899 EB	261,000	125	150	200	325	—

KM# 765 20 KRONOR
8.9606 g., 0.9000 Gold .2593 oz. **Obv:** Large head

Date	Mintage	F	VF	XF	Unc	BU
1900 EB	104,000	125	150	215	400	—

TRADE COINAGE

KM# 716 CAROLIN (10 Francs)
3.2258 g., 0.9000 Gold .0933 oz.

Date	Mintage	F	VF	XF	Unc	BU
1868	33,000	65.00	125	225	400	—
1869	31,000	65.00	125	250	450	—
1871	5,153	120	225	350	675	—
1871	Inc. above	175	350	675	950	—
Note: Larger ear						
1872	12,000	100	200	325	600	—
1872	Inc. above	225	400	550	850	—
Note: Larger ear						

KM# 542 DUCAT
3.5000 g., 0.9760 Gold .1098 oz. **Ruler:** Gustaf IV Adolf

Date	Mintage	VG	F	VF	XF	Unc
1801 OL	3,100	200	475	1,000	2,000	—
1801 OL	3,100	200	475	1,000	2,000	—
1802 OL	4,827	180	350	750	1,450	—
1802 OL	4,827	180	350	750	1,450	—
1803 OL	7,300	175	325	725	1,400	—
1804 OL	8,700	180	350	750	1,450	—
1805 OL	13,000	150	300	675	1,250	—
1806 OL	14,000	150	300	675	1,250	—
1807 OL	11,000	125	285	625	1,150	—
1808 OL	33,000	125	285	625	1,150	—
1809 OL	21,000	125	285	625	1,150	—

KM# 562 DUCAT
3.5000 g., 0.9760 Gold .1098 oz.

Date	Mintage	VG	F	VF	XF	Unc
1801 OL	900	500	1,100	2,250	4,250	—

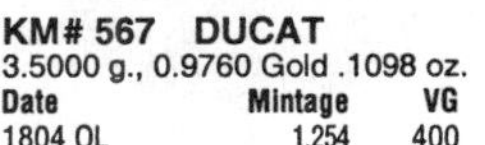

KM# 567 DUCAT
3.5000 g., 0.9760 Gold .1098 oz.

Date	Mintage	VG	F	VF	XF	Unc
1804 OL	1,254	400	950	1,900	3,750	—

KM# 581 DUCAT
3.5000 g., 0.9760 Gold .1098 oz.

Date	Mintage	VG	F	VF	XF	Unc
1810 OL	14,000	150	325	600	1,075	—
1811 OL	9,750	175	400	650	1,175	—
1812 OL	16,000	150	325	600	1,075	—
1813 OL	26,000	150	325	600	1,075	—
1814 OL	22,000	150	325	650	1,075	—

KM# 582 DUCAT
3.5000 g., 0.9760 Gold .1098 oz. **Subject:** Dalarna Mines Commemorative

Date	Mintage	VG	F	VF	XF	Unc
1810 OL	1,322	300	650	1,250	2,450	—

KM# 591 DUCAT
3.5000 g., 0.9760 Gold .1098 oz.

Date	Mintage	VG	F	VF	XF	Unc
1815 OL	8,060	150	325	650	1,175	—
1816 OL	6,130	175	375	700	1,300	—
1817 OL	5,673	200	425	800	1,500	—

KM# 594 DUCAT
3.5000 g., 0.9760 Gold .1098 oz.

Date	Mintage	VG	F	VF	XF	Unc
1818 OL	6,389	100	225	500	900	—
1819 OL	1,828	425	850	1,650	2,350	—
1820 LB	7,248	125	350	750	1,275	—
1821 LB	19,000	100	225	500	900	—
1822 CB	5,222	100	250	550	950	—
1823 AG	3,155	300	650	1,250	2,350	—
1824 CB Rare	3,370	—	—	—	—	—
1825 CB	8,127	100	250	550	975	—
1826 CB	4,126	200	500	1,000	2,150	—
1827/6 CB	4,579	100	250	550	950	—
1828 CB	5,150	100	225	450	850	—
1829 CB	5,642	110	300	650	1,300	—

KM# 628 DUCAT
3.5000 g., 0.9760 Gold .1098 oz.

Date	Mintage	VG	F	VF	XF	Unc
1830 CB	5,269	90.00	200	375	850	—
1831 CB	3,917	100	225	550	1,075	—
1832 CB	2,082	100	275	650	1,300	—
1833 CB	2,310	100	275	650	1,200	—
1834 CB	3,142	90.00	200	400	975	—

KM# 628a DUCAT
3.4856 g., 0.9760 Gold .1094 oz.

Date	Mintage	VG	F	VF	XF	Unc
1835 CB	7,622	90.00	200	375	900	—
1836 CB Rare	1,947	—	—	—	—	—
1837 CB	13,000	80.00	175	350	750	—

Date	Mintage	VG	F	VF	XF	Unc
1838 AG	15,000	80.00	175	350	750	—
1839 AG	10,000	80.00	175	350	750	—
1840 AG	1,840	125	300	700	1,500	—
1841 AG	13,000	80.00	175	350	800	—
1842 AG	30,000	80.00	175	350	700	—
1843 AG	74,000	75.00	160	325	540	—

KM# 662 DUCAT
3.4856 g., 0.9760 Gold .1094 oz. **Obv:** Large head of Oscar I right

Date	Mintage	VG	F	VF	XF	Unc
1844 AG Rare	946	—	—	—	—	—
1845/4 AG	46,000	125	300	600	650	—

KM# 668 DUCAT
3.4856 g., 0.9760 Gold .1094 oz. **Obv:** Smaller head

Date	Mintage	VG	F	VF	XF	Unc
1845/4 AG	Inc. above	75.00	160	350	800	—
1845 AG	Inc. above	70.00	150	275	700	—
1846 AG	22,000	70.00	150	275	475	—
1847/4 AG	18,000	80.00	165	300	450	—
1847 AG	Inc. above	70.00	150	275	475	—
1848 AG	37,000	70.00	150	275	475	—
1849/4 AG	14,000	80.00	165	300	650	—
1849 AG	Inc. above	70.00	150	275	450	—
1850 AG	20,000	70.00	200	375	750	—
1851 AG	16,000	70.00	150	275	450	—
1852 AG	27,000	70.00	150	275	450	—
1853 AG	13,000	70.00	200	375	750	—
1854 AG	20,000	70.00	150	250	450	—
Note: Small AG						
1854 AG	Inc. above	70.00	150	250	450	—
Note: Large AG						
1855 AG	18,000	70.00	150	250	450	—
1856 ST	12,000	70.00	200	350	750	—
1857 ST	27,000	70.00	150	275	450	—
Note: Small ST						
1857 ST	Inc. above	70.00	150	250	420	—
Note: Large ST						
1858 ST	41,000	70.00	150	250	420	—
1859 ST	31,000	70.00	150	275	485	—

KM# 709 DUCAT
3.4856 g., 0.9760 Gold .1094 oz.

Date	Mintage	VG	F	VF	XF	Unc
1860 ST	58,000	65.00	125	275	425	—
1861/0 ST	38,000	70.00	140	325	425	—
1861 ST	Inc. above	65.00	125	275	425	—
1862 ST	42,000	65.00	125	275	425	—
1863 ST	37,000	55.00	100	250	425	—
1864/3 ST	38,000	75.00	140	325	450	—
1864 ST Small L. A.	Inc. above	65.00	125	275	425	—
1864 ST Larger L. A.	Inc. above	65.00	125	275	425	—
1865 ST Large year and ST	39,000	65.00	125	275	425	—
1865 ST Smaller year and ST	Inc. above	65.00	125	275	425	—
1866 ST	32,000	65.00	125	275	425	—
Note: Large ST						
1866 ST	Inc. above	65.00	125	275	425	—
Note: Smaller ST						
1867 ST	11,000	65.00	125	275	450	—
1867 TS	Inc. above	125	325	750	1,500	—
1868 ST	9,398	70.00	150	300	425	—
Note: Small ST						
1868 ST	Inc. above	70.00	150	300	600	—
Note: Larger ST						

KM# 629 2 DUCAT
7.0000 g., 0.9860 Gold .2219 oz.

Date	Mintage	VG	F	VF	XF	Unc
1830 CB Rare	2	—	—	—	—	—
1836 CB	1,500	275	700	1,400	2,150	—
1837 CB	1,989	275	700	1,400	2,150	—
1838 AG Rare	1,000	—	—	—	—	—
1839 AG	2,200	350	800	1,550	2,650	—
1842 AG Rare	1,546	—	—	—	—	—
1843 AG	2,159	250	650	1,300	1,950	—

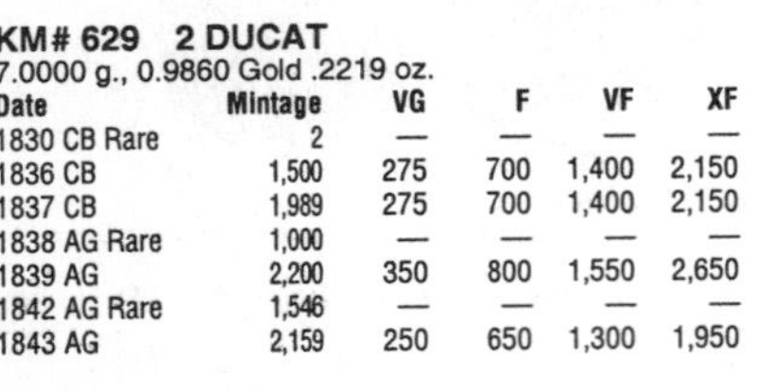

KM# 680 2 DUCAT
7.0000 g., 0.9860 Gold .2219 oz.

Date	Mintage	VG	F	VF	XF	Unc
1850 AG	819	400	800	1,800	2,600	—
1852 AG Rare	386	—	—	—	—	—
1857 ST	763	375	700	1,375	1,725	—

KM# 645 4 DUCAT
13.9424 g., 0.9760 Gold .4376 oz.

Date	Mintage	VG	F	VF	XF	Unc
1837 CB	1,625	550	1,100	2,000	3,000	—
1838 AG	625	600	1,200	2,150	3,500	—
1839 AG	2,000	450	950	2,000	3,500	—
1841 AG Rare	2,084	—	—	—	—	—
1843 AG	4,405	400	850	1,500	2,600	—

KM# 670 4 DUCAT
13.9424 g., 0.9760 Gold .4376 oz.

Date	Mintage	VG	F	VF	XF	Unc
1846 AG	400	700	1,400	2,500	3,750	—
1850 AG	507	500	1,000	2,000	3,200	—
1852 AG Rare	2	—	—	—	—	—

MEDALLIC COINAGE

Largesse Money

Largesse is defined as a generous giving. The throwing of coins to the people is believed to have begun with Gustavus Vasa I (1528). It became the practice to throw coins to the people at coronations and royal funerals, while more important persons were presented with medals to commemorate the occasion.

Specially struck largesse coins of a somewhat uniform size and weight began with Carl X Adolf coronation in 1654. The coins from 1654 until and including the Coronation piece of Gustaf III (1772) are of a 2 mark denomination. The pieces after that date thru Carl XIV funeral piece of 1844 are of a one-third Riksdaler denomination. It was due to the unseemly conduct of the people and the resultant deaths of some, that after this issue the practice of throwing the coins to the public was discontinued and instead they were distributed to the garrison and honored guests and carried no monetary designation. However, it may be noted that these subsequent issues with no relation to the monetary system were circulated as coin of the realm.

KM# M55 1/3 RIKSDALER
Silver **Subject:** Coronation of Carl XIII

Date	Mintage	VG	F	VF	XF	Unc
1809	—	8.50	18.00	35.00	90.00	—

KM# M56.1 1/3 RIKSDALER
Silver **Subject:** Funeral of Queen Sofia Magdalena **Obv:** Large bust, E. below

Date	Mintage	VG	F	VF	XF	Unc
1813	—	12.00	25.00	50.00	100	—

KM# M56.2 1/3 RIKSDALER
Silver **Subject:** Funeral of Queen Sofia Magdalena **Obv:** Small bust, without E.

Date	Mintage	VG	F	VF	XF	Unc
1813	—	15.00	30.00	60.00	120	—

KM# M57 1/3 RIKSDALER
Silver **Subject:** Funeral of Carl XIII **Obv:** Head right **Rev:** Crowns on globe

Date	Mintage	VG	F	VF	XF	Unc
1818 Rare	—	—	—	—	—	—

KM# M58 1/3 RIKSDALER
Silver **Rev:** Crowns on cushion

Date	Mintage	VG	F	VF	XF	Unc
1818	—	8.00	20.00	40.00	85.00	—

KM# M59 1/3 RIKSDALER
Silver **Rev:** Curl on far shoulder

Date	Mintage	VG	F	VF	XF	Unc
1818	—	8.00	20.00	40.00	85.00	—

KM# M60 1/3 RIKSDALER
Silver **Subject:** Coronation of Carl XIV John

Date	Mintage	F	VF	XF	Unc	BU
1818	—	20.00	40.00	90.00	150	—

KM# M61 1/3 RIKSDALER
Silver **Subject:** Funeral of Queen Hedwig Elisabeth Charlotte

Date	Mintage	F	VF	XF	Unc	BU
1818	—	30.00	60.00	125	180	—

KM# M62 1/3 RIKSDALER
Silver **Subject:** Funeral of Carl XIV John

Date	Mintage	F	VF	XF	Unc	BU
1844	—	20.00	32.50	60.00	110	—

KM# M63 1/3 RIKSDALER
Silver **Subject:** Funeral of Oscar I **Obv:** Head left **Rev:** Three-towered church

Date	Mintage	F	VF	XF	Unc	BU
1859	3,200	12.50	27.50	55.00	100	—

KM# M64 1/3 RIKSDALER

Silver **Subject:** Coronation of Carl XV

Date	Mintage	F	VF	XF	Unc	BU
1860	3,200	12.50	27.50	55.00	100	—

KM# M65 1/3 RIKSDALER

Silver **Subject:** Coronation of Oscar II

Date	Mintage	F	VF	XF	Unc	BU
1873	—	20.00	32.50	60.00	85.00	—

PATTERNS

Including off metal strikes

KM#	Date	Mintage	Identification	Mkt Val
PnC1	1812	—	Skilling. Copper. Prev. KMPn1.	—
PnA2	1818	—	1/4 Skilling. Copper. Overstruck on earlier coins. Prev. KMPn2.	—
PnA3	1818	—	Ducat. Tin. Prev. KMPn3.	—
PnA4	1822	—	Riksdaler. Copper. Prev. KMPn4.	2,000
PnA5	1822	—	Riksdaler. Silver. Struck in collar. Prev. KMPn5.	6,000
PnA6	1826	—	1/2 Skilling. Copper. Struck in collar. Prev. KMPn6.	750
PnA7	1826	—	1/2 Skilling. Tin. Prev. KMPn7.	500
PnA8	1826	—	Skilling. Copper. 30 mm. Prev. KMPn8.	750
PnA9	1826	—	Skilling. Copper. 28 mm. Prev. KMPn9.	750
PnA10	1826	—	Skilling. Tin. Prev. KMPn10.	500
PnA11	1827	—	1/3 Riksdaler. Copper. Prev. KMPn11.	—
PnA12	1827	—	1/3 Riksdaler. Copper. Lettered edge. Prev. KMPn12.	—
PnA13	1829	—	1/12 Riksdaler. Copper. Prev. KMPn13.	—
Pn14	1829	—	1/12 Riksdaler. Silver. Thick planchet.	500
Pn15	1829	—	1/12 Riksdaler. Silver. Thin planchet.	350
Pn16	1829 CB	—	1/6 Riksdaler. Silver.	700

KM#	Date	Mintage	Identification	Mkt Val
Pn17	1829 CB	—	1/3 Riksdaler. Silver.	1,500
Pn18	1829 CB	—	Riksdaler. Silver.	2,500
Pn19	ND(1829)	—	2/3 Riksdaler. Copper.	400
Pn20	ND(1829)	—	2/3 Riksdaler. Silver.	500
Pn21	1830 CB	—	12 Skilling. Silver.	900
Pn22	1830 CB	—	1/2 Daler. Silver.	650
Pn23	1830 CB	—	1/2 Daler. Silver. Small planchet.	650
Pn24	1830 CB	—	Daler. Silver.	900
Pn26	1830	—	Carolin/32 Skillingar. Gold.	—
Pn27	1830	—	Carolin/32 Skillingar. Gold.	—
Pn28	1830	—	2 Carolin/32 Skillingar. Gold. Value changed from 1 to 2.	—
Pn29	ND(1830)	—	1/10 Carolin. Gold.	750
Pn30	ND(1930)	—	1/4 Carolin. Gold.	750
Pn31	ND(1830)	—	1/2 Carolin. Gold.	750
Pn32	ND(1830)	—	Carolin. Gold.	1,200
Pn33	ND(1830)	—	2 Carolin. Gold.	1,500
Pn25	1830 CB	—	2 Daler. Silver.	900
Pn34	1831	—	1/6 Skilling. Copper.	250
Pn35	1831 CB	—	1/3 Riksdaler. Silver.	800
Pn36	1833	—	1/6 Skilling. Copper.	600
Pn37	1833	—	Skilling. Copper.	1,000
Pn38	1834 CB	—	1/2 Riksdaler. Silver.	—
Pn39	1834 CB	—	Riksdaler. Silver. Plain edge.	1,000
Pn40	1834 CB	—	Riksdaler. Silver. Lettered edge.	1,000
Pn41	1834 CB	—	2 Riksdaler. Silver.	—
Pn42	1834	—	4 Riksdaler. Silver. Lettered edge.	4,500
Pn43	ND(1834)	—	2 Skilling. Copper.	1,500
Pn44	1839	—	4 Skilling. Copper.	1,000
Pn45	1843	—	2 Skilling. Copper.	1,000
Pn46	1844	—	2/3 Skilling. Copper.	900
Pn47	1844	—	4 Skilling. Copper.	1,000
Pn48	ND(CXIXJ)	—	Non-Denominated. Copper.	900
Pn49	ND(CXIVJ)	—	Non-Denominated. Copper.	900
Pn50	1844	—	4 Skilling. Copper. Plain edge.	1,800
Pn51	1844	—	4 Skilling. Copper. Reeded edge.	1,500

KM#	Date	Mintage	Identification	Mkt Val
Pn52	1844	—	4 Skilling. Copper. Plain edge.	700
Pn53	1844	—	4 Skilling. Copper. Reeded edge.	800
Pn56	ND(1844)	—	Cent. Copper.	650
Pn57	ND(1844)	—	2 Cents. Copper.	900
Pn58	ND(1844)	—	5 Cents. Copper.	900
Pn59	ND(1844)	—	5 Cents. Copper. Thick planchet.	1,000
Pn60	ND(1844)	—	10 Cents. Copper.	1,250
Pn61	1845	—	2 Skilling. Copper.	—
Pn62	1845	—	4 Skilling. Copper.	—
Pn63	1845	—	1/16 Riksdaler. Silver.	1,200
Pn64	ND(1845)	—	1/16 Riksdaler. Head on both sides.	—
Pn65	ND(c.1848)	—	5 Penningar. Copper.	—
Pn66	ND(c.1848)	—	10 Penningar. Copper.	—
Pn67	ND(c.1852)	—	4 Skilling. Silver.	350
Pn68	ND(c.1852)	—	4 Skilling. Silver.	350
Pn69	1853	—	Ore. Copper.	300
Pn70	1853	—	Ore. Copper.	300

KM#	Date	Mintage	Identification	Mkt Val
Pn71	1853	—	2 Ore. Copper. Plain edge.	550
Pn72	1853	—	2 Ore. Copper. Reeded edge.	550
Pn73	ND(c.1854)	—	1/2 Ore. Copper.	225
Pn74	ND(c.1854)	—	1/2 Ore. Copper. "150 Rd"	225
Pn75	ND(c.1854)	—	1/2 Ore. Copper. "125 Rd"	250
Pn76	ND(c.1854)	—	1/2 Ore. Copper. Blank planchet with punched value	—
Pn77	ND(c.1854)	—	Ore. Copper. 150 Rd	150
Pn78	ND(c.1854)	—	Ore. Copper. Blank planchet with punched value.	—
Pn79	1854	—	2 Ore. Copper. Date on reverse.	—
Pn80	ND(c.1854)	—	2 Ore. Copper. 150 Rd	650
Pn81	ND(c.1854)	—	2 Ore. Copper. Thick planchet.	750
Pn82	ND(c.1854)	—	5 Ore. Copper. "200 Rd"	650
Pn83	ND(c.1854)	—	5 Ore. Copper. "250 Rd"	650
Pn84	ND(c.1854)	—	5 Ore. Copper. "250 Rd"; thick planchet.	650
Pn85	ND(c.1854)	—	5 Ore. Copper. Blank with punched value.	—
Pn86	ND(c.1854)	—	10 Ore. Copper. "200 R"	900
Pn87	ND(c.1854)	—	10 Ore. Copper. "250 Rd"	900
PnA88	1855 AG	—	Riksdaler. Silver.	—
Pn88	1880	—	2 Kronor. Gold center. Silver outer limit.	—
Pn89	1880	—	2 Kronor. Silver. 15.1000 g.	—
Pn90	1880	—	5 Kronor. Gold. 15.5000 g. Grams on reverse.	—
Pn91	1880	—	5 Kronor. Gold. 16.0000 g. Grams on reverse.	—
Pn92	1880	—	5 Kronor. Gold. 16.5000 g. Grams on reverse.	—
Pn93	1881	—	Krona. Gold center. Silver outer limit.	—
Pn94	1881	—	Krona. Silver outer limit. 5.9500 g.	—
Pn95	ND(c.1890)	—	5 Ore. Bronze. "3" denomination.	—
Pn96	1892	—	2 Ore. Aluminum. KM#746.	—
Pn97	1892	—	2 Kronor. Aluminum. KM#761.	—
Pn98	1900	—	20 Kronor. Bronze. KM#765.	—

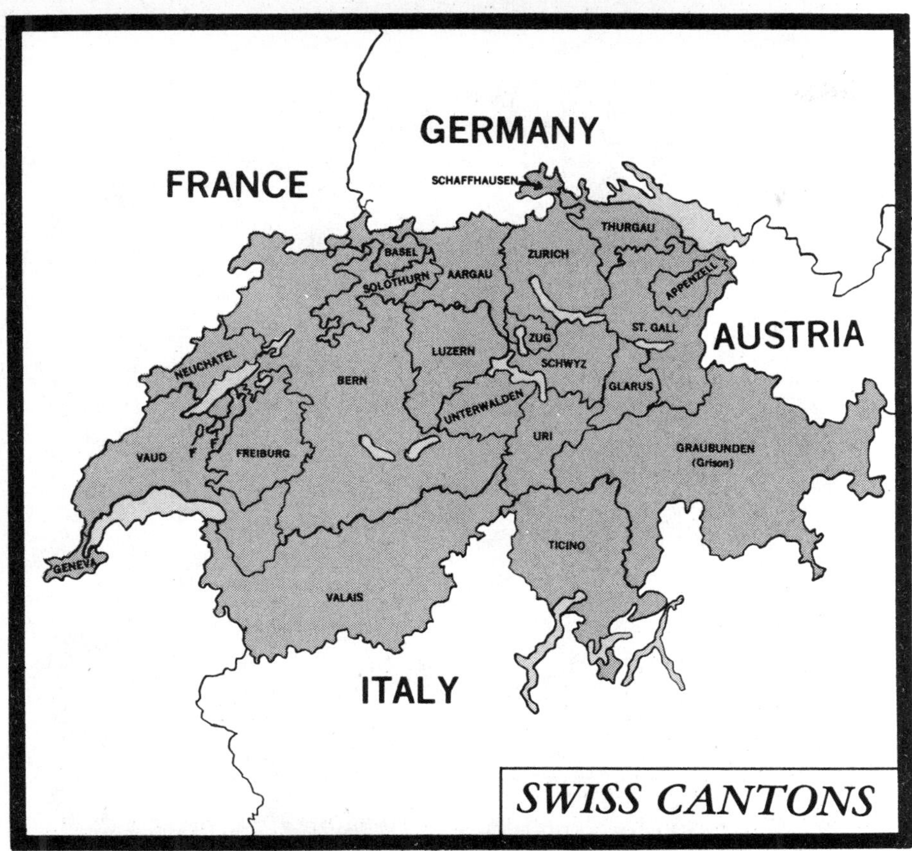

In Switzerland, canton is the name given to each of the 23 states comprising the Swiss Federation. The origin of the cantons is rooted in the liberty-loving instincts of the peasants of Helvetia.

After the Romans departed Switzerland to defend Rome against the barbarians, Switzerland became, in the Middle Ages, a federation of fiefs of the Holy Roman Empire. In 888 it was again united by Rudolf of Burgundy, a minor despot, and for 150 years Switzerland had a king. Upon the death of the last Burgundian king, the kingdom crumbled into a loose collection of feudal fiefs ruled by bishops and ducal families who made their own laws and levied their own taxes. Eventually this division of rule by arbitrary despots became more than the freedom-loving and resourceful peasants could bear. The citizens living in the remote valleys of Uri, Schwyz (from which Switzerland received its name) and Unterwalden decided to liberate themselves from all feudal obligations and become free.

On Aug. 1, 1291, the elders of these three small states met on a tiny heath known as the Rutli on the shores of the Lake of Lucerne and negotiated an eternal pact' which recognized their right to local self-government, and pledged one another assistance against any encroachment upon these rights. The pact was the beginning of the Everlasting League' and the foundation of the Swiss Confederation.

CANTONAL MINT MARKS OF SWITZERLAND

Mint Mark	Canton	Mint
A., B.	Geneva	Geneva 1847, Auguste Bovet
A., B.	Graubunden	Geneva 1842, Antoine Bovy
A-B	Graubunden	Private coiner 1836, antoine Bovy
A-B	Graubunden	Geneva 1842, Antoine Bovy
B	Basel	Basel 1826, Bel-Bessiere
B	Glarus	Unknown site 1806-14
B	Graubunden	Beren 1820
B	Graubunden	Private coiner 1826
B	Luzern	Luzern 1807-14, Bruppacher
B	Schwyz	Schwyz or Aargau 1810
B	Zurich	Zurich 1806-13, Bruckmann
BEL	Basel	Basel 1826, Bel-Bessiere
BEL	Freiburg	Freiburg 1830-46, Bel-Bessiere
BEL	Vaud	Lausanne 1826-34, Bel-Bessiere
D	Zurich	Stuttgart 1842-48
DB	Schwyz	Schwyz 1843-46
F	Glarus	Unknown site 1806-07
G	Geneva	Geneva An 8-13
H	Geneva	Geneva 1817, Hoyer
H	Schwyz	Schwyz or Aargau 1810-11
HB	Graubunden	Private coiner 1836, Bruppacher
K	St. Gall	St. Gall 1807-17, Kukler
M	Aargau	Aargau 1807-08, Meyer
M	Schwyz	Aargau or Schwyz 1844
N	Graubunden	Bern 1825, Nett
SIBEER	Vaud	Lausanne 1845, Siber
Star	Ticino	Luzern 1813

AARGAU

Argau, Argovie

Located in north central Switzerland. Was named after the river Aar. Was admitted to the Swiss Confederation in 1803.

MONETARY SYSTEM

10 Rappen = 4 Kreuzer = 1 Batzen

10 Batzen = 1 Frank

CANTON

STANDARD COINAGE

KM# 15 RAPPEN

Billon

Date	Mintage	F	VF	XF	Unc	BU
1809	44,000	25.00	45.00	80.00	150	200
1811	39,000	8.00	17.50	30.00	60.00	75.00
1816	—	8.00	17.50	30.00	60.00	75.00

KM# 18 RAPPEN

Billon **Rev:** Wreath of stars and flowers

Date	Mintage	F	VF	XF	Unc	BU
1810	20,000	25.00	50.00	100	200	275

KM# 11 2 RAPPEN

Billon

Date	Mintage	F	VF	XF	Unc	BU
1808	92,000	5.00	10.00	17.50	45.00	60.00
1811	—	10.00	25.00	40.00	65.00	100
1812	—	5.00	10.00	20.00	45.00	60.00
1813	—	5.00	10.00	20.00	45.00	60.00
1814	—	4.00	7.00	15.00	25.00	40.00
1816	—	5.00	10.00	20.00	45.00	60.00

KM# 25 2-1/2 RAPPEN

Billon **Obv:** Concordance cross

Date	Mintage	F	VF	XF	Unc	BU
1831	—	7.00	17.50	35.00	60.00	85.00

KM# 24 5 RAPPEN

Billon **Obv:** Concordance cross

Date	Mintage	F	VF	XF	Unc	BU
1829	1,000	10.00	17.00	35.00	75.00	100
1831	—	10.00	17.00	35.00	75.00	100

KM# 8.1 1/2 BATZEN

Billon **Obv:** Aargau shield **Note:** Varieties exist.

Date	Mintage	F	VF	XF	Unc	BU
1807	—	15.00	50.00	80.00	150	200
1808	—	15.00	50.00	80.00	150	200
1809	—	10.00	25.00	60.00	120	150
1811	—	10.00	25.00	60.00	120	150
1815	—	10.00	25.00	60.00	120	150

KM# 8.2 1/2 BATZEN

Billon **Note:** Crude style.

Date	Mintage	F	VF	XF	Unc	BU
1807	—	15.00	50.00	80.00	150	200

KM# 5 BATZEN

Billon **Obv:** Oval arms **Obv. Legend:** CANTON AARGAU **Rev:** value and date within wreath

Date	Mintage	F	VF	XF	Unc	BU
1805	1,000	50.00	150	250	350	450

KM# 6 BATZEN

Billon **Obv. Legend:** CANTON ARGAU

Date	Mintage	F	VF	XF	Unc	BU
1806	—	65.00	150	275	425	650

KM# 7 BATZEN

Billon **Obv:** Pointed arms with garlands

Date	Mintage	F	VF	XF	Unc	BU
1806	—	40.00	100	200	325	425

KM# 9.1 BATZEN
Billon **Note:** Varieties exist.

Date	Mintage	F	VF	XF	Unc	BU
1807	132,000	15.00	35.00	60.00	125	165
1808	184,000	12.00	25.00	65.00	115	165
1809	350,000	15.00	27.50	75.00	125	175
1810	215,000	12.00	25.00	65.00	115	165
1811	60,000	12.00	25.00	65.00	115	165
1816	—	25.00	75.00	125	250	350

KM# 9.2 BATZEN
Billon **Note:** Crude style.

Date	Mintage	F	VF	XF	Unc	BU
1807	—	15.00	35.00	75.00	125	165

KM# 12 BATZEN
Billon **Obv. Legend:** CANTON ARGAU **Rev:** Value and date within leaved branches

Date	Mintage	F	VF	XF	Unc	BU
1808	—	75.00	150	250	600	800

KM# 21 BATZEN
Billon **Rev:** Concordance cross within quatrelobe, all within beaded circle

Date	Mintage	F	VF	XF	Unc	BU
1826	—	10.00	20.00	40.00	80.00	100

KM# 22 BATZEN
Billon **Rev:** Cross within quatrelobe

Date	Mintage	F	VF	XF	Unc	BU
1826	—	25.00	50.00	100	175	250

KM# 10 5 BATZEN
Silver

Date	Mintage	F	VF	XF	Unc	BU
1807 M	250	250	400	800	1,200	1,600
1808 M	114,000	75.00	150	250	350	500

KM# 13.1 5 BATZEN
Silver

Date	Mintage	F	VF	XF	Unc	BU
1808	—	50.00	100	200	375	600
1809	84,000	30.00	60.00	110	150	200
1810	171,000	20.00	40.00	85.00	125	200

KM# 13.2 5 BATZEN
Silver

Date	Mintage	F	VF	XF	Unc	BU
1811	65,000	20.00	40.00	85.00	125	200

KM# 13.3 5 BATZEN
Silver

Date	Mintage	F	VF	XF	Unc	BU
1812	73,000	125	200	350	750	1,000
1814	—	125	250	400	900	1,200
1815	—	20.00	40.00	80.00	125	185

KM# 23 5 BATZEN
Silver

Date	Mintage	F	VF	XF	Unc	BU
1826	508,000	12.50	25.00	70.00	95.00	125

KM# 14 10 BATZEN
Silver **Obv:** Arms within laurel and palm wreath

Date	Mintage	F	VF	XF	Unc	BU
1808	3,884	60.00	100	300	600	800
1809	9,842	60.00	100	250	400	500
1818	3,223	75.00	125	300	650	900

KM# 16 10 BATZEN
Silver **Obv:** Arms within laurel wreath

Date	Mintage	F	VF	XF	Unc	BU
1809	Inc. above	75.00	150	400	800	1,100

KM# 17 20 BATZEN
Silver

Date	Mintage	F	VF	XF	Unc	BU
1809	14,000	75.00	150	300	450	600

KM# 20 4 FRANK
Silver

Date	Mintage	F	VF	XF	Unc	BU
1812	2,527	200	400	600	800	1,000

PATTERNS

Including off metal strikes

KM#	Date	Mintage	Identification	Mkt Val
Pn1	1809	80	20 Batzen. Silver.	3,500

APPENZELL

Located in northeast Switzerland, completely surrounded by the canton of St. Gall. The name was derived from "Abbot's Cell". Achieved independence from the abbots of St. Gall in the period 1377/1411. Divided by religious differences into two half cantons, Ausser-Rhoden(Protestant) and Inner-Rhoden (Catholic). Both were joined to the Canton of Santis 1797-1803, but regained their independent status in 1803.

MONETARY SYSTEM
4 Pfenning = 1 Kreuzer
10 Rappen = 4 Kreuzer = 1 Batzen
10 Batzen = 1 Franken

AUSSER RHODEN

Protestant

STANDARD COINAGE

KM# 11 PFENNIG
Copper

Date	Mintage	F	VF	XF	Unc	BU
1816	66,000	60.00	125	165	—	—

KM# 10 KREUZER
Billon

Date	Mintage	F	VF	XF	Unc	BU
1813	86,000	10.00	20.00	50.00	100	145

KM# 5 1/2 BATZEN
Billon

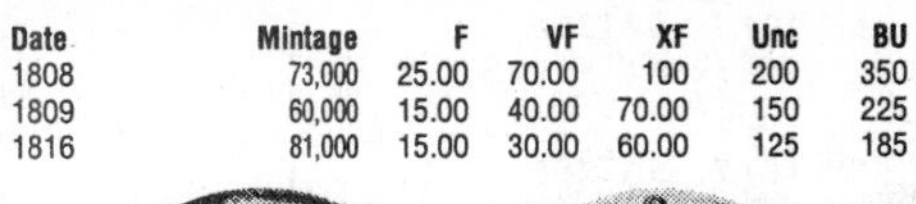

Date	Mintage	F	VF	XF	Unc	BU
1808	73,000	25.00	70.00	100	200	350
1809	60,000	15.00	40.00	70.00	150	225
1816	81,000	15.00	30.00	60.00	125	185

KM# 6 BATZEN
Billon

Date	Mintage	F	VF	XF	Unc	BU
1808	266,000	15.00	30.00	60.00	120	175
1816	203,000	15.00	30.00	60.00	120	175

KM# 7 1/2 FRANKEN
Silver

Date	Mintage	F	VF	XF	Unc	BU
1809	6,534	90.00	200	400	500	900

KM# 8 2 FRANKEN
Silver

Date	Mintage	F	VF	XF	Unc	BU
1812	1,861	150	300	500	650	850

KM# 9 4 FRANKEN
Silver

Date	Mintage	F	VF	XF	Unc	BU
1812	2,357	200	400	600	800	1,500

KM# 12 4 FRANKEN
Silver

Date	Mintage	F	VF	XF	Unc	BU
1816	1,850	200	425	650	1,200	1,750

BASEL

Basilea

A bishopric in northwest Switzerland, founded in the 5th century. The first coinage was c.1000AD. During the Reformation Basel became Protestant and the bishop resided henceforth in the town of Porrentruy. The Congress of Vienna gave the territories of the Bishopric to Bern. Today they form the Canton Jura and the French speaking part of Bern.

MONETARY SYSTEM

After 1803

10 Rappen = 1 Batzen
10 Batzen = 1 Frank

CANTON

STANDARD COINAGE

KM# 201 RAPPEN
Billon

Date	Mintage	F	VF	XF	Unc	BU
1810	—	5.00	10.00	17.50	30.00	40.00
1818	—	5.00	10.00	17.50	30.00	40.00

KM# 202 2 RAPPEN
Billon

Date	Mintage	F	VF	XF	Unc	BU
1810	—	5.00	10.00	20.00	40.00	60.00
1818	—	5.00	10.00	20.00	40.00	60.00

KM# 204 5 RAPPEN
Billon

Date	Mintage	F	VF	XF	Unc	BU
1826 B	—	7.50	15.00	40.00	70.00	100

KM# 205 5 RAPPEN
Billon **Obv:** Oval shield

Date	Mintage	F	VF	XF	Unc	BU
1826	—	100	200	400	900	1,300

KM# 206 5 RAPPEN
Billon **Obv:** Value in exergue

Date	Mintage	F	VF	XF	Unc	BU
1826	—	100	200	400	900	1,300

KM# 197 1/2 BATZEN
Billon

Date	Mintage	F	VF	XF	Unc	BU
1809	—	10.00	15.00	45.00	75.00	100

KM# 196 BATZEN
Billon **Note:** As a Canton.

Date	Mintage	F	VF	XF	Unc	BU
1805	—	30.00	65.00	120	225	300
1806	—	20.00	35.00	85.00	125	200
1809	—	7.00	17.50	75.00	90.00	125
1810	—	7.00	17.50	75.00	90.00	125

KM# 195 BATZEN
Billon **Note:** Under the Republic.

Date	Mintage	F	VF	XF	Unc	BU
1805	—	50.00	100	175	275	375

KM# 207 BATZEN
Billon

Date	Mintage	F	VF	XF	Unc	BU
1826	—	150	250	500	950	1,500

KM# 208 BATZEN
Billon

Date	Mintage	F	VF	XF	Unc	BU
1826 B	—	8.00	15.00	35.00	75.00	100

KM# 198 3 BATZEN
Silver

Date	Mintage	F	VF	XF	Unc	BU
1809	—	5.00	10.00	30.00	60.00	75.00
1810	—	7.00	15.00	50.00	75.00	100

KM# 199 5 BATZEN
Silver

Date	Mintage	F	VF	XF	Unc	BU
1809	—	20.00	40.00	75.00	110	150
1810	—	12.50	30.00	60.00	90.00	125

KM# 209 5 BATZEN
Silver **Obv:** BATZEN

Date	Mintage	F	VF	XF	Unc	BU
1826	—	15.00	35.00	75.00	135	175

KM# 210 5 BATZEN
Silver **Obv:** BATZn

Date	Mintage	F	VF	XF	Unc	BU
1826	—	75.00	150	200	350	500

PATTERNS

Including off metal strikes

KM#	Date	Mintage	Identification	Mkt Val
Pn4	1826	—	5 Batzen. Silver.	1,350
PnA4	1826	—	5 Rappen.	950

BERN

A city and canton in west central Switzerland. It was founded as a military post in 1191 and became an imperial city with the mint right in 1218. It was admitted to the Swiss Confederation as a canton in 1353.

CANTON

REFORM COINAGE

Commencing 1803

KM# 172 RAPPEN
Billon **Obv. Legend:** CANTON BERN

Date	Mintage	F	VF	XF	Unc	BU
1811	—	5.00	12.00	18.00	27.00	35.00
1829	—	10.00	20.00	35.00	55.00	75.00

KM# 175 RAPPEN
Billon **Obv. Legend:** REPUBL. BERN

Date	Mintage	F	VF	XF	Unc	BU
1818	—	5.00	12.00	18.00	27.00	35.00
1819	—	5.00	12.00	18.00	27.00	35.00
1836	—	5.00	12.00	18.00	27.00	35.00

KM# 171 2 RAPPEN
Billon

Date	Mintage	F	VF	XF	Unc	BU
1809	—	10.00	20.00	40.00	85.00	125

KM# 173 2-1/2 RAPPEN
Billon

Date	Mintage	F	VF	XF	Unc	BU
1811	114,000	5.00	12.00	20.00	30.00	40.00

KM# 192 5 RAPPEN
Billon **Rev:** Wide cross within beaded inner circle

Date	Mintage	F	VF	XF	Unc	BU
1826	—	4.00	6.00	20.00	30.00	40.00

KM# 193 5 RAPPEN
Billon **Rev:** Wide cross without inner beaded circle

Date	Mintage	F	VF	XF	Unc	BU
1826	—	10.00	20.00	30.00	55.00	75.00

KM# 176 1/2 BATZEN
Billon

Date	Mintage	F	VF	XF	Unc	BU
1818	—	10.00	30.00	60.00	100	150
1824	—	20.00	50.00	100	150	200

KM# 177 BATZEN
Billon

Date	Mintage	F	VF	XF	Unc	BU
1818	—	7.00	12.50	30.00	45.00	65.00
1824	—	8.00	15.00	35.00	50.00	75.00

KM# 194.1 BATZEN
Billon **Obv. Legend:** Denomination as BATZ

Date	Mintage	F	VF	XF	Unc	BU
1826	—	4.00	6.00	20.00	35.00	45.00

KM# 194.2 BATZEN
Billon **Rev. Legend:** Denomination as BAZ

Date	Mintage	F	VF	XF	Unc	BU
1826	—	7.00	15.00	35.00	55.00	75.00

Note: These are found overstruck on 1 Batzen, KM#87

KM# 195.1 2-1/2 BATZEN
Silver **Obv. Legend:** Denomination as BATZ

Date	Mintage	F	VF	XF	Unc	BU
1826	—	10.00	20.00	40.00	55.00	75.00

KM# 195.2 2-1/2 BATZEN
Silver **Obv. Legend:** Denomination as BAZ

Date	Mintage	F	VF	XF	Unc	BU
1826	—	15.00	30.00	60.00	95.00	125

KM# 170 5 BATZEN
Silver

Date	Mintage	F	VF	XF	Unc	BU
1808	—	20.00	45.00	70.00	90.00	115
1810	—	20.00	45.00	70.00	90.00	115
1811	—	80.00	125	275	350	450
1818	—	25.00	50.00	90.00	125	160

KM# 196.1 5 BATZEN
Silver **Obv. Legend:** Denomination as BATZ

Date	Mintage	F	VF	XF	Unc	BU
1826	—	15.00	30.00	50.00	80.00	120

KM# 196.2 5 BATZEN
Silver **Obv. Legend:** Denomination as BAZ

Date	Mintage	F	VF	XF	Unc	BU
1826	—	35.00	70.00	150	225	300

KM# 196.3 5 BATZEN
Silver **Obv:** Denomination in exergue

Date	Mintage	F	VF	XF	Unc	BU
1826	—	50.00	100	200	300	450

KM# 174 FRANK
Silver

Date	Mintage	F	VF	XF	Unc	BU
1811	11,000	75.00	150	300	500	650

KM# 198 2 FRANKEN
Silver

Date	Mintage	F	VF	XF	Unc	BU
1835	—	100	200	325	525	700

KM# 190 4 FRANKEN
Silver

Date	Mintage	F	VF	XF	Unc	BU
1823	—	250	650	900	1,500	2,500

KM# 199 4 FRANKEN
Silver

Date	Mintage	F	VF	XF	Unc	BU
1835	—	150	300	425	750	1,200

KM# 163 DUPLONE
7.6400 g., 0.9000 Gold .2210 oz. **Obv:** Crowned pointed shield **Rev:** Standing Swiss

Date	Mintage	F	VF	XF	Unc	BU
1819	—	—	2,000	3,000	5,000	—
1829	—	—	2,000	3,000	6,000	—

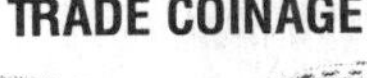

TRADE COINAGE

KM# 155.1 4 DUCAT
14.0000 g., 0.9860 Gold .4438 oz. **Obv:** Crowned supported arms **Rev:** Small denomination and date

Date	Mintage	VG	F	VF	XF	Unc
1825	—	1,500	2,800	4,000	7,000	8,500

COUNTERSTAMPED COINAGE

40 Batzen (BZ)

During the period 1816-1819 an estimated 660,000 French Ecus of Louis XV and Louis XVI 1726-93 and 6 Livres dated 1793-1794 along with 40 Batzen and 4 Franken of the Helvetian Republic were counterstamped with a bear and 40 BZ on shields.

Approximately ninety percent of the counterstamped pieces were melted by 1851. It is estimated some 5,000 pieces or less still exist.

KM# 178 40 BATZEN
Silver **Counterstamp:** Bern arms/40BZ **Note:** Counterstamp on France Louis XV Ecu, C#42.

CS Date	Host Date	Good	VG	F	VF	XF
(1816)	(1726-41)	65.00	100	150	250	400

KM# 179 40 BATZEN
Silver **Counterstamp:** Bern arms/40BZ **Note:** Counterstamped on France Louis XV Ecu, C#47.

CS Date	Host Date	Good	VG	F	VF	XF
(1816)	(1740-71)	65.00	100	150	250	400

KM# 180 40 BATZEN
Silver **Counterstamp:** Bern arms/40BZ **Note:** Counterstamp on France Louis XV Ecu, C#47a.

CS Date	Host Date	Good	VG	F	VF	XF
(1816)	(1770-74)	65.00	100	150	250	400

KM# 181 40 BATZEN
Silver **Counterstamp:** Bern arms/40BZ **Note:** Counterstamp on France Louis XVI Ecu, C#78.

CS Date	Host Date	Good	VG	F	VF	XF
(1816)	(1774-92)	65.00	100	150	250	400

KM# 182 40 BATZEN
Silver **Counterstamp:** Bern arms/40BZ **Note:** Counterstamped on France Louis XVI Constitutional Ecu, C#93.

CS Date	Host Date	Good	VG	F	VF	XF
(1816)	(1792-93)	150	225	250	600	900

KM# 183 40 BATZEN
Silver **Counterstamp:** Bern arms/40BZ **Note:** Counterstamped on France 6 Livres, C#123.

CS Date	Host Date	Good	VG	F	VF	XF
(1816)	(1793-94)	250	400	650	1,250	2,000

KM# 184 40 BATZEN
Silver **Counterstamp:** Bern arms/40BZ **Note:** Counterstamped on Helvetia 40 Batzen, KM#41.

CS Date	Host Date	Good	VG	F	VF	XF
(1816)	(1798)	—	—	—	—	—

Note: Reported, not confirmed

KM# 185 40 BATZEN
Silver **Counterstamp:** Bern arms/40BZ **Note:** Counterstamped on Helvetia 40 Batzen, KM#4.2.

CS Date	Host Date	Good	VG	F	VF	XF
(1816)	(1798)	—	—	—	—	—

Note: Reported, not confirmed

KM# 186 40 BATZEN
Silver **Counterstamp:** Bern arms/40BZ **Note:** Counterstamped on Helvetia 4 Franken, KM#10.

CS Date	Host Date	Good	VG	F	VF	XF
(1816)	(1799-1801)	—	—	—	—	—

Note: Reported, not confirmed

PATTERNS

Including off metal strikes

KM#	Date	Mintage	Identification	Mkt Val
Pn20	1804	—	Batzen. Billon.	1,100

KM#	Date	Mintage	Identification	Mkt Val
Pn21	1825	—	Batzen. Billon. Cross in circle.	600

KM#	Date	Mintage	Identification	Mkt Val
Pn23	1825	—	5 Batzen. Silver.	900

KM#	Date	Mintage	Identification	Mkt Val
Pn22	1825	—	Batzen. Billon. Cross without circle.	—

KM#	Date	Mintage	Identification	Mkt Val
Pn24	1826	—	Concordiataler. Silver.	6,000

KM#	Date	Mintage	Identification	Mkt Val
Pn25	1838	100	Cent. Copper.	500
Pn26	1838	I.A.	Cent. Copper Silvered.	900

FREIBURG

Friburg, Fribourg, Freyburg

A canton and city located in western Switzerland. The city was founded in 1178 and obtained the mint right in 1422. It joined the Swiss Confederation in 1481. During the Helvetian Republic period it was known as Sarine Et Broyebut changed the name back to Freiburg in 1803.

CANTON

STANDARD COINAGE

KM# 81 2-1/2 RAPPEN
Billon **Obv:** Arms, value below

Date	Mintage	F	VF	XF	Unc	BU
1827	—	5.00	7.50	15.00	25.00	35.00

KM# 91 2-1/2 RAPPEN
Billon **Obv:** Pointed arms **Rev:** Value and date within oak wreath

Date	Mintage	F	VF	XF	Unc	BU
1846 BEL	—	5.00	7.50	15.00	25.00	35.00

KM# 70 5 RAPPEN
Billon

Date	Mintage	F	VF	XF	Unc	BU
1806	—	15.00	30.00	60.00	100	150

KM# 82 5 RAPPEN
Billon **Obv:** Shield, date in legend

Date	Mintage	F	VF	XF	Unc	BU
1827	—	10.00	17.00	25.00	35.00	45.00
1828	—	10.00	17.00	25.00	35.00	45.00

KM# 87 5 RAPPEN
Billon **Obv:** Shield **Rev:** Wide cross, date in legend

Date	Mintage	F	VF	XF	Unc	BU
1830 BEL	—	8.00	17.00	25.00	40.00	50.00
1831 BEL	—	8.00	17.00	25.00	40.00	50.00

KM# 73 1/2 BATZEN
Billon

Date	Mintage	F	VF	XF	Unc	BU
1810	—	15.00	25.00	45.00	85.00	110
1811	—	10.00	20.00	40.00	65.00	85.00

KM# 71 BATZEN
Billon

Date	Mintage	F	VF	XF	Unc	BU
1806	—	10.00	30.00	50.00	100	150

KM# 74 BATZEN
Billon

Date	Mintage	F	VF	XF	Unc	BU
1810	—	10.00	30.00	60.00	120	170

KM# 75 BATZEN
Billon

Date	Mintage	F	VF	XF	Unc	BU
1811	—	10.00	30.00	50.00	100	150

KM# 83 BATZEN
Billon **Obv:** Shield, value as 1 BAZ in exergue

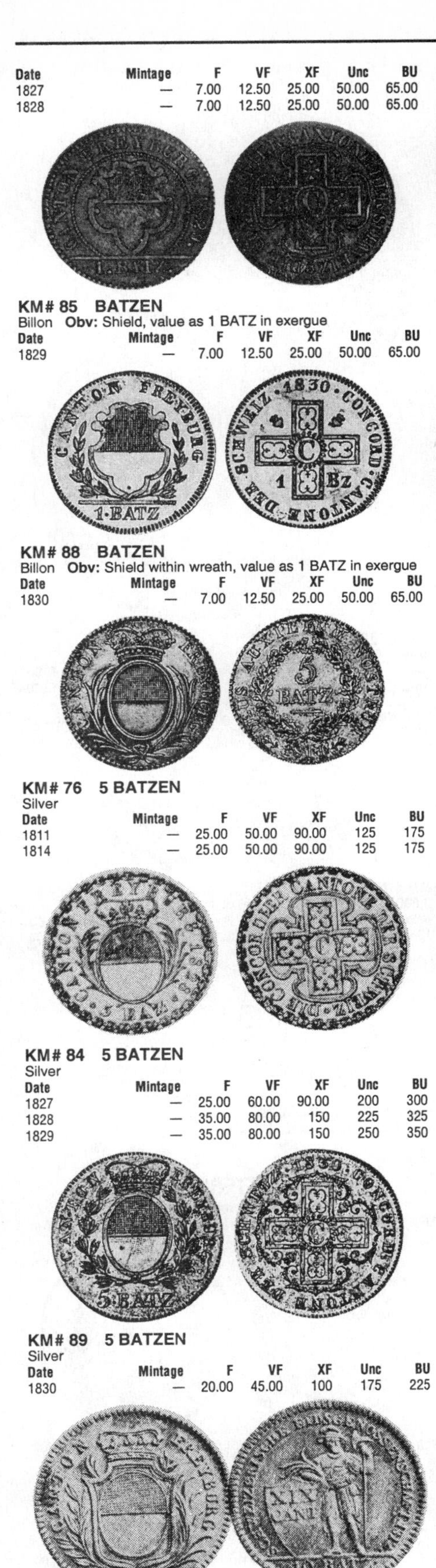

Date	Mintage	F	VF	XF	Unc	BU
1827	—	7.00	12.50	25.00	50.00	65.00
1828	—	7.00	12.50	25.00	50.00	65.00

KM# 85 BATZEN
Billon **Obv:** Shield, value as 1 BATZ in exergue

Date	Mintage	F	VF	XF	Unc	BU
1829	—	7.00	12.50	25.00	50.00	65.00

KM# 88 BATZEN
Billon **Obv:** Shield within wreath, value as 1 BATZ in exergue

Date	Mintage	F	VF	XF	Unc	BU
1830	—	7.00	12.50	25.00	50.00	65.00

KM# 76 5 BATZEN
Silver

Date	Mintage	F	VF	XF	Unc	BU
1811	—	25.00	50.00	90.00	125	175
1814	—	25.00	50.00	90.00	125	175

KM# 84 5 BATZEN
Silver

Date	Mintage	F	VF	XF	Unc	BU
1827	—	25.00	60.00	90.00	200	300
1828	—	35.00	80.00	150	225	325
1829	—	35.00	80.00	150	250	350

KM# 89 5 BATZEN
Silver

Date	Mintage	F	VF	XF	Unc	BU
1830	—	20.00	45.00	100	175	225

KM# 77 10 BATZEN
Silver

Date	Mintage	F	VF	XF	Unc	BU
1811	4,907	85.00	175	375	600	750

KM# 78 10 BATZEN
Silver

Date	Mintage	F	VF	XF	Unc	BU
1812	Inc. above	75.00	150	300	500	800

KM# 79 4 FRANKEN
Silver

Date	Mintage	F	VF	XF	Unc	BU
1813	2,429	200	375	650	1,100	1,450

PATTERNS

Including off metal strikes

KM#	Date	Mintage	Identification	Mkt Val
Pn7	1811	—	Batzen. Silver. KM#75.	—

GENEVA

A canton and city in southwestern Switzerland. The city became a bishopric c.400 AD and was part of the Burgundian Kingdom for 500 years. They became completely independent in 1530. In 1798 they were occupied by France but became independent again in 1813. They joined the Swiss Confederation in 1815.

MINT OFFICIALS' INITIALS

Initial	Date	Name
A-B		Auguste Bovet
H		Hoyer

MONETARY SYSTEM
1814-1838

12 Deniers = 4 Quarts = 1 Sol
12 Sols = 1 Florin
12 Florins, 9 Sols = 1 Thaler
35 Florins = 1 Pistole

CANTON

REFORM COINAGE

1814-1838

KM# 115 6 DENIERS
Billon

Date	Mintage	F	VF	XF	Unc	BU
1817	—	3.00	5.00	10.00	20.00	30.00

KM# 115a 6 DENIERS
Silver **Note:** Presentation strike.

Date	Mintage	F	VF	XF	Unc	BU
1817	—	—	—	100	150	—

KM# 118 6 DENIERS
Billon

Date	Mintage	F	VF	XF	Unc	BU
1819	—	3.00	5.00	10.00	20.00	30.00
1825	—	5.00	10.00	15.00	25.00	35.00
1833	—	3.00	5.00	7.00	15.00	25.00

KM# 118a 6 DENIERS
Silver **Note:** Presentation strike.

Date	Mintage	F	VF	XF	Unc	BU
1819	—	—	—	100	150	—
1825	—	—	—	115	175	—
1833	—	—	—	100	150	—

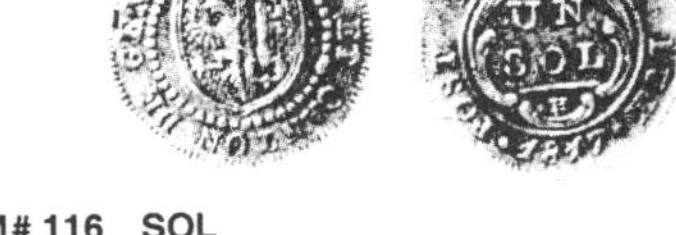

KM# 116 SOL
Billon

Date	Mintage	F	VF	XF	Unc	BU
1817 H	—	2.00	4.00	8.00	16.00	22.00

KM# 116a SOL
Silver **Note:** Presentation strike.

Date	Mintage	F	VF	XF	Unc	BU
1817 H	—	—	—	80.00	135	—

KM# 119 SOL
Billon

Date	Mintage	F	VF	XF	Unc	BU
1819	—	2.00	4.00	8.00	16.00	22.00

KM# 119a SOL
Billon

Date	Mintage	F	VF	XF	Unc	BU
1819	—	—	—	85.00	135	—

KM# 120 SOL
Billon

Date	Mintage	F	VF	XF	Unc	BU
1825	—	2.00	4.00	8.00	15.00	20.00
1833	—	2.00	4.00	8.00	15.00	20.00

KM# 120a SOL
Silver **Note:** Presentation strike.

Date	Mintage	F	VF	XF	Unc	BU
1825	—	—	—	85.00	135	—
1833	—	—	—	85.00	135	—

KM# 117 1-1/2 SOL
Billon

Date	Mintage	F	VF	XF	Unc	BU
1817 H	—	4.00	7.00	12.00	20.00	30.00

KM# 121 1-1/2 SOL
Billon

Date	Mintage	F	VF	XF	Unc	BU
1825	—	4.00	7.00	12.00	20.00	30.00

KM# 121a 1-1/2 SOL
Silver **Note:** Presentation strike.

Date	Mintage	F	VF	XF	Unc	BU
1825	—	—	—	130	200	—

DECIMAL COINAGE

100 Centimes = 1 Franc

KM# 125 CENTIME
Billon

Date	Mintage	F	VF	XF	Unc	BU
1839	325,000	2.50	4.50	7.00	12.00	20.00

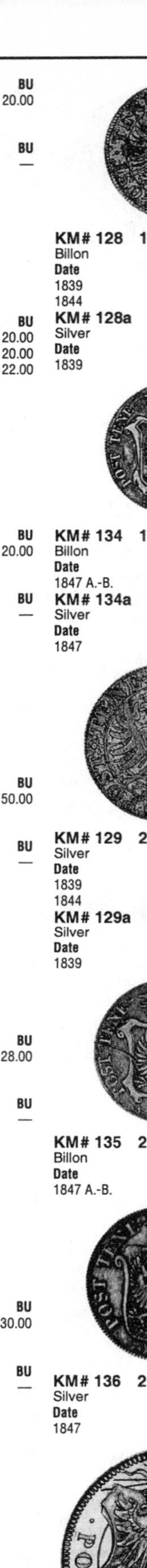

KM# 125a CENTIME
Silver

Date	Mintage	F	VF	XF	Unc	BU
1839	—	—	—	80.00	125	—

KM# 130 CENTIME
Copper

Date	Mintage	F	VF	XF	Unc	BU
1840	—	2.50	4.50	7.00	12.00	20.00
1844	—	2.50	4.50	7.00	12.00	20.00
1846	—	3.50	5.00	8.00	14.00	22.00

KM# 132 CENTIME
Copper

Date	Mintage	F	VF	XF	Unc	BU
1847	—	2.50	4.50	7.00	12.00	20.00

KM# 132a CENTIME
Silver

Date	Mintage	F	VF	XF	Unc	BU
1847	—	—	—	80.00	125	—

KM# 126 2 CENTIMES
Billon

Date	Mintage	F	VF	XF	Unc	BU
1839	78,000	5.00	10.00	20.00	35.00	50.00

KM# 126a 2 CENTIMES
Silver

Date	Mintage	F	VF	XF	Unc	BU
1839	—	—	—	200	300	—

KM# 127 4 CENTIMES
Billon

Date	Mintage	F	VF	XF	Unc	BU
1839	331,000	2.50	4.50	9.00	18.00	28.00

KM# 127a 4 CENTIMES
Silver

Date	Mintage	F	VF	XF	Unc	BU
1839	—	—	—	115	175	—

KM# 131 5 CENTIMES
Billon

Date	Mintage	F	VF	XF	Unc	BU
1840	—	2.50	5.00	10.00	20.00	30.00

KM# 131a 5 CENTIMES
Silver

Date	Mintage	F	VF	XF	Unc	BU
1840	—	—	—	45.00	75.00	—

KM# 133 5 CENTIMES
Billon **Obv:** Arms on shield

Date	Mintage	F	VF	XF	Unc	BU
1847 A.-B.	Inc. above	2.50	5.00	7.00	15.00	25.00

KM# 133a 5 CENTIMES
Silver

Date	Mintage	F	VF	XF	Unc	BU
1847	—	—	—	130	200	—

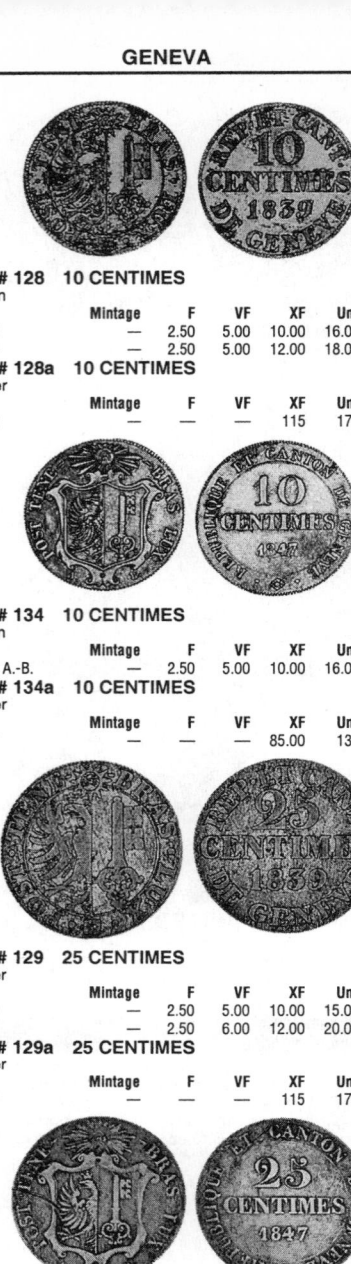

KM# 128 10 CENTIMES
Billon

Date	Mintage	F	VF	XF	Unc	BU
1839	—	2.50	5.00	10.00	16.00	27.50
1844	—	2.50	5.00	12.00	18.00	30.00

KM# 128a 10 CENTIMES
Silver

Date	Mintage	F	VF	XF	Unc	BU
1839	—	—	—	115	175	—

KM# 134 10 CENTIMES
Billon

Date	Mintage	F	VF	XF	Unc	BU
1847 A.-B.	—	2.50	5.00	10.00	16.00	27.50

KM# 134a 10 CENTIMES
Silver

Date	Mintage	F	VF	XF	Unc	BU
1847	—	—	—	85.00	135	—

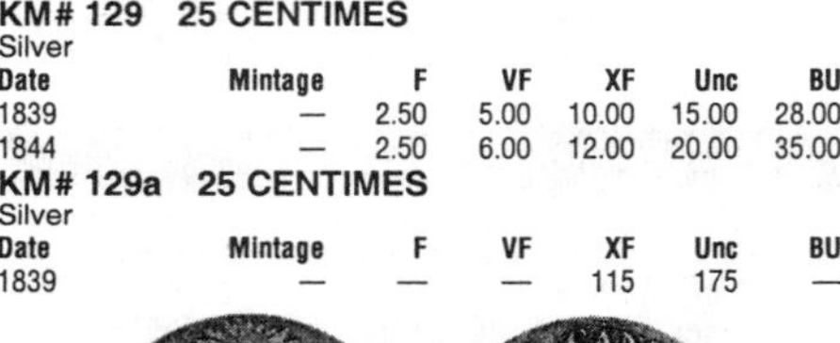

KM# 129 25 CENTIMES
Silver

Date	Mintage	F	VF	XF	Unc	BU
1839	—	2.50	5.00	10.00	15.00	28.00
1844	—	2.50	6.00	12.00	20.00	35.00

KM# 129a 25 CENTIMES
Silver

Date	Mintage	F	VF	XF	Unc	BU
1839	—	—	—	115	175	—

KM# 135 25 CENTIMES
Billon

Date	Mintage	F	VF	XF	Unc	BU
1847 A.-B.	—	2.50	5.00	10.00	20.00	35.00

KM# 136 25 CENTIMES
Silver

Date	Mintage	F	VF	XF	Unc	BU
1847	—	—	—	115	175	—

KM# 137 5 FRANCS
Silver

Date	Mintage	F	VF	XF	Unc	BU
1848	1,176	60.00	120	200	350	750

KM# 138 10 FRANCS
Silver **Obv:** Geneva arms

Date	Mintage	F	VF	XF	Unc	BU
1848	385	200	400	650	1,000	1,800
1851	678	250	450	900	1,500	—

Note: The 1851 date was not a legal tender issue and is considered a Shooting Thaler.

KM# 139 10 FRANCS
3.8000 g., 0.7500 Gold 0.0916 oz.

Date	Mintage	F	VF	XF	Unc	BU
1848	336	375	650	1,250	1,500	2,000

KM# 140 20 FRANCS
7.6000 g., 0.7500 Gold .1833 oz.

Date	Mintage	F	VF	XF	Unc	BU
1848	3,421	250	400	800	1,100	1,400

PATTERNS

Including off metal strikes

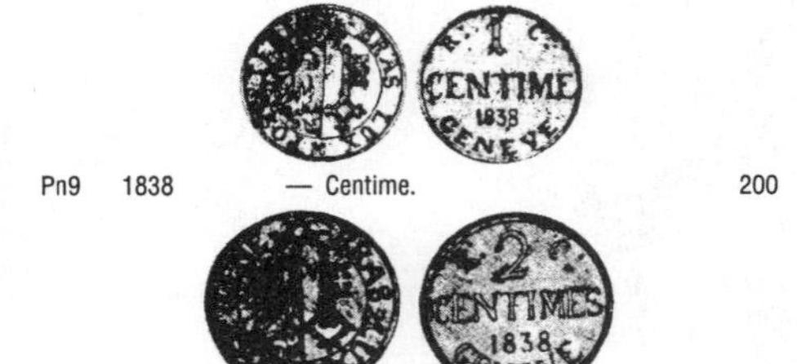

KM#	Date	Mintage	Identification	Mkt Val
Pn8	1831	—	42 Sols.	1,500
Pn9	1838	—	Centime.	200
Pn10	1838	—	2 Centimes.	200

KM#	Date	Mintage Identification	Mkt Val
Pn11	1838	— 5 Centimes.	200
Pn12	1838	— 10 Centimes.	500

KM#	Date	Mintage Identification	Mkt Val
Pn13	1838	— 25 Centimes.	500

KM#	Date	Mintage Identification	Mkt Val
Pn14	1846	— Centime.	200

GLARUS

A canton in eastern Switzerland. Independence was gained in c.1390 but from 1798-1803 it was occupied by the French. They rejoined the Swiss Confederation in1803.

MONETARY SYSTEM
3 Rappen = 1 Schilling
100 Rappen = 1 Frank

CANTON

STANDARD COINAGE

KM# 10 SCHILLING
Billon

Date	Mintage	F	VF	XF	Unc	BU
1806 F	—	25.00	100	275	400	525
1807 F	—	35.00	120	300	450	575

KM# 13 SCHILLING
Billon **Obv:** Shield with garlands

Date	Mintage	F	VF	XF	Unc	BU
1808	—	25.00	100	275	400	525
1809	—	25.00	75.00	225	325	400
1811	—	20.00	50.00	125	225	300
1812	—	20.00	50.00	125	225	300
1813	—	20.00	50.00	125	225	300

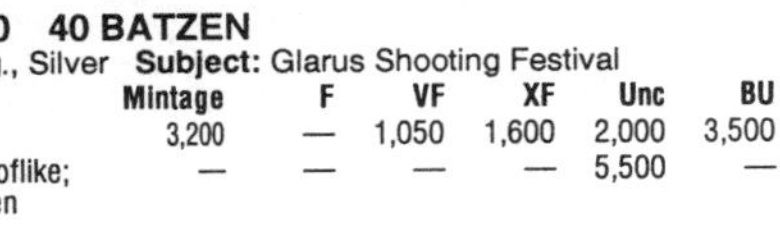

KM# 15 SCHILLING
Billon **Obv:** Shield in branches

Date	Mintage	F	VF	XF	Unc	BU
1809	—	20.00	60.00	175	300	375
1810	—	400	800	1,200	2,000	2,500

KM# 11 3 SCHILLING
Billon

Date	Mintage	F	VF	XF	Unc	BU
1806	134,000	60.00	150	400	600	750

KM# 14 3 SCHILLING
Billon

Date	Mintage	F	VF	XF	Unc	BU
1808	—	50.00	100	275	400	525
1812	—	60.00	125	325	450	600

KM# 16 3 SCHILLING
Billon

Date	Mintage	F	VF	XF	Unc	BU
1809	—	60.00	125	325	450	600
1810	—	50.00	100	275	400	525
1814	—	50.00	100	275	400	525

KM# 12 15 SCHILLING
Silver

Date	Mintage	F	VF	XF	Unc	BU
1806 B	7,067	250	525	1,000	1,250	1,500
1807 B	Inc. above	200	450	800	1,000	1,250
1811 B	Inc. above	350	650	1,100	1,600	2,000
1813 B	Inc. above	300	600	1,000	1,450	1,800
1814 B	Inc. above	250	550	950	1,150	1,400

KM# 20 40 BATZEN
0.9000 g., Silver **Subject:** Glarus Shooting Festival

Date	Mintage	F	VF	XF	Unc	BU
1847	3,200	—	1,050	1,600	2,000	3,500
1847 Prooflike; Specimen	—	—	—	—	5,500	—

GRAUBUNDEN

The largest and most easterly of the Swiss Cantons. The district was set up in the reign of Roman Emperor Augustus and was one of the various factions sparring for power in the 14th and 15th centuries. The name is derived from "Grey League". The first coins were issued in c.1600. They joined the Swiss Confederation in 1803.

MINTMASTERS INITIALS
A-B - Bouey
H.B. – Bruppacher

MONETARY SYSTEM
15 Rappen = 6 Bluzger = 1 Schweizer Batzen
10 Schweizer Batzen = 1 Frank
16 Franken = 1 Duplone

CANTON

STANDARD COINAGE

KM# 5 1/6 BATZEN
Billon **Obv:** Three oval shield draped with garland **Rev:** Value within wreath **Note:** Spelled BATZEN.

Date	Mintage	F	VF	XF	Unc	BU
1807	58,000	7.00	15.00	30.00	50.00	65.00
1820	480,000	15.00	25.00	50.00	75.00	120

KM# 16 1/6 BATZEN
Billon **Obv:** Three oval shields **Rev:** Value within wreath **Note:** Spelled BAZEN.

Date	Mintage	F	VF	XF	Unc	BU
1842 A.B.	172,000	6.00	12.50	30.00	50.00	65.00

KM# 6 1/2 BATZEN
Billon **Obv:** Three oval shields, date below **Rev:** Value within wreath

Date	Mintage	F	VF	XF	Unc	BU
1807	75,000	20.00	40.00	80.00	125	165
1820 B	60,000	20.00	40.00	90.00	135	185

KM# 9 1/2 BATZEN
Billon **Obv:** Three oval shields **Rev:** Value and date within wreath

Date	Mintage	F	VF	XF	Unc	BU
1812	100,000	30.00	75.00	165	300	400

KM# 13 1/2 BATZEN
Billon **Obv:** Three shield divided by circular wreath **Rev:** Value and date within wreath

Date	Mintage	F	VF	XF	Unc	BU
1836 A-B	212,000	15.00	30.00	60.00	90.00	120
1842 A-B	162,000	10.00	20.00	35.00	60.00	75.00

KM# 7 BATZEN
Billon **Obv:** Three oval shields, date in exergue **Rev:** Value within wreath

Date	Mintage	F	VF	XF	Unc	BU
1807	56,000	10.00	30.00	65.00	100	150

KM# 11 BATZEN
Billon **Obv:** Three oval shields, date below **Rev:** Value within wreath

Date	Mintage	F	VF	XF	Unc	BU
1820 B	50,000	10.00	30.00	65.00	100	150
1826 B	50,000	15.00	35.00	90.00	175	235

KM# 15 BATZEN
Billon **Obv:** Three shields around circle, wreath between **Rev:** Value and date within wreath **Note:** 1 on reverse breaks top of wreath.

Date	Mintage	F	VF	XF	Unc	BU
1836	99,000	15.00	25.00	50.00	90.00	135
1842 A-B	100,000	10.00	25.00	50.00	90.00	135

KM# 14 BATZEN
Billon **Obv:** Three shields in circle with wreath between **Rev:** Value within wreath **Note:** 1 on reverse below (within) top of wreath.

Date	Mintage	F	VF	XF	Unc	BU
1836 HB	Inc. above	40.00	85.00	175	350	450

KM# 8 5 BATZEN
Silver **Obv:** Three oval shields, date below **Rev:** Value within wreath

Date	Mintage	F	VF	XF	Unc	BU
1807	6,398	50.00	95.00	150	300	375
1820	16,000	50.00	95.00	150	300	375
1826	—	75.00	125	180	350	450

KM# 12 10 BATZEN
Silver **Obv:** Three oval shields, palm branches below **Rev:** Value and date within circular wreath

Date	Mintage	F	VF	XF	Unc	BU
1825 N	2,000	150	250	450	650	1,000

KM# 17 4 FRANKEN
0.8000 Silver **Obv:** Three oval shields **Rev:** Swiss arms on flags, rifles and branches

Date	Mintage	F	VF	XF	Unc	BU
1842	6,000	200	350	575	850	1,200
1842 Specimen	—	—	—	—	—	2,400

KM# 10 16 FRANKEN
7.6400 g., 0.9000 Gold 0.2211 oz. **Obv:** Three shields in circle, wreath between **Rev:** Value and date within wreath

Date	Mintage	F	VF	XF	Unc	BU
1813	100	1,500	3,500	6,000	8,000	9,500

LUZERN

Lucerne

Luzern is a canton and city in central Switzerland. The city grew around the Benedictine Monastery which was founded in 750. They joined the Swiss Confederation as the 4th member in 1332. Few coins were issued before the1500s.

MINT OFFICIALS' INITIALS

Initial	Date	Name
B	1794-1807	Bruppacher

CITY

STANDARD COINAGE

KM# 76 ANGSTER
Copper **Note:** Similar to Rappen, KM#96.

Date	Mintage	F	VF	XF	Unc	BU
1804	—	25.00	85.00	150	225	300
1811	—	7.00	17.50	30.00	45.00	60.00
1823	—	5.00	9.00	13.00	18.00	28.00
1832	—	5.00	9.00	13.00	18.00	28.00
1834	—	5.00	9.00	13.00	18.00	28.00

KM# 117 ANGSTER
Copper **Obv:** Shield **Rev:** Value within wreath

Date	Mintage	F	VF	XF	Unc	BU
1839	—	5.00	9.00	13.00	18.00	28.00
1843	—	5.00	7.00	12.00	17.00	25.00

KM# 75 RAPPEN
Copper **Note:** Similar to KM#96.

Date	Mintage	F	VF	XF	Unc	BU
1804	—	5.00	7.50	12.50	18.00	28.00

KM# 96 RAPPEN
Copper

Date	Mintage	F	VF	XF	Unc	BU
1804	—	5.00	7.50	12.50	18.00	28.00

KM# 115 RAPPEN
Copper **Obv:** Shield in wreath **Rev:** Value in wreath **Note:** Denomination as RAPPEN or RAPEN.

Date	Mintage	F	VF	XF	Unc	BU
1831	—	5.00	7.50	12.50	18.00	28.00

KM# 116 RAPPEN
Copper

Date	Mintage	F	VF	XF	Unc	BU
1834	—	5.00	7.50	12.50	18.00	28.00

KM# 118 RAPPEN
Copper **Obv:** Shield **Rev:** Value and date within circle wreath

Date	Mintage	F	VF	XF	Unc	BU
1839	—	5.00	7.50	12.50	18.00	28.00

KM# 119 RAPPEN
Copper **Obv:** Shield **Rev:** Value and date within oak wreath

Date	Mintage	F	VF	XF	Unc	BU
1839	—	4.00	6.50	12.50	18.00	28.00
1843	—	4.00	6.50	12.50	18.00	28.00
1844	—	4.00	6.50	12.50	18.00	28.00
1845	—	4.00	6.50	12.50	20.00	30.00
1846	—	4.00	6.50	12.50	18.00	28.00

KM# 106 1/2 BATZEN - 5 RAPPEN
Billon **Obv:** Shield within wreath **Rev:** Dual value within circular wreath

Date	Mintage	F	VF	XF	Unc	BU
1813	—	10.00	25.00	50.00	80.00	110

KM# 95 BATZEN - 10 RAPPEN
Billon **Obv:** Shield, 1 BAZ on exergue **Rev:** Value and date within laurel wreath

Date	Mintage	F	VF	XF	Unc	BU
1803	—	15.00	40.00	70.00	120	150

KM# 97 BATZEN - 10 RAPPEN
Billon **Obv:** Shield within wreath, 1 BAZ in exergue **Rev:** Value within oak wreath

Date	Mintage	F	VF	XF	Unc	BU
1804	—	7.50	15.00	40.00	80.00	120
1806	—	10.00	20.00	40.00	80.00	120

KM# 99 BATZEN - 10 RAPPEN
Billon **Obv:** Shield within baroque frame **Obv. Legend:**

MONETA•REIPUB•LUCERNENSIS **Rev:** Value and date within oak wreath

Date	Mintage	F	VF	XF	Unc	BU
1805	—	10.00	20.00	40.00	80.00	120

KM# 101 BATZEN - 10 RAPPEN
Billon **Obv:** Shield with garland **Rev:** Value within wreath

Date	Mintage	F	VF	XF	Unc	BU
1807	—	5.00	12.50	35.00	75.00	110
1808	—	5.00	12.50	35.00	75.00	110
1809	—	5.00	12.50	35.00	75.00	110
1810	—	5.00	12.50	35.00	75.00	110
1811	—	5.00	12.50	35.00	75.00	110

KM# 107 BATZEN - 10 RAPPEN
Billon **Obv:** Shield within palm wreath **Rev:** Dual denomination within circular oak wreath

Date	Mintage	F	VF	XF	Unc	BU
1813	—	5.00	12.50	35.00	75.00	110

KM# 110 2-1/2 BATZEN
Silver **Obv:** Shield within palm wreath **Obv. Legend:** RESPUBLICA LUCERNENSIS

Date	Mintage	F	VF	XF	Unc	BU
1815	—	25.00	50.00	90.00	150	200

KM# 111 2-1/2 BATZEN
Silver **Obv:** Shield within palm wreath **Obv. Legend:** CANTON LUZERN

Date	Mintage	F	VF	XF	Unc	BU
1815	—	10.00	20.00	35.00	80.00	120

KM# 100 5 BATZEN
Silver **Obv:** Crowned shield within wreath **Rev:** Value and date within oak wreath

Date	Mintage	F	VF	XF	Unc	BU
1806	—	25.00	75.00	135	200	300

KM# 104 5 BATZEN
Silver **Obv:** Crowned shield within laurel and palm wreath **Rev:** Value and date within laurel wreath

Date	Mintage	F	VF	XF	Unc	BU
1810	—	20.00	40.00	90.00	150	200

Note: 1811 dates are fakes.

KM# 108 5 BATZEN
Silver **Obv:** Crowned shield within laurel wreath **Rev:** Value and date within laurel wreath

Date	Mintage	F	VF	XF	Unc	BU
1813	—	20.00	40.00	90.00	150	200
1814	—	20.00	40.00	90.00	150	200

KM# 112 5 BATZEN
Silver **Obv:** Crowned shield within palm wreath **Rev:** Value within palm wreath

Date	Mintage	F	VF	XF	Unc	BU
1815	—	20.00	40.00	90.00	150	200
1816	—	20.00	40.00	90.00	150	200

KM# 105 10 BATZEN (1 Franken)
Silver **Obv:** Crowned shield within palm wreath

Date	Mintage	F	VF	XF	Unc	BU
1811	—	225	450	700	1,000	1,500
1812	—	45.00	100	200	375	550

KM# 113 40 BATZEN
Silver **Obv:** Crowned shield within palm wreath **Rev:** Value within laurel and oak wreath

Date	Mintage	F	VF	XF	Unc	BU
1816	3,107	175	350	750	1,100	1,400
1817	3,989	250	425	775	1,150	1,450

KM# 109 4 FRANKEN
Silver **Obv:** Crowned shield within palm wreath

Date	Mintage	F	VF	XF	Unc	BU
1813	—	125	250	500	800	1,100
1814	44,000	75.00	150	300	500	650

KM# 98 10 FRANKS
Gold **Obv:** Crowned garlanded shield, date in exergue

Date	Mintage	F	VF	XF	Unc	BU
1804	—	350	700	950	1,400	1,800

KM# 102 20 FRANKS
Gold **Obv:** Crowned garlanded shield, value in exergue

Date	Mintage	F	VF	XF	Unc	BU
1807 B	—	900	2,000	3,000	4,500	6,000

NEUCHATEL

Nuenberg

A canton on the west central border of Switzerland. The first coins (bracteates) were struck in the 11th century. They were under Prussian rule from 1707 to 1806. France occupied the canton from 1806-1815. They reverted to Prussia until 1857, when they became a full member of the Swiss Confederation.

NOTE: For coins previously listed here dated 1707-1806, see German States, Prussia.

RULERS
Prussian, 1707-1806
Alexandre Berthier, Prince, 1806-1814
Prussian, 1814-1857

MONETARY SYSTEM
4 Kreuzer = 1 Batzen
7 Kreuzer = 1 Piecette
21 Batzen = 1 Gulden
2 Gulden = 1 Thaler

CANTON
Prussian Administration
STANDARD COINAGE

KM# 64 1/2 KREUZER
Billon

Date	Mintage	F	VF	XF	Unc	BU
1802	—	40.00	125	200	300	400
1803	—	125	250	400	600	800

KM# 62 KREUZER
Billon

Date	Mintage	F	VF	XF	Unc	BU
1802	—	12.00	25.00	60.00	90.00	120
1803	—	5.00	9.00	14.00	20.00	30.00

KM# 66 KREUZER
Billon

Date	Mintage	F	VF	XF	Unc	BU
1807	—	5.00	8.00	16.00	30.00	50.00
1808	—	5.00	8.00	16.00	30.00	50.00

KM# 71 KREUZER
Billon

Date	Mintage	F	VF	XF	Unc	BU
1817	303,000	5.00	9.00	14.00	20.00	35.00
1818	Inc. above	7.50	10.00	15.00	25.00	35.00

KM# 57 1/2 BATZEN
Billon **Obv. Legend:** F.W. III. BOR. REX. P ...

Date	Mintage	F	VF	XF	Unc	BU
1803	—	5.00	8.00	20.00	30.00	50.00

KM# 55 1/2 BATZEN
Billon **Obv:** Legend, crowned arms **Obv. Legend:** F.G. BOR. REX. PR ... **Rev:** Cross

Date	Mintage	VG	F	VF	XF	Unc
1803	—	3.00	5.00	9.00	20.00	35.00

KM# 67 1/2 BATZEN
Billon **Rev:** Value: DEMI BATZ

Date	Mintage	F	VF	XF	Unc	BU
1807	—	7.50	12.50	25.00	45.00	70.00

KM# 68.1 1/2 BATZEN
Billon **Rev:** Value: 1/2 BATZ

Date	Mintage	F	VF	XF	Unc	BU
1807	—	5.00	10.00	25.00	40.00	65.00
1808	—	5.00	10.00	25.00	40.00	65.00
1809	—	5.00	10.00	25.00	40.00	65.00

KM# 68.2 1/2 BATZEN
Billon **Rev:** Value: 2/1 BATZ

Date	Mintage	F	VF	XF	Unc	BU
1807	—	—	—	—	—	—

KM# 65 BATZEN
Billon **Note:** Varieties exist.

Date	Mintage	F	VF	XF	Unc	BU
1806	—	12.50	20.00	35.00	65.00	90.00
1807	—	5.00	10.00	20.00	40.00	65.00
1808	—	5.00	10.00	20.00	40.00	65.00
1809	—	5.00	10.00	20.00	40.00	65.00
1810	—	12.50	20.00	50.00	90.00	135

KM# 69 BATZEN
Billon

Date	Mintage	F	VF	XF	Unc	BU
1807	—	5.00	10.00	20.00	40.00	65.00
1808	—	5.00	10.00	20.00	40.00	65.00

PATTERNS

Including off metal strikes

KM#	Date	Mintage	Identification	Mkt Val

Pn14	1814	—	2 Francs. Copper.	—
Pn15	1814	—	2 Francs. Silver.	1,400
			 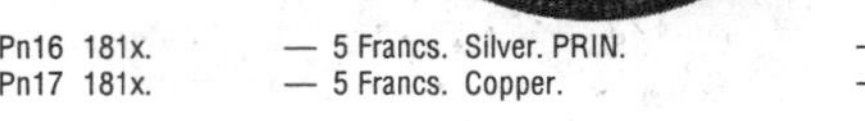	
Pn16	181x.	—	5 Francs. Silver. PRIN.	—
Pn17	181x.	—	5 Francs. Copper.	—

Pn18	181x.	—	5 Francs. Copper. PRINCE. Restruck at the end of the 19th Century.	700

SAINT GALL

St. Gallen

A canton in northeast Switzerland which completely surrounds the canton of Appenzell. It joined the Swiss Confederation in 1803.

MINT OFFICIALS' INITIALS

Initial	Date	Name
K	1808-17	?

MONETARY SYSTEM
4 Pfennig = 1 Kreuzer
4 Kreuzer = 1 Batzen
10 Batzen = 1 Frank

CITY

A city located in northeast Switzerland which was built to protect the abbey. It became a free city in 1311 and gained independence from the Abbots in 1457. The first coins were struck in the 1400s and the last ones in 1790.

STANDARD COINAGE

KM# 100 PFENNIG
Billon **Note:** Uniface, arms on concave planchet.

Date	Mintage	F	VF	XF	Unc	BU
ND	151,000	5.00	10.00	15.00	35.00	60.00

KM# 108 2 PFENNIG
Billon

Date	Mintage	F	VF	XF	Unc	BU
1808	—	60.00	120	200	300	400

KM# 109 1/2 KREUZER
Billon

Date	Mintage	F	VF	XF	Unc	BU
1808 K	111,000	7.50	12.00	30.00	55.00	85.00
1809 K	118,000	7.50	12.00	30.00	55.00	85.00
1810 K	101,000	7.50	12.00	30.00	55.00	85.00
1811 K	99,000	7.50	12.00	30.00	55.00	85.00
1812 K	175,000	7.50	12.00	30.00	55.00	85.00
1813 K	149,000	7.50	12.00	30.00	55.00	85.00
1814 K	114,000	7.50	12.00	30.00	55.00	85.00
1815 K	136,000	7.50	12.00	30.00	55.00	85.00
1816 K	238,000	7.50	12.00	30.00	55.00	85.00
1817 K	—	7.50	12.00	30.00	55.00	85.00

KM# 101 KREUZER
Billon

Date	Mintage	F	VF	XF	Unc	BU
1807 K	162,000	12.00	25.00	60.00	90.00	150
1808 K	202,000	12.00	25.00	60.00	90.00	150

KM# 102 KREUZER
Billon

Date	Mintage	F	VF	XF	Unc	BU
1807	—	65.00	125	200	325	450
Note: Mintage included in KM#101						
1809 K	160,000	5.00	10.00	20.00	40.00	65.00
1810 K	146,000	5.00	10.00	20.00	40.00	65.00
1811 K	106,000	5.00	10.00	20.00	40.00	65.00
1812 K	135,000	5.00	10.00	20.00	40.00	65.00
1813 K	102,000	5.00	10.00	20.00	40.00	65.00
1815 K	1,116,000	5.00	10.00	20.00	40.00	65.00
1816 K	135,000	5.00	10.00	20.00	40.00	65.00

KM# 103 1/2 BATZEN
Billon

Date	Mintage	F	VF	XF	Unc	BU
1807	110,000	10.00	20.00	35.00	75.00	100
1810 K	290,000	5.00	7.50	15.00	35.00	60.00
1811 K	349,000	5.00	7.50	15.00	35.00	60.00
1812 K	252,000	5.00	7.50	15.00	35.00	60.00
1813 K	154,000	5.00	7.50	15.00	35.00	60.00
1814 K	140,000	5.00	7.50	15.00	35.00	60.00
1815 K	181,000	5.00	7.50	15.00	35.00	60.00
1816 K	134,000	5.00	7.50	15.00	35.00	60.00
1817 K	—	12.50	20.00	45.00	90.00	125

KM# 104 1/2 BATZEN

Billon **Note:** Some varieties of KM#104 do not have the initial K.

Date	Mintage	F	VF	XF	Unc	BU
1807 K	Inc. above	8.00	15.00	35.00	65.00	100
1808 K	Inc. above	5.00	10.00	25.00	50.00	80.00
1809 K	Inc. above	5.00	10.00	25.00	50.00	80.00
1810 K	Inc. above	8.00	15.00	30.00	45.00	75.00

KM# 105 BATZEN

Billon

Date	Mintage	F	VF	XF	Unc	BU
1807 K	63,000	10.00	20.00	45.00	75.00	135
1808 K	133,000	5.00	7.50	25.00	50.00	90.00
1809 K	187,000	10.00	20.00	45.00	75.00	120

KM# 106 BATZEN

Billon

Date	Mintage	F	VF	XF	Unc	BU
1807	Inc. above	15.00	30.00	60.00	90.00	150

KM# 110 BATZEN

Billon **Obv:** Date **Rev:** Value: 1 BATZEN **Note:** Many varieties of KM#110 are known, including some without the K initial.

Date	Mintage	F	VF	XF	Unc	BU
1810 K	259,000	5.00	7.50	22.00	45.00	70.00
1811 K	319,000	5.00	7.50	22.00	45.00	70.00
1812 K	341,000	5.00	7.50	22.00	45.00	70.00
1813 K	—	5.00	7.50	22.00	45.00	70.00
1814 K	229,000	5.00	7.50	22.00	45.00	70.00
1815 K	1,008,000	5.00	7.50	22.00	45.00	70.00
1816 K	68,000	5.00	7.50	22.00	45.00	70.00
1817 K	—	15.00	30.00	75.00	100	150

KM# 107 6 KREUZER

Billon **Obv:** Arms in oak branches **Rev:** Value and date in oak branches **Note:** Overstruck on 6 Kreuzer (1760-97) of the Günzburg Mint

Date	Mintage	F	VF	XF	Unc	BU
1807	4,510	55.00	110	185	285	400

KM# 111 5 BATZEN

Silver **Obv:** Date in exergue

Date	Mintage	F	VF	XF	Unc	BU
1810 K	—	20.00	35.00	85.00	145	220
1811 K	—	30.00	45.00	110	175	250

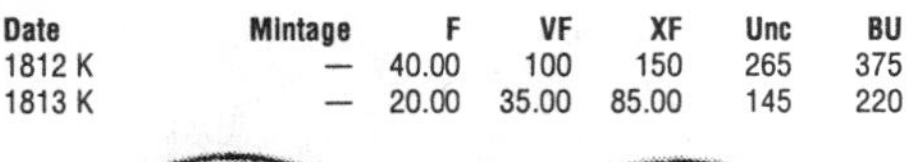

Date	Mintage	F	VF	XF	Unc	BU
1812 K	—	40.00	100	150	265	375
1813 K	—	20.00	35.00	85.00	145	220

KM# 113 5 BATZEN

Silver

Date	Mintage	F	VF	XF	Unc	BU
1813 K	—	20.00	35.00	85.00	145	220
1814 K	—	20.00	35.00	85.00	145	220
1817 K	—	35.00	50.00	125	185	275

KM# 114 5 BATZEN

Silver

Date	Mintage	F	VF	XF	Unc	BU
1817 K	—	35.00	50.00	125	185	275

KM# 112 1/2 FRANKEN

Silver

Date	Mintage	F	VF	XF	Unc	BU
1810 K	759	750	2,000	3,500	6,500	8,500

SCHAFFHAUSEN

A canton located on the north central border of Switzerland. The first coins, which were issued in the 13th century were known as "Ram Bracteates". It joined the Swiss Confederation in 1501.

MONETARY SYSTEM

4 Kreuzer = 1 Batzen

CANTON

STANDARD COINAGE

KM# 65 KREUZER

Billon

Date	Mintage	F	VF	XF	Unc	BU
1808	216,000	25.00	60.00	100	150	220

KM# 66 1/2 BATZEN

Billon

Date	Mintage	F	VF	XF	Unc	BU
1808	80,000	20.00	30.00	100	175	250

KM# 68 1/2 BATZEN

Billon

Date	Mintage	F	VF	XF	Unc	BU
1809	30,000	22.00	35.00	125	225	325

KM# 67 BATZEN

Billon

Date	Mintage	F	VF	XF	Unc	BU
1808	64,000	30.00	65.00	125	225	325

KM# 69 BATZEN

Billon **Rev:** Value: 1 BATZEN

Date	Mintage	F	VF	XF	Unc	BU
1809	15,000	22.50	40.00	100	150	250

SCHWYZ

Schwytz, Suitensis

A canton in central Switzerland. In 1291 it became one of the three cantons that would ultimately become the Swiss Confederation and were known as the "Everlasting League". The first coinage was issued in1624.

MINT OFFICIALS' INITIALS

Initial	Date	Name
DB	1843-46	?
H	1810-11	?
M	1844	?

MONETARY SYSTEM

240 Angster = 120 Rappen
= 40 Schillinge = 1 Gulden
4 Kreuzer = 1 Batzen
40 Batzen = 3 Gulden = 1 Thaler
12 Gulden = 1 Duplone

CANTON

STANDARD COINAGE

KM# 55 ANGSTER
Copper **Obv:** Oval arms within wreath **Rev:** Value and date **Note:** Varieties exist.

Date	Mintage	F	VF	XF	Unc	BU
1810	—	5.00	7.50	15.00	25.00	40.00
1811	—	5.00	7.50	15.00	25.00	40.00
1812	—	5.00	7.50	15.00	25.00	40.00
1813	—	10.00	20.00	30.00	50.00	75.00
1814	—	7.50	14.00	22.50	30.00	45.00
1815	—	10.00	20.00	30.00	50.00	75.00
1816	—	5.00	7.50	15.00	25.00	40.00
1821	—	12.50	20.00	30.00	50.00	75.00
1827	—	12.50	20.00	30.00	50.00	75.00
1838	—	12.50	20.00	30.00	50.00	75.00
1843	—	5.00	7.50	12.50	25.00	40.00
1845	—	5.00	7.50	12.50	25.00	40.00
1846	—	5.00	7.50	12.50	25.00	40.00

KM# 59 RAPPEN
Copper **Obv:** Oval shield within wreath **Rev:** Value and date within wreath **Note:** Many varieties exist, including some with value 1 RAPEN and mint mark B.

Date	Mintage	F	VF	XF	Unc	BU
1811	—	5.00	12.50	17.50	25.00	40.00
1812	—	3.00	5.00	9.00	16.00	25.00
1815	—	3.00	5.00	9.00	16.00	25.00
1845	—	3.00	5.00	8.00	15.00	22.00
1846	—	5.00	12.00	17.00	25.00	40.00

KM# 60 RAPPEN
Copper **Obv:** Shield within wreath **Rev:** Value and date within thin wreath

Date	Mintage	F	VF	XF	Unc	BU
1811	—	5.00	12.00	17.50	25.00	40.00
1812	—	3.00	5.00	9.00	16.00	25.00

KM# 65 RAPPEN
Copper **Obv:** Shield within wreath **Rev:** Value and date within wreath

Date	Mintage	F	VF	XF	Unc	BU
1815	—	3.00	5.00	9.00	16.00	25.00
1816	—	7.50	12.00	17.00	25.00	40.00
1843	—	3.00	5.00	9.00	16.00	25.00
1844	—	7.50	12.00	17.00	25.00	40.00
1845	—	3.00	5.00	9.00	16.00	25.00
1846	—	5.00	12.00	17.00	25.00	40.00

KM# 62 2 RAPPEN
Billon **Obv:** Shield **Rev:** Value and date within wreath **Note:** Many varieties exist, including some with the value as 2 RAPEN and mint mark B.

Date	Mintage	F	VF	XF	Unc	BU
1811	—	5.00	12.00	18.00	25.00	40.00
1812	—	3.00	7.00	10.00	17.00	28.00
1813	—	3.00	7.00	10.00	17.00	28.00
1814	—	3.00	7.00	10.00	17.00	28.00
1815	—	3.00	7.00	10.00	17.00	28.00
1842	—	10.00	20.00	30.00	50.00	75.00
1843	—	3.00	7.00	10.00	17.00	28.00
1843 DB	—	3.00	7.00	10.00	17.00	28.00
1844 DB	—	8.00	12.50	20.00	30.00	50.00
1845 DB	—	3.00	7.00	10.00	17.00	28.00
1846 DB	—	3.00	7.00	10.00	17.00	28.00

KM# 61 2 RAPPEN
Billon **Obv:** Shield within wreath **Rev:** Value and date within wreath **Note:** Varieties of these coins are known with value as 2 RAPEN.

Date	Mintage	F	VF	XF	Unc	BU
1811	—	12.00	25.00	50.00	90.00	125
1812	—	12.00	25.00	50.00	90.00	125
1813	—	12.00	25.00	50.00	90.00	125

KM# 56 2/3 BATZEN
Billon **Obv:** Shield within wreath **Rev:** Value and date within wreath

Date	Mintage	F	VF	XF	Unc	BU
1810	—	12.50	35.00	65.00	125	175
1811	—	12.50	35.00	65.00	100	150

KM# 63 2/3 BATZEN
Billon **Obv:** Shield in wreath **Rev. Legend:** 2/3 BATZEN

Date	Mintage	F	VF	XF	Unc	BU
1812	—	45.00	85.00	120	175	225

KM# 64 2/3 BATZEN
Billon **Rev. Legend:** 2/3 BATZ

Date	Mintage	F	VF	XF	Unc	BU
1812	—	50.00	125	175	300	400

KM# 57 2 BATZEN
Billon

Date	Mintage	F	VF	XF	Unc	BU
1810 H	—	60.00	120	165	250	350

KM# 58 4 BATZEN
Silver **Obv:** Shield in laurel wreath **Rev:** Value and date in wreath, legend around **Note:** Varieties exist with the value as 4 BATZ.

Date	Mintage	F	VF	XF	Unc	BU
1810 M	—	300	600	1,000	2,500	4,000
1811 M	—	70.00	150	275	500	700

TRADE COINAGE

KM# 66 DUCAT
3.5000 g., 0.9860 Gold 0.111 oz. **Obv:** Lion rampant supporting shield **Rev:** Legend and date within wreath **Note:** Given as a winner's prize at a shooting meeting.

Date	Mintage	F	VF	XF	Unc	BU
1844 M	50	3,000	5,000	7,000	9,000	12,000

SOLOTHURN

Solodornensis, Soleure

A canton in northwest Switzerland. Bracteates were struck in the 1300s even though the mint right was not officially granted until 1381. They joined the Swiss Confederation in 1481.

CANTON

STANDARD COINAGE

KM# 71 RAPPEN
Billon **Obv:** Shield within wreath **Rev:** Legend and date within circular wreath

Date	Mintage	F	VF	XF	Unc	BU
1813	—	15.00	30.00	50.00	85.00	125

KM# 85 2-1/2 RAPPEN
Billon **Obv:** Shield **Rev:** Wide cross

Date	Mintage	F	VF	XF	Unc	BU
1830	—	5.00	12.00	20.00	30.00	45.00

KM# 72 KREUZER
Billon **Obv:** Shield within wreath **Rev:** Value and date within wreath

Date	Mintage	F	VF	XF	Unc	BU
1813	—	5.00	12.00	20.00	30.00	45.00

KM# 78 5 RAPPEN
Billon **Obv:** Shield **Rev:** Wide cross in quatrelobe

Date	Mintage	F	VF	XF	Unc	BU
1826	—	20.00	30.00	50.00	85.00	125

KM# 65 BATZEN - 10 RAPPEN
Billon **Obv:** Shield with S-O flanking, within beaded circle; date in exergue **Rev:** Dual values within beaded circle

Date	Mintage	F	VF	XF	Unc	BU
1805	—	15.00	30.00	50.00	100	150

KM# 66 BATZEN - 10 RAPPEN
Billon **Obv:** Shield with garlanded at top all in pellet circle, date in exergue **Rev:** Dual values within beaded circle

Date	Mintage	F	VF	XF	Unc	BU
1807	—	60.00	100	200	300	425

KM# 67 BATZEN - 10 RAPPEN
Billon **Obv:** Shield within pellet circle, date in exergue **Rev:** Value within beaded circle

Date	Mintage	F	VF	XF	Unc	BU
1808	—	15.00	30.00	50.00	100	—
1809	—	15.00	30.00	50.00	100	150
1810	—	5.00	12.50	30.00	65.00	90.00
1811	—	5.00	12.50	30.00	65.00	90.00

KM# 79 BATZEN - 10 RAPPEN
Billon **Obv:** Shield, value in exergue **Rev:** Wide cross within quatrelobe

Date	Mintage	F	VF	XF	Unc	BU
1826	—	10.00	20.00	30.00	60.00	75.00

KM# 80 BATZEN - 10 RAPPEN
Billon **Obv:** Shield, value in exergue **Rev:** Wide cross in quatrelobe

Date	Mintage	F	VF	XF	Unc	BU
1826	—	5.00	12.50	25.00	45.00	60.00

KM# 81 2-1/2 BATZEN
Silver **Obv:** Crowned shield within wreath **Rev:** Wide cross within quatrelobe

Date	Mintage	F	VF	XF	Unc	BU
1826	—	20.00	40.00	75.00	110	150

KM# 68 5 BATZEN
Silver **Obv:** Crowned oval shield within wreath **Rev:** Value within circular wreath

Date	Mintage	F	VF	XF	Unc	BU
1809	—	75.00	150	300	550	1,100
1811	—	40.00	75.00	125	200	300

KM# 82 5 BATZEN
Silver **Obv:** Crowned oval shield within wreath, value as 5 BATZ below **Rev:** Wide cross within quatrelobe

Date	Mintage	F	VF	XF	Unc	BU
1826	—	25.00	50.00	90.00	125	175

KM# 83 5 BATZEN
Silver **Obv:** Crowned oval shield in wreath, value as 5 BAZ below **Rev:** Wide cross in quatrelobe

Date	Mintage	F	VF	XF	Unc	BU
1826	—	30.00	75.00	110	150	225

KM# 70 FRANK
Silver **Obv:** Crowned shield within wreath

Date	Mintage	F	VF	XF	Unc	BU
1812	2,000	200	350	500	750	1,250

KM# 73 4 FRANKEN
Silver **Obv:** Crowned shield within wreath

Date	Mintage	F	VF	XF	Unc	BU
1813	250	350	500	850	1,500	2,000

KM# 74 8 FRANKEN
3.8200 g., 0.9000 Gold 0.1105 oz. **Obv:** Crowned shield within wreath

Date	Mintage	F	VF	XF	Unc	BU
1813	106	2,000	4,000	6,000	7,500	10,000

KM# 75 16 FRANKEN
7.6400 g., 0.9000 Gold 0.2211 oz. **Obv:** Crowned shield within wreath

Date	Mintage	F	VF	XF	Unc	BU
1813	150	2,500	5,000	7,000	9,000	12,000

KM# 76 32 FRANKEN
15.2800 g., 0.9000 Gold 0.4421 oz. **Obv:** Crowned shield within wreath **Rev:** Standing knight supporting shield, value in exergue

Date	Mintage	F	VF	XF	Unc	BU
1813	—	—	—	17,500	20,000	—

THURGAU

Thurgovie

A canton in northeast Switzerland. They were ruled by the Swiss Confederates beginning c. 1460 until 1798. In 1803 they joined the Swiss Confederation.

MONETARY SYSTEM
4 Kreuzer = 1 Schweizer Batzen
10 Batzen = 1 Frank

CANTON

STANDARD COINAGE

KM# 1 1/2 KREUZER
Billon **Obv:** Shield within wreath **Rev:** Value and date within wreath

Date	Mintage	F	VF	XF	Unc	BU
1808	100,000	75.00	150	300	450	650

KM# 2 KREUZER
Billon **Obv:** Shield within wreath **Rev:** Value and date within wreath

Date	Mintage	F	VF	XF	Unc	BU
1808	99,000	25.00	45.00	85.00	120	200

KM# 3 1/2 BATZEN
Billon **Obv:** Shield within wreath **Rev:** Value and date within wreath

Date	Mintage	F	VF	XF	Unc	BU
1808	149,000	20.00	40.00	75.00	120	165

KM# 4 BATZEN
Billon **Obv:** Shield within wreath **Rev:** Value and date within wreath

Date	Mintage	F	VF	XF	Unc	BU
1808	232,000	20.00	40.00	90.00	150	225
1809	Inc. above	20.00	40.00	90.00	150	225

KM# 5 5 BATZEN
Billon **Obv:** Shield within wreath **Rev:** Value and date within wreath

Date	Mintage	F	VF	XF	Unc	BU
1808	2,580	200	375	625	900	1,250

TICINO

Tessin

A canton in southeast Switzerland. They were previously known as the Lombard vassal state of Bellinzona. They joined the Swiss Confederation in 1803.

MONETARY SYSTEM
12 Denari = 1 Soldo
20 Soldi = 1 Franco

CANTON

STANDARD COINAGE

KM# 5 3 DENARI
Copper **Obv:** Round shield within circle wreath **Rev:** Value within wreath

Date	Mintage	F	VF	XF	Unc	BU
1814	417,000	9.00	15.00	27.50	55.00	85.00
1835	598,000	9.00	15.00	27.50	50.00	75.00

KM# 9 3 DENARI
Copper **Obv:** Shield within wreath **Rev:** Value and date within wreath

Date	Mintage	F	VF	XF	Unc	BU
1841	322,000	9.00	15.00	27.50	60.00	90.00

KM# 1 6 DENARI
Copper **Obv:** Shield within wreath **Rev:** Value and date within wreath

Date	Mintage	F	VF	XF	Unc	BU
1813	280,000	9.00	15.00	32.50	55.00	80.00
1835	364,000	12.00	25.00	40.00	70.00	100
1841	241,000	9.00	15.00	32.50	55.00	80.00

KM# 2 3 SOLDI
Billon **Obv:** Shield, wreath above, garland in exergue **Rev:** Value and date within wreath

Date	Mintage	F	VF	XF	Unc	BU
1813 with star	1,405,000	20.00	40.00	90.00	125	165
1813 without star	Inc. above	10.00	25.00	60.00	90.00	125
1835	323,000	5.00	12.50	35.00	60.00	100
1838	514,000	5.00	12.50	35.00	60.00	100
1841	243,000	5.00	12.50	35.00	60.00	100

KM# 7 1/4 FRANCO
Silver **Obv:** Shield within wreath **Rev:** Value within wreath

Date	Mintage	F	VF	XF	Unc	BU
1835	58,000	50.00	100	185	275	350

KM# 8 1/2 FRANCO
Silver **Obv:** Shield within wreath **Rev:** Value within wreath

Date	Mintage	F	VF	XF	Unc	BU
1835	44,000	50.00	125	375	650	900

KM# 3 FRANCO
Silver **Obv:** Shield within wreath **Rev:** Knight standing next to shield

Date	Mintage	F	VF	XF	Unc	BU
1813	5,920	175	350	600	900	1,200
Note: With star (Lucerne)						
1813	Inc. above	125	250	550	850	1,100
Note: Without star (Berne).						

KM# 4 2 FRANCHI
Silver **Obv:** Shield within wreath **Rev:** Knight standing beside shield

Date	Mintage	F	VF	XF	Unc	BU
1813	4,150	500	1,150	1,650	2,200	3,500
Note: With star (Lucerne).						
1813	Inc. above	300	650	1,100	1,600	2,250
Note: Without star (Berne).						

KM# 6 4 FRANCHI
Silver **Obv:** Shield within wreath **Rev:** Knight standing beside shield

Date	Mintage	F	VF	XF	Unc	BU
1814 with star	7,921	300	600	1,100	2,000	2,500
1814 without star	Inc. above	250	500	800	1,500	2,250

UNTERWALDEN

Subsilvania

A canton in central Switzerland which was one of the three original cantons which became the Swiss Confederation in 1291. It is made up of two half cantons - Nidwalden and Obwalden. They had their own coinage beginning in the1500s.

MONETARY SYSTEM
4 Kreuzer = 1 Batzen
10 Batzen = 1 Frank

CANTON
Nidwalden

STANDARD COINAGE

KM# A11 1/2 BATZEN
Billon **Obv:** Shield within wreath **Rev:** Value and date within wreath

Date	Mintage	F	VF	XF	Unc	BU
1811	12,000	50.00	110	200	300	400

KM# A12 BATZEN - 10 RAPPEN
Billon **Obv:** Shield within wreath and pellet circle **Rev:** Dual values within circular wreath

Date	Mintage	F	VF	XF	Unc	BU
1811	12,000	50.00	110	200	300	450

KM# A13 5 BATZEN
Billon **Obv:** Shield within wreath **Rev:** Value and date within oak wreath

Date	Mintage	F	VF	XF	Unc	BU
1811	3,600	150	350	550	850	1,050

CANTON
Obwalden

STANDARD COINAGE

KM# 51 1/2 BATZEN
Billon **Obv:** Oval shield within palm wreath **Rev:** Value and date within wreath

Date	Mintage	F	VF	XF	Unc	BU
1812	—	45.00	75.00	175	300	400

KM# 52 BATZEN
Billon **Obv:** Shield within palm wreath, all within pellet circle **Rev:** Value within geometric wreath

Date	Mintage	F	VF	XF	Unc	BU
1812	—	45.00	75.00	175	300	400

KM# 53 5 BATZEN
Billon **Obv:** Shield within wreath **Rev:** Value and date within wreath

Date	Mintage	F	VF	XF	Unc	BU
1812	—	100	300	500	800	1,000

URI

Uranie

A canton in central Switzerland. It is one of the three original cantons which became the Swiss Confederation in 1291. They had their own coinage from the early 1600s until 1811.

MONETARY SYSTEM
10 Rappen = 1 Batzen
10 Batzen = 1 Frank

CANTON

STANDARD COINAGE

KM# 40 RAPPEN

Billon

Date	Mintage	F	VF	XF	Unc	BU
1811	19,000	50.00	100	150	250	400

KM# 41 1/2 BATZEN

Billon

Date	Mintage	F	VF	XF	Unc	BU
1811	15,000	45.00	75.00	150	250	350

KM# 42 BATZEN - 10 RAPPEN

Billon

Date	Mintage	F	VF	XF	Unc	BU
1811	20,000	50.00	75.00	175	250	350

KM# 43 2 BATZEN

Silver

Date	Mintage	F	VF	XF	Unc	BU
1811	4,995	100	200	350	500	700

KM# 44 4 BATZEN

Silver

Date	Mintage	F	VF	XF	Unc	BU
1811	3,510	125	250	450	700	950

VAUD

Waadt

A canton in southwest Switzerland. They had possession of Bern from 1536 until 1798. They joined the Swiss Confederation in 1803.

MINTMASTERS INITIALS

BEL - Bel Bessiere, 1827-1831

MONETARY SYSTEM

10 Rappen = 1 Batz
10 Batz = 1 Franc
4 Francs = 1 Thaler

CANTON

STANDARD COINAGE

KM# 5 RAPPEN

Billon **Obv:** Shield in wreath **Rev:** Value and date within circle wreath

Date	Mintage	F	VF	XF	Unc	BU
1804	211,000	30.00	65.00	100	150	200

KM# 12 RAPPEN

Billon **Obv:** Shield within wreath **Rev:** Value and date within wreath

Date	Mintage	F	VF	XF	Unc	BU
1807	Inc. above	15.00	25.00	45.00	70.00	95.00

KM# 14 2-1/2 RAPPEN

Billon **Obv:** Shield **Rev:** Value within wreath

Date	Mintage	F	VF	XF	Unc	BU
1809	230,000	10.00	20.00	40.00	60.00	100

KM# 18 2-1/2 RAPPEN

Billon **Obv:** Shield **Rev:** Value within wreath

Date	Mintage	F	VF	XF	Unc	BU
1816	—	7.00	14.00	30.00	50.00	90.00

KM# 6 1/2 BATZEN - 5 RAPPEN

Billon **Obv:** Shield within fine pellet circle **Rev:** Dual values within wreath

Date	Mintage	F	VF	XF	Unc	BU
1804	2,962,000	5.00	10.00	25.00	40.00	60.00
1805	Inc. above	5.00	10.00	25.00	40.00	60.00
1806	Inc. above	5.00	10.00	25.00	40.00	60.00
1807	Inc. above	5.00	10.00	25.00	40.00	60.00
1808	Inc. above	15.00	30.00	50.00	80.00	120
1809	—	5.00	10.00	25.00	35.00	45.00
1810	—	5.00	10.00	25.00	35.00	45.00
1811	—	5.00	10.00	25.00	35.00	45.00
1813	—	5.00	10.00	25.00	35.00	45.00
1814	—	5.00	10.00	25.00	35.00	45.00
1816	—	10.00	20.00	35.00	45.00	65.00
1817	—	5.00	10.00	25.00	35.00	45.00
1818	—	8.00	20.00	40.00	50.00	60.00
1819	—	8.00	20.00	40.00	50.00	60.00

KM# 7 BATZEN - 10 RAPPEN

Billon **Obv:** Shield within fine pellet circle, date in exergue **Rev:** Dual values within wreath

Date	Mintage	F	VF	XF	Unc	BU
1804	—	40.00	90.00	150	250	350

KM# 8 BATZEN - 10 RAPPEN

Billon **Obv:** Shield within wreath, all within fine pellet circle, date in exergue **Rev:** Dual values within wreath

Date	Mintage	F	VF	XF	Unc	BU
1804	—	5.00	12.50	30.00	50.00	75.00
1805	—	5.00	12.50	30.00	50.00	75.00
1806	—	5.00	12.50	30.00	50.00	75.00
1807	—	5.00	12.50	30.00	50.00	75.00
1808	—	150	250	500	750	1,200
1809	—	25.00	40.00	70.00	120	145
1810	—	5.00	10.00	22.00	40.00	60.00
1811	—	5.00	10.00	22.00	40.00	60.00
1812	—	5.00	10.00	22.00	40.00	60.00
1813	—	5.00	10.00	22.00	40.00	60.00
1814	—	5.00	10.00	22.00	40.00	60.00
1815	—	5.00	10.00	22.00	40.00	60.00
1816	—	5.00	10.00	22.00	40.00	60.00
1817	—	5.00	10.00	22.00	40.00	60.00
1818	—	5.00	10.00	22.00	40.00	60.00
1819	—	5.00	10.00	22.00	40.00	60.00
1820	—	9.00	15.00	30.00	60.00	80.00

KM# 20 BATZEN - 10 RAPPEN

Billon **Obv:** Shield within wreath, value in exergue **Rev:** Wide cross within ornate border **Note:** Varieties exist.

Date	Mintage	F	VF	XF	Unc	BU
1820	—	—	—	—	—	—
1826	—	30.00	80.00	150	250	350
1827 BEL	—	7.00	15.00	30.00	50.00	90.00
1828	—	7.00	15.00	30.00	50.00	90.00
1828 BEL	—	7.00	15.00	30.00	50.00	90.00
1829 BEL	—	7.00	15.00	30.00	50.00	90.00
1830 BEL	—	7.00	15.00	30.00	50.00	90.00
1831	—	7.00	15.00	30.00	50.00	90.00
1832 BEL	—	7.00	15.00	30.00	50.00	90.00
1834 BEL	—	10.00	25.00	50.00	75.00	100

KM# 9 5 BATZEN

Silver **Obv:** Shield, date in exergue **Rev:** Value wihtin wreath

Date	Mintage	F	VF	XF	Unc	BU
1804	1,692	200	450	700	1,000	1,500

KM# 11 5 BATZEN

Silver **Obv:** Shield within wreath **Rev:** Value within vine wreath

Date	Mintage	F	VF	XF	Unc	BU
1805	—	125	185	260	425	600
1806	—	125	185	260	425	600

KM# 13 5 BATZEN

Silver **Obv:** Shield within wreath **Rev:** Value within wreath

Date	Mintage	F	VF	XF	Unc	BU
1807	—	25.00	50.00	75.00	150	250
1810	—	20.00	40.00	75.00	125	200
1811	—	20.00	35.00	70.00	120	200
1812	—	20.00	40.00	75.00	125	200
1813	—	20.00	40.00	75.00	125	200
1814	—	30.00	70.00	125	200	300

KM# 21.1 5 BATZEN

Silver **Obv:** Shield within wreath, value below **Rev:** Wide cross within fancy quatrelobe

Date	Mintage	F	VF	XF	Unc	BU
1826	—	20.00	50.00	80.00	125	200
1827 BEL	—	12.00	30.00	50.00	90.00	125
1828 BEL	—	12.00	30.00	50.00	90.00	125
1829 BEL	—	15.00	35.00	60.00	100	150
1830 BEL	—	15.00	35.00	60.00	100	150
1831 BEL	—	15.00	35.00	60.00	100	150

KM# 21.2 5 BATZEN
Silver **Obv:** Shield within wreath, value below **Rev:** Wide cross within ornate quatrelobe

Date	Mintage	F	VF	XF	Unc	BU
1827 BEL	—	12.00	30.00	50.00	90.00	125

KM# 10 10 BATZEN
Silver **Obv:** Shield, date in exergue **Rev:** Value within oak wreath

Date	Mintage	F	VF	XF	Unc	BU
1804	1,234	250	450	700	1,100	1,600

KM# 15 10 BATZEN
Silver **Obv:** Shield within wreath, date in exergue **Rev:** Knight standing beside shield, value in exergue

Date	Mintage	F	VF	XF	Unc	BU
1810	1,234	60.00	125	200	350	500
1811	2,963	60.00	125	200	350	500

KM# 19 10 BATZEN
Silver **Obv:** Shield within wreath, date in exergue **Rev:** Knight standing beside shield, value in exergue

Date	Mintage	F	VF	XF	Unc	BU
1823	6,198	40.00	90.00	150	275	450

KM# 16 20 BATZEN
Silver **Obv:** Shield within wreath, date in exergue **Rev:** Knight standing beside shield, value in exergue

Date	Mintage	F	VF	XF	Unc	BU
1810	6,590	65.00	150	300	400	650
1811	Inc. above	65.00	150	300	400	650

KM# 17 40 BATZEN
Silver **Obv:** Shield within wreath, date in exergue **Rev:** Knight standing beside shield, value in exergue **Note:** 616 pieces were melted in 1851.

Date	Mintage	F	VF	XF	Unc	BU
1812	2,485	150	300	500	750	1,150

KM# 22 FRANC
Silver **Obv:** Shield within wreath, date below **Rev:** Knight standing beside shield **Note:** Struck to commemorate a Shooting Festival held on August 10, 1845. It has legal tender status.

Date	Mintage	F	VF	XF	Unc	BU
1845	8,626	30.00	50.00	100	200	—

COUNTERSTAMPED COINAGE

KM# 23 39 BATZEN
Silver **Note:** Counterstamped on France Louis XV Ecu, C#42.

CS Date	Host Date	Good	VG	F	VF	XF
(1816)	(1726-41)	—	600	1,000	1,500	—

KM# 24 39 BATZEN
Silver **Note:** Counterstamped on France Louis XV Ecu, C#47.

CS Date	Host Date	Good	VG	F	VF	XF
(1816)	(1740-71)	—	600	1,000	1,500	—

KM# 25 39 BATZEN
Silver **Note:** Counterstamped on France Louis XV Ecu, #C47a.

CS Date	Host Date	Good	VG	F	VF	XF
(1816)	(1770-74)	—	600	1,000	1,500	—

KM# 26 39 BATZEN
Silver **Note:** Counterstamped on France Louis XVI Ecu, C#78.

CS Date	Host Date	Good	VG	F	VF	XF
(1816)	(1774-92)	—	600	1,000	1,500	—

KM# 27 39 BATZEN
Silver **Note:** Counterstamped on France Louis XVI Constitutional Ecu, C#93.

CS Date	Host Date	Good	VG	F	VF	XF
(1816)	(1792-93)	—	1,000	2,000	4,000	—

KM# 28 39 BATZEN
Silver **Note:** Counterstamped on France 6 Livres, C#123.

CS Date	Host Date	Good	VG	F	VF	XF
(1816)	(1793-94)	—	1,500	3,000	6,500	—

PATTERNS

(Including off metal strikes)

KM#	Date	Mintage	Identification	Mkt Val
Pn1	1804	—	1/2 Batzen - 5 Rappen. Billon. Shield within circle. value and date within wreath.	—
Pn2	1830	—	1/4 Franc. Silver. Shield within wreath. Value and date within wreath.	—

ZUG

Tugium, Tugiensis

A canton in central Switzerland. They joined the Swiss Confederation in 1352 and had their own coinage from1564 to 1805.

MONETARY SYSTEM
6 Angster = 3 Rappen
= 1 Schilling = 1 Assis

CANTON

STANDARD COINAGE

KM# 61 ANGSTER
Copper **Obv:** Arms in branches **Rev:** Date, value in cartouche

Date	Mintage	VG	F	VF	XF	Unc
1804	—	40.00	70.00	150	250	400

KM# 63 RAPPEN
Copper **Obv:** Arms in branches **Rev:** Date, value in cartouche

Date	Mintage	VG	F	VF	XF	Unc
1805	—	3.00	5.00	15.00	40.00	75.00

ZURICH

Thicurinae, Thuricensis, Ticurinae, Turicensis

A canton in north central Switzerland. It was the mint for the dukes of Swabia in the 10th and 11th centuries. The mint right was obtained in 1238. The first coinage struck were bracteates and the last coins were struck in 1848. It joined the Swiss Confederation in 1351.

MINTMASTER'S INITIAL
B - Bruckmann

CANTON

REFORM COINAGE

Commencing 1803

KM# 180 3 HALLER
Billon **Obv:** Round shield within laurel and palm wreath **Rev:** value within frame

Date	Mintage	F	VF	XF	Unc	BU
ND (1827-41)	3,518,000	4.00	7.00	10.00	14.00	18.00

KM# 181 3 HALLER
Billon **Obv:** Round shield in laurel and palm wreath **Rev:** Value as HALER, within frame

Date	Mintage	F	VF	XF	Unc	BU
ND (1827-41)	Inc. above	5.00	8.50	12.00	15.00	20.00

KM# 194 RAPPEN
Billon **Obv:** Shield within laurel wreath **Rev:** value and date within wreath

Date	Mintage	F	VF	XF	Unc	BU
1842	—	3.00	6.00	17.50	27.00	35.00
1844	—	8.00	15.00	28.00	40.00	60.00
1845	—	3.00	6.00	17.50	27.00	35.00
1846	—	65.00	225	400	600	750
1848	—	3.00	7.50	15.00	22.50	30.00

KM# 195 2 RAPPEN
Billon **Obv:** Shield within oak and laurel wreath **Rev:** Value and date within oak wreath

Date	Mintage	F	VF	XF	Unc	BU
1842 D	460,000	5.00	12.50	20.00	32.00	45.00

KM# 182 10 SCHILLINGS
Silver **Obv:** Shield **Rev:** Legend and date in frame within laurel and palm wreath, value below in oval

Date	Mintage	F	VF	XF	Unc	BU
ND (1806)	—	30.00	60.00	125	175	225
1807 B	—	45.00	100	200	300	400
1808 B	—	12.50	27.50	50.00	75.00	110
1809 B	—	12.50	27.50	50.00	75.00	110
1810 B	—	15.00	30.00	65.00	125	175
1811 B	—	12.50	27.50	50.00	75.00	110

KM# 184 8 BATZEN
Silver **Obv:** Shield within laurel and palm wreath **Rev:** Value and date within laurel wreath

Date	Mintage	F	VF	XF	Unc	BU
1810 B	108,000	40.00	70.00	150	210	275
1814 B	Inc. above	50.00	90.00	165	235	325

KM# 185 10 BATZEN
Silver **Obv:** Shield with wreath above and garland at sides, value in exergue **Rev:** Legend and date within laurel wreath

Date	Mintage	F	VF	XF	Unc	BU
1812 B	28,000	60.00	100	150	225	300

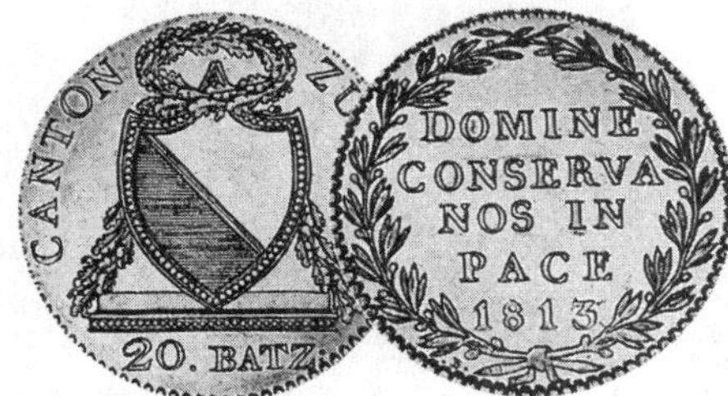

KM# 186 20 BATZEN
Silver **Obv:** Shield with wreath above and garland at sides, value in exergue **Rev:** Legend and date within thin laurel wreath, four berries at bottom

Date	Mintage	F	VF	XF	Unc	BU
1813 B	—	60.00	125	225	350	400

KM# 187 20 BATZEN
Silver **Obv:** Shield with wreath above and garland at sides, value in exergue **Rev:** Legend and date within thin wreath, 2 berries below date

Date	Mintage	F	VF	XF	Unc	BU
1813	—	60.00	125	225	350	400

KM# 188 20 BATZEN
Silver **Obv:** Shield with wreath above, long garland at sides, value in exergue **Rev:** Legend and date within thin wreath, two berries below

Date	Mintage	F	VF	XF	Unc	BU
1813	—	75.00	125	225	375	450

KM# 192 20 BATZEN
Silver **Obv:** Shield with wreath above and garland at sides, value in exergue **Rev:** Legend and date within open wreath

Date	Mintage	F	VF	XF	Unc	BU
1826	—	100	175	250	425	600

KM# 189 40 BATZEN
Silver **Obv:** Shield with wreath above and garland at sides, value in exergue **Rev:** Legend and date within laurel wreath. Large date, four berries at bottom

Date	Mintage	F	VF	XF	Unc	BU
1813	—	75.00	125	250	350	450

KM# 190 40 BATZEN
Silver **Obv:** Shield with wreath above, garland at sides, date in exergue. 19mm wide shield. **Rev:** Legend and date within wreath. Small date, 2 berries below

Date	Mintage	F	VF	XF	Unc	BU
1813 B	—	75.00	125	250	350	450

KM# 191 40 BATZEN
Silver **Obv:** Shield with wreath above, garland at sides, value in exergue. 18mm wide shield **Rev:** Legend and date within wreath. Small date, two berries below

Date	Mintage	F	VF	XF	Unc	BU
1813 B	—	75.00	125	250	350	450

TRADE COINAGE

KM# A185 DUCAT
3.5000 g., 0.9860 Gold 0.111 oz.

Date	Mintage	F	VF	XF	Unc	BU
1810 B	—	700	900	1,200	2,000	2,500

MEDALLIC COINAGE

KM# M2 DUCAT
3.5000 g., 0.9860 Gold 0.111 oz. **Obv:** Bust r. of Magister Zwingli **Rev:** 9-line legend and date

Date	Mintage	F	VF	XF	Unc	BU
1819	—	—	300	400	600	800

PATTERNS

Including off metal strikes

KM#	Date	Mintage	Identification	Mkt Val

KM#	Date	Mintage	Identification	Mkt Val
Pn8	1811	—	1/2 Kreuzer. Billon. Shield within wreath. Value within border.	—

KM#	Date	Mintage	Identification	Mkt Val
Pn9	1842	—	Kreuzer. Billon. Shield within wreath. Value and date within wreath.	—

The Swiss Confederation, located in central Europe north of Italy and south of Germany, has an area of 15,941 sq. mi. (41,290 sq. km.).

Switzerland, the habitat of lake dwellers in prehistoric times, was peopled by the Celtic Helvetians when Julius Caesar made it a part of the Roman Empire in 58 B.C. After the decline of Rome, Switzerland was invaded by Teutonic tribes, who established small temporal holdings which in the Middle Ages, became a federation of fiefs of the Holy Roman Empire. As a nation, Switzerland originated in 1291 when the districts of Nidwalden, Schwyz and Uri united to defeat Austria and attain independence as the Swiss Confederation. After acquiring new cantons in the 14th century, Switzerland was made independent from the Holy Roman Empire by the 1648 Treaty of Westphalia. The revolutionary armies of Napoleonic France occupied Switzerland and set up the Helvetian Republic, 1798-1803. After the fall of Napoleon, the Congress of Vienna, 1815, recognized the independence of Switzerland and guaranteed its neutrality. The Swiss Constitutions of 1848 and 1874 established a union modeled upon that of the United States.

MINT MARKS

A - Paris
AB - Strasbourg
B - Bern
B. - Brussels 1874
BA - Basel
BB - Strasbourg
S – Solothurn

NOTE: The coinage of Switzerland has been struck at the Bern Mint since 1853 with but a few exceptions. All coins minted there carry a B' mint mark through 1969, except for the 2-Centime and 2-Franc values where the mintmark was discontinued after 1968. In 1968 and 1969some issues were struck at both Bern (B) and in London (no mint mark).

MONETARY SYSTEM

10 Rappen = 1 Batzen
10 Batzen = 1 Franc
16 Franken = 1 Duplone

HELVETIAN REPUBLIC

DECIMAL COINAGE

100 Rappen (Centimes) = 1 Franc

KM# A11 RAPPEN

Billon **Obv:** Fasces in branches **Rev:** Value in wreath

Date	Mintage	F	VF	XF	Unc	BU
1801	—	5.00	10.00	22.50	40.00	60.00
1802	—	7.50	15.00	25.00	45.00	70.00

KM# A6 1/2 BATZEN

Billon

Date	Mintage	F	VF	XF	Unc	BU
1802	—	12.00	22.00	55.00	90.00	125
1803	—	12.00	22.00	50.00	90.00	115

KM# A8 BATZEN

Billon **Obv:** Legend in wreath **Obv. Legend:** HELVET.REPUBL **Rev:** Similar to 1 Rappen, KM#11

Date	Mintage	F	VF	XF	Unc	BU
1801B	—	12.50	22.50	60.00	90.00	125
1802B	—	12.50	22.50	60.00	90.00	125
1803B	—	12.50	22.50	60.00	90.00	125

KM# A9 5 BATZEN

Silver **Obv:** Standing Swiss holding flag **Rev:** Value within wreath

Date	Mintage	F	VF	XF	Unc	BU
1802B	—	250	400	700	950	1,300

KM# A1 10 BATZEN

Silver **Obv:** Standing Swiss holding flag **Rev:** Value within wreath

Date	Mintage	F	VF	XF	Unc	BU
1801B	—	75.00	175	400	650	800

KM# A10 4 FRANKEN

Silver **Note:** Dav. #1772.

Date	Mintage	F	VF	XF	Unc	BU
1801B	—	225	400	650	900	1,250

CONFEDERATION

Confoederatio Helvetica

MONETARY SYSTEM

100 Rappen (Centimes) = 1 Franc

DECIMAL COINAGE

100 Rappen (Centimes) = 1 Franc

KM# 3.1 RAPPEN

Bronze **Obv:** Cross in shield

Date	Mintage	F	VF	XF	Unc	BU
1850A	2,270,000	24.00	60.00	95.00	125	175
1851A	2,730,000	10.00	20.00	35.00	65.00	90.00
1853B thick cross	2,008,000	20.00	40.00	85.00	125	175
1853B thin cross	Inc. above	700	1,100	1,600	220	2,700
1855B	500,000	175	300	450	600	750
1856B	2,500,000	5.00	15.00	30.00	60.00	85.00
1857B	1,587,000	20.00	40.00	65.00	90.00	120
1863B	501,000	115	225	300	400	600
1864B	501,000	115	235	325	425	600
1866B	1,000,000	45.00	90.00	135	180	225
1868B	2,000,000	5.00	15.00	30.00	45.00	65.00
1870B	500,000	70.00	125	175	225	300
1872B	2,080,000	7.50	18.00	25.00	40.00	60.00
1875B	975,000	20.00	45.00	65.00	90.00	120
1876B	1,000,000	18.00	45.00	60.00	75.00	100
1877B	923,000	18.00	40.00	55.00	70.00	95.00
1878B	981,000	18.00	40.00	55.00	70.00	95.00
1879B	998,000	18.00	40.00	55.00	70.00	95.00
1880B	992,000	16.00	35.00	45.00	70.00	95.00
1882B	1,000,000	12.00	25.00	35.00	50.00	70.00
1883B	1,000,000	10.00	20.00	30.00	40.00	55.00
1884B	1,000,000	8.00	17.50	32.50	42.50	40.00
1887B	1,504,000	6.00	15.00	22.50	35.00	45.00
1889B	500,000	40.00	95.00	125	200	250
1890B	1,000,000	8.00	20.00	27.00	37.50	45.00
1891B Thick cross	2,000,000	8.00	20.00	25.00	40.00	48.00
1891B Thin cross	Inc. above	8.00	17.50	25.00	40.00	48.00
1892B	1,000,000	8.00	20.00	27.00	40.00	55.00
1894B	1,000,000	8.00	22.00	30.00	45.00	65.00
1895B	2,000,000	4.00	6.00	12.00	18.00	24.00
1896B	36	—	—	—	4,000	5,000
1897B	500,000	15.00	30.00	40.00	60.00	80.00
1898B	1,500,000	4.00	8.00	12.00	18.00	25.00
1899B	1,500,000	4.00	8.00	12.00	18.00	25.00
1900B	2,000,000	4.00	8.00	12.00	18.00	25.00

KM# 4.1 2 RAPPEN

Bronze **Obv:** Thick cross in shield

Date	Mintage	F	VF	XF	Unc	BU
1850A	7,290,000	2.00	7.00	17.50	30.00	40.00
1851A	3,720,000	1.50	8.00	17.50	30.00	40.00
1866B	1,000,000	5.00	10.00	17.50	40.00	60.00
1870B	540,000	18.00	35.00	60.00	80.00	100
1875B	984,000	3.00	8.00	14.00	25.00	35.00
1879B	990,000	3.00	7.00	12.00	25.00	35.00
1883B	1,000,000	2.00	7.00	12.00	20.00	30.00
1886B	1,000,000	1.50	5.00	10.00	20.00	30.00
1888B	500,000	12.00	30.00	45.00	65.00	85.00
1890B	1,000,000	1.50	5.00	9.00	15.00	22.00

KM# 4.2 2 RAPPEN
Bronze **Obv:** Thin cross in shield

Date	Mintage	F	VF	XF	Unc	BU
1893B	2,000,000	1.00	4.00	6.00	9.00	12.00
1896B Rare	20	—	—	—	4,000	5,000
1897B	487,000	10.00	24.00	35.00	50.00	65.00
1898B	500,000	8.00	21.00	30.00	40.00	50.00
1899B	1,000,000	3.00	6.00	10.00	17.00	24.00
1900B	1,000,000	3.00	7.00	11.00	17.00	24.00

KM# 5 5 RAPPEN
Billon

Date	Mintage	F	VF	XF	Unc	BU
1850BB	7,970,000	4.00	12.00	25.00	55.00	80.00
1850AB	Inc. above	30.00	120	400	600	800
1850	Inc. above	250	600	1,200	1,600	2,200
1851BB	12,042,000	100	250	500	850	1,200
1872B	1,213,000	10.00	25.00	45.00	60.00	75.00
1873B	1,622,000	10.00	20.00	32.00	48.00	65.00
1874B	1,700,000	10.00	20.00	32.00	48.00	65.00
1876B	989,000	20.00	45.00	60.00	95.00	125
1877B	978,000	24.00	50.00	75.00	100	135

KM# 26 5 RAPPEN
Copper-Nickel

Date	Mintage	F	VF	XF	Unc	BU
1879B	1,000,000	5.00	12.00	30.00	70.00	110
1880B	2,000,000	2.00	6.00	12.50	45.00	60.00
1881B	2,000,000	2.00	5.00	10.00	25.00	45.00
1882B	3,000,000	1.00	3.00	10.00	25.00	45.00
1883B	3,000,000	1.00	3.00	10.00	22.00	40.00
1884B	2,000,000	2.00	6.00	12.50	30.00	50.00
1885B	3,000,000	1.00	2.50	10.00	20.00	32.00
1887B	500,000	12.00	35.00	100	225	325
1888B	1,500,000	2.00	5.00	10.00	25.00	40.00
1889B	500,000	12.00	32.00	100	250	350
1890B	1,000,000	4.00	10.00	20.00	45.00	65.00
1891B	1,000,000	3.00	10.00	25.00	75.00	110
1892B	1,000,000	3.00	10.00	20.00	65.00	95.00
1893B	2,000,000	0.50	1.50	8.00	20.00	32.00
1894B	2,000,000	0.50	1.50	7.00	20.00	30.00
1895B	2,000,000	0.50	1.50	7.00	20.00	30.00
1896B Rare	16	—	—	—	4,000	5,000
1897B	500,000	4.00	10.00	25.00	70.00	100
1898B	2,500,000	0.50	1.50	9.00	21.00	30.00
1899B	1,500,000	3.50	9.00	20.00	45.00	65.00
1900B	2,000,000	1.00	3.00	7.50	20.00	30.00
1902B T over L in HELVETICA	Inc. above	—	20.00	60.00	100	150

KM# 6 10 RAPPEN
Billon

Date	Mintage	F	VF	XF	Unc	BU
1850BB	8,780,000	4.00	17.50	40.00	75.00	105
1851BB	4,530,000	14.00	50.00	110	275	375
1871B	844,000	20.00	35.00	60.00	85.00	110
1873B	1,398,000	12.00	25.00	40.00	65.00	85.00
1875B	174,000	275	500	650	850	1,100
1876B	1,962,000	12.00	25.00	38.00	57.00	70.00

KM# 7 20 RAPPEN
Billon

Date	Mintage	F	VF	XF	Unc	BU
1850BB	11,559,783	5.00	17.50	45.00	95.00	125
1851BB	Inc. above	50.00	160	400	850	1,200
1858B	1,547,860	7.00	25.00	50.00	100	150
1859B	2,775,965	4.00	10.00	27.50	50.00	70.00

KM# 29 20 RAPPEN
Nickel

Date	Mintage	F	VF	XF	Unc	BU
1881B	1,000,000	1.50	4.00	17.00	45.00	65.00
1883B	2,500,000	0.50	1.50	15.00	42.00	60.00
1884B	4,000,000	0.50	1.00	10.00	22.00	35.00
1885B	3,000,000	0.50	1.00	12.00	30.00	45.00
1887B	500,000	2.50	8.00	35.00	95.00	145
1891B	1,000,000	0.50	1.00	10.00	40.00	60.00
1893B	1,000,000	0.50	1.00	10.00	40.00	60.00
1894B	1,000,000	0.50	1.00	10.00	35.00	48.00
1896B	1,000,000	0.50	1.00	10.00	35.00	48.00
1897B	500,000	1.00	4.00	20.00	125	185
1898B	500,000	3.00	6.00	25.00	100	135
1899B	500,000	2.00	5.00	20.00	100	135
1900B	1,000,000	0.50	1.00	7.50	40.00	65.00

KM# 8 1/2 FRANC
2.5000 g., 0.9000 Silver .0723 oz.

Date	Mintage	F	VF	XF	Unc	BU
1850A	4,500,000	40.00	100	175	350	500
1850A Specimen	—	—	—	—	1,500	—
1851A	Inc. above	35.00	75.00	150	350	500
1851A Specimen	—	—	—	—	1,500	—

KM# 23 1/2 FRANC
2.5000 g., 0.8350 Silver .0671 oz.

Date	Mintage	F	VF	XF	Unc	BU
1875B	1,000,000	12.50	55.00	150	350	500
1875B Specimen	—	—	—	—	1,500	—
1877B	1,000,000	12.50	60.00	200	500	700
1877B Specimen	—	—	—	—	1,800	—
1878B	1,000,000	17.50	70.00	200	500	700
1878B Specimen	—	—	—	—	2,400	—
1879B	1,000,000	10.00	30.00	100	250	375
1879B Specimen	—	—	—	—	1,500	—
1881B	1,000,000	4.00	20.00	75.00	250	350
1881B Specimen	—	—	—	—	1,500	—
1882B	1,000,000	5.00	40.00	100	275	400
1882B Specimen	—	—	—	—	1,500	—
1894B	800,000	10.00	40.00	75.00	135	200
1894B Specimen	—	—	—	—	900	—
1896B Specimen; Rare	28	—	—	—	12,000	15,000
1898B	1,600,000	1.00	2.50	15.00	50.00	75.00
1898B Specimen	—	—	—	—	600	—
1899B	400,000	2.00	7.50	60.00	150	225
1899B Specimen	—	—	—	—	1,500	—
1900B	400,000	3.00	12.00	60.00	175	250
1900B Specimen	—	—	—	—	1,500	—
1946B Medal alignment	Inc. above	50.00	100	150	200	300

KM# 9 FRANC
5.0000 g., 0.9000 Silver .1447 oz.

Date	Mintage	F	VF	XF	Unc	BU
1850A	5,750,000	40.00	100	200	300	450
1850A Specimen	—	—	—	—	1,800	—
1851A	Inc. above	50.00	110	225	350	500
1851A Specimen	—	—	—	—	1,800	—
1857B	526	2,400	4,000	7,000	10,000	13,500
1857B Specimen, Rare	—	—	—	—	—	—

KM# 9a FRANC
5.0000 g., 0.8000 Silver .1286 oz.

Date	Mintage	F	VF	XF	Unc	BU
1860B	515,000	75.00	175	500	1,200	1,800
1860B Specimen	—	—	—	—	3,600	—
1861B	3,002,000	12.50	35.00	75.00	250	350
1861B Specimen	—	—	—	—	1,800	—

KM# 24 FRANC
5.0000 g., 0.8350 Silver .1342 oz.

Date	Mintage	F	VF	XF	Unc	BU
1875B	1,036,000	6.00	40.00	135	400	700
1875B Specimen	—	—	—	—	3,000	—
1876B	2,500,000	3.00	15.00	75.00	250	400
1876B Specimen	—	—	—	—	2,400	—
1877B	2,520,000	2.50	20.00	100	300	450
1877B Specimen	—	—	—	—	2,400	—
1880B	944,000	3.00	45.00	150	800	1,200
1880B Specimen	—	—	—	—	3,600	—
1886B	1,000,000	1.50	10.00	50.00	125	200
1886B Specimen	—	—	—	—	1,500	—
1887B	1,000,000	1.50	10.00	50.00	125	175
1887B Specimen	—	—	—	—	1,200	—
1894A	1,200,000	1.50	10.00	50.00	125	200
1894A Specimen	—	—	—	—	1,050	—
1896B Specimen; Rare	28	—	—	—	12,000	15,000
1898B	400,000	2.00	7.00	50.00	200	300
1898B Specimen	—	—	—	—	1,800	—
1899B	400,000	2.00	7.00	50.00	200	300
1899B Specimen	—	—	—	—	1,800	—
1900B	400,000	2.50	7.00	50.00	200	300
1900B Specimen	—	—	—	—	1,800	—

KM# 10 2 FRANCS
10.0000 g., 0.9000 Silver .2894 oz.

Date	Mintage	F	VF	XF	Unc	BU
1850A	2,500,000	110	210	325	600	900
1850A Specimen	—	—	—	—	3,000	—
1857B	622	3,000	4,500	7,500	10,000	14,000
1857B Specimen	—	—	—	—	—	—

KM# 10a 2 FRANCS
10.0000 g., 0.8000 Silver .2572 oz.

Date	Mintage	F	VF	XF	Unc	BU
1860B	2,000,760	25.00	60.00	200	600	800
1860B Specimen	—	—	—	—	3,000	—
1862B	1,000,000	35.00	80.00	250	800	1,100
1862B Specimen	—	—	—	—	3,000	—
1863B	500,000	110	225	600	1,250	1,700
1863B Specimen	—	—	—	—	4,800	—

KM# 21 2 FRANCS
10.0000 g., 0.8350 Silver .2685 oz.

Date	Mintage	F	VF	XF	Unc	BU
1874B	1,000,000	4.00	25.00	275	600	800
1874B Specimen	—	—	—	—	3,600	—
1875B	983,250	6.00	40.00	300	800	1,250
1875B Specimen	—	—	—	—	4,500	—
1878B	1,500,000	4.00	15.00	150	500	750
1878B Specimen	—	—	—	—	3,000	—
1879B	517,750	7.00	40.00	650	2,500	4,000
1879B Specimen	—	—	—	—	12,000	—
1886B	1,000,000	2.50	12.00	100	400	600
1886B Specimen	—	—	—	—	3,000	—
1894A	700,000	3.00	12.00	125	400	600

Date	Mintage	F	VF	XF	Unc	BU
1894A Specimen	—	—	—	—	2,400	—
1896B Specimen	20	—	—	—	20,000	25,000

KM# 11 5 FRANCS
25.0000 g., 0.9000 Silver .7234 oz.

Date	Mintage	F	VF	XF	Unc	BU
1850A	500,000	125	200	300	750	1,000
1850A Specimen	—	—	—	—	6,000	—
1851A	Inc. above	90.00	150	250	500	750
1851A Specimen	—	—	—	—	6,000	—
1873B	30,500	550	900	1,750	2,500	3,200
1873B Specimen	—	—	—	—	9,000	—
1874B.	195,650	75.00	150	250	500	700
Note: The dot after the B is for Brussels. For coins dated 1855 see Shooting Talers						
1874B. Specimen	—	—	—	—	6,000	—
Note: The dot after the B is for Brussels. For coins dated 1855 see Shooting Talers						
1874B	196,000	60.00	120	200	400	600
1874B Specimen	—	—	—	—	6,000	—
1884	4	—	—	—	—	—

KM# 34 5 FRANCS
25.0000 g., 0.9000 Silver .7234 oz.

Date	Mintage	F	VF	XF	Unc	BU
1888B	25,000	200	350	900	2,000	2,800
1888B Specimen	—	—	—	—	7,500	—
1889B	225,000	50.00	90.00	250	500	700
1889B Specimen	—	—	—	—	4,500	—
1890B	305,000	50.00	85.00	200	500	700
1890B Specimen	—	—	—	—	4,500	—
1891B	150,000	65.00	130	300	800	1,100
1891B Specimen	—	—	—	—	4,500	—
1892B	190,000	50.00	90.00	250	600	850
1892B Specimen	—	—	—	—	4,500	—
1894B	34,000	275	500	1,400	3,000	4,000
1894B Specimen	—	—	—	—	12,000	—
1895B	46,000	200	300	900	1,700	2,400
1895B Specimen	—	—	—	—	9,000	—
1896B	2,000	10,000	15,000	25,000	37,500	50,000
1896B Specimen; Rare	—	—	—	—	—	—
1900B	33,000	325	500	1,400	2,200	3,000
1900B Specimen	—	—	—	—	9,000	—

KM# 31.1 20 FRANCS
6.4516 g., 0.9000 Gold .1867 oz. **Edge:** Reeded

Date	Mintage	F	VF	XF	Unc	BU
1883	250,000	—	—	75.00	90.00	150

KM# 31.3 20 FRANCS
6.4516 g., 0.9000 Gold .1867 oz. **Edge:** DOMINUS XXX PROVIDEBIT XXXXXXXXXX

Date	Mintage	F	VF	XF	Unc	BU
1886	250,000	—	—	75.00	90.00	150
1887B	176	—	—	—	25,000	35,000
1888B	4,224	—	3,500	4,500	6,000	8,000
1889B	100,000	—	80.00	80.00	125	200
1890B	125,000	—	—	75.00	90.00	150
1891B	100,000	—	—	75.00	90.00	160
1892B	100,000	—	—	75.00	90.00	160
1893B	100,000	—	—	75.00	90.00	160
1893B	25	—	—	—	—	30,000

Date	Mintage	F	VF	XF	Unc	BU
Note: Struck of bright Valaisan gold from Gondo with a small cross punched in the center of the Swiss cross						
1894B	121,000	—	—	75.00	90.00	150
1895B	200,000	—	—	75.00	90.00	150
1895B	19	—	—	—	—	30,000
Note: Struck of bright Valaisan gold from Gondo with a small cross punched in the center of the Swiss cross						
1896B	400,000	—	—	75.00	90.00	150

KM# 31.2 20 FRANCS
6.4516 g., 0.9000 Gold .1867 oz. **Edge:** DOMINUS XXX /XXXXXXXXXX PROVIDEBIT

Date	Mintage	F	VF	XF	Unc	BU
1896B Reported, not confirmed	Inc. above	—	—	—	—	—

KM# 35.1 20 FRANCS
6.4516 g., 0.9000 Gold .1867 oz.

Date	Mintage	F	VF	XF	Unc	BU
1897B	400,000	—	BV	75.00	95.00	120
1897B Rare	29	—	—	—	—	—
Note: Struck of bright Valaisan gold from Gondo with a small cross punched in the center of the Swiss cross						
1898B	400,000	—	BV	75.00	95.00	120
1899B	300,000	—	BV	75.00	95.00	120
1900B	400,000	—	BV	75.00	95.00	120

COMMEMORATIVE COINAGE

Shooting Festival

The listings which follow have traditionally been categorized in many catalogs as "Swiss Shooting Thalers". Technically, all are medallic issues rather than "coins", excepting the Solothurn issue of 1855. According to the Swiss Federal Finance Department, the issue was legally equal to the then current silver 5 Francs issue to which it was identical in design, aside from bearing an edge inscription which read, EIDGEN FREISCHIESSEN SOLOTHURN (National Shooting Fest Solothurn). For subsequent issues, denominations have been indicated with government consent (though they) were not given legal tender status. The presence of the denomination was intended to indicate these talers were of the same weight and fineness as (Prescribed for) legal tender coins. Two generally associated "Shooting Festival" coins of earlier dates - 1842 Graubunden and 1847 Glarus - will be found incorporated in the listings for these cantons, as they were issued prior to the Swiss confederation of 1848. Values for exceptional quality BU examples will command a premium over the prices listed.

KM# S3 5 FRANCS
0.8350 Silver **Issuer:** Solothurn **Edge Lettering:** EIDGEN FREISCHIESEN SOLOTHURN 1855 **Note:** Similar to KM#11 but with edge lettering.

Date	Mintage	F	VF	XF	Unc	BU
1855	3,000	—	600	1,200	2,500	3,500
1855 Specimen	—	—	—	—	—	9,000

KM# S4 5 FRANCS
0.8350 Silver **Issuer:** Bern

Date	Mintage	F	VF	XF	Unc	BU
1857	5,195	—	150	250	450	700
1857 Specimen	—	—	—	—	—	3,000

KM# S5 5 FRANCS
0.8350 Silver **Issuer:** Zurich

Date	Mintage	F	VF	XF	Unc	BU
1859	6,000	—	80.00	150	300	450
1859 Specimen	—	—	—	—	—	2,400

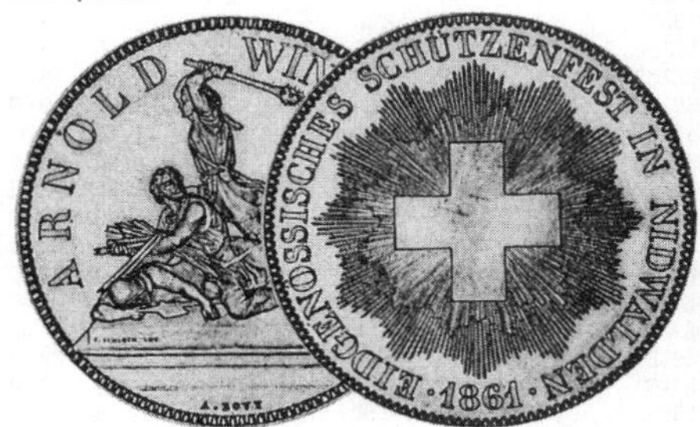

KM# S6 5 FRANCS
0.8350 Silver **Issuer:** Stans in Nidwalden

Date	Mintage	F	VF	XF	Unc	BU
1861	6,000	—	115	200	350	500
1861 Speciemn	—	—	—	—	—	2,400

KM# S7 5 FRANCS
0.8350 Silver **Issuer:** La Chaux-De-Fonds in Neuchatel

Date	Mintage	F	VF	XF	Unc	BU
1863	6,000	—	100	200	400	550
1863 Specimen	—	—	—	—	—	2,400

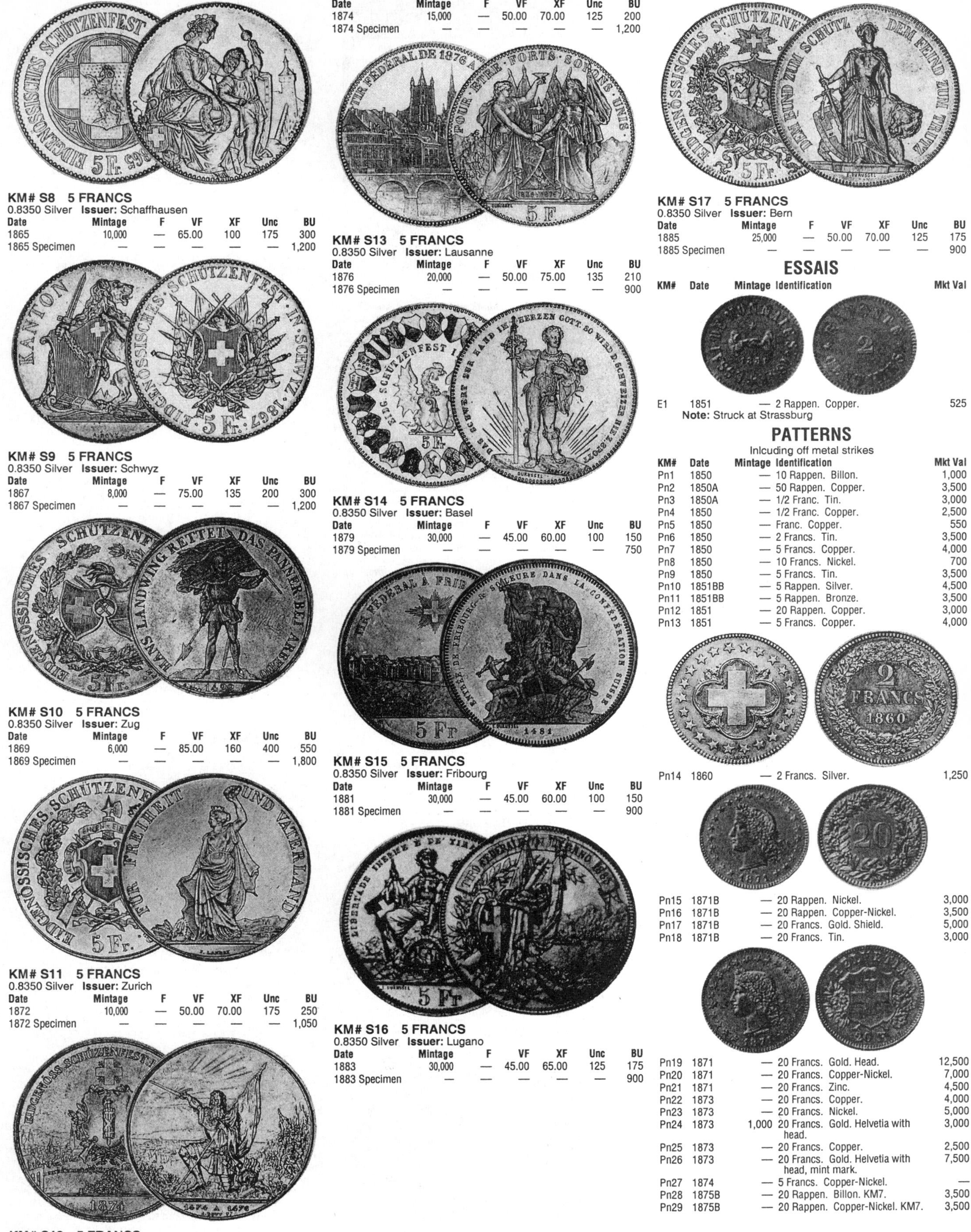

KM# S8 5 FRANCS
0.8350 Silver **Issuer:** Schaffhausen

Date	Mintage	F	VF	XF	Unc	BU
1865	10,000	—	65.00	100	175	300
1865 Specimen	—	—	—	—	—	1,200

KM# S9 5 FRANCS
0.8350 Silver **Issuer:** Schwyz

Date	Mintage	F	VF	XF	Unc	BU
1867	8,000	—	75.00	135	200	300
1867 Specimen	—	—	—	—	—	1,200

KM# S10 5 FRANCS
0.8350 Silver **Issuer:** Zug

Date	Mintage	F	VF	XF	Unc	BU
1869	6,000	—	85.00	160	400	550
1869 Specimen	—	—	—	—	—	1,800

KM# S11 5 FRANCS
0.8350 Silver **Issuer:** Zurich

Date	Mintage	F	VF	XF	Unc	BU
1872	10,000	—	50.00	70.00	175	250
1872 Specimen	—	—	—	—	—	1,050

KM# S12 5 FRANCS
0.8350 Silver **Issuer:** St. Gallen

Date	Mintage	F	VF	XF	Unc	BU
1874	15,000	—	50.00	70.00	125	200
1874 Specimen	—	—	—	—	—	1,200

KM# S13 5 FRANCS
0.8350 Silver **Issuer:** Lausanne

Date	Mintage	F	VF	XF	Unc	BU
1876	20,000	—	50.00	75.00	135	210
1876 Specimen	—	—	—	—	—	900

KM# S14 5 FRANCS
0.8350 Silver **Issuer:** Basel

Date	Mintage	F	VF	XF	Unc	BU
1879	30,000	—	45.00	60.00	100	150
1879 Specimen	—	—	—	—	—	750

KM# S15 5 FRANCS
0.8350 Silver **Issuer:** Fribourg

Date	Mintage	F	VF	XF	Unc	BU
1881	30,000	—	45.00	60.00	100	150
1881 Specimen	—	—	—	—	—	900

KM# S16 5 FRANCS
0.8350 Silver **Issuer:** Lugano

Date	Mintage	F	VF	XF	Unc	BU
1883	30,000	—	45.00	65.00	125	175
1883 Specimen	—	—	—	—	—	900

KM# S17 5 FRANCS
0.8350 Silver **Issuer:** Bern

Date	Mintage	F	VF	XF	Unc	BU
1885	25,000	—	50.00	70.00	125	175
1885 Specimen	—	—	—	—	—	900

ESSAIS

KM#	Date	Mintage	Identification	Mkt Val
E1	1851	—	2 Rappen. Copper.	525

Note: Struck at Strassburg

PATTERNS

Inlcuding off metal strikes

KM#	Date	Mintage	Identification	Mkt Val
Pn1	1850	—	10 Rappen. Billon.	1,000
Pn2	1850A	—	50 Rappen. Copper.	3,500
Pn3	1850A	—	1/2 Franc. Tin.	3,000
Pn4	1850	—	1/2 Franc. Copper.	2,500
Pn5	1850	—	Franc. Copper.	550
Pn6	1850	—	2 Francs. Tin.	3,500
Pn7	1850	—	5 Francs. Copper.	4,000
Pn8	1850	—	10 Francs. Nickel.	700
Pn9	1850	—	5 Francs. Tin.	3,500
Pn10	1851BB	—	5 Rappen. Silver.	4,500
Pn11	1851BB	—	5 Rappen. Bronze.	3,500
Pn12	1851	—	20 Rappen. Copper.	3,000
Pn13	1851	—	5 Francs. Copper.	4,000
Pn14	1860	—	2 Francs. Silver.	1,250
Pn15	1871B	—	20 Rappen. Nickel.	3,000
Pn16	1871B	—	20 Rappen. Copper-Nickel.	3,500
Pn17	1871B	—	20 Francs. Gold. Shield.	5,000
Pn18	1871B	—	20 Francs. Tin.	3,000
Pn19	1871	—	20 Francs. Gold. Head.	12,500
Pn20	1871	—	20 Francs. Copper-Nickel.	7,000
Pn21	1871	—	20 Francs. Zinc.	4,500
Pn22	1873	—	20 Francs. Copper.	4,000
Pn23	1873	—	20 Francs. Nickel.	5,000
Pn24	1873	1,000	20 Francs. Gold. Helvetia with head.	3,000
Pn25	1873	—	20 Francs. Copper.	2,500
Pn26	1873	—	20 Francs. Gold. Helvetia with head, mint mark.	7,500
Pn27	1874	—	5 Francs. Copper-Nickel.	—
Pn28	1875B	—	20 Rappen. Billon. KM7.	3,500
Pn29	1875B	—	20 Rappen. Copper-Nickel. KM7.	3,500

KM#	Date	Mintage	Identification	Mkt Val
Pn30	NDB	—	20 Rappen. Copper-Nickel.	3,500
Pn31	NDB	—	20 Rappen. Billon.	3,500
Pn32	1876	—	5 Rappen. Copper-Nickel.	5,000
Pn33	1881B	—	20 Rappen. Copper-Nickel.	2,000
Pn34	1883	—	20 Francs. Gold.	15,000
Pn35	1894A	—	1/2 Franc. Silver.	6,000
Pn36	1894A	—	Franc. Silver.	10,000
Pn37	1894A	—	2 Francs. Silver.	10,000
Pn38	1897	—	20 Francs. Copper-Nickel.	1,400
Pn39	1897B	12	20 Francs. Gold.	35,000

MINT SETS

KM#	Date	Mintage	Identification	Issue Price	Mkt Val
MS1	1896 (9)	—	KM3.1, 4.2, 21, 23-24, 26-27, 29, 34 Rare	—	—

THAILAND

The Kingdom of Thailand (formerly Siam), a constitutional monarchy located in the center of mainland southeast Asia between Burma and Laos, has an area of 198,457mi. (514,000 sq. km.).

The history of The Kingdom of Siam, the only country in south and southeast Asia that was never colonized by an European power, dates from the 6th century A.D. when Thai people started to migrate into the area. A process that accelerated with the Mongol invasion of China in the 13th century. After 400 years of sporadic warfare with the neighboring Burmese, King Taskin won the last battle in 1767. He founded a new capital, Dhonburi, on the west bank of the Chao Praya River. King Rama I moved the capital to Bangkok in 1782,thus initiating the so-called Bangkok Period of Siamese coinage characterized by Pot Duang money (bullet coins) stamped with regal symbols.

The Thai were introduced to the Western world by the Portuguese, who were followed by the Dutch, British and French. Rama III of the present ruling dynasty negotiated a treaty of friendship and commerce with Britain in 1826, and in 1896 the independence of the kingdom was guaranteed by an Anglo-French accord.

In 1909 Siam ceded to Great Britain its suzerain rights over the dependencies of Kedah, Kelantan, Trengganu and Perlis, Malay states situated in southern Siam just north of British Malaya which eliminated any British jurisdiction in Siam proper.

RULERS

Rama I (Phra Buddha Yodfa Chulalok), 1782-1809
Rama II (Phra Buddha Lert La Nabhalai), 1809-1824
Rama III (Phra Nang Klao), 1824-1851
Rama IV (Phra Chom Klao 'Mongkut'), 1851-1868
Rama V (Phra Maha Chulalongkorn), 1868-1910

MONETARY SYSTEM

Old currency system

2 Solos = 1 Att
2 Att = 1 Sio (Pai)
2 Sio = 1 Sik
2 Sik = 1 Fuang
2 Fuang = 1 Salung (not Sal'ung)
4 Salung = 1 Baht
4 Baht = 1 Tamlung
20 Tamlung = 1 Chang

MINT MARKS

UNITS OF OLD THAI CURRENCY

Chang -	ชั่ง	Sik -	ซีก
Tamlung -	ตำลึง	Sio (Pai) -	เสี้ยว
Baht -	บาท	Att -	อัฐ
Salung -	สลึง	Solos -	โสพส
Fuang -	เฟื้อง		

H-Heaton Birmingham

DATING

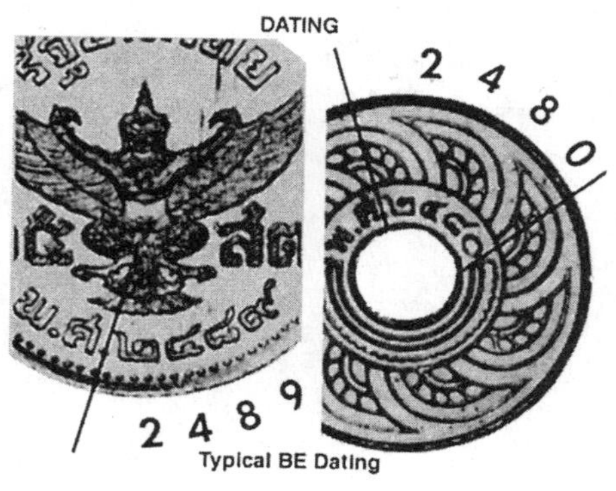

Typical BE Dating

Typical BE Dating

Typical CS Dating

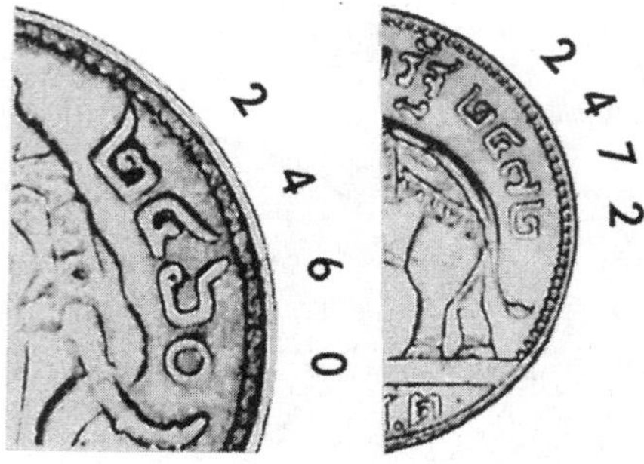

NOTE: Sometimes the era designator *BE* or *CS* will actually appear on the coin itself.

Denomination

2-1/2 (Satang)   RS Dating

DATE CONVERSION TABLES

B.E. date - 543 = A.D. date
Ex: 2516 - 543 = 1973

R.S. date + 1781 = A.D. date
Ex: 127 + 1781 = 1908

C.S. date + 638 = A.D. date
Ex 1238 + 638 = 1876

Primary denominations used were 1 Baht, 1/4 and 1/8 Baht up to the reign of Rama IV. Other denominations are much scarcer.

BULLET COINAGE

Gold and silver "bullet" coins have been a medium of exchange since medieval times. Interesting enough is the fact that a 1 Baht bullet made of gold will weigh the same as a 1 Baht bullet in silver. The reason for this is that Baht originally was a weight not a denomination. It was a coinage weight only until the time of Rama VII, (1925-1935) and now it is a weight and also a denomination (as far as standard weight coins are concerned). Usually 1 gold Baht was equal to 16 silver Baht on an exchange basis.

BULLET WEIGHTS

Grams

Baht	1/2 Baht	1/4 Baht	1/8 Baht
15.40	7.70	3.85	1.92

1/16 Baht	1/32 Baht	1/64 Baht
0.96	0.48	0.24

Chopmarks exist on bullet coins as they do on many other coins that have traveled on their way through the Orient. One must be careful not to mistake a money changers chopmark for the regular dynastic marks on the bullet. Some chopmarks are rather simple in design while others appear to be rather elaborate.

DYNASTIC MARKS

Chakra

The Chakra, symbol of the God Vishnu, is the mark of the Bangkok Dynasty. It varies slightly in design between issues, being very ornate on ceremonial issues.

RAMA I

1782-1809

Tri — Unalom

The trident, the symbol of the Hindu God, Siva, used as the first mark of Rama I. The unalom is an ornamented conch shell, used as the second mark of Rama I.

RAMA II

1809-1824

Krut

A facing Krut, half man – half bird, used as the mark of Rama II.

RAMA III

1824-1851

Krut Sio — Prasat — Dok Mai

The Krut bird to left, used as the first mark of Rama III. The Prasat, the palace used as second mark of Rama III. The Dok Mai was a flower used as third mark of Rama III.

Bai Matum — Ruang Puang — Arrow Head

The Bai Matum is a bale-fruit tree used as the fourth mark of Rama III. The Ruang Puang is a beehive used as the fifth mark of Rama III. Very similar to Dok Mai, having only 1 dot below the point used as the sixth mark of Rama III.

Chaleo

A symbol of varied meanings. In this instance it is believed to represent a charm to ward off evil spirits, found as a seventh mark on bullet coinage of Rama III.

RAMA IV

1851-1868

P'ra Tao — Mongkut

The P'ra Tao or royal water pot was used as the first mark of Rama IV. The Royal Siamese Crown was used as the second mark of Rama IV.

RAMA V

1868-1880

P'ra Kieo Cho 1876 — Rampeuy 1880

The Royal Coronet worn on the top knot of the Royal Princess on ceremonial occasions. First used on the occasion of the funeral of Princess Charoenkamol Suksawadi who died in 1874. The Thai flower was on a ceremonial issue along with an ornate crown of 2 vessels in memory of Somdet Pira Deb Sirindhra, the mother of Rama V and commemorating his age, dated CS1242.

MARKET VALUATIONS

Market valuations are primarily based on the quality and condition of the countermarks found on bullet coinage.

KINGDOM OF SIAM

until 1939

BULLET COINAGE

SILVER POT DUANG

C# 120 1/128 BAHT

0.1200 g., Silver **Ruler:** Rama IV Phra Chom Klao 'Mongkut'

Date	Mintage	VG	F	VF	XF	Unc
ND P'ra Tao	—	—	—	—	—	—

Note: Confirmed as an unofficial hill tribe piece only. This weight never issued as a official coin.

C# 121 1/2 PAI (1/64 Baht)

Silver **Ruler:** Rama IV Phra Chom Klao 'Mongkut' **Note:** Observed weight range 0.24-0.26 gram.

Date	Mintage	VG	F	VF	XF	Unc
ND P'ra Tao	—	50.00	100	200	250	—

C# 1 PAI (1/32 Baht)

Silver **Ruler:** Rama I **Note:** Observed weight range 0.44-0.56 gram.

Date	Mintage	VG	F	VF	XF	Unc
ND Tri Rare	—	20.00	30.00	50.00	100	—

C# 8 PAI (1/32 Baht)

Silver **Ruler:** Rama I **Note:** Observed weight range 0.44-0.56 gram.

Date	Mintage	VG	F	VF	XF	Unc
ND Unalom Rare	—	20.00	30.00	50.00	100	—

C# 42 PAI (1/32 Baht)

Silver **Ruler:** Rama III Phra Nang Klao **Note:** Observed weight range 0.44-0.56 gram.

Date	Mintage	VG	F	VF	XF	Unc
ND Prasat	—	20.00	30.00	50.00	100	—

C# 51 PAI (1/32 Baht)

Silver **Ruler:** Rama III Phra Nang Klao **Note:** Observed weight range 0.44-0.56 gram.

Date	Mintage	VG	F	VF	XF	Unc
ND Dok Mai	—	20.00	30.00	50.00	100	—

C# 61 PAI (1/32 Baht)

Silver **Ruler:** Rama III Phra Nang Klao **Note:** Observed weight range 0.44-0.56 gram.

Date	Mintage	VG	F	VF	XF	Unc
ND Bai Matum	—	20.00	30.00	50.00	100	—

C# 71 PAI (1/32 Baht)

Silver **Ruler:** Rama III Phra Nang Klao **Note:** Observed weight range 0.44-0.56 gram.

Date	Mintage	VG	F	VF	XF	Unc
ND Ruang Puang	—	20.00	30.00	50.00	100	—

C# 81 PAI (1/32 Baht)

Silver **Ruler:** Rama III Phra Nang Klao **Note:** Observed weight range 0.44-0.56 gram.

Date	Mintage	VG	F	VF	XF	Unc
ND Arrowhead	—	20.00	30.00	50.00	100	—

C# 122 PAI (1/32 Baht)

Silver **Ruler:** Rama IV Phra Chom Klao 'Mongkut' **Note:** Observed weight range 0.44-0.56 gram.

Date	Mintage	VG	F	VF	XF	Unc
ND P'ra Tao	—	10.00	15.00	20.00	30.00	—

C# 2 SONG PAI (1/16 Baht)

Silver **Ruler:** Rama I **Note:** Observed weight range 0.80-1.06 grams.

Date	Mintage	VG	F	VF	XF	Unc
ND Tri	—	17.50	27.50	50.00	100	—

C# 9 SONG PAI (1/16 Baht)

Silver **Ruler:** Rama I **Note:** Observed weight range 0.80-1.06 grams.

Date	Mintage	VG	F	VF	XF	Unc
ND Unalom	—	20.00	30.00	50.00	100	—

C# 16 SONG PAI (1/16 Baht)

Silver **Ruler:** Rama II Phra Buddha Lert La Nabhalai **Note:** Observed weight range 0.80-1.06 grams.

Date	Mintage	VG	F	VF	XF	Unc
ND Krut	—	—	—	—	—	—

Note: No examples of this type have been confirmed.

C# 43 SONG PAI (1/16 Baht)

Silver **Ruler:** Rama III Phra Nang Klao **Note:** Observed weight range 0.80-1.06 grams.

Date	Mintage	VG	F	VF	XF	Unc
ND Prasat	—	6.00	10.00	20.00	50.00	—

C# 52 SONG PAI (1/16 Baht)

Silver **Ruler:** Rama III Phra Nang Klao **Note:** Observed weight range 0.80-1.06 grams.

Date	Mintage	VG	F	VF	XF	Unc
ND Dok Mai	—	5.00	6.00	10.00	20.00	—

C# 62 SONG PAI (1/16 Baht)

Silver **Ruler:** Rama III Phra Nang Klao **Note:** Observed weight range 0.80-1.06 grams.

Date	Mintage	VG	F	VF	XF	Unc
ND Bai Matum	—	5.00	8.00	12.00	20.00	—

C# 72 SONG PAI (1/16 Baht)

Silver **Ruler:** Rama III Phra Nang Klao **Note:** Observed weight range 0.80-1.06 grams.

Date	Mintage	VG	F	VF	XF	Unc
ND Ruang Puang	—	5.00	8.00	12.00	20.00	—

C# 82 SONG PAI (1/16 Baht)

Silver **Ruler:** Rama III Phra Nang Klao **Note:** Observed weight range 0.80-1.06 grams.

Date	Mintage	VG	F	VF	XF	Unc
ND Arrowhead	—	5.00	8.00	12.00	20.00	—

C# 123 SONG PAI (1/16 Baht)

Silver **Ruler:** Rama IV Phra Chom Klao 'Mongkut' **Note:** Observed weight range 0.80-1.06 grams.

Date	Mintage	VG	F	VF	XF	Unc
ND P'ra Tao	—	3.00	5.00	8.50	12.50	—

C# 133 SONG PAI (1/16 Baht)

Silver **Ruler:** Rama IV Phra Chom Klao 'Mongkut' **Note:** Observed weight range 0.80-1.06 grams.

Date	Mintage	VG	F	VF	XF	Unc
ND Mongkut	—	6.00	10.00	17.50	50.00	—

C# 3 FUANG (1/8 Baht)

Silver **Ruler:** Rama I **Note:** Observed weight range 1.60-2.01 grams.

Date	Mintage	VG	F	VF	XF	Unc
ND Tri	—	15.00	25.00	37.50	—	—

C# 10 FUANG (1/8 Baht)

Silver **Ruler:** Rama I **Note:** Observed weight range 1.60-2.01 grams.

Date	Mintage	VG	F	VF	XF	Unc
ND Unalom	—	15.00	25.00	37.00	—	—

C# 17 FUANG (1/8 Baht)

Silver **Ruler:** Rama II Phra Buddha Lert La Nabhalai **Note:** Observed weight range 1.60-2.01 grams.

Date	Mintage	VG	F	VF	XF	Unc
ND Krut	—	20.00	35.00	50.00	—	—

C# 44 FUANG (1/8 Baht)

Silver **Ruler:** Rama III Phra Nang Klao **Note:** Observed weight range 1.60-2.01 grams.

Date	Mintage	VG	F	VF	XF	Unc
ND Prasat	—	6.00	10.00	15.00	25.00	—

C# 44.1 FUANG (1/8 Baht)

Silver **Ruler:** Rama III Phra Nang Klao **Note:** Observed weight range 1.60-2.01 grams.

Date	Mintage	VG	F	VF	XF	Unc
ND Prasat and Unalom	—	50.00	80.00	100	300	—

C# 44.2 FUANG (1/8 Baht)

Silver **Ruler:** Rama III Phra Nang Klao **Note:** Observed weight range 1.60-2.01 grams.

Date	Mintage	VG	F	VF	XF	Unc
ND Prasat and Krut	—	50.00	80.00	100	300	—

C# 53 FUANG (1/8 Baht)

Silver **Ruler:** Rama III Phra Nang Klao **Note:** Observed weight range 1.60-2.01 grams.

Date	Mintage	VG	F	VF	XF	Unc
ND Dok Mai	—	5.00	8.00	12.00	20.00	—

C# 63 FUANG (1/8 Baht)

Silver **Ruler:** Rama III Phra Nang Klao **Note:** Observed weight range 1.60-2.01 grams.

Date	Mintage	VG	F	VF	XF	Unc
ND Bai Matum	—	4.00	7.00	10.00	16.00	—

C# 73 FUANG (1/8 Baht)

Silver **Ruler:** Rama III Phra Nang Klao **Note:** Observed weight range 1.60-2.01 grams.

Date	Mintage	VG	F	VF	XF	Unc
ND Ruang Puang	—	4.00	7.00	10.00	16.00	—

C# 83 FUANG (1/8 Baht)

Silver **Ruler:** Rama III Phra Nang Klao **Note:** Observed weight range 1.60-2.01 grams.

Date	Mintage	VG	F	VF	XF	Unc
ND Arrowhead	—	4.00	7.00	11.00	17.00	—

C# 124 FUANG (1/8 Baht)

Silver **Ruler:** Rama IV Phra Chom Klao 'Mongkut' **Note:** Observed weight range 1.60-2.01 grams.

Date	Mintage	VG	F	VF	XF	Unc
ND P'ra Tao	—	3.00	5.00	8.00	13.00	—

C# 134 FUANG (1/8 Baht)

Silver **Ruler:** Rama IV Phra Chom Klao 'Mongkut' **Note:** Observed weight range 1.60-2.01 grams.

Date	Mintage	VG	F	VF	XF	Unc
ND Mongkut	—	3.00	5.00	8.00	13.00	—

C# 4 SALU'NG (1/4 Baht)

Silver **Ruler:** Rama I **Note:** Observed weight range 3.60-4.00 grams.

Date	Mintage	VG	F	VF	XF	Unc
ND Tri Rare	—	50.00	100	150	350	—

C# 11 SALU'NG (1/4 Baht)

Silver **Ruler:** Rama I **Note:** Observed weight range 3.60-4.00 grams.

Date	Mintage	VG	F	VF	XF	Unc
ND Unalom	—	15.00	25.00	37.00	65.00	—

C# 18 SALU'NG (1/4 Baht)
Silver **Ruler:** Rama II Phra Buddha Lert La Nabhalai **Note:** Observed weight range 3.60-4.00 grams.

Date	Mintage	VG	F	VF	XF	Unc
ND Krut	—	100	200	300	450	—

C# 45 SALU'NG (1/4 Baht)
Silver **Ruler:** Rama III Phra Nang Klao **Note:** Observed weight range 3.60-4.00 grams.

Date	Mintage	VG	F	VF	XF	Unc
ND Prasat	—	6.00	10.00	15.00	25.00	—

C# 54 SALU'NG (1/4 Baht)
Silver **Ruler:** Rama III Phra Nang Klao **Note:** Observed weight range 3.60-4.00 grams.

Date	Mintage	VG	F	VF	XF	Unc
ND Dok Mai	—	6.00	10.00	15.00	25.00	—

C# 64 SALU'NG (1/4 Baht)
Silver **Ruler:** Rama III Phra Nang Klao **Note:** Observed weight range 3.60-4.00 grams.

Date	Mintage	VG	F	VF	XF	Unc
ND Bai Matum	—	5.00	8.00	12.00	20.00	—

C# 74 SALU'NG (1/4 Baht)
Silver **Ruler:** Rama III Phra Nang Klao **Note:** Observed weight range 3.60-4.00 grams.

Date	Mintage	VG	F	VF	XF	Unc
ND Ruang Puang	—	5.00	9.00	13.00	22.00	—

C# 84 SALU'NG (1/4 Baht)
Silver **Ruler:** Rama III Phra Nang Klao **Note:** Observed weight range 3.60-4.00 grams.

Date	Mintage	VG	F	VF	XF	Unc
ND Arrowhead	—	5.00	9.00	13.00	22.00	—

C# 125 SALU'NG (1/4 Baht)
Silver **Ruler:** Rama IV Phra Chom Klao 'Mongkut' **Note:** Observed weight range 3.60-4.00 grams.

Date	Mintage	VG	F	VF	XF	Unc
ND P'ra Tao	—	5.00	8.00	12.00	20.00	—

C# 135 SALU'NG (1/4 Baht)
Silver **Ruler:** Rama IV Phra Chom Klao 'Mongkut' **Note:** Observed weight range 3.60-4.00 grams.

Date	Mintage	VG	F	VF	XF	Unc
ND Mongkut	—	5.00	8.00	12.00	20.00	—

C# 5 2 SALU'NG (1/2 Baht)
Silver **Ruler:** Rama I **Note:** Observed weight range 7.40-7.70 grams.

Date	Mintage	VG	F	VF	XF	Unc
ND Tri	—	50.00	100	150	350	—

C# 12 2 SALU'NG (1/2 Baht)
Silver **Ruler:** Rama I **Note:** Observed weight range 7.40-7.70 grams.

Date	Mintage	VG	F	VF	XF	Unc
ND Unalom	—	50.00	100	150	350	—

C# 19 2 SALU'NG (1/2 Baht)
Silver **Ruler:** Rama II Phra Buddha Lert La Nabhalai **Note:** Observed weight range 7.40-7.70 grams.

Date	Mintage	VG	F	VF	XF	Unc
ND Krut	—	100	300	400	500	—

C# 46 2 SALU'NG (1/2 Baht)
Silver **Ruler:** Rama III Phra Nang Klao **Note:** Observed weight range 7.40-7.70 grams.

Date	Mintage	VG	F	VF	XF	Unc
ND Prasat	—	7.00	12.00	18.00	30.00	—

C# 55 2 SALU'NG (1/2 Baht)
Silver **Ruler:** Rama III Phra Nang Klao **Note:** Observed weight range 7.40-7.70 grams.

Date	Mintage	VG	F	VF	XF	Unc
ND Dok Mai	—	100	250	350	500	—

C# 65 2 SALU'NG (1/2 Baht)
Silver **Ruler:** Rama III Phra Nang Klao **Note:** Observed weight range 7.40-7.70 grams.

Date	Mintage	VG	F	VF	XF	Unc
ND Bai Matum	—	100	200	300	450	—

C# 136 2 SALU'NG (1/2 Baht)
Silver **Ruler:** Rama IV Phra Chom Klao 'Mongkut' **Note:** Observed weight range 7.40-7.70 grams.

Date	Mintage	VG	F	VF	XF	Unc
ND Mongkut	—	20.00	30.00	40.00	50.00	—

C# 136.1 2 SALU'NG (1/2 Baht)
Silver **Ruler:** Rama IV Phra Chom Klao 'Mongkut' **Note:** Observed weight range 7.40-7.70 grams.

Date	Mintage	VG	F	VF	XF	Unc
ND Mongkut and Prasat	—	50.00	100	150	300	—

C# A1 BAHT
Silver **Ruler:** Rama I **Note:** Observed weight range 14.86-15.43 grams.

Date	Mintage	VG	F	VF	XF	Unc
ND Tri	—	15.00	20.00	30.00	60.00	75.00

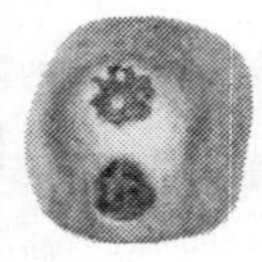

C# 13 BAHT
Silver **Ruler:** Rama I **Note:** Observed weight range 14.86-15.43 grams.

Date	Mintage	VG	F	VF	XF	Unc
ND Unalom	—	15.00	20.00	30.00	60.00	75.00

C# 20 BAHT
Silver **Ruler:** Rama II Phra Buddha Lert La Nabhalai **Note:** Observed weight range 14.86-15.43 grams.

Date	Mintage	VG	F	VF	XF	Unc
ND Krut	—	15.00	20.00	25.00	50.00	—

C# 39 BAHT
Silver **Ruler:** Rama III Phra Nang Klao **Note:** Observed weight range 14.86-15.43 grams.

Date	Mintage	VG	F	VF	XF	Unc
ND Chaleo	—	1,000	1,500	2,000	—	—

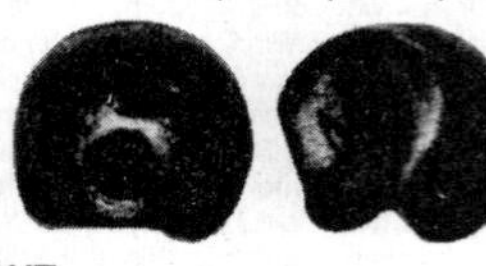

C# 47 BAHT
Silver **Ruler:** Rama III Phra Nang Klao **Note:** Observed weight range 14.86-15.43 grams.

Date	Mintage	VG	F	VF	XF	Unc
ND Prasat	—	15.00	20.00	25.00	40.00	—

C# 56 BAHT
Silver **Ruler:** Rama III Phra Nang Klao **Note:** Observed weight range 14.86-15.43 grams.

Date	Mintage	VG	F	VF	XF	Unc
ND Dok Mai	—	100	200	300	450	—

C# 66 BAHT
Silver **Ruler:** Rama III Phra Nang Klao **Note:** Observed weight range 14.86-15.43 grams.

Date	Mintage	VG	F	VF	XF	Unc
ND Bai Matum	—	100	200	300	450	—

C# 127 BAHT
Silver **Ruler:** Rama IV Phra Chom Klao 'Mongkut' **Note:** Observed weight range 14.86-15.43 grams.

Date	Mintage	VG	F	VF	XF	Unc
P"ra Tao	—	—	—	—	—	—

Note: Confirmed cnly as a Fantasy piece.

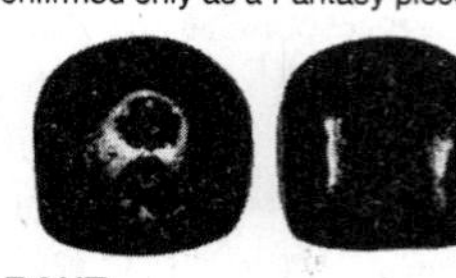

C# 137.1 BAHT
Silver **Ruler:** Rama IV Phra Chom Klao 'Mongkut' **Note:** Observed weight range 14.86-15.43 grams.

Date	Mintage	VG	F	VF	XF	Unc
ND Mongkut	—	17.00	28.00	40.00	60.00	—

C# 137.2 BAHT
Silver **Ruler:** Rama IV Phra Chom Klao 'Mongkut' **Note:** Observed weight range 14.86-15.43 grams.

Date	Mintage	VG	F	VF	XF	Unc
ND Mongkut and Prasat	—	100	120	150	200	—

C# 177 BAHT
Silver **Ruler:** Rama V Phra Maha Chulalongkorn **Subject:** Death of Princess Charoen Kamon Suk Sawad **Note:** Observed weight range 14.86-15.43 grams.

Date	Mintage	VG	F	VF	XF	Unc
ND P"ra Kieo Rare	—	—	—	—	—	—

C# 48 1-1/2 BAHT
23.1000 g., Silver **Ruler:** Rama III Phra Nang Klao

Date	Mintage	VG	F	VF	XF	Unc
ND Prasat Rare	—	—	—	—	—	—

C# 14 2 BAHT
Silver **Ruler:** Rama I **Note:** Observed weight range 29.90-30.60 grams. Thought by some to be a fantasy.

Date	Mintage	VG	F	VF	XF	Unc
ND Unalom Rare	—	4,000	4,500	6,000	8,000	—

C# 21 2 BAHT
Silver **Ruler:** Rama II Phra Buddha Lert La Nabhalai **Note:** Observed weight range 29.90-30.60 grams.

Date	Mintage	VG	F	VF	XF	Unc
ND Krut	—	—	—	—	—	—

Note: No examples are currently known.

C# 49 2 BAHT
Silver **Ruler:** Rama III Phra Nang Klao **Note:** Observed weight range 29.90-30.60 grams.

Date	Mintage	VG	F	VF	XF	Unc
ND Prasat	—	—	1,500	3,000	6,000	8,000

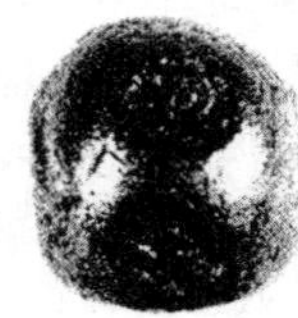

C# 138 2 BAHT
Silver **Ruler:** Rama IV Phra Chom Klao 'Mongkut' **Countermark:** Eight dots in Chakra **Note:** Observed weight range 29.90-30.60 grams.

Date	Mintage	VG	F	VF	XF	Unc
ND Mongkut	—	120	160	250	425	600

C# 138.1 2 BAHT
Silver **Ruler:** Rama IV Phra Chom Klao 'Mongkut' **Countermark:** Six blades in Chakra **Note:** Observed weight range 29.90-30.60 grams.

Date	Mintage	VG	F	VF	XF	Unc
ND Mongkut	—	150	225	325	600	800

C# 138.2 2 BAHT
Silver **Ruler:** Rama IV Phra Chom Klao 'Mongkut' **Countermark:** Eight blades in Chakra, elaborate design **Note:** Observed weight range 29.90-30.60 grams.

Date	Mintage	VG	F	VF	XF	Unc
ND Mongkut Restrike	—	200	300	400	650	800

C# 188 2 BAHT
Silver **Ruler:** Rama V Phra Maha Chulalongkorn **Subject:** Cremation of Somdet P'ra Deb Sirindhra **Note:** Observed weight range 29.90-30.60 grams.

Date	Mintage	VG	F	VF	XF	Unc
CS1242(1880) Cho Rampevy	—	225	335	450	750	1,000

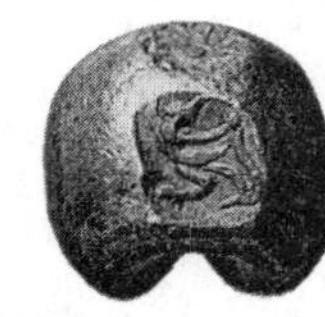

C# 31 2-1/2 BAHT
38.5000 g., Silver **Ruler:** Rama III Phra Nang Klao **Note:** Three varieties exist.

Date	Mintage	VG	F	VF	XF	Unc
ND Krut Sio	—	250	375	550	850	1,500

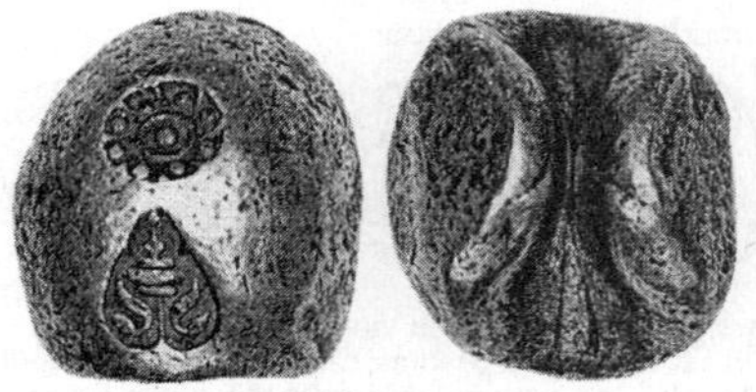

C# 139.1 TAMLUNG (4 Baht)
Silver **Ruler:** Rama IV Phra Chom Klao 'Mongkut' **Countermark:** Eight dots in Chakra **Note:** Observed weight range 60.00-61.00 grams.

Date	Mintage	VG	F	VF	XF	Unc
ND Mongkut	—	225	350	475	1,000	1,500

C# 139.2 TAMLUNG (4 Baht)
Silver **Ruler:** Rama IV Phra Chom Klao 'Mongkut' **Countermark:** Seven dots in Chakra **Note:** Observed weight range 60.00-61.00 grams.

Date	Mintage	VG	F	VF	XF	Unc
ND Mongkut	—	200	300	450	1,000	1,500

C# 189 TAMLUNG (4 Baht)
Silver **Ruler:** Rama V Phra Maha Chulalongkorn **Subject:** Cremation of Somdet P'ra Deb Sirindhra **Note:** Observed weight range 60.00-61.00 grams.

Date	Mintage	VG	F	VF	XF	Unc
CS1242 Cho Rampevy	—	250	365	850	2,500	4,500

C# 32 4-1/2 BAHT
Silver **Ruler:** Rama III Phra Nang Klao

Date	Mintage	VG	F	VF	XF	Unc
ND Krut Sio	—	—	—	—	—	—

Note: Confirmed only as a fantasy piece.

C# 33 8 BAHT
123.2000 g., Silver **Ruler:** Rama III Phra Nang Klao

Date	Mintage	VG	F	VF	XF	Unc
ND Krut Sio	—	—	—	—	—	—

Note: Confirmed only as a fantasy piece.

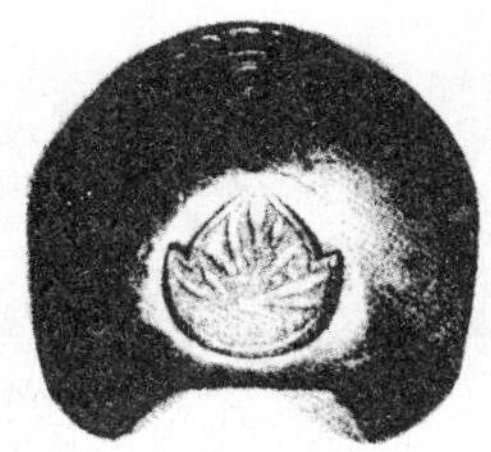

C# 190 2-1/2 TAMLUNG (10 Baht)
154.0000 g., Silver **Ruler:** Rama V Phra Maha Chulalongkorn **Subject:** Cremation of Somdet P'ra Deb Sirindhra

Date	Mintage	VG	F	VF	XF	Unc
CS1242 Cho Rampevy	—	500	650	1,000	2,000	5,000

C# 191 5 TAMLUNG (20 Baht)
308.0000 g., Silver **Ruler:** Rama V Phra Maha Chulalongkorn **Subject:** Cremation of Somdet P'ra Deb Sirindhra

Date	Mintage	VG	F	VF	XF	Unc
CS1242 Cho Rampevy	—	—	—	3,200	5,000	10,000

C# 192 1/2 CHANG (10 Tamlung)
616.0000 g., Silver **Ruler:** Rama V Phra Maha Chulalongkorn **Subject:** Cremation of Somdet P'ra Deb Sirindhra

Date	Mintage	VG	F	VF	XF	Unc
CS1242 Cho Rampevy	—	—	—	5,500	7,500	20,000

C# 140.1 CHANG (20 Tamlung)
Silver, 65 mm. **Ruler:** Rama IV Phra Chom Klao 'Mongkut' **Note:** Chakra wheel engraved turning counterclockwise. Illustration reduced. Weight varies: 1185.00-1232.00 grams.

Date	Mintage	VG	F	VF	XF	Unc
ND Mongkut	—	—	—	12,500	25,000	60,000

C# 140.2 CHANG (20 Tamlung)
Silver **Ruler:** Rama IV Phra Chom Klao 'Mongkut' **Note:** Chakra wheel engraved turning clockwise. Weight varies: 1185.00-1232.00 grams.

Date	Mintage	VG	F	VF	XF	Unc
ND Mongkut	—	—	—	12,500	25,000	60,000

C# 193 CHANG (20 Tamlung)
Silver **Ruler:** Rama V Phra Maha Chulalongkorn **Subject:** Cremation of Somdet P'ra Deb Sirindhra

Date	Mintage	VG	F	VF	XF	Unc
CS1242 Cho Rampevy	—	—	—	15,000	30,000	60,000

BULLET COINAGE

Gold Pot Duang

C# 152 1/32 GOLD BAHT
0.4800 g., Gold **Ruler:** Rama IV Phra Chom Klao 'Mongkut'

Date	Mintage	VG	F	VF	XF	Unc
ND P'ra Tao	—	250	850	1,500	2,000	—

C# 162 1/32 GOLD BAHT
0.4800 g., Gold **Ruler:** Rama IV Phra Chom Klao 'Mongkut'

Date	Mintage	VG	F	VF	XF	Unc
ND Mongkut	—	—	—	—	—	—

Note: No examples of this type have been confirmed.

C# 92 1/16 GOLD BAHT
0.9600 g., Gold **Ruler:** Rama III Phra Nang Klao

Date	Mintage	VG	F	VF	XF	Unc
ND Prasat	—	75.00	120	350	500	700

C# 153 1/16 GOLD BAHT
0.9600 g., Gold **Ruler:** Rama IV Phra Chom Klao 'Mongkut'

Date	Mintage	VG	F	VF	XF	Unc
ND P'ra Tao	—	100	150	375	550	700

C# 163 1/16 GOLD BAHT
0.9600 g., Gold **Ruler:** Rama IV Phra Chom Klao 'Mongkut'

Date	Mintage	VG	F	VF	XF	Unc
ND Mongkut	—	70.00	100	325	500	700

C# 93 1/8 GOLD BAHT
1.9600 g., Gold **Ruler:** Rama III Phra Nang Klao

Date	Mintage	VG	F	VF	XF	Unc
ND Prasat	—	125	200	500	900	1,500

C# 103 1/8 GOLD BAHT
1.9600 g., Gold **Ruler:** Rama III Phra Nang Klao

Date	Mintage	VG	F	VF	XF	Unc
ND Dok Mai	—	150	200	450	650	800

C# 113 1/8 GOLD BAHT
1.9600 g., Gold **Ruler:** Rama III Phra Nang Klao

Date	Mintage	VG	F	VF	XF	Unc
ND Bai Matum	—	150	200	450	650	800

C# 154 1/8 GOLD BAHT
1.9600 g., Gold **Ruler:** Rama IV Phra Chom Klao 'Mongkut'

Date	Mintage	VG	F	VF	XF	Unc
ND P'ra Tao	—	100	175	350	550	700

C# 155 1/4 GOLD BAHT
3.8500 g., Gold **Ruler:** Rama IV Phra Chom Klao 'Mongkut'

Date	Mintage	VG	F	VF	XF	Unc
ND P'ra Tao	—	200	400	675	800	1,000

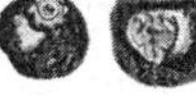

C# 165 1/4 GOLD BAHT
3.8500 g., Gold **Ruler:** Rama IV Phra Chom Klao 'Mongkut'

Date	Mintage	VG	F	VF	XF	Unc
ND Mongkut	—	250	425	700	800	1,000

C# 105 1/2 GOLD BAHT
7.7000 g., Gold **Ruler:** Rama III Phra Nang Klao

Date	Mintage	VG	F	VF	XF	Unc
ND Dok Mai Rare	—	—	—	—	—	—

C# 166 1/2 GOLD BAHT
7.7000 g., Gold **Ruler:** Rama IV Phra Chom Klao 'Mongkut'

Date	Mintage	VG	F	VF	XF	Unc
ND Mongkut	—	250	400	900	2,000	2,500

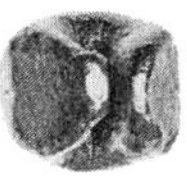

C# 96 GOLD BAHT
15.4000 g., Gold **Ruler:** Rama III Phra Nang Klao

Date	Mintage	VG	F	VF	XF	Unc
ND Prasat	—	900	1,800	4,250	7,500	10,000

C# 167 GOLD BAHT
15.4000 g., Gold **Ruler:** Rama IV Phra Chom Klao 'Mongkut'

Date	Mintage	VG	F	VF	XF	Unc
ND Mongkut	—	800	1,650	3,000	5,000	6,500

C# 167.5 1-1/2 GOLD BAHT (Met Kanoon)
23.1000 g., Gold **Ruler:** Rama IV Phra Chom Klao 'Mongkut'

Date	Mintage	VG	F	VF	XF	Unc
ND Mongkut	—	—	—	—	20,000	—

Note: Unlike other bullet coins this does not have its ends hammered into the normal bullet configuration

C# 168 2 GOLD BAHT
30.8000 g., Gold **Ruler:** Rama IV Phra Chom Klao 'Mongkut'

Date	Mintage	VG	F	VF	XF	Unc
ND Mongkut	—	—	—	15,000	20,000	—

C# 169 4 GOLD BAHT
61.6000 g., Gold **Ruler:** Rama IV Phra Chom Klao 'Mongkut'

Date	Mintage	VG	F	VF	XF	Unc
ND Mongkut Rare	—	—	—	—	—	—

TRANSITIONAL COINAGE

A series of hammered flat coinage ordered by Rama IV to alleviate a shortage in small bullet coinage while awaiting arrival of the modern coinage presses from England.

C# 172 GOLD 1/2 FUANG
1.0000 g., Gold **Ruler:** Rama IV Phra Chom Klao 'Mongkut' **Obv:** "Chakra" above royal crown and "P'ra Tao" at left and right **Note:** Uniface.

Date	Mintage	VG	F	VF	XF	Unc
ND(c.1856) Rare	—	—	—	—	—	—

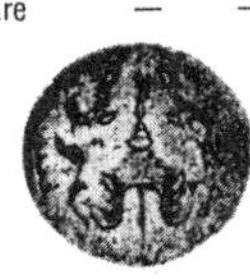

C# 173 FUANG
2.0000 g., Silver **Ruler:** Rama IV Phra Chom Klao 'Mongkut' **Obv:** Royal crown **Rev. Legend:** "Krungthep" (Bangkok)

Date	Mintage	VG	F	VF	XF	Unc
ND(c.1856) Rare	—	—	—	—	—	—

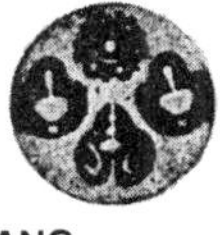

C# 170 FUANG
1.8500 g., Silver **Ruler:** Rama IV Phra Chom Klao 'Mongkut' **Obv:** "Chakra" above royal crown and "P'ra Tao" at left and right **Note:** Uniface.

Date	Mintage	VG	F	VF	XF	Unc
ND(c.1856)	—	250	425	600	1,500	—

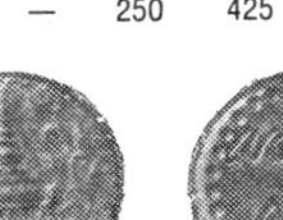

C# 175 GOLD FUANG
1.8000 g., Gold **Ruler:** Rama IV Phra Chom Klao 'Mongkut' **Obv:** Royal crown **Rev. Legend:** "Krungthep" (Bangkok)

Date	Mintage	VG	F	VF	XF	Unc
ND(c.1856) Rare	—	—	—	—	—	—

Note: Taisei-Baldwin-Gillio Singapore sale 3-96 AU realized $42,000

C# 174 SALUNG
3.7000 g., Silver **Ruler:** Rama IV Phra Chom Klao 'Mongkut' **Obv:** Royal crown **Rev. Legend:** "Krungthep" (Bangkok)

Date	Mintage	VG	F	VF	XF	Unc
ND(c.1856) Rare	—	—	—	—	—	—

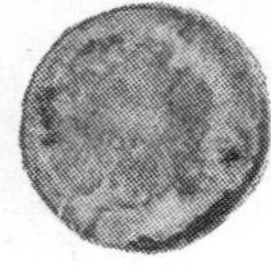

C# 171 SALUNG
3.7000 g., Silver **Ruler:** Rama IV Phra Chom Klao 'Mongkut' **Obv:** "Chakra" above royal crown and "P'ra Tao" at left and right **Note:** Uniface.

Date	Mintage	VG	F	VF	XF	Unc
ND(c.1856)	—	300	500	700	1,000	—

C# 176 GOLD SALUNG
3.8000 g., Gold **Ruler:** Rama IV Phra Chom Klao 'Mongkut' **Obv:** Royal crown **Rev. Legend:** "Krungthep" (Bangkok)

Date	Mintage	VG	F	VF	XF	Unc
ND(c.1856) Rare	—	—	—	—	—	—

COUNTERMARKED TRADE COINAGE

Foreign trade brought in quantities of Latin American silver 8 reales which were not widely accepted by the public. As a result many were then officially countermarked with the royal marks "Chakra and Mongkut" in the period 1858-60 to guarantee their current exchange value.

C# 141.1 DOLLAR
0.9030 g., Silver **Countermark:** "Chakra" and "Mongkut" **Note:** Countermark on Mexico Chihuahua 8 Reales, KM#377.2.

Date	Mintage	Good	VG	F	VF	XF
ND(1831-57)	—	350	600	1,000	1,500	—

C# 141.4 DOLLAR
0.9030 g., Silver **Countermark:** "Chakra" and "Mongkut" **Note:** Countermark on Mexico Durango 8 Reales, KM#377.4.

Date	Mintage	Good	VG	F	VF	XF
ND(1825-57)	—	400	700	1,150	1,650	—

C# 141.6 DOLLAR
0.9030 g., Silver **Countermark:** "Chakra" and "Mongkut" **Note:** Countermark on Mexico Guanajanto 8 Reales, KM#377.8.

Date	Mintage	Good	VG	F	VF	XF
ND(1825-57)	—	300	550	950	1,450	—

C# 141.8 DOLLAR
0.9030 g., Silver **Countermark:** "Chakra" and "Mongkut" **Note:** Countermark on Mexico City 8 Reales, KM#377.10.

Date	Mintage	Good	VG	F	VF	XF
ND(1824-57)	—	300	550	950	1,450	—

C# 141.11 DOLLAR
0.9030 g., Silver **Countermark:** "Chakra" and "Mongkut" **Note:** Countermark on Mexico Zacatecas 8 Reales, KM#377.13.

Date	Mintage	Good	VG	F	VF	XF
ND(1825-57)	—	400	700	1,150	1,650	—

C# 141.14 DOLLAR
0.9030 g., Silver **Countermark:** "Chakra" and "Mongkut" **Note:** Countermark on Peru Cuzco 8 Reales, KM#142.4.

Date	Mintage	Good	VG	F	VF	XF
ND(1830-34)	—	1,000	2,000	20,000	30,000	—

Note: The "Mongkut" countermark illustrated is believed to be a modern fabrication

C# 141.17 DOLLAR
0.9030 g., Silver **Countermark:** "Chakra" and "Mongkut" **Note:** Countermark on Peru Lima 8 Reales, KM#142.10.

Date	Mintage	Good	VG	F	VF	XF
ND(1841-55)	—	450	800	1,250	1,750	—

C# 141.20 DOLLAR
0.9030 g., Silver **Countermark:** "Chakra" and "Mongkut" **Note:** Countermark on Philippines countermarked 8 Reales, KM#129.

Date	Mintage	Good	VG	F	VF	XF
ND(1825-57) Rare	—	—	—	—	—	—

TOKEN COINAGE

Produced in England as samples for a medium to replace the circulating cowries; They met disfavor with Rama III and were never adopted.

KM# Tn1 2 KEPING
Copper **Ruler:** Rama III Phra Nang Klao **Obv. Legend:** "Muang Thai" (Thailand) **Rev:** Elephant

Date	Mintage	F	VF	XF	Unc	BU
CS1197(1835)	500	—	—	1,000	2,000	—
CS1197(1835) Proof	—	Value: 3,000				

KM# Tn1a 2 KEPING
Gilt Copper **Ruler:** Rama III Phra Nang Klao

Date	Mintage	F	VF	XF	Unc	BU
CS1197(1835)	—	—	—	—	2,500	—

KM# Tn2 2 KEPING
Gilt Copper **Ruler:** Rama III Phra Nang Klao **Rev:** Lotus

Date	Mintage	F	VF	XF	Unc	BU
CS1197(1835)	500	—	—	900	1,850	—
CS1197(1835) Proof	—	Value: 2,750				

STANDARD COINAGE

Y# 17 1/2 ATT (1 Solot)
Copper **Ruler:** Rama V Phra Maha Chulalongkorn

Date	Mintage	F	VF	XF	Unc	BU
CS1236(1874)	—	1.00	2.00	9.00	45.00	—
CS1244(1882)	2,560,000	1.00	2.00	9.00	45.00	—
CS1244(1882) Proof	—	Value: 200				

Y# 17a 1/2 ATT (1 Solot)
Copper-Nickel **Ruler:** Rama V Phra Maha Chulalongkorn **Note:** Thought by some to be a pattern.

Date	Mintage	F	VF	XF	Unc	BU
CS1244(1882)	—	75.00	150	300	1,000	—

Y# 21 1/2 ATT (1 Solot)
Bronze **Ruler:** Rama V Phra Maha Chulalongkorn

Date	Mintage	F	VF	XF	Unc	BU
CS1249 (1887)	—	1.50	2.50	8.50	85.00	—
RS109 (1890)	10,240,000	1.50	2.50	8.50	85.00	—
RS118 (1899)	—	1.50	2.50	8.50	85.00	—
RS118 (1899) Proof	—	Value: 1,250				

Y# 5 1/16 FUANG (1 Solot)
Tin **Ruler:** Rama IV Phra Chom Klao 'Mongkut' **Note:** Dark color and crude rims. Usually plain edge. Rotated dies are common.

Date	Mintage	VG	F	VF	XF	Unc
ND(1862)	—	2.00	5.00	20.00	50.00	300

Y# 16 1/16 FUANG (1 Solot)
Tin **Ruler:** Rama IV Phra Chom Klao 'Mongkut'

Date	Mintage	VG	F	VF	XF	Unc
ND(1868)	—	5.00	10.00	20.00	45.00	195

Y# 6.1 1/8 FUANG (1 Att)
Tin **Ruler:** Rama IV Phra Chom Klao 'Mongkut' **Obv:** Large elephant **Rev:** Lower row of jewels in crown between lines **Edge:** Reeded **Note:** Dark color.

Date	Mintage	VG	F	VF	XF	Unc
ND(1862)	—	1.50	4.00	9.00	18.00	200

Y# 6.2 1/8 FUANG (1 Att)
Tin **Ruler:** Rama IV Phra Chom Klao 'Mongkut' **Rev:** Lower row of jewels in crown enclosed

Date	Mintage	VG	F	VF	XF	Unc
ND(1862)	—	10.00	15.00	20.00	50.00	200

Y# 6.3 1/8 FUANG (1 Att)
Tin **Ruler:** Rama IV Phra Chom Klao 'Mongkut' **Obv:** Small elephant **Rev:** Lower row of jewels in crown between lines

Date	Mintage	VG	F	VF	XF	Unc
ND(1862)	—	1.50	4.00	9.00	18.00	200

Y# 6.4 1/8 FUANG (1 Att)
Tin **Ruler:** Rama IV Phra Chom Klao 'Mongkut' **Rev:** Lower row of jewels in crown enclosed **Note:** Rotated dies are common.

Date	Mintage	VG	F	VF	XF	Unc
ND(1862)	—	15.00	20.00	40.00	80.00	200

Y# 18 1/2 PAI (1/64 Baht)
Copper **Ruler:** Rama V Phra Maha Chulalongkorn

Date	Mintage	F	VF	XF	Unc	BU
CS1236(1874)	—	1.50	2.50	10.00	80.00	—
CS1238(1876)	—	1.50	2.50	10.00	80.00	—
CS1244(1882)	15,300,000	1.50	2.50	10.00	80.00	—
CS1244(1882) Proof	—	Value: 275				

Y# 22 1/2 PAI (1/64 Baht)
Bronze **Ruler:** Rama V Phra Maha Chulalongkorn **Note:** Full red uncirculated coins of this type carry a substantial premium.

Date	Mintage	F	VF	XF	Unc	BU
CS1249 (1887)	—	1.50	2.50	8.50	100	—
RS109 (1890)	10,240,000	3.50	5.00	30.00	170	—
RS114 (1895)	5,120,000	3.50	5.00	30.00	170	—
Note: Exists with large (greater than 1mm) and small (less than 1mm) numerals						
RS115 (1896)	—	3.50	5.00	30.00	170	—
RS118 (1899)	—	3.50	5.00	30.00	170	—
RS118 (1899) Proof	1,899	Value: 850				

Y# 1 1/4 FUANG (1/32 Baht = 1 Sio)
Copper **Ruler:** Rama IV Phra Chom Klao 'Mongkut' **Note:** Crude, thick planchet (2.5mm).

Date	Mintage	VG	F	VF	XF	Unc
ND(1865)	—	15.00	35.00	75.00	150	—

Y# 1a 1/4 FUANG (1/32 Baht = 1 Sio)
Brass **Ruler:** Rama IV Phra Chom Klao 'Mongkut'

Date	Mintage	VG	F	VF	XF	Unc
ND(1865)	—	15.00	40.00	80.00	150	—

Y# 3 1/4 FUANG (1/32 Baht = 1 Sio)
Brass **Ruler:** Rama IV Phra Chom Klao 'Mongkut' **Note:** Thin planchet (1.5mm). Rotated dies are common.

Date	Mintage	VG	F	VF	XF	Unc
ND(1866)	—	15.00	35.00	65.00	125	—

Y# 2a 1/2 FUANG (1/16 Baht = 1 Sik)
Brass **Ruler:** Rama IV Phra Chom Klao 'Mongkut'

Date	Mintage	VG	F	VF	XF	Unc
ND(1865)	—	12.00	25.00	55.00	135	—

Y# 2 1/2 FUANG (1/16 Baht = 1 Sik)
Copper **Ruler:** Rama IV Phra Chom Klao 'Mongkut' **Note:** Thick planchet (3mm). Crude, plain edges.

Date	Mintage	VG	F	VF	XF	Unc
ND(1865)	—	10.00	20.00	45.00	125	—

Y# 4 1/2 FUANG (1/16 Baht = 1 Sik)
Brass **Ruler:** Rama IV Phra Chom Klao 'Mongkut' **Note:** Thin planchet (1.5mm). Rotated dies are common.

Date	Mintage	VG	F	VF	XF	Unc
ND(1866)	—	12.00	25.00	85.00	200	—

Y# 19 2 ATT (1/32 Baht = 1 Sio)
Copper **Ruler:** Rama V Phra Maha Chulalongkorn

Date	Mintage	F	VF	XF	Unc	BU
CS1236(1874)	—	2.00	4.00	15.00	125	—
CS1238(1876)	—	2.00	4.00	15.00	120	—
CS1244(1882)	10,200,000	2.00	4.00	15.00	120	—

Y# 23 2 ATT (1/32 Baht = 1 Sio)
Bronze **Ruler:** Rama V Phra Maha Chulalongkorn **Note:** Varieties in numeral size and rotated dies exist. Full red uncirculated coins of this type carry a substantial premium.

Date	Mintage	F	VF	XF	Unc	BU
CS1249 (1887)	—	1.50	3.00	25.00	150	—
RS107 (1888)	—	1.50	3.00	25.00	160	—
RS108 (1889)	—	1.50	3.00	25.00	160	—
RS109 (1890)	5,120,000	1.50	3.00	25.00	160	—
RS114 (1895)	—	1.50	3.00	25.00	160	—
RS115 (1896)	—	1.50	3.00	25.00	160	—
RS118 (1899)	—	1.50	3.00	25.00	160	—
RS119 (1900)	735,000	1.50	3.00	25.00	250	—

Y# 20 4 ATT (1/16 Baht = 1 Sik)
Copper **Ruler:** Rama V Phra Maha Chulalongkorn

Date	Mintage	F	VF	XF	Unc	BU
CS1238(1876)	—	20.00	60.00	185	600	—
Note: Frequently counterfeited						

Y# 8 FUANG (1/8 Baht)
1.9400 g., Silver **Ruler:** Rama IV Phra Chom Klao 'Mongkut' **Note:** Thick flan. Denomination indicated by number of stars outside chakra; 1 star = 1/8 Baht.

Date	Mintage	F	VF	XF	Unc	BU
ND(1860)	—	4.00	9.00	40.00	150	—

Y# 8a FUANG (1/8 Baht)
0.9000 g., 1.9400 Gold **Ruler:** Rama IV Phra Chom Klao 'Mongkut' **Edge:** Reeded **Note:** Thin flan.

Date	Mintage	F	VF	XF	Unc	BU
ND(1864)	—	800	1,600	3,000	5,000	—

Y# 28 FUANG (1/8 Baht)
1.8900 g., Silver **Ruler:** Rama IV Phra Chom Klao 'Mongkut'

Date	Mintage	F	VF	XF	Unc	BU
ND(1869)	—	4.00	8.00	45.00	160	—

Y# 32 FUANG (1/8 Baht)
1.8900 g., Silver **Ruler:** Rama V Phra Maha Chulalongkorn

Date	Mintage	F	VF	XF	Unc	BU
ND(1876-1900)	—	3.00	7.00	30.00	90.00	—
ND(1876-1900) Proof	—	Value: 2,500				

Y# 32b FUANG (1/8 Baht)
Gold **Ruler:** Rama V Phra Maha Chulalongkorn

Date	Mintage	F	VF	XF	Unc	BU
ND(1876)	—	800	1,600	3,500	6,000	—

Y# 7.1 1/16 BAHT (1 Sik)
1.0000 g., Silver **Ruler:** Rama IV Phra Chom Klao 'Mongkut' **Note:** Thick flan.

Date	Mintage	F	VF	XF	Unc	BU
ND(1860)	—	15.00	30.00	125	400	—

Y# 7.2 1/16 BAHT (1 Sik)
1.0000 g., Silver **Ruler:** Rama IV Phra Chom Klao 'Mongkut' **Obv:** Smaller crown **Rev:** Larger elephant

Date	Mintage	F	VF	XF	Unc	BU
ND(1860)	—	20.00	35.00	150	475	—

Y# 7a 1/16 BAHT (1 Sik)
1.0000 g., 0.9000 Gold **Ruler:** Rama IV Phra Chom Klao 'Mongkut' **Edge:** Reeded

Date	Mintage	F	VF	XF	Unc	BU
ND(1864)	—	—	—	—	—	—

Y# 9 SALU'NG (1/4 Baht)
3.7100 g., Silver **Ruler:** Rama IV Phra Chom Klao 'Mongkut' **Note:** Denomination indicated by number of stars outside chakra; 2 stars = 1/4 Baht.

Date	Mintage	F	VF	XF	Unc	BU
ND(1860)	—	12.00	25.00	120	—	—

Y# 9a SALU'NG (1/4 Baht)
Gold **Ruler:** Rama IV Phra Chom Klao 'Mongkut'

Date	Mintage	F	VF	XF	Unc	BU
ND(1864)	—	—	—	—	—	—

Y# 29 SALU'NG (1/4 Baht)
3.8200 g., Silver **Ruler:** Rama IV Phra Chom Klao 'Mongkut'

Date	Mintage	F	VF	XF	Unc	BU
ND(1869)	—	8.00	17.50	80.00	300	—

Y# 33 SALU'NG (1/4 Baht)
3.8200 g., Silver **Ruler:** Rama IV Phra Chom Klao 'Mongkut'

Date	Mintage	F	VF	XF	Unc	BU
ND(1876-1900)	—	6.00	15.00	45.00	175	—
ND(1876-1900) Proof	—	Value: 3,000				

Y# 10.1 2 SALU'NG (1/2 Baht)
7.5400 g., Silver **Ruler:** Rama IV Phra Chom Klao 'Mongkut' **Note:** Denomination indicated by number of stars outside chakra; 4 stars = 1/2 Baht.

Date	Mintage	F	VF	XF	Unc	BU
ND(1860)	—	35.00	110	200	500	—

Y# 10.2a 2 SALU'NG (1/2 Baht)
7.5500 g., Gold **Ruler:** Rama IV Phra Chom Klao 'Mongkut'

Date	Mintage	F	VF	XF	Unc	BU
ND(1864) Rare	—	—	—	—	—	—

Note: Spink-Taisei Auction #15, 9-93 Unc. realized $23,000

Y# 15.5 2 SALU'NG (1/2 Baht)
7.5500 g., Gold **Ruler:** Rama V Phra Maha Chulalongkorn **Edge:** Reeded

Date	Mintage	F	VF	XF	Unc	BU
ND(1894)	—	—	—	—	—	—

Y# 11 BAHT
15.4500 g., 0.9000 Silver .4470 oz. **Ruler:** Rama IV Phra Chom Klao 'Mongkut' **Note:** Denomination indicated by number of stars outside chakra; 8 stars = 1 Baht.

Date	Mintage	F	VF	XF	Unc	BU
ND(1860)	—	15.00	25.00	125	340	—

Y# 11a BAHT
15.2500 g., Gold **Ruler:** Rama IV Phra Chom Klao 'Mongkut'

Date	Mintage	F	VF	XF	Unc	BU
ND(1864) Rare	—	—	—	—	—	—

Note: Spink-Taisei Auction #15, 9-93 Unc. realized $34,000

Y# 31 BAHT
Silver **Ruler:** Rama IV Phra Chom Klao 'Mongkut'

Date	Mintage	F	VF	XF	Unc	BU
ND(1869)	—	15.00	25.00	120	350	—

Y# 34 BAHT
Silver **Ruler:** Rama V Phra Maha Chulalongkorn

Date	Mintage	F	VF	XF	Unc	BU
ND(1876-1900)	—	5.00	10.00	40.00	185	—
ND(1876-1900) Proof	—	Value: 6,000				

Y# 12 2 BAHT
30.2000 g., 0.9000 Silver .8738 oz. **Ruler:** Rama IV Phra Chom Klao 'Mongkut' **Note:** Denomination indicated by number of stars outside chakra; 16 stars = 1 Baht.

Date	Mintage	F	VF	XF	Unc	BU
ND(c.1863)	—	175	375	650	1,500	—

Y# 12a 2 BAHT
30.3000 g., Gold **Ruler:** Rama IV Phra Chom Klao 'Mongkut'

Date	Mintage	F	VF	XF	Unc	BU
ND(1864) Rare	—	—	—	—	—	—

Note: Spink-Taisei Auction #15, 9-93 Unc. realized $44,000

Y# 13 POT DUENG (2-1/2 Baht)
2.2000 g., 0.9970 Gold **Ruler:** Rama IV Phra Chom Klao 'Mongkut' **Rev:** Crude elephant

Date	Mintage	F	VF	XF	Unc	BU
ND(1863)	—	800	1,500	2,500	4,000	—

Y# 13.5 POT DUENG (2-1/2 Baht)
Gold **Ruler:** Rama V Phra Maha Chulalongkorn **Rev:** Refined elephant

Date	Mintage	F	VF	XF	Unc	BU
ND(1894)	—	600	1,000	1,800	2,600	—

Y# 13.1 POT DUENG (2-1/2 Baht)
Gold **Ruler:** Rama V Phra Maha Chulalongkorn **Note:** Weight varies: 1.90-2.00 grams.

Date	Mintage	F	VF	XF	Unc	BU
ND(1894)	—	650	1,250	2,000	2,800	—

Y# A12 TAMLUNG (4 Baht)
60.4000 g., 0.9000 Silver 1.7477 oz. **Ruler:** Rama IV Phra Chom Klao 'Mongkut' **Subject:** 60th Birthday of Rama IV **Edge:** Plain

Date	Mintage	F	VF	XF	Unc	BU
ND(1864) Rare	—	—	—	—	—	—

Note: Spink-Taisei Auction #15, 9-93 Unc. realized $16,000

Y# A12a TAMLUNG (4 Baht)
60.7700 g., 0.9970 Gold **Ruler:** Rama IV Phra Chom Klao 'Mongkut'

Date	Mintage	F	VF	XF	Unc	BU
ND(1864) Rare	—	—	—	—	—	—

Note: Spink-Taisei Auction #4, 2-88, XF specimen realized $74,800

Y# 14 PIT (4 Baht)
0.9970 Gold 3.40 oz. **Ruler:** Rama IV Phra Chom Klao 'Mongkut' **Rev:** Crude elephant **Edge:** Reeded

Date	Mintage	F	VF	XF	Unc	BU
ND(1863)	—	1,000	1,500	2,300	4,000	—

Y# 14.5 PIT (4 Baht)
0.9970 Gold **Ruler:** Rama V Phra Maha Chulalongkorn **Rev:** Refined elephant **Note:** Weight varies: 3.65-4.00 grams.

Date	Mintage	F	VF	XF	Unc	BU
ND(1894)	—	1,000	1,600	2,500	3,500	—

Y# 15 TOT (8 Baht)
6.8000 g., 0.9970 Gold **Ruler:** Rama IV Phra Chom Klao 'Mongkut' **Rev:** Crude elephant **Edge:** Reeded

Date	Mintage	F	VF	XF	Unc	BU
ND(1863)	—	1,250	2,500	4,500	10,000	—

Y# 15.1 TOT (8 Baht)
Gold **Ruler:** Rama V Phra Maha Chulalongkorn **Note:** Weight varies: 7.30-8.00 grams.

Date	Mintage	F	VF	XF	Unc	BU
ND(1894)	—	1,000	1,750	2,800	6,500	—

Y# 15.6 TOT (8 Baht)
Gold **Ruler:** Rama V Phra Maha Chulalongkorn **Rev:** Refined elephant

Date	Mintage	F	VF	XF	Unc	BU
ND(1896)	—	—	—	—	—	—

Note: Reported, not confirmed

DECIMAL COINAGE

25 Satang = 1 Salung; 100 Satang = 1 Baht

Y# 24 2-1/2 SATANG
Copper-Nickel **Ruler:** Rama V Phra Maha Chulalongkorn

Date	Mintage	F	VF	XF	Unc	BU
RS116(1897)H	5,080,000	—	3.00	5.00	10.00	—

Note: Issued in 1898 although dated RS116 (1897)

RS116(1897)H Proof	—	Value: 25.00

Y# 25 5 SATANG
Copper-Nickel **Ruler:** Rama V Phra Maha Chulalongkorn

Date	Mintage	F	VF	XF	Unc	BU
RS116(1897)H	5,080,000	—	10.00	15.00	40.00	—

Note: Issued in 1898 although dated RS116 (1897)

RS116(1897)H Proof	—	Value: 75.00

Y# 26 10 SATANG
Copper-Nickel **Ruler:** Rama V Phra Maha Chulalongkorn

Date	Mintage	F	VF	XF	Unc	BU
RS116(1897)H	3,810,000	—	20.00	50.00	150	—
RS116(1897)H Proof	—	Value: 185				

Y# 27 20 SATANG
Copper-Nickel **Ruler:** Rama V Phra Maha Chulalongkorn

Date	Mintage	F	VF	XF	Unc	BU
RS116(1897)H	3,126,000	—	10.00	22.00	55.00	—

PRESENTATION COINAGE

Bannakin (Royal Gift) Coins

KM# 11 FUANG (1/8 Baht)
2.0000 g., Silver **Ruler:** Rama IV Phra Chom Klao 'Mongkut' **Obv:** Larger crown **Edge:** Plain **Note:** Similar to 1/8 Baht, Y#8.

Date	Mintage	F	VF	XF	Unc	BU
ND(1857-58)	—	—	1,000	2,000	3,000	—

KM# 12 SALU'NG (1/4 Baht)
3.9000 g., Silver **Ruler:** Rama IV Phra Chom Klao 'Mongkut' **Edge:** Plain

Date	Mintage	F	VF	XF	Unc	BU
ND(1857-58)	—	—	3,000	4,000	6,000	—

KM# 13 1/2 BAHT
Silver **Ruler:** Rama IV Phra Chom Klao 'Mongkut' **Edge:** Plain

Date	Mintage	F	VF	XF	Unc	BU
ND(1857-58) Rare	—	—	—	—	—	—

Note: The total mintage for KM#11-13 equalled 840 Baht

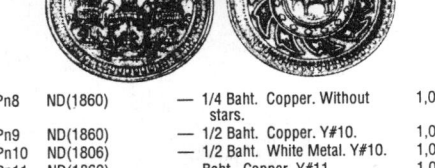

KM# 14 BAHT
15.5000 g., Silver **Ruler:** Rama IV Phra Chom Klao 'Mongkut' **Edge:** Milled

Date	Mintage	F	VF	XF	Unc	BU
ND(1857-58)	2,400	—	4,000	5,000	6,000	—
ND(c.1868) Rare	—	—	—	—	—	—

Note: Spink-Taisei Auction #4, Feb. 1988, realized $20,125

Y# B34 BAHT
Silver **Ruler:** Rama V Phra Maha Chulalongkorn **Subject:** Queen's Royal Mint Visit **Obv:** RS date 116 added in field **Obv. Legend:** "Rong Krasab" (Royal Mint)

Date	Mintage	F	VF	XF	Unc	BU
RS116(1897)	—	—	—	5,000	15,000	—

KM# A10 POT DUENG (2-1/2 Baht)
2.1500 g., Gold **Ruler:** Rama IV Phra Chom Klao 'Mongkut'

Date	Mintage	F	VF	XF	Unc	BU
ND(1857-58) Rare	—	—	—	—	—	—

PATTERNS

Including off metal strikes

KM#	Date	Mintage	Identification	Mkt Val
Pn1	ND(1857-58)	—	1/8 Baht. Copper. KM11.	—
Pn2	ND(1860)	—	1/16 Baht. Copper. Y#7.	1,000
Pn3	ND(1860)	—	1/16 Baht. White Metal. Y#7.	1,000
Pn4	ND(1860)	—	1/8 Baht. Copper. Y#8.	1,000
Pn5	ND(1860)	—	1/8 Baht. White Metal. Y#8.	1,000
Pn6	ND(1860)	—	1/4 Baht. Copper. Y#9.	1,000
Pn7	ND(1860)	—	1/4 Baht. White Metal. Y#9.	1,000

KM#	Date	Mintage	Identification	Mkt Val
Pn8	ND(1860)	—	1/4 Baht. Copper. Without stars.	1,000
Pn9	ND(1860)	—	1/2 Baht. Copper. Y#10.	1,000
Pn10	ND(1806)	—	1/2 Baht. White Metal. Y#10.	1,000
Pn11	ND(1860)	—	Baht. Copper. Y#11.	1,000
Pn12	ND(1860)	—	Baht. White Metal. Y#11.	1,500

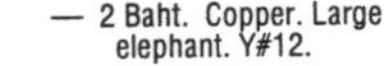

KM#	Date	Mintage	Identification	Mkt Val
Pn13	ND(1860)	—	2 Baht. Copper. Large elephant. Y#12.	2,000
Pn14	ND(1860)	—	2 Baht. White Metal. Y#12.	3,000

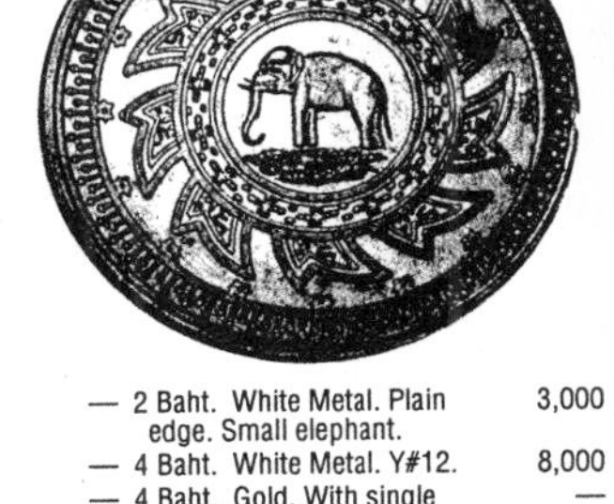

KM#	Date	Mintage	Identification	Mkt Val
Pn15	ND(1860)	—	2 Baht. White Metal. Plain edge. Small elephant.	3,000
Pn16	ND(1860)	—	4 Baht. White Metal. Y#12.	8,000
Pn17	ND(1860)	—	4 Baht. Gold. With single outline around Thai legend. Y#A12a.	—
Pn18	ND(1868)	—	1/16 Baht. Silver.	1,000
Pn19	ND(1868)	—	1/16 Baht. Copper.	600
Pn20	ND(1868)	—	1/8 Baht. Silver.	1,000
Pn21	ND(1868)	—	1/8 Baht. Copper.	800

KM#	Date	Mintage	Identification	Mkt Val
Pn22	ND(1868)	—	1/4 Baht. Silver.	3,000
Pn23	ND(1868)	—	1/4 Baht. Copper.	2,000
Pn24	ND(1868)	—	1/2 Baht. Silver.	—
Pn25	ND(1868)	—	1/2 Baht. Copper.	2,000
Pn26	ND(1868)	—	1/2 Baht. Nickel.	3,000

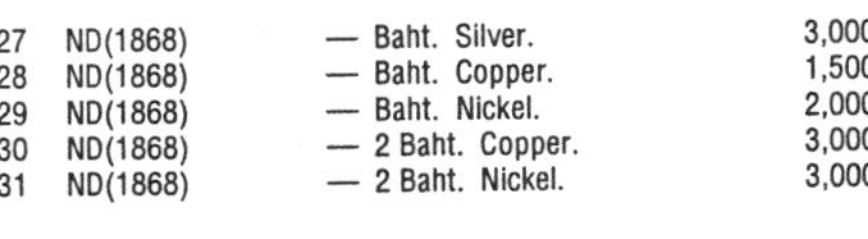

KM#	Date	Mintage	Identification	Mkt Val
Pn27	ND(1868)	—	Baht. Silver.	3,000
Pn28	ND(1868)	—	Baht. Copper.	1,500
Pn29	ND(1868)	—	Baht. Nickel.	2,000
Pn30	ND(1868)	—	2 Baht. Copper.	3,000
Pn31	ND(1868)	—	2 Baht. Nickel.	3,000

KM#	Date	Mintage	Identification	Mkt Val

KM#	Date	Mintage	Identification	Mkt Val
Pn32	ND(1868)	—	4 Baht. Copper.	8,000
Pn33	ND(1876)	—	Baht. Copper.	2,000
Pn34	ND(1876)	—	Baht. White Metal.	2,000

KM#	Date	Mintage	Identification	Mkt Val
Pn35	ND(1877)	—	2 Baht. Silver.	25,000
Pn36	ND(1877)	—	2 Baht. Copper.	10,000
Pn37	ND(1877)	—	2 Baht. Bronzed Copper.	10,000
Pn38	ND(1877)	—	2 Baht. White Metal.	10,000

KM#	Date	Mintage	Identification	Mkt Val
Pn39	CS1249(1887)	—	2 Att. Nickel. Y#23.	1,200
Pn40	RS114(1895)	—	1/2 Att. Nickel.	800

KM#	Date	Mintage	Identification	Mkt Val
Pn41	RS114(1895)	—	Att. Nickel.	800
Pn42	RS114(1895)	—	2 Att. Nickel.	3,000
Pn43	RS115(1896)	—	Att. Nickel.	1,200
Pn44	RS118(1899)	—	1/2 Att. Tin. Y#21	—
Pn45	RS118(1899)	—	Att. Tin. Y#22.	—
Pn46	RS118(1899)	—	2 Att. Tin. Y#23.	—

JARING

(Jering)

All coins of Jaring are uniface

One of the 7 provinces cut out of Patani State after the uprising of 1830/31. It lies on the east coast of the Malay peninsula. The uniface tin coins were made from 1845 to 1894.

TITLES

Jering

PROVINCE

HAMMERED COINAGE

KM# 1.1 PITIS

Tin **Note:** Arabic legend: "Ini Pitis Jering Sanat 1261".

Date	Mintage	Good	VG	F	VF	XF
AH1261	—	10.00	20.00	40.00	80.00	—

KM# 1.2 PITIS

3.0000 g., Tin

Date	Mintage	Good	VG	F	VF	XF
AH1280	—	10.00	20.00	40.00	80.00	—

KM# 2 PITIS

Tin **Note:** Arabic legend: "Ini Pitis Balad Jarin Sanat 1297".

Date	Mintage	Good	VG	F	VF	XF
AH1297(1897)	—	10.00	15.00	40.00	80.00	—

KM# 3 PITIS

Tin **Note:** Arabic legend: "Hadha al-Diwan al-Raj al-Adil Fi Balad al-Jarin 1302".

Date	Mintage	Good	VG	F	VF	XF
AH1302(1884)	—	11.50	22.50	45.00	90.00	—
AH1312(1894)	—	11.50	22.50	45.00	90.00	—

KM# 3a PITIS

Tin **Note:** Crude imitation of KM#3.

Date	Mintage	Good	VG	F	VF	XF
ND	—	7.50	15.00	25.00	50.00	—

LEGEH

Ligeh, Ligor, Langkat

One of the inland provinces cut out of Patani State. Coins attributable to Legeh run from 1840 to 1893. Siam again assumed control in 1902.

TITLES

دار السلام

Dar es-Salam

نكري لغكه

Negri Ligkeh

PROVINCE

HAMMERED COINAGE

KM# 1 PITIS

Tin **Obv. Legend:** "Pitis Negeri Langkat Dar al-Salam" **Rev. Legend:** "Malik al Adil Khalifat al-Mu'minin" **Note:** Legends in Arabic.

Date	Mintage	Good	VG	F	VF	XF
ND	—	13.50	27.50	55.00	95.00	—

Note: For a piece dated 1256, sometimes attributed to Legeh, see KM#4 of Kelantan (Malaysia)

KM# 2 PITIS
Tin **Obv. Legend:** "al-Sultan al-Muzaffar Daulat Langkat Khalifat" **Rev. Legend:** "al-Shamar Wal-Qamar Fi Rabi al-Awal Sanat 1307" **Note:** Legends in Arabic.

Date	Mintage	Good	VG	F	VF	XF
AH1307	—	9.00	18.00	40.00	80.00	—
AH1313	—	—	—	—	—	—

Note: Reported, not confirmed

PATANI

Pattani

Patani (Pattani), a former Malay state in the Malay peninsula, is a small province or changwat' of Thailand (Siam) on the eastern side of peninsula Thailand near the border of Malaya, has an area of 777 sq. mi. (2,012 sq.km.) and a population of about 275,000. After the 1830/31 uprising it was one of 7 provinces administered by Siam through Malayan governors. Patani was the most prolific coin issuer of the Siamese period having made coins periodically from 1845 to 1891. Formerly ruled by a Moslem Rajah subject to Siam.

TITLES

خليفة الكرم

Khalifa(t) al-Karam

الفطاني

al-Patani

PROVINCE

HAMMERED COINAGE

KM# 1 PITIS
Tin **Obv. Legend:** "Ini Pitis Belanja Raja Patani" **Rev. Legend:** "Khalifat al-Mu'minin Sanat 1261" **Note:** Legends in Arabic.

Date	Mintage	Good	VG	F	VF	XF
AH1261	—	7.50	15.00	25.00	45.00	—

KM# 2 PITIS
Tin **Obv. Legend:** "al-Sultan al-Azam Wa Khalifat al-Karam" **Rev. Legend:** "al-Malik al-Balad al-Patani al-Imami 1284" **Note:** Legends in Arabic.

Date	Mintage	Good	VG	F	VF	XF
AH1284	—	7.50	15.00	25.00	45.00	—

KM# 3 PITIS
Tin **Obv. Legend:** "al-Sultan al-Patani Sanat 1297" **Rev. Legend:** "Wa Khalifat al-Karim" **Note:** Legends in Arabic.

Date	Mintage	Good	VG	F	VF	XF
AH1297	—	7.50	15.00	25.00	45.00	—

KM# 4 PITIS
Tin **Obv. Legend:** "al-Matsaraf Fi Balad al-Patania Sanat 1301" **Rev. Legend:** "Zarb FI Harat al-Daulat Azza Nasrahu" **Note:** Legends in Arabic. Reverse legend incuse.

Date	Mintage	Good	VG	F	VF	XF
AH1301	—	12.50	20.00	30.00	50.00	—

KM# 5 PITIS
Tin **Obv. Legend:** "al-Matsaraf Fi Balad al-Patani Sanat 1309" **Rev. Legend:** "Ini Pitis Belanja di-Dalam Negri Patani" **Note:** Legends in Arabic. Reverse legend in relief.

Date	Mintage	Good	VG	F	VF	XF
AH1309	—	7.50	15.00	25.00	45.00	—

KM# 50 KUPANG
Gold **Obv:** Bull standing to left **Rev. Legend:** "Malik al-Adil" **Note:** Reverse legend in Arabic in two lines.

Date	Mintage	F	VF	XF	Unc	BU
ND(1800-50)	—	45.00	50.00	65.00	90.00	—

KM# 51 KUPANG
Gold **Obv:** Bull standing to left **Rev. Legend:** "al-Adil" **Note:** Reverse legend in Arabic.

Date	Mintage	F	VF	XF	Unc	BU
ND(1800-50)	—	45.00	50.00	65.00	90.00	—

KM# 52 KUPANG
Gold **Obv:** Bull standing to left **Rev. Legend:** "Malik al-Adil" **Note:** Reverse legend in Arabic in three lines.

Date	Mintage	F	VF	XF	Unc	BU
ND(1800-50)	—	45.00	50.00	65.00	90.00	—

KM# 53 KUPANG
Gold **Obv:** Bull standing to left **Rev. Legend:** "Asma Adil" **Note:** Reverse legend in Arabic.

Date	Mintage	F	VF	XF	Unc	BU
ND(1800-50)	—	45.00	50.00	65.00	90.00	—

KM# 54 KUPANG
Gold **Obv:** Bull standing to right **Rev. Legend:** "Malik al-Adil" **Note:** Reverse legend in Arabic in two lines.

Date	Mintage	F	VF	XF	Unc	BU
ND(1800-50)	—	60.00	85.00	115	150	—

KM# 55 KUPANG
Gold **Obv:** Eight-pointed star **Rev. Legend:** "Malik al-Adil" **Note:** Reverse legend in Arabic.

Date	Mintage	F	VF	XF	Unc	BU
ND(1800-50)	—	50.00	60.00	80.00	120	—

KM# 56 KUPANG
Gold **Obv:** Six-pointed star **Rev. Legend:** "Malik al-Adil" **Note:** Reverse legend in Arabic.

Date	Mintage	F	VF	XF	Unc	BU
ND(1800-50)	—	45.00	50.00	65.00	90.00	—

KM# 57 KUPANG
Gold **Obv:** Four-petalled flower **Rev. Legend:** "Malik al-Adil" **Note:** Reverse legend in Arabic.

Date	Mintage	F	VF	XF	Unc	BU
ND(1800-50)	—	50.00	60.00	75.00	100	—

KM# 58 KUPANG
Gold **Obv. Legend:** "Dama Shah" **Rev. Legend:** "Binaqdi Sahibi" **Note:** Legends in Arabic.

Date	Mintage	F	VF	XF	Unc	BU
ND(1800-50)	—	50.00	60.00	75.00	100	—

KM# 59 KUPANG
Gold **Obv. Legend:** "Shah Adil" **Rev. Legend:** "Malik al-Adil" **Note:** Legends in Arabic.

Date	Mintage	F	VF	XF	Unc	BU
ND(1800-50)	—	50.00	60.00	75.00	100	—

KM# 60 KUPANG
Gold **Obv. Legend:** "al-Julus Kelantan" **Rev. Legend:** "al-Mutawakkilu Ala Liah" **Note:** Legends in Arabic.

Date	Mintage	F	VF	XF	Unc	BU
ND(1800-50)	—	50.00	60.00	75.00	100	—

KM# 61 KUPANG
Gold **Obv. Legend:** "Aqam'u'd-Din" **Rev. Legend:** "Malik al-Adil" **Note:** Legends in Arabic.

Date	Mintage	F	VF	XF	Unc	BU
ND(1800-50)	—	50.00	60.00	75.00	100	—

KM# 62 KUPANG
Gold **Obv. Legend:** "Shah Alam" **Rev. Legend:** "Malik al-Adil" **Note:** Legends in Arabic.

Date	Mintage	F	VF	XF	Unc	BU
ND(1800-50)	—	50.00	60.00	75.00	100	—

KM# 63 KUPANG
Gold **Obv. Legend:** "Sultan" **Rev. Legend:** "Mu'azzam Shah" **Note:** Legends in Arabic.

Date	Mintage	F	VF	XF	Unc	BU
ND(1800-50)	—	60.00	70.00	90.00	130	—

KM# 64 KUPANG
Gold **Obv. Legend:** "Sultan Muhammad" **Rev. Legend:** "Mu'azzam Shah" **Note:** Legends in Arabic.

Date	Mintage	F	VF	XF	Unc	BU
ND(1800-50)	—	60.00	70.00	90.00	130	—

KM# 65 KUPANG
Gold **Obv. Legend:** "al-Julus Kelantan" **Rev. Legend:** "Khalifata'r-Rahman" **Note:** Legends in Arabic.

Date	Mintage	F	VF	XF	Unc	BU
ND(1800-50)	—	40.00	50.00	70.00	100	—

REMAN

Rhaman

Another of the inland provinces cut from Patani State. Only a single type tin coin is presently known from Reman. This piece was minted about 1890.

TITLES

Rehman

PROVINCE

HAMMERED COINAGE

KM# 1 PITIS
Tin **Note:** Uniface. Retrograde Arabic legend: "Ini Pitis Rahman Raja Melayu".

Date	Mintage	Good	VG	F	VF	XF
ND(c.1890)	—	12.50	25.00	50.00	90.00	—

SAI

Saiburi, Teluban

Sai is one of the provinces on the east coast of Malaya cut from the state of Patani. The tin Pitis of this province were made from c.1870 to 1891 and are distinctive in that they have a reverse that bears no legend. It carries only a decorative motif.

TITLES

al-Saiwi

PROVINCE

HAMMERED COINAGE

KM# 1 PITIS
Tin **Obv. Legend:** "Malik al-Adil Fi Blad al-Saiwi 1290" **Note:** Legend in Arabic.

Date	Mintage	Good	VG	F	VF	XF
AH1290	—	12.50	22.50	35.00	65.00	—

KM# 2 PITIS
Tin **Obv. Legend:** "al-Dawlat al-Khairiyat Fi Balad al-Saiwi 1307"
Note: Legend in Arabic.

Date	Mintage	Good	VG	F	VF	XF
AH1307	—	12.50	22.50	35.00	65.00	—

Note: A number of Chinese token issues are tentatively assigned to the Patani state of Jala (Jalor)

SINGGORA

Songkhla

Singgora (modern Songkhla) was an important seaport and trading center on the Gulf of Siam on the eastern side of peninsular Thailand and just a few miles north of the border with Malaya. It borders Patani province to the southeast. Songkhla remains a key commercial center today. Its rare coinage from the early 19th century features Arabic legends on obverse and chinese characters on reverse, clearly indicating the influence of Chinese traders in its economy.

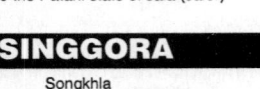

Negri Singgora

PROVINCE

HAMMERED COINAGE

KM# 1 PITIS
Tin **Obv:** Arabic legend including mint name **Rev:** Chinese characters

Date	Mintage	Good	VG	F	VF	XF
ND Rare	—	—	—	—	—	—

KM# 2 PITIS
Tin **Obv:** Arabic legend with mint name and date **Rev:** Chinese characters

Date	Mintage	Good	VG	F	VF	XF
AH1241 Rare	—	—	—	—	—	—

TIBET

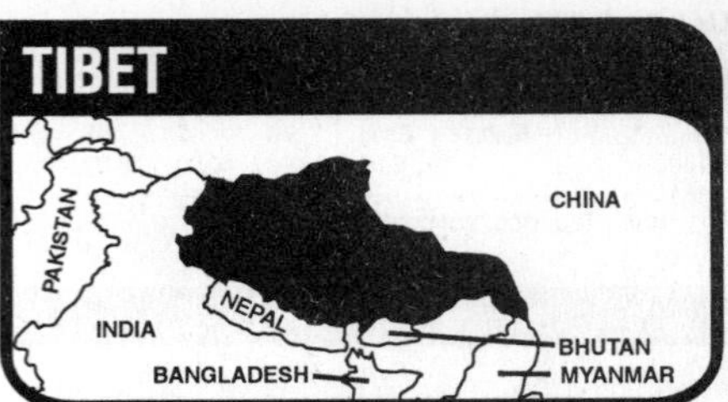

Tibet, an autonomous region of China located in central Asia between the Himalayan and Kunlun Mts. has an area of 471,660 sq. mi. (1,221,599 sq. km.).

Lamaism, a form of Buddhism, developed in Tibet in the 8th century. From that time until the 1900s, the Tibetan rulers virtually isolated the country from the outside world. The British in India achieved some influence in the early 20th century.

The first coins to circulate in Tibet were those of neighboring Nepal from about 1570. Shortly after 1720, the Nepalese government began striking specific issues for use in Tibet. These coins had a lower silver content than those struck for use in Nepal and were exchanged with the Tibetans for an equal weight in silver bullion. Around 1763 the Tibetans struck their own coins for the first time in history. The number of coins struck at that time must have been very small. Larger quantities of coins were struck by the Tibetan government mint, which opened in 1791 with the permission of the Chinese. Operations of this mint however were suspended two years later. The Chinese opened a second mint in Lhasa in 1792. It produced a coinage until 1836. Shortly thereafter, the Tibetan mint was reopened and the government of Tibet continued to strike coins until 1953.

DATING

Based on the Tibetan calendar, Tibetan coins are dated by the cycle which contains 60 years. To calculate the western date use the following formula: Number of cycles -1, x 60 + number of years + 1026. Example 15th cycle 25th year = 1891 AD. Example: 15th cycle, 25th year 15 - 1 x 60 + 25 + 1026 = 1891AD.

13/30 = 1776	14/30 = 1836	15/30 = 1896
13/40 = 1786	14/40 = 1846	15/40 = 1906
13/50 = 1796	14/50 = 1856	15/50 = 1916
13/60 = 1806	14/60 = 1866	15/60 = 1926
14/10 = 1816	15/10 = 1876	16/10 = 1936
14/20 = 1826	15/20 = 1886	16/20 = 1946

Certain Sino-Tibetan issues are dated in the year of reign of the Emperor of China.

MONETARY SYSTEM

15 Skar = 1-1/2 Sho = 1 Tangka
10 Sho = 1 Srang

TANGKA

16(th)CYCLE 2(nd)YEAR = 1928AD

16(th) CYCLE 7(th) YEAR = 1933AD

1	༡	གཅིག་
2	༢	གཉིས་
3	༣	གསུམ་
4	༤	བཞི་
5	༥	ལྔ་
6	༦	དྲུག་
7	༧	བདུན་
8	༨	བརྒྱད་
9	༩	དགུ་
10	༡༠	བཅུ་ or བཅུ་ཐམ་པ་
11	༡༡	བཅུག་ or བཅུ་གཅིག་
12	༡༢	བཅུས་ or བཅུ་གཉིས་
13	༡༣	བཅུམ་ or བཅུ་གསུམ་
14	༡༤	བཅུ་བཞི་
15	༡༥	བཅོ་ལྔ་
16	༡༦	བཅུ་དྲུག་
17	༡༧	བཅུ་བདུན་
18	༡༨	བཅོ་བརྒྱད་
19	༡༩	བཅུ་དགུ་
20	༢༠	ཉི་ཤུ
21	༢༡	ཉི་ཤུ་རྩ་གཅིག་ or ཉེར་གཅིག་
22	༢༢	ཉེར་གཉིས་
23	༢༣	ཉེར་གསུམ་
24	༢༤	ཉེར་བཞི་
25	༢༥	ཉེར་ལྔ་
26	༢༦	ཉེར་དྲུག་
27	༢༧	ཉེར་བདུན་
28	༢༨	ཉེར་བརྒྱད་

THEOCRACY

SINO-TIBETAN COINAGE

Hammered

C# 85 SHO

3.7000 g., Silver, 30 mm. **Ruler:** Chia Ch'ing **Rev:** "One Miscal" in Manchu script added **Note:** This is the only trilingual coin from Tibet. Legends in Tibetan, Manchu and Chinese.

Date	Mintage	Good	VG	F	VF	XF
CD6(1801)	—	800	1,150	1,500	2,000	—

C# 83.2 SHO

Silver **Ruler:** Chia Ch'ing **Obv:** Without four clouds **Rev:** Four clouds **Note:** Size varies: 24.5-28 mm.

Date	Mintage	Good	VG	F	VF	XF
CD8(1803)	—	30.00	50.00	80.00	120	—
CD9(1804)	—	30.00	50.00	80.00	120	—

Note: Years 8 and 9, unlike all other Shos, lack the four obverse "clouds"

C# 83.3 SHO

Silver **Ruler:** Chia Ch'ing **Obv:** Without four clouds **Rev:** Three clouds with six characters at top to upper right **Note:** 24.5-28mm, 3.2-5g.

Date	Mintage	Good	VG	F	VF	XF
CD8(1803)	—	25.00	45.00	70.00	110	—

C# 83.1 SHO

Silver **Obv:** Four clouds **Rev:** Four clouds **Note:** Size varies: 25-29mm. Weight varies: 3.00-3.80 grams. Prev. C83.

Date	Mintage	Good	VG	F	VF	XF
CD24(1819)	—	20.00	35.00	55.00	90.00	—
CD25(1820)	—	15.00	25.00	35.00	55.00	—

C# 93 SHO

Silver **Ruler:** Tao Kuang

Date	Mintage	Good	VG	F	VF	XF
CD1(1821)	—	40.00	65.00	115	160	—
CD2(1822)	—	15.00	25.00	40.00	60.00	—
CD3(1823)	—	15.00	25.00	40.00	60.00	—
CD4(1824)	—	30.00	50.00	80.00	120	—
CD15(1835)	—	50.00	70.00	110	180	—
CD16(1836)	—	50.00	70.00	110	180	—

Note: Varieties exist in ornamentation, inscription styles as well as in number of dots (Obverse: 26, 27, 28, 30, 31; Reverse: 22, 24, 25, 26, 28, 30)

TIBETAN COINAGE

Hammered

C# 60.5 "KONG-PAR" TANGKA

Silver **Ruler:** Tao Kuang **Obv:** Sun and moon above date arch **Rev:** N has six dots, without three dots above date **Note:** Weight varies: 5.-5.60 g.

Date	Mintage	Good	VG	F	VF	XF
CD13-46(ca.1820s)	—	18.00	30.00	50.00	80.00	—

C# 60.2 "KONG-PAR" TANGKA

Silver **Ruler:** Tao Kuang **Obv:** Sun and moon above date arch **Rev:** N has six dots **Note:** Weight varies: 5.00-5.60 grams.

Date	Mintage	Good	VG	F	VF	XF
CD13-46(ca.1820s)	—	18.00	30.00	50.00	80.00	—

Note: It is believed that this type was struck in the 1820's; A variety with reversed symbols on the reverse exist. An obverse variety w/o three dots above the figures for the date exists.

C# 60.3 "KONG-PAR" TANGKA

Silver **Ruler:** Tao Kuang **Obv:** Crescent and three dots above date arch **Rev:** N has five or six dots; SE endless knot rounded **Note:** Weight varies: 4.20-5.60 grams.

Date	Mintage	Good	VG	F	VF	XF
CD13-46(ca.1860)	—	18.00	30.00	50.00	80.00	—

Note: It is believed that this type was struck in the early 1860's; Numerous varieties exist including one with missing date

C# 60.4 "KONG-PAR" TANGKA

Silver **Ruler:** Tao Kuang **Rev:** N four dots; SE knot composed of for to thirteen boxes

Date	Mintage	Good	VG	F	VF	XF
CD13-46(ca.1860s)	—	4.00	7.00	13.00	25.00	—

Note: It is believed that this type was struck in the early 1860's; Numerous varieties exist including one with missing date arch on obverse

C# A13.2 "KONG-PAR" TANGKA

Silver **Rev:** Two circles around lotus

Date	Mintage	Good	VG	F	VF	XF
CD15-24(1890)	—	250	300	425	550	—

C# A13.1 "KONG-PAR" TANGKA

Silver **Note:** Weight varies: 3.60-5.20 grams.

Date	Mintage	Good	VG	F	VF	XF
CD15-24(1890)	—	3.00	4.00	7.00	12.00	—
CD15-25(1891)	—	5.00	8.00	12.00	20.00	—

Note: Varieties of reverse exist including 2 fish at 1 o'clock swimming in counter clockwise direction (both years)

C# 27 "KONG-PAR" TANGKA

Silver **Note:** Weight varies: 3.60-5.20 grams.

Date	Mintage	Good	VG	F	VF	XF
CD15-28(1894)	—	12.00	20.00	30.00	45.00	—
CD15-30(1896)	—	20.00	30.00	45.00	60.00	—

Note: In addition to the above meaningful (probably) dates, the following meaningless ones exist: 13-16, 13-31, 13-92, 16-16, 16-61, 16-64, 16-69, 16-92, 16-93, 92-34, 92-39, 96-61, (sixes may be reversed threes and nines reversed ones)

GA-DEN TANGKA COINAGE

Hammered

The Ga-den Tangkas are among the most common and perhaps most beautiful of all Tibetan silver coins. The obverse shows a stylized Lotus flower within a circle surrounded by the 8 Buddhist lucky symbols in radiating petals. The reverse shows an 8-petalled wheel (flower) within a star surrounded by a Tibetan inscription (reading Ga-den Palace, victorious in all directions), which is broken up into 8 oval frames. The Ga-den Palace is the former residence of the Dala Lamas, located in Drepung Monastery near Lhasa. On Tibetan coins the name "Ga-den Palace" is used as epithet for "Tibetan Government". Compass directions indicate the location of the Buddhist emblems.

Numbers for Obverse Types A & B

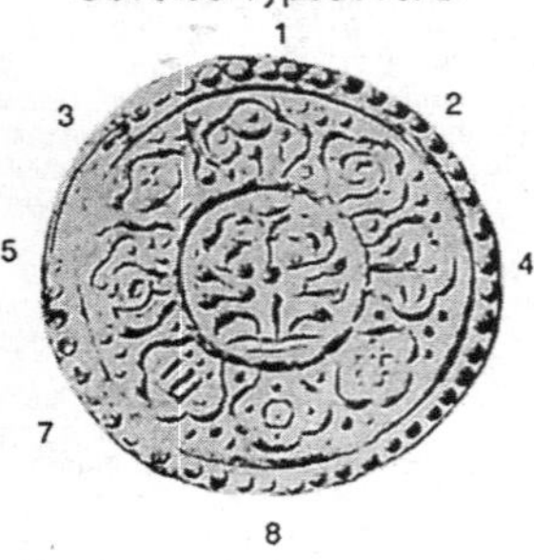

Numbers for Obverse Types C thru H

1. Umbrella of sovereignty.
2. Two golden fish of good fortune.
3. Amphora of ambrosia.
4. Lotus.
5. Conch shell.
6. Emblem of endless birth.
7. Banner of victory.
8. Wheel of empire.

Reverse - All Types

དགའ་	dGa'	*Ga-*
ལྡན་	lDan	*den*
ཕྱོགས་	Phyogs	*Tschog-*
ལས་	Las	*le*
རྣམ་	rNam	*Nam-*
རྒྱལ་	rGyal	*gyel*

Based on the ornamentation in the outer angles between the petals on both sides of the coin, the Ga-Den Tangkas can be differentiated in the following 8 types, A-H.

Type	Outer Obv.	Water-line	Outer Rev.	Rev. Ctr.
A	⁖	None	﹏	Pellet
B	⁖	2 lines	﹏	3 Crescents
C	⁖	1 line	﹏	2 Crescents
D	⁘	1 line	⁖	2 Crescents
E	﹏	1 line	⁖	2 Crescents
F	•	1 line	⁖	2 Crescents
G	None	1 line	none	2 Crescents
H	•	1 line	•	3 Crescents

Within these types, changes in the order, design, and style of the 8 lucky signs or significant errors constitute subtypes. The sutypes appearing in this catalog are not the only ones. Some subtypes show a wide range of styles and die varieties. Weights given include 95 percent of the indicated types.

Error strikes with muled reverses exist. Specimens of Types D, E, and F with lumps are known, reportedly containing gold, probably used by high lamas in their offerings.

Obverse

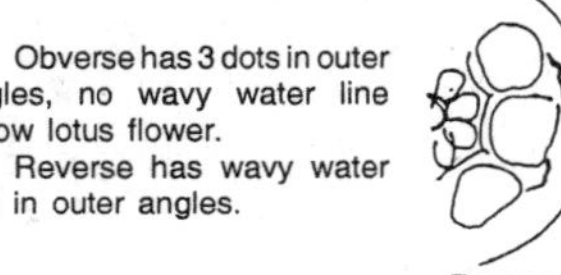

Obverse has 3 dots in outer angles, no wavy water line below lotus flower.

Reverse has wavy water line in outer angles.

Reverse

Y# A13.1 TANGKA

Silver **Obv:** No wavy water line below 3 separate lotus stems, fish (NE) swim clockwise **Note:** Weight varies: 5.08-5.22 grams.

Date	Mintage	Good	VG	F	VF	XF
ND(ca.1840)	—	15.00	25.00	40.00	60.00	—

Note: One variety has the reverse central flower buds solid rather than hollow

Y# A13.2 TANGKA

Silver **Obv:** Lotus stems joined, cruder style, fish (NE) swim clockwise and counterclockwise **Note:** Weight varies: 5.08-5.22 grams.

Date	Mintage	Good	VG	F	VF	XF
ND(ca.1840)	—	15.00	25.00	40.00	60.00	—

Obverse has 3 dots in outer angles, double wavy water line below lotus flower.

Reverse has wavy water line in outer angles.

Obverse

Reverse

Y# B13.1 TANGKA

Silver **Obv:** Doubled wavy water line below sytlized lotus, fish swim counterclockwise **Note:** Type B. Weight varies: 4.4-4.6 grams. Smaller flan.

Date	Mintage	Good	VG	F	VF	XF
ND(ca.1880)	—	5.00	7.00	11.00	18.00	—

Y# B13.2 TANGKA

Silver **Obv:** Four dots (SW), boxy base (NW)

Date	Mintage	Good	VG	F	VF	XF
ND(ca.1882)	—	3.00	4.50	7.00	12.00	—

Y# B13.3 TANGKA

Silver **Rev:** Outer angles, hook opposite dot

Date	Mintage	Good	VG	F	VF	XF
ND(ca.1885)	—	15.00	25.00	35.00	55.00	—

Y# B13.4 TANGKA

Silver **Obv:** Single line base (NW)

Date	Mintage	Good	VG	F	VF	XF
ND(ca.1888)	—	3.00	5.00	8.00	14.00	—

Y# B13.5 TANGKA

Silver **Obv:** No dots (W)

Date	Mintage	Good	VG	F	VF	XF
ND(ca.1891)	—	3.00	5.00	7.00	14.00	—

Y# B13.6 TANGKA

Silver **Obv:** Emblems rotated 90 degrees counterclockwise in relation to central design

Date	Mintage	Good	VG	F	VF	XF
ND(ca.1892)	—	125	175	250	325	—

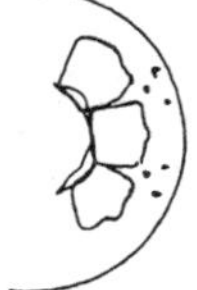

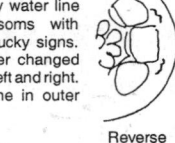

Obverse has 3 dots in outer angles, single wavy water line below lotus blossoms with changed order of lucky signs. Style of lotus flower changed with 3 small leaves left and right.

Wavy water line in outer angles.

Obverse

Reverse

Y# C13.1 TANGKA

Silver **Rev:** Central wheel spokes extend to octagon **Note:** Weight varies: 4.40-4.60 grams.

Date	Mintage	VG	F	VF	XF	Unc
ND(ca.1895-96)	—	4.00	6.00	9.00	13.50	—

Y# C13.2 TANGKA

Silver **Rev:** Spokes do not extend

Date	Mintage	Good	VG	F	VF	XF
ND(ca.1895)	—	3.50	5.00	7.00	14.00	—

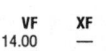

Obverse and reverse have 3 dots in outer angles. The obverse has single wavy water line below lotus flower.

Obverse Reverse

Y# D13.1 TANGKA
Silver **Obv:** Dots rising (N) **Note:** Weight varies: 4.6-4.8 grams.

Date	Mintage	Good	VG	F	VF	XF
ND(ca.1896)	—	3.00	4.50	7.00	12.00	—

Y# D13.2 TANGKA
Silver **Obv:** Dots hanging (N), five dots (NW)

Date	Mintage	Good	VG	F	VF	XF
ND(ca.1897)	—	3.00	4.50	7.00	12.00	—

Y# D13.3 TANGKA
Silver **Obv:** Eight dots (NW)

Date	Mintage	Good	VG	F	VF	XF
ND(ca.1898)	—	3.00	4.50	7.00	12.00	—

Y# D13.4 TANGKA
Silver **Obv:** (W) resembles (N)

Date	Mintage	Good	VG	F	VF	XF
ND(ca.1899)	—	3.00	4.50	7.00	12.00	—

Y# D13.5 TANGKA
Silver **Obv:** Seven dots around lotus center uniform edge and thickness

Date	Mintage	Good	VG	F	VF	XF
ND(ca.1899)	—	75.00	100	150	225	—

Obverse has wavy water line in outer angles. New style lotus without 3 small leaves to left and right.

Reverse has 3 dots in outer angles, wheel with spokes.

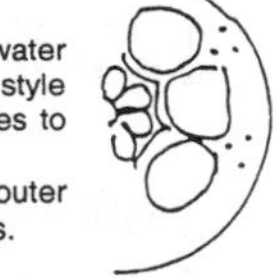

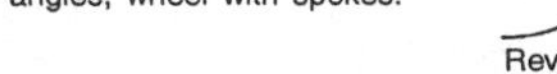

Obverse Reverse

Y# E13.1 TANGKA
Silver **Obv:** Dot to left and right of lotus **Note:** Weight varies: 4.60-4.80 grams. Prev. Y#13.4.

Date	Mintage	VG	F	VF	XF	Unc
ND(ca.1899-1907)	—	3.00	4.00	7.00	12.00	—

Y# E13.2 TANGKA
Silver **Obv:** Similar to Y#E13.1

Date	Mintage	Good	VG	F	VF	XF
ND(ca.1899-1907)	—	150	250	400	600	—

PATTERNS

Including off metal strikes

KM#	Date	Mintage	Identification	Mkt Val
Pn1	ND (1851-61)	—	1/2 Sho. Silver. Hsien Feng	—
Pn2	ND(1851-61)	—	Sho. Silver. Hsien Feng	—

TIMOR

COLONY

COUNTERMARKED COINAGE

100 Avos = 1 Pataca

KM# 8.1 8 REALES
Silver **Countermark:** Maltese cross **Note:** Countermark on Mexico, Chihuahua 8 Reales, KM#377.2.

CM Date	Host Date	Good	VG	F	VF	XF
ND(1900)	1890	75.00	125	200	325	—
Note: Other dates 1891, 1892, 1893, 1894, 1895 1896 are reported but mints are unknown						
ND(1900)	1890MM	75.00	125	200	325	—

KM# 8.2 8 REALES
Silver **Countermark:** Maltese cross **Note:** Countermark on Mexico, Potosi 8 Reales, KM#377.2

CM Date	Host Date	Good	VG	F	VF	XF
ND(1900)	1886LC	100	165	275	450	—

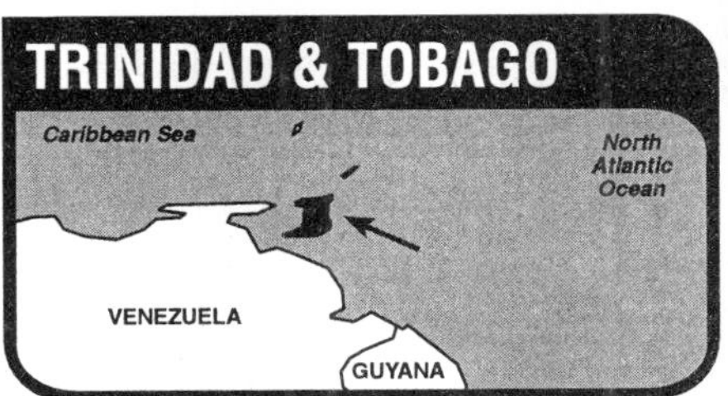

The Republic of Trinidad and Tobago is situated 7 miles (11 km.) off the coast of Venezuela, has an area of 1,981 sq. mi. (5,130 sq. km.) and a population of *1.2 million. Capital: Port-of-Spain. The island of Trinidad contains the world's largest natural asphalt bog. Birds of Paradise live on little Tobago, the only place outside of their native New Guinea where they can be found in a wild state. Petroleum and petroleum products are the mainstay of the economy. Petroleum products, crude oil and sugar are exported.

Columbus discovered Trinidad and Tobago in 1498. Trinidad remained under Spanish rule from the time of its settlement in 1592 until its capture by the British in 1797. It was ceded to the British in 1802. Tobago was occupied at various times by the French, Dutch and English before being ceded to Britain in 1814. Trinidad and Tobago were merged into a single colony in 1888. The colony was part of the Federation of the West Indies until Aug. 31, 1962, when it became independent. A new constitution establishing a republican form of government was adopted on Aug. 1, 1976. Trinidad and Tobago is a member of the Commonwealth of Nations. The President is Chief of State. The Prime Minister is Head of Government.

RULERS
British, until 1976

MONETARY SYSTEM
100 Cents = 1 Dollar

COLONIAL

CUT & COUNTERMARKED COINAGE

KM# A3 3 PENCE
Silver **Note:** Cut quarter segment from Spanish Colonial 1 Real

Date	Mintage	Good	VG	F	VF	XF
ND(1804)	—	20.00	30.00	50.00	85.00	—

KM# A6 6 PENCE
Silver **Note:** Cut half segment from Spanish Colonial 1 Real

Date	Mintage	Good	VG	F	VF	XF
ND(1804)	—	20.00	30.00	50.00	85.00	—

KM# A9 SHILLING
Silver **Countermark:** T **Note:** Countermark on 1/8 or 1/9 cut of Spanish or Spanish Colonial 8 Reales. Weight varies: 3.00-3.31 grams.

Date	Mintage	Good	VG	F	VF	XF
ND(1798-1801)	—	400	500	850	1,250	—

Note: The attribution of this type has been questioned

KM# A10 SHILLING
2.9800 g., Silver **Countermark:** T **Note:** Countermark on center plug cut from Spanish or Spanish Colonial 8 Reales, C#26.

Date	Mintage	Good	VG	F	VF	XF
ND(1811)	25,000	120	150	260	425	—

KM# A13 9 SHILLINGS
Silver **Countermark:** T **Note:** Countermark on holed Spanish or Spanish Colonial 8 Reales.

Date	Mintage	Good	VG	F	VF	XF
ND(1811)	25,000	400	500	750	1,000	—

KM# A14 9 SHILLINGS
Silver **Note:** Similar to K#13 but without T countermark.

Date	Mintage	Good	VG	F	VF	XF
ND(1811)	Inc. above	300	400	600	850	—

TOKEN COINAGE

KM# Tn2 FARTHING
Copper **Issuer:** J. G. D'ade & Co.

Date	Mintage	VG	F	VF	XF	Unc
ND(1874)	10,000	100	225	450	750	—

KM# Tn3 1/2 STAMPEE
Copper **Issuer:** H. E. Rapseys

Date	Mintage	VG	F	VF	XF	Unc
ND(1860)	—	100	200	400	650	—

KM# Tn1.1 1/2 PENNY
Copper **Issuer:** Francois Declos **Countermark:** FD **Note:** Countermark on various types of 1/2 Penny size coins including French Colonial.

Date	Mintage	VG	F	VF	XF	Unc
ND(1854-74)	—	25.00	50.00	75.00	125	—

KM# Tn1.2 1/2 PENNY
Copper **Issuer:** Francois Declos **Countermark:** FD **Note:** Countermark on H. E. Rapseys 1/2 Stampee, Tn3.

Date	Mintage	VG	F	VF	XF	Unc
ND(1854-74)	—	50.00	100	175	275	—

TUNISIA

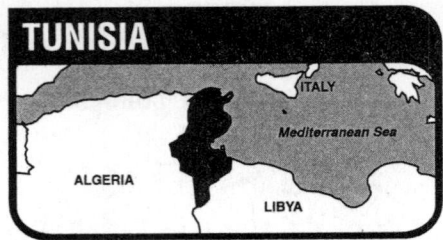

Tunisia, located on the northern coast of Africa between Algeria and Libya, has an area of 63,170sq. mi. (163,610 sq. km.).

Tunisia, settled by the Phoenicians in the 12th century B.C., was the center of the seafaring Carthaginian empire. After the total destruction of Carthage, Tunisia became part of Rome's African province. It remained a part of the Roman Empire (except for the 439-533 interval of Vandal conquest) until taken by the Arabs, 648, who administered it until the Turkish invasion of 1570. Under Turkish control, the public revenue was heavily dependent upon the piracy of Mediterranean shipping, an endeavor that wasn't abandoned until 1819 when a coalition of powers threatened appropriate reprisal. Deprived of its major source of income, Tunisia underwent a financial regression that ended in bankruptcy, enabling France to establish a protectorate over the country in 1881.

MINT MARKS
A - Paris, AH1308/1891-AH1348/1928
(a) - Paris, privy marks, AH1349/1929-AH1376/1957

FRENCH PROTECTORATE

Muhammad al-Sadio Bey
1881-82AD

HAMMERED COINAGE

KM# 201 8 KHARUB
1.6000 g., Silver, 18.5 mm.

Date	Mintage	F	VF	XF	Unc
AH1299	—	200	400	750	1,250

KM# 202 PIASTRE
3.2000 g., Silver

Date	Mintage	F	VF	XF	Unc
AH1299	—	200	400	750	1,250

KM# 203 2 PIASTRES
6.4000 g., Silver, 26.5 mm.

Date	Mintage	F	VF	XF	Unc
AH1299	—	200	400	750	1,250

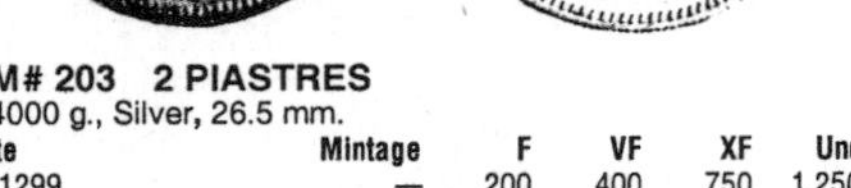

KM# 200 25 PIASTRES
4.9200 g., 0.9000 Gold .1424 oz. AGW, 20 mm.

Date	Mintage	F	VF	XF	Unc
AH1298	—	100	250	500	750
AH1300	—	150	300	600	950

KM# 204 50 PIASTRES
9.8400 g., 0.9000 Gold .2847 oz. AGW, 26 mm.

Date	Mintage	F	VF	XF	Unc
AH1299	—	300	400	650	1,000

Ali Bey
AH1299-1320/1882-1902AD

HAMMERED COINAGE

KM# 205 8 KHARUB
1.6000 g., Silver

Date	Mintage	F	VF	XF	Unc
AH1300	—	15.00	25.00	55.00	115
AH1301	—	15.00	25.00	55.00	115
AH1302	—	15.00	25.00	55.00	115
AH1303	—	15.00	25.00	55.00	115
AH1304	—	15.00	25.00	55.00	115
AH1305	—	15.00	25.00	55.00	115
AH1306	—	15.00	25.00	55.00	115
AH1307	—	15.00	25.00	55.00	115
AH1308	—	15.00	25.00	55.00	115

KM# 206 PIASTRE
3.2000 g., Silver

Date	Mintage	F	VF	XF	Unc
AH1300	—	18.00	30.00	75.00	155
AH1301	—	18.00	30.00	75.00	155
AH1302	—	18.00	30.00	75.00	155
AH1303	—	18.00	30.00	75.00	155
AH1304	—	18.00	30.00	75.00	155
AH1305	—	18.00	30.00	75.00	155
AH1306	—	18.00	30.00	75.00	155
AH1307	—	18.00	30.00	75.00	155
AH1308	—	18.00	30.00	75.00	155

KM# 215 PIASTRE
3.2000 g., Silver **Note:** Modified design.

Date	Mintage	F	VF	XF	Unc
AH1308	—	20.00	35.00	75.00	150

KM# 207 2 PIASTRES
6.4000 g., Silver

Date	Mintage	F	VF	XF	Unc
AH1300	—	30.00	50.00	125	275
AH1301	—	30.00	50.00	125	275
AH1302	—	30.00	50.00	125	275
AH1303	—	30.00	50.00	125	275
AH1304	—	30.00	50.00	125	275
AH1305	—	30.00	50.00	125	275
AH1306	—	30.00	50.00	125	275
AH1307	—	30.00	50.00	125	275
AH1308	—	30.00	50.00	125	275

KM# 210 2 PIASTRES
6.4000 g., Silver **Note:** Modified design.

Date	Mintage	F	VF	XF	Unc
AH1308	—	40.00	70.00	125	275

KM# 208 4 PIASTRES
12.8000 g., Silver

Date	Mintage	F	VF	XF	Unc
AH1300	—	30.00	50.00	150	325
AH1301	—	30.00	50.00	150	325
AH1302	—	30.00	50.00	150	325
AH1303	—	30.00	50.00	150	325
AH1304	—	30.00	50.00	150	325
AH1305	—	30.00	50.00	150	325
AH1306	—	30.00	50.00	150	325

Date	Mintage	F	VF	XF	Unc
AH1307	—	30.00	50.00	150	325
AH1308	—	30.00	50.00	150	325

KM# 216 4 PIASTRES
12.8000 g., Silver **Note:** Modified design.

Date	Mintage	F	VF	XF	Unc
AH1308	—	40.00	70.00	180	350

KM# 209 25 PIASTRES
4.9200 g., 0.9000 Gold .1424 oz. AGW

Date	Mintage	F	VF	XF	Unc
AH1300	—	85.00	110	150	250
AH1302	—	85.00	110	150	250

KM# A212 25 PIASTRES (15 Francs)
4.9200 g., 0.9000 Gold .1424 oz. AGW **Obv:** Value"15F" below Arabic legend

Date	Mintage	F	VF	XF	Unc
AH1304	80,000	85.00	110	175	300

KM# 214 25 PIASTRES (15 Francs)
4.9200 g., 0.9000 Gold .1424 oz. AGW **Rev:** Modified design

Date	Mintage	F	VF	XF	Unc
AH1307A	52,000	85.00	110	175	300
AH1308A	120,000	85.00	110	175	300
AH1308A	—	Value: 2,000			

KM# 212 25 PIASTRES (15 Francs)
4.9200 g., 0.9000 Gold .1424 oz. AGW **Obv:** Value"15-F" divided by Arabic legend

Date	Mintage	F	VF	XF	Unc
AH1308	Inc. above	85.00	110	175	300

KM# 213 50 PIASTRES
9.8400 g., 0.9000 Gold .2847 oz. AGW

Date	Mintage	F	VF	XF	Unc
AH1304	—	200	350	500	750

KM# 211 100 PIASTRES
19.6800 g., 0.9000 Gold .5695 oz. AGW

Date	Mintage	F	VF	XF	Unc
AH1303	—	300	600	1,000	1,500

DECIMAL COINAGE

100 Centimes = 1 Franc

The following coins all bear French inscriptions on one side, Arabic on the other, and usually have both AH and AD dates. Except for KM#246-48, they are struck in the name of the Tunisian Bey.

KM# 219 CENTIME
Bronze **Obv. Legend:** "Ali"

Date	Mintage	F	VF	XF	Unc
AH1308	500,000	3.00	6.00	12.00	28.00

KM# 220 2 CENTIMES
Bronze **Obv. Legend:** "Ali"

Date	Mintage	F	VF	XF	Unc
AH1308//1891 A	1,000,000	1.25	2.25	5.00	15.00

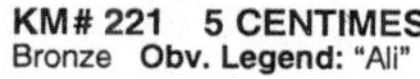

KM# 221 5 CENTIMES
Bronze **Obv. Legend:** "Ali"

Date	Mintage	F	VF	XF	Unc
AH1308//1891 A	4,300,000	1.00	2.00	7.00	25.00
AH1308//1891 A Proof	—	Value: 50.00			
AH1309//1892 A	1,192,000	1.25	2.50	8.00	25.00
AH1310//1893 A	1,008,000	1.50	3.00	10.00	28.00

KM# 222 10 CENTIMES
Bronze **Obv. Legend:** "Ali"

Date	Mintage	F	VF	XF	Unc
AH1308//1891 A	2,600,000	2.00	4.00	8.00	25.00
AH1309//1892 A	1,374,000	2.00	4.00	10.00	28.00
AH1310//1892 A	—	35.00	75.00	125	200
AH1310//1893 A	26,000	35.00	75.00	125	200

KM# 223 50 CENTIMES
2.5000 g., 0.8350 Silver .0671 oz. ASW **Obv. Legend:** ALI

Date	Mintage	F	VF	XF	Unc
AH1308/1891A	1,470,000	8.00	15.00	25.00	50.00
AH1309/1892A	1,000	—	—	100	175
AH1310/1893A	1,000	—	—	100	175
AH1311/1893A	—	—	—	100	175
AH1311/1894A	1,000	—	—	100	175
AH1313/1895A	1,000	—	—	100	175
AH1314/1896A	1,000	—	—	100	175
AH1315/1897A	1,000	—	—	100	175
AH1316/1898A	1,000	—	—	100	175
AH1317/1899A	1,000	—	—	100	175
AH1318/1900A	1,000	—	—	100	175

KM# 224 FRANC
5.0000 g., 0.8350 Silver .1342 oz. ASW **Obv. Legend:** ALI

Date	Mintage	F	VF	XF	Unc
AH1308/1891A	1,575,000	10.00	20.00	35.00	50.00
AH1309/1892A	1,575,000	10.00	20.00	35.00	50.00
AH1310/1893A	703	—	—	135	225
AH1311/1894A	703	—	—	135	225
AH1313/1895A	703	—	—	135	225
AH1314/1896A	703	—	—	135	225
AH1315/1897A	703	—	—	135	225
AH1316/1898A	703	—	—	135	225
AH1317/1899A	703	—	—	135	225
AH1318/1900A	703	—	—	135	225

KM# 225 2 FRANCS
10.0000 g., 0.8350 Silver .2685 oz. ASW **Obv. Legend:** ALI

Date	Mintage	F	VF	XF	Unc
AH1308/1891A	595,000	10.00	20.00	35.00	70.00
AH1309/1892A	432,000	10.00	20.00	35.00	70.00
AH1310/1893A	300	—	—	150	250
AH1311/1893A	—	—	—	150	250
AH1311/1894A	300	—	—	150	250
AH1313/1895A	300	—	—	150	250
AH1314/1896A	300	—	—	150	250
AH1315/1897A	300	—	—	150	250
AH1316/1898A	300	—	—	150	250
AH1317/1899A	300	—	—	150	250
AH1318/1900A	300	—	—	150	250

KM# 226 10 FRANCS
3.2258 g., 0.9000 Gold .0933 oz. AGW **Obv. Legend:** ALI

Date	Mintage	F	VF	XF	Unc
AH1308/1891A	400,000	—	50.00	70.00	100
AH1308/1891A Proof	—	Value: 1,250			
AH1309/1892A	83	—	—	450	850
AH1310/1893A	83	—	—	450	850
AH1311/1894A	83	—	—	450	850
AH1313/1895A	83	—	—	450	850
AH1314/1896A	83	—	—	450	850
AH1315/1897A	83	—	—	450	850
AH1316/1898A	83	—	—	450	850
AH1317/1899A	83	—	—	450	850
AH1318/1900A	83	—	—	450	850

KM# 227 20 FRANCS
6.4516 g., 0.9000 Gold .1867 oz. AGW **Obv. Legend:** ALI

Date	Mintage	F	VF	XF	Unc
AH1308/1891A	400,000	—	BV	85.00	110
AH1308/1891 Proof	—	Value: 1,500			
AH1309/1892	937,000	—	BV	85.00	110
AH1310/1892A	Inc. above	—	BV	85.00	110
AH1310/1893A	35,000	—	BV	85.00	110
AH1311/1894A	20	—	—	550	1,000
AH1313/1895A	20	—	—	550	1,000
AH1314/1896A	20	—	—	550	1,000
AH1315/1897A	164,000	—	BV	85.00	110
AH1316/1898A	150,000	—	BV	85.00	110
AH1316/1899A	150,000	—	BV	85.00	110
AH1318/1900A	150,000	—	BV	85.00	110

PATTERNS

Including off metal strikes

KM#	Date	Mintage	Identification	Mkt Val
Pn13	AH1305	—	25 Piastres. Gold. KM#212.	700

TUNIS

Tunis, the capital and major seaport of Tunisia, existed in the Carthaginian era, but its importance dates only from the Moslem conquest, following which it became a major center of Arab power and prosperity. Spain seized it in 1535, lost it in 1564, retook it in 1573 and ceded it to the Turks in 1574. Thereafter the history of Tunis merged with that of Tunisia.

RULERS

Ottoman, until 1881

LOCAL RULERS

Hammuda Pasha II,
AH1196-1229/1782-1813AD
'Uthman,
AH1229-1230/1813-1814AD
Mahmud Pasha,
AH1230-1239/1814-1824AD
Husayn II,
AH1239-1251/1824-1835AD
Mustapha,
AH1251-1253/1835-1837AD
Ahmad I Pasha,
AH1253-1271/1837-1855AD
Muhammad Bey,
AH1271-1276/1855-1859AD
Ali Bey, AH1299-1320/1882-1902AD

NOTE: All coins struck until AH1298/1881AD bear the name of the Ottoman Sultan; the name of the Bey of Tunis was added in AH1272/1855AD. After AH1298, when the French established their protectorate, only the Bey's name appears on the coin until AH1376/1956AD.

MINT

تونس

Tunis

With exceptions noted in their proper place, all coins were struck at Tunis prior to AH1308/1891AD. Thereafter, all coins were struck at Paris with mint mark A until 1928, symbols of the mint from 1929-1957.

MONETARY SYSTEM

1847-1871

1 Burbe (Bourbe) = 104 Fals = 1 Riyal Sebili (Piastre)
1 Asper = 52 Nasri = 1 Riyal Sebili
16 Kharub (Caroub) = 1 Riyal Sebili
3 1/4 Nasri = 1 Kharub = 1/16 Riyal Sebili
6 1/2 Nasri = 2 Kharub = 1/8 Riyal Sebili
13 Nasri = 4 Kharub = 1/4 Riyal Sebili

Arabic name	French name	Value
Qafsi of Fals	Bourbine	1/12 Nasri
Raqiq	(Burben)	
Fals	Bourbe	6 Qafsi or 1/2 Nasri
Nasri	Asper	1/52 Riyal
Kharub	Caroub	1/16 Riyal
1/8 Riyal	1/8 Piastre	1 Kharub
1/4 Riyal	1/4 Piastre	4 Kharub
1/2 Riyal	1/2 Piastre	8 Kharub
Riyal	Piastre	16 Kharub

OTTOMAN EMPIRE

Selim III
AH1203-22/1789-1807AD

HAMMERED COINAGE

KM# 75 NASRI
Billon, 9x9 mm. **Obv. Legend:** "Sultan Selim" **Rev:** Date and mint **Shape:** Square

Date	Mintage	Good	VG	F	VF	XF
AH1216	—	30.00	60.00	100	150	—

KM# 74 4 KHARUB
4.0000 g., Billon

Date	Mintage	Good	VG	F	VF	XF
AH1216	—	50.00	100	150	250	—
AH1217	—	50.00	100	150	250	—

KM# 73 8 KHARUB
Billon, 27-28 mm. **Note:** Varieties of ornamentation exist. 7.10-7.70 grams. Similar to 1 Piastre, KM#72.

Date	Mintage	Good	VG	F	VF	XF
AH1216	—	15.00	25.00	42.00	85.00	—
AH1217	—	15.00	25.00	42.00	85.00	—
AH1218	—	15.00	25.00	42.00	85.00	—
AH1219	—	15.00	25.00	42.00	85.00	—
AH1220	—	15.00	25.00	42.00	85.00	—
AH1221	—	15.00	25.00	42.00	85.00	—
AH1222	—	15.00	25.00	42.00	85.00	—

KM# 72.2 PIASTRE
Billon **Rev:** Mint above date within ornamental frame **Note:** Varieties of ornamentation exist. 14.90-16.00 grams.

Date	Mintage	Good	VG	F	VF	XF
AH1216	—	18.00	30.00	50.00	95.00	—
AH1217	—	18.00	30.00	50.00	95.00	—
AH1218	—	18.00	30.00	50.00	95.00	—
AH1219	—	18.00	30.00	50.00	95.00	—
AH1220	—	18.00	30.00	50.00	95.00	—
AH1221	—	18.00	30.00	50.00	95.00	—
AH1222	—	18.00	30.00	50.00	95.00	—

Mustafa IV
AH1222-23/1807-08AD

HAMMERED COINAGE

KM# 78 4 KHARUB
3.5000 g., Billon, 21 mm. **Note:** Similar to 1 Piastre, KM#72.

Date	Mintage	Good	VG	F	VF	XF
AH1223	—	100	200	400	650	—

KM# 76 8 KHARUB
7.5000 g., Billon, 27 mm.

Date	Mintage	Good	VG	F	VF	XF
AH1222	—	125	225	450	750	—
AH1223	—	125	225	450	750	—

KM# 77 PIASTRE
16.0000 g., Billon, 35 mm.

Date	Mintage	Good	VG	F	VF	XF
AH1222	—	100	175	300	500	—
AH1223	—	100	175	300	500	—

Mahmud II
AH1223-25/1808-39AD

HAMMERED COINAGE

KM# 85 BURBEN
0.8000 g., Copper

Date	Mintage	Good	VG	F	VF	XF
AH1230	—	15.00	35.00	75.00	125	—
AH1231	—	15.00	35.00	75.00	125	—
AH1232	—	15.00	35.00	75.00	125	—

KM# 83 NASRI
0.2000 g., Billon, 8 mm. **Shape:** Square

Date	Mintage	Good	VG	F	VF	XF
AH1228	—	30.00	60.00	120	250	—
AH1229	—	30.00	60.00	120	250	—

KM# 91 KHARUB
Billon **Note:** Weight varies: 0.60-0.70 grams.

Date	Mintage	Good	VG	F	VF	XF
AH1229	—	—	—	—	—	—
AH1241	—	6.00	10.00	17.50	30.00	—
AH1242	—	6.00	10.00	17.50	30.00	—
AH1249	—	3.00	5.00	10.00	22.00	—
AH1250	—	3.00	5.00	10.00	22.00	—
AH1251	—	3.00	5.00	10.00	22.00	—
AH1252	—	3.00	5.00	10.00	22.00	—
AH1253	—	3.00	5.00	10.00	22.00	—
AH1254	—	3.00	5.00	10.00	22.00	—
AH1255	—	3.00	5.00	10.00	22.00	—

KM# 92 2 KHARUB
1.3000 g., Billon, 16 mm.

Date	Mintage	Good	VG	F	VF	XF
AH1243	—	20.00	30.00	60.00	85.00	—
AH1244	—	20.00	30.00	60.00	85.00	—

KM# 81 4 KHARUB
3.5000 g., Billon, 21 mm.

Date	Mintage	Good	VG	F	VF	XF
AH1223	—	30.00	60.00	120	200	—
AH1228	—	30.00	60.00	120	200	—
AH1231	—	30.00	60.00	120	200	—

KM# 88 4 KHARUB
2.5000 g., Billon, 20 mm.

Date	Mintage	Good	VG	F	VF	XF
AH1240	—	10.00	20.00	50.00	100	—
AH1241	—	10.00	20.00	50.00	100	—
AH1242	—	10.00	20.00	50.00	100	—
AH1243	—	10.00	20.00	50.00	100	—
AH1245	—	10.00	20.00	50.00	100	—
AH1246	—	10.00	20.00	50.00	100	—
AH1249	—	10.00	20.00	50.00	100	—
AH1250	—	10.00	20.00	50.00	100	—
AH1252	—	10.00	20.00	50.00	100	—
AH1253	—	10.00	20.00	50.00	100	—
AH1254	—	10.00	20.00	50.00	100	—
AH1255	—	10.00	20.00	50.00	100	—

KM# 84 8 KHARUB
7.5000 g., Billon, 27 mm.

Date	Mintage	Good	VG	F	VF	XF
AH1228	—	40.00	75.00	150	185	—
AH1229	—	40.00	75.00	150	185	—
AH1230	—	40.00	75.00	150	185	—
AH1231	—	40.00	75.00	150	185	—
AH1232	—	40.00	75.00	150	185	—
AH1233	—	40.00	75.00	150	185	—

KM# 89 8 KHARUB
5.0000 g., Billon, 26 mm.

Date	Mintage	Good	VG	F	VF	XF
AH1240	—	10.00	20.00	50.00	100	—
AH1241	—	10.00	20.00	50.00	100	—
AH1242	—	10.00	20.00	50.00	100	—
AH1243	—	10.00	20.00	50.00	100	—
AH1244	—	10.00	20.00	50.00	100	—
AH1245	—	10.00	20.00	50.00	100	—
AH1246	—	10.00	20.00	50.00	100	—
AH1247	—	10.00	20.00	50.00	100	—
AH1248	—	10.00	20.00	50.00	100	—
AH1251	—	10.00	20.00	50.00	100	—
AH1252	—	10.00	20.00	50.00	100	—
AH1253	—	10.00	20.00	50.00	100	—
AH1254	—	10.00	20.00	50.00	100	—

KM# 82 PIASTRE
16.0000 g., Billon

Date	Mintage	Good	VG	F	VF	XF
AH1225	—	20.00	40.00	70.00	115	—
AH1226	—	20.00	40.00	70.00	115	—
AH1227	—	20.00	40.00	70.00	115	—
AH1228	—	20.00	40.00	70.00	115	—
AH1229	—	20.00	40.00	70.00	115	—
AH1230	—	20.00	40.00	70.00	115	—
AH1231	—	20.00	40.00	70.00	115	—
AH1232	—	20.00	40.00	70.00	115	—
AH1233	—	25.00	50.00	80.00	125	—
AH1234	—	40.00	75.00	125	175	—

KM# 90 PIASTRE
Billon **Note:** Weight varies: 11.00-11.50 grams. Varieties in ornamentation exist.

Date	Mintage	Good	VG	F	VF	XF
AH1240	—	10.00	15.00	25.00	50.00	—
AH1241	—	10.00	15.00	25.00	50.00	—
AH1242	—	10.00	15.00	25.00	50.00	—
AH1243	—	10.00	15.00	25.00	50.00	—
AH1244	—	10.00	15.00	25.00	50.00	—
AH1245	—	10.00	15.00	25.00	50.00	—
AH1246	—	10.00	15.00	25.00	50.00	—
AH1247	—	10.00	15.00	25.00	50.00	—
AH1248	—	10.00	15.00	25.00	50.00	—
AH1249	—	10.00	15.00	25.00	50.00	—
AH1250	—	10.00	15.00	25.00	50.00	—
AH1251	—	10.00	15.00	25.00	50.00	—
AH1252	—	10.00	15.00	25.00	50.00	—
AH1253	—	10.00	15.00	25.00	50.00	—
AH1254	—	10.00	15.00	25.00	50.00	—
AH1255	—	10.00	15.00	25.00	50.00	—

KM# 86 2 PIASTRES
27.4000 g., Billon, 39 mm.

Date	Mintage	Good	VG	F	VF	XF
AH1232	—	—	—	—	—	—

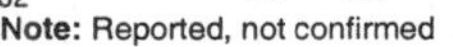

Note: Reported, not confirmed

KM# 93 2 PIASTRES
23.0000 g., Billon, 39 mm.

Date	Mintage	Good	VG	F	VF	XF
AH1244	—	45.00	75.00	150	200	—
AH1245	—	45.00	75.00	150	200	—
AH1246	—	45.00	75.00	150	200	—
AH1248	—	75.00	125	175	350	—

KM# 87 SULTANI
0.9860 Gold, 20 mm. **Note:** Weight varies: 2.50-3.20 grams.

Date	Mintage	F	VF	XF	Unc
AH1236	—	200	300	425	600

Sultan Abdul Mejid
AH1255-77/1839-61AD

PRE-REFORM COINAGE

KM# 97 4 KHARUB
2.7700 g., Billon, 20 mm.

Date	Mintage	Good	VG	F	VF	XF
AH1256	—	50.00	80.00	200	400	—

KM# 98 8 KHARUB
5.0000 g., Billon, 26 mm.

Date	Mintage	Good	VG	F	VF	XF
AH1256	—	50.00	80.00	200	400	—

KM# 96 PIASTRE
11.0000 g., Billon, 32 mm.

Date	Mintage	Good	VG	F	VF	XF
AH1255	—	35.00	60.00	150	200	—

REFORM COINAGE

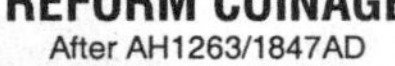

After AH1263/1847AD

KM# 101 FALS
1.0000 g., Copper

Date	Mintage	Good	VG	F	VF	XF
AH1263	—	2.00	4.00	10.00	20.00	—
AH1264	—	2.00	4.00	10.00	20.00	—
AH1265	—	2.00	4.00	10.00	20.00	—
AH1266	—	2.00	4.00	10.00	20.00	—
AH1267	—	2.00	4.00	10.00	20.00	—

KM# 102 NASRI
2.0000 g., Copper

Date	Mintage	Good	VG	F	VF	XF
AH1263	—	2.00	4.00	7.00	15.00	—
AH1264	—	2.00	4.00	7.00	15.00	—
AH1265	—	2.00	4.00	7.00	15.00	—
AH1266	—	2.00	4.00	7.00	15.00	—
AH1267	—	2.00	4.00	7.00	15.00	—

KM# 103.1 3 NASRI
5.5000 g., Copper **Edge:** Reeded

Date	Mintage	Good	VG	F	VF	XF
AH1263	—	4.00	8.00	15.00	30.00	—

KM# 103.2 3 NASRI
5.5000 g., Copper **Edge:** Plain

Date	Mintage	Good	VG	F	VF	XF
AH1264	—	2.50	4.00	7.50	15.00	—
AH1265	—	2.50	4.00	7.50	15.00	—
AH1266	—	2.50	4.00	7.50	15.00	—
AH1267	—	2.50	4.00	7.50	15.00	—
AH1268	—	2.50	4.00	7.50	15.00	—
AH1269	—	2.50	4.00	7.50	15.00	—

KM# 104.1 6 NASRI
11.5000 g., Copper **Edge:** Reeded

Date	Mintage	Good	VG	F	VF	XF
AH1263	—	8.00	15.00	35.00	50.00	—

KM# 104.2 6 NASRI
11.5000 g., Copper **Edge:** Plain

Date	Mintage	Good	VG	F	VF	XF
AH1263	—	4.00	8.00	15.00	25.00	—
AH1264	—	2.00	4.00	10.00	20.00	—
AH1265	—	2.00	4.00	10.00	20.00	—
AH1266	—	2.00	4.00	10.00	20.00	—
AH1267	—	2.00	4.00	10.00	20.00	—
AH1268	—	2.00	4.00	10.00	20.00	—
AH1269	—	1.00	2.00	5.00	12.00	—
AH1270	—	6.00	10.00	20.00	30.00	—
AH1271	—	6.00	10.00	20.00	30.00	—

KM# 106 2 PIASTRES

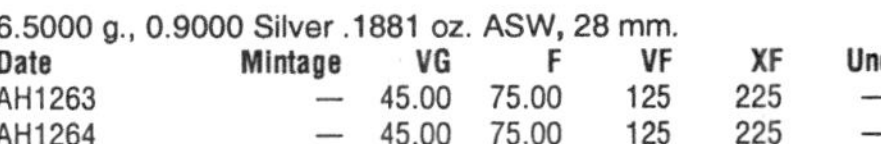

6.5000 g., 0.9000 Silver .1881 oz. ASW, 28 mm.

Date	Mintage	VG	F	VF	XF	Unc
AH1263	—	45.00	75.00	125	225	—
AH1264	—	45.00	75.00	125	225	—

KM# 109 2 PIASTRES
6.5000 g., 0.9000 Silver .1881 oz. ASW **Note:** Modified design.

Date	Mintage	VG	F	VF	XF	Unc
AH1267	—	40.00	67.50	100	185	—

KM# 107 5 PIASTRES
16.0000 g., 0.9000 Silver .4630 oz. ASW, 33 mm.

Date	Mintage	VG	F	VF	XF	Unc
AH1263	—	150	225	325	550	—
AH1264	—	150	225	325	550	—

KM# 108 5 PIASTRES
16.0000 g., 0.9000 Silver .4630 oz. ASW **Note:** Modified design.

Date	Mintage	VG	F	VF	XF	Unc
AH1265	—	50.00	80.00	140	250	—
AH1266	—	20.00	32.50	50.00	85.00	—
AH1267	—	20.00	32.50	50.00	85.00	—
AH1268	—	22.50	37.50	60.00	100	—
AH1269	—	50.00	80.00	140	250	—
AH1270	—	50.00	80.00	140	250	—
AH1271	—	20.00	32.50	50.00	85.00	—

Sultan Abdul Mejid with Muhammad Bey
AH1272-76/1856-59AD

HAMMERED COINAGE

KM# 112.1 3-1/4 NASRI
5.8000 g., Copper

Date	Mintage	Good	VG	F	VF	XF
AH1272	—	4.50	7.50	15.00	30.00	—
AH1273	—	4.50	7.50	15.00	30.00	—

KM# 112.2 3-1/4 NASRI
5.8000 g., Copper **Note:** Thick legend.

Date	Mintage	Good	VG	F	VF	XF
AH1272	—	4.50	7.50	15.00	30.00	—
AH1274	—	4.50	7.50	15.00	30.00	—

KM# 113.2 6 NASRI (6 Asper)
11.6000 g., Copper **Note:** Thick legend.

Date	Mintage	Good	VG	F	VF	XF
AH1273	—	2.75	4.50	10.00	20.00	—
AH1272	—	2.75	4.50	10.00	20.00	—
AH1274	—	2.75	4.50	10.00	20.00	—

KM# 113.1 6 NASRI (6 Asper)
11.6000 g., Copper **Note:** Thin legend.

Date	Mintage	Good	VG	F	VF	XF
AH1272	—	2.75	4.50	10.00	20.00	—
AH1273	—	2.75	4.50	10.00	20.00	—

KM# 115.1 13 NASRI
23.0000 g., Copper

Date	Mintage	Good	VG	F	VF	XF
AH1272	—	5.00	8.50	12.50	25.00	—
AH1273	—	5.00	8.50	12.50	25.00	—

KM# 115.2 13 NASRI
23.0000 g., Copper **Note:** Thick legend.

Date	Mintage	Good	VG	F	VF	XF
AH1273	—	5.00	8.50	12.50	25.00	—
AH1274	—	5.00	8.50	12.50	25.00	—
AH1275	—	6.00	10.00	15.00	30.00	—

KM# 132 2 KHARUB
0.4000 g., Silver

Date	Mintage	Good	VG	F	VF	XF
AH1273	—	10.00	18.00	50.00	90.00	—
AH1274	—	10.00	18.00	50.00	90.00	—
AH1275	—	10.00	18.00	50.00	90.00	—
AH1276	—	10.00	18.00	50.00	90.00	—

KM# 134.1 2 KHARUB
Silver **Note:** Thick legend.

Date	Mintage	Good	VG	F	VF	XF
AH1273	—	6.00	10.00	20.00	40.00	—
AH1274	—	6.00	10.00	20.00	40.00	—
AH1275	—	3.00	6.00	12.00	25.00	—
AH1276	—	5.00	8.00	15.00	30.00	—

KM# 134.2 2 KHARUB
Silver **Note:** Thin legend.

Date	Mintage	Good	VG	F	VF	XF
AH1276	—	12.00	18.00	28.00	45.00	—

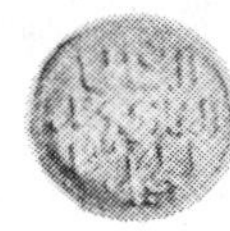 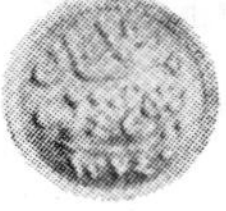

KM# 135 4 KHARUB
0.8000 g., Silver

Date	Mintage	VG	F	VF	XF	Unc
AH1274	—	20.00	35.00	100	150	—
AH1275	—	20.00	35.00	100	150	—

KM# 136 8 KHARUB
1.6000 g., Silver

Date	Mintage	VG	F	VF	XF	Unc
AH1274	—	20.00	45.00	100	180	—
AH1275	—	20.00	45.00	100	180	—

KM# 117.1 PIASTRE
3.2000 g., Silver **Note:** Thick legend.

Date	Mintage	VG	F	VF	XF	Unc
AH1272	—	25.00	40.00	100	180	—
AH1273	—	25.00	40.00	100	180	—

KM# 117.2 PIASTRE
3.2000 g., Silver **Note:** Thin legend.

Date	Mintage	VG	F	VF	XF	Unc
AH1272	—	25.00	40.00	100	180	—

KM# 118.1 2 PIASTRES
6.4000 g., Silver **Note:** Thick legend.

Date	Mintage	VG	F	VF	XF	Unc
AH1272	—	30.00	60.00	150	250	—

KM# 118.2 2 PIASTRES
6.4000 g., Silver **Note:** Thin legend.

Date	Mintage	VG	F	VF	XF	Unc
AH1272	—	30.00	60.00	150	270	—

KM# 119 3 PIASTRES
9.6000 g., Silver

Date	Mintage	VG	F	VF	XF	Unc
AH1272	—	100	150	300	450	—

KM# 120 4 PIASTRES
12.8000 g., Silver, 31 mm.

Date	Mintage	VG	F	VF	XF	Unc
AH1272	—	100	180	450	750	—

KM# 121 5 PIASTRES
16.0000 g., Silver, 33 mm.

Date	Mintage	VG	F	VF	XF	Unc
AH1272	—	150	300	800	1,200	—
AH1273	—	150	300	800	1,200	—
AH1274	—	150	300	800	1,200	—

KM# 122 5 PIASTRES
0.9800 g., 0.9000 Gold .0284 oz. AGW, 12 mm.

Date	Mintage	VG	F	VF	XF	Unc
AH1272	—	22.50	30.00	70.00	125	—
AH1273	—	22.50	30.00	70.00	125	—
AH1274	—	22.50	30.00	70.00	125	—
AH1275	—	22.50	30.00	70.00	125	—

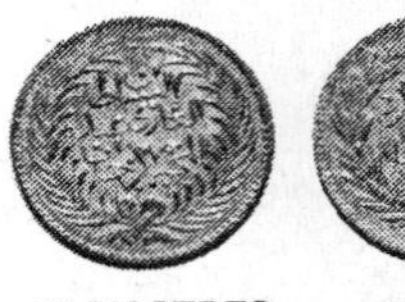 

KM# 123 10 PIASTRES
1.7700 g., 1.0000 Gold .0569 oz. AGW

Date	Mintage	VG	F	VF	XF	Unc
AH1272	—	35.00	55.00	90.00	150	—

KM# 124 10 PIASTRES
1.9700 g., 0.9000 Gold .0570 oz. AGW

Date	Mintage	VG	F	VF	XF	Unc
AH1272	—	35.00	55.00	90.00	150	—
AH1274	—	35.00	55.00	90.00	150	—

KM# 125 20 PIASTRES
3.5500 g., 1.0000 Gold .1141 oz. AGW, 21 mm.

Date	Mintage	VG	F	VF	XF	Unc
AH1272	—	100	125	200	400	—

KM# 133 25 PIASTRES
4.9200 g., 0.9000 Gold .1424 oz. AGW, 20 mm.

Date	Mintage	VG	F	VF	XF	Unc
AH1273	—	125	150	250	400	—
AH1274	—	125	150	250	400	—
AH1275	—	125	150	250	400	—

KM# 126 40 PIASTRES
7.1000 g., 1.0000 Gold .2283 oz. AGW, 26 mm.

Date	Mintage	VG	F	VF	XF	Unc
AH1272	—	135	175	300	525	—

KM# 127 50 PIASTRES
9.8400 g., 0.9000 Gold .2847 oz. AGW

Date	Mintage	VG	F	VF	XF	Unc
AH1272	—	175	200	300	500	—
AH1273	—	175	200	300	500	—
AH1274	—	175	200	300	500	—
AH1275	—	175	200	300	500	—

KM# 128 80 PIASTRES
14.2100 g., 1.0000 Gold .4569 oz. AGW, 31 mm.

Date	Mintage	VG	F	VF	XF	Unc
AH1272	—	325	450	900	1,200	—

KM# 129 100 PIASTRES
17.7100 g., 1.0000 Gold .5694 oz. AGW, 33 mm.

Date	Mintage	VG	F	VF	XF	Unc
AH1272	—	400	600	925	1,400	—

KM# 130 100 PIASTRES
19.6800 g., 0.9000 Gold .5695 oz. AGW

Date	Mintage	VG	F	VF	XF	Unc
AH1272	—	375	500	700	1,150	—
AH1273	—	375	500	700	1,150	—
AH1274	—	375	500	700	1,150	—

COUNTERMARKED COINAGE

AH1275/1858AD

KM# 105 KHARUB
Copper **Countermark:** Arabic "1" **Note:** Countermark on 6 Nasri. Large and small countermarks exist.

CM Date	Host Date	Good	VG	F	VF	XF
ND	AH1263	4.00	8.00	16.00	32.00	—
ND	AH1264	4.00	8.00	16.00	32.00	—
ND	AH1265	4.00	8.00	16.00	32.00	—
ND	AH1266	4.00	8.00	16.00	32.00	—
ND	AH1267	4.00	8.00	16.00	32.00	—
ND	AH1268	4.00	8.00	16.00	32.00	—
ND	AH1269	4.00	8.00	16.00	32.00	—
ND	AH1270	—	—	—	—	—
	Note: Reported, not confirmed					
ND	AH1271	4.00	8.00	16.00	32.00	—

KM# 114.1 KHARUB
Copper **Countermark:** Arabic "1" **Note:** Countermark on 6-1/2 Nasri, KM#113.1.

CM Date	Host Date	Good	VG	F	VF	XF
ND	AH1272	4.00	8.00	16.00	32.00	—
ND	AH1273	4.00	8.00	16.00	32.00	—

KM# 114.2 KHARUB
Copper **Countermark:** Arabic "1" **Note:** Countermark on 6-1/2 Nasri, KM#113.2. Large and small countermarks exist.

CM Date	Host Date	Good	VG	F	VF	XF
ND	AH1272	4.00	8.00	16.00	32.00	—
ND	AH1273	4.00	8.00	16.00	32.00	—
ND	AH1274	4.00	8.00	16.00	32.00	—

KM# 116.1 2 KHARUB
Copper **Countermark:** Arabic "2" **Note:** Countermark on 13 Nasri, KM#115.1.

CM Date	Host Date	Good	VG	F	VF	XF
ND	AH1272	4.00	8.00	16.00	32.00	—
ND	AH1273	4.00	8.00	16.00	32.00	—
ND	AH1274	4.00	8.00	16.00	32.00	—

KM# 116.2 2 KHARUB
Copper **Countermark:** Arabic "2" **Note:** Countermark on 13 Nasri, KM#115.2.

CM Date	Host Date	Good	VG	F	VF	XF
ND	AH1273	4.00	8.00	16.00	32.00	—
ND	AH1274	4.00	8.00	16.00	32.00	—
ND	AH1275	4.00	8.00	16.00	32.00	—

Sultan Abdul Mejid with Muhammad al-Sadiq Bey

AH1276-77/1859-1860AD

HAMMERED COINAGE

KM# 137.1 2 KHARUB
23.0000 g., Copper **Note:** Thin legend.

Date	Mintage	VG	F	VF	XF	Unc
AH1276	—	10.00	20.00	35.00	80.00	—

KM# 137.2 2 KHARUB
23.0000 g., Copper **Note:** Thick legend.

Date	Mintage	VG	F	VF	XF	Unc
AH1276	—	10.00	20.00	35.00	80.00	—

KM# 142 8 KHARUB
1.6000 g., Silver, 18 mm.

Date	Mintage	VG	F	VF	XF	Unc
AH1276	—	60.00	100	250	450	—
AH1277	—	60.00	100	250	450	—

KM# 143 PIASTRE
3.2000 g., Silver, 22 mm.

Date	Mintage	VG	F	VF	XF	Unc
AH1278 (sic)	—	75.00	150	300	500	—

KM# 138 2 PIASTRES
6.4000 g., Silver

Date	Mintage	VG	F	VF	XF	Unc
AH1276 Rare	—	—	—	—	—	—

KM# 139 25 PIASTRES
4.9000 g., Gold, 20 mm.

Date	Mintage	VG	F	VF	XF	Unc
AH1276	—	125	200	325	650	—

KM# 140 50 PIASTRES
9.8000 g., Gold, 26 mm.

Date	Mintage	VG	F	VF	XF	Unc
AH1276	—	150	300	500	750	—

KM# 141 100 PIASTRES
19.7000 g., Gold, 33 mm.

Date	Mintage	VG	F	VF	XF	Unc
AH1276	—	1,000	1,250	1,500	2,000	—

Sultan Abdul Aziz with Muhammad al-Sadiq Bey

AH1276-93/1860-76AD

HAMMERED COINAGE

KM# 153 1/4 KHARUB
1.0000 g., Copper

Date	Mintage	VG	F	VF	XF	Unc
AH1281	3,200,000	4.00	6.00	10.00	20.00	—

KM# 171 1/4 KHARUB
1.5000 g., Copper

Date	Mintage	VG	F	VF	XF	Unc
AH1289	—	5.00	8.00	30.00	60.00	—

KM# 154 1/2 KHARUB
1.8000 g., Copper

Date	Mintage	VG	F	VF	XF	Unc
AH1281	3,200,000	1.00	2.00	4.00	8.00	—

KM# 172 1/2 KHARUB
3.2000 g., Copper

Date	Mintage	VG	F	VF	XF	Unc
AH1289	—	2.50	8.00	20.00	40.00	—

KM# 155 KHARUB
3.5000 g., Copper

Date	Mintage	VG	F	VF	XF	Unc
AH1281	5,600,000	1.00	2.00	6.00	10.00	—

KM# 173 KHARUB
6.2000 g., Copper

Date	Mintage	VG	F	VF	XF	Unc
AH1289	—	1.50	2.25	8.00	20.00	—
AH1290	—	2.25	3.50	10.00	25.00	—

KM# 157 2 KHARUB
12.9000 g., Copper **Note:** Slightly thinner planchets exist.

Date	Mintage	VG	F	VF	XF	Unc
AH1281	—	—	—	—	—	—
Note: Reported, not confirmed						
AH1283	—	2.50	6.00	15.00	25.00	—
Note: Three varieties of inscription exist for AH1283						
AH1284	—	—	—	—	—	—
Note: Reported, not confirmed						

KM# 156 2 KHARUB
7.5000 g., Copper **Note:** Thick and thin planchets exist.

Date	Mintage	VG	F	VF	XF	Unc
AH1281	12,000,000	0.75	1.25	4.00	12.00	—

KM# 174 2 KHARUB
Copper **Note:** Weight varies: 12.00-12.50 grams.

Date	Mintage	VG	F	VF	XF	Unc
AH1289	—	1.75	3.00	6.00	12.50	—
AH1290	—	3.50	6.00	12.50	30.00	—

KM# 158 4 KHARUB
15.0000 g., Copper

Date	Mintage	VG	F	VF	XF	Unc
AH1281	12,000,000	3.00	6.00	10.00	20.00	—
AH1283	—	25.00	40.00	60.00	125	—

KM# 159 8 KHARUB
30.0000 g., Copper

Date	Mintage	VG	F	VF	XF	Unc
AH1281	10,000,000	2.00	5.00	10.00	20.00	—

Note: KM#153-156, 158 and 159 were struck at the Heaton Mint, Birmingham, and are relatively common in higher grades

KM# 160 8 KHARUB
1.8000 g., 0.9000 Silver 0.0559 oz. ASW

Date	Mintage	VG	F	VF	XF	Unc
AH1281	—	30.00	50.00	100	150	—
AH1282	—	30.00	50.00	100	150	—
AH1283	—	30.00	50.00	100	150	—
AH1284	—	30.00	50.00	100	150	—
AH1285	—	30.00	50.00	100	150	—
AH1286	—	30.00	50.00	100	150	—

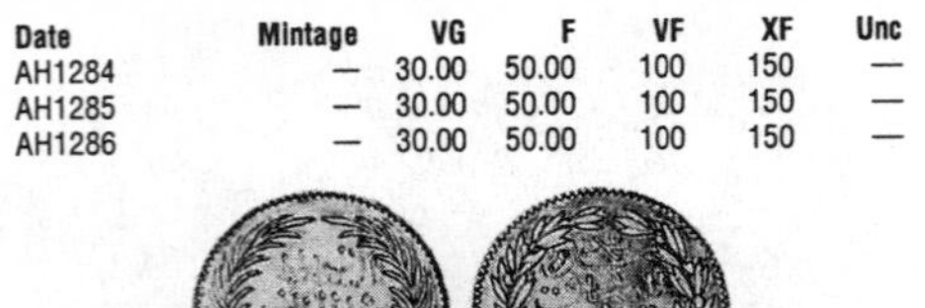

KM# 160a 8 KHARUB
1.8000 g., 0.8350 Silver .0483 oz. ASW

Date	Mintage	VG	F	VF	XF	Unc
AH1287	—	30.00	50.00	100	150	—
AH1288	—	30.00	50.00	100	150	—
AH1289	—	15.00	25.00	50.00	100	—
AH1290	—	30.00	50.00	100	150	—
AH1291	—	30.00	50.00	100	150	—
AH1292	—	30.00	50.00	100	150	—
AH1293	—	30.00	50.00	100	150	—

KM# 145 PIASTRE
3.2000 g., 0.9000 Silver .0926 oz. ASW

Date	Mintage	VG	F	VF	XF	Unc
AH1279	—	10.00	15.00	35.00	65.00	—
AH1280	—	20.00	35.00	60.00	100	—
AH1281	—	20.00	35.00	60.00	100	—
AH1282	—	20.00	35.00	60.00	100	—
AH1284	—	20.00	35.00	60.00	100	—

KM# 145a PIASTRE
3.2000 g., 0.8350 Silver .0859 oz. ASW

Date	Mintage	VG	F	VF	XF	Unc
AH1287	—	20.00	35.00	60.00	100	—
AH1288	—	20.00	35.00	60.00	100	—
AH1289	—	5.00	9.00	20.00	50.00	—
AH1290	—	6.00	10.00	25.00	60.00	—
AH1291	—	20.00	35.00	60.00	100	—
AH1292	—	20.00	35.00	60.00	100	—
AH1293	—	20.00	35.00	60.00	100	—

KM# 147 2 PIASTRES
6.4000 g., 0.9000 Silver .1852 oz. ASW

Date	Mintage	VG	F	VF	XF	Unc
AH1279	—	30.00	60.00	100	150	—
AH1280	—	30.00	60.00	100	150	—
AH1282	—	30.00	60.00	100	150	—
AH1283	—	30.00	60.00	100	150	—
AH1284	—	30.00	60.00	100	150	—

KM# 161 2 PIASTRES
6.2700 g., Silver

Date	Mintage	VG	F	VF	XF	Unc
AH1281 Paris Proof	—	Value: 375				

Note: Without name of the Bey of Tunis - possibly a pattern

KM# 147a 2 PIASTRES
6.4000 g., 0.8350 Silver .1718 oz. ASW

Date	Mintage	VG	F	VF	XF	Unc
AH1287	—	30.00	60.00	100	150	—
AH1288	—	30.00	60.00	100	150	—
AH1289	—	20.00	25.00	50.00	90.00	—
AH1290	—	20.00	25.00	50.00	90.00	—
AH1291	—	30.00	60.00	100	150	—
AH1292	—	30.00	60.00	100	150	—
AH1293	—	30.00	60.00	100	150	—

KM# 166 3 PIASTRES
9.6000 g., Silver, 30 mm.

Date	Mintage	VG	F	VF	XF	Unc
AH1288	—	100	150	250	400	—

KM# 167 4 PIASTRES
12.8000 g., 0.8350 Silver .3436 oz. ASW

Date	Mintage	VG	F	VF	XF	Unc
AH1288	—	20.00	40.00	95.00	180	—
AH1290	—	12.00	25.00	50.00	100	—
AH1291	—	12.00	25.00	50.00	100	—
AH1292	—	15.00	30.00	80.00	150	—
AH1293	—	15.00	30.00	80.00	150	—

KM# 175 4 PIASTRES
12.8000 g., 0.8350 Silver .3436 oz. ASW **Obv:** KM#186 **Rev:** KM#167 **Note:** Mule.

Date	Mintage	VG	F	VF	XF	Unc
AH1292	—	35.00	65.00	120	210	—

KM# 162 5 PIASTRES
0.9800 g., 0.9000 Gold .0284 oz. AGW

Date	Mintage	VG	F	VF	XF	Unc
AH1281	—	20.00	30.00	50.00	100	—
AH1281 Proof	—	Value: 150				

KM# 164 5 PIASTRES
16.0000 g., 0.9000 Silver .4630 oz. ASW, 33 mm.

Date	Mintage	VG	F	VF	XF	Unc
AH1281	—	100	150	250	325	—
AH1282	—	100	150	250	325	—
AH1288	—	100	150	250	325	—
AH1290	—	100	150	250	325	—
AH1291	—	100	150	250	325	—
AH1293	—	100	150	250	325	—

KM# 169 5 PIASTRES
0.9800 g., 0.9000 Gold .0284 oz. AGW

Date	Mintage	VG	F	VF	XF	Unc
AH1288	—	20.00	30.00	50.00	90.00	—
AH1289	—	20.00	30.00	50.00	90.00	—
AH1290	—	20.00	30.00	50.00	90.00	—
Note: Varieties exist						
AH1291	—	20.00	30.00	50.00	90.00	—
Note: Varieties exist						
AH1292	—	25.00	40.00	60.00	100	—

KM# 150 10 PIASTRES
1.9700 g., 0.9000 Gold .0570 oz. AGW

Date	Mintage	VG	F	VF	XF	Unc
AH1280	—	40.00	60.00	80.00	180	—
AH1281	—	40.00	60.00	80.00	180	—
AH1281 Proof	—	Value: 300				
AH1284	—	40.00	60.00	80.00	180	—
AH1287	—	40.00	60.00	80.00	180	—
AH1288	—	40.00	60.00	80.00	180	—

KM# 148 25 PIASTRES
4.9200 g., 0.9000 Gold .1424 oz. AGW

Date	Mintage	VG	F	VF	XF	Unc
AH1278	—	100	150	225	300	—
AH1279	—	100	150	225	300	—
AH1280	—	100	150	225	300	—
AH1281	—	100	150	225	300	—
AH1281 Proof	—	Value: 400				
AH1282 Rare	—	—	—	—	—	—
AH1283	—	100	150	225	300	—
AH1284 Rare	—	—	—	—	—	—
AH1285	—	100	150	225	300	—

Date	Mintage	VG	F	VF	XF	Unc
AH1286 Rare	—	—	—	—	—	—
AH1287	—	100	150	225	300	—
AH1288	—	100	150	225	300	—
AH1289	—	100	125	165	250	—
AH1290	—	100	125	165	250	—
AH1291	—	100	125	165	250	—

KM# 152 50 PIASTRES
9.8400 g., 0.9000 Gold .2847 oz. AGW

Date	Mintage	VG	F	VF	XF	Unc
AH1280	—	200	225	285	500	—
AH1281	—	200	225	275	350	—
AH1281 Proof	—	Value: 550				
AH1286	—	200	225	275	350	—
AH1288	—	200	225	275	350	—
AH1293	—	250	275	350	450	—

KM# 149 100 PIASTRES
19.6800 g., 0.9000 Gold .5695 oz. AGW

Date	Mintage	VG	F	VF	XF	Unc
AH1279	—	375	575	950	2,000	—
AH1280	—	375	575	950	2,000	—
AH1281	—	375	575	950	2,000	—
AH1281 Proof	—	Value: 3,200				
AH1283	—	375	575	950	2,000	—
AH1285	—	375	575	950	2,000	—
AH1286	—	375	575	950	2,000	—

Note: KM#148-150, 152, 161, 162, 164 and 166, dated AH1281, were all struck at Tunis, from dies produced at the Heaton Mint in Birmingham, hence their obvious superiority

Sultan Murad V with Muhammad al-Sadiq Bey
AH1293/1876AD

HAMMERED COINAGE

KM# 176 4 PIASTRES
12.8000 g., Silver

Date	Mintage	VG	F	VF	XF	Unc
AH1293 Rare	—	—	—	—	—	—

KM# 177 25 PIASTRES
4.9200 g., 0.9000 Gold .1424 oz. AGW, 20 mm.

Date	Mintage	VG	F	VF	XF	Unc
AH1293	—	300	500	850	1,500	—

Sultan Abdul Hamid II with Muhammad al-Sadiq Bey
AH1293-99/1876-82AD

HAMMERED COINAGE

KM# 180 2 KHARUB
12.5000 g., Copper, 31 mm.

Date	Mintage	VG	F	VF	XF	Unc
AH1293	—	12.50	20.00	45.00	85.00	—

KM# 188 8 KHARUB
1.5000 g., Silver **Obv:** Without "al-Ghazi"

Date	Mintage	VG	F	VF	XF	Unc
AH1293	—	60.00	125	250	375	—
AH1294	—	60.00	125	250	375	—

KM# 181 8 KHARUB
1.5000 g., Silver **Obv:** "al-Ghazi"

Date	Mintage	VG	F	VF	XF	Unc
AH1294	—	37.50	75.00	150	275	—
AH1295	—	30.00	60.00	125	225	—
AH1296	—	37.50	75.00	150	275	—

Date	Mintage	VG	F	VF	XF	Unc
AH1297	—	37.50	75.00	150	275	—
AH1298	—	37.50	75.00	150	275	—

KM# 182 PIASTRE
3.2000 g., Silver, 22.5 mm. **Obv:** Without "al-Ghazi"

Date	Mintage	VG	F	VF	XF	Unc
AH1293	—	35.00	75.00	150	300	—
AH1294	—	35.00	75.00	150	300	—

KM# 189 PIASTRE
3.2000 g., Silver **Obv:** "al-Ghazi" added

Date	Mintage	VG	F	VF	XF	Unc
AH1294	—	35.00	75.00	150	300	—
AH1295	—	35.00	75.00	150	300	—
AH1296	—	35.00	75.00	150	300	—
AH1297	—	35.00	75.00	150	300	—
AH1298	—	35.00	75.00	150	300	—

KM# 184 2 PIASTRES
6.4000 g., Silver, 26.5 mm.

Date	Mintage	VG	F	VF	XF	Unc
AH1293	—	40.00	70.00	150	300	—
AH1294	—	40.00	70.00	150	300	—

KM# 191 2 PIASTRES
6.4000 g., Silver **Obv:** "al-Ghazi" added

Date	Mintage	VG	F	VF	XF	Unc
AH1294	—	40.00	70.00	150	300	—
AH1297	—	60.00	100	175	350	—

KM# 186 4 PIASTRES
12.8000 g., Silver, 31 mm. **Obv:** Without "al-Ghazi"

Date	Mintage	VG	F	VF	XF	Unc
AH1293	—	20.00	60.00	125	250	—
AH1294	—	20.00	60.00	125	250	—

KM# 193 4 PIASTRES
12.8000 g., Silver **Obv:** "al-Ghazi" added

Date	Mintage	VG	F	VF	XF	Unc
AH1294	—	20.00	60.00	125	250	—
AH1295	—	20.00	60.00	125	250	—
AH1296	—	20.00	60.00	125	250	—
AH1297	—	20.00	60.00	125	250	—

KM# 195 5 PIASTRES
0.9800 g., 0.9000 Gold .0284 oz. AGW, 12.5 mm.

Date	Mintage	VG	F	VF	XF	Unc
AH1294	—	40.00	75.00	150	250	—

KM# 199 10 PIASTRES
1.9700 g., 0.9000 Gold .0570 oz. AGW

Date	Mintage	VG	F	VF	XF	Unc
AH1295	—	—	—	—	—	—

KM# 196 25 PIASTRES
4.9200 g., 0.9000 Gold .1424 oz. AGW

Date	Mintage	VG	F	VF	XF	Unc
AH1294	—	85.00	110	175	250	—
AH1295	—	85.00	110	175	250	—
AH1296	—	85.00	110	175	250	—
AH1297	—	85.00	110	175	250	—
AH1298 Rare	—	—	—	—	—	—

KM# 197 50 PIASTRES
9.8400 g., 0.9000 Gold .2847 oz. AGW, 26 mm. **Obv:** Without "al-Ghazi"

Date	Mintage	VG	F	VF	XF	Unc
AH1294 Rare	—	—	—	—	—	—

KM# 198 50 PIASTRES
9.8400 g., 0.9000 Gold .2847 oz. AGW, 26 mm. **Obv:** "al-Ghazi" added

Date	Mintage	VG	F	VF	XF	Unc
AH1295 Rare	—	—	—	—	—	—
AH1297	—	150	200	250	350	—

KM# A199 100 PIASTRES
19.6800 g., 0.9000 Gold .5695 oz. AGW, 33 mm.

Date	Mintage	VG	F	VF	XF	Unc
AH1295	—	—	—	—	—	—

Note: Reported, not confirmed

COUNTERMARKED COINAGE
AH1295/1878AD

KM# 183 PIASTRE
3.2000 g., Silver **Countermark:** Star **Note:** Countermark on KM#182.

CM Date	Host Date	Good	VG	F	VF	XF
ND	AH1293	—	35.00	60.00	100	150
ND	AH1294	—	35.00	60.00	100	150

KM# 146 PIASTRE
3.2000 g., Silver **Countermark:** Star **Note:** Countermark on KM#145a.

CM Date	Host Date	Good	VG	F	VF	XF
ND	AH1289	—	10.00	20.00	40.00	70.00
ND	AH1290	—	10.00	20.00	40.00	70.00
ND	AH1291	—	10.00	20.00	40.00	70.00
ND	AH1292	—	10.00	20.00	40.00	70.00

KM# 192 2 PIASTRES
6.4000 g., Silver **Countermark:** Star **Note:** Countermark on KM#191.

CM Date	Host Date	Good	VG	F	VF	XF
ND	AH1294	—	35.00	75.00	150	300

KM# 165 2 PIASTRES
6.2700 g., Silver **Countermark:** Star **Note:** Countermark on 2 Piastres KM#147a.

CM Date	Host Date	Good	VG	F	VF	XF
ND	AH1295	—	10.00	20.00	45.00	75.00
ND	AH1290	—	10.00	20.00	45.00	75.00
ND	AH1291	—	10.00	20.00	45.00	75.00
ND	AH1292	—	10.00	20.00	45.00	75.00
ND	AH1293	—	10.00	20.00	45.00	75.00

KM# 185 2 PIASTRES
6.4000 g., Silver, 26.5 mm. **Countermark:** Star **Note:** Countermark on KM#184.

CM Date	Host Date	Good	VG	F	VF	XF
ND	AH1293	—	35.00	75.00	150	300
ND	AH1294	—	35.00	75.00	150	300

KM# 187 4 PIASTRES
0.8350 Silver .3436 oz. ASW **Countermark:** Star **Note:** Countermark on KM#186.

CM Date	Host Date	Good	VG	F	VF	XF
ND	AH1293	—	20.00	35.00	75.00	150
ND	AH1294	—	20.00	35.00	75.00	150

KM# 168 4 PIASTRES
0.8350 Silver .3436 oz. ASW, 31 mm. **Countermark:** Star **Note:** Countermark on KM#167.

CM Date	Host Date	Good	VG	F	VF	XF
ND	AH1290	—	25.00	50.00	100	150
ND	AH1291	—	25.00	50.00	100	150
ND	AH1292	—	25.00	50.00	100	150
ND	AH1293	—	25.00	50.00	100	150

KM# 194 4 PIASTRES
0.8350 Silver .3436 oz. ASW **Countermark:** Star **Note:** Countermark on KM#193.

CM Date	Host Date	Good	VG	F	VF	XF
ND	AH1294	—	20.00	35.00	75.00	150

KM# 163 5 PIASTRES
0.9800 g., 0.9000 Gold .0284 oz. AGW **Countermark:** Star **Note:** Countermark on KM#162.

CM Date	Host Date	Good	VG	F	VF	XF
ND	AH1295	—	20.00	30.00	50.00	100

KM# 170 5 PIASTRES
0.9800 g., 0.9000 Gold .0284 oz. AGW **Countermark:** Star
Note: Countermark on KM#169.

CM Date	Host Date	Good	VG	F	VF	XF
ND	AH1288	—	20.00	35.00	60.00	100
ND	AH1289	—	20.00	35.00	60.00	100
ND	AH1290	—	20.00	35.00	60.00	100
ND	AH1291	—	20.00	35.00	60.00	100

KM# 151 10 PIASTRES
1.9700 g., 0.9000 Gold .0570 oz. AGW **Countermark:** Star
Note: Countermark on KM#150.

CM Date	Host Date	Good	VG	F	VF	XF
ND	AH1281	—	45.00	70.00	85.00	135
ND	AH1288	—	45.00	70.00	85.00	135

PATTERNS

Including off metal strikes

KM#	Date	Mintage	Identification	Mkt Val
Pn1	AH1255	—	Kharub. Copper.	375

KM#	Date	Mintage	Identification	Mkt Val
Pn2	AH1255	—	2 Kharub. Copper.	375

KM#	Date	Mintage	Identification	Mkt Val
Pn3	AH1255	—	4 Kharub. Copper.	450
Pn4	AH1270	—	1/4 Piastre. Billon.	300
Pn5	AH1270	—	1/2 Piastre. Billon.	300
Pn6	AH1270	—	Piastre. Silver.	300
Pn7	AH1281	—	2 Piastres. Copper. KM#161.	450
Pn8	AH1281	—	5 Piastres. Copper. KM#162.	250
Pn9	AH1281	—	10 Piastres. Copper. KM#150	250
Pn10	AH1281	—	25 Piastres. Copper. KM#148.	250
Pn11	AH1281	—	50 Piastres. Copper. KM#152.	325
Pn12	AH1281	—	100 Piastres. Copper. KM#149.	375

PROOF SETS

KM#	Date	Mintage	Identification	Issue Price	Mkt Val
PS1	1864 (AH1281) (5)	—	KM#148-150, 152, 162	—	4,750

TURKEY

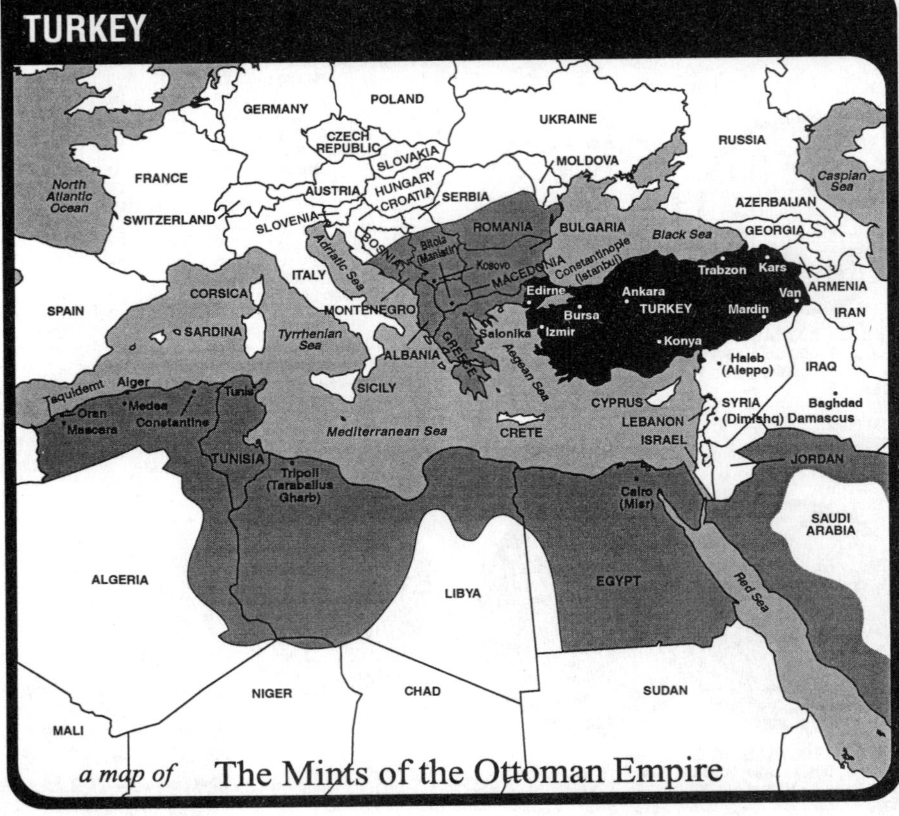

The Republic of Turkey, a parliamentary democracy of the Near East located partially in Europe and partially in Asia between the Black and the Mediterranean Seas, has an area of 301,382 sq. mi. (780,580 sq. km.).

The Ottoman Turks, a tribe from Central Asia, first appeared in the early 13th century, and by the 17th century had established the Ottoman Empire which stretched from the Persian Gulf to the southern frontier of Poland, and from the Caspian Sea to the Algerian plateau. The defeat of the Turkish navy by the Holy League in 1571, and of the Turkish forces besieging Vienna in 1683, began the steady decline of the Ottoman Empire which, accelerated by the rise of nationalism, contracted its European border, and by the end of World War I deprived it of its Arab lands

RULERS

Selim III, AH1203-1222/1789-1807AD
Mustafa IV, AH1222-1223/1807-1808AD
Mahmud II, AH1223-1255/1808-1839AD
Abdul Mejid, AH1255-12771839-1861AD
Abdul Aziz, AH1277-1293/1861-1876AD
Murad V, AH1293/1876AD
Abdul Hamid II, AH1293-1327/1876-1909AD

MINT NAMES

بغداد
Baghdad
See Iraq-Mesopotamia

بروسة
Bursa
(Brusah)

قسطنتنيه
Constantine (Constaniyah, Qusantinah) See Algeria-Algiers

قسطنطنية
Constantinople
(Qustantiniyah)

دمشق
Damascus
(Damask) See Syria

ادرنة
Edirne
(Adrianople)

Erevan
(Erewan, Revan, Yerevan)

كنجه
Ganjah (Ganja)

حلب
Halab
(Aleppo) See Syria

اسلامبول or اسلامبول
Islambul
Istanbul

الجزاير
Jaza'Ir
(See Algeria-Algiers)

كارآمد
Kara Amid
(Amid)

قوصوه
Kosova

مناستر
Manistir

المعسكر
al-Mascara
See Algeria-Algiers

مديه
Medea
See Algeria-Algiers

مكه
Makkah (Mecca)
See Saudi Arabia

مصر
Misr
See Egypt

روان
Revan
(Erevan, now Yerevan)
See Armenia

سلانيك
Salonika
(Selanik, Saloniki)

تاقدمت
Taqidemt
See Algeria-Algiers

طرابلس
Tarabalus
See Libya-Tripoli

طرابلس غرب
Tarabalus Gharb
See Libya-Tripoli

تفليس
Tiflis
See Georgia

تونس
Tunis
See Tunisia-Tunis

وان
Van
(Wan)

MONETARY EQUIVALENTS

3 Akche = 1 Para
5 Para = Beshlik (Beshparalik)
10 Para = Onluk
20 Para = Yirmilik
30 Para = Zolota
40 Para = Kurush (Piastre)
1-1/2 Kurush (Piastres) = Altmishlik

MONETARY SYSTEM

Silver Coinage
40 Para = 1 Kurush (Piastre)
2 Kurush (Piastres) = 1 Ikilik
2-1/2 Kurush (Piastres) = Yuzluk
3 Kurush (Piastres) = Uechlik
5 Kurush (Piastres) = Beshlik
6 Kurush (Piastres) = Altilik

Gold Coinage
100 Kurush (Piastres) = 1 Turkish Pound (Lira)

This system has remained essentially unchanged since its introduction by Ahmad III in 1688, except that the Asper and Para have long since ceased to be coined. The Piastre, established as a crown-sized silver coin approximately equal to the French Ecu of Louis XIV, has shrunk to a tiny copper coin, worth about 1/15 of a U.S. cent. Since the establishment of the Republic in 1923, the Turkish terms, Kurus and Lira, have replaced the European names Piastres and Turkish Pounds.

MINT VISIT ISSUES

From time to time, certain cities of the Ottoman Empire, such as Bursa, Edirne, Kosova, Manistir and Salonikawere honored by having special coins struck at Istanbul, but with inscriptions stating that they were struck in the city of honor. These were produced on the occasion of the Sultan's visit to that city. The coins were struck in limited, but not small quantities, and were probably intended for distribution to the notables of the city and the Sultan's own followers. Because they were of the same size and type as the regular circulation issues struck at Istanbul, many specimens found their way into circulation and worn or mounted specimens are found today, although some have been preserved in XF or better condition. Mintage statistics are not known.

MONNAIE DE LUXE

In the 23rd year of the reign of Abdul Hamid II, two parallel series of gold coins were produced, regular mint issues and monnaies de luxe', which were intended primarily for presentation and jewelry purposes. The Monnaie de Luxe' were struck to a slightly less weight and the same fineness as regular issues, but were broader and thinner, and from more ornate dies.

Coins are listed by type, followed by a list of reported years. Most of the reported years have never been confirmed and other years may also exist. Mintage figures are known for the AH1293 and 1327 series, but are unreliable and of little utility.

Although some years are undoubtedly much rarer than others, there is at present no date collecting of Ottoman gold and therefore little justification for higher prices for rare dates.

There is no change in design in the regular series. Only the toughra, accessional date and regnal year vary. The deluxe series show ornamental changes. The standard coins generally do not bear the denomination.

INITIAL LETTERS

Letters, symbols and numerals were placed on coins during the reigns of Mustafa II (1695) until Selim III(1789). They have been observed in various positions but the most common position being over *bin* in the third row of the obverse.

HONORIFIC TITLES

El Ghazi

Reshat

The first coinage of Abdul Hamid II has a flower right of the toughra while the second coinage has *el Ghazi* (The Victorious). The first coinage of Mohammad Reshat Vhas *Reshat* right of the toughra while his second coinage has *el Ghazi.*

OTTOMAN EMPIRE

Selim III

AH1203-22/1789-1807AD

MILLED COINAGE

Silver Third Issue

Light coinage based on a Kurush weighing approximately 12.80g. with second toughra.

KM# 486 PARA
0.4650 Silver **Mint:** Islambul **Note:** Weight varies 0.24-0.48 grams.

Date	Mintage	VG	F	VF	XF	Unc
AH1203//14	—	0.75	1.25	6.00	12.00	—
AH1203//15	—	0.75	1.25	6.00	12.00	—
AH1203//16	—	0.75	1.25	6.00	12.00	—
AH1203//17	—	0.75	1.25	6.00	12.00	—
AH1203//18	—	0.75	1.25	6.00	12.00	—
AH1203//19	—	2.00	4.00	12.00	30.00	—

KM# 489 5 PARA
0.4650 Silver **Mint:** Islambul **Note:** Weight varies 1.35-1.75 grams.

Date	Mintage	VG	F	VF	XF	Unc
AH1203//14	—	6.50	10.00	25.00	40.00	—
AH1203//15	—	6.50	10.00	25.00	40.00	—
AH1203//16	—	6.50	10.00	25.00	40.00	—
AH1203//17	—	6.50	10.00	25.00	40.00	—
AH1203//18	—	6.50	10.00	25.00	40.00	—
AH1203//19	—	10.00	15.00	35.00	75.00	—

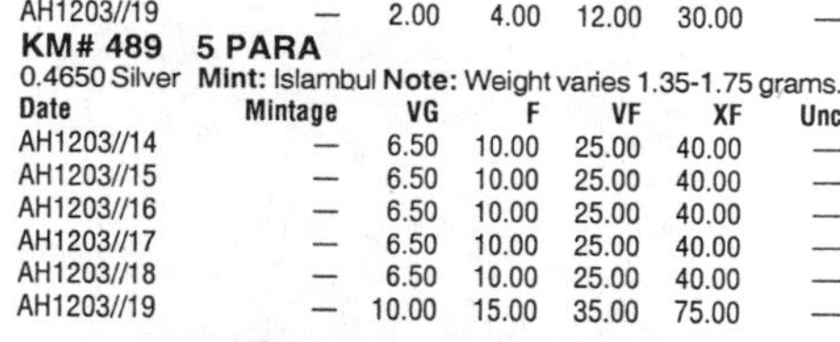

KM# 492 10 PARA
0.4650 Silver **Mint:** Islambul **Note:** Weight varies 2.4-3.5 grams.

Date	Mintage	VG	F	VF	XF	Unc
AH1203//14	—	4.00	8.00	17.50	35.00	—
AH1203//15	—	4.00	8.00	17.50	35.00	—
AH1203//16	—	4.00	8.00	17.50	35.00	—
AH1203//17	—	4.00	8.00	17.50	35.00	—
AH1203//18	—	4.00	8.00	17.50	35.00	—
AH1203//19	—	8.00	15.00	25.00	55.00	—

KM# 495 20 PARA
0.4650 Silver **Mint:** Islambul **Note:** Weight varies 6-6.2 grams.

Date	Mintage	VG	F	VF	XF	Unc
AH1203//15	—	50.00	100	190	350	—
AH1203//16	—	50.00	100	190	350	—
AH1203//19 Rare	—	—	—	—	—	—

KM# 507 YUZLUK
0.4650 Silver **Mint:** Islambul **Note:** Weight varies 31-32.9 grams. Dav. #334.

Date	Mintage	VG	F	VF	XF	Unc
AH1203//14	—	10.00	12.00	25.00	40.00	—
AH1203//15	—	10.00	12.00	25.00	50.00	—
AH1203//16	—	10.00	12.00	25.00	55.00	—
AH1203//17	—	10.00	12.00	25.00	70.00	—
AH1203//18	—	30.00	40.00	60.00	110	—
AH1203//19	—	50.00	75.00	150	350	—

KM# 498 KURUSH
0.4650 Silver **Mint:** Islambul **Note:** Weight varies 12.3-13 grams.

Date	Mintage	VG	F	VF	XF	Unc
AH1203//14	—	20.00	30.00	60.00	125	—
AH1203//15	—	25.00	35.00	70.00	150	—
AH1203//16	—	25.00	35.00	70.00	150	—
AH1203//17	—	25.00	35.00	70.00	150	—
AH1203//18	—	25.00	35.00	70.00	150	—
AH1203//19	—	150	250	400	750	—

KM# 504 2 KURUSH
0.4650 Silver **Mint:** Islambul **Note:** Weight varies 25.2-25.6 grams. Dav. #335.

Date	Mintage	VG	F	VF	XF	Unc
AH1203//14	—	10.00	12.00	30.00	45.00	—
AH1203//15	—	10.00	12.00	30.00	45.00	—
AH1203//16	—	10.00	12.00	30.00	45.00	—
AH1203//17	—	10.00	12.00	30.00	45.00	—
AH1203//18	—	30.00	75.00	100	200	—
AH1203//19	—	75.00	150	250	400	—

Gold Issues

KM# 510 1/4 ZERI MAHBUB
Gold **Rev. Inscription:** "Azza Nasara" **Mint:** Islambul **Note:** Weight varies 0.5-0.6 grams. Dav. #334.

Date	Mintage	VG	F	VF	XF	Unc
AH1203//14	—	25.00	35.00	50.00	75.00	—
AH1203//15	—	25.00	35.00	50.00	75.00	—
AH1203//16	—	25.00	35.00	50.00	75.00	—
AH1203//17	—	25.00	35.00	50.00	75.00	—

Note: With "Azza Nasara."

KM# 517 1/2 ZERI MAHBUB
Gold **Mint:** Islambul **Note:** Weight varies 1.10-1.20 grams. Second toughra.

Date	Mintage	VG	F	VF	XF	Unc
AH1203//14	—	40.00	65.00	80.00	100	—
AH1203//15	—	40.00	65.00	80.00	100	—
AH1203//16	—	40.00	65.00	80.00	100	—
AH1203//17	—	40.00	65.00	80.00	100	—
AH1203//18	—	50.00	80.00	120	180	—
AH1203//19	—	100	200	300	400	—

KM# 523 ZERI MAHBUB
2.4000 g., Gold, 21 mm. **Mint:** Islambul **Note:** Reduced size.

Date	Mintage	VG	F	VF	XF	Unc
AH1203//14	—	50.00	75.00	90.00	120	—
AH1203//15	—	50.00	75.00	90.00	120	—
AH1203//16	—	50.00	75.00	90.00	120	—
AH1203//17	—	50.00	75.00	90.00	120	—
AH1203//18	—	50.00	75.00	90.00	120	—
AH1203//19	—	50.00	75.00	90.00	120	—

KM# 514 1/4 ALTIN (Findik)
0.9000 g., Gold **Mint:** Islambul **Note:** Plain borders.

Date	Mintage	VG	F	VF	XF	Unc
AH1203//14	—	25.00	35.00	50.00	70.00	—
AH1203//15	—	25.00	35.00	50.00	70.00	—
AH1203//16	—	25.00	35.00	50.00	70.00	—
AH1203//17	—	25.00	35.00	50.00	70.00	—
AH1203//18	—	25.00	35.00	50.00	70.00	—
AH1203//19	—	30.00	50.00	75.00	125	—

KM# 520 1/2 ALTIN
Gold **Mint:** Islambul **Note:** Weight varies 0.75-0.8 grams.

Date	Mintage	VG	F	VF	XF	Unc
AH1203//18	—	60.00	90.00	130	185	—

KM# 527 ALTIN
3.4500 g., Gold **Mint:** Islambul

Date	Mintage	VG	F	VF	XF	Unc
AH1203//17	—	60.00	85.00	130	185	—
AH1203//18	—	60.00	85.00	130	185	—
AH1203//19	—	60.00	85.00	130	185	—

Mustafa IV
AH1222-23/1807-08AD
HAMMERED COINAGE
Copper Issue

KM# 534 MANGIR
2.7000 g., Copper **Mint:** Qustantiniyah

Date	Mintage	VG	F	VF	XF	Unc
AH1222//1	—	—	—	—	—	—

Silver Issues

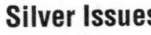

KM# 536 PARA
0.4000 g., 0.4650 Silver **Mint:** Qustantiniyah

Date	Mintage	VG	F	VF	XF	Unc
AH1222//1	—	25.00	35.00	50.00	80.00	—
AH1222//2	—	35.00	50.00	70.00	100	—

KM# 537 5 PARA
1.5000 g., 0.4650 Silver **Mint:** Qustantiniyah

Date	Mintage	VG	F	VF	XF	Unc
AH1222//1	—	50.00	90.00	200	350	—
AH1222//2	—	60.00	140	350	500	—

KM# 538 10 PARA
3.1400 g., 0.4650 Silver **Mint:** Qustantiniyah

Date	Mintage	VG	F	VF	XF	Unc
AH1222//1	—	40.00	90.00	200	300	—
AH1222//2	—	50.00	100	350	500	—

KM# 540.1 2 ZOLOTA
0.4650 Silver **Mint:** Qustantiniyah **Note:** Weight varies: 18.00-19.45 grams.

Date	Mintage	VG	F	VF	XF	Unc
AH1222//1	—	600	1,000	2,000	3,000	—

KM# 540.2 2 ZOLOTA
0.4650 Silver **Obverse:** Ornaments flank regnal year **Mint:** Qustantiniyah **Note:** Weight varies: 18.00-19.45 grams.

Date	Mintage	VG	F	VF	XF	Unc
AH1222//1	—	—	—	—	3,000	—

KM# 540.3 2 ZOLOTA
0.4650 Silver **Obverse:** Ornaments encircle regnal year **Mint:** Qustantiniyah **Note:** Weight varies: 18.00-19.45 grams.

Date	Mintage	VG	F	VF	XF	Unc
AH1222//1	—	—	—	—	3,000	—

KM# 539 KURUSH
0.4650 Silver **Mint:** Qustantiniyah **Note:** Weight varies: 12.65-12.95 grams.

Date	Mintage	VG	F	VF	XF	Unc
AH1222//1	—	250	600	800	1,000	—
AH1222//2	—	300	700	1,000	1,500	—

KM# 541 2 KURUSH
0.4650 Silver **Mint:** Qustantiniyah **Note:** Weight varies: 24.95-26.10 grams.

Date	Mintage	VG	F	VF	XF	Unc
AH1222//1	—	500	850	1,750	2,500	—

KM# 542 2-1/2 KURUSH
32.8000 g., 0.4650 Silver **Mint:** Qustantiniyah

Date	Mintage	VG	F	VF	XF	Unc
AH1222//1	—	650	1,100	1,750	2,500	—

Gold Issues

KM# 544 1/2 ZERI MAHBUB
1.2000 g., Gold **Mint:** Qustantiniyah

Date	Mintage	VG	F	VF	XF	Unc
AH1222//1	—	60.00	100	175	250	—
AH1222//2	—	60.00	100	200	300	—

KM# 545 ZERI MAHBUB
2.3500 g., Gold **Mint:** Qustantiniyah

Date	Mintage	VG	F	VF	XF	Unc
AH1222//1	—	90.00	200	300	400	—
AH1222//2	—	125	300	400	500	—

KM# 543.1 1/4 ALTIN
0.7700 g., Gold **Mint:** Qustantiniyah

Date	Mintage	VG	F	VF	XF	Unc
AH1222//1	—	40.00	60.00	100	150	—
AH1222//2	—	45.00	65.00	120	175	—

KM# 543.2 1/4 ALTIN
0.7700 g., Gold, 13.4 mm. **Reverse:** Inscription added at top **Rev. Inscription:** "Azz Nasrahuc" **Mint:** Qustantiniyah **Note:** Reduced size.

Date	Mintage	VG	F	VF	XF	Unc
AH1223//14	—	50.00	70.00	125	185	—

KM# 546 ALTIN
3.2000 g., Gold **Mint:** Qustantiniyah

Date	Mintage	VG	F	VF	XF	Unc
AH1222//1	—	70.00	100	120	170	—
AH1222//2	—	90.00	120	140	200	—

Mahmud II
AH1223-55/1808-39AD

HAMMERED COINAGE

Copper Issue

KM# 547 MANGIR
Copper **Mint:** Van

Date	Mintage	VG	F	VF	XF	Unc
AH1225	—	50.00	60.00	70.00	115	—
AH1231	—	50.00	60.00	70.00	115	—
AH1238	—	50.00	60.00	70.00	115	—

MILLED COINAGE

Silver First Issue - Years 1-2

The silver currency of the reign of Mahmud II is characterized by frequent change of standard, so that the Piastre (Kurus), which began with 5.90g of pure silver, had dropped to only .56g in the lower denominations (token currency) and .94g in the higher (actual currency). From time to time, the fineness, diameter, weight and type of the coins were changed, with the result that it is difficult, and not very neaningful, to atempt to trace individual denominations through the 32 years of his reign. For that reason, following Craig and others, the coins are grouped by standards of weight, fineness, or size. Changes in fineness, weight, and size are regularly indicated, as are distinguishing features whenever necessary for the proper identification of coins. The tolerance on Mahmud;s silver coinage was considerable, particularly on the smaller denominations, and the weights listed are approximate. During the 15th-16th years of his reign,m Mahmud II obtained the title ADLI - just. which was inscribed to the right of his toughra.

KM# 550 AKCE
0.4650 Silver **Mint:** Qustantiniyah **Note:** Weight varies: 0.10-0.16 grams.

Date	Mintage	VG	F	VF	XF	Unc
AH1223//1	—	6.00	15.00	35.00	70.00	—
AH1223//2	—	6.00	15.00	35.00	70.00	—

KM# 551 PARA
0.3200 g., 0.4650 Silver **Mint:** Qustantiniyah

Date	Mintage	VG	F	VF	XF	Unc
AH1223//1	—	4.00	15.00	25.00	40.00	—
AH1223//2	—	4.00	15.00	25.00	40.00	—

KM# 552 5 PARA
0.4650 Silver **Mint:** Qustantiniyah **Note:** Weight varies: 1.50-1.60 grams.

Date	Mintage	VG	F	VF	XF	Unc
AH1223//1	—	8.00	30.00	55.00	80.00	—
AH1223//2	—	8.00	30.00	55.00	80.00	—

KM# 553 10 PARA
0.4650 Silver **Mint:** Qustantiniyah **Note:** Weight varies: 2.80-3.20 grams. Two obverse varieties exist.

Date	Mintage	VG	F	VF	XF	Unc
AH1223//1	—	10.00	30.00	60.00	90.00	—
AH1223//2	—	12.00	35.00	70.00	100	—

KM# 549 30 PARA
9.5300 g., 0.4650 Silver **Mint:** Qustantiniyah

Date	Mintage	VG	F	VF	XF	Unc
AH1223//1 Unique	—	—	—	—	—	—

KM# 554 KURUSH
0.4650 Silver **Mint:** Qustantiniyah **Note:** Weight varies: 12.00-13.18 grams.

Date	Mintage	VG	F	VF	XF	Unc
AH1223//1	—	100	300	550	800	—
AH1223//2	—	150	350	650	850	—

Silver Second Issue - Years 2-14

KM# 556 AKCE
0.4650 Silver **Mint:** Qustantiniyah **Note:** Weight varies: 0.10-0.12 grams.

Date	Mintage	VG	F	VF	XF	Unc
AH1223//5	—	2.50	10.00	30.00	50.00	—
AH1223//10	—	2.50	10.00	30.00	50.00	—
AH1223//12	—	2.50	10.00	30.00	50.00	—

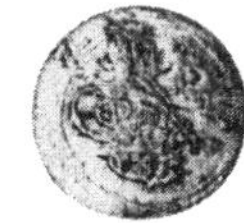

KM# 557 PARA
0.4650 Silver **Mint:** Qustantiniyah **Note:** Weight varies: 0.18-0.26 grams.

Date	Mintage	VG	F	VF	XF	Unc
AH1223//3	—	1.00	3.00	5.00	10.00	—
AH1223//4	—	1.00	3.00	5.00	10.00	—
AH1223//5	—	1.00	3.00	5.00	10.00	—
AH1223//6	—	1.00	3.00	5.00	10.00	—
AH1223//7	—	1.00	3.00	5.00	10.00	—
AH1223//8	—	1.00	3.00	5.00	10.00	—
AH1223//9	—	1.00	3.00	5.00	10.00	—
AH1223//10	—	1.00	3.00	5.00	10.00	—
AH1223//11	—	1.00	3.00	5.00	10.00	—
AH1223//12	—	1.00	3.00	5.00	10.00	—
AH1223//13	—	1.00	3.00	5.00	10.00	—
AH1223//14	—	1.00	3.00	5.00	10.00	—

KM# 558 5 PARA
0.4650 Silver **Mint:** Qustantiniyah **Note:** Weight varies: 1.01-1.20 grams.

Date	Mintage	VG	F	VF	XF	Unc
AH1223//3	—	5.00	10.00	30.00	45.00	—
AH1223//4	—	5.00	10.00	30.00	45.00	—
AH1223//5	—	5.00	10.00	30.00	45.00	—
AH1223//6	—	5.00	10.00	30.00	45.00	—
AH1223//7	—	5.00	10.00	30.00	45.00	—
AH1223//8	—	5.00	10.00	30.00	45.00	—
AH1223//9	—	5.00	10.00	30.00	45.00	—
AH1223//10	—	5.00	10.00	30.00	45.00	—
AH1223//11	—	5.00	10.00	30.00	45.00	—
AH1223//12	—	5.00	10.00	30.00	45.00	—
AH1223//13	—	5.00	10.00	30.00	45.00	—
AH1223//14	—	5.00	10.00	30.00	45.00	—

KM# 559 10 PARA
0.4650 Silver **Mint:** Qustantiniyah **Note:** Weight varies: 2.10-2.50 grams.

Date	Mintage	VG	F	VF	XF	Unc
AH1223//3	—	4.00	10.00	25.00	40.00	—
AH1223//4	—	4.00	10.00	25.00	40.00	—
AH1223//5	—	4.00	10.00	25.00	40.00	—
AH1223//6	—	4.00	10.00	25.00	40.00	—
AH1223//7	—	4.00	10.00	25.00	40.00	—
AH1223//8	—	4.00	10.00	25.00	40.00	—
AH1223//9	—	4.00	10.00	25.00	40.00	—
AH1223//10	—	4.00	10.00	25.00	40.00	—
AH1223//11	—	4.00	10.00	25.00	40.00	—
AH1223//12	—	4.00	10.00	25.00	40.00	—
AH1223//13	—	4.00	10.00	25.00	40.00	—
AH1223//14	—	4.00	10.00	25.00	40.00	—

KM# 560 KURUSH
9.6000 g., 0.4650 Silver **Mint:** Qustantiniyah

Date	Mintage	VG	F	VF	XF	Unc
AH1223//3	—	12.00	20.00	40.00	75.00	—
AH1223//4	—	12.00	20.00	40.00	75.00	—
AH1223//5	—	12.00	20.00	40.00	75.00	—
AH1223//6	—	12.00	20.00	40.00	75.00	—
AH1223//7	—	12.00	20.00	40.00	75.00	—

Date	Mintage	VG	F	VF	XF	Unc
AH1223//8	—	12.00	20.00	40.00	75.00	—
AH1223//9	—	12.00	20.00	40.00	75.00	—
AH1223//10	—	12.00	20.00	40.00	75.00	—
AH1223//11	—	12.00	20.00	40.00	75.00	—
AH1223//12	—	12.00	20.00	40.00	75.00	—
AH1223//13	—	12.00	20.00	40.00	75.00	—

Silver Third Issue - Years 3-11

KM# 562 KURUSH
0.7300 Silver **Mint:** Qustantiniyah **Note:** Weight varies: 4.60-5.20 grams.

Date	Mintage	VG	F	VF	XF	Unc
AH1223//3	—	175	300	500	850	—

KM# 563 2-1/2 KURUSH
0.7300 Silver **Mint:** Qustantiniyah **Note:** Weight varies: 12.50-13.20 grams.

Date	Mintage	VG	F	VF	XF	Unc
AH1223//3	—	100	175	350	600	—
AH1223//4	—	100	175	350	600	—
AH1223//5	—	100	175	350	600	—
AH1223//6	—	100	175	350	600	—
AH1223//7	—	100	175	350	600	—
AH1223//8	—	100	175	350	600	—
AH1223//9	—	100	175	350	600	—
AH1223//10	—	175	300	550	800	—
AH1223//11	—	350	600	850	1,250	—

KM# 564 5 KURUSH
0.7300 Silver **Mint:** Qustantiniyah **Note:** Weight varies: 24.00-26.00 grams.

Date	Mintage	VG	F	VF	XF	Unc
AH1223//3	—	20.00	30.00	55.00	90.00	—
AH1223//4	—	20.00	30.00	50.00	85.00	—
AH1223//5	—	20.00	30.00	50.00	85.00	—
AH1223//6	—	20.00	30.00	50.00	85.00	—
AH1223//7	—	20.00	30.00	50.00	85.00	—
AH1223//8	—	20.00	30.00	75.00	110	—
AH1223//9	—	20.00	30.00	75.00	110	—
AH1223//10	—	100	150	225	350	—
AH1223//11	—	275	400	650	1,000	—

Silver Fourth Issue - Years 14-15

KM# 566 PARA
0.1500 g., 0.4650 Silver **Obverse:** Without flower behind toughra **Mint:** Qustantiniyah

Date	Mintage	VG	F	VF	XF	Unc
AH1223//14	—	1.25	2.50	6.00	12.00	—
AH1223//15	—	1.25	2.50	6.00	12.00	—

KM# 567 5 PARA
0.8500 g., 0.4650 Silver, 18 mm. **Mint:** Qustantiniyah

Date	Mintage	VG	F	VF	XF	Unc
AH1223//14	—	7.00	15.00	50.00	80.00	—

KM# 568 10 PARA
0.4650 Silver, 22 mm. **Mint:** Qustantiniyah **Note:** Weight varies: 1.60-1.80 grams.

Date	Mintage	VG	F	VF	XF	Unc
AH1223//14	—	5.00	10.00	35.00	60.00	—
AH1223//15	—	10.00	20.00	50.00	100	—

KM# 569 KURUSH
5.5000 g., 0.4650 Silver, 32 mm. **Mint:** Qustantiniyah

Date	Mintage	VG	F	VF	XF	Unc
AH1223//14	—	25.00	35.00	75.00	150	—
AH1223//15	—	45.00	60.00	100	175	—

KM# 570 2 KURUSH
0.4650 Silver **Mint:** Qustantiniyah **Note:** Some coins have stars above and below outlined regnal year box. Weight varies: 11.50-13.40 grams.

Date	Mintage	VG	F	VF	XF	Unc
AH1223//14	—	25.00	50.00	100	200	—
AH1223//15	—	30.00	60.00	120	225	—

Silver Fifth Issue - Years 15-16

KM# 572 PARA
0.7300 Silver **Edge:** Plain **Mint:** Qustantiniyah **Note:** With flowers behind toughra. Varieties exist. Weight varies: 0.14-0.17 grams.

Date	Mintage	VG	F	VF	XF	Unc
AH1223//15	—	1.50	3.00	6.00	15.00	—
AH1223//16	—	1.50	3.00	6.00	15.00	—

KM# 573 5 PARA
0.8000 g., 0.7300 Silver **Edge:** Reeded **Mint:** Qustantiniyah

Date	Mintage	VG	F	VF	XF	Unc
AH1223//15	—	8.00	17.50	40.00	60.00	—
AH1223//16	—	7.50	15.00	35.00	50.00	—

KM# 574 10 PARA
1.6000 g., 0.7300 Silver **Edge:** Reeded **Mint:** Qustantiniyah

Date	Mintage	VG	F	VF	XF	Unc
AH1223//15	—	7.50	15.00	20.00	35.00	—
AH1223//16	—	7.50	15.00	20.00	35.00	—

KM# 575 KURUSH
6.1500 g., 0.7300 Silver **Edge:** Reeded **Mint:** Qustantiniyah

Date	Mintage	VG	F	VF	XF	Unc
AH1223//15	—	20.00	30.00	50.00	100	—
AH1223//16	—	20.00	30.00	50.00	100	—

KM# 576 2 KURUSH
0.7300 Silver **Edge:** Reeded **Mint:** Qustantiniyah **Note:** Weight varies: 12.00-13.00 grams.

Date	Mintage	VG	F	VF	XF	Unc
AH1223//15	—	10.00	18.00	40.00	70.00	—
AH1223//16	—	10.00	20.00	45.00	80.00	—

Silver Sixth Issue - Years 16-21

KM# 578 PARA
0.6000 Silver **Mint:** Qustantiniyah **Note:** Weight varies: 0.15-0.20 grams.

Date	Mintage	VG	F	VF	XF	Unc
AH1223//17	—	1.50	3.00	9.00	18.00	—
AH1223//18	—	1.50	3.00	9.00	18.00	—
AH1223//19	—	1.50	3.00	9.00	18.00	—
AH1223//20	—	1.50	3.00	9.00	18.00	—
AH1223//21	—	1.50	3.00	9.00	18.00	—

KM# A579 5 PARA
Silver **Mint:** Qustantiniyah **Note:** Flower on obverse exists with two and three buds.

Date	Mintage	VG	F	VF	XF	Unc
AH1223//18	—	—	—	—	—	—

KM# C579 10 PARA
Silver **Mint:** Qustantiniyah **Note:** Weight varies 1.6 - 1.8 grams; size varies 20 - 21 mm.

Date	Mintage	Good	VG	F	VF	XF
AH1223//18	—	—	—	—	—	—

KM# B579 30 PARA
2.9800 g., Silver **Mint:** Qustantiniyah

Date	Mintage	VG	F	VF	XF	Unc
AH1223//16	—	4.00	6.00	15.00	30.00	—

KM# 579 30 PARA
0.6000 Silver **Mint:** Qustantiniyah **Note:** Weight varies: 3.00-3.40 grams.

Date	Mintage	VG	F	VF	XF	Unc
AH1223//17	—	4.00	6.00	15.00	30.00	—
AH1223//18	—	4.00	6.00	15.00	30.00	—
AH1223//19	—	4.00	6.00	15.00	30.00	—
AH1223//20	—	4.00	6.00	15.00	30.00	—
AH1223//21	—	4.00	6.00	15.00	35.00	—

KM# 580 60 PARA
0.6000 Silver **Mint:** Qustantiniyah **Note:** Weight varies: 5.60-6.25 grams.

Date	Mintage	VG	F	VF	XF	Unc
AH1223//16	—	8.00	12.00	25.00	40.00	—
AH1223//17	—	5.00	8.00	16.00	25.00	—
AH1223//18	—	5.00	8.00	16.00	25.00	—
AH1223//19	—	5.00	8.00	16.00	25.00	—
AH1223//20	—	5.00	8.00	16.00	25.00	—
AH1223//21	—	5.00	8.00	16.00	25.00	—

Note: This coin occurs frequently in high grade

Silver Seventh Issue - Years 21-22

KM# 582 AKCE
Silver **Mint:** Qustantiniyah

Date	Mintage	VG	F	VF	XF	Unc
AH1223//21	—	3.00	5.00	7.00	15.00	—

KM# 583 20 PARA
0.8000 g., 0.8330 Silver **Mint:** Qustantiniyah

Date	Mintage	VG	F	VF	XF	Unc
AH1223//21	—	4.00	6.00	9.00	15.00	—
AH1223//22	—	20.00	35.00	60.00	100	—

Note: This coin occurs frequently in high grade, also with open and closed rosettes on obverse and reverse

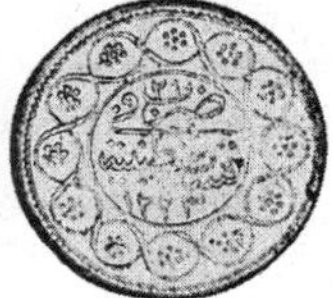

KM# 584 KURUSH
0.8330 Silver **Mint:** Qustantiniyah **Note:** Weight varies: 1.40-1.60 grams.

Date	Mintage	VG	F	VF	XF	Unc
AH1223//21	—	5.00	6.50	11.00	20.00	—
AH1223//22	—	25.00	35.00	60.00	100	—

Note: This coin occurs frequently in high grade, also with open and closed rosettes on obverse and reverse

Silver Eighth Issue - Years 22-25

Coins of the eighth series are readily distinguished from the ninth series, as they lack the dot or rosette below the inner wreath that appears on the ninth series. In the eighth and ninth series, with the exception of the Para, all coins have the word Adli (the Just) to the right of the toughra, sometimes with vertical mark below. The Para is distinguished only by date, however. Many coins are debased with a silver wash.

KM# 586 PARA
0.1000 g., 0.2200 Silver **Mint:** Qustantiniyah

Date	Mintage	VG	F	VF	XF	Unc
AH1223//22	—	1.00	2.25	3.50	8.00	—
AH1223//23	—	1.00	2.25	3.50	8.00	—
AH1223//42	—	2.00	3.00	4.50	10.00	—
Note: Error for 24						
AH1223//24	—	1.00	2.25	3.50	8.00	—
AH1223//25	—	2.00	3.00	4.50	10.00	—

KM# 587 10 PARA
0.8000 g., 0.2200 Silver, 17 mm. **Mint:** Qustantiniyah

Date	Mintage	VG	F	VF	XF	Unc
AH1223//22	—	2.00	6.00	15.00	35.00	—
AH1223//23	—	2.00	6.00	15.00	35.00	—
AH1223//24	—	2.00	6.00	15.00	35.00	—
AH1223//25	—	2.00	6.00	15.00	35.00	—

KM# 588 20 PARA
0.2200 Silver **Mint:** Qustantiniyah **Note:** Weight varies: 1.40-1.80 grams.

Date	Mintage	VG	F	VF	XF	Unc
AH1223//21 Rare	—	—	—	—	—	—
AH1223//22	—	1.00	2.00	5.00	12.00	—
AH1223//23	—	1.00	2.00	5.00	12.00	—
AH1223//24	—	1.00	2.00	5.00	12.00	—
AH1223//25	—	1.00	2.00	5.00	12.00	—

KM# 590 100 PARA (2-1/2 Kurush)
0.2200 Silver **Mint:** Qustantiniyah **Note:** Weight varies: 7.20-7.80 grams.

Date	Mintage	VG	F	VF	XF	Unc
AH1223//22	—	4.75	7.50	11.00	25.00	—
AH1223//23	—	3.50	5.00	8.00	15.00	—
AH1223//24	—	3.50	5.00	8.00	15.00	—
AH1223//25	—	3.50	5.00	8.00	15.00	—

KM# 589 KURUSH
0.2200 Silver **Mint:** Qustantiniyah **Note:** Weight varies: 2.60-3.00 grams.

Date	Mintage	VG	F	VF	XF	Unc
AH1223//22	—	2.75	3.00	6.25	15.00	—
AH1223//23	—	2.75	3.00	6.25	15.00	—
AH1223//24	—	2.75	3.00	6.25	15.00	—
AH1223//25	—	2.75	3.00	6.25	15.00	—

KM# 591 5 KURUSH
0.2200 Silver **Mint:** Qustantiniyah **Note:** Weight varies: 15.00-16.00 grams.

Date	Mintage	VG	F	VF	XF	Unc
AH1223//22	—	3.00	5.00	12.50	25.00	—
AH1223//23	—	3.00	5.00	12.50	25.00	—
AH1223//24	—	3.00	5.00	12.50	25.00	—
AH1223//25	—	3.00	5.00	15.00	30.00	—

Silver Ninth Issue - Years 25-32

Rosette or dot added beneath inner wreath on obverse and reverse except on 1 Akce and 1 Para.

KM# 593 AKCE
0.1700 Silver **Mint:** Qustantiniyah **Note:** Weight varies: 0.04-0.07 grams.

Date	Mintage	VG	F	VF	XF	Unc
AH1223//25	—	5.00	10.00	25.00	55.00	—
AH1223//26	—	2.50	4.00	15.00	40.00	—
AH1223//27	—	2.50	4.00	15.00	40.00	—

KM# 594 PARA
0.1700 Silver **Mint:** Qustantiniyah **Note:** Weight varies: 0.08-0.15 grams.

Date	Mintage	VG	F	VF	XF	Unc
AH1223//26	—	1.00	1.50	2.75	7.00	—
AH1223//27	—	0.75	1.25	2.00	5.00	—
AH1223//28	—	0.75	1.25	2.00	5.00	—
AH1223//29	—	0.75	1.25	2.00	5.00	—
AH1223//30	—	0.75	1.25	2.00	5.00	—
AH1223//31	—	0.75	1.25	2.00	5.00	—
AH1223//32	—	0.75	1.25	2.00	5.00	—

KM# 595 10 PARA
0.1700 Silver **Mint:** Qustantiniyah **Note:** Weight varies: 0.50-0.75 grams.

Date	Mintage	VG	F	VF	XF	Unc
AH1223//25	—	2.00	3.00	5.00	12.50	—
AH1223//26	—	5.00	7.50	10.00	18.50	—
AH1223//27	—	2.00	3.00	5.00	12.50	—
AH1223//28	—	2.00	3.00	5.00	12.50	—
AH1223//29	—	2.00	3.00	5.00	12.50	—

Date	Mintage	VG	F	VF	XF	Unc
AH1223//30	—	2.00	3.00	5.00	12.50	—
AH1223//31	—	2.00	3.00	5.00	12.50	—
AH1223//32	—	2.00	3.00	5.00	12.50	—

KM# 596 20 PARA
0.1700 Silver **Mint:** Qustantiniyah **Note:** Weight varies: 1.35-1.60 grams.

Date	Mintage	VG	F	VF	XF	Unc
AH1223//25	—	2.00	2.50	4.00	10.00	—
AH1223//26	—	2.00	2.50	4.00	10.00	—
AH1223//27	—	2.00	2.50	4.00	10.00	—
AH1223//28	—	2.00	2.50	4.00	10.00	—
AH1223//29	—	2.00	2.50	4.00	10.00	—
AH1223//30	—	2.00	2.50	4.00	10.00	—
AH1223//31	—	2.00	2.50	4.00	10.00	—
Note: Years 26 and 31 are easily confused						
AH1223//32	—	2.00	2.50	4.00	10.00	—

KM# 597 KURUSH
0.1700 Silver **Mint:** Qustantiniyah **Note:** Weight varies: 2.60-3.00 grams.

Date	Mintage	VG	F	VF	XF	Unc
AH1223//25	—	3.50	5.00	8.00	17.50	—
AH1223//26	—	3.50	5.00	8.00	17.50	—

KM# 598 KURUSH
0.1700 Silver **Mint:** Qustantiniyah **Note:** Weight varies: 6.40-7.80 grams.

Date	Mintage	VG	F	VF	XF	Unc
AH1223//25	—	3.00	4.50	9.00	18.50	—
AH1223//26	—	3.00	4.50	9.00	18.50	—

KM# 599 5 KURUSH
0.1700 Silver **Mint:** Qustantiniyah **Note:** Weight varies: 13.00-16.00 grams.

Date	Mintage	VG	F	VF	XF	Unc
AH1223//25	—	4.00	7.00	12.50	25.00	—
AH1223//26	—	4.00	7.00	12.50	25.00	—

Silver Tenth Issue - Years 26-32

KM# 601 1-1/2 KURUSH
0.4350 Silver **Mint:** Qustantiniyah **Note:** Weight varies: 2.60-3.00 grams.

Date	Mintage	VG	F	VF	XF	Unc
AH1223//26	—	4.00	6.00	12.00	25.00	—
AH1223//27	—	3.50	5.00	10.00	20.00	—
AH1223//28	—	3.50	5.00	10.00	20.00	—
AH1223//29	—	3.50	5.00	10.00	20.00	—
AH1223//30	—	3.50	5.00	10.00	20.00	—
AH1223//31	—	3.50	5.00	10.00	20.00	—
AH1223//32	—	3.50	5.00	10.00	20.00	—

KM# 602 3 KURUSH
0.4350 Silver **Mint:** Qustantiniyah **Note:** Weight varies: 5.60-6.20 grams.

Date	Mintage	VG	F	VF	XF	Unc
AH1223//26	—	5.00	7.50	12.00	25.00	—
AH1223//27	—	4.50	6.00	10.00	20.00	—
AH1223//28	—	4.50	6.00	10.00	20.00	—
AH1223//29	—	4.50	6.00	10.00	20.00	—
AH1223//30	—	4.50	6.00	10.00	20.00	—
AH1223//31	—	4.50	6.00	10.00	20.00	—
AH1223//32	—	4.50	6.00	10.00	20.00	—

KM# 603 6 KURUSH
0.4350 Silver **Mint:** Qustantiniyah **Note:** Weight varies: 11.00-13.00 grams.

Date	Mintage	VG	F	VF	XF	Unc
AH1223//26	—	6.00	8.00	15.00	40.00	—
AH1223//27	—	6.00	8.00	15.00	30.00	—
AH1223//28	—	6.00	8.00	15.00	30.00	—
AH1223//29	—	6.00	8.00	15.00	30.00	—
AH1223//30	—	6.00	8.00	15.00	30.00	—
AH1223//31	—	6.00	8.00	15.00	30.00	—
AH1223//32	—	6.50	9.00	17.50	32.50	—

Gold Zeri Mahbub Issues

Zeri Mahbub - Beloved Gold Series

The obverse of all denominations consists of a toughra, with mint name and date below on the 1 and 1/2 Zeri Mahbub only. The reverse of the 1 and 1/2 bears a four-line inscription; the reverse of the 1/4, the mint and date

FIRST TYPE:

Lily on 1 and 1/2 Zeri Mahbub, branch with one rose on the 1/4 Zeri Mahbub.

SECOND TYPE:

Rose replaces lily on 1 and 1/2 Zeri Mahbub, branch with 2 roses replaces branch with one rose on the 1/4 Zeri Mahbub.

KM# 605 1/4 ZERI MAHBUB
Gold **Mint:** Qustantiniyah **Note:** First type; Weight varies: 0.70-0.80 grams.

Date	Mintage	VG	F	VF	XF	Unc
AH1223//1	—	15.00	20.00	30.00	40.00	—
AH1223//2	—	15.00	20.00	30.00	40.00	—
AH1223//3	—	15.00	25.00	40.00	60.00	—
AH1223//4	—	15.00	20.00	30.00	40.00	—
AH1223//5	—	15.00	20.00	30.00	40.00	—

KM# 608 1/4 ZERI MAHBUB
Gold **Mint:** Qustantiniyah **Note:** Second type; Weight varies: 0.75-0.79 grams.

Date	Mintage	VG	F	VF	XF	Unc
AH1223//6	—	15.00	20.00	30.00	45.00	—
AH1223//7	—	15.00	20.00	30.00	45.00	—
AH1223//8	—	15.00	20.00	30.00	45.00	—
AH1223//9	—	15.00	20.00	30.00	45.00	—
AH1223//10	—	15.00	20.00	30.00	45.00	—
AH1223//11	—	15.00	20.00	35.00	50.00	—
AH1223//12	—	15.00	20.00	35.00	50.00	—
AH1223//13	—	15.00	20.00	35.00	50.00	—
AH1223//14	—	15.00	20.00	35.00	50.00	—

KM# 606 1/2 ZERI MAHBUB
Gold **Mint:** Qustantiniyah **Note:** First type; Weight varies: 1.10-1.20 grams.

Date	Mintage	VG	F	VF	XF	Unc
AH1223//1	—	35.00	50.00	70.00	90.00	—
AH1223//2	—	35.00	50.00	70.00	90.00	—
AH1223//3	—	35.00	50.00	70.00	90.00	—
AH1223//4	—	35.00	50.00	70.00	90.00	—
AH1223//5	—	35.00	50.00	70.00	90.00	—

KM# 609 1/2 ZERI MAHBUB
Gold, 18 mm. **Mint:** Qustantiniyah **Note:** Second type; Weight varies: 1.10-1.20 grams.

Date	Mintage	VG	F	VF	XF	Unc
AH1223//8	—	40.00	60.00	80.00	100	—
AH1223//12	—	40.00	60.00	80.00	100	—

KM# 607 ZERI MAHBUB
Gold **Mint:** Qustantiniyah **Note:** First type; Weight varies: 2.30-2.40 grams.

Date	Mintage	VG	F	VF	XF	Unc
AH1223//1	—	50.00	75.00	100	150	—
AH1223//2	—	50.00	75.00	100	150	—
AH1223//5	—	150	275	400	750	—

KM# 610 ZERI MAHBUB
Gold **Mint:** Qustantiniyah **Note:** Second type; Weight varies: 2.30-2.40 grams.

Date	Mintage	VG	F	VF	XF	Unc
AH1223//6	—	40.00	75.00	85.00	125	—
AH1223//7	—	40.00	75.00	85.00	125	—
AH1223//8	—	40.00	75.00	85.00	125	—
AH1223//9	—	40.00	75.00	85.00	125	—
AH1223//10	—	40.00	75.00	85.00	125	—
AH1223//11	—	40.00	75.00	85.00	125	—
AH1223//12	—	40.00	75.00	85.00	125	—
AH1223//14	—	40.00	75.00	85.00	125	—
AH1223//15	—	40.00	75.00	85.00	125	—

Gold Rumi Issue

Characterized by a flower right of toughra and an ornamental border, consisting of a wavy line hexagon, on both sides.

KM# 612 1/2 RUMI ALTIN
1.2000 g., Gold **Mint:** Qustantiniyah

Date	Mintage	VG	F	VF	XF	Unc
AH1223//10	—	75.00	100	125	175	—
AH1223//11	—	75.00	100	125	175	—
AH1223//12	—	75.00	100	125	175	—
AH1223//13	—	75.00	100	125	175	—

KM# 613 RUMI ALTIN
2.4000 g., Gold **Mint:** Qustantiniyah

Date	Mintage	VG	F	VF	XF	Unc
AH1223//10	—	200	250	300	350	—

KM# 614 2 RUMI ALTIN
Gold **Mint:** Qustantiniyah **Note:** Weight varies: 4.70-4.80 grams.

Date	Mintage	VG	F	VF	XF	Unc
AH1223//8	—	80.00	100	125	200	—
AH1223//9	—	80.00	100	125	200	—
AH1223//10	—	80.00	100	125	200	—
AH1223//11	—	80.00	100	125	200	—
AH1223//12	—	80.00	100	125	200	—
AH1223//13	—	80.00	100	125	200	—
AH1223//14	—	80.00	125	150	225	—

New Gold Rumi Issues

Similar to the Rumi series, except the wavy borders are replaced by an inscription containing the name and titles of Mahmud II

KM# 616 RUMI ALTIN
2.4000 g., Gold, 23 mm. **Mint:** Qustantiniyah

Date	Mintage	VG	F	VF	XF	Unc
AH1223//9	—	—	—	—	—	—
Note: Reported, not confirmed						
AH1223//10	—	40.00	50.00	90.00	125	—
AH1223//11	—	40.00	50.00	90.00	125	—
AH1223//12	—	40.00	50.00	90.00	125	—
AH1223//13	—	40.00	50.00	90.00	125	—
AH1223//14	—	40.00	50.00	90.00	125	—
AH1223//15	—	40.00	50.00	90.00	125	—

KM# 617 2 RUMI ALTIN
Gold **Mint:** Qustantiniyah **Note:** Weight varies: 4.70-4.80 grams.

Date	Mintage	VG	F	VF	XF	Unc
AH1223//9	—	100	125	150	200	—
AH1223//10	—	100	125	150	200	—

Date	Mintage	VG	F	VF	XF	Unc
AH1223//11	—	100	125	150	200	—
AH1223//12	—	100	125	150	200	—

Gold El-Aliye Surre Issues

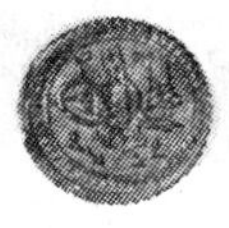

KM# 619 1/4 SURRE ALTIN
0.4800 g., Gold **Mint:** Darulhilafe

Date	Mintage	VG	F	VF	XF	Unc
AH1223//15 (1822)	—	30.00	50.00	100	150	—
AH1223//16 (1823)	—	30.00	50.00	100	150	—

KM# 620 1/2 SURRE ALTIN
0.7800 g., Gold, 15-16 mm. **Mint:** Darulhilafe

Date	Mintage	VG	F	VF	XF	Unc
AH1223//15	—	40.00	60.00	150	250	—
AH1223//16	—	40.00	60.00	150	250	—

KM# 621 SURRE ALTIN
1.5600 g., Gold **Mint:** Darulhilafe

Date	Mintage	VG	F	VF	XF	Unc
AH1223//15	—	60.00	85.00	110	150	—
AH1223//16	—	60.00	85.00	110	150	—

Gold Esseniye Surre Issues

KM# 623 1/4 SURRE ALTIN
0.4800 g., Gold **Mint:** Darulhilafe

Date	Mintage	VG	F	VF	XF	Unc
AH1223//15	—	30.00	45.00	100	150	—

KM# 624 1/4 SURRE ALTIN
0.7800 g., Gold **Mint:** Darulhilafe

Date	Mintage	VG	F	VF	XF	Unc
AH1223//15	—	50.00	75.00	200	300	—

KM# 625 SURRE ALTIN
1.5000 g., Gold **Mint:** Darulhilafe

Date	Mintage	VG	F	VF	XF	Unc
AH1223//15	—	60.00	90.00	150	225	—

Unnamed Gold Issues

The following type does not fit into any of the recognized series

KM# 627 1/4 ALTIN
0.5800 g., Gold **Mint:** Qustantiniyah **Note:** Considered a 1/4 Zeri Mahbub. "Azze Nasaru" above mint name.

Date	Mintage	VG	F	VF	XF	Unc
AH1223//13	—	15.00	20.00	40.00	60.00	—
AH1223//14	—	15.00	20.00	40.00	60.00	—
AH1223//15	—	15.00	20.00	40.00	60.00	—

Gold Adli Issues

These types are similar to the Zeri Mahbub series, except the word "Adli" replaces the flower right of the toughra

KM# 629 1/4 ADLI ALTIN
Gold **Mint:** Qustantiniyah **Note:** Weight varies: 0.40-0.45 grams.

Date	Mintage	VG	F	VF	XF	Unc
AH1223//16	—	20.00	30.00	75.00	125	—
AH1223//17	—	20.00	30.00	75.00	125	—

KM# 630 1/2 ADLI ALTIN
Gold **Mint:** Qustantiniyah **Note:** Weight varies: 0.75-0.85 grams.

Date	Mintage	VG	F	VF	XF	Unc
AH1223//15	—	45.00	60.00	75.00	90.00	—
AH1223//16	—	—	—	—	—	—
Note: Reported, not confirmed						
AH1223//17	—	45.00	60.00	75.00	90.00	—
AH1223//18	—	45.00	60.00	75.00	90.00	—
AH1223//19	—	45.00	60.00	75.00	90.00	—
AH1223//20	—	45.00	60.00	75.00	90.00	—
AH1223//21	—	45.00	60.00	75.00	90.00	—
AH1223//22	—	45.00	60.00	75.00	90.00	—
AH1223//23	—	45.00	60.00	75.00	90.00	—
AH1223//24	—	—	—	—	—	—
Note: Reported, not confirmed						
AH1223//25	—	45.00	60.00	75.00	90.00	—
AH1223//26	—	—	—	—	—	—
Note: Reported, not confirmed						
AH1223//27	—	45.00	60.00	75.00	90.00	—
AH1223//28	—	—	—	—	—	—
Note: Reported, not confirmed.						
AH1223//29	—	45.00	60.00	75.00	90.00	—
AH1223//30	—	45.00	60.00	75.00	90.00	—
AH1223//31	—	45.00	60.00	75.00	90.00	—
AH1223//32	—	45.00	60.00	75.00	90.00	—

KM# 631 ADLI ALTIN
Gold **Mint:** Qustantiniyah **Note:** Weight varies: 1.50-1.60 grams.

Date	Mintage	VG	F	VF	XF	Unc
AH1223//15	—	30.00	40.00	90.00	135	—
AH1223//17	—	30.00	40.00	90.00	135	—
AH1223//18	—	30.00	40.00	90.00	135	—
AH1223//19	—	30.00	40.00	90.00	135	—
AH1223//20	—	30.00	40.00	90.00	135	—

New Gold Adli Issues

The toughra appears on the obverse, with the mint name and date on the reverse, additional legends around and the mint name "Qustantinyah" has epithet "Al-Mahrusa" added

KM# 633 1/4 NEW ADLI ALTIN
Gold **Mint:** Qustantiniyah **Note:** Weight varies: 0.38-0.43 grams.

Date	Mintage	VG	F	VF	XF	Unc
AH1223//15	—	10.00	20.00	30.00	45.00	—
AH1223//17	—	10.00	20.00	30.00	45.00	—
AH1223//18	—	10.00	20.00	30.00	45.00	—
AH1223//19	—	10.00	20.00	30.00	45.00	—
AH1223//20	—	10.00	20.00	30.00	45.00	—
AH1223//21	—	10.00	20.00	30.00	45.00	—
AH1223//22	—	10.00	20.00	30.00	45.00	—
AH1223//23	—	10.00	20.00	30.00	45.00	—
AH1223//24	—	10.00	20.00	40.00	55.00	—

KM# 632 1/4 NEW ADLI ALTIN
Gold **Mint:** Qustantiniyah **Note:** Weight varies: 0.38-0.43 grams.

Date	Mintage	VG	F	VF	XF	Unc
AH1223//17	—	10.00	20.00	30.00	45.00	—

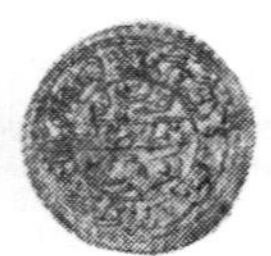

KM# 634 1/2 NEW ADLI ALTIN
0.7800 g., Gold **Mint:** Qustantiniyah

Date	Mintage	VG	F	VF	XF	Unc
AH1223//16	—	30.00	40.00	50.00	75.00	—
AH1223//17	—	30.00	40.00	50.00	75.00	—
AH1223//18	—	30.00	40.00	50.00	75.00	—
AH1223//19	—	30.00	40.00	50.00	75.00	—
AH1223//20	—	30.00	40.00	50.00	75.00	—
AH1223//21	—	—	—	—	—	—

Note: Reported, not confirmed

KM# 635 NEW ADLI ALTIN
1.5800 g., Gold **Mint:** Qustantiniyah

Date	Mintage	VG	F	VF	XF	Unc
AH1223//16	—	27.50	40.00	60.00	80.00	—
AH1223//17	—	27.50	40.00	60.00	80.00	—
AH1223//18	—	27.50	40.00	60.00	80.00	—
AH1223//19	—	27.50	40.00	60.00	80.00	—
AH1223//20	—	27.50	40.00	60.00	80.00	—
AH1223//21	—	—	—	—	—	—
Note: Reported, not confirmed						
AH1223//22	—	—	—	—	—	—

Note: Reported, not confirmed

Gold Hayriye Issues

This type is similar to the New Adli series, but in place of the legend around the edge, there are alternating ovals of inscription and branches

KM# 637 1/2 HAYRIYE ALTIN
0.8600 g., Gold **Mint:** Qustantiniyah

Date	Mintage	VG	F	VF	XF	Unc
AH1223//21	—	25.00	35.00	45.00	65.00	—
AH1223//22	—	25.00	35.00	45.00	65.00	—
AH1223//23	—	25.00	35.00	45.00	65.00	—
AH1223//24	—	25.00	35.00	45.00	65.00	—
AH1223//25	—	25.00	35.00	45.00	65.00	—
AH1223//26	—	25.00	35.00	45.00	65.00	—

KM# 638 HAYRIYE ALTIN
1.7300 g., Gold **Mint:** Qustantiniyah

Date	Mintage	VG	F	VF	XF	Unc
AH1223//21	—	30.00	35.00	45.00	90.00	—
AH1223//22	—	30.00	35.00	45.00	90.00	—
AH1223//23	—	30.00	35.00	45.00	90.00	—
AH1223//24	—	30.00	35.00	45.00	90.00	—
AH1223//25	—	30.00	35.00	45.00	90.00	—
AH1223//26	—	—	—	—	—	—

Note: Reported, not confirmed

KM# 639 2 HAYRIYE ALTIN
3.5500 g., Gold **Mint:** Qustantiniyah

Date	Mintage	VG	F	VF	XF	Unc
AH1223//21	—	100	125	150	200	—

Gold New Yeni Issues

The New Yeni series is found in one denomination, distinguished by a starlike wavy pattern around the edge

KM# 641 1/4 NEW ALTIN (Yeni Rubiye)
Gold, 12 mm. **Mint:** Qustantiniyah **Note:** Weight varies: 0.26-0.31 grams.

Date	Mintage	VG	F	VF	XF	Unc
AH1223//24	—	15.00	25.00	40.00	55.00	—
AH1223//25	—	15.00	25.00	40.00	55.00	—
AH1223//26	—	15.00	25.00	40.00	55.00	—
AH1223//27	—	15.00	25.00	40.00	55.00	—
AH1223//28	—	15.00	25.00	40.00	55.00	—
AH1223//29	—	—	—	—	—	—
Note: Reported, not confirmed						
AH1223//30	—	17.50	22.50	25.00	30.00	—

Gold Cedid Mahmudiye Issues

This type is similar to the Hayriye, but with ovals of inscriptions and branches replaced by a wreath design

KM# 643 1/4 CEDID MAHMUDIYE
Gold **Mint:** Qustantiniyah **Note:** Weight varies: 0.38-0.40 grams.

Date	Mintage	VG	F	VF	XF	Unc
AH1223//26	—	15.00	25.00	35.00	45.00	—
AH1223//27	—	15.00	25.00	35.00	45.00	—
AH1223//28	—	15.00	25.00	35.00	45.00	—
AH1223//29	—	15.00	25.00	35.00	45.00	—
AH1223//30	—	15.00	25.00	35.00	45.00	—
AH1223//31	—	15.00	25.00	35.00	45.00	—
AH1223//32	—	15.00	25.00	35.00	45.00	—

KM# 644 1/2 CEDID MAHMUDIYE
Gold **Mint:** Qustantiniyah **Note:** Weight varies: 0.70-0.80 grams.

Date	Mintage	VG	F	VF	XF	Unc
AH1223//26	—	20.00	30.00	45.00	65.00	—
AH1223//27	—	20.00	30.00	45.00	65.00	—
AH1223//28	—	20.00	30.00	45.00	65.00	—
AH1223//29	—	20.00	30.00	45.00	65.00	—
AH1223//30	—	20.00	30.00	45.00	65.00	—
AH1223//31	—	20.00	30.00	45.00	65.00	—
AH1223//32	—	20.00	30.00	45.00	65.00	—

KM# 645 CEDID MAHMUDIYE
Gold **Mint:** Qustantiniyah **Note:** Weight varies: 1.58-1.60 grams.

Date	Mintage	VG	F	VF	XF	Unc
AH1223//26	—	30.00	40.00	55.00	75.00	—
AH1223//27	—	30.00	40.00	55.00	75.00	—
AH1223//28	—	30.00	40.00	55.00	75.00	—
AH1223//29	—	30.00	40.00	55.00	75.00	—
AH1223//30	—	30.00	40.00	55.00	75.00	—
AH1223//31	—	30.00	40.00	55.00	75.00	—
AH1223//32	—	30.00	40.00	55.00	75.00	—

Gold Mint Visit Issues

The gold coins continued to be struck to the weights and finenesses of the old Ottoman system, but were tariffed at the going price of gold. The same continues to hold true today. Both regular and the "Monnaie de Luxe" series were produced.

KM# 647 1/2 HAYRIYE ALTIN
0.8800 g., Gold **Mint:** Edirne

Date	Mintage	VG	F	VF	XF	Unc
AH1223//24	—	60.00	100	150	250	—

KM# 648 HAYRIYE ALTIN
1.8000 g., Gold **Mint:** Edirne

Date	Mintage	VG	F	VF	XF	Unc
AH1223//24	—	100	120	150	200	—

KM# 649 2 HAYRIYE ALTIN
3.5500 g., Gold **Mint:** Edirne

Date	Mintage	VG	F	VF	XF	Unc
AH1223//24	—	175	225	275	350	—

Abdul Mejid
AH1255-77/1839-61AD
MILLED COINAGE
Gold Issues

KM# 677 25 KURUSH
1.8040 g., 0.9170 Gold .0532 oz. AGW **Mint:** Qustantiniyah

Date	Mintage	VG	F	VF	XF	Unc
AH1255//17	—	25.00	35.00	65.00	110	—
AH1255//18	—	25.00	35.00	65.00	110	—
AH1255//19	—	25.00	35.00	65.00	110	—
AH1255//20	—	25.00	35.00	65.00	110	—
AH1255//21	—	25.00	35.00	65.00	110	—
AH1255//22	—	25.00	35.00	65.00	110	—
AH1255//23	—	25.00	35.00	65.00	110	—

KM# 678 50 KURUSH
3.6080 g., 0.9170 Gold .1064 oz. AGW **Mint:** Qustantiniyah

Date	Mintage	VG	F	VF	XF	Unc
AH1255//6	—	BV	50.00	70.00	110	—
AH1255//7	—	BV	50.00	70.00	110	—
AH1255//8	—	BV	50.00	70.00	110	—
AH1255//9	—	BV	50.00	70.00	110	—
AH1255//10	—	BV	50.00	70.00	110	—
AH1255//11	—	BV	50.00	70.00	110	—
AH1255//12	—	BV	50.00	70.00	110	—
AH1255//13	—	BV	50.00	70.00	110	—
AH1255//15	—	BV	50.00	70.00	110	—
AH1255//16	—	BV	50.00	70.00	110	—
AH1255//17	—	BV	50.00	70.00	110	—
AH1255//20	—	1,750	2,500	3,500	5,000	—
AH1255//22	—	1,750	2,500	3,500	5,000	—

KM# 679 100 KURUSH
7.2160 g., 0.9170 Gold .2128 oz. AGW **Mint:** Qustantiniyah

Date	Mintage	VG	F	VF	XF	Unc
AH1255//5	—	—	BV	100	115	—
AH1255//6	—	—	BV	100	115	—
AH1255//7	—	—	BV	100	115	—
AH1255//8	—	—	BV	100	115	—
AH1255//9	—	—	BV	100	115	—
AH1255//10	—	—	BV	100	115	—
AH1255//11	—	—	BV	100	115	—
AH1255//12	—	—	BV	100	115	—
AH1255//13	—	—	BV	100	115	—
AH1255//14	—	—	BV	100	115	—
AH1255//15	—	—	BV	100	115	—
AH1255//16	—	—	BV	100	115	—
AH1255//17	—	—	BV	100	115	—
AH1255//18	—	—	BV	100	115	—
AH1255//19	—	—	BV	100	115	—
AH1255//20	—	—	BV	100	115	—
AH1255//21	—	—	BV	100	115	—
AH1255//22	—	—	BV	100	115	—
AH1255//23	—	—	BV	100	115	—

KM# 680 250 KURUSH
18.0400 g., 0.9170 Gold .5319 oz. AGW **Mint:** Qustantiniyah

Date	Mintage	VG	F	VF	XF	Unc
AH1255//7	—	250	275	450	650	—
AH1255//18	—	250	275	450	650	—
AH1255//22	—	2,000	3,000	4,000	6,000	—

Note: This is the first Ottoman coin to bear a numeral denomination, the 250 is at 6 o'clock on the obverse

KM# 681 500 KURUSH
36.0800 g., 0.9170 Gold 1.0638 oz. AGW **Mint:** Qustantiniyah

Date	Mintage	VG	F	VF	XF	Unc
AH1255//18	9,140	BV	525	750	1,100	—
AH1255//20	—	2,000	3,000	4,000	6,000	—
AH1255//22	—	2,000	3,000	4,000	6,000	—

Gold Mint Visit Issues

The gold coins continued to be struck to the weights and finenesses of the old Ottoman system, but were tariffed at the going price of gold. The same continues to hold true today. Both regular and the "Monnaie de Luxe" series were produced.

KM# 682 50 KURUSH
3.6080 g., 0.9170 Gold .1064 oz. AGW **Subject:** Mint Visit Coinage **Mint:** Edirne

Date	Mintage	VG	F	VF	XF	Unc
AH1255//8	10,000	—	250	375	550	1,150

KM# 683 100 KURUSH
7.2160 g., 0.9170 Gold .2128 oz. AGW **Subject:** Mint Visit Coinage **Mint:** Edirne

Date	Mintage	VG	F	VF	XF	Unc
AH1255//8	10,000	—	300	525	700	1,400

Pre-Reform

These issues are of standard, fineness and denominations of silver coinage similar to the ninth (1, 10 and 20 Para) and the tenth (1 1/2, 3 and 6 Kurush) series of Mahmud II (KM#594-596, 601-603)

KM# 651 PARA
Billon **Mint:** Qustantiniyah **Note:** Weight varies: 0.14-0.20 grams.

Date	Mintage	VG	F	VF	XF	Unc
AH1255//1	—	1.50	2.25	3.00	5.00	—
AH1255//2	—	1.50	2.25	3.00	5.00	—
AH1255//3	—	2.50	4.00	5.00	7.50	—
AH1255//4	—	1.50	2.25	3.00	5.00	—
AH1255//5	—	1.50	2.25	3.00	5.00	—
AH1255//6	—	7.50	10.00	15.00	20.00	—

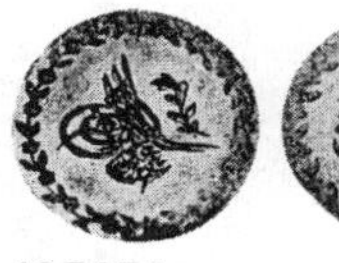

KM# 652 10 PARA
Billon **Mint:** Qustantiniyah **Note:** Weight varies: 0.60-0.80 grams.

Date	Mintage	VG	F	VF	XF	Unc
AH1255//1	—	2.00	3.00	4.00	7.50	—
AH1255//2	—	2.00	3.00	4.00	7.50	—
AH1255//3	—	3.00	4.00	5.00	8.00	—
AH1255//4	—	2.00	3.00	4.00	7.50	—
AH1255//5	—	2.00	3.00	4.00	7.50	—

KM# 653 20 PARA
Billon **Mint:** Qustantiniyah **Note:** Weight varies: 1.35-1.60 grams.

Date	Mintage	VG	F	VF	XF	Unc
AH1255//1	—	0.50	1.00	2.50	4.00	—
AH1255//2	—	1.50	2.50	4.00	7.50	—
AH1255//3	—	1.50	2.50	4.00	7.50	—
AH1255//4	—	1.00	2.00	3.50	5.00	—
AH1255//5	—	2.00	3.00	5.00	9.00	—

KM# 660 1/2 ZERI MAHBUB
0.8000 g., Gold **Reverse:** Four-line inscription **Mint:** Qustantiniyah

Date	Mintage	VG	F	VF	XF	Unc
AH1255//1	—	45.00	60.00	75.00	100	—
AH1255//2	—	45.00	60.00	75.00	100	—
AH1255//3	—	45.00	60.00	75.00	100	—
AH1255//4	—	45.00	60.00	75.00	100	—
AH1255//5	—	45.00	60.00	75.00	100	—
AH1255//6	—	75.00	100	120	200	—

KM# 657 1/4 MEMDUHIYE ALTIN
Gold **Mint:** Qustantiniyah **Note:** Weight varies: 0.38-0.40 grams.

Date	Mintage	VG	F	VF	XF	Unc
AH1255//1	—	17.50	25.00	35.00	55.00	—
AH1255//2	—	17.50	25.00	35.00	55.00	—
AH1255//3	—	17.50	25.00	35.00	55.00	—
AH1255//4	—	17.50	25.00	35.00	55.00	—
AH1255//5	—	17.50	25.00	35.00	55.00	—

KM# 658 1/2 MEMDUHIYE ALTIN
Gold **Mint:** Qustantiniyah **Note:** Weight varies: 0.78-0.80 grams.

Date	Mintage	VG	F	VF	XF	Unc
AH1255//1	—	40.00	50.00	60.00	80.00	—
AH1255//2	—	40.00	50.00	60.00	80.00	—
AH1255//3	—	40.00	50.00	60.00	80.00	—
AH1255//4	—	40.00	50.00	60.00	80.00	—
AH1255//5	—	40.00	50.00	60.00	80.00	—

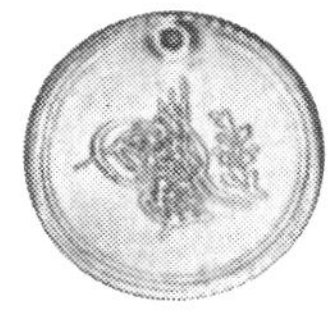

KM# 659 MEMDUHIYE ALTIN
Gold **Mint:** Qustantiniyah **Note:** Weight varies: 1.58-1.60 grams.

Date	Mintage	VG	F	VF	XF	Unc
AH1255//1	—	45.00	55.00	75.00	150	—
AH1255//2	—	45.00	55.00	75.00	150	—
AH1255//3	—	45.00	55.00	75.00	150	—
AH1255//4	—	45.00	55.00	75.00	150	—
AH1255//5	—	45.00	55.00	75.00	150	—

Note: The Memduhiye issue of Abdul Mejid was of the same fineness, weight and diameter as the Mahmudiye issue of Mahmud II; Although officially valued at 20 Piastres, the actual value of the Memduhiye Altin varied with the relative prices of gold and silver

KM# 654 1-1/2 KURUSH
Silver **Mint:** Qustantiniyah **Note:** Weight varies: 2.60-3.00 grams.

Date	Mintage	VG	F	VF	XF	Unc
AH1255//1	—	6.00	8.50	13.00	19.00	—
AH1255//2	—	5.00	6.50	12.00	18.00	—
AH1255//3	—	7.00	9.00	14.00	20.00	—
AH1255//4	—	5.00	6.50	12.00	18.00	—
AH1255//5	—	5.00	6.50	12.00	18.00	—

KM# 655 3 KURUSH
Silver **Mint:** Qustantiniyah **Note:** Weight varies: 5.60-6.20 grams.

Date	Mintage	VG	F	VF	XF	Unc
AH1255//1	—	20.00	40.00	100	150	—
AH1255//2	—	45.00	75.00	150	200	—
AH1255//3	—	100	200	275	350	—
AH1255//4	—	100	200	275	350	—

KM# 656 6 KURUSH
Silver **Mint:** Qustantiniyah **Note:** Weight varies: 12.42-13.00 grams.

Date	Mintage	VG	F	VF	XF	Unc
AH1255//1	—	40.00	50.00	75.00	150	—
AH1255//2	—	80.00	120	200	325	—
AH1255//4 Rare	—	—	—	—	—	—

STANDARD COINAGE

KM# 665.1 PARA
Copper **Mint:** Qustantiniyah **Note:** Weight varies: 1.00-1.10 grams. Thick planchet.

Date	Mintage	VG	F	VF	XF	Unc
AH1255//8	1,000,000	2.00	4.00	10.00	20.00	—
AH1255//9	375,000	5.00	10.00	30.00	50.00	—
AH1255//10	1,250,000	3.00	5.00	12.00	25.00	—
AH1255//11	165,000	2.00	4.00	8.00	15.00	—
AH1255//12	1,600,000	2.00	4.00	8.00	15.00	—
AH1255//13	800,000	2.00	3.00	6.00	12.00	—
AH1255//14	300,000	4.00	6.00	15.00	25.00	—
AH1255//15	700,000	3.00	6.00	12.00	20.00	—
AH1255//16	3,400,000	3.00	6.00	12.00	20.00	—

KM# 665.2 PARA
Copper **Mint:** Qustantiniyah **Note:** Weight varies: 0.80-0.90 grams. Medium planchet.

Date	Mintage	VG	F	VF	XF	Unc
AH1255//16	Inc. above	0.50	1.00	1.75	5.00	—
AH1255//17	800,000	1.00	3.00	6.00	10.00	—
AH1255//18	4,500,000	0.75	1.50	2.50	5.00	—

KM# 665.3 PARA
Copper **Mint:** Qustantiniyah **Note:** Weight varies: 0.50-0.60 grams. Thin planchet.

Date	Mintage	VG	F	VF	XF	Unc
AH1255//18	Inc. above	0.50	1.00	2.50	5.00	—
AH1255//19	2,500,000	0.25	0.50	1.25	2.50	—

Note: The thin planchet coin of "year 16" is actually year 19 with broken 9

Date	Mintage	VG	F	VF	XF	Unc
AH1255//21	2,000,000	10.00	20.00	45.00	70.00	—

KM# 666.1 5 PARA
Copper **Mint:** Qustantiniyah **Note:** Weight varies: 4.90-6.00 grams. Thick planchet.

Date	Mintage	VG	F	VF	XF	Unc
AH1255//7	—	7.50	15.00	20.00	50.00	—
AH1255//8	1,000,000	1.00	2.00	7.50	15.00	—
AH1255//9	300,000	10.00	20.00	50.00	100	—
AH1255//10	800,000	1.50	3.00	6.00	15.00	—
AH1255//11	2,542,000	1.50	3.00	6.00	15.00	—
AH1255//12	3,680,000	0.75	1.25	5.00	15.00	—
AH1255//13	4,640,000	0.75	1.25	5.00	15.00	—
AH1255//14	3,400,000	0.75	1.25	8.00	25.00	—
AH1255//15	5,060,000	0.75	1.25	8.00	25.00	—

KM# 666.2 5 PARA
Copper **Mint:** Qustantiniyah **Note:** Weight varies: 3.70-4.20 grams. Medium planchet.

Date	Mintage	VG	F	VF	XF	Unc
AH1255//15	Inc. above	2.00	4.00	20.00	40.00	—
AH1255//16	6,300,000	0.50	1.00	2.00	10.00	—
AH1255//17	6,500,000	0.50	1.00	2.00	10.00	—

KM# 666.3 5 PARA
Copper **Mint:** Qustantiniyah **Note:** Weight varies: 2.50-3.30 grams. Thin planchet.

Date	Mintage	VG	F	VF	XF	Unc
AH1255//18	2,000,000	1.25	2.75	15.00	25.00	—
AH1255//19	9,300,000	0.50	1.00	2.00	10.00	—
AH1255//20	10,060,000	0.50	1.00	2.00	10.00	—
AH1255//21	6,200,000	0.50	1.00	2.00	10.00	—

KM# 667.1 10 PARA
Copper **Mint:** Qustantiniyah **Note:** Weight varies: 9.00-12.80 grams. Thick planchet.

Date	Mintage	VG	F	VF	XF	Unc
AH1255//15	750,000	5.00	15.00	30.00	75.00	—

KM# 667.2 10 PARA
Copper **Mint:** Qustantiniyah **Note:** Weight varies: 7.50-8.20 grams. Medium planchet.

Date	Mintage	VG	F	VF	XF	Unc
AH1255//16	9,120,000	0.75	1.50	3.75	12.00	—
AH1255//17	9,110,000	0.75	1.50	3.75	12.00	—
AH1255//18	1,900,000	1.25	2.50	5.00	15.00	—

KM# 667.3 10 PARA
Copper **Mint:** Qustantiniyah **Note:** Weight varies: 4.90-5.70 grams. Thin planchet.

Date	Mintage	VG	F	VF	XF	Unc
AH1255//17	Inc. above	2.50	5.00	6.50	15.00	—
AH1255//18	Inc. above	1.25	2.50	5.00	15.00	—
AH1255//19	33,600,000	0.35	0.75	2.00	12.00	—
AH1255//20	20,800,000	0.35	0.75	2.00	12.00	—
AH1255//21	7,500,000	0.35	0.75	2.00	12.00	—

KM# 669 20 PARA
0.6013 g., 0.8300 Silver .0160 oz. ASW **Mint:** Qustantiniyah

Date	Mintage	VG	F	VF	XF	Unc
AH1255//9	400,000	3.00	6.00	25.00	60.00	—
AH1255//10	910,000	2.50	5.00	15.00	25.00	—
AH1255//11	390,000	2.00	4.00	15.00	25.00	—
AH1255//12	270,000	3.75	7.50	20.00	35.00	—
AH1255//13	230,000	4.50	9.00	40.00	75.00	—
AH1255//14	180,000	3.75	7.50	15.00	25.00	—
AH1255//15	240,000	4.00	8.00	30.00	50.00	—
AH1255//16	270,000	2.50	5.00	15.00	25.00	—
AH1255//17	170,000	5.00	10.00	40.00	75.00	—
AH1255//18	260,000	2.00	4.00	20.00	35.00	—
AH1255//19	900,000	2.00	4.25	20.00	35.00	—
AH1255//20	150,000	2.00	4.25	15.00	25.00	—
AH1255//21	250,000	4.25	8.50	15.00	25.00	—
AH1255//22	190,000	4.25	8.50	15.00	25.00	—
AH1255//23	620,000	50.00	150	300	500	—

KM# 668.1 20 PARA
Copper **Mint:** Qustantiniyah **Note:** Weight varies: 14.00-16.00 grams. Thick planchet. Varieties exist.

Date	Mintage	VG	F	VF	XF	Unc
AH1255//10	—	—	—	—	—	—
AH1255//16	4,350,000	1.25	2.50	5.00	15.00	—
AH1255//17	2,050,000	2.00	4.00	7.50	20.00	—

KM# 668.2 20 PARA
Copper **Mint:** Qustantiniyah **Note:** Weight varies: 10.00-11.00 grams. Thin planchet.

Date	Mintage	VG	F	VF	XF	Unc
AH1255//17	Inc. above	1.00	2.00	4.50	15.00	—
AH1255//19	1,200,000	1.00	2.00	4.50	15.00	—
AH1255//20	3,000,000	1.00	2.00	4.50	15.00	—
AH1255//21	8,400,000	0.50	1.00	3.00	15.00	—

KM# 670 40 PARA
Copper **Mint:** Qustantiniyah **Note:** Varieties exist in the size of year.

Date	Mintage	VG	F	VF	XF	Unc
AH1255//17	1,450,000	2.50	5.00	7.50	30.00	—
AH1255//17 Proof	—	—	—	—	—	—
AH1255//18	3,950,000	1.50	3.25	8.00	30.00	—
AH1255//19	11,300,000	1.25	2.50	6.50	30.00	—
AH1255//20	14,030,000	1.25	2.50	6.50	30.00	—
AH1255//21	9,300,000	1.25	2.50	6.50	30.00	—
AH1255//22	4,140,000	2.50	5.00	10.00	35.00	—
AH1255//23	—	50.00	75.00	100	150	—

KM# 671 KURUSH
1.2027 g., 0.8300 Silver .0321 oz. ASW **Mint:** Qustantiniyah
Note: Varieties exist in size of year.

Date	Mintage	VG	F	VF	XF	Unc
AH1255//6	—	20.00	30.00	50.00	100	—
AH1255//7	650,000	1.00	2.00	6.00	12.00	—
AH1255//8	1,420,000	1.00	2.00	6.00	12.00	—
AH1255//9	910,000	1.00	2.00	6.00	12.00	—
AH1255//10	970,000	1.00	2.50	7.00	15.00	—
AH1255//11	1,040,000	1.00	2.50	7.00	15.00	—
AH1255//12	1,100,000	1.00	2.50	7.00	15.00	—
AH1255//13	820,000	1.00	2.50	7.00	15.00	—
AH1255//14	790,000	1.00	2.50	7.00	15.00	—
AH1255//15	960,000	1.00	3.00	8.00	20.00	—
AH1255//16	1,220,000	1.00	2.50	7.00	15.00	—
AH1255//17	810,000	7.00	15.00	30.00	75.00	—
AH1255//18	720,000	1.50	4.00	10.00	25.00	—
AH1255//19	2,270,000	1.00	3.00	8.00	20.00	—
AH1255//20	1,165,000	1.00	3.00	8.00	20.00	—
AH1255//21	1,405,000	1.00	2.50	7.00	15.00	—
AH1255//22	825,000	1.00	3.00	8.00	20.00	—
AH1255//23	755,000	5.00	10.00	20.00	50.00	—

KM# 672 2 KURUSH
2.4055 g., 0.8300 Silver .0642 oz. ASW **Mint:** Qustantiniyah

Date	Mintage	VG	F	VF	XF	Unc
AH1255//7	1,035,000	1.00	2.00	6.00	12.00	—
AH1255//8	1,150,000	1.00	2.00	6.00	12.00	—
AH1255//9	530,000	1.00	3.00	8.00	20.00	—
AH1255//10	543,000	1.50	4.00	10.00	25.00	—
AH1255//11	695,000	1.50	4.00	10.00	20.00	—
AH1255//12	685,000	1.50	5.00	12.00	25.00	—
AH1255//13	540,000	1.50	5.00	12.00	25.00	—
AH1255//14	280,000	5.00	10.00	25.00	50.00	—
AH1255//15	300,000	1.50	5.00	12.00	25.00	—
AH1255//16	510,000	1.50	5.00	12.00	25.00	—
AH1255//19	275,000	20.00	40.00	65.00	135	—
AH1255//20	105,000	15.00	30.00	50.00	115	—
AH1255//21 Rare	—	—	—	—	—	—

KM# 673 5 KURUSH
6.0130 g., 0.8300 Silver .1605 oz. ASW **Mint:** Qustantiniyah
Note: Varieties in size of year exist.

Date	Mintage	VG	F	VF	XF	Unc
AH1255//6	1,347,000	2.00	4.00	10.00	22.50	—
AH1255//7	2,612,000	2.00	4.00	10.00	22.50	—
AH1255//8	362,000	2.00	4.00	10.00	22.50	—
AH1255//9	240,000	2.50	5.00	12.00	30.00	—
AH1255//10	252,000	3.00	6.00	15.00	40.00	—
AH1255//11	314,000	2.50	4.50	17.00	35.00	—
AH1255//12	452,000	2.50	4.50	15.00	35.00	—
AH1255//13	498,000	2.50	4.50	15.00	35.00	—
AH1255//14	354,000	2.50	4.50	15.00	35.00	—
AH1255//15	680,000	2.00	4.00	10.00	22.50	—
AH1255//16	972,000	2.00	4.00	10.00	22.50	—
AH1255//17	206,000	2.50	4.50	15.00	35.00	—
AH1255//18	218,000	2.50	4.50	15.00	35.00	—
AH1255//19	384,000	2.50	4.50	15.00	35.00	—
AH1255//20	310,000	2.50	4.50	15.00	35.00	—
AH1255//21	324,000	2.50	4.50	15.00	35.00	—
AH1255//22	214,000	2.50	4.50	15.00	35.00	—
AH1255//23	120,000	5.00	10.00	22.50	50.00	—

KM# 674 10 KURUSH
12.0270 g., 0.8300 Silver .3210 oz. ASW **Mint:** Qustantiniyah

Date	Mintage	VG	F	VF	XF	Unc
AH1255//6	338,000	15.00	35.00	80.00	150	—
AH1255//7	12,000	350	500	800	1,100	—
AH1255//9 Rare	—	—	—	—	—	—
AH1255//13 Rare	—	—	—	—	—	—

KM# 675 20 KURUSH
24.0550 g., 0.8300 Silver .6419 oz. ASW **Reverse:** Small inscription **Mint:** Qustantiniyah

Date	Mintage	VG	F	VF	XF	Unc
AH1255//6	2,013,000	9.00	15.00	20.00	45.00	—
AH1255//7	740,000	9.00	15.00	20.00	45.00	—
AH1255//8	1,671,000	9.00	15.00	20.00	45.00	—
AH1255//9	3,125,000	8.00	12.00	18.00	40.00	—
AH1255//10	1,020,000	9.00	15.00	20.00	45.00	—
AH1255//11	815,000	9.00	15.00	20.00	45.00	—
AH1255//12	684,000	9.00	15.00	20.00	45.00	—
AH1255//13	485,000	9.00	15.00	20.00	45.00	—
AH1255//14	633,000	9.00	15.00	20.00	45.00	—
AH1255//15	797,000	9.00	15.00	20.00	45.00	—

KM# 676 20 KURUSH
24.0550 g., 0.8300 Silver .6419 oz. ASW **Reverse:** Large inscription **Mint:** Qustantiniyah

Date	Mintage	VG	F	VF	XF	Unc
AH1255//8	Inc. above	—	—	—	—	—
AH1255//15	Inc. above	9.00	15.00	20.00	45.00	—
AH1255//16	320,000	9.00	15.00	20.00	45.00	—
AH1255//17	410,000	10.00	15.00	30.00	55.00	—
AH1255//18	340,000	12.00	20.00	35.00	70.00	—
AH1255//19	201,000	40.00	75.00	125	200	—
AH1255//20	103,000	12.00	20.00	35.00	75.00	—
AH1255//21	513,000	9.00	15.00	30.00	60.00	—
AH1255//22	624,000	9.00	15.00	30.00	60.00	—
AH1255//23	317,000	25.00	40.00	80.00	150	—

Abdul Aziz
AH1277-93/1861-76AD

MILLED COINAGE
Gold Issues

KM# 694 25 KURUSH
1.8040 g., 0.9170 Gold .0532 oz. AGW **Mint:** Qustantiniyah

Date	Mintage	VG	F	VF	XF	Unc
AH1277//1	52,000	27.50	32.50	40.00	60.00	—
AH1277//2	86,000	27.50	32.50	40.00	60.00	—
AH1277//3	89,000	27.50	32.50	40.00	60.00	—
AH1277//4	69,000	27.50	32.50	40.00	60.00	—
AH1277//5	67,000	27.50	32.50	40.00	60.00	—
AH1277//6	73,000	27.50	32.50	40.00	60.00	—
AH1277//7	116,000	27.50	32.50	40.00	60.00	—
AH1277//9	177,000	27.50	32.50	40.00	60.00	—
AH1277//11	65,000	27.50	32.50	40.00	60.00	—
AH1277//12	122,000	27.50	32.50	40.00	60.00	—
AH1277//13	152,000	27.50	32.50	40.00	60.00	—
AH1277//15	17,000	32.50	45.00	60.00	100	—

KM# 695 50 KURUSH
3.6080 g., 0.9170 Gold .1064 oz. AGW **Mint:** Qustantiniyah

Date	Mintage	VG	F	VF	XF	Unc
AH1277//1	5,800	65.00	125	250	350	—
AH1277//2	—	65.00	125	250	350	—
AH1277//3	—	1,750	2,500	3,500	5,000	—
AH1277//7	2,000	60.00	85.00	150	250	—
AH1277//8	2,000	—	—	—	—	—
Note: Reported, not confirmed						
AH1277//9	25,000	60.00	85.00	150	250	—

KM# 696 100 KURUSH
7.2160 g., 0.9170 Gold .2128 oz. AGW **Mint:** Qustantiniyah

Date	Mintage	VG	F	VF	XF	Unc
AH1277//1	2,347,000	—	BV	100	115	—
AH1277//2	3,129,000	—	BV	100	115	—
AH1277//3	478,000	—	BV	100	115	—
AH1277//4	628,000	—	BV	100	115	—
AH1277//5	561,000	—	BV	100	115	—
AH1277//6	330,000	—	BV	100	115	—
AH1277//7	1,491,000	—	BV	100	115	—
AH1277//8	495,000	—	BV	100	115	—
AH1277//9	1,570,000	—	BV	100	115	—
AH1277//10	304,000	—	BV	100	115	—
AH1277//11	866,000	—	BV	100	115	—
AH1277//12	372,000	—	BV	100	115	—
AH1277//13	246,000	—	BV	100	115	—
AH1277//14	286,000	—	BV	100	115	—
AH1277//15	3,600	110	120	160	200	—

KM# 697 250 KURUSH
18.0400 g., 0.9170 Gold .5319 oz. AGW **Mint:** Qustantiniyah

Date	Mintage	VG	F	VF	XF	Unc
AH1277//1	3,880	325	425	800	1,250	—
AH1277//5	—	375	525	900	1,550	—
AH1277//7	2,800	300	400	600	1,000	—
AH1277//8	30,000	250	325	450	650	—
AH1277//9	8,000	250	350	500	700	—

KM# 698 500 KURUSH
36.0800 g., 0.9170 Gold 1.0638 oz. AGW **Mint:** Qustantiniyah

Date	Mintage	VG	F	VF	XF	Unc
AH1277//1	3,180	525	700	1,000	1,400	—
AH1277//3	1,580	600	800	1,250	1,750	—
AH1277//5	—	800	1,000	1,750	2,500	—
AH1277//7	21,000	BV	525	650	950	—
AH1277//8	71,000	BV	525	650	950	—
AH1277//9	74,000	BV	525	650	950	—
AH1277//10	30,000	BV	525	650	950	—
AH1277//11	36,000	BV	525	650	950	—
AH1277//13	59,000	BV	525	650	950	—

MILLED COINAGE
Gold Mint Visit Issues

The gold coins continued to be struck to the weights and finenesses of the old Ottoman system, but were tariffed at the going price of gold. The same continues to hold true today. Both regular and the "Monnaie de Luxe" series were produced.

KM# 706 25 KURUSH
1.8040 g., 0.9170 Gold .0532 oz. AGW **Subject:** Mint Visit Coinage **Mint:** Bursa

Date	Mintage	VG	F	VF	XF	Unc
AH1277//1	4,800	—	150	300	450	650

KM# 707 50 KURUSH
3.6080 g., 0.9170 Gold .1064 oz. AGW **Subject:** Mint Visit Coinage **Mint:** Bursa

Date	Mintage	VG	F	VF	XF	Unc
AH1277//1	2,476	—	200	400	650	1,000

KM# 708 100 KURUSH
7.2160 g., 0.9170 Gold .2128 oz. AGW **Subject:** Mint Visit Coinage **Mint:** Bursa

Date	Mintage	VG	F	VF	XF	Unc
AH1277//1	9,737	—	400	650	1,000	1,600

STANDARD COINAGE

KM# 685 5 PARA
Copper **Mint:** Qustantiniyah

Date	Mintage	VG	F	VF	XF	Unc
AH1277//1	—	2.25	5.00	12.50	20.00	—

KM# 699 5 PARA
Copper **Mint:** Qustantiniyah

Date	Mintage	VG	F	VF	XF	Unc
AH1277//4	16,000,000	—	1.00	3.00	5.00	10.00

KM# 686 10 PARA
Copper **Mint:** Qustantiniyah

Date	Mintage	VG	F	VF	XF	Unc
AH1277//1	—	3.00	4.00	10.00	20.00	—

KM# 700 10 PARA
Copper **Mint:** Qustantiniyah

Date	Mintage	VG	F	VF	XF	Unc
AH1277//4	8,000,000	—	1.00	3.00	5.00	10.00
AH1277//4 Proof	—	Value: 125				

KM# 687 20 PARA
Copper **Mint:** Qustantiniyah

Date	Mintage	VG	F	VF	XF	Unc
AH1277//1	—	4.00	5.00	12.50	25.00	—

KM# 688 20 PARA
0.6013 g., 0.8300 Silver .0160 oz. ASW **Mint:** Qustantiniyah

Date	Mintage	VG	F	VF	XF	Unc
AH1277//1	420,000	3.50	6.00	12.00	25.00	—
AH1277//2	850,000	3.50	6.00	12.00	25.00	—
AH1277//3	1,570,000	3.50	6.00	12.00	25.00	—
AH1277//4	930,000	25.00	50.00	100	150	—
AH1277//5	740,000	3.50	6.00	12.00	25.00	—
AH1277//6	520,000	5.00	10.00	17.50	40.00	—
AH1277//7	350,000	7.50	15.00	30.00	60.00	—

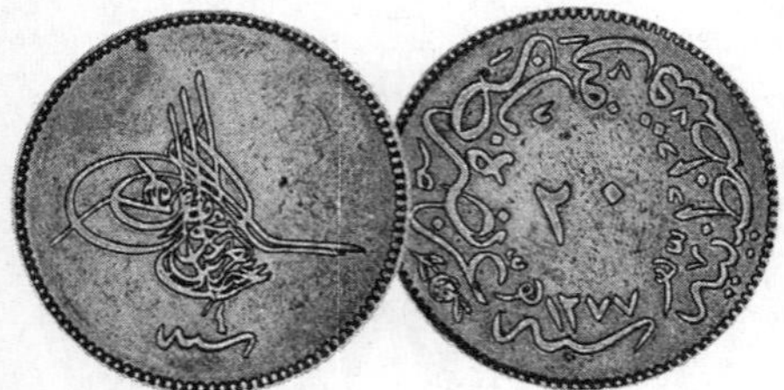

KM# 701 20 PARA
Copper **Mint:** Qustantiniyah

Date	Mintage	VG	F	VF	XF	Unc
AH1277//4	4,000,000	—	1.00	2.50	6.00	12.00
AH1277//4 Proof	—	Value: 175				

KM# 689 40 PARA
1.2027 g., 0.8300 Silver .0321 oz. ASW **Mint:** Qustantiniyah

Date	Mintage	VG	F	VF	XF	Unc
AH1277//1	545,000	2.00	3.00	10.00	25.00	—
AH1277//2	2,245,000	2.00	3.00	7.50	20.00	—
AH1277//3	1,370,000	2.00	3.00	7.50	20.00	—
AH1277//4	900,000	2.00	3.00	7.50	20.00	—
AH1277//5	685,000	2.00	3.00	7.50	20.00	—
AH1277//7	535,000	35.00	75.00	100	200	—

KM# 702 40 PARA
Copper **Mint:** Qustantiniyah

Date	Mintage	VG	F	VF	XF	Unc
AH1277//4	2,000,000	—	3.00	9.00	15.00	30.00

KM# 703 KURUSH
1.2027 g., 0.8300 Silver .0321 oz. ASW **Subject:** Mint Visit Coinage **Mint:** Bursa

Date	Mintage	F	VF	XF	Unc
AH1277//1 (1861)	40,000	200	300	500	1,000

KM# 690 2 KURUSH
2.4055 g., 0.8300 Silver .0642 oz. ASW **Mint:** Qustantiniyah

Date	Mintage	VG	F	VF	XF	Unc
AH1277//1	55,000	25.00	50.00	100	200	—
AH1277//2	65,000	45.00	90.00	200	400	—
AH1277//3	235,000	20.00	35.00	75.00	125	—
AH1277//5	135,000	40.00	75.00	125	250	—
AH1277//5 Proof	—	Value: 1,500				

KM# 704 2 KURUSH
2.4055 g., 0.8300 Silver .0642 oz. ASW **Subject:** Mint Visit Coinage **Mint:** Bursa

Date	Mintage	VG	F	VF	XF	Unc
AH1277//1	40,000	—	150	225	400	800

KM# 691 5 KURUSH
6.0130 g., 0.8300 Silver .1605 oz. ASW **Mint:** Qustantiniyah

Date	Mintage	VG	F	VF	XF	Unc
AH1277//1	16,000	2.50	4.00	8.50	20.00	—
AH1277//2	280,000	5.00	10.00	17.50	35.00	—
AH1277//3	288,000	2.50	4.00	8.50	20.00	—
AH1277//4	280,000	2.50	4.00	8.50	20.00	—
AH1277//5	242,000	2.50	4.00	8.50	20.00	—
AH1277//6	342,000	2.50	4.00	8.50	20.00	—
AH1277//7	248,000	2.50	4.00	8.50	20.00	—
AH1277//8	20,000	70.00	130	225	350	—
AH1277//9	50,000	2.50	4.00	8.50	20.00	—
AH1277//10	230,000	2.50	4.00	8.50	20.00	—
AH1277//11	126,000	2.50	4.00	8.50	20.00	—
AH1277//12	186,000	2.50	4.00	8.50	20.00	—
AH1277//13	284,000	2.50	4.00	8.50	20.00	—
AH1277//14	202,000	5.00	10.00	17.50	35.00	—
AH1277//15	154,000	10.00	20.00	35.00	70.00	—

KM# 705 5 KURUSH
6.0130 g., 0.8300 Silver .1605 oz. ASW **Subject:** Mint Visit Coinage **Mint:** Bursa

Date	Mintage	VG	F	VF	XF	Unc
AH1277//1	18,000	—	125	200	350	550

KM# 692 10 KURUSH
12.0270 g., 0.8300 Silver .3210 oz. ASW **Mint:** Qustantiniyah

Date	Mintage	VG	F	VF	XF	Unc
AH1277//1	—	20.00	50.00	100	200	—
AH1277//2	280,000	50.00	100	200	350	—
AH1277//5 Proof	—	Value: 6,000				

KM# 693 20 KURUSH
24.0550 g., 0.8300 Silver .6419 oz. ASW **Reverse:** Similar to Y#22 **Mint:** Qustantiniyah **Note:** Varieties exist in size of accession date.

Date	Mintage	VG	F	VF	XF	Unc
AH1277//1	1,055,000	9.00	15.00	20.00	40.00	—
AH1277//2	3,106,000	9.00	15.00	20.00	40.00	—
AH1277//3	257,000	12.00	20.00	35.00	70.00	—
AH1277//4	234,000	15.00	25.00	50.00	100	—
AH1277//5	387,000	10.00	18.00	25.00	50.00	—
AH1277//6	314,000	9.00	15.00	20.00	40.00	—
AH1277//7	640,000	9.00	15.00	20.00	40.00	—
AH1277//8	1,457,000	9.00	15.00	20.00	40.00	—
AH1277//9	859,000	9.00	15.00	20.00	40.00	—
AH1277//10	528,000	9.00	15.00	20.00	40.00	—
AH1277//11	530,000	9.00	15.00	20.00	40.00	—
AH1277//12	233,000	9.00	15.00	20.00	40.00	—
AH1277//12 Proof	—	Value: 1,000				
AH1277//13	514,000	9.00	15.00	20.00	40.00	—
AH1277//14	584,000	9.00	15.00	20.00	40.00	—
AH1277//15	4,034,000	9.00	15.00	20.00	40.00	—

Murad V
AH1293/1876AD

MILLED COINAGE
Gold Issues

KM# 713 25 KURUSH
1.8040 g., 0.9170 Gold .0532 oz. AGW **Obverse:** Crescent above toughra **Mint:** Qustantiniyah

Date	Mintage	VG	F	VF	XF	Unc
AH1293//1	14,000	100	175	300	450	—

KM# 714 50 KURUSH
3.6080 g., 0.9170 Gold .1064 oz. AGW **Obverse:** Crescent above toughra **Mint:** Qustantiniyah

Date	Mintage	VG	F	VF	XF	Unc
AH1293//1	4,500	300	500	750	1,250	—

KM# 715 100 KURUSH
7.2160 g., 0.9170 Gold .2128 oz. AGW **Obverse:** Crescent above toughra **Mint:** Qustantiniyah

Date	Mintage	VG	F	VF	XF	Unc
AH1293//1	7,700	BV	110	175	250	—

STANDARD COINAGE

KM# 710 KURUSH
1.2027 g., 0.8300 Silver .0321 oz. ASW **Obverse:** Without flower right of toughra **Mint:** Qustantiniyah

Date	Mintage	VG	F	VF	XF	Unc
AH1293//1	280,000	75.00	125	175	300	—

KM# 711 5 KURUSH
6.0130 g., 0.8300 Silver .1605 oz. ASW **Obverse:** Without flower right of toughra **Mint:** Qustantiniyah

Date	Mintage	VG	F	VF	XF	Unc
AH1293//1	20,000	100	150	250	400	—

KM# 712 20 KURUSH
24.0550 g., 0.8300 Silver .6419 oz. ASW **Obverse:** Without flower right of toughra **Mint:** Qustantiniyah

Date	Mintage	VG	F	VF	XF	Unc
AH1293//1	128,000	25.00	45.00	60.00	100	—

Note: Beware of specimens of KM#722 altered to appear as a piece of Murad; the toughra is very different

SULTANATE

Abdul Hamid II

AH1293-1327/1876-1909AD

MILLED COINAGE

Gold Issues

KM# 745 12-1/2 KURUSH
0.8770 g., 0.9170 Gold .0258 oz. AGW **Series:** Monnaie de Luxe **Obverse:** Toughra **Mint:** Qustantiniyah **Note:** Struck at Qustantiniyah.

Date	Mintage	VG	F	VF	XF	Unc
AH1293//25	720	40.00	70.00	100	180	—
AH1293//28	800	40.00	70.00	100	180	—
AH1293//29	12,000	20.00	30.00	45.00	75.00	—
AH1293//30	13,000	20.00	30.00	45.00	75.00	—
AH1293//31	24,000	20.00	30.00	45.00	75.00	—

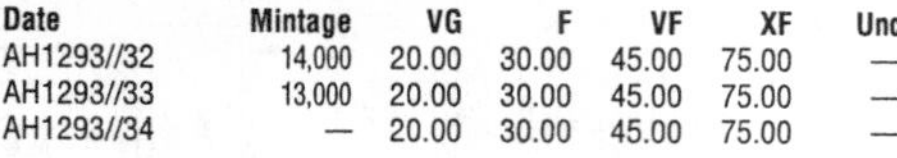

Date	Mintage	VG	F	VF	XF	Unc
AH1293//32	14,000	20.00	30.00	45.00	75.00	—
AH1293//33	13,000	20.00	30.00	45.00	75.00	—
AH1293//34	—	20.00	30.00	45.00	75.00	—

KM# 723 25 KURUSH
1.8040 g., 0.9170 Gold .0532 oz. AGW **Obverse:** Flower right of toughra **Mint:** Qustantiniyah

Date	Mintage	VG	F	VF	XF	Unc
AH1293//1 Rare	—	—	—	—	—	—
AH1293//2 Rare	3,600	—	—	—	—	—
AH1293//3	5,400	50.00	100	150	200	—
AH1293//4	3,600	50.00	100	150	200	—
AH1293//5	—	50.00	100	125	175	—
AH1293//6	9,340	50.00	100	125	175	—

KM# 729 25 KURUSH
1.8040 g., 0.9170 Gold .0532 oz. AGW **Obverse:** Toughra; "el-Ghazi" to right **Note:** Struck at Qustantiniyah.

Date	Mintage	VG	F	VF	XF	Unc
AH1293//6 Rare	560	—	—	—	—	—
AH1293//7	49,000	BV	27.50	35.00	45.00	—
AH1293//8	4,600	BV	27.50	40.00	50.00	—
AH1293//9	6,000	BV	27.50	40.00	50.00	—
AH1293//10	6,800	BV	27.50	40.00	50.00	—
AH1293//11	36,000	BV	27.50	35.00	45.00	—
AH1293//12	36,000	BV	27.50	35.00	45.00	—
AH1293//13	40,000	BV	27.50	35.00	45.00	—
AH1293//14	52,000	BV	27.50	35.00	45.00	—
AH1293//15	12,000	BV	27.50	35.00	45.00	—
AH1293//16	2,000	BV	27.50	45.00	60.00	—
AH1293//17	40,000	BV	27.50	35.00	45.00	—
AH1293//18	14,000	BV	27.50	35.00	45.00	—
AH1293//19	59,000	BV	27.50	35.00	45.00	—
AH1293//20	43,000	BV	27.50	35.00	45.00	—
AH1293//21	38,000	BV	27.50	35.00	45.00	—
AH1293//22	36,000	BV	27.50	35.00	45.00	—
AH1293//23	52,000	BV	27.50	35.00	45.00	—
AH1293//24	43,000	BV	27.50	35.00	45.00	—
AH1293//25	57,000	BV	27.50	35.00	45.00	—
AH1293//26	48,000	BV	27.50	35.00	45.00	—
AH1293//27	99,000	BV	27.50	35.00	45.00	—
AH1293//28	77,000	BV	27.50	35.00	45.00	—
AH1293//29	102,000	BV	27.50	35.00	45.00	—
AH1293//30	156,000	BV	27.50	35.00	45.00	—
AH1293//31	58,000	BV	27.50	35.00	45.00	—
AH1293//32	112,000	BV	27.50	35.00	45.00	—
AH1293//33	16,000	BV	27.50	35.00	45.00	—
AH1293//34	—	BV	27.50	35.00	45.00	—

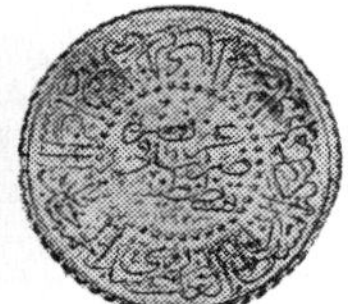

KM# 739 25 KURUSH
1.7540 g., 0.9170 Gold .0517 oz. AGW **Series:** Monnaie de Luxe **Obverse:** Toughra; "el-Ghazi" to right **Note:** Struck at Qustantiniyah.

Date	Mintage	VG	F	VF	XF	Unc
AH1293//18 Rare	—	—	—	—	—	—
AH1293//23	26,000	50.00	65.00	75.00	95.00	—
AH1293//24	17,000	50.00	65.00	75.00	95.00	—
AH1293//25	—	50.00	65.00	75.00	95.00	—
AH1293//26	4,300	50.00	65.00	75.00	95.00	—
AH1293//27	7,620	50.00	65.00	75.00	95.00	—
AH1293//28	9,268	50.00	65.00	75.00	95.00	—
AH1293//29	7,600	50.00	65.00	75.00	95.00	—
AH1293//30	26,056	50.00	65.00	75.00	95.00	—
AH1293//31	27,964	50.00	65.00	75.00	95.00	—
AH1293//32	39,192	50.00	65.00	75.00	95.00	—
AH1293//33	41,696	50.00	65.00	75.00	95.00	—
AH1293//34	17,728	50.00	65.00	75.00	95.00	—

KM# 724 50 KURUSH
3.6080 g., 0.9170 Gold .1064 oz. AGW **Obverse:** Flower right of toughra **Mint:** Qustantiniyah

Date	Mintage	VG	F	VF	XF	Unc
AH1293//1	5,700	75.00	100	150	300	—
AH1293//3	200	120	250	425	850	—
AH1293//6	8,200	100	200	350	750	—

KM# 731 50 KURUSH
3.6080 g., 0.9170 Gold .1064 oz. AGW **Obverse:** Toughra; "el-Ghazi" to right **Mint:** Qustantiniyah **Note:** Struck at Qustantiniyah.

Date	Mintage	VG	F	VF	XF	Unc
AH1293//7	6,500	BV	50.00	65.00	95.00	—
AH1293//8	2,000	BV	55.00	70.00	100	—
AH1293//9	3,000	BV	55.00	70.00	100	—
AH1293//10	6,000	BV	50.00	65.00	95.00	—
AH1293//11	14,000	BV	50.00	60.00	90.00	—
AH1293//12	3,600	BV	55.00	70.00	100	—
AH1293//13	5,000	BV	50.00	65.00	95.00	—
AH1293//14	8,000	BV	50.00	65.00	95.00	—
AH1293//15	6,000	BV	50.00	65.00	95.00	—
AH1293//16	2,000	BV	55.00	70.00	100	—
AH1293//17	13,000	BV	50.00	60.00	90.00	—
AH1293//18	6,000	BV	50.00	65.00	95.00	—
AH1293//19	11,000	BV	50.00	60.00	90.00	—
AH1293//20	18,000	BV	50.00	60.00	90.00	—
AH1293//21	12,000	BV	50.00	60.00	90.00	—
AH1293//22	13,000	BV	50.00	60.00	90.00	—
AH1293//23	18,000	BV	50.00	60.00	90.00	—
AH1293//24	10,000	BV	50.00	60.00	90.00	—
AH1293//25	15,000	BV	50.00	60.00	90.00	—
AH1293//26	14,000	BV	50.00	60.00	90.00	—
AH1293//27	14,000	BV	50.00	60.00	90.00	—
AH1293//28	33,000	BV	50.00	60.00	90.00	—
AH1293//29	24,000	BV	50.00	60.00	90.00	—
AH1293//30	66,000	BV	50.00	60.00	90.00	—
AH1293//31	59,000	BV	50.00	60.00	90.00	—
AH1293//32	48,000	BV	50.00	60.00	90.00	—
AH1293//33	16,000	BV	50.00	60.00	90.00	—
AH1293//34	—	BV	50.00	60.00	90.00	—

KM# 740 50 KURUSH
3.5080 g., 0.9170 Gold .1034 oz. AGW **Series:** Monnaie de Luxe **Obverse:** Toughra; "el-Ghazi" to right **Note:** Struck at Qustantiniyah.

Date	Mintage	VG	F	VF	XF	Unc
AH1293//18 Rare	—	—	—	—	—	—
AH1293//23	14,000	50.00	75.00	90.00	140	—
AH1293//24	8,980	50.00	75.00	90.00	140	—
AH1293//25	—	50.00	75.00	90.00	140	—
AH1293//26	4,820	50.00	75.00	90.00	140	—
AH1293//27	5,436	50.00	75.00	90.00	140	—
AH1293//28	6,630	50.00	75.00	90.00	140	—
AH1293//29	8,660	50.00	75.00	90.00	140	—
AH1293//30	14,924	50.00	75.00	90.00	140	—
AH1293//31	18,813	50.00	75.00	90.00	140	—
AH1293//32	22,460	50.00	75.00	90.00	140	—
AH1293//33	27,542	50.00	75.00	90.00	140	—
AH1293//34	12,886	50.00	75.00	90.00	140	—

KM# 725 100 KURUSH
7.2160 g., 0.9170 Gold .2128 oz. AGW **Obverse:** Flower right of toughra **Mint:** Qustantiniyah

Date	Mintage	VG	F	VF	XF	Unc
AH1293//1	77,000	110	150	200	275	—
AH1293//2	415,000	110	150	200	275	—
AH1293//3	97,000	110	150	200	275	—
AH1293//4	1,530	150	200	300	400	—
AH1293//6	220,000	110	150	200	275	—

KM# 730 100 KURUSH
7.2160 g., 0.9170 Gold .2128 oz. AGW **Obverse:** Toughra; "el-Ghazi" to right **Note:** Struck at Qustantiniyah.

Date	Mintage	VG	F	VF	XF	Unc
AH1293//6	1,220	—	BV	110	125	—
AH1293//7	415,000	—	BV	100	115	—
AH1293//8	18,000	—	BV	100	115	—
AH1293//9	23,000	—	BV	100	115	—
AH1293//10	572,000	—	BV	100	115	—
AH1293//11	255,000	—	BV	100	115	—
AH1293//12	2,000	—	BV	110	125	—
AH1293//13	2,000	—	BV	110	125	—
AH1293//14	18,000	—	BV	100	115	—
AH1293//15	2,000	—	BV	110	125	—
AH1293//16	722,000	—	BV	100	115	—
AH1293//17	3,350	—	BV	110	125	—
AH1293//18	165,000	—	BV	100	115	—
AH1293//19	3,000	—	BV	110	125	—
AH1293//20	728,000	—	BV	100	115	—
AH1293//21	4,400	—	BV	110	125	—
AH1293//22	186,000	—	BV	100	115	—
AH1293//23	225,000	—	BV	100	115	—
AH1293//24	2,850	—	BV	110	125	—
AH1293//25	3,000	—	BV	110	125	—
AH1293//26	2,000	—	BV	150	180	—
AH1293//27	48,000	—	BV	120	150	—
AH1293//28	865,000	—	BV	100	115	—
AH1293//29	1,026,000	—	BV	100	115	—
AH1293//30	1,644,000	—	BV	100	115	—
AH1293//31	2,748,000	—	BV	100	115	—
AH1293//32	1,952,000	—	BV	100	115	—
AH1293//33	963,000	—	BV	100	115	—
AH1293//34	—	—	100	200	250	—

KM# 741 100 KURUSH
7.0160 g., 0.9170 Gold .2068 oz. AGW **Series:** Monnaie de Luxe **Obverse:** Toughra; "el-Ghazi" to right **Note:** Struck at Qustantiniyah.

Date	Mintage	VG	F	VF	XF	Unc
AH1293//18 Rare	—	—	—	—	—	—
AH1293//23	10,000	BV	100	135	190	—
AH1293//24	9,600	BV	100	135	190	—
AH1293//25	—	BV	100	135	190	—
AH1293//26	3,635	BV	100	135	190	—
AH1293//27	5,590	BV	100	135	190	—
AH1293//28	9,870	BV	100	135	190	—
AH1293//29	13,638	BV	100	135	190	—
AH1293//30	18,129	BV	100	135	190	—
AH1293//31	22,796	BV	100	135	190	—
AH1293//32	31,126	BV	100	135	190	—
AH1293//33	42,667	BV	100	135	190	—
AH1293//34	18,716	BV	100	135	190	—

KM# 726 250 KURUSH
18.0400 g., 0.9170 Gold .5319 oz. AGW **Obverse:** Flower right of toughra **Mint:** Qustantiniyah

Date	Mintage	VG	F	VF	XF	Unc
AH1293//1	120	600	1,000	1,600	2,000	—

KM# 732 250 KURUSH
18.0400 g., 0.9170 Gold .5319 oz. AGW **Obverse:** Toughra; "el-Ghazi" to right **Mint:** Qustantiniyah **Note:** Struck at Qustantiniyah.

Date	Mintage	VG	F	VF	XF	Unc
AH1293//11	—	BV	250	300	450	—
AH1293//12	—	BV	250	300	450	—
AH1293//13	—	BV	250	300	450	—
AH1293//14	—	BV	250	300	450	—
AH1293//15	—	BV	250	300	450	—
AH1293//16	—	BV	250	300	450	—
AH1293//17	—	BV	250	300	450	—
AH1293//18	—	BV	250	300	450	—
AH1293//19	—	BV	250	300	450	—
AH1293//20	—	BV	250	300	450	—
AH1293//21	—	BV	250	300	450	—
AH1293//22	—	BV	250	300	450	—
AH1293//23	—	BV	250	300	450	—
AH1293//24	—	BV	250	300	450	—
AH1293//25	—	BV	250	300	450	—
AH1293//26	1,428	BV	250	300	450	—
AH1293//27	1,450	BV	250	300	450	—
AH1293//28	7,027	BV	250	300	450	—
AH1293//29	7,522	BV	250	300	450	—
AH1293//30	7,522	BV	250	300	450	—
AH1293//31	4,900	BV	250	300	450	—
AH1293//32	8,729	BV	250	300	450	—
AH1293//33	2,669	BV	230	275	450	—
AH1293//34	1,420	BV	230	275	450	—

KM# 742 250 KURUSH
17.5400 g., 0.9170 Gold .5169 oz. AGW **Series:** Monnaie de Luxe **Obverse:** Toughra; "el-Ghazi" to right **Note:** Struck at Qustantiniyah.

Date	Mintage	VG	F	VF	XF	Unc
AH1293//24	—	BV	250	375	600	—
AH1293//25	—	BV	275	400	600	—
AH1293//26	1,544	BV	275	400	600	—
AH1293//27	1,538	BV	275	400	600	—
AH1293//28	1,770	BV	275	400	600	—
AH1293//29	1,520	BV	275	400	600	—
AH1293//30	1,631	BV	275	400	600	—
AH1293//31	1,922	BV	275	400	600	—
AH1293//32	1,778	BV	275	400	600	—
AH1293//33	2,650	BV	275	400	600	—
AH1293//34 Rare	931	—	—	—	—	—

KM# 727 500 KURUSH
36.0800 g., 0.9170 Gold 1.0638 oz. AGW **Obverse:** Flower right of toughra **Mint:** Qustantiniyah

Date	Mintage	VG	F	VF	XF	Unc
AH1293//1	220	BV	525	675	950	—
AH1293//2	5,580	BV	500	650	900	—
AH1293//3	54,000	BV	450	600	850	—
AH1293//4	60	BV	550	700	1,000	—
AH1293//6	2,600	BV	500	650	900	—

KM# 733 500 KURUSH
36.0800 g., 0.9170 Gold 1.0638 oz. AGW **Obverse:** Toughra; "el-Ghazi" to right **Mint:** Qustantiniyah **Note:** Struck at Qustantiniyah.

Date	Mintage	VG	F	VF	XF	Unc
AH1293//11	200	BV	500	550	750	—
AH1293//12	200	BV	500	550	750	—
AH1293//13	200	BV	500	550	750	—
AH1293//14	200	BV	500	550	750	—
AH1293//15	200	BV	500	550	750	—
AH1293//16	15,000	BV	450	500	700	—
AH1293//17	200	BV	500	550	750	—
AH1293//18	200	BV	500	550	750	—
AH1293//19	200	BV	500	550	750	—
AH1293//20	200	BV	500	550	750	—
AH1293//21	200	BV	500	550	750	—
AH1293//22	200	BV	500	500	750	—
AH1293//23	15,000	BV	450	525	700	—
AH1293//24	8,048	BV	475	550	725	—
AH1293//25	11,000	BV	500	550	750	—
AH1293//26	8,765	BV	500	550	750	—
AH1293//27	22,000	BV	500	550	750	—
AH1293//28	36,000	BV	500	550	750	—
AH1293//29	17,000	BV	500	550	750	—
AH1293//30	33,000	BV	500	550	750	—
AH1293//31	41,000	BV	500	550	750	—
AH1293//32	33,000	BV	500	550	750	—
AH1293//33	16,000	BV	500	550	750	—
AH1293//34	—	BV	500	550	750	—

STANDARD COINAGE

KM# 728 5 PARA
Copper **Obverse:** Toughra **Mint:** Qustantiniyah

Date	Mintage	VG	F	VF	XF	Unc
AH1293//2 Rare	—	—	—	—	—	—
AH1293//3	—	0.25	0.50	3.00	10.00	—
AH1293//4	—	0.25	0.50	3.00	10.00	—

KM# 743 5 PARA
1.0023 g., 0.1000 Silver .0032 oz. ASW **Obverse:** Toughra; "el-Ghazi" to right **Mint:** Qustantiniyah **Note:** Struck at Qustantiniyah.

Date	Mintage	VG	F	VF	XF	Unc
AH1293//25	3,336,000	0.25	0.50	1.25	4.00	—
AH1293//26	—	0.25	0.50	1.25	4.00	—
AH1293//27	—	0.25	0.50	1.25	4.00	—
AH1293//28	—	0.50	1.00	3.00	12.00	—
AH1293//30	—	6.00	12.00	20.00	40.00	—

KM# 744 10 PARA
2.0046 g., 0.1000 Silver .0064 oz. ASW **Obverse:** Toughra; "el-Ghazi" to right **Mint:** Qustantiniyah **Note:** Struck at Qustantiniyah.

Date	Mintage	VG	F	VF	XF	Unc
AH1293//25	3,492,000	0.25	0.50	1.00	4.00	—
AH1293//26	—	0.25	0.50	1.00	4.00	—
AH1293//27	—	0.25	0.50	1.00	4.00	—
Note: Varieties exist in size of regnal year 27						
AH1293//28	—	0.25	0.50	1.50	6.00	—
AH1293//30	—	1.00	2.00	5.00	15.00	—

KM# 717 20 PARA
0.6013 g., 0.8300 Silver .0160 oz. ASW **Obverse:** Flower right of toughra **Mint:** Qustantiniyah

Date	Mintage	VG	F	VF	XF	Unc
AH1293//1	110,000	25.00	50.00	100	175	—
AH1293//4	50,000	40.00	100	200	300	—

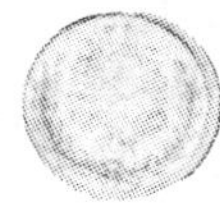

KM# 734 20 PARA
0.6013 g., 0.8300 Silver .0160 oz. ASW **Obverse:** "el Ghazi" right of toughra **Mint:** Qustantiniyah

Date	Mintage	VG	F	VF	XF	Unc
AH1293//8	350,000	5.00	7.50	15.00	35.00	—

KM# 718 KURUSH
1.2027 g., 0.8300 Silver .0321 oz. ASW **Obverse:** Flower right of toughra **Mint:** Qustantiniyah

Date	Mintage	VG	F	VF	XF	Unc
AH1293//1	345,000	40.00	75.00	150	250	—
AH1293//2	20,000	50.00	100	175	300	—
AH1293//4	45,000	40.00	75.00	150	250	—

KM# 735 KURUSH
1.2027 g., 0.8300 Silver .0321 oz. ASW **Obverse:** Toughra; "el-Ghazi" to right **Mint:** Qustantiniyah **Note:** Varieties exist in the size of year and inscription. Struck at Qustantiniyah.

Date	Mintage	VG	F	VF	XF	Unc
AH1293//8	210,000	1.00	1.75	3.50	7.00	—
AH1293//9	600,000	1.00	2.00	3.00	5.00	—
AH1293//11	8,830,000	1.00	2.00	3.00	5.00	—
AH1293//13	130,000	4.00	10.00	20.00	35.00	—
AH1293//16	4,000,000	1.00	2.00	3.00	5.00	—
AH1293//17	6,440,000	1.00	2.00	3.00	5.00	—
AH1293//18	40,000	5.00	15.00	30.00	50.00	—
AH1293//19	3,070,000	1.00	2.00	3.00	5.00	—
AH1293//20	4,122,000	1.00	2.00	3.00	5.00	—
AH1293//21	40,000	3.00	7.50	15.00	30.00	—
AH1293//22	3,979,000	1.00	2.00	3.00	5.00	—
AH1293//23	3,760,000	1.00	2.00	3.00	5.00	—
AH1293//24	2,041,000	1.00	2.00	3.00	5.00	—
AH1293//25	84,000	3.00	7.50	15.00	30.00	—
AH1293//26	55,000	3.00	7.50	15.00	30.00	—
AH1293//27	9,945,000	1.00	2.00	3.00	5.00	—
AH1293//28	16,139,000	1.00	2.00	3.00	5.00	—
AH1293//29	7,076,000	1.00	2.00	3.00	5.00	—
AH1293//30	707,000	2.00	4.00	8.00	15.00	—
AH1293//31	1,366,000	1.00	2.00	3.00	5.00	—
AH1293//32	1,140,000	1.00	2.00	3.00	5.00	—
AH1293//33	1,700,000	1.00	2.00	3.00	5.00	—
AH1293//34	—	40.00	60.00	115	225	—

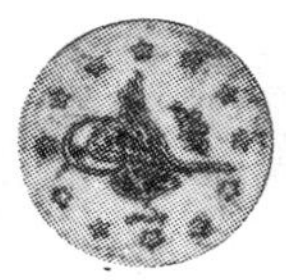

KM# 719 2 KURUSH
2.4055 g., 0.8300 Silver .0642 oz. ASW **Obverse:** Flower right of toughra **Mint:** Qustantiniyah

Date	Mintage	VG	F	VF	XF	Unc
AH1293//1	10,000	250	500	800	1,500	—

KM# 736 2 KURUSH
2.4055 g., 0.8300 Silver .0642 oz. ASW **Obverse:** Toughra; "el-Ghazi" to right **Mint:** Qustantiniyah **Note:** Varieties exist in the size of toughra and year. Struck at Qustantiniyah.

Date	Mintage	VG	F	VF	XF	Unc
AH1293//8	103,000	2.00	2.50	5.00	10.00	—
AH1293//9	605,000	1.75	2.75	4.50	8.00	—
AH1293//11	5,115,000	1.50	2.00	4.00	7.00	—
AH1293//12	325,000	1.75	2.75	4.50	8.00	—
AH1293//13	30,000	15.00	22.50	35.00	75.00	—
AH1293//16	980,000	1.50	2.00	4.00	7.00	—
AH1293//17	3,736,000	1.50	2.00	4.00	7.00	—
AH1293//18	23,000	15.00	25.00	35.00	75.00	—
AH1293//19	3,507,000	1.50	2.00	4.00	7.00	—
AH1293//20	3,370,000	1.50	2.00	4.00	7.00	—
AH1293//21	21,000	15.00	25.00	35.00	75.00	—
AH1293//22	2,980,000	1.50	2.00	4.00	7.00	—
AH1293//23	3,139,000	1.50	2.00	4.00	7.00	—
AH1293//24	1,490,000	1.75	2.25	4.50	8.00	—
AH1293//25	14,000	15.00	25.00	35.00	75.00	—
AH1293//26	17,000	15.00	25.00	35.00	75.00	—
AH1293//27	4,689,000	1.50	2.00	4.00	7.00	—
AH1293//28	7,567,000	1.50	2.00	4.00	7.00	—
AH1293//29	7,775,000	1.50	2.00	4.00	7.00	—
AH1293//30	1,366,000	1.50	2.00	4.00	7.00	—
AH1293//31	3,014,000	1.50	2.00	4.00	7.00	—
AH1293//32	1,625,000	1.50	2.00	4.00	7.00	—
AH1293//33	2,173,000	1.50	2.00	4.00	7.00	—
AH1293//34	—	45.00	90.00	140	200	—

KM# 720 5 KURUSH
6.0130 g., 0.8300 Silver .1605 oz. ASW **Obverse:** Flower right of toughra **Mint:** Qustantiniyah

Date	Mintage	VG	F	VF	XF	Unc
AH1293//1	42,000	50.00	100	150	250	—
AH1293//2	14,000	30.00	60.00	100	200	—
AH1293//3	16,000	10.00	20.00	35.00	75.00	—
AH1293//4	269,000	7.50	15.00	30.00	60.00	—

KM# 737 5 KURUSH
6.0130 g., 0.8300 Silver .1605 oz. ASW **Obverse:** Toughra; "el-Ghazi" to right **Note:** Varieties exist in the size of toughra, inscription, and date. Struck at Qustantiniyah.

Date	Mintage	VG	F	VF	XF	Unc
AH1293//8	82,000	4.00	8.00	11.00	17.50	—
AH1293//9	614,000	2.00	3.50	5.00	9.50	—
AH1293//11	1,788,000	2.00	3.50	5.00	9.50	—
AH1293//12	1,880,000	2.00	3.50	5.00	9.50	—
AH1293//13	2,182,000	2.00	3.50	5.00	9.50	—
AH1293//14	380,000	2.00	3.50	5.00	9.50	—
AH1293//24	126,000	2.00	3.75	6.50	10.00	—
AH1293//15	194,000	2.00	4.00	6.00	12.00	—
AH1293//16	914,000	2.00	3.50	5.00	9.50	—
AH1293//17	1,337,000	2.00	3.50	5.00	9.50	—
AH1293//18	12,000	20.00	35.00	55.00	85.00	—
AH1293//19	31,000	10.00	20.00	35.00	60.00	—
AH1293//20	162,000	4.00	7.50	12.00	20.00	—
AH1293//21	18,000	15.00	30.00	45.00	75.00	—
AH1293//22	8,000	15.00	30.00	45.00	75.00	—
AH1293//23	7,000	15.00	30.00	45.00	75.00	—
AH1293//25	13,000	15.00	30.00	45.00	75.00	—
AH1293//26	8,000	15.00	30.00	45.00	75.00	—
AH1293//27	16,000	15.00	30.00	45.00	75.00	—
AH1293//28	6,000	15.00	30.00	45.00	75.00	—
AH1293//29	7,000	15.00	30.00	45.00	75.00	—
AH1293//30	38,000	5.00	10.00	15.00	30.00	—
AH1293//31	Inc. above	3.50	4.50	7.00	15.00	—
AH1293//31/0	3,175,000	6.00	13.00	25.00	35.00	—
AH1293//32	3,334,000	2.00	3.25	4.50	9.50	—
AH1293//33	907,000	3.00	5.00	9.00	16.00	—
AH1293//34	—	50.00	80.00	110	200	—

KM# 721 10 KURUSH
12.0270 g., 0.8300 Silver .3210 oz. ASW **Obverse:** Flower right of toughra **Mint:** Qustantiniyah

Date	Mintage	VG	F	VF	XF	Unc
AH1293//1	4,000	125	200	300	500	—
AH1293//3	5,000	12.50	25.00	50.00	100	—

KM# 738 10 KURUSH
12.0270 g., 0.8300 Silver .3210 oz. ASW **Obverse:** Toughra; "el-Ghazi" to right **Note:** Struck at Qustantiniyah.

Date	Mintage	VG	F	VF	XF	Unc
AH1293//12	—	25.00	50.00	100	175	—
AH1293//13	161,000	5.00	10.00	20.00	45.00	—
AH1293//20	34,000	25.00	50.00	100	175	—
AH1293//31	51,000	20.00	40.00	75.00	125	—
AH1293//32	575,000	7.50	12.50	18.00	30.00	—
AH1293//33	273,000	6.00	10.00	20.00	35.00	—

KM# 722 20 KURUSH
24.0550 g., 0.8300 Silver .6419 oz. ASW **Obverse:** Flower right of toughra **Reverse:** Similar to KM#712 **Mint:** Qustantiniyah

Date	Mintage	VG	F	VF	XF	Unc
AH1293//1	1,402,000	BV	12.00	25.00	40.00	—
AH1293//2	1,357,000	BV	12.00	20.00	35.00	—
AH1293//3	5,940,000	BV	12.00	20.00	35.00	—

PATTERNS

Including off metal strikes

KM#	Date	Mintage	Identification	Mkt Val
Pn1	AH1223//22	—	10 Kurush. Silver.	—
Pn2	AH1223/22	—	10 Kurush. Silver.	—
Pn4	AH1223//1	—	30 Para. Silver.	—
Pn5	AH1223//1	—	60 Para. Silver.	—
Pn6	AH1223//1	—	80 Para. Silver.	—
Pn7	AH1223//1	—	100 Para. Silver.	—
Pn3	AH1223//1	—	20 Para. Silver.	—

UNITED STATES OF AMERICA

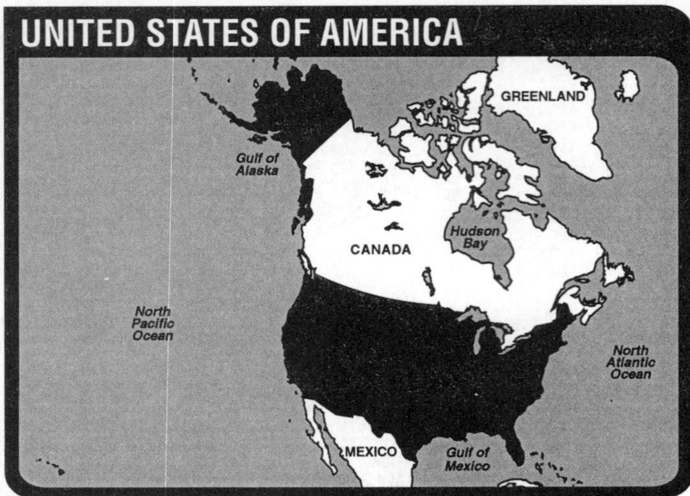

The United States of America as politically organized, under the Articles of Confederation consisted of the 13 original British-American colonies; New Hampshire, Massachusetts, Rhode Island, Connecticut, New York, New Jersey, Pennsylvania, Delaware, Virginia, North Carolina, South Carolina, Georgia and Maryland. Clustered along the eastern seaboard of North American between the forests of Maine and the marshes of Georgia. Under the Article of Confederation, the United States had no national capital: Philadelphia, where the "United States in Congress Assembled", was the "seat of government". The population during this political phase of America's history (1781-1789) was about 3 million, most of whom lived on self-sufficient family farms. Fishing, lumbering and the production of grains for export were major economic endeavors. Rapid strides were also being made in industry and manufacturing by 1775, the (then) colonies were accounting for one-seventh of the world's production of raw iron.

On the basis of the voyage of John Cabot to the North American mainland in 1497, England claimed the entire continent. The first permanent English settlement was established at Jamestown, Virginia, in 1607. France and Spain also claimed extensive territory in North America. At the end of the French and Indian Wars (1763), England acquired all of the territory east of the Mississippi River, including East and West Florida. From 1776 to 1781, the States were governed by the Continental Congress. From 1781 to 1789, they were organized under the Articles of Confederation, during which period the individual States had the right to issue money. Independence from Great Britain was attained by the American Revolution in 1776. The Constitution which organized and governs the present United States was ratified on Nov. 21, 1788.

MINT MARKS

C – Charlotte, N.C., 1838-61
CC – Carson City, NV, 1870-93
D – Dahlonega, GA, 1838-61
D – Denver, CO, 1906-present
O – New Orleans, LA, 1838-1909
P – Philadelphia, PA, 1793-present
S – San Francisco, CA, 1854-present
W – West Point, NY, 1984-present

CIRCULATION COINAGE

CENT

Draped Bust Cent

KM# 22 COPPER 29 mm. 10.9800 g. **Designer:** Robert Scot **Notes:** The "stemless" variety does not have stems extending from the wreath above and on both sides of the fraction on the reverse. The 1801 "3 errors" variety has the fraction on the reverse reading "1/000," has only one stem extending from the wreath above and on both sides of the fraction on the reverse, and "United" in "United States of America" appears as "linited."

Stems

Stemless

Date	Mintage	G-4	VG-8	F-12	VF-20	XF-40	MS-60
1801	1,362,837	36.00	65.00	125	280	1,000	—
1801 3 errors	Inc. above	85.00	300	700	1,500	5,500	—
1802	3,435,100	34.00	55.00	110	225	775	2,250
1803	2,471,353	34.00	55.00	110	225	775	2,250
1804	96,500	1,300	2,000	2,600	3,200	7,000	—
1804 Restrike of 1860	—	325	450	500	600	900	1,100
1805	941,116	37.00	60.00	125	300	875	2,450
1806	348,000	39.00	75.00	125	350	1,100	4,700
1807	727,221	31.00	53.00	110	225	775	2,250
1807/6 large 7/6	—	34.00	55.00	125	250	1,275	—
1807/6 small 7/6	—	1,500	2,500	3,900	5,000	—	—

Classic Head Cent

KM# 39 COPPER 29 mm. 10.8900 g. **Designer:** John Reich

Date	Mintage	G-4	VG-8	F-12	VF-20	XF-40	MS-60
1808	1,109,000	80.00	150	250	575	1,200	3,600
1809	222,867	90.00	175	420	1,300	2,650	6,300
1810	1,458,500	36.00	70.00	200	550	1,100	3,850
1811	218,025	90.00	150	400	1,000	1,500	7,000
1811/10	Inc. above	90.00	175	440	1,200	2,200	—
1812	1,075,500	36.00	65.00	180	525	975	2,800
1813	418,000	60.00	95.00	375	600	1,200	—
1814	357,830	36.00	65.00	180	530	975	2,800

Coronet Cent

KM# 45 COPPER 28-29 mm. 10.8900 g. **Designer:** Robert Scot **Notes:** The 1817 strikes have either 13 or 15 stars on the obverse.

Date	Mintage	G-4	VG-8	F-12	VF-20	XF-40	MS-60
1816	2,820,982	14.00	25.00	50.00	100.00	175	420
1817 13 stars	3,948,400	12.50	16.00	24.00	56.00	120	275
1817 15 stars	Inc. above	16.00	25.00	45.00	125	350	1,550
1818	3,167,000	12.50	16.00	24.00	56.00	125	250
1819	2,671,000	12.50	16.00	23.00	63.00	120	275
1820	4,407,550	12.50	16.00	23.00	63.00	120	275
1821	389,000	25.00	38.00	250	400	1,500	6,000
1822	2,072,339	12.50	16.00	32.00	84.00	195	575
1823 Included in 1824 mintage	—	90.00	150	310	690	2,750	—
1823/22 Included in 1824 mintage	—	80.00	110	300	675	2,450	—
1823 Restrike	—	700	550	675	800	900	1,300
1824	1,262,000	14.00	23.00	38.00	145	350	625
1824/22	Inc. above	17.00	30.00	56.00	225	975	—
1825	1,461,100	13.00	16.00	35.00	110	300	840
1826	1,517,425	12.50	16.00	26.00	84.00	175	700
1826/25	Inc. above	16.00	40.00	75.00	175	600	1,800
1827	2,357,732	12.50	16.00	23.00	75.00	135	385
1828	2,260,624	12.50	16.00	26.00	84.00	175	425
1829	1,414,500	12.50	16.00	22.00	100.00	140	425
1830	1,711,500	12.50	16.00	22.00	70.00	135	385
1831	3,359,260	12.50	16.00	22.00	63.00	125	315
1832	2,362,000	12.50	16.00	22.00	63.00	125	315
1833	2,739,000	12.50	16.00	22.00	56.00	120	265
1834	1,855,100	12.50	16.00	22.00	56.00	140	250
1835	3,878,400	12.50	16.00	22.00	56.00	91.00	225
1836	2,111,000	13.00	16.00	24.00	60.00	105	250
1837	5,558,300	12.50	16.00	22.00	51.00	91.00	300
1838	6,370,200	12.50	16.00	22.00	51.00	91.00	225
1839	3,128,661	12.50	16.00	22.00	51.00	105	350
1839/36	Inc. above	400	500	700	1,500	3,900	—

Braided Hair Cent

KM# 67 COPPER 27.5 mm. 10.8900 g. **Designer:** Christian Gobrecht **Notes:** 1840 and 1842 strikes are known with both small and large dates, with little difference in value. 1855 and 1856 strikes are known with both slanting and upright 5s in the date, with little difference in value. A slightly larger Liberty head and larger reverse lettering were used beginning in 1843. One 1843 variety uses the old obverse with the new reverse.

Date	Mintage	G-4	VG-8	F-12	VF-20	XF-40	MS-60
1840	2,462,700	11.00	14.00	17.00	38.00	70.00	475
1841	1,597,367	14.00	18.00	22.00	44.00	80.00	440
1842	2,383,390	11.00	15.00	17.00	38.00	70.00	425
1843	2,425,342	11.00	15.00	17.00	38.00	75.00	445
1843 obverse 1842 with reverse of 1844	Inc. above	12.00	15.00	21.00	38.00	80.00	350
1844	2,398,752	11.00	15.00	16.00	22.00	54.00	215
1844/81	Inc. above	25.00	50.00	75.00	100.00	200	600
1845	3,894,804	11.00	15.00	16.00	20.00	44.00	225
1846	4,120,800	11.00	15.00	16.00	20.00	44.00	225
1847	6,183,669	11.00	15.00	16.00	20.00	44.00	160
1848	6,415,799	11.00	15.00	16.00	20.00	44.00	160

Date	Mintage	G-4	VG-8	F-12	VF-20	XF-40	MS-60
1849	4,178,500	11.00	15.00	16.00	28.00	60.00	275
1850	4,426,844	11.00	15.00	16.00	20.00	44.00	160
1851	9,889,707	11.00	15.00	16.00	20.00	41.00	160
1851/81	Inc. above	20.00	15.00	35.00	80.00	150	500
1852	5,063,094	11.00	15.00	16.00	20.00	41.00	160
1853	6,641,131	11.00	15.00	16.00	20.00	41.00	160
1854	4,236,156	11.00	15.00	16.00	20.00	41.00	160
1855	1,574,829	14.00	18.00	20.00	26.00	50.00	170
1856	2,690,463	12.00	15.00	17.00	22.00	42.00	160
1857	333,456	40.00	63.00	72.50	85.00	110	250

Flying Eagle Cent

KM# 85 COPPER-NICKEL 19 mm. 4.6700 g. **Designer:** James B. Longacre **Notes:** On the large-letter variety of 1858, the "A" and "M" in "America" are connected at their bases; on the small-letter variety, the two letters are separated.

Large letters
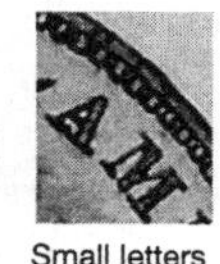
Small letters

Date	Mintage	G-4	VG-8	F-12	VF-20	XF-40	AU-50	MS-60	MS-65	Prf-65
1856	Est. 2,500	6,000	7,250	7,800	9,600	10,500	11,500	13,500	58,000	24,500
1857	17,450,000	20.00	24.00	33.00	44.00	125	165	285	3,750	29,000
1858/7	—	65.00	90.00	175	390	750	1,500	2,500	75,000	—
1858 large letters	24,600,000	20.00	24.00	34.00	45.00	130	180	300	3,750	23,500
1858 small letters	Inc. above	20.00	24.00	33.00	44.00	125	175	290	3,800	30,000

Indian Head Cent

KM# 87 COPPER-NICKEL 19 mm. 4.6700 g. **Designer:** James B. Longacre

Date	Mintage	G-4	VG-8	F-12	VF-20	XF-40	AU-50	MS-60	MS-65	Prf-65
1859	36,400,000	12.00	15.00	21.00	42.50	100.00	175	215	3,200	5,000

Indian Head Cent
Shield added at top of wreath

KM# 90 COPPER-NICKEL 19 mm. 4.6700 g. **Designer:** James B. Longacre

Date	Mintage	G-4	VG-8	F-12	VF-20	XF-40	AU-50	MS-60	MS-65	Prf-65
1860	20,566,000(1,000)	10.00	12.50	16.00	25.00	53.50	80.00	150	1,000	3,900
1861	10,100,000	19.50	30.00	41.00	52.50	90.00	160	180	1,000	7,150
1862	28,075,000	7.50	9.00	10.00	14.50	27.50	55.00	80.00	1,000	2,100
1863	49,840,000	7.50	9.00	10.00	11.00	24.00	54.00	72.50	1,000	3,200
1864	13,740,000	15.00	20.00	34.00	47.50	70.00	92.50	150	1,250	3,200

Indian Head Cent

KM# 90a BRONZE 19 mm. 3.1100 g. **Designer:** James B. Longacre **Notes:** The 1864 "L" variety has the designer's initial in Liberty's hair to the right of her neck.

Date	Mintage	G-4	VG-8	F-12	VF-20	XF-40	AU-50	MS-60	MS-65	Prf-65
1864	39,233,714	6.00	12.00	20.00	37.50	60.00	75.00	90.00	325	4,300
1864 L	Inc. above	50.00	65.00	130	170	260	310	400	1,650	110,000
1865	35,429,286	6.00	10.00	17.50	23.00	35.00	50.00	80.00	450	1,550
1866	9,826,500	40.00	48.00	60.00	90.00	175	210	240	1,250	950
1867	9,821,000	40.00	53.00	70.00	100.00	175	210	240	1,250	1,050
1868	10,266,500	37.50	40.00	65.00	100.00	150	180	220	1,000	985
1869/9	6,420,000	115	140	300	410	590	650	775	1,800	—
1869	Inc. above	58.50	85.00	220	300	400	475	510	1,650	950
1870	5,275,000	42.50	70.00	200	280	375	440	515	1,600	1,075
1871	3,929,500	60.00	100.00	230	285	380	400	425	2,550	1,100
1872	4,042,000	67.50	135	375	425	575	700	775	4,100	1,100
1873	11,676,500	21.00	30.00	46.00	75.00	150	190	215	1,300	850
1874	14,187,500	15.00	17.50	35.00	55.00	95.00	125	170	700	800
1875	13,528,000	15.00	28.00	50.00	65.00	95.00	135	175	800	1,500
1876	7,944,000	27.00	35.00	62.50	125	200	265	315	1,100	925
1877	852,500	550	750	1,150	1,550	2,000	2,600	2,850	8,750	4,900
1878	5,799,850	26.00	36.00	60.00	135	225	265	315	900	490
1879	16,231,200	7.00	11.00	16.00	33.00	65.00	72.50	75.00	350	450
1880	38,964,955	4.00	6.00	8.00	11.00	25.00	37.50	60.00	350	435
1881	39,211,575	4.00	5.00	7.00	10.00	18.00	30.00	40.00	330	425
1882	38,581,100	4.00	6.00	8.00	11.00	18.00	30.00	37.50	330	425
1883	45,589,109	3.00	4.50	7.00	10.00	16.00	24.00	38.50	330	425
1884	23,261,742	4.00	6.00	8.00	14.00	27.00	38.00	65.00	500	425
1885	11,765,384	6.00	8.00	15.00	29.00	54.00	65.00	95.00	750	425

Date	Mintage	G-4	VG-8	F-12	VF-20	XF-40	AU-50	MS-60	MS-65	Prf-65
1886	17,654,290	4.00	6.00	30.00	65.00	120	175	200	1,250	460
1887	45,226,483	2.00	3.00	4.00	6.00	15.00	28.00	50.00	395	475
1888	37,494,414	2.00	2.50	4.00	7.00	20.00	28.00	42.00	950	525
1889	48,869,361	1.75	2.20	2.50	4.00	10.00	27.00	35.00	395	450
1890	57,182,854	1.50	1.80	2.50	4.00	10.00	22.00	35.00	395	500
1891	47,072,350	1.70	2.25	3.00	4.50	10.00	22.00	35.00	400	520
1892	37,649,832	2.00	2.25	3.00	5.00	16.00	20.00	34.00	395	525
1893	46,642,195	1.70	2.25	3.00	5.00	10.00	22.00	30.00	340	540
1894	16,752,132	4.00	6.00	12.00	20.00	45.00	55.00	70.00	375	525
1895	38,343,636	1.75	2.00	3.00	6.00	12.00	22.00	32.00	200	475
1896	39,057,293	1.50	2.00	2.75	5.00	10.00	21.00	33.00	230	425
1897	50,466,330	1.50	2.00	2.25	4.00	10.00	20.00	30.00	200	425
1898	49,823,079	1.50	2.00	2.25	3.00	10.00	20.00	30.00	200	425
1899	53,600,031	1.50	1.80	2.00	3.00	10.00	18.00	27.50	140	415
1900	66,833,764	1.40	1.70	2.00	4.00	12.00	20.00	25.00	175	425

2 CENTS

KM# 94 COPPER-TIN-ZINC 23 mm. 6.2200 g. **Designer:** James B. Longacre **Notes:** The motto "In God We Trust" was modified in 1864, resulting in small-motto and large-motto varieties for that year.

Date	Mintage	G-4	VG-8	F-12	VF-20	XF-40	AU-50	MS-60	MS-65	Prf-65
1864 small motto	19,847,500	110	150	200	350	550	625	800	2,250	45,000
1864 large motto	Inc. above	14.50	15.00	18.50	25.00	34.00	65.00	70.00	500	1,400
1865	13,640,000	14.50	15.00	18.50	25.00	34.00	65.00	70.00	500	850
1866	3,177,000	14.50	17.00	20.00	28.00	34.00	65.00	70.00	630	850
1867	2,938,750	16.00	21.00	30.00	38.50	47.50	85.00	125	550	850
1868	2,803,750	16.00	20.00	30.00	38.50	52.50	95.00	135	625	850
1869	1,546,000	17.50	21.50	32.50	40.00	60.00	110	150	650	850
1870	861,250	19.00	26.00	36.00	50.00	90.00	135	235	750	850
1871	721,250	22.50	27.50	41.00	60.00	110	165	240	750	850
1872	65,000	250	315	390	580	760	840	960	2,900	900
1873 proof	Est. 1,100	1,000	1,150	1,200	1,250	1,300	1,500	—	—	2,200

SILVER 3 CENTS

Silver 3 Cents - Type 1
No outlines in star

KM# 75 0.7500 SILVER 0.0193 oz. ASW. 14 mm. 0.8000 g. **Designer:** James B. Longacre

Date	Mintage	G-4	VG-8	F-12	VF-20	XF-40	AU-50	MS-60	MS-65	Prf-65
1851	5,447,400	23.50	30.00	31.00	35.00	60.00	145	160	900	—
1851O	720,000	30.00	35.00	36.00	72.50	125	220	310	2,400	—
1852	18,663,500	23.50	30.00	31.00	35.00	60.00	145	160	900	—
1853	11,400,000	23.50	30.00	31.00	35.00	60.00	145	160	900	—

Silver 3 Cents - Type 2
Three outlines in star

KM# 80 0.9000 SILVER 0.0218 oz. ASW. 14 mm. 0.7500 g. **Designer:** James B. Longacre

Date	Mintage	G-4	VG-8	F-12	VF-20	XF-40	AU-50	MS-60	MS-65	Prf-65
1854	671,000	23.50	30.00	31.00	42.50	95.00	225	350	3,300	33,500
1855	139,000	30.00	40.00	53.50	95.00	150	280	500	9,500	15,000
1856	1,458,000	23.50	30.00	31.00	52.50	90.00	190	275	4,300	15,500
1857	1,042,000	23.50	30.00	31.00	46.00	90.00	240	300	3,300	13,500
1858	1,604,000	23.50	30.00	31.00	42.50	90.00	190	240	3,300	6,400

Silver 3 Cents - Type 3
Two outlines in star

KM# 88 0.9000 SILVER 0.0218 oz. ASW. 14 mm. 0.7500 g. **Designer:** James B. Longacre

Date	Mintage	G-4	VG-8	F-12	VF-20	XF-40	AU-50	MS-60	MS-65	Prf-65
1859	365,000	21.50	25.00	30.00	39.00	60.00	135	160	850	2,150
1860	287,000	21.50	25.00	30.00	40.00	66.00	135	160	850	4,000
1861	498,000	21.50	25.00	30.00	37.50	60.00	135	165	850	1,800
1862	343,550	21.50	25.00	30.00	45.00	60.00	135	160	850	1,400
1863	21,460	315	340	350	360	400	500	675	2,250	1,350
1863/62 proof only; Rare	Inc. above	450	500	550	625	650	675	—	—	5,000
1864	12,470	300	340	350	360	400	500	610	1,700	1,350

Date	Mintage	G-4	VG-8	F-12	VF-20	XF-40	AU-50	MS-60	MS-65	Prf-65
1865	8,500	375	375	425	450	465	500	675	1,650	1,350
1866	22,725	310	340	350	365	400	435	625	1,900	1,325
1867	4,625	375	400	435	450	465	500	675	2,750	1,300
1868	4,100	375	400	435	450	465	500	675	5,750	1,400
1869	5,100	375	400	435	450	465	500	675	2,150	1,400
1869/68 proof only; Rare	Inc. above	—	—	—	—	—	—	—	—	—
1870	4,000	360	390	420	440	450	480	800	4,700	1,350
1871	4,360	375	400	435	450	465	500	675	1,650	1,450
1872	1,950	400	435	460	500	510	600	775	5,400	1,350
1873 proof only	600	650	675	700	725	750	850	—	—	1,800

NICKEL 3 CENTS

KM# 95 COPPER-NICKEL 17.9 mm. 1.9400 g. **Designer:** James B. Longacre

Date	Mintage	G-4	VG-8	F-12	VF-20	XF-40	AU-50	MS-60	MS-65	Prf-65
1865	11,382,000	14.00	15.00	16.00	20.00	27.00	46.00	85.00	920	6,000
1866	4,801,000	14.00	15.00	16.00	20.00	27.00	46.00	85.00	640	1,550
1867	3,915,000	14.00	15.00	16.00	20.00	27.00	46.00	85.00	800	1,450
1868	3,252,000	14.00	15.00	16.00	20.00	27.00	46.00	85.00	640	1,400
1869	1,604,000	14.00	15.00	16.00	20.00	27.00	55.00	110	760	1,050
1870	1,335,000	14.00	15.00	16.00	22.00	29.00	55.00	115	760	1,500
1871	604,000	14.00	15.00	16.00	20.00	29.00	56.00	120	800	1,200
1872	862,000	14.00	15.00	16.00	20.00	27.00	55.00	120	1,100	1,050
1873	1,173,000	14.00	15.00	16.00	20.00	29.00	55.00	115	1,325	1,050
1874	790,000	14.00	15.00	16.00	20.00	27.00	56.00	120	1,000	950
1875	228,000	14.00	15.00	16.00	20.00	33.00	66.50	150	825	1,500
1876	162,000	15.00	16.00	18.50	26.00	36.00	85.00	170	1,700	1,000
1877 proof	Est. 900	950	975	1,000	1,025	1,050	1,100	—	—	2,550
1878 proof	2,350	465	475	480	485	490	500	—	—	900
1879	41,200	50.00	58.50	77.00	85.00	95.00	125	250	760	525
1880	24,955	77.00	88.00	100.00	115	135	160	280	780	525
1881	1,080,575	13.50	14.00	16.00	20.00	27.00	45.00	85.00	700	525
1882	25,300	75.00	80.00	92.50	100.00	115	145	260	1,025	565
1883	10,609	145	160	200	225	280	300	385	4,200	560
1884	5,642	300	330	475	485	490	500	780	5,600	550
1885	4,790	375	395	540	550	575	630	795	2,300	590
1886 proof	4,290	250	260	270	275	290	300	—	—	575
1887/6 proof	7,961	300	310	320	330	350	360	—	—	710
1887	Inc. above	225	265	275	290	325	400	485	1,200	1,050
1888	41,083	37.50	46.00	50.00	55.00	70.00	110	225	700	525
1889	21,561	65.00	80.00	100.00	105	115	120	265	775	525

HALF DIME

Draped Bust Half Dime
Heraldic eagle

KM# 34 0.8920 **SILVER** 0.0388 oz. ASW. 16.5 mm. 1.3500 g. **Designer:** Robert Scot

Date	Mintage	G-4	VG-8	F-12	VF-20	XF-40	MS-60
1801	33,910	775	1,150	1,600	2,800	5,000	15,000
1802	13,010	17,500	25,000	40,000	65,000	85,000	185,000
1803 Large 8	37,850	750	950	1,300	2,000	4,000	9,000
1803 Small 8	Inc. above	950	1,400	1,900	3,000	5,500	11,500
1805	15,600	900	1,250	1,650	2,500	5,500	27,500

Liberty Cap Half Dime

KM# 47 0.8920 **SILVER** 0.0388 oz. ASW. 15.5 mm. 1.3500 g. **Designer:** William Kneass **Notes:** Design modifications in 1835, 1836 and 1837 resulted in variety combinations with large and small dates, and large and small "5C." inscriptions on the reverse.

Date	Mintage	G-4	VG-8	F-12	VF-20	XF-40	AU-50	MS-60	MS-65
1829	1,230,000	25.00	36.00	48.00	75.00	140	250	350	2,650
1830	1,240,000	25.00	36.00	48.00	75.00	140	250	350	2,650
1831	1,242,700	25.00	36.00	48.00	75.00	140	250	350	2,600
1832	965,000	25.00	36.00	48.00	75.00	140	250	350	2,600
1833	1,370,000	25.00	36.00	48.00	75.00	140	250	350	2,650
1834	1,480,000	25.00	36.00	48.00	75.00	140	250	350	2,600
1835 lg. dt., lg. 5C.	2,760,000	25.00	36.00	48.00	75.00	140	250	350	2,600
1835 lg. dt., sm. 5C	Inc. above	25.00	36.00	48.00	75.00	140	250	350	2,600
1835 sm. dt., lg. 5C	Inc. above	25.00	36.00	48.00	75.00	140	250	350	2,600
1835 sm. dt., sm. 5C	Inc. above	25.00	36.00	48.00	75.00	140	250	350	2,600
1836 lg. 5C.	1,900,000	25.00	36.00	48.00	75.00	140	250	350	2,600
1836 sm. 5C.	Inc. above	25.00	36.00	48.00	75.00	140	250	350	2,600
1837 lg. 5C.	2,276,000	25.00	36.00	48.00	75.00	140	250	350	3,500
1837 sm. 5C.	Inc. above	33.00	40.00	55.00	100.00	200	450	950	8,750

Seated Liberty Half Dime
No stars around rim

KM# 60 0.9000 **SILVER** 0.0388 oz. ASW. 15.5 mm. 1.3400 g. **Designer:** Christian Gobrecht **Notes:** A design modification in 1837 resulted in small-date and large-date varieties for that year.

Date	Mintage	G-4	VG-8	F-12	VF-20	XF-40	AU-50	MS-60	MS-65
1837 small date	Inc. above	26.00	35.00	53.00	100.00	185	375	600	3,400
1837 large date	Inc. above	25.00	35.00	53.00	100.00	210	375	600	3,250
1838O	70,000	80.00	125	225	400	750	1,450	2,000	—

Seated Liberty Half Dime
Stars around rim. No drapery

KM# 62.1 0.9000 **SILVER** 0.0388 oz. ASW. 15.5 mm. 1.3400 g. **Designer:** Christian Gobrecht **Notes:** The two varieties of 1838 are distinguished by the size of the stars on the obverse. The 1839-O with reverse of 1838-O was struck from rusted reverse dies. The result is a bumpy surface on this variety's reverse.

Date	Mintage	G-4	VG-8	F-12	VF-20	XF-40	AU-50	MS-60	MS-65
1838 large stars	2,255,000	12.00	13.50	16.00	25.00	60.00	150	240	2,250
1838 small stars	Inc. above	18.00	27.50	45.00	100.00	175	300	650	3,850
1839	1,069,150	13.50	15.00	18.00	29.00	65.00	160	250	2,500
1839O	1,034,039	14.00	16.00	19.00	31.00	70.00	170	550	5,500
1839O reverse 1838O	—	375	575	750	1,200	2,250	3,500	—	—
1840	1,344,085	14.00	16.00	19.00	25.00	60.00	140	240	2,100
1840O	935,000	15.00	17.00	27.00	40.00	80.00	210	700	—

Seated Liberty Half Dime
Drapery added to Liberty's left elbow

KM# 62.2 0.9000 **SILVER** 0.0388 oz. ASW. 15.5 mm. 1.3400 g. **Designer:** Christian Gobrecht **Notes:** In 1840 drapery was added to Liberty's left elbow. Varieties for the 1848 Philadelphia strikes are distinguished by the size of the numerals in the date.

Date	Mintage	G-4	VG-8	F-12	VF-20	XF-40	AU-50	MS-60	MS-65
1840	Inc. above	25.00	40.00	75.00	125	225	350	450	300
1840O	Inc. above	35.00	60.00	115	190	450	1,250	6,500	—
1841	1,150,000	11.00	12.00	14.00	24.00	55.00	115	150	1,250
1841O	815,000	12.50	15.00	22.50	42.00	110	275	650	6,500
1842	815,000	11.00	12.00	14.00	24.00	55.00	115	150	1,750
1842O	350,000	30.00	45.00	75.00	225	500	1,250	2,500	—
1843	1,165,000	11.00	12.00	14.00	24.00	50.00	110	150	1,350
1844	430,000	11.00	12.00	14.00	24.00	50.00	110	150	1,150
1844O	220,000	75.00	105	175	450	950	1,900	5,400	—
1845	1,564,000	11.00	12.00	14.00	22.00	50.00	110	150	1,150
1845/1845	Inc. above	12.00	13.00	15.00	24.00	50.00	115	160	1,200
1846	27,000	300	450	750	1,150	2,250	3,600	7,500	—
1847	1,274,000	11.00	12.00	14.00	20.00	55.00	110	160	1,150
1848 medium date	668,000	12.00	13.00	15.00	25.00	60.00	115	210	2,600
1848 large date	Inc. above	20.00	30.00	45.00	65.00	135	275	450	4,000
1848O	600,000	19.00	25.00	33.00	50.00	110	265	400	1,950
1849/8	1,309,000	14.00	20.00	25.00	50.00	100.00	180	375	1,800
1849/6	Inc. above	12.00	13.00	15.00	40.00	85.00	175	375	1,500
1849	Inc. above	11.00	12.00	14.00	20.00	50.00	110	175	1,650
1849O	140,000	29.00	40.00	95.00	225	475	975	1,950	14,000
1850	955,000	11.00	12.00	14.00	20.00	50.00	115	150	1,400
1850O	690,000	13.00	16.00	25.00	50.00	110	275	675	4,000
1851	781,000	11.00	12.00	14.00	20.00	50.00	110	150	1,500
1851O	860,000	12.00	15.00	20.00	35.00	95.00	185	500	3,750
1852	1,000,500	11.00	12.00	14.00	20.00	50.00	110	150	1,150
1852O	260,000	23.00	32.00	65.00	135	275	475	750	10,000
1853	135,000	28.00	36.00	56.00	100.00	185	350	650	3,000
1853O	160,000	225	265	375	675	1,350	2,750	4,800	25,000

Seated Liberty Half Dime
Arrows at date

KM# 76 0.9000 **SILVER** 0.0362 oz. ASW. 1.2400 g. **Designer:** Christian Gobrecht

Date	Mintage	G-4	VG-8	F-12	VF-20	XF-40	AU-50	MS-60	MS-65	Prf-65
1853	13,210,020	11.00	12.00	14.00	17.00	50.00	120	190	1,850	35,000
1853O	2,200,000	12.00	14.00	16.00	25.00	65.00	135	275	3,500	—
1854	5,740,000	10.50	12.00	14.00	17.00	45.00	110	185	1,850	16,000
1854O	1,560,000	11.00	13.00	15.00	23.00	60.00	145	250	4,250	—
1855	1,750,000	11.00	13.00	15.00	18.00	47.00	115	190	1,950	18,000
1855O	600,000	15.00	20.00	30.00	55.00	135	235	600	4,000	—

Seated Liberty Half Dime

Arrows at date removed

KM# A62.2 0.9000 **SILVER** 0.0362 oz. ASW. 1.2400 g. **Designer:** Christian Gobrecht **Notes:** On the 1858/inverted date variety, the date was engraved into the die upside down and then re-engraved right side up. Another 1858 variety has the date doubled.

Date	Mintage	G-4	VG-8	F-12	VF-20	XF-40	AU-50	MS-60	MS-65	Prf-65
1856	4,880,000	10.50	12.00	14.00	18.00	45.00	95.00	140	1,650	15,000
1856O	1,100,000	11.00	13.00	15.00	38.00	80.00	250	550	2,000	—
1857	7,280,000	10.00	12.00	14.00	18.00	45.00	95.00	150	1,550	5,500
1857O	1,380,000	11.00	13.00	18.00	33.00	55.00	180	325	1,800	—
1858	3,500,000	10.50	12.00	14.00	18.00	55.00	175	300	1,700	5,500
1858 inverted date	Inc. above	25.00	40.00	60.00	90.00	175	275	650	2,600	—
1858 double date	Inc. above	45.00	60.00	90.00	175	285	425	700	—	—
1858O	1,660,000	11.00	13.00	16.00	36.00	65.00	135	265	1,600	—
1859	340,000	11.00	13.00	20.00	34.00	70.00	135	225	1,550	4,000
1859O	560,000	12.00	14.00	23.00	40.00	110	200	240	1,700	—

Seated Liberty Half Dime

"United States of America" replaced stars

KM# 91 0.9000 **SILVER** 0.0362 oz. ASW. 1.2400 g. **Designer:** Christian Gobrecht **Notes:** In 1860 the legend "United States of America" replaced the stars on the obverse.

Date	Mintage	G-4	VG-8	F-12	VF-20	XF-40	AU-50	MS-60	MS-65	Prf-65
1860	799,000	11.00	13.00	15.00	17.00	30.00	65.00	125	1,150	1,850
1860O	1,060,000	12.00	14.00	16.00	18.00	36.00	75.00	175	1,450	—
1861	3,361,000	11.00	13.00	15.00	17.00	30.00	65.00	125	1,175	2,500
1861/0	Inc. above	20.00	30.00	55.00	125	260	360	500	4,000	—
1862	1,492,550	12.00	14.00	16.00	20.00	33.00	68.00	135	1,150	1,650
1863	18,460	190	225	275	375	475	550	700	1,650	1,700
1863S	100,000	25.00	35.00	50.00	75.00	150	295	700	2,500	—
1864	48,470	325	425	500	600	800	1,000	1,250	2,250	1,750
1864S	90,000	50.00	65.00	100.00	150	250	450	700	3,750	—
1865	13,500	325	400	450	550	650	875	1,000	1,950	1,750
1865S	120,000	25.00	35.00	50.00	75.00	135	375	800	—	—
1866	10,725	350	450	550	650	800	1,000	1,250	2,550	1,700
1866S	120,000	25.00	35.00	50.00	75.00	135	285	450	5,000	—
1867	8,625	450	550	675	800	900	1,100	1,300	2,250	1,750
1867S	120,000	25.00	35.00	50.00	75.00	135	295	550	3,850	—
1868	89,200	55.00	70.00	110	170	250	375	570	2,400	1,750
1868S	280,000	20.00	25.00	30.00	40.00	55.00	125	300	3,250	—
1869	208,600	20.00	25.00	30.00	40.00	55.00	125	235	1,500	1,750
1869S	230,000	18.00	22.00	29.00	35.00	50.00	115	325	4,000	—
1870	536,600	18.00	22.00	29.00	35.00	50.00	125	175	1,200	1,650
1870S unique	—	—	—	—	—	—	—	—	—	—
Note: 1870S, Superior Galleries, July 1986, brilliant uncirculated, $253,000.										
1871	1,873,960	11.00	13.00	15.00	17.00	32.00	65.00	120	1,250	1,650
1871S	161,000	25.00	30.00	45.00	60.00	85.00	175	250	2,450	—
1872	2,947,950	11.00	13.00	15.00	18.00	32.00	65.00	120	1,200	1,650
1872S mint mark in wreath	837,000	11.00	13.00	15.00	18.00	32.00	65.00	120	1,200	—
1872S mint mark below wreath	Inc. above	11.00	13.00	15.00	18.00	32.00	65.00	120	1,200	—
1873	712,600	11.00	13.00	15.00	20.00	35.00	70.00	125	1,300	1,750
1873S	324,000	20.00	25.00	30.00	39.00	50.00	90.00	150	1,350	—

5 CENTS

Shield Nickel

Rays between stars

KM# 96 COPPER-NICKEL 20.5 mm. 5.0000 g. **Designer:** James B. Longacre

Date	Mintage	G-4	VG-8	F-12	VF-20	XF-40	AU-50	MS-60	MS-65	Prf-65
1866	14,742,500	25.00	35.00	47.50	62.50	150	225	250	2,600	3,400
1867	2,019,000	32.50	43.50	55.00	77.50	190	275	335	3,800	75,000

Shield Nickel

No rays between stars

KM# 97 COPPER-NICKEL 5.0000 g.

Date	Mintage	G-4	VG-8	F-12	VF-20	XF-40	AU-50	MS-60	MS-65	Prf-65
1867	28,890,500	15.00	16.50	19.00	25.00	37.50	62.50	100.00	850	2,750
1868	28,817,000	15.00	16.50	19.00	25.00	37.50	62.50	100.00	800	1,400
1869	16,395,000	15.00	16.50	19.00	25.00	40.00	62.50	100.00	750	1,025
1870	4,806,000	19.00	21.50	37.50	42.50	62.50	105	150	1,250	1,275
1871	561,000	55.00	67.50	90.00	125	200	235	520	1,475	1,075
1872	6,036,000	19.00	23.50	40.00	50.00	62.50	105	160	960	750
1873	4,550,000	20.00	26.00	38.50	47.50	62.50	95.00	160	1,250	800
1874	3,538,000	23.50	32.50	50.00	62.50	77.50	100.00	165	120	850
1875	2,097,000	26.00	37.50	62.50	80.00	100.00	140	200	1,800	1,750
1876	2,530,000	23.50	31.00	55.00	75.00	96.00	130	185	1,000	950
1877 proof	Est. 900	1,300	1,350	1,500	1,800	1,850	1,950	—	—	3,000
1878 proof	2,350	575	625	715	850	890	960	—	—	1,050
1879	29,100	315	430	530	560	600	650	750	1,700	790
1880	19,995	410	515	625	750	1,100	1,700	3,450	27,500	650
1881	72,375	210	275	375	425	515	625	715	1,525	630
1882	11,476,600	15.00	16.75	19.25	25.00	37.50	62.50	100.00	650	600
1883	1,456,919	16.50	20.50	27.50	33.50	47.50	75.00	115	650	570
1883/2	—	135	185	260	300	515	625	775	3,750	—

Liberty Nickel

"Cents" below "V"

KM# 112 COPPER NICKEL 5.0000 g.

Date	Mintage	G-4	VG-8	F-12	VF-20	XF-40	AU-50	MS-60	MS-65	Prf-65
1883	16,032,983	11.00	13.50	29.00	40.00	70.00	95.00	125	625	500
1884	11,273,942	15.00	21.50	32.00	38.50	70.00	105	160	1,900	550
1885	1,476,490	480	530	675	775	875	1,150	1,300	4,800	950
1886	3,330,290	185	235	340	440	575	675	750	4,500	525
1887	15,263,652	8.00	12.00	32.00	45.00	70.00	95.00	120	1,200	520
1888	10,720,483	22.00	35.00	50.00	90.00	140	165	215	1,400	520
1889	15,881,361	7.00	11.00	25.00	37.00	52.50	95.00	130	900	520
1890	16,259,272	7.00	16.00	23.50	35.00	56.00	100.00	152.5	1,700	600
1891	16,834,350	6.00	7.50	18.00	28.00	60.00	88.00	145	1,050	520
1892	11,699,642	6.00	7.50	20.00	30.00	58.50	100.00	130	1,425	520
1893	13,370,195	6.00	8.00	18.00	28.00	60.00	95.00	122.5	1,140	520
1894	5,413,132	10.00	25.00	80.00	140	190	250	285	1,300	500
1895	9,979,884	5.00	8.00	25.00	40.00	60.00	100.00	135	2,000	600
1896	8,842,920	8.00	16.00	39.00	50.00	75.00	125	150	1,900	600
1897	20,428,735	3.00	6.00	14.00	26.00	40.00	65.00	95.00	1,050	600
1898	12,532,087	2.00	4.50	9.50	21.00	36.00	70.00	140	1,200	500
1899	26,029,031	2.00	3.00	9.00	18.00	28.00	54.00	94.00	600	500
1900	27,255,995	2.00	3.00	8.00	18.00	35.00	70.00	88.00	600	500

DIME

Draped Bust Dime

Heraldic eagle

KM# 31 0.8920 **SILVER** 0.0775 oz. ASW. 19 mm. 2.7000 g. **Designer:** Robert Scot **Notes:** The 1798 overdates have either 13 or 16 stars on the obverse. Varieties of the regular 1798 strikes are distinguished by the size of the 8 in the date. The 1805 strikes have either 4 or 5 berries on the olive branch held by the eagle.

Date	Mintage	G-4	VG-8	F-12	VF-20	XF-40	MS-60
1801	34,640	650	850	1,300	2,500	4,500	—
1802	10,975	950	1,400	2,000	3,000	6,000	17,500
1803	33,040	550	700	950	1,500	3,600	—
1804 13 stars	8,265	1,400	1,900	2,650	5,500	13,500	—
1804 14 stars	Inc. above	1,600	2,100	3,000	6,000	15,000	—
1805 4 berries	120,780	450	650	800	1,050	2,100	5,000
1805 5 berries	Inc. above	700	1,000	1,300	1,800	2,700	5,250
1807	165,000	450	650	800	1,050	2,100	5,000

Liberty Cap Dime

KM# 42 0.8920 **SILVER** .0775 oz. ASW. 18.8 mm. 2.7000 g. **Designer:** John Reich **Notes:** Varieties of the 1814, 1821 and 1828 strikes are distinguished by the size of the numerals in the dates. The 1820 varieties are distinguished by the size of the 0 in the date. The 1823 overdates have either large E's or small E's in "United States of America" on the reverse.

Date	Mintage	G-4	VG-8	F-12	VF-20	XF-40	AU-50	MS-60	MS-65
1809	51,065	150	250	450	800	1,400	3,000	4,500	22,500
1811/9	65,180	90.00	165	275	650	1,100	2,000	4,000	22,500
1814 small date	421,500	60.00	70.00	120	475	700	1,000	2,000	8,000
1814 large date	Inc. above	29.00	35.00	55.00	200	400	800	1,100	8,000
1820 large O	942,587	26.00	33.00	55.00	150	375	750	1,050	8,000
1820 small O	Inc. above	26.00	33.00	55.00	175	425	750	1,050	8,000
1821 large date	1,186,512	26.00	33.00	60.00	150	375	750	1,050	8,000
1821 small date	Inc. above	26.00	33.00	55.00	175	400	750	1,050	8,000

Date	Mintage	G-4	VG-8	F-12	VF-20	XF-40	AU-50	MS-60	MS-65
1822	100,000	425	600	1,100	1,700	3,000	6,000	10,000	—
1823/22 large E's	440,000	26.00	33.00	50.00	150	375	750	1,050	8,000
1823/22 small E's	Inc. above	26.00	33.00	50.00	150	375	750	1,050	8,000
1824/22 mintage undetermined	—	30.00	50.00	150	400	750	1,500	2,500	—
1825	510,000	26.00	33.00	50.00	150	450	900	1,250	8,000
1827	1,215,000	26.00	33.00	50.00	140	375	775	1,050	8,000
1828 large date	125,000	80.00	110	175	375	750	1,275	3,000	—

Liberty Cap Dime

KM# 48 SILVER 18.5 mm. **Designer:** John Reich **Notes:** The three varieties of 1829 strikes and two varieties of 1830 strikes are distinguished by the size of "10C." on the reverse. On the 1833 "high 3" variety, the last 3 in the date is higher than the first 3. The two varieties of the 1834 strikes are distinguished by the size of the 4 in the date.

Date	Mintage	G-4	VG-8	F-12	VF-20	XF-40	AU-50	MS-60	MS-65
1828 small date	Inc. above	30.00	45.00	75.00	195	475	775	1,750	—
1829 very large 10C.	770,000	35.00	45.00	85.00	150	375	600	1,500	—
1829 large 10C.	—	26.00	30.00	40.00	75.00	270	400	725	8,000
1829 medium 10C.	Inc. above	26.00	30.00	40.00	70.00	270	400	725	8,000
1829 small 10C.	Inc. above	26.00	30.00	40.00	70.00	270	400	725	8,000
1829 curl base 2	—	3,200	5,000	7,500	—	—	—	—	—
1830 large 10C.	510,000	26.00	30.00	38.00	65.00	260	375	675	8,000
1830 small 10C.	Inc. above	26.00	30.00	38.00	65.00	260	375	675	8,000
1830/29	Inc. above	35.00	60.00	115	250	500	775	1,500	—
1831	771,350	26.00	30.00	38.00	65.00	260	375	675	6,000
1832	522,500	26.00	30.00	38.00	65.00	260	375	675	6,500
1833	485,000	26.00	30.00	38.00	65.00	260	375	675	6,700
1834	635,000	26.00	30.00	38.00	65.00	260	375	675	6,500
1835	1,410,000	26.00	30.00	38.00	65.00	260	375	675	6,500
1836	1,190,000	26.00	30.00	38.00	65.00	260	375	675	6,500
1837	1,042,000	26.00	30.00	38.00	65.00	260	375	675	6,600

Seated Liberty Dime
No stars around rim

KM# 61 0.9000 **SILVER** 0.0773 oz. ASW. 17.9 mm. 2.6700 g. **Designer:** Christian Gobrecht **Notes:** The two 1837 varieties are distinguished by the size of the numerals in the date.

Date	Mintage	G-4	VG-8	F-12	VF-20	XF-40	AU-50	MS-60	MS-65
1837 small date	Inc. above	29.00	40.00	75.00	275	550	750	1,100	6,500

Seated Liberty Dime
Stars around rim. No drapery

KM# 63.1 0.9000 **SILVER** 0.0773 oz. ASW. 17.9 mm. 2.6700 g. **Obv. Designer:** Christian Gobrecht **Notes:** The two 1838 varieties are distinguished by the size of the stars on the obverse. The 1838 "partial drapery" variety has drapery on Liberty's left elbow. The 1839-O with reverse of 1838-O variety was struck from rusted dies. This variety has a bumpy surface on the reverse.

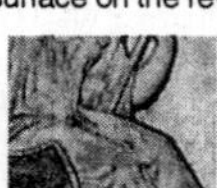
Without drapery

Date	Mintage	G-4	VG-8	F-12	VF-20	XF-40	AU-50	MS-60	MS-65
1838 small stars	1,992,500	25.00	30.00	50.00	80.00	165	350	600	—
1838 large stars	Inc. above	12.50	15.00	18.00	25.00	63.50	195	275	8,500
1838 partial drapery	Inc. above	30.00	45.00	65.00	125	195	325	550	—
1839	1,053,115	12.50	15.00	18.00	35.00	70.00	170	265	2,500
1839O	1,323,000	12.50	15.00	20.00	45.00	85.00	300	1,250	—
1839O reverse 1838O	—	145	200	350	550	950	—	—	—
1840	1,358,580	12.50	15.00	20.00	30.00	60.00	170	300	2,500
1840O	1,175,000	13.00	14.50	40.00	70.00	125	295	975	—

Seated Liberty Dime
Drapery added to Liberty's left elbow

KM# 63.2 0.9000 **SILVER** 0.0773 oz. ASW. 17.9 mm. 2.6700 g. **Designer:** Christian Gobrecht

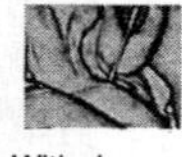
With drapery

Date	Mintage	G-4	VG-8	F-12	VF-20	XF-40	AU-50	MS-60	MS-65
1840	Inc. above	35.00	50.00	95.00	185	350	1,250	—	—
1841	1,622,500	12.00	15.00	18.00	23.00	50.00	175	260	2,550
1841O	2,007,500	12.00	15.00	15.00	30.00	65.00	250	1,500	—
1841O large O	Inc. above	600	900	1,200	2,500	—	—	—	—
1842	1,887,500	12.00	15.00	18.00	22.00	45.00	175	260	2,550
1842O	2,020,000	12.00	18.00	30.00	75.00	225	1,350	2,900	—
1843	1,370,000	12.00	15.00	18.00	22.00	45.00	175	260	2,550
1843/1843	—	12.00	15.00	18.00	30.00	75.00	200	295	—
1843O	150,000	35.00	65.00	125	275	800	2,250	—	—
1844	72,500	275	350	550	800	1,450	2,200	3,000	—
1845	1,755,000	12.00	15.00	18.00	22.00	45.00	120	260	2,550
1845/1845	Inc. above	12.00	15.00	35.00	55.00	100.00	175	—	—
1845O	230,000	22.00	35.00	70.00	200	550	1,350	—	—
1846	31,300	200	225	300	400	950	2,250	—	—
1847	245,000	19.00	25.00	40.00	75.00	150	350	950	—
1848	451,500	17.00	20.00	25.00	45.00	85.00	185	750	7,050
1849	839,000	12.00	15.00	18.00	28.00	60.00	140	500	7,050
1849O	300,000	20.00	30.00	45.00	120	235	750	—	—
1850	1,931,500	12.00	15.00	18.00	22.00	55.00	120	260	2,550
1850O	510,000	18.00	25.00	35.00	70.00	160	475	1,250	—
1851	1,026,500	12.00	15.00	18.00	22.00	60.00	120	325	—
1851O	400,000	18.00	25.00	35.00	75.00	175	500	1,500	—
1852	1,535,500	12.00	15.00	18.00	22.00	50.00	120	290	2,550
1852O	430,000	22.00	30.00	45.00	125	235	550	1,800	—
1853	95,000	70.00	100.00	130	195	300	475	800	—

Seated Liberty Dime
Arrows at date

KM# 77 0.9000 **SILVER** 0.0721 oz. ASW. 2.4900 g. **Designer:** Christian Gobrecht

Date	Mintage	G-4	VG-8	F-12	VF-20	XF-40	AU-50	MS-60	MS-65	Prf-65
1853	12,078,010	8.00	9.00	10.00	14.00	45.00	125	330	2,500	31,500
1853O	1,100,000	11.00	14.00	20.00	45.00	145	400	900	—	—
1854	4,470,000	8.75	9.25	10.00	15.00	45.00	125	330	2,500	31,500
1854O	1,770,000	10.00	11.00	14.00	25.00	75.00	175	600	—	—
1855	2,075,000	8.75	9.25	14.00	20.00	55.00	150	350	3,800	31,500

Seated Liberty Dime
Arrows at date removed

KM# A63.2 0.9000 **SILVER** 0.0721 oz. ASW. 2.4900 g. **Designer:** Christian Gobrecht **Notes:** The two 1856 varieties are distinguished by the size of the numerals in the date.

Date	Mintage	G-4	VG-8	F-12	VF-20	XF-40	AU-50	MS-60	MS-65	Prf-65
1856 small date	5,780,000	12.00	15.00	18.00	22.00	32.00	115	250	7,050	38,000
1856 large date	Inc. above	12.00	15.00	18.00	25.00	65.00	175	475	—	—
1856O	1,180,000	12.00	15.00	20.00	35.00	85.00	175	500	—	—
1856S	70,000	160	225	325	500	1,200	1,750	—	—	—
1857	5,580,000	12.00	15.00	18.00	22.00	32.00	100.00	260	2,500	3,400
1857O	1,540,000	12.00	15.00	18.00	25.00	65.00	200	350	—	—
1858	1,540,000	12.00	15.00	20.00	35.00	55.00	145	260	2,500	3,400
1858O	290,000	19.00	25.00	40.00	85.00	165	275	800	—	—
1858S	60,000	135	200	300	425	975	1,400	—	—	—
1859	430,000	16.00	20.00	25.00	45.00	70.00	140	350	—	3,400
1859O	480,000	16.00	20.00	25.00	45.00	80.00	225	550	—	—
1859S	60,000	150	225	325	500	1,350	3,000	—	—	—
1860S	140,000	30.00	40.00	55.00	135	300	800	—	—	—

Seated Liberty Dime
"United States of America" replaced stars

KM# 92 0.9000 **SILVER** 0.0721 oz. ASW. 2.4900 g. **Obv. Designer:** Christian Gobrecht **Notes:** The 1873 "closed-3" and "open-3" varieties are distinguished by the amount of space between the upper left and lower left serifs of the 3 in the date.

Date	Mintage	G-4	VG-8	F-12	VF-20	XF-40	AU-50	MS-60	MS-65	Prf-65
1860	607,000	15.00	22.00	29.00	31.00	55.00	125	275	—	1,400
1860O	40,000	350	475	875	1,650	3,500	5,500	—	—	—
1861	1,884,000	12.00	15.00	17.00	20.00	35.00	65.00	125	—	1,400
1861S	172,500	50.00	85.00	145	275	400	900	—	—	—
1862	847,550	12.00	15.00	19.00	25.00	45.00	65.00	150	—	1,400
1862S	180,750	40.00	60.00	95.00	175	350	775	—	—	—
1863	14,460	350	450	600	700	875	1,100	1,300	—	1,400
1863S	157,500	30.00	40.00	75.00	125	275	550	1,200	—	—
1864	11,470	350	450	575	650	775	1,000	1,200	—	1,400
1864S	230,000	28.00	35.00	60.00	95.00	225	425	1,200	—	—
1865	10,500	400	500	650	750	900	1,100	1,250	—	1,400
1865S	175,000	35.00	45.00	75.00	125	300	850	—	—	—
1866	8,725	450	550	700	800	975	1,200	1,800	—	1,750
1866S	135,000	40.00	50.00	85.00	145	325	675	1,900	—	—
1867	6,625	550	700	950	1,100	1,450	1,600	1,800	—	1,750
1867S	140,000	40.00	50.00	85.00	145	295	625	1,200	—	—
1868	464,000	18.00	22.00	29.00	39.00	80.00	175	300	—	1,400
1868S	260,000	25.00	35.00	50.00	85.00	165	300	600	—	—
1869	256,600	25.00	35.00	45.00	75.00	135	250	600	—	1,400
1869S	450,000	20.00	25.00	35.00	45.00	75.00	175	400	—	—
1870	471,000	18.00	22.00	30.00	40.00	50.00	80.00	150	—	1,400
1870S	50,000	275	350	450	550	675	950	2,000	—	—
1871	907,710	16.00	20.00	25.00	33.00	55.00	160	300	—	1,400
1871CC	20,100	1,400	1,850	2,950	4,000	7,500	10,500	—	—	—
1871S	320,000	35.00	55.00	75.00	130	195	350	900	—	—
1872	2,396,450	12.00	15.00	17.00	20.00	31.00	95.00	175	—	1,400

Date	Mintage	G-4	VG-8	F-12	VF-20	XF-40	AU-50	MS-60	MS-65	Prf-65
1872CC	35,480	425	650	975	1,950	5,500	—	—	—	—
1872S	190,000	40.00	60.00	80.00	150	235	450	1,100	—	—
1873 closed 3	1,568,600	12.00	15.00	18.00	27.00	50.00	100.00	200	—	1,400
1873 open 3	Inc. above	22.00	30.00	40.00	60.00	110	225	650	—	—
1873CC	12,400	—	—	—	—	—	—	—	—	—

Note: 1873-CC, Heritage Sale, April 1999, MS-64, $632,500.

Seated Liberty Dime
Arrows at date

KM# 105 0.9000 **SILVER** 0.0724 oz. ASW. 2.5000 g. **Designer:** Christian Gobrecht

Date	Mintage	G-4	VG-8	F-12	VF-20	XF-40	AU-50	MS-60	MS-65	Prf-65
1873	2,378,500	12.00	15.00	25.00	50.00	150	350	500	4,500	4,500
1873CC	18,791	1,400	1,850	2,950	4,000	8,500	—	—	—	—
1873S	455,000	20.00	30.00	40.00	70.00	190	320	1,500	—	—
1874	2,940,700	12.00	15.00	17.50	50.00	150	315	500	4,500	4,500
1874CC	10,817	3,500	5,500	8,000	12,500	25,000	—	—	—	—
1874S	240,000	60.00	75.00	100.00	160	250	450	1,500	—	—

Seated Liberty Dime
Arrows at date removed

KM# A92 0.9000 **SILVER** 0.0724 oz. ASW. 2.5000 g. **Designer:** Christian Gobrecht **Notes:** On the 1876-CC doubled-obverse variety, doubling appears in the words "of America" in the legend.

Date	Mintage	G-4	VG-8	F-12	VF-20	XF-40	AU-50	MS-60	MS-65	Prf-65
1875	10,350,700	12.00	15.00	17.00	20.00	22.00	60.00	125	2,250	4,600
1875CC mint mark in wreath	4,645,000	12.00	15.00	17.00	20.00	37.50	90.00	160	2,700	—
1875CC mint mark under wreath	Inc. above	12.00	15.00	22.50	37.50	65.00	165	235	3,000	—
1875S mint mark in wreath	9,070,000	20.00	25.00	30.00	43.00	65.00	125	225	3,100	—
1875S mint mark under wreath	Inc. above	12.00	15.00	17.50	25.00	35.00	70.00	125	1,100	—
1876	11,461,150	12.00	15.00	17.00	20.00	24.00	60.00	110	1,100	1,200
1876CC	8,270,000	12.00	15.00	17.00	20.00	30.00	60.00	175	—	—
1876CC doubled obverse	Inc. above	14.00	20.00	30.00	80.00	135	300	500	—	—
1876S	10,420,000	12.00	15.00	17.00	20.00	35.00	85.00	165	1,100	—
1877	7,310,510	12.00	15.00	17.00	20.00	23.00	60.00	110	1,100	1,200
1877CC	7,700,000	12.00	15.00	17.00	20.00	35.00	75.00	175	—	—
1877S	2,340,000	14.00	18.00	20.00	30.00	50.00	105	225	—	—
1878	1,678,800	12.00	15.00	17.00	20.00	30.00	60.00	110	1,100	1,200
1878CC	200,000	60.00	75.00	125	190	300	475	775	3,900	—
1879	15,100	225	250	300	350	425	525	675	1,750	1,500
1880	37,335	185	215	250	300	350	400	500	1,750	1,500
1881	24,975	200	225	275	325	400	500	650	2,500	1,600
1882	3,911,100	12.00	15.00	17.00	20.00	27.00	60.00	110	1,100	1,200
1883	7,675,712	12.00	15.00	17.00	20.00	24.00	60.00	110	1,100	1,200
1884	3,366,380	12.00	15.00	17.00	20.00	27.00	60.00	110	1,100	1,200
1884S	564,969	30.00	35.00	45.00	55.00	125	200	500	—	—
1885	2,533,427	12.00	15.00	17.00	20.00	27.00	60.00	110	1,100	1,200
1885S	43,690	350	475	725	1,450	2,200	2,950	3,750	—	—
1886	6,377,570	12.00	15.00	17.00	20.00	22.00	60.00	110	1,100	1,200
1886S	206,524	50.00	70.00	80.00	125	175	280	600	—	—
1887	11,283,939	12.00	15.00	17.00	20.00	22.00	60.00	110	1,100	1,200
1887S	4,454,450	12.00	15.00	17.00	22.00	38.00	80.00	110	1,100	—
1888	5,496,487	12.00	15.00	17.00	20.00	22.00	60.00	110	1,100	1,200
1888S	1,720,000	12.00	15.00	17.00	25.00	40.00	95.00	200	—	—
1889	7,380,711	12.00	15.00	17.00	20.00	22.00	60.00	110	1,100	1,200
1889S	972,678	14.00	18.00	25.00	45.00	70.00	150	475	4,500	—
1890	9,911,541	12.00	15.00	17.00	20.00	22.00	60.00	110	1,100	1,200
1890S	1,423,076	12.00	15.00	20.00	50.00	85.00	155	400	4,900	—
1891	15,310,600	12.00	15.00	17.00	20.00	22.00	60.00	110	1,100	1,200
1891O	4,540,000	12.00	15.00	17.00	20.00	24.00	70.00	175	1,750	—
1891O /horizontal O	Inc. above	65.00	95.00	125	175	225	400	—	—	—
1891S	3,196,116	12.00	15.00	17.00	20.00	24.00	75.00	225	1,650	—
1891S/S	Inc. above	25.00	30.00	40.00	85.00	135	250	—	—	—

Barber Dime

KM# 113 0.9000 **SILVER** 0.0724 oz. ASW. 17.9 mm. 2.5000 g. **Designer:** Charles E. Barber **Notes:** Commonly called "Barber dime."

Date	Mintage	G-4	VG-8	F-12	VF-20	XF-40	AU-50	MS-60	MS-65	Prf-65
1892	12,121,245	4.25	5.75	16.00	22.00	24.00	70.00	95.00	700	1,450
1892O	3,841,700	7.50	11.50	25.00	44.00	50.00	72.50	145	1,200	—
1892S	990,710	55.00	95.00	175	195	245	260	395	3,600	—
1893	3,340,792	6.40	11.00	16.00	24.00	35.00	67.50	150	950	1,450
1893O	1,760,000	25.00	39.00	110	125	150	160	295	3,200	—
1893S	2,491,401	9.50	18.00	25.00	35.00	55.00	115	275	4,200	—
1894	1,330,972	16.00	29.00	100.00	120	145	165	250	1,200	1,450

Date	Mintage	G-4	VG-8	F-12	VF-20	XF-40	AU-50	MS-60	MS-65	Prf-65
1894O	720,000	50.00	85.00	190	235	330	640	1,200	10,500	—
1894S	24	—	—	—	—	—	—	—	—	—

Note: 1894S, Eliasberg Sale, May 1996, Prf-64, $451,000.

Date	Mintage	G-4	VG-8	F-12	VF-20	XF-40	AU-50	MS-60	MS-65	Prf-65
1895	690,880	67.50	120	300	415	485	535	675	2,700	2,000
1895O	440,000	315	465	715	1,000	1,950	3,300	6,000	16,000	—
1895S	1,120,000	36.00	44.00	120	160	195	230	465	7,500	—
1896	2,000,762	9.00	20.00	50.00	67.50	83.00	105	145	1,450	1,450
1896O	610,000	67.50	120	275	330	400	600	1,000	7,200	—
1896S	575,056	75.00	140	285	275	345	500	740	3,500	—
1897	10,869,264	2.00	3.35	6.40	12.00	24.00	65.00	120	650	1,450
1897O	666,000	60.00	100.00	250	315	400	550	925	4,500	—
1897S	1,342,844	20.00	30.00	90.00	95.00	120	200	400	4,000	—
1898	16,320,735	2.00	2.75	6.40	10.00	21.50	65.00	95.00	690	1,450
1898O	2,130,000	8.00	18.00	80.00	100.00	200	200	435	4,000	—
1898S	1,702,507	5.50	12.00	27.00	35.00	58.50	115	335	3,700	—
1899	19,580,846	2.45	2.75	6.40	9.50	20.00	65.00	95.00	670	1,450
1899O	2,650,000	5.75	14.50	67.50	90.00	125	215	360	4,700	—
1899S	1,867,493	6.00	12.00	19.50	24.00	40.00	85.00	300	490	—
1900	17,600,912	2.50	4.00	6.40	10.00	21.50	65.00	95.00	800	1,450
1900O	2,010,000	14.00	33.00	95.00	125	200	345	570	5,800	—
1900S	5,168,270	4.00	4.50	10.00	12.50	23.50	72.50	150	1,750	—

20 CENTS

KM# 109 0.9000 **SILVER** 0.1447 oz. ASW. 22 mm. 5.0000 g. **Designer:** William Barber

Date	Mintage	G-4	VG-8	F-12	VF-20	XF-40	AU-50	MS-60	MS-65	Prf-65
1875	39,700	85.00	100.00	135	165	220	360	575	5,500	9,500
1875S	1,155,000	80.00	82.50	85.00	115	165	285	465	5,000	—
1875CC	133,290	100.00	120	150	220	325	520	725	9,500	—
1876	15,900	110	125	215	270	350	470	650	5,200	9,500
1876CC	10,000	—	—	—	—	—	—	—	—	—

Note: 1876CC, Eliasberg Sale, April 1997, MS-65, $148,500. Heritage 1999 ANA, MS-63, $86,500.

Date	Mintage	G-4	VG-8	F-12	VF-20	XF-40	AU-50	MS-60	MS-65	Prf-65
1877 proof	510	1,400	1,600	1,900	2,100	2,300	2,500	—	—	10,000
1878 proof	600	1,200	1,400	1,650	1,800	1,900	2,000	—	—	9,500

QUARTER

Draped Bust Quarter
Heraldic eagle

KM# 36 0.8920 **SILVER** .1935 oz. ASW. 27.5 mm. 6.7400 g. **Designer:** Robert Scot

Date	Mintage	G-4	VG-8	F-12	VF-20	XF-40	AU-50	MS-60	MS-65
1804	6,738	2,000	2,400	3,500	5,000	11,000	20,000	43,000	110,000
1805	121,394	200	275	500	950	1,600	3,500	5,000	62,000
1806	206,124	200	275	500	900	1,450	3,300	4,650	46,500
1806/5	Inc. above	225	375	650	1,400	2,500	4,000	6,250	62,500
1807	220,643	200	275	500	925	1,700	3,400	4,650	48,500

Liberty Cap Quarter
"E Pluribus Unum" above eagle

KM# 44 0.8920 **SILVER** 0.1935 oz. ASW. 27 mm. 6.7400 g. **Designer:** John Reich **Notes:** Varieties of the 1819 strikes are distinguished by the size of the 9 in the date. Varieties of the 1820 strikes are distinguished by the size of the 0 in the date. One 1822 variety and one 1828 variety have "25" engraved over "50" in the denomination. The 1827 restrikes were produced privately using dies sold as scrap by the U.S. Mint.

Date	Mintage	G-4	VG-8	F-12	VF-20	XF-40	AU-50	MS-60	MS-65
1815	89,235	55.00	70.00	175	475	1,000	1,650	2,750	25,000
1818	361,174	50.00	65.00	150	450	900	1,500	2,500	16,000
1818/15	Inc. above	55.00	70.00	200	575	1,100	1,750	2,800	20,000
1819 small 9	144,000	55.00	65.00	150	425	875	1,500	2,500	22,000
1819 large 9	Inc. above	55.00	65.00	150	425	875	1,500	2,500	22,000
1820 small 0	127,444	60.00	75.00	150	425	875	1,500	2,500	28,000
1820 large 0	Inc. above	50.00	65.00	150	425	875	1,500	2,500	25,000
1821	216,851	50.00	60.00	150	450	675	1,250	1,850	16,500
1822	64,080	65.00	90.00	200	550	1,200	2,000	3,750	—
1822 25/50C.	Inc. above	1,500	3,000	4,250	7,000	12,500	19,000	—	—
1823/22	17,800	10,000	14,000	20,000	30,000	40,000	55,000	—	—

Date	Mintage	G-4	VG-8	F-12	VF-20	XF-40	AU-50	MS-60	MS-65
Note: 1823/22, Superior, Aug. 1990, Proof, $62,500.									
1824/2 mintage unrecorded	—	80.00	130	350	850	1,900	3,500	6,250	—
1825/22	168,000	70.00	100.00	200	500	1,100	1,900	2,800	22,500
1825/23	Inc. above	50.00	65.00	140	425	875	1,500	2,500	16,500
1825/24	Inc. above	50.00	65.00	140	425	875	1,500	2,500	16,500
1827 original	4,000	—	—	—	—	—	—	—	—
Note: Eliasberg, April 1997, VF-20, $39,600.									
1827 restrike	Inc. above	—	—	—	—	—	—	—	—
Note: 1827 restrike, Eliasberg, April 1997, Prf-65, $77,000.									
1828	102,000	50.00	65.00	140	375	775	1,600	2,850	19,500
1828 25/50C.	Inc. above	150	325	550	1,050	1,850	4,000	8,500	—

Liberty Cap Quarter

"E Pluribus Unum" removed from above eagle

KM# 55 0.8920 **SILVER** 24.3 mm. **Designer:** William Kneass **Notes:** Varieties of the 1831 strikes are distinguished by the size of the lettering on the reverse.

Date	Mintage	G-4	VG-8	F-12	VF-20	XF-40	AU-50	MS-60	MS-65
1831 small letter	398,000	55.00	65.00	75.00	120	350	850	1,000	13,500
1831 large letter	Inc. above	55.00	65.00	75.00	120	350	850	1,000	18,500
1832	320,000	55.00	65.00	75.00	120	350	850	1,000	16,000
1833	156,000	55.00	65.00	75.00	120	350	850	1,000	13,500
1834	286,000	55.00	65.00	75.00	120	350	850	1,000	13,500
1835	1,952,000	55.00	65.00	75.00	120	350	850	1,000	13,500
1836	472,000	55.00	65.00	75.00	120	350	850	1,000	14,500
1837	252,400	55.00	65.00	75.00	120	350	850	1,000	13,500
1838	832,000	55.00	65.00	75.00	120	350	850	1,000	14,750

Seated Liberty Quarter

No drapery

KM# 64.1 0.9000 **SILVER** 0.1934 oz. ASW. 24.3 mm. 6.6800 g. **Designer:** Christian Gobrecht

Date	Mintage	G-4	VG-8	F-12	VF-20	XF-40	AU-50	MS-60	MS-65
1838	Inc. above	18.00	25.00	35.00	65.00	300	550	1,250	23,000
1839	491,146	20.00	28.00	35.00	65.00	275	550	1,250	25,000
1840O	425,200	14.00	25.00	45.00	110	375	575	1,350	30,000

Seated Liberty Quarter

Drapery added to Liberty's left elbow

KM# 64.2 0.9000 **SILVER** 0.1934 oz. ASW. 24.3 mm. 6.6800 g. **Designer:** Christian Gobrecht **Notes:** Two varieties for 1842 and 1842-O are distinguished by the size of the numerals in the date. 1852 obverse dies were used to strike the 1853 no-arrows variety, with the 2 being recut to form a 3.

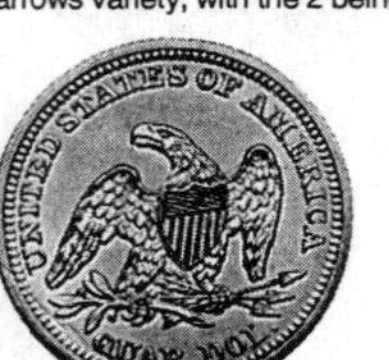

Date	Mintage	G-4	VG-8	F-12	VF-20	XF-40	AU-50	MS-60	MS-65
1840	188,127	30.00	55.00	80.00	125	225	350	950	12,000
1840O	Inc. above	29.00	39.00	70.00	115	250	450	1,000	—
1841	120,000	75.00	90.00	120	185	300	385	750	11,000
1841O	452,000	16.00	27.00	50.00	85.00	165	350	700	10,000
1842 small date	88,000	—	—	—	—	—	—	—	—
Note: 1842 small date, Eliasberg, April 1997, Prf-63, $66,000.									
1842 large date	Inc. above	85.00	120	170	275	350	800	1,250	—
1842O small date	769,000	425	650	1,100	1,850	4,000	—	—	—
1842O large date	Inc. above	16.00	20.00	30.00	45.00	125	300	—	4,000
1843	645,600	16.00	20.00	27.00	37.00	55.00	150	400	3,500
1843O	968,000	20.00	28.00	42.00	100.00	275	750	2,000	11,000
1844	421,200	17.00	22.00	30.00	40.00	65.00	160	450	5,000
1844O	740,000	16.00	24.00	37.50	60.00	115	275	1,000	6,000
1845	922,000	16.00	20.00	27.00	37.00	50.00	150	450	5,000
1846	510,000	19.00	23.00	36.50	50.00	75.00	160	475	6,000
1847	734,000	16.00	20.00	27.00	37.00	50.00	150	425	5,000
1847O	368,000	27.00	40.00	60.00	120	275	700	1,900	—
1848	146,000	40.00	55.00	100.00	185	225	375	1,000	10,000
1849	340,000	18.00	22.00	36.00	65.00	125	275	750	9,000
1849O mintage unrecorded	—	425	600	1,000	1,700	2,900	5,750	—	—
1850	190,800	35.00	45.00	75.00	110	150	275	800	—
1850O	412,000	20.00	30.00	50.00	100.00	150	450	1,300	—
1851	160,000	60.00	75.00	125	225	285	400	850	8,500
1851O	88,000	150	265	375	575	1,000	2,250	4,000	—
1852	177,060	50.00	60.00	100.00	185	225	350	500	4,800
1852O	96,000	175	250	350	595	1,200	3,500	8,000	—
1853 recut date	44,200	350	500	700	900	1,200	1,600	2,600	9,000

Seated Liberty Quarter

Arrows at date Rays around eagle

KM# 78 0.9000 **SILVER** 0.1800 oz. ASW. 24.3 mm. 6.2200 g. **Designer:** Christian Gobrecht

Date	Mintage	G-4	VG-8	F-12	VF-20	XF-40	AU-50	MS-60	MS-65	Prf-65
1853	15,210,020	15.00	20.00	27.50	45.00	150	275	950	19,000	90,000
1853/4	Inc. above	40.00	65.00	100.00	200	275	750	1,750	—	—
1853O	1,332,000	18.00	35.00	50.00	100.00	275	1,100	2,750	—	—

Seated Liberty Quarter

Rays around eagle removed

KM# 81 0.9000 **SILVER** .1934 oz. ASW. 24.3 mm. 6.6800 g. **Designer:** Christian Gobrecht **Notes:** The 1854-O "huge O" variety has an oversized mint mark.

Date	Mintage	G-4	VG-8	F-12	VF-20	XF-40	AU-50	MS-60	MS-65	Prf-65
1854	12,380,000	15.00	20.00	27.50	35.00	75.00	225	440	7,500	17,500
1854O	1,484,000	17.00	24.00	35.00	60.00	125	300	1,750	—	—
1854O huge O	Inc. above	—	—	—	—	—	—	—	—	—
1855	2,857,000	15.00	20.00	27.50	35.00	75.00	225	440	8,500	18,500
1855O	176,000	50.00	75.00	110	240	475	950	2,750	—	—
1855S	396,400	40.00	60.00	80.00	225	500	1,250	2,000	—	—

Seated Liberty Quarter

Arrows at date removed

KM# A64.2 0.9000 **SILVER** 0.1800 oz. ASW. 24.3 mm. 6.2200 g. **Designer:** Christian Gobrecht

Date	Mintage	G-4	VG-8	F-12	VF-20	XF-40	AU-50	MS-60	MS-65	Prf-65
1856	7,264,000	15.00	20.00	27.50	35.00	60.00	145	290	4,250	15,000
1856O	968,000	20.00	30.00	40.00	60.00	110	250	1,000	8,500	—
1856S	286,000	45.00	65.00	110	250	450	900	2,200	—	—
1856S/S	Inc. above	70.00	100.00	185	375	875	1,250	—	—	—
1857	9,644,000	15.00	20.00	27.50	35.00	60.00	145	290	4,000	9,500
1857O	1,180,000	15.00	20.00	29.00	40.00	80.00	275	975	—	—
1857S	82,000	100.00	145	250	400	600	950	2,750	—	—
1858	7,368,000	15.00	20.00	27.50	35.00	60.00	160	300	4,000	6,500
1858O	520,000	25.00	30.00	45.00	70.00	135	360	1,350	—	—
1858S	121,000	60.00	100.00	175	275	650	1,250	—	—	—
1859	1,344,000	17.00	24.00	30.00	40.00	75.00	175	375	6,000	7,000
1859O	260,000	25.00	30.00	50.00	80.00	150	400	1,000	15,000	—
1859S	80,000	100.00	135	225	450	1,350	2,500	—	—	—
1860	805,400	18.00	22.00	28.00	33.00	60.00	160	500	—	5,250
1860O	388,000	20.00	30.00	40.00	55.00	100.00	275	1,200	—	—
1860S	56,000	175	325	575	900	3,500	6,000	—	—	—
1861	4,854,600	16.00	19.00	27.00	32.00	55.00	150	290	4,200	5,500
1861S	96,000	80.00	125	235	400	1,250	2,750	—	—	—
1862	932,550	18.00	22.00	33.00	40.00	65.00	165	300	4,350	5,350
1862S	67,000	80.00	125	200	300	700	1,600	2,750	—	—
1863	192,060	30.00	45.00	60.00	120	185	300	650	4,350	5,500
1864	94,070	75.00	100.00	135	200	300	400	650	5,000	5,500
1864S	20,000	375	575	875	1,250	2,350	3,750	7,000	—	—
1865	59,300	75.00	100.00	150	200	290	375	875	9,500	5,500
1865S	41,000	100.00	135	200	350	650	1,250	2,350	11,500	—
1866 unique	—	—	—	—	—	—	—	—	—	—

Seated Liberty Quarter

"In God We Trust" above eagle

KM# 98 0.9000 **SILVER** 0.1800 oz. ASW. 24.3 mm. 6.2200 g. **Designer:** Christian Gobrecht **Notes:** The 1873 closed-3 and open-3 varieties are distinguished by the amount of space between the upper left and lower left serifs in the 3.

Date	Mintage	G-4	VG-8	F-12	VF-20	XF-40	AU-50	MS-60	MS-65	Prf-65
1866	17,525	450	575	700	950	1,200	1,500	2,250	7,500	3,000

Date	Mintage	G-4	VG-8	F-12	VF-20	XF-40	AU-50	MS-60	MS-65	Prf-65
1866S	28,000	250	325	550	900	1,450	2,000	3,000	—	—
1867	20,625	225	300	450	625	800	975	1,200	—	2,450
1867S	48,000	275	350	600	900	1,350	1,700	—	—	—
1868	30,000	185	250	325	400	500	650	900	7,000	3,450
1868S	96,000	80.00	100.00	185	300	625	1,350	2,000	—	—
1869	16,600	325	425	550	675	775	950	1,275	—	2,500
1869S	76,000	90.00	115	225	375	700	1,400	2,400	16,000	—
1870	87,400	55.00	80.00	125	200	285	375	850	6,000	2,750
1870CC	8,340	3,800	5,500	8,000	12,000	16,000	25,000	35,000	—	—
1871	119,160	40.00	65.00	75.00	150	195	350	650	6,000	2,500
1871CC	10,890	2,250	3,800	5,500	9,500	14,500	25,000	40,000	—	—
1871S	30,900	300	450	550	800	1,100	1,850	3,000	10,000	—
1872	182,950	30.00	40.00	80.00	110	155	300	600	6,500	2,500
1872CC	22,850	650	850	1,500	2,950	5,900	7,500	14,000	—	—
1872S	83,000	900	1,250	1,650	2,100	3,500	4,500	7,500	—	—
1873 closed 3	212,600	150	225	325	525	600	1,000	2,000	—	2,600
1873 open 3	Inc. above	30.00	42.50	80.00	120	175	250	450	5,000	—
1873CC 6 known	4,000	—	75,000	—	—	—	—	—	—	—

Note: 1873CC, Heritage, April 1999, MS-62, $106,375.

Seated Liberty Quarter

Arrows at date

KM# 106 0.9000 **SILVER** 0.1808 oz. ASW. 24.3 mm. 6.2500 g. **Designer:** Christian Gobrecht

Date	Mintage	G-4	VG-8	F-12	VF-20	XF-40	AU-50	MS-60	MS-65	Prf-65
1873	1,271,700	16.00	23.00	30.00	60.00	200	400	775	4,250	8,000
1873CC	12,462	2,250	3,500	5,250	8,500	14,500	18,000	35,000	—	—
1873S	156,000	25.00	40.00	85.00	140	275	550	1,200	8,000	—
1874	471,900	20.00	26.00	40.00	70.00	220	420	850	4,000	6,750
1874S	392,000	23.00	30.00	50.00	110	240	425	900	4,500	—

Seated Liberty Quarter

Arrows at date removed

KM# A98 0.9000 **SILVER** 0.1808 oz. ASW. 24.3 mm. 6.2500 g. **Designer:** Christian Gobrecht
Notes: The 1876-CC fine-reeding variety has a more finely reeded edge.

Date	Mintage	G-4	VG-8	F-12	VF-20	XF-40	AU-50	MS-60	MS-65	Prf-65
1875	4,293,500	14.00	17.00	25.00	30.00	50.00	135	225	1,600	2,300
1875CC	140,000	60.00	90.00	175	300	550	850	1,600	15,000	—
1875S	680,000	25.00	36.00	67.00	110	175	275	575	3,200	—
1876	17,817,150	14.00	17.00	25.00	30.00	50.00	135	225	1,600	2,250
1876CC	4,944,000	17.00	20.00	30.00	40.00	70.00	150	325	3,600	—
1876CC fine reeding	Inc. above	18.00	28.00	33.00	42.00	72.00	150	325	3,600	—
1876S	8,596,000	16.00	19.00	25.00	30.00	50.00	135	225	2,000	—
1877	10,911,710	14.00	17.00	25.00	30.00	50.00	135	225	1,600	2,250
1877CC	4,192,000	18.00	28.00	33.00	42.00	72.00	150	325	2,000	—
1877S	8,996,000	14.00	17.00	25.00	30.00	50.00	135	225	1,600	—
1877S / horizontal S	Inc. above	32.00	48.00	75.00	125	225	375	650	—	—
1878	2,260,800	16.00	18.00	28.00	34.00	55.00	145	250	2,750	2,300
1878CC	996,000	19.00	29.00	45.00	85.00	110	150	450	3,500	—
1878S	140,000	150	185	285	350	600	850	1,450	—	—
1879	14,700	190	235	285	325	400	485	575	1,700	2,250
1880	14,955	190	235	285	325	400	485	575	1,600	2,250
1881	12,975	200	250	300	350	425	500	600	1,650	2,200
1882	16,300	200	250	300	350	425	500	600	1,850	2,200
1883	15,439	210	265	315	365	435	525	625	2,450	2,200
1884	8,875	325	400	485	585	675	750	850	1,900	2,200
1885	14,530	210	265	315	365	435	525	625	2,600	2,200
1886	5,886	500	600	700	800	900	1,000	1,250	2,600	2,400
1887	10,710	300	350	400	485	585	625	750	2,350	2,200
1888	10,833	250	300	350	400	475	550	650	2,000	2,350
1888S	1,216,000	15.00	20.00	27.50	30.00	60.00	160	245	2,450	—
1889	12,711	225	285	325	385	450	500	625	1,750	2,350
1890	80,590	65.00	85.00	100.00	125	200	300	425	—	2,350
1891	3,920,600	15.00	20.00	27.50	30.00	60.00	160	245	1,750	2,350
1891O	68,000	150	225	325	550	950	1,250	3,000	14,500	—
1891S	2,216,000	16.00	22.00	29.00	65.00	52.50	185	275	2,400	—

Barber Quarter

KM# 114 0.9000 **SILVER** 0.1809 oz. ASW. 24.3 mm. 6.2500 g. **Designer:** Charles E. Barber

Date	Mintage	G-4	VG-8	F-12	VF-20	XF-40	AU-50	MS-60	MS-65	Prf-65
1892	8,237,245	5.25	6.75	22.50	40.00	70.00	120	185	1,100	2,000
1892O	2,640,000	8.00	15.00	37.50	50.00	87.50	135	300	1,650	—
1892S	964,079	21.50	43.50	75.00	100.00	150	300	480	4,850	—
1893	5,484,838	5.00	7.00	26.00	36.00	67.50	120	210	1,750	2,000
1893O	3,396,000	6.25	7.00	27.50	46.00	82.50	160	275	1,900	—
1893S	1,454,535	11.00	25.00	55.00	100.00	130	300	480	8,400	—
1894	3,432,972	5.00	7.50	31.50	45.00	90.00	135	250	1,550	2,000
1894O	2,852,000	7.00	10.00	38.00	58.50	100.00	200	340	3,000	—
1894S	2,648,821	7.50	11.00	38.00	58.50	100.00	205	315	3,000	—
1895	4,440,880	5.50	8.00	30.00	38.00	75.00	135	230	1,900	2,000
1895O	2,816,000	7.00	12.50	40.00	62.50	110	225	400	2,750	—
1895S	1,764,681	10.00	18.00	48.50	82.50	110	240	400	4,000	—
1896	3,874,762	5.00	6.50	25.00	37.50	77.50	135	235	1,600	2,000
1896O	1,484,000	9.60	27.50	92.50	235	375	650	850	7,750	—
1896S	188,039	535	780	1,250	1,925	3,300	4,500	5,600	3,850	—
1897	8,140,731	5.00	6.25	21.50	33.50	71.50	120	185	1,100	2,000
1897O	1,414,800	10.00	25.00	80.00	200	375	625	800	3,750	—
1897S	542,229	80.00	100.00	225	275	400	700	1,000	7,000	—
1898	11,100,735	5.00	6.25	22.50	33.50	71.50	120	185	1,100	2,000
1898O	1,868,000	8.00	19.00	65.00	125	235	415	625	10,000	—
1898S	1,020,592	7.00	15.00	42.50	55.00	72.50	200	400	7,200	—
1899	12,624,846	5.00	6.25	22.50	33.50	71.50	120	185	1,100	2,000
1899O	2,644,000	7.00	13.50	32.50	51.50	96.00	265	400	3,350	—
1899S	708,000	15.00	26.00	70.00	85.00	125	250	440	3,700	—
1900	10,016,912	6.00	8.00	21.50	33.50	71.50	135	185	1,100	2,000
1900O	3,416,000	8.50	21.50	62.50	100.00	125	335	585	3,800	—
1900S	1,858,585	7.25	13.00	38.00	55.00	75.00	130	385	5,400	—

HALF DOLLAR

Draped Bust Half Dollar

Heraldic eagle

KM# 35 0.8920 **SILVER** 0.3869 oz. ASW. 32.5 mm. 13.4800 g. **Designer:** Robert Scot **Notes:** The two varieties of the 1803 strikes are distinguished by the size of the 3 in the date. The several varieties of the 1806 strikes are distinguished by the style of 6 in the date, size of the stars on the obverse, and whether the stem of the olive branch held by the reverse eagle extends through the claw.

Date	Mintage	G-4	VG-8	F-12	VF-20	XF-40	MS-60
1801	30,289	225	300	700	1,500	5,000	35,000
1802	29,890	225	300	700	1,500	4,500	40,000
1803 small 3	188,234	150	170	300	600	1,500	8,500
1803 large 3	Inc. above	125	150	250	500	1,000	9,000
1805	211,722	125	150	250	550	1,050	9,000
1805/4	Inc. above	190	300	500	1,000	2,500	26,000
1806 round-top 6, large stars	839,576	125	150	190	450	1,100	6,000
1806 round-top 6, small stars	Inc. above	125	140	180	450	1,100	6,250
1806 knobbed 6, stem not through claw	—	—	35,000	40,000	50,000	65,000	—
1806 pointed-top 6, stem not through claw	Inc. above	115	130	250	340	1,000	5,750
1806 pointed-top 6, stem through claw	Inc. above	120	150	250	340	1,000	5,750
1806/5	Inc. above	125	160	275	500	1,400	8,000
1806 /inverted 6	Inc. above	200	350	600	1,200	2,100	15,000
1807	301,076	120	150	250	340	1,000	5,750

Bust Half Dollar

"50 C." below eagle

KM# 37 0.8920 **SILVER** 0.3869 oz. ASW. 32.5 mm. 13.4800 g. **Designer:** John Reich **Notes:** There are three varieties of the 1807 strikes. Two are distinguished by the size of the stars on the obverse. The third was struck from a reverse die that had a 5 cut over a 2 in the "50C" denomination. Two varieties of the 1811 are distinguished by the size of the 8 in the date. A third has a period between the 8 and second 1 in the date. One variety of the 1817 has a period between the 1 and 7 in the date. Two varieties of the 1819/18 overdate are distinguished by the size of the 9 in the date. Two varieties of the 1820 are distinguished by the size of the date. On the 1823 varieties, the "broken 3" appears to be almost separated in the middle of the 3 in the date; the "patched 3" has the error repaired; the "ugly 3" has portions of its detail missing. The 1827 "curled-2" and "square-2" varieties are distinguished by the numeral's base -- either curled or square. Among the 1828 varieties, "knobbed 2" and "no knob" refers to whether the upper left serif of the digit is rounded. The 1830 varieties are distinguished by the size of the 0 in the date. The four 1834 varieties are distinguished by the sizes of the stars, date and letters in the inscriptions. The 1836 "50/00" variety was struck from a reverse die that had "50" recut over "00" in the denomination.

Date	Mintage	G-4	VG-8	F-12	VF-20	XF-40	AU-50	MS-60	MS-65
1807 small stars	750,500	65.00	105	200	475	800	3,500	5,900	35,000
1807 large stars	Inc. above	60.00	100.00	180	475	800	3,500	5,500	—
1807 50/20 C.	Inc. above	55.00	92.50	140	250	500	2,100	4,000	30,000
1807 bearded goddess	—	300	500	900	1,500	2,750	7,500	—	—
1808	1,368,600	50.00	57.50	65.00	100.00	260	600	1,800	15,000
1808/7	Inc. above	52.50	62.50	92.50	160	330	900	1,850	17,500
1809	1,405,810	50.00	57.50	65.00	100.00	210	525	1,600	15,000
1810	1,276,276	52.50	57.50	66.00	100.00	175	475	1,550	13,000
1811 small 8	1,203,644	52.50	60.00	65.00	100.00	140	375	800	7,500
1811 large 8	Inc. above	50.00	57.50	62.50	95.00	150	500	1,000	8,500
1811 dated 18.11	Inc. above	55.00	60.00	80.00	150	300	800	2,100	12,000
1812	1,628,059	52.50	60.00	65.00	100.00	150	340	775	7,500
1812/1 small 8	Inc. above	53.50	61.00	90.00	160	250	700	2,000	12,000
1812/1 large 8	Inc. above	1,350	1,900	3,500	4,850	7,500	15,500	—	—
1813	1,241,903	52.50	60.00	65.00	100.00	165	500	1,250	11,000
1813 50/UNI reverse	1,241,903	55.00	62.50	92.50	135	300	900	1,900	12,000
1814	1,039,075	52.50	60.00	66.00	100.00	165	500	1,350	9,800
1814/3	Inc. above	62.50	75.00	110	150	275	850	2,000	16,500
1815/2	47,150	840	11,500	1,550	1,900	3,000	4,750	11,000	60,000
1817	1,215,567	52.50	60.00	66.00	90.00	160	385	900	10,000
1817/3	Inc. above	80.00	125	175	385	800	1,800	3,750	43,500
1817/4	—	50,000	60,000	115,000	145,000	190,000	240,000	—	—
1817 dated 181.7	Inc. above	54.00	62.50	70.00	100.00	175	650	1,500	12,500
1818	1,960,322	52.50	60.00	66.00	85.00	135	375	900	8,500
1818/7	Inc. above	60.00	72.50	85.00	105	160	700	1,500	11,000
1819	2,208,000	52.50	60.00	66.00	85.00	125	375	900	9,000
1819/8 small 9	Inc. above	57.50	62.50	75.00	100.00	200	550	1,300	1,150
1819/8 large 9	Inc. above	57.50	62.50	75.00	100.00	200	550	1,300	11,500
1820 small date	751,122	53.50	61.00	75.00	145	260	650	1,500	12,500
1820 large date	Inc. above	53.50	61.00	75.00	125	250	660	1,350	12,000
1820/19	Inc. above	62.50	75.00	85.00	150	300	900	2,000	15,000
1821	1,305,797	52.50	60.00	66.00	80.00	140	525	1,200	9,750
1822	1,559,573	52.50	60.00	66.00	85.00	125	300	750	7,700
1822/1	Inc. above	60.00	68.50	92.50	150	250	800	1,750	11,000
1823	1,694,200	47.50	52.50	57.50	66.00	110	300	825	7,500
1823 broken 3	Inc. above	55.00	66.00	92.50	140	360	900	1,750	12,000
1823 patched 3	Inc. above	52.50	62.50	85.00	115	180	400	1,300	13,500
1823 ugly 3	Inc. above	53.50	67.50	88.00	135	235	900	1,700	14,000
1824	3,504,954	47.50	52.50	66.00	75.00	110	260	650	7,500
1824/21	Inc. above	52.50	60.00	66.00	85.00	150	400	1,000	8,000
1824 1824/various dates	Inc. above	52.50	60.00	70.00	125	200	750	1,750	12,000
1825	2,943,166	47.50	52.50	66.00	75.00	110	260	550	7,000
1826	4,004,180	47.50	52.50	66.00	75.00	110	260	550	7,000
1827 curled 2	5,493,400	47.50	52.50	66.00	100.00	130	345	900	8,500
1827 square 2	Inc. above	47.50	52.50	60.00	75.00	110	260	650	7,500
1827/6	Inc. above	57.50	68.50	80.00	100.00	150	375	975	9,000
1828 curled-base 2, no knob	3,075,200	47.50	52.50	66.00	75.00	110	260	650	7,000
1828 curled-base 2, knobbed 2	Inc. above	47.50	52.50	66.00	85.00	120	270	700	7,250
1828 small 8s, square-base 2, large letters	Inc. above	47.50	52.50	66.00	75.00	110	260	550	6,250
1828 small 8s, square-base 2, small letters	Inc. above	52.50	70.00	95.00	135	220	720	1,200	9,500
1828 large 8s, square-base 2	Inc. above	48.50	52.50	66.00	75.00	110	260	750	9,000
1829	3,712,156	45.00	50.00	53.50	60.00	100.00	250	600	9,000
1829/7	Inc. above	47.50	57.50	67.50	85.00	165	330	925	11,750
1830 small letter rev.	4,764,800	45.00	50.00	53.50	60.00	100.00	250	500	7,000
1830 large letter rev.	Inc. above	1,250	1,850	2,250	3,300	4,500	7,500	—	—
1831	5,873,660	45.00	50.00	53.50	60.00	100.00	250	500	7,000
1832 small letters	4,797,000	45.00	50.00	53.50	60.00	100.00	250	575	7,000
1832 large letters	Inc. above	45.00	50.00	64.00	90.00	155	315	700	7,500
1833	5,206,000	45.00	50.00	53.50	60.00	100.00	250	575	7,000
1834 small date, large stars, small letters	6,412,004	45.00	50.00	53.50	60.00	100.00	250	575	7,000
1834 small date, small stars, small letters	Inc. above	45.00	50.00	53.50	60.00	100.00	250	575	7,000
1834 large date, small letters	Inc. above	45.00	50.00	53.50	60.00	100.00	250	575	7,000
1834 large date, large letters	Inc. above	45.00	50.00	53.50	60.00	100.00	250	575	7,000
1835	5,352,006	45.00	50.00	53.50	60.00	100.00	275	600	9,000
1836	6,545,000	45.00	50.00	53.50	60.00	100.00	250	500	7,000
1836 50/00	Inc. above	55.00	80.00	100.00	185	300	800	1,750	10,000

Bust Half Dollar

"50 Cents" below eagle

KM# 58 0.9000 **SILVER** 0.3867 oz. ASW. 30 mm. 13.3600 g. **Designer:** Christian Gobrecht

Date	Mintage	G-4	VG-8	F-12	VF-20	XF-40	AU-50	MS-60	MS-65
1836	1,200	700	1,000	1,200	1,500	2,250	3,200	6,000	40,000
1837	3,629,820	50.00	60.00	75.00	110	165	325	750	12,500

Bust Half Dollar

"Half Dol." below eagle

KM# 65 0.9000 **SILVER** 0.3867 oz. ASW. 30 mm. 13.3600 g. **Designer:** Christian Gobrecht

Date	Mintage	G-4	VG-8	F-12	VF-20	XF-40	AU-50	MS-60	MS-65
1838	3,546,000	50.00	60.00	75.00	110	165	475	825	17,000
1838O proof only	Est. 20	85,000	105,000	115,000	125,000	150,000	180,000	—	—
1839	1,392,976	56.00	66.00	82.50	115	185	375	990	30,000
1839O	178,976	135	215	300	400	675	1,200	2,500	45,000

Seated Liberty Half Dollar

KM# 68 0.9000 **SILVER** .3867 oz. ASW. 30.6 mm. 13.3600 g. **Designer:** Christian Gobrecht **Notes:** The 1839 varieties are distinguished by whether there's drapery extending from Liberty's left elbow. One variety of the 1840 strikes has smaller lettering; another used the old reverse of 1838. Varieties of 1842 and 1846 are distinguished by the size of the numerals in the date.

Date	Mintage	G-4	VG-8	F-12	VF-20	XF-40	AU-50	MS-60	MS-65
1839 no drapery from elbow	Inc. above	38.00	65.00	110	315	725	1,650	4,500	150,000
1839 drapery	Inc. above	20.00	30.00	50.00	75.00	145	265	450	—
1840 small letters	1,435,008	23.00	32.00	47.50	67.00	110	350	575	8,250
1840 reverse 1838	Inc. above	125	175	250	325	575	1,100	2,900	12,000
1840O	855,100	23.00	28.00	45.00	80.00	125	275	430	—
1841	310,000	39.00	49.00	80.00	130	200	300	1,100	5,700
1841O	401,000	19.00	28.00	44.00	75.00	125	250	550	5,900
1842 small date	2,012,764	35.00	42.00	60.00	110	185	325	1,300	12,000
1842 large date	Inc. above	18.00	28.00	43.00	52.00	100.00	175	1,250	12,000
1842O small date	957,000	650	850	1,400	2,250	4,000	—	—	—
1842O large date	Inc. above	22.00	29.00	48.00	115	225	750	1,750	—
1843	3,844,000	17.00	28.00	43.00	52.00	100.00	180	350	4,500
1843O	2,268,000	17.00	28.00	43.00	60.00	115	250	550	—
1844	1,766,000	17.00	28.00	43.00	52.00	100.00	210	350	4,500
1844O	2,005,000	18.00	28.00	43.00	52.00	100.00	225	525	—
1844/1844O	Inc. above	500	775	1,000	1,375	2,300	4,900	—	—
1845	589,000	30.00	40.00	60.00	110	200	375	900	—
1845O	2,094,000	18.00	28.00	43.00	52.00	125	240	550	—
1845O no drapery	Inc. above	25.00	35.00	65.00	115	185	375	750	—
1846 medium date	2,210,000	18.00	28.00	43.00	52.00	100.00	200	500	9,000
1846 tall date	Inc. above	22.00	30.00	60.00	85.00	145	250	650	12,000
1846 /horizontal 6	Inc. above	175	235	300	400	575	1,000	2,500	—
1846O medium date	2,304,000	18.00	28.00	43.00	52.00	100.00	225	550	12,000
1846O tall date	Inc. above	135	245	325	575	950	2,000	3,600	—
1847/1846	1,156,000	2,000	2,750	3,200	4,250	6,500	—	—	—
1847	Inc. above	25.00	35.00	55.00	70.00	115	250	480	9,000
1847O	2,584,000	18.00	28.00	43.00	52.00	95.00	250	640	7,000
1848	580,000	40.00	60.00	85.00	170	265	475	1,000	9,000
1848O	3,180,000	18.00	28.00	43.00	52.00	110	285	750	9,000
1849	1,252,000	26.00	40.00	55.00	90.00	150	365	1,250	9,000
1849O	2,310,000	17.00	28.00	43.00	60.00	110	250	650	9,000
1850	227,000	275	325	400	500	675	1,000	1,500	—
1850O	2,456,000	20.00	28.00	45.00	80.00	135	275	650	9,000
1851	200,750	425	500	700	900	1,000	1,250	1,950	—
1851O	402,000	37.00	45.00	75.00	105	175	300	675	9,000
1852	77,130	400	500	650	850	1,000	1,200	1,650	—
1852O	144,000	100.00	125	200	350	525	1,050	1,850	—

Date	Mintage	G-4	VG-8	F-12	VF-20	XF-40	AU-50	MS-60	MS-65
1853O mintage unrecorded	—	—	—	—	—	—	—	—	—

Note: 1853O, Eliasberg Sale, 1997, VG-8, $154,000.

Seated Liberty Half Dollar
Arrows at date Rays around eagle

KM# 79 0.9000 **SILVER** 0.3600 oz. ASW. 12.4400 g. **Designer:** Christian Gobrecht

Date	Mintage	G-4	VG-8	F-12	VF-20	XF-40	AU-50	MS-60	MS-65	Prf-65
1853	3,532,708	17.00	27.00	40.00	90.00	250	505	1,700	21,500	—
1853O	1,328,000	21.00	32.00	50.00	125	290	700	2,100	21,500	—

Seated Liberty Half Dollar
Rays around eagle removed

KM# 82 0.9000 **SILVER** 0.3600 oz. ASW. 12.4400 g. **Designer:** Christian Gobrecht

Date	Mintage	G-4	VG-8	F-12	VF-20	XF-40	AU-50	MS-60	MS-65	Prf-65
1854	2,982,000	17.00	28.00	43.00	55.00	100.00	270	675	8,000	—
1854O	5,240,000	17.00	28.00	43.00	55.00	100.00	270	600	8,000	—
1855	759,500	23.00	33.00	45.00	75.00	150	325	1,200	8,000	22,500
1855/4	Inc. above	35.00	60.00	80.00	125	225	400	1,500	—	—
1855O	3,688,000	17.00	28.00	43.00	55.00	100.00	270	650	8,000	—
1855S	129,950	250	350	600	1,300	2,400	6,000	—	—	—

Seated Liberty Half Dollar
Arrows at date removed

KM# A68 0.9000 **SILVER** 0.3600 oz. ASW. 12.4400 g. **Designer:** Christian Gobrecht

Date	Mintage	G-4	VG-8	F-12	VF-20	XF-40	AU-50	MS-60	MS-65	Prf-65
1856	938,000	19.00	31.00	43.00	55.00	90.00	195	425	6,500	12,500
1856O	2,658,000	17.00	28.00	43.00	52.00	90.00	190	385	12,500	—
1856S	211,000	85.00	120	160	260	475	1,250	3,500	19,000	—
1857	1,988,000	17.00	28.00	43.00	52.00	90.00	190	385	5,150	12,500
1857O	818,000	21.00	31.00	43.00	65.00	125	275	885	12,500	—
1857S	158,000	100.00	120	145	285	575	975	3,500	19,000	—
1858	4,226,000	17.00	28.00	43.00	52.00	90.00	190	385	6,500	12,500
1858O	7,294,000	17.00	28.00	43.00	52.00	90.00	190	385	12,500	—
1858S	476,000	25.00	35.00	50.00	95.00	185	400	950	12,500	—
1859	748,000	17.00	28.00	43.00	60.00	110	200	650	6,600	5,500
1859O	2,834,000	17.00	28.00	43.00	50.00	90.00	190	450	6,500	—
1859S	566,000	25.00	38.00	55.00	85.00	215	375	750	12,500	—
1860	303,700	25.00	35.00	47.50	80.00	110	350	1,000	6,500	5,500
1860O	1,290,000	17.00	28.00	43.00	52.00	90.00	190	450	5,150	—
1860S	472,000	20.00	30.00	50.00	75.00	130	245	850	12,500	—
1861	2,888,400	17.00	28.00	43.00	52.00	90.00	190	440	5,150	5,500
1861O	2,532,633	18.00	29.00	50.00	65.00	100.00	190	450	5,150	—
1861S	939,500	18.00	29.00	43.00	60.00	110	195	975	9,500	—
1862	253,550	28.00	40.00	55.00	95.00	175	285	750	5,150	5,500
1862S	1,352,000	18.00	29.00	43.00	65.00	110	195	460	9,000	—
1863	503,660	20.00	32.00	43.00	75.00	130	250	750	5,150	5,500
1863S	916,000	18.00	29.00	43.00	60.00	100.00	195	460	9,000	—
1864	379,570	29.00	35.00	60.00	95.00	175	250	750	5,150	5,500
1864S	658,000	18.00	28.00	45.00	60.00	115	215	675	9,000	—
1865	511,900	28.00	37.00	55.00	85.00	135	275	750	5,150	5,500
1865S	675,000	18.00	29.00	43.00	60.00	100.00	235	500	9,000	—
1866 proof, unique	—	—	—	—	—	—	—	—	—	—
1866S	60,000	90.00	135	215	375	795	1,500	5,000	—	—

Seated Liberty Half Dollar
"In God We Trust" above eagle

KM# 99 0.9000 **SILVER** 0.3600 oz. ASW. 12.4400 g. **Designer:** Christian Gobrecht **Notes:** In 1866 the motto "In God We Trust" was added to the reverse. The "closed-3" and "open-3" varieties are distinguished by the amount of space between the upper and lower left serifs of the 3.

Date	Mintage	G-4	VG-8	F-12	VF-20	XF-40	AU-50	MS-60	MS-65	Prf-65
1866	745,625	18.00	27.00	45.00	70.00	110	225	350	4,800	3,750
1866S	994,000	19.00	29.00	45.00	60.00	100.00	275	650	5,000	—
1867	449,925	25.00	35.00	55.00	90.00	145	250	350	4,800	3,750
1867S	1,196,000	19.00	29.00	40.00	60.00	100.00	250	350	7,000	—
1868	418,200	35.00	49.00	80.00	135	225	300	525	7,100	3,750
1868S	1,160,000	19.00	29.00	41.00	60.00	110	250	350	7,000	—
1869	795,900	19.00	29.00	41.00	60.00	110	190	385	4,600	3,750
1869S	656,000	20.00	29.00	41.00	60.00	120	265	600	7,000	—
1870	634,900	21.00	31.00	42.00	70.00	125	250	475	7,000	3,750
1870CC	54,617	800	1,200	1,750	2,900	10,000	—	—	—	—
1870S	1,004,000	19.00	31.00	45.00	70.00	125	275	575	7,000	—
1871	1,204,560	18.00	29.00	41.00	60.00	110	165	350	7,000	3,750
1871CC	153,950	200	325	600	1,200	1,950	10,000	15,000	—	—
1871S	2,178,000	18.00	29.00	41.00	55.00	110	215	400	7,000	—
1872	881,550	18.00	29.00	40.00	55.00	110	195	430	2,850	3,750
1872CC	272,000	70.00	100.00	200	325	1,500	4,000	8,000	50,000	—
1872S	580,000	28.00	33.00	60.00	110	185	375	975	7,000	—
1873 closed 3	801,800	23.00	30.00	50.00	90.00	135	250	500	4,500	3,750
1873 open 3	Inc. above	2,200	2,700	4,100	5,500	7,500	—	—	—	—
1873CC	122,500	170	225	325	800	1,500	2,500	4,100	9,000	3,750
1873S no arrows	5,000	—	—	—	—	—	—	—	—	—

Note: 1873S no arrows, no specimens known to survive.

Seated Liberty Half Dollar
Arrows at date

KM# 107 0.9000 **SILVER** 0.3618 oz. ASW. 12.5000 g. **Designer:** Christian Gobrecht

Date	Mintage	G-4	VG-8	F-12	VF-20	XF-40	AU-50	MS-60	MS-65	Prf-65
1873	1,815,700	18.00	27.00	40.00	85.00	210	400	850	17,500	9,000
1873CC	214,560	115	220	335	725	1,700	2,400	5,700	42,000	—
1873S	233,000	42.50	62.50	100.00	200	375	675	2,200	40,000	—
1874	2,360,300	18.00	27.00	40.00	85.00	210	400	850	12,750	9,000
1874CC	59,000	400	550	950	1,500	2,500	4,500	8,000	—	—
1874S	394,000	30.00	40.00	70.00	160	315	600	1,600	—	—

Seated Liberty Half Dollar
Arrows at date removed

KM# A99 0.9000 **SILVER** 0.3618 oz. ASW. 12.5000 g. **Designer:** Christian Gobrecht

Date	Mintage	G-4	VG-8	F-12	VF-20	XF-40	AU-50	MS-60	MS-65	Prf-65
1875	6,027,500	17.00	25.00	39.00	47.00	70.00	160	425	3,500	3,200
1875CC	1,008,000	20.00	34.00	53.00	95.00	185	300	540	5,450	—
1875S	3,200,000	17.00	26.00	40.00	47.00	80.00	165	340	2,700	—
1876	8,419,150	17.00	25.00	39.00	45.00	70.00	160	340	5,300	3,200
1876CC	1,956,000	18.00	30.00	48.00	85.00	175	275	560	4,200	—
1876S	4,528,000	17.00	25.00	39.00	45.00	70.00	160	340	2,700	—
1877	8,304,510	17.00	25.00	39.00	45.00	70.00	160	340	2,700	3,750
1877CC	1,420,000	18.00	33.00	43.00	75.00	145	275	630	3,250	—
1877S	5,356,000	17.00	25.00	39.00	45.00	70.00	160	340	2,700	—
1878	1,378,400	20.00	28.00	36.00	55.00	115	170	425	3,650	3,200
1878CC	62,000	375	525	875	1,250	2,750	5,000	7,000	42,500	—
1878S	12,000	15,000	17,500	22,000	27,500	33,000	40,000	52,500	125,000	—
1879	5,900	295	325	375	425	525	600	825	2,900	3,250
1880	9,755	275	310	365	415	500	575	800	2,900	3,250
1881	10,975	275	300	350	400	485	550	800	2,900	3,250
1882	5,500	350	400	425	500	585	650	850	3,600	3,250
1883	9,039	275	310	365	415	500	575	800	2,900	3,250

Date	Mintage	G-4	VG-8	F-12	VF-20	XF-40	AU-50	MS-60	MS-65	Prf-65
1884	5,275	375	425	450	550	600	675	825	2,900	3,250
1885	6,130	350	400	425	500	585	650	800	2,900	3,250
1886	5,886	375	425	475	575	625	700	850	4,800	3,250
1887	5,710	450	500	575	650	750	800	900	2,900	3,250
1888	12,833	280	310	365	400	485	550	800	2,900	3,250
1889	12,711	275	300	350	400	485	550	800	2,900	3,250
1890	12,590	285	310	365	415	500	550	800	3,250	3,250
1891	200,600	50.00	60.00	80.00	115	165	290	500	3,250	3,250

Barber Half Dollar

KM# 116 0.9000 **SILVER** 0.3618 oz. ASW. 30.6 mm. 12.5000 g. **Designer:** Charles E. Barber

Date	Mintage	G-4	VG-8	F-12	VF-20	XF-40	AU-50	MS-60	MS-65	Prf-65
1892	935,245	27.50	38.50	65.00	115	190	285	415	3,000	3,300
1892O	390,000	275	350	440	485	525	590	850	4,200	—
1892O micro O	—	2,000	3,750	4,500	7,000	10,000	17,500	—	55,000	—
1892S	1,029,028	230	325	380	440	550	610	900	5,250	—
1893	1,826,792	17.50	25.00	67.50	120	200	315	525	5,250	3,300
1893O	1,389,000	32.50	55.00	95.00	180	300	380	550	10,500	—
1893S	740,000	135	180	275	410	480	550	1,200	27,500	—
1894	1,148,972	25.00	41.00	96.00	135	250	360	485	3,300	3,300
1894O	2,138,000	18.50	27.50	85.00	130	250	325	520	7,500	—
1894S	4,048,690	15.00	22.00	62.50	105	210	340	450	12,250	—
1895	1,835,218	15.00	20.00	67.50	110	200	315	580	3,500	3,300
1895O	1,766,000	18.50	32.50	90.00	155	200	365	580	7,850	—
1895S	1,108,086	25.00	46.00	105	195	285	375	565	9,000	—
1896	950,762	20.00	23.00	82.50	135	250	330	550	6,000	3,400
1896O	924,000	32.50	45.00	160	235	410	675	1,500	13,000	—
1896S	1,140,948	80.00	125	180	300	425	580	1,350	11,500	—
1897	2,480,731	10.00	12.00	43.50	92.50	152.5	315	450	4,300	3,300
1897O	632,000	100.00	200	435	775	1,000	1,225	1,675	8,250	—
1897S	933,900	135	195	315	475	790	1,050	1,450	8,750	—
1898	2,956,735	11.00	13.00	37.50	85.00	160	325	425	3,650	3,300
1898O	874,000	27.50	67.50	200	315	465	550	1,150	12,000	—
1898S	2,358,550	18.50	40.00	67.50	125	225	360	950	10,000	—
1899	5,538,846	12.50	13.00	35.00	90.00	152.5	310	425	4,800	3,900
1899O	1,724,000	20.00	30.00	70.00	130	250	360	640	8,250	—
1899S	1,686,411	19.00	30.00	67.50	115	200	350	645	7,000	—
1900	4,762,912	13.00	14.50	35.00	85.00	152.5	305	420	4,300	3,300
1900O	2,744,000	13.50	19.50	49.00	125	270	365	850	16,500	—
1900S	2,560,322	13.00	13.50	46.00	100.00	200	310	640	12,500	—

DOLLAR

Draped Bust Dollar

Heraldic eagle

KM# 32 0.8920 **SILVER** 0.7737 oz. ASW. 39-40 mm. 26.9600 g. **Designer:** Robert Scot **Notes:** The "close" and "wide" varieties of 1802 refer to the amount of space between the numerals in the date.

Date	Mintage	F-12	VF-20	XF-40	AU-50	MS-60	MS-63
1801	54,454	1,175	1,825	2,850	4,600	20,000	40,000
1801 proof restrike	—	—	—	—	—	—	—
1802/1 close	Inc. above	1,350	2,050	3,300	6,000	15,500	—
1802/1 wide	Inc. above	1,350	2,050	3,300	6,000	15,500	—
1802 close, perfect date	Inc. above	1,200	1,850	2,900	4,650	15,500	—
1802 wide, perfect date	Inc. above	1,175	1,825	2,850	4,600	16,500	—
1802 proof restrike, mintage unrecorded	—	—	—	—	—	—	—
1803 large 3	85,634	1,225	1,925	3,000	5,400	15,500	37,500
1803 small 3	Inc. above	1,350	2,050	3,300	6,000	16,500	38,500
1803 proof restrike, mintage unrecorded	—	—	—	—	—	—	—
1804 15 known	—	—	—	—	1,000,000	—	—

Note: 1804, Childs Sale, Aug. 1999, Prf-68, $4,140,000.

Gobrecht Dollar

"C. Gobrecht F." below base Eagle flying left amid stars

KM# 59.1 0.9000 **SILVER** 0.7736 oz. ASW. 38.1 mm. 26.7300 g. **Obv. Designer:** Christian Gobrecht

Date	Mintage	VF-20	XF-40	AU-50	Prf-
1836	1,000	3,750	4,750	—	12,500

"C. Gobrecht F." below base Eagle flying in plain field

KM# 59.2 0.9000 **SILVER** 0.7736 oz. ASW. 38.1 mm. 26.7300 g. **Obv. Designer:** Christian Gobrecht.

Date	Mintage	VF-20	XF-40	AU-50	Prf-
1836 Restrike	—	—	—	—	—

"C. Gobrecht F." on base

KM# 59a.1 0.9000 **SILVER** 0.7736 oz. ASW. 38.1 mm. 26.7300 g.

Date	Mintage	VF-20	XF-40	AU-50	Prf-
1836	600	—	—	—	—

"C. Gobrecht F." on base Eagle flying left amid stars

KM# 59a.2 0.9000 **SILVER** 0.7736 oz. ASW. 38.1 mm. 26.7300 g.

Date	Mintage	VF-20	XF-40	AU-50	Prf-
1836 Restrike	—	—	—	—	—

Designer's name omitted Eagle in plain field

KM# 59a.3 0.9000 **SILVER** 0.7736 oz. ASW. 38.1 mm. 26.7300 g.

Date	Mintage	VF-20	XF-40	AU-50	Prf-
1839	300	—	—	—	—

Seated Liberty Dollar

No motto above eagle

KM# 71 0.9000 **SILVER** 0.7736 oz. ASW. 38.1 mm. 26.7300 g. **Designer:** Christian Gobrech

Date	Mintage	G-4	VG-8	F-12	VF-20	XF-40	AU-50	MS-60	MS-63	MS-65	Prf-
1840	61,005	160	180	225	300	525	750	1,750	12,500	—	
1841	173,000	145	165	210	250	360	625	1,500	4,200	42,500	
1842	184,618	145	165	210	250	350	600	1,100	3,750	24,000	
1843	165,100	145	165	210	250	350	625	1,400	4,350	24,000	
1844	20,000	180	245	300	385	500	850	3,000	7,000	44,500	
1845	24,500	200	260	285	350	550	800	4,850	17,000	—	
1846	110,600	145	165	225	275	385	625	1,450	4,650	30,000	
1846O	59,000	150	250	300	475	1,250	3,000	12,000	24,500	—	
1847	140,750	145	165	210	250	350	600	950	3,500	26,500	
1848	15,000	220	300	425	550	750	1,500	3,000	7,500	40,000	
1849	62,600	165	190	250	325	400	700	1,650	4,600	32,500	
1850	7,500	400	635	750	900	1,000	2,000	4,500	13,000	47,500	
1850O	40,000	250	300	375	650	1,275	2,850	6,250	15,500	55,000	
1851	1,300	4,000	5,000	8,000	9,500	13,500	21,500	27,500	35,000	60,000	
1852	1,100	3,800	4,800	7,500	8,500	11,500	21,500	26,500	33,500	55,000	
1853	46,110	185	235	285	375	600	850	2,350	6,500	26,500	
1854	33,140	1,000	1,200	1,600	2,350	3,650	4,850	7,000	9,800	24,500	
1855	26,000	800	1,150	1,400	1,900	2,950	3,800	6,500	15,000	—	
1856	63,500	400	500	600	750	975	1,650	3,450	6,500	—	
1857	94,000	375	475	550	750	950	1,300	2,750	4,200	27,500	
1858 proof	Est. 800	2,250	2,650	3,350	4,200	5,500	6,250	9,000	12,000	—	

Note: Proof Only restruck in later years.

Date	Mintage	G-4	VG-8	F-12	VF-20	XF-40	AU-50	MS-60	MS-63	MS-65	Prf-
1859	256,500	180	220	300	450	600	850	1,800	5,000	15,000	13,5
1859O	360,000	145	175	220	275	375	600	950	2,600	32,000	
1859S	20,000	235	300	400	600	1,350	3,000	8,000	25,500	60,000	
1860	218,930	165	200	275	350	475	600	1,100	2,600	26,000	13,5
1860O	515,000	145	165	210	250	350	550	900	2,500	15,000	
1861	78,500	440	500	650	800	1,000	1,500	2,800	4,600	22,500	13,5
1862	12,090	450	525	675	850	950	1,600	2,750	5,000	34,500	13,5
1863	27,660	325	375	450	550	1,200	2,350	3,800	11,250	1,400	13,5
1864	31,170	240	265	315	425	600	1,200	2,300	4,600	20,000	13,5
1865	47,000	225	245	290	400	560	1,150	2,150	4,450	32,500	13,5
1866 2 known without motto	—	—	—	—	—	—	—	—	—	—	

Seated Liberty Dollar

"In God We Trust" above eagle

KM# 100 0.9000 **SILVER** 0.7736 oz. ASW. 38.1 mm. 26.7300 g. **Designer:** Christian Gobrecht
Notes: In 1866 the motto "In God We Trust" was added to the reverse above the eagle.

Date	Mintage	G-4	VG-8	F-12	VF-20	XF-40	AU-50	MS-60	MS-63	MS-65	Prf-65
1866	49,625	175	220	285	400	550	900	1,650	2,900	23,500	7,000
1867	47,525	170	215	265	415	525	875	1,500	3,000	24,500	7,000
1868	162,700	165	205	245	375	475	850	1,600	6,000	33,500	7,000
1869	424,300	155	195	235	325	440	650	1,450	3,350	24,500	7,000
1870	416,000	165	185	225	320	440	600	1,400	2,750	24,500	7,000
1870CC	12,462	275	345	500	800	1,450	3,000	9,500	20,000	38,500	—
1870S 12-15 known	—	30,000	—	—	—	—	—	—	—	—	—

Note: 1870S, Eliasberg Sale, April 1997, EF-45 to AU-50, $264,000.

Date	Mintage	G-4	VG-8	F-12	VF-20	XF-40	AU-50	MS-60	MS-63	MS-65	Prf-65
1871	1,074,760	155	190	265	340	425	600	1,100	2,600	21,500	7,000
1871CC	1,376	1,650	2,500	3,750	5,750	8,950	18,500	41,000	96,000	150,000	—
1872	1,106,450	150	190	265	340	425	600	1,100	2,600	21,500	7,000
1872CC	3,150	900	1,250	1,750	2,850	4,250	8,500	18,500	35,000	—	—
1872S	9,000	220	285	400	575	1,100	2,750	8,500	23,500	—	—
1873	293,600	145	165	215	240	350	575	1,125	2,750	21,500	7,000
1873CC	2,300	3,250	4,750	6,500	9,000	16,000	30,000	63,500	110,000	—	—
1873S none known	700	—	—	—	—	—	—	—	—	—	—

Trade Dollar

KM# 108 0.9000 **SILVER** 0.7878 oz. ASW. 38.1 mm. 27.2200 g. **Designer:** William Barber

Date	Mintage	G-4	VG-8	F-12	VF-20	XF-40	AU-50	MS-60	MS-65	Prf-65
1873	397,500	100.00	110	125	165	250	325	1,000	12,000	12,000
1873CC	124,500	175	200	300	450	700	1,200	2,100	80,000	—
1873S	703,000	130	145	160	180	260	375	1,200	25,000	—
1874	987,800	120	130	150	185	240	340	700	15,000	12,000
1874CC	1,373,200	80.00	90.00	105	165	240	350	1,000	40,000	—
1874S	2,549,000	70.00	80.00	95.00	120	165	250	675	30,000	—
1875	218,900	260	350	425	525	675	800	1,850	13,000	6,500
1875CC	1,573,700	80.00	90.00	105	130	200	375	900	40,000	—
1875S	4,487,000	60.00	70.00	85.00	100.00	120	210	500	7,000	—
1875S/CC	Inc. above	275	325	400	525	695	1,100	1,900	—	—
1876	456,150	70.00	80.00	100.00	125	165	400	675	7,500	6,500
1876CC	509,000	150	175	220	250	375	500	2,100	75,000	—
1876S	5,227,000	60.00	70.00	85.00	100.00	120	210	475	10,000	—
1877	3,039,710	60.00	70.00	85.00	105	130	210	525	16,000	19,000
1877CC	534,000	150	175	210	260	370	600	1,275	70,000	—
1877S	9,519,000	60.00	70.00	85.00	100.00	120	210	475	8,000	—
1878 proof	900	—	—	—	1,100	1,300	1,500	—	—	22,000
1878CC	97,000	425	525	675	850	1,750	2,100	5,500	67,500	—
1878S	4,162,000	60.00	70.00	85.00	100.00	120	210	475	7,000	—
1879 proof	1,541	—	—	—	900	950	1,100	—	—	22,000
1880 proof	1,987	—	—	—	900	950	1,100	—	—	19,500
1881 proof	960	—	—	—	950	1,000	1,250	—	—	20,000
1882 proof	1,097	—	—	—	950	1,000	1,250	—	—	20,000
1883 proof	979	—	—	—	1,100	1,200	1,400	—	—	20,000
1884 proof	10	—	—	—	—	—	—	—	—	—

Note: 1884, Eliasberg Sale, April 1997, Prf-66, $396,000.

Date	Mintage	G-4	VG-8	F-12	VF-20	XF-40	AU-50	MS-60	MS-65	Prf-65
1885 proof	5	—	—	—	—	—	—	—	—	—

Note: 1885, Eliasberg Sale, April 1997, Prf-65, $907,500.

Morgan Dollar

KM# 110 0.9000 **SILVER** 0.7736 oz. ASW. 38.1 mm. 26.7300 g. **Designer:** George T. Morgan
Notes: "65DMPL" values are for coins grading MS-65 deep-mirror prooflike. The 1878 "8 tail feathers" and "7 tail feathers" varieties are distinguished by the number of feathers in the eagle's tail. On the "reverse of 1878" varieties, the top of the top feather in the arrows held by the eagle is straight across and the eagle's breast is concave. On the "reverse of 1879 varieties," the top feather in the arrows held by the eagle is slanted and the eagle's breast is convex. The 1890-CC "tail-bar variety has a bar extending from the arrow feathers to the wreath on the reverse, the result of a die gouge.

8 tail feathers

7 tail feathers

7 over 8 tail feathers

Date	Mintage	VG-8	F-12	VF-20	XF-40	AU-50	MS-60	MS-63	MS-64	MS-65	65DMPL	Prf-65
1878 8 tail feathers	750,000	23.00	24.00	25.50	27.50	45.00	125	160	435	1,400	6,300	7,500
1878 7 tail feathers, reverse of 1878	Inc. above	16.00	17.50	20.00	22.00	40.00	56.00	95.00	390	1,500	6,300	—
1878 7 tail feathers, reverse of 1879	Inc. above	16.00	17.50	19.50	22.00	40.00	67.50	140	640	3,000	8,800	9,000
1878 7 over 8 tail feathers	9,759,550	19.00	20.00	21.50	28.00	50.00	125	350	550	3,350	14,500	—
1878CC	2,212,000	90.00	92.50	95.00	100.00	110	220	410	640	2,000	3,450	—
1878S	9,744,000	15.50	17.50	19.50	21.50	33.00	46.00	70.00	105	285	2,250	—
1879	14,807,100	13.50	13.00	15.00	16.50	20.00	30.00	60.00	135	1,250	6,950	6,000
1879CC	756,000	95.00	100.00	300	540	1,250	2,700	6,250	8,500	25,000	65,000	—
1879O	2,887,000	13.50	13.00	15.00	17.00	20.50	72.50	180	480	3,300	16,500	—
1879S reverse of 1878	9,110,000	14.00	17.00	25.00	30.00	50.00	90.00	360	1,450	8,300	22,000	—
1879S reverse of 1879	9,110,000	14.00	13.00	16.00	17.00	21.00	40.00	42.50	63.50	165	450	—
1880	12,601,335	14.00	13.50	15.00	17.00	20.00	30.00	55.00	115	800	3,450	5,900
1880CC reverse of 1878	591,000	90.00	105	115	185	245	480	625	1,100	3,000	11,000	—
1880CC reverse of 1879	591,000	110	145	150	220	300	480	515	800	1,450	3,650	—
1880O	5,305,000	13.50	13.00	15.00	16.75	20.50	60.00	385	2,000	24,000	70,000	—
1880S	8,900,000	14.00	14.50	15.00	17.00	21.00	33.00	46.00	63.50	165	450	—
1881	9,163,975	14.00	14.50	15.00	17.00	20.00	30.00	55.00	150	850	13,750	6,250
1881CC	296,000	270	290	300	345	370	500	495	625	850	1,450	—
1881O	5,708,000	13.50	13.00	15.00	16.50	20.00	30.00	48.00	160	1,650	15,000	—
1881S	12,760,000	13.50	13.00	15.00	16.50	20.00	30.00	46.00	63.50	165	450	—
1882	11,101,100	13.50	13.00	15.00	17.00	20.00	30.00	46.00	63.50	450	4,100	5,900
1882CC	1,133,000	90.00	92.50	95.00	96.00	100.00	215	220	270	500	725	—
1882O	6,090,000	13.00	13.00	15.00	16.75	20.00	32.50	46.00	75.00	800	4,200	—
1882S	9,250,000	13.50	13.00	15.00	16.50	25.00	33.00	46.00	63.50	165	1,100	—
1883	12,291,039	13.50	13.00	15.00	16.50	20.00	30.00	46.00	63.50	170	760	5,900
1883CC	1,204,000	90.00	95.00	100.00	102.5	105	210	220	250	425	830	—
1883O	8,725,000	13.50	14.00	15.00	16.50	20.00	30.00	46.00	65.00	165	575	—
1883S	6,250,000	13.50	16.00	17.00	33.00	165	500	2,750	4,850	22,000	94,500	—
1884	14,070,875	13.50	14.00	15.00	16.50	20.00	30.00	46.00	63.50	300	2,200	5,900
1884CC	1,136,000	90.00	92.50	95.00	96.00	100.00	205	220	250	425	600	—
1884O	9,730,000	13.50	14.00	15.00	16.50	20.00	30.00	46.00	63.50	165	670	—
1884S	3,200,000	14.00	15.00	17.50	41.50	280	4,500	26,000	110,000	200,000	220,000	—
1885	17,787,767	13.50	14.00	14.50	16.50	20.00	30.00	46.00	60.00	165	570	5,900
1885CC	228,000	340	350	390	415	450	585	565	980	1,450	1,450	—
1885O	9,185,000	13.50	14.00	14.50	16.50	20.00	30.00	46.00	63.50	165	490	—
1885S	1,497,000	17.50	21.50	27.50	41.00	125	185	250	600	1,950	16,500	—
1886	19,963,886	13.50	14.00	14.50	16.50	20.00	30.00	46.00	62.00	165	575	5,900
1886O	10,710,000	13.50	14.00	14.50	18.00	80.00	505	4,000	8,000	215,000	283,500	—
1886S	750,000	24.00	28.00	48.50	57.50	95.00	240	450	675	3,200	16,500	—
1887	20,290,710	14.00	14.50	15.00	17.50	20.00	30.00	46.00	63.50	165	530	5,900
1887O	11,550,000	13.50	14.50	14.75	17.00	22.00	54.00	105	425	4,100	8,500	—
1887S	1,771,000	14.50	15.00	17.50	20.00	39.00	100.00	285	750	4,000	27,000	—
1888	19,183,833	13.50	13.50	14.50	16.50	20.00	30.00	46.00	63.50	215	2,350	6,000
1888O	12,150,000	13.50	14.50	16.00	17.00	20.00	30.00	46.00	64.50	460	1,600	—
1888S	657,000	44.00	72.50	80.00	110	130	240	440	850	3,500	10,500	—
1889	21,726,811	13.50	14.00	14.50	16.50	20.00	29.00	46.00	62.00	310	2,950	5,900
1889CC	350,000	625	900	1,500	3,500	6,500	18,500	32,000	5,150	315,000	285,000	—
1889O	11,875,000	13.50	14.00	15.00	17.50	30.00	140	465	900	5,550	14,500	—
1889S	700,000	33.50	46.00	55.00	63.50	87.50	200	440	575	1,950	7,550	—
1890	16,802,590	13.50	14.00	15.00	16.50	20.00	30.00	50.00	115	2,300	12,500	5,900
1890CC	2,309,041	90.00	92.50	15.00	160	210	350	850	2,300	6,300	9,750	—
1890CC tail bar	Inc. above	135	145	180	500	900	1,600	4,000	8,500	—	9,800	—
1890O	10,701,000	13.50	14.00	15.00	18.00	24.00	56.00	110	340	1,750	7,500	—
1890S	8,230,373	13.50	14.00	15.00	16.50	20.00	56.00	110	300	1,050	8,200	—
1891	8,694,206	13.50	14.00	15.00	16.50	21.50	51.00	135	575	7,500	25,000	5,900
1891CC	1,618,000	90.00	92.50	95.00	160	210	345	850	1,350	5,000	20,000	—

Date	Mintage	VG-8	F-12	VF-20	XF-40	AU-50	MS-60	MS-63	MS-64	MS-65	65DMPL	Prf-65
1891O	7,954,529	13.50	14.00	15.00	18.00	34.00	135	350	750	9,000	21,500	—
1891S	5,296,000	13.50	14.00	15.00	19.50	24.00	60.00	125	275	1,300	7,250	—
1892	1,037,245	16.50	18.00	18.50	30.00	72.50	150	400	1,000	4,000	15,750	5,900
1892CC	1,352,000	110	125	160	415	550	825	2,100	2,800	11,000	27,000	—
1892O	2,744,000	14.50	19.00	19.50	30.00	60.00	160	325	700	5,250	27,000	—
1892S	1,200,000	19.50	21.50	46.00	170	1,750	34,000	57,500	96,000	170,000	170,000	—
1893	378,792	115	135	140	175	225	540	1,150	1,900	7,500	38,000	5,900
1893CC	677,000	195	265	550	1,700	2,250	3,150	7,800	13,500	47,500	85,000	—
1893O	300,000	180	240	350	600	1,000	1,500	6,750	20,000	215,000	201,500	—
1893S	100,000	2,400	3,400	5,000	7,800	23,000	80,000	100,000	250,000	400,000	380,000	—
1894	110,972	1,000	1,100	1,250	1,800	2,600	3,750	5,800	8,900	31,500	44,000	6,500
1894O	1,723,000	43.50	50.00	62.50	115	315	550	3,750	8,500	50,000	56,500	—
1894S	1,260,000	34.00	47.50	68.50	115	525	595	1,150	1,850	5,750	19,000	—
1895 proof only	12,880	21,000	27,500	29,000	33,500	36,000	—	—	—	—	—	65,000
1895O	450,000	330	440	580	900	1,650	13,500	37,500	100,000	225,000	—	—
1895S	400,000	190	275	335	460	1,650	2,600	4,850	7,150	20,000	40,500	—
1896	9,967,762	12.50	16.00	16.25	16.50	20.00	29.00	46.00	67.50	230	975	5,900
1896O	4,900,000	13.00	16.00	16.50	18.00	190	940	7,350	46,000	185,000	170,000	—
1896S	5,000,000	17.50	27.00	47.50	160	625	1,250	3,000	4,000	16,000	25,000	—
1897	2,822,731	13.00	16.00	16.25	17.00	20.00	30.00	46.00	63.50	260	2,900	5,900
1897O	4,004,000	13.50	16.00	16.50	24.00	110	650	5,500	15,500	50,000	56,500	—
1897S	5,825,000	13.50	16.00	16.50	17.50	24.00	56.00	115	170	700	1,700	—
1898	5,884,735	16.00	16.50	16.50	17.50	20.00	30.00	46.00	63.50	265	1,075	5,900
1898O	4,440,000	13.00	16.00	16.50	17.00	20.00	30.00	46.00	63.50	165	510	—
1898S	4,102,000	18.00	20.00	22.50	31.00	80.00	260	465	890	2,500	11,250	—
1899	330,846	28.50	45.00	53.50	62.50	77.50	125	265	415	850	2,250	6,000
1899O	12,290,000	15.00	16.00	16.50	19.00	21.00	30.00	45.00	63.50	165	825	—
1899S	2,562,000	15.00	18.75	25.00	38.50	95.00	325	480	750	2,150	8,600	—
1900	8,880,938	13.00	15.00	16.00	18.00	20.00	30.00	46.00	63.50	210	11,000	5,900
1900O	12,590,000	13.00	25.00	16.00	20.00	24.00	32.00	46.00	63.50	165	3,000	—
1900O/CC	Inc. above	21.50	23.00	34.00	47.50	120	230	675	1,250	2,750	19,000	—
1900S	3,540,000	16.00	17.00	19.50	36.00	83.00	275	400	500	1,575	9,450	—

GOLD

Liberty Head - Type 1

KM# 73 0.9000 **GOLD** 0.0484 oz. AGW. 13 mm. 1.6720 g. **Designer:** James B. Longacre **Notes:** On the "closed wreath" varieties of 1849, the wreath on the reverse extends closer to the numeral 1.

Date	Mintage	F-12	VF-20	XF-40	AU-50	MS-60
1849 open wreath	688,567	100.00	140	190	225	450
1849 closed wreath	Inc. above	100.00	135	185	210	365
1849C closed wreath	11,634	800	950	1,250	1,900	8,000
1849C open wreath	Inc. above	—	—	—	—	—
1849D open wreath	21,588	950	1,150	1,600	1,950	5,000
1849O open wreath	215,000	120	150	230	310	700
1850	481,953	100.00	135	190	200	340
1850C	6,966	800	950	1,250	2,250	7,500
1850D	8,382	950	1,150	1,650	2,600	8,500
1850O	14,000	185	245	350	725	2,700
1851	3,317,671	100.00	135	190	200	250
1851C	41,267	800	950	1,250	1,600	4,900
1851D	9,882	950	1,150	1,600	2,000	5,400
1851O	290,000	135	160	200	230	725
1852	2,045,351	100.00	135	190	200	245
1852C	9,434	800	950	1,250	1,600	3,800
1852D	6,360	950	1,150	1,600	2,150	8,500
1852O	140,000	115	140	230	320	1,100
1853	4,076,051	100.00	135	190	200	245
1853C	11,515	800	950	1,250	1,750	5,000
1853D	6,583	950	1,150	1,600	2,400	8,500
1853O	290,000	130	160	210	225	600
1854	736,709	100.00	135	190	200	250
1854D	2,935	950	1,150	2,000	5,300	11,000
1854S	14,632	245	290	420	700	2,100

Indian Head - Type 2

KM# 83 0.9000 **GOLD** 0.0484 oz. AGW. 15 mm. 1.6720 g. **Designer:** James B. Longacre

Date	Mintage	F-12	VF-20	XF-40	AU-50	MS-60
1854	902,736	210	280	415	550	3,300
1855	758,269	210	280	415	550	3,300
1855C	9,803	800	1,100	3,000	8,500	24,500
1855D	1,811	3,000	4,250	8,250	22,000	48,000
1855O	55,000	330	400	540	1,250	6,750
1856S	24,600	440	725	1,200	2,200	7,700

Indian Head - Type 3

KM# 86 0.9000 **GOLD** 0.0484 oz. AGW. 15 mm. 1.6720 g. **Designer:** James B. Longacre **Notes:** The 1856 varieties are distinguished by whether the 5 in the date is slanted or upright. The 1873 varieties are distinguished by the amount of space between the upper left and lower left serifs in the 3.

Date	Mintage	F-12	VF-20	XF-40	AU-50	MS-60	Prf-65
1856 upright 5	1,762,936	125	145	195	225	465	—
1856 slanted 5	Inc. above	130	140	190	210	260	50,000
1856D	1,460	2,200	3,400	5,400	7,500	30,000	—
1857	774,789	110	135	190	210	260	31,000
1857C	13,280	800	950	1,400	2,750	10,500	—
1857D	3,533	950	1,150	1,750	3,650	10,000	—
1857S	10,000	250	500	600	1,100	5,600	—
1858	117,995	110	135	190	215	265	27,500
1858D	3,477	950	1,150	1,500	2,750	10,000	—
1858S	10,000	280	375	500	1,150	5,000	—
1859	168,244	110	135	190	205	260	16,000
1859C	5,235	800	950	1,500	3,100	9,000	—
1859D	4,952	950	1,150	1,500	2,850	10,000	—
1859S	15,000	185	225	480	1,000	5,000	—
1860	36,668	110	135	190	205	280	14,500
1860D	1,566	2,000	2,500	3,800	6,000	15,000	—
1860S	13,000	280	325	465	700	2,250	—
1861	527,499	110	135	190	205	265	13,500
1861D mintage unrecorded	—	4,600	6,400	9,000	16,500	28,000	—
1862	1,361,390	110	135	190	205	260	14,500
1863	6,250	370	425	825	1,600	3,650	16,500
1864	5,950	270	350	440	750	950	16,000
1865	3,725	270	350	550	700	1,450	16,000
1866	7,130	275	360	425	650	900	16,000
1867	5,250	300	400	485	600	1,100	16,000
1868	10,525	250	275	400	465	900	16,500
1869	5,925	315	335	520	800	1,000	15,000
1870	6,335	245	270	385	475	850	14,000
1870S	3,000	280	440	725	1,100	2,150	—
1871	3,930	245	270	365	450	700	16,500
1872	3,530	245	275	350	440	850	16,500
1873 closed 3	125,125	300	400	750	900	1,600	—
1873 open 3	Inc. above	110	135	190	200	260	—
1874	198,820	110	135	190	200	260	16,500
1875	420	1,600	1,850	3,650	4,700	5,900	32,500
1876	3,245	220	275	345	440	600	15,500
1877	3,920	140	175	330	440	900	16,500
1878	3,020	175	200	350	450	600	14,000
1879	3,030	160	180	270	315	500	12,500
1880	1,636	140	160	200	225	440	12,500
1881	7,707	140	160	200	225	425	10,500
1882	5,125	150	170	200	225	425	8,500
1883	11,007	140	160	200	225	425	8,500
1884	6,236	135	150	200	225	415	8,500
1885	12,261	140	160	200	225	400	8,500
1886	6,016	140	160	200	225	400	8,500
1887	8,543	140	160	200	225	400	8,500
1888	16,580	140	160	200	225	400	8,500
1889	30,729	140	160	200	225	400	8,500

$2.50 (QUARTER EAGLE)

GOLD

Liberty Cap

KM# 27 0.9160 **GOLD** 0.1289 oz. AGW. 20 mm. 4.3700 g. **Designer:** Robert Scot **Notes:** The 1804 varieties are distinguished by the number of stars on the obverse.

Date	Mintage	F-12	VF-20	XF-40	MS-60
1802/1	3,035	4,350	6,250	7,500	20,000
1804 13-star reverse	3,327	23,500	31,250	70,000	200,000
1804 14-star reverse	Inc. above	4,350	6,250	7,250	20,000
1805	1,781	4,350	6,250	7,250	20,000
1806/4	1,616	4,500	6,350	7,500	21,000
1806/5	Inc. above	5,600	8,000	11,500	70,000
1807	6,812	4,350	6,250	7,250	18,500

Turban Head

KM# 40 0.9160 **GOLD** 0.1289 oz. AGW. 20 mm. 4.3700 g. **Designer:** John Reich

Date	Mintage	F-12	VF-20	XF-40	MS-60
1808	2,710	22,500	28,000	34,000	80,000

Turban Head

KM# 46 0.9160 **GOLD** 0.1289 oz. AGW. 18.5 mm. 4.3700 g. **Designer:** John Reich

Date	Mintage	F-12	VF-20	XF-40	MS-60
1821	6,448	5,000	6,250	7,500	20,000
1824/21	2,600	5,000	6,250	7,250	18,500

Date	Mintage	F-12	VF-20	XF-40	MS-60
1825	4,434	5,000	6,250	7,250	15,500
1826/25	760	5,250	6,500	8,000	31,500
1827	2,800	5,350	7,000	8,500	19,000

Turban Head

KM# 49 0.9160 **GOLD** 0.1289 oz. AGW. 18.2 mm. 4.3700 g. **Designer:** John Reich

Date	Mintage	F-12	VF-20	XF-40	MS-60
1829	3,403	4,600	5,500	6,500	12,500
1830	4,540	4,600	5,500	6,500	12,500
1831	4,520	4,600	5,500	6,500	12,500
1832	4,400	4,600	5,500	6,500	12,500
1833	4,160	4,600	5,500	6,600	12,750
1834	4,000	7,000	9,750	15,500	33,500

Classic Head

KM# 56 0.8990 **GOLD** 0.1209 oz. AGW. 18.2 mm. 4.1800 g. **Designer:** William Kneass

Date	Mintage	VF-20	XF-40	AU-50	MS-60	MS-65
1834	112,234	325	465	700	2,000	24,000
1835	131,402	325	465	700	2,250	31,000
1836	547,986	325	465	700	2,000	27,500
1837	45,080	415	650	1,175	3,250	32,500
1838	47,030	325	465	800	2,000	27,000
1838C	7,880	1,200	2,000	6,100	23,500	50,000
1839	27,021	360	650	1,440	4,250	—
1839C	18,140	1,100	2,200	3,500	22,500	—
1839D	13,674	1,125	2,800	6,000	21,000	—
1839O	17,781	500	925	1,500	5,600	—

Coronet Head

KM# 72 0.9000 **GOLD** 0.121 oz. AGW. 18 mm. 4.1800 g. **Designer:** Christian Gobrecht **Notes:** Varieties for 1843 are distinguished by the size of the numerals in the date. One 1848 variety has "Cal." inscribed on the reverse, indicating it was made from California gold. The 1873 "closed-3" and "open-3" varieties are distinguished by the amount of space between the upper left and lower left serifs in the 3 in the date.

Date	Mintage	F-12	VF-20	XF-40	AU-50	MS-60	Prf-65
1840	18,859	150	180	850	2,950	6,000	—
1840C	12,822	650	1,100	1,600	4,700	13,000	—
1840D	3,532	800	2,400	8,000	15,500	35,000	—
1840O	33,580	225	270	800	1,700	10,000	—
1841	—	—	50,000	90,000	95,000	—	—
1841C	10,281	650	1,100	1,600	3,250	18,500	—
1841D	4,164	850	1,650	3,850	9,900	25,000	—
1842	2,823	500	900	2,900	6,500	20,000	140,000
1842C	6,729	700	1,300	2,800	7,500	27,000	—
1842D	4,643	900	1,650	3,350	11,750	36,500	—
1842O	19,800	220	350	1,100	2,400	11,000	—
1843	100,546	150	170	220	325	1,150	140,000
1843C small date	26,064	1,100	2,150	5,000	8,400	22,000	—
1843C large date	Inc. above	600	1,100	1,600	3,100	8,500	—
1843D small date	36,209	700	1,250	1,850	2,750	9,500	—
1843O small date	288,002	150	180	240	350	1,600	—
1843O large date	76,000	200	250	450	1,600	7,000	—
1844	6,784	225	400	850	1,900	7,250	140,000
1844C	11,622	600	1,100	1,850	6,250	19,000	—
1844D	17,332	650	1,250	1,850	2,650	7,800	—
1845	91,051	180	245	300	440	1,150	140,000
1845D	19,460	650	1,250	1,850	2,750	13,000	—
1845O	4,000	525	950	2,000	5,900	16,000	—
1846	21,598	200	275	500	850	5,500	140,000
1846C	4,808	650	1,250	3,500	8,500	18,750	—
1846D	19,303	650	1,250	1,850	2,500	10,500	—
1846O	66,000	170	280	400	1,050	6,100	—
1847	29,814	140	220	360	825	3,400	—
1847C	23,226	600	1,100	1,600	2,300	6,500	—
1847D	15,784	650	1,250	1,850	2,500	10,000	—
1847O	124,000	150	220	375	1,000	3,500	—
1848	7,497	315	500	850	1,700	6,000	125,000
1848 "Cal."	1,389	6,000	10,000	20,000	29,000	40,000	—
1848C	16,788	600	1,100	1,650	2,800	14,000	—
1848D	13,771	650	1,250	1,850	2,750	10,000	—
1849	23,294	200	275	475	900	2,500	—
1849C	10,220	600	1,100	1,750	5,000	23,500	—
1849D	10,945	650	1,250	1,850	3,500	16,000	—
1850	252,923	140	170	215	350	1,100	—
1850C	9,148	600	1,100	1,600	2,400	17,500	—
1850D	12,148	650	1,250	1,850	3,150	11,500	—
1850O	84,000	160	225	450	1,150	4,750	—
1851	1,372,748	135	170	200	225	325	—
1851C	14,923	600	1,100	1,600	4,400	12,000	—
1851D	11,264	650	1,250	1,850	3,800	12,000	—
1851O	148,000	140	185	215	900	4,650	—
1852	1,159,681	135	170	200	225	325	—
1852C	9,772	600	1,100	1,700	4,250	19,000	—
1852D	4,078	700	1,300	2,550	7,250	17,000	—
1852O	140,000	145	185	300	950	5,000	—
1853	1,404,668	135	170	200	225	350	—
1853D	3,178	950	1,700	3,250	4,900	18,500	—
1854	596,258	135	170	200	225	350	—
1854C	7,295	600	1,100	2,000	5,000	14,750	—
1854D	1,760	1,750	2,750	5,000	11,000	27,500	—
1854O	153,000	140	170	215	415	1,500	—
1854S	246	32,500	43,500	80,000	185,000	300,000	—
1855	235,480	135	170	200	225	350	—
1855C	3,677	700	1,350	3,000	6,000	25,000	—
1855D	1,123	1,750	3,250	7,500	18,500	48,500	—
1856	384,240	135	170	200	225	380	9,500
1856C	7,913	650	1,150	2,200	4,400	15,500	—
1856D	874	3,500	6,400	9,800	2,500	72,500	—
1856O	21,100	150	200	700	1,250	7,700	—
1856S	71,120	145	195	360	900	4,400	—
1857	214,130	135	170	200	225	380	78,000
1857D	2,364	650	1,250	2,500	3,750	13,000	—
1857O	34,000	145	195	350	1,000	4,400	—
1857S	69,200	145	195	330	850	5,500	—
1858	47,377	135	170	235	350	1,250	62,500
1858C	9,056	600	1,100	1,600	2,900	9,250	—
1859	39,444	135	170	250	400	1,250	62,500
1859D	2,244	900	1,650	2,900	4,750	20,000	—
1859S	15,200	180	425	900	2,500	6,500	—
1860	22,675	135	170	245	450	1,100	33,500
1860C	7,469	600	1,100	1,800	3,650	22,500	—
1860S	35,600	160	250	675	1,150	4,000	—
1861	1,283,878	135	170	200	230	325	33,000
1861S	24,000	175	350	900	2,900	7,250	—
1862	98,543	145	190	300	500	1,250	33,000
1862/1	Inc. above	450	900	1,750	3,300	8,000	—
1862S	8,000	400	850	2,100	4,250	17,000	—
1863	30	—	—	—	—	—	80,000
1863S	10,800	300	500	1,500	3,200	13,500	—
1864	2,874	2,500	5,500	11,000	22,000	37,500	27,000
1865	1,545	2,400	4,650	7,250	19,000	36,500	31,500
1865S	23,376	150	215	610	1,200	4,400	—
1866	3,110	650	1,200	3,500	6,000	11,500	25,000
1866S	38,960	170	300	650	1,500	6,250	—
1867	3,250	185	365	800	1,150	4,800	27,000
1867S	28,000	150	250	600	1,600	4,000	—
1868	3,625	170	220	400	650	1,600	27,000
1868S	34,000	135	190	290	1,000	4,000	—
1869	4,345	150	230	450	715	3,000	23,000
1869S	29,500	135	215	440	775	5,000	—
1870	4,555	150	220	400	725	3,650	23,500
1870S	16,000	135	200	400	750	4,750	—
1871	5,350	150	230	325	575	2,200	23,500
1871S	22,000	135	185	275	525	2,200	—
1872	3,030	200	400	750	1,000	4,650	22,000
1872S	18,000	135	190	400	900	4,300	—
1873 closed 3	178,025	135	170	200	250	515	22,500
1873 open 3	Inc. above	135	165	195	240	285	—
1873S	27,000	135	225	400	850	2,750	—
1874	3,940	150	240	365	700	2,100	33,000
1875	420	1,750	3,500	5,000	8,000	12,500	43,500
1875S	11,600	135	180	300	750	3,350	—
1876	4,221	160	275	6,400	900	3,300	21,000
1876S	5,000	145	225	500	950	3,300	—
1877	1,652	250	380	750	1,050	3,000	21,500
1877S	35,400	135	160	195	230	615	—
1878	286,260	135	160	195	225	275	34,000
1878S	178,000	135	160	195	225	340	—
1879	88,990	135	160	195	225	275	21,500
1879S	43,500	135	195	275	525	215	—
1880	2,996	160	200	335	600	1,300	21,000
1881	691	850	1,850	2,800	4,350	9,000	19,000
1882	4,067	150	210	290	400	675	15,000
1883	2,002	150	220	440	975	2,300	15,500
1884	2,023	150	210	400	590	1,500	16,000
1885	887	400	700	1,750	2,350	4,400	15,500
1886	4,088	150	190	260	425	1,100	16,500
1887	6,282	150	175	245	325	700	16,500
1888	16,098	140	165	225	270	325	15,000
1889	17,648	150	165	200	250	325	17,500
1890	8,813	150	180	225	280	500	14,000
1891	11,040	150	165	200	230	400	14,000
1892	2,545	155	175	235	325	725	15,000
1893	30,106	145	165	190	225	280	14,000
1894	4,122	155	170	225	325	750	13,500
1895	6,199	135	160	205	275	395	12,500
1896	19,202	135	160	195	225	285	12,500
1897	29,904	135	160	195	225	285	12,500
1898	24,165	135	160	195	225	285	12,500
1899	27,350	135	160	195	225	285	12,500
1900	67,205	135	160	250	340	425	12,500

$3

GOLD

KM# 84 0.9000 **GOLD** 0.1452 oz. AGW. 20.5 mm. 5.0150 g. **Designer:** James B. Longacre **Notes:** The 1873 "closed-3" and "open-3" varieties are distinguished by the amount of space between the upper left and lower left serifs of the 3 in the date.

Date	Mintage	VF-20	XF-40	AU-50	MS-60	MS-65	Prf-65
1854	138,618	675	1,000	1,350	2,450	15,500	125,000
1854D	1,120	8,000	14,000	25,500	65,000	—	—
1854O	24,000	950	1,750	3,000	16,500	55,000	—
1855	50,555	700	1,000	1,300	2,400	30,000	125,000
1855S	6,600	1,000	2,000	5,000	22,000	—	—
1856	26,010	700	1,000	1,400	2,400	27,000	85,000
1856S	34,500	750	1,150	2,000	9,000	50,000	—
1857	20,891	700	1,000	1,400	3,000	32,500	62,500
1857S	14,000	800	1,750	4,500	15,500	—	—
1858	2,133	800	1,450	2,600	7,000	35,000	62,500
1859	15,638	700	1,000	1,400	2,550	18,500	45,000
1860	7,155	750	1,000	1,400	3,150	21,000	46,000
1860S	7,000	850	1,550	6,100	14,000	—	—
1861	6,072	750	1,025	1,600	3,300	27,000	46,000
1862	5,785	750	1,000	1,600	3,300	28,000	46,500
1863	5,039	800	1,150	1,600	3,400	20,000	40,000
1864	2,680	800	1,050	1,600	3,300	29,000	40,000
1865	1,165	1,150	2,200	4,500	7,500	40,000	40,000
1866	4,030	850	1,000	1,600	3,300	27,500	40,000
1867	2,650	850	1,000	1,800	3,350	28,000	40,000
1868	4,875	700	950	1,500	2,800	22,000	38,000
1869	2,525	825	1,000	1,700	3,650	34,500	40,000
1870	3,535	725	1,000	1,750	3,700	40,000	47,000
1870S unique	—	—	—	—	—	—	—
Note: Est. value, $1.25 million, AU50 cleaned, Bass Collection.							
1871	1,330	825	1,150	1,700	3,700	27,500	47,000
1872	2,030	750	1,000	1,500	3,250	35,000	33,000
1873 open 3, proof only	25	3,300	5,000	8,700	—	—	65,000
1873 closed 3, mintage unknown	—	4,000	6,000	10,000	—	—	40,000
1874	41,820	650	950	1,300	2,300	12,500	38,000
1875 proof only	20	20,000	28,000	47,500	—	—	175,000
1876	45	5,500	10,000	14,000	—	—	50,000
1877	1,488	1,200	2,700	5,000	11,500	67,000	42,000
1878	82,324	650	1,000	1,300	2,500	11,000	47,500
1879	3,030	700	1,000	1,500	2,400	12,000	32,000
1880	1,036	750	1,600	2,000	2,800	15,500	31,000
1881	554	1,200	2,250	4,000	5,250	22,500	25,000
1882	1,576	850	1,000	1,750	3,000	20,000	25,000
1883	989	800	1,300	20,000	3,200	18,000	24,000
1884	1,106	1,150	1,500	2,200	2,750	22,000	24,000
1885	910	1,150	1,500	2,250	3,300	22,500	25,000
1886	1,142	1,100	1,700	2,100	4,000	35,000	24,000
1887	6,160	700	1,000	1,600	2,800	14,000	24,000
1888	5,291	750	1,000	1,500	2,450	13,000	24,000
1889	2,429	725	1,000	1,400	2,500	13,500	24,000

$5 (HALF EAGLE)

GOLD

Liberty Cap

KM# 19 0.9160 **GOLD** 0.258 oz. AGW. 25 mm. 8.7500 g. **Designer:** Robert Scot **Notes:** 1806 varieties are distinguished by whether the top of the 6 has a serif.

Date	Mintage	F-12	VF-20	XF-40	MS-60
1802/1	53,176	2,750	3,300	3,700	8,700
1803/2	33,506	2,750	3,300	3,700	8,700
1804 small 8	30,475	2,750	3,300	3,700	8,700
1804 large 8	Inc. above	2,750	3,300	3,700	9,600
1805	33,183	2,750	3,300	3,700	8,600
1806 pointed 6	64,093	2,800	3,350	3,750	9,000
1806 round 6	Inc. above	2,750	3,300	3,700	8,600
1807	32,488	2,750	3,300	3,700	8,700

Turban Head

Capped draped bust

KM# 38 0.9160 **GOLD** 0.258 oz. AGW. 25 mm. 8.7500 g. **Designer:** John Reich **Notes:** The 1810 varieties are distinguished by the size of the numerals in the date and the size of the 5 in the "5D." on the reverse. The 1811 varieties are distinguished by the size of the 5 in the "5D." on the reverse.

Date	Mintage	F-12	VF-20	XF-40	MS-60
1807	51,605	2,000	2,400	3,150	6,800
1808	55,578	2,000	2,400	3,150	6,900
1808/7	Inc. above	3,100	3,300	3,750	12,000
1809/8	33,875	2,000	2,400	3,150	6,900
1810 small date, small 5	100,287	9,600	22,500	35,000	102,500
1810 small date, large 5	Inc. above	2,100	2,400	3,200	7,000
1810 large date, small 5	Inc. above	13,500	25,000	37,000	124,000
1810 large date, large 5	Inc. above	2,000	2,400	3,150	6,800
1811 small 5	99,581	2,000	2,400	3,150	6,800
1811 large 5	Inc. above	1,950	2,350	3,100	7,000
1812	58,087	2,000	2,400	3,150	6,800

Turban Head

Capped head

KM# 43 0.9160 **GOLD** 0.258 oz. AGW. 25 mm. 8.7500 g. **Designer:** John Reich **Notes:** 1820 varieties are distinguished by whether the 2 in the date has a curved base or square base and by the size of the letters in the reverse inscriptions. 1832 varieties are distinguished by whether the 2 in the date has a curved base or square base and by the number of stars on the reverse. 1834 varieties are distinguished by whether the 4 has a serif at its far right.

Date	Mintage	F-12	VF-20	XF-40	MS-60
1813	95,428	2,400	2,750	3,400	7,800
1814/13	15,454	2,500	2,800	3,500	9,800
1815	635	—	—	—	—
Note: 1815, private sale, Jan. 1994, MS-61, $150,000					
1818	48,588	2,475	2,750	3,400	8,000
1819	51,723	9,600	16,500	275,000	62,000
1820 curved-base 2, small letters	263,806	2,450	2,800	3,600	10,500
1820 curved-base 2, large letters	Inc. above	2,500	3,000	3,750	20,000
1820 square-base 2	Inc. above	2,450	2,800	3,600	10,500
1821	34,641	5,800	13,500	20,000	72,000
1822 3 known	—	55,000	1,000,000	1,500,000	—
Note: 1822, private sale, 1993, VF-30, $1,000,000.					
1823	14,485	2,500	3,400	4,700	16,000
1824	17,340	5,000	10,000	16,000	38,000
1825/21	29,060	5,150	8,250	12,000	38,000
1825/24	Inc. above	—	—	250,000	350,000
Note: 1825/4, Bowers & Merena, March 1989, XF, $148,500.					
1826	18,069	3,600	7,500	9,300	25,000
1827	24,913	5,600	9,600	12,250	34,000
1828/7	28,029	15,000	27,500	41,000	125,000
Note: 1828/7, Bowers & Merena, June 1989, XF, $20,900.					
1828	Inc. above	5,500	12,500	19,000	65,000
1829 large planchet	57,442	15,000	27,500	50,000	110,000
Note: 1829 large planchet, Superior, July 1985, MS-65, $104,500.					
1829 small planchet	Inc. above	37,500	50,000	82,500	140,000
Note: 1829 small planchet, private sale, 1992 (XF-45), $89,000.					
1830 small "5D."	126,351	14,500	17,500	21,000	40,000
1830 large "5D."	Inc. above	14,500	17,500	21,000	40,000
1831	140,594	14,500	17,500	21,000	42,500
1832 curved-base 2, 12 stars	157,487	45,000	65,000	125,000	—
1832 square-base 2, 13 stars	Inc. above	14,500	17,500	21,000	40,000
1833	193,630	14,500	17,500	21,000	40,000
1834 plain 4	50,141	14,500	17,500	21,000	40,000
1834 crosslet 4	Inc. above	14,500	17,500	21,000	40,000

Classic Head

KM# 57 0.8990 **GOLD** 0.2418 oz. AGW. 22.5 mm. 8.3600 g. **Designer:** William Kneass **Notes:** 1834 varieties are distinguished by whether the 4 has a serif at its far right.

Date	Mintage	VF-20	XF-40	AU-50	MS-60	MS-65
1834 plain 4	658,028	390	550	890	2,850	48,000
1834 crosslet 4	Inc. above	1,650	2,750	5,500	20,000	—
1835	371,534	390	560	960	3,150	70,000
1836	553,147	390	550	890	2,900	70,000

ate	Mintage	VF-20	XF-40	AU-50	MS-60	MS-65
837	207,121	390	585	1,200	3,500	75,000
838	286,588	390	5,500	890	3,700	58,000
838C	17,179	1,900	3,850	12,500	38,500	—
838D	20,583	1,500	3,400	8,250	23,000	—

Coronet Head
No motto above eagle

:M# 69 0.9000 GOLD 0.242 oz. AGW. 21.6 mm. 8.3590 g. **Designer:** Christian Gobrecht **Notes:** arieties for the 1842 Philadelphia strikes are distinguished by the size of the letters in the reverse scriptions. Varieties for the 1842-C and -D strikes are distinguished by the size of the numerals in e date. Varieties for the 1843-O strikes are distinguished by the size of the letters in the reverse scriptions.

ate	Mintage	F-12	VF-20	XF-40	MS-60	Prf-65
839	118,143	250	275	480	4,000	—
39/8 curved date	Inc. above	275	325	700	2,250	—
39C	17,205	700	1,450	2,700	24,000	—
39D	18,939	700	1,450	2,200	22,000	—
40	137,382	190	235	360	3,700	—
40C	18,992	700	1,450	2,600	25,000	—
40D	22,896	700	1,450	2,000	15,000	—
400	40,120	200	325	850	11,000	—
41	15,833	210	375	1,750	10,500	—
41C	21,467	650	1,400	1,925	18,500	—
41D	30,495	700	1,450	1,925	14,500	—
410 2 known	50	—	—	—	—	—
42 small letters	27,578	165	345	1,100	1,375	—
42 large letters	Inc. above	300	750	2,000	11,000	—
42C small date	28,184	4,500	9,000	23,000	125,000	—
42C large date	Inc. above	650	1,400	2,000	18,000	—
42D small date	59,608	700	1,450	1,925	15,000	—
42D large date	Inc. above	1,000	2,200	5,800	48,000	—
420	16,400	450	1,000	3,000	22,000	—
43	611,205	170	220	260	1,850	—
43C	44,201	650	1,375	1,925	12,500	—
43D	98,452	650	1,450	1,925	12,500	—
430 small letters	19,075	250	500	1,400	20,000	—
430 large letters	82,000	175	250	1,125	12,000	—
44	340,330	150	220	240	2,000	—
44C	23,631	650	1,375	3,000	22,000	—
44D	88,982	700	1,450	1,925	11,000	—
440	364,600	175	250	375	4,000	—
45	417,099	150	220	240	2,000	—
45D	90,629	700	1,450	1,925	12,000	—
450	41,000	200	410	750	9,900	—
46	395,942	150	220	240	2,400	—
46C	12,995	700	1,450	2,900	22,500	—
46D	80,294	700	1,450	1,925	12,000	—
460	58,000	200	375	960	11,500	—
47	915,981	150	220	250	1,650	—
47C	84,151	650	1,375	1,925	13,000	—
47D	64,405	700	1,450	1,925	10,000	—
470	12,000	1,925	7,500	9,600	26,000	—
48	260,775	150	225	275	1,500	—
48C	64,472	650	1,375	1,925	19,250	—
48D	47,465	700	1,450	1,925	14,500	—
49	133,070	150	220	270	2,750	—
49C	64,823	650	1,375	1,925	13,500	—
49D	39,036	700	1,450	1,925	14,000	—
50	64,491	185	275	600	3,700	—
50C	63,591	650	1,375	1,925	12,000	—
50D	43,984	700	1,450	1,925	27,500	—
51	377,505	150	220	240	2,800	—
51C	49,176	650	1,375	1,925	16,500	—
51D	62,710	700	1,450	1,925	15,000	—
510	41,000	275	565	1,500	12,000	—
52	573,901	150	220	245	1,250	—
52C	72,574	650	1,375	1,925	6,750	—
52D	91,584	700	1,450	1,925	12,500	—
53	305,770	150	220	240	1,500	—
53C	65,571	650	1,375	1,925	8,500	—
53D	89,678	700	1,450	1,925	10,000	—
54	160,675	150	220	250	2,000	—
54C	39,283	650	1,375	1,925	14,000	—
54D	56,413	700	1,450	1,925	10,500	—
540	46,000	200	300	525	8,250	—
54S	268	—	—	—	—	—
e: 1854S, Bowers & Merena, Oct. 1982, AU-55, $170,000.						
55	117,098	140	220	235	1,800	—
55C	39,788	650	1,375	2,000	15,000	—
55D	22,432	700	1,450	1,925	16,500	—
550	11,100	275	650	2,100	20,000	—
55S	61,000	200	390	975	15,500	—
56	197,990	150	220	240	2,300	—
56C	28,457	650	1,375	1,925	20,000	—
56D	19,786	700	1,450	1,925	11,000	—
560	10,000	330	650	1,250	12,500	—
56S	105,100	175	300	625	6,900	—
57	98,188	150	220	240	1,600	123,500
57C	31,360	650	1,375	1,925	9,000	—
57D	17,046	700	1,450	1,925	13,000	—
570	13,000	325	640	1,400	17,000	—
57S	87,000	180	300	525	9,600	—

Date	Mintage	F-12	VF-20	XF-40	MS-60	Prf-65
1858	15,136	150	240	550	3,850	190,000
1858C	38,856	650	1,375	1,925	10,000	—
1858D	15,362	700	1,450	1,925	12,500	—
1858S	18,600	300	700	2,350	30,000	—
1859	16,814	185	325	625	7,250	—
1859C	31,847	650	1,375	1,925	15,000	—
1859D	10,366	700	1,450	1,925	14,500	—
1859S	13,220	500	1,250	3,500	29,000	—
1860	19,825	175	275	575	2,700	100,000
1860C	14,813	650	1,375	2,200	15,000	—
1860D	14,635	700	1,450	2,000	17,000	—
1860S	21,200	400	1,100	2,100	25,000	—
1861	688,150	150	220	245	1,200	100,000
1861C	6,879	700	1,850	3,900	25,000	—
1861D	1,597	2,400	4,400	7,000	53,500	—
1861S	18,000	450	1,000	4,500	36,500	—
1862	4,465	300	700	1,850	20,000	96,000
1862S	9,500	1,600	3,000	6,300	62,000	—
1863	2,472	450	1,200	3,750	27,500	90,000
1863S	17,000	600	1,450	3,900	35,500	—
1864	4,220	350	630	1,850	14,500	72,000
1864S	3,888	2,300	5,000	16,000	55,000	—
1865	1,295	500	1,300	4,100	20,000	82,500
1865S	27,612	450	1,300	2,400	20,000	—
1866S	9,000	700	1,650	4,000	40,000	—

Coronet Head
"In God We Trust" above eagle

KM# 101 0.9000 **GOLD** 0.242 oz. AGW. 21.6 mm. 8.3590 g. **Designer:** Christian Gobrecht **Notes:** The 1873 "closed-3" and "open-3" varieties are known and are distinguished by the amount of space between the upper left and lower left serifs of the 3 in the date.

Date	Mintage	VF-20	XF-40	AU-50	MS-60	MS-63	MS-65	Prf-65
1866	6,730	800	1,650	3,500	16,500	—	—	70,000
1866S	34,920	900	2,600	8,000	25,000	—	—	—
1867	6,920	500	1,700	3,700	11,500	—	—	70,000
1867S	29,000	1,300	2,700	8,000	34,500	—	—	—
1868	5,725	650	1,000	3,500	11,000	—	—	70,000
1868S	52,000	400	1,550	4,000	20,000	—	—	—
1869	1,785	925	2,400	3,500	17,500	33,500	—	65,000
1869S	31,000	500	1,750	4,000	26,000	—	—	—
1870	4,035	800	2,000	2,850	18,000	—	—	75,000
1870CC	7,675	5,000	13,000	26,000	110,000	137,500	200,000	—
1870S	17,000	950	2,600	8,250	29,000	—	—	—
1871	3,230	950	1,850	3,300	12,500	—	—	70,000
1871CC	20,770	1,100	3,300	11,000	60,000	—	—	—
1871S	25,000	500	1,000	3,150	13,000	—	—	—
1872	1,690	850	1,925	3,000	15,000	20,000	—	60,000
1872CC	16,980	1,100	4,800	20,000	60,000	—	—	—
1872S	36,400	445	800	3,600	13,000	—	—	—
1873 closed 3	49,305	180	225	400	1,175	6,500	24,000	70,000
1873 open 3	63,200	180	215	350	850	3,800	—	—
1873CC	7,416	2,200	12,500	27,500	60,000	—	—	—
1873S	31,000	525	1,400	3,250	22,000	—	—	—
1874	3,508	660	1,675	2,500	12,500	26,000	—	66,000
1874CC	21,198	800	1,700	9,500	38,000	—	—	—
1874S	16,000	640	2,100	4,600	22,500	—	—	—
1875	220	34,000	45,000	60,000	200,000	—	—	185,000
1875CC	11,828	1,400	4,400	11,500	52,000	—	—	—
1875S	9,000	675	2,250	4,800	16,500	32,500	—	—
1876	1,477	1,100	2,500	4,125	11,000	14,500	55,000	60,000
1876CC	6,887	1,200	5,000	14,000	46,500	82,500	165,000	—
1876S	4,000	2,000	3,600	9,500	30,000	—	—	—
1877	1,152	900	2,750	4,000	13,750	29,000	—	75,000
1877CC	8,680	1,000	3,300	11,000	52,500	—	—	—
1877S	26,700	400	650	1,400	9,200	—	—	—
1878	131,740	160	190	240	425	2,000	—	50,000
1878CC	9,054	3,000	7,200	20,000	60,000	—	—	—
1878S	144,700	165	190	3,000	675	4,250	—	—
1879	301,950	165	180	225	400	2,000	12,000	55,000
1879CC	17,281	525	1,375	3,000	2,200	—	—	—
1879S	426,200	180	225	240	825	3,300	—	—
1880	3,166,436	160	175	180	220	840	7,500	54,000
1880CC	51,017	425	770	1,375	9,900	—	—	—
1880S	1,348,900	160	175	180	220	800	5,750	—
1881	5,708,802	160	175	180	220	775	4,800	54,000
1881/80	Inc. above	330	600	750	1,500	4,500	—	—
1881CC	13,886	515	1,400	6,750	22,500	60,000	—	—
1881S	969,000	160	175	180	220	775	7,150	—
1882	2,514,568	160	175	180	220	800	6,150	54,000
1882CC	82,817	390	550	800	7,500	40,000	—	—
1882S	969,000	160	175	180	220	800	4,500	—
1883	233,461	160	175	200	260	1,200	—	40,000
1883CC	12,958	450	1,000	3,200	18,000	—	—	—
1883S	83,200	200	240	300	1,000	2,950	—	—
1884	191,078	170	200	220	650	2,250	—	35,000
1884CC	16,402	550	975	3,000	17,000	—	—	—
1884S	177,000	170	200	215	360	2,000	—	—
1885	601,506	160	175	180	220	825	4,800	35,000
1885S	1,211,500	160	175	180	220	790	4,000	—
1886	388,432	160	175	180	230	1,100	5,600	44,000
1886S	3,268,000	160	175	180	220	790	4,500	—

Date	Mintage	VF-20	XF-40	AU-50	MS-60	MS-63	MS-65	Prf-65
1887	87	—	14,500	20,000	—	—	—	130,000
1887S	1,912,000	160	175	180	220	825	4,800	—
1888	18,296	175	230	300	550	1,550	—	28,000
1888S	293,900	175	200	320	1,200	4,000	—	—
1889	7,565	280	4,400	515	1,100	2,400	—	29,000
1890	4,328	400	475	550	2,200	6,500	—	27,000
1890CC	53,800	330	385	560	1,175	5,000	55,000	—
1891	61,413	170	200	225	450	1,900	5,400	28,000
1891CC	208,000	315	415	525	750	3,150	31,500	—
1892	753,572	160	175	180	220	880	7,000	30,000
1892CC	82,968	315	400	575	1,500	6,000	33,500	—
1892O	10,000	515	1,000	1,375	3,300	—	—	—
1892S	298,400	180	195	220	525	3,300	—	—
1893	1,528,197	160	175	180	220	790	3,900	34,000
1893CC	60,000	315	450	770	1,400	6,350	—	—
1893O	110,000	225	315	480	950	6,500	—	—
1893S	224,000	170	200	210	230	825	9,000	—
1894	957,955	160	175	180	220	790	2,000	35,000
1894O	16,600	200	360	570	1,300	5,500	—	—
1894S	55,900	240	375	575	2,900	10,000	—	—
1895	1,345,936	160	175	180	220	790	4,500	29,000
1895S	112,000	200	275	400	3,150	6,500	26,000	—
1896	59,063	160	175	175	235	9,750	4,500	30,000
1896S	155,400	200	240	300	1,150	6,000	24,500	—
1897	867,883	160	175	180	220	825	4,500	35,000
1897S	354,000	175	210	235	865	5,150	—	—
1898	633,495	160	175	180	225	885	6,000	30,000
1898S	1,397,400	175	200	210	230	950	—	—
1899	1,710,729	160	175	180	220	790	3,600	30,000
1899S	1,545,000	170	180	185	230	1,000	9,600	—
1900	1,405,730	160	175	180	220	790	3,600	30,000
1900S	329,000	170	190	200	230	900	14,000	—
1907	626,192	160	175	180	220	790	3,600	23,000

$10 (EAGLE)

GOLD

Liberty Cap

Heraldic eagle

KM# 30 0.9160 **GOLD** 0.5159 oz. AGW. 33 mm. 17.5000 g. **Designer:** Robert Scot **Notes:** The 1798/97 varieties are distinguished by the positioning of the stars on the obverse.

Date	Mintage	F-12	VF-20	XF-40	MS-60
1801	44,344	7,500	8,900	10,000	20,000
1803	15,017	7,500	9,000	10,000	21,000
1804	3,757	7,700	9,250	10,250	34,500

Coronet Head

Old-style head No motto above eagle

KM# 66.1 0.9000 **GOLD** 0.4839 oz. AGW. 27 mm. 16.7180 g. **Designer:** Christian Gobrecht

Date	Mintage	F-12	VF-20	XF-40	MS-60	Prf-65
1838	7,200	800	1,100	2,900	35,500	—
1839 large letters	38,248	800	1,000	1,950	30,000	—

Coronet Head

New-style head No motto above eagle

KM# 66.2 0.9000 **GOLD** 0.4839 oz. AGW. 27 mm. 16.7180 g. **Designer:** Christian Gobrecht **Notes:** The 1842 varieties are distinguished by the size of the numerals in the date.

Date	Mintage	F-12	VF-20	XF-40	MS-60	Prf-65
1839 small letters	Inc. above	800	1,500	3,500	30,000	—
1840	47,338	300	400	650	10,000	—
1841	63,131	300	385	500	9,500	—
1841O	2,500	1,100	2,200	5,000	30,000	—
1842 small date	81,507	275	375	650	16,500	—
1842 large date	Inc. above	250	325	475	9,200	—
1842O	27,400	250	370	500	22,500	—
1843	75,462	250	370	500	19,000	—
1843O	175,162	250	370	475	11,500	—
1844	6,361	800	1,350	2,700	16,750	—
1844O	118,700	245	325	475	15,000	—
1845	26,153	290	600	775	14,000	—
1845O	47,500	250	380	650	16,500	—
1846	20,095	410	625	900	20,000	—
1846O	81,780	250	425	770	14,750	—
1847	862,258	240	300	350	3,000	—
1847O	571,500	250	325	375	4,850	—
1848	145,484	260	340	375	4,300	—
1848O	38,850	325	525	1,050	14,000	—
1849	653,618	240	300	350	3,400	—
1849O	23,900	375	710	2,100	21,000	—
1850	291,451	240	300	380	3,600	—
1850O	57,500	285	380	880	—	—
1851	176,328	275	325	475	5,150	—
1851O	263,000	250	315	440	5,750	—
1852	263,106	240	300	350	4,200	—
1852O	18,000	375	650	1,100	19,000	—
1853	201,253	240	300	350	3,500	—
1853O	51,000	285	325	485	12,500	—
1854	54,250	290	320	400	6,000	—
1854O small date	52,500	290	375	675	10,500	—
1854O large date	Inc. above	375	475	875	—	—
1854S	123,826	275	325	410	5,500	—
1855	121,701	250	300	350	4,150	—
1855O	18,000	400	625	1,250	20,000	—
1855S	9,000	700	1,250	2,100	29,500	—
1856	60,490	250	300	350	4,200	—
1856O	14,500	375	725	1,250	9,800	—
1856S	68,000	250	320	500	8,500	—
1857	16,606	325	490	850	12,000	—
1857O	5,500	600	975	1,850	18,000	—
1857S	26,000	300	375	950	9,500	—
1858	2,521	2,600	4,650	7,250	32,000	—
1858O	20,000	300	440	750	9,000	—
1858S	11,800	825	1,450	3,100	34,000	—
1859	16,093	325	390	750	10,500	—
1859O	2,300	1,850	3,800	8,200	47,500	—
1859S	7,000	1,000	1,800	4,500	40,000	—
1860	15,105	300	420	775	8,000	—
1860O	11,100	410	575	1,100	8,250	—
1860S	5,000	1,400	3,250	6,100	40,500	—
1861	113,233	250	300	350	3,600	—
1861S	15,500	690	1,600	2,950	32,500	—
1862	10,995	265	515	1,000	13,500	—
1862S	12,500	675	1,750	2,950	37,000	—
1863	1,248	2,400	3,650	10,000	42,500	—
1863S	10,000	625	1,600	3,350	24,000	—
1864	3,580	775	1,600	4,200	17,500	—
1864S	2,500	2,300	4,900	12,500	50,000	—
1865	4,005	875	1,950	3,500	31,500	—
1865S	16,700	1,700	5,350	10,500	45,000	—
1865S /inverted 186	—	1,250	2,850	6,100	47,000	—
1866S	8,500	950	2,400	3,300	44,000	—

Coronet Head

New-style head "In God We Trust" above eagle

KM# 102 0.9000 **GOLD** 0.4839 oz. AGW. 27 mm. 16.7180 g. **Designer:** Christian Gobrecht **Notes:** The 1873 "closed-3" and "open-3" varieties are distinguished by the amount of space between the upper left and lower left serifs of the 3 in the date.

Date	Mintage	VF-20	XF-40	AU-50	MS-60	MS-63	MS-65	Prf-65
1866	3,780	775	1,650	3,500	15,500	—	—	75,000
1866S	11,500	1,550	3,400	6,400	23,000	—	—	—
1867	3,140	1,500	2,600	4,800	26,000	—	—	75,000
1867S	9,000	2,000	5,200	8,900	40,000	—	—	—
1868	10,655	500	750	1,700	15,000	—	—	60,000
1868S	13,500	1,250	2,100	3,800	24,000	—	—	—
1869	1,855	1,400	2,800	5,400	27,500	—	—	—
1869S	6,430	1,500	2,500	6,250	25,000	—	—	—
1870	4,025	800	1,175	2,350	17,000	—	—	60,000
1870CC	5,908	9,000	22,000	42,000	90,000	—	—	—
1870S	8,000	1,100	2,500	6,500	32,000	—	—	—
1871	1,820	1,450	2,400	4,000	19,500	—	—	75,000
1871CC	8,085	2,150	4,950	16,500	53,500	—	—	—
1871S	16,500	1,075	1,500	5,700	26,000	—	—	—
1872	1,650	2,200	3,600	9,500	16,500	32,000	—	60,000
1872CC	4,600	3,000	8,800	20,000	55,000	—	—	—
1872S	17,300	550	850	1,800	22,000	—	—	—
1873 closed 3	825	4,500	9,500	17,500	55,000	—	—	60,000
1873CC	4,543	5,000	12,000	26,000	57,500	—	—	—
1873S	12,000	950	1,950	4,750	24,500	—	—	—

Date	Mintage	VF-20	XF-40	AU-50	MS-60	MS-63	MS-65	Prf-65
1874	53,160	240	265	315	1,850	8,750	—	60,000
1874CC	16,767	850	2,500	8,000	40,000	—	—	—
1874S	10,000	1,150	3,250	6,800	39,500	—	—	—
1875	120	38,000	53,000	80,000	95,000	—	—	185,000

Note: 1875, Akers, Aug. 1990, Proof, $115,000.

Date	Mintage	VF-20	XF-40	AU-50	MS-60	MS-63	MS-65	Prf-65
1875CC	7,715	3,700	8,800	25,000	65,000	—	—	—
1876	732	3,500	4,750	15,000	55,000	—	—	60,000
1876CC	4,696	3,200	6,500	20,500	50,000	—	—	—
1876S	5,000	1,250	2,000	5,500	38,000	—	—	—
1877	817	2,100	3,800	8,500	—	—	—	—
1877CC	3,332	2,300	4,750	14,000	47,000	—	—	—
1877S	17,000	500	700	2,200	22,500	—	—	—
1878	73,800	220	265	285	900	4,800	—	60,000
1878CC	3,244	3,600	7,500	14,000	47,000	—	—	—
1878S	26,100	450	550	1,650	15,000	—	—	—
1879	384,770	200	220	315	665	2,850	—	50,000
1879/78	Inc. above	300	400	700	800	900	—	—
1879CC	1,762	6,500	12,000	21,750	60,000	—	—	—
1879O	1,500	2,300	3,750	10,000	28,750	—	—	—
1879S	224,000	200	220	250	1,100	7,750	—	—
1880	1,644,876	210	225	250	280	2,250	—	45,000
1880CC	11,190	475	700	1,450	12,500	—	—	—
1880O	9,200	415	700	1,200	12,750	—	—	—
1880S	506,250	200	230	315	415	3,300	—	—
1881	3,877,260	200	225	240	275	800	—	45,000
1881CC	24,015	360	515	950	6,500	18,500	—	—
1881O	8,350	375	650	1,250	6,750	—	—	—
1881S	970,000	200	225	240	350	—	—	—
1882	2,324,480	200	225	240	270	800	—	41,500
1882CC	6,764	950	1,300	3,000	13,000	35,000	—	—
1882O	10,820	375	575	1,200	7,700	16,750	—	—
1882S	132,000	200	230	240	350	4,200	—	—
1883	208,740	200	225	240	300	1,300	—	41,500
1883CC	12,000	425	700	2,350	12,500	35,000	—	—
1883O	800	2,950	6,800	9,500	33,500	—	—	—
1883S	38,000	200	250	340	1,100	6,900	—	—
1884	76,905	190	225	250	750	2,600	—	46,000
1884CC	9,925	600	950	2,250	10,750	34,000	—	—
1884S	124,250	210	220	235	525	6,500	—	—
1885	253,527	210	220	230	375	2,750	—	43,000
1885S	228,000	210	225	250	375	3,600	6,500	—
1886	236,160	210	225	250	375	1,800	—	42,500
1886S	826,000	200	225	250	340	1,000	—	—
1887	53,680	200	225	295	800	3,800	—	37,000
1887S	817,000	200	225	240	315	1,950	—	—
1888	132,996	225	235	315	700	4,500	—	38,500
1888O	21,335	225	250	275	515	4,500	—	—
1888S	648,700	210	225	240	300	1,950	—	—
1889	4,485	575	700	1,100	2,700	6,800	—	43,000
1889S	425,400	210	220	240	350	1,400	4,200	—
1890	58,043	225	275	300	700	3,900	7,750	37,500
1890CC	17,500	385	450	650	2,000	13,500	—	—
1891	91,868	225	250	275	325	1,900	—	32,500
1891CC	103,732	350	400	515	750	4,200	—	—
1892	797,552	210	225	250	285	1,150	12,000	37,500
1892CC	40,000	350	450	625	3,100	8,000	—	—
1892O	28,688	250	275	300	400	2,500	—	—
1892S	115,500	210	220	250	360	2,950	—	—
1893	1,840,895	200	210	235	275	695	—	34,500
1893CC	14,000	425	625	1,450	6,200	14,500	—	—
1893O	17,000	260	315	350	625	5,100	—	—
1893S	141,350	220	230	250	440	2,750	—	—
1894	2,470,778	210	225	250	265	725	11,500	35,000
1894O	107,500	225	260	360	900	4,750	—	—
1894S	25,000	260	385	875	3,500	8,800	—	—
1895	567,826	200	210	240	280	775	8,800	33,000
1895O	98,000	220	230	280	480	3,500	—	—
1895S	49,000	225	300	600	2,250	9,000	—	—
1896	76,348	200	220	260	300	1,475	—	31,500
1896S	123,750	215	265	450	2,500	10,500	—	—
1897	1,000,159	200	215	250	285	685	6,500	35,000
1897O	42,500	225	265	335	700	2,000	—	—
1897S	234,750	200	250	335	870	3,300	—	—
1898	812,197	200	215	255	285	900	3,800	35,000
1898S	473,600	205	235	250	350	2,200	—	—
1899	1,262,305	200	220	245	285	650	2,800	31,000
1899O	37,047	230	275	325	550	2,700	—	—
1899S	841,000	200	235	265	320	1,300	—	—
1900	293,960	200	225	230	300	650	7,750	30,500
1900S	81,000	210	275	350	850	3,800	—	—
1903O	112,771	225	250	295	375	1,875	—	—

$20 (DOUBLE EAGLE)

GOLD

Liberty

"Twenty D." below eagle. No motto above eagle

KM# 74.1 0.9000 **GOLD** 0.9677 oz. AGW. 34 mm. 33.4360 g. **Designer:** James B. Longacre

Date	Mintage	VF-20	XF-40	AU-50	MS-60	MS-63	MS-65	Prf-65
1849 unique, in Smithsonian collection	1	—	—	—	—	—	—	—
1850	1,170,261	700	1,150	260	6,700	46,500	—	—
1850O	141,000	850	1,400	7,500	33,000	—	—	—
1851	2,087,155	650	700	925	3,200	20,000	—	—
1851O	315,000	750	925	1,650	17,000	—	—	—
1852	2,053,026	650	720	900	3,300	13,000	—	—
1852O	190,000	775	925	1,800	15,000	—	—	—
1853	1,261,326	650	720	925	4,400	21,000	—	—
1853O	71,000	750	1,200	2,500	25,000	—	—	—
1854	757,899	650	715	925	5,850	21,000	—	—
1854O	3,250	29,000	57,500	110,000	330,000	—	—	—
1854S	141,468	700	825	1,300	3,800	12,000	40,000	—
1855	364,666	650	725	1,150	8,250	—	—	—
1855O	8,000	2,350	5,750	17,500	75,000	—	—	—
1855S	879,675	650	675	1,100	7,200	15,000	—	—
1856	329,878	675	725	1,150	8,900	22,500	—	—
1856O	2,250	41,500	75,000	120,000	425,000	—	—	—
1856S	1,189,750	650	725	1,150	5,500	11,500	33,000	—
1857	439,375	650	675	900	3,400	26,000	—	—
1857O	30,000	1,050	1,750	4,250	27,500	115,000	—	—
1857S	970,500	650	700	950	4,800	7,150	—	—
1858	211,714	700	925	1,250	4,950	36,000	—	—
1858O	35,250	1,375	2,000	1,800	26,500	—	—	—
1858S	846,710	650	725	1,000	9,250	—	—	—
1859	43,597	960	2,100	4,000	31,500	—	—	—
1859O	9,100	3,400	6,750	17,000	82,500	—	—	—
1859S	636,445	650	675	1,000	4,950	—	—	—
1860	577,670	650	675	950	4,000	20,000	—	—
1860O	6,600	3,200	6,000	17,500	89,000	—	—	—
1860S	544,950	650	675	1,000	6,000	20,000	—	—
1861	2,976,453	650	675	950	2,500	9,500	36,000	—
1861O	17,741	2,400	4,000	13,750	90,000	—	—	—
1861S	768,000	650	720	1,600	8,500	30,000	—	—

Liberty

Paquet design

KM# 93 0.9000 **GOLD** 0.9677 oz. AGW. 33.4360 g. **Notes:** In 1861 the reverse was redesigned by Anthony C. Paquet, but it was withdrawn soon after its release. The letters in the inscriptions on the Paquet-reverse variety are taller than on the regular reverse.

Date	Mintage	VF-20	XF-40	AU-50	MS-60	MS-63	MS-65	Prf-65
1861S	Inc. above	11,000	22,500	34,000	170,000	—	—	—

Note: 1861S Paquet reverse, Bowers & Merena, Nov. 1988, MS-67, $660,000.

Liberty

Longacre design resumed

KM# A74.1 0.9000 **GOLD** 0.9677 oz. AGW. 33.4360 g.

Date	Mintage	VF-20	XF-40	AU-50	MS-60	MS-63	MS-65	Prf-65
1862	92,133	925	1,450	2,900	15,500	33,000	—	—
1862S	854,173	650	775	1,600	10,000	—	—	—
1863	142,790	720	880	1,850	17,000	35,000	—	—
1863S	966,570	650	800	1,400	7,500	30,000	—	—
1864	204,285	775	1,000	1,750	14,000	—	—	—
1864S	793,660	650	675	1,700	6,600	—	—	—
1865	351,200	650	700	1,000	6,000	25,000	—	—
1865S	1,042,500	650	715	1,000	4,000	6,600	17,500	—
1866S	Inc. below	1,650	2,850	11,000	60,000	—	—	—

Liberty

"Twenty D." below eagle. "In God We Trust" above eagle

KM# 74.2 0.9000 **GOLD** 0.9677 oz. AGW. 34 mm. 33.4360 g. **Designer:** James B. Longacre **Notes:** The 1873 "closed-3" and "open-3" varieties are known and are distinguished by the amount of space between the upper left and lower left serif in the 3 in the date.

Date	Mintage	VF-20	XF-40	AU-50	MS-60	MS-63	MS-65	Prf-65
1866	698,775	675	825	1,300	4,800	28,500	—	—
1866S	842,250	625	700	1,250	15,500	—	—	—
1867	251,065	625	650	925	2,400	20,000	—	—
1867S	920,750	625	725	1,600	14,000	—	—	—
1868	98,600	925	1,150	2,000	10,000	40,000	—	—
1868S	837,500	625	750	1,200	8,500	—	—	—
1869	175,155	700	950	1,250	6,000	21,000	—	—
1869S	686,750	625	650	1,100	5,300	30,000	—	—
1870	155,185	750	1,000	1,650	9,000	—	—	—
1870CC	3,789	85,000	115,000	240,000	675,000	—	—	—
1870S	982,000	650	675	925	5,000	24,000	—	—
1871	80,150	825	960	1,500	4,000	26,000	—	—
1871CC	17,387	6,000	9,600	19,000	50,000	—	—	—
1871S	928,000	625	750	750	4,400	22,000	—	—
1872	251,880	650	675	740	2,700	25,000	—	—
1872CC	26,900	1,900	2,400	5,500	27,500	—	—	—
1872S	780,000	625	740	715	3,000	24,000	—	—
1873 closed 3	Est. 208,925	675	800	1,100	2,600	—	—	—
1873 open 3	Est. 1,500,900	625	650	660	990	11,000	—	—
1873CC	22,410	2,250	3,500	6,000	30,000	100,000	—	—
1873S	1,040,600	625	650	660	1,500	21,000	—	—
1874	366,800	625	650	660	1,150	20,000	—	—
1874CC	115,085	1,100	1,500	2,400	8,500	—	—	—
1874S	1,214,000	625	650	660	1,375	26,000	—	—
1875	295,740	625	650	660	1,000	11,000	—	—
1875CC	111,151	1,100	1,300	1,500	2,300	17,500	—	—
1875S	1,230,000	625	650	660	1,000	16,500	—	—
1876	583,905	625	650	660	990	11,500	—	—
1876CC	138,441	1,100	1,300	1,650	4,500	35,000	—	—
1876S	1,597,000	625	650	660	990	11,500	—	—

Liberty

"Twenty Dollars" below eagle

KM# 74.3 0.9000 **GOLD** 0.9677 oz. AGW. 33.4360 g.

Date	Mintage	VF-20	XF-40	AU-50	MS-60	MS-63	MS-65	Prf-65
1877	397,670	585	590	600	825	5,250	—	—
1877CC	42,565	1,250	1,550	2,300	16,500	—	—	—
1877S	1,735,000	585	590	600	750	12,500	—	—
1878	543,645	585	590	600	675	5,600	—	—
1878CC	13,180	2,000	2,800	4,600	26,000	—	—	—
1878S	1,739,000	585	590	600	750	22,000	—	—
1879	207,630	585	590	600	1,000	125,000	—	—
1879CC	10,708	2,000	3,000	5,750	30,000	—	—	—
1879O	2,325	4,500	6,750	15,000	75,000	120,000	—	—
1879S	1,223,800	585	590	600	1,375	—	—	—
1880	51,456	585	590	600	3,000	16,500	—	—
1880S	836,000	585	590	600	950	16,000	—	—
1881	2,260	4,500	6,750	13,750	44,000	—	—	105,000
1881S	727,000	585	590	600	850	17,500	—	—
1882	630	7,000	15,000	28,000	66,000	135,000	—	—
1882CC	39,140	1,150	1,375	1,900	6,500	—	—	—
1882S	1,125,000	585	590	600	750	16,000	—	—
1883 proof only	92	—	—	10,000	—	—	—	—
1883CC	59,962	1,100	1,250	1,650	4,000	20,000	—	—
1883S	1,189,000	585	590	600	675	8,500	—	—
1884 proof only	71	—	—	10,000	—	—	—	150,000
1884CC	81,139	1,100	1,300	1,600	2,750	—	—	—
1884S	916,000	585	590	600	675	7,000	—	—
1885	828	6,500	8,500	11,000	35,000	—	—	—
1885CC	9,450	2,100	3,000	5,500	11,000	—	—	—
1885S	683,500	585	590	600	675	7,000	—	—
1886	1,106	8,250	11,500	30,000	45,000	55,000	—	67,000
1887	121	—	—	8,000	—	—	—	85,000
1887S	283,000	585	590	600	675	14,000	—	—
1888	226,266	585	590	600	675	4,500	32,000	—
1888S	859,600	585	590	600	675	5,500	—	—
1889	44,111	625	650	700	750	11,000	—	57,500
1889CC	30,945	1,250	1,450	2,100	3,400	15,000	—	—
1889S	774,700	585	590	600	675	6,750	—	—
1890	75,995	585	590	600	675	5,500	—	27,000
1890CC	91,209	1,100	1,400	1,400	2,300	27,500	—	—
1890S	802,750	585	590	600	675	8,500	—	—
1891	1,442	3,300	5,000	8,500	40,000	—	—	62,500
1891CC	5,000	3,500	5,000	7,500	15,000	44,000	—	—
1891S	1,288,125	585	590	600	650	3,350	—	—
1892	4,523	1,150	1,650	2,600	5,500	18,500	—	55,000
1892CC	27,265	1,200	1,400	2,000	3,300	25,000	—	—
1892S	930,150	585	590	600	650	4,000	—	—
1893	344,339	585	590	600	650	2,400	—	60,000
1893CC	18,402	1,400	1,750	2,000	3,000	15,000	—	—
1893S	996,175	585	590	600	650	3,850	—	—
1894	1,368,990	585	590	600	650	1,500	—	55,000
1894S	1,048,550	585	590	600	650	2,400	—	—
1895	1,114,656	585	590	600	650	1,300	11,500	54,000
1895S	1,143,500	585	590	600	650	2,400	12,500	—
1896	792,663	585	590	600	650	2,000	11,500	49,000
1896S	1,403,925	585	590	600	650	2,150	—	—
1897	1,383,261	585	590	600	650	1,350	—	55,000
1897S	1,470,250	585	590	600	650	1,350	9,600	—
1898	170,470	585	590	625	675	4,800	—	49,000
1898S	2,575,175	585	590	600	650	1,300	12,000	—
1899	1,669,384	585	590	600	650	1,000	8,500	49,000
1899S	2,010,300	585	590	600	650	1,800	12,500	—
1900	1,874,584	585	590	600	650	900	6,000	49,000
1900S	2,459,500	585	590	600	650	2,300	—	—

CONFEDERATE STATES of AMERICA

The Confederate States of America (1861-1865) was a federal republic constituted by the 11 Southern states which seceded from the United States after the election of Abraham Lincoln as President. In the order of their secession, the 11 members of the Confederate States of America were South Carolina, Mississippi, florida, Alabama, Georgia, Louisiana, Texas, Arkansas, North Carolina, Virginia, and Tennessee.

The seceded states had left the Union separately and were in effect separate nations, each too small to withstand economic pressures or attack by the Union Army. On Feb. 4, 1861, delegations from South Carolina, Mississippi, Florida, Alabama, Georgia, and Louisiana, Texas arrived later – met in Montgomery, Alabama to organize a Southern nation dedicated to states' rights and the protection of slavery. A provisional government was formed and Jefferson Davis was elected President. The secession crisis precipitated the Civil War – officially known as the War of the Rebellion and, in the South, as the War Between the States – which ended in Union victory and the collapse of the Confederate States of America. The secession states were eventually readmitted to the Union.

To finance the war, both the Confederacy and its constituent states issued paper currency, the redemption of which is specifically forbidden by Section 4 of the 14th which is specifically forbidden by Section 4 of the 14th Amendment to the U.S. Constitution. WATERMARKS "NY" "TEN" "FIVE" "CSA" in block letters, "CSA" in Script letters. "J. WHATMAN 1862" "HODGKINSON & CO. WOOKEY HOLE MILL" "CSA" in block letters with wavy borderline.

MONETARY SYSTEM
1 Dollar = 100 Cents

PATTERNS

(INCLUDING OFF METAL STRIKES)

KM#	Date	Mintage	Identification	Mkt Val
Pn2	1861	—	1/2 Dollar. 0.9000 Silver. Restrikes exist.	—
Pn1	1861	12	Cent. Copper-Nickel. Restrikes exist in other metals.	15,000

HAWAII

Hawaii, the 50th state, consists of eight main islands and numerous smaller islets of coral and volcanic origin. Situated in the central Pacific Ocean, 2400 miles from San Francisco, the Hawaiian archipelago has an area of 6,450 sq. mi. Capital: Honolulu. The principal sources of income are in order: tourism, defense, and agriculture.

The islands, originally populated by Polynesians from the Society Islands, were rediscovered by British navigator Capt. James Cook in 1778. He named them the Sandwich Islands. King Kamehameha I (the Great) united the islands under one kingdom which endured until 1893, when Queen Lilioukalani was deposed and a provisional government established. This was followed in 1894 by a republic which governed Hawaii until 1898, when the islands were ceded to the United States. Hawaii was organized as a territory in 1900, and attained statehood on August 21, 1959.

RULERS

Kamehameha I, 1795-1819
Kamehameha II, 1819-1824
Kamehameha III, 1825-1854
Kamehameha IV, 1854-1863
Kamehameha V, 1863-1872
Lunalilo, 1873-1874
Kalakaua, 1874-1891
Liliuokalani, 1891-1893
Provisional Government, 1893-1894
Republic, 1894-1898
Annexed to U.S., 1898-1900
Territory, 1900-1959

MONETARY SYSTEM

100 Hapa Haneri – Akahi Dala
100 Cents – 1 Dollar (Dala)

KINGDOM

STANDARD COINAGE

KM# 1a CENT
Copper

Date	Mintage	VG	F	VF	XF	Unc
1847 Plain 4, 13 berries (6 left, 7 right)	100,000	175	250	325	550	1,000

KM# 1b CENT
Copper

Date	Mintage	VG	F	VF	XF	Unc
1847 Plain 4, 15 berries (8 left, 7 right)	Inc. above	175	250	325	550	1,000

KM# 1f CENT
Copper

Date	Mintage	VG	F	VF	XF	Unc
1847 Plain 4, 15 berries (7 left, 8 right)	Inc. above	550	800	1,500	2,000	—

KM# 1c CENT
Copper

Date	Mintage	VG	F	VF	XF	Unc
1847 Plain 4, 17 berries (8 left, 9 right)	Inc. above	175	250	325	550	1,200

KM# 1d CENT
Copper

Date	Mintage	VG	F	VF	XF	Unc
1847 Crosslet 4, 15 berries (7 left, 8 right)	Inc. above	150	225	325	500	1,000

KM# 1e CENT
Copper

Date	Mintage	VG	F	VF	XF	Unc
1847 Crosslet 4, 18 berries (9 left, 9 right)	Inc. above	250	400	550	750	6,000

KM# 2 5 CENTS (Pattern)
Nickel

Date	Mintage	VG	F	VF	XF	Unc
1881	200	2,500	3,500	5,500	7,500	12,500

Note: All original specimens of this pattern were struck on thin nickel planchets, presumably in Paris and ave "MAILLECHORT" stamped on the edge. In the early 1900's, deceptive replicas of the issue were produced in Canada, on thick and thin nickel and aluminum, and thin copper planchets (thick about 2.7 to 3.1mm; thin about 1.4 to 1.7mm). The original patterns can be easily distiguished from the replicas, because on the former, a small cross surmounts the crown on the reverse; on the replicas the c

KM# 3 10 CENTS (Umi Keneta)
2.5000 g., 0.9000 Silver .0724 oz.

Date	Mintage	VG	F	VF	XF	Unc
1883	250,000	40.00	55.00	85.00	250	900
1883 Proof	26	Value: 7,500				

KM# 4a 1/8 DOLLAR (Hapawalu)
Copper **Note:** Pattern issue.

Date	Mintage	VG	F	VF	XF	Unc
1883 Proof	18	Value: 9,000				

KM# 4 1/8 DOLLAR (Hapawalu)
0.9000 Silver **Note:** Pattern issue.

Date	Mintage	VG	F	VF	XF	Unc
1883 Proof	20	Value: 25,000				

KM# 5 1/4 DOLLAR (Hapaha)
6.2200 g., 0.9000 Silver .1800 oz.

Date	Mintage	VG	F	VF	XF	Unc
1883	500,000	35.00	45.00	60.00	90.00	200
1883/1383	Inc. above	40.00	50.00	80.00	125	275
1883 Proof	26	Value: 7,500				

KM# 5a 1/4 DOLLAR (Hapaha)
Copper **Note:** Pattern issue.

Date	Mintage	VG	F	VF	XF	Unc
1883 Proof	18	Value: 5,000				

KM# 6 1/2 DOLLAR (Hapalua)
12.5000 g., 0.9000 Silver .3618 oz.

Date	Mintage	VG	F	VF	XF	Unc
1883	700,000	70.00	95.00	135	250	975
1883 Proof	26	Value: 8,000				

KM# 6a 1/2 DOLLAR (Hapalua)
Copper **Note:** Pattern issue.

Date	Mintage	VG	F	VF	XF	Unc
1883 Proof	18	Value: 6,000				

KM# 7 DOLLAR (Akahi Dala)
26.7300 g., 0.9000 Silver .7736 oz.

Date	Mintage	VG	F	VF	XF	Unc
1883	500,000	225	255	400	750	4,000
1883 Proof	26	Value: 9,000				

KM# 7a DOLLAR (Akahi Dala)
Copper **Note:** Pattern issue.

Date	Mintage	VG	F	VF	XF	Unc
1883 Proof	18	Value: 9,000				

Note: Official records indicate the following quantities of the above issues were redeemed and melted: KM#1 - 88,305; KM#3 - 79; KM#5 - 257,400; KM#6 - 612,245; KM#7 - 453,652. That leaves approximate net mintages of: KM#1 - 11,600; KM#3 - 250,000; KM#5 (regular date) - 202,600, (overdate) 40,000; KM#6 - 87,700; KM#7 - 46,300.

US TERRITORIAL GOLD

Territorial gold pieces (also referred to as "Private" and "Pioneer" gold) are those struck outside the U.S. Mint and not recognized as official issues by the federal government. The pieces so identified are of various shapes, denominations, and degrees of intrinsic value, and were locally required because of the remoteness of the early gold fields from a federal mint and/or an insufficient quantity of official coinage in frontier areas.

The legality of these privately issued pieces derives from the fact that federal law prior to 1864 prohibited a state from coining money, but did not specifically deny that right to an individual, providing that the privately issued coins did not closely resemble those of the United States.

In addition to coin-like gold pieces, the private minters of the gold rush days also issued gold in ingot and bar form. Ingots were intended for circulation and were cast in regular values and generally in large denominations. Bars represent a miner's deposit after it had been assayed, refined, cast into convenient form (generally rectangular), and stamped with the appropriate weight, fineness, and value. Although occasionally cast in even values for the convenience of banks, bars were more often of odd denomination, and when circulated were rounded off to the nearest figure. Ingots and bars are omitted from this listing.

Georgia and North Carolina

The first territorial gold pieces were struck in 1830 by **Templeton Reid**, a goldsmith and assayer who established a private mint at Gainesville, Georgia, at the time gold was being mined on a relatively large scale in Georgia and North Carolina. Reid's pieces were issued in denominations of $2.50, $5, and $10. Except for an undated variety of the $10 piece, all are dated 1830.

The southern Appalachians were also the scene of a private gold minting operation conducted by Christopher Bechtler Sr., his son August, and nephew Christopher Jr. The Bechtlers, a family of German metallurgists, established a mint at Rutherfordton, North Carolina, which produced territorial gold coins for a longer period than any other private mint in American history. Christopher Bechtler Sr. ran the Bechtler mint from July 1831 until his death in 1842, after which the mint was taken over by his son August who ran it until 1852.

The Bechtler coinage includes but 3 denominations -- $1, $2.50, and $5 - but they were issued in a wide variety of weights and sizes. The coinage is undated, except for 3 varieties of the $5 piece which carry the inscription "Aug. 1, 1834" to indicate that they conform to the new weight standard adopted by the U.S. Treasury for official gold coins. **Christopher Bechtler Sr.** produced $2.50 and $5 gold coins for Georgia, and $1, $2.50, and $5 coins for North Carolina. The dollar coins have the distinction of being the first gold coins of that denomination to be produced in the United States. While under the supervision of **August Bechtler**, the Bechtler mint issued $1 and $5 coins for North Carolina.

California

Norris, Grieg & Norris produced the first territorial gold coin struck in California, a $5 piece struck in 1849 at Benicia City, though it bears the imprint of San Francisco. The coining facility was owned by Thomas H. Norris, Charles Greig, and Hiram A. Norris, members of a New York engineering firm. A unique 1850 variety of this coin has the name STOCKTON beneath the date, instead of SAN FRANCISCO.

Early in 1849, John Little Moffat, a New York assayer, established an assay office at San Francisco in association with Joseph R. Curtis, Philo H. Perry, and Samuel Ward. The first issues of the **Moffat & Co.** assay office consisted of rectangular $16 ingots and assay bars of various and irregular denominations. In early August, the firm began striking $5 and $10 gold coins which resemble those of the U.S. Mint in design, but carry the legend S.M.V. (Standard Mint Value) CALIFORNIA GOLD on the reverse. Five-dollar pieces of the same design were also issued in 1850.

On Sept. 30, 1850, Congress directed the Secretary of the Treasury to establish an official Assay Office in California. Moffat & Co. obtained a contract to perform the duties of the U.S. Assay Office. **Augustus Humbert**, a New York watchcase maker, was appointed U.S. Assayer of Gold in California. Humbert stamped the first octagonal coin-ingots of the Provisional Government Mint on Jan. 31, 1851. The $50 pieces were accepted at par with standard U.S. gold coins, but were not officially recognized as coins. Officially, they were designated as "ingots." Colloquially, they were known as slugs, quintuple eagles, or 5-eagle pieces.

The $50 ingots failed to alleviate the need of California for gold coins. The banks regarded them as disadvantageous to their interests and utilized them only when compelled to do so by public need or convenience. Being of sound value, the ingots drove the overvalued $5, $10, and $20 territorial gold coins from circulation, bringing about a return to the use of gold dust for everyday transactions. Eventually, the slugs became so great a nuisance that they were discounted 3 percent when accepted. This unexpected turn of events forced Moffat & Co. to resume the issuing of $10 and $20 gold coins in 1852. The $10 piece was first issued with the Moffat & Co. imprint on Liberty's coronet, and later with the official imprint of Augustus Humbert on reverse. The $20 piece was issued with the Humbert imprint.

On Feb. 14, 1852, John L. Moffat withdrew from Moffat & Co. to enter the diving bell business, and Moffat & Co. was reorganized as the **United States Assay Office of Gold**, composed of Joseph R. Curtis, Philo H. Perry, and Samuel Ward. The U.S. Assay Office of Gold issued gold coins in denominations of $50 and $10 in 1852, and $20 and $10 in 1853. With the exception of the $50 slugs, they carry the imprint of the Assay Office on reverse. The .900 fine issues of this facility reflect an attempt to bring the issues of the U.S. Assay Office into conformity with the U.S. Mint standard.

The last territorial gold coins to bear the imprint of Moffat & Co. are $20 pieces issued in 1853, after the retirement of John L. Moffat. These coins do not carry a mark of fineness, and generally assay below the U.S. Mint standard.

Templeton Reid, previously mentioned in connection with the private gold issues of Georgia, moved his coining equipment to California when gold was discovered there, and in 1849 issued $10 and $25 gold pieces. No specimens are available to present-day collectors. The only known $10 piece is in the Smithsonian Collection. The only known specimen of the $25 piece was stolen from the U.S. Mint Cabinet Collection in 1858 and was never recovered.

Little is known of the origin and location of the **Cincinnati Mining & Trading Co.** It is believed that the firm was organized in the East and was forced to abandon most of its equipment while enroute to California. A few $5 and $10 gold coins were struck in 1849. Base metal counterfeits exist.

The **Massachusetts & California Co.** was organized in Northampton, Mass., in May 1849 by Josiah Hayden, S. S. Wells, Miles G. Moies, and others. Coining equipment was taken to San Francisco where $5 gold pieces were struck in 1849. The few pieces extant are heavily alloyed with copper.

Wright & Co., a brokerage firm located in Portsmouth Square, San Francisco, issued an undated $10 gold piece in the autumn of 1849 under the name of **Miners' Bank**. Unlike most territorial gold pieces, the Miners' Bank eagle was alloyed with copper. The coinage proved to be unpopular because of its copper-induced color and low intrinsic value. The firm was dissolved on Jan. 14, 1850.

In 1849, Dr. **J. S. Ormsby** and Major William M. Ormsby struck gold coins of $5 and $10 denominations at Sacramento under the name of Ormsby & Co. The coinage, which is identified by the initials J. S. O., is undated. Ormsby & Co. coinage was greatly over-valued, the eagle assaying at as little as $9.37.

The **Pacific Co.** of San Francisco issued $5 and $10 gold coins in 1849. The clouded story of this coinage is based on conjecture. It is believed that the well-struck pattern coins of this type were struck in the East by the Pacific Co. that organized in Boston and set sail for California on Feb. 20, 1849, and that the crudely hand-struck pieces were made by the jewelry firm of Broderick and Kohler after the dies passed into their possession. In any event, the intrinsic value of the initial coinage exceeded face value, but by the end of 1849, when they passed out of favor, the coins had been debased so flagrantly that the eagles assayed for as little as $7.86.

Dubosq & Co., a Philadelphia jewelry firm owned by Theodore Dubosq Sr. and Jr. and Henry Dubosq, took melting and coining equipment to San Francisco in 1849, and in 1850 issued $5 and $10 gold coins struck with dies allegedly made by U.S. Mint Engraver James B. Longacre. Dubosq & Co. coinage was immensely popular with the forty-niners because its intrinsic worth was in excess of face value.

The minting equipment of David C. Broderick and Frederick D. Kohler (see Pacific Co.) was acquired in May 1850 by San Francisco jewelers George C. Baldwin and Thomas S. Holman, who organized a private minting venture under the name of **Baldwin & Co**. The firm produced a $5 piece of Liberty Head design and a $10 piece with Horseman device in 1850. Liberty Head $10 and $20 pieces were coined in 1851. Baldwin & Co. produced the first $20 piece issued in California.

Schultz & Co. of San Francisco, a brass foundry located in the rear of the Baldwin & Co. establishment, and operated by Judge G. W. Schultz and William T. Garratt, issued $5 gold coins from early 1851 until April of that year. The inscription "SHULTS & CO." is a misspelling of SCHULTZ & CO.

Dunbar & Co. of San Francisco issued a $5 gold piece in 1851, after Edward E. Dunbar, owner of the Calif3ornia Bank in San Francisco, purchased the coining equipment of the defunct Baldwin & Co.

The San Francisco-based firm of **Wass, Molitor & Co.** was owned by 2 Hungarian exiles, Count S. C. Wass and A. P. Molitor, who initially founded the firm as a gold smelting and assaying plant. In response to a plea from the commercial community for small gold coins, Wass, Molitor & Co. issued $5 and $10 gold coins in 1852. The $5 piece was coined with small head and large head varieties, and the $10 piece with small head, large head, and small close-date varieties. The firm produced a second issue of gold coins in 1855, in denominations of $10, $20, and $50.

The U.S. Assay Office in California closed its doors on Dec. 14, 1853, to make way for the newly established San Francisco Branch Mint. The Mint, however, was unable to start immediate quantity production due to the lack of refining acids. During the interim, John G. Kellogg, a former employee of Moffat & Co., and John Glover Richter, a former assayer in the U.S. Assay Office, formed **Kellogg & Co.** for the purpose of supplying businessmen with urgently needed coinage. The firm produced $20 coins dated 1854 and 1855, after which Augustus Humbert replaced Richter and the enterprise reorganized as Kellogg & Humbert Melters, Assayers & Coiners. Kellogg & Humbert endured until 1860, but issued coins, $20 pieces, only in 1855.

Oregon

The Oregon Exchange Co., a private mint located at Oregon City, Oregon Territory, issued $5 and $10 pieces of local gold in 1849. The initials K., M., T., A., W. R. C. (G on the $5 piece), and S. on the obverse represent the eight founders of the **Oregon Exchange Co.**: William Kilborne, Theophilus Magruder, James Taylor, George Abernathy, William Willson, William Rector, John Campbell, and Noyes Smith. Campbell is erroneously represented by a G on the $5 coin. For unknown reasons, the initials A and W are omitted from the $10 piece. O.T. (Oregon Territory) is erroneously presented as T.O. on the $5 coin.

Utah

In 1849, the **Mormons** settled in the Great Salt Lake Valley of Utah and established the Deseret Mint in a small adobe building in Salt Lake City. Operating under the direct supervision of Brigham Young, the Deseret Mint issued $2.50, $5, $10, and $20 gold coins in 1849. Additional $5 pieces were struck in 1850 and 1860, the latter in a temporary mint set up in Barlow's jewelry shop. The Mormon $20 piece was the first of that denomination to be struck in the United States. The initials G.S.L.C.P.G. on Mormon coins denotes "Great Salt Lake City Pure Gold." It was later determined that the coinage was grossly deficient in value, mainly because no attempt was made to assay or refine the gold.

Colorado

The discovery of gold in Colorado Territory was accompanied by the inevitable need for coined money. Austin M. Clark, Milton E. Clark, and Emanuel H. Gruber, bankers of Leavenworth, Kansas, moved to Denver where they established a bank and issued $2.50, $5, $10, and $20 gold coins in 1860 and 1861. To protect the holder from loss by abrasion, **Clark, Gruber & Co.** made their coins slightly heavier than full value required. The 1860 issues carry the inscription PIKE'S PEAK GOLD on reverse. CLARK, GRUBER & CO. appears on the reverse of the 1861 issues, and PIKE'S PEAK on the coronet of Liberty. The government purchased the plant of Clark, Gruber & Co. in 1863 and operated it as a federal Assay Office until 1906.

In the summer of 1861, **John Parsons**, an assayer whose place of business was located in South Park at the Tarryall Mines, Colorado, issued undated gold coins in the denominations of $2.50 and $5. They, too, carry the inscription PIKE'S PEAK GOLD on reverse.

J. J. Conway & Co., bankers of Georgia Gulch, Colorado operated the Conway Mint for a short period in 1861. Undated gold coins in the denominations of $2.50, $5, and $10 were issued. A variety of the $5 coin does not carry the numeral 5 on reverse. The issues of the Conway Mint were highly regarded for their scrupulously maintained value.

NOTE: The above introduction is organized chronologically by geographical region. However, for ease of use the following listings appear alphabetically by state and issuer, except for small California gold.

Small California Gold

During the California gold rush a wide variety of U.S. and foreign coins were used for small change, but only limited quantities of these coins were available. Gold dust was in common use, although this offered the miner a relatively low value for his gold.

By 1852 California jewelers had begun to manufacture 25¢, 50¢ and $1 gold pieces in round and octagonal shapes. Makers included M. Deriberpe, Antoine Louis Nouizillet, Isadore Routhier, Robert B. Gray, Pierre Frontier, Eugene Deviercy, Herman J. Brand, and Herman and Jacob Levison. Reuben N. Hershfield and Noah Mitchell made their coins in Leavenworth, Kansas and most of their production was seized in August 1871. Herman Kroll made California gold coins in New York City in the 1890s. Only two or three of these companies were in production at any one time. Many varieties bear the makers initials. Frontier and his partners made most of the large Liberty Head, Eagle reverse, and Washington Head design types. Most of the small Liberty Head types were made first by Nouizillet and later by Gray and then the Levison brothers and lastly by the California Jewelry Co. Coins initialed "G.G." are apparently patterns made by Frontier and Deviercy for the New York based firm of Gaime, Guillemot & Co.

Most of the earlier coins were struck from gold alloys and had an intrinsic value of about 50-60 percent of face value. They were generally struck from partially hubbed dies and with reeded collars. A few issues were struck with a plain collar or a collar with reeding on only 7 of the 8 sides. Many issues are too poorly struck or too thin to have a clear and complete image of the collar. The later coins and some of the earlier coins were struck from laminated or plated gold planchets, or from gold plated silver planchets. Most of the last dates of issue are extremely thin and contain only token amounts of gold.

Circumstantial evidence exists that the coins issued through 1856 circulated as small change. The San Francisco mint was established in 1854, and by 1856 it had ramped up its production enough to satisfy the local need for small change. However, some evidence exists that these small gold coins may have continued to circulate on occasion through to 1871. After 1871, the gold content of the coins dramatically decreases and it is very unlikely that any of these last issues circulated.

Although the Private Coinages Act of 1864 outlawed all private coinage, this law was not enforced in California and production of small denominated gold continued through 1882. In the spring of 1883, Col. Henry Finnegass of the U.S. Secret Service halted production of the denominated private gold pieces. Nondenominated tokens (lacking DOLLARS, CENTS or the equivalent) were also made during this latter period, sometimes by the same manufacturing jeweler using the same obverse die and the same planchets as the small denomination gold coins. Production of these tokens continues to this day, with most issues made after the 1906 earthquake and fire being backdated to 1847-1865 and struck from brass or gold plated brass planchets.

Approximately 25,000 pieces of California small denomination gold coins are estimated to exist, in a total of over 500 varieties. A few varieties are undated, mostly gold rush era pieces; and a few of the issues are backdated, mostly those from the 1880's. This listing groups varieties together in easily identified categories. The prices quoted are for the most common variety in each group. UNC prices reflect the median auction prices realized of MS60 to MS62 graded coins. BU prices reflect the median auction prices realized of MS63 to MS64 graded coins. Pre-1871 true MS-65 coins are rare and sell for substantial premiums over the prices on this list. Post-1871 coins are rarely found with wear and often have a cameo proof appearance. Auction prices realized are highly volatile and it is not uncommon to find recent records of sales at twice or half of the values shown here. Many of the rarity estimates published in the 1980s and earlier have proven to be too high, so caution is advised when paying a premium for a rare variety. In addition, many varieties that have a refined appearance command higher prices than equivalent grade but scarcer varieties that have a more crude appearance.

Several counterfeits of California Fractional Gold coins exist. Beware of 1854 and 1858 dated round 1/2 dollars, and 1871 dated round dollars that have designs that do not match any of the published varieties. Beware of reeded edge Kroll coins being sold as originals (see the listings below).

For further information consult "California Pioneer Fractional Gold" by W. Breen and R.J. Gillio and "The Brasher Bulletin" the official newsletter of The Society of Private and Pioneer Numismatists.

FRACTIONAL AND SMALL SIZE GOLD COINAGE

CALIFORNIA

1/4 DOLLAR (OCTAGONAL)

KM# 1.1 Obverse: Large Liberty head **Reverse:** Value and date within beaded circle

Date	XF	AU	Unc	BU
1853	100.	150	200	300
1854	100.	150	250	350
1855	100.	150	250	350
1856	100.	150	260	375

KM# 1.10 Obverse: Oriental Liberty head above date **Reverse:** 1/4 CALDOLL withn wreath

Date	XF	AU	Unc	BU
1881	—	—	1,000	3,000

KM# 1.11 Obverse: Large Liberty head above 1872 **Reverse:** Value and 1871 within wreath

Date	XF	AU	Unc	BU
1872-71	—	—	1,000	3,000

KM# 1.2 Reverse: Value and date within wreath

Date	XF	AU	Unc	BU
1859	65.	110	200	450
1864	75.	125	250	400
1866	75.	125	250	400
1867	65.	110	250	400
1868	70.	125	200	350
1869	70.	125	200	350
1870	65.	110	200	350
1871	65.	110	200	350

KM# 1.3 Obverse: Large Liberty head above date **Reverse:** Value and CAL within wreath

Date	XF	AU	Unc	BU
1872	65.	110	250	400
1873	50.	85.00	175	300

KM# 1.4 Obverse: Small Liberty head **Reverse:** Value and date within beaded circle

Date	XF	AU	Unc	BU
1853	125.	250	325	425

KM# 1.5 Obverse: Small Liberty head above date **Reverse:** Value within wreath

Date	XF	AU	Unc	BU
1854	125.	250	300	350

KM# 1.6 Obverse: Small Liberty head **Reverse:** Value and date within wreath

Date	XF	AU	Unc	BU
1855	—	—	—	—
1856	—	—	—	—
1857 Plain edge	—	—	—	—
Note: Kroll type date				
1857 Reeded edge	—	—	—	—
Note: Kroll type date				
1860	—	—	—	—
1870	—	—	—	—

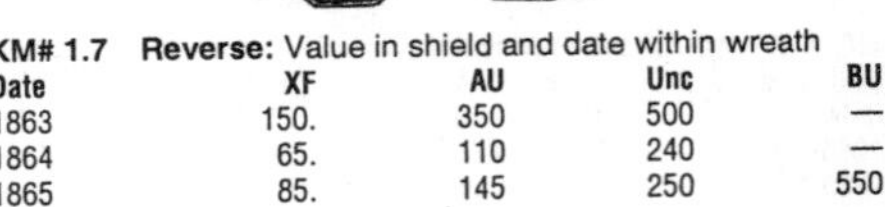

KM# 1.7 Reverse: Value in shield and date within wreath

Date	XF	AU	Unc	BU
1863	150.	350	500	—
1864	65.	110	240	—
1865	85.	145	250	550

Date	XF	AU	Unc	BU
1866	85.	145	250	400
1867	75.	125	200	400
1868	75.	125	200	—
1869	75.	125	190	300
1870	75.	125	200	350

KM# 1.8 Obverse: Small Liberty head above date **Reverse:** Value and CAL within wreath

Date	XF	AU	Unc	BU
1870	65.	110	200	300
1871	65.	110	175	250
1871	65.	110	175	250
1873	175.	250	400	—
1874	65.	110	175	275
1875/3	350.	700	1,000	—
1876	65.	110	200	300

KM# 1.9 Obverse: Goofy Liberty head **Reverse:** Value and date within wreath

Date	XF	AU	Unc	BU
1870	85.	145	200	300

KM# 2.1 Obverse: Large Indian head above date **Reverse:** Value within wreath

Date	XF	AU	Unc	BU
1852	100.	175	240	450
Note: Back dated issue				
1868	100.	175	240	450
Note: Back dated issue				
1874	85.	160	220	400
Note: Back dated issue				
1876	85.	160	220	400
1880	75.	150	200	350
1881	85.	160	220	400

KM# 2.2 Reverse: Value and CAL within wreath

Date	XF	AU	Unc	BU
1872	65.	110	210	300
1873/2	200.	350	550	800
1873	90.	160	250	350
1874	65.	110	210	300
1875	90.	160	250	350
1876	90.	160	250	350

KM# 2.3 Obverse: Small indian head above date

Date	XF	AU	Unc	BU
1875	90.	160	250	350
1876	90.	160	250	500
1881	—	—	500	1,100

KM# 2.4 Obverse: Aztec indian head above date

Date	XF	AU	Unc	BU
1880	65.	110	210	300

KM# 2.6 Obverse: Dumb indian head above date **Reverse:** Value and CAL within wreath

Date	XF	AU	Unc	BU
1881	—	—	650	—

KM# 2.7 Obverse: Young indian head above date **Reverse:** Value within wreath

Date	XF	AU	Unc	BU
1881	—	—	450	—

KM# 2.8 Reverse: Value and CAL within wreath

Date	XF	AU	Unc	BU
1882	—	—	500	750

KM# 3 Obverse: Washington head above date

Date	XF	AU	Unc	BU
1872	—	—	400	950

1/4 DOLLAR (ROUND)

KM# 4 Obverse: Defiant eagle above date **Reverse:** 25¢ within wreath

Date	XF	AU	Unc	BU
1854	11,000.	22,000	33,000	44,000

KM# 5.1 Obverse: Large Liberty head **Reverse:** Value and date within wreath

Date	XF	AU	Unc	BU
1853	400.	700	1,000	1,500
1854	150.	250	400	600
1859	70.	120	225	275
1865	90.	160	250	350
1866	—	—	200	300
1867	—	—	200	300
1868	—	—	200	300
1870	—	—	200	300
1871	—	—	200	300

KM# 5.2 Obverse: Large Liberty head above date **Reverse:** Value and CAL within wreath

Date	XF	AU	Unc	BU
1871	—	—	200	275
1872	—	—	200	275
1873	—	—	180	260

KM# 5.3 Obverse: Small Liberty head **Reverse:** 25¢ in wreath

Date	XF	AU	Unc	BU
	1,000.	1,650	2,450	3,500

KM# 5.4 Reverse: 1/4 DOLL. or DOLLAR and date in wreath

Date	XF	AU	Unc	BU
	90.	150	200	350

Note: Rare counterfeit exists

KM# 5.5 Reverse: Value in shield and date within wreath

Date	XF	AU	Unc	BU
1863	80.	160	200	—

KM# 5.6 Obverse: Small Liberty head above date **Reverse:** Value and CAL within wreath

Date	XF	AU	Unc	BU
	100.	175	500	—
1870	80.	160	200	250
1871	80.	160	200	250
1871	—	—	210	350
1873	—	—	300	500
1874	—	—	300	500
1875	—	—	250	475
1876	—	—	225	450

KM# 5.7 Obverse: Goofy Liberty head **Reverse:** Value and date within wreath

Date	XF	AU	Unc	BU
1870	110.	160	220	250

KM# 5.8 Obverse: Liberty head with H and date below **Reverse:** Value and CAL in wreath

Date	XF	AU	Unc	BU
1871	80.	125	160	250

KM# 6.1 Obverse: Large indian head above date **Reverse:** Value within wreath

Date	XF	AU	Unc	BU
1852	—	—	200	300
Note: Back dated issue				
1868	—	—	250	375
Note: Back dated issue				
1874	—	—	190	275
Note: Back dated issue				
1876	—	—	200	325
1878/6	—	—	200	300
1880	—	—	200	325
1881	—	—	200	325

KM# 6.2 Reverse: Value and CAL within wreath

Date	XF	AU	Unc	BU
1872/1	—	—	200	300
1873	—	—	180	275
1874	—	—	180	275
1875	—	—	200	300
1876	—	—	200	300

KM# 6.3 Obverse: Small indian head above date

Date	XF	AU	Unc	BU
1875	75.	125	250	400
1876	65.	110	200	350
1881 Rare	—	—	—	—

KM# 6.4 Obverse: Young indian head above date

Date	XF	AU	Unc	BU
1882	400.	725	1,225	1,750

KM# 7 Obverse: Washington head above date

Date	XF	AU	Unc	BU
1872	—	—	600	900

1/2 DOLLAR (OCTAGONAL)

KM# 8.1 Obverse: Liberty head above date **Reverse:** 1/2 DOLLAR in beaded circle, CALIFORNIA GOLD around circle

Date	XF	AU	Unc	BU
1853	165.	280	350	450
1854	110.	225	285	350
Note: Rare counterfeit exists				
1854	165.	280	350	450
1856	165.	285	365	450

KM# 8.10 Obverse: Goofy Liberty head **Reverse:** Value and date within wreath

Date	XF	AU	Unc	BU
1870	55.	110	200	300

KM# 8.11 Obverse: Oriental Liberty head above date **Reverse:** 1/2 CALDOLL within wreath

Date	XF	AU	Unc	BU
1881	250.	450	750	1,150

KM# 8.2 Reverse: Small eagle with rays ("peacock")

Date	XF	AU	Unc	BU
1853	400.	600	1,000	1,500

KM# 8.3 Obverse: Large Liberty head **Reverse:** Large eagle with date

Date	XF	AU	Unc	BU
1853	750.	1,350	2,250	—

KM# 8.4 **Reverse:** Value and date within wreath

Date	XF	AU	Unc	BU
1859	—	130	200	275
1866	—	200	300	400
1867	—	130	225	300
1868	—	130	225	300
1869	—	130	250	350
1870	—	130	250	350
1871	—	130	225	300

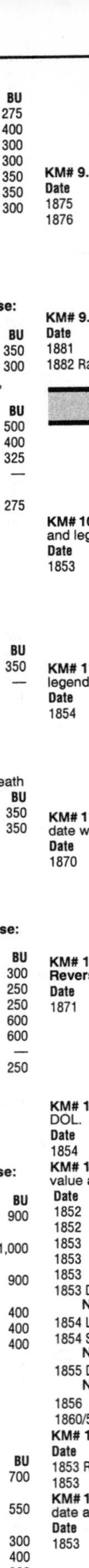

KM# 8.5 **Obverse:** Large Liberty head above date **Reverse:** Value and CAL within wreath

Date	XF	AU	Unc	BU
1872	—	130	250	350
1873	—	130	225	300

KM# 8.6 **Obverse:** Liberty head **Reverse:** Date in wreath, HALF DOL. CALIFORNIA GOLD around wreath

Date	XF	AU	Unc	BU
1854	100.	250	350	500
1855	90.	200	300	400
1856	90.	200	265	325
1856	165.	350	1,100	—
Note: Back date issue struck in 1864				
1868	60.	110	185	275
Note: Kroll type date				

KM# 8.7 **Obverse:** Small Liberty head **Reverse:** HALF DOLLAR and date in wreath

Date	XF	AU	Unc	BU
1864	—	175	275	350
1870	—	175	275	—

KM# 8.8 **Reverse:** CAL. GOLD HALF DOL and date in wreath

Date	XF	AU	Unc	BU
1869	—	175	200	350
1870	—	175	200	350

KM# 8.9 **Obverse:** Small Liberty head above date **Reverse:** Value and CAL in wreath

Date	XF	AU	Unc	BU
1870	55.	110	200	300
1871	55.	110	200	250
1871	55.	100.00	165	250
1873	85.	200	300	600
1874	85.	200	300	600
1875	250.	475	1,000	—
1876	55.	110	200	250

KM# 9.1 **Obverse:** Large indian head above date **Reverse:** Value within wreath

Date	XF	AU	Unc	BU
1852	—	—	500	900
Note: Back dated issue				
1868	—	—	650	1,000
Note: Back dated issue				
1874	—	175	500	900
Note: Back dated issue				
1876	—	—	300	400
1880	—	—	300	400
1881	—	—	300	400

KM# 9.2 **Reverse:** Value and CAL within wreath

Date	XF	AU	Unc	BU
1852	—	—	450	700
Note: Back dated issue				
1868	—	—	260	550
Note: Back dated issue				
1872	—	—	200	300
1873/2	—	—	200	400
1873	—	—	200	300
1874/3	—	—	250	350
1874	—	—	200	300
1875	—	—	250	425
1876	—	—	250	400
1878/6	—	—	250	400
1880	—	—	500	1,000
1881	—	—	250	400

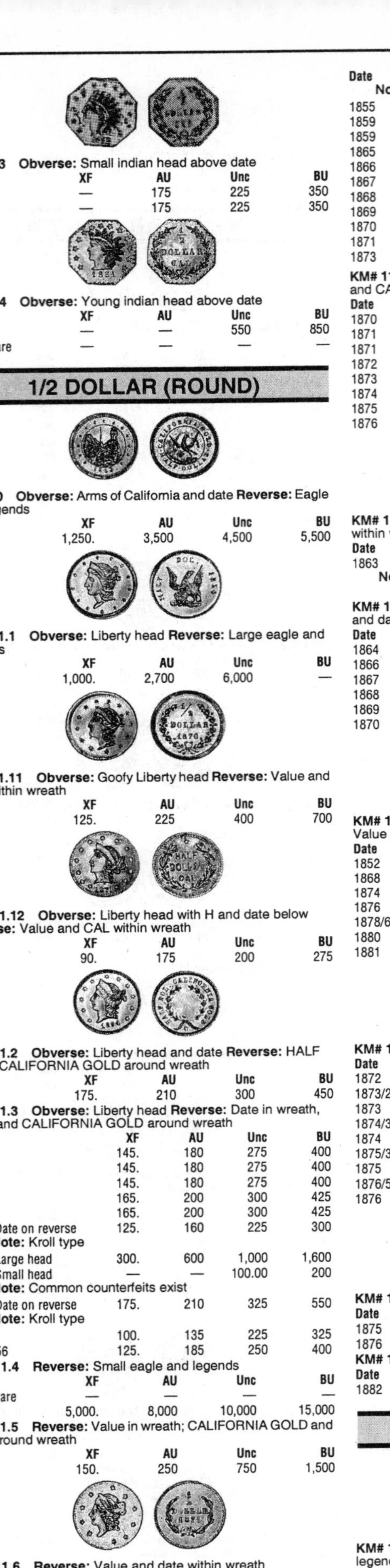

KM# 9.3 **Obverse:** Small indian head above date

Date	XF	AU	Unc	BU
1875	—	175	225	350
1876	—	175	225	350

KM# 9.4 **Obverse:** Young indian head above date

Date	XF	AU	Unc	BU
1881	—	—	550	850
1882 Rare	—	—	—	—

1/2 DOLLAR (ROUND)

KM# 10 **Obverse:** Arms of California and date **Reverse:** Eagle and legends

Date	XF	AU	Unc	BU
1853	1,250.	3,500	4,500	5,500

KM# 11.1 **Obverse:** Liberty head **Reverse:** Large eagle and legends

Date	XF	AU	Unc	BU
1854	1,000.	2,700	6,000	—

KM# 11.11 **Obverse:** Goofy Liberty head **Reverse:** Value and date within wreath

Date	XF	AU	Unc	BU
1870	125.	225	400	700

KM# 11.12 **Obverse:** Liberty head with H and date below **Reverse:** Value and CAL within wreath

Date	XF	AU	Unc	BU
1871	90.	175	200	275

KM# 11.2 **Obverse:** Liberty head and date **Reverse:** HALF DOL. CALIFORNIA GOLD around wreath

Date	XF	AU	Unc	BU
1854	175.	210	300	450

KM# 11.3 **Obverse:** Liberty head **Reverse:** Date in wreath, value and CALIFORNIA GOLD around wreath

Date	XF	AU	Unc	BU
1852	145.	180	275	400
1852	145.	180	275	400
1853	145.	180	275	400
1853	165.	200	300	425
1853	165.	200	300	425
1853 Date on reverse	125.	160	225	300
Note: Kroll type				
1854 Large head	300.	600	1,000	1,600
1854 Small head	—	—	100.00	200
Note: Common counterfeits exist				
1855 Date on reverse	175.	210	325	550
Note: Kroll type				
1856	100.	135	225	325
1860/56	125.	185	250	400

KM# 11.4 **Reverse:** Small eagle and legends

Date	XF	AU	Unc	BU
1853 Rare	—	—	—	—
1853	5,000.	8,000	10,000	15,000

KM# 11.5 **Reverse:** Value in wreath; CALIFORNIA GOLD and date around wreath

Date	XF	AU	Unc	BU
1853	150.	250	750	1,500

KM# 11.6 **Reverse:** Value and date within wreath

Date	XF	AU	Unc	BU
Rare	—	—	—	—
1854	850.	2,000	—	—
Note: Common counterfeit without FD beneath truncation				
1855	155.	300	450	600
1859	140.	250	350	500
1859	—	150	175	250
1865	—	150	225	350
1866	—	165	250	400
1867	—	150	225	350
1868	—	165	250	400
1869	—	165	250	400
1870	—	132	225	350
1871	—	125	200	300
1873	—	170	250	450

KM# 11.7 **Obverse:** Liberty head above date **Reverse:** Value and CAL within wreath

Date	XF	AU	Unc	BU
1870	—	125	250	400
1871	—	125	250	400
1871	—	200	400	—
1872	—	—	250	400
1873	—	200	400	1,000
1874	—	125	250	750
1875	—	125	300	800
1876	—	100.00	250	—

KM# 11.8 **Obverse:** Liberty head **Reverse:** Value and date within wreath, CALIFORNIA GOLD outside

Date	XF	AU	Unc	BU
1863	265.	425	675	950
Note: This issue is a rare Kroll type. All 1858 dates of this type are counterfeits				

KM# 11.9 **Obverse:** Liberty head **Reverse:** HALF DOLLAR and date in wreath

Date	XF	AU	Unc	BU
1864	100.	165	250	350
1866	200.	330	500	700
1867	100.	165	250	350
1868	100.	165	250	350
1869	125.	200	300	—
1870	—	200	350	—

KM# 12.1 **Obverse:** Large indian head above date **Reverse:** Value within wreath

Date	XF	AU	Unc	BU
1852	—	—	350	675
1868	—	—	300	600
1874	—	—	300	600
1876	—	—	200	250
1878/6	—	—	300	450
1880	—	—	250	400
1881	—	—	250	400

KM# 12.2 **Reverse:** Value and CAL within wreath

Date	XF	AU	Unc	BU
1872	—	—	200	300
1873/2	—	—	350	650
1873	—	—	200	300
1874/3	—	—	300	450
1874	—	—	200	300
1875/3	—	—	200	300
1875	—	—	300	500
1876/5	—	—	200	300
1876	—	—	340	600

KM# 12.3 **Obverse:** Small indian head above date

Date	XF	AU	Unc	BU
1875	100.	165	250	450
1876	75.	100.00	200	300

KM# 12.4 **Obverse:** Young indian head above date

Date	XF	AU	Unc	BU
1882	—	350	850	—

DOLLAR (OCTAGONAL)

KM# 13.1 **Obverse:** Liberty head **Reverse:** Large eagle and legends

Date	XF	AU	Unc	BU
	1,000.	1,500	2,000	4,000
1853	3,000.	3,500	5,500	—

Date	XF	AU	Unc	BU
1854	1,000.	1,500	2,000	4,000

KM# 13.2 Reverse: Value and date in beaded circle; CALIFORNIA GOLD, initials around circle

Date	XF	AU	Unc	BU
1853	275.	500	750	1,100
1853	450.	800	1,100	—
1853	300.	450	900	—
1853	275.	450	750	1,200
1854	450.	800	1,100	—
1854	300.	500	900	1,600
1855	350.	600	900	—
1856	2,100.	3,300	5,000	—
1863 Reeded edge	150.	225	325	500
1863 Plain edge	—	—	40.00	80.00

Note: Reeded edge 1863 dates are Kroll types, while plain edge examples are Kroll restrikes

KM# 13.3 Reverse: Value and date inside wreath; legends outside wreath

Date	XF	AU	Unc	BU
1854 Rare	—	—	—	—

Note: Bowers and Marena sale 5-99, XF $9,775

Date	XF	AU	Unc	BU
1854	275.	500	750	1,100
1855	275.	500	750	1,100
1858	150.	250	350	600

Note: 1858 dates are Kroll types

Date	XF	AU	Unc	BU
1859	1,900.	—	—	—
1860	—	450	750	100.00
1868	—	450	750	1,100
1869	—	350	6,600	900
1870	—	350	600	900
1871	—	300	400	850

KM# 13.5 Obverse: Liberty head above date **Reverse:** Value and date within wreath; CALIFORNIA GOLD around wreath

Date	XF	AU	Unc	BU
1871	—	350	600	900
1874	—	3,000	—	—
1875	—	3,000	—	—
1876	—	2,000	—	—

KM# 14.1 Obverse: Large indian head above date **Reverse:** 1 DOLLAR inside wreath; CALIFORNIA GOLD around wreath

Date	XF	AU	Unc	BU
1872	—	350	600	900
1873/2	—	400	700	1,100
1873	—	600	750	—
1874	—	525	850	1,300
1875	—	475	600	1,000
1876/5	—	700	1,000	1,300

KM# 14.2 Obverse: Small indian head above date **Reverse:** 1 DOLLAR CAL inside wreath

Date	XF	AU	Unc	BU
1875	700.	900	1,200	—
1876	—	1,000	1,400	—

KM# 14.3 Reverse: 1 DOLLAR inside wreath; CALIFORNIA GOLD around wreath

Date	XF	AU	Unc	BU
1876	—	500	750	—

DOLLAR (ROUND)

KM# 15.1 Obverse: Liberty head **Reverse:** Large eagle and legends

Date	XF	AU	Unc	BU
1853 Rare	—	—	—	—

Note: Superior sale Sept. 1987 MS-63 $35,200

KM# 15.2 Reverse: Value and date inside wreath; CALIFORNIA GOLD around wreath

Date	XF	AU	Unc	BU
1854	3,000.	5,500	—	—
1854	5,000.	7,500	—	—
1854 Rare	—	—	—	—

Note: Superior sale Sept. 1988 Fine $13,200

Date	XF	AU	Unc	BU
1857 2 known	—	—	—	—
1870	500.	1,250	2,000	—

Date	XF	AU	Unc	BU
1871	850.	1,450	2,500	—

Note: Coutnerfeits reported

KM# 15.3 Obverse: Liberty head above date **Reverse:** Value inside wreath; CALIFORNIA GOLD around wreath

Date	XF	AU	Unc	BU
1870	500.	1,000	1,400	2,000
1871	500.	1,000	1,400	2,000

KM# 15.4 Obverse: Goofy Liberty head **Reverse:** Value and date inside wreath; CALIFORNIA GOLD around wreath

Date	XF	AU	Unc	BU
1870	400.	1,000	1,500	—

KM# 16 Obverse: Large indian head above date **Reverse:** Value inside wreath; CALIFORNIA GOLD outside wreath

Date	XF	AU	Unc	BU
1872	650.	1,100	1,800	2,400

U.S. TERRITORIAL GOLD COINAGE

CALIFORNIA

BALDWIN & COMPANY

5 DOLLARS

KM# 17

Date	XF	AU	Unc	BU
1850	10,000.	—	25,000	—

10 DOLLARS

KM# 18

Date	XF	AU	Unc	BU
1850	48,500.	—	85,000	—

Note: Bass Sale May 2000, MS-64 $149,500

KM# 19

Date	Fine	VF	XF	Unc
1851	9,000	14,500	28,500.	50,000

20 DOLLARS

KM# 20

Date	Fine	VF	XF	Unc
1851	—	—	—	—

Note: Stack's Superior Sale Dec. 1988, XF-40 $52,800; Beware of copies cast in base metals

BLAKE & COMPANY

20 DOLLARS

KM# 21

Date	Fine	VF	XF	Unc
1855 Rare	—	—	—	—

Note: Many modern copies exist

J. H. BOWIE

5 DOLLARS

KM# 22

Date	Fine	VF	XF	Unc
1849 Rare	—	—	—	—

Note: Americana Sale Jan. 2001, AU-58 $253,000

CINCINNATI MINING AND TRADING COMPANY

5 DOLLARS

KM# 23

Date	Fine	VF	XF	Unc
1849 Rare	—	—	—	—

10 DOLLARS

KM# 24

Date	Fine	VF	XF	Unc
1849 Rare	—	—	—	—

Note: Brand Sale 1984, XF $104,500

DUBOSQ & COMPANY

5 DOLLARS

KM# 26

Date	Fine	VF	XF	Unc
1850	25,000	42,500	—	—

10 DOLLARS

KM# 27

Date	Fine	VF	XF	Unc
1850	25,000	45,000	65,000.	—

DUNBAR & COMPANY

5 DOLLARS

KM# 28

Date	Fine	VF	XF	Unc
1851	22,500	32,500	55,000.	—

Note: Spink & Son Sale 1988, AU $62,000

AUGUSTUS HUMBERT / UNITED STATES ASSAYER

10 DOLLARS

KM# 29.1 **Note:** AUGUSTUS HUMBERT imprint.

Date	Fine	VF	XF	Unc
1852/1	2,000	3,500	5,500.	15,000
1852	1,500	2,500	4,750.	11,500

KM# 29.2 **Note:** Error: IINITED.

Date	Fine	VF	XF	Unc
1852/1 Rare	—	—	—	—
1852 Rare	—	—	—	—

20 DOLLARS

KM# 30

Date	Fine	VF	XF	Unc
1852/1	4,500	6,000	9,500.	—

Note: Mory Sale June 2000, AU-53 $13,800; Garrett Sale Mar. 1980, Humberts Proof $325,000; Private Sale May 1989, Humberts Proof (PCGS Pr-65) $1,350,000; California Sale Oct. 2000, Humberts Proof (PCGS Pr-65) $552,000

50 DOLLARS

KM# 31.1 **Obverse:** 50 D C 880 THOUS, eagle **Reverse:** 50 in center

Date	Fine	VF	XF	Unc
1851	9,500	12,000	22,000.	—

KM# 31.1a **Obverse:** 887 THOUS

Date	Fine	VF	XF	Unc
1851	6,000	9,000	17,500.	37,500

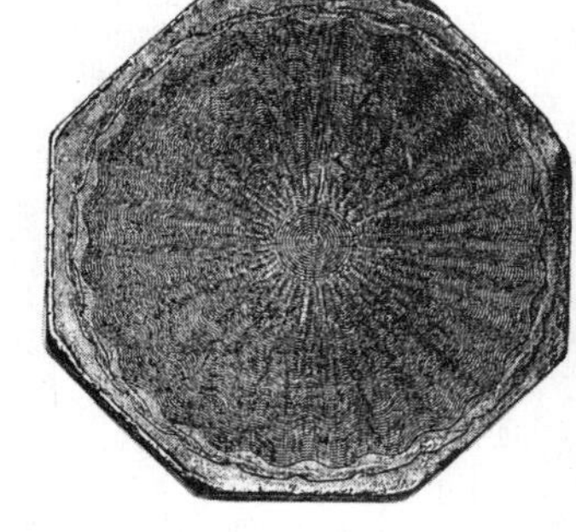

KM# 31.2 **Obverse:** 880 THOUS **Reverse:** Without 50

Date	Fine	VF	XF	Unc
1851	5,000	8,000	16,500.	35,500

KM# 31.2a **Obverse:** 887 THOUS

Date	Fine	VF	XF	Unc
1851	—	14,500	25,000.	—

KM# 31.3 **Note:** ASSAYER inverted.

Date	Fine	VF	XF	Unc
1851 Unique	—	—	—	—

KM# 31.4 **Obverse:** 880 THOUS **Reverse:** Rays from central star

Date	Fine	VF	XF	Unc
1851 Unique	—	—	—	—

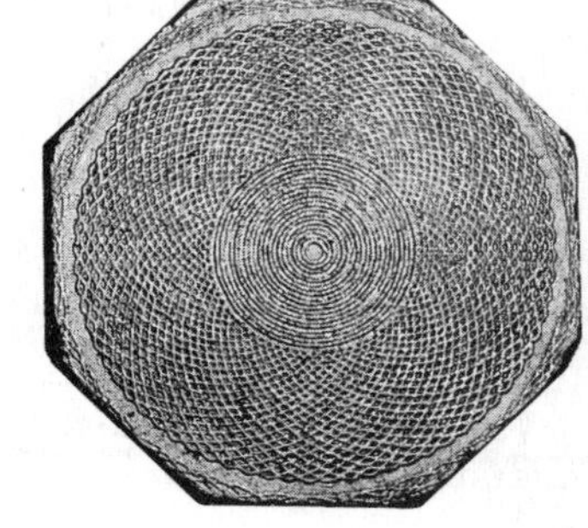

KM# 32.1 **Obverse:** 880 THOUS **Reverse:** "Target"

Date	Fine	VF	XF	Unc
1851	5,000	8,000	16,000.	35,000

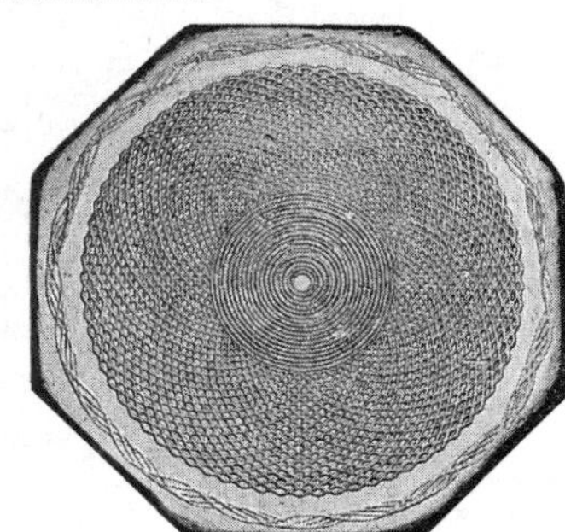

KM# 32.1a Obverse: 887 THOUS

Date	Fine	VF	XF	Unc
1851	5,000	8,000	16,000.	35,000

Note: Garrett Sale March 1980, Humberts Proof $500,000

KM# 32.2 Reverse: Small design

Date	Fine	VF	XF	Unc
1851	5,000	8,000	16,000.	—
1852	4,500	7,500	18,500.	40,000

Note: Bloomfield Sale December 1996, BU $159,500

KELLOGG & COMPANY

20 DOLLARS

KM# 33.1 Obverse: Thick date **Reverse:** Short arrows

Date	Fine	VF	XF	Unc
1854	1,200	2,000	4,000.	17,500

KM# 33.2 Obverse: Medium date

Date	Fine	VF	XF	Unc
1854	1,200	2,000	4,000.	17,500

KM# 33.3 Obverse: Thin date

Date	Fine	VF	XF	Unc
1854	1,200	2,000	4,000.	17,500

KM# 33.4 Reverse: Long arrows

Date	Fine	VF	XF	Unc
1854	1,200	2,000	4,000.	17,500
1855	1,200	2,250	4,250.	18,500

Note: Garrett Sale March 1980 Proof $230,000

KM# 33.5 Reverse: Medium arrows

Date	Fine	VF	XF	Unc
1855	1,200	2,250	4,250.	18,500

KM# 33.6 Reverse: Short arrows

Date	Fine	VF	XF	Unc
1855	1,200	2,250	4,250.	18,500

50 DOLLARS

KM# 34

Date	Fine	VF	XF	Unc
1855	—	—	—	—

Note: Heritage ANA Sale August 1977, Proof $156,500

MASSACHUSETTES AND CALIFORNIA COMPANY

5 DOLLARS

KM# 35

Date	Fine	VF	XF	Unc
1849 Rare Proof	40,000	65,000	—	—

MINERS BANK

10 DOLLARS

KM# 36

Date	Fine	VF	XF	Unc
(1849)	—	8,500	17,500.	45,000

Note: Garrett Sale March 1980, MS-65 $135,000

KM# 36a

Date	Fine	VF	XF	Unc
(1849)	—	—	—	—

Note: Rare, as most specimens have heavy copper alloy

MOFFAT & COMPANY

5 DOLLARS

KM# 37.1

Date	Fine	VF	XF	Unc
1849	1,000	1,500	3,500.	12,000

KM# 37.2 Reverse: Die break at DOL

Date	Fine	VF	XF	Unc
1849	1,000	1,500	3,500.	12,000

KM# 37.3 Reverse: Die break on shield

Date	Fine	VF	XF	Unc
1849	1,000	1,500	3,500.	12,000

KM# 37.4 Reverse: Small letters

Date	Fine	VF	XF	Unc
1850	1,100	1,650	4,200.	14,000

KM# 37.5 Reverse: Large letters

Date	Fine	VF	XF	Unc
1850	1,100	1,650	4,200.	14,000

Note: Garrett Sale March 1980, MS-60 $21,000

10 DOLLARS

KM# 38.1 Reverse: Value: TEN DOL., arrow below period

Date	Fine	VF	XF	Unc
1849	1,650	3,500	6,000.	15,000

KM# 38.2 Reverse: Arrow above period

Date	Fine	VF	XF	Unc
1849	1,650	3,500	6,000.	15,000

KM# 38.3 Reverse: Value: TEN D., large letters

Date	Fine	VF	XF	Unc
1849	2,250	5,000	7,500.	16,500

KM# 38.4 Reverse: Small letters

Date	Fine	VF	XF	Unc
1849	—	5,000	7,500.	16,500

KM# 39.1 **Note:** MOFFAT & CO. imprint, wide date

Date	Fine	VF	XF	Unc
1852	2,500	5,500	10,000.	20,000

KM# 39.2 **Note:** Close date. Struck by Augustus Humbert.

Date	Fine	VF	XF	Unc
1852	2,000	4,250	9,000.	18,500

20 DOLLARS

KM# 40 **Note:** Struck by Curtis, Perry, & Ward.

Date	Fine	VF	XF	Unc
1853	2,150	3,750	6,000.	16,500

NORRIS, GREIG, & NORRIS

HALF EAGLE

KM# 41.1 **Reverse:** Period after ALLOY

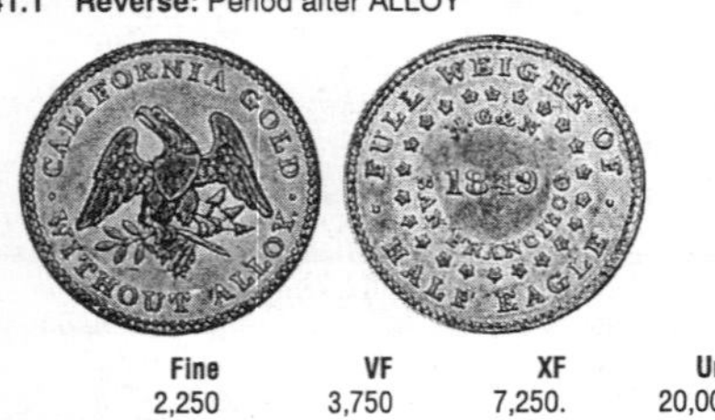

Date	Fine	VF	XF	Unc
1849	2,250	3,750	7,250.	20,000

KM# 41.2 **Reverse:** Without period after ALLOY

Date	Fine	VF	XF	Unc
1849	2,250	3,750	7,250.	20,000

KM# 41.3 **Reverse:** Period after ALLOY

Date	Fine	VF	XF	Unc
1849	1,750	3,000	6,750.	20,000

KM# 41.4 **Reverse:** Without period after ALLOY

Date	Fine	VF	XF	Unc
1849	1,750	3,000	6,750.	20,000

KM# 42 **Obverse:** STOCKTON beneath date

Date	Fine	VF	XF	Unc
1850 Unique	—	—	—	—

J. S. ORMSBY

5 DOLLARS

KM# 43.1

Date	Fine	VF	XF	Unc
(1849) Unique	—	—	—	—

KM# 43.2

Date	Fine	VF	XF	Unc
(1849) Unique	—	—	—	—

Note: Superior Auction 1989, VF $137,500

10 DOLLARS

KM# 44

Date	Fine	VF	XF	Unc
(1849) Rare	—	—	—	—

Note: Garrett Sale March 1980, F-12 $100,000; Ariagno Sale June 1999, AU-50 $145,000

PACIFIC COMPANY

5 DOLLARS

KM# 45

Date	Fine	VF	XF	Unc
1849 Rare	—	—	—	—

Note: Garrett Sale March 1980, VF-30 $180,000

10 DOLLARS

KM# 46.1

Date	Fine	VF	XF	Unc
1849 Rare	—	—	—	—

Note: Waldorf Sale 1964, $24,000

KM# 46.2

Date	Fine	VF	XF	Unc
1849 Rare	—	—	—	—

1 DOLLAR

KM# A45

Date	Fine	VF	XF	Unc
(1849) Unique	—	—	—	—

Note: Mory Sale June 2000, EF-40 $57,500

TEMPLETON REID

10 DOLLARS

KM# 47

Date	Fine	VF	XF	Unc
1849 Unique	—	—	—	—

20 DOLLARS

KM# 48

Date	Fine	VF	XF	Unc
1849 Unknown	—	—	—	—

Note: Only known specimen of above stolen from U.S. Mint in 1858 and never recovered; also see listings under Georgia

SCHULTZ & COMPANY

5 DOLLARS

KM# 49

Date	Fine	VF	XF	Unc
1851	—	36,800	50,000.	—

UNITED STATES ASSAY OFFICE OF GOLD

10 DOLLARS

KM# 50.1 **Obverse:** TEN DOLS 884 THOUS **Reverse:** O of OFFICE below I of UNITED

Date	Fine	VF	XF	Unc
1852	—	—	—	—

Note: Garrett Sale March 1980, MS-60 $18,000

KM# 51.2 **Reverse:** O below N, strong beads

Date	Fine	VF	XF	Unc
1852	1,750	2,500	3,850.	9,500

KM# 51.3 **Reverse:** Weak beads

Date	Fine	VF	XF	Unc
1852	1,750	2,500	3,850.	9,500

KM# 52 **Obverse:** TEN D, 884 THOUS

Date	Fine	VF	XF	Unc
1853	5,000	7,750	14,500.	—

KM# 52a **Obverse:** 900 THOUS

Date	Fine	VF	XF	Unc
1853	2,700	4,200	6,500.	—

Note: Garrett Sale March 1980, MS-60 $35,000

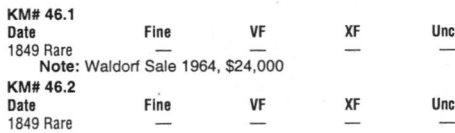

20 DOLLARS

KM# 53 Obverse: 884/880 THOUS

Date	Fine	VF	XF	Unc
1853	8,500	12,500	17,500.	23,500

KM# 53a Obverse: 900/880 THOUS

Date	Fine	VF	XF	Unc
1853	1,550	2,750	4,250.	10,000

Note: 1853 Liberty Head listed under Moffat & Company

50 DOLLARS

KM# 54 Obverse: 887 THOUS

Date	Fine	VF	XF	Unc
1852	4,000	6,500	13,500.	26,500

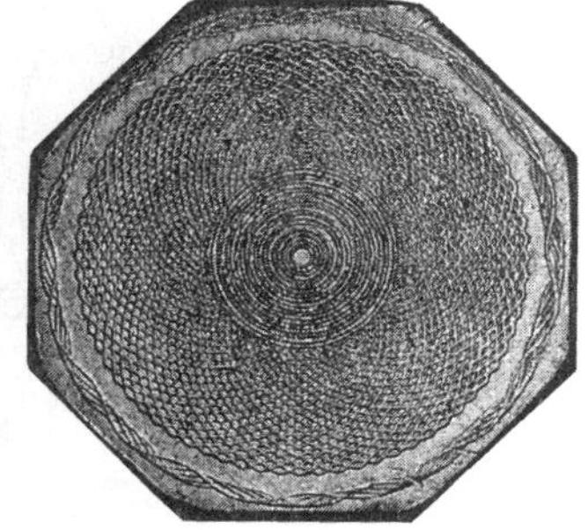

KM# 54a Obverse: 900 THOUS

Date	Fine	VF	XF	Unc
1852	5,000	7,000	14,500.	28,500

WASS, MOLITOR & COMPANY

5 DOLLARS

KM# 55.1 Obverse: Small head, rounded bust

Date	Fine	VF	XF	Unc
1852	2,000	4,000	6,750.	16,500

KM# 55.2 Note: Thick planchet.

Date	Fine	VF	XF	Unc
1852 Unique	—	—	—	—

KM# 56 Obverse: Large head, pointed bust

Date	Fine	VF	XF	Unc
1852	2,000	4,500	8,500.	17,500

10 DOLLARS

KM# 57 Obverse: Long neck, large date

Date	Fine	VF	XF	Unc
1852	2,750	5,000	8,500.	15,500

KM# 58 Obverse: Short neck, wide date

Date	Fine	VF	XF	Unc
1852	1,500	2,650	5,500.	13,500

KM# 59.1 Obverse: Short neck, small date

Date	Fine	VF	XF	Unc
1852 Rare	—	—	—	—

Note: Eliasberg Sale May 1996, EF-45 $36,300; S.S. Central America Sale December 2000, VF-30 realized $12,650

KM# 59.2 Obverse: Plugged date

Date	Fine	VF	XF	Unc
1855	6,000	8,000	12,500.	28,500

20 DOLLARS

KM# 60 Obverse: Large head

Date	Fine	VF	XF	Unc
1855 Rare	—	—	—	—

KM# 61 Obverse: Small head

Date	Fine	VF	XF	Unc
1855	7,000	11,000	20,000.	—

50 DOLLARS

KM# 62

Date	Fine	VF	XF	Unc
1855	—	—	—	—

Note: Bloomfield Sale December 1996, BU $170,500

COLORADO

CLARK, GRUBER & COMPANY

2-1/2 DOLLARS

KM# 63

Date	Fine	VF	XF	Unc
1860	750	1,300	2,500.	8,500

Note: Garrett Sale March 1980, MS-65 $12,000

KM# 64.1

Date	Fine	VF	XF	Unc
1861	850	1,500	2,750.	11,500

KM# 64.2 **Note:** Extra high edge.

Date	Fine	VF	XF	Unc
1861	850	1,750	3,500.	12,500

5 DOLLARS

KM# 65

Date	Fine	VF	XF	Unc
1860	1,000	1,750	3,000.	9,200

Note: Garrett Sale March 1980, MS-63 $9,000

KM# 66

Date	Fine	VF	XF	Unc
1861	1,500	2,500	4,500.	13,500

10 DOLLARS

KM# 67

Date	Fine	VF	XF	Unc
1860	2,750	3,750	8,000.	21,500

KM# 68

Date	Fine	VF	XF	Unc
1861	1,500	2,500	4,500.	15,500

20 DOLLARS

KM# 69

Date	Fine	VF	XF	Unc
1860	25,000	55,000	75,000.	100,000

Note: Eliasberg Sale May 1996, AU $90,200; Schoonmaker Sale June a997, VCF $62,700

KM# 70

Date	Fine	VF	XF	Unc
1861	7,000	10,000	21,500.	—

J. J. CONWAY

2-1/2 DOLLARS

KM# 71

Date	Fine	VF	XF	Unc
(1861)	—	45,000	70,000.	—

5 DOLLARS

KM# 72.1

Date	Fine	VF	XF	Unc
(1861) Rare	—	—	—	—

Note: Brand Sale June 1984, XF-40 $44,000

KM# 72.2 **Reverse:** Numeral 5 omitted

Date	Fine	VF	XF	Unc
(1861) Unique	—	—	—	—

10 DOLLARS

KM# 73

Date	Fine	VF	XF	Unc
(1861) Rare	—	60,000	—	—

JOHN PARSONS

2-1/2 DOLLARS

KM# 74

Date	Fine	VF	XF	Unc
(1861) Rare	—	—	—	—

Note: Garrett Sale March 1980, VF-20 $85,000

5 DOLLARS

KM# 75

Date	Fine	VF	XF	Unc
(1861) Rare	—	—	—	—

Note: Garrett Sale March 1980, VF-20 $100,000

GEORGIA

CHRISTOPHER BECHTLER

2-1/2 DOLLARS

KM# 76.1 **Reverse:** GEORGIA, 64 G, 22 CARATS

Date	Fine	VF	XF	Unc
	1,650	2,650	5,000.	10,000

KM# 76.2 **Reverse:** GEORGIA, 64 G, 22 CARATS, even 22

Date	Fine	VF	XF	Unc
	1,850	2,850	5,500.	11,500

5 DOLLARS

KM# 77 Obverse: RUTHERF **Reverse:** 128 G, 22 CARATS

Date	Fine	VF	XF	Unc
	2,000	3,500	5,500.	11,500

KM# 78.1 Obverse: RUTHERFORD

Date	Fine	VF	XF	Unc
	2,000	3,750	6,000.	12,500

KM# 78.2 Reverse: Colon after 128 G:

Date	Fine	VF	XF	Unc
	—	20,000	30,000.	—

Note: Akers Pittman Sale October 1997, VF-XF $26,400

TEMPLETON REID

2-1/2 DOLLARS

KM# 79

Date	Fine	VF	XF	Unc
1830	12,500	32,500	55,000.	—

5 DOLLARS

KM# 80

Date	Fine	VF	XF	Unc
1830 Rare	—	—	—	—

Note: Garrett Sale November 1979, XF-40 $200,000

10 DOLLARS

KM# 81 Obverse: With date

Date	Fine	VF	XF	Unc
1830 Rare	—	—	—	—

KM# 82 Obverse: Undated

Date	Fine	VF	XF	Unc
(1830) Rare	—	—	—	—

Note: Also see listings under California

NORTH CAROLINA

AUGUST BECHTLER

DOLLAR

KM# 83.1 Reverse: CAROLINA, 27 G. 21C.

Date	Fine	VF	XF	Unc
	450	650	1,150.	2,950

KM# 83.2

Date	Fine	VF	XF	Unc
	450	650	1,150.	2,950

KM# 84 Reverse: CAROLINA, 134 G. 21 CARATS

Date	Fine	VF	XF	Unc
	1,750	3,500	6,000.	12,500

KM# 85 Reverse: CAROLINA, 128 G. 22 CARATS

Date	Fine	VF	XF	Unc
	3,000	5,500	8,000.	15,000

KM# 86 Reverse: CAROLINA, 141 G: 20 CARATS

Date	Fine	VF	XF	Unc
	2,750	4,850	7,500.	14,500

Note: Proof restrikes exist from original dies; in the Akers Pittman Sale October 1997, an example sold for $14,300

CHRISTOPHER BECHTLER

DOLLAR

KM# 87 Obverse: CAROLINA, N reversed **Reverse:** 28 G.

Date	Fine	VF	XF	Unc
	900	1,200	1,700.	3,750

KM# 88.1 Obverse: N. CAROLINA **Reverse:** 28 G centered without star

Date	Fine	VF	XF	Unc
	1,500	2,200	3,500.	8,000

KM# 88.2 Obverse: N. CAROLINA **Reverse:** 28 G high without star

Date	Fine	VF	XF	Unc
	2,500	4,500	6,500.	12,000

KM# 89 Obverse: N. CAROLINA **Reverse:** 30 G.

Date	Fine	VF	XF	Unc
	850	1,200	2,750.	5,500

2-1/2 DOLLARS

KM# 90.1 Reverse: CAROLINA, 67 G. 21 CARATS

Date	Fine	VF	XF	Unc
	1,250	2,250	5,500.	11,500

KM# 90.2 Reverse: 64 G 22 CARATS, uneven 22

Date	Fine	VF	XF	Unc
	1,450	2,850	6,000.	12,000

KM# 90.3 Reverse: Even 22

Date	Fine	VF	XF	Unc
	1,650	3,000	6,500.	12,500

KM# 91 Reverse: CAROLINA, 70 G. 20 CARATS

Date	Fine	VF	XF	Unc
	1,650	3,000	6,750.	18,500

Note: Bowers and Merena Long Sale May 1995, MS-63 $31,900

KM# 92.1 Obverse: NORTH CAROLINA, 20 C. 75 G. **Reverse:** RUTHERFORD in a circle, border of large beads

Date	Fine	VF	XF	Unc
	—	7,500	11,500.	25,000

KM# 92.2 Obverse: NORTH CAROLINA, without 75 G, wide 20 C.

Date	Fine	VF	XF	Unc
	2,800	5,000	7,000.	14,500

KM# 92.3 Obverse: Narrow 20 C

Date	Fine	VF	XF	Unc
	2,800	5,000	7,000.	14,500

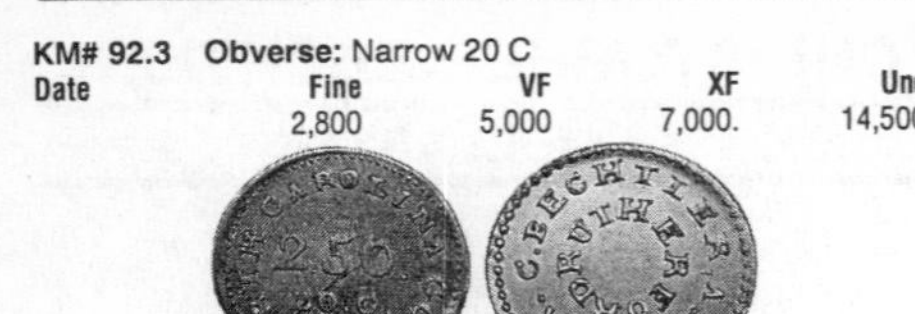

KM# 93.1 Obverse: NORTH CAROLINA without 75 G, CAROLINA above 250 instead of GOLD

Date	Fine	VF	XF	Unc
Unique	—	—	—	—

KM# 93.2 Obverse: NORTH CAROLINA, 20 C **Reverse:** 75 G, border finely serrated

Date	Fine	VF	XF	Unc
	4,500	7,500	10,500.	—

5 DOLLARS

KM# 94 Reverse: CAROLINA, 134 G. star 21 CARATS

Date	Fine	VF	XF	Unc
	1,650	3,250	6,000.	11,000

KM# 95 Reverse: 21 above CARATS, without star

Date	Fine	VF	XF	Unc
Unique	—	—	—	—

KM# 96.1 Obverse: RUTHERFORD **Reverse:** CAROLINA, 140 G. 20 CARATS

Date	Fine	VF	XF	Unc
1834	1,750	3,750	6,500.	11,500

KM# 96.2

Date	Fine	VF	XF	Unc
1834	2,000	4,000	7,000.	12,500

KM# 97.1 Obverse: RUTHERF **Reverse:** CAROLINA. 140 G. 20 CARATS; 20 close to CARATS

Date	Fine	VF	XF	Unc
1834	1,800	3,850	6,750.	12,000

KM# 97.2 Reverse: 20 away from CARATS

Date	Fine	VF	XF	Unc
1834	2,500	6,500	11,500.	—

KM# 98 Obverse: RUTHERF **Reverse:** CAROLINA, 141 G, 20 CARATS

Date	Fine	VF	XF	Unc
Proof restrike	—	—	—	15,500

KM# 99.1 Reverse: NORTH CAROLINA, 150 G, below 20 CARATS

Date	Fine	VF	XF	Unc
	2,800	4,500	8,500.	18,500

KM# 99.2 Reverse: Without 150 G

Date	Fine	VF	XF	Unc
	3,200	6,000	10,000.	20,000

OREGON

OREGON EXCHANGE COMPANY

5 DOLLARS

KM# 100

Date	Fine	VF	XF	Unc
1849	10,000	18,500	33,350.	—

10 DOLLARS

KM# 101

Date	Fine	VF	XF	Unc
1849	20,000	40,000	65,000.	—

UTAH

MORMON ISSUES

2-1/2 DOLLARS

KM# 102

Date	Fine	VF	XF	Unc
1849	4,000	7,000	13,500.	24,500

5 DOLLARS

KM# 103

Date	Fine	VF	XF	Unc
1849	4,000	7,000	12,000.	23,500

KM# 104

Date	Fine	VF	XF	Unc
1850	4,500	7,500	15,000.	25,500

KM# 105

Date	Fine	VF	XF	Unc
1860	6,500	12,000	25,000.	37,500

10 DOLLARS

KM# 106

Date	Fine	VF	XF	Unc
1849 Rare	—	—	—	—

Note: Heritage ANA Sale July 1988, AU $93,000

20 DOLLARS

KM# 107

Date	Fine	VF	XF	Unc
1849	22,500	47,500	85,000.	—

PATTERNS (Pn)

The United States pattern section contains Judd cross reference numbers and selected descriptive references from the 6th edition of *United States Pattern, Experimental and Trial Pieces* edited by Abe Kosoff from the original edition by J. Hewitt Judd, M.D. Copyright 1977, 1959 Western Publishing Company, Inc. Used by permission.

Market values established in this section are based on auction results gleened from *Auction Prices Realized*, an annual compilation of U.S. auction firm sales edited by Bob Wilhite and Tom Michael and published by Krause Publications of Iola, Wisconsin. Due to the wide variance in grade amongst U.S. patterns, these values represent only an average example of the type. To determine values for patterns of greater or lesser quality the serious collector may wish to research the market trend of a given type over time by using several volumes of *Auction Prices Realized* as well as original auction catalogs.

DENOMINATION EQUIVALENTS

10 Cent = Dime
25 Cent = Quarter Dollar
50 Cent = Half Dollar
Dollar = Silver Dollar
Gold Dollar = Gold Dollar
2-1/2 Dollar = Quarter Eagle
5 Dollar = Half Eagle
10 Dollar = Eagle
20 Dollar = Double Eagle

NOTE: Photographs are representative of the type group, and not always the particular listing that it appears above.

KM#	Date	Mintage	Identification	Mkt.Val.
Pn14	1803	—	5 Dollar, Copper, reeded edge, restrikes from rusty dies, J27	—
Pn15	1804	—	1 Cent, Tin, plain edge, restrike, J28	—
Pn16	1804	—	5 Dollar, Silver, reeded edge, restrike, J29	Rare
Pn17	1804	—	5 Dollar, Silver, plain edge, restrike, J30	Unique

NOTE: Bowers Harry W. Bass Jr. sale 5-99, MS-65 realized $13,800.

KM#	Date	Mintage	Identification	Mkt.Val.
Pn18	1804	—	5 Dollar, Copper, reeded edge, restrike, J31	—
Pn19	1804	—	5 Dollar, Tin, restrike, J32	—
Pn20	1804	4 known	10 Dollar (Eagle), Gold, obv: plain 4 in date, rev: beaded border, J33	—
Pn21	1804	4-5 struck	10 Dollar, Silver, reeded edge, J34	13,500.
Pn22	1804	—	10 Dollar, Silver, plain edge, J34a	—
Pn23	1805	—	2-1/2 Dollar (Quarter Eagle), Copper reeded edge, restrike, J35	—
Pn24	1805	—	5 Dollar, Silver, restrike, J36	2750.
Pn25	1805	—	5 Dollar, Copper, restrike, J37	2250.
Pn26	1805	—	5 Dollar, Tin, restrike, J38	2200.
Pn27	1806	—	1 Cent, Copper, obv: die of the quarter, rev: 1807 cent, plain edge, restrike mule, J38a	—
Pn28	1808	—	5 Dollar, Silver, reeded edge, restrike, J39	—
Pn29	1808	—	5 Dollar, Silver, plain edge, restrike, J40	—
Pn30	1810	2	1 Cent, White Metal, restrike, J41	7500.
Pn31	1810	—	50 Cent, Copper, plain edge, restrike, J42	5000.
Pn32	1810	—	50 Cent, Brass, plain edge, J42a	—
Pn33	1810	—	50 Cent, Brass, plain edge, restrike, J43	5000.
Pn34	1814	3 known	50 Cent, Platinum, J44	Rare
Pn35	1818	—	1 Cent, Silver, obv: die of the quarter, restrike, J45	Unique
Pn36	1823	12	1 Cent, Silver, plain edge, restrike, J46	—
Pn37	1823	—	1 Cent, Copper, plain edge, restrike, J46a	750.00
Pn38	1823	—	50 Cent, Copper, reeded edge, restrike, J47	—
Pn39	1827	4-5 known	25 Cent, Copper, rev: die of 1819, restrike, J48	27,600.
Pn40	1831	—	2-1/2 Dollar, Silver, reeded edge, J49	Unique
Pn41	1834	2 known	2-1/2 Dollar, Copper, reeded edge, J50	Rare
Pn42	1834	—	5 Dollar, Copper, plain edge, J51	3000.
Pn43	1834	—	5 Dollar, Copper, plain edge, J51a	400.00

NOTE: The authenticity of this piece has been questioned.

KM#	Date	Mintage	Identification	Mkt.Val.
Pn44	1836	—	2 Cent, Billon, plain edge, J52	2750.
Pn45	1836	—	2 Cent, Billon, reeded edge, J53	3200.
Pn46	1836	—	2 Cent, Copper, plain edge, J54	2250.
Pn47	1836	—	2 Cent, Copper, reeded edge,	
Pn47			J55	1850.
Pn48	1836	—	2 Cent, White Metal, plain edge, J56	1850.
Pn49	1836	—	2 Cent, White Metal, reeded edge, J56a	2000.

KM#	Date	Mintage	Identification	Mkt.Val.
Pn50	1836	1,200 est.	50 Cent, Silver, reeded edge, J57	2300.
Pn51	1836	18	1 Dollar, Silver, plain edge, name above date, stars, J58	99,000.
Pn51a	1836	—	1 Dollar, Silver, restrike from cracked reverse die, J58a	28,750.
Pn52	1836	—	1 Dollar, Copper, plain edge, J59	121,000.

KM#	Date	Mintage	Identification	Mkt.Val.
Pn53	1836	1,000	1 Dollar, Silver, plain edge, coin turn, name on base, stars, J60	7000.
Pn53a	1836	600	1 Dollar, Silver, plain edge, medal turn, J60	8000.
Pn53b	1836	—	1 Dollar, Silver, plain edge, restrikes from cracked reverse, J60a	4500.
Pn54	1836	—	1 Dollar, Silver, reeded edge, restrike, J61	—
Pn55	1836	—	1 Dollar, Copper, plain edge, restrike, J62	—
Pn56	1836	—	1 Dollar, Silver, plain edge, name above date, no stars, restrike, J63	35,000.
Pn57	1836	—	1 Dollar, Copper, plain edge, restrike, J64	12,500.
Pn58	1836	—	1 Dollar, Silver, plain edge, name on base, no stars, restrike, J65	35,000.
Pn59	1836	—	1 Dollar, Copper, plain edge, restrike, J66	12,500.

KM#	Date	Mintage	Identification	Mkt.Val.
Pn60	1836	5	1 Gold Dollar, Gold, coin turn, plain edge, J67	10,000.
Pn61	1836	—	1 Gold Dollar, Gold alloyed w/Silver, medal turn, plain edge, J68	12,000.
Pn62	1836	—	1 Gold Dollar, Silver, plain edge, J69	4850.
Pn62a	1836	—	1 Gold Dollar, Silver Gilt, plain edge, J69a	4850.
Pn63	1836	—	1 Gold Dollar, Copper, plain edge, J70	4750.
Pn63a	1836	—	1 Gold Dollar, Copper Gilt, plain edge, J70a	4750.
Pn64	1836	—	1 Gold Dollar, Oroide, plain edge, J71	—

KM#	Date	Mintage	Identification	Mkt.Val.
Pn65	1838	—	50 Cent, Silver, reeded edge, J72	3500.

KM#	Date	Mintage	Identification	Mkt.Val.
Pn66	1838	2-3 known	50 Cent, Silver, reeded edge, 143 reeds, J73	10,000.
Pn66a	1838	—	50 Cent, Silver, reeded edge, 152 reeds, restrike, J73a	3750.
Pn67	1838	—	50 Cent, Copper, reeded edge, restrike, J74	1500.
Pn68	1838	1 known	50 Cent, Silver, reeded edge, J75	—
Pn69	1838	1 known	50 Cent, Silver, plain edge, curved date, LIBERTY incuse, 206 gr, J76	—
Pn69a	1838	—	50 Cent, Silver, plain edge, straight date, 192 gr, restrike, J76	6500.
Pn69b	1838	—	50 Cent, Silver, reeded edge, straight date, 192 gr, restrike, J76a	6500.
Pn70	1838	1 known	50 Cent, Copper, plain edge, straight date, J77	8650.
Pn70a	1838	—	50 Cent, Copper, plain edge, restrike from rusted die, J77a	4000.
Pn71	1838	2-3 known	50 Cent, Copper, reeded edge, straight date, rusted die, J78	12,500.
Pn72	1838	2 known	50 Cent, Silver, reeded edge, curved date, LIBERTY raised, J79	—
Pn73	1838	3 known	50 Cent, Silver, reeded edge, straight date, restrike, J79a	9000.
Pn74	1838	—	50 Cent, Silver, reeded edge, LIBERTY incuse, J79a	7000.
Pn75	1838	—	50 Cent, Silver, reeded edge, straight date, restrike, J80	7500.
Pn76	1838	—	50 Cent, Copper, reeded edge, restrike, J81	6500.
Pn77	1838	2 known	50 Cent, Silver, reeded edge, curved date, J82	—
Pn77a	1838	1 known	50 Cent, Silver, plain edge, restrike, J82a	10,000.
Pn78	1838	1 known	50 Cent, Silver, reeded edge, J83	—

KM#	Date	Mintage	Identification	Mkt.Val.
Pn79	1838	—	1 Dollar, Silver, reeded edge, no name on base, J84	36,800.
Pn79a	1838	—	1 Dollar, Silver, reeded edge, restrike, rev: w/o stars, J84a	17,500.
Pn80	1838	—	1 Dollar, Silver, plain edge, restrike, J85	15,500.
Pn81	1838	—	1 Dollar, Copper, reeded edge, J86	Rare
Pn82	1838	—	1 Dollar, Copper, plain edge, restrike, J87	14,500.

KM#	Date	Mintage	Identification	Mkt.Val.
Pn83	1838	—	1 Dollar, Silver, plain edge, no name on base, rev: w/stars restrike, J88	Rare
Pn84	1838	—	1 Dollar, Copper, plain edge, restrike, J89	Rare
Pn85	1838	—	1 Dollar, Copper, reeded edge, restrike, J90	Rare
Pn86	1839	—	50 Cent, Silver, reeded edge, restrike, J91	4500.
Pn87	1839	—	50 Cent, Silver, reeded edge, restrike, J92	—

KM#	Date	Mintage	Identification	Mkt.Val.
Pn88	1839	7 known	50 Cent, Silver, reeded edge, J93	6000.
Pn89	1839	—	50 Cent, Copper, reeded edge, J94	—
Pn90	1839	—	50 Cent, Silver, reeded edge, 152 reeds, J95	12,000.
Pn91	1839	—	50 Cent, Copper, reéded edge, J96	5000.

KM#	Date	Mintage	Identification	Mkt.Val.
Pn92	1839	—	50 Cent, Silver, reeded edge, restrike, 146 reeds, J97	12,000.
Pn93	1839	—	50 Cent, Copper, reeded edge, restrike, J98	11,550.
Pn94	1839	2 known	50 Cent, Silver, reeded edge, 143 reeds, J99	37,500.
Pn95	1839	2 known	50 Cent, Silver, reeded edge, restrike, J100	37,500.
Pn95a	1839	—	50 Cent, Silver, reeded edge, J100a	—
Pn96	1839	1 known	50 Cent, Silver, plain edge, J101	42,500.
Pn97	1839	—	50 Cent, Silver, reeded edge, 152 reeds, restrike, J102	5500.
Pn98	1839	—	50 Cent, Copper, reeded edge, 152 reeds, restrike, J103	5500.

KM#	Date	Mintage	Identification	Mkt.Val.
Pn99	1839	300	1 Dollar, Silver, reeded edge, no name or stars, J104	15,400.
Pn99a	1839	—	1 Dollar, Silver, restrike, medal turn, J104a	10,000.
Pn99b	1839	—	1 Dollar, Silver, restrike, coin turn, J104b	10,000.
Pn100	1839	—	1 Dollar, Silver, plain edge, J105	17,600.
Pn101	1839	—	1 Dollar, Copper, reeded edge, J106	Rare
Pn102	1839	—	1 Dollar, Copper, plain edge, J107	Rare
Pn103	1839	—	1 Dollar, Silver, plain edge, no name, rev: w/stars, restrike, J108	Rare
Pn104	1839	—	1 Dollar, Silver, plain edge, J109	Unique
Pn105	ND(1840)	—	25 Cent, Brass, broad planchet, J110	Unique
Pn106	1846	Unique	2-1/2 Dollar, Copper, reeded edge, J110a	3650.

KM#	Date	Mintage	Identification	Mkt.Val.
Pn107	1849	—	3 Cent, Silver & Copper, (50-50) reeded edge, 22 gr, J111	3000.
Pn107a	1849	—	3 Cent, Silver & Copper, (50-50) restrike, J111a	3000.
Pn108	1849	—	3 Cent, Silver & Copper, (60-40) reeded edge, 18.5 g, J112	3250.

KM#	Date	Mintage	Identification	Mkt.Val.
Pn109	ND(1849)	—	3 Cent, Silver-Copper, plain edge, J113	3000.
Pn109a	ND(1849)	—	3 Cent, Silver-Copper, plain edge, restrike, J113a	3000.

KM#	Date	Mintage	Identification	Mkt.Val.
Pn110	ND(1849)	—	3 Cent, Copper-Nickel, plain edge, restrike, J114	3000.
Pn111	1849	—	1 Gold Dollar, plain edge, 25.8 gr, J115	8750.
Pn112	1849	3 known	1 Gold Dollar, Silver, Gold plated, J116	5500.
Pn113	1849	1 known	20 Dollar, Gold, reeded edge, J117	Rare
Pn114	1849	—	20 Dollar, Brass Gilt, reeded edge, J118	Unique

KM#	Date	Mintage	Identification	Mkt.Val.
Pn115	1850	—	1 Cent, Billon, plain edge, w/hole, J119	1350.
Pn116	1850	—	1 Cent, Billon, plain edge, w/o hole, restrike, J120	650.00
Pn117	1850	—	1 Cent, Copper, plain edge, w/hole, J121	2000.
Pn118	1850	—	1 Cent, Copper, plain edge, w/o hole, restrike, J122	1650.
Pn119	1850	—	1 Cent, Copper-Nickel, plain edge, w/hole, J123	2250.
Pn120	1850	—	1 Cent, Copper-Nickel, plain edge, w/o hole, restrike, J124	2500.

KM#	Date	Mintage	Identification	Mkt.Val.
Pn121	1850	—	1 Cent, White Metal, plain edge, w/hole, J124a	3500.

KM#	Date	Mintage	Identification	Mkt.Val.
Pn122	1850	—	3 Cent, Silver, plain edge, 12.75 gr, J125	3000.
Pn122a	1850	—	3 Cent, Silver, plain edge, restrike, J125a	1500.
Pn123	ND(1850)	2 known	20 Dollar, Silver, reeded edge, J126	Rare

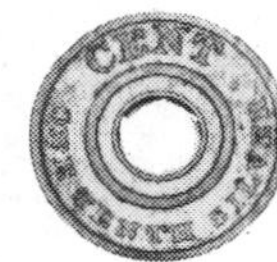

KM#	Date	Mintage	Identification	Mkt.Val.
Pn124	ND(1851)	—	1 Cent, Billon, plain edge, w/hole, J127	1650.
Pn124a	ND(1851)	—	1 Cent, Billon, plain edge, w/large hole, J127a	1650.
Pn125	ND(1851)	—	1 Cent, Billon, plain edge, w/o hole, restrike, J128	1900.
Pn125a	ND(1851)	—	1 Cent, Billon, reeded edge, w/o hole, thin, restrike, J128a	1900.
Pn125b	ND(1851)	—	1 Cent, Billon, reeded edge, w/o hole, thick, restrike, J128a	1900.
Pn126	ND(1851)	—	1 Cent, Copper, plain edge, w/hole, J129	1750.

KM#	Date	Mintage	Identification	Mkt.Val.
Pn126a	ND(1851)	—	1 Cent, Copper, plain edge, w/o hole, restrike, J130	2365.
Pn127	ND(1851)	—	1 Cent, Copper-Nickel, reeded edge, w/o hole, restrike, J131	2350.
Pn127a	ND(1851)	—	1 Cent, Nickel, reeded edge, w/o hole, J131a	2400.

NOTE: Examples of Pn127 & 127a exist silver plated.

KM#	Date	Mintage	Identification	Mkt.Val.
Pn128	1851	5 known	1 Dollar, Copper, reeded edge, restrike, J132	5000.

KM#	Date	Mintage	Identification	Mkt.Val.
Pn129	1852	—	1 Dollar, Nickel, reeded edge, J133	6500.

KM#	Date	Mintage	Identification	Mkt.Val.
Pn130	1852	—	1 Dollar, Copper, reeded edge, restrike, J134	6000.
Pn131	1852	6 known	1 Gold Half Dollar, Gold, reeded edge, 13 gr, J135	9000.
Pn132	1852	4 known	1 Gold Dollar, Gold, reeded edge, 25.8 gr, J136	10,000.

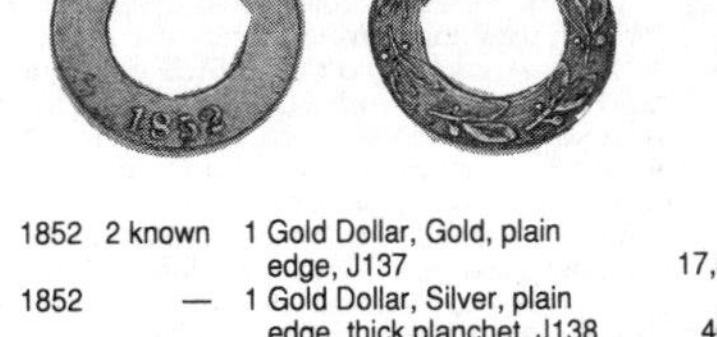

KM#	Date	Mintage	Identification	Mkt.Val.
Pn133	1852	2 known	1 Gold Dollar, Gold, plain edge, J137	17,500.
Pn134	1852	—	1 Gold Dollar, Silver, plain edge, thick planchet, J138	4000.
Pn134a	1852	—	1 Gold Dollar, Silver, plain edge, thin planchet, J138	5000.
Pn135	1852	—	1 Gold Dollar, Copper, plain edge, J139	2350.
Pn136	1852	—	1 Gold Dollar, Copper-Nickel, plain edge, J140	2500.
Pn137	1852	—	1 Gold Dollar, Nickel, plain edge, J140a	3250.

KM#	Date	Mintage	Identification	Mkt.Val.
Pn138	1852	—	1 Gold Dollar, Gold, plain edge, J141	Rare
Pn139	1852	—	1 Gold Dollar, Silver, plain edge, J142	Rare
Pn140	1852	—	1 Gold Dollar, Copper, plain edge, J143	2800.

KM#	Date	Mintage	Identification	Mkt.Val.
Pn141	1852	—	1 Gold Dollar, Nickel, plain edge, J144	Unique
Pn142	1852	—	1 Gold Dollar, Gold, plain edge, thick planchet, 25.8 gr, J145	15,500.
Pn142a	1852	—	1 Gold Dollar, Gold, plain edge, thin planchet, J145	10,000.
Pn143	1852	5 known	1 Gold Dollar, Silver, plain edge, J146	6000.
Pn144	1852	—	1 Gold Dollar, Copper, plain edge, J147	3750.
Pn145	1852	—	1 Gold Dollar, Copper-Nickel, plain edge, J148	3750.
Pn146	1852	—	1 Gold Dollar, Nickel, plain edge, thin planchet, J148a	2750.
Pn147	1852	—	1 Gold Dollar, Brass, plain edge, J148b	7000.

NOTE: Restrikes exist from cracked dies. Gilt examples also exist.

KM#	Date	Mintage	Identification	Mkt.Val.
Pn148	1853	—	1 Cent, German Silver (40% Nickel), reeded edge, J149	2150.
Pn148a	1853	—	1 Cent, German Silver (30% Nickel), reeded edge, thick planchet, J150	5000.
Pn148b	1853	—	1 Cent, German Silver (30% Nickel), reeded edge, thin planchet, J150	4500.
Pn149	1853	—	1 Cent, Nickel-Copper (60-40), reeded edge, J151	1150.
Pn150	1853	—	1 Cent, German Silver, plain edge, J152	850.00
Pn151	1853	—	1 Cent, Nickel, plain edge, w/o hole, thick planchet, J152a	850.00
Pn152	1853	—	1 Cent, Nickel, plain edge, w/hole, thin planchet, J152b	850.00
Pn153	1853	—	3 Cent, Silver, plain edge, J153	Unique
Pn154	1853	—	1 Dollar, Copper, reeded edge, restrike, J154	3750.
Pn155	1854	2 known	1/2 Cent, Copper-Nickel, plain edge, J155	Rare

KM#	Date	Mintage	Identification	Mkt.Val.
Pn156	1854	—	1 Cent, German Silver (40% Nickel), reeded edge, J156	1650.
Pn157	1854	—	1 Cent, German Silver (30% Nickel), reeded edge, J157	1650.
Pn158	1854	—	1 Cent, Nickel-Copper (40-60), reeded edge, J158	2850.
Pn159	1854	—	1 Cent, Copper, reeded edge, J159	2200.

KM#	Date	Mintage	Identification	Mkt.Val.
Pn160	1854	—	1 Cent, Copper, plain edge, 100 gr, J160	1750.

KM#	Date	Mintage	Identification	Mkt.Val.
Pn161	1854	—	1 Cent, Bronze, plain edge, 96 gr, J161	1150.
Pn161a	1854	—	1 Cent, Bronze, restrike from damaged die, J161	1250.
Pn162	1854	—	1 Cent, Oroide, plain edge, J162	2750.

KM#	Date	Mintage	Identification	Mkt.Val.
Pn163	1854	—	1 Cent, Copper, plain edge, 100 gr, J163	1850.
Pn164	1854	—	1 Cent, Bronze, plain edge, 96 gr, J164	3200.
Pn164a	1854	—	1 Cent, Bronze, restrike from damaged dies, J164	2200.
Pn165	1854	—	1 Cent, Copper, plain edge, restrike, J165	Rare
Pn166	1854	—	1 Cent, Copper, plain edge, 100 gr, J165a	—
Pn166a	1854	—	1 Cent, Copper, restrike from clashed dies, J165a	—
Pn167	1854	—	1 Cent, Bronze, plain edge, J165b	3000.
Pn167a	1854	—	1 Cent, Bronze, restrike from clashed dies, J165b	3000.
Pn168	1854	—	1/2 Dime, German Silver, plain edge, J166	—

KM#	Date	Mintage	Identification	Mkt.Val.
Pn169	1855	—	1 Cent, Copper, plain edge, 100 gr, J167	1750.
Pn169a	1855	—	1 Cent, Copper, plain edge, 115 gr, restrike, J167	1550.
Pn170	1855	—	1 Cent, Pure Nickel, plain edge, J167a	—
Pn171	1855	—	1 Cent, Bronze, plain edge, 96 gr, J168	1650.
Pn171a	1855	—	1 Cent, Bronze, plain edge, 115 gr, restrike, J168	1350.
Pn172	1855	—	1 Cent, Oroide, plain edge, J169	—
Pn173	1855	—	1 Cent, Copper-Nickel (80-20), plain edge, J170	2250.
Pn174	1855	—	1 Cent, Copper-Nickel (60-40), plain edge, J171	1450.

KM#	Date	Mintage	Identification	Mkt.Val.
Pn175	1855	—	1 Cent, Copper, plain edge, J172	2500.
Pn176	1855	—	1 Cent, Bronze, plain edge, J173	2250.
Pn177	1855	—	1 Cent, Oroide, plain edge, J174	—
Pn178	1855	—	1 Cent, Nickel, J174a	4500.
Pn179	1855	—	50 Cent, Aluminum, reeded edge, J175	Unique
Pn180	1855	—	1 Gold Dollar, White Metal, plain edge, J175a	Unique
Pn181	1855	—	10 Dollar, Copper, reeded edge, restrike, J176	Rare

KM#	Date	Mintage	Identification	Mkt.Val.
Pn182	1856	—	1/2 Cent, Copper-Nickel, plain edge, J177	2850.

KM#	Date	Mintage	Identification	Mkt.Val.
Pn183	1856	—	1 Cent, Copper-Nickel, plain edge, J178	3500.
Pn184	1856	—	1 Cent, Copper, plain edge, J179	5000.

KM#	Date	Mintage	Identification	Mkt.Val.
Pn185	1856	—	1 Cent, Copper-Nickel, plain edge, J180	5000.
Pn186	1856	—	1 Cent, Copper, plain edge, J181	5000.
Pn187	1856	—	1 Cent, Bronze, plain edge, J182	5250.
Pn188	1856	—	1 Cent, Nickel, plain edge, J183	5250.

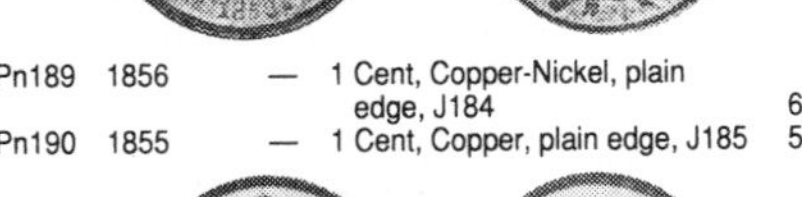

KM#	Date	Mintage	Identification	Mkt.Val.
Pn189	1856	—	1 Cent, Copper-Nickel, plain edge, J184	6500.
Pn190	1855	—	1 Cent, Copper, plain edge, J185	5500.

KM#	Date	Mintage	Identification	Mkt.Val.
Pn191	1857	—	1 Cent, Copper-Nickel, plain edge, J186	6250.
Pn192	1857	—	1 Cent, Copper, plain edge, J187	4250.
Pn193	1857	—	1 Cent, Nickel, plain edge, J187a	5000.
Pn194	1857	—	25 Cent, Copper, reeded edge, J188	2650.
Pn195	1857	—	2-1/2 Dollar, Copper, reeded edge, J189	3500.
Pn196	ND(1857)	1 known	20 Dollar, Copper, plain edge, J190	8500.
Pn197	1858	—	1 Cent, Copper-Nickel, plain edge, J191	2550.
Pn197a	1858	—	1 Cent, Copper-Nickel, restrike from rusty dies, J191	1150.
Pn198	1858	—	1 Cent, Copper-Nickel, plain edge, J192	2000.

KM#	Date	Mintage	Identification	Mkt.Val.
Pn199	1858	—	1 Cent, Copper-Nickel, plain edge, J193	2250.
Pn200	1858	—	1 Cent, Copper-Nickel, broad planchet, plain edge, J194	Unique
Pn201	1858	—	1 Cent, Copper, plain edge, J195	Unique

KM#	Date	Mintage	Identification	Mkt.Val.
Pn202	1858	—	1 Cent, Copper-Nickel, J196	3500.
Pn203	1858	—	1 Cent, Copper-Nickel, J197	4500.

KM#	Date	Mintage	Identification	Mkt.Val.
Pn204	1858	—	1 Cent, Copper-Nickel, J198	2250.
Pn205	1858	—	1 Cent, Copper-Nickel, broad planchet, plain edge, J199	4500.
Pn206	1858	—	1 Cent, Copper-Nickel, plain edge, J200	Rare
Pn207	1858	—	1 Cent, Copper-Nickel, plain edge, J201	Rare

KM#	Date	Mintage	Identification	Mkt.Val.
Pn208	1858	—	1 Cent, Copper-Nickel, plain edge, J202	1200.

KM#	Date	Mintage	Identification	Mkt.Val.
Pn209	1858	—	1 Cent, Copper-Nickel, plain edge, J203	1500.

KM#	Date	Mintage	Identification	Mkt.Val.
Pn210	1858	—	1 Cent, Copper-Nickel, plain edge, J204	1850.
Pn211	1858	—	1 Cent, Copper, plain edge, J205	3000.
Pn212	1858	—	1 Cent, Copper-Nickel, plain edge, J206	1550.
Pn213	1858	—	1 Cent, Copper, plain edge, J207	2250.
Pn214	1858	—	1 Cent, Nickel, plain edge, J207a	3000.

KM#	Date	Mintage	Identification	Mkt.Val.
Pn215	1858	—	1 Cent, Copper-Nickel, plain edge, thick planchet, J208	1450.
Pn215a	1858	—	1 Cent, Copper-Nickel, plain edge, thin planchet, J208	900.00
Pn216	1858	—	1 Cent, Copper, plain edge, J209	4500.
Pn217	1858	—	1 Cent, Bronze, plain edge, J210	5000.

KM#	Date	Mintage	Identification	Mkt.Val.
Pn218	1858	—	1 Cent, Copper-Nickel, plain edge, J211	1000. 1250.

KM#	Date	Mintage	Identification	Mkt.Val.
Pn219	1858	—	1 Cent, Copper-Nickel, plain edge, J212	1150.

KM#	Date	Mintage	Identification	Mkt.Val.
Pn220	1858	—	1 Cent, Copper-Nickel, plain	

KM#	Date	Mintage	Identification	Mkt.Val.
Pn220			edge, J213	1150.
Pn221	1858	—	1 Cent, Copper-Nickel, broad planchet, plain edge, J214	8250.
Pn222	1858	—	1 Cent, Copper, plain edge, J215	—
Pn223	1858	—	1 Cent, Copper-Nickel, broad planchet, plain edge, J216	—
Pn224	1858	—	1 Cent, Copper, plain edge, J217	—
Pn225	1858	—	1 Cent, Nickel, J217a	—
Pn226	1858	—	1 Cent, Copper, plain edge, J218	—
Pn227	1858	—	1 Cent, Nickel alloy, plain edge, J218a	—
Pn228	1858	—	1 Cent, Copper-Nickel, plain edge, J219	11,550.
Pn229	1858	—	1 Cent, Copper-Nickel, plain edge, J220	Unique
Pn230	1858	—	25 Cent, Silver, reeded edge, J221	4500.
Pn231	1858	—	50 Cent, Silver, reeded edge, J222	Rare
Pn232	1858	—	50 Cent, Copper, reeded edge, defaced, J223	Unique
Pn233	1858	—	1 Gold Dollar, Gold, reeded edge, J224	Unique
Pn234	1858	—	1 Gold Dollar, Copper, reeded edge, J225	6500.
Pn235	1859	—	1 Cent, Copper-Nickel, plain edge, J226	1150.
Pn236	1859	—	1 Cent, Copper-Nickel, plain edge, J227	1200.
Pn237	1859	—	1 Cent, Copper-Nickel, plain edge, J228	1000.
Pn238	1859	—	1 Cent, Copper, plain edge, J229	1150.
Pn239	1859	—	1 Cent, Copper, plain edge, J230	1100.
Pn240	1859	—	1 Cent, Bronze, plain edge, J231	1550.
Pn241	1859	—	1 Cent, Lead, plain edge, J231a	—
Pn242	1859	—	1/2 Dime, Silver, reeded edge, J232	10,000.
Pn243	1859	—	10 Cent, Silver, reeded edge, J233	11,500.
Pn244	1859	—	25 Cent, Silver, reeded edge, J234	5000.
Pn245	1859	—	50 Cent, Silver, reeded edge, J235	1350.
Pn246	1859	—	50 Cent, Copper, reeded edge, J236	1750.
Pn247	1859	—	50 Cent, Silver, reeded edge, J237	1500.
Pn248	1859	—	50 Cent, Copper, reeded edge, J238	1750.

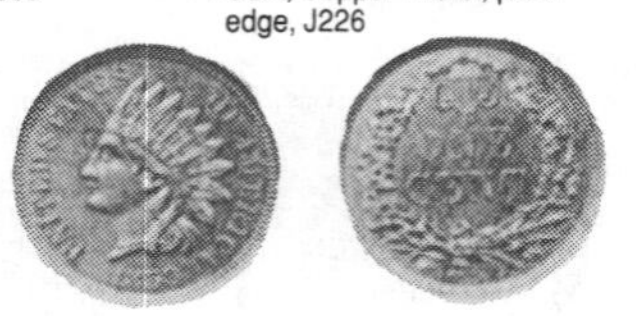

KM#	Date	Mintage	Identification	Mkt.Val.
Pn249	1859	—	50 Cent, Silver, reeded edge, J239	1350.
Pn250	1859	—	50 Cent, Copper, reeded edge, J240	2750.
Pn251	1859	—	50 Cent, Silver, reeded edge, J241	2250.
Pn252	1859	—	50 Cent, Copper, reeded edge, J242	2000.
Pn253	1859	—	50 Cent, Silver, reeded edge, J243	2000.
Pn254	1859	—	50 Cent, Copper, reeded edge, J244	1750.
Pn255	1859	—	50 Cent, Silver, reeded edge, J245	2650.
Pn256	1859	—	50 Cent, Copper, reeded edge, J246	3650.
Pn257	1859	—	50 Cent, Silver, reeded edge, J247	2400.
Pn258	1859	—	50 Cent, Copper, reeded edge, J248	2200.
Pn259	1859	—	50 Cent, Silver, reeded edge, J249	2400.
Pn260	1859	—	50 Cent, Copper, reeded edge, J250	2200.
Pn261	1859	—	50 Cent, Silver, reeded edge, J251	2350.
Pn262	1859	—	50 Cent, Copper, reeded edge, J252	2150.
Pn263	1859	—	50 Cent, Silver, reeded edge, J253	2800.
Pn264	1838(1859)	2 known	50 Cent, Silver, reeded edge, J254	—
Pn265	1838(1859)	3 known	50 Cent, Copper, reeded edge, J255	4000.
Pn266	1859	—	1 Gold Dollar, Copper, reeded edge, J256	3000.
Pn267	1859	—	20 Dollar, Copper, reeded edge, J257	5200.
Pn267a	1859	—	20 Dollar, Copper Bronzed, reeded edge, J257	5000.
Pn267b	1859	—	20 Dollar, Copper Gilt, reeded edge, J257	9500.
Pn268	1859	—	20 Dollar, Copper, reeded edge, J258	5500.
Pn268a	1859	—	20 Dollar, Copper Gilt, reeded edge, J258	5500.
Pn269	1859	—	20 Dollar, Copper, reeded edge, J259	—
Pn270	1859	—	20 Dollar, Copper, reeded edge, J260	—
Pn270a	1859	—	20 Dollar, Copper Gilt, reeded	

KM#	Date	Mintage	Identification	Mkt.Val.
Pn270a			edge, J260	17,250.
Pn271	1859	—	20 Dollar, Copper, reeded edge, J261	—
Pn271a	1859	—	20 Dollar, Copper Gilt, reeded edge, J261	12,500.
Pn272	1859	—	20 Dollar, Copper, reeded edge, J262	6000.
Pn272a	1859	—	20 Dollar, Copper Gilt, reeded edge, J262	6000.
Pn273	1859	—	20 Dollar, Copper, reeded edge, J263	6350.
Pn274	ND(1860)	—	1 Cent, Copper-Nickel, plain edge, J264	—
Pn275	1860	—	1 Cent, Copper, plain edge, J265	1000.
Pn276	1860	—	1 Cent, Copper-Nickel, plain edge, J266	—
Pn277	1860	100	1/2 Dime, Silver, reeded edge, J267	5000.
Pn278	1860	—	2-1/2 Dollar, Copper-Nickel, J268	—
Pn279	1860	—	50 Cent, Copper, reeded edge, J269	—
Pn280	1857//1860	—	2-1/2 Dollar, Copper, reeded edge, J270	4500.
Pn281	1860	—	5 Dollar, Gold, reeded edge, J271	Rare
Pn282	1860	—	5 Dollar, Copper, reeded edge, J272	4000.
Pn282a	1860	—	5 Dollar, Copper Gilt, reeded edge, J272	4500.
Pn283	1860	—	20 Dollar, Gold, reeded edge, J272a	Unique
Pn284	1860	—	20 Dollar, Copper, reeded edge, J273	18,500.
Pn284a	1860	—	20 Dollar, Copper Gilt, reeded edge, J273	18,500.
Pn285	1861	—	1 Cent, Copper, plain edge, J274	—
Pn286	1861	—	25 Cent, Copper, reeded edge, J275	3500.
Pn287	1861	—	25 Cent, Copper-Nickel, reeded edge, J276	3500.
Pn288	1861	—	50 Cent, Silver, reeded edge, J277	5300.
Pn289	1861	—	50 Cent, Copper, reeded edge, J278	3500.
Pn290	1861	—	50 Cent, Silver, reeded edge, J279	3000.
Pn291	1861	—	50 Cent, Copper, reeded edge, J280	4200.
Pn291a	1861	—	50 Cent, Copper Bronzed, reeded edge, J280	4000.
Pn292	1861	—	2-1/2 Dollar, Silver, reeded edge, J281	8100.
Pn293	1861	—	2-1/2 Dollar, Copper, reeded edge, J282	5000.
Pn294	1861	—	5 Dollar, Copper, reeded edge, J283	4250.
Pn294a	1861	—	5 Dollar, Copper Bronzed, reeded edge, J283	4150.
Pn294b	1861	—	5 Dollar, Copper Gilt, reeded edge, J283	2850.
Pn295	1861	—	10 Dollar, Gold, reeded edge, J284	Rare
Pn296	1861	—	10 Dollar, Copper, reeded edge, J285	4000.
Pn297	1861	—	10 Dollar, Copper Bronzed, reeded	

KM#	Date	Mintage	Identification	Mkt.Val.
Pn297			edge, J285	3250.
Pn297a	1861	—	10 Dollar, Copper Gilt, reeded edge, J285	2850.
Pn298	1861	—	10 Dollar, Gold, reeded edge, J286	Rare
Pn299	1861	—	10 Dollar, Copper, reeded edge, J287	4250.
Pn300	1861	—	10 Dollar, Copper Bronzed, reeded edge, J287	4000.
Pn300a	1861	—	10 Dollar, Copper Gilt, reeded edge, J287	4000.
Pn301	1861	—	20 Dollar, Copper, J288	11,550.
Pn301a	1861	—	20 Dollar, Copper Gilt, J288	11,550.
Pn302	1861	—	20 Dollar, Copper, reeded edge, J289	Unique
Pn303	1862	—	1 Cent, Copper, plain edge, J290	2000.
Pn304	1862	—	1 Cent, Copper-Nickel, reeded edge, J291	2000.
Pn305	1862	—	1 Cent, Oroide, plain edge, J292	—
Pn306	1862	—	50 Cent, Silver, reeded edge, J293	2250.
Pn307	1862	—	50 Cent, Copper, reeded edge, J294	1250.
Pn308	1862	—	50 Cent, Silver, reeded edge, J295	2500.
Pn309	1862	—	50 Cent, Copper, reeded edge, J296	3550.
Pn310	1862	—	10 Dollar, Copper, reeded edge, J297	2350.
Pn310a	1862	—	10 Dollar, Copper Bronzed, reeded edge, J297	3250.
Pn311	1862	—	10 Dollar, Copper, reeded edge, J298	3500.
Pn311a	1862	—	10 Dollar, Copper Bronzed, reeded edge, J298	3450.
Pn311b	1862	—	10 Dollar, Copper Gilt, reeded edge, J298	2750.
Pn312	1863	—	1 Cent, Bronze, plain edge, J299	1000.
Pn313	1863	—	1 Cent, Copper-Nickel, reeded edge, J300	1650.
Pn314	1863	3 known	1 Cent, Bronze, plain edge, J301	10,450.
Pn315	1863	—	1 Cent, Copper-Nickel, plain edge, J302	20,900.
Pn316	1863	—	1 Cent, Oroide, plain edge, J303	—
Pn317	1863	2 known	1 Cent, Aluminum, plain edge, J304	—
Pn318	1863	—	2 Cent, Bronze, thick planchet, plain edge, J305	2450.
Pn318a	1863	—	2 Cent, Bronze, thin planchet, plain edge, J305	1850.
Pn319	1863	—	2 Cent, Copper-Nickel, plain edge, J306	2000.
Pn320	1863	—	2 Cent, Oroide, plain edge, J307	—
Pn321	1863	—	2 Cent, Aluminum, plain edge, J308	—
Pn322	1863	—	2 Cent, Bronze, plain edge, J309	2500.
Pn323	1863	—	2 Cent, Copper-Nickel, plain edge, J310	2750.
Pn324	1863	—	2 Cent, Aluminum, plain edge, J311	5000.
Pn325	1863	—	2 Cent, Bronze, plain edge, 96 gr, J312	2000.
Pn326	1863	—	2 Cent, Copper, plain edge, 106 gr, J312a	2000.
Pn327	1863	—	2 Cent, Copper-Nickel, plain edge, J313	2200.
Pn328	1863	—	2 Cent, Aluminum, plain edge, J314	—
Pn329	1863	—	2 Cent, Aluminum, plain edge, small motto, J314a	—
Pn330	1863	—	2 Cent, Bronze, plain edge, J315	4500.
Pn331	1863	—	2 Cent, Bronze, plain edge, J316	8500.
Pn332	1863	—	2 Cent, Copper-Nickel, plain edge, J317	—
Pn333	1863	—	2 Cent, Aluminum, plain edge, J318	6500.
Pn334	1863	—	3 Cent, Bronze, plain edge, 144 gr, J319	2000.
Pn334a	1863	—	3 Cent, Bronze, plain edge, 119 gr, restrike, J319	1850.
Pn335	1863	—	3 Cent, Aluminum, plain edge, J320	5750.
Pn336	1863	—	3 Cent, Copper, plain edge, J321	4500.
Pn337	1863	—	3 Cent, Aluminum, plain edge, J322	3250.
Pn338	1863	—	1/2 Dime, Copper, reeded edge, J323	3750.
Pn339	1863	—	1/2 Dime, Aluminum, reeded edge, J324	2500.
Pn340	1863	—	10 Cent, Silver, plain edge, J325	1650.
Pn341	1863	—	10 Cent, Silver, reeded edge, J325a	—
Pn342	1863	—	10 Cent, Copper-Silver (75-25), reeded edge, thin planchet, 25.25 g, J326	3750.
Pn342a	1863	—	10 Cent, Copper-Silver (75-25), reeded edge, thick planchet, 38.35 gr, J326	4000.
Pn343	1863	—	10 Cent, Copper-Silver (75-25), plain edge, J326a	2500.
Pn344	1863	—	10 Cent, Aluminum, plain edge, 11 gr, J327	2000.
Pn345	1863	—	10 Cent, Aluminum-Silver (97-3), reeded edge, 8 gr, J328	1800.
Pn346	1863	—	10 Cent, Tin, plain edge, 20.5 gr, J329	2150.
Pn347	1863	—	10 Cent, Tin-Copper (97-3), 25 gr, J330	6500.
Pn348	1863	—	10 Cent, Nickel, reeded edge, J330a	4000.
Pn349	1863	—	10 Cent, Silver-Nickel, reeded edge, J331	—
Pn350	1863	—	10 Cent, Copper, reeded edge, J331a	—
Pn351	1863	—	10 Cent, Nickel, J331b	3575.
Pn352	1863	—	10 Cent, Aluminum, plain edge, J332	2750.
Pn353	1863	—	10 Cent, Copper, reeded edge, J333	1600.
Pn354	1863	—	10 Cent, Aluminum, reeded edge, J334	2200.
Pn355	1863	—	25 Cent, Silver, reeded edge, J335	2450.
Pn356	1863	—	25 Cent, Copper, reeded edge, J336	3000.
Pn357	1863	—	25 Cent, Aluminum, reeded edge, J337	3500.
Pn358	1863	—	50 Cent, Silver, reeded edge, J338	1750.
Pn359	1863	—	50 Cent, Copper, reeded edge, J339	1750.
Pn360	1863	—	50 Cent, Silver, reeded edge, J340	2750.
Pn361	1863	—	50 Cent, Copper, reeded edge, J341	2150.
Pn362	1863	—	50 Cent, Silver, reeded edge, J342	2750.
Pn363	1863	—	50 Cent, Copper, reeded edge, J343	2500.
Pn364	1863	—	50 Cent, Aluminum, reeded edge, J344	2750.
Pn365	1863	—	1 Dollar, Silver, reeded edge, J345	27,500.
Pn366	1863	—	1 Dollar, Copper, reeded edge, J346	11,500.
Pn367	1863	—	1 Dollar, Aluminum, reeded edge, J347	10,850.
Pn368	1863	—	1 Dollar, Copper, reeded edge, J348	3000.
Pn369	1863	—	10 Dollar, Gold, reeded edge, J349	Rare
Pn370	1863	—	10 Dollar, Copper, reeded edge, J350	3000.
Pn371	1863	—	10 Dollar, Gold, reeded edge, J351	Rare
Pn372	1863	—	10 Dollar, Copper, reeded edge, J352	3000.
Pn373	1864	—	1 Cent, Copper-Aluminum (13:1), plain edge, 39 gr, J353	1800.
Pn374	1864	—	1 Cent, Copper-Aluminum (19:1), plain edge, J354	4250.
Pn375	1864	—	1 Cent, Copper-Aluminum (9:1), plain edge, 40 gr, J355	1800.
Pn376	1864	—	1 Cent, Bronze, thin planchet, J355a	4150.
Pn377	1864	—	1 Cent, Copper-Tin (9:1), plain edge, 45 gr, J356	2750.
Pn378	1864	—	1 Cent, Copper, thick planchet, plain edge, J356a	1450.
Pn379	1864	—	1 Cent, Copper, plain edge, J357	2250.
Pn380	1864	—	1 Cent, Copper-Nickel, plain edge, thick planchet, J358	2250.
Pn380a	1864	—	1 Cent, Copper-Nickel, plain edge, thin planchet, J358a	2000.
Pn381	1864	—	1 Cent, Nickel, plain edge, J359	—
Pn382	1864	—	1 Cent, Oroide, plain edge, J360	—
Pn383	1864	2	1 Cent, Aluminum, plain edge, J361	2250.
Pn384	1864	—	1 Cent, Composition, plain edge, J361a	6500.
Pn385	1864	—	1 Cent, Copper-Nickel, plain edge, J362	—
Pn386	1864	—	2 Cent, Copper, plain edge, J363	2000.
Pn387	1864	—	2 Cent, Copper-Nickel, plain edge, large planchet, J364	—
Pn388	1864	—	2 Cent, Aluminum, plain edge, J365	—
Pn389	1864	—	2 Cent, Bronze, plain edge, J366	2750.
Pn390	1864	—	2 Cent, Copper, plain edge, J367	2750.
Pn391	1864	—	2 Cent, Copper-Nickel, plain edge,	

KM#	Date	Mintage	Identification	Mkt.Val.
Pn391			J368	—
Pn392	1864	—	2 Cent, Aluminum, plain edge, J369	—
Pn393	1864	—	2 Cent, Copper, plain edge, J370	3000.
Pn394	1864	—	2 Cent, Copper-Nickel, plain edge, J371	1350.
Pn395	1864	—	2 Cent, Aluminum, plain edge, J372	—
Pn396	1864	—	2 Cent, Nickel, plain edge, J372a	—
Pn397	1864	—	2 Cent, Copper, plain edge, J373	—
Pn398	1864	—	2 Cent, Copper-Nickel, plain edge, J374	—
Pn399	1864	—	3 Cent, Copper, plain edge, J375	5000.
Pn400	1864	—	3 Cent, Aluminum, plain edge, J376	5000.
Pn401	1864	—	3 Cent, Nickel, plain edge, J377	—
Pn402	1864	—	1/2 Dime, Copper, reeded edge, J378	2000.
Pn403	1864	—	1/2 Dime, Aluminum, reeded edge, J379	—
Pn404	1864	—	1/2 Dime, Nickel, reeded edge, J380	—
Pn405	1864	—	10 Cent, Copper, reeded edge, J381	2250.
Pn406	1864	—	10 Cent, Aluminum, reeded edge, J382	6000.
Pn407	1864	—	10 Cent, Nickel, reeded edge, J383	6000.
Pn408	1864	—	25 Cent, Silver, reeded edge, J384	3500.
Pn409	1864	—	25 Cent, Copper, reeded edge, J385	2800.
Pn410	1864	—	25 Cent, Silver, reeded edge, J386	4500.
Pn411	1864	—	25 Cent, Copper, reeded edge, J387	2500.
Pn412	1864	—	25 Cent, Aluminum, reeded edge, J388	7500.
Pn413	1864	—	25 Cent, Nickel, reeded edge, J389	9500.
Pn414	1864	—	25 Cent, Copper, reeded edge, J390	—
Pn415	1864	—	50 Cent, Silver, reeded edge, J391	6875.
Pn416	1864	—	50 Cent, Copper, reeded edge, J392	4500.
Pn417	1864	—	50 Cent, Aluminum, reeded edge, J393	5000.
Pn418	1864	—	50 Cent, Nickel, reeded edge, J394	Unique
Pn419	1864	—	50 Cent, Aluminum, reeded edge, J395	3500.
Pn420	1864	—	1 Dollar, Silver, reeded edge, J396	27,500.
Pn421	1864	—	1 Dollar, Copper, reeded edge, J397	—
Pn422	1864	—	1 Dollar, Aluminum, reeded edge, J398	Rare
Pn423	1864	—	1 Dollar, Nickel, reeded edge, J399	Rare
Pn424	1864	—	3 Dollar, Copper, reeded edge, J400	—
Pn425	1864	—	3 Dollar, Copper-Nickel, reeded edge, J401	—
Pn426	1864	—	3 Dollar, Nickel, reeded edge, J402	—
Pn427	1865	—	1 Cent, Copper, plain edge, J403	2500.
Pn428	1865	—	1 Cent, Copper, reeded edge, thin planchet, J403	3000.
Pn428a	1865	—	1 Cent, Copper, reeded edge, thick planchet, J403a	3250.

KM#	Date	Mintage	Identification	Mkt.Val.
Pn429	1865	—	1 Cent, Copper-Nickel, plain edge, thin planchet, J404	3250.
Pn429a	1865	—	1 Cent, Copper-Nickel, plain edge, thick planchet, J404	3500.
Pn430	1865	—	1 Cent, Copper-Nickel, reeded edge, thin planchet, J405	3750.
Pn430a	1865	—	1 Cent, Copper-Nickel, reeded edge, thick planchet, J405	4000.
Pn431	1865	—	1 Cent, Nickel, plain edge, J406	2250.
Pn432	1865	2 known	1 Cent, Nickel-Silver, plain edge, J406a	2000.
Pn433	1865	—	2 Cent, Copper-Silver, plain edge, J407	1750.
Pn434	1865	—	2 Cent, Copper, plain edge, J408	2000.
Pn434a	1865	—	2 Cent, Copper, Silvered, plain edge, J408	3000.
Pn435	1865	—	2 Cent, Copper-Nickel, plain edge, J409	3750.
Pn436	1865	—	2 Cent, Nickel, plain edge, J409a	—
Pn437	1865	—	2 Cent, Silver, plain edge, J409b	—
Pn438	1865	—	3 Cent, Nickel, plain edge, J410	1850.
Pn439	1865	—	3 Cent, Copper, plain edge, J411	1000.
Pn440	1865	—	3 Cent, Aluminum, plain edge, J412	—
Pn441	1865	—	3 Cent, Copper, plain edge, J413	1250.
Pn442	1865	—	3 Cent, Oroide, plain edge, J414	—
Pn443	1865	—	3 Cent, Aluminum, plain edge, J414a	2250.
Pn444	1865	—	3 Cent, Copper, plain edge, J415	2000.

KM#	Date	Mintage	Identification	Mkt.Val.
Pn445	1865	—	5 Cent, Nickel, plain edge, J416	5500.
Pn446	1865	—	5 Cent, Copper, plain edge, J417	3000.
Pn447	1865	—	5 Cent, Nickel, plain edge, J418	3550.
Pn448	1865	—	5 Cent, Copper, plain edge, J419	3550.
Pn449	1865	—	1/2 Dime, Copper, reeded edge, J420	4000.
Pn450	1865	—	10 Cent, Copper, reeded edge, J421	3250.
Pn451	1865	—	10 Cent, Nickel, reeded edge, J422	3750.
Pn452	1865	—	25 Cent, Silver, reeded edge, J423	3575.
Pn453	1865	—	25 Cent, Copper, reeded edge, J424	4000.
Pn454	1865	—	25 Cent, Silver & Copper, reeded edge, J424a	—

KM#	Date	Mintage	Identification	Mkt.Val.
Pn455	1865	—	25 Cent, Silver, reeded edge, J425	4250.
Pn456	1865	—	25 Cent, Copper, reeded edge, J426	4850.
Pn457	1865	—	25 Cent, Aluminum, reeded edge, J427	4850.
Pn458	1865	—	25 Cent, Copper, J428	—

KM#	Date	Mintage	Identification	Mkt.Val.
Pn459	1865	—	50 Cent, Silver, reeded edge, J429	4650.
Pn460	1865	—	50 Cent, Copper, reeded edge, J430	3250.
Pn461	1865	—	50 Cent, Aluminum, reeded edge, J431	3750.

KM#	Date	Mintage	Identification	Mkt.Val.
Pn462	1865	—	50 Cent, Copper, reeded edge, J432	2750.
Pn463	1865	—	50 Cent, Aluminum, reeded edge, J433	4000.
Pn464	1865	—	1 Dollar, Silver, reeded edge, J434	12,000.
Pn465	1865	—	1 Dollar, Copper, reeded edge, J435	9000.
Pn466	1865	—	1 Dollar, Aluminum, reeded edge, J436	9000.
Pn467	1865	—	1 Dollar, Copper, reeded edge, J437	4000.
Pn468	1865	—	1 Gold Dollar, Copper, reeded edge, J438	5750.
Pn469	1865	—	2-1/2 Dollar, Copper, reeded edge, J439	3000.
Pn470	1865	2 known	3 Dollar, Gold, reeded edge, J440	14,950.
Pn471	1865	—	3 Dollar, Copper, reeded edge, J441	4400.
Pn472	1865	1 known	3 Dollar, Silver, reeded edge, J441a	—
Pn473	1865	—	3 Dollar, Copper, reeded edge, J442	—
Pn474	1865	—	3 Dollar, Copper-Nickel, reeded edge, J443	—
Pn475	1865	—	3 Dollar, Nickel, reeded edge, J444	—
Pn476	1865	—	3 Dollar, Bronze, reeded edge, J444a	—
Pn477	1865	2 known	5 Dollar, Gold, reeded edge, J445	Rare
Pn478	1865	—	5 Dollar, Copper, reeded edge, J446	5250.
Pn479	1865	—	5 Dollar, Copper, reeded edge, J447	5250.
Pn480	1865	—	5 Dollar, Aluminum, reeded edge, J448	6000.
Pn481	1865	2 known	10 Dollar, Gold, reeded edge, J449	Rare
Pn482	1865	—	10 Dollar, Copper, reeded edge, J450	6500.
Pn483	1865	—	10 Dollar, Copper, reeded edge, J451	6000.

KM#	Date	Mintage	Identification	Mkt.Val.
Pn484	1865	2 known	20 Dollar, Gold, reeded edge, J452	Rare
Pn485	1865	—	20 Dollar, Copper, reeded edge, J453	9000.
Pn486	1865	—	20 Dollar, Copper Gilt, reeded edge, J453	—
Pn487	1865	—	20 Dollar, Copper, reeded edge, J454	—
Pn488	1866	—	1 Cent, Copper, plain edge, J455	2150.
Pn489	1866	—	1 Cent, Copper-Nickel, plain edge, J456	2150.
Pn490	1866	—	1 Cent, Nickel, plain edge, J457	2250.
Pn491	1866	—	2 Cent, Copper-Nickel, plain edge, J458	—
Pn492	1866	—	2 Cent, Nickel, plain edge, J459	2000.
Pn493	1866	—	3 Cent, Copper, plain edge, J460	1500.

KM#	Date	Mintage	Identification	Mkt.Val.
Pn494	1866	—	5 Cent, Nickel, plain edge, J461	1800.
Pn495	1866	—	5 Cent, Copper, plain edge, J462	4000.
Pn496	1866	—	5 Cent, Copper-Nickel, plain edge, J463	3000.

KM#	Date	Mintage	Identification	Mkt.Val.
Pn497	1866	—	5 Cent, Nickel, plain edge, J464	4500.
Pn498	1866	—	5 Cent, Copper, plain edge, J465	8500.
Pn499	1866	—	5 Cent, Bronze, plain edge, J466	7150.
Pn500	1866	—	5 Cent, Silver, plain edge, J466a	—

KM#	Date	Mintage	Identification	Mkt.Val.
Pn501	1866	—	5 Cent, Nickel, plain edge, J467	3000.
Pn502	1866	—	5 Cent, Copper, plain edge, J468	3000.
Pn503	1866	—	5 Cent, Bronze, plain edge, J469	2500.

KM#	Date	Mintage	Identification	Mkt.Val.
Pn504	1866	—	5 Cent, Nickel, plain edge, J470	3200.
Pn505	1866	—	5 Cent, Copper, plain edge, J471	3000.
Pn506	1866	—	5 Cent, Bronze, plain edge, J472	3200.

KM#	Date	Mintage	Identification	Mkt.Val.
Pn507	1866	—	5 Cent, Nickel, plain edge, J473	2500.
Pn508	1866	—	5 Cent, Copper, plain edge, J474	2500.
Pn509	1866	—	5 Cent, Bronze, plain edge, J475	2500.

KM#	Date	Mintage	Identification	Mkt.Val.
Pn510	1866	1 known	5 Cent, Nickel, plain edge, J476	—
Pn511	1866	2 known	5 Cent, Copper, plain edge, J477	6500.
Pn512	1866	1 known	5 Cent, Brass, plain edge, J478	—
Pn513	1866	3 known	5 Cent, White Metal, plain edge, J479	6000.
Pn514	1866	—	5 Cent, Nickel, plain edge, J480	Unique
Pn515	1866	—	5 Cent, Nickel, plain edge, J481	4000.
Pn516	1866	—	5 Cent, Copper, plain edge, J482	4500.
Pn517	1866	—	5 Cent, Nickel, plain edge, J483	5750.
Pn518	1866	—	5 Cent, Copper, plain edge, J484	5500.
Pn519	1866	—	5 Cent, Bronze, plain edge, J485	8000.

KM#	Date	Mintage	Identification	Mkt.Val.
Pn520	1866	—	5 Cent, Nickel, plain edge, J486	6000.
Pn521	1866	—	5 Cent, Copper, plain edge, J487	4000.
Pn522	1866	—	5 Cent, Bronze, plain edge, J488	4850.

KM#	Date	Mintage	Identification	Mkt.Val.
Pn523	1866	—	5 Cent, Nickel, plain edge, J489	2500.
Pn524	1866	—	5 Cent, Copper, plain edge, J490	3250.
Pn525	1866	—	5 Cent, Bronze, plain edge, J491	3250.

KM#	Date	Mintage	Identification	Mkt.Val.
Pn526	1866	—	5 Cent, Nickel, plain edge, J492	4500.
Pn527	1866	—	5 Cent, Copper, plain edge, J493	4500.

KM#	Date	Mintage	Identification	Mkt.Val.
Pn528	1866	—	5 Cent, Nickel, plain edge, J494	7500.
Pn529	1866	—	5 Cent, Copper, plain edge, J495	7150.
Pn530	1866	—	5 Cent, Bronze, plain edge, J496	7150.

KM#	Date	Mintage	Identification	Mkt.Val.
Pn531	1866	—	5 Cent, Nickel, plain edge, J497	4500.
Pn532	1866	—	5 Cent, Copper, plain edge, J498	5250.
Pn533	1866	—	5 Cent, Bronze, plain edge, J499	5250.
Pn534	1866	—	5 Cent, Nickel, plain edge, J500	—
Pn535	1866	—	5 Cent, Nickel, plain edge, J501	4650.
Pn536	1866	—	5 Cent, Copper, plain edge, J502	4650.
Pn537	1866	—	5 Cent, Bronze, plain edge, J503	4650.
Pn538	1866	—	5 Cent, Nickel, plain edge, J504	3350.
Pn539	1866	—	5 Cent, Copper, plain edge, J505	2750.
Pn540	1866	—	5 Cent, Bronze, plain edge, J506	2750.

KM#	Date	Mintage	Identification	Mkt.Val.
Pn541	1866	—	5 Cent, Nickel, plain edge, J507	3150.
Pn542	1866	—	5 Cent, Copper, plain edge, J508	2500.
Pn543	1866	—	5 Cent, Bronze, plain edge, J509	3000.
Pn544	1866	—	5 Cent, White Metal, J509a	3000.
Pn545	1866	—	5 Cent, Copper, plain edge, J510	—
Pn546	1866	—	5 Cent, Bronze, plain edge, J511	—
Pn547	1866	—	5 Cent, Steel, plain edge, J512	—
Pn548	1866	—	5 Cent, Nickel, plain edge, J513	—
Pn549	1866	—	5 Cent, Copper, plain edge, J514	—

KM#	Date	Mintage	Identification	Mkt.Val.
Pn550	1866	—	5 Cent, Brass, plain edge, J515	—
Pn551	1866	—	5 Cent, Nickel, plain edge, J516	2250.
Pn552	1866	—	5 Cent, Copper, plain edge, J517	2750.
Pn553	1866	—	5 Cent, Silver, plain edge, J518	4500.
Pn554	1866	—	5 Cent, Brass, plain edge, J519	4000.

KM#	Date	Mintage	Identification	Mkt.Val.
Pn555	1866	—	5 Cent, Lead, plain edge, J520	1750.

KM#	Date	Mintage	Identification	Mkt.Val.
Pn556	1866	—	5 Cent, Silver, plain edge, J521	—
Pn557	1866	—	5 Cent, Copper, plain edge, J522	4000.
Pn558	1866	—	5 Cent, Brass, plain edge, J523	4000.
Pn559	1866	—	5 Cent, White Metal, plain edge, J524	4000.
Pn559a	1866	—	5 Cent, Nickel, plain edge, J524a	7750.
Pn560	1866	—	5 Cent, Copper, plain edge, J525	8500.
Pn561	1866	—	5 Cent, White Metal, plain edge, J526	4000.
Pn562	1866	—	5 Cent, Nickel, plain edge, J527	—
Pn563	1866	—	5 Cent, Nickel, plain edge, J528	—
Pn564	1866	—	5 Cent, Nickel, plain edge, J529	—
Pn565	1866	—	5 Cent, White Metal, plain edge, J530	5000.
Pn566	1866	—	5 Cent, Nickel, plain edge, J531	5000.
Pn567	1866	—	5 Cent, Nickel, plain edge, J531a	5000.
Pn568	1866	—	5 Cent, White Metal, plain edge, J532	7500.
Pn569	1866	—	5 Cent, Copper, plain edge, J533	—
Pn570	1866	—	10 Cent, Nickel, reeded edge, J534	3500.
Pn571	1866	—	10 Cent, Silver Nickel, reeded edge, J535	3000.
Pn572	1866	—	25 Cent, Silver, reeded edge, J536	Unique
Pn573	1866	—	25 Cent, Copper, reeded edge, J537	5000.
Pn574	1866	—	50 Cent, Silver, reeded edge, J538	Unique
Pn575	1866	—	50 Cent, Copper, reeded edge, J539	1750.
Pn576	1866	2 known	1 Dollar, Silver, reeded edge, J540	Rare
Pn577	1866	—	1 Dollar, Copper, reeded edge, J541	5000.
Pn578	1866	—	2-1/2 Dollar, Nickel, reeded edge, J542	5200.
Pn579	1866	—	3 Dollar, Nickel, reeded edge, J543	5300.
Pn580	1866	—	3 Dollar, Aluminum, reeded edge, J544	—
Pn581	1866	1 known	5 Dollar, White Metal, plain edge, J545	Rare
Pn582	1866	—	5 Dollar, Copper, reeded edge, J546	3500.
Pn583	1866	1 known	5 Dollar, White Metal, plain edge, J547	4500.
Pn584	1866	—	10 Dollar, Copper, reeded edge, J548	4850.
Pn585	1866	—	20 Dollar, Copper, reeded edge, J549	7000.
Pn585a	1866	—	20 Dollar, Copper, Gilt, reeded edge, J549	7000.
Pn586	1867	—	1 Cent, Copper, plain edge, J550	2250.
Pn587	1867	—	1 Cent, Copper-Nickel, plain edge, J551	—
Pn588	1867	—	1 Cent, Nickel, plain edge, J552	2500.
Pn589	1867	—	1 Cent, Oroide, plain edge, J553	—
Pn590	1867	—	2 Cent, Copper, plain edge, J554	2000.
Pn591	1867	—	2 Cent, Copper-Nickel, plain edge, J555	—
Pn592	1867	—	2 Cent, Nickel, plain edge, J556	2250.
Pn593	1867	—	2 Cent, Oroide, plain edge, J557	2000.
Pn594	1867	—	3 Cent, Copper, plain edge, J558	2650.

KM#	Date	Mintage	Identification	Mkt.Val.
Pn595	1867	—	3 Cent, Oroide, plain edge, J559	—
Pn596	1867	—	3 Cent, Copper, plain edge, J560	2000.

KM#	Date	Mintage	Identification	Mkt.Val.
Pn597	1867	—	5 Cent, Aluminum, plain edge, J561	1850.
Pn598	1867	—	5 Cent, Aluminum, reeded edge, J562	2150.
Pn599	1867	—	5 Cent, Copper, plain edge, J563	—
Pn600	1867	—	5 Cent, Copper, reeded edge, J564	2500.
Pn601	1867	—	5 Cent, Nickel, plain edge, J565	—

KM#	Date	Mintage	Identification	Mkt.Val.
Pn602	1867	—	5 Cent, Nickel, plain edge, J566	2150.
Pn603	1867	—	5 Cent, Copper, plain edge, J567	2250.
Pn604	1867	—	5 Cent, Copper, plain edge, J568	—
Pn605	1867	1 known	5 Cent, Nickel, plain edge, J569	—
Pn606	1867	—	5 Cent, Nickel, plain edge, J570	1750.
Pn607	1867	—	5 Cent, Copper, plain edge, J571	2000.
Pn608	1867	—	5 Cent, Copper, plain edge, J572	3500.

KM#	Date	Mintage	Identification	Mkt.Val.
Pn609	1867	—	5 Cent, Copper, plain edge, J573	2650.

KM#	Date	Mintage	Identification	Mkt.Val.
Pn610	1867	2 known	5 Cent, Copper, plain edge, J573a	5000.
Pn611	1867	—	5 Cent, White Metal, plain edge, J574	—
Pn612	1867	—	5 Cent, Nickel, plain edge, J575	—
Pn613	1867	—	5 Cent, Nickel, plain edge, J576	—
Pn614	1867	—	5 Cent, Nickel, plain edge, J577	—
Pn615	1867	—	5 Cent, Nickel, plain edge, J578	—
Pn616	1867	—	5 Cent, Copper, plain edge, J578a	—
Pn617	1867	—	5 Cent, Silver, plain edge, J579	—
Pn618	1867	—	5 Cent, Nickel, plain edge, J580	—
Pn619	1867	—	5 Cent, White Metal, plain edge, J581	—
Pn620	1867	—	5 Cent, Nickel, plain edge, J582	2750.
Pn621	1867	—	5 Cent, Silver, plain edge, J583	2750.
Pn622	1867	—	5 Cent, White Metal, plain edge, J584	—
Pn622a	1867	—	5 Cent, Nickel, plain edge, J584a	9350.
Pn623	1867	—	5 Cent, White Metal, plain edge, J585	3000.
Pn624	1867	—	1/2 Dime, Copper, reeded edge, J586	2750.

KM#	Date	Mintage	Identification	Mkt.Val.
Pn625	1867	—	10 Cent, Copper, reeded edge, J587	5000.
Pn626	1867	—	10 Cent, Nickel, reeded edge, J588	4250.
Pn627	1867	—	10 Cent, Silver-Nickel, reeded edge, J589	—
Pn628	1867	—	25 Cent, Copper, reeded edge, J590	3000.
Pn629	1867	—	50 Cent, Copper, reeded edge, J591	3250.

KM#	Date	Mintage	Identification	Mkt.Val.
Pn630	1867	—	1 Dollar, Copper, reeded edge, J592	4500.
Pn631	1867	5	1 Dollar, Brass, reeded edge, J593	7000.
Pn632	1867	—	1 Gold Dollar, Copper, reeded edge, J594	—
Pn633	1867	—	2-1/2 Dollar, Copper, reeded edge, J595	5500.
Pn634	1867	—	3 Dollar, Copper, reeded edge, J596	5250.
Pn635	1867	—	3 Dollar, Nickel, reeded edge, J597	18,400.
Pn636	1867	—	3 Dollar, Silver, reeded edge, J598	6500.
Pn637	1867	—	5 Dollar, Copper, reeded edge, J599	4000.
Pn638	1867	—	5 Dollar, Nickel, reeded edge, J600	4000.

KM#	Date	Mintage	Identification	Mkt.Val.
Pn639	1867	2 known	5 Dollar, Nickel, plain edge, J601	7150.
Pn640	1867	—	10 Dollar, Copper, reeded edge, J602	6850.
Pn641	1867	—	10 Dollar, Nickel, reeded edge, J603	7000.
Pn642	1867	—	20 Dollar, Copper, reeded edge, J604	10,350.
Pn643	1868	—	1 Cent, Nickel, plain edge, J605	2000.
Pn644	1868	—	1 Cent, Copper, plain edge, J606	2500.
Pn645	1868	—	1 Cent, Aluminum, plain edge, J607	2750.

KM#	Date	Mintage	Identification	Mkt.Val.
Pn646	1868	—	1 Cent, Nickel, plain edge, J608	1600.
Pn647	1868	—	1 Cent, Copper, plain edge, J609	2000.

KM#	Date	Mintage	Identification	Mkt.Val.
Pn648	1868	—	1 Cent, Nickel, plain edge, J610	6500.
Pn649	1868	—	1 Cent, Copper, plain edge, J611	16,100.
Pn650	1868	—	1 Cent, Aluminum, plain edge, J612	2650.
Pn651	1868	—	2 Cent, Nickel, plain edge, J613	3000.
Pn652	1868	—	2 Cent, Aluminum, plain edge, J614	3000.

KM#	Date	Mintage	Identification	Mkt.Val.
Pn653	1868	—	3 Cent, Nickel, plain edge, J615	2250.
Pn654	1868	—	3 Cent, Copper-Nickel, plain edge, J615a	1750.
Pn655	1868	—	3 Cent, Copper, plain edge, J616	2000.
Pn656	1868	—	3 Cent, Aluminum, plain edge, J617	2000.
Pn657	1868	—	3 Cent, Aluminum, plain edge, J617a	—
Pn658	1868	2 known	3 Cent, Copper, plain edge, J617b	—
Pn659	1868	—	3 Cent, Copper-Nickel, plain edge, J617c	—

KM#	Date	Mintage	Identification	Mkt.Val.
Pn660	1868	—	3 Cent, Nickel, plain edge, J618	1450.
Pn661	1868	—	3 Cent, Copper, plain edge, J619	2750.
Pn662	1868	—	3 Cent, Aluminum, plain edge, J620	1750.
Pn663	1868	—	3 Cent, Aluminum, plain edge, J620a	—
Pn664	1868	—	3 Cent, Aluminum, plain edge, J621	1700.
Pn665	1868	—	3 Cent, Aluminum, plain edge, J622	1850.

KM#	Date	Mintage	Identification	Mkt.Val.
Pn666	1868	—	5 Cent, Nickel, plain edge, J623	1250.

KM#	Date	Mintage	Identification	Mkt.Val.
Pn667	1868	—	5 Cent, Nickel, broad planchet, plain edge, J624	2450.
Pn668	1868	—	5 Cent, Nickel, broad planchet, reeded edge, J625	6500.
Pn669	1868	—	5 Cent, Copper, plain edge, J626	2000.
Pn670	1868	—	5 Cent, Copper, broad planchet, plain edge, J627	3000.
Pn671	1868	—	5 Cent, Copper, broad planchet, reeded edge, J628	3000.
Pn672	1868	—	5 Cent, Aluminum, plain edge, J629	3750.

KM#	Date	Mintage	Identification	Mkt.Val.
Pn673	1868	—	5 Cent, Nickel, plain edge, J630	4500.

KM#	Date	Mintage	Identification	Mkt.Val.
Pn674	1868	—	5 Cent, Copper, plain edge, J631	5500.
Pn675	1868	—	5 Cent, Copper, plain edge, J632	—
Pn676	1868	—	5 Cent, Aluminum, plain edge, J632a	Rare

KM#	Date	Mintage	Identification	Mkt.Val.
Pn677	1868	—	5 Cent, Nickel, plain edge, J633	1350.
Pn678	1868	—	5 Cent, Copper, plain edge, J634	1750.
Pn679	1868	—	5 Cent, Copper, plain edge, J635	3200.
Pn680	1868	—	5 Cent, Aluminum, plain edge, J636	3000.
Pn681	1868	—	1/2 Dime, Copper, plain edge, J637	2750.
Pn682	1868	—	1/2 Dime, Nickel, plain edge, J638	2000.
Pn683	1868	—	1/2 Dime, Aluminum, plain edge, J639	3000.
Pn684	1868	—	10 Cent, Silver, reeded edge, J640	—
Pn685	1868	—	10 Cent, Nickel, reeded edge, J641	3000.
Pn686	1868	—	10 Cent, Copper, reeded edge, J642	3750.
Pn687	1868	—	10 Cent, Silver, reeded edge, J643	3000.
Pn688	1868	—	10 Cent, Nickel, reeded edge, J644	3750.
Pn689	1868	—	10 Cent, Copper, plain edge, J645	4500.
Pn690	1868	—	10 Cent, Aluminum, plain edge, J646	3250.

KM#	Date	Mintage	Identification	Mkt.Val.
Pn691	1868	—	10 Cent, Nickel, plain edge, J647	3000.
Pn692	1868	—	10 Cent, Copper, plain edge, J648	2800.
Pn693	1868	—	10 Cent, Aluminum, reeded edge, J649	5000.
Pn694	1868	—	25 Cent, Aluminum, reeded edge, J650	6000.
Pn695	1868	—	50 Cent, Aluminum, reeded edge, J651	7000.
Pn696	1868	—	1 Dollar, Aluminum, reeded edge, J652	7500.
Pn697	1868	—	1 Gold Dollar, Aluminum, reeded edge, J653	8000.
Pn698	1868	—	2-1/2 Dollar, Aluminum, reeded edge, J654	8500.
Pn699	1868	—	3 Dollar, Aluminum, reeded edge, J655	9000.

KM#	Date	Mintage	Identification	Mkt.Val.
Pn700	1868	—	5 Dollar, Copper, reeded edge, J656	7000.
Pn700a	1868	—	5 Dollar, Copper Gilt, reeded edge, J656	7250.
Pn701	1868	—	5 Dollar, Copper, plain edge, J657	4750.
Pn702	1868	—	5 Dollar, Aluminum, reeded edge, J658	4750.
Pn703	1868	—	5 Dollar, Alluminum, plain edge, J659	4750.
Pn704	1868	—	5 Dollar, Aluminum, reeded edge, J660	4500.

KM#	Date	Mintage	Identification	Mkt.Val.
Pn705	1868	4 known	10 Dollar, Gold, reeded edge, J661	Rare
Pn706	1868	—	10 Dollar, Copper, reeded edge, J662	4750.
Pn706a	1868	—	10 Dollar, Copper Gilt, reeded edge, J662	4600.
Pn707	1868	—	10 Dollar, Aluminum, reeded edge, J663	4250.
Pn708	1868	—	10 Dollar, Aluminum, reeded edge, J664	4850.
Pn709	1868	—	20 Dollar, Aluminum, reeded edge, J665	7000.

KM#	Date	Mintage	Identification	Mkt.Val.
Pn710	1869	—	1 Cent, Nickel, plain edge, J666	1650.
Pn711	1869	—	1 Cent, Copper, plain edge, J667	3000.
Pn712	1869	—	1 Cent, Copper, plain edge, J668	1650.
Pn713	1869	—	1 Cent, Copper-Nickel, plain edge, J669	3250.
Pn714	1869	—	1 Cent, Nickel, plain edge, J670	1850.
Pn715	1869	—	1 Cent, Aluminum, plain edge, J671	1650.
Pn716	1869	—	2 Cent, Copper, plain edge, J672	4000.
Pn717	1869	—	2 Cent, Nickel, plain edge, J673	—
Pn718	1869	—	2 Cent, Aluminum, plain edge, J674	4000.
Pn719	1869	—	2 Cent, Copper-Aluminum, plain edge, J674a	3950.
Pn720	1869	—	2 Cent, Silver-Copper, plain edge, J675	—
Pn721	1869	—	3 Cent, Nickel, plain edge, J676	1750.
Pn722	1869	—	3 Cent, Copper, plain edge, J677	2500.
Pn723	1869	—	3 Cent, Copper, plain edge, J678	2450.
Pn724	1869	—	3 Cent, Aluminum, plain edge, J679	2200.
Pn725	1869	—	3 Cent, Copper, plain edge, J680	2000.
Pn726	1869	—	3 Cent, Nickel, plain edge, J681	—
Pn727	1869	—	3 Cent, Aluminum, plain edge, J682	2200.
Pn728	1869	—	5 Cent, Nickel, plain edge, J683	6650.

KM#	Date	Mintage	Identification	Mkt.Val.
Pn729	1869	—	5 Cent, Nickel, plain edge, J684	2150.
Pn730	1869	—	5 Cent, Copper, plain edge, J685	2150.
Pn731	1869	—	5 Cent, Nickel, plain edge, J686	—
PnA732	1869	—	5 Cent, Nickel, obv. as Pn731, rev. bust right Washington	10,450.
Pn732	1869	—	5 Cent, Copper, plain edge, J687	6500.
Pn733	1869	—	5 Cent, Aluminum, plain edge, J688	6000.
Pn734	1869	—	5 Cent, Steel, plain edge, J689	Unique
Pn735	1869	—	5 Cent, Nickel, plain edge, J690	—
Pn736	1869	—	5 Cent, Nickel, plain edge, J691	Unique
Pn737	1869	—	1/2 Dime, Copper, reeded edge, J692	2000.
Pn738	1869	—	1/2 Dime, Aluminum, reeded edge, J693	1550.
Pn739	1869	—	1/2 Dime, Nickel, reeded edge, J694	2750.
Pn740	1869	—	1/2 Dime, Nickel, plain edge, J695	2750.

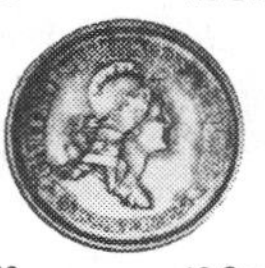

KM#	Date	Mintage	Identification	Mkt.Val.
Pn741	1869	—	10 Cent, Silver, reeded edge, J696	1150.
Pn742	1869	—	10 Cent, Silver, plain edge, J697	1150.
Pn743	1869	—	10 Cent, Copper, reeded edge, J698	1000.
Pn744	1869	—	10 Cent, Copper, plain edge, J699	2850.
Pn745	1869	—	10 Cent, Aluminum, reeded edge, J700	3750.
Pn746	1869	—	10 Cent, Aluminum, reeded edge, J701	3250.

KM#	Date	Mintage	Identification	Mkt.Val.
Pn747	1869	—	10 Cent, Silver, reeded edge, J702	1150.
Pn748	1869	—	10 Cent, Silver, plain edge, J703	2700.
Pn749	1869	—	10 Cent, Copper, reeded edge, J704	3000.
Pn750	1869	—	10 Cent, Copper, plain edge, J705	1750.
Pn751	1869	—	10 Cent, Aluminum, reeded edge, J706	1500.
Pn752	1869	—	10 Cent, Aluminum, plain edge, J707	1850.

KM#	Date	Mintage	Identification	Mkt.Val.
Pn753	1869	—	10 Cent, Silver, reeded edge, J708	1250.
Pn754	1869	—	10 Cent, Silver, plain edge, J709	1250.
Pn755	1869	—	10 Cent, Copper, reeded edge, J710	1650.
Pn756	1869	—	10 Cent, Copper, plain edge, J711	1650.
Pn757	1869	—	10 Cent, Aluminum, reeded edge, J712	1650.
Pn758	1869	—	10 Cent, Aluminum, plain edge, J713	1650.

KM#	Date	Mintage	Identification	Mkt.Val.
Pn759	1869	—	10 Cent, Silver-Nickel, reeded edge, J714	2500.
Pn760	1869	—	10 Cent, Copper, reeded edge, J715	2500.

KM#	Date	Mintage	Identification	Mkt.Val.
Pn761	1869	—	10 Cent, Silver-Nickel-Copper, reeded edge, J716	1800.
Pn762	1869	3 known	10 Cent, Silver, reeded edge, J716a	3500.
Pn763	1869	—	10 Cent, Copper, reeded edge, J717	2500.
Pn764	1869	—	10 Cent, Copper-Nickel (75-25), reeded edge, J717a	—
Pn765	1869	—	10 Cent, Copper, reeded edge, J718	4000.
Pn766	1869	—	10 Cent, Aluminum, reeded edge, J719	4000.

KM#	Date	Mintage	Identification	Mkt.Val.
Pn767	1869	—	10 Cent, Nickel, reeded edge, J720	3000.

KM#	Date	Mintage	Identification	Mkt.Val.
Pn768	1869	—	25 Cent, Silver, reeded edge, J721	1250.
Pn769	1869	—	25 Cent, Silver, plain edge, J722	2000.
Pn770	1869	—	25 Cent, Copper, reeded edge, J723	2200.
Pn771	1869	—	25 Cent, Copper, plain edge, J724	2200.
Pn772	1869	—	25 Cent, Aluminum, reeded edge, J725	2200.
Pn773	1869	—	25 Cent, Aluminum, plain edge, J726	1650.

KM#	Date	Mintage	Identification	Mkt.Val.
Pn774	1869	—	25 Cent, Silver, reeded edge, J727	1750.
Pn775	1869	—	25 Cent, Silver, plain edge, J728	1850.
Pn776	1869	—	25 Cent, Copper, reeded edge, J729	1250.
Pn777	1869	—	25 Cent, Copper, plain edge, J730	1250.
Pn778	1869	—	25 Cent, Aluminum, reeded edge, J731	1800.
Pn779	1869	—	25 Cent, Aluminum, plain edge, J732	1800.

KM#	Date	Mintage	Identification	Mkt.Val.
Pn780	1869	—	25 Cent, Silver, reeded edge, J733	1450.
Pn781	1869	—	25 Cent, Silver, plain edge, J734	3650.
Pn782	1869	—	25 Cent, Copper, reeded edge, J735	1200.
Pn783	1869	—	25 Cent, Copper, plain edge, J736	1500.
Pn784	1869	—	25 Cent, Aluminum, reeded edge, J737	1000.
Pn785	1869	—	25 Cent, Aluminum, plain edge, J738	1000.
Pn786	1869	—	25 Cent, Copper, reeded edge, J739	1500.
Pn787	1869	—	25 Cent, Aluminum, reeded edge, J740	1500.
Pn788	1869	—	25 Cent, Aluminum, plain edge, J741	—

KM#	Date	Mintage	Identification	Mkt.Val.
Pn789	1869	—	50 Cent, Silver, reeded edge, J742	2000.
Pn790	1869	—	50 Cent, Silver, reeded edge, J742a	Rare
Pn791	1869	—	50 Cent, Silver, plain edge, J743	2200.
Pn792	1869	—	50 Cent, Copper, reeded edge, J744	2550.
Pn793	1869	—	50 Cent, Copper, plain edge, J745	3250.
Pn794	1869	—	50 Cent, Aluminum, reeded edge, J746	2250.
Pn795	1869	—	50 Cent, Aluminum, plain edge, J747	3650.
Pn796	1869	—	50 Cent, Silver, reeded edge, w/o "B", J747a	—

KM#	Date	Mintage	Identification	Mkt.Val.
Pn797	1869	—	50 Cent, Silver, reeded edge, J748	1650.
Pn798	1869	—	50 Cent, Silver, plain edge, J749	2650.

KM#	Date	Mintage	Identification	Mkt.Val.
Pn799	1869	—	50 Cent, Copper, reeded edge, J750	2850.
Pn800	1869	—	50 Cent, Copper, reeded edge, J751	2500.
Pn801	1869	—	50 Cent, Aluminum, reeded edge, J752	2500.
Pn802	1869	—	50 Cent, Aluminum, plain edge, J753	2200.
Pn803	1869	—	50 Cent, Brass, reeded edge, J753a	Unique

KM#	Date	Mintage	Identification	Mkt.Val.
Pn804	1869	—	50 Cent, Silver, reeded edge, J754	1650.
Pn805	1869	—	50 Cent, Silver, plain edge, J755	1850.
Pn806	1869	—	50 Cent, Copper, reeded edge, J756	1500.
Pn807	1869	—	50 Cent, Copper, plain edge, J757	2000.
Pn808	1869	—	50 Cent, Aluminum, reeded edge, J758	3600.
Pn809	1869	—	50 Cent, Aluminum, plain edge, J759	3200.
Pn810	1869	—	50 Cent, Brass, reeded edge, J759a	Unique
Pn811	1869	—	50 Cent, Copper, reeded edge, J760	3650.
Pn812	1869	—	50 Cent, Aluminum, reeded edge, J761	4650.
Pn813	1869	—	50 Cent, Nickel, reeded edge, J762	6000.
Pn814	1869	—	1 Dollar, Copper, reeded edge, J763	4250.
Pn815	1869	—	1 Dollar, Aluminum, reeded edge, J764	4250.
Pn816	1869	—	1 Dollar, Nickel, reeded edge, J765	4500.
Pn817	1869	—	1 Gold Dollar, Copper, reeded edge, J766	—
Pn818	1869	—	1 Gold Dollar, Aluminum, reeded edge, J767	4500.
Pn819	1869	—	1 Gold Dollar, Nickel, reeded edge, J768	4500.
Pn820	1869	—	2-1/2 Dollar, Copper, reeded edge, J769	4500.
Pn821	1869	—	2-1/2 Dollar, Aluminum, reeded edge, J770	5750.
Pn822	1869	—	2-1/2 Dollar, Nickel, reeded edge, J771	—
Pn823	1869	—	3 Dollar, Copper, reeded edge, J772	4250.
Pn824	1869	—	3 Dollar, Aluminum, reeded edge, J773	3950.
Pn825	1869	—	3 Dollar, Nickel, reeded edge, J774	—
Pn826	1869	—	5 Dollar, Copper, reeded edge, J775	2250.
Pn827	1869	—	5 Dollar, Aluminum, reeded edge, J776	1950.
Pn828	1869	—	5 Dollar, Nickel, reeded edge, J777	—
Pn829	1869	—	5 Dollar, Brass, reeded edge, J778	Unique
Pn830	1869	—	10 Dollar, Copper, thick planchet, reeded edge, J779	5500.
Pn830a	1869	—	10 Dollar, Copper Bronzed, thick planchet, reeded edge, J779a	5000.
Pn830b	1869	—	10 Dollar, Copper, thin planchet, reeded edge, J779	5500.
Pn830c	1869	—	10 Dollar, Copper Bronzed, thin planchet, reeded edge, J779	5000.
Pn831	1869	—	10 Dollar, Aluminum, reeded edge, J780	6000.
Pn832	1869	—	10 Dollar, Copper, reeded edge, J781	5000.
Pn833	1869	—	10 Dollar, Aluminum, reeded edge, J782	5750.
Pn834	1869	—	10 Dollar, Nickel, reeded edge, J783	—
Pn835	1869	—	20 Dollar, Copper, reeded edge, J784	5000.
Pn836	1869	—	20 Dollar, Aluminum, reeded edge, J785	5000.
Pn837	1869	—	20 Dollar, Nickel, reeded edge, J786	—
Pn838	1870	—	1 Cent, Copper, plain edge, J787	3000.
Pn839	1870	—	1 Cent, Aluminum, plain edge, J788	3000.
Pn840	1870	—	1 Cent, Nickel, plain edge, J789	—
Pn841	1870	—	2 Cent, Copper, plain edge, J790	5000.
Pn842	1870	—	2 Cent, Aluminum, plain edge, J791	5000.
Pn843	1870	—	2 Cent, Nickel, plain edge, J792	—
Pn844	1870	—	2 Cent, Silver-Copper, plain edge, J793	6000.
Pn845	1870	—	3 Cent, Copper, plain edge, J794	3000.
Pn846	1870	—	3 Cent, Aluminum, plain edge, J795	3000.

KM#	Date	Mintage	Identification	Mkt.Val.
Pn847	1870	—	3 Cent, Silver, plain edge, J796	4500.
Pn848	1870	—	3 Cent, Silver, reeded edge, J797	3500.
Pn849	1870	—	3 Cent, Copper, plain edge, J798	2500.
Pn850	1870	—	3 Cent, Copper, reeded edge, J799	2750.
Pn851	1870	—	3 Cent, Aluminum, plain edge, J800	2500.
Pn852	1870	—	3 Cent, Aluminum, reeded edge, J801	2500.
Pn853	1870	—	3 Cent, Copper, plain edge, J802	3200.
Pn854	1870	—	3 Cent, Aluminum, plain edge, J803	3200.
Pn855	1870	—	3 Cent, Nickel, plain edge, J804	—
Pn856	1870	—	3 Cent, Brass, plain edge, J804a	—
Pn857	1870	—	5 Cent, Copper, plain edge, J805	3200.
Pn858	1870	—	5 Cent, Aluminum, plain edge, J806	3250.
Pn859	1870	—	5 Cent, Nickel, plain edge, J807	—
Pn860	1870	—	5 Cent, Steel, plain edge, J808	Unique

KM#	Date	Mintage	Identification	Mkt.Val.
Pn861	1870	—	1/2 Dime, Silver, reeded edge, J809	2550.
Pn862	1870	—	1/2 Dime, Silver, plain edge, J810	3200.
Pn863	1870	—	1/2 Dime, Copper, reeded edge, J811	4200.
Pn864	1870	—	1/2 Dime, Copper, plain edge, J812	1650.
Pn865	1870	—	1/2 Dime, Aluminum, reeded edge, J813	1850.
Pn866	1870	—	1/2 Dime, Aluminum, plain edge, J814	1850.

KM#	Date	Mintage	Identification	Mkt.Val.
Pn867	1870	—	1/2 Dime, Silver, reeded edge, J815	2500.
Pn868	1870	—	1/2 Dime, Silver, plain edge, J816	2000.
Pn869	1870	—	1/2 Dime, Copper, reeded edge, J817	1750.
Pn870	1870	—	1/2 Dime, Copper, plain edge, J818	2150.
Pn871	1870	—	1/2 Dime, Aluminum, reeded edge, J819	1850.
Pn872	1870	—	1/2 Dime, Aluminum, plain edge, J820	1850.
Pn873	1870	—	1/2 Dime, Copper, reeded edge, J821	3500.
Pn874	1870	—	1/2 Dime, Copper, plain edge, J822	—
Pn875	1870	—	1/2 Dime, Aluminum, reeded edge, J823	3500.
Pn876	1870	—	1/2 Dime, Nickel, reeded edge, J824	—
Pn877	1870	—	10 Cent, Silver, reeded edge, J825	3550.
Pn878	1870	—	10 Cent, Silver, plain edge, J826	2000.
Pn879	1870	—	10 Cent, Copper, reeded edge, J827	1800.
Pn880	1870	—	10 Cent, Copper, plain edge, J828	2000.
Pn881	1870	—	10 Cent, Aluminum, reeded edge, J829	3000.
Pn882	1870	—	10 Cent, Aluminum, plain edge, J830	3000.
Pn883	1870	—	10 Cent, Silver, reeded edge, J831	2000.
Pn884	1870	—	10 Cent, Silver, plain edge, J832	2000.
Pn885	1870	—	10 Cent, Copper, reeded edge, J833	1850.
Pn886	1870	—	10 Cent, Copper, plain edge, J834	2250.
Pn887	1870	—	10 Cent, Aluminum, reeded edge, J835	3500.
Pn888	1870	—	10 Cent, Aluminum, plain edge, J836	3500.

KM#	Date	Mintage	Identification	Mkt.Val.
Pn889	1870	—	10 Cent, Silver, reeded edge, J837	1500.
Pn890	1870	—	10 Cent, Silver, plain edge, J838	1750.
Pn891	1870	—	10 Cent, Copper, reeded edge, J839	4500.
Pn892	1870	—	10 Cent, Copper, plain edge, J840	5200.
Pn893	1870	—	10 Cent, Aluminum, reeded edge, J841	3000.
Pn894	1870	—	10 Cent, Aluminum, plain edge, J842	2800.
Pn895	1870	—	10 Cent, Silver, reeded edge, J843	3650.
Pn896	1870	—	10 Cent, Silver, plain edge, J844	1800.
Pn897	1870	—	10 Cent, Copper, reeded edge, J845	2000.
Pn898	1870	—	10 Cent, Copper, plain edge, J846	1800.
Pn899	1870	—	10 Cent, Aluminum, reeded edge, J847	2800.
Pn900	1870	—	10 Cent, Aluminum, plain edge, J848	2800.

KM#	Date	Mintage	Identification	Mkt.Val.
Pn901	1870	—	10 Cent, Silver, reeded edge, J849	1250.
Pn902	1870	—	10 Cent, Silver, plain edge, J850	1750.
Pn903	1870	—	10 Cent, Copper, reeded edge, J851	1600.
Pn904	1870	—	10 Cent, Copper, plain edge, J852	1500.
Pn905	1870	—	10 Cent, Aluminum, reeded edge, J853	2000.
Pn906	1870	—	10 Cent, Aluminum, plain edge, J854	2000.

KM#	Date	Mintage	Identification	Mkt.Val.
Pn907	1870	—	10 Cent, Silver, reeded edge, J855	5600.
Pn908	1870	—	10 Cent, Silver, plain edge, J856	5400.
Pn909	1870	—	10 Cent, Copper, reeded edge, J857	2750.
Pn910	1870	—	10 Cent, Copper, plain edge, J858	2000.
Pn911	1870	—	10 Cent, Aluminum, reeded edge, J859	3250.
Pn912	1870	—	10 Cent, Aluminum, plain edge, J860	3250.
Pn913	1870	—	10 Cent, Silver, reeded edge, J861	1600.
Pn914	1870	—	10 Cent, Silver, plain edge, J862	3750.
Pn915	1870	—	10 Cent, Copper, reeded edge, J863	1850.
Pn916	1870	—	10 Cent, Copper, plain edge, J864	3200.
Pn917	1870	—	10 Cent, Aluminum, reeded edge, J865	2200.
Pn918	1870	—	10 Cent, Aluminum, plain edge, J866	2550.

KM#	Date	Mintage	Identification	Mkt.Val.
Pn919	1870	—	10 Cent, Silver, reeded edge, J867	2150.
Pn920	1870	—	10 Cent, Silver, plain edge, J868	2750.
Pn921	1870	—	10 Cent, Copper, reeded edge, J869	5250.
Pn922	1870	—	10 Cent, Copper, plain edge, J870	5500.
Pn923	1870	—	10 Cent, Aluminum, reeded edge, J871	5500.
Pn924	1870	—	10 Cent, Aluminum, plain edge, J872	5500.
Pn925	1870	—	10 Cent, Copper, reeded edge, J873	2500.
Pn926	1870	—	10 Cent, Aluminum, reeded edge, J874	4750.
Pn927	1870	—	10 Cent, Nickel, reeded edge, J875	—
Pn928	1870	—	25 Cent, Silver, reeded edge, J876	3200.
Pn929	1870	—	25 Cent, Silver, plain edge, J877	4000.
Pn930	1870	—	25 Cent, Copper, reeded edge, J878	5250.
Pn931	1870	—	25 Cent, Copper, plain edge, J879	2650.
Pn932	1870	—	25 Cent, Aluminum, reeded edge, J880	5250.
Pn933	1870	—	25 Cent, Aluminum, plain edge, J881	5250.

KM#	Date	Mintage	Identification	Mkt.Val.
Pn934	1870	—	25 Cent, Silver, reeded edge, J882	3000.
Pn935	1870	—	25 Cent, Silver, plain edge, J883	3000.
Pn936	1870	—	25 Cent, Copper, reeded edge, J884	1850.
Pn937	1870	—	25 Cent, Copper, plain edge, J885	2850.
Pn938	1870	—	25 Cent, Aluminum, reeded edge, J886	3000.
Pn939	1870	—	25 Cent, Aluminum, plain edge, J887	3000.
Pn940	1870	—	25 Cent, Silver, reeded edge, J888	1750.
Pn941	1870	—	25 Cent, Silver, plain edge, J889	2750.
Pn942	1870	—	25 Cent, Copper, reeded edge, J890	2250.
Pn943	1870	—	25 Cent, Copper, plain edge, J891	2250.
Pn944	1870	—	25 Cent, Aluminum, reeded edge, J892	3300.
Pn945	1870	—	25 Cent, Aluminum, plain edge, J893	3300.

KM#	Date	Mintage	Identification	Mkt.Val.
Pn946	1870	—	25 Cent, Silver, reeded edge, J894	1850.
Pn947	1870	—	25 Cent, Silver, plain edge, J895	2450.
Pn948	1870	—	25 Cent, Copper, reeded edge, J896	3000.
Pn949	1870	—	25 Cent, Copper, plain edge, J897	3000.
Pn950	1870	—	25 Cent, Aluminum, reeded edge, J898	1200.
Pn951	1870	—	25 Cent, Aluminum, plain edge, J899	1200.
Pn952	1870	—	25 Cent, Silver, reeded edge, J900	1350.

KM#	Date	Mintage	Identification	Mkt.Val.
Pn953	1870	—	25 Cent, Silver, plain edge, J901	2850.
Pn954	1870	—	25 Cent, Copper, reeded edge, J902	1500.
Pn955	1870	—	25 Cent, Copper, plain edge, J903	3000.
Pn956	1870	—	25 Cent, Aluminum, reeded edge, J904	3250.
Pn957	1870	—	25 Cent, Aluminum, plain edge, J905	3250.
Pn958	1870	—	25 Cent, Silver, reeded edge, J906	1500.

KM#	Date	Mintage	Identification	Mkt.Val.
Pn959	1870	—	25 Cent, Silver, plain edge, J907	2250.
Pn960	1870	—	25 Cent, Copper, reeded edge, J908	2450.
Pn961	1870	—	25 Cent, Copper, plain edge, J909	2450.
Pn962	1870	—	25 Cent, Aluminum, reeded edge, J910	2850.
Pn963	1870	—	25 Cent, Aluminum, plain edge, J911	4000.

KM#	Date	Mintage	Identification	Mkt.Val.
Pn964	1870	—	25 Cent, Silver, reeded edge, J912	2500.
Pn965	1870	—	25 Cent, Silver, plain edge, J913	2000.
Pn966	1870	—	25 Cent, Copper, reeded edge, J914	1850.
Pn967	1870	—	25 Cent, Copper, plain edge, J915	4600.
Pn968	1870	—	25 Cent, Aluminum, reeded edge, J916	2650.
Pn969	1870	—	25 Cent, Aluminum, plain edge, J917	2750.
Pn970	1870	—	25 Cent, Silver, reeded edge, J918	1850.
Pn971	1870	—	25 Cent, Silver, plain edge, J919	2000.
Pn972	1870	—	25 Cent, Copper, reeded edge, J920	2650.
Pn973	1870	—	25 Cent, Copper, plain edge, J921	2650.
Pn974	1870	—	25 Cent, Aluminum, reeded edge, J922	3350.
Pn975	1870	—	25 Cent, Aluminum, plain edge, J923	3250.
Pn976	1870	—	25 Cent, Copper, reeded edge, J924	3500.
Pn977	1870	—	25 Cent, Aluminum, reeded edge, J925	3500.
Pn978	1870	—	25 Cent, Nickel, reeded edge, J926	—
Pn979	1870	—	50 Cent, Silver, reeded edge, J927	6500.
Pn980	1870	—	50 Cent, Silver, reeded edge, LIBERTY raised, J927a	—
Pn981	1870	—	50 Cent, Silver, plain edge, J928	6750.
Pn982	1870	—	50 Cent, Copper, reeded edge, J929	6000.
Pn983	1870	—	50 Cent, Copper, reeded edge, LIBERTY raised, J929a	—
Pn984	1870	—	50 Cent, Copper. plain edge, J930	6000.
Pn985	1870	—	50 Cent, Aluminum, reeded edge, J931	5500.
Pn986	1870	—	50 Cent, Aluminum, plain edge, J932	5500.

KM#	Date	Mintage	Identification	Mkt.Val.
Pn987	1870	—	50 Cent, Silver, reeded edge, J933	3000.
Pn988	1870	—	50 Cent, Silver, plain edge, J934	3250.
Pn989	1870	—	50 Cent, Copper, reeded edge, J935	3500.
Pn990	1870	—	50 Cent, Copper, plain edge, J936	2550.
Pn991	1870	—	50 Cent, Aluminum, reeded edge, J937	3750.
Pn992	1870	—	50 Cent, Aluminum, plain edge, J938	3750.

KM#	Date	Mintage	Identification	Mkt.Val.
Pn993	1870	—	50 Cent, Silver, reeded edge, J939	1750.
Pn994	1870	—	50 Cent, Silver, plain edge, J940	1450.
Pn995	1870	—	50 Cent, Copper, reeded edge, J941	3000.
Pn996	1870	—	50 Cent, Copper, plain edge, J942	3000.
Pn997	1870	—	50 Cent, Aluminum, reeded edge, J943	3250.
Pn998	1870	—	50 Cent, Aluminum, plain edge, J944	3250.
Pn999	1870	—	50 Cent, Silver, reeded edge, J945	1500.
Pn1000	1870	—	50 Cent, Silver, plain edge, J946	3250.
Pn1001	1870	—	50 Cent, Copper, reeded edge, J947	4850.
Pn1002	1870	—	50 Cent, Copper, plain edge, J948	5000.
Pn1003	1870	—	50 Cent, Aluminum, reeded edge, J949	5000.
Pn1004	1870	—	50 Cent, Aluminum, plain edge, J950	5000.
Pn1005	1870	—	50 Cent, Silver, reeded edge, J951	1500.
Pn1006	1870	—	50 Cent, Silver, plain edge, J952	1500.
Pn1007	1870	—	50 Cent, Copper, reeded edge, J953	5000.
Pn1008	1870	—	50 Cent, Copper, plain edge, J954	5000.
Pn1009	1870	—	50 Cent, Aluminum, reeded edge, J955	4500.
Pn1010	1870	—	50 Cent, Aluminum, plain edge, J956	4750.

KM#	Date	Mintage	Identification	Mkt.Val.
Pn1011	1870	—	50 Cent, Silver, reeded edge, J957	1500.
Pn1012	1870	—	50 Cent, Silver, plain edge, J958	2200.
Pn1013	1870	—	50 Cent, Copper, reeded edge, J959	3850.
Pn1014	1870	—	50 Cent, Copper, plain edge, J960	4500.
Pn1015	1870	—	50 Cent, Aluminum, reeded edge, J961	4500.
Pn1016	1870	—	50 Cent, Aluminum, plain edge, J962	4500.
Pn1017	1870	—	50 Cent, Silver, reeded edge, J963	5500.
Pn1018	1870	—	50 Cent, Silver, plain edge, J964	5500.
Pn1019	1870	—	50 Cent, Copper, reeded edge, J965	5500.
Pn1020	1870	—	50 Cent, Copper, plain edge, J966	5500.
Pn1021	1870	—	50 Cent, Aluminum, reeded edge, J967	6000.
Pn1022	1870	—	50 Cent, Aluminum, plain edge, J968	6000.
Pn1023	1870	—	50 Cent, Silver, reeded edge, J969	4500.
Pn1024	1870	—	50 Cent, Silver, plain edge, J970	4750.
Pn1025	1870	—	50 Cent, Copper, reeded edge, J971	4500.
Pn1026	1870	—	50 Cent, Copper, plain edge, J972	4750.
Pn1027	1870	—	50 Cent, Aluminum, reeded edge, J973	5000.
Pn1028	1870	—	50 Cent, Aluminum, plain edge, J974	5000.
Pn1029	1870	—	50 Cent, Silver, reeded edge, J975	5000.
Pn1030	1870	—	50 Cent, Silver, plain edge, J976	5000.
Pn1031	1870	—	50 Cent, Copper, reeded edge,	

KM#	Date	Mintage	Identification	Mkt.Val.
Pn1031			J977	4000.
Pn1032	1870	—	50 Cent, Copper, plain edge, J978	3450.
Pn1033	1870	—	50 Cent, Aluminum, reeded edge, J979	5000.
Pn1034	1870	—	50 Cent, Aluminum, plain edge, J980	5000.
Pn1035	1870	—	50 Cent, Silver, reeded edge, J981	3000.
Pn1036	1870	—	50 Cent, Silver, plain edge, J982	3450.
Pn1037	1870	—	50 Cent, Copper, reeded edge, J983	4500.
Pn1038	1870	—	50 Cent, Copper, plain edge, J984	3750.
Pn1039	1870	—	50 Cent, Aluminum, reeded edge, J985	4750.
Pn1040	1870	—	50 Cent, Aluminum, plain edge, J986	4750.

KM#	Date	Mintage	Identification	Mkt.Val.
Pn1041	1870	—	50 Cent, Silver, reeded edge, J987	4000.
Pn1042	1870	—	50 Cent, Silver, plain edge, J988	4000.
Pn1043	1870	—	50 Cent, Copper, reeded edge, J989	3500.
Pn1044	1870	—	50 Cent, Copper, plain edge, J990	6500.
Pn1045	1870	—	50 Cent, Aluminum, reeded edge, J991	5000.
Pn1046	1870	—	50 Cent, Aluminum, plain edge, J992	5300.
Pn1047	1870	—	50 Cent, Copper, reeded edge, J993	5000.
Pn1048	1870	—	50 Cent, Aluminum, reeded edge, J994	5000.
Pn1049	1870	—	50 Cent, Nickel, reeded edge, J995	—
Pn1050	1870	—	50 Cent, Copper-Nickel, J995a	—

KM#	Date	Mintage	Identification	Mkt.Val.
Pn1051	1870	—	1 Dollar, Silver, reeded edge, J996	4850.
Pn1052	1870	—	1 Dollar, Silver, plain edge, J997	4500.
Pn1053	1870	—	1 Dollar, Copper, reeded edge, J998	4000.
Pn1054	1870	—	1 Dollar, Copper, plain edge, J999	3250.
Pn1055	1870	—	1 Dollar, Aluminum, reeded edge, J1000	5000.
Pn1056	1870	—	1 Dollar, Aluminum, plain edge, J1001	5000.
Pn1057	1870	—	1 Dollar, Silver, reeded edge, J1002	4500.
Pn1058	1870	—	1 Dollar, Silver, plain edge, J1003	3500.
Pn1059	1870	—	1 Dollar, Copper, reeded edge, J1004	8500.

KM#	Date	Mintage	Identification	Mkt.Val.
Pn1060	1870	—	1 Dollar, Copper, plain edge, J1005	3500.
Pn1061	1870	—	1 Dollar, Aluminum, reeded edge, J1006	5000.
Pn1062	1870	—	1 Dollar, Aluminum, plain edge, J1007	5000.
Pn1063	1870	—	1 Dollar, Silver, reeded edge, J1008	5500.
Pn1064	1870	—	1 Dollar, Silver, plain edge, J1009	11,500.
Pn1065	1870	—	1 Dollar, Copper, reeded edge, J1010	6000.
Pn1066	1870	—	1 Dollar, Copper, plain edge, J1011	6000.
Pn1067	1870	—	1 Dollar, Aluminum, reeded edge, J1012	6000.
Pn1068	1870	—	1 Dollar, Aluminum, plain edge, J1013	6000.

KM#	Date	Mintage	Identification	Mkt.Val.
Pn1069	1870	—	1 Dollar, Silver, reeded edge, J1014	3500.
Pn1070	1870	—	1 Dollar, Silver, plain edge, J1015	2750.
Pn1071	1870	—	1 Dollar, Copper, reeded edge, J1016	4650.
Pn1072	1870	—	1 Dollar, Copper, plain edge, J1017	3500.
Pn1073	1870	—	1 Dollar, Aluminum, reeded edge, J1018	8500.
Pn1074	1870	—	1 Dollar, Aluminum, plain edge, J1019	8250.
Pn1075	1870	—	1 Dollar, Copper, reeded edge, J1020	12,100.
Pn1076	1870	—	1 Dollar, Aluminum, reeded edge, J1021	—
Pn1077	1870	—	1 Dollar, Nickel, reeded edge, J1022	17,000.
Pn1078	1870	—	1 Gold Dollar, Copper, reeded edge, J1023	—
Pn1079	1870	—	1 Gold Dollar, Aluminum, reeded edge, J1024	—
Pn1080	1870	—	1 Gold Dollar, Nickel, reeded edge, J1025	—
Pn1081	1870	—	2-1/2 Dollar, Copper, reeded edge, J1026	3750.
Pn1082	1870	—	2-1/2 Dollar, Aluminum, reeded edge, J1027	3550.
Pn1083	1870	—	2-1/2 Dollar, Nickel, reeded edge, J1028	—
Pn1084	1870	—	3 Dollar, Copper, reeded edge, J1029	6000.
Pn1085	1870	—	3 Dollar, Aluminum, reeded edge, J1030	8500.
Pn1086	1870	—	3 Dollar, Nickel, reeded edge, J1031	7500.
Pn1087	1870	—	5 Dollar, Copper, reeded edge, J1032	7000.
Pn1088	1870	—	5 Dollar, Aluminum, reeded edge, J1033	—
Pn1089	1870	—	5 Dollar, Nickel, reeded edge, J1034	—
Pn1090	1870	—	10 Dollar, Copper, reeded edge, J1035	—
Pn1091	1870	—	10 Dollar, Aluminum, reeded edge, J1036	—
Pn1092	1870	—	10 Dollar, Nickel, reeded edge, J1037	—
Pn1093	1870	—	20 Dollar, Copper, reeded edge, J1038	16,500.
Pn1093a	1870	—	20 Dollar, Copper Gilt, reeded edge, J1038	9750.
Pn1094	1870	—	20 Dollar, Aluminum, reeded edge, J1039	—
Pn1095	1870	—	20 Dollar, Nickel, reeded edge, J1040	—
Pn1096	1871	—	1 Cent, Copper, plain edge, J1041	—
Pn1097	1871	—	1 Cent, Aluminum, plain edge, J1042	—
Pn1098	1871	—	2 Cent, Copper, plain edge, J1043	1250.
Pn1099	1871	—	2 Cent, Aluminum, plain edge, J1044	7000.
Pn1100	1871	—	3 Cent, Copper, plain edge, J1045	2500.
Pn1101	1871	—	3 Cent, Aluminum, plain edge, J1046	2500.
Pn1102	1871	—	3 Cent, Copper, plain edge, J1047	3000.
Pn1103	1871	—	3 Cent, Nickel, plain edge, J1048	Unique
Pn1104	1871	—	3 Cent, Aluminum, plain edge, J1049	3000.

KM#	Date	Mintage	Identification	Mkt.Val.
Pn1105	1871	—	5 Cent, Nickel, plain edge, J1050	1650.
Pn1106	1871	—	5 Cent, Copper, plain edge, J1051	1650.
Pn1106a	1871	—	5 Cent, Copper, Silver plated, plain edge, J1051	1850.
Pn1107	1871	—	5 Cent, Aluminum, plain edge, J1052	5000.

KM#	Date	Mintage	Identification	Mkt.Val.
Pn1108	1871	—	5 Cent, Nickel, plain edge, J1053	2000.
Pn1109	1871	—	5 Cent, Copper, plain edge, J1054	1500.
Pn1110	1871	—	5 Cent, Aluminum, plain edge, J1055	3750.
Pn1111	1871	—	5 Cent, Copper, plain edge, J1056	3000.
Pn1112	1871	—	5 Cent, Aluminum, plain edge, J1057	5000.
Pn1113	1871	—	5 Cent, Steel, plain edge, J1058	Unique
Pn1114	1871	—	1/2 Dime, Silver, reeded edge, J1059	3150.
Pn1115	1871	—	1/2 Dime, Copper, reeded edge, J1060	4200.
Pn1116	1871	—	1/2 Dime, Aluminum, reeded edge, J1061	4500.
Pn1117	1871	—	1/2 Dime, Silver, reeded edge, J1062	4500.
Pn1118	1871	—	1/2 Dime, Copper, reeded edge, J1063	6000.
Pn1119	1871	—	1/2 Dime, Aluminum, reeded edge, J1064	7500.
Pn1120	1871	—	1/2 Dime, Silver, reeded edge, J1065	4500.
Pn1121	1871	—	1/2 Dime, Copper, reeded edge, J1066	3650.
Pn1122	1871	—	1/2 Dime, Aluminum, reeded edge, J1067	7500.
Pn1123	1871	—	1/2 Dime, Silver, reeded edge, J1068	2750.
Pn1124	1871	—	1/2 Dime, Copper, reeded edge, J1069	2850.
Pn1125	1871	—	1/2 Dime, Aluminum, reeded edge, J1070	—
Pn1126	1871	—	1/2 Dime, Copper, reeded edge, J1071	1750.
Pn1127	1871	—	1/2 Dime, Aluminum, reeded edge, J1072	—
Pn1128	1871	—	1/2 Dime, Nickel, reeded edge, J1073	4850.
Pn1129	1871	—	10 Cent, Silver, reeded edge, J1074	6000.
Pn1130	1871	—	10 Cent, Copper, reeded edge, J1075	2550.
Pn1131	1871	—	10 Cent, Aluminum, reeded edge, J1076	7000.
Pn1132	1871	—	10 Cent, Silver, reeded edge, J1077	3500.
Pn1133	1871	—	10 Cent, Copper, reeded edge, J1078	4500.
Pn1134	1871	—	10 Cent, Aluminum, reeded edge, J1079	550.00
Pn1135	1871	—	10 Cent, Silver, reeded edge, J1080	1450.
Pn1136	1871	—	10 Cent, Copper, reeded edge, J1081	4200.
Pn1137	1871	—	10 Cent, Aluminum, reeded edge, J1082	2250.
Pn1138	1871	—	10 Cent, Nickel, reeded edge, J1083	—
Pn1139	1871	—	10 Cent, Silver, reeded edge, J1084	4000.
Pn1140	1871	—	10 Cent, Copper, reeded edge, J1085	2250.
Pn1141	1871	—	10 Cent, Aluminum, reeded edge, J1086	—
Pn1142	1871	—	10 Cent, Copper, reeded edge, J1087	2750.
Pn1143	1871	—	10 Cent, Aluminum, reeded edge, J1088	3000.
Pn1144	1871	—	10 Cent, Nickel, reeded edge, J1089	3550.
Pn1145	1871	—	25 Cent, Silver, reeded edge, J1090	—
Pn1146	1871	—	25 Cent, Copper, reeded edge, J1091	5000.
Pn1147	1871	—	25 Cent, Aluminum, reeded edge, J1092	6000.
Pn1148	1871	—	25 Cent, Silver, reeded edge, J1093	5000.
Pn1149	1871	—	25 Cent, Copper, reeded edge, J1094	4500.
Pn1150	1871	—	25 Cent, Aluminum, reeded edge, J1095	—
Pn1151	1871	—	25 Cent, Silver, reeded edge, J1096	5000.
Pn1152	1871	—	25 Cent, Copper, reeded edge, J1097	4200.
Pn1153	1871	—	25 Cent, Aluminum, reeded edge, J1098	12,650.
Pn1154	1871	—	25 Cent, Silver, reeded edge, J1099	5000.
Pn1155	1871	—	25 Cent, Copper, reeded edge, J1100	4650.
Pn1156	1871	—	25 Cent, Aluminum, reeded edge, J1101	—
Pn1157	1871	—	25 Cent, Copper, reeded edge, J1102	2750.
Pn1158	1871	—	25 Cent, Aluminum, reeded edge, J1103	4000.
Pn1159	1871	—	25 Cent, Nickel, reeded edge, J1104	—
Pn1160	1871	—	50 Cent, Silver, reeded edge, J1105	6750.
Pn1161	1871	—	50 Cent, Copper, reeded edge, J1106	6875.
Pn1162	1871	—	50 Cent, Aluminum, reeded edge, J1107	7000.
Pn1163	1871	—	50 Cent, Silver, reeded edge, J1108	—
Pn1164	1871	—	50 Cent, Copper, reeded edge, J1109	6500.
Pn1165	1871	—	50 Cent, Aluminum, reeded edge, J1110	8500.
Pn1166	1871	—	50 Cent, Silver, reeded edge, J1111	4850.
Pn1167	1871	—	50 Cent, Copper, reeded edge, J1112	6000.
Pn1168	1871	—	50 Cent, Aluminum, reeded edge, J1113	7000.
Pn1169	1871	—	50 Cent, Silver, reeded edge, J1114	6000.
Pn1170	1871	—	50 Cent, Copper, reeded edge, J1115	3300.
Pn1171	1871	—	50 Cent, Aluminum, reeded edge, J1116	5000.
Pn1172	1871	—	50 Cent, Copper, reeded edge, J1117	4500.
Pn1173	1871	—	50 Cent, Aluminum, reeded edge, J1118	6500.
Pn1174	1871	—	50 Cent, Nickel, reeded edge, J1119	Unique
Pn1175	1871	—	1 Dollar, Silver, reeded edge, J1120	14,300.
Pn1176	1871	—	1 Dollar, Silver, plain edge, J1121	7000.
Pn1177	1871	—	1 Dollar, Copper, reeded edge, J1122	7500.
Pn1178	1871	—	1 Dollar, Copper, plain edge, J1123	7500.
Pn1179	1871	—	1 Dollar, Aluminum, reeded edge, J1124	15,400.
Pn1180	1871	—	1 Dollar, Aluminum, plain edge, J1125	Rare
Pn1181	1871	—	1 Dollar, Silver, reeded edge, J1126	7500.
Pn1182	1871	—	1 Dollar, Silver, plain edge, J1127	6000.
Pn1183	1871	—	1 Dollar, Copper, reeded edge, J1128	6000.
Pn1184	1871	—	1 Dollar, Copper, plain edge, J1129	6000.
Pn1185	1871	—	1 Dollar, Aluminum, reeded edge, J1130	7000.
Pn1186	1871	4 known	1 Dollar, Aluminum, plain edge, J1131	19,000.
Pn1187	1871	—	1 Dollar, Copper, reeded edge, J1132	—
Pn1188	1871	—	1 Dollar, Copper, plain edge, J1132a	—
Pn1189	1871	—	1 Dollar, Silver, reeded edge, J1133	19,000.
Pn1190	1871	—	1 Dollar, Silver, plain edge, J1134	6000.
Pn1191	1871	—	1 Dollar, Copper, reeded edge, J1135	4650.
Pn1192	1871	—	1 Dollar, Copper, plain edge, J1136	4500.
Pn1193	1871	—	1 Dollar, Aluminum, reeded edge, J1137	6000
Pn1194	1871	—	1 Dollar, Aluminum, plain edge, J1138	6000
Pn1195	1871	—	1 Dollar, Silver, reeded edge, J1138a	—
Pn1196	1871	—	1 Dollar, Aluminum, reeded edge, J1138b	—
Pn1197	1871	—	1 Dollar, Silver, reeded edge, J1139	6500
Pn1198	1871	—	1 Dollar, Silver, plain edge, J1140	6500
Pn1199	1871	—	1 Dollar, Copper, reeded edge, J1141	7000
Pn1200	1871	—	1 Dollar, Copper, plain edge, J1142	5000
Pn1201	1871	—	1 Dollar, Aluminum, reeded edge, J1143	7000
Pn1202	1871	—	1 Dollar, Aluminum, plain edge, J1144	7000
Pn1203	1871	—	1 Dollar, Silver, reeded edge, J1145	7500
Pn1204	1871	—	1 Dollar, Silver, plain edge, J1146	7500
Pn1205	1871	—	1 Dollar, Copper, reeded edge, J1147	5000
Pn1206	1871	—	1 Dollar, Copper, plain edge, J1148	5500.
Pn1207	1871	—	1 Dollar, Aluminum, reeded edge, J1149	7150.
Pn1208	1871	—	1 Dollar, Aluminum, plain edge, J1150	4500.
Pn1209	1871	—	1 Dollar, Copper, reeded edge, J1151	4000.
Pn1210	1871	—	1 Dollar, Aluminum, reeded edge, J1152	4000.
Pn1211	1871	—	1 Dollar, Nickel, reeded edge, J1153	—
Pn1212	1871	—	Commercial Dollar, Silver, reeded edge, J1154	7500
Pn1213	1871	—	Commercial Dollar, Silver, plain edge, J1155	8000.
Pn1214	1871	—	Commercial Dollar, Copper, reeded edge, J1156	—
Pn1215	1871	—	Commercial Dollar, Copper, plain edge, J1157	—
Pn1216	1871	—	Commercial Dollar, Silver, reeded edge, J1158	—
Pn1217	1871	—	Commercial Dollar, Copper, reeded edge, J1159	—
Pn1218	1871	—	Commercial Dollar, Silver, reeded edge, J1160	—
Pn1219	1871	—	1 Gold Dollar, Copper, reeded edge, J1161	3450.
Pn1220	1871	—	1 Gold Dollar, Aluminum, reeded edge, J1162	4000.
Pn1221	1871	—	1 Gold Dollar, Nickel, reeded edge, J1163	5000.
Pn1222	1871	—	2-1/2 Dollar, Copper, reeded edge, J1164	3750.
Pn1223	1871	—	2-1/2 Dollar, Aluminum, reeded edge, J1165	4000.
Pn1224	1871	—	2-1/2 Dollar, Nickel, reeded edge, J1166	5000.
Pn1225	1871	—	3 Dollar, Copper, reeded edge, J1167	4800.
Pn1226	1871	—	3 Dollar, Aluminum, reeded edge, J1168	5000.
Pn1227	1871	—	3 Dollar, Nickel, reeded edge, J1169	5500.
Pn1228	1871	—	5 Dollar, Copper, reeded edge, J1170	4650.
Pn1229	1871	—	5 Dollar, Aluminum, reeded edge, J1171	5750.
Pn1230	1871	—	5 Dollar, Nickel, reeded edge, J1172	4750.

KM#	Date	Mintage	Identification	Mkt.Val.
Pn1231	1871	—	10 Dollar, Copper, reeded edge, J1173	3000.
Pn1232	1871	—	10 Dollar, Aluminum, reeded edge, J1174	6500.
Pn1233	1871	—	10 Dollar, Nickel, reeded edge, J1175	5000.
Pn1234	1871	—	20 Dollar, Copper, reeded edge, J1176	4000.
Pn1235	1871	—	20 Dollar, Aluminum, reeded edge, J1177	6000.
Pn1236	1871	—	20 Dollar, Nickel, reeded edge, J1178	6500.
Pn1237	1872	—	1 Cent, Copper, plain edge, J1179	3000.
Pn1238	1872	—	1 Cent, Copper-Nickel, plain edge, J1180	—
Pn1239	1872	—	1 Cent, Aluminum, plain edge, J1181	5000.
Pn1240	1872	—	1 Cent, Nickel, plain edge, J1182	—
Pn1241	1872	—	2 Cent, Copper, plain edge, J1183	3250.
Pn1242	1872	—	2 Cent, Aluminum, plain edge, J1184	3750.
Pn1243	1872	—	3 Cent, Copper, plain edge, J1185	3450.
Pn1244	1872	—	3 Cent, Aluminum, plain edge, J1186	3500.
Pn1245	1872	—	3 Cent, Copper, plain edge, J1187	3250.
Pn1246	1872	—	3 Cent, Aluminum, plain edge, J1188	6500.
Pn1247	1872	—	5 Cent, Copper, plain edge, J1189	3250.
Pn1248	1872	—	5 Cent, Aluminum, plain edge, J1190	3750.
Pn1249	1872	—	1/2 Dime, Copper, reeded edge, J1191	3250.
Pn1250	1872	—	1/2 Dime, Aluminum, reeded edge, J1192	3750.
Pn1251	1872	—	10 Cent, Copper, reeded edge, J1193	3000.
Pn1252	1872	—	10 Cent, Aluminum, reeded edge, J1194	3500.

KM#	Date	Mintage	Identification	Mkt.Val.
Pn1253	1872	—	25 Cent, Silver, reeded edge, J1195	18,400.
Pn1254	1872	—	25 Cent, Copper, reeded edge, J1196	—
Pn1255	1872	—	25 Cent, Aluminum, reeded edge, J1197	—
Pn1256	1872	—	25 Cent, Copper, reeded edge, J1198	3500.
Pn1257	1872	—	25 Cent, Aluminum, reeded edge, J1199	4000.

KM#	Date	Mintage	Identification	Mkt.Val.
Pn1258	1872	—	50 Cent, Silver, reeded edge, J1200	20,350.
Pn1259	1872	—	50 Cent, Copper, reeded edge, J1201	19,550.
Pn1260	1872	—	50 Cent, Aluminum, reeded edge, J1202	12,650.
Pn1261	1872	—	50 Cent, Copper, reeded edge, J1203	4000.
Pn1262	1872	—	50 Cent, Aluminum, reeded edge, J1204	4750.
Pn1263	1872	—	1 Dollar, Silver, reeded edge, J1205	—
Pn1264	1872	—	1 Dollar, Copper, reeded edge, J1206	36,000.
Pn1265	1872	—	1 Dollar, Aluminum, reeded edge, J1207	19,800.
Pn1266	1872	—	1 Dollar, Silver, reeded edge, J1208	16,100.
Pn1267	1872	—	1 Dollar, Silver, plain edge, J1209	Rare

KM#	Date	Mintage	Identification	Mkt.Val.
Pn1268	1872	—	1 Dollar, Copper, reeded edge, J1210	7000.
Pn1269	1872	—	1 Dollar, Aluminum, reeded edge, J1211	8500.
Pn1270	1872	—	Commercial Dollar, Silver, reeded edge, J1212	5500.
Pn1271	1872	—	Commercial Dollar, Silver, plain edge, J1213	6500.

KM#	Date	Mintage	Identification	Mkt.Val.
Pn1272	1872	—	Commercial Dollar, Silver, reeded edge, J1214	10,350.
Pn1273	1872	—	Commercial Dollar, Silver, plain edge, J1215	8450.
Pn1274	1872	—	Commercial Dollar, Copper, reeded edge, J1216	5750.
Pn1275	1872	—	Commercial Dollar, Copper, plain edge, J1217	5500.
Pn1276	1872	—	Commercial Dollar, Aluminum, reeded edge, J1218	—
Pn1277	1872	—	Commercial Dollar, Silver, reeded edge, J1219	11,000.
Pn1278	1872	—	Commercial Dollar, Copper, reeded edge, J1219a	Unique
Pn1279	1872	—	Trade Dollar, Silver, reeded edge, J1220	5000.
Pn1280	1872	—	Trade Dollar, Copper, reeded edge, J1221	9350.
Pn1281	1872	—	Trade Dollar, Aluminum, reeded edge, J1222	—
Pn1282	1872	—	Trade Dollar, Silver, reeded edge, J1223	16,100.

KM#	Date	Mintage	Identification	Mkt.Val.
Pn1283	1872	—	1 Gold Dollar, Gold, reeded edge, J1224	Unique
Pn1284	1872	—	1 Gold Dollar, Copper, reeded edge, J1225	9000.
Pn1285	1872	—	1 Gold Dollar, Aluminum, reeded edge, J1226	19,000.
Pn1286	1872	—	1 Gold Dollar, Copper, reeded edge, J1227	7000.
Pn1287	1872	—	1 Gold Dollar, Aluminum, reeded edge, J1228	7500.
Pn1288	1872	—	1 Gold Dollar, Silver, reeded edge, J1229	Unique

KM#	Date	Mintage	Identification	Mkt.Val.
Pn1289	1872	—	2-1/2 Dollar, Gold, reeded edge, J1230	Unique
Pn1290	1872	—	2-1/2 Dollar, Copper, reeded edge, J1231	11,000.
Pn1291	1872	—	2-1/2 Dollar, Aluminum, reeded edge, J1232	15,000.
Pn1292	1872	—	2-1/2 Dollar, Copper, reeded edge, J1233	5000.
Pn1293	1872	—	2-1/2 Dollar, Aluminum, reeded edge, J1234	7000.

KM#	Date	Mintage	Identification	Mkt.Val.
Pn1294	1872	—	3 Dollar, Gold, reeded edge, J1235	Unique
Pn1295	1872	—	3 Dollar, Copper, reeded edge, J1236	12,000.
Pn1296	1872	—	3 Dollar, Aluminum, reeded edge, J1237	20,125.
Pn1297	1872	—	3 Dollar, Copper, reeded edge, J1238	4250.
Pn1298	1872	—	3 Dollar, Aluminum, reeded edge, J1239	6500.

KM#	Date	Mintage	Identification	Mkt.Val.
Pn1299	1872	—	5 Dollar, Gold, reeded edge, J1240	Unique
Pn1300	1872	—	5 Dollar, Copper, reeded edge, J1241	5000.
Pn1301	1872	—	5 Dollar, Aluminum, reeded edge, J1242	13,500.
Pn1302	1872	—	5 Dollar, Copper, reeded edge, J1243	4000.
Pn1303	1872	—	5 Dollar, Aluminum, reeded edge, J1244	14,500.

KM#	Date	Mintage	Identification	Mkt.Val.
Pn1304	1872	—	10 Dollar, Gold, reeded edge, J1245	Unique
Pn1305	1872	—	10 Dollar, Copper, reeded edge, J1246	16,000.
Pn1306	1872	—	10 Dollar, Aluminum, reeded edge, J1247	15,000.
Pn1307	1872	—	10 Dollar, Copper, reeded edge, J1248	4650.
Pn1308	1872	—	10 Dollar, Aluminum, reeded edge, J1249	9000.

KM#	Date	Mintage	Identification	Mkt.Val.
Pn1309	1872	—	20 Dollar, Gold, reeded edge, J1250	Unique
Pn1310	1872	—	20 Dollar, Copper, reeded edge, J1251	14,500.
Pn1311	1872	—	20 Dollar, Aluminum, reeded edge, J1252	45,000.
Pn1312	1872	—	20 Dollar, Copper, reeded edge, J1253	—
Pn1312a	1872	—	20 Dollar, Copper Gilt, reeded edge, J1253	5350.
Pn1313	1872	—	20 Dollar, Aluminum, reeded edge, J1254	—
Pn1314	1873	—	1 Cent, Copper, plain edge, J1255	3500.
Pn1315	1873	—	1 Cent, Aluminum, plain edge, J1256	3450.
Pn1316	1873	—	1 Cent, Nickel, plain edge, J1257	—
Pn1317	1873	—	2 Cent, Copper, plain edge, J1258	—
Pn1318	1873	—	2 Cent, Aluminum, plain edge, J1259	—
Pn1319	1873	—	3 Cent, Copper, plain edge, J1260	3500.
Pn1320	1873	—	3 Cent, Aluminum, plain edge, J1261	7000.
Pn1321	1873	—	3 Cent, Copper, plain edge, J1262	3150.
Pn1322	1873	—	3 Cent, Aluminum, plain edge, J1263	3250.
Pn1323	1873	—	5 Cent, Copper, plain edge, J1264	3150.
Pn1324	1873	—	5 Cent, Aluminum, plain edge, J1265	3250.
Pn1325	1873	—	1/2 Dime, Copper, reeded edge, J1266	3150.
Pn1326	1873	—	1/2 Dime, Aluminum, reeded edge,	

KM#	Date	Mintage	Identification	Mkt.Val.
Pn1326			J1267	3250.
Pn1327	1873	—	10 Cent, Copper, reeded edge, J1268	3650.
Pn1328	1873	—	10 Cent, Aluminum, reeded edge, J1269	3250.
Pn1329	1873	—	25 Cent, Copper, reeded edge, J1270	2850.
Pn1330	1873	—	25 Cent, Aluminum, reeded edge, J1271	3250.
Pn1331	1873	—	50 Cent, Copper, reeded edge, J1272	5550.
Pn1332	1873	—	50 Cent, Aluminum, reeded edge, J1273	5750.
Pn1333	1873	—	1 Dollar, Copper, reeded edge, J1274	12,650.
Pn1334	1873	—	1 Dollar, Aluminum, reeded edge, J1275	4000.

KM#	Date	Mintage	Identification	Mkt.Val.
Pn1335	1873	—	Trade Dollar, Silver, reeded edge, J1276	4000.
Pn1336	1873	—	Trade Dollar, Silver, plain edge, J1277	4000.
Pn1337	1873	—	Trade Dollar, Copper, reeded edge, J1278	5500.
Pn1338	1873	—	Trade Dollar, Aluminum, reeded edge, J1279	6500.
Pn1339	1873	—	Trade Dollar, White Metal, plain edge, J1280	6500.

KM#	Date	Mintage	Identification	Mkt.Val.
Pn1340	1873	—	Trade Dollar, Silver, reeded edge, J1281	4500.
Pn1341	1873	—	Trade Dollar, Silver, plain edge, J1282	6500.
Pn1342	1873	—	Trade Dollar, Copper, reeded edge, J1283	7000.
Pn1343	1873	—	Trade Dollar, Aluminum, reeded edge, J1284	7500.
Pn1344	1873	—	Trade Dollar, Copper, reeded edge, J1285	—
Pn1345	1873	—	Trade Dollar, Aluminum, reeded edge, J1286	—
Pn1346	1873	—	Trade Dollar, White Metal, plain edge, J1287	—
Pn1347	1873	—	Trade Dollar, Copper, reeded edge, J1288	—
Pn1348	1873	—	Trade Dollar, Copper, reeded edge, J1289	—
Pn1349	1873	—	Trade Dollar, Silver, reeded edge, J1290	—
Pn1350	1873	—	Trade Dollar, Silver, plain edge, J1291	—
Pn1351	1873	—	Trade Dollar, White Metal, plain edge, J1292	—
Pn1352	1873	—	Trade Dollar, Silver, reeded edge, J1293	3250.
Pn1353	1873	—	Trade Dollar, Silver, plain edge, J1294	4500.
Pn1354	1873	—	Trade Dollar, Copper, reeded edge, J1295	8250.
Pn1355	1873	—	Trade Dollar, Copper, plain edge, J1296	8500.
Pn1356	1873	—	Trade Dollar, Aluminum, reeded edge, J1297	—
Pn1357	1873	—	Trade Dollar, White Metal, plain edge, J1298	—
Pn1358	1873	—	Trade Dollar, White Metal, plain edge, J1299	—
Pn1359	1873	—	Trade Dollar, Silver, reeded edge, J1300	10,000.
Pn1360	1873	—	Trade Dollar, Copper, reeded edge, J1301	11,550.
Pn1361	1873	—	Trade Dollar, Copper, plain edge, J1302	12,500.
Pn1362	1873	—	Trade Dollar, Aluminum, reeded edge, J1303	—
Pn1363	1873	—	Trade Dollar, White Metal, plain edge, J1304	—
Pn1364	1873	—	Trade Dollar, Silver, reeded edge, J1304a	Unique
Pn1365	1873	4 pcs.	Trade Dollar, Copper, reeded edge, J1305	Rare
Pn1366	1873	—	Trade Dollar, White Metal, plain edge, J1306	—
Pn1367	1873	—	Trade Dollar, White Metal, plain edge, J1307	—
Pn1368	1873	—	Trade Dollar, Silver, J1308	—
Pn1369	1873	—	Trade Dollar, White Metal, plain edge, J1309	6500.
Pn1370	1873	—	Trade Dollar, Silver, reeded edge, J1310	4000.
Pn1371	1873	—	Trade Dollar, Silver, plain edge, J1311	5500.
Pn1372	1873	—	Trade Dollar, Copper, reeded edge, J1312	6000.
Pn1373	1873	—	Trade Dollar, Aluminum, reeded edge, J1313	—
Pn1374	1873	—	Trade Dollar, White Metal, plain edge, J1314	—
Pn1375	1873	—	Trade Dollar, Silver, reeded edge, J1315	3850.
Pn1376	1873	—	Trade Dollar, Silver, plain edge, J1316	4650.
Pn1377	1873	—	Trade Dollar, Copper, reeded edge, J1317	5500.
Pn1378	1873	—	Trade Dollar, Aluminum, reeded edge, J1318	6500.
Pn1379	1873	—	Trade Dollar, White Metal, plain edge, J1319	6500.
Pn1380	1873	—	Trade Dollar, Silver, reeded edge, J1320	Rare
Pn1381	1873	—	Trade Dollar, Copper, reeded edge, J1321	Rare
Pn1382	1873	—	Trade Dollar, Silver, reeded edge, J1322	3500.
Pn1383	1873	—	Trade Dollar, Silver, plain edge, J1323	4250.
Pn1384	1873	—	Trade Dollar, Copper, reeded edge, J1324	4000.
Pn1385	1873	—	Trade Dollar, Aluminum, reeded edge, J1325	6500.
Pn1386	1873	—	Trade Dollar, White Metal, plain edge, J1326	6500.
Pn1387	1873	—	Trade Dollar, Silver, reeded edge, J1326a	Rare
Pn1388	1873	—	Trade Dollar, White Metal, plain edge, J1326b	Rare
Pn1389	1873	—	Trade Dollar, Copper, reeded edge, J1327	5500.
Pn1390	1873	—	Trade Dollar, Aluminum, reeded edge, J1328	—
Pn1391	1873	—	Trade Dollar, White Metal, plain edge, J1329	—
Pn1392	1873	—	Trade Dollar, Tin, reeded edge, J1330	—
Pn1393	1873	—	1 Gold Dollar, Copper, reeded edge, J1331	5750.
Pn1394	1873	—	1 Gold Dollar, Aluminum, reeded edge, J1332	10,350.
Pn1395	1873	—	2-1/2 Dollar, Copper, reeded edge, J1333	3750.
Pn1396	1873	—	2-1/2 Dollar, Aluminum, reeded edge, J1334	3350.
Pn1397	1873	—	3 Dollar, Copper, reeded edge, J1335	6650.
Pn1397a	1873	—	3 Dollar, Copper Gilt, reeded edge, J1335	5350.
Pn1398	1873	—	3 Dollar, Aluminum, reeded edge, J1336	5550.
Pn1399	1873	2 known	5 Dollar, Gold, reeded edge, J1337	Rare
Pn1400	1873	—	5 Dollar, Copper, reeded edge, J1338	6500.
Pn1401	1873	—	5 Dollar, Aluminum, reeded edge, J1339	5000.
Pn1402	1873	—	5 Dollar, Copper, reeded edge, J1340	2875.
Pn1403	1873	—	5 Dollar, Aluminum, reeded edge, J1341	4600.
Pn1404	1873	—	10 Dollar, Copper, reeded edge, J1342	3700.
Pn1405	1873	—	10 Dollar, Aluminum, reeded edge, J1343	7200.
Pn1406	1873	—	20 Dollar, Copper, reeded edge, J1344	5350.
Pn1407	1873	—	20 Dollar, Aluminum, reeded edge, J1345	8650.
Pn1408	1874	—	1 Cent, Copper, plain edge, J1346	2250.
Pn1409	1874	—	1 Cent, Aluminum, plain edge, J1347	3250.
Pn1410	1874	—	3 Cent, Copper, plain edge, J1348	2250.
Pn1411	1874	—	3 Cent, Aluminum, plain edge, J1349	3250.
Pn1412	1874	—	5 Cent, Copper, plain edge, J1350	2250.
Pn1413	1874	—	5 Cent, Aluminum, plain edge, J1351	3250.
Pn1414	1874	—	10 Cent, Copper, reeded edge, J1352	2500.
Pn1415	1874	—	10 Cent, Aluminum, reeded edge, J1353	3750.

KM#	Date	Mintage	Identification	Mkt.Val.
Pn1416	1874	—	20 Cent, Silver, plain edge, J1354	2650.
Pn1417	1874	—	20 Cent, Copper, plain edge, J1355	3250.
Pn1418	1874	—	20 Cent, Aluminum, plain edge, J1356	3450.
Pn1419	1874	—	20 Cent, Silver, plain edge, J1357	—
Pn1420	1874	—	20 Cent, Nickel, plain edge, J1358	6000.
Pn1421	1874	—	25 Cent, Copper, reeded edge, J1359	8000.
Pn1422	1874	—	25 Cent, Aluminum, reeded edge, J1360	9000.
Pn1423	1874	—	50 Cent, Copper, reeded edge, J1361	9500.
Pn1424	1874	—	50 Cent, Aluminum, reeded edge, J1362	10,000.
Pn1425	1874	—	Trade Dollar, Copper, reeded edge, J1363	11,275.
Pn1426	1874	—	Trade Dollar, Aluminum, reeded edge, J1364	4300.
Pn1427	1874	—	1 Gold Dollar, Copper, reeded edge, J1365	7500.
Pn1428	1874	—	1 Gold Dollar, Aluminum, reeded edge, J1366	—
Pn1429	1874	—	2-1/2 Dollar, Copper, reeded edge, J1367	4500.
Pn1430	1874	—	2-1/2 Dollar, Aluminum, reeded edge, J1368	4750.
Pn1431	1874	—	3 Dollar, Copper, reeded edge, J1369	5000.
Pn1432	1874	—	3 Dollar, Aluminum, reeded edge, J1370	6350.
Pn1433	1874	—	5 Dollar, Copper, reeded edge, J1371	4850.
Pn1434	1874	—	5 Dollar, Copper, reeded edge, J1372	4750.
Pn1435	1874	2 known	10 Dollar, Gold, reeded edge, J1373	201,250.
Pn1436	1874	—	10 Dollar, Copper, reeded edge, J1374	11,000.
Pn1436a	1874	—	10 Dollar, Copper Gilt, reeded edge, J1374	7000.
Pn1437	1874	—	10 Dollar, Copper, plain edge, J1375	11,500.
Pn1437a	1874	—	10 Dollar, Copper Gilt, plain edge, J1375	6350.

KM#	Date	Mintage	Identification	Mkt.Val.
Pn1438	1874	—	10 Dollar, Aluminum, reeded edge, J1376	35,000.
Pn1439	1874	—	10 Dollar, Nickel, reeded edge,	

KM#	Date	Mintage	Identification	Mkt.Val.
Pn1439			J1377	8000.
Pn1440	1874	—	10 Dollar, Nickel, plain edge, J1378	8000.
Pn1441	1874	—	10 Dollar, Copper, reeded edge, J1379	5550.
Pn1442	1874	—	10 Dollar, Aluminum, reeded edge, J1380	5000.
Pn1443	1874	—	20 Dollar, Copper, reeded edge, J1381	4500.
Pn1444	1874	—	20 Dollar, Aluminum, reeded edge, J1382	5000.
Pn1445	1875	—	1 Cent, Copper, plain edge, J1383	2500.
Pn1446	1875	—	1 Cent, Aluminum, plain edge, J1384	2750.
Pn1447	1875	—	3 Cent, Copper, plain edge, J1385	2800.
Pn1448	1875	—	3 Cent, Aluminum, plain edge, J1386	5000.
Pn1449	1875	—	5 Cent, Copper, plain edge, J1387	7750.
Pn1450	1875	—	5 Cent, Aluminum, plain edge, J1388	7000.
Pn1451	1875	—	1/2 Dime, Aluminum, reeded edge, J1389	—
Pn1452	1875	—	10 Cents, Copper, reeded edge, J1390	2250.
Pn1453	1875	—	10 Cent, Aluminum, reeded edge, J1391	2500.

KM#	Date	Mintage	Identification	Mkt.Val.
Pn1454	1875	—	20 Cent, Silver, plain edge, J1392	3500.
Pn1455	1875	—	20 Cent, Copper, plain edge, J1393	4000.
Pn1456	1875	—	20 Cent, Aluminum, plain edge, J1394	5000.
Pn1457	1875	—	20 Cent, Nickel, plain edge, J1395	4750.
Pn1458	1875	—	20 Cent, Silver, Silver, plain edge, J1396	3500.
Pn1459	1875	—	20 Cent, Copper, plain edge, J1397	3750.
Pn1460	1875	—	20 Cent, Aluminum, plain edge, J1398	4000.

KM#	Date	Mintage	Identification	Mkt.Val.
Pn1461	1875	—	20 Cent, Silver, plain edge, J1399	3750.
Pn1462	1875	—	20 Cent, Copper, plain edge, J1400	3500.
Pn1463	1875	—	20 Cent, Aluminum, plain edge, J1401	—
Pn1464	1875	—	20 Cent, Nickel, plain edge, J1402	4750.

KM#	Date	Mintage	Identification	Mkt.Val.
Pn1465	1875	—	20 Cent, Silver, plain edge, J1403	4250.
Pn1466	1875	—	20 Cent, Copper, plain edge, J1404	4250.
Pn1467	1875	—	20 Cent, Aluminum, plain edge, J1405	5750.
Pn1468	1875	—	20 Cent, White Metal, plain edge, J1406	—

KM#	Date	Mintage	Identification	Mkt.Val.
Pn1469	1875	—	20 Cent, Silver, plain edge, J1407	4000.
Pn1470	1875	—	20 Cent, Copper, plain edge, J1408	3550.
Pn1471	1875	—	20 Cent, Aluminum, plain edge, J1409	—
Pn1472	1875	—	20 Cent, Nickel, plain edge, J1410	4000.
Pn1473	1875	—	20 Cent, Silver, plain edge, J1411	3500.
Pn1474	1875	—	20 Cent, Copper, plain edge, J1412	3250.
Pn1475	1875	—	20 Cent, Aluminum, plain edge, J1413	4650.
Pn1476	1875	—	20 Cent, Copper, plain edge, J1414	3000.
Pn1477	1875	—	20 Cent, Aluminum, plain edge, J1415	3750.
Pn1478	1875	—	25 Cent, Copper, reeded edge, J1416	2000.
Pn1479	1875	—	25 Cent, Aluminum, reeded edge, J1417	2200.
Pn1480	1875	—	50 Cent, Copper, reeded edge, J1418	2000.

KM#	Date	Mintage	Identification	Mkt.Val.
Pn1481	1875	—	50 Cent, Aluminum, reeded edge, J1419	2200.
Pn1482	1875	6	1 Dollar, Silver, reeded edge, J1420	8500.
Pn1483	1875	8	1 Dollar, Copper, reeded edge, J1421	6500.
Pn1484	1875	2	1 Dollar, Aluminum, reeded edge, J1422	—

KM#	Date	Mintage	Identification	Mkt.Val.
Pn1485	1875	6	Trade Dollar, Silver, reeded edge, J1423	9200.
Pn1486	1875	8	Trade Dollar, Copper, reeded edge, J1424	6500.
Pn1487	1875	3	Trade Dollar, Aluminum, reeded edge, J1425	—
Pn1488	1875	—	Trade Dollar, Silver, reeded edge, J1426	—
Pn1489	1875	—	Trade Dollar, Copper, reeded edge, J1427	8000.
Pn1490	1875	—	Trade Dollar, Aluminum, reeded edge, J1428	—
Pn1491	1875	—	Trade Dollar, White Metal, reeded edge, J1429	—
Pn1492	1875	—	Trade Dollar, Copper, reeded edge, J1430	16,100.
Pn1493	1875	—	Trade Dollar, Aluminum, reeded edge, J1431	7500.
Pn1494	1875	—	1 Gold Dollar, Copper, reeded edge, J1432	7000.
Pn1494a	1875	—	1 Gold Dollar, Copper Gilt, reeded edge, J1432	4500.
Pn1495	1875	—	1 Gold Dollar, Aluminum, reeded edge, J1433	—
Pn1496	1875	—	2-1/2 Dollar, Copper, reeded edge, J1434	7000.
Pn1496a	1875	—	2-1/2 Dollar, Copper Gilt, reeded edge, J1434	6750.
Pn1497	1875	—	2-1/2 Dollar, Aluminum, reeded edge, J1435	10,350.
Pn1498	1875	—	3 Dollar, Copper, reeded edge, J1436	7000.
Pn1498a	1875	—	3 Dollar, Copper Gilt, reeded edge, J1436	6750.
Pn1499	1875	—	3 Dollar, Aluminum, reeded edge, J1437	10,500.

KM#	Date	Mintage	Identification	Mkt.Val.
Pn1500	1875	2 known	5 Dollar, Gold, reeded edge, J1438	Rare
Pn1501	1875	—	5 Dollar, Copper, reeded edge, J1439	6350.
Pn1502	1875	—	5 Dollar, Aluminum, reeded edge, J1440	Rare
Pn1503	1875	—	5 Dollar, White Metal, J1440a	Rare
Pn1504	1875	—	5 Dollar, Copper, reeded edge, J1441	8250.
Pn1504a	1875	—	5 Dollar, Copper Gilt, reeded edge, J1441	6750.
Pn1505	1875	—	5 Dollar, Aluminum, reeded edge, J1442	—
Pn1505a	1875	—	5 Dollar, Aluminum Gilt, reeded edge, J1442	—
Pn1506	1875	2 known	10 Dollar, Gold, reeded edge, J1443	Rare
Pn1507	1875	—	10 Dollar, Copper, reeded edge, J1444	6750.
Pn1507a	1875	—	10 Dollar, Copper Gilt, reeded edge, J1444	6750.
Pn1508	1875	—	10 Dollar, Aluminum, reeded edge, J1445	Rare
Pn1509	1875	—	10 Dollar, White Metal, J1445a	Rare

KM#	Date	Mintage	Identification	Mkt.Val.
Pn1510	1875	—	10 Dollar, Copper, reeded edge, J1446	9200.
Pn1510a	1875	—	10 Dollar Copper Gilt, reeded edge, J1446	4375.
Pn1511	1875	—	10 Dollar, Aluminum, reeded edge, J1447	—
Pn1512	1875	—	20 Dollar, Copper, reeded edge, J1448	7500.
Pn1513	1875	—	20 Dollar, Aluminum, reeded edge, J1449	9775.
Pn1514	1876	—	1 Cent, Aluminum, plain edge, J1450	2000.
Pn1515	1876	3 known	1 Cent, Nickel, plain edge, J1451	2000.
Pn1516	1876	—	10 Cent, Copper, reeded edge, J1452	2000.
Pn1517	1876	—	10 Cent, Nickel, reeded edge, J1453	2000.
Pn1518	1876	—	20 Cent, Copper, plain edge, J1454	5775.
Pn1519	1876	—	25 Cent, Copper, reeded edge, J1455	4500.
Pn1520	1876	2 known	50 Cent, Copper, reeded edge, J1456	6600.
Pn1521	1876	2 known	1 Dollar, Silver, reeded edge, J1457	Rare
Pn1522	1876	—	1 Dollar, Copper, plain edge, J1458	—
Pn1523	1876	—	1 Dollar, Copper, reeded edge, J1458a	16,100.
Pn1524	1876	2 known	1 Dollar, Silver, reeded edge, J1459	29,900.
Pn1525	1876	—	1 Dollar, Copper, reeded edge, J1460	6500.
Pn1526	1876	—	1 Dollar, Copper, plain edge, J1461	9775.
Pn1527	1876	2 known	1 Dollar, Silver, reeded edge, J1462	Rare
Pn1528	1876	—	1 Dollar, Copper, reeded edge, J1463	15,500.
Pn1529	1876	2 known	1 Dollar, Copper, plain edge, J1463a	12,500.
Pn1530	1876	—	1 Dollar, Silver, reeded edge, J1464	Rare
Pn1531	1876	—	1 Dollar, Copper, reeded edge, J1465	10,350.
Pn1532	1876	—	1 Dollar, Copper, plain edge, J1466	Rare
Pn1533	1876	5 known	1 Dollar, Silver, reeded edge, J1467	22,000.
Pn1534	1876	—	1 Dollar, Copper, reeded edge, J1468	10,350.
Pn1535	1876	—	1 Dollar, Copper, plain edge, J1469	—
Pn1536	1876	—	1 Dollar, Silver, reeded edge, J1470	19,550.
Pn1537	1876	—	1 Dollar, Copper, reeded edge, J1471	Rare
Pn1538	1876	2 known	1 Dollar, Silver, reeded edge, J1472	Rare
Pn1539	1876	4 known	1 Dollar, Copper, reeded edge, J1473	16,100.
Pn1540	1876	2 known	Trade Dollar, Silver, reeded edge, J1474	Rare
Pn1541	1876	—	Trade Dollar, Copper, reeded edge, J1475	21,850.
Pn1542	1876	—	Trade Dollar, Copper, reeded edge, J1476	4750.
Pn1543	1876	—	Trade Dollar, Aluminum, reeded edge, J1477	—
Pn1544	1876	—	1 Gold Dollar, Copper, reeded edge, J1478	4250.
Pn1545	1876	—	1 Gold Dollar, Aluminum, reeded edge, J1479	—
Pn1546	1876	—	2-1/2 Dollar, Copper, reeded edge, J1480	4750.
Pn1547	1876	—	2-1/2 Dollar, Aluminum, reeded edge, J1481	—
Pn1548	1876	—	3 Dollar, Copper, reeded edge, J1482	5775.
Pn1549	1876	—	3 Dollar, Aluminum, reeded edge, J1483	—
Pn1550	1876	—	5 Dollar, Copper, reeded edge, J1484	4850.
Pn1551	1876	—	5 Dollar, Aluminum, reeded edge, J1485	—
Pn1552	1876	—	10 Dollar, Copper, reeded edge, J1486	4650.
Pn1553	1876	—	10 Dollar, Aluminum, reeded edge, J1487	—
Pn1554	1876	—	20 Dollar, Gold, reeded edge, J1488	Unique
Pn1555	1876	—	20 Dollar, Copper, reeded edge, J1489	14,950.
Pn1555a	1876	—	20 Dollar, Copper Gilt, reeded edge, J1489	4850.
Pn1556	1876	—	20 Dollar, Gold, reeded edge, J1490	Unique
Pn1557	1876	—	20 Dollar, Copper, reeded edge, J1491	8500.
Pn1558	1876	—	20 Dollar, Copper Gilt, plain	

KM#	Date	Mintage	Identification	Mkt.Val.
Pn1558			edge, J1492	Unique
Pn1559	1876	—	20 Dollar, Copper, reeded edge, J1493	29,000.
Pn1560	1876	—	20 Dollar, Aluminum, reeded edge, J1494	—
Pn1561	1877	—	1 Cent, Copper-Nickel, plain edge, J1495	—
Pn1562	1877	—	1 Cent, Nickel, plain edge, J1496	2750.

KM#	Date	Mintage	Identification	Mkt.Val.
Pn1563	1877	—	10 Cent, Silver, reeded edge, (may not exist), J1497	—
Pn1564	1877	—	10 Cent, Copper, reeded edge, J1498	4250.
Pn1565	1877	—	10 Cent, Copper Silvered, reeded edge, J1498	4550.
Pn1566	1877	—	25 Cent, Silver, reeded edge, J1499	—
Pn1567	1877	—	25 Cent, Copper, reeded edge, J1500	4000.
Pn1568	1877	—	25 Cent, Copper Silvered, reeded edge, J1500	4000.
Pn1569	1877	—	50 Cent, Silver, reeded edge, J1501	Rare
Pn1570	1877	—	50 Cent, Copper, reeded edge, J1502	—

KM#	Date	Mintage	Identification	Mkt.Val.
Pn1571	1877	—	50 Cent, Silver, reeded edge, J1503	22,000.
Pn1572	1877	—	50 Cent, Silver, reeded edge, J1504	27,600.
Pn1573	1877	—	50 Cent, Copper, reeded edge, J1505	5150.

KM#	Date	Mintage	Identification	Mkt.Val.
Pn1574	1877	—	50 Cent, Silver, reeded edge, J1506	10,000.
Pn1575	1877	2 known	50 Cent, Copper, reeded edge, J1507	Rare
Pn1576	1877	—	50 Cent, Silver, reeded edge, J1508	Rare
Pn1577	1877	—	50 Cent, Copper, reeded edge, J1509	5550.
Pn1578	1877	—	50 Cent, Silver, reeded edge, J1509a	Rare
Pn1579	1877	—	50 Cent, Copper, plain edge, J1509b	—
Pn1580	1877	—	50 Cent, Silver, reeded edge, J1509c	—

KM#	Date	Mintage	Identification	Mkt.Val.
Pn1581	1877	—	50 Cent, Silver, reeded edge, J1510	26,450.
Pn1582	1877	—	50 Cent, Copper, reeded edge, J1511	Rare
Pn1583	1877	—	50 Cent, Silver, reeded edge, J1512	21,850.
Pn1584	1877	—	50 Cent, Copper, reeded edge, J1513	5750.

KM#	Date	Mintage	Identification	Mkt.Val.
Pn1585	1877	—	50 Cent, Silver, reeded edge, J1514	18,400.
Pn1586	1877	—	50 Cent, Copper, reeded edge, J1515	12,650.
Pn1587	1877	—	50 Cent, Silver, reeded edge, J1516	25,300.
Pn1588	1877	—	50 Cent, Copper, reeded edge, J1517	10,000.
Pn1589	1877	—	50 Cent, Silver, reeded edge, (may not exist), J1518	—
Pn1590	1877	—	50 Cent, Copper Silvered, reeded edge, J1518a	Unique
Pn1591	1877	—	50 Cent, Copper, reeded edge, J1519	11,500.
Pn1592	1877	—	50 Cent, Silver, reeded edge, J1520	Rare
Pn1593	1877	—	50 Cent, Copper, reeded edge, J1521	12,650.
Pn1594	1877	—	50 Cent, Silver, reeded edge, J1522	11,500.
Pn1595	1877	—	50 Cent, Copper, reeded edge, J1523	12,650.
Pn1596	1877	—	50 Cent, Silver, reeded edge, J1523a	Unique
Pn1597	1877	—	50 Cent, Copper, reeded edge, J1523b	Rare
Pn1598	1877	—	50 Cent, Silver, reeded edge, J1524	12,650.
Pn1599	1877	—	50 Cent, Copper, reeded edge, J1525	10,000.

KM#	Date	Mintage	Identification	Mkt.Val.
Pn1600	1877	—	50 Cent, Silver, reeded edge, J1526	28,000.
Pn1601	1877	—	50 Cent, Copper, reeded edge, J1527	Rare
Pn1602	1877	—	50 Cent, Silver, reeded edge, J1528	Rare
Pn1603	1877	—	50 Cent, Copper, reeded edge, J1529	Rare
Pn1604	1877	—	50 Cent, Silver, reeded edge, J1530	18,400.
Pn1605	1877	—	50 Cent, Copper, reeded edge, J1531	17,250.
Pn1606	1877	—	50 Cent, Silver, reeded edge, (may not exist), J1532	—
Pn1607	1877	3 known	50 Cent, Copper, reeded edge, J1533	5500.
Pn1608	1877	—	50 Cent, Silver, reeded edge, J1534a	Unique
Pn1609	1877	2 known	50 Cent, Copper, reeded edge, J1534	13,800.
Pn1610	1877	—	50 Cent, Silver, reeded edge, J1535	8150.
Pn1611	1877	—	50 Cent, Copper, reeded edge, J1536	12,650.

KM#	Date	Mintage	Identification	Mkt.Val.
Pn1612	1877	—	50 Cent, Silver, reeded edge, J1537	Rare
Pn1613	1877	—	50 Cent, Copper, reeded edge, J1538	6500.
Pn1614	1877	—	50 Cent, Silver, reeded edge, J1539	11,500.
Pn1615	1877	—	50 Cent, Copper, reeded edge, J1539a	14,950.

KM#	Date	Mintage	Identification	Mkt.Val.
Pn1616	1877	—	50 Cent, Silver, reeded edge, J1540	17,250.
Pn1617	1877	—	50 Cent, Copper, reeded edge, J1541	10,000.
Pn1618	1877	—	50 Cent, Silver, reeded edge, (may not exist), J1541a	—
Pn1619	1877	3 known	50 Cent, Copper, reeded edge, J1541b	Rare
Pn1620	1877	—	1 Dollar, Copper, reeded edge, J1542	10,000.
Pn1621	1877	—	1 Dollar, Copper, reeded edge, J1543	11,500.
Pn1622	1877	—	1 Dollar, Copper, reeded edge, J1544	16,100.
Pn1623	1877	—	1 Dollar, Copper Silvered, reeded edge, J1544	9500.
Pn1624	1877	—	10 Dollar, Copper, reeded edge, J1545	6000.
Pn1624a	1877	—	10 Dollar, Copper Gilt, reeded edge, J1545	Rare
Pn1625	1877	—	50 Dollar, Gold, reeded edge, J1546	Unique

KM#	Date	Mintage	Identification	Mkt.Val.
Pn1626	1877	—	50 Dollar, Copper, reeded edge, J1547	120,000.
Pn1626a	1877	—	50 Dollar, Copper Gilt, reeded edge, J1547	Rare
Pn1627	1877	—	50 Dollar, Gold, reeded edge, J1548	Unique
Pn1628	1877	—	50 Dollar, Copper, reeded edge, J1549	Rare
Pn1628a	1877	—	50 Dollar, Copper Gilt, reeded edge, J1549	Rare

KM#	Date	Mintage	Identification	Mkt.Val.
Pn1629	1878	—	1 Dollar, Silver, reeded edge, J1550	6000.
Pn1630	1878	—	1 Dollar, Silver, reeded edge,	

KM#	Date	Mintage	Identification	Mkt.Val.
n1630			rev: lg. stars, J1550a	4500.
n1631	1878	—	1 Dollar, Copper, reeded edge, J1551	8500.
n1632	1878	—	1 Dollar, Silver, reeded edge, J1552	7150.
n1633	1878	—	1 Dollar, Copper, reeded edge, J1553	7150.
n1634	1878	—	1 Dollar, Silver, reeded edge, J1554	5000.
n1635	1878	—	1 Dollar, Copper, reeded edge, J1555	7000.
n1636	1878	—	1 Dollar, Aluminum, reeded edge, J1556	—
n1637	1878	—	1 Dollar, White Metal, reeded edge, J1556a	—
n1638	1878	13 pcs.	Goloid Dollar, Goloid, reeded edge, J1557	2450.
n1639	1878	—	Goloid Dollar, Silver, reeded edge, J1558	8500.
n1639a	1878	—	Goloid Dollar, Silver, light weight reeded edge, J1558	2850.
n1640	1878	—	Goloid Dollar, Copper, reeded edge, J1559	4850.

KM#	Date	Mintage	Identification	Mkt.Val.
n1641	1878	4 known	Goloid Dollar, Goloid, reeded edge, J1560	5550.
n1642	1878	—	Goloid Dollar, Silver, reeded edge, J1561	—
n1643	1878	—	Goloid Dollar, Copper, reeded edge, J1562	3450.

KM#	Date	Mintage	Identification	Mkt.Val.
n1644	1878	—	Goloid Metric Dollar, Goloid, reeded edge, J1563	2550.
n1645	1878	—	Goloid Metric Dollar, Silver, reeded edge, J1564	4200.
n1645a	1878	—	Goloid Metric Dollar, Silver, light weight restrike, reeded edge, J1564	2200.
n1646	1878	—	1 Dollar, Copper, reeded edge, J1565	10,120.

KM#	Date	Mintage	Identification	Mkt.Val.
n1647	1878	2 known	2-1/2 Dollar, Gold, reeded edge, J1566	115,500.
n1648	1878	—	2-1/2 Dollar, Copper, reeded edge, J1567	7000.
n1648a	1878	—	2-1/2 Dollar, Copper Gilt, reeded edge, J1567	4375.
n1649	1878	—	5 Dollar, Copper, reeded edge, J1568	9000.
n1649a	1878	—	5 Dollar, Copper Gilt, reeded edge, J1568	5750.
n1650	1878	—	5 Dollar, Copper, Gilt, Rev: W/o pellets, reeded edge, J1568a	4000.
n1651	1878	—	5 Dollar, Copper, reeded edge, J1569	5750.
n1651a	1878	—	5 Dollar, Copper Gilt, reeded edge, J1569	4850.
n1652	1878	—	5 Dollar, Gold, reeded edge, J1570	Unique

KM#	Date	Mintage	Identification	Mkt.Val.
Pn1653	1878	—	5 Dollar, Copper, reeded edge, J1571	5500.
Pn1654	1878	—	5 Dollar, Gold, reeded edge, J1572	Unique
Pn1655	1878	—	5 Dollar, Copper, reeded edge, J1573	5500.

KM#	Date	Mintage	Identification	Mkt.Val.
Pn1656	1878	—	5 Dollar, Copper, reeded edge, J1574	6500.
Pn1656a	1878	—	5 Dollar, Copper Gilt, reeded edge, J1574	4650.
Pn1657	1878	—	5 Dollar, Brass, reeded edge, J1574a	Rare
Pn1556	1878	—	5 Dollar, Gold, reeded edge, J1575	Rare
Pn1659	1878	—	5 Dollar, Copper, reeded edge, J1576	7650.
Pn1659a	1878	—	5 Dollar, Copper Gilt, reeded edge, J1576	9775.
Pn1660	1878	—	5 Dollar, Gold, reeded edge, J1577	Rare
Pn1661	1878	—	5 Dollar, Copper, reeded edge, J1578	4000.
Pn1661a	1878	—	5 Dollar, Copper Gilt, reeded edge, J1578	4500.
Pn1662	1878	—	10 Dollar, Gold, plain edge, J1579	Rare
Pn1663	1878	—	10 Dollar, Copper, thin planchet, reeded edge, J1580	6500.
Pn1663a	1878	—	10 Dollar, Copper, thick planchet, reeded edge, J1580	4650.
Pn1663b	1878	—	10 Dollar, Copper Gilt, reeded edge, J1580	34,500.

KM#	Date	Mintage	Identification	Mkt.Val.
Pn1664	1878	—	10 Dollar, Gold, reeded edge, J1581	Rare
Pn1665	1878	—	10 Dollar, Copper, reeded edge, J1582	6500.
Pn1666	1879	—	1 Cent, Nickel, plain edge, J1583	Rare

KM#	Date	Mintage	Identification	Mkt.Val.
Pn1667	1879	—	10 Cent, Silver, reeded edge, J1584	8000.
Pn1668	1879	—	10 Cent, Copper, reeded edge, J1585	7000.

KM#	Date	Mintage	Identification	Mkt.Val.
Pn1669	1879	—	10 Cent, Silver, reeded edge, J1586	4000.
Pn1670	1879	—	10 Cent, Copper, reeded edge, J1587	4000.
Pn1671	1879	—	10 Cent, Silver, reeded edge, J1588	8000.
Pn1672	1879	—	10 Cent, Silver, reeded edge, J1589	3750.

KM#	Date	Mintage	Identification	Mkt.Val.
Pn1673	1879	—	25 Cent, Silver, reeded edge, J1590	14,300.
Pn1674	1879	—	25 Cent, Copper, reeded edge, J1591	11,000.
Pn1675	1879	—	25 Cent, White Metal, reeded edge, J1592	Rare

KM#	Date	Mintage	Identification	Mkt.Val.
Pn1676	1879	—	25 Cent, Silver, reeded edge, J1593	19,800.
Pn1677	1879	—	25 Cent, Copper, reeded edge, J1594	11,500.
Pn1678	1879	—	25 Cent, White Metal, reeded edge, J1594a	Rare
Pn1679	1879	—	25 Cent, White Metal, plain edge, J1595	Rare
Pn1680	1879	—	25 Cent, White Metal, plain edge, J1596	Unique

KM#	Date	Mintage	Identification	Mkt.Val.
Pn1681	1879	—	50 Cent, Silver, reeded edge, J1597	7000.
Pn1682	1879	—	50 Cent, Copper, reeded edge, J1598	9500.

KM#	Date	Mintage	Identification	Mkt.Val.
Pn1683	1879	—	50 Cent, Silver, reeded edge, J1599	8500.
Pn1684	1879	—	50 Cent, Copper, reeded edge, J1600	8250.
Pn1685	1879	—	50 Cent, Silver, reeded edge, J1601	7500.

KM#	Date	Mintage	Identification	Mkt.Val.
Pn1686	1879	—	50 Cent, Copper, reeded edge, J1602	8000.
Pn1687	1879	—	1 Dollar, Silver, reeded edge, J1603	35,650.
Pn1688	1879	—	1 Dollar, Copper, reeded edge, J1604	17,500.
Pn1689	1879	—	1 Dollar, Silver, reeded edge, J1605	—
Pn1690	1879	—	1 Dollar, Copper, reeded edge, J1606	6500.
Pn1691	1879	—	1 Dollar, White Metal, reeded edge, J1607	Rare
Pn1692	1879	—	1 Dollar, Silver, reeded edge, J1608	35,200.
Pn1693	1879	—	1 Dollar, Copper, reeded edge, J1609	18,975.
Pn1694	1879	—	1 Dollar, Lead, reeded edge, J1610	—
Pn1695	1879	—	1 Dollar, Silver, reeded edge, J1611	8000.
Pn1696	1879	—	1 Dollar, Copper, reeded edge,	

KM#	Date	Mintage	Identification	Mkt.Val.
Pn1696			J1612	6500.
Pn1697	1879	—	1 Dollar, Silver, reeded edge, J1613	7500.
Pn1698	1879	—	1 Dollar, Copper, reeded edge, J1614	4750.
Pn1699	1879	—	1 Dollar, Silver, reeded edge, J1615	12,650.

KM#	Date	Mintage	Identification	Mkt.Val.
Pn1700	1879	—	1 Dollar, Copper, reeded edge, J1616	9200.

KM#	Date	Mintage	Identification	Mkt.Val.
Pn1701	1879	—	Metric Dollar, Silver Alloy, 25 g, reeded edge, J1617	3000.
Pn1702	1879	—	Metric Dollar, Silver, light etching, lt. restrike, J1618	2000.
Pn1703	1879	—	Metric Dollar, Copper, reeded edge, J1619	5400.
Pn1704	1879	—	Metric Dollar, Aluminum, reeded edge, J1620	—
Pn1705	1879	—	Metric Dollar, Lead, reeded edge, J1621	—
Pn1706	1879	—	Metric Dollar, Silver Alloy, reeded edge, J1622	8650.
Pn1707	1879	—	Metric Dollar, Copper, reeded edge, J1623	5500.
Pn1708	1879	—	Metric Dollar, Aluminum, reeded edge, J1624	—
Pn1709	1879	—	Metric Dollar, White Metal, reeded edge, J1625	—

KM#	Date	Mintage	Identification	Mkt.Val.
Pn1710	1879	—	Goloid Metric Dollar, Goloid, 14 g, reeded edge, J1626	3500.
Pn1711	1879	—	Goloid Metric Dollar, Silver, reeded edge, J1627	3200.
Pn1712	1879	—	Goloid Metric Dollar, Copper, reeded edge, J1628	7000.
Pn1713	1879	—	Goloid Metric Dollar, Aluminum, reeded edge, J1629	7500.
Pn1714	1879	—	Goloid Metric Dollar, Lead, reeded edge, J1630	—
Pn1715	1879	—	Goloid Metric Dollar, Goloid, 14 g, reeded edge, J1631	8000.
Pn1716	1879	—	Goloid Metric Dollar, Copper, reeded edge, J1632	7200.
Pn1717	1879	—	Goloid Metric Dollar, Aluminum, reeded edge, J1633	9200.
Pn1718	1879	—	Goloid Metric Dollar, White Metal, reeded edge, J1634	6000.

KM#	Date	Mintage	Identification	Mkt.Val.
Pn1719	1879	415	4 Dollar Stella, Gold, 109 g, reeded edge, J1635	69,000.
Pn1720	1879	—	4 Dollar Stella, Gold, restrike, 103-109 g, worn obv. die, J1636	34,500.
Pn1721	1879	—	4 Dollar Stella, Copper, reeded edge, J1636	9000.

KM#	Date	Mintage	Identification	Mkt.Val.
Pn1722	1879	—	4 Dollar Stella, Aluminum, reeded edge, J1637	39,100.

KM#	Date	Mintage	Identification	Mkt.Val.
Pn1723	1879	10	4 Dollar Stella, Gold, reeded edge, J1638	310,000.
Pn1724	1879	—	4 Dollar Stella, Copper, reeded edge, J1639	11,550.
Pn1725	1879	—	4 Dollar Stella, Aluminum, reeded edge, J1640	Rare
Pn1726	1879	—	4 Dollar Stella, White Metal, reeded edge, J1641	Rare
Pn1727	1879	—	Metric 20 Dollar, Copper, reeded edge, J1642	Unique
Pn1728	1879	4 known	Metric 20 Dollar, Gold, 540.5 g, reeded edge, J1643	258,750.
Pn1728a	1879	—	Metric 20 Dollar, Gold, restrike, 516 g, reeded edge, J1643	—
Pn1729	1879	—	Metric 20 Dollar, Copper, reeded edge, J1644	—
Pn1730	1880	—	Metric Dollar, Silver Alloy, reeded edge, J1645	4900.
Pn1731	1880	—	Metric Dollar, Copper, reeded edge, J1646	6350.
Pn1732	1880	—	Metric Dollar, Aluminum, reeded edge, J1647	10,175.

KM#	Date	Mintage	Identification	Mkt.Val.
Pn1733	1880	—	Metric Dollar, Silver Alloy, reeded edge, J1648	5750.
Pn1734	1880	—	Metric Dollar, Copper, reeded edge, J1649	5650.
Pn1735	1880	—	Metric Dollar, Aluminum, reeded edge, J1650	7500.

KM#	Date	Mintage	Identification	Mkt.Val.
Pn1736	1880	—	Goloid Metric Dollar, Goloid, reeded edge, J1651	5350.
Pn1737	1880	—	Goloid Metric Dollar, Copper, reeded edge, J1652	6350.
Pn1738	1880	—	Goloid Metric Dollar, Aluminum, reeded edge, J1653	17,250.
Pn1739	1880	—	Goloid Metric Dollar, Goloid, reeded edge, J1654	8650.
Pn1740	1880	—	Goloid Metric Dollar, Copper, reeded edge, J1655	8000.
Pn1741	1880	—	Goloid Metric Dollar, Aluminum, reeded edge, J1656	—

KM#	Date	Mintage	Identification	Mkt.Val.
Pn1742	1880	15	4 Dollar Stella, Gold, reeded edge, J1657	143,750.
Pn1743	1880	—	4 Dollar Stella, Copper, reeded edge, J1658	9000.
Pn1744	1880	—	4 Dollar Stella, Aluminum, reeded edge, J1659	15,125.

KM#	Date	Mintage	Identification	Mkt.Val.
Pn1745	1880	10	4 Dollar Stella, Gold, reeded edge, J1660	368,000.
Pn1746	1880	—	4 Dollar Stella, Copper, reeded edge, J1661	36,800.
Pn1746a	1880	—	4 Dollar Stella, Copper Gilt, reeded edge, J1661	37,500.
Pn1747	1880	—	4 Dollar Stella, Aluminum, J1662	18,400.
Pn1748	1880	—	5 Dollar, Copper, reeded edge, J1663	6500.
Pn1749	1881	—	1 Cent, Nickel, plain edge, J1664	—

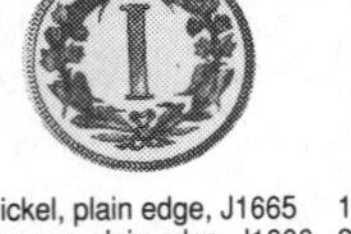

KM#	Date	Mintage	Identification	Mkt.Val.
Pn1750	1881	—	1 Cent, Nickel, plain edge, J1665	1850.
Pn1751	1881	—	1 Cent, Copper, plain edge, J1666	2450.
Pn1752	1881	—	1 Cent, Aluminum, plain edge, J1667	2750.

KM#	Date	Mintage	Identification	Mkt.Val.
Pn1753	1881	—	3 Cent, Nickel, plain edge, J1668	2800.
Pn1754	1881	—	3 Cent, Copper, plain edge, J1669	2200.
Pn1755	1881	—	3 Cent, Aluminum, plain edge, J1670	4000.
Pn1756	1881	—	5 Cent, Nickel, plain edge, J1671	2750.
Pn1757	1881	—	5 Cent, Copper, plain edge, J1672	2850.
Pn1758	1881	—	5 Cent, Aluminum, plain edge, J1673	4500.
Pn1759	1881	—	5 Cent, Nickel, plain edge, J1674	Unique
Pn1760	1882	—	5 Cent, Nickel, plain edge, J1675	Rare
Pn1761	1882	—	5 Cent, Copper, plain edge, J1676	Rare
Pn1762	1882	—	5 Cent, Nickel, plain edge, J1677	4000.
Pn1763	1882	—	5 Cent, Copper, plain edge, J1678	3500.
Pn1764	1882	—	5 Cent, Aluminum, plain edge, J1679	5000.

KM#	Date	Mintage	Identification	Mkt.Val.
Pn1765	1882	—	5 Cent, Nickel, plain edge, J1680	2500.
Pn1766	1882	—	5 Cent, Copper, plain edge, J1681	3250.
Pn1767	1882	—	5 Cent, Aluminum, plain edge, J1682	3750.
Pn1768	1882	—	5 Cent, Nickel, 5 equally spaced bars on edge, J1683	10,350.
Pn1769	1882	—	5 Cent, Nickel, plain edge, J1684	2000
Pn1770	1882	—	5 Cent, Copper, plain edge, J1685	2000.
Pn1771	1882	—	5 Cent, Aluminum, plain edge, J1686	6000.
Pn1772	1882	—	5 Cent, Nickel, plain edge, J1687	1500.
Pn1773	1882	—	5 Cent, Copper, plain edge, J1688	—
Pn1774	1882	—	5 Cent, Aluminum, plain edge, J1689	2750

KM#	Date	Mintage	Identification	Mkt.Val.
Pn1775	1882	—	5 Cent, Nickel, plain edge, J1690	9500
Pn1776	1882	—	5 Cent, Copper, plain edge, J1691	2500
Pn1777	1882	—	5 Cent, Aluminum, plain edge, J1692	4650

KM#	Date	Mintage	Identification	Mkt.Val.
Pn1778	1882	—	5 Cent, Nickel, plain edge, J1693	5300.
Pn1779	1882	—	5 Cent, Copper, plain edge, J1694	6000.
Pn1779a	1882	—	5 Cent, Copper, small thin planchet, plain edge, J1694a	2000.
Pn1780	1882	—	5 Cent, Aluminum, plain edge, J1695	5200.
Pn1781	1882	—	5 Cent, White Metal, plain edge, J1696	Rare
Pn1782	1882	—	5 Cent, Nickel, 5 equally spaced bars on edge, J1697	13,800.

KM#	Date	Mintage	Identification	Mkt.Val.
Pn1783	1882	—	25 Cent, Silver, reeded edge, J1698	26,450.
Pn1784	1882	—	25 Cent, Copper, reeded edge, J1699	Rare
Pn1785	1882	—	50 Cent, Silver, reeded edge, J1700	12,100.
Pn1786	1882	—	50 Cent, Copper, reeded edge, J1701	14,500.

KM#	Date	Mintage	Identification	Mkt.Val.
Pn1787	1882	—	1 Dollar, Silver, reeded edge, J1702	27,500.
Pn1788	1882	—	1 Dollar, Copper, reeded edge, J1703	24,200.
Pn1789	1882	—	1 Dollar, Copper, reeded edge, J1703a	8750.
Pn1790	1882	—	Trade Dollar, Copper, reeded edge, J1703b	Rare

KM#	Date	Mintage	Identification	Mkt.Val.
Pn1791	1883	—	5 Cent, Pure Nickel, plain edge, J1704	2750.
Pn1792	1883	—	5 Cent, Nickel, plain edge, J1705	2750.
Pn1793	1883	—	5 Cent, Aluminum, plain edge, J1706	3000.
Pn1794	1883	—	5 Cent, Nickel, plain edge, J1706a	Unique
Pn1795	1883	—	5 Cent, Pure Nickel, plain edge, J1707	2650.
Pn1796	1883	—	5 Cent, Nickel, plain edge, J1708	—
Pn1797	1883	—	5 Cent, Aluminum, plain edge, J1709	3750.

KM#	Date	Mintage	Identification	Mkt.Val.
Pn1798	1883	—	5 Cent, Nickel, plain edge, J1710	3000.
Pn1799	1883	—	5 Cent, Aluminum, plain edge, J1711	2200.

KM#	Date	Mintage	Identification	Mkt.Val.
Pn1800	1883	—	5 Cent, Nickel, plain edge, J1712	2550.
Pn1801	1883	—	5 Cent, Aluminum, plain edge, J1713	—

KM#	Date	Mintage	Identification	Mkt.Val.
Pn1802	1883	—	5 Cent, Nickel, plain edge, J1714	2650.
Pn1803	1883	—	5 Cent, Copper, plain edge, J1715	4600.
Pn1804	1883	—	5 Cent, Aluminum, plain edge, J1716	—

KM#	Date	Mintage	Identification	Mkt.Val.
Pn1805	1883	—	5 Cent, Nickel, plain edge, J1717	2650.
Pn1806	1883	—	5 Cent, Copper, plain edge, J1718	9000.
Pn1807	1883	—	5 Cent, Aluminum, plain edge, J1719	3000.

KM#	Date	Mintage	Identification	Mkt.Val.
Pn1808	1883	—	5 Cent, Aluminum, plain edge, J1720	—
Pn1809	1883	—	Trade Dollar, Copper, reeded edge, J1720a	—

KM#	Date	Mintage	Identification	Mkt.Val.
Pn1810	1884	—	1 Cent, Nickel, plain edge, J1721	1850.
Pn1811	1884	—	1 Cent, Aluminum, plain edge, J1722	3500.
Pn1812	1884	—	1 Cent, White Metal, plain edge, J1723	Rare
Pn1813	1884	—	1 Cent, Nickel Alloy, plain edge, J1723a	Rare

KM#	Date	Mintage	Identification	Mkt.Val.
Pn1814	1884	—	5 Cent, Nickel, plain edge, J1724	3000.
Pn1815	1884	—	5 Cent, Aluminum, plain edge, J1725	3500.
Pn1816	1884	—	5 Cent, White Metal, plain edge, J1726	—
Pn1817	1884	—	5 Cent, Aluminum, plain edge, J1727	—
Pn1818	1884	—	10 Cent, Copper, reeded edge, J1728	—
Pn1819	1884	—	25 Cent, Copper, reeded edge, J1729	—
Pn1820	1884	—	50 Cent, Copper, reeded edge, J1730	—
Pn1821	1884	—	1 Dollar, Copper, reeded edge, J1731	1650.
Pn1822	1884	—	Trade Dollar, Copper, reeded edge, J1732	—
Pn1823	1884	—	Trade Dollar, Copper Silvered, reeded edge, J1732	—
Pn1824	1884	—	Gold Dollar, Copper, reeded edge, J1733	—
Pn1825	1884	—	2-1/2 Dollar, Copper, reeded edge, J1734	—
Pn1826	1884	—	3 Dollar, Copper, reeded edge, J1735	8250.
Pn1827	1884	—	5 Dollar, Copper, reeded edge, J1736	—
Pn1828	1884	—	10 Dollar, Copper, reeded edge, J1737	—
Pn1829	1884	—	20 Dollar, Copper, reeded edge, J1738	—

KM#	Date	Mintage	Identification	Mkt.Val.
Pn1830	1885/3	—	1 Cent, Silver, plain edge, J1740	2550.
Pn1830a	1885/3	—	1 Cent, Silver, w/o hole, plain edge, J1740a	Rare
Pn1831	1885	—	3 Cent, Aluminum, plain edge, J1741	6500.

KM#	Date	Mintage	Identification	Mkt.Val.
Pn1832	1885	—	5 Cent, Silver, plain edge, J1742	3000.
Pn1833	1885	—	5 Cent, Aluminum, plain edge, J1743	4000.
Pn1834	1885	—	10 Cent, Aluminum, reeded edge, J1744	4000.
Pn1835	1885	—	25 Cent, Aluminum, reeded edge, J1745	4000.
Pn1836	1885	—	50 Cent, Aluminum, reeded edge, J1746	3750.
Pn1837	1885	—	1 Dollar, Silver, lettered edge, J1747	4500.
Pn1838	1885	—	1 Dollar, Copper, lettered edge, J1748	4500.
Pn1839	1885	—	1 Dollar, Aluminum, lettered edge, J1749	4750.
Pn1840	1885	—	1 Dollar, Aluminum, reeded edge, J1750	8000.
Pn1841	1885	—	1 Dollar, Copper, reeded edge, J1750a	8500.
Pn1842	1885	—	1 Gold Dollar, Aluminum, reeded edge, J1751	—
Pn1843	1885	—	2-1/2 Dollar, Aluminum, reeded edge, J1752	—
Pn1844	1885	—	3 Dollar, Aluminum, reeded edge, J1753	4750.
Pn1845	1885	—	5 Dollar, Aluminum, reeded edge, J1754	—
Pn1846	1885	—	10 Dollar, Aluminum, reeded edge, J1755	—
Pn1847	1885	—	20 Dollar, Aluminum, reeded edge, J1756	—
Pn1848	1890	—	1 Cent, Copper, plain edge, J1757	4000.
Pn1849	1890	—	1 Cent, Copper-Nickel, plain edge, J1758	4650.
Pn1850	1890	—	1 Cent, Aluminum, plain edge, J1759	5000.
Pn1851	1891	2 known	10 Cent, Silver, reeded edge, J1760	Rare
Pn1852	1891	2 known	25 Cent, Silver, reeded edge, J1761	Rare
Pn1853	1891	2 known	50 Cent, Silver, reeded edge, J1762	Rare
Pn1854	1891	2 known	50 Cent, Silver, reeded edge, J1763	Rare
Pn1855	1891	2 known	50 Cent, Silver, reeded edge, J1764	Rare
Pn1856	1891	2 known	50 Cent, Silver, reeded edge, J1765	Rare
Pn1857	1891	3 known	50 Cent, Silver, reeded edge, J1766	Rare

KM#	Date	Mintage	Identification	Mkt.Val.
Pn1858	1896	—	1 Cent, Nickel Alloy, plain edge, J1767	1275.
Pn1859	1896	—	1 Cent, Pure Nickel, plain edge, J1767a	1750.
Pn1860	1896	—	1 Cent, Bronze, plain edge, J1768	2250.
Pn1861	1896	—	1 Cent, Aluminum, plain edge, J1769	2500.

KM#	Date	Mintage	Identification	Mkt.Val.
Pn1862	1896	—	5 Cent, Nickel Alloy, plain edge, J1770	1750.
Pn1863	1896	—	5 Cent, Pure Nickel, plain edge, J1771	2200.
Pn1864	1896	—	5 Cent, Aluminum, plain edge, J1772	1750.

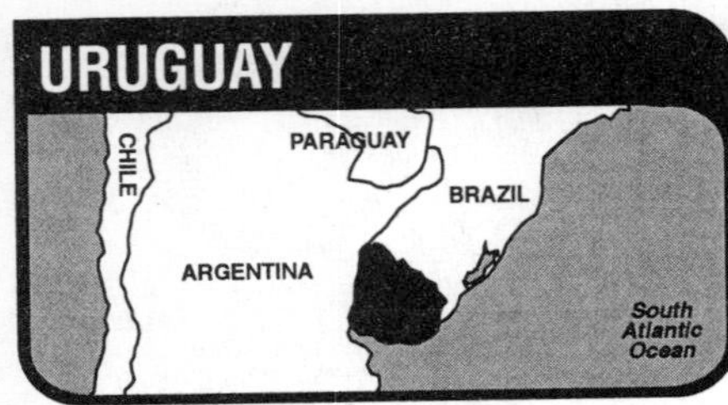

The Oriental Republic of Uruguay (so called because of its location on the east bank of the Uruguay River) is situated on the Atlantic coast of South America between Argentina and Brazil. This South American country has an area of 68,536 sq. mi.(176,220 sq. km.). Capital: Montevideo. Uruguay was discovered in 1516 by Juan Diaz de Solis, a Spaniard, but settled by the Portuguese who founded Colonia in 1680. Spain contested Portuguese possession and, after a long struggle, gained control of the country in 1778. During the general South American struggle for independence, Uruguay's first attempt was led by Gaucho soldier Jose Gervasio Artigas leading the Banda Oriental which was quelled by Spanish and Portuguese forces in 1811. The armistice was soon broken and Argentine force from Buenos Aires cast off the Spanish bond in the Plata region in 1814 only to be reconquered by the Portuguese from Brazil in the struggle of 1816-20. Revolt flared anew in 1825 and independence was reasserted in 1828 with the help of Argentina. The Uruguayan Republic was established in1830.

MINT MARKS

A - Paris, Berlin, Vienna
(a) Paris, privy marks only
D - Lyon (France)
H - Birmingham
Mx, Mo - Mexico City
(p) - Poissy, France
So - Santiago (Small O above S)
(u) – Utrecht

MONETARY SYSTEM

100 Centesimo = 1 Peso

DECIMAL COINAGE

KM# 11 CENTESIMO
5.0000 g., Bronze **Obv:** Radiant sun face **Rev:** Value in circle within wreath

Date	Mintage	F	VF	XF	Unc	BU
1869A	1,000,000	1.00	2.00	12.00	40.00	—
1869H	1,000,000	1.00	2.00	12.00	40.00	—

KM# 12 2 CENTESIMOS
10.0000 g., Bronze **Obv:** Radiant sun face **Rev:** Value in circle within wreath

Date	Mintage	F	VF	XF	Unc	BU
1869A	3,000,000	1.00	2.50	15.00	45.00	—
1869H	2,000,000	1.00	2.50	15.00	45.00	—

KM# 13 4 CENTESIMOS
20.0000 g., Bronze **Obv:** Radiant sun face **Rev:** Value in circle within wreath

Date	Mintage	F	VF	XF	Unc	BU
1869A	2,000,000	2.50	6.00	18.00	75.00	—

Date	Mintage	F	VF	XF	Unc	BU
1869H	6,250,000	2.50	6.00	18.00	60.00	—
1869H Specimen	—	Value: 200				

KM# 1 5 CENTESIMOS
4.2500 g., Copper **Obv:** Radiant sun face **Rev:** Value in circle within wreath

Date	Mintage	VG	F	VF	XF	Unc
1840	1,500	125	250	400	650	—
1844/0	—	95.00	190	325	475	—
1854/40	—	20.00	30.00	50.00	100	—

KM# 6 5 CENTESIMOS
4.3500 g., Copper **Obv:** Radiant sun face **Rev:** Value in circle within wreath

Date	Mintage	VG	F	VF	XF	Unc
1855	—	75.00	125	225	500	—

KM# 8 5 CENTESIMOS
Copper **Obv:** Radiant sun face **Rev:** Value in circle within wreath

Date	Mintage	F	VF	XF	Unc	BU
1857D	—	6.00	12.00	28.00	65.00	—

KM# 14 10 CENTESIMOS
2.5000 g., 0.9000 Silver .0723 oz. **Obv:** Flags flank shield of arms **Rev:** Value within wreath

Date	Mintage	F	VF	XF	Unc	BU
1877A	3,000,000	3.50	6.00	10.00	35.00	—
Note: Privy mark anchor points left						
1877A	Inc. above	50.00	75.00	150	400	—
Note: Privy mark anchor points right						
1877A Proof	—	—	—	—	—	—
1893/77So	—	—	—	—	—	—
1893	—	50.00	70.00	110	250	—
Note: Without mint mark						
1893So	1,000,000	2.50	7.00	15.00	50.00	—

KM# 2.1 20 CENTESIMOS
28.0000 g., Copper **Obv:** Radiant sun face **Rev:** Value in circle within wreath, small design **Note:** 2.75 millimeter thick planchet.

Date	Mintage	VG	F	VF	XF	Unc
1840	2,125	20.00	60.00	110	300	—

KM# 2.2 20 CENTESIMOS
21.0000 g., Copper **Note:** Reduced weight, 1.75 millimeter thick planchet.

Date	Mintage	VG	F	VF	XF	Unc
1843/40	—	25.00	70.00	120	325	—
1844	—	35.00	85.00	165	400	—

KM# 2.3 20 CENTESIMOS
21.0000 g., Copper **Obv:** Radiant sun face **Rev:** Value in circle within wreath, small design

Date	Mintage	VG	F	VF	XF	Unc
1854	—	20.00	40.00	80.00	200	—

KM# 7 20 CENTESIMOS
21.0000 g., Copper **Obv:** Radiant sun face **Rev:** Value in circle within wreath, large design

Date	Mintage	VG	F	VF	XF	Unc
1854	—	22.00	50.00	100	285	—
1855	—	20.00	45.00	85.00	275	—

KM# 9 20 CENTESIMOS
21.3000 g., Copper **Obv:** Radiant sun face **Rev:** Value in circle within wreath

Date	Mintage	F	VF	XF	Unc	BU
1857D	—	5.00	10.00	22.00	75.00	—

KM# 15 20 CENTESIMOS
5.0000 g., 0.9000 Silver .1446 oz. **Obv:** Shield in wreath, flags flanking behind **Rev:** Value in wreath

Date	Mintage	F	VF	XF	Unc	BU
1877A	1,500,000	3.00	5.00	12.00	45.00	—
1877A Proof	—	—	—	—	—	—
1893/73So	750,000	5.00	7.50	15.00	65.00	—

KM# 3 40 CENTESIMOS
Copper **Obv:** Male sunface **Rev:** Value in circle within wreath

Date	Mintage	VG	F	VF	XF	Unc
1844	—	40.00	80.00	150	300	—

KM# 4 40 CENTESIMOS
Copper **Obv:** Female sunface

Date	Mintage	VG	F	VF	XF	Unc
1844	—	175	375	750	1,250	—

Note: There are at least 12 different obverse and reverse die varieties known for KM #4.

KM# 10 40 CENTESIMOS
Copper

Date	Mintage	F	VF	XF	Unc	BU
1857D	—	5.00	10.00	45.00	125	—

KM# 16 50 CENTESIMOS
12.5000 g., 0.9000 Silver .3617 oz.

Date	Mintage	F	VF	XF	Unc	BU
1877A	400,000	6.00	8.00	22.00	125	—
1877A Proof	—	—	—	—	—	—
1893/73So	500,000	6.00	8.00	20.00	100	—
1894 large letters	800,000	6.00	8.00	20.00	90.00	—

KM# 5 PESO
27.0000 g., 0.8750 Silver .7596 oz. **Note:** Exists with both coin and medal reverse alignments.

Date	Mintage	F	VF	XF	Unc	BU
1844	1,500	200	350	750	1,850	—

KM# 17 PESO
25.5000 g., 0.9170 Silver .7518 oz.

Date	Mintage	F	VF	XF	Unc	BU
1877A	300,000	22.00	42.00	100	400	—
1877A Proof	—	Value: 4,000				

KM# 17a PESO
25.0000 g., 0.9000 Silver .7235 oz.

Date	Mintage	F	VF	XF	Unc	BU
1878A	100,000	125	350	800	1,500	—
Note: 43,200 melted after sea salvage.						
1893/73So	500,000	25.00	50.00	100	400	—
1893So	Inc. above	20.00	35.00	85.00	375	—
1893	600,000	18.00	30.00	75.00	325	—
1895	1,000,000	15.00	25.00	65.00	300	—

REPUBLIC

COUNTERSTAMPED COINAGE

KM# 18 PESO
Silver **Series:** F.A.O

CS Date	Host Date	Good	VG	F	VF	XF
	1895	—	—	75.00	135	245

Note: Dies were made in the Paysandu area of Uruguay, and Brazil 2,000 reis were overstruck to create an 1895 1 peso coin. These coins are considered by some to be a contemporary counterfeit and probably have no official standing

ESSAIS

KM#	Date	Mintage	Identification	Mkt Val

KM#	Date	Mintage	Identification	Mkt Val
E1	1856	—	40 Centesimos. KM10.	—

KM#	Date	Mintage	Identification	Mkt Val
E2	1869	—	100 Centesimos. Silver. Liberty head.	—

KM#	Date	Mintage	Identification	Mkt Val
E3	1869	—	100 Centesimos. Silver. Arms.	—

PATTERNS

Including off metal strikes

KM#	Date	Mintage	Identification	Mkt Val
Pn1	1844	—	Peso. Lead.	—
Pn2	1854	—	40 Reales. Gold. 8.7500 g.	—
PnA3	1869	—	2 Centesimos. Bronze.	—
Pn3	1869	—	4 Centesimos. Bronze.	—
Pn4	1869	—	100 Centesimos. Silver.	—
Pn5	1869A	—	Centesimo. Silver. KM11.	—
Pn6	1869H	—	Centesimo. Silver. KM11.	—
Pn7	1869A	—	Centesimo. Gold. KM11.	—
Pn8	1869H	—	Centesimo. Gold. KM11.	—

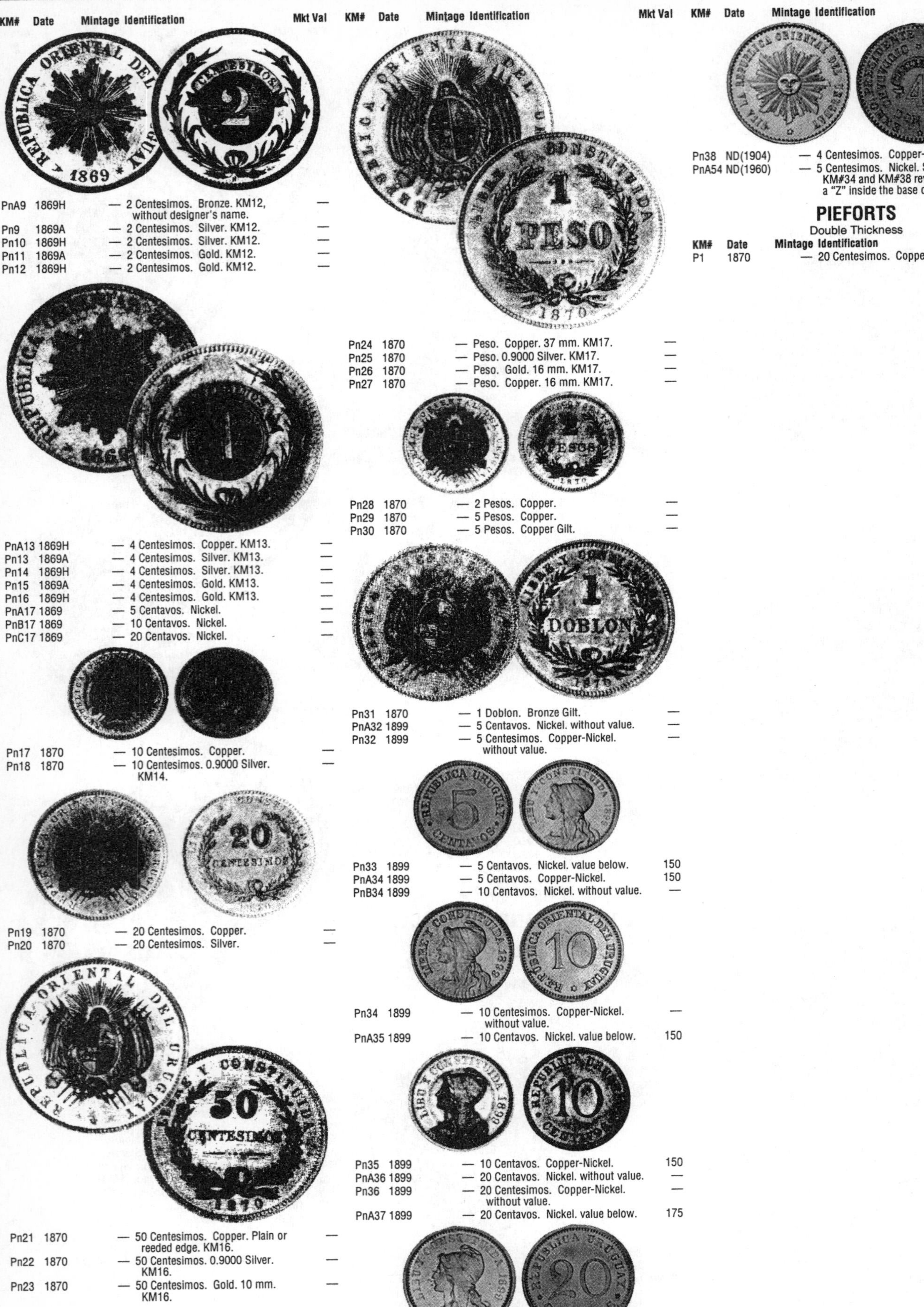

KM#	Date	Mintage	Identification	Mkt Val
PnA9	1869H	—	2 Centesimos. Bronze. KM12, without designer's name.	—
Pn9	1869A	—	2 Centesimos. Silver. KM12.	—
Pn10	1869H	—	2 Centesimos. Silver. KM12.	—
Pn11	1869A	—	2 Centesimos. Gold. KM12.	—
Pn12	1869H	—	2 Centesimos. Gold. KM12.	—
PnA13	1869H	—	4 Centesimos. Copper. KM13.	—
Pn13	1869A	—	4 Centesimos. Silver. KM13.	—
Pn14	1869H	—	4 Centesimos. Silver. KM13.	—
Pn15	1869A	—	4 Centesimos. Gold. KM13.	—
Pn16	1869H	—	4 Centesimos. Gold. KM13.	—
PnA17	1869	—	5 Centavos. Nickel.	—
PnB17	1869	—	10 Centavos. Nickel.	—
PnC17	1869	—	20 Centavos. Nickel.	—
Pn17	1870	—	10 Centesimos. Copper.	—
Pn18	1870	—	10 Centesimos. 0.9000 Silver. KM14.	—
Pn19	1870	—	20 Centesimos. Copper.	—
Pn20	1870	—	20 Centesimos. Silver.	—
Pn21	1870	—	50 Centesimos. Copper. Plain or reeded edge. KM16.	—
Pn22	1870	—	50 Centesimos. 0.9000 Silver. KM16.	—
Pn23	1870	—	50 Centesimos. Gold. 10 mm. KM16.	—
Pn24	1870	—	Peso. Copper. 37 mm. KM17.	—
Pn25	1870	—	Peso. 0.9000 Silver. KM17.	—
Pn26	1870	—	Peso. Gold. 16 mm. KM17.	—
Pn27	1870	—	Peso. Copper. 16 mm. KM17.	—
Pn28	1870	—	2 Pesos. Copper.	—
Pn29	1870	—	5 Pesos. Copper.	—
Pn30	1870	—	5 Pesos. Copper Gilt.	—
Pn31	1870	—	1 Doblon. Bronze Gilt.	—
PnA32	1899	—	5 Centavos. Nickel. without value.	—
Pn32	1899	—	5 Centesimos. Copper-Nickel. without value.	—
Pn33	1899	—	5 Centavos. Nickel. value below.	150
PnA34	1899	—	5 Centavos. Copper-Nickel.	150
PnB34	1899	—	10 Centavos. Nickel. without value.	—
Pn34	1899	—	10 Centesimos. Copper-Nickel. without value.	—
PnA35	1899	—	10 Centavos. Nickel. value below.	150
Pn35	1899	—	10 Centavos. Copper-Nickel.	150
PnA36	1899	—	20 Centavos. Nickel. without value.	—
Pn36	1899	—	20 Centesimos. Copper-Nickel. without value.	—
PnA37	1899	—	20 Centavos. Nickel. value below.	175
Pn37	1899	—	20 Centavos. Copper-Nickel.	175
Pn38	ND(1904)	—	4 Centesimos. Copper-Nickel.	225
PnA54	ND(1960)	—	5 Centesimos. Nickel. Similar to KM#34 and KM#38 reverses. With a "Z" inside the base of the 5.	—

PIEFORTS

Double Thickness

KM#	Date	Mintage	Identification	Mkt Val
P1	1870	—	20 Centesimos. Copper.	350

UZBEKISTAN

Uzbekistan (formerly the Uzbek S.S.R.), is bordered on the north by Kazakhstan, to the east by Kirghizia and Tajikistan, on the south by Afghanistan and on the west by Turkmenistan. The republic is comprised of the regions of Andizhan, Bukhara, Dzhizak, Ferghana, Kashkadar, Khorezm (Khiva), Namangan, Navoi, Samarkand, Surkhan-.Darya, Syr-Darya, Tashkent and the Karakalpak Autonomous Republic. It has an area of 172,741 sq. mi. (447,400 sq. km.). Capital: Tashkent.

In 1853, Ak-Mechet ("White Mosque", renamed Perovsk, later Kzyl Orda), was conquered by the Russians, and the following year the fortress of Vermoye (later Alma-Ata)was established. On July 29, 1867, Gen. C.P. Kaufmann was appointed governor general of Turkestan with headquarters in Tashkent. On July 5 Mozaffar ed-Din, emir of Bukhara, signed a treaty making his country a Russian vassal state with much-reduced territory. Khiva was conquered by Gen.N.N. Golovachev, and on Aug. 24, 1873, Khan Mohammed Rakhim Kuli had to become a vassal of Russia. Furthermore, all his possessions east of the Amu Darya were annexed to the Turkestan governor-generalship. The khanate of Khokand was suppressed and on March 3, 1876, became the Fergana province. On the eve of WW I, Khiva and Bukhara were enclaves within a Russian Turkestan divided into five provinces or oblasti. The czarist government did not attempt to Russify the indigenous Turkic or Tajik populations. The revolution of March 1917 created a confused situation in the area. In Tashkent there was a Turkestan committee of the provisional government; a Communist-controlled council of workers', soldiers' and peasants' deputies; also a Moslem Turkic movement, Shuro-i-Islamiya, and a young Turkestan or Jaddidi (Renovation) party. The last named party claimed full political autonomy for Turkestan and the abolition of the emirate of Bukhara and the khanate of Khiva.

Monetary System

100 Tiyin = 1 Som

KHANATE OF BUKHARA

Bukhara, a city and former emirate in southern Russian Turkestan, formed part (Sogdiana) of the Seleucid empire after the conquest of Alexander the Great and remained an important regional center, sometimes city state, until the 19th century. It became virtually a Russian vassal state in 1868 as a consequence of the Czarist invasion of 1866, following which it gradually became a part of Russian Turkestan and then part of Uzbekistan S.S.R., now Uzbekistan.

RULERS

Haidar Tora,
AH1215-1242/1800-1826AD
Hussain Sayyid,
AH1242/1826AD
Nasrullah,
AH1242-1277/1826-1860AD
Muzaffar al-Din,
AH1277-1284/1860-1867AD
Russian Vassal,
AH1284-1336/1868-1917AD

MINT NAME

Bukhara

MONETARY SYSTEM

10 Falus = 1 Tenga

Haidar Tora
AH1215-1242/1800-1826 AD
HAMMERED COINAGE

KM# 31 FALUS

Copper **Note:** Obverse and reverse legends.

Date	Mintage	Good	VG	F	VF	XF
AH1221	—	12.00	18.00	25.00	35.00	—
AH1228	—	12.00	18.00	25.00	35.00	—
AH1229	—	12.00	18.00	25.00	35.00	—
AH1241	—	12.00	18.00	25.00	35.00	—
AH1242	—	12.00	18.00	25.00	35.00	—

KM# 41 FALUS

Copper **Obv:** Legend **Rev:** Legend

Date	Mintage	Good	VG	F	VF	XF
AH1232	—	10.00	15.00	20.00	25.00	—

KM# A42 FALUS

Copper

Date	Mintage	Good	VG	F	VF	XF
AH1242	—	15.00	20.00	30.00	40.00	—

KM# 62 FALUS

Copper **Rev:** Fish

Date	Mintage	Good	VG	F	VF	XF
AH1241	—	—	20.00	30.00	40.00	—

KM# 33 2 FULUS

Silver

Date	Mintage	VG	F	VF	XF	Unc
AH1227	—	8.00	15.00	25.00	50.00	—
AH1228	—	8.00	15.00	25.00	50.00	—

KM# 28 TENGA

Silver **Note:** Weight varies: 2.50-3.00 grams. Border varieties exist.

Date	Mintage	VG	F	VF	XF	Unc
AH1216	—	8.00	15.00	25.00	45.00	—
AH1217	—	8.00	15.00	25.00	45.00	—
AH1223//1217	—	9.00	16.50	27.50	50.00	—
AH1226	—	8.00	15.00	25.00	45.00	—
AH1228//1215	—	9.00	16.50	27.50	50.00	—
AH1229	—	9.00	16.50	27.50	50.00	—
AH1230//1229	—	9.00	16.50	27.50	50.00	—
AH1230//1231	—	9.00	16.50	27.50	50.00	—
AH1231//1216	—	9.00	16.50	27.50	50.00	—
AH1231//1230	—	9.00	16.50	27.50	50.00	—
AH1232//1231	—	9.00	16.50	27.50	50.00	—
AH1233//1218	—	9.00	16.50	27.50	50.00	—
AH1233//1233	—	9.00	16.50	27.50	50.00	—
AH1234	—	8.00	15.00	25.00	45.00	—
AH1235	—	8.00	15.00	25.00	45.00	—
AH1236	—	8.00	15.00	25.00	45.00	—
AH1237//1234	—	9.00	16.50	27.50	50.00	—
AH1237//1236	—	9.00	16.50	27.50	50.00	—

KM# 43 TILLA

Gold **Obv:** Circular border **Obv. Inscription:** "Ma'sum Ibn Daniyal" **Rev:** Circular border

Date	Mintage	VG	F	VF	XF	Unc
AH1229	—	75.00	100	150	200	—
AH1231	—	75.00	100	150	200	—
AH1232//1233	—	75.00	100	150	200	—
AH1233	—	75.00	100	150	200	—
AH1234	—	75.00	100	150	200	—
AH1235	—	75.00	100	150	200	—

KM# 27 TILLA

Gold **Obv:** Teardrop **Rev:** Circle

Date	Mintage	VG	F	VF	XF	Unc
AH1217//1216	—	95.00	120	175	250	—
AH1218	—	85.00	110	160	220	—
AH1219//1218	—	120	175	250	—	—
AH1219	—	85.00	110	160	220	—
AH1220//1216	—	95.00	120	175	250	—

KM# 30 TILLA

Gold **Rev:** Octagon

Date	Mintage	VG	F	VF	XF	Unc
AH1221	—	100	150	225	325	—
AH1222	—	100	150	225	325	—
AH1225	—	100	150	225	325	—
AH1226	—	100	150	225	325	—
AH1227	—	100	150	225	325	—
AH1229	—	100	150	225	325	—

KM# 32 TILLA

Gold **Obv:** Teardrop **Rev:** Circle

Date	Mintage	VG	F	VF	XF	Unc
AH1225	—	75.00	100	150	200	—

KM# 34 TILLA

Gold **Obv:** Teardrop border **Obv. Inscription:** "Ma'sum Ibn Daniyal"

Date	Mintage	VG	F	VF	XF	Unc
AH1229	—	85.00	110	160	220	—
AH1230//1229	—	95.00	120	175	250	—
AH1230	—	85.00	110	160	220	—
AH1231	—	85.00	110	160	220	—
AH1233//1033 (sic)	—	95.00	120	175	250	—
AH1233//1232	—	95.00	120	175	250	—
AH1234	—	85.00	110	160	220	—

KM# 52 TILLA

Gold **Obv. Inscription:** "Ma'sum Ibn Daniyal"

Date	Mintage	VG	F	VF	XF	Unc
AH1235	—	75.00	100	150	200	—
AH1236//1235	—	75.00	100	150	200	—
AH1236	—	75.00	100	150	200	—
AH1239//1240	—	85.00	110	175	250	—
AH1241	—	75.00	100	150	200	—

Hussain Sayyid
AH1242/1826 AD
HAMMERED COINAGE

KM# 61 TENGA

Silver

Date	Mintage	VG	F	VF	XF	Unc
AH1241//1242	—	20.00	50.00	75.00	100	—

Nasrullah
AH1242-1277/1826-1860
HAMMERED COINAGE

KM# 66 FALUS

Brass

Date	Mintage	VG	F	VF	XF	Unc
AH1244	—	10.00	20.00	35.00	70.00	—

KM# 64 TENGA

Silver **Obv. Inscription:** "Haidar Tora"

Date	Mintage	VG	F	VF	XF	Unc
AH1243//1242	—	50.00	70.00	100	135	—
AH1244	—	50.00	70.00	100	135	—

Date	Mintage	VG	F	VF	XF	Unc
AH1247/1244	—	50.00	70.00	100	135	—
AH1275//1273	—	50.00	70.00	100	135	—
AH1275//1274	—	50.00	70.00	100	135	—
AH1277//1276	—	50.00	70.00	100	135	—

Anonymous

HAMMERED COINAGE

KM# 67.1 PUL (Fulus)

Copper Or Brass **Note:** Previous KM#67.

Date	Mintage	Good	VG	F	VF	XF
AH1277	—	12.00	18.00	25.00	35.00	—
AH1281	—	12.00	18.00	25.00	35.00	—
AH1284	—	12.00	18.00	25.00	35.00	—
AH1285	—	12.00	18.00	25.00	35.00	—

Emir Abd Al-Ahad

AH1303-1328/1886-1910AD

HAMMERED COINAGE

KM# 63 TENGA

Silver **Note:** Varieties exist; weight varies 3.06-3.25 grams; size varies 11-18 mm; die varieties exist with and without date on reverse; Struck in the name of late Emir Haydar; Previous #Y2.

Date	Mintage	Good	VG	F	VF	XF
AH1301//1300	—	—	20.00	30.00	45.00	60.00
AH1242	—	—	8.50	15.00	30.00	45.00
AH1244	—	—	8.50	15.00	30.00	45.00
AH1245	—	—	8.50	15.00	30.00	45.00
AH1247	—	—	8.50	15.00	30.00	45.00
AH1248	—	—	8.50	15.00	30.00	45.00
AH1249	—	—	8.50	15.00	30.00	45.00
AH1250	—	—	8.50	15.00	30.00	45.00
AH1255	—	—	8.50	15.00	30.00	45.00
AH1257	—	—	8.50	15.00	30.00	45.00
AH1258	—	—	8.50	15.00	30.00	45.00
AH1261	—	—	10.00	20.00	40.00	75.00
AH1263	—	—	8.50	15.00	30.00	45.00
AH1265	—	—	8.50	15.00	30.00	45.00
AH1267	—	—	8.50	15.00	30.00	45.00
AH1269	—	—	8.50	15.00	30.00	45.00
AH1271	—	—	8.50	15.00	30.00	45.00
AH1273	—	—	8.50	15.00	30.00	45.00
AH1275	—	—	8.50	15.00	30.00	45.00
AH1276	—	—	8.50	15.00	30.00	45.00
AH1277	—	—	8.50	15.00	30.00	45.00
AH1278	—	—	7.00	13.50	25.00	40.00
AH1278//1279	—	—	20.00	30.00	45.00	60.00
AH1278//1279	—	—	20.00	30.00	45.00	60.00
AH1279	—	—	7.00	13.50	25.00	40.00
AH1280//1279	—	—	20.00	30.00	45.00	60.00
AH1281//1280	—	—	20.00	30.00	45.00	60.00
AH1281	—	—	7.00	13.50	25.00	40.00
AH1282	—	—	7.00	13.50	25.00	40.00
AH1283	—	—	7.00	13.50	25.00	40.00
AH1284	—	—	7.00	13.50	25.00	40.00
AH1285	—	—	7.00	13.50	25.00	40.00
AH1293//1283	—	—	20.00	30.00	45.00	60.00
AH1293//1284	—	—	20.00	30.00	45.00	60.00
AH1293	—	—	7.00	13.50	25.00	40.00
AH1293//1294	—	—	20.00	30.00	45.00	60.00
AH1294//1293	—	—	20.00	30.00	45.00	60.00
AH1294//1296	—	—	20.00	30.00	45.00	60.00
AH1294	—	—	7.00	13.50	25.00	40.00
AH1295	—	—	20.00	30.00	45.00	60.00
AH1297//1296	—	—	20.00	30.00	45.00	60.00
AH1296	—	—	7.00	13.50	25.00	40.00
AH1297//1298	—	—	20.00	30.00	45.00	60.00
AH1297	—	—	7.00	13.50	25.00	40.00
AH1298	—	—	7.00	13.50	25.00	40.00
AH1299//1297	—	—	20.00	30.00	45.00	60.00
AH1299//1298	—	—	20.00	30.00	45.00	60.00
AH1299	—	—	7.00	13.50	25.00	40.00
AH1300//1254	—	—	20.00	30.00	45.00	60.00
AH1300//1299	—	—	20.00	30.00	45.00	60.00
AH1301//1299	—	—	20.00	30.00	45.00	60.00
AH1301//1300	—	—	10.00	16.50	27.50	40.00
AH1300	—	—	7.00	13.50	25.00	40.00
AH1301	—	—	7.00	13.50	25.00	40.00
AH1303	—	—	7.00	13.50	25.00	40.00
AH1304//1303	—	—	20.00	30.00	45.00	60.00
AH1305//1304	—	—	10.00	16.50	27.50	40.00
AH1304	—	—	6.50	12.50	20.00	30.00
AH1305	—	—	6.50	12.50	20.00	30.00
AH1306//1299	—	—	10.00	16.50	27.50	40.00
AH1306//1305	—	—	10.00	16.50	27.50	40.00
AH1306//1307	—	—	10.00	16.50	27.50	40.00
AH1306//1308	—	—	10.00	16.50	27.50	40.00
AH1306	—	—	6.50	12.50	20.00	30.00
AH1307	—	—	6.50	12.50	20.00	30.00
AH1308//1309	—	—	20.00	30.00	45.00	60.00
AH1308//1307	—	—	10.00	16.50	27.50	40.00
AH1309//1304	—	—	10.00	16.50	27.50	40.00
AH1308	—	—	6.50	12.50	20.00	30.00
AH1309//1310	—	—	20.00	30.00	45.00	60.00
AH1309	—	—	6.50	12.50	20.00	30.00
AH1310//1311	—	—	10.00	16.50	27.50	40.00
AH1310//1311	—	—	20.00	30.00	45.00	60.00
AH1310//1315	—	—	10.00	16.50	27.50	40.00
AH1310	—	—	6.50	12.50	20.00	30.00
AH1311	—	—	6.50	12.50	20.00	30.00
AH1315	—	—	6.50	12.50	20.00	30.00
AH1316	—	—	6.50	12.50	20.00	30.00

KM# 65 TILLA

4.5500 g., Gold **Note:** Struck in the name of late Ma'sum Ghazi (Emir Shah Murad); Die varieties exist with and without date on reverse; Previous #Y3.

Date	Mintage	Good	VG	F	VF	XF
AH1243//1242	—	—	85.00	110	165	225
AH1243	—	—	75.00	100	150	200
AH1244//1245	—	—	85.00	110	165	225
AH1244	—	—	75.00	100	150	200
AH1246	—	—	75.00	100	150	200
AH1247//1244	—	—	85.00	110	165	225
AH1247/6//1246	—	—	85.00	110	165	225
AH1248	—	—	75.00	100	150	200
AH1254	—	—	75.00	100	150	200
AH1255//1254	—	—	85.00	110	165	225
AH1255	—	—	75.00	100	150	200
AH1256//1254	—	—	85.00	110	165	225
AH1256//1255	—	—	85.00	110	165	225
AH1256	—	—	75.00	100	150	200
AH1257//1258	—	—	85.00	110	165	225
AH1857//1261	—	—	75.00	100	150	200
AH1264	—	—	75.00	100	150	200
AH1265//1266	—	—	85.00	110	165	225
AH1272//1275	—	—	85.00	110	165	225
AH1273//1243(sic)	—	—	85.00	110	165	225
AH1273//1274	—	—	75.00	100	150	200
AH1273//1275	—	—	75.00	100	150	200
AH1278	—	—	70.00	90.00	120	175
AH1279	—	—	70.00	90.00	120	175
Note: Date combination of AH1279 obverse and AH1285 reverse is reported.						
AH1283	—	—	70.00	90.00	120	175
AH1284	—	—	70.00	90.00	120	175
AH1285	—	—	70.00	90.00	120	175
AH1289	—	—	70.00	90.00	120	175
AH1291	—	—	60.00	85.00	120	175
AH1294	—	—	60.00	85.00	120	175
AH1296//1300	—	—	75.00	100	150	200
AH1296	—	—	60.00	85.00	120	175
AH1297	—	—	60.00	85.00	120	175
AH1298//1298	—	—	75.00	100	150	200
AH1299	—	—	60.00	85.00	120	175
AH1303	—	—	75.00	100	135	185
AH1306	—	—	75.00	100	135	185
AH1309	—	—	75.00	100	135	185
AH1315	—	—	75.00	100	135	185
AH1316	—	—	75.00	100	135	185

KHANATE OF KHIVA (KHWAREZM)

Khwarezm (Khiva), a historical region, once a great kingdom under the names of Chorasmia, Khwarezm and Gurganj (Urgench), is located in the lower stream and the delta of the Amu Darya River, east of the Caspian Sea and south of the Aral Sea. Russia established relations with Khwarezm (Khiva Khanate) in the 17th century, occupied it in 1873, and annexed it in 1875. Revolution concentrated Russia's preoccupation elsewhere during 1917 and Khiva seized this opportunity to declare its independence. It was able to sustain this status for a scant two years. By 1919 the Soviet regime had reestablished control over the region and extinguished the independent state. In AH1338/1920AD it was proclaimed Khorezm People's Soviet Republic and later became part of the Uzbekistan S.S.R. (Qaraqalpaq Autonomous Republic), now Uzbekistan.

RULERS

Muhammad Rahim,
AH1221-1241/1805-1825AD
Allah Quli,
AH1241-1258/1825-1842AD
Rahim Quli,
AH1258-1261/1842-1845AD
Muhammad Amin,
AH1261-1271/1845-1855AD
Qutlugh Muhammad,
AH1271-1272/1855-1856AD
Sayyid Muhammad Khan,
AH1272-1282/1856-1864AD
Sayid Muhammad Rahim
AH1282-1289/1864-1872AD
Sayid Muhammad Rahim, Russian vassal,
AH1290-1313/1873-1896AD

MINT NAMES

خوارزم

Khwarezm

KHANATE OF KHIVA

Muhammad Rahim

AH1221-1241 / 1805-1825 AD

HAMMERED COINAGE

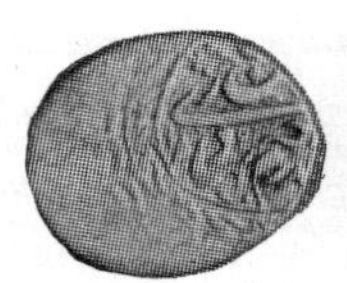

C# 40 TENGA

3.0000 g., Silver

Date	Mintage	VG	F	VF	XF	Unc
AH1232	—	20.00	30.00	50.00	85.00	—
AH1235	—	20.00	30.00	50.00	85.00	—

Allah Quli

AH1241-1258 / 1825-1842 AD

HAMMERED COINAGE

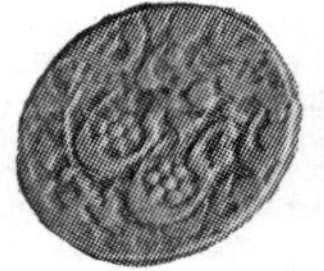

C# 50 TENGA

3.0000 g., Silver **Note:** Varieites exist.

Date	Mintage	VG	F	VF	XF	Unc
AH1247	—	20.00	30.00	50.00	85.00	—
AH1248	—	20.00	30.00	50.00	85.00	—
AH1258	—	20.00	30.00	50.00	85.00	—

Muhammad Amin

AH1261-1271 / 1845-1855 AD

HAMMERED COINAGE

C# 60 TENGA

3.0000 g., Silver

Date	Mintage	VG	F	VF	XF	Unc
AH1262	—	18.00	25.00	40.00	75.00	—
AH1263	—	18.00	25.00	40.00	75.00	—
AH1264	—	18.00	25.00	40.00	75.00	—
AH1265	—	18.00	25.00	40.00	75.00	—
AH1266	—	18.00	25.00	40.00	75.00	—
AH1267	—	18.00	25.00	40.00	75.00	—
AH1268	—	18.00	25.00	40.00	75.00	—
AH1269	—	18.00	25.00	40.00	75.00	—

C# 60a TENGA

3.0000 g., Silver **Rev:** Two borders enclose legend

Date	Mintage	VG	F	VF	XF	Unc
ND	—	18.00	25.00	40.00	75.00	—

C# 65 1/2 TILLA

Gold

Date	Mintage	VG	F	VF	XF	Unc
AH1261	—	200	350	550	800	—
AH1265	—	200	350	550	800	—

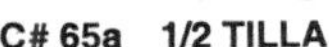

C# 65a 1/2 TILLA

Gold

Date	Mintage	VG	F	VF	XF	Unc
AH1270	—	200	350	550	800	—
AH1271	—	200	350	550	800	—

Qutlugh Muhammad

AH1271-1272 / 1855-1856 AD

HAMMERED COINAGE

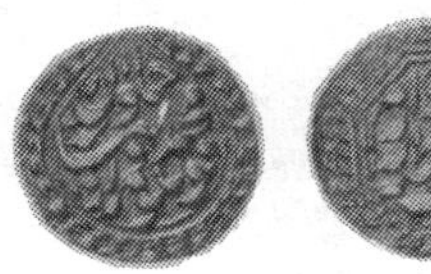

Y# A1 1/2 TILLA

Gold

Date	Mintage	VG	F	VF	XF	Unc
AH1271	—	250	450	750	1,100	—
AH1272	—	250	450	750	1,100	—

Sayyid Muhammad Khan

AH1272-1282 / 1856-1864 AD

HAMMERED COINAGE

Y# 1 FALUS

Copper **Note:** Border varieties exist.

Date	Mintage	VG	F	VF	XF	Unc
AH1272	—	20.00	35.00	50.00	75.00	—
AH1274	—	20.00	35.00	50.00	75.00	—
AH1275	—	20.00	35.00	50.00	75.00	—
AH1277	—	20.00	35.00	50.00	75.00	—
AH1278	—	20.00	35.00	50.00	75.00	—
AH1279	—	20.00	35.00	50.00	75.00	—
AH1280	—	20.00	35.00	50.00	75.00	—

Y# 2 TENGA

3.0000 g., Silver **Obv:** Date in center **Rev:** Ornamented

Date	Mintage	VG	F	VF	XF	Unc
AH1273	—	20.00	30.00	45.00	75.00	—
AH1274	—	20.00	30.00	45.00	75.00	—
AH1275	—	20.00	30.00	45.00	75.00	—
AH1276	—	20.00	30.00	45.00	75.00	—
AH1277	—	20.00	30.00	45.00	75.00	—
AH1278	—	20.00	30.00	45.00	75.00	—
AH1279	—	20.00	30.00	45.00	75.00	—
AH1280	—	20.00	30.00	45.00	75.00	—
AH1281	—	20.00	30.00	45.00	75.00	—
AH1288	—	20.00	30.00	45.00	75.00	—

Note: AH1288 dated strikes are posthumous issues

Y# A3 TILLA

Gold

Date	Mintage	VG	F	VF	XF	Unc
AH1276	—	275	450	700	1,000	—
AH1277	—	275	450	700	1,000	—

Sayyid Muhammad Rahim

AH1282-1328 / 1865-1910 AD

HAMMERED COINAGE

Y# 3 FALUS

Copper **Note:** Varieties exist. AH1290-1311 date strikes are posthumous issues.

Date	Mintage	VG	F	VF	XF	Unc
AH1286	—	12.50	25.00	50.00	80.00	—
AH1290	—	12.50	25.00	50.00	80.00	—
AH1308	—	12.50	25.00	50.00	80.00	—
AH1310	—	12.50	25.00	50.00	80.00	—
AH1311	—	12.50	25.00	50.00	80.00	—

Y# 6 TENGA

Silver **Note:** Two distinct varieties of obverse inscription (legend distribution) exist. AH1294-1313 dated strikes are posthumous issues.

Date	Mintage	VG	F	VF	XF	Unc
AH1282	—	15.00	20.00	30.00	45.00	—
AH1283	—	15.00	20.00	30.00	45.00	—
AH1284//1283	—	20.00	28.00	40.00	60.00	—
AH1284	—	15.00	20.00	30.00	45.00	—
AH1285	—	15.00	20.00	30.00	45.00	—
AH1287	—	18.00	25.00	42.50	70.00	—
AH1288	—	15.00	20.00	30.00	45.00	—
AH1294	—	18.00	25.00	42.50	70.00	—
AH1294//1295	—	18.00	25.00	42.50	70.00	—
AH1296//1297	—	18.00	25.00	42.50	70.00	—
AH1298	—	18.00	25.00	42.50	70.00	—
AH1301	—	18.00	25.00	42.50	70.00	—
AH1303	—	18.00	25.00	42.50	70.00	—
AH1305//1306	—	18.00	25.00	42.50	70.00	—
AH1305	—	18.00	25.00	42.50	70.00	—
AH1306	—	18.00	25.00	42.50	70.00	—
AH1307	—	18.00	25.00	42.50	70.00	—
AH1308	—	18.00	25.00	42.50	70.00	—
AH1311	—	18.00	25.00	42.50	70.00	—
AH1312	—	18.00	25.00	42.50	70.00	—
AH1313	—	18.00	25.00	42.50	70.00	—

KHOQAND

Khoqand, a town and former khanate in eastern Turkestan, was a powerful state in the 18th century. Russian superiority in the area was recognized following the holy war of 1875 and was annexed in 1875. It regained its independence briefly during 1918-1920 and became a Soviet Peoples Republic briefly between 1920-1924, and finally was absorbed into Uzbekistan S.S.R., now Uzbekistan.

RULERS

Muhammad Ali Khan,
AH1238-1256/1822-1840AD
Sher Ali,
AH1258-1261/1842-1845AD
Muhammad Khudayar Khan, 1st reign,
AH1261-1275/1845-1858AD
Malla Khan,
AH1275-1278/1858-1862AD
Shah Murad,
AH1278-1279/1862AD
Muhammad Khudayar Khan, 2nd reign,
AH1279-1280/1862-1863AD
Sayyid Sultan,
AH1280-1282/1863-1865AD
Muhammad Khudayer Khan, 3rd reign,
AH1282-1292/1865-1875AD
Independent until AH1283/1866AD
Russian Vassal AH1283-1293/ 1866-1876AD
Nasir al-Din,
AH1292-1293/1875-1876AD
Annexed To Russia, 1875-1876AD
Muhammad Fulad, Rebel,
AH1292-1293/1875-1876AD

MINT NAMES

Until AH1257, the coinage of Khoqand was struck at two mints.

Fe - Fergana(t)

Kd – Khoqand

STATE

Muhammad Ali Khan

AH1238-56/1822-40AD

STANDARD COINAGE

C# 60 PUL

Copper

Date	Mintage	VG	F	VF	XF	Unc
AH1249 Kd	—	20.00	35.00	50.00	75.00	—

C# 63 PUL

Copper

Date	Mintage	VG	F	VF	XF	Unc
AH1252 Fa	—	35.00	60.00	100	150	—

C# 65 TENGA

Silver **Note:** Borders on obverse and reverse vary.

Date	Mintage	VG	F	VF	XF	Unc
AH1241	—	15.00	30.00	60.00	90.00	—
AH1243	—	15.00	30.00	60.00	90.00	—
AH1244	—	15.00	30.00	60.00	90.00	—
AH1245	—	15.00	30.00	60.00	90.00	—
AH125x	—	15.00	30.00	60.00	90.00	—
ND Kd	—	15.00	30.00	60.00	90.00	—

C# 67 TILLA

Gold

Date	Mintage	VG	F	VF	XF	Unc
AH1247 Fa Rare	—	—	—	—	—	—

C# 68 TILLA

Gold

Date	Mintage	VG	F	VF	XF	Unc
AH1252	—	75.00	100	175	265	—
AH1254	—	75.00	100	175	265	—
AH1255	—	75.00	100	175	265	—
AH1256	—	75.00	100	175	265	—
AH1257	—	75.00	100	175	265	—

Note: AH1257 dated strikes are posthumous issues

Sher Ali

AH1258-61/1842-45AD

STANDARD COINAGE

KM# A70 FALUS

Copper

Date	Mintage	VG	F	VF	XF	Unc
AH1259	—	—	—	—	—	—

C# 78 TILLA

Gold

Date	Mintage	VG	F	VF	XF	Unc
AH1259//1258	—	100	125	225	300	—
AH1259	—	80.00	100	225	300	—
AH1260	—	80.00	100	225	300	—

Muhammad Khudayar Khan, 1st reign

AH1261-75/1845-58AD

STANDARD COINAGE

C# 87 PUL

Copper

Date	Mintage	VG	F	VF	XF	Unc
AH1265	—	15.00	18.00	25.00	35.00	—
AH1269	—	15.00	18.00	25.00	35.00	—

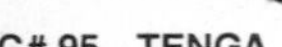

C# 95 TENGA

Silver

Date	Mintage	VG	F	VF	XF	Unc
AH1266//1268	—	30.00	40.00	60.00	100	—
AH1266	—	20.00	30.00	45.00	80.00	—
AH1269	—	20.00	30.00	45.00	80.00	—
AH1270	—	20.00	30.00	45.00	80.00	—
AH1271	—	20.00	30.00	45.00	80.00	—
AH1272	—	20.00	30.00	45.00	80.00	—
AH1273	—	20.00	30.00	45.00	80.00	—
AH1274	—	20.00	30.00	45.00	80.00	—
AH1275	—	20.00	30.00	45.00	80.00	—

C# 100 TILLA

Gold

Date	Mintage	VG	F	VF	XF	Unc
AH1260	—	100	140	170	225	—
AH1261//1264	—	125	175	200	250	—
AH1261	—	100	140	170	225	—
AH1262//1261	—	125	175	200	250	—
AH1263	—	100	140	170	225	—
AH1264	—	100	140	170	225	—
AH1265	—	100	140	170	225	—
AH1266	—	100	140	170	225	—
AH1270	—	100	140	170	225	—
AH1272	—	100	140	170	225	—

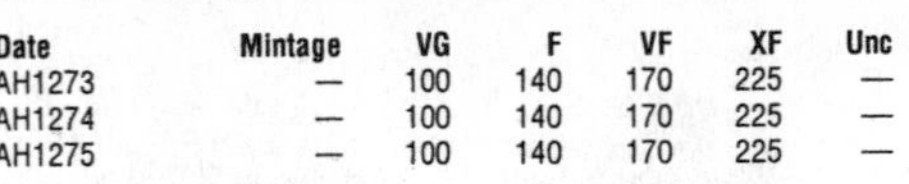

Date	Mintage	VG	F	VF	XF	Unc
AH1273	—	100	140	170	225	—
AH1274	—	100	140	170	225	—
AH1275	—	100	140	170	225	—

C# 100.5 TILLA

Gold **Obv:** New title

Date	Mintage	VG	F	VF	XF	Unc
AH1261//1262	—	125	275	425	600	—
AH1265	—	125	275	425	600	—

Muhammad Malla Khan

AH1275-78/1858-62AD

STANDARD COINAGE

C# 112 PUL

Copper

Date	Mintage	VG	F	VF	XF	Unc
AH1277	—	12.00	20.00	35.00	60.00	—

C# 115 TENGA

Silver

Date	Mintage	VG	F	VF	XF	Unc
AH1275	—	20.00	40.00	50.00	85.00	—
AH1276	—	20.00	40.00	50.00	85.00	—
AH1277	—	20.00	40.00	50.00	85.00	—

C# 118 TILLA

Gold

Date	Mintage	VG	F	VF	XF	Unc
AH1275	—	100	140	170	225	—
AH1276	—	100	140	170	225	—
AH1277	—	100	140	170	225	—
AH1278	—	100	140	170	225	—

Shah Murad

AH1278-79/1862AD

STANDARD COINAGE

C# 128 TILLA

Gold

Date	Mintage	VG	F	VF	XF	Unc
AH1278	—	100	150	250	350	—

Muhammad Khudayar Khan, 2nd reign

AH1279-80/1862-63AD

STANDARD COINAGE

C# 130 TENGA

Silver **Obv:** Teardrop border **Rev:** Teardrop border

Date	Mintage	VG	F	VF	XF	Unc
AH1279	—	30.00	60.00	100	150	—

C# 135 TILLA

Gold

Date	Mintage	VG	F	VF	XF	Unc
ND	—	—	—	—	—	—

Note: Reported, not confirmed

Sayyid Sultan

AH1280-82/1863-65AD

STANDARD COINAGE

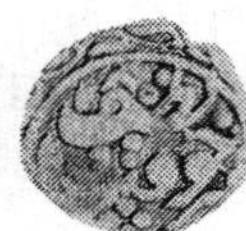

C# 140 TENGA

Silver

Date	Mintage	VG	F	VF	XF	Unc
AH1280	—	30.00	45.00	75.00	150	—
AH1281	—	30.00	45.00	75.00	150	—
AH1285	—	30.00	45.00	75.00	150	—

Note: AH1285 dated strikes are posthumous issues

C# 145 TILLA

Gold

Date	Mintage	VG	F	VF	XF	Unc
AH1280	—	100	140	170	225	—
AH1281	—	100	140	170	225	—

Muhammad Khudayer Khan, 3rd reign

AH1282-92/1865-75AD

STANDARD COINAGE

C# 148 PUL

Copper

Date	Mintage	VG	F	VF	XF	Unc
AH1287	—	15.00	25.00	40.00	70.00	—

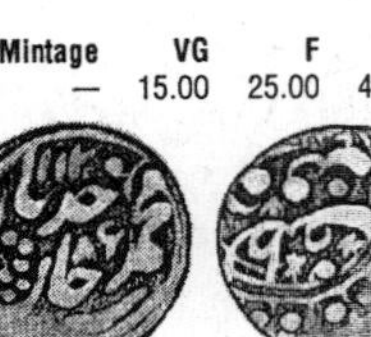

C# 151 TENGA

Silver

Date	Mintage	VG	F	VF	XF	Unc
AH1282	—	20.00	30.00	45.00	80.00	—
AH1283	—	20.00	30.00	45.00	80.00	—
AH1284	—	20.00	30.00	45.00	80.00	—
AH1285	—	20.00	30.00	45.00	80.00	—
AH1286	—	20.00	30.00	45.00	80.00	—
AH1287	—	20.00	30.00	45.00	80.00	—
AH1289	—	20.00	30.00	45.00	80.00	—
AH1291	—	20.00	30.00	45.00	80.00	—
AH1292	—	20.00	30.00	45.00	80.00	—

C# 152 TENGA

Silver **Obv. Inscription:** "Muhammad Malla Khan"

Date	Mintage	VG	F	VF	XF	Unc
AH1289	—	30.00	50.00	80.00	100	—

Note: This is a posthumous issue

C# 155 TILLA

Gold **Obv. Inscription:** "Muhammad Malla Khan"

Date	Mintage	VG	F	VF	XF	Unc
AH1282	—	90.00	120	160	190	—
AH1283	—	90.00	120	160	190	—
AH1285	—	90.00	120	160	190	—
AH1288	—	90.00	120	160	190	—
AH1289	—	90.00	120	160	190	—

Muhammad Fulad, Rebel

AH1292-93/1875-76AD

STANDARD COINAGE

C# 105 TENGA

Silver

Date	Mintage	VG	F	VF	XF	Unc
AH1292	—	20.00	30.00	40.00	65.00	—
AH1293	—	20.00	30.00	40.00	65.00	—

Nasir al-Din

AH1292-93/1875-76AD

STANDARD COINAGE

C# 165 TILLA

Gold

Date	Mintage	VG	F	VF	XF	Unc
AH1292	—	—	—	—	—	—

Note: Reported, not confirmed

VENEZUELA

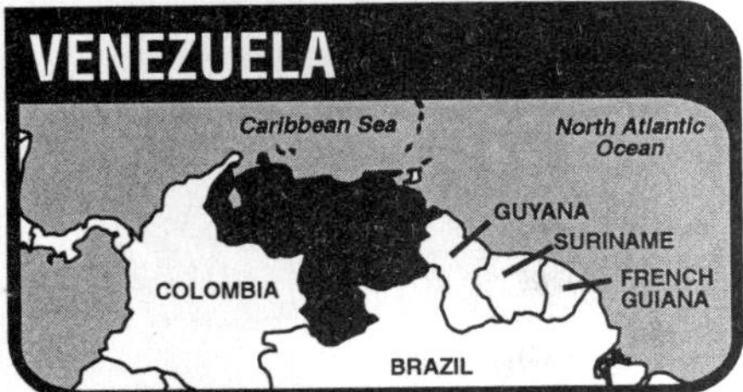

Venezuela ("Little Venice"), located on the northern coast of South America between Colombia and Guyana, has an area of 352,145 sq. mi.(912,050 sq. km.).

Columbus discovered Venezuela on his third voyage in 1498. Initial exploration did not reveal Venezuela to be a land of great wealth. An active pearl trade operated on the offshore islands and slavers raided the interior in search of Indians to be sold into slavery, but no significant mainland settlements were made before 1567 when Caracas was founded. Venezuela, the home of Bolivar, was among the first South American colonies to rebel against Spain in 1810. The declaration of Independence of Venezuela was signed by seven provinces which are represented by the seven stars of the Venezuelan flag. Coinage of Caracas and Margarita use the seven stars in their designs. These original provinces were: Barcelona, Barinas, Caracas, Cumana, Margarita, Merida and Trujillo. The Provinces of Coro, Guyana and Maracaibo were added to Venezuela during the Independence War. Independence was attained in 1821 but not recognized by Spain until 1845. Together with Ecuador, Panama and Colombia, Venezuela was part of "Gran Colombia" until 1830, when it became a sovereign and independent state.

RULERS

Spanish, until 1810
Spanish and Independent, 1810-1823
Republic, 1823-present

MINT MARKS

A - Paris
(a) - Paris, privy marks only
(aa) - Altena
(b) - Berlin
(bb) - Brussels
(cc) - Canada
(c) - Caracas
(d) - Denver
H, Heaton - Heaton, Birmingham
(l) - London
(m) - Madrid
(mm) - Mexico
(o) - Ontario
(p) - Philadelphia
(s) - San Francisco
(sc) - Schwerte - Vereinigte Deutsche Nickelwerke
(w) - Werdohl - Vereinigte Deutsche Metalwerke

MONETARY SYSTEM

16 Reales = 1 Escudo
8 Reales = 1 Peso

REPUBLIC OF VENEZUELA

DECIMAL COINAGE

10 Centavos = 1 Real; 10 Reals = 1 Peso

Y# 1 1/4 CENTAVO

3.0000 g., Copper, 19.25 mm. **Obv:** Head of Liberty facing right, initials below **Obv. Legend:** REPUBLICA DE VENEZUELA **Rev:** Value and date within two branches **Edge:** Diagonally reeded edge

Date	Mintage	F	VF	XF	Unc	BU
1843(l)	3,841,957	7.50	25.00	60.00	200	600
Note: W.W. below Liberty head						
1852H	2,000,000	10.00	60.00	170	300	800
Note: H below Liberty head, diameter 19mm, weight 2.9 grams						

Y# 4 1/4 CENTAVO

2.7000 g., Copper, 18.5 mm. **Obv:** Head of Liberty facing right **Rev:** Value and date within two branches **Edge:** Diagonally reeded edge

Date	Mintage	F	VF	XF	Unc	BU
1852(l)	4,000,000	5.00	25.00	60.00	200	800

Y# 2 1/2 CENTAVO

6.0000 g., Copper, 23 mm. **Obv:** Head of Liberty facing right, initials below **Obv. Legend:** REPUBLICA DE VENEZUELA **Rev:** Value and date within two branches **Edge:** Diagonally reeded edge

Date	Mintage	F	VF	XF	Unc	BU
1843(l)	960,020	9.50	40.00	140	250	700
Note: W.W. below Liberty head						
1843(l) Proof	—	Value: 900				
Note: W.W. below Liberty head						
1852H	500,000	15.00	85.00	350	550	1,000
Note: H below Liberty head, weight 5.7 grams						

Y# 5.1 1/2 CENTAVO

5.4000 g., Copper, 22 mm. **Obv:** Head of Liberty facing right **Obv. Legend:** REPUBLICA DE VENEZUELA **Rev:** Value and date within two branches **Note:** 24 berries

Date	Mintage	F	VF	XF	Unc	BU
1852(l)	1,000,000	9.50	55.00	160	250	500

Y# 5.2 1/2 CENTAVO

5.4000 g., Copper **Note:** 23 berries

Date	F	VF	XF	Unc	BU
1852(l)	28.50	120	300	500	800

Y# 3.1 CENTAVO

12.1000 g., Copper, 32 mm. **Obv:** Head of Liberty facing right, W. Wyon below **Obv. Legend:** REPUBLICA DE VENEZUELA **Rev:** Value and date within two branches **Edge:** Diagonally reeded edge **Note:** Slant-top 1.

Date	Mintage	F	VF	XF	Unc	BU
1843(l)	480,010	35.00	80.00	170	400	800
1843(l) Proof	—	Value: 1,000				

Y# 3.2 CENTAVO

11.4000 g., Copper, 31.5 mm. **Obv:** Head of Liberty facing right, Heaton below **Obv. Legend:** REPUBLICA DE VENEZUELA **Rev:** Value and date within two branches **Edge:** Diagonally reeded edge **Note:** Flat-top 1.

Date	Mintage	F	VF	XF	Unc	BU
1852H	250,000	20.00	70.00	200	400	600
1852H Proof	—	Value: 750				

Y# 6 CENTAVO

10.9000 g., Copper, 30.5 mm. **Obv:** Head of Liberty facing right **Rev:** Value and date within two branches **Edge:** Diagonally reeded edge

Date	Mintage	F	VF	XF	Unc	BU
1852(l)	500,000	10.00	25.00	85.00	200	500
1852(l) Proof	—	Value: 600				

Y# 7 CENTAVO
7.5000 g., Copper, 25 mm. **Obv:** Draped bust of Liberty facing right, HEATON on truncation **Rev:** Value and date within two branches **Edge:** Diagonally reeded edge

Date	Mintage	F	VF	XF	Unc	BU
1858 LIBERTAD incuse	2,000,000	5.00	12.00	35.00	100	400
1858 Proof, LIBERTAD incuse	—	Value: 500				
1858 LIBERTAD in relief	Inc. above	5.00	15.00	40.00	120	400
1858 Proof, LIBERTAD in relief	—	Value: 500				
1862	1,500,000	5.00	12.00	35.00	100	400
1863	500,000	9.00	25.00	70.00	175	500

Y# 8 1/2 REAL
1.1500 g., 0.9000 Silver .0333 oz. **Note:** Similar to 2 Reales Y#10, but value shown as 1-1/2 Real, erroneously.

Date	Mintage	F	VF	XF	Unc	BU
1858A	40,270	150	275	785	1,400	2,500

Y# 9 REAL
2.3000 g., 0.9000 Silver .0666 oz. **Note:** Similar to 2 Reales, Y#10.

Date	Mintage	F	VF	XF	Unc	BU
1858A	42,698	100	200	520	1,200	3,000

Y# 10 2 REALES
4.6000 g., 0.9000 Silver .1331 oz.

Date	Mintage	F	VF	XF	Unc	BU
1858A	29,990	150	275	1,000	2,250	5,000

Y# 11 5 REALES
11.5000 g., 0.9000 Silver .3328 oz.

Date	Mintage	F	VF	XF	Unc	BU
1858A	26,120	200	335	1,150	2,500	4,000

Y# A11 10 REALES
Silver

Date	F	VF	XF	Unc	BU
1863A	—	—	8,000	12,000	15,000

Note: Almost entire issue melted, estimated 200 pcs. survived

REFORM COINAGE

1871-1879; 100 Centavos = 1 Venezolano

Y# 25 CENTAVO
Copper-Nickel

Date	Mintage	F	VF	XF	Unc	BU
1876(p)	8,000,000	6.00	15.00	45.00	150	500
1876(p) Proof	—	Value: 550				
1877(p)	2,000,000	8.00	20.00	55.00	200	600
1877(p) Proof	—	Value: 650				

Y# 26 2-1/2 CENTAVOS
Copper-Nickel

Date	Mintage	F	VF	XF	Unc	BU
1876(p)	1,500,000	15.00	30.00	120	250	600
1876(p) Proof	—	Value: 650				
1877(p)	500,000	17.50	35.00	140	300	700
1877(p) Proof	—	Value: 750				

Y# 12.1 5 CENTAVOS
1.2500 g., 0.8350 Silver .0336 oz. **Rev:** Bolivar head left, serifed A as mint mark

Date	Mintage	F	VF	XF	Unc	BU
1874A	800,000	5.00	15.00	35.00	125	350
1874A Proof	—	Value: 500				
1876A	520,000	9.00	20.00	50.00	175	450
1876A Proof	—	Value: 700				

Y# 12.2 5 CENTAVOS
1.2500 g., 0.8350 Silver .0336 oz. **Rev:** Bolivar head left, unserifed A as mint mark

Date	F	VF	XF	Unc	BU
1874A	5.00	15.00	35.00	125	350
1876A	9.00	20.00	50.00	175	450

Y# 13.1 10 CENTAVOS
2.5000 g., 0.8350 Silver .0671 oz. **Rev:** Bolivar head left, serifed A as mint mark

Date	Mintage	F	VF	XF	Unc	BU
1874A	800,000	10.00	25.00	60.00	125	400
1874A Proof	—	Value: 600				
1876A	280,000	25.00	70.00	160	225	500

Y# 13.2 10 CENTAVOS
2.5000 g., 0.8350 Silver .0671 oz. **Rev:** Bolivar head left, unserifed A as mint mark

Date	F	VF	XF	Unc	BU
1874A	10.00	25.00	60.00	125	400
1876A	25.00	70.00	160	225	500

Y# 14 20 CENTAVOS
5.0000 g., 0.8350 Silver .1342 oz.

Date	Mintage	F	VF	XF	Unc	BU
1874A Small A	400,000	25.00	50.00	130	250	450
1874A Large A	Inc. above	25.00	50.00	130	250	450
1876A	136,000	50.00	100	300	450	600

Y# 15 50 CENTAVOS
12.5000 g., 0.8350 Silver .3356 oz.

Date	Mintage	F	VF	XF	Unc	BU
1873A	200,000	60.00	140	600	950	2,000
1874A	200,000	60.00	140	600	950	2,000
1876A	158,000	60.00	140	600	950	2,000

Y# 16 VENEZOLANO
25.0000 g., 0.9000 Silver .7234 oz.

Date	Mintage	F	VF	XF	Unc	BU
1876A	35,000	80.00	200	1,000	3,500	10,000
1876A Proof	—	Value: 12,000				

Y# 17 5 VENEZOLANOS
8.0645 g., 0.9000 Gold .2333 oz.

Date	Mintage	F	VF	XF	Unc	BU
1875A	69,000	100	150	200	500	800

REFORM COINAGE

1896; 100 Centimos = 1 Bolivar

Y# 27 5 CENTIMOS
Copper-Nickel

Date	Mintage	F	VF	XF	Unc	BU
1896(b)	4,000,000	0.50	2.00	17.00	75.00	150

Y# 28 12-1/2 CENTIMOS
Copper-Nickel **Note:** Varieties exist.

Date	Mintage	F	VF	XF	Unc	BU
1896(b)	6,000,000	1.00	4.00	25.00	150	300

Y# 19.1 1/5 BOLIVAR
1.0000 g., 0.8350 Silver .0268 oz. **Obv:** Shield, crude letters in legend

Date	Mintage	VG	F	VF	XF	Unc
1879(bb)	125,000	120	200	300	700	3,000

Y# 19.2 1/5 BOLIVAR
1.0000 g., 0.8350 Silver .0268 oz. **Obv:** Shield, refined letters in legend

Date	VG	F	VF	XF	Unc
1879(bb)	120	170	300	700	3,000

Note: Coin recalled and many melted upon issuance of the 1/4 Bolivar in 1894

Y# 20 1/4 BOLIVAR
1.2500 g., 0.8350 Silver .0336 oz.

Date	Mintage	F	VF	XF	Unc	BU
1894A	2,000,000	2.00	3.50	8.50	40.00	200
1900(a)	407,000	5.00	14.00	28.00	120	300

Y# 21 1/2 BOLIVAR
2.5000 g., 0.8350 Silver .0671 oz.

Date	Mintage	F	VF	XF	Unc	BU
1879(bb)	200,000	40.00	100	330	800	2,000
1886(c) High second 8	300,000	20.00	50.00	150	400	1,000
1886(c) Low second 8	Inc. above	20.00	50.00	150	400	1,000
1887(c)	310,000	50.00	100	250	600	1,500
1888(c)	230,000	400	600	1,100	2,000	5,000
1889(c)	80,000	2,500	4,000	6,000	12,000	—
1893A	500,000	15.00	30.00	70.00	300	1,000
1900A	600,000	20.00	50.00	175	500	1,000
1900(a)	—	35.00	55.00	220	800	1,500

Y# 22 BOLIVAR
5.0000 g., 0.8350 Silver .1342 oz.

Date	Mintage	F	VF	XF	Unc	BU
1879(bb)	375,000	28.00	85.00	500	1,200	2,000
1886A Rare	—	—	—	—	—	—
1886(c) Wide date	600,000	22.00	65.00	250	800	1,500
1886(c) Narrow date	Inc. above	22.00	70.00	260	1,000	2,000
1887(c)	280,000	125	350	1,000	1,500	3,000
1888(c)	197,000	150	400	1,100	3,000	5,000
1889(c)	118,000	100	250	850	2,000	3,000
1893(a)	500,000	15.00	45.00	150	400	700
1900(a)	380,000	20.00	55.00	150	650	1,250

Y# 23 2 BOLIVARES
10.0000 g., 0.8350 Silver .2685 oz.

Date	Mintage	F	VF	XF	Unc	BU
1879(bb)	375,000	25.00	80.00	400	950	2,000
1886(c) Knobbed 6	240,000	40.00	150	900	3,500	6,000
1886(c) Pointed 6	Inc. above	40.00	150	900	3,500	6,000
1887(c) High second 8	200,000	11.50	50.00	200	600	2,000
1887(c) Low second 8	Inc. above	11.50	50.00	200	600	2,000
1888(c)	141,000	55.00	200	750	1,850	5,000
1889(c)	50,000	75.00	225	800	2,500	5,000
1894(a)	250,000	16.50	45.00	300	800	1,800
1900(a)	350,000	15.00	35.00	150	500	1,500

Y# 24.1 5 BOLIVARES
25.0000 g., 0.9000 Silver .7234 oz. **Obv:** Date on ribbon right of arms 28 DE MARZO DE 1864

Date	Mintage	F	VF	XF	Unc	BU
1879(bb)	250,000	15.00	90.00	450	1,400	4,000
1886(c) Normal date	470,000	12.00	35.00	200	700	2,000
1886(c) Low second 8	Inc. above	12.00	35.00	200	700	2,000
1886(c) Tight 8's	Inc. above	12.00	35.00	200	700	2,000
1886(c) Without accent on Bolivar	Inc. above	12.00	35.00	200	700	2,000
1887(c)	500,000	12.00	40.00	300	1,200	2,500
1888(c) High second 8	281,000	12.00	40.00	300	1,200	3,000
1888(c) Low second 8	Inc. above	12.00	40.00	300	1,200	3,000
1889(c)	329,000	12.00	40.00	300	1,200	3,000

Y# 24.2 5 BOLIVARES
25.0000 g., 0.9000 Silver .7234 oz. **Obv:** Date on ribbon right of arms 13 DE APRIL DE 1864

Date	Mintage	F	VF	XF	Unc	BU
1900(a)	270,000	12.00	28.00	150	700	1,500

Y# 32 20 BOLIVARES
6.4516 g., 0.9000 Gold .1867 oz.

Date	Mintage	F	VF	XF	Unc	BU
1879(bb)	41,000	BV	100	150	400	650
1880(bb) 1 and 8 close	84,000	BV	100	110	300	600
1880(bb) 1 and 8 apart	Inc. above	BV	100	110	300	600
1880(bb) Tight 8's	Inc. above	BV	100	110	300	600
1886(c) High 6	23,000	BV	130	150	200	500
1886(c) Low 6	Inc. above	BV	130	150	200	500
1887(c)	132,000	125	175	250	600	1,000
1888/6(c)	81,000	100	150	200	450	800
1888(c)	Inc. above	110	160	220	500	1,000

Y# 34 100 BOLIVARES
32.2580 g., 0.9000 Gold .9334 oz.

Date	Mintage	F	VF	XF	Unc	BU
1886(c) Normal date	4,250	BV	600	700	1,000	1,500
1886(c) 8 and 6 close	Inc. above	BV	600	700	1,000	1,500
1886(c) 8 and 6 apart	Inc. above	BV	600	700	1,000	1,500
1887(c)	28,000	BV	600	700	1,000	1,500
1888(c)	32,000	BV	600	700	1,000	1,500
1889(c)	23,000	BV	600	700	1,000	1,500

ESSAIS

KM#	Date	Mintage	Identification	Mkt Val
E1	1863	—	Centavo. Copper. E below bow.	300
E2	1863	—	2 Centavos. Copper. E below bow.	400
E3	1863	—	1/2 Real. Silver. Plain edge.	13,000
E4	1863	—	Real. Silver. Plain edge.	13,000
E5	1863	—	2 Reales. Silver. Plain edge.	13,000
E6	1863	—	4 Reales. Silver.	13,000
E7	1863	—	10 Reales. Silver.	15,000
E8	1863	—	10 Reales. Silver. Plain edge.	15,000
E9	1868	—	Centavo. Nickel.	500
E10	1873	—	2-1/2 Centavos. Nickel.	—
E11	1873	—	5 Centavos. Silver. Reeded edge.	2,500
E12	1873	—	10 Centavos. Silver.	2,500
E13	1873	—	50 Centavos. Silver.	5,000
E14	1874	—	20 Centavos. Silver.	2,500
E15	1874	—	Venezolano. Silver. Plain edge. 13 de APRIL 1864 at lower right	10,000

KM#	Date	Mintage	Identification	Mkt Val
E16	1874	—	Venezolano. 0.9000 Silver. 28 DE MARZO 1864 at lower right	10,000
E17	1875	—	Venezolano. Gold-Plated Copper.	15,000
EA18	1875	—	Venezolano. 0.9000 Gold.	20,000

Note: Akers Pittman sale 8-99, very choice Proof realized $18,400

KM#	Date	Mintage	Identification	Mkt Val
E19	1875	—	5 Venezolanos. Gold-Plated Copper.	15,000

KM#	Date	Mintage	Identification	Mkt Val
E20	1875	—	5 Venezolanos. 0.9000 Gold.	15,000

Note: Akers Pittman sale 8-99, very choice Proof realized $20,700

KM#	Date	Mintage	Identification	Mkt Val
E21	1875	—	10 Venezolanos. Gold-Plated Copper.	25,000
E22	1875	—	10 Venezolanos. 0.9000 Gold.	25,000
E23	1876	—	20 Venezolanos. Gold-Plated Copper.	15,000
E24	1875	—	20 Venezolanos. 0.9000 Gold.	15,000
E25	1876	—	Centavo. Copper.	800
E26	1991(c)	—	1300 Bolivares. Copper. M1, thin planchet	—
E27	1991(c)	—	1300 Bolivares. Copper. M1, thick planchet.	—

PATTERNS

Including off metal strikes

KM#	Date	Mintage	Identification	Mkt Val
Pn1	1843	—	1/4 Centavo. Plain edge. Thick planchet, medal rotation.	2,000
Pn2	1843	—	1/4 Centavo. Diagonal edge reeding, coin rotation.	2,000
Pn3	1843	—	1/4 Centavo. Plain edge. Coin rotation.	2,000
Pn4	1843	—	1/2 Centavo. Plain edge. Thick planchet, medal rotation.	2,500
Pn5	1843	—	1/2 Centavo. Diagonal edge reeding, coin rotation.	2,500
Pn6	1843	—	1/2 Centavo. Plain edge. Coin rotation (not confirmed).	—
Pn7	1843	—	Centavo. Plain edge. Thick planchet, medal rotation.	1,200
Pn8	1843	—	Centavo. Diagonal edge reeding, coin rotation.	3,000
Pn9	1843	—	Centavo. Plain edge. Coin rotation.	2,000
Pn10	1852H	—	1/4 Centavo. Plain edge.	1,600
Pn11	1852	—	1/4 Centavo. Plain edge.	1,600
Pn12	1852H	—	1/2 Centavo. Plain edge.	1,000
Pn13	1852	—	1/2 Centavo. Plain edge. Thick planchet.	1,500
Pn14	1852H	—	1/2 Centavo. Nickel. Double reverse, Y#2.	1,700
Pn15	1852	—	1/2 Centavo. Plain edge. Thin planchet.	1,000
Pn16	1852H	—	1/2 Centavo. Copper. Double reverse, Y#2.	1,100
Pn17	1852	—	1/2 Centavo. Copper. Double reverse.	1,000
Pn18	1852H	—	Centavo. Plain edge. Medal rotation.	3,000
Pn19	1852	—	Centavo. Coin rotation.	2,000
Pn20	1852H	—	Centavo. Thick planchet, coin rotation.	2,000
Pn21	1852	—	Centavo. Bronze.	1,500
Pn22	1852H	—	Centavo. Nickel.	2,000
Pn23	1852	—	Centavo. Double reverse, piefort.	1,500
Pn24	1852H	—	Centavo. Nickel. Plain edge. Double reverse, Y#3.2.	650
Pn25	1852	—	Centavo. Nickel. Double reverse.	600
Pn26	1852H	—	Centavo. Copper. Plain edge. Double reverse.	600
Pn27	1852	—	Centavo. Copper. Double reverse.	550

KM#	Date	Mintage	Identification	Mkt Val
Pn28	1858H	—	Centavo. Copper. Y7.	300
Pn29	1858H	—	Centavo. Copper-Nickel-Zinc. Y7.	750
Pn30	1858	—	Centavo. Copper. Plain edge. Incuse.	1,000
Pn31	1858	—	Centavo. Plain edge. High relief.	750
Pn32	1858	—	Centavo. Copper. Plain edge. Incuse.	1,500
Pn33	1858	—	Centavo. Plain edge. Thick planchet.	800
Pn34	1858	—	Centavo. Plain edge. Thin planchet, incuse.	300
Pn35	1858	—	Centavo. Reeded edge.	1,000
Pn36	1858	—	Centavo. Very thin planchet, incuse.	300
Pn37	1858	—	Centavo. Double reverse, Y#7.	600
Pn38	1858	—	Centavo. Nickel. Plain edge. Incuse.	1,000
Pn39	1858	—	Centavo. Nickel.	1,000
Pn40	1858	—	Centavo. Nickel. Plain edge. Incuse.	1,000
Pn41	1858	—	Centavo. Bronze.	1,000
Pn42	1862	—	Centavo. Copper. Plain edge.	1,600
Pn43	1863	—	Centavo. Nickel. Plain edge. Incuse, double reverse.	1,000

KM#	Date	Mintage	Identification	Mkt Val
Pn44	1875	—	10 Venezolanos. 0.9000 Gold.	—

Note: Akers Pittman sale 8-99, choice Proof realized $25,300+

KM#	Date	Mintage	Identification	Mkt Val
Pn45	1876	—	Centavo. Copper. Y#25.	800
Pn46	1888	—	50 Bolivares. 0.9000 Gold.	—

Note: Baldwin's Auction 12-99, realized $37,500

TRIAL STRIKES

KM#	Date	Mintage	Identification	Mkt Val
TS1	ND(1875)	—	Venezolano. Gilt Copper. Bolivar. Retrograde 20C.	7,500
TS2	1875	—	Venezolano. Gilt Copper. Retrograde 20C. Standard arms.	7,500
TS3	ND(1875)	—	5 Venezolanos. Gilt Copper. Bolivar.	—
TS4	1875	—	5 Venezolanos. Gilt Copper. Standard arms.	—
TS5	ND(1875)	—	10 Venezolanos. Gilt Copper. Bolivar. Retrograde 50F.	—

KM#	Date	Mintage	Identification	Mkt Val
TS6	1875	—	10 Venezolanos. Gilt Copper. Retrograde 50F. Standard arms.	—
TS7	ND(1875)	—	20 Venezolanos. Gilt Copper. Bolivar. Retrograde. B. EPREUVGE 100.F.1855.	—
TS8	1875	—	20 Venezolanos. Gilt Copper. Standard arms, retrograde. B. EPREUVE 100F.1855.	—

BARINAS

The name of Barinas is used to identify the colonial coins minted from 1817 to 1824 by General Jose Antonio Paez in the west-central south Venezuela in different towns such as Achaguas and Caujaral, which are commonly known as Yagual and Chipi-chipis, both from the province of Barinas.

ACHAGUAS

NECESSITY COINAGE

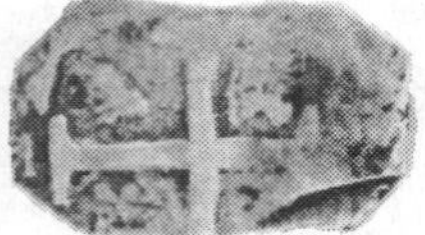

KM# 1 2 REALES (El Yagual)
0.4020 Silver **Note:** Weight range 3.58-4.93g.

Date	Good	VG	F	VF	XF
781(1817)	450	600	825	1,000	—

CAUJARAL

NECESSITY COINAGE

KM# 2 REAL (Chipi-chipi)
Silver **Note:** Weight range 0.95-2.20g. Many locally produced counterfiets exist.

Date	Good	VG	F	VF	XF
124	60.00	90.00	125	200	—
127	60.00	90.00	125	200	—
142	60.00	90.00	125	200	—
143	60.00	90.00	125	200	—
145	60.00	90.00	125	200	—
152	60.00	90.00	125	200	—
156	60.00	90.00	125	200	—
157	60.00	90.00	125	200	—
158	60.00	90.00	125	200	—
161	60.00	90.00	125	200	—
162	60.00	90.00	125	200	—
173	60.00	90.00	125	200	—
177	60.00	90.00	125	200	—
181	60.00	90.00	125	200	—
700	60.00	90.00	125	200	—
1241	85.00	115	165	255	—
1791	90.00	125	180	255	—
1811	90.00	125	180	255	—
1814	90.00	125	180	255	—
1926 (sic)	90.00	125	180	255	—
1941 (sic)	90.00	125	180	255	—
1991	90.00	125	180	255	—

CARACAS

This province surrounds the national capital also named Caracas. Spain opened the first mint in Venezuela in that city in November 1802. Coins were made initially from 1802 to 1805. Caracas rebelled on April 19, 1810, and the Spanish retreated, but retook the city in July 1812 and Royalist coinage resumed. Copper and silver coins were struck through 1821, when Bolivar's troops defeated the Spanish.

ROYALIST

ROYALIST COINAGE

C# 1 1/8 REAL
2.0000 g., Copper **Note:** Diameter range 18-20mm. Beware of counterfeits.

Date	Mintage	Good	VG	F	VF	XF
1802	59,000	300	600	1,000	1,500	—
1804	19,000	1,000	1,500	2,200	3,000	—
1805	100,000	200	300	500	900	—
1814	12,000	500	750	1,250	2,000	—
1817	4,500	1,500	2,000	3,250	5,500	—
1818	94,000	50.00	100	200	300	400

Large date

Small date

C# 2 1/4 REAL
Copper **Note:** Beginning around 1813, average planchet size begins to diminish. Diameter range 21-25mm. Weight range 2.0-3.1g. Beware of counterfeits.

Date	Mintage	Good	VG	F	VF	XF
1802	14,000	850	1,250	2,500	4,000	—
1804	6,589	1,700	2,200	4,500	7,000	—
1805	70,000	400	600	1,100	1,600	—
1813	10,000	35.00	60.00	120	200	—
1814/3	40,000	10.00	25.00	60.00	85.00	—
1814	Inc. above	8.00	15.00	50.00	75.00	—
1816	750,000	6.00	12.00	45.00	65.00	—
1817 Large date	490,000	3.00	5.00	10.00	20.00	—
1817 Small date	1,640,000	2.00	3.50	9.00	17.50	—
1818	2,240,000	2.00	3.50	9.00	17.50	—
1821	650,000	5.00	10.00	25.00	50.00	—

ROYALIST AND/OR REPUBLICAN COINAGE

C# 12 REAL (Macuquina)
Silver **Note:** Weight range 2.20-3.11g. Cob style - Caracas shape.

Date	Good	VG	F	VF	XF
42(1)	100	215	300	500	750
182	100	235	350	600	875
721	100	235	350	600	875
781	100	215	300	500	750
931	90.00	185	265	450	585

C# 13.1 2 REALES (Macuquinas)
Silver **Note:** Approximately .200-.600 fine. Diameter range 22-26mm. Weight range 4.50-5.80g. Cob style - Caracas shape.

Date	Good	VG	F	VF	XF
142	75.00	135	220	345	—
152	150	270	360	500	—
172	60.00	115	200	325	—
174	90.00	165	280	385	—
182	55.00	100	170	280	—
183	150	275	360	500	—
184	50.00	100	155	265	—
281	120	215	325	440	—
471	60.00	115	200	325	—
741	60.00	115	200	325	—
751	60.00	115	200	325	—
781	60.00	115	200	325	—

C# 13.2 2 REALES (Macuquinas)
Silver **Note:** Approximately .200-.650 fine. Diameter range 22-25mm. Weight range 4.50-5.80g. Round style. Varieties exist in the shape, placement and design of most obverse and reverse features of these coins.

Date	Good	VG	F	VF	XF
186	120	200	340	475	—
816	60.00	115	200	315	—
1816	100	175	300	—	—
817	60.00	115	200	315	—
1817	100	175	300	—	—

ROYALIST COINAGE

Resumed

C# 5.1 REAL
Silver **Rev:** Lion in upper left of cross **Note:** Approximately .700 fine. Weight range 2.45-3.25g. Diameter range 19-21mm.

Date	Mintage	Good	VG	F	VF	XF
1817 BS	6,500	2,000	2,500	4,000	8,000	—
1818 BS	14,000	150	300	450	800	—

C# 5.2 REAL
Silver **Rev:** Castle in upper left of cross **Note:** Approximately .700 fine. Weight varies 2.45-3.25 grams.

Date	Mintage	Good	VG	F	VF	XF
1817 BS	Inc. above	2,000	2,500	4,000	8,000	—
1820 BS	11,000	500	650	1,200	2,200	—
1821 BS	8,000	600	800	1,300	2,900	—

C# 6.1 2 REALES (Morilleros)
Silver **Rev:** Lion in upper left of cross **Note:** Size varies 23-26 millimeters; weight varies 4.3-5.3 grams. For similar coin without "F.7" on reverse, see Republican Coinage under Gran Colombia.

Date	Mintage	Good	VG	F	VF	XF
1817 BS	76,000	60.00	90.00	230	400	—
1818 BS	777,000	10.00	15.00	25.00	50.00	—
1819/8 BS	1,450,000	10.00	15.00	25.00	50.00	—
1819 BS	Inc. above	10.00	15.00	25.00	50.00	—
1820 BS	755,000	15.00	20.00	40.00	85.00	—
1821 BS	110,000	20.00	40.00	70.00	100	—

C# 6.2 2 REALES (Morilleros)
Silver **Rev:** Castle in upper left of cross

Note: Size varies 23-25 millimeters; weight varies 4.3-5.3 grams. Beware of contemporary counterfeits struck in German silver, (copper-nickel-zinc alloy). These are valued at roughly 25-30% of genuine silver pieces. For similar coins without F.7 on reverse see Republican Coinage, under Gran Columbia.

Date	Good	VG	F	VF	XF
1817 BS	60.00	90.00	230	400	—
1818 BS	10.00	15.00	25.00	50.00	—
1820 BS	15.00	20.00	40.00	85.00	—
1821 BS	20.00	40.00	70.00	100	—

C# 7.1 4 REALES
Silver **Rev:** Lion in upper left of cross **Note:** Weight varies 9.50-10.30 grams.

Date	Mintage	Good	VG	F	VF	XF
1819 BS	18,000	375	600	1,200	2,000	—

C# 7.2 4 REALES
Silver **Rev:** Castle in upper left of cross **Note:** Weight varies 9.50-10.30 grams; die varieties exist.

Date	Mintage	Good	VG	F	VF	XF
1819 BS	Inc. above	375	600	1,200	2,000	—
1820 BS	29,000	375	600	1,200	2,000	—

REPUBLICAN COINAGE
1812

19 refers to 19 April, 1810, the date of the Declaration of Independence

C# 21 1/8 REAL
2.5000 g., Copper, 24 mm.

Date	Mintage	Good	VG	F	VF	XF
1812(c)	7,000	300	500	800	1,200	2,500

C# 22 1/4 REAL
3.0000 g., Copper **Note:** Diameter range 26-30mm.

Date	Mintage	Good	VG	F	VF	XF
1812(c)	30,000	25.00	50.00	100	200	800

C# 25 1/2 REAL
1.2000 g., Silver, 16 mm. **Obv:** Large "1/2" **Note:** Approximately .700 fine.

Date	Mintage	Good	VG	F	VF	XF
Ano 2(c)	16,000	750	1,350	2,300	3,500	5,000

C# 26 REAL
2.4000 g., Silver, 20 mm. **Note:** Approximately .700 fine.

Date	Mintage	Good	VG	F	VF	XF
Ano 2(c)	20,000	800	1,500	2,200	3,500	4,500

UNDER GRAN COLOMBIA

REPUBLICAN COINAGE

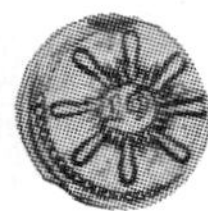

C# 31 1/4 REAL
Silver **Note:** Approximately .500 fine. Diameter range 11.5-15mm. Weight range 0.4-0.65g.

Date	Mintage	Good	VG	F	VF	XF
1821(c)	90,000	135	185	380	850	2,000
1822(c)	540,000	50.00	110	235	430	1,000

C# 34 1/4 REAL
Silver, 12 mm. **Note:** Approximately .500 fine. Weight range 4.8-5.5g.

Date	Mintage	Good	VG	F	VF	XF
1829(c)	750,000	12.50	20.00	40.00	80.00	250
1830(c)	650,000	13.50	22.50	45.00	85.00	300

C# 36 2 REALES
Silver **Rev:** Cross between 2 rosettes **Note:** Approximately .700 fine. Diameter range 23-24mm. Weight range 4.30-4.72g.

Date	Mintage	Good	VG	F	VF	XF
1818(1830) BS	268,000	18.50	26.50	42.50	80.00	200

Note: Sometimes found struck over cut down Spanish De Vellon 4 Reales, KM#137

PATTERNS
Including off metal strikes

KM#	Date	Mintage	Identification	Mkt Val
Pn3	1812(c)	—	Real. Silver. REPUB instead of REP.	—

KM#	Date	Mintage	Identification	Mkt Val
Pn4	1829 O	—	1/2 Real. Silver.	—

GUAYANA

Coinage for this province in eastern Venezuela was authorized by an act of October 26, 1813. This was to alleviate the coin shortage caused by the isolation of the province from other Spanish forces.

ROYALIST

ROYALIST COINAGE

C# 40 1/4 REAL
2.0000 g., Copper **Note:** Diameter range 18-19mm.

Date	Good	VG	F	VF	XF
1813	600	900	1,300	3,000	—

C# 41.1 1/2 REAL
3.0000 g., Copper **Obv:** Solid castle **Rev:** Solid lion **Note:** Large flan with diameters ranging from 26.1-30mm. Varieties exist with outlined castle and outlined lion.

Date	Good	VG	F	VF	XF
1813	30.00	50.00	120	240	—
1814	7.00	13.00	28.00	48.00	—

C# 41.2 1/2 REAL
Copper **Note:** Small flan with diameters ranging from 22-26mm. These types generally have only partial dates visibile, examples with full clear dates command a premium, while examples with no traces of date showing are worth significantly less.

Date	Good	VG	F	VF	XF
ND(1814-17) Date off flan	1.75	2.50	3.75	5.00	—
1814	6.00	11.00	22.00	45.00	—
1815	5.00	10.00	18.50	38.00	—
1816	4.50	9.00	15.00	30.00	—
1817	4.50	9.00	15.00	30.00	—

MARACAIBO

A province in northwestern Venezuela includes the city of Maracaibo, situated on the channel between Lake Maracaibo and the Caribbean. This crude coinage was presumably necessary because of the temporary isolation of local Royalist forces from the main Spanish armies. The coins of Maracaibo were struck by order dated March 13, 1813 by Fernando Mijares, Captain General of the Province of Maracaibo.

PROVINCE
ROYALIST COINAGE

KM# 1 1/4 REAL
Copper **Obv:** Lion **Rev:** Denomination

Date	Good	VG	F	VF	XF
ND(1813)	40.00	85.00	120	260	—

KM# 2 2/4 REAL
Copper **Obv:** Crowned arms **Rev:** Denomination **Note:** Varieties exist.

Date	Good	VG	F	VF	XF
ND(1813)	37.50	80.00	145	275	—

KM# 3 1/2 REAL
Copper **Obv:** Bust right **Rev:** Monogram **Note:** Unaccepted by the public and plagued w/counterfeits, these pieces were withdrawn late in 1813.

Date	Good	VG	F	VF	XF
1813	135	250	385	550	—

KM# 4 2 REALES
Silver **Obv:** Cross with lions and castles **Rev:** Pillars with denomination above, date below and 8VI in center

Date	Good	VG	F	VF	XF
38	180	285	550	800	—
181	180	285	550	800	—

KM# 5 2 REALES
Silver **Obv:** Cross with lions and castles **Rev:** Pillars with denomination above, date below and LVS in center. **Note:** It has been reported that a total of 70,000 2 Reales were struck in 1814. This may represent the entire combined mintage for all dates of KM#4 and KM#5.

Date	Good	VG	F	VF	XF
182	180	285	550	800	—
1813	180	285	550	800	—
1814	180	285	550	800	—

MARGARITA

Margarita is an island north of Venezuela, which at the beginning of the Independence War, had trade relations with the other islands of the Caribbean where Spanish coins valued in Maravedis were used. 2 weeks after the April 19, 1810 Declaration of Independence by Caracas, Margarita joined that declaration.

REPUBLIC
REPUBLICAN COINAGE

KM# 1 4 MARAVEDIS
Copper **Obv:** 3 men in a boat, sun aabove **Obv. Legend:** MARGARITA PERLA PRECIOSA **Rev:** Denomination encircled with 7 stars **Rev. Legend:** DA FX DIA 4 DE MAIO 1810

Date	Good	VG	F	VF	XF
1810 Rare	—	—	—	—	—

Note: The 4 in the center of the reverse design of this type may represent; a denomination, making it a coin, or the Margarita Independence declaration date, making it a medal. Both theories have been proposed and further study is required

TACHIRA STATE

San Cristobal

A city in Tachira State in Western Venezuela, located in the mountains at the southwest end of Cordillera de Merida and south of Lake Maracaibo, near the Colombian border.

ESTADO TACHIRA
STATE COINAGE

KM# S1 2 REALES
Bronze **Note:** With R. below 2.

Date	VG	F	VF	XF	Unc
1872	175	300	500	1,200	2,500

KM# S2 2 REALES
Bronze **Note:** With star below 2.

Date	VG	F	VF	XF	Unc
1872 Rare	—	—	—	—	—

LEPER COLONIES

MARACAIBO LAZARETO NACIONAL

In 1826 Simon Bolivar authorized the establishment of Lazareto Maracaibo on Burro Island in Lake Maracaibo. Over time this became a large leper colony maintained by the Venezuelan Government, where hundreds of people suffering from Hansen's disease were cared for. To provide a monetary system and prevent regular coinage, handled by lepers, to re-circulate in the general population, the Venezuelan Government created a special currency. These coins had value only on the island until 30 years ago, when the illness was almost fully extinguished in South America and medical research revealed that little risk was invloved in handling these coins. The first issues under the name Lazareto Nacional Maracaibo were struck in the late 1880's and the final series was issued in 1916.

LEPROSARIUM COINAGE

KM# L1 1/4 REAL
Copper

Date	VG	F	VF	XF	Unc
1897 Rare	—	—	—	—	—

KM# L2 1/8 BOLIVAR
Copper

Date	VG	F	VF	XF	Unc
1898 Rare	—	—	—	—	—

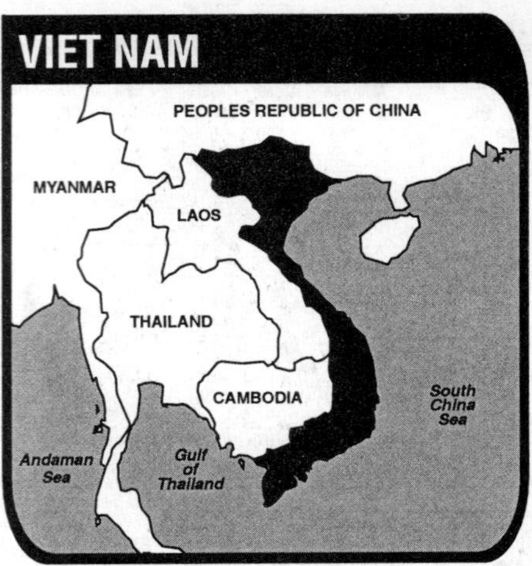

In 207 B.C. a Chinese general set up the Kingdom of Nam-Viet on the Red River. This kingdom was overthrown by the Chinese under the Han Dynasty in 111 B.C., where upon the country became a Chinese province under the name of Giao-Chi, which was later changed to Annam or peaceful or pacified South. Chinese rule was maintained until 968, when the Vietnamese became independent until 1407 when China again invaded Viet Nam. The Chinese were driven out in 1428 and the country became independent and named Dai-Viet. Gia Long renamed the country Dai Namin 1802.

After the French conquered Dai Nam, they split the country into three parts. The South became the Colony of Cochin china; the North became the Protectorate of Tonkin; and the central became the Protectorate of Annam. The emperors were permitted to have their capital in Hue and to produce small quantities of their coins, presentation pieces, and bullion bars. Annam had an area of 57,840 sq. mi. (141,806 sq. km.) and a population of about 6 million. Chief products of the area are silk, cinnamon and rice. There are important mineral deposits in the mountainous inland.

United Dai Nam

EMPERORS

寶興
Bao Hung, 1801-02

嘉隆
Gia Long, 1802-20

明命
Minh Mang, 1820-41

紹治
Thieu Tri, 1841-41

嗣德
Tu Duc, 1848-83

建福
Kien Phuc, 1883-84

咸宜
Ham Nghi, 1884-85

Protectorate of Annam

EMPERORS

同慶
Dong Khanh, 1885-88

成泰
Thanh Thai, 1888-1907

REBELS and INVADERS

治元
Tri Nguyen, 1831-34

元隆
Nguyen Long, 1832-33

IDENTIFICATION

Khai 啓

寶 *Bao* *Thong* 通

Dinh 

Khai Dinh Thong Bao

The square holed cash coins of Vietnam are easily identified by reading the characters top-bottom (emperor's name) and right-left (Thong Bao general currency). The character at right will change with some emperors.

CYCLICAL DATES

	庚	辛	壬	癸	甲	乙	丙	丁	戊	己
戌	1850 1910		1862 1922		1874 1934		1886 1946		1838 1898	
亥		1851 1911		1863 1923		1875 1935		1887 1947		1839 1899
子	1840 1900		1852 1912		1864 1924		1876 1936		1888 1948	
丑		1841 1901		1853 1913		1865 1925		1877 1937		1889 1949
寅	1830 1890		1842 1902		1854 1914		1866 1926		1878 1938	
卯		1831 1891		1843 1903		1855 1915		1867 1927		1879 1939
辰	1880 1940		1832 1892		1844 1904		1856 1916		1868 1928	
巳		1881 1941		1833 1893		1845 1905		1857 1917		1869 1929
午	1870 1930		1882 1942		1834 1894		1846 1906		1858 1918	
未		1871 1931		1883 1943		1835 1895		1847 1907		1859 1919
申	1860 1920		1872 1932		1884 1944		1836 1896		1848 1908	
酉		1861 1921		1873 1933		1885 1945		1837 1897		1849 1909

NOTE: This table has been adapted from *Chinese Bank Notes* by Ward Smith and Brian Matravers.

Cyclical dates consist of a pair of characters one of which indicates the animal associated with that year. Every 60 years, this pair of characters is repeated. The first character of a cyclical date corresponds to a character in the first row of the chart above. The second character is taken from the column at left. In this catalog where a cyclical date is used, the abbreviation CD appears before the A.D. date.

Annamese silver and gold coins were sometimes dated according to the year of the emperor's reign. In this case, simply add the year of reign to the year in which the reign would be 1849 (1847 plus 3 = 1850 -1 = 1849 or 1847 = 1; 1848 = 2; 1849 = 3). In this catalog the A.D. date appears in parenthesis followed by the year of reign.

NUMERALS

NUMBER	CONVENTIONAL	FORMAL	COMMERCIAL
1	一 元	壹 弌	〡
2	二	弍 貳	〢
3	三	叁 弎	〣
4	四	肆	〤
5	五	伍	〥
6	六	陸	〦
7	七	柒	〧
8	八	捌	〨
9	九	玖	〩
10	十	拾 什	十
20	十 二 or 廿	拾貳	〢十
25	五 十 二 or 五廿	伍拾貳	〢十〥
30	十 三 or 卅	拾叁	〣十
100	百 一	佰壹	〡百
1,000	千 一	仟壹	〡千
10,000	萬 一	萬壹	〡万
100,000	萬十 億 一	萬拾 億壹	十万
1,000,000	萬百一	萬佰壹	〡百 万

NOTE: This table has been adapted from "Chinese Bank Notes" by Ward Smith and Brian Matravers.

MONETARY SYSTEM

COPPER and ZINC

10 Dong (zinc) = 1 Dong (copper)
600 Dong (zinc) = 1 Quan (string of cash)
Approx. 2600 Dong (zinc) = 1 Piastre

NOTE: Ratios between metals changed frequently, therefore the above is given as an approximate relationship.

SILVER and GOLD

2-1/2 Quan = 1 Lang
10 Tien (Mace) = 1 Lang (Tael)
14 to 17 Piastres (silver) = 1 Piastre (gold)
14 to 17 Lang (silver) = 1 Lang (gold)

The real currency of Dai Nam and An Nam consisted of copper and zinc coins similar to Chinese cash-style coins and were called sapeques and dongs by the French.

The smaller gold pieces saw a limited circulation, mainly among the local merchants and foreign traders. The larger gold pieces were used mainly for hoarding, while most of these were intended as rewards and gifts. Many of these gold pieces appear to have been struck from silver coin dies or vice-versa.

The fineness of the gold and silver pieces varied considerably. The silver and gold dragon coins with the streaked edges were intended to be equivalent to the Mexican and Spanish Colonial 8 Reales (Dollar/Piastre) and 8 Escudos, and their minor denominations, but the silver normally exchanged for much less because their fineness usually ranged from .500 to .700 fine. The gold and silver coins with other designs and smooth edges are generally considered as presentation pieces but some did appear in circulation when their owners came upon hard times. Their fineness usually ranges from .500 to .999. Authentic gold of all designs are rarely found below .850 fine.

Only a few Vietnamese silver and gold pieces are inscribed with their weight and fineness and therefore must be weighed and tested. It should be remembered that Phan, Tien and Lang are weights and not denominations. The pieces inscribed with Van and Quan are money of account terms but could be considered the first Vietnamese denominations. The Vietnamese ignored these terms and exchanged them and all other metallic forms at the prevailing market value of their intrinsic weight and not their inscribed or total weight. Without testing devices or a specific gravity setup, you will only be able to determine the total weight of your piece. For the pieces described in this catalog without weights or terms inscribed on them, they are classified by their total weight. The following table will assist you to determine your pieces Phan, Tien or Lang weight:

PHAN SYSTEM

1 Phan	.3778 grams
5 Phan (or 1/2 Tien)	1.8892 grams
10 Phan (or 1 Tien)	3.7783 grams

TIEN SYSTEM

1/2 Tien (or 5 Phan)	1.8892 grams
1 Tien (or 10 Phan)	3.7783 grams
1/1/2 Tien	5.6675 grams
2 Tien	7.5566 grams
2-1/2 Tien (or 1/4 Lang)	9.4458 grams
3 Tien	11.3349 grams
4 Tien	15.1132 grams
5 Tien (or 1/2 Lang)	18.8915 grams
6 Tien	22.6698 grams
7 Tien	26.4481 grams
8 Tien	30.2264 grams
9 Tien	34.0047 grams
10 Tien (or 1 Lang)	37.7830 grams

LANG SYSTEM

1/2 Lang (or 5 Tien)	18.8915 grams
1 Lang (or 10 Tien)	37.7783 grams
5 Lang	188.9150 grams
10 Lang	377.8300 grams
50 Lang	1889.15 grams
100 Lang	3778.30 grams

NOTE: The Van and Quan pieces are denominations for fiat money. A 10 Van coin was officially worth 10 full weight 1 Tien coins of copper, but, of course, weighed less and less during the inflationary times of their period of issue. The 3 Quan silver bar was officially worth 3 full weight strings of copper coins. The weight of these Van and Quan coins and bars varied considerably and are specified at their listing. The heavier weight pieces are generally the earliest issues with the lighter ones the latest.

PALACE ISSUES

Canh-thinh, 1792-1801

Craig #53 "1 Mach or 60 Dong"
Obverse inscription:
"Canh-thinh Thong-bao"
Reverse: Dragon at left, two fish at right.

There are many dollar size and larger copper and brass tokens with obverses similar to the small square holed cash coins listed here with eight, four, or two characters or dragon and fish on the reverse. These were believed to have been given as gifts or bestowed as rewards and circulated to some extent although they do not carry any designation of weight or denomination. The large 130-135mm square holed circular copper pieces with the emperor's name on the obverse and an 8 character legend reverse were displayed in respect of the current emperor. They had a nominal 'trade value' of 600 sapeques as quoted by Bernard J. Permar in *"Catalogue of Annam Coins,* 968-1955".

NOTE: Sch#'s are in reference to Albert Schroeder's *Annam, Etudes Numismatiques* or to the same numbering system used in *Gold and Silver Coins of Annam"*, by Bernard Permar and John Novak.

CHARACTER IDENTIFICATION

(Reading left to right)

The Vietnamese used Chinese-style characters for official documents and coins and bars. Some were modified to their liking and will sometimes not match the Chinese character for the same word. The above identification and this table will translate most of the Vietnamese characters (Chinese-style) on their coins and bars described herein.

Chinese/French
Vietnamese/English

An Nam = name of the French protectorate

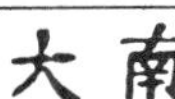

Dai Nam = name of the country under Gia Long's Nguyen dynasty

越南

Dai Viet = name of the country under the later Le dynasty

越南

Viet Nam = name used briefly during Minh Mang's reign and became the modern name of the country

河内

Ha Noi = city and province in north Dai NamTonkin

Noi Thang = court treasury in the capital of Hue

Nien = year

造
Tao = made

銀
Ngan = silver

金
Kim = gold

錢
Tien = a weight of about 3.78 grams

兩
Lang = a weight of about 37.78 grams

貫
Quan = a string of cash-style coins

分
Phan = a weight of about .38 grams

文
Van = cash-style coins

中平
Trung Binh = a name of weight standard

PROVINCIAL DESIGNATORS
(Reading right to left)

An Giang	江安
Bac Ninh	寧北
Binh Dinh	定平
Can Than	申庚
Dinh Tuong	商定
Gia Dinh	定嘉
Hung Yen	遠興
Lang Son	山諒
Nghe An	安清 or 安乂
Phu Yen	燕虎
Quang Nam	南廣
Quang Yen	義廣
Son Tay	西山
Thai Nguyen	原太

SOUTH DAI VIET

CAST COINAGE

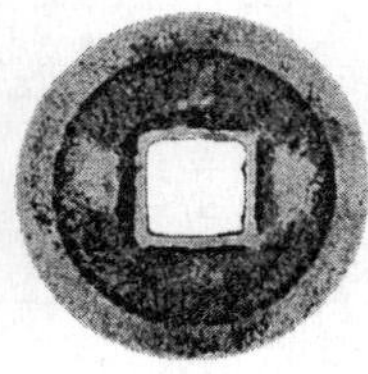

KM# 160.1 PHAN
Cast Brass **Ruler:** Canh Thinh **Rev:** Plain **Note:** Craig #51.1.

Date	Good	VG	F	VF	XF
ND(1792-1801)	3.00	5.00	8.00	15.00	—

Note: Examples are reported to exist in tin (by Toda)

KM# 160.2 PHAN
Cast Brass **Ruler:** Canh Thinh **Rev:** Crescent left, dot right **Note:** Craig #51.2.

Date	Good	VG	F	VF	XF
ND(1792-1801)	5.00	8.00	15.00	25.00	—

KM# 161 PHAN
Cast Brass **Ruler:** Canh Thinh **Obv:** Double rim **Note:** Craig #51.3.

Date	Good	VG	F	VF	XF
ND(1792-1801)	4.00	7.00	11.00	17.00	—

KM# 162.1 PHAN
Cast Brass **Ruler:** Canh Thinh **Obv:** Double rim **Rev:** Double rim **Note:** Craig #51.4.

Date	Good	VG	F	VF	XF
ND(1792-1801)	5.00	8.00	15.00	25.00	—

Note: Examples are reported to exist in tin (by Toda)

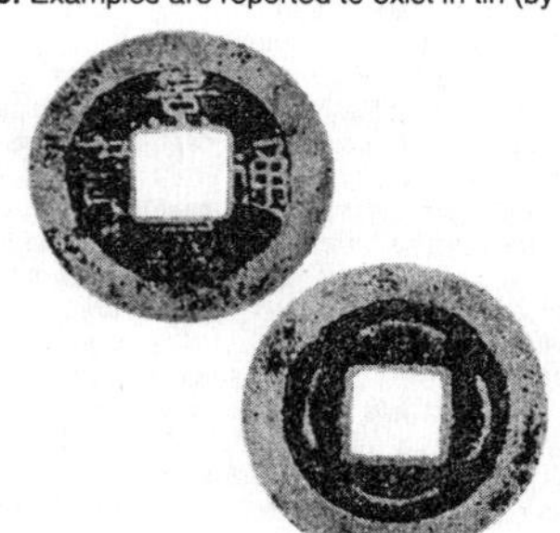

KM# 162.2 PHAN
Cast Brass **Ruler:** Canh Thinh **Rev:** Four crescents, tips inward **Note:** Craig #51.5; size varies 22 - 23 mm.

Date	Good	VG	F	VF	XF
ND(1792-1801)	4.00	8.00	12.00	20.00	—

KM# 162.3 PHAN
Cast Brass **Ruler:** Canh Thinh **Rev:** Four bumps next to inner rim **Note:** Craig #51.6.

Date	Good	VG	F	VF	XF
ND(1792-1801)	6.00	10.00	15.00	30.00	—

KM# 163 PHAN
Cast Brass **Ruler:** Canh Thinh **Rev:** Numeral one at bottom **Note:** Craig #51.7.

Date	Good	VG	F	VF	XF
ND(1792-1801)	6.00	10.00	15.00	30.00	—

KM# 164 PHAN
Cast Brass **Ruler:** Canh Thinh **Obv:** "Dai Bao", Bao abbreviated **Note:** Craig #52.1; Schroeder #477.

Date	Good	VG	F	VF	XF
ND(1792-1801)	8.00	12.00	20.00	35.00	—

KM# 165 PHAN
Cast Brass **Ruler:** Canh Thinh **Obv:** "Dai Bao, Bao" abbreviated, double rim **Rev:** Double rim **Note:** Craig #52.2.

Date	Good	VG	F	VF	XF
ND(1792-1801)	12.00	17.50	25.00	40.00	—

KM# 167 PHAN
Cast Brass **Ruler:** Bao Hung **Rev:** Plain **Note:** Prev. Craig #57.

Date	Good	VG	F	VF	XF
ND(1801-02) Rare	—	—	—	—	—

UNITED DAI NAM

CAST COINAGE

Rebel Issues

KM# 250 PHAN
Cast Copper Alloys **Ruler:** Nguyen Long **Obv:** Conventional "Nguyen" **Note:** Nung Rebellion; Previous Craig #138.2.

Date	Good	VG	F	VF	XF
ND(1823-33)	10.50	18.00	30.00	45.00	—

KM# 248 PHAN
Cast Copper Alloys **Ruler:** Tri Nguyen **Obv. Inscription:** "Tri Nguyen Thong Bao" **Rev:** Dot left, crescent right **Note:** Nguy Khoi Rebellion; Craig #137.

Date	Good	VG	F	VF	XF
ND(1831-34)	8.50	13.50	21.50	35.00	—

KM# 251 PHAN
Cast Copper Alloys **Ruler:** Nguyen Long **Obv:** Cursive "Nguyen" **Rev:** Double rim **Note:** Nung Rebellion, Craig #139.1.

Date	Good	VG	F	VF	XF
ND(1832-33)	10.50	18.00	30.00	45.00	—

KM# 249 PHAN
Cast Copper Alloys **Ruler:** Nguyen Long **Obv. Legend:** "Nguyen Long Thong Bao, cursive Nguyen" **Note:** Nung Rebellion; Craig #138.1.

Date	Good	VG	F	VF	XF
ND(1832-33)	8.50	13.50	21.50	35.00	—

KM# 252 PHAN
Cast Copper Alloys **Ruler:** Nguyen Long **Rev:** Character "Ch'ang" right **Note:** Nung Rebellion; Craig #139.2.

Date	Good	VG	F	VF	XF
ND(1832-33)	10.50	18.00	30.00	45.00	—

CAST COINAGE

KM# 171.3 PHAN
Copper Alloys **Ruler:** Gia Long **Rev:** Crescent at top and bottom

Date	Good	VG	F	VF	XF
ND(1802-20)	4.50	7.50	12.50	20.00	—

KM# 169a.1 PHAN

Copper Alloys **Ruler:** Gia Long **Note:** Craig #61.3; varieties exist with dot appearing at any of the 4 sides of the square hole in center.

Date	Good	VG	F	VF	XF
ND(1802-20)	2.00	3.50	5.50	9.00	—

KM# 169a.2 PHAN

Copper Alloys **Ruler:** Gia Long **Rev:** Circle at bottom **Note:** Craig #61.3a.

Date	Good	VG	F	VF	XF
ND(1802-20)	2.00	3.50	5.50	9.00	—

KM# 170 PHAN

Copper Alloys **Ruler:** Gia Long **Obv:** Double rim **Note:** Craig #61.3b.

Date	Good	VG	F	VF	XF
ND(1802-20)	2.00	3.50	5.50	9.00	—

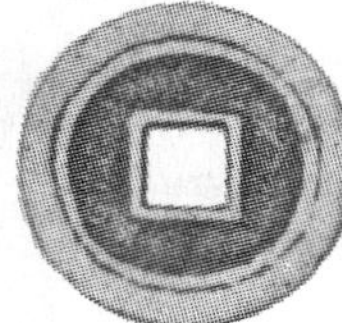

KM# 171.1 PHAN

Copper Alloys **Ruler:** Gia Long **Obv:** Double rim **Rev:** Double rim **Note:** Craig #61.3c.

Date	Good	VG	F	VF	XF
ND(1802-20)	2.00	3.50	5.50	9.00	—

KM# 171.2 PHAN

Copper Alloys **Ruler:** Gia Long **Rev:** Crescent, dot right **Note:** Craig #61.4.

Date	Good	VG	F	VF	XF
ND(1802-20)	4.50	7.50	12.50	20.00	—

KM# 169b PHAN

Cast Zinc **Ruler:** Gia Long **Rev:** Plain **Note:** Craig #73.

Date	Good	VG	F	VF	XF
ND(1802-20)	4.50	7.50	12.50	20.00	—

KM# 169a PHAN

Copper Alloys **Ruler:** Gia Long **Note:** Reduced size; Craig #61.2; size varies 22.6 - 23.8 grams mm.

Date	Good	VG	F	VF	XF
ND(1802-20)	0.85	1.50	2.75	4.50	—

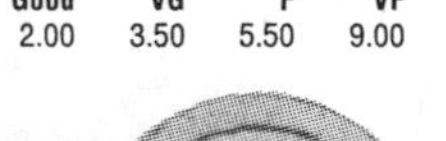

KM# 169 PHAN

Copper Alloys **Ruler:** Gia Long **Rev:** Plain **Note:** Schroeder #113; Craig #61.1, size varies 24 - 26 mm.

Date	Good	VG	F	VF	XF
ND(1802-20)	1.25	2.00	3.50	6.00	—

KM# 182c PHAN

Cast Zinc **Ruler:** Minh Mang **Rev:** Plain **Note:** Craig #79.

Date	Good	VG	F	VF	XF
ND(1820-41)	1.25	2.00	3.50	8.00	—

KM# 182 PHAN

Cast Copper Alloys **Ruler:** Minh Mang **Rev:** Plain **Note:** Craig #81.1; size varies 24.5 - 26 mm.

Date	Good	VG	F	VF	XF
ND(1820-41)	1.00	1.75	2.75	4.50	—

KM# 182a PHAN

Cast Copper Alloys **Ruler:** Minh Mang **Note:** Craig #81.2; size varies 22.7 - 24 mm.

Date	Good	VG	F	VF	XF
ND(1820-41)	0.75	1.25	2.00	3.50	—

KM# 182b PHAN

Cast Copper Alloys, 21 mm. **Ruler:** Minh Mang **Note:** Craig #81.3.

Date	Good	VG	F	VF	XF
ND(1820-41)	0.75	1.25	2.00	3.50	—

KM# 253b PHAN

Cast Zinc **Ruler:** Thieu Tri **Note:** Craig #140.

Date	Good	VG	F	VF	XF
ND(1841-47)	2.75	4.50	7.50	12.50	—

KM# 253 PHAN

Cast Copper Alloys **Ruler:** Thieu Tri **Note:** Craig #141.1; size varies 24 - 25 mm.

Date	Good	VG	F	VF	XF
ND(1841-47)	0.60	1.00	1.75	3.00	—

KM# 253a PHAN

Cast Copper Alloys **Ruler:** Thieu Tri **Note:** Reduced size; size varies 23 - 23.8 mm; Craig #141.2.

Date	Good	VG	F	VF	XF
ND(1841-47)	0.60	1.00	1.75	3.00	—

KM# 378a PHAN

Cast Copper Alloys, 22-23.8 mm. **Ruler:** Tu Duc **Note:** Reduced size; size varies 22 - 23.8 mm; Craig #201.2.

Date	Good	VG	F	VF	XF
ND(1848-83)	1.25	2.00	3.50	6.00	—

KM# 378 PHAN

Cast Copper Alloys **Ruler:** Tu Duc **Note:** Size varies 24-25 mm; Craig #201.1.

Date	Good	VG	F	VF	XF
ND(1848-83)	1.25	2.00	3.50	6.00	—

KM# 601 PHAN

Cast Zinc **Ruler:** Kien Phuc **Obv. Inscription:** "Kien Phuc Thong Bao" **Note:** Schroeder #415; Craig #271.1.

Date	Good	VG	F	VF	XF
ND(1883-84)	18.50	30.00	50.00	80.00	—

KM# 602 PHAN

Cast Zinc **Ruler:** Kien Phuc **Obv:** "Phuc" written differently **Note:** Schroeder #416; Craig #271.2.

Date	Good	VG	F	VF	XF
ND(1883-84)	18.50	30.00	50.00	80.00	—

KM# 173 CASH (6 Phan)

Cast Copper Alloys **Ruler:** Gia Long **Rev:** "Luc Phan" in seal script **Note:** Craig #62; size varies 21 - 23 mm.

Date	Good	VG	F	VF	XF
ND(1802-20)	2.75	4.50	7.50	12.50	—

KM# 173a CASH (7 Phan)

Cast Zinc **Ruler:** Gia Long **Rev:** "That Phan" **Note:** Craig #63; Schroeder #441.

Date	Good	VG	F	VF	XF
ND(1802-20)	5.50	9.00	15.00	25.00	—

KM# 380a 6 VAN

Cast Copper Alloys, 23 mm. **Ruler:** Tu Duc **Note:** Craig #202.1; Schroeder #302.

Date	Good	VG	F	VF	XF
ND(1848-83)	1.25	2.00	3.50	6.00	—

KM# 380 6 VAN

Cast Copper Alloys, 24-26 mm. **Ruler:** Tu Duc **Rev:** "Luc Van" **Note:** Craig #202; Schroeder #303; size varies 24 - 26 mm.

Date	Good	VG	F	VF	XF
ND(1848-83)	1.25	2.00	3.50	6.00	—

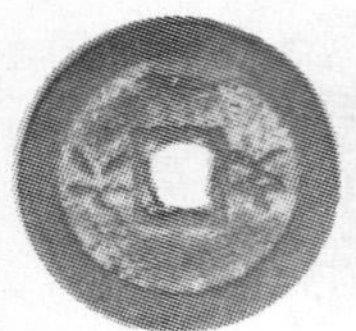

KM# A606 6 VAN
Cast Copper Alloys **Ruler:** Ham Nghi **Note:** Craig #282.

Date	Good	VG	F	VF	XF
ND(1884-85)	35.00	60.00	100	165	—

KM# 382 8 VAN
Cast Zinc **Ruler:** Tu Duc **Rev:** Plain **Note:** Craig #191.

Date	Good	VG	F	VF	XF
ND(1848-83)	2.00	3.50	5.50	9.00	—

KM# 383.1 8 VAN
Cast Zinc **Ruler:** Tu Duc **Rev:** Large "Ha Noi" **Note:** Craig #192.1; Schroeder #298.

Date	Good	VG	F	VF	XF
ND(1848-83)	5.00	8.50	13.50	21.50	—

KM# 384 8 VAN
Cast Zinc **Ruler:** Tu Duc **Rev:** "Son Tay" **Note:** Craig #192.2; Schroeder #299.

Date	Good	VG	F	VF	XF
ND(1848-83)	6.00	10.00	16.50	25.00	—

KM# 383.2 8 VAN
Cast Zinc **Ruler:** Tu Duc **Rev:** Small "Ha Noi" **Note:** Schroeder #297.

Date	Good	VG	F	VF	XF
ND(1848-83)	5.00	8.50	13.50	21.50	—

KM# 175 10 VAN
Cast Zinc **Ruler:** Gia Long **Rev:** Four Chinese characters "Tang... Shih Wen" **Note:** Craig #65.

Date	Good	VG	F	VF	XF
ND(1802-20)	11.50	18.50	30.00	50.00	—

KM# 386 10 VAN
6.0000 g., Cast Zinc **Ruler:** Tu Duc **Obv. Inscription:** "Tu Duc Bao Sao" **Rev. Inscription:** "Chuan Thap Van" **Note:** Craig #204; Schroeder #310.

Date	Good	VG	F	VF	XF
ND(1848-83)	11.50	18.50	30.00	50.00	—

KM# 387 10 VAN
Cast Zinc **Ruler:** Tu Duc **Obv. Inscription:** "Tu Duc Bao Sao" **Rev. Inscription:** "Chuan Nhat Thap Van" **Note:** Craig #204a; Schroeder #304.

Date	Good	VG	F	VF	XF
ND(1848-83)	11.50	18.50	30.00	50.00	—

KM# 389 20 VAN
12.0000 g., Cast Copper Or Brass **Ruler:** Tu Duc **Obv. Inscription:** "Tu Duc Bao Sao" **Rev. Inscription:** "Chuan Nhi Thap Van" **Note:** Craig #205; Schroeder #305.

Date	Good	VG	F	VF	XF
ND(1848-83)	70.00	100	140	200	—

KM# 391 30 VAN
16.4000 g., Cast Copper Or Brass **Ruler:** Tu Duc **Obv. Inscription:** "Tu Duc Bao Sao" **Rev. Inscription:** "Chuan Tam Thap Van" **Note:** Craig #205.5; Schroeder #306.

Date	Good	VG	F	VF	XF
ND(1848-83)	85.00	120	170	240	—

KM# 393 40 VAN
Cast Copper Or Brass **Ruler:** Tu Duc **Obv. Inscription:** "Tu Duc Bao Sao" **Rev. Inscription:** "Chuan Tu Thap Van" **Note:** Craig #206; Schroeder 307.

Date	Good	VG	F	VF	XF
ND(1848-83)	85.00	120	170	240	—

KM# 395 50 VAN
27.2000 g., Cast Copper Or Brass **Ruler:** Tu Duc **Obv. Inscription:** "Tu Duc Bao Sao" **Rev. Inscription:** "Chuan Ngu Thap Van" **Note:** Craig #206.5; Schroeder #308.

Date	Good	VG	F	VF	XF
ND(1848-83)	70.00	100	140	200	—

KM# 397a 60 VAN
38.2000 g., Cast Copper Or Brass, 43 mm. **Ruler:** Tu Duc **Obv. Inscription:** "Tu Duc Bao Sao" **Rev. Inscription:** "Chuan Luc Thap Van" **Note:** Craig #207.1; Schroeder #309.

Date	Good	VG	F	VF	XF
ND(1848-83)	42.50	60.00	85.00	120	—

KM# 397 60 VAN
Cast Copper Or Brass **Ruler:** Tu Duc **Obv. Inscription:** "Tu Duc Bao Sao" **Note:** Craig #207.2; size varies 47-49 mm.

Date	Good	VG	F	VF	XF
ND(1848-83)	42.50	60.00	85.00	120	—

SILVER MILLED COINAGE

The silver dragon coins with crude oblique milled edges are considered to be those in imitation of the Mexican/Spanish Colonial 8 Reales (Dollar/Piastre) coins and its minor denominations. The smooth edge silver dragon coins and those with square center holes are considered presentation pieces. Each coin is compared to the Weight System table in the introduction and assigned the respective Tien or Lang designation corresponding to its actual weight in grams.

VIRTUES

1 Tien - Viet Tu (benignity)

2 Tien - Viet Hein (gratitude)

3 Tien - Viet lang (kindness)

4 Tien - Viet De (respect)

5 Tien - Viet Ngai (justice)

6 Tien - Viet Thinh (obedience)

7 Tien - Viet Hue (benevolence)

8 Tien - Viet Thuan (submissiveness)

9 Tien - Viet Nhan (humanity)

1 Lang - Viet Trung (faithfulness)

KM# 255 1/2 TIEN
1.8000 g., Silver **Ruler:** Thieu Tri **Obv. Inscription:** "Thieu Tri Thong Bao" **Rev:** Blank **Note:** Schroeder #257.

Date	VG	F	VF	XF	Unc
ND(1841-47)	30.00	60.00	100	175	—

Note: This type was used as a presentation piece and was not meant for general circulation

KM# 399 1/2 TIEN
1.5000 g., Silver **Ruler:** Tu Duc **Obv. Inscription:** "Tu Duc Thong Bao" **Note:** Schroeder #367.

Date	Mintage	VG	F	VF	XF	Unc
ND(1848-83)	1	27.50	55.00	90.00	160	—

Note: This type was used as a presentation piece and was not meant for general circulation

KM# 400 1/2 TIEN
1.5000 g., Silver **Ruler:** Tu Duc **Obv. Inscription:** "Su Dan Phu Tho" **Note:** Schroeder #367B.

Date	VG	F	VF	XF	Unc
ND(1848-83)	30.00	60.00	100	175	—

KM# 183 TIEN
4.5000 g., Silver **Ruler:** Minh Mang **Obv. Inscription:** "Ming Mang Thong Bao" **Note:** Schroeder #180.

Date	VG	F	VF	XF	Unc
ND(1820-41)	30.00	60.00	100	175	—

Note: This type was used as a presentation piece and was not meant for general circulation

KM# 257.2 TIEN
3.8000 g., Silver, 22 mm. **Ruler:** Thieu Tri **Rev:** Sun, moon and five planets **Note:** Clouds deviating in style.

Date	VG	F	VF	XF	Unc
ND(1841-47)	27.50	55.00	90.00	160	—

KM# A264 TIEN
Silver **Ruler:** Thieu Tri **Rev:** Fan (mirror image)

Date	VG	F	VF	XF	Unc
ND(1841-47)	35.00	70.00	120	200	—

KM# 256 TIEN
3.6000 g., Silver **Ruler:** Minh Mang **Obv. Inscription:** "Thieu Tri Thong Bao" **Rev. Inscription:** "Nhat Nguyen" **Note:** Schroeder #250.

Date	VG	F	VF	XF	Unc
ND(1841-47)	30.00	60.00	100	175	—

KM# 264 TIEN
3.8000 g., Silver **Ruler:** Thieu Tri **Obv. Inscription:** "Thieu Tri Thong Bao" **Rev:** Two scepters and two swastikas **Note:** Schroeder #256.

Date	VG	F	VF	XF	Unc
ND(1841-47)	32.50	65.00	110	200	—

KM# 257.1 TIEN
Silver **Ruler:** Thieu Tri **Rev:** Sun, moon and five planets **Note:** Schroeder #262. Weight varies: 3.70-4.00 grams.

Date	VG	F	VF	XF	Unc
ND(1841-47)	27.50	55.00	90.00	160	—

KM# 258 TIEN
Silver **Ruler:** Thieu Tri **Obv. Inscription:** "Thieu Tri" **Rev:** Scepter and swastika **Note:** Schroeder #264. Weight varies: 3.60-4.00 grams.

Date	VG	F	VF	XF	Unc
ND(1841-47)	27.50	55.00	90.00	160	—

KM# 259 TIEN
Silver **Ruler:** Thieu Tri **Rev:** Mirror image of KM#258 **Note:** Schroeder #265.

Date	VG	F	VF	XF	Unc
ND(1841-47)	27.50	55.00	90.00	160	—

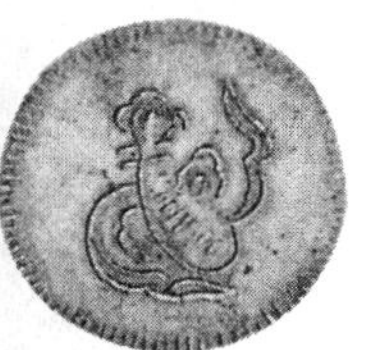

KM# 260 TIEN
4.0000 g., Silver **Ruler:** Thieu Tri **Obv. Inscription:** "Thieu Tri" **Rev:** Guitar **Note:** Schroeder #266A.

Date	VG	F	VF	XF	Unc
ND(1841-47)	35.00	70.00	120	200	—

KM# 261 TIEN
3.7000 g., Silver **Ruler:** Thieu Tri **Rev:** Inscription above Three Plenties **Rev. Inscription:** "Tam Da" **Note:** Schroeder #267.

Date	VG	F	VF	XF	Unc
ND(1841-47)	30.00	60.00	100	170	—

KM# 262.1 TIEN
Silver **Ruler:** Thieu Tri **Rev:** Flaming sun clockwise **Note:** Schroeder #287A.

Date	VG	F	VF	XF	Unc
ND(1841-47)	21.50	42.50	70.00	125	—

KM# 263 TIEN
Silver **Ruler:** Thieu Tri **Rev:** Fan **Note:** Schroeder #291A.

Date	VG	F	VF	XF	Unc
ND(1841-47)	35.00	70.00	120	200	—

KM# 262.2 TIEN
Silver **Ruler:** Thieu Tri **Rev:** Flaming sun counter-clockwise

Date	VG	F	VF	XF	Unc
ND(1841-47)	21.50	42.50	70.00	125	—

KM# 403 TIEN
3.7000 g., Silver **Ruler:** Tu Duc **Rev:** Sun, moon, and five planets **Note:** Schroeder #352.

Date	VG	F	VF	XF	Unc
ND(1848-83)	27.50	55.00	90.00	160	—

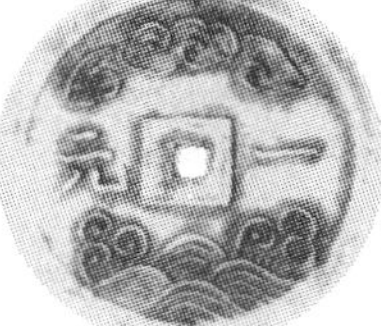

KM# 402 TIEN
3.5000 g., Silver **Ruler:** Tu Duc **Obv. Inscription:** "Tu Duc Thong Bao" **Rev:** Inscription, cosmic evolution **Rev. Inscription:** "Nhat Nguyen" **Note:** Schroeder #353.

Date	VG	F	VF	XF	Unc
ND(1848-83)	30.00	60.00	100	175	—

KM# 404 TIEN
3.7400 g., Silver **Ruler:** Tu Duc **Rev:** Legend between two stylized fish **Rev. Inscription:** "Nhat Duc" **Note:** Schroeder #354.1.

Date	VG	F	VF	XF	Unc
ND(1848-83)	27.50	55.00	90.00	160	—

KM# 405 TIEN
4.5000 g., Silver **Ruler:** Tu Duc **Rev:** Inscription between two goldfish **Rev. Inscription:** "Nhat Duc" **Note:** Schroeder #354.2.

Date	VG	F	VF	XF	Unc
ND(1848-83)	27.50	55.00	90.00	160	—

KM# 406 TIEN
3.8000 g., Silver **Ruler:** Tu Duc **Rev:** Inscription between sun, moon, and clouds **Rev. Inscription:** "Nhi Duc" **Note:** Schroeder #355B.

Date	VG	F	VF	XF	Unc
ND(1848-83)	30.00	60.00	100	175	—

KM# 407 TIEN
3.8000 g., Silver **Ruler:** Tu Duc **Obv:** Small characters **Rev:** Small characters, inscription above Three Plenties **Rev. Inscription:** "Tam Da" **Note:** Schroeder #357.1.

Date	VG	F	VF	XF	Unc
ND(1848-83)	35.00	70.00	120	200	—

KM# 408 TIEN
3.8000 g., Silver **Ruler:** Tu Duc **Obv:** Large characters **Rev:** Large characters **Note:** Schroeder #357.2.

Date	VG	F	VF	XF	Unc
ND(1848-83)	35.00	70.00	120	200	—

KM# 409 TIEN
3.6000 g., Silver **Ruler:** Tu Duc **Rev:** Two swastikas and two scepters which look like flowers **Note:** Schroeder #361.

Date	VG	F	VF	XF	Unc
ND(1848-83)	32.50	65.00	130	225	—

KM# 410 TIEN
3.7000 g., Silver **Ruler:** Tu Duc **Rev:** Inscription between Four Precious Objects **Rev. Inscription:** "Tu Bao" **Note:** Schroeder #362.

Date	VG	F	VF	XF	Unc
ND(1848-83)	35.00	70.00	120	200	—

KM# 411 TIEN
3.3000 g., Silver **Ruler:** Tu Duc **Rev:** The Five Precious Objects **Note:** Schroeder #363.

Date	VG	F	VF	XF	Unc
ND(1848-83)	30.00	60.00	100	175	—

KM# 412 TIEN
Silver **Ruler:** Tu Duc **Rev:** Eight Precious Objects **Note:** Schroeder #364. Weight varies: 3.50-3.70 grams.

Date	VG	F	VF	XF	Unc
ND(1848-83)	30.00	60.00	100	175	—

Note: There are three varieties of this coin based upon the placement of the symbols

KM# 413 TIEN
3.8000 g., Silver **Ruler:** Tu Duc **Rev:** Inscription on dragon **Rev. Inscription:** "Nhat Tien Viet Tu" **Note:** Schroeder #377.

Date	VG	F	VF	XF	Unc
ND(1848-83)	30.00	60.00	100	175	—

KM# 414 TIEN
3.9000 g., Silver **Ruler:** Tu Duc **Rev:** Sun, moon, and five planets **Note:** Schroeder #386.

Date	VG	F	VF	XF	Unc
ND(1848-83)	27.50	55.00	90.00	160	—

KM# 415 TIEN
4.0000 g., Silver **Ruler:** Tu Duc **Rev:** Inscription above Three Plenties **Rev. Inscription:** "Tam Da" **Note:** Schroeder #387.

Date	VG	F	VF	XF	Unc
ND(1848-83)	27.50	55.00	90.00	160	—

KM# 416 TIEN
4.5000 g., Silver **Ruler:** Tu Duc **Rev:** Scepter and swastika **Note:** Schroeder #388.

Date	VG	F	VF	XF	Unc
ND(1848-83)	35.00	70.00	120	200	—

KM# 417 TIEN
3.8000 g., Silver **Ruler:** Tu Duc **Rev:** Horn **Note:** Schroeder #389.

Date	VG	F	VF	XF	Unc
ND(1848-83)	32.50	65.00	110	180	—

KM# 418 TIEN
3.5000 g., Silver **Ruler:** Tu Duc **Rev:** Five Precious Objects **Note:** Schroeder #390.

Date	VG	F	VF	XF	Unc
ND(1848-83)	27.50	55.00	90.00	160	—

KM# 184 1-1/2 TIEN
Silver **Ruler:** Minh Mang **Obv. Inscription:** "Minh Mang" **Note:** Schroeder #189. Weight varies: 5.00-6.00 grams.

Date	VG	F	VF	XF	Unc
ND(1820-41)	27.50	55.00	90.00	160	—

KM# 266 1-1/2 TIEN
5.6300 g., Silver **Ruler:** Thieu Tri **Obv. Legend:** "Thieu Tri" **Note:** Schroeder #266B.

Date	VG	F	VF	XF	Unc
ND(1841-47)	32.50	65.00	110	180	—

KM# 421 1-1/2 TIEN
5.3000 g., Silver **Ruler:** Tu Duc **Rev. Inscription:** "Su Dan Phu Tho" **Note:** Schroeder #351C

Date	VG	F	VF	XF	Unc
ND(1848-83)	35.00	70.00	120	200	—

KM# 420 1-1/2 TIEN
5.2000 g., Silver **Ruler:** Tu Duc **Obv. Inscription:** "Tu duc Thong Bao" **Rev. Inscription:** "Phu Tho Da Nam" **Note:** Schroeder #358.

Date	VG	F	VF	XF	Unc
ND(1848-83)	35.00	70.00	120	200	—

KM# 269 2 TIEN
7.5000 g., Silver **Ruler:** Thieu Tri **Rev:** Two facing dragons **Note:** Schroeder #240.

Date	VG	F	VF	XF	Unc
ND(1841-47)	45.00	90.00	150	250	—

KM# 268 2 TIEN
7.6000 g., Silver **Ruler:** Thieu Tri **Obv. Inscription:** "Thieu Tri Thong Bao" **Rev:** Inscription between sun, moon, and clouds **Rev. Inscription:** "Nhi Nghi" **Note:** Schroeder #251.

Date	VG	F	VF	XF	Unc
ND(1841-47)	30.00	60.00	100	175	—

KM# 426 2 TIEN
7.3000 g., Silver **Ruler:** Tu Duc **Rev:** Two facing dragons

Date	VG	F	VF	XF	Unc
ND(1848-83)	42.50	90.00	150	250	—

KM# 423 2 TIEN
7.6000 g., Silver **Ruler:** Tu Duc **Obv. Inscription:** "Tu Duc Thong Bao" **Rev. Inscription:** "Su Dan Phu Tho" **Note:** Schroeder #351B

Date	VG	F	VF	XF	Unc
ND(1848-83)	30.00	60.00	100	175	—

KM# 424 2 TIEN
6.6000 g., Silver **Ruler:** Tu Duc **Obv. Inscription:** "Tu Duc Thong Bao" **Rev:** Inscription between sun, moon, and clouds **Rev. Inscription:** "Nhi Nghi" **Note:** Schroeder #355.

Date	VG	F	VF	XF	Unc
ND(1848-83)	42.50	90.00	150	250	—

KM# 425 2 TIEN
7.3000 g., Silver **Ruler:** Tu Duc **Rev:** Inscripton on dragon **Rev. Inscription:** "Nhi Tien Viet Hien" **Note:** Schroeder #378.

Date	VG	F	VF	XF	Unc
ND(1848-83)	45.00	90.00	150	250	—

KM# 186 3 TIEN
Silver **Ruler:** Minh Mang **Obv. Inscription:** "Minh Mang Thong Bao" **Rev:** Dragon **Note:** Schroeder #184. Weight varies: 13.30-13.70 grams.

Date	VG	F	VF	XF	Unc
ND(1820-41)	67.50	135	225	375	—

KM# 187.1 3 TIEN
Silver **Ruler:** Minh Mang **Obv:** Large inscription **Note:** Schroeder #185. Weight varies: 13.30-13.70 grams.

Date	VG	F	VF	XF	Unc
ND//14 (1833)	67.50	135	225	375	—

KM# 187.2 3 TIEN
Silver **Ruler:** Minh Mang **Obv:** Small inscription **Note:** Schroeder #186. Weight varies: 13.30-13.70 grams.

Date	VG	F	VF	XF	Unc
ND//15 (1834)	67.50	135	225	375	—

KM# 274 3 TIEN
13.3000 g., Silver **Ruler:** Thieu Tri **Obv. Inscription:** "Thieu Tri Thong Bao" **Rev:** Two facing dragons **Note:** Schroeder #239.

Date	VG	F	VF	XF	Unc
ND(1841-47)	70.00	140	240	400	—

KM# 277 3 TIEN
11.9000 g., Silver **Ruler:** Thieu Tri **Rev:** Inscription above Three Longevities **Rev. Inscription:** "Tam Tho" **Note:** Schroeder #252.

Date	VG	F	VF	XF	Unc
ND(1841-47)	67.50	135	225	375	—

KM# 276 3 TIEN
13.3400 g., Silver **Ruler:** Thieu Tri **Rev:** Large dragon **Note:** Schroeder #259.

Date	VG	F	VF	XF	Unc
ND(1841-47)	67.50	135	225	375	—

KM# 275 3 TIEN
13.5000 g., Silver **Ruler:** Thieu Tri **Obv. Inscription:** "Thieu Tri Thong Bao" **Rev:** Small dragon **Note:** Schroeder #260.

Date	VG	F	VF	XF	Unc
ND(1841-47)	67.50	135	225	375	—

KM# 435 3 TIEN

13.1000 g., Silver **Ruler:** Tu Duc **Rev:** Flaming sun between two facing dragons wtih long tails **Note:** Schroeder #347.1.

Date	VG	F	VF	XF	Unc
ND(1848-83)	70.00	140	240	400	—

KM# 436 3 TIEN

13.1000 g., Silver **Ruler:** Tu Duc **Rev:** Two facing daragons with short tails **Note:** Schroeder #347.2.

Date	VG	F	VF	XF	Unc
ND(1848-83)	70.00	140	240	400	—

KM# 437 3 TIEN

13.1000 g., Silver **Ruler:** Tu Duc **Rev:** Clouds below dragons' long tails **Note:** Schroeder #347.3.

Date	VG	F	VF	XF	Unc
ND(1848-83)	70.00	140	240	400	—

KM# 438 3 TIEN

13.1000 g., Silver **Ruler:** Tu Duc **Note:** Schroeder #369.

Date	VG	F	VF	XF	Unc
ND(1848-83)	67.50	135	225	375	—

KM# 439 3 TIEN

13.4500 g., Silver, 32.2 mm. **Ruler:** Tu Duc **Edge:** Plain **Note:** Schroeder #369A.

Date	VG	F	VF	XF	Unc
ND(1848-83)	45.00	90.00	150	250	—

KM# 440 3 TIEN

12.4000 g., Silver **Ruler:** Tu Duc **Obv:** Dot in center of sun **Note:** Schroeder #370.

Date	VG	F	VF	XF	Unc
ND(1848-83)	45.00	90.00	150	250	—

KM# 433 3 TIEN

11.9000 g., Silver **Ruler:** Tu Duc **Rev:** Inscription on facing dragon **Rev. Inscription:** "Long Van" **Note:** Schroeder #373.

Date	VG	F	VF	XF	Unc
ND(1848-83)	70.00	140	240	400	—

KM# 434 3 TIEN

11.3000 g., Silver **Ruler:** Tu Duc **Rev:** Inscription on dragon **Rev. Inscription:** "Tam Tien Viet Lang" **Note:** Schroeder #379.

Date	VG	F	VF	XF	Unc
ND(1848-83)	70.00	140	240	400	—

KM# 442 3 TIEN

12.4000 g., Silver **Ruler:** Tu Duc **Obv:** Large characters **Rev:** Inscription above the Three Longevities **Rev. Inscription:** "Tam Tho" **Note:** Schroeder #407A.

Date	VG	F	VF	XF	Unc
ND(1848-83)	50.00	100	175	300	—

KM# 443 3 TIEN

12.4000 g., Silver **Ruler:** Tu Duc **Obv:** Small legend characters **Rev:** Finer style **Note:** Schroeder #407B.

Date	VG	F	VF	XF	Unc
ND(1848-83)	50.00	100	175	300	—

KM# 444 3 TIEN

12.4000 g., Silver **Ruler:** Tu Duc **Rev:** One hill at bottom **Note:** Schroeder #407C.

Date	VG	F	VF	XF	Unc
ND(1848-83)	50.00	100	175	300	—

KM# 445 3 TIEN
12.4000 g., Silver **Ruler:** Tu Duc **Rev:** Large tree **Note:** Schroeder #407D.

Date	VG	F	VF	XF	Unc
ND(1848-83)	50.00	100	175	300	—

KM# 446 3 TIEN
12.4000 g., Silver **Ruler:** Tu Duc **Rev:** Dragon **Note:** Schroeder #414.

Date	VG	F	VF	XF	Unc
ND(1848-83)	50.00	100	175	300	—

KM# 278 4 TIEN
15.5000 g., Silver **Ruler:** Thieu Tri **Obv:** Inscription between bird and dragon **Obv. Inscription:** "Phan Long Lau Phu Phung Duc" **Note:** Schroeder #246.

Date	VG	F	VF	XF	Unc
ND(1841-47)	70.00	140	240	400	—

KM# 279 4 TIEN
15.5000 g., Silver **Ruler:** Thieu Tri **Obv. Inscription:** "Thieu Tri Thong Bao" **Rev:** Inscription between Four Perfections **Rev. Inscription:** "Tu My" **Note:** Schroeder #254.

Date	VG	F	VF	XF	Unc
ND(1841-47)	62.50	125	225	375	—

KM# 450 4 TIEN
15.0000 g., Silver **Ruler:** Tu Duc **Rev:** Inscription between Two Perfections **Rev. Inscription:** "Tu My"

Date	VG	F	VF	XF	Unc
ND(1848-83)	70.00	140	240	400	—

KM# 451 4 TIEN
15.0000 g., Silver **Ruler:** Tu Duc **Rev:** Finer style

Date	VG	F	VF	XF	Unc
ND(1848-83)	70.00	140	240	400	—

KM# 448 4 TIEN
15.5000 g., Silver **Ruler:** Tu Duc **Obv. Inscription:** "Tu duc Thong Bao" **Rev. Inscription:** "Su Dan Phu Tho" **Note:** Schroeder #351.

Date	VG	F	VF	XF	Unc
ND(1848-83)	62.50	125	225	375	—

KM# 449 4 TIEN
15.0000 g., Silver **Ruler:** Tu Duc **Rev:** Inscription on dragon **Rev. Inscription:** "Tu Tien Viet De" **Note:** Schroeder #380.

Date	VG	F	VF	XF	Unc
ND(1848-83)	70.00	140	240	400	—

KM# 188 5 TIEN
19.0000 g., Silver **Ruler:** Minh Mang **Obv. Inscription:** "Minh Mang Thong Bao" **Rev:** Inscription on facing dragon **Rev. Inscription:** "Long Van" **Note:** Schroeder #188.

Date	VG	F	VF	XF	Unc
ND(1820-41)	70.00	140	240	400	—

KM# 281 5 TIEN
19.0000 g., Silver **Ruler:** Thieu Tri **Obv. Inscription:** "Thieu Tri Thong Bao, Van the Binh Lai" **Note:** Schroeder #242.

Date	VG	F	VF	XF	Unc
ND(1841-47)	80.00	160	275	450	—

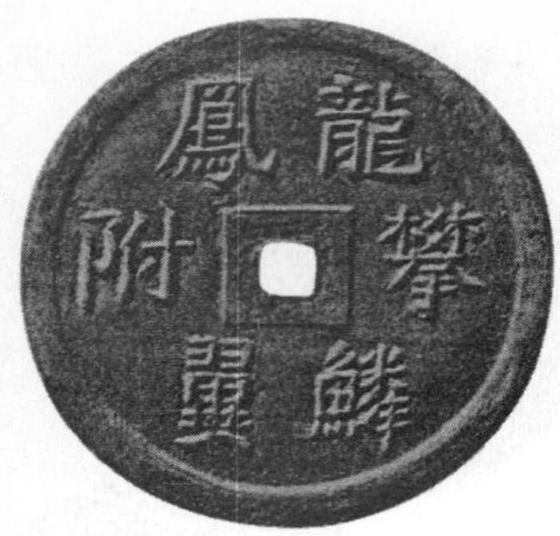

KM# 282 5 TIEN
19.2000 g., Silver **Ruler:** Thieu Tri **Obv:** Inscription between bird and dragon **Obv. Inscription:** "Thieu Tri" **Rev. Inscription:** "Phan Long Lau Phu Phung Duc" **Note:** Schroeder #243.

Date	VG	F	VF	XF	Unc
ND(1841-47)	80.00	160	275	450	—

KM# 283 5 TIEN
Silver **Ruler:** Thieu Tri **Obv. Inscription:** "Thieu Tri Thong Bao, Trieu Dan Lai Chi" **Rev:** Facing dragon **Note:** Schroeder #247. Weight varies: 18.50-19.00 grams.

Date	VG	F	VF	XF	Unc
ND(1841-47)	70.00	140	240	400	—

KM# 284 5 TIEN
Silver **Ruler:** Thieu Tri **Obv. Inscription:** "Thieu Tri Thong Bao" **Rev. Inscription:** "Phu Tho Da Nam" **Note:** Schroeder #253. Weight varies: 17.00-18.50 grams.

Date	VG	F	VF	XF	Unc
ND(1841-47)	70.00	140	240	400	—

KM# 285 5 TIEN
Silver **Ruler:** Thieu Tri **Rev:** Inscription between five bats **Rev. Inscription:** "Ngu Phuc" **Note:** Schroeder #255. Weight varies: 17.00-18.50 grams.

Date	VG	F	VF	XF	Unc
ND(1841-47)	80.00	160	275	450	—

KM# 286 5 TIEN
19.0000 g., Silver **Ruler:** Thieu Tri **Rev:** Inscription around facing dragon **Rev. Inscription:** "Long Van Khe Hoi" **Note:** Schroeder #261.

Date	VG	F	VF	XF	Unc
ND(1841-47)	80.00	160	275	450	—

KM# 453.1 5 TIEN
26.6000 g., Silver **Ruler:** Tu Duc **Obv. Inscription:** "Tu Duc Thong Bao" **Rev:** Two small facing dragons **Note:** Schroeder #347A.

Date	VG	F	VF	XF	Unc
ND(1848-83)	100	200	325	550	—

KM# 455 5 TIEN
18.0000 g., Silver **Ruler:** Tu Duc **Obv:** Large characters **Obv. Inscription:** "Tu Duc Thong Bao, Trieu Dan Lai Chi" **Rev:** Narrow faced dragon **Note:** Schroeder #349.1.

Date	VG	F	VF	XF	Unc
ND(1848-83)	70.00	140	240	400	—

KM# 456.1 5 TIEN
18.0000 g., Silver **Ruler:** Tu Duc **Obv:** Small characters **Rev:** Round-faced dragon **Note:** Schroeder #349.2.

Date	VG	F	VF	XF	Unc
ND(1848-83)	70.00	140	240	400	—

KM# 457.1 5 TIEN
18.9000 g., Silver **Ruler:** Tu Duc **Obv. Inscription:** "Tu Duc Thong Bao" **Rev:** Inscription between five bats **Rev. Inscription:** "Ngu Phuc" **Note:** Schroeder #359.

Date	VG	F	VF	XF	Unc
ND(1848-83)	80.00	160	275	450	—

KM# 458 5 TIEN
18.5000 g., Silver **Ruler:** Tu Duc **Obv:** Small sun at center **Rev:** Small sun at center, Inscription on facing dragon **Rev. Inscription:** "Long Van" **Note:** Schroeder #372.1.

Date	VG	F	VF	XF	Unc
ND(1848-83)	80.00	160	275	450	—

KM# 459 5 TIEN
18.5000 g., Silver **Ruler:** Tu Duc **Obv:** Large sun at center **Rev:** Large sun at center **Note:** Schroeder #372.2.

Date	VG	F	VF	XF	Unc
ND(1848-83)	80.00	160	275	450	—

KM# 457.2 5 TIEN
18.9000 g., Silver **Ruler:** Tu Duc **Obv. Inscription:** "Tu Duc Thong Bao" **Rev:** Inscription between 5 bats deviating in style, waves on hilltops below center bat **Note:** Schroeder #359.

Date	Good	VG	F	VF	XF
ND(1848-83)	—	80.00	160	275	450

KM# 460 5 TIEN
Silver **Ruler:** Tu Duc **Obv:** Flaming sun at center **Rev:** Inscription around facing dragon **Rev. Inscription:** "Long Van Khe Hoi" **Note:** Schroeder #374.1. Weight varies: 18.90-20.00 grams.

Date	VG	F	VF	XF	Unc
ND(1848-83)	80.00	160	275	450	—

KM# 461 5 TIEN
Silver **Ruler:** Tu Duc **Rev:** Inscription around facing dragon, cloud below "Hoi" at left **Note:** Schroeder #374.2. Weight varies: 18.90-20.00 grams.

Date	VG	F	VF	XF	Unc
ND(1848-83)	80.00	160	275	475	—

KM# 462 5 TIEN
18.8000 g., Silver **Ruler:** Tu Duc **Rev:** Inscription on dragon **Rev. Inscription:** "Ngu Tien Viet Ngai" **Note:** Schroeder #381.

Date	VG	F	VF	XF	Unc
ND(1848-83)	80.00	160	275	450	—

KM# 463 5 TIEN
17.0000 g., Silver **Ruler:** Tu Duc **Rev. Inscription:** "Phu Tho Da Nam" **Note:** Schroeder #408A.

Date	VG	F	VF	XF	Unc
ND(1848-83)	70.00	140	240	400	—

KM# 454 5 TIEN
26.6000 g., Silver **Ruler:** Tu Duc **Obv. Inscription:** "Tu Duc Thong Bao, Van The Vinh Lai" **Note:** Schroeder #A348.

Date	VG	F	VF	XF	Unc
ND(1848-83)	80.00	160	275	450	—

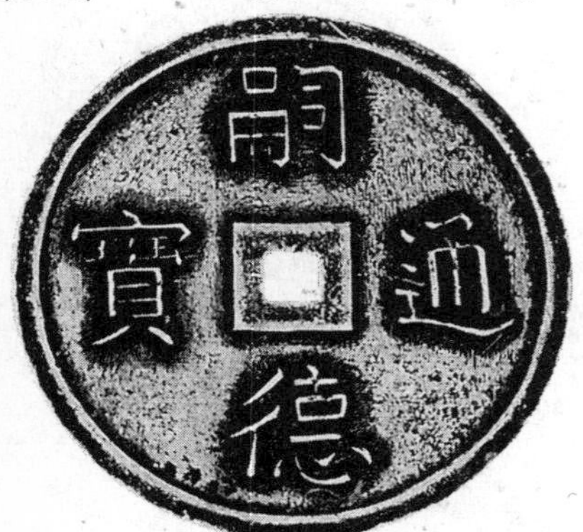

KM# 453.2 5 TIEN
26.0000 g., Silver **Ruler:** Tu Duc **Obv. Inscription:** "Tu Duc Thong Bao" **Rev:** Two large facing dragons **Note:** Schroeder #347B.

Date	VG	F	VF	XF	Unc
ND(1848-83)	100	200	325	550	—

KM# 456.2 5 TIEN
18.0000 g., Silver **Ruler:** Tu Duc **Rev:** Small characters **Note:** Schroeder #349.3

Date	VG	F	VF	XF	Unc
ND(1848-83)	70.00	140	240	400	—

KM# 465 6 TIEN
23.0000 g., Silver **Ruler:** Tu Duc **Obv. Inscription:** "Tu Duc Thong Bao" **Rev:** Inscription on dragon **Rev. Inscription:** "Luc Tien Viet Thinh" **Note:** Schroeder #382.

Date	VG	F	VF	XF	Unc
ND(1848-83)	100	200	350	600	—

KM# 190 7 TIEN
Silver, 35 mm. **Ruler:** Minh Mang **Obv:** Inscription around large sun **Obv. Inscription:** "Minh Mang Thong Bao" **Rev:** Small dragon **Note:** Schroeder #181A. Weight varies: 26.30-26.70 grams. Plain edge silver dragon coins are considered as medallic or presentation pieces while the crude oblique milled edge versions were meant for circulation for most emperors.

Date	VG	F	VF	XF	Unc
ND(1820-41)	140	280	450	750	—

KM# 191 7 TIEN
Silver, 40-42 mm. **Ruler:** Minh Mang **Obv:** Large sun **Rev:** Large dragon **Note:** Schroeder #181B. Weight varies: 26.66-27.42 grams.

Date	VG	F	VF	XF	Unc
ND(1820-41)	140	280	450	600	—

KM# 194 7 TIEN
Silver **Ruler:** Minh Mang **Obv:** Large sun **Rev:** Large dragon **Note:** Schroeder #181.

Date	VG	F	VF	XF	Unc
ND//13 (1832)	90.00	180	300	500	—

KM# 195 7 TIEN
Silver **Ruler:** Minh Mang **Obv:** Small sun **Rev:** Large dragon **Note:** Schroeder #182, 183, 183A.

Date	VG	F	VF	XF	Unc
ND//14 (1833)	70.00	140	240	400	—
ND//15 (1834)	40.00	80.00	150	250	—
ND//16 (1835)	90.00	180	300	500	—

KM# 288 7 TIEN
Silver **Ruler:** Thieu Tri **Obv. Inscription:** "Thieu Tri Thong Bao" **Rev:** Two facing dragons **Note:** Schroeder #238. Weight varies: 25.80-26.40 grams.

Date	VG	F	VF	XF	Unc
ND(1841-47)	175	350	600	1,000	—

KM# 289 7 TIEN
Silver **Ruler:** Thieu Tri **Obv:** Inscription between bird and dragon **Obv. Inscription:** "Thieu Tri" **Rev. Inscription:** "Phan Long Lan Phu Phung Duc" **Note:** Schroeder #244. Weight varies: 26.40-28.50 grams.

Date	VG	F	VF	XF	Unc
ND(1841-47)	90.00	180	300	500	—

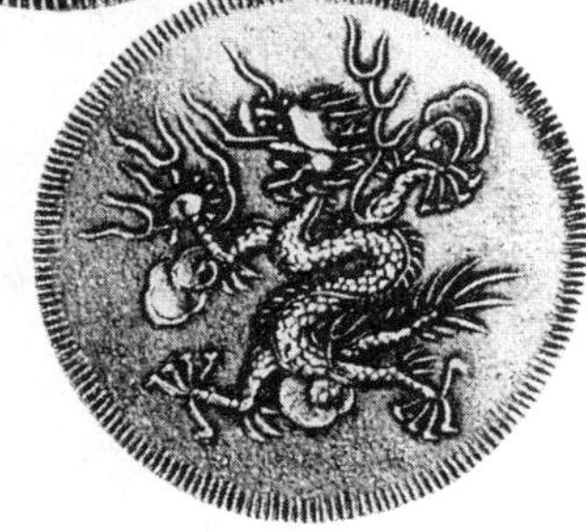

KM# 290 7 TIEN
26.5000 g., Silver, 40.5 mm. **Ruler:** Thieu Tri **Obv:** Large Characters **Obv. Inscription:** "Thieu Tri Thong Bao" **Rev:** Small dragon left **Note:** Schroeder #258.1.

Date	VG	F	VF	XF	Unc
ND(1841-47)	70.00	140	240	400	—

KM# 293 7 TIEN
26.5000 g., Silver **Ruler:** Thieu Tri **Obv:** Flaming sun at center **Rev:** Inscription around facing dragon **Rev. Inscription:** "Long Van Khe Hoi" **Note:** Schroeder #261.

Date	VG	F	VF	XF	Unc
ND(1841-47)	125	250	450	750	—

KM# 291 7 TIEN
26.5000 g., Silver **Ruler:** Thieu Tri **Obv:** Small characters **Rev:** Large dragon left **Note:** Schroeder #258.2.

Date	VG	F	VF	XF	Unc
ND(1841-47)	90.00	180	300	500	—

KM# 292 7 TIEN
26.5000 g., Silver **Ruler:** Thieu Tri **Rev:** Dragon right **Note:** Schroeder #258A.

Date	VG	F	VF	XF	Unc
ND(1841-47)	100	200	350	600	—

KM# 468 7 TIEN
Silver **Ruler:** Tu Duc **Rev:** Ornate sun between two small facing dragons **Note:** Schroeder #347C.

Date	VG	F	VF	XF	Unc
ND(1848-83)	150	300	500	850	—

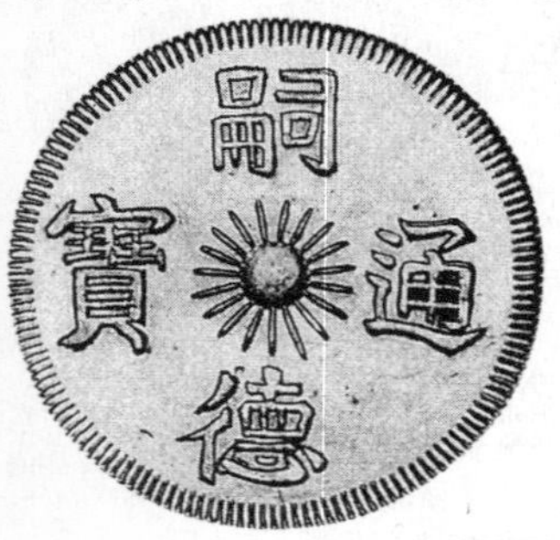

KM# 469 7 TIEN
26.2000 g., Silver **Ruler:** Tu Duc **Rev:** Dragon left **Note:** Schroeder #368.

Date	VG	F	VF	XF	Unc
ND(1848-83)	70.00	140	240	400	—

KM# 470 7 TIEN
26.5000 g., Silver **Ruler:** Tu Duc **Rev:** Inscription on facing dragon **Rev. Inscription:** "Long Van" **Note:** Schroeder #371.

Date	VG	F	VF	XF	Unc
ND(1848-83)	100	200	350	600	—

KM# 471 7 TIEN
26.0000 g., Silver **Ruler:** Tu Duc **Rev:** Inscription on dragon **Rev. Inscription:** "That Tien Viet Hue" **Note:** Schroeder #383.

Date	VG	F	VF	XF	Unc
ND(1848-83)	150	300	500	850	—

KM# 467 7 TIEN
26.6000 g., Silver **Ruler:** Tu Duc **Obv. Inscription:** "Tu duc Thong Bao" **Rev:** Plain sun between two large facing dragons **Note:** Size varies: 51-53 mm; Schroeder #347B.

Date	VG	F	VF	XF	Unc
ND(1848-83)	150	300	500	850	—

KM# 473 8 TIEN
30.5000 g., Silver **Ruler:** Tu Duc **Obv. Inscription:** "Tu Duc Thong Bao" **Rev:** Inscription on dragon **Rev. Inscription:** "Bat Tien Viet Thuan" **Note:** Schroeder #384.

Date	VG	F	VF	XF	Unc
ND(1848-83)	150	300	500	850	—

KM# 475 9 TIEN
34.2000 g., Silver **Ruler:** Tu Duc **Obv. Inscription:** "Tu Duc Thong Bao" **Rev:** Inscription on dragon **Rev. Inscription:** "Cuu Tien Viet Nhan" **Note:** Schroeder #385.

Date	VG	F	VF	XF	Unc
ND(1848-83)	165	325	575	950	—

KM# 271 1/4 LANG
9.2000 g., Silver **Ruler:** Thieu Tri **Obv. Inscription:** "Thieu Tri Thong Bao, Trieu Dan Lai Chi" **Rev:** Dragon **Note:** Schroeder #249.

Date	VG	F	VF	XF	Unc
ND(1841-47)	50.00	100	175	300	—

KM# 272 1/4 LANG
9.6000 g., Silver **Ruler:** Thieu Tri **Obv:** Inscription around flaming sun **Obv. Inscription:** "Thieu Tri Thong Bao" **Rev:** Inscription around dragon **Rev. Inscription:** "Long Van Khe Hoi" **Note:** Schroeder #261B.

Date	VG	F	VF	XF	Unc
ND(1841-47)	62.50	125	200	350	—

KM# 428 1/4 LANG
9.4000 g., Silver **Ruler:** Tu Duc **Obv. Inscription:** "Tu Duc Thong Bao, Trieu Dan Lai Chi" **Rev:** Simple dragon **Note:** Schroeder #350.1.

Date	VG	F	VF	XF	Unc
ND(1848-83)	50.00	100	175	300	—

KM# 429 1/4 LANG
9.4000 g., Silver **Ruler:** Tu Duc **Rev:** Round-faced dragon with streamers **Note:** Schroeder #350.2.

Date	VG	F	VF	XF	Unc
ND(1848-83)	50.00	100	175	300	—

KM# 430 1/4 LANG
9.4000 g., Silver **Ruler:** Tu Duc **Rev:** Ornate dragon **Note:** Schroeder #350.3.

Date	VG	F	VF	XF	Unc
ND(1848-83)	50.00	100	175	300	—

KM# 431 1/4 LANG
Silver **Ruler:** Tu Duc **Obv:** Inscription around flaming sun **Obv. Inscription:** "Tu Duc Thong Bao" **Rev:** Inscription around dragon **Rev. Inscription:** "Long Van Khe Hoi" **Note:** Schroeder #375. Weight varies: 9.50-9.80 grams.

Date	VG	F	VF	XF	Unc
ND(1848-83)	62.50	125	200	350	—

KM# 192 LANG
38.0000 g., Silver, 38 mm. **Ruler:** Minh Mang **Obv:** Inscription around small sun **Obv. Inscription:** "Minh Mang Thong Bao" **Rev:** Inscription on facing dragon **Rev. Inscription:** "Long Van" **Note:** Schroeder #187.

Date	VG	F	VF	XF	Unc
ND(1820-41)	120	240	400	650	—

KM# 193 LANG
38.0000 g., Silver, 40 mm. **Ruler:** Minh Mang **Obv:** Large sun at center **Rev:** Large sun at center **Note:** Schroeder #187A.

Date	VG	F	VF	XF	Unc
ND(1820-41)	135	270	450	750	—

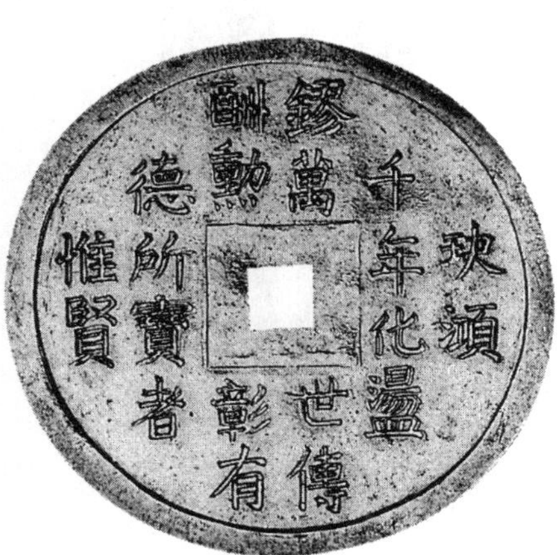

KM# 295 LANG
Silver, 63 mm. **Ruler:** Thieu Tri **Obv. Inscription:** "Thieu Tri Thong Bao, Van The Vinh Lai" **Note:** Schroeder #241. Illustration reduced. Weight varies: 38.00-38.80 grams.

Date	VG	F	VF	XF	Unc
ND(1841-47)	165	325	525	950	—

KM# 477 LANG
37.3000 g., Silver, 66 mm. **Ruler:** Tu Duc **Obv. Inscription:** "Tu Duc Thong Bao, Van The Vinh Lai" **Note:** Schroeder #348. Illustration reduced.

Date	VG	F	VF	XF	Unc
ND(1848-83)	165	325	575	950	—

KM# 478 LANG
37.2000 g., Silver **Ruler:** Tu Duc **Obv. Inscription:** "Tu Duc Thong Bao" **Rev:** Inscription on facing dragon **Rev. Inscription:** "Long Van" **Note:** Schroeder #371.

Date	VG	F	VF	XF	Unc
ND(1848-83)	135	270	450	700	—

KM# 479 LANG
37.4000 g., Silver **Ruler:** Tu Duc **Rev:** Inscription on dragon **Rev. Inscription:** "Nhat Lang Viet Trung" **Note:** Schroeder #376.

Date	VG	F	VF	XF	Unc
ND(1848-83)	225	450	750	1,250	—

SILVER BAR COINAGE

Quan System

KM# 498 1/2 QUAN
Silver **Ruler:** Tu Duc **Note:** Schroeder #338. Weight unknown.

Date	VG	F	VF	XF	Unc
ND(1848-83)	42.50	70.00	100	150	—

KM# 500 7/10 QUAN
3.5000 g., Silver **Ruler:** Tu Duc **Note:** Schroeder #339.

Date	VG	F	VF	XF	Unc
ND(1848-83)	60.00	100	140	200	—

KM# 502 QUAN
Silver **Ruler:** Tu Duc **Note:** Schroeder #340. Weight varies: 5.00-5.28 grams.

Date	VG	F	VF	XF	Unc
ND(1848-83)	50.00	85.00	120	175	—

KM# 504 1-1/2 QUAN
Silver **Ruler:** Tu Duc **Note:** Schroeder #341. Weight varies: 7.50-8.00 grams.

Date	VG	F	VF	XF	Unc
ND(1848-83)	60.00	100	140	200	—

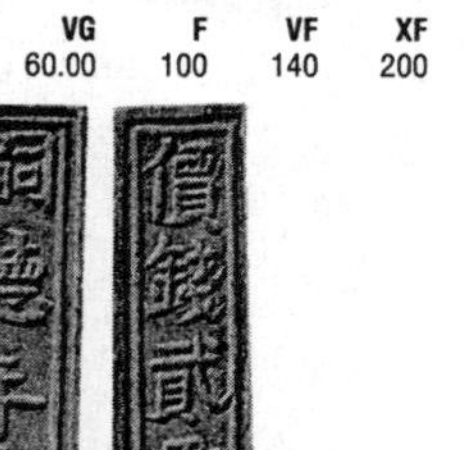

KM# 506 2 QUAN
10.5000 g., Silver **Ruler:** Tu Duc **Note:** Schroeder #342.

Date	VG	F	VF	XF	Unc
ND(1848-83)	65.00	110	160	225	—

KM# 507 2 QUAN
Silver **Ruler:** Tu Duc **Note:** Schroeder #345. Similar to KM#506, but thinner characters. Weight varies: 10.30-10.50 grams.

Date	VG	F	VF	XF	Unc
ND(1848-83)	75.00	125	175	250	—

KM# 509 2-1/2 QUAN
Silver **Ruler:** Tu Duc **Note:** Schroeder #343. Weight varies: 13.00-13.50 grams.

Date	VG	F	VF	XF	Unc
ND(1848-83)	85.00	140	200	275	—

KM# 511 3 QUAN
Silver **Ruler:** Tu Duc **Note:** Schroeder #344. Weight varies: 15.92-16.20 grams. Thick characters.

Date	VG	F	VF	XF	Unc
ND(1848-83)	90.00	150	210	300	—

KM# 513 3 QUAN
15.4000 g., Silver **Ruler:** Tu Duc **Obv:** Double borders, thin characters **Rev:** Double borders, thin characters **Note:** Schroeder #346.

Date	VG	F	VF	XF	Unc
ND(1848-83)	150	275	425	650	—

BULLION SILVER BARS

All of the bars described here are inscribed with their weight, except the 10 Lang ""banana bars"", and many contain a date or the name of the province in which they were made.

KM# 197 TIEN
Silver **Ruler:** Minh Mang **Note:** Schroeder #174. Weight varies: 3.80-3.90 grams.

Date	VG	F	VF	XF	Unc
ND(1820-41)	45.00	75.00	100	150	—

KM# 198 TIEN
4.2000 g., Silver **Ruler:** Minh Mang **Note:** Schroeder #175.

Date	VG	F	VF	XF	Unc
ND(1820-41)	45.00	75.00	100	150	—

KM# A481 TIEN
3.8000 g., Silver **Ruler:** Tu Duc **Obv. Inscription:** "Tu Duc Nien Tao" **Rev. Inscription:** "That Mach" **Note:** Schroeder #339.

Date	VG	F	VF	XF	Unc
ND(1848-83)	45.00	75.00	100	150	—

KM# 481 1-1/2 TIEN
Silver **Ruler:** Tu Duc **Obv. Inscription:** "Tu Duc Nien Tao" **Note:** Schroeder #340. Weight varies: 5.00-5.20 grams.

Date	VG	F	VF	XF	Unc
ND(1848-83)	45.00	75.00	100	150	—

KM# 199 2 TIEN
8.0000 g., Silver **Ruler:** Minh Mang **Note:** Schroeder #176.

Date	VG	F	VF	XF	Unc
ND(1820-41)	50.00	85.00	120	175	—

KM# 483 2 TIEN
Silver **Ruler:** Tu Duc **Issuer:** Court Treasury **Rev:** Five characters **Note:** Schroeder #331. Weight varies: 7.00-7.50 grams.

Date	VG	F	VF	XF	Unc
ND(1848-83)	50.00	85.00	1,120	175	—

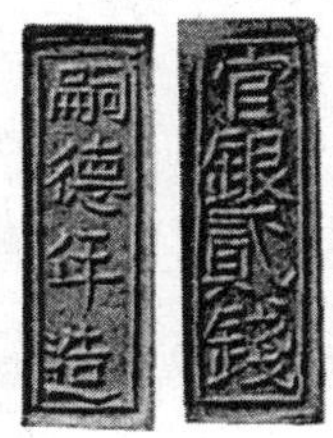

KM# 485 2 TIEN
6.8000 g., Silver **Ruler:** Tu Duc **Rev:** Four characters **Note:** Schroeder #335.

Date	VG	F	VF	XF	Unc
ND(1848-83)	50.00	85.00	120	175	—

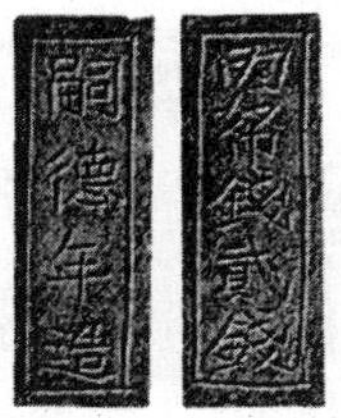

KM# 484 2 TIEN
7.9000 g., Silver **Ruler:** Tu Duc **Issuer:** Court Treasury **Rev:** Error, third and fifth characters the same **Note:** Schroeder #337.

Date	VG	F	VF	XF	Unc
ND(1848-83)	50.00	85.00	120	175	—

KM# 200 3 TIEN
11.6000 g., Silver **Ruler:** Minh Mang **Note:** Schroeder #177.

Date	VG	F	VF	XF	Unc
ND(1820-41)	75.00	125	175	250	—

KM# 487 3 TIEN
10.2000 g., Silver **Ruler:** Tu Duc **Issuer:** Court Treasury **Note:** Schroeder #332.

Date	VG	F	VF	XF	Unc
ND(1848-83)	75.00	125	175	250	—

KM# 201 4 TIEN
15.4000 g., Silver **Ruler:** Minh Mang **Note:** Schroeder #178.

Date	VG	F	VF	XF	Unc
ND(1820-41)	85.00	140	200	300	—

KM# 297 4 TIEN
15.5000 g., Silver **Ruler:** Thieu Tri **Issuer:** Court Treasury **Note:** Schroeder #236.

Date	VG	F	VF	XF	Unc
ND(1841-47)	85.00	140	200	300	—

KM# 489 4 TIEN
15.0000 g., Silver **Ruler:** Tu Duc **Issuer:** Court Treasury **Note:** Schroeder #333.

Date	VG	F	VF	XF	Unc
ND(1848-83)	85.00	140	200	300	—

KM# 177 5 TIEN
Silver **Ruler:** Gia Long **Rev:** Inscription at top **Rev. Inscription:** "Trung Binh" **Note:** Schroeder #122. Weight unknown.

Date	VG	F	VF	XF	Unc
ND(1802-20)	100	175	250	350	—

KM# 178 5 TIEN
Silver **Ruler:** Gia Long **Rev:** Four characters **Note:** Schroeder #122A. Weight unknown.

Date	VG	F	VF	XF	Unc
ND(1802-20)	100	175	250	350	—

KM# 202 5 TIEN
19.0000 g., Silver **Ruler:** Minh Mang **Rev:** Four characters **Note:** Schroeder #179.

Date	VG	F	VF	XF	Unc
ND(1820-41)	100	175	250	350	—

KM# 299 5 TIEN
19.2000 g., Silver **Ruler:** Thieu Tri **Issuer:** Court Treasury **Rev:** Five characters **Note:** Schroeder #237.

Date	VG	F	VF	XF	Unc
ND(1841-47)	100	175	250	350	—

KM# 491 5 TIEN
19.0000 g., Silver **Ruler:** Thieu Tri **Issuer:** Court Treasury **Note:** Schroeder #334.

Date	VG	F	VF	XF	Unc
ND(1848-83)	100	175	250	350	—

KM# 180.2 LANG
Silver **Ruler:** Gia Long **Note:** Large characters; Schroeder #120; weight varies 38.13-38.55 grams; Similar to KM#180.1, but edge inscriptions are reversed.

Date	Good	VG	F	VF	XF
ND(1802-1820)	—	60.00	100	140	200

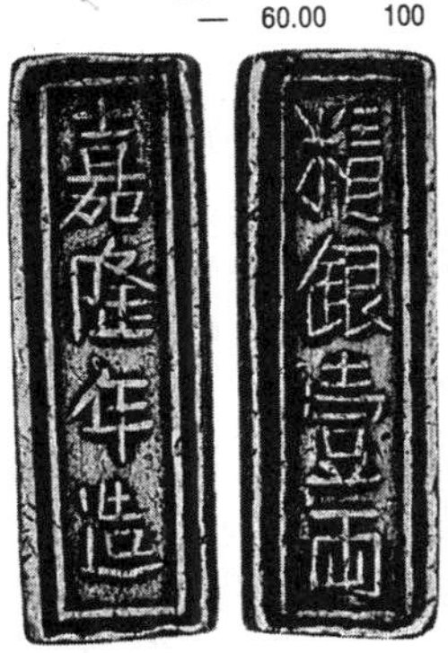

KM# 179 LANG
37.9400 g., Silver **Ruler:** Gia Long **Note:** Large characters. Schroeder #118. Produced as a common form of bullion well into the 20th century.

Date	VG	F	VF	XF	Unc
ND(1802-20)	25.00	40.00	55.00	80.00	—

KM# 180.1 LANG
Silver **Ruler:** Gia Long **Note:** Small characters. Schroeder #119. Weight varies: 38.13-38.55 grams.

Date	VG	F	VF	XF	Unc
ND(1802-20)	60.00	100	140	200	—

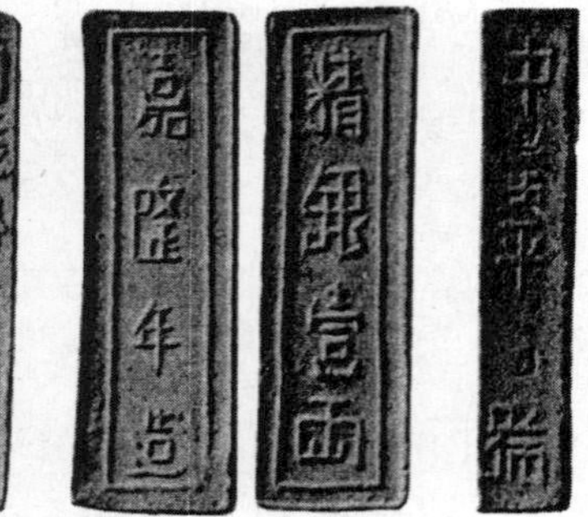

KM# 180.3 LANG
Silver **Ruler:** Gia Long **Note:** Small characters, Swastica between edge inscription "Trung" and "Binh Hieu"; Schroeder #121; weight varies 38.13 - 38.55 grams.

Date	Good	VG	F	VF	XF
ND(1802-20)	—	60.00	100	140	200

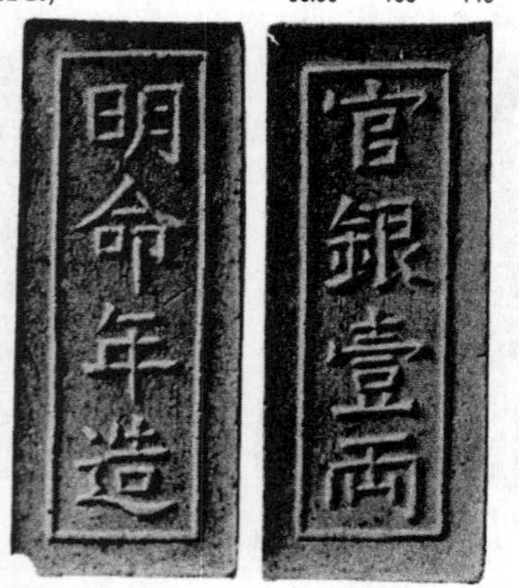

KM# 203 LANG
Silver **Ruler:** Minh Mang **Note:** Schroeder #169. Weight varies: 38.13-38.55 grams. Size varies: 57.2-57.8 millimeters.

Date	VG	F	VF	XF	Unc
ND(1820-41)	75.00	125	175	250	—

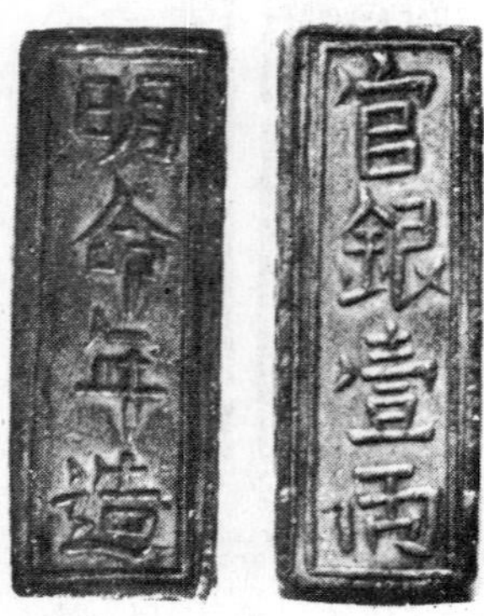

KM# 204 LANG
Silver **Ruler:** Minh Mang **Note:** Weight unknown; size: 41 millimeters.

Date	VG	F	VF	XF	Unc
ND(1820-41)	60.00	100	140	200	—

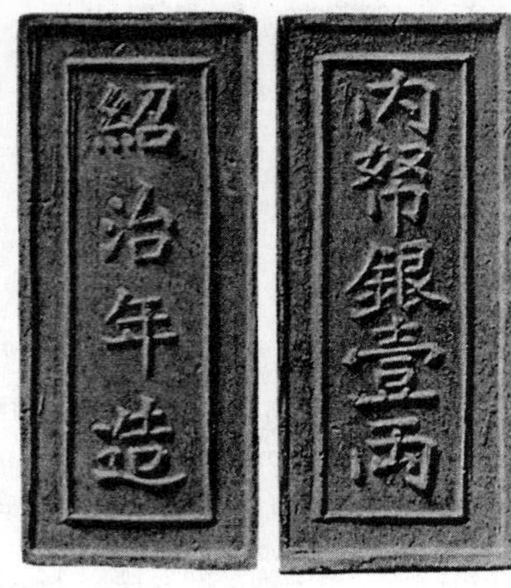

KM# 301 LANG
38.0000 g., Silver **Ruler:** Thieu Tri **Issuer:** Court Treasury **Note:** Schroeder #219.

Date	VG	F	VF	XF	Unc
ND(1841-47)	75.00	125	185	275	—

KM# 302 LANG
38.0000 g., Silver **Ruler:** Thieu Tri **Rev. Inscription:** "Gia Dinh"

Date	VG	F	VF	XF	Unc
CD1844	100	175	250	350	—

KM# 494 LANG
38.0000 g., Silver **Ruler:** Tu Duc **Rev:** "Binh Dinh" on edge **Note:** Schroeder #320A.

Date	VG	F	VF	XF	Unc
ND(1848-83)	60.00	100	140	200	—

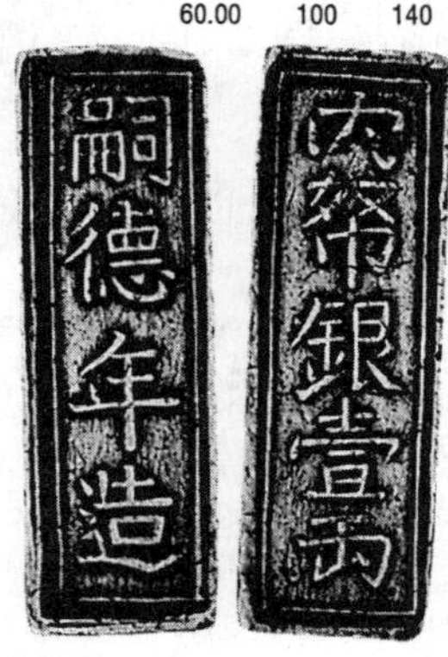

KM# 493 LANG
Silver **Ruler:** Tu Duc **Subject:** Court Treasury **Note:** Schroeder #324B. Weight varies: 37.43-38.33 grams. Produced as a common form of bullion well into the 20th century.

Date	VG	F	VF	XF	Unc
ND(1848-83)	25.00	40.00	55.00	80.00	—

KM# 586 LANG
Silver **Ruler:** Tu Duc **Rev:** "Dinh Tuong" on edge **Note:** Schroeder #320B. Weight unknown.

Date	VG	F	VF	XF	Unc
CD1859	100	175	250	350	—

KM# 587 LANG
38.2900 g., Silver **Ruler:** Tu Duc **Rev:** "Phu Yen" on edge **Note:** Schroeder #320C; size: 57 milllimeters.

Date	VG	F	VF	XF	Unc
CD1859	100	175	250	350	—

KM# 588 LANG
Silver **Ruler:** Tu Duc **Note:** Schroeder #323. "Canh Than".

Date	VG	F	VF	XF	Unc
CB1860	100	175	250	350	—

KM# 592 LANG
Silver **Ruler:** Tu Duc **Rev:** Legend at top **Rev. Legend:** "Phu Yen" **Note:** Schroeder #322. Weight unknown.

Date	VG	F	VF	XF	Unc
CD1861	100	175	250	350	—

KM# 591 LANG
38.6900 g., Silver **Ruler:** Tu Duc **Obv:** Date **Rev:** "Binh Dinh" at top **Note:** Schroeder #321; size: 58 mm.

Date	VG	F	VF	XF	Unc
CD1861	100	175	250	350	—

KM# 596 LANG
37.0000 g., Silver **Ruler:** Tu Duc **Obv:** Date **Rev. Inscription:** "An Giang" **Note:** Schroeder #324.

Date	VG	F	VF	XF	Unc
CD1863	150	250	350	500	—

KM# 205 5 LANG
Silver **Ruler:** Minh Mang **Note:** Schroeder #170. Weight varies: 181.00-191.00 grams.

Date	VG	F	VF	XF	Unc
ND(1820-41)	200	350	500	700	—

KM# 304 5 LANG
Silver **Ruler:** Thieu Tri **Subject:** Court Treasury **Note:** Schroeder #220. Weight varies: 186.00-191.00 grams; size: 40x92 mm; Illustration reduced.

Date	VG	F	VF	XF	Unc
ND(1841-47)	200	350	500	700	—

KM# 181 10 LANG
Silver **Ruler:** Gia Long **Note:** Curved series. Approximate weight: 385 grams. Top with two four-character rectangular markings.

Date	VG	F	VF	XF	Unc
ND(1802-20)	75.00	125	185	275	—

KM# 206 10 LANG
Silver **Ruler:** Minh Mang **Issuer:** Court Treasury **Note:** Curved series. Schroeder #171. Similar to Schroeder #173; Approximately 385 grams; size: 28 x 116 mm; Illustration reduced.

Date	VG	F	VF	XF	Unc
CD1832	300	500	700	1,000	—

KM# 207 10 LANG
Silver **Ruler:** Minh Mang **Note:** Curved series. Similar to KM#210. "Quang An"; approximately 385 grams.

Date	VG	F	VF	XF	Unc
CD1832	300	500	700	1,000	—

KM# 209 10 LANG
Silver **Ruler:** Minh Mang **Note:** Curved series. Similar to KM#210. Approximately 385 grams.

Date	VG	F	VF	XF	Unc
CD1833	300	500	700	1,000	—

KM# 208 10 LANG
Silver **Ruler:** Minh Mang **Issuer:** Court Treasury **Note:** Curved series; Schroeder #172; Approximately 385 grams; size: 28 x 115 mm; Illustration reduced.

Date	VG	F	VF	XF	Unc
CD1833	300	500	700	1,000	—

KM# 210 10 LANG
Silver **Ruler:** Minh Mang **Note:** Curved series. Schroeder #173. "Son Tay"; Approximately 385 grams; size: 27 x 108 mm; Illustration reduced.

Date	VG	F	VF	XF	Unc
CD1837	300	500	700	1,000	—

KM# A210 10 LANG
0.8500 Silver **Ruler:** Minh Mang **Note:** Schroeder #192; approximately 385 grams; curved series; "Noi Thang"; Illustration reduced.

Date	Good	VG	F	VF	XF
CD1837	—	300	500	700	1,000

KM# 306 10 LANG
Silver **Ruler:** Thieu Tri **Issuer:** Court Treasury **Note:** Flat Series. Schroeder #221; size: 42x115 mm; approximately 385 grams; Illustration reduced to 50% actual size.

Date	VG	F	VF	XF	Unc
ND(1841-47)	250	425	600	850	—

KM# 363 10 LANG
Silver **Ruler:** Thieu Tri **Rev:** Inscription at top **Rev. Inscription:** "Hung Yen" **Note:** Flat Series. Schroeder #222; size: 45x120 mm; approximately 385.00 grams.

Date	VG	F	VF	XF	Unc
CD1844	250	425	600	850	—

KM# 364 10 LANG
Silver **Ruler:** Thieu Tri **Rev:** Inscription at top **Rev. Inscription:** "Binh Dinh" **Note:** Flat Series. Schroeder #223; approximately 385 grams.

Date	VG	F	VF	XF	Unc
CD1844	250	425	600	850	—

KM# 375 10 LANG
Silver **Ruler:** Thieu Tri **Rev:** Inscription at top **Rev. Inscription:** "Hung Yen" **Note:** Flat Series; approximately 385 grams.

Date	VG	F	VF	XF	Unc
CD1844	250	425	600	850	—

KM# 376 10 LANG
Silver **Ruler:** Thieu Tri **Rev:** Legend at top **Rev. Legend:** "Son Tay" **Note:** Flat Series; approximately 385 grams.

Date	VG	F	VF	XF	Unc
CD1844	250	425	600	850	—

KM# 366 10 LANG
Silver **Ruler:** Thieu Tri **Rev:** Inscription at top **Rev. Inscription:** "Son Tay" **Note:** Flat Series. Schroeder #224; approximately 385 grams

Date	VG	F	VF	XF	Unc
CD1845	250	425	600	850	—

KM# 367 10 LANG
385.0000 g., Silver **Ruler:** Thieu Tri **Rev:** Inscription at top **Rev. Inscription:** "Quang Nam" **Note:** Flat Series. Schroeder #225. 48x120 millimeters; approximately 385 grams.

Date	VG	F	VF	XF	Unc
CD1846	250	425	600	850	—

KM# 369 10 LANG
Silver **Ruler:** Thieu Tri **Rev:** Inscription at top **Rev. Inscription:** "Din Nam" **Note:** Flat Series. Illustration reduced; approximately 385 grams.

Date	VG	F	VF	XF	Unc
CD1846	250	—	600	850	—

KM# 368 10 LANG
Silver **Ruler:** Thieu Tri **Rev:** Inscription at top **Rev. Inscription:** "Son Tay" **Note:** Flat Series; approximately 385 grams.

Date	VG	F	VF	XF	Unc
CD1846	250	425	600	850	—

KM# 373 10 LANG
Silver **Ruler:** Thieu Tri **Rev:** Inscription at top **Rev. Inscription:** "Son Tay" **Note:** Flat Series. Schroeder #229; approximately 385 grams.

Date	VG	F	VF	XF	Unc
CD1847	250	425	600	850	—

KM# 374 10 LANG
Silver **Ruler:** Thieu Tri **Rev:** Inscription at top **Rev. Inscription:** "Gia Dinh" **Note:** Flat Series. Schroeder #230; approximately 385 grams.

Date	VG	F	VF	XF	Unc
CD1847	250	425	600	850	—

KM# 370 10 LANG
Silver **Ruler:** Thieu Tri **Rev:** Inscription at top **Rev. Inscription:** "Hung Yen" **Note:** Flat Series. Schroeder #226. 46x120 millimeters; approximately 385 grams.

Date	VG	F	VF	XF	Unc
CD1847	250	425	600	850	—

KM# 371 10 LANG
Silver **Ruler:** Thieu Tri **Rev:** Inscription at top **Rev. Inscription:** "Lang Sun" **Note:** Flat Series. Schroeder #227; approximately 385 grams.

Date	VG	F	VF	XF	Unc
CD1847	250	425	600	850	—

KM# 372 10 LANG
Silver **Ruler:** Thieu Tri **Rev:** Inscription at top **Rev. Inscription:** "Bac Ninh" **Note:** Flat Series. Schroeder #228; approximately 385 grams.

Date	VG	F	VF	XF	Unc
CD1847	250	425	600	850	—

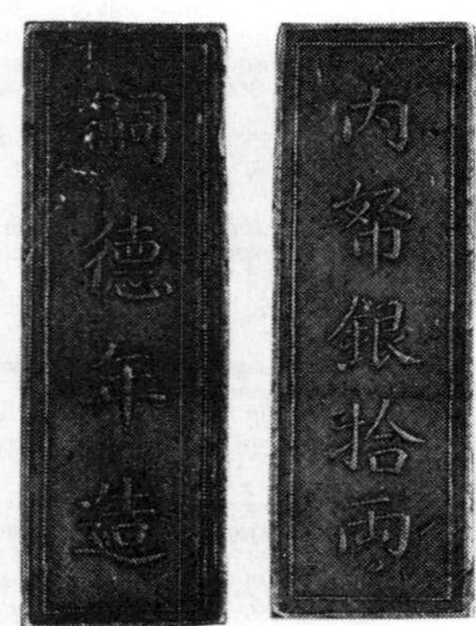

KM# 496 10 LANG
382.5000 g., Silver **Ruler:** Tu Duc **Issuer:** Court Treasury **Rev:** Inscription at top **Rev. Inscription:** "Son Tay" **Note:** Flat Series. Schroeder #329. 34x100 millimeters; approximately 385 grams; Illustration reduced.

Date	VG	F	VF	XF	Unc
ND(1848-83)	250	425	600	850	—

KM# 495 10 LANG
383.0000 g., Silver **Ruler:** Tu Duc **Note:** Top with two four-character rectangular markings. Produced as a common form of bullion into the 20th century; approximately 385 grams; curved series.

Date	VG	F	VF	XF	Unc
ND(1848-83)	75.00	125	185	275	—

Note: 10 Lang curved "banana bars" of these types without any characters on their top surfaces but with various markings on their ends and sides were also produced as a common form of bullion into the 20th century

KM# 589 10 LANG
383.0000 g., Silver **Ruler:** Tu Duc **Note:** Curved series. Schroeder #325. "Thai Nguyen"; approximately 385 grams; Similar to KM#210.

Date	VG	F	VF	XF	Unc
CD1860	275	450	625	900	—

KM# 594 10 LANG
383.0000 g., Silver **Ruler:** Tu Duc **Note:** Curved series. Schroeder #326. "Binh Dinh"; approximately 385 grams; Similar to KM#210.

Date	VG	F	VF	XF	Unc
CD1861	275	450	625	900	—

KM# 598 10 LANG
383.0000 g., Silver **Ruler:** Tu Duc **Note:** Curved series. Schroeder #327. "Son Tay". Similar to KM#210.

Date	VG	F	VF	XF	Unc
CD1880	275	450	625	900	—

KM# 599 10 LANG
383.0000 g., Silver **Ruler:** Tu Duc **Note:** Curved series. Schroeder #328. Similar to KM#210. "Nghe An"; approximately 385 grams.

Date	VG	F	VF	XF	Unc
CD1882	275	450	625	900	—

KM# 308 20 LANG
765.5000 g., Silver **Ruler:** Thieu Tri **Issuer:** Court Treasury **Obv:** Inscription framed within ornate border of dragons **Rev:** Inscription framed within ornate border of bats **Note:** Flat Series. Schroeder #231; size: 49x122 mm.

Date	VG	F	VF	XF	Unc
ND(1841-47) Rare	—	—	—	—	—

KM# 310 30 LANG
1149.0000 g., Silver **Ruler:** Thieu Tri **Note:** Flat Series. Schroeder #232; size: 55x127 mm. Similar to 20 Lang, KM#308.

Date	VG	F	VF	XF	Unc
ND(1841-47) Rare	—	—	—	—	—

KM# 312 40 LANG
1528.0000 g., Silver **Ruler:** Thieu Tri **Note:** Flat Series. Schroeder #233; size: 60x130 mm. Similar to 20 Lang, KM#308.

Date	VG	F	VF	XF	Unc
ND(1841-47) Rare	—	—	—	—	—

KM# 314 50 LANG
1915.0000 g., Silver **Ruler:** Thieu Tri **Note:** Flat Series. Schroeder #234; size: 65x140 mm. Similar to 20 Lang, KM#308.

Date	VG	F	VF	XF	Unc
ND(1841-47) Rare	—	—	—	—	—

KM# 316 100 LANG
3831.0000 g., Silver **Ruler:** Thieu Tri **Note:** Flat Series. Schroeder #235; size: 77x160 mm. Similar to 20 Lang, KM#308.

Date	VG	F	VF	XF	Unc
ND(1841-47) Rare	—	—	—	—	—

GOLD MILLED COINAGE

KM# 318 1/2 TIEN
1.8000 g., Gold **Ruler:** Thieu Tri **Obv. Inscription:** "Thieu Tri Thong Bao" **Rev:** Blank **Note:** Schroeder #257.

Date	VG	F	VF	XF	Unc
ND(1841-47)	150	275	425	650	—

KM# 212 TIEN
Gold **Ruler:** Minh Mang **Obv. Inscription:** "Minh Mang Thong Bao" **Rev:** Five planets **Note:** Schroeder #209.1. Weight varies: 3.65-4.00 grams.

Date	VG	F	VF	XF	Unc
ND(1820-41)	300	550	850	1,350	—

KM# 213 TIEN
Gold **Ruler:** Minh Mang **Rev:** Mirror image **Note:** Schroeder #209.2.

Date	VG	F	VF	XF	Unc
ND(1820-41)	300	550	850	1,350	—

KM# 320 TIEN
Gold **Ruler:** Thieu Tri **Obv. Inscription:** "Thieu Tri Thong Bao" **Rev. Inscription:** "Nhat Nguyen" **Note:** Schroeder #250B.

Date	VG	F	VF	XF	Unc
ND(1841-47)	350	650	1,100	1,750	—

KM# A328 TIEN
4.0000 g., Gold **Ruler:** Thieu Tri **Rev:** Fan-mirror image

Date	VG	F	VF	XF	Unc
ND(1841-47)	325	600	950	1,450	—

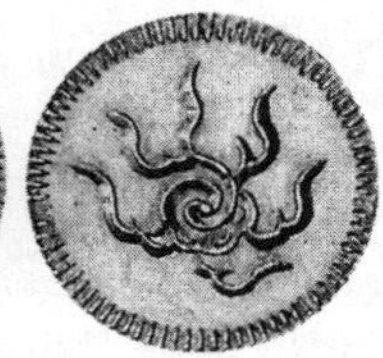

KM# 321 TIEN
Gold **Ruler:** Thieu Tri **Rev:** Flaming sun with lower flames right **Note:** Schroeder #287.1.

Date	VG	F	VF	XF	Unc
ND(1841-47)	325	600	950	1,450	—

KM# 322 TIEN
Gold **Ruler:** Thieu Tri **Rev:** Flaming sun with lower flames left **Note:** Schroeder #287.2.

Date	VG	F	VF	XF	Unc
ND(1841-47)	325	600	950	1,450	—

KM# 323 TIEN
3.8000 g., Gold **Ruler:** Thieu Tri **Rev:** Scepter and swastika **Note:** Schroeder #288.

Date	VG	F	VF	XF	Unc
ND(1841-47)	325	600	950	1,450	—

KM# 324 TIEN
4.0000 g., Gold **Ruler:** Thieu Tri **Rev:** Guitar **Note:** Schroeder #289.1.

Date	VG	F	VF	XF	Unc
ND(1841-47)	325	600	950	1,450	—

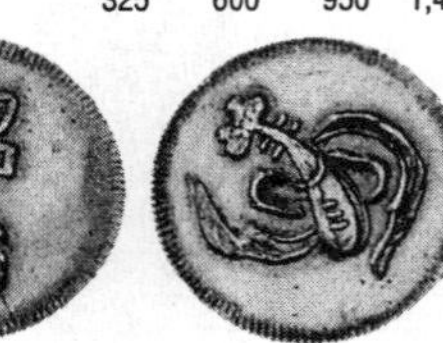

KM# 325 TIEN
Gold **Ruler:** Thieu Tri **Rev:** Mirror image **Note:** Schroeder #289.2.

Date	VG	F	VF	XF	Unc
ND(1841-47)	—	—	—	1,800	—

KM# 326 TIEN
Gold **Ruler:** Thieu Tri **Rev:** Horn **Note:** Schroeder #290.

Date	VG	F	VF	XF	Unc
ND(1841-47)	325	600	950	1,450	—

KM# 327 TIEN
3.8000 g., Gold **Ruler:** Thieu Tri **Rev:** Fan **Note:** Schroeder #291.

Date	VG	F	VF	XF	Unc
ND(1841-47)	325	600	950	1,450	—

KM# 329 TIEN
4.2000 g., Gold **Ruler:** Thieu Tri **Rev:** Clappers **Note:** Schroeder #293.

Date	VG	F	VF	XF	Unc
ND(1841-47)	325	600	950	1,450	—

KM# 330 TIEN
4.0000 g., Gold **Ruler:** Thieu Tri **Rev:** Books **Note:** Schroeder #294.

Date	VG	F	VF	XF	Unc
ND(1841-47)	325	600	950	1,450	—

KM# 331 TIEN
3.8000 g., Gold **Ruler:** Thieu Tri **Rev:** "Tam Da" above the Three Plenties **Note:** Schroeder #295.

Date	VG	F	VF	XF	Unc
ND(1841-47)	325	600	950	1,450	—

KM# 328 TIEN
4.0000 g., Gold **Ruler:** Thieu Tri **Rev:** Calabash **Note:** Schroeder #292.

Date	VG	F	VF	XF	Unc
ND(1841-47)	325	600	950	1,450	—

KM# 515 TIEN
3.7000 g., Gold **Ruler:** Tu Duc **Rev. Inscription:** "Nhat Nguyen" **Note:** Schroeder #353B.

Date	VG	F	VF	XF	Unc
ND(1848-83)	—	1,350	2,000	3,000	—

KM# 516 TIEN
3.8000 g., Gold **Ruler:** Tu Duc **Rev:** Inscription on dragon **Rev. Inscription:** "Nhat Nguyen Tien Viet Tu" **Note:** Schroeder #377.

Date	VG	F	VF	XF	Unc
ND(1848-83)	325	600	950	1,450	—

KM# 517 TIEN
Gold **Ruler:** Tu Duc **Rev:** Sun, moon, and five planets **Note:** Schroeder #386A.

Date	VG	F	VF	XF	Unc
ND(1848-83)	325	600	950	1,450	—

KM# 518 TIEN
Gold **Ruler:** Tu Duc **Rev:** Scepter and swastika **Note:** Schroeder #388B.

Date	VG	F	VF	XF	Unc
ND(1848-83)	650	1,100	1,800	3,000	—

KM# 215 1-1/2 TIEN
5.7000 g., Gold **Ruler:** Minh Mang **Obv. Inscription:** "Minh Mang" **Rev:** Five Precious symbols **Note:** Schroeder #211. Weight varies: 5.40-6.50 grams.

Date	VG	F	VF	XF	Unc
ND(1820-41)	350	650	1,000	1,600	—

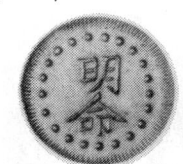

KM# 216 1-1/2 TIEN
5.7000 g., Gold **Ruler:** Minh Mang **Rev:** Eight Precious symbols **Note:** Schroeder #212.

Date	VG	F	VF	XF	Unc
ND(1820-41)	350	650	1,000	1,600	—

KM# 217 1-1/2 TIEN
5.7000 g., Gold **Ruler:** Minh Mang **Rev:** Mirror image **Note:** Schroeder #213.

Date	VG	F	VF	XF	Unc
ND(1820-41)	350	650	1,000	1,600	—

KM# 520 1-1/2 TIEN
5.6000 g., Gold **Ruler:** Tu Duc **Obv. Inscription:** "Tu Duc Thong Bao" **Rev. Inscription:** "Su Dan Phu Tho" **Note:** Schroeder #406.

Date	VG	F	VF	XF	Unc
ND(1848-83)	350	650	950	1,450	—

KM# 219 2 TIEN
7.8000 g., Gold **Ruler:** Minh Mang **Obv. Inscription:** "Minh Mang" **Rev:** Inscription above the Three Plenties **Rev. Inscription:** "Tam Da" **Note:** Schroeder #210.

Date	VG	F	VF	XF	Unc
ND(1820-41)	350	650	1,000	1,600	—

KM# 333 2 TIEN
Gold **Ruler:** Thieu Tri **Obv. Inscription:** "Thieu Tri Thong Bao" **Rev:** Inscription between sun and moon **Rev. Inscription:** "Nhi Nghi" **Note:** Schroeder #281.

Date	VG	F	VF	XF	Unc
ND(1841-47)	350	650	1,000	1,600	—

KM# 522 2 TIEN
7.3000 g., Gold **Ruler:** Tu Duc **Obv. Inscription:** "Tu Duc Thong Bao" **Rev:** Inscription on dragon **Rev. Inscription:** "Nhi Tien Viet Hien" **Note:** Schroeder #378.

Date	VG	F	VF	XF	Unc
ND(1848-83)	350	650	1,000	1,600	—

KM# 523 2 TIEN
Gold **Ruler:** Tu Duc **Rev:** Flaming sun between facing dragons **Note:** Schroeder #402B.

Date	VG	F	VF	XF	Unc
ND(1848-83)	400	750	1,150	1,750	—

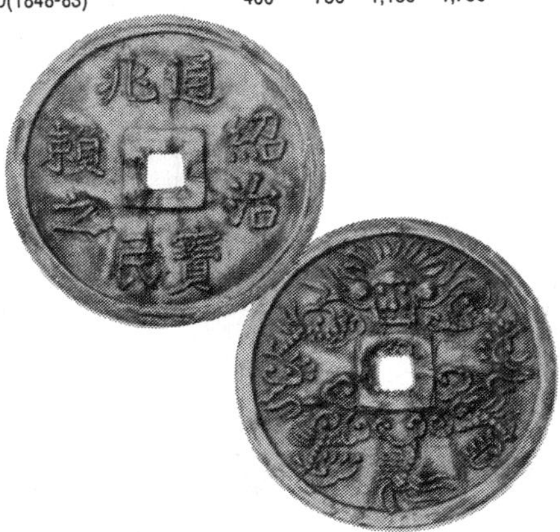

KM# 335 2-1/2 TIEN
8.9000 g., Gold **Ruler:** Thieu Tri **Obv. Inscription:** "Thieu Tri Thong Bao" **Rev:** Facing dragon **Note:** Schroeder #280B.

Date	VG	F	VF	XF	Unc
ND(1841-47)	—	—	—	3,250	—

KM# 525 2-1/2 TIEN
8.9000 g., Gold **Ruler:** Tu Duc **Obv. Inscription:** "Thieu Tri Thong Bao, Trieu Dan Lai Chi" **Rev:** Inscription around facing dragon **Rev. Inscription:** "Long Van Khe Hoi" **Note:** Schroeder #375.

Date	VG	F	VF	XF	Unc
ND(1848-83)	400	700	1,150	1,700	—

KM# 221 3 TIEN
Gold **Ruler:** Minh Mang **Obv:** Large sun, large inscription **Obv. Inscription:** "Minh Mang thong Bao" **Note:** Schroeder #207. Weight varies: 11.50-13.30 grams.

Date	VG	F	VF	XF	Unc
ND(1820-41)	550	1,000	1,700	2,600	—

KM# 226 3 TIEN
Gold **Ruler:** Minh Mang **Obv:** Small sun, large inscription **Note:** Schroeder #208.

Date	VG	F	VF	XF	Unc
ND//14 (1833)	550	1,000	1,700	2,600	—

KM# 227 3 TIEN
Gold **Ruler:** Minh Mang **Obv:** Small sun, medium inscription **Note:** Schroeder #206C.

Date	VG	F	VF	XF	Unc
ND15 (1834)	550	1,000	1,700	2,600	—

KM# 229 3 TIEN
Gold **Ruler:** Minh Mang **Obv:** Small sun, small inscription **Note:** Schroeder #206D.

Date	VG	F	VF	XF	Unc
ND16 (1835)	—	—	2,000	—	—

KM# 337 3 TIEN
13.5400 g., Gold **Ruler:** Thieu Tri **Obv. Inscription:** "Thieu Tri Thong Bao" **Rev:** Large dragon **Note:** Schroeder #285.

Date	VG	F	VF	XF	Unc
ND(1841-47)	550	1,000	1,700	2,600	—

KM# 338 3 TIEN
13.5400 g., Gold **Ruler:** Thieu Tri **Rev:** Small dragon left **Note:** Schroeder #286.

Date	VG	F	VF	XF	Unc
ND(1841-47)	550	1,000	1,700	2,600	—

KM# 529 3 TIEN
11.2000 g., Gold **Ruler:** Tu Duc **Rev:** Inscription on facing dragon **Rev. Inscription:** "Long Van" **Note:** Schroeder #373B.

Date	VG	F	VF	XF	Unc
ND(1848-83)	600	1,100	1,900	2,900	—

KM# 530 3 TIEN
11.3000 g., Gold **Ruler:** Tu Duc **Rev:** Inscription on facing dragon **Rev. Inscription:** "Tam Tien Viet Lang" **Note:** Schroeder #379B.

Date	VG	F	VF	XF	Unc
ND(1848-83)	550	1,000	1,700	2,600	—

KM# 528 3 TIEN
11.0000 g., Gold **Ruler:** Tu Duc **Rev:** Inscription above Three Longevities **Rev. Inscription:** "Tam Thao" **Note:** Schroeder #407.

Date	VG	F	VF	XF	Unc
ND(1848-83)	600	1,100	1,900	2,900	—

KM# 527 3 TIEN
13.2400 g., Gold **Ruler:** Tu Duc **Obv. Inscription:** "Tu duc Thong Bao" **Note:** Schroeder #413.

Date	VG	F	VF	XF	Unc
ND(1848-83)	550	1,000	1,700	2,600	—

KM# 535 4 TIEN
15.0000 g., Gold **Ruler:** Tu Duc **Rev:** Inscription on dragon **Rev. Inscription:** "Tu Tien Viet De" **Note:** Schroeder #380.

Date	VG	F	VF	XF	Unc
ND(1848-83)	650	1,200	2,100	3,200	—

KM# 536 4 TIEN
13.1600 g., Gold **Ruler:** Tu Duc **Rev:** Flaming sun between facing dragons **Note:** Schroeder #402C.

Date	VG	F	VF	XF	Unc
ND(1848-83)	—	—	—	7,000	—

KM# 532 4 TIEN
14.7000 g., Gold **Ruler:** Tu Duc **Obv. Inscription:** "Tu duc Thong Bao" **Rev. Inscription:** "Su Dan Phu Tho" **Note:** Schroeder #406.

Date	VG	F	VF	XF	Unc
ND(1848-83)	650	1,200	2,100	3,200	—

KM# 533 4 TIEN
Gold **Ruler:** Tu Duc **Obv:** Large characters **Rev:** Inscription between the Four Perfections **Rev. Inscription:** "Tu My" **Note:** Schroeder #409.1. Weight varies: 14.50-15.20 grams.

Date	VG	F	VF	XF	Unc
ND(1848-83)	650	1,200	2,100	3,200	—

KM# 534 4 TIEN
Gold **Ruler:** Tu Duc **Obv:** Small characters **Rev:** Finer style **Note:** Schroeder #409.2.

Date	VG	F	VF	XF	Unc
ND(1848-83)	650	1,200	2,100	3,200	—

KM# 223 5 TIEN
19.2000 g., Gold **Ruler:** Minh Mang **Obv. Inscription:** "Minh Mang Thong Bao" **Rev. Inscription:** "Phu Tho Da Nam" **Note:** Schroeder #205.

Date	VG	F	VF	XF	Unc
ND(1820-41)	1,000	2,000	—	5,000	—

KM# 340 5 TIEN
17.6100 g., Gold **Ruler:** Thieu Tri **Obv. Inscription:** "Thieu Tri Thong Bao" **Rev. Inscription:** "Phu Tho Da Nam" **Note:** Schroeder #253B.

Date	VG	F	VF	XF	Unc
ND(1841-47)	1,100	2,200	3,500	5,500	—

KM# 341 5 TIEN
19.5000 g., Gold **Ruler:** Thieu Tri **Obv. Inscription:** "Thieu Tri Thong Bao, Van The Vinh Lai" **Note:** Schroeder #279.

Date	VG	F	VF	XF	Unc
ND(1841-47)	1,100	—	3,500	5,500	—

KM# 538 5 TIEN
Gold **Ruler:** Tu Duc **Obv. Inscription:** "Tu Duc Thong Bao" **Rev:** Inscription around dragon **Rev. Inscription:** "Long Van Khe Hoi" **Note:** Schroeder #374B. Weight varies: 18.00-20.00 grams.

Date	VG	F	VF	XF	Unc
ND(1848-83)	950	1,850	3,100	4,850	—

KM# 544 5 TIEN
18.8000 g., Gold **Ruler:** Tu Duc **Rev:** Inscription on dragon **Rev. Inscription:** "Ngu Tien Viet Ngai" **Note:** Schroeder #381.

Date	VG	F	VF	XF	Unc
ND(1848-83)	1,000	2,000	3,250	5,000	—

KM# 542 5 TIEN
19.2200 g., Gold **Ruler:** Tu Duc **Obv. Inscription:** "Tu Duc Thong Bao, Van The Vinh Lai" **Note:** Schroeder #404.

Date	VG	F	VF	XF	Unc
ND(1848-83)	1,100	2,200	3,500	5,500	—

KM# 541 5 TIEN
19.0000 g., Gold **Ruler:** Tu Duc **Obv. Inscription:** "Tu Duc Thong Bao, Trieu Dan Lai Chi" **Rev:** Facing dragon **Note:** Schroeder #405.

Date	VG	F	VF	XF	Unc
ND(1848-83)	1,000	2,000	3,250	5,000	—

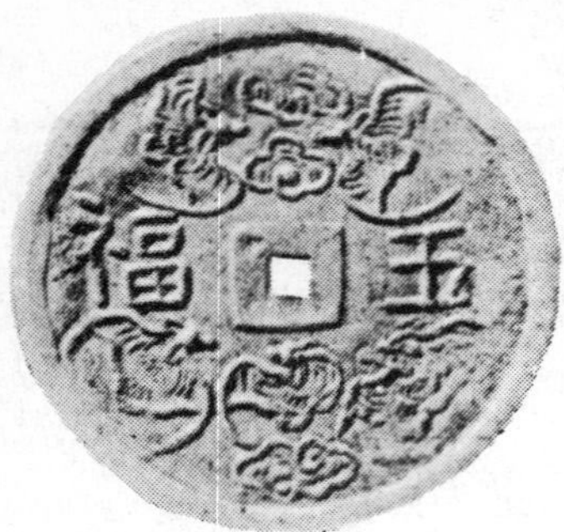

KM# 543 5 TIEN
18.0000 g., Gold **Ruler:** Tu Duc **Obv. Inscription:** "Tu Duc Thong Bao" **Rev:** Inscription and five bats **Rev. Inscription:** "Ngu Phuc" **Note:** Schroeder #410.

Date	VG	F	VF	XF	Unc
ND(1848-83)	1,000	2,000	3,250	5,000	—

KM# 539 5 TIEN
18.9000 g., Gold **Ruler:** Tu Duc **Obv:** Sun with eight rays at center **Rev:** Inscription on facing dragon **Rev. Inscription:** "Long Van" **Note:** Schroeder #414C.

Date	VG	F	VF	XF	Unc
ND(1848-83)	950	1,850	3,100	4,850	—

KM# 540 5 TIEN
18.2400 g., Gold **Ruler:** Tu Duc **Obv:** Sun with twelve rays at center **Note:** Schroeder #414D.

Date	VG	F	VF	XF	Unc
ND(1848-83)	950	1,850	3,100	4,850	—

KM# 546 6 TIEN
23.0000 g., Gold **Ruler:** Tu Duc **Obv. Inscription:** "Tu Duc Thong Bao" **Rev:** Inscription on dragon **Rev. Inscription:** "Luc Tien Viet Thinh" **Note:** Schroeder #382.

Date	VG	F	VF	XF	Unc
ND(1848-83)	1,100	2,200	3,500	5,500	—

KM# 224 7 TIEN
Gold **Ruler:** Minh Mang **Obv. Inscription:** "Minh Mang Thong Bao" **Rev:** Large dragon left **Note:** Weight varies: 26.50-27.50 grams.

Date	VG	F	VF	XF	Unc
ND(1820-40)	1,100	2,200	3,500	5,500	—

KM# 225 7 TIEN
Gold **Ruler:** Minh Mang **Obv. Inscription:** "Minh Mang Thong Bao" **Rev:** Large dragon

Date	VG	F	VF	XF	Unc
ND//13 (1832)	1,100	2,200	3,500	5,500	—

KM# 228 7 TIEN
Gold **Ruler:** Minh Mang **Obv. Inscription:** "Minh Mang Thong Bao" **Rev:** Large dragon left **Note:** Schroeder #206.

Date	VG	F	VF	XF	Unc
ND//15 (1834)	1,100	2,200	3,500	5,500	—

KM# 230 7 TIEN
Gold **Ruler:** Minh Mang **Obv. Inscription:** "Minh Mang Thong Bao" **Rev:** Large dragon **Note:** Schroeder #206B.

Date	VG	F	VF	XF	Unc
ND//16 (1835)	1,100	2,200	3,500	5,500	—

KM# 345 7 TIEN
26.7500 g., Gold **Ruler:** Thieu Tri **Rev:** Flaming sun between facing dragons **Note:** Schroeder #278.

Date	VG	F	VF	XF	Unc
ND(1841-47)	1,100	2,200	3,500	5,500	—

KM# 343 7 TIEN
Gold **Ruler:** Thieu Tri **Obv. Inscription:** "Thieu Tri Thong Bao" **Rev:** Dragon left **Note:** Schroeder #283. Weight varies: 26.60-27.00 grams.

Date	VG	F	VF	XF	Unc
ND(1841-47)	1,100	2,200	3,500	5,500	—

KM# 344 7 TIEN
Gold **Ruler:** Thieu Tri **Rev:** Dragon right **Note:** Schroeder #284. Weight varies: 28.15-28.20 grams.

Date	VG	F	VF	XF	Unc
ND(1841-47)	1,150	2,250	3,750	5,750	—

KM# 548 7 TIEN
Gold **Ruler:** Tu Duc **Obv:** Dentilated border **Obv. Inscription:** "Tu Duc Thong Bao" **Rev:** Dentilated border, dragon left **Note:** Schroeder #368B.

Date	VG	F	VF	XF	Unc
ND(1848-83)	1,150	2,250	3,750	5,750	—

KM# 553 7 TIEN
26.0000 g., Gold **Ruler:** Tu Duc **Rev:** Inscription on dragon **Rev. Inscription:** "That Tien Viet Hue" **Note:** Schroeder #383B.

Date	VG	F	VF	XF	Unc
ND(1848-83)	1,150	2,250	3,750	5,750	—

KM# 551 7 TIEN
Gold **Ruler:** Tu Duc **Obv:** Small characters **Rev:** Small, thin, curved facing dragons **Note:** Schroeder #402.1. Weight varies: 26.45-27.00 grams.

Date	VG	F	VF	XF	Unc
ND(1848-83)	1,150	2,250	3,750	5,750	—

KM# 552 7 TIEN
Gold **Ruler:** Tu Duc **Obv:** Large characters **Rev:** Large, thick facing dragons **Note:** Schroeder #402.2. Weight varies: 26.45-27.00 grams.

Date	VG	F	VF	XF	Unc
ND(1848-83)	1,150	2,250	3,750	5,750	—

KM# 549 7 TIEN
26.8000 g., Gold **Ruler:** Tu Duc **Obv:** Pearled border **Rev:** Pearled border **Note:** Schroeder #411.

Date	VG	F	VF	XF	Unc
ND(1848-83)	1,150	—	3,750	5,750	—

KM# 550 7 TIEN
26.2000 g., Gold **Ruler:** Tu Duc **Rev:** Inscription on facing dragon **Rev. Inscription:** "Long Van" **Note:** Schroeder #414B.

Date	VG	F	VF	XF	Unc
ND(1848-83)	1,100	2,200	3,500	5,500	—

KM# 555 8 TIEN
30.5000 g., Gold **Ruler:** Tu Duc **Obv. Inscription:** "Tu Duc Thong Bao" **Rev:** Inscription on dragon **Rev. Inscription:** "Bat Tien Viet Thuan" **Note:** Schroeder #384B.

Date	VG	F	VF	XF	Unc
ND(1848-83)	1,300	2,500	4,500	6,500	—

KM# 557 9 TIEN
Gold **Ruler:** Tu Duc **Obv. Inscription:** "Tu Duc Thong Bao" **Rev:** Inscription on dragon **Rev. Inscription:** "Cuu Tien Viet Nhan" **Note:** Schroeder #385B. Weight varies: 34.07-34.20 grams.

Date	VG	F	VF	XF	Unc
ND(1848-83)	1,400	2,800	5,000	7,500	—

KM# 561 LANG
37.4000 g., Gold **Ruler:** Tu Duc **Rev:** Inscription on dragon **Rev. Inscription:** "Nhat Lang Viet Trung" **Note:** Schroeder #376B.

Date	VG	F	VF	XF	Unc
ND(1848-83)	2,700	5,400	9,000	13,500	—

KM# 559 LANG
Gold **Ruler:** Tu Duc **Obv. Inscription:** "Tu Duc Thong Bao, Van The Vinh Lai" **Note:** Schroeder #403. Weight varies: 37.70-38.00 grams.

Date	VG	F	VF	XF	Unc
ND(1848-83)	2,800	5,600	9,200	14,500	—

KM# 560.1 LANG
Gold **Ruler:** Tu Duc **Obv:** Sun with 10 rays **Obv. Inscription:** "Tu Duc Thong Bao" **Rev:** Inscription on facing dragon, Sun with 11 rays **Rev. Inscription:** "Long Van" **Note:** Schroeder #414. Weight varies: 37.00-37.690 grams.

Date	VG	F	VF	XF	Unc
ND(1848-83)	2,600	5,200	8,000	12,500	—

KM# 560.2 LANG
Gold **Ruler:** Tu Duc **Obv:** Sun with 16 rays **Obv. Inscription:** "Tu Duc Thong Bao" **Rev:** Inscription on facing dragon, Sun with 16 rays **Note:** Weight varies: 37 - 37.69 grams.

Date	VG	F	VF	XF	Unc
ND(1848-83)	2,600	5,200	8,000	12,500	—

BULLION GOLD BARS

KM# 232 TIEN
Gold **Ruler:** Minh Mang **Note:** Schroeder #200. Weight unknown.

Date	VG	F	VF	XF	Unc
ND(1820-41)	300	600	900	1,500	—

KM# 347 TIEN
3.9000 g., 0.8500 Gold **Ruler:** Thieu Tri **Issuer:** Court Treasury **Note:** Schroeder #273. Fineness on edge.

Date	VG	F	VF	XF	Unc
ND(1841-47)	300	600	900	1,500	—

KM# 563 TIEN
Gold **Ruler:** Tu Duc **Issuer:** Court Treasury **Note:** Schroeder #397. Weight unknown.

Date	VG	F	VF	XF	Unc
ND(1848-83)	300	600	900	1,500	—

KM# 233 2 TIEN
Gold **Ruler:** Minh Mang **Note:** Schroeder #201. Weight unknown.

Date	VG	F	VF	XF	Unc
ND(1820-41)	325	650	1,000	1,650	—

KM# 349 2 TIEN
7.5000 g., 0.8500 Gold **Ruler:** Thieu Tri **Issuer:** Court Treasury **Note:** Schroeder #274. Fineness on edge.

Date	VG	F	VF	XF	Unc
ND(1841-47)	350	700	1,150	2,000	—

KM# 565 2 TIEN
Gold **Ruler:** Tu Duc **Issuer:** Court Treasury **Note:** Schroeder #398. Weight unknown. Fineness on edge.

Date	VG	F	VF	XF	Unc
ND(1848-83)	350	700	1,150	2,000	—

KM# 234 3 TIEN
Gold **Ruler:** Minh Mang **Note:** Schroeder #202. Weight unknown.

Date	VG	F	VF	XF	Unc
ND(1820-41)	500	1,000	1,750	2,700	—

KM# 351 3 TIEN
11.3000 g., Gold **Ruler:** Thieu Tri **Note:** Schroeder #275.

Date	VG	F	VF	XF	Unc
ND(1841-47)	500	1,000	1,750	2,700	—

KM# 567 3 TIEN
Gold **Ruler:** Tu Duc **Issuer:** Court Treasury **Note:** Schroeder #399. Weight unknown.

Date	VG	F	VF	XF	Unc
ND(1848-83)	500	1,000	1,750	2,700	—

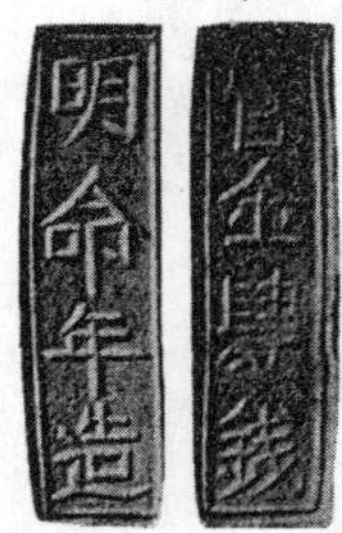

KM# 235 4 TIEN
Gold **Ruler:** Minh Mang **Note:** Schroeder #203. Weight unknown.

Date	VG	F	VF	XF	Unc
ND(1820-41) Rare	—	—	—	—	—

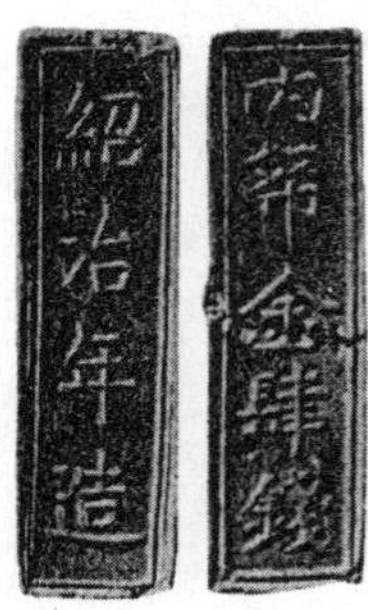

KM# 236 4 TIEN
15.2500 g., 0.8500 Gold **Ruler:** Minh Mang **Issuer:** Court Treasury **Note:** Schroeder #276.

Date	VG	F	VF	XF	Unc
ND(1841-47) Rare	—	—	—	—	—

KM# 569 4 TIEN
Gold **Ruler:** Tu Duc **Issuer:** Court Treasury **Note:** Schroeder #400. Weight unknown. Fineness on edge.

Date	VG	F	VF	XF	Unc
ND(1848-83) Rare	—	—	—	—	—

KM# 237 5 TIEN
Gold **Ruler:** Minh Mang **Note:** Schroeder #204. Weight unknown.

Date	VG	F	VF	XF	Unc
ND(1820-41) Rare	—	—	—	—	—

KM# 353 5 TIEN
18.8500 g., 0.8500 Gold **Ruler:** Thieu Tri **Issuer:** Court Treasury **Note:** Schroeder #277. Fineness on edge.

Date	VG	F	VF	XF	Unc
ND(1841-47) Rare	—	—	—	—	—

KM# 571 5 TIEN
Gold **Ruler:** Tu Duc **Issuer:** Court Treasury **Note:** Schroeder #401. Fineness on edge. Weight unknown.

Date	VG	F	VF	XF	Unc
ND(1848-83) Rare	—	—	—	—	—

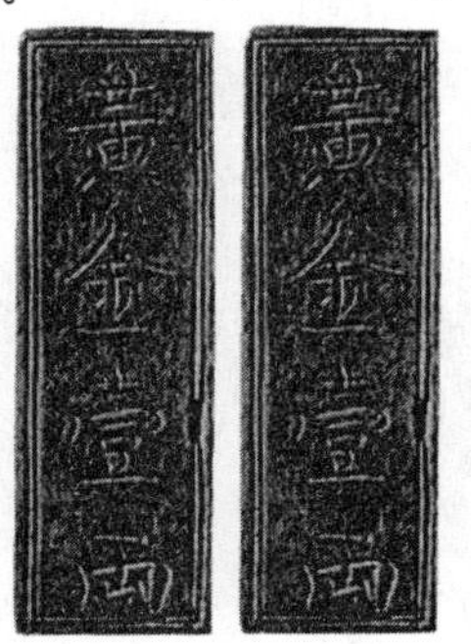

KM# 238 LANG
0.8500 Gold **Ruler:** Minh Mang **Note:** Schroeder #190. Very crude. Weight unknown.

Date	VG	F	VF	XF	Unc
ND(1820-41) Rare	—	—	—	—	—

KM# 355 LANG
Gold **Ruler:** Thieu Tri **Issuer:** Court Treasury **Note:** Schroeder #268.

Date	VG	F	VF	XF	Unc
ND(1841-47) Rare	—	—	—	—	—

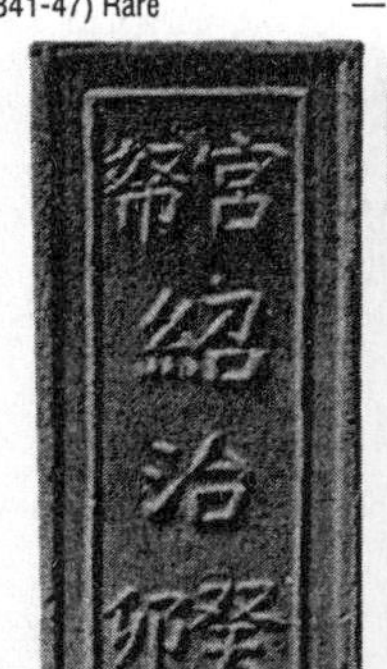

KM# 359 LANG
Gold **Ruler:** Thieu Tri **Issuer:** Court Treasury **Note:** Schroeder #269. Fineness on edge.

Date	VG	F	VF	XF	Unc
CD1843 Rare	—	—	—	—	—

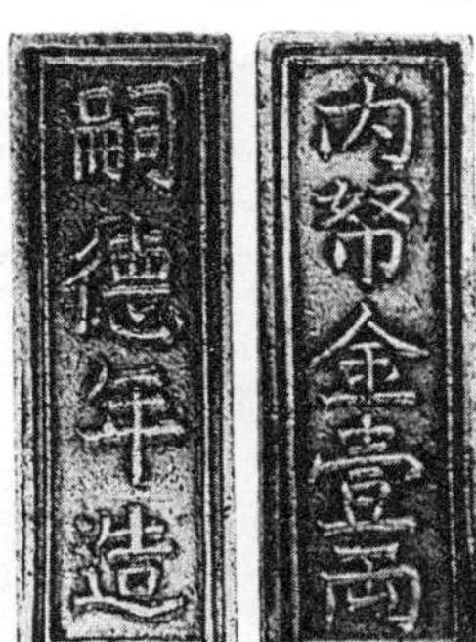

KM# 573 LANG
37.4000 g., 0.9500 Gold **Ruler:** Tu Duc **Issuer:** Court Treasury **Note:** Schroeder #391. Fineness on edge.

Date	VG	F	VF	XF	Unc
ND(1848-83) Rare	—	—	—	—	—

Note: Stack's NYINC sale 12/89 virtual Uncirculated realized $8250

KM# 574 LANG
0.8500 Gold **Ruler:** Tu Duc **Issuer:** Court Treasury **Note:** Schroeder #392. Fineness on edge.

Date	VG	F	VF	XF	Unc
ND(1848-83) Rare	—	—	—	—	—

KM# 239 5 LANG
0.8500 Gold **Ruler:** Minh Mang **Note:** Schroeder #191. Weight unknown. Fineness on edge.

Date	VG	F	VF	XF	Unc
ND(1820-41) Rare	—	—	—	—	—

KM# 576 5 LANG
190.2500 g., Gold **Ruler:** Tu Duc **Issuer:** Court Treasury **Note:** Schroeder #394. Fineness on edge; illustration reduced, actual size: 28.5 x 82 mm.

Date	VG	F	VF	XF	Unc
ND(1848-83) Rare	—	—	—	—	—

KM# 240 10 LANG
0.8500 Gold **Ruler:** Minh Mang **Issuer:** Court Treasury **Note:** Schroeder #192. Fineness on edge. Weight unknown. Similar to 10 Lang, Schroeder #173.

Date	VG	F	VF	XF	Unc
CD1837 Rare	—	—	—	—	—

KM# 357 10 LANG
382.4000 g., 0.7500 Gold **Ruler:** Thieu Tri **Issuer:** Court Treasury **Note:** Schroeder #270. Fineness on edge; illustration reduced, Actual size: 43x108 mm.

Date	VG	F	VF	XF	Unc
ND(1841-47) Rare	—	—	—	—	—

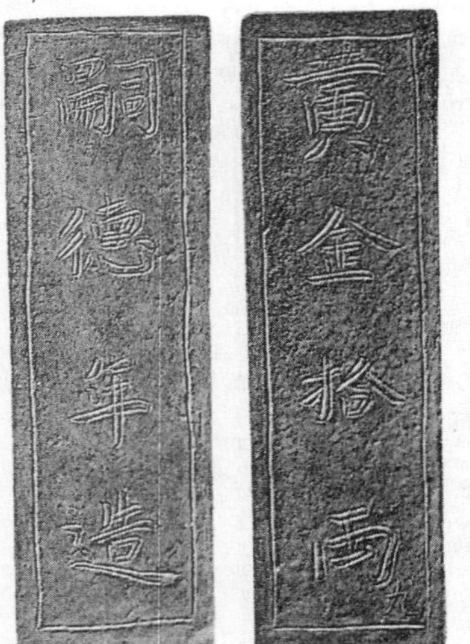

KM# 578 10 LANG
0.9000 Gold **Ruler:** Tu Duc **Rev:** Four characters **Note:** Schroeder #396. Fineness on edge; size: 30x100 mm. All inscriptions engraved.

Date	VG	F	VF	XF	Unc
ND(1848-83) Rare	—	—	—	—	—

KM# 582 10 LANG
Gold **Ruler:** Tu Duc **Obv. Legend:** "Bac Ninh" **Rev:** Two characters (engraved) plus hallmark **Note:** Schroeder #395.

Date	VG	F	VF	XF	Unc
CB1849 Rare	—	—	—	—	—

KM# 241 30 LANG
0.7500 Gold **Ruler:** Minh Mang **Obv. Inscription:** "Dai Nam Nguyen Bao" **Note:** Schroeder #193. Weight unknown; illustration reduced, actual size: 43x101 mm. Fineness on edge. Similar to 40 Lang.

Date	VG	F	VF	XF	Unc
ND(1840)/21 Rare	—	—	—	—	—

KM# 243 40 LANG
0.9000 Gold **Ruler:** Minh Mang **Obv. Inscription:** "Viet Nam Nguyen Bao" **Note:** Schroeder #194; size: 43x112 mm. Fineness on edge.

Date	VG	F	VF	XF	Unc
ND(1820-41) Rare	—	—	—	—	—

KM# 242 40 LANG
0.7500 Gold **Ruler:** Minh Mang **Obv. Inscription:** "Dai Nam Nguyen Bao" **Note:** Schroeder #195. Weight unknown; size: 43x107 mm. Fineness on edge. Illustration reduced.

Date	VG	F	VF	XF	Unc
ND(1840)/21 Rare	—	—	—	—	—

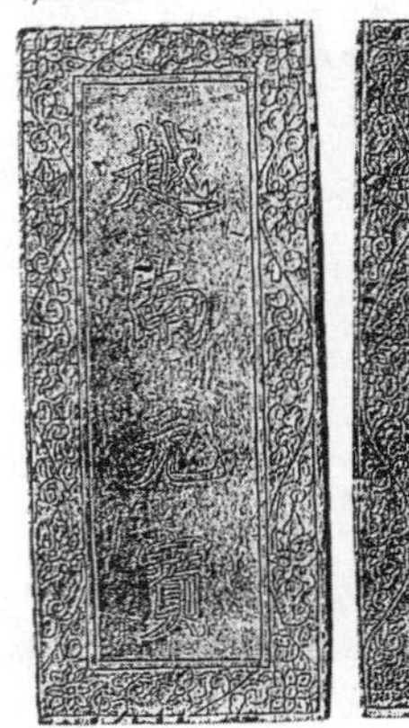

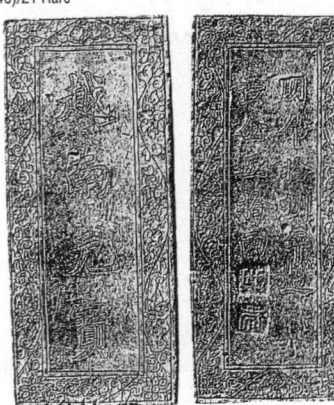

KM# 246 50 LANG
0.7500 Gold **Ruler:** Minh Mang **Obv. Inscription:** "Viet Nam Nguyen Bao" **Note:** Schroeder #196. Weight unknown; illustration reduced, actual size: 48x118 mm. Fineness on edge.

Date	VG	F	VF	XF	Unc
ND(1837)/18 Rare	—	—	—	—	—

KM# 247 50 LANG
0.8000 Gold **Ruler:** Minh Mang **Obv:** Inscription framed within ornate border **Obv. Inscription:** "Dai Nam Nguyen Bao" **Rev:** Inscription framed within ornate border **Note:** Schroeder #197; size: 49x115 mm. Fineness on edge.

Date	VG	F	VF	XF	Unc
ND(1838)/19 Rare	—	—	—	—	—

KM# 360 50 LANG
1917.3500 g., 0.7000 Gold **Ruler:** Thieu Tri **Issuer:** Court Treasury **Note:** Schroeder #271. Fineness on edge, illustration reduced.

Date	VG	F	VF	XF	Unc
CD1843 Rare	—	—	—	—	—

KM# 244 100 LANG
0.8500 Gold **Ruler:** Minh Mang **Obv:** Inscription framed in ornate border, small characters **Obv. Inscription:** "Viet Nam Nguyen Bao" **Rev:** Inscription framed within ornate border **Note:** Schroeder #198. Weight unknown. Fineness on edge; size: 59x138 mm.

Date	VG	F	VF	XF	Unc
ND(1833)/14 Rare	—	—	—	—	—

KM# 245 100 LANG
0.8500 Gold **Ruler:** Minh Mang **Note:** Schroeder #199. Similar to KM#244, but large characters on obverse.

Date	VG	F	VF	XF	Unc
ND(1833)/14 Rare	—	—	—	—	—

KM# 361 100 LANG
3831.0000 g., 0.7000 Gold **Ruler:** Thieu Tri **Issuer:** Court Treasury **Obv:** Inscription framed within ornate border **Rev:** Inscription framed within ornate border **Note:** Schroeder #272. Fineness on edge. Illustration reduced; size: 78x146 mm.

Date	VG	F	VF	XF	Unc
CD1843 Rare	—	—	—	—	—

REBEL CAST COINAGE

The status of the large copper and brass 60 Van pieces of Canh Hung is debatable, but most experts believe them to be presentation pieces or weights. Many fabrications exist.

KM# 604 PHAN
Cast Copper Alloys **Ruler:** Ham Nghi **Obv. Inscription:** "Ham Nghi Thong Bao" **Rev:** Plain **Note:** Craig #281.

Date	Good	VG	F	VF	XF
ND(1884-85)	35.00	60.00	100	165	—

TRADE COINAGE

KM# 580 7 TIEN 2 PHAN (Dollar)
Silver **Ruler:** Tu Duc **Rev. Inscription:** "That Tien Nhi Phan" **Note:** Originally considered fantasies, it has now been determined these were issued for payment of the war ransom to France in April 1865.

Date	VG	F	VF	XF	Unc
ND1865)	90.00	180	300	500	—

FRENCH PROTECTORATE OF ANNAM

HAMMERED COINAGE

KM# 630 3 TIEN
Silver **Ruler:** Thanh Thai **Obv. Inscription:** "Thanh Thai Thong Bao" **Rev:** Dragon **Note:** Schroeder #428.

Date	Good	VG	F	VF	XF
ND(1888-1907)	—	70.00	140	240	400

CAST COINAGE

KM# 606 PHAN
Cast Copper Alloys, 26 mm. **Ruler:** Dong Khanh **Note:** Schroeder #418; Craig #301.2; size varies 25 - 26 mm.

Date	Good	VG	F	VF	XF
ND(1885-88)	11.50	18.50	30.00	50.00	—

KM# 606a PHAN
Cast Copper Alloys **Ruler:** Dong Khanh **Note:** Schroeder #419; Craig #301.1; Size varies: 23-24 mm.

Date	Good	VG	F	VF	XF
ND(1885-88)	2.75	4.50	7.50	12.50	—

KM# 626 PHAN
Cast Copper Alloys **Ruler:** Thanh Thai **Obv. Inscription:** "Thanh Thai Thong Bao" **Rev:** Plain
Note: Y#1.

Date	Good	VG	F	VF	XF
ND(1888-1907)	2.00	3.50	5.50	9.00	—

KM# 628 10 VAN
Cast Copper Alloys **Ruler:** Thanh Thai **Obv. Inscription:** "Thanh Thai Thong Bao" **Rev. Inscription:** "Thap Van" **Note:** Y#2.

Date	Good	VG	F	VF	XF
ND(1888-1907)	0.50	0.75	1.25	2.50	—

SILVER MILLED COINAGE

The silver dragon coins with crude oblique milled edges are considered to be those in imitation of the Mexican/Spanish Colonial 8 Reales (Dollar/Piastre) coins and its minor denominations. The smooth edge silver dragon coins and those with square center holes are considered presentation pieces. Each coin is compared to the Weight System table in the introduction and assigned the respective Tien or Lang designation corresponding to its actual weight in grams.

VIRTUES

1 Tien - Viet Tu (benignity)

2 Tien - Viet Hein (gratitude)

3 Tien - Viet lang (kindness)

4 Tien - Viet De (respect)

5 Tien - Viet Ngai (justice)

6 Tien - Viet Thinh (obedience)

7 Tien - Viet Hue (benevolence)

8 Tien - Viet Thuan (submissiveness)

9 Tien - Viet Nhan (humanity)

1 Lang - Viet Trung (faithfulness)

KM# 609.2 2 TIEN
Silver **Ruler:** Dong Khanh **Obv:** Small characters **Rev:** Inscription between sun, moon and clouds **Rev. Inscription:** "Nhi Nghi" **Note:** Schroeder #425A.

Date	Good	VG	F	VF	XF
ND(1885-88)	—	45.00	90.00	150	250

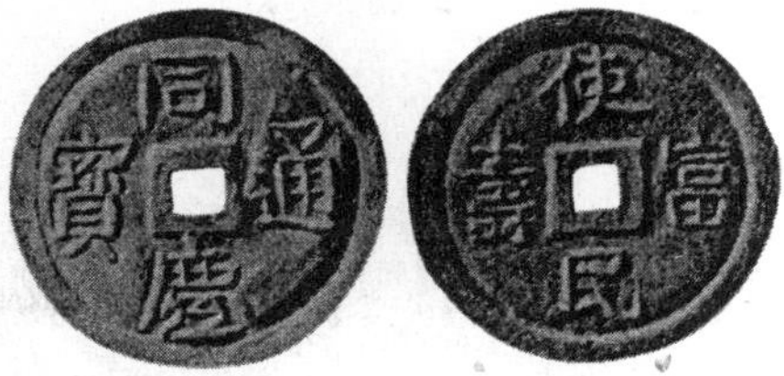

KM# 608 2 TIEN
Silver **Ruler:** Dong Khanh **Obv. Inscription:** "Dong Khanh Thong Bao" **Rev. Inscription:** "Su Dan Phu Tho" **Note:** Schroeder #420.

Date	VG	F	VF	XF	Unc
ND(1885-88)	45.00	90.00	150	250	—

KM# 609.1 2 TIEN
Silver **Ruler:** Dong Khanh **Obv:** Large characters **Rev:** Inscription between sun, moon and clouds **Rev. Inscription:** "Nhi Nghi" **Note:** Schroeder #425A.

Date	VG	F	VF	XF	Unc
ND(1885-88)	45.00	90.00	150	250	—

KM# 613 3 TIEN
10.2000 g., Silver **Ruler:** Dong Khanh **Obv. Inscription:** "Dong Khanh Thong Bao" **Rev. Inscription:** "Su Dan da Nam" **Note:** Schroeder #421.

Date	Good	VG	F	VF	XF
ND(1885-88)		62.50	125	225	375

KM# 615 4 TIEN
15.0000 g., Silver **Ruler:** Dong Khanh **Obv. Inscription:** "Dong Khanh Thong Bao" **Rev:** Inscription between Four Perfections **Rev. Inscription:** "Tu My"

Date	VG	F	VF	XF	Unc
ND(1885-88)	80.00	160	275	450	—

KM# 611 1/4 LANG
8.8000 g., Silver **Ruler:** Dong Khanh **Obv:** Inscription around flaming sun **Obv. Inscription:** "Dong Khanh Thong Bao" **Rev:** Inscription around dragon **Rev. Inscription:** "Long Van Khe Hoi" **Note:** Schroeder #422.

Date	VG	F	VF	XF	Unc
ND(1885-88)	62.50	125	200	350	—

Note: Later issues after the French colonial coinage was introduced in 1885 are considered awards for various services

BULLION SILVER BARS

All of the bars described here are inscribed with their weight, except the 10 Lang ""banana bars"", and many contain a date or the name of the province in which they were made.

KM# 617 LANG
37.7000 g., 0.7000 Silver **Ruler:** Dong Khanh **Issuer:** Court Treasury **Note:** Schroeder #423. Very crude. Fineness inscribed on edge.

Date	VG	F	VF	XF	Unc
ND(1885-88)	75.00	125	175	250	—

KM# 632 LANG
Silver, 65 mm. **Ruler:** Thanh Thai **Obv. Inscription:** "Than Thai Thong Bao" **Rev. Inscription:** "Van The Vinh Lai" **Note:** Schroeder #431. Weight unknown.

Date	VG	F	VF	XF	Unc
ND(1888-1907)	175	350	600	1,000	—

KM# 658 LANG
Silver **Ruler:** Khai Dinh **Note:** Date on edge. Weight unknown.

Date	VG	F	VF	XF	Unc
CD1919	75.00	125	185	275	—

KM# 659 LANG
Silver **Ruler:** Khai Dinh **Note:** Date on edge. Weight unknown.

Date	VG	F	VF	XF	Unc
CD1922	75.00	125	185	275	—

GOLD MILLED COINAGE

KM# 619 1/2 TIEN
1.8000 g., Gold **Ruler:** Dong Khanh **Obv. Inscription:** "Dong Khanh Thong Bao" **Rev:** Blank **Note:** Schroeder #424.

Date	VG	F	VF	XF	Unc
ND(1885-88)	150	275	425	650	—

KM# 634 TIEN
3.9000 g., Gold **Ruler:** Thanh Thai **Obv. Inscription:** "Thanh Thai Thong Bao" **Rev. Inscription:** "Nhat Nguyen" **Note:** Schroeder #432.

Date	Good	VG	F	VF	XF
ND(1888-1907)	—	325	600	950	1,450

KM# 621 1-1/2 TIEN
Gold **Ruler:** Dong Khanh **Obv. Inscription:** "Dong Kanh Thong Bao" **Rev:** Inscription between moon and sun **Rev. Inscription:** "Nhi Nghi" **Note:** Schroeder #425.1. Weigt varies: 6-40-6.90 grams.

Date	VG	F	VF	XF	Unc
ND(1885-88)	240	450	750	1,150	—

KM# 622 1-1/2 TIEN
Gold **Ruler:** Dong Khanh **Rev:** Inscription between sun and moon **Rev. Inscription:** "Nhi Nghi" **Note:** Schroeder #425.2.

Date	VG	F	VF	XF	Unc
ND(1885-88)	240	450	750	1,150	—

KM# 636 1-1/2 TIEN
6.6000 g., Gold **Ruler:** Thanh Thai **Obv. Inscription:** "Thanh Thai Thong Bao" **Rev:** Inscription between moon and sun **Rev. Inscription:** "Nhi Nghi" **Note:** Schroeder #435.

Date	Good	VG	F	VF	XF
ND(1888-1907)	—	240	450	750	1,150

KM# 638 3 TIEN
Gold **Ruler:** Thanh Thai **Obv. Inscription:** "Thanh Thai Thong Bao" **Rev:** Dragon **Note:** Weight varies: 10.50-12.40 grams. Schroeder #433.

Date	VG	F	VF	XF	Unc
ND(1888-1907)	1,000	2,000	3,250	5,000	—

KM# 639 3 TIEN
Gold **Ruler:** Thanh Thai **Obv. Inscription:** "Thanh Thai Thong Bao" **Rev:** Dragon above three Longevities **Rev. Inscription:** "Tam Tho" **Note:** Weight varies: 10.00-10.50 grams. Schroeder #436.

Date	VG	F	VF	XF	Unc
ND(1888-1907)	550	1,000	1,700	2,600	—

KM# 641 4 TIEN
14.5000 g., Gold **Ruler:** Thanh Thai **Obv. Inscription:** "Tu My" **Rev:** Inscription between Four Perfections **Note:** Schroeder #437.

Date	VG	F	VF	XF	Unc
ND(1888-1907)	650	1,200	2,100	3,200	—

KM# 643 5 TIEN
15.4800 g., Gold **Ruler:** Thanh Thai **Obv. Legend:** "Than Thai Thong Bao" **Rev:** Dragon

Date	VG	F	VF	XF	Unc
ND(1888-1907)	600	1,200	2,000	3,000	—

KM# 645 6 TIEN
23.0000 g., Gold **Ruler:** Thanh Thai **Obv. Inscription:** "Thanh Thai Thong Bao" **Rev:** Large dragon **Note:** Schroeder #382A.

Date	VG	F	VF	XF	Unc
ND(1888-1907)	1,100	2,200	3,500	5,500	—

KM# 647 LANG
Gold **Ruler:** Thanh Thai **Obv:** Inscription: "Thanh-thai Thong-bao" at right, "Van The Vinh Lai" at left **Note:** Weight unknown. Schroeder #431.

Date	VG	F	VF	XF	Unc
ND(1888-1907)	3,000	5,700	9,500	15,000	—

BULLION GOLD BARS

KM# 624 LANG
0.8500 Gold **Ruler:** Dong Khanh **Issuer:** Court Treasury **Note:** Schroeder #423. Crude.

Date	VG	F	VF	XF	Unc
ND(1885-88) Rare	—	—	—	—	—

KM# 650 LANG
0.8000 Gold **Ruler:** Thanh Thai **Issuer:** Court Treasury **Obv. Inscription:** "Thanh-thai Nien-tao" **Rev. Inscription:** "Noi Thang Kim Nhat Lang" **Note:** Fineness on edge; Schroeder #429.

Date	VG	F	VF	XF	Unc
ND(1888-1907) Rare	—	—	—	—	—

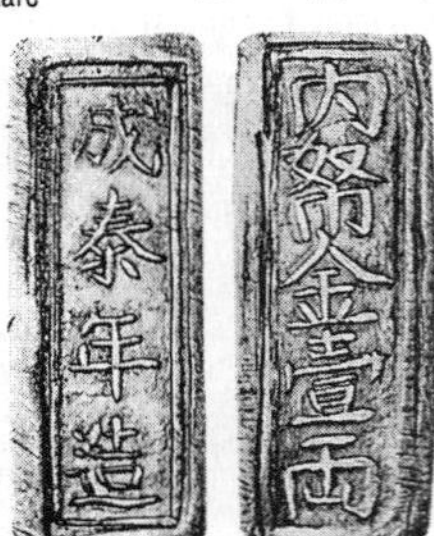

KM# 649 LANG
0.8500 Gold **Ruler:** Thanh Thai **Issuer:** Court Treasury **Obv. Inscription:** "Thanh-thai Nien-tao" **Rev. Inscription:** "Noi Thang Kim Nhat Lang" **Note:** Fineness on edge; weight varies: 36.10-36.70 grams; Schroeder#429.

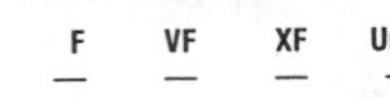

Date	VG	F	VF	XF	Unc
ND(1888-1907) Rare	—	—	—	—	—

ZANZIBAR

The British protectorate of Zanzibar and adjacent small islands, located in the Indian Ocean 22 miles (35 km.) off the coast of Tanganyika, comprised a portion of British East Africa. Zanzibar was also the name of a sultanate which included the Zanzibar and Kenya protectorates. Zanzibar has an area of 637 sq. mi. (1,651 sq. km.). Chief city: Zanzibar. The islands are noted for their cloves, of which Zanzibar is the world's foremost producer.

Zanzibar came under Portuguese control in 1503, was conquered by the Omani Arabs in 1698, became independent of Oman in 1860, and (with Pemba) came under British control in 1890.

TITLES

زنجباراه

Zanjibara

RULERS

Sultan Barghash Ibn Sa'Id,
1870-1888AD

MONETARY SYSTEM

64 Pysa (Pice) = 1 Rupee
136 Pysa = 1 Ryal (to 1908)
100 Cents = 1 Rupee (to 1909)

SULTANATE

STANDARD COINAGE

KM# 1 PYSA
Copper

Date	Mintage	F	VF	XF	Unc	BU
AH1299	4,640,000	5.00	15.00	40.00	110	—
AH1299 Proof	—	Value: 300				

KM# 7 PYSA
Copper

Date	Mintage	F	VF	XF	Unc	BU
AH1304	18,680,000	8.00	20.00	50.00	150	—
AH1304 Proof	—	Value: 450				

KM# 2 1/4 RIYAL
Silver

Date	F	VF	XF	Unc	BU
AH1299 Rare	—	—	—	—	—

KM# 3 1/2 RIYAL
Silver

Date	F	VF	XF	Unc	BU
AH1299 Rare	—	—	—	—	—

KM# 4 RIYAL
Silver

Date	Mintage	F	VF	XF	Unc	BU
AH1299	60,000	125	225	350	650	—

KM# 5 2-1/2 RIYALS
Gold

Date	F	VF	XF	Unc	BU
AH1299	—	—	—	25,000	—

KM# 6 5 RIYALS
Gold

Date	Mintage	F	VF	XF	Unc	BU
AH1299	2,000	—	—	8,000	15,000	—

PATTERNS

Including off metal strikes

KM#	Date	Mintage	Identification	Mkt Val
Pn1	AH1299	—	Riyal. Copper. KM#4.	—

HEJIRA DATE CONVERSION CHART

JEHIRA DATE CHART

HEJIRA (Hijira, Hegira), the name of the Muslim era (A.H. = Anno Hegirae) dates back to the Christian year 622 when Mohammed "fled" from Mecca, escaping to Medina to avoid persecution from the Koreish tribemen. Based on a lunar year the Muslim year is 11 days shorter.

*=Leap Year (Christian Calendar)

AH Hejira	AD Christian Date
1010	1601, July 2
1011	1602, June 21
1012	1603, June 11
1013	1604, May 30
1014	1605, May 19
1015	1606, May 19
1016	1607, May 9
1017	1608, April 28
1018	1609, April 6
1017	1608, April 28
1018	1609, April 6
1019	1610, March 26
1020	1611, March 16
1021	1612, March 4
1022	1613, February 21
1023	1614, February 11
1024	1615, January 31
1025	1616, January 20
1026	1617, January 9
1027	1617, December 29
1028	1618, December 19
1029	1619, December 8
1030	1620, November 26
1031	1621, November 16
1032	1622, November 5
1033	1623, October 25
1034	1624, October 14
1035	1625, October 3
1036	1626, September 22
1037	1627, Septembe 12
1038	1628, August 31
1039	1629, August 21
1040	1630, July 10
1041	1631, July 30
1042	1632, July 19
1043	1633, July 8
1044	1634, June 27
1045	1635, June 17
1046	1636, June 5
1047	1637, May 26
1048	1638, May 15
1049	1639, May 4
1050	1640, April 23
1051	1641, April 12
1052	1642, April 1
1053	1643, March 22
1054	1644, March 10
1055	1645, February 27
1056	1646, February 17
1057	1647, February 6
1058	1648, January 27
1059	1649, January 15
1060	1650, January 4
1061	1650, December 25
1062	1651, December 14
1063	1652, December 2
1064	1653, November 22
1065	1654, November 11
1066	1655, October 31
1067	1656, October 20
1068	1657, October 9
1069	1658, September 29
1070	1659, September 18
1071	1660, September 6
1072	1661, August 27
1073	1662, August 16
1074	1663, August 5
1075	1664, July 25
1076	1665, July 14
1077	1666, July 4
1078	1667, June 23
1079	1668, June 11
1080	1669, June 1
1081	1670, May 21
1082	1671, may 10
1083	1672, April 29
1084	1673, April 18
1085	1674, April 7

AH Hejira	AD Christian Date
1086	1675, March 28
1087	1676, March 16*
1088	1677, March 6
1089	1678, February 23
1090	1679, February 12
1091	1680, February 2*
1092	1681, January 21
1093	1682, January 10
1094	1682, December 31
1095	1683, December 20
1096	1684, December 8*
1097	1685, November 28
1098	1686, November 17
1099	1687, November 7
1100	1688, October 26*
1101	1689, October 15
1102	1690, October 5
1103	1691, September 24
1104	1692, September 12*
1105	1693, September 2
1106	1694, August 22
1107	1695, August 12
1108	1696, July 31*
1109	1697, July 20
1110	1698, July 10
1111	1699, June 29
1112	1700, June 18
1113	1701, June 8
1114	1702, May 28
1115	1703, May 17
1116	1704, May 6*
1117	1705, April 25
1118	1706, April 15
1119	1707, April 4
1120	1708, March 23*
1121	1709, March 13
1122	1710, March 2
1123	1711, February 19
1124	1712, Feburary 9*
1125	1713, January 28
1126	1714, January 17
1127	1715, January 7
1128	1715, December 27
1129	1716, December 16*
1130	1717, December 5
1131	1718, November 24
1132	1719, November 14
1133	1720, November 2*
1134	1721, October 22
1135	1722, October 12
1136	1723, October 1
1137	1724, September 19
1138	1725, September 9
1139	1726, August 29
1140	1727, August 19
1141	1728, August 7*
1142	1729, July 27
1143	1730, July 17
1144	1731, July 6
1145	1732, June 24*
1146	1733, June 14
1147	1734, June 3
1148	1735, May 24
1149	1736, May 12*
1150	1737, May 1
1151	1738, April 21
1152	1739, April 10
1153	1740, March 29*
1154	1741, March 19
1155	1742, March 8
1156	1743, Febuary 25
1157	1744, February 15*
1158	1745, February 3
1159	1746, January 24
1160	1747, January 13
1161	1748, January 2
1162	1748, December 22*
1163	1749, December 11
1164	1750, November 30
1165	1751, November 20
1166	1752, November 8*
1167	1753, October 29
1168	1754, October 18
1169	1755, October 7
1170	1756, September 26*
1171	1757, September 15
1172	1758, September 4
1173	1759, August 25
1174	1760, August 13*
1175	1761, August 2
1176	1762, July 23

AH Hejira	AD Christian Date
1177	1763, July 12
1178	1764, July 1*
1179	1765, June 20
1180	1766, June 9
1181	1767, May 30
1182	1768, May 18*
1183	1769, May 7
1184	1770, April 27
1185	1771, April 16
1186	1772, April 4*
1187	1773, March 25
1188	1774, March 14
1189	1775, March 4
1190	1776, February 21*
1191	1777, February 91
1192	1778, January 30
1193	1779, January 19
1194	1780, January 8*
1195	1780, December 28*
1196	1781, December 17
1197	1782, December 7
1198	1783, November 26
1199	1784, November 14*
1200	1785, November 4
1201	1786, October 24
1202	1787, October 13
1203	1788, October 2*
1204	1789, September 21
1205	1790, September 10
1206	1791, August 31
1207	1792, August 19*
1208	1793, August 9
1209	1794, July 29
1210	1795, July 18
1211	1796, July 7*
1212	1797, June 26
1213	1798, June 15
1214	1799, June 5
1215	1800, May 25
1216	1801, May 14
1217	1802, May 4
1218	1803, April 23
1219	1804, April 12*
1220	1805, April 1
1221	1806, March 21
1222	1807, March 11
1223	1808, February 28*
1224	1809, February 16
1225	1810, Febauary 6
1226	1811, January 26
1227	1812, January 16*
1228	1813, Janaury 26
1229	1813, December 24
1230	1814, December 14
1231	1815, December 3
1232	1816, November 21*
1233	1817, November 11
1234	1818, October 31
1235	1819, October 20
1236	1820, October 9*
1237	1821, September 28
1238	1822, September 18
1239	1823, September 18
1240	1824, August 26*
1241	1825, August 16
1242	1826, August 5
1243	1827, July 25
1244	1828, July 14*
1245	1829, July 3
1246	1830, June 22
1247	1831, June 12
1248	1832, May 31*
1249	1833, May 21
1250	1834, May 10
1251	1835, April 29
1252	1836, April 18*
1253	1837, April 7
1254	1838, March 27
1255	1839, March 17
1256	1840, March 5*
1257	1841, February 23
1258	1842, February 12
1259	1843, February 1
1260	1844, January 22*
1261	1845, January 10
1262	1845, December 30
1263	1846, December 20
1264	1847, December 9
1265	1848, November 27*
1266	1849, November 17
1267	1850, November 6

AH Hejira	AD Christian Date
1268	1851, October 27
1269	1852, October 15*
1270	1853, October 4
1271	1854, September 24
1272	1855, September 13
1273	1856, September 1*
1274	1857, August 22
1275	1858, August 11
1276	1859, July 31
1277	1860, July 20*
1278	1861, July 9
1279	1862, June 29
1280	1863, June 18
1281	1864, June 6*
1282	1865, May 27
1283	1866, May 16
1284	1867, May 5
1285	1868, April 24*
1286	1869, April 13
1287	1870, April 3
1288	1871, March 23
1289	1872, March 11*
1290	1873, March 1
1291	1874, February 18
1292	1875, Febuary 7
1293	1876, January 28*
1294	1877, January 16
1295	1878, January 5
1296	1878, December 26
1297	1879, December 15
1298	1880, December 4*
1299	1881, November 23
1300	1882, November 12
1301	1883, November 2
1302	1884, October 21*
1303	1885, October 10
1304	1886, September 30
1305	1887, September 19
1306	1888, September 7*
1307	1889, August 28
1308	1890, August 17
1309	1891, August 7
1310	1892, July 26*
1311	1893, July 15
1312	1894, July 5
1313	1895, June 24
1314	1896, June 12*
1315	1897, June 2
1316	1898, May 22
1317	1899, May 12
1318	1900, May 1
1319	1901, April 20
1320	1902, april 10
1321	1903, March 30
1322	1904, March 18*
1323	1905, March 8
1324	1906, February 25
1325	1907, February 14
1326	1908, February 4*
1327	1909, January 23
1328	1910, January 13
1329	1911, January 2
1330	1911, December 22
1332	1913, November 30
1333	1914, November 19
1334	1915, November 9
1335	1916, October 28*
1336	1917, October 17
1337	1918, October 7
1338	1919, September 26
1339	1920, September 15*
1340	1921, September 4
1341	1922, August 24
1342	1923, August 14
1343	1924, August 2*
1344	1925, July 22
1345	1926, July 12
1346	1927, July 1
1347	1928, June 20*
1348	1929, June 9
1349	1930, May 29
1350	1931, May 19
1351	1932, May 7*
1352	1933, April 26
1353	1934, April 16
1354	1935, April 5
1355	1936, March 24*
1356	1937, March 14
1357	1938, March 3
1358	1939, February 21
1359	1940, February 10*

AH Hejira	AD Christian Date
1360	1941, January 29
1361	1942, January 19
1362	1943, January 8
1363	1943, December 28
1364	1944, December 17*
1365	1945, December 6
1366	1946, November 25
1367	1947, November 15
1368	1948, November 3*
1369	1949, October 24
1370	1950, October 13
1371	1951, October 2
1372	1952, September 21*
1373	1953, September 10
1374	1954, August 30
1375	1955, August 20
1376	1956, August 8*
1377	1957, July 29
1378	1958, July 18
1379	1959, July 7
1380	1960, June 25*
1381	1961, June 14
1382	1962, June 4
1383	1963, May 25
1384	1964, May 13*
1385	1965, May 2
1386	1966, April 22
1387	1967, April 11
1388	1968, March 31*
1389	1969, march 20
1390	1970, March 9
1391	1971, February 27
1392	1972, February 16*
1393	1973, February 4
1394	1974, January 25
1395	1975, January 14
1396	1976, January 3*
1397	1976, December 23*
1398	1977, December 12
1399	1978, December 2
1400	1979, November 21
1401	1980, November 9*
1402	1981, October 30
1403	1982, October 19
1404	1984, October 8
1405	1984, September 27*
1406	1985, September 16
1407	1986, September 6
1409	1987, August 26
1409	1988, August 14*
1410	1989, August 3
1411	1990, July 24
1412	1991, July 13
1413	1992, July 2*
1414	1993, June 21
1415	1994, June 10
1416	1995, May 31
1417	1996, May 19*
1418	1997, May 9
1419	1998, April 28
1420	1999, April 17
1421	2000, April 6*
1422	2001, March 26
1423	2002, March 15
1424	2003, March 5
1425	2004, February 22*
1426	2005, February 10
1427	2006, January 31
1428	2007, January 20
1429	2008, January 10*
1430	2008, December 29
1431	2009, December 18
1432	2010, December 8
1433	2011, November 27*
1434	2012, November 15
1435	2013, November 5
1436	2014, October 25
1437	2015, October 15*
1438	2016, October 3
1439	2017, September 22
1440	2018, September 12
1441	2019, September 11*
1442	2020, August 20
1443	2021, August 10
1444	2022, July 30
1445	2023, July 19*
1446	2024, July 8
1447	2025, June 27
1448	2026, June 17
1449	2027, June 6*
1450	2028, May25